Twenty-Ninth Edition
Blue Book
of Gun Values™
by S.P. Fjestad

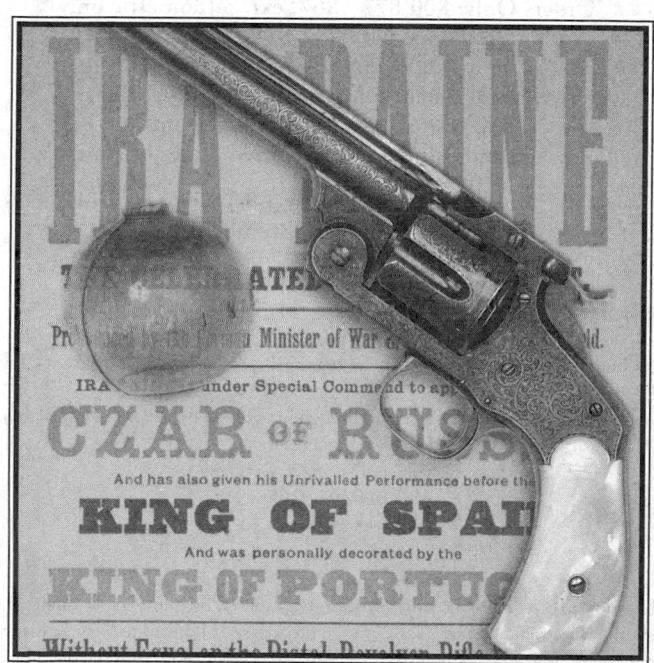

$39.95
Publisher's Softcover Suggested List Price

NRA Special Limited Edition
Suggested List Price - $39.95 (limited quantities)

Publisher's Limited Edition Hardcover
Suggested List Price - $75.00 (limited quantities)

2

Publisher's Note:

This book is the result of nonstop and continuous firearms research obtained by attending and/or participating in trade shows, gun shows, auctions, and also communicating with contributing editors, gun dealers, collectors, company historians, and other knowledgeable industry professionals worldwide each year. This book represents an analysis of prices for which collectible firearms have actually been selling during that period at an average retail level. Although every reasonable effort has been made to compile an accurate and reliable guide, gun prices may vary significantly (especially auction prices) depending on such factors as the locality of the sale, the number of sales we were able to consider, and economic conditions. Accordingly, no representation can be made that the guns listed may be bought or sold at prices indicated, nor shall the author or publisher be responsible for any error made in compiling and recording such prices and related information.

All Rights Reserved
Copyright 2008
Blue Book Publications, Inc.
8009 34th Avenue South, Suite 175
Minneapolis, MN 55425 U.S.A.

Orders Only: 800-877-4867, ext. 3 (domestic only)
Phone No.: 952-854-5229
Fax No.: 952-853-1486
General Email: support@bluebookinc.com
Web site: www.bluebookinc.com
Published and printed in the United States of America

ISBN 10: 1-886768-75-7
ISBN 13: 978-1-886768-75-8

Library of Congress ISSN number - 1524-6043

Electronic Access ID Code - 29032508
Distributed in part to the book trade by Ingram Book Company and Baker & Taylor.

Distributed throughout Europe by *Deutsches Waffen Journal*
Rudolf-Diesel-Strasse 46
Blaufelden, D-74572 Germany
Fax No.: 011-497-919566919
Website: www.dwj-verlag.de

TABLE OF CONTENTS

GENERAL INFORMATION

While many of you have probably dealt with our company for years, it may be helpful for you to know a little bit more about our operation, including information on how to contact us regarding our various titles, software programs, and other informational services.

Blue Book Publications, Inc.
8009 34th Avenue South, Suite 175
Minneapolis, MN 55425 USA
Phone No.: 952-854-5229 • Orders Only (domestic and Canada): 800-877-4867
Fax No.: 952-853-1486 (available 24 hours a day)
Web site: www.bluebookinc.com

General Email: bluebook@bluebookinc.com - we check our email at 9am, 12pm, and 4pm M - F (excluding major U.S. holidays). Please refer to individual email addresses listed below with phone extension numbers.

To find out the latest information on our products including availability and pricing and consumer related services, and up-to-date industry information (blog trade show recaps with photos/captions, upcoming events, feature articles, etc.), please check our web site, as it is updated on a regular basis. Surf us - you'll have fun!

Since our phone system is equipped with voice mail, you may also wish to know extension numbers which have been provided below:

Ext. 10 - Beth Schreiber
(beths@bluebookinc.com)
Ext. 11 - Katie Sandin
(katies@bluebookinc.com)
Ext. 12 - John Andraschko
(johnand@bluebookinc.com)
Ext. 13 - S.P. Fjestad
(stevef@bluebookinc.com)
Ext. 15 - Clint Schmidt
(clints@bluebookinc.com)
Ext. 16 - John Allen
(johna@bluebookinc.com)

Ext. 17 - Zach Fjestad
(zachf@bluebookinc.com)
Ext. 18 - Tom Stock
(toms@bluebookinc.com)
Ext. 19 - Cassandra Faulkner
(cassandraf@bluebookinc.com)
Ext. 22 - Kelsey Fjestad
(kelseyf@bluebookinc.com)
Ext. 24 - Ricky McNamara
(rickm@bluebookinc.com)

Office hours are: 8:30am - 5:00pm CST, Monday - Friday.

Additionally, an after-hours message service is available for ordering. All orders are processed within 24 hours of receiving them, assuming payment and order information is correct. Depending on the product, we typically ship either DHL, UPS, Media Mail, or Priority Mail. Expedited shipping services are also available domestically for an additional charge. Please contact us directly for an expedited shipping quotation.

All correspondence regarding technical information/values on guns or guitars is answered in a FIFO (first in, first out) system. That means that letters, faxes, and email are answered in the order in which they are received, even though some people think that their emails take preference over everything else. Please refer to our policy regarding gun questions and appraisals on page 20 for more information.

Online subscriptions and individual downloads for the *Blue Book of Gun Values, Blue Book of Modern Black Powder Arms, Blue Book of Airguns, Blue Book of Electric Guitars, Blue Book of Acoustic Guitars*, and the *Blue Book of Guitar Amplifiers* are available.

As this edition goes to press, the following titles/products are currently available, unless otherwise specified:

Blue Book of Gun Values, 29th Edition by S.P. Fjestad

Blue Book of Guns Inventory Software Program CD-ROM (ISP) (inventory software program which includes updated databases from 29th Edition *Blue Book of Gun Values*, 5th Edition *Blue Book of Modern Black Powder Arms* and 7th Edition *Blue Book of Airguns*)

Black Powder Reproductions & Replicas by Dennis Adler

5th Edition Blue Book of Modern Black Powder Arms by John Allen

Gianfranco Pedersoli - Master Engraver by Dag Sundseth, edited by S.P. Fjestad & Elena Micheli-Lamboy

7th Edition Blue Book of Airguns by Dr. Robert Beeman & John Allen

The Ammo Encyclopedia by Michael Bussard

American Gunsmiths, 2nd Edition by Frank Sellers

Parker Gun Identification & Serialization, compiled by Charlie Price and edited by S.P. Fjestad

Blue Book of Pool Cues, 3rd Edition, by Brad Simpson

Blue Book of Electric Guitars, 11th Edition, by Zach Fjestad, edited by S.P. Fjestad

Blue Book of Acoustic Guitars, 11th Edition, by Zach Fjestad, edited by S.P. Fjestad

Blue Book of Guitar Amplifiers, 3rd Edition, by Zach Fjestad, edited by S.P. Fjestad

Blue Book of Guitars CD-ROM

Blue Book of Guitar Amplifiers CD-ROM

If you would like to get more information about any of the above publications/products, simply check our web site: www.bluebookinc.com.

We would like to thank all of you for your business in the past - you are the reason we are successful. Our goal remains the same - to give you the best products, the most accurate and up-to-date information for the money, and the highest level of customer service available in today's marketplace. If something's right, tell the world over time. If something's wrong, please tell us immediately - we'll make it right.

MEET THE STAFF

Many of you may want to know what the person on the other end of the telephone/fax/email looks like, so here are the faces that go with the voices and emails.

S.P. Fjestad - Author/Publisher

Cassandra Faulkner
Executive Editor

John B. Allen
Author & Associate
Editor Arms Division

Dave Kosowski
Copy Editor

MEET THE STAFF

Tom Stock
CFO

Clint Schmidt
Art Director

John Andraschko
Technology Director

Beth Schreiber
Operations Manager

Katie Sandin
Operations

Kelsey Fjestad
Operations/Proofing

Sara Lange
Operations/Proofing

Ricky McNamara
Operations/Shipping

Zachary R. Fjestad
Author/Editor Guitar &
Amp Division

O n many collectible antique and discontinued guns, the professionals listed below typically specialize within a certain company, trademark, or configuration, and their expertise and knowledge obtained and shared within these specific areas has helped this publication tremendously over the years. These people are truly experts within their field(s) and deserve much of the credit on older makes/models.

If you feel that you have an important correction, revision, or addition, please submit them by letter, fax, or email - sorry, we can't do this over the telephone. Once received, we will review the information, and if accepted, you will see it not only in the next edition of the *Blue Book of Gun Values*, but will also be updated online quarterly. We rely on your reader feedback to help make this publication stay more accurate and up-to-date.

Once again, the people listed below are to be thanked for their contributions, and more importantly, sharing their knowledge. Without them, this new 29th Edition would have been a lot thinner, and you wouldn't be as well informed and up-to-date.

Leonardo M. Antaris, M.D.
David Kosowski
Rodney Herrmann
Bill Mullins
John Stimson, Jr.
Lowell Pauli
Randy Shuman
Wilmer Kellogg
Michael Kelly
Sal Raimondi
Greg Martin
Glen Jensen of Browning
Frank Pycha III
Tony Palermo
Larry Stewart
Rick Nahas
Larry Baer
Anthony Vanderlinden
Dennis Dawson
H.M. Shirley
Roy Marcot
Gene Myszkowski
G. Brad Sullivan
Stephen Wang
Steve Engleson
John Gyde
Don Grove
Bruce Hart
Michael Gerulat
James W. Whitcomb
Don "Duck" Combs
Gene Weicht
Robert Rayburn
Ron Lough
Richard Littlefield
Keith Bernkrant from
   European American
   Armory
Bill Allen
George C. Carlson
Jay Dewing - Dewing's Fly &
   Gun Shop
Nick Razau - Jaqua's
Crosnoe's Guns
Dietrich Apel

Jim Supica
Richard Machniak
Lynn Oliver
Bill Goforth
Jim Hauff
Kevin Cherry
Gurney Brown
Keith Kearcher
Elena Micheli-Lamboy
Jay Hansen
Carol and the late Don
   Wilkerson
Charles Layson
Jim Ellis
Mark Murray-Flutter -
   National Firearms Centre
Tom Covault
Jean Verney-Carron
Bertram O'Neill, Jr.
Richard Spurzem
Gary Chatham
John Houchins
Rob Blank
Bob Ball
John Groenewold
C. Lee Newton
William R. Mook
Jim Jasken
Ian Skennerton
Joe Gillenwater
John T. Callahan
Kurt House
Peter Powell - William Powell
   & Son
Jack Heath - retired
   Remington historian
James A. Buelow
John Lacy
Axel Eichendorff
Chad Hiddleson
Don Anderson
Charlie Price
Glen Mattox
Jim Gentile
Robert Weiss

Rick Crosier
Morris Hallowell IV
John Kopec
Orvin Olson
Tom Turpin
John Picchetti
Steve Barnett
J.B. Wood
Jack Lesher
Richard Skeuse of Parker
   Reproductions
Martin J. Lane
Jim King
John Dougan
Harry Klein
Rick Maples
Dwight Van Brunt & Aaron
   Cummins from Kimber
Karl Lippard
Peter Horn II - The Beretta
   Gallery
Paul Roberts from J. Roberts
   & Sons
Dieter Krieghoff
Warren Weider
Kathleen Hoyt - Colt historian
Paul Pluff - Smith & Wesson
Einar Hoff - Merkel USA
Jackie Love - Browning
Rob Johansen - SKB
Margaret Sheldon from
   Sturm, Ruger & Co.
Linda Powell & Pam from
   Remington Arms. Co
R.L. Wilson
Dave Wills
Charles Semmer
Thomas Mintner
Major Mark Rendina
David M. Rachwal
LeRoy Merz
Brad Taylor
Dennis Adler

ACKNOWLEDGEMENTS

Robert (Doc) Adelman aka, "mad" rocket scientist
Daniel Sheil, Jr.
Dr. Robert & Toshika Beeman (Honorary)
Paul Warden from America Remembers
George Fram, Victor & Cheryl Havlin - Mossberg Collectors Association
Doug Turnbull
Jim Spacek
Marv Adams
Edmund Goldshinsky of Marlin Firearms
Paolo & Luciano Amadi and their Venetian apartment
T. Rees Day
Thad Scott
Larry "Iron" Orr
Jack Enlund
Francis Kennedy
Michael Radford
Charles Wagner
Bob PalmerRon McGhie - Browning Custom Shop
Mike Streitbeck
Jay Huber

Harold Pedersen
Dr. Joseph Eisenlauer
Brook Davis
CWO Ric Cameron
Barry Delong
Hal Hamilton
Dan Shuck
R.W. Elliot
Tor Karstensen
Richard Dee Hanks, Jon W. Miller, MD, Maylene Rabeneck, Arley J. Wallace, Jerry Watson, Brad Adams, Bill Bryant & the High Standard Collectors Association
Gail Foster, Alvin Olson & the Minnesota Weapons Collectors Association
The Buffalo Bill Historical Center in Cody, WY, including David Kennedy, Warren Newman, Jesi Bennett and Connie Miller
F.E. "Pete" Wall
David Noll
Dean Rinehart
A.O. Salvo

Jim Foral
Nigel Beaumont, Peter Blaine, and crew - J. Purdey & Sons
Holland & Holland - Daryl Greatrex, Roger Mitchell (ret.), Robert Pearson, David Winks (ret.), David Cruz, Guy Davies, and Russell Wilkin
Col. (ret.) R.D. Whittington
Robert and Barb White
Browning Collectors Association
German Gun Collectors Association
Mannlicher Collectors Association
L.C. Smith Collectors Association
Ruger Collectors Association (RCA)
Colt Collectors Association (CCA)
Remington Society of America
Marlin Firearms Collectors Association, Ltd.

IN REMEMBERANCE TO OUR FALLEN COMRADES-IN-ARMS

It's always difficult adding names to this box, and unfortunately this year, there have been too many.

- Herb Glass Sr., an excellent competition shooter, and world-renowned firearms scholar and dealer, who perhaps did more than anyone else in the last half of the 20th century to place firearms into major museum exhibits, and take them to the next level on an art form basis.
- Louis Imperato, chairman of Henry Repeating Arms Company, was very influential in the development of Colt black powder reproductions and replicas.
- Dr. David Avery, a dentist from McKinney, TX, who had me in his chair once during an emergency toothache. A longtime contributing editor, he became one of the largest handgun dealers in Texas. He was also the first Blue Book distributor to break the 1,000 book mark. I'll miss you, Doc!
- Ron Stilwell, previous president of Colt and noted firearms industry consultant, who never had a bad word to say about anybody.
- William Powell, who was one of the more interesting people I have ever known. He could recite poetry as easily as point out minor engineering changes on S&W hand ejector models. A true Renaissance man, whenever big Bill Powell came to our table, we knew we were in for a treat, and about to learn something.
- Ted Szabo, co-founder of Para-Ordnance and its chief designer, who took Browning's M1911 design to a higher level with many innovations.
- Frank Sellers, whose encyclopedic knowledge of antiques never failed to amaze me, and the firearms expert for PBS' Antiques Roadshow. Once, at a Las Vegas Antique Arms show, he sold an attorney "160 square feet of handguns" to decorate his offices.
- George Sodini. A unique individual, George could usually be found at one of the better steak houses following a trade show. At one time, he sold books for Stoeger's, and always had an interesting story or two regarding his expeditions around the world. Thanks Mike, for carrying on his torch!

Chevalier Ira Paine

Chevalier Ira Paine was born circa 1841 in Providence, RI. He became a prominent minstrel after high school, and then joined a successful quartet, which quickly gained a considerable reputation, especially with Mr. Paine as its vibrant impresario. His large physique, quick wit, booming voice, and theatrical skills made him very popular with audiences up and down the east coast.

As good as he was inside performing on stage, he was even better outside enjoying his other career as an exhibition shooter. Ira Paine may have been the world's finest all-around shot during his 25 years as a shooting entertainer, and was a deadly shot whether using a pistol, revolver, rifle, or shotgun. Some of his most chronicled feats involved his public challenges with Capt. Adam Bogartus, the legendary late 19th century shotgun shooter. Even though Paine narrowly lost more of these live pigeon shoots than he won, it was never by more than two birds. Whenever these two personalities faced off, the prize money was typically $1,000, a fortune at the time.

It is important to remember that during the late 19th century, shooting exhibitions were a very popular spectator sport, especially in rural areas, where people cheered on their favorite shooters and guns, no different than NASCAR fans today supporting their drivers and cars.

With a dueling pistol, he could regularly cut his business card in half when put on its edge 30 feet from the muzzle. He also used rifles and shotguns with equal dexterity and accuracy during his exhibitions, which became so popular by America's 1876 Centennial, he started taking his show to Europe. On foreign soil, his theatrical skills served him well while entertaining kings, queens, czars, prime ministers, and other famous personalities. It was during one of these overseas shooting exhibitions where he met his future wife, who was one of the most beautiful actresses to adorn London's stages at the time.

The cover gun is a Smith & Wesson special order New Model No. 3 Frontier Target in .44-40 WCF cal. A factory letter from Mr. Roy Jinks, the Smith & Wesson historian, verifies this revolver left the factory on Feb. 17, 1887, and was delivered to Ira Paine. Records indicate this special revolver was shipped with blue finish, a 6 ½ in. barrel with fixed rear target sight, had checkered pearl grips, and was factory engraved by Gustav Young, one of America's most famous and prolific engravers at the time. Furthermore, a post-it note stuck on the bottom of the letter from Mr. Jinks states, "Great gun, important gun, Ira Paine, the great exhibition shooter. R.J."

The glass ball target (most were amber colored) was originally invented by Paine, and was used as a substitute for live pigeons during most shooting exhibitions circa 1876-1886. This short target glass ball era came to an end when clay pigeons were perfected and became a satisfactory substitute for live bird rings and glass balls. Always the showman wanting to give his audiences more visual excitement, Paine stuffed many of his target balls with feathers, which when squarely hit, blew feathers in a three foot diameter, which the crowds never seemed to get enough of. While his competitors may have regarded him as a real "Paine-in-the-glass", when he died in 1889 at the age of 48, the world lost one of the greatest shooting entertainers of all time.

Gun on back cover is an S&W Model No. 1 Third Issue, in .22 rimfire cal. with nickel finish, walnut grips, and factory engraving. Leather purse case with clasp is a very rare and desirable accessory.

- S.P. Fjestad

Credits:
Cover guns, catalogs/brochures, and accoutrements - Mr. Dale Peterson from the MWCA
Cover design and layout - S.P. Fjestad & Clint Schmidt
Cover photography - Clint Schmidt

Dieter Krieghoff (l) and S.P. Fjestad, shown holding Krieghoff's newest and most innovative design, the Semprio slide action rifle, at a recent SCI Show.

Welcome to the 29th edition! First of all, thanks for buying or using this newest 29th edition, the most comprehensive and up-to-date book ever published on firearms and their values. Both segments of the firearms industry, currently manufactured firearms and older, discontinued guns including antiques, seem to be in good shape at the moment. However, there seems to be some dark clouds forming out west, and an apparent storm could be on its way. More on that shortly.

At 2,176 pages, this is the fattest *Blue Book of Gun Values* ever, with more information and pricing included for your benefit. Unlike previous editions where the Forewords have been written or sent in from airplanes, various European countries, taxis and trains, this edition's final two pages is being written from the carpeted third step of the small, elevated home office at the Ranch, where over 13,000 hours have been logged on this ever-changing database.

Over the last 3-4 years, many values on collectible firearms have changed radically, thanks in part to a much larger percentage of these firearms being bought and sold at auction houses and online. More than a few dealers and collectors have told me that you almost can't overprice really good merchandise any more, and a seasoned contributing editor recently told me "Steve, on really minty major trademark models, I have no clue what real values are anymore." Will this trend continue? Answering that question requires a good look at our present economic situation, what factors will be involved in the supply and demand economics in the next few years, and vigorously rubbing my crystal ball. Here's what we need to consider:

A COUNTRY ON THE ROPES?

America is in trouble - maybe bigger trouble than we may think. If it was a company, not a country, we would have probably been in bankruptcy court 3-4 years ago. The current national debt is closing in on ten trillion dollars, thanks to the outgoing administration's insatiable thirst for more money, and Congress, who enabled the out of control spending by increasing the U.S. debt limit five times since 2001. The only way the U.S. is going to recover economically is to pay off our debt and return to a balanced federal budget, but I'm not sure if the feds in Washington, D.C. are willing to make the painful sacrifices necessary to accomplish this. While states are constitutionally required to balance their budgets, the federal government can put as much red ink in the ledger books as it wants, while the rest of us watch in disappointed bewilderment.

How much money is ten trillion dollars? It's approximately $33,333 for every man, woman and child in the U.S. If all 469 of America's billionaires agreed to give their entire assets to bail out our federal deficit, it would account for only 16% of the total! Bill Gates and Warren Buffett combined couldn't even put a dent on the interest, which would mostly go to China. Here are the vital signs of a bad economy in need of help:

- The dollar is so frail and weak, it deserves to be airlifted to the closest financial ICU.
- Gold is at an all-time high, and interest rates are very low, and falling. This is about as healthy as your blood pressure being 165/110.
- The war has steamrolled us financially. We cannot afford the mess we're in, and no one in power has a magic bullet on how to get us out - unusual, especially in an election year.
- Real estate has tanked as an investment. Have you tried to get one of those pre-approved home equity loans recently?
- Unemployment is up. Many of America's manufacturing jobs have been relocated to the Pacific Rim - especially China, and we're not going to get them back.
- Lack of new construction has torpedoed many other sub-industries, and everybody from electricians to tile layers is feeling the pinch.
- The stock market is justifiably bearish, and it should be. In this case, the always hungry grizzly bear continues to devour many late reacting, nervous sellers like they're tasty snacks.
- Some farm commodities are now out of sight, created in part because of the heavily subsidized ethanol industry boondoggle, which has resulted in overgrowing corn, creating a shortage of wheat and other small grains. $15+ for a bushel of wheat? Something's drastically wrong.

Maybe the worst thing that has happened since the Bush administration took over is that all the good will America had after 9/11 is gone - completely squandered. No one feels sorry or has compassion for us any more. Maybe the worst questions I get overseas which really stick in my craw are, "Why don't your elected politicians in Washington listen to what you voters want? Don't you care about what their fiscal irresponsibility is doing to your country?" How do you answer questions like that?

WILL ROCKY MAKE ANOTHER COMEBACK?

There's so much economic bad news, it's almost impossible to try and look at the flip side. For one thing, new and more restrictive firearms laws have generally been absent during the Bush administration, and after the Crime Bill sunset in 2004, the firearms industry became unthrottled in producing many configurations that were no longer banned. Even though most of that good news is now behind us, demand for paramilitary styled configurations is still very high. Sales for new sporting rifles and shotguns remain constant, even though today's marketplace in long guns is rapidly being controlled by the lower priced Turkish and Russian alternatives. The sales of new handguns also remain strong, although no one seems to be bragging about record sales.

The most generalized comment I have heard after attending 5 recent gun/trade shows is that everyone feels confident that the new gun marketplace will remain strong through the first quarter of 2009, and then all bets are off. If federal anti-gun politics/legislation reappears after that, it will spur demand on certain configurations, no different than in the past. Unfortunately, a short term spike created by anti-gun legislation is never good in the long term for the firearms industry, or our constitutionally guaranteed gun rights.

As mentioned earlier, the marketplace for better quality collectible firearms has been on fire for the past 3-4 years. Yet, most average guns have not appreciated in value. Many newer auction buyers would rather spend more to get a really top condition specimen than lower their sights on something mediocre and worn-out looking. A lot of people don't realize that supply and demand economics on collectible firearms can be segregated by condition factors. On truly mint condition, original makes/models, there is very little supply and a lot of demand, while on below average guns, there seems to be a glut of supply, with the only demand factor being shooting value. Moral to the story? Same as it's always been - buy as much original condition as you can afford in a major trademark and model. I've been preaching this for years, and it's never been truer.

Barbara Fausti, with her sisters Giovanna and Elena in the background, shown with one of Fausti's high grade Italian O/U shotguns.

In closing, maybe the best advice I can give you for the next 12 months is don't overpay, borrow money, or be in a hurry to buy a good gun. If you want to learn more about the implications behind that statement, please refer to my blog, entitled "Will the Real Price Stand Up?" It's humorous, but based on today's real world gun economics.

I would like to thank our entire talented staff, who goes through this annual literary rite of passage every March. Publishing 2,176 pages in less than 30 days requires a lot of horsepower, torque, and traction. At the end, it's extremely rewarding knowing that you've created the best product of its type available. Don't forget that all of the information within these pages is also available online, either by subscription or individual download, and much of it is free! Thanks for all your help and support over the years, and start getting ready for next year's 30th Anniversary edition - it's going to be a monster!

Sincerely,

S.P. Fjestad
Author & Publisher

PS - If you have any interest in fine engraving (and not just guns), you need to buy *Gianfranco Pedersoli - Master Engraver*, one of the world's finest master engravers (see pages 70-71). Inventory is limited, so don't wait until it's too late! Please visit our website for sample pages and ordering information - www.bluebookinc.com

HOW TO USE THIS BOOK

The prices listed in this 29th Edition of the *Blue Book of Gun Values* are based on national average retail prices for both modern and antique firearms, and some accessories/acoutrements. **This is not a firearms wholesale pricing guide. More importantly, do not expect to walk into a gun/pawn shop or gun show and think that the proprietor/dealer/collector should pay you the retail price listed within this text for your gun(s).** Resale offers on many models could be anywhere from near retail to 20%-50% less than the values listed, depending upon locality, desirability, dealer inventory, and profitability. In other words, if you want to receive 100% of the price (retail value), then you have to do 100% of the work (become the retailer, which also includes assuming 100% of the risk).

Percentages of original condition (with corresponding values) are listed between 10%-100% for most antiques (unless configuration, rarity, and age preclude upper conditions), and 60%-100% on most modern firearms since condition below 60% is seldom encountered (or purchased). Please consult our revised, 80-page Photo Percentage Grading System™ (PPGS) located on pages 33-110 to learn more about the condition of your firearm(s). Since condition is the overriding factor in price evaluation, study these photos and captions carefully to learn more about the condition of your specimen(s).

Please refer to the Abbreviations section for a complete listing of abbreviations used within this text. Also, an expanded Glossary explains most firearms terminology. Updated ATF regional information is also provided in this edition. You may also want to check out the Store Brand Cross-Over List, since hundreds of makes and models are cross-referenced. A Proof Marks section may also help you identify and date many European firearms. If you wish to contact current manufacturers, importers, and/or some distributors, please refer to the Trademark Index for listings and contact information, which includes websites and email addresses whenever possible.

Since the 29th Edition is now nearly 2,200 pages, it may be easier to zero in on a particular manufacturer and category (pistols, rifles, shotguns, etc.) by referring to the updated Index. For trademarks and companies with more than one configuration of firearms, individual category names are listed alphabetically. Alphabetical tabs are located on the tops of the pages next to the page number and heading, making it easier to find all the information you want quickly. Sidebar black markers are also provided, enabling you to zero in on an alphabetical section. As in previous editions, the NRA condition standards and grading criteria have been included to make the conversion to percentages easier (see page 31). This will be especially be helpful when evaluating antiques. Additionally, NRA condition standards are represented in the PPGS.

To find a model in this text, first look under the name of the manufacturer, trademark, brand name, and in some cases, the importer (please consult the Index if necessary). Next, find the correct category name(s) (Commemoratives, Pistols, Rifles, Shotguns, etc.). When applicable, antiques will appear before modern guns, and are typically listed in chronological sequence.

Once you find the correct model or sub-model under its respective subheading, determine the specimen's percentage of original condition (see the Photo Percentage Grading System™ on pages 33-110) and find the corresponding percentage column showing the price. Commemoratives or special/limited editions will generally appear last under a manufacturer's heading. For those of you who would like to make notes within this publication, there may be a Notes Page at the end of each alphabetical section allowing you room for notes and miscellaneous observations. For the sake of simplicity, the following organizational framework has been adopted throughout this publication.

1. Alphabetical names are located on the top of right-facing, odd-numbered pages and appear as follows:

S SECTION

2. Trademark, manufacturer, brand name, importer, or organization is listed in bold face type alphabetically, like this:

BROWNING, DPMS, SAKO, DUCKS UNLIMITED

3.   Manufacturer/trademark information is listed directly beneath the trademark heading: **Current manufacturer established in 1917, and located in Eibar, Spain. Currently imported and distributed by by Anglo American Sporting Agency, located in Corona del Mar, CA, H.G. Lomas Gunmakers, located in Elkhart Lake, WI, New England Custom Gun Service, Ltd. (NECG), located in Plainfield, NH; John F. Rowe, located in Enid, OK; and by Fieldsport, located in Traverse City, MI.**

4.   Manufacturer notes may appear next under individual heading descriptions and can be differentiated by the following typeface:

Bettinsoli manufactures fine quality O/U shotguns, express rifles, and combination guns, with certain models private labeled under the Franchi trademark in the U.S., and manufactured under the Bettinsoli name in Europe. Please contact the factory directly for more information (see Trademark Index).

5.   The next classification is the category name (normally, in alphabetical sequence) in uppercase lettering (inside a screened gray box) referring mostly to a firearm's configuration:

REVOLVERS: SAA, 1873-1940 MFG.

6.   A further sub-classification may appear under a category name, as depicted below. These are sub-categories of a major category name, and, again, appear in alphabetical order whenever possible.

AR-15, Post-Ban, Mfg. Sept. 12, 1994 - Present

7.   Following a category or sub-category name, a category note may follow to help explain the category, and/or provide limited information on models and values. This appears as follows:

Due to Colt's current military contracts, the commercial availability of AR-15s and variations listed below has been somewhat limited in recent years.

During 2007, Colt released the M-5 Military Carbine and the LE 10-20, with 11 1/2, 14 1/2, or 16 in. barrel. These guns are only available for military and law enforcement.

8.   Model names appear flush left, are bold faced, and are in uppercase lettering either in chronological order (normally) or alphabetical order (sometimes, the previous model name and/or close subvariation will appear at the end in parentheses) and are listed under the individual category names. Examples include:

MATCH H-BAR (R6601), SERVICE MASTER, BOSS MODEL, HI-POWER

9.   Model descriptions are denoted by the following typeface and usually include the following information:

- calibers, gauges/bore, action type, barrel length(s), finish(es), weight, and other descriptive data are further categorized adjacent to model names in this typeface. This is where most of the information is listed for each specific model including identifiable features and possibly some production data, including quantity, date of manufacture, and discontinuance date, if known.

10. Variations (and possible production periods) within a model appear as sub-models – they are differentiated from model names by an artistic icon ✻ prefix, are indented, and are in uppercase and lowercase type, as follows:

   ✻ *KS-5 Special, Mark VII .44 Mag. Desert Eagle Stainless Steel, Model 147EL*
   This is usually followed by a short description of that sub-model. These sub-model descriptions have the same typeface as the model descriptions:
- additional sub-model information could include finishes, calibers, barrel lengths, special order features, and other production data specific for that sub-model.

11. Also included is yet another layer of model/information nomenclature differentiating sub-models from variations of sub-models or a lower hierarchy of sub-model information. These items are indented from the sub-models, and have the icon ❖ graphic, for example:

    ❖ **Citori Grade I, Model 147EL Sporter, Hi-Cap Limited .45, SP-10 Camo**
    A description for this level of sub-model information may appear next to the sub-entry, and uses the same typeface as model and sub-model descriptions shown above.

12. Model notes and information appear in smaller type, generally after the price line, and should be read since they contain important, critical, and/or up-to-date information, like the following:

    This model is NOT a re-designed Ithaca Mag-10 and parts are not interchangeable. The SP-10 is a new design.

13. Extra features/special orders that can add or subtract value are placed either under category names, model/submodel descriptions, and pricing lines. These individual lines appear bolder than other descriptive typeface, like the following:

    Add $1,200 for .375 H&H cal. (open sights only).
    Subtract approx. 35%-50% for nickel finish, depending on original condition.
    On many guns less than twenty years old, these add/subtract items indicate the original factory pricing for that model's option, either added or subtracted from the last MSR.

14. On many discontinued models/variations after 1985, the following line will appear under the price line or model description, indicating the last manufacturer's suggested retail price flush right on the page, like this:

    Last MSR was $899.

15. Grading lines normally appear at the top of each page, and in the middle if price lines change. If you are uncertain as to how to properly grade a particular firearm, please refer to the all-new, digital color Photo Percentage Grading System™ (PPGS) on pages 33-110 for more assistance. The most commonly encountered grading line (shown with typical price line underneath) in this text is for 100%-60% condition factors:

GRADING - PPGS™	100%	98%	95%	90%	80%	70%	60%
	$2,650	$2,350	$2,000	$1,750	$1,500	$1,350	$1,200

Antique grading lines have additional values listed for 100%-10% and also 80%-10%. Examples (with price lines) are as follows:

100%	98%	95%	90%	80%	70%	60%	50%	40%	30%	20%	10%
$1,750	$1,500	$1,250	$1,050	$925	$825	$750	$675	$600	$550	$450	$350
N/A	N/A	$12,000	$10,000	$8,250	$7,000	$6,200	$5,400	$4,500	$3,750	$3,000	$2,300

When "N/A" (Not Applicable) is listed instead of a value, this indicates that this particular model is not encountered enough in those condition factors to warrant a price - especially true on antiques.

Most commemorative/limited edition grading and price lines will appear as follows:

GRADING - PPGS™	100%	Issue Price	Qty. Made
	$2,450	$600	200

In some cases, an organization's or company's listing (i.e. Ducks Unlimited, the National Wild Turkey Federation, etc.) of guns will appear as follows:

Model	Manufacturer	Qty.	Year	Issue Price
Model 12 Repro, 28 ga.	Browning	1,000	1995	N/A

16. Price line formats are as follows – when the price line shown below (with proper grading line) is encountered,

GRADING - PPGS™	100%	98%	95%	90%	80%	70%	60%
MSR $795	$695	$625	$550	$500	$450	$400	$350
MSR N/A	$1,325	$1,100	$885	$825	$760	$700	$640
No MSR	$850	$700	$650	$600	$550	$500	$400

it automatically indicates that the gun is currently manufactured, and the MSR is shown left of the 100% column. Following this are the 100%-60% values. **This 100% price is the national average price a consumer will typically expect to pay for that model in NIB unfired condition.** 100% specimens without boxes, warranties, etc., that are currently manufactured may be discounted slightly (5%-20%, depending on the desirability of make and model). **This 100% price on currently manufactured guns also assumes not previously sold at retail. In a few cases, a "N/A" may follow the MSR, indicating that its MSR is not available. Some companies are no longer publishing MSRs, and in this case, a No MSR is listed first in the pricing line.**

GRADING - PPGS™	100%	98%	95%	90%	80%	70%	60%

17. When a currently manufactured or discontinued limited mfg./special edition firearm with or without retail pricing is encountered, it typically will not have prices listed from 90%-60%, but rather N/As (Not Applicable), as these lower condition factors are seldom encountered. The price lines will appear as follows in this case:

MSR $1,995		$1,850	$1,675	$9,500	N/A	N/A	N/A	N/A
		$875	$750	$625	N/A	N/A	N/A	N/A

18. A price line with seven values listed, as represented below, indicates a discontinued, out-of-production model with values shown for 100%-60% conditions. In the past, values were not been provided on stainless steel guns in less than 60% condition, because of recent manufacture. Since many stainless steel models are now over 20 years old, complete pricing down to 60% is now provided. Because stainless steel is almost impervious to visible wear, a 80% - 60% model must be determined by the condition of its action and barrel (i.e., how much it has been shot/used), in addition to grip wear. Values are normally not listed for 50%-10% condition factors, since these lower conditions are seldom encountered on recently discontinued models. Examples include:

$47,500	$43,000	$38,000	$34,000	$30,000	$26,500	$23,000
N/A	$3,250	$2,850	$2,425	$2,000	$1,650	$1,350

Values for conditions under 60% will typically be no less than 50% (1/2) of the 60% price, unless the gun has been shot to a point where the action may be loose or questionable. Obviously, no "MSR" will appear in the left margin, but a last manufacturer's suggested retail price may appear flush right below the price line, automatically indicating a discontinued gun, like this:

Last MSR was $1,299.

19. Early Winchester lever action models will have two price lines - one will list values from 100%-10%, while the other one will give you value ranges in Above Average, Average, and Below Average condition factors. These value range price lines appear as follows:

$14,500 - $21,000 (Above Ave.) $10,000 - $13,500 (Average) $7,500 - $9,750 (Below Ave.)

An explanation of what to look for in these three condition ranges will precede this information in that section.

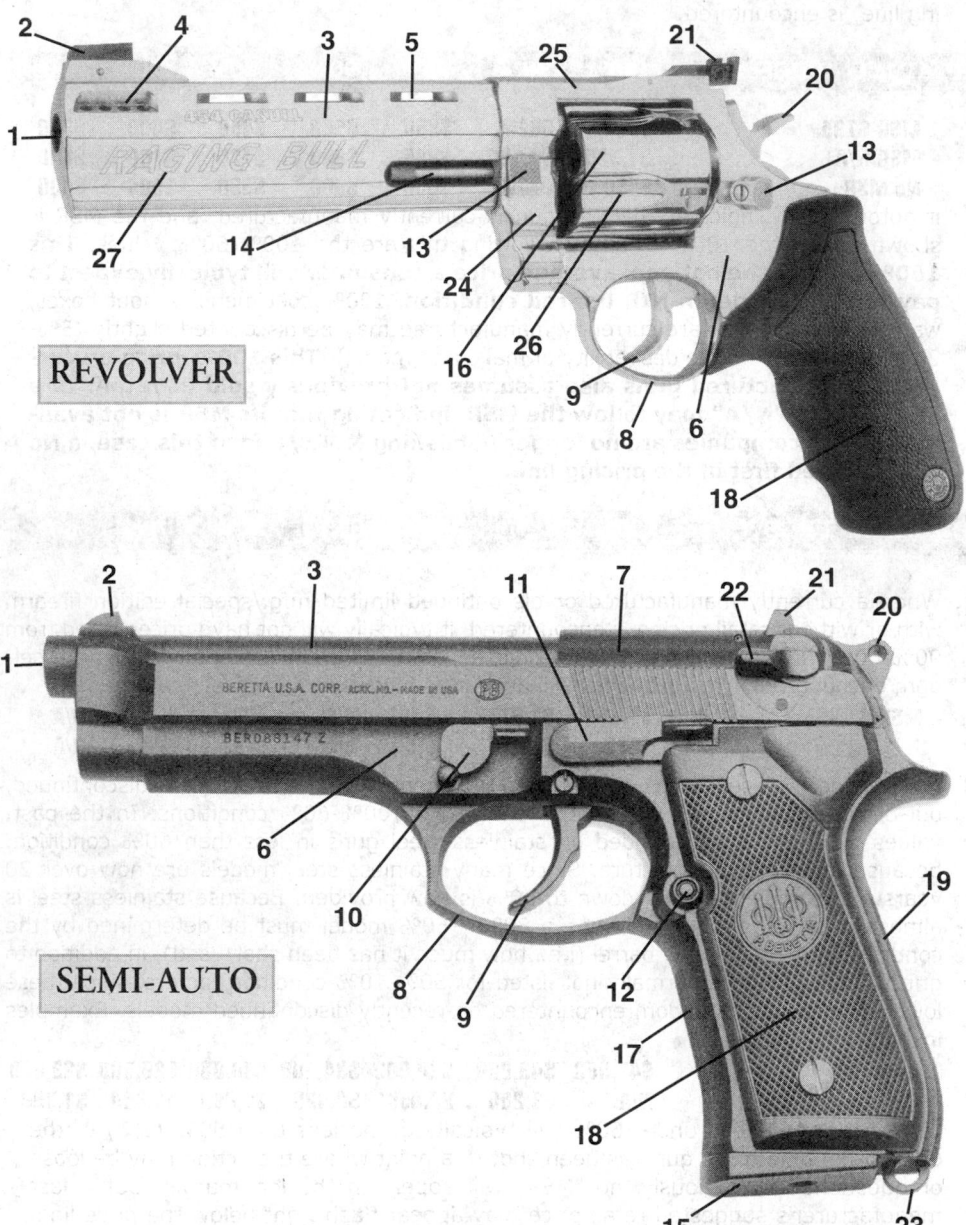

REVOLVER

SEMI-AUTO

1. Muzzle	10. Takedown Lever	19. Rear Grip Strap
2. Front Sight	11. Slide Release Lever	20. Hammer
3. Barrel	12. Magazine Release Button	21. Rear Sight
4. Gas Ports	13. Cylinder Release Latch	22. Safety Lever
5. Ventilated Rib	14. Extractor Rod	23. Lanyard Loop
6. Frame	15. Magazine	24. Crane
7. Slide	16. Cylinder	25. Top Strap
8. Trigger Guard	17. Front Grip Strap	26. Cylinder Flute
9. Trigger	18. Grip	27. Full Length Barrel Shroud

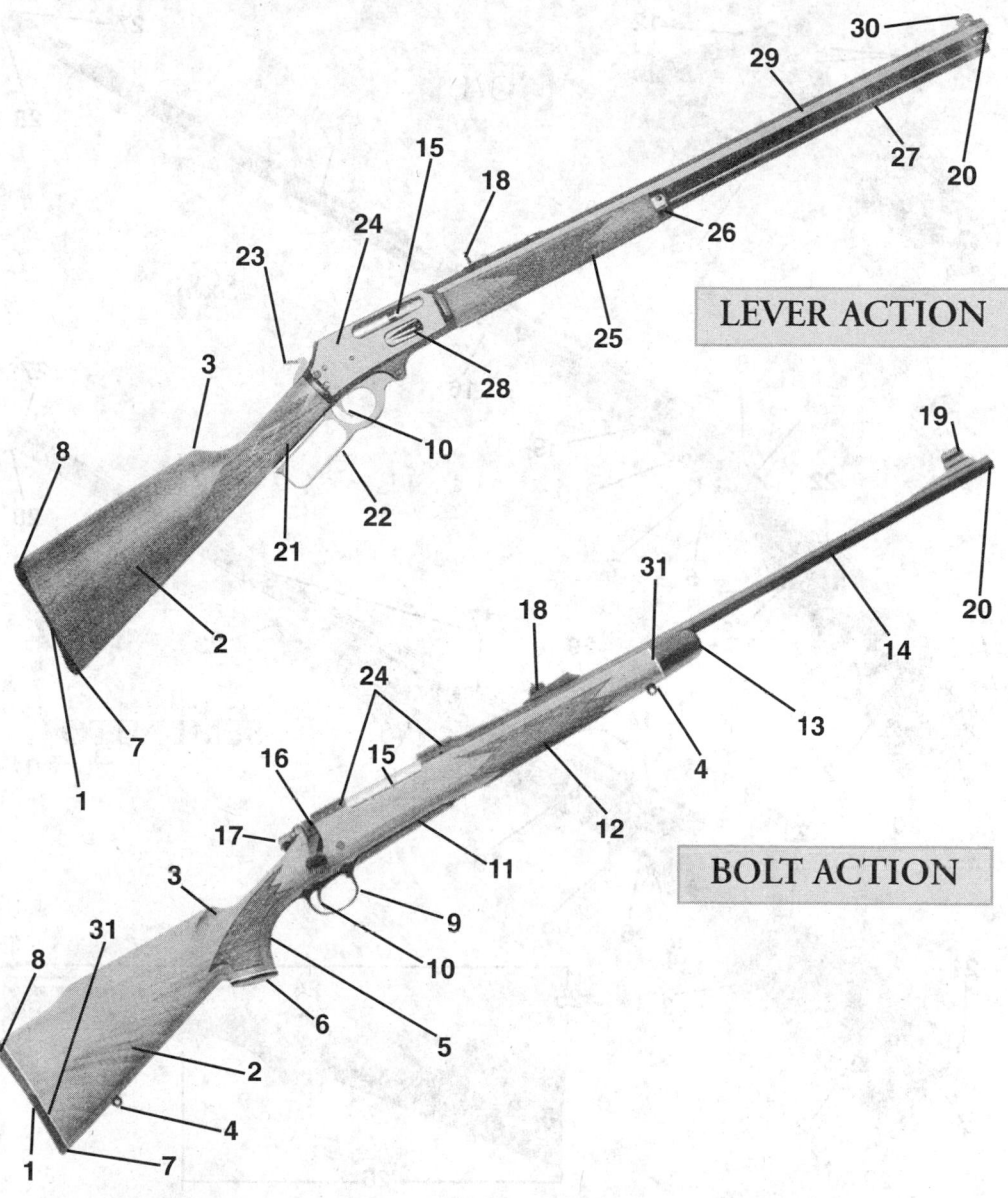

LEVER ACTION

BOLT ACTION

1. Buttplate	12. Forend	23. Hammer
2. Buttstock	13. Forend Cap	24. Receiver
3. Comb	14. Barrel	25. Forearm
4. Sling Swivel Stud	15. Bolt	26. Forearm Cap
5. Semi-Pistol Grip	16. Bolt Handle	27. Magazine Tube
6. Pistol Grip Cap	17. Safety Button	28. Loading Port
7. Toe	18. Rear Sight	29. Octagon Barrel
8. Heel	19. Hooded-Ramp Front Sight	30. Blade Front Sight
9. Trigger Guard	20. Muzzle	31. Spacer
10. Trigger	21. Straight Grip	
11. Floor Plate	22. Lever	

ANATOMY OF A SHOTGUN

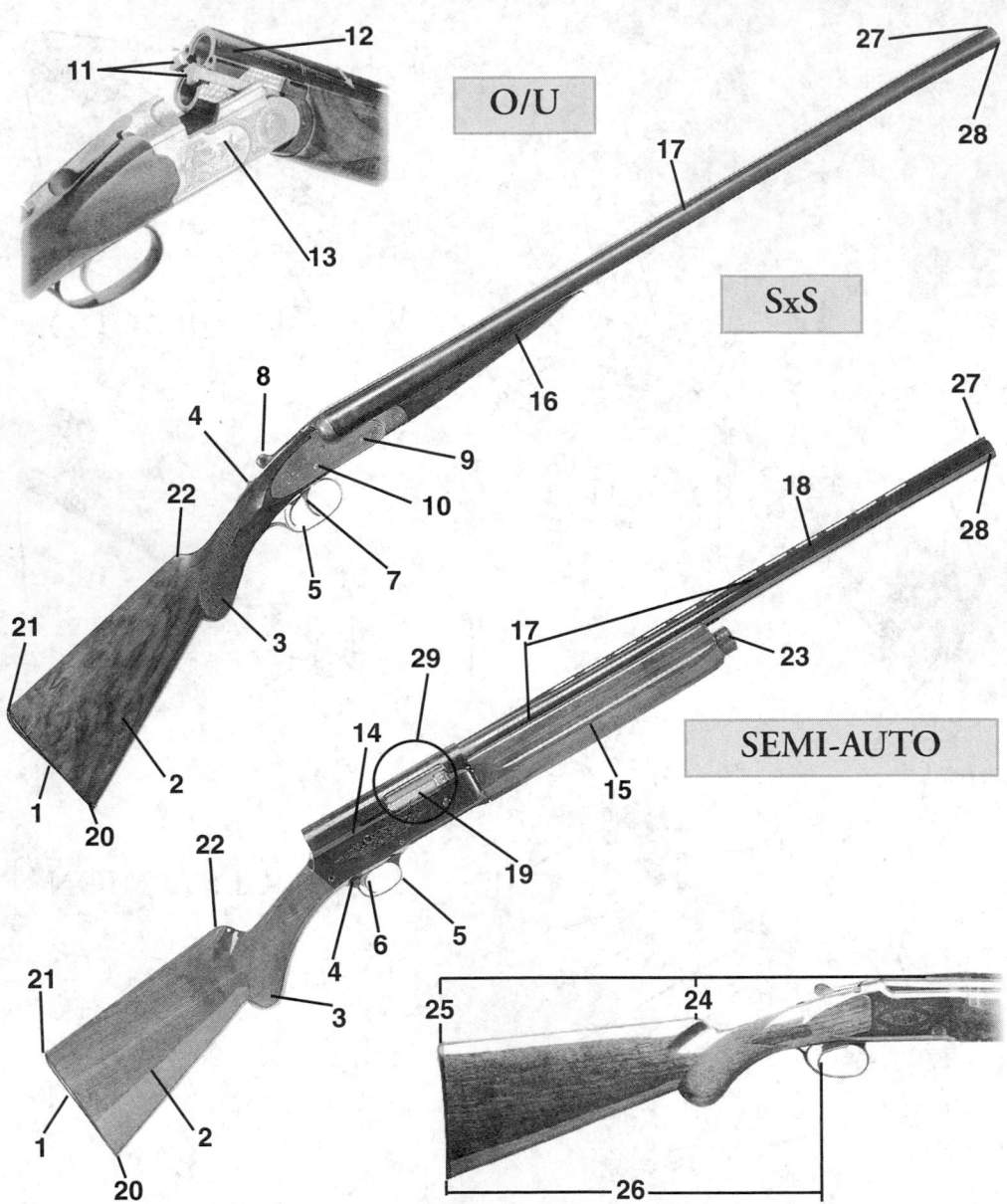

O/U

SxS

SEMI-AUTO

1. Buttplate	11. Ejectors or Extractors	21. Heel
2. Buttstock	12. Breech/Chamber	22. Comb (fluted)
3. Rounded Pistol Grip	13. Scalloped Boxlock Action	23. Magazine Tube Cap
4. Safety Button	14. Receiver	24. Drop at Comb
5. Trigger Guard	15. Forearm	25. Drop at Heel
6. Trigger	16. Splinter Forearm	26. Length of Pull (LOP)
7. Double Triggers	17. Barrel(s)	27. Front Sight Bead
8. Top Opening Lever	18. Ventilated Rib	28. Muzzle
9. Frame	19. Breech Block	29. Ejection Port
10. Side Plate	20. Toe	

Over the course of many editions, we've had many referral requests for buying, selling, or trading firearms. As Blue Book Publications, Inc. is a publisher, not a gun shop, this service is designed to link you up with the right companies and/or individuals. There is no charge for this service, nor do we receive a commission (a thank you would be appreciated, however!). The goal is for you to get hooked up with the right people. Our established international network of reliable dealers and collectors allows your particular buy or sell request to be referred to the right company/individual based on both your region and area of collectibility. All replies are treated strictly confidentially.

Correspondence and replies should be directed to:

> **Blue Book Publications, Inc.**
> **Attn: John Allen**
> **8009 34th Ave. So., Ste. 175 o Minneapolis, MN 55425 USA**
> **Phone: 952-854-5229, ext. 16 • Fax: 952-853-1486**
> **Email: guns@bluebookinc.com**
> **Use "Referral" in the subject line or it may get deleted.**

Courtesy Heym Waffenfabrik AG

GUN QUESTIONS/APPRAISALS POLICY

Whether we wanted it or not, Blue Book Publications, Inc. has ended up in the driver's seat as the clearinghouse for gun information. Because the volume of gun questions now requires full-time attention, we have developed a standardized policy that will enable us to provide you with the service you have come to expect from Blue Book Publications, Inc. To that end, we have extended all of these services to our website (www.bluebookinc.com).

To ensure that the research department can answer every gun question with an equal degree of thoroughness, a massive firearms library of well over 1,000 volumes, hundreds of both new and old factory brochures, price sheets, and dealer inventory listings are maintained and constantly updated. It's a huge job, and we answer every question like we could go to court on it.

POLICY FOR GUN QUESTIONS

The charge is $10 per gun question, payable by a major credit card. All gun questions are answered on a first-come, first-served basis, guaranteeing that everyone will be treated equally. All pricing requests will be given within a value range only. Gun question telephone/fax hours are 1:00 p.m. to 4:00 p.m., M-F, CST, no exceptions please. If we are not available by phone, please leave a voicemail. You must provide us with all the necessary gun information if you want an accurate answer. For email questions (firearms inquiries) please refer to www.bluebookinc.com. Letter questions (preferred, with photos) will also be answered in the order of arrival. Make sure you include the proper return address and phone number.

APPRAISAL INFORMATION

Written appraisals will be performed only if the following criteria are met:
We must have good quality photos with a complete description, including manufacturer's name, model, gauge/caliber, barrel length, and other pertinent information. On some firearms (depending on the trademark and model), a factory letter may be necessary. Our charge for a written appraisal is 2% of the appraised value with a minimum charge of $20 per gun. Please allow 2-3 weeks response time per appraisal request.

ADDITIONAL SERVICES

Individuals requesting a photocopy of a particular page or section from any edition for insurance or reference purposes will be billed at $5 per page, up to 5 pages, and $3.50 per page thereafter.

TURNAROUND TIME

Our goal is to answer most telephone, mail, email, or faxed gun questions in less than 7 business days, unless we're away attending trade/gun shows. This also assumes that all information needed to process the question(s) is initially provided, otherwise delays will occur.

Please direct all gun questions and appraisals to:
Blue Book Publications, Inc.
Attn: Research Dept.
8009 34th Ave. S., Suite 175
Minneapolis, MN 55425 USA
Phone: 952-854-5229, ext. 16
Fax: 952-853-1486 • www.bluebookinc.com
Email: guns@bluebookinc.com
Use "Firearm Inquiry" in the subject line or it may get deleted.

**ACT TODAY AND GET NRA'S
MULTI-TOOL
A $24.95 VALUE — FREE!**

Insure Your Gun Rights
JOIN **NRA**

Right now, your hunting and shooting traditions are under attack in Congress, courts, state legislatures and the U.N. NRA membership is the only insurance policy that protects your firearm freedoms.

Save $10 and join today for only $25!

XR012415

MR/MRS/MS _____

ADDRESS _____

CITY _____ STATE _____ ZIP _____

E-MAIL _____ D.O.B. _____

CHOOSE ONE MAGAZINE:
❑ AMERICAN RIFLEMAN ❑ AMERICAN HUNTER ❑ AMERICA'S 1ST FREEDOM

PAYMENT TYPE: ❑ CHECK OR MONEY ORDER - *FOR $25 PAYABLE TO NRA*

CREDIT CARD: ❑ VISA ❑ MASTERCARD ❑ AMEX ❑ DISCOVER

CARD NUMBER:

_ _ _ _ _ _ _ _ _ _ _ _ _ _ _ _   EXP. DATE: _ _ / _ _

SIGNATURE _____

To join instantly call 1-800-672-0004

MAIL THIS APPLICATION TO: **NATIONAL RIFLE ASSOCIATION • C/O RECRUITING DEPARTMENT
11250 WAPLES MILL RD • FAIRFAX, VA 22030**

CONTRIBUTIONS, GIFTS OR MEMBERSHIP DUES MADE OR PAID TO THE NATIONAL RIFLE ASSOCIATION ARE NOT REFUNDABLE OR TRANSFERABLE AND ARE NOT DEDUCTIBLE AS CHARITABLE CONTRIBUTIONS FOR FEDERAL INCOME TAX PURPOSES. $3.75 of annual membership dues are designated for magazine. This membership offer cannot be combined with any other discounts or offers. Please allow 4 - 6 weeks for processing of membership. International memberships: add $5 for Canadian and $10 for all other countries. Insurance benefits are subject to conditions contained in the master policy on file at NRA headquarters at the time a claim arises.

National Firearms Museum

The only museum dedicated to telling our story of freedom and the American experience through firearms…the NATIONAL FIREARMS MUSEUM

As a firearms owner, the National Firearms Museum accurately tells your story through 85 educational exhibits displaying over 2,000 historic and rare firearms.

Your TAX-DEDUCTIBLE GIFT to the NATIONAL FIREARMS MUSEUM ENDOWMENT will help guarantee that future generations will be able to learn of America's constitutional rights and firearms heritage.

The NRA Foundation

Teach Freedom...™

INVEST IN THE FUTURE OF THE SHOOTING SPORTS

The NRA Foundation is a 501(c)(3) charitable organization that supports a wide range of firearm-related public service activities of the National Rifle Association and other groups that promote the continuation of America's firearms heritage. Since 1990, the foundation has awarded 17,000 grants for $112 million nationwide. More than half have been invested in youth programs — the future of the shooting sports.

Through The NRA Foundation Endowment, you can make a gift to secure these traditions for generations. The endowment establishes a permanent base of funding for shooting sports programs, ensuring their continuation and expansion forever. The NRA Foundation National Firearms Museum Endowment is an example of a program that gun collectors might want to support through any one of a variety of charitable giving programs.

Your tax-deductible donation to The NRA Foundation is truly an investment in the future of the shooting sports. You are invited to join us in our commitment to promote safety and conservation, teach the responsible use of firearms, and protect our American firearms traditions by making a tax-deductible gift to The NRA Foundation.

For more information, please contact:
The NRA Foundation
11250 Waples Mill Road ★ Fairfax, VA 22030
www.nrafoundation.org ★ 1-877 NRA GIVE

THE HILL IS OUR BASE

(NOTHING REPLACES BEING THERE)

Since 1989, the Congressional Sportsmen's Foundation has been solidifying the sportsmen's base camp. Our mission is to champion hunting, angling, and trapping issues with elected officials.

With our feet on the streets of Washington, DC and our eyes our on the issues, CSF provides the ultimate protection against legislative attacks and delivers victories for sportsmen and women in the political arena.

While you are in the field or on the water, CSF is scoping the political landscape and keeping the fires burning on all fronts for sportsmen.

Learn more about CSF's victories for sportsmen and how federal legislation impacts your passion for the outdoors, visit www.sportsmenslink.org.

CONGRESSIONAL SPORTSMEN'S FOUNDATION

Looking for the best place to hunt and shoot?
Point and click.

If it involves hunting or shooting, you'll find it right here. Huntandshoot.org is the largest, most comprehensive online resource for finding the best places and services, planning your next adventure, learning how to get started, you name it. A site you'll only occasionally visit? Hardly – this site is about to become your favorite bookmark.

www.huntandshoot.org Go ahead, give it a shot.

DUCKS UNLIMITED
Photo courtesy of Ducks Unlimited

Quality time with family and friends doesn't just happen around the dinner table.

Introduce newcomers to the hunting activities you love and win yourself $1,000.

As a hunter you're in a unique position to also be a mentor. By sharing your knowledge and enthusiasm with a friend or loved one, by spending quality time in the great outdoors with a newcomer to your sport, you earn trust and admiration. You can also earn $1,000 in prizes.

Ask someone to STEP OUTSIDE and introduce them to the sport you love. Then tell us about it. You'll be automatically entered to **win one of five $1,000 prizes.** It's a great incentive to bond with those you enjoy spending time with. It's also the perfect way to support and promote the great outdoors and your passion for outdoor sports.

Join us. STEP OUTSIDE with family and friends and show them just how great the great outdoors can be.

Visit HuntandShoot.org/STEPOUTSIDE for more details.

STEP OUTSIDE

National SHOOTING SPORTS Foundation • ALWAYS SHOOTING FOR MORE

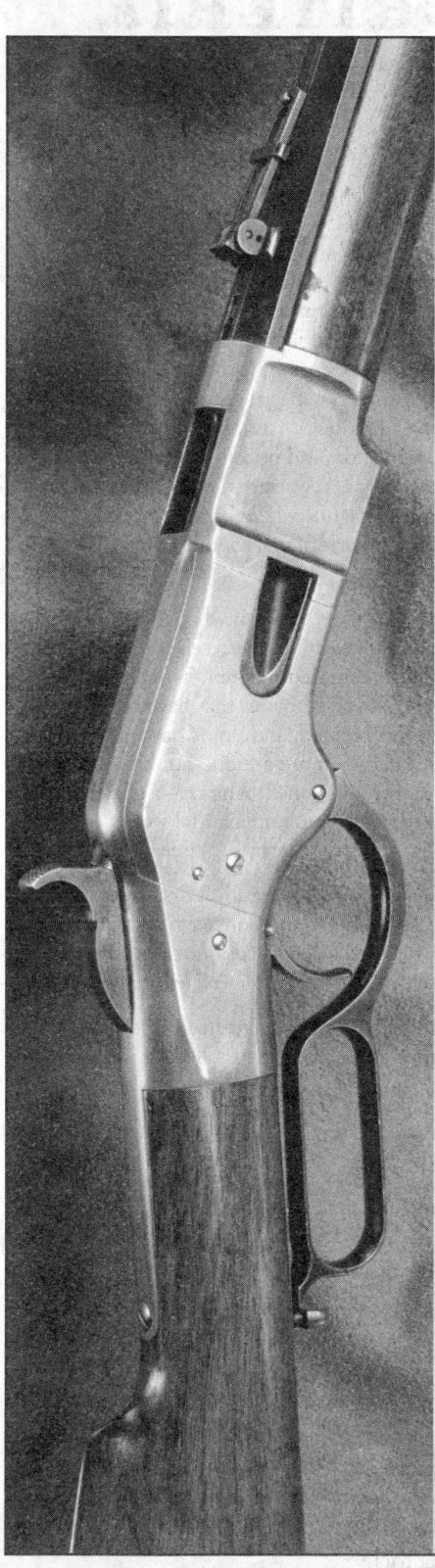

GRADING CRITERIA

The old, NRA method of firearms grading - relying upon adjectives such as "Excellent" or "Fair" - has served the firearms community for a many years. Today's dealers/collectors, especially those who deal in modern guns, have turned away from the older subjective system. There is too much variance within some of the older subjective grades, therefore making accurate grading difficult.

Most dealers and collectors are now utilizing what is essentially an objective method for deciding the condition of a gun: THE PERCENTAGE OF ORIGINAL FACTORY FINISH(ES) REMAINING ON THE GUN. After looking critically at a variety of firearms and carefully studying the Photo Percentage Grading System™ (pages 33-110), it will soon become evident whether a gun has 98%, 90%, 70% or less finish remaining. Remember, sometimes an older gun described as NIB can actually be 98% or less condition, simply because of the wear accumulated by taking it in and out of the box and being handled too many times. Commemoratives are especially prone to this problem. Of course, factors such as quality of finish(es), engraving (and other embellishments), special orders/features, historical significance and/or provenance, etc. can and do affect prices immensely. Also, it seems that every year bore condition becomes more important in the overall grading factor (and price) of both collectible and desirable major trademarks such as Winchester, Remington, Sharps, Schuetzens, older Springfields etc. Because of this, bore condition must be listed separately for those guns where it makes a difference in value. Never pay a premium for condition that isn't there. Remember, original condition still beats everything else to the bank.

Every gun's unique condition factor - and therefore the price - is best determined by the percentage of original finish(es) remaining, with the key consideration being the overall frame/receiver finish. The key word here is "original," for if anyone other than the factory has refinished the gun, its value as a collector's item has been diminished, with the exception of rare and historical pieces that have been properly restored. Every year, top quality restorations have become more accepted, and prices have gone up proportionately with the quality of the workmanship. Also popular now are antique finishes, and a new question has come up, "what is 100% antique finish on new reproductions?" Answer - a gun that started out as new, and then has been aged to a lower condition factor to duplicate natural wear and tear.

CAREFULLY STUDY THE HIGH QUALITY DIGITAL IMAGES AND READ THE CAPTIONS ON PAGES 33-110. Note where the finishes of a firearm typically wear off first. These are usually places where the gun accumulates wear from holster/case rubbing, and contact with the hands or body over an extended period of time. A variety of firearms have been shown in four-color to guarantee that your "sampling rate" for observing finishes with their correct colors is as diversified as possible.

It should be noted that the older a collectible firearm is, the smaller the percentage of original finish one can expect to find. Some very old and/or very rare firearms are acceptable to collectors in almost any condition!

For your convenience, NRA Condition Standards are listed on page 31. Converting from this grading system to percentages can now be done accurately. Remember the price is wrong if the condition factor isn't right!

PHOTO PERCENTAGE GRADING SYSTEM CONVERSION GUIDELINES

New/Perfect 100% condition with or without box. 100% on currently manufactured firearms assumes NIB condition and not sold previously at retail.

Mint typically 98%-99% condition, depending on the age of the firearm. Probably sold previously at retail, and may have been shot occasionally.

Excellent 95%+ - 98% condition (typically).

Very Good 80% - 95% condition (should be all original).

Good 60% - 80% condition (should be all original).

Fair 20% - 60% condition (may or may not be original, but must function properly and shoot).

Poor under 20% condition (shooting not a factor).

The NRA conditions listed below have been provided as guidelines to assist the reader in converting and comparing condition factors to the Photo Percentage Grading System™ (see pages 33-110). NRA antique and modern condition standards are now represented in the PPGS - please refer to pages 33-69 (handguns) and 72-110 (long guns). In order to use this book correctly, the reader is urged to examine these images of NRA condition standards. Once the gun's condition has been accurately assessed, only then can values be accurately ascertained.

NRA MODERN CONDITION DESCRIPTIONS

New - not previously sold at retail, in same condition as current factory production.

Perfect - in new condition in every respect.

Excellent - new condition, used but little, no noticeable marring of wood or metal, bluing near perfect (except at muzzle or sharp edges).

Very Good - in perfect working condition, no appreciable wear on working surfaces, no corrosion or pitting, only minor surface dents or scratches.

Good - in safe working condition, minor wear on working surfaces, no broken parts, no corrosion or pitting that will interfere with proper functioning.

Fair - in safe working condition, but well worn, perhaps requiring replacement of minor parts or adjustments which should be indicated in advertisement, no rust, but may have corrosion pits which do not render article unsafe or inoperable.

NRA ANTIQUE CONDITION DESCRIPTIONS

Factory New - all original parts; 100% original finish; in perfect condition in every respect, inside and out.

Excellent - all original parts; over 80% original finish; sharp lettering, numerals and design on metal and wood; unmarred wood; fine bore.

Fine - all original parts; over 30% original finish; sharp lettering, numerals and design on metal and wood; minor marks in wood; good bore.

Very Good - all original parts; none to 30% original finish; original metal surfaces smooth with all edges sharp; clear lettering, numerals and design on metal; wood slightly scratched or bruised; bore disregarded for collectors firearms.

Good - less than 20% original finish, some minor replacement parts; metal smoothly rusted or lightly pitted in places, cleaned or reblued; principal lettering, numerals and design on metal legible; wood refinished, scratched, bruised or minor cracks repaired; in good working order.

Fair - less than 10% original finish, some major parts replaced; minor replacement parts may be required; metal rusted, may be lightly pitted all over, vigorously cleaned or reblued; rounded edges of metal and wood; principal lettering, numerals and design on metal partly obliterated; wood scratched, bruised, cracked or repaired where broken; in fair working order or can be easily repaired and placed in working order.

Poor - little or no original finish remaining, major and minor parts replaced; major replacement parts required and extensive restoration needed; metal deeply pitted; principal lettering, numerals and design obliterated, wood badly scratched, bruised, cracked or broken; mechanically inoperative, generally undesirable as a collector's firearm.

THE PPGS
FIREARMS GRADING MADE EASY

The next 80 pages with captions are easily the most important in this book. If you carefully study all the images, and thoroughly read the accompanying captions, the following color pages will help you accurately determine condition better than anything that's ever been printed or written. This revised Photo Percentage Grading System (PPGS) includes images of both NRA new and antique condition factors, in addition to all the 100%-10% percentage conditions for revolvers, pistols, rifles, and shotguns.

After seventeen editions, the Photo Percentage Grading System™ has now become the industry standard for visibly ascertaining various condition factors based on a percentage system. The 29th Edition also retains the "PPGS-o-meters" whenever possible, so you can get a quick fix on condition factors. Computer savvy readers will be pleased to know that this expanded 29th Edition PPGS™ is also included free of charge on our website at www.bluebookinc.com.

Condition factors pictured (indicated by PPGS-o-meters), unless otherwise noted, refer to the percentage of a gun's remaining finish(es), including blue, case colors, nickel, or another type of original finish remaining on the frame/receiver. On older guns, describing the receiver/frame finish accurately is absolutely critical to ascertain an accurate grade, which will determine the correct value.

Additional percentages of condition may be used to describe other specific parts of a gun (i.e. barrel, wood finish, plating, magazine tube, etc.). Percentages of patina/brown or other finish discoloration factors must also be explained separately when necessary, and likewise be interpolated accurately. **With antiques, the overall percentage within this text is NOT an average of the various condition factors, but, again, refers to the overall original condition of the frame/receiver. Being able to spot original condition has never been more important, especially when the prices get into four, five, and six figures.** Remember, the price is wrong if the condition factor isn't right.

Now, more than ever, it takes a well-trained sense of sight, hearing, touch, and smell, and a corresponding connection to the most powerful computer ever built, a trained human brain, to accurately fingerprint a gun's correct condition factor. Regardless of how much knowledge you've accumulated from books, websites, auction catalogs, dealer listings, etc., you're still in potential danger as a buyer if you can't figure out a gun's condition factor(s) accurately. More than anything else, an older gun's overall condition must "add up" (i.e., a well-used L.C. Smith SxS with almost no case colors remaining should not have mint-looking barrels, and a crispy looking Broomhandle should not have faded straw colors and/or worn grips).

While the 29th Edition's Photo Percentage Grading System™ certainly isn't meant to be the Last Testament on firearms grading, it hopefully goes a lot further than anything else published on the subject. Once you've accumulated the experience necessary to grade guns accurately, a ten-second "CAT scan" is usually all the time that is needed to zero in on each gun's unique condition factor.

In closing, the publisher wishes to express his thanks and gratitude to Pat Hogan & Rock Island Auctions, and Dr. Leonardo Antaris, M.D. for authorizing the use of their digital images for the Photo Percentage Grading System™ (PPGS™).

Sincerely,

S.P. Fjestad
Author & Publisher *Blue Book of Gun Values*™

Twenty-Ninth Edition *Blue Book of Gun Values*™

***Photo Percentage Grading System*™**

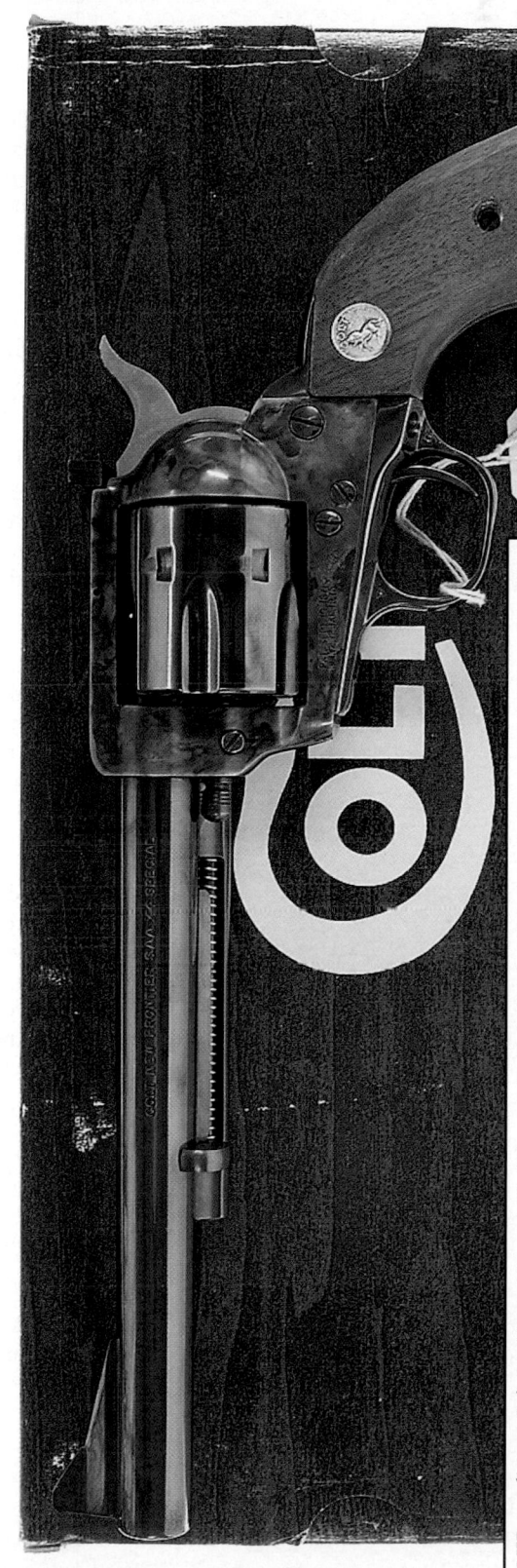

REVOLVERS: PPGS CONDITION FACTORS

NIB condition, Colt SAA New Frontier (3rd Generation), .44 Spl., 7½ in. barrel, ser. no. 07109NF - mfg. 1980. Colt 3rd Generation New Frontier SAAs were manufactured 1978-1981, and this gun sold new for $431.95, $57.45 more than the Standard Model SAA with fixed sights and walnut grips w/colt medalion. Note brilliant case colors on flattop frame, adj. rear sight, elevated front sight, and two-piece plain walnut grips with Colt medallions - all New Frontier distinctive features. This SAA appears unfired with no problems, and also includes the hanging tag, original numbered brown box matching the gun, and all factory paperwork. Every year, original boxes become more important when determining value for major trademark firearms. Remember - there is a big difference in the value of "boxed" guns (especially with pre-WWII mfg.) between an original box numbered to the gun (most desirable), an original non-matching or unnumbered box from the same circa (less desirable), a factory box for a different model or circa (add for box only), or an outright fake (recent reproduction that adds no value). So be careful before paying a premium for a firearm advertised as "includes box", as it could mean almost anything.

REVOLVERS: PPGS CONDITION FACTORS

Photo Percentage Grading System™

Mint condition (99%+), **Smith & Wesson Model 48-3**, .22 Mag, cal., 4 in. barrel, ser. no. 11K8792 - mfg. 1977. While mint condition means "as new", may have been previously sold at retail", it can be trickier than you think to understand, especially with revolvers. This S&W could easily be advertised and sold as NIB, since the original owner claims his wife never shot the gun (this could actually be true!). Closer inspection reveals light striations (also called drag marks) between the cylinder lockup notches, which occurred while cocking the hammer more than a few times in the past. Once vertical striations and notch wear (more apparent on blue finish than on nickel) occurs between the cylinder notches, many dealers and collectors automatically knock the condition factor down to mint or 98%, even if the revolver is truly unfired. So what's the moral to the story? While it's entirely possible for a "NIB" gun to be in less than 100% original condition due to improper storage and handling, a 100% condition factor guarantees new condition. Also note scuffing and edge wear on older S&W box, brilliant case colors on trigger/hammer, mint checkered grips with medallions, and pinned barrel (indicating pre-1981 mfg.).

Twenty-Ninth Edition *Blue Book of Gun Values*™

Twenty-Ninth Edition Blue Book of Gun Values™

Photo Percentage Grading System™

98% condition, cased Smith & Wesson Model 29-2, .44 Mag. cal., 4 in. barrel, ser. no. N480732 - mfg. 1978. Recently manufactured revolvers with a nickel finish or manufactured from stainless steel do not visibly show as much wear as their blued counterparts, even though they may have as much or more use. Note the vertical drag line between the cylinder lockup notches and slight muzzle wear, plus correct case colored hammer and trigger. This model in blue finish with 6 1/2 in. barrel was preferred by Clint Eastwood's character Dirty Harry, and due to its popularity, Model 29 pricing doubled the factory MSR price ($270 in 1978) during the 1970s. Two-piece checkered grips with medallions appear perfect, and S&W wood presentation case was an extra $30 accessory at the time. Any factory accessories that were originally included or available through special order will always add to a gun's desirability.

REVOLVERS: PPGS CONDITION FACTORS

REVOLVERS: PPGS CONDITION FACTORS

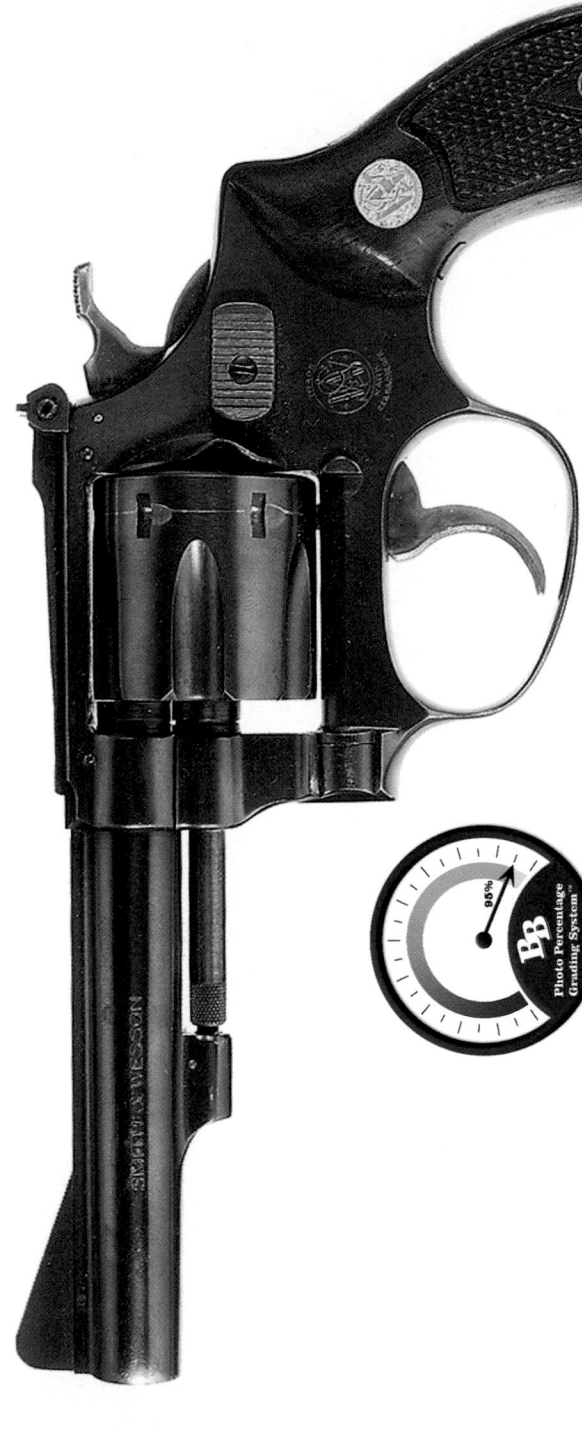

Photo Percentage Grading System™

95% condition, Smith & Wesson Model 34, .22 LR cal., 4 in. barrel, ser. no. 191 - mfg. 1954. 95% on newer mfg. revolvers typically means minor barrel muzzle wear, indicating holster use and a more noticeable wear line between the cylinder lock cutouts. Flat latch cylinder release indicates early mfg., and is worth 25% more than later mfg. Note round butt grip configuration with S&W medallions inset in slightly worn walnut grips with diamond checkering. Careful observation also reveals slight wear on frame and cylinder edges. Bluing is still bright, with several small areas of slight discoloration – case colors on hammer/trigger are near perfect. Whenever a revolver in this condition is encountered, the bore should be near perfect, and the action tight and in tune. Overall, a nice example of early S&W quality that can still be used and purchased for a reasonable price.

Twenty-Ninth Edition *Blue Book of Gun Values*™

Twenty-Ninth Edition *Blue Book of Gun Values*™

Photo Percentage Grading System™

REVOLVERS: PPGS CONDITION FACTORS

90% condition, **Sturm-Ruger Single Six**, .22 LR and .22 Mag. cal. cylinders, 6½ in. barrel, ser. no. 260-95611 - mfg. 1985. You might initially think that this gun's condition is actually better than the 95% S&W on the preceding page. Note that the trigger guard has been chipped and damaged, certainly not indicative of normal wear. Careful observation reveals pitting and metal discoloration on the frame (top and front), hammer, and loading gate (bad), in addition to serious drag marks between the cylinder lock up notches, which indicates a lot of shooting. Original wood grips also show finish wear and scratching. This revolver is a good example of a 90% condition factor with problems, as opposed to a 90% revolver with normal bluing wear. The areas of pitting, freckling, finish discoloration, etc. need to be measured similarly as regular wear when determining the correct condition, and are actually more detrimental to value than normal wear in the same condition factor.. This shooter with problems is worth less than an 80% specimen with ordinary wear, and its only salvation is the original box.

Photo Percentage Grading System™

80% condition, Smith & Wesson .455 Hand Ejector 2nd Model with Canadian proofmarks, .455 Mark II cal., 6½ in. barrel, ser. no. 54318 - mfg. circa 1916. This gun might have made 90% condition if it wasn't for the barrel wear next to frame. Closer examination reveals an earlier area of small barrel pitting that apparently someone overcleaned to the point where it wore off the bluing around the pitting. Also note some discoloration in the barrel bluing, scratches and nicks on barrel, frame, and cylinder, and four exposed frame screws. Checkered wooden grips with S&W medallions show some wear, but hammer/trigger case colors are excellent. Note the lanyard ring on the bottom of the grip frame, standard for this model. While unseen in image, this specimen has both the Commonwealth "BNP" (British Nitro Proof), and Canadian crossed flags, indicating military usage.

Twenty-Ninth Edition Blue Book of Gun Values™

Twenty-Ninth Edition Blue Book of Gun Values™

Photo Percentage Grading System™

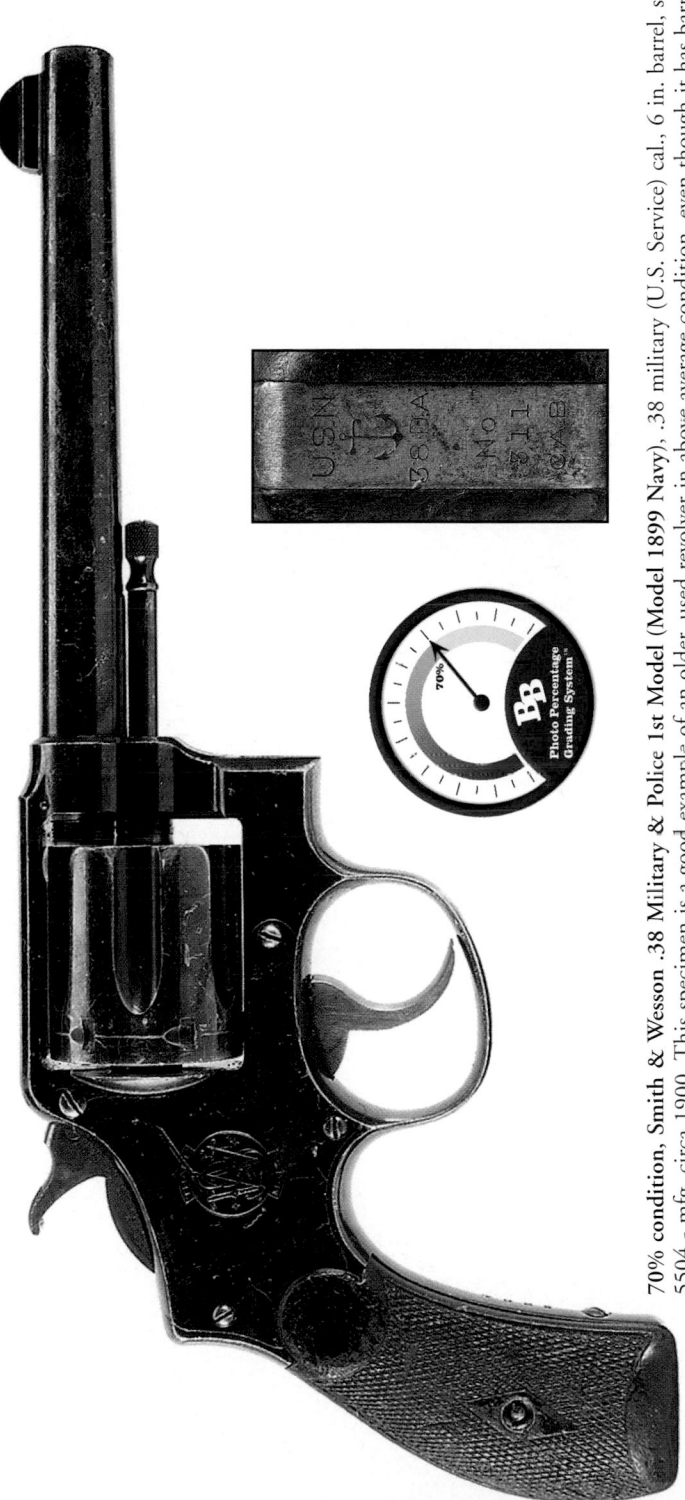

70% condition, Smith & Wesson .38 Military & Police 1st Model (Model 1899 Navy), .38 military (U.S. Service) cal., 6 in. barrel, ser. no. 5504 - mfg. circa 1900. This specimen is a good example of an older, used revolver in above average condition, even though it has barrel and cylinder discoloration and pitting (brown areas) and worn grips (the diamond pattern around the screw is barely visible). This particular revolver is one of 1,000 that were purchased by the U.S. Navy. Inset photo of bottom of grip frame reveals seven line markings with U.S. Navy markings (note anchor) and "CAB" inspector marks. Considering this U.S. Navy Contract model was typically subjected to sea conditions, including salt corrosion, most specimens today are in it is condition factor or worse. Even with this much finish wear, however, the action remains very tight, and the bore is still bright with very little corrosion.

REVOLVERS: PPGS CONDITION FACTORS

60% condition, engraved Spanish copy of Smith & Wesson .32-20 WCF Hand Ejector, .32-20 WCF cal., 6 in. barrel, ser. no. M12256 - mfg. circa 1920s. This revolver's condition factor is based on the amount of original gold plating remaining, which originally covered 100% of the metal surfaces. Observe areas which typically accumulate the least amount of wear on a revolver – the cylinder flutes, bottom of barrel underneath unshrouded ejector rod, upper part of frame, and crane (yoke). Thin gold plating explains the wear on the barrel and lower frame. Mother-of-pearl grips are probably original, but notice the gap between the arched portion of the grip and the frame. If this was an original factory engraved S&W, someone would care, and pay accordingly, but as a Spanish copy with little or no collectibility, this gun gets priced as a fancy shooter.

Photo Percentage Grading System™

Twenty-Ninth Edition *Blue Book of Gun Values*™

Twenty-Ninth Edition *Blue Book of Gun Values*™

Photo Percentage Grading System™

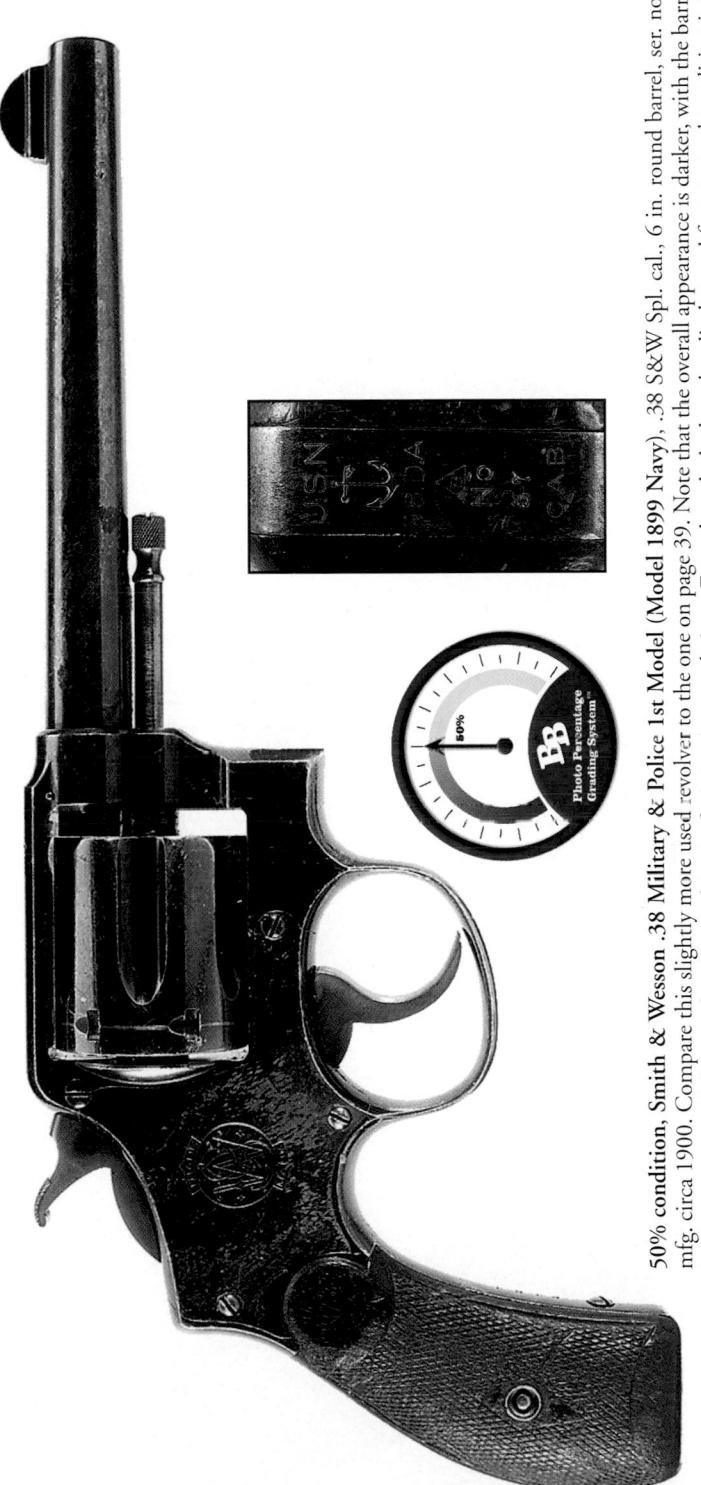

REVOLVERS: PPGS CONDITION FACTORS

50% condition, Smith & Wesson .38 Military & Police 1st Model (Model 1899 Navy), .38 S&W Spl. cal., 6 in. round barrel, ser. no. 5151 - mfg. circa 1900. Compare this slightly more used revolver to the one on page 39. Note that the overall appearance is darker, with the barrel showing more wear, and the rear frame scratching and pitting is very obvious. Even though the barrel, cylinder, and frame metal condition is less than the previous page, the case colors on the hammer and trigger are actually better on this revolver. Again, note the inset with USN and anchor signature. The checkered grips are also in worse condition. Nice, straight slots on frame screw heads on this and the previous revolver indicate this revolver has probably never been taken apart. Older original revolvers in this condition factor or less typically show more pitting and bluing discoloration.

40% condition, Smith & Wesson .38 Military & Police 1st Model (Model 1899 Navy), .38 S&W Spl. cal., 6 in. barrel, ser. no. 5043 - mfg. circa 1900. This Model 1899 Navy would be at least 70% overall, if it wasn't for the major finish deterioration on the rear of the frame – note the brown patina and pitting in back of the S&W logo. Barrel, frame, cylinder scratches, nicks, and gouges are also typical of this condition factor. The ejector rod has also turned a brown patina. As you can see, each gun is unique once you get down to these lower condition factors, and each revolver component (barrel, frame, cylinder, grips, case colors, trigger/hammer) has to be taken into consideration before the overall condition factor can be accurately established. In cases where finish wear is excessive on a single part, it is usually prudent to mention/describe that lower condition factor/problem separately.

Photo Percentage Grading System™

Twenty-Ninth Edition *Blue Book of Gun Values*™

Twenty-Ninth Edition *Blue Book of Gun Values*™

Photo Percentage Grading System™

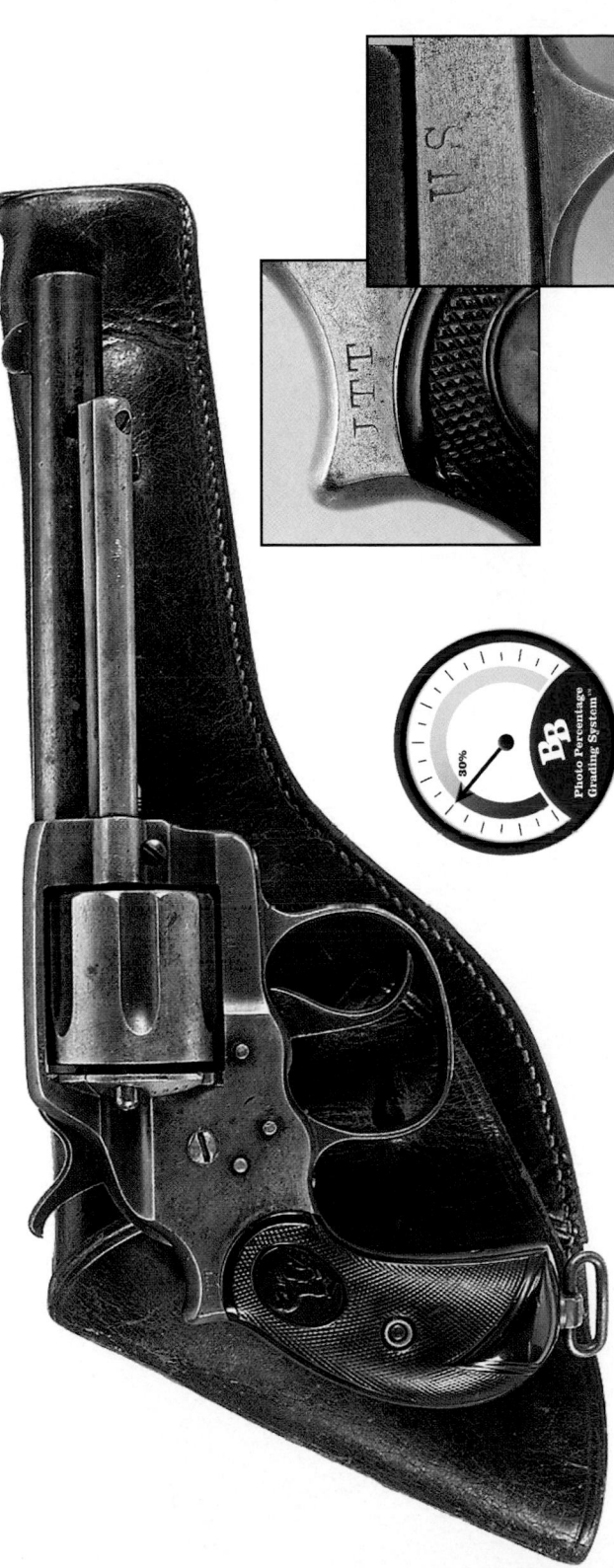

30% condition, U.S. Colt Alaskan Model 1878/1902, .45 LC cal., 6 in. round barrel, ser. no. 45317 - mfg. 1900. Notice how the overall condition of this revolver is approximately in 10% less condition than the S&W on the preceding page. This military marked specimen, which includes "RAC" on left side and "JTT" (John T. Thompson, of Thompson machine gun fame) inspector initials on right side, also has a U.S. property marking. Observe the smooth, overall brownish patina finish, while the barrel exhibits overall pitting, even though the bore is excellent. Note traces of bright barrel blue next to and in front of ejector rod assembly. Screw heads look original, and grips with rampant Colt inserts are worn proportionately with the rest of this gun's finish. Oversize trigger and trigger guard, in addition to the lanyard ring, are distinguishing features of this U.S. military contract model, allowing soldiers to fire it with mittened or gloved hands.

REVOLVERS: PPGS CONDITION FACTORS

20% condition, Colt Model 1901 New Army & Navy, .38 LC cal., 6 in. barrel, ser. no. 2822 - mfg. 1892. Compare the overall finish on this revolver to the one on page 43. This gun's finish has turned mostly brown patina, with the only bright bluing remaining in protected areas (cylinder flutes and front of frame). Note the rust inside of cylinder flutes and upper front portion of frame. Closer examination reveals that frame screws have been amateurishly removed. "RAC" marked grips show moderate wear, but are original, and free of major dings and cracks. This revolver's value is enhanced somewhat because it still has a very tight action and bright bore, which is very important to collectors of older revolvers. Many handgun collectors would rather have a no-problem gun in this condition than one in 50% condition, but with major pitting, a dark bore, and other problems. The original holster and belt accompany this well-worn specimen.

Photo Percentage Grading System™

Photo Percentage Grading System™

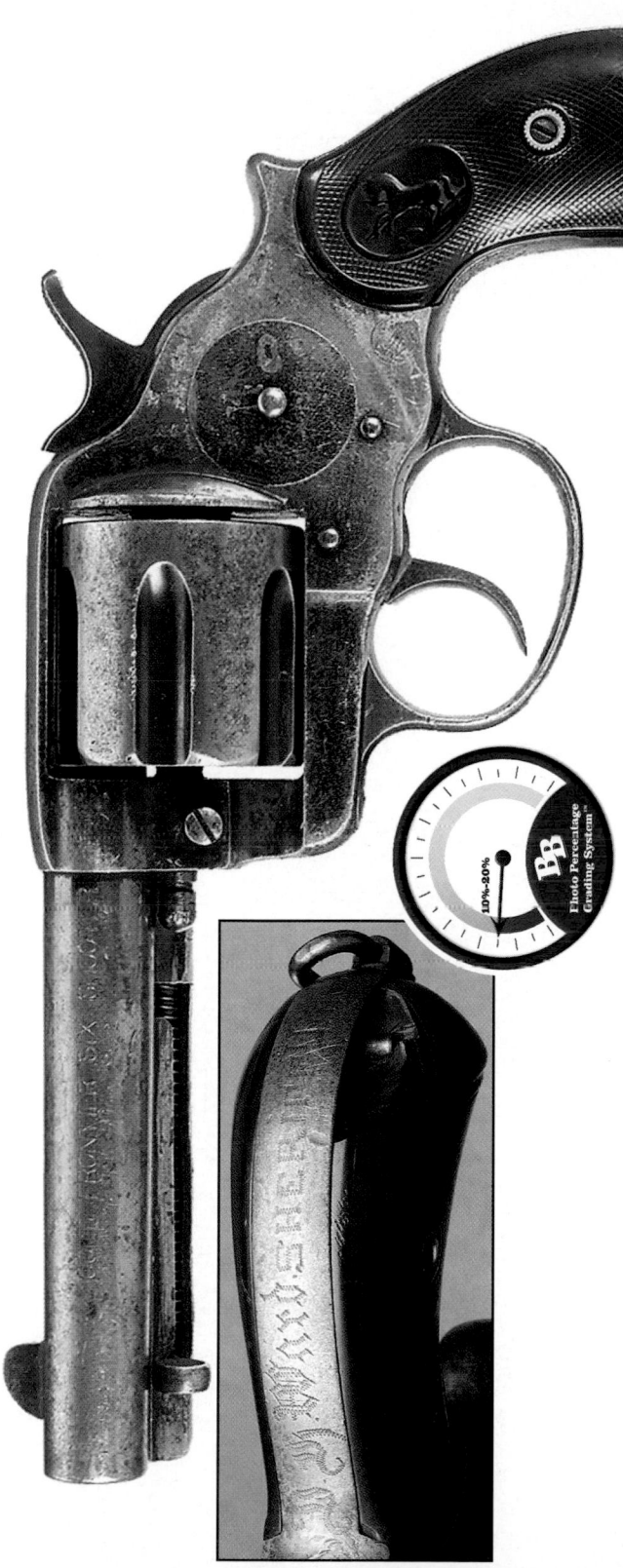

REVOLVERS: PPGS CONDITION FACTORS

10%-20% condition, inscribed Colt Model 1878 DA Frontier Six Shooter, .44-40 WCF cal., 4¾ in. barrel, ser. no. 34108 - mfg. 1894. If the condition factor is less than this, it won't make much of a price difference anyway. Almost all metal surfaces have either no finish or a slight brown patina - note the exterior of cylinder was severely rusted in the past, but cylinder flutes retain a nice brown patina finish. This particular gun's salvation is the 17 pages of documentation that are provided, proving it belonged to "G.H. Ward Sheriff Vinta Co.", the sheriff who captured Butch Cassidy and delivered him to prison - note backstrap inscription. Any gun with a documented, sterling provenance has to be appraised individually. The auction estimate on this revolver was $1,500-$2,500, the Blue Book price range is $555-$685 (for a normal gun), and when the final auction (2007) gavel sounded, it sold for $3,450, including 15% buyer's premium!

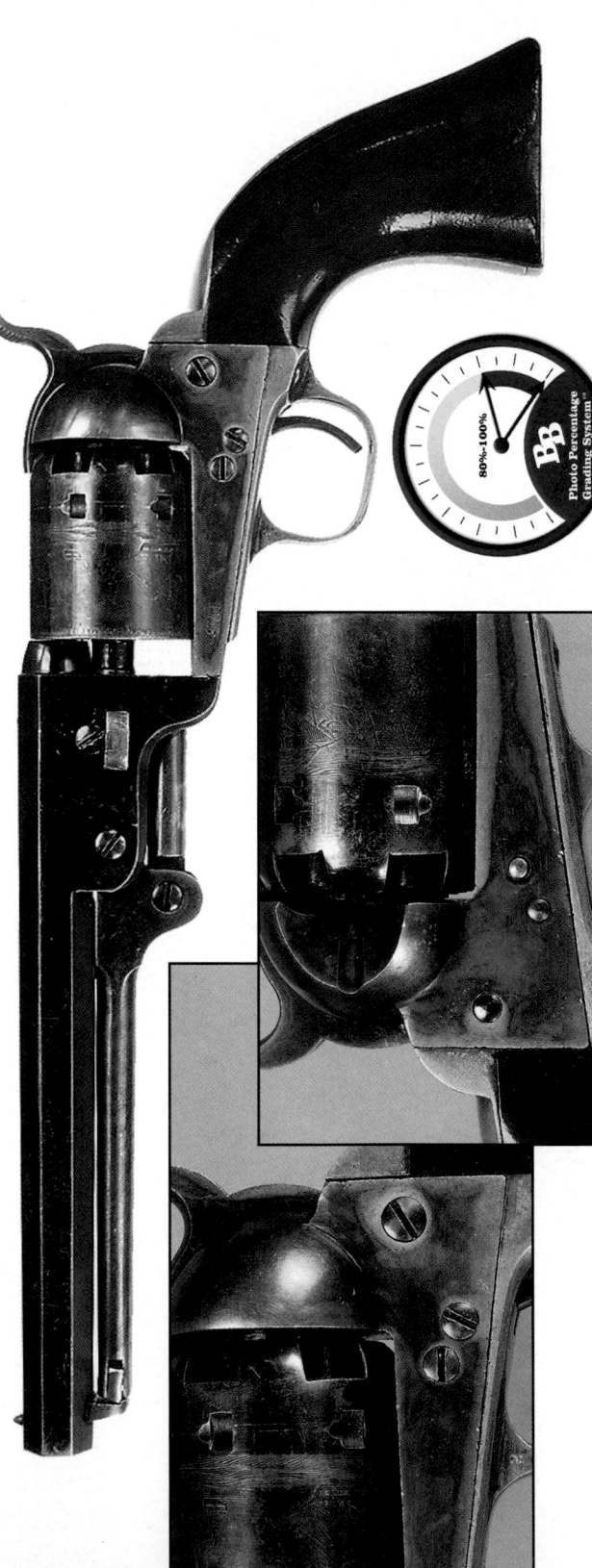

NRA Excellent (over 80% condition), inscribed Colt Model 1851 Navy Fourth Model, .36 cal. percussion, 7½ in. octagon barrel, ser. no. 127080/2 - mfg. 1862. This commercial Colt 1851 Navy was manufactured during the Civil War (1861-1865), and has the late New York barrel address. The frame, barrel, trigger guard, and backstrap all have matching 127080/2 serial numbers, indicating this gun was one of a two-gun presentation set. The backstrap is inscribed "To Major Hill, 45th Reg't OVI" (Ohio Volunteer Infantry). Also verifying this revolver's authenticity is a tintype (older photograph) of Major Hill, his saber and Colt 1851 Navy (not shown). Note the barrel and loading lever retain most of the original finish, strong frame case colors, fire blued untampered frame screws, and excellent original wood grips, all adding up to the NRA Excellent condition factor this revolver deserves. Blue Book value without provenance – approx. $4,500. Auction (2007) price – $11,500.

Photo Percentage Grading System™

Twenty-Ninth Edition *Blue Book of Gun Values*™

Twenty-Ninth Edition *Blue Book of Gun Values*™

Photo Percentage Grading System™

REVOLVERS: NRA ANTIQUE CONDITIONS

NRA Fine (30%-80% condition), Remington New Model Army, .44 cal. percussion, 8 in. octagon barrel, ser. no. 19329 - mfg. circa 1866. Overall, a nice, no problem Remington revolver retaining approx. 40%-50% original finish. Octagon barrel retains much of its bright bluing on the flats, while edges are shiny. Most of the frame and unfluted cylinder have turned a nice brown patina, while two-piece grips show normal handling marks with tiny chips. Action remains tight, and this revolver does not have the "New Model" markings used in later manufacture. While some of these guns were converted into .44 rimfire, this specimen retains its original percussion configuration. Also note the brass trigger guard and excellent condition of the screw heads. Since NRA Fine condition covers everything from 30%-80%, this revolver represents the middle of the NRA Fine condition range. Guns in better condition than this generally retain more bright blue, while guns in worse condition will have more patina.

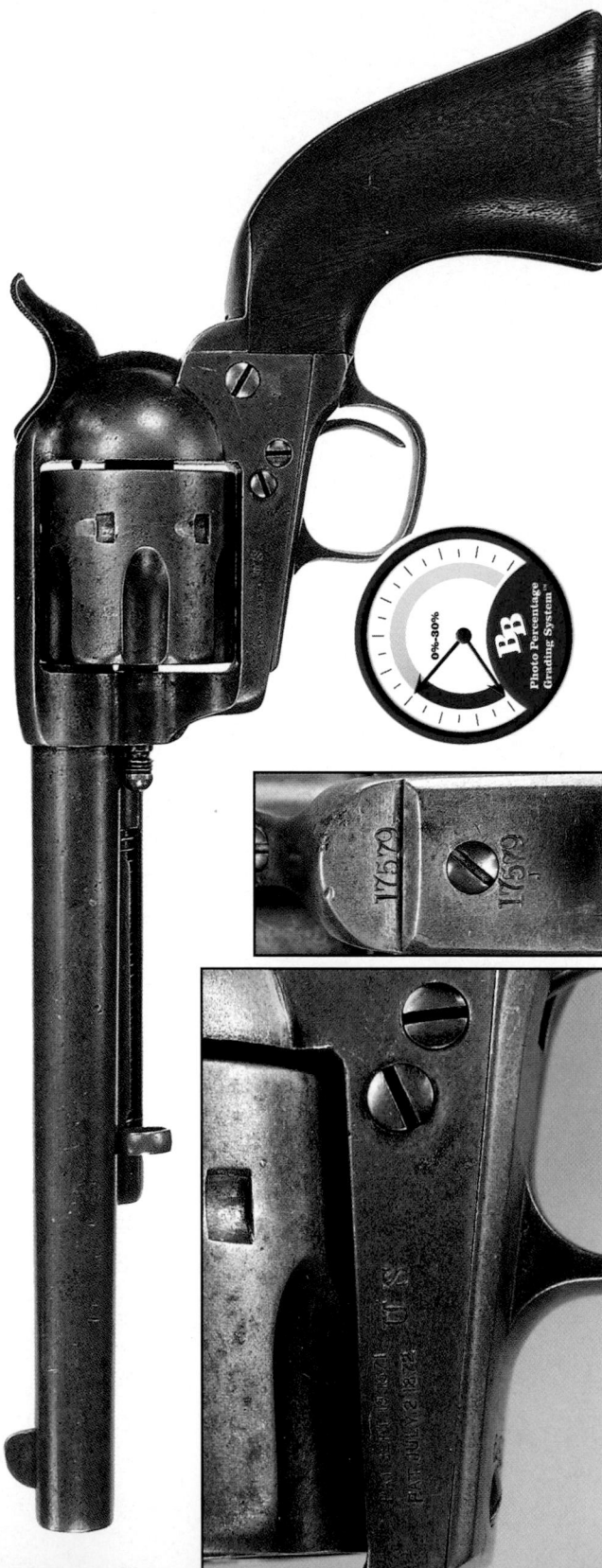

Photo Percentage Grading System™

NRA Very Good (0%-30% condition), U.S. Colt SAA Cavalry Model 1873, .45 Colt cal., ser. no. 17579 - mfg. 1875. Except for protected areas, this gun's original blue and case colored finishes have turned a smooth greyish-brown patina. One-piece walnut grips are fine, with only minor scratches, and matching serial numbers are on all visible components. Note how serial numbers are marked on the frame and trigger guard in the macro image. On 1st Generation SAAs, it always pays to inspect the numbers very carefully, since they were stamped with a rotating roll die. Not only should all the serial numbers look the same, but they should also retain the same vertical positioning in all three areas. Other macro image of "U.S." property stamp marking becomes very important, since revolvers in this serial range were probably issued as replacements to the 7th Cavalry after the Battle of Little Big Horn.

Twenty-Ninth Edition *Blue Book of Gun Values*™

Photo Percentage Grading System™

NRA Good, Colt Model 1849 Pocket, .31 cal. percussion, 6 in. octagon barrel, ser. no. 181985 - mfg. 1860. Note how the finish on this revolver (10%-20%) has turned an overall plum patina, as opposed to the bright bluing and case colors remaining on the 1851 Navy on page 46. Dark areas on barrel and frame indicate major areas of earlier pitting. Brass trigger guard and frame, originally silver plated, indicate that this revolver is a first type, as the second type has steel grip straps. The cylinder has been filed and renumbered to match the two line address, while the grips have been revarnished over the dents and scratches. Screws look good, and this gun's overall condition suggests that it was never abused during its shooting career. This revolver's operating mechanism still functions smoothly, even though the bore is somewhat dark and lightly pitted.

REVOLVERS: NRA ANTIQUE CONDITIONS

REVOLVERS: NRA ANTIQUE CONDITIONS

NRA Fair, Colt Model 1849 Pocket, .31 cal. percussion, 4 in. octagon barrel, ser. no. 186127 - mfg. 1861. The first thing you may note while comparing this gun to the one on the previous page, is that the trigger guard and backstraps are steel instead of brass, indicating that this model is a second type of the 1849 Pocket Model. Finish has turned to a grey/brown patina overall, and metal surfaces have many dings, gouges, and scratches in addition to some previous pitting. While unseen, the backstrap has been filed to remove dents, and the grips are worn at the high spots, but retain almost half their varnish. Several frame screws have been replaced, and the action is in good condition overall. The only NRA condition factor worse than than this is Poor (not pictured), which means that both major and minor parts have been replaced, metal surfaces are deeply pitted, the mechanism is inoperative, and generally the gun is undesirable as a collector's firearm.

Photo Percentage Grading System™

Twenty-Ninth Edition Blue Book of Gun Values™

Twenty-Ninth Edition Blue Book of Gun Values™

Photo Percentage Grading System™

NIB condition, Colt MK IV Series 70 Government Model, .45 ACP cal., 5 in. barrel, ser. no. 32386B70 - mfg. 1979. When encountered in NIB condition, semi-automatic pistols by design show less wear than revolvers. Even though a pistol may be unfired, its semi-auto action may have been racked many times, and this type of inspection use doesn't show up as wear as with the revolver. This Colt Series 70 Government Model with nickel finish has never been more desirable, and NIB specimens like this one are now priced over $1,250. Note the older brown Colt box with scuff marks and edge wear, indicating that this pistol, for whatever reasons, has done some traveling, even though it remains unfired. NIB condition also means that everything that was supplied with the gun originally is still in the box/case, including the instruction manual, warranty card, lock (if applicable), and other factory materials.

PISTOLS: PPGS CONDITION FACTORS

PISTOLS: PPGS CONDITION FACTORS

Mint condition, Mauser Banner Bolo Broomhandle, 7.63mm Mauser cal., 3.9 in. barrel, ser. no. 658391, mfg. circa 1926. If you are a condition freak, it doesn't get much better than this! Mauser made over one million broomhandles, and nearly 300,000 (serial numbered from 515xxx-793xxx) were late post-WWI Mauser Banner Bolos whose features included a shorter barrel and the smaller configured grip. The vast majority of Bolos were rust blued with fire blued small parts. On many early Mauser broomhandles, most of the small parts were struck with a matching assembly number. Once completed, the guns were shipped with a matching shoulder stock (not shown) that allowed the attached pistol to be used as a carbine. Although common from the standpoint of production, most ended up in China where they were "used hard and put away wet." In today's market, it is very difficult to find a gun like this one that is all matching with more than 99% finish and a perfect bore.

Photo Percentage Grading System™

Twenty-Ninth Edition *Blue Book of Gun Values*™

Twenty-Ninth Edition Blue Book of Gun Values™

Photo Percentage Grading System™

PISTOLS: PPGS CONDITION FACTORS

98% condition, Fabrique Nationale (F.N.). **Hi-Power**, 9mm Para. cal., 4 ¾ in. barrel, ser. no. 54066 - mfg. circa early 1950s. Those of you who can tell the difference in coloring between the various bluing techniques will immediately recognize this gun as being rust-blued, correct for this post-WWII F.N. pistol, as is the ring hammer. Even a little bit of additional holster wear on the front of the slide and frame would knock this specimen out of its 98% condition factor. A big plus is that the front grip strap does not show any wear or even light freckling, an indication that this pistol has spent a lot more time in its W. German police issue holster than in someone's hands. Walnut grip checkering is almost perfect, and light cleaning would probably remove the dirt/light corrosion in the slide serrations. Note definitive Belgian proof marks on slide and frame, fixed sights, and the light metal blotching in middle of top slide legend. Original issue black leather holster also adds value to this pistol.

PISTOLS: PPGS CONDITION FACTORS

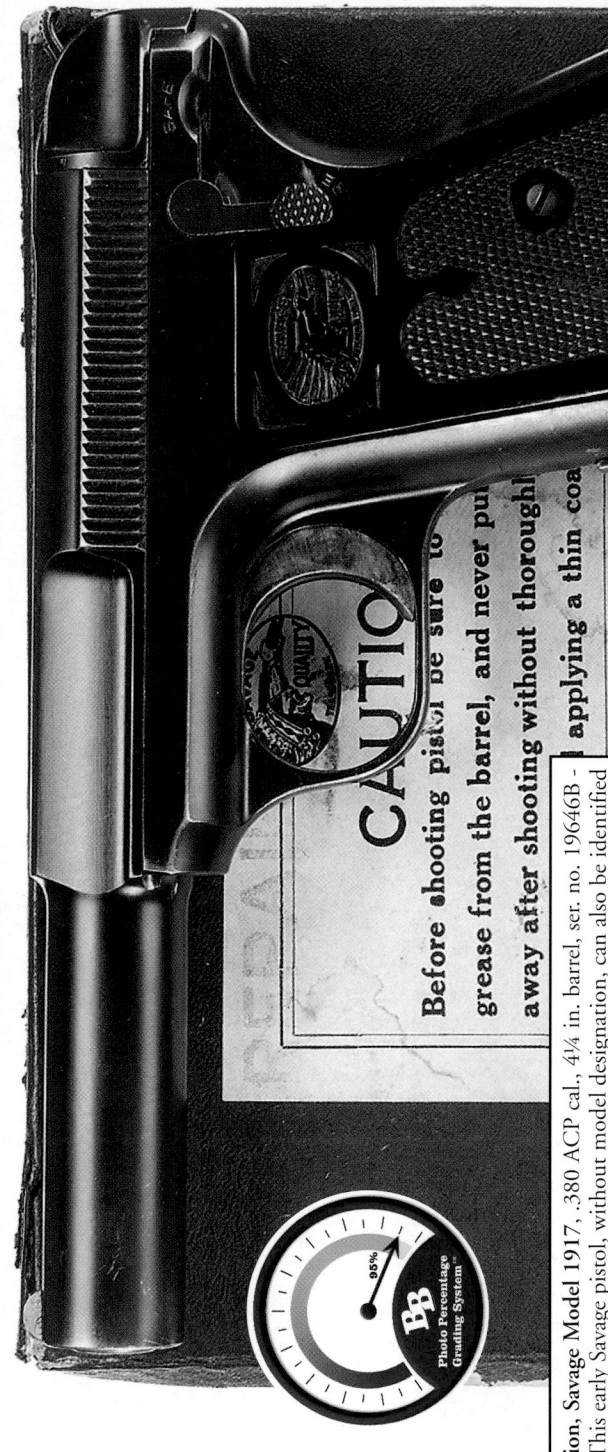

Photo Percentage Grading System™

95% condition, Savage Model 1917, .380 ACP cal., 4¼ in. barrel, ser. no. 19646B - mfg. 1920. This early Savage pistol, without model designation, can also be identified by its caliber, hammer spur, and trapezoid grips. Notice there is more wear on the sharp metal edges, especially around lower front grip strap. Case colors on trigger remain vivid and black rubber grips show light scratching. Manufactured during the first year of America's prohibition, the original black cardboard box helps this pistol's value. Clean, major trademark, no problem pistols like this one with its superior original condition, have traditionally been no downside risk investments for their owners. Maybe the best part about 95% condition is that you can actually enjoy shooting these guns once in a while, without negatively affecting the value, if properly maintained.

Twenty-Ninth Edition *Blue Book of Gun Values™*

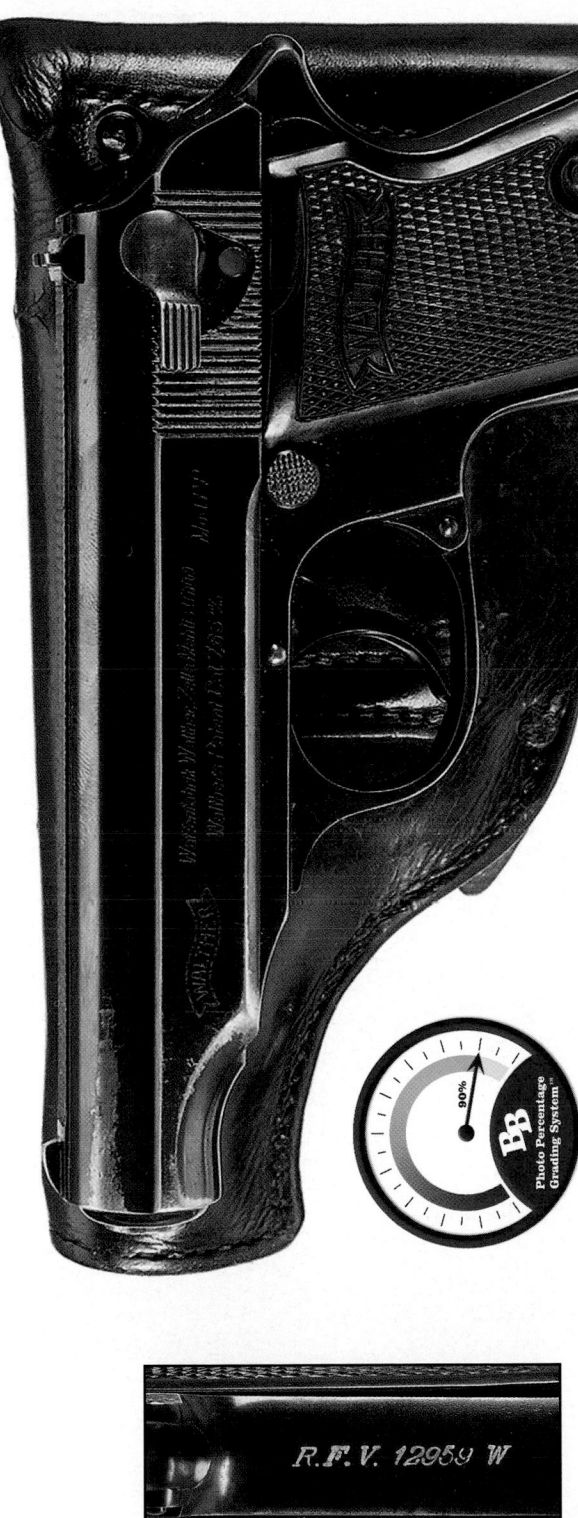

PISTOLS: PPGS CONDITION FACTORS

90% condition, Walther PP w/R.F.V. marking and holster, 7.65mm (.32 ACP) cal., 3¾ in. barrel, ser. no. 986819. Mfg. circa late 1930's. Most of the wear on this pistol has accumulated at the front of the frame and barrel, indicating a lifetime of holster usage. Metal surfaces in back of the trigger guard are an easy 95%. R.F.V. backstrap marking (see inset) indicate this pistol was made for Hitler's Reich Finance Administration. Crown N proof-marks indicate pre-April, 1940 mfg. The unmarked holster contains an extra magazine. Original black plastic grips show limited usage and are in excellent condition. Perfect action and crisp bore enhance this gun's value. The original, early Walther Models PP and smaller PPK are still benchmarks for quality, reliability, and design. The Walther PP was the world's first double action pistol, and pre-war and WWII production has become very collectible. And don't forget, the legendary James Bond carried a PPK for decades.

PISTOLS: PPGS CONDITION FACTORS

80% condition, Walther P.38 Pistol code AC-45 w/holster, 9mm Para. cal., 4 7/8 in. barrel, ser. no. 2622b. This P.38 double action pistol was manufactured towards the end of the war during 1945. The AC-45 code (not shown, left side of slide) designates Walther production (byf was Mauser, and cyq was Spreewerke), and the polishing, bluing, and overall finish were not up to par with earlier manufacture during 1938-1944. During the end of WWII, the Germans were taking quality control shortcuts to get pistols into the hands of the ever decreasing number of desperate German soldiers. Close examination reveals machine cutter lines on both the barrel and side of slide. Also note metal scratching and thinning of the blue in trigger guard area. Not visible in this image is the wear on front grip strap and lower trigger guard, retaining almost no original blue, which decreases this pistol's condition another 10%. Black grips are excellent, and original holster is stamped with the "WaA36" code.

Photo Percentage Grading System™

Twenty-Ninth Edition Blue Book of Gun Values™

Photo Percentage Grading System™

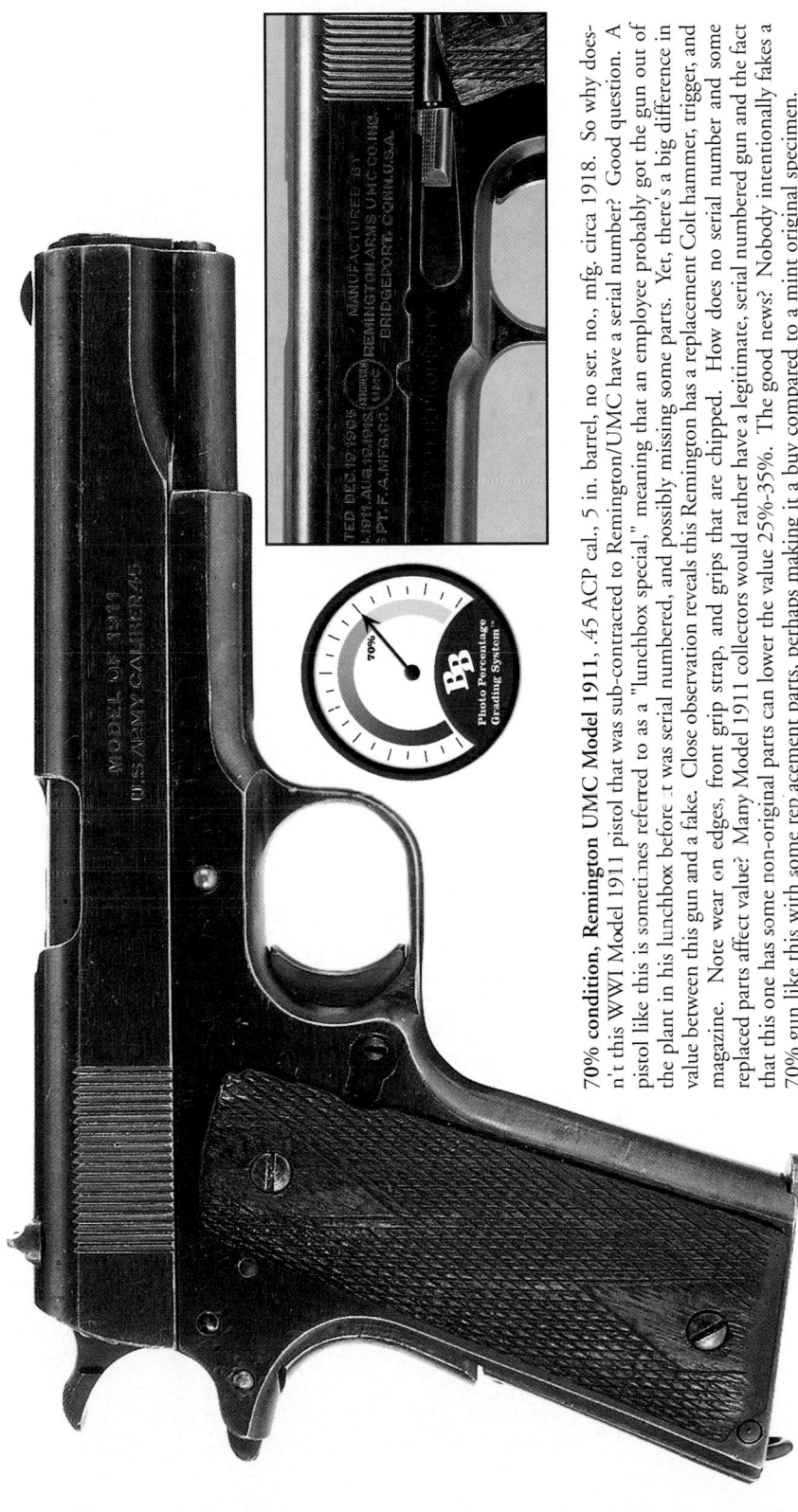

70% condition, Remington UMC Model 1911, .45 ACP cal., 5 in. barrel, no ser. no., mfg. circa 1918. So why doesn't this WWI Model 1911 pistol that was sub-contracted to Remington/UMC have a serial number? Good question. A pistol like this is sometimes referred to as a "lunchbox special," meaning that an employee probably got the gun out of the plant in his lunchbox before it was serial numbered, and possibly missing some parts. Yet, there's a big difference in value between this gun and a fake. Close observation reveals this Remington has a replacement Colt hammer, trigger, and magazine. Note wear on edges, front grip strap, and grips that are chipped. How does no serial number and some replaced parts affect value? Many Model 1911 collectors would rather have a legitimate, serial numbered gun and the fact that this one has some non-original parts can lower the value 25%-35%. The good news? Nobody intentionally fakes a 70% gun like this with some replacement parts, perhaps making it a buy compared to a mint original specimen.

PISTOLS: PPGS CONDITION FACTORS

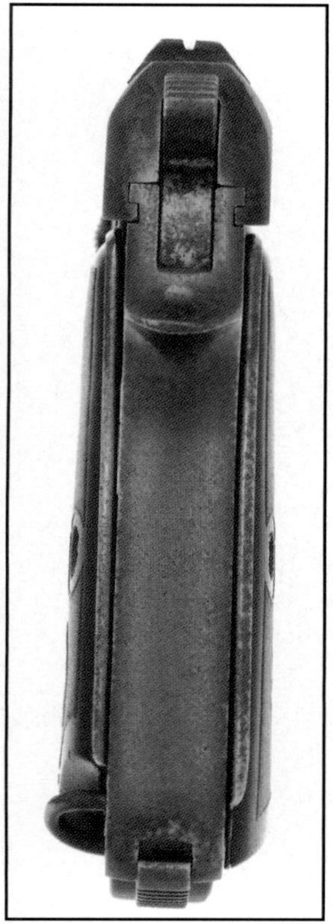

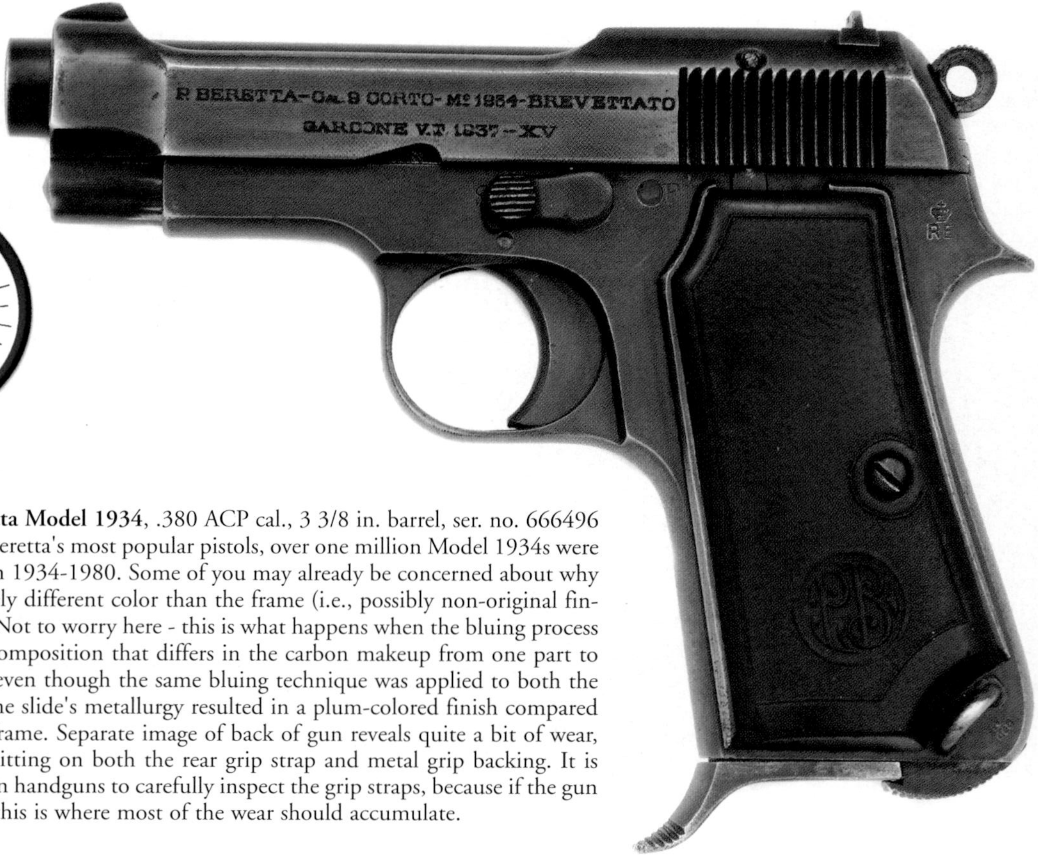

PISTOLS: PPGS CONDITION FACTORS

60% condition, Beretta Model 1934, .380 ACP cal., 3 3/8 in. barrel, ser. no. 666496 - mfg. 1937. One of Beretta's most popular pistols, over one million Model 1934s were manufactured between 1934-1980. Some of you may already be concerned about why the slide is a completely different color than the frame (i.e., possibly non-original finish or replaced slide). Not to worry here - this is what happens when the bluing process interacts with metal composition that differs in the carbon makeup from one part to another. In this case, even though the same bluing technique was applied to both the slide and the frame, the slide's metallurgy resulted in a plum-colored finish compared to the normal blued frame. Separate image of back of gun reveals quite a bit of wear, corrosion, and light pitting on both the rear grip strap and metal grip backing. It is especially important on handguns to carefully inspect the grip straps, because if the gun was extensively used, this is where most of the wear should accumulate.

Photo Percentage Grading System™

Twenty-Ninth Edition *Blue Book of Gun Values*™

50% condition, Mauser Standard Pre-War Commercial Broomhandle w/Stock, 7.63mm Mauser cal., 5½ in. barrel, ser. no. 95950 - mfg. circa 1909. If only someone would have taken better care of this Broomhandle during its lifetime. The barrel shows a lot of serious pitting, and you can see what happens if you get the steel wool (maybe sandpaper in this case) out and get aggressive! Receiver rail is almost completely shiny, and magazine well housing in front of trigger guard is very scratched, and has serious pitting on the bottom. Grips are worn, but match this Broomhandle's overall condition factor. Stock is original, but has been broken and poorly repaired – also, it does not match. Action is mechanically tight, and bore is very good. This is a classic example of a very collectible pistol losing over 65% of its potential value because the owner(s) didn't give it some TLC when it needed it the most.

Photo Percentage Grading System™

40% condition, Colt Model 1905, .45 ACP cal., 4 7/8 in. barrel, ser. no. 1656 - mfg. early 1907. As you can see, this gun has problems. Note the original bright bluing on frame, but overall grey finish on slide, indicating that someone acid cleaned this gun thoroughly in the past, probably trying to clean up the heavy pitting on the right side (not shown). Since the frame is one condition factor (thinning blue), and the slide is a totally different condition (grey patina), this pistol's overall condition factor had to be interpolated based on the overall appearance. Note heavy frame scratching next to grips. Grip straps are also worn and grey, and left wood grip has a crack above the top screw. Action is mechanically good, and all parts are original. This gun has lost most of its collector value because of its altered condition and poor eye appeal.

Twenty-Ninth Edition *Blue Book of Gun Values*™

Twenty-Ninth Edition *Blue Book of Gun Values*™

Photo Percentage Grading System™

PISTOLS: PPGS CONDITION FACTORS

30% condition, Colt Model 1905, .45 ACP cal., 4 7/8 in. barrel, ser. no. 3730 - mfg. 1909. Most of this pistol's lifetime is behind it. Note how the original bluing has turned a dark grey patina. the front of the slide is shiny, and there is pitting throughout the slide. Frame has also turned to a mostly brown patina, and some bluing remains in protected areas. The grip straps are very worn and have turned grey, while the checkered, revarnished grips also show a lot of wear. Action is mechanically okay. This gun is a good example of when value is determined almost completely by collectibility, not shootability. 500 of this model were factory slotted for a shoulder stock (this one isn't), making it a rare configuration that automatically adds 50% to the pistol's value, regardless of condition. Most pistols in this condition factor are not very collectible, but this rare Colt is an exception.

PISTOLS: PPGS CONDITION FACTORS

20% condition, Colt Model 1905, 45 ACP cal., 4 7/8 in. barrel, ser. no. 1840 - mfg. 1907. We know what you're think-ing – how did the front of this gun become so pitted? Even CSI undergraduates will quickly figure out what happened in this case. At one point (maybe several), the gun and its holster got very wet. Unfortunately, the gun was stored in the wet holster, and witness the results. Serious pitting is an understatement to describe the wear on the front and rear of this unfor-tunate pistol. The only thing this gun still has going for it is that it can still claim originality and functionality. Grips are well-worn, and the points are long gone on the checkering. Rampant Colt logo is still visible on rear of slide. The only original finish remaining on this gun is in the protected area on the upper frame around the radiused grips.

Photo Percentage Grading System™

Twenty-Ninth Edition *Blue Book of Gun Values*™

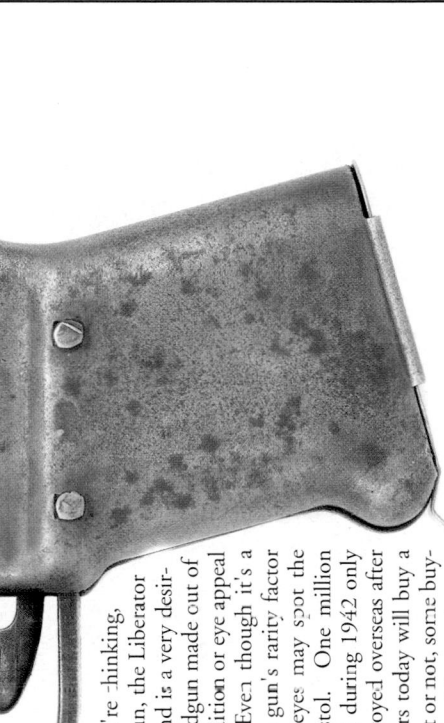

10% condition, Liberator single shot pistol, .45 ACP cal., 4 in. smoothbore barrel, no ser. no., mfg. 1942. I know what you're thinking, and it's wrong! While appearing to be Uncle Ernie's long lost toy gun, the Liberator was originally designed for resistance fighters in Europe and Asia, and is a very desirable WWII contract pistol. So how can a poorly manufactured handgun made out of pot metal that's been riveted and spot-welded together with no condition or eye appeal possibly be worth a lot more than a nice WWII Colt 1911A1? Even though it's a weirdo, the Liberator is a classic example of what happens when a gun's rarity factor overrules everything else when determining desirability. Trained eyes may spot the shiny replacement floorplate - a common occurrence on this pistol. One million Liberators were made in less than 11 weeks (one every 6.6 seconds) during 1942 only at a cost of $1.73 each, and most of the guns ended up being destroyed overseas after the war. None were issued to U.S. troops, and as a result, collectors today will buy a Liberator in virtually any condition, as long as it's original. Believe it or not, some buyers at major auctions are paying over $5,000 for an average condition Liberator!

NRA Modern New Condition (100%), Browning Hi-Power, 9mm Para. cal., 4 5/8 in. barrel, ser. no. 245NV56269, mfg. 1995. The Hi-Power was John M. Browning's last pistol design, and production began in Belgium during 1935. It was immediately accepted, and many military contracts followed shortly. Being a venerable work horse for decades, the HP is still in action around the world today, and its design and functionality are truly ageless. This silver chrome finished HP variation with gold trigger, molded rubber grips with Browning medallions, adj. rear sight, and parkerized small parts was manufactured by F.N. in Herstal, Belgium, and shipped to Portugal for assembly and packaging. Even though NRA Modern New condition generally means not previously sold at retail on currently manufactured guns, this pistol was never fired by its original owner, nor does it show any wear. It is entirely possible for a NIB, unfired gun to accumulate wear if it has been displayed, handled, holstered, improperly stored, or overcleaned. This condition factor means NIB in every respect, with no excuses.

Photo Percentage Grading System™

NRA Modern Perfect Condition (Mint - 99%), High Standard Model A, .22 LR cal., 4½ in. barrel, ser. no. 91591, mfg. late 1941. If you're a .22 cal. pistol collector and like condition, it doesn't get much better than this wartime, boxed High Standard Model A with original receipt from Abercrombie & Fitch. NRA Perfect translates into mint condition in every respect, and this gun certainly qualifies, perhaps test fired only, spending most of its life in the slightly tattered yellow and black two-piece box. Observe the checkered walnut grips with no wear on sharp points, perfect bluing with no wear on edges or end of barrel, and unturned screws still aligned. The older the gun, the harder it is to find one in this condition factor. On many older and desirable collectible firearms, values can double over NRA Excellent. Approximately 7,300 Model As were manufactured circa 1938-1942, but less than a handful may still remain in this condition with original box and bill of sale.

PISTOLS: NRA MODERN CONDITIONS

PISTOLS: NRA MODERN CONDITIONS

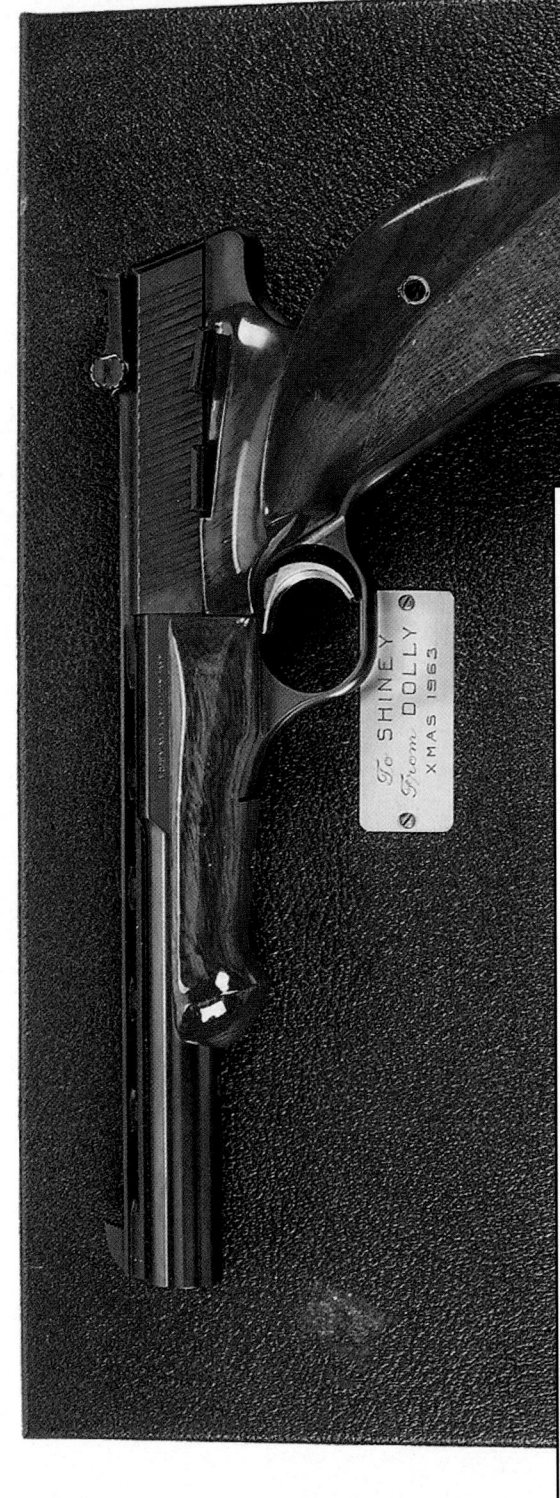

To SHINEY
From DOLLY
XMAS 1963

Photo Percentage Grading System™

NRA Modern Excellent Condition (95%-98%), cased Browning Medallist, .22 LR cal., 6¾ in. barrel, ser. no. 30491T3 - mfg. 1963. This beautiful Browning Medallist in NRA Excellent condition must have made Shiney happy after Santa (Dolly) delivered it during Xmas of 1963! This cased target pistol has always been popular due to its ergonomically enhanced French walnut checkered grips with thumbrest, separate forend, VR barrel, and unique case with accessories. Obviously, Shiney didn't take a shine to shooting this gun, as there is no visible exterior wear. Even the corners of the vinyl covered presentation case are perfect, and the inside contains the original cartridge block, three barrel weights, and folding screwdriver. During the mid-1990's, Medallists like this were selling in the $575-$650 range – now they're in the $1,00-$1,200 range. Whenever possible, pay a little bit more for NIB or mint condition – you'll get it back in spades when you sell.

Twenty-Ninth Edition *Blue Book of Gun Values™*

NRA Modern Very Good Refinished Condition (80%-95%), Webley & Scott MK I, .455 Webley auto cal., 5 in. barrel, ser. no. 100407, mfg. 1913. Normally, refinished guns are not pictured in the PPGS, except when they can provide the reader information on condition which can be useful. Notice how the white marker has enhanced a soft, nearly polished off slide legend. This relatively rare, pre-WWI English pistol has been poorly reblued and polished at an earlier date. Note the previous pitting on the frame and barrel, which was poorly polished (observe horizontal slide serrations and rounded corners on slide), then cheaply refinished by hot dipping it into a bluing tank. Rubber grips also show wear, with light cracking, and the action also needs some adjustment. Unfortunately, this pistol's collector value has been virtually ruined, but will provide someone who is not concerned about originality, and is looking for a "buy." The problem is, a badly refinished gun like this very rarely goes up in value.

PISTOLS: NRA MODERN CONDITIONS

Photo Percentage Grading System™

NRA Modern Good Condition (60%-80%), Mauser 42 Code Luger, 9mm Para. cal., 4 in. barrel, ser. no. 9746y, mfg. 1939. The best compliment you can give this Nazi-period WWII Luger is that it's all original, and except for condition, there are no major problems. Wear on this pistol is where it should be-on the sideplate, barrel, and gripstraps-due to holster wear and usage. Also note pitting on barrel, lower sideplate, and top of slide. All parts are matching, with the exception of a correct, aluminum base magazine. In today's Luger marketplace, original condition is everything when determining value, and many collectors will pay a premium for the quality of early wartime manufacture. While this pistol's value is currently in the $1,150 range, a mint specimen with original holster and two matching mags (be wary of pistol refinishing and renumbered magazines) may sell for over $4,000!

Twenty-Ninth Edition *Blue Book of Gun Values*™

NRA Modern Fair Condition (20%-60%), CZ Model 27, 7.65mm cal., 4 ¾ in., ser. no. 414459, mfg. circa 1944. Manufactured in late WWII, with not a lot of time left for proper polishing and finishing (note rough horizontal machining marks on slide), this semi-auto pistol originally had a thin phosphate finish, which has turned into a grayish patina overall. Marked with the "WaA76" Waffenampt code on the frame, this Nazi-era pistol could probably tell some interesting stories about its life. Note the plastic grips with the circle CZ logo, indicating manufacture in Czechoslovakia. Observe finish discoloring on trigger and around the trigger guard. In its current condition factor, most collectors would pass on this gun, but this little WWII-era pistol has no major problems, and would still make an inexpensive, decent shooter. When condition lower than this is encountered, it won't make much difference on the price, as it's already bottomed out based on its shooting value.

GIANFRANCO PEDERSOLI
Master Engraver

by Dag Sundseth

Edited by S.P. Fjestad & Elena Micheli-Lamboy

While there can be some spirited discussion as to which country makes the finest long arms produced currently, there can be no argument about who has the highest concentration of master engravers. It's Italy, where these artists are called "Maestro Incisori". One of the country's finest is Gianfranco Pedersoli, whose extraordinary engraving career has spanned over 45 years, and his unique style has graced guns for Beretta, Fabbri, F.lli Rizzini, Famars, Piotti, and many other best quality custom gun makers.

This new *Gianfranco Pedersoli - Master Engraver* is a 212-page, deluxe hardbound color book featuring stunning images and first person captions of his best works, in addition to separate chapters on engraved knives and jewelry. Don't miss this first in a series, oversized publication (9x12 in.) on of one of the world's premier engravers.

Available in either standard edition for $65.00 or limited deluxe slipcased edition for $150. To order or to get more information, including sample pages, please visit www.bluebookinc.com, or call toll free domestically: 800-877-4867, ext. 3. Don't wait until it's too late!

"Both Ivo and myself have known Gianfranco Pedersoli for years, and as one of Italy's finest master engravers, many of our customers have requested that Pedersoli perform the engraving on their special order Fabbris. Being able to execute any type or style of engraving at its highest level is also a tremendous advantage for him. While famous for his masks and grotesques, perhaps his greatest asset is being able to successfully combine elaborate ornamentation with perfectly created figures and animals, all with a high degree of detail and imagination. We are very proud of the engraving Pedersoli has done for Fabbri, and our customers couldn't be more pleased."
- Tullio Fabbri, Fabbri s.n.c.

Twenty-Ninth Edition
Blue Book of Gun Values™ *2008*

S	APRIL					S
		1	2	3	4	5
6	7	8	9	10	11	12
13	14	15	16	17	18	19
20	21	22	23	24	25	26
27	28	29	30			

S	MAY					S
			1	2	3	
4	5	6	7	8	9	10
11	12	13	14	15	16	17
18	19	20	21	22	23	24
25	26	27	28	29	30	31

S	JUNE					S
1	2	3	4	5	6	7
8	9	10	11	12	13	14
15	16	17	18	19	20	21
22	23	24	25	26	27	28
29	30					

S	JULY					S
		1	2	3	4	5
6	7	8	9	10	11	12
13	14	15	16	17	18	19
20	21	22	23	24	25	26
27	28	29	30	31		

S	AUGUST					S
					1	2
3	4	5	6	7	8	9
10	11	12	13	14	15	16
17	18	19	20	21	22	23
24	25	26	27	28	29	30
31						

S	SEPTEMBER					S
	1	2	3	4	5	6
7	8	9	10	11	12	13
14	15	16	17	18	19	20
21	22	23	24	25	26	27
28	29	30				

S	OCTOBER					S
		1	2	3	4	
5	6	7	8	9	10	11
12	13	14	15	16	17	18
19	20	21	22	23	24	25
26	27	28	29	30	31	

S	NOVEMBER					S
						1
2	3	4	5	6	7	8
9	10	11	12	13	14	15
16	17	18	19	20	21	22
23	24	25	26	27	28	29
30						

S	DECEMBER					S
	1	2	3	4	5	6
7	8	9	10	11	12	13
14	15	16	17	18	19	20
21	22	23	24	25	26	27
28	29	30	31			

Twenty-Ninth Edition
Blue Book of Gun Values™ *2009*

S	JANUARY					S
				1	2	3
4	5	6	7	8	9	10
11	12	13	14	15	16	17
18	19	20	21	22	23	24
25	26	27	28	29	30	31

S	FEBRUARY					S
1	2	3	4	5	6	7
8	9	10	11	12	13	14
15	16	17	18	19	20	21
22	23	24	25	26	27	28

S	MARCH					S
1	2	3	4	5	6	7
8	9	10	11	12	13	14
15	16	17	18	19	20	21
22	23	24	25	26	27	28
29	30	31				

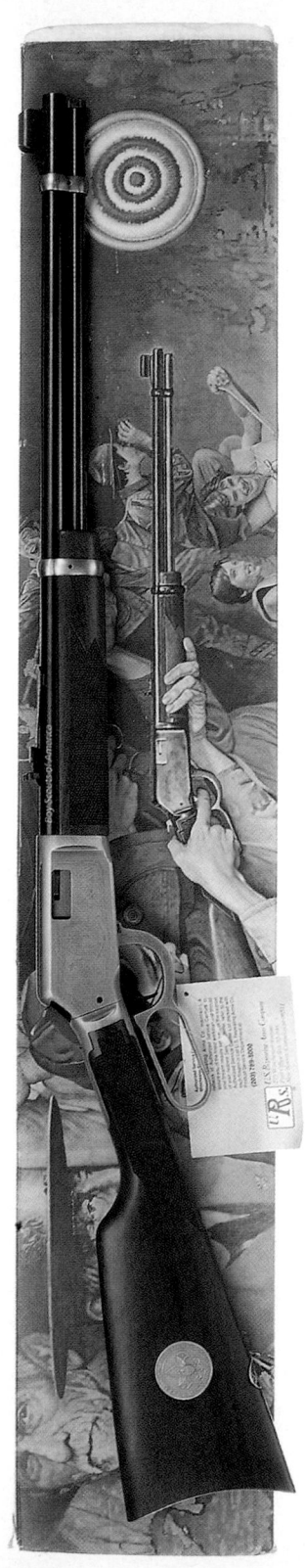

NIB condition, Winchester Model 9422 Boy Scouts of America Commemorative, .22 LR cal., 20 in. round barrel, ser. no. BSA3002 - mfg. 1985. With commemoratives, it is very important to have the box(es), paperwork (including warranty card), and any other accessories/accoutrements that came with the gun when it left the factory. Since most commemoratives are never used or shot, proper storage is the key to keeping them truly NIB - this becomes especially important on silver, gold, or bright nickel finishes, since they have a tendency to naturally tarnish. Commemoratives and limited editions that have been shot and don't have the original box or paperwork are nothing more than fancy shooters most of the time and are priced accordingly with little or no premium. Because the commemorative consumer is now more in charge (consumers now own most of the guns since distributor/dealer inventories are depleted) than during the 1960s-1980s, commemorative firearms values are possibly as strong as they have ever been. When the supply side of commemorative economics has to be purchased from knowledgeable collectors or savvy dealers and demand stays the same or increases slightly, prices have no choice but to go up. If and when the manufacturers crank up the commemorative production runs again (and it won't be like the good old days), the old marketplace characteristics may reappear. Until then, however, the commemorative marketplace remains steady, with values having become more predictable. Manufacturers today are focusing their efforts more on special/limited editions rather than factory commemoratives, as these variations are typically subcontracted by other companies and organizations, which means the manufacturers get paid faster without the extra expense of advertising and marketing. Two versions of this model, the Boy Scout (15,000 mfg. - original issue price was $495) and the Eagle Scout (1,000 mfg. - original issue price was $1,710), were manufactured to commemorate the Boy Scouts 75th Anniversary in 1985. Some well-heeled Eagle Scouts at the time paid as much as $5,000 to get an Eagle Scout model! In today's marketplace, an NIB Boy Scout model is valued at $1,000, while the Eagle Scout is $6,000, more than double its original 1985 MSR.

Photo Percentage Grading System™

Twenty-Ninth Edition *Blue Book of Gun Values™*

Twenty-Ninth Edition Blue Book of Gun Values™

Photo Percentage Grading System™

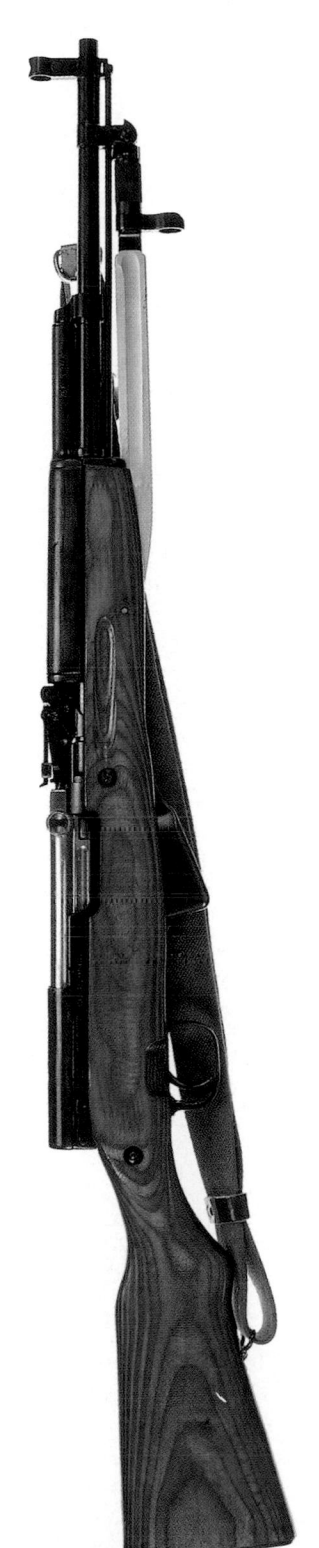

Mint Condition, Russian SKS, 7.62x39mm Russian cal., 20 in. barrel, ser. no. Hh1244 (Cyrillic lettering), mfg. date unknown. The SKS semi-auto rifle was adopted by the Soviet military in 1949, two years after the select-fire AK-47. Most of the recently imported Russian SKSs came from military stockpiles, and were refurbished at the Tula Arms Works. Today, the most collectible SKS models are East German, North Korean, or North Vietnam manufacture. This particular Russian manufactured configuration with brown laminated stock, tilting blade style bayonet, and canvas sling became very popular before the Crime Bill was enacted in September of 1994. During this time period, Chinese imports starting flooding the marketplace, reducing the prices of all SKS rifles, despite the fact that the more recent Chinese imports are typically of poor quality with thumbhole stocks. Although millions of SKSs have been imported over the years, NIB examples like this Russian manufactured specimen are actually getting harder to find, and prices are going up slightly.

RIFLES: PPGS CONDITION FACTORS

RIFLES: PPGS CONDITION FACTORS

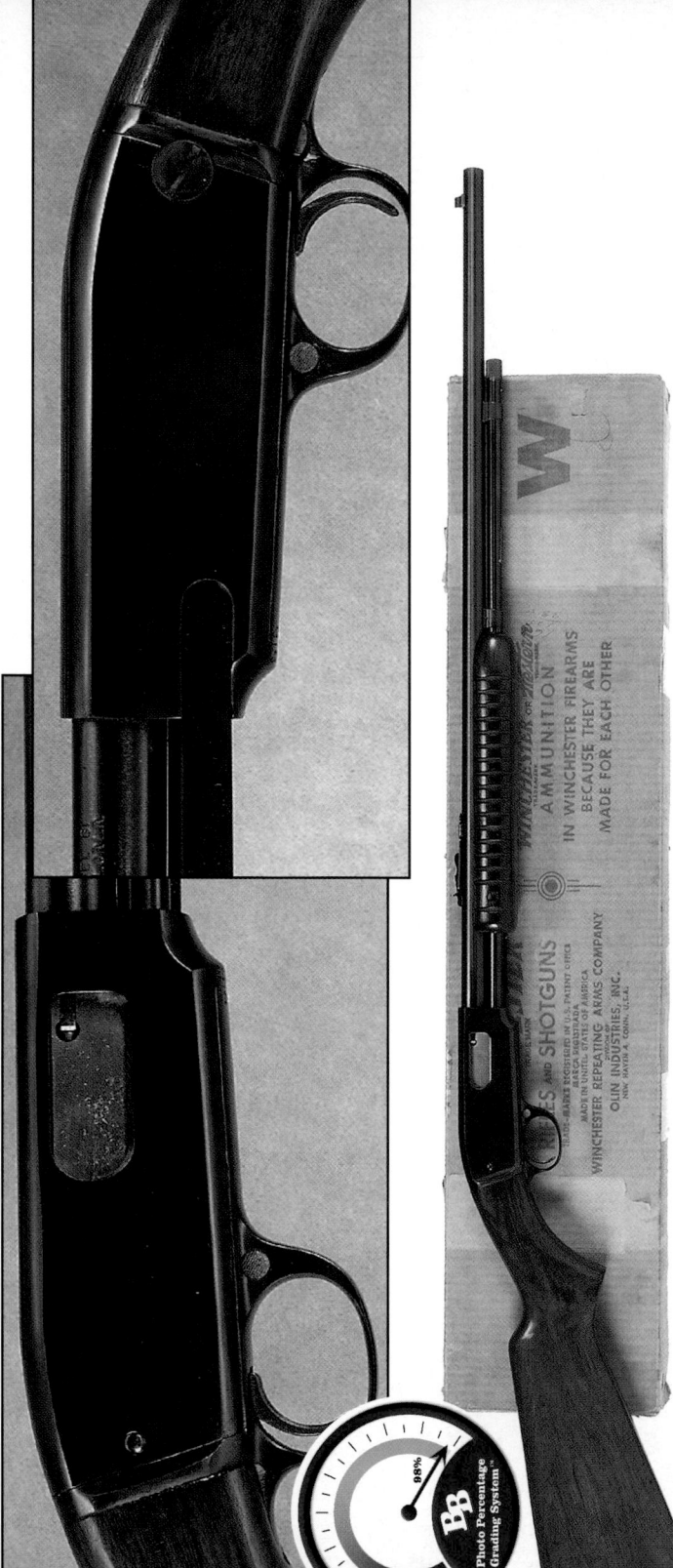

98% Condition, Winchester Model 61 slide action, .22 S-L-LR cal., 24 in. round barrel, ser. no. 212207, mfg. 1956. This Winchester may be unfired, but close observation will reveal some light dents and scratches in both the stock and forearm, indicating careless handling and in-box wear. There is virtually no bluing wear on the metal surfaces, and the grooved receiver for scope mount indicates late production, which is actually more desirable than a rifle without grooving. Even the breech block shows no vertical scratching, indicating little or no use. While the original box is somewhat tattered and has some tape marks, unfortunately, in recent years fake cardboard boxes for the Winchester Models 61, 62, and 63 have been appearing in the secondary marketplace. Since original boxes and hanging tags can add quite a bit of value to a 95%+ gun, be wary when buying these models with an "original" box.

Photo Percentage Grading System™

Twenty-Ninth Edition *Blue Book of Gun Values™*

RIFLES: PPGS CONDITION FACTORS

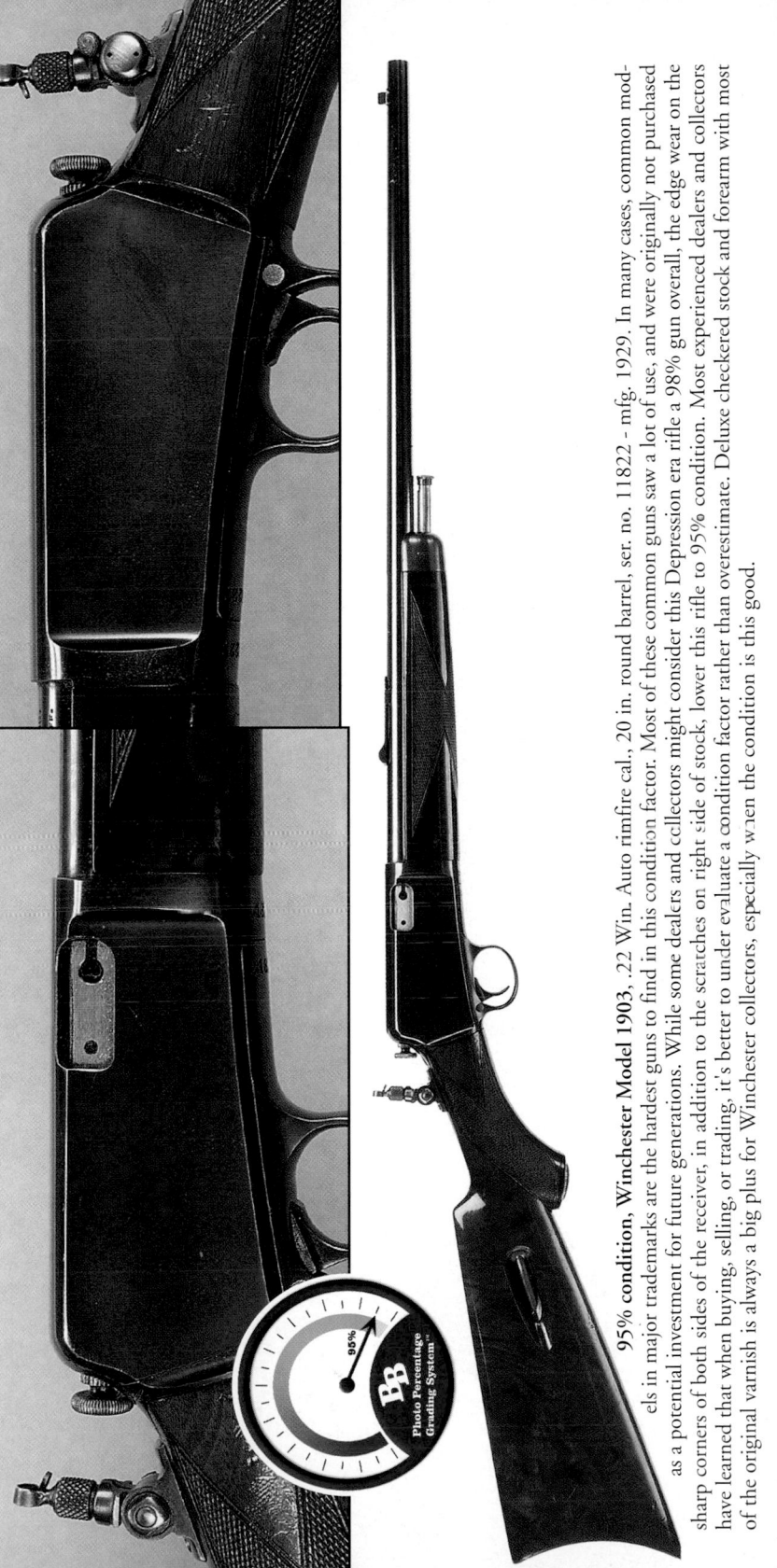

95% condition, Winchester Model 1903, .22 Win. Auto rimfire cal., 20 in. round barrel, ser. no. 11822 - mfg. 1929. In many cases, common models in major trademarks are the hardest guns to find in this condition factor. Most of these common guns saw a lot of use, and were originally not purchased as a potential investment for future generations. While some dealers and collectors might consider this Depression era rifle a 98% gun overall, the edge wear on the sharp corners of both sides of the receiver, in addition to the scratches on right side of stock, lower this rifle to 95% condition. Most experienced dealers and collectors have learned that when buying, selling, or trading, it's better to under evaluate a condition factor rather than overestimate. Deluxe checkered stock and forearm with most of the original varnish is always a big plus for Winchester collectors, especially when the condition is this good.

RIFLES: PPGS CONDITION FACTORS

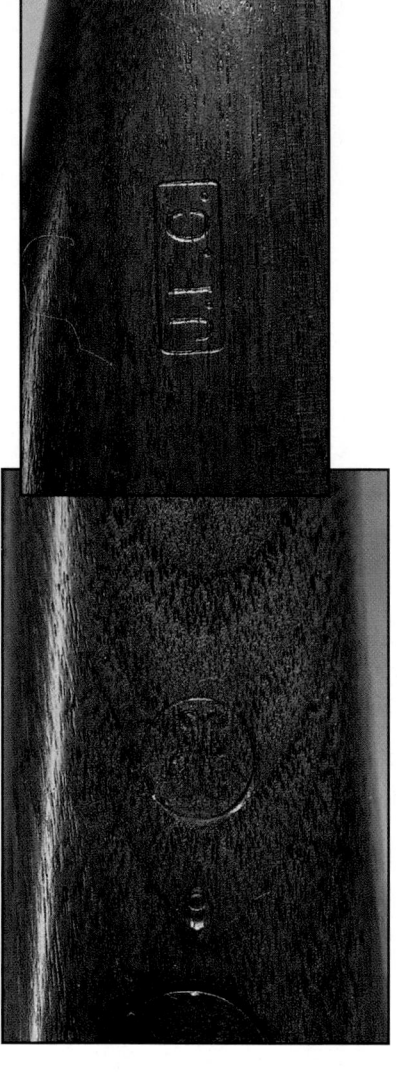

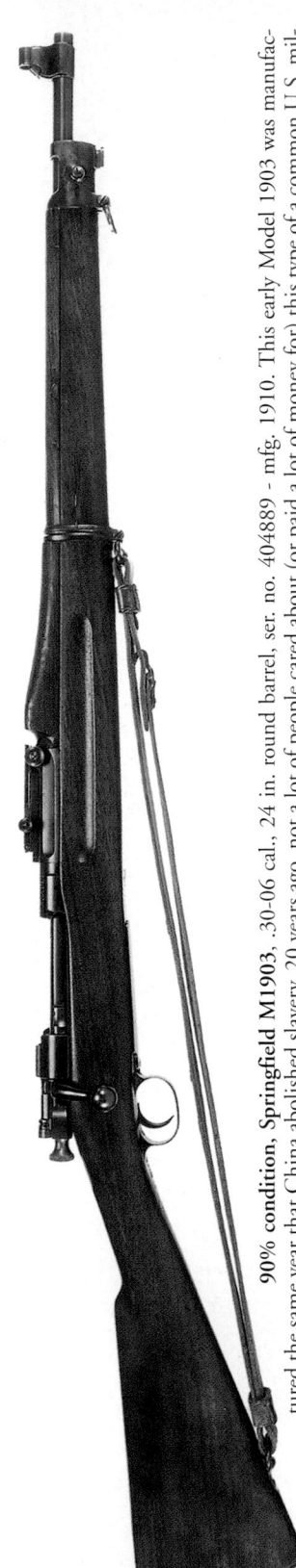

90% condition, Springfield M1903, .30-06 cal., 24 in. round barrel, ser. no. 404889 - mfg. 1910. This early Model 1903 was manufactured the same year that China abolished slavery. 20 years ago, not a lot of people cared about (or paid a lot of money for) this type of a common U.S. military rifle - that's not the case today. Note the blue and color case hardened metal finishes. It has nice original wood with no problems and "J.F.C." final inspector mark (for J.F. Coyle) in block letters inside rectangle in addition to script "P" in circle proof stamped on underside stock wrist. More than anything else, originality is the key when determining value on this type of 20th century U.S. military rifle - knowing what to look for in proofs/markings, how the original markings appear, and where to find them are absolutely critical when evaluating this rifle's value. Sling is an early RIA 1904 pattern.

Photo Percentage Grading System™

Twenty-Ninth Edition *Blue Book of Gun Values™*

Twenty-Ninth Edition Blue Book of Gun Values™

Photo Percentage Grading System™

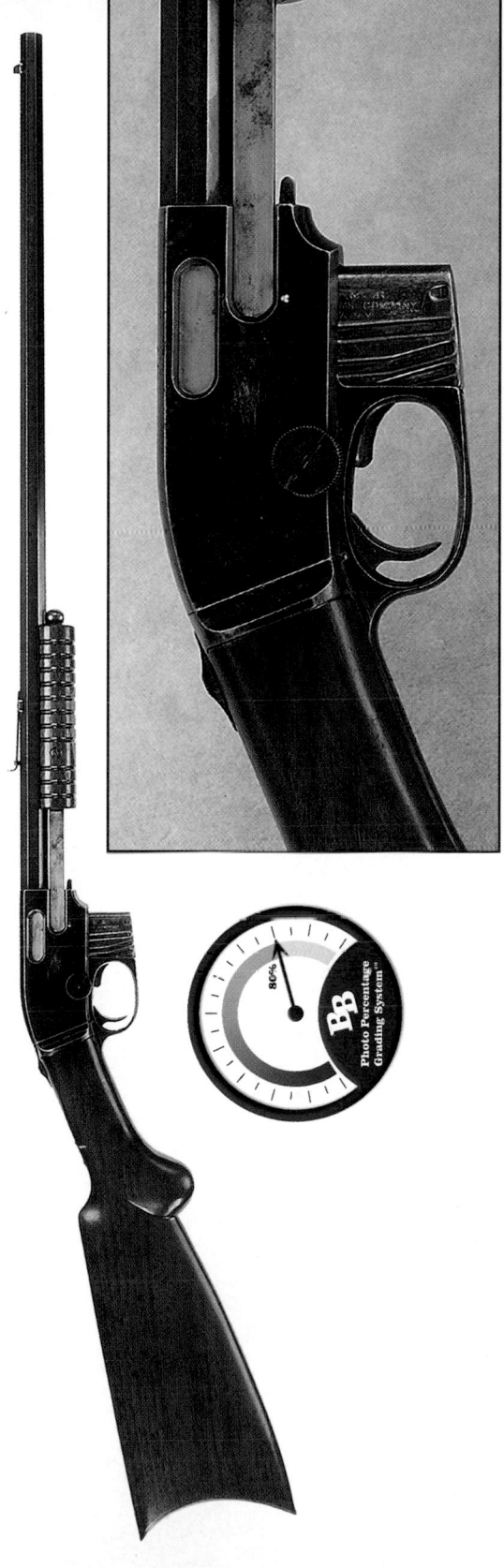

80% condition, Savage **Model 1903 slide action**, .22 S-L-LR cal., 24 in. octagon barrel, ser. no. 79070 - mfg. circa 1907. On most early 20th century .22 cal. slide action rifles such as this one which were inexpensively priced when new (typically $10-$15), the hardest thing to find now is superior original condition. Even at 80%, this rifle is probably still in better condition than the vast majority of original slide actions available at the time. Note wear on edges of frame that still retains most of its bright bluing, and small areas of scattered rust on the shiny slide rail and frame. The 7-shot detachable magazine with vertical markings located on front of trigger guard has also faded and turned a light plum color - consistent with the rest of this gun's overall wear. Barrel bluing also shows light fading and perhaps some over aggressive cleaning. Uncheckered rounded pistol stock with crescent buttplate and eleven groove forearm retain most of the original varnish. If this rifle was in 95% condition, the value would double, and it would be easier to sell.

RIFLES: PPGS CONDITION FACTORS

RIFLES: PPGS CONDITION FACTORS

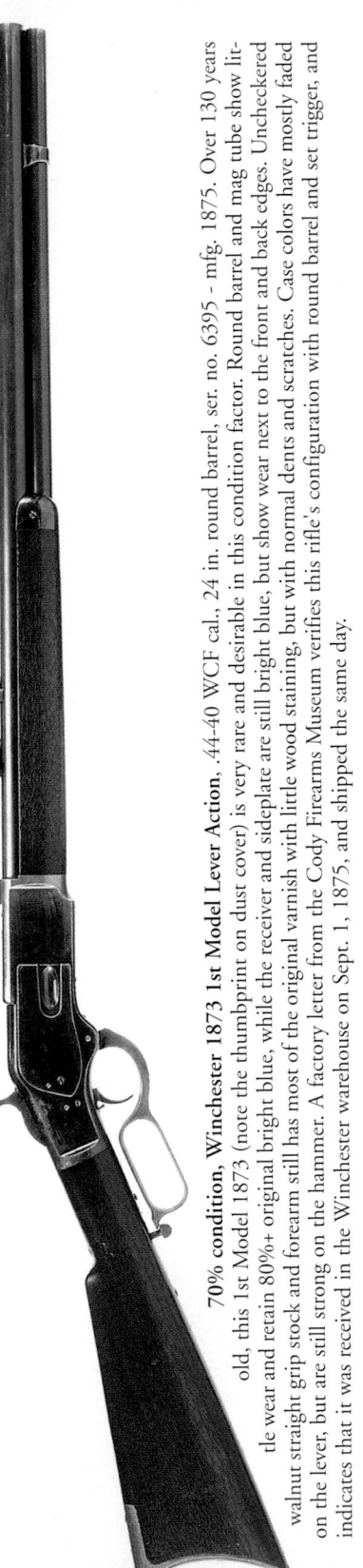

70% condition, Winchester 1873 1st Model Lever Action, .44-40 WCF cal., 24 in. round barrel, ser. no. 6395 - mfg. 1875. Over 130 years old, this 1st Model 1873 (note the thumbprint on dust cover) is very rare and desirable in this condition factor. Round barrel and mag tube show little wear and retain 80%+ original bright blue, while the receiver and sideplate are still bright blue, but show wear next to the front and back edges. Uncheckered walnut straight grip stock and forearm still has most of the original varnish with little wood staining, but with normal dents and scratches. Case colors have mostly faded on the lever, but are still strong on the hammer. A factory letter from the Cody Firearms Museum verifies this rifle's configuration with round barrel and set trigger, and indicates that it was received in the Winchester warehouse on Sept. 1, 1875, and shipped the same day.

Photo Percentage Grading System™

Twenty-Ninth Edition *Blue Book of Gun Values*™

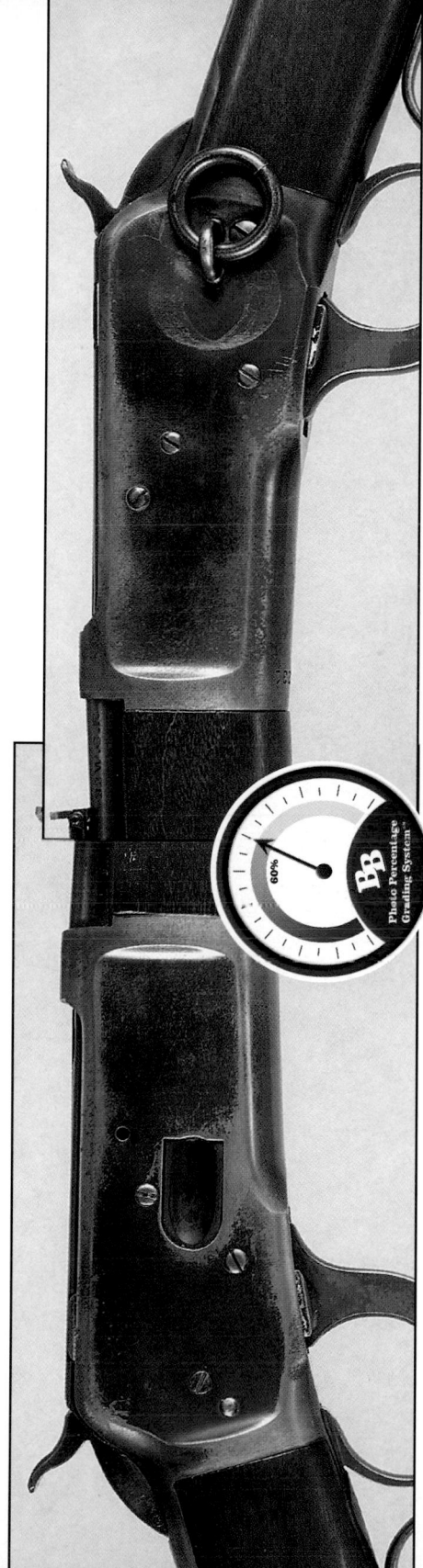

RIFLES: PPGS CONDITION FACTORS

79

60% condition, Winchester Model 1892 Saddle Ring Carbine, .32-20 WCF cal., 20 in. round barrel, ser. no. 917231 - mfg. late 1922. Compare the overall condition of this Model - 892 to the Winchester Model 1873 on the preceding page, and you'll observe approximately 10% less original condition. Notice how top, bottom, front, and rear of receiver have worn, turning silver with light brown patina, while the receiver sides retain a lot of the original bright bluing. The receiver on this carbine was refinished some time ago (note slightly rounded edges), and helps to explain its current wear pattern. Saddle ring imprint on rear left side of receiver is normal, and barrel band has turned mostly grey. Uncheckered straight grip walnut stock shows signs of light cleaning, but is still flush with metal. Action remains mechanically perfect, and its overall good eye appeal help elevate its value to above that of a poor reblue.

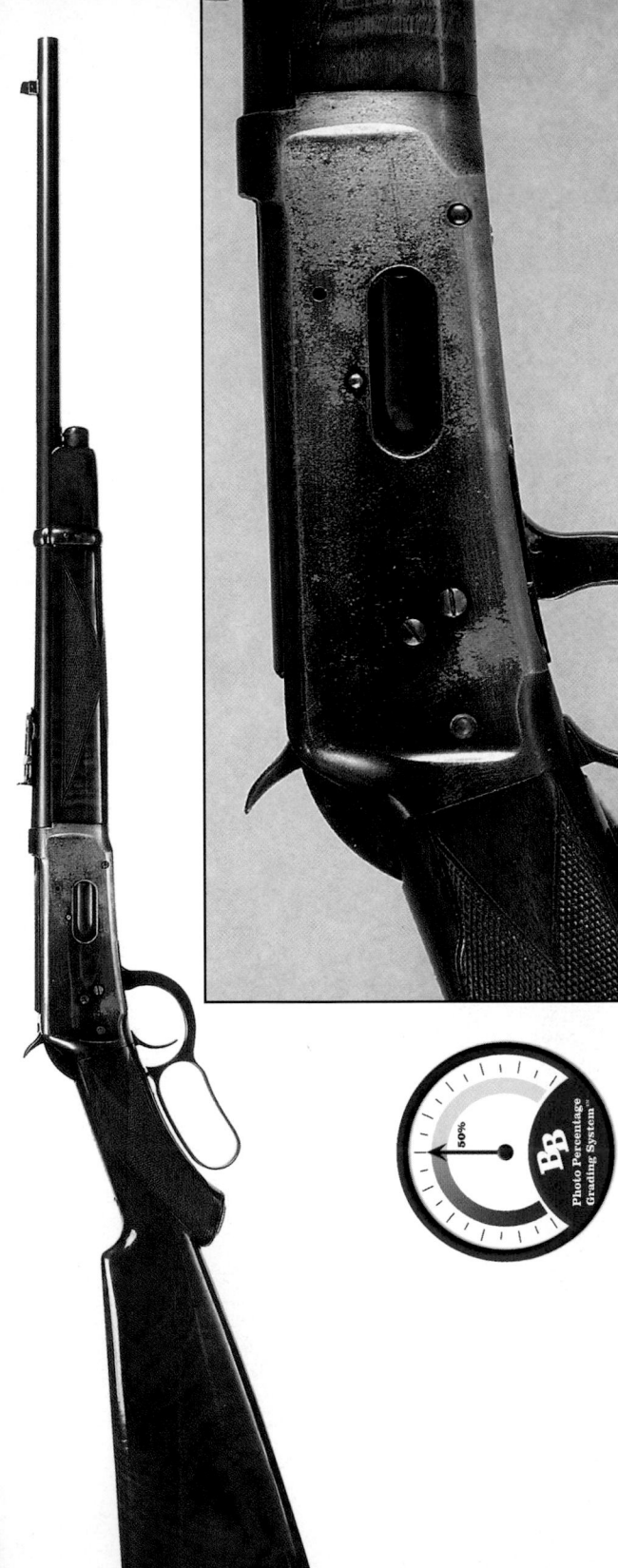

50% condition, Winchester Model 1894 Deluxe Saddle Ring Carbine, .30-30 Win. cal., 20 in. round barrel, ser. no. 582407 - mfg. 1911. Even in this condition factor, this Model 1894 deluxe saddle ring carbine is very desirable, with auction pricing now controlling the final premium paid on most major trademark firearms! Nickel steel barrel with ladder type rear sight and half magazine still has 95%+ original bluing, while the receiver has had much of its bluing flake off. Do not confuse receiver flaking with normal wear and usage - some Winchester lever action rifles can be almost unfired, but show similar frame wear as this specimen. Flaking occurred because the bluing did not adhere properly on guns with a high nickel content in the steel. Deluxe checkered walnut stock with steel shotgun buttplate may have been resprayed at a later date, but the varnish is in excellent condition, and matches the condition of the forearm.

Twenty-Ninth Edition Blue Book of Gun Values™

Photo Percentage Grading System™

Photo Percentage Grading System™

Twenty-Ninth Edition Blue Book of Gun Values™

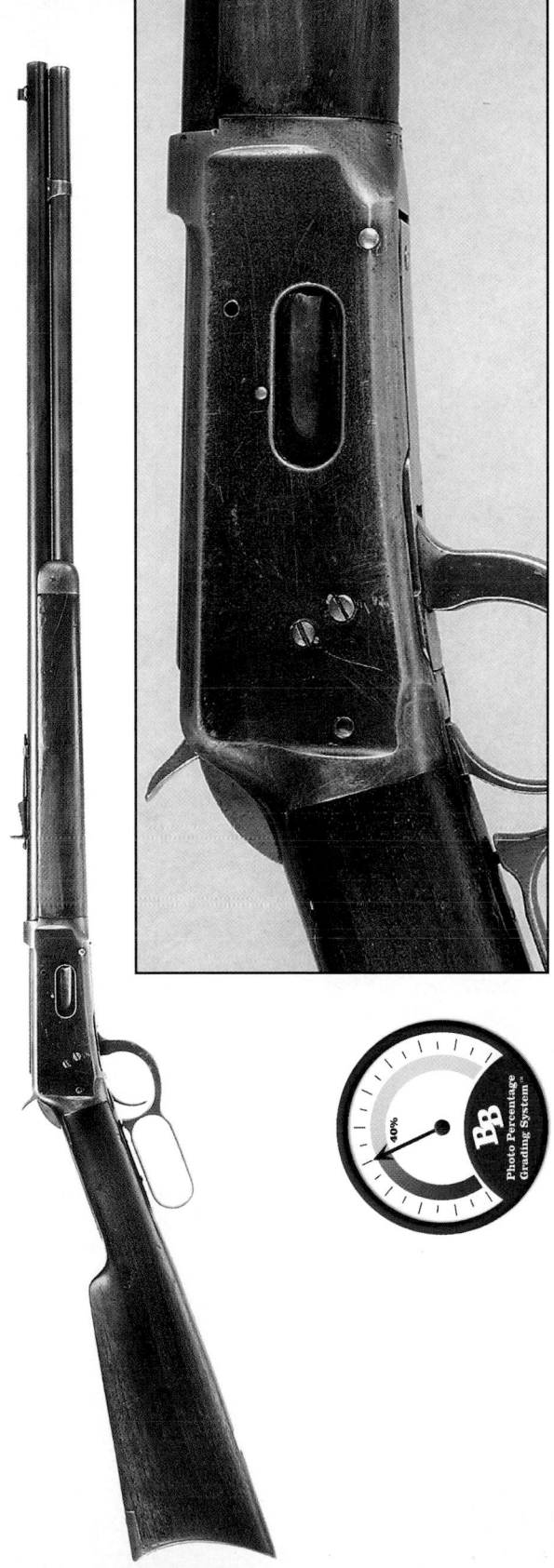

40% condition, Winchester Model 1894 Lever Action, .32 Win. Spl. cal., 26 in. round barrel, ser. no. 875560 - mfg. 1920. In the gun business, this is what you call a gun's condition factors "adding up" correctly. This plain Jane Model 1894 with 25 in. barrel is a study on what to look for when evaluating an older rifle. Note how the nickel steel barrel still has much of its bright blue, while the mag tube has turned a brown patina overall. Metal forearm cap is mostly shiny, and matches the condition on the receiver and wood. Flat receiver sides still have a lot of bright bluing left, especially at rear – also note how the loading gate finish looks good. The original stock wood and varnish has darkened somewhat, especially next to the receiver (normal) and the forearm shows normal use in the right areas. The receiver screw heads look good, and again, this Winchester still has a lot of eye appeal.

RIFLES: PPGS CONDITION FACTORS

RIFLES: PPGS CONDITION FACTORS

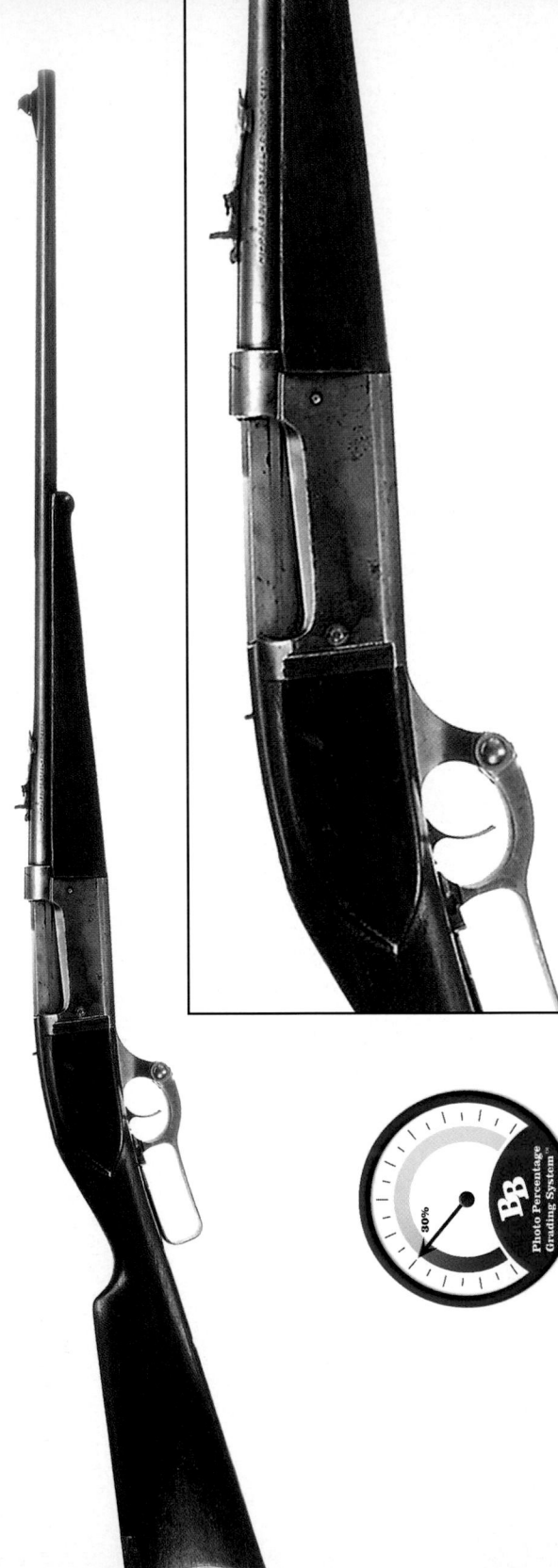

Photo Percentage Grading System™

30% condition, Savage Model 1899 Lever Action, .300 Sav. cal., 24 in. round barrel, ser. no. 324301 - mfg. 1929. If this rifle could talk, you'd probably be listening to a lot of interesting older deer hunting tales. Mostly shiny receiver shows previous polishing, while thinning barrel wear indicates this lever action has been on many previous hunting trips. Uncheckered straight grip walnut stock has turned somewhat dark due to oil staining and handling, and has some dings and scratches. While unseen, serious cracks in the stock have been repaired, and some pitting is present on both the frame and the barrel. Lever is also mostly shiny, attesting to the years of use. This rifle in this condition has now reached shooter status only, since most collectors want better condition in this type of common model. In other words, figure out its price as a shooter, and don't pay a penny more.

Twenty-Ninth Edition Blue Book of Gun Values™

Photo Percentage Grading System™

Twenty-Ninth Edition Blue Book of Gun Values™

RIFLES: PPGS CONDITION FACTORS

20% condition, Winchester Model 1906 Slide Action, .22 S-L-LR cal., 20 in. round barrel, ser. no. 256876 - mfg. 1926. Two of Winchester's most popular slide action .22 cal. rifles, the Models 1890 and 1906, enjoyed tremendous popularity between 1890-1932, with almost 1.7 million manufactured. Yet, a mint specimen of either model is very rare and only infrequently encountered. This Model 1906 is in below average condition, with the receiver having turned a dark brown patina, and showing major areas of pitting. Barrel has also turned an overall brown patina, while the mag tube and action bar are nickel plated. Stock and forearm have been revarnished, and do not match the rest of this gun's condition. Action remains tight, while bore is good. This rifle's value has bottomed out in this condition factor, and has limited desirability for Winchester collectors wanting better condition.

RIFLES: PPGS CONDITION FACTORS

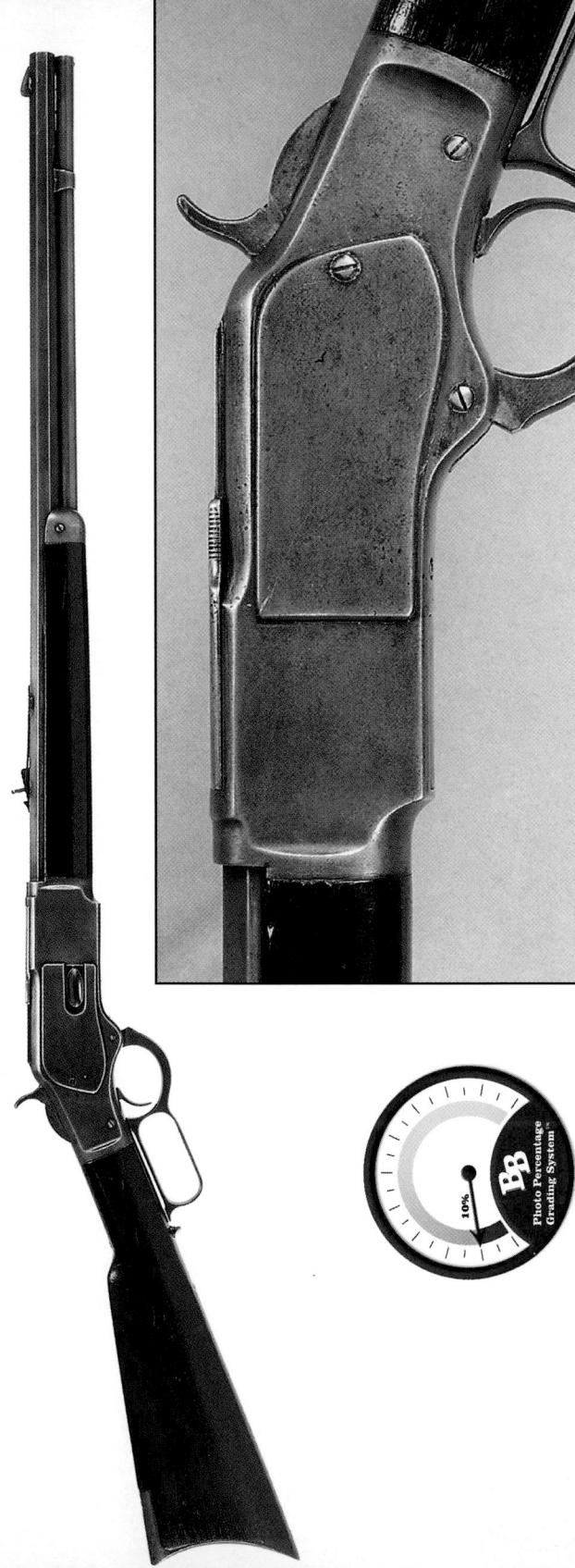

10% condition, Winchester 3rd Model 1873 Lever Action, .32-20 WCF cal., 24 in. octagon barrel, ser. no. 354761B - mfg. 1890. This Model 1873 is a good example of an antique rifle's original finish having turned a smooth grey brown patina overall (compare the finish on this gun to the one on page 78). Even though this gun has little original finish left, it does not have major problems like severe pitting, replaced non-original parts, or damaged/cracked wood, even though the stock and forearm have been previously revarnished. All markings remain sharp, the action is mechanically okay, and the bore is fair. Many Winchester collectors would still rather have a no problem, original rifle like this than a 40% overall specimen with major finish problems and alterations. This specimen would be considered an entry-level model for collecting, based on its condition and originality.

Photo Percentage Grading System™

Twenty-Ninth Edition *Blue Book of Gun Values*™

Twenty-Ninth Edition Blue Book of Gun Values™

Photo Percentage Grading System™

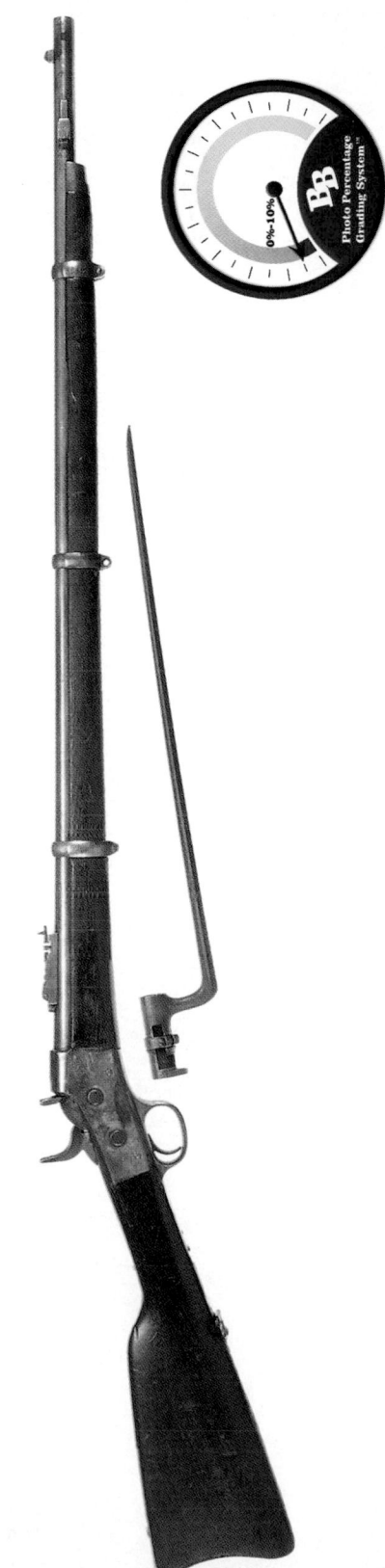

RIFLES: PPGS CONDITION FACTORS

0%-10% Condition, Remington Rolling Block w/bayonet, .43 Spanish cal., 33 7/8 in. round barrel, no ser. no., mfg. circa late 19th century. This well-worn Remington Rolling Block rifle made under contract for the Spanish government is a good example of how a gun's value can be reduced to almost nothing if there is very little original condition remaining. The metal finish has turned a grayish patina, with quite a bit of rusting and pitting on the receiver. The stock is also battered, and note that the ramrod and front sling swivel are missing. The bore is as dark as the oil-soaked wood, but at least it has the original bayonet. Remington made hundreds of thousands of rolling block rifles in various configurations and calibers for many countries, and the remaining majority now look like this. While a mint original specimen is both rare and desirable, a contract rolling block in this condition has lost most of its desirability and eye appeal. Typically priced under $250, these contract rifles, in many obsolete calibers, can no longer be considered even as shooters.

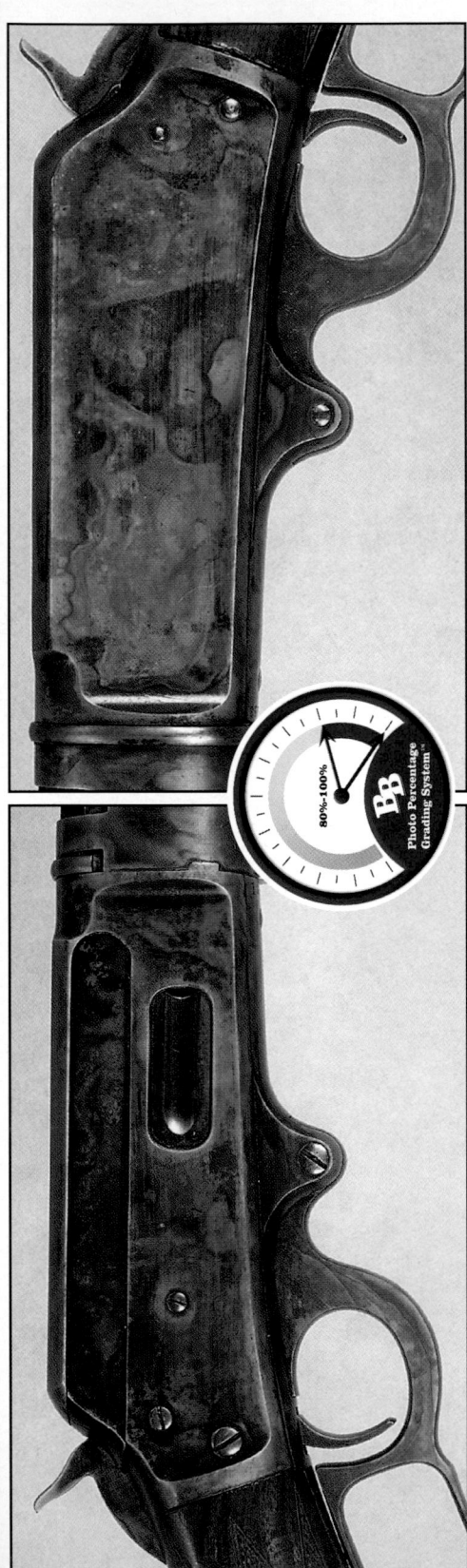

NRA Antique Excellent (over 80% condition), Marlin Model 1893 Takedown, .38-55 cal., 30 in. octagon barrel, ser. no. 136493 - mfg. 1896. This special order Marlin rifle, manufactured the same year as the introduction of the motion picture, had a base price of $13. Special features on this gun include a 30 in. octagon barrel ($5 up charge), take down feature ($4 up charge), and extra select walnut with B checkering ($20 up charge) - bringing the total up to $42! Note the vivid case colors on both sides of the receiver, featuring predominately mottled blues and greens. Barrel and magazine tube bluing are above 95%, and checkered Circassian walnut stock and forearm retain most of the original varnish. Once you start adding up what these special orders/features can do to a major trademark gun in this type of superior original condition in today's marketplace, the price tag gets turbo charged in a hurry!

Photo Percentage Grading System™

Twenty-Ninth Edition *Blue Book of Gun Values™*

NRA Antique Fine (30%-80% condition), Engraved Marlin Model 1889 Deluxe Lever Action, .32-20 WCF cal., 24 in. octagon barrel, ser. no. 69896 - mfg. June 18, 1892. As a general rule of thumb, engraved guns appear to have less case colors than non-engraved standard models. Extensive engraving on any case colored rifle actually subdues the case colors somewhat, as the scrollwork tends to break up the overall patern. Note how front and rear receiver edges have become shiny with light freckling, and how wood to metal fit is perfect. Also note that the case colored lever has coloration left only in the protected area where it pivots. Hammer case colors are nice, and match the overall condition factor of this fine rifle. While some dealers and collectors may refer to this condition as Very Fine, this term is not a proper NRA Antique condition factor.

RIFLES: NRA ANTIQUE CONDITIONS

RIFLES: NRA ANTIQUE CONDITIONS

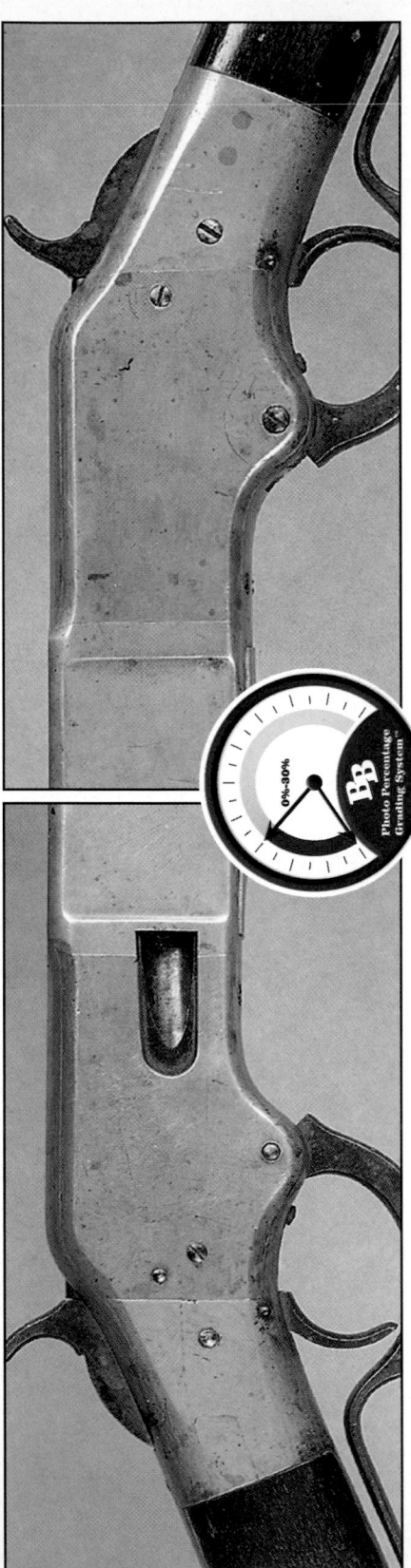

NRA Antique Very Good Condition (0%-30%), Winchester Model 1866 4th Model lever action, .44 cal., 24 in. octagon barrel, ser. no. 150724, mfg. 1879. Winchester lever action aficionados will immediately recognize this rifle as a 4th Model, with its distinctive steel forend cap and crescent buttplate. The barrel and magazine tube bluing have turned a brownish-gray patina, and notice the barrel wear on the sharp edges. The condition of the brass frame is critical when evaluating this model, and note the mustard coloring and sharp edges-many of these were sanded or polished to make them look newer. The stock may have been lightly sanded at an earlier date, but overall, this is a very nice Model 1866 4th Model. Antique Winchester lever actions like this one used to be commonly seen at most major gun shows, but in recent years, can mainly be found either at auctions or from specialized high end dealers and collectors.

Photo Percentage Grading System™

Twenty-Ninth Edition Blue Book of Gun Values™

Twenty-Ninth Edition *Blue Book of Gun Values*™

Photo Percentage Grading System™

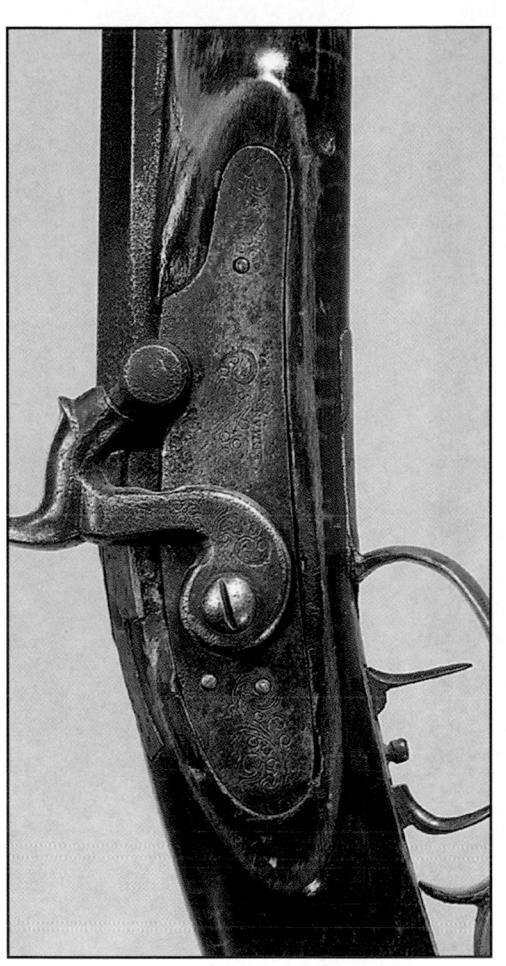

NRA Antique Good Condition (0%-20%), Leman Lancaster half-stock percussion rifle, .40 cal., 36 in. octagon barrel, no. ser. no., mfg. date unknown. Even though this gun is not listed in this publication, this percussion rifle manufactured in Lancaster County, PA, has been included to portray this NRA Antique condition factor. Note that the metal surfaces, including the lock, have turned a rust-brown patina, with major pitting around the breech. The stock has also been refinished, artifically striped, and repaired several times around the barrel and beside the lock. Brass/silver furniture and mother-of-pearl inlays appear to be original and in good shape. This condition factor takes into consideration pitting, minor replacement parts, and wood refinishing, but in good working order. In general, the older and more common the gun, the less likely it will be found in over NRA Antique Fine condition. Collectors prefer originality over anything else once an older gun like this reaches this condition factor.

RIFLES: NRA ANTIQUE CONDITIONS

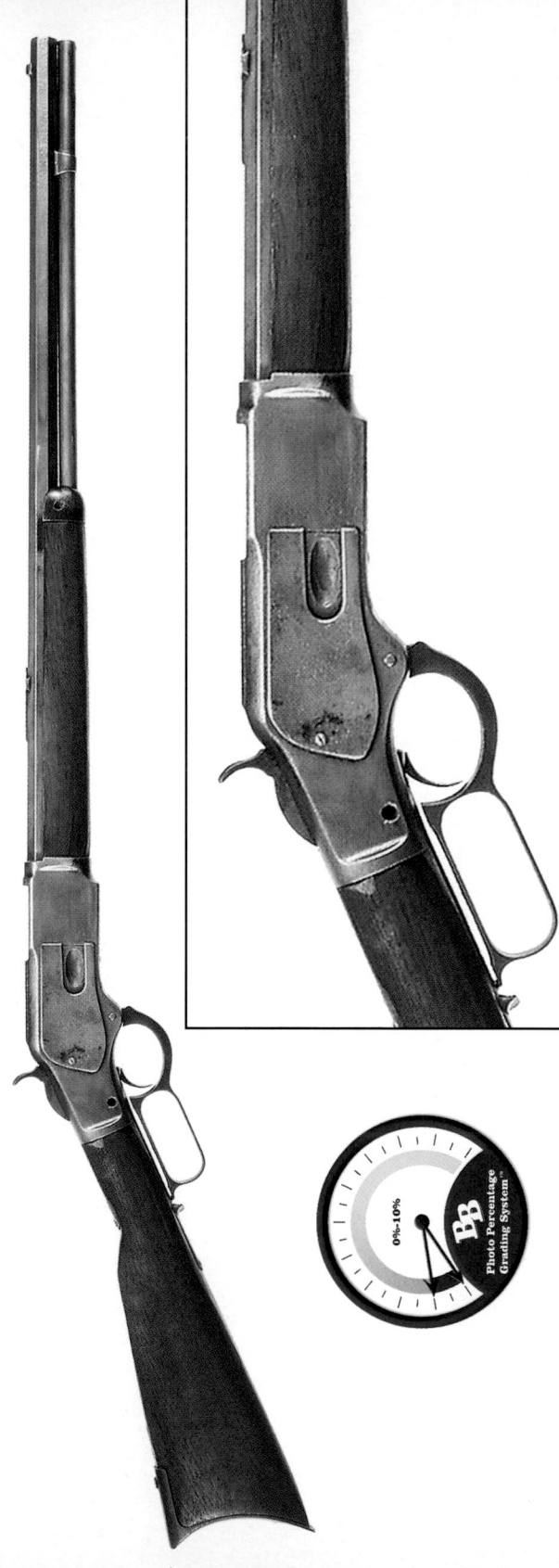

NRA Antique Fair Condition (0-10% or less). Altered Winchester Model 1873 Lever Action, .32-20 WCF cal., 24 in. octagon barrel, ser. no. 167428 - mfg. 1884. Except for the forearm cap, there is no original finish remaining on either the receiver, barrel, or magazine tube. This gun has had all its metal surfaces polished and is also missing major parts such as the dust cover, receiver screws, and rear sight. Both the stock and the forearm are crude replacements, and fit poorly to the metal. This rifle (or what's left of it) constitutes 0-10% condition (NRA Poor). So what's it worth? The answer is, add up values for the individual parts, and don't include the stock or forearm. In this case, the total is approx. $400, still cheaper than a modern reproduction. Unfortunately, most guns in this condition factor never become more desirable (or expensive) as junk will always be junk, and gets priced accordingly!

Photo Percentage Grading System™

Twenty-Ninth Edition *Blue Book of Gun Values*™

Twenty-Ninth Edition *Blue Book of Gun Values*™

Photo Percentage Grading System™

NRA Antique Poor Condition (no original finish remaining), Spanish percussion blunderbuss, .50 cal., 16½ in. part-octagon barrel, no ser. no., mfg. circa 1840-1860. What's an unlisted blunderbuss doing in this section? Trying to give you an idea of what a gun looks like towards the end of its altered life (and family members need to be notified). The marking on top of the barrel is "Fa ARRATE EIBAR" in silver, indicating manufacture in northern Spain in the historic Eibar region. This gun probably started life as a percussion rifle, but the rifled barrel was belled out at a later date to resemble a blunderbuss. Some lock parts have also been replaced, and the ramrod is missing. The barrel is now deeply pitted, and appears to have gone through a fire. As a result, this gun is almost totally non-original, and "wall hanger" probably describes it more accurately than anything else. An interior decorator would probably pay a premium for this type of historic "art décor"!

RIFLES: NRA ANTIQUE CONDITIONS

SHOTGUNS: PPGS CONDITION FACTORS

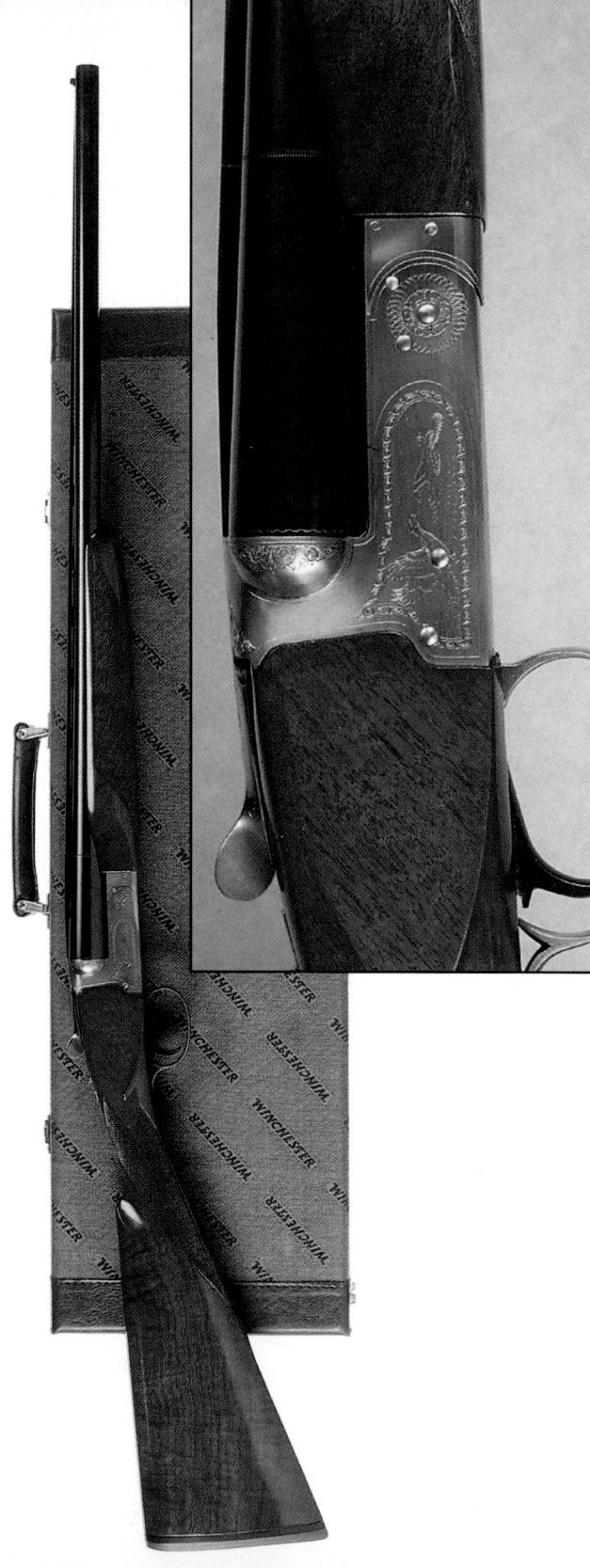

NIB condition, Winchester Model 23 Cased Pigeon Grade Lightweight SxS, 20 ga., 25½ in. vent. rib barrels., ser. no. PKW 204779 - mfg. circa 1984. This Pigeon Grade SxS model was manufactured by Miroku in Japan until 1986. The good news is its NIB condition factor, short barrels with open choking (bored IC/M), English straight grip stock, and it's a 20 ga., not a 12. The bad news is that it doesn't have choke tubes, which became standard in 1986. Correct Winchester green canvas case with leather ends is also original to this gun and adds approximately $200-$250 of value. Small gauge shotguns, especially 28 ga. and .410 bore, have outperformed the rest of the gauges as an investment by a significant margin in recent times. Conversely, common makes/models in 12 ga. without choke tubes are getting less desirable each year, and one contributing editor recently commented that without choke tubes, it is the "kiss of death" when selling.

Photo Percentage Grading System™

Twenty-Ninth Edition *Blue Book of Gun Values*™

Twenty-Ninth Edition *Blue Book of Gun Values*™

SHOTGUNS: PPGS CONDITION FACTORS

Mint condition, Ithaca Model 5E Knick Single Barrel Trap w/gold inlays, 12 ga., 32 in. round barrel, ser. no. 402059T - mfg. circa 1931. Experienced shotgun traders and savvy collectors will tell you to be careful when buying used trap shotguns, especially if they're older. Trap guns are manufactured specifically to shoot a lot of shotshells within a relatively short period of competition. Because of this, action wear can accumulate long before wear is visible on the outside of the gun. Always focus on how tight (or loose) the action is, and if the top opening lever is still on the right side of center on upper tang. This nice Ithaca 5E Knick Model has almost no bluing or case color wear, factory engraving and gold bird inlays, definitive of the model. The uncut stock has a replacement Pachmayr recoil pad, typical on trap guns where dimensions are critical and tailored to the individual.

98% condition, Boxed L.C. Smith Field Grade SxS Long Range Waterfowl, 12 ga., 32 in. round barrels, ser. no. 86110 - mfg. circa 1925. Even though this shotgun is both new and unfired, normal storage wear, cleaning, and occasional assembly have all accumulated enough wear to knock this gun's condition factor down to 98%. Original L.C. Smith case colors do not get any better than this - look at the vivid blues and greens surrounded by greyish/brown swirls compared to the examples on pages 101 and 106. Also note unstained, light colored, checkered standard grade walnut stock and forearm, and tight wood to metal fit around side-plates. When a desirable gun's condition factor is this good, the value may double or even triple the 90% value. L.C. Smith only had one level of quality - the best, regardless of the grade. Stock and splinter forearm show virtually no wear. In many cases, a 98%+ condition specimen of a factory's most common model is the hardest to find, since most of them were heavily used. Original box is somewhat tattered, and has water staining.

Photo Percentage Grading System™

Twenty-Ninth Edition *Blue Book of Gun Values™*

Twenty-Ninth Edition Blue Book of Gun Values™

Photo Percentage Grading System™

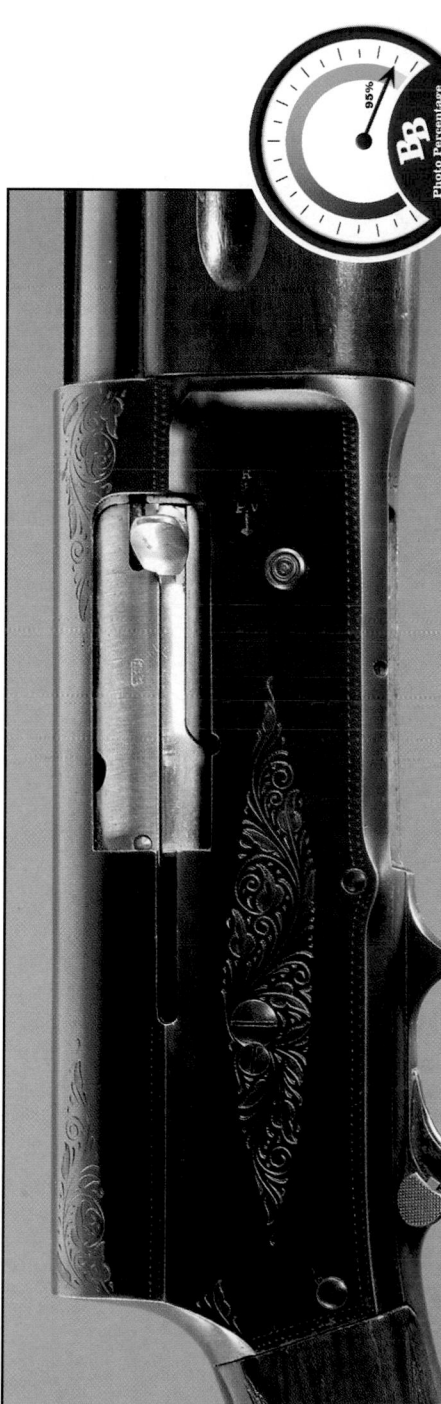

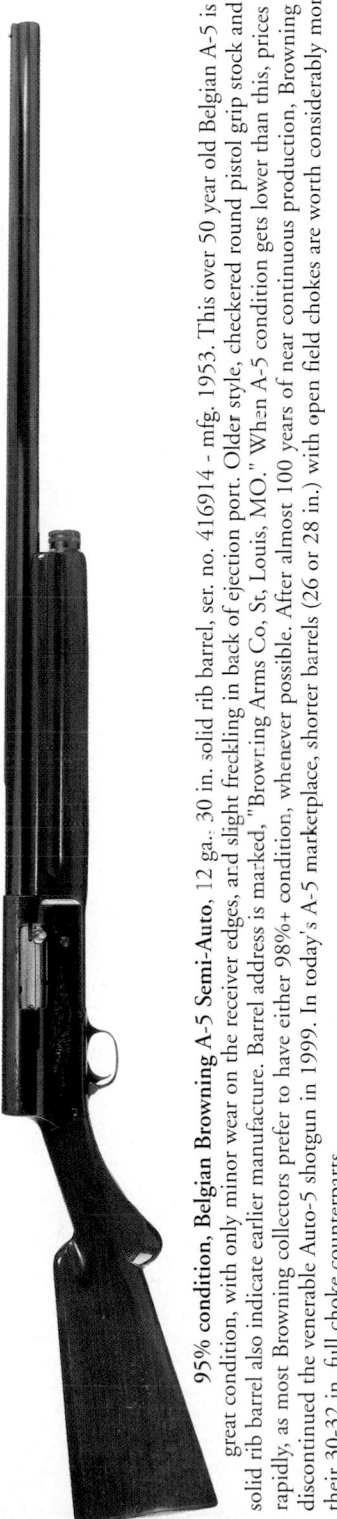

95% condition, Belgian Browning A-5 Semi-Auto, 12 ga., 30 in. solid rib barrel, ser. no. 416914 - mfg. 1953. This over 50 year old Belgian A-5 is still in great condition, with only minor wear on the receiver edges, and slight freckling in back of ejection port. Older style, checkered round pistol grip stock and 30 in. solid rib barrel also indicate earlier manufacture. Barrel address is marked, "Browning Arms Co, St, Louis, MO." When A-5 condition gets lower than this, prices fall off rapidly, as most Browning collectors prefer to have either 98%+ condition, whenever possible. After almost 100 years of near continuous production, Browning finally discontinued the venerable Auto-5 shotgun in 1999. In today's A-5 marketplace, shorter barrels (26 or 28 in.) with open field chokes are worth considerably more than their 30-32 in. full choke counterparts.

SHOTGUNS: PPGS CONDITION FACTORS

SHOTGUNS: PPGS CONDITION FACTORS

90% condition, Belgian Browning A-5 Sweet Sixteen, 16 ga., 28 in. barrel, ser. no. S14514 - mfg. 1954. Note the additional wear around the lower receiver edges on this Browning compared to the one on page 95. This Sweet Sixteen A-5 is referred to as a round knob, long tang variation, indicating that the pistol grip is rounded (mfg. 1952-1976), instead of flat, and the lower tang is longer than recent manufacture. Note blonde French walnut stock and forearm, typical for this period of production. This is a good example of what a rarer variation of a common model can do to the price tag. While the frequently encountered 12 ga. A-5 with 30 in. solid matted rib barrel on page 95 currently has a retail value of $500, this rarer Sweet 16 in 90% condition can top $1,500. This same model in 100% condition retails in the $800 range. This rarer Sweet 16 in 90% condition currently has a retail value of $1,500, even more if with the original box!

Photo Percentage Grading System™

Twenty-Ninth Edition *Blue Book of Gun Values™*

Photo Percentage Grading System™

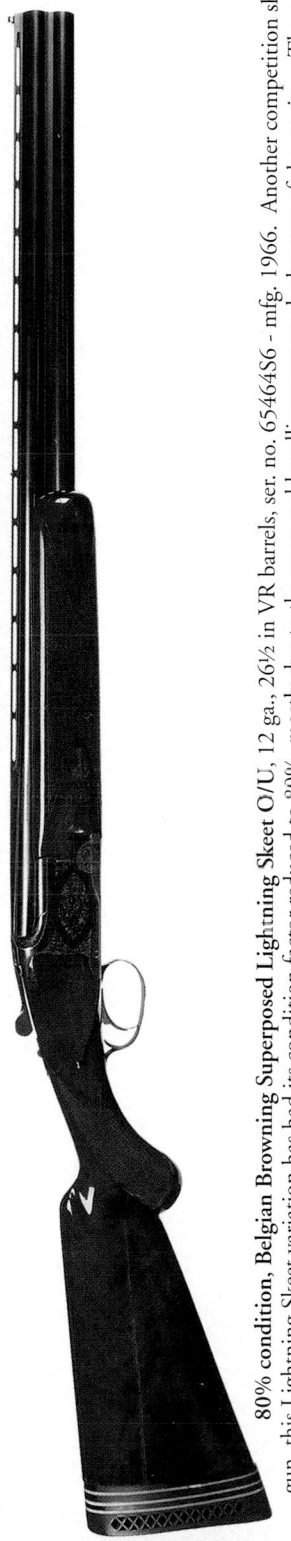

80% condition, Belgian Browning Superposed Lightning Skeet O/U, 12 ga., 26½ in VR barrels, ser. no. 65464S6 - mfg. 1966. Another competition shotgun, this Lightning Skeet variation has had its condition factor reduced to 80%, mostly due to the carry and handling wear on the bottom of the receiver. The stock has some scratches, dings, light gouges, and a non-factory Steinburg recoil pad with three spacers kill this gun's eye appeal for collectors. Of major concern to all Browning collectors is if the original stock has been cut to accept a recoil device (read that subtract $500). If a pad has been added, but the stock remains the original factory length and is unaltered, the value diminishes only slightly. This gun's action falls open by itself after using the opening lever, but is not loose. The Superposed was one of John Browning's last designs, with production beginning in 1931 in Belgium.

SHOTGUNS: PPGS CONDITION FACTORS

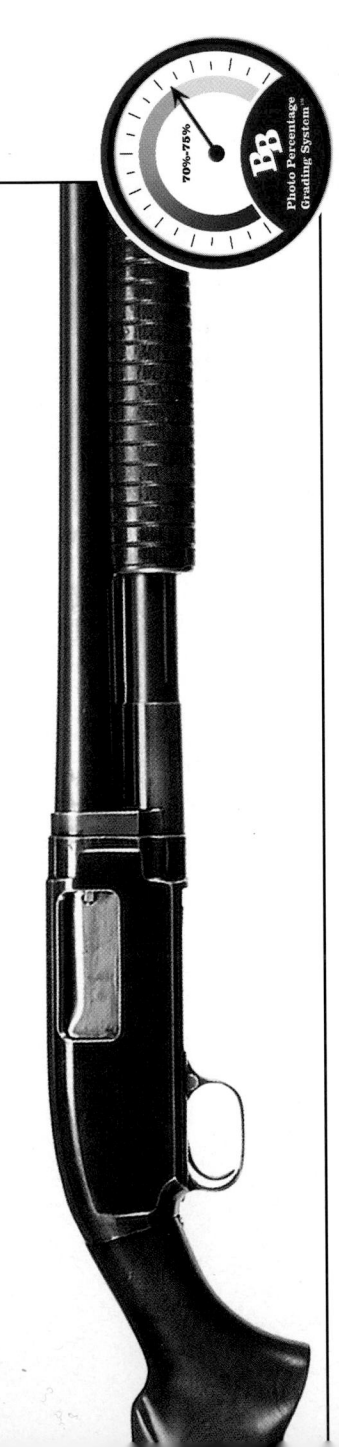

70%-75% condition, Winchester Model 12 Slide Action, 12 ga., 28 in. round barrel, ser. no. 902723, mfg. 1941. Very few shotgun models are found in such a wide array of condition factors as the Model 12 Winchester. It's pretty hard for any shotgun enthusiast not to have a Model 12 somewhere in his/her gun vault. This particular shotgun shows normal wear, but no abuse. While some dealers and collectors might grade this gun at 80% based on the receiver and barrel bluing, the wear on the mag tube and ring at end of barrel assembly knock this shotgun's condition down to approx. 70%-75%. Stock has a Pachmayr rubber vent. replacement recoil pad with spacers, but has not been cut. Horizontal striations and dulling on breech block indicate this shotgun has pumped out more than a few ounces of lead (hopefully, no steel!) in its lifetime.

Photo Percentage Grading System™

Twenty-Ninth Edition *Blue Book of Gun Values*™

Twenty-Ninth Edition Blue Book of Gun Values™

Photo Percentage Grading System™

SHOTGUNS: PPGS CONDITION FACTORS

60% condition, Winchester Model 12 Slide Action, 12 ga., 30 in. round barrel, ser. no. 219576 - mfg. early Jan., 1919. When a shotgun gets down to this condition factor, normally the barrel also shows visible wear, as seen on this shotgun. Note how receiver, barrel, and mag. tube have also started to turn a brownish patina. Scuffed breech block and horizontal wear line on mag tube tell this shotgun's shooting story. The stock has been sanded – note how light it is in the back, but gets dark where it joins the receiver (compare to Model 12 on page 98). Most of this gun's value must be determined by its worth as a reliable shooter, since the 12 ga./30 in. full choke barrel is the most common Model 12 configuration. The smaller gauges, especially the 28 ga. and .410 bore, are always more desirable than a 12 ga. in any shotgun model.

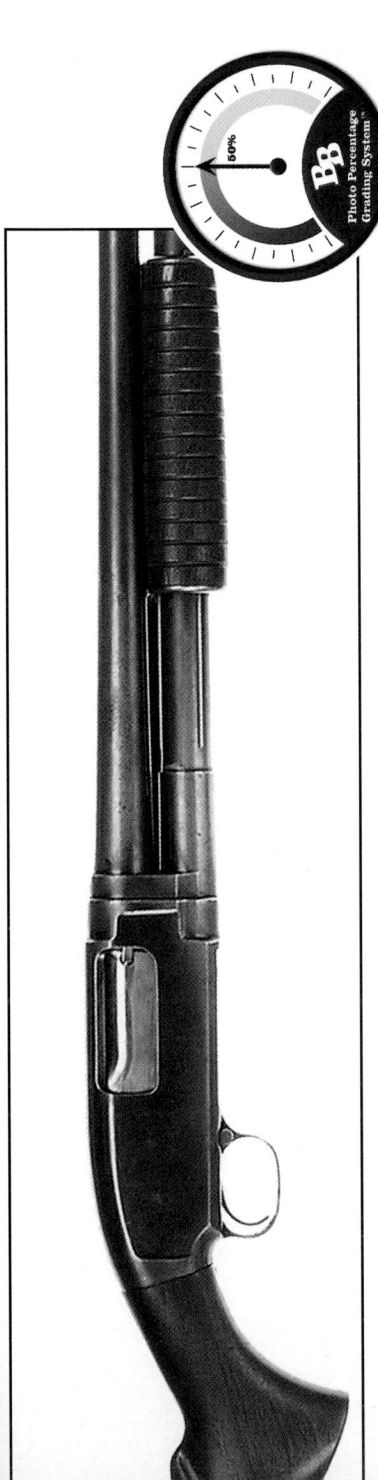

50% condition, Winchester Model 12 Slide Action, 16 ga., 28 in. round barrel, ser. no. 886875 - mfg. 1941. This is a good example of a well used, no problem Model 12. All the major components (wood, receiver, barrel, and mag tube) are worn in all the right places, as well as not worn in all the right places. When barrel wear reaches this type of brown patina condition, the rest of the gun should look even more worn, as the barrel was normally not handled that much during usage. The mag tube is equally worn, and the original stock and forearm reveal the right amount of original varnish to match the rest of the gun. Recently, 16 ga. guns have made a comeback in terms of collectibility, and are now priced slightly above the 12 ga. – if original condition is 95% or better.

Twenty-Ninth Edition *Blue Book of Gun Values*™

Photo Percentage Grading System™

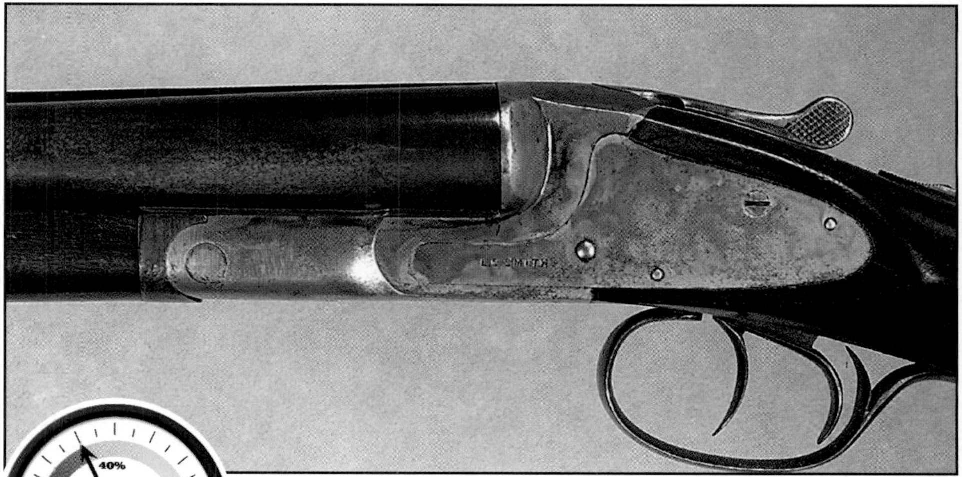

Twenty-Ninth Edition *Blue Book of Gun Values*™

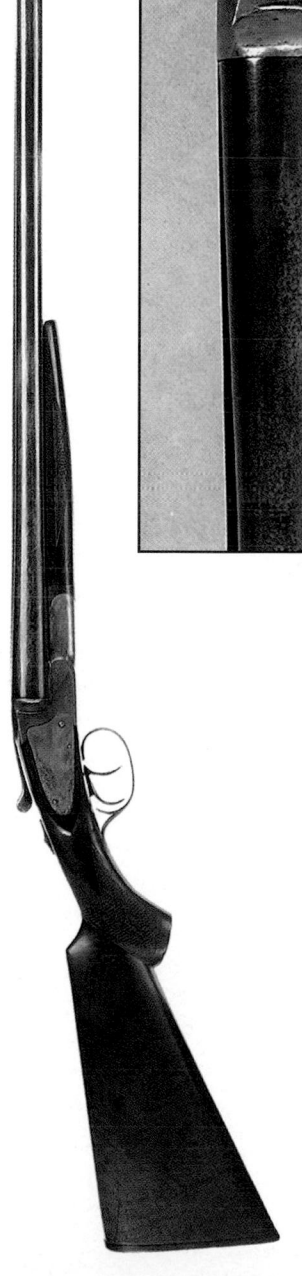

40% Condition, L.C. Smith Field Grade SxS, 12 ga., 30 in. barrels, ser. no. 125367 - mfg. circa 1905. The overall condition of this 100-year-old L.C. Smith is a good example of the individual condition factors of the wood finish, frame case colors, and barrel bluing wearing equally. Which means no one or two condition factors are a lot better or a lot worse than the others - very important when evaluating older guns for originality. Compare mottled case colors on frame, mostly visible around protected areas, to the vivid patterns depicted on page 94. Checkered Field Grade stock and forearm have darkened somewhat, but do not show major cracks, nicks, or gouges. Bluing on barrels is starting to fade to a patina, but overall, this is a nice original Field Grade L.C. Smith with tight action. Often times, American major trademark Field Grade or Standard Models (including A.H. Fox, Ithaca, Lefever, Parker, Remington, and L.C. Smith) are the hardest models to find in superior original condition, since they were typically used (and possibly abused) the most.

30% Condition, Colt Model 1883 hammerless, 10 ga., 30 in. barrels, ser. no. 2520, mfg. 1887. While Colt certainly isn't known for its 19th century shotguns, they were every bit as good as the Parkers, L.C. Smiths, Lefevers, Remingtons, etc., at the time, and cost as much or more. This 10 ga. with damascus barrels is still in above average condition when compared to other remaining specimens. Less than 7,400 of this model were manufactured between 1883 and 1895, and former U.S. President Grover Cleveland shot one regularly in 8 ga., which weighed over 12 lbs! Faded case colors remain in a few protected areas, the English walnut stock and forearm have a few scratches, yet the checkering retains its entire pattern and shows little wear. The damascus barrels have turned an overall dull gray patina throughout, and the bores are still shiny. The action is tight, and because of its originality with no problems, many Colt and/or SxS shotgun collectors would be more than glad to add this gun to their collections.

Twenty-Ninth Edition Blue Book of Gun Values™

Photo Percentage Grading System™

Twenty-Ninth Edition *Blue Book of Gun Values*™

Photo Percentage Grading System™

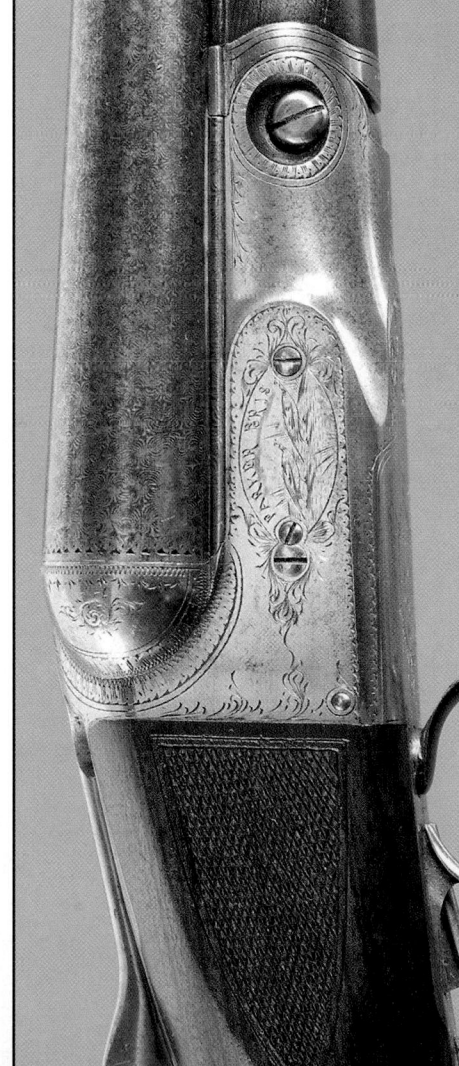

10%-20% condition, Parker GH Grade Hammerless damascus SxS, 12 ga., 30 in. barrels, ser. no. 115310 - mfg. 1903. This older Parker has more problems than you may have already seen. Stock and forearm have been refinished, and Parker aficionados have already spotted the non-original checkering on the stock side panels. Slotted hinge pin should also be on left side of gun, and does not align properly, indicating a replacement put in from the wrong side. Note that almost all the original frame case colors are gone, and this shotgun's frame may have been previously polished, as some of the engraving has thinned out in areas. The damascus hammerless barrels still show great patterning, and double triggers are to be expected on the Model GH, which retailed for approximately $80 when new, $25 more with ejectors. Parker shotguns have continued to lead the domestic SxS marketplace price appreciation, with pricing for strong, original condition guns in smaller gauges (20 ga. and less) going well above auction reserve levels. But don't forget that originality has always been Polar North for Parker shotgun collectors.

SHOTGUNS: PPGS CONDITION FACTORS

SHOTGUNS: PPGS CONDITION FACTORS

0%-10% Condition, Remington Model 1900 damascus SxS, 12 ga., 30 in. barrels, ser. no. 316534, mfg. circa 1901. In terms of condition, it doesn't get much worse than this, and even if it did, it wouldn't make any difference on the value (or lack of it). Major problems include poorly installed hardware store bolt in stock above trigger guard (probably put in after the stock chipped on both sides), forearm lock no longer works (note plastic tie around barrels), rusted/pitted frame, loose action, and partially cleaned damascus barrels. If this shotgun could talk, it would probably need a psychiatrist to help tell its entire painful story! With no eye appeal and major condition problems, this Remington also doesn't have any shooting value unless a gunsmith extensively went through it, and it wouldn't be worth it. Falling into the rusty iron/kindling category, this gun's value has been under $100 for quite some time, and the problem is, that will never change. Trash will always be trash!

Photo Percentage Grading System™

Twenty-Ninth Edition *Blue Book of Gun Values*™

Photo Percentage Grading System™

NRA Antique Excellent Refinished Condition (over 80%), Parker DHE hammerless SxS, 12 ga., 28 in. barrels, ser. no. 139955, mfg. 1907. This Parker's original configuration (not originality) can be verified in *Parker Gun Identification & Serialization.* Factory records indicate that it left the Meriden plant as a Grade 3 with titanic steel barrels and ejectors (DHE), hammerless action, straight grip stock, and had 28 in. barrels on a No. 2 frame. The Beavertail forearm is not original, the stock has been recheckered, and a non-factory recoil pad has also been added. The refinished case colors resemble the factory's, and the reblued barrels also have good color. Action is still tight, and as you can see, the engraving is still very sharp. With originality being Polar North for Parker collectors, how do you determine value on a shotgun like this? If this gun was all original, and in 95% condition overall, its value would be in the $12,500-$15,000 range (and easy to sell!). This non-original DHE in this type of refurbished condition would probably be in the $3,750-$5,000 range, or less than half of an original.

SHOTGUNS: NRA ANTIQUE CONDITIONS

NRA Antique Fine Condition (30%-80%), L.C. Smith **Grade IIE SxS**, 12 ga., 30 in. barrels, ser. no. 210689, mfg. early 1909. This older L.C. Smith, manufactured by Hunter Arms Company in Fulton, NY is a typical example of the condition factor you'll find on older, pre-WWI major trademark American shotguns. The exception is the barrels, which have obviously been reblued and do not match the overall condition of this SxS. Original case colors have mottled/faded over the years, and there appears to be some surface pitting on the front part of the lower frame. Original stock appears to have no cracks around the sidelock mechanism (unusual for an L.C. Smith of this vintage), and the splinter forearm checkering has almost disappeared. This shotgun's single trigger and ejectors will raise its value approximately 65%. Overall, compare the case colors on this L.C. Smith to the 40% and 98% condition L.C. Smiths in the Shotguns: PPGS Condition Factors section. Originality and strong frame case colors are everything when determining value on America's major trademark SxS shotguns.

Photo Percentage Grading System™

Twenty-Ninth Edition *Blue Book of Gun Values*™

NRA Antique Very Good Condition (0%-30%), Lefever Arms Company G Grade SxS hammerless, 12 ga., 30 in. barrels, no ser. no., mfg. circa 1890. This shotgun qualifies for this condition factor because there are still traces of case colors on the frame in protected areas. Original metal surfaces are smooth with sharp edges, the wood is slightly scratched or bruised, and the bore condition is disregarded. Yet, this SxS retains some eye appeal because nothing has been replaced, and the wood and metal condition factors match each other. Also, the action remains tight, and it is possible that this gun could still be shot if it was inspected by a competent gunsmith. The solid rubber recoil pad has become deformed after decades of sitting in a gun cabinet, where the weight of the gun will eventually flatten out the pad. Overall, American SxS collectors would rather have an original gun in this condition than a Fine example with problems.

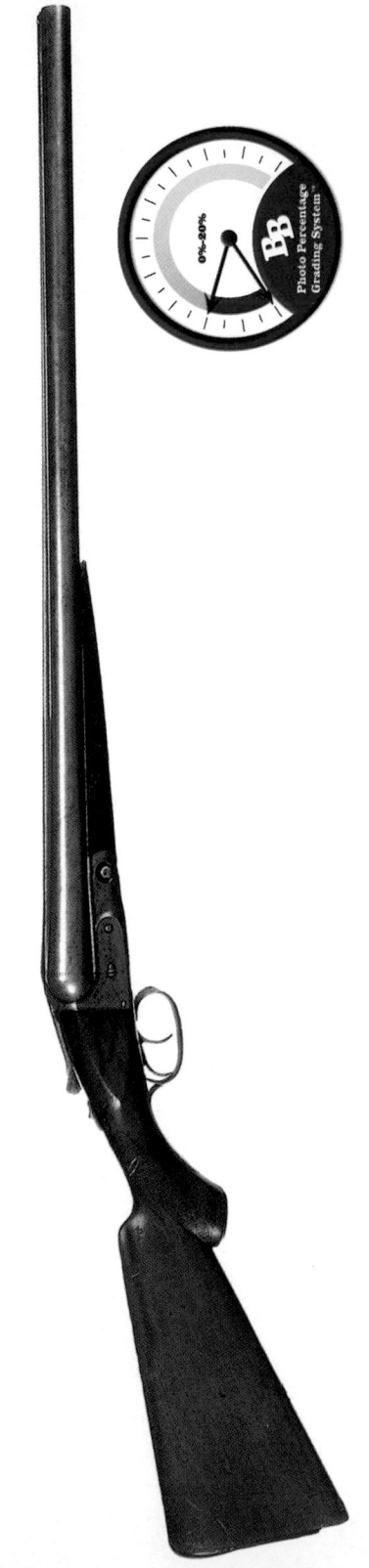

NRA Antique Good Condition (0%–20%), Parker VH SxS hammerless, 12 ga., 26 1/8 in. barrels, ser. no. 111718, mfg. 1902. So what's wrong with this description? If you're a Parker collector, 26 1/8 in. barrels immediately raise a red flag, as they have been shortened from the original factory 30 in. length. Cut barrels on Parkers are a very negative alteration, seriously affecting a Parker's value, regardless of grade. Other problems include stock gouging/chipping, and only a portion of the broken buttplate remains. Original frame and barrel finish are gone and have turned an overall grayish patina. Action still remains tight (no surprise there), and this gun may still be shootable, but must be inspected carefully first. With over 242,000 Parkers manufactured between 1866 and 1938 (Remington took over production 1934-1938), this is a good example of how a lot of them look today—well used, and almost worn out. Most people, including many serious collectors, have never seen an original mint condition Parker—they are that rare!

Twenty-Ninth Edition *Blue Book of Gun Values*™

***Photo Percentage Grading System*™**

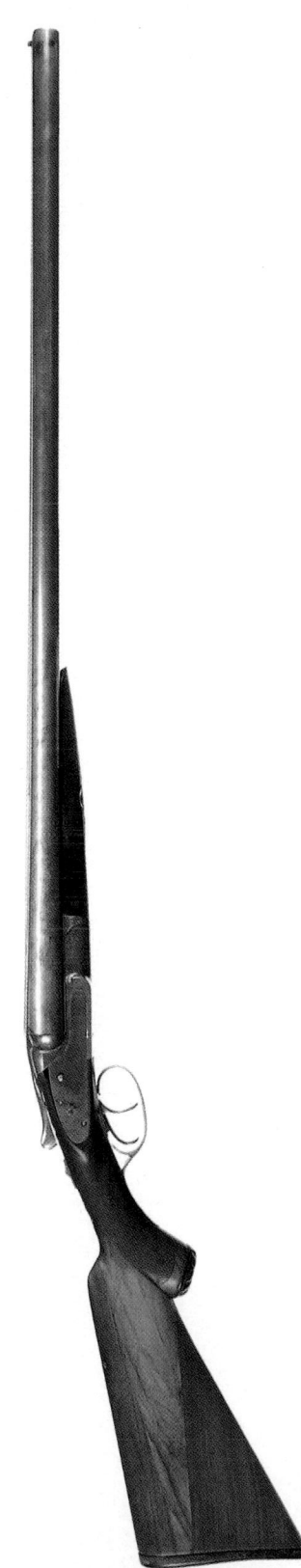

NRA Antique Fair Condition (no finish, some major parts replaced), Lefever G Grade SxS, 12 ga., 30 in. barrels, ser. no. 18725, mfg. 1893. As you can see, with NRA Antique grading factors, once you get down to Good, Fair, or Poor, there isn't a lot of difference when it comes to eye appeal, as guns in this condition are typically not that desirable. The biggest problem with this gun is that the stock was shattered at an earlier date, and a large replacement chunk with non-matching grain has been added. This gun's action is loose, and no metal finish remains on either the barrels or frame. The bores are also dark and pitted (i.e., don't shoot). Close observation will also reveal that the wood surrounding the sidelock is very thin, and appears to have been sanded. Overall, this gun's Fair condition and non-originality have bottomed out its value. Unfortunately, hundreds of similar surviving examples are in this condition factor, which explains why a really good original example is so rare (and expensive) in today's SxS marketplace.

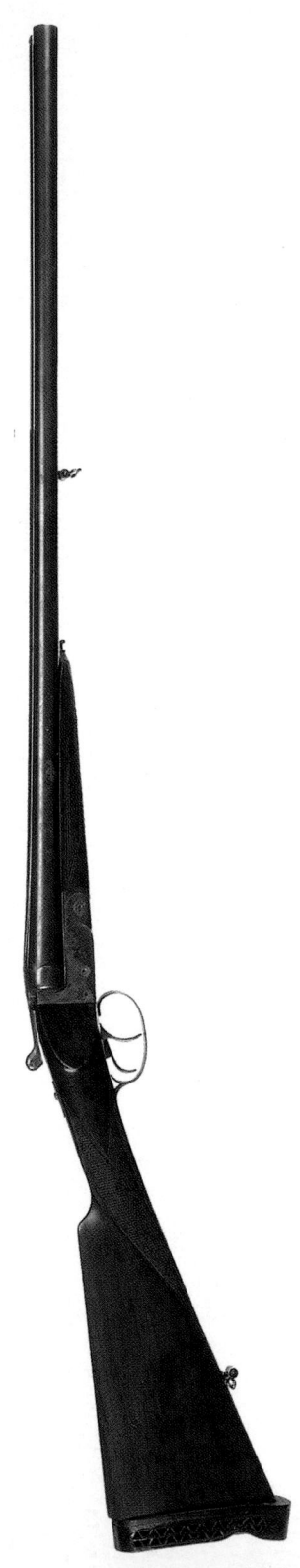

NRA Antique Poor Condition (no finish w/replacement parts), French SxS, 16 ga., 28 in. barrels, ser. no. 1513, mfg. circa 1910-1920. This is truly a no-name shotgun, as no manufacturer's name or marking appears anywhere on this gun—only the proofmarks indicate French production. Probably manufactured by spec, this boxlock is only chambered for 2 9/16 in. cartridges, and still has its sling swivels. There is virtually no eye appeal with this shotgun, and the crudely installed recoil pad and major dents on left barrel (not shown) further hurt this gun's overall desirability factor. So how do you determine the value of a gun like this which basically can no longer be shot, and needs to be hidden in the back of your gun cabinet when your friends come over? The answer is thousands of shotguns in this type of condition that are virtually unknown might be rare, but the only thing rarer is the person who might buy it. In other words, don't pay over $125, since in this case, even the parts aren't worth anything, as virtually no one is going to have a similar make, model, and gauge.

Photo Percentage Grading System™

Twenty-Ninth Edition *Blue Book of Gun Values*™

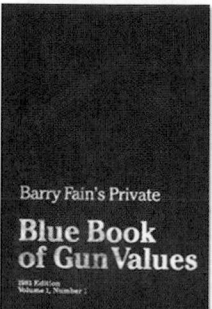

1st Edition (Vol. I, No. I)
1981

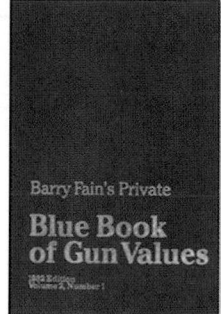

2nd Edition (Vol. II, No. I)
1982

3rd Edition (Vol. II, No. II)
1982

4th Edition
1983

5th Edition
1984

6th Edition
1985

7th Edition
1986

8th Edition
1987

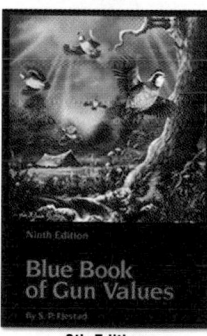

9th Edition
1988

10th Edition
1989

11th Edition
1990

12th Edition
1991

13th Edition
1992

14th Edition
1993

15th Edition
1994

16th Edition
1995

OLDER EDITIONS

17th Edition
1996

18th Edition
1997

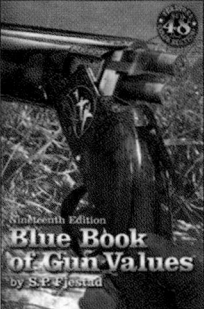

19th Edition
1998

20th Edition
1999

21st Edition
2000

22nd Edition
2001

23rd Edition
2002

24th Edition
2003

25th Edition
2004

26th Edition
2005

27th Edition
2006

28th Edition
2007

Many of you may want to pick up older editions to start or complete a collection. The rule of thumb is that the older an edition is, the harder it is to find, and the more expensive it will be. Books may be signed with an inscription and/or dated if you'd like. We do carry some older editions in stock, but the inventory can change daily. For more information, availability, condition, and pricing contact Kelsey at ext. 22 or email her at: support@bluebookinc.com

Blue Book Publications, Inc.
1-800-877-4867
www.bluebookinc.com

A SECTION

A.A.

Previously manufactured by Azanza & Arrizabalaga, located in Eibar, Spain.

GRADING - PPGS™	100%	98%	95%	90%	80%	70%	60%

PISTOLS: SEMI-AUTO

A.A. - 7.65mm cal., semi-auto pistol, slide marked "Azanza & Arrizabalaga Model 1916, A.A." in oval on frame.

	100%	98%	95%	90%	80%	70%	60%
	$235	$200	$165	$135	$115	$85	$75

REIMS - 6.35mm or 7.65mm cal., semi-auto pistol, copies of M1906 Browning, marked "1914 Model".

	100%	98%	95%	90%	80%	70%	60%
	$185	$150	$130	$110	$90	$70	$50

A.A.A.

Previously manufactured by Aldazabal, located in Spain.

PISTOLS: SEMI-AUTO

M1919 - 7.65mm cal., semi-auto pistol.

	100%	98%	95%	90%	80%	70%	60%
	$110	$100	$85	$70	$65	$60	$55

A.A. ARMS INC.

Previous manufacturer located in Monroe, NC until 1999.

CARBINES: SEMI-AUTO

AR9 CARBINE - similar action to AP9, except has carbine length barrel and side-folding metal stock. Banned 1994.

	100%	98%	95%	90%	80%	70%	60%
	$750	$625	$550	$475	$400	$350	$300

PISTOLS: SEMI-AUTO

AP9 MINI-SERIES PISTOL - 9mm Para. cal., semi-auto blowback paramilitary design, phosphate/blue or nickel finish, 2 barrel lengths, 10- (C/B 1994) or 20*-shot mag. Disc. 1999, parts cleanup during 2000.

	100%	98%	95%	90%	80%	70%	60%
	$210	$185	$165	$150	$135	$125	$115

Last MSR was $245.

> Add $20 for nickel finish.
> Add $200 for AP9 long barrel Target Model (banned 1994).

A & B HIGH PERFORMANCE FIREARMS

Previous competition pistol manufacturer located in Arvin, CA.

PISTOLS: SEMI-AUTO

LIMITED CLASS - 9mm Para. or .38 Super cal., single action, competition M1911-styled action, STI frame, Ultimatch bull barrel, Caspian slide, Bo-Mar adj. rear sight, blue or chrome finish.

	100%	98%	95%	90%	80%	70%	60%
	$1,875	$1,600	$1,375	$1,150	$925	$700	$550

Last MSR was $1,875.

OPEN CLASS - 9mm Para. or .38 Super cal., single action, competition M1911-styled action, STI frame, Ultimatch or Hybrid compensated barrel, Caspian slide, C-More scope, blue or chrome finish.

	100%	98%	95%	90%	80%	70%	60%
	$2,800	$2,300	$1,875	$1,600	$1,375	$1,000	$750

Last MSR was $2,800.

A.R. SALES

Previous manufacturer located in South El Monte, CA, circa 1968-1977.

PISTOLS: SEMI-AUTO

HANDGUN - .45 ACP cal., semi-auto patterned after Colt Model 1911 Govt., less weight than normal Colt .45.

	100%	98%	95%	90%	80%	70%	60%
	$295	$250	$225	$205	$175	$155	$145

RIFLES: SEMI-AUTO

RIFLE: MARK IV SPORTER - .308 Win. cal., semi-auto, M-14 style action, clip-fed, adj. sights. Approx. 200 mfg.

	100%	98%	95%	90%	80%	70%	60%
	$725	$650	$575	$500	$450	$400	$350

ADC

Current pistol manufacturer and customizer located in Gardone, Italy. Consumer direct sales.

ADC manufactures high quality custom pistols, mainly of M1911 design. ADC also provides a complete range of customizing and gunsmithing services. Please contact the company directly for more information (see Trademark Index).

AFC

Previously manufactured by Auguste Francotte located in Liege, Belgium, 1912-1914.

PISTOLS: SEMI-AUTO

SEMI-AUTO PISTOL - 6.35mm cal., 6-shot mag., frame marked "Francotte Liege."

	100%	98%	95%	90%	80%	70%	60%
	$275	$250	$220	$165	$140	$110	$85

A. J. ORDNANCE

Previous manufacturer located in Covina, CA.

PISTOLS: SEMI-AUTO

THOMAS - .45 ACP cal., semi-auto, double action only, 6 shot, 3 1/2 in. barrel, fixed sights, checkered plastic grips, delayed blowback action, stainless steel barrel. Disc. mid-1970s.

	100%	98%	95%	90%	80%	70%	60%
	$600	$525	$450	$400	$350	$300	$250

Add 50% for chrome or stainless steel.

A K S (AK-47, AK-74, & AKM COPIES)

Select fire paramilitary design rifle originally designed in Russia (initials refer to Avtomat Kalashnikova, 1947). The AK-47 was officially adopted by Russia in 1949. Russian-manufactured select fire AK-47s have not been manufactured since the mid-1950s. Semi-auto AK-47 and AKM clones are currently manufactured by several arsenals in China including Norinco and Poly Technologies, Inc. (currently illegal to import), in addition to being manufactured in other countries including the Czech Republic, Bulgaria, Russia, Egypt, and Hungary. On April 6th, 1998, recent "sporterized" variations (imported 1994-1998) with thumbhole stocks were banned by presidential order. Beginning in 2000, AK-47s were being assembled in the U.S., using both newly manufactured and older original military parts and components.

AK-47s are not rare - over 100 million have been manufactured by Russia and China since WWII.

AK/AK-47/AKM HISTORY & RECENT IMPORTATION

Since the early 1950s, the AK/AK-47/AKM series of select fire rifles has been the standard issue military rifle of the former Soviet Union and its satellites. It continues to fulfill that role reliably today. The AK series of rifles, from the early variants of the AK-47 through the AKM and AK-74, is undoubtedly the most widely used military small arms design in the world. Developed by Mikhail Kalashnikov (the AK stands for Avtomat Kalashnikova) in 1946, the AK went into full production in 1947 in Izhevsk, Russia. In 1953, the milled receiver was put into mass production. Since then, variants of the original AK-47 have been manufactured by almost every former Soviet bloc country and some free world nations, including Egypt. The AK action is the basis for numerous other weapons, including the RPK (Ruchnoy Pulemyot Kalashnikova).

The AK-47 was replaced in 1959 by the AKM, and retained the same basic design. The rifle was simply updated to incorporate easier and more efficient production methods, using a stamped, sheet metal receiver that was pinned and riveted in place, rather than a milled receiver. Other changes included a beavertail forearm, muzzle compensator, and an anti-bounce device intended to improve controllability and increase accuracy.

The AK was designed to be, and always has been, a "peasant-proof" military weapon. It is a robust firearm, both in design and function. Its record on the battlefields around the world is impressive, rivaled only by the great M1 Garand of the U.S. or bolt rifles such as the English Mark III Enfield. The original AK-47 prototypes are on display in the Red Army Museum in Moscow.

All of the current semi-auto AK "clones" are copies of the AKM's basic receiver design and internal components minus the full-auto parts. The Saiga rifle (see separate listing), manufactured by the Izhevsk Machining Plant, in Izhevsk, Russia, is the sole Russian entry into this market. It is available in the standard 7.62x39 mm, 5.45x39 mm (disc.) and 20 gauge or .410 bore. Molot (hammer) JSC also exports semi-automatic AKs to the U.S. under the trade name Vepr. (see separate listing). Both the Saiga and Vepr. are imported and distributed by Robinson Armaments. Molot was the home of the PPSh-41 sub-machine gun during WWII, and also manufactured the RPK and the RPK-74. Other AK European manufacturers include companies in the Czech Republic, Bulgaria, and the former Yugoslavia. The Egyptian-made Maahdi AK clones were also available in the U.S. market.

Interest in the Kalashnikov design is at an all-time high due to the availability of high quality military AK-74, AKS-74, AKS-74U, and RPK-74 parts kits. Some models, such as those produced by Marc Krebs, are of very high quality. Currently, it is hard to go to a gun show or page through a buy/sell firearms magazine and not see a variety of parts, accessories, and high capacity magazines available for the variety of AK variants. For shooters, the value represented by these guns is undeniable for the price point.

Values for almost all of the imported AK clones are based solely on their use as sporting or target rifles. Fit and finish varies by country and importer. Most fall on the "low" side. Interest peaked prior to the passage of the 1994 Crime Bill and both AK clones and their "high capacity" magazines were bringing a premium for a short period of time in 1993 and 1994. However, interest waned during 1995-97, and the reduced demand lowered prices. In November of 1997, the Clinton Administration instituted an "administrative suspension" on all import licenses for these types of firearms in order to do a study on their use as "sporting firearms."

On April 6th, 1998, the Clinton Administration, in the political wake of the Jonesboro tragedy, banned the further import of 58 "assault-type" rifles, claiming that these semi-automatics could not be classified as sporting weapons - the AK-47 and most related configurations were included. During 1997, firearms importers obtained permits to import almost 600,000 reconfigured rifles - approximately only 20,000 had entered the country when this ban took effect. When the ban began, applications were pending to import an additional 1,000,000 guns. Previously, thumbhole-stocked AK Sporters were still legal for import, and recent exporters included the Czech Republic, Russia, and Egypt.

RIFLES: SEMI-AUTO, AK-47, AK-74, & AKM MODELS

"AK-47" technically designates the original select fire (semi-automatic or fully automatic), Russian-made military rifle with a milled receiver. Recent semi-automatic "clones" normally have stamped receivers and are technically designated AKMs. Recently manufactured AK-47 clones refer to rifles with milled receivers. Chinese importation stopped during late 1990. Also refer to separate listings under Poly Technologies, Inc., Norinco, Federal Ordnance, B-West, K.B.I., Sentinel Arms, American Arms, Inc., and others who have recently imported this configuration.

GRADING - PPGS™	100%	98%	95%	90%	80%	70%	60%

AK-47 (AKM) RECENT IMPORTS - 7.62x39mm (most common cal., former Russian M43 military), 5.45x39mm (Romanian mfg. or Saiga/MAK - recent mfg. only), or .223 Rem. cal., semi-auto Kalashnikov action, stamped (most common) or milled receiver, typically 16 1/2 in. barrel, 5-shot, 10-shot, or 30*-shot (C/B 1994) mag., wood or synthetic stock and forearm except on folding stock model, recent importation (1994-early 1998) mostly had newer "sporterized" fixed stocks with thumbholes, may be supplied with bayonet, sling, cleaning kit, patterned after former military production rifle of China and Russia.

	100%	98%	95%	90%	80%	70%	60%
Current U.S. assembly MSR N/A	$495	$425	$325	$295	$250	$230	$210
Bulgarian mfg.	$525	$425	$325	$275	$240	$220	$200
Egyptian mfg. (recent import)	$345	$275	$225	$185	$165	$130	$115
Romanian mfg. (recent import)	$335	$285	$260	$240	$220	$200	$180
Yugoslavian mfg.	$525	$425	$325	$275	$240	$220	$200
Hungarian mfg.	$525	$425	$325	$275	$240	$220	$200
Czech mfg.	$525	$425	$325	$275	$240	$220	$200
Bulgarian mfg.	$525	$425	$325	$275	$240	$220	$200

Add 10-15% for 5.45x39 mm cal. on Eastern European mfg. (non-recent import).
Add 20% for older folding stock variations.

Recent U.S. assembly refers to an original stamped European (mostly FEG) or milled receiver with U.S. assembly, using either new parts or matched, older unused original Eastern European-manufactured parts (BATF 922.R compliant). This newest generation of AK-47s is high quality overall, and cannot be sold in California. Check city and state laws regarding high capacity magazine compliance.

AK-74 - 5.45x39mm cal., semi-auto action based on the AKM, imported from Bulgaria and other previous Eastern bloc countries, in addition to recent assembly in the U.S., using FEG receivers, Bulgarian parts sets, and additional U.S.-made components.

	100%	98%	95%	90%	80%	70%	60%
Bulgarian mfg.	$450	$375	$315	$275	$240	$220	$200
Recent U.S. assembly	$495	$425	$325	$295	$250	$230	$210

A M A C

See the "Iver Johnson" section in this text. AMAC stands for American Military Arms Corporation. Manufactured in Jacksonville, AR. AMAC ceased operations in early 1993.

AMP TECHNICAL SERVICE GmbH

Previous manufacturer located in Puchheim, Germany. Previously imported and distributed exclusively beginning in 2001 by CQB Products, located in Tustin, CA.

RIFLES: BOLT ACTION

DSR-1 - .300 Win. Mag., .308 Win., or .338 Lapua cal., bolt action, bull pup design with in-line stock, receiver is made from aluminum, titanium, and polymers, internal parts are stainless steel, two-stage adj. trigger, 4- or 5-shot mag., 25.6 Lothar Walther fluted barrel with muzzlebrake and vent. shroud, includes bipod, ambidextrous 3-position safety, 13 lbs. Imported 2002-2004.

$7,295	$6,300	$5,200	$4,100	$3,000	$2,500	$2,000

Last MSR was $7,795.

Add $100 for .300 Win. Mag. cal.
Add $300 for .338 Lapua cal.

GRADING - PPGS™	100%	98%	95%	90%	80%	70%	60%

A M T

Current trademark manufactured beginning late 2004 by Crusader Gun Company, Inc., located in Houston, TX. Previous trademark manufactured by Galena Industries Inc. located in Sturgis, SD, 1999-Jan. 2001. Previously located in Irwindale, CA until 1998. From 1998-2001, all AMTs manufactured by Galena Industries Inc. had a lifetime warranty, which is now void. Also see Irwindale Arms, Inc. and Auto-Mag for older, discontinued models.

Galena Industries phased out the use of the AMT name, but continued to use the individual model names until 2001.

During 2005, Crusader Gun Company Inc. acquired the previous tooling of AMT - Auto Mag., and plans to reintroduce the following models: Auto Mag II, Auto Mag III, AutoMag IV, the Back Up .380, and the Back Up .45. As this edition went to press, production on these models was just beginning. Please contact the company directly for more information, including availability and pricing on these re-released models (see Trademark Index).

PISTOLS: SEMI-AUTO

From 1999 to 2001, AMT began using Millett sights exclusively. Between 1993 and 1998, AMT changed from white outline Millett adjustable sights to an adjustable three-dot (white) system manufactured by LPA in Italy. Early production pistols were made in El Monte, CA, and are marked "El Monte."

LIGHTNING - .22 LR cal., semi-auto, stainless steel only, 5 (bull only), 6 1/2, 8 1/2, 10 1/2, or 12 1/2 (disc. 1987) in. bull or tapered barrels, adj. sights and trigger, pistol based on semi-auto Ruger action, tapered barrels. 23,903 were mfg. 1984-87.

$350	$200	$150	$120	$105	$90	$80

Last MSR was $289.

This model featured a frame grooved for scope mounts, Clark trigger, Millett sights, and either Pachmayr rubber or Wayland wood grips as standard equipment.

✳ *Lightning Bull's Eye Regulation Target* - similar to 6 1/2 in. Lightning with bull barrel, except has vent. rib, wood grips, extended rear sight. Mfg. 1986 only.

$425	$350	$285	$225	$175	$140	$125

Last MSR was $436.

BABY AUTOMAG - .22 LR cal., semi-auto, stainless steel only, 8 1/2 in. vent. rib barrel, Millett adj. sights, smooth walnut grips, 1,001 mfg.

$750	$650	$550	$460	$395	$335	$285

AUTOMAG II - .22 Mag. cal., stainless steel only, 3 3/8 (Compact Model, disc., limited mfg.), 4 1/2 (disc., limited mfg.), or 6 in. barrel, gas-assisted action, white outline Millett adj. sights, grooved Lexan grips, 7- (Compact) or 9-shot mag., 24-32 oz. Mfg. 1987-2001, reintroduced late 2004.

MSR $695	$575	$425	$350	$300	$250	$200	$175

Subtract approx. 25% for 3 3/8 or 4 1/2 in. barrel.

AUTOMAG III - .30 Carbine or 9mm Win. Mag. (mfg. 1993 only) cal., stainless steel, 6 3/8 in. barrel, patterned after Colt Govt. Model, white outline Millett adj. sights, grooved Lexan grips, 8-shot mag., 43 oz. Mfg. 1992-2001, 2007 re-release date.

MSR N/A	$530	$445	$335	$265	$230	$195	$170

Last MSR was $549.

GRADING - PPGS™	100%	98%	95%	90%	80%	70%	60%

AUTOMAG IV - 10mm (disc. 1993) or .45 Win. Mag. cal., 6 1/2 (.45 Win. Mag. only) or 8 5/8 (disc. 1993) in. barrel, 7 or 8-shot mag., Millett adj. sights, stainless steel, 46 oz. Mfg. 1992-2001, 2007 re-release date.

MSR N/A	$530	$445	$325	$265	$230	$195	$170

AUTOMAG V - .50 AE cal., stainless steel, 6 1/2 in. barrel, gas venting system reduces recoil, 5-shot mag., 46 oz. Mfg. 1993-95.

	$815	$700	$625	$515	$450	$375	$325

Last MSR was $900.

AUTOMAG 440 - .440 Cor-Bon cal., special order only. Mfg. 1999-2001.

	$775	$650	$550	$460	$395	$335	$285

Last MSR was $899.

JAVELINA - 10mm cal., semi-auto, 7 in. barrel, 8-shot mag., Millett adj. sights, wraparound neoprene grips, wide adj. trigger, long grip safety, 48 oz. Mfg. 1992 only.

	$560	$460	$360	$285	$250	$215	$185

Last MSR was $676.

BACKUP PISTOL - .22 LR (disc. 1987), .357 Sig. (new 1996), .380 ACP, .38 Super (new 1995), 9mm Para. (new 1995), .40 S&W (new 1995), .400 Cor-Bon (new 1997), or .45 ACP (new 1995) cal., semi-auto, choice of traditional double action (disc. 1992) or double action only (new 1992), 2 1/2 (.22 LR or .380 ACP) or 3 in. barrel, stainless steel, Lexan grips, 5-shot (.380 ACP or .40 S&W), 6-shot, or 8-shot (.22 LR) mag., 18 (.380 ACP only) or 23 oz. Older disc. walnut grip models are worth a slight premium. In 1992, AMT reengineered this model and removed all external levers, production resumed again late 2004.

✳ *Backup Pistol Small Frame* - .22 LR (limited production) or .380 ACP cal. (disc. 2000, reintroduced 2004).

MSR $349	$295	$225	$140	$110	$100	$85	$75

    Add approx. 10% for .22 LR cal.

✳ *Backup Pistol Large Frame* - 9mm Para. (disc. 2006), .357 SIG, .38 Super, .40 S&W, .400 Cor-Bon, or .45 ACP cal.

MSR $489	$420	$300	$225	$150	$125	$110	$95

    Add $110 for .400 Cor-Bon cal.
    Subtract approx. 15% for 9mm Para.

BACKUP PISTOL II - .380 ACP cal., single action, semi-auto, stainless steel, 2 1/2 in. barrel, 5-shot finger extension mag., black carbon fiber grips, 18 oz. Mfg. 1993-98.

	$295	$225	$150	$120	$105	$90	$80

Last MSR was $369.

.45 ACP STANDARD GOVERNMENT MODEL - .45 ACP cal., similar to Colt semi-auto Govt. Model, stainless steel, 5 in. barrel, fixed rear sight, loaded chamber indicator, adj. trigger, wraparound neoprene grips, 38 oz. Disc. 1999.

	$325	$275	$225	$175	$140	$125	$105

Last MSR was $399.

HARDBALLER II - .45 ACP cal., similar to Colt Gold Cup Model, stainless steel, 5 in. barrel, adj. Millett rear sight, serrated rib, loaded chamber indicator, adj. trigger, wraparound neoprene grips, 38 oz. Disc. 2001.

	$400	$325	$250	$195	$165	$140	$120

Last MSR was $499.

    Add $280 for 7 in. Hardballer conversion kit (disc. 1997).

GRADING - PPGS™	100%	98%	95%	90%	80%	70%	60%

* *Hardballer II Longslide* - similar to Hardballer II, except 7 in. barrel, longer slide assembly, and also available in .400 Cor-Bon (named .400 Accelerator, new 1998), 46 oz. Disc. 2001.

	$425	$320	$250	$195	$165	$140	$120

Last MSR was $549.

Add $50 for .400 Cor-Bon (.400 Accelerator) cal.
Add $300 for 5 in. Longslide conversion kit (disc. 1997).

COMMANDO - .40 S&W cal., 4 in. barrel. Mfg. 1998-2001.

	$400	$325	$250	$195	$165	$140	$120

Last MSR was $499.

SKIPPER - .45 ACP cal., re-released in 1991 with choice of .40 S&W or .45 ACP cal., similar to Hardballer, except approx. 1 in. shorter slide on pre-1984 mfg., 4 1/4 in. barrel, checkered walnut grips, matte finish stainless steel, Millett adj. rear sight, 7-shot mag., 33 oz. Disc. 1991.

	$350	$285	$250	$195	$165	$140	$120

Last MSR was $450.

COMBAT SKIPPER - similar to Skipper, but with fixed sights. Disc. 1984.

	$375	$330	$295	$240	$210	$180	$155

BULL'S EYE TARGET MODEL - .40 S&W cal., similar to Hardballer with 5 in. barrel, 8-shot mag., adj. Millett sights, wraparound neoprene grips, 38 oz. Mfg. 1991 only.

	$400	$340	$295	$240	$210	$180	$155

Last MSR was $500.

"ON DUTY" DOUBLE ACTION - 9mm Para., .40 S&W, or .45 ACP (new late 1994) cal., stainless steel slide and barrel, 4 1/2 in. barrel, 10-shot (C/B 1994), 15*-shot (9mm Para.), 11*-shot (.40 S&W), or 9-shot (.45 ACP) mag., 3-dot sighting system, anodized aluminum frame, trigger disconnect safety with inertia firing pin, carbon fiber grips, 32 oz. Mfg. 1991-94.

	$385	$295	$250	$195	$165	$140	$120

Last MSR was $470.

Add $60 for .45 ACP cal.

In 1992, this model became available with either traditional double action with decocking lever or double action only with safety.

RIFLES: BOLT ACTION

AMT rifles were discontinued in 1998.

BOLT ACTION STANDARD SINGLE SHOT - 11 various cals., post-1964 push-feed action, pre-1964 3-position side safety, cone breech, composite stock, cryogenically treated stainless steel barrel w/o sights, 8 1/2 lbs. Mfg. 1996-97.

	$825	$650	$450	$385	$335	$280	$235

Last MSR was $1,500.

BOLT ACTION DELUXE SINGLE SHOT - 11 various cals., Mauser-type controlled feeding, short, medium, or long right-hand or left-hand action, pre-1964 3-position side safety and claw-type extractor, cryogenically treated stainless steel barrel w/o sights, custom Kevlar stock, approx. 8 1/2 lbs. Mfg. 1996 only.

	$995	$800	$600	$495	$430	$365	$315

Last MSR was $2,400.

GRADING - PPGS™	100%	98%	95%	90%	80%	70%	60%

BOLT ACTION STANDARD REPEATER - 21 various cals., post-1964 push-feed action, Mauser-type mag., pre-1964 3-position side safety, Model 70-type trigger, composite stock, cryogenically treated stainless steel barrel w/o sights. 8 1/2 lbs. Mfg. 1996 only.

	$800	$625	$500	$430	$375	$315	$270

Last MSR was $1,110.

BOLT ACTION DELUXE REPEATER - similar features to Bolt Action Deluxe Single Shot, except has Mauser-type mag. Mfg. 1996 only.

	$1,000	$800	$650	$540	$465	$385	$335

Last MSR was $1,596.

RIFLES: SEMI-AUTO

LIGHTNING (25/22) - .22 LR cal., semi-auto based on Ruger 10-22 action, stainless steel, 30-shot mag., 17 1/2 in. bull or tapered barrel, nylon pistol grip handle and forearm, folding stock with recoil pad or youth stock, fixed sights, 6 lbs. Mfg. 1986-93.

	$220	$175	$150	$120	$105	$90	$80

Last MSR was $296.

SMALL GAME HUNTER (SGH) - .22 LR cal., same mechanical action as Lightning, except has matte black nylon stock with checkered forearm and grip, 22 in. barrel, 10-shot mag., no sights. Removable recoil pad allows storage in stock. 6 lbs. Mfg. 1986-93.

	$230	$190	$160	$125	$110	$90	$80

Last MSR was $300.

SMALL GAME HUNTER II - similar to Small Game Hunter, except has match grade 22 in. heavyweight full-floating barrel, 10-shot rotary mag., black fiberglass nylon stock, no sights, 6 lbs. Mfg. 1993 only.

	$230	$190	$160	$125	$110	$90	$80

Last MSR was $300.

Add $70 for 17 1/2 in. stainless steel barrel.
Add $150 for 22 1/2 in. stainless steel match grade barrel.

CHALLENGE EDITION (I, II, III) - .22 LR cal., semi-auto target variation featuring McMillan fiberglass stock, 16 1/4 (choice of 6 in. barrel weight extension or 3 in. muzzle brake, new 1997), 18, 20 (mfg. 1994-96), or 22 (mfg. 1994-96) in. floating stainless steel bull barrel, custom designed or Jewell (new 1997) trigger, custom order through AMT's Custom Shop. Mfg. 1994-98.

	$800	$600	$450	$385	$335	$280	$235

Last MSR was $1,296.

Subtract $200 without Jewell trigger.
Add $144 for 16 1/4 barrel with 3 in. muzzle brake (Challenge Edition II, new 1997).
Add $85 for 16 1/4 barrel with 6 in. barrel extension (Challenge Edition III).

* *Challenge Edition Elite With Bloop Tube* - features 16 1/4 in. barrel with a 6 in. bloop tube extension enabling increased bullet velocity with muzzle heavy characteristics, McMillan fiberglass STC stock. Mfg. 1996-98.

	$925	$700	$550	$460	$395	$335	$285

Last MSR was $1,498.

Subtract $255 if without compensator.

SPORTER EDITION - .22 LR cal., 16 1/2, 18, 20, or 22 in. tapered sporter barrel, McMillan fiberglass sporter stock. Mfg. 1996 only.

	$650	$525	$400	$335	$290	$245	$215

Last MSR was $900.

GRADING - PPGS™	100%	98%	95%	90%	80%	70%	60%

HUNTER EDITION I - .22 LR cal., 18, 20, or 22 in. regular barrel with injection-molded sporter stock. Mfg. 1996 only (replaced with Hunter Edition II).

	$550	$425	$300	$240	$210	$180	$155

Last MSR was $800.

HUNTER EDITION II - .22 LR cal., 22 in. tapered sporter barrel with 2 lb. Jewell trigger, McMillan synthetic sporter stock. Mfg. 1997-98.

	$750	$575	$425	$360	$315	$260	$225

Last MSR was $1,354.

FLY SWATTER I - .22 LR cal., 16 1/2 in. regular barrel with injection molded (1996 only) or Hogue over-molded (new 1997) sporter stock. Mfg. 1996-97.

	$575	$450	$325	$265	$230	$195	$170

Last MSR was $822.

FLY SWATTER II - similar to Fly Swatter I, except has 3 in. muzzle brake. Mfg. 1997 only.

	$675	$475	$350	$285	$250	$215	$185

Last MSR was $936.

BR-50 ACCELERATOR EDITION - .22 LR cal., features 16 1/4 (new 1998) or 16 1/2 (disc. 1997) in. bull barrel with 3 in. muzzle brake (new 1998), McMillan bench rest stock, Hoehn barrel tuner (disc. 1997), and Jewell trigger. Mfg. 1997-98.

	$795	$600	$450	$385	$335	$280	$235

Last MSR was $1,440.

ACCULITE EDITION RIFLE - .22 LR cal., features 18 in. Magnum Research graphite barrel with muzzle brake, thumbhole sporter stock, adj. Jewell trigger, 4 3/4 lbs. Mfg. 1998 only.

	$750	$575	$425	$360	$315	$260	$225

Last MSR was $1,321.

INTIMIDATOR EDITION RIFLE - .22 LR cal., 16 1/4 Shilen select match grade barrel with 6 in. bloop tube, adj. Jewell trigger, 6 1/4 lbs. Mfg. 1998 only.

	$875	$625	$475	$415	$360	$300	$255

Last MSR was $1,581.

MAGNUM HUNTER - .22 Mag. cal., semi-auto, 20 in. free-floating barrel, stainless steel, 10-shot straight stacked mag., no sights, drilled and tapped for Weaver 87-A scope base, black synthetic stock, 6 lbs. Mfg. 1995-98.

	$375	$295	$225	$175	$140	$125	$105

Last MSR was $459.

TARGET RIFLE SEMI-AUTO - .22 LR cal., button rifled cryogenically treated barrel with target crown, choice of Fajen laminate or Hogue composite stock, 10-shot mag., one-piece receiver with integral Weaver mount, 7 1/2 lbs. Mfg. 1997-98.

	$425	$350	$275	$225	$195	$165	$140

Last MSR was $549.

Add $50 for Fajen laminate stock.

AR-7 INDUSTRIES, LLC

Previous manufacturer 1998-2004, and located in Geneseo, IL. Previously located in Meriden, CT, from 1998 to early 2004.

≡≡**AR-7**≡≡

In February 2004, AR-7 Industries LLC was purchased by ArmaLite, Inc., and recent manufacture was in Geneseo, IL.

GRADING - PPGS™	100%	98%	95%	90%	80%	70%	60%

RIFLES: BOLT ACTION

AR-7 TAKEDOWN - .22 LR cal., bolt action variation of the AR-7 Explorer rifle, similar takedown/storage configuration, 2 1/2 lbs. Advertised 2002 only.

While advertised during 2002, this model was never manufactured.

RIFLES: SEMI-AUTO

AR-7 EXPLORER RIFLE - .22 LR cal., takedown barrelled action stores in synthetic stock which floats, 8-shot mag., aperture rear sight, 16 in. barrel (synthetic barrel with steel liner), black matte finish on AR-7, silvertone on AR-7S (disc. 2000), camouflage finish on AR-7C, two-tone (silver receiver with black stock and barrel) on AR-7T (disc. 2000), walnut finish on AR-W (mfg. 2001-2002), stowed length 16 1/2 in., 2 1/2 lbs. Mfg. late 1998-2004.

	$175	$150	$125	$110	$100	$90	$80

Last MSR was $200.

Add $15 for camouflage or walnut finish.

This model was also previously manufactured by Survival Arms, Inc. and Charter Arms - see individual listings for information.

AR-7 SPORTER (AR-20) - .22 LR cal., 16 1/2 in. steel barrel with vent. aluminum shroud, metal skeleton fixed stock with pistol grip, 8 (new 2001) or 16 shot "flip clip" (optional) mag., 3.85 lbs. Mfg. late 1998-2004.

	$175	$150	$125	$110	$100	$90	$80

Last MSR was $200.

Add $100 for sporter conversion kit (includes aluminum shrouded barrel, pistol grip stock, and 16 shot flip clip).

This model was also previously manufactured by Survival Arms, Inc. - see individual listing for information.

AR-7 TARGET - .22 LR cal., 16 in. bull barrel with 7/8 in. cantilever scope mount, tube stock with pistol grip, 8-shot mag., 3-9x40mm compact rubber armored scope was optional, 5.65 lbs. Mfg. 2002-2004.

	$195	$175	$150	$125	$105	$95	$80

Last MSR was $210.

Add $60 for compact scope.

ASAI AG (ADVANCED SMALL ARMS INDUS-TRIES)

Previous manufacturer located in Solothurn, Switzerland 1994-2004. Previously imported until 2000 by Magnum Research, Inc. located in Minneapolis, MN.

PISTOLS: SEMI-AUTO

ONE PRO.45 - 9mm Para. (limited mfg. in Europe, never imported into the U.S.), .40 S&W (limited mfg. in Europe, never imported into the U.S.), .400 Cor-Bon (conversion only), or .45 ACP cal., SA or DA, 3 (disc. 1998) or 3 3/4 in. barrel with polygonal rifling, steel or alloy (not imported into U.S.) frame, black contoured synthetic grips, black or two-tone (less than 10 mfg.) finish, 10-shot mag., includes plastic case, extra 10 shot mag., and cleaning kit, 25 or 31 oz. Imported mid-1997 through 2000.

	$595	$485	$410	$360	$330	$300	$275

Last MSR was $699.

Add $209 for .400 Cor-Bon conversion kit without compensator.
Add $249 for .45 ACP or .400 Cor-Bon conversion kit with extended barrel, compensator, and recoil spring guide.

GRADING - PPGS™	100%	98%	95%	90%	80%	70%	60%

AWA USA

Current importer established during late 2004 and located in Hialeah, FL.

AWA USA purchased the remaining assets of American Western Arms, Inc. in late 2004, and became the importer of guns manufactured by AWA International, Inc. in Brescia, Italy.

HANDGUNS

1873 CLASSIC SAA/1884 BISLEY - .357 Mag. or .45 LC cal., 4 3/4 or 5 1/2 in. barrel, Bisley style, blue, Turnbull color case hardened, nickel, or hard chrome finish, walnut grips. Importation began 2007.

	MSR $440	$395	$360	$330	$295	$250	$200	$150

Add $125 for color case hardened frame or $195 for nickel or hard chrome finish.

1873 ULTIMATE SAA - .32-20 WCF, .38-40 WCF, .44 Spl., .357 Mag., .44-40 WCF, or .45 LC cal., 4 3/4, 5 1/2, or 7 1/2 in. barrel, blue, Turnbull color case hardened, nickel, or hard chrome finish, walnut grips, coil main spring. Importation began 2007.

	MSR $600	$525	$450	$400	$350	$300	$250	$200

Add $125 for color case hardened frame or $195 for nickel or hard chrome finish.

LIGHTNINGBOLT SLIDE ACTION - .45 LC cal., 12 in. round barrel, 5 shot, walnut stock and forearm, blade front sight, available in high polish blue, color case hardened, hard chrome, or nickel finish. Importation began 2007.

	MSR $1,000	$895	$750	$625	$500	$400	$300	$225

Add $150 for color case hardened frame or $300 for nickel or hard chrome finish.

RIFLES: SLIDE ACTION

LIGHTNING RIFLE - .32-20 WCF, .38 Spl., .38-40 WCF, .44-40 WCF, or .45 LC cal., 20 or 24 in. round or octagon barrel, patterned after the original Colt Lightning model, choice of blue, color case hardened, white (hard chrome, brush nickel, or polished nickel) or black frame, standard or limited edition wood stock. Importation began 2007.

	MSR $850	$775	$675	$600	$525	$450	$375	$300

Add $40 for octagon barrel.
Add $200 for color case hardened frame.
Add $450 for White Lightning with either hard chrome or brushed/polished nickel finish.
Add $525 for Black Lightning w/black chrome finish.
Add $450 for limited edition model (1 of 500).

A-SQUARE COMPANY

Current manufacturer located in Glenrock, WY beginning late 2007. Previously located in Jeffersonville, IN 2003-2007. A-Square Company is a wholly owned subsidiary of JISTA, LLC. Previously located in Bedford KY until 2002, Louisville, KY until 2000, and in Madison, IN until 1991.

A-SQUARE

A-Square also offers different grades of walnut, different metal finishes, and various sights and scope rings as special orders. Custom calibers are also available by special order.

A-Square also manufactures ammunition at a facility located in Chamberlain, SD.

RIFLES: BOLT ACTION

Add $350 for A-Grade walnut, add $650 for AAA-Grade fancy walnut, add $500 for English walnut (disc.), add $100 for accent package (disc.), add $550 for black synthetic stock (disc.), add $600 for weather-impervious package (disc.), add $350 for 3-leaf steel express sights, add $300 for royal high gloss blue finish (disc. 1995, add $150 for high gloss polymer wood finish (disc. 2002), or $550 for .505 Gibbs or .577 Tyrannosaur cal.

GRADING - PPGS™	100%	98%	95%	90%	80%	70%	60%

HANNIBAL MODEL - most cals. available, bolt action built on a P-17 Enfield receiver, 22-26 in. barrel, deluxe oil finished walnut with pistol grip and recoil pad, Teflon coated metal, choice of barrel length and LOP, 9-11 1/4 lbs. New 1986.

MSR $3,500	$3,250	$2,850	$2,400	$2,100	$1,875	$1,725	$1,575

HAMILCAR MODEL - various cals. available, smaller variation of the Hannibal model featuring slimmer design gained by not needing the reinforcement for heavy Mag. cals., 4/5/6/7-shot mag., cocks on opening, 8-8 1/2 lbs. New 1994.

MSR $3,500	$3,250	$2,850	$2,400	$2,100	$1,875	$1,725	$1,575

CAESAR MODEL - most cals. available, bolt action built on a Remington M-700 receiver until 1993, Sako L-V actions were utilized beginning 1993, 22-26 in. barrel, select walnut with pistol grip and recoil pad, primarily a left-handed action with right-handed action a special order, 9-10 3/4 lbs. New 1986.

MSR $3,500	$3,250	$2,850	$2,400	$2,100	$1,875	$1,725	$1,575

GENGHIS KHAN MODEL - .22-250 Rem., .243 Win., .25-06, or 6mm Rem. cal., features Winchester pre-1964 Model 70 action, heavy tapered barrel, Coil-Chek stock helps reduce recoil, designed for varmint hunting. New 1995.

MSR $3,500	$3,200	$2,850	$2,400	$2,100	$1,875	$1,725	$1,575

A T C S A

Previously manufactured by Armas De Tiro Y Casa located in Spain.

REVOLVERS

COLT POCKET PISTOL COPY - revolver, .38 cal., 6-shot.

	$155	$140	$110	$100	$90	$75	$65

SINGLE SHOT REVOLVER - target pistol.

	$195	$165	$145	$110	$100	$90	$75

ATA ARMS

Current shotgun manufacturer located in Istanbul, Turkey. Currently imported (private label only) by Tristar, located in N. Kansas City, MO, and by K.B.I., located in Harrisonburg, PA.

SHOTGUNS

ATA Arms manufactures a complete line of good quality semi-automatic and slide-action shotguns in various configurations. Please contact the importers directly for more information, including model availability and U.S. pricing.

AYA (AGUIRRE Y ARANZABAL)

Current manufacturer established in 1917, and located in Eibar, Spain. Currently imported and distributed by by Anglo American Sporting Agency, located in Corona del Mar, CA, H.G. Lomas Gunmakers, located in Elkhart Lake, WI, New England Custom Gun Service, Ltd. (NECG), located in Plainfield, NH; John F. Rowe, located in Enid, OK; and by Fieldsport, located in Traverse City, MI; Previously imported by William Larkin Moore 1969-1978 (with Agoura, CA import marking) and 1978-1986 (with West Lake, CA import marking). Diarm also manufactured AYAs circa 1986-1988 in Eibar, Spain. Retail and dealer sales by importer and AYA select distributors.

AYA-manufactured shotguns can be identified by serialization. Serial numbers over 600,001 with barrel flats marked "Arms de Chasse" or "Scotia Group" are post-1988 AYA manufactured while specimens numbered under 600,000 may have been manufactured by Diarm circa 1986-1989. Diarm manufacture is not covered by the AYA warranty, nor is the resale the same as values listed below.

Please refer to the AYA and Spanish year of mfg. date codes under Serialization in the back of this text for more information on AYA shotguns.

SHOTGUNS: O/U

AYA also manufactured a Coral boxlock, both in standard and deluxe configurations. The Excelsior sidelock model was also available (2007 MSR price range was $3,800 - $4,600). The MD Series O/U models complete their European line (2007 MSR was $4,100 - $7,300).

Add 5% for gauges smaller than 12 ga.
Add 5% for 3 in. magnum chambers.

AUGUSTA - 12 ga. only, deluxe O/U sidelock, arabesque engraving in deep relief, select walnut.

This model has been imported off and on over the years and the importers should be contacted directly for current pricing information and availability.

CORAL "A" - 12 or 16 ga., boxlock action with Kersten cross bolt, vent. rib, ejectors, double triggers. Disc. 1985.

$1,275	$1,050	$875	$775	$695	$625	$560

Last MSR was $2,195.

CORAL "B" - similar to Coral A, except for coin-wash engraved receiver. Disc. 1985.

$1,395	$1,100	$925	$820	$720	$650	$595

Last MSR was $2,450.

MODEL 37 SUPER - 12, 16, or 20 ga., various barrel lengths and chokes, vent. rib, sidelock, auto ejector, elaborate engraving, high grade wood. Merkel-style action. Prices below reflect older models. Disc.

12 ga.	$3,000	$2,500	$2,100	$1,900	$1,700	$1,500	$1,250
16 ga.	$3,250	$2,600	$2,000	$1,700	$1,500	$1,350	$1,150
20 ga.	$3,500	$2,750	$2,200	$1,900	$1,700	$1,600	$1,475

* *New Model 37 A/B/C* - game scene engraved, detachable sidelock action, nickel steel receiver. This model has been imported off and on over the years.

Please contact the importers directly for pricing information and availability on this model.

MODEL 77 - 12 ga. only, Merkel-style O/U sidelock with Greener crossbolt, deluxe engraving checkering. Disc. 1985.

$3,100	$2,750	$2,500	$2,255	$2,030	$1,805	$1,600

Last MSR was $4,100.

MODEL 79 "A" - 12 ga. only, boxlock with double-locking lugs, sel. trigger, ejectors. Disc. 1985.

$1,275	$1,075	$965	$880	$790	$705	$640

Last MSR was $1,595.

MODEL 79 "B" - similar to Model 79 "A," only more elaborate engraving. Disc. 1985.

$1,395	$1,200	$1,085	$990	$890	$790	$695

Last MSR was $1,795.

MODEL 79 "C" - similar to Model 79 "B," only more elaborate engraving, double triggers on request. Disc. 1985.

$2,050	$1,825	$1,605	$1,460	$1,315	$1,165	$1,000

Last MSR was $2,650.

GRADING - PPGS™	100%	98%	95%	90%	80%	70%	60%

SHOTGUNS: SxS

Current retail values on the AYA shotguns listed below could vary somewhat from importer to importer. For the following models, please use these guidelines for special orders and/or features.

On current models listed below, add 5% to values if other than 12 ga. or Mag. chambers.
Add $1,050 for SNT or approx. $1,180 for SST on recently manufactured guns.
Add $1,968 for self-opening action.
Add approx. 40% for extra set of barrels.

BILL HANUS BIRDGUN - 16, 20 (disc. 2005), or 28 ga., similar wood, fit, checkering, and finish as the No. 53 sidelock, except is Anson & Deeley boxlock, patterned after the Westley Richards game gun, individual frames proportionate to ga., 27 (28 ga.) or 28 (16 ga.) in. barrels with fixed open chokes, case colored receiver with moderate engraving, SST (disc.) or DT, ejectors, includes leather-covered handguard, splinter forearm, straight grip. Imported 1997-2007.

	$2,650	$2,150	$1,750	$1,450	$1,100	$875	$700

Last MSR was $2,995.

This model was available only through Bill Hanus Birdguns LLC. Stocks bent for cast-on and leather-covered decelerator pads were also available at additional cost.

BOLERO - similar to Matador, with non-selective single trigger and extractors. Disc. 1984.

	$450	$395	$350	$300	$275	$250	$220

COUNTRYMAN GAME GUN - 12 or 20 ga. Imported 1998-2002.

	$2,050	$1,650	$675	$525	$450	$410	$365

Last MSR was $2,295.

IBERIA - 12 or 20 ga., 3 in., boxlock, double triggers, plain walnut. Disc. 1984.

	$495	$450	$395	$350	$300	$265	$230

IBERIA II - 12 or 16 ga., 28 in. barrels, 2 3/4 in. chamber only, double triggers, plain walnut. Mfg. 1984-85 only.

	$550	$475	$425	$365	$300	$265	$230

Last MSR was $570.

MATADOR - 10, 12, 16, 20, 28 ga., or .410 bore, 26, 28, or 30 in. barrel, various chokes, Anson & Deeley boxlock, auto ejectors, beavertail forearm, SST, checkered pistol grip stock. Mfg. 1955-63.

	$550	$475	$375	$325	$275	$225	$200

Add 10% for 20 ga. or 20% for .410 bore or 28 ga.

MATADOR NO. 2 - similar to Matador, with vent. rib, 12 or 20 ga. only. Disc.

	$675	$575	$475	$375	$300	$250	$200

Add 10% for 20 ga.

MATADOR NO. 3A - 12 or 20 ga., 3 in. chamber in 20 ga. only, boxlock, vent. rib, ejectors, SST. Disc. 1985.

	$795	$675	$575	$495	$440	$385	$335

Last MSR was $1,235.

Add 10% for 20 ga.

SENIOR - 12 ga. only, self opener, engraved sidelock action, select walnut. Top-of-the-line quality, made to special order only. Lighter upland version also available. Disc. 1987.

	$15,500	$12,000	$10,000	$8,000	$6,500	$5,500	$4,500

Last MSR was $21,000.

GRADING - PPGS™	100%	98%	95%	90%	80%	70%	60%

NO. 1 - 12, 16, 20, 28 ga. or .410 bore, full sidelock action, straight grip, ejectors, DTs, elaborate fine scroll engraving. Importation disc. 1987, resumed in 1991.

MSR $9,900		$7,995	$6,500	$5,250	$4,100	$3,250	$2,750	$2,250

Add approx. $400 for rounded action.

✳ *No. 1 DeLuxe* - features bold foliate engraving.

MSR $14,200		$11,000	$8,500	$6,750	$5,500	$4,000	$3,000	$2,500

Add approx. $200 for rounded action.

✳ *No. 1 DeLuxe English* - exhibition quality wood and engraved by Geoff Moore, English metal finish, custom order only.

This shotgun is specifically made for A.S.I., and is sold exclusively in the U.K. marketplace. Please contact A.S.I. for more information, including availability and prices (see Trademark Index).

NO. 2 - 12, 16, 20, 28 ga., or .410 bore, 3 in. chambers, English-style sidelock, ejector, cocking indicators, DTs. Importation disc. 1987, resumed 1991.

MSR $4,800		$4,100	$3,325	$2,700	$2,000	$1,650	$1,275	$1,000

Add $400 for rounded action.

✳ *No. 2 Bill Hanus Dreamgun Sidelock* - features Boss rounded action, built per individual custom order, 10 month delivery. Imported 2003-2007.

		$5,500	$4,750	$3,200	$2,600	$1,950	$1,500	$1,200

Last MSR was $5,950.

This model was only available from Bill Hanus Birdguns LLC.

NO. 3-A - 12, 16, 20, 28 ga., or .410 bore, boxlock, extractors, double triggers. Disc. 1985.

		$675	$575	$495	$450	$400	$375	$350

Last MSR was $850.

Add 25%-35% for 28 ga. or .410 bore.

NO. 4 - 12, 16, 20, 28 ga., or .410 bore, 3 in. chambers, English-style straight stock, boxlock action, ejectors, double trigger, straight grip stock, standard wood, Importation disc. 1987, resumed 1991.

MSR $2,300		$2,000	$1,675	$1,250	$1,000	$850	$600	$500

✳ *No. 4/53* - similar to No. 4, except has No. 53 wood upgrade. Importation disc. 1987, resumed 1991.

MSR $2,900		$2,425	$2,000	$1,575	$1,250	$1,000	$875	$725

Add approx. $200 for No. 4/53S (includes wood upgrade, SNT, and round knob pistol grip, disc.).

NO. 4 DELUXE - 12, 20, 28 ga. or .410 bore, English-style, boxlock, ejector, stock, forearm, trigger to order. Importation disc. 1985, resumed 1991.

MSR $4,400		$3,900	$3,250	$2,700	$2,150	$1,650	$1,450	$1,200

XXV BOXLOCK (BL) - 12, 20, 28 ga. or .410 bore, similar to No. 4 Deluxe, except 25 in. barrels, Churchill rib. Importation disc. 1986, resumed 1991-2005.

		$2,550	$2,175	$1,750	$1,450	$1,250	$1,000	$875

Last MSR was $2,950.

Add approx. $1,509 for extra set of barrels.

XXV SIDELOCK (SL) - 12, 16, 20 (disc. 1997), 28 (disc. 1997) ga., or .410 bore (disc. 1997), sidelock ejector, 25 in. barrels, Churchill rib. stock, forearm, trigger to order. Importation disc. 1986, resumed 1991-2005.

		$4,000	$3,350	$2,550	$2,100	$1,650	$1,275	$1,000

Last MSR was $4,750.

Add approx. 15% for 28 ga. or .410 bore.
Add approx. $1,720 for extra set of barrels.

GRADING - PPGS™	100%	98%	95%	90%	80%	70%	60%

NO. 53 - 12, 16 (disc. 1997), or 20 ga., engraved sidelock ejector, sideclips, third lock. Stock, forearm, trigger to order. Importation disc. 1986, resumed 1991.

MSR $5,900	$5,000	$4,00	$3,175	$2,650	$2,000	$1,500	$1,250

NO. 56 - 12, 16 (disc. 1997), or 20 (disc. 1999) ga., sidelock action-engraved, ejectors, sel. trigger. Importation disc. 1985, resumed 1991.

MSR $11,600	$9,250	$7,750	$6,500	$5,250	$4,000	$3,250	$2,750

NO. 106 - 12, 16, or 20 ga., English-style boxlock, double trigger, pistol grip, 28 in. barrels. Disc. 1985.

	$550	$475	$400	$360	$320	$300	$275

Last MSR was $585.

Add 20% for 16 or 20 ga.

107-LI - 12 or 16 ga., English-style boxlock, double trigger, straight grip, light English scroll engraving. Disc. 1985.

	$775	$650	$550	$495	$450	$400	$350

Last MSR was $745.

MODEL 116 - 12, 16, or 20 ga., 27-30 in. barrels, any choke, hand detachable H&H sidelocks, double triggers, engraved, select checkered walnut pistol grip stock. Disc. 1985.

	$1,500	$1,275	$1,075	$925	$800	$700	$600

Last MSR was $1,125.

MODEL 117 - 10, 12, 16, or 20 ga., 3 in. chambers, 26-30 in. barrels, any choke, hand-detachable H&H sidelocks, ejectors, SST, engraved, select checkered walnut pistol grip stock. Disc. 1986.

	$1,750	$1,500	$1,225	$1,075	$925	$800	$700

Last MSR was $1,075.

MODEL 117 QUAIL UNLIMITED - 12 ga. only, 26 in. barrels choked IC/M with 3 in. chambers, upgraded wood and checkering, high gloss bluing, gold colored ST, engraved by Baron Technologies in PA, only 42 mfg. for Quail Unlimited of North America.

	$1,650	$1,400	$1,150	$975	$875	$800	$725

This model had a retail price of $1,700 but was made available to Quail Unlimited members for approx. $1,200.

MODEL 210 - 12 or 16 ga., boxlock, exposed hammers, double triggers, plain walnut, light engraving. Disc. 1985.

	$795	$675	$550	$475	$435	$395	$350

Last MSR was $900.

MODEL 711 SIDELOCK - sidelock action. Mfg. 1985 only.

	$1,450	$1,250	$1,075	$925	$800	$700	$600

Last MSR was $1,250.

ABADIE

Previous trademark of Portuguese military revolvers manufactured by several Belgian makers.

REVOLVERS

MODEL 1878 (OFFICER'S MODEL) - 9.1mm cal., solid frame revolver, 6 shot, ejector rod, officer's issue A.

	$220	$195	$165	$130	$120	$110	$100

MODEL 1886 (TROOPER'S MODEL) - similar to 1878, but larger, trooper issue A.

	$195	$175	$160	$120	$110	$100	$90

100%	98%	95%	90%	80%	70%	60%	50%	40%	30%	20%	10%

ABBEY, GEORGE T.

Previous manufacturer of percussion and breechloading firearms located in Utica, NY from 1845-1852, and Chicago, IL from 1852-1874.

RIFLES: PERCUSSION

PERCUSSION RIFLE

* *Percussion Rifle .44 cal.* - 32 in. octagon barrel.

100%	98%	95%	90%	80%	70%	60%	50%	40%	30%	20%	10%
$605	$550	$470	$415	$370	$340	$305	$275	$250	$220	$195	$165

* *Percussion Rifle .44 cal.* - octagon barrel, brass trimmed.

$770	$735	$695	$605	$550	$485	$450	$405	$365	$330	$275	$220

* *Percussion Rifle .44 cal.* - 31 in. side-by-side barrels.

$1,210	$1,100	$880	$770	$715	$650	$595	$550	$515	$475	$430	$360

* *Percussion Rifle .44 cal.* - O/U, brass trimmed.

$1,485	$1,295	$1,130	$990	$910	$855	$770	$715	$660	$605	$495	$330

ABBEY, F.J. & COMPANY

Previous manufacturer of muzzle and breech loading shotguns and rifles located in Chicago, IL, 1858-1878.

RIFLES: PERCUSSION

PERCUSSION RIFLE - several variations.

$605	$550	$470	$415	$360	$305	$275	$250	$210	$175	$145	$110

SHOTGUNS: PERCUSSION

PERCUSSION SHOTGUN - several variations.

$800	$715	$635	$550	$470	$415	$360	$320	$285	$250	$210	$155

ABBIATICO & SALVINELLI (FAMARS)

Please refer to the Famars di Abbiatico & Salvinelli srl listing.

ACCU-MATCH INTERNATIONAL INC.

Previous handgun and pistol parts manufacturer located in Mesa, AZ circa 1996.

GRADING - PPGS™	100%	98%	95%	90%	80%	70%	60%

PISTOLS: SEMI-AUTO

ACCU-MATCH PISTOL - .45 ACP cal., patterned after the Colt Govt. 1911, competition pistol features stainless steel construction with 5 1/2 in. match grade barrel with 3 ports, recoil reduction system, 8-shot mag., 3-dot sight system. Approx. 160 mfg. 1996 only.

$795	$700	$625	$550	$450	$375	$325

Last MSR was $840.

ACCU-TEK

Current trademark manufactured by Excel Industries, Inc., located in Chino, CA. Distributor and dealer direct sales.

PISTOLS: SEMI-AUTO

MODEL AT-25 - .25 ACP cal., single action, 2 1/2 in. barrel, 7-shot mag. with finger extension, similar design to AT-32, stainless steel, aluminum, or alloy construction with choice of stainless, satin aluminum, or black finish, 11 (Model AT-25AL) or 18 (Model AT-25B, disc.) oz. Mfg. 1992-95.

$150	$125	$105	$90	$80	$70	$60

Last MSR was $182.

This model was available in satin aluminum (Model AT-25AL) or black (Model AT-25SSB) finish.

GRADING - PPGS™	100%	98%	95%	90%	80%	70%	60%

MODEL AT-32SS - .32 ACP cal., single action design, 2 1/2 in. barrel, 5-shot mag. with finger extension, alloy (disc. 1991) or stainless steel (new 1992) construction, black synthetic grips, manual safety with firing pin block and trigger disconnect, side mag. release, exposed hammer, satin aluminum (disc. 1991) finish, 1 lb. Mfg. in U.S. 1990-2003.

		$190	$155	$120	$100	$80	$70	$60

Last MSR was $239.

Add $5 for black finish (Model AT-32SSB).

MODEL AT-380II (SS/SSB) - .380 ACP cal., similar to Model AT-32, except has 2 3/4 in. barrel, 6-shot mag., black grips, alloy (disc. 1991) or stainless steel construction, 23 1/2 oz. New 1990.

MSR $249		$195	$160	$120	$100	$90	$80	$70

Add $5 for black finish (Model AT-380SSB, disc. 1999).

BL-380 - .380 ACP cal., double action only, carbon steel, black finish, compact size, two 5 shot mags., lockable case. Mfg. 1997-99.

		$165	$140	$120	$100	$90	$80	$70

Last MSR was $199.

MODEL HC-380 (SS) - .380 ACP cal., single action semi-auto, stainless steel, 2 1/2 in. barrel, 10 (C/B 1994) or 13*-shot mag., warp-around grips, manual safety with firing pin block and trigger disconnect, exposed hammer, includes two 13 shot mags., lock and hard case, 26 oz. Mfg. 1993-2003, reintroduced 2007.

MSR $285		$230	$180	$145	$125	$115	$100	$90

Add $5 for black finish (Model HC-380B, mfg. 1995-99).

MODEL AT-9SS - 9mm Para. cal., double action only, stainless steel, 3.2 in. barrel, 8-shot mag., firing pin block with no external safety, black or brushed stainless finish, 3-dot sights adj. for windage, 28 oz. Mfg. 1995-96 only.

		$260	$205	$165	$135	$115	$100	$85

Last MSR was $317.

BL-9 - 9mm Para. cal., double action only, carbon steel, black finish, ultra compact size, includes two 5 shot mags., and lockable case. Mfg. 1997-2002.

		$195	$150	$120	$95	$80	$70	$60

Last MSR was $232.

CP-9SS - 9mm Para. cal., double action only, stainless steel, black finish, compact size, 8-shot mag. Mfg. 1997-99.

		$220	$165	$125	$100	$85	$70	$65

Last MSR was $265.

MODEL XL-9SS - 9mm Para. cal, double action only, stainless steel, 3 in. barrel, 5-shot mag., black pebble finished grips, 3-dot adj. sights, 24 oz. Mfg. 1999-2003.

		$215	$170	$125	$100	$85	$70	$65

Last MSR was $267.

MODEL AT-40SS - .40 S&W cal., double action only, 3.2 in. barrel, 7-shot mag., firing pin block with no external safety, black or brushed stainless finish, 3-dot sights adj. for windage, 28 oz. Mfg. 1995-96 only.

		$260	$205	$165	$130	$110	$95	$75

Last MSR was $317.

CP-40SS - .40 S&W cal., 7-shot mag., otherwise similar to CP-9SS. Mfg. 1997-99.

		$220	$165	$125	$100	$85	$70	$60

Last MSR was $265.

GRADING - PPGS™	100%	98%	95%	90%	80%	70%	60%

MODEL AT-45SS - .45 ACP cal., similar to Model AT-40SS, except has 6-shot mag., stainless only, 28 oz. Mfg. 1996 only.

	$265	$210	$165	$130	$110	$95	$75

Last MSR was $327.

CP-45SS - .45 ACP cal., 6-shot mag., otherwise similar to CP-40SS. Mfg. 1997-99.

	$220	$165	$125	$100	$85	$70	$60

Last MSR was $265.

ACCURACY INTERNATIONAL LTD.

Current rifle manufacturer located in Hampshire, England since 1978. Currently imported beginning 2006 by TacPro Shooting Center, located in Mingus, TX. Previously imported by Accuracy International North America, located in Orchard Park, NY until circa 2005. Previously located 1998-2005 in Oak Ridge, TN. Previously imported until 1998 by Gunsite Training Center, located in Paulden, AZ.

RIFLES: BOLT ACTION

In addition to the models listed below, Accuracy International also makes military and law enforcement rifles, including the SR98 Australian, G22 German, and the Dutch SLA.

On Models AE, AW, AWP, and AWM listed below, many options and configurations are available which will add to the base prices listed.

Add $210 for Picatinny rail on all currently manufactured rifles.

AE MODEL - .308 Win. cal., similar to AWP Model, 5-shot mag., 24 in. stainless barrel, Harris bipod attachment point, four sling attachment points, Picatinny rail. New 2002.

MSR $3,200		$2,950	$2,500	$2,250	$1,950	$1,675	$1,425	$1,200

Add $175 for adj. cheekpiece or $515 for adj. cheekpiece and folding stock.

AW MODEL - .243 Win. (new 2000) or .308 Win. cal., precision bolt action featuring 20, 24, or 26 in. 1:12 twist stainless steel barrel with or w/o muzzle brake, 3-lug bolt, 10-shot detachable mag., green synthetic folding (military/LE only) thumbhole adj. stock, AI bipod, 14 lbs. Importation began 1995.

MSR $5,300		$4,750	$4,250	$3,650	$3,150	$2,650	$2,150	$1,800

Add $376 for AW-F Model (disc. 2002).
Add $225 for muzzle brake or for fluted barrel.

AWP MODEL - similar to AW Model, except has 20 or 24 in. barrel w/o muzzle brake, 15 lbs. Imported 1995-2007.

	$4,250	$3,650	$3,150	$2,650	$2,150	$1,800	$1,500

Last MSR was $4,600.

Add $310 for AWP-F Model (disc. 2002).

AWM MODEL (SUPER MAGNUM) - .300 Win. Mag. or .338 Lapua cal., 6-lug bolt, 26 or 27 in. 1:9/1:10 twist stainless steel fluted barrel with muzzle brake, 5-shot mag., 15 1/2 lbs. Importation began 1995.

MSR $5,900		$5,600	$5,100	$4,675	$3,800	$2,950	$2,500	$1,750

Add $100 for .338 Lapua cal.
Add $324 for AWM-F Model (disc. 2002).

PALMAMASTER - .308 Win. cal., available with either NRA prone or UIT style stock, 30 in. stainless steel fluted barrel, designed for competition shooting, laminate stock. Disc. 2002.

	$2,600	$2,350	$2,100	$1,900	$1,700	$1,500	$1,250

Last MSR was $2,850.

GRADING - PPGS™	100%	98%	95%	90%	80%	70%	60%

CISMMASTER - .22 BR, 6mm BR, .243 Win., .308 Win., 6.5x55mm, or 7.5x55mm cal., designed for slow and rapid fire international and military shooting competition, 10-shot mag., 2-stage trigger. Disc. 2002.

	100%	98%	95%	90%	80%	70%	60%
	$3,175	$2,850	$2,600	$2,350	$2,100	$1,900	$1,700

Last MSR was $3,480.

VARMINT RIFLE - .22 Middlested, .22 BR, .22-250 Rem., .223 Rem., 6mm BR, .243 Win., .308 Win., or 7mm-08 Rem. cal., features 26 in. fluted stainless steel barrel. Mfg. 1997-2002.

	100%	98%	95%	90%	80%	70%	60%
	$3,200	$2,725	$2,350	$1,950	$1,675	$1,475	$1,300

Last MSR was $3,650.

AW50 - .50 BMG, advanced ergonomic design, features built-in anti-recoil system, 5-shot mag., adj. third supporting leg, folding stock, 35 lbs. New 1998.

MSR $13,000	100%	98%	95%	90%	80%	70%	60%
	$12,000	$10,250	$8,750	$7,500	$6,250	$4,950	$3,750

ACHA
Previous manufacturer located in Eibar, Spain until 1936.

PISTOLS: SEMI-AUTO

MODEL 1916 - 6.35mm cal., semi-auto pistol, 7-shot mag., 1905 Browning copy.

	100%	98%	95%	90%	80%	70%	60%
	$250	$185	$130	$90	$80	$70	$60

ATLAS - 6.35mm cal., semi-auto pistol, 6-shot mag., slide marked ATLAS, 1905 Browning copy.

	100%	98%	95%	90%	80%	70%	60%
	$200	$165	$125	$95	$75	$65	$50

LOOKING GLASS - 6.35mm or 7.65mm cal., 6-shot mag., blue or nickel, 1905 Browning copy, slide marked "Looking Glass," many variations.

	100%	98%	95%	90%	80%	70%	60%
	$235	$170	$130	$100	$85	$70	$55

Add 50% for extended grip.

ACME
Previous trade name of Davenport Arms Company Shotguns, Maltby Henley & Co. Revolvers, and Merwin Hulbert & Co. Owl Head Revolvers.

100%	98%	95%	90%	80%	70%	60%	50%	40%	30%	20%	10%

REVOLVERS

SEVEN SHOT REVOLVER - .22 short rimfire cal., single action.

100%	98%	95%	90%	80%	70%	60%	50%	40%	30%	20%	10%
$360	$310	$240	$185	$165	$150	$120	$110	$100	$90	$65	$55

FIVE SHOT REVOLVER - .32 short rimfire cal., single action.

100%	98%	95%	90%	80%	70%	60%	50%	40%	30%	20%	10%
$360	$320	$255	$200	$175	$160	$120	$110	$100	$90	$65	$55

ACME ARMS
Previous trade name for Cornwall Hardware Co., NY.

REVOLVERS

SEVEN SHOT - .22 short rimfire cal., single action.

100%	98%	95%	90%	80%	70%	60%	50%	40%	30%	20%	10%
$275	$250	$210	$185	$165	$155	$140	$125	$110	$90	$85	$75

FIVE SHOT - .32 short rimfire cal., single action.

100%	98%	95%	90%	80%	70%	60%	50%	40%	30%	20%	10%
$285	$255	$215	$195	$175	$165	$145	$120	$100	$90	$85	$75

100%	98%	95%	90%	80%	70%	60%	50%	40%	30%	20%	10%

SHOTGUNS: SxS

SIDE-BY-SIDE - 12 ga., damascus barrel.

100%	98%	95%	90%	80%	70%	60%	50%	40%	30%	20%	10%
$275	$240	$195	$165	$145	$125	$110	$95	$65	$60	$50	$45

ACME HAMMERLESS

Previously manufactured by Hopkins & Allen, for Hulbert Brothers, 1893.

REVOLVERS

FIVE SHOT - .32 or .38 centerfire cal., double action, top break, non-ejecting.

100%	98%	95%	90%	80%	70%	60%	50%	40%	30%	20%	10%
$145	$125	$100	$90	$80	$70	$60	$50	$40	$30	$20	$15

Also known as Forehand Model 1891, can be hammer or hammerless.

ACTION (M.S.)

Previously manufactured by Modesto Santos, located in Eibar, Spain.

GRADING - PPGS™	100%	98%	95%	90%	80%	70%	60%

PISTOLS: SEMI-AUTO

MODEL 1915 - 7.65mm cal., semi-auto pistol (French Military).

100%	98%	95%	90%	80%	70%	60%
$245	$175	$140	$105	$90	$75	$65

MODEL 1920 - 6.35mm cal., semi-auto pistol, slide marked "Action".

100%	98%	95%	90%	80%	70%	60%
$195	$150	$110	$85	$65	$45	$40

ACTION ARMS LTD.

Previous firearms importer and distributor until 1994, located in Philadelphia, PA.

Only Action Arms Models AT-84S, AT-88S, and the Model B Sporter will be listed under this heading. Galil, Timberwolf, and Uzi trademarks can be located in their respective sections.

CARBINES: SEMI-AUTO

MODEL B SPORTER - 9mm Para. cal., patterned after the original Uzi Model B Sporter, 16.1 in. barrel, closed breech, thumbhole stock with recoil pad, 10-shot mag., adj. rear sight, 8.8 lbs. Limited importation from China 1994 only.

100%	98%	95%	90%	80%	70%	60%
$550	$475	$435	$385	$335	$295	$275

Last MSR was $595.

PISTOLS: SEMI-AUTO

AT-84S - 9mm Para. cal., selective double action design, patterned after the CZ-75, 4.8 in. barrel, 15-shot mag., originally introduced in 1985.

100%	98%	95%	90%	80%	70%	60%
$470	$415	$385	$360	$330	$275	$220

The AT-84S Series was manufactured in Switzerland by Industrial Technology & Machines A.G. and was sold by Action Arms between June of 1987 and 1989. Serial number range is 01201- 06000. No P or H models were ever mfg. in this series (2 or 3 prototypes only).

AT-88S - 9mm or .41 Action Express (available early 1990) cal., selective double action design patterned after CZ-75, 4.8 in. barrel, 15 shot (9mm) or 10 shot (.41 AE) mag., can be "cocked and locked," fixed sights, blue metal, walnut grips, 35.3 oz. Introduced in 1987 with limited production samples imported in 1989.

100%	98%	95%	90%	80%	70%	60%
$500	$450	$395	$360	$330	$275	$220

A very small quantity of AT-88Ss (various configurations) were made by I.T.M. of Switzerland and finishes included all blue, all chrome, or two-tone. These pistols may exhibit both I.T.M. and A.A.L. markings. More recent manufacture was performed by Sphinx-Muller of Switzerland. These pistols were manufactured by Sphinx-Muller, renamed the AT-2000 Series and previously imported by Sile Distributors.

GRADING - PPGS™	100%	98%	95%	90%	80%	70%	60%

RIFLES: SLIDE ACTION

TIMBERWOLF - see separate listing in T section.

ACTION LEGENDS MFG., INC.

Previous manufacturer, importer, and distributor until circa 2006 and located in Houston, TX.

RIFLES

MODEL 888 M1 CARBINE - .22 LR or .30 Carbine cal., 18 in. barrel, mfg. from new original M1 parts and stock and unused GI parts, 10-, 15-, or 30-shot mag., choice of birch or walnut stock, parkerized finish, metal or wood handguard, 5 1/2 lbs.

$575	$425	$300	$225	$175	$150	$125	

Last MSR was $650.

Add $11 for .22 LR cal.
Add $31 for walnut/metal forearm or $47 for walnut/wood forearm.

MODEL 1903 SPRINGFIELD - .30-06 cal. 24 in. barrel, bolt action, mfg. from new and original GI parts, 5-shot mag., parkerized finish, wood stock, canvas sling. While previously advertised at a $950 MSR, only a few prototypes were manufactured.

ADAMS

Previously manufactured by Deane, Adams, & Deane, located in London, England.

100%	98%	95%	90%	80%	70%	60%	50%	40%	30%	20%	10%

REVOLVERS: PERCUSSION

MODEL 1851 .38 CAL. - .38 cal., double action, 4 1/2 in. barrel.

100%	98%	95%	90%	80%	70%	60%	50%	40%	30%	20%	10%
$1,375	$1,265	$1,100	$990	$855	$745	$690	$605	$550	$440	$385	$330

Add approx. 25% for case and accessories.

MODEL 1851 .44 CAL. - .44 cal., double action, 6 in. barrel.

100%	98%	95%	90%	80%	70%	60%	50%	40%	30%	20%	10%
$935	$880	$800	$690	$550	$495	$440	$395	$340	$305	$275	$255

Add approx. 25% for case and accessories.

MODEL 1851 .50 CAL. - .50 cal., Dragoon, double action, 8 in. barrel.

100%	98%	95%	90%	80%	70%	60%	50%	40%	30%	20%	10%
$1,375	$1,265	$1,100	$990	$855	$715	$690	$605	$550	$385	$360	$340

Add 25% for case and accessories.

ADAMS, JOSEPH

Previous manufacturer located in Birmingham, England.

PISTOLS: FLINTLOCK

OFFICER MODEL - .65 cal., flintlock pistol, Brown Bess.

100%	98%	95%	90%	80%	70%	60%	50%	40%	30%	20%	10%
$2,850	$2,500	$2,250	$2,000	$1,800	$1,600	$1,400	$1,100	$900	$825	$725	$600

ADAMY, GEBR. JAGDWAFFEN

Current manufacturer and retailer established circa 1921 and located in Suhl, Germany. Limited importation by New England Custom Gun Service, located in Plainfield, NH. The Adamy gunmaking tradition goes back to 1820, and sixth and seventh generation descendants are currently building guns.

Adamy Jadgwaffen currently specializes in custom-made break open rifles, drillings, and combination guns, SxS and O/U shotguns, and double rifles featuring an Anson & Deeley boxlock action or H&H type sidelocks. Since all guns are made to custom order, please contact New England Custom Gun Service (current importer) directly for more information.

GRADING - PPGS™	100%	98%	95%	90%	80%	70%	60%

ADCO SALES INC.

Current importer of Diamond shotguns manufactured by Vega in Istanbul, Turkey, and accessory manufacturer established circa 1981, and currently located in Woburn, MA. Dealer sales.

SHOTGUNS: O/U

DIAMOND DOUBLE FIELD GRADE - 12 or 20 ga., 3 in. chambers, boxlock action, extractors, includes choke tubes, checkered walnut stock and forearm. Importation began 2007.

MSR $449	$380	$330	$285	$250	$215	$180	$160

Add $20 for single trigger.
Add $100 for target grade with wide VR (12 ga. only, disc. 2007).

DIAMOND IMPERIAL - 12 or 20 ga., 3 in. chambers, boxlock action, SST, ejectors, 26 or 28 in. barrels with choke tubes, checkered fine Turkish walnut stock and forearm. Importation began 2007.

MSR $639	$545	$460	$415	$385	$350	$325	$300

Add $20 for 20 ga.

DIAMOND FOLDING MODEL - 28 ga. or .410 bore, DT, folding boxlock action. Limited importation 2007.

	$550	$495	$450	$400	$350	$300	$275

Last MSR was $629.

DIAMOND DOUBLE ELITE SERIES - 12 or 20 ga., 26 or 28 in. barrels, uncheckered pistol grip walnut stock, blue receiver with light engraving, 5 choke tubes, deluxe ST, extractors. New 2008.

MSR $579	$495	$410	$365	$330	$295	$260	$235

Add $40 for 20 ga.

SHOTGUNS: SxS

DH12 COACH GUN - 12 ga., exposed hammers, DT, 20 in. barrels with or w/o choke tubes, checkered walnut stock and splinter forearm. Importation began 2006.

MSR $599	$500	$415	$365	$330	$295	$260	$235

Add $20 for choke tubes or Field Gun with 28 in. barrels.

DIAMOND DOUBLE FIELD GRADE - 12, 16 (2006 only), or 20 ga., exposed hammers or hammerless, 28 in. barrels with choke tubes, extractors. Importation began 2006.

MSR $449	$380	$330	$285	$250	$215	$180	$160

Add $10 for 16 (disc.) or 20 ga.

DIAMOND DOUBLE HEIRLOOM SERIES - 12 ga., exposed hammers, includes choke tubes. Importation began 2007.

MSR $899	$775	$650	$550	$495	$450	$400	$350

DIAMOND FOLDING MODEL - .410 bore, 3 in. chambers, DT, folding boxlock action. Limited importation 2007.

	$550	$495	$450	$400	$350	$300	$275

Last MSR was $629.

SHOTGUNS: SEMI-AUTO

All semi-auto shotguns were mfg. in Turkey.

GRADING - PPGS™	100%	98%	95%	90%	80%	70%	60%

GOLD SERIES - 12 ga., 3 in. chamber, gas operated, 24 (slug gun, non-rifled, includes open sights) or 28 in. VR barrel with 3 choke tubes, semi-humpback style, anodized alloy frame with gold etching, rotary bolt, grey trigger guard, choice of black synthetic or checkered Turkish walnut stock with recoil pad, and forearm. Imported 2001-2006.

	100%	98%	95%	90%	80%	70%	60%
	$450	$375	$325	$295	$270	$235	$200

Last MSR was $549.

Subtract $50 for black synthetic stock and forearm.

DIAMOND IMPERIAL SERIES - 12 or 20 ga., 3 (20 ga.) or 3 1/2 (12 ga.) in. chamber, 24 (slug, 12 ga.), 26 (20 ga. only), or 28 in. VR barrel with 3 chokes (except slug), features rotary bi-lateral bolt, deluxe checkered stock and forearm. Imported 2003-2004.

	100%	98%	95%	90%	80%	70%	60%
	$425	$350	$300	$250	$225	$200	$175

Last MSR was $499.

Subtract $20 for slug variation.

DIAMOND ELITE SERIES - 12 ga., 3 in. chamber, gas operated, similar to Gold Series, except has engraved receiver with choice of 22 (slug), 24, 26, or 28 in. VR barrel with 3 choke tubes, deluxe checkered walnut stock and forearm. Imported 2001-2006.

	100%	98%	95%	90%	80%	70%	60%
	$375	$330	$295	$260	$230	$200	$175

Last MSR was $449.

DIAMOND PANTHER SERIES - 12 ga., 3 in. chamber, gas operated, similar to Diamond Elite Series, except has black synthetic stock and forearm, 20 (slug), 20 regular, or 28 in. barrel with 3 choke tubes. Imported 2002-2006.

	100%	98%	95%	90%	80%	70%	60%
	$335	$280	$260	$240	$225	$200	$175

Last MSR was $399.

Add $20 for walnut stock and forearm (new 2003).

MARINER MODEL (SILVER SERIES) - 12 ga., 3 in. chamber, gas operated, 20 (slug, new 2003) or 22 in. VR barrel, anodized alloy frame receiver with high strength satin silver metal finish, checkered walnut stock and forearm. Imported 2002-2006.

	100%	98%	95%	90%	80%	70%	60%
	$425	$350	$300	$250	$225	$200	$175

Last MSR was $499.

SHOTGUNS: SINGLE SHOT

DIAMOND FOLDING MODEL - 12 ga. or .410 bore, folding barrel design, folding operating lever is in front of trigger guard. Limited importation 2007.

	100%	98%	95%	90%	80%	70%	60%
	$165	$130	$110	$95	$80	$70	$60

Last MSR was $199.

Add $60 for .410 bore.

SHOTGUNS: SLIDE ACTION

All Adco slide action shotguns were manufactured in Turkey.

GOLD ELITE SERIES - 12 ga., 3 in. chamber, 24 (slug gun, non-rifled, includes open sights) or 28 in. VR barrel with 3 choke tubes, semi-humpback style, anodized alloy frame, choice of black synthetic or checkered Turkish walnut stock with recoil pad, and forearm. 7 lbs. Imported 2001-2006.

	100%	98%	95%	90%	80%	70%	60%
	$300	$250	$205	$175	$160	$145	$120

Last MSR was $379.

Subtract $60 for black synthetic stock and forearm.

GRADING - PPGS™	100%	98%	95%	90%	80%	70%	60%

DIAMOND IMPERIAL SERIES - 12 ga., 3 1/2 in. chamber, 28 in. VR barrel with 3 chokes, deluxe checkered stock and forearm. Imported 2003-2006.

	$335	$280	$260	$240	$225	$200	$175

Last MSR was $399.

DIAMOND ELITE SERIES - 12 ga., 3 in. chamber, similar to Gold Elite Series, except has engraved receiver with choice of 20 (slug), regular 20 (disc. 2002), 24, or 28 in. VR barrel with 3 choke tubes, deluxe checkered walnut stock and forearm. Imported 2001-2006.

	$280	$240	$200	$175	$160	$145	$120

Last MSR was $359.

DIAMOND PANTHER SERIES - 12 ga., 3 in. chamber, similar to Diamond Elite Series, except has black synthetic stock and forearm, 18 1/2 (slug), 20 (disc. 2002), 22 (slug, new 2003), or 28 in. barrel with 3 choke tubes. Imported 2001-2006.

	$200	$165	$145	$135	$115	$105	$95

Last MSR was $239.

Subtract $30 for 18 1/2 in. slug variation.

MARINER MODEL - 12 ga., 3 in. chamber, choice of 18 1/2 plain or 22 in VR barrel with chokes, 5-shot mag., black synthetic stock and forearm. Imported 2003-2006.

	$250	$225	$200	$175	$150	$135	$110

Last MSR was $319.

ADIRONDACK ARMS COMPANY

Previous manufacturer located in Plattsburgh, NY, 1870-1874.

Magazine loaded repeating rifle, .44 cal., brass or iron frame, later model, may also be marked A.S. Babbitt, Plattsburgh, N.Y., absorbed by Winchester in 1874, then discontinued. This rifle was designed in 1870 and patented by Orvill M. Robinson in Upper Jay, NY. It was available in .30 and .44 cal. rimfire versions without a wood forend and had a high cyclic rate of fire. Original models were made in Plattsburgh, NY, at which time A.S. Babbitt became one of several additional partners. In 1872, Robinson was granted a patent for a second model rifle. It was similar to the Model 1870, except a wood forend was added and the operating mechanism was changed considerably. Following these improvements, Mr. Oliver Winchester contacted Mr. Robinson and purchased the entire Robinson company, discontinuing manufacture.

100%	98%	95%	90%	80%	70%	60%	50%	40%	30%	20%	10%

RIFLES

EARLY MODEL - finger holds on hammer.

$2,400	$2,100	$1,750	$1,450	$1,325	$1,200	$1,075	$975	$875	$775	$675	$600

LATE MODEL - action worked by buttons top of receiver mid-section.

$2,200	$1,950	$1,675	$1,300	$1,200	$1,100	$975	$875	$775	$675	$550	$495

ADLER

Previously manufactured by Engelbrecht & Wolff located in Blasii, Germany, 1905-1907.

GRADING - PPGS™	100%	98%	95%	90%	80%	70%	60%

PISTOLS: SEMI-AUTO

SEMI-AUTO PISTOL - 7mm Adler cal., 8-shot mag., cocking lever on top of frame.

	$5,000	$4,000	$3,000	$2,500	$2,000	$1,495	$1,100

GRADING - PPGS™	100%	98%	95%	90%	80%	70%	60%

ADVANTAGE ARMS USA, INC.

Previous manufacturer located in St. Paul, MN, and distributed by Wildfire Sports, Inc. also located in St. Paul, MN. Advantage Arms USA, Inc. was sold and moved to Tucson, AZ, with the new name of New Advantage Arms, Inc. (see separate listing).

DERRINGERS

MODEL 422 - .22 LR or 22 Mag. cal., 4 barrel double action derringer, rotating firing pin, this model is patterned after the Mossberg "Brownie," 2 1/2 in. barrel, high grade alloy frame and barrel, 4 shot, available in blue, nickel, or QPQ (heat treated but appears blue) finish, 15 oz. Mfg. 1986-87 only.

$150	$135	$115	$105	$95	$85	$75

Last MSR was $166.

Add 15% for .22 Mag. cal.
Add $6 for nickel finish.
Add $11 for QPQ finish.

AETNA

Previous trademark manufactured by Harrington & Richardson located in Worchester, MA.

Type: single action revolvers, all of the same general size and configuration, solid frame, spur trigger, so-called "Suicide Specials" during their day.

100%	98%	95%	90%	80%	70%	60%	50%	40%	30%	20%	10%

REVOLVERS

AETNA NO. 2 - .32 rimfire cal., 5 shot.

100%	98%	95%	90%	80%	70%	60%	50%	40%	30%	20%	10%
$330	$275	$245	$215	$190	$175	$160	$145	$120	$95	$80	$60

AETNA NO. 2 1/2 - .32 rimfire cal., 5 shot.

100%	98%	95%	90%	80%	70%	60%	50%	40%	30%	20%	10%
$330	$275	$245	$215	$190	$175	$160	$145	$120	$95	$80	$60

MODEL 1876 - .22, .32, or .38 rimfire cal., 5 (.38 or .32 cal.) or 7 shot.

100%	98%	95%	90%	80%	70%	60%	50%	40%	30%	20%	10%
$330	$275	$245	$215	$190	$175	$160	$145	$120	$95	$80	$60

AETNA ARMS COMPANY

Previous manufacturer located in New York, 1869-1883.

Single action pocket revolver, blue or nickel, birdshead grip, copy of S&W Models 1-3, models marked "ALLING" are worth a slight premium.

REVOLVERS

SEVEN SHOT - .22 rimfire cal.

100%	98%	95%	90%	80%	70%	60%	50%	40%	30%	20%	10%
$250	$235	$210	$195	$175	$165	$155	$130	$110	$95	$90	$65

FIVE SHOT - .32 rimfire cal.

100%	98%	95%	90%	80%	70%	60%	50%	40%	30%	20%	10%
$230	$220	$205	$175	$165	$155	$145	$120	$105	$90	$75	$55

AGNER

Previous trademark manufactured by Saxhoj Products Inc. in Denmark. Imported until 1986 by Beeman Arms, Inc. located in Santa Rosa, CA.

GRADING - PPGS™	100%	98%	95%	90%	80%	70%	60%

PISTOL: SEMI-AUTO

MODEL M 80 - .22 LR cal. only, stainless steel, semi-auto target pistol, new design features unique security key safety feature, adj. French walnut grips, dry fire mechanism, 5.9 in. barrel, 5-shot mag., limited production, 2.4 lbs. Imported 1981-86.

	100%	98%	95%	90%	80%	70%	60%
	$1,125	$1,040	$950	N/A	N/A	N/A	N/A

Last MSR was $1,295.

Add $100 for left-hand action.

AIR MATCH

Previously imported by Kendall International, located in Paris, KY.

PISTOLS: SINGLE SHOT

AIR MATCH 500 - .22 LR cal. match single shot pistol, target grips, adj. front counterweight, 10 1/2 in. barrel. Imported 1984-86.

	100%	98%	95%	90%	80%	70%	60%
	$550	$495	$450	$425	$395	$360	$330

Last MSR was $788.

AJAX ARMY

Previously distributed by E.C. Meacham Co., maker unknown, circa 1880s.

100%	98%	95%	90%	80%	70%	60%	50%	40%	30%	20%	10%

REVOLVERS

SINGLE ACTION - .44 rimfire cal., spur trigger, solid frame.

100%	98%	95%	90%	80%	70%	60%	50%	40%	30%	20%	10%
$550	$440	$360	$315	$275	$255	$230	$210	$185	$170	$155	$140

AKKAR

Current shotgun manufacturer located in Istanbul, Turkey. Currently imported by K.B.I., located in Harrisburg, PA.

Akkar manufacturers slide action, semi-auto, and O/U shotguns under a variety of trademarks, including Akkar, Altay, Apache, Karatay, M-2000, Commanchi, Maxi-Mag, Churchill, and Poseidon. Currently, Akkar manufactures private label slide action and semi-auto shotguns for K.B.I., Inc.

AKRILL, E.

Previously manufactured in France, circa mid-1800s.

RIFLES: FLINTLOCK

FLINTLOCK RIFLE - .69 cal., breech loaded, damascus octagon barrel.

100%	98%	95%	90%	80%	70%	60%	50%	40%	30%	20%	10%
$3,300	$2,750	$2,200	$1,980	$1,460	$1,320	$1,240	$1,075	$935	$800	$745	$660

ALAMO RANGER

Previous manufacturer located in Spain.

GRADING - PPGS™	100%	98%	95%	90%	80%	70%	60%

REVOLVERS

REVOLVER - .38 Spl. cal., Spanish copy of Colt Model 1929.

	100%	98%	95%	90%	80%	70%	60%
	$140	$120	$110	$100	$90	$85	$75

ALASKA

Previous trademark manufactured by Hood Firearms Company, Norwich, CT, 1873-1884. These inexpensive utilitarian revolvers were dubbed "Suicide Specials" in their day.

100%	98%	95%	90%	80%	70%	60%	50%	40%	30%	20%	10%

REVOLVERS

SINGLE ACTION - .22 rimfire cal, 7 shot, spur trigger, solid frame.

100%	98%	95%	90%	80%	70%	60%	50%	40%	30%	20%	10%
$275	$220	$195	$145	$140	$125	$110	$100	$90	$75	$70	$65

FIVE SHOT - .32 Short rimfire cal.

100%	98%	95%	90%	80%	70%	60%	50%	40%	30%	20%	10%
$220	$195	$160	$155	$150	$140	$125	$105	$95	$85	$75	$70

ALASKAN COMMEMORATIVES

The following is a complete chronological listing of Alaskan special and limited editions.

GRADING - PPGS™	100%	Issue Price	Qty. Made

COMMEMORATIVES, SPECIAL EDITIONS, & LIMITED MFG.

1967 ALASKAN PURCHASE CENTENNIAL WINCHESTER 94 CARBINE - see listing under Winchester Commemoratives.

1967 ALASKA PURCHASE CENTENNIAL CONTENDER - .22 Hornet and .357 Mag. cal., Thompson Contender with 2 barrels, ser. no. range beginning with C0001.
Issue price is unknown and rarity precludes accurate secondary market pricing.

1976 ALASKA PIPELINE COMMEMORATIVE - .45 LC cal., Colt SAA, cased with Kershaw knife.

	100%	Issue Price	Qty. Made
	$1,495	$800	801

1981 ALASKA STATE TROOPER 40TH ANNIVERSARY - .357 Mag. cal., Smith & Wesson Model 19-5, 4 in. barrel, cased with belt buckle and patch.

	100%	Issue Price	Qty. Made
	$850	$500	250

1984 STATE OF ALASKA SILVER ANNIVERSARY EDITION - .44 Mag. cal., Smith & Wesson Model 29-3, 6 in. barrel, cased with bronze brown bear and ivory grips with scrimshaw AK state seal and silver engraving.

	100%	Issue Price	Qty. Made
	$12,250	$10,000	10

1984 ALASKA SILVER ANNIVERSARY - .44 Mag. cal., Smith & Wesson Model 29-3, 6 in. barrel, cased with gold engraving.

	100%	Issue Price	Qty. Made
	$1,500	$1,195	300

1984 ALASKA STATEHOOD 25TH ANNIVERSARY - .338 Win. Mag. cal., Winchester Model 70XTR, sterling silver engraving.

	100%	Issue Price	Qty. Made
	$1,100	$1,080	500

1984 ALASKA 25TH ANNIVERSARY - .357 Mag. cal., Colt Python, 6 in. barrel, engraved brown bear with gold lettering and numbers, cased.

	100%	Issue Price	Qty. Made
	$1,000	$500	200

1988 IDITAROD "1 OF 1,000" - .44 Mag. cal., Smith & Wesson Model 629-1, 6 in. barrel, cased with laser-etched box, while a thousand were planned, only 500 were mfg.

	100%	Issue Price	Qty. Made
	$995	$775	500

1988 ALASKA SERIES "TOKLAT" SPECIAL - .45 Win. Mag. cal., LAR mfg. Grizzly Mag., mfg. for Great Northern Guns in Anchorage, AK, cased with plaque.

	100%	Issue Price	Qty. Made
	$1,800	$1,195	20

1990 ALASKA "GUIDE" SERIES - .454 Casull cal., Freedom Arms mfg. for Great Northern Guns in Anchorage, AK, 5 1/2 in. barrel, Custom Field Grade, engraved handle.

	100%	Issue Price	Qty. Made
	$1,900	$1,300	25

GRADING - PPGS™	100%	Issue Price	Qty. Made

1991 ALASKA "MASTER GUIDE" SERIES - .454 Casull cal., Freedom Arms mfg. for Great Northern Guns in Anchorage, AK, 5 1/2 in. barrel, Custom Premier Grade, engraved handle.

$2,200	$1,600	26

1997 ALASKA IDITAROD TRAPPER SILVER ANNIVERSARY EDITION - .45 LC cal., Win. Mod. 94 Trapper rifle, 24Kt. gold engraving, extensive laser carved stock and forearm with musher and dog team, cased.

$4,950	$2,495	149

1997 ALASKA IDITAROD SINGLE ACTION SILVER ANNIVERSARY EDITION - .45 LC cal., Colt SAA, 24Kt. gold engraving with Iditarod logo and trail scenes, cased.

$4,950	$2,495	149

1998 ALASKA "KLONDIKE" COMMEMORATIVE GRADE I - .30-30 Win. cal., Winchester Model 94, 24 in. round barrel, roll engraved with Klondike scene on receiver, sponsored by the Alaskan Gun Collectors Association.

$550	$550	450

✳ *1998 Alaska "Klondike" Commemorative Hi-Grade* - similar to Grade I, except has gold-plated receiver.

$1,000	$1,000	100

1998 ALASKA GOLD RUSH (1898-1998) CENTENNIAL - .38-55 WCF cal., Winchester Model 94 rifle, featuring 24Kt. gold engraving, serial numbered, silver medallion inlayed in stock, and extensive laser carving on stock and forearm, cased. New 1998.

$6,500	$2,795	25

2000 ALASKA AMERICAN BALD EAGLE LIMITED EDITION - .45-70 Govt. cal., Marlin Model 1895SS lever action rifle, 24Kt. gold etching of American eagle, extensive laser etched stock and forearm with Alaska and eagle scenes, includes special glass display case and leather carrying case.

N/A	$2,750	10 per state

2000 ALASKA MILLENNIUM RIFLE - .45 LC cal., Winchester Model 1866 Sporting Rifle mfg. by Uberti, cased with silver and gold presentation numbered buckle, features 24Kt. gold engraving with symbols representing events in U.S. history.

N/A	$2,495	10 per state

2000 ALASKA MILLENNIUM REVOLVER - .44 cal., Colt Model 1860 mfg. by Colt, cased, 24Kt. gold engraved with Statue of Freedom, "Don´t Tread On Me" "One Nation, Under God, Indivisible with Liberty and Justice for All."

N/A	$1,895	10 per state

2001 JOE REDDINGTON SR. "FATHER OF THE IDITAROD" - .45 LC cal., Winchester Model 1866 lever action carbine mfg. by Uberti, 24Kt. gold engraved map of the 1,049 mile Iditarod Trail, "Last Great Race."

N/A	$2,750	82

2001 80th ANNIVERSARY ANCHORAGE POLICE DEPARTMENT - 12 ga., Remington Model 870 in riot configuration, mfg. by Remington, special combat sights, extended mag., 24Kt. gold engraved receiver, cased with officer's badge, personalized for owner officer, honors the fallen officers of the Anchorage Police Dept. from 1921-2001.

N/A	$1,895	100

GRADING - PPGS™	100%	Issue Price	Qty. Made

2002 ALASKA TRIBUTE TO OLD GLORY LIMITED EDITION - .45 LC cal., Winchester Model 94, featuring 24Kt. gold engraving, extensive laser carved stock and forearm, commemorates history of American flag, cased.

	N/A	$2,995	10 per state

2002 ALASKA 9-11 LIBERTY RIFLE EDITION - .22 LR cal., semi-auto, featuring 24Kt. gold uncirculated NY quarter placed in buttstock, laser engraved stock with Twin Towers, the Pentagon, and bald eagle, mfg. by Sturm Ruger.

	N/A	$500	500 per state

ALCHEMY ARMS COMPANY

Previous manufacturer located in Auburn, WA, 1999-circa 2006.

GRADING - PPGS™	100%	98%	95%	90%	80%	70%	60%

PISTOLS: SEMI-AUTO

SPECTRE STANDARD ISSUE (SI) - 9mm Para., .40 S&W, or .45 ACP cal., single action full size design, hammerless firing mechanism, linear action trigger, keyed internal locking device, aluminum receiver with 4 1/2 in. match grade stainless steel barrel and slide, tactical rail, various silver/black finishes, lowered ejection port, 10-shot double column mag, 32 oz. Mfg. 2000-2006.

	$675	$585	$525	$465	$415	$350	$300

Last MSR was $749.

SPECTRE SERVICE GRADE (SG & SGC) - similar to Spectre Standard Issue, except does not have tactical rail and rounded trigger guard, SGC is Commander style with 4 in. barrel and weighs 27 oz. Mfg. 2000-2006, SGC mfg. 2001-2006.

	$675	$585	$525	$465	$415	$350	$300

Last MSR was $749.

SPECTRE TITANIUM EDITION (TI/TIC) - similar to Spectre Series, except features a titanium slide with aluminum receiver, 22 (TIC is Commander style) or 24 oz. Mfg. 2000-2006.

	$895	$775	$675	$575	$500	$450	$395

Last MSR was $999.

ALDAZABAL

Previously manufactured by Aldazabal, Leturiondo & Cia., located in Spain.

PISTOLS: SEMI-AUTO

SEMI-AUTOMATIC PISTOL - 7.65mm cal., 7 shot, Eibar style.

$195	$165	$110	$100	$90	$75	$65

ALERT

Previous trademark manufactured by Hood Firearms Company, Norwich, CT, 1873-1881. These revolvers were dubbed "Suicide Specials" in their day.

100%	98%	95%	90%	80%	70%	60%	50%	40%	30%	20%	10%

REVOLVERS

SINGLE ACTION - .22 rimfire cal., 7 shot, spur trigger, solid frame.

$220	$195	$165	$145	$130	$125	$110	$100	$90	$75	$70	$65

FIVE SHOT - .32 Short rimfire cal.

$170	$165	$160	$155	$150	$140	$125	$105	$95	$85	$75	$70

GRADING - PPGS™	100%	98%	95%	90%	80%	70%	60%

ALESSANDRI, LOU, AND SON

Previous custom rifle manufacturer located in Rehoboth, MA 1975-circa 1998.

Lou Alessandri and Son were noted for their top-quality custom rifles (bolt action and side-by-side). Double rifles started at $18,500, while Express bolt actions started at $5,600. All guns were custom built per individual specifications and a wide variety of special order options were available. In addition to building custom rifles, Lou Alessandri and Son also offered a complete line of high-quality cleaning kits and related accessories. To determine the used value of a Lou Alessandri & Son rifle, the configuration has to be evaluated carefully (caliber, grade of wood, embellishments, and overall desirability).

ALEXANDER ARMS LLC

Current manufacturer located in Radford, VA. Dealer and military sales.

RIFLES: SEMI-AUTO

.50 BEOWULF - .50 Beowulf cal., AR-15 styling, shoots 300-400 grain bullet at approx. 1,800 feet per second, forged upper and lower receiver, 7-shot mag., rotary locking bolt and gas delay mechanism, various configurations include Entry ($1,197 MSR), Over Match kit ($1,300 MSR), Over Match Plus kit ($1,439 MSR), Over Match Tactical kit ($1,605 MSR), Precision Entry ($1,349 MSR), Precision kit ($1,277 MSR), AWS ($1,370 MSR), and Law Enforcement (POR). New 2002.

* *Beowulf Overwatch .50* - similar to .50 Beowulf, except has 24 in. stainless steel barrel, extended range model, shoots 334 grain bullet at approx. 2,000 feet per second, 9 1/4 lbs. Mfg. 2004-2005.

$1,550	$1,350	$1,150	$950	$800	$700	$600

Last MSR was $1,789.

GENGHIS - 5.45x39mm cal., M-4 styling with 16 in. stainless steel barrel, forged upper and lower receiver, 10-shot mag., various configurations with last MSRs include Entry ($1,066 MSR), Over Match kit ($1,158 MSR), Over Match Plus kit ($1,267 MSR), Over Match Tactical kit ($1,372 MSR). Mfg. 2002-2005.

6.5 GRENDEL - 6.5 Grendel cal., M-4 styling with 18 1/2, 19, 20, or 24 in. stainless steel barrel, 10-shot mag., various configurations include Entry ($1,469 MSR), Tactical ($1,027 MSR), Hunter ($1,369 MSR), AWS (starting at $1,499 MSR, 19 or 24 in. barrel), and GDMR ($3,299 MSR). New 2004.

* *Grendel Overwatch 6.5* - 6.5 Grendel cal., 24 in. stainless steel barrel with match chamber, extremely accurate, forged and hard anodized upper and lower receiver. MSR on this model starts at $1,499. New 2004.

ALEXIA

Previous trademark manufactured by Hopkins & Allen, located in Norwich, CT, 1867-1915.

Also known as: Blue Jacket, Captain Jack, Chichester, Defender, Dictator, Monarch, Mountain Eagle, Hopkins & Allen, Towers Police Safety, and Universal.

100%	98%	95%	90%	80%	70%	60%	50%	40%	30%	20%	10%

REVOLVERS

The revolvers listed below are single action design, solid frame, spur trigger - they were an inexpensive vest pocket pistol issued under numerous names for private companies, octagon barrel.

.22 RIMFIRE - 7 shot.

$165	$160	$155	$145	$130	$125	$110	$100	$90	$75	$70	$65

100%	98%	95%	90%	80%	70%	60%	50%	40%	30%	20%	10%

.32 SHORT RIMFIRE - 5 shot.

100%	98%	95%	90%	80%	70%	60%	50%	40%	30%	20%	10%
$170	$165	$160	$155	$150	$140	$125	$105	$95	$85	$75	$70

SINGLE ACTION .38 SHORT RIMFIRE - 5 shot.

100%	98%	95%	90%	80%	70%	60%	50%	40%	30%	20%	10%
$195	$180	$170	$165	$160	$145	$140	$120	$110	$100	$90	$85

.41 SHORT RIMFIRE - 5 shot.

100%	98%	95%	90%	80%	70%	60%	50%	40%	30%	20%	10%
$220	$210	$205	$195	$180	$170	$160	$145	$125	$110	$100	$90

ALFA

Previous trademark manufactured by Armero Especialistas Reunidas, located in Eibar, Spain, circa 1920.

All revolvers are marked "Alfa" on grips.

GRADING - PPGS™	100%	98%	95%	90%	80%	70%	60%

REVOLVERS

EARLY MODEL - .32, .38, or .44 cal., copies of S&W No. 2 by O. Hermanos.

100%	98%	95%	90%	80%	70%	60%
	$145	$130	$120	$110	$105	$95	$75

Add 50% for .44 cal.

LATE MODEL - .22 LR, .32 S&W, or .38 S&W cal., copies of Colt Police Positive and S&W Military and Police.

100%	98%	95%	90%	80%	70%	60%
	$160	$150	$130	$120	$110	$100	$90

ALFA PROJ

Current manufacturer established during 1993, and located in Brno, Czech Republic. Currently imported beginning 2007 by Trail Blazin' Innovations (starter guns only), located in Houston, TX. Previously imported during 2006 by GunX, LLC, located in Shelton, CT.

Alfa Proj marked handguns are of good quality and utilitarian manufacture, and are currently available in both double action revolvers and semi-auto pistols. Alfa Proj also manufactures blank starter revolvers. Additionally, Alfa Proj manufactures revolver carbines and rifles. Most of these guns are not currently imported into the U.S. Please contact the importer directly for more information and U.S. availability (see Trademark Index).

ALKARTASUNA FABRICA DE ARMAS, S.A.

Previous manufacturer located in Guernica, Spain.

PISTOLS: SEMI-AUTO

ALKARTASUNA CARTRIDGE COUNTER - 6.35mm cal., 7 shot, left grip panel cartridge counter, loaded indicator, grip safety.

100%	98%	95%	90%	80%	70%	60%
	$450	$350	$275	$225	$175	$150	$125

ALKARTASUNA RUBY AUTOMATIC - 7.65mm cal., 2 variations - more common is the "Ruby" type, 9 shot, 3 5/8 in. barrel, blue, fixed sights, checkered wood or hard rubber grips, used by French Army in WWI and WWII. Mfg. 1917-22.

100%	98%	95%	90%	80%	70%	60%
	$325	$235	$165	$110	$65	$55	$45

Add 25% for extended barrel.

ALLEN & THURBER

Previous manufacturer/trademark originally located in Grafton, Mass. Ethan Allen started many plants to keep up with expanding business after 1832. Listed below is a chronological order of the firms constituting the family dynasty founded by Ethan Allen.

GRADING - PPGS™	100%	98%	95%	90%	80%	70%	60%

E. Allen - Grafton, Mass. 1832-1837
Allen & Thurber - Grafton, Mass. 1837-1842
Allen & Thurber - Norwich, Conn. 1842-1847
Allen & Thurber - Worcester, Mass. 1847-1854
Allen, Thurber, & Co. - Worcester, Mass. 1854-1856
Allen & Wheelock - Worcester, Mass. 1856-1865
E. Allen & Co. - Worcester, Mass. 1865-1871
Forehand & Wadsworth - Worcester, Mass. 1871-1890
Forehand Arms Co. - Worcester, Mass. 1890-1902

No other 19th-century American firm produced a wider variety of firearms than did Ethan Allen & subsidiaries. In 1902, the Forehand Arms Co. was sold to Hopkins & Allen.

Please refer to the Hopkins & Allen section for approximate values.

ALLEN FIREARMS

Previous importer located in Santa Fe, NM importing A. Uberti Firearms until early in 1987. After Allen Firearms closed, Cimarron F.A. Mfg. Co. located in Houston, TX purchased the remaining inventory (in addition to ordering new products under their name).

Allen Firearms was formerly called Western Arms and manufactured both modern and black powder reproduction firearms and accessories patterned after famous older models. Only modern cartridge guns will be shown in this section.

Rather than provide a complete listing of Allen Firearms models, the following rules usually apply. Since Allen Firearms imported A. Uberti firearms, the Uberti section in this text should be referenced for current values regarding models with similar configurations. Collectibility to date has been limited on most Allen Firearms models, and as a rule, up-to-date values on this trademark are established by current importation prices of Uberti firearms. A complete listing of older Allen Firearms models can be found in Blue Book editions Eleven and Twelve. The models listed below are provided since Uberti is not currently manufacturing them.

RIFLES: REPRODUCTIONS

SHARPS/GEMMER SPORTING RIFLE - .45-70 Govt. cal. only, copy of the famous Sharps rifle. Introduced 1985.

$575	$515	$430	$375	$320	$295	$270

Last MSR was $599.

1979 JUSTIN CENTENNIAL COMMEMORATIVE - includes specially engraved 1866 sporting rifle and 1873 single action revolver (7 1/2 in. barrel) with gold-plated parts and inlay. Both guns are chambered for .44-40 cal. Also includes special hand signed pair of Justin boots, serial numbered belt buckle and presentation oak case. All serial numbers are matching.

MODEL 1873 1 of 1,000 - .44-40 cal, special wood, only 1,000 manufactured. Disc. 1985.

$1,400	$1,200	$1,000	$875	$750	$625	$500

Last MSR was $1,500.

ALMAR

Current trademark of private label Turkish shotguns sold by S. Alamanos & Co. O.E., located in Athens, Greece.

Almar is a private label of shotguns in various configurations manufactured in Turkey. To date, these guns have had little, if any, U.S. importation. Please contact the company directly for more information, including U.S. availability and pricing (see Trademark Index).

GRADING - PPGS™	100%	98%	95%	90%	80%	70%	60%

ALPHA ARMS INC.

Previous manufacturer located in Flower Mound, TX from 1983-1987.
Retail price included custom hard case.

RIFLES: BOLT ACTION

Many special order options including an octagonal barrel, various finishes, special sights, and deluxe wood were available at extra cost on the models listed below. These options, while not listed separately by price, will add value to the prices shown below. All Alpha Arms rifles were manufactured under stringent quality control.

ALPHA CUSTOM - available in most calibers from .222 Rem. through .338 Win. Mag., many other calibers available on special order, 3-position Model 70 type safety, 60 degree bolt, 20 to 24 in. Douglas barrel, limited production, right-hand or left-hand, deluxe checkered Claro walnut standard, approx. 6 lbs. Mfg. 1984-87.

$1,525	$1,200	$975	$850	$725	$640	$560

Last MSR was $1,735.

ALPHA GRAND SLAM - same general specifications as the Alpha Custom, except comes standard with laminated wood stock, fluted bolt and non-glare matte finished metal parts, right-hand or left-hand, approx. 6 1/2 lbs. Mfg. 1985-87.

$1,200	$950	$875	$750	$650	$600	$525

Last MSR was $1,465.

ALPHA ALASKAN - .308 Win., .350 Rem. Mag., .358 Win., or .458 Win. Mag. cal., action is similar to Alpha Grand Slam, except barrel, receiver, bolt and safety are stainless steel, right-hand or left-hand, Nitex coated small parts, approx. 6 3/4-7 1/2 lbs. Mfg. 1985-87.

$1,525	$1,200	$975	$850	$725	$640	$560

Last MSR was $1,735.

ALPHA BIG-FIVE - .300 H&H thru .375 H&H or .458 Win. Mag. cal., reinforced stock and decelerator recoil pad. Mfg. 1987 only.

$1,575	$1,250	$1,050	$895	$750	$640	$560

Last MSR was $1,795.

ALPINE INDUSTRIES

Previous manufacturer located in Los Angeles, CA.

Alpine Industries was a commercial M1 carbine manufacturer that produced approximately 17,000 guns between 1962-1965. Guns were made with newly manufacturerd cast receivers with military surplus parts.

AMERICA REMEMBERS

Current organization located in Ashland, VA, that privately commissions historical, limited/special editions in conjunction with various manufacturers. Previously located in Mechanicsville, VA until 1999.

America Remembers is a private non-governmental organization dedicated to the remembrance of notable Americans and important historical American events. Along with its affiliates, the Armed Forces Commemorative Society®, American Heroes and Legends®, and the United States Society of Arms and Armour®, the company produces special issue limited edition firearms. America Remembers purchased the antique arms division of the U.S. Historical Society on April 1, 1994. Older U.S.H.S. firearms can be located in the U section of this text.

LIMITED/SPECIAL EDITIONS

Values listed below reflect America Remembers most recent issue prices. These do not necessarily represent secondary marketplace prices. No other values are listed since

Model	Manufacturer	Qty.	Year	Issue Price

America Remembers limited edition firearms do not appear that frequently in the secondary marketplace. This is because America Remembers typically sells to consumers directly, without involving normal gun dealers and distributors. Because of this consumer direct sales program, many gun dealers do not have a working knowledge about what America Remembers firearms are currently selling for. The publisher suggests that those people owning America Remembers Limited/Special Editions contact America Remembers (See Trademark Index) for current information, including secondary marketplace liquidity.

While not specifically mentioned, the firearms listed below all have various degrees of ornamentation and other embellishments (including some inscriptions).

Please refer to the *Blue Book of Modern Black Powder Arms* by John Allen (also available online) for more information and prices on America Remembers black powder models. *Black Powder Reproductions & Replicas* by Dennis Adler is also an invaluable source for most black powder reproductions and replicas, and includes hundreds of color images on most popular makes/models, provides manufacturer/trademark histories, and up-to-date information on related items/accessories for black powder shooting - www.bluebookinc.com

HANDGUNS

REVOLVERS: SINGLE ACTION

Model	Manufacturer	Qty.	Year	Issue Price
* *American Indian Tribute SAA.45 LC*	Uberti	300	N/A	$1,795
* *Buffalo Bill Sesquicentennial SAA .45 LC*	Uberti	500	N/A	$1,500
* *Doc Holliday SAA .45 LC*	Uberti	200	N/A	$1,895
* *Interpol SAA .45 LC*	Colt	154	N/A	$4,500
* *Gene Autry Cowboy Edition SAA*	Uberti	1,000	N/A	$1,695
* *Gene Autry Premier Colt SAA*	Colt	100	N/A	$5,250
* *George Jones SA .45 LC*	Uberti	950	N/A	$1,795
* *Herb Jeffries Tribute .45 LC*	Uberti	500	N/A	$1,695
* *Hopalong Cassidy Cowboy SAA*	Uberti	950	N/A	$1,795
* *Hopalong Cassidy Premier Colt SAA*	Colt	100	N/A	$4,500
* *James Arness SA Revolver*	Colt/Uberti	250	N/A	$1,995
* *Roy Rogers & Dale Evans SAA*	Colt	250	N/A	$3,295
* *Seventh Cavalry SAA Tribute*	Uberti	500	N/A	$1,795
* *Sitting Bull SA Revolver .45 Colt*	Colt/Uberti	300	N/A	$1,995
* *Tom Mix Tribute SAA .45 LC*	Uberti	200	N/A	$1,895
* *Tom Mix Premier Edition .45 LC*	Colt	50	N/A	$3,295
* *Travis Tritt SAA .45 LC*	Uberti	500	N/A	$1,795
* *Ruger and His Guns Classic .44 Magnum*	Ruger	400	N/A	$1,995
* *Ruger and His Guns Premier .44 Magnum*	Ruger	100	N/A	$3,595
* *Clayton Moore SAA .45 LC*	Uberti	500	N/A	$1,995
* *Geronimo Colt Cowboy SA .45 LC*	Colt	100	N/A	$1,995
* *Heroic Indian Leaders SAA .44 Spl.*	Colt	50	N/A	$3,195
* *Arms Frank & Jesse James Tribute .45 LC Schofield Cavalry Model*	Navy	100	N/A	$1,695
* *Elvis Western Tribute SA .45 LC*	Colt/Uberti	300	N/A	$1,995
* *Roy Rogers "Happy Trails to You" SA .45*	Colt/Uberti	250	N/A	$2,195
* *Texas Ranger Tribute SA .45 LC*	Colt/Uberti	300	N/A	$2,195
* *West Point Bicentennial Colt Cowboy SA .45*	Colt	300	N/A	$2,195
* *Gene Autry Tribute SA .45 LC*	Colt/Uberti	150	N/A	$2,195
* *U.S. Cavalry Association Tribute SA .45 LC*	Colt/Uberti	300	N/A	$2,195

Model	Manufacturer	Qty.	Year	Issue Price
✳ Native American Legends Tribute Model 3 Schofield .45	S&W	100	N/A	$3,195
✳ Gen. George S. Patton, Jr. SA .45	Colt/Uberti	500	N/A	$2,295
✳ American Cattlebrand Tribute SA .45	Colt	100	N/A	$4,995
✳ Legends In Steel SA .45 LC	Colt	250	N/A	$2,995
✳ Elvis Presley Taking Care of Business .357 Mag.	S&W	500	N/A	$2,195
✳ Richard Petty Silver SA .45	Uberti	1,000	N/A	$1,675
✳ Doc Holliday & Kate Haroney SAA .45 LC	Uberti	300	N/A	$2,195

SEMI-AUTOS: .45 ACP

Model	Manufacturer	Qty.	Year	Issue Price
✳ Army Air Corp. Tribute	Colt	300	N/A	$1,895
✳ American Eagle Tribute	Colt	2,500	N/A	$1,995
✳ American Patriot Tribute	Colt	N/A	N/A	$1,695
✳ Army Air Forces Tribute	Colt	500	N/A	$1,500
✳ Audie Murphy Tribute	Colt	1,000	N/A	$1,895
✳ Chuck Yeager Tribute	Colt	1,000	N/A	$1,995
✳ Ernie Irvan Tribute	Colt	250	N/A	$1,895
✳ Leatherneck Tribute Pistol	Colt	300	N/A	$1,895
✳ Navajo Code Talkers Yellowhorse (w/knife)	Colt	300	N/A	$3,000
✳ Pacific Naval Tribute	Auto-Ordnance	500	N/A	$1,500
✳ Pearl Harbor Tribute Pistol	Colt	500	N/A	$1,995
✳ Purple Heart Tribute Pistol	Colt	250	N/A	$1,895
✳ VJ-Day Tribute	Colt	250	N/A	$1,495
✳ West Point Tribute	Colt	300	N/A	$1,995
✳ West Point WWII Tribute Pistol	Colt	500	N/A	$1,995
✳ Wings of Freedom-USAF 50th Anniversary Tribute	Colt	250	N/A	$1,695
✳ VFW 100th Anniversary	Colt	500	N/A	$1,695
✳ Special Operations Associations Tribute	Colt	250	N/A	$1,995
✳ Spirit of America Tribute Pistol	Colt	911	N/A	$1,795
✳ Berlin Airlift Golden Anniversary Tribute	Colt	250	N/A	$1,795
✳ Elvis Tribute Pistol	Colt	300	N/A	$1,995
✳ VFW Korean War Tribute	Colt	300	N/A	$1,795
✳ NRA Tribute Pistol	Colt	300	N/A	$2,195
✳ U.S. Army 20th Century Tribute	Colt	300	N/A	$1,995
✳ VFW Vietnam War Tribute	Colt	300	N/A	$2,195
✳ Colt Patriotic Tribute	Colt	500	N/A	$1,995
✳ Gen. George S. Patton Jr. Tribute	Colt	500	N/A	$2,195
✳ WWII Golden Anniversary Marine Pacific Tribute	Colt	500	N/A	$1,500
✳ Operation Iraqi Freedom Tribute 92FS Semi-Auto 9mm	Beretta	300	N/A	$2,195
✳ Special Operations Association Vietnam Tribute Browning Hi-Power Captain	Browning	250	N/A	$1,995
✳ Colt Legacy Tribute	Colt	300	N/A	$1,995
✳ Ranger Spirit Tribute	Colt	300	N/A	$1,995

Model	Manufacturer	Qty.	Year	Issue Price
✳ Air Force Academy 50th Anniversary Tribute	Colt	300	N/A	$1,995
✳ Navajo Code Talkers Tribute	Colt	300	N/A	$2,195
✳ Army Air Forces WWII Golden Anniversary	Colt	500	N/A	$1,500
✳ Don't Give Up the Ship Tribute	Colt	1,997	N/A	$1,795
✳ John Wayne Tribute	Colt	3,500	N/A	$2,295
✳ Leatherneck Vietnam Tribune	Colt	500	N/A	$2,195
✳ CAF Legends of the Sky	Colt	300	N/A	$2,195
✳ Tex Hill Tribute	Colt	200	N/A	$1,995
✳ Founding Fathers 2nd Amendment Tribute	Colt	500	N/A	$1,995
✳ Colt Proud To Be An American Tribute	Colt	500	N/A	$1,995
✳ VFW "Defenders of Freedom" Tribute	Colt	500	N/A	$1,995

RIFLES

Model	Manufacturer	Qty.	Year	Issue Price
✳ Model 94 (.22 LR) King Richard Tribute	Winchester	200	N/A	$1,495
✳ Model 94 (.30-30) American Eagle Tribute	Winchester	500	N/A	$1,895
✳ Model 94 (.30-30) American Wildlife Tribute	Winchester	300	N/A	$1,895
✳ Model 94 (.30-30)B. Bill Sesqui. Tribute	Winchester	300	N/A	$1,895
✳ Model 94 (.30-30) Babe Ruth Tribute	Winchester	300	N/A	$1,895
✳ Model 94 (.30-30) Bruce Boxleitner Tribute	Winchester	100	N/A	$1,895
✳ Model 94 (.30-30) California Sesquicentennial	Winchester	150	N/A	$1,495
✳ Model 94 (.30-30) C.M. Russell Tribute	Winchester	300	N/A	$1,895
✳ Model 94 (.30-30) Cherokee Trail of Tears Tribute	Winchester	300	N/A	$1,795
✳ Model 94 (.30-30) Cochise Tribute Rifle	Winchester	300	N/A	$1,895
✳ Model 94 (.30-30) Dale Berry Tribute	Winchester	300	N/A	$1,850
✳ Model 94 (.30-30) Davey Allison Tribute	Winchester	500	N/A	$1,895
✳ Model 94 (.30-30) Deer Hunter Tribute	Winchester	300	N/A	$1,795
✳ Model 94 (.30-30) Dennis Weaver Tribute	Winchester	100	N/A	$1,895
✳ Model 94 (.30-30) Elvis and Graceland Tribute	Winchester	1,000	N/A	$1,995
✳ Model 94 (.30-30) Field & Stream Tribute	Winchester	300	N/A	$1,595
✳ Model 94 (.30-30) Wrangler Ft. Worth Tribute	Winchester	300	N/A	$1,895
✳ Model 94 (.30-30) Gene Autry Tribute	Winchester	300	N/A	$2,100
✳ Model 94 (.30-30) George Jones Tribute	Winchester	300	N/A	$1,995
✳ Model 94 (.30-30) Great North American Rodeo	Winchester	500	N/A	$1,895
✳ Model 94 (.30-30) Heroic Indian Leaders Tribute	Winchester	300	N/A	$1,650
✳ Model 94 (.30-30) Hopalong Cassidy Tribute	Winchester	500	N/A	$1,850
✳ Model 94 (.30-30) Leatherneck Sportsman Tribute	Winchester	300	N/A	$1,995
✳ Model 94 (.30-30) Roy Rogers Tribute	Winchester	300	N/A	$2,100
✳ Model 94 Roy Rogers & Gabby Hayes .45 LC	Winchester	300	N/A	$1,895

Model	Manufacturer	Qty.	Year	Issue Price
✳ Model 94 (.30-30) Rusty Wallace Tribute	Winchester	1,000	N/A	$1,895
✳ Model 94 (.30-30) Tennessee Ernie Ford Tribute	Winchester	100	N/A	$1,895
✳ Model 94 (.30-30) Terry Labonte Tribute	Winchester	1,000	N/A	$1,895
✳ Model 94 (.30-30) Texas Motor Speedway	Winchester	500	N/A	$1,795
✳ Model 94 (.30-30) Ty Murray Tribute	Winchester	500	N/A	$1,895
✳ Model 94 (.30-30) U.S. Cavalry Association Tribute	Winchester	300	N/A	$1,995
✳ Model 94 (.30-30) Tribute to Yellowstone National Park	Winchester	125	N/A	$1,895
✳ Model 336CS (.30-30) Whitetail Trophy	Marlin	500	N/A	$1,595
✳ Model 336CS (.30-30) Whitetail Hunter Tribute	Marlin	300	N/A	$1,395
✳ Model 336CS (.30-30) Whitetail Deer Trophy	Marlin	300	N/A	$1,595
✳ Model 1894 (.45 LC) White Buffalo Spirit Tribute	Marlin	300	N/A	$1,895
✳ Model 94 (.45 LC) American Cowboy Tribute	Winchester	200	N/A	$2,795
✳ Model 94 (.45 LC) American Indian Tribute	Winchester	300	N/A	$1,250
✳ Model 94 (.45 LC) Citation Bass Tribute	Winchester	300	N/A	$1,495
✳ Model 94 (.45 LC) Darrell Waltrip 25th Anniversary	Winchester	750	N/A	$1,795
✳ Model 94 (.45 LC) Monte Hale Tribute	Winchester	300	N/A	$1,895
✳ Model 94 (.45 LC) Rex Allen Tribute	Winchester	500	N/A	$1,895
✳ Model 94 (.45 LC) Clint Walker Tribute	Winchester	300	N/A	$1,895
✳ Model 92 (.45 LC) Lawmen & Outlaws of the Wild West	Winchester	300	N/A	$1,850
✳ Model 336CS (.30-30) American Hunter Tribute	Marlin	300	N/A	$1,695
✳ Model 1873 (.44-40) Buffalo Bill´s Wild West Tribute	Uberti	300	N/A	$1,995
✳ Model 1873 (.44-40) Scouts of the Western Frontier	Uberti	300	N/A	$1,995
✳ Model 1873 (.44-40) Wild West Exhibition Shooters Tribute	Uberti	300	N/A	$1,795
✳ Model 1873 (.44-40) Wild West Frontier Tribute	Uberti	125	N/A	$1,695
✳ Model 94 (.30-30) Wrangler Gene Autry, Smiley Burnette, & Pat Buttram Tribute	Winchester	300	N/A	$1,895
✳ Model 94 (.30-30) Iron Eyes Cody Tribute	Winchester	300	N/A	$1,895
✳ Model 94 (.30-30) James Arness Tribute	Winchester	250	N/A	$1,995
✳ Model 94 (.30-30) NRA Tribute	Winchester	300	N/A	$1,850
✳ Model 94 (.30-30) Nolan Ryan Tribute	Winchester	324	N/A	$1,850
✳ Model 94 (.30-30) Tribute to the Rough Riders	Winchester	300	N/A	$1,895
✳ Model 94 (.30-30) Richard Boone Tribute	Winchester	250	N/A	$1,895
✳ Model 94 (.30-30) Richard Farnsworth Tribute	Winchester	100	N/A	$1,895

Model	Manufacturer	Qty.	Year	Issue Price
✱ Model 94 (.30-30) Texas Ranger 175th Anniversary Tribute	Winchester	300	N/A	$1,950
✱ Model 94 (.30-30) Texas Trophy Hunters	Winchester	250	N/A	$1,895
✱ Henry (.44-40) A Nation Reunited: Civil War Tribute	Uberti	300	N/A	$1,895
✱ Model 1873 (.45 LC) Wyatt Earp Sesquicentennial Tribute	Uberti	300	N/A	$1,995
✱ Model 1894 (.45 LC) Cowboy Limited Roy Rogers/Dale Evans & Dusty Rogers Tribute	Marlin	300	N/A	$1,895
✱ Model 94 (.30-30) Audie Murphy Tribute	Winchester	250	N/A	$1,995
✱ Model 94 (.30-30) Frederic Remington Art Museum Tribute	Winchester	300	N/A	$1,895
✱ Model 94 (.30-30) National Cowboy Hall of Fame	Winchester	300	N/A	$1,895
✱ Model 94 (.30-30) Travis Tritt Tribute	Winchester	300	N/A	$1,895
✱ Model 94 (.30-30) 101 Ranch Western Tribute	Winchester	300	N/A	$1,895
✱ Model 1873 (.44-40) Heroes of Texas Tribute	Uberti	300	N/A	$2,195
✱ Model 1866 (.44-40) Yellow Boy American Buffalo Tribute	Uberti	300	N/A	$1,995
✱ Henry Civil War Cavalry Leaders Tribute (.44-40)	Uberti	300	N/A	$2,195
✱ Henry Mort Künstler Civil War Tribute (.44-40)	Uberti	300	N/A	$2,195
✱ Henry Quanah Parker Red River War Tribute (.44-40)	Uberti	300	N/A	$2,295
✱ Henry Sons of Confederate Veterans (.44-40)	Uberti	300	N/A	$2,195
✱ Henry (.44-40) West Point Civil War Tribute	Uberti	300	N/A	$1,995
✱ Henry (.44-40) West Point Civil War Union Leaders	Uberti	500	N/A	$2,295
✱ Henry (.44-40) West Point Civil War Confederate Leader	Uberti	500	N/A	$2,295
✱ Model 94 (.30-30) Progressive Farmer/Rural Sportsman Whitetail Deer Tribute	Winchester	300	N/A	$1,695
✱ Model 94 (.30-30) Virginia Deer Hunters Whitetail Deer Tribute	Winchester	50	N/A	$1,795
✱ Henry (.44-40) Gettysburg Tribute	Uberti	500	N/A	$2,295
✱ American Indian Tribute Henry (.44-40)	Uberti	500	N/A	$2,295
✱ Chisholm Trail Tribute Model 1873 Sporting	Uberti	300	N/A	$2,195
✱ Legends of the Old West Tribute Model 1866 Yellow Boy (.44-40)	Uberti	500	N/A	$2,195
✱ Red Man 100th Anniversary Tribute Model 94 (.30-30)	Winchester	100	N/A	$1,995
✱ NRA Tribute M1 Garand Rifle (.30-06)	Springfield Armory	300	N/A	$2,995
✱ Mule Deer Foundation Tribute BAR (.30-06)	Browning	300	N/A	$2,195

Model	Manufacturer	Qty.	Year	Issue Price
✳ BAR Semi-Auto (.30-06) Rocky Mt. Elk Tribute	Browning	300	N/A	$2,195
✳ Model 94 Frank McCarthy American West Tribute (.30-30)	Winchester	300	N/A	$1,995
✳ Model 94 Clayton Moore Tribute (.30-30)	Winchester	300	N/A	$1,995
✳ Leatherneck Tribute M1 Garand (.30-06)	Springfield Armory	300	N/A	$2,995
✳ Model 94 (.30-30) American Whitetails Van Gilder Tribute	Winchester	300	N/A	$1,795
✳ Model 1873 (.44-40) Battle of Little Bighorn Tribute	Uberti	500	N/A	$2,295
✳ Model 1873 Billy the Kid Tribute	Uberti	300	N/A	$2,295
✳ Henry (.44-40) Frank McCarthy American Buffalo Tribute	Uberti	300	N/A	$2,295
✳ Model 94 Gambling Legends Tribute	Winchester	1,000	N/A	$1,995
✳ Model 94 (.30-30) Gary Cooper Tribute	Winchester	250	N/A	$1,895
✳ Model 94 (.30-30) George Jones 50th Anniversary Tribute	Winchester	100	N/A	$1,995
✳ Model 94 (.45 Colt) Hopalong Cassidy Trails End Tribute	Winchester	300	N/A	$2,195
✳ Rolling Block (.45-70) James-Younger Northfield Bank Raid Tribute	Pedersoli	500	N/A	$2,595
✳ Henry (.44-40) Mort Kunstler Lee-Jackson Tribute	Uberti	300	N/A	$2,295
✳ Henry (.44-40) NRA Tribute	Uberti	300	N/A	$2,295
✳ Model 94 (.30-30) Pancho Villa Tribute	Winchester	300	N/A	$1,895
✳ Carbine (.56-50) Sons of Confederate Veterans Tribute to the Confederacy	Spencer	300	N/A	$2,495
✳ Model 1873 (.44-40) Texas Ranger Tribute	Uberti	300	N/A	$2,295
✳ Model 94 (.30-30) U.S. Marshals Tribute	Winchester	500	N/A	$1,995
✳ West Point M1 Garand	Springfield Armory	300	N/A	$2,995
✳ Model 1873 (.44-40) Winning the West Tribute	Uberti	1,000	N/A	$2,295
✳ Model 336C (.30-30) Whitetail Deer Tribute	Marlin	300	N/A	$1,895
✳ Model 1866 (.44-40) Spirit of the Wild Tribute	Uberti	300	N/A	$2,195
✳ Henry (.44-40) Bozeman Trail Tribute	Uberti	300	N/A	$2,295
✳ Model 1873 Carbine (.45 LC) John Wayne Tribute	Uberti	3,500	N/A	$2,495
✳ Thompson Semi-Auto (.45 ACP) G-Men/J. Edgar Hoover Tribute	Auto-Ordnance	750	N/A	$2,995

SHOTGUNS

Model	Manufacturer	Qty.	Year	Issue Price
✳ Model 870 Wingmaster (12 ga.) Ned & Dale Jarrett	Remington	750	N/A	$1,595
✳ Law & Order (12 ga.) double-hammered shotgun	SIACE	100	N/A	$3,000
✳ Model 870 (12 ga.) Remington Deer Hunter Tribute	Remington	300	N/A	$1,495

Model	Manufacturer	Qty.	Year	Issue Price
* Model 870 (12 ga.) Remington Waterfowl Tribute	Remington	300	N/A	$1,795
* Model BPS (12 ga.) Texas Sportsman Tribute	Browning	250	N/A	$1,695
* Model 870 (12 ga.) Wingmaster Ducks Unlimited Tribute	Remington	300	N/A	$1,795
* Model 11-87 (12 ga.) Ducks Unlimited Flyways Tribute	Remington	300	N/A	$1,995
* John Wayne Coach Shotgun (12 ga.)	Baikal	2,500	N/A	$1,795
* Red Label (20 ga.) Wildlife Forever 15th Anniversary Tribute	Ruger	100	N/A	$2,495
* Nat'l Wild Turkey Fed. 30th Anniversary Tribute Model 11-87 Premier (12 ga.)	Remington	300	N/A	$1,995
* Model BPS (12 ga.) Ducks Unlimited Duck Hunter Tribute	Browning	300	N/A	$1,995
* Model BPS (12 ga.) Jamestown 400th Anniversary Tribute	Browning	400	N/A	$1,995
* Model 1878 (12 ga.) Doc Holliday OK Corral Tribute	TTN	300	N/A	$1,995

AMERICAN ARMS

Previous manufacturer located in Garden Grove, CA.

GRADING - PPGS™	100%	98%	95%	90%	80%	70%	60%

PISTOLS: SEMI-AUTO

EAGLE 380 - .380 ACP cal. only, stainless steel semi-auto, copy of Walther PPK/S, 6-shot mag., 3 1/4 in. barrel, limited production, 20 oz.

	100%	98%	95%	90%	80%	70%	60%
	$400	$250	$215	N/A	N/A	N/A	N/A

Last MSR was $289.

Add $25 for case.
Add $50 for case and belt buckle.
Add $25 for black teflon finish (disc. 1985).

AMERICAN ARMS CO.

Previous manufacturer located in Boston, MA from 1870-1901 and Milwaukee, WI. from 1893-1904. American Arms Co. was acquired by Marlin in 1901.

100%	98%	95%	90%	80%	70%	60%	50%	40%	30%	20%	10%

DERRINGERS

O/U DESIGN - .22 Short R.F., .32 Short R.F., or .41 Short R.F. cal., Wheeler Pat. Action, brass frame, spur trigger.

100%	98%	95%	90%	80%	70%	60%	50%	40%	30%	20%	10%
$800	$750	$700	$650	$600	$550	$500	$450	$395	$325	$250	$175

SHOTGUNS: SxS

HAMMERLESS MODEL - 12 ga., semi-hammerless.

100%	98%	95%	90%	80%	70%	60%	50%	40%	30%	20%	10%
$600	$550	$500	$450	$350	$275	$225	$175	$150	$125	$100	$75

WHITMORE PATENT - 10 or 12 ga., hammerless, checkering.

100%	98%	95%	90%	80%	70%	60%	50%	40%	30%	20%	10%
$685	$625	$575	$520	$460	$400	$340	$270	$200	$150	$125	$100

Add 10% for 10 ga. (2 7/8 in. chambers).

SINGLESHOT - 12 ga., semi-hammerless, damascus barrel.

100%	98%	95%	90%	80%	70%	60%	50%	40%	30%	20%	10%
$260	$225	$200	$175	$150	$125	$90	$70	$50	$40	$30	$20

GRADING - PPGS™	100%	98%	95%	90%	80%	70%	60%

AMERICAN ARMS, INC.

Previous importer and manufacturer located in North Kansas City, MO, until 2000. American Arms imported various Spanish shotguns (Indesal, Lanber, Norica, and Zabala Hermanos), Italian shotguns including F. Stefano, several European pistols and rifles, and Sites handguns (1990-2000) mfg. in Torino, Italy. This company also manufactured several pistols in North Kansas City, MO. For more information and pricing on Norica airguns previously imported by American Arms, please refer to the *Blue Book of Airguns* by Dr. Robert Beeman & John Allen (also available online).

In late 2000, TriStar Sporting Arms, Ltd. acquired the parts inventory for some models previously imported by American Arms, Inc. Original warranties from American Arms do not apply to TriStar Sporting Arms, Ltd.

COMBINATION GUNS

RS COMBO - choice of .222 Rem. or .308 Win. rifle barrel under 12 ga. barrel, engraved boxlock frame with antique silver finish, DTs, 24 in. VR barrels with shotgun choke tubes, rifle sights, grooved for scope mounting, Monte Carlo stock, 7 lbs. 14 oz. Imported 1989 only.

$675	$595	$550	$495	$450	$420	$385

Last MSR was $749.

PISTOLS: SEMI-AUTO

MODEL TT-9MM TOKAREV - 9mm Para. cal., semi-auto single action, 4 1/2 in. barrel, 9-shot mag., hammer block external safety, 31 oz. Imported 1988-89 only.

$250	$230	$210	$195	$180	$170	$160

Last MSR was $289.

This model is patterned after the Tokarev action and was made from machined steel parts in Yugoslavia.

MODEL EP-380 - .380 ACP cal., semi-auto double action, stainless steel, 3 1/2 in. barrel, 7-shot mag., wood checkered grips, adj. rear sight, 25 oz. Imported 1988-90 only.

$375	$325	$250	$195	$165	$140	$120

Last MSR was $449.

This model was made in West Germany.

MODEL PK-22 CLASSIC - .22 LR cal., semi-auto double action, styled after Govt. .45 ACP, 3 1/3 in. barrel, 8 shot finger extension mag., black polymer grips, 22 oz. Mfg. 1988-96.

$165	$140	$115	$100	$90	$80	$70

Last MSR was $199.

This model was made in North Kansas City, MO. It has patented safety features such as external hammer block and internal blocking of the firing pin until the trigger is pulled.

MODEL CX-22 CLASSIC - .22 LR cal., style patterned after Walther PPK, 3 1/3 in. barrel, 8 shot finger extension mag., 22 oz. Mfg. 1990-95.

$175	$145	$125	$110	$100	$90	$80

Last MSR was $213.

This model was made in North Kansas City, MO. It has patented safety features such as external hammer block and internal blocking of the firing pin until the trigger is pulled.

✱ *Model CXC-22* - similar to CX-22 Classic, except has chrome slide. Mfg. in 1990 only.

$170	$150	$125	$110	$100	$90	$80

Last MSR was $189.

GRADING - PPGS™	100%	98%	95%	90%	80%	70%	60%

MODEL PX-22/25 CLASSIC - .22 LR or .25 ACP (mfg. 1991 only) cal., compact variation of the Model CX-22, 2 3/4 in. barrel, 7 shot finger extension mag., 15 oz. New 1989, PX-25 was mfg. 1991 only, PX-22 was disc. 1995.

	$175	$145	$125	$110	$100	$90	$80

Last MSR was $206.

This model was made in North Kansas City, MO. It has patented safety features such as external hammer block and internal blocking of the firing pin until the trigger is pulled.

MODEL P-98 CLASSIC - .22 LR cal., semi-auto double action patterned after Walther P.38, 5 in. barrel, 8-shot mag., blue/black finish, grooved wraparound grips, 26 oz. Mfg. 1990-96.

	$170	$145	$125	$110	$100	$90	$80

Last MSR was $209.

ESCORT - .380 ACP cal., double action only, 3 3/8 in. barrel, 7-shot mag., unique thin profile, matte stainless steel, soft polymer grips, polygonal rifling, 19 oz. Mfg. 1995-97.

	$285	$230	$200	$185	$170	$160	$150

Last MSR was $349.

SABRE - while this model was advertised, it was never mfg.

SPECTRE - 9mm Para., .40 S&W (mfg. 1991 only), or .45 ACP (new 1993) cal., semi-auto double action, 6 in. barrel with polygonal rifling, 30-shot mag., ambidextrous safety, decocking lever, adj. sights, 4 1/2 lbs., mfg. in Italy by Sites. Imported 1990-93.

	$500	$325	$275	$240	$200	$185	$170

Last MSR was $429.

Add $28 for .45 ACP cal.

This model was previously imported by F.I.E. located in Hialeah, FL (1989-1990).

AUSSIE SEMI-AUTO - 9mm Para. or .40 S&W cal., semi-auto double action, polymer frame with nickeled steel slide and 4 3/4 in. barrel, 10-shot mag., features 5 safeties, open slide after last shot, 23 oz. Limited importation from Spain 1996 only.

	$350	$250	$225	$200	$185	$170	$160

Last MSR was $425.

REVOLVERS: SAA

REGULATOR MODEL - .357 Mag., .44-40, or .45 LC cal., 4 3/4, 5 1/2 (new 1993), or 7 1/2 in. barrel, reproduction of the Colt Peacemaker, featuring brass trigger guard and back strap, fixed sights, half-cock and hammer block safeties, blade front, grooved rear sights, color case hardened frame and blue barrel/cylinder or nickel finish (imported 1999 only in .45 LC cal.), walnut grips, 35 oz. Mfg. by Uberti. Imported 1992-2000.

	$270	$230	$200	$185	$170	$160	$150

Last MSR was $320.

Add $55 for nickel finish (disc. 1999).
Add $40 for dual cylinder set (.44-40/.44 Spl. or .45 LC/.45 ACP). Disc. 1998.

* *Regulator Model Deluxe* - similar to Regulator Model, except .45 LC cal. only, all blue charcoal finish (mfg. 1996-97) or color case hardened frame (new 1998), case hardened (pre-1993) or blue (post-1993) steel trigger guard and back strap. Importation disc. 1992, resumed 1994-2000.

	$315	$260	$215	$190	$170	$160	$150

Last MSR was $365.

Add $70 for dual cylinder set (.44-40/.44 Spl. or .45 LC/.45 ACP). Disc. 1992.

GRADING - PPGS™	100%	98%	95%	90%	80%	70%	60%

✳ *Regulator Model Buckhorn* - .44 Mag cal., 4 3/4, 6, or 7 1/2 in. barrel, otherwise similar to Regulator Model, 44 oz. Imported 1993-96.

	$305	$255	$205	$185	$170	$160	$150

Last MSR was $379.

Add $10 for Target variation (flattop and adj. rear sight). Imported 1994 only.

✳ *Regulator Model Storekeeper* - .44-40 WCF or .45 LC cal., 4 in. barrel, smooth walnut curved grips, nickel or B/H nickel finish, 31 oz. Imported 1999 only.

	$320	$265	$215	$190	$170	$160	$150

Last MSR was $375.

Add $44 for B/H nickel finish.

UBERTI BISLEY - .45 LC cal., patterned after the Colt Bisley, case hardened steel frame, 4 3/4, 5 1/2, or 7 1/2 in. barrel with fixed sights, hammer block safety. Imported 1997-98 only.

	$425	$340	$275	$215	$190	$170	$160

Last MSR was $475.

UBERTI .454 SAA - .454 cal., 6 SR or 7 1/2 in. top-ported barrel, hammer block safety, satin nickel finish, custom hardwood grips, wide trigger, adj. rear sight. Imported 1996-97 only.

	$750	$625	$550	$495	$465	$435	$375

Last MSR was $869.

SILVERADO - .357 Mag., .44 Mag., or .45 LC cal., 4 3/4, 5 1/2, or 7 1/2 barrel, brushed nickel finish, unfluted cylinder, laminated charcoal grips. Mfg. by Uberti, imported 1999-2000.

	$345	$285	$220	$195	$170	$160	$150

Last MSR was $409.

RIFLES: O/U

SILVER EXPRESS - 8x57JRS or 9.3x74R cal., O/U boxlock design, gold SNT, monoblock 28 in. separated barrels, manual safety, silver finished receiver with light engraving, skipline checkered walnut stock and forearm, approx. 7 3/4 lbs. Limited importation 1999-2000.

	$1,800	$1,625	$1,500	$1,375	$1,250	$1,125	$1,000

Last MSR was $1,949.

RIFLES: REPRODUCTIONS

MODEL 1860 HENRY REPLICA - .44-40 WCF or .45 LC cal., 24 1/4 in. blue or white finish (new 1999) barrel, 9 1/4 lbs. Mfg. by Uberti, importation disc. 2000.

	$835	$625	$525	$425	$360	$320	$260

Last MSR was $940.

Add $50 for white barrel finish.

✳ *Model 1860 Henry Trapper Replica* - similar to the Henry Replica, except has 18 1/2 in. barrel, 8 lbs. Imported 1999-2000.

	$835	$625	$525	$425	$360	$320	$260

Last MSR was $940.

Add $50 for white barrel finish.

MODEL 1866 WINCHESTER REPLICA - .44-40 WCF or .45 LC cal., 19 (Carbine) or 24 1/4 (Rifle) in. barrel, approx. 8 lbs. Mfg. by Uberti, importation disc. 2000.

	$650	$550	$460	$375	$300	$250	$200

Last MSR was $730.

Subtract $20 for Carbine variation (Yellowboy).

GRADING - PPGS™	100%	98%	95%	90%	80%	70%	60%

MODEL 1873 WINCHESTER REPLICA - .44-40 WCF or .45 LC cal., 24 1/4 or 30 (new 1999) in. octagon barrel, case colored receiver, approx. 8 1/4 lbs. Mfg. by Uberti, importation disc. 2000.

	$775	$625	$525	$425	$360	$320	$260

Last MSR was $860.

Add $80 for 30 in. barrel.

* *Model 1873 Deluxe Winchester Replica* - similar to Model 1873 Winchester Replica, except has better quality checkered pistol grip stock and forearm. Disc. 1997.

	$1,100	$775	$625	$500	$425	$350	$275

Last MSR was $1,299.

MODEL 1885 SINGLE SHOT HIGH WALL - .45-70 Govt. cal., 28 in. round barrel, color case hardened frame, 8.82 lbs. Mfg. by Uberti, imported 1998-2000.

	$700	$575	$495	$395	$350	$300	$260

Last MSR was $810.

SHARPS CAVALRY CARBINE - .45-70 Govt. cal., 22 in. heavy round barrel, case colored action, blue barrel with adj. rear ladder sight, DST, uncheckered walnut stock and forearm, 8 lbs. 3 oz. Imported 1999-2000.

	$625	$525	$450	$400	$360	$330	$300

Last MSR was $660.

SHARPS FRONTIER CARBINE - similar to Cavalry Carbine, except has regular barrel with barrel band and single trigger, 7 lbs. 13 oz. Imported 1999-2000.

	$615	$535	$450	$400	$360	$330	$300

Last MSR was $675.

SHARPS 1874 SPORTING RIFLE - .45-70 Govt. or .45-120 black powder cartridge, 28 in. octagon barrel, checkered walnut stock and forearm, DST, 9 lbs. 3 oz. Imported 1999-2000.

	$635	$535	$450	$400	$360	$330	$300

Last MSR was $685.

* *Sharps 1874 Deluxe Sporting Rifle* - similar to Sharps 1874 Sporting Rifle, except has brown barrel finish. Imported 1999-2000.

	$650	$545	$460	$410	$360	$330	$300

Last MSR was $705.

RIFLES: SEMI-AUTO

MODEL ZCY 308 - .308 Win. cal., gas operated semi-auto AK-47 type action, Yugoslavian mfg. Imported 1988 only.

	$775	$650	$550	$450	$400	$375	$350

Last MSR was $825.

MODEL AKY 39 - 7.62x39mm cal., gas operated semi-auto AK-47 type action, teakwood fixed stock and grip, flip up Tritium night front sight and rear, Yugoslavian mfg. Imported 1988-89 only.

	$650	$550	$495	$440	$395	$350	$300

Last MSR was $559.

This model was supplied with sling and cleaning kit.

* *Model AKF 39 Folding Stock* - 7.62x39mm cal., folding stock variation of the Model AKY-39. Imported 1988-89 only.

	$725	$625	$550	$475	$425	$375	$325

Last MSR was $589.

GRADING - PPGS™	100%	98%	95%	90%	80%	70%	60%

EXP-64 SURVIVAL RIFLE - .22 LR cal., semi-auto, takedown rifle stores in over-size synthetic stock compartment, 21 in. barrel, 10-shot mag., open sights, receiver grooved for scope mounting, cross bolt safety, 40 in. overall length, 7 lbs. Imported 1989-90 only.

	$150	$135	$125	$115	$105	$95	$85

Last MSR was $169.

MINI-MAX - .22 LR cal., semi-auto, 18 3/4 in. barrel, wood or black synthetic stock, 10-shot mag., adj. rear sight, 4 1/3 lbs. Imported in 1990 only.

	$85	$75	$65	$55	$45	$40	$35

Last MSR was $99.

Add $6 for wood stock.

SM 64 TD SPORTER - .22 LR cal., semi-auto, takedown barrel, 21 in. barrel, checkered walnut finished hardwood stock and forend, hooded front sight and adj. rear sight, 7 lbs. Imported 1989-90 only.

	$130	$115	$105	$95	$85	$75	$65

Last MSR was $149.

SHOTGUNS: O/U

American Arms imported Spanish shotguns manufactured by Zabala Hermanos, Lanber, and Indesal. Italian shotguns were also imported and mfg. by Stefano Fausti (Models Silver, Waterfowl, and Turkey Special). American Arms also imported Franchi Black Magic semi-auto and O/U shotguns until 1998. These shotguns will appear under the Franchi section in this text. Older Diarm models have been listed below.

LINCE - 12 or 20 ga., 3 in. chambers, boxlock with Greener crossbolt, various barrel lengths and chokings, available in either blue or shiny chrome finish, SST, VR, ejectors. Imported 1986 only.

	$510	$400	$380	$360	$340	$320	$300

Last MSR was $610.

Add $70 for choke tubes.

SILVER MODEL - 12 or 20 ga. only, similar to Lince Model, except has brushed aluminum finished receiver, no engraving. Imported 1986-87 only.

	$495	$450	$390	$360	$330	$300	$285

Last MSR was $545.

Add $50 for multi-chokes.

SILVER I - similar to Silver Model, except also available in 28 ga. or .410 bore (both new 1988), single selective trigger became standard in 1988, extractors, engraved frame, fixed chokes, recoil pad. Imported 1986-2000.

	$535	$430	$350	$300	$285	$270	$255

Last MSR was $649.

Add $30 for 28 ga. or .410 bore.
Engraved frame became standard in 1987.

SILVER II - similar to Silver I, except is supplied with choke tubes, deluxe walnut, and ejectors, 16 ga. new 1999. Imported 1987-2000.

	$660	$560	$475	$400	$360	$330	$300

Last MSR was $769.

Add $46 for 28 ga. or .410 bore (fixed chokes only).

✱ *Silver II Lite (Silver Upland Lite)* - 12, 20, or 28 ga. (disc. 1995), 3 in. chambers (except for 28 ga.), 26 in. VR barrels, with Franchoke tubes (except for 28 ga.), SST, ejectors, engraved frame with antique silver finish, checkered walnut stock and forearm, 5 3/4-6 1/4 lbs. Imported 1994-98.

	$800	$660	$550	$485	$440	$400	$360

Last MSR was $925.

✳ *Silver II Small Gauge Combo* - includes either 20/28 ga. (new 1997) or 28 ga./ .410 bore barrels. Imported 1989-2000.

	$1,080	$925	$750	$625	$550	$495	$450

Last MSR was $1,239.

SILVER LITE - 12 or 20 ga., 2 3/4 in. chambers, boxlock action, 26 in. vent. barrels with VR and choke tubes, blue alloy receiver, SST, ejectors, gold trigger, checkered walnut stock and forearm, 5 lbs. 14 oz. or 6 (12 ga.) lbs., mfg. by Lanber. Imported 1990-92.

	$625	$535	$460	$400	$360	$330	$300

Last MSR was $749.

SILVER HUNTER - 12 or 20 ga., steel boxlock action, SST, extractors, monoblock VR 26 or 28 (12 ga. only) in. barrels with 2 choke tubes, checkered walnut stock and forearm. Imported 1999 only.

	$550	$450	$375	$315	$285	$270	$255

Last MSR was $629.

SILVER SPORTING - 12 ga. or 20 ga. (new 1996), Sporting Clay model, boxlock action, 28, 29 (new 1999), or 30 (new 1993) in. ported vent. barrels with channelled broadway VR, choke tubes, and elongated forcing cones, nickel finished engraved receiver, SST, ejectors, figured walnut stock and forearm with handcut checkering, 7 lbs. 6 oz. Mfg. by Lanber, imported 1990-2000. 1993 manufacture by Pedersoli.

	$835	$680	$550	$485	$440	$400	$360

Last MSR was $965.

SILVER SKEET - 12 ga. only, similar appearance to Silver Sporting, 26 or 28 (new 1993) in. ported vent. barrels with raised VR, 4 choke tubes, recoil pad, 7 lbs. 6 oz. Imported 1992-93 only.

	$790	$685	$575	$495	$450	$400	$360

Last MSR was $899.

SILVER TRAP - similar appearance to Silver Sporting, 30 in. ported barrels with raised VR, 4 choke tubes, recoil pad, trap stock dimensions, 7 3/4 lbs. Imported 1992-1993 only.

	$790	$685	$575	$495	$450	$400	$360

Last MSR was $899.

STERLING/BRISTOL - 12 or 20 ga., 3 in. chambers, boxlock with Greener crossbolt and false side plates, various barrel lengths and choke tubes, chrome finished receiver with moderate game scene engraving, SST, VR, ejectors. Imported 1986-89.

	$695	$550	$495	$450	$400	$375	$350

Last MSR was $825.

Until 1989, this model was designated the Bristol. In 1988, the engraving pattern was changed from game scene to elaborate scroll type.

SIR - 12 or 20 ga., 3 in. chambers, sidelock with Greener crossbolt, various barrel lengths and chokings, chrome finished receiver with game scene engraving, ST, VR, ejectors, deluxe checkered pistol grip stock and forearm. Imported 1986 only.

	$1,100	$900	$750	$675	$610	$565	$520

Last MSR was $1,090.

   Add $75 for choke tubes.

GRADING - PPGS™	100%	98%	95%	90%	80%	70%	60%

ROYAL - 12 or 20 ga., 3 in. chambers, sidelock with Greener crossbolt, various barrel lengths and chokings, chrome finished receiver with elaborate scroll engraving, ST, VR, ejectors, oil finished deluxe checkered pistol grip and forearm. Imported 1986-87 only.

	$1,595	$1,310	$1,080	$960	$850	$750	$675

Last MSR was $1,730.

Add $65 for choke tubes.

EXCELSIOR - 12 or 20 ga., 3 in. chambers, sidelock with Greener crossbolt, various barrel lengths and chokings, chrome finished receiver with elaborate deep relief engraving and multiple gold inlays, ST, VR, ejectors, oil finished deluxe checkered pistol grip and forearm. Imported 1986-87 only.

	$1,775	$1,510	$1,250	$1,100	$975	$885	$780

Last MSR was $1,925.

Add $70 for choke tubes.

WS/WT - O/U (SILVER) 12 WATERFOWL/TURKEY SPECIAL - 12 ga. only, Mag. chambers (3 1/2 in. was added in 1989), 24 (Turkey - disc. 1996), 26 (Turkey) or 28 (Waterfowl) in. barrels with choke tubes, SST, ejectors, parkerized metal finish, matte finished stock and forearm, Mossy Oak Breakup camo pattern began 1997 for Turkey Special, sling swivels, recoil pad, approx. 7 lbs. Imported 1987-2000.

	$650	$550	$460	$395	$360	$330	$300

Last MSR was $799.

Add $86 for Camo Turkey Model (WT/OU Camo 12, Breakup camo pattern, new 1997).

✳ *WS/WT O/U 10 ga. Waterfowl* - 10 ga. Mag., double triggers, extractors, matte finishes similar to 12 ga. Waterfowl, beavertail forearm. Imported 1988-89 only.

	$750	$625	$550	$495	$450	$390	$360

Last MSR was $829.

WT-O/U10 TURKEY SPECIAL - 10 ga., 3 1/2 in. Mag., 26 in. barrels with choke tubes, SST (became standard in 1990), extractors, recoil pad, non-glare metal finish, 9 lbs. 10 oz. Imported 1988-2000.

	$865	$695	$550	$500	$450	$390	$360

Last MSR was $995.

F.S. 200 - 12 ga., trap or skeet model, 26 or 32 in. separated barrels only, SST, ejectors, boxlock with Greener crossbolt, black or chromed receiver, checkered walnut stock and forearm. Imported 1986-87 only.

	$690	$560	$500	$450	$410	$375	$350

Last MSR was $835.

F.S. 300 - 12 ga., trap or skeet model, 26, 30, or 32 in. separated barrels only, SST, ejectors, boxlock with Greener crossbolt and false side plates lightly engraved, chromed receiver, checkered walnut stock and forearm. Imported 1986 only.

	$825	$675	$610	$555	$510	$470	$440

Last MSR was $995.

F.S. 400 - 12 ga., trap or skeet model, 26, 30, or 32 in. separated barrels only, ST, ejectors, sidelock with Greener crossbolt, lightly engraved chromed receiver, checkered walnut stock and forearm. Imported 1986 only.

	$1,145	$945	$860	$800	$740	$680	$620

Last MSR was $1,360.

F.S. 500 - same specifications as F.S. 400. Importation disc. 1985.

	$1,175	$950	$860	$795	$730	$660	$595

Last MSR was $1,360.

GRADING - PPGS™	100%	98%	95%	90%	80%	70%	60%

SHOTGUNS: SxS

American Arms imported Spanish shotguns manufactured by Zabala Hermanos and Grulla. Older discontinued Diarm models will also be shown in this section.

GENTRY/YORK - 12, 16 (disc. 1990), 20, 28 ga., or .410 bore, 3 in. chambers, boxlock, ejectors (extractors after 1986), double or SST (became standard in 1992), chromed receiver features fine scroll engraving, fixed chokes, pistol grip stock with recoil pad and beavertail forearm. Imported 1986-2000.

	$625	$475	$375	$300	$280	$260	$240

Last MSR was $750.

   Add $45 for 28 ga. or .410 bore.

Before 1988 this model was designated York (case coloring began 1988, silver finish began 1993). DTs were supplied with 28 ga. or .410 bore 1990-2000.

BRITTANY - 12 or 20 ga., boxlock action, 25 (20 ga. only, disc. 1996), 26, or 27 (12 ga. only, disc. 1996) in. barrels, SST, ejectors, matted solid rib, choke tubes, engraved case colored frame, checkered walnut straight grip stock with recoil pad and semi-beavertail forearm, 6 1/2 or 7 lbs. Imported 1989-2000.

	$725	$575	$485	$435	$400	$375	$350

Last MSR was $885.

The wood finish was changed in this model from oil to semi-gloss in 1991.

SHOGUN - 10 ga., 3 1/2 in. chambers, boxlock, ejectors, double triggers, chromed receiver features fine scroll engraving. Imported 1986 only.

	$440	$350	$325	$300	$280	$260	$240

Last MSR was $525.

DERBY - 12, 20, 28 (disc. 1991) ga., or .410 bore (disc. 1991) ga., 3 in. chambers, sidelock, ejectors, double (disc. 1989) or SNT, chromed receiver features fine scroll engraving, fixed chokes, straight grip walnut stock and forearm. Imported 1986-94.

	$1,150	$975	$050	$750	$625	$500	$425

Last MSR was $1,039.

   Add 10% for 28 ga. or .410 bore (disc. 1991).
   Subtract 10% for DT.
   Add approx. 50%-60% for 2-barrel set (20 and 28 ga. - approx. 300 sets mfg.) - disc. 1990.

This model featured a case-colored receiver between 1988-90 and was changed to coin finish in late 1991. At the same time, the wood finish was changed from oil to semi-gloss.

GRULLA NO. 2 - 12, 20, 28 ga., or .410 bore, hand fitted sidelock action, 26 or 28 in. barrels, DTs, ejectors, fixed chokes, concave rib, case colored receiver with elaborate engraving, deluxe English-style straight stock and splinter forearm (checkered and hand rubbed), between 5 3/4-6 1/4 lbs. Imported 1989-2000.

This model was individually handcrafted with less than 800 mfg. each year. Before going to a special order basis, this model retailed for $3,099 (1994).

   ✳ *Grulla No. 2 Small Gauge Set* - includes choice of 20/28 ga. or 28 ga./.410 bore barrel combination (26 in. fixed choke barrels). Imported 1989-95.

	$3,600	$3,000	$2,375	$2,000	$1,650	$1,325	$1,150

Before going to a special order basis, this combination last retailed for $4,219 (1994/5).

WS/SS 10 WATERFOWL SPECIAL - 10 ga. only, 3 1/2 in. chambers, 32 in. barrels, DTs, parkerized finish, sling swivels and camouflaged sling, extractors, fixed chokes, recoil pad, 11 lbs. 3 oz. Imported 1987-93.

	$560	$500	$440	$400	$375	$350	$325

Last MSR was $639.

GRADING - PPGS™	100%	98%	95%	90%	80%	70%	60%

WT/SS 10 - 10 ga. only, 3 1/2 in. chambers, similar to TS/SS 12, except as 28 in. barrels with multi-chokes. Imported 1998-2000.

	$775	$650	$550	$450	$400	$375	$350

Last MSR was $860.

TS/SS 10/12 TURKEY SPECIAL - 10 (disc. 1995) or 12 ga., 3 or 3 1/2 in. chambers (3 1/2 in. 12 ga. introduced in 1989), 26 in. barrels only, double triggers, parkerized finish, dull finish stock and forearm, sling swivels, recoil pad, choke tubes, 7 lbs. 6 oz. or 10 lbs. 13 oz. (10 ga.). Imported 1987-2000.

	$665	$550	$450	$400	$375	$350	$325

Last MSR was $799.

This model in 12 ga. was supplied with a SST.

SHOTGUNS: SEMI-AUTO

PHANTOM FIELD - 12 ga. only, 3 in. chamber, gas operated, 24, 26, or 28 in. VR barrel with 3 choke tubes, black synthetic or checkered walnut stock and forearm, blue finish. Imported 1999-2000.

	$395	$360	$330	$275	$250	$225	$200

Last MSR was $439.

✳ *Phantom HP* - similar to Phantom Field with synthetic stock and forearm, except has 19 in. threaded barrels for external choke tubes, swivel studs, and extended mag. Imported 1999-2000.

	$400	$365	$330	$275	$250	$225	$200

Last MSR was $449.

SHOTGUNS: SINGLE SHOT

SINGLE SHOT MODEL - 12, 20 ga., or .410 bore, 3 in. chamber non-exposed hammer, pistol grip stock, non-reflective finish. Imported 1988-89 only.

	$90	$80	$70	$60	$55	$50	$45

Last MSR was $99.

✳ *Single Shot Model Camper Special* - 12, 20 ga., or .410 bore, 3 in. chamber folding design, 21 in. barrel, pistol grip. Imported 1988-89 only.

	$95	$80	$70	$60	$55	$50	$45

Last MSR was $107.

✳ *Single Shot Model Slugger* - 12 or 20 ga., 24 in. slug shotgun barrel with adj. rear sight and blade front, recoil pad. Imported 1989 only.

	$100	$85	$75	$65	$55	$50	$45

Last MSR was $115.

✳ *Single Shot Model Youth* - 20 ga. or .410 bore, 26 in. barrel, 12 1/2 in. stock dimensions, recoil pad. Imported 1989 only.

	$100	$85	$75	$65	$55	$50	$45

Last MSR was $115.

✳ *Single Shot Model Combo* - interchangeable rifle and shotgun barrels, choice of .22 Hornet/12 ga. with 28 in. barrel or .22 LR/20 ga. with 26 in. barrel, includes fitted hard case. Imported 1989 only.

	$195	$165	$130	$115	$100	$90	$80

Last MSR was $235.

✳ *Single Shot Model 10 Ga.* - 10 ga. only, 3 1/2 in. chambers, 26 in. multi-choke or 32 in. full fixed choke barrel, non-exposed hammer, non-reflective finish. Imported 1988-89 only.

	$135	$115	$95	$80	$70	$60	$55

Last MSR was $149.

Add $30 for multi-chokes (26 in. barrel).

GRADING - PPGS™	100%	98%	95%	90%	80%	70%	60%

AMERICAN BARLOCK WONDER

Previous trademark manufactured by Crescent Arms for Sears Roebuck & Co.

SHOTGUNS: SxS

SIDE-BY-SIDE - various gauges, hammerless or outside hammer, damascus or steel barrels.

	100%	98%	95%	90%	80%	70%	60%
	$240	$225	$200	$175	$140	$100	$75

Add 15% for steel barrels, smaller gauges.

SINGLE SHOT - various gauges, hammer, steel barrel.

	100%	98%	95%	90%	80%	70%	60%
	$125	$115	$100	$90	$75	$60	$50

Add 35% for smaller gauges.

AMERICAN CUSTOM GUNMAKERS GUILD, INC. (ACGG)

The American Custom Gunmakers Guild is an organization of craftsmen who specialize in high quality custom work on firearms. Guild members share a common bond toward the betterment of fine custom firearms and the skills needed to achieve as near perfection in the field of gunmaking as possible.

There are two basic types of membership, Regular and Associate. Each Regular Member has passed an examination of his work by his fellow members as part of the application process. The privileges of Regular membership include the right to use the ACGG logo with the word "Member", use the ACGG Hallmark, vote at the annual meeting, the quarterly *Gunmaker* magazine, a discount on Guild publications, and the option to rent a display table at the annual show in Reno, NV. Current ACGG Regular members can be found by visiting the web site (see Trademark Index).

Associate membership is open to all who have an interest in custom guns. The benefits of Associate membership include free admission to the annual exhibition, the quarterly *Gunmaker* magazine, a membership card, and a discount on Guild publications.

The Guild's bylaws stress creative ability and practicing good business ethics.

The annual Firearms Engravers and Gunmakers Exhibition is the most visible activity of the ACGG. This winter event in Reno, Nevada offers the public the unique opportunity to see America's finest firearm craftsmanship and meet the individual makers. This gathering of ACGG members provides a forum to share technical expertise, honor exemplary work and accept and induct new members, and conduct association business.

The American Custom Gunmakers Guild has created a registry for custom guns which have been built by Guild members who Hallmark their work with the Guild logo. Certificates of Hallmark are provided by the Guild's Historian which describe and document the firearm's origin.

For collectors, these documents verify the work of a gunmaker through research of photographs, records, receipts, or other documentation.

For more information about this organization, please contact them directly (see Trademark Index).

AMERICAN DERRINGER CORPORATION

Current manufacturer located in Waco, TX since 1980. Distributor and dealer sales.

DERRINGERS: STAINLESS STEEL

MODEL 1 - available in over 55 cals. including .22 LR through .45-70 Govt., also 2 1/2 in. .410 shot shell, O/U stainless steel derringer, top break action, satin or high polish finish, 3 in. barrels, automatic barrel selection, hammer block type safety, 15 oz., spur trigger, rosewood grips. New 1980.

GRADING - PPGS™	100%	98%	95%	90%	80%	70%	60%

* **Model 1 Regular Cals.** - most cals. between .22 LR and .40 S&W.

MSR $500	$415	$350	$275	$225	$175	$140	$100

     Add $55 for high polish finish.
     Add approx. $140 for .22 Hornet (disc. 1989).
     Add $170 for .223 Rem. or $140 for .30-30 Win. cal. (disc. 2003).

* **Model 1 Larger Cals.** - typically .44 Spl. - .45-70 Govt. cal.

MSR $575	$475	$385	$315	$250	$200	$150	$100

     Add $55 for high polish finish.
     Add $70 for .41 Mag., .44 Mag., or .45 Win. Mag. cal.

This model can be ordered with special ser. nos. and other custom features at additional cost(s).

* **Model 1 Engraved** - limited mfg., mostly special ordered.

Please contact the factory regarding a price quotation for this special order model.

* **Model 1 Millennium 2000 Series** - .45 LC/.410 shotshell only, 3 in. barrel, 15,000 mfg. beginning 1998 in various configurations including Gambler and Cowboy.

                       The 2003 MSR on this model was $470.

Please contact the factory regarding a price quotation for this special order model.

* **Model 1 United We Stand Commemorative** - .45 LC/.410 shotshell only, 3 in. barrel, choice of custom grips, includes red, white and blue presentation case. Limited mfg. 2002-2003.

$355	$285	$230	$175	N/A	N/A	N/A

                       Last MSR was $450.

American Derringer Corporation donated a portion of the proceeds from this commemorative to the post-9/11 recovery effort.

LADY DERRINGER - available in various cals. between .22 LR - .45 LC, and .45 LC/.410 shotshell cal., O/U top break action, 3 in. barrel, high polish stainless steel, spur trigger, scrimshawed synthetic ivory grips, handfitted action allowing easy cocking, with French styled leatherette display case, 15 1/2 oz. New 1990.

Please contact the factory regarding a price quotation for this model.

* **Lady Derringer Deluxe Engraved** - similar to Deluxe Grade, except hand engraved with circa 1880 patterns. Disc. 1994.

$650	$515	$400	$335	$290	$245	$215

                       Last MSR was $750.

Mother-of-pearl grips and personalized engraving were available as extra cost options on this model.

* **Lady Derringer 14Kt. Gold Engraved** - entire Derringer manufactured out of a 14Kt. gold bar (contains approx. 20 oz. of 14Kt. gold and 3 oz. of stainless steel), custom engraved with diamond sights, special order only until late 1993.

N/A	N/A	N/A	N/A	N/A	N/A	N/A

                       Last MSR was $100,000.

* **Millenium Lady Derringer** - similar to Model 1 Millenium 2000 Series. Disc.

$390	$290	$210	$160	$130	$115	$95

                       Last MSR was $470.

LADY DERRINGER II - .22 LR (disc.), .32 ACP (disc.), .38 Spl., or .22 Mag. (disc.) cal., O/U pivot design with double action, aluminum frame, trigger guard stops at trigger bottom, 1/2 lb. Mfg. 1999-2003.

$395	$290	$210	N/A	N/A	N/A	N/A

                       Last MSR was $480.

GRADING - PPGS™	100%	Issue Price	Qty. Made

MODEL 1 TEXAS COMMEMORATIVE - .38 Spl., .44-40, or .45 LC cal., similar to Model 1 except has brass frame, stainless steel barrel, and stag grips.

.44-40 cal	$395	$440	N/A
.45 cal.	$415	$470	N/A
.32 Mag	$205	$255	500+
.38 Spl.	$340	$385	N/A
.22 LR (mfg. 1991-92)	$200	$238	500
.41 Rimfire (not shootable)	$235	$295	500
Fully engraved model	$695	$750	limited

Add $25 for special serial number on the .45 LC cal. model.

American Derringer is making the Texas Commemorative on a limited basis - please contact the factory directly for a price quotation on this model.

125TH ANNIVERSARY - special edition 125th anniversary variation with pistol case. Disc. 1993.

.44-40 or .45 cal.	$285	$320	500
.38 Spl.	$185	$225	500
Deluxe engraved model	$650	$750	limited

GRADING - PPGS™	100%	98%	95%	90%	80%	70%	60%

MODEL 3 - .32 Mag. (new 1990 - limited availability) or .38 Spl. cal., single shot, 2 1/2 in. barrel, 8 1/2 oz., spur trigger, rosewood grips. Disc. 1994.

$95	$70	$55	$45	$40	$35	$30

Last MSR was $120.

MODEL 4 - .357 Mag., .357 Max., .44 Mag. (disc. 2003), .45 ACP, .45-70 Govt. (disc. 2003), or .45 LC cal. on upper barrel, 3 in. .410 shotshell lower barrel, O/U derringer combination pistol, 4 1/10 in. barrel, rosewood grips, 16 1/2 oz. New 1985.

MSR $570	$475	$350	$275	$200	$165	$135	$105

Add $75 for oversized grips.
Add $105 for .44 Mag. cal. (oversized grips became standard 1997, disc. 2003).
Add $150 for .45-70 Govt. cal. in both barrels (disc. 2003).

This model was also available on special order in either .50-70 or .50 Saunders cal. (new 1989 - single shot only). MSR was $395.

* *Model 4 Engraved* - .45 LC/.410 shotshell cal., allow 12 weeks for delivery. New 1997.

Please contact the factory directly for a price quotation on this special order model.

* *Model 4 Alaskan Survival Model* - similar to Model 4, except .45-70 Govt. cal. top barrel, and choice of .44 Mag. (disc.), .45 LC, or .45 LC/.410 shotshell lower barrel.

MSR $695	$625	$400	$325	$275	$240	$185	$155

Add $60 for high polish finish.

MODEL 6 - .22 Mag. (disc.), .357 Mag., .45 LC, .45 ACP, or .45 LC/.410 shotshell cal., O/U, 6 in. barrel, 21 oz. Available in high polish, satin, or grey matte finish (standard). New 1986.

MSR $550	$425	$300	$250	$215	$165	$135	$100

Add $45 for .45 cals.
Add $13 for satin finish (disc. 1994).
Add $70 for high polish finish.
Add $50 for oversized grips (disc. 1994, reinstated 1998-99).

* *Model 6 Engraved* - .45 LC/.410 shotshell cal., allow 12 weeks for delivery. New 1997.

Please contact the factory directly for a price quotation on this special order model.

GRADING - PPGS™	100%	98%	95%	90%	80%	70%	60%

MODEL 7 - .22 LR (disc.), .22 Mag. (mfg. 1992-2003), .32 H&R Mag. (disc.), .38 Spl., .38 S&W (disc. 1989), .380 ACP, (disc.) or .44 Spl. (disc.) cal., O/U, same basic specifications as Model 1, except ultra lightweight (7 1/2 oz.).

	100%	98%	95%	90%	80%	70%	60%
MSR $595	$480	$375	$310	$260	$215	$170	$140

✳ *Model 7 .44 Special Cal.* - .44 Spl. cal. only. Disc.

		98%	95%	90%	80%	70%	60%
	$500	$440	$370	$315	$270	$230	$200

Last MSR was $585.

MODEL 8 - .45 LC/.410 shotshell cal., O/U, 8 in. barrel, nickel finish, grooved grips, 24 oz. New 1997.

	100%	98%	95%	90%	80%	70%	60%
MSR $695	$540	$400	$335	$285	$235	$180	$140

Add $80 for high polish finish.

✳ *Model 8 Engraved* - .45 LC/.410 shotshell cal. Limited mfg. 1997-98 only.

	100%	98%	95%	90%	80%	70%	60%
	$1,675	$1,300	$975	$860	$700	$600	$500

Last MSR was $1,917.

MODEL 10 - .38 Spl. (new 1995), .45 ACP, .45 LC, or .45 LC/.410 shotshell (disc. 1997), O/U, 3 in. stainless barrels, aluminum frame and barrel, matte grey finish, 7 1/2 oz. New 1988.

	100%	98%	95%	90%	80%	70%	60%
MSR $550	$425	$300	$250	$215	$165	$135	$100

Add $45 for .45 cals.

MODEL 11 - .22 LR (mfg. 1995-2003), .22 Mag. (mfg. 1995-2003), .32 H&R Mag. (mfg. 1995-2003), .380 ACP (mfg. 1995-2003), or .38 Spl. cal., same basic specifications as Model 1, matte grey finish, only 11 oz.

	100%	98%	95%	90%	80%	70%	60%
MSR $550	$425	$300	$250	$215	$165	$135	$100

RIMFIRE DOUBLE ACTION - .22 LR or .22 Mag. cal., 3 1/2 in. O/U barrels, double action trigger, dual extraction, hammerless, blue finish with black synthetic grips, 11 oz. Mfg. 1990-95.

	100%	98%	95%	90%	80%	70%	60%
	$145	$115	$95	$85	$80	$75	$70

Last MSR was $170.

This O/U Derringer was patterned after the original High Standard design.

DS .22 MAG. - .22 Mag. cal., 3 in. barrel, stainless steel with blue finish, 11 oz. Special order beginning 1998.

Please contact the factory directly for a price quotation on this model.

DA 38 DOUBLE ACTION - .22 LR (mfg. 1996-2003), .357 Mag. (new 1991), .38 Spl., 9mm Para., or .40 S&W (new 1993) cal., 3 in. O/U barrels, satin stainless steel with aluminum grip frame, double action trigger design, hammerblock thumb safety, choice of checkered rosewood, walnut, or other hardwood grips, 14 1/2 oz. New 1990.

	100%	98%	95%	90%	80%	70%	60%
MSR $550	$425	$300	$250	$215	$165	$135	$100

Add $45 for .357 Mag. or .40 S&W cal.
Add $15 for Lady Derringer Model (scrimshawed synthetic ivory grips, .38 Spl. only. Mfg. 1992-94).

MINI-COP - .22 Mag. cal., 4 shot double action design, stainless steel construction, patterned after the original Mini-Cop mfg. in Torrance, CA. Mfg. 1990-94.

	100%	98%	95%	90%	80%	70%	60%
	$250	$220	$185	$140	$120	$100	$85

Last MSR was $313.

4-BARREL DERRINGER - .22 LR, .38 Spl., or .357 Mag. cal., double action, similar design to Mini-Cop, semi-matte finish, 28 oz. While advertised beginning 1991 at $425, only a few prototypes were manufactured during 1997.

GRADING - PPGS™	100%	98%	95%	90%	80%	70%	60%

CUSTOM TARGET MODELS - .38 Spl. Wadcutter or 9mm Federal (disc.) cal., mfg. for End of Trail Derringer Match, limited production. Mfg. 1990-92.

	$695	$575	$475	$415	$360	$300	$255

Last MSR was $750.

PISTOLS: PEN DESIGN

MODEL 2 PEN PISTOL - .22 LR, .25 ACP, or .32 ACP cal., unique hinged action allows pen to be converted into a legal pistol within two seconds, folding design, 2 in. barrel, cocks on opening action, firing pin block grip safety, brushed stainless finish, 5 oz. Mfg. 1993-94.

	$145	$120	$100	$95	$90	$80	$75

Last MSR was $203.

Add $24 for .32 ACP cal.

PISTOLS: SEMI-AUTO

STANDARD MODEL

✳ *Standard Model .25 Mag. Cal.* - .25 Mag., semi-auto single action, less than 100 manufactured in stainless steel only.

	$500	$400	$300	$240	$210	$180	$155

✳ *Standard Model .25 ACP Cal.* - .25 ACP, semi-auto single action, less than 400 manufactured in stainless steel, less than 50 in blue steel.

	100%	98%	95%	90%	80%	70%	60%
Stainless	$400	$300	$250	$195	$165	$140	$120
Blue	$550	$400	$325	$265	$230	$195	$170

LM-5 - .25 ACP, .32 Mag. (disc. 1997), or .380 ACP (mfg. 1998-99) cal., compact stainless semi-auto, single action, 2 1/4 in. barrel, hammerless, wood grips, 4- (.32 Mag. or .380 ACP) or 5- (.25 ACP) shot mag., 15 oz. Limited mfg. since 1997.

The 2003 MSR on this model was $353.

Add $27 for .32 Mag. cal. (disc. 1997).
Please contact the factory directly for a price quotation on this model.

✳ *LM-5 .380 ACP* - limited mfg., disc. 1999.

	$365	$295	$215	$165	$140	$115	$100

Last MSR was $425.

PISTOLS: SLIDE-ACTION

LM-4 (SEMMERLING) - .45 ACP cal., 2 in. barrel, super compact, thumb activated slide mechanism, blue finish, 4-shot mag., 24 oz., very limited manufacture since 1998.

The 2003 MSR on this model was $2,655.

Please contact the factory directly for a price quotation on this special order model.

AMERICAN FIREARMS MANUFACTURING CO., INC.

Previous manufacturer located in San Antonio, TX between 1972 and 1974.

DERRINGERS

AMERICAN .38 SPL. - .38 Spl. cal., O/U configuration, approx. 3,000-4,000 mfg. 1972-74.

	$200	$165	$135	$110	$90	$75	$65

AMERICAN .380 AUTOMATIC - .380 ACP cal., 8 shot, 3 1/2 in. barrel, stainless steel, smooth walnut grips, approx. 10 mfg. 1972-74.

	$700	$500	$300	$240	$210	$180	$155

GRADING - PPGS™	100%	98%	95%	90%	80%	70%	60%

PISTOLS: SEMI-AUTO

AMERICAN .25 AUTOMATIC - .25 ACP cal., 8 shot, 2 1/10 in. barrel, smooth walnut grips. Mfg. 1966-74.

	100%	98%	95%	90%	80%	70%	60%
Stainless	$195	$180	$165	N/A	N/A	N/A	N/A
Blue	$165	$150	$140	$120	$100	$90	$85

AMERICAN FRONTIER FIREARMS MFG., INC.

Previous manufacturer located in Aguanga, CA 1995-2000.

American Frontier Firearms Mfg., Inc. manufactured a line of replica metallic cartridge firing revolvers (black powder or smokeless). These revolvers were manufactured in .22 LR, .32 Spl., .38 Spl., .44 Russian, or .45 LC. During 2000, AFF developed a new cartridge, a .44 A.F.F. It can be used in revolvers firing .44-40 WCF, .44 Russian, .44 Spl., and .44 Mag. It also meets current S.A.S.S. specifications.

REVOLVERS: CARTRIDGE CONVERSIONS & OPEN TOPS

Production on these models was mid-1997 through 2000. Revolvers were supplied with standard finish high polish blue steel parts, color case hardened hammer and/or trigger, silver plated or blue backstrap and trigger guard, and varnished walnut grips. Special orders were also available featuring simulated ivory grips, special finishes, and engraving options. Some models and variations had very limited production, due to problems procuring high quality parts.

1851 NAVY RICHARDS CONVERSION - .38 Spl., .38 LC, .44 Russian, or .44-40 WCF cal., 4 3/4, 5 1/2, or 7 1/2 in. octagon barrel, roll engraved cylinder, blue steel finish, varnished walnut grips. No ejector rod.

$695	$550	$375	$325	$295	$265	$235

Last MSR was $795.

1851 NAVY RICHARDS & MASON CONVERSION - .38 Spl., .38 LC, .44 Russian, or .44-40 WCF cal., 4 3/4, 5 1/2, or 7 1/2 in. octagon barrel with Mason ejector assembly, roll engraved cylinder, blue steel finish, varnished walnut grips.

$695	$550	$375	$325	$295	$265	$235

Last MSR was $795.

1858 REMINGTON NEW ARMY CAVALRY MODEL - .38 Spl., .44-40 WCF or .45 LC cal., 7 1/2 in. barrel with ejector assembly, blue steel finish, color case hardened hammer, varnished walnut grips.

$715	$575	$475	$375	$325	$275	$225

Last MSR was $795.

1858 REMINGTON NEW ARMY ARTILLERY MODEL - .38 Spl., .44-40 WCF and .45 LC cal., 5 1/2 in. barrel with ejector assembly, blue steel finish, color case hardened hammer, varnished walnut grips.

$715	$575	$475	$375	$325	$275	$225

Last MSR was $795.

1858 REMINGTON ORIGINAL FACTORY-TYPE CONVERSION - .38 Spl., .44-40 WCF, or .45 LC cal., 5 1/2 or 7 1/2 in. barrels, original loading lever and no gate or ejector assembly, blue steel finish, color case hardened hammer, varnished walnut grips.

$715	$575	$475	$375	$325	$275	$225

Last MSR was $795.

POCKET REMINGTON - .22 LR, .32 S&W Short, or .38 Spl. cal., 3 1/2 in. barrel with or without ejector rod or gate, blue steel finish, color case hardened hammer, varnished walnut grips.

$425	$375	$325	$275	$225	$185	$165

Last MSR was $495.

GRADING - PPGS™	100%	98%	95%	90%	80%	70%	60%

1860 ARMY RICHARDS CONVERSION - .38 Spl., .38 LC, or .44-40 WCF cal., 4 3/4, 5 1/2, or 7 1/2 in. round barrel, with or without ejector assembly, roll engraved cylinder, blue steel finish, silver plated trigger guard, varnished walnut grips.

	$695	$550	$375	$325	$295	$265	$235

Last MSR was $795.

1861 NAVY RICHARDS CONVERSION - .38 Spl., or .38 LC cal., 4 1/2 or 7 1/2 in. round barrel with ejector assembly, blue steel finish, silver plated backstrap and trigger guard, varnished walnut grips.

	$695	$550	$375	$325	$295	$265	$235

Last MSR was $795.

POCKET NAVY RICHARDS & MASON CONVERSION - .32 S&W Short cal., 4 1/2 in. octagon barrel with ejector assembly, blue steel finish, silver plated backstrap and trigger guard, color case hardened trigger and hammer, varnished walnut grips.

	$465	$375	$325	$275	$225	$185	$165

Last MSR was $495.

1871-72 OPEN-TOP FRONTIER MODEL - .38 Spl., .38 LC, or .44-40 WCF cal., 4 3/4, 5 1/2, or 7 1/2 in. round barrel with ejector assembly, blue steel finish, varnished walnut grips.

	$695	$550	$375	$325	$295	$265	$235

Last MSR was $795.

* *1871-72 Open-Top Tiffany Model* - similar to 1871-72 Standard Model, except has engraved gold/silver finished Tiffany grips and also available with 4 3/4 in. barrel. Mfg. 2001.

	$995	$895	$700	$525	$450	$395	$350

Last MSR was $1,200.

AMERICAN GUN CO.

Previous trademark manufactured by Crescent Firearms Co. and distributed by H. & D. Folsom Co.

REVOLVERS

REVOLVER - .32 S&W cal., 5 shot, double action, top break-open action.

	N/A	$175	$160	$140	$120	$95	$65

SHOTGUNS: SxS

SxS - various gauges, hammer or hammerless, damascus or steel barrels.

	N/A	$240	$225	$200	$175	$140	$100

Add 15% for small gauges or steel barrels.

AMERICAN HISTORICAL FOUNDATION, THE

Current organization which privately commissions historical commemoratives in conjunction with leading manufacturers and craftsmen around the world. The Foundation is located in Ashland, VA. Previously located in Richmond, VA. During 2005, the assets of the Foundation were acquired by America Remembers, located in Ashland, VA. Direct-to-consumer sales only. Delivery to local FFL holder.

The Foundation's limited/special edition models are not all manufactured at one time. Rather, guns are fabricated as demand dictates. Limited editions include guns by Colt, Winchester, Browning, Dan Wesson, Auto-Ordnance/Thompson, Sturm Ruger, Holland & Holland, Walther, Smith & Wesson, Mauser, and Beretta.

LIMITED/SPECIAL EDITIONS

AHF consumers include members, history buffs, veterans, museums, and other interested parties who normally keep these items for a considerable time period, and very few are sold in the secondary marketplace annually. Because of this consumer direct sales program, many non-AHF consumers and gun dealers do not have a working knowledge on current pricing for AHF firearms.

The publisher suggests that those people who want more information about American Historical Foundation's Commemorative Issue firearms contact AHF directly (see Trademark Index), or visit their website: www.ahfrichmond.com. Additionally, information on most AHF offerings manufactured between 1988 and 1997 can be found in the 20th and earlier editions of the *Blue Book of Gun Values.*

AMERICAN HUNTING RIFLES, INC. (AHR)

Current manufacturer established in 1998 and located in Corvallis, MT since 2007. Previously located in Hamilton, MT, 1998-2006.

RIFLES: BOLT ACTION

CZ-550 actions are also available individually. Prices range from $450-$575.

CLASSIC 550 - standard and various Howell proprietary cals., CZ 550 double square bridge standard action, controlled feed claw extractor, 25 in. chrome-moly sporter barrel, also available in optional stainless steel, blue finish, black fiberglass or optional walnut stock with Decelerator recoil pad. New 1999.

MSR $1,895	$1,725	$1,375	$1,075	$900	$775	$650	$550

Add $75 for stainless steel barrel.
Add $220 for integral and removable muzzle brake, with protective cap.

VARMINT 550 PRO - .220 Howell, .220 Swift, .22-250 Rem., .30-06, or .308 Win. cal., CZ 550 double square bridge standard action, 26 in. stainless heavy barrel, SST, black fiberglass stock with Decelerator recoil pad. Mfg. 2001-2007.

$1,650	$1,325	$1,050	$900	$775	$650	$550

Last MSR was $1,795.

SAFARI 550 - various Mag. cals., similar to Classic 550, except has Magnum action with integral scope mounts, oil finished fancy walnut stock, trigger guard safety. New 2001.

MSR $3,995	$3,600	$3,250	$2,675	$2,075	$1,725	$1,450	$1,175

SAFARI 550 DGR - various standard Mag. cals. from .404 Jeffery - .600 Overkill, similar to Safari 550, except has 3-position safety, extra fancy wood, and banded front sling attachment. New 2001.

MSR $4,495	$4,100	$3,625	$3,125	$2,625	$2,075	$1,625	$1,400

Pricing is for base model only.

.700 AHR - .700 AHR cal., Granite Mt. Arms magnum action, hand checkered AAA fancy walnut stock, African blackwood forend tip and grip cap, fixed folding sight, AHR X-brake, custom serial number, custom hand engraving, custom LOP. Limited mfg. beginning 2008.

Prices for this model start at $11,500.

AMERICAN INDUSTRIES

Please refer to the Calico section in this text.

GRADING - PPGS™	100%	98%	95%	90%	80%	70%	60%

AMERICAN INTERNATIONAL CORP.

Previous manufacturer and importer located in Salt Lake City, UT, circa 1972-1984. American International was a wholly owned subsidiary of ARDCO (American Research & Development). ARDCO's previous name was American Mining & Development. American International imported firearms from Voere, located in Kufstein, Austria. American Arms International (AAI) was another subsidiary of ARDCO.

In 1979, after American International Corp. had dissolved, AAI resumed production using mostly Voere parts. After running out of Voere parts, late production featured U.S. mfg. receivers (can be recognized by not having a pivoting barrel retainer slotted on the bottom of the receiver). American Arms International declared bankruptcy in 1984.

CARBINES: SEMI-AUTO

AMERICAN 180 AUTO CARBINE (M-1) - .22 LR cal., a specialized design for para-military use, 177 round drum mag., 16 1/2 in. barrel, aperture sight, high impact plastic stock and forearm, aluminum alloy reciever with black finish. Semi-auto variation mfg. 1979-c.1984. Total Voere production (denoted by A prefix serial number) between 1972 and 1979 was 2,300 carbines (includes both full and semi-auto versions). Later mfg. was marked either M-1 (semi-auto) or M-2 (fully auto). "B" serial number prefix was introduced in 1980, and barrel markings were changed to "Amer Arms Intl, SLC, UT."

$725	$600	$475	$375	$350	$325	$295

Add $550 for Laser Lok System - first commercially available laser sighting system.
Add approx. $300 for extra drum mag. and winder (fragile and subject to breakage).

AMERICAN LEGACY FIREARMS

Current company located in Ft. Collins, CO.

American Legacy Firearms is a company that specializes in special/limited edition and unique firearms based on currently manufactured trademarks. Please contact the company directly for more information, including pricing and model availability (see Trademark Index).

AMERICAN LEGENDS

Previous trademark of some handguns manufactured by IAI. Please refer to the IAI section in this text.

AMERICAN SPIRIT ARMS CORP.

Previous rifle and components manufacturer 1998-2005, and located in Tempe, AZ. Previously located in Scottsdale, AZ.

RIFLES: SEMI-AUTO

Add $25 for green furniture, $65 for black barrel finish, $75 for fluted barrel, $125 for porting, $119 for two-stage match trigger, and $55 for National Match sights on .223 cal. models listed below.

ASA 24 IN. BULL BARREL FLATTOP RIFLE - .223 Rem. cal., patterned after AR-15, forged steel lower receiver, forged aluminum flattop upper receiver, 24 in. stainless steel bull barrel, free floating aluminum handguard, includes Harris bipod. Mfg. 1999-2005.

$850	$700	$625	$550	$500	$450	$400

Last MSR was $950.

ASA 24 IN. BULL BARREL A2 RIFLE - similar to ASA Bull Barrel Flattop, except features A2 upper receiver with carrying handle and sights. Mfg. 1999-2005.

$875	$725	$650	$565	$500	$450	$400

Last MSR was $980.

GRADING - PPGS™	100%	98%	95%	90%	80%	70%	60%

OPEN MATCH RIFLE - .223 Rem. cal., 16 in. fluted and ported stainless steel match barrel with round shroud, flattop without sights, forged upper and lower receiver, two-stage match trigger, upgraded pistol grip, individually tested, USPSA/IPSC open class legal. Mfg. 2001-2005.

	$1,350	$1,100	$950	$825	$725	$650	$525

Last MSR was $1,500.

LIMITED MATCH RIFLE - .223 Rem. cal., 16 in. fluted stainless steel match barrel with round shroud with staggered hand grip, National Match front and rear sights, two-stage match trigger, upgraded pistol grip, individually tested, USPSA/IPSC open class legal. Mfg. 2001-2005.

	$1,175	$975	$825	$725	$650	$525	$475

Last MSR was $1,300.

DCM SERVICE RIFLE - .223 Rem. cal., 20 in. stainless steel match barrel with ribbed free floating shroud, National Match front and rear sights, two-stage match trigger, pistol grip, individually tested. Mfg. 2001-2005.

	$1,175	$975	$825	$725	$650	$525	$475

Last MSR was $1,300.

ASA 16 IN. M4 RIFLE - .223 Rem. cal., features non-collapsible stock and M4 handguard, 16 in. barrel with muzzlebrake, aluminum flattop upper receiver. Mfg. 2002-2005.

	$795	$700	$625	$525	$450	$400	$350

Last MSR was $905.

ASA 20 IN. A2 RIFLE - .223 Rem. cal., features A2 receiver and 20 in. National Match barrel. Mfg. 1999-2005.

	$765	$640	$565	$500	$425	$350	$300

Last MSR was $820.

ASA CARBINE WITH SIDE CHARGING RECEIVER - .223 Rem. cal., features aluminum side charging flattop upper receiver, M4 handguard, 16 in. NM barrel with slotted muzzlebrake. Mfg. 2002-2004.

	$865	$750	$650	$565	$500	$450	$400

Last MSR was $970.

C.A.R. POST-BAN 16 IN. CARBINE - .223 Rem. cal., non-collapsible stock, Wilson 16 in. National Match barrel. Mfg. 1999-2005.

	$775	$650	$575	$500	$450	$400	$350

Last MSR was $830.

ASA 16 IN. BULL BARREL A2 INVADER - .223 Rem. cal., similar to ASA 24 in. Bull Barrel rifle, except has 16 in. stainless steel barrel. Mfg. 1999-2005.

	$860	$725	$630	$550	$500	$450	$400

Last MSR was $955.

ASA 9MM A2 CAR CARBINE - 9mm Para. cal., forged upper and lower receiver, non-collapsible CAR stock, 16 in. Wilson heavy barrel w/o muzzlebrake, with birdcage flash hider (pre-ban) or muzzlebrake (post-ban), includes 9mm conversion block, 25 shot modified Uzi mag. Mfg. 2002-2005.

	$860	$725	$630	$550	$500	$450	$400

Last MSR was $950.

Add $550 per extra 25 shot mag.

ASA 9MM FLATTOP CAR RIFLE - 9mm Para. cal., similar to A2 CAR Rifle, except has is flattop w/o sights. Mfg. 2002-2005.

	$860	$725	$630	$550	$500	$450	$400

Last MSR was $950.

GRADING - PPGS™	100%	98%	95%	90%	80%	70%	60%

ASA 16 IN. TACTICAL RIFLE - .308 Win. cal., 16 in. stainless steel air gauged regular or match barrel, side charging handle, Hogue pistol grip, guaranteed 1/2 in. MOA, individually tested, 8 3/4 lbs. Mfg. 2002-2005.

	$1,475	$1,200	$995	$850	$750	$650	$525

Last MSR was $1,675.

Add $515 for Match Rifle (includes fluted and ported barrel, 2 stage trigger, and hard chromed bolt and carrier).

ASA 24 IN. MATCH RIFLE - .308 Win. cal., 24 in. stainless steel air gauged match barrel with or w/o fluting/porting, side charging handle, Hogue pistol grip, guaranteed 1/2 in. MOA, individually tested, approx. 12 lbs. Mfg. 2002-2005.

	$1,475	$1,200	$995	$850	$750	$650	$525

Last MSR was $1,675.

Add $515 for Match Rifle (includes fluted and ported barrel, 2 stage trigger, and hard chromed bolt and carrier).

AMERICAN WESTERN ARMS, INC.

Previous trademark and importer 1999-2004, and located in Delray Beach, FL. During late 2004, the remaining assets of this company were sold and a new company was established as AWA USA in Hialeah, FL. SAA revolver components were manufactured in the former Armi San Marco factory in Italy (now AWA International, Inc.), and assembled in the U.S. This plant was thoroughly updated during 2000 with all new tooling, stringent quality control, and now has bone colored case hardening in house. Dealer sales.

Please refer to AWA USA listing for current information.

AWA International Inc. purchased American Western Arms, Inc. in 2000, along with Classic Old West Styles (COWS) and Millenium Leather.

Please refer to the *Blue Book of Modern Black Powder Arms* by John Allen (now online also) for more information and prices on American Western Arms' lineup of modern black powder models.

Black Powder Reproductions & Replicas by Dennis Adler is also an invaluable source for most black powder reproductions and replicas, and includes hundreds of color images on most popular makes/models, provides manufacturer/trademark histories, and up-to-date information on related items/accessories for black powder shooting - www.bluebookinc.com

REVOLVERS: CARTRIDGE CONVERSIONS & OPEN TOP

1851 NAVY RICHARDS-TYPE CARTRIDGE CONVERSION - .38 Spl., .38 LC, or .44-40 WCF, 5 1/2 or 7 1/2 in. octagon barrel, color case hardened frame and hammer. Disc. 2000.

	$650	$525	$450	$375	$300	$225	$200

Last MSR was $750.

1860 ARMY RICHARDS-TYPE CARTRIDGE CONVERSION - .38 Spl., .38 LC, or .44-40 WCF, 5 1/2 or 8 in. round barrel, color case hardened frame and hammer. Disc. 2000.

	$650	$525	$450	$375	$300	$225	$200

Last MSR was $750.

1861 NAVY RICHARDS-TYPE CARTRIDGE CONVERSION - .38 Spl., .38 LC, or .44-40 WCF, 5 1/2 or 7 1/2 in. round barrel, color case hardened frame and hammer. Disc. 2000.

	$650	$525	$450	$375	$300	$225	$200

Last MSR was $750.

GRADING - PPGS™	100%	98%	95%	90%	80%	70%	60%

1872 OPEN TOP - .38 Spl., .38 LC, or .44-40 WCF, 5 1/2 or 7 1/2 in. round barrel, color case hardened frame and hammer. Disc. 2000.

	$650	$525	$450	$375	$300	$225	$200

Last MSR was $750.

REVOLVERS: SINGLE ACTION

PEACEKEEPER (MODEL 1) - .32-20 WCF (special order), .38-40 WCF (special order), .357 Mag., .44 Spl. (special order), .44-40 WCF, or .45 LC cal., 3, 3 1/2 (Sheriff), 4, 4 3/4, 5 1/2, 7 1/2, 10 (Buntline), or 12 (Buntline) in. barrel, charcoal case colored receiver, blue finish, black powder or cross-pin frame, beveled cylinder, original hammer design w/o transfer bar safety, 2-line patent dates, 1st Generation Colt style hard rubber grips, assembled in America. While original prototypes were developed in 2000, actual importation was late 2000-2003.

	$725	$600	$550	$500	$460	$430	$400

Last MSR was $835.

Add $35 for Sheriff, Thunderer, Birdshead, or Cavalry/Artillery configurations.
Add $165 for bright nickel finish.
Add $1,450 for grade A (25% coverage), $1,750 for grade B (50% coverage), $1,920 for grade C (75% coverage), or $2,240 for grade D (100% coverage) engraving - nickel finish only.
Add $90 for dual cylinder.

LONGHORN - .357 Mag., .44-40 WCF, or .45 LC cal., 3 1/2 (Sheriff), 4 3/4, 5 1/2, or 7 1/2 in. barrel, case colored receiver, blue finish, one-piece walnut grips, 2 line address, assembled in America. Imported 2001-2003.

	$435	$375	$340	$315	$285	$260	$230

Last MSR was $495.

Add $30 for Sheriff or Birdshead/Thunderer Model.
Add $100 for nickel finish.

CLASSIC - .357 Mag. or .45 LC cal. only, flat main spring, 4 3/4 or 5 1/2 in. barrel, blue frame, one piece smooth walnut grips, two line patent dates, 5-5 1/2 lb. trigger. Imported 2003-2004.

	$385	$340	$315	$285	$260	$230	$200

Last MSR was $440.

Add $125 for Turnbull case colors.
Add $195 for nickel or hard chrome finish.

＊*Classic Bisley* - similar to Classic, except has Bisley configuration frame. Imported 2004 only.

	$450	$395	$350	$315	$285	$260	$230

Last MSR was $520.

Add $125 for Turnbull case colors.
Add $195 for nickel or hard chrome finish.

ULTIMATE - .32-20 WCF, .38-40 WCF, .357 Mag., .44-40 WCF, .44 Spl., or .45 LC cal., coil suspension main spring, 3, 3 1/2, 4, 4 1/2, 5 1/2, or 7 1/2 in. barrel, blue frame, one piece smooth walnut grips. Imported 2003-2004.

	$525	$450	$395	$350	$315	$285	$260

Last MSR was $600.

Add $125 for Turnbull case colors.
Add $195 for nickel or hard chrome finish.

GRADING - PPGS™	100%	98%	95%	90%	80%	70%	60%

RIFLES: LEVER ACTION

1892 CARBINE/RIFLE - .357 Mag., .44-40 WCF, or .45 LC cal., 20 (short rifle - octagon, carbine - round) or 24 1/2 octagon barrel, blue finish, uncheckered walnut stock and forearm. Limited importation from Italy late 2000 only.

	$625	$525	$450	$395	$350	$300	$250

Last MSR was $695.

LIGHTNING CARBINE/RIFLE - .32-20 WCF, .38 Spl., .38-40 WCF, .44-40 WCF, or .45 LC cal., patterned after the Colt Lightning rifle, firing pin block safety, blue finish, 20 (carbine) or 24 in. round or octagon barrel, engraved receiver with AWA logo, walnut stock and forearm. Imported 2003-2004.

	$745	$625	$575	$500	$460	$430	$400

Last MSR was $850.

Add $40 for octagon barrel.
Add $350 for White Lightning Model (polished steel receiver.)
Add $300 for case colored hardened finish.

✳ *Lightning Carbine/Rifle Limited Edition* - similar to regular Lightning Carbine/Rifle, except has engraved chrome receiver and select walnut stock, only 500 mfg. Imported 2003-2004.

	$1,075	$900	$775	$650	$575	$500	$460

Last MSR was $1,200.

SHOTGUNS: SXS

HAMMERLESS COACHGUN - while initially advertised during 2000, this model never went into production.

AMTEC 2000, INC.

Previous trademark incorporating Erma Werke (German) and H & R 1871 (U.S.) companies located in Gardner, MA until 1999. Amtec 2000, Inc. previously imported the Erma SR 100 rifle (see listing in Erma Suhl section).

REVOLVERS

5 SHOT REVOLVER - .38 S&W cal., 5 shot double action, swing-out cylinder, 2 or 3 in. barrel, transfer bar safety, Pachmayr composition grips, high polish blue, matte electroless nickel, or stainless steel construction, fixed sights, approx. 25 oz., 200 mfg. 1996-99, all were distributed and sold in Europe only (no U.S. pricing).

ANCIENS ETABLISSEMENTS PIEPER

Please refer to the Bayard section in this text for Bayard Models 1908, 1923, and 1930. In addition, Bergmann-Bayard Models 1908 and 1910 mfg. in Gaggenau, Germany will appear under the Bergman heading.

ANGEL ARMS INC.

Previous manufacturer located in Hayward, CA, 1998-2001.

PISTOLS: SEMI-AUTO

The pistols listed below were designed to shoot a unique integrated case projectile (ICP). These projectiles were hollow, contained the powder charge, and since the case was the projectile, there was no ejection.

MODEL 1000 SE GUN ONE - .45 ICP (Integrated Case Projectile) cal., unique semi-auto design, mag tube is located on top of 6 in. fixed barrel.
While advertised, this model never went into production. $1,900 was the projected MSR.

MODEL QT 427 ZMR - .427 ICP (Integrated Case Projectile) cal., break open action, 5 shot tube or 10 shot staggered mag, 3 1/2 in. barrel, located underneath clear mag tube, 5 oz., compact size.
While advertised, this model never went into production. $900 was the projected MSR.

ANSCHÜTZ

DIE MEISTER MACHER

Current manufacturer (J. G. Anschütz, GmbH & Co. KG) established in 1856 and currently located in Ulm, Germany. Sporting rifles are currently being imported beginning 2006 by Merkel USA, located in Trussville, AL. Target/competition rifles are currently being imported by various distributors (see Trademark Index). Sporting rifles were imported 1996-2003 by Tristar Sporting Arms. Ltd., located in N. Kansas City, MO. Previously distributed until 2000 by Go Sportsmens Supply, located in Billings, MT. Previously imported and distributed through 1995 in the U.S. by Precision Sales International Inc., located in Westfield, MA.

Anschütz was founded by Julius Gottfried Anschütz in 1856, and located in Zella-Mehlis, Germany until 1945. WWII nearly ended the company. Members of the Anschütz family were evacuated to West Germany after the war, while the company's possesions were expropriated and dismantled. Brothers Max & Rudolf Anschütz, grandsons of Julius, re-established the company in Ulm after WWII. In 1968, Max Anschütz turned over general management to his son Dieter, who now shares it with his son, Jochen. The management of the company remains a family business.

For more information and current pricing on both new and used Anschütz airguns, please refer to the *Blue Book of Airguns* by Dr. Robert Beeman & John Allen (now online also).

PISTOLS: BOLT ACTION

Anschütz also manufactured an MSP Pistol Series with ergonomic stock for the silhouette shooters. This series was designed for target shooting. All currently produced Anschütz pistols are delivered with a keyed security gun lock.

MODEL 1416P/1451P (EXEMPLAR) - .22 LR cal., bolt action, Match 64 left-hand action (for right-hand shooters), approx. 7 (original Silhouette Model, mfg. 1994-95) or 10 in. barrel, single shot (Model 1451P, new 1997) or repeater with 5-shot mag. (Model 1416P), two-stage trigger, adj. rear sight, receiver grooved for scope, contoured grip and forestock are stippled, 3 1/3 lbs., also available for left-hand shooters. Mfg. 1987-97.

$395	$345	$295	$250	$225	$200	$180

Last MSR was $470.

Add $17 for single shot (Model 1451P).
Add $110 for right-hand action (for left-hand shooters).
This model was previously designated the Exemplar until 1996.

❋ *Exemplar Magnum* - while advertised in 1987, only one .22 Mag. was manufactured.

❋ *Exemplar XIV* - .22 LR cal., similar to Exemplar, except has 14 in. barrel, 4.15 lbs. Imported 1988-95.

$450	$370	$300	$250	$225	$200	$180

Last MSR was $562.

❋ *Exemplar Hornet* - .22 Hornet cal., 5-shot mag., Match 54 left-hand action, 10 in. barrel, grooved and tapped w/o sights, 4.35 lbs. Imported 1988-95.

$835	$685	$575	$525	$475	$415	$365

Last MSR was $995.

This model may also be marked M-1730MSPE Field.

MODEL 1416 MSPR/MSPE - .22 LR cal., silhouette variation of the Exemplar pistol, MSPR designates repeater, MSPE designates single shot. Mfg. 1997 only.

$1,100	$875	$750	$625	$525	$450	$375

Last MSR was $1,260.

GRADING - PPGS™	100%	98%	95%	90%	80%	70%	60%

MODEL 64P - .22 LR or .22 Mag. (disc. 2001) cal., right-hand Match 64 bolt action, 10 in. barrel drilled and tapped (sights not included), weather proof "Choate" Rynite stock with stippling, 2-stage trigger, 4- (.22 Mag.) or 5-shot mag., 3 1/2 lbs. Mfg. 1998-2003.

	$445	$385	$335	$285	$240	$200	$180

Last MSR was $509.

> **Add 10% for .22 Mag. cal. (Model 64P Mag., disc. 2001).**
> **Add $73 for accessory sight set.**

✳ *Model 64LP* - .22 LR cal., left-hand Match 64 bolt action, 12 in. drilled and tapped barrel (sights not included), "Choate" Rynite stock with stippling, two-stage trigger, 5-shot mag., approx. 3 1/2 lbs. Imported 2003-2004.

	$495	$400	$350	$300	$275	$235	$200

Last MSR was $602.

MODEL 17LP - .17 HMR cal., 4-shot mag., otherwise similar to Model 64LP. Imported 2003-2004.

	$535	$450	$400	$350	$300	$250	$225

Last MSR was $651.

MODEL 1730 MSPE FIELD - .22 Hornet cal., 9.3 in. barrel, single shot, target stock with ventilated forend, ergonomic grips, left handed bolt, 54 Match action, drilled and tapped. Importation disc.

	$1,140	$900	$750	$625	$525	$450	$375

RIFLES: BOLT ACTION, DISC.

Sile Distributors located in NY acted as an import agent during the early 1960s which can be identified by Sile barrel markings. Savage imported Anschütz rifles were available from 1963-1981 and also have Savage/Anschütz barrel markings. While some of those models might not be listed below, refer to models of similar caliber and quality that are listed to ascertain values.

During the period when Savage was importing Anschütz rifles, certain models in the Anschütz line were designated either "Savage-Anschütz" or "Anschütz-Savage" for sales by Savage in the U.S. Conversely, certain models manufactured by Savage were designated "Anschütz-Savage" for sale by Anschütz in Europe. Some of these models did not have any modifications but others were restocked, supplied with different sights, and had other different features from their original counterparts. In most cases, the original model numbers were used. Some "Anschütz-Savage" rifles have made their way into the U.S. While somewhat rare, these rifles are typically based on the Savage Model 110 action. They are not as desirable as those "Savage-Anschütz" marked rifles utilizing the superior Anschütz actions. Anschütz also manufactured between 1,000-2,000 rifles utilizing SAKO actions in .222 Rem. cal. in the late 50s-early 60s. These guns will approximate values shown on the discontinued centerfire models listed below.

Currently, Anschütz offers 3 different actions. The 1451 action is Anschütz's entry level action, which is lightweight in design, utilizes cam cocking, and has a lateral sliding safety. The 1451 action is currently used in the Models 1451 D KL, 1451 R Sporter Target, and 1451 Target. The Match 64 utilizes a cam cocking system with claw extractor and ejector, grooved receiver, and sliding safety on the right side behind the bolt. The Model 64 match action is used on the Model 1416 and variations, 1418, 64MP R, 1516, 1517 D Classic, 1517 D HB Classic, 1517 D Monte Carlo, 1517 M PR, and the Model 64 Target pistol. The Match 54 is Anschütz's top-of-the-line action, and features dual locking lugs on the bolt which are seated eccentricaly in the receiver, allowing more support for improved stock bedding. It also features a cam cocking bolt, 2 position pivot rear safety, and is drilled and tapped. The Match 54 action is currently utilized on the 1710 series, 1712D, 1717, 1720, 1730 series, 1733, and 1740 Models.

The models below have been listed in numerical sequence.

GRADING - PPGS™	100%	98%	95%	90%	80%	70%	60%

MARK 10 TARGET RIFLE - .22 LR cal., single shot. 26 in. heavy barrel, adj. sights, globe front, target stock with full pistol grip, adj. palm stop. Mfg. 1963-81.

	$425	$365	$335	$295	$260	$230	$210

MODEL 54 SPORTER - .22 LR cal., Match 54 action, 5-shot mag., 24 in. round tapered barrel, Monte Carlo roll-over cheekpiece, folding leaf sight, checkered pistol grip. Mfg. 1963-81.

	$750	$675	$625	$525	$450	$400	$360

MODEL 54M - similar to Model 54 Sporter, except .22 Mag. cal.

	$850	$750	$675	$575	$500	$435	$395

MODEL MATCH 64 - .22 LR cal., Match 64 action, single shot, 26 in. barrel, hardwood stock with stipled ergonomic pistol grip, adj. pad, grooved receiver, approx. 8 lbs. Disc.

	$575	$500	$450	$400	$350	$295	$250

Subtract $150 if w/o correct Anschütz micrometer sights (front and rear).

MODEL 141 - .22 LR cal., 5-shot mag., 23 in. round tapered barrel, Monte Carlo stock, folding leaf sight. Disc.

	$400	$350	$300	$250	$200	$180	$160

✷ *Model 141M (Mag.)* - similar to Model 141, except .22 Mag. cal.

	$495	$425	$350	$275	$225	$200	$180

MODEL 153 - .222 Rem. cal., 24 in. barrel, folding leaf rear sight, French walnut stock, rosewood forend tip and pistol grip cap. Mfg. 1963-81.

	$850	$750	$675	$575	$475	$400	$375

MODEL 153-S - similar to Model 153, 24 in. barrel, double set triggers.

	$950	$850	$775	$625	$525	$425	$400

MODEL 164 - .22 LR cal., 5-shot mag., 23 in. round tapered barrel, Monte Carlo stock, folding leaf sight. Mfg. 1963-81.

	$450	$400	$350	$300	$250	$200	$160

MODEL 164M - similar to Model 164, except .22 Mag. cal.

	$500	$450	$375	$325	$275	$210	$180

MODEL 184 - .22 LR cal., 21 1/2 in. barrel, Monte Carlo combination, checkered pistol grip, Schnabel forend, folding leaf sight. Mfg. 1963-1981.

	$495	$435	$375	$325	$275	$210	$180

MODEL 1400 - .22 LR cal., regular barrel, with sights. Disc.

	$350	$320	$290	$260	$230	$210	$195

MODEL 1407 I.S.U. MATCH 54 - .22 LR cal., heavy barrel, match two-stage trigger, stippled walnut stock and forearm with aluminum rail, aperture sights. Disc.

	$650	$550	$475	$400	$350	$300	$260

Last MSR was approx. $530.

MODEL 1408 - .22 LR cal., heavy barrel, no sights. Disc.

	$450	$375	$325	$275	$235	$210	$195

Add $150 for 1408 ED Model.

MODEL 1411 MATCH 54 - .22 LR cal., prone position target model, heavy barrel, aperture sights, side safety, fast lock time, adj. cheekpiece. Disc.

	$650	$550	$475	$400	$350	$300	$260

Last MSR was approx. $575.

Subtract $150 if w/o correct Anschütz micrometer sights (front and rear).

GRADING - PPGS™	100%	98%	95%	90%	80%	70%	60%

MODEL 1413 SUPER MATCH 54 - .22 LR cal., top-of-the-line free style international target rifle, adj. cheekpiece and curved buttplate, heavy target barrel with aperture sights. Disc.

	$825	$725	$625	$525	$425	$375	$325

Last MSR was approx. $875.

Subtract $150 if w/o correct Anschütz micrometer sights (front and rear).

MODEL 1418 - .22 LR cal., sporter variation, previous importation by Savage Arms.

	$375	$325	$275	$225	$200	$175	$150

MODEL 1418 MANNLICHER - .22 LR cal., hunting model, fine checkering, 5-shot mag.

	$825	$750	$650	$550	$450	$375	$325

MODEL 1450 - .22 LR cal., Sporter, 5-shot mag.

	$450	$375	$325	$275	$225	$200	$175

MODEL 1518 MANNLICHER - deluxe model of Model 1418.

	$950	$850	$725	$625	$525	$450	$350

MODEL 1574 SPORTER - .22 Mag., .222 Rem., .22-250 Rem., .223 Rem., .243 Win., or .308 Win. cal. Mfg. by Krico (Kriegeskorte) located at Stuttgart and distributed by Anschütz, approx. 1,000 imported during 1970-73.

	$795	$695	$595	$540	$485	$430	$375

MODEL 1807 - .22 LR cal., replacement for the Model 1407 Match 54, for I.S.U. and NRA shooting, 26 in. barrel, Match 54 action, 10 lbs. Disc.

	$495	$425	$350	$300	$250	$225	$200

RIFLES: BOLT ACTION SPORTER, .17 RIMFIRE - RECENT MFG.

MODEL 1502D HB CLASSIC - .17 Mach 2 cal., features Model 64 action with single stage trigger, 5-shot mag., checkered walnut stock, choice of regular or grooved beavertail forend, heavy barrel w/o sights. Imported 2005-2006.

	$695	$595	$550	$495	$450	$415	$385

Last MSR was $790.

Add $46 for beavertail forend.

MODEL 1517D CLASSIC - .17 HMR cal., features Model 64 action with single stage trigger, 4-shot mag., checkered walnut stock with or w/o Monte Carlo cheekpiece, 23 in. regular or heavy barrel, 5 1/2 or 6.2 (heavy barrel) lbs. Importation began 2003.

MSR $949	$795	$675	$600	$525	$475	$435	$395

Add $21 for Monte Carlo stock (disc. 2006).
Add $51 for left-hand Match 64 action (new 2004).
Add $40 for Model 1517D HB with heavy barrel and grooved beavertail forend (new 2005).

* *Model 1517 MP R Multi-Purpose* - .17 HMR cal., 25 1/2 in. heavy match barrel, two-stage trigger, no sights, hardwood Monte Carlo stock with beavertail forend, 9 lbs. Importation began 2003.

MSR $1,079	$895	$745	$625	$550	$475	$425	$395

Add $60 for stainless steel barrel (new 2007).

MODEL 1702D HB CLASSIC - .17 Mach 2 cal., Match 54 action, 23 in. heavy barrel w/o sights, 5-shot mag., checkered walnut stock and forend, match grade single stage adj. trigger, 7.3 lbs. Imported 2005-2006.

	$1,300	$1,075	$875	$750	$650	$550	$450

Last MSR was $1,512.

GRADING - PPGS™	100%	98%	95%	90%	80%	70%	60%

MODEL 1713 SILHOUETTE - .17 HMR cal., 21.6 in. barrel w/o sights, Monte Carlo stock, Meistergrade features. New 2008.

MSR $2,199	$1,775	$1,475	$1,100	$900	$800	$700	$600

MODEL 1717D KL (CUSTOM) - .17 HMR cal., features Match 54 action, 23 in. barrel, no sights, Monte Carlo stock with pistol grip cap and Schnabel forend, 7.3 lbs. Importation began late 2002.

MSR $1,869	$1,525	$1,225	$1,000	$875	$750	$650	$550

Add $330 for Meistergrade (select walnut and gold etched trigger guard).

✱ *Model 1717 S-BR* - .17 HMR cal., features 22 in. target barrel w/o sights. New 2008.

MSR $1,349	$1,095	$950	$825	$700	$600	$500	$425

MODEL 1717D CLASSIC - .17 HMR cal., features Match 54 action, 4-shot mag., 23 in. regular or heavy barrel, no sights, 8 lbs. New 2002.

MSR $1,739	$1,450	$1,250	$975	$850	$725	$600	$525

Add $340 for Meistergrade (select walnut and gold etched trigger guard).

MODEL 1717 SILHOUETTE SPORTER - .17 HMR cal., Monte Carlo stock with adj. LOP and two-stage trigger. Importation began 2008.

MSR $1,999	$1,625	$1,275	$1,050	$850	$750	$600	$525

RIFLES: BOLT ACTION SPORTER, .22 LR - RECENT MFG.

All currently produced Anschütz rifles are delivered with a keyed security gun lock. Current manufactured Anschütz rifles use the following alphabetical suffixes when describing factory features and options. D = single stage trigger, G = threaded barrel, HB = heavy barrel, KL = folding leaf sight, KV = heavy tangent sight, L = left-hand action, MP = Multi-Purpose, R = repeater, and ST = double set trigger.

KADETT - .22 LR cal., bolt action, youth dimensions, 22 in. barrel, 5-shot clip mag., folding leaf rear sight, single stage trigger, grooved receiver, checkered hard-wood stock, 5 1/2 lbs. Mfg. 1987 only.

	$235	$200	$180	$165	$150	$135	$120

Last MSR was $265.

ACHIEVER - .22 LR cal., bolt action, 19 1/2 in. barrel, single shot, folding leaf rear sight, two-stage trigger, grooved receiver, stippled hard-wood stock with vented forearm and adj. length of pull, 5 1/4 lbs. Mfg. 1987-95.

	$340	$280	$230	$205	$185	$165	$150

Last MSR was $399.

✱ *Achiever ST* - .22 LR cal., 2000 MK single shot action, slide safety, two-stage trigger, adj. length of pull stock, target sights, approx. 6 1/2 lbs. Mfg. 1994-95.

	$415	$360	$315	$260	$230	$205	$185

Last MSR was $485.

MODEL WOODCHUCKER - .22 LR cal., similar to Model 1449D Youth, sold exclusively by R.S.R. Wholesale.

	$210	$185	$165	$150	$135	$120	$110

MODEL 64MP - .22 LR cal., repeater, 5-shot mag., 21.2 regular (disc. 2002) or 25 1/2 (new 2003) in. drilled and tapped heavy match steel or stainless steel (mfg. 2000-2003) barrel, two-stage trigger, uncheckered walnut stained stock and beavertail forend, adj. rubber buttplate. Importation began 1999.

MSR $979	$825	$650	$525	$425	$325	$250	$225

Add $50 for stainless steel barrel (disc. 2003, reintroduced 2007).
Add $49 for left-hand action (disc. 2006).
Subtract approx. $75 if w/o swivel rail.

GRADING - PPGS™	100%	98%	95%	90%	80%	70%	60%

✳ *Model 64R Sporter Target* - .22 LR cal., repeater, Match 64 action, two-stage match trigger, 21.4 in. match grade barrel, checkered hardwood stock, 10-shot mag., adj. buttplate and stainless steel rail. Importation began 2004.

	MSR $1,049	$875	$700	$575	$450	$350	$300	$250

This model replaced the Model 1451 Sport Target during 2004.

✳ *Model 64 S BR* - .22 LR cal., features 20 in. target barrel w/o sights. New 2008.

	MSR $1,349	$1,095	$950	$825	$700	$600	$500	$425

MODEL 1416D CUSTOM (LUXUS) - .22 LR cal., Match 64 action, 22 1/2 in. barrel, 5 or 10-shot mag., cam cocking system on recent mfg., checkered Monte Carlo walnut stock, folding leaf sight, 6 lbs. 2 oz. Disc. 2007.

	$715	$575	$475	$375	$300	$250	$225

Last MSR was $819.

Add $40 for left-hand action.

This model utilizes the Match 64 action, similar to the Anschütz Model 1403 Target.

✳ *Model 1416D Fiberglass* - similar to Model 1416D Custom, except has McMillan fiberglass stock in hunter brown color and includes roll-over cheekpiece and checkered Wundhammer swell pistol grip, 5 1/4 lbs. Imported 1991 only.

	$755	$650	$575	$525	$475	$415	$365

Last MSR was $842.

MODEL 1416D CLASSIC - same specifications as Model 1416D Custom, except straight hardwood stock.

	MSR $899	$775	$625	$500	$400	$325	$275	$240

Add $50 for left-hand action (Model 1416LD).
Add $28 for iron sights (disc. 2006).

✳ *1416D Classic Heavy Barrel* - similar to Model 1416D Classic, except has heavy barrel and no sights, grooved beavertail forend became standard 2005. Mfg. 2000-2001, reintroduced 2003.

	MSR $919	$785	$635	$500	$400	$325	$275	$240

MODEL 1418D - .22 LR cal., Match 64 action, Mannlicher full stock, skipline checkering, 19 3/4 in. barrel, same action as Model 1416D, 5 lbs. 5 oz. Importation disc. 1995, resumed 1998-2003.

	$915	$800	$700	$575	$495	$425	$360

Last MSR was $1,014.

Add $40 for set trigger (mfg. 1985-89).

MODEL 1448D - .22 Clay Bird cal., Model 1451 action, 22 1/2 in. smooth bore barrel w/o sights, repeater, 5-shot mag., checkered walnut stained stock and forend. Imported 1999-2001.

	$295	$265	$240	$220	$200	$185	$170

Last MSR was $349.

MODEL 1449D YOUTH - .22 LR cal., bolt action design, youth dimensions, 16 1/4 in. tapered barrel with adj. rear sight, receiver is grooved for scope mounting, 5-shot mag. with single shot adapter available, European hardwood stock, 12 1/4 in. trigger pull, 3 1/2 lbs. Imported 1990-91 only.

	$210	$185	$165	$150	$135	$120	$110

Last MSR was $249.

MODEL 1451 E/R SPORTER/TARGET - .22 LR cal., single shot (Model 1451E) or 5 shot repeater (Model 1451R), Model 1451 action, sporter target model w/o front sight, 22 (new 1998) or 22 3/4 (disc. 1997) in. barrel w/o sights, stippled pistol grip wood stock and vent. forend (with or w/o beavertail), 6 1/2 lbs. Mfg. 1996-2001.

$435	$395	$360	$330	$300	$280	$260

Last MSR was $485.

Subtract approx. $100 for Model 1451E (single shot).
Add $110 for Model 1451 Junior Super Target (single shot only).

* **Model 1451R Sporter Target Prisma** - .22 LR cal., 5 shot repeater, entry level cam cocking, claw extractor, and recessed bolt face, sliding safety, fully adj. stipled hardwood stock, 22 in. target barrel, grooved receiver, optional micrometer sights, 6.3 lbs. Imported 2001-2003.

$455	$415	$385	$350	$325	$300	$275

Last MSR was $515.

This model was replaced by the Model 64R Sporter Target.

* **Model 1451ST-R** - .22 LR cal., repeater, 5-shot mag., drilled and tapped 22 in. barrel w/o sights, cam cocking system, 2-stage trigger, uncheckered walnut stained hardwood stock. Imported 1999-2001.

$435	$395	$360	$330	$300	$280	$260

Last MSR was $485.

* **Model 1451D Custom** - similar to Model 1451D Classic, except has walnut stock with Monte Carlo cheekpiece, Schnabel forend, and sling swivels, 5 lbs. Mfg. 1998-2001.

$430	$395	$360	$330	$300	$280	$260

Last MSR was $480.

* **Model 1451D Classic (Super)** - .22 LR cal., 5 shot, 22 3/4 in. barrel with front sights, grooved receiver, walnut finished straight hardwood stock, 5 lbs. Mfg. 1996-2001.

$335	$280	$245	$210	$175	$160	$150

Last MSR was $398.

This model was designated the 1451 Super during 1996-97.

MODEL 1466D REPEATER - .22 LR cal., 24 in. conically tapered barrel with open sights, grooved receiver, checkered Monte Carlo walnut stock and forend. Imported 1996 only.

$660	$525	$435	$375	$315	$260	$235

Last MSR was $766.

MODEL 1710D CUSTOM (1700D) - .22 LR cal., Match 54 action, 5-shot mag., 23 3/4 (new 1998) or 24 (disc. 1997) in. regular (new 1998) or heavy (disc. 1997) barrel, folding rear sight, single or two-stage trigger (Model 1710 KL, mfg. 2003, reintroduced 2007), Monte Carlo stock with roll-over cheekpiece and skipline checkering, 6 1/2 - 7 1/4 lbs.

MSR $1,759							
	$1,450	$1,150	$875	$700	$600	$500	$400

Add $320 for Meistergrade (select walnut and gold etched trigger guard - disc. 1996, resumed 1998 w/o gold trigger guard).

This model was designated 1422D until 1989 when it was changed to the Model 1700D with some modifications. In 1996, model nomenclature changed from Model 1700D Custom to the Model 1710D Custom. The Model 1400D Meistergrade was disc. 1987 - the last advertised retail price was $930.

The Model 1700D Custom employs the Anschütz Match 54 action.

GRADING - PPGS™	100%	98%	95%	90%	80%	70%	60%

✳ *Model 1700D Graphite* - similar to Model 1700D Custom, except has McMillan black graphite reinforced stock with Monte Carlo roll-over cheekpiece, includes sling and swivels, 22 in. barrel, 7 1/4 lbs. Imported 1991-95.

	$1,130	$885	$760	$650	$550	$450	$375

Last MSR was $1,299.

1710D CLASSIC - same general specifications as 1700D/1710D Custom, regular straight stock, choice of regular (disc. 2003), heavy (new 1999), or heavy stainless (mfg. 2000-2003) barrel, open sights (disc. 1994), 7.3-8 lbs. Disc. 1994. Importation resumed 1998.

MSR $1,649	$1,375	$1,125	$925	$800	$700	$600	$475

Add $320 for Meistergrade (select walnut and gold etched trigger guard, disc. 1994, reintroduced 2000).

This model was also available as a 2000 Signature Series - includes high polish bluing, select American black walnut, "1 of 200" and "Dieter Anschütz 2000" signature in 24Kt. gold on bottom of trigger guard, aluminum case, and dated certificate at no extra charge.

This model was designated 1422DCL Classic until 1989 when it was changed to the Model 1700D Classic with some modifications. The Model 1422DCL Classic Meistergrade was disc. 1987 - the last advertised retail price was $875. In 1998, this model was reintroduced as the Model 1710D Classic.

MODEL 1700D FEATHERWEIGHT (FWT) - similar to Model 1700D Custom, except has matte black McMillan fiberglass stock configured like the Custom Model, 22 in. barrel, no sights, 6 1/4 lbs. Imported 1989-95.

	$1,075	$895	$775	$650	$550	$450	$375

Last MSR was $1,230.

✳ *Model 1700D Featherweight Deluxe* - similar specification to the Model 1700D Featherweight, except has skip-line checkered Fibergrain synthetic stock with realistic wood grain. Imported 1990-95.

	$1,235	$1,050	$875	$775	$650	$550	$450

Last MSR was $1,460.

MODEL 1700D BAVARIAN - .22 LR cal., 24 in. barrel, 5-shot mag., checkered European style stock with European Monte Carlo cheekpiece and schnabel forend, 7 1/2 lbs. Mfg. 1988-95.

	$1,165	$935	$775	$650	$550	$450	$375

Last MSR was $1,364.

Add $199 for Meistergrade variation (select walnut).

MODEL 1710 CLASSIC HIGH GRADE - .22 LR cal., 23 in. stainless steel heavy barrel w/o sights, 150th Anniversary model featuring Anschutz 150 year logo carved in premium walnut stock, wood bolt handle, founder's logo in gold on trigger guard, original Germania 1901 logo on barrel, two different styles of carving/checkering, limited mfg. beginning 2007.

MSR $2,299	$1,995	$1,775	$1,525	$1,350	$1,175	$950	$775

MODEL 1712D - .22 LR cal., current top-of-the-line sporter rifle with deluxe walnut. Imported 1997-98 only.

	$1,300	$1,100	$895	$775	$650	$550	$450

Last MSR was $1,495.

MODEL 1712 SILHOUETTE SPORTER - .22 LR cal., similar to Model 1712D, except has Monte Carlo stock with adj. LOP and two-stage trigger. Importation began 2003.

MSR $1,759	$1,450	$1,100	$925	$775	$650	$550	$450

MODEL 1717 SILHOUETTE - .22 LR cal., 21.6 in. barrel w/o sights, Monte Carlo stock, Meistergrade features. New 2008.

MSR $2,079	$1,675	$1,400	$1,100	$900	$800	$700	$600

DIE MEISTERMACHER - .22 LR cal., Match 54 action, top-of-the-line model, limited edition of 25 guns, select wood, extra polish on metal parts, hand-lapped barrel, with numerous gold inlays including Olympic wreath. Mfg. 1985.

	$2,750	$2,000	$1,600	N/A	N/A	N/A	N/A

Last MSR was $2,475.

This variation sold out in late 1988.

RIFLES: BOLT ACTION SPORTER, .22 MAG. - RECENT MFG.

All currently produced Anschütz rifles are delivered with a keyed security gun lock. Current manufactured Anschütz rifles use the following alphabetical suffixes when describing factory features and options. D = single stage trigger, G = threaded barrel, HB = heavy barrel, KL = folding leaf sight, KV = heavy tangent sight, L = left-hand action, MP = Multi-Purpose, R = repeater, and ST = double set trigger.

MODEL 1516D CUSTOM (LUXUS) - similar to Model 1416D, except .22 Mag. cal., 4-shot mag., 6 lbs. 2 oz. Importation disc. 2003.

	$630	$530	$465	$385	$335	$275	$250

Last MSR was $717.

This model utilizes the Match 64 action, similar to the Anschütz Model 1403 Target. In 1996, model nomenclature changed from the Model 1516D Custom to Model 1516D Luxus and during 1998, it changed back to Model 1516D Custom.

∗ *1516D/DCL Classic* - same specifications as Model 1516D Custom, except regular hardwood stained stock, regular or heavy (new 2000) barrel.

MSR $919	$785	$635	$500	$400	$325	$275	$240

MODEL 1518D (LUXUS) - .22 Mag. cal., otherwise similar to Model 1418D (Mannlicher stock), 4-shot mag., 5 1/2 lbs. Importation disc. 1995, reintroduced 1997, nomenclature was changed to Model 1518D in 1997, disc. 2001.

	$895	$795	$675	$550	$440	$375	$325

Last MSR was $987.

Add $50 for set trigger (disc. 1995).

MODEL 1720D CUSTOM (1700D) - .22 Mag. cal., bolt action, 5-shot mag., 23 3/4 (new 1998) or 24 (disc. 1991) in. regular (new 1998) or heavy (disc. 1991) barrel, iron sights, Monte Carlo stock with skipline checkering, 6 lbs. 10 oz. to 7 1/4 lbs. Importation disc. 1991, resumed 1998, disc. 2001.

	$995	$875	$750	$650	$550	$450	$375

Last MSR was $1,104 for the Model 1720D Custom. Last MSR was $1,229 for the Model 1700D.

Add $174 for Meistergrade variation (select walnut).

This model was designated 1522D until 1989 and then reintroduced as the Model 1700D with some modifications. The Model 1522D Custom Meistergrade was disc. 1985 - last advertised retail price was $678. In 1998, this model was reintroduced as the 1720D Custom.

MODEL 1700D/1720D CLASSIC - same general specifications as 1700D Custom, straight regular stock, choice of heavy (new 1999), or regular diameter barrel. Importation disc. 1991, resumed 1998, disc. 2001.

	$900	$795	$700	$625	$525	$425	$350

Last MSR was $1,021 for the Model 1720D Classic. Last MSR was $1,199 for the Model 1700D Classic.

Add $174 for Meistergrade variation (select walnut).

This model was designated 1522DCL until 1989 and then reintroduced as the Model 1700D with some modifications. In 1998, this model was reintroduced as the 1720D Classic. The Model 1522DCL Classic Meistergrade was disc. 1985 - the last advertised retail price was $660.

GRADING - PPGS™	100%	98%	95%	90%	80%	70%	60%

MODEL 1700D BAVARIAN - .22 Mag. cal., 24 in. barrel, clip mag., checkered European style stock with European Monte Carlo cheekpiece and schnabel forend, 7 1/2 lbs. Mfg. 1988-95.

	$1,165	$935	$775	$650	$550	$450	$375

Last MSR was $1,364.

Add $199 for Meistergrade variation (select walnut).

RIFLES: BOLT ACTION SPORTER, CENTERFIRE - RECENT MFG.

All currently produced Anschütz rifles are delivered with a keyed security gun lock. Current manufactured Anschütz rifles use the following alphabetical suffixes when describing factory features and options. D = single stage trigger, G = threaded barrel, HB = heavy barrel, KL = folding leaf sight, KV = heavy tangent sight, L = left-hand action, MP = Multi-Purpose, R = repeater, and ST = double set trigger.

MODEL 1433D - .22 Hornet cal., special order only, Match 54 target action, Mannlicher full stock, 4-shot mag. Disc. 1986.

	$995	$840	$740	$640	$525	$425	$350

Last MSR was $826.

Add 5% for set trigger (new 1985).

MODEL 1730D KL CUSTOM (1700D) - .22 Hornet cal., 24 in. barrel, folding leaf sight, Monte Carlo stock with skipline checkering and rosewood grip cap, 4-shot mag., 7 3/4 lbs. Model 1432D was disc. 1987, and the Model 1700D was introduced 1989.

MSR $1,979	$1,625	$1,300	$1,100	$900	$800	$700	$600

Add $220 for Meistergrade variation (select walnut).

This model will be discontinued during 2008.

This model was designated 1432D until 1987 and then reintroduced 1989 as the Model 1700D with some modifications. In 1996, model nomenclature changed from the Model 1700D Custom to the Model 1730D Custom. The Model 1432D Custom Meistergrade was disc. 1986 - the last advertised retail price was $770.

The 1700D Custom comes standard with the Anschütz Match 54 action.

✳ *Model 1700D Graphite* - similar to Model 1700D Custom, except has McMillan black graphite reinforced stock with Monte Carlo roll-over cheekpiece, includes sling and swivels, 22 in. barrel, 7 1/4 lbs. Imported 1995 only.

	$1,235	$1,025	$840	$725	$625	$525	$425

Last MSR was $1,478.

MODEL 1730D CLASSIC (1700D) - .22 Hornet cal., same general specifications as 1700D Custom, except regular stock and 23 1/2 (1432DCL), 5 shot, 23 3/4 regular, heavy (new 1999) - 1730D, or heavy stainless (imported 2001-2002), or 24 (1700D) in. barrel. Disc. 1994, reintroduced 1998.

MSR $1,869	$1,575	$1,250	$975	$825	$700	$600	$500

Last MSR was $1,395 on the Model 1700D Classic.

Add $210 for Meistergrade variation (select walnut).

Add $77 for heavy stainless barrel (disc. 2002).

This model will be discontinued during 2008.

This model was designated 1432D until 1987, and then reintroduced 1989 as the Model 1700D with some modifications. In 1998, this model was reintroduced as the Model 1730D Classic. This model comes standard with the Anschütz Match 54 action.

MODEL 1700D BAVARIAN - .22 Hornet or .222 Rem. cal., 24 in. barrel, 5-shot mag., checkered European style stock with European Monte Carlo cheekpiece and schnabel forend, 7 1/2 lbs. Mfg. 1988-95.

	$1,325	$1,050	$900	$775	$650	$550	$425

Last MSR was $1,364.

Add approx. $200 for Meistergrade variation (select walnut).

MODEL 1733D - .22 Hornet cal., Mannlicher full stock featuring skipline checkering, European walnut, and rosewood Schnabel tip, 19 3/4 in. barrel with hooded front sight, 6 lbs. 6 oz. Imported 1993-95, reintroduced 1998-2002, limited mfg. through 2008..

MSR $1,899	$1,595	$1,275	$975	$825	$700	$600	$500

MODEL 1740D CUSTOM (1700D) - .222 REM. - .222 Rem. cal., 3 shot, otherwise similar to Model 1700D Custom, except is also available with 23 3/4 in. barrel. Importation disc. 2006.

	$1,450	$1,175	$1,050	$850	$750	$650	$550

Last MSR was $1,729. Last MSR was $909 on the Model 1532D.

Add $270 for Meistergrade variation (select walnut).

This model was designated 1532D until 1987 and then reintroduced 1989 as the Model 1700D with some modifications. In 1996, model nomenclature changed from the Model 1700D Custom to the Model 1740D Custom. The Model 1532D MG Custom Meistergrade was disc. 1986 - the last advertised retail price was $770.

MODEL 1740D CLASSIC (1700D) - similar to Model 1700D Custom, except regular stock. Disc. 1994, reintroduced 1998-2006.

	$1,375	$1,125	$900	$775	$675	$575	$475

Last MSR was $1,621. Last MSR was $849 on the Model 1532DCL. Last MSR was $1,395 on the Model 1700D Classic.

Add $274 for Meistergrade variation (select walnut).
Add $77 for heavy stainless barrel (disc. 2002).

This model was designated 1532DCL until 1987 and then reintroduced 1989 as the Model 1700D with some modifications. In 1998, this model was reintroduced as the 1740D Classic.

MODEL 1743D - .222 Rem. cal., Mannlicher full stock variation of the Model 1740D, 6.8 lbs. Imported 1997-2001.

	$1,225	$1,000	$850	$750	$625	$500	$400

Last MSR was $1,373.

MODEL 1533 - .222 Rem. cal., open sights, checkered walnut stock. Disc. 1994.

	$795	$725	$660	$600	$550	$475	$400

RIFLES: BOLT ACTION, SILHOUETTE

Currently imported Anschütz silhouette rifles can vary somewhat in price, depending on the distributor and inventory. All currently produced Anschütz rifles are delivered with a keyed security gun lock.

MODEL 2013 SUPER-MATCH FREE RIFLE (BR-50) - .22 LR cal., single shot, 20 in. heavy barrel, no sights, black synthetic stock with adj. cheekpiece and widened forend ("ANSCHÜTZ BR-50" is stenciled on sides), 15.4 lbs. Limited importation 1994-98.

	$2,225	$1,750	$1,375	$1,050	$900	$725	$625

Last MSR was $2,880.

Add $300 for color laminate stock (mfg. 1997-98 only).

Model nomenclature changed from the BR-50 to the Model 2013 in 1997.

MODEL 64S RIFLE - .22 LR cal., single shot, 26 in. round barrel, beavertail forearm, adj. single stage trigger, aperture sights, target stock with Wundhammer swell grip and adj. buttplate, checkered pistol grip. Mfg. 1963-1981.

	$475	$425	$375	$325	$285	$240	$220

Subtract 15% if without sights (Model 64).

This model was available in left-hand or right-hand action.

MODEL 64MS/MP R - .22 LR cal., single shot (Model 64MS, disc. 1996) or 5 shot repeater (Model 64MS R), silhouette target model, 21 1/4 in. barrel, no sights, Wundhammer swell stippled pistol grip beechwood stock, adj. trigger, 8 lbs.

MSR N/A	$800	$700	$600	$500	$400	$325	$275

Add $50 for left-hand action (disc.).

This variation employs a Match 64 action. R suffix nomenclature started 1997, S suffix began 2003.

✳ *Model 64MS - FWT* - similar to Model 64MS, except single stage trigger, 6 1/4 lbs. Disc. 1988.

$550	$475	$425	$350	$325	$260	$230

Last MSR was $596.

MODEL 54.18MS - .22 LR cal., silhouette target model, 22 in. barrel, Match 54 single shot action, walnut Wundhammer stock is stippled on pistol grip and entire forearm, no sights, 8 lbs. 6 oz. Disc. 1997.

$1,295	$1,075	$895	$760	$650	$550	$475

Last MSR was $1,579.

Add $96 for left-hand action.

This model employs the Super Match 54 action.

✳ *Model 54.18MS ED* - same action as Model 54.18MS, except has 19 1/4 in. barrel 7/8 in. diameter) with 14 1/4 in. extension tube, 3 removable muzzle weights. Disc. 1988.

$1,075	$900	$775	$675	$575	$485	$410

Last MSR was $1,215.

Add $100 for left-hand action.

MODEL 54.18MS REP - similar to Model 54.18MS, except has repeating action, 5-shot mag., regular beechwood plain stock with or w/o, thumbhole, vented forend, or black, grey, or tan-green swirl synthetic stock, 7 3/4 lbs.

MSR N/A	$1,750	$1,500	$1,250	$995	$875	$750	$625

Add $75 for synthetic stock.
Add approx. $175 for wood stock, with or w/o thumbhole.

This model features a Super Match 54 action with clip mag. This model was introduced in 1989 with a wood stock and a retail price of $1,650. In 1990, the stock was changed to a synthetic McMillan fiberglass finished in grey. Currently, it is available with beechwood or synthetic stock.

✳ *Model 54.18MS REP Deluxe* - deluxe version of the Model 54.18MS REP featuring Fibergrain McMillan stock with advanced thumbhole design and stippled checkering. Imported 1990-97.

$2,035	$1,600	$1,275	$1,025	$915	$785	$695

Last MSR was $2,450.

RIFLES: BOLT ACTION MATCH, RECENT MFG.

All currently manufactured Anschütz match/target and biathlon rifles listed in the following sections are imported by Champion's Choice, Inc., Champions Shooter's Supply, Creedmoor Sports and Gunsmithing, Inc., unless otherwise noted. These match/target models will vary somewhat in price, depending on the features, options, and availability. Typically, there are no MSRs on match rifles. All currently produced Anschütz match rifles are delivered with a keyed security gun lock.

MODEL 2000 MK - .22 LR cal., single shot match, 26 in. barrel, aperture sights, 7 1/2 lbs. Disc. 1988.

$340	$290	$250	$210	$180	$160	$145

Last MSR was $400.

MODEL 1403D - .22 LR cal., improved Model 64S match rifle, single shot, no sights, adj. trigger, 8 lbs. 6 oz. Importation disc. in 1990.

| | $600 | $525 | $450 | $360 | $300 | $260 | $225 |

Last MSR was $700.

Add $50 for left-hand action (disc. 1988).

MODEL 1803D - .22 LR cal., Match 64 action, 25 1/2 in. target barrel, single stage adj. trigger, blond finished wood with dark stippling on pistol grip and forearm, adj. cheekpiece and buttplate, 8.6 lbs. Imported 1987-93.

| | $850 | $725 | $625 | $525 | $430 | $365 | $310 |

Last MSR was $1,012.

Add $70 for left-hand action (disc. 1989).

MODEL 1808D RT/1808MS R (RUNNING TARGET) - .22 LR cal., single shot running target model, 19 (w/o barrel weights) - 32 1/2 in. barrel, adj. stock, cheekpiece, trigger, heavy beavertail forend, no sights, muzzle barrel weights, 9 1/4 lbs. Importation disc. 1998.

| | $1,850 | $1,400 | $1,075 | $950 | $800 | $695 | $595 |

Last MSR was $2,220.

Add $50 for left-hand action (disc. 1991).
Subtract 20% for earlier models (Model 1808D RT and Model 1808 ED-Super).

This model was previously designated Model 1808D RT from 1991-96, and also the Model 1808 ED-Super during 1990 and earlier mfg.

MODEL 1808MS R - .22 LR cal., 5 shot repeater designed for metallic silhouette shooting, 19.2 in. barrel w/o sights, thumbhole Monte Carlo stock with grooved forearm featuring "ANSCHÜTZ" in panel scene, approx. 8 lbs. Importation began 1998.

| MSR $1,916 | | $1,695 | $1,450 | $1,175 | $1,025 | $900 | $800 | $700 |

This sporting model is distributed by Acusport Corp., Zander's Sporting Goods, Inc., and Ellett Brothers.

MODEL 1813 SUPER MATCH - .22 LR cal., top-of-the-line competition model with sophisticated adj. cheekpiece, buttplate, trigger, pistol grip, and palm rest, Super Match 54 action, stippled walnut stock with thumbhole grip, 15.4 lbs. Mfg. 1979-88.

| | $1,850 | $1,600 | $1,400 | $1,200 | $975 | $875 | $775 |

This model previously held all the Olympic and world records. The model nomenclature was changed to Model 1913 Super Match in 1988.

MODEL 1903D - .22 LR cal., similar specifications to the Model 1803D, except has new improved target stock and adj. cheekpiece made from walnut finished European hardwood, color laminated stock mfg. 1995-98, full length stippled checkering on forend and contoured pistol grip, fully adj. new style buttplate, 9.9 lbs. New 1990.

| MSR N/A | | $875 | $800 | $725 | $625 | $525 | $450 | $375 |

Add $130 for color laminated stock (disc. 1998).

MODEL 1907 - .22 LR cal., single shot match "I.S.U." model, 26 in. button-rifled barrel, prone and position shooting, removable cheekpiece, adj. buttplate, hand stippled stock with ventilated forearm and choice of beechwood (new 1997) walnut, blond laminated (disc.), or color laminated (mfg. 1995-96) wood stock, 10 1/2 lbs.

| MSR N/A | | $1,795 | $1,525 | $1,325 | $1,100 | $900 | $775 | $650 |

Add $125 for left-hand action.
Add $130 for stainless steel barrel.
Add approx. $700 for aluminum stock.
Add $125 for quick adj. cheekpiece (disc.).
Add $125 for color laminated stock (disc.).

This model is also available with an Anschütz stock no. 2213 blue laminate (Alu Color), featuring the most recent technology in stock innovation.

This variation was designated Model 1807 before 1989.

GRADING - PPGS™	100%	98%	95%	90%	80%	70%	60%

MODEL 1909 - target variation of the Model 1910 Super Match II, limited importation 1997-98 only.

	$1,925	$1,550	$1,225	$1,025	$895	$785	$695

Last MSR was $2,480.

MODEL 1910 SUPER MATCH II - .22 LR cal., single shot, 27 1/4 in. barrel, diopter sights, thumbhole stock is fully adj., 12 lbs., model down from 1813 (or 1913), special order only - limited quantities imported until 1998.

	$2,150	$1,750	$1,475	$1,100	$900	$725	$625

Last MSR was $2,967.

Add $149 for left-hand action.
Subtract 20% for Model 1810.

This variation was designated as Model 1810 before 1988.

MODEL 1911 PRONE MATCH - .22 LR cal., single shot match prone rifle, 27 1/4 in. barrel, beechwood stock with adj. cheekpiece, buttplate, no sights, 11.9 lbs.

MSR N/A	$1,865	$1,550	$1,200	$995	$925	$825	$700

Add $99 for stainless steel barrel.
Add $100 for left-hand action (disc. 1993).
Subtract 20% for Model 1811.

This variation was designated Model 1811 before 1988.

MODEL 1912 LADIES SPORT RIFLE - .22 LR cal., designed for new ladies I.S.S.F. standards, features 1907 barreled action w/o sights, walnut stock with shorter dimensions, 11.4 lbs. Importation began 1999.

MSR N/A	$2,175	$1,850	$1,575	$1,350	$1,100	$975	$825

Add $336 for aluminum stock.
Add $135 for left-hand action.

MODEL 1913 SUPER MATCH FREE RIFLE - .22 LR cal., single shot, top-of-the-line match rifle, every possible refinement, international diopter sights, 27 1/4 in. button rifled barrel, hand and palm rest, wood (disc. 2007) or blue aluminum Alu Color (new 2000) stock, 15 1/2 lbs.

MSR N/A	$2,475	$2,075	$1,750	$1,500	$1,225	$1,050	$925

Add $130 for stainless steel barrel.
Add approx. $125 for aluminum stock.

This variation was designated Model 1813 before 1988 (see separate listing).

MODEL 2007 ISSF STANDARD - .22 LR cal., ISSF model, featuring 19 3/4 in. standard or heavy (new 2001) barrel with 8 in. detachable front tube allowing for different sights and counter-weights (total barrel length with tube is 27 1/4 in.), adj. cheekpiece and rubber buttplate, grooved and vented forearm, choice of blond (disc. 2000), walnut, or blue aluminum Alu Color (new 2001) stock, Match 54 action, 12 lbs. New 1992.

MSR N/A	$2,525	$2,250	$1,875	$1,550	$1,325	$1,100	$965

Add $135 for stainless steel barrel.
Add approx. $520 for Acu Color aluminum stock, right-or left-hand.

This model underwent significant engineering changes during 1994, including a heavier receiver.

MODEL 2012 LADIES SPORT RIFLE - .22 LR cal., utilizes 2007 rectangular receiver barreled action designed for new ladies ISSF rules, smaller dimensions, walnut stock, 11.4 lbs. Importation began 1999.

MSR N/A	$3,295	$2,850	$2,525	$2,100	$1,775	$1,475	$1,200

GRADING - PPGS™	100%	98%	95%	90%	80%	70%	60%

MODEL 2013 SUPER MATCH "SPECIAL" - .22 LR cal., top-of-the-line international target rifle featuring 19 3/4 in. standard or heavy (new 2001) barrel with 8 in. detachable front tube allowing for different sights and counter-weights (total barrel length with tube is 27 1/4 in.), top grain walnut, color laminate, or Acu-Color aluminum stock with adj. hand rest, palm rest, cheekpiece, and elaborate metal buttplate, Match 54 action, 15.4 lbs. New 1992.

MSR N/A	$3,000	$2,600	$2,275	$1,900	$1,600	$1,250	$1,025

> Add $135 for stainless steel barrel.

This model underwent significant engineering changes during 1994.

✳ *Model 2013 BR-50 (Benchrest)* - .22 LR cal., developed especially for benchrest competition, trigger can be adjusted for either light single or two-stage action, 19.6 in. barrel, uncheckered walnut stock with wide forend, 10.3 lbs. Importation began 1999.

MSR N/A	$2,175	$1,825	$1,475	$1,250	$975	$850	$725

RIFLES: BOLT ACTION, BIATHLON

MODEL 64R BIATHLON - .22 LR cal., repeater, 5-shot mag., Match 64 action, 21.2 in. barrel, match trigger, hardwood stock with adj. cheekpiece and buttplate, right-or left-hand action, 7.9 lbs. Importation began 2004.

MSR N/A	$925	$825	$750	$675	$600	$525	$450

MODEL 1450B - .22 LR cal., 2000 MK action, 19 1/2 in. barrel, European hardwood with vent. forearm and adj. buttplate, aperture sights, 5 lbs. Mfg. 1993 only.

	$650	$550	$450	$375	$300	$260	$230

> *Last MSR was $765.*

MODEL 1403B - .22 LR cal., Match 64 action, 21 1/2 in. barrel, blonde finished European hardwood with stippled pistol grip, Biathlon design allows 4 mags. to be stored in a housing attached to the forend on right side, entry level Biathlon gun, 8 1/2 lbs. Mfg. 1990-92.

	$850	$730	$660	$525	$450	$375	$335

> *Last MSR was $998.*

MODEL 1827B - .22 LR cal., biathlon rifle, carries four 5 shot mags. in stock, special biathlon features, 21 1/2 in. barrel, limited mfg.

	$1,875	$1,550	$1,225	$1,025	$895	$785	$695

> *Last MSR was $2,457.*

> Add $120 for left-hand action (disc. 1989).

In 1990, the stock design was changed permitting 8 mags. to be stored in two housings attached to both the stock and forend on right side.

✳ *Model 1827BT Fortner* - same general specifications as Model 1827B, except has Fortner straight pull-through bolt action, color laminated stock became available 1995, blue or stainless barrel, 8.8 lbs. New 1986.

MSR N/A	$2,375	$2,100	$1,800	$1,675	$1,425	$1,175	$925

> Add $125 for stainless steel barrel.
> Subtract $200 for standard blue barrel.

In 1990, the stock design was changed permitting 8 mags. to be stored in two housings attached to both the stock and forend on right side.

RIFLES: SEMI-AUTO

MODEL 520/61 - .22 LR cal., semi-auto, 24 in. barrel, 10-shot mag., Monte Carlo stock, 6 1/2 lbs. Disc. 1983.

	$295	$250	$215	$175	$150	$130	$120

GRADING - PPGS™	100%	98%	95%	90%	80%	70%	60%

MARK 525 SPORTER RIFLE - .22 LR cal., semi-auto, 24 in. barrel, 10-shot mag., adj. rear sight, Monte Carlo stock, 6 1/2 lbs. Imported 1984-95.

	$495	$425	$365	$315	$265	$225	$185

Last MSR was $547.

This model is still manufactured, but is not currently imported into the U.S.

* *Mark 525 Carbine* - similar to Mark 525 Rifle, except has 20 in. barrel. Importation disc. 1986.

	$425	$365	$325	$265	$225	$200	$175

SHOTGUNS: O/U

Anschütz marked O/U shotguns were manufactured by Miroku of Japan and distributed in Germany only. Several grades of these shotguns were manufactured and while rarely seen in the U.S., values approximate other Miroku O/Us of similar quality and features ($650-$1,000 assuming 95% or better condition).

ANZIO IRONWORKS CORP.

Current manufacturer established during 2000, and located in St. Petersburg, FL. Anzio Ironworks has been making gun parts and accessories since 1994. Dealer and consumer sales.

RIFLES: BOLT ACTION

.50 BMG SINGLE SHOT TAKEDOWN MODEL - .50 BMG cal., modified bullpup configuration, tube stock with 2 in. buttpad, 17 in. barrel with match or military chambering and muzzle brake, automatic ambidextrous safety and decocking mechanism, takedown action allowing disassembly in under 25 seconds, adj. target trigger, inclined mounting rail, cased, 25 lbs. Mfg. 2000-2002.

	$2,350	$2,000	$1,800	$1600	$1,400	$1,200	$1,000

Last MSR was $2,500.

Add $150 for 29 in. barrel or $1,050 for 29 in. barrel assembly.

.50 BMG SINGLE SHOT TITANIUM TAKEDOWN MODEL - .50 BMG cal., modified bullpup configuration, tube stock, 16 In. barrel with match or military chambering and muzzlebrake, automatic ambidextrous safety and decocking mechanism, interrupted thread lockup, takedown action allowing disassembly in under 12 seconds, adj. target trigger, Picatinny rail mount, cased, 11 lbs. Limited mfg. 2002 only.

	$2,995	$2,600	$2,350	$2,000	$1,800	$1600	$1,400

Last MSR was $3,200.

Add $250 for 29 in. barrel, $350 for custom barrel length to 45 in., or $1,050 for 29 in. barrel assembly.

.50 BMG SINGLE SHOT MODEL - .50 BMG cal., laminated wood stock, butter knife bolt handle, bolt complete with ejector and extractor, parkerized finish, inclined mounting rail, 17 in. barrel with match or military chambering and muzzlebrake, 21 lbs. Limited mfg. 2002 only.

	$2,500	$2,200	$1,950	$1,675	$1,400	$1,200	$1,000

Last MSR was $2,750.

Add $150 for 29 in. barrel or $250 for custom barrel length to 45 in.

.50 BMG SINGLE SHOT MODEL - .50 BMG cal., 29 1/2 in. Lothar Walther match grade barrel, AR-15 trigger and safety, fixed metal buttstock with shrouded barrel and optional muzzle brake, 22 lbs. Mfg. 2003-2006.

	$1,800	$1,625	$1,400	$1,200	$1,000	$900	$800

Last MSR was $1,995.

GRADING - PPGS™	100%	98%	95%	90%	80%	70%	60%

SINGLE SHOT MODEL W/ TAKEDOWN BARREL - .50 BMG or .338 Lapua cal., similar to single shot model, except features a 20 minute incline rail, heavier receiver, match grade stainless steel takedown barrel with clamshell muzzle brake, .5 MOA guaranteed. New 2005.

	100%	98%	95%	90%	80%	70%	60%
MSR $4,200	$3,675	$3,150	$2,750	$2,400	$2,100	$1,900	$1,700

Add $500 for .338 Lapua cal.

.50 BMG LIGHTWEIGHT REPEATER MODEL - .50 BMG cal., lightweight model with 18 in. Lothar Walther fluted target barrel with 3 (standard) or 5 shot detachable mag., titanium muzzle brake, scope rail, bipod, and sling, 13 1/2 lbs. New 2003.

	100%	98%	95%	90%	80%	70%	60%
MSR $4,995	$4,500	$3,950	$3,300	$2,775	$2,350	$2,125	$1,850

Add $705 for takedown model.

ANZIO .50 BMG STANDARD REPEATER - .50 BMG cal., 18 or 26 in. barrel, similar to .50 Lightweight Repeater Model, except does not have barrel/receiver fluting, and is not available with titanium muzzle brake/bolt handle. New 2004.

	100%	98%	95%	90%	80%	70%	60%
MSR $3,995	$3,475	$2,850	$2,400	$2,000	$1,750	$1,500	$1,350

MAG. FED RIFLE - 14.5mm, 20mm (requires $200 transfer tax in states where legal), or Anzio .20-50 cal., single shot or repeater, 49 in. match grade fluted take down barrel, detachable 3 shot box mag., titanium firing pin, bipod, scope rail, customer choice duracoat finish, oversized bolt handle. New 2008.

	100%	98%	95%	90%	80%	70%	60%
MSR $11,900	$11,900	$9,950	$8,750	$8,000	$7,250	$6,500	$5,750

Add $1,100 for handguard, freefloating barrel and adj. bipod.
Add $3,200 for muzzlebrake.
Subtract $2,100 for single shot.

APACHE

Previous trademark manufactured by Ojanguren Y Vidosa located in Eibar, Spain.

PISTOLS: SEMI-AUTO

SEMI-AUTO - 6.35mm cal., clip fed.

	100%	98%	95%	90%	80%	70%	60%
	$225	$190	$160	$140	$120	$95	$75

ARCUS CO.

Current trademark of handguns manufactured in Bulgaria and currently imported by Century International Arms, located in Boca Raton, FL. Previously imported until 2000 by Miltex, Inc., located in Waldorf, MD.

PISTOLS: SEMI-AUTO

MODEL 94/94 COMPACT - 9mm Para. cal., SA or DA (disc. 2000), 4 (compact), 4 3/4 or 5 1/4 (disc. 2000) in. barrel, 10-shot mag., choice of blue (disc.), two-tone, or silver matte (disc.) metal finish, rubber or molded synthetic (disc. 2000) grips, 32-35 oz. Imported 1998-2000, reimported beginning 2003.

	100%	98%	95%	90%	80%	70%	60%
No MSR	$310	$255	$225	$200	$180	$160	$150

MODEL 98DA/98DAC - 9mm Para. cal., SA/DA, duo-tone finish, 10-shot mag., soft rubber grips with finger grooves, 32 oz. Limited importation since 2002.

	100%	98%	95%	90%	80%	70%	60%
No MSR	$295	$250	$225	$200	$180	$160	$150

ARLINGTON ORDNANCE

Previous importer located in Westport, CT until 1996. Formerly located in Weston, CT.

GRADING - PPGS™	100%	98%	95%	90%	80%	70%	60%

CARBINES & RIFLES: SEMI-AUTO

M1 GARAND RIFLE - .30-06 cal., these Garands were imported from Korea in used condition, various manufacturers, with import stamp. Imported 1991-96.

	$675	$550	$500	$475	$450	$400	$350

Add $40 for stock upgrade (better wood).

* *Arsenal Restored M1 Garand Rifle* - .30-06 or .308 Win. cal., featured new barrel, rebuilt gas system, and reinspected components. Mfg. 1994-96.

	$750	$600	$550	$500	$475	$450	$400

Add 5% for .308 Win. cal.

TROPHY GARAND - .308 Win. cal. only, action was original mil-spec., included new barrel and checkered walnut stock and forend, recoil pad. Mfg. 1994-96.

	$825	$725	$625	$550	$475	$425	$375

Last MSR was $695.

T26 TANKER - .30-06 or .308 Win. cal., included new barrel and other key components, updated stock finish. Mfg. 1994-96.

	$750	$650	$550	$475	$425	$375	$350

.30 CAL. CARBINE - .30 Carbine cal., 18 in. barrel, imported from Korea in used condition, various manufacturers, with import stamp. Imported 1991-1996.

	$625	$550	$475	$425	$375	$325	$300

Add approximately $55 for stock upgrade (better wood).

MODEL FIVE CARBINE - while advertised, this model never went into production.

ARMALITE

Previous manufacturer located in Costa Mesa, CA, approx. 1959-1973.

RIFLES: SEMI-AUTO

AR-7 EXPLORER - .22 LR cal., 16 in. aluminum barrel with steel liner, aperture sight, take down action and barrel stores in hollow plastic stock in either brown (rare), black, or multi-color, gun will float, designed by Gene Stoner, mfg. 1959-73 by Armalite, 1973-90 by Charter Arms, 1990-97 by Survival Arms located in Cocoa, FL and current mfg. beginning 1997 by Henry Repeating Arms Co. located in Brooklyn, NY, and AR-7 Industries, LLG, located in Meriden, CT, starting 1998.

	100%	98%	95%	90%	80%	70%	60%
Black/Multi-color stock	$250	$215	$190	$160	$140	$120	$100
Brown stock	$425	$365	$300	$240	$185	$165	$145

Some unusual early Costa Mesa AR-7 variations have been observed with ported barrels, extendable wire stock, hooded front sight, and hollow pistol grip containing cleaning kit, perhaps indicating a special military contract survival weapon.

AR-7 CUSTOM - similar to AR-7 Explorer, only with custom walnut stock including cheekpiece, pistol grip. Mfg. 1964-70.

	$285	$250	$225	$200	$190	$180	$170

AR-180 - .223 Rem. cal., semi-auto, gas operated, 18 1/4 in. barrel, folding stock. Manufactured by Armalite in Costa Mesa, CA, 1969-1972, Howa Machinery Ltd., Nagoya, Japan 1972 and 1973, and by Sterling Armament Co. Ltd., Dagenham, Essex, England.

	100%	98%	95%	90%	80%	70%	60%
Sterling Mfg.	$1,500	$1,395	$1,250	$1,100	$1,000	$900	$850
Howa Mfg.	$1,950	$1,750	$1,650	$1,500	$1,350	$1,150	$1,000
Costa Mesa Mfg.	$1,950	$1,850	$1,750	$1,600	$1,450	$1,300	$1,200

GRADING - PPGS™	100%	98%	95%	90%	80%	70%	60%

SHOTGUNS: SEMI-AUTO

AR-17 - 12 ga., semi-auto, 24 in. barrel, interchangeable choke tubes, recoil operated, high strength aluminum barrel and receiver, plastic stock and forearm, either gold anodized or black finish. Only 2,000 mfg. 1964-65.

	$750	$575	$475	$400	$350	$295	$200

ARMALITE, INC.

Current manufacturer located in Geneseo, IL. New manufacture began in 1995 after Eagle Arms, Inc. purchased the ArmaLite trademarks. The ArmaLite trademark was originally used by Armalite (no relation to ArmaLite, Inc.) during mfg. in Costa Mesa, CA, approx. 1959-1973 (see Armalite listing above). Dealer and distributor sales.

PISTOLS: SEMI-AUTO

MODEL AR-24 ULTIMATE - 9mm Para. cal., full size (24-15) or compact (24K-13) frame, 10, 13, or 15 shot mag., with or w/o adj. sight, black parkerized finish, checkered polymer grips. Mfg. by Sarzsilmaz in Turkey. Importation began 2007.

MSR $559	$475	$425	$375	$325	$275	$250	$225

Add $70 for adj. sight (C suffix).

RIFLES: BOLT ACTION

AR-30M - .300 Win. Mag., .308 Win., or .338 Lapua cal., scaled down AR-50, repeater, Shilen modified single stage trigger, w/o muzzle brake, 5 shot detachable mag., 26 in. barrel, 12 lbs. New 2003.

MSR $1,460	$1,275	$1,100	$925	$825	$725	$600	$500

Add $155 for .338 Lapua cal.

AR-50 - .50 BMG cal., single shot bolt action with octagonal receiver integrated into a skeletonized aluminum stock with adj. cheekpiece and recoil pad, 31 in. tapered barrel w/o sights and sophisticated muzzle brake (reduces felt recoil to approx. .243 Win. cal.), removable buttstock, right or left-hand action, single stage trigger, 33.2 lbs. New 1999.

MSR $2,999	$2,600	$2,200	$1,900	$1,700	$1,500	$1,250	$1,100

During 2004, this model was produced with a special commemorative stamp notation on the left side of the receiver.

RIFLES: SEMI-AUTO

All ArmaLite semi-auto rifles have a limited lifetime warranty.

Add $100 for stainless steel barrel on those AR-10 models which are available with that option.
Add $180 for National Match trigger where applicable.
Add $100 for black stock, forearm, and pistol grip where applicable.
Add $150 for 100% Realtree Hardwoods or Advantage Classic camo finish.

AR-10 SERIES - semi-auto paramilitary design, various configurations, with or w/o sights and carry handle, choice of standard green, black (new 1999), or camo finish, supplied with two 10 shot mags. (until 2004), current mfg. typically ships with one 10 round and one 20 round mag. New late 1995.

✱ **AR-10B Rifle** - .308 Win. cal., patterned after the early Armalite AR-10 rifle, featuring tapered M16 handguards, pistol grip, distinctive charging bolt on top inside of carry handle (cannot be scoped), original brown color, 20 in. barrel, 9 1/2 lbs. New 1999.

MSR $1,698	$1,495	$1,225	$1,075	$975	$875	$750	$675

GRADING - PPGS™	100%	98%	95%	90%	80%	70%	60%

✴ AR-10T Rifle - .243 Win. (disc. 2003), .300 RSUM (new 2004, Ultra Mag Model), or .308 Win. cal., features 24 in. stainless 1:10 twist heavy barrel, two-stage NM trigger, smooth green or black fiberglass handguard tube, stock, and pistol grip, Picatinny rail, w/o sights or carry handle, 10.4 lbs.

MSR $2,126	$1,860	$1,550	$1,300	$1,100	$995	$875	$750

Add $214 for AR-10T Ultra in .300 RSUM cal.

✴ AR-10T Carbine (Navy Model) - .308 Win. cal., similar to AR-10T Rifle, except has 16 in. stainless barrel and match trigger, 8 1/2 lbs. Disc. 2004.

$1,825	$1,525	$1,275	$1,075	$995	$875	$750

Last MSR was $2,080.

✴ AR-10A4 Rifle (SPR - Special Purpose Rifle) - .243 Win. (disc. 2003) or .308 Win. cal., features 20 in. chrome-lined 1:10 twist barrel, removable front sight, green or black furniture, Picatinny rail, w/o carry handle, approx. 9 lbs.

MSR $1,506	$1,325	$1,075	$900	$800	$700	$600	$525

✴ AR-10A4 Carbine - .308 Win. cal., similar to AR-10A4 Rifle, except has 16 in. barrel, 8.4 lbs.

MSR $1,506	$1,325	$1,075	$900	$800	$700	$600	$525

Add $414 for SIR system (modular receiver sleeving system, mfg. 2004-2006).

✴ AR-10A2 Infantry Model Rifle - .243 Win. (disc. 2003) or .308 Win. cal., features 20 in. chrome-lined 1:10 barrel, includes fixed sights and carry handle, 9.4 lbs.

MSR $1,506	$1,325	$1,075	$900	$800	$700	$600	$525

✴ AR-10A2 Carbine - .308 Win. cal., similar to AR-10A2 Rifle, except has 16 in. barrel, 8.7 lbs.

MSR $1,506	$1,325	$1,075	$900	$800	$700	$600	$525

Add $74 for 4-way quad rail on front of forearm (new 2004).

✴ AR-10SOF (Special Operation Forces) Carbine - .308 Win. cal., available in either A2 or A4 configurations, fixed tube stock, 16 in. barrel, black finish only. Mfg. 2003-2004.

$1,250	$1,075	$900	$800	$700	$600	$525

Last MSR was $1,503.

Add $52 for A2 configuration (includes Picatinny rail).

✴ AR-10 Super SASS Carbine/Rifle - .308 Win. cal., adj. gas system, AAC supressor (military or law enforcement) or mock AAC supressor, floating rail system with rail covers, Magpul adj. buttstock, 20 shot mag., black finish, available with various accessories.

MSR $2,828	$2,400	$2,150	$1,875	$1,525	$1,250	$1,050	$925

M4A1C CARBINE - features 16 in. chrome-lined 1:9 twist heavy barrel with National Match sights and detachable carrying handle, grooved barrel shroud, 7 lbs. Disc. 1997.

$840	$725	$640	$560	$500	$450	$415

Last MSR was $935.

M4C CARBINE - similar to M4A1C Carbine, except has non-removable carrying handle and fixed sights, 7 lbs. Disc. 1997.

$785	$675	$600	$550	$500	$450	$415

Last MSR was $870.

M15 RIFLE/CARBINE VARIATIONS - .223 Rem. cal., various configurations, barrel lengths, sights, and other features.

✴ M15A2 National Match Rifle - features 20 in. stainless steel NM sleeved 1:8 twist barrel with National Match sights and NM two-stage trigger, grooved barrel shroud, 9 lbs.

MSR $1,472	$1,255	$1,050	$875	$775	$675	$595	$525

This model is also available with black stock, forearm, and pistol grip at no extra charge.

GRADING - PPGS™	100%	98%	95%	90%	80%	70%	60%

* **M15A2 Golden Eagle** - similiar to M15A2 National Match Rifle, except has 20 in. heavy barrel, 9.4 lbs. Limited mfg. 1998 only.

	$1,200	$975	$850	$750	$675	$595	$525

Last MSR was $1,350.

* **M15A2 Service Rifle** - includes 20 in. chrome-lined 1:9 twist barrel, fixed sights and carrying handle, 8.2 lbs.

MSR $1,100	$950	$775	$675	$575	$500	$450	$415

* **M15A2 Carbine** - similar to M15A2 Service Rifle, except has 16 in. barrel, 7 lbs.

MSR $1,100	$950	$775	$675	$575	$500	$450	$415

* **M15A4 SPR (Special Purpose Rifle)** - includes 20 in. chrome-lined H-Bar 1:9 twist barrel with National Match sights, Picatinny rail, detachable carry handle, grooved barrel shroud, 7.9 lbs.

MSR $1,100	$950	$775	$675	$575	$500	$450	$415

* **M15A4 Carbine** - similar to M15A4 Special Purpose Rifle, except has 16 in. barrel, 7 lbs.

MSR $1,100	$950	$775	$675	$575	$500	$450	$415

Subtract $60 for fixed front sight w/detachable carry handle.

* **M15A4 SPR II National Match (Special Purpose Rifle)** - similar to M15A4 SPR, except has triple lapped rifled barrel, strengthed floating barrel sleeve and two-stage match trigger, green or black furniture. Mfg. 2003-2005.

	$1,250	$1,050	$875	$800	$700	$600	$500

Last MSR was $1,472.

* **M15SOF (Special Operation Forces) Carbine** - .223 Rem. cal., available in either A2 or A4 configurations, fixed tube stock, 16 in. barrel, black finish only. Mfg. 2003-2004.

	$950	$775	$675	$600	$525	$475	$450

Last MSR was $1,084.

Add $69 for A2 configuration (includes Picatinny rail).

* **M15ARTN** - .223 Rem. cal., 20 in. stainless steel barrel, National Match trigger, green or black finish. New 2004.

MSR $1,322	$1,130	$925	$825	$700	$600	$500	$450

* **M15A4T Rifle (Eagle Eye)** - 24 in. stainless steel 1:8 twist heavy barrel, two-stage trigger, smooth green or black fiberglass hand guard, Picatinny front sight rail but w/o sights and carrying handle, 9.2 lbs. Disc. 2005, reintroduced 2007.

MSR $1,504	$1,325	$1,075	$900	$800	$700	$600	$525

* **M15A4T Carbine (Eagle Eye)** - features 16 in. stainless steel 1:9 twist heavy barrel, picatinny rail, smooth fiberglass handguard tube, two-stage trigger, 7.1 lbs. Mfg. 1997-2004.

	$1,225	$995	$850	$775	$675	$595	$525

Last MSR was $1,383.

* **M15A4 Predator** - similar to M15A4T Eagle Eye, except has 1:12 twist barrel. Disc. 1996.

	$1,215	$985	$850	$750	$675	$595	$525

Last MSR was $1,350.

* **M15A4 Action Master** - includes 20 in. stainless steel 1:9 twist barrel, two-stage trigger, muzzle brake, Picatinny flattop design w/o sights or carrying handle, 9 lbs. Disc. 1997.

	$1,050	$900	$800	$700	$625	$565	$500

Last MSR was $1,175.

GRADING - PPGS™	100%	98%	95%	90%	80%	70%	60%

AR-180B - .223 Rem. cal., polymer lower receiver with formed sheet metal upper, standard AR-15 trigger group/magazine, incorporates the best features of the M15 (lower group with trigger and mag. well) and early AR-180 (gas system allowing operating gases to be kept outside the receiver) rifles, 19.8 in. barrel with integral muzzle brake, 6 lbs. New 2003.

MSR $750	$675	$600	$525	$475	$425	$400	$375

For more information on the original ArmaLite AR-180 and variations, please refer to the previous ArmaLite listing.

ARMAMENT TECHNOLOGY

Previous firearms manufacturer located in Halifax, Nova Scotia, Canada 1988-2003.

Armament Technology discontinued making bolt action rifles in 2003. Currently, the company is distributing optical rifle sights only.

RIFLES: BOLT-ACTION

AT1-C24 TACTICAL RIFLE - .308 Win. or .300 Win. Mag. (disc. 2000) cal., similar to AT1-M24, except has detachable mag., adj. cheekpiece and buttstock for LOP, includes 3.5-10X 30mm tactical scope and Mil-Spec shipping case, 1/2" MOA guaranteed, 14.9 lbs. Mfg. 1998-2003.

		$4,095	$3,650	$2,775	$2,250	$1,825	$1,500	$1,275

Last MSR was $4,195.

AT1-C24B TACTICAL RIFLE - .308 Win. cal., similar to AT1-C24, except is not available in left-hand, 15.9 lbs. Mfg. 2001-2003.

		$4,250	$3,750	$2,850	$2,300	$1,850	$1,525	$1,300

Last MSR was $4,695.

AT1-M24 TACTICAL RIFLE - .223 Rem. (new 1998), .308 Win., or .300 Win. Mag. (disc. 2000) cal., bolt action, tactical rifle with competition tuned right-hand or left-hand Rem. 700 action, stainless steel barrel, Kevlar reinforced fiberglass stock, Harris bipod, matte black finish, competition trigger, 1/2" MOA guaranteed, 14.9 lbs. Disc. 2003.

		$4,350	$3,850	$2,850	$2,350	$1,900	$1,600	$1,350

Last MSR was $4,495.

ARMAMENT TECHNOLOGY CORP.

Previous manufacturer located in Las Vegas, NV between 1972 and 1978.

RIFLES: SEMI-AUTO

In addition to the models listed below, ATC also manufactured a select fire pistol named "Firefly II."

MODEL 4 POCKET RIFLE - .22 LR cal., semi-auto action (supplied by Mossberg), 5 in. barrel, shortened rifle (18 1/2 in. overall length) with cut stock, 7-shot mag., approx. 450 mfg., approx. 3 lbs.

	$350	$295	$260	$230	$195	$175	$150

MODEL 6 - full length variation of the Model 4, Mossberg Model 453-T with ATC trademarks, approx. 12 mfg., approx. 5 1/2 lbs.

	$125	$100	$85	$75	$65	$55	$45

M-2 FIREFLY - 9mm Para. cal., featured a unique gas delayed blowback action, paramilitary configuration, collapsible stock, very limited mfg., 4 3/4 lbs.

	$695	$625	$550	$475	$395	$350	$295

GRADING - PPGS™	100%	98%	95%	90%	80%	70%	60%

ARMAS AZOR, S.A.

Previous manufacturer of double rifles located in Eibar, Spain. Previously imported 1994-1997 by Armes De Chasse located in Hertford, NC.

RIFLES: SxS, SIDELOCK

The models listed below are English styled sidelock double rifles. Gold inlay and custom engraving prices were quoted per individual request.

AFRICA MARK I - available in most cals. between 9.3 X 74R and .375 H&H, nominal engraving and select grade wood.

Previous retail prices ranged between $8,000 and $10,000.

AFRICA MARK II - available in most cals. between 9.3 X 74R and .375 H&H, African game scene engraving and superior grade wood.

Previous retail prices ranged between $10,000 and $12,000.

AFRICA MARK III - available in most cals. between 9.3 X 74R and .470 NE Mag., intricate scroll engraving, cartridge trap, top tang, and superior quality grade wood.

Previous retail prices ranged between $13,000 and $18,000.

SHOTGUNS: SxS, SIDELOCK

SIDELOCK MODEL - 12 ga.-.410 bore, English-style sidelock game gun.

$3,275	$2,700	$2,200	$1,750	$1,500	$1,250	$995

Last MSR was $3,500.

ARMERIA DE MADRID, LA

Current long gun manufacturer located in Madrid, Spain. No current U.S. importation.

La Armeria manufactures high quality bolt action rifles based on the Mauser 98 action in .270 Win., .30-06, 9.3x62mm, .375 H&H, .338 Win. Mag., .300 Win. Mag., or .416 Rigby cal. Many options are available and prices start at $18,000. Single shot rifles are available beginning at $20,000. Express double rifles come in a variety of options and configurations, and are available in pairs beginning at $30,000.

La Armeria also manufactures high quality SxS shotguns in 12, 16, 20, 28 ga. or .410 bore, with fine exhibition quality wood and hand engraving in a variety of styles. Prices begin at $30,000 for a pair.

Please contact the company for available options, a price quotation, and delivery time (see Trademark Index).

ARMES DE CHASSE LLC

Current importer and distributor located in Norfolk, VA. Previously located in Hertford, NC.

SHOTGUNS: SxS

ALBEMARLE GAME GUN SIDELOCK - 12, 16 (special order only), 20, 28 ga., or .410 bore (new 2001), H&H style detachable sidelock action, Purdey style bolt, DT with articulated front trigger, 26, 27, or 28 in. barrels with concave solid rib, ejectors, checkered oil finished walnut English or pistol grip stock and forearm (base price includes custom stock dimensions), extensive lockplate engraving, 5 3/4 (20 ga.) or 6 7/8 (12 ga.) lbs. Spanish importation from 1999-2005.

$3,100	$2,650	$2,195	$1,800	$1,500	$1,200	$995

Last MSR was $3,525.

Add 10% for 28 ga. or .410 bore.
Add $1,050 for extra set of barrels.
Add $1,525 for Grade A fine scroll engraving.
Add $1,330 for Grade A black and gold option (mfg. 2000-2003).
Add $1,310 for Grade B ribbon and scroll engraving.
Add $1,100 Grade C game scene engraving.
Add $135 for left-hand.

GRADING - PPGS™	100%	98%	95%	90%	80%	70%	60%

ALBEMARLE GAME GUN BOXLOCK - 12, 16 (special order only), 20, 28 ga., or .410 bore, H&H style boxlock action, DT, ejectors, old silver or case hardened action, beavertail or semi-beavertail forend available. Importation began 2003.

	$2,350	$2,150	$1,875	$1,525	$1,200	$995	$875

Last MSR was $2,635.

Add $135 for left-hand.
Add 10% for 28 ga.or .410 bore.

ARMES PIERRE ARTISAN ETS. (P. CHAPUIS)

Previous manufacturer located in St. Bonnet Le Chateau, France.

Armes Pierre Artisan manufactured high quality double rifles and shotguns on a custom order basis. Each gun should be appraised individually, and values will depend on the quality and desirability of the custom features.

ARMI PERUGINI-VISINI

Please refer to P section.

ARMI SALVINELLI

Current manufacturer established in 1975, and located in Marcheno, Italy. Currently imported by Cherry's, located in Greensboro, NC.

Armi Salvinelli manufactures high quality O/U competition and hunting shotguns. Please contact the importer directly for more information, including pricing and availability (see Trademark Index).

ARMI SAN PAOLO

Previous manufacturer located in Concesio, Italy.

During 2002, Armi San Paolo changed its name to Euroarms Italia. Please refer to Euroarms Italia listing for current information.

REVOLVERS

Armi San Paolo manufactured double action .22 and .38 cal. revolvers in both 2 and 6 in. barrel lengths. These revolvers were manufactured in Concesio, Italy under license from J.P. Sauer & Sohn. Assuming 95%+ condition, these handguns are currently priced in the $150-$225 range.

ARMI SPORT

Current manufacturer established in 1958, and located in Brescia, Italy. Currently distributed by various U.S. companies (please refer to Trademark Index).

Armi Sport also manufactures a complete line of percussion and flintlock blackpowder reproductions and replicas, including both pistols and rifles. For more information on these replicas, please refer to the *Blue Book of Modern Black Powder Arms* by John Allen.

RIFLES: REPRODUCTIONS

Armi Sport manufactures top quality reproductions of famous rifles/carbines, including the Model 1874 Deluxe Sharps Sporting rifle in various configurations and cals., including .45-70, the Model 1865 Spencer Carbine in .45 Schofield, .44 Russian, or .56-50 cal., and the Model 1892 lever action takedown rifle and carbine. Please refer to the distributors listing for current information on these models, including U.S. pricing and availability (see Trademark Index).

ARMINEX LTD.

Previous manufacturer located in Scottsdale, AZ.

PISTOLS: SEMI-AUTO

TRI-FIRE - .45 ACP cal., single action auto, interchangeable barrels allow caliber conversion. Available in 5, 6, or 7 (disc. 1984) in. stainless barrel lengths, no grip safety, steel frame construction, ambidextrous thumb safety (on Target

GRADING - PPGS™	100%	98%	95%	90%	80%	70%	60%

and Presentation only), smooth walnut grips, 38 oz. Approx. 400 mfg. between 1981 and 1985.

	$750	$650	$475	$400	$375	$350	$325

Last MSR was $396.

Add $50 if presentation cased.
Add approx. $130/conversion unit.

✳ *Tri-Fire Target Model* - same specifications as Tri-Fire, except has 6 or 7 (disc. 1984) in. barrel. Very limited mfg.

	$850	$725	$550	$450	$400	$360	$330

Last MSR was $448.

ARMINIUS

Current trademark of revolvers manufactured by Weihrach, located in Mellrichstadt, Germany. No current U.S. importation. Previously manufactured in Zella-Mehlis, Germany beginning circa 1922 through the mid-1970s.

PISTOLS: SINGLE SHOT

MODEL 1 - .22 LR cal., target model, adj. sights.

	$275	$210	$195	$165	$155	$140	$110

MODEL 2 - similar to Model 1, except has set trigger.

	$340	$255	$225	$190	$170	$155	$140

REVOLVERS

Currently manufactured Arminius revolvers are not individually listed, since they are not currently imported into the U.S. There are however, many models, including combat, sport, and target variations. Calibers include .22 LR. .22 Mag., .32 S&W Wadcutter, .357 Mag., and .38 Spl.

MODEL 3 - .25 ACP cal., folding trigger, hammerless.

	$175	$135	$125	$105	$100	$90	$80

MODEL 8 - .320 Revolver cal., folding trigger, hammerless.

	$175	$135	$125	$105	$100	$90	$80

MODEL 9 - .32 ACP cal.

	$185	$140	$130	$115	$105	$95	$85

MODEL 10 - .32 ACP cal., hammerless.

	$165	$125	$120	$100	$95	$85	$75

TARGET - .22 LR cal.

	$90	$70	$65	$55	$50	$45	$45

ARMITAGE INTERNATIONAL, LTD.

Previous manufacturer until 1990 located in Seneca, SC.

PISTOLS: SEMI-AUTO

SCARAB SKORPION - 9mm Para. Cal., paramilitary design patterned after the Czech Model 61, direct blow back action, 4.63 in. barrel, matte black finish, 12 shot (standard) or 32 shot (optional) mag., 3 1/2 lbs. Mfg. in U.S. 1989-90 only.

	$625	$550	$475	$400	$350	$300	$260

Last MSR was $400.

Add $45 for threaded flash hider or imitation suppressor.
Only 602 Scarab Skorpions were manufactured during 1989-90.

ARMORY USA L.L.C.

Current manufacturer/importer located in Houston, TX. Previous company name was Arsenal USA LLC.

RIFLES: SEMI-AUTO

Armory USA, LLC produces a variety of AK-47/AKM/AK-74 semi-auto rifles. Early rifles used Bulgarian milled receivers, later versions were built using sheet metal receivers made in Hungary by FEG.

During 2004, Armory USA began production of 1.6mm thick U.S. made AK receivers, which are sold as both receivers and complete rifles. Production of 1mm thick receivers began in Jan. 2005. Models not listed here may have been assembled by other manufacturers using these receivers. During 2004, Armory USA began assembling rifles at a new factory in Kazanlak, Bulgaria. Some components are made in the U.S., in compliance with the BATF. Please refer to the Arsenal USA listing for pre-2004 manufactured/imported rifles.

MODEL SSR-56-2 - 7.62x39mm cal., Armory USA made 1.6mm receiver wall thickness, Poly-Tec barrel assembly, Bulgarian internal parts. Approx. 400 mfg. during 2004.

	$575	$500	$450	$400	$350	$300	$250

Last MSR was $500.

MODEL AMD-63-2 UP - 7.62x39mm cal., Armory USA made 1.6mm receiver wall thickness, Hungarian parts, underfolding buttstock. Approx. 125 mfg. 2004.

	$700	$650	$600	$500	$450	$400	$350

Last MSR was $600.

MODEL SSR-85C-2 - 7.62x39mm cal., assembled in Bulgaria, marked "ISD Ltd", blond wood and black polymer furniture. Imported beginning 2004.

MSR $550	$500	$450	$400	$300	$250	$200	$150

Add $100 for sidefolding buttstock (Model SSR-85C-2 SF).

MODEL SSR-74-2 - 5.45x39mm cal., assembled in Bulgaria, marked "ISD Ltd", blond wood and black polymer furniture. Imported beginning 2005.

MSR $550	$500	$450	$400	$300	$250	$200	$150

ARMS CORPORATION OF THE PHILIPPINES

Please refer to the Armscor listing in this section.

ARMS MORAVIA, LTD.

Current European importer/exporter of firearms and accessories located in Ostrava, Czech Republic. Previously imported into the United States by Anderson & Richardson Arms Co., located in Ft. Worth, TX until 2001.

Arms Moravia Ltd. exports a wide variety of European trademarks, including their own line of pistols.

ARMS RESEARCH ASSOCIATES

Previous manufacturer until 1991, located in Stone Park, IL.

CARBINES: SEMI-AUTO

KF SYSTEM - 9mm Para. cal., paramilitary design carbine, 18 1/2 in. barrel, vent. barrel shroud, 20- or 36-shot mag., matte black finish, 7 1/2 lbs., select fire-class III transferable only.

	$395	$350	$300	$275	$250	$230	$210

Last MSR was $379.

ARMS TECH LTD.

Previous manufacturer located in Phoenix, AZ 1987-1998.

RIFLES: SEMI-AUTO

SUPER MATCH INTERDICTION POLICE MODEL - .243 Win., .300 Win. Mag., or .308 Win. (standard) cal., features 22 in. free floating Schnieder or Douglas air gauged stainless steel barrel, gas operation, McMillan stock, updated trigger group, detachable box mag., 13 1/4 lbs. Limited mfg. 1996-98.

$3,950	$3,650	$3,300	$3,000	$2,750	$2,350	$2,000

Last MSR was $4,800.

ARMSAN

Current shotgun manufacturer located in Istanbul, Turkey.

Armsan manufactures good quality O/U, SxS and semi-auto shotguns. Armsan is currently making a private label 20 ga. semi-auto shotgun for Mossberg. Please contact the company directly for more information, including pricing and U.S. availability (see Trademark Index).

ARMSCO

Previous North American importer and distributor of Huglu shotguns located in Des Plaines, IL. Please refer to the Huglu section for more information.

ARMSCOR

Current trademark of firearms manufactured by Arms Corporation of the Philippines (manufacturing began 1952) established in 1995. Currently imported and distributed by Armscor Precision International (full line), located in Las Vegas, NV beginning 2001, and by K.B.I., Inc. located in Harrisburg, PA beginning 1995. Previously imported by Ruko located in Buffalo, NY until 1995 and by Armscorp Precision Inc. located in San Mateo, CA until 1991.

In 1991, the importation of Arms Corporation of the Philippines firearms was changed to Ruko Products, Inc., located in Buffalo, NY. Barrel markings on firearms imported by Ruko Products, Inc. state "Ruko-Armscor" instead of the older "Armscorp Precision" barrel markings. All Armscorp Precision, Inc. models were discontinued in 1991.

The models listed below also provide cross-referencing for older Armscorp Precision and Ruko imported models.

PISTOLS: SEMI-AUTO

M-1911-A1 FS (FULL SIZE STANDARD) - .45 ACP cal., patterned after the Colt Govt. Model, 7-shot mag. (2 provided), 5 in. barrel, parkerized (disc. 2001), blue (new 2002), two-tone (new 2002), or stainless steel (new 2002), skeletonized combat hammer and trigger, front and rear slide serrations, hard rubber grips, 38 oz. Imported 1996-97, reintroduced 2001.

MSR $399		$350	$300	$280	$260	$240	$220	$200

Add $31 for two-tone finish.
Add $75 for stainless steel.

This model is also available in a high capacity configuration (Model 1911-A2 HC, 13 shot mag., $519 MSR).

M-1911-A1 MS (COMMANDER) - .45 ACP cal., Commander configuration with 4 in. barrel, otherwise similar to M-1911 A1 Standard, rear slide serrations only. Importation began 2001.

MSR $408		$360	$300	$280	$260	$240	$220	$200

Add $37 for two-tone finish.
Add $90 for stainless steel.

GRADING - PPGS™	100%	98%	95%	90%	80%	70%	60%

M-1911-A1 CS (OFFICER) - .45 ACP cal., officer's configuration with 3 1/2 in. barrel, checkered hardwood grips, 2.16 lbs. Importation began 2002.

MSR $423	$370	$310	$285	$265	$245	$220	$200

   Add $52 for two-tone finish.
   Add $105 for stainless steel.

M-1911-A1 MEDALLION SERIES - 9mm Para., .40 S&W, or .45 ACP cal., 5 in. barrel, customized model including many shooting enhancements, match barrel, hand fitted slide and frame, choice of checkered wood or Pachmayr grips, available in either Standard or Tactical variation, blue, two-tone or chrome finish. Importation began 2002.

MSR $539	$445	$350	$310	$285	$260	$240	$220

   Add $129 for Tactical Model, add $198 for Tactical Model two-tone, or $203 for Tactical Model chrome.

REVOLVERS

MODEL 200 (DC) REVOLVER - .38 Spl. cal., 6 shot, double action, 2 1/2 (importation disc.), 4 (new 1998) or 6 (new 1998, importation disc.) in. barrel with shroud, transfer bar safety, combat style rubber grips, blue finish only, fixed rear sight, 26 oz. Imported 1996-99, reintroduced 2001.

MSR $156	$145	$125	$105	$90	$75	$65	$60

   Add approx. $6 for 4 in. barrel or $16 for 6 in. barrel (disc.)

MODEL 202 REVOLVER - similar to Model 200, except does not have barrel shroud. Importation began 2001.

MSR $156	$135	$115	$100	$85	$75	$65	$60

MODEL 206 REVOLVER - similar to Model 200, except has 2 in. barrel, 24 oz. Importation began 2001.

MSR $180	$160	$125	$105	$90	$75	$65	$60

MODEL 210 REVOLVER - similar to Model 200, except has 4 in. VR barrel, and adj. rear sight, 28 oz. Importation began 2001.

MSR $196	$175	$150	$125	$105	$90	$75	$65

RIFLES: BOLT ACTION

M-12Y/12-TY - .22 LR cal., bolt action, single shot, youth model with 18 3/8 in. barrel. Imported 1997 only, reintroduced during 2001.

	$95	$80	$70	$60	$50	$40	$35

Last MSR was $109.

M-14P - .22 LR cal., bolt action, 10-shot mag., 23 in. barrel, open sights, hooded bead ramp front sight and leaf type rear sight, 6 lbs. Disc. 1997.

	$95	$75	$60	$50	$45	$40	$35

Last MSR was $129.

   A youth model was also available with shorter dimensions at no extra charge (M-14Y).

   ✳ *M-14-D* - .22 LR cal., bolt action, similar to M-14P, except has adj. rear sight and checkered mahogany stock. Importation disc. 1995.

	$105	$85	$70	$60	$50	$45	$40

Last MSR was $139.

M-1400LW - .22 LR cal., similar action to M-14P, except has checkered stock and Schnabel forend, 10-shot mag., hard rubber pad, 6 lbs. Imported 1990-92.

	$185	$165	$150	$135	$120	$105	$95

Last MSR was $219.

✳ *M-1400S* - .22 LR cal., similar to M-1500(S), except has 10-shot mag., 6.7 lbs. Imported 1996-97.

	100%	98%	95%	90%	80%	70%	60%
	$175	$125	$100	$75	$65	$55	$50

Last MSR was $224.

✳ *M-1400 (SC-Super Classic)* - .22 LR cal., otherwise similar to M-1500SC, except has 10-shot mag. and 23 in. barrel, 6 lbs. Imported 1990-97, reintroduced 2001.

MSR $242	$200	$150	$110	$85	$70	$60	$55

Add $18 for stainless steel construction (new 2002).

✳ *M-1400E* - .22 LR cal., 6- or 10-shot mag., similar to M-1400, except has checkered stock and Scnabel forend, hard rubber pad, fiber optic front sight and adj. rear sight. Importation began 2004.

As this edition went to press, prices had yet to be established on this model.

✳ *M-1400 Sportster* - .22 LR cal., similar to M-1400E, except has competition type stock and scalloped forearm, Monte Carlo style butt with cheekpiece. Importation began 2004.

As this edition went to press, prices had yet to be established on this model.

M-1500S - .22 Mag. cal., deluxe bolt action, 5-shot mag., 21 1/2 or 22 5/8 in. barrel, checkered mahogany stock, open sights, 7 lbs. Disc. 1997, reintroduced 2001.

	$145	$125	$110	$95	$85	$75	$65

Last MSR was $160.

✳ *M-1500LW (Lightweight)* - similar to M-1500, except has lightweight classic European styled stock made of checkered American Walnut, with buttpad. Imported 1990-92.

	$190	$170	$150	$135	$120	$105	$95

Last MSR was $229.

✳ *M-1500 (SC-Super Classic)* - checkered American Walnut stock with hard rubber pad and Monte Carlo cheekpiece, hardwood forend tip, engine turned bolt, 7 lbs. Imported 1990-97, reintroduced 2001.

MSR $260	$215	$165	$120	$100	$85	$70	$60

Subtract $3 for stainless steel.

M-1800S (CLASSIC) - .22 Hornet cal., 5-shot mag., double locking lugs, checkered hardwood stock, adj. rear sight, 6.6 lbs. Imported 1996-97.

	$250	$225	$200	$180	$165	$150	$135

Last MSR was $358.

✳ *M-1800SC (Super Classic)* - similar to M-1800S, except has checkered walnut stock with forend tip, and high polish bluing, 7 1/4 lbs. Imported 1996-97, reintroduced during 2001.

	$285	$260	$240	$220	$200	$185	$170

Last MSR was $323.

RIFLES: SEMI-AUTO

M-1600 - .22 LR cal., semi-auto, 10- or 15- (disc.) shot mag., 18 in. barrel, copy of the Armalite M16, ebony stock, 5 1/4 lbs.

MSR $205	$170	$130	$100	$80	$65	$55	$50

✳ *M-1600R* - similar to M-1600, except has stainless steel retractable buttstock and vent. barrel hood, 7 1/4 lbs. Importation disc. 1995.

	$155	$115	$95	$75	$65	$55	$50

Last MSR was $199.

M-20 - .22 LR cal., 10-shot mag., deluxe checkered hardwood stock and forend, blue or stainless steel. Importation began 2002.

MSR $245	$205	$155	$110	$85	$70	$60	$55

Add $15 for stainless steel construction (new 2002).

M-20P - .22 LR cal., semi-auto, 15-shot mag., 20 3/4 in. barrel, open sights, 5 1/2 lbs. Disc. 1997, reintroduced during 2001.

	$100	$80	$60	$50	$45	$40	$35

Last MSR was $120.

✱ **M-20C** - similar to M-20P, except has carbine style stock, barrel band, and curved steel buttplate, 16 1/2 in. barrel, 5 1/4 lbs. Previously available from K.B.I. only, disc. 2001.

	$130	$100	$80	$60	$50	$45	$40

Last MSR was $159.

✱ **M-20D** - .22 LR cal., 22 in. barrel, 10- or 15-shot mag., checkered hardwood stock and forend, 6 1/2 lbs. Importation began 2002.

MSR $245	$205	$155	$110	$85	$70	$60	$55

Add $15 for stainless steel construction (new 2002).

M-2000(S) - same specifications as M-20P, except has checkered mahogany stock and adj. rear sight. Disc. 1997.

	$140	$120	$95	$75	$60	$55	$50

Last MSR was $213.

✱ **M-2000SC (Super Classic)** - similar to M-2000, except has checkered American Walnut stock with cheekpiece and hardwood forend tip, engine turned bolt, 6 lbs. Imported 1990-97.

	$270	$215	$175	$140	$110	$95	$85

Last MSR was $340.

M-50S - .22 LR cal., semi-auto design, 16 1/2 in. shrouded barrel, 25- or 30-shot mag., uncheckered mahogany stock, 6 1/2 lbs. Disc. 1995.

	$155	$115	$95	$75	$65	$50	$45

Last MSR was $209.

M-AK22(S) - .22 LR cal., semi-auto, copy of the famous Russian Kalashnikov AK-47 rifle, 18 1/2 in. barrel, 10- or 15- (disc.) shot mag., mahogany stock and forearm, 7 lbs.

MSR $224	$185	$165	$145	$120	$95	$85	$80

✱ **M-AK22(F)** - similar to M-AK22, except has metal folding stock, and 30-shot mag. Disc. 1995.

	$275	$225	$185	$150	$115	$95	$80

Last MSR was $299.

SHOTGUNS: SLIDE ACTION

M-30 F (INTERCHANGEABLE CHOKES) - 12 ga. only, 28 in. plain barrel with 3 choke tubes, 5-shot mag., uncheckered stock and forearm. Disc. 1999.

	$225	$190	$160	$140	$120	$95	$85

Last MSR was $269.

✱ **M-30 D/IC (Deluxe)** - similar to Model M30 IC, except has checkered walnut stock and forearm with recoil pad. Importation reintroduced during 2001 only.

	$180	$155	$125	$110	$95	$85	$75

Last MSR was $208.

M-30 DG (DEER GUN) - 12 ga. only, law enforcement version of M-30, 20 in. plain barrel, iron sights, 7-shot mag., approx. 7 lbs. Disc. 1999, reintroduced during 2001.

	$165	$140	$120	$100	$85	$75	$70

Last MSR was $195.

M-30SAS1 - 12 ga. only, riot configuration with 20 in. barrel and vent. barrel shroud, and speedfeed 4-shot (disc.) or regular synthetic buttstock and forearm, 6-shot mag., matte finish, 8 lbs. Mfg. 1996-99, reintroduced 2001.

MSR $211	$180	$155	$130	$110	$95	$85	$75

Add $56 for Speedfeed stock (new 2002).

M-30 R6/R8 (RIOT) - 12 ga. only, similar to M-30DG, except has front bead sight only, 5- or 7-shot mag., cyl. bore. Disc. 1999, reintroduced 2001.

MSR $181	$155	$135	$110	$90	$80	$75	$70

Add $7 for 7 shot mag.

M-30BG - 12 ga. only, 18 1/2 in. barrel, 5-shot mag., polymer pistol grip and forearm. Importation began 2004.

As this edition went to press, prices had yet to be established on this model.

M-30F/FS - similar to M-30BG, except has additional folding metal stock unit.

MSR $211	$180	$155	$130	$110	$95	$85	$75

M30 C (COMBO) - 12 ga., 20 in. barrel, 5-shot mag., unique detachable black synthetic buttstock that separates, allowing pistol grip only operation. Disc. 1995.

	$210	$175	$145	$120	$100	$90	$80

Last MSR was $289.

M30 RP (COMBO) - 12 ga. only, same action as M-30 DG, interchangeable black pistol grip, 18 1/4 in. plain barrel w/front bead sight, 6 1/4 lbs. Disc. 1995.

	$210	$175	$145	$120	$100	$90	$80

Last MSR was $289.

ARMSCORP USA, INC.

Previous manufacturer and importer located in Baltimore, MD. Currently Armscorp USA deals in parts only.

PISTOLS: SEMI-AUTO

HI POWER - 9mm Para. cal., patterned after Browning design, 4 2/3 in. barrel, military finish, 13-shot mag., synthetic checkered grips, spur hammer, 2 lbs. mfg. in Argentina, imported 1989-90 only.

	$395	$350	$295	$275	$250	$225	$200

Last MSR was $450.

Add $15 for round hammer.
Add $50 for hard chrome finish w/combat grips (disc. 1989).

✳ *Hi Power Compact Detective HP* - similar to Hi Power, except has 3 1/2 in. barrel, 1.9 lbs. Mfg. 1989 only.

	$395	$350	$295	$275	$250	$225	$200

Last MSR was $475.

SD-9 - 9mm Para. cal., double action only, blowback mechanism, 3.07 in. barrel, 6-shot mag., frame is fabricated mostly of heavy gauge sheet metal stampings, chamber indicator, limited Israeli mfg., 1 1/2 lbs. Imported 1989-90 only.

	$350	$250	$230	$210	$195	$180	$170

Last MSR was $350.

This pistol has also been manufactured by Sirkis Industries - refer to their section.

GRADING - PPGS™	100%	98%	95%	90%	80%	70%	60%

P22 - .22 LR cal., patterned after the Colt Woodsman, 4 or 6 in. barrel, 10-shot mag., checkered wood grips, mfg. in Argentina. Imported 1989-90 only.

	$190	$150	$130	$115	$100	$95	$85

Last MSR was $225.

RIFLES: SEMI-AUTO

M-14 RIFLE (NORINCO PARTS) - .308 Win. cal., 20-shot mag., newly mfg. M-14 using Norinco parts, wood stock. Mfg. 1991-92 only.

	$925	$850	$750	$675	$575	$475	$375

Last MSR was $688.

M-14R RIFLE (USGI PARTS) - .308 Win. cal., 10- (C/B 1994) or 20*-shot mag., newly manufactured M-14 using original excellent condition forged G.I. parts including USGI fiberglass stock with rubber recoil pad. Mfg. 1986-2006.

	$1,625	$1,375	$1,100	$975	$825	$700	$550

Last MSR was $1,895.

Add $80 for medium weight National Match walnut stock (M-14RNS).
Add $25 for G.I. buttplate (disc.).
Add $45 for USGI birch stock (M-14RNSB, disc.).

M-14 BEGINNING NATIONAL MATCH - .308 Win. cal., mfg. from hand selected older USGI parts, except for new receiver and new USGI air gauged premium barrel, guaranteed to shoot 1 1/4 in. group at 100 yards. Mfg. 1993-96.

	$1,750	$1,350	$1,050	$925	$825	$725	$625

Last MSR was $1,950.

M-14 NMR (NATIONAL MATCH) - .308 Win. cal., built in accordance with A.M.T.U. mil. specs., 3 different barrel weights to choose from, NM rear sight system, calibrated mag., leather sling, guaranteed 1 MOA. Mfg. 1987-2006.

	$2,425	$1,875	$1,500	$1,150	$950	$825	$700

Last MSR was $2,850.

M-21 MATCH RIFLE - .308 Win. cal., NM rear lugged receiver, choice of McMillan fiberglass or laminated wood stock, guaranteed 1 MOA.

	$3,125	$2,550	$1,975	$1,650	$1,300	$995	$825

Last MSR was $3,595.

T-48 FAL ISRAELI PATTERN RIFLE - .308 Win. cal., mfg. in the U.S. to precise original metric dimensions (parts are interchangeable with original Belgium FAL), forged receiver, hammer forged chrome lined mil-spec. 21 in. barrel (standard or heavy) with flash suppressor, adj. front sight, aperture rear sight, 10 lbs. Imported 1990-92.

	$1,325	$1,150	$975	$825	$750	$650	$550

Last MSR was $1,244.

This model was guaranteed to shoot within 2.5 MOA with match ammunition.

* *T-48 FAL L1A1 Pattern* - .308 Win. cal., fully enclosed forend with vents, 10 lbs. Imported 1992 only.

	$1,325	$1,150	$975	$825	$750	$650	$550

Last MSR was $1,181.

Add $122 for wood handguard sporter model (limited supply).

T-48 BUSH MODEL - similar to T-48 FAL, except has 18 in. barrel, 9 3/4 lbs. Mfg. 1990 only.

	$1,225	$1,050	$925	$775	$625	$525	$465

Last MSR was $1,250.

FRHB - .308 Win. cal., Israeli mfg. with heavy barrel and bipod. Imported 1990 only.

	100%	98%	95%	90%	80%	70%	60%
	$1,725	$1,450	$1,150	$975	$875	$795	$725

Last MSR was $1,895.

FAL - .308 Win. cal., Armscorp forged receiver, 21 in. Argentinian rebuilt barrel, manufactured to military specs., supplied with one military 20-shot mag., aperture rear sight, 10 lbs. Mfg. 1987-89.

	$1,425	$1,200	$1,050	$875	$750	$650	$550

Last MSR was $875.

> **Subtract $55 if without flash hider.**
> **Add $75 for heavy barrel with bipod (14 lbs.).**
> **Add $400 (last retail) for .22 LR conversion kit.**
> This model was guaranteed to shoot within 2.5 MOA with match ammunition.

✳ *FAL Bush Model* - similar to FAL, except has 18 in. barrel with flash suppressor, 9 3/4 lbs. Mfg. 1989 only.

	$1,950	$1,800	$1,675	$1,575	$1,500	$1,250	$1,000

Last MSR was $900.

✳ *FAL Para Model* - similar to FAL Bush Model, except has metal folding stock, leaf rear sight. Mfg. 1989 only.

	$2,150	$1,900	$1,800	$1,700	$1,500	$1,400	$1,300

Last MSR was $930.

✳ *FAL Factory Rebuilt* - factory (Argentine) rebuilt FAL without flash suppressor in excellent condition with Armscorp forged receiver, 9 lbs. 10 oz. Disc. 1989.

	$1,475	$1,250	$995	$825	$750	$575	$495

Last MSR was $675.

> **Add 20% for heavy barrel variation manufactured in Argentina under license from F.N.**

M36 ISRAELI SNIPER RIFLE - .308 Win. cal., gas operated semi-auto, Bullpup configuration, 22 in. free floating barrel, Armscorp M14 receiver, 20-shot mag., includes flash suppressor and bipod, 10 lbs. Civilian offering 1989 only.

	$2,900	$2,500	$2,275	$2,050	$1,900	$1,775	$1,600

Last MSR was $3,000.

EXPERT MODEL - .22 LR cal., semi-auto, 20.9 in. barrel, 10-shot mag., wood stock with one-screw takedown, iron sights with grooved receiver, 5.1 lbs. New 1989.

	$195	$150	$125	$115	$105	$95	$85

Last MSR was $225.

ARM SPORT LLC

Current conversion manufacturer and customizer located in Eastlake, CO.

Gunsmith R.L. Millington specializes in authentic, hand-built conversions of Colt and Remington black powder pistols to metallic cartridge, custom engraving, refinishing, and antique refinishing.

CARTRIDGE CONVERSIONS

All prices listed are for conversion work only. Current calibers include .32 S&W Short, .38 S&W, .38 LC, .38 Spl., .44-40 WCF, and .45 LC. Antiquing and period-style engraving are options. Currently, Arms Sport LLC is charging $875 for converting the 1839 Texas Paterson, Colt Pocket Dragoon (Wells-Fargo Model), 1851 Navy, 1861 Navy, and 1862 Pocket Navy/1862 Pocket Police, $895 for the 1847 Walker/Dragoon Models and the 1860 Army, $565 for the 1858 Remington Army, $785 for the Remington Navy, and $365 for the Remington Pocket Pistol.

ARMSPORT, INC.

Previous importer and distributor located in Miami, FL. Armsport imported shotguns (various configurations, mfg by Sarsilmaz of Turkey) until 2000. Armsport, Inc. imported a revolver and offered a complete line of accessories (snap caps, scope rings, and cleaning kits).

For a complete listing of older Armsport, Inc. models, please refer to the 20th - 21st Editions, the current *Blue Book of Gun Values* CD-ROM, or the online version of the *Blue Book of Gun Values*.

ARMY & NAVY

Previous department stores established in the United Kingdom circa 1871, with headquarters in London, England.

The Army & Navy trademark was originally established circa 1871 by a group of Army & Navy officers, and maintained its trademark until 2005, when it was renamed House of Fraser Victoria. In addition to selling domestic goods, the London store also sold guns using the Army & Navy trademark, manufactured by many respected English firms, including Webley & Scott, W.J. Jeffery, and others. These long guns (mostly shotguns, circa 1870s-pre WWII) were offered in a variety of both hammer and hammerless configurations, which included both plain boxlocks and special order sidelocks with elaborate engraving and deluxe wood. A few double rifles were also manufactured in various calibers. Because of the variety of guns that the Army & Navy department stores offered its customers, these guns need to be appraised individually for correct values. A general guideline is that average condition 12 ga. boxlocks sell in the $750-$2,000 range, sidelocks with nice engraving and no problems typically start at $1,750 and can exceed $5,000 for best quality, cased specimens.

ARNOLD ARMS CO., INC.

Previous rifle manufacturer located in Arlington, WA, 1994-2001.

In addition to making a series of accurate rifles built on their own Apollo action, Arnold Arms Co. also built rifles on Remington, Ruger, Sako, or Winchester actions. All Arnold Arms rifles had a written guarantee on accuracy (1/2 in. group or less at 100 yards with handloads), and a 5-year limited warranty. Any Arnold Arms warranty is now void. The company also made proprietary cartridges in 6mm Arnold, .257 Arnold, .270 Arnold, .300 Arnold, .338 Arnold, or .458 Arnold.

ARRIETA, S.L.

Current manufacturer established circa 1928 and located in Elgoibar, Spain. Currently imported by several importers including Wingshooting Adventures, Quality Arms, Griffin & Howe, William Larkin Moore, and Orvis (see separate listing). Previously imported by New England Arms.

More information can be obtained on the Arrieta models listed below by contacting the importers listed above.

RIFLES: SxS

Arrieta rifles have had limited U.S. importation in the past. Please contact the importers directly for more information, including availability and pricing on these models (see Trademark Index).

R-1 - 7x65R, 8x57JRS, or 9.3x74R cal., true sidelock, ejectors, quarter rib barrel with express rear sight.

MSR N/A	$19,000	$16,250	$13,250	$10,750	$9,350	$7,400	$6,200

R-2 - similar to R-1, except has more elaborate H&H style engraving, elongated tangs, and choice of English or reinforced pistol grip with metal cap, ejectors.

MSR N/A	$23,500	$19,000	$17,750	$15,500	$12,950	$10,450	$9,250

GRADING - PPGS™	100%	98%	95%	90%	80%	70%	60%

R-3 - similar to R-1, except includes .375 H&H, .470 NE, .500 NE cal.
This model has a current MSR of $35,900.

SHOTGUNS: SxS

The models listed below are essentially custom ordered per individual specifications - delivery time is approx. 12 months.

All Arrieta shotguns have frames scaled to individual gauges. Standard gauges are 12 & 16. Most models are available with either color case hardened or coin finished frames. Many factory upgrades and custom options/special orders are available from the individual importers - please contact them directly for availability and current pricing on these special orders.

On the models listed below, there are four different types of sidelock actions. One is used on the Model 550. Another is used on Models 557, 578, and 871. A third is used on Models 590 and 595 (designed for heavy use). Finally, the best quality is used on Models 600-903, except for Model 900 (557 action), and Model 871. All Arrieta actions are assisted opening, except the Models 557, 570, 578, and 871.

MSRs may vary somewhat from importer to importer.

> **Add 10% for small gauges (20, 24, 28, 32 ga., or .410 bore).**
> **Add approx. $1,290 for single trigger depending on action.**
> **Add 10% for matched pair.**
> **Add 10% for rounded action on standard models (except Models 871 and 872).**
> **Extra barrels are priced from $1,500-$2,500/set depending on model.**
> **Add $310 for pistol grip or semi-pistol grip stock or beavertail forearm.**
> **Add $700-$2,500 for wood upgrade, depending on model.**

"BOSS" ROUND BODY - all gauges, Boss pattern best quality engraving, includes $1,500 wood upgrade.

	100%	98%	95%	90%	80%	70%	60%
MSR N/A	N/A	$8,250	$7,150	$5,950	$5,200	$4,400	$3,600

557 - 12, 16, or 20 ga., Demi-Bloc steel barrels, detachable engraved sidelocks, double triggers, ejectors.

		98%	95%	90%	80%	70%	60%
MSR $4,500		$4,150	$3,850	$3,350	$2,350	$1,750	$1,250	$925

570 - 12, 16, or 20 ga., similar to 560 (non-standard model), except has non-detachable sidelocks.

MSR $5,500		$4,975	$4,650	$4,175	$3,475	$2,450	$1,825	$1,375

578 - 12, 16, or 20 ga., similar to 570, except is fine English scrollwork engraved.

MSR $6,200		$5,750	$5,225	$4,550	$3,950	$3,000	$2,100	$1,525

600 - 12, 16, or 20 ga., top-of-the-line self-opening action, very ornate engraving throughout.

MSR $9,900		$8,600	$7,400	$6,175	$5,275	$4,150	$3,300	$2,550

601 - all gauges, sidelock action with nickel plating, ejectors, SST, self-opening action, border engraving.

MSR $9,160		$8,725	$7,500	$6,250	$5,300	$4,175	$3,300	$2,550

801 - all gauges, Holland-style detachable sidelocks, self-opening action standard, ejectors, coin-wash finish, finest Churchill style engraving.

MSR $14,275		$12,750	$10,500	$9,300	$8,300	$7,300	$6,325	$5,275

802 - 12, 16, or 20 ga., similar to 801 only non-detachable sidelocks, finest Holland-style engraving.

MSR $14,275		$12,750	$10,500	$9,300	$8,300	$7,300	$6,325	$5,275

803 - all gauges, similar to 801, finest Purdey-style engraving.

MSR $11,900		$9,750	$8,750	$7,500	$6,300	$5,400	$4,250	$3,500

GRADING - PPGS™	100%	98%	95%	90%	80%	70%	60%

871 - all gauges, rounded frame sidelock action with Demi-Bloc barrels, scroll engraved, ejectors, DTs.

MSR $6,670 $6,000 $5,200 $4,500 $3,425 $2,750 $2,200 $1,750

872 - all gauges, rounded frame sidelock action with Demi-Bloc barrels, elaborate scroll engraving with third lever fastener.

MSR $17,850 $15,500 $12,500 $10,750 $9,000 $7,250 $6,000 $5,250

873 - all gauges, sidelock action with Demi-Bloc barrels, game scene engraving, ejectors, SST.

MSR $16,275 $15,500 $13,750 $11,000 $9,250 $8,000 $7,250 $6,325

874 - all gauges, sidelock action with Demi-Bloc barrels, action is gold line engraved.

MSR $13,125 $12,250 $11,000 $9,500 $8,300 $7,300 $6,325 $5,275

875 - all gauges, top-of-the-line quality, built to individual customer specs. only, elaborate engraving with gold inlays.

MSR $19,850 $18,275 $17,500 $14,550 $11,000 $9,250 $8,100 $7,250

931 - all gauges, self-opening action, elaborate engraving, H&H selective ejectors.

MSR $31,000 $27,950 $24,500 $18,750 $15,250 $11,250 $9,259 $8,100

ARRIZABALAGA, PEDRO

Current manufacturer located in Eibar, Spain since 1940. Currently imported and distributed by Harry Marx Hi-Grade Imports located in Gilroy, CA, and by William Larkin Moore, located in Scottsdale, AZ. Previously imported by New England Arms Corp. located in Kittery Point, ME.

Arrizabalaga manufactures best quality guns only, carefully made to individual customer specifications. Shotguns listed below have Demi-Bloc, chopper lump barrels and self-opening hand-detachable locks as standard features. The models listed below are essentially custom ordered per individual specifications - delivery time is approximately 12-18 months.

SHOTGUNS: SxS

Add 5% of MSRs for matched pair.
Add $4,500 per extra set of same gauge barrels.
Add $900 for 28 ga.
Add $1,700 for .410 bore.
Add $2,100 for single non-selective trigger.
Add $700 for beavertail forearm.
Add $900 for pistol grip stock.

HEAVY SCROLL MODEL - all gauges, sidelock action, elaborate engraving, deluxe oil finished stock and forearm.

MSR $20,700 $18,750 $15,750 $13,000 $10,250 $7,550 $5,850 $5,000

ENGLISH SCROLL MODEL - all gauges, sidelock action, English scroll engraving, deluxe oil finished walnut stock and forearm.

MSR $22,000 $19,750 $16,500 $13,500 $10,500 $7,550 $5,850 $5,000

MODEL DELUXE - all gauges, limited importation.

MSR N/A   N/A $12,750 $10,000 $8,350 $6,250 $5,250 $5,000

BOSS STYLE ROUND ACTION MODEL - all gauges, features English Boss-style scroll engraving.

MSR $22,700 $20,000 $16,750 $13,500 $10,500 $7,550 $5,850 $5,000

Add $700 for Luxe engraving.

GRADING - PPGS™	100%	98%	95%	90%	80%	70%	60%

SPECIAL MODEL - all gauges, sidelock top-of-the-line model, best quality wood and engraving.

MSR N/A	N/A	$17,000	$14,750	$10,350	$9,100	$8,000	$6,000

ARSENAL, BULGARIA

Current manufacturer located in Bulgaria. Currently imported by Arsenal, Inc., located in Las Vegas, NV. Previously imported exclusively in 1994-96 by Sentinel Arms located in Detroit, MI. For currently imported models, please refer to the Arsenal, Inc. listing.

The artillery arsenal in Rousse began in 1878, and was managed by Russian officers until 1884, when a Bulgarian was appointed the director. In 1891, the factory was transferred to Sofia, and was renamed the Sofia Artillery Arsenal until the entire facility was moved to Kazanlak in 1924. At that point, the name was changed to the State Military Factory. After WWII, the arsenal diversified into civilian production, and its nickname was "Factory 10." In 1958, the first AK-47 under Russian license came off the assembly line, and in 1982, the one millionth AK-47 had been manufactured.

PISTOLS: SEMI-AUTO

MAKAROV MODEL - 9mm Makarov cal., 3 2/3 in. barrel, 8-shot mag., black synthetic grips, blue finish. Disc. 1996.

	$185	$165	$125	$115	$105	$95	$85

RIFLES: SEMI-AUTO

BULGARIAN SA-93 - 7.62x39mm cal., Kalashnikov milled action with hardwood thumbhole stock, 16.3 in. barrel, 5-shot detachable mag., 9 lbs. Disc. 1996.

	$525	$440	$350	$275	$225	$200	$175

✳ *Bulgarian SA-93L* - 7.62x39mm cal., similar to Bulgarian SA-93 except has 20 in. barrel, with or without optics, 9 lbs. Disc. 1996.

	$595	$525	$450	$395	$350	$295	$250

Add $145 with optics.

BULGARIAN SS-94 - 7.62x39mm cal., Kalashnikov action featuring single shot operation, thumbhole hardwood stock, 5-shot detachable mag., 9 lbs. Disc. 1996.

	$475	$395	$325	$275	$225	$190	$180

ARSENAL INC.

Current importer of non-military Arsenal 2000 JSCo (Bulgarian Arsenal), established during 2001 and located in Las Vegas, NV. Dealer and distributor sales.

RIFLES: SEMI-AUTO

Arsenal Inc. is the exclusive licensed manufacturer of various Arsenal Bulgaria AK style/ design rifles conforming 100% to Arsenal Bulgaria specifications and manufacturing procedures. Models are built on forged and milled recievers with the CNC technology, and feature solid, under-folding or side folding stock.

SA M-5 SERIES - .223 Rem. cal., patterned after the AK-47, 16.3 in. barrel, black (SA M-5) or green (SA M-5G, disc. 2005) synthetic furniture with pistol grip, approx. 8.1 lbs. New 2003.

MSR $800		$710	$545	$450	$375	$325	$300	$275

Add $75 for SA M-5 R with scope rail (new 2007).
Add $10 for SA M-5G (disc. 2005).
Add $75 for SA M-5S with scope rail (limited edition, disc. 2005).
Add $80 for SA M-5SG (disc. 2005).

GRADING - PPGS™	100%	98%	95%	90%	80%	70%	60%

SA M-7 SERIES - 7.62x39mm cal., milled receiver, also available in carbine, otherwise similar to SA M-5. New 2003.

MSR $800	$715	$540	$460	$410	$355	$325	$295

Add $170 for SA M-7 R with scope rail (new 2007).
Add $35 for SA M-7S with scope rail.
Add $5 for SA M-7G with OD green furniture.
Add $40 for SA M-7SG with scope rail.

SA M-7 CLASSIC - 7.62x39mm cal., features blonde wood stock, pistol grip and forearm, double stack magazine, heavy barrel and slanted gas block, Warsaw Pact buttstock, less than 200 mfg. 2001-2002, reintroduced 2007.

MSR $1,200	$795	$650	$525	$400	$350	$325	$295

SA M-7 A1/SA M-7 A1 R - 7.62x39mm cal., milled receiver, front sight block w/bayonet lug, 24mm flash hider, cleaning rod, accessory lug, black polymer furnite, NATO buttstock. New 2007.

MSR $960	$850	$700	$625	$550	$500	$450	$400

Add $75 for SA M-7 A1 R w/scope rail.

SA M-7 SF - 7.62x39mm cal., U.S. mfg., milled receiver, front sight block with bayonet lug, 24mm flash hider, cleaning rod, accessory lug, black polymer furniture, right side folding stock, ambidextrous safety, scope rail. New 2007.

MSR $1,300	$1,025	$875	$750	$650	$575	$515	$475

SA M-7 SFC/SA M-7 SFK - 7.62x39mm cal., U.S. mfg., milled receiver, front sight/gas block combination with 24mm thread protector, cleaning rod, black polymer furniture, right side folding tubular buttstock, ambidextrous safety, scope rail. New 2007.

MSR $1,425	$1,200	$1,025	$875	$750	$650	$575	$515

Add $150 for SA M-7 SFK model with short gas system and laminated wood Krinkov handguards.

SA RPK-7 - 7.62x39mm cal., paddle style buttstock, folding bi-pod, no scope rail, otherwise similar to SA RPK-5 S. Limited edition 2003-2005, reintroduced 2007.

MSR $1,250	$995	$875	$750	$650	$575	$515	$475

Add $75 for SA RPK-7 R with scope rail.

SA RPK-5 (S) - .223 Rem. cal., features blonde wood stock, RPK heavy barrel, 14mm muzzle threads, pistol grip and forearm, 23 1/4 in. barrel with folding tripod, approx. 11 lbs. Limited edition 2003-2005, reintroduced 2007.

MSR $1,250	$1,075	$900	$750	$650	$575	$515	$475

Add $75 for SA RPK-5 R model with scope rail.

SAS M-7 - 7.62x39mm cal., U.S. mfg., authentic semi-auto version of Bulgarian model AR M1F with vertical gas block and ATF-approved fixed metal underfolding-style stock. New 2004.

MSR $1,250	$1,075	$900	$750	$650	$575	$515	$475

SAS M-7 CLASSIC - 7.62x39mm cal., U.S. mfg., authentic semi-auto version of Russian 1953 Model AKS-47 with slant gas block and ATF-approved fixed metal underfolding-style stock, blond furniture, heavy barrel. Limited edition 2001-2002, reintroduced 2007.

MSR $1,275	$1,000	$850	$725	$650	$575	$515	$475

SLR 101 S - 7.62x39mm cal., similar to SA M-7, except has black thumbole synthetic stock, available in polymer black (SLR 101SB1) or polymer OD Green (SLR 101SG1). Mfg. 2003-2005.

	$335	$275	$240	$210	$185	$170	$155

Last MSR was $410.

Add $100 for SLR 101SB1.
Add $110 for SLR 101SG1.

GRADING - PPGS™	100%	98%	95%	90%	80%	70%	60%

SLR 101SB/SG - 7.62x39mm cal., double stack mag., features side mount scope rail, 16 in. barrel, standard military stock configuration. Mfg. 2004-2005.

	100%	98%	95%	90%	80%	70%	60%
	$525	$450	$375	$295	$250	$200	$185

Last MSR was $655.

    Add $45 for SG Model with green polymer.

SLR-105 SERIES - 5.45x39.5mm cal., stamped receiver, cleaning rod, black polymer furniture, NATO buttstock. New 2007.

	100%	98%	95%	90%	80%	70%	60%
MSR $475	$395	$325	$275	$250	$200	$175	$150

    Add $50 for SLR-105 R with scope rail.
    Add $150 for SLR-105 A1 model with front sight block, bayonet lug and 24mm muzzle brake.
    Add $200 for SLR-105 A1 R model with scope rail.

SLR-106 SERIES - 5.56 NATO cal., stamped receiver, left-side folding stock, 24mm muzzle brake, bayonet lug, accessory lug, stainless steel heat shield, two-stage trigger. New 2007.

	100%	98%	95%	90%	80%	70%	60%
MSR $800	$710	$545	$450	$375	$325	$300	$275

    Add $80 for SLR-106 FR with scope rail.
    Add $99 for Desert Sand stock.
    Add $199 for SLR-106 U Model with short gas system front sight block/gas combination and black furniture.
    Add $80 for SLT-106 U Model with scope rail (SLR-106 UR).
    Add $179 for SLR-106 Model with removable muzzle attachment.
    Subtract $19 for original metal left-side folding stock.

SLR-107 SERIES - 7.62x39mm cal., stamped receiver, left-side folding stock, 24mm flash hider, bayonet lug, accessory lug, stainless steel heat shield, two-stage trigger. New 2008.

	100%	98%	95%	90%	80%	70%	60%
MSR $799	$710	$545	$450	$375	$325	$300	$275

    Add $80 for SLR-107 FR with scope rail.
    Add $326 for SLR-107 UR Model with short gas system front sight block/gas combination, black furniture, and scope rail.
    Add $180 for SLR-107 CR Model with removable muzzle attachment.

ARSENAL USA LLC

Previous manufacturer/importer from 1999-2004, and located in Houston, TX. During September 2004, Arsenal USA LLC changed its name to Armory USA L.L.C. Please refer to this listing for currently manufactured rifles.

RIFLES: SEMI-AUTO

MODEL SSR-99 - 7.62x39mm cal., Bulgarian milled receiver and parts, black polymer furniture. Less than 300 mfg. 1999-2000.

	100%	98%	95%	90%	80%	70%	60%
	$625	$550	$500	$450	$400	$350	$300

Last MSR was $600.

MODEL K-101 - .223 Rem. cal., Bulgarian milled receiver and parts, black polymer furniture. Less than 200 mfg. 1999-2000.

	100%	98%	95%	90%	80%	70%	60%
	$625	$550	$500	$450	$400	$350	$300

Last MSR was $600.

MODEL SSR-99P - 7.62x39mm cal., Bulgarian milled receiver and parts, with rare Polish grenade launching variant parts, Polish wood furniture. Less than 500 mfg. 1999-2001.

	100%	98%	95%	90%	80%	70%	60%
	$625	$550	$500	$450	$400	$350	$300

Last MSR was $600.

GRADING - PPGS™	100%	98%	95%	90%	80%	70%	60%

MODEL SSR-85B - 7.62x39mm cal., Hungarian FEG receiver and Polish AKM parts, blond Hungarian wood furniture, small number produced using ITM U.S. made receiver. Approx. 1,200 mfg. 2000-2003.

	$600	$550	$500	$450	$400	$350	$325

Last MSR was $450.

MODEL AMD-63 - 7.62x39mm cal., Hungarian FEG receiver and Polish AKM parts, unique metal lower handguard with pistol grip. 200 mfg. 2000-2003.

	$625	$550	$500	$450	$400	$350	$300

Last MSR was $600.

MODEL SSR-56 - 7.62x39mm cal., Hungarian FEG receiver, Poly-Tec barrel assembly and Bulgarian internal parts. Approx. 500 mfg. 2002-2003.

	$500	$450	$400	$350	$300	$250	$225

Last MSR was $450.

ART MANIFACTTURA ARMI

Current longarm manufacturer located in Gardone, Italy. Currently imported beginning 2004 by William Larkin Moore, located in Scottsdale, AZ. Art Manifacttura Armi manufactures high quality custom long guns, including rifles and shotguns. Please contact the importer (see Trademark Index) directly for more information, including availability and pricing.

Currently imported models include a SxS Anson & Deely boxlock action with rose and scroll engraving, a H&H type sidelock SxS shotgun with choice of H&H or Purdey style engraving, and a SxS sidelock rifle in .375 H&H, .470 NE, or .500 NE cal., with rose and scroll engraving. All models are POR. Please contact the importer directly for more information, including pricing and delivery time (see Trademark Index).

ASP

Previously manufactured customized variation of a S&W Model 39-2 semi-auto pistol (or related variations) manufactured by Armament Systems and Procedures located in Appleton, WI.

PISTOLS: SEMI-AUTO

ASP - 9mm Para. cal., compact double action semi-auto, features see-through grips with cut-away mag. making cartridges visible, Teflon coated, re-contoured lightened slide, combat trigger guard, spurless hammer, and mostly painted Guttersnipe rear sight (no front sight), supplied with 3 mags., 24 oz. loaded. Approx. 3,000 mfg. until 1981.

	$1,500	$1,275	$1,050	$875	$775	$695	$625

Add $200 for Tritium filled Guttersnipe.

This pistol is marked "ASP" on the magazine extension.

* *ASP Quest For Excellence* - special edition, marked "Quest for Excellence". Included buffalo horn grips, presentation book case and letter opener. Approx. 100 mfg.

	$3,150	$2,700	$2,400	$2,050	$1,775	$1,525	$1,275

REVOLVERS

ASP REVOLVER - .44 Spl. cal., conversion from a Ruger Speed or Security Six, 5 shot. Less than 100 mfg., unmarked.

	$1,275	$1,075	$950	$875	$775	$700	$650

ASPREY

Previous long gun manufacturer located in London, England. While established in 1781, Asprey manufactured high quality shotguns and rifles 1990-99. During 1998, the name was changed to Asprey & Garrard. Guns are currently manufactured by William & Son, located in London, England.

Please refer to the William & Son listing for currently manufactured models.

GRADING - PPGS™	100%	98%	95%	90%	80%	70%	60%

ASTRA

Previous manufacturer located in Guernica, Spain. Astra was one of the oldest and most widely recognized trademarks in Spain, with a history dating back to 1908. Though arms were manufactured for many years by Unceta y Compania, S.A., located in Guernica, Spain, corporate reorganization resulted in renaming the same firm Astra Sport, S.A. (1995-1997), and Astra Sport Guerniquesa de Mecanizado Tratamiento y Montaje de Armas, S.A. (1997-1998).

Although Astra had hoped to acquire Star patents and relocate to a smaller facility, these efforts were not successful. Foreclosure sealed the factory doors in July, 1998, and all inventory, including the "factory collection", was released for sale in 1999.

PISTOLS: SEMI-AUTO

MODEL 1911 - .25 ACP or .32 ACP cal., semi-auto, may have external or internal hammer.

$365	$265	$175	$135	$115	$100	$85

Add 50% if with external hammer.

MODEL 1915/1916 - .32 ACP cal., semi-auto.

$350	$265	$175	$135	$115	$100	$85

Note: Models 1915/1916 were later referred to as Model 100 Special.

CAMPO GIRO 1913 - 9mm Largo cal., mfg. 1913-14. Ser. No. range 1-1,300.

$5,000	$4,000	$3,000	$2,250	$1,750	$1,200	$750

Add 10% for matching magazine.

CAMPO GIRO 1913-1916 - 9mm Largo cal., mfg. 1915-19. Serial number range 1-13,625.

$2,750	$2,250	$1,750	$1,250	$950	$750	$500

Add 10% if fit with horn logo grips.
Add 10% for matching magazine.

MODEL 200 FIRECAT AUTOMATIC PISTOL - .25 ACP cal., 2 1/4 in. barrel, 6 shot, blue, plastic grips. Mfg. 1920-68.

$295	$220	$165	$145	$125	$110	$100

100% prices assume N.I.B. condition.
Add 50% for engraved M-200.

MODEL 300 - .32 ACP or .380 ACP cal., semi-auto.

$850	$650	$450	$325	$225	$180	$150

Add 20% for Nazi-proofed .380 ACP pistols.
Add 100% for lightly engraved M-300.
Add 200% for deeply engraved M300 model with salesman sample grips.

MODEL 400 AUTOMATIC PISTOL - 9mm Largo cal., 9 shot, 6 in. barrel, blue, fixed sights, plastic grips. Mfg. 1921-1945.

$650	$500	$350	$275	$225	$175	$125

Add 200% for Navy variation.
Add 100% for Nazi accepted specimens.
Serial range of Nazi accepted specimens (no markings) is S/N 92,851-98,850.
This particular model in reworked configuration has recently been imported in large quantities.

✳ *Model 400 Copies Marked "F. Ascaso"* - close copy of the Astra Model 400, produced by the Spanish Republican forces during the later part of the Spanish Civil War, F. Ascaso marked (un-numbered) mags., salt blue, estimated production is approx. 8,000, has identifying logo on slide and grip panels, and base of magazine.

$1,000	$750	$550	$450	$350	$255	$225

GRADING - PPGS™	100%	98%	95%	90%	80%	70%	60%

✱ *Model 400 Copies Marked R.E. (Republica Espagnola)* - serial number range to approx. 15,000, has identifying logo on forward slide and grip panels.

	$850	$650	$450	$350	$210	$170	$125

Add $200 if pistol is fit with wood serrated grips having brass "RE" medallion.

MODEL 600 MOD. AUTOMATIC - 9mm Para. cal., 8 shot, 5 1/4 in. barrel, blue, fixed sights, wood or plastic grips. Mfg. 1944-45.

	$500	$425	$325	$250	$200	$175	$150

Add 100% for Nazi Waffenamt proofing (serial range 1-10,500).

MODEL 700 SPECIAL - .32 ACP cal., semi-auto.

	$1,500	$1,250	$1,000	$800	$650	$525	$400

MODEL 800 CONDOR AUTOMATIC - 9mm Para. cal., similar to Model 600, except has exposed hammer. Mfg. 1958-65.

	$1,850	$1,500	$1,200	$900	$800	$700	$600

Add 20% if NIB with accessories.

MODEL 900 - 7.63 Mauser cal., Broomhandle copy, parts non-interchangeable with Mauser. Mfg. from 1928-36.

	$3,250	$2,500	$2,000	$1,500	$1,000	$750	$500

Add $650 for non-matching shoulder stock.
Add $900 for matching stock.
Add 50% for early Bolo grip variation.
Add 20% for specimens with Japanese characters.

MODEL 902 - 7.63 Mauser cal., semi-auto, similar to Model 900 except 20-shot mag. Beware of fakes - usually created by welding up selective fire pistols.

	$20,000	$16,000	$12,500	$10,000	$7,500	$5,000	$3,500

Add $1,500 for original "booted" stock.
Subtract 60% for selective fire version.

MACHINE PISTOLS - class III, transferrable only, 10 or 20 shot detachable mag., several variations.

	$10,000	$8,500	$7,000	$6,000	$5,000	$3,750	$2,500

MODEL 3000 POCKET AUTOMATIC - .32 ACP or .380 ACP cal., 4 in. barrel, fixed sights, blue, plastic grips. Mfg. 1947-1956.

	$750	$600	$400	$300	$250	$200	$150

Add 75% for engraved M3002.
Add 150% for deeply engraved M3003.

MODEL 1000 OR 1000 SPECIAL - .32 ACP cal., semi-auto, extended frame to hold 12-shot mag.

	$950	$700	$500	$400	$300	$255	$225

MODEL 2000 CUB - .22 short or .25 ACP cal., 2 1/4 in. barrel, fixed sights, blue, plastic grips, also chrome finish, mfg. 1954-98, U.S. importation stopped by GCA 68. Astra also made 2000 Model 2000 Cubs for Colt called Jr. Model (see Colt section).

	$300	$225	$140	$115	$95	$85	$75

Add 25% for chrome finish.
Add 50% for engraved M-2000.

MODEL 2000 CAMPER - .22 short cal. only, similar to Model 2000 Cub, with 4 in. barrel. Mfg. 1955-1960.

	$350	$275	$200	$160	$125	$90	$70

Add 10% if in original box.

GRADING - PPGS™	100%	98%	95%	90%	80%	70%	60%

CONSTABLE - .22 LR (10 shot, disc. 1990), .32 ACP (8 shot, disc. 1984), or .380 ACP (7 shot) cal., double action, exposed hammer, 3 1/2 in. barrel, fixed sight, blue or chrome (disc.) finish, plastic grips. Imported 1965-91.

	$325	$295	$250	$225	$200	$175	$150

Last MSR was $380.

Add $10 for chrome finish or wood grips (disc. in 1990).
Add 10% for .22 LR cal.

✳ *Constable Stainless* - .380 ACP cal. only, stainless version of the Constable. Mfg. 1986 only.

	$550	$450	$400	$350	$285	$250	$215

Last MSR was $345.

✳ *Constable Sport* - similar to Constable, except has 6 in. barrel, blue finish only, 35 oz. Mfg. 1986-87 only.

	$450	$350	$300	$250	$200	$165	$150

Last MSR was $330.

✳ *Constable Blue Engraved* - blue engraved. Importation disc. 1987.

	$550	$450	$350	$285	$250	$200	$175

Last MSR was $375.

Add $20 for .22 LR or checkered wood grips.

✳ *Constable Chrome Engraved* - chrome engraved. Importation disc. 1987.

	$500	$425	$350	$285	$250	$200	$175

Last MSR was $390.

Add $20 for .22 LR or checkered wood grips.

CONSTABLE A-60 - .380 ACP cal., double action, 3 1/2 in. barrel, 13-shot mag., ambidextrous safety, adj. rear sight, blue finish only. Imported 1986-91.

	$395	$325	$280	$245	$220	$185	$160

Last MSR was $475.

MODEL A-70 - 9mm Para. or .40 S&W cal., single action, 3 1/2 in. barrel, steel frame and slide, 7- (.40 S&W) or 8- (9mm Para.) shot mag., compact design, dual safeties, 3-dot sights, matte blue or nickel (new 1993) finish, 25 3/4 oz. Imported 1991-96.

	$300	$250	$225	$200	$185	$170	$160

Last MSR was $358.

Add $29 for nickel finish.

✳ *Model A-70 Stainless* - stainless steel variation of the Model A-70. Mfg. 1994 only.

	$500	$400	$300	$250	$195	$165	$140

Last MSR was $435.

MODEL A-75 - 9mm Para., .40 S&W, or .45 ACP (new 1994) cal., action similar to Model A-70, except has selective double action with a decocking lever, steel or aluminum (9mm Para. only) frame. Importation began 1993.

✳ *Model A-75 9mm Para or .40 S&W* - choice of blue or nickel steel frame or lightweight aluminum frame (23 1/2 oz.), 7- (.40 S&W) or 8- (9mm Para.) shot mag. Disc. 1998.

	$325	$285	$240	$210	$185	$170	$160

Last MSR was $303.

Add $17 for nickel finish.
Add $20 for lightweight model (aluminum frame).

✳ *Model A-75 .45 ACP* - blue or nickel finish, 7-shot mag. Disc. 1998.

	$350	$275	$225	$200	$175	$160	$150

Last MSR was $358.

Add $23 for nickel finish.

GRADING - PPGS™	100%	98%	95%	90%	80%	70%	60%

✳ *Model A-75 Stainless* - stainless steel variation of the Model A-75. Mfg. 1994 only.

	$375	$325	$295	$240	$210	$180	$155

Last MSR was $485.

MODEL A-80 - 9mm Para, .38 Super (disc.), or .45 ACP cal., double action, semi-auto, 15-shot mag. (9 for .45 ACP), 3 3/4 in. barrel. Imported 1982-89.

	$350	$320	$285	$265	$240	$210	$185

Last MSR was $425.

Add $35 for chrome finish (disc.).
.38 Super cal. in chrome finish will command a premium (10%-20%).

MODEL A-90 - 9mm Para. or .45 ACP cal., 1986 designation for Model A-80 with updated slide mounted safety and pushbutton mag. release, 3 3/4 in. barrel, 14-shot mag. (9mm), or 8-shot (.45 ACP), blue only, approx. 48 oz. Imported 1986-90, replaced by Model A-100.

	$450	$375	$295	$275	$245	$225	$200

Last MSR was $500.

MODEL A-100 - 9mm Para., .40 S&W, or .45 ACP cal., replaced the Model A-90 in 1990, with similar specifications, blue or nickel finish, re-engineered 1993 incorporating increased mag. capacity, 10 (C/B 1994), 17*/9mm, 12*/.40 S&W, or 9 shot/.45 ACP, approx. 29 oz. Imported 1990-97.

	$400	$325	$295	$275	$245	$225	$175

Last MSR was $351.

Add $22 for nickel finish.
A small number of pistols with an extended slide were made for the Turkish police - add 50%.

MODEL 4000 FALCON - .22 LR, .32 ACP, or .380 ACP cal., 4 in. barrel, fixed sights, blue, plastic grips, exposed hammer. Mfg. 1956-86.

	$600	$475	$330	$260	$235	$200	$150

Last MSR was $340.

Add 50% for .22 cal.
Add 10% for .380 ACP.
Add 100% for engraved Model-4000 Falcon.

✳ *Model 4000 Tri-cal. Kit* - includes frame and 3 barrels (.22 LR, .32 ACP, and .380 ACP cals.), may have rust blue, salt blue, or chromed (rare) finish, less than 200 mfg.

	$1,500	$1,250	$1,000	$750	$600	$500	$450

Subtract 15% if not in factory box.

REVOLVERS

CADIX DOUBLE ACTION REVOLVER - .22 LR cal., 9 shot, .38 Spl., 5 shot, 4 or 6 in. barrel, adj. sights, blue, plastic grips. Mfg. 1960-68.

	$225	$175	$150	$125	$110	$85	$55

Add 25% for early variation with single piece grip.

.357 D/A REVOLVER - .357 Mag. cal., 6 shot, 3, 4, 6, or 8 1/2 in. barrel, adj. sights, blue, checkered wood grips. Mfg. 1972-88.

	$250	$215	$185	$170	$155	$140	$125

Last MSR was $295.

Add 50% for 8 1/2 in. barrel.

✳ *.357 D/A Revolver Stainless Steel* - 4 in. barrel only. Disc. 1987.

	$295	$265	$215	$165	$125	$110	$95

Last MSR was $330.

GRADING - PPGS™	100%	98%	95%	90%	80%	70%	60%

LARGE CAL. D/A REVOLVER - .41 Mag. (disc. 1985), .44 Mag., or .45 LC (disc. 1987) cal., 6 shot, 6 or 8 1/2 in. (.44 Mag. only) barrels. Mfg. 1980-87.

	$325	$295	$250	$200	$180	$170	$160

Last MSR was $315.

✳ *Large Cal. D/A Revolver Stainless Steel* - .44 Mag. cal. only, 6 in. barrel only, 2 1/2 lbs. Importation disc. 1993.

	$375	$325	$275	$235	$200	$165	$140

Last MSR was $450.

CONVERTIBLE REVOLVER - 9mm Para. cal. with extra .357 Mag. cal. cylinder, 6 shot, 3 in. barrel, blue only, checkered walnut grips, 2 1/4 lbs. Imported 1986-1993.

	$395	$350	$300	$250	$200	$180	$160

Last MSR was $395.

TERMINATOR - .44 Mag. or .44 Spl. (disc.) cal., 6 shot, adj. rear sight, Roberts rubber grips, 2 3/4 in. shrouded barrel only. Inventories were depleted in 1989.

	100%	98%	95%	90%	80%	70%	60%
Blue finish	$325	$250	$200	$175	$160	$150	$140
Stainless steel	$350	$275	$225	$175	$140	$125	$105

Last MSR for Blue finish was $250. Last MSR for Stainless Steel was $275.

These models were distributed by John Jovino, located in Yonkers, NY.

ATKIN, GRANT & LANG LTD.

Current gunmaker established in 1960, and located in Hertfordshire, England. Atkin, Grant & Lang is the parent company that owns the trademarks of Henry Atkin, Stephen Grant and Joseph Lang. Please refer to these individual trademarks listed separately.

ATKIN, HENRY

Current trademark established in 1877 and currently manufactured by Atkin Grant & Lang, Ltd. located in Hertfordshire, England. Henry Atkin Ltd. joined with Grant & Lang during 1960, forming Atkin Grant & Lang Ltd. No current U.S. importation.

Atkin Grant & Lang Ltd. provide a useful historical research service on older Henry Atkin shotguns and rifles. The charge for this service is £25 per gun, and the company will give you all pertinent factory information regarding the history.

SHOTGUNS: SxS

Prices on Henry Atkin shotguns do not include VAT or importation costs. Please contact the company directly (see Trademark Index) for more information, including availability, delivery time, and a price quotation.

Add 10% for matched pairs.

BOXLOCK MODEL - 28 (2 mfg.) or 20 (3 mfg.) ga., very limited millenium edition.

This model is POR from the factory, based on an individual custom order.

SIDELOCK MODEL - 12, 20 ga., or .410 bore, best quality sidelock ejector model with opening assist.

This model is POR from the factory, based on an individual custom order.

AUSTRALIAN AUTOMATIC ARMS PTY. LTD.

Previous manufacturer located in Tasmania, Australia. Previously imported and distributed by California Armory, Inc. located in San Bruno, CA.

GRADING - PPGS™	100%	98%	95%	90%	80%	70%	60%

PISTOLS: SEMI-AUTO

SAP - .223 Rem. cal., semi-auto paramilitary design pistol, 10 1/2 in. barrel, 20-shot mag., fiberglass stock and forearm, 5.9 lbs. Imported 1986-93.

	$795	$700	$600	$550	$500	$475	$450

Last MSR was $799.

RIFLES: SEMI-AUTO

SAR - .223 Rem. cal., semi-auto paramilitary design rifle, 16 1/4 or 20 in. (new 1989) barrel, 5- or 20-shot M-16 style mag., fiberglass stock and forearm, 7 1/2 lbs. Imported 1986-89.

	$1,000	$900	$850	$800	$775	$750	$700

Last MSR was $663.

Add $25 for 20 in. barrel.

This model was also available in fully automatic version (AR).

SAC - .223 Rem. cal., semi-auto paramilitary design carbine, 10 1/2 in. barrel, 20-shot mag., fiberglass stock and forearm, 6.9 lbs. New 1986.

This model was available to class III dealers and law enforcement agencies only.

SP - .223 Rem. cal., semi-auto, sporting configuration, 16 1/4 or 20 in. barrel, wood stock and forearm, 5 or 20 shot M-16 style mag., 7 1/4 lbs. Imported late 1991-93.

	$850	$750	$650	$600	$550	$500	$475

Last MSR was $879.

Add $40 for wood stock.

AUSTRALIAN INTERNATIONAL ARMS

Current manufacturer and exporter located in Brisbane, Australia. Previously, Australian International Arms worked in cooperation with ADI Limited Lithgow, formerly Small Arms Factory, known for its SMLE No. I MKIII and L1A1 rifles. AIA now manufactures its products through outsourcing to its designs and specifications. Currently imported in North America by Marstar Canada, located in Ontario, Canada. Previously imported and distributed until 2004 by Tristar Sporting Arms, Ltd., located in N. Kansas City, MO.

RIFLES: BOLT ACTION, ENFIELD SERIES

M10-A1 - 7.62x39mm cal., features a redesigned and improved No. 4 MK2 action, parkerized finish, all new components, teak furniture with No. 5 Jungle Carbine style stock with steel or brass buttplate, 20 in. chrome lined barrel with recoil break, adj. front sight, 10 shot mag., Picatinny rail, 8.3 lbs. Importation began 2007.

As this edition went to press, prices had yet to be established on this model.

✷ *M10-A2* - 7.62x39mm cal., similar to M10A2, except has No. 8 style forend, Monte Carlo stock, and 16.1 in. chrome lined barrel. Limited importation 2003-2004 by Tristar.

	$575	$500	$425	$350	$300	$275	$250

Last MSR was $659.

M10-B1 - .308 Win. cal., features a redesigned and improved No. 4 MK2 action, matte blue finish, all new components, teak furniture with sporter carbine style stock and steel buttplate, 22 in. barrel, adj. fron sight, 10 shot mag., Picatinny rail, 8.3 lbs. Importation began 2006.

MSR $675	$575	$500	$425	$350	$300	$275	$250

✷ *M10-B2* - .308 Win. cal., similar to M10-B1, except has brass buttplate, gloss blue finish, 25 in. chrome lined bull barrel, and bipod stud, 10.5 lbs. Importation began 2006.

MSR $760	$650	$525	$425	$350	$300	$275	$225

GRADING - PPGS™	100%	98%	95%	90%	80%	70%	60%

✳ *M10-B3* - .308 Win. cal., similar to M10-B1, except has chrome steel buttplate, gloss blue finish, and 22 in. lightweight barrel, 7 1/2 lbs. Limited importation began 2006.

MSR $1,000		$900	$800	$700	$600	$500	$425	$350

NO.4 MK IV - .308 Win. cal., parkerized finish, 25.2 in. chrome lined medium weight barrel, teak furniture with steel buttplate, 9.1 lbs. Prototype only imported by Tristar. Limited importation beginning 2006.

MSR $675		$575	$500	$425	$350	$300	$275	$250

Add $440 for walnut stock, glass bedded target barrel, elevated Picatinny rail, and accessories (disc.).

M 42 - .308 Win. cal., 27.6 in. barrel with mahogany stock and extra cheekpiece, blue printed action, bright metal/barrel finish, includes Picatinny rail, 8.2 lbs. Imported 2003-2004.

		$1,125	$950	$800	$650	$550	$450	$350

Last MSR was $1,295.

SHOTGUNS: LEVER ACTION

MODEL 1887 - 12 ga., 2 3/4 in. chamber, uncheckered oil finished walnut stock and forearm, blue finish, steel buttplate, 5 shot, exposed hammer with half cock, 22 in. barrel, 8 3/4 lbs. Approx. 100 units mfg. by ADI Lithgow before discontinuance due to ADI technical and quality control problems. Dealer sample importation only 2003-2004.

		$995	$850	$750	$650	$600	$550	$500

Last MSR was $1,195.

AUTAUGA RIFLES, INC.

Previous manufacturer located in Prattville, AL 1996-2002. In 2000, Autauga Arms, Inc. changed their name to Autauga Rifles, Inc.

PISTOLS: SEMI-AUTO

AUTAUGA MKII 32 - .32 ACP cal., double action only, 2 in. barrel, hammerless, blow-back-type action, 6-shot mag., stainless steel, black polymer grips, 3/4 lb. 3,200 mfg. 1996-2000.

		$325	$225	$185	$140	$120	$100	$85

Last MSR was $399.

Early guns did not have the MKII designation.

RIFLES: BOLT ACTION

Autauga Rifles, Inc. manufactured a complete line of precision bolt action rifles that were special ordered per individual customer specifications. Configurations included hunting, long range competition, law enforcement and military tactical rifles. Complete packages included rifle, optics, hardware, and cleaning equipment. Standard rifle prices varied from $2,500-$3,500, depending on options. Rifles were supplied with a Pelican 1750 case.

AUTO MAG

Previously manufactured (circa 1971-1982) by Auto Mag. Corp. and TDE Corp. Recent manufacture (Harry Sanford Commemorative) was produced by Galena Industries, located in Sturgis, SD.

Less than 9,000 Auto Mags were produced by all manufacturers. All pistols originally had all stainless steel mags.

Short recoil rotary bolt system made entirely of stainless steel. Most pistols were sold in .44 AMP cal., although .357 AMP was also a popular factory option.

A unique handgun, the Auto Mag was never a commercial success due to high manufacturing costs and initial functioning problems (mostly attributed to hand loading all the ammo - once factory ammo became available, reliability improved significantly). Initial reaction to Dirty Harry's use of this weapon in the movie "Sudden Impact" (1983), as well as Burt Reynolds in "Malone" (1987) made prices escalate considerably, but most values appear to have stabilized since 1989. Be aware of fakes - especially of the XP variety (re-serialized, re-stamped, location of markings, etc.). Also, the ease of barrel swapping should be considered when deciding on a potential purchase. Auto Mags were never Mag-Na-Ported from the factory (only The Custom 100 Series). Non-original Mag-Na-Porting actually detracts from the values listed below, since it is a non-factory alteration.

Serial number ranges for the various models are as follows: Pasadena mfg. - A0000 through A03700. TDE North Hollywood - mostly A02500 through A05015, although some were marked with very low serial numbers. TDE El Monte mfg. - A05016 through A08300. (Note: these numbers should only be used as a guideline - as the company named changed, serial numbers overlapped.)

Although High Standard claimed to be the national sales distributor in 1974 and 1975 and had flyers saying this to be so, Lee E. Jurras and Associates, Inc. was actually the exclusive world wide distributor. Despite this, High Standard records show sales of 1045 Auto Mags.

High Standard catalog numbers are: 9346 for .44 AMP, and 9347 for .357 AMP. High Standard sold 134 Auto Mags with an "H" prefix. Serial numbers between H1 and H198, with one at H1566 and three between H17,219-H17,222. 108 of these were .44 AMP and 26 were .357 AMP. High Standard also sold 911 Auto Mags between serial numbers A05278-A07637. 777 of these were .44 AMP and 108 were .357 AMP. The "H" prefix guns remain a collectors' item and command a 25% premium over values listed below. It is estimated that an additional 300 barrels were marked High Standard.

DE/OMC marked pistols - B00001 through B00370 are known as the "B" series or solid bolt models (only 370 manufactured). This "B" series also commands collector premiums.

AMT manufactured the last two lots of Auto Mags; the first was the "C" series and was basically the same as the "B" except that only 50 guns were fabricated. The "B" Series was manufactured in 1979. Serial numbered C00001-C00050 "C" Series was manufactured in 1979, and the "Last" Series was manufactured in 1982. The last Auto Mags made by AMT were appropriately serial numbered LAST 1 through LAST 50. These guns had the reputation of being the poorest quality but do carry collector premiums. One interesting variation is the North Hollywood "two-line" model. Also, the first .357 cal. pistols manufactured did not have the words AUTO MAG appearing on the gun. These are also collectors' items.

In addition to the above calibers, a very few non-factory .22, .25 and .30 LMP (Lomont Magnum Pistols) cal. prototypes were fabricated by Kent Lomont. These specimens will usually demand a premium over the values listed below. Also, some barrels and pistols were made in Covina, CA.

PISTOLS: SEMI-AUTO

ORIGINAL PASADENA - .44 AMP cal. only, 6 1/2 in. VR barrel, ser. no. A0001 - A3,300.

$2,500	$2,300	$1,995	$1,735	$1,495	$1,215	$1,000

This model is generally regarded as having the most quality, as all components were milled from Carpenter 455 stainless steel stock.

TDE NORTH HOLLYWOOD - ser. no. range A3,400 - A05015.

✳ *TDE North Hollywood .44 AMP* - 6 1/2 in. VR barrel, initial guns were mfg. from existing Pasadena parts, later mfg. required new components made by TDE.

$2,275	$1,850	$1,700	$1,500	$1,235	$1,030	$855

Quality on this model goes down in later mfg. (some small parts are not stainless). Because of this, higher serial numbered guns in this model are less desirable.

✳ *TDE North Hollywood .357 AMP* - two line address, there are no factory records verifying this caliber, and most were assembled with spare barrels.

$1,850	$1,600	$1,450	$1,275	$1,040	$900	$725

GRADING - PPGS™	100%	98%	95%	90%	80%	70%	60%

TDE EL MONTE - ser. no. range A05016-A08300.

   ✻ *TDE El Monte .44 AMP* - 6 1/2 VR, 8 1/2, or 10 1/2 in. tapered barrel.

	100%	98%	95%	90%	80%	70%	60%
	$2,000	$1,700	$1,600	$1,410	$1,160	$980	$800

   ✻ *TDE El Monte .357 AMP* - 6 1/2 VR, 8 1/2, or 10 1/2 in. tapered barrel.

	$1,750	$1,600	$1,450	$1,275	$1,040	$900	$855

HIGH STANDARD - "H" prefixed serial numbers, approx. 132 mfg. by TDE with High Standard markings.

	$2,250	$2,100	$1,850	$1,620	$1,335	$1,115	$930

LEE JURRAS STANDARD MODELS - see listings below, custom features would vary from presentation grade polishing of barrel and frame to exotic wood or micarta grips.

   ✻ *LEJ Standard Automag* - .357 AMP or .44 AMP cal., 6 1/2 w/VR, 8 1/2, or 10 1/2 in. non-rib barrel, TDE markings, lion's head logo. 1,100-1,200 mfg. 1974-76 by Lee Jurras & Associates. - Lee Jurras Custom Models included the 100 (listed below), 200 International (12 mfg.), 300 Alaskan (9 mfg.), 400 Backpacker (5 mfg.), 500 Grizzly (5 mfg.), 600 Condor (2 mfg.), and Metallic Silouhette (2 mfg.). Because of the rarity factor, these models with 12 or less mfg. are difficult to price accurately, and must be evaluated and appraised individually.

	$2,225	$2,050	$1,775	$1,560	$1,280	$1,070	$885

Lee Jurras added his Lion's head logo (1974-1976) on TDE manufactured guns. There were also a very limited quantity of original shoulder stocks (less than 12), and were available for the International and Alaskan models only - extreme rarity precludes accurate price evaluation.

Several other calibers and variations were marketed through Lee Jurras including one-of-a-kind exotics like a .30 cal. Cougar with 12 in. barrel and highly polished metal.

LEE JURRAS CUSTOM MODELS

   ✻ *LEJ Custom Model 100* - .357 AMP, .41 JMP (Jurras Magnum Pistol), or .44 AMP cal., 6 1/2 in. VR or 8 1/2 non-rib (only 10 mfg. in each cal.) polished magna-ported barrel, custom laminated wood grips, special carrying case. 100 mfg. in each cal.

	$3,150	$2,850	$2,350	$2,065	$1,860	$1,430	$1,175

TDE/OMC "B" SERIES - 6 1/2 VR or 10 in. barrel, ser. no. range B00001-B00370.

	$2,250	$2,100	$1,850	$1,620	$1,335	$1,115	$930

AMT "C" SERIES - 6 1/2 VR or 10 in. barrel, ser. no. range C00001-C00050.

	$2,250	$2,100	$1,850	$1,620	$1,335	$1,115	$930

Note: guns were cased (plastic attache style) with accessories. Collector caution - over the years, the foam in these plastic cases can break down, and may cause discoloration and pitting on the gun. Original Auto-Mag ammo (only original mfg. by CDM in Mexico and Norma in Sweden) is currently selling for approx. $75-$95 a box. Starline now has .44 AMP brass, and Cor-bon loaded .44 AMP ammo also - new 2001.

HARRY SANFORD COMMEMORATIVE AUTO MAG - .44 AMP cal., Automag, Inc. commemorative reissue, "STURGIS, SD" barrel address with Harry Sanford signature on left rear of slide, cased. 1,000 pistols were scheduled to be mfg., but only approx. 300 actually completed by Galena Industries 1999-2000.

	$2,750	$2,300	$1,995	N/A	N/A	N/A	N/A

Last MSR was $2,750.

AUTO-ORDNANCE CORP.

Current manufacturer with facilities located in Worcester, MA, and corporate offices in Blauvelt, NY. Auto-Ordnance Corp. became a division of Kahr Arms in 1999. Auto-Ordnance Corp. was a division of Gun Parts Corp. until 1999. Previously located in West Hurley, NY. Consumer, dealer and distributor sales.

   Auto-Ordnance Corp. manufactures an exact reproduction of the original 1927 Thompson machine gun. They are currently available from Kahr Arms in semi-auto only since

GRADING - PPGS™	100%	98%	95%	90%	80%	70%	60%

production ceased on fully automatic variations (Model 1928 and M1) in 1986 (mfg. 1975-1986 including 609 M1s). All guns currently manufactured utilize the Thompson trademark, are manufactured in the U.S. and come with a lifetime warranty.

PISTOLS: SEMI-AUTO

During 1997, Auto Ordnance discontinued all calibers on the pistols listed below, except for .45 ACP cal. or 9mm Para. Slide kits were available for $179. Also, conversion units (converting .45 ACP to .38 Super or 9mm Para.) were available for $195.

All current Auto Ordnance 1911 Models include a spent case, plastic case, and cable lock.

1911 COMPETITION - .38 Super (1996 only) or .45 ACP cal., competition features include compensated barrel, commander hammer, flat mainspring housing, white 3-dot sighting system, beavertail grip safety, black textured wraparound grips. Mfg. 1993-96.

	$530	$415	$375	$330	$300	$285	$270

Last MSR was $636.

Add $10 for .38 Super cal.

1911 THOMPSON CUSTOM - .45 ACP cal., stainless steel or aluminum (Lightweight model, new 2005) construction, Series 80 design, 5 in. barrel, Thompson bullet logo on left side of double serrated slide, 7-shot mag., grip safety, checkered laminate grips with medallion, skeletonized trigger, combat hammer, low profile sights, 31 1/2 (Lightweight) or 39 oz. Mfg. 2004-2007.

	$675	$560	$480	$410	$350	$300	$275

Last MSR was $775.

1911 A1 STANDARD/COMPACT STANDARD - .38 Super (disc. 1996), 9mm Para. (disc. 1996), .40 S&W (mfg. 1991-93), 10mm (mfg. 1991-96), or .45 ACP cal., 4 1/4 (.45 ACP only, Compact Standard Model), 4 1/2 (.40 S&W cal. only) or 5 (Standard Model) in. barrel, 7-shot mag., single action, parts interchange with the original Colt Govt. Model, blue or nickel finish, checkered plastic grips, 39 oz. Disc. 2005.

	$450	$370	$295	$255	$235	$225	$215

Last MSR was $592.

Add $28 for satin nickel (mfg. 1990-96) or $37 for duo-tone (mfg. 1992-96) finish (.45 ACP only).

* *1911 A1 WWII Parkerized* - .45 ACP cal., no frills variation of the 1911 A1, military parkerizing, G.I. detailing with military style roll stamp, plastic or checkered walnut (disc. 2001, reintroduced 2007) grips, and lanyard loop. New 1992.

MSR $627	$495	$395	$315	$275	$235	$225	$215

Add $35 for wood grips (new 2007).

* *1911 A1 Standard 80* - .45 ACP cal., features firing pin block in slide, 5 in. barrel, otherwise similar to 1911 A1 Standard. Mfg. 2004-2007.

	$465	$375	$310	$255	$235	$225	$215

Last MSR was $609.

* *1911 A1 Deluxe 80* - .38 Super (disc. 1996), 9mm Para. (disc. 1996), or .45 ACP cal., 5 in. barrel, 3-dot sights, wraparound grips, 39 oz. Mfg. 1991-2006.

	$480	$385	$315	$260	$240	$225	$215

Last MSR was $615.

* *1911 A1 General* - .38 Super (mfg. 1996 only) or .45 ACP cal., 4 1/2 in. barrel with full length recoil guide system, 7-shot mag., blue finish, 3-dot fixed Millett sights, black rubber wraparound grips, Commander styling, 37 oz. Mfg. 1992-98.

	$385	$315	$255	$235	$225	$215	$200

Last MSR was $465.

GRADING - PPGS™	100%	98%	95%	90%	80%	70%	60%

* *1911 A1 Custom High Polish* - .45 ACP cal., 8-shot mag., 5 in. barrel, custom combat hammer, beavertail grip safety, rosewood grips with medallions, 3-dot sights, flat mainspring housing, Videcki speed trigger, 39 oz. Mfg. 1997-99.

	$485	$395	$325	$265	$235	$225	$215

Last MSR was $585.

MODEL ZG-51 "PIT BULL" - .45 ACP cal. only, compact variation of the 1911 A1, 3 5/8 in. standard (disc. 1996) or 4 3/8 in. compensated (new 1997) barrel, 7-shot mag., 36 oz. Mfg. 1988-99.

	$385	$310	$255	$235	$225	$215	$200

Last MSR was $470.

THOMPSON 1927A-1 DELUXE - .45 ACP cal., single action, blow back design, 10 1/2 in. finned barrel, grooved walnut forearm with sling swivel, blade front sight, adj. rear sight, 50 shot drum mag, also accepts 30 shot stick, 10 shot stick and 100 shot drum magazines, approx. 6 lbs. New 2008.

MSR $1,117	$895	$750	$625	$550	$475	$400	$350

Add $577 for 100 shot drum mag.

This model is marked "Model of 1927A-1" and "Thompson Semi-Automatic Carbine" on the left side and Auto-Ordnance Corporation on the right side.

RIFLES: SEMI-AUTO

The Auto-Ordnance Thompson replicas listed below are currently supplied with a 15, 20, or 30 shot stick mag. Tommy Guns are not currently legal in CA or CT.

Thompson
Auto-Ordnance Corporation

Add the following for currently manufactured Thompson 1921 A-1 models:
Add $70 for 30 shot stick mag.
Add $193 for 10 shot drum mag. (they resemble the older 50 shot L-type drum) - new 1994.
Add $299 for 50* shot drum mag. or $577 for 100* shot drum mag. (mfg. 1990-93, reintroduced 2006).
Add $157 for factory violin case or $181 for hard case.

THOMPSON M1 CARBINE (.45 ACP CAL.) - .45 ACP cal., combat model, 16 1/2 in. smooth barrel w/o compensator, 30 shot original surplus mag., side-cocking lever, matte black finish, walnut stock, pistol grip, and grooved horizontal forearm, current mfg. will not accept drum mags., 11 1/2 lbs. New 1986.

MSR $1,205	$950	$775	$575	$475	$350	$295	$265

* *Thompson 1927 M1-C Lightweight* - similar to M1 Carbine, except receiver is made of a lightweight alloy, current mfg. accepts drum mags., 9 1/2 lbs. Mfg. 2001-2002, reintroduced 2005.

MSR $962	$775	$650	$525	$400	$325	$295	$275

During 2006, this model incorporated a large machined radius on the bottom of the receiver to improve magazine insertion.

AUTO-ORDNANCE M1-CARBINE (.30 CAL.) - .30 Carbine cal., birch or walnut (standard beginning 2008) stock, 18 in. barrel, all new parts, parkerized reciever, metal handguard, aperture rear sight and bayonet lug, 10 (new 2005) or 15-shot mag., 5.4 lbs. New 2004.

MSR $814	$675	$550	$450	$350	$300	$275	$250

* *Auto-Ordnance M1 Carbine Paratrooper* - .30 Carbine cal., similar to .30 cal. M1 Carbine, except has folding stock, walnut handguard, parkerized finish, 15 shot mag. New 2008.

MSR $965	$775	$650	$525	$400	$325	$295	$275

GRADING - PPGS™	100%	98%	95%	90%	80%	70%	60%

* **Auto-Ordnance M1 Carbine Tactical** - .30 Carbine cal., similar to .30 cal. M1 carbine, except has black polymer folding stock, metal handguard, 15 shot mag. New 2008.

MSR $792	$650	$525	$425	$350	$300	$275	$250

AUTO-ORDNANCE 1927 A-1 STANDARD - .45 ACP cal., 16 in. plain barrel, solid steel construction, standard military sight, walnut stock and horizontal forearm. Disc. 1986.

	$570	$490	$430	$360	$315	$290	$270

Last MSR was $575.

THOMPSON 1927 A-1 DELUXE CARBINE - 10mm (mfg. 1991-93) or .45 ACP cal., 16 1/2 in. finned barrel with compensator, includes one 30 shot original surplus mag., current mfg. accepts drum mags., solid steel construction, matte black finish, adj. rear sight, walnut stock, pistol grip, and finger grooved forearm grip, 13 lbs.

MSR $1,282	$975	$750	$600	$475	$375	$295	$275

Add $392 for detachable buttstock and horizontal foregrip (new 2007).

During 2006, design changes included a more authentic spherical cocking knob, improved frame to receiver fit, and a large machined radius at the bottom of the receiver to help with magazine insertion.

* **Thompson 1927 A-1C Lightweight Deluxe** - .45 ACP cal., similar to 1927 A-1 Deluxe, except receiver made of a lightweight alloy, currently shipped with 30 shot stick mag. (where legal), current mfg. accepts drum mags., 9 1/2 lbs. New 1984.

MSR $1,034	$875	$725	$550	$450	$375	$295	$275

* **Thompson 1927 A-1 Presentation Walnut Carbine** - .45 ACP cal., similar to 1927 A-1 Deluxe, except has presentation grade walnut buttstock, pistol grip, and foregrip, supplied with plastic case. Limited mfg. 2003.

	$850	$675	$525	$425	$350	$325	$295

Last MSR was $1,121.

* **Thompson 1927 A-1 Deluxe .22 LR Cal.** - .22 LR cal., very limited mfg., 30-shot mag. standard.

	$1,100	$995	$925	$800	$700	$650	$575

THOMPSON 1927 A-1 COMMANDO - .45 ACP cal., 16 1/2 in. finned barrel with compensator, 30-shot mag., black finished stock and forearm, parkerized metal, black nylon sling, 13 lbs. New 1997.

MSR $1,259	$985	$750	$575	$450	$375	$295	$275

During 2006, this model incorporated a spherical cocking knob.

THOMPSON SBR - .45 ACP cal., 10 1/2 in. finned barrel, closed bolt, blue metal finish, pistol grip forearm, 30-shot mag., 12 lbs. New 2004.

MSR $1,855	$1,600	$1,375	$1,150	$975	$850	$725	$600

Add $452 for detachable buttstock and horizontal foregrip (new 2007).

This carbine model may only be shipped from the factory to a Class II manufacturer or Class III dealer.

THOMPSON M1 SBR - .45 ACP cal., 10 1/2 in. barrel, closed bolt, blue metal finish, regular forearm, 30-shot mag., 12 lbs. New 2004.

MSR $1,779	$1,500	$1,300	$1,125	$925	$800	$700	$600

This carbine model may only be shipped from the factory to a Class II manufacturer or Class III dealer.

GRADING - PPGS™	100%	98%	95%	90%	80%	70%	60%

1927 A5 PISTOL/CARBINE - .45 ACP cal., 13 in. finned barrel, alloy construction, overall length 26 in., 10- (C/B 1994) shot mag., 7 lbs. Mfg. disc. 1994.

	$1,050	$925	$825	$750	$650	$600	$500

Last MSR was $765.

1927 A3 - .22 CAL. - .22 LR cal., 16 or 18 in. finned barrel with compensator, alloy frame and receiver, fixed or detachable walnut stock, pistol grip, and forearm pistol grip, 7 lbs. Mfg. disc. 1994.

	$995	$875	$750	$650	$550	$500	$450

Last MSR was $510.

AUTO-POINTER

Previous trademark manufactured by Yamamoto Co. Formerly imported by Sloans.

SHOTGUNS: SEMI-AUTO

SEMI-AUTO SHOTGUN - 12 or 20 ga., gas operated. Disc.

	$275	$240	$220	$195	$180	$160	$145

AXTELL RIFLE CO.

Current rifle manufacturer located in Sheridan, MT. Distributed by The Riflesmith Inc., located in Sheridan, MT. Consumer direct sales.

RIFLES: REPRODUCTIONS

New Model 1877 Sharps reproductions are available for both long-range and sporting rifles listed below in the following black powder calibers: .40-50, .40-70, .40-90, .45-70 Govt., .45-90, and .45-100 cal. The Riflesmith Inc. should be contacted (see Trademark Index) directly for accessories and/or engraving options. MSRs and 100% value do not include federal excise tax.

    Add $275 for bull hide rifle case.

NUMBER ONE CREEDMOOR - features 34 in. Rigby style barrel, choice of high-grade black or English checkered walnut stock and forearm with ebony inlays. Long range sights. 10 lbs.

MSR $4,700	$4,700	$3,950	$3,500	$3,025	$2,500	$2,000	$1,575

C-EXPRESS - top-of-the-line model with double set triggers, 32 or 34 in. 1/2 round, 1/2 octagon barrel, select walnut checkered stock, deluxe front and rear sights, approx. 13 lbs.

MSR $5,300	$5,300	$4,350	$3,750	$3,150	$2,600	$2,100	$1,650

NUMBER TWO LONG RANGE - choice of 30-34 in. Rigby style barrel, select black or English checkered walnut stock and forearm. Long range sights.

MSR $4,300	$4,300	$3,300	$3,050	$2,525	$2,000	$1,650	$1,300

OVERBAUGH SCHUETZEN - features 26-30 in. octagon barrel, double-set triggers, Schuetzen buttplate with cheekpiece, palm rest, short-range sights, 11-14 lbs.

MSR $4,900	$4,900	$3,850	$3,450	$2,700	$2,125	$1,700	$1,300

LOWER SPORTER - 28 or 30 in. octagon barrel, double-set triggers, steel buttplate with straight grip, standard rifle weight of 9 lbs.

MSR $3,100	$3,100	$2,350	$1,825	$1,400	$1,050	$825	$700

LOWER BUSINESS - 28 in. contoured round barrel, double-set triggers, black walnut stock has steel shotgun buttplate with straight grip, hunter tang, blade front sights, approx. 8 1/2 lbs.

MSR $2,950	$2,950	$2,225	$1,725	$1,350	$995	$825	$700

B SECTION

BSA GUNS LIMITED

Current manufacturer and trademark established in 1861 and located in Birmingham, England. BSA (Birmingham Small Arms) currently manufactures airguns only. English-made BSA firearms were imported until 1985 by Precision Sports from Ithaca, NY and 1986 by BSA Guns Ltd., located in Grand Prairie, TX. Imported and distributed until 1989 by Samco Global Arms, Inc., located in Miami, FL.

For more information and current pricing on both new and used BSA airguns, please refer to the *Blue Book of Airguns* by Dr. Robert Beeman & John Allen (also available online).

GRADING - PPGS™	100%	98%	95%	90%	80%	70%	60%

RIFLES: BOLT ACTION

Importation of all BSA rimfire and centerfire rifles was disc. 1987.

MAJESTIC FEATHERWEIGHT DELUXE - .243 Win., .270 Win., .308 Win., or .30-06 cal., bolt action, 22 in. barrel, folding sight, checkered European style stock. Mfg. 1959-65.

	100%	98%	95%	90%	80%	70%	60%
	$395	$350	$220	$195	$180	$165	$145
.458 Mag.	$445	$375	$305	$275	$220	$210	$200

MAJESTIC DELUXE - .222 Rem., .22 Hornet, .243 Win., 7x57mm, .308 Win., or .30-06 cal., heavier barrel.

	100%	98%	95%	90%	80%	70%	60%
	$395	$300	$300	$275	$250	$165	$145

Add 100% for .22 Hornet cal.

MONARCH DELUXE - similar to Majestic Deluxe, but American design stock. Mfg. 1965-74.

	100%	98%	95%	90%	80%	70%	60%
	$395	$275	$250	$220	$195	$180	$165

MONARCH DELUXE VARMINT - similar to Monarch Deluxe, except .222 Rem. or .243 Win. cal., 24 in. heavy barrel. Disc.

	100%	98%	95%	90%	80%	70%	60%
	$395	$315	$275	$250	$210	$195	$180

MARTINI ISU MATCH .22 - .22 LR cal. only, single shot, bolt action, similar to CFT Model. Disc. 1985.

	100%	98%	95%	90%	80%	70%	60%
	$825	$700	$600	$530	$475	$435	$400

Last MSR was $1,000.

Add $100 for Mk. V.H.B. Model.

CF-2 ACTION - .222 Rem., .22-250 Rem., .243 Win., 6.5x55mm, 7x57mm, 7x64mm, 7mm Rem. Mag., .270 Win., .308 Win., .30-06, or .300 Win. Mag. cal., bolt action, barrel length 23-26 in., 7 1/2-8 lbs. CF-2 nomenclature designates an action rather than a model. The following are CF-2 actioned models.

Add $70 for double set trigger option on the following models.

✳ *CF-2 Action Sporter/Classic* - same cals. as above, checkered oil finished walnut stock. Imported 1986-87.

	100%	98%	95%	90%	80%	70%	60%
	$395	$275	$250	$225	$210	$195	$180

Last MSR was $360.

Sporter Model features Monte Carlo stock, rosewood capped forearm and pistol grip stock, and swivels.

✳ *CF-2 Action Classic Varminter* - .222 Rem. - .243 Win. cals. only, heavy barrel, matte finish, with swivels. Imported 1986 only.

	100%	98%	95%	90%	80%	70%	60%
	$395	$275	$250	$225	$210	$190	$175

Last MSR was $345.

GRADING - PPGS™	100%	98%	95%	90%	80%	70%	60%

✱ *CF-2 Action Heavy Barrel Model* - .222 Rem., .22-250 Rem., or .243 Win. cal., approx. 9 lbs., no sights.

	100%	98%	95%	90%	80%	70%	60%
	$375	$300	$260	$240	$225	$210	$180

Last MSR was $410.

✱ *CF-2 Action Carbine Model* - 20 in. barrel. Disc. 1985.

	$495	$375	$300	$270	$250	$225	$200

Last MSR was $480.

✱ *CF-2 Action Stutzen Rifle* - Mannlicher style full length stock, same general specifications as Sporter/Classic, 20 1/2 in. barrel. Not available in 7mm Rem. Mag. or .300 Win. Mag. cal.

	$595	$400	$325	$300	$275	$250	$225

Last MSR was $385.

✱ *CF-2 Action Regal Custom* - similar to Sporter Model, except has slim classic European style stock with Schnabel forend, deluxe walnut with extra checkering, ebony forend cap, engraved action and floorplate. Limited importation 1986 only.

	$875	$795	$685	$590	$550	$500	$450

Last MSR was $950.

This model was custom-made by special order only.

CFT TARGET RIFLE - 7.62mm cal., single shot, bolt action, globe front and aperture rear sights, 26 1/2 in. barrel, 11 lbs. Disc. 1987.

	$675	$590	$550	$500	$450	$400	$360

Last MSR was $780.

RIFLES: SINGLE SHOT

NO. 12 MARTINI - .22 LR cal., 29 in. barrel, target sights, straight stock, pre-WWII.

	$725	$600	$500	$425	$350	$300	$275

MILITARY MARTINI HENRY (MODELS 1871 & 1885) - various cals., pre-WWII mfg. many configurations and barrel lengths. Pricing takes into consideration most commonly encountered types with no engraving or special orders.

	100%	98%	95%	90%	80%	70%	60%
Post-1900 mfg.	$900	$700	$500	$450	$400	$365	$335
Pre-1899 mfg.	$650	$550	$475	$400	$350	$300	$250

MARTINI CADET - various cals., mostly military issue, many thousands previously imported into the U.S. from England, many have been sporterized or modified.

	$725	$600	$500	$425	$350	$300	$275

✱ *Martini Cadet Australian Junior* - .310 cal., mfg. by BSA and W.W. Greener, Francotte patent one-piece take out action, various rear sight configurations, some have been coverted to modern cartridges.

	$550	$475	$375	$325	$275	$235	$200

MODEL 15 - similar to No. 12 Martini, except pistol grip stock, better grade target sights, pre-WWII.

	$725	$600	$500	$425	$350	$300	$275

CENTURION MATCH RIFLE - similar to Model 15, except Centurion guarantee 1 1/2 in. grouping at 100 yards, 24 in. barrel, pre-WWII.

	$800	$675	$550	$475	$425	$350	$300

MATCH 12/15 - similar to Model 15, except made after WWII.

	$725	$600	$500	$425	$350	$300	$275

MODEL 12/15 - heavy barrel.

	$725	$600	$500	$425	$350	$300	$275

MODEL 13 - lighter version of No. 12 Martini.

	$725	$600	$500	$425	$350	$300	$275

GRADING - PPGS™	100%	98%	95%	90%	80%	70%	60%

MODEL 13 SPORTER - similar to Model 13, except has sport sights.

	100%	98%	95%	90%	80%	70%	60%
	$725	$600	$500	$425	$350	$300	$275
.22 Hornet	$950	$825	$725	$625	$525	$425	$325

MARTINI INTERNATIONAL MATCH - .22 LR cal., 29 in. heavy barrel, international sights. Mfg. 1950-53.

$825	$700	$600	$475	$400	$350	$325

INTERNATIONAL LIGHT - 26 in. lightweight barrel.

$775	$675	$550	$450	$400	$350	$325

INTERNATIONAL MKII - improved trigger, ejectors and stock design. Mfg. 1953-59.

$950	$825	$700	$600	$550	$500	$450

INTERNATIONAL MKIII - longer action, floating barrel. Mfg. 1959-67.

$995	$875	$750	$650	$600	$550	$500

INTERNATIONAL ISU - modeled to meet ISU standards, 28 in. barrel. Mfg. 1968-disc.

$1,000	$875	$750	$650	$600	$550	$500

INTERNATIONAL MARK V - similar to ISU, but heavier barrel, mfg. 1976-disc.

$1,000	$875	$750	$650	$600	$550	$500

SHOTGUNS

BSA Imports, located in Ft. Lauderdale, FL, imported O/U, SxS, and semi-auto shotguns from 2004-2006 which were manufactured in Turkey and utilized the BSA logo/trademark. BSA also manufactured SxS boxlock shotguns in various grades. Normally encountered in 12 ga. with DTs and extractors, these shotguns are of good quality and are typically encountered in the secondary market in the $250-$500 range, assuming standard grade.

SILVER EAGLE O/U - 12 or 20 ga., 3 in. chambers, 26 or 28 in. barrels, multi-chokes, hand-checkered Turkish walnut stock, blue receiver, gold SST, extractors (Silver Eagle) or ejectors (Silver Eagle II). Imported 2004-2006.

$395	$360	$330	$295	$260	$230	$200

Last MSR was $489.

Add $100 for ejectors (Silver Eagle II).

FALCON O/U - 12 or 20 ga., 3 in. chambers, boxlock action, 26, 28, or 30 in. barrels, Beretta style multichokes, laser-checkered field walnut stock with Schnabel forend, ejectors, case colored engraved receiver, gold SST. Imported 2004-2006.

$1,000	$900	$800	$700	$600	$500	$400

Last MSR was $1,199.

SPORTING O/U - 12 ga., 2 3/4 in. chambers, 28 or 30 in. ported barrels, multichokes, checkered walnut target stock, ejectors, silver finished engraved receiver, triggerguard, safety and opening lever, gold SST. Imported 2004-2006.

$1,025	$950	$825	$725	$625	$525	$425

Last MSR was $1,249.

CLASSIC SxS - 12, 16, 20, 28 ga. or .410 bore, 2 3/4 (16 or 28 ga.) or 3 in. chambers, 26 or 28 in. barrels with Beretta style choke tubes, checkered select walnut stock with Prince of Wales pistol grip, ejectors, case colored hardened receiver, gold SST, semi-beavertail forend. Imported 2004-2006.

$1,065	$975	$850	$750	$650	$550	$450

Last MSR was $1,299.

ROYAL SxS - 12 or 20 ga., 3 in. chambers, 26 or 28 in. barrels with Beretta style choke tubes, checkered select walnut stock. Imported 2005-2006.

$1,225	$1,075	$975	$850	$750	$650	$550

Last MSR was $1,499.

GRADING - PPGS™	100%	98%	95%	90%	80%	70%	60%

200/300 SERIES SEMI-AUTO - 12, 16, 20, 28 ga. or .410 bore, 2 3/4 (16, 28 ga. or .410 bore), 3 or 3 1/2 (Model 312 only) in. chamber, 24 (Model 312 only), 26 or 28 in. barrels, vent. rib, multichokes, synthetic or checkered Turkish walnut stock, blue receiver, gold trigger, drilled and tapped, firing pin block. Imported 2004-2006.

	$325	$285	$250	$225	$200	$175	$150

Last MSR was $399.

Add $60 for wood stock.
Add $30 for 16 or 28 ga. or .410 bore.
Add $20 for 3 1/2 in. chamber.
This model was manufactured by Matsan in Turkey, and was also available in a 20 ga. at no extra charge.

B-WEST

Previous importer/distributor located in Tucson, AZ, until 1997.

B-West previously imported rifles (including AK-47 clones, the Saiga, Dragunov, etc.), the IJ series .380 ACP Makarov pistol, and the Daewoo DP-51 semi-auto pistol.

BAFORD ARMS, INC.

Previous manufacturer located in Bristol, TN. Previously distributed by C.L. Reedy & Associates, Inc. located in Melbourne, FL.

DERRINGERS

THUNDER DERRINGER - .44 Spl. cal./.410 shotshell, single shot, tip-up action, 3 in. barrel, blue finish steel finish, spur trigger, wood grips. Introduced late 1988 with limited mfg. until 1991, when production permanently ceased.

	$130	$110	$95	$90	$85	$80	$75

Last MSR was $130.

Add $90 for interchangeable barrel kit.
Interchangeable pistol barrels are chambered in various calibers between .22 Short and 9mm Para. There are two types: one fits flush while the other facilitates a scope mounting.

PISTOLS: SEMI-AUTO

MODEL 35 FIRE POWER - 9mm Para. cal., semi-auto single action, patterned after the Browning Hi-Power, total stainless steel construction, 4 3/4 in. barrel, combat hammer and safety, Pachmayr grips, removable barrel bushing, Millett Mk. II sights, 14-shot mag., 32 oz. Introduced late 1988 with limited mfg. until 1993.

	$500	$425	$350	$285	$250	$215	$185

Last MSR was $550.

BAIKAL

Current trademark of products manufactured by the Russian Federal State Unitary Plant "Izhevsky Mechanichesky Zavod" (FSUP IMZ). Baikal SxS and O/U hunting guns (including air guns) are imported and distributed exclusively beginning 2005 by U.S. Sporting Goods, located in Rockledge, FL. Many Baikal shotguns and rifles are being sold domestically by Remington under the Spartan Gunworks trademark. See listings under Spartan Gunworks for more information.

Previously imported from late 1998 until 2004 by European American Armory Corp., located in Sharpes, FL, and from 1993-96 by Big Bear, located in Dallas, TX.

Please contact the importer directly for more information and pricing on Baikal firearms.

Baikal (the name of a lake in Siberia) was one of the key holding companies from the former Soviet Union, specializing in the production of firearms, and science intensive, complex electronic equipment.

The company was founded in 1942 as part of the Russian National Defense Industry. At that time, the plant produced world renowned Tokarev TT pistols. Upon conclusion of WWII, the company expanded its operation to include non-military weapons (O/U, SxS, and single barrel shotguns). FSUP IMZ is one of the world's largest manufacturers of mili-

GRADING - PPGS™	100%	98%	95%	90%	80%	70%	60%

tary and non-military weapons. The total amount of guns that are produced by the FSUP IMZ is 680,000 units per year. The products range from various smoothbore guns, including slide action and self-loading models, rifled and combination guns, to a full array of sporting, civil, and combat pistols, including the internationally famous Makarov pistol. Since 2000, Baikal has produced a new pistol for the Russian Army that was developed by the enterprise designers and named after the group's leader - the Yarygin pistol.

FSUP IMZ features efficient manufacturing capacity and unique intellectual potential of qualified engineers-and-technicians staff. The FSUP IMZ is also undertaking the task of reintroducing the world to the "Russian Custom Gunsmith." There is a gunsmith school at the factory area for custom, one-of-a-kind hand engraved shotguns and rifles. The guns produced by the school feature high-quality assembly, attractive appearance and high functional quality according to the best traditions of Russian gunmakers.

In the past, Baikal shotguns have had limited importation into the U.S. 1993 marked the first year that Baikals were officially (and legally) imported into the U.S. because of Russia's previous export restrictions domestically. In prior years, however, a few O/Us have been seen for sale and have no doubt been imported into this country one at a time. Currently produced Baikals are noted for their good quality at low-level costs.

N/As have replaced MSRs on certain models below, indicating the most recent importation by EAA.

COMBINATION GUNS

IZH-94 O/U - 12 or 20 (new 2001) ga. over various cals. (domestic and metric), 3 in. chamber, boxlock action, 23 1/2 in. separated barrels with express sights, DT, extractors, fixed or screw-in chokes, checkered walnut stock and forearm, approx. 7 1/4 lbs.

MSR N/A	$425	$375	$335	$300	$275	$250	$235

This model was also sold in the U.S. under the model name SPR94.

* *IZH-94 .410 Bore/Rimfire* - .410 bore with 3 in. chamber over choice of .17 HMR, .22 LR or .22 Mag. cal., 23 1/2 in. barrel, extractors, single trigger, walnut stock and forearm. Importation began 2003.

MSR N/A	$175	$140	$130	$125	$120	$115	$110

This model was also sold in the U.S. under the model names IZH94 Rimfire and SPR94 Rimfire.

PISTOLS: SEMI-AUTO

IZH-35M - 22 LR cal., semi-auto target pistol featuring fully adj. walnut ergonomic target grip, 6 in. hammer forged barrel, adj. trigger assembly, integral grip safety, 5-shot mag., cocking indicator and detachable scope mount, 2.3 lbs. Importation began 2000.

MSR N/A	$425	$385	$335	$300	$275	$250	$225

U.S. options on this gun includes manual lever safety, side-located push-button mag. catch, slide retainer and removable scope base (not available in standard European version).

IZH-70 (IJ-70) - .380 ACP or 9x18 Makarov cal., double action semi-auto, all steel blue construction, 4 in. barrel, slide mounted safety with decocking, fully adj. target sights, choice of two 8-shot (IJ- 70), two 10-shot (C/B 1994, Model IJ-70-HC), or two 12*-shot mag., holster and cleaning rod, checkered plastic grips, 25 oz. Disc. 1996.

	$175	$150	$135	$120	$105	$95	$85

Last MSR was $199.

Add $40 for IJ-70-HC (High Capacity).
Add $50 for .380 ACP cal.
Add $10 for nickel finish (disc.).

This model was also imported under the model name Baikal 442.

GRADING - PPGS™	100%	98%	95%	90%	80%	70%	60%

RIFLES: O/U

IZH-94 EXPRESS - .222 Rem., .223 Rem., .30-06, .308 Win., 6.5x55mm, or 7.62x39mm cal., DT, extractors, mono bloc construction, 24 in. barrels with express sights, checkered walnut stock and forearm, 8.3 lbs. Importation began 2001.

MSR N/A	$450	$395	$365	$335	$295	$280	$265

RIFLES: SxS

MP-221 - .223 Rem., .270 Win., .30-06, .308 Win., or .45-70 Govt. cal., 23 1/2 in. barrel, boxlock monobloc action, DT, adj. barrel regulation, 11mm scope rail, checkered walnut stock and forearm with sling swivels, extractors, vent. recoil pad, 7 1/2 lbs. Importation began 2003.

MSR N/A	$525	$425	$365	$335	$295	$280	$265

This model was also sold in the U.S. under the name SPR22.

RIFLES: SINGLE BARREL

IZH-18MH - .222 Rem., .243 Win., .270 Win., 7.62x39mm, .308 Win., or .30-06 cal., boxlock action, 23 1/2 in. barrel with extractor, underlever action next to triggerguard, checkered walnut stock with vent. recoil pad, sling swivels, iron sights or scope rail, 6.8 lbs. Importation began 2003.

MSR N/A	$190	$165	$145	$130	$120	$110	$105

This model has also been sold in the U.S. under the names IZH018MN and SPR-18.

SHOTGUNS: O/U, RECENT IMPORTATION

IZH-27 - 12, 16, 20, 28 ga., or .410 bore, 3 in. chambers (2 3/4 in. on 16 or 28 ga.) boxlock action, 26 or 28 in. VR barrels with (standard on 12 and 20 ga.) or w/o chokes, monobloc receiver, walnut checkered stock (with or w/o Monte Carlo) and forearm, extractors or ejectors, blue or nickel finish (new 2001), SST. Importation began 1999.

MSR N/A	$400	$350	$295	$265	$225	$200	$190

    Add $10 for 16 or 20 ga.
    Add $34 for 28 ga. or .410 bore.
    Add $224 for 20 ga. 2 barrel set.
    Add $24 for nickel finish.
    Add $80 for nickel finish with barrel porting (12 ga. only, disc. 2003).

E nomenclature indicates ejectors. 1C indicates single trigger. This model has also been sold in the U.SD. under the model names SPR310 (SST) and SPR320 (DT).

✱ *IZH-27 Sporting* - 12 or 20 ga., 3 in. chambers, SST, ejectors, ported 29 1/2 in. barrels with MC-3 chokes, wide rib, nickel finished frame. Importation began 2004.

MSR N/A	$525	$450	$400	$350	$295	$265	$225

MP 233 SPORTING - 12 ga. only, 3 in. chambers, 26, 28, or 29 1/2 in. unported (disc.) or ported barrels with multi-chokes and wide VR, removable trigger group, SST, ejectors, checkered walnut stock and forearm, includes carrying case, 7.2 lbs. Importation began 1999.

MSR N/A	$775	$650	$575	$500	$460	$430	$395

SHOTGUNS: SxS, RECENT IMPORTATION

The following Bounty Hunters are available in either 12 or 20 ga., include 3 in. chambers, are designed for cowboy action shooting, with choice of hammers or hammerless action, SST, DT (disc.), or double selective triggers, 20 in. barrels with or w/o choke tubes, hardwood or walnut stock and forearm, engraved receiver, extractors, and weigh approx. 7 lbs.

GRADING - PPGS™	100%	98%	95%	90%	80%	70%	60%

IZH-43 FIELD MODEL - 12 or 20 ga., double triggers, extractors, 20, 26 (disc.), or 28 in. barrels. Disc. 1996.

	$235	$200	$160	$130	$105	$95	$75

Last MSR was $299.

Add $20 for 20 in. barrels bored C/C.

IZH-43 TRADITIONAL HUNTING MODEL - 12, 16, 20, 28 ga., or .410 bore, Anson & Deeley style boxlock action with monobloc, SST, 24, 26, or 28 in. barrels with or w/o (28 ga. and .410 bore) choke tubes, checkered walnut stock and forearm, approx. 7 lbs. Importation began 1999.

MSR N/A	$340	$295	$250	$220	$185	$165	$150

Add $30 for 16, 20, 28 ga., or .410 bore.
Add $20 for nickel finish (new 2004).

This model has been sold in the U.S. under the model names SPR210 (SST), SPR220 (DT), and Stevens Upland Sporter 411.

✱ *IZH-43 2 Barrel Set* - includes both 20 and 28 ga. barrels. Importation began 2000.

MSR N/A	$515	$465	$415	$375	$345	$315	$290

✱ *IZH-43 Traditional Bounty Hunter* - 12, 20 ga., or .410 bore (mfg. 2001-2002), 2 3/4 in. chambers, hammerless, 20 in. barrels with choice of cyl./cyl. bore or multichokes, nickel receiver (new 2004), DT or SST, hardwood or walnut stock. Importation began 2000.

MSR N/A	$275	$235	$205	$185	$165	$150	$145

Add $20 for nickel receiver.
Add $40-$50 for walnut stock and forearm.
Add $50-$60 for SST.
Add $159 for .45-70 cal. barrel inserts (only if shotgun is 12 ga., has 2 3/4 in. chambers, and 20 in. barrels with choke tubes).

IZH-43K EXTERNAL HAMMERS - 12 or 20 (disc.) ga., similar to IZH-43 Hunting Model, except has engraved sideplates and external cocking hammers, approx. 6.3 lbs. Importation began 2000.

MSR N/A	$330	$290	$260	$235	$215	$200	$195

Add $20 for choke tubes.
Add $20 for external firing pins.

✱ *IZH-43K External Hammer 2 Barrel Set* - includes both 20 and 28 ga. barrels. Imported 2000 only.

	$550	$500	$460	$420	$395	$360	$330

Last MSR was $639.

✱ *IZH-43K Bounty Hunter Traditional* - 12 or 20 (disc. 2002) ga., 20 in. barrels with choice of cyl./cyl. bore or multichokes. Importation began 2000.

MSR N/A	$285	$260	$225	$200	$180	$165	$150

Add $40 for multichokes or $50 for multichokes and SST.
Add $10 for external firing pins and traditional sideplates.
Add $159 for .45-70 cal. barrel inserts (only if shotgun is 12 ga., has 2 3/4 in. chambers, and 20 in. barrels with choke tubes).

✱ *IZH-43KH External Hammers* - 20 ga., 20 or 28 in. barrels with screw-in chokes, sideplates.

MSR N/A	$330	$290	$260	$235	$215	$200	$195

This model has also been sold in the U.S. under the model name SPR220F.

MP-213 - 12 ga. only, 3 in. chambers, hammerless, SST (disc. 2000) or double selective triggers, ejectors, removable trigger assembly, 20 (Coach Gun), 24, 26, or 28 in. monobloc barrels with choke tubes, checkered walnut stock and forearm, includes carrying case, approx. 7 lbs. Disc.

	$795	$675	$595	$525	$450	$400	$360

Add $159 for .45-70 cal. barrel inserts (only if shotgun is 12 ga., has 2 3/4 in. chambers, and 20 in. barrels with choke tubes).

GRADING - PPGS™	100%	98%	95%	90%	80%	70%	60%

SHOTGUNS: SEMI-AUTO, RECENT IMPORTATION

MP-151 - 12 ga., 3 in. chamber, 26 or 28 in. plain barrel with 2 choke tubes, black synthetic or checkered walnut Monte Carlo stock, tube or detachable box (available late 1999) mag., approx. 7.8 lbs. Imported 1999 only.

	$275	$235	$215	$195	$180	$165	$150

Last MSR was $310.

MP-153 - 12 ga. only, 3 1/2 in. chamber, 24 (new 2001), 26 or 28 in. VR barrel with choke tubes, black synthetic or walnut stock and forearm, approx. 8 lbs. Importation began 2000.

MSR N/A	$395	$360	$320	$285	$235	$200	$190

    Add $30 for MC-4 choke tubes (24 in. barrel only).
    Subtract $110 for black synthetic stock and forearm.

This model has also been sold in the U.S. under the model name SPR453.

SHOTGUNS: SINGLE SHOT, RECENT IMPORTATION

IZH-18M-M - 12, 16, 20 ga., or .410 bore, hammerless, 24 (Youth), 26, 28 or 29 1/2 in. barrel with fixed or multichokes (12 or 20 ga. only, new 2001), ejector (IZH-18EM-M), blue or nickel (new 2001) finish, decocking/cocking lever on rear of triggerguard, cocking indicator, hardwood or walnut (new 2001) stock and forearm, trigger block safety, approx. 5 1/2 lbs. Importation began 1998.

MSR N/A	$90	$75	$65	$55	$45	$35	$30

    Add $10 for Youth Model (20 ga. or .410 bore only).
    Add $110 for nickel finished receiver (IZH-18 Max) with MC-3 multichokes and walnut stock and forearm.

This model has also been sold in the U.S. under the model name SPR100.

✳ *IZH-18 Sporting* - 12 or 20 (new 2004) ga., 28 (20 ga.) 29 1/2 in. VR barrel with porting, rubber butt pad, wide rib, ejector, screw-in choke, nickel finish, Monte Carlo stock. Importation began 2002.

MSR N/A	$235	$200	$160	$135	$110	$95	$80

SHOTGUNS: SLIDE ACTION, RECENT IMPORTATION

IZH-81 - 12 ga. only, 3 in. chamber, 5 shot box mag., 20, 26, or 28 in. plain or VR barrel with (26 or 28 in. barrel only) or w/o choke tubes, hardwood or walnut (disc. 1999) stock and corncob style forearm, blue finish. Imported 1999-2000.

	$235	$190	$170	$160	$145	$135	$125

Last MSR was $269.

    Add $17 for walnut stock (disc.1999).
    Add $68 for VR barrel (walnut stock only).

MP-133 - 12 ga., 3 1/2 in. chamber, 20, 24 (new 2001), 26, or 28 in. VR barrel with choke tubes (not available with 20 in. barrel), walnut stock and forearm, approx. 7 lbs. Importation began 2000.

MSR N/A	$295	$230	$195	$185	$155	$145	$135

BAILONS GUNMAKERS LIMITED

Previous manufacturer located in Birmingham, England until 1993, when operations ceased. Inquiries regarding this trademark (including repairs) should be directed to Guthrie Consulting (see Trademark Index for listing).

RIFLES: BOLT ACTION

HUNTING RIFLE - various cals., modified Mauser bolt action, barrel length to suit from 18 to 30 in., set triggers or match, Habicht Telescope sight (magnification and reticle to suit), engraving, and types of finishes are at optional cost, prices below reflect standard rifle with no options. Imported 1986-1993.

	$2,495	$2,250	$1,995	$1,775	$1,625	$1,450	$1,300

Last MSR was $2,750.

100%	98%	95%	90%	80%	70%	60%	50%	40%	30%	20%	10%

BAKER, W.H. & CO.

Previous manufacturer located in Syracuse, NY circa 1878-1883.

Originally started by William H. and Ellis L. Baker circa 1878. During this time, Leroy H. and Lyman C. Smith financed the new company, W.H. Baker & Co. Circa 1880, L.C. Smith bought the interest from the two Baker partners and continued production with markings reading "L.C. Smith and Co., Maker of the Baker Gun" on the rib and "Baker Pat." on the locks. Smith decided to drop the Baker name in 1883, but continued to manufacture this gun and a shotgun/rifle combination gun in Syracuse, NY until 1888. At this point, the company was sold to the Hunter Brothers and this new company, Baker Gun & Forging Co., began making both the New Baker shotguns (see separate listing below) and the Ithaca gun. The company was sold to the Hunter Brothers circa 1888, and the Hunter Arms Company made L.C. Smith shotguns for approximately 60 years, at which point the Marlin Firearms Company bought the business during the early 1940s.

Baker guns were originally 10 or 12 ga., and unusual in that the opening mechanism was operated by pressing forward on the front trigger. While relatively rare, most original Baker guns (including the shotgun/rifle) do not have a lot of original finish remaining. Most specimens are priced in the $400-$850 range, assuming finish is less than 10%. If condition is better than 40%, guns have to be evaluated individually for accurate pricing.

THE BAKER GUN & FORGING CO.

Previous trademark manufactured 1877-1888 by W.H. Baker & Co. and L.C. Smith Maker in Syracuse, NY. See L.C. Smith section in this book for listings of the Baker patented 3-barrel and 2-barrel guns.

This section covers the popular hammer and hammerless guns manufactured 1887-1919 by the Baker Gun & Forging Company, (founded by William H. & Ellis L. Baker) in Syracuse and Batavia, NY and the H&D Folsom Arms Co. 1920-1930 in Norwich, CT. These guns sold in substantial quantities (approx. 190,000) and they attracted a strong and devoted following.

The Baker sidelock shotgun is considered an "American Best" and is recognized as one of America's Classic shotguns manufactured during that era, like the L.C. Smith, Parker, LeFever, Fox and Ithaca. Collector interest in these high quality sidelock shotguns is on the rise.

The very popular Baker Paragon grade hammerless shotguns were made to customer order and the company went to great lengths to accommodate the customer's taste in engraving, finish and specifications.

Therefore, no two guns are exactly alike. Paragon guns with damascus barrels in 80% or better original condition without pitting, reboring or polishing out are of almost equal value with the Krupp barrel guns.

All 'Baker Grade' guns were available with the Extra Draw Lug and Baker's famous Firing Pin Block Safeties. The 'Batavia Grade' guns did not have these features.

The *Blue Book of Gun Values* strongly recommends an expert examination and appraisal when comtemplating the purchase of a high grade Baker in 80% or better original condition.

Add 33% for 16 ga. on all grades.

Add $200-$300 for auto ejectors as shown.

Add $500 for single selective trigger all grades valued at $1,500 or more or 33% for values less than $1,500.

SHOTGUNS: SXS, BAKER HAMMER-LONDON TWIST OR DAMASCUS, MFG. 1897-1916

MODEL "D" 1897 - sidelock twist bar London action, extra draw lug.

100%	98%	95%	90%	80%	70%	60%	50%	40%	30%	20%	10%
N/A	N/A	$1,500	$1,250	$1,100	$1,000	$900	$800	$750	$700	$675	$650

Add $200 for damascus barrels.

100%	98%	95%	90%	80%	70%	60%	50%	40%	30%	20%	10%

NEW BAKER 1887-1896 - boxlock twist London action.

| N/A | N/A | $900 | $750 | $650 | $600 | $550 | $500 | $450 | $400 | $375 | $350 |

SHOTGUNS: SXS, BATAVIA GRADE, SIDELOCK, HAMMERLESS-DAMASCUS OR FLUID STEEL, MFG. 1898-1930

BATAVIA LEADER - London twist, later guns had special steel barrels, plain wood and finish.

| N/A | N/A | $1,000 | $850 | $700 | $600 | $550 | $500 | $450 | $400 | $350 | $300 |

Add $200 for damascus barrels (Batavia Damascus) and $200 for auto ejectors (Batavia ejector).

BATAVIA SPECIAL - similar to Leader model, homo-tensil steel.

| N/A | N/A | $800 | $650 | $550 | $500 | $450 | $400 | $350 | $300 | $275 | $250 |

BLACK BEAUTY - similar to Batavia Special model, cockrill steel, black oxide metal finish.

| N/A | N/A | $800 | $650 | $550 | $500 | $450 | $400 | $350 | $300 | $275 | $250 |

Add $200 for ejectors.

BLACK BEAUTY SPECIAL - special steel, line engraving, upgraded wood, checkering and finish.

| N/A | N/A | $1,300 | $1,150 | $1,000 | $900 | $800 | $750 | $700 | $650 | $600 | $550 |

SHOTGUNS: SXS, BAKER GRADE, SIDELOCK, HAMMERLESS-DAMASCUS OR FLUID STEEL, MFG. 1890-1923

Baker Grade hammerless guns were made in 10, 12 & 16 gauges with 26, 28, 30 & 32 in. barrels. Guns with Damascus barrels are of almost equal value if the Damascus barrels are in 80%+ original condition without pitting, reboring or polishing out. The A and B grades were mfg. 1890-1910; R and S grades 1905-1915. The Paragon, Krupp, Pigeon and Deluxe grades were made in the Standard Model between 1892-1919. The Paragon, Expert and Deluxe grades were also made in the Model NN style with the L.C. Smith style rotary locking bolt 1909-1915 and the Greener style crossbolt 1915-1919.

S GRADE - fluid tempered steel, plain line and scroll engraving.

| N/A | N/A | $1,800 | $1,300 | $1,100 | $1,000 | $900 | $800 | $700 | $650 | $600 | $550 |

Add $300 for ejectors.

R GRADE - three rod damascus or Krupp steel barrels, dog and bird on locks with line and some scroll engraving, better wood and finish.

| N/A | N/A | $2,400 | $1,900 | $1,600 | $1,350 | $1,250 | $1,150 | $1,100 | $900 | $850 | $800 |

Add $500 for Krupp barrels or $300 for ejectors.

B GRADE - London twist, good line and scroll engraving with dog or bird on locks, better wood and finish than Leader model.

| N/A | N/A | $2,000 | $1,500 | $1,300 | $1,100 | $1,000 | $900 | $800 | $750 | $700 | $650 |

Add 25% for early models with elaborate game scene engraving.

A GRADE - three rod damascus or Krupp steel barrels, same engraving as B Grade, better wood and finish.

| N/A | N/A | $2,400 | $1,900 | $1,600 | $1,350 | $1,250 | $1,150 | $1,100 | $900 | $850 | $800 |

Add 25% for early models with elaborate game scene engraving.
Add $500 for Krupp barrels.

PARAGON GRADE - very fine damascus or Krupp barrels, fine scroll and game scene engraving, best quality wood, checkering and finish, special order only to customer specifications.

| N/A | N/A | $4,000 | $3,500 | $3,000 | $2,700 | $2,500 | $2,300 | $2,100 | $1,900 | $1,700 | $1,500 |

Add $300 for ejectors.

KRUPP GRADE (N) - Krupp barrels, finer scroll and game scene engraving, better wood, checkering, and finish, most had straight stocks.

| N/A | N/A | $4,500 | $4,000 | $3,500 | $3,000 | $2,800 | $2,500 | $2,300 | $2,100 | $1,900 | $1,700 |

Add $300 for ejectors.

100%	98%	95%	90%	80%	70%	60%	50%	40%	30%	20%	10%

PIGEON GRADE (L) - Holland special steel barrels, elaborate scroll and game scene engraving, fancy wood, checkering, and finish.

| N/A | N/A | $5,500 | $4,750 | $4,250 | $3,750 | $3,500 | $3,000 | $2,800 | $2,600 | $2,400 | $2,200 |

Add $300 for ejectors.

EXPERT GRADE - Holland special steel barrels, ejectors standard, finest scroll and game scene engraving, fancy checkering, wood and finish.

| N/A | N/A | $6,000 | $5,250 | $4,750 | $4,250 | $4,000 | $3,500 | $3,300 | $3,100 | $2,900 | $2,700 |

DELUXE GRADE - Sir Joseph Whitworth fluid compressed steel barrels, highest quality full coverage scroll and game scene engraving, checkering, wood, and finish.

| N/A | N/A | $10,000 | $9,000 | $8,000 | $7,000 | $6,750 | $6,500 | $6,250 | $6,00 | $5,750 | $5,500 |

Add $300 for ejectors.

SHOTGUNS: SINGLE BARREL TRAP, BOXLOCK, HAMMERLESS, FLUID STEEL, MFG. 1909-1923

The Baker SBT guns were of the highest quality. Made in 12 ga. only with 30, 32, 34 inch barrels in 3 grades. They were offered with vent ribs, auto ejectors, single triggers, stocks with cheek piece and Monte Carlo shapes. The two highest grades had the famous Baker firing pin blocks safety. The *Blue Book of Gun Values* recommends an expert appraisal when contemplating the purchase of a high grade SBT Baker in 80% or better original condition.

STERLING GRADE - line border and scroll engraving, semi-fancy wood, neatly checkered.

| N/A | N/A | $1,500 | $1,350 | $1,200 | $1,100 | $1,000 | $900 | $800 | $700 | $650 | $600 |

ELITE GRADE - elaborate scroll engraving, fancy wood and checkering.

| N/A | N/A | $2,500 | $2,150 | $2,000 | $1,900 | $1,800 | $1,700 | $1,600 | $1,500 | $1,350 | $1,300 |

SUPERBA GRADE - ornate scroll and game scene engraved, finest wood and checkering.

| N/A | N/A | $4,000 | $3,600 | $3,400 | $3,200 | $3,000 | $2,800 | $2,600 | $2,500 | $2,400 | $2,300 |

BALLARD ARMS, LLC

Current rifle manufacturer located in Cody, WY, since 1996. Previously named Ballard Rifles LLC until 2006. Dealer and consumer direct sales.

GRADING - PPGS™	100%	98%	95%	90%	80%	70%	60%

RIFLES: SINGLE SHOT

All Ballard rifles feature receivers milled from solid stock, hand polished barrels, and authentic "packed" case hardening. Many custom features are also available - contact the factory directly for availability and pricing. In addition to the standard models listed (up to 12 months delivery time), special order models include No. 1 Silhouette ($3,275 MSR), No. 2 Sporting ($3,450 last MSR), No. 4 Perfection ($3,260 MSR), No. 5 1/2 Montana ($3,510 MSR), No. 6 Schuetzen ($3,625 MSR), No. 8 Union Hill ($3,575 MSR), Schoyen Schuetzen ($3,750 MSR), No. 3 Gallery ($2,950 MSR), and No. 3F Fine Gallery ($3,475 MSR). Allow up to 12 months for delivery.

BALLARD 1 1/2 HUNTER'S RIFLE - available in 7 cals. between .22 LR - .50-70, single trigger, unchecked stock and forearm, S style lever action, 9 3/4 - 10 1/2 lbs.

| | MSR $2,950 | | $2,600 | $2,275 | $2,050 | $1,875 | $1,575 | $1,325 | $1,075 |

BALLARD 1 3/4 FAR WEST RIFLE - available in 8 cals. between .32-40 WCF - .50-90 SS, patterned after the original Ballard Far West Model, 30 or 32 in. standard or heavyweight octagon barrel, double set triggers, ring style lever, 9 3/4 - 10 1/2 lbs.

| | MSR $3,260 | | $2,850 | $2,500 | $2,200 | $2,075 | $1,750 | $1,425 | $1,150 |

GRADING - PPGS™	100%	98%	95%	90%	80%	70%	60%

BALLARD NO. 5 PACIFIC - available in 9 cals. between .32-40 WCF - .50-90 SS, includes under-barrel wiping rod, otherwise similar to No. 1 3/4 Far West Rifle.

MSR $3,510	$3,125	$2,750	$2,350	$2,100	$1,775	$1,450	$1,175

BALLARD NO. 4 1/2 MID RANGE - available in 5 cals. between .32-40 WCF - .45-110, configured for black powder cartridge silhouette, half-round, half-octagon 30 or 32 in. standard or heavyweight barrel, single or double set triggers, pistol grip stock, full loop lever, hard rubber Ballard buttplate, Vernier tang sight. 10 3/4 - 11 1/2 lbs.

MSR $3,190	$2,800	$2,475	$2,200	$1,975	$1,750	$1,425	$1,150

BALLARD NO. 7 LONG RANGE - available in 5 cals. between .40-65 Win. - .45-110, designed for long range shooting, half-round, half-octagon 32 or 34 in. standard or heavyweight barrel, other features similar to Ballard No. 4 1/2 Mid Range.

MSR $3,190	$2,800	$2,475	$2,200	$1,975	$1,750	$1,425	$1,150

WINCHESTER MODEL 1885 HIGH WALL - various cals., exact copy of original Winchester Model 1885 (parts interchange), 30 or 32 in. octagon barrel, ST with small lever, case colored receiver, uncheckered straight grip walnut stock and foream, approx. 9 lbs. New 2001.

MSR $2,950	$2,600	$2,275	$2,050	$1,875	$1,575	$1,325	$1,075

Add $250 for Special Sporting Model.
Add $800 for Helm Schuetzen Model.

✱ *Winchester Model 1885 High Wall Deluxe* - similar to Model 1885 High Wall, except has deluxe checkered pistol grip stock with shotgun buttplate and forearm, double set triggers, 32 in. No. 4 barrel, aperture sights, 11 lbs. Mfg. 2001-2005.

	$3,250	$2,775	$2,350	$2,100	$1,775	$1,450	$1,175

Last MSR was $3,675.

Add $75 for Express Model.

BALLESTER MOLINA/RAGAUD (HAFDASA)

Previous trademark of semi-auto pistols manufactured by Hispano Argentino Fabricade Automoviles SA (Hafdasa).

PISTOLS: SEMI-AUTO

The Ballester-Molina was an attempt to market a less expensive alternative to the Colt Model 1927, which was an Argentina-made licensed copy of the Colt Model 1911. During the first three years of production, the pistol was marked "Ballester-Ragaud", and later marked "Ballester-Molina". Although the Ballester-Molina .45 ACP is virtually the same size and shape as the Colt Model 1911, only the barrel and grips are interchangable.

BALLESTER-MOLINA/RAGAUD - .45 ACP or .22 LR (training version) cal., 5 in. barrel, patterned after the Colt M-1911A1 except has pinned trigger, is without grip safety, has different sear mechanism, and distinctive pattern retracting grooves in slide, issued to the Argentine Military and Police (marked on slide), also sold commercially in Latin America, ser. no. stamped on hilt next to magazine floor plate, some also marked with property numbers. Approx. 90,000 - 110,000 mfg. 1937-1953.

	$625	$550	$500	$400	$360	$330	$300

Add 100% for .22 LR cal. training model.

During WWII the British purchased between 10,000 - 15,000 Ballester-Molinas in .45 ACP cal. for both the British military and clandestine activities. These are marked with a B prefix before the serial number. Pistol marked "Ejercito" are Army issue and pistols marked "Armada" are navy issue (this would include the Marines and the Coast Guard). Slides may be marked with various federal and police agencies and issue numbers (not to be confused with the serial number).

Guns marked "Cal. .45" or "11.25mm" will shoot .45 ACP ammo.

Pistols were exported to Columbia, Bolivia, Ecuador, Peru, Uruguay, and Venezuela.

GRADING - PPGS™	100%	98%	95%	90%	80%	70%	60%

BALTIMORE ARMS COMPANY
Previous manufacturer of SxS shotguns located in Baltimore, MD circa 1895-1902.

SHOTGUNS: SxS

STYLE 1 - this variation does not have the improved Hollenbeck barrel locking mechanism characterized by the eye-shaped hole in the top rib extension. Mfg. 1895-1900.

There are 4 grades of Baltimore Arms Company shotguns: Field, Grade A, Grade B, and Grade C. Prices generally range from $295 to $1,500 depending on condition and grade.

STYLE 2 - this variation has the improved barrel locking mechanism and is patent date marked "FEB. 13, 1900" on the water table. Mfg. 1900-02.

There are 4 grades of Baltimore Arms Company shotguns: Field, Grade A, Grade B, and Grade C. Prices generally range from $295 to $2,000 depending on condition and grade.

BANSNER'S ULTIMATE RIFLES, L.L.C.
Current custom rifle manufacturer established during 1981 and located in Adamstown, PA. In 2000, the company name changed from Bansner's Gunsmithing Specialities to Bansner's Ultimate Rifles, L.L.C. Consumer direct sales.

RIFLES: BOLT ACTION

All Bansner's UR rifles up to approx. June 1, 1999 have either Remington 700 or Winchester post-64 claw extractor actions. After this approx. date, Bansner´s started using its own proprietary action, and during 2005, released the Sharpshooter model with Nesika Bay action.

All MSRs listed below do not include excise tax.

ULTIMATE ONE - various cals. and configurations including different metal finishes and special orders, Rem. 700 (disc. 1999), Win. post-64 Model 70 (disc. 1999), Bansner's custom action by Nesika beginning 2004, exclusive action was mfg. by McMillan Bros. Rifle Co., Inc. (steel or stainless steel, mfg. 2001-2003), Douglas premium air gauged (disc.) or Lilja fluted barrel with M-50 muzzle brake, large extractor, plunger ejector, 3 lbs. custom tuned trigger, custom color synthetic stock with Pachmayr decelerator pad, includes Talley custom scope bases and rings, various weights.

MSR $5,195	$4,650	$3,475	$2,825	$2,350	$1,950	$1,700	$1,450

Add $325 for 3 position Model 70 style safety or Lazzeroni calibers (disc. 2007).

ULTIMATE SAFARI HUNTER - various dangerous game cals., Lilja Precision stainless steel 24 in. barrel, scalloped action based on the M-70 Classic (disc.), or Dakota 76 CRF action, M-50 muzzle brake, synthetic stock with Pachmayr decelerator pad, matte black teflon metal finish. New 2003.

MSR $6,195	$5,700	$5,150	$3,700	$3,000	$2,350	$2,000	$1,700

SHARPSHOOTER - various cals., Nesika Bay action, Lilja Precision medium to heavy weight match grade fluted barrel (customer choice of length), with recessed crown, Jewell trigger, brown wood laminate pillar bedded and reinforced fiberglass stock with palm swell, "Ti" polymer K-Kote metal finish, ebony forend tip, inletted swivel studs. Mfg. 2005-2007.

	$7,900	$6,850	$5,900	$4,950	$4,000	$3,250	$2,750

Last MSR was $8,495.

ULTIMATE OVIS SHEEP HUNTER - various cals., Rem. 700 action (disc.) or Banser's custom lightweight stainless steel action (new 2007), accurized, turned outside, fluted bolt, skeletonized bolt handle, alloy ADL trigger guard, Jewell trigger, Lilja Precision barrel, fiberglass stock, 5 1/4 lbs.

MSR $5,195	$4,650	$3,475	$2,825	$2,350	$1,950	$1,700	$1,450

ULTIMATE VARMINT HUNTER - various cals., Rem. 700 action, accurized and polished, Jewell varmint trigger, Lilja Precision stainless steel barrel, "Ti" K-Kote metal finish, fully bedded fiberglass stock, Pachmayr Decelerator pad.

MSR $4,995	$4,550	$3,550	$2,900	$2,350	$1,950	$1,700	$1,450

GRADING - PPGS™	100%	98%	95%	90%	80%	70%	60%

ALPINE HUNTER - .300 WSM cal. only, Howa 1500 action, milled receiver, fluted barrel, muzzle brake, tuned trigger, fully bedded fiberglass stock, Pachmayr Decelerator pad, Ti K-Kote metal finish.

MSR $2,395	$2,150	$1,900	$1,625	$1,400	$1,200	$1,000	$800

ALASKAN HUNTER - various cals., Rem. 700 action, accurized, scalloped and polished receiver, fluted bolt, skeletonized handle, alloy ADL trigger guard, Lilja Precision barrel, fiberglass stock, Pachmayr Decelerator pad, approx. 5 lbs. Disc. 2004.

	$3,525	$2,900	$2,450	$2,050	$1,875	$1,675	$1,450

Last MSR was $3,895.

ULTIMATE RIFLE - various cals., Rem. 700 or Win. 70 action, accurized and polished, 3 lbs. trigger pull, Lilja Precision stainless steel barrel, fully bedded fiberglass stock, Pachmayr Decelerator pad. Disc. 2004.

	$2,995	$2,600	$2,300	$2,000	$1,800	$1,600	$1,400

Last MSR was $3,300.

HIGH TECH SERIES - various cals., Howa 1500 steel or stainless steel action with factory barrel and Bansner's synthetic stock with Pachmayr Decelerator pad. Mfg. 1997-2004.

	$965	$835	$725	$625	$575	$500	$450

Last MSR was $1,050.

Add $100 for all stainless steel.

ULTIMATE/TRADITIONAL CLASSIC - various cals., custom Dakota 76 controlled round feed claw extractor action with custom floorplate and inside bow release, Lilja Precision match grade hand lapped barrel, choice of matte blue or "Ti" polymer K-Kote metal finish, synthetic stock, Pachmayer decelerator pad. New 2005.

MSR $4,895	$4,450	$3,475	$2,850	$2,350	$1,950	$1,700	$1,450

LIMITED EDITION SERIES - various cals., customized Bansner's (new 2004) or Rem. 700 action with scalloped receiver, fluted bolt body and Jewell trigger, Gentry 3-position safety, synthetic stock with choice of black or silver coated teflon metal, 25-50 of each limited edition beginning 2003.

Please contact the company directly regarding pricing on these limited editions.

25TH ANNIVERSARY MODEL - customer chosen caliber and barrel contour, stainless steel action with custom engraving, sequential serial number, Lilja Precision match grade barrel, Jewell trigger, fiberglass Sheep Hunter stock, Pachmayr Decelerator pad, includes custom aluminum case and black sling. Only 25 to be mfg. beginning late 2005.

This model has a MSR of $7,995.

BARRETT FIREARMS MANUFACTURING, INC.

Current manufacturer located in Murfreesboro, TN. Dealer direct sales.

RIFLES: BOLT ACTION

MODEL 90 - .50 BMG cal., bolt action design, 29 in. match grade barrel with muzzle brake, 5 shot detachable box mag., includes extendible bi-pod legs, scope optional, 22 lbs. Mfg. 1990-95.

	$3,450	$2,950	$2,400	$2,150	$1,875	$1,600	$1,500

Last MSR was $3,650.

Add $1,150 for Swarovski 10X scope and rings.

MODEL 95M - .50 BMG cal., bolt action design, 29 in. match grade barrel with high efficiency muzzle brake, 5 shot detachable box mag., includes extendible bi-pod legs, M19 optics rail, scope optional, includes carrying case, 22 1/2 lbs. New 1995.

MSR $6,000	$5,495	$4,995	$3,950	$2,900	$2,425	$1,875	$1,600

GRADING - PPGS™	100%	98%	95%	90%	80%	70%	60%

MODEL 99 - .416 Barrett (.32 in. barrel only) or .50 BMG cal., single shot bolt action, 25 or 29 in lightweight fluted, or 32 in. heavy barrel with muzzle brake, straight through design with pistol grip and bi-pod, M1913 optics rail, black, brown, or silver finish, 21-25 lbs. New 1999.

	MSR $4,000	$3,650	$3,150	$2,550	$2,000	$1,825	$1,550	$1,250

Subtract $100 for .50 BMG cal. with 25 in. barrel.
Subtract $200 for .50 BMG cal. with 29 or 32 in. barrel.

RIFLES: SEMI-AUTO

MODEL 82 RIFLE - .50 BMG cal., semi-auto recoil operation, 33-37 in. barrel, 11 shot mag., 2,850 FPS muzzle velocity, scope sight only, parkerized finish, 35 lbs. Mfg. 1985-87.

$4,350	$3,950	$3,450	$2,700	$2,150	$1,800	$1,500

Last MSR for consumers was $3,180 in 1985.

This model underwent design changes since initial production. Only 115 were mfg. starting with ser. no. 100.

MODEL 82A1 - .50 BMG cal., paramilitary design w/short recoil operating system, variant of the original Model 82, back-up iron sights provided and fitted hard case, 20 or 29 (new late 1989) or 33 (disc. 1989) in. barrel, 10 shot detachable mag., 32 1/2 lbs. for 1989 and older mfg., approx. 30 lbs. for 1990 mfg. and newer. Current mfg. includes elevated M1913 optics rail, watertight case and cleaning kit.

MSR $8,050	$7,450	$6,400	$5,400	$4,450	$3,800	$3,250	$2,700

Add $360 for pack-mat backpack case (new 1999).
Add $275 for camo backpack carrying case (disc.).
Add $1,325 for Swarovski 10X scope and rings (disc.).

This model boasts official U.S. military rifle (M107) status following government procurement during Operation Desert Storm. In 1992, a new "arrowhead" shaped muzzle brake was introduced to reduce recoil.

MODEL 98 - .338 Lapua Mag. cal., 10 shot box mag., 24 in. match grade barrel with muzzle brake, bi-pod, 15 1/2 lbs.

While advertised during mid-1999, this model was never produced.

MODEL M468 - 6.8 Rem. SPC cal., aluminum upper and lower receiver, 16 in. barrel with muzzle brake, 5, 10, or 30 shot mag., dual spring extractor system, folding front and rear sight, gas block, two-stage trigger, integrated rail system, choice of full or telescoping 4-position stock, 8 lbs. New 2005.

MSR $2,700	$2,400	$2,050	$1,675	$1,375	$1,175	$995	$875

Add $1,590 for Model M468 upper conversion kit.

BAR-STO

Previous manufacturer located in Palms, CA. Bar-Sto still manufactures barrels and firearms-related accessories.

PISTOLS: SEMI-AUTO

BAR-STO .25 ACP PISTOL - .25 ACP cal., patterned after the Baby Browning, brushed stainless steel finish, walnut grips, approx. 250 manufactured in circa 1974.

$195	$165	$125	$100	$85	$70	$65

BARTOLOT, WERNER

Current custom gun manufacturer located in Hermagor, Austria. Direct sales only.
Werner Bartolot manufactures very high quality SxS and O/U double rifles, drillings, and single shot rifles. Please contact the company for more information, including availability and an individual price quotation (see Trademark Index).

GRADING - PPGS™	100%	98%	95%	90%	80%	70%	60%

BATTAGLIA, MAURO

Current manufacturer established in 1992 and located in Ravenna, Italy. No current U.S. importation.

Mauro Battaglia manufactures custom order high quality SxS shotguns. He also manufactures a sidelock action with new, unique design. Please contact the factory directly for more information.

BAUER FIREARMS CORPORATION

Previous manufacturer located in Fraser, MI circa 1971-1984.

DERRINGERS

THE RABBIT - .22 LR cal. and .410 bore, combination gun, all metal construction, O/U configuration. Mfg. 1982-84.

	$125	$100	$90	$80	$70	$60	$50

PISTOLS: SEMI-AUTO

BAUER .25 ACP - .25 ACP cal., 2 1/2 in. barrel, 6 shot, fixed sights, checkered walnut or pearlite grips. Mfg. 1972-84.

	$150	$130	$110	$95	$75	$65	$60

Note: These guns are identical to the Baby Browning, except stainless steel.

* *Bauer .25 ACP Bicentennial Model* - .25 ACP cal., engraved with buckle in display case.

	$300	$200	$150	$120	$105	$90	$80

BAYARD

Previously manufactured by Anciens Etablissements Pieper located in Herstal, Belgium.

Even though Bayard Models 1908, both 1923s, and 1930 were manufactured only by Anciens Etablissements Pieper of Herstal, Belgium, these pistols are listed under this heading as they are most commonly referred to by this trademark designation.

PISTOLS: SEMI-AUTO

.25 ACP and .380 ACP cals. are more rare than the .32 ACP, and will command a 20%+ premium above values listed unless indicated differently.

MODEL 1908 POCKET AUTOMATIC - .25 ACP, .32 ACP, or .380 ACP cal., 6 shot, 2 1/4 in. barrel, fixed sights, blue, hard rubber grips.

	$350	$250	$165	$100	$85	$70	$55

Add 10% for .25 ACP cal.
Add 25% if marked with Imperial Eagle.
Add 200% if factory engraved.

MODEL 1923 POCKET AUTOMATIC - .25 ACP cal., 2 1/2 in. barrel, blue, fixed sights, checkered hard rubber grips.

	$350	$295	$225	$170	$140	$125	$95

BAYARD 1923 POCKET AUTOMATIC - .32 ACP or .380 ACP cal., 6 shot, 3 5/16 in. barrel, fixed sights, blue, checkered hard rubber grips.

	$375	$295	$225	$170	$140	$125	$95

Add 100% for .380 ACP cal.

BAYARD 1930 POCKET AUTOMATIC - slight modification of 1923.

	$350	$250	$200	$170	$145	$120	$95

BECAS

Current trademark of shotguns manufactured by Molot, JSC, located in the Kirov Region, Russia.

Becas semi-automatic and slide action shotguns have had little or no importation into the U.S. Please contact the factory for more information (see Trademark Index), including U.S. model availability.

GRADING - PPGS™	100%	98%	95%	90%	80%	70%	60%

BEEMAN OUTDOOR SPORTS

Previous importer and distributor located in Santa Rosa, CA.

On April 1, 1993, Beeman Precision Arms, Inc. was split into two independent companies: Beeman Precision Airguns, a division of S/R Industries (Maryland Corp.), located in Huntington Beach, CA retains worldwide distribution of Beeman airguns and accessories. Beeman Outdoor Sports, a Division of Robert's Precision Arms, Inc., located in Santa Rosa, CA distributed Feinwerkbau firearms until 1995.

Beeman Precision Arms, Inc. was a large importer, primarily specializing in high quality European air rifles and pistols. Firearms trademarks previously distributed in the U.S. include the following trademarks: Agner (disc. 1986), Erma (disc. 1985), FAS (disc. 1987), Fabarm (disc. 1985), Feinwerkbau, Korth (disc. 1990), Krico (disc. 1988), Unique (disc. 1991), and Weihrauch (disc.). These trademarks appear under their respective alphabetical headings.

For more information and current pricing on both new and used Beeman Precision Airguns, please refer to the *Blue Book of Airguns* by Dr. Robert Beeman & John Allen (also available online).

The following firearms were manufactured to Beeman specifications, and are therefore listed under the Beeman Outdoor Sports heading.

PISTOLS: SEMI-AUTO

BEEMAN MP-08 - .380 ACP cal., Luger type toggle action, 3 1/2 in. barrel, 6-shot mag., blue, 1.4 lbs. Mfg. 1968-90.

$395	$335	$275	$240	$185	$145	$115

Last MSR was $390.

In 1988, Beeman took over importation of these two models (MP-08 and P-08). These revised models have new Luger style checkered walnut grips and 3 1/2 in. barrel. Previous variations had plastic grips.

BEEMAN P-08 - .22 LR cal., Luger type toggle action, 8-shot mag., 3.8 in. barrel, blue, checkered walnut grips, 1.9 lbs. Mfg. 1969-90.

$395	$335	$275	$240	$185	$145	$115

Last MSR was $390.

PISTOLS: SINGLE SHOT

MODEL SP/SPX - .22 LR cal., designed for silhouette shooting, 10 in. heavy bull barrel, blue metal parts, birchwood stocks and forearm, aperture sights, 3.9 lbs. Disc. 1994.

$625	$550	$475	$425	$375	$330	$295

Last MSR was $700.

Only a few of these models were actually delivered.

﹡*Model SPX Deluxe* - similar to Model SPX, except has matte chrome metal finish, hand stippled walnut grips, and Anschütz rear sight. Limited mfg. 1993-94.

$800	$725	$650	$575	$500	$425	$350

Last MSR was $900.

SP STANDARD - .22 LR cal., sidelever action, 8, 10, 12, or 15 in. barrel, adj. sights and walnut grips, single shot. Made in W. Germany. Imported 1985-86 only.

$250	$220	$180	$170	$160	$150	$140

Last MSR was $250.

Add $10 or $30 for 12 or 15 in. barrel respectively.

SP DELUXE - similar to SP Standard, except has forearm, about 3 1/2 lbs. Made in W. Germany. Imported 1985-86 only.

$275	$240	$200	$185	$170	$155	$145

Last MSR was $300.

Add $10 for 12 or $30 for 15 in. barrel.

GRADING - PPGS™	100%	98%	95%	90%	80%	70%	60%

BEHOLLA PISTOL

Previously manufactured by Becker & Hollander located in Suhl, Germany.

PISTOLS: SEMI-AUTO

BEHOLLA POCKET AUTOMATIC - .32 ACP cal., 7 shot, 2.9 in. barrel, blue, serrated wood or rubber grips, mfg. 1915-20, from 1920-25 the same gun was mfg. by Stenda-Werke.

$225	$170	$150	$135	$120	$100	$90

BENELLI

Current manufacturer established in 1967, and located in Urbino, Italy. Benelli USA was formed during late 1997, and is currently importing all Benelli shotguns and rifles. Benelli pistols (and air pistols) are currently imported by Larry's Guns, located in Portland, ME beginning 2003. Company headquarters are located in Accokeek, MD. Shotguns were previously imported 1983-1997 by Heckler & Koch, Inc., located in Sterling, VA. Handguns were previously imported until 1997 by European American Armory, located in Sharpes, FL, in addition to Sile Distributors, Inc., until 1995, located in New York, NY, and Saco, located in Arlington, VA.

For more information on Benelli air pistols, please refer to the *Blue Book of Airguns* by Dr. Robert Beeman and John Allen (also available online)

PISTOLS: SEMI-AUTO

Models B-77, B-80, and MP3S were previously imported by Sile Distributors. Models MP90S and MP95E Atlanta were imported by Benelli USA until 2002. Beginning 2003, Benelli pistols are exclusively imported by Larry's Guns, located in Portland, ME.

MODEL B-76 - 9mm Para. cal., selective double action, all steel, 4 1/4 in. barrel, 8 shot mag., 34 oz. Importation disc. in 1990.

$400	$375	$335	$295	$245	$225	$210

Last MSR was $428.

MODEL B-76S TARGET - 9mm Para. cal., similar to B-76, except has 5 1/2 in. barrel, target grips, and adj. rear sights. Importation disc. 1990.

$550	$475	$425	$395	$350	$325	$300

Last MSR was $595.

MODEL B-77 - .32 ACP cal., selective double action, all steel, 4 1/4 in. barrel, 8-shot mag. Importation disc. 1995.

$395	$350	$295	$255	$225	$200	$180

Last MSR was $385.

MODEL B-80 - .30 Luger cal., selective double action, all steel, 4 1/4 in. barrel, 8 shot mag., 34 oz. Importation disc. 1995.

$395	$350	$295	$255	$225	$200	$180

Last MSR was $385.

MODEL B-80S TARGET - similar to B-80, except has 5 1/2 in. barrel, target grips, and adj. rear sights. Importation disc. 1995.

$500	$450	$375	$325	$295	$275	$250

Last MSR was $572.

MODEL MP3S - .32 S&W Long Wadcutter cal., target variation with 5 1/2 in. barrel, high gloss bluing, target grips, and adj. rear sights. Importation disc. 1995.

$550	$450	$375	$325	$295	$275	$250

Last MSR was $785.

MODEL MP90S WORLD CUP - .22 S (disc.), .22 LR, or .32 S&W Wadcutter (disc. 1999) cal., 4.4 in. barrel, blue finish, target pistol featuring forward assisted breech bolt mechanism, anatomic grips, and adj. weight, 5 (disc.), 6 or 9

GRADING - PPGS™	100%	98%	95%	90%	80%	70%	60%

(optional) shot mag., 2.4 lbs. Imported 1992-2002, and again beginning 2003.

MSR N/A $1,165 $995 $875 $750 $650 $600 $550

     Add $123 for .32 S&W Wadcutter cal.

Conversion kits were previously available for this model at an extra charge.

MODEL MP95E ATLANTA - .22 LR or .32 S&W Wadcutter (disc. 1999, reintroduced 2006) cal., 4.4 in. barrel, features inertial recoiling mass system, integral Weaver style base mount, 5 (disc.), 6 or 9 (optional) shot mag., adj. trigger assembly, fully adj. sight, modular firing system, blue or matte chrome finish, smooth laminate (chrome finish only) or choice of checkered adj. (disc.) or non-adj. walnut grips, 2 1/2 lbs. Imported late 1994-2002, and again beginning 2003.

MSR N/A $741 $625 $550 $500 $450 $400 $375

     Add $53 for chrome finish.
     Add $117 for .32 S&W Wadcutter cal.

This model was originally designated as Model MP95.

RIFLES: SEMI-AUTO

R1 STANDARD CARBINE/RIFLE - .270 WSM (new 2005), .30-06, .308 Win., .300 WSM (new 2005), or .300 Win. Mag. cal., features auto-regulating gas operated (ARGO) system and rotating 3 lug bolt, 20 (carbine, .30-06 or .300 Win. Mag. only), 22, or 24 (.300 Win. Mag. and WSM cals.) in. barrel with cryogenic treatment and interchangeable rear rib, detachable 3 or 4 shot mag., optional sights, forearm is fixed to the alloy receiver, drilled and tapped, Picatinny rail included, available in black or nickel plated (Europe only) receiver finish, optional APG HD camo treatment (.30-06 cal. and synthetic stock only, new 2007), black ComforTech synthetic with grip tight inserts (new 2006, .30-06, .270 WSM, .300 WSM or .300 Win. Mag. cal.) or checkered walnut Monte Carlo stock and forearm, recoil pad is cut into the stock (adj., with shims), ambidextrous safety, approx. 7 lbs. New 2002.

MSR $1,290 $1,050 $885 $750 $650 $550 $450 $400

     Add $175 for ComforTech synthetic stock.
     Add $305 for camo.

This model is designated the Argo in Europe.

SHOTGUNS: SEMI-AUTO, 1985-OLDER

Benelli semi-auto 3rd generation (inertia recoil) shotguns were imported starting in the late 1960s. The receivers were mfg. of light aluminum alloy - the SL-80 Model 121 had a semi-gloss, anodized black finish, the Model 123 had an ornate photo-engraved receiver, the Model Special 80 had a brushed, white nickel-plated receiver, and the Model 121 M1 had a matte finish receiver, barrel, and stock. All 12 ga. SL-80 Series shotguns will accept 2 3/4 or 3 in. shells, and all SL-80 Series 12 ga. Models have interchangeable barrels (except the 121 M1) with 4 different model receivers (121, 121 M1, 123, and Special 80). All 4 models had fixed choke barrels.

The SL-80 Series shotguns were disc. during 1985, and neither H&K nor Benelli USA has parts for these guns. Some misc. parts still available for the 12 ga. from Gun Parts Corp. (see Trademark Index for more information).

Approx. 50,000 SL-80 series shotguns were mfg. before discontinuance - choke markings (located on side or underneath barrel) are as follows: * full choke, ** imp. mod., *** mod., **** imp. cyl. SL-80 series guns used the same action (much different than current mfg.) and all had the split receiver design. Be aware of possible wood cracking where the barrel rests on the thin area of the forend and also on the underside of the buttstock behind trigger guard. When buying or selling an SL-80 Series shotgun, be aware that when comparing the SL-80 Series with the newer action Benellis (post 1985), there is a big difference between the action, design changes, and actual selling prices in today's marketplace. The SL80s are much lower priced than current production Benellis.

Since the late 1980s, the Benelli SL-80 series marketplace has dropped sharply, and relatively few guns have been traded during the new millennium. In the past five years, there have been an increasing number of SL-80 guns for sale that have had unresolved mechanical problems. Parts are scarce and high priced. Wood and trigger assembly groups for most models are no longer available. In 2005, there was an increase in the number of SL-80 guns sold that were "new-in-the-box." Sales of "used guns" continue to be poor, especially if less than 98% condition. Buyers clearly have become more discriminating when considering the purchase of a SL-80 series shotgun.

100% values within this section assume NIB condition.
Subtract 5% for "SACO" importation (Saco was located in Arlington, VA).

SL-80 SERIES MODEL SL-121V - 12 ga., field grade, 26, or 28 in. fixed choke VR barrel, anodized and black semi-gloss finish on lower receiver. Disc. 1985.

	$395	$340	$300	$275	$240	$185	$160

Last MSR was $397.

SL-80 SERIES MODEL SL-121/SL-122 SLUG - 12 ga., features Monte Carlo stock and flat bottom Trap Grade beavertail forearm, 21 1/16 cyl. bore barrel, fixed open ring rear iron sights and fixed front ramp, 5 shot mag., recoil pad, 7 lbs. 3 oz. Disc. 1985.

	$385	$360	$325	$300	$230	$185	$160

Last MSR was $434.

SL-80 SERIES MODEL SL-123V - 12 ga., stylish field grade, receiver Ergal special aluminum alloy with photo engraving, 26 or 28 in. VR barrel with various chokes, approx. 6 lbs. 13 oz. Disc. 1985.

	$420	$365	$350	$325	$225	$200	$185

Last MSR was $464.

Add $20 for trap stock, $10 for beavertail forearm and $25 for skeet barrel.

The only difference between the SL-123V and SL-121V is the photo engraved receiver. The SL-123V was at times referred to as the deluxe model when compared to with the SL-121V. Both models were field grade shotguns.

EX-L - 12 ga., similar in appearance to the Model SL123V, except has hand-engraved receiver, very limited mfg. with unpredictable premiums over Model SL123V.

SL-80 SERIES MODEL 121 M1 POLICE/MILITARY - 12 ga. only, similar in appearance to the Super 90 M1, hardwood stock, 7 shot mag., matte metal and wood finish, most stocks had adj. lateral sling attachment inside of buttstock, 18 3/4 in. barrel. Disc. 1985.

	$395	$350	$300	$285	$250	$225	$195

Since many of this model were sold to the police and military, used specimens should be checked carefully for excessive wear and/or possible damage.

MODEL 80 SPECIAL SKEET/TRAP - 12 ga. only, 28 in. VR with mod. choke and phosphorescent bead sight, has trap/skeet Monte Carlo grade/style wood stock with recoil pad, lower receiver is nickel plated, 7 lbs. 10 oz. Disc. 1986.

	$465	$395	$350	$295	$250	$225	$195

Last MSR was $531.

Trap guns should have high comb trap stock and trap grade forearm (not field grade/style wood). Trap guns should also be inspected carefully for internal wear before buying/selling.

SL-80 SERIES MODEL SL201 FIELD GRADE - 20 ga., 26 in. VR barrel bored mod., black anodized lower receiver, approx. 5 lbs. 10 oz., mfg. in France for Benelli. Disc. 1985.

	$385	$360	$340	$300	$240	$185	$165

Last MSR was $399.

GRADING - PPGS™	100%	98%	95%	90%	80%	70%	60%

BRI-BENELLI SL-80 123 SLUG GUN - 12 ga. only, custom designed, premium slug gun featuring SL-80 Series action and drilled and tapped rifle bored barrel by E. R. Shaw Barrel Co., assembled by BRI in the U.S., Monte Carlo stock with beavertail forend, approx. 25 guns total mfg. 1986-87.

	$1,895	$1,275	$1,025	$875	$750	$625	$525

Subtract 40% if w/o trap style beavertail forend and Monte Carlo stock.
Original issue price on this model was $750-$850. These specimens are marked "BRI-Benelli" on barrel. No warranties exist on this model.

SHOTGUNS: SEMI-AUTO, 1986-NEWER

Extra barrels (non-slug) for the currently manufactured models are typically priced in the $335-$565 range, depending on the model. Unless indicated otherwise, all currently manufactured Benelli shotguns utilize a red bar front sight, and are equipped with a patented Benelli keyed chamber lock.

M1 FIELD (SUPER 90) - 12 (disc. 2005) or 20 (new 2001) ga., 3 in. chamber, inertia recoil operating system, alloy receiver, 21 (mfg. 1990-2005, 12 ga. only), 24 (new 1990), 26, or 28 (disc. 2005) in. vent. rib barrel and 3-shot mag., includes 5 screw in choke tubes, satin walnut (mfg. 1994-2005) or black polymer stock, Turkey Models include steady-grip with built-in stock pistol grip (mfg. 2003-2005) or regular pistol grip, red fiber optic front sight, matte finish, 100% Realtree X-tra Brown (mfg. 1997-2001) or Advantage Timber HD (new 2001) camo coverage, approx. 5.8 (20 ga.) or 7.2 (12 ga.) lbs. Disc. 2006.

	$825	$700	$600	$450	$375	$335	$300

Last MSR was $1,030.

Subtract $30 for 12 ga.
Add $15 for satin walnut stock (12 ga., 26 or 28 in. barrel only, disc. 2005).
Add $120 for Advantage Timber HD camo finish.
Add $195 for Turkey configuration with 24 in. barrel, steady-grip and 100% Timber HD camo coverage (disc. 2005).
Add $100 for Turkey configuration with 24 in. barrel and Timber HD camo finish (disc. 2004).
Add $95 for Realtree Xtra Brown camo finish (disc. 2001).
Add $60 for 11 oz. mercury recoil reducer (synthetic stock only).
Add $20 for left-hand action (mfg. 2000-2003, available in synthetic and camo, 12 ga. only).
During 2000, Benelli improved this model with a stepped VR and oversized safety.
This model was available with an extended magazine tube (26 or 28 in. barrel only).

M1 FIELD SLUG (SUPER 90) - 12 (disc. 2004) or 20 (new 2004) ga., 3 in. chamber, incorporates improvements on the Benelli action, including rotating Montefeltro bolt system, 19 3/4 cyl. bore (disc. 1997) or 24 (new 1998) in. rifled barrel with iron sights (disc. 1997, reintroduced 2001), drilled and tapped beginning 1998, 3 (new 1998) or 7 (disc. 1997) shot mag., Realtree Xtra Brown camo (mfg. 2000-2001), Advantage Timber HD (new 2002) camo, or black fiberglass stock and forearm, 6 1/2 - 7.6 lbs. Mfg. 1986-2006.

	$895	$700	$600	$475	$375	$335	$300

Last MSR was $1,105.

Add $110 for Advantage Timber HD camo finish.
Add $105 for Realtree Xtra brown camo finish (disc. 2001).
Subtract 15% for 19 3/4 cyl. bore barrel with iron sights.

M1 DEFENSE (SUPER 90) - similar to Super 90 Slug, except has pistol grip stock, 7.1 lbs. Disc. 1998.

	$685	$525	$395	$325	$300	$270	$250

Last MSR was $851.

Add $41 for ghost-ring sighting system.

M1 PRACTICAL (SUPER 90) - 12 ga. only, 3 in. chamber, 26 in. plain barrel with muzzle brake, designed for IPSC events, extended 8 shot mag. tube, oversized safety, speed loader, larger bolt handle, Milspec adj. ghost-ring sight and Picatinny rail, black regular synthetic stock and forearm, matte metal finish, includes 3 choke tubes, 7.6 lbs. Mfg. 1998-2004.

	$925	$825	$750	$625	$525	$450	$400

Last MSR was $1,285.

M1 TACTICAL (SUPER 90) - 12 ga. only, 3 in. chamber, 18 1/2 in. barrel, fixed rifle or ghost-ring sighting system, available with synthetic pistol grip or standard buttstock, includes 3 choke tubes, 5 shot mag., 6.7 - 7 lbs. Mfg. 1993-2004.

	$725	$650	$575	$450	$375	$335	$300

Last MSR was $975.

Add $50 for ghost-ring sighting system.
Add $50-$65 for pistol grip stock.

✳ *M1 Tactical M* - similar to M1 Tactical, except has military ghost-ring sights and standard synthetic stock, 7.1 lbs. Mfg. 1999-2000.

	$725	$595	$435	$375	$315	$275	$250

Last MSR was $960.

Add $10 for pistol grip stock.

M1 ENTRY (SUPER 90) - 12 ga. only, includes 14 in. barrel, choice of synthetic pistol grip or standard stock, choice of rifle or ghost-ring sights, 5 shot mag. (2 shot extension), approx. 6.7 lbs. Mfg. 1992-2006.

	$810	$675	$585	$450	$395	$340	$310

Add $15 for synthetic pistol grip stock.
Add $65 for ghost-ring sighting system.

This model required special licensing (special tax stamp) for consumers, and was normally available to law enforcement/military only.

M1 SPORTING SPECIAL (SUPER 90) - 12 ga., 18 1/2 in. barrel, matte black finish, includes ghost ring sighting system, 6 1/2 lbs. Mfg. 1993-97.

	$750	$650	$550	$450	$395	$340	$310

Last MSR was $924.

M2 FIELD - 12 or 20 (new 2007) ga., 3 in. chamber, similar operating system as the M1, redesigned receiver, trigger guard, and safety, 3 shot mag., red fiber optic front sight, short forearm with large magazine cap, includes ComforTech stock system with two gel pads that reduce recoil (not available w/walnut stock), 21 (Turkey), 24 (Turkey, with steady-grip), 26, or 28 in. VR barrel with cryo treatment, satin walnut, synthetic, or choice of 100% coverage Advantage Max-4 HD, APG HD (new 2007), or Advantage Timber HD (disc. 2007) camo stock, 6.9 - 7.2 lbs. New 2004.

MSR $1,170	$995	$800	$675	$550	$425	$350	$325

Add $60 for black synthetic stock w/ComforTech and forearm.
Add $195 for 100% camo coverage.
Add $225 for 24 in. barrel with steady-grip Turkey configuration (new 2005).
Add $195 for Turkey configuration with pistol grip and 100% camo coverage.
Add $95 for left hand action w/black synthetic stock or $210 for left-hand action w/camo.
Add $60 for 20 ga.

✳ *M2 Field Super Slug* - 12 or 20 ga., 24 in. rifled barrel with open sights, choice of black synthetic ComforTech stock and forearm, or 100% camo coverage, 7.3 lbs. New 2004.

MSR $1,300	$1,195	$825	$675	$525	$400	$350	$300

Add $120 for camo coverage.

GRADING - PPGS™	100%	98%	95%	90%	80%	70%	60%

M2 PRACTICAL - 12 ga. only, 3 in. chamber, 26 in. compensated barrel with ghost ring sights, designed for IPSC competition, 8 shot mag., Picatinny rail. Limited importation 2005.

		$1,095	$900	$800	$650	$550	$475	$425

Last MSR was $1,335.

M2 TACTICAL - 12 ga. only, 3 in. chamber, 18 1/2 in. barrel with choice of pistol grip, regular stock, or ComforTech stock configuration, matte finish, 5 shot mag., AirTouch checkering pattern on stock and forearm, open rifle or ghost ring sights, 6.7-7 lbs. New 2005.

MSR $1,200		$1,125	$825	$675	$550	$475	$425	$375

Add $100 for ghost ring sights w/ComforTech stock.
Subtract $100 for tactical open rifle sights.

M3 CONVERTIBLE AUTO/PUMP (SUPER 90) - 12 ga. only, 3 in. chamber, defense configuration incorporating convertible (fingertip activated) pump or semi-auto action, 19 3/4 in. cyl. bore barrel with ghost ring or rifle (disc. 2007) sights, 5 shot mag., choice of standard black polymer stock or integral pistol grip (disc. 1996, reintroduced 1999), approx. 7.3 lbs. New 1989.

MSR $1,380		$1,195	$925	$825	$750	$675	$575	$475

Add $110 for folding stock (mfg. 1990-disc.) - only available as a complete gun.
Add $340 for Model 200 Laser Sight System with bracket (disc.).
Subtract approx. 10% for rifle sights (disc. 2007).

M4 TACTICAL - 12 ga. only, consumer version of the U.S. Military M4, 3 in. chamber, includes auto-regulating gas operating (ARGO) system, dual stainless self cleaning pistons, 4 shot mag., matte black phosphated metal standard, or 100% Desert camo coverage (except for pistol grip, new 2007), 18 1/2 in. barrel with ghost ring sights, pistol grip, or non-collapsible (disc. 2004) stock and forearm, includes Picatinny rail, approx. 7.8 lbs. Importation began late 2003.

MSR $1,625		$1,395	$1,100	$950	$825	$725	$650	$600

Add $130 for 100% desert camo coverage (new 2007).

M1014 LIMITED EDITION - similar to M4, except only available with non-collapsible stock, U.S. flag engraved on receiver, 8 lbs. Limited edition of 2,500 mfg. 2003-2004.

	$1,375	$1,100	$950	$825	$725	$650	$600

Last MSR was $1,575.

MONTEFELTRO STANDARD HUNTER (SUPER 90) - 12 or 20 (new 1993) ga., 3 in. chamber, aluminum alloy receiver, rotary bolt, 21 (disc. 1997), 24, 26, or 28 (12 ga. only) in. VR barrel with 5 choke tubes, matte black metal or 100% Realtree camo (20 ga. only, mfg. 1998-2000) finish, checkered walnut stock and forearm with choice of high gloss (disc. 1997) or satin finish, 4 shot mag., approx. 5 1/2 (20 ga.) or 7.1 lbs. New 1988.

MSR $1,140		$975	$775	$675	$575	$475	$425	$375

Add $100 for 100% Realtree camo finish on 20 ga. only (disc.).
Add $10 for left-hand action (12 ga., 26 or 28 in. barrel only).
Add $10 for shortened stock with 12 1/2 in. LOP, approx. 5 1/2 lbs. (20 ga. only, new 1999).

* *Montefeltro Grade II* - 12 or 20 (disc. 2005) ga., 26 in. VR barrel with 5 chokes, red fiber optic front sight, includes upgraded select walnut and gold accents, 5 1/2 (20 ga.) or 6.9 (12 ga.) lbs. Mfg. 2004-2006.

		$1,050	$875	$750	$600	$525	$450	$395

Last MSR was $1,220.

* *Montefeltro Silver* - 12 or 20 ga., 3 in. chamber, 4 shot mag., features nickel/blue receiver with etched game scenes, 26 (20 ga.) or 28 (12 ga.) in. VR barrel with choke tubes, AA grade satin finished checkered walnut stock and forearm, 5.6 or 6.9 lbs. New 2007.

MSR $1,575		$1,350	$1,050	$875	$750	$650	$550	$475

* *Montefeltro Limited Edition (Super 90)* - 20 ga. only, nickel plated lower receiver with etched gold highlights, 26 in. VR barrel. Limited mfg. 1995-96.

	100%	98%	95%	90%	80%	70%	60%
	$1,825	$1,400	$1,225	$995	$875	$750	$625

Last MSR was $2,080.

* *Montefeltro Turkey Gun* - similar to Montefeltro Standard Hunter except has 24 in. VR barrel with 3 choke tubes, satin finish wood only, 7 lbs. Imported 1989 only.

	100%	98%	95%	90%	80%	70%	60%
	$650	$575	$500	$450	$415	$365	$310

Last MSR was $675.

* *Montefeltro Uplander* - similar to Montefeltro Turkey Gun except has 21 or 24 in. VR barrel with 3 choke tubes, satin finish wood only, 7 lbs. Mfg. 1989-92.

	100%	98%	95%	90%	80%	70%	60%
	$650	$575	$500	$450	$415	$365	$310

Last MSR was $799.

* *Montefeltro Slug Gun* - deer gun configuration with 19 3/4 in. slug barrel. Disc. 1992.

	100%	98%	95%	90%	80%	70%	60%
	$650	$500	$475	$425	$400	$350	$310

Last MSR was $799.

ULTRALIGHT - 12 ga., 2 3/4 or 3 in. chamber, 24 or 26 (new 2007) in. VR blue barrel, WeatherCoat stock, 2 shot mag., featherweight alloy receiver, shortened mag. tube and forearm, raised carbon fiber target rib, 6 lbs. Importation began 2006.

MSR $1,445		$1,175	$950	$825	$725	$625	$525	$450

CORDOBA - 12 or 20 ga., 3 in. chamber, 28 or 30 in. 10mm ported VR cyro barrel with extended choke tubes, 4 shot mag., matte black finish, black synthetic ComforTech stock with grip tight panels and dimple checkering, or Max 4 HD (12 ga. only, 28 in. barrel, rifle sights, new 2007) camo coverage, 7.2 lbs. New 2005.

MSR $1,770		$1,495	$1,200	$995	$875	$750	$650	$600

Add $120 for Max 4 HD camo (new 2007).

SPORT MODEL - 12 ga., 3 in. chamber, one piece blued alloy receiver, 26 (disc. 1999, reintroduced during 2001 only) or 28 in. barrel with 5 choke tubes and 2 removable and interchangeable carbon fiber vent. ribs, 4 shot mag., adj. butt pad and buttstock, satin finished select checkered walnut stock and forearm, "Benelli" outlined in red on matte finished receiver side, approx. 7.1 lbs. Mfg. 1997-2002.

		$1,125	$895	$750	$575	$500	$450	$400

Last MSR was $1,375.

SPORT II - 12 or 20 ga., 3 in. chamber, one piece satin nickel finished alloy receiver, blued, 26 (disc. 2004), 28, or 30 (new 2005) in. cryogenically treated ported barrel with 5 extra long (not flush with barrel) choke tubes, twin bead sights, 4 shot mag., gel recoil pad with stock spacer kit provided, satin finished select checkered walnut stock and forearm, "Sport II" on receiver side, approx. 7 7/8 lbs. Importation began 2003.

MSR $1,605		$1,365	$1,050	$850	$750	$625	$550	$475

SUPERSPORT - 12 or 20 ga., 3 in. chamber, dimpled black carbon fiber stock and forearm with AirTouch recoil reduction system, 4 shot mag. (shell view feature in 20 ga. only), 28 or 30 in. ported VR barrel with Cryo treatment and extended Cryo choke tubes, twin bead sights, satin nickel receiver finish with "Supersport" on right side, 7.9 lbs. New 2004.

MSR $1,870		$1,595	$1,225	$975	$850	$750	$650	$600

LEGACY MODEL - 12 or 20 (new 1999) ga., 3 in. chamber, 24 (20 ga. only), 26 or 28 (12 ga. only) in. VR barrel with 5 choke tubes and red bar front sight with bead midsight, 4 shot mag., engraved nickel finished alloy lower or all alloy (20 ga. only) receiver, cartridge drop lever, select AA checkered walnut stock with vent. recoil pad and forearm, stock shim kit provided, mfg. to commemorate the 30th Anniversary of Benelli shotgun manufacturing, approx. 5.8 lbs. or 7 1/2 lbs. New 1998.

MSR $1,625		$1,375	$1,050	$875	$750	$675	$600	$525

GRADING - PPGS™	100%	98%	95%	90%	80%	70%	60%

* Legacy Limited Edition - 12 or 20 ga., features acid etched engraving with gold filled game scenes, only 250 of each ga. mfg. for the new millennium only, deluxe checkered walnut stock and forearm. Limited mfg. 2000 only.

	$1,750	$1,475	$850	$675	$600	$500	$450

Last MSR was $1,600.

Add 20% to individual prices for a 2 gun set with matching serial numbers (NIB only).

* Legacy Sport - 12 ga. only, 3 in. chamber, 30 in. ported VR barrel with choke tubes, AA grade satin finished walnut stock. New 2008.

MSR $2,160	$1,850	$1,595	$1,225	$975	$850	$750	$650

RAFFAELLO SERIES - 12 ga., 3 in. chamber, 26 in. VR barrel with choke tubes, higher grade model with three different levels of embellishments and checkered select walnut stock and forearm, 4 shot mag., available through Benelli World Class dealers only, 7.4 lbs. Importation began late 2005.

* Raffaello Standard - unengraved black receiver with Raffaello marked on right side.

MSR $1,800	$1,550	$1,300	$1,025	$875	$775	$675	$600

* Raffaello Deluxe - features etched fine scroll engraving with game scenes on coin finished lower receiver, fancy walnut.

MSR $2,200	$1,925	$1,625	$1,300	$1,100	$950	$875	$750

* Raffaello Legacy - features fine scroll engraved with gold inlaid birds and animals on coin finished lower receiver, deluxe walnut with wood buttplate.

MSR $2,600	$2,275	$1,900	$1,500	$1,250	$1,100	$925	$850

EXCLUSIVE LIMITED EDITION - 12 (available only as a set) or 20 ga., 3 in. chamber, 26 in. VR barrel with choke tubes, satin finished checkered walnut stock and forearm, silver receiver with light scroll and game bird inlays, 4 shot mag., red bar sights, silver "E" inset pistol grip cap, 6 lbs. Importation began 2007, available through World Class dealers only.

MSR $2,600	$2,275	$1,900	$1,500	$1,250	$1,100	$925	$850

ELITE LIMITED EDITION SET - 12 and 20 ga., 3 in. chamber, 26 in. VR barrel with choke tubes, oil finished checkered walnut stock and forearm, silver receiver with scroll engraving, gold borders and game bird inlays, 4 shot mag., 5.8 (20 ga.) - 7.4 lbs. Importation began 2007, available through World Class dealers only.

MSR $4,300	$3,850	$3,400	$3,100	$2,800	$2,600	$2,350	$2,100

EXECUTIVE SERIES - 12 ga. only, 3 in. chamber, features engraved all-steel greyed lower receiver by Giovanelli, mid-rib barrel bead, high polish upper receiver and barrel bluing, extra select grade walnut with standard stock dimensions, 5 choke tubes, and other accessories, choice of 21 (disc.), 24 (disc.), 26, or 28 in. VR barrel, approx. 7 3/4 lbs. Importation began 1996, available through World Class dealers only.

* Executive Grade I (Type I)

MSR $6,900	$5,875	$4,950	$3,925	$3,500	$2,950	$2,500	$2,100

* Executive Grade II (Type II)

MSR $7,800	$6,750	$5,600	$4,400	$3,800	$3,250	$2,725	$2,400

* Executive Grade III (Type III)

MSR $8,800	$7,750	$6,550	$4,775	$4,100	$3,450	$3,000	$2,650

BLACK EAGLE - 12 ga., 3 in. chamber, Montefeltro action, similar to Montefeltro Super 90 Standard Hunter except has black synthetic regular or pistol grip stock and forearm, 21 (disc. 1990), 24 (disc. 1990), 26, or 28 (new 1990) in. VR barrel with 3 choke tubes, right-hand only. Originally imported 1989-90, resumed 1997 only.

	$800	$675	$550	$450	$375	$315	$285

Last MSR was $992.

This configuration changed to competition in 1991 (see Black Eagle Competition Model).

✳ *Black Eagle Competition Model* - 12 ga. only, designed for competition shooting with action adj. for lighter loads, silver finished etched lower receiver, 26 or 28 in. VR barrel with 5 choke tubes and wrench provided, includes buttstock drop adjustment kit. Mfg. 1991-97.

100%	98%	95%	90%	80%	70%	60%
$875	$775	$675	$550	$475	$375	$300

Last MSR was $1,229.

✳ *Black Eagle 1994 Limited Edition* - 12 ga. only, features 26 in. VR barrel with extra fancy grade checkered walnut and gold inlays on receiver sides, 1,000 mfg. 1994-95 only with special serialization.

100%	98%	95%	90%	80%	70%	60%
$1,500	$1,300	$1,150	$995	$875	$750	$625

Last MSR was $2,000.

✳ *Black Eagle Slug Gun* - 12 ga., 24 in. rifled barrel with receiver scope mount. Imported 1990-91 only.

100%	98%	95%	90%	80%	70%	60%
$735	$625	$500	$425	$365	$315	$285

Last MSR was $859.

SUPER BLACK EAGLE - 12 ga. only, 3 1/2 in. chamber, updated Montefeltro action accepts all 12 ga. loads, right or left-hand (new 1999) action, upper steel/lower alloy receiver, 24, 26, or 28 in. VR barrel with 5 choke tubes and wrench provided, 3 shot mag., choice of matte finish and satin wood stock, blue finish and high gloss wood finish (26 or 28 in. barrel only, disc. 2004), or 100% coverage Advantage Timber HD (new 2002), or Realtree X-tra Brown camo. (mfg. 1997-2001) finish on polymer stock and forearm, Turkey Models include steady-grip with built-in stock pistol grip (new 2003) or regular pistol grip with 24 in. barrel, red fiber optic front sight with metal bead sight, black synthetic stock and forearm with matte metal finish was introduced in 1993, vent. recoil pad, includes buttstock drop adjustment kit, approx. 7.4 lbs. Mfg. 1991-2005.

100%	98%	95%	90%	80%	70%	60%
$1,075	$825	$725	$625	$525	$475	$425

Last MSR was $1,305.

Add $95 for camo finish (Turkey Models).
Add $95 for 100% coverage Realtree camo wood/metal finish (disc. 2001).
Add $10 for satin walnut stock and forearm (26 or 28 in. barrel only).
Add $45 for 11 oz. mercury recoil reducer (synthetic stock only).
Add $75 for left-hand action for either black synthetic stock/forearm or full coverage camo finish (disc. 2004).
Add $180 for Turkey configuration with 24 in. barrel, steady-grip, and 100% camo coverage.

✳ *Super Black Eagle Limited Edition* - 12 ga. only, features 26 in. VR barrel with extra fancy grade checkered walnut and gold inlays on nickel plated receiver sides, 1,000 mfg. beginning 1997 with special serialization, 7.4 lbs. Disc. 1999.

100%	98%	95%	90%	80%	70%	60%
$1,825	$1,500	$1,225	$995	$875	$750	$625

Last MSR was $2,095.

✳ *Super Black Eagle Limited Edition 10th Anniversary* - 12 ga., 3 1/2 in. chamber, 26 in. barrel, matte finish, wildlife engraving on both sides of receiver featuring two turkeys and three geese, gold inlays similar to Executive Type III with "Super Black Eagle Tenth Anniversary" on left, "1 of 500", and "SBE10XXX" special serialization on right, 500 mfg. 2002.

100%	98%	95%	90%	80%	70%	60%
$2,250	$1,950	$1,650	$1,325	$1,050	$900	$800

✳ *Super Black Eagle Slug Gun* - 12 ga., 3 in. chamber, includes 24 in. rifled barrel with adj. rifle sights, drilled and tapped receiver, choice of matte or camo metal finish, choice of black polymer (new 1993), satin finished wood, or 100% Advantage Timber HD (new 2002) or Realtree X-tra Brown camo (mfg. 2000-2001), 7.6 lbs. Mfg. 1992-2003.

100%	98%	95%	90%	80%	70%	60%
$1,110	$910	$775	$650	$575	$475	$425

Last MSR was $1,335.

Add $10 for wood stock.

GRADING - PPGS™	100%	98%	95%	90%	80%	70%	60%

Add $125 for Advantage Timber HD camo finish.
Add $100 for Realtree X-tra Brown camo finish (disc. 2001).

SUPER BLACK EAGLE I - 12 ga. only, 3 1/2 in. chamber, 24, 26, or 28 in. barrel, choice of satin walnut wood with matte metal finish, synthetic, Advantage Max-4 HD camo (100% coverage), Advantage Timber HD (100% coverage), or steady-grip (Turkey, 24 in. barrel only) with Advantage Timber HD, red fiber optic front sight with bead metal sight, 3 shot mag. Mfg. 2005.

	$1,100	$925	$800	$650	$550	$500	$450

Last MSR was $1,333.

Add $67 for satin walnut stock and forearm.
Add $120 for camo finish.
Add $200 for Turkey configuration with steady-grip stock.

✳ *Super Black Eagle I Slug* - 12 ga. only, 24 in. smoothbore barrel, satin walnut stock and forearm, matte metal finish, 3 shot mag., adj. rifle sights. Mfg. 2005.

	$1,185	$950	$825	$700	$600	$475	$425

Last MSR was $1,465.

SUPER BLACK EAGLE II - 12 ga. only, 3 1/2 in. chamber, action similar to Super Black Eagle, with or w/o ComforTech recoil reduction in stock with two gel pads, 3 shot mag., 24 (Turkey, with steady grip), 26, or 28 in. VR barrel with cryogenic treatment, larger trigger guard, AirTouch checkering on stock and shortened forearm, choice of satin finished walnut, black synthetic, or 100% coverage of Advantage Max-4 HD, APG HD (new 2007) or Advantage Timber HD camo, approx. 7.2 lbs. New 2004.

MSR $1,485	$1,275	$1,025	$875	$775	$675	$550	$500

Add $65 for ComforTech stock.
Add $100 for left-hand action with ComforTech stock system.
Add $35 for left-hand action (disc. 2005).
Add $205 for steady grip (pistol grip) stock (Turkey configuration with APG HD camo).
Add $205 for camo.

✳ *Super Black Eagle II Slug* - 12 ga. only, 24 in. barrel with rifled bore and adj. sights, includes Picatinny rail, choice of satin walnut stock and forearm or black synthetic stock, ComforTech became standard 2007, or 100% camo coverage of Timber HD or APG HD, approx. 7.4 lbs. New 2004.

MSR $1,550	$1,325	$1,025	$875	$700	$650	$550	$500

Add $180 for 100% camo treatment.
Add $75 for black synthetic ComforTech stock and forearm.

✳ *Super Black Eagle II Flyway Limited Edition* - four variations include: the Atlantic, Mississippi, Central, and Pacific Flyways, roll engraved satin grey receiver finish with four gold duck/goose inlays (each Flyway has four different inlays), select checkered walnut stock and forearm, 7.2 lbs. 175 of each Flyway manufactured 2004.

	$1,795	$1,500	$1,275	$1,000	$875	$800	$725

Last MSR was $2,130.

SHOTGUNS: SLIDE-ACTION

All currently manufactured Benelli shotguns are equipped with a patented Benelli keyed chamber lock.

NOVA - 12 or 20 (new 2001) ga., 3 (20 ga. only) or 3 1/2 in. chamber, unique design allows stock and internal metal receiver "shell" to be molded in one unit, utilizing a glass polymer matrix, Montefeltro rotating bolt, dual action bars, 24 (Turkey only), 26, or 28 in. VR barrel with 3 choke tubes and red fiberoptic front sight, 3 (3 1/2 in. shells) or 4 shot mag., matte metal finish, choice of black synthetic, full coverage Realtree X-tra brown (disc. 2002), Advantage Max-4 HD, APG HD (new 2007), or Advantage Timber HD (mfg. 2001-2007, 20 ga.

GRADING - PPGS™	100%	98%	95%	90%	80%	70%	60%

only until 2002) camo stock and forearm with grooved hand ribs, mag. shell stop button in bottom of forearm, approx. 6 1/2 (20 ga.) or 8 lbs. New 1999.

MSR $390		$330	$265	$225	$210	$190	$180	$170

Add $65 for Realtree X-tra brown full camo finish (12 ga. only, disc. 2002).
Add $95 for full camo coverage.
Add $20 for 20 ga.
Add $95 for 24 in. barrel with 100% camo coverage (Turkey Model).
Add $30 for 20 ga. Youth Model with 13 in. LOP.
Add $60 for 2 (12 ga.) or $45 for 4 (20 ga. only) shot magazine extension.
Add $105 for recoil reducer - 10 oz. (disc.) or 14 oz. mercury, installed in stock with reduction tube operation (12 ga.).

✳ *Nova Tactical (Special Purpose Smooth Bore)* - 12 ga. only, 3 1/2 in. chamber, similar action to Nova, features 18 1/2 in. cyl. bore barrel with choice of rifle or ghost ring (new 2000) sights, black synthetic stock and forearm only, 7.2 lbs. New 1999.

MSR $365		$315	$250	$215	$200	$185	$170	$155

Add $40 for ghost ring sights.

✳ *Nova H20* - 12 ga. only, 3 1/2 in. chamber, 18 1/2 in. matte nickel finished barrel, mag. tube, trigger group, and inner metal parts, black synthetic stock and forearm, open rifle sights, 4 shot mag., 7.2 lbs. Importation began 2003.

MSR $575		$495	$395	$350	$300	$255	$225	$200

✳ *Nova Entry* - 12 ga. only, 14 in. barrel, choice of ghost ring or open rifle sights, black synthetic stock and forearm, 4 shot mag., approx. 6.9 lbs. Importation began 2003.

MSR N/A		$295	$265	$235	$220	$215	$200	$185

Add $30 for ghost ring sights.
This model is available to law enforcement or military only.

✳ *Nova Slug* - 12 or 20 ga., 3 in. chamber, features 24 in. rifled bore drilled and tapped barrel with open rifle sights, black synthetic or 100% coverage Advantage Timber HD camo stock and forearm, 8.1 lbs. Mfg. 2000-2006.

		$445	$390	$355	$315	$285	$260	$240

Last MSR was $535.

Add $90 for Advantage Timber HD camo.

❖ **Nova Slug & Field Combo** - 12 or 20 ga., 3 in. chamber, combo features 24 in. rifled bore drilled and tapped barrel with extra 26 in. field barrel, open rifle sights, black synthetic or 100% coverage Advantage Timber HD camo stock and forearm, 8.1 lbs. Mfg. 2000-2007.

		$460	$400	$365	$325	$290	$260	$240

Last MSR was $560.

SUPERNOVA - 12 ga. only, 3 1/2 in. chamber, 24, 26, or 28 in. VR barrel with choke tubes, choice of matte synthetic, APG HD (new 2007) Advantage Max-4 HD or Advantage Timber HD (disc. 2007) 100% camo coverage, includes ComforTech stock system. New 2006.

MSR $485		$395	$350	$300	$265	$230	$200	$180

Add $95 for 100% camo coverage.

✳ *SuperNova Steady-Grip* - features 24 in. barrel with steady-grip (full pistol grip), choice of matte finish or APG HD (new 2007) or Advantage Timber HD (disc. 2007) camo. New 2006.

MSR $500		$415	$365	$320	$280	$250	$230	$195

Add $95 for camo.

GRADING - PPGS™	100%	98%	95%	90%	80%	70%	60%

❋ *SuperNova Tactical* - features 18 in. barrel with choice of ComforTech or pistol grip synthetic stock, matte finish or Desert camo (new 2007, pistol grip only), choice of rifle or ghost ring sights. New 2006.

MSR $445		$380	$325	$285	$240	$210	$180	$165

Add $10 for pistol grip stock.
Add $15 for ghost ring sights.
Add $130 for Desert camo w/pistol grip and ghost ring sights (new 2007).

❋ *SuperNova Slug* - 12 ga., 2 3/4 or 3 in. chamber, features 24 in. rifled bore drilled and tapped barrel with adj. rifle sights, black synthetic or 100% coverage APG HD camo stock and forearm, 8.1 lbs. New 2007.

MSR $645		$525	$450	$400	$350	$300	$260	$240

Add $130 for 100% camo coverage.
Add $10 for Field & Slug combo with extra 26 in. Field barrel (mfg. 2007 only).

BENSON FIREARMS LTD.

Previous importer for guns manufactured by Aldo Uberti in Italy. Previously imported and distributed from 1987-1989 by Benson Firearms Ltd. located in Seattle, WA. Benson Firearms Ltd. combined with A. Uberti USA Inc. in early 1989 and discontinued importation.

Benson Firearms can be differentiated from other A. Uberti imports by the "Benson Firearms Seattle, WA" barrel marking.

Rather than provide a complete listing of Benson Firearms models, the following rules usually apply. Since Benson Firearms imported A. Uberti firearms, the Uberti section in this text should be referenced for current values regarding models with similar configurations. Collectibility to date has been limited on most Benson Fireams models, and as a rule, up-to-date values on this trademark are established by current importation prices of Uberti firearms. A complete listing of older Benson Firearms models can be found in the 11th and 12th Editions of the *Blue Book of Gun Values*.

BENTON & BROWN FIREARMS, INC.

Previous manufacturer located in Fort Worth, TX and Delhi, LA circa 1993-1996.

RIFLES: BOLT ACTION

MODEL 93 - available in 15 cals. between .243 Win. and .375 H&H Mag., patterned after the Model R-84 Blaser, takedown, free floating 22 or 24 in. barrels, right- or left-hand action, checkered walnut stock and forearm, 7-8 1/2 lbs. New 1993.

		$1,875	$1,550	$1,225	$1,100	$995	$875	$750

Last MSR was $2,075.

Subtract $200 for fiberglass stock.
Add $450 per interchangeable barrel.

BERETTA, DR. FRANCO

Previous manufacturer located in Concesio (Brescia), Italy until 1994.

SHOTGUNS: O/U, BLACK DIAMOND SERIES

Black Diamond target guns were imported exclusively by Double M Shooting Sports until 1988.

FIELD MODEL - 12, 16, 20, 28 ga., or .410 bore, variety of chokes, coin finish receiver.

		$595	$550	$495	$450	$395	$365	$335

Last MSR was $960.

GRADE ONE - 12, 16, 20, 28 ga., or .410 bore, variety of chokes, coin finish receiver with acid etched engraving, French walnut. Trap or skeet model also available, except in 16 ga.

		$1,020	$900	$810	$720	$630	$570	$525

Last MSR was $1,440.

GRADING - PPGS™	100%	98%	95%	90%	80%	70%	60%

GRADE TWO - 12, 16, 20, 28 ga., or .410 bore, variety of chokes, coin finish receiver with moderate engraving, French walnut. Trap or skeet model also available, except in 16 ga.

	$1,475	$1,320	$1,200	$1,080	$930	$815	$750

Last MSR was $2,040.

GRADE THREE - 12, 16, 20, 28 ga., or .410 bore, variety of chokes, coin finish receiver with scrollwork engraving, French walnut. Trap or skeet model also available, except in 16 ga.

	$2,100	$1,920	$1,775	$1,560	$1,410	$1,200	$1,035

Last MSR was $3,000.

GRADE FOUR - 12, 16, 20, 28 ga., or .410 bore, variety of chokes, coin finish receiver with elaborate engraving, French walnut. Trap or skeet model also available, except in 16 ga.

	$2,500	$2,250	$1,950	$1,650	$1,375	$1,125	$995

Last MSR was $3,960.

SKEET SET - includes 12, 20, 28 ga., and .410 bore barrels, available in Grades One through Four.

Multiply values on Grades One - Four by 275% for 4 ga. skeet sets.

SHOTGUNS: O/U, SxS, & SINGLE BARREL, RECENT MFG.

GAMMA STANDARD O & U - 12, 16, or 20 ga., 26 or 28 in. barrels, coin finish receiver with extensive engraving, Italian walnut. Imported 1984-88.

	$400	$360	$330	$300	$275	$260	$240

Last MSR was $445.

Add $83 with single trigger and ejectors.

✳ *Gamma Standard* - with interchangeable choke tubes. Importation disc. 1993.

	$825	$695	$525	$425	$325	$250	$195

Last MSR was $1,000.

Add 20% for auto ejectors.
Add $100 for single trigger.
Add 36% for Gamma Trap or Skeet variation (ST).

GAMMA DELUXE O & U - 12, 16, or 20 ga., 26 or 28 in. barrels, coin finish receiver with extensive engraving, Italian walnut. Imported 1984-88.

	$445	$405	$370	$350	$325	$300	$275

Last MSR was $480.

Add $84 with single trigger and ejectors.

✳ *Gamma Deluxe* - with interchangeable choke tubes. Importation disc. 1988.

	$635	$570	$530	$490	$450	$420	$390

Last MSR was $685.

GAMMA TARGET O & U - 12 ga. only, SST, ejectors, Wundhammer swell pistol grip, English walnut stock and beavertail forearm. Imported 1986-88.

	$550	$505	$455	$410	$370	$350	$325

Last MSR was $595.

ALPHA STANDARD O & U - 12, 16, or 20 ga., 26 or 28 in. barrels, coin finish receiver with extensive engraving, Italian walnut. Imported 1984-88, resumed 1993.

	$720	$650	$525	$450	$375	$300	$250

Last MSR was $780.

Add 18% for auto ejectors.
Add $100 for single trigger.

GRADING - PPGS™	100%	98%	95%	90%	80%	70%	60%

ALPHA DELUXE O & U - 12, 16, or 20 ga., 26 or 28 in. barrels, coin finish receiver with extensive engraving, sling swivels, Italian walnut. Imported 1984-88.

	$395	$355	$330	$300	$275	$250	$230

Last MSR was $435.

Add $75 with single trigger and ejectors.
Add $80 for interchangeable choke tubes (disc. 1985).

AMERICA STANDARD O & U - .410 bore only, 26 or 28 in. barrels, coin finish receiver with extensive engraving, Italian walnut. Imported 1984-88.

	$305	$280	$265	$240	$215	$205	$190

Last MSR was $335.

Add $85 for Deluxe model.

EUROPA O & U - .410 bore only, 26 in. barrels, coin finish receiver with some engraving, Italian walnut. Imported 1984-88.

	$275	$250	$235	$220	$210	$200	$185

Last MSR was $295.

Add $95 for Deluxe model (disc. 1985).

FRANCIA STANDARD SxS - .410 bore only, double triggers, extractors, checkered walnut. Imported 1986-88.

	$235	$220	$210	$200	$185	$175	$160

Last MSR was $255.

Add $19 for Deluxe Model.

OMEGA STANDARD SxS - 12, 16, or 20 ga., 26 or 28 in. barrels, coin finish receiver with extensive engraving, Italian walnut. Imported 1984-93.

	$780	$695	$550	$450	$375	$300	$250

Last MSR was $880.

Add 32% for auto ejectors.
Add 10% for single trigger (disc. 1985).

MILANO O/U - 9mm Flobert, folding design. Imported 1993 only.

	$380	$330	$295	$250	$210	$180	$150

Last MSR was $420.

VERONA/BERGAMO SxS - 9mm Flobert, folding design, Bergamo model has hammers, Verona model is hammerless. Imported 1993 only.

	$270	$225	$180	$140	$115	$95	$75

Last MSR was $300.

BRESCIA SINGLE BARREL - 9mm Flobert, folding design. Imported 1993 only.

	$175	$150	$130	$110	$90	$70	$55

Last MSR was $200.

BETA SINGLE BARREL - 12, 16, 20, 24, 28, 32 ga., or .410 bore, single barrel field gun, VR, chrome finish receiver, folding design. Imported 1985-93.

	$215	$185	$160	$145	$135	$125	$115

Last MSR was $240.

Add 10% for VR.

SHOTGUNS: SEMI-AUTO

ARIETE STANDARD - 12 ga. only, gas operated, 2 3/4 or 3 in. chamber, various barrel lengths, with or without choke tubes, aluminum receiver, checkered stock and forearm, approx. 6.9 lbs. Imported 1993 only.

	$995	$795	$525	$425	$325	$250	$195

Last MSR was $1,180.

Add $20 for 3 in. mag. variation.

GRADING - PPGS™	100%	98%	95%	90%	80%	70%	60%

SHOTGUNS: SLIDE ACTION

ARIETE - 12 ga. only, 3 in. chamber, various barrel lengths without VR, twin action bars, matte finish, recoil pad. Imported 1993 only.

$780	$695	$550	$450	$375	$300	$250

Last MSR was $880.

BERETTA

Current manufacturer located in Brescia, Italy, 1526-present—company name in Italy is Fabbrica d´Armi Pietro Beretta—in Accokeek, MD, 1978 to date. Beretta U.S.A. Corp. was formed in 1977 and is located in Accokeek, MD. Beretta U.S.A. Corp. has been importing Beretta Firearms exclusively since 1980. 1970-1977 manufacture was imported exclusively by Garcia. Distributor and dealer direct sales.

Beretta is one of the world's oldest family owned industrial firms, having started business in 1526. In addition to Beretta owning Benelli & Franchi, the company also purchased Sako and Tikka Companies in late 1999, Aldo Uberti & Co. in 2000, and Burris Optics in 2002. Beretta continues to be a leader in firearms development and safety, and shooters attest to the reliability of their weapons worldwide.

For more information and current pricing on both new and used Beretta precision airguns, please refer to the *Blue Book of Airguns* by Dr. Robert Beeman & John Allen (also available online).

PISTOLS: SEMI-AUTO, PRE-WWII MFG.

MODEL 1915 - .32 or 9mm Glisenti cal., Beretta's first military pistol, exaggerated slide stop, safety on rear of tang, checkered wood grips, 7 shot mag., serial range 1-16,000.

$1,250	$900	$750	$600	$500	$400	$300

9mm Para. cal. is not interchangeable and potentially dangerous if interchanged with 9mm Glisenti cal.

MODEL 1915-1917 - later 7.65mm cal. variation, 8 shot mag., exaggerated slide stops, wood grips, sold commercially and to the military. A few marked "RM" were issued to the Italian Navy, ser. no. range 16,000-72,000. Mfg. 1917-21.

$750	$600	$450	$350	$275	$225	$175

Add 100% if Navy issue.

MODEL 1922 - successor to the Model 1915-1917, mfg. with more open slide and modern slide stop, wood or pressed metal grips, ser. no. range 200,000-243,000. Mfg. 1922-1932.

$700	$550	$450	$350	$275	$225	$175

Add 100% if Navy issue.

MODEL 1923 - 9mm Glisenti cal., 8 shot, 4 in. barrel, fixed sights, usually with pressed steel grips, less frequently smooth wood with PB emblem, occasionally slotted for shoulder stock. Most were purchased by the Italian Army and marked "RE," ser. no. range 300,000-310,400. Mfg. 1923-26.

$1,750	$1,500	$1,200	$1,000	$750	$500	$350

Add 25% if slotted for shoulder stock.

MODEL 1919 - .25 ACP cal., SA, 8 shot mag., offered in several variations. First type in serial range 100,000-156,000, subsequent improvement involved changing the disconnector and left panel in the range 156,000-185,000.

$375	$325	$275	$225	$195	$165	$135

MODEL 1926 - similar to Model 1919, except fit with wood panels bearing an encircled PB. Approx. 11,000 pistols were mfg. in ser. no. range 187,000-198,000.

$350	$315	$270	$220	$190	$160	$130

GRADING - PPGS™	100%	98%	95%	90%	80%	70%	60%

MODEL 1926-31 - similar to Model 1926, except has small modifications in the slide, grips are no longer impressed with the PB monogram, interrupted serial range from 198,000-200,000 and 600,000-601,000.

	$325	$310	$265	$215	$190	$160	$125

MODEL 318 - .25 ACP cal., 2 1/2 in. barrel, fixed sights, blue, modifications in the slide legend, grip configuration, and magazine floor plate. Limited production during 1936-37, in ser. no. range 609,000-615,000.

	$275	$240	$215	$180	$160	$140	$120

Add 50%-100% for engraved and plated variations if in 98%+ original condition.
Embellished variations of the Model 318 included the Model 319 (engraved/blue), Model 320 (engraved/nickel plated) and Model 321 (engraved/gold plated).

MODEL 418 - .25 ACP cal., fixed sights, similar to Model 318, but with loaded indicator and grip safety (early type is semi-circular, late type is curved), occasionally was made with an alloy frame, popular pistol mfg. 1937-1961 with minor modifications. Later guns are suffixed with the letters A, B, and C, 178,000 mfg.

	$250	$225	$200	$175	$155	$135	$120

Add 50%-100% for engraved and plated variations if in 98%+ original condition.
Embellished variations of the Model 418 included the Model 419 (engraved blue), Model 420 (engraved nickel), and Model 421 (engraved gold plated).

MODEL 1932 - 7.65mm cal., two variations including straight and curved rear grip strap, smooth wood grips bearing PB monogram (commercial) or RM monogram (Italian Navy). 8,000 mfg. in ser. no. range 400,000-408,000.

	$2,750	$2,000	$1,500	$1,000	$750	$500	$400

MODEL 1934 - 7.65mm or .380 ACP cal., (9mm Corto cal.), 3 3/8 in. barrel, fixed sights, blue, plastic grips, Italy's service weapon in WWII, one of the most common Beretta pistols - over one million manufactured between 1934-80, many of the military pistols have a parkerized finish, usually fit with metal-backed grips, later guns have an alphabetical prefix. Post-war production (1946) serial numbers start with C00001.

	$550	$425	$325	$275	$200	$175	$150

Add 10% for high polish, unless post-war production.
Add 20% for Italian Air Force.
Add 300% for post-war commercial deluxe pistols which were engraved, gold plated, and cased with a spare mag. and cleaning brush.

MODEL 1935 - similar to the Model 1934, except 7.65mm cal., 3 1/2 in. barrel, fixed sights, blue, plastic grips, the wartime model had poor finish, a small number were fit with an experimental slide safety in the ser. no. range 500,xxx, military issue was often parkerized. 525,000 mfg. 1935-67.

	$425	$375	$325	$275	$200	$175	$150

Add 10% for high polish, unless post-war production.
Add 300% for post-war commercial deluxe pistols which were engraved, gold plated, and cased with a spare mag. and cleaning brush.

PISTOLS: SEMI-AUTO, POST WWII MFG.

100% values on below listed models assume NIB condition.

MODEL 948 - .22 LR cal., 3 1/2 or 6 in. barrel, fixed sights, hammer.

	$175	$150	$125	$100	$75	$60	$50

MODEL 949 OLYMPIC TARGET - .22 S or LR cal., 8 3/4 in. barrel, target sights, adj. barrel weights, blue, muzzle brake, checkered wood grips with thumbrest. Limited mfg. 1959-64.

	$660	$550	$495	$385	$305	$250	$195

MODEL 950CC MINX M2 - .22 short cal., hinged 2 3/8 in. barrel, fixed sights, blue, plastic grips. Mfg. 1955-disc.

	$135	$115	$105	$95	$85	$75	$70

MODEL 950CC SPECIAL MINX M4 - similar to M2, with 4 in. barrel.

	100%	98%	95%	90%	80%	70%	60%
	$135	$115	$105	$95	$85	$75	$70

MODEL 950B JETFIRE - similar to M2, in .25 ACP cal.

	$150	$120	$105	$95	$85	$75	$70

MODEL 951 BRIGADIER - 9mm Para. cal., 4 1/2 in. barrel, fixed sights, blue, plastic grips, current Italian service pistol and immediate predecessor to the M92 Series. Mfg. 1952-disc.

	$285	$235	$195	$175	$150	$130	$115

Add $350 for "Egyptian" (denoted by EC prefix) or "Israeli" Model.

MODEL 20 - .25 ACP cal., double action, alloy frame, 9 shot, 2 1/2 in. barrel, plastic or walnut grips, 10.9 oz. Disc. 1985.

	$160	$140	$125	$115	$95	$85	$75

Last MSR was $214.

MODEL 70 PUMA OR COUGAR - .32 ACP or .380 ACP cal., 3 1/2 in. barrel, fixed or adj. sights, blue, plastic grips, .32 Puma alloy frame, .380 Cougar steel frame. Disc.

	$215	$180	$165	$150	$130	$110	$90

Add 10% for .380 ACP cal.

MODEL 70T - .32 ACP cal., similar to Model 70, target sights. Disc.

	$275	$250	$220	$195	$165	$150	$140

MODEL 70S - .22 LR or .380 ACP cal., single action, 3 1/2 in. barrel, 9 shot, blue finish, plastic grips, weight .22 cal. - 18 oz., .380 ACP - 23 oz., steel frame, .22 LR has adj. rear sight. Disc. 1985.

	$240	$210	$185	$170	$155	$140	$125

Last MSR was $295.

MODEL 71 JAGUAR - .22 LR cal. version of Model 70, alloy frame, also referred to as the Jaguar Plinker pistol. Disc.

	$220	$195	$180	$160	$150	$140	$120

MODEL 72 JAGUAR - similar to Model 71 Jaguar, except includes extra 6 in. barrel. Disc.

	$275	$230	$200	$180	$160	$150	$140

MODEL 75 JAGUAR - similar to Model 71 Jaguar.

	$220	$195	$180	$160	$150	$140	$120

MODEL 76P-76W TARGET PISTOL - .22 LR cal., single action, 11 shot, steel frame, 6 in. barrel, adj. sights, blue finish, thumbrest plastic grips (76-P). Disc. 1985.

	$345	$300	$275	$245	$220	$195	$170

Last MSR was $395.

Add $40 for thumbrest wood grips (Model 76-W).

MODEL 80 - .22 short cal., target pistol with limited importation into the U.S.

	$750	$675	$595	$550	$495	$450	$395

MODEL 81P-81W - .32 ACP cal., double action, 13 shot, 3.8 in. barrel, fixed sights, blue. Imported 1976-84.

	$300	$250	$225	$195	$175	$155	$135

Add $90 for nickel finish.
Add $20 for wood grips (W suffix).

MODEL 82W - .32 ACP cal., double action, more compact than Model 81, 10 shot, walnut grips, 17 oz. Importation disc. 1984.

	$295	$250	$225	$195	$175	$155	$135

Add $75 for nickel finish.

GRADING - PPGS™	100%	98%	95%	90%	80%	70%	60%

MODEL 84B - .380 ACP cal., double action, brown wood or plastic grips, 13 shot mag., blue finish, fixed sights. Disc.

	$295	$250	$225	$195	$175	$155	$135

MODEL 84W-EL - similar to Model 84 but specially engraved, select walnut grips. Presentation case. Disc. 1984.

	$1,025	$770	$720	$615	$565	$520	$460

MODEL 86P-86W - .380 ACP cal. only, double action, tip-up 4 1/3 in. barrel, 8 shot mag., plastic or walnut grips, 23 oz. While this model was advertised, it was never released.

MSR was $480 in 1986, walnut grips were $80 extra (86-W).

MODEL 90 DOUBLE ACTION AUTOMATIC - .32 ACP cal., 3 5/8 in. barrel, fixed sights, blue, plastic grips. Mfg. 1969-83.

	$275	$195	$175	$155	$130	$110	$95

Add 25% if without external slide latch.

MODEL 100 - .32 ACP cal., fixed sights. Disc.

	$250	$220	$195	$165	$150	$140	$130

MODEL 101 - similar to Model 70T, except in .22 LR. Disc.

	$250	$220	$195	$165	$150	$140	$130

MODEL 102 - .22 LR cal., target pistol, single action, steel/alloy construction, plastic grips, 10 shot mag. with finger extension, adj. rear sight. Disc.

	$325	$250	$220	$195	$165	$150	$140

PISTOLS: SEMI-AUTO, RECENT AND CURRENT MFG.

On Beretta's large frame pistols, alphabetical suffixes refer to the following: F Model - double/single action system with external safety decocking lever, G Model - double/single action system with external decocking only lever, D Model - double action only without safety lever, DS Model - double action only with external safety lever. The models in this section appear in numerical sequence.

MODEL 21(A)-W BOBCAT - .22 LR or .25 ACP cal., double action, alloy frame, 7 (.22 LR) or 8 (.25 ACP) shot mag., 2.4 in. barrel, plastic or walnut (EL Model, disc. 2000) grips, 11 1/2 oz.

✳ *Model 21(A)-W Blue Finish*

	$240	$195	$150	$130	$115	$95	$85

Last MSR was $300.

Add approx. $75 for engraving and wood grips (EL Model, disc. 2000).

✳ *Model 21(A)-W Nickel Finish* - disc. 2000.

	$255	$215	$165	$140	$130	$115	$95

Last MSR was $322.

✳ *Model 21(A)-W Matte Finish* - matte finished metal, plastic grips. New 1992.

MSR $300	$240	$195	$150	$130	$115	$95	$85

This model is manufactured by Beretta U.S.A. Corp. in Accokeek, MD.

✳ *Model 21(A)-W Stainless Steel (Inox)* - similar to Model 21 Bobcat, except is .22 LR only, stainless steel with plastic grips, approx. 11 1/2 oz. New 2000.

MSR $375	$285	$225	$185	$150	$120	$110	$100

✳ *Model 21(A)-W Lady Beretta* - .22 LR cal. only, similar to Model 21-W, except is specially serial numbered and has gold etching on top of frame and slide sides. Supplied with a blue velvet drawstring bag. 1990 issue.

	$245	$185	$160	$140	$130	$115	$100

Last MSR was $285.

This model was sold exclusively by Lew Horton Distributing Co.

MODEL U22 NEOS - .22 LR cal., single action, unique design features modular construction and modern styling, matte black finish, 10 shot mag., 4 1/2 or 6 in. barrel with sights incorporated into integral full length sight rail, various colored grips with interchangeable rubber inlays in aqua, grey, or blue (black standard), 31 1/2 or 36 oz. New 2002.

MSR $250	$210	$185	$160	$140	$120	$100	$90

This model is also available in a carbine kit, which includes a 16 in. barrel and skeletonized buttstock. Current MSR is $282 (not legal in CA).

* *Model U22 Neos Inox* - similar to Model U22 Neos, except slide and barrel are stainless steel. New 2002.

MSR $350	$285	$235	$195	$160	$130	$110	$100

MODEL U22 NEOS DLX - .22 LR cal., similar to Model U22 Neos, except includes adj. trigger and interchangeable front and rear sights (six included), 6 or 7 1/2 in. barrel, laser engraved "U22 NEOS" on slide. Mfg. mid-2003-2007.

$280	$230	$200	$170	$145	$125	$110

Last MSR was $350.

* *Model U22 Neos DLX Inox* - similar to U22 Neos DLX, except is stainless steel. Mfg. mid-2003-2007.

$310	$255	$215	$185	$145	$130	$110

Last MSR was $375.

MODEL 71 - .22 LR cal., single action, 8 shot, 6 in. barrel, plastic grips with thumbrest, finger extension mag. Imported 1987 only.

$190	$160	$140	$130	$115	$95	$85

Last MSR was $215.

MODEL 84 CHEETAH - .380 ACP cal., single/double action semi-auto, 3.82 in. barrel, alloy frame, steel slide, 10 (C/B 1994) or 13* (reintroduced late 2004) shot staggered mag., firing pin block, ambidextrous manual safety (also used as a decocking lever), low-profile 3-dot sights, curved trigger guard, plastic or wood (available with nickel finish) grips, blue (disc.), Bruniton, or nickel (disc. 2001, reintroduced 2004) finish, 23.3 oz.

MSR $700	$525	$425	$350	$300	$250	$210	$190

Add $30 for wood grips (Model 84W, disc. 2001).
Add $50 for nickel finish (Model 84FS, includes checkered wood grips).

* *Model 84F* - similar specifications to the Model 84P-84W, except patterned after the Model 92F Govt. Model, matte black Bruniton finish, squared off trigger guard, plastic or wood grips, 23 oz. Mfg. 1990 only.

$395	$330	$300	$270	$240	$210	$190

Last MSR was $479.

MODEL 85 CHEETAH - .380 ACP cal., same general specifications as the Model 84, except slimmer profile because of 8 shot straight line mag., Model 85P has plastic grips, 21.9 oz.

MSR $650	$500	$400	$350	$300	$250	$200	$175

Add $100 for nickel finish (includes wood grips, disc. 2001, reintroduced 2004).
Add $33 for wood grips with blue finish (Model 85W - disc. 2000).

* *Model 85F* - similar specifications to the Model 85P-85W, except patterned after the Model 92F Govt. Model, matte black Bruniton finish, squared off trigger guard, plastic or wood grips, 21.8 oz. Mfg. in 1990 only.

$375	$300	$270	$240	$210	$190	$175

Last MSR was $440.

Add $25 for wood grips.

GRADING - PPGS™	100%	98%	95%	90%	80%	70%	60%

MODEL 86 CHEETAH - .380 ACP cal., single/double action semi-auto with 4.4 in. tip-up barrel, 8 shot mag., checkered walnut grips, matte Bruniton finish, fixed sights, gold trigger, 23.3 oz. Imported 1991-2004.

	$500	$390	$320	$250	$225	$190	$175

Last MSR was $615.

MODEL 87 CHEETAH - .22 LR cal., single/double action semi-auto, 7 shot mag., 3.82 or 6 in. target barrel with counterweight (disc. 1994), blue finish, wood grips, 20 oz. (3.82 in. barrel). Importation began 1986.

MSR $700	$525	$425	$350	$300	$250	$210	$190

* *Model 87 Target* - single action only target variation of the Model 87 with 5.9 in. barrel, 10 shot mag., 23.3 (older mfg.) or 41 (new mfg.) oz. Disc. 1994, reintroduced 2000.

MSR $775	$650	$500	$400	$350	$300	$265	$235

This model was reintroduced in 2000, and now features adj. rear target sight, integral scope base rail that is machined on the aluminum barrel sleeve, and Bruniton finish with anodized aluminum frame.

MODEL 89 GOLD STANDARD - .22 LR cal., single action target semi-auto, matte Bruniton black finish on metal parts, 6 in. barrel, 10 shot mag., anatomical wood grips, adj. sights, 41 oz. Imported 1988-2000.

	$630	$510	$410	$360	$310	$275	$250

Last MSR was $802.

MODEL 90-TWO TYPE F - 9mm Para. or .40 S&W cal., 4.9 in. barrel, single/double action, matte metal finish, removable single piece wraparound grip in two sizes, internal recoil buffer and captive recoil sping guide assembly, low profile fixed sights, 10, 12 (.40 S&W cal.), or 17 (9mm Para. cal.) shot mag., lower accessories rail with cover, 32 1/2 oz. New 2006.

MSR $700	$600	$525	$450	$375	$330	$300	$275

MODEL 950 JETFIRE (BS) - .22 Short (disc. 1992) or .25 ACP cal., single action, alloy frame, 8 shot (.25 cal. only) or 6 shot mag., tip-up 2 1/2 and 4 in. (.22 S only) barrel, plastic grips, thumb safety, matte (new 1992, plastic grips only), blue or nickel finish, 9.9 oz. Disc. 2002.

	$180	$140	$115	$100	$90	$80	$70

Last MSR was $226.

Add $22 for blue finish (disc. 1999).
Add $80 for nickel finish (disc. 1999).
This model is manufactured by Beretta U.S.A. Corp. in Accokeek, MD.

* *Model 950 Jetfire Stainless (Inox)* - similar to Model 950 BS, except is stainless steel. Mfg. 2000-2002.

	$210	$150	$120	$100	$85	$70	$65

Last MSR was $267.

* *Model 950 EL* - same general specifications as Model 950 BS, only with wood grips and gold plated parts. Disc. 1999.

	$275	$230	$200	$180	$165	$150	$135

Last MSR was $337.

MODEL 3032 TOMCAT - .32 ACP cal., similar to Model 21 Bobcat, except has 2.45 in. barrel, 7 shot mag., choice of matte or blue (disc. 2007) finish, plastic grips, regular or Tritium AO Big Dot Express (new 2002) sights, approx. 14 1/2 oz., mfg. by Beretta U.S.A. New 1996.

MSR $400	$315	$235	$200	$175	$150	$135	$120

Add $25 for blue finish (disc. 2007).
Add $150 for laser grips (new 2008).
Add $75 for Alley Cat package - includes Tritium AO Big Dot Express sights and in-the-pants Alcantara synthetic holster.

GRADING - PPGS™	100%	98%	95%	90%	80%	70%	60%

✳ *Model 3032 Tomcat Stainless (Inox)* - similar to Model 3032 Tomcat, except has stainless steel slide and barrel, grey anodized alloy frame, 15.8 oz. New 2000.

MSR $500	$385	$325	$250	$200	$175	$150	$125

✳ *Model 3032 Tomcat Titanium* - similar to Model 3032 Tomcat, except has titanium frame, blue finish only, 16.9 oz. Mfg. 2001-late 2002.

	$460	$360	$310	N/A	N/A	N/A	N/A

Last MSR was $589.

MODEL 8000 COUGAR F/D - 9mm Para. cal., single/double (Model 8000 Cougar F) or DA (Model 8000 Cougar D, disc. 2000) only, short recoil system with 3.6 in. rotating barrel, 10 or 13 (became option late 2004) shot mag., fixed sights, anodized aluminum alloy frame, black plastic grips, Bruniton matte black finish, 32.6 oz. Mfg. 1995-2005.

	$665	$575	$440	$385	$335	$300	$275

Last MSR was $800.

✳ *Model 8000 Mini Cougar* - similar to Model 8000 Cougar, except overall height has been reduced to 4 1/2 in. and weight is 27.6 oz. Mfg. 1998-2003.

	$600	$545	$415	$375	$330	$300	$275

Last MSR was $709.

✳ *Model 8000L Cougar* - similar to Model 8000F Cougar, except has shortened grip, 10 or 13 (optional late 2004) shot double stack mag., 28.2 oz. Mfg. 2003-2005.

	$665	$575	$440	$385	$335	$300	$275

Last MSR was $800.

✳ *Model 8000 Cougar (Inox)* - similar to Model 8000F Cougar, except is stainless steel. Limited mfg. 2004 only.

	$715	$575	$450	$385	$335	$280	$235

Last MSR was $875.

MODEL 8040 COUGAR F/D - .40 S&W cal., single/double (Model 8040 Cougar F) or DA (Model 8040 Cougar D, disc. 2000) only, short recoil system with 3.6 in. rotating barrel, 10 or 11 (became optional late 2004) shot mag., fixed sights, anodized aluminum alloy frame, Bruniton matte black finish, 32.4 oz. Mfg. 1995-2005.

	$665	$575	$440	$385	$335	$300	$275

Last MSR was $800.

✳ *Model 8040 Cougar (Inox)* - similar to Model 8040F Cougar, except is stainless steel. Limited mfg. 2004 only.

	$715	$575	$450	$385	$335	$280	$235

Last MSR was $875.

✳ *Model 8040 Mini Cougar* - similar to Model 8040 Cougar, except overall height has been reduced to 4 1/2 in. and weight is 27.6 oz., supplied with 8 and extended 10 shot mag. Mfg. 1998-2003.

	$600	$545	$415	$375	$330	$300	$275

Last MSR was $709.

MODEL 8045 COUGAR F/D - .45 ACP cal., 8 shot mag., otherwise similar to Models 8000 and 8040, 32 oz. Mfg. 1998-2004, D Model disc. 2002.

	$710	$560	$450	$395	$345	$300	$275

Last MSR was $860.

Subtract approx. $25 for Model 8045 Cougar D (DA only, disc. 2002).

✳ *Model 8045 Mini Cougar D/F* - similar to Model 8045 Cougar, except overall height has been reduced to 4 1/2 in. and weight is 27.6 oz, supplied with 6 shot mag. Importation began 1999, D Model disc. 2002, F disc. in 2003.

	$635	$515	$435	$385	$340	$300	$275

Last MSR was $764.

Subtract approx. $25 for Model 8045 Mini-Cougar D (DA only, disc. 2002).

GRADING - PPGS™	100%	98%	95%	90%	80%	70%	60%

MODEL 8357 COUGAR F - .357 Sig cal., single/double action, 5 1/2 in. barrel, blue finish with plastic grips, 10 shot mag., 32.4 oz. Mfg. 2001-2004.

	$665	$575	$450	$395	$350	$300	$275

Last MSR was $800.

MODEL 9000S TYPE F/D - 9mm Para. or .40 S&W cal., single/double (Model 9000S Type F) or DA only (Model 9000S Type D, disc. 2003), 3 1/2 in. tilt barrel, 10 or 12 (9mm Para. only, optional late 2004) shot mag., spurless (Type D only) or external (Type F) hammer, ambidextrous safety with hammer decocking, sub-compact pistol utilizing state of the art ergonomic design by Giugiaro Design, matte black techno-polymer frame, overmolded rubber grip, cased, approx. 26 1/2 oz. Mfg. 2000-2005.

	$410	$330	$285	$260	$240	$220	$200

Last MSR was $485.

Add $24 for B-Lok safety system using key lock (mfg. 2003, Type F only).

MODEL PX4 STORM - 9mm Para, .40 S&W cal., or .45 ACP (new 2007) cal., single/double action, 4 in. barrel, polymer frame, locked breech with rotating barrel system, matte black finish with plastic grips, Pronox sights, 10, 14 (.40 S&W cal.) or 17 (9mm Para. cal.) shot mag., accessory rail on lower frame, approx. 27 1/2 oz. New mid-2005.

MSR $575		$450	$365	$310	$260	$220	$195	$175

Add $50 for .45 ACP cal. (new 2007).
Add $400 for PX4 Storm SD .45 ACP w/extended barrel and brown polymer frame.

The trigger mechanism of this gun can be customized to four different configurations: Type F (single/double action decocker and manual safety), Type D (DAO with spurless hammer, LE only), Type G (single/double action decocker with no manual safety, LE only), or Type C (constant action, spurless hammer, LE only). Values are for Type F model only.

* *Model PX4 Storm Sub-Compact* - 9mm Para. or .40 S&W cal., 10 or 13 (9mm Para. cal. only) shot mag., similar to Model PX4 Storm, except has sub-compact frame, includes three backstraps, 26 oz. New 2007.

MSR $575		$450	$365	$310	$260	$220	$195	$175

Pistols: Semi-Auto, Model 92 & Variations - 5.9 in. barrel

MODEL 92 COMBAT - similar to Model 92, except has 5.9 in. target barrel, blue finish, plastic grips, only 50 imported into the U.S. for competition.

	$775	$625	$475	$300	$255	$240	$220

Pistols: Semi-Auto, Model 92 & Variations - 4.9 in. barrel

MODEL 92 (FIRST SERIES) - 4.9 in. barrel, early production Model 92s had a flat slide, frame mounted safety, and mag. release button at base of pistol grip. Production of the M92 was approx. 5,000 pistols. Originally mfg. 1976. Disc.

	$750	$600	$450	$300	$255	$240	$220

MODEL 92S (SECOND SERIES) - similar to Model 92, except has a slide mounted firing pin safety. Disc.

	$575	$475	$375	$300	$250	$240	$220

MODEL 92SB-P (THIRD SERIES) - 9mm Luger cal., double action, 15 shot mag., 4.9 in. barrel, fixed sights, alloy frame, high-polish blue finish, plastic grips (Model 92SB-P), conventionally located push button magazine release, ambidextrous safety, 34 1/2 oz. Mfg. 1980-85.

	$525	$425	$395	$350	$325	$295	$270

Last MSR was $600.

* *Model 92SB-W* - similar to above, only with wood grips. Disc. 1985.

	$550	$450	$400	$355	$330	$290	$260

Last MSR was $620.

GRADING - PPGS™	100%	98%	95%	90%	80%	70%	60%

MODEL 92D - 9mm Para. cal., double action only, otherwise similar to Model 92F, except does not have a manual safety lever, includes black plastic grips, 3-dot sights, 33.8 oz. Introduced 1992 - disc. 1998.

		$475	$400	$350	$300	$250	$210	$190

Last MSR was $586.

Add $90 for Tritium (new 1994) sight system.
Add 10% for Trijicon (disc.) sights.

MODEL 92FS & 92F - 9mm Para. cal., official U.S. military variation of 92 Series, 4.9 in. barrel, alloy frame, steel slide, 10 (C/B 1994), or 15* (reintroduced late 2004, optional) shot mag., chamber loaded indicator, matte black Bruniton or olive drab (mfg. 2004) finish, squared off trigger guard to facilitate two-hand shooting, extended mag. base, choice of regular or 3-dot sights (new 1991), approx 34 1/2 oz. Model 92F-P has plastic grips. Model 92F-W has wood grips. New 1984.

MSR $600		$525	$450	$400	$370	$330	$300	$275

Add $25 for olive drab finish (mfg. 2004 only).
Add $24 for B-Lok safety system using key lock (mfg. 2003 only).
Add $462 for .22 LR conversion kit (includes slide, barrel, spring, follower, and .22 LR mag., new 2002).
Add approx. $20 for checkered wood grips (Model 92F-W, disc. 1998).
Add approx. $80 for Tritium sight system (mfg. 1994-98).
Add 10% for Trijicon (disc.) sights.
Add approx. $175 for gold engraving/accenting (Model EL-3, 92F-W only, disc. 1998).
Add $395 for 9mm Competition Conversion Kit (mfg. 1992-98).

The Model 92FS incorporates a slide retaining pin engineering change not included in the Model 92F.

The U.S. military on January 15, 1985 announced that the M9 military variation of the commercial Model 92F would replace the Colt Govt. Model .45 ACP as the standard government issue sidearm. Because of domestic political pressures, Congress requested that a new sidearm competition be conducted again in 1988. The result of this second trial was that the Department of the Army announced on May 22, 1989 that Beretta had won again. This military contract with Beretta U.S.A. Corp. initially involved over 320,000 Model M9s (military designation for the commercial Model 92F) manufactured for U.S. military consumption in the 1990s. Actual delivery of commercial Model 92s began in January of 1986, while M9 delivery to U.S. Armed Forces exceeded 430,000 units, and was completed in 1999.

✳ Model 92FS & 92F Stainless (Inox) - similar to Model 92F/92FS, except is mfg. from stainless steel, satin finish with plastic grips, 3-dot sights, initially released to law enforcement agencies only, this model was commercially manufactured in quantity. Reintroduced 2008.

MSR $700		$595	$500	$425	$385	$340	$310	$285

Add $180 for laser grips (new 2004).
Add $24 for B-Lok safety system using key lock (mfg. 2003 only).
Add approx. $20 for wood grips (disc. 1998).
Add approx. $90 for Trijicon (1993 only) or Tritium (mfg. 1994-98) sight system.

MODEL 92FS BRIGADIER - similar to the Model 92FS, except has heavier slide to reduce felt recoil, wraparound rubber grips, and 3-dot sights, 35.3 oz. Mfg. 1999-2005.

		$650	$525	$425	$385	$335	$300	$275

Last MSR was $795.

✳ Model 92FS Brigadier Stainless (Inox) - similar to Model 92FS Brigadier, except is stainless steel, 35.3 oz. Mfg. 2000-2005.

		$690	$575	$475	$415	$360	$300	$255

Last MSR was $845.

MODEL 92FS B.A.T.S. - 9mm Para. cal., 4.9 in. barrel, features black matte Bruniton finish and textured rubber wraparound grips with finger grooves, package includes both 10 and 15 shot mags., Airlight knife, aluminum carrying case, 34.4 oz. Limited mfg. late 2000 only.

	$665	$550	$465	$415	$360	$300	$275

Last MSR was $785.

MODEL 92FS VERTEC - 9mm Para. cal., single/double action, features vertical grip design, special short reach trigger, thin dual textured grip panels, and integral accessory rail on lower frame, removable front sight, beveled 10-shot mag., Bruniton finish, 32.2 oz. Mfg. 2002-2005.

	$635	$495	$440	$385	$340	$300	$275

Last MSR was $760.

Add $25 for B-Lok safety system using key lock (mfg. 2003).

＊ *Model 92FS Vertec Stainless (Inox)* - stainless variation of the Model 92FS Vertec. Mfg. 2002-2005.

	$670	$525	$425	$360	$315	$260	$225

Last MSR was $825.

Add $170 for laser grips (new 2004).
Add $25 for B-Lok safety system using key lock (mfg. 2003).

MODEL 92 BLACK INOX - 9mm Para. cal., single/double action, features black stainless slide and stipled, finger groove plastic grips. Limited mfg. 2002 only.

	$610	$485	$390	$325	$280	$240	$200

Last MSR was $734.

MODEL 92 BILLENIUM - 9mm Para. cal., single action only, frame mounted safety, contoured steel frame with checkered grip straps and contoured carbon fiber grips, interchangeable sights, oversize mag. release button, unique slide serrations and Billenium engraving, nickel alloy surface treatment finish, includes deluxe lockable carrying case, 43.3 oz. Limited mfg. in Italy of 2,000 during 2002-2003.

	$1,100	$900	$750	$650	$575	$500	$425

Last MSR was $1,429.

MODEL 92 STEEL I - 9mm Para. cal., single action only or SA/DA, plastic grips, features all-steel construction, frame mounted safety, nickel alloy finish, includes two 10-shot mags., 41.1 oz. Mfg. 2004-2005.

	$1,295	$1,150	$900	$825	$750	$675	$595

Last MSR was $1,600.

MODEL 92FS YEAR 2000 - 9mm Para. cal., 4.9 in. barrel, matte black Bruniton finish, features rosewood laminate grips with Beretta "trident" logo on brass medallions. 2,000 mfg. during 2000 only.

	$615	$500	$450	$400	$350	$300	$275

Last MSR was $726.

MODEL 92F-ELS - deluxe variation of the Model 92F featuring high polish stainless steel finish with gold highlights on trim, frame etchings, and small parts, plastic grips. Mfg. 1992-94.

	$685	$550	$425	$360	$315	$260	$225

Last MSR was $790.

MODEL 92F/FS "UNITED WE STAND" LIMITED EDITION - 9mm Para. cal., features laser etched gold American flag and "United We Stand" slide lettering, Bruniton finish, black plastic grips. Mfg. limited to 2001 (Model 92F) and 3,900 (Model 92FS) pistols in late 2001-early 2002.

	$625	$560	$485	$425	$375	$300	$275

Last MSR $734.

Beretta USA made a donation from the proceeds of this model to the NYPD Foundation and the Survivor's Fund of the National Capitol Region.

GRADING - PPGS™	100%	98%	95%	90%	80%	70%	60%

MODEL 92FS 470th ANNIVERSARY LIMITED EDITION - features stainless steel construction with mirror polished finish, smooth select walnut grips with inlaid gold plated medallions, gold filled engraving with Dr. Ugo Gussalli-Beretta's signature, 470th Anniversary logos, only 470 mfg. (with "1 of 470" gold filled on each gun) beginning 1999, lockable walnut case. Disc. 2004.

	100%	98%	95%	90%	80%	70%	60%
	$1,950	$1,575	$1,100	$985	$795	$675	$565

Last MSR was $2,217.

MODEL 92F/FS "DESERT STORM" SPECIAL EDITION - 9mm Para. cal., features U.S. Central Command seal, marked "Official Sidearm U.S. Armed Forces" on left side of slide, right side is marked "DESERT STORM", stamped "15 January 1991-11 April 1991", special ser. no. Approx. 8,000 mfg. 1991-92.

	100%	98%	95%	90%	80%	70%	60%
	$625	$560	$485	$425	$375	$300	$275

Last MSR was $660.

MODEL 92F DELUXE - deluxe model featuring gold or silver plating and elaborate engraving. Importation began 1993.

MSR $5,750	$4,950	$3,750	$2,500	$2,180	$1,965	$1,565	$1,250

This model is available at the Beretta Galleries or select Beretta Premium dealers only.

MODEL 92G - 9mm Para. cal., identical to the Model 92F, except features a spring loaded decocking lever that safely lowers the hammer allowing fire-ready when unholstering the pistol. New 1990.

The Model 92G is sold to law enforcement agencies only and prices are slightly higher than the standard Model 92FS. This pistol has been used by French Gendarmes since 1987.

MODEL 92G-SD - 9mm Para. cal., similar to Model 92G, except has an integral accessory rail machined into frame in front of trigger guard for sighting devices, Bruniton finish, 10 shot mag., Tritium sights, 35.3 oz. Mfg. 2003-2005.

	100%	98%	95%	90%	80%	70%	60%
	$955	$745	$585	$510	$450	$400	$350

Last MSR was $1,175.

MODEL 92F WITH U.S. M9 MARKED SLIDE/FRAME - 9mm Para. cal., approx. 2,000 mfg. with special serial no. range, "BER" prefix, government assembly numbers on frame, slide, hammer, mag. etc. Mfg. for the Armed Forces Reserve shooters, identical to military M9, except for serial number.

	100%	98%	95%	90%	80%	70%	60%
	$1,000	$900	$800	$725	$650	$575	$500

MODEL 92FS OPERATION ENDURING FREEDOM - 9mm Para. cal., M9 U.S. Army edition, two 10 shot mags., "BER" prefix, 2,500 mfg. 2003 only.

	100%	98%	95%	90%	80%	70%	60%
	$625	$500	$425	$360	$315	$260	$225

Last MSR was $712.

M9 LIMITED STANDARD EDITION - commercial limited edition of the U.S. Govt. M9 military pistol, features gold inscribed slide legend "The First Decade 1985-1995", Air Force or Marine Corps emblems on right slide side, 10,000 mfg. during 1995-97.

	100%	98%	95%	90%	80%	70%	60%
	$600	$475	$425	$360	$315	$260	$225

Last MSR was $643.

 ✳ *M9 Limited Deluxe Edition* - features checkered walnut grips, gold-plated hammer, grip screws, and mag. release button. Disc. 1997.

	100%	98%	95%	90%	80%	70%	60%
	$695	$525	$475	$415	$360	$300	$255

Last MSR was $750.

M9 SPECIAL EDITION - patterned after the U.S. Armed Forces M9, special M9-XXXX ser. no. range, one 15 shot mag. (pre-1994 mfg.), dot and post sight system, M9 military packaging including Army operator's manual, Bianchi M12 holster, mag. pouch, and web pistol belt. Mfg. 1998-2000.

	100%	98%	95%	90%	80%	70%	60%
	$850	$700	$550	$460	$395	$335	$285

Last MSR was $861.

At a recent 2007 Rock Island Auction Co. auction a 98-99% condition example sold for $805.

M9 20TH ANNIVERSARY - 9mm Para. cal., special edition for 20th anniversary of the U.S. government M9, 10 or 15 shot mag. New 2006.

| MSR $600 | $525 | $450 | $400 | $370 | $330 | $300 | $275 |

M9A1 - 9mm Para. cal., single/double action, features accessory rail on lower frame and serrated grip straps, 10 or 15 shot mag., 3-dot sights, 35.3 oz. New 2006.

| MSR $700 | $595 | $500 | $425 | $385 | $340 | $310 | $285 |

Pistols: Semi-Auto, Model 92 & Variations - 4.7 in. barrel

MODEL 92FS INOX TACTICAL - 9mm Para. cal., 4.7 in. barrel, features satin matte finished stainless steel slide and alloy frame, rubber grips, Tritium sights. Mfg. 1999-2000.

| | $695 | $560 | $480 | $425 | $375 | $325 | $295 |

Last MSR was $822.

MODEL 92FS BORDER MARSHAL - 9mm Para. cal., commercial equivalent of the I.N.S. (Immigration & Naturalization Service) government contract, 4.7 in. barrel, heavy duty steel slide, Tritium sights, Border Marshal engraving on the slide. Mfg. 1999-2000.

| | $670 | $560 | $480 | $425 | $375 | $325 | $295 |

Last MSR was $802.

MODEL 92G ELITE IA (BRIGADIER) - 9mm Para. cal., similar to Model 92FS Brigadier, except has 4.7 in. stainless barrel and many standard I.D.P.A. competition features including front and rear serrated slide, skeletonized hammer, and removable three-dot sighting system, plastic grips, includes Elite engraving on slide, 35.3 oz. Mfg. 1999-2005.

| | $725 | $585 | $495 | $425 | $360 | $300 | $275 |

Last MSR was $875.

* *Model 92G Elite II (Brigadier)* - similar to Model 92G Elite, except has stainless steel slide with black "Elite II" markings, target barrel crown, extended mag. release, optimized trigger mechanism, front and back strap checkering, low profile Novak rear sight, 35 oz. Mfg. mid-2000-2005.

| | $815 | $635 | $530 | $450 | $385 | $325 | $295 |

Last MSR was $985.

Pistols: Semi-Auto, Model 92 & Variations - 4.3 in. barrel

MODEL 92D CENTURION - 9mm Para. cal., compact variation with 4.3 in. barrel, plastic grips only, without safety, choice of 3 dot or Tritium sights. Mfg. 1994-98.

| | $460 | $360 | $300 | $250 | $210 | $190 | $175 |

Last MSR was $586.

Add $90 for Tritium sights.

MODEL 92SB-P COMPACT - similar to Model 92SB, except has 4.3 in. barrel, 14 shot, plastic grips (Model 92SB-P), rarer when frontstrap has curved lip, 31 oz. Disc. 1985.

| | $500 | $440 | $385 | $345 | $310 | $285 | $260 |

Last MSR was $620.

Add $60 for nickel finish.

* *Model 92SB-W Compact* - similar to above only with wood grips. Disc. 1985.

| | $525 | $465 | $395 | $355 | $335 | $300 | $280 |

Last MSR was $635.

GRADING - PPGS™	100%	98%	95%	90%	80%	70%	60%

MODEL 92F/92FS COMPACT - similar to Model 92F, except has 4.3 in. barrel and 13 shot mag., plastic or wood grips, 31 1/2 oz. While temporarily suspended in 1986, production was resumed 1989-93.

	$550	$450	$415	$375	$335	$300	$275

Last MSR was $625.

Add $20 for checkered walnut grips (Model 92F Wood).
Add $65 for Trijicon sight system.

* *Model 92F Compact "M"* - similar to Model 92F Compact, except has 8 shot straight line mag., plastic grips only. Imported 1990-93.

	$550	$450	$415	$375	$335	$300	$275

Last MSR was $625.

Add $65 for Trijicon sight system.
Approx. 1,200 92SBM Models were imported in the 1980s.

MODEL 92F & 92FS CENTURION - similar to Model 92F, except has compact barrel slide unit with full size frame, 4.3 in. barrel, choice of plastic or wood grips, 3 dot sight system, same length as Model 92F Compact, 10 (C/B 1994) or 15* shot mag., 33.2 oz. Mfg. 1992-98.

	$525	$435	$395	$365	$335	$300	$275

Last MSR was $613.

Add approx. $20 for checkered walnut grips (Model 92F Wood).
Add $90 for Tritium sight system (mfg. 1994-98).
Add 10% for Trijicon sights (disc.).

MODEL 92FS COMPACT - 9mm Para. cal., similar to Model 92 Compact Type M, except has 10 shot staggered mag., 35.3 oz. Mfg. 1999-2003.

	$575	$465	$415	$370	$335	$300	$275

Last MSR was $691.

* *Model 92FS Compact Stainless (Inox)* - similar to Model 92FS Compact, except is stainless steel. Mfg. 2000-2003.

	$620	$490	$395	$325	$275	$235	$200

Last MSR was $748.

* *Model 92FS Custom Carry* - 9mm Para. cal., 4.3 in. barrel, shortened grip, low profile control levers, left side only safety lever, blue only, 10 shot staggered mag., plastic grips. Mfg. 1999-2000.

	$550	$450	$400	$365	$335	$300	$275

Last MSR was $655.

* *Model 92FS Custom Carry II (Type M)* - 9mm Para. cal., similar dimensions as Custom Carry, except is stainless steel construction with black components and black slide markings, Novak low profile 3-dot sights, 8 shot single stack mag., 30.9 oz. Mfg. 2000.

	$560	$455	$410	$345	$295	$245	$215

Last MSR was $669.

MODEL 92 TYPE M COMPACT - same features as the Model 92FS, except has 4.3 in. barrel, overall height is 5.3 in., Bruniton matte finish, choice of single/double or double action only (disc. 1998), plastic grips, single column 8 shot mag., 30.9 oz. Mfg. 1998-2003.

	$575	$465	$415	$370	$335	$300	$275

Last MSR was $691.

Add approx. $90 for Tritium sight system (disc. 1998).
Subtract approx. $25 for double action only (disc. 1998).

* *Model 92 Type M Compact Stainless (Inox)* - similar to Model 92 Type M, except is stainless steel. Mfg. 2000-2003.

	$615	$475	$395	$340	$295	$245	$215

Last MSR was $748.

GRADING - PPGS™	100%	98%	95%	90%	80%	70%	60%

Pistols: Semi-Auto, Model 96 & Variations, Recent Mfg.

The models in this section appear in approximate chronological sequence.

MODEL 96D - .40 S&W cal., 4.9 in. barrel, double action only variation of the Model 96F, no safety, 3 dot sight system, 33.8 oz. Introduced 1992 - disc. 1998.

	$460	$360	$300	$250	$210	$190	$175

Last MSR was $586.

Add $90 for Tritium sight system (new 1994).
Add $65 for Trijicon sights (disc.).

✳ *Model 96D Centurion* - similar to Model 96D, except is compact variation with 4.3 in. barrel, 3-dot sights. Mfg. 1994-98.

	$460	$360	$300	$250	$210	$190	$175

Last MSR was $586.

Add $90 for Tritium sight system.

MODEL 96, 96F, & 96FS - .40 S&W cal., similar to Model 92F, 4.9 in. barrel, plastic grips only, flared grip with grip strap serrations, Bruniton matte black finish, 3 dot sight system, 10 or 11 (optional) shot mag., 34.4 oz. Mfg. 1992-2005.

	$595	$475	$420	$380	$335	$300	$275

Last MSR was $715.

Add $24 for B-Lok safety system with key lock (mfg. 2003).
Add $91 for Tritium sight system (mfg. 1994-99).
Add 10% for Trijicon sights (disc.).
Current model nomenclature for this pistol is the Model 96.

✳ *Model 96, 96FS Stainless (Inox)* - stainless variation of the Model 96FS, rubber grips, 34.4 oz. Mfg. 1999-2005.

	$650	$525	$425	$360	$315	$260	$225

Last MSR was $795.

Add $24 for B-Lok safety system with key lock (mfg. 2003).
Current model nomenclature for this pistol is the Model 96 Inox.

✳ *Model 96F Compact* - 4.3 in. barrel, 10 shot mag., 3-dot sights, plastic grips, approx. 32 oz. Mfg. 2000-2003.

	$580	$465	$415	$370	$335	$300	$275

Last MSR was $691.

While advertised during the 1990s, this gun finally went into production during 2000.

✳ *Model 96F Compact Stainless (Inox)* - similar to Model 96F Compact, except is stainless steel. Mfg. 2000-2003.

	$620	$500	$415	$370	$335	$300	$275

Last MSR was $748.

✳ *Model 96F Centurion* - similar to Model 96F, except has 4.3 in. barrel, 33.2 oz. Mfg. 1992-99.

	$525	$435	$395	$365	$335	$300	$275

Last MSR was $613.

Add $91 for Tritium sight system (new 1994).

✳ *Model 96 Stainless (Inox) "United We Stand" Limited Edition* - 40 S&W cal., features laser etched gold American flag and "United We Stand" slide lettering. Mfg. limited to 3,900 pistols in late 2001 - early 2002.

	$625	$560	$485	$425	$365	$305	$260

Last MSR was $734.

Beretta USA made a donation from the proceeds of this model to the NYPD Foundation and the Survivor's Fund of the National Capitol Region.

✳ *Model 96FS B.A.T.S.* - .40 S&W cal., 4.9 in. barrel, features black matte Bruniton finish and textured rubber wraparound grips with finger grooves, package includes both 10 and 11 shot mags., Airlight knife, aluminum carrying case, 34.4 oz. Limited mfg. mid-2000 only.

	$665	$550	$465	$415	$360	$300	$275

Last MSR was $785.

✳ *Model 96G Elite IA (Brigadier)* - .40 S&W cal., similar to Model 96 Brigadier, except has 4.7 in. stainless barrel and many standard I.D.P.A. competition features including front and rear serrated slide, skeletonized hammer, and removable 3-dot sighting system, plastic grips, includes Elite engraving on slide. Mfg. 1999-2005.

	$725	$575	$480	$420	$350	$300	$275

Last MSR was $875.

✳ *Model 96G Elite II (Brigadier)* - similar to Model 96G Elite, except has stainless steel slide with black "Elite II" markings, target barrel crown, extended mag. release, optimized trigger mechanism, front and back strap checkering, low profile Novak rear sight, 35.3 oz. Mfg. mid-2000-2005.

	$815	$625	$525	$450	$385	$325	$295

Last MSR was $985.

MODEL 96G-SD - .40 S&W cal., similar to Model 92G that allows ready-fire, except has an integral accessory rail machined into frame in front of trigger guard for sighting devices, Bruniton finish, 10 shot mag., Tritium sights, 35.3 oz. Mfg. 2003-2005.

	$955	$725	$625	$525	$450	$400	$350

Last MSR was $1,175.

MODEL 96 STEEL I - .40 S&W cal., single action only or SA/DA, plastic grips, features all steel construction, nickel alloy frame, slim vertical grip, frame mounted safety, includes two 10-shot mags. Mfg. 2004-2005.

	$1,295	$1,140	$950	$825	$750	$675	$595

Last MSR was $1,600.

MODEL 96 COMBAT - .40 S&W cal., single action only, similar to Model 96 Stock, except has factory tuned trigger, 4.9 (new 1998) or 5.9 in. barrel with weight and fully adj. rear target sight, aluminum or plastic grips. Mfg. in Italy 1997-2001.

	$1,350	$1,060	$900	$775	$625	$550	$495

Last MSR was $1,735.

Add approx. $250 for 5.9 in. barrel (previously available as a Combat Combo).

MODEL 96 VERTEC - .40 S&W cal., single/double action, 4.9 in. barrel, features vertical grip design, special short reach trigger, thin dual textured grip panels, and integral accessory rail on lower frame, removable front sight, beveled 10 shot mag., Bruniton finish, 32.2 oz. Mfg. 2002-2005.

	$635	$495	$440	$385	$340	$300	$275

Last MSR was $760.

Add $25 for B-Lok safety system with key lock (mfg. 2003).

✳ *Model 96 Vertec Stainless (Inox)* - stainless variation of the Model 96 Vertec. Mfg. 2002-2005.

	$670	$530	$430	$365	$320	$260	$225

Last MSR was $825.

Add $25 for B-Lok safety system with key lock (mfg. 2003).

MODEL 96 BLACK INOX - .40 S&W cal., single/double action, features black stainless slide and stippled, finger groove plastic grips. Limited mfg. 2002 only.

	$610	$485	$390	$325	$285	$240	$210

Last MSR was $734.

GRADING - PPGS™	100%	98%	95%	90%	80%	70%	60%

MODEL 96 BORDER MARSHAL - .40 S&W cal., commercial equivalent of the I.N.S. (Immigration & Naturalization Service) government contract, 4.7 in. barrel, heavy duty steel slide, Tritium sights, Border Marshal engraving on the slide. Mfg. 1999-2000.

	$670	$560	$480	$425	$375	$325	$295

Last MSR was $802.

MODEL 96 BRIGADIER - similar to Model 96FS, except has heavier slide to reduce felt recoil, wraparound rubber grips, and 3-dot sights, 35.3 oz. Mfg. 1999-2005.

	$660	$510	$440	$385	$335	$300	$275

Last MSR was $795.

＊ *Model 96 Brigadier Stainless (Inox)* - similar to Model 96 Brigadier, except is stainless steel. New 2000.

	$680	$530	$425	$360	$315	$260	$225

Last MSR was $845.

MODEL 96 CUSTOM CARRY - .40 S&W cal., 4.3 in. barrel, shortened grip, low profile control levers, left side only safety lever, blue only, 10 shot staggered mag., plastic grips. Mfg. 1999-2000.

	$550	$450	$400	$365	$335	$300	$275

Last MSR was $655.

MODEL 96 STOCK - .40 S&W cal., designed for practical shooting competition, includes accurized barrel bushing, 4.9 in. barrel, competition frame mounted ambidextrous safety, 3 interchangeable front sights, checkered front and back grip straps, aluminum grips, beveled mag. well, cased with two mags. and tool kit, 35 oz. Mfg. 1997-99, limited quantities remained into 2000.

	$1,200	$995	$865	$725	$600	$550	$495

Last MSR was $1,407.

REVOLVERS: SINGLE ACTION

Beretta's SAA revolvers are manufactured in Italy by Aldo & C. Uberti S.r.l., which was purchased by Beretta in 2000.

LARAMIE - .38 Spl. or .45 LC cal., patterned after S&W Model 1870 Schofield, 5 or 6 1/2 in. barrel, 6-shot, blued finish with case colored hammer and triggerguard, smooth walnut grips with Beretta medallions, top-break, approx. 37-43 oz. New 2005.

MSR $1,200		$1,025	$795	$750	$650	$550	$475	$375

Add $175 for nickel finish or 6 1/2 in. barrel.

STAMPEDE SAA - .357 Mag., .44-40 WCF (mfg. 2003), or .45 LC cal., patterned after the Colt SAA, transfer bar and half-cock safeties, 6 shot, 4 3/4, 5 1/2, or 7 1/2 in. barrel, various finishes, approx. 37 oz. Mfg. by Uberti beginning mid-2003.

＊ *Stampede SAA Blue* - features blue finish with case colored frame and black polymer grips.

MSR $600		$475	$395	$340	$300	$270	$240	$220

＊ *Stampede SAA Brushed Nickel* - features brushed nickel finish with smooth walnut grips with Beretta medallions and fire blued frame screws.

MSR $650		$515	$425	$350	$315	$285	$255	$230

＊ *Stampede SAA Old West* - .357 Mag. (new 2008) or .45 LC cal., features distressed Old West finish, 4 3/4 or 5 1/2 in. barrel. New 2007.

MSR $675		$525	$465	$415	$365	$325	$280	$250

GRADING - PPGS™	100%	98%	95%	90%	80%	70%	60%

✳ *Stampede SAA Bisley* - features Bisley styled grips/frame and reked hammer, blue or nickel finish. New 2005.

| MSR $650 | $515 | $425 | $350 | $315 | $285 | $255 | $230 |

Add $50 for nickel finish.

✳ *Stampede Buntline Carbine* - .45 LC cal., 18 in. blue barrel, replica of the Buntline revolver, transfer bar safety, 6 shot, hooked trigger guard, brass crescent buttplate, satin walnut stock with gold Beretta medallions. New 2007.

| MSR $850 | $750 | $650 | $575 | $500 | $425 | $350 | $275 |

✳ *Stampede SAA Stainless (Inox)* - .45 LC cal. only, features stainless steel construction, otherwise similar to Stampede. Mfg. 2004-2007.

| | $455 | $380 | $325 | $265 | $230 | $195 | $170 |

Last MSR was $575.

✳ *Stampede SAA Marshal* - .357 Mag. or .45 LC cal., 3 1/2 in. barrel, birdshead grips, blue or Old West (.45 LC cal. only) finish. New 2004.

| MSR $650 | $515 | $425 | $350 | $315 | $285 | $255 | $230 |

Add $50 for Old West finish (new 2007).

✳ *Stampede SAA Deluxe* - features charcoal blue metal finish, case colored frame and deluxe smooth walnut grips.

| MSR $675 | $525 | $460 | $415 | $365 | $320 | $275 | $250 |

✳ *Stampede SAA Patton* - .45 LC cal., features charcoal blue metal finish, engraved case colored frame, light gold accents, simulated ivory grips. Mfg. 2005-2006.

| | $925 | $800 | $700 | $600 | $525 | $450 | $375 |

Last MSR was $1,095.

This model was also available as a set - MSR was $2,190.

✳ *Stampede SAA Matched Pairs* - .45 LC cal. only, wood grips with Beretta medallions, 5 1/2 in. barrel, case colored frame, available with Philadelphia Centennial laser engraving (Philadelphia) or German silver trigger guard and backstrap (Gemini), paired serial numbers. New 2007.

❖ **Stampede Gemini Matched Pair**

| MSR $1,350 | $1,175 | $1,025 | $900 | $800 | $700 | $650 | $600 |

❖ **Stampede Philadelphia Centennial Matched Pair**

| MSR $2,100 | $1,775 | $1,550 | $1,325 | $1,100 | $950 | $850 | $750 |

RIFLES: BOLT ACTION, RECENT MFG.

MODEL 500 CUSTOM - .222 Rem., .223 Rem., .243 Win., .270 Win., .30-06, or .308 Win. cal., 3 action lengths, 24 in. barrel, iron sights, checkered walnut stock with recoil pad. Importation was resumed 1988 only.

| | $595 | $530 | $450 | $395 | $350 | $315 | $275 |

Last MSR was $725.

Add 10%-15% for .223 Rem. cal.

✳ *Model 500 S* - similar to Model 500, except is equipped with iron sights. Imported 1986 only.

| | $615 | $560 | $460 | $400 | $350 | $315 | $275 |

Last MSR was $700.

✳ *Model 500 DL* - same specifications as Model 500, only better walnut and light engraving. Disc. 1986.

| | $1,395 | $1,260 | $1,000 | $875 | $795 | $725 | $650 |

Last MSR was $1,595.

Add 10%-15% for .223 Rem. cal.

GRADING - PPGS™	100%	98%	95%	90%	80%	70%	60%

❊ *Model 500 DLS* - similar to Model 500 DL, except is equipped with iron sights. Imported 1986 only.

	$1,420	$1,285	$1,020	$875	$795	$725	$650

Last MSR was $1,625.

❊ *Model 500 EELL* - same specifications as Model 500 DL, only select walnut and more engraving. Disc. 1986.

	$1,550	$1,260	$1,150	$1,000	$875	$800	$725

Last MSR was $1,745.

Add 10%-15% for .223 Rem. cal.

❊ *Model 500 EELLS* - similar to Model 500 EELL, except is equipped with iron sights. Imported 1986 only.

	$1,575	$1,425	$1,200	$1,120	$875	$800	$725

Last MSR was $1,785.

MODEL 501 - .243 Win. or .308 Win. cal., medium bolt action, 6 shot, 23 in. barrel, no sights, checkered walnut stock. Disc. 1986.

	$595	$530	$465	$395	$350	$315	$275

Last MSR was $665.

❊ *Model 501 S* - similar to Model 501, except is equipped with iron sights. Imported 1986 only.

	$615	$560	$460	$400	$350	$315	$275

Last MSR was $700.

❊ *Model 501 DL* - same specifications as Model 501, only better walnut and light engraving. Disc. 1986.

	$1,395	$1,260	$1,000	$875	$795	$725	$650

Last MSR was $1,575.

❊ *Model 501 DLS* - sImilar to Model 501 DL, except is equipped with iron sights. Imported 1986 only.

	$1,420	$1,285	$1,020	$875	$795	$725	$650

Last MSR was $1,625.

❊ *Model 501 EELL* - same specifications as Model 501 DL, only select walnut and more engraving. Disc. 1986.

	$1,550	$1,260	$1,150	$1,000	$875	$800	$725

Last MSR was $1,745.

❊ *Model 501 EELLS* - similar to Model 501 EELL, except is equipped with iron sights. Imported 1986 only.

	$1,575	$1,425	$1,200	$1,120	$875	$800	$725

Last MSR was $1,785.

MODEL 502 - .30-06, .270 or 7mm Rem. Mag. cal., long bolt action, 5 or 6 shot, 24 in. barrel, no sights, checkered walnut stock. Disc. 1986.

	$625	$565	$490	$440	$395	$360	$330

Last MSR was $710.

❊ *Model 502 S* - similar to Model 502, except is equipped with iron sights. Imported 1986 only.

	$650	$595	$525	$460	$395	$360	$330

Last MSR was $745.

❊ *Model 502 DL* - same specifications as Model 502, only better walnut and light engraving. Also available in .375 H&H Mag. Disc. 1986.

	$1,495	$1,310	$1,175	$1,025	$900	$775	$695

Last MSR was $1,640.

* *Model 502 DLS* - similar to Model 502, except is equipped with iron sights. Imported 1986 only.

	100%	98%	95%	90%	80%	70%	60%
	$1,410	$1,325	$1,175	$1,025	$900	$775	$695

Last MSR was $1,660.

* *Model 502 EELL* - same specifications as Model 502 DL, only select walnut and more engraving. Also available in .375 H&H Mag. Disc. 1986.

	$1,575	$1,425	$1,200	$1,120	$875	$800	$725

Last MSR was $1,785.

* *Model 502 EELLS* - similar to Model 502 EELL, except is equipped with iron sights. Imported 1986 only.

	$1,575	$1,425	$1,200	$1,120	$875	$800	$725

Last MSR was $1,785.

MATO SYNTHETIC - .270 Win., .280 Rem., .30-06, .300 Win. Mag., .338 Win. Mag., .375 H&H, or 7mm Rem. Mag. cal., 23.6 in. barrel, composite black synthetic stock with integral bedding block, Mauser style 98 action with controlled round feeding, 3-position safety, ergonomic bolt handle, 3 or 4 shot detachable box mag., adj. trigger, black satin metal finish, mfg. in the U.S., 8 lbs. Mfg. 1997-2002.

	$975	$825	$750	$675	$575	$495	$400

Last MSR was $1,117.

Add $357 for .375 H&H cal. (includes muzzle brake and iron sights).

* *Mato Deluxe* - same cals. as the standard model, features deluxe checkered walnut with ebony forend tip, cased, 7.9 lbs. Mfg. 1997-2002.

	$2,025	$1,575	$1,150	$995	$825	$675	$600

Last MSR was $2,470.

Add $325 for .375 H&H cal. (includes muzzle brake and iron sights).

* *Mato Deluxe Safari Grade* - .375 H&H cal. only, elaborately hand engraved with best quality wood. Available through Beretta Premium dealers only. Disc. 2002.

	$14,750	$12,500	$10,250	$8,000	$6,750	$5,500	$4,350

Last MSR was $16,500.

RIFLES: LEVER ACTION

1873 RENEGADE SHORT RIFLE - .357 Mag. or .45 LC cal., 20 in. octagon barrel. New 2008.

MSR $1,200	$1,050	$875	$725	$600	$500	$425	$375

MODEL 1876 RIFLE - .45-75 WCF cal., 28 in. octagon barrel with full mag., case colored receiver. New 2008.

MSR $1,625	$1,350	$1,125	$900	$775	$675	$575	$500

RIFLES: SEMI-AUTO, RECENT MFG.

BM-59 M-1 GARAND - with original Beretta M1 receiver, only 200 imported into the U.S.

	$2,450	$2,300	$1,900	$1,700	$1,500	$1,300	$1,175

Last MSR was $2,080.

BM-62 - similar to BM-59, except has flash suppressor and is Italian marked.

	$2,550	$2,300	$1,800	$1,600	$1,400	$1,200	$1,075

AR-70 - .222 Rem. or .223 Rem. cal., semi-auto paramilitary design rifle, 5-, 8-, or 30-shot mag., diopter sights, epoxy finish, 17.72 in. barrel, 8.3 lbs.

	$1,925	$1,675	$1,375	$1,150	$1,025	$850	$750

Last MSR was $1,065.

1989 Federal legislation banned the importation of this model into U.S.

GRADING - PPGS™	100%	98%	95%	90%	80%	70%	60%

CX4 STORM CARBINE - 9mm Para. (92 Carbine), .40 S&W (96 Carbine) or .45 ACP (8045 Carbine) cal., blowback single action, Giugiaro design featuring paramilitary styling with one-piece matte black synthetic stock with thumbhole, rubber recoil pad and stock cheekpiece, top, bottom, and side Picatinny rails, ghost ring sights, 16.6 in. hammer forged barrel, reversible crossbolt safety, mag. button, bolt handle, and ejection port, 8- (.45 ACP cal.), 10, 11 (8000 and 8040 models, new 2005), 15 (92 or 96 carbine, new 2005), or 17 (92 Carbine) shot mag. (accepts Models 92, 96, 8000, 8040, and 8045 pistol mags.), 29.7 in. overall length, 5 3/4 lbs. New mid-2003.

MSR $825	$715	$500	$450	$400	$350	$325	$300

Add $95 for 92 Carbine package (includes scope, 9mm Para., (disc. 2005) or .40 S&W cal).
Add $50 for top rail (only available in 9mm Para. or .40 S&W cal., mfg. 2006-2007).
This model is available in many variations - 8045 (.45 ACP), 92 Carbine (8000, 9mm Para.), 92 Carbine package (w/ scope), and 96 Carbine (8040, .40 S&W).

RX4 STORM CARBINE - .223 Rem. cal., gas operating, available in collapsible five position telescoping stock or sporter style stock with optional pistol grip, black matte finish, ghost ring sights, includes 5 and 10 shot AR-15 style magazines. New 2007.

MSR $1,100	$925	$800	$700	$600	$525	$450	$400

RIFLES: O/U, CUSTOM

Current high grade Beretta O/U and SxS rifles are sold only by premium grade franchised Beretta dealers. For a listing of these dealers, contact a Beretta Gallery (see Trademark Index).

MODEL S686/S689 SILVER SABLE - .30-06, 9.3x74R, or .444 cal. (disc. 1995), boxlock action, single or double (special order only) triggers. Importation began 1995.

MSR $4,200	$3,500	$3,000	$2,700	$2,200	$2,000	$1,800	$1,550

Add $500 for 9.3x74R cal.

MODEL S689 GOLD SABLE - 9.3x74R or 30-06 cal., boxlock action, nickel (disc. 1985) or case hardened (new 1986) receiver, double triggers, 23 in. barrels, auto ejectors, sling swivels, 7.7 lbs.

MSR $5,950	$4,875	$4,250	$3,750	$2,950	$2,350	$1,900	$1,600

Add $500 for 9.3x74R cal.
Add approx. $2,000 for scope and quick detachable claw mounts.

MODEL S686/S689 EELL DIAMOND SABLE - .30-06, 9.3x74R, or .444 Marlin cal., moderate engraving. New 1995.

MSR $12,750	$10,500	$8,750	$7,750	$6,750	$5,975	$5,325	$4,700

Add $1,250 for an extra set of 20 ga. barrels with forearm.
Add approx. $2,000 for scope and quick detachable claw mounts.

SSO EXPRESS - .375 H&H or .458 Win. Mag. cal., sidelock action, case hardened receiver, double triggers, 23 in. barrels, auto ejectors, 11 lbs., cased. Importation disc. 1989.

	$12,500	$9,500	$8,250	$6,950	$6,100	$5,600	$4,875

Last MSR was $17,533.

Add $425 for claw mounts.

SSO5 EXPRESS - similar to SSO Express except has more elaborate engraving and better walnut.

	$14,250	$11,750	$8,750	$7,500	$6,750	$6,100	$5,600

Last MSR was $19,600.

SSO6 EXPRESS CUSTOM SIDELOCK - 9.3x74R, .375 H&H, or .458 Win. Mag. cal., next to top-of-the-line sidelock double rifle, individually built to the customer's specifications, cased. New 1990.

MSR $39,500	$32,750	$21,850	$16,000	$12,250	$9,750	$8,750	$7,000

Add $6,750 for extra set of barrels.
Add approx. $2,000 for scope mounts for Zeiss 4x32mm scope.

GRADING - PPGS™	100%	98%	95%	90%	80%	70%	60%

* *SS06 EELL Gold Custom* - same cals. as SS06 Express, features multiple gold inlays and best quality wood.

MSR $45,500		$37,250	$25,000	$18,500	$14,000	$11,500	$9,000	$7,500

Add $6,750 for extra set of barrels.
Add approx. $25,000-$45,000 for upgraded master engraving.
Add approx. $2,000 for scope mounts for Zeiss 4x32mm scope.

RIFLES: SxS, CUSTOM

MODEL 455 SIDE-BY-SIDE - .375 H&H, .416 Rigby, .458 Win. Mag., .470 NE, or .500 3 in. NE cal., top of the line sidelock double rifle, individually built to the customer's specifications, cased. New 1990.

MSR $55,650		$46,250	$36,500	$28,500	$24,000	$19,250	$16,000	$13,000

Add approx. $2,000 for scope mounts for Zeiss 4x32mm scope.

* *Model 455 EELL* - similar cals. as Model 455 SxS, top-of-the-line custom side-lock double rifle featuring every refinement of the gunmaker's art, cased.

Add approx. $2,000 for scope mounts for Zeiss 4x32mm scope.
MSR on this model ranges from $76,500-$125,000, depending on amount of engraving and the engraver.

RIFLES: SLIDE ACTION

GOLD RUSH CARBINE/RIFLE - .357 Mag. or .45 LC cal., patterned after Colt Lightning model with improved feeding system and hammer block safety, 20 (carbine), 24 1/4, or 26 (mfg. 2005) in. round or octagon barrel, 10-15 shot full mag., case colored receiver, blued barrel/mag. tube, checkered straight grip stock with Beretta medallions and forearm, adj. sights, 6 1/2 - 7 1/2 lbs. Importation began 2005.

MSR $1,375		$1,195	$1,050	$925	$800	$675	$550	$475

Add $475 for deluxe model with oil finished deluxe walnut stock with fish scale checking, charcoal blued barrel and mag. tube, and jeweled hammer. Add $50 for rifle configuration.

SHOTGUNS: O/U, DISC.

BL-1 - 12 ga., 26, 28, or 30 in. barrels with fixed chokes, blued receiver/barrel finish, boxlock, extractors, double triggers, checkered pistol grip stock, approx. 7 lbs. Mfg. 1968-73.

		$395	$350	$250	$200	$180	$170	$150

BL-2 - similar to BL-1, except with single selective trigger, more engraving.

		$400	$375	$325	$275	$250	$200	$150

BL-2 STAKE-OUT - riot configuration with 18 in. barrels, DT, blue finish, approx. 6,000 mfg.

		$400	$350	$285	$200	$175	$150	$125

BL-2/S - similar to BL-2, with vent. rib and speed trigger. Mfg. 1974-76.

		$475	$425	$365	$295	$275	$225	$200

BL-3 - also available in 20 or 28 ga., blued receiver/barrel finish, similar to BL-2, with more engraving and vent. rib., 6-7 1/4 lbs. Mfg. 1968-1976.

		$600	$550	$475	$425	$375	$335	$300

Add 50% for 28 ga., if original condition is 90%+.

BL-3 SKEET

		$600	$550	$475	$425	$375	$335	$300

Subtract 10% for 26 in. barrels.

BL-3 TRAP

		$550	$500	$450	$395	$350	$300	$250

GRADING - PPGS™	100%	98%	95%	90%	80%	70%	60%

BL-4 - 12, 20, or 28 ga., 3 in. chambers (12 and 20 ga. only), blued receiver/barrel finish, deluxe version of BL-3, more engraving, better wood, and ejectors, 6-7 1/4 lbs.

	$850	$700	$575	$450	$375	$325	$275

Add 10% for 20 ga.
Add 25% for 28 ga.

BL-4 SKEET

	$700	$650	$525	$425	$350	$300	$250

Subtract 10% for 26 in. barrels.

BL-4 TRAP

	$600	$550	$475	$400	$350	$300	$250

BL-5 - 12, 20, or 28 ga., higher grade version of BL-4 with more engraving, matte grey reciever with blued barrels, full pistol grip stock.

	$900	$775	$675	$600	$500	$450	$400

Add 10% for 20 ga.
Add 25% for 28 ga.

BL-5 SKEET

	$875	$750	$650	$575	$475	$425	$375

Subtract 10% for 26 in. barrels.

BL-5 TRAP

	$875	$750	$650	$575	$475	$425	$375

BL-6 - 12, 20, or 28 ga., boxlock with coin finished scroll engraved sideplates, deluxe checkered walnut stock with full pistol grip and slender forearm, ejectors, SST.

	$1,175	$995	$850	$750	$650	$550	$450

Add 10% for 20 ga.
Add 25% for 28 ga.

BL-6 SKEET

	$1,000	$900	$800	$700	$600	$550	$500

Subtract 10% for 26 in. barrels.

BL-6 TRAP

	$1,000	$900	$725	$625	$525	$475	$425

MODEL S55 B - 12 or 20 ga., 26, 28, or 30 in. barrels, various chokes, boxlock, extractors, selective trigger, checkered pistol grip stock. Disc.

	$550	$500	$475	$440	$385	$330	$300

Add 10% for 20 ga.

MODEL S56 E - similar to S55B, with engraved receiver and auto ejectors. Disc.

	$750	$700	$675	$650	$600	$550	$500

Add 10% for 20 ga.

MODEL S58 SKEET - similar to S56E, with 26 in. Bohler steel barrels, skeet bore, wide vent. rib, skeet.

	$775	$725	$650	$550	$495	$445	$395

Subtract 10% for 26 in. barrels.

MODEL S58 TRAP - similar to S58 Skeet, with 30 in. barrels, imp. mod. and full choke, Monte Carlo stock with pad.

	$600	$550	$525	$495	$450	$410	$365

SILVER SNIPE - 12, 20 or 28 ga., 26, 28, or 30 in. barrels, boxlock, extractors, trigger optional, checkered pistol grip stock. Mfg. 1955-67.

	$700	$650	$595	$550	$475	$425	$395

Add 10% for 20 ga.
Add 25% for 28 ga.

GRADING - PPGS™	100%	98%	95%	90%	80%	70%	60%

* *Silver Snipe SST* - with vent. rib and SST.

	100%	98%	95%	90%	80%	70%	60%
	$700	$675	$650	$595	$550	$495	$450

Add 10% for 20 ga.
Add 25% for ejectors.
Add 25% for 28 ga.

GOLDEN SNIPE - similar to Silver Snipe, with auto ejectors and vent. rib standard.

	$900	$800	$700	$600	$550	$500	$425

Add 10% for 20 ga.
Add 25% for 28 ga.

* *Golden Snipe SST* - with SST.

	$1,075	$900	$800	$700	$600	$550	$500

Add 10% for 20 ga.
Add 25% for 28 ga.

MODEL (S)57 E - higher quality version of Golden Snipe. Mfg. 1955-67.

	$900	$800	$700	$600	$550	$500	$425

Add 10% for 20 ga.
Add 25% for 28 ga.

* *Model (S)57 E SST* - with single selective trigger.

	$1,075	$900	$800	$700	$600	$550	$500

Add 10% for 20 ga.
Add 25% for 28 ga.

ASE MODEL - 12 or 20 ga., light border scroll engraving, mfg. approx. 1947-64.

	100%	98%	95%	90%	80%	70%	60%
12 ga.	$1,600	$1,400	$1,200	$1,050	$875	$750	$600
20 ga.	$2,400	$2,200	$1,875	$1,600	$1,400	$1,200	$900

ASEL MODEL - 12 or 20 ga., 26, 28, or 30 in. barrels, various chokes, single trigger, receiver moderately engraved, checkered pistol grip stock, auto ejectors. Mfg. 1947-1964.

	100%	98%	95%	90%	80%	70%	60%
12 ga.	$2,375	$1,975	$1,600	$1,375	$1,050	$875	$750
20 ga.	$3,950	$3,500	$3,000	$2,500	$2,000	$1,675	$1,375

ASEELL MODEL - 12 or 20 ga., full coverage engraving, rare, very limited mfg.

	100%	98%	95%	90%	80%	70%	60%
12 ga.	$4,000	$3,500	$3,000	$2,500	$2,000	$1,675	$1,325
20 ga.	$7,400	$6,500	$5,750	$5,000	$4,250	$3,500	$2,750

GRADE 100 - 12 ga., 26, 28, or 30 in. barrels, any choke, sidelock, double trigger, auto ejectors, checkered pistol grip or straight stock.

	$1,550	$1,300	$1,100	$900	$775	$695	$575

MODEL 200 - similar to 100, with chrome lined bores and action parts, higher quality engraving.

	$2,000	$1,875	$1,650	$1,375	$1,100	$875	$750

MODEL 680 - 12 ga. only, competition trap and skeet model, boxlock, various chokes. Mono-trap model available. Silver finish receiver, hand engraved, premium walnut. Disc.

	$900	$850	$800	$700	$600	$550	$500

Add approx. $300 for 2 barrel combo. package.

SHOTGUNS: O/U, FIELD - RECENT MFG.

All models listed in this category are field grade configuration regardless of model nomenclature.
All currently manufactured Berettas in this category include hardshell cases.
BERETTA CHOKES AND THEIR CODES (ON REAR LEFT-SIDE OF BARREL)
* designates full choke (F).
** designates improved modified choke (IM).
*** designates modified choke (M).

**** designates improved cylinder choke (IC).

SK designates skeet (SK).

***** designates cylinder bore (CYL).

During 2003, Beretta introduced X-Tra Wood on stocks and forearms of select models. X-Tra Wood is a patented and exclusive Beretta wood enhancement finish where average wood is encapsulated with a waterproof film which resembles best quality Circassian walnut. Normal checkering is possible, and all X-tra Wood stocks are marked clearly on the bottom of the pistol grip cap. It can also be refinished through a special refinishing program available with Beretta USA.

Note: values are for unaltered guns.

> **Subtract 20% on the following factory multi-choke models if w/o newer Beretta Optima-chokes (12 ga. only, became standard 2003).**

MODEL 685 - 12 or 20 ga. 2 3/4 or 3 in. chambers, matte chromed receiver, extractors, single trigger. Disc. 1986.

$575	$525	$460	$420	$360	$320	$295

Last MSR was $875.

MODEL 686 WHITE ONYX FIELD (ONYX) - 12, 20, or 28 (new 2003) ga., 2 3/4 (28 ga. only) or 3 in. chambers, boxlock action, 26 or 28 in. barrels with multi-chokes, matte blue metal (disc. 2003) or Dura-Jewel satin nickel alloy (new 2003, became standard 2004) frame, choice of standard pistol grip or English straight (disc. 1999) stock with gloss (new 1999), matte (disc. 2003) or X-Tra (standard beginning 2004) wood finish, single trigger, ejectors, approx. 6.2 or 6.8 lbs. New 1988.

MSR $1,925	$1,525	$1,050	$825	$650	$550	$480	$425

> **Add $154 for deluxe wood upgrade (mfg. 2001-2002, included case).**
> **Add $25 for left-hand (disc.).**
> **Subtract 10% for matte blue finish.**

✳ *Model 686 White Onyx Waterfowler Magnum* - 12 ga. only, similar to Model S686 Onyx, except has 3 1/2 in. chambers, 28 in. barrels only, matte wood and metal finish. Mfg. 1993, reintroduced 1996-2003.

$995	$950	$800	$675	$600	$550	$495

Last MSR was $1,648.

✳ *Model 686 Onyx Essential* - 12 ga. only, 3 in. chambers, 26 or 28 in. VR separated barrels with choke tubes, checkered high-gloss walnut stock and forearm, matte finished metal, 6.7 lbs. Mfg. 1994-96.

$795	$700	$575	$475	$400	$350	$300

Last MSR was $1,186.

> **Subtract 10% for 26 in. barrels.**

✳ *Model S686 Onyx Silver Essential* - 12 ga. only, 3 in. chambers, 26 or 28 in. VR separated barrels with choke tubes, checkered matte finished walnut stock and forearm, matte chrome finished receiver, 6.7 lbs. Imported 1997-98 only.

$795	$700	$575	$475	$400	$350	$300

Last MSR was $1,070.

> **Subtract 10% for 26 in. barrels.**

✳ *Model 686 Onyx Quail Unlimited Covey Limited Edition* - 12 (disc. 2002) 20, or 28 (new 2003) ga., similar to Model 686 Onyx, except includes 6 quail inlays in 24Kt. gold on receiver sides and Quail Unlimited logo on bottom of receiver, marked "1 of 750," deluxe checkered high gloss stock and forearm, cased with 5 choke tubes, 750 of each ga. Mfg. 2002-2004.

$1,400	$1,275	$850	$775	$675	$600	$475

Last MSR was $2,000.

This model was available through Beretta Showcase Dealers only.

GRADING - PPGS™	100%	98%	95%	90%	80%	70%	60%

✳ Model 686 Onyx Ringneck Pheasants Forever Limited Edition - 12 or 20 ga., similar to Onyx Model 686 Quail Unlimited, except includes multiple ringneck pheasant inlays in 24Kt. gold on receiver sides and Pheasants Forever logo on bottom of receiver, marked "1 of 500," deluxe checkered high gloss stock and forearm, cased with 5 choke tubes, 500 of each ga. Mfg. 2003-2004.

	$1,400	$1,275	$900	$775	$700	$525	$475

Last MSR was $2,027.

ULTRALIGHT 687 (686/ONYX) - 12 ga. only, 2 3/4 in. chambers, Ergal alloy receiver reinforced with titanium plate, electroless nickel finish receiver with game scene engraving (new 1998, restyled 2002 with several gold inlays) or matte black finish on receiver (disc. 1997) and 26 (disc. 2001) or 28 in. VR barrels, choice of English (new 2001) straight or pistol grip checkered walnut stock and forearm, matte (new 2001, restyled) or gloss wood finish, choke tubes, gilded lettering and logo (disc. 1997), gold SST, ejectors, very light weight, 5 lbs. 11 oz. Importation began 1992.

MSR $2,075		$1,775	$1,450	$1,175	$875	$775	$650	$575

Add approx. $150 for deluxe wood upgrade (includes case, mfg. 2001 only).
Subtract approx. 10%-15% if with matte black finish, depending on condition.

This model is discontinued as a 686 Series.

✳ Ultralight Deluxe (Onyx) - 12 ga. only, 2 3/4 in. chambers, similiar to 1998 Model 686 Ultralight, except has gold game scene engraving and select walnut stock and forearm. Mfg. began 1998.

MSR $2,450		$2,075	$1,700	$1,325	$1,000	$900	$800	$695

ONYX PRO - 12, 20, or 28 ga., 2 3/4 (28 ga.only) or 3 in. chambers, matte blue finish with Dura-Jewel treatment on receiver, X-Tra wood finish on stock and forearm, Gel-tek recoil pad, gold trigger, TruGlo sights, includes case and 5 choke tubes, 6.8 lbs. (12 ga.). Imported 2003-2006.

	$1,650	$1,300	$1,125	$950	$800	$650	$575

Last MSR was $1,875.

✳ Onyx Pro 3.5 - 12 ga., 3 1/2 in. chambers, otherwise similar to Onyx Pro, 6.9 lbs. Imported 2003-2006.

	$1,650	$1,325	$1,150	$975	$825	$675	$595

Last MSR was $1,975.

WHITEWING - 12 or 20 ga., 3 in. chambers, 26 or 28 in. separated VR barrels and MC3 choke tubes, similar to Model 686 Silver Essential, except has checkered gloss finish walnut stock and silver polished receiver with game scene engraving, 6.7 lbs. Mfg. 1999-2003.

	$1,025	$900	$800	$725	$600	$485	$350

Last MSR was $1,332.

BLACKWING - similar to Whitewing, except has matte black receiver finish, lower stock dimensions, and Schnabel forearm. Mfg. 2002-2003.

	$1,095	$950	$875	$750	$650	$525	$400

Last MSR was $1,332.

MODEL 686(L) SILVER PERDIZ - 12 (disc. 1990), 20 (disc. 1990), or 28 ga., field model, boxlock action, various barrels/ chokes, ejectors, single trigger, engraved silver finished receiver, special walnut, pistol or straight grip stock, fixed chokes disc. 1987. Importation disc. 1994.

	$925	$775	$600	$500	$475	$425	$375

Last MSR was $1,355.

Subtract 20% with fixed chokes (disc.).
Add 20% for 28 ga.

❋ *Model 686 Silver Pigeon S & Silver Pigeon (Silver Perdiz)* - 12, 20, or 28 (mfg. 1995-2001, reintroduced 2004) ga. or .410 bore (new 2005), 3 in. chambers (except for 28 ga.), 26 or 28 in. VR barrels with choke tubes, choice of polished (new 1999) or regular nickel finished receiver with scroll engraving, gold trigger, gloss finish checkered pistol grip or straight grip (disc. 1999) walnut stock and forearm, supplied with carrying case, 5 choke tubes, recoil pad and sling swivels beginning 2004, includes hardshell case, 6.8 lbs. New 1992.

MSR $2,350	$1,950	$1,475	$1,300	$1,000	$825	$700	$600

Add $153 for deluxe wood upgrade (Silver Pigeon only, 12 or 20 ga. only, includes case, mfg. 2001-2002).

Add $100 for King Ranch model with special cowboy and western engraving motifs (new 2006).

Add $25 for left-hand (disc. 2007).

During 1996, the model nomenclature was changed from the Silver Perdiz to the Silver Pigeon.

❋ *Model 686 Silver Pigeon S (Silver Perdiz) and 686 Silver Pigeon Combo* - similar to Model 686 Onyx, except is supplied with 1 set each of 20 ga. (28 in.) and 28 ga. (26 in.) barrels, includes carrying case, 5 choke tubes, recoil pad, and sling swivels, polished receiver became standard 1999. Introduced 1986.

MSR $3,175	$2,775	$2,300	$1,800	$1,525	$1,250	$1,000	$875

Subtract 10% for 26 in. barrels.

MODEL S686 EL GOLD PERDIZ - 12 or 20 ga., 3 in. chambers, boxlock action with floral scroll engraved sideplates, silver receiver finish, 26 or 28 (20 ga. only beginning 1997) VR in. barrels with choke tubes, gold SST, checkered walnut stock and forearm, cased, approx. 6.8 lbs. Mfg. 1992-97.

	$1,600	$1,350	$1,150	$950	$875	$800	$695

Last MSR was $1,930.

Add 10% for 20 ga.

Subtract 10% for 26 in. barrels.

MODEL S687(L) SILVER PIGEON - 12 (disc. 1999) or 20 ga., 3 in. chambers, boxlock, various barrels/chokes, ejectors, game scene engraved nickel finished receiver, gloss finished select walnut stock and forearm, approx. 6.8 lbs., fitted case was optional. Disc. 2000.

	$1,395	$1,275	$1,125	$975	$875	$750	$695

Last MSR was $2,255.

Subtract 30% without multi-chokes (disc.).

Subtract 10% for 26 in. barrels.

The "L" suffix model nomenclature was disc. 1996.

MODEL S687 SILVER PIGEON II - 12 or 20 ga., similar to Model S687 Silver Pigeon, except has deep relief engraved game scenes on receiver sides and oil finished (matte) walnut stock and forearm, 26 or 28 in. VR barrels with MC3 choke tubes. New 1999.

MSR $2,750	$2,375	$1,875	$1,625	$1,300	$1,025	$925	$825

❋ *Model S687 Silver Pigeon II Combo* - includes 1 set each of 28 ga. and 20 ga. with 28 in. barrels, cased with 5 choke tubes. Importation began 2003.

MSR $3,750	$3,125	$2,300	$1,950	$1,775	$1,525	$1,300	$1,075

MODEL 687 SILVER PIGEON III - 12, 20, or 28 ga., 26 or 28 in. VR barrels, engraved boxlock action with game scenes, select checkered walnut stock and forearm, Gel-Tek recoil pad, gold SST, TruGlo front sight, 6.8 lbs. New 2004.

MSR $2,975	$2,550	$1,975	$1,700	$1,325	$1,050	$925	$825

Add $25 for left-hand (disc. 2007).

GRADING - PPGS™	100%	98%	95%	90%	80%	70%	60%

MODEL 687 SILVER PIGEON IV - 12, 20, or 28 ga., 2 3/4 (28 ga. only) or 3 in. chambers, black metal finished receiver with full coverage scroll engraving and 4 gold bird inlays, 26 or 28 in. barrels, checkered oil finished walnut stock with Gel-Tek recoil pad, TruGlo front sight, includes molded case with 5 choke tubes, 6.8 lbs. (12 ga.). Importation began 2003.

MSR $3,150	$2,725	$2,175	$1,800	$1,400	$1,050	$875	$825

> Add $225 for King Ranch model with special cowboy and western engraving motifs (new 2006, only available in 20 or 28 ga.).

MODEL 687 SILVER PIGEON V - 12, 20, 28 ga., or .410 bore (new 2005), 26 or 28 in. barrels, case colored finished receiver with gold bird inlays, 28 ga. is on a true "baby frame," upgraded select oil finished checkered straight grip English (not available in 12 ga.) or pistol grip walnut stock and forearm, gold SST, Gel-Tek recoil pad, Schnabel forend, 6.8 lbs., includes hardshell case. New 2004.

MSR $3,575	$2,900	$2,400	$2,000	$1,550	$1,300	$1,075	$925

MODEL 687 DU - 12 (1990 release) or 20 ga., mfg. for DU dinner gun auctions and membership, prices may vary significantly from region to region.

	$1,200	$1,050	$925	$800	$700	$575	$475

> Add 10% for 20 ga.

MODEL 687 BLACK & GOLD TERCENTENNIAL - 12 ga. only, 2 3/4 in. chambers, 28 in. barrels with fixed F/M chokes, bottom of blued receiver features special 1680-1980 Tercentennial logo, inlaid (with gold) and engraved by Giovanelli (signed), ser. no. 001-300.

	$1,800	$1,675	$1,500	$1,225	$995	$900	$800

MODEL 687 TERCENTENNIAL COMMEMORATIVE - 12 ga. only, 2 3/4 in. chambers, 28 in. barrels, engraved and signed by Giovanelli, with ducks and woodcocks on sides of grey finished frame, oil finished walnut stock and forearm, ser. no. 001-200.

	$1,800	$1,675	$1,500	N/A	N/A	N/A	N/A

MODEL 687 L ONYX - 12 or 20 ga., 3 in. chambers, same game scene engraving as standard Model 687 L, except has Onyx blackened receiver, multi-chokes standard. Mfg. 1990 only.

	$1,150	$1,000	$900	$750	$650	$575	$525

> *Last MSR was $1,590.*

> Add 10% for 20 ga.

MODEL 687 GOLDEN ONYX - 12 or 20 ga., 3 in. chambers, similar to Model 686 Onyx, except has more engraving, better walnut, and several gold inlays. Imported 1988-89 only.

	$1,375	$1,275	$995	$825	$700	$650	$575

> *Last MSR was $1,800.*

> Add 15% for 20 ga.
> Subtract 10% for 26 in. barrels.

MODEL S687 EL GOLD PIGEON - same general specifications as Model 687L, except also available in 28 ga. (new 1990) or .410 (new 1990) bore, 20 ga. disc. 2001, 2 3/4 or 3 in. chambers, boxlock with gold inlaid game scene on sideplates, highly figured walnut, and more engraving, oval nameplate, approx. 6.8 lbs, cased. Disc. 2002.

	$2,600	$2,200	$1,950	$1,575	$1,350	$1,150	$1,000

> *Last MSR was $4,099.*

> Add $100 for 28 ga.
> Subtract 10% for 26 in. barrels.

GRADING - PPGS™	100%	98%	95%	90%	80%	70%	60%

✳ *Model 687 EL DU* - 28 ga. or .410 bore, small frame, released 1992 for DU auctions and membership.

	$2,300	$2,000	$1,800	$1,550	$1,400	$1,200	$1,050

MODEL S687 EL GOLD PIGEON II - 12, 20, 28 ga., or .410 bore, similar to EL Gold Pigeon, except features deep relief engraving on sideplates, 6.8 lbs., cased. Mfg. 2001-2006.

	$4,325	$3,525	$3,150	$2,625	$2,050	$1,800	$1,500

Last MSR was $5,095.

✳ *S687 Gold Pigeon II Combo* - includes either 20 and 28 ga. barrels or 28 ga. and .410 bore barrels, cased with 5 choke tubes. Imported 2003-2007.

	$5,475	$4,375	$3,800	$3,200	$2,825	$2,475	$2,050

Last MSR was $6,400.

MODEL 687 EL ONYX - 12 or 20 ga., 3 in. chambers, simulated sidelock plates with classic scroll engraving. Mfg. 1990 only.

	$1,895	$1,700	$1,500	$1,350	$1,075	$950	$800

Last MSR was $2,660.

Subtract 10% for 26 in. barrels.

MODEL S687 EELL DIAMOND PIGEON - 12, 20, 28 ga. or .410 bore (new 2003), boxlock action, silver receiver with full sideplates and hand engraved game scenes, 26 or 28 in. VR barrels, 3 in. (except 28 ga.) chambers and gold plated trigger, cased, multi-chokes introduced 1988, 6.8 lbs.

MSR $7,000	$6,150	$4,400	$3,675	$3,100	$2,500	$2,000	$1,650

Add $500 for King Ranch model with special cowboy and western engraving motifs (new 2006).
Add 10%-20% for earlier mfg. with hand chased engraving (non-machine engraved), depending on condition.
Subtract 20% if without multi-chokes.
Subtract 10% for 26 in. barrels.

This model is also available with a straight grip English stock at no extra charge (20 ga. only). If hand engraved, the engraver's name will be next to the trigger guard.

✳ *Model S687 EELL Combo* - includes either 20 and 28 ga. or 28 ga. and .410 bore multi-choke 26 or 28 in. barrels, cased. Limited importation.

MSR $8,500	$7,200	$6,000	$5,300	$4,400	$3,725	$3,100	$2,600

Subtract 20% for fixed chokes.
Multi-chokes became standard in 1991.

✳ *Model S687 EELL Gallery Edition* - 12, 20, 28 ga., or .410 bore, available as a pair (optional) or 2 barrel sets, featuring special engraving and upgraded wood with oil finish. New 2000.

Prices range from $7,250 -$8,750 for single guns and 2 barrel sets, depending on ga. and options. Pairs start at $16,675. Available at Beretta Galleries only.

MODEL S687 EXTRA - 12, 20, 28 ga., or .410 bore, available in pairs or 2 barrel sets (special order only), features special engraving and upgraded wood with oil finish. New 2001.

Prices start at $7,875 for Field Model, and vary depending on ga. and options. Pairs start at approx. $16,675. Available at Beretta Premium dealers only.

MODEL ASE 90 PIGEON - 12 ga. only, 28 in. fixed choke (IM/F) vent. barrels with VR, new design features nickel-chromium-molybdenum receiver with special hardening and cross bolt engaging 2 monobloc lugs, detachable trigger grouping, V-shaped main springs, cold hammered barrels, choice of silver or blue receiver with gold etching and no engraving, top quality checkered walnut stock and forearm with vent. recoil pad, choke tubes, 7 lbs. 13 oz., cased. Imported 1992-94.

	$3,650	$3,225	$2,950	$2,650	$2,300	$2,000	$1,750

Last MSR was $8,070.

GRADING - PPGS™	100%	98%	95%	90%	80%	70%	60%

SHOTGUNS: O/U, SKEET - RECENT MFG.

Full descriptions for the following models may be found under the corresponding model numbers in the Field Shotguns category.

Note: values are for unaltered guns.

Subtract 20% on the following factory multi-choke models if w/o newer Beretta Optima-chokes (12 ga. only, became standard 2003).

MODEL S682 GOLD SKEET - 12, 20 (disc. 1991), 28 ga. (disc. 1988), or .410 bore (disc. 1988), competition skeet model, 26 (disc.) or 28 in. barrels, boxlock, skeet chokes, silver finish (disc.) or Greystone (titanium nitrate) receiver, hand engraved, premium walnut, cased. Mfg. 1984-99.

$1,400	$1,300	$1,275	$1,025	$900	$800	$700

Last MSR was $2,850.

Subtract 20% for 26 in. barrels.
Subtract 20% for fixed chokes.
Subtract 20% for silver finish.

* *Model S682 Gold Skeet With Adj. Stock* - similar to Model S682 Gold Skeet, except has fully adj. stock, allowing the comb, drop, and cast to be adjusted per shooter. Imported 1999-2000.

$1,600	$1,500	$1,450	$1,350	$1,075	$950	$825

Last MSR was $3,515.

* *Model S682 Gold E Skeet* - 12 ga. only, 28 or 30 in. VR barrels with Optima-Bore and Optima-Choke, adj. stock with memory system, dual color finished receiver with engraved merging circular lines and gold highlights, including trigger, deluxe wide checkered stock and Schnabel forearm with gloss wood finish, 7.6 lbs. New 2001.

MSR $4,425		$3,750	$3,150	$2,775	$2,425	$2,000	$1,650	$1,425

* *Model 682 Super Skeet* - 12 ga. only, 28 in. VR barrels bored SK/SK featuring factory porting, stock has separate adj. comb cheekpiece. Mfg. 1991-95.

$1,500	$1,300	$1,200	$1,100	$1,050	$900	$800

Last MSR was $3,006.

* *Model 682 Skeet Deluxe* - similar to Model 682, except deluxe walnut and elaborate engraving. Disc. 1986.

$1,850	$1,700	$1,550	$1,250	$1,050	$900	$800

Last MSR was $3,000.

* *Model 682 2-Barrel Skeet Set* - 12 ga. only, two barrel set bored for skeet and sporting clays competition. Imported 1988 only.

$2,400	$2,150	$2,000	$1,850	$1,600	$1,400	$1,300

Last MSR was $6,650.

Subtract 25% if w/o choke tubes.

* *Model 682 4-Ga. Skeet Set* - four barrel skeet set comes with interchangeable barrels (28 in.) in 12, 20, 28 gauges, and .410 bore. Imported 1985-95.

$3,300	$3,100	$3,000	$2,850	$2,500	$2,175	$1,900

Last MSR was $6,037.

Subtract 10% for silver frame.

MODEL S686 SKEET SILVER PERDIZ/SILVER PIGEON - 12 ga. only, 28 in. VR barrels bored SK/SK, checkered walnut stock and forearm, Silver Perdiz was disc. 1996 and featured silver finish, while Silver Pigeon nomenclature began 1997 and features nickel finish, 7.6 lbs. Imported 1994-98.

$825	$775	$700	$675	$625	$550	$480

Last MSR was $1,795.

GRADING - PPGS™	100%	98%	95%	90%	80%	70%	60%

MODEL S687 EELL SKEET DIAMOND PIGEON - 12 ga. only, fixed chokes, 28 in. barrels, elaborate game scene engraving on sideplates, cased. Disc. 2002.

	$2,750	$2,500	$2,250	$2,000	$1,800	$1,500	$1,250

Last MSR was $4,984.

✴ *Model S687 EELL Skeet Diamond Pigeon With Adj. Stock* - similar to Model S687 EELL Skeet Diamond Pigeon, except has fully adj. stock, allowing the comb, drop, and cast to be adjusted per shooter. Imported 1999-2004.

	$4,600	$4,200	$3,950	$3,750	$3,250	$2,600	$2,150

Last MSR was $6,207.

✴ *Model S687 EELL 4-Ga. Skeet Set* - 4 ga. skeet set, cased. Imported 1988-1998.

	$5,000	$4,600	$4,200	$3,750	$3,400	$2,900	$2,450

Last MSR was $8,405.

DT10 TRIDENT SKEET - 12 ga. only, 3 in. chambers, 28 or 30 in. vent. barrels with target VR, specially designed skeet gun featuring removable adj. trigger group, massive crossbolt locking system, Optima-choke competition choke tubes, Optima-Bore internal barrel configuration, specific point of impact, and unique distribution of mass that helps target acquisition and eliminate muzzle rise, adj. walnut stock with memory system, carbon reinforced frame, 7.9 lbs. New 2000.

MSR $7,400		$6,300	$4,800	$4,450	$4,000	$3,600	$3,150	$2,550

MODEL ASE 90 GOLD SKEET - 12 ga. only, 28 in. fixed choke vent. barrels with VR, similar action and specifications as the Model ASE 90 Pigeon, except has more elaborate hand scroll engraving and extra fine wood, 7.6 lbs., cased. Mfg. 1992-99.

	$3,600	$3,400	$3,250	$3,000	$2,750	$2,500	$2,250

Last MSR was $12,060.

SHOTGUNS: O/U, SPORTING CLAYS - RECENT MFG.

These variations have been specifically designed for sporting clay target shooting. All of the following models have 3 in. chambers, unless specified otherwise. Full descriptions for the following models may be found under the corresponding model numbers in the Field Shotguns category.

Subtract 10% for 28 in. barrels on all used Sporting models in this section.

Subtract 20% on the following factory multi-choke models if w/o newer Beretta Optima-chokes (12 ga. only, became standard 2003).

MODEL S682 CONTINENTAL COURSE - 12 ga. only, 2 3/4 in. chambers, 28 or 30 (disc. 1995) in. VR barrels with multi-chokes, designed for English Sporting Clays courses, previously was Model Super Sport with tapered rib, cased. Mfg. 1993-97.

	$1,400	$1,300	$1,200	$975	$875	$775	$675

Last MSR was $2,345.

MODEL S682 GOLD SPORTING - 12 or 20 (mfg. 1992-94) ga., similar specifications to Model 682 Skeet, 2 3/4 in. chambers, 28, 30 (new 1989), or 31 (new 1997) in. unported or ported (new 1995) VR barrels, except over-field stock dimensions and hand engraved silver (disc.) or Greystone (titanium nitrate) finished receiver, cased, 7.6 lbs. Multi-chokes are standard. Disc. 2000.

	$1,650	$1,500	$1,250	$1,075	$950	$875	$800

Last MSR was $3,100.

Add $500 for extra set of 12 ga. barrels (combo. package - mfg. 1990-94).

✴ *Model S682 Gold E Sporting* - 12 ga. only, 28, 30, or 32 in. VR barrels with Optima-Bore and Optima-Choke, dual color finished receiver with engraved merging circular lines and gold highlights, including trigger, select wide checkered stock and Schnabel forearm with gloss wood finish, approx. 7.6 lbs. New 2001.

MSR $3,975		$3,275	$2,700	$2,275	$1,900	$1,650	$1,425	$1,200

GRADING - PPGS™	100%	98%	95%	90%	80%	70%	60%

MODEL 682 SUPER SPORTING - 12 ga. only, 2 3/4 in. chambers, 28 or 30 in. VR ported (new 1993) barrels with multi-chokes and tapered rib, otherwise similar to Model 682 Sporting, cased, 7.6 lbs. Imported 1989-95.

		$1,500	$1,375	$1,250	$1,100	$950	$875	$800

Last MSR was $3,017.

Beginning 1993, this model featured a special fully adj. stock and LOP.

MODEL 682 LTD - 12 ga. only, 30 or 32 in. barrels, limited edition mfg. 2006.

	$4,100	$3,600	$3,175	$2,775	$2,300	$2,000	$1,650

Last MSR was $5,075.

MODEL 686 SPORTING/SPECIAL SPORTING - 12 ga. only, 3 in. chambers, deluxe checkered walnut stock and forearm with over-field dimensions, 28 or 30 (new 1991) in. barrels only, multi-chokes standard. Mfg. 1987-92.

	$1,200	$1,100	$925	$825	$675	$625	$550

Last MSR was $1,940.

The Model 686 Special Sporting is marked "Model S686 Special," and the barrels are marked "Sporting."

* *Model S686 Silver Pigeon (Silver Perdiz) Sporting* - 12 or 20 (disc. 2000) ga., 28 or 30 in. VR barrels with multi-chokes, 7.7 lbs. Mfg. 1993-2002.

	$1,300	$1,175	$995	$850	$725	$650	$575

Last MSR was $1,931.

Add $139 for deluxe wood upgrade (includes case, mfg. 2001-2002).

Until 1994, this model was named the Model 686 Hunter Sport. Between 1994-95, this model was named the S686 Silver Perdiz, and beginning 1996, this model was again renamed to the 686 Silver Pigeon Sporting.

* *Model 686 E Sporting* - 12, 20 or 28 ga., 3 in. chambers, 28 (20 ga. only) or 30 in. VR barrels with 5 chokes, improved styling, oil finished walnut stock and Schnabel forearm, includes accessories, 5 choke tubes, and carrying case, 7.7 lbs. Mfg. 2001-2004.

	$1,475	$1,275	$1,075	$975	$850	$750	$650

Last MSR was $2,008.

* *Model 686 Silver Perdiz/S686 Silver Pigeon Sporting Combo* - 12 ga., includes extra set of 30 in. barrels. Model 686 Silver Perdiz was manufactured 1991-95, Model S686 Silver Pigeon was manufactured 1997-99.

	$1,925	$1,700	$1,475	$1,250	$1,025	$900	$800

Last MSR was $2,210. Last MSR was $2,687 for the 686 Silver Perdiz Combo.

MODEL 686 COLLECTION SPORT - 12 ga. only, features multi-colored checkered wood stock and forearm, 28 in. VR barrels, 7.7 lbs. Mfg. 1996 only.

	$900	$775	$650	$550	$475	$400	$350

Last MSR was $1,499.

MODEL 686 ONYX SPORTING - 12 ga. only, 28 or 30 in. vent. fixed choke barrels with VR, high luster blue finish with gold lettering on receiver sides. Mfg. 1992 only.

	$900	$775	$650	$550	$475	$400	$350

Last MSR was $1,940.

* *Model 686 Onyx Sporting w/Multi-chokes* - 12 ga. only, 28 or 30 in. VR barrels with multi- chokes, matte wood finish, choice of semi-matte black (disc. 1998) or polished black receiver with "P. Beretta" engraved in gold, 7.7 lbs. Mfg. 1993-2002.

	$995	$900	$775	$595	$525	$460	$415

Last MSR was $1,639.

Add $139 for deluxe wood upgrade (includes case, mfg. 2001-2002).

✱ *Model 686 English Course* - 12 ga. only, features 28 in. VR barrels and special reverse tapered VR with special sighting plane designed for English courses. Mfg. 1991-92.

| | $995 | $895 | $775 | $675 | $600 | $500 | $400 |

Last MSR was $2,015.

MODEL 686 WHITE ONYX SPORTING - 12 ga. only, 30 or 32 in. VR barrels, nickel alloy finish, gold SST, oil finished checkered select walnut stock and forearm, black rubber recoil pad, Schnabel forend, 7-8 1/2 lbs. New 2004.

| MSR $2,025 | $1,725 | $1,375 | $1,100 | $900 | $800 | $700 | $600 |

MODEL S687(L) SILVER PIGEON (SILVER PERDIZ) SPORTING - 12 or 20 ga. only, deluxe checkered walnut stock and forearm with over-field dimensions, game scene engraved, 28 or 30 (12 ga. only) in. barrels, multi-chokes standard. Mfg. 1987-2001.

| | $1,450 | $1,350 | $1,215 | $975 | $875 | $775 | $675 |

Last MSR was $2,363.

✱ *Model 687 Silver Pigeon Sporting Combo* - 12 ga., includes set of 28 and 30 in. barrels. Mfg. 2002 only.

| | $1,850 | $1,725 | $1,600 | $1,400 | $1,200 | $1,000 | $875 |

Last MSR was $3,151.

✱ *Model 687 English Course* - 12 ga. only, features 28 in. VR barrels and special reverse tapered VR with special sighting plane designed for English courses. Mfg. 1991-92.

| | $1,500 | $1,400 | $1,300 | $1,075 | $975 | $895 | $800 |

Last MSR was $2,630.

MODEL S687 SILVER PIGEON II SPORTING - 12, 20 (new 2002), or 28 ga. (new 2002), features deep relief game scene engraving on receiver sides, matte oil finished select walnut stock and forearm, 28, 30, or 32 (12 ga. only, new 2002) in. barrels with choke tubes, Optima-Bore choking with extended Optima-chokes became standard on 12 ga. in 2003, 7.7 lbs. Importation began 1999.

| MSR $2,950 | $2,500 | $1,875 | $1,675 | $1,475 | $1,275 | $995 | $875 |

Subtract 20% if w/o Optima chokes.

MODEL S687 SILVER PIGEON III SPORTING - 12 ga. only, 30 or 32 in. VR barrels, select checkered walnut stock and forearm, game scene engraving on receiver sides, floral and scroll engraving on bottom of receiver and trigger guard, approx. 8 lbs. New 2004.

| MSR $3,175 | $2,675 | $1,975 | $1,725 | $1,525 | $1,300 | $1,100 | $900 |

MODEL S687 EL GOLD PIGEON SPORTING - 12 ga. only, 28 or 30 in. VR barrels with multi-chokes (non-Optima), 7.7 lbs. Mfg. 1993-2001.

| | $2,650 | $1,900 | $1,675 | $1,450 | $1,250 | $1,050 | $875 |

Last MSR was $4,182.

MODEL S687 EL GOLD PIGEON II SPORTING - 12, 20 (new 2003), 28 ga., or .410 bore (new 2003), similar to Model S687 Gold Pigeon Sporting, except features deep relief engraving on sideplates, also available in 28 ga. and 32 in. barrels beginning 2002, Optima-Bore choking with flush Optima-chokes became standard on 12 ga. in 2003. Mfg. 2001-2006.

| | $4,350 | $3,750 | $3,300 | $2,850 | $2,350 | $2,025 | $1,600 |

Last MSR was $5,495.

✱ *Model 687 EL Gold Pigeon II Sporting 20 ga./.410 Bore* - includes set of 20 ga. and .410 bore barrels, cased. Imported 2003 only.

| | $4,500 | $4,000 | $3,350 | $2,850 | $2,350 | $1,975 | $1,625 |

Last MSR was $6,071.

GRADING - PPGS™	100%	98%	95%	90%	80%	70%	60%

✳ *Model 687 EL Gold Pigeon II Sporting Combo* - 28 ga. and .410 bore, includes set of 30 in. barrels. Mfg. 2002-2007.

	$5,600	$4,900	$4,050	$3,500	$3,175	$2,800	$2,375

Last MSR was $6,600.

MODEL S687 EELL DIAMOND PIGEON SPORTING - 12, 20 (disc. 1992, reintroduced 2003), 28 (new 2003) ga. or .410 bore (new 2003), features fine scroll engraving on receiver and sideplates, deluxe checkered walnut stock and forearm with over-field dimensions, 28, 30 (new 1995), or 32 (new 2002) in. barrels only, Optima-Bore choking with flush Optima-chokes became standard on 12 ga. in 2003 or with multi-chokes, cased, 7.6 lbs. New 1987.

MSR $7,475	$6,525	$5,550	$4,675	$3,850	$2,950	$2,300	$1,875

Add $1,500 for extra set of barrels (combo. package - 1990 mfg. only).
Subtract 10% if w/o Optima-chokes.

DT10 TRIDENT SPORTING - 12 ga. only, 3 in. chambers, 28, 30, or 32 in. vent. barrels with target VR, specially designed sporting gun featuring removable adj. trigger group, massive crossbolt locking system, Optima-choke competition choke tubes, Optima-Bore internal barrel configuration, specific point of impact, and unique distribution of mass that helps target acquisition and eliminate muzzle rise, deluxe checkered walnut stock and Schnabel forearm, carbon reinforced frame, cased, approx. 8 lbs. New 2000.

MSR $6,775	$6,100	$5,125	$4,150	$3,600	$3,200	$2,900	$2,375

✳ *DT10 Trident L Sporting* - 12 ga., 30 or 32 in. barrels, floral engraved receiver and trigger guard, palm swell, adj. trigger. New 2004.

MSR $8,925	$7,575	$6,600	$5,450	$4,700	$3,950	$3,300	$2,600

✳ *DT10 Trident EELL Sporting* - 12 ga., 30 or 32 in. barrels, hand engraved, upgraded wood. New 2004.

MSR $12,995	$11,000	$9,650	$8,250	$7,000	$6,000	$5,000	$4,000

This model is available by special order through Beretta Galleries only.

MODEL ASE 90 GOLD SPORTING CLAYS - 12 ga. only, 28, 30, or 31 (new 1997) in. vent. barrels with VR, similar action and specifications to Model ASE 90 Pigeon, 7 1/2 lbs., cased. Mfg. 1992-99.

		$3,800	$3,600	$3,400	$3,250	$3,000	$2,850	$2,500

Last MSR was $12,145.

SHOTGUNS: O/U, TRAP - RECENT MFG.

Note: values are for unaltered trap guns.

Subtract 20% on the following factory multi-choke models if w/o newer Beretta Optima-chokes (12 ga. only, became standard 2003).
Subtract 10% for 28 in. barrels on used Trap models.

MODEL S682 GOLD TRAP (GOLD X) - 12 ga. only, competition trap model, Greystone (titanium nitrate) or Bruniton finish (matte black, disc.), 30 or 32 in. barrels with or w/o choke tubes (became standard 1996), adj. trigger, supplied with case, 8.8 lbs. Mfg. 1985-2000.

	$1,650	$1,350	$1,200	$1,050	$900	$775	$650

Last MSR was $3,100.

Subtract 15% for Bruniton finish.
Subtract 20% if w/o choke tubes.

✳ *Model S682 Mono/Top Combo Trap (Gold X)* - 12 ga. only, supplied with mono under or upper single barrel and O/U barrel sets, multi-chokes became standard 1996. Otherwise same specifications as Model S682 Gold Trap. Cased. Disc. 2000.

	$2,000	$1,850	$1,700	$1,600	$1,400	$1,200	$1,000

Last MSR was $4,085.

Subtract 15% for Bruniton finish.

GRADING - PPGS™	100%	98%	95%	90%	80%	70%	60%

✳ *Model S682 Gold Trap Adjustable Stock* - 12 ga. only, features Monte Carlo style stock with adj. comb, 30 or 32 in. barrels, 8.8 lbs. Mfg. 1998-2000.

		$1,700	$1,600	$1,550	$1,475	$1,250	$1,050	$895

Last MSR was $3,625.

Add $985 for combo package (includes extra set of 34 in. barrels).

✳ *Model 682 Mono* - single under-barrel trap model, high post vent. rib, 32 or 34 in. barrel. Imported 1985-88.

		$1,250	$1,100	$1,000	$900	$800	$700	$600

Last MSR was $1,890.

Subtract if w/o choke tubes.

✳ *Model S682 Gold Trap Live Bird (Pigeon Trap)* - 12 ga. only, includes features for international style pigeon and competition shooters including international style stock, standard or flat (new 1995) VR, and mid-rib sights, Greystone (new 1991) or matte black (disc.) metal finish, semi-gloss American walnut stock, light scroll engraving, sliding trigger, includes multi-chokes, cased, 8.8 lbs. Imported 1990-98.

		$1,700	$1,625	$1,325	$1,175	$950	$895	$800

Last MSR was $2,910.

Subtract 15% for matte black.

✳ *Model 682 Gold X Trap Mono (Top Single)* - 12 ga. only, single over-barrel trap model, 32 or 34 in. barrel. Imported 1986-95.

		$1,400	$1,275	$1,150	$925	$850	$775	$675

Last MSR was $2,734.

Subtract 10% if w/o choke tubes.
Multi-chokes became standard in 1989.

✳ *Model 682 Unsingle Trap* - 12 ga. only, single under-barrel trap model with 32 in. high post VR, optional choke tubes. Imported 1992-94.

		$1,495	$1,350	$1,150	$925	$850	$775	$675

Last MSR was $2,650.

Subtract 10% if w/o choke tubes.

MODEL S682 (GOLD X) SUPER TRAP - 12 ga. only, competition trap model, 30 in. barrels, step tapered rib, factory porting, LOP, and separate stock cheekpiece are adjustable, cased. Imported 1991-95.

		$1,800	$1,650	$1,375	$1,050	$900	$800	$700

Last MSR was $2,907.

✳ *Model S682 Top Mono Super Trap (Gold X)* - 12 ga. only, single over-barrel trap model, 32 or 34 in. barrel with choice of fixed or multi-chokes. Imported 1991-95.

		$1,550	$1,375	$1,200	$1,050	$900	$800	$700

Last MSR was $3,083.

Subtract 10% for 32 in. barrel.
Subtract 10% for fixed choke.

✳ *Model S682 Gold Super Trap Top Combo (Gold X)* - 12 ga. only, supplied with upper single barrel and O/U barrel sets. Otherwise same specifications as Model 682 Super Trap, multi-chokes became standard 1996, cased. Imported 1991-97.

		$2,200	$1,950	$1,825	$1,650	$1,400	$1,125	$895

Last MSR was $4,040.

MODEL S682 GOLD E TRAP - 12 ga. only, 30 or 32 in. VR barrel with Optima-Bore and Optima-Choke, adj. stock with memory system, dual color finished receiver with engraved merging circular lines and gold highlights, including trigger, deluxe wide checkered stock with gloss wood finish, 7.6 lbs. New 2001.

MSR $4,425		$3,750	$3,150	$2,775	$2,425	$2,000	$1,650	$1,425

Add $400 for bottom single configuration.

GRADING - PPGS™	100%	98%	95%	90%	80%	70%	60%

✳ *Model S682 Gold E Trap Combo Top/Bottom* - 12 ga. only, includes 30 (scarce, disc. 2001), 32 (disc. 2002) or 34 (new 2002) in. mono top or bottom barrel and choice of 30 or 32 in. O/U barrels, cased. New 2001.

MSR $5,575	$4,675	$3,950	$3,550	$3,075	$2,625	$2,275	$1,850

Add $500 for bottom single combo.

MODEL S682 LTD. - 12 ga. only, 32 or 34 in. barrel, includes adj. stock. Limited edition mfg. 2006.

$5,400	$4,900	$4,475	$4,200	$3,850	$3,600	$3,300

Last MSR was $6,775.

MODEL S686 SILVER PIGEON TRAP - 12 ga. only, low-profile action, 30 in. VR barrels with 3/8 in. flat rib, matte wood finish, choke tubes, nickel finished receiver with scroll engraving, 7.7 lbs. Mfg. 1997-99.

$1,095	$925	$750	$625	$525	$460	$415

Last MSR was $1,795.

✳ *Model S686 Silver Pigeon Trap Top Mono* - 12 ga. only, single over-barrel trap model, 32 or 34 in. barrel with multi-chokes, gloss wood finish, 8.14 lbs. Mfg. 1998-2002.

$1,000	$900	$775	$650	$550	$475	$415

Last MSR was $1,869.

MODEL 686 INTERNATIONAL TRAP - 12 ga. only, 30 in. VR barrels bored IM/F, checkered walnut stock and forearm. Imported 1994 only.

$900	$800	$725	$650	$550	$500	$460

Last MSR was $1,300.

MODEL S687 EELL DIAMOND PIGEON TRAP (X TRAP) - 12 ga. only, boxlock action with engraved black (new 1992) or silver (disc. 1991) finished side plates, Monte Carlo stock with recoil pad, 30 in. barrels with choke tubes, cased, 8.8 lbs. Disc. 1999.

$2,750	$2,475	$2,150	$1,875	$1,650	$1,475	$1,200

Last MSR was $4,815.

✳ *Model S687 EELL Diamond Pigeon Trap Top Mono* - 12 ga. only, single over-barrel trap model, 32 or 34 in. barrel, fixed chokes standard. Imported 1988-92, resumed 1996, disc. 1999.

$2,500	$2,250	$2,000	$1,850	$1,700	$1,425	$1,150

Last MSR was $5,060.

Subtract $20% for non-Optima multi-chokes.

✳ *Model S687 EELL Diamond Pigeon X Bottom Mono Trap Combo* - 12 ga. only, supplied with 30 or 32 in. O/U barrels and a mono trap bottom barrel. Imported 1986-1988, resumed 1994-95.

$3,500	$3,150	$2,725	$2,500	$2,250	$2,000	$1,725

Last MSR was $4,984.

Add 5% for multi-chokes.

✳ *Model S687 EELL Diamond Pigeon X Top Mono Trap Combo* - 12 ga. only, supplied with 30 or 32 in. O/U barrels and a mono trap upper barrel, multi-chokes became standard 1995. Mfg. 1988-1997.

$3,850	$3,350	$3,000	$2,800	$2,650	$2,475	$2,175

Last MSR was $6,070.

MODEL ASE 90 GOLD TRAP - 12 ga. only, 30 in. vent. barrels with VR, similar action and specifications to Model ASE 90 Pigeon, 8.2 lbs., cased with extra trigger group, multi-chokes became standard 1995. Mfg. 1992-99.

$4,250	$4,000	$3,750	$3,250	$2,750	$2,450	$2,250

Last MSR was $12,145.

Add $1,000 for Trap Combo package.
Subtract 10% if w/o choke tubes.
Subtract $250 if w/o extra trigger assembly.

GRADING - PPGS™	100%	98%	95%	90%	80%	70%	60%

DT10 TRIDENT TRAP - 12 ga. only, 3 in. chambers, 30 or 32 in. vent. barrels with target VR, specially designed trap gun featuring removable adj. trigger group, massive crossbolt locking system, Optima-choke competition choke tubes, Optima-Bore internal barrel configuration, specific point of impact, and unique distribution of mass that helps target acquisition and eliminate muzzle rise, adj. walnut stock with memory system, carbon reinforced frame, 8.8 lbs., cased. New 2000.

MSR $7,400	$6,325	$4,750	$4,050	$3,500	$2,950	$2,500	$2,025

* *DT10 Trident Trap Top Single* - includes 34 in. top single barrel, cased. New 2000.

MSR $7,400	$6,325	$4,750	$4,050	$3,500	$2,950	$2,500	$2,025

* *DT10 Trident Trap Bottom Single* - includes 34 in. bottom single barrel with adj. rib, cased. New 2004.

MSR $8,025	$6,900	$5,600	$4,700	$3,950	$3,275	$2,750	$2,250

* *DT10 Trident Trap Combo* - includes choice of 30 or 32 in. O/U barrels and a 34 in. top single barrel, cased. New 2000.

MSR $10,475	$9,000	$7,550	$6,800	$6,050	$5,500	$4,500	$4,000

* *DT10 Trident Trap Bottom Single Combo* - includes 34 in. bottom single barrel and choice of 30 or 32 in. O/U barrels, rib on bottom single barrel is adj. for point of impact, cased. New 2001.

MSR $10,875	$9,500	$7,150	$6,075	$5,425	$4,750	$4,000	$3,450

SHOTGUNS: O/U, CUSTOM GRADE - RECENT MFG.

Current high grade Beretta O/U and SxS shotguns are sold only by premium grade franchised Beretta dealers. For a listing of these dealers, contact a Beretta Gallery (see Trademark Index).

Where applicable, Beretta's new SST, with selector switch built into safety, is more desirable than older manufacture utilizing the disc. single, non-selective trigger. Subtract 10%-15% for older style non-selective single trigger.

ROYAL PIGEON (GALLERY SPECIAL) - 12 or 20 ga., non-sideplated Mode 600 action, hand engraved in the EELL style, upgraded wood, made especially for Beretta Galleries. 40 mfg. in each gauge beginning 2004.

MSR $5,950	$5,250	$4,550	$4,100	$3,550	$3,200	$2,800	$2,400

ASEL - 12 or 20 ga., best SO grade boxlock with vintage 1960s action, SO grade hand finished wood, Boehler Antinit steel barrels, 28 mfg. in 20 ga. (2004-2005), 300 mfg. in 12 ga. New 2004.

12 ga. MSR $14,500	$12,250	$10,500	$9,000	$7,500	$6,000	$5,000	$4,500
20 ga.	$22,250	$18,500	$14,000	$10,500	$9,500	$8,500	$7,500

Last MSR was $25,750.

Pairs on this model are available for $59,225.

ASE GOLD - see individual models with descriptions under Skeet, Sporting Clays, and Trap category names.

ASE 90 DE LUXE - 12 ga. only, specifications furnished by customer, deep scroll engraving signed by the engraver, upgraded wood, Sporting or Field Model, cased. New 1996.

MSR $24,500	$20,500	$15,000	$10,750	$8,750	$7,250	$6,000	$5,000

JUBILEE - 12, 20, 28 ga., or .410 bore, choice of Field or Sporting Clays configuration, signed scroll or game scene engraving, upgraded wood, tru-oil finish, and hand polished details throughout, cased. New 1998.

MSR $14,850	$12,450	$8,250	$6,100	$4,750	$3,100	$2,780	$2,500

* *Jubilee Matched Pair* - available with consecutive serial numbers, made to special order, cased. New 2002.

MSR $31,650	$25,000	$20,000	$15,000	$11,750	$7,000	$6,500	$5,000

GRADING - PPGS™	100%	98%	95%	90%	80%	70%	60%

SO-1 - 12 ga. only, entry level SO model, sidelock action with greener crossbolt, ejectors, DT, checkered walnut stock and forearm, perimeter engraving only, various configurations. Mfg. circa 1935-disc.

	100%	98%	95%	90%	80%	70%	60%
	$3,250	$2,950	$2,600	$2,250	$1,850	$1,725	$1,600

SO-2 - 12 ga., 26-30 in. barrels, sidelock, any chokes, vent. rib, auto ejectors, SST, checkered stock in various configurations (field, skeet, or trap), grades differ in wood, engraving, and finish, cased. SO series mfg. beginning 1948.

MSR $4,750	$3,995	$2,950	$2,350	$1,950	$1,675	$1,475	$1,250

SO-3 - 2nd grade of the SO series.

MSR $6,250	$4,500	$3,550	$3,200	$2,800	$2,400	$2,100	$1,850

SO-3 EL - grade-up from SO-3 with better wood and engraving.

MSR $7,750	$6,250	$4,250	$3,600	$3,050	$2,500	$2,200	$1,950

SO-3 EELL - best quality model, custom specifications, choice of engraving motifs.

MSR $14,750	$13,500	$8,750	$7,500	$6,250	$5,250	$4,750	$3,950

Add $2,000 for master engraving.

SO-4 - 12 ga., sidelock, available in field, skeet, or trap configurations, custom specs., fluorescent sights, wide rib, cased. Disc. 1987, reintroduced 2001.

MSR $6,500	$5,650	$4,750	$4,225	$3,650	$3,250	$2,800	$2,400

SO-5 COMPETITION - best quality O/U, extensively engraved, top quality checkered walnut stock (semi-pistol grip) and forearm, available in either Trap, Skeet, or Sporting configurations, leather cased, limited importation.

MSR $25,000	$19,750	$12,500	$9,250	$7,450	$6,000	$5,200	$4,500

Add $5,900 for extra set of barrels.
Add $3,500 for Trap Combo set (disc.).

SO-5 EELL - next to top-of-the-line model, available in either Trap, Skeet, or Sporting Clays configuration, custom built to customer dimensions.

MSR $15,000	$13,750	$9,250	$7,750	$6,250	$5,250	$4,750	$3,950

SO-6 COMPETITION - 12 ga. only high quality O/U, extensively scroll engraved, top quality checkered walnut stock (semi-pistol grip) and forearm, choice of Field (reintroduced during 1998), Trap, Skeet, or Sporting Clays configuration, built to customer specifications, leather cased, limited importation. Disc. 2002.

	$16,650	$13,500	$10,750	$8,500	$7,450	$6,350	$5,100

Last MSR was $23,900.

Add $6,250 for extra set of barrels.

SO-6 EL FIELD GRADE - 12 ga. only, available with rose and scroll engraving, 28, 30, or 32 in. barrels. New 2003.

MSR $27,500	$24,250	$19,750	$15,000	$11,000	$9,750	$8,750	$7,500

SO-6 EELL - 12 ga., current next to top-of-the-line model, field dimensions, custom built to customer specifications, leather cased.

MSR $40,000	$35,000	$30,000	$23,250	$18,000	$13,500	$11,000	$9,500

Add $6,250 for extra set of barrels.

Special engraving options are available on this model for an additional charge - contact the Gallery directly for pricing.

SO-6 EESS - 12 ga., features green enamel sideplates with diamond inlays. New 1998.

MSR $84,000	$77,500	$65,000	$52,000	$45,000	$39,000	$32,000	$26,500

✳ *SO-6 EESS w/o Diamonds* - features red or blue enamel sideplates, w/o diamonds. New 1998.

MSR $51,000	$40,000	$35,000	$27,250	$21,250	$16,750	$12,750	$10,750

GRADING - PPGS™	100%	98%	95%	90%	80%	70%	60%

SO-9 - 12, 20, 28 ga., or .410 bore, top-of-the-line sidelock model until 2003, 1990 was the first time the SO series was offered in smaller gauges, 28 ga. or .410 bore models have smaller proportionate frames. New 1990.

MSR $46,725	$35,000	$27,500	$20,500	$16,000	$12,000	$9,200	$7,000

Add $6,275 for extra set of barrels.
Add 10%-25% for well-known engravers.
Subtract 10% for 12 ga. on used specimens.

✳ *SO-9 EELL Special* - top-of-the-line O/U model, retail prices range from $55,000- $110,000, depending on individual custom-order engraving options.

SO-10 - top-of-the-line O/U sidelock model, barrels made of nickel, chromium, and molybdenum steel. Limited availability beginning late 2003.

MSR $75,000	$67,000	$52,000	$40,000	$30,000	$21,000	$16,000	$12,000

Pairs are available for $138,000. Any level of engraving is available on this model in 20 ga. through 2005. 28 ga. or .410 bore models will be available in 2006. Please contact the Beretta Gallery directly for more information about this model.

✳ *SO-10 EELL Special* - top-of-the-line O/U model, extra engraving.

Prices for single guns, depending on the amount of engraving, range from $96,500 - $300,000. Pairs are available from $212,000 to $400,000, depending on the amount of engraving. Please contact the Beretta Gallery directly for more information regarding availability and options.

GIUBILEO - 12 or 20 ga., 28, 30, or 32 in. barrels with Optima chokes, premium walnut oil finished stock and checkered forearm, coin finished boxlock engraved action with sideplates, scroll engraved receiver with P. Beretta logo, single trigger, available in Sporting configuration and combo, 6.6 - 7.3 lbs. New 2007.

MSR $14,000	$12,750	$10,250	$8,750	$7,800	$6,900	$6,000	$5,000

SHOTGUNS: SxS, RECENT MFG.

Subtract 20% on the following factory multi-choke models if w/o newer Beretta Optima-chokes (12 ga. only, became standard 2003).

MODEL 409 PB - 12, 16, 20, or 28 ga., 27, 28, and 30 in. barrels, various chokes, double triggers, plain extractors, checkered pistol grip stock. Mfg. 1934-1964.

12 or 16 ga.	$825	$725	$625	$550	$495	$440	$385
20 ga.	$1,250	$1,100	$975	$850	$775	$700	$625
28 ga.	$1,675	$1,400	$1,175	$925	$825	$750	$650

MODEL 410 E - higher quality, auto ejector version of 409 PB.

12 ga.	$1,275	$1,000	$895	$775	$675	$575	$475
20 ga.	$1,750	$1,550	$1,275	$1,000	$895	$775	$675
28 ga.	$3,775	$3,300	$2,800	$2,275	$1,800	$1,450	$1,100

MODEL 410 - similar to 410 E, except 10 ga. Mag., 32 in. barrel, full choke, heavier construction. Mfg. 1934-81.

	$1,200	$995	$880	$795	$700	$625	$550

MODEL 411 E - similar to 409 PB, with false sideplates and finer finishing. Mfg. 1934-64.

12 ga.	$2,000	$1,750	$1,350	$1,050	$895	$775	$675
20 ga.	$2,750	$2,325	$1,750	$1,300	$1,000	$895	$775
28 ga.	$4,250	$3,775	$3,300	$2,800	$2,275	$1,800	$1,450

MODEL 424-426 - 12 and 20 ga. (Model 426 only), 26 and 28 in. barrels, various chokes, boxlock, extractors, double triggers, light engraving, checkered straight stock.

	$1,195	$1,095	$975	$875	$750	$650	$600

Add $115 for Model 426.
Add 25% for 20 ga.

GRADING - PPGS™	100%	98%	95%	90%	80%	70%	60%

MODEL 426 E - similar to 424, with auto ejectors, SST, select wood and more intricate engraving, silver pigeon inlay. Disc. 1983.

	100%	98%	95%	90%	80%	70%	60%
	$1,495	$1,300	$1,200	$1,075	$850	$775	$675

MODEL 625 - 12 or 20 ga., 26-30 in. barrels, various chokes, boxlock, extractors, DTs or SST, light engraving, checkered straight stock. Imported 1984-86.

	$1,000	$925	$850	$775	$650	$600	$550

Last MSR was $835.

Add 25% for 20 ga.
Add 15% for SST.

MODEL GR-2 - 12 or 20 ga., 26 and 28 in. barrels, various chokes, boxlock, extractors, double triggers, checkered pistol grip stock. Mfg. 1968-76.

	$900	$800	$700	$600	$400	$330	$275

Add 25% for 20 ga.

MODEL GR-3 - similar to GR-2, with select wood and more engraving. Mfg. 1968-1976.

	$1,095	$995	$800	$550	$475	$425	$375

Add 25% for 20 ga.

MODEL GR-4 - similar to GR-3, with auto ejectors. Mfg. 1968-1976.

	$1,300	$1,200	$1,075	$900	$775	$675	$600

Add 25% for 20 ga.

SILVER HAWK - 12 ga. Mag. (3 in. chambers) or 10 ga. Mag. (3 1/2 chambers) with double triggers and extractors. Disc. 1967.

	$795	$700	$600	$400	$300	$275	$250

Subtract 10% for 10 ga.

SILVER HAWK FEATHERWEIGHT - 12, 16, 20, or 28 ga., 26-32 in. barrels, high solid rib, various chokes, single or double triggers, checkered pistol grip stock, beavertail forearm. Disc. 1967.

	100%	98%	95%	90%	80%	70%	60%
Double trigger	$800	$700	$600	$450	$400	$350	$300
Single trigger	$900	$800	$700	$550	$500	$450	$400

Add 25% for 20 ga.
Add 50% for 28 ga.

MODEL 470 SILVER HAWK (RECENT MFG.) - 12 or 20 ga., 3 in. chambers, 26 or 28 in. barrels with choice of fixed or multi-chokes (new 1999), satin chrome receiver finish, selector lever on forearm allows either automatic ejection or mechanical extraction, straight grip stock with matte finish, 5.9 or 6 1/2 lbs. Mfg. 1998-2002.

	$1,950	$1,700	$1,475	$1,300	$1,175	$1,025	$875

Last MSR was $2,596.

Add 15% for 20 ga.
Add $130 for multi-chokes (new 1999).

MODEL 470 EL - 12 or 20 ga., 3 in. chambers, 26 (20 ga. only) or 28 in. barrels with Optima-Chokes (12 ga. only) or MC3 multichokes, case colored boxlock receiver with 4 gold inlays (doves and ducks) on sideplates, selector lever on forearm allows either automatic ejection or mechanical extraction, deluxe straight grip stock and splinter forearm with oil finish, 5.9 or 6 1/2 lbs. Mfg. 2002-2006.

	$4,500	$4,350	$4,000	$3,750	$3,550	$3,200	$2,800

Last MSR was $6,495.

This model is available only through select Beretta Showcase dealers.

MODEL 471 SILVER HAWK - 12 or 20 ga., 3 in. chambers, 26 or 28 in. barrels with multi-chokes or Optima-Chokes, engraved satin chrome or color case hardened receiver finish, selector lever on forearm allows either automatic ejection or mechanical extraction, ST, choice of straight grip or pistol grip stock with matte finish, beavertail or splinter forearm (fixed chokes only), 5.9 or 6 1/2 lbs. New 2003.

MSR $3,750	$3,325	$2,700	$2,275	$1,875	$1,600	$1,400	$1,100

> Add $625 for color case hardened frame with straight grip stock and splinter forearm (IC/IM fixed chokes only)

MODEL 471 EL - 12 or 20 ga., 3 in. chambers, 26 or 28 in. VR barrels, color case hardened receiver with gold accents, satin finished wood. New 2005.

MSR $8,350	$7,150	$6,000	$4,950	$4,250	$3,650	$3,150	$2,750

MODEL 626 FIELD - 12 or 20 (disc. 1987) ga., 2 3/4 in. chambers, 26 and 28 in. barrels, various chokes, boxlock, ejectors, single trigger, moderate engraving, pistol grip or straight checkered stock. Imported 1984-88.

	$1,195	$1,050	$875	$795	$675	$600	$550

Last MSR was $995.

> Add 25% for 20 ga.

MODEL 626 ONYX - 12 or 20 ga., 3 in. chambers, 26 or 28 (new 1990) in. VR barrels with multi-chokes, matte finished metal parts, select checkered walnut stock and forearm. Imported 1988-93.

	$1,650	$1,350	$1,100	$925	$825	$750	$650

Last MSR was $1,870.

✷ *Model 626 Onyx Magnum* - 12 ga. only, 3 1/2 in. chambers. Mfg. 1990-92.

	$1,650	$1,250	$1,050	$925	$825	$750	$650

Last MSR was $1,870.

MODEL 627 EL FIELD - 12 and 20 (disc. 1987) ga., 2 3/4 (disc. 1990) or 3 in. (became standard in 1991) chambers, 26 and 28 in. barrels, various chokes, boxlock, ejectors, single trigger, extensive engraving, pistol grip or straight checkered stock, cased. Imported 1985-93.

	$2,250	$2,000	$1,800	$1,500	$1,275	$1,000	$900

Last MSR was $3,270.

> Subtract 10% for fixed chokes and 2 3/4 in. chambers.
> Add 25% for 20 ga.

✷ *Model 627 EL Sport* - similar to Model 627 EL Field, except 12 ga. only, knurled rib, sporting clays dimensions. Importation disc. 1988.

	$2,500	$2,200	$1,900	$1,625	$1,350	$1,100	$925

Last MSR was $1,995.

> Add 10% for 20 ga.

MODEL 627 EELL - 12 or 20 (disc. 1987) ga., 2 3/4 (disc.) or 3 (12 ga. only) in. chambers, 26 or 28 in. barrels, various chokes, boxlock, ejectors, single trigger, elaborate engraving, pistol grip or straight English checkered stock, cased. Imported 1985-1993.

	$4,300	$3,675	$3,150	$2,700	$2,350	$1,975	$1,825

Last MSR was $5,405.

> Add 10% for 20 ga.
> Add 10% for 28 in. barrels.
> Subtract 10% if fixed chokes only.

Multi-chokes became standard in 1991.

SHOTGUNS: SxS, CUSTOM GRADE

Current Custom grade Beretta O/U and SxS shotguns are sold only by premium grade franchised Beretta dealers. For a listing of these dealers, contact a Beretta Gallery (see Trademark Index).

GRADING - PPGS™	100%	98%	95%	90%	80%	70%	60%

Where applicable, Beretta's new SST, with selector switch built into safety, is more desirable than older manufacture utilizing the disc. single, non-selective trigger. Also, hand chased engraving on earlier mfg. (can be denoted by engraver's signature next to trigger guard) is more desirable, and may add a 10% premium, depending on condition.

MODEL 450 SERIES - 12 ga. only, built to individual customer order, various levels of engraving. Disc.

   ✳ *Model 450 EL* - incorporates H&H type sidelocks.

	$8,000	$7,350	$5,900	$5,350	$4,750	$4,200	$3,600

   ✳ *Model 450 EELL* - features third fastener with H&H type sidelocks.

	$9,995	$8,000	$7,500	$6,000	$5,500	$4,850	$4,300

SO-1 - 12 ga. only, entry level sidelock model with light engraving, ejectors, DT standard, cased with accessories. Mfg. 1934-disc.

	$2,750	$2,300	$2,000	$1,800	$1,600	$1,400	$1,250

SO-2 - 12 ga. only, similar to the SO-1 except has movable Monobloc shoulders and fore-end, an engraved release lever, and English-style engraving. Mfg. 1930s-disc.

	$3,750	$3,350	$3,000	$2,800	$2,575	$2,200	$1,995

SO-3 - 12 ga. only, similar to the SO-2 except does not have swivels and plastic buttplate; instead has select walnut stock/forearm, floral motif engraving, and hand-finished diamond checkering. Mfg. 1930s-disc.

	$4,300	$3,950	$3,600	$3,000	$2,700	$2,400	$2,100

   ✳ *SO-3 EL* - similar to the SO-3 except has superior engraving, specially selected walnut, detachable sidelocks, simple screw takedown, and matted hand-knurled ventilated rib. Mfg. circa 1930s-disc.

	$4,995	$4,400	$4,000	$3,600	$3,200	$2,800	$2,400

   ❖ *SO-3 EELL* - similar to the SO-3 EL except has gold-plated interior parts, trigger, and locking pin, ivory bead front sight, and best quality engraving signed by artist. Mfg. 1930s-disc.

	$5,650	$5,100	$4,750	$4,200	$3,750	$3,250	$2,700

SO-4 - standard engraving motifs and custom stock dimensions, DT standard. Mfg. 1968-mid-1980s.

	$4,400	$4,000	$3,650	$3,050	$2,750	$2,450	$2,100

SO-6 - same general specifications and embellishments as the SO series O/U guns, but SxS, removable sidelocks, elaborate scroll engraving, cased with accessories. Mfg. 1988-disc.

	$7,250	$6,500	$5,925	$5,300	$4,700	$4,250	$3,850

   ✳ *SO-6 EELL* - similar to the SO-6 except has master engraved floral and traditional game scene, finest burl walnut. Mfg. 1988-disc.

	$8,250	$7,250	$6,300	$5,500	$5,000	$4,500	$4,000

SO-7 - top of the line SxS, finest quality wood, more elaborate engraving. Disc.

	$8,950	$7,950	$6,875	$6,000	$5,250	$4,600	$4,000

MODEL 451 SERIES - 12 ga., totally hand-made, sidelock action, ejectors, scroll engraving. Custom made to order with fitted luggage case, various grades have increasing embellishments in EL Models.

   ✳ *Model 451* - disc. 1987.

	$6,250	$5,500	$4,875	$4,600	$4,300	$3,995	$3,600

Last MSR was $12,375.

   ✳ *Model 451 E* - 12 ga. only, double triggers, specifications furnished by individual customer. Limited importation since 1989.

MSR $7,250	$6,750	$6,200	$5,500	$4,750	$4,000	$3,500	$2,750

   Add approx. 40% for extra set of barrels.
   Add $750 for SST (disc.).

GRADING - PPGS™	100%	98%	95%	90%	80%	70%	60%

✳ *Model 451 EL* - limited importation, temporarily disc. 1984.
  MSR $15,250 — $14,500 $7,750 $6,750 $5,600 $5,000 $4,500 $4,100

✳ *Model 451 EELL* - top-of-the-line for Model 451, choice of engraving motifs per customer specifications. Disc. 1987, reintroduced 1989.
  MSR $18,500 — $16,750 $8,500 $7,500 $6,500 $5,750 $5,150 $4,600

MODEL 452 CUSTOM - 12 ga. only, next to top-of-the-line side-by side shotgun featuring H&H style detachable locks, built to customer's specifications, leather cased. New 1990.
  MSR $35,000 — $28,750 $15,750 $11,750 $8,750 $6,650 $5,500 $4,500
  Add $6,275 for extra set of barrels.

✳ *Model 452 EELL Custom* - 12 ga. only, top-of-the-line custom sidelock model featuring every refinement, built to customer's specifications, leather cased. Importation began 1992.
  MSR $46,500 — $38,950 $21,000 $15,750 $11,750 $9,000 $6,750 $5,600
  Add $6,275 for extra set of barrels.
  Add approx. $8,500-$43,500 for special master engraving options.

MODEL 470 EL CUSTOM - 12 or 20 ga., mfg. by Beretta's custom shop per individual order, custom case hardened frame with 24Kt. bird inlays, upgraded wood with oil finish. New 1999.
  MSR $9,350 — $8,250 $7,000 $5,750 $3,600 $2,800 $2,300 $1,800

MODEL JUBILEE II (MODEL 470 EELL) - 12 or 20 ga., scroll or game scene engraving signed by the engraver, select SO quality wood with Tru-oil finish, includes suede case, also available in pairs. New 1999.
  MSR $15,250 — $13,750 $9,250 $7,750 $6,250 $5,250 $4,750 $3,950
  Pairs are available in this model for $35,075.
  This model was designated the Model 470 EELL through 1999.

GIUBILEO II - 12 or 20 ga., 3 in. chambers, 26 or 28 in. barrels with fixed chokes, oil finished premium English straight grip style walnut stock and checkered forearm, coin finished engraved boxlock action with sideplates, scroll and floral engraving, 6 1/2 lbs. New 2007.
  MSR $15,250 — $13,950 $11,500 $9,500 $8,000 $6,500 $5,750 $4,950

SHOTGUNS: SINGLE BARREL, DISC.

MARK II TRAP - 12 ga., 32 or 34 in. wide vent. rib, full choke, boxlock with auto ejector, Monte Carlo stock, recoil pad. Mfg. 1972-76.
  $495 $425 $400 $360 $330 $295 $260

MODEL FS-1 SINGLE BARREL - 12, 16, 20, 28 ga., or .410 bore, 26 or 28 in. barrels, full choke, checkered semi-pistol grip, under lever break open, folds to length of barrel (also known as Companion).
  $175 $150 $125 $110 $100 $90 $80
  Subtract 20% for 12 ga.

TR-1 TRAP - 12 ga., 32 in. full choke barrel, under lever break open, Monte Carlo pistol grip stock with pad, engraved. Mfg. 1968-71.
  $275 $250 $220 $195 $140 $110 $100

TR-2 TRAP - similar to TR-1, with high rib. Mfg. 1969-73.
  $290 $260 $230 $205 $150 $120 $110

MODEL 412 - 12, 20, 28 ga., or .410 bore, monobloc construction, folding action, sling swivels, checkered walnut stock and forearm, 5 lbs. Importation disc. 1988.
  $190 $170 $125 $100 $85 $70 $60
  Last MSR was $215.

GRADING - PPGS™	100%	98%	95%	90%	80%	70%	60%

VANDALIA SPECIAL TRAP - 12 ga., sidelock action with crossbolt, fixed choke, coin finished receiver, light scroll hand engraving with borders, cased with accessories, never offically introduced or released commercially. 6 mfg. circa 1997.

	$4,600	$3,850	$3,150	$2,500	$2,180	$1,965	$1,565

SHOTGUNS: SLIDE ACTION, MFG. 1960-1996

MODEL SL-2 - 12 ga., 26, 28, or 30 in. barrels, various chokes, vent. rib, checkered pistol grip stock. Mfg. 1968-71.

	$300	$275	$250	$220	$195	$165	$140

SILVER PIGEON - 12 ga., various chokes, light engraving.

	$250	$200	$175	$160	$150	$140	$130

GOLD PIGEON - 12 ga., various chokes, vent. rib, engraved.

	$475	$375	$310	$275	$240	$215	$195

Add $200 for deluxe models.

RUBY PIGEON - 12 ga., various chokes, vent. rib, elaborately engraved, special deluxe walnut.

	$600	$475	$395	$350	$295	$260	$230

SHOTGUNS: SEMI-AUTO

It is possible on some of the following models to have production variances occur including different engraving motifs, stock configurations and specifications, finishes, etc. These have occurred when Beretta changed from production of one model to another. Also, some European and English distributors have sold their excess inventory through Beretta U.S.A., creating additional variations/configurations that are not normally imported domestically. While sometimes rare, these specimens typically do not command premiums over Beretta's domestic models.

The following Beretta semi-auto models have been listed in numerical sequence, if possible, disregarding any alphabetical suffix or prefix.

BERETTA CHOKES AND THEIR CODES (ON REAR LEFT-SIDE OF BARREL)

* designates full choke (F).

** designates improved modified choke (IM).

*** designates modified choke (M).

**** designates improved cylinder choke (IC).

SK designates skeet (SK).

***** designates cylinder bore (CYL).

Note: values are for unaltered guns.

Subtract 10% on the following factory multi-choke models if w/o newer Beretta Optima-chokes (12 ga. only, became standard 2003).

MODEL 60 - 12 ga., 2 3/4 in. chamber, gas operated with piston rod, 3 shot mag., 24, 26, or 28 in. plain barrel, approx. 7 lbs. Mfg. 1956-1960.

	$295	$260	$240	$220	$200	$185	$170

Add 10% for Model 60 Deluxe with special embellishments.

MODEL 61 - 12 ga., improved version of the Model 60 with recoil spring located in stock, chromium plated action and fine engraving, 24, 26, or 28 in. VR barrel. Mfg. approx. 1961-1965.

	$335	$295	$260	$235	$210	$195	$175

SILVER LARK - 12 ga., various chokes.

	$295	$260	$240	$220	$200	$185	$170

GOLD LARK - 12 ga., vent. rib, light scroll engraving, select walnut.

	$480	$400	$325	$260	$230	$210	$195

RUBY LARK - 12 ga., vent. rib, heavy engraving, deluxe walnut.

	$675	$550	$475	$395	$350	$295	$260

GRADING - PPGS™	100%	98%	95%	90%	80%	70%	60%

MODEL AL-1 - 12 and 20 ga., semi-auto gas operated, 26, 28, and 30 in. plain barrel, various chokes, checkered pistol grip stock. Mfg. 1971-73.

| | $385 | $360 | $330 | $305 | $250 | $195 | $165 |

MODEL AL-2 - 12 or 20 ga., 26, 28, or 30 in. barrels, vent. rib, various chokes, gas operated, checkered pistol grip stock. Mfg. 1973-75.

| | $330 | $305 | $275 | $250 | $220 | $195 | $165 |

MODEL AL-2 SKEET - similar to AL-2, with 26 in. wide rib skeet bored barrel. Mfg. 1973-75.

| | $395 | $360 | $320 | $275 | $220 | $200 | $185 |

MODEL AL-2 TRAP - similar to AL-2, with 30 in. full choke barrel, wide rib, Monte Carlo stock, with recoil pad. Mfg. 1973-75.

| | $375 | $345 | $315 | $285 | $250 | $195 | $165 |

MODEL AL-2 MAGNUM - 12 or 20 ga., 3 in. chamber, heavier action bar, 28 and 30 in. mod. or full choke. Mfg. 1973-75.

| | $415 | $385 | $330 | $275 | $250 | $230 | $210 |

MODEL AL-3 - continuation of the AL-2 series. Mfg. 1975-1976.

	100%	98%	95%	90%	80%	70%	60%
Field grade	$395	$360	$330	$260	$240	$220	$190
Magnum grade	$395	$350	$300	$275	$250	$230	$210
Skeet grade	$400	$360	$330	$260	$240	$220	$190
Trap grade	$385	$350	$295	$250	$225	$210	$185

MODEL AL-3 DELUXE TRAP - similar to AL-3, with fully engraved receiver, premium grade wood. Mfg. 1975-76.

| | $600 | $550 | $500 | $450 | $425 | $400 | $375 |

MODEL UGB25 XCEL TRAP - 12 ga., 2 3/4 in. chamber, unique two shot (second shell is located outside receiver on cartridge carrier), break open action featuring short recoil operating system, rising lock block system, light alloy black receiver with gold lettering, 30 or 32 in. three alloy steel barrel with Optima-Bore, competition front sight, laser-checkered walnut stock with adj. comb, gold trigger, button safety, Gel-tek recoil pad, 7.7-9 lbs. Prototypes were introduced late 2004, but regular production started late 2007.

| MSR $3,875 | $3,350 | $2,650 | $2,275 | $1,950 | $1,700 | $1,500 | $1,300 |

MODEL ES100 PINTAIL (VITTORIA) - 12 ga., 3 in. chamber, uses Montefeltro short action, 24, 26, or 28 (new 1999) in. VR barrel, matte black metal finish, choice of matte finished wood (disc. 1998) or black synthetic stock and forearm (new 1999), includes sling swivels, 7.3 lbs. Mfg. 1993-2001, reintroduced 2003 only.

| | $425 | $400 | $375 | $350 | $325 | $275 | $250 |

Last MSR was $682.

In 1999, this model was renamed the ES 100 Pintail (with synthetic stock).

* *Model ES100 Camouflage* - 12 ga. only, features 100% Advantage Wetlands, Realtree Hardwoods HD (new 2003), or Mossy Oak Shadowgrass (new 2003) coverage, 28 in. VR barrel only, 7.3 lbs. Mfg. 2000-2003.

| | $450 | $400 | $375 | $330 | $280 | $250 | $230 |

Last MSR was $777.

* *Model ES100 Rifled Slug (Pintail Rifled Slug)* - 12 ga., 3 in. chamber, 24 in. rifled barrel with drilled and tapped upper receiver, barrel and upper receiver are permanently joined, anti-glare matte black metal finish, choice of matte finished wood (disc. 1998) or black synthetic (new 1999) stock and forearm, includes swivels, 7 lbs. Mfg. 1998-2001, reintroduced 2003 only.

| | $495 | $425 | $375 | $330 | $280 | $250 | $230 |

Last MSR was $749.

Add $148 for combo package (includes extra 28 in. smooth bore barrel with MC3 choke, mfg. 2001).
In 1999, the model nomenclature changed from Pintail Rifled Slug to ES100 Rifled Slug.

GRADING - PPGS™	100%	98%	95%	90%	80%	70%	60%

✳ *Model ES100 Pintail Slug (Vittoria)* - 12 ga. only, 24 in. slug barrel, includes rifle sights and rifle choke tubes, 7 lbs. Imported 1993-95.

	$495	$425	$375	$325	$280	$250	$230

Last MSR was $700.

✳ *Model ES100 NWTF Special Camouflage (Pintail)* - 12 ga. only, 24 in. VR barrel with 3 dot TruGlo fiberoptic sight system, includes Briley extended extra-full choke tube and 3 standard Mobilchoke tubes, features Mossy Oak Break-up treatment on synthetic stock and forearm, black matte anti-glare finish on metal components, includes nylon sling. Limited mfg. 1999, reintroduced 2002 only (limited mfg.).

	$600	$550	$475	$375	$325	$290	$265

Last MSR was $966.

MODEL 300/301 - continuation of the AL-3 series, scroll engraved receiver. Mfg. approx. 1968-82.

	100%	98%	95%	90%	80%	70%	60%
Field grade	$395	$360	$330	$260	$240	$220	$190
Magnum grade	$395	$385	$330	$275	$250	$230	$210
Skeet grade	$395	$360	$330	$260	$240	$220	$190
Trap grade	$385	$350	$295	$250	$225	$210	$185

Beretta changed model nomenclature rapidly during the Model 300 Series. In approx. 10 months, the evolution of this model had progressed from the 300 to 303 Series. Beginning with the Model 303, all receivers were milled with a 3 in. ejection port window.

MODEL 301 SLUG GUN - 22 in. barrel, with sights. Disc.

	$395	$360	$330	$305	$265	$230	$190

MODEL 302 - 12 or 20 ga., self-compensating gas operation semi-auto, designed for both 2 3/4 and 3 in. shells, available with interchangeable chokes, slug barrel, trap and skeet models (disc.), VR, mag. cut-off. Mfg. 1982-87. This model was superceded by the Model 303.

	$395	$365	$340	$310	$280	$255	$225

Last MSR was $480.

Add $30 for multi-choke set.

✳ *Model 302 Super Lusso* - same specifications as Model A302, but includes hand engraved receiver, many gold plated parts, and stock and forearm made from presentation grade walnut. Disc. 1986.

	$1,700	$1,500	$1,250	$1,025	$900	$800	$700

Last MSR was $2,500.

MODEL A-303 FIELD - 12 (disc. 1993) or 20 ga., 2 3/4 or 3 in. chambers, same gas operation as the Model 302, 26 or 28 in. VR barrel, high-strength alloy receiver, select wood with choice pistol grip or straight English stock, beavertail forearm, multi-chokes became standard 1987. Disc. 1996.

	$450	$400	$375	$335	$300	$270	$240

Last MSR was $799.

Subtract 20% if without multi-chokes.
Subtract $20 for straight grip English stock.

✳ *Model A-303 Upland* - 12 (disc. 1993) or 20 ga., 2 3/4 or 3 in. chamber, 24 in. VR barrel with multi-chokes, English style straight stock, approx. 7 lbs. Importation began 1989. Disc. 1996.

	$450	$400	$380	$335	$300	$270	$240

Last MSR was $772.

✳ *Model A-303 Waterfowl/Turkey* - 12 ga. only, 3 in. chamber, choice of 24, 26, 28, or 30 in. VR barrel, matte finished wood and metal, multi-chokes are standard. Imported 1991 only.

	$450	$400	$380	$335	$300	$270	$240

Last MSR was $665.

GRADING - PPGS™	100%	98%	95%	90%	80%	70%	60%

✴ *Model A-303 Sporting* - 12 (disc. 1994) or 20 (new 1991) ga. only, 2 3/4 in. chambers, sporting clay dimensions, 28 or 30 (12 ga. only) in. VR barrel with multi-chokes. Mfg. 1988-96.

	$495	$450	$425	$375	$325	$300	$275

Last MSR was $822.

Subtract 10% for 28 in. barrel.

✴ *Model A-303 Skeet* - 12 (disc. 1994) or 20 ga., 26 in. VR barrel with fixed skeet choking. Importation disc. 1995.

	$400	$375	$350	$315	$275	$250	$225

Last MSR was $736.

✴ *Model A-303 Super Skeet* - 12 ga. only, 28 in. VR fixed choke barrel, features factory porting, adj. LOP, and adj. separate cheekpiece on stock. Mfg. 1991-92.

	$425	$375	$350	$315	$280	$240	$200

Last MSR was $1,160.

✴ *Model A-303 Trap* - 12 ga. only, 30 or 32 in. VR barrel with fixed choking or multi-chokes. Importation disc. 1994.

	$450	$400	$380	$350	$325	$300	$275

Last MSR was $735.

Add $40 for multi-chokes (with Monte Carlo stock).

✴ *Model A-303 Super Trap* - 12 ga. only, 30 or 32 in. VR multi-choke barrel with step tapered rib, features factory porting, adj. LOP, and adj. separate cheek-piece on stock. Mfg. 1991-92.

	$550	$525	$500	$450	$425	$365	$300

Last MSR was $1,210.

✴ *Model A-303 Slug* - 12 or 20 ga., 3 in. chamber (12 ga. only), 22 in. cylinder bore barrel, iron sights. Importation disc. 1991.

	$395	$350	$325	$300	$275	$265	$240

Last MSR was $665.

✴ *Model A-303 Youth* - 20 ga. only, 2 3/4 or 3 (disc.) in. chamber, 24 in. VR barrel with multi-chokes, shortened stock, approx. 6 lbs. Mfg. 1988-96.

	$400	$375	$350	$325	$300	$270	$240

Last MSR was $772.

MODEL A304 LARK - 12 ga., 2 3/4 in. chamber, 20 (Silver Slug), 22 (Silver Slug), 24, 26, 28, or 30 in. barrel, vent. rib (except Silver Slug model), Mobilchoke or cylinder (Silver Slug) bore, ambidextrous safety, crossbolt, checkered walnut pistol grip stock and semi-beavertail forend, black recoil pad, black matte finished receiver with light scroll work, gold trigger, available in Silver Lark, Silver Slug, or Gold Lark. Mfg. 1994-disc.

	$450	$400	$375	$335	$300	$270	$240

Add 10% for Silver Lark with scroll engraved black receiver.
Add 20% for White or Black A304 Gold Lark Model with gold filled P. Beretta signature and game scene engraving.

MODEL AL390 FIELD SILVER MALLARD - 12 or 20 (new 1997) ga. only, 3 in. chamber, features new gas system that will accept all 2 3/4 and 3 in. shotshells, single stainless steel piston with self regulating valve, mag. cut-off on left side of receiver, 22 slug (12 ga. only, new 1994), 24, 26, 28, or 30 (12 ga. only) in. VR barrel with Mobilchoke system, choice of gloss or matte (includes sling swivels) wood finish on lightly engraved receiver, adj. checkered walnut stock, gold trigger, 6.4 (20 ga.) or 7.2 (12 ga.) lbs. Mfg. 1992-99.

	$495	$450	$415	$350	$300	$270	$240

Last MSR was $860.

Add $25 for 20 ga.
Subtract $25 for 24 in. barrel.

Beginning 1997, Beretta introduced the "AL" Series of the 390, which is the lightweight variation of the 390. Prior to 1997, this model was designated the A390 Series.

GRADING - PPGS™	100%	98%	95%	90%	80%	70%	60%

* **Model AL390 Field Deluxe Gold Mallard** - similar to Model 390 Field, except has gold accents on receiver frame, including a gold inlaid snipe, setter, and P. Beretta signature, deluxe walnut, 7.2 lbs. Mfg. 1993-99.

	$595	$550	$460	$400	$360	$320	$285

Last MSR was $1,025.

    Add $30 for 20 ga.

* **Model AL390 Lioness Limited Edition** - 12 ga. only, 28 in. VR barrel with MC3 choke tubes, deluxe checkered walnut stock and forearm. Limited mfg. 2002.

	$2,450	$1,950	$1,600	$1,410	$1,160	$980	$800

Last MSR was $2,969.

* **Model AL390 Silver Mallard Synthetic** - 12 ga. only, 3 in. chamber, 24, 26, 28, or 30 in. barrel with multi-choke, black synthetic stock and forearm with sling swivels, matte finish, approx. 7.2 lbs. Mfg. 1996-99.

	$450	$425	$400	$350	$300	$270	$240

Last MSR was $885.

* **Model AL390 Silver Mallard Camouflage** - 12 ga. only, 3 in. chamber, Advantage camo finish on entire gun, 24 or 28 in. VR barrel with choke tubes, synthetic stock and forearm, 7.2 lbs. Mfg. 1997-99.

	$450	$425	$400	$375	$300	$270	$240

Last MSR was $1,020.

* **Model AL390 Silver Mallard Slug** - 12 ga. only, 3 in. chamber, 22 in. non-rifled barrel with slug choke, gloss wood finish, adj. rear sight, approx. 6.8 or 7.4 (Model A390) lbs. Mfg. 1995-97.

	$450	$425	$400	$350	$300	$270	$240

Last MSR was $860.

* **Model AL390 Silver Mallard Youth** - 20 ga. only, 3 in. chamber, gloss wood finish, 24 in. VR barrel only with choke tubes, features youth stock dimensions, 6.4 lbs. Mfg. 1997-99.

	$450	$425	$400	$350	$300	$270	$240

Last MSR was $885.

* **Model AL390 NWTF Special Camouflage** - 12 ga. only, 3 in. chamber, 24 in. VR barrel with 3 dot TruGlo fiber optic sight system, includes Briley extended extra-full choke tube and 3 standard Mobilchoke tubes, full Realtree X-tra Brown camo treatment (including synthetic stock and forearm), includes camo nylon sling. Special Edition released during 1999 only.

	$525	$500	$475	$450	$425	$400	$375

Last MSR was $1,105.

❖ **Model AL390 NWTF Special Synthetic** - similar to NWTF Special Camouflage, except has matte black anti-glare finish. Mfg. 1999 only.

	$495	$450	$400	$365	$315	$275	$240

Last MSR was $970.

* **Model AL390 NWTF Special Youth** - 20 ga. only, 3 in. chamber, 24 in. barrel, shorter stock dimensions with 13 1/2 LOP, matte finished wood stock and forearm, matte black metal anti-glare finish. Mfg. 1999 only.

	$525	$500	$425	$350	$300	$270	$240

Last MSR was $910.

MODEL AL390 SPORT SPORTING - 12 or 20 (new 1997) ga., 3 in. chamber, designed for sporting clays competition, similar to Model 390 Sport Skeet, 28 or 30 (12 ga. only) in. VR ported or unported barrel with choke tube, 6.8 (20 ga.) or 7.6 (12 ga.) lbs. Imported 1995-99.

	$495	$450	$425	$400	$325	$275	$240

Last MSR was $925.

GRADING - PPGS™	100%	98%	95%	90%	80%	70%	60%

❋ *Model AL390 Sport Sporting Collection* - 12 or 20 (Youth Model) ga., 3 in. chamber, 26 (20 ga. only), 28 in. VR barrel with multi-choke, features multi-colored, gloss finished stock and forearm, 6.7 (20 ga.) or 7.6 (12 ga.) lbs. Mfg. 1998-99.

	$525	$475	$450	$400	$325	$275	$240

Last MSR was $965.

The 20 ga. in this model is a youth model with 13 1/2 LOP.

❋ *Model AL390 Sport Sporting Gold* - 12 ga. only, 28 or 30 in. VR barrel with multi-chokes, gloss finished wood, gold engraved receiver, 7.6 lbs. Mfg. 1997-99.

	$725	$650	$575	$525	$495	$460	$425

Last MSR was $1,145.

Subtract 10% for 28 in. barrel.

❋ *Model AL390 Sport Sporting Diamond* - 12 ga. only, 3 in. chamber, silver sided receiver with multiple gold inlays, EELL quality stock and forearm with oil finish, matte 28 or 30 in. barrel with multi-chokes, oval nameplate on stock, 7.6 lbs. Mfg. 1998-99.

	$2,000	$1,650	$1,450	$1,275	$1,200	$995	$825

Last MSR was $3,075.

Subtract 10% for 26 in. barrel.

❋ *Model AL390 Sport Sporting Youth* - 20 ga. only, 3 in. chamber, matte finished checkered stock and forearm, 26 in. VR barrel only with choke tubes, features youth stock dimensions (13 1/2 LOP), 6.7 lbs. Imported 1997-98 only.

	$500	$475	$450	$375	$300	$270	$240

Last MSR was $900.

MODEL AL390 SPORT SKEET - 12 ga. only, 3 in. chamber, 26 (disc.) or 28 in. SK bored VR barrel, matte finish on wood and metal, black rubber recoil pad, 7.6 lbs. Imported 1995-99.

	$425	$400	$375	$350	$300	$270	$240

Last MSR was $890.

❋ *Model AL390 Sport Super Skeet* - 12 ga. only, 28 in. skeet choke VR ported barrels, includes adj. stock comb and LOP (using 3 different recoil pads) approx. 8.1 lbs. Mfg. 1993-99.

	$495	$450	$400	$375	$300	$270	$240

Last MSR was $1,160.

MODEL AL390 SPORT TRAP - 12 ga. only, 3 in. chamber, 30 or 32 in. VR barrel, matte finish on wood and metal, black rubber recoil pad, 7.8 or 8 1/4 (A390) lbs. Imported 1995-99.

	$495	$450	$400	$375	$300	$270	$240

Last MSR was $890.

❋ *Model AL390 Sport Trap Super* - 12 ga. only, 30 or 32 in. VR multi-choke ported barrels, adj. stock comb and LOP, approx. 8 lbs. Mfg. 1993-97.

	$600	$500	$450	$400	$375	$325	$295

Last MSR was $1,215.

MODEL AL391 URIKA - 12 or 20 ga., 3 in. chamber, features new self-compensating gas valve and receiver recoil absorber for internal shock reduction, satin finished checkered walnut stock and forearm, gas valve is located on the front bottom of the forearm, alloy receiver with thin design, cold hammer forged barrel, black anodized metal surfaces, gold trigger, beginning 2003, all 12 ga. AL391 Urika include Optima-Bore overbored barrels with flush Optima-Choke plus tubes, molded synthetic case included, 6.3-7.3 lbs. New 2000.

✳ *Model AL391 Urika Standard* - 12 or 20 ga., 24 (20 ga. only), 26, 28, or 30 (12 ga. only, disc. 2005) in. VR barrel, available in synthetic stock beginning 2004 at no charge, approx. 5.95 (20 ga.) or 7 1/4 lbs. Mfg. 2000-2006.

$940	$825	$725	$625	$500	$400	$350

Last MSR was $1,050.

✳ *Model AL391 Urika Synthetic Optima* - 12 ga. only, 24 (disc. 2003), 26, 28, or 30 (disc. 2003) in. VR barrel with matte finish, features black synthetic stock with oversized grip area for a secure grip and recoil absorption and forearm, Optima-Chokes became standard in 2004, approx. 7 1/4 lbs. Mfg. 2000-2006.

$895	$795	$695	$600	$475	$400	$350

Last MSR was $998.

Subtract 20% for Mobilchokes.

✳ *Model AL391 Urika Camouflage* - 12 ga. only, choice of 100% Hardwoods Green HD (mfg. 2003), RealTree Hardwoods HD (24 in. barrel only, turkey configuration), Max-4 HD (new 2004), or Advantage Wetlands camo (28 in. barrel only, waterfowl configuration, mfg. 2003) finish, with oversized stock grip, approx. 7 1/4 lbs. Mfg. 2000-2006.

$1,025	$825	$700	$625	$525	$425	$350

Last MSR was $1,175.

✳ *Model AL391 Urika Youth* - 20 ga. only, 24 in. VR barrel only, shortened walnut stock and regular forearm, 5.95 lbs. Mfg. 2000-2006.

$940	$825	$725	$625	$500	$400	$350

Last MSR was $1,050.

✳ *Model AL391 Urika Gold* - 12 or 20 ga., similar to Model AL391 Urika Standard, except has deluxe checkered walnut stock and forearm, choice of black (standard) or partial silver (lightweight configuration, 12 ga. only) receiver finish, multiple gold receiver inlays, 26 or 28 in. VR barrel, jewelled bolt, 5.9 (20 ga.), 6.6 (12 ga. lightweight), or approx. 7 1/4 lbs. Mfg. 2000-2002.

$795	$725	$625	$495	$400	$350	$300

Last MSR was $1,213.

✳ *Model AL391 Urika Covey Quail Unlimited* - 20 ga., matte black receiver with multiple gold quail inlays, deluxe checkered walnut stock and forearm, marked "1 of 1000." 1,000 mfg. 2003-2004.

$825	$775	$700	$650	$600	$500	$425

Last MSR was $1,336.

✳ *Model AL391 Urika Ringneck Pheasants Forever* - 12 ga., matte black receiver with multiple gold pheasant inlays, deluxe checkered walnut stock and forearm, includes Gel-Tek recoil pad and Optima-Bore chokes, marked "1 of 1000." 1,000 mfg. 2003-2004.

$995	$895	$825	$775	$675	$550	$450

Last MSR was $1,377.

MODEL AL391 URIKA SPORTING - 12 or 20 ga., 3 in. chamber, gas operating system the same as Model Al391 Urika Standard, 28 or 30 in. wide VR barrel with 2 beads, features special competition checkered walnut sporting stock with rounded solid rubber recoil pad, satin black receiver with silver markings, gold trigger, Mobilchoke tubes are standard on 20 ga., Optima-Bore chokes with flush Optima choke tubes became standard in 12 ga. during 2003 (AL391 Urika Sporting Optima), molded synthetic case included, 5.95 or 7.3 lbs. Mfg. 2000-2006.

$1,025	$825	$725	$650	$575	$475	$375

Last MSR was $1,250.

GRADING - PPGS™	100%	98%	95%	90%	80%	70%	60%

✳ *Model AL391 Urika Gold Sporting* - similar to Model AL391 Urika Gold, except has deluxe walnut stock and forearm, with choice of black (disc.) or silver receiver and gold accents. Mfg. 2000-2006.

| | $1,300 | $1,050 | $875 | $775 | $650 | $550 | $450 |

Last MSR was $1,500.

✳ *Model AL391 Urika Diamond Sporting* - 12 ga. only, 3 in. chamber, silver sided receiver with multiple gold inlays, EELL quality stock and forearm with oil finish, matte 28 in. barrel with MC4 multi-chokes, oval nameplate on stock, 7.6 lbs. Mfg. 2002 only.

| | $2,000 | $1,850 | $1,700 | $1,525 | $1,200 | $995 | $775 |

Last MSR was $3,139.

MODEL AL391 URIKA TRAP OPTIMA - 12 ga. only, 30 or 32 in. wide VR barrel with 2 beads, Monte Carlo stock with special trap recoil pad, satin black receiver with glossy side panels and silver markings, gold trigger, Optima-Bore chokes with flush Optima choke tubes became standard in 12 ga. during 2003, molded synthetic case included, 7 1/4 lbs. Mfg. 2000-2006.

| | $1,000 | $800 | $725 | $675 | $600 | $500 | $400 |

Last MSR was $1,250.

✳ *Model AL391 Urika Trap Gold* - similar to Model AL391 Urika Trap, except has black receiver with gold filled Beretta logo and P. Beretta signature, jewelled bolt and carrier, 7 1/4 lbs. Mfg. 2000-2002.

| | $995 | $850 | $725 | $565 | $450 | $415 | $395 |

Last MSR was $1,254.

MODEL AL391 URIKA PARALLEL TARGET RL/SL - 12 ga. only, similar to Model AL391 Urika Trap, except features a Monte Carlo stock with parallel comb and reduced grip radius, RL suffix designates shorter LOP and slimmer grip, molded synthetic case included, 7 1/4 lbs. Mfg. 2000-2006.

| | $995 | $825 | $725 | $675 | $600 | $500 | $400 |

Last MSR was $1,250.

MODEL AL391 TEKNYS - 12 or 20 ga., 3 in. chamber, multi-colored receiver with unique asymetrical patterns, X-tra Wood stock with Gel-Tek recoil pad, anti-glare receiver top, TruGlo Tru-bead front sight, choice of Optima-Bore or Mobilchokes (20 ga.), includes molded case with 5 choke tubes, 5.9 (20 ga.) or 7.3 (12 ga.) lbs. Imported 2003-2005.

| | $1,250 | $900 | $775 | $650 | $525 | $425 | $375 |

Last MSR was $1,425.

✳ *Model AL391 Teknys Gold* - 12 or 20 ga., 3 in. chamber, receiver has engraved hunting scenes, jewelled breech bolt and carrier, checkered deluxe walnut stock and forearm with green colored enamel inserts in rear receiver and front of stock, includes Gel-Tek recoil pad, and stock recoil reducer. Importation began 2003.

| MSR $1,825 | | $1,475 | $1,150 | $1,025 | $925 | $850 | $750 | $550 |

Add $150 for King Ranch model with ranch stable engraving and rope bordered logo (new 2006).

✳ *Model AL391 Teknys Gold Sporting* - 12 or 20 ga., similar to Model AL391 Teknys Gold, except has two-tone dark grey receiver with blue enamel inserts on stock and receiver, interchangeable rib, improved forearm checkering pattern, includes Gel-Tek recoil pad and stock recoil reducer, deluxe checkered walnut stock and forearm, includes hard case, 6.6 (20 ga.) or 7.9 (12 ga.) lbs. Importation began 2003.

| MSR $1,850 | | $1,600 | $1,225 | $1,095 | $950 | $800 | $675 | $550 |

GRADING - PPGS™	100%	98%	95%	90%	80%	70%	60%

✳ *Model AL391 Teknys Gold Trap* - 12 ga. only, 30 or 32 in. VR barrel, oil finished checkered walnut stock, gold trigger, Gel-Tek recoil pad, includes hardshell case. Importation began 2004.

MSR $1,950	$1,725	$1,325	$1,150	$1,000	$850	$725	$625

✳ *Model AL391 Teknys Gold Target* - 12 ga. only, 30 in. VR barrel with interchangable VRs and Optima-Plus choking, includes 8 1/2 oz. recoil reducer, deluxe checkered walnut stock w/adj. comb, satin nickel finished reciever with blue enamel accents on back of frame and stock. New 2007.

MSR $2,150	$1,850	$1,575	$1,300	$1,100	$975	$825	$725

MODEL AL391 XTREMA2 3.5 (AL 391 EXTREMA 3.5) - 12 ga. only, 3 1/2 in. chamber, features Gel-Tek recoil pad, spring mass and bolt travel recoil reducers lower felt recoil up to 20%, 24, 26, or 28 in. VR barrel with Optima-Choke Plus and Optima-Bore, gas operating system with rotating locking bolt, black synthetic stock and forearm with rubber inserts for firm control instead of traditional checkering, grooved receiver, removable trigger grip, includes carrying case, 7.8 lbs. New 2002.

MSR $1,100	$975	$850	$775	$675	$575	$500	$450

Add $500 for KO configuration (Kick-off recoil reduction).
This model's nomenclature changed to Xtrema2 during 2005.

✳ *Model AL391 Xtrema2 Camouflage (AL391 Extreme Camouflage)* - 12 ga. only, similar operating system to Model AL391 Xtrema 3.5, choice of 100% RealTree Hardwoods HD (24 in. barrel only, turkey configuration, disc. 2006), RealTree All-Purpose (new 2007), Max-4 HD (new 2004, 30 in. barrel only), Advantage Timber HD camo (26 in. barrel only, disc. 2004) or Advantage Wetlands (26 or 28 in. barrel, disc. 2004) finish, 7.8 lbs. New 2002.

MSR $1,250	$1,050	$900	$800	$675	$575	$500	$450

Add $450 for KO configuration (Kick-off recoil reduction).

✳ *Model AL391 Xtrema2 Slug* - 12 ga. only, 24 in. rifle bore barrel, Optima-Bore choke. Mfg. 2005-2007.

	$1,275	$995	$875	$775	$675	$575	$475

Last MSR was $1,450.

Add $150 for KO configuration (Kick-off recoil reduction).

MODEL AL391 URIKA 2 - 12 or 20 ga., 3 in. chamber, features an improved gas system which is both faster and self-cleaning, various configurations. New 2007.

✳ *Model AL391 Urika 2 Standard* - 12 or 20 ga., features Beretta's new proprietary X-Tra grain wood enhancement on stock and forearm, 26 or 28 in. barrel w/ choice of Optima or Mobilechokes, fine line scroll engraving on receiver.

MSR $1,300	$1,100	$875	$725	$650	$550	$450	$400

✳ *Model AL391 Urika 2 Youth* - 20 ga., 24 in. barrel, similar to Standard, except has shorter dimensions.

MSR $1,300	$1,100	$875	$725	$650	$550	$450	$400

✳ *Model AL391 Urika 2 Synthetic* - 12 ga., similar to Standard model, except features black synthetic stock, available with or w/o Kick-Off recoil reducer (two shock absorbers).

MSR $875	$795	$700	$625	$550	$475	$400	$325

Add $375 for Kick-Off recoil reduction.
Add $75 for Urika 2 Synthetic Sporting Model w/Kick-Off (new 2008).

✳ *Model AL391 Urika 2 Camo* - 12 ga., similar to Standard model, except features Advantage Max-4 or Realtree AP camo treatment, with or w/o Kick-Off recoil reducer.

MSR $975	$875	$750	$675	$600	$525	$450	$375

Add $375 for Kick-Off recoil reduction.

GRADING - PPGS™	100%	98%	95%	90%	80%	70%	60%

✳ *Model AL391 Urika 2 Gold* - 12 or 20 ga., oil finished wood stock and forend, engraved recevier with gold game bird inlays.

MSR $1,450	$1,250	$925	$775	$650	$550	$475	$425

✳ *Model AL391 Urika 2 Sporting* - 12 or 20 ga., 28 or 30 in. barrel w/either Optima (12 ga.) or Mobilechokes (20 ga.) choke tubes, features Beretta X-Tra Grain wood enhancement on stock and forearm.

MSR $1,350	$1,125	$950	$850	$725	$600	$500	$425

Add $350 for AL391 Urika 2 Gold Sporting (12 ga. only, includes gold inlays on receiver).

✳ *Model AL391 Urika 2 Parallel* - 12 ga., 28, 30, or 32 in. VR barrel with Optima-Plus choke system, X-Tra Grain wood enhancement on stock and forearm, available in RL (Youth) or SL configurations.

MSR $1,350	$1,125	$950	$850	$725	$600	$500	$425

Add $350 for AL391 Urika 2 Gold Parallel (includes gold inlays on receiver).

MODEL 1200 FIELD - 12 ga., inertia recoil system, 28 in. VR barrels with multi-chokes, checkered European walnut stock and forearm (pre-1989), matte black polymer stock and forearm (starting 1989), recoil pad, 4 shot mag., approx. 8 lbs. Imported 1984-1989.

	$375	$350	$300	$275	$250	$225	$200

Last MSR was $580.

✳ *Model 1200 Riot* - 12 ga. only, 2 3/4 or 3 in. chamber, 20 in. cyl. bore barrel with iron sights, extended mag. Imported 1989-90 only.

	$400	$375	$350	$295	$250	$225	$200

Last MSR was $660.

MODEL 1201 FIELD MAGNUM - 12 ga., 3 in. chamber, short recoil blowback action, 24, 26, or 28 in. VR barrel with multi-chokes (2), matte black polymer stock and forearm. Imported 1989-94.

	$500	$395	$340	$285	$250	$225	$200

Last MSR was $625.

The Model 1201 can be differentiated from the Model 1200 by stock spacers to adjust length.

✳ *Model 1201 FP (Riot)* - 12 ga., riot configuration featuring 18 (new 1997) or 20 (disc. 1996) in. cylinder bore barrel, 5 shot mag, choice of adj. rifle sights (disc.), Tritium sights (disc. 1998) or ghost ring (new 1999, Tritium front sight insert) sights, matte wood (disc.) or black synthetic stock and forearm, matte metal finish (disc.), 6.3 lbs. Mfg. 1991-2004.

	$725	$595	$500	$400	$300	$250	$200

Last MSR was $890.

Add $80 for Tritium sights (mfg. 1997-98).
Add $45 for pistol grip configuration (Model 1201 FPG3 - mfg. 1994 only).

MODEL AL3901 - 12 or 20 (new 2003) ga., 3 in. chamber, 24 (new 2003), 26 (new 2003), or 28 in. VR barrel with MC3 multi-chokes, choice of regular or shortened (Model AL3901RL) charcoal grey synthetic checkered wood, or Mossy Oak New Break-Up (new 2003), or Mossy Oak New Shadowgrass (new 2003) camo covered stock and forearm, gold trigger, matte metal finish, reversible crossbolt safety, 7 1/2 lbs. Mfg. 2002-2003.

	$450	$425	$375	$335	$280	$250	$230

Last MSR was $730.

Add $50 for camo finish.
This model was available through Beretta Showcase Dealers only.

GRADING - PPGS™	100%	98%	95%	90%	80%	70%	60%

MODEL 3901 SERIES - 12 or 20 ga., 3 in. chamber, 26 or 28 in. VR barrel with MC3 choke tubes, available in five configurations, including Citizen (synthetic stock), Statesman, Ambassador (X-Tra wood, disc. 2006), Target RL (12 ga. only, IC choke, shorter dimensions w/12-13 in. LOP and adj. comb, new 2006), or Rifled Slug (12 ga. only, 24 in. rifled slug barrel, new 2006), gas operating system, 26 or 28 in. steel alloy hammer forged barrel, Mobilchoke, removable trigger group, mfg. in America. New 2005.

	100%	98%	95%	90%	80%	70%	60%
MSR $750	$650	$575	$500	$425	$375	$325	$275

Add $150 for Statesman configuration.
Add $200 for Ambassador configuration (disc. 2006).
Add $150 for Target RL model.
Add $50 for Rifled Slug Model (disc. 2007).

COMMEMORATIVES

MODEL A-303 DUCKS UNLIMITED - 12 or 20 ga., D.U. serialization, 5,500 mfg. in 12 ga. 1986-87, 3,500 mfg. in 20 ga. 1987-88.

	100%	98%	95%	90%	80%	70%	60%
12 ga.	$525	$450	$350	$285	$250	$215	$185
20 ga.	$575	$475	$375	$315	$270	$230	$200

These D.U. Models had no retail pricing from Beretta. Rather, they were auctioned off at D.U. dinners, and as a result, prices could vary substantially from region to region.

MODEL 687 O/U SHOTGUN TERCENTENNIAL - 12 ga., SST and ejectors. Limited production, only 300 manufactured.

100%	98%	95%	90%	80%	70%	60%
$2,500	$1,950	$1,400	$1,235	$1,000	$870	$700

MODEL 84 PISTOL TERCENTENNIAL - commemorative, only 300 manufactured. Fully engraved with gold inlays. Presentation case. Only 100 imported to U.S.

100%	98%	95%	90%	80%	70%	60%
$1,450	$1,100	$850	$740	$620	$515	$440

BERGMANN

Previous manufacturer located in Gaggenau, Germany circa 1892-1944. Re-established in 1931 under Bergmann Erben.

100%	98%	95%	90%	80%	70%	60%	50%	40%	30%	20%	10%

PISTOLS: SEMI-AUTO

Prices established are for original guns with matching parts.

MODEL 1894 (ANTIQUE) - 8mm "Bergmann Schmeisser" cal. Extremely rare.

100%	98%	95%	90%	80%	70%	60%	50%	40%	30%	20%	10%
N/A	N/A	$18,500	$16,000	$12,000	$8,000	$7,500	$7,000	$6,500	$6,000	$5,500	$5,000

MODEL 1896-NO. 2 - 5mm cal., smaller type frame.

100%	98%	95%	90%	80%	70%	60%	50%	40%	30%	20%	10%
$3,500	$3,000	$2,500	$2,000	$1,500	$1,250	$1,000	$800	$700	$600	$550	$500

Add 50% for "folding trigger" version.

MODEL 1896-NO. 3 - 6.5mm cal. 80mm barrel.

100%	98%	95%	90%	80%	70%	60%	50%	40%	30%	20%	10%
$4,000	$3,250	$2,500	$2,250	$1,850	$1,500	$1,200	$900	$800	$700	$600	$565

Add 10% for early pistols without extractors and narrow grips.
Add 20% if hexagonal chamber.
Add 100% for target variation.

MODEL 1896-NO. 4 - 8mm cal., military contract. Rarely seen.

100%	98%	95%	90%	80%	70%	60%	50%	40%	30%	20%	10%
$4,950	$4,250	$3,500	$3,000	$2,200	$1,500	$1,200	$1,000	$900	$800	$700	$600

MODEL 1897-NO. 5 - 7.8mm cal., commercial manufacture. May be fit with shoulder stock.

100%	98%	95%	90%	80%	70%	60%	50%	40%	30%	20%	10%
$8,500	$7,000	$5,500	$4,500	$3,500	$2,500	$2,000	$1,500	$1,000	$900	$800	$700

Add 200% for long barrel carbine version.
Add 100% if fit with shoulder stock, add another 20% to total if matching stock.

100%	98%	95%	90%	80%	70%	60%	50%	40%	30%	20%	10%

BERGMANN SIMPLEX - 8mm cal., 2.7 in. barrel, 10 shot mag., scaled down design, first and most common variation has mag. release button in front of mag. housing, later and much scarcer version has push button mag. release mounted on side of frame. Mfg. circa 1901-1914.

* *Bergmann Simplex First Variation*

100%	98%	95%	90%	80%	70%	60%	50%	40%	30%	20%	10%
$3,500	$3,250	$3,000	$2,750	$2,500	$2,250	$2,000	$1,850	$1,650	$1,475	$1,350	$1,225

* *Bergmann Simplex Second Variation*

100%	98%	95%	90%	80%	70%	60%	50%	40%	30%	20%	10%
$4,500	$4,250	$3,900	$3,650	$3,300	$3,050	$2,750	$2,350	$2,100	$1,800	$1,600	$1,475

BERGMANN MARS MODEL 1903 - .30 or 9mm Bergmann cal.

100%	98%	95%	90%	80%	70%	60%	50%	40%	30%	20%	10%
$6,500	$5,000	$4,000	$3,000	$2,500	$2,000	$1,750	$1,500	$1,250	$1,100	$750	$500

Add 100% if fit with shoulder stock.
Add 25% if .30 caliber (first 100 pistols).

MODEL 2 - .25 cal., small frame.

100%	98%	95%	90%	80%	70%	60%	50%	40%	30%	20%	10%
$350	$295	$260	$240	$215	$180	$160	$135	$115	$95	$80	$65

Add $100 for Model 2A.

MODEL 3 - .25 cal., small frame.

100%	98%	95%	90%	80%	70%	60%	50%	40%	30%	20%	10%
$350	$295	$260	$240	$215	$180	$160	$135	$115	$95	$80	$65

Add $100 for Model 3A.

ERBEN - .25 cal., Models I, II, and Special (.32 cal.).

100%	98%	95%	90%	80%	70%	60%	50%	40%	30%	20%	10%
$450	$400	$350	$300	$250	$215	$180	$160	$135	$115	$95	$80

PISTOLS: SEMI-AUTO - BERGMANN-BAYARD

Even though the below listed Bergmann-Bayard models were manufactured only by Anciens Etablissements Pieper of Herstal, Belgium, these pistols are listed under this heading as they are most commonly referred to by this trademark designation.

MODEL 1908 STANDARD COMMERCIAL - 9mm Bergmann/Bayard cal., identified by a mounted knight on the left magazine housing and is without finger cuts at base of magazine housing.

100%	98%	95%	90%	80%	70%	60%	50%	40%	30%	20%	10%
$2,250	$1,850	$1,500	$1,250	$1,000	$800	$700	$600	$500	$400	$350	$300

Add 25% if backstrap is slotted for shoulder stock.
Add $3,500 for excellent original leather/wood shoulder stock.

MODEL 1908 SPANISH CONTRACT - 9mm Bergmann/Bayard cal., total contract was for 3,000 pistols, can be identified from standard commercial pistols by the Spanish military acceptance stamp struck on the receiver.

100%	98%	95%	90%	80%	70%	60%	50%	40%	30%	20%	10%
$2,000	$1,750	$1,500	$1,250	$1,000	$800	$700	$600	$500	$400	$350	$300

MODEL 1910 STANDARD COMMERCIAL - 9mm Bergmann/Bayard cal., mechanically similar to Model 1908 Standard Commercial except has finger cuts in bottom of magazine housing, circular grooves are present on each side of magazine base.

100%	98%	95%	90%	80%	70%	60%	50%	40%	30%	20%	10%
$1,750	$1,500	$1,250	$1,000	$800	$700	$600	$500	$400	$350	$300	$250

MODEL 1910 DANISH GOVERNMENT CONTRACT - 9mm Bergmann/Bayard cal., Trolit grips were used for the original conversion, followed later by wood replacements, total contract was for 4,840 pistols with delivery mfg. 1911-1914. This variation can be identified from the usual commercial pistols by the Danish proof mark on the left receiver side and Danish inventory number on right side of receiver.

100%	98%	95%	90%	80%	70%	60%	50%	40%	30%	20%	10%
$1,500	$1,200	$900	$750	$600	$450	$400	$360	$335	$310	$285	$260

Subtract 20% if converted and overstamped M.1910/21.

MODEL 1910/21 TOJHUS - 9mm Bergmann/Bayard cal., these pistols are marked "Haerens Tojhus" and are numbered from 1-900, original grips were black Trolit, replacement grips are either all smooth or with checkered circles above and below grip screw.

100%	98%	95%	90%	80%	70%	60%	50%	40%	30%	20%	10%
$2,500	$2,200	$2,000	$1,750	$1,450	$1,100	$900	$800	$700	$600	$500	$400

This contract was manufactured by the Danish Royal Arsenal located in Copenhagen.

100%	98%	95%	90%	80%	70%	60%	50%	40%	30%	20%	10%

MODEL 1910/21 RUSTKAMMER - 9mm Bergmann/Bayard cal., pistols are marked "Haerens Rustkammer", and numbered 901-2204, grip replacements are the same as noted for Haerens Tojhus.

$2,250	$1,850	$1,500	$1,250	$1,000	$800	$700	$600	$500	$400	$350	$300

This contract was manufactured by the Danish Royal Arsenal located in Copenhagen.

WAYNE BERGQUIST CUSTOM PISTOLS

Current custom pistolsmith and gun dealer located in Naples, FL. The company should be contacted directly (see Trademark Index for current information) regarding its limited production custom pistol models.

BERNARDELLI, VINCENZO

Current trademark of guns mostly manufactured in Turkey, with headquarters located in Brescia, Italy beginning mid-2002. No current U.S. importation. Previously manufactured from 1721 to August, 1997 in Gardone, VT, Italy. Previously imported and distributed until 1997 by Armsport, Inc. located in Miami, FL. Previously imported and distributed by Magnum Research, Inc. located in Minneapolis, MN (1989-1992), Quality Arms, Inc. located in Houston, TX, Armes De Chasse located in Chadds Ford, PA, Stoeger located in New York, NY, and Action Arms, Ltd. located in Philadelphia, PA.

There is some confusion on the Bernardelli trademark as there have been three different companies (Pietro Bernardelli, Vincenzo Bernardelli, and Santini Bernardelli) that have produced firearms. During the late 1980s, there were quite a lot of Pietro Bernardellis that were "dumped" in the American marketplace - these guns do not have the quality of Vincenzo Bernardelli and are not covered within the scope of this text.

The Vincenzo Bernardelli trademark was purchased in early 2002, and many of the older discontinued models are once again back into production, in addition to some new models. Please contact the company directly for more information, including domestic model availability, pricing, and current importation (see Trademark Index).

GRADING - PPGS™	100%	98%	95%	90%	80%	70%	60%

COMBINATION GUNS

MODEL 190 - 12, 16, or 20 ga. under .243 Win., .30-06, or .308 Win. cal., combination rifle/shotgun, boxlock action, DTs, extractors. Imported 1989 only.

			$1,295	$1,025	$895	$800	$700	$600	$525

Last MSR was $1,393.

Add $700 for extra set of 12 ga. O/U barrels.

MODEL COMB 2000 - 12, 16, or 20 ga. under choice of rifle cals., ejectors, set trigger. Imported 1990-97.

			$2,300	$1,550	$1,075	$875	$750	$675	$575

Last MSR was $2,920.

Add $621 for extra set of O/U shotgun barrels (Model COMB 2000S - disc.).

MODEL 120 - 12 ga. over choice of 12 cals., deluxe checkered walnut stock and forearm, iron sights, double triggers, vent. recoil pad, coin washed receiver with light engraving.

			$1,950	$1,585	$1,300	$1,050	$850	$760	$650

Last MSR was $2,411.

Add $130 for extra set of shotgun barrels.

PISTOLS: SEMI-AUTO

VEST POCKET MODEL - .25 ACP cal., 2 1/8 in. barrel, fixed sights, blue, bakelite grips. Mfg. 1945-48.

			$250	$195	$165	$140	$110	$90	$65

GRADING - PPGS™	100%	98%	95%	90%	80%	70%	60%

BABY SEMI-AUTO - .22 S or L cal., 2 1/8 in. barrel, fixed sights, blue, bakelite grips. Mfg. 1949-68.

| | $250 | $175 | $150 | $130 | $100 | $90 | $80 |

SPORTER MODEL - .22 LR cal., 6, 8, or 10 in. barrels, target sights, blue, wood grips. Mfg. 1949-68.

| | $305 | $275 | $220 | $165 | $140 | $110 | $85 |

MODEL 60 - .22 LR cal., .32 ACP, or .380 ACP cal., 3 1/2 in. barrel, fixed sights, blue, bakelite grips. Mfg. 1959-disc.

| | $220 | $195 | $180 | $165 | $155 | $135 | $120 |

This model was not imported domestically.

MODEL 68 - .22 short or .22 LR cal., vest pocket model, 6 shot, bakelite grips, 8 1/2 oz. Disc.

| | $140 | $120 | $110 | $100 | $90 | $80 | $70 |

This model was not imported domestically.

MODEL 80 - .22 LR or .380 ACP cal., 3 1/2 in. barrel, adj. sights, blue, thumbrest plastic grips. Imported 1968-88.

| | $185 | $160 | $150 | $140 | $130 | $115 | $100 |

  Add $5 for .380 ACP.

Note: This model was produced to conform to import regulations of GCA 1968. Importation of this model was disc. 1988.

MODEL USA - .22 LR, .32 ACP (disc.), or .380 ACP. cal., semi-auto, single action, steel frame, loaded chamber indicator, adj. sights, target bakelite grips, 7 shot (.380 ACP) or 10 shot (.22 LR) mag. Disc. 1997.

| | $380 | $295 | $250 | $215 | $185 | $165 | $145 |

Last MSR was $425.

  Add $60 for chrome finish.

This model has the same technical specifications as the Model 60.

MODEL AMR - .22 LR, .32 ACP (disc.), or .380 ACP cal., similar action to USA Model except has 6 in. barrel and adj. rear sight. Disc. 1994.

| | $395 | $325 | $275 | $225 | $185 | $165 | $145 |

Last MSR was $445.

MODEL 90 SPORT TARGET - .22 LR cal. or .32 ACP, similar to Model 80, with 6 in. barrel. Imported 1968-88.

| | $210 | $185 | $170 | $155 | $140 | $120 | $110 |

Last MSR was $245.

MODEL 69 TARGET - .22 LR cal., target semi-auto, single action, 5.9 in. heavy barrel, 10 shot mag., wraparound checkered wood grips, 38 oz.

| | $575 | $475 | $400 | $350 | $275 | $225 | $185 |

Last MSR was $660.

This model was previously designated Model 100.

MODEL 100 TARGET - .22 LR cal., 5.9 in. barrel, adj. sight, blue, checkered wood, thumbrest grips, cased. Imported 1968-88.

| | $395 | $325 | $295 | $260 | $225 | $190 | $175 |

Last MSR was $360.

P-ONE - 9mm Para. or .40 S&W cal., double action, 10 shot mag., choice of matte black or chrome finish. Imported 1993-97.

| | $580 | $495 | $400 | $360 | $330 | $295 | $265 |

Last MSR was $684.

  Add $36 for chrome finish.
  Add $36 for wood grips.

GRADING - PPGS™	100%	98%	95%	90%	80%	70%	60%

∗ P-One Compact - compact variation of the P-One. Disc. 1997.

	$595	$500	$400	$360	$330	$295	$265

Last MSR was $702.

Add $48 for chrome finish.
Add $48 for wood grips.

MODEL P010 TARGET - .22 LR cal., single action, 5.9 in. barrel, adj. sights and trigger, matte black finish, large anatomic walnut stippled grips with thumbrest, 10 shot mag., 40 1/2 oz. Imported 1989-92, re-introduced 1995-97.

	$675	$575	$495	$425	$375	$325	$275

Last MSR was $768.

Add $132 for wood case and two sets of weights.

MODEL P018 - 7.65mm (disc. 1988), .380 ACP (mfg. 1993-94), or 9mm Para. cal., double action, semi-auto, steel construction, 4 7/8 in. barrel, 10 (C/B 1994) or 16∗ shot mag., black plastic (standard) or walnut checkered (disc. 1992) grips, blue (disc.), black (new 1994), or chrome finish, 36 oz. Imported 1985-96.

	$485	$400	$350	$300	$275	$250	$230

Last MSR was $560.

Add $40 for walnut grips (disc. 1992).
Add $60 for chrome finish.
Add $30 for carrying case w/combination lock (disc. 1989).

This model was extensively redesigned in 1989 and included a "cocked and locked" feature, thumb mag. release, loaded chamber indicator, as well as other improvements.

∗ Model P018 Compact - .380 ACP or 9mm Para. cal., similar to Model P018 except has 4 in. barrel and 10 (C/ B 1994) or 14∗ shot mag., approx. 2 lbs. Imported 1989-96.

	$545	$430	$375	$310	$275	$250	$230

Last MSR was $610.

Add $55 for chrome finish.

This model was also redesigned in 1989 to incorporate the same features as the Model P018.

PRACTICAL VB - 9x21mm cal., comp. gun built for IPSC competition, various configurations, black or matte chrome finish, 2, 4, or 6 port compensating system. Mfg. 1993-97.

	$1,100	$925	$775	$675	$575	$475	$400

Last MSR was $1,260.

Add $60 for 4 port compensator.
Add $60 for chrome finish.

∗ Practical VB Customized - state-of-the-art competition pistol featuring 4+2 port compensating system. Mfg. 1993-97.

	$1,775	$1,325	$1,100	$975	$850	$725	$600

Last MSR was $1,920.

Add $60 for chrome finish.

RIFLES: DOUBLE

EXPRESS VB - various cals., side-by-side sidelock action, ejectors, single or double triggers. Imported 1990-97.

	$5,475	$4,100	$3,400	$2,725	$2,275	$1,900	$1,600

Last MSR was $6,000.

Add $1,000 for Deluxe Model (double triggers).

GRADING - PPGS™	100%	98%	95%	90%	80%	70%	60%

EXPRESS 2000 - .30-06, 7x65R, 8x57JRS, or 9.3x74R cal., O/U boxlock design, single or double trigger, extractors, checkered walnut stock and forearm. Imported 1994-97.

	$2,600	$1,995	$1,600	$1,275	$1,100	$975	$875

Last MSR was $3,192.

Add $130 for single trigger.

MINERVA EXPRESS - various cals., exposed hammers, extractors, double triggers, moderate engraving. Imported 1995-97.

	$4,975	$3,850	$3,250	$2,725	$2,275	$1,900	$1,600

Last MSR was $5,850.

RIFLES: SEMI-AUTO

CARBINA .22 - .22 LR cal., blow back action. Imported 1990-97.

	$575	$375	$295	$210	$170	$150	$135

Last MSR was $720.

SHOTGUNS: FOLDING MODELS

SINGLE BARREL - 12, 16, 20, 24, 28, 32 ga., or .410 bore, gun folds in half. Importation disc. 1990.

	$230	$185	$150	$135	$125	$115	$100

Last MSR was $265.

DOUBLE BARREL - 12 and 16 ga., gun folds in half, double triggers. Previously available in Europe only.

	$570	$430	$370	$315	$285	$260	$230

SHOTGUNS: O/U

MODEL 115 HUNTING - 12 ga. only, boxlock action, monobloc frame, inclined plane lockings, blue receiver, single trigger, ejectors. Importation disc. 1989.

	$1,770	$1,425	$1,225	$1,000	$895	$750	$650

Last MSR was $1,915.

✳ *Model 115S* - similar to 115, except moderate engraving.

	$2,150	$1,925	$1,745	$1,500	$1,250	$1,025	$950

Last MSR was $2,500.

✳ *Model 115L* - similar to 115S, except extensive scroll engraving on silver finish receiver.

	$2,600	$2,375	$2,050	$1,750	$1,450	$1,100	$850

Last MSR was $3,170.

✳ *Model 115E* - sideplate, boxlock action, ejector, bulino game scene engraving.

	$4,650	$4,125	$3,600	$3,100	$2,650	$2,200	$1,800

Last MSR was $5,200.

MODEL 115 TARGET - 12 ga. only, same specifications as Model 115, except trap dimensions. Importation disc. 1989.

	$1,800	$1,595	$1,375	$1,175	$1,000	$895	$750

Last MSR was $2,160.

✳ *Model 115S* - same specifications as 115 Target, except light engraving. Importation disc. 1992.

	$3,275	$2,425	$1,825	$1,500	$1,250	$1,025	$895

Last MSR was $3,920.

This model was available in either Pigeon, Skeet, Sporting Clays, or Trap configuration.

＊ *Model 115L* - similar to 115S, except extensive scroll engraving on silver finish receiver. Importation disc. 1990.

	100%	98%	95%	90%	80%	70%	60%
	$3,700	$2,995	$2,600	$2,375	$2,050	$1,750	$1,450

Last MSR was $4,201.

＊ *Model 115E* - same specifications as 115S, except with extensively engraved sideplates. Importation disc. 1990.

	100%	98%	95%	90%	80%	70%	60%
	$5,950	$4,800	$4,125	$3,600	$3,100	$2,650	$2,200

Last MSR was $6,827.

＊ *Model 115S Trap/Skeet* - 12 ga. only, available in Trap or Skeet configuration, ejectors, single trigger. Disc. 1997.

	100%	98%	95%	90%	80%	70%	60%
	$3,250	$2,450	$1,825	$1,425	$995	$875	$725

Last MSR was $3,780.

＊ *Model 115S Sporting Clays* - 12 ga. only, SST, ejectors, choke tubes. Imported 1995-97.

	100%	98%	95%	90%	80%	70%	60%
	$3,875	$3,350	$2,775	$2,100	$1,750	$1,500	$1,350

Last MSR was $4,200.

MODEL 190 TARGET - 12 ga, SST, ejectors, engraved silver receiver, select checkered walnut stock and forearm. Imported 1986-89.

	100%	98%	95%	90%	80%	70%	60%
	$1,425	$1,095	$925	$800	$700	$600	$525

Last MSR was $1,572.

＊ *Model 190 MC* - similar to Model 190 Target except has Monte Carlo stock. Imported 1989 only.

	100%	98%	95%	90%	80%	70%	60%
	$1,000	$825	$700	$600	$525	$475	$450

Last MSR was $1,155.

＊ *Model 190 Special* - 12 ga. only, similar to Model 190 Target, except has better walnut and engraving. Imported 1988-89.

	100%	98%	95%	90%	80%	70%	60%
	$1,335	$1,000	$895	$800	$700	$600	$525

Last MSR was $1,456.

Add $75 for single trigger (Model 190 Special MS).

These variations are hunting models.

MODEL 192 FIELD - 12 ga. only, single or double triggers, ejectors, choke tubes optional. Imported 1995-97.

	100%	98%	95%	90%	80%	70%	60%
	$1,175	$895	$750	$650	$550	$450	$375

Last MSR was $1,425.

Add $65 for single trigger.
Add $200 for choke tubes.
Add $350 for 192 Special (includes double triggers, ejectors).

MODEL 192 MS COMPETITION - 12 ga. only, ejectors, selective or non-selective triggers, multi-chokes standard on Sporting Clays Model. Mfg. 1990-97.

	100%	98%	95%	90%	80%	70%	60%
	$1,725	$1,475	$1,150	$925	$775	$675	$575

Last MSR was $1,930.

Add $120 for SST.
Add $200 for choke tubes.
Add $485 for Special Sport.

This model was available in either Pigeon, Skeet, Sporting Clays, Special Sport, or Trap configuration.

MODEL 192 MS-MC HUNTING - 12 ga. only, boxlock action with engraved coin finished receiver, 3 in. chambers, ejectors, SST, 26 3/4 or 28 in. VR barrels with choke tubes, steel shot compatible. Imported 1990-1992.

	100%	98%	95%	90%	80%	70%	60%
	$1,400	$995	$825	$700	$600	$525	$475

Last MSR was $1,833.

GRADING - PPGS™	100%	98%	95%	90%	80%	70%	60%

✳ *Model 192 MS-MC-WF* - waterfowler variation which includes 3 1/2 in. chambers, 3 choke tubes, and SST. Imported 1990 only.

| | $1,275 | $950 | $875 | $775 | $675 | $575 | $500 |

Last MSR was $1,444.

MODEL 200 LIGHTWEIGHT MS - 12 ga. only, silver grey finished receiver with game scene engraving, ejectors, DTs. Imported 1988-89, resumed 1993-97.

| | $1,325 | $975 | $850 | $725 | $650 | $550 | $450 |

Last MSR was $1,525.

MODEL 220 MS HUNTING - 12 or 20 ga., silver grey finished receiver with engraving. Mfg. 1988-97.

| | $1,350 | $995 | $850 | $725 | $650 | $550 | $450 |

Last MSR was $1,560.

Add $75 for SST.
Add $180 for 12 ga. slug variation with DTs (new 1994).
Add $700 for extra set of 12 ga. barrels (disc. 1990).

This model was available with either a pistol grip or English grip (straight) stock.

MODEL LUCK - 12 ga., ejectors, boxlock action, choice of double or single trigger. Imported 1994-97.

| | $1,450 | $995 | $725 | $650 | $550 | $450 | $375 |

Last MSR was $1,795.

Add $275 for single trigger.

SATURNO MS-MC COMPETITION - 12 ga. only, sporter configuration, boxlock action with lightly engraved side plates, ejectors, DTs. Imported 1991-97.

| | $2,325 | $1,725 | $1,150 | $925 | $775 | $675 | $575 |

Last MSR was $2,760.

This model was available in either Pigeon, Skeet, Sporting Clays, or Trap configuration.

SATURNO MS-MC HUNTING - 12 ga. only, boxlock action with lightly engraved side plates, ejectors, SST, includes multi-chokes. Imported 1991-92.

| | $2,275 | $1,525 | $1,050 | $875 | $750 | $695 | $600 |

Last MSR was $2,609.

ORIONE S - 12 ga., double Purdey lock, VR, ejectors, engraved nickel finish receiver. Importation disc. 1989.

| | $1,175 | $1,025 | $860 | $760 | $650 | $560 | $510 |

Last MSR was $1,425.

ORIONE L - similar to Orione S, single trigger, finer engraving, English or pistol-type select walnut stock. Importation disc. 1989.

| | $1,285 | $1,125 | $950 | $840 | $750 | $650 | $550 |

Last MSR was $1,550.

ORIONE E - top-of-the-line, deep relief engraving. Importation disc. 1989.

| | $1,375 | $1,200 | $1,020 | $900 | $820 | $710 | $650 |

Last MSR was $1,660.

SHOTGUNS: SxS

Bernardelli side-by-side shotguns were manufactured with straight grip, English style stocks with pistol grip available as a special order. Importation of Bernardelli shotguns was inconsistent over the years.

A wide variety of special order options was available on these shotguns.

Barrel choke markings for V. Bernardelli shotguns are as follows; Full: *, Impr. Mod: **, Mod: ***, Impr. Cyl: ****, Cylinder: CL.

MODEL 110 - 12 ga., trap or skeet model, separated barrels, high post rib.

| | $2,000 | $1,500 | $1,300 | $1,100 | $1,000 | $900 | $800 |

GRADING - PPGS™	100%	98%	95%	90%	80%	70%	60%

MODEL 110 EXTRA0 - similar to Model 110, except engraved.

	100%	98%	95%	90%	80%	70%	60%
	$3,021	$2,265	$1,970	$1,665	$1,510	$1,360	$1,210

S. UBERTO 1 GAMECOCK - 12, 16, 20, or 28 ga., 25 3/4 in. imp. cyl. and mod., 27 1/2 in. full and mod., hammerless, boxlock, extractors, two triggers, English style stock, checkered.

	$853	$635	$605	$550	$495	$440	$415

Add 20% for ejectors.

BRESCIA HAMMER DOUBLE BARREL - 12, 16, or 20 ga., 25 3/4, 27 1/2 and 29 1/2 in. mod. and full, 12 ga., 25 1/2 in. imp. cyl. and mod., sidelock, extractors, two triggers, straight English stock, splinter forearm, checkered. Importation disc.

	$1,495	$1,150	$800	$600	$500	$400	$350

Last MSR was $2,482.

ITALIA HAMMER DOUBLE BARREL - similar to Brescia, except higher grade engraving and wood. Importation disc.

	$1,750	$1,300	$925	$700	$600	$500	$450

Last MSR was $2,844.

ITALIA EXTRA HAMMER - 12, 16, or 20 ga., hammer double. Top-of-the-line hammer model. Importation disc.

	$6,400	$3,150	$2,200	$1,650	$1,375	$1,050	$800

Last MSR was $7,861.

MODEL 112 - 12 ga., entry-level model with extractors and DTs. Imported 1989 only.

	$850	$750	$675	$625	$550	$495	$450

Last MSR was $998.

Add $65 for single trigger (Model 112 M - disc.).

MODEL 112 E - 12 ga., Anson & Deeley action, light engraving. Importation disc. 1989.

	$995	$850	$775	$695	$625	$550	$495

Last MSR was $1,108.

MODEL 112 SI/S (EM) - similar to Model 112E, except has single or double triggers. Disc. 1997.

	$1,795	$1,000	$825	$725	$650	$550	$450

Last MSR was $2,100.

Add $174 for ejectors.
Add $138 for ST.
Add $420 for choke tubes.

* *Model 112 EM - MC* - similar to Model 112 EM, except has 3 in. chambers and 5 choke tubes. Imported 1990-92.

	$1,600	$1,000	$850	$775	$675	$575	$495

Last MSR was $1,971.

* *Model 112 EM-MC-WF* - includes 3 1/2 in. chambers, waterfowl model with matte finish, single trigger and 3 choke tubes. Importation disc. 1990.

	$1,275	$975	$850	$775	$675	$575	$495

Last MSR was $1,444.

S. UBERTO 1 - 12, 16, 20, or 28 ga., Anson & Deeley action, Purdey locks, light engraving, case hardened receiver, double triggers, extractors.

	$1,050	$900	$800	$700	$625	$550	$495

Last MSR was $1,164.

Add $65 for single trigger (Model S. Uberto 1M).

* *S. Uberto 1E* - similar to S. Uberto 1, except with ejectors. Importation disc. 1990.

	$1,175	$950	$850	$740	$650	$565	$495

Last MSR was $1,357.

Add $65 for single trigger (Model S. Uberto 1EM).

GRADING - PPGS™	100%	98%	95%	90%	80%	70%	60%

S. UBERTO 2 - 12, 16, 20, and 28 ga.'s, Anson & Deeley action, Purdey locks, light scroll engraving, silver finished receiver, double triggers, extractors. Importation disc. 1989, resumed 1993-97.

	$1,375	$1,150	$875	$725	$650	$550	$450

Last MSR was $1,580.

Add $35 for single trigger (Model S. Uberto 2M - disc.).

✳ *S. Uberto 2E* - similar to S. Uberto 2, except with ejectors. Disc. 1997.

	$1,525	$1,300	$1,050	$875	$725	$650	$550

Last MSR was $1,710.

Add $80 for single trigger (Model S. Uberto 2EM - disc.).

S. UBERTO FS - 12, 16, 20, or 28 ga., Purdey locks, relief engraved with hunting scenes on silver finished receiver, double triggers, extractors. Importation disc. 1989, resumed 1993-97.

	$1,695	$1,450	$1,125	$895	$750	$675	$575

Last MSR was $1,915.

Add $65 for single trigger (Model S. Uberto FSM - disc. 1989).

✳ *S. Uberto FSE* - similar to S. Uberto FS, except with ejectors. Importation disc. 1989.

	$1,375	$1,100	$975	$850	$750	$625	$550

Last MSR was $1,537.

Add $65 for single trigger (Model S. Uberto FSEM).

ROMA 3 - similar to S. Uberto, double triggers, extractors, false sideplates, case hardened receiver. Importation disc. 1989, resumed 1993-97.

	$1,425	$1,200	$895	$775	$675	$575	$475

Last MSR was $1,625.

Add $65 for single trigger (Model Roma 3M - disc.).

✳ *Roma 3E* - similar to Roma 3, except with ejectors. Disc. 1997.

	$1,550	$1,325	$1,050	$875	$725	$650	$550

Last MSR was $1,770.

Add $80 for single trigger (Model Roma 3EM - disc.).

ROMA 4 - more deluxe model than Roma 3, false sideplates, scroll engraved, silver finished receiver. Importation disc. 1989.

	$1,250	$1,025	$900	$800	$700	$625	$550

Last MSR was $1,439.

Add $65 for single trigger (Model Roma 4M).

✳ *Roma 4E* - similar to Roma 4, except with ejectors. Disc. 1997.

	$1,775	$1,475	$1,150	$925	$775	$675	$575

Last MSR was $2,000.

Add $80 for single trigger (Model Roma 4EM - disc.).

ROMA 6 - 12, 16, 20, or 28 ga., fully engraved sideplates with hunting scenes, Purdey locks, silver finish receiver, single trigger, finely figured English walnut. Importation disc. 1989.

	$1,395	$1,150	$975	$875	$775	$675	$600

Last MSR was $1,619.

Add $175 for single trigger (Model Roma 6M).

✳ *Roma 6E* - similar to Roma 6, except with ejectors, 16 ga. was disc. 1989. Disc. 1997.

	$2,400	$1,825	$1,475	$1,150	$925	$775	$675

Last MSR was $2,880.

Add $180 for single trigger (Model Roma 6EM).

GRADING - PPGS™	100%	98%	95%	90%	80%	70%	60%

ROMA 7 - 12 ga., ejectors, grade up from the Roma 6. Imported 1994-97.

	$3,200	$2,200	$1,675	$1,375	$995	$875	$750

Last MSR was $3,840.

ROMA 8 - 12 ga., ejectors, grade up from the Roma 7. Imported 1994-97.

	$3,700	$2,700	$1,950	$1,675	$1,375	$995	$875

Last MSR was $4,740.

ROMA 9 - 12 ga., ejectors, grade up from the Roma 8. Imported 1994-97.

	$4,550	$3,200	$2,500	$1,950	$1,675	$1,375	$995

Last MSR was $5,520.

ELIO - 12 ga. only, lightweight, extractors, fine English style scroll engraving on silver finish receiver. Importation disc. 1989.

	$1,125	$925	$850	$740	$650	$565	$475

Last MSR was $1,238.

    Add $65 for single trigger (Model Elio M).

✱ *Elio E* - similar to Elio, except with ejectors. Importation disc. 1989.

	$1,200	$1,000	$895	$795	$695	$595	$500

Last MSR was $1,353.

    Add $65 for single trigger (Model Elio EM).

SLUG GUN - 12 ga. only, 23 3/4 in. slug bored barrels, extractors, Anson & Deeley action, Purdey locks, lightly engraved, silver finish receiver. Importation disc. 1990.

	$1,325	$1,000	$895	$795	$695	$595	$500

Last MSR was $1,575.

    Add $65 for single trigger (Model Slug M).

SLUG LUSSO - 12 ga. only, 23 3/4 in. slug bored barrels, sideplates, with extensive engraving featuring hunting scenes, cheekpiece, ejectors, silver finished receiver. Importation disc. 1992.

	$2,325	$1,550	$1,200	$995	$875	$750	$650

Last MSR was $2,793.

    Add $80 for single trigger (Model Slug Lusso M).
This model was previously designated Slug Deluxe (1988 or earlier).

HEMINGWAY - 12, 20, or 28 (new 1992) ga., boxlock action, coin finished receiver with game scene engraving, 23 1/2 in. barrels, DTs, deluxe checkered walnut stock and forearm, 6 1/4 lbs. Disc. 1997.

	$2,050	$1,500	$1,050	$875	$750	$675	$575

Last MSR was $2,520.

    Add $70 for single trigger.
    Add $120 for single selective trigger.

HEMINGWAY DE LUXE - similar to Hemingway, except is also available in 16 ga. and has sideplates, better wood, and more engraving. Disc. 1997.

	$2,350	$1,750	$1,150	$925	$775	$675	$575

Last MSR was $2,874.

    Add $126 for single trigger (Model Hemingway De Luxe M).

LAS PALOMAS PIGEON - 12 ga. live pigeon gun, single trigger, special dimensions for live pigeon shooting. Disc. 1997.

	$3,125	$2,550	$2,000	$1,700	$1,375	$995	$875

Last MSR was $3,700.

    Add $750 for Pigeon Model (includes single trigger).

HOLLAND V.B. LISCIO - 12 ga. only, Holland type sidelocks, light engraving, silver finish receiver, single trigger, ejectors, select walnut. Disc. 1997.

	$10,350	$5,300	$4,450	$3,900	$3,350	$2,850	$2,400

Last MSR was $12,600.

GRADING - PPGS™	100%	98%	95%	90%	80%	70%	60%

HOLLAND V.B. INCISO - 12 ga. only, H&H sidelock action, Purdey locks, various barrel lengths, single trigger, ejectors, straight or pistol grip stock, 100% engraved on coin finished receiver. Importation disc. 1992.

$10,700 $7,000 $5,500 $4,700 $4,200 $3,500 $3,000

Last MSR was $12,929.

HOLLAND V.B. LUSSO - 12 ga. only, H&H sidelock action, Purdey locks, various barrel lengths, single trigger, ejectors, straight or pistol grip stock, same features as Holland V.B. Inciso, only extra select wood and game scene engraving. Importation disc. 1992.

$8,900 $7,900 $6,500 $5,200 $4,750 $4,000 $3,450

Last MSR was $14,377.

HOLLAND V.B. EXTRA - 12 ga. only, H&H style action, any barrel length and choke, double triggers, auto ejectors, straight or pistol grip stock, 100% engraved on coin finished receiver. Prices are completely dependent upon individual customer specifications. Values are for engraving pattern No. 3. Importation disc. 1992.

$13,250 $9,700 $7,450 $6,150 $5,200 $4,600 $3,950

Last MSR was $16,549.

Add $1,034 for engraving pattern No. 4.
Add $4,551 for engraving pattern No. 12.
Add $8,895 for engraving pattern No. 20.
Add $621 for single trigger.

Older specimens ordered before 1992 could have values considerably lower than those listed.

HOLLAND V.B. GOLD - top-of-the-line model, made to individual order. Very limited production and ultra-rare. Importation disc. 1992.

$47,500 $32,500 $24,000 $18,500 $13,000 $11,500 $9,950

Last MSR was $57,922.

Older specimens ordered before 1992 could have values considerably lower than those listed.

SHOTGUNS: SEMI-AUTO

MODEL 9MM FLOBERT - 9mm Flobert cal. (rimfire shot cartridge), 24.4 In. smooth bore barrel, 3-shot mag., steel receiver, walnut stock and forearm with sling and swivels, 5 lbs. 3 oz. Disc. 1997.

$385 $265 $175 $150 $125 $105 $95

Last MSR was $474.

BERSA

Current manufacturer established circa 1958 and located in Ramos Mejia, Argentina. Currently distributed exclusively by Eagle Imports, Inc. located in Wanamassa, NJ. Previously imported and distributed before 1988 by Rock Island Armory located in Geneseo, IL, Outdoor Sports Headquarters, Inc. located in Dayton, OH, and R.S.A. Enterprises, Inc. located in Ocean, NJ. Distributor sales only.

PISTOLS: SEMI-AUTO

THUNDER 9 - 9mm Para. cal., double action semi-auto, 3 1/2 in. barrel, 10- (C/B 1994) or 14* shot mag., ambidextrous manual safety and decocking lever, automatic firing pin safety, 3-dot sights, aluminum frame, wraparound matte black polymer grips, link-free locked breech design, non-glare matte blue, satin nickel (new 1995), or duo-tone (new 1995) finish. Imported 1993-95.

$400 $335 $295 $265 $235 $210 $190

Last MSR was $475.

Add $17 for duo-tone finish.
Add $50 for satin nickel finish.

GRADING - PPGS™	100%	98%	95%	90%	80%	70%	60%

THUNDER 22 (MODEL 23) - .22 LR cal., double action semi-auto, 9-shot mag., 3 1/2 in. barrel, black polymer (new 1997) or walnut (disc. 1996) grips, 24 1/2 oz. Imported 1988-98.

	$230	$195	$155	$125	$115	$105	$95

Last MSR was $265.

Add $17 for satin nickel finish.

THUNDER 380 - .380 ACP cal., double action, 3 1/2 in. barrel, fixed sights, 7 shot mag., deep blue, satin nickel, duo-tone (disc. 1995) finish, rubber grips, 25 3/4 oz. Imported 1995-98.

	$235	$195	$155	$130	$115	$105	$95

Last MSR was $275.

Add $16 for satin nickel.
Add $16 for duo-tone finish (disc. 1995).

✳ *Thunder 380 Deluxe* - .380 ACP cal., 9-shot mag., black polymer grips, extended slide release and mag. bottom, polished blue, 3-dot sights, 23 oz. New 1997.

MSR $336	$270	$230	$170	$125	$115	$105	$95

✳ *Thunder 380 Plus* - similar to Thunder 380, except has 15 shot mag. Mfg. 1995-1997.

	$265	$210	$165	$130	$115	$105	$95

Last MSR was $316.

Add $32 for satin nickel finish.
Add $17 for duo-tone finish.

THUNDER 380 SERIES (95) - .380 ACP cal., double action, 3 1/2 in. barrel, fixed sights, 7, 8 (Concealed Carry) or 15 (new 2006) shot mag., matte blue, satin nickel, matte plus (new 2007) or duotone (3,000 mfg. 2001, reintroduced 2008) finish, black polymer grips, 23 oz. New 1995.

MSR $310	$250	$200	$155	$130	$115	$105	$95

Add $5 for Concealed Carry Model (new 2005).
Add $26 for satin nickel finish.
Add $81 for 15 shot mag. (Bersa .380 Plus, matte finish only).
Subtract $16 for duo-tone finish.

THUNDER 9MM ULTRA-COMPACT SERIES - 9mm Para. cal., double action, ultra-compact dimensions, choice of matte blue, nickel, duo-tone (new 2008), or stainless steel, 9, 13 (new 2006), or 17 shot mag. New 2004.

MSR $402	$335	$295	$265	$240	$215	$185	$160

Add $58 for stainless steel (disc. 2008).
Add $10 for 17 shot mag. (nickel finish only beginning 2008).
Add $27 for duo-tone finish.

THUNDER 40 ULTRA-COMPACT SERIES - .40 S&W cal., similar to Thunder 9mm, 10 (disc. 2006) or 13 shot mag. New late 2004.

MSR $409	$340	$295	$265	$240	$215	$185	$160

Add $42 for stainless steel (disc.).
Add $10 for nickel finish (new 2006).

THUNDER 45 ULTRA-COMPACT SERIES - .45 ACP cal., double action, ultra compact configuration, 3.6 in. barrel, skeletonized hammer, loaded chamber indicator, 7 shot mag., choice of matte, duo tone (mfg. 2003, reintroduced 2008), stainless steel (mfg. 2004-2007), or satin nickel finish, 27 oz. Importation began 2003.

MSR $402	$335	$295	$265	$240	$215	$185	$160

Add $43 for satin nickel finish.
Add $58 for stainless steel (disc. 2007).
Add $27 for duo-tone finish.

GRADING - PPGS™	100%	98%	95%	90%	80%	70%	60%

MODEL 83 - .380 ACP cal., double action semi-auto, 3 1/2 in. barrel, blue or satin nickel finish, custom walnut grips, 6-shot mag., 24 1/2 oz. Imported 1988-94.

	$235	$180	$150	$125	$115	$105	$95

Last MSR was $288.

Add $34 for satin nickel finish.

MODEL 85 - .380 ACP cal., similar specifications to Model 83 except has 12- or 13-shot mag., 30 1/2 oz. Imported 1988-94.

	$285	$245	$220	$195	$170	$150	$130

Last MSR was $340.

Add $47 for satin nickel finish.

MODEL 86 - .380 ACP cal., blue matte or nickel finish, undercover model, wrap-around rubber grips, 12-shot mag. Imported 1991-94.

	$315	$265	$225	$200	$170	$150	$130

Last MSR was $375.

Add $29 for nickel finish.

MODEL 90 - 9mm Para. cal., single action, semi-auto, steel frame, checkered walnut grips, 13-shot mag., deep blue finish. Imported 1990-91 only.

	$325	$280	$250	$220	$195	$170	$150

Last MSR was $384.

MODEL 223 - .22 LR cal., single action semi-auto, 10-shot mag., 3 1/2 in. barrel, blue finish, squared-off trigger guard, nylon grips. Importation disc. 1987.

	$200	$170	$150	$125	$115	$105	$95

Last MSR was $239.

MODEL 224 - similar to Model 223, except has 4 in. barrel. Imported 1987 only.

	$200	$170	$150	$125	$115	$105	$95

Last MSR was $239.

MODEL 225 - similar to Model 223, except has 5 in. barrel and 10-shot mag. Disc. 1987.

	$155	$135	$125	$115	$105	$95	$85

Last MSR was $170.

MODEL 226 - similar to Model 225, except has 6 in. barrel. Importation disc. 1987.

	$200	$170	$150	$125	$115	$105	$95

Last MSR was $239.

MODEL 323 - .32 ACP cal., single action semi-auto, 8-shot mag., thumbrest plastic grips, 25 oz. Disc. 1987.

	$105	$95	$85	$75	$65	$55	$45

Last MSR was $125.

MODEL 383 - .380 ACP cal., single or double action semi-auto, 3 1/2 in. barrel, blue finish, nylon grips, 7-shot mag. Importation disc. 1988.

	$120	$95	$90	$80	$70	$60	$50

Last MSR was $188 for single action. Last MSR was $239 for double action.

Add $15 for double action.

BERTUZZI, F.LLI

Current manufacturer located in Gardone, VT, Italy since 1886. Current distributed by Dewing's Fly & Gun Shop, located in W. Palm Beach, FL. Previously imported and distributed by New England Arms Corp. located in Kittery Point, ME.

Bertuzzi makes only best quality sidelock O/U and SxS shotguns, both with and w/o external hammers. Only 40-50 guns are mfg. annually, and all are custom ordered per individual specifications. Please contact the distributor directly for more information and current pricing.

SHOTGUNS: O/U

Beginning 2008, Bertuzzi is no longer providing price quotations on current models, since the company already has a 5 year back order situation. Base values listed below reflect the most recent available pricing (2007).

ZEUS - 12 ga., sidelock, auto ejector, deluxe engraving, deluxe wood checkering, SST. Importation disc. 1994.

> This model was available on special order only. Retail prices generally ranged from $18,500-$27,500.

ZEUS EXTRA LUSSO - 12, 16, or 20 ga., sidelock, auto ejector, deluxe wood, deluxe checkering and engraving, SST. Disc. 2002.

> This model was available on special order only. Prices generally ranged $35,000+.

ZEUS BOSS SYSTEM - 12 or 20 ga., features Boss locking system. Importation began 1995.

> Prices start at $45,000.

ZEUS SEAGULL WINGS - elaborate O/U model with hinged swing open locks, all internal surfaces polished and engraved, exhibition wood, trigger plate action with lockplates exposed from a switch on the safety. Very limited mfg., approx. 1-2 guns per year.

> Base model not including engraving is $135,000.
> Add 10% for small frame.
> Add 20% for matched pairs.

Engraving prices will vary depending on style and engraver. Delivery time is approx. 4 years.

SHOTGUNS: SxS

Beginning 2008, Bertuzzi is no longer providing price quotations on current models, since the company already has a 5 year back order situation. Base values listed below reflect the most recent available pricing (2007).

MODEL ORIONE - 12 , 16, 20, or 28 ga., round boxlock action, DT or ST, ejectors, chopper lump barrels, base price includes English scroll engraving, deluxe Turkish walnut, and custom stock dimensions.

> This model has a current MSR of $27,950.
> Add 10% for small frame.
> Add 20% for matched pairs.

Additional engraving styles are available on this model - price will vary on style and engraver. Delivery time is approx. 2 years.

VENERE BEST QUALITY SIDELOCK - various gauges, best quality sidelock model, ejectors, many options and engraving styles available, standard engraving is English rose and scroll.

> Base model has a MSR of $31,950.
> Add 10% for small frame.
> Add 20% for matched pair.

Additional engraving options available - price will vary depending on style and engraver. Delivery time is approx. 2 years.

VENERE SEAGULL WINGS - elaborate model with hinged swing open locks, all internal surfaces polished and engraved, exhibition wood, trigger plate action with lockplates exposed from switch on safety, very limited mfg., approx. 1-2 guns per year.

> Base model not including engraving has a MSR of $75,000.
> Add 10% for small frame.
> Add 20% for matched pair.

Engraving prices will vary depending on style and engraver. Delivery time is approx. 2 years.

ARIETE HAMMER GUN - all gauges, upper tang safety, double triggers, fine quality engraving.

> Prices start at $19,500. The self-cocking, auto-ejector mechanism is popular in this model and prices can vary between $20,000-$40,000.

GRADING - PPGS™	100%	98%	95%	90%	80%	70%	60%

BESCHI, MARIO

Previous manufacturer until circa 1983 located in Italy.

SHOTGUNS: O/U

BOXLOCK MODEL - 12 or 20 ga., standard model with light engraving.

$3,000	$2,600	$2,300	$1,950	$1,600	$1,300	$995

SHOTGUNS: SxS

EXTRA LUSSO SIDELOCK - 12 or 20 ga., elaborate game scene engraving.

	100%	98%	95%	90%	80%	70%	60%
12 ga.	$12,000	$10,750	$9,250	$8,000	$6,750	$5,500	$4,250
20 ga.	$12,000	$10,750	$9,250	$8,000	$6,750	$5,500	$4,250

BOXLOCK MODEL - prices assume moderate engraving.

$1,650	$1,475	$1,300	$1,050	$850	$650	$500

BETTINSOLI, TARCISIO, Srl

Current manufacturer located in Brescia, Italy. Currently imported on a private label basis by Franchi. Distributed in Europe by Bignami, located in Bolzano, Italy.

Bettinsoli manufactures fine quality O/U shotguns, express rifles, and combination guns, with certain models private labeled under the Franchi trademark in the U.S., and manufactured under the Bettinsoli name in Europe. Please contact the factory directly for more information (see Trademark Index).

BIG BEAR ARMS & SPORTING GOODS INC.

Previous firearms importer located in Carrollton, TX 1992-1999, specializing in the importation of both Russian military surplus and new firearms. Limited inventories remained through 2000.

PISTOLS: SEMI-AUTO

IZH-70 MAKAROV - .380 ACP or 9mm Makarov cal., 8-shot mag., current mfg. from Russia. Imported 1994-99.

$265	$185	$155	$135	$115	$100	$90

Last MSR was $325.

RIFLES: SEMI-AUTO

SAIGA SPORTER RIFLE - 7.62x39mm cal., semi-auto with improved Kalashnikov design, checkered hardwood (disc.) or synthetic stock and forearm, 5- or 10- (disc.) shot mag. Imported 1996-99.

$575	$400	$325	$250	$225	$200	$175

Last MSR was $750.

Add $169 for 3.5X scope and mount.

SHOTGUNS

SAIGA SEMI-AUTO - .410 bore, 3 in. chamber, paramilitary configuration. Imported 1996-99.

$425	$350	$295	$250	$200	$180	$165

Last MSR was $499.

IJ-27 O/U - 12 ga., 2 3/4 in. chambers. Imported 1995-99.

$425	$350	$295	$250	$200	$180	$165

Last MSR was $499.

IJ-39E O/U - 12 ga., 2 3/4 in. chambers. Imported 1995-99.

$760	$600	$495	$400	$360	$330	$295

Last MSR was $895.

GRADING - PPGS™	100%	98%	95%	90%	80%	70%	60%

IJ-43 SxS - 12 ga., 2 3/4 in. chambers. Imported 1995-99.

			100%	98%	95%	90%	80%	70%	60%
			$325	$250	$200	$175	$155	$145	$135

Last MSR was $399.

BIG HORN ARMS CORP.
Previous manufacturer located in Watertown, SD.

PISTOLS: SINGLE SHOT

TARGET PISTOL - .22 Short cal. only, unique action permitting auto. ejection, ambidextrous stock made of molded Tufflex with carvings, 26 oz. Approx. 1,200 mfg. Disc. in the late 1960s.

$175	$150	$135	$125	$115	$105	$95

SHOTGUNS: SINGLE SHOT

LIL´ MAGNUM SHOTGUN - .410 diameter reloadable shot cartridge, single shot open bolt operation, included reloading equipment, approx. 2,000 mfg. in the late 1960s.

$125	$100	$75	$65	$55	$50	$45

BIGHORN RIFLE CO.
Previous manufacturer located in Orem, UT.

PISTOLS: BOLT ACTION

BIGHORN PISTOL - .22 LR cal., bolt action design.

Lack of information on this pistol precludes accurate pricing.

RIFLES: BOLT ACTION

BIGHORN RIFLE - Mauser action, choice of calibers, custom made bolt action of high quality, interchangeable barrels (gun was supplied with 2 barrels), adj. trigger, deluxe walnut stock, many custom options. Mfg. 1984 only.

$2,100	$1,800	$1,600	$1,400	$1,200	$1,000	$850

BILL HANUS BIRDGUNS LLC
Current dealer and importer located in Newport, OR. Bill Hanus has sold private label models from AYA (see listings under AYA), Browning (16 ga. Citoris), CZ, and Fabarm. Previously, he had his own private label model manufactured by Armas Ugartechea (see separate listing) located in Eibar, Spain until 1997. Please contact the company directly for more information, including availability, delivery time, and pricing (see Trademark Index).

BINGHAM, LTD.
Previous manufacturer located in Norcross, GA circa 1976-1985.

RIFLES: BOLT ACTION

BANTAM - .22 LR or 22 Mag. cal., bolt action single shot, 18 1/2 in. barrel. Disc. 1985.

$110	$90	$75	$65	$55	$45	$40

Last MSR was $120.

RIFLES: SEMI-AUTO

PPS 50 - .22 LR cal. only, blowback action, 50 round drum mag., standard model has Beechwood stock. Disc. 1985.

$250	$225	$195	$180	$145	$135	$125

Last MSR was $230.

Add 15% for deluxe model with walnut stock.

Add 20% for Duramil model with chrome finish and walnut stock.

This model was styled after the Soviet WWII Model PPSh Sub Machine Gun.

GRADING - PPGS™	100%	98%	95%	90%	80%	70%	60%

AK-22 - .22 LR cal. only, blowback action, styled after AK-47, 15 shot mag. standard, 29 shot mag. available. Standard model has beechwood stock. Disc. 1985.

	$250	$225	$195	$180	$145	$135	$125

Last MSR was $230.

Add $20 for Deluxe model with walnut stock.

GALIL-22 - .22 LR cal. only, patterned after Galil semi-auto paramilitary design rifle. Disc.

	$250	$225	$195	$180	$145	$135	$125

FG-9 - 9mm Para. cal., blowback action, semi-auto paramilitary design carbine, 20 1/2 in. barrel.

While advertised during 1984, this gun never went into production.

BITTNER

Previously manufactured by Gustav Bittner located in Vieprty, Bohemia (Austria, Hungary), circa 1893.

PISTOLS

BITTNER MODEL 1893 - 7.7mm Bittner cal., pistol with hand activated repeater mechanism, box magazine, checkered grips, limited manufacture circa 1893.

	N/A	$5,500	$4,250	$3,000	$2,400	$1,900	$1,500

BLAND, THOMAS & SONS GUNMAKERS LTD.

Current manufacturer located in England since 1840. This firm was purchased in 1990 by Woodcock Hill located in Benton, PA. Manufacturer direct sales only.

Woodcock Hill should be contacted directly (address listed in Trademark Index) for more information (including current models and prices) regarding Thomas Bland & Sons firearms. Prices will vary depending on the exchange rate between the pound/dollar.

Record checks by serial number on all Thomas Bland & Sons rifles and shotguns are also available.

RIFLES: CUSTOM

Double rifles are available in almost all calibers and specifications. Prices vary between $10,000-$75,000 depending upon configuration, finish, and accessories. Bolt action rifles are available in any type of action, most popular calibers, and other special options. The bolt action models are not manufactured in England, and Woodcock Hill should be contacted directly for pricing. Prices vary, depending on configuration.

SHOTGUNS: CUSTOM

Boxlock, sidelock SxS and O/U best quality shotguns are available in all gauges, and pricing can vary depending upon configuration, finish, and accessories.

BLASER

Blaser

Currently manufactured by Blaser Jagdwaffen GmbH in Isny im Allgäu, Germany. Currently imported and distributed beginning late 2006 by Blaser USA, located in Stevensville, MD. Previously imported and distributed 2002-2006 by SIG Arms located in Exeter, NH, and circa 1988-2002 by Autumn Sales Inc. located in Fort Worth, TX. Dealer sales.

The Blaser Company was founded in 1963 by Horst Blaser. In 1986, the company was taken over by Gerhard Blenk. During 1997, the company was sold to SIG. In late 2000, SIG Arms AG, the firearms portion of SIG, was purchased by SAN Swiss Arms AG, a newly formed company whose investors have a background in textiles. This new group initially included 6 independently operational companies - Blaser Jadgwaffen GmbH, Hämmerli AG, Mauser, B.R. Rizzini, J.P. Sauer & Sohn GmbH, SIG-Sauer, and SAN

Swiss Arms AG. The restructured Blaser group now includes the primary factories of Blaser (Germany) and SIG-Blaser (Switzerland), in addition to much outsourcing in the smaller Blaser operations located in Lichtenstein, Ungarn (Hungary), and Bulgaria. Blaser currently makes approx. 20,000 rifles annually, with most being sold in Europe. During 2003, Blaser manufactured the No. 100,000 R-93 Model, after producing this straight pull bolt action for less than a decade.

Current SAN Swiss Arms AG trademarks include: Blaser, Mauser, Sauer rifles, and Sig-Sauer pistols. Please refer to these individual company listings for current information, importation and pricing.

Blaser Jagdwaffen also manufactures a large variety of rifles, drillings, and combination guns for the European market that are not imported domestically.

PISTOLS: BOLT ACTION

R-93 HHS (HUNTING HANDGUN SYSTEM) - various cals. between .222 Rem. - .375 H&H, features R93 right or left-hand straight pull bolt action, 14 in. hammer forged free floating barrel (interchangeable), matte black receiver with choice of wood, case colored, or game scene sideplates, Turkish walnut stock and pistol grip, 3-4 shot mag., 5 lbs. Limited importation 2004-2006.

	$2,475	$2,050	$1,775	$1,500	$1,350	$1,200	$1,025

Last MSR was $2,900.

Add $200 for left-hand bolt assembly.
Add $900 per interchangeable barrel.

RIFLES: BOLT ACTION

The R-93 rifle system's biggest advantage is its component interchangeability. Both barrels and bolt heads/assemblies can be quickly changed to make the R-93 a very versatile rifle platform. Many special orders and features are available from the factory, and please contact Blaser USA directly for additional information, including pricing and availability (see Trademark Index).

Add $153 for left-hand action available on currently manufactured R-93 models.
Add $1,167 for rimfire conversion kit (.17 HMR, .22 LR, or .22 Mag. cal., includes barrel, magazine, bolt assembly, and bolt catch insert). New 2008.
Add $396 for semi-weight configuration on currently manufactured standard R-93 models.
Add $556 for match grade configuration on currently manufactured standard R-93 models.
Beginning late 2006, Blaser began offering graded wood between grades 3-11. There are many ways in which to upgrade wood, so please contact the importer directly regarding wood upgrade pricing based on the model selected.

R-84 - .22-250 Rem. (disc. 1993), .243 Win., 6mm Rem., .25-06 Rem., .270 Win., .280 Rem., or .30-06 standard cals., .257 Wby. Mag., .264 Win. Mag., 7mm Rem. Mag., .300 Win. Mag., .300 Wby. Mag., .338 Win. Mag., or .375 H&H cal., 23 or 24 (Mag. cals. only) in. interchangeable barrel, scroll engraving on receiver, short bolt action with 60 degree rotation, checkered Turkish walnut stock and forearm, approx. 7 lbs. Mfg. 1988-94.

	$2,100	$1,575	$1,275	$1,050	$950	$850	$775

Last MSR was $2,300.

Add $50 for left-hand action.
Add $600 per interchangeable barrel (w/scope mounts).
This model has the scope mounted directly to the barrel (and not the receiver). Since the scope mounts are on the barrel extension, this takedown rifle is unique in that it does not require re-zeroing when the rifle is reassembled, regardless of caliber change.

✱ *R-84 Deluxe* - features a better grade of Turkish walnut with a North American game scene engraved on receiver, silver pistol grip cap with animal scene engraving.

	$2,375	$2,025	$1,650	$1,200	$1,000	$925	$825

Last MSR was $2,600.

Add $50 for left-hand action.

❋ *R-84 Super Deluxe* - best grade Turkish walnut with receiver featuring African game scene engraving (animals are in gold and silver), and silver pistol grip cap with gold animal engraving.

$2,675	$2,225	$1,775	$1,300	$1,100	$975	$895

Last MSR was $2,950.

Add $50 for left-hand action.

R-93 CLASSIC - available in various domestic (.22-250 Rem. - .416 Rem. Mag.) and European (6.5x55mm and 7x57mm currently) calibers, 22, 24 (Mag. cals.), or 27 1/2 (disc.) in. barrel, unique patented rifle features straight pull bolt action (0 degree bolt lift), 360 degree radial locking system eliminates bolt rotation, unique safety offering cartridge in chamber capability, 3 shot mag, features interchangeable barrel system and newly designed bolt, searfree trigger mechanism, matte finished nickel receiver with engraving, non-glare "black velvet" barrel finish, integrated low scope mounts standard (1994-97 only), custom gun case with combination lock became standard 1998, 6 1/2 - 7 lbs. Importation began 1994, R-93 Classic introduced 1998, disc. May, 2002.

$2,600	$2,200	$1,850	$1,675	$1,500	$1,375	$1,250

Last MSR was $2,950.

Add $595 per interchangeable barrel (w/o mounts).

IMPORTANT RECALL NOTICE - During 2002, Blaser issued an important recall on all R93 rifles due to a potential problem with the trigger assembly. All R93 rifles must be returned to SIG Arms for inspection and possible trigger assembly replacement. Blaser request that consumers contact SIG Arms directly, not your local dealer. Please call 1-877-442-7671 for more information regarding this important safety recall on the Model R93 only.

During 1998, this model's nomenclature changed to the R-93 Classic. Scope mounts are no longer included. Between 1994-97, this model retailed for approx. $2,800 and a Deluxe Grade was available for $3,100, while the Super Deluxe Grade retailed for $3,500.

❋ *Model R-93 Classic Safari* - .416 Rem. Mag. cal., features 24 in. heavy barrel, open sights, large forearm, 9 1/2 lbs., this model was renamed the R-93 Classic in 1998. Imported 1994-2002.

$3,575	$3,100	$2,650	$2,275	$1,825	$1,350	$1,150

Last MSR was $4,140.

R-93 LUXUS - available in 20 calibers from .222 Rem. - .375 H&H., similar to the R-93 Classic, except has Grade 4 wood and ebony forend tip, available in right or left-hand action, case not included. New 2002.

MSR $4,326		$3,900	$3,450	$2,700	$2,200	$1,850	$1,525	$1,350

Add $700 for Luxus Plus Model with upgraded wood, black receiver and choice of color case hardened steel, wood, or animal sideplates (mfg. 2005-2007).

❋ *R-93 Luxus Safari* - .375 H&H or .416 Rem Mag. cal., similar to R-93 Classic Safari, except has higher quality walnut and ebony forend tip, available in right or left-hand action, case not included. New 2002.

MSR $5,470		$4,875	$4,450	$3,700	$3,150	$2,400	$2,100	$1,800

R-93 SUPER LUXUS - various cals., oil finished Grade 6 stock, engraved sideplates with animals and different styles of engraving are optional. New 2007.

Base price on this special order model is $9,917.

R-93 ATTACHE - various cals., features premium walnut stock and forearm with receiver wood panel inserts, wood bolt knob, ebony forearm tip, fluted barrel, current mfg. includes Grade 7 walnut, includes case, approx. 6 1/2 lbs. New 1998.

MSR $5,990		$5,400	$4,850	$4,350	$3,700	$3,200	$2,600	$2,025

R-93 OCTAGON - various cals., Grade 6 wood, black receiver with wooden sideplates, full octagon barrel.

MSR $7,883		$7,100	$6,000	$5,000	$4,000	$3,250	$2,650	$2,475

R-93 GRAND LUXE - various cals., deluxe model with high grade checkered Grade 5 stock and forearm, fully hand engraved receiver with sideplates (various styles available), 3 shot mag, 6 1/2 - 7 lbs. Mfg. 1999-2003, reintroduced 2007.

MSR $7,972	$7,100	$6,000	$5,000	$4,000	$3,250	$2,650	$2,475

Last MSR during 2003 was $5,160.

R-93 LRS 2 (LONG RANGE SPORTER 2) - .22-250 Rem. (disc. 2004, reintroduced 2008), .223 Rem., .243 Win. (new 2008), .308 Win., .300 Win. Mag. (mfg. 2000-2007), .338 Lapua (mfg. 2000-2006), 6.5x55mm (new 2005), or 6mm Norma BR (new 2005) cal., competition styled long range sporter with adj. trigger and stock, 5 or 10 (disc. 1999) shot removable box mag, free floating fluted barrel, many competition features, 10.4 lbs. New 1999.

MSR $3,733	$3,350	$2,925	$2,500	$2,000	$1,675	$1,400	$1,200

Add 10% for .338 Lapua cal. (disc. 2006).
Add $1,254 per interchangeable barrel (w/o mounts).
Add $1,600 for Package II or $2,600 for Package II in .338 Lapua cal. or $1,600 for Package III (includes Leupold scope, mounts, muzzle brake, bi-pod, and hard carry case). Disc. 2006.

R-93 TACTICAL 2 - .300 Win. Mag., .308 Win. or .338 Lapua cal., fluted barrel with muzzle brake, Picatinny rails on top of receiver and forearm over barrel, straight pull, ambidextrous pistol grip polymer stock with adj. buttplate and cheekpiece, black finish throughout, includes bipod, 12 lbs. Importation began 2007.

MSR $4,256	$3,775	$3,350	$2,925	$2,500	$2,100	$1,850	$1,475

Add $309 for .338 Lapua cal.

This model is distributed by Sig Sauer, located in Exeter, NH.

R-93 SYNTHETIC - available in 21 cals. between .22-250 Rem. - .416 Rem. Mag., also available by special order in the same European cals. as the Model R-93 Repeater, features one-piece conventional black, wood grain (new 2004), or Mossy Oak camo (new 2004) synthetic stock, 22 or 26 in. barrel, without scope mounts and rings, 6 1/2 - 7 lbs. Mfg. 1998-2006.

	$1,800	$1,450	$1,150	$1,000	$875	$775	$675

Last MSR was $2,100.

Add $400 for black synthetic Safari Model in .375 H&H or .416 Rem. Mag.
Add $600 for wood grain or camo stock.

Add $700 per interchangeable barrel (w/o mounts) in standard cals.

R-93 VARMINT - various cals., fluted match barrel, adj. comb, integrated rail, beavertail forend, removable sling swivels, Grade 3 wood. Importation began 2007.

MSR $4,844	$4,350	$3,875	$3,425	$2,950	$2,500	$2,000	$1,650

Add $306 for bi-pod.

∗ **R-93 Varmint Success** - similar to Varmint model, except has one-piece wood thumbhole stock. New 2008.

MSR $6,438	$5,850	$5,350	$4,800	$4,300	$3,550	$3,100	$2,475

R-93 PROFESSIONAL - various cals., one-piece dark green synthetic stock with black thermo-elastic inlays, ergonomic pistol grip and rubber recoil pad, also available in Mossy Oak or orange camo. Importation began 2007.

MSR $3,031	$2,675	$2,300	$1,950	$1,550	$1,300	$1,100	$975

Add $1,134 for Professional Tracking model with open sights and detachable sling swivels.
Add $379 for camo coverage.

The basic Professional model is also available as a receiver, stock, and bolt assembly - MSR is $2,055 or $1,458 for receiver and stock.

GRADING - PPGS™	100%	98%	95%	90%	80%	70%	60%

R-93 LX - similar cals. as Model R-93 Synthetic, features checkered walnut stock and forearm, coin finished stippled receiver sides, without scope mounts and rings, 6 1/2 - 7 lbs. Mfg. 1998-2002.

	$1,750	$1,425	$1,195	$1,000	$875	$795	$695

Last MSR was $1,990.

Add $275 for Safari LX Model in .416 Rem. Mag. cal.
Add $595 per interchangeable barrel (w/o mounts).

R-93 PRESTIGE - similar to R-93 LX, except receiver has fine scroll engraving, and Grade 3 wood, case not included. New 2002.

MSR $3,177	$2,775	$2,400	$1,950	$1,550	$1,225	$975	$850

Add $977 for Prestige Safari Model in .375 H&H or .416 Rem. Mag. cal. (disc. 2007).

R-93 EXCLUSIVE - various cals., high quality oil finished Grade 7 walnut stock, engraved sideplates, trigger guard, and bolt assembly, various levels of engraving available. Importation began 2007.

Base price on this special order model is $14,390.

R-93 SUPER EXCLUSIVE - various cals., similar to Exclusive, except has gold line engraving with deeper relief and Grade 8 stock and forearm.

Base price on this special order model is $21,908.

R-93 IMPERIAL - various cals., top-of-the-line R-93 model, Grade 9 wood, highest quality engraving with gold line and animal scenes, engraved bolt assembly and trigger guard, wood ball on bolt handle, titanium trigger and bolt head. Importation began 2007.

Base price on this special order model is $30,810.

R-93 STUTZEN - various cals, octagon barrel, full two-piece Grade 4 stock, sling swivels, various configurations available. Importation began 2007.

MSR $6,716	$6,000	$5,400	$4,800	$4,350	$3,750	$3,250	$2,400

This model is also available in the following special order configutations: Stutzen Attache ($8,464 MSR), Stutzen Grand Luxe ($9,835 MSR), Stutzen Super Luxus ($11,780 MSR), Stutzen Exclusive ($16,251 MSR), Stutzen Super Exclusive ($23,771 MSR), and the Stutzen Imperial ($32,676 MSR).

ULTIMATE BOLT ACTION - .22-250 Rem., .243 Win., .25-06 Rem., .270 Win., .308 Win., .30-06, 7x57mm, 7x64mm, .264 Win. Mag., 7mm Rem. Mag., .300 Win. Mag., .338 Win. Mag., or .375 H&H cal., unique bolt action design with 60 degree bolt throw, interchangeable barrel capability, 3 locking lugs, safety lever cocks and uncocks the firing pin spring, exposed hammer, aluminum receiver, 22 or 24 in. barrel, single set trigger, silver finished receiver has light engraving, select checkered walnut stock and forearm, 6 3/4 lbs. Extra interchangeable barrels were $545 each, extra bolt heads were $175 each. Mfg. 1985-89.

	$1,350	$1,100	$975	$925	$825	$750	$675

Last MSR was $1,495.

All models were available in left-hand version at no extra charge.

ULTIMATE BOLT ACTION - SPECIAL ORDER - all of the following models may have been ordered with a buttstock cartridge trap - add $250-$500 depending on model. Mfg. was disc. 1989 on all models.

✳ *Ultimate Deluxe* - similar to Ultimate, except better wood and game scene engraving.

	$1,425	$1,175	$1,000	$950	$850	$775	$700

Last MSR was $1,595.

✳ *Ultimate Deluxe Carbine* - .243 Win. or .308 Win. cal. only, 19 1/2 in. barrel with full length forearm. New 1986.

	$1,600	$1,375	$1,150	$1,000	$900	$825	$750

Last MSR was $1,800.

GRADING - PPGS™	100%	98%	95%	90%	80%	70%	60%

✳ *Ultimate Super Deluxe* - similar to Ultimate Deluxe, except features better wood and game scene engraving. New 1986.

	$3,750	$3,250	$2,900	$2,600	$2,300	$2,100	$1,850

Last MSR was $4,030.

✳ *Ultimate Exclusive* - similar to Ultimate Super Deluxe, except features better wood and game scene engraving. New 1986.

	$4,850	$4,300	$3,500	$2,975	$2,600	$2,275	$1,975

Last MSR was $5,655.

Add $700 per interchangeable barrel.

✳ *Ultimate Super Exclusive* - similar to Ultimate Exclusive, except features better wood and game scene engraving. New 1986.

	$7,700	$6,800	$5,750	$4,700	$3,950	$3,450	$2,950

Last MSR was $8,905.

Add $950 per interchangeable barrel.

✳ *Ultimate Royal* - best quality Ultimate, featuring Bavarian cheekpiece and checkering/carving on stock and forearm, elaborate game scene engraving, gold plated hammer. New 1986.

	$9,000	$7,500	$6,750	$6,000	$5,375	$4,600	$4,000

Last MSR was $11,500.

Add $1,200 per interchangeable barrel.

RIFLES: SxS

S2 - various cals. between .22 Hornet - .308 Win., including various metric cals., scalloped boxlock action false sideplates (higher grades only), 22.6 or 24 in. free floating barrels with quarter rib and iron sights, interchangeable barrels, easily regulated, tilting lock block, manual cocking safety, checkered Turkish walnut stock and forearm (Grade 1 standard), approx. 7.7 lbs for standard cals. Limited importation 2004-2005, reintroduced 2007.

MSR $6,792	$6,200	$5,650	$5,100	$4,600	$4,100	$3,600	$3,000

Add $4,390 for extra set of standard cal. barrels.

This model is also available in higher grades by special order, including the S2 Luxus ($7,707 MSR), S2 Super Luxus ($12,759 w/sideplates), S2 Exclusive ($16,596 MSR), S2 Super Exclusive ($21,820 MSR), and the S2 Imperial $30,978 MSR). Previously available in S2 Royal (last MSR was $29,000).

✳ *S2 Safari* - .375 H&H, .470 NE, .416 Rem. Mag. (disc.), .416 NE, or .500 NE cal., 24.4 in. barrel, Grade 1 wood standard, similar to S2 model, except has Monte Carlo stock with cheekpiece, kickstop in buttstock, rubber recoil pad and half beavertail forend.

MSR $9,449	$8,750	$7,950	$7,300	$6,400	$5,800	$5,100	$4,650

Add $5,721 for extra set of standard cal. barrels.

This model is also available in higher grades by special order, including the S2 Safari Luxus ($10,363 MSR), S2 Safari Super Luxus ($15,416 w/sideplates), S2 Safari Exclusive ($19,252 MSR), S2 Safari Super Exclusive ($24,482 MSR), and the S2 Safari Imperial ($33,647MSR).

RIFLES: SINGLE SHOT

MODEL BL 820 - various American and European cals., falling block action, adj. trigger, 26 1/2 in. barrel, available in Standard to Royal configurations. Mfg. 1982-89.

Standard Model	$1,550	$1,300	$1,075	$925	$800	$700	$600

Last MSR was 2,900 DM.

Add 30% for Royal configuration.

GRADING - PPGS™	100%	98%	95%	90%	80%	70%	60%

MODEL K77 A - .22-250 Rem., .243 Win., 6.5x55mm, .270 Win., 7x57R, 7x65R, or .30-06 standard cals., 7mm Rem. Mag., .300 Win. Mag. or .300 Wby. Mag. cal., break open action, 23 or 24 in. barrel, 3 piece take down, upper tang safety, checkered walnut stock and forearm, engraved silver finished receiver, sling swivels, 5 1/2 lbs. Imported 1988-90.

	$2,000	$1,675	$1,475	$1,300	$1,100	$925	$800

Last MSR was $2,280.

Add $50 for Mag. calibers.
Add $730-$778 per interchangeable barrel.

K95 PRESTIGE - .222 Rem., .22 Hornet (new 2006), .243 Win., .25-06 Rem. (new 2006), .270 Win., .308 Win., .30-06, 7mm Rem. Mag., .300 Win. Mag., or .300 Wby. Mag. cal., break open action, 22 (standard cals.) or 25 (Mag. cals.) in. barrel, upper tang safety/cocking lever, 3 piece takedown, checkered Grade 3 stock and forearm, scroll engraved sideplates, sling swivels. Importation began 2000.

MSR $4,132		$3,800	$3,595	$3,350	$2,725	$2,150	$1,600	$1,425

Add $1,208 for interchangable barrel.
Add $2,327 for octagonal barrel.

The following special order models are available in K95 Prestige configuration: K95 Attache (Grade 7 wood, MSR $8,081), K95 Super Luxus (Grade 6 wood, MSR $10,571), K95 Baronesse (Grade 7 wood, MSR $14,441), K95 Exclusive (Grade 7 wood, MSR $15,082), K95 Super Exclusive (Grade 8 wood, MSR $19,347), and the K95 Imperial (Grade 9 wood, MSR $28,800).

K95 LUXUS - similar to K95 Prestige, except has Grade 4 checkered stock and forearm, engraved sideplates and receiver. Importation began 2000.

MSR $4,776		$4,325	$3,875	$3,300	$2,850	$2,350	$1,975	$1,600

Add $1,208 for interchangable barrel.
Add $2,327 for octagonal barrel.

K95 STUTZEN LUXUS - various cals., features engraved aluminum frame, 20 in. octagon barrel and full length forearm, deluxe checkered Turkish Grade 4 wood, iron sights, 6 lbs. Importation began 2004.

MSR $7,220		$6,650	$6,000	$5,250	$4,400	$3,850	$3,350	$2,700

Add $2,384 for interchangable barrel.

The following special order models are available in K95 Stutzen configuration: K95 Attache (Grade 7 wood, MSR $8,639), K95 Super Luxus (Grade 6 wood, MSR $12,339), K95 Baronesse (Grade 7 wood, MSR $14,999), K95 Exclusive (Grade 7 wood, MSR $16,852), K95 Super Exclusive (Grade 8 wood, MSR $21,117), and the K95 Imperial (Grade 9 wood, MSR $30,568).

SHOTGUNS: O/U

F3 GAME STANDARD - 12 or 20 (new 2008) ga., 3 in. chambers, boxlock action with satin oxide finish, SST, ejectors, 27, 28, or 29 in. VR barrels with 2 Briley choke tubes, similar to Competition model, except has Schnabel forearm, Grade 4 wood, 7.3 lbs. New 2007.

MSR $6,011		$5,550	$4,875	$4,300	$3,650	$3,150	$2,500	$2,150

Add $3,175 per extra O/U barrel assembly.

This model is also available in the following special order configurations: Attache (Grade 7 wood, $8,493 MSR), Baroness (Grade 7 wood, $12,371 MSR), Luxus (Grade 5 wood, $7,570 MSR), Super Luxus (Grade 6 wood, $10,923 MSR), Exclusive (Grade 7 wood, MSR $14,247), Super Exclusive (Grade 8 wood, MSR $18,861), and the Imperial (Grade 9 wood, MSR $28,283).

F3 COMPETITION STANDARD - 12 ga. only, 3 in. chambers, boxlock action with monobloc barrels, SST, ejectors, Grade 4 wood, various VR barrel lengths with 5 Briley Spectrum extended chokes, greyed receiver finish, 8-8.4 lbs. New 2005.

MSR $6,508		$5,850	$5,100	$4,400	$3,750	$3,250	$2,600	$2,250

Add $3,553 per O/U barrel assembly.

This model is also available in additional higher grades, including the Attache (Grade 7 wood, $8,821 MSR), Luxus (Grade 5 wood, MSR $8,067), Super Luxus (Grade 6 wood, MSR $11,593 MSR), Baroness (Grade 7 wood, $12,868 MSR), Exclusive (Grade 7 wood, $14,830 MSR),

GRADING - PPGS™	100%	98%	95%	90%	80%	70%	60%

Super Exclusive (Grade 8 wood, $19,443 MSR), and the Imperial (Grade 9 wood, $28,864 MSR). Previously available in F3 Competition Royal ($25,895 last MSR).

F3 AMERICAN SKEET - similar to F3 Competition, except has choice of heavy or lightweight 30 in. barrels, 2 Briley choke tubes, approx. 8.2 lbs. New 2007.

MSR $6,508		$5,850	$5,100	$4,400	$3,750	$3,250	$2,600	$2,250

Add $3,677 for extra barrels.
Add $124 for heavy barrels (4 lbs., 7 oz.).

This model is also available in additional higher grades, including the Attache (Grade 7 wood, $8,639 MSR), Luxus (Grade 5 wood, MSR $8,067), Super Luxus (Grade 6 wood, MSR $11,420 MSR), Baroness (Grade 7 wood, $12,868 MSR), Exclusive (Grade 7 wood, $14,638 MSR), Super Exclusive (Grade 8 wood, $19,252 MSR), and the Imperial (Grade 9 wood, $28,674 MSR).

F3 AMERICAN TRAP - similar to F3 Competition, except has 30 in. barrels, also available as Unsingle with 34 in. barrel, approx. 8.1 lbs. New 2007.

MSR $7,238		$6,500	$5,500	$4,750	$3,950	$3,450	$2,800	$2,350

Add $4,283 for extra O/U or Unsingle barrel.

This model is also available in additional higher grades, including the Attache (Grade 7 wood, $9,369 MSR), Luxus (Grade 5 wood, MSR $8,797), Super Luxus (Grade 6 wood, MSR $12,150 MSR), Baroness (Grade 7 wood, $13,496), Exclusive (Grade 7 wood, $15,402 MSR), Super Exclusive (Grade 8 wood, $20,015 MSR), and the Imperial (Grade 9 wood, $29,436 MSR).

BLEIKER, HEINRICH

Current rifle manufacturer located in Buetschwil, Switzerland. No current U.S. importation.

RIFLES: BOLT ACTION

Please contact the factory directly for more information, including current U.S. availability on the following and other custom models (see Trademark Index).

CHALLENGER - .22 LR cal., Bleiker action featuring minimum firing pin resonance and precise head space clearance, super match trigger, match barrel, many options available. New 2002.

Please contact the factory directly for current pricing on this model.

MATCH RIFLE - 6mm BR, .308 Win., or 7.5x55mm Swiss cal., Bleiker alloy action featuring titanium hardening/coating, integrated magazine, super match trigger, match barrel, many options available, including different colors. New 2002.

Please contact the factory directly for current pricing on this model.

BLOW

Current trademark of guns manufactured by Ücyildiz Silah Sanayi Tic Ltd. Sti., located in Istanbul Turkey. No current U.S. importation.

Ücyildiz Silah Sanayi Tic Ltd. Sti. manufactures a wide variety of semi-auto pistols, slide action and semi-auto shotguns. These guns have had little or no importation into the U.S. The company should be contacted directly for more information, including pricing and availablility (see Trademark Index).

BLUEGRASS ARMORY

Current rifle manufacturer located in Richmond, KY. Consumer direct sales.

RIFLES: BOLT ACTION

VIPER MODEL - .50 BMG cal., single shot action with 3-lug bolt, 29 in. chrome moly steel barrel with muzzle brake, one-piece frame with aluminum stock (choice of gray, OD green, or black), incorporates Picatinny rail, includes detachable bipod, approx. 24 lbs. New 2003.

MSR $2,995		$2,550	$2,150	$1,900	$1,700	$1,550	$1,400	$1,250

GRADING - PPGS™	100%	98%	95%	90%	80%	70%	60%

BOBCAT WEAPONS INC.

Previous manufacturer from April, 2003-circa 2006 and located in Mesa, AZ. During late 2006, the company name was changed to Red Rock Arms. Please refer to the R section for current information and pricing.

RIFLES: SEMI-AUTO

BW-5 MODEL - 9mm Para cal., paramilitary design, stamped steel or polymer (Model BW-5 FS) lower receiver, roller lock bolt system with delayed blowback, 16 1/2 in. stainless steel barrel, choice of black, desert tan, OD green, or camo stock, pistol grip, and forearm, Model BW-5 FS has fake supressor, paddle mag. release and 8 7/8 in. barrel, 10 shot mag., approx. 6.4 lbs. Mfg. 2003-2006.

	$1,175	$995	$875	$800	$725	$650	$575

Last MSR was $1,350.

Add $275 for Model BW-5 FS.

BOHICA

Previous manufacturer and customizer located in Sedalia, CO, circa 1993-94.

RIFLES: SEMI-AUTO

M16-SA - .223 Rem., .50 AE, or various custom cals., AR-15 style, 16 or 20 in. barrel, A-2 sights, standard handguard, approx. 950 were mfg. through September 1994.

	$1,375	$1,225	$1,000	$850	$725	$600	$525

Add $100 for flat-top receiver with scope rail.
Add $65 for two-piece, free floating handguard.

In addition to the rifles listed, Bohica also manufactured a M16-SA Match variation (retail was $2,295, approx. 10 mfg.), a pistol version of the M16-SA in both 7 and 10 in. barrel (retail was $1,995, approx. 50 mfg.), and a limited run of M16-SA in .50 AE cal. (retail was $1,695, approx. 25 mfg.).

BOITO

Previous manufacturer located in Brazil. Previously imported by F.I.E. Corp. located in Hialeah, FL.

Boito shotguns were inexpensive, utilitarian shotguns that are shootable, but not collectible. Because of this, prices typically range between $75 - $175, depending on the gauge and condition.

BOND ARMS, INC.

Current manufacturer located in Granbury, Texas beginning 1998.

DERRINGERS: O/U

A key entry internal safety locking device was introduced for all Defender models beginning in 2000. This device locks the preexisting crossbolt safety in the on-safe position.

Add $15 for left-handed configuration.
Add $139 per extra set of 3 in. barrels, $159 for 3 1/2 in. barrels or $189 for 4 1/4 in. barrels.

TEXAS DEFENDER - 9mm Para., .32 H&R Mag., .357 Mag., .357 Max., .40 S&W, .44 Mag., .45 ACP, or .45 LC/.410 shot shell cals., O/U design, 3 in. barrels with spring loaded extractors, stainless steel, removable trigger guard, rebounding hammer, crossbolt safety, spring loaded cammed locking lever, 21 oz. New 1998.

MSR $389	$310	$250	$195	$145	$120	$110	$95

CENTURY 2000 DEFENDER (C2K) - .410 bore/.45 LC cal. with 2 1/2 in. chambers and 3 in. barrels, or .410 bore with 3 in. chambers and 3 1/2 in. barrels. New 1999.

MSR $404	$325	$265	$200	$150	$120	$110	$95

GRADING - PPGS™	100%	98%	95%	90%	80%	70%	60%

COWBOY DEFENDER - similar cals. as Texas Defender, designed specifically for cowboy action shooting, w/o trigger guard. New 2000.

MSR $389	$310	$250	$195	$145	$120	$110	$95

SUPER DEFENDER - .450 AutoBond cal., 3 in. barrels, rosewood grips, stainless steel construction, 20 oz. Limited mfg. 2003-2004.

	$300	$245	$195	$145	$120	$110	$95

Last MSR was $369.

SNAKE SLAYER - .410 bore/.45 LC cal. with 3 in. chambers and 3 1/2 in. barrels, features larger grip frame with laser carved "Bond Arms" and logo on grips, 22 oz. New 2005.

MSR $455	$380	$300	$250	$195	$165	$140	$120

SNAKE SLAYER IV - similar to the Snake Slayer, except has 4 1/4 in. barrels. and 23 1/2 oz. New mid-2006.

MSR $485	$400	$320	$255	$195	$165	$140	$120

RANGER - .410 bore/.45 LC cal., 4 1/4 in. barrel, black ash extended grips with star. New 2008.

MSR $599	$525	$465	$410	$365	$295	$250	$200

PISTOLS: SEMI-AUTO

.450 AUTOBOND - .450 AutoBond/.45 ACP cal., based on Colt 1911 design, full size frame, 5 in. barrel.

While advertised during 2003, this model never went into production.

BORCHARDT

Previous pistol design originating in Germany circa 1894-1897.

PISTOLS: SEMI-AUTO

Prices below assume matching parts and original condition.

MODEL 1893 - 7.65mm Borchardt cal., original Luger design, 6 1/2 in. barrel, blue finish with fire-blue small parts, checkered walnut grips, 8 shot mag., distinguished by elongated spring mechanism housing located behind the toggle assembly, may include accessories (mags., holster, stock) and/ or case.

✳ *Model 1893 Ludwig Loewe Mfg.* - serial numbered 1-1104.

	$21,000	$17,325	$14,700	$11,550	$9,725	$7,875	$6,300

Original stocks (with attached leather holster) are priced starting at $5,000.

❖ **Model 1893 Ludwig Lowe Mfg. Cased With Accessories** - original cased gun was supplied with matching shoulder stock, detachable cheekpiece, leather holster, 3 regular mags. and a hold-open mag., plus tools.

	$43,325	$34,125	$28,875	$23,100	$17,100	$14,175	$11,275

✳ *Model 1893 DWM Mfg.* - starting approx. 1895, serial numbered 1105-3000.

	$20,225	$17,000	$14,450	$11,300	$8,925	$7,350	$5,775

Original stocks (with attached leather holster) are priced starting at $4,750.

❖ **Model 1893 DWM Mfg. Cased With Accessories** - original cased gun was supplied with shoulder stock, detachable cheekpiece, leather holster, 3 regular mags. and a hold-open mag., plus tools.

	$41,500	$33,350	$28,100	$23,100	$17,075	$13,650	$11,025

BOROVNIK, LUDWIG KG

Current long gun manufacturer located in Ferlach, Austria.

Ludwig Borovnik manufactures long guns by custom order only. Please contact him directly for more information (see Trademark Index).

BOSIS, LUCIANO

Current manufacturer located in Travagliato, Italy. Currently distributed exclusively by Dewing's Fly & Gun Shop, located in W. Palm Beach, FL. Currently imported by British Sporting Arms Ltd., located in Millsbrook, NY. Previously imported by Old Friends Hunting & Shooting Co., located in Livingston, MT, New England Arms, located in Kittery Point, ME and by William Larkin Moore & Co., located in Scottsdale, AZ.

All Luciano Bosis guns are manufactured on a custom order only basis. Annual production is approx. 25 best quality guns. Delivery time is approx. 9 months to one year. Please contact the distributor directly for current availability and pricing.

SHOTGUNS

Add €350 for SST on boxlock and hammer models listed below.
Add 10% for 28 ga. or 20% for .410 bore on the Michaelangelo O/U and Queen SxS.

MICHAELANGELO O/U - 12, 16, 20, 28 ga., or .410 bore, pinned Boss style sidelock action, chopper lump barrels, scaled frame, supplied in the white, exhibition quality Turkish walnut, w/o engraving, optional case.

Add 10% for matched pair.

This model has a MSR of €51,000, w/o engraving.
Base price is for gun in-the-white.

✻ *Michaelangelo O/U Extra* - 12, 16, 20, 28 ga., or .410 bore, pinless Boss style sidelock action, 28 in. chopper lump barrels, scaled frame, best quality Turkish walnut and engraving.

Add 10% for pairs.

Please contact Dewing's directly for a price quotation on this model.

WILD O/U - various gauges, boxlock action with optional sideplates, 100% handmade stock and forearm with no CNC operations, normal or optional bluing, regular or round action, engraving per customer specifications, supplied in-the-white. New 2008.

Add €6,000 for sideplates.
Add €350 for SST.

This model has a current MSR of €20,000 w/o engraving.
Base price is for model in-the-white.

HAMMER GUN SxS - 12 ga., sidelock back action, regular or round action, stock and forearm are handmade, engraving depends on customer specifications, supplied in-the-white.

This model has a MSR of €31,000, w/o engraving.
Base price is for model in-the-white.

QUEEN SxS - 12, 16, 20, 28 ga., or .410 bore, H&H type sidelock action, hand forged 27 in. chopper lump barrels, w/o engraving, supplied in-the-white.

Add 10% for pairs.

This model has a MSR of €46,000, w/o engraving.
Base price is for model in-the-white.

COUNTRY SxS - 12, 16, 20, 28 ga., or .410 bore, Anson & Deeley type scalloped boxlock action, hand forged 27 in. chopper lump barrels, DT, checkered deluxe English straight grip stock and forearm.

Add 10% for 28 ga. or .410 bore (w/o engraving).
Add 10% for matched pair.
Add €6,000 for sideplates.

This model has a MRS of €21,000, w/o engraving.
Base price is for model in-the-white.

BOSS & CO., LTD.

Current manufacturer located in London, England 1812 to date. Direct sales from the manufacturer only.

Boss manufactures some of the world's finest shotguns and rifles (best quality guns only). Their shotguns and rifles have always been custom built per individual order.

Approximately 10,000 have been manufactured to date. The following are basic models (does not include special orders, optional engraving patterns, and other possible options). Prices indicated below for manufacturer's suggested retail and 100% condition factors are listed in English pounds. All new prices do not include English VAT. Delivery time for new guns is approx. 3 years. Values for used guns in 98%-60% condition factors are priced in U.S. dollars.

RIFLES: BOLT ACTION

BOSS BOLT ACTION - .270 Win. or .275 Rigby (disc.) cal., Mauser action with Walther premium sporter barrel, Win. Model 70 three-position side safety, box mag., includes mounts and Zeiss scope.

MSR N/A	N/A	$13,000	$11,500	$7,750	$6,500	$5,500	$4,500

This model has very limited manufacture, and Boss should be contacted directly for a firm price quotation.

RIFLES: O/U & SxS, CUSTOM

Boss Express O/U double rifles are quoted per individual request only. Current base price for the .375 H&H cal. starts at £130,000 (w/o VAT), larger calibers up to .700 NE are also available at additional cost. Approx. 12 1/2 lbs. Older double rifles must be appraised individually. The Boss SxS rifle starts at £90,000 (w/o VAT). These models have had very limited manufacture.

SHOTGUNS: CUSTOM

Add 25% for self-opening action (extremely rare on small gauges).
Add 50% for 20 ga. on older mfg.
Add 100% for 28 ga. or .410 bore (very rare) on older mfg.

BOSS O/U - 12, 16, 20, 28 ga., or .410 bore standard, barrel lengths and chokes to specifications, shell-framed sidelock, auto ejectors, double triggers or single non-selective, English straight stock standard to specifications, VR or pistol grip stock optional, best English bouquet & scroll fine engraving, limited production.

MSR £75,000		£75,000	$80,000	$70,000	$62,500	$55,000	$47,500	$40,000

Add £5,000 for 28 ga. or .410 bore on current mfg.

Note: above values represent base gun only and are w/o VAT. Any additional engraving (tight bouquet and scroll is the traditional standard) and/or special orders will add considerably to the above prices.

BOSS SxS - all gauges, barrel lengths and chokes to specifications, bar-action sidelock, easy open/close action (not self-opening), square or rounded action, checkered stock, pistol grip (optional) or straight grip stock, single (patented 3 pull system) or double triggers, splinter or beavertail (optional) forearm, best English bouquet & scroll engraving, limited production.

MSR £55,000		£55,000	$60,000	$50,000	$45,000	$40,000	$35,000	$30,000

Add £5,000 for 28 ga. or .410 bore on current mfg.

Note: above values represent base gun only, and are w/o VAT. Any additional engraving (tight rose and scroll is the traditional standard) and/or special orders will add considerably to the above prices.

ROBERTSON O/U - 12 or 20 ga., boxlock action, fitted sideplates, single trigger, ejectors, 28 or 30 in. rota-hammer forged monobloc barrels, available with or w/o top rib, oil finished French walnut stock, six point multi-locking feature, hand engraved, color case hardened receiver. New 2005.

MSRs on this model range from £10,000 - £14,000.
Note: above MSRs represent base gun only and are w/o VAT.

GRADING - PPGS™	100%	98%	95%	90%	80%	70%	60%

ROBERTSON SxS - 12 or 20 ga., Anson & Deeley boxlock action, fitted sideplates, top tang safety, ejectors, single trigger, 28 or 30 in. barrels, Boss style concave rib, oil finished French walnut stock with splinter forearm, hand engraved, color case hardened receiver. New 2005.

MSRs on this model range from £6,000 - £10,000.

Note: above MSRs represent base gun only and are w/o VAT.

BOSWELL, CHARLES

Current manufacturer established in 1869, and located in London, England. Consumer direct sales.

Charles Boswell was not only a fine gunmaker but an expert shot in the sport of live pigeon shooting and accordingly specialized in the building of high quality competition shotguns and rifles. Chris Batha acquired the company name, records, and goodwill in January of 2004 and continues the heritage of building best guns of superior craftsmanship and outstanding quality of shotguns and rifles in all gauges and calibers.

All new prices do not include English VAT. Delivery time for new guns 12 to 18 months.

In 1988, Charles Boswell was purchased by U.S. interests and Cape Horn International (previously Cape Horn Outfitters) located in Charlotte, NC, was retained to sell and manufacture the Boswell Guns in the U.S. In addition to acquiring their entire inventory of English manufactured firearms, Charles Boswell fabricated new shotguns and double rifles in the U.S. using the best materials including English lock mechanisms and retained the Charles Boswell Co. trademark. Every gun was custom ordered to an individual client's requirements/specifications. Previously imported by Saxon Arms, Ltd., located in Clearwater, FL.

The most collectible Boswell guns are both pre-war and post-war, up to 1988.

RIFLES: BOLT ACTION

BOLT ACTION RIFLE - all standard calibers, built on Mauser or Mannlicher action, 3/4 rib with standard and two folding leaf rear sight, Finest well figured hand checkered Turkish walnut, with pistol grip and cheekpiece. Delivered in leather motor case with accessories.

MSR for a base model is $22,500.

Pinless, scopes, Kurz or Magnum actions are available by individual quotation.

RIFLES: SxS

SIDELOCK DOUBLE RIFLE - all standard calibers, best quality reinforced sidelock ejector with pinless lock plates, folding leaf rear sight on 3/4 rib, finest well figured hand checkered Turkish walnut, with pistol grip and cheekpiece. Delivered in leather motor case with accessories.

MSR for base model is $71,950.

Deluxe and game scene engraving is POR.

BOXLOCK RIFLE - .300 Express, .375 H&H, .458 Win. Mag., or .500 NE cal., made to individual order, choice of game scene engraving, Anson & Deeley boxlock actions, select European hybrid walnut, double triggers, leather cased. Disc. 1996.

$17,500	$17,150	$16,625	$15,750	$14,000	$12,250	$10,500

Last MSR was $35,000.

Add 40% for .458 Win. Mag. cal. or 50% for .500 NE cal.

∗ *Boxlock Rifle .600 Nitro Express*

This model was priced by quotation only. A .600 NE sold for $123,000 in 1991. Disc. 1996.

SIDELOCK RIFLE - .300 Express, .375 H&H, or .458 Win. Mag. cal., made to individual order, choice of game scene engraving, H&H sidelock action, select European hybrid walnut, double triggers, leather cased. Disc. 1996.

$35,000	$29,500	$25,000	$20,000	$16,500	$13,250	$10,750

Last MSR was $65,000.

Add 40% for .375 H&H cal. or 50% for .458 Win. Mag. cal.

GRADING - PPGS™	100%	98%	95%	90%	80%	70%	60%

✳ Sidelock Rifle .600 Nitro Express

	100%	98%	95%	90%	80%	70%	60%
	$65,000	$55,000	$45,000	$37,500	$30,000	$25,000	$19,950

Last MSR was $125,000.

SHOTGUNS: O/U, SIDELOCK

MERLIN - 12, 16, 20, 28 ga., or .410 bore, best quality sidelock ejector, pinless lock plates, single or double triggers, finest well figured hand checkered Turkish walnut. Delivered in leather motor case with accessories.
MSR for base model is $59,950.

PENDRAGON - 20 gauge only, best quality sideplate ejector pinless lock plates, trigger plate model with Boss style forend iron, finest well figured hand checkered Turkish walnut. Delivered in leather motor case with accessories.
MSR for base model is $30,000.

SHOTGUNS: SxS

MERLIN SIDELOCK MODEL - 12, 16, 20, 28 ga., or .410 bore, best quality sidelock ejector, pinless lock plates, single or double triggers, finest well figured hand checkered Turkish walnut. Delivered in leather motor case with accessories.
MSR for base model is $52,950.

BOXLOCK MODEL - previously made to individual order, choice of engraving - including game scenes with gold, Anson & Deeley boxlock actions, select European hybrid walnut, double triggers, leather cased. While each shotgun was priced per individual special order, the below listed prices represented standard features and embellishments. Disc. 1996.

✳ Boxlock Model Best Quality

	100%	98%	95%	90%	80%	70%	60%
	$5,500	$4,750	$4,150	$3,550	$3,150	$2,650	$2,000

Last MSR was $9,500.

✳ Boxlock Model Deluxe Grade - game scene engraved.

	100%	98%	95%	90%	80%	70%	60%
	$6,750	$5,250	$4,500	$4,000	$3,550	$3,000	$2,500

Last MSR was $10,500.

Add $900 for single trigger.
Add $2,800 for extra set of barrels.
Add $2,200 for 28 ga. or .410 bore.

FEATHERWEIGHT MONARCH GRADE - lavishly engraved with gold game scenes, lightweight model, specifications per individual customer special order. Mfg. 1989-96.

✳ Featherweight Monarch Grade Boxlock Model

	100%	98%	95%	90%	80%	70%	60%
	$9,750	$7,350	$6,000	$5,000	$4,400	$3,750	$3,150

Last MSR was $12,500.

✳ Featherweight Monarch Grade Sidelock Model

	100%	98%	95%	90%	80%	70%	60%
	$16,500	$14,000	$12,000	$9,750	$8,500	$7,250	$6,250

Last MSR was $25,000.

SIDELOCK MODEL - previously made to individual order, choice of game scene engraving, H&H sidelock action, select European hybrid walnut, double triggers, leather cased, while each shotgun was priced per individual special order, the below listed values represented standard features and embellishments.

	100%	98%	95%	90%	80%	70%	60%
	$11,750	$9,450	$8,250	$7,000	$6,000	$5,000	$4,000

Last MSR was $17,500.

Add $4,000 for smaller gauges except .410 bore - add $5,000.
Add $2,800 for extra set of barrels.
Add $2,800 for extra set of .410 bore barrels.
Subtract 50% for post-1988 mfg.

BOWEN, BRUCE & COMPANY

Current shotgun manufacturer established 1996 and located in Sturgis, SD. Consumer direct sales only. Bruce Bowen & Company is a division of NIP Manufacturing, Inc.

SHOTGUNS: SINGLE SHOT

BOWEN TRAP GUN - 12 ga. only, unique break open action similar to Seitz trap gun, 32, 33, 34, or 35 in. fixed full choke barrel with four different rib configurations, allowing for four different points of impact, both release and pull triggers included, deluxe checkered walnut with either regular or Monte Carlo stock, individually made per customer's specifications, 9 lbs.

The base price for the Bowen Trap Gun is $16,500 for fixed rib and $13,500 for adj. rib. Please contact the factory directly for a firm price quotation with various options and a delivery date.

BOY'S RIFLES

Rifle configuration generally denoting small caliber single shot rifles designed for youth circa 1890-early 1940s.

U.S. Boy's rifles are generally single-shot, small caliber, rimfire rifles. The era of Boy's rifles is considered to be from 1890 to the beginning of the US involvement in World War II in the early 1940s.

Many Boy's rifles are not marked with the maker's name, model, or caliber. Therefore, identification and evaluation should be left to an expert in the field for those unmarked guns. Many are clearly marked and are familiar to many gun enthusiasts. Many marked Boy's rifles are included in this book, e.g., Remington No 4, Quackenbush Safety Rifles, Winchester Thumb Trigger, Stevens Favorite, etcetera. Unfortunately, due to various circumstances, many brands of Boys rifles are not listed in this book, such as the various Hamilton guns, Davenport, Page Lewis, Meriden, Heal, Nicholson, Clive, etcetera.

In the beginning, Boys rifles were all single shot and mostly falling block. Later when the bolt action became common, Boys rifles started to appear with bolt actions. Then even later, repeaters started to emerge as Boy's rifles.

The most common caliber was .22 rimfire in all cartridge lengths. Some were available in .25 or .32 rimfire.

Most Boy's rifles were cheaply made and, therefore, barely safe. Those that have seen excessive wear or have a loose action are definitely not safe to be used with modern ammunition. They were designed to be inexpensive so young boys could afford them. Most were of diminutive size to suit young boys and girls. Most were made in the northeast and midwestern parts of the US.

It is not uncommon to find these in rough condition with poor bores. This is primarily due to the low quality steel used, lack of proper care by youngsters, and lack of proper cleaning (many Boy's rifles were used with black powder and/or corrosive powders) and are only worth a few dollars in this type of condition. However, one in excellent or close to like new condition with box and literature can command many thousands of dollars.

The publisher would like to thank Mr. John Groenewold for providing this information.

BRAZIER, JOSEPH, LTD.

Current manufacturer established in circa 1700 and currently located in West Sussex, England. Currently represented in the U.S. by Joseph Brazier, Ltd - Karl Lippard, gunmaker, located in Colorado Springs, CO.

This firm was founded in approx. 1702 by William Brazier, Gunmaker, London (1721-1753), and was continued by his son, John Brazier, also of London, from 1741-1769. Benjamin Brazier was established in Wolverhampton from 1818-1835. Joseph Brazier was listed as a gun and lock maker at the same address (9 Brick Kiln Street) during 1827. From 1834 to 1887, the address was "The Ashes" on Great Brick Kiln Street, Wolverhampton. By 1838, the firm was also making implements, and had been appointed lock makers to the East India Company and the Board of Ordnance. In 1849, Joseph's elder son, also named Joseph, was made a partner, and the firm became known as Joseph Brazier & Son. By 1851, younger son Richard Brazier was made a partner, and the firm was renamed J & R Brazier. This company exhibited locks and accessories at the Great Exhibition of 1851.

During this same time, J & R Brazier was making gun furniture, sights, bullets, moulds, and breech loading actions. In 1855, Joseph Brazier patented a lever ramrod for Adams self-cocking pistols (No. 760) (single action later converted to double action), and the Adams revolvers, which he made under license. During 1858, Richard Brazier patented a loading device (No. 1593), and at least one revolver using this patent was made; the name engraved on the revolver was "Joseph Brazier & Son", which implied that Richard had died, and the firm's name had reverted.

By 1859, Joseph Brazier Jr. registered two designs, the first (No. 1056) was for a spring clamp, and the second (No. 1068) was for a lock vice. In 1864, Joseph Brazier Jr. reportedly patented a snap action breech loading mechanism (patent not traced). By 1872, the firm was classified as gun barrel makers, and in 1874 (as well as 1879-1880), the firm was recognized as gunmakers - breech loading. After 1874, the firm changed its name to Joseph Brazier & Sons, most likely indicating Joseph Sr. had retired after taking his sons into the business as partners. During 1876, the firm purchased a license to manufacture Anson & Deeley's famous patent boxlock. In 1887, William Mansfield Jr. became a senior partner, and the company moved from "The Ashes Works" to Lord Street. Mansfield was a lock maker on Lord Street from 1875-1896 and during 1887 under the name J. Brazier & Sons, patented the "Galwey Brazier Improved Game Scorer", which fitted into the forend or stock of a shotgun. By 1896, William Mansfield either retired or died, and G. Brazier together with W. Cashmore patented a safety for a hammerless gun.

It appears that after 1896, the Brazier family regained control of their family's business. Around 1920, the firm, which had approx. 26 employees, was bought by Edwin Chilton of Wolverhampton, and Brazier named locks continued to be made until 1978, when Chilton closed down the company. After 1978, Joseph Brazier, was registered as Magnum Arms Company Ltd. at 46 Newhampton Rd. West, Wolverhampton, West Midlands. In 1983, Joseph Brazier Ltd. was registered as a limited company, and by 1993 was acquired and incorporated.

Today, Joseph Brazier manufactures complete guns, gunlocks for the HMS Victory, firearms locks, parts, accessories, and new technology Solid Solid one piece barrels for the trade. The firm also offers state of the art engineering services to the English gunmaking trade and is an engineering consultant to 14 major firearms manufacturers.

For more information on the current line of Joseph Brazier Ltd. guns, please contact the U.S. representative directly, including information about importation, availability and pricing. All firearms are designed by Karl Lippard Designs.

HANDGUNS

.357 Mag. cal. revolvers in stainless steel start at $2,050. Semi-auto 1911 A1 style pistols are available in a variety of configurations and begin at $5,000.

RIFLES

A boxlock double rifle in .470 NE cal. is available starting at $13,500.

SHOTGUNS

Brazier boxlock SxS shotguns are available in 20 or 28 ga., with DTs, ejector and full hand engraving for $10,500.
A sidelock O/U Best gun is available in 12, 20, or 28 ga. and start at $22,500 and $25,000 if with Solid Solid barrels.

BREDA MECCANICA BRESCIANA

Current manufacturer located in Brescia, Italy. Previous company name was Ernesto Breda. Currently imported beginning 2007 by Legacy Sports International located in Reno, NV. Previously imported beginning 2002-2005 by Tristar, located in No. Kansas City, MO. Previously imported 2000-2001 by Gryphon International, located in Kansas City, MO, and by Diana Imports Co., located in San Francisco, CA. Dealer direct sales.

GRADING - PPGS™	100%	98%	95%	90%	80%	70%	60%

SHOTGUNS: O/U

VEGA SPECIAL - 12 or 20 ga., boxlock action, 26 or 28 in. barrels, single trigger, ejectors, blue only.

	$575	$495	$460	$440	$400	$375	$350

Last MSR was $650.

VEGA SPECIAL TRAP - 12 ga. only, boxlock action, triggers and locks designed for competition shooting, 30 or 32 in. barrels, single trigger, ejectors, blue only.

	$885	$820	$760	$720	$675	$635	$575

Last MSR was $1,114.

VEGA LUSSO - 12 ga. only, scalloped boxlock action, 3 in. chambers, SST, ejectors, 26 or 28 in. VR barrels, coin finished receiver with light perimeter engraving, deluxe checkered Circassian walnut stock and forearm. Imported 2001-2002.

	$1,695	$1,375	$1,100	$975	$850	$725	$600

Last MSR was $1,858.

SIRIO STANDARD - 12 or 20 ga., boxlock action, 26 or 28 in. barrels, single trigger, ejectors, blue only, action extensively engraved. Also available in skeet model (28 in. barrels).

	$2,000	$1,850	$1,630	$1,480	$1,320	$1,200	$1,050

Last MSR was $2,225.

PEGASO HUNTER - 12 or 20 ga., boxlock action, 3 in. chambers, 26, 28 (12 ga. only), or 30 (Sporting Clays only) in. VR barrels with 7mm (Hunter) or 11mm (Sporting Clays) rib, 5 interchangeable chokes, removable trigger group, engraved silver steel (Hunter Model) or blue finished (Sporting Clays), inertia SST, oil finished deluxe walnut stock and forearm, approx. 7-7 1/2 lbs. Imported 2004 only.

	$2,400	$2,050	$1,850	$1,650	$1,425	$1,200	$950

Last MSR was $2,739.

* *Pegaso Sporting Clays* - features upgraded wood, Breda logos in 24Kt. gold, removable trigger group, supplied with ABS fitted case. Imported 2004 only.

	$3,300	$2,875	$2,400	$2,050	$1,700	$1,450	$1,200

Last MSR was $3,644.

PEGASO HUNTING - 12 or 20 ga., 3 in. chambers, 28 in. blued VR barrels with three flush choke tubes, boxlock stainless steel receiver, SST, ejectors, checkered pistol grip stock and forearm, 6.2 - 6.8 lbs. Limited importation 2007.

	$2,400	$2,000	$1,850	$1,650	$1,425	$1,200	$950

Last MSR was $2,729.

PEGASO SPORTING - 12 or 20 ga., 3 in. chambers, 28 in. blued VR barrels with three flush choke tubes, blue boxlock receiver, SST, ejectors, checkered pistol grip stock and forearm, 7.9 lbs. Limited importation 2007.

	$3,100	$2,600	$2,300	$2,000	$1,700	$1,400	$1,125

Last MSR was $3,509.

PEGASO TRAP - 12 or 20 ga., 3 in. chambers, 28 in. blued VR barrels with three flush choke tubes, chrome plated boxlock receiver, checkered pistol grip stock and forearm, SST, ejectors, 7.8 lbs. Limited importation 2007.

	$3,100	$2,600	$2,300	$2,000	$1,700	$1,400	$1,125

Last MSR was $3,509.

GRADING - PPGS™	100%	98%	95%	90%	80%	70%	60%

SHOTGUNS: SxS

ANDROMEDA SPECIAL - 12 ga. only, single trigger, ejectors, select checkered walnut, satin finish receiver with elaborate engraving.

	$640	$550	$480	$420	$365	$300	$250

Last MSR was $685.

SHOTGUNS: SEMI-AUTO

Values in this section are based on the most recent importation, and N/As signify there are no current MSRs.

Add approx. 5% for vent. rib on those discontinued models below where applicable.
Add approx. 10% for choke tubes on discontinued models.

GOLD SERIES - 12 or 20 (lightweight) ga., 2 3/4 in. chamber, 25 or 27 in. barrels, recoil operated, interchangeable choke tubes on recent mfg., vent. rib is standard.

* *Antares Standard* - all steel construction. Importation disc. 1988.

	$440	$375	$340	$310	$285	$260	$240

Last MSR was $495.

* *Argus* - lightweight standard, weighs only 6.6 lbs. Importation disc. 1988.

	$450	$380	$340	$310	$285	$260	$240

Last MSR was $510.

* *Aries* - Magnum, 3 in. chambers, 7.9 lbs. Importation disc. 1988.

	$460	$395	$350	$320	$295	$270	$250

Last MSR was $525.

STANDARD - 12 ga., 2 3/4 in. chamber, recoil operated, 25 or 27 in. barrel, lightly engraved, interchangeable choke tubes on recent mfg. Disc.

	$300	$275	$255	$230	$215	$200	$180

GRADE 1 - 12 ga., similar to standard, except with fancier wood and engraving.

	$575	$530	$485	$440	$410	$380	$350

GRADE 2 - 12 ga., exceeds Grade 1 on embellishments.

	$685	$620	$560	$500	$460	$420	$375

GRADE 3 - 12 ga., top-of-the-line semi-auto.

	$850	$790	$700	$640	$590	$540	$480

MAGNUM MODEL - 12 ga. only, chambered for 3 in. shells.

	$470	$415	$380	$350	$315	$290	$265

ALTAIR SPECIAL - 12 ga., 2 3/4 in. chamber, gas operated, 25 or 27 in. barrel, alloy construction, interchangeable choke tubes on recent mfg., vent. rib is standard, choice of blue or chromed receiver.

	$440	$375	$340	$310	$285	$260	$240

Last MSR was $495.

ALTAIR - 12 or 20 ga., 3 in. chamber, gas operated, two-tone (disc.) or blue alloy receiver finish with 28 in. VR barrel and three choke tubes, checkered walnut stock and forearm, 5.7 - 6.1 lbs. Importation began 2007.

MSR $1,320	$1,150	$950	$850	$725	$625	$550	$475

ASTRO - 12 (disc. 2002) or 20 ga., 3 in. chamber, inertia movement action, 22 (slug), 24, 26, 28, or 30 in. VR barrel with choke tube, choice of black synthetic, Advantage camo, or Circassian walnut stock (recoil pad on 20 ga. only) and forearm. Imported 2001-2004.

	$1,050	$825	$675	$600	$525	$450	$425

Last MSR was $1,215.

Add $100 for Advantage camo coverage (disc. 2002).

ASTROLUX - similar to Astro, except has two-tone receiver with engraving and deluxe checkered Circassian walnut stock and forearm. Imported 2001-2002.

	$1,475	$1,200	$995	$875	$750	$625	$550

Last MSR was $1,665.

ERMES SERIES (2000/2000 L) - 12 ga., 3 in. chamber, inertia recoil operating system, aluminum alloy receiver, nickel plated or blue (lower receiver only) finish, 24, 26, or 28 in. barrel with choke tube, deluxe checkered Circassian walnut stock and forearm. Imported 2001-2005.

	N/A	$925	$800	$700	$600	$500	$400

Last MSR was $1,339.

Add $417 for Ermes 2000 L with nickel finished receiver.

✴ *Ermes Silver* - similar to Ermes 2000, except has engraved nickel plated silver finish on lower receiver. Imported 2002-2005.

	N/A	$1,200	$975	$825	$700	$575	$495

Last MSR was $1,834.

✴ *Ermes Gold* - similar to Ermes 2000, except has nickel plated silver finish with engraving and 24Kt. animal gold inlays on lower receiver. Imported 2002-2005.

	N/A	$1,325	$1,075	$900	$775	$650	$550

Last MSR was $2,060.

MIRA - 12 ga. only, 3 in. chamber, gas operated, Ergal aluminum alloy receiver, choice of annodized black metal or Advantage camo finish, 22 (slug), 24, 26, 28, or 30 in. VR barrel with choke tube, Circassian walnut or black synthetic (disc. 2002) stock and forearm. Imported 2001-2005.

	N/A	$700	$625	$550	$450	$375	$325

Last MSR was $938.

Subtract 10% for black synthetic stock and forearm.
Add $12 for Sporting Clays configuration.

GRIZZLY - 12 ga., 3 1/2 in. chamber, inertia operation with rotary bolt, 28 in. VR barrel with choke tubes, choice of matte black receiver/barrel finish or 100% Advantage Timber HD camo, sling swivels, includes fitted case, 7 1/2 lbs. Imported 2004, resumed during 2007.

MSR $1,826		$1,495	$1,250	$1,050	$900	$800	$700	$600

Add $295 for 100% camo coverage.

ARIES 2 - 12 ga. only, 2 3/4 in. chamber, gas operated, engraved two-tone receiver, 28 or 30 in. VR barrel, deluxe checkered Circassian walnut stock and forearm. Limited importation 2001 only.

	$815	$725	$595	$550	$495	$445	$395

Last MSR was $925.

ECHO - 12 or 20 ga., 3 in. chamber, intertia mechanism, blue, bronze, or nickel finished receiver with accents, 28 in. VR barrel and three choke tubes, grooved/checkered walnut stock and forearm, 6 - 6 1/2 lbs. Importation began 2007.

MSR $1,897		$1,550	$1,275	$1,050	$900	$800	$700	$600

Add $317 for nickel finished receiver.
Add $72 for bronze finished receiver.

XANTHOS - 12 ga., 3 in. chamber, inertia operation, 28 in. VR blue barrel with three choke tubes, receiver colors include blue, grey, or chrome with accents, deluxe checkered walnut stock and forearm, 6 1/2 lbs. Importation began 2007.

MSR $2,309		$1,995	$1,750	$1,500	$1,250	$995	$850	$750

Add $142 for grey receiver with colored accents.
Add $1,097 for chrome receiver with colored accents.

BREEDING, RYAN

Current custom rifle manufacturer located in Nampa, ID. Previously located in Palmdale, CA.

RIFLES: BOLT ACTION

Ryan Breeding specializes in making high quality, custom built rifles in .22-.585 cal. On his safari rifles in larger cals., he features a 4 shot mag. and shorter barrel (19 in. - 24 in.) with optional muzzle brake. Please contact Ryan Breeding directly for more information, including pricing and availability.

BREN 10

Previous trademark manufactured 1983-1986 by Dornaus & Dixon Ent., Inc., located in Huntington Beach, CA.

Bren 10 magazines played an important part in the failure of these pistols to be accepted by consumers. Originally, Bren magazines were not shipped in some cases until a year after the customer received his gun. The complications arising around manufacturing a reliable dual caliber magazine domestically led to the downfall of this company. For this reason, original Bren 10 magazines are currently selling for $125-$150 if new (watch for fakes).

PISTOLS: SEMI-AUTO

Note: the Bren 10 shoots a Norma factory loaded 10mm auto. cartridge. Ballistically, it is very close to a .41 Mag. Bren pistols also have unique power seal rifling, with five lands and grooves. While in production, Bren pistols underwent (4) engineering changes, the most important probably being re-designing the floorplate of the magazine, thus preventing mag. shifting while undergoing recoil.

100% values in this section assume NIB condition. Subtract 10% without box/manual.

BREN 10 STANDARD MODEL - 10mm cal. only, semi-auto selective double action design, blue slide/silver frame finish, 5 in. barrel, 11 shot, stainless steel frame, usually supplied with two mags. although early mfg. did not include a mag. because of design problems, "83SM" ser. no. prefix. Mfg. 1984-86.

$1,775	$1,450	$950	$700	$600	$475	$395

Last MSR was $500.

Add $600 for .45 conversion unit.

Be wary of Standard Models with wooden cases and conversion kits - they are fakes!

BREN 10 MILITARY/POLICE MODEL - 10mm cal. only, identical to standard model, except has all black finish, "83MP" ser. no. prefix. Mfg. 1984-86.

$1,875	$1,550	$1,050	$950	$650	$475	$395

Last MSR was $550.

BREN 10 SPECIAL FORCES MODEL - 10mm cal. only, commercial version of the military pistol submitted to the U.S. gov´t. Model D has dark finish. Model L has light finish, "SFD" ser. no. prefix on Model D, "SFL" ser. no. prefix on Model L. Disc. 1986.

Dark finish - Model D	$1,950	$1,550	$1,050	$775	$550	$475	$395
Light finish - Model L	$2,250	$1,775	$1,150	$950	$700	$575	$475

Last MSR was $600.

BREN 10 DUAL-MASTER PRESENTATION MODEL - 10mm and .45 ACP cal., supplied with extra slide and barrel (numbered to gun) to accommodate the .45 ACP, same mags. (two) for both cals., extra fine finish, light scroll engraving, with wood presentation case, "83DM" ser. no. prefix, less than 50 mfg. Disc. 1986.

$4,200	$3,600	$2,950	$1,750	$1,000	$800	$700

Last MSR was $800.

Be wary of Standard Models with wooden cases and conversion kits - they are fakes!

GRADING - PPGS™	100%	98%	95%	90%	80%	70%	60%

BREN 10 JEFF COOPER COMMEMORATIVE - 10mm cal. only, while 2,000 were annnounced for mfg., sources believe that approx. 13 were actually made, 22Kt. gold plated detailing, laser engraved stocks, special presentation chest. Disc. 1986.

	$5,500	$5,000	$4,600	N/A	N/A	N/A	N/A

Last MSR was $2,000.

MARKSMAN MODEL - .45 ACP cal., 250 mfg. (in its own ser. range) for a retail shop in Chicago called "The Marksman," action similar to Bren 10 Standard Model, "MSM" ser. no. prefix.

	$1,100	$750	$600	$500	$350	$200	$150

Add $750 for 10mm conversion unit.
Add $200 for original nylon carrying case marked "Marksman."

BRETTON-GAUCHER

Current manufacturer established in 2000, and located in Saint-Etienne, France. No current U.S. importation. Previously imported and distributed by Mandall Shooting Supplies, Inc. located in Scottsdale, AZ.

The Bretton trademark was established in 1934, and specialized in Baby lightweight shotguns. Gaucher dates back to 1834, and specialized in Express double rifles. The two companies merged in 2000.

RIFLES

Bretton-Gaucher manufactures a variety of single-shot and small caliber rifles, in addition to Express double rifles. To date, these guns have had little or no importation into the U.S. Please contact the factory directly for more information, including pricing and availability.

SHOTGUNS: O/U

All Bretton shotguns are extremely lightweight and well balanced because of their unique design (permitting total disassembly including barrels) and use of various composition alloys.

BABY STANDARD (SPRINT MODEL) - 12 or 20 ga. only, sliding breech action allows barrels to move straight forward, 27 1/2 In. separated barrels, double triggers, side opening lever, blue action and barrels, recoil pad, checkered walnut stock and forearm, 4.8 lbs. Limited importation.

MSR N/A		$995	$885	$700	$625	$575	$475	$430

Prices reflect most recent importation information.

SPRINT DELUXE - 12, 16 (disc.), or 20 ga., action similar to Baby Standard, engraved coin finished receiver, 27 1/2 in. separated barrels, deluxe checkered walnut stock and forearm, extremely lightweight, 4.8 lbs. Limited importation.

MSR N/A		$895	$725	$625	$575	$475	$430	$395

Last MSR was $975.

FAIR PLAY MODEL - 12 or 20 ga., differs from Sprint Models in that action pivots like normal O/U, 27 1/2 in. separated barrels, lightweight construction, 4.8 lbs. Limited importation.

MSR N/A		$966	$850	$675	$625	$575	$475	$430

Add $64 for Fair Play Limited Model.

BRIGNOLI, SILVIO

Current retailer and manufacturer established in 1965 and located in Brescia, Italy. No current U.S. importation.

Silvio Brignoli manufactures a boxlock SxS shotgun in most gauges. Please contact the company directly for more information, including pricing and availability (see Trademark Index).

GRADING - PPGS™	100%	98%	95%	90%	80%	70%	60%

BRILEY

Current trademark of choke tubes manufactured by Briley Manufacturing Inc., and located in Houston, TX. Briley has produced both pistols and rifles, including those listed, in addition to manufacturing a complete line of top quality shotgun barrel tubes and chokes since 1976. Additionally, beginning late March, 2006, Briley Manufacturing began importing and distributing Mauser Models 98 and 03 bolt action rifles from Germany. Please refer to the Mauser section for more information.

PISTOLS: SEMI-AUTO

FANTOM - 9mm Para., .38 Super, .40 S&W, or .45 ACP cal., features Caspian aluminum wide body frame, Briley match barrel, and many competition features, hot blue slide finish and armor coated frame, 8 or 10 shot mag, black synthetic grips, approx. 22-24 oz. Mfg. 1998-2003.

$1,675	$1,300	$1,075	$875	$750	$625	$575

Last MSR was $1,900.

Add $95 for hard chrome finish.
Add $75 for night sights.
Add $350 for 2 port barrel compensator.

ADVANTAGE - 9mm Para., .40 S&W, or .45 ACP cal., features 5 in. Briley match barrel, checkered walnut grips and front grip strap, hot blue finish. Mfg. 1998-2004.

$1,495	$1,250	$1,050	$875	$750	$625	$575

Last MSR was $1,650.

Add $175 for hard chrome finish.
Add $100 for stainless steel (new 2000).

VERSATILITY PLUS - 9mm Para., .40 S&W, or .45 ACP cal., features steel or stainless steel (new 2000) 1911 Govt. length modular or Caspian frame, 5 in. barrel, checkered black synthetic grips and front grip strap, squared off trigger guard, hot blue finish. Mfg. 1998-2004.

$1,625	$1,300	$1,050	$875	$725	$600	$550

Last MSR was $1,850.

Add $175 for hard chrome finish.
Add $175 for stainles steel (new 2000).

SIGNATURE SERIES - .40 S&W cal. only, similar to Versatility Plus. Mfg. 1998-2004.

$1,975	$1,650	$1,325	$1,125	$900	$775	$625

Last MSR was $2,250.

Add $175 for hard chrome finish.

PLATE MASTER - 9mm Para. or .38 Super cal., features 1911 Govt. length frame, Briley TCII titanium barrel compensator, Briley scope mount, and other competition features, hot blue finish. Mfg. 1998-2004.

$1,675	$1,325	$1,075	$895	$775	$625	$575

Last MSR was $1,895.

Add $175 for hard chrome finish.

EL PRESIDENTE - 9mm Para. or .38 Super cal., top-of-the-line competition model with Briley quad compensator with side ports, checkered synthetic grips and front grip strap, squared off trigger guard. Mfg. 1998-2004.

$2,250	$1,925	$1,625	$1,325	$1,075	$875	$750

Last MSR was $2,550.

Add $175 for hard chrome finish.

RIFLES: BOLT ACTION

Briley began importing and distributing Mauser Models 98 and 03 bolt action rifles in early 2006. Please refer to the Mauser section for current information.

GRADING - PPGS™	100%	98%	95%	90%	80%	70%	60%

TRANS PECOS - .22-250 Rem., .243 Win., .260 Rem., .308 Win., or 7mm-08 Rem. cal., solid aluminum frame fits metal to metal with barreled action, bench rest grade Jewell trigger, match grade L. Walther barrel, 3 lug 45 degree one-piece bolt, choice of black synthetic (single shot) or checkered high gloss stock and forearm (repeater). Mfg. 1998-2002.

	$3,200	$2,750	$2,275	$1,950	$1,775	$1,525	$1,250

Last MSR was $3,495.

Subtract $500 for single shot action.

This model is guaranteed to shoot 1/2 in. groups at 100 yards with factory ammo.

RIFLES: SEMI-AUTO

HUNTER - .22 LR cal., utilizes Ruger 10/22 action, 21 1/2 in. tapered match stainless steel barrel with crown, Hogue rubber or wood stock, 10 shot mag., includes Briley integral scope mount, approx. 6 1/4 - 6 5/8 lbs.

	$550	$475	$395	$360	$330	$300	$285

Last MSR was $600.

Add $250 for wood stock.
Add $100 for fluted barrel.

✳ *Hunter Magnum* - .22 Mag. cal., similar to Hunter, except is 9 shot mag. and 21 1/2 in. bull barrel. Disc. 2003.

	$750	$575	$475	$425	$375	$325	$295

Last MSR was $850.

Add $250 for walnut or laminate stock.
Add $100 for fluted barrel.

SPORTER - .17 HMR (new 2006) or .22 LR cal., similar to Hunter, except has 18 1/2 or 21 1/2 in. match stainless steel bull barrel with crown, Hogue rubber, brown laminate, or uncheckered walnut sporter stock, 10 shot mag., approx. 6 1/2 lbs.

	$550	$475	$395	$360	$330	$300	$285

Last MSR was $600.

Add $250 for laminate or sporter style walnut stock.
Add $100 for fluted barrel.

BMG - .22 LR cal., 17 in. match stainless steel bull barrel with target crown, includes 3 1/2 lbs. adj. match barrel weights, choice of Hogue rubber, brown laminate sporter, or walnut sporter stock, 10 shot mag., designed for match grade ammunition only.

	$675	$600	$525	$465	$425	$385	$350

Last MSR was $750.

Add $250 for laminate or sporter style walnut stock.

BRITARMS

Previous trademark manufactured by Berdan Gunmakers Ltd. located in England. Previously imported and distributed until 1994 by Mandall Shooting Supplies, Inc. located in Scottsdale, AZ. Previously by Action Arms Ltd. (1982-1983) located in Philadelphia, PA.

Britarms Target Pistols had very limited importation into the U.S. While Britarms manufactured other models, only the Model 2000 is listed since it was formally imported through U.S. firms.

PISTOLS: SEMI-AUTO

MODEL 2000 (MK II) - .22 LR cal., standard fire target semi-auto pistol, adj. trigger and rear sight, anatomical adj. grips, 5.82 in. barrel, 5 shot mag., 3 lbs., limited importation, including approx. 2000 through Action Arms Ltd.

	$995	$825	$700	$625	$550	$495	$450

Last MSR was $1,295.

This model features a bolt hold-open mechanism which serves as a manual safety to allow importation.

BRNO ARMS (ZBROJOVKA BRNO)

Currently manufactured by Zbrojovka Brno located in Brno, Czech Republic (formerly Czechoslovakia) since 1918. Limited U.S. importation. Brno 98 bolt action rifles and actions were imported by EAA Corp, located in Sharpes, FL until 2002. Also previously imported and distributed by Euro-Imports, located in El Cajon, CA until 2001 and by Bohemia Arms located in Fountain Valley, CA until 1997. Brno rifles, shotguns, and combination guns produced at the Brno factory were previously imported and distributed by Magnum Research Inc. located in Minneapolis, MN (c. 1994-1996). In the early '50s, Brno rifles were imported by Continental Arms Corp. located in New York City. Pragotrade located in Ontario, Canada also imports this trademark for Canada currently (and exclusively). Previously imported by T.D. Arms located in New Baltimore, MD.

As more history is becoming available on this important European trademark, the following biographical sketch will provide some information. Circa 1918, some military personnel took over the controlling interest of the Austro-Hungarian armament shop in Brno, Czechoslovakia, renaming it The State Armament and Engineering Works. Approximately a year later, the name was changed to Czechoslovak State Armament Works. The former provinces of Bohemia and Moravia had long been firearms manufacturing centers within their regions. Prior to 1924, this firm was involved mainly with Mauser Model 98 type rifles (both assembly and mfg.).

Pistol manufacture was tranferred from Brno to Ceská Zbrojovka, located in Strakonice, Czechoslovakia, circa 1923. During 1964-1966, the Czech government transferred the production of long guns from Zbrojovka Brno to Ceská Zbrojovka Uhersky Brod. During the 1970s & 1980s, the arms production of Zbrojovka Brno accounted for less than 3% of its total capacity. The activities of this company were deverted into the production of typewriters, diesel motors, and automatic machine tools. While many firearm designs originated in Brno, Zbrojovka Brno was not the manufacturer. Because of this, the long guns manufactured in the mid-1960s, including the ZKK 600 - 602 series and ZKM rimfires, were manufactured in CZ Uhersky Brod. Because of the Czech government's decision to merge manufacture within both companies, the Brno trademark was also used by Ceská Zbrojovka Uhersky Brod.

This relationship was terminated in 1983, when both companies became part of the Agrozet conglomerate. While confusing, the arms utlizing the Brno trademark were not produced in Brno during this time. All firearms exported from Czechoslovakia at the time carried the Brno logo, and most of them were manufactured by Ceská Zbrojovka Uhersky Brod.

Since many of the models listed below have not been imported since 2002, N/As will appear in place of MSRs on those recent imports.

CZ PISTOLS & RIFLES

See separate listing under CZ in this text.

PISTOLS: SEMI-AUTO

MODEL ZBP-99 - 9mm Para. or .40 S&W cal., double action.
While advertised in 1998, this gun never went into production.

REVOLVERS

ZKR 551 - .32 S&W Long or .38 Spl. cal., double action, fixed access 6 shot cylinder, adj. sights, checkered wood grips with thumb rest, 6 in. barrel, approx. 2 lbs. Importation began 1999.

MSR N/A		$1,375	$1,100	$978	$875	$775	$675	$600

RIFLES: BOLT ACTION

The Brno Lightweight Sporter was introduced in the late 1930s. A small quantity was manufactured during pre-war and WWII. Most production occured between 1946-1955. Total production of this model was approx. 40,000+ units. A design change was implemented at approximately serial number 23,000, at which time the receiver was changed to a double square bridge dovetailed to accept scope mounts.

Earlier mfg. had a rounded receiver and some had claw type scope mounts installed. These guns were referenced as Models 21 and 22 domestically, but no model designation appears on the gun. Available cals. were 6.5x57mm, 7x57mm, 7x64mm, 8x57mm, or 8x60mm. Configuration was small ring Mauser 98 receiver with double set trigger(s), butterknife bolt, checkered walnut pistol grip stock (half or full length), with cheekpiece and sling swivels, late production incorporated four variations and two barrel lengths (20.5 or 23.6 in.).

All currently manufactured Brno firearms have a 3 year guarantee.

Brno rifles may be dated by the two digit date beside their proofmarks.

HORNET SPORTER (MODEL ZKW 465) - .22 Hornet cal., miniature Mauser action, 22 3/4 in. barrel, 5 shot clip mag., 3-leaf express sight, double set trigger(s), checkered pistol grip stock, also called Z-B Mauser, serial range noted is 00,111-37,393, approx. 40,000 mfg. between 1948-1973.

$1,200	$925	$750	$625	$500	$400	$295

There are few examples in .218 Bee and .222 Rem. cal. - premiums can be added.

This model was redesigned with a subsequent designation of ZKB 680 Fox in approx. 1975.

MODEL ZG-47 - .270 Win., .30-06, 7x57mm, 7x64mm, 8x64S, 8x57mm, 9.3x62mm, or 10.75x68mm cal., large ring Mauser 98 action with 20mm dovetails on receiver ring and bridge, single trigger, hinged floorplate, rollover type safety and bolt handle designed for low scope mounting, 23 1/2 in. barrel, checkered pistol grip walnut stock with sling swivels and Schnabel forend, approx. serial range is 0-20,000, mfg. and exported world-wide between 1956-62 (approx.).

$1,125	$895	$725	$600	$495	$395	$295

Early specimens of this model are marked "BRNO MADE IN CZECHOSLOVAKIA". This model is generally regarded as being one of the finest rifles that Brno has manufactured.

MODEL G 33-40 - 8mm cal., mfg. between 1940-42, prices below assume sporterized condition.

$350	$295	$260	$230	$200	$175	$150

MODEL 21H - 6.5x57mm, 7x57mm, 7x64mm (scarce), 8x57mm, or 8x60mm cal., featherweight style design of the small ring Mauser type action, with (post-1949) or without 20mm dovetails on receiver ring and bridge, 20 1/2 or 23 in. barrel, butterknife style bolt handle, double set triggers, 2-leaf rear sight, checkered pistol grip walnut stock with cheekpiece and plastic buttplate/grip cap, small Schnabel forend, sling swivels included, noted serialization is 14,410-40,098, mfg. approx. 1946-55.

$1,200	$925	$750	$625	$500	$400	$295

This model was available in 4 different variations: short barrel/short stock, short barrel/full length stock, long barrel/short stock, long barrel/full length stock. The left receiver rail on these models is marked "ZBROJOVKA BRNO, NARODNI PODNIK".

MODEL 22F - similar to 21H, with full length stock. Disc.

$1,400	$1,100	$925	$800	$675	$550	$475

MODEL 1 - .22 LR cal., 22 3/4 in. barrel, 3-leaf sight, 5 shot clip mag., checkered pistol, 6 lbs. Mfg. 1946-57.

$595	$540	$485	$405	$375	$320	$265

GRADING - PPGS™	100%	98%	95%	90%	80%	70%	60%

MODEL 2 - similar to Model 1, with checkered deluxe walnut stock.

	$635	$570	$515	$430	$405	$350	$295

MODEL 3 - .22 LR cal., target rifle model with 27 1/2 in. heavy barrel, adj. click target sights, 5 shot clip mag., plain target style stock with large swivels, 9 1/2 lbs. Mfg. 1949-56.

	$635	$570	$515	$430	$405	$350	$295

MODEL 4 - similar to Model 3, except has improved trigger design and safety. Mfg. 1957-62.

	$700	$635	$570	$515	$430	$405	$350

MODEL 5 - similar to Model 1, except has improved trigger design and safety. Mfg. 1957-73.

	$650	$570	$515	$430	$405	$350	$295

BRNO 98 STANDARD - .243 Win., .270 Win., .30-06, .308 Win., .300 Win. Mag., 6.5x55mm SE, 7mm Rem. Mag. (new 2000), 7x57mm, 7x64mm, 8x57 JS, or 9.3x62mm cal., Mauser 98 style action, 23.6 in. barrel with or without iron sights, checkered walnut stock with Bavarian cheekpiece, or synthetic stock (disc.) and forearms (new 2002) single or set trigger, 7 1/4 lbs.

MSR N/A	$525	$425	$350	$315	$285	$260	$225

    Subtract approx. $150 for synthetic stock (disc.).
    Add $52 for Mag. cals.
    Add $83 for single set trigger.
    Add $22 for Battue ramp sights.

✳ *Brno 98 Mannlicher* - similar to Brno 98 Standard, except has full length stock and set trigger.

MSR N/A	$695	$550	$475	$385	$350	$315	$295

    Add $60 for Mag. cals.

MODEL ZOM-451 - .22 LR cal., straight pull bolt action, limited importation by Century International Arms during 1998.

MODEL ZKM-451 - .22 LR cal. Importation began 1995.

MSR N/A	$215	$200	$185	$170	$155	$140	$125

    Add $62 for Lux Model (deluxe checkered wood).

MODEL ZKM-452 - please refer to the CZ listing in this text for current information (current mfg. is by CZ).

MODEL ZKM-456 LUX SPORTER - .22 LR cal., bolt action, 5 or 10 shot mag., 24.4 in. barrel, folding rear sight, blue finish, beechwood stock with pistol grip, 6.8 lbs. Imported 1992-98.

	$315	$260	$215	$175	$155	$135	$120

Last MSR was $370.

    Add $18 for micrometer rear sight (ZKM-456 MI).

✳ *Model 456 L/LK Target* - .22 LR cal., Target variation of the ZKM-456 Lux featuring 25 or 28 in. barrel with adj. front and rear sights, 10.1 lbs. Imported 1992-98.

	$305	$250	$210	$170	$150	$130	$115

Last MSR was $358.

    Add $7 for 25 in. barrel.

✳ *Model 456 Match Single Shot* - .22 LR cal., designed for UIT competition at 50 M, features 27 1/2 in. barrel, adj. cheekpiece and buttplate, aperture sights, 9.9 lbs. Imported 1992-98.

	$375	$335	$280	$250	$215	$175	$155

Last MSR was $459.

ZKK 600 - please refer to the CZ listing in this text for current information (current mfg. is by CZ).

GRADING - PPGS™	100%	98%	95%	90%	80%	70%	60%

ZKK 601 - please refer to the CZ listing in this text for current information (current mfg. was by CZ).

ZKK 602 - please refer to the CZ listing in this text for current information (current mfg. is by CZ).

ZKB 680 (FOX II) - .22 Hornet or .222 Rem. (disc.) cal., 23 1/2 in. barrel, 5 shot mag., set triggers, 5 lbs. 12 oz. Importation disc. 1991.

	$445	$380	$340	$295	$255	$230	$200

Last MSR was $499.

RIFLES: O/U

ZH-344, 348, & 349 - 7x57R (Model ZH-344), 7x65R (Model ZH-348), or 8x57JRS (Model ZH-349) cal., 23.6 in. VR barrels, double triggers, skip line checkering, sling swivels, approx. 7 1/2 lbs. Importation began 1998.

MSR N/A	$1,100	$978	$875	$775	$675	$600	$550

Add $324-$357 per additional set of shotgun barrels, $418 per additional rifle barrel, and $829 for additional Mag. cal. rifle barrels.

SUPER EXPRESS - 7x65R, 9.3x/4R, .375 H&H, or .458 Win. Mag. (disc.) cal., sidelock action with Kersten breech crossbolt, hand engraved, skipline checkering, approx. 9 lbs. Importation disc. 1992.

	$3,450	$2,875	$2,300	$1,875	$1,600	$1,375	$1,200

Last MSR was $3,900.

This model previously could be ordered with 6 different types of engraving options. They were: Grade I - add $2,060, Grade II - add $1,030, Grade III - add $1,545, Grade IV - add $1,030, Grade V - add $620, Grade VI - add $660.

SUPER SAFARI - 7x64R, .375 H&H Mag., or 9.3x74R cal., action derived from the Super Express, sidelock, DT with set trigger built in, adj. point of impact, 23.6 in. barrels with open sights, deluxe skipline checkered walnut stock and forearm with vent. recoil pad, approx. 9 lbs. Imported 1992-disc.

	$2,375	$1,975	$1,675	$1,450	$1,225	$1,000	$900

MODEL 803 - various cals., includes set trigger.

MSR N/A	$1,350	$1,175	$1,000	$875	$750	$650	$550

RIFLES: SEMI-AUTO

ZKM-611 - .17 HMR (new 2006), .22 Mag. cal., 20 1/2 in. barrel, 6, 10 (C/B 1994), or 12* shot mag., black metal finish, beechwood (new 1996) or checkered walnut stock and forend, grooved receiver, 6.2 lbs.

MSR N/A	$440	$395	$350	$300	$265	$230	$200

Add $70 for walnut stock (disc. 1999).

MODEL 581 - .22 LR cal., semi-auto, select walnut stock, adj. sights, 5 shot mag. Disc.

	$600	$540	$495	$440	$395	$350	$295

RIFLES: SINGLE SHOT

ZK-05 - various cals., upgraded variation of the ZK-99, set trigger, many other design improvements.

MSR N/A	$575	$475	$400	$330	$285	$240	$200

ZK 99 - various cals., break open action with top lever, quarter rib on barrel, checkered walnut stock with cheekpiece and Schnabel forearm, includes swivels and slings, 5 3/4 lbs. Importation began 2000.

MSR N/A	$875	$725	$625	$550	$500	$450	$400

GRADING - PPGS™	100%	98%	95%	90%	80%	70%	60%

MODEL ZKB-110 - .22 Hornet, .222 Rem., 5.6x52R, 5.6x50R Mag., 6.5x57R (disc. 1999), 7x57R (disc. 1999), or 8x57JRS (disc. 1999) cal., single shot break open rifle/shotgun, top lever opening, 23.6 in. barrel, uncheckered (Standard Model) or checkered walnut stock with Bavarian cheekpiece and forearm (Lux Model), includes sling swivels, 6 lbs. Importation began 1998.

MSR N/A	$225	$185	$160	$140	$120	$110	$100

    Add $77 for ZKB-110 Lux Model.
    Add $205 for ZKB-110 Super Lux Model (new 2000).
    Add $48 for 7x57R or 8x57JRS cal. (disc. 1999).
    Add $132 (standard) or $142 (Lux) for an interchangeable 12 ga. shotgun barrel.

SHOTGUNS/COMBINATIONS GUNS: O/U

The following models were imported and distributed by Euro-Imports, located in El Cajon, CA.

ZH-300 SHOTGUN - 12 ga. only, double triggers with rear trigger doubling as single trigger, 27 1/2 in. barrels, 7 lbs. Imported 1986-92.

$530	$430	$395	$360	$330	$300	$275

Last MSR was $599.

This model was available in skeet, trap, or field configuration.

ZH-301 FIELD SHOTGUN - 12 or 16 ga. field, 27 1/2 in. barrels, optional Monte Carlo stock (disc.).

MSR N/A	$600	$475	$375	$315	$240	$200	$180

    Add $20 for Monte Carlo stock.

ZH-302 SKEET SHOTGUN - 12 ga., skeet model, 26 in. barrels, optional Monte Carlo stock (disc.).

MSR N/A	$650	$515	$375	$300	$250	$225	$195

    Add $20 for Monte Carlo stock.

ZH-303 TRAP SHOTGUN - 12 ga., trap model, 30 in. barrels, optional Monte Carlo stock (disc.).

MSR N/A	$650	$515	$375	$300	$250	$225	$195

    Add $20 for Monte Carlo stock.

ZH-300 SERIES COMBINATION GUNS - 7x57R x 12 ga. (ZH-304), 6x52R x 12 ga. (ZH-305), 6x50R Mag. x 12 ga. (ZH-306), .22 Hornet x 12 ga. (ZH-307), 7x65R x 12 ga. (ZH-308), 8x57JRS x 12 ga. (ZH-309), 7x57R x 16 ga. (ZH-324), 7x65R x 16 ga. (ZH-328), combination rifle/shotgun, optional adj. trigger and Monte Carlo stock. Importation disc. 1994 - reintroduced 1999.

MSR N/A	$695	$575	$425	$350	$300	$250	$195

    Add $73 for cheekpiece and set trigger.
    Add $35 for adj. trigger (disc.).
    Add $20 for Monte Carlo stock (disc.).

ZH 300 Series over and unders are unique in that they permit 8 different interchangeable barrels including rifle and shotgun sets, interrupter on double trigger, blued action, engraving, diamond checkered walnut.

MODEL ZH-300 COMBO SET - Model ZH-300 style engraving and features, equipped with 8 interchangeable barrels that include various O/U configurations including shotgun/shotgun and shotgun/rifle configurations in various gauges and cals. Imported 1986-91.

$2,950	$2,600	$2,250	$2,000	$1,800	$1,600	$1,450

Last MSR was $3,500.

MODEL 500/501 SHOTGUN - 12 ga. only, 28 in. VR barrels, double or single (disc. 1999) trigger.

MSR N/A	$845	$725	$625	$525	$425	$350	$295

    Add $50 for single trigger (disc. 1999).

GRADING - PPGS™	100%	98%	95%	90%	80%	70%	60%

✳ *Model 500 Combo Set* - shotgun/rifle set comprised of 4 barrels including 12 ga. over barrels with choice of 5.6x52R (disc.), 7x57R, 7x65R, or 12 ga. under barrels (in either field, skeet, or trap chokings), sling swivels, set trigger on rifle/shotgun combo, chemically engraved, about 7 1/2 lbs. Imported 1987-91.

	$1,925	$1,625	$1,400	$1,200	$1,075	$950	$825

Last MSR was $2,169.

This model was available in limited quanitity.

MODEL 502 SERIES COMBINATION GUN - 12 ga. only, ejectors, combination shotgun/rifle available in .222 Rem., .243 Win., .30-06, .308 Win., and 4 metric cals., fixed choke, acid etched engraving, skipline checkering and cheekpiece. New 1986.

MSR N/A	$1,050	$850	$695	$600	$525	$425	$350

Add $699 for interchangeable 12 ga. shotgun barrels (new 1998).

BS-571/572 SHOTGUN/COMBINATION GUN - 12 ga. only, boxlock action with ejectors, 6x65R (disc.) or 7x65R rifle cal. only. Limited importation 1992-95.

	$825	$700	$600	$550	$475	$425	$375

Last MSR was $995.

Add approx. $115 for rifle/shotgun (12 ga. only) combination (Model 572).

MODEL 571 SUPER SERIES - 12 ga. field, skeet, and trap configuration as well as combination shotgun/rifle in 12 ga. x 7x57R or 7x65R cal. Importation disc. 1991.

	$800	$700	$640	$590	$550	$515	$475

Last MSR was $899.

Add $70 for single trigger or trap/skeet configuration (disc.).
Add $700 for extra set of 12 ga. field barrels.
Add $1,101 for hand engraving.

✳ *Model 571 Super Combo* - 3 barrel set including 12 ga., 7x57R, and 7x65R barrels. Imported 1987-90.

	$1,925	$1,640	$1,425	$1,250	$1,100	$1,000	$925

Last MSR was $2,169.

MODEL 801 SERIES SHOTGUN - 12 ga. only, 2 3/4 or 3 in. chambers, ejectors, SST, machine engraved receiver, checkered walnut stock and forearm, VR barrels with or without choke tubes, left-hand version in various configurations that include field, sporting, trap, and skeet available at no additional charge.

MSR N/A	$875	$750	$625	$550	$495	$450	$395

Add $276 for Sporting Model with 4 interchangeable choke tubes.

MODEL 802 COMBINATION GUN - 12 ga., 3 in. chamber, various American and metric cals., includes set trigger, extractors, machined engraved receiver, checkered walnut stock and forearm, interchangeable barrels.

MSR N/A	$1,000	$875	$750	$675	$600	$525	$450

SHOTGUNS: SxS

ZP-49 - 12 ga. only, ejectors, double triggers, true sidelock, Purdey-type top bolt, cocking indicators, walnut stock, swivels. Imported 1986-91.

	$535	$460	$420	$385	$350	$320	$290

Last MSR was $589.

Add $20 for engraving.

ZP-149 - similar to ZP-49, except has game scene engraving on sideplates, choice of English or pistol grip stock. Imported 1986-98.

	$575	$495	$425	$350	$300	$250	$225

Last MSR was $676.

Add $23 for pistol grip stock.

GRADING - PPGS™	100%	98%	95%	90%	80%	70%	60%

ZP-349 - 12 ga. only, extractors, double triggers, true sidelock, Purdey-type top bolt, cocking indicators, walnut stock with cheek piece, beavertail forearm, swivels, 7.3 lbs. Imported 1986 only.

	100%	98%	95%	90%	80%	70%	60%
	$450	$390	$360	$325	$300	$270	$250

Last MSR was $520.

Add $20 for engraving.

SHOTGUNS: SINGLE SHOT

ZBK 100 - 12 or 20 ga., 3 in. chamber, walnut stock and forearm. Importation began 1999.

MSR N/A	$180	$160	$140	$120	$105	$95	$85

BROCKMAN'S CUSTOM GUNSMITHING

Current custom rifle manufacturer and gunsmith established in 1986, and located in Gooding, Idaho. Consumer direct sales only.

Brockman's Custom Gunsmithing manufactures a wide variety of custom bolt action rifles typically based on Win. Model 70, Rem. Model 700, Dakota, or Nesika action. Please contact the company directly to find out more about their wide variety of custom rifles and gunsmithing services.

RIFLES: BOLT ACTION

Specific models and/or configurations include the Universal Hunter (complete gun base price $2,895), Dangerous Game (last MSR $2,450, disc. 2001), Premier Practical (base price $3,495), Model 70 Classic Practical (base price $2,995), Working Rifle (base price $3,195), Ladies rifles (base price was $2,100-$2,895 - disc. 2000), Scout rifles (last MSR $1,995 - disc. 2000), .50 Beowulf-Brockman (disc., base price was $995, includes case), and other handcrafted custom bolt action rifles.

RIFLES: LEVER ACTION

Brockman's modifies general purpose lever action rifles based on the Marlin 1895G/SS actions, including the Beast (base price $2,476), the SOB (is based on shorter and lighter Beast, disc. 2004, last MSR was $1,995), Master Guide Package (base price $1,291), and the Super Guide Package (base price $1,839).

BROLIN ARMS, INC.

Previous importer of handguns (FEG mfg.), rifles (older Mauser military, see Mauser listing), shotguns (Chinese mfg.), and airguns from 1995 to 1999. Previously located in Pomona, CA, until 1999, and in La Verne, CA until 1997.

PISTOLS: SEMI-AUTO, SINGLE ACTION

LEGEND SERIES MODEL L45 - .45 ACP cal., patterned after the Colt 1911 Government Model, features include throated match 5 in. barrel, polished feed ramp, flared ejection port, beveled mag. well, flattop slide, flat mainspring housing, front strap high relief cut, aluminum lightweight extended trigger, high visibility sights, 7 shot mag., commander style hammer and checkered walnut grips, 38 oz. Mfg. 1995-98.

	$425	$365	$325	$295	$275	$250	$225

Last MSR was $500.

* *Legend Series Model L45C (Compact)* - similar to Model L45, except has 4 in. barrel, 35 oz. Mfg. 1995-98.

	$440	$380	$330	$295	$275	$250	$225

Last MSR was $520.

✳ *Legend Series Model L45T* - features standard frame with compact slide, 4 in. barrel, 36 oz. Mfg. 1997-98.

	100%	98%	95%	90%	80%	70%	60%
	$440	$380	$330	$295	$275	$250	$225

Last MSR was $520.

PATRIOT SERIES MODEL P45 COMP - .45 ACP cal., similar to Legend Series Model L45, except has one-piece match 4 in. barrel with integral dual port compensator, 7 shot mag., Millett or Novak combat sights (new 1997), test target provided, choice of blue or satin (frame only) finish, 38 oz. Mfg. 1996-97 only.

	$585	$475	$415	$365	$325	$285	$250

Last MSR was $649.

> Add $70 for Novak combat sights (new 1997).
> Add $20 for T-tone finish (frame only).

✳ *Patriot Series Model P45C (Compact)* - .45 ACP cal., similar to Model P45 Comp, except has 3 1/4 in. barrel with integral conical lock-up system, 34 1/2 oz. Mfg. 1996-97.

	$610	$495	$425	$375	$325	$285	$250

Last MSR was $689.

> Add $70 for Novak combat sights.
> Add $20 for T-tone finish (frame only).

✳ *Patriot Series Model P45T* - features standard frame with compact slide, 3 1/4 in. barrel, 35 1/2 oz. Mfg. 1997 only.

	$620	$500	$425	$375	$325	$285	$250

Last MSR was $699.

> Add $60 for Novak combat sights (new 1997).
> Add $10 for T-tone finish (frame only).

PRO STOCK MODEL COMPETITION PISTOL - .45 ACP cal., competition pistol featuring most state-of-the-art competitive improvements, 5 in. barrel, 8 shot mag., blue or satin (frame only) finish, signature wood grips, 40 oz. Mfg. 1996-97.

	$685	$550	$475	$415	$360	$295	$260

Last MSR was $779.

> Add $20 for T-tone finish (frame only).

✳ *Pro Comp Model Competition Pistol* - similar to Pro Stock Model, except has 4 in. dual port compensated heavy match barrel, blue or satin (frame only) finish, 40 oz. Mfg. 1996-97.

	$800	$650	$525	$435	$375	$325	$295

Last MSR was $919.

> Add $10 for T-tone finish (frame only).

TAC 11 - .45 ACP cal., 5 in. conical barrel w/o bushing, beavertail grip safety, 8 shot mag., T-tone or blue finish, Novak low profile combat or Tritium sights, black rubber contour grips, 37 oz. Mfg. 1997-98.

	$595	$485	$425	$365	$325	$285	$250

Last MSR was $670.

> Add $90 for Tritium sights (disc. 1997).

✳ *Tac 11 Compact* - similar to Tac 11, except has shorter barrel. Mfg. 1998 only.

	$610	$495	$435	$365	$325	$285	$250

Last MSR was $690.

> Add $60 for hard-chrome finish.

GRADING - PPGS™	100%	98%	95%	90%	80%	70%	60%

GOLD SERIES - .45 ACP cal., 5 in. barrel w/o barrel bushing and supported chamber, IPSC configuration with many features, adj. aluminum trigger, front and rear slide serations, stainless steel construction with choice of natural stainless or blue stainless finish. Limited mfg. 1998 only.

	$715	$625	$525	$440	$385	$325	$280

Last MSR was $800.

PISTOLS: SEMI-AUTO, DOUBLE ACTION

The following models had limited manufacture 1998 only.

TAC SERIES SERVICE MODEL - .45 ACP cal., full sized double action service pistol, single/double action, 8 shot single column mag., front and rear slide serations, combat style trigger guard, royal or satin blue finish, low profile 3-dot sights. Mfg. 1998 only.

	$360	$315	$285	$260	$240	$220	$200

Last MSR was $400.

Add $20 for royal blue finish.

TAC SERIES FULL SIZE MODEL - 9mm Para., .40 S&W, or .45 ACP cal., similar to Tac Series Service Model, except longer barrel, checkered walnut or plastic grips, 8 (.45 ACP only) or 10 shot mag. Mfg. 1998 only.

	$360	$315	$285	$260	$240	$220	$200

Last MSR was $400.

Add $20 for royal blue finish.

TAC SERIES COMPACT MODEL - 9mm Para. or .40 S&W cal., shortened barrel/slide with full size frame, 10 shot mag. Mfg. 1998 only.

	$360	$315	$285	$260	$240	$220	$200

Last MSR was $400.

Add $20 for royal blue finish.

TAC SERIES BANTAM MODEL - 9mm Para. or .40 S&W cal., super compact size, single/double action with concealed hammer, all steel construction, 3-dot sights. Mfg. 1998 only.

	$360	$315	$285	$260	$240	$220	$200

Last MSR was $399.

BANTAM MODEL - 9mm Para. or .40 S&W cal., single or double action, super compact size, concealed hammer, all steel construction, 3-dot sights, royal blue or matte finish. Limited mfg. by FEG 1999 only.

	$360	$315	$285	$260	$240	$220	$200

Last MSR was $399.

PISTOLS: CUSTOM

Brolin Arms manufactured a small quantity of high performance M1911 based custom combat and competition pistols during 1998 only. The Formula Z Model Custom Combat Model retail price range was $1,300-$1,600, the Formula One RS Limited Class Competition Model was priced at $2,000-$2,300, and the Formula One RZ Competition Race Gun Model topped the line at $2,450-$2,750.

SHOTGUNS: SEMI-AUTO

MODEL BL-12 - 12 ga. only, 3 in. chamber, 18 1/2 (security) or 28 (field) in. VR barrel with 3 choke tubes (Beretta compatible), satin blue finish, choice of wood or synthetic stock and forearm. Mfg. 1998 only.

	$375	$325	$300	$280	$260	$240	$220

Last MSR was $430.

GRADING - PPGS™	100%	98%	95%	90%	80%	70%	60%

MODEL SAS-12 - 12 ga. only, 2 3/4 in. chamber, 24 in. barrel with IC choke tube, 3 (standard) or 5 shot (disc. late 1998) detachable box mag., synthetic stock and forearm, gas operated. Mfg. 1998-99.

	$445	$385	$335	$300	$280	$260	$240

Last MSR was $499.

Add $39 for extra 3 or 5 (disc.) shot mag.

SHOTGUNS: SLIDE ACTION

Brolin shotguns were manufactured in China through Hawk Industries, and were unauthorized copies of the Remington Model 870. Most of these slide action models were distributed by Interstate Arms, and it is thought that Norinco or China North Industries were connected to the manufacturer during the importation of these shotguns.

FIELD SERIES - 12 ga. only, 3 in. chamber, 24, 26, 28, or 30 in. VR barrel with mod. choke tube, steel receiver and aluminum trigger guard, choice of black synthetic or wood stock, bead sights, 5 shot mag., matte finish, 7.3 lbs. Mfg. 1997-98.

	$195	$170	$155	$140	$130	$120	$110

Last MSR was $240.

✳ *Field Combo* - includes choice of extra 12 ga. 18 1/2 or 22 in. barrel, choice of regular or pistol grip stock. Mfg. 1997-98.

	$230	$195	$175	$155	$140	$130	$120

Last MSR was $270.

Add approx. $25 for rifled deer barrel.

LAWMAN MODEL - 12 ga. only, 3 in. chamber, action patterned after the Rem. Model 870 (disc. 1998) or the Ithaca Model 37 (new 1999) 18 1/2 in. barrel, choice of bead, rifle (disc. 1998), or ghost ring (disc. 1998) sights, matte (disc. 1998), nickel (disc. 1997), royal blue (new 1998), satin blue (new 1998) or hard chrome finish, black synthetic or hardwood stock and forearm, 7 lbs. Mfg. in China 1997-99.

	$165	$155	$145	$135	$125	$115	$105

Last MSR was $189.

Add $20 for nickel finish (disc. 1997).
Add $20 for hard chrome finish.
Add $20 for ghost ring sights.

SLUG SPECIAL - 12 ga. only, 3 in. chamber, choice of 18 1/2 or 22 in. barrel with either rifle sights, ghost ring, or cantilevered scope mount, wood or synthetic stock, choice of fixed IC choke, 4 in. extended rifled choke, or fully rifled barrel, 5 shot mag. Mfg. 1998 only.

	$230	$180	$165	$150	$140	$130	$120

Last MSR was $270.

Add $10 for rifled barrel.
Add $20 for cantilevered scope mount.

SLUGMASTER - 12 ga. only, 3 in. chamber, action patterned after the Model 37 Ithaca, bottom ejection, choice of royal blue metal finish with wood stock or satin blue metal with synthetic stock, rifle sights, mfg. in China. Limited importation 1999 only.

	$165	$155	$145	$135	$125	$115	$105

Last MSR was $189.

TURKEY SPECIAL - 12 ga. only, 3 in. chamber, 22 in. VR barrel with extra-full extended turkey choke, choice of wood or synthetic stock. Mfg. 1998 only.

	$215	$165	$155	$145	$135	$125	$115

Last MSR was $250.

GRADING - PPGS™	100%	98%	95%	90%	80%	70%	60%

BRONCO

Previous trademark manufactured by Echave Y Arizmendi, located in Eibar, Spain.

PISTOLS: SEMI-AUTO

MODEL 1918 POCKET AUTOMATIC - 7.65mm cal., 6 shot, 2 1/2 in. barrel, fixed sights, blue, hard rubber grips. Mfg. 1918-25.

	$175	$150	$100	$80	$70	$60	$50

VEST POCKET AUTOMATIC - 6.35mm cal., small frame. Disc.

	$160	$125	$110	$95	$80	$60	$40

A.A. BROWN & SONS

Current long gun manufacturer established in 1930 and located in Birmingham, England.

A.A. Brown & Sons manufactures high quality SxS English sidelock ejector shotguns in all gauges with many options available. For more information, including pricing, VAT, customer options, availability and delivery time, please contact the company directly (see Trademark Index).

DAVID MCKAY BROWN (GUNMAKERS) LTD.

Current long gun manufacturer established in 1967 and located in Bothwell, Glasgow, Scotland. Available through U.S. agents, Griffin & Howe, New York City and Bernardsville, NJ, Wingshooting Adventures, located in Coopersville, MI, or the manufacturer directly.

Makers of Scottish Round Action SxS and O/U shotguns and rifles (approx. 30 guns mfg. annually). David McKay Brown apprenticed with Alex Martin Ltd. and John Dickson & Son before establishing his own gunmaking company. All guns made to customer order on round sidelock actions. Delivery approximately 12 months, depending on the configuration.

Prices indicated below for manufacturer's suggested retail and 100% condition factors are listed in English pounds. Values for used guns in 98%-60% condition factors are priced in U.S. dollars.

RIFLES: CUSTOM, SxS

Please contact the agent/importer directly for a firm quotation on a SxS double rifle.

SHOTGUNS: CUSTOM

Add £250 for Pistol/Prince of Wales grip.
Add £1,000 for .410 bore.
Add £750 for single non-selective trigger.
Add £2,050 - £3,300 for scroll engraving, depending on type.

SxS SHOTGUN - 12, 16, 20, 28 ga., or .410 bore, features rounded case colored action, double triggers, custom order only.

MSR £26,000	£26,000	$31,450	$25,250	$19,250	$15,750	$13,000	$11,000

O/U SHOTGUN - 12, 16, 20, 28 ga., or .410 bore, features rounded case colored action, double triggers, custom order only.

MSR £33,000	£33,000	$41,250	$34,000	$28,750	$23,250	$19,000	$14,750

ED BROWN CUSTOM, INC.

Current rifle manufacturer established during 2000 and located in Perry, MO.

RIFLES: BOLT ACTION

The following MSRs represent each model's base price, with many options available at additional charge. Beginning 2006, all M-702 actions were disc. in favor of Ed Brown's new

Model 704 controlled feed action with spring-loaded extractor integral with the bolt. All currently manufactured rifles have stainless steel barrels and the entire rifle is coated with Generation III black coating (new 2007).

702 DENALI - various short and long action cals., designed as lightweight mountain hunting rifle, 22, 23 (disc.), or 24 in. lightweight barrel, glass bedded McMillian sporter stock with checkering and recoil pad, 3 position safety, 7 3/4 lbs. Mfg. 2002-2004.

$2,895	$2,350	$1,800	$1,500	$1,200	$975	$725

Last MSR was $2,895.

702 OZARK - various cals., lightweight hunting rifle utilizing Ed Brown custom short action, steel trigger guard and floorplate, 3 position safety, checkered lightweight fiberglass stock, match grade, hand lapped 21 in. barrel, approx. 6 1/2 lbs. Disc. 2003.

$2,800	$2,300	$1,775	$1,500	$1,200	$975	$725

Last MSR was $2,800.

BUSHVELD - various short and long action cals., dangerous game rifle utilizing Ed Brown custom action, match grade 24 in. medium or heavyweight barrel, McMillan fiberglass stock with cheekpiece and recoil pad, approx. 8 1/2-9 lbs.

MSR $2,995		$2,995	$2,425	$1,850	$1,500	$1,200	$975	$725

Add $300 for .416 Rem. Mag or .458 Lott cals. (disc. 2005).

EXPRESS - .375 H&H, .416 Rem. Mag., .458 Lott cal., dangerous game rifle utilizing Ed Brown custom M-704 fully controlled feed action, 4 shot internal mag, 24 in. barrel with iron sights and barrel band, Shilen trigger, hand-bedded McMillan fiberglass stock with Monte Carlo cheekpiece and Pachmayer Decelerator recoil pad, approx. 9-10 lbs. New 2006.

MSR $3,695		$3,695	$3,125	$2,750	$2,400	$2,100	$1,800	$1,500

SAVANNA - various long and short action cals., hunting rifle utilizing Ed Brown custom action, McMillan checkered fiberglass stock with steel trigger guard and floor plate, Talley rings and bases, 24 or 26 in. match grade barrel, approx. 7.5-8 lbs.

MSR $3,195		$3,195	$2,575	$1,975	$1,600	$1,300	$1,000	$875

Add $100 for muzzle brake.

DAMARA - various cals., lightweight hunting rifle with Ed Brown short repeater action, 23 in. barrel and ultra-lightweight McMillan graphite stock with Pachmayr Decelerator pad,, 6.1 lbs. New 2004.

MSR $3,295		$3,295	$2,675	$2,050	$1,650	$1,350	$1,050	$900

Add $100 for Mag. cals. with muzzle brake.

VARMINT/COMPACT VARMINT - various varmint cals., features Ed Brown short action with steel trigger guard and adj. trigger., match grade 22 (new 2006, compact variation), 24 (Varmint), or 26 (optional, disc.) barrel, hand bedded McMillian fiberglass stock and recoil pad, approx. 9 lbs.

MSR $3,195		$3,195	$2,575	$1,975	$1,600	$1,300	$1,000	$875

702 LIGHT TARGET (TACTICAL) - .223 Rem. or .308 Win. cal., features Ed Brown short repeater action, aluminum trigger guard and floorplate, 21 in. match grade barrel, includes Talley scope mounts, approx. 8 3/4 lbs. Disc. 2005.

$2,495	$2,000	$1,650	$1,350	$1,100	$925	$825

Last MSR was $2,495.

A3 TACTICAL - various cals., top-of-the-line sniper weapon, 26 in. heavyweight match grade hand lapped barrel, Shilen trigger, McMillan fiberglass A-3 tactical stock, 11 1/4 lbs.

MSR $2,995		$2,995	$2,425	$1,875	$1,550	$1,225	$1,000	$850

GRADING - PPGS™	100%	98%	95%	90%	80%	70%	60%

A5 TACTICAL - .300 Win. Mag. or .308 Win. cal., features adj. McMillan A-5 tactical stock, 5 shot detachable mag., black finish, Shilen trigger, 12 1/2 lbs. New 2008.

MSR $3,495	$3,495	$2,825	$2,150	$1,700	$1,400	$1,100	$950

M40A2 MARINE SNIPER - .30-06 or .308 Win. cal., 24 in. match grade barrel, special McMillan GP fiberglass tactical stock with recoil pad, Woodlands camo is molded into stock, this model is a duplicate of the original McMillan Marine Sniper rifle used in Vietnam, except for the Ed Brown action, 9 1/4 lbs. New 2002.

MSR $2,995	$2,995	$2,425	$1,875	$1,550	$1,225	$1,000	$850

ED BROWN PRODUCTS, INC.

Current components and pistol manufacturer established during 1988 located in Perry, MO.

Ed Brown Products

PISTOLS: SEMI-AUTO

Add $100 for stainless steel frame and blue slide.
Add $200 for 100% stainless steel construction (new 2002, .45 ACP cal. only).
Add $75 for ambidextrous safety.
Add $200 for Generation III black coating (new 2007).

CLASSIC CUSTOM - .45 ACP cal., M1911 style, top-of-the-line model with highest level of cosmetic finishing, 5 in. barrel, incorporates all custom Ed Brown features, including slide and frame, choice of blue/blue, stainless/blue, or stainless/stainless frame and slide, exotic checkered cocobolo wood grips, adj. Bo-Mar rear sight, custom made per individual order, 39 oz.

MSR $2,895	$2,750	$2,300	$1,950	$1,700	$1,500	$1,250	$995

CLASS A LIMITED - available in 8 cals., M1911 style, basic custom pistol and features all custom Ed Brown accessories, including slide and frame, 7 shot mag., 4.25 (Commander) or 5 in. barrel length, Hogue exotic grips, 34 or 39 oz. Disc. 2003.

	$2,250	$1,900	$1,550	$1,300	$1,100	$900	$800

Last MSR was $2,250.

Add $100 for stainless steel frame and all lower parts.
Add $100 for Novak night sights.

COMMANDER BOBTAIL - various cals., M1911 style, carry configuration, features round butt variation of the Class A Limited frame, incorporating frame and grip modifications, including a special housing w/o checkering, 4 1/4 in. barrel, Hogue exotic wood grips, 34 oz. Disc. 2003.

	$2,350	$1,975	$1,625	$1,350	$1,125	$925	$825

Last MSR was $2,350.

EXECUTIVE TARGET - .45 ACP cal., similar to Executive Elite, except modified for target and range shooting, adj. Bo-Mar rear sight, 5 in. barrel, single stack mag., ambidextrous safety, matte finish, cocobolo diamond checkered grips, approx. 34 oz. New 2006.

MSR $2,370	$2,370	$1,975	$1,625	$1,350	$1,125	$925	$825

EXECUTIVE ELITE - .45 ACP cal., M1911 style, 5 in. barrel, choice of all blue, stainless blue, or full stainless slide/barrel, features Hardcore components, flared and lowered ejection port, Commander style hammer, 25 LPI checkering on front and rear grip strap, beveled mag. well, Novak low mount sights, checkered cocobolo wood grips, 34 oz. New 2004.

MSR $2,195	$2,195	$1,875	$1,525	$1,275	$1,075	$900	$800

EXECUTIVE CARRY - .45 ACP cal., similar to Executive Elite, except has 4 1/4 in. barrel and Bobtail grip, 34 oz. New 2004.

MSR $2,295	$2,295	$1,950	$1,600	$1,325	$1,125	$925	$825

GRADING - PPGS™	100%	98%	95%	90%	80%	70%	60%

KOBRA - .45 ACP cal., M1911 style, 7 shot, 5 in. barrel, features metal "snakeskin" treatment on frame, mainspring housing and slide, fixed Novak low mount night sights, exotic wood grips, 39 oz. New 2002.

MSR $1,995		$1,995	$1,750	$1,375	$1,200	$1,050	$900	$800

KOBRA CARRY - .45 ACP cal., M1911 style, 4 1/4 in. barrel, features round butt (Bobtail) and metal "snakeskin" treatment on frame, mainspring housing and slide, fixed Novak low mount night sights, 34 oz. New 2002.

MSR $2,095		$2,095	$1,825	$1,425	$1,225	$1,075	$925	$825

SPECIAL FORCES - .45 ACP cal., M1911 style, 7 shot mag, 5 in. barrel, Commander style hammer, special ChainLink treatment on front and rear grip straps, checkered diamond pattern cocobolo grips, fixed Novak Lo-Mount dovetail night sights, Generation III black coating applied to all metal surfaces, 38 oz. New 2006.

MSR $1,995		$1,995	$1,750	$1,375	$1,200	$1,050	$900	$800

JIM WILSON SPECIAL LIMITED EDITION - .45 ACP cal., features black frame with Jim Wilson signature on slide, smooth Tru-Ivory grips, 7 shot mag., 38 oz. Limited mfg. 2007.

		$2,295	$1,950	$1,600	$1,325	$1,125	$925	$825

Last MSR was $2,295.

JEFF COOPER COMMEMORATIVE LIMITED EDITION - .45 ACP cal., 5 in. barrel, Govt. style, forged frame and slide, matte finish, square cutt serrations on rear of slide, Jeff Cooper signature on slide, fixed Novak low mount dovetail rear sight, dovetail front sight, 7 shot mag., exhibition grade cocobolo grips with Jeff Cooper pen and sword logo, includes ltd. ed. leather bound copy of *Principles of Self Defense*, 38 oz. Ltd. mfg. beginning 2008.

MSR $2,295		$2,295	$1,950	$1,600	$1,325	$1,125	$925	$825

BROWN PRECISION, INC.

Current manufacturer established in 1968, and located in Los Molinos, CA. Previously manufactured in San Jose, CA. Consumer direct sales.

Brown Precision Inc. manufactures rifles primarily using Remington or Winchester actions and restocks them using a combination of Kevlar, Fiberglass and Graphite (wrinkle finish) to save weight. Stock colors are green, brown, grey, black, camo brown, camo green, or camo grey. Chet Brown pioneered the concept of the fiberglass rifle stock in 1968.

PISTOLS: BOLT ACTION

CUSTOM XP-100 HIGH COUNTRY - various cals., includes highly tuned XP-100 single shot action with Shilen stainless match grade barrel, electroless nickel or Teflon finish, fiberglass stock. Limited mfg. 1993-96.

		$1,550	$1,375	$1,150	$950	$775	$650	$525

Last MSR was $1,690.

RIFLES: BOLT ACTION

Brown Precision will also stock a rifle from a customer supplied action. This process includes a Brown Precision stock, custom glass bedding, recoil pad, stock finish, etc. Prices range from $895-$995.

GRADING - PPGS™	100%	98%	95%	90%	80%	70%	60%

CUSTOM HIGH COUNTRY - various cals. within the following factory barreled actions, choice of Rem. 700 ADL/BDL, Model 7, Ruger 77 (disc.), or Win. Model 70 push feed (disc.), or Winchester Model 70 Classic with controlled round feeding action and custom trigger guard, fiberglass/Kevlar stock (various colors), electroless nickel or Teflon metal finish, sling swivels and pad. New 1975.

MSR $4,395	$3,750	$3,200	$2,650	$2,200	$1,775	$1,500	$1,350

    Add $300 for left-hand action.
    Add $135 for cryogenic barrel treatment.
    Add $600 for take down action (new 2006).
    Subtract approx. $800 for Ruger M77 action and steel barrel.
    Subtract $1,000 if action is supplied by customer.

Beginning 2006, this model's standard features include a choice of a fully blueprinted Winchester Model 70 (controlled round feeding), Rem. Model 700, or Rem. Model 7 action, and a match grade stainless steel barrel.

＊*Custom High Country ES II* - similar to Custom High Country, except includes cryogenic barrel treatment and speed lock firing pin spring, includes 60 rounds of custom ammo. Disc. 2003.

	$3,400	$2,650	$2,100	$1,725	$1,400	$1,125	$995

Last MSR was $3,995.

    Add $100 for Rem. 700 BDL or Model 7 action.
    Add $300 for stainless steel Rem. 700 BDL action.
    Add $500 for Win. Model 70 Classic action with controlled round feeding.
    Add $300 for left-hand action.
    Subtract $700 if action is supplied by customer.

HIGH COUNTRY YOUTH RIFLE - various cals., choice of Rem. Model 7 or 700 factory barreled action, fiberglass stock. Mfg. 1993-2000.

	$1,250	$1,050	$825	$700	$550	$495	$440

Last MSR was $1,435.

    Add $145 for lengthening stock.

BROWN PRECISION WINCHESTER 70 - .270 Win. or .30-06 cal., 22 in. featherweight barrel, camo stock in four colors with black recoil pad, 6 1/4 lbs. Mfg. 1989-92.

	$650	$575	$475	$425	$385	$325	$300

Last MSR was $750.

    Add $20 for 7mm Rem. Mag. (24 in. sporter barrel).

BLASER BOLT ACTION RIFLE - standard Camex Blaser cals. and action, fiberglass stock and nickel plated barrel. Disc. 1989.

	$1,395	$1,150	$995	$875	$750	$675	$600

Last MSR was $1,395.

MODEL 7 SUPER LIGHT - .223 Rem., .243 Win., 6mm Rem., 7mm-08 Rem., or .308 Win. cal., Model 7 action, 18 in. factory barrel, no sights, 5 lbs. 4 oz. Disc. 1992.

	$995	$900	$750	$650	$575	$500	$450

Last MSR was $1,059.

This model could have been special ordered with similar options from the Custom High Country Model, with the exception of left-hand action.

LAW ENFORCEMENT SELECTIVE TARGET - .308 Win. cal., Model 700 Varmint action with 20, 22, or 24 in. factory barrel, O.D. green camouflage treatment. Disc. 1992.

	$995	$900	$750	$650	$575	$500	$450

Last MSR was $1,086.

This model could have been special ordered with similar options from the Custom High Country Model, with the exception of left-hand action.

TACTICAL ELITE - various cals. and custom features, customized per individual order. New 1997.

	100%	98%	95%	90%	80%	70%	60%
MSR $4,595	$4,000	$3,350	$2,800	$2,300	$1,850	$1,600	$1,400

Add $675 for 3 way adj. buttplate.
Subtract $1,100 if action is supplied by customer.

PRO/LIGHT VARMINTER - various cals., includes custom tuned Rem. Model 700 ADL action, Shilen match stainless steel barrel. New 1993, Light Varminter new 2006.

	100%	98%	95%	90%	80%	70%	60%
MSR $3,795	$3,275	$2,900	$2,400	$2,050	$1,750	$1,500	$1,350

Add $300 for left-hand action.
Add $600 for optional Rem. Model 40-XB action with target trigger.
Subtract $1,000 if action is supplied by customer.

PRO HUNTER - available in over 25 cals., Model 700 ADL action is standard, match grade stainless steel barrel, dull electroless nickel, blue, or teflon finish, express sights, synthetic stock (four different colors). New 1988.

	100%	98%	95%	90%	80%	70%	60%
MSR $4,895	$4,300	$3,650	$3,000	$2,450	$1,975	$1,700	$1,550

Add $100 for left-hand action.
Subtract $1,000 if action is supplied by customer.

✳ *Pro Hunter Elite* - various cals., custom tuned Winchester Model 70 Super Grade action with controlled feed claw extractor, includes many custom order features. New 1993.

	100%	98%	95%	90%	80%	70%	60%
MSR $5,495	$4,800	$4,000	$3,300	$2,650	$2,100	$1,800	$1,600

Add $695 for drop box trigger guard (allows additonal round in mag.).
Subtract $1,000 if action is supplied by customer.
Add $600 for take down action.

In late 1991, improvements were made including decelerator recoil pad, barrel band swivel, and speed lock firing pin spring.

THE UNIT - .270 Win., .300 Win. Mag., .300 Wby. Mag., .338 Win. Mag., 7mm-08 Rem., 7mm Rem. Mag., or 7mm STW cal., Rem. 700 BDL or Win. Mod. 70 controlled feed action, various lengths match grade stainless steel barrel with cryogenic treatment, Teflon or electroless nickel finish, Brown Precision Kevlar or graphite reinforced fiberglass stock, includes 60 rounds of custom ammo. Limited mfg. 2001 only.

	100%	98%	95%	90%	80%	70%	60%
	$3,225	$2,500	$2,000	$1,650	$1,350	$1,125	$995

Last MSR was $3,795.

Add $500 for Win. Model 70 Super Grade action with controlled round feeding.
Add $200 for left-hand action.
Subtract $600 if action was supplied by customer.

SUPER BOLT RIMFIRE - .22 LR or .22 Mag. cal., modified Ruger 77/22 action, 20 in. heavy Shilen match grade steel or stainless steel barrel, extended mag. release, choice of lightweight fiberglass or Kevlar stock, blue or silver metal finish, 6 1/2 lbs, disc. 2005.

	100%	98%	95%	90%	80%	70%	60%
	$1,600	$1,200	$925	$825	$675	$600	$550

Last MSR was $1,895.

Add $100 for stainless steel barrel.
Add $200 for stainless steel action & barrel.

RIFLES: SEMI-AUTO

CUSTOM TEAM CHALLENGER - .22 LR cal., modified Ruger 10/22 action, 20 in. heavy Shilen match grade steel or stainless steel barrel, extended mag. release, choice of lightweight fiberglass or Kevlar stock, blue or silver metal finish, disc. 2005.

	100%	98%	95%	90%	80%	70%	60%
	$1,350	$1,075	$825	$675	$550	$450	$400

Last MSR was $1,595.

Add $100 for stainless steel barrel.
Add $200 for stainless steel barrel & action.

BROWNING

Current manufacturer with U.S. headquarters located in Morgan, UT. Browning guns originally were manufactured in Ogden, UT, circa 1880. Browning firearms are manufactured by Fabrique Nationale in Herstal and Liège, Belgium. Beginning 1976, Browning also contracted Miroku of Japan and A.T.I. in Salt Lake City, UT to manufacture both long arms and handguns. In 1992, Browning (including F.N.) was acquired by GIAT of France. During late 1997, the French government received $82 million for the sale of F.N. Herstal from the Walloon business region surrounding Fabrique Nationale in Belgium.

BROWNING

The category names within the Browning section have been arranged in an alphabetical format: - PISTOLS (& variations), RIFLES (& variations), SHOTGUNS (& variations), SPECIAL EDITIONS, COMMEMORATIVES & LIMITED MFG.

The author would like to express his sincere thanks to the Browning Collector's Association, including members Rodney Hermann, H.M. Shirley, Richard Spurzem, Jim King, Bert O'Neill, Jr., Anthony Vanderlinden, and Gary Chatham for continuing to make their important contributions to the Browning section.

BROWNING HISTORY

The Browning firm, first known as J.M. Browning & Bro., was established in Ogden, Utah about 1880. Later known as Browning Brothers and Browning Arms Company (BAC), the firm actually manufactured only one gun - the Model 1878 Single Shot which was John M.'s first patent. Winchester bought the production and distribution rights to this gun in 1883, bringing it out as the Winchester M1885. From that time until 1900, Mr. Browning sold Winchester the exclusive rights to 31 rifles and 13 shotguns, of which Winchester produced only 7 rifles (M1885SS: the lever actions M1886, 1892, 1894 and 1895: and the slide action .22s M1890 and 1906) and 3 shotguns (M1887, M1893 and M1897). The other models were bought from Browning simply to keep them out of the hands of other arms makers.

John M. Browning, perhaps the greatest firearms inventor the world has ever known, was directly responsible for an estimated 80 separate firearms that evolved from his 128 patents. During his most prolific period from 1894 to 1910, Browning sold the rights to his rifles, semi-auto pistols, shotguns and machine guns to Winchester, Remington, Colt and Stevens in this country and to Fabrique Nationale (Belgium) for sale outside the U.S. Every Colt and F.N. semi-auto pistol is based on a Browning patent. In 1902, Browning broke off relations with Winchester when the company refused to negotiate a royalty arrangement for his new semi-auto shotgun (A-5). Browning took the prototype to F.N. F.N. has produced numerous automatic pistols, 3 rifles and 2 shotguns designed by John M. Browning and is still a major producer of arms sold by Browning in the U.S. and by F.N. distributors worldwide.

Our American military was armed for many years with Browning designed weaponry, not the least of which is the venerable "Old Slabside" 1911 Govt. Model .45 ACP. Today, the firm that bears the Browning name still stands at the forefront with the other makers of fine sporting firearms.

BROWNING FACTS

Note: Between 1966-1971 Browning used a salt-curing process to speed the drying time needed for their walnut stock blanks. Unfortunately, the salt would be released from the wood and oxidize the metal surface(s) after a period of time. These guns, especially bolt action rifles in all grades, some BARs, Superposed shotguns, and T-bolt models should be examined carefully around the edges of the wood for signs of freckling and rust. Discount values on guns which show tell-tale characteristics of salt corrosion 25%-40%, depending on how bad rusting has occurred. Check screws and wood under buttplate as well. Original Superposed owners of salt wood guns who still have their warranty card are still eligible for Browning factory refurbishing of affected parts only without charge. Otherwise, Browning has a standardized charge for each model.

Since the inception and standardization of steel shot for hunting purposes, the desirability factor of shotguns has changed considerably. On newer manufacture, choke tubes are now expected for most shooters, and shotguns without choke tubes must be discounted somewhat. Browning does not recommend using steel shot in any Superposed (B-25) or older Belgian Auto-5 barrels.

GRADING - PPGS™	100%	98%	95%	90%	80%	70%	60%

BROWNING VALUES INFORMATION

Editor's Note: It is important to note the differences in values of Browning firearms manufactured in Belgium by F.N. and those made recently in Japan by Miroku. We feel that these values are somewhat higher because of collector interest in Belgian guns, and not as the result of any inferiority of the quality of Browning guns made anywhere else.

AS A FINAL NOTE: Most post-war Brownings are collectible only if in 95% or better condition as most models have relatively high mfg. and are not that old. Condition under 95% is normally very shootable, but not as collectible and values for 95% or less condition could be lower than shown in some areas.

All add-ons or deductions on Browning's currently manufactured models reflect retail pricing without any discounting. On higher grade Browning firearms that are engraved, signed specimens by FN's master engravers Funken, J. Baerten, Vrancken, and Watrin will command premiums over the values listed.

BROWNING SERIALIZATION

In addition to the Belgian Browning serialization listed in the back of this text, the following codes will determine the year and origin of those guns made from 1975 to date. The 2 letters in the middle of the serial number are the code designations for year of manufacture. They represent the following: RV - 1975, RT - 1976, RR - 1977, RP - 1978, RN - 1979, PM - 1980, PZ - 1981, PY - 1982, PX - 1983, PW - 1984, PV - 1985, PT -1986, PR - 1987, PP - 1988, PN - 1989, NM - 1990, NZ - 1991, NY - 1992, NX - 1993, NW - 1994, NV - 1995, NT - 1996, NR - 1997, NP - 1998, NN - 1999, MM - 2000, MZ - 2001, MY - 2002, MX - 2003, MW - 2004, MV - 2005, MU - 2006, MT - 2007, MS - 2008,and MR 2009.

Since most Brownings use a 3-digit model identification code (appearing first on European or U.S. mfg. guns and last on Japanese mfg.), both where and when the specimen was made can easily be determined (i.e. ser. no. 611RP2785 would be a Model B-2000 made in Belgium, and assembled in Portugal during 1978 with 2785 being the ser. no. Ser. no. 01479PX368 indicates a B-SS 20 ga. mfg. in Japan in 1983).

BROWNING CUSTOM SHOP

Browning's Custom Shop in Herstal, Belgium, continues to make a wide variety of firearms, a number of which have limited importation into the U.S. Current Custom Shop Superposed prices and model information have been provided in the Superposed section. For more information on the Browning Custom Shop's additional offerings, please look under the various category names availability and current pricing. Please refer to Browning's web site at www.browning.com for more information on the wide variety of firearms available from the Browning Custom Shop in Belgium, or contact Browning directly.

PISTOLS: SEMI-AUTO, F.N. PRODUCTION UNLESS OTHERWISE NOTED

MODEL 1899-FN - 7.65mm cal., first Belgian Browning, 4 in. barrel, similar to later M-1900 but w/o safety markings or lanyard ring, almost 15,000 mfg. 1899-1901.

$950	$800	$700	$650	$550	$500	$450

Add 15% for guns manufactured in 1899 (ser. nos. 1-3900, without "A" prefix or suffix).
Add 50% for factory nickel finish (nickel finish with blue trigger and blue safety lever) - if 95% condition or better.
Add $500 for factory presentation case with accessories.

MODEL 1900-FN - 7.65mm cal., 4 in. barrel, standard safety markings are in French: Feu and Sur. 724,500 mfg. 1900-14.

$800	$625	$525	$475	$395	$275	$225

Add 50% for factory nickel finish (nickel finish with blue trigger and safety lever) - if 95% condition or better.
Add $500 for factory presentation case with accessories.
Add $750 for Imperial Russian contract (crossed rifles marking on blue or nickel guns).
Add $100 for Imperial German contracts with German safety markings (Feuer & Sicher).
Add $100 minimum for special contract or retailer markings.

GRADING - PPGS™	100%	98%	95%	90%	80%	70%	60%

MODEL 1903-FN - 9mm Browning Long cal., 5 in. barrel. 58,400 mfg. 1903-27.

	$850	$750	$550	$500	$450	$400	$350

Add 100% if slotted to accept shoulder stock - beware of fakes.
Add $150 minimum for special contract or retailers markings.

This variation was also manufactured with a detachable shoulder stock. This accessory is rare and can add $1,000-$1,250 (shoulder stock w/o extended magazine) or $1,650-$1,850 (shoulder stock with extended magazine) to the values listed.

MODEL 1905-FN (VEST POCKET) - 6.35mm cal. (.25 ACP), dubbed "Vest Pocket" model, 2 in. barrel, manufactured by Fabrique Nationale, Herstal, Belgium. 1,086,133, mfg. 1906 to circa 1949.

　❋ *Model 1905-FN First Variation* - no slide lock/safety lever.

	$575	$475	$375	$325	$275	$225	$175

Add 50% for factory nickel finish (nickel finish with blue trigger and blue safety lever) - if 95% condition or better.
Add $500 for factory presentation case.
Add $750 for Imperial Russian contract (crossed rifles marking on blue or nickel guns).

　❋ *Model 1905-FN Second Variation* - post 1908, with slide lock/safety lever.

	$500	$375	$275	$225	$175	$125	$100

Add 50% for factory nickel finish (nickel finish with blue trigger and blue safety lever) - if 95% condition or better.
Add $500 for factory presentation case.
Add $750 for Imperial Russian contract (crossed rifles marking on blue or nickel guns).
Add $100 minimum for special contract or retailers markings.

MODEL 1907 HUSQVARNA MFG. - 9mm Browning Long cal., identical to FN Browning 1903, mfg. by Husqvarna in Sweden to supply the Swedish military. Mfg. started in 1917 because the FN Browning 1903 was not available from Belgium during WWI, produced 1917-1942. Most were arsenal refinished in Sweden featuring a dull blue finish over sandblasted metal. Many were imported into the U.S. and converted to .380 ACP cal. in the U.S.

	$625	$550	$500	$450	$400	$375	$350

Add 50% for original early factory high polish blue finish.
Add 15% for early "Browning's Patent" slide legend.
Add 10% for "System Browning" slide legend.
Subtract 40% for .380 ACP conversion.

MODEL 1910-FN (MODEL 1955) - 7.65mm (.32 ACP) or Browning 9mm short (.380 ACP) cal., 4 in. barrel. FN manufacture. 701,266 mfg. 1912-1983.

	$495	$395	$300	$275	$250	$195	$150

Add 20% if BAC marked and 7.65mm cal., or if FN marked and .380 ACP cal.
Add $100 minimum for special contract or retailer markings.

This model is also referred to as the Model 1910/55. BAC marked pistols were imported 1954-1968. Importation ceased after the 1968 GCA.

　❋ *Model 1955 Renaissance* - Renaissance engraved model. Most often encountered with BAC slide legend, rarely encountered in the U.S. with "Fabrique Nationale" slide legend.

	$2,100	$1,650	$1,350	N/A	N/A	N/A	N/A

Add $100 for original Browning case.

MODEL 1922 OR 10/22 FN - 7.65mm (.32 ACP) or .380 ACP cal., 4 1/2 in. barrel, Model 10/22 and 1922 are the same. The Model 1910 was modified by FN technicians for sale to the Yugoslav military in 1922, includes a longer barrel, larger frame and magazine. Made primarily for police and military contracts, it was also sold in France, Holland, Greece, Germany, Turkey, and many other nations. Several hundred thousand were mfg. during the Nazi occupation of FN during 1940-44. Most common variations are wartime WaA140 marked pistols.

	$425	$375	$350	$300	$275	$225	$200

GRADING - PPGS™	100%	98%	95%	90%	80%	70%	60%

Add 150% if .380 ACP and WaA613 marked on triggerguard.
Add 100% if .32 ACP and WaA613 marked.
Add 30% if WaA103 marked.
Add 25% for post liberation "A" prefix ser. no.
Add at least $100 for special prewar contract markings.
Subtract 10% for common WaA140 wartime marked pistols.

FN "BABY" MODEL - 6.35mm (.25 ACP) cal., 2 in. barrel, w/o grip safety or slide lock lever, imported under BAC trademark from 1954-68+ in standard blue finish, lightweight nickel and alumnium frame, and engraved Renaissance models. Over 510,000 mfg. 1931-83. Reintroduced during the 1990s for the European market.

✴ *FN "Baby" Model: FN Marked* - slide marked "Fabrique Nationale", blue finish standard.

	$550	$475	$400	$350	$250	$200	$150

Add 10% for pre-war production (ser. no. 1-50140).
Add $100 for original cardboard or plastic box with extras.
Add $500 for prewar factory presentation case.

✴ *FN "Baby" Model: BAC Marked* - slide marked "Browning Arms Co.", blue finish standard.

	$450	$375	$300	$225	$200	$175	$150

Add $50-$100 for original box and manual, or $25-$50 for original BAC pouch and manual.

✴ *FN "Baby" Model: Lightweight Model* - nickel or aluminum (introduced 1954) frame, with pearl grips.

	$500	$400	$350	$300	$250	$225	$200

✴ *FN "Baby" Model: Renaissance Model* - engraved, satin grey finish.

	$1,950	$1,500	$1,000	$850	$700	$600	$500

FN/BROWNING MODEL 10/71 - .380 ACP cal., 4 1/2 in. barrel, modified version of Model 1922 (10/22)in .380 ACP cal., grip safety, includes target sights and grips in addition to incorporating a magazine finger tip extension designed to comply with GCA of 1968. Sold in U.S. by BAC 1970-1974 as the "Standard .380," still mfg. by FN as Model 125.

	$550	$475	$450	$400	$375	$350	$300

✴ *FN/Browning Model 10/71 Renaissance Model*

	$2,150	$1,750	$1,400	$1,200	$1,000	$750	$600

MODEL 1935 HI-POWER (HP) - 9mm Para. cal., 13 shot mag., 4 21/32 in. barrel, Browning's last pistol design, mfg. 1935 to date in variations for commercial, military, and police use in over 68 countries, first imported under BAC trademark in 1954.

Please refer to the Fabrique Nationale section of this book for pre-1954 variations (including pre-WWII, WWII, and earlier commercial models), as well as contemporary production of those variations not imported by BAC.

HI-POWER: POST-1954 MFG. - 9mm Para. or .40 S&W (new 1995) cal., similar to FN model 1935, has BAC slide marking, 10 (C/B 1994) or 13* shot mag., 4 5/8 in. barrel, polished blue finish, checkered walnut grips, fixed sights, molded grips were introduced in 1986 (disc. in 2000), ambidextrous safety was added to all models in 1989, approx. 32 (9mm Para.) or 35 (.40 S&W) oz., mfg. by FN in Belgium, imported 1954-2000, reintroduced 2002.

GRADING - PPGS™	100%	98%	95%	90%	80%	70%	60%

✱ *Hi-Power Standard - Polished Blue Finish* - includes fixed front and lateral adj. rear sight.

MSR $922	$750	$600	$500	$425	$375	$350	$325

> **Add 50% for ring hammer and internal extractor.**
> **Add 10% for ring hammer and external extractor (post 1962 mfg.).**
> **Add 30% for thumb print feature.**
> **Add 10% for T-prefix serial number.**

Major identifying factors of the Hi-Power are as follows: the "Thumb-Print" feature was mfg. from the beginning through 1958. Old style internal extractor was mfg. from the beginning through 1962, the "T" SN prefix (T-Series start visible extractor) was mfg. 1963-mid-1970s for all U.S. imports by BAC, 69C through 77C S/N prefixes were mfg. 1969-1977. Rounded type Ring Hammers with new external extractor were mfg. from 1962-1972 (for U.S. imports by BAC, much later on FN marked pistols). Spur Hammers have been mfg. 1972-present, and the "245" S/N prefix has been mfg. 1977-present.

Older specimens in original dark green, maroon, or red/black plastic boxes were mfg. 1954-1965 and are scarce - add $100+ in value. Black pouches (circa 1965-1968, especially with gold metal zipper) will also command a $25-$50 premium, depending on condition.

✱ *Hi-Power with Adj. Sights*

MSR $988	$795	$625	$525	$450	$400	$375	$350

✱ *Hi-Power Mark III* - 9mm Para. or .40 S&W (mfg. 1994-2000, reintroduced 2003) cal., non-glare matte blue (disc. 2005) or black epoxy (new 2006) finish, ambidextrous safety, tapered dovetail rear fixed sight, two-piece molded grips, Mark III designation became standard in 1994, approx. 35 oz. Imported 1985-2000, reintroduced 2002.

MSR $897	$675	$550	$450	$400	$350	$325	$300

This model's finish may be confused with some other recent imports which have a "black" painted finish. These black finish guns are painted rather than blue, and some parties have been selling them as original military FNs.

✱ *Hi-Power Silver Chrome Finish* - 9mm Para. or .40 S&W (new 1995) cal., entire gun finished in silver chrome, includes adj. sights and Pachmayr rubber grips, 36 (9mm Para.) or 39 (.40 S&W) oz. Assembled in Portugal, and imported 1991-2000.

		$700	$625	$550	$500	$425	$400	$375

Last MSR was $718.

> **Add 50% for circa 1980 Belgian model marked "Made in Belgium."**

✱ *Hi-Power Practical Model* - 9mm Para. or .40 S&W (new 1995) cal., features blue (disc. 2005) or black epoxy slide, silver-chromed frame finish, wraparound Pachmayr rubber grips, round style serrated hammer, and choice of adj. sights (new 1993) or removable front sight, 36 (9mm Para.) or 39 (.40 S&W) oz. Imported 1990-2000, reintroduced 2002-2006.

		$695	$575	$510	$450	$425	$400	$375

Last MSR was $863.

> **Add $58 for adj. sights (disc. 2000).**

✱ *Hi-Power Nickel/Silver Chrome Finish* - not to be confused with stainless steel (never offered in the Hi-Power), this nickel/silver chrome finish is different from the silver chrome finish released in 1991, gold trigger, checkered walnut grips. Approx. 11,609 mfg. 1980-85.

		$750	$625	$550	$500	$425	$400	$375

Last MSR was $525.

> **Add 50% for circa 1980 Belgian model marked "Made in Belgium."**

GRADING - PPGS™	100%	98%	95%	90%	80%	70%	60%

✳ *Hi-Power .30 Luger cal.* - .30 Luger cal., mfg. for European sales (most are marked BAC on slide), approx. 1,500 imported late 1986-89, similar specifications as 9mm Para. model.

	$800	$700	$550	$500	$425	$395	$350

This model was never cataloged for sale by BAC in the U.S. A few earlier specimens have been noted with F.N. markings and ring hammer.

✳ *Hi-Power GP Competition* - 9mm Para. cal., competition model with 6 in. barrel, detent adj. rear sight, rubber wraparound grips, front counterweight, improved barrel bushing, decreased trigger pull, approx. 36 1/2 oz.

	$995	$895	$725	$600	$550	$500	$450

The original GP Competition came in a black plastic case w/accesories and is more desirable than later imported specimens which were computer serial numbered and came in a styrofoam box. Above prices are for older models - subtract 10% if newer model (computer serial numbered). This model was never cataloged for sale by BAC in the U.S., and it is not serviced by Browning.

✳ *Hi-Power Tangent Rear Sight* - 9mm Para. cal., manufactured from 1965-78. Adj. rear sight to 500 meters. A total of approx. 7,000 were imported by Browning Arms Co. Early pistols are designated by "T" prefix and were mfg. 1964-69, later pistols mfg. 1972-76, had spur hammers and followed the 69C-76C ser. no. prefixes.

	$1,000	$925	$800	$600	$475	$400	$375

   Add $100 for "T" prefix.
   Add $50 for original pouch and instruction manual.

✳ *Hi-Power Tangent Capitan Polished Blue Finish* - 9mm Para. cal., features 50-500 meter tangent rear sight, blue finish with walnut grips, slide is marked "Made in Belgium, Assembled in Portugal", 32 oz. Imported 1993-2000.

	$750	$650	$600	$500	$400	$350	$300

Last MSR was $764.

✳ *Hi-Power Tangent Rear Sight & Slotted* - 9mm Para. cal., variation with grip strap slotted to accommodate shoulder stock. Early pistols had "T" prefixes. Later pistols had spur hammers and are in the serial range 73CXXXX-74CXXXX.

	$1,550	$1,300	$1,100	$900	$775	$650	$525

   Add $200 if with "T" prefix.
   Add $50 for original pouch and instruction booklet.

This variation will command a premium; beware of fakes, however (carefully examine slot milling and look for ser. no. in 3 places).

Vektor Arms in N. Salt Lake, UT, imported this model again in limited quantities circa 2004 with both the "245" and seldolm seen "511" (includes wide trigger, loaded chamber indicator and external spring mags.) ser. no. prefixes. These guns are not arsenal refinished or refurbished, and were sold in NIB condition, with two 13 shot mags. Original oricing was $895 for the "245" prefix, and $995 for the "511" prefix.

BCA EDITION HI-POWER - 9mm Para. cal., limited edition made specifically for the Browning Collectors Association in 1980, approx. 100 were delivered.

	$795	$650	$500	N/A	N/A	N/A	N/A

GOLD LINE HI-POWER - 9mm Para. cal., blue finish with gold line perimeter engraving.

	$5,000	$4,000	$2,950	N/A	N/A	N/A	N/A

Check this model carefully for factory originality - including the ring hammer, engraving and bluing, as most models encountered are reproductions.

GRADING - PPGS™	100%	98%	95%	90%	80%	70%	60%

RENAISSANCE HI-POWER - 9mm Para. cal., extensive scroll engraving on grey silver slide and frame, synthetic pearl grips, gold plated trigger. Disc. approx. 1978.

	100%	98%	95%	90%	80%	70%	60%
Round Hammer/fixed sights	$3,795	$3,250	$2,950	N/A	N/A	N/A	N/A
Spur Hammer/fixed sights	$2,775	$2,475	$1,950	N/A	N/A	N/A	N/A

    Add $100 for internal extractor (pre-1962 mfg.)
    Add $100 for "Thumb Print."
    Add $50 for original pouch and booklet.
    Add $600 for older individual blue leatherette European case.
    Add $300-$500 for coin finish, depending on condition.

Target sights do not affect the value of this model significantly.

Currently, the Browning Custom Shop in Belgium is making the following Renaissance models: Dore ($6,066 MSR), Nickele ($5,970 MSR), L1 ($4,163 MSR), I1 ($5,250 MSR), and the B2 ($4,350 MSR).

HI-POWER: CUSTOM SHOP MODELS - Currently, the Browning Custom Shop in Belgium is making the following Hi-Power custom shop models: Renaissance "Or" or Gold, Renaissance Argentor Silver, L1, and B2. MSRs for these models fluctuate due to currency exchanges and are best obtained from Browning at the time of ordering.

CASED RENAISSANCE SET - one pistol each in .25 ACP, .380 ACP (rarest cal. of the three), and 9mm Para. cal., Hi-Power Renaissance models in walnut or black vinyl case, ser. no. not related to other calibers. Offered 1954-1969.

	100%	98%	95%	90%	80%	70%	60%
	$7,500	$6,500	$4,500	N/A	N/A	N/A	N/A

    Add 30% for coin finish/high polish in early walnut case.
    Add $100 for "St. Louis" slide address.
    Add $150 for old style Hi-Power extractor.

All original Renaissance cased sets had a Ring Hammer 9mm Para. Hi-Power. The .380 ACP cal. is the rarest of this set, and will bring $2,500 if new.

CASED GRADE I (BLUE) SET - one pistol each in .25 ACP, .380 ACP, and 9mm Para. cal., Hi-Power Grade I Models in walnut or black vinyl case, ser. no. not related to other calibers.

	100%	98%	95%	90%	80%	70%	60%
	$2,250	$1,900	$1,500	N/A	N/A	N/A	N/A

    Add $100 for walnut presentation case.
    Add $100 for thumbprint.
    Add $100 for "St. Louis" slide address.
    Add $100 for old style Hi-Power extractor.

All original Grade I blue cased sets had a Ring Hammer 9mm Para. Hi-Power.

CENTENNIAL MODEL HI-POWER - similar to fixed sight Hi-Power, chrome plated with inscription "Browning Centennial/1878-1978", engraved on side, checkered walnut grips with "B" in circle, cased, 3,500 mfg. in 1978. Original issue price was $495.

	100%	98%	95%	90%	80%	70%	60%
	$1,000	$900	$750	N/A	N/A	N/A	N/A

CENTENAIRRE MODEL HI-POWER 1 OF 100 - 9mm Para. cal., unique pattern chemically etched, signed by the engraver, checkered walnut grips with border. 100 mfg. during 1989 - approx. half were sold in U.S., the other half in Europe.

	100%	98%	95%	90%	80%	70%	60%
	$5,000	$4,000	$3,250	N/A	N/A	N/A	N/A

LOUIS XVI MODEL - 9mm Para., chemically etched throughout in leaf scroll patterns, satin finish, checkered grips, walnut case. Disc. 1984.

	100%	98%	95%	90%	80%	70%	60%
	$1,400	$1,200	$900	N/A	N/A	N/A	N/A

CLASSIC HI-POWER SERIES - 9mm Para. cal., less than 2,500 manufactured in Classic model and under 350 manufactured in Gold Classic. Both editions feature multiple engraved scenes, and a special silver grey finish, presentation grips, cased. Mfg. 1984-86.

	100%	98%	95%	90%	80%	70%	60%
	$1,150	$1,000	$850	N/A	N/A	N/A	N/A

Last MSR was $1,000.

GRADING - PPGS™	100%	98%	95%	90%	80%	70%	60%

✳ *Gold Classic Hi-Power* - 5 gold inlays, select walnut grips are both checkered and carved. Less than 500 mfg. 1984-86.

	$2,300	$2,000	$1,700	N/A	N/A	N/A	N/A

Last MSR was $2,000.

125th ANNIVERSARY HI-POWER - 9mm Para. cal., silver nitride finish with scroll engraving, gold enhanced 125th Browning Anniversary logo with image of John M. Browning in gold on slide, 10 shot mag., fixed sights, smooth oil finished walnut grips. 125 mfg. 2003-2004 only.

	$1,450	$1,125	$850	N/A	N/A	N/A	N/A

Last MSR was $1,516.

BROWNING DOUBLE ACTION - this model was first listed in the Browning catalog in 1985 but was never imported commercially. The advertised 1985 retail price was $494.

BDM/BPM/BRM SINGLE/DOUBLE ACTION - 9mm Para. cal., double mode design featuring slide selector allowing choice between pistol (true double action operation) or revolver mode (full hammer decocking after each shot), available in double mode, single mode (BPM-D decocker, mfg. 1997), or double action only (BRM-DAO, mfg. 1997), dual purpose decocking lever/safety, 4.73 in. barrel, 10 (C/B 1994) or 15* shot mag., matte blue finish, black molded wraparound grips, unique breech block allows visible cartridge inspection, adj. rear sight, 31 oz., mfg. in U.S. 1991-97.

	$500	$450	$400	$350	$300	$280	$260

Last MSR was $551.

This model features hammer block and firing pin block safeties.

✳ *BDM Practical* - similar to Standard BDM, except has matte blue slide and silver chrome frame. Mfg. 1997-98.

	$500	$400	$365	$330	$300	$280	$260

Last MSR was $571.

✳ *BDM Silver Chrome* - similar to Standard BDM, except has silver chrome finish. Only 119 mfg. in 1997 only.

	$550	$450	$400	$350	$300	$280	$260

Last MSR was $571.

FN DA 9 - 9mm Para. cal., choice of double action or double action only, 4 5/8 in. barrel, molded rubber grips, 10 shot mag., 31 oz. Mfg. by FN. While advertised in 1996, this model was never imported commercially - the retail price was listed at $613.

PRO-9/PRO-40 - 9mm Para or .40 S&W cal., single/double action, 4 in. barrel, 10, 14 (.40 S&W cal. only), or 16 (9mm Para. cal. only) shot mag., ambidextrous decocking and safety, black polymer frame with satin stainless steel slide, under barrel accessory rail, interchangeable backstrap inserts, fixed sights only, 30 (9mm Para.) or 33 oz. Mfg. in the U.S. by FNH USA 2003-2006.

	$525	$430	$370	$350	$315	$295	$260

Last MSR was $641.

Please refer to FNH USA handgun listing for current manufacture.

BDA-380 - .380 ACP cal., double action, 10 (C/B 1994) or 14* shot, 3 13/16 in. barrel, fixed sights, smooth walnut grips, 23 oz., introduced 1978 - recent production was by Beretta. Disc. 1997.

	100%	98%	95%	90%	80%	70%	60%
Blue finish	$525	$450	$395	$325	$275	$225	$200
Nickel finish	$595	$495	$450	$350	$295	$250	$225

Last MSR was $564 and $607 for Nickel finish.

GRADING - PPGS™	100%	98%	95%	90%	80%	70%	60%

BDA MODEL - 9mm Para. (9 shot, 2,740 mfg.), .38 Super (752 mfg.), or .45 ACP (7 shot) cal., mfg. from 1977-80 by Sig-Sauer of W. Germany (same as Sig-Sauer 220).

	100%	98%	95%	90%	80%	70%	60%
9mm Para.	$550	$450	$375	$295	$250	$225	$200
.38 Super	$650	$575	$495	$450	$390	$350	$300
.45 ACP	$600	$500	$400	$325	$275	$250	$225

NOMAD MODEL - .22 LR cal., 10 shot, 4 1/2 and 6 3/4 in. barrels, steel or alloy frame, adj. sights, blue finish, black plastic grips. Mfg. 1962-74 by FN.

	$450	$375	$325	$300	$225	$200	$175

    Add 10% for alloy frame.

CHALLENGER MODEL - .22 LR cal., 10 shot, 4 1/2 and 6 3/4 in. barrels, steel frame, adj. sights, checkered walnut or plastic (mfg. 1974 only) wraparound grips, gold plated trigger. Mfg. 1962-75 by FN.

	$525	$475	$400	$350	$300	$275	$250

    Add 10% for late production plastic grips.

* *Challenger Renaissance* - engraved satin nickel finish, 437 mfg. total (121 with 4 1/2 in. barrel, and 316 with 6 3/4 in. barrel).

	$2,950	$2,250	$1,700	N/A	N/A	N/A	N/A

* *Challenger Gold Line* - blue finish, gold line border on perimeter of frame surfaces, 293 mfg. total (147 with 4 1/2 in. barrel, and 146 with 6 3/4 in. barrel).

	$2,950	$2,250	$1,700	N/A	N/A	N/A	N/A

CHALLENGER II - .22 LR cal., Salt Lake City mfg., 6 3/4 in. barrel, steel frame, plastic impregnated hardwood grips, 38 oz. Mfg. 1975-82.

	$325	$300	$275	$250	$200	$175	$150

* *Challenger II BCA Commemorative* - .22 LR cal., mfg. to commemorate BCA's fourth anniversary.

	$475	$450	$400	N/A	N/A	N/A	N/A

CHALLENGER III - .22 LR cal., Salt Lake City mfg., 5 1/2 in. bull barrel, 11 shot, alloy frame, adj. sights, 35 oz. Mfg. 1982-85.

	$240	$200	$175	$145	$135	$120	$110

Last MSR was $240.

CHALLENGER III SPORTER - similar to Challenger III, except 6 3/4 in. round barrel, wide trigger, 29 oz. Mfg. 1982-85.

	$240	$200	$175	$145	$135	$120	$110

Last MSR was $240.

MEDALIST MODEL - .22 LR cal., 6 3/4 in. barrel, vent. rib, adj. target sights and barrel weights (3 supplied), blue finish, target walnut grips with thumbrest, dry-fire mechanism, 46 oz., cased. Mfg. 1964-1975 by FN.

	$1,350	$1,200	$1,000	$900	$800	$700	$600

    Subtract 15%-25% if without case and accessories, depending on condition.

11 Renaissance pistols were mfg. 1962-67 with full coverage engraving, and 382 were mfg. 1970-75 w/o full coverage engraving, early production guns were coin finished and later ones were satin chrome. Mfg. by FN 1964-75.

The BAC edition was a special order (not regular production), featured full coverage engraving, and was sold in 1986.

* *Medalist Gold Line* - 407 mfg. 1963.

	$3,150	$2,750	$2,250	N/A	N/A	N/A	N/A

* *Medalist Renaissance Model* - 11 pistols were mfg. 1962-1967 with full coverage engraving, and 382 were mfg. 1970-1975 w/o full coverage engraving, early production guns were coin finished and later ones were satin chrome. Mfg. by FN 1964-1975.

	$3,500	$3,000	$2,500	N/A	N/A	N/A	N/A

* *Medalist BAC Engraved Edition* - this BAC edition was a special order (not regular production), featured full coverage engraving. 60 mfg. 1986 only.

	100%	98%	95%	90%	80%	70%	60%
	$4,000	$3,000	$2,500	N/A	N/A	N/A	N/A

INTERNATIONAL MEDALIST - target variation model manufactured 1977-80, 5.9 in. barrel, only 681 made with BAC markings and blue finish. Currently manufactured by FN in the parkerized international configuration.

	100%	98%	95%	90%	80%	70%	60%
	$750	$650	$550	$450	$350	$300	$275
Early Model	$1,050	$900	$725	$625	$500	$425	$350

BUCK MARK STANDARD URX - .22 LR cal., 10 shot mag., 5 1/2 in. bull barrel, aluminum frame, composite grips with skipline checkering (disc. 1990), molded rubber grips (mfg. 1991-2006), or URX grips (ambidextrous with finger grooves, new 2006, became standard during 2007), adj. sights, gold trigger, matte blue finish, 34-36 oz. New 1985.

	100%	98%	95%	90%	80%	70%	60%
MSR $380	$290	$240	$195	$165	$145	$125	$110

Add $58 for nickel finish (mfg. 1991-2005).
Subtract approx. 10% for composite or molded rubber grips.
Buck Mark models are manufactured in Salt Lake City, UT.

* *Buck Mark Standard Stainless URX* - similar to Buck Mark Standard, except stainless steel, 34 oz. New 2005.

	100%	98%	95%	90%	80%	70%	60%
MSR $419	$310	$265	$225	$190	$165	$145	$125

Subtract 10% for molded rubber grips (mfg. 2005-2006).

BUCK MARK MICRO STANDARD URX - similar to Buck Mark Standard, except has 4 in. barrel, choice of standard or nickel finish, URX grips became standard 2007, 32 oz. New 1992.

	100%	98%	95%	90%	80%	70%	60%
MSR $380	$290	$240	$195	$165	$145	$125	$110

Add $58 for nickel finish (disc. 2005).
Subtract approx. 10% for composite or molded grips.

* *Buck Mark Micro Standard Stainless URX* - similar to Buck Mark Micro Standard, except stainless steel, URX grips became standard 2007, 34 oz. New 2005.

	100%	98%	95%	90%	80%	70%	60%
MSR $419	$310	$265	$225	$190	$165	$145	$125

* *Buck Mark Micro Plus* - similar to Micro Buck Mark, except has ambidextrous contoured laminated wood grips, nickel (new 1996) or blue finish. Disc. 2001.

	100%	98%	95%	90%	80%	70%	60%
	$265	$210	$155	$135	$120	$110	$100

Last MSR was $350.

Add $33 for nickel finish.

BUCK MARK CHALLENGE - .22 LR cal., features smaller grip circumference for smaller hands, smooth (disc.) or checkered walnut grips with medallions, matte blue finish, 5 1/2 in. lightweight barrel, Pro-Target sights, 25 oz. New 1999.

	100%	98%	95%	90%	80%	70%	60%
MSR $381	$290	$240	$195	$165	$145	$125	$110

* *Buck Mark Micro Challenge* - similar to Buck Mark Challenge, except has 4 in. barrel. 23 oz. Mfg. 1999-2000.

	100%	98%	95%	90%	80%	70%	60%
	$250	$200	$150	$120	$110	$100	$90

Last MSR was $311.

BUCK MARK CAMPER - .22 LR cal., features 5 1/2 in. heavy barrel, ambidextrous molded black composite grips, matte blue or satin nickel finish, Pro-Target sights, 34 oz. New 1999.

	100%	98%	95%	90%	80%	70%	60%
MSR $315	$240	$195	$160	$120	$100	$95	$85

Add $33 for satin nickel finish (disc. 2005).

* *Buck Mark Camper Stainless* - similar to Buck Mark Camper, except stainless steel, 34 oz. New 2005.

	100%	98%	95%	90%	80%	70%	60%
MSR $345	$260	$210	$175	$135	$110	$95	$75

Add $10 for Camper Stainless URX model with fiber optic sights (new 2008, available from Full Line Browning dealers only).

GRADING - PPGS™	100%	98%	95%	90%	80%	70%	60%

BUCK MARK HUNTER - .22 LR cal., features 7 1/4 in. round heavy barrel with integral scope base, Truglo front sight, smooth cocobolo target grips, matte blue finish, 38 oz. New 2005.

MSR $408	$310	$240	$180	$135	$110	$100	$90

BUCK MARK PLUS UDX - similar to Buck Mark Standard, except has uncheckered laminated wood (disc. 2006) grips, or walnut ambidextrous DX Ultragrips (new 2007), Tru-Glo Marble front sight (new 2002), and choice of high polish blue or nickel (mfg. 1996-2006), 34 oz. Mfg. 1987-2007.

	$325	$275	$225	$175	$150	$125	$110

Last MSR was $425.

Add approx. 10% for nickel finish (disc. 2006).

✳ *Buck Mark Field Plus UDX (Classic Plus)* - similar to Buck Mark Plus, except has rosewood grips (disc. 2006) or DX Ultragrips (new 2007), and Tru-Glo Marble front sight. Mfg. 2002-2007.

	$325	$275	$225	$175	$150	$125	$110

Last MSR was $425.

This model was available from Full-Line dealers only.

✳ *Buck Mark Plus Stainless UDX* - similar to Buck Mark Plus, except has stainless steel barrel/slide, choice of black or brown UDX laminate grips, 34 oz. Mfg. 2007.

	$325	$275	$225	$175	$150	$125	$110

Last MSR was $425.

Add $36 for black laminate grips.

BUCK MARK BULLSEYE TARGET - .22 LR cal., Bullseye model featuring 16 click per turn Pro-Target rear sight, 7 1/4 in. fluted barrel, matte blue finish, adj. trigger pull, contoured rosewood target or wraparound finger groove (disc.) grips, 10 shot mag., 36 oz. Mfg. 1996-2005.

	$440	$325	$260	$200	$165	$140	$125

Last MSR was $604.

✳ *Buck Mark Bullseye Target Stainless* - similar to Buck Mark Bullseye Target, except is stainless steel and has laminated rosewood grips, 39 oz. New 2006.

MSR $689	$520	$395	$320	$265	$215	$175	$150

✳ *Buck Mark Bullseye Standard* - similar to Buck Mark Bullseye Target, except has molded composite ambidextrous grips, 36 oz. Mfg. 1996-2006.

	$355	$280	$220	$180	$160	$145	$125

Last MSR was $468.

BUCK MARK BULLSEYE URX - .22 LR cal., 7 1/4 in. fluted barrel, matte blue finish, URX ambidextrous grips with finger grooves, 39 oz. New 2006.

MSR $522	$395	$325	$270	$215	$185	$165	$150

BUCK MARK 5.5 TARGET - .22 LR cal., same action as Buck Mark, 5 1/2 in. barrel with serrated top rib allowing adj. sight positioning, target sights, matte blue finish, choice of contoured walnut (disc. 2004), cocobolo (became standard 2005), or walnut wraparound finger groove grips (new 1992-disc.), 35 oz. New 1990.

MSR $521	$385	$315	$265	$215	$185	$165	$135

Add $54 for nickel finish (mfg. 1994-2000).

✳ *Buck Mark 5.5 Gold Target* - similar to 5.5 Target, except has gold anodized frame and top rib. Mfg. 1991-99.

	$355	$275	$220	$180	$160	$140	$125

Last MSR was $477.

GRADING - PPGS™	100%	98%	95%	90%	80%	70%	60%

BUCK MARK 5.5 FIELD - same action and barrel as the Target 5.5, except sights are designed for field use, anodized blue finish, contoured walnut grips, choice of contoured walnut, cocobolo (became standard 2005), or walnut wraparound finger groove grips (new 1992-disc.), 35 1/2 oz. New 1991.

MSR $547		$400	$325	$270	$215	$185	$165	$135

BUCK MARK LITE SPLASH URX - .22 LR cal., 5 1/2 or 7 1/4 in. round barrel, aluminum barrel and receiver feature gold splash anodizing, URX grips standard, adj. sights with TruGlo fiber optic front sight, 28 or 30 oz. New 2006.

MSR $469		$355	$280	$225	$175	$150	$135	$120

Add $17 for 7 1/4 in. barrel.

BUCK MARK CONTOUR URX - .22 LR cal., 5 1/2 or 7 1/4 in. specially contoured steel or alloy (Lite) sleeved barrel with full length scope base, matte blue finish, URX grips, adj. rear sight, 28-36 oz. (Contour Lite variation is 8 oz. less than standard). New 2006.

MSR $442		$325	$260	$195	$160	$135	$120	$110

Add $16 for 7 1/4 in. barrel.

Add $38 for Contour Lite variation (alloy sleeved barrel, 8 oz. less than steel).

BUCK MARK VARMINT - .22 LR cal., same action as Buck Mark, 9 7/8 in. barrel with serrated top rib allowing adj. sight positioning, laminated wood grips, choice of contoured walnut or walnut wraparound finger groove grips (new 1992), optional detachable forearm, matte blue, 48 oz. Mfg. 1987-99.

		$315	$255	$200	$175	$155	$135	$120

Last MSR was $403.

BUCK MARK SILHOUETTE - .22 LR cal., silhouette variation of the Buck Mark, 9 7/8 in. bull barrel with serrated top rib allowing adj. sight positioning, hooded target sights, laminated wood stocks and forearm, choice of contoured walnut or walnut wraparound finger groove grips (new 1992), matte blue, 53 oz. Mfg. 1987-99.

		$360	$285	$230	$195	$170	$150	$135

Last MSR was $448.

⁕ *Buck Mark Unlimited Silhouette (Match)* - similar to Silhouette Model featuring 14 in. barrel with set back front sight, choice of contoured walnut or walnut wraparound finger groove grips (new 1992), 64 oz. Mfg. 1991-99.

		$425	$330	$270	$230	$195	$170	$150

Last MSR was $536.

BUCK MARK COMMEMORATIVE - features 6 3/4 in. Challenger style tapered barrel, white bonded ivory grips with scrimshaw style patterning including "1 of 1,000 Commemorative Model" on sides, matte blue finish, gold trigger, 30 1/2 oz. 1,000 mfg. 2001 only.

		$350	$300	$250	N/A	N/A	N/A	N/A

Last MSR was $437.

RIFLES: BOLT ACTION

MODEL 52 LIMITED EDITION - .22 LR cal., virtually identical to the original Winchester Model 52C Sporter, except for minor safety enhancements, bolt action, 24 in. drilled and tapped barrel, 5 shot detachable mag., pistol grip walnut stock with oil style finish, deep blue finish, adj. trigger, two-position safety, 7 lbs. 5,000 mfg. 1991-92.

		$650	$600	$525	N/A	N/A	N/A	N/A

Last MSR was $500.

MODEL BBR - .25-06 Rem., .270 Win., .30-06, 7mm Mag., .300 Win. Mag. or .338 Win. Mag. cal., short action available in .22-250 Rem., 243 Win., 257 Roberts, 7mm- 08 Rem., or 308 Win. cal., 24 in. standard or heavy barrel, 60 degree throw, fluted bolt, adj. trigger, hidden detachable mag., no sights, checkered pistol grip, Monte Carlo stock. Mfg. 1978-84 by Miroku.

	$525	$425	$375	$325	$275	$240	$220

Some rare production calibers will add premiums to the values listed (i.e., add 50% for .243 Win. cal.).

BBR RIFLE ELK ISSUE - 7mm Rem. Mag. cal., bolt action rifle, 1,000 manufactured, deeply blue receiver which has multiple animals gold inlaid, high grade walnut stock and forearm feature skipline checkering. Disc. 1986.

	$1,400	$1,100	$925	N/A	N/A	N/A	N/A

Last MSR was $1,395.

T-BOLT SPORTER/TARGET (NEW MFG.) - .17 HMR (new 2008), .22 LR, or .22 Mag. (new 2008) cal., original straight pull action with enlarged bolt handle, 22 in. free floating medium sporter or heavy target barrel, 10 shot double helix rotary mag., blued steel receiver, satin finish sporter or target (w/cheekpiece) walnut stock with cut checkering, sling studs, gold trigger, no sights, top tang safety, 4 lbs., 14 oz. or 5 1/2 lbs. New 2006.

MSR $649		$515	$465	$410	$365	$320	$280	$240

Add $50 for target/varmint configuration (new 2007).
Add $50 for .17 HMR or .22 Mag. cal. in sporter configuration, $19 for target/varmint.

＊ *T-Bolt Composite Sporter/Target (New Mfg.)* - similar to T-Bolt Sporter/Target, except has matte black composite stock, includes sling swivels, choice of 22 in. medium (sporter) or heavy target (target/varmint) barrel, approx. 4 1/2 (sporter) or 5 lbs., 2 oz. (target/varmint). New 2008.

MSR $649		$515	$465	$410	$365	$320	$280	$240

Add $50 for target/varmint configuration (new 2007).
Add $50 for .17 HMR or .22 Mag. cal. in sporter configuration, $19 for target/varmint.

T-BOLT T-1 - .22 LR cal., straight pull bolt action, 5 shot mag., 22 in. barrel, adj. rear sight, 5 1/2 lbs., plain pistol grip stock. Mfg. 1965-1974 by FN.

	$525	$450	$350	$325	$275	$250	$225

Add 10%-15% for left-hand model (mfg. 1967-1974 only).
An aperture rear sight was standard for the first nine years of production.

T-BOLT T-2 - similar to T-1, only with select checkered walnut stock (lacquer finished), pinned front sight blade, 24 in. barrel, 6 lbs.

	$725	$550	$450	$375	$325	$300	$275

Add 10%-15% for left-hand model (mfg. 1969-74 only).

＊ *T-Bolt T-2 Late Production* - features oil finished stock, press fit plastic front sight, and Browning computerized serialization.

	$525	$425	$325	$300	$250	$225	$200

FN HIGH-POWER MODEL - .222 Rem. (Sako action), .222 Rem. Mag. (Sako action), .22-250 Rem. (Sako action), .243 Win., .257 Roberts, .264 Win. Mag., .270 Win., .284 Win. (Sako action), .30-06, .308 Win., 7mm Mag., .300 Win. Mag., .308 Norma Mag., .300 H&H, .338 Win. Mag., .375 H&H, or .458 Win. Mag. cal., standard Mauser type action with either short or long (more desirable) extractor, 22 or 24 in. (heavy available) barrel, folding leaf sight, checkered pistol grip stock. Mfg. 1960-1974 by FN.

The .243 Win. and .308 Win. cals. were built on the small ring Mauser action prior to using the Sako medium action.
Note: Grades differ in engraving, finish, checkering, and grade of wood. It should be noted that the salt wood problem is more common in these high powered models. Guns should be checked carefully for rust below wood surfaces.

GRADING - PPGS™	100%	98%	95%	90%	80%	70%	60%

✳ *FN High-Power Safari Grade Basic Model* - basic model with blue finish.

Standard cals.	$1,395	$1,195	$950	$725	$550	$475	$425
Mag. cals.	$1,595	$1,425	$1,175	$825	$650	$575	$475
.257 Roberts	$2,350	$1,750	$1,450	$1,175	$800	$700	$625
.308 Norma Mag.	$1,750	$1,450	$1,250	$995	$725	$650	$550
.375 H&H/.338 Win. Mag.	$1,750	$1,450	$1,250	$995	$725	$650	$550

Add 15% for Magnum long extractor models.

Between 1963 and 1974, Browning also offered short and medium barrelled actions in the Safari, Medallion and Olympian Grades. These models have Sako barrelled actions and were stocked by FN. Medium weight barrels could also be ordered.

✳ *FN High-Power Safari Grade Short Sako Action* - Short Sako Action - short action, .222 Rem. or .222 Rem. Mag. cal.

	$1,575	$1,300	$850	$625	$525	$450	$400

✳ *FN High-Power Safari Grade Medium Sako Action* - Medium Sako Action - medium action, .22-250 Rem., .243 Win., .284 Win. or .308 Win. cal.

	$1,325	$1,000	$800	$675	$550	$500	$450

Add 75% for .284 Win. cal. (mfg. 1965-76).

In .284 Win. cal., only 162 rifles were mfg. in Safari Grade, 29 in Medallion Grade, and 10 in Olympian Grade.

✳ *FN High-Power Medallion Grade* - features select figured walnut with skipline checkering, rosewood grip and forearm caps, blue/black lustre bluing, receiver and barrel portion scroll engraved, ram's head engraved on floor plate.

	$2,750	$2,400	$2,000	$1,600	$1,325	$1,050	$875

Add 10%-50% for rare calibers, depending on rarity.
Add 15% for Mag. cals. with long extractor.
Caliber rarity is as follows: .30-06 (least rare), .300 H&H, .375 H&H long extractor, .264 Win. Mag., .222 Rem./.222 Rem. Mag., .284 Win. (rarest).
This model was also available with a Sako short or medium action - cals. are the same as listed for the Sako Safari.

✳ *FN High-Power Olympian Grade* - top-of-the-line model featuring highly figured walnut stock that is both checkered and carved. Receiver, floor plate, and trigger guard are chrome plated in a satin finish that has deep relief animal scenes engraved, as well as deep scroll work on other metal parts.

	$7,000	$6,000	$5,000	$4,000	$3,250	$2,650	$2,150

Add 10%-50% for rare calibers, depending on the rarity.
Add 15% for Mag. cals. with long extractor.
Caliber rarity is as follows: .30-06 (least rare), .308 Norm. Mag., .300 H&H, .375 H&H long extractor, .264 Win. Mag., .222 Rem./.222 Rem. Mag., .284 Win. (rarest).
This model was also available with a Sako short or medium action - cals. are the same as listed for the Sako Safari.

At a recent 2007 Rock Island Auction Co. auction a 98-99% condition example in .22-250 cal. sold for $10,350.

ACERA MODEL - .30-06 or .300 Win. Mag. cal., features straight pull action, Teflon coated breech block face, 7 lug bolt, 22 or 24 (.300 Win. Mag.) in. barrel, available w/o sights, with sights (disc. 1999), or with BOSS, detachable box mag., checkered walnut stock, gloss metal finish, 7 lbs. 3 oz. - 7 lbs. 9 oz. Mfg. 1999-2000, reintroduced during 2002 only.

	$820	$745	$660	$600	$550	$495	$450

Last MSR was $896.

Add $34 for .300 Win. Mag. cal.
Add $24 for iron sights (disc. 1999).
Add $80 for barrel BOSS (.30-06 cal. mfg. 2002 only).

GRADING - PPGS™	100%	98%	95%	90%	80%	70%	60%

RIFLES: BOLT ACTION, CENTERFIRE A-BOLT I SERIES

A-BOLT HUNTER MODEL I - available in .25-06 Rem., .270 Win., .280 Rem. (new 1988), .30-06, 7mm Rem. Mag., .300 Win. Mag., or .338 Win. Mag. cal. in long action, short action available in .223 Rem. (new 1988), .22-250 Rem., .243 Win., .257 Roberts, .284 Win. (new 1989), 7mm-08 Rem., or .308 Win. cal., 3 or 4 shot mag., matte blue finish, 3 lug rotary bolt locking, 22 (short action only), 24 in. (disc. 1987), or 26 in. barrel (new 1988 - long action Mag. cals. only), 60 degree bolt throw, adj. trigger, hidden detachable mag., with or without sights, top tang thumb safety, checkered pistol grip stock, 6 lbs. 3 oz. - 7 lbs. 11oz. Mfg. 1985-93 by Miroku. Replaced by A-Bolt Model II in 1994.

	$415	$340	$295	$265	$240	$225	$210

Last MSR was $510.

Add $65 for open sights.

* ✱ *A-Bolt Hunter Medallion Model* - same A-Bolt specifications, except also available in .375 H&H cal., features better grade walnut stock with rosewood pistol grip and forend cap, synthetic floor plate, high lustre bluing, no sights. Disc. 1993. Replaced by A-Bolt Medallion Model II in 1994.

	$475	$385	$330	$290	$265	$250	$235

Last MSR was $597.

Add $25 for left-hand action (avail. in long action cals. only).
Add $100 for .375 H&H cal. (open sights only).
Left-hand action available in .25-06 Rem., .270 Win., .280 Rem., .30-06, 7mm Rem. Mag., .300 Win. Mag., .338 Win. Mag., or .375 H&H cal.

* ✱ *A-Bolt Hunter Micro Medallion Model* - .223 Rem. (new 1988), .22-250 Rem., .243 Win., .257 Roberts, .284 Win., .308 Win., or 7mm-08 Rem. cal., scaled down variation of the A-Bolt Hunter Model, 20 in. barrel, short action only, 13 5/16 in. LOP, 3 shot mag., no sights, 6 lbs. 3 oz. for short action. Mfg. 1988-93. Replaced by A-Bolt Micro Medallion Model II in 1994.

	$475	$385	$330	$290	$265	$250	$235

Last MSR was $597.

* ✱ *A-Bolt Hunter Gold Medallion Model* - .270 Win., .30-06, .300 Win. Mag. (new 1993), or 7mm Rem. Mag. cal., similar to Medallion Model, except has extra select walnut stock with continental style cheekpiece, gold lettering and light engraving, no sights. Mfg. 1988-93. Replaced by A- Bolt Gold Medallion Model II in 1994.

	$670	$535	$430	$360	$330	$300	$265

Last MSR was $810.

* ✱ *A-Bolt Hunter Euro-Bolt* - .22-250 Rem., .243 Win., .270 Win., .30-06, .308 Win., or 7mm Rem. Mag. cal., features European styling including Schnabel style forearm, rounded rear receiver, Mannlicher style bolt, European cheekpiece on satin finished checkered stock, low-lustre bluing, hinged floor plate with removable mag., cocking indicator, upper tang thumb activated safety, 6 lbs. 14 oz. - 7 lbs. 6 oz. (Mag.). Mfg. 1993-96.

	$600	$475	$395	$350	$300	$265	$250

Last MSR was $700.

* ✱ *A-Bolt Hunter Stainless Stalker* - .22-250 Rem. (left-hand only, new 1993), .25-06 Rem., .270 Win., .280 Rem., .30- 06, 7mm Rem. Mag., .300 Win. Mag., .338 Win. Mag. or .375 H&H (new 1990) cal., action and barrel are stainless steel, matte black graphite fiberglass composite stock, dull stainless finish, no sights, 6 lbs. 11 oz. - 7 lbs. 3 oz. Mfg. 1987-93. Replaced by Stainless Stalker II in 1994.

	$575	$430	$350	$285	$250	$215	$185

Last MSR was $665.

Add $100 for .375 H&H cal.
Add $20 for left-hand action.
Originally, this model was offered in .270 Win., .30-06, or 7mm Rem. Mag. cal. only.

GRADING - PPGS™	100%	98%	95%	90%	80%	70%	60%

✳ *A-Bolt Hunter Camo Stalker* - .270 Win., .30-06, or 7mm Rem. Mag. cal., laminated black and green wood stock, matte finish on metal parts, no sights. Mfg. 1987-89.

	$400	$340	$310	$285	$250	$230	$215

Last MSR was $483.

✳ *A-Bolt Hunter Composite Stalker* - .25-06 Rem., .270 Win., .280 Rem., .30-06, 7mm Rem. Mag., .300 Win. Mag., or .338 Win. Mag. cal., black graphite fiberglass composite stock, matte non-glare metal finish, 6 lbs. 11 oz. - 7 lbs. 3 oz. Mfg. 1988-93. Replaced by Composite Stalker II in 1994.

	$410	$340	$295	$265	$240	$225	$210

Last MSR was $525.

A-BOLT BIGHORN SHEEP ISSUE - .270 Win. cal. only, 22 in. barrel, high grade walnut stock with gloss finish and skipline checkering, deep relief engraving on receiver barrel, floorplate, and trigger guard, two 24Kt. inlays depicting bighorn sheep. 600 mfg. 1986-87 only.

	$975	$750	$625	$515	$450	$375	$325

Last MSR was $1,365.

A-BOLT PRONGHORN ISSUE - .243 Win. cal., presentation grade walnut with skipline checkering and pearl borders, receiver and barrel engraving, multiple gold inlays on receiver top and floor plate. 500 mfg. 1987 only.

	$925	$725	$600	$495	$430	$365	$315

Last MSR was $1,302.

RIFLES: BOLT ACTION, CENTERFIRE A-BOLT II SERIES

The A-Bolt II Series was introduced in 1994, and differs from the original A-Bolt variations (disc. 1993) in that a new anti-blnd bolt featuring a non-rotating bolt sleeve has been incorporated In addltlon to an Improved trigger system. Consumers also may have their name/inscription engraved on the flat bolt-face on any A- Bolt II Series variation for an additional $25. Browning introduced the BOSS (ballistic optimizing shooting system) in 1994 as an option on A-Bolt rifles, except Micro-Medallion models. It is available with ported BOSS (results in approx. 30% less recoil) or unported (designated BOSS-CR, for conventional recoil) muzzle brake.

A-BOLT HUNTER MODEL II - available in various cals. between .22-250 Rem. - .338 Win. Mag., .270 WSM and 7mm WSM cals. (new 2002), .300 WSM (new 2001), or .325 WSM (new 2005) cal., 22, 23 (.300 WSM cal. only), 24, or 26 in. barrel with (disc. 1998) or w/o open sights, walnut stock with gloss finish, top tang safety, low lustre bluing, 60 degree bolt throw, right hand action was disc. during 2007, except for Full Line dealer model, 6 lbs. 7 oz. - 7 lbs. 3 oz.

MSR $765		$595	$475	$395	$310	$250	$225	$210

Subtract approx. $40 for right hand action (disc. 2007).
Add $31 for Mag. cals.

Add $75 for Full-line dealer model featuring Monte Carlo stock and gold trigger, WSM and WSSM (mfg. 2007 only) cals. only, new 2007.
Add approx. $60 for open sights (available in 8 cals., disc. 1998).

✳ *A-Bolt Hunter Model II WSSM* - .223 WSSM, .25 WSSM (new 2004), or .243 WSSM cal., 3 shot mag., super short action, 21 or 22 (new 2004) in. barrel, walnut stock with satin finish and smaller dimensions, 6 1/4 lbs. Mfg. 2003-2007.

	$600	$500	$425	$375	$325	$280	$240

Last MSR was $770.

GRADING - PPGS™	100%	98%	95%	90%	80%	70%	60%

✳ *A-Bolt Hunter Model II with BOSS* - same cals. as Hunter Model II until 1999, available only in .22- 250 Rem., .243 Win., .270 Win., .280 Rem., .30-06, or .308 Win. cal. during 1999, features 22 or 26 (Mag. cals. only, disc. 1998) in. barrel with BOSS. Mfg. 1994-99.

	$525	$435	$365	$300	$260	$235	$215

Last MSR was $617.

A-BOLT HUNTER FIELD II (CLASSIC HUNTER) - .270 Win. (disc. 2001), .270 WSM (new 2002), .30-06 (disc. 2001), .300 Win. Mag. (disc. 2001), .300 WSM (new 2002), .325 WSM (new 2005) 7mm Rem. Mag. (disc. 2001), or 7mm WSM (new 2002) cal., 22 (disc. 2001), 23 (new 2002, WSM cals. only), or 26 (disc. 2001) in. barrel, 3-5 shot mag., features low-lustre bluing and select checkered satin finished Monte Carlo walnut stock and forend, approx. 6 1/2 - 7 1/4 lbs. Mfg. 1999-2006.

	$655	$540	$445	$375	$315	$275	$250

Last MSR was $808.

This model was available to Full-line and Medallion dealers only.

✳ *A-Bolt Hunter Field II WSSM (Classic Hunter)* - .223 WSSM, .25 WSSM (new 2004), or .243 WSSM cal., 3 shot mag., super short action, 22 in. barrel, satin finished Monte Carlo walnut stock with palm swell and double bordered checkering, low lustre bluing, 6 1/4 lbs. Mfg. 2003-2006.

	$695	$575	$475	$375	$325	$290	$265

Last MSR was $829.

This model was available to Full-line and Medallion dealers only.

A-BOLT RMEF SPECIAL HUNTER - .325 WSM cal., similar to Medallion Model II, except has satin finished Monte Carlo stock and special RMEF logo insert on floorplate. New 2007.

MSR $864	$695	$550	$475	$395	$325	$290	$265

A-BOLT NRA WILDLIFE CONSERVATION COLLECTION - .243 Win. cal., 22 in. barrel, blue finish, features NRA Heritage logo laser engraved in satin finished walnut stock, approx. 6 1/2 lbs. Limited mfg. 2006-2007.

	$670	$555	$450	$375	$325	$280	$250

Last MSR was $813.

A-BOLT MICRO HUNTER II - .22 Hornet, .22-250 Rem., .223 Rem. (mfg. 2000-2005), .243 Win., .260 Rem. (disc. 2001), .270 WSM (new 2003), 7mm WSM (new 2003), .300 WSM (new 2003), .325 WSM (new 2005), .308 Win., or 7mm-08 Rem. cal., 3 shot mag., features shorter LOP and 20 or 22 in. barrel w/o sights, checkered walnut stock and forend, approx. 6 1/4 lbs. New 1999.

MSR $712	$545	$435	$350	$295	$245	$225	$210

Add $31 for Mag. cals.
Add $31 for left-hand action (new 2003).

A-BOLT MEDALLION MODEL II - available in various cals. between .22-250 Rem. (disc.) - .375 H&H, similar to Medallion Model with A-Bolt II improvements, without sights, except for .375 H&H cal. (open sights standard), gloss finished walnut stock with rosewood grip and forend caps, right hand action w/o BOSS was disc 2007, 6 lbs. 7 oz. - 7 lbs. 1 oz. New 1994.

MSR $871	$690	$565	$460	$370	$300	$275	$250

Add $31 for all Mag. cals., including WSM.
Subtract approx. $50 for right hand action w/o BOSS (disc. 2007).

GRADING - PPGS™	100%	98%	95%	90%	80%	70%	60%

✳ *A-Bolt Medallion Model II WSSM* - .223 WSSM, .25 WSSM (new 2004), or .243 WSSM cal., 3 shot mag., super short action, 22 in. barrel, engraved receiver, Monte Carlo gloss finished walnut stock with rosewood pistol grip and forend caps, palm swell and double bordered checkering, no sights, low lustre bluing, 6 1/4 lbs. Mfg. 2003-2007.

	$695	$575	$475	$425	$385	$365	$335

Last MSR was $872.

✳ *A-Bolt Medallion Model II with BOSS* - various cals. between .223 WSSM - .375 H&H, similar to Medallion Model II, ecept has 22, 23 (new 2002, WSM cals. only) or 26 in. BOSS barrel. New 1994.

MSR $919	$740	$600	$495	$425	$385	$365	$335

Add $31 for normal Mag. and WSM cals. or $51 for WSSM (disc. 2007) cals.
Add $32 for left-hand action (disc. 2005).

✳ *A-Bolt Micro Medallion Model II* - .22 Hornet, .22-250 Rem., .223 Rem., .243 Win., 7mm-08 Rem., .284 Win. (disc. 1997), or .308 Win. cal., similar to Micro Medallion Model with A-Bolt II improvements, 20 or 22 (.22 Hornet only) in. barrel without sights, 6 lbs. Mfg. 1994-98.

	$525	$465	$400	$350	$300	$275	$250

Last MSR was $636.

A-BOLT CUSTOM TROPHY II - .270 Win., .30-06, .300 Win. Mag., or 7mm Rem. Mag. cal., features 24 or 26 (Mag. cals. only) in. octagon barrel with gold band at muzzle, no sights, gold outlines on barrel and receiver, checkered select American walnut stock with shadowline cheekpiece and skeleton pistol grip, approx. 7 1/2 lbs. Mfg. 1998-2000.

	$1,150	$925	$800	$660	$525	$450	$375

Last MSR was $1,428.

A-BOLT GOLD MEDALLION MODEL II - .270 Win., .30-06, .300 Win. Mag. or 7mm Rem. Mag. cal., similar to Gold Medallion Model, except has A-Bolt II improvements, 22 or 26 in. barrel, approx. 7 1/2 lbs. Mfg. 1994-98.

	$695	$595	$450	$375	$335	$300	$265

Last MSR was $855.

✳ *A-Bolt Gold Medallion Model II with BOSS* - mfg. 1994-97.

	$750	$625	$525	$450	$375	$325	$285

Last MSR was $916.

A-BOLT WHITE GOLD MEDALLION MODEL II - .270 WSM (new 2004), .270 Win., .30-06, .300 Win. Mag., .300 WSM (new 2004), .325 WSM (new 2005), 7mm WSM (new 2004), or 7mm Rem. Mag. cal., stainless steel receiver and 22, 23 (new 2004), or 26 in. barrel, gold engraving, checkered high gloss Monte Carlo walnut stock with rosewood cap on forend and pistol grip, 6 lbs. 6 oz. - 7 lbs. 11 oz. New 1999.

MSR $1,202	$970	$750	$600	$500	$425	$360	$300

Add $30 for Mag. cals.

✳ *A-Bolt White Gold Medallion II RMEF* - 7mm Rem. Mag. (disc. 2006) or .325 WSM (new 2007) cal., similar to White Gold Medallion, includes RMEF logo on pistol grip cap, gold engraved, stainless steel receiver and 26 in. barrel, select walnut stock, contrasting spacers and rosewood caps on forend and pistol grip, continental style cheekpiece and sling swivels, 7 lbs., 11 oz. Limited edition beginning 2003.

MSR $1,312	$1,045	$785	$630	$515	$450	$375	$325

✳ *A-Bolt White Gold Medallion II with BOSS* - similar to White Gold Medallion, except has barrel with BOSS, and not available in WSM cals. Disc. 2006.

	$985	$765	$610	$500	$435	$375	$320

Last MSR was $1,235.

Add $28 for non-WSSM Mag. cals.

A-BOLT ECLIPSE HUNTER II WITH BOSS - .22-250 Rem. (disc. 1999), .243 Win. (disc. 1997), .270 Win., .30-06, .308 Win. (disc. 2000), or 7mm Rem. Mag. cal., features laminated thumbhole wood stock with cheekpiece, long action, 22 or 26 (7mm Rem. Mag. only) in. barrel with BOSS, approx. 7 1/2 lbs. New 1996.

	100%	98%	95%	90%	80%	70%	60%
MSR $1,180	$930	$750	$585	$485	$375	$325	$285

    Add $31 for Mag. cal.

✱ *A-Bolt Eclipse Varmint II with BOSS* - .22-250 Rem., .223 Rem., or .308 Win. cal., 24 in. heavy barrel with BOSS, 4 shot mag., otherwise similar to Eclipse Model, approx. 9 lbs. Mfg. 1996-99.

		98%	95%	90%	80%	70%	60%
	$810	$655	$535	$455	$375	$325	$285

Last MSR was $969.

A-BOLT ECLIPSE M-1000 II - .22-250 Rem. (new 2006), .270 WSM, 7mm WSM, .300 WSM, or .308 Win. (new 2006) cal., features 26 in. heavy blue or stainless steel bull barrel, 3 shot mag., 9 lbs. 14 oz. New 2004.

	100%	98%	95%	90%	80%	70%	60%
MSR $1,100	$885	$700	$575	$475	$375	$315	$275

    Add $214 for stainless steel action and bull barrel.
    Add $30 for WSM cals.

✱ *A-Bolt Eclipse M-1000 II with BOSS* - .22-250 Rem. (new 2006), .300 Win. Mag., .308 Win. (new 2006), .270 WSM (new 2006), 7mm WSM (new 2006), or .300 WSM (new 2006) cal., features special 26 in. heavy target barrel, refined trigger system, 10 lbs.

	100%	98%	95%	90%	80%	70%	60%
MSR $1,181	$960	$750	$600	$475	$385	$335	$285

    Add $214 for stainless steel receiver/barrel.
    Add $31 for Mag. cals.

A-BOLT VARMINT II WITH BOSS - .22-250 Rem., .223 Rem., or .308 Win. (new 1995) cal., features A-Bolt II improvements, 22 in. heavy barrel with BOSS, blue/gloss or satin/matte (new 1995, .223 Rem. disc. 1999) finish, black laminated wood stock with checkering, palm swell, and solid recoil pad, without sights, 9 lbs. Mfg. 1994-2000.

		98%	95%	90%	80%	70%	60%
	$715	$600	$465	$380	$335	$300	$265

Last MSR was $879.

A-BOLT EURO-BOLT II - .243 Win., .270 Win., .30-06, .308 Win., or 7mm Rem. Mag. cal., similar to Euro-Bolt with A-Bolt II improvements, 22 or 26 (7mm Rem. Mag. only) in. barrel w/o sights, 6 lbs. 7 oz. - 7 lbs. 3 oz. (Mag.). Mfg. 1994-96.

		98%	95%	90%	80%	70%	60%
	$625	$510	$410	$355	$300	$265	$250

Last MSR was $824.

✱ *A-Bolt Euro-Bolt II with BOSS* - .243 Win., .270 Win., or .308 Win. cal., 22 in. barrel with BOSS, 6 lbs. 7 oz.

		98%	95%	90%	80%	70%	60%
	$725	$600	$500	$425	$350	$325	$295

Last MSR was $922.

A-BOLT STAINLESS STALKER II - similar to Stainless Stalker with A-Bolt improvements, available in various cals, between .22-250 Rem. - .375 H&H, .223 Rem. reintroduced during 2004 in SSA only, no sights, right hand action w/o Boss was disc. 2007, 6 lbs. 1 oz. - 7 lbs. 3 oz. New 1994.

	100%	98%	95%	90%	80%	70%	60%
MSR $963	$785	$565	$400	$325	$285	$240	$205

    Add $30 for normal Mag. or WSM cals.
    Subtract approx. $50 for right hand action (disc. w/o Boss 2007).

✱ *A-Bolt Stainless Stalker II WSSM* - .223 WSSM, .25 WSSM (new 2004), or .243 WSSM cal., 3 shot mag., super short action, 21 (disc.) or 22 in. barrel, walnut stock with satin finish and smaller dimensions, 6 lbs., 1 oz. Mfg. 2003-2007.

		98%	95%	90%	80%	70%	60%
	$790	$585	$425	$350	$300	$250	$215

Last MSR was $966.

✳ A-Bolt Stainless Stalker II with BOSS - various cals. between .22-250 Rem. and .375 H&H, 22, 23 (new 2002, .300 WSM cal. only), 24 (.375 H&H cal. only) 26 (Mag. cals. only) in. barrel with BOSS.

MSR $1,015	$830	$615	$475	$415	$360	$300	$250

Add $31 for normal Mag. or WSM cals., or $51 for WSSM cals. (mfg. 2004-2007).
Add $29 for left-hand action.

A-BOLT CARBON FIBER STAINLESS STALKER II - .22-250 Rem. or .300 Win. Mag. cal., features Christensen lightweight 22 or 26 in. carbon fiber barrel with steel liner, stainless steel action, black synthetic stock, 4 or 5 shot mag., approx. 6 1/4 or 7 1/4 lbs. Mfg. 2000-2001.

$1,475	$1,225	$975	$860	$700	$600	$500

Last MSR was $1,750.

A-BOLT COMPOSITE STALKER II - various cals. between .22-250 Rem. - .338 Win. Mag., similar to Composite Stalker with A-Bolt II improvements, 22, 23 (WSM cals. only), 24, or 26 (Mag. cals. only) in. barrel without sights, 6 lbs. 1 oz. - 7 lbs. 3 oz. Mfg. 1994-2007.

$545	$420	$345	$285	$240	$225	$210

Last MSR was $719.

Add $30 for all Mag. cals.

✳ A-Bolt Composite Stalker II WSSM - .223 WSSM, .25 WSSM (new 2004), or .243 WSSM cal., 3 shot mag., super short action, 21 (disc.) or 22 in. barrel, black composite stock with matte blued metal and smaller dimensions, 6.1 lbs. Mfg. 2003-2007.

$650	$535	$435	$380	$335	$295	$260

Last MSR was $770.

✳ A-Bolt Composite Stalker II with BOSS - various cals., 22, 23 (WSM cals. only), or 26 (Mag. cals. only) in. barrel with BOSS.

MSR $815	$655	$535	$415	$345	$290	$250	$225

Add $31 for standard Mag. and WSM cals., or $51 for WSSM cals. (mfg. 2004-2007).

A-BOLT VARMINT STALKER II - .22-250 Rem. or .223 Rem. (SSA only beginning 2004) cal., 24 or 26 (.22-250 Rem. cal. only) in. heavy barrel, features Dura-Touch armor coated composite stock with slight palm swell, matte blue metal, 4 or 6 shot mag., approx. 7 3/4 lbs. New 2002.

MSR $895	$715	$575	$450	$360	$300	$255	$230

✳ A-Bolt Varmint Stalker II WSSM - .223 WSSM, .25 WSSM (new 2004), or .243 WSSM cal., 3 shot mag., super short action, 21 (mfg. 2003 only) or 24 (new 2004) in. barrel, features Dura-Touch armor coated composite stock with slight palm swell, matte blue metal, 7 lbs., 13 oz. Mfg. 2003-2007.

$745	$580	$475	$395	$335	$295	$275

Last MSR was $928.

A-BOLT II MOUNTAIN TI - .243 Win. (new 2006), .308 Win. (new 2006), 7mm-08 Rem. (new 2006), .270 WSM, .300 WSM, 7mm WSM, .223 WSSM (mfg. 2005), .243 WSSM (mfg. 2005), .25 WSSM (mfg. 2005), or .325 WSM (new 2006) cal., features titanium short action receiver with composite bolt sleeve and stainless steel 23 in. barrel, fiberglass Bell & Carlson stock with Mossy Oak New Break-Up camo and Dura-Touch armor coating, Pachmayr Decelerator recoil pad, approx. 5 1/2 lbs. New 2004.

MSR $1,706	$1,375	$1,085	$875	$760	$625	$525	$450

Add $30 for WSM cals.

GRADING - PPGS™	100%	98%	95%	90%	80%	70%	60%

A-BOLT II GREYWOLF - .25-06 Rem., .270 Win., .280 Rem., .30-06, .300 Win. Mag., .338 Win. Mag., or 7mm Rem. Mag. cal., stainless steel, classic sporter with select walnut stock. Limited mfg. during 1994 only.

	$850	$675	$595	N/A	N/A	N/A	N/A

Last MSR was $935.

RIFLES: BOLT ACTION, CENTERFIRE X-BOLT SERIES

The X-Bolt Series was introduced during 2008, and features a new three-lever Feather trigger system that is adjustable from 3-5 lbs. It also has a 3-4 shot detachable rotary mag., 60-degree bolt lift, top safety with bolt unlock button feature, free floating barrel, X-lock scope mounting system (four screws per base, instead of two), and a soft recoil pad using Inflex technology. The various models listed all have these features.

X-BOLT HUNTER - various cals. in both short and long action, satin finished walnut stock with checkering, low lustre blue finish, 22-26 in. barrel (depending on caliber) w/o sights, 6 2/3 - 7 lbs. New 2008.

MSR $799	$625	$525	$435	$385	$335	$295	$260

Add $50 for standard Mag. or WSM cals.

X-BOLT MEDALLION - similar to X-Bolt Hunter, except has a gloss finished walnut stock with rosewood pistol grip and forend caps. New 2008.

MSR $899	$725	$575	$450	$400	$350	$300	$275

Add $50 for standard Mag. or WSM cals.

X-BOLT COMPOSITE - similar cals. as X-Bolt Hunter, features matte black composite stock with palm swell and DuraTouch Armor coating, matte blued steel receiver and barrel, 22-26 in. barrel w/o sights, 6 lbs. 5 oz. - 6 lbs. 13 oz. New 2008.

MSR $799	$625	$525	$435	$385	$335	$295	$260

Add $50 for standard Mag. or WSM cals.

X-BOLT STAINLESS STALKER - similar to X-Bolt Composite, except has matte finished stainless steel receiver and barrel. New 2008.

MSR $999	$825	$625	$500	$425	$375	$350	$325

Add $50 for regular Mag. or WSM cals.

RIFLES: BOLT ACTION, RIMFIRE A-BOLT SERIES

A-BOLT GRADE I RIMFIRE - .22 LR or .22 Mag. (new 1989) cal., 60 degree bolt throw, 22 in. barrel, checkered walnut stock and forearm or laminated stock (scarce - approx. 1,500 mfg., 390 had no sights), 5 or 15 (optional) shot mag., adj. trigger, available with or without open sights, 5 lbs. 9 oz. Mfg. 1986-96.

✳ *A-Bolt Grade I .22 LR cal.*

	$440	$395	$325	$300	$225	$200	$175

Last MSR was $425.

Add $14 for open sights.
A 15 shot mag. was also available for this model at $45 retail.

✳ *A-Bolt Grade I .22 Win. Mag. cal.*

	$465	$410	$350	$325	$250	$225	$200

Last MSR was 493.

Add $21 for open sights.

A-BOLT GOLD MEDALLION RIMFIRE - .22 LR cal. only, similar to A-Bolt, except has high grade select walnut stock checkered 22 lines per inch, rosewood pistol and forend cap, high gloss finish, gold filled lettering and moderate engraving, solid recoil pad. Mfg. 1988-96.

	$495	$450	$375	$325	$270	$240	$225

Last MSR was $567.

GRADING - PPGS™	100%	98%	95%	90%	80%	70%	60%

RIFLES: LEVER ACTION

BL-17 - .17 Mach 2 cal., otherwise similar to the BL-22, 5 lbs., 2 oz. New 2005.

✳ *BL-17 Grade I* - uncheckered stock with choice of blued or nickel (BL-17 Field) receiver, blued trigger. Mfg. 2005.

	$420	$300	$250	$200	$150	$110	$100

Last MSR was $484.

Add $32 for nickel.

✳ *BL-17 Grade II* - features choice of engraved blued or nickel (Field) receiver, gold trigger, checkered stock and forearm. Mfg. 2005.

	$440	$335	$265	$215	$185	$150	$125

Last MSR was $524.

Add $53 for nickel.

✳ *BL-17 Grade II Field Octagon* - similar to BL-22 Classic/Field octagon, 5 lbs., 6 oz., mfg. 2005 by Miroku.

	$650	$550	$475	$425	$365	$310	$260

Last MSR was $744.

BL-22 GRADE I - .22 S, L, and LR cal., 20 in. barrel, short throw (33 degree) lever, folding leaf sight, 15 shot (LR) mag., blue finish, exposed hammer, Western style gloss finished uncheckered stock and forearm, 5 lbs. Mfg. 1970-2003 by Miroku.

	$375	$310	$275	$210	$175	$160	$140

Last MSR was $436.

✳ *BL-22 Grade I (Classic/Field)* - similar to BL-22 Grade I, except has choice of gloss or satin finished stock and forearm, blue or nickel (new 2005) receiver. New 1999, mfg. by Miroku.

MSR $494	$390	$275	$225	$175	$135	$110	$100

Add $35 for satin nickel finished frame and satin finished stock (Field, new 2005).

The satin nickel model is available through Full-Line and Medallion dealers only.

✳ *BL-22 Grade I NRA* - similar to BL-22 Grade I, except has NRA logo laser engraved in stock. Mfg. 2006-2007.

	$400	$280	$225	$170	$135	$110	$100

Last MSR was $514.

BL-22 GRADE II - same general specifications as BL-22, except scroll engraved blue receiver and deluxe high gloss checkered walnut stock and forearm. Disc. 2003.

	$400	$350	$300	$235	$200	$175	$150

Last MSR was $494.

✳ *BL-22 Grade II (Classic/Field)* - similar to BL-22 Grade II, except has choice of gloss or satin finished stock and forearm, engraved blue or nickel (new 2005) receiver. New 1999, mfg. by Miroku.

MSR $567	$440	$325	$250	$195	$145	$125	$115

Add $33 for satin nickel receiver and satin finished stock and forearm (Field, new 2005).

This model is available through Full-Line and Medallion dealers only.

✳ *BL-22 Grade II Classic/Field Octagon* - features 24 in. octagon barrel and silver nitride finished receiver with scroll engraving, adj. buckhorn rear sight, checkered satin finished stock and forearm, 5 1/4 lbs. New 2004, mfg. by Miroku.

MSR $786	$630	$535	$460	$415	$350	$300	$250

This model is available through Full-Line and Medallion dealers only.

GRADING - PPGS™	100%	98%	95%	90%	80%	70%	60%

MODEL 53 DELUXE LIMITED EDITION - .32-20 WCF cal. (round nose or hollow point bullets only), patterned after the original Winchester Model 53 (redesigned Model 1892), 7 shot tube mag., high polished blue metal, open sights, 22 in. tapered barrel, high grade checkered walnut stock featuring full pistol grip cap and shotgun style metal buttplate, 6 1/2 lbs. Only 5,000 mfg. in 1990.

	$795	**$525**	**$425**	**N/A**	**N/A**	**N/A**	**N/A**

Last MSR was $675.

MODEL 65 GRADE I LIMITED EDITION - .218 Bee cal., patterned after the Winchester Model 65, round tapered 24 in. barrel, open sights (hooded front), blue metal finish, 7 shot tube mag., uncheckered pistol grip stock and semi-beavertail forearm, metal buttplate, 6 3/4 lbs. 3,500 total mfg. for Grade I in 1989 only, inventory depleted in 1990.

	$550	**$425**	**$375**	**N/A**	**N/A**	**N/A**	**N/A**

Last MSR was $550.

✳ *Model 65 High Grade* - greyed receiver (and lever) with scroll engraving and gold plated animals, gold plated trigger, deluxe checkered walnut stock and semi-beavertail forearm. 1,500 total mfg. in 1989, inventory depleted in 1990.

	$850	**$775**	**$700**	**N/A**	**N/A**	**N/A**	**N/A**

Last MSR was $850.

MODEL 71 LIMITED EDITION CARBINE - .348 Win. cal., reproduction of the Winchester Model 71 Carbine, 20 in. barrel, open sights, 4 shot mag., 8 lbs. New 1987 with inventory depleted in 1990.

✳ *Model 71 Limited Edition Carbine Grade I* - uncheckered satin finished walnut stock and forearm. 4,000 mfg. 1986-87 only.

	$725	**$600**	**$525**	**N/A**	**N/A**	**N/A**	**N/A**

Last MSR was $600.

✳ *Model 71 Limited Edition Carbine High Grade* - deluxe checkered walnut stock and forearm with high gloss finish, scroll engraved-grey receiver with gold inlays and trigger. 3,000 mfg. 1986-87 only.

	$950	**$775**	**$650**	**N/A**	**N/A**	**N/A**	**N/A**

Last MSR was $980.

MODEL 71 LIMITED EDITION RIFLE - .348 Win. cal., reproduction of the Winchester Model 71 Rifle, 24 in. barrel, open sights, 4 shot mag., 8 lbs. 2 oz. Mfg. 1986-87 only with inventory depleted in 1990.

✳ *Model 71 Grade I Rifle* - uncheckered satin finished walnut stock and forearm. 3,000 mfg. 1986-87 only.

	$795	**$650**	**$550**	**N/A**	**N/A**	**N/A**	**N/A**

Last MSR was $600.

✳ *Model 71 High Grade Rifle* - deluxe checkered walnut stock and forearm with high gloss finish, scroll engraved-grey receiver with gold inlays and trigger. 3,000 mfg. 1986-87 only.

	$1,100	**$875**	**$775**	**N/A**	**N/A**	**N/A**	**N/A**

Last MSR was $980.

MODEL BLR 81 SHORT ACTION - .22-250 Rem., .222 Rem. (disc. 1989), .223 Rem., .243 Win., .257 Roberts (disc. 1992), 7mm-08 Rem., .284 Win. (disc. 1994), .308 Win., or .358 Win. (disc. 1992) cal., steel receiver, rotary bolt locking lugs, 20 in. barrel with band, 3 (.284 Win. only) or 4 shot detachable mag., adj. rear sight, checkered straight grip stock, recoil pad, approx. 7 lbs, no sights optional 1988-89.

.243 Win. and .308 Win. cals. are the most popular in this model.

GRADING - PPGS™	100%	98%	95%	90%	80%	70%	60%

✱ *Model BLR 81 USA* - .243 Win. or .308 Win. cal., this model was originally sched- uled to be manufactured by TRW in Cleveland, OH for Browning. Originally assembled in 1966, these rifles are considered prototypes as they were never sold through regular channels and at one time were scheduled to be destroyed. Approx. 50-250 of these rifles exist, some still NIB.

	$995	$895	$750	$600	$550	$500	$450

This variation has a 2-line legend on the right side marked "MADE IN USA" and "PATENT PENDING".

✱ *Model BLR 81 Belgian* - .243 Win. or .308 Win. cal., mfg. was moved to FN in Belgium with original assembly beginning 1969 and concluding in 1973. This FN model included a number of small dimensioning and engraving changes.

	$875	$750	$625	$500	$425	$375	$325

✱ *Model BLR 81 Japan* - cals. as noted above (except .358 cal. was added 1976), mfg. was moved to Miroku in Japan 1974-1980. Early guns during 1974 had stocks with impressed checkering. By 1975, cut checkering and gloss wood fin- ish was used on stocks and forearms.

	$700	$550	$475	$400	$375	$325	$275

Last MSR was $550.

Add $40 without sights (scarce).

✱ *Model BLR 81 Short Action* - cals. as noted above, mfg. 1981-95 by Miroku in Japan.

	100%	98%	95%	90%	80%	70%	60%
Standard cals.	$600	$550	$425	$375	$285	$250	$225
.257 Roberts	$825	$750	$600	$475	$350	$275	$250
.284 Win./.358 Win.	$825	$750	$600	$475	$350	$275	$250
.222 Rem.	$1,400	$1,275	$825	$650	$595	$500	$425

Last MSR was $550.

MODEL BLR 81 LONG ACTION - .270 Win., .30-06, or 7mm Rem Mag. cal., incor- porates distinct design changes, 22 or 24 in. barrel, approx. 8 1/2 lbs. Mfg. 1991-95 by Miroku.

	$650	$525	$425	$350	$300	$275	$250

Last MSR was $580.

NEW MODEL LIGHTNING BLR (SHORT ACTION) - .22-250 Rem., .223 Rem. (disc. 1998), .243 Win., 7mm-08 Rem., or .308 Win. cal., rotary bolt locking lugs, 20 in. barrel w/o barrel band, similar action as the BLR 81, but features aluminum alloy receiver, checkered pistol grip stock and forearm, rack and pinion geared slide, fold down hammer, trigger travels with lever, 3-5 shot detachable mag., adj. rear sight, approx. 6 1/2 lbs. Mfg. by Miroku late 1995 - 2002.

	$575	$450	$375	$325	$250	$195	$165

Last MSR was $681.

NEW MODEL LIGHTNING BLR (LONG ACTION) - .270 Win., .30-06, .300 Win. Mag. (new 1997), or 7mm Rem. Mag. cal., 22 or 24 (Mag. cals.) in. barrel, approx. 7 1/4 - 7 3/4 lbs. Mfg. by Miroku 1995-2002.

	$600	$465	$375	$300	$250	$215	$175

Last MSR was $721.

BLR LIGHTWEIGHT ´81 (SHORT ACTION) - .22-250 Rem., .243 Win., .270 WSM (new 2004), 7mm-08 Rem., .325 WSM (pistol grip only, new 2005), .300 WSM (new 2004), 7mm WSM (new 2004), .308 Win., .358 Win., .450 Marlin cal., 20 or 22 (WSM cals. only) in. barrel with barrel band, solid or takedown (new 2007) action, aluminum alloy receiver, choice of checkered Model 81 styled straight grip and forearm with gloss finish or checkered, gloss finished pistol grip with Schnabel forearm w/o barrel band (new 2005) stock, sling swivels (pistol grip only), rack and pinion geared slide with rotating breech head, fold

GRADING - PPGS™	100%	98%	95%	90%	80%	70%	60%

down hammer, trigger travels with lever, 3-4 shot detachable mag., adj. rear sight, approx. 6 1/2 - 7 lbs. Mfg. by Miroku beginning 2003.

MSR $784	$595	$445	$375	$325	$300	$275	$250

Add $75 for WSM cals. (new 2004).
Add $36 for checkered pistol grip stock and Schnabel forearm (new 2005).
Add $73 for takedown action (new 2007).
Add $70 for one-piece scope mount (new 2007).

BLR LIGHTWEIGHT '81 (LONG ACTION) - .270 Win., .30-06, .300 Win. Mag., or 7mm Rem. Mag. cal., 22 or 24 in. barrel, 7 1/4 or 7 3/4 lbs. Mfg. by Miroku beginning 2003.

MSR $831	$645	$485	$430	$380	$325	$300	$275

Add $36 for checkered pistol grip stock and Schnabel forearm (new 2005).
Add $73 for takedown action (new 2007).

MODEL 1886 LIMITED EDITION GRADE I RIFLE - .45-70 Govt. cal. only, patterned after the Winchester Model 1886, blue receiver, 26 in. octagon barrel, 8 shot full mag., crescent buttplate, 8 shot full term mag., open sights. 7,000 mfg. 1986 only.

	$1,325	$1,050	$850	N/A	N/A	N/A	N/A

Last MSR was $578.

✳ *Model 1886 Limited Edition High Grade Rifle* - same general specifications as Model 1886, except has checkered high grade walnut stock and forearm, greyed steel receiver, with game scene engraving including elk and American Bison, gold accenting with "1 of 3,000" engraved on top of barrel. 3,000 mfg. 1986 only.

	$1,875	$1,450	$1,050	N/A	N/A	N/A	N/A

Last MSR was $935.

✳ *Model 1886 Montana Centennial Rifle* - similar to Model 1886 High Grade. 2,000 mfg. 1986 only to commemorate Montana Centennial.

	$1,875	$1,450	$1,050	N/A	N/A	N/A	N/A

Last MSR was $935.

MODEL 1886 LIMITED EDITION GRADE I CARBINE - .45-70 Govt. cal. only, saddle ring carbine, patterned after the Winchester Model 1886 Carbine, blue receiver, 22 in. round barrel, 7 shot full mag., crescent buttplate, open sights. 7,000 total mfg. 1992-93.

	$900	$750	$575	N/A	N/A	N/A	N/A

Last MSR was $750.

✳ *Model 1886 Limited Edition High Grade Carbine* - same general specifications as Model 1886, except has checkered high grade walnut stock and forearm, greyed steel receiver, with game scene engraving including bear and elk, gold accenting, 3,000 total mfg. 1992-93.

	$1,475	$1,050	$800	N/A	N/A	N/A	N/A

Last MSR was $1,175.

B-92 CARBINE - .357 Mag. or .44 Rem. Mag. cal., 20 in. barrel, patterned after the Winchester Model 92, 11 shot mag. (tubular), blue finish. Disc. 1986.

	$550	$450	$395	$300	$250	$225	$200

Last MSR was $342.

Add 15% for .357 Mag. cal.

✳ *B-92 Centennial* - .44 Mag. cal., 6,000 mfg. in 1978.

	$595	$495	$450	N/A	N/A	N/A	N/A

Last MSR was $220.

✳ *B-92 BCA Commemorative* - mfg. to commemorate BCA's third anniversary.

	$595	$495	$450	N/A	N/A	N/A	N/A

GRADING - PPGS™	100%	98%	95%	90%	80%	70%	60%

MODEL 1895 LIMITED EDITION GRADE I - .30/40 Krag or .30-06 cal. only, patterned after the Winchester Model 1895, blue receiver, 24 in. barrel, 4 shot mag.(box type), select walnut, rear buckhorn sight, 8 lbs. Mfg. 1984 only.

	100%	98%	95%	90%	80%	70%	60%
.30/40 Krag	$650	$550	$450	N/A	N/A	N/A	N/A
.30-06	$700	$600	$475	N/A	N/A	N/A	N/A

Production totaled 6,000 in the .30-06 cal. and 2,000 in .30/40 Krag for this model.

✱ *Model 1895 Limited Edition High Grade* - same general specifications as Model 1895, except gold plated game scenes on satin finish receiver, gold trigger, and finely checkered select French walnut.

	100%	98%	95%	90%	80%	70%	60%
	$1,475	$1,050	$850	N/A	N/A	N/A	N/A

Production totaled 1,000 in the .30-06 cal. and 1,000 in .30/40 Krag for this model.

RIFLES: O/U

Currently, the Browning Custom Shop in Belgium is making the following double rifles: CCS Herstal ($14,449 MSR), CCS25 B2E ($20,199 MSR), CCS Africa ($15,266 MSR, disc. 2005), Bavarian ($25,149 MSR), CCS25 D5G ($43,665 MSR), and the M1 ($57,498 MSR).

EXPRESS RIFLE - .270 Win., .30-06 cal., or 9.3x74R cal., Superposed Superlight style action. 24 in. barrels, checkered straight grip stock and forearm, auto ejectors, Fleur-de-lis engraving, single trigger, folding leaf rear sight, 6 lbs. 14 oz., cased. Disc. 1986.

	100%	98%	95%	90%	80%	70%	60%
	$4,950	$4,400	$3,950	$3,650	$3,300	$3,100	$2,900

Last MSR was $3,125.

GRADE I CONTINENTAL SET - includes .30-06 O/U rifle barrels with extra set of 20 ga. O/U shotgun barrels (26 1/2 in.), rifle barrels are 24 in., 20 ga. frame, SST, ejectors, blue receiver with scroll engraving, straight grip checkered stock and forearm, supplied with 2 barrel takedown case. Mfg. 1978-86.

	100%	98%	95%	90%	80%	70%	60%
	$6,500	$5,750	$5,000	$4,500	$4,000	$3,600	$3,200

RIFLES: SEMI-AUTO, .22 LR

Miroku manufactured .22s can be determined by year of manufacture in the following manner: RV suffix - 1975, RT - 1976, RR - 1977, RP - 1978, RN - 1979, PM - 1980, PZ - 1981, PY - 1982, PX - 1983, PW - 1984, PV - 1985, PT -1986, PR - 1987, PP - 1988, PN - 1989, NM - 1990, NZ - 1991, NY - 1992, NX - 1993, NW - 1994, NV - 1995, NT - 1996, NR - 1997, NP - 1998, NN - 1999, MM - 2000, MZ - 2001, MY - 2002, MX - 2003, MW - 2004, MV - 2005, MU - 2006, MT - 2007, MS - 2008, MR - 2009.

Currently, the Browning Custom Shop in Belgium is making the following .22 LR cal. semi-auto models: Grade II ($4,000 MSR), and the Grade III ($6,100 MSR).

AUTO RIFLE GRADES I - VI - .22 LR or .22 short (disc.) cal., takedown design, 10 shot (16 for .22 short) tube mag. in buttstock, 19 1/4 in. barrel for all .22 LR, .22 shorts had various barrel lengths according to mfg. year: 19 1/4 in. for 1956, 22 3/8 in. for 1957, and 22 in. from 1958 until general production was disc. in 1983, checkered pistol grip stock, semi-beavertail forearm, stock has hole machined halfway to allow partial filling of tube mag., adj. folding rear or earlier wheel sight, Grades differ in finish, amount of engraving, and grade of wood, 4 3/4-5 3/4 lbs. Early top loaders were mfg. from 1914 until approx. 1955. Modern loader mfg. 1956 to 1974 by FN Belgium. Mfg. beginning 1976 by Miroku in Japan.

✱ *Auto Rifle Grade I - FN*

	100%	98%	95%	90%	80%	70%	60%
	$725	$625	$500	$400	$325	$300	$250

Add 50% for guns in .22 Short cal., if in 95% or better condition.
Add 25% for wheel sight guns if in 95% or better condition.
Add at least $50 for original box and manual.

FN Postwar Grade Is have a lightly engraved blue steel receiver, checkered walnut, blue trigger, and a variety of rear sights.

GRADING - PPGS™	100%	98%	95%	90%	80%	70%	60%

* *Auto Rifle Grade I - Miroku* - approx. 5 1/4 lbs.

MSR $574	$445	$345	$275	$230	$185	$160	$140

* *Auto Rifle Grade II - FN*

	$1,325	$1,150	$825	$600	$550	$500	$450

Add $100 for guns initialed by the engraver.
Add $200 for guns fully signed by the engraver.
Add 35% for Grade II with wheel sight.

FN Grade IIs have grey receiver, deluxe wood with finer checkering, gold plated trigger, and engraving depicting two squirrels and two prairie dogs. Unsigned, signed, or initialed by engraver.

* *Auto Rifle Grade II - Miroku* - disc. 1984.

	$695	$600	$475	$375	$325	$275	$250

* *Auto Rifle Grade III - FN*

	$3,350	$2,750	$2,250	$1,775	$1,350	$1,100	$850

Add 15% for guns signed by the engraver.

FN Grade IIIs have coin finish or grey chromed receiver, extra deluxe walnut with skipline checkering, gold plated trigger, and more elaborate game scene engraving usually featuring a dog flushing ducks or upland game. Signed or unsigned by engraver (Funken, J. Baerten, Vrancken, and Watrin will command premiums over values listed). A few were also special ordered with blue finish and special engraving - these command an extra premium.

* *Auto Rifle Grade III - Miroku* - disc. 1983.

	$1,395	$1,075	$950	$800	$700	$600	$500

Add 15% for guns signed by the engraver.
Add 30% for "transition" guns signed by FN engravers with barrels and boxes marked "Made in Japan."

* *Auto Rifle Grade VI - Miroku* - game scene engraved with gold plating, choice of blue or greyed receiver, deluxe walnut. New 1987.

MSR $1,251	$975	$785	$600	$460	$400	$340	$300

Add at least 50% for small run of .22 Short Grade VI mfg. during 2003.

* *Auto Rifle Grade VI 125th Anniversary Miroku* - features silver nitride receiver with gold enhanced 125th Anniversary logo and delicate scroll engraving. 500 mfg. 2003-2004.

	$1,275	$1,050	$825	N/A	N/A	N/A	N/A

Last MSR was $1,271.

BAR-22 - .22 LR cal., 20 1/4 in. barrel, 15 shot tube mag., folding leaf sight, high polish steel receiver, checkered pistol grip stock, 5 lbs. 13 oz. Mfg. 1977-85 by Miroku.

	$600	$550	$475	$400	$300	$250	$200

Last MSR was $245.

BAR-22 GRADE II - engraved model of BAR-22 featuring game scenes on silver greyed steel receiver, select French walnut. Disc. 1985.

	$995	$825	$725	$575	$450	$350	$250

Last MSR was $350.

BUCK MARK RIFLE - .22 LR cal., Buck Mark pistol blowback action, 18 in. tapered barrel with Hi-Viz fiber optic sights (Sporter Rifle), heavy barrel w/o sights (Target or Field Target Rifle), or carbon composite barrel (disc. 2006), includes intergral scope rail, uncheckered walnut or grey laminate (new 2002, no sights) Monte Carlo stock that attaches to non-detachable, one-piece skeletonized and enclosed rear grip assembly, seperate forearm, 10 shot mag., 3 lbs., 10 oz. (Classic Carbon), 4 lbs. 6 oz. (Sporter) or approx. 5 1/2 lbs. (Target & Classic Target) New 2001.

MSR $612	$465	$335	$280	$240	$200	$160	$150

Add $19 for grey laminate stock (Classic/Field Target Rifle, new 2002).
Add $95 for carbon composite barrel (disc. 2006).

The Buck Mark Classic/Field Target & Classic/Field Carbon Rifles are available through Full-Line and Medallion dealers only.

GRADING - PPGS™	100%	98%	95%	90%	80%	70%	60%

RIFLES: SEMI-AUTO, BAR SERIES

Currently, the Browning Custom Shop in Belgium is making the following BAR custom shop rifles: Grade 4 VB ($14,333 MSR), Grade 4 PH ($14,333 MSR), and the Grade D (disc. 2006, last $6,543 MSR).

BROWNING PATENT 1900 - please refer to model listing under F.N.

BAR SEMI-AUTO - .243 Win., .270 Win., .280 Rem. (new 1990), .308 Win., or .30-06 cal. available in standard model, Mag. cals. include 7mm Rem., .300 Win., and .338 Win. Mag. (reintroduced 1990), gas operated, blued steel receiver, 22 or 24 (Mag. only) in. barrel, rotary bolt with seven lugs, folding leaf sight, walnut stock. Grades differ in engraving, finish, and grade of wood, in 1993, to celebrate the 25th Anniversary of the BAR, Browning introduced the BAR MK II Safari (see model listing), approx. 7 lbs. 6 oz. New 1967 (includes BAR MK II).

Add 20% for FN mfg. and assembled BARs (marked "Made in Belgium").
Add 10% for .338 Win. Mag. cal. (FN mfg. only).

Note: Original .338s were limited production, mostly seen in the deluxe Grade II only. During the last year of FN .338 production, several were delivered in a Grade I by FN. Although being rarer than the Grade II, it is not as desirable. The following prices are for Portugese assembled guns, manufactured by FN, and are so stamped on the barrel.

✳ *BAR Grade I* - standard grade without engraving, blue finish. Ordering this model without sights became an option in 1988. Disc. 1992.

	100%	98%	95%	90%	80%	70%	60%
	$695	$575	$500	$450	$400	$350	$300

Last MSR was $633.

Add 15% for .280 Rem. cal. if in 98%+ condition.
Subtract $16 without sights.

FN mfg. and assembled Grade Is can be denoted by light scroll engraving on the receiver.

✳ *BAR Grade I Magnum* - standard grade without engraving, with recoil pad, 8 lbs. 6 oz. Disc. 1992.

	100%	98%	95%	90%	80%	70%	60%
	$725	$600	$525	$475	$425	$375	$325

Last MSR was $680.

Subtract $16 without sights.

Ordering this gun without sights became an option in 1988.

✳ *BAR Grade II* - blue receiver, engraved with big game heads. Mfg. 1967-74.

	100%	98%	95%	90%	80%	70%	60%
	$975	$850	$750	$650	$525	$495	$450

This model was previously designated Deluxe.

✳ *BAR Grade II Magnum* - magnum version of Grade II. Mfg. 1967-74.

	100%	98%	95%	90%	80%	70%	60%
	$1,075	$950	$875	$750	$650	$575	$550

✳ *BAR Grade III* - features antelope and deer game scenes etched on greyed steel receiver, select checkered stock and forearm. Disc. 1984.

	100%	98%	95%	90%	80%	70%	60%
	$1,375	$1,200	$975	$775	$650	$595	$550

✳ *BAR Grade III Magnum* - magnum version of Grade III, features elk and moose game scenes. Disc. 1984.

	100%	98%	95%	90%	80%	70%	60%
	$1,500	$1,325	$1,050	$900	$800	$700	$650

✳ *BAR Grade IV* - engraved satin finish greyed receiver depicts big game animal scenes and trigger guard, carved borders on checkering. Disc. 1989.

	100%	98%	95%	90%	80%	70%	60%
	$2,000	$1,800	$1,600	$1,425	$1,200	$1,100	$925

Last MSR was $1,670.

✳ *BAR Grade IV Magnum* - magnum version of Grade IV. Disc. 1984.

	100%	98%	95%	90%	80%	70%	60%
	$2,175	$2,000	$1,725	$1,550	$1,325	$1,200	$1,000

Last MSR was $1,720.

GRADING - PPGS™	100%	98%	95%	90%	80%	70%	60%

* *BAR Grade V* - more elaborate engraving than Grade IV, with gold inlays. Mfg. 1971-74.

	100%	98%	95%	90%	80%	70%	60%
	$5,325	$4,850	$4,500	$4,150	$3,600	$3,100	$2,650

* *BAR Grade V Magnum* - magnum version of Grade V.

	100%	98%	95%	90%	80%	70%	60%
	$5,700	$5,150	$4,750	$4,250	$3,700	$3,200	$2,750

BAR NORTH AMERICAN DEER RIFLE ISSUE - .30-06 cal. only, BAR style action with silver grey finish and engraved action, 600 total production, walnut cased with accessories. Disc. 1983 but were sold through 1989.

	100%	98%	95%	90%	80%	70%	60%
	$3,800	$3,450	$2,900	$2,650	$2,400	$2,050	$1,850

Last MSR was $3,550.

BAR MK II SAFARI - .22-250 Rem. (mfg. as prototype only during 1997), .25-06 Rem. (new 1997), .243 Win., .270 Win., .30-06, .308 Win., .270 Wby. Mag. (mfg. 1996-2000), 7mm Rem. Mag., .300 Win. Mag., or .338 Win. Mag. cal., improved BAR action featuring redesigned bolt release, new gas operating system, and reduced recoil, removable trigger assembly, 22, 23 (WSM cals. only), or 24 (Mag. cals. only) in. barrel with (adj. for windage and elevation) or without sights, BOSS became optional 1994, and is available with ported BOSS, which results in approx. 30% less recoil, or unported (designated BOSS-CR, for conventional recoil) muzzle brake, blue finish with scroll engraved receiver, checkered walnut stock and forearm, gold trigger, detachable 3 (.300 WSM cal. only), 4 (Mag. cals. only) or 5 shot box mag., approx. 7 lbs. 6 oz. except for Mag. cals. (8 lbs. 6 oz.). Mfg. by FN in Belgium. New 1993.

MSR $1,030	$850	$635	$500	$425	$385	$350	$325

   Add $92 for Mag. cals.
   Add $19 for open sights (not available in .270 Wby. Mag., disc.).

The new BAR MK II Safari does not have interchangeable magazine capability with the older pre-1993 BARs.

* *BAR Classic Mark II Safari* - .270 Win. (disc. 2001), .270 WSM (new 2003), .30-06 (disc. 2001), 7mm Rem. Mag., (disc. 2001), 7mm WSM (new 2003), .300 Win. Mag. (disc. 2001), or .300 WSM (new 2002) cal., similar to BAR Mark II Safari, except has satin finished checkered stock and forearm, 7 lbs. 6 oz. or 8 lbs. 6 oz. Mfg. 1999-2003.

	$785	$610	$520	$430	$380	$335	$310

Last MSR was $908.

   Subtract approx. 10% for non-Mag. cals.
   Add $17 for open sights (disc. 2000).

This model is available to Full-line and Medallion dealers only.

* *BAR Mark II Safari with BOSS* - .243 Win. (disc. 1999), .308 Win. (disc. 1999), .270 Win., .270 WSM (new 2003), .30-06, 7mm Rem. Mag., 7mm WSM (new 2003), .300 Win. Mag., .300 WSM (new 2003), .338 Win. Mag. cal., similar to BAR MK II Safari, with BOSS (ballistic optimizing shooting system) accurizing adj. assembly on barrel end, no sights, approx. 7 1/2 or 8 1/2 lbs. New 1994.

MSR $1,145	$950	$750	$650	$550	$475	$425	$385

   Add $92 for Mag. and WSM cals.

* *BAR Mark II Lightweight* - .243 Win., .270 Win., .30-06, .308 Win., 7mm Rem. Mag. (new 1999), .300 Win. Mag. (new 1999), or .338 Win. Mag. (new 1999) cal., features alloy receiver and 20 or 24 (Mag. cals. only) in. barrel, matte wood and barrel finish, open sights, 7 lbs. 2 oz. or 7 lbs. 12 oz. Mfg. 1997-2003.

	$710	$545	$450	$395	$355	$330	$310

Last MSR was $850.

   Add $77 for Mag. cals. (new 1999).

GRADING - PPGS™	100%	98%	95%	90%	80%	70%	60%

❋ *BAR MK II Lightweight with BOSS* - 7mm Rem. Mag., .300 Win. Mag., or .338 Win. Mag. (disc. 1999) cal., similar to BAR Mark II Lightweight, except has 24 in. barrel with BOSS, 8 lbs., 6 oz. Mfg. 1999-2000.

	$800	$625	$525	$445	$385	$350	$310

Last MSR was $939.

❋ *BAR MK II Lightweight Stalker* - .243 Win., .270 Win., .270 WSM (new 2003), .30-06, .308 Win., 7mm Rem. Mag. (disc. 2004), 7mm WSM (new 2003), .300 Win. Mag., .300 WSM (new 2002), or .338 Win. Mag. cal., similar to BAR Mark II Safari, except has aluminum alloy receiver and checkered black synthetic stock and forearm, matte metal finish, 20, 22, 23 (new 2002, WSM cals. only), or 24 (Mag. cals. only) in. barrel with open sights, 7 lbs. 2 oz. - 7 lbs. 12 oz. New 2001.

MSR $1,022	$850	$635	$500	$425	$385	$350	$325

Add $93 for Mag. or WSM cals.

❖ **BAR MK II Lightweight Stalker with BOSS** - .270 WSM (new 2003), 7mm Rem. Mag., 7mm WSM (new 2003), .300 Win. Mag., .300 WSM (new 2002), or .338 Win. Mag. cal., similar to BAR Mark II Stalker, except has 23 (new 2002, WSM cals. only) or 24 in. barrel with BOSS, approx. 7 3/4 lbs. Mfg. 2001-2003.

	$835	$650	$540	$450	$395	$350	$325

Last MSR was $981.

❋ *BAR MK II High Grade* - .270 Win., .30-06, .300 Win. Mag., or 7mm Rem. Mag. cal., satin finished receiver with either whitetail/mule deer or moose/elk etched game scenes and gold border, checkered high grade gloss finished walnut stock and forearm, no sights, 7 lbs. 6 oz. or 8 lbs. 6 oz. Mfg. 2001-2003.

	$1,475	$1,015	$795	$675	$565	$465	$415

Last MSR was $1,856.

Add $58 for Mag. cals.

❋ *BAR MK II Grade III* - features Grade III engraving pattern. Mfg. by the FN custom shop 1996-99.

	$3,100	$1,875	$1,375	$1,000	$775	$675	$575

Last MSR was $3,754.

❋ *BAR MK II Grade IV* - features Grade IV engraving pattern. Mfg. by the FN custom shop beginning 1996.

	$3,180	$1,930	$1,400	$1,025	$795	$675	$575

Last MSR was $3,859.

BAR SHORTTRAC - .243 Win., .270 WSM, .300 WSM, .308 Win., or 7mm WSM cal., features new styling with aluminum alloy gas operated short action receiver and composite trigger guard and mag. floorplate, 22 or 23 in. hammer forged barrel w/o sights, mfg. in Belgium, drilled and tapped, checkered satin finished walnut stock supplied with 6 adj. shims and squared off forearm, 3 or 4 shot detachable mag., 6 lbs., 10 oz (regular cals.) or 7 1/4 lbs. (WSM cals.). New 2004.

MSR $1,026	$850	$635	$500	$425	$385	$350	$325

Add $92 for WSM cals.
Add $40 for left-hand model with left-side ejection port.

❋ *BAR Shorttrac Stalker* - similar to BAR Shorttrac, except has matte black metal finish and black composite stock and forearm. New 2006.

MSR $1,043	$865	$650	$515	$425	$385	$350	$325

Add $93 for WSM cals.

❋ *BAR Shorttrac Camo* - similar to BAR Shorttrac, except has 100% Mossy Oak New Break Up camo coverage. New 2007.

MSR $1,163	$995	$795	$675	$550	$475	$425	$375

Add $93 for WSM cals.

GRADING - PPGS™	100%	98%	95%	90%	80%	70%	60%

BAR LONGTRAC - .270 Win., .30-06, .300 Win. Mag., or 7mm Rem. Mag. cal., similar to BAR Shorttrac, except has long action, 7 or 7 1/2 lbs. New 2004.

MSR $1,026	$850	$635	$500	$425	$385	$350	$325

Add $92 for WSM cals.
Add $40 for left-hand model with left-side ejection port.

∗ *BAR Longtrac Stalker* - similar to BAR Longtrac, except has matte black metal finish and black composite stock and forearm. New 2006.

MSR $1,043	$865	$650	$515	$425	$385	$350	$325

Add $92 for WSM cals.

∗ *BAR Longtrac Camo* - similar to BAR Longtrac, except has 100% Mossy Oak New Break Up camo coverage. New 2007.

MSR $1,163	$995	$795	$675	$550	$475	$425	$375

Add $93 for WSM cals.

RIFLES: SEMI-AUTO, FAL & CAL SERIES

FN manufactured FALs and CALs imported by BAC can be found under the Fabrique Nationale heading.

Above Average	Average	Below Average

RIFLES: SINGLE SHOT

MODEL 1878 STANDARD - various cals., J.M. Browning's first patent, falling block action, fewer than 600 made (highest known ser. no. is 542) by Browning Brothers in Ogden, Utah between 1878-1883, octagon barrel marked "Browning Bros. Ogden, Utah USA" plain wood stock and forearm with and without pistol grips, crescent steel buttplate, with or without ramrod, several receiver configurations, a very few were made in the deluxe model, seldom found in better than average used condition, with or w/o serial number. Approx. only 100 have survived - Browning Arms Co. & the Winchester Museum have no factory records on this model.

$50,000 - $40,000	$35,000 - $30,000	$25,000 - $20,000

Add 50% for Deluxe Rifle (checkered stock and forearm), 10% for Early Rifle with Sharps Borchardt type lever, 40% for Early Rifle stamped "Ogden, U.T.", 20% for any caliber other than .40-70 SS or .45-70 Govt., 25% for Late Model with rammer rod under barrel held by two thimbles (known as "Montana Model").
Subtract 20% if the original sights have been removed or replaced incorrectly.

Please refer to the grading explanation for Winchester lever actions regarding descriptions for the above condition factors.

Calibers in this model are listed from rarest to most commonly encountered: .50-70 Govt., .45 Sharps, .44 Rem., .40-90 Sharps, .44-77 Sharps, .45-70 Govt., and .40-70 Sharps Straight.

This model is rare since approx. only 550 were mfg. (approx. ser. range 1-550). This patent was sold to Winchester, which became their Model 1885 single shot. To date, less than 100 original Model 1878s have been encountered indicating a high mortality rate (most remaining specimens are in poor original condition). An inherent weakness of the original design was the way the stock attached to the action - Winchester later corrected this design flaw. A few remaining examples are not serial numbered. Barter guns are rifles that have Browning stamped actions and barrels of an older gunsmith's identity.

GRADING - PPGS™	100%	98%	95%	90%	80%	70%	60%

MODEL B-78 - .22-250 Rem., 6mm Rem., .243 Win. (only 671 mfg.), .25-06 Rem., 7mm Mag., .30-06, or .45-70 Govt. cal., 24 or 26 in. round or octagon barrel, lever activated falling block, no sights except .45- 70 Govt., checkered walnut stock, approx. 24,000 mfg. 1973-1982.

	$1,375	$1,150	$950	$825	$650	$475	$350

Add 25% for .243 Win. cal.
The Model B-78 was reintroduced as the Model 1885 in 1985.

GRADING - PPGS™	100%	98%	95%	90%	80%	70%	60%

MODEL 1885 HIGH WALL - .22-250 Rem., .223 Rem. (disc. 1994), .270 Win., .30-06, 7mm Rem. Mag., .45-70 Govt., or .454 Casull (new 1998) cal., falling block action, sear safety, 28 in. octagonal barrel, adj. trigger, no sights, checkered walnut stock and Schnabel forearm, exposed hammer, gold trigger, approx. 8 3/4 lbs. Mfg. 1985-2001.

	$1,375	$1,075	$925	$800	$650	$550	$475

Last MSR was $1,027.

This model is equipped with open sights in .45-70 Govt. and .454 Casull cals.

MODEL 1885 LOW WALL - .22 Hornet, .223 Rem. (disc. 2000), .243 Win. (disc. 2000), or .260 Rem. (new 1999) cal., action patterned after the Winchester Low Wall receiver, 24 in. barrel, adj. trigger, features thinner 24 in. barrel, 6 1/4 lbs. Mfg. 1995-2001.

	$1,175	$995	$875	$725	$600	$525	$450

Last MSR was $997.

MODEL 1885 HIGH WALL TRADITIONAL HUNTER - .30-30 Win., .38-55 WCF or .45-70 Govt. cal., High-Wall action, 30 in. octagon barrel with ejector, blue receiver, rear tang aperture sight, crescent buttplate, checkered stock and forearm, approx. 9 lbs. Mfg. 1997-2000. - .45-70 Govt. cal., features delicate scroll receiver engraving and gold enhanced 125th anniversary logo with gold border. 500 mfg. 2003-2004 only.

	$1,275	$1,075	$950	$850	$725	$600	$525

Last MSR was $1,220.

✻ *Model 1885 High Wall Traditional Hunter 125th Anniversary*

	$1,675	$1,350	$1,000	N/A	N/A	N/A	N/A

Last MSR was $1,516.

MODEL 1885 LOW WALL TRADITIONAL HUNTER - .357 Mag., .44 Mag., or .45 LC cal., 24 in. half-round, half-octagon barrel, case colored receiver and buttplate, gold bead front, semi-buckhorn rear, and upper tang aperture sights, 6 1/2 lbs. Mfg. 1998-2001.

	$1,300	$1,150	$925	$800	$675	$550	$475

Last MSR was $1,289.

MODEL 1885 BPCR (BLACK POWDER CARTRIDGE) - .40-65 Win. (black powder only) or .45-70 Govt. (black powder or smokeless) cal., case colored high wall action, 30 in. half-round, half-octagon barrel, checkered pistol grip stock with shotgun butt, w/o ejector system and shell deflector, vernier tang rear sight and globe front sight with spirit level, approx. 11 lbs. Mfg. 1996-2001.

	$1,900	$1,600	$1,300	$1,100	$950	$825	$700

Last MSR was $1,766.

✻ *Model 1885 BPCR Creedmoor* - .45-90 cal., blue receiver, 34 in. half-round, half-octagon barrel with globe front and aperture rear tang sights, 11 3/4 lbs. Mfg. 1998-99.

	$1,900	$1,600	$1,300	$1,100	$950	$825	$700

Last MSR was $1,764.

RIFLES: SLIDE ACTION

BPR - .243 Win., .270 Win., .30-06, .308 Win., .300 Win. Mag., or 7mm Rem. Mag. cal., 7 lug rotary bolt, blue alloy receiver, 22 or 24 (Mag. cals. only) in. barrel with open sights, features downward camming slide action assembly, checkered walnut stock and forend, cross-bolt safety, 3 or 4 shot mag., approx. 7 lbs. 3 oz. Mfg. 1997-2001.

	$695	$625	$550	$455	$400	$360	$330

Last MSR was $725.

Add $55 for Mag. cals.

GRADING - PPGS™	100%	98%	95%	90%	80%	70%	60%

BPR-22 - .22 LR or .22 Mag. cal., short-stroke action, 20 1/4 in. barrel, 11 shot tube mag., mfg. 1977-82.

	$325	$250	$200	$160	$140	$130	$100

✳ *BPR-22 Grade II* - similar to BPR-22, only engraved action, select walnut.

	$525	$400	$350	$275	$230	$200	$175

     Add 10% for .22 Mag. cal.

TROMBONE MODEL - .22 LR cal. only, slide action with tube mag., fixed sights, takedown, 24 in. barrel, hammerless, with either FN or U.S. (rare) barrel address, approx. 150,000 Grade Is were mfg. total.

✳ *Trombone Model w/FN Barrel Address* - most common variation.

	$1,250	$1,050	$850	$600	$450	$350	$300

✳ *Trombone Model w/BAC Barrel Markings* - approx. 3,200 Grade Is were imported by BAC during the late 1960s.

	$1,575	$1,250	$1,000	$750	$600	$475	$400

✳ *Trombone Model Grade I* - limited mfg. for the BCA circa 1985, 30 mfg. total, with only 10 sold individually, engraved by Custom Shop at FN for wholesaler.

	$1,750	$1,400	$1,175	N/A	N/A	N/A	N/A

✳ *Trombone Grades I & II 2 Gun Set* - limited mfg. for the BCA circa 1985, 10 set mfg. total, available in 2 gun set.

	$3,750	$2,950	$2,300	N/A	N/A	N/A	N/A

✳ *Trombone Grades I, II, & III 3 Gun Set* - 10 sets mfg. for BCA circa 1985.

	$6,950	$5,500	$4,500	N/A	N/A	N/A	N/A

SHOTGUNS: BOLT ACTION, A-BOLT SERIES

A-BOLT SHOTGUN MODEL - 12 ga. only, 3 in. chamber, 2 shot mag., same bolt system as A-Bolt II Rifle, 22 or 23 in. barrel (rifled or Invector with rifled tube), available in Stalker Model with graphite fiberglass composite stock or Hunter Model with select satin finished walnut stock, dull matte finished barrel and receiver, top tang safety, choice of no sights (new 1996) or adj. rear sight, drilled and tapped receiver, approx. 7 lbs. Mfg. by Miroku 1995-98.

✳ *A-Bolt Stalker Model Shotgun*

	$995	$800	$650	$525	$475	$440	$400

Last MSR was $720.

     Add $45 for open sights.
     Add $150 for rifled barrel.

✳ *A-Bolt Hunter Model Shotgun*

	$995	$800	$650	$525	$475	$440	$400

Last MSR was $805.

     Add $40 for open sights.
     Add $150 for rifled barrel.

SHOTGUNS: O/U

CYNERGY SERIES - 12, 20 (new 2005), 28 (new 2005) ga. or .410 bore (new 2007), silver nitride finished receiver, features new MonoLock hinge system allowing low receiver profile, mechanical striker based SST, reverse striker ignition system (triple trigger system included on Sporting models), backbored and ported vent. barrels with VR, Invector-Plus chokes, choice of wood or composite (12 ga. only) stock and forearm, solid, vent., or Inflex recoil pad, impact ejectors. New 2004.

❊ *Cynergy Field* - 12 (disc. 2006), 20, or 28 ga., 2 3/4 (28 ga. only) or 3 in. chambers, 26 or 28 in. non-ported barrels with 5/16 in. slanted VR, flush choke tubes, silver nitride finished receiver with clay pigeon motif, checkered Grade I walnut or non-glare black composite (disc. 2006) stock and forearm, stock has adj. comb with built in Inflex recoil pad system allowing LOP adjustment, approx. 6 1/4 - 7 1/2 lbs. Mfg. 2004-2007.

	$1,495	$1,200	$950	$875	$775	$700	$625

Last MSR was $2,062.

Subtract approx. 10% for composite stock and forearm.

❊ *Cynergy Sporting* - 12 (disc. 2006), 20, 28 ga., 2 3/4 in. chambers, 28, 30, or 32 in. ported barrels with tapered VR (non-tapered 5/16 in. rib on 28 ga.), Hi-Viz fiber optic front sight, silver nitride receiver with clay pigeon motif, oil finished checkered walnut (with or w/o adj. comb) or black composite (12 ga. only, disc. 2006) stock and forearm, stock has adj. comb with built in Inflex recoil pad system allowing LOP adjustment (disc. 2006), extended choke tubes, approx. 6 1/2 - 8 lbs. Mfg. 2004-2007.

	$2,000	$1,700	$1,525	$1,275	$1,050	$875	$800

Last MSR was $3,080.

Add 25% for adj. comb (mfg. 2006 only).
Subtract approx. 20% for composite stock and forearm.

❊ *Cynergy Classic Sporting* - 12, 20 (new 2007), 28 ga. (new 2007) or .410 bore (new 2007), 2 3/4 in. chambers, 28, 30, or 32 in. ported barrels with extended choke tubes, features traditional oil finished walnut stock with solid recoil pad and Schnabel forearm, etched Browning logo on receiver sides, approx. 7 3/4 - 8 lbs. New 2006.

MSR $3,296	$2,725	$2,325	$2,000	$1,700	$1,475	$1,275	$1,050

Add $36 for 20, 28 ga. or .410 bore.
Add $298 for adj. comb (new 2007).

❊ *Cynergy Euro Sporting* - 12 or 20 (new 2008) ga., 2 3/4 in. chambers, 28, 30, or 32 in. VR barrels with porting and extended choke tubes, features traditional checkered oil finished walnut stock and Schnabel forearm, or black composite (adj. comb only) stock with Inflex recoil pad, approx. 6 1/4 - 8 lbs. New 2007.

MSR $3,501	$2,875	$2,425	$2,050	$1,750	$1,500	$1,275	$1,050

Add $342 for adj. comb with oil finished walnut stock and Schnabel forearm.
Subtract $36 for 20 ga.
Subtract $206 for adj. comb black composite stock and forearm.

❊ *Cynergy Classic Trap* - 12 ga. only, 2 3/4 in. chambers, 30 or 32 in. VR barrels with porting, extended Invector-Plus chokes and Hi-Viz fiber optic front sight, checkered walnut stock with or w/o adj. comb and competition forearm, vent. recoil pad, approx. 8 3/4 lbs. New 2007.

MSR $3,329	$2,750	$2,325	$2,000	$1,700	$1,475	$1,275	$1,050

Add $290 for adj. comb.

❊ *Cynergy Classic Trap Unsingle Combo* - 12 ga. only, includes choice of 32 or 34 in. ported single barrel and choice of 30 or 32 in. O/U ported barrels with adj. top rib, gloss finished Grade III/VI walnut stock with adj. comb and semi-beavertail forearm with finger grooves, includes aluminum case, approx. 8 3/4 lbs. New 2008.

MSR $4,942	$4,150	$3,125	$2,400	$1,875	$1,500	$1,275	$1,050

GRADING - PPGS™	100%	98%	95%	90%	80%	70%	60%

* *Cynergy Classic Field* - 12, 20 (new 2007), 28 ga. (new 2007), or .410 bore (new 2007), 3 in. chambers, features traditional satin finished walnut stock with standard vent. recoil pad and Schnabel forearm, etched mallard and pheasant on receiver sides, approx. 6 1/4 - 7 3/4 lbs. New 2006.

MSR $2,252	$1,775	$1,325	$1,050	$925	$800	$700	$625

    Add $14 for 20, 28 ga. or .410 bore.

* *Cynergy Classic Field Grade III* - 12 or 20 ga., 3 in. chambers, similar to Classic Field, except has gloss finished upgraded wood (Grade III/Grade IV) and fully engraved receiver. New 2007.

MSR $3,295	$2,725	$2,350	$2,000	$1,725	$1,475	$1,275	$1,050

    Add $33 for 20 ga.

* *Cynergy Classic Field Grade VI* - similar to Classic Field Grade III, except has upgraded wood (Grade V/VI), fully engraved receiver with multiple gold inlays. New 2007.

MSR $4,925	$3,850	$3,350	$2,875	$2,350	$1,975	$1,700	$1,475

    Add $16 for 20 ga.

* *Cynergy Feather* - 12, 20 (new 2008), 28 (new 2008) ga. or .410 bore (new 2008), 3 in. chambers, choice of checkered black composite stock with adj. comb or checkered satin-finished walnut stock and Schnabel forearm, Inflex recoil pad, 26 or 28 in. barrels with flush Invector-Plus choke tubes, approx. 5 - 7 lbs. New 2007.

MSR $2,430	$1,875	$1,400	$1,075	$950	$825	$750	$650

    Add $17 for 20, 28 ga. or .410 bore.
    Subtract $64 for black adj. composite stock and forearm (12 ga. only).

SHOTGUNS: O/U, CITORI HUNTING SERIES

All Citori shotguns which incorporate the Invector choke tube system may be used with steel shot. Invector Plus choke tubes are designed for backbored barrels. DO NOT USE Standard Invector choke tubes in barrels marked for the Invector Plus choking system.

    Subtract $100 for 26 in. barrels on used guns.

CITORI HUNTING MODELS - 12, 16 (mfg. 1986-89), 20, 28 ga. (disc. 1994) or .410 bore (disc. 1994), 26, 28, or 30 in. barrels, various chokes, boxlock, auto ejectors, SST, vent. rib, features checkered semi-pistol grip stock with grooved semi-beavertail forearm, grades differ in amount of engraving, finish, and wood. Invector chokes became standard in 1988, Invector Plus chokes became standard 1995 on 12 or 20 ga., 6 lbs. 9 oz. - 8 lbs. 5 oz. Mfg. 1973-2001 by Miroku.

* *Citori Hunting Grade I 12 or 20 ga.* - blue finish with light scroll engraving beginning 1978.

    ❖ **Citori Hunting Grade I Earlier Mfg. without Invector Choking**

	$950	$800	$700	$600	$575	$500	$450

    Add 15% for 16 ga. if in 90%+ original condition.
    Add approx. 40% for extra 20 ga. barrels originally ordered with gun.

    ❖ **Citori Grade I Hunter Model w/Invector Choking** - recent mfg. with Invector Choking, 12 or 20 ga., 3 in. chambers, 20 ga. available with Standard Invector or Invector Plus (new 1994) choking system, Invector Plus choking standard on recently mfg. 12 and 20 ga., 6 lbs. 9 oz. - 8 lbs. 5 oz. Disc. 2001.

	$1,150	$950	$825	$700	$650	$575	$525

    Last MSR was $1,486.

    Add $100 for Invector Plus choke tubes.

* *Citori Hunting Grade I Smaller Gauges*

    ❖ **Citori Hunting Grade I 28 ga. or .410 bore** - without Invector choking. Disc. 1994.

	$1,075	$900	$750	$650	$600	$550	$500

    Last MSR was $1,097.

GRADING - PPGS™	100%	98%	95%	90%	80%	70%	60%

✱ *Citori Hunting Grade II* - 12, 20, 28 ga., or .410 bore. Mfg. 1978-1983.

	$1,200	$1,000	$800	$650	$600	$550	$500

✱ *Citori Hunting Grade III* - 12, 16 (mfg. 1986-89), 20, 28 ga. (disc. 1994), or .410 bore (disc. 1994), greyed steel receiver with engraved game scenes featuring grouse (20 ga.) and ducks (12 ga.), Invector chokes standard, Invector Plus became standard in 12 ga. in 1994. Mfg. 1985-95.

	$1,900	$1,600	$1,300	$1,000	$800	$700	$600

Last MSR was $1,875.

Add 15% for 16 ga. if in 90%+ original condition.
Add 15%-25% for 28 ga. or .410 bore (both disc. 1989).
Subtract $200 for standard Invector chokes.

✱ *Citori Hunting Grade V* - 12, 20, 28 ga., or .410 bore, extensive deep relief engraving with game scenes on satin grey receiver. Disc. 1984.

	$2,400	$2,050	$1,850	$1,525	$1,300	$1,150	$995

Add 20% for 28 ga.

✱ *Citori Hunting Grade VI* - 12, 16 (mfg. 1986-89), 20, 28 ga. (disc. 1992), or .410 bore (disc. 1989), blue or greyed receiver with extensive engraving including multiple gold inlays, Standard Invector (12 ga. disc. 1993) or Invector Plus chokes. Mfg. 1985-95.

	$2,600	$2,200	$1,900	$1,600	$1,350	$1,225	$1,100

Last MSR was $2,715.

Add 15% for 16 ga. if in 90%+ original condition.
Add 15%-25% for 28 ga.
Subtract $200 for standard Invector chokes.

✱ *Citori Hunting 3 1/2 in. Magnum Model* - 12 ga., 3 1/2 in. chambers, 28 or 30 in. VR barrels with back-bored Invector plus choke tubes, with recoil pad, approx. 8 lbs. 9 oz. Mfg. 1989-2000.

	$1,250	$950	$825	$695	$600	$550	$495

Last MSR was $1,563.

✱ *Citori Sporting Hunter* - 12 or 20 ga., 3 or 3 1/2 (12 ga. only) in. chambers, 26, 28, or 30 (12 ga. only) in. barrels with Invector Plus choking, configured for both hunting and sporting clays shooting, Superposed style forearm, contoured recoil pad, front and center bead sights, gloss or satin (3 1/2 in. only) wood finish, 6 lbs. 9 oz. - 8 lbs. 9 oz. Mfg. 1998-2001.

	$1,250	$950	$825	$695	$600	$550	$495

Last MSR was $1,607.

✱ *Citori Satin Hunter* - 12 ga. only, 3 or 3 1/2 (disc. 2000) in. chambers, 26, 28, or 30 (3 1/2 in. Mag. only, disc. 1998) in. VR backbored barrels with Invector Plus choking, features satin wood finish, approx. 8 1/4 lbs. Mfg. 1998-2001.

	$1,150	$895	$700	$600	$500	$450	$375

Last MSR was $1,535.

✱ *Citori Upland Special* - 12, 16 (mfg. 1989 only), or 20 ga. (2 3/4 in. chambers), shortened checkered straight grip walnut stock (14 in. LOP) and Schnabel forearm, 24 in. barrels, blue finish, Invector (12 ga. disc. 1993) or Invector Plus choking, 6-6 3/4 lbs. Mfg. 1984-2000.

	$1,195	$975	$725	$625	$500	$450	$375

Last MSR was $1,514.

Add 15% for 16 ga. if in 90%+ original condition.
Subtract $200 for Invector choking.

✱ *Citori White Upland Special* - 12 or 20 ga., 2 3/4 in. chambers, similar to Upland Special, except features silver nitride finished receiver, 6 1/8 or 6 1/2 lbs. Mfg. 2000-2001.

	$1,250	$1,000	$875	$750	$650	$600	$550

Last MSR was $1,583.

GRADING - PPGS™	100%	98%	95%	90%	80%	70%	60%

CITORI SUPERLIGHT MODELS - 12, 16, 20, 28 ga., or .410 bore, 2 3/4 in. chambers except for .410 bore, English stock, oil finish, Invector chokes became standard in 1988, Invector Plus became standard 1995 for 12 or 20 ga., approx. 5 lbs., 11 oz. - 6 3/4 lbs. New 1983.

✳ *Citori Superlight Grade I 12, 16, or 20 ga.*

❖ **Citori Superlight Grade I Earlier Mfg. without Invector Choking**

	100%	98%	95%	90%	80%	70%	60%
	$995	$850	$750	$650	$600	$550	$500

❖ **Citori Superlight Grade I w/Invector Choking** - recent mfg. with Invector Choking 12 or 20 ga., 20 ga. available with Standard Invector or Invector Plus (new 1994, became standard 1995) choking system, Invector Plus choking standard on recently mfg. 12 ga. Disc. 2002.

	100%	98%	95%	90%	80%	70%	60%
	$1,250	$1,025	$850	$750	$675	$600	$525

Last MSR was $1,590.

Subtract $200 for Standard Invector choking in 12 or 20 ga.

✳ *Citori Superlight Grade I Smaller Gauges*

❖ **Citori Superlight Grade I 28 ga. or .410 bore** - without Invector choking until 1993, Invector choking became an option in 1994 and standard in 1995. Disc. 2002.

	100%	98%	95%	90%	80%	70%	60%
	$1,300	$1,100	$875	$775	$700	$625	$550

Last MSR was $1,666.

Subtract $200 if without Invector choke tubes.

✳ *Citori Superlight Feather* - 12 or 20 (new 2002) ga., 2 3/4 in. chambers, greyed alloy receiver, 26 in. Invector choked VR barrels, gloss finished straight grip English stock and scaled down Schnabel forearm, 5 3/4 or 6 1/4 lbs. New 1999.

	100%	98%	95%	90%	80%	70%	60%
MSR $2,098	$1,600	$1,350	$1,025	$885	$715	$610	$515

✳ *Citori Superlight Grade III* - same gauges as Grade I, Standard Invector on 12 or 20 (disc.) ga. or Invector Plus (standard in 12 ga. beginning 1994) chokes. Mfg. 1986-2002.

	100%	98%	95%	90%	80%	70%	60%
	$1,800	$1,400	$1,100	$900	$800	$700	$600

Last MSR was $2,300.

Add $270 for 28 ga. or .410 bore (disc. 1997).
Subtract $300 if without Invector choke tubes or $200 for standard Invector choke tubes.

✳ *Citori Superlight Grade V* - sideplate available. Disc. 1984.

	100%	98%	95%	90%	80%	70%	60%
	$2,400	$2,100	$1,800	$1,425	$1,250	$1,075	$900

✳ *Citori Superlight Grade VI* - older mfg. has Invector chokes standard (option on 28 ga. or .410 bore beginning 1994) or Invector Plus (standard and available in 12 or 20 ga. only) chokes, choice of blue or grey (new 1996) receiver finish. Mfg. 1983-2002.

	100%	98%	95%	90%	80%	70%	60%
	$2,750	$2,350	$2,000	$1,700	$1,450	$1,325	$1,200

Last MSR was $3,510.

Subtract 10% for 28 ga. or .410 bore without choke tubes.
Subtract $200 for standard Invector choke tubes.
Add $270 for 28 ga. or .410 bore with Standard Invector choking.

✳ *Citori Superlight Grade VI Sideplate* - 20 ga. only. Disc.

	100%	98%	95%	90%	80%	70%	60%
	$3,350	$2,750	$2,250	$1,950	$1,825	$1,650	$1,475

CITORI SPORTER MODELS - similar to Citori Superlight, except with 3 in. chambers, 26 in. barrels, various chokes, straight grip stock, Schnabel forearm. Disc. 1983.

	100%	98%	95%	90%	80%	70%	60%
	$1,100	$900	$825	$700	$600	$550	$500

Add 10% for 28 ga. or .410 bore.

✳ *Citori Sporter Grade II* - 12, 20, 28 ga., or .410 bore.

	100%	98%	95%	90%	80%	70%	60%
	$1,350	$1,100	$1,000	$965	$880	$770	$715

Add 10% for 28 ga.

GRADING - PPGS™	100%	98%	95%	90%	80%	70%	60%

✳ *Citori Sporter Grade V* - 12, 20, 28 ga., or .410 bore.

	$2,400	**$2,100**	**$1,800**	**$1,600**	**$1,450**	**$1,300**	**$1,150**

Add 10% for 28 ga.

CITORI LIGHTNING MODELS - 12, 16 (disc. 1989), 20, 28 ga., or .410 bore, 2 3/4 (28 ga. only), or 3 in. (standard on 12 ga., 20 ga., and .410 bore) chamber, 26, 28, or 30 (disc.) in. barrels, Invector chokes standard on newer mfg. smaller ga.'s, Invector Plus became standard 1995 for 12 or 20 ga., boxlock, auto ejectors, SST, vent. rib, features checkered round knob pistol grip stock and slimmer forearm, grades differ in amount of engraving, finish, and quality of wood, approx. 6.5-8 lbs. Introduced 1988.

✳ *Citori Lightning Grade I 12, 16 or 20 ga.*

❖ **Citori Lightning Grade I Earlier Mfg. w/o Invector Choking** - without Invector Choking.

	$995	**$850**	**$750**	**$650**	**$600**	**$550**	**$500**

Add 15% for 16 ga.

❖ **Citori Lightning Grade I w/Invector Choking** - 12 or 20 ga., current mfg. with Invector Choking, 12 or 20 ga., Invector (disc. 1994) or Invector Plus choking (became standard on 12 ga. in 1994, 20 ga. in 1995), gloss finished walnut stock and forearm, 6 1/2 - 8 lbs.

MSR $1,763	**$1,425**	**$1,100**	**$850**	**$725**	**$600**	**$500**	**$460**

Subtract 10% for Standard Invector choking.

This model was supplied with scroll engraving with rosette design until 2004. Beginning 2004, standard engraving is high relief, intricate, and sculpted.

✳ *Citori Lightning Grade I Smaller Gauges* - 28 ga. or .410 bore, without Invector choking until 1993, Invector choking became an option in 1994, standard in 1995.

MSR $1,831	**$1,475**	**$1,150**	**$900**	**$775**	**$700**	**$600**	**$550**

Subtract $200 if without Standard Invector choking.

✳ *Citori Lightning Grade III* - 12, 16 (disc. 1989), or 20 ga., greyed steel receiver with engraved game scenes (mallards/pheasants on 12 ga., quail/grouse on 20 ga.), older mfg. may or may not have Invector choking, Invector Plus choking is now standard on 12 or 20 ga. Mfg. 1988-2004.

	$1,865	**$1,350**	**$1,035**	**$850**	**$675**	**$600**	**$550**

Last MSR was $2,464.

Subtract 10% if without Invector choking.
Add 15% for 16 ga. (disc. 1989).

❖ **Citori Lightning Grade III 28 ga. or .410 bore** - features quail and grouse scene engraving. Disc. 2004.

	$1,950	**$1,675**	**$1,500**	**$1,375**	**$1,250**	**$1,175**	**$995**

Last MSR was $2,754.

✳ *Citori Lightning Grade IV* - 12 or 20 ga., high relief engraving on grey receiver (pheasants on left, mallards on right on 12 ga., quail and grouse on 20 ga.) triggerguard and tang screws, high gloss finished walnut stock and forearm. New 2005.

MSR $2,822	**$2,375**	**$1,700**	**$1,225**	**$950**	**$750**	**$625**	**$550**

❖ **Citori Lightning Grade IV 28 ga. or .410 bore** - features quail and grouse inlays.

MSR $3,160	**$2,700**	**$2,125**	**$1,850**	**$1,675**	**$1,425**	**$1,200**	**$995**

✳ *Citori Lightning Grade VI* - 12, 16 (disc. 1989), 20 ga., blue or greyed receiver with extensive deep relief engraving with 7 gold inlays, including mallards/pheasants on receiver sides. Disc. 2004.

	$2,825	**$2,400**	**$2,000**	**$1,650**	**$1,450**	**$1,225**	**$1,050**

Last MSR was $3,797.

Add 15% for 16 ga. (disc. 1989).

GRADING - PPGS™	100%	98%	95%	90%	80%	70%	60%

❖ **Citori Lightning Grade VI 28 ga. or .410 bore** - disc. 2004.

	$3,075	$2,550	$2,100	$1,750	$1,550	$1,325	$1,100

Last MSR was $4,090.

✳ *Citori Lightning Grade VII* - 12 or 20 ga., deep relief engraving on grey or blue receiver, triggerguard, top tang, takedown lever and bracket, 24Kt. gold bird inlays (two flushing ringnecks and pointer on right side with three mallards on left side on 12 ga., quail and grouse on 20 ga.), high gloss finished walnut stock and forearm. New 2005.

MSR $4,487	$3,800	$2,625	$1,825	$1,450	$1,250	$1,025	$950

❖ **Citori Lightning Grade VII 28 ga. or .410 bore** - features quail and grouse inlays.

MSR $4,832	$4,125	$2,775	$2,550	$2,050	$1,650	$1,400	$1,175

CITORI LIGHTNING FEATHER - 12 or 20 (new 2000) ga., 3 in. chambers, greyed alloy receiver with dovetailed steel breechface and steel hinge pin, 26 or 28 in. Invector Plus choked VR barrels, select checkered round knob walnut stock and forearm with gloss finish, vent. recoil pad, approx. 6 1/4 - 7 lbs. Mfg. 1999-2007.

	$1,695	$1,200	$925	$775	$550	$475	$450

Last MSR was $1,944.

✳ *Citori Lightning Feather Combo* - includes set of 27 in. 20 ga. (3 in. chambers) and 28 ga. barrels with Invector Plus (20 ga.) and standard Invector (28 ga.) chokes, includes luggage case, approx. 6 1/4 lbs. New 2000.

MSR $3,286	$2,800	$2,225	$1,950	$1,675	$1,400	$1,175	$995

CITORI GRAN LIGHTNING (GL) MODEL - 12, 20, 28 ga. (new 1994), or .410 bore (new 1994) only, 2 3/4 (28 ga. only) or 3 in. chambers, similar to Lightning Model, except has Grade III walnut stock and forearm with satin/oil finish, includes recoil pad, 26 or 28 in. barrels, Invector chokes standard on newer mfg. smaller ga.'s, Invector Plus became standard 1995 for 12 or 20 ga., 6 1/4 - 8 lbs. Mfg. 1990-2005.

	$1,925	$1,675	$1,375	$1,100	$975	$850	$725

Last MSR was $2,429.

    Add $128 for 28 ga. or .410 bore.

    Subtract $200 for standard Invector chokes on 12 or 20 ga.

    Beginning 2004, high relief intricate sculpted engraving replaced rosette, scroll type engraving.

CITORI WHITE LIGHTNING - 12, 20, 28 (new 2000) ga., or .410 bore (new 2000), 3 in. chambers, silver nitride receiver with engraving, satin wood finish with round pistol grip stock and vent recoil pad, 26 or 28 in. VR barrels with Invector Plus choking, 6 lbs. 7 oz - 8 lbs. 2 oz. New 1998.

MSR $1,836	$1,595	$1,250	$900	$725	$600	$550	$500

    Add $83 for .28 ga. or .410 bore (new 2000).

    Beginning 2004, high relief intricate sculpted engraving replaced rosette, scroll type engraving.

CITORI MICRO LIGHTNING - 20 ga. only, 2 3/4 in. chambers, 24 in. VR barrels, Invector (disc. 1993) or Invector Plus (new 1994) choking, 13 3/4 LOP (1/2 in. shorter), 6 lbs. 3 oz. Mfg. 1991-2001.

✳ *Citori Micro Lightning Grade I*

	$1,250	$1,000	$850	$750	$650	$575	$525

Last MSR was $1,591.

    Subtract 10% for standard Invector choking.

✳ *Citori Micro Lightning Grade III* - Invector (disc. 1993) or Invector Plus choking. Mfg. 1993-94.

	$1,600	$1,300	$1,175	$950	$825	$700	$550

Last MSR was $1,850.

    Subtract $200 for Standard Invector choking.

GRADING - PPGS™	100%	98%	95%	90%	80%	70%	60%

✳ *Citori Micro Lightning Grade VI* - Mfg. 1993-94.

	$2,025	$1,725	$1,500	$1,250	$1,025	$900	$825

Last MSR was $2,680.

Subtract $200 for standard Invector choking.

CITORI CLASSIC LIGHTNING GRADE I - 12 or 20 ga., 3 in. chambers, 26 or 28 in. vent. rib barrels, Invector Plus chokes, silver nitride receiver with Grade I Superposed engraving, Grade II/III oil finished slender lightning style walnut stock and forearm with vent. recoil pad, 6 lbs. 10 oz. - 8 lbs., 2 oz. Mfg. 2005-2007.

	$1,600	$1,300	$1,100	$850	$725	$650	$500

Last MSR was $1,968.

CITORI CLASSIC LIGHTNING FEATHER GRADE I - 12 or 20 ga., 3 in. chambers, 26 or 28 in. vent. rib barrels, Invector Plus chokes, lightweight alloy receiver with high relief sculpted engraving, Grade II/III satin finished lightning style stock and Schnabel forearm, vent. recoil pad, 6 lbs. 3 oz. - 7 lbs. Mfg. 2005-2006.

	$1,650	$1,350	$1,100	$850	$725	$650	$550

Last MSR was $1,991.

CITORI SUPER LIGHTNING GRADE I - 12 or 20 ga., 3 in. chambers, 26 or 28 in. vent. rib barrels, Invector Plus chokes, deep blue receiver with gold border accents, Grade II/III gloss finished lightning style stock with buttplate and Schnabel forearm, 6 lbs. 7 oz. - 8 lbs. 2 oz. Mfg. 2005-2007.

	$1,500	$1,200	$1,000	$825	$700	$600	$500

Last MSR was $1,941.

CITORI 525 FIELD - 12 (disc. 2007), 20, 28 (new 2003) ga. or .410 bore (new 2003), 3 in. chambers (except 28 ga.), engraved silver nitride receiver, 26 or 28 in. unported barrels featuring VR with forward angled posts, pronounced walnut pistol grip stock with European comb, flush fit Invector Plus choke tubes, oil finished European checkered stock with vent recoil pad, Schnabel forearm, 6 lbs. 6 oz. - 8 lbs. New 2002.

MSR $2,144	$1,800	$1,300	$1,150	$850	$725	$625	$525

Add $31 for 28 ga. or .410 bore.
Subtract $50 for 12 ga.

CITORI 525 FIELD GRADE III - 12 ga. only, 3 in. chambers, similar to 525 Field, excpet has Grade III/VI wood and more engraving, includes case, approx. 8 lbs. Mfg. 2007.

	$2,000	$1,450	$1,225	$900	$775	$675	$575

Last MSR was $2,532.

CITORI 525 FEATHER - 12 , 20 (new 2008), 28 (new 2008) ga. or .410 bore (new 2008), 3 in. chambers, silver nitride alloy receiver featuring high relief engraving, traditional oil finished checkered stock and Schnabel forearm, approx. 6 1/4 lbs. New 2007.

MSR $2,278	$1,900	$1,325	$1,175	$900	$775	$650	$550

Add $17 for 28 ga. or .410 bore.

CITORI ESPRIT - 12 ga. only, 3 in. chambers, 28 in. barrels with VR and 3 choke tubes, features removable and interchangeable sideplates, satin finished receiver, choice of scroll or pointer engraving scenes, gold enhancements are optional, 8 1/4 lbs. Mfg. 2002-2003.

	$1,950	$1,350	$1,025	$875	$725	$625	$550

Last MSR was $2,502.

CITORI PRIVILEGE - 12 or 20 (new 2001) ga., 3 in. chambers, boxlock with extensively hand engraved sideplates, silver finished receiver, 26 or 28 in. barrels with 5/16 in. VR and Invector Plus choking, approx. 8 lbs. Mfg. 2000-2003.

$4,775	$4,075	$3,450	$2,875	$2,475	$2,025	$1,750

Last MSR was $5,537.

CITORI 625 FIELD - 12 ga. only, 3 in. chambers, 26 or 28 in. VR barrels with Vector Pro choking system with extended forcing cones, gloss finished Grade II/III special cut checkered walnut stock and Schnabel forearm, vent recoil pad, silver nitride finished receiver with etched engraving, approx. 7 3/4 lbs. New 2008.

MSR $2,299	$1,925	$1,325	$1,175	$900	$775	$650	$550

SHOTGUNS: O/U, CITORI SKEET

Subtract 10%-15% for all Skeet models with 26 in. barrels.

CITORI SKEET/SPECIAL SKEET MODELS - 12, 20, 28 ga., or .410 bore, same action as Citori Field, only with high post target rib (standard 1985), 26 and 28 in. skeet barrels, recoil pad, Invector chokes became standard in 1990 in 12 and 20 ga., Invector Plus chokes with ported barrels were an option during 1992 and became standard on the 12 ga. in 1994. in 1994, new Special Skeet models were introduced during 1995 with decreased weight (1/4 lb. lighter) and better swing/balance characteristics.

✳ *Citori Skeet Grade I*

❖ **Citori Skeet Grade I 12 or 20 Ga.** - Invector Plus choking, high-post target rib, and ported barrels became standard in 1994, 7 1/4 - 8 lbs. Disc. 2000.

$1,295	$1,095	$995	$800	$625	$575	$500

Last MSR was $1,742.

Add $100 for factory adj. comb (mfg. 1995-98).
Subtract 10% if without Invector Plus chokes.
Subtract 30% for fixed chokes.
Add approx. 40% for extra 20 ga. skeet barrels originally ordered with gun.
Add $50 for 20 ga.

Earlier mfg. skeet guns had a low profile, wide VR.

❖ **Citori Skeet Grade I Smaller Gauges** - 28 ga. or .410 bore, 6 lbs. 15 oz. Disc. 1999.

$1,400	$1,000	$850	$650	$550	$500	$450

Last MSR was $1,627.

Subtract 20% if without Invector chokes.

✳ *Citori Skeet Grade II* - 12, 20, 28 ga., or .410 bore, high rib. Disc. 1983.

$1,100	$935	$825	$740	$690	$650	$600

✳ *Citori Skeet Grade III* - 12, 20, 28 ga., or .410 bore, Invector chokes originally in 12 and 20 ga. and became an option on 28 ga. and .410 bore in 1994. Mfg. 1986-99.

❖ **Citori Skeet Grade III 12 or 20 Ga.** - Invector Plus choking, high-post target rib, and ported barrels became standard in 1994. Disc. 1999.

$1,600	$1,300	$975	$795	$650	$550	$495

Last MSR was $2,310.

Add $100 for factory adj. comb (mfg. 1995-98).
Subtract 10% if w/o Invector Plus choke system.

❖ **Citori Skeet Grade III Smaller Gauges** - 28 ga. or .410 bore. Disc. 1999.

$1,895	$1,495	$1,000	$825	$675	$595	$550

Last MSR was $2,316.

Subtract 20% if without standard Invector choking (new 1994).

✳ *Citori Skeet Grade V* - 12, 20, 28 ga., or .410 bore, high rib. Disc. 1984.

$2,300	$1,950	$1,750	$1,500	$1,250	$1,050	$850

Add 20% for 20 ga. or 30% for 28 ga.or .410 bore.

GRADING - PPGS™	100%	98%	95%	90%	80%	70%	60%

✳ *Citori Skeet Grade VI* - Skeet gauges, choice of blue or grey finished receiver with multi gold inlays, deluxe walnut. Disc. 1995.

❖ **Citori Skeet Grade VI 12 Ga** - Invector Plus choking, high-post target rib, and ported barrels became standard in 1994.

	$2,200	$1,900	$1,600	$1,100	$960	$875	$825

Last MSR was $2,555.

Subtract 10% if w/o Invector Plus choke system.

❖ **Citori Skeet Grade VI Smaller Gauges** - 20, 28 ga., or .410 bore, 20 ga. available with standard Invector choking, 28 ga. and .410 bore are choked SK/SK.

	$2,400	$2,000	$1,700	$1,100	$960	$875	$825

Last MSR was $2,518.

✳ *Citori Skeet Golden Clays (GC)* - 12, 20, 28 ga., or .410 bore, 26 or 28 in. ported VR barrels, Invector Plus choking, Skeet features, satin grey receiver with Grade VI level of engraving and gold inlays depicting a transitional hunting to clay pigeon scene. Disc. 1993-99.

❖ **Citori Skeet Golden Clays 12 or 20 Ga.** - Invector (disc. 1995) or Invector Plus choking, high-post target rib, and ported barrels (12 ga. only).

	$2,725	$2,400	$2,250	$2,000	$1,650	$1,300	$1,000

Last MSR was $3,434.

Add $100 for factory adj. comb (mfg. 1995-98).
Subtract approx. 20% if without Invector Plus choking.

❖ **Citori Skeet Golden Clays Smaller Gauges** - 28 ga. or .410 bore, standard Invector or fixed SK/SK choking.

	$2,725	$2,400	$2,250	$2,000	$1,650	$1,300	$1,000

Last MSR was $3,356.

Subtract approx. 20% with fixed choking.

CITORI XS SKEET - 12 or 20 (new 2001) ga., 2 3/4 in. chambers, ported 28 or 30 in. vent. barrels with raised 5/16 in. VR and Invector Plus choking, silver nitride receiver with gold accents, checkered walnut stock available with or without adj. comb, features similar to the Ultra XS Sporting Model, Hi-Viz fiber optic front sight, includes triple trigger system, approx. 7 - 8 1/4 lbs. New 2000.

MSR $2,659	$2,300	$1,750	$1,450	$1,200	$1,000	$675	$575

Add $300 for adj. comb.

This model's nomenclature was changed from Ultra XS Skeet to Citori XS Skeet in 2002.

CITORI 3-GAUGE SKEET SETS - supplied with one 20 ga. frame, 1 removable forearm, and 3 barrels consisting of 20, 28 ga. and .410 bore, cased. Mfg. 1987-96.

✳ *Citori 3-Gauge Skeet Set Grade I* - with high post target rib, standard Invector choking became standard 1994.

	$2,650	$2,200	$1,900	$1,450	$1,275	$1,050	$975

Last MSR was $3,100.

✳ *Citori 3-Gauge Skeet Set Grade III* - with high post target rib, available with standard Invector choking (new 1994) or fixed SK/SK chokes.

	$3,400	$2,600	$2,100	$1,550	$1,395	$1,250	$1,125

Last MSR was $3,900.

Subtract 20% for fixed SK/SK chokes.

✳ *Citori 3-Gauge Skeet Set Grade VI* - with high post target rib, fixed SK/SK chokes only. Disc. 1994.

	$3,600	$2,800	$2,300	$1,775	$1,600	$1,400	$1,275

Last MSR was $3,990.

GRADING - PPGS™	100%	98%	95%	90%	80%	70%	60%

✳ *Citori 3-Gauge Skeet Set Golden Clays* - features Golden Clays accents and engraving, standard Invector choking. Mfg. 1994-95 only.

	$4,250	$3,075	$2,600	$2,100	$1,900	$1,750	$1,600

Last MSR was $5,100.

CITORI 4-GAUGE SKEET SETS - supplied with one 12 ga. frame, 1 removable forearm, and 4 barrels consisting of 12, 20, 28 ga., and .410 bore, cased. Imported 1985 only.

✳ *Citori 4-Gauge Skeet Set Grade I* - with high post target rib, choice of standard Invector (new 1994) or fixed SK/SK choking.

	$3,500	$2,850	$2,400	$1,975	$1,800	$1,775	$1,600

Last MSR was $4,450.

Subtract 10% for fixed SK/SK choking.

✳ *Citori 4-Gauge Skeet Set Grade III* - with high post target rib, choice of standard Invector (new 1994) or fixed SK/SK choking.

	$4,250	$3,250	$2,700	$2,250	$1,950	$1,800	$1,700

Last MSR was $5,450.

Subtract 20% for fixed SK/SK choking.

✳ *Citori 4-Gauge Skeet Set Grade VI* - with high post target rib, fixed SK/SK choking only. Disc. 1994.

	$4,600	$3,350	$2,775	$2,300	$2,100	$2,000	$1,900

Last MSR was $5,225.

✳ *Citori 4-Gauge Skeet Set Golden Clays* - features Golden Clays accents and engraving, standard Invector choking. Mfg. 1994 only.

	$5,650	$4,100	$3,300	$2,600	$2,350	$2,100	$1,975

Last MSR was $6,750.

SHOTGUNS: O/U, CITORI SPORTING CLAYS

All sporting clays models mfg. after 1994 have the Triple Trigger System which includes 3 interchangeable trigger shoes.

Subtract 10% for 28 in. barrels on used guns.

CITORI 325 GRADE II - 12 or 20 ga., 28, 30, or 32 (12 ga. only) in. 10mm VR barrels with Invector Plus choking, 12 ga. has ported barrels, European styling featuring checkered walnut stock and Schnabel forearm, greyed nitrous finished receiver, top tang safety, SST, ejectors, 6 lbs. 12 oz. - 7 lbs. 15 oz. Mfg. 1993-94.

	$1,195	$995	$850	$715	$575	$495	$450

Last MSR was $1,625.

CITORI 325 GOLDEN CLAYS - 12 or 20 ga., 28, 30, or 32 in. ported (12 ga. only) or unported (20 ga. only) VR barrels, Invector Plus choking, Model 325 Grade II features, satin grey receiver with engraving and gold inlays depicting a transitional hunting to clay pigeon scene. Mfg. 1994 only.

	$2,450	$2,050	$1,450	$1,150	$975	$875	$825

Last MSR was $3,030.

CITORI 425 SPORTING CLAYS GRADE I - 12 or 20 ga., 28, 30, or 32 (disc. 2000 - 12 ga. only, adj. comb) in. 10mm VR barrels with Invector Plus choking, 12 ga. has ported barrels, with or without adj. comb (disc. 2000), European styling featuring checkered walnut stock and Schnabel forearm, mono-bloc action with greyed nitrous finished receiver, top tang safety, SST, ejectors, solid pad, approx. 6 3/4 - 8 lbs. Mfg. 1995-2001.

	$1,625	$1,200	$1,000	$825	$725	$625	$525

Last MSR was $2,006.

Add $231 for adj. comb.

GRADING - PPGS™	100%	98%	95%	90%	80%	70%	60%

CITORI 425 GOLDEN CLAYS - 12 or 20 ga., 28, 30, or 32 (disc. 1999) in. ported (12 ga. only) or unported (20 ga. only) VR barrels, with (disc. 1998) or without adj. comb, Invector Plus choking, Model 425 Grade I features, satin grey receiver with engraving and gold inlays depicting a transitional hunting to clay pigeon scene, 6 lbs., 13 oz. - 7 lbs., 14 oz. Mfg. 1995-2001.

| | $2,725 | $2,400 | $2,250 | $2,000 | $1,650 | $1,300 | $1,000 |

Last MSR was $3,977.

Add $100 for factory adj. comb (disc. 1998).

CITORI 425 WSSF - 12 ga. only, special dimensions for Women's Shooting Sports Foundation, features painted turquoise finish with WSSF logo on stock or natural walnut finish (new 1997), 7 1/4 lbs. Mfg. 1995-99.

| | $1,750 | $1,300 | $1,100 | $925 | $800 | $675 | $550 |

Last MSR was $1,855.

CITORI 525 SPORTING - 12, 20, 28 (new 2003) ga., or .410 bore (new 2003), 2 3/4 or 3 (.410 bore) in. chambers, 28, 30, or 32 (new 2003) in. vent. barrels with 8-11 mm (12 ga. only) or 10 mm (20 ga. only) width canted VR and porting (12 or 20 ga. only), silver nitride receiver finish with high relief engraving, Hi-Viz Pro-Comp sights, redesigned stock, includes full set of Midas Grade Invector Plus choke tubes (non-flush), oil finished European style checkered Grade III/IV walnut stock with palm swell and forearm, approx. 7-8 1/2 lbs. New 2002.

| MSR $3,035 | $2,600 | $1,925 | $1,450 | $1,050 | $895 | $775 | $675 |

Add $11 for 28 ga. or .410 bore.
Add $298 for adj. comb stock (mfg. 2004-2007, 12 or 20 ga.).

✳ *Citori 525 Sporting Grade I* - 12 ga. only, 3 in. chambers, 28, 30, or 32 in. ported barrels, silver nitride receiver with light 525 style field engraving, oil finished Grade I American walnut stock and Schnabel forearm, right hand palm swell, tapered floating rib, triple trigger system, three flush Invector-Plus choke tubes, Hi-Viz Pro-Comp sight, approx. 8 lbs. Mfg. 2005-2007.

| | $1,900 | $1,400 | $1,125 | $925 | $775 | $675 | $575 |

Last MSR was $2,461.

CITORI 525 GOLDEN CLAYS - 12, 20, 28 (new 2003) ga. or .410 bore (new 2003), similar features to the Model 525 Sporting, except has oil finished Grade V/VI walnut stock with solid pad and Schnabel forearm, engraving pattern that depicts the transistion of a game bird into a clay bird in 24Kt. gold, includes 5 Midas Grade Invector Plus choke tubes (non-flush), 7-8 1/2 lbs. Mfg. 2002-2007.

| | $3,975 | $3,000 | $2,300 | $1,850 | $1,500 | $1,250 | $995 |

Last MSR was $4,722.

Add $215 for 28 ga. or .410 bore.

CITORI 625 SPORTING - 12 ga., 2 3/4 in. chambers, 28, 30, or 32 in. ported VR barrels with extended Vector Pro choking system, checkered gloss finished Grade III/IV walnut stock with or w/o adj. comb and Schnabel forearm, triple trigger system, Hi-Viz fiber optic front sight, silver nitride finished receiver with gold accents, approx. 7 3/4 - 8 1/2 lbs. New 2008.

| MSR $3,299 | $2,850 | $2,300 | $2,000 | $1,700 | $1,400 | $1,200 | $1,000 |

Add $200 for adj. comb.

CITORI 802 EXTENDED SWING (ES) SPORTING - 12 ga. only, 2 3/4 in. chambers, features 28 in. ventilated ported VR barrels (low post, 6.2mm wide) which accept either Invector Plus 2 or 4 stainless steel extension tubes (extends barrels to 30 or 32 in.), adj. pull trigger, slimmer checkered and Schnabel forearm, 7 lbs. 5 oz. Mfg. 1996-2001.

| | $1,295 | $1,095 | $975 | $800 | $700 | $600 | $550 |

Last MSR was $2,063.

CITORI GTI GRADE I - 12 ga. only, 28 or 30 in. barrel with 13mm vent. rib and barrels, red lettering on receiver during 1989 only - changed to gold lettering and borders with Browning logo in 1990, checkered stock and semi-beavertail forearm, ported barrels were introduced 1990 and became standard 1992, Invector chokes standard, back-bored Invector plus chokes became standard in 1990, approx. 8 lbs. Mfg. 1989-94.

$1,100	$950	$850	$700	$625	$550	$475

Last MSR was $1,450.

> **Subtract $100 for standard chokes.**
> **Add $35 for Signature Painted Model.**

The Signature Painted Model includes special paint treatment on stock and forearm featuring Browning logos and trademark - new 1993.

CITORI GTI GOLDEN CLAYS - 12 ga. only, 28, 30, or 32 in. ported VR barrels, Invector Plus choking, GTI features, satin grey receiver with Grade VI level of engraving and gold inlays depicting a transitional hunting to clay pigeon scene. Mfg. 1993-94.

$2,350	$1,950	$1,600	$1,300	$1,050	$925	$825

Last MSR was $2,930.

CITORI GRADE I SPECIAL SPORTING - 12 ga. only, 2 3/4 in. chambers, target dimensions, high-post tapered rib, 28, 30, or 32 in. barrels, full pistol grip with palm swell, adj. comb became optional in 1994, approx. 8 lbs. 3 oz. Mfg. 1989-99.

$1,195	$925	$775	$635	$525	$495	$450

Last MSR was $1,636.

> **Add $100 for factory adj. comb.**
> **Add $35 for Signature Painted Model (disc. 1994).**
> **Add $800 for 2 barrel set (28 and 30 in. barrels), disc. 1990.**

The Signature Painted Model includes special paint treatment on stock and forearm featuring Browning logos and trademark - mfg. 1993-94.
Ported barrels were new in 1990 and became standard in 1992.
In 1990, the Grade I designation was added to this model. Changes include back-bored barrels with Invector plus choke tubes.

CITORI SPECIAL SPORTING GOLDEN CLAYS (GC) - 12 ga. only, 28, 30, or 32 in. ported barrels with high- post VR, Invector Plus choking, Special Sporting features, satin grey receiver with Grade VI level of engraving and gold inlays depicting a transitional hunting to clay pigeon scene. Mfg. 1993-98.

$2,000	$1,800	$1,500	$1,175	$995	$875	$825

Last MSR was $3,203.

> **Add $100 for factory adj. comb.**

CITORI GRADE I SPECIAL SPORTING PIGEON GRADE - 12 ga. only, Invector Plus choking and ported barrels, higher grade of Special Sporting model featuring higher grade walnut and gold line receiver accents. Mfg. 1993-94.

$1,395	$1,150	$950	$800	$700	$625	$550

Last MSR was $1,630.

CITORI ULTRA SPORTER - 12 ga. only, 28, 30, or 32 in. barrels with vent rib separating barrels, low tapered 13- 10mm VR, blue or grey (new 1996) receiver with gold accents, satin finished checkered pistol grip stock and forearm, Invector Plus choking, 7 lbs. 10 oz. - 8 lbs. 4 oz. Mfg. 1995-99.

$1,400	$1,050	$875	$750	$575	$495	$450

Last MSR was $1,800.

> **Add $210 for adj. comb (disc. 1998).**

This model was designated GTI until 1995.

✳ *Citori Ultra Sporter Golden Clays (GC)* - 12 ga. only, features better wood and satin finished engraved receiver with gold inlays clay target scene. Mfg. 1995-99.

	$2,200	$1,900	$1,700	$1,500	$1,275	$1,075	$925

Last MSR was $3,396.

Add $210 for adj. comb (disc. 1997).

CITORI FEATHER XS SPORTING - 12, 20, 28 ga., or .410 bore, 2 3/4 in. chambers (3 in. standard on .410 bore), 28 or 30 in. vent. barrels with tapered VR (12 ga. only) and Invector Plus choking on 12 and 20 ga. (standard Invector on 28 ga. and .410 bore, 28 in. barrels), alloy receiver with dovetailed steel breechface and hinge pin, satin finished checkered walnut pistol grip stock with Schnabel forearm, Hi-Viz comp. sighting system (includes 8 interchangeable colored light pipes), Nitex receiver finish, includes triple trigger system (3 interchangeable trigger shoes), 6 lbs. (28 ga. or .410 bore) - approx. 7 lbs. (12 ga., 30 in. barrels). Mfg. 2000-2002.

$1,700	$1,375	$1,150	$995	$875	$775	$675

Last MSR was $2,311.

CITORI XS GOLDEN CLAYS - 12 or 20 ga. only, similar to 525 Golden Clays, except has traditional checkering pattern and 1/2 - 3/8 in. width VR, includes 3 choke tubes. Mfg. 2002-2003.

$3,150	$2,600	$2,050	$1,650	$1,400	$1,150	$925

Last MSR was $3,914.

CITORI XS SPORTING (ULTRA) - 12, 20, 28 ga. (disc. 2003) or .410 bore (disc. 2003), greyed steel receiver with silver nitride finish, 24Kt. gold accents and light engraving, 28, 30, or 32 (new 2003) in. barrels, with or w/o (30 in. barrels only) barrel porting, 12 ga. features flush Invector Plus choking and right-hand palm swell, Hi-Viz Pro-Comp sight, triple trigger system, select checkered walnut stock with satin finish and Schnabel forearm, 6 lbs. 5 oz. - 8 lbs. Mfg. 1999-2007.

$1,900	$1,600	$1,300	$995	$875	$750	$650

Last MSR was $2,597.

Add 10% for 28 ga. or .410 bore.

CITORI GRAND PRIX SPORTER - 12 ga. only, 2 3/4 in. chambers, steel receiver with silver nitride finish and gold enhanced engraving, 28, 30, or 32 in. VR ported barrels with extended Invector-Plus Midas Grade choke tubes and Hi-Viz fiber optic front sight, oil finished checkered pistol grip walnut stock and Schnabel forearm, select ejector system allows for either ejection or manual extraction, cased, approx. 8 1/4 lbs. New 2007.

MSR $3,236	$2,650	$2,250	$1,750	$1,500	$1,200	$1,050	$925

CITORI LIGHTNING SPORTING (GRADE I) - 12 ga. only, features 3 in. chambers, rounded pistol grip, Lightning style forearm, choice of high or low post VR, standard or adj. (new 1995) comb stock, "Lightning Sporting Clays Edition" inscribed and gold-filled on receiver, triple trigger system, 28 in. ported or 30 in. ported or unported (disc.) barrels, approx. 8 1/2 lbs. Mfg. 1989-2004.

$1,300	$1,045	$885	$765	$650	$550	$495

Last MSR was $1,794.

Add $100 for adj. comb (disc. 1998).
Subtract $100 for low rib.

The Signature Painted Model includes special paint treatment on stock and forearm featuring Browning logos and trademark - mfg. 1993-94.

Ported barrels were new in 1990 and became standard in 1992.

Between 1990-2000, the Grade I designation was added to this model. Changes include back-bored barrels with Invector plus choke tubes.

✻ *Citori Lightning Sporting Golden Clays (GC)* - 12 ga. only, 28, 30, or 32 (disc.) in. ported barrels with choice of low or high-post VR, standard or adj. (new 1995) comb stock, Invector Plus choking, Lightning Sporting features, satin grey receiver with Grade VI level of engraving and gold inlays depicting a transitional hunting to clay birds scene, approx. 8 1/2 lbs. Mfg. 1993-98.

	$2,495	$2,000	$1,550	$1,400	$1,175	$1,000	$875

Last MSR was $3,092.

Add $100 for factory adj. comb.
Subtract $100 for low post rib.

CITORI GRADE I LIGHTNING SPORTING PIGEON GRADE - 12 ga. only, higher grade model featuring higher grade walnut and gold line receiver accents. Mfg. 1993-94.

	$1,395	$1,050	$850	$700	$575	$495	$450

Last MSR was $1,566.

Subtract $100 for low post rib.

CITORI SPORTING HUNTER - please refer to description and pricing under Shotguns: O/U Citori Hunting Series category.

CITORI XS SPECIAL - 12 ga. only, 2 3/4 in. chambers, 30 or 32 in. vent. barrels, silver nitride receiver with XS Special engraving, satin finished stock with adj. comb and semi-beavertail forearm, regular or high-post (new 2007) floating 8-11mm tapered rib, includes triple trigger system and 5 Midas Grade Invector Plus chokes (non-flush), approx. 8 3/4 lbs. New 2004.

MSR $2,980	$2,525	$1,900	$1,575	$1,150	$950	$850	$750

CITORI GTS GRADE I - 12 ga. only, 3 in. chambers, 28 or 30 in. 10mm VR barrels with flush Invector-Plus choke tubes, steel silver nitride finished receiver with game bird transforming into clay target engraving, oil finished checkered Grade II/III walnut pistol grip stock and Schnabel forearm, Hi-Viz front sight, includes case, approx. 8 1/4 lbs. New 2007.

MSR $2,210	$1,875	$1,300	$975	$800	$700	$600	$500

CITORI GTS HIGH GRADE - similar to Grade I, except has gold game bird/clay target engraving. New 2007.

MSR $4,056	$3,250	$2,675	$2,250	$1,875	$1,575	$1,300	$1,175

CITORI ULTRA XS PRESTIGE - 12 ga., similar to Citori GTS High Grade, except has gloss oil finished adj. stock and gold accented Ultra XS special engraving, ported barrels, Hi-Viz fiber optic sight, includes case, approx. 8 lbs. New 2008.

MSR $4,477	$3,800	$2,625	$1,825	$1,450	$1,250	$1,025	$950

CITORI TRAP MODELS - 12 ga., similar to Standard Citori, 30 or 32 in. barrels, trap chokes, Monte Carlo stock, recoil pad. Invector chokes became standard in 1988, Invector Plus chokes with ported barrels became an option in 1992, and were made standard in 1993, new Special Trap models were introduced during 1995 with decreased weight (1/4 lb. lighter) and better swing/balance characteristics. Mfg. 1974-current.

✻ *Citori Trap Grade I* - w/o choke tube, mfg. 1974-78.

	$900	$800	$750	$650	$525	$495	$450

✻ *Citori Grade I Special Trap* - approx. 8 1/2 lbs. Mfg. 1995-99.

	$1,395	$975	$795	$650	$525	$495	$450

Last MSR was $1,658.

Add $100 for factory adj. comb.
Subtract 20% without Invector chokes or high rib.

GRADING - PPGS™	100%	98%	95%	90%	80%	70%	60%

＊ *Citori Trap Combination Set* - Grade I only, 32 in. O/U and 34 in. single barrel, or extra set of barrels in same ga., cased. Disc.

	$1,295	$1,100	$975	$900	$825	$775	$725

Add approx. 40% for extra 20 ga. barrels originally ordered with gun.

＊ *Citori Grade I Plus Trap* - features adj. rib and stock, back-bored barrels, Invector Plus choke system. Mfg. 1990-94.

	$1,900	$1,525	$1,225	$995	$700	$600	$500

Last MSR was $2,005.

Add 5% for ported barrels.

In 1991 this model included a travel vault gun case at no extra charge. Subtract $50 for older mfg. without travel case.

＊ *Citori Grade I Plus Trap Combo* - includes ported barrels with Invector Plus choking and extra standard single ported barrel, luggage case. Mfg. 1992-94.

	$2,775	$2,475	$2,100	$1,900	$1,700	$1,500	$1,250

Last MSR was $3,435.

＊ *Citori Plus Trap Golden Clays* - 12 ga. only, 30 or 32 in. ported VR barrels, Invector Plus choking, Trap features, satin grey receiver with Grade VI level of engraving and gold inlays depicting a transitional hunting to clay birds scene. Mfg. 1993-94.

	$3,000	$2,600	$2,000	$1,600	$1,400	$1,200	$995

Last MSR was $3,435.

＊ *Citori Plus Trap Golden Clays Combo* - includes O/U ported barrels with Invector Plus choking and extra standard single ported barrel, luggage case. Mfg. 1993-94.

	$4,425	$3,300	$2,775	$2,250	$1,925	$1,800	$1,700

Last MSR was $5,200.

＊ *Citori XT Trap* - 12 ga. only, features greyed receiver with 24Kt. gold accents and light engraving, triple trigger system (includes 3 interchangeable triggers for 1/8 in. adj. on LOP), 30 or 32 in. vent. backbored barrels with high-post VR, checkered high gloss Monte Carlo walnut stock and forearm, right hand palm swell, Hi-Viz front sight, waffle-style recoil pad, approx. approx. 8 1/2 lbs. New 1999.

MSR $2,486	$2,100	$1,625	$1,250	$1,050	$825	$700	$500

Add $299 for adj. comb.

＊ *Citori XT Trap Gold* - 12 ga. only, 2 3/4 in. chambers, features intricate "Golden Clays" engraving with game bird/clay bird, Grade V/VI American walnut stock and semi-beavertail forearm, vented 30 or 32 in. ported barrels with high post VR and Invector Plus choke system with five flush Midas Grade chokes, adj. comb, adj. GraCoil recoil reduction system, triple trigger system, Hi-Viz Pro-Comp sight with mid-bead, approx. 9 lbs. New 2005.

MSR $4,612	$3,900	$2,800	$2,000	$1,500	$1,175	$1,000	$875

＊ *Citori Trap Pigeon Grade* - 12 ga. only, features extra deluxe walnut, Invector Plus ported barrels, and receiver gold accents. Mfg. 1993-94.

	$1,715	$1,250	$950	$800	$700	$600	$500

Last MSR was $2,225.

＊ *Citori Trap Signature Painted* - 12 ga. only, features painted red/black stock with Browning logos on stock and forearm, Invector Plus ported barrels. Mfg. 1993-94.

	$1,595	$1,200	$940	$800	$700	$600	$500

Last MSR was $2,065.

＊ *Citori Trap Grade II* - high post rib. Mfg. 1978-1983.

	$1,200	$900	$800	$740	$690	$650	$600

GRADING - PPGS™	100%	98%	95%	90%	80%	70%	60%

✳ *Citori Trap Grade III* - 12 ga. only, high post rib, Invector Plus choking and ported barrels became standard in 1994. Mfg. 1986-99.

	$1,895	$1,600	$1,300	$995	$825	$600	$525

Last MSR was $2,310.

Add $100 for factory adj. comb.
Subtract 10% if without Invector Plus chokes or ported barrels.

✳ *Citori Trap Grade V* - high post rib. Mfg. 1978-1984.

	$1,595	$1,300	$1,000	$880	$795	$710	$620

✳ *Citori Trap Grade VI* - 12 ga. only, Invector chokes became standard in 1985, Invector Plus chokes became standard in 1994. Disc. 1994.

	$1,995	$1,600	$1,300	$1,100	$960	$875	$825

Last MSR was $2,555.

Subtract $150 if without Invector Plus chokes or ported barrels.
Subtract $250 for fixed chokes.

✳ *Citori Trap Golden Clays (GC)* - 12 ga. only, 30 or 32 in. ported VR barrels, Invector Plus choking, Trap features, Monte Carlo or regular stock, satin grey receiver with Grade VI level of engraving and gold inlays depicting a transitional hunting to clay pigeon scene. Mfg. 1993-99.

	$2,750	$2,400	$2,100	$1,750	$1,500	$1,250	$1,025

Last MSR was $3,434.

Add $220 for adj. comb (new 1995).

CITORI XS PRO-COMP - 12 ga. only, 2 3/4 in. chambers, 28 or 30 in. vent. and ported VR barrels with spreader chokes, adj. comb, beavertail forearm, GraCoil recoil reduction system, right-hand palm swell, triple trigger system, features removable tungsten alloy forearm weight which approximates the same weight as barrel tubes, also has removable front barrel weight to adj. the swing through, approx. 9 lbs. Mfg. 2002-2004.

	$2,500	$2,100	$1,800	$1,425	$1,100	$975	$850

Last MSR was $4,027.

SHOTGUNS: O/U, SUPERPOSED GENERAL INFO & CHOKE CODES

SUPERPOSED MODEL - 12, 20 (introduced circa 1948-49), 28 ga. (introduced 1960) or .410 bore (introduced 1960), 26 1/2, 28, 30, or 32 in. barrels, various chokes, boxlock, auto ejectors, various trigger combinations (single & double), checkered pistol grip stock, mfg. 1931-40 and 1948-76 by FN, grades differ in amount of engraving, inlays, general quality of workmanship and wood.

NOTE: The use of steel shot is NOT recommended in any Superposed Series manufactured in Belgium (B-25 variations).

BROWNING CHOKES AND THEIR CODES (MARKED NEXT TO EJECTORS)

* designates full choke (F).
*- designates improved modified choke (IM).
** designates modified choke (M).
**- designates improved cylinder choke (IC).
**$ designates skeet (SK).
*** designates cylinder bore (CYL).

SKEET MODELS were available in every ga. and grade.

TRAP MODELS were available in every grade in 12 ga. only.

BROADWAY TRAP MODELS (mfg. 1961-75) featured a 5/8 in. wide vent. rib and were also available in every grade.

Please refer to the new expanded Browning Superposed serialization section in this text for determining year of manufacture.

GRADING - PPGS™	100%	98%	95%	90%	80%	70%	60%

SUPERPOSED: 1931-1940 MFG. (PRE-WWII)

Early pre-war guns had long slender forearms with a metal plate at the front called a horseshoe plate. Approx. circa 1936, the forearm was changed to the one used post war - smaller with a transverse bolt to hold the forearm on. The earlier forearm had a long bolt that ran from front to back through the metal plate to hold the forearm on. The earlier transverse bolts were recessed into the sides of the forearms. Later the head and fastener on the other side of the forearm were flush with the wood.

Pre-war cases were manufactured in black or brown, with a textured surface called elephant hide, in leather or tex leather. Insides were lined with grey or blue cloth, and the Browning brass label was on the inside top of the case, not the outside. Depending on original condition, these cases sell in the $200-$400 range - single barrel cases are more common than multi-barrel ones. Extra barrels (same ga. only) could be ordered with the original gun, and were supplied in a Browning hard case.

Very few pre-war Pigeon, Diana, and Midas Grades were signed by the engraver.

Add approx. 35%-50% per extra set of barrels (same ga. only), depending on condition.
Subtract 10%-25% for recoil pad (depending on originality, deterioration, and condition).

SUPERPOSED STANDARD GRADE/GRADE I/LIGHTNING - 12 ga. only, boxlock action, blue w/border receiver engraving until 1938, when a simple small center rosette engraving pattern was introduced, 4 trigger options until 1938, when the barrel selector was moved to the top tang, trigger options included: double normal, selective single with the selector on the bottom next to the trigger, twin single, and non- selective single, Standard model nomenclature was changed to Grade I during 1938, in addition to changing the trigger to SST with the barrel selector on the top tang, raised hollow or ventilated rib, Lightning Model introduced during 1936 in Standard grade with striped barrels - ribs were extra cost. Original buttplates featured intertwined twin circles and were made of horn.

12 ga.	N/A	$2,200	$1,650	$1,325	$1,050	$900	$825

Original buttplates with unaltered (uncut) stock are very important to collectors for this period of Superposed manufacture.

First year production Superposed will command a premium (approx. ser. no. range 1-2,000). The twin single trigger is also very desirable for collectors.

Recoil pads were an extra option during this time, and even though they might be factory installed, they are not desirable to collectors, and as a result, prices could be reduced substantially based on pad deterioration. Pad makers included: Jostam, Hawkins, Noshoc, D&W, and Black Diamond - these pads were $5 options pre-WWII.

SUPERPOSED PIGEON GRADE - grey receiver with 2 pigeons on either side, these earlier guns had larger engraved pigeons than later production (1960 and later). Mfg. 1931-40.

12 ga.	N/A	$4,800	$4,050	$3,250	$2,475	$1,750	$1,550

The Pigeon Grade style of engraving is the only pre-war style that was continued after WWII.

SUPERPOSED DIANA GRADE - grey receiver with lighter style, delicate European style engraving, boars and stags were pictured in the 1931 catalog, but dogs and birds could also be special ordered at no additional cost until 1936, after which it became extra cost, dogs and birds engraving are more common than boars and stag. Mfg. 1931-40.

12 ga.	N/A	$7,100	$5,800	$4,400	$3,700	$3,050	$2,200

The Diana Grade was changed dramatically in post-WWII production.

SUPERPOSED MIDAS GRADE - featured gold inlaid pigeons with outstretched wings on blue frame sides and bottom plus trigger guard. This Germanic syle engraving also exhibited multiple gold escutcheons and gold lining, ejector trip rods, ejector hammers and firing pins are also 18Kt. gold plated, finest checkered walnut.

12 ga.	N/A	$8,500	$7,100	$5,800	$4,000	$3,300	$2,700

The Midas Grade was changed dramatically in post-WWII production.

GRADING - PPGS™	100%	98%	95%	90%	80%	70%	60%

SUPERPOSED: 1948-1960 MFG. (POST-WWII)

Model nomenclature was changed from pre-war designations to Grades I-VI. During this period, extra barrels could only be ordered in the same gauge as the original gun. Hardshell cases from this era are referred to as Tolex cases - they have blue velvet lining, and a brass Browning label on the outside top.

Engraved guns signed by Browning's top engravers (Funken, Vrancken, Watrin, Doyen, Müller, and Magis) will command a premium over unsigned guns. Felix Funken retired in 1960, and died in 1966.

On most Superposed with added recoil pads, the stock has usually been cut to keep the LOP the same. The correct LOP on a Superposed is 14 1/4 inches, with or w/o a recoil pad.

The twin circle buttplate was always horn, and was used on very early post war guns until 1949-1950.

Barrel addresses appeared as follows: circa 1947-1958 "St. Louis, M.O." (earliest BAC markings) or "St. Louis, Missouri", 1959-1968 "St. Louis, Missouri and Montreal P.Q.", 1969-1975 "Morgan, Utah and Montreal, P.Q.". Make sure barrel address date matches year of mfg. (see listings in the back of this text).

The original factory configuration of almost all Superposed shotguns can be verified by grade, gauge/bore, and barrel length. To obtain information on a specific Belgian Superposed serial number, please contact the Browning historian directly (refer to Trademark Index for more information).

> Add approx. 35%-50% per extra set of barrels (same ga. only), depending on condition.
> Add $200-$300 for correct Tolex hardshell case with paperwork.
> Subtract $150-$500 for non-original recoil pads on Grade I models, depending on condition.
> Subtract $250-$750 for non-original recoil pads on the higher grades, depending on condition.
> Special order Superposed with non-standard factory engraving, checkered buttstocks, 3 piece forearms, and other special orders will command premiums over standard configurations.

SUPERPOSED GRADE I STANDARD WEIGHT - 12 or 20 ga. (3 in. chambers were introduced in the 12 ga. during 1955, and in 20 ga. during 1957), otherwise similar to pre-war mfg., blue finish and triggers until 1955, gold trigger(s) became standard in 1955, raised (standard until 1959) or vent. rib only beginning in 1959, round knob long tang (RKLT) stock configuration, this earlier period of mfg. also featured smaller, narrower forearms and thinner pistol grip stock with horn buttplate (can be determined by the rounded "g" in Browning, not square), early post-war production had similar pre-WWII minimal engraving until circa 1952-53, more standard engraving continued through 1955, when Grade I models featured considerably more engraving, post-war 12 ga. serialization began at approx. 17,100, and with 200 on 20 ga. Mfg. 1948-60.

	100%	98%	95%	90%	80%	70%	60%
12 ga.	N/A	$1,825	$1,525	$1,125	$950	$850	$775
20 ga.	N/A	$3,350	$2,825	$2,350	$1,625	$1,325	$1,150

Grade I models had 3 levels of standard engraving coverage.

* *Superposed Grade I Lightning Hunting Model* - 12 or 20 ga., 6 oz. lighter than Standard Weight. Introduced in all Grades beginning 1956.

	100%	98%	95%	90%	80%	70%	60%
12 ga.	N/A	$1,825	$1,525	$1,125	$950	$850	$775
20 ga.	N/A	$3,375	$2,850	$2,375	$1,625	$1,325	$1,150

* *Superposed Grade I Magnum* - 12 ga. only, 3 in. chambers, 28, 30, or 32 (rare) in. barrels with raised or vent. rib, recoil pad standard, introduced in all Grades in 1955.

	100%	98%	95%	90%	80%	70%	60%
	N/A	$1,850	$1,575	$1,150	$975	$875	$800

This model with 30 or 32 (rare) in. barrels is now popular again, as Sporting Clays shooters like this desirable configuration.

GRADING - PPGS™	100%	98%	95%	90%	80%	70%	60%

✳ *Superposed Grade I Trap Standard Weight Model* - 12 ga. only, various configurations, Introduced 1952.

	N/A	$1,825	$1525	$1,125	$950	$850	$775

Pre-war trap guns and those manufactured post-war until approx. 1955 were virtually indistinguishable from field guns as they had field style forearms, round knob (semi-pistol grip) and long tangs. The only way to tell the difference is they had a longer LOP (14 1/2 in.) and a shorter drop at the heel - 1 3/4 in. vs. 2 1/2 in. for field stocks. These early trap guns did not come with recoil pads. Between 1956-1960, trap guns had the forearm changed to semi-beavertail. These late guns with semi-beavertail forearms are very desirable today due to their rarity and overall desirability.

SUPERPOSED GRADE II - featured pre-war Pigeon Grade engraving with large pigeons, some early post- war mfg. were signed by Funken.

12 ga.	N/A	$4,200	$3,150	$2,100	$1,800	$1,675	$1,550
20 ga.	N/A	$7,300	$5,700	$4,400	$3,525	$2,750	$1,975

SUPERPOSED GRADE III - 12 or 20 ga., European style engraving, commonly referred to as "fighting cocks," pheasants on right side, fighting cocks on left, most were signed by the engraver.

12 ga.	N/A	$4,800	$3,500	$2,350	$2,000	$1,800	$1,650
20 ga.	N/A	$8,700	$7,250	$6,300	$4,950	$4,100	$3,000

SUPERPOSED GRADE IV - 12 or 20 ga., features deeper European style engraving with dogs and foxes, most were signed by the engraver.

12 ga.	N/A	$7,000	$5,500	$4,000	$3,250	$2,350	$1,900
20 ga.	N/A	$11,500	$9,500	$7,500	$5,250	$3,500	$2,950

SUPERPOSED GRADE V - 12 or 20 ga., features deeper engraving than pre-war Diana Grade, pheasants and ducks on receiver, most were signed by the engraver - Doyen was prevalent on this model.

12 ga.	N/A	$6,800	$5,600	$3,850	$2,750	$2,200	$1,975
20 ga.	N/A	$9,500	$8,500	$6,100	$4,950	$3,850	$3,300

SUPERPOSED GRADE VI - 12 or 20 ga., engraving pattern similar to later production Midas Grade, almost all of these were signed by Müller. Introduced in July, 1957, changed in 1960, limited production, and rarest of the 6 grades.

12 ga.	N/A	$9,250	$6,500	$5,000	$4,000	$3,500	$2,800
20 ga.	N/A	$16,500	$11,750	$8,750	$7,250	$5,000	$4,200

SUPERPOSED:1960-1976 MFG.

In early 1960, a major change was made in the manner in which the various grades of Superposed were designated. The Roman numerals used in the 1950s were dropped, and Browning once again returned to names. The Pigeon, Diana, and Midas names used for pre-war designations were brought back and replaced the Grade II, Grade V, and Grade VI respectively. Grades III & IV were dropped and replaced by the Pointer. The Grade I remained unchanged.

The Broadway Trap Model was introduced in 1961. Browning's lifetime Superposed warranty began in 1963. During 1965, the Hydro Coil stock (1 year only) and barrel Super Tubes were introduced. During 1966, a major change was implemented to save money when Browning switched from a long tang to short tang. During 1970-71, the stock configuration was once again changed to a full pistol grip (referred to as flat knob), and the long tang was brought back. Also at this time, mechanical triggers were implemented vs. the older inertial design, and silver solder vent. ribs vs. tin solder. As a result, this period of Superposed manufacture was mechanically better and more reliable. The Superlight Model was introduced in 12 ga. during 1967, 20 ga. during 1969, and became available in all Grades beginning in 1971. All gauge Skeet sets became available in all Grades during 1972.

During late 1966, Browning's salt wood problems began to emerge, and continued until 1972. Most experts have never seen a long tang salt gun, and therefore believe that almost 100% of the salt guns had short tangs. Depending on the damage (it can vary a lot), values for salt dam-

GRADING - PPGS™	100%	98%	95%	90%	80%	70%	60%

aged guns can be reduced as much as 50% (heavy pitting and original salt wood). Those salt guns that have been restocked by Browning are accepted by the shooting fraternity, and can command as much as 90% of the value of non-salt original guns. To determine if a Superposed has salt damage, examine carefully any gun where the serial number is within the 1966-1971 production range (please refer to the Browning Superposed serialization section), and carefully inspect the wood around the buttplate, forearm, and where the wood joins the receiver metal for any telltale rusting or pitting.

Engraved guns signed by Browning's top engravers (Funken, Vrancken, Watrin, Magis, Müeller, and J. Baerten) will command a premium over unsigned guns. Also, more and more Super-posed models are appearing with Angelo Bee's signature (while non-factory, Mr. Bee's work is universally recognized. He engraved in Belgium at FN from 1951-1974.) Louis Vrancken and Andre Watrin took over as heads of the engraving department in 1960.

The following values are for 1960-1976 Superposed production non-salt damaged guns. Most desirable period of mfg. is 1960-1966 (round knob, long tang, pre-salt). Guns made during 1972-1976 (FKLT) are worth more than RKST. Lowest values are for 1966-1971 mfg. (round/flat knob, short tang - should be inspected carefully for potential salt wood problems).

Barrel addresses appeared as follows: circa 1947-1958 "St. Louis, M.O." (earliest BAC markings) or "St. Louis, Missouri", 1959-1968 "St. Louis, Missouri and Montreal P.Q.", 1969-1975 "Morgan, Utah and Montreal, P.Q." Make sure barrel address date matches year of mfg. (see listings in the back of this text).

The original factory configuration of almost all Superposed shotguns can be verified by grade, gauge/bore, and barrel length. To obtain information on a specific Belgian Superposed serial number, please contact the Browning historian directly (refer to Trademark Index for more information).

SUPERPOSED WITH EXTRA BARREL(S) OR SUPER-TUBES - The Superposed could be special ordered from the factory in the following combinations: 12 or 20 ga. with one extra set of barrels in same ga., 12 ga. with one extra set in 20 ga., 12 or 20 ga. with two extra barrel sets of same ga., 20 ga. with one extra set in either 28 ga. or .410 bore, 20 ga. with both 28 ga. and .410 bore barrel sets, and 28 ga. with extra set of .410 bore barrels. Super-Tubes were adapt-able on 12 ga. guns only; came from the factory cased with accessories, 16 1/2 in. long, factory installation.

Add 40%-50% of the gun's value for each Grade I extra barrel set(s). For higher grades, add approx. $1,000-$2,500 per barrel set, depending on grade.

Add $250 for Super-Tubes - available for 12 ga. only, introduced in 1965.

Add $400 for Super-Tube Set - 3 ga. set (20, 28 ga., and .410 bore).

Subtract $150-$500 for non-original recoil pads on Grade I models, depending on condition.

Subtract $250-$750 for non-original recoil pads on higher grades, depending on condition.

SUPERPOSED VARIATIONS - On most Superposed with added recoil pads, the stock has usually been cut to keep the LOP the same. The correct LOP on a Superposed is 14 1/4 inches (14 1/2 in. on Trap & New Style Skeet), with or w/o a factory recoil pad, unless special ordered from the factory. Except for the Superlight Model, individual configurations have not been broken out on the Pigeon, Pointer, Diana, and Midas grades, but values will be similar to each other in most cases.

Subtract approx. 25%-40% for salt wood (depending on extent of damage).

Subtract 10% for new style Skeet configuration on models.

Subtract 15%-20% for Broadway Trap Model.

Special order Superposed with non-standard factory engraving, checkered buttstocks, 3 piece forearms, and other special orders will command premiums over standard configurations.

SUPERPOSED GRADE I STANDARD WEIGHT & LIGHTNING - 12, 20, 28 ga., or .410 bore (the 28 ga. & .410 bore were not cataloged until 1960), 28 ga. and .410 bore were built on a 20 ga. frame, the buttplate was changed from horn to plastic during 1961, 12 and 20 ga. Lightning Models were approx. 6 oz. lighter than Standard Weight.

	100%	98%	95%	90%	80%	70%	60%
12 ga.	$2,250	$1,775	$1,450	$1,050	$900	$825	$750

GRADING - PPGS™	100%	98%	95%	90%	80%	70%	60%
20 ga.	$3,950	$3,400	$2,800	$2,200	$1,550	$1,275	$1,100
28 ga.	$6,500	$5,500	$4,250	$3,250	$2,650	$2,300	$2,100
.410 Bore	$5,500	$4,500	$3,500	$3,000	$2,200	$1,475	$1,225

Subtract 10%-15% for Grade I Standardweight (12 ga. only).
Add 20%-25% for round knob, long tang stock variations (pre-1966), unless Skeet choked.

✳ *Superposed Grade I Magnum* - 12 ga. only, 3 in. chambers, 28, 30, or 32 (rare) in. barrels with vent. rib, recoil pad standard.

12 ga.	$1,850	$1,500	$1,100	$1,000	$825	$775	$725

This model with 30 or 32 (very rare) in. barrels is now popular again, as Sporting Clays shooters like this desirable configuration.

✳ *Superposed Grade I Superlight* - 12 (mfg. 1967-1976), 20 (1969-1976), 28 (very rare, approx. 12-14 mfg.) ga. or .410 bore (mfg. 1970-76) features lightweight construction and straight grip stock. During 1971, the Superlight was offered in all Grades.

Add 20%-40% over Standardweight and Lightning values, depending on condition and overall desirability.
A Quail Unlimited limited edition was also available in the Superlight Series, add 10%-15% if in 98%+ original condition.
Add 100% for 28 ga.

✳ *Superposed Grade I Skeet/New Model Skeet* - 12, 20, 28 ga. or .410 bore, 26 1/2 or 28 in. VR barrels with fixed SK/SK chokes, New Model Skeet was introduced during 1968, and was available in both Standard and Lightning weights in 12 and 20 ga., this New Model featured a flat bottom pistol grip stock with factory vent. recoil pad and beavertail forearm, pre-'68 mfg. was basically a hunting model with skeet chokes. Mfg. circa 1950s-1976.

12 ga.	$1,675	$1,400	$1,100	$950	$825	$750	$700
20 ga.	$2,450	$2,100	$1,700	$1,250	$975	$850	$775
28 ga.	$4,500	$3,500	$2,750	$2,250	$1,550	$1,275	$1,100
.410 bore	$2,800	$2,400	$1,950	$1,450	$1,100	$925	$850

Add approx. 10%-15% for pre 1968 mfg. (w/o beavertail forearm and recoil pad.)
Subtract 20% for 26 in. (New Skeet style) barrels.

✳ *Superposed Grade I Four Gauge Skeet Set* - includes 12, 20, 28 ga. and .410 bore barrels, 26 1/2 or 28 in. VR barrels, 12 ga. frame, single removable beavertail forearm, includes fitted luggage case. Mfg. 1972-76.

	$5,250	$4,950	$4,500	$4,150	$3,850	$3,350	$2,650

Subtract 20% for 26 in. (New Skeet style) barrels.

✳ *Superposed Grade I Trap Model (Lightning and Broadway)* - 12 ga. only, FKLT, Trap dimension stock with recoil pad, semi-beavertail forearm, 30 or 32 (rare in Lightning model) in. barrels with either standard 5/16 in. VR (Lightning) or 5/8 in. Broadway VR, first cataloged in 1961, this new Lightning Model Trap was approx. 6 oz. lighter than previous mfg., front and center ivory bead sights standard, 14 3/8 in. LOP, Broadway is approx. 1 lbs. heavier than Lightning with same length barrels.

	$1,850	$1,500	$1,100	$1,000	$825	$750	$700

SUPERPOSED PIGEON GRADE -12, 20, 28 ga. or .410 bore, features a silver grey receiver with 2 smaller flying pigeons surrounded by fine scroll engraving on each side of the frame, receiver bottom and tangs also exhibit fine scroll work. Disc. 1974.

12 ga.	$5,500	$3,850	$2,900	$2,000	$1,700	$1,570	$1,485
20 ga.	$8,000	$6,750	$5,250	$3,600	$2,650	$2,100	$1,850
28 ga.	$11,000	$9,000	$7,800	$6,000	$4,500	$3,500	$2,500
.410 bore	$8,000	$6,750	$5,500	$4,200	$3,300	$2,800	$2,200

Add 20%-25% for round knob, long tang stock variations (pre-1966), unless Skeet choked.
Subtract 20% for newer Skeet style model with beavertail forearm and recoil pad.
Between 1948-1960, this model was designated the Grade II.

✴ Superposed Pigeon Grade Superlight - 12 (mfg. 1967-1976), 20 (1969-1976), 28 (very rare, approx. 7-9 mfg.) ga. or .410 bore (mfg. 1970-76) features lightweight construction and straight grip stock. During 1971, the Superlight was offered in all Grades.

> **Add 40% over standard Pigeon Grade values, depending on condition and overall desirability. Add 60% for 28 ga.**

SUPERPOSED POINTER GRADE - features engraved silver grey receiver with a pointer on one side, and a setter on the other, select checkered walnut, early production was engraved by Funken, while the final design was executed by Vrancken. Mfg. 1959-disc. 1966, except for special orders.

	100%	98%	95%	90%	80%	70%	60%
12 ga.	$8,750	$6,850	$5,500	$4,150	$3,100	$2,200	$1,800
20 ga.	$15,000	$12,500	$9,250	$7,600	$6,000	$5,000	$3,750
28 ga. (rare)	$20,000	$17,000	$14,750	$12,500	$8,000	$5,000	$3,800
.410 bore (rare)	$17,500	$14,000	$12,250	$9,250	$6,000	$4,600	$3,500

> **Add 40% for round knob, long tang stock variations (pre-1966), unless Skeet choked (add 50% if 28 ga.).**
> **Subtract 20% for newer Skeet style model with beavertail forearm and recoil pad.**

✴ Superposed Pointer Grade Superlight - this model was available by special order only, and was never cataloged by BAC (approx. 10-12 mfg. in 28 ga.).

> **Add 40% over standard Pointer Grade values, depending on condition and overall desirability add 50% if 28 ga.).**

SUPERPOSED DIANA GRADE - deeper engraving with duck and pheasant game scenes - similar to 1948-60 mfg. Grade V. Disc. 1976.

	100%	98%	95%	90%	80%	70%	60%
12 ga.	$7,750	$6,500	$4,300	$2,750	$2,450	$2,200	$1,975
20 ga.	$12,500	$9,250	$8,150	$5,950	$4,850	$3,650	$3,150
28 ga.	$19,995	$16,750	$13,750	$9,500	$7,350	$5,750	$4,750
.410 bore	$13,750	$10,500	$8,500	$6,550	$5,000	$4,200	$3,650

> **Add 40% for round knob, long tang stock variations (pre-1966) (add 50% if 28 ga.).**
> **Subtract 20% for newer Skeet style model with beavertail forearm and recoil pad.**

Between 1948-1960, this model was designated the Grade V.

✴ Superposed Diana Grade Superlight - 12 (mfg. 1967-76), 20 (1969-76), 28 (very rare, approx. 8-10 mfg.) ga. or .410 bore (mfg. 1970-76) features lightweight construction and straight grip stock. During 1971, the Superlight was offered in all Grades.

> **Add approx. 25%-40% over standard Diana Grade values, depending on condition and overall desirability (add 60% if 28 ga.).**

SUPERPOSED MIDAS GRADE - features new design by Vrancken with deep relief scroll engraving with gold inlaid ducks and pheasants on frame sides and a quail on the bottom, ejector trip rods, ejector hammers, and firing pins are also 18Kt. gold plated, best quality walnut with fine checkering. Disc. 1976.

	100%	98%	95%	90%	80%	70%	60%
12 ga.	$12,500	$10,500	$8,750	$6,250	$5,000	$4,000	$3,500
20 ga.	$19,500	$16,500	$14,000	$11,750	$8,750	$7,250	$5,000
28 ga.	$25,000	$22,000	$19,000	$16,500	$12,500	$9,000	$7,350
.410 bore	$19,500	$16,500	$14,000	$11,750	$8,750	$7,250	$5,000

> **Add 40% for round knob, long tang stock variations (pre-1966), unless Skeet choked (add 50% if 28 ga.).**
> **Subtract 20% for newer Skeet style model with beavertail forearm and recoil pad.**

Between 1948-1960, this model was designated the Grade VI.

✴ Superposed Midas Grade Superlight - 12 (mfg. 1967-76), 20 (1969-76), 28 (very rare, approx. 9 mfg.) ga. or .410 bore (mfg. 1970-76) features lightweight construction and straight grip stock. During 1971, the Superlight was offered in all Grades.

> **Add approx. 25%-40% over standard Midas Grade values, depending on condition and overall desirability (add 50% for 28 ga.).**

SUPERPOSED BICENTENNIAL SUPERLIGHT - specially engraved limited edition Model, 51 mfg. - one for each state and Washington, D.C. Left side has U.S. Flag, bald eagle and state emblem inlaid in gold. Right side has gold inlaid hunter and turkey. Blue receiver, fancy checkered English stock, Schnabel forend, velvet lined wood case. Made 1976 by FN.

	100%	98%	95%	90%	80%	70%	60%
	$11,500	$9,000	$7,500	N/A	N/A	N/A	N/A

SUPERPOSED EXPOSITION/EXHIBITION MODEL - this specially manufactured Superposed saw limited production from pre-WWII through 1976. There are true exhibition models and a "C" series. Most "C" series did not have carved stocks, and were a special BAC sale of FN guns which did not sell well in Europe. True exhibition guns had gold lettering on the barrels in most cases, and many also had carved stocks. These guns were made for a very special reason, purpose, or person. Prices usually start in the 5 digit level - the C Series is typically priced between $20,000-$30,000, and true Exhibition guns can get much more expensive, depending on how elaborate the embellishments are.

SUPERPOSED PRESENTATION MODELS (P1-P4) - custom made versions of the Lightning Field, Super Light, Trap, and Skeet guns, specifications the same as Standard models, with differences in finish, engraving and inlay(s), and grade of wood and checkering. These guns were introduced by FN in 1977 and were disc. after 1984. Gauge premiums below refer to Models P1-P3.

   Add 50% for 20 ga.
   Add 75% for 28 ga.
   Add 40% for .410 bore.
   Add $1,500of the gun's value for each P1 extra barrel set(s). For higher grades, add approx. $1,500-$2,500 per barrel set, depending on grade.
   Subtract 25% for P Series Trap Models.
   Subtract 25% for P Series Broadway Trap Models.
   Subtract 20% for P Series Skeet 12 and 20 ga. guns.

Since P Series Superposed were disc. in 1985, collector interest has increased substantially. Interestingly, the P series models are rarer than most of the pre-1976 high grade Superposed models.

✳ *Superposed Presentation 1* - silver grey or blue receiver, oak leaf and fine scroll engraved, choice of 6 different animal scenes.

	100%	98%	95%	90%	80%	70%	60%
	$3,300	$2,500	$2,100	$1,850	$1,500	$1,250	$1,000

✳ *Superposed Presentation 1 w/gold inlays* - similar to Presentation 1, only with gold inlays.

	$4,750	$3,500	$3,000	$2,100	$1,825	$1,700	$1,500

✳ *Superposed Presentation 2* - silver grey or blue receiver, high relief engraving, choice of 3 different sets of game scenes.

	$4,800	$4,000	$2,750	$2,050	$1,825	$1,700	$1,500

✳ *Superposed Presentation 2 w/gold inlays* - similar to Presentation 2, only with gold inlays.

	$7,000	$6,000	$4,200	$2,150	$1,925	$1,750	$1,550

✳ *Superposed Presentation 3* - silver grey or blue receiver, more elaborate high relief engraving with choice of partridges, mallards, or geese depicted on frame sides in 18Kt. gold.

	$9,000	$7,500	$5,500	$3,750	$3,200	$2,875	$2,300

✳ *Superposed Presentation 4* - features engraved side plates in either silver grey or blue finish, hand engraved game scenes include waterfowl on right frame side, 5 pheasants on left frame side, 2 quail on receiver bottom, and a retriever's head on trigger guard. Extra figure walnut stock and forearm.

	$8,000	$6,900	$5,250	$4,000	$3,350	$2,950	$2,375

   Add 30% for 20 ga., 70% for 28 ga., or 50% for .410 bore.

GRADING - PPGS™	100%	98%	95%	90%	80%	70%	60%

✳ *Superposed Presentation 4 w/gold inlays* - similar to Presentation 4, only with game scenes inlaid in 18Kt. gold.

	$12,000	$10,500	$8,700	$6,000	$4,250	$3,650	$2,950

Add 50% for 20 ga., 75% for 28 ga., or 50% for .410 bore.

SUPERPOSED PRESENTATION SERIES SUPERLITE (PI - PIV) - available in various configurations including multi-barrel sets.

✳ *Superposed Presentation I Superlite w/Gold* - G, H, I, J, K, or L style engraving.

	100%	98%	95%	90%	80%	70%	60%
12 ga. (25 mfg.)	$6,000	$5,500	$4,500	$3,200	$3,000	$2,500	$2,200
20 ga. (80 mfg.)	$9,000	$7,600	$6,600	$5,300	$4,000	$3,200	$2,600
28 ga. (38 mfg.)	$11,000	$9,800	$9,000	$7,500	$6,000	$4,000	$3,400
.410 bore (47 mfg.)	$8,500	$7,500	$6,500	$5,500	$4,000	$3,200	$2,600

Add $1,500 per extra barrel.
Add 40% for an all option gun (checkered buttstock, oil finish, three piece forend, rare).
Add 15% for J. Baerten signed gun (rare).
Subtract 35% for Trap or Skeet Models.
Subtract 30% for A, B, C, D, E, or F models w/o gold.

✳ *Superposed Presentation II Superlite* - P, Q, or R style engraving.

	100%	98%	95%	90%	80%	70%	60%
12 ga. (23 mfg.)	$8,500	$8,000	$7,000	$6,000	$4,200	$3,100	$2,000
20 ga. (93 mfg.)	$11,000	$10,000	$9,000	$7,000	$6,000	$5,000	$3,000
28 ga. (57 mfg.)	$13,000	$12,000	$9,500	$8,500	$6,500	$5,500	$4,500
.410 bore (44 mfg.)	$11,000	$10,000	$9,000	$7,000	$5,500	$4,500	$3,500

Add $1,500 per extra barrel.
Add 40% for an all option gun (checkered buttstock, oil finish, three piece forend, rare).
Add 15% for J. Baerten signed gun (rare).
Subtract 35% for Trap or Skeet Models.
Subtract 30% for M, N, or O models w/o gold.

✳ *Superposed Presentation III Superlite* - S, T, or U style engraving.

	100%	98%	95%	90%	80%	70%	60%
12 ga. (16 mfg.)	$11,500	$10,500	$9,000	$7,500	$5,200	$4,600	$3,500
20 ga. (85 mfg.)	$16,500	$15,000	$12,000	$9,000	$6,500	$5,100	$4,000
28 ga. (36 mfg.)	$19,000	$17,500	$15,000	$12,500	$9,200	$7,700	$6,200
.410 bore (37 mfg.)	$14,000	$13,000	$11,000	$8,500	$7,200	$5,700	$4,500

Add $2,000 per extra barrel.
Add 30% for an all option gun (checkered buttstock, oil finish, three piece forend).
Add 25% for an all option FKLT gun (very rare).
Add 15% for J. Baerten signed gun (rare).
Subtract 35% for Trap or Skeet Models.

✳ *Superposed Presentation IV Superlite w/Gold* - W style engraving.

	100%	98%	95%	90%	80%	70%	60%
12 ga. (14 mfg.)	$18,000	$17,000	$15,000	$12,500	$10,200	$8,100	$6,000
20 ga. (44 mfg.)	$22,000	$20,000	$16,500	$13,000	$9,500	$7,100	$5,750
28 ga. (20 mfg.)	$27,000	$25,000	$21,000	$16,000	$13,000	$11,000	$9,250
.410 bore (35 mfg.)	$19,000	$18,000	$15,000	$13,000	$11,000	$9,000	$7,100

Add $2,500 per extra barrel.
Add 30% for an all option gun (checkered buttstock, oil finish, three piece forend).
Add 25% for an all option FKLT gun (very rare).
Add 15% for J. Baerten signed gun (rare).
Subtract 35% for Trap or Skeet Models.

Subtract 35% for plain models w/o gold.

LIEGE (FN B-26) - 12 ga., 26 1/2, 28 or 30 in. barrels, various chokes, boxlock, auto ejectors, non- selective single trigger, vent. rib, checkered pistol grip stock. Approx. 10,000 mfg. 1973-75 by FN.

	$1,325	$1,050	$850	$685	$610	$570	$540

This model is also known as the B-26.

GRADING - PPGS™	100%	98%	95%	90%	80%	70%	60%

GRAND LIEGE - similar to Liege, except has deluxe checkered walnut stock and forearm, and engraved receiver. Disc.

	$1,650	$1,225	$1,000	$850	$750	$700	$650

B-26 - with BAC markings. Mfg. 1973-75.

	$1,250	$1,000	$825	$685	$610	$570	$540

B-27 - F.N. manufactured modified B-26, imported into the U.S. in 1984, same action as Liege (B 26), blue or satin finished receiver with light engraving, no BAC markings and never cataloged.

✳ *B-27 Standard Game* - 28 in. barrels, 9/32 in. vent. rib, pistol grip stock, Schnabel forearm, SST, blue receiver, choking M/F only.

	$1,325	$1,050	$850	$685	$610	$570	$540

Also available in Skeet model with gold "Browning" logo on blue receiver. Prices are the same.

✳ *B-27 Deluxe Game (Grade II)* - similar to Standard Grade, except has 30 in. barrels, better wood and English scroll engraved satin finished receiver, choking M/F only.

	$1,425	$1,100	$1,000	$850	$750	$650	$550

✳ *B-27 Grand Deluxe Game* - 28 in. IC/IM & M/F choked barrels, game scene engraved, signed by the engraver, 90% receiver coverage.

	$1,575	$1,200	$1,075	$900	$775	$660	$595

This model was also available in a Trap configuration - values are about the same as above.

✳ *B-27 Deluxe Skeet* - similar to Deluxe Game (Grade II), except is designed for skeet shooting.

	$1,325	$1,050	$850	$685	$610	$570	$540

International Skeet is also available at same price; hand fit pistol grip with stippling and International Type recoil pad.

✳ *B-27 Deluxe Trap* - similar to Deluxe Game (Grade II), except is configured for trap shooting.

	$1,325	$1,050	$850	$685	$610	$570	$540

✳ *B-27 City of Liege Commemorative* - limited edition of 250 units manufactured to commemorate the 1,000th anniversary of the city of Liege, cased. Only 29 imported into the U.S.

	$1,750	$1,500	$1,225	N/A	N/A	N/A	N/A

ST-100 - 12 ga., Belgian mfg., O/U trap configuration with separated barrels and adj. point of impact, manufactured 1979-81 for European sale mostly, floating VR, ST, deluxe checkered walnut stock and forearm, non-BAC model.

	$3,500	$2,750	$2,000	$1,850	$1,200	$975	$825

SUPERPOSED WATERFOWL SERIES - 12 ga., 500 made of each issue, 7 gold inlays with extensive engraving on French Grey receiver, lightning action, 28 in. barrels, checkered buttstock, full-length walnut case, factory inventories were depleted on Mallard, Pintail, and Black Duck Issues in 1989.

Add 20% for 3 gun set with same serial number.

✳ *Superposed Waterfowl 1981 Mallard Issue*

	$9,500	$7,500	$6,000	N/A	N/A	N/A	N/A

Last MSR was $7,000.

This issue was sold out in 1988.

✳ *Superposed Waterfowl 1982 Pintail Issue*

	$9,500	$7,500	$6,000	N/A	N/A	N/A	N/A

Last MSR was $7,000.

✳ *Superposed Waterfowl 1983 Black Duck Issue*

	$9,500	$7,500	$6,000	N/A	N/A	N/A	N/A

Last MSR was $8,800.

GRADING - PPGS™	100%	98%	95%	90%	80%	70%	60%

SUPERPOSED SHOTGUN: 1983-86 MFG. - 12 or 20 ga. In 1983, Browning announced renewed production of the famous Belgian "Superposed" O/U in Grade I only. Available in Lightning or Superlight models, 3 in. chambers in Lightning 20 ga., 26 1/2 or 28 in. barrels. Belgian manufactured from 1983-86.

* *Superposed Shotgun Grade I (1983-86 mfg.)* - limited mfg., not compatible with steel shot, featured select walnut stock/forearm and extra engraving.

	100%	98%	95%	90%	80%	70%	60%
Lightning	$2,800	$2,150	$1,550	$950	$800	$675	$550
Superlight	$3,750	$3,300	$2,750	$1,850	$1,400	$1,000	$850

Last MSR was $1,995.

    Add 25% for 20 ga.

SUPERPOSED CLASSIC SERIES - 20 ga. only, 26 in. barrels, less than 2,500 manufactured in Classic model and under 350 manufactured in Gold Classic. Both editions feature multiple engraved scenes and a special silver grey finish. Select American walnut featuring oil finish. Available 1986 only.

	100%	98%	95%	90%	80%	70%	60%
	$4,000	$3,350	$2,750	N/A	N/A	N/A	N/A

Last MSR was $2,000.

* *Superposed Gold Classic* - 8 gold inlays, select walnut forearm and stock are both checkered and carved, many were shipped back to Belgium due to poor sales domestically. Available 1986 only.

	100%	98%	95%	90%	80%	70%	60%
	$7,250	$6,000	$4,150	N/A	N/A	N/A	N/A

Last MSR was $6,000

SHOTGUNS: O/U, SUPERPOSED HIGH GRADES: 1985-PRESENT

Browning, in 1985, resumed production of the Superposed in Pigeon, Pointer, Diana, and Midas grades. They were available in 12 and 20 ga. only, in either a Lightning or Superlight configuration. These higher grades were custom ordered from the factory with delivery ranging from 8 to more than 12 months. Custom options could be special ordered on each grade with corresponding prices being higher than shown below. B-25 engraving patterns on these various grades will nearly duplicate those styles manufactured before 1976. Skeet models were not available.

Be wary of non-factory upgraded Superposed higher grade models. These upgraded guns have very nice workmanship, but are valued at approx. 50% less than a factory guns in similar grade/gauge, and barrel length. Non-factory engraving has been done by: R. Capece, Dubois, Diet, and Bee. It is strongly advised to get a factory letter from Glen Jensen in the Browning Historical Dept. to guarantee the original configuration of a Superposed.

Superposed: Custom Shop Current Pricing & Models

In 2000, Browning changed the nomenclature of their B-25 shotgun Series. Prices reflect current custom shop MSRs. These new boxlock grades include: Special Woodcock $23,749, Special Duck $23,916, Special Pigeon $25,049, Trap Evolution 2 $23,899, Traditionnel $24,049, Sporting 207 Gold 25 $23,382, US Model B $20,866, Diana UK $31,082, and Grades B11 - $20,716 (disc. 2003, reintroduced 2006), B12 - $20,833 (disc. 2003, reintroduced 2006), B2G - $20,949 (disc. 2003, reintroduced 2004), C11 - $29,565, C12 - $30,549, C1G - $28,082, C2G - $30,682, D11 - $41,415, D12 - $40,882, D2L $44,248, D4G $45,082, D5G - $46,165, Special Automn - $49,165, Cheverny - $57,081.

Additionally, the Browning Custom Shop also offers the following shotguns in various grades with engraved sideplates: Grade II - $23,234 (disc. 2003), C2S - $41,082, Grade E1 - $56,798, Grade F1 - $58,331, Grade I1 - $57,831, Grade M1 - $60,131, Grade M2 - $57,831, Special Perdrix - $73,214, Windsor Or - $70,131, Chenonceau - $74,664, Cheverny - $76,330, D5G Sideplate - $73,747, and the Special Automn $73,080. These new grades are special order only through the Browning Custom Shop.

Grade I Traditional, Pigeon Grade, Pointer Grade, Diana Grade, and Midas Grade Superposed are listed separately under the B-25 model listing.

GRADING - PPGS™	100%	98%	95%	90%	80%	70%	60%

Add 20% for 20 ga. on previously owned models.
Add approx. $1,250 for a previously owned extra set of barrels.
Add $6,479 - $11,954 per extra set of barrels on currently manufactured Superposed models, depending on the grade.

B-25 - 12 or 20 ga. only, original Superposed Model manufactured entirely from parts fabricated in Herstal, Belgium. Also available in Superlight configuration. This older nomenclature series was discontinued domestically in 1999, but the Custom Shop is still producing these grades.

✳ *B-25 Grade I Traditional*

	100%	98%	95%	90%	80%	70%	60%
	$15,550	N/A	N/A	N/A	N/A	N/A	N/A

Last MSR was $19,433.

✳ *B-25 Pigeon Grade*
MSR $25,049

	$20,000	N/A	N/A	N/A	N/A	N/A	N/A

✳ *B-25 Pointer C Grade*
MSR $27,416

	$21,950	N/A	N/A	N/A	N/A	N/A	N/A

✳ *B-25 Diana C Grade*
MSR $28,916

	$23,150	N/A	N/A	N/A	N/A	N/A	N/A

✳ *B-25 Midas D Grade*
MSR $35,832

	$28,650	N/A	N/A	N/A	N/A	N/A	N/A

B-25 125th ANNIVERSARY - 12 ga. only, 2 3/4 in. chamber, 28 in. VR barrels with fixed M/F chokes and 8mm rib, Lightning style stock and forearm with oil finish and black buttplate, case colored receiver with gold border and gold enhanced 125th Anniversary logo. 10 mfg. 2003 only.

	$13,750	$5,250	$3,750	N/A	N/A	N/A	N/A

Last MSR was $15,219.

B-125 - 12 or 20 ga. only, retains all the features of the original Superposed, except parts were subcontracted worldwide to decrease production costs and were assembled "in the white" at Herstal's Custom Gun Shop in Belgium, choice of three different engraving styles and two receiver finishes. Mfg. 1988-2003.

✳ *B-125 Hunting Model* - available in either Hunting Lightning or Superlight configuration.

❖ **B-125 Hunting Model w/"A" Style Engraving** - blue frame with border engraving featuring Browning logo engraved on each side.

	$3,400	$2,750	$2,150	$1,700	$1,450	$1,275	$1,050

Last MSR was $3,925.

❖ **B-125 Hunting Model w/"B" Style Engraving** - coin finished frame with smaller game scene engravings.

	$3,700	$3,100	$2,250	$1,800	$1,500	$1,300	$1,100

Last MSR was $4,360.

❖ **B-125 Hunting Model w/"C" Style Engraving** - coin finished frame with elaborate scroll work and game scene engraving.

	$4,100	$3,475	$2,450	$1,900	$1,600	$1,400	$1,200

Last MSR was $4,903.

✳ *B-125 Sporting Clays Model* - 12 ga. only, designed for sporting clays competition and included Invector-Plus choke tube system.

❖ **B-125 Sporting Clays Model w/"A" Style Engraving** - blue frame with border engraving featuring Browning logo engraved on each side.

	$3,400	$2,750	$2,150	$1,700	$1,450	$1,275	$1,050

Last MSR was $3,925.

GRADING - PPGS™	100%	98%	95%	90%	80%	70%	60%

❖ **B-125 Sporting Clays Model w/"B" Style Engraving** - coin finished frame with smaller game scene engravings.

	$3,700	$3,100	$2,250	$1,800	$1,500	$1,300	$1,100

Last MSR was $4,360.

❖ **B-125 Sporting Clays Model w/"C" Style Engraving** - coin finished frame with elaborate scroll work and game scene engraving.

	$4,100	$3,475	$2,450	$1,900	$1,600	$1,400	$1,200

Last MSR was $4,903.

✳ *B-125 Trap Model* - standard F-1 style engraving.

	$4,950	$3,550	$2,325	$1,750	$1,450	$1,275	$1,050

Last MSR was $5,452.

SHOTGUNS: SxS

The Browning Custom Shop in Herstal, Belgium currently offers several SxS sidelock models manufactured by Lebeau-Courally. Models include the LC1 (blued receiver, $17,516 MSR), and LC2 (coin finished receiver, $22,799 MSR).

B-SS - 12 or 20 ga., 26, 28, or 30 in. barrels, various chokes, engraved boxlock action, auto ejectors, checkered pistol grip walnut stock, beavertail forearm, SST. Mfg. 1971-88 by Miroku.

	100%	98%	95%	90%	80%	70%	60%
12 ga.	$1,175	$1,000	$850	$725	$650	$550	$450
20 ga.	$2,250	$2,000	$1,775	$1,525	$1,300	$1,100	$950

Last MSR was $775.

Early guns had a single non-selective trigger (silver plated) - subtract 10%.

✳ *B-SS Grade II* - satin greyed steel receiver featuring an engraved pheasant, duck, quail, and dogs. Disc. 1983.

	$3,100	$2,650	$2,250	$1,775	$1,350	$1,100	$925

B-SS SPORTER - 12 or 20 ga., straight grip stock, longer lower tang, slimmed down beavertail forearm, oil finish, 26 or 28 in. barrels. Disc. 1988.

	$2,000	$1,750	$1,500	$1,225	$950	$800	$650

Last MSR was $775.

Add 50% for 20 ga., if in 95%+ condition.

✳ *B-SS Sporter Grade II* - satin greyed steel receiver featuring an engraved pheasant, duck, quail and dogs. Disc. 1983.

	$3,150	$2,700	$2,225	$1,800	$1,350	$1,100	$925

Add 50% for 20 ga., if in 95%+ condition.

✳ *B-SS "Bottle" Sporter Set* - 12 and 20 ga., wild turkey and wood duck inlays on 12 ga., wood ducks only on 20 ga., straight grip sporter stock, shoulders are sculpted and engraved, Exhibition grade walnut, engraving was done in Belgium by custom shop, cased in Browning Airways case. Less than 100 mfg. circa 1976.

	100%	98%	95%	90%	80%	70%	60%
Set	$6,950	$6,500	$5,850	$5,250	$4,600	$4,000	$3,450
12 ga.	$2,750	$2,400	$2,100	$1,850	$1,600	$1,400	$1,200
20 ga.	$3,250	$2,950	$2,650	$2,300	$2,000	$1,800	$1,600

This model got its nickname from a Mr. Bottles Sporting Goods store in Wichita, KS, who special ordered 100 sets of these guns circa 1976.

B-SS SIDELOCK - 12 or 20 ga., engraved sidelock action in satin grey finish, ST, 26 or 28 in. barrels, English select walnut stock, splinter forend. Mfg. 1983-88 in Miroku in Japan.

	100%	98%	95%	90%	80%	70%	60%
12 ga.	$3,750	$3,300	$2,725	$2,275	$1,875	$1,500	$1,250
20 ga.	$4,995	$4,300	$3,650	$2,900	$2,300	$1,875	$1,500

Last MSR was $2,000.

GRADING - PPGS™	100%	98%	95%	90%	80%	70%	60%

SHOTGUNS: SEMI-AUTO, A-5 1903-1998 MFG.

BROWNING CHOKES AND THEIR CODES (ON REAR LEFT-SIDE OF BARREL)
* designates full choke (F).
*- designates improved modified choke (IM).
** designates modified choke (M).
**- designates improved cylinder choke (IC).
**$ designates skeet (SK).
*** designates cylinder bore (CYL).
INV. designates barrel is threaded for Browning Invector choke tube system.
INV. PLUS designates back-bored barrels.
Miroku manufactured A-5s can be determined by year of manufacture in the following manner:
RV suffix - 1975, RT - 1976, RR - 1977, RP - 1978, RN - 1979, PM - 1980, PZ - 1981, PY - 1982,
PX - 1983, PW - 1984, PV - 1985, PT - 1986, PR - 1987, PP - 1988, PN - 1989, NM - 1990, NZ -
1991, NY - 1992, NX - 1993, NW - 1994, NV - 1995, NT - 1996, NR - 1997, NP - 1998.
Browning resumed importation from F.N. in 1946. On November 26, 1997, Browning announced
that the venerable Auto-5 would finally be discontinued. Final shipments were made in February,
1998. Over 3 million A-5s were mfg. by F.N. in all configurations between 1903-1976. 1976-1998
mfg. was by Miroku.
NOTE: Barrels are interchangeable between older Belgian A-5 models and recent Japanese A-
5s mfg. by Miroku, if the gauge and chamber length are the same. A different barrel ring design
and thicker barrel wall design might necessitate some minor sanding of the inner forearm on the
older model, but otherwise, these barrels are fully interchangeable.
NOTE: The use of steel shot is recommended ONLY in those recent models manufactured in
Japan - NOT in the older Belgian variations.
Recoil operation, scroll engraved receiver, 1946-1951 mfg. has safety in front of triggerguard.
1951-1976 mfg. has crossbolt safety behind the trigger. Post-war 16 ga. Imports by Browning
are chambered for 2 3/4 in., and have either a horn (disc. 1964) or plastic (1962-1976) buttplate,
high luster wood finish (disc. 1962) or glossy lacquer (1962-1976) finish. Walnut buttstock has
either round knob pistol grip (disc. 1967) or flat knob (new 1967). In today's A-5 marketplace, 16
and 20 ga. guns with shorter barrels and open chokes are more desirable than a 30 in. 12 ga.
gun with full choke barrel.
The publisher would like to thank Mr. H.M. Shirley, Jr. for his contributions to the A-5 section.

> **Add 10%-15% for NIB condition on Belgian mfg. A-5 models only, depending on desirability.**
>
> **Add 10-15% for the round knob (rounded pistol grip knob on stock, pre-1967 mfg.) variation on FN models only, depending on desirability.**
>
> **Add $200-$375 per additional barrel, depending on the gauge, barrel length, choke, and condition (smaller gauge open chokes are the most desirable).**

AUTO-5 STANDARD - 1903-1940 MFG. - 12 ga. (introduced in Sept., 1903, Browning discontinued imports Dec., 1903), 16 ga. (introduced in 1909, but not in the U.S.), in 1923, Browning resumed importing both 12 and 16 ga. in four grades that differ in engraving, inlays, and grade of wood, both gauges were available with 26-32 in. barrel, recoil operated, 4 shot mag. with cutoff, various chokes, checkered pistol grip stock, horn buttplate, also available in a 3 shot version with shorter magazine tube to limit capacity to 3 rounds from 1932-1940. Importation temporarily ceased in 1940 with the German occupation of Belgium, ser. no. range 1-224,596 (12 ga.) and 1-126,175 (16 ga.).

	100%	98%	95%	90%	80%	70%	60%
Grade 1	$725	$625	$500	$375	$325	$285	$250
Solid matte rib	$800	$725	$600	$475	$375	$325	$285
With vent. rib	$875	$775	$675	$575	$465	$375	$325
Grade 2 (disc.1937)	$1,425	$1,175	$950	$825	$725	$650	$575
Solid matte rib	$1,650	$1,450	$1,150	$950	$760	$685	$625
With vent. rib	$1,850	$1,625	$1,325	$1,050	$825	$775	$675
Grade 3 (disc. 1940)	$2,825	$2,500	$2,200	$1,950	$1,600	$1,375	$1,095

GRADING - PPGS™	100%	98%	95%	90%	80%	70%	60%
Solid matte rib	$3,050	$2,675	$2,350	$2,100	$1,750	$1,500	$1,195
With vent. rib	$3,375	$2,925	$2,575	$2,300	$2,000	$1,700	$1,350
Grade 4 (disc. 1940)	$4,250	$3,800	$3,400	$3,050	$2,550	$2,050	$1,650
Solid matte rib	$4,525	$4,175	$3,750	$3,350	$2,975	$2,350	$2,050
Grade 4 w/vent. rib	$4,900	$4,300	$4,100	$3,200	$2,800	$2,300	$2,100

Subtract 25% for pre-WWII 16 ga. A-5s chambered for 2 9/16 in. shells.

Early models with safety mounted in front of trigger guard are not as desirable as there are potential safety problems inherent in the design.

Pre-WWII 16 ga. A-5s could be chambered for 2 9/16 in. shells. These shotguns are considerably less desirable than 16 ga. A-5s chambered for 2 3/4 in. modern shotshells. Since some guns have been modified to 2 3/4 in., careful inspection is advised before purchasing or shooting. The 2 9/16 chambered guns can be modified by the Browning Service Dept. to accept 2 3/4 in. shells if so desired.

"AMERICAN BROWNING" AUTO-5 - 12, 16, or 20 ga., Remington-produced model of the Auto-5, very similar to the Remington Model 11, except with Browning logo, mag. cut-off, and different engraving, over 38,000 mfg. in 12 ga. (ser. no. range B5000- B43129), over 14,000 in 16 ga. (ser. no. range A5000-A19450), and 11,000 in 20 ga. (ser. no. range C5000- C16152), stocks have Remington style round knob pistol grip. Mfg. 1940-47.

	$595	$475	$400	$350	$300	$275	$250

Add 10% for vent. rib and/or 20 ga.

An easy way to identify this configuration is to look for the "A", "B", or "C" prefix on the left side of receiver.

AUTO-5 STANDARDWEIGHT - 12 (disc. 1970) or 16 (disc. 1964) ga., 26-32 in. barrel, various chokes, checkered walnut stock and forearm, between 7 1/3-8 lbs. Browning resumed importation from F.N. in 1946.

	100%	98%	95%	90%	80%	70%	60%
Plain barrel	$625	$525	$450	$375	$325	$295	$250
Matted rib (solid)	$795	$650	$550	$450	$375	$325	$295
Vent rib	$995	$825	$675	$550	$475	$425	$395

Subtract 20% for front safety.

Note: Watch for cracked forearms on all A-5 models (due to barrel recoil.)

Barrel addresses appeared as follows: circa 1930-1958 "St. Louis, M.O.", 1959-1968 "St. Louis, Missouri and Montreal P.Q.", 1969-1976 "Morgan, Utah and Montreal, P.Q.". Barrels are serial numbered to the gun until 1953. Make sure barrel address date matches year of mfg. (see listings in the back of this text).

AUTO-5 LIGHTWEIGHT (LIGHT 12 & LIGHT 20) - 12 (new 1947) or 20 (new 1958) ga., recoil operated, 26, 28, or 30 in. barrel, various chokes, gold plated trigger, checkered pistol grip round knob (disc. 1967) or flat knob (mfg. 1967-1976) stock, approx. 10 oz. lighter than Standard weight.

	100%	98%	95%	90%	80%	70%	60%
FN model	$775	$650	$525	$450	$390	$370	$340
FN-vent. rib	$1,150	$925	$735	$630	$525	$470	$415

Add 40% for 20 ga.

Subtract 30% for Cutts or Polychoke.

✳ *Auto-5 Light 12 Miroku* - 12 ga. only, 22, 26, 28, or 30 in. VR (became standard 1986) barrel with Invector choke system, approx. 8-8 1/2 lbs. Mfg. 1976-Feb. 1998.

	$825	$630	$550	$490	$435	$385	$330

Last MSR was $840.

Subtract 10% without Invector chokes.

✳ *Auto-5 Light 20 Miroku* - 20 ga. only, 2 3/4 in. chamber, similar to original Belgian Light 20, VR, 22 (new 1995), 26, or 28 in. barrel, Invector chokes standard until 1993, Invector Plus choking became standard 1994, 6 lbs. 12 oz - 7 lbs. 2 oz. Mfg. 1987-1997.

	$950	$750	$625	$525	$450	$400	$350

Last MSR was $840.

AUTO-5 MAGNUM - 12 (new 1958) or 20 (new 1967) ga., 3 in. chamber, 26, 28, 30, or 32 in. barrels, various chokes, VR or etched, 8 1/2 - 9 lbs. Mfg. 1958-1976 by FN, 1976-Feb. 1998 by Miroku.

	100%	98%	95%	90%	80%	70%	60%
FN model.	$875	$775	$650	$525	$450	$395	$365
FN-vent. rib.	$1,150	$975	$850	$750	$650	$550	$450

    Add 15% for 20 ga.

Between 1976-1985 approx. 2,000 Belgian 12 ga. A-5 Mags. were imported into the U.S. These late models can be differentiated by serialization - also, slight premiums may be asked.

✷ *Auto-5 Mag. Miroku* - 12 or 20 ga., VR barrel with Invector choke system until 1993, Invector Plus choking became standard 1994, 8 1/2 - 9 lbs. Disc. 1997.

	100%	98%	95%	90%	80%	70%	60%
	$925	$775	$650	$575	$495	$425	$375

Last MSR was $866.

    Subtract 10% without Invector chokes.

AUTO-5 STALKER - 12 ga. only, 2 3/4 (Light-12) or 3 (Mag. Stalker) in. chamber, 22 (Light-12 only), 26, 28, or 30, or 32 (Mag. only) in. VR barrel with Invector chokes, black matte finish graphite-fiberglass stock and forearm, matte finished metal, recoil pad, 8 lbs. 1 oz. - 8 lbs. 13 oz. Mfg. by Miroku 1992-1997.

	100%	98%	95%	90%	80%	70%	60%
	$850	$650	$550	$495	$435	$395	$335

Last MSR was $840.

    Add approx. $100 for Mag. Stalker.

AUTO-5 BUCK SPECIAL - 12, 16, or 20 ga., included Lightweight, Standardweight, and Magnum Models, 24 in. barrel, slug bore, adj. sight, optional sling studs and sling, between 1985-88, Buck Special barrels were available at additional cost. Introduced in 1962, mfg. by F.N. until 1976, and by Miroku from 1976-1984, and again in 1989.

✷ *Auto-5 Buck Special FN Mfg. 12 Ga.*

	100%	98%	95%	90%	80%	70%	60%
	$1,195	$975	$875	$750	$675	$495	$430

    Add 30% for Sweet 16 model.
    Add 25% for 20 ga.

This model was made in Light 12, Standard 12, 3 in. Mag. 12, Sweet 16, Standard 16, Lightweight 20 and Lightweight 20 Mag. (new 1967) configurations.

✷ *Auto-5 Buck Special Miroku Model* - mfg. 1989-97.

	100%	98%	95%	90%	80%	70%	60%
	$825	$675	$575	$500	$415	$375	$330

Last MSR was $829.

AUTO-5 SKEET - 12, 16, or 20 ga., Lightweight models with 26 or 28 in. skeet bored, vent. rib barrel. Pre 1976 mfg. by F.N., 1976-1983 mfg. by Miroku.

✷ *Auto-5 Skeet FN Mfg.*

	100%	98%	95%	90%	80%	70%	60%
	$1,050	$850	$675	$575	$500	$395	$350

    Add 20% for vent. rib.
    Add 20% for 20 ga.

✷ *Auto-5 Skeet Miroku Model*

	100%	98%	95%	90%	80%	70%	60%
	$895	$775	$625	$550	$490	$435	$385

    Add 20% for 20 ga.

AUTO-5 TRAP MODEL - 12 ga. only, similar to Standard, 30 in. full vent. rib barrel, 8 1/2 lbs., mfg. by FN until 1970.

	100%	98%	95%	90%	80%	70%	60%
	$1,150	$995	$825	$750	$650	$550	$450

GRADING - PPGS™	100%	98%	95%	90%	80%	70%	60%

AUTO-5 SWEET 16 - 16 ga., 2 9/16 in. chamber from 1937-1940, and 2 3/4 in. chamber from 1947-1975, similar configuration to Lightweight, 12 and 20 ga., gold plated trigger, 10 oz. lighter than Standardweight Model 16 ga., 1937-1940 mfg. Sweet Sixteens were available in pre-war Grades I, III, and IV. Mfg. 1937-1975 by F.N.

	100%	98%	95%	90%	80%	70%	60%
Plain Barrel	$1,075	$950	$825	$725	$625	$500	$425
Solid Matte Rib	$1,650	$1,300	$1,075	$950	$825	$700	$600
Vent. Rib	$2,100	$1,650	$1,225	$1,050	$875	$775	$675

Subtract 20% for front safety.
Subtract 20% for 2 9/16 in. chamber.

✳ *Auto-5 Sweet 16 Miroku* - 16 ga. only, similar to original Belgian Sweet 16, VR, Invector choke standard. Mfg. 1987-92.

	100%	98%	95%	90%	80%	70%	60%
	$1,295	$1,075	$975	$825	$725	$575	$500

Last MSR was $720.

AUTO-5 TWO MILLIONTH COMMEMORATIVE - 12 ga., 2,500 mfg., 1971-74 mfg., special walnut, engraving, high-lustre bluing, cased with Browning book. Issue price was $550-$700, serial range 2,000,000-1 to 2,000,000-2,500.

	100%	98%	95%	90%	80%	70%	60%
	$2,500	$1,750	$1,200	N/A	N/A	N/A	N/A

AUTO-5 POLICE CONTRACT - 12 ga. only, 5 or 8 (factory extended) shot mag., black enamel finish on receiver and barrel, can be recognized by the European "POL" police markings below serial number, 24 in. barrel. Imported in limited quantities during 1999.

	100%	98%	95%	90%	80%	70%	60%
5 shot mag.	N/A	$550	$525	$495	$450	$400	$375
8 shot mag.	N/A	$1,200	$995	$895	$795	$750	$650

A-5 CLASSIC SERIES - 12 ga., 5,000 mfg. in Classic model, 500 mfg. in Gold Classic. Both editions feature game scenes, John M. Browning's profile, and other inscriptions, special silver grey finished receiver. Introduced 1984.

✳ *A-5 Gold Classic Model* - features 5 inlays depicting duck hunting scenes. Mfg. 1986 with inventory depleted 1989.

	100%	98%	95%	90%	80%	70%	60%
	$5,750	$3,900	$2,650	N/A	N/A	N/	N/A

Last MSR was $6,500.

✳ *A-5 Classic Model* - no inlays. Factory inventories were depleted in 1987.

	100%	98%	95%	90%	80%	70%	60%
	$2,000	$1,200	$995	N/A	N/A	N/A	N/A

Last MSR was $1,260.

FN CENTENARY EDITION - 12 or 16 ga., limited production mfg. 1989 to commemorate the 100th anniversary of FN, available for worldwide FN sales and not limited to Browning.

✳ *FN Centenary Edition 12 ga.* - 2 3/4 in. chamber, 28 in. VR barrel, Mod. choke, more engraving than a standard A-5, gold relief FN logo on left side of receiver, high grade French walnut flat knob pistol grip stock, 20 LPI checkering, ser. no. CENT 211 001 - 100, 100 mfg.

	100%	98%	95%	90%	80%	70%	60%
	$2,500	$1,750	$1,175	N/A	N/A	N/A	N/A

Last MSR was $2,100.

✳ *FN Centenary Edition 16 ga.* - 2 3/4 in. chamber, 26 in. VR barrel, Mod. choke, ornate engraving with gold relief inlay (24 Kt.), commemorative FN medallion on left side of receiver, high grade French walnut flat knob pistol grip stock, 25 LPI checkering, ser. no. CENT 221 001 - 010, 10 mfg.

	100%	98%	95%	90%	80%	70%	60%
	$7,500	$5,750	$4,250	N/A	N/A	N/A	N/A

Last MSR was $6,855.

GRADING - PPGS™	100%	98%	95%	90%	80%	70%	60%

A-5 BCA COMMEMORATIVE - 12 ga., 3 in. Mag., round knob, Belgian mfg., 1984 issue price was $595.

	$1,350	$1,050	$875	N/A	N/A	N/A	N/A

A-5 DU 50TH ANNIVERSARY

　❋ *A-5 DU Light 12* - 12 ga. only, 5,500 mfg. in 1987 only for Ducks Unlimited chapters throughout North America. Prices will fluctuate greatly from chapter to chapter as these guns were auctioned to the highest bidder. Receiver is specially engraved and has "Fiftieth Year" depicted on right side of receiver, deluxe checkered stock and forearm, grey finished receiver.

	$1,395	$995	$750	N/A	N/A	N/A	N/A

　❋ *A-5 DU Sweet 16* - 16 ga. only, companion 1988-89 DU auction gun, 4,500 mfg. 1988 only.

	$2,000	$1,550	$1,100	N/A	N/A	N/A	N/A

　❋ *A-5 DU Light 20* - 20 ga. only, companion 1990 DU auction gun, 4,500 mfg. 1990 only.

	$1,825	$1,495	$1,075	N/A	N/A	N/A	N/A

A-5 FINAL TRIBUTE - 12 ga. only, limited edition of 1,000 guns, features elaborate engraving on white receiver, the last of the A-5 semi-autos. Mfg. 1999 only, sellout occurred during 2000.

	$2,650	$2,300	$1,950	N/A	N/A	N/A	N/A

Last MSR was $1,330.

SHOTGUNS: SEMI-AUTO, DOUBLE AUTO MODELS

Add 10% for NIB condition on the following models.

STANDARD DOUBLE AUTO - 12 ga. only, 2 shot, 26, 28, or 30 in. barrel, various chokes, checkered pistol grip stock and forearm, blued steel receiver, approx. 7 1/2 lbs. Mfg. 1952-1960.

	$750	$600	$500	$425	$350	$300	$250
w/vent. rib or raised rib barrel	$850	$725	$625	$550	$450	$350	$300

LIGHTWEIGHT DOUBLE AUTO - similar to Standard Model, except has hiduminum (aircraft alloy) frame, anodized in velvet grey, dragon black, autumn brown, and forest green, appro. 6 3/4 lbs. Approx. 67,000 (all variations) mfg. 1952-56.

	$750	$600	$500	$425	$350	$300	$250
w/vent. rib. or raised rib	$850	$725	$625	$550	$450	$350	$300

Add 25% for autumn brown or forest green receiver.
Add 100%+ for all other colors (rare, only a few mfg.).

TWELVETTE DOUBLE AUTO - similar to Lightweight model, except has "Twelvette" stamped above loading port. Mfg. 1957-1971.

	$750	$600	$500	$450	$400	$350	$300
w/vent. rib or raised rib	$850	$725	$625	$550	$450	$350	$300

Add 25% for autumn brown or forest green receiver.
Add 100%+ for all other colors (rare, only a few mfg.).

TWENTYWEIGHT DOUBLE AUTO - similar to Twelvette, but 3/4 pound lighter, jet black finish with engraving accented with gold foil, "Twentyweight" stamped above loading port, 26 1/2 in. barrel only. Mfg. 1957-1971.

	$825	$675	$575	$500	$425	$375	$300
w/vent. rib	$925	$775	$650	$575	$525	$450	$395

SHOTGUNS: SEMI-AUTO, MISC. - RECENT MFG.

BROWNING CHOKES AND THEIR CODES (ON REAR LEFT-SIDE OF BARREL)
* designates full choke (F).

GRADING - PPGS™	100%	98%	95%	90%	80%	70%	60%

*- designates improved modified choke (IM).
** designates modified choke (M).
**- designates improved cylinder choke (IC).
**$ designates skeet (SK).
*** designates cylinder bore (CYL).

Add $195-$375 per additional barrel, depending on the condition and configuration.

B/2000 STANDARD - 12 or 20 ga. (new 1975), 26, 28, or 30 in. barrel, various chokes, vent. rib, gas operated, checkered pistol grip stock, Belgian manufactured but assembled in Portugal, approx. 115,000 imported (approx. 95,000 in 12 ga., and 20,000 in 20 ga.) into the U.S. between 1974-83.

	$425	$395	$350	$325	$300	$275	$250

Last MSR was $475.

Add 20% for 20 ga.

This model could be converted to accept 3 in. Mag. shotshells by simply installing a barrel chambered for 3 in. shells.

Even though production on this model ceased in 1979, assembly and sales were not discontinued until 1983.

B/2000 MAGNUM - similar to B/2000 Auto Shotgun, except with 3 in. chambered barrel (all receivers were the same), recoil pad, vent. rib.

	$450	$425	$375	$350	$325	$300	$275

B/2000 SKEET - similar to Standard, with 26 in. skeet bored barrel, floating vent. rib, skeet stock, pad.

	$425	$395	$350	$325	$300	$275	$250

B/2000 TRAP - similar to Standard, with 30 or 32 in. barrel bored F or IM, floating rib, Monte Carlo trap stock.

	$425	$395	$350	$325	$300	$275	$250

B/2000 BUCK SPECIAL - 12 or 20 ga., barrel sights on 24 in. barrel.

	$425	$395	$350	$325	$300	$275	$250

1976 CANADIAN OLYMPICS B2000 - 12 ga., 100 manufactured in 1976 for Canadian sales only, high polish blue with multiple gold inlays including Olympic crest, 30 in. barrel, cased. Issue price was $1,295.

	$1,495	$1,095	$850	N/A	N/A	N/A	N/A

MODEL B-80 - 12 or 20 ga., 3 in. capability by changing barrel, gas operation, 4 shot, hunting models use choice of steel or aluminum receiver, anodized aluminum was used in the Superlight (12 ga. mfg. 1984 only), 6 to 8 lbs. 1 oz. Buck special disc. 1984. Components manufactured by Beretta of Italy and finished and assembled FN's plant in Portugal. Mfg. 1981-late 1988, final inventory was sold in 1991. Invector chokes became standard in 1985.

	$450	$375	$325	$295	$275	$250	$230

Last MSR was $562.

Add 10% for Invector chokes.

Steel frames were reintroduced into production again in 1988.

✳ *Model B-80 Upland Special* - 12 or 20 ga., 2 3/4 in. chamber, 22 in. vent. rib barrel, straight grip stock, Invector chokes. Mfg. 1986-88.

	$525	$450	$395	$350	$325	$300	$275

Last MSR was $562.

MODEL B 80 DU COMMEMORATIVE - mfg. for American DU Chapters (The Plains and others), price fluctuates greatly as collector support is sometimes limited. Unless new, this model's values approximate those of the regular Model B-80. If NIB, values recently have been in the $795-$995 range.

GRADING - PPGS™	100%	98%	95%	90%	80%	70%	60%

A-500 (R) HUNTING - 12 ga. only, 3 in. chamber, new design utilizing short recoil system with a four- lug rotary bolt design, capable of shooting all 12 gauge loads interchangeably, magazine cut-off, 26, 28, or 30 in. VR barrel with Invector chokes standard, 24 in. barrel on Buck Special (fixed choke), high polished blue finish with red accents on receiver sides, gold trigger, checkered semi-pistol grip walnut stock with vent. recoil pad, 7 lbs. 11 oz. - 8 lbs. 1 oz. Mfg. 1987-93.

	$525	$450	$395	$350	$325	$300	$275

Last MSR was $560.

Add $33 for Buck Special variation (Invector chokes).

This model features fewer moving parts than many other semi-auto shotguns due to the short recoil operating system. From 1987-90, this model was the Model A-500 - R suffix was added in 1991.

A-500G HUNTING - similar to A-500, except is gas operated, distinguishable by "A-500G" in gold accents on receiver, capable of shooting all 2 3/4 or 3 in. shells interchangeably, approx. 8 lbs. Mfg. 1990-93.

	$575	$495	$425	$375	$340	$325	$295

Last MSR was $653.

A Buck Special variation was mfg. until 1992. No premiums currently exist.

✳ *A-500G Sporting Clays* - 12 ga. only, Sporting Clays variation with 30 in. VR barrel, 8 lbs. 2 oz. Mfg. 1992-93.

	$575	$495	$425	$375	$340	$325	$295

Last MSR was $653.

GOLD 3 IN. HUNTER - 12 or 20 ga., 3 in. chamber, self-cleaning piston rod gas action with self-regulation, alloy receiver with non-glare black finish and "Gold Hunter" on receiver side, 26, 28, or 30 (12 ga. only, disc. 2001) in. VR Invector Plus (12 ga. only) or Invector (20 ga. only) choked barrel with high polish bluing, cross-bolt safety, gloss finish checkered walnut stock and forearm with recoil pad (vent on 12 ga.), includes 3 choke tubes, 6 lbs. 12 oz. - 7 lbs. 10 oz. Parts mfg. in Belgium and final assembly in Portugal. Mfg. 1994-2005.

	$825	$575	$450	$375	$300	$275	$250

Last MSR was $1,025.

Do not use 12 ga. 3 1/2 in. chambered barrels on either a 2 3/4 or 3 in. receiver, or vice versa.

✳ *Gold Superlite Hunter* - 12 or 20 ga., similar to Gold 3 in. Hunter, except has new alloy magazine, "Gold SL" on receiver sides, 6 lbs. 7 oz. - 7 lbs., 15 oz. New 2006.

MSR $1,161	$975	$750	$535	$425	$325	$275	$250

GOLD 3 1/2 IN. HUNTER - 12 ga., 3 1/2 in. chamber, 24 (mfg. 2002-2003), 26, 28, or 30 (disc. 2003) in. VR barrel with Invector Plus choking, otherwise similar to Gold Hunter, 3-4 shot mag., approx. 7 3/4 lbs. Mfg. 1998-2005.

	$985	$725	$600	$550	$450	$375	$335

Last MSR was $1,190.

✳ *Gold 3 1/2 In. Superlite Hunter* - 12 ga., similar to Gold 3 1/2 in. Hunter, except has new alloy magazine, "Gold SL" engraved on receiver sides, approx. 7 1/4 lbs. Mfg. 2006-2007.

	$1,075	$900	$700	$525	$425	$350	$300

Last MSR was $1,279.

✳ *Gold 3 1/2 In. Turkey/Waterfowl Hunter* - similar to Gold 3 1/2 in. Hunter, full coverage (including barrel) Mossy Oak Break-Up camo finish, 24 in. VR barrel with extra full choke tube, 7 1/4 lbs. Mfg. 1999-2000.

	$875	$695	$600	$500	$425	$375	$335

Last MSR was $1,038.

✳ *Gold 3 1/2 In. NWTF Mossy Oak Break-Up* - 12 ga. only, 3 1/2 in. chamber, 24 in. VR barrel with 4 chokes tubes and Hi-Viz sight, full coverage Mossy Oak Break-Up camo pattern, Dura Touch armor coating became standard 2003, 7 1/4 lbs. Mfg. 2001-2002.

	100%	98%	95%	90%	80%	70%	60%
	$875	$695	$600	$525	$450	$385	$335

Last MSR was $1,221.

✳ *Gold 3 1/2 In. Mossy Oak New Break-Up/New Shadow Grass* - similar to Gold 3 1/2 in. Hunter, choice of full coverage (including barrel) Mossy Oak Break-Up, New Break-Up (standard beginning 2004) or Shadow Grass camo finish, 24 (Mossy Oak Break-Up only, disc. 2001), 26 (Mossy Oak Shadow Grass only), or 28 (Mossy Oak Shadow Grass only) in. VR backbored barrel with Invector Plus choke tubes, Dura-Touch armor coating became standard 2003, approx. 7 1/2 lbs. Mfg. 1999-2007.

	100%	98%	95%	90%	80%	70%	60%
	$900	$750	$650	$600	$500	$400	$350

Last MSR was $1,359.

✳ *Gold 3 1/2 In. Mossy Oak Duck Blind* - 12 ga. only, similar to Gold Mossy Oak New Break-Up, except has Mossy Oak Duck Blind camo coverage. Mfg. 2007.

	100%	98%	95%	90%	80%	70%	60%
	$900	$750	$650	$600	$500	$400	$350

Last MSR was $1,359.

✳ *Gold 3 1/2 In. NWTF Ultimate Turkey Gun* - 12 ga. only, similar to Gold NWTF Mossy Oak New Break-Up, except has extended full strut turkey tube and neoprene sling, 7 1/4 lbs. Mfg. 2003-2007.

	100%	98%	95%	90%	80%	70%	60%
	$1,100	$900	$725	$675	$600	$500	$450

Last MSR was $1,469.

GOLD FIELD HUNTER (CLASSIC) - similar to Gold Hunter, except has semi-hump back receiver design, magazine cutoff, adj. comb, and satin finished wood, 26 or 28 in. VR barrel. Mfg. 1999-2005.

	100%	98%	95%	90%	80%	70%	60%
	$800	$575	$450	$375	$300	$275	$250

Last MSR was $1,025.

This model was available through Full-line and Medallion dealers only.

✳ *Gold Superlite Field Hunter* - 12 or 20 ga., similar to Gold 3 in. Superlite Hunter, except is semi-humpback design, approx. 6 1/2 - 7 lbs. Mfg. 2006-2007.

	100%	98%	95%	90%	80%	70%	60%
	$1,025	$725	$525	$400	$300	$275	$250

Last MSR was $1,105.

✳ *Gold Turkey/Waterfowl Hunter Camo* - similar to Gold Hunter, full coverage (including barrel) Mossy Oak Break-Up camo finish, 24 in. VR barrel with Hi-Viz sights and extra full choke tube, 7 lbs. Mfg. 1999-2000.

	100%	98%	95%	90%	80%	70%	60%
	$750	$500	$400	$350	$295	$275	$250

Last MSR was $867.

✳ *Gold Mossy Oak New Break-Up/Shadow Grass* - 12 ga., similar to Gold 3 in. Hunter, choice of full coverage (including barrel) Mossy Oak New Break-Up or New Shadow Grass camo finish (New became standard in 2004), 24 (Mossy Oak Break-Up only, disc. 2004), 26, or 28 in. VR back-bored barrel with Invector Plus choke tubes, Dura-Touch armor coating became standard 2003, approx. 7 1/2 - 7 3/4 lbs. Mfg. 1999-2007.

	100%	98%	95%	90%	80%	70%	60%
	$850	$700	$525	$450	$325	$285	$250

Last MSR was $1,150.

✳ *Gold Mossy Oak Duck Blind* - 12 ga. only, similar to Gold Mossy Oak New Break-Up, except has Mossy Oak Duck Blind camo coverage. Mfg. 2007.

	100%	98%	95%	90%	80%	70%	60%
	$850	$700	$525	$450	$325	$285	$250

Last MSR was $1,150.

GRADING - PPGS™	100%	98%	95%	90%	80%	70%	60%

* *Gold NWTF Mossy Oak New Break-Up* - 12 ga. only, 3 in. chamber, drilled and tapped receiver, 24 in. VR barrel with 4 chokes tubes and Hi-Viz sight, full coverage Mossy Oak New Break-up camo pattern, Dura-Touch armor coating became standard 2003, 7 lbs. Mfg. 2001-2007.

	$850	$700	$575	$450	$375	$300	$250

Last MSR was $1,226.

* *Gold Classic High Grade Hunter* - 12 (disc. 2001) or 20 ga. (new 2002), similar to Gold Classic Hunter, except has nickel finished receiver featuring multiple gold inlays with ducks and dogs (disc.) or doves and quail (current) and light scroll engraving, deluxe checkered gloss finished walnut stock and forearm, 28 in. barrel only, 6 lbs. 14 oz. Mfg. 1999-2004.

	$1,575	$1,250	$1,050	$875	$725	$625	$550

Last MSR was $1,838.

This model was available through Full-line and Medallion dealers only.

GOLD MICRO - 20 ga. only, 3 in. chamber, 24 (new 2002) or 26 in. VR barrel, features shorter stock (13 7/8 LOP) and lighter weight, 6 lbs., 10 oz. Mfg. 2001-2005.

	$775	$575	$450	$375	$300	$275	$250

Last MSR was $1,025.

* *Gold Superlite Micro* - 20 ga. only, 3 in. chamber, 26 in. VR barrel, features shorter stock (13 7/8 LOP) and lighter weight, 6 lbs., 3 oz. Mfg. 2006-2007.

	$750	$650	$525	$400	$300	$275	$250

Last MSR was $1,105.

GOLD UPLAND SPECIAL - 12 or 20 ga., 3 in. chamber, 24 or 26 (20 ga. only) in. VR barrel, checkered satin finished straight grip stock, 6 3/4 (20 ga.) or 7 lbs. Mfg. 2001-2005.

	$750	$550	$425	$375	$300	$275	$250

Last MSR was $1,025.

GOLD FUSION - 12 or 20 (new 2002) ga., 3 in. chamber, 26, 28, or 30 (12 ga. only, new 2002) in. wide profile lightweight VR barrel with 5 Invector Plus chokes and Hi-Viz Pro-Comp sight system, checkered oil finished Turkish walnut stock and forearm, shim adj. stock system, alloy mag. tube, includes hardshell case, 6.25 - 7 lbs. Mfg. 2001-2007.

	$900	$650	$550	$400	$350	$295	$260

Last MSR was $1,152.

* *Gold Fusion High Grade* - 12 or 20 ga., 3 in. chamber, silver nitride receiver with engraving and gold inlays (mallards and lab on 12 ga., quail and pointer on 20 ga.), 26, 28, or 30 in. barrel with five interchangeable Invector Plus chokes, high grade Turkish walnut stock and forearm, shim adj. stock system with 1/4 in. adj. range, Hi-Viz TriComp sight system, includes hard case, 6 lbs., 6 oz. - 7 lbs. Mfg. 2005-2007.

	$1,825	$1,300	$1,125	$950	$850	$725	$625

Last MSR was $2,137.

GOLD EVOLVE - 12 ga. only, 3 in. chamber, features updated engraved receiver, magazine cap, and canted VR design, 26, 28, or 30 in. barrel, includes shim adj. stock system, newly designed checkered satin finished walnut stock and forearm, alloy mag. tube, Hi-Viz Pro-Comp sight system, approx. 7 lbs. Mfg. 2004-2007.

	$900	$650	$525	$425	$335	$285	$250

Last MSR was $1,220.

GRADING - PPGS™	100%	98%	95%	90%	80%	70%	60%

✴ *Gold Evolve Sporting* - 12 ga. only, similar to Gold Evolve, except has 2 3/4 in. chamber, 28 or 30 in. ported barrel, gold receiver accents, includes case, approx. 7 lbs. Mfg. 2006-2007.

	$950	$700	$550	$450	$350	$300	$250

Last MSR was $1,287.

Subtract 10% for 28 in. barrel on used guns.

GOLD DEER HUNTER - 12 or 20 (new 2001) ga., 3 in. chamber, 22 in. barrel with choice of 5 in. rifled Invector choke (disc. 1998) or rifled plain barrel, checkered satin finished stock and forearm, cantilevered scope mount, sling swivels, 6 3/4 (20 ga.) or 7 3/4 lbs. Mfg. 1997-2007.

	$900	$650	$525	$400	$325	$285	$250

Last MSR was $1,154.

Subtract approx. 10% for rifled choke tube (disc. 1998).

✴ *Gold Deer Hunter with Mossy Oak Break-Up Camo* - 12 ga., similar to Gold Deer Hunter, except has full Mossy Oak Break-Up or New Break-Up (standard 2004) camo coverage, rifled barrel standard. Mfg. 1999-2007.

	$950	$750	$625	$550	$450	$365	$335

Last MSR was $1,242.

GOLD 3 IN. STALKER - 12 ga., similar to Gold Hunter (3 in. chamber), except has checkered black composite stock and forearm with sling swivels, approx. 7 3/8 lbs. Mfg. 1998-2007.

	$800	$625	$475	$375	$300	$275	$250

Last MSR was $1,001.

✴ *Gold 3 In. Stalker Field (Classic)* - similar to Gold Stalker, except has semi-hump back receiver design, magazine cutoff and adj. comb, 26 or 28 in. VR barrel. Mfg. 1999-2007.

	$800	$625	$475	$375	$300	$275	$250

Last MSR was $1,001.

This model was available through Full-line and Medallion dealers only.

✴ *Gold 3 In. Turkey/Waterfowl Stalker* - similar to Gold Stalker, except has 24 in. VR barrel with extra full choke tube, Hi-Viz sights, matte non-glare wood and finish, 7 lbs. Mfg. 1999-2000.

	$800	$625	$475	$350	$300	$275	$250

Last MSR was $850.

✴ *Gold 3 In. NWTF Stalker* - 12 ga. only, 3 in. chamber, 24 in. VR barrel with 3 chokes tubes and Hi-Viz sight, 7 lbs. Mfg. 2001-2002.

	$635	$475	$415	$350	$295	$275	$250

Last MSR was $744.

✴ *Gold 3 In. Rifled Deer Stalker* - 12 ga. only, 22 in. rifled barrel, cantilevered scope mount, sling swivels, 7 3/4 lbs. Mfg. 1997-2007.

	$850	$625	$475	$395	$340	$295	$265

Last MSR was $1,108.

GOLD 3 1/2 IN. STALKER - 12 ga., 3 1/2 in. chamber, 26, 28, or 30 (disc. 2002) in. VR barrel with Invector Plus choking, otherwise similar to Gold Stalker, 3-4 shot mag., approx. 7 lbs. 10 oz. Mfg. 1998-2007.

MSR $1,171	$985	$725	$625	$525	$425	$375	$335

✴ *Gold 3 1/2 In. Turkey/Waterfowl Stalker* - similar to Gold 3 1/2 Stalker, except has 24 in. VR barrel with extra full choke tube, matte non-glare wood and finish, 7 1/4 lbs. Mfg. 1999-2000.

	$800	$650	$595	$500	$420	$375	$335

Last MSR was $1,022.

GRADING - PPGS™	100%	98%	95%	90%	80%	70%	60%

GOLD SPORTING CLAYS - 12 ga. only, similar specs as the Gold Hunter, except has 2 3/4 in. chamber, 28 or 30 in. ported barrel with Invector Plus choking, gloss finished walnut stock and forearm, adj. stock shims, Hi-Viz front sight, approx. 7 3/4 lbs. New 1996.

MSR $1,184	$1,000	$650	$500	$400	$325	$285	$260

This model is supplied standard with 2 interchangeable gas pistons for light or heavy loads.

✱ *Gold Golden Clays* - 12 ga. only, 2 3/4 in. chamber, engraved coin finished alloy receiver with gold accents and game birds, new scroll motif was introduced during 2005, deluxe satin finished checkered walnut stock and forearm, 28 or 30 in. VR ported barrel with Hi-Viz Tri-Comp front sight and mid-bead, approx. 7 3/4 lbs. New 1999.

MSR $1,941	$1,650	$1,225	$950	$850	$750	$650	$550

Subtract approx. 10% if with older engraving motif (non-scroll, disc. 2004).

✱ *Gold Sporting Ladies/Youth* - similar to Gold Sporting Clays, except has shorter 13 1/2 in. LOP stock, 28 in. barrel only, approx. 7 1/2 lbs. New 1999.

MSR $1,184	$1,000	$650	$500	$400	$325	$285	$260

❖ **Gold Golden Clays Ladies/Youth** - similar to Gold Sporting Ladies/Youth, except features coin finished receiver with "golden clays" rose motif and gold enhancements, satin finished select walnut stock and forearm. Mfg. 2005-2007.

$1,575	$1,175	$925	$850	$750	$650	$550

Last MSR was $1,848.

GOLD NRA SPORTING - 12 ga. only, 2 3/4 in. chamber, similar to Gold Sporting Clays, except has NRA logo/banner on left side of receiver, approx. 7 3/4 lbs. Mfg. 2006-2007.

$985	$625	$475	$375	$325	$285	$260

Last MSR was $1,160.

This model was supplied standard with 2 interchangeable gas pistons for light or heavy loads.

BSA 10 - while advertised, this gun had its model nomenclature changed to the Gold 10 Ga. before mfg. started.

GOLD LIGHT 10 GA. HUNTER/STALKER - 10 ga. Mag., 3 1/2 in. chamber, short stroke self-cleaning gas action, 4 shot mag., steel (disc. 2000) or aluminum (new 2001) receiver, choice of high polish (Hunter Model, disc. 2000), dull finish (Stalker Model, disc. 1999, reintroduced 2000) bluing, 24 (NWTF Model only with Break-Up, new 2001), 26, 28, or 30 (disc. 2001) in. VR standard Invector choke barrel, available with either high-gloss checkered walnut (Hunter, disc. 2002) stock/forearm, matte black fiberglass (Stalker, disc. 1998, reintroduced 2000-2003) stock/forearm, or choice of 100% camo treatment in Shadow Grass (disc. 2003), Break-Up (mfg. 2001-2003), New Shadow Grass (new 2005),Mossy Oak Duck Blind (new 2007), or New Break-Up (new 2004), vent recoil pad, Dura-Touch armor coating became standard for camo finishes during 2003, approx. 9 1/2 lbs. (aluminum receiver) or 10 lbs. 10 oz. (steel receiver, disc. 2000), mfg. by Miroku, Japan. New 1994.

MSR $1,390	$1,175	$875	$750	$625	$525	$450	$400

Add $116 for the NWTF Model with Mossy Oak New Break-Up.
Add 10% for extra 24 in. turkey barrel.
Subtract approx. 10% for matte black fiberglass stock and forearm.
Subtract 10% for steel receiver.

During 1999-2001, this model was packaged to include an extra 24 in. turkey barrel.

SILVER 3 IN. HUNTER - 12 or 20 ga., 3 in. chamber, semi-humpback design, silver finished aluminum alloy receiver, gas operating system similar to Gold Hunter, 26, 28, or 30 in. VR barrel, checkered satin finished stock and forearm with vent. recoil pad, includes three choke tubes, approx. 7 3/8 lbs. New 2006.

MSR $979	$825	$650	$525	$425	$350	$300	$250

GRADING - PPGS™	100%	98%	95%	90%	80%	70%	60%

SILVER MICRO - 20 ga., 3 in. chamber, 26 in. VR barrel, lightweight aluminum alloy receiver, semi-humpback design, satin finished walnut stock and forearm, compact dimensions for smaller shooters, three Invector Plus choke tubes, 6 lbs., 3 oz. New 2008.

MSR $979	$825	$650	$525	$425	$350	$300	$250

SILVER SPORTING MICRO - 12 ga., 2 3/4 in. chamber, 28 in. VR ported barrel, lightweight aluminum alloy receiver, semi-humpback design, satin finished walnut stock and forearm, features 13 3/4 in. LOP adj. in 1/4 in. increments using three included adj. spacers, premium Pachmayr Decelerator pad, three Invector Plus chokes, 7 lbs. New 2008.

MSR $1,132	$975	$800	$700	$600	$500	$400	$350

SILVER LIGHTNING 3 IN. - 12 ga., 3 in. chamber, 26 or 28 in. VR barrel, silver finished aluminum alloy receiver, semi-humpback design, gloss finished Lightning style walnut stock, three Invector Plus choke tubes, approx. 7 1/2 lbs. New 2008.

MSR $996	$840	$660	$525	$425	$350	$300	$250

This model is available only through Browning Full Line and Medallion dealers.

SILVER 3 IN. NWTF MOSSY OAK NEW BREAK-UP - 12 ga., 3 in. chamber, 24 in. VR barrel, aluminum alloy receiver, composite stock and forearm with Dura-Touch Armor coating and 100% Mossy Oak New Break-Up camo treatment, NWTF logo, Hi-Viz 4 in 1 fiber optic sight, three Invector Plus choke tubes, 7 lbs. New 2008.

MSR $1,151	$995	$775	$675	$575	$450	$400	$350

SILVER RIFLED DEER MOSSY OAK NEW BREAK-UP - 12 ga., 3 in. chamber, 22 in. rifled deer barrel, aluminum alloy receiver, composite stock and forearm with Dura-Touch Armor coating and 100% Mossy Oak New Break-Up camo treatment, cantilever scope mount, 7 lbs., 12 oz. New 2008.

MSR $1,199	$1,025	$775	$675	$575	$450	$400	$350

SILVER RIFLED DEER STALKER/SATIN - 12 ga., 3 in. chamber, 22 in. rifled deer barrel, choice of non-glare matte black finish composite stock and forearm (Stalker) or satin finished walnut stock with Dura-Touch Armor coating, cantilever scope mount, 7 lbs., 12 oz. New 2008.

MSR $1,069	$895	$700	$600	$500	$425	$375	$325

Add $50 for satin finished walnut stock and forearm with matte grey finished receiver.

SILVER 3 1/2 IN. HUNTER/STALKER - 12 ga. only, 26 or 28 in. barrel, choice of wood or black composite stock and forearm, Stalker has matte black metal finish, includes three choke tubes, approx. 7 1/2 lbs. New 2006.

MSR $1,076	$895	$700	$600	$500	$425	$375	$325

Add $52 for walnut stock and foream (Silver Hunter).

✶ *Silver 3 1/2 In. Mossy Oak Camo* - 12 ga. only, similar to Silver 3 1/2 In. Hunter/Stalker, except has choice of 100% Mossy Oak New Break-Up, Mossy Oak Duck Blind (new 2007), or New Shadowgrass (mfg. 2006 only) camo finish, 7 1/2 lbs. New 2006.

MSR $1,212	$1,025	$800	$700	$600	$500	$400	$325

SILVER LIGHTNING 3 1/2 IN. - 12 ga., similar to Silver Lightning 3 In., except has 3 1/2 in. chamber. New 2008.

MSR $1,147	$995	$775	$675	$575	$450	$400	$350

This model is available only through Browning Full Line and Medallion dealers.

GRADING - PPGS™	100%	98%	95%	90%	80%	70%	60%

SILVER 3 1/2 IN. NWTF MOSSY OAK NEW BREAK UP - 12 ga., 3 1/2 in. chamber, 24 in. barrel, aluminum alloy receiver, composite stock and forearm with Dura-Touch Armor coating and 100% Mossy Oak New Break-Up camo treatment, NWTF logo, Hi-Viz 4 in 1 fiber optic sight, three Invector Plus choke tubes, 7 1/4 lbs. New 2008.

MSR $1,295	$1,100	$750	$650	$550	$475	$425	$375

SHOTGUNS: SINGLE BARREL, BT-99 & BT-100

BT-99 STANDARD TRAP GUN - 12 ga., 32 or 34 in. vent. rib barrel, mod., imp. mod., or full choke, boxlock, auto ejector, checkered pistol grip with Monte Carlo or conventional style stock, beavertail forearm. Invector chokes became standard in 1986 and ported barrel with Invector Plus chokes and back boring became standard in 1992. Values below assume Invector Plus choking with ported barrel. Mfg. 1968-94 by Miroku.

	$995	$850	$700	$600	$550	$500	$450

Last MSR was $1,288.

Subtract $125 without Invector chokes or ported barrels.

* **BT-99 2 Barrel Set** - without Invector choking or barrel porting. Disc. 1983.

	$1,150	$995	$850	$750	$700	$650	$600

* **BT-99 Stainless** - features all stainless construction with Invector Plus ported 32 or 34 in. black VR barrel. Mfg. 1993-94.

	$1,500	$1,200	$1,000	$700	$575	$495	$450

Last MSR was $1,738.

* **BT-99 Current Mfg.** - choice of 32 or 34 in. back bored unported barrel with 11/32 in. high post rib and one full Invector Plus choke tube, satin finished conventional or adj. comb stock, beavertail forearm, ejector only, 8 lbs. 5 oz. New 2001.

MSR $1,438	$1,225	$895	$750	$600	$500	$425	$395

Add $294 for factory adj. comb stock.

* **BT-99 Micro** - 30 or 32 in. high post VR barrel, similar to BT-99, except has shortened 13 3/4 LOP, approx. 7 3/4 lbs. New 2004.

MSR $1,452	$1,125	$885	$750	$600	$500	$425	$395

* **BT-99 Pigeon Grade** - features higher grade walnut and gold receiver accents, Invector chokes and ported barrels. Mfg. 1993-94.

1978-1985 mfg.	$1,700	$1,500	$1,200	$1,100	$650	$575	$525
	$1,395	$1,150	$875	$600	$525	$495	$450

Last MSR was $1,505.

Older Pigeon Grade guns featured a satin grey receiver with deep relief, engraved pigeons in a fleur-de-lis background.

* **BT-99 Signature Painted** - features painted red/black stock with Browning logos on stock and forearm, Invector Plus ported barrels. Mfg. 1993-94.

	$1,250	$1,050	$900	$700	$600	$500	$330

Last MSR was $1,323.

* **BT-99 Golden Clays** - features gloss finished Grade V/Grade VI wood and gold outline receiver and inlays depicting a transitional hunting to clay pigeon scene, current mfg. includes ported barrel, adj. comb and LOP, and GraCoil recoil reduction, approx. 9 lbs. Mfg. 1994, reintroduced 2003.

MSR $3,759	$3,175	$2,125	$1,500	$1,150	$975	$875	$795

Subtract 15% for older mfg. w/o current features.

BT-99 PLUS GRADE I - similar to BT-99, except has adj. rib to control point of impact and new recoil reduction system that reduces felt recoil by 50%, stock has adj. comb and buttplate (recoil pad), back-bored barrel, Invector chokes, 8 3/4 lbs. Mfg. 1989-94.

		$1,775	$1,525	$1,275	$1,100	$1,000	$800	$700

Last MSR was $1,835.

> **Add 5% for ported barrel.**
>
> In 1990, the Grade I designation was added to this model. In 1991, this model was supplied with a travel vault gun case as standard equipment. Older mfg. will not have these cases as an original accessory.
>
> Beginning 1991, a Micro Plus Model was introduced that incorporates smaller dimensions (shorter stock and choice of shorter barrel). Values are the same as listed.

✱ *BT-99 Plus Stainless Grade I* - features all stainless construction with Invector Plus ported 32 or 34 in. black VR barrel. Mfg. 1993-94.

		$1,950	$1,725	$1,425	$1,255	$1,020	$885	$715

Last MSR was $2,240.

> Beginning 1991, a Micro Plus Model was introduced that incorporates smaller dimensions (shorter stock and choice of shorter barrel). Values are the same as listed.

✱ *BT-99 Plus Pigeon Grade Grade I* - features higher grade walnut and gold receiver accents, Invector chokes and ported barrels. Mfg. 1993-disc.

		$1,875	$1,600	$1,250	$1,100	$895	$785	$630

Last MSR was $2,065.

> Beginning 1991, a Micro Plus Model was introduced that incorporates smaller dimensions (shorter stock and choice of shorter barrel). Values are the same.

✱ *BT-99 Plus Signature Painted Grade I* - features painted red/black stock with Browning logos on stock and forearm, Invector Plus ported barrels. Mfg. 1993-94.

		$1,750	$1,525	$1,250	$1,100	$895	$785	$630

Last MSR was $1,890.

> Beginning 1991, a Micro Plus Model was introduced that incorporates smaller dimensions (shorter stock and choice of shorter barrel). Values are the same.

✱ *BT-99 Plus Golden Clays Grade I* - features high-grade wood and gold outline receiver and inlays depicting a transitional hunting to clay pigeon scene. Mfg. 1994 only.

		$2,700	$2,350	$2,050	$1,850	$1,700	$1,550	$1,395

Last MSR was $3,205.

> Beginning 1991, a Micro Plus Model was introduced that incorporates smaller dimensions (shorter stock and choice of shorter barrel). Values are the same.

BT-99 MAX - 12 ga. only, choice of blue steel with engraving or stainless steel barrel, receiver, and trigger guard, 32 or 34 in. high post VR ported barrel, thin forearm with finger grooves, select walnut pistol grip stock (regular or Monte Carlo) with high gloss finish, ejector/ extractor selector, no safety, approx. 8 lbs. 10 oz. Mfg. 1995-96.

		$1,300	$1,000	$800	$600	$525	$495	$450

Last MSR was $1,496.

> **Add $400 for stainless steel.**

BT-99 GRADE III - similar to BT-99, except has silver nitride receiver finished with gold accents, gloss finished Grade III/IV Monte Carlo stock with beavertail forend, ported barrel, approx. 8 1/2 lbs. New 2008.

MSR $2,226		$1,900	$1,325	$1,125	$950	$850	$750	$650

> **Add $269 for adj. comb.**

BT-100 STANDARD TRAP GUN - 12 ga. only, 32 or 34 in. steel high-post ported Invector Plus or fixed choked (F) barrel, without safety, choice of blue or stainless steel receiver, removable trigger assembly, ejector selector (either ejects or extracts) adj. comb and thumbhole stock (disc. 1999) are optional, approx. 8 lbs. 10 oz. Mfg. 1995-2002.

$1,800	$1,600	$1,300	$795	$575	$495	$450

Last MSR was $2,266.

Subtract approx. 10% for fixed choke.
Add $100 for adj. comb.
Add $558 for replacement trigger assembly (blue or stainless).

✳ *BT-100 Stainless* - features stainless steel barrel, receiver, trigger guard and top lever. Disc. 2002.

$2,210	$1,800	$1,600	$1,000	$815	$695	$580

Last MSR was $2,742.

Subtract approx. 10% for fixed choke.
Add $100 for adj. comb.
Add $558 for replacement trigger assembly (blue or stainless).

BT-100 SATIN (LOW LUSTRE) - features 32 or 34 in. Invector Plus barrel, satin/low lustre metal/wood finish, conventional type stock without Monte Carlo, quick removable trigger with adj. trigger pull, 8 lbs. 10 oz. Mfg. 1998-2000.

$1,400	$1,200	$1,000	$775	$650	$575	$495

Last MSR was $1,684.

SHOTGUNS: SINGLE BARREL, RECOILLESS TRAP

RECOILLESS SINGLE BARREL TRAP - 12 ga., special bolt action design that eliminates 72% of felt recoil, 27 (also available in Micro Model) or 30 in. high-post vent. rib Invector Plus choked back-bored barrel, rib adjusts for 3 points of impact (3, 6, or 9 in.), stock has adj. pull (2 sizes) and comb height, anodized receiver, no safety, approx. 8 1/2 lbs. Mfg. 1994-96.

$995	$850	$750	$650	$525	$500	$450

Last MSR was $1,995.

The Micro Model featured a 27 in. barrel and shorter length of pull.

✳ *Recoilless Single Barrel Trap Signature Painted* - features painted red/black stock with Browning logos on stock and forearm, Invector Plus ported barrels. Mfg. 1994 only.

$895	$825	$725	$625	$525	$500	$450

Last MSR was $1,900.

SHOTGUNS: SLIDE ACTION

Do not use BPS barrels chambered for 3 1/2 in. shotshells on a BPS 3 in. receiver or vice versa.

BPS HUNTER/FIELD MODEL - 12, 16 (new 2008), 20, or 28 (new 1994) ga. or .410 bore (new 2000), 2 3/4 (28 ga. only) or 3 in. chamber, bottom ejection, double action bars, top tang safety, 5 shot capacity, vent. rib, all steel receiver with variety of finishes, receiver engraving became standard 1991 and was disc. during 1998, 20 and 28 ga. are approx. 1/2 lb. lighter than 12 ga. Field Models, Invector or Invector Plus (new 1994 in 20 ga.) choking, various barrel lengths, Invector Plus choking became standard 1995 (except 28 ga.), back bored barrels on 12 and 20 ga. BPS Models (except Game guns) became standard during 2003, 6 3/4 lbs. - 8 lbs. 3 oz. Mfg. by Miroku. New 1977.

MSR $529	$455	$350	$285	$225	$200	$185	$170

Add $36 for 16, 28 ga., or .410 bore.
Subtract 10% if without Invector Plus choke tubes.

* *BPS Stalker Model* - 12 ga. only, 3 in. chamber, all metal parts have a dull matte finish, non-glare black synthetic composite stock and forearm, 24 (mfg. 1999-2000), 26, 28, or 30 in. VR barrel, approx. 8 lbs. New 1987.

MSR $512	$435	$325	$265	$225	$200	$185	$170

* *BPS Camouflage* - 12 or 20 (disc. 2006) ga., 3 in. chamber, features Mossy Oak Shadow Grass (disc. 2006), Mossy Oak Duck Blind (new 2007), Mossy Oak Break-Up (mfg. 2000-2003), or New Break-Up (new 2004) full camo treatment, 24 (standard model disc., or NWTF Model with Mossy Oak Break-Up camo - new 2001), 26, or 28 in. barrel, Dura-Touch armor coating became standard during 2003, approx. 8 lbs. New 1999.

MSR $636	$550	$395	$345	$310	$275	$245	$215

Add $32 for NWTF Model with 24 in. barrel with New Mossy Oak Break-Up camo treatment.

* *BPS Pigeon Grade* - 12 ga. only, 3 in. chamber, features high grade walnut and gold trimmed receiver, 26 or 28 in. VR barrel with Invector chokes, 7 lbs. 10 oz. Mfg. 1992-98.

$550	$465	$395	$350	$310	$290	$275

Last MSR was $603.

* *BPS Upland Special* - 12, 16 (new 2008), or 20 ga., 2 3/4 (16 ga.) or 3 in. chamber, 22 (12 and 20 ga.), 24, or 26 in. VR barrel, straight grip satin finished stock and forearm, Invector (pre-1994) or Invector Plus (new 1994, standard 1995) choking, 6 3/4 or 7 1/2 lbs. New 1985.

MSR $529	$455	$350	$285	$225	$200	$185	$170

Add $37 for 16 ga.
Subtract 10% if without Invector Plus choke tubes.

* *BPS Turkey Special* - 12 ga. only, 3 in. chamber, 20 1/2 in. lightened barrel, non-glare walnut stock, matte finished barrel and receiver, receiver is drilled and tapped for scope base, rifle-style stock dimensions, sling swivels, new extra-full Invector choke tube, 7 lbs. 8 oz. Mfg. 1992-2001.

$400	$340	$275	$240	$215	$190	$175

Last MSR was $500.

* *BPS Micro Model* - 20 ga. only, 22 in. vent. rib barrel, pistol grip stock (13 1/4 LOP), Invector Plus choking (includes 3 chokes), 6 3/4 lbs. New 2001.

MSR $529	$455	$345	$285	$225	$200	$185	$170

* *BPS Micro - Youth and Ladies Model* - 20 ga. only, 22 in. vent. rib barrel, straight grip shortened stock (13 1/4 LOP), Invector (pre-1994) or Invector Plus (new 1994, standard 1995) choking, 6 3/4 lbs. Mfg. 1986-2002.

$385	$300	$260	$225	$200	$185	$170

Last MSR was $473.

Subtract 10% if without Invector Plus choke tubes.

* *BPS Deer Hunter/Special (DG, DS or DH)* - 12 or 20 (new 2007) ga., 3 in. chamber, 20 1/2 (disc. 2000) or 22 in. barrel with 5 in. rifled choke tube or rifled barrel (DH, cantilever scope mount with satin finish only, new 1997), iron sights, scope mount base, choice of gloss (DG, disc. 1997) or satin (DS, disc. 2000) finish checkered stock with recoil pad and forearm, sling swivels, polished or matte finished metal, approx. 7 1/2 lbs. New 1992.

MSR $655	$565	$410	$325	$255	$220	$195	$175

Subtract approx. 10% for rifled choke tube.
Add $16 for 20 ga. (new 2007).

* *BPS Deer Camo* - 12 or 20 ga., 3 in. chamber, 22 in. rifled barrel with cantilever scope mount, 100% Mossy Oak New Break-Up camo coverage, approx. 7 1/2 lbs. New 2007.

MSR $676	$570	$415	$330	$255	$220	$195	$175

Add $106 for 20 ga.

GRADING - PPGS™	100%	98%	95%	90%	80%	70%	60%

✴ *BPS Buck Special* - 12 or 20 (disc. 1984) ga., 3 in. chamber, 24 in. cyl. bore barrel, iron sights, 7 lbs. 10 oz. Reintroduced 1988-disc. 1998.

		$335	$275	$230	$200	$185	$175	$160

Last MSR was $409.

BPS MAGNUM HUNTER/STALKER 12 GA. 3 1/2 IN. - 12 ga., 3 1/2 in. chamber, 24 (disc. 1997, reintroduced 1999-2000 - Stalker only), 26, 28, or 30 (disc. 1997) in. barrel with Invector chokes and vent. rib, 4 shot mag., 7 3/4 lbs. Hunter 3 1/2 in. Model disc. 2002.

MSR $632		$540	$415	$350	$315	$275	$245	$215

In 1990, the back-bored Invector plus choke tube system became standard in 12 ga. 3 1/2 in. chamber only.

✴ *BPS Camo Magnum Hunter* - 12 ga., similar to Magnum Hunter or Stalker 12 ga., features Mossy Oak Shadow Grass (disc. 2006), Mossy Oak Duck Blind (new 2007), or Mossy Oak Break-Up (new 2000) full camo treatment, 24 (standard model disc., or NWTF Model with Mossy Oak Break-Up camo - new 2001), 26, or 28 in. VR barrel, Dura-Touch armor coating became standard during 2003, approx. 7 3/4 - 9 1/4 lbs. New 1999.

MSR $752		$650	$516	$450	$375	$325	$300	$275

Add $54 for NWTF Model with 24 in. barrel (12 ga., available in Mossy Oak Break-Up only beginning 2000).

✴ *BPS Magnum Hunting Waterfowl* - 10 ga., 3 1/2 in. Mag. with choice of 28 or 30 in. matte finished VR barrel with standard Invector choking, features higher grade walnut and gold trimmed receiver with Waterfowl outlined, approx. 9 lbs. 6 oz. Mfg. 1993-98.

		$615	$500	$400	$375	$350	$315	$285

Last MSR was $750.

✴ *BPS Magnum 3 1/2 In. Buck Special* - 10 or 12 (disc. 1994) ga., 3 1/2 in. chambers, 24 in. cyl. bore barrel, 7 lbs. 10 oz. Mfg. 1990-97.

		$500	$450	$400	$370	$335	$310	$290

Last MSR was $677.

BPS MAGNUM HUNTER/STALKER 10 GA. - 10 ga., 3 1/2 in. chamber, currently available in either Stalker (black synthetic stock and forearm), or camo (choice of Mossy Oak New Break-Up, Mossy Oak Duck Blind (new 2007) or New Shadowgrass (disc. 2006) with Dura-Touch coating configuration, 10 1/2 lbs. Disc. 2001, reintroduced 2004.

MSR $632		$550	$435	$365	$325	$275	$245	$215

Add $120 for 100% camo coverage.

✴ *BPS 10 ga. NWTF* - features 24 in. VR barrel with HiViz TriViz fiber optic sights and extra full XF extended turkey choke tube, 100% Mossy Oak New Break-Up camo coverage, NWTF logo on synthetic stock, 10 lbs., 3 oz.

MSR $806		$685	$515	$450	$375	$325	$275	$225

BPS TRAP MODEL - 12 ga., 30 in. barrel. Disc. 1984 but trap barrels were available separately for several years.

		$360	$300	$270	$230	$210	$190	$170

BPS TRAP (CURRENT MFG.) - 12 ga. only, 2 3/4 in. chamber, features dark grey receiver with full coverage engraving, 30 in. VR barrel with HiViz front sight, checkered satin finished Monte Carlo walnut stock and forearm, magazine cut-off, approx. 8 1/2 lbs. New 2007.

MSR $683		$580	$435	$330	$265	$220	$195	$175

✴ *BPS Micro Trap* - 12 ga. only, similar to BPS Trap, except has 28 in. VR barrel and 13 3/4 LOP. New 2007.

MSR $683		$580	$435	$330	$265	$220	$195	$175

GRADING - PPGS™	100%	98%	95%	90%	80%	70%	60%

BPS WILD TURKEY FEDERATION COMMEMORATIVE - only 500 manufactured. Disc. 1991.

	100%	98%	95%	90%	80%	70%	60%
	$495	$395	$325	N/A	N/A	N/A	N/A

BPS PACIFIC EDITION DU - limited mfg., DU serialization, cased.

	100%	98%	95%	90%	80%	70%	60%
	$595	$475	$350	$285	$250	$215	$185

BPS COASTAL DU - limited mfg., DU serialization, cased.

	100%	98%	95%	90%	80%	70%	60%
	$595	$475	$350	$285	$250	$215	$185

BPS WATERFOWL DELUXE - 12 ga. Mag., gold trigger and etching, Invector chokes, limited mfg.

	100%	98%	95%	90%	80%	70%	60%
	$625	$525	$450	$385	$335	$280	$235

MODEL 12 LIMITED EDITION SERIES

✳ *Model 12 Limited Edition Grade I 20 Ga.* - 20 ga. only, 2 3/4 in. chamber only, reproduction of the famous Winchester Model 12 with slight design improvements, 26 in. VR barrel bored modified, 5 shot mag., high post floating rib, walnut stock and forearm with semi-gloss finish, take down, serialization format similar to 28 ga., 7 lbs. 1 oz. 8,000 mfg. in 1988 with inventory depleted 1990.

	100%	98%	95%	90%	80%	70%	60%
	$775	$650	$525	N/A	N/A	N/A	N/A

Last MSR was $735.

✳ *Model 12 Limited Edition Grade V 20 Ga.* - similar specifications to Grade I, except has select walnut checkered 22 lines per inch with high gloss finish, extensive game scene engraving including multiple gold inlays serialization format similar to 28 ga. 4,000 mfg. 1988 only.

	100%	98%	95%	90%	80%	70%	60%
	$1,350	$1,125	$900	N/A	N/A	N/A	N/A

Last MSR was $1,187.

✳ *Model 12 Limited Edition Grade I 28 Ga.* - 28 ga. only, similar to Grade I 20 Ga., except in 28 ga., 26 in. VR modified choke barrel, 5 digit ser. no. with NM872 suffix. 7,000 mfg. 1991-92.

	100%	98%	95%	90%	80%	70%	60%
	$1,050	$875	$700	N/A	N/A	N/A	N/A

Last MSR was $772.

✳ *Model 12 Limited Edition Grade V 28 ga.* - 28 ga. only, similar to Grade V 20 ga., except in 28 ga., 26 in. VR modified choke barrel, 5 digit ser. no. with NM972 suffix. 5,000 mfg. 1991-92.

	100%	98%	95%	90%	80%	70%	60%
	$1,675	$1,350	$1,000	N/A	N/A	N/A	N/A

Last MSR was $1,246.

MODEL 42 LIMITED EDITION

✳ *Model 42 Limited Edition Grade I* - .410 bore, 3 in. chamber, reproduction of the Winchester Model 42 with slight design improvements, 26 in. VR full choke barrel, select walnut stock, 5 digit ser. no. with NZ882 suffix, 6 lbs. 12 oz. 6,000 mfg. late 1991-1993.

	100%	98%	95%	90%	80%	70%	60%
	$895	$775	$550	N/A	N/A	N/A	N/A

Last MSR was $800.

✳ *Model 42 Limited Edition Grade V* - .410 bore, engraving and embellishments similar to the Model 12 Grade V, 5 digit ser. no. with NZ982 suffix, 6,000 mfg. late 1991-1993.

	100%	98%	95%	90%	80%	70%	60%
	$1,495	$1,225	$925	N/A	N/A	N/A	N/A

Last MSR was $1,360.

SPECIAL EDITIONS, COMMEMORATIVES, & LIMITED MFG.

Please refer to the *Blue Book of Modern Black Powder Arms* by John Allen (now online also) for more information and prices on Browning black powder rifles.

GRADING - PPGS™	100%	98%	95%	90%	80%	70%	60%

BICENTENNIAL 1876-1976 SET - .45-70 Govt. cal., Model 78 rifle with specially engraved receiver, silver finish, fancy wood, cased, with engraved knife and medallion, 1,000 sets mfg. in 1976. Issue price - $1,500.

	$1,875	$1,425	$925	N/A	N/A	N/A	N/A

CENTENNIAL O/U RIFLE/SHOTGUN - 20 ga. O/U shotgun w/extra set of .30-06 O/U rifle barrels. Shotgun barrels are 26 1/2 in., rifle barrels are 24 in., SST, ejectors, elaborate scroll engraved receiver with 2 gold inlays, straight grip special oil finished walnut stock and forearm, deluxe walnut full-length case. 500 mfg. 1978 only.

	$6,250	$5,750	$4,950	N/A	N/A	N/A	N/A

Last MSR was $7,000.

CENTENNIAL SET - complete Browning set mfg. in 1978, includes the Centennial O/U rifle/shotgun, 9mm Hi-Power, B92 .44 Mag., Mountain Rifle, and a set of three knives.

	$8,250	$7,000	$5,750	N/A	N/A	N/A	N/A

1 OF 50 BICENTENNIAL RIFLE - .30-06 cal., Model 78 single shot with 26 in. octagon barrel, includes special engraving by Neil Hartliep (non-factory), extra fine walnut, 4X wide angle scope, special luggage case. 50 mfg. (one for each state) durlng 1976 only and sold by silent mail order bidding (minimum bid was $3,100 in 1976).

As very few specimens are bought or sold each year, pricing is rather unpredictable. A few specimens have been sold in the $6,000 range recently. Remember, the work on this gun was subcontracted by Centennial Guns (division of Frigon Guns located in Clay Center, KS).

BUCK MARK COMMEMORATIVE PISTOL - features 6 3/4 in. Challenger style tapered barrel, white bonded ivory grips with scrimshaw style patterning including "1 of 1,000 Commemorative Model" on sides, matte blue finish, gold trigger, 30 1/2 oz. 1,000 mfg. 2001-2002.

	$335	$275	$225	N/A	N/A	N/A	N/A

Last MSR was $437.

BRUCHET

Current manufacturer located in Saint Etienne, France. Distributed exclusively from 1982-1989 by Wes Gilpin located in Dallas, TX. In 1989, Bruchet was able to get permission to use the older Darne trademark and all new manufacture will be entered under the Darne listing.

Paul Bruchet has been manufacturing his shotguns patterned after the Darne action since 1981, following his tenure at Darne as line foreman until 1979 (at which time the Darne plant closed). These new Bruchet Models were designated "A" or "B". All shotguns were totally hand made with approx. 50 guns being mfg. each year.

Since Paul Bruchet was able to retain the Darne trademark in 1989, please refer to the Darne section in this text for current manufacture.

SHOTGUNS: SxS

MODEL A - 12, 16, 20, 28 ga., or .410 bore, small key opening, ejectors, double triggers only, basically 4 variations (1, 1A, 2, and 2A), wide assortment of customer specified special orders.

Retail values were as follows: Model 1A started at under $2,000, the Model 2 started at $3,000, and the Model 2A started at $3,500. Each additional grade represented more embellishments and better grade of walnut. Magnum chambers could be ordered at a small surcharge. Importation began 1982, values represent the last published retail prices from 1989.

MODEL B - 12, 16, 20, 28 ga., or .410 bore, large key opening, self-opening (assisted) action, ejectors, double triggers only, basically special ordered to individual customer specifications.

Retail values were as follows: Model B started at $5,800 and included deluxe carrying case. Each additional upgrade represented more embellishments and a better grade of walnut. Magnum chambers could be ordered at a small surcharge. Importation began 1982, values represent the last published retail prices from 1989.

BRÜGGER & THOMET

Curret manufacturer located in Thun, Switzerland. Currently imported by D.S.A., located in Barrington, IL.

Brüegger & Thomet manufactures a wide variety of high quality paramilitary style semi-auto pistols and rifles. Currently imported models include the TP-9 semi-auto tactical pistol with a MSR of $1,250. Please contact the importer directly for more information (see Trademark Index).

BRYCO ARMS

Previous manufacturer located in Irvine, CA until 2003. Previously distributed by Jennings Firearms, Inc. located in Carson City, NV.

PISTOLS: SEMI-AUTO, SINGLE ACTION

MODEL T-22 - while advertised during 1997 at a retail price of $179, this model was never produced.

MODEL J-25 - .25 ACP cal., aluminum alloy frame, 2 1/2 in. barrel, single action, synthetic ivory, walnut, or black combat grips, positive safety, 11 oz. Mfg. 1988-95, reintroduced 1999.

$65	$55	$45	$40	$35	$30	$30

Last MSR was $79.

This model was available in either satin nickel, bright chrome, or black teflon finish.

MODEL M-32/M-38 - .22 LR (disc.), .32 ACP, or .380 ACP cal., semi-auto single action, 2.8 in. barrel, pressure cast fabrication using non-ferrous alloy, chrome or blue finish, black combat grips, 16 oz. Mfg. 1991-disc.

$65	$50	$40	$35	$30	$30	$30

Last MSR was $79.

Add $20 for .380 ACP cal.

MODEL M-48 - .22 LR, .32 ACP, or .380 ACP cal., semi-auto single action, 4 in. barrel, larger frame variation of the M-38, chrome or blue finish, black combat grips, 24 oz. Mfg. 1991-95.

$85	$75	$65	$55	$50	$45	$40

Last MSR was $96.

MODEL M-5 - .380 ACP or 9mm Para. cal., 3 1/4 in. barrel, 10 or 12 shot mag., blue or nickel finish, black synthetic grips, 36 oz. Disc. 1995.

$85	$75	$65	$55	$50	$45	$40

Last MSR was $100 for the .380 ACP, $119 for 9mm Para.

Add $15 for 9mm Para. cal.

MODEL M-59 - .380 ACP or 9mm Para. cal., 4 in. barrel, 10 shot mag., blue or nickel finish, black synthetic grips, 36 oz. Disc. 1995.

$95	$85	$75	$70	$65	$60	$55

Last MSR was $119.

Add $15 for 9mm Para. cal.

JENNINGS NINE - 9mm Para. cal., single action, redesigned model 59, frame mounted ejector, contour grips, loaded chamber indicator, 30 oz. Mfg. 1997-2003.

$120	$100	$85	$75	$65	$55	$50

Last MSR was $145.

BUDISCHOWSKY

Previous manufacturer located in Mt. Clemens, MI.

PISTOLS: SEMI-AUTO

TP-70 - .22 LR cal., double action, 2 1/2 in. barrel, stainless steel, fixed sights, plastic grips. Mfg. 1973-77.

$440	$385	$330	$265	$230	$195	$175

GRADING - PPGS™	100%	98%	95%	90%	80%	70%	60%

TP-70 - similar to TP-70, except .25 ACP cal. Mfg. 1973-77.

	$330	$275	$220	$175	$140	$125	$105

Note: In 1977, Norton Arms marketed this pistol. Quality of workmanship is not on par with the early Budischowsky and values are approx. 35% less.

SEMI-AUTO PISTOL - .223 Rem. cal., 11 5/8 in. barrel, 20 or 30 shot mag., fixed sights, a novel paramilitary designed type pistol.

	$470	$415	$385	$360	$305	$250	$220

RIFLES: SEMI-AUTO

PARAMILITARY DESIGN RIFLE - .223 Rem. cal., semi-auto, 18 in. barrel, wood paramilitary stock.

	$505	$440	$415	$385	$330	$275	$250

PARAMILITARY DESIGN RIFLE W/FOLDING STOCK

	$575	$500	$450	$425	$395	$360	$330

BULLARD REPEATING ARMS COMPANY

Previous manufacturer located in Springfield, MA, circa 1882-1891.

Designed by prolific inventor James Bullard, the design, quality, and workmanship of Bullard rifles rivaled those of any competitor during the 1880s. Bullard made two basic rifles: a lever action repeater and a single shot. The repeater was made in two frame styles: large and small. The single shot was also made in two basic styles; solid frame and detachable-interchangeable barrel model. Total production is estimated at 2,800 rifles.

The author would like to thank Mr. Gene Weicht for providing information and values for this section.

100%	98%	95%	90%	80%	70%	60%	50%	40%	30%	20%	10%

RIFLES: LEVER ACTION

LEVER ACTION REPEATER - rack and pinion style lever activated mechanism, mag. mounted under barrel, loaded through underside of action while lever was opened, blue finish with various parts (including receiver) sometimes case hardened, approx. 1,700 mfg.

✳ *Lever Action Large Frame* -.45-70 Govt., .45-75, .50-95, .40-70 Bullard, .40-75 Bullard, .40-90 Bullard, .45-85 Bullard or .50-115 Bullard cal., 26 or 28 in. round, octagon, or part round barrel, crescent steel or hard rubber buttplates with elk motif, ser. no. range 1-1,500 and 2,000-3,000.

N/A	N/A	$3,500	$3,050	$2,425	$2,100	$1,950	$1,750	$1,475	$1,325	$1,125	$975

Add 25% for .40-90 Bullard, .50-95, or .50-115 Bullard cal.

Add 25% for deluxe checkered wood with pistol grip.

Various military and experimental models are found in this frame size and will command significant premiums.

Large frame repeating rifles up to ser. no. 113 will be marked "Bullard Repeating Arms Association". Ser. no. 114-4067 will be marked Bullard Repeating Arms Company.

✳ *Lever Action Small Frame* - .32-40 Bullard or .38-45 Bullard cal., (other calibers cataloged, but essentially unknown), 24, 26, or 28 in. round, octagon or part round barrel, crescent steel or hard rubber buttplates with turkey motif, ser. no. range 1,500-2,000. Approx. 500 mfg.

N/A	N/A	$3,000	$2,500	$2,175	$1,850	$1,650	$1,400	$1,175	$1,050	$950	$850

Add 25% for deluxe checkered wood with pistol grip.

Add 40% for any caliber other than .32-40 and .38-45.

Although the small frame saw less production and is scarcer than the large frame repeater, it is not as desirable among collectors, and is typically priced less than a large frame model.

100%	98%	95%	90%	80%	70%	60%	50%	40%	30%	20%	10%

RIFLES: SINGLE SHOT

SINGLE SHOT MODEL - thin receiver with full lever, similar in appearance to small frame repeater action, except shorter (several part will interchange), 26, 28, or 30 in. round, octagon, or part round barrel, blue finish with various parts sometimes case hardened (including receiver), crescent steel or hard rubber (turkey motifs) buttplates, ser. no. range 3,500-4,100. Approx. 600 mfg.

    * *Single Shot Solid Frame* - wide variety of cals. from .22 rimfire to .50 cal., (.22 and .32-40 are most common), made in both frame sizes.

100%	98%	95%	90%	80%	70%	60%	50%	40%	30%	20%	10%
N/A	N/A	$3,150	$2,700	$2,300	$1,975	$1,800	$1,650	$1,450	$1,300	$1,150	$1,025

    * *Single Shot Detachable-interchangeable Barrel Model* - same cals. as small frame model with two frame sizes - small (.38 cal. and smaller) and large (usually .40 cal. and larger, but some small calibers were mfg.), interchangeable barrels could not be switched between the two frame sizes, barrel and breech detach from action.

100%	98%	95%	90%	80%	70%	60%	50%	40%	30%	20%	10%
N/A	N/A	$3,050	$2,600	$2,200	$1,900	$1,725	$1,600	$1,400	$1,275	$1,125	$1,000

    Add 15% for large frame models in less than .40 cal.
    Add 30% for .50 cals.
    Add 30% for extra barrel with forend (numbers matching).
    Add 30% for Schuetzen model.
    Add 25% for deluxe checkered wood with pistol grip.
    Values are for models with original sights and no stock alterations - subtract 15% if not original.

BULLSEYE GUN WORKS

Previous manufacturer located in Miami, FL circa 1954-1959.

CARBINES

Bullseye Gun Works initially started as a gun shop circa 1954, and several years later, they started manufacturing M1 carbines using their own receivers and barrels. Approx. 2,000 - 2,500 were manufactured with their name on the receiver side until the company was reorganized as Universal Firearms Corporation circa late 1950s. Values are typically in the $200 - $350 range, depending on originality and condition.

BUL TRANSMARK LTD.

Current manufacturer located in Tel Aviv, Israel. Currently imported beginning 2003 by K.B.I., located in Harrisburg, PA. Previously imported and distributed in North America during 2002 by EAA Corp., located in Sharpes, FL. Previously imported and distributed 1997-2001 by International Security Academy (ISA) located in Los Angeles, CA, and from 1996-1997 by All America Sales, Inc. located in Memphis, TN. Dealer sales only.

PISTOLS: SEMI-AUTO

Please refer to the Charles Daly section in this text for current information and prices on Bul Transmark pistols (domestic imports are marked Charles Daly beginning 2004). Non-domestic Bul Pistols are typically marked Bul M-5 on left side of slide except for the Cherokee and Storm models. M-5 frame kits were previously available at $399 retail.

BUL IMPACT - while advertised during 1999, this model was never produced.

BUL STORM & COMPACT - while advertised during 1999, this model was never produced.

GRADING - PPGS™	100%	98%	95%	90%	80%	70%	60%

BUL 1911 GOVERNMENT (M-5 STANDARD) - .38 Super (disc.), 9mm Para. (disc.), .40 S&W (disc.), or .45 ACP cal., single action, 5 in. barrel, polymer double column frame, steel slide, aluminum speed trigger, checkered front and rear grip straps, blue or chrome (new 2000) finished slide, 10 shot staggered mag., 31-33 oz. Imported 1995-2000, reintroduced 2002-2003.

	$525	$450	$375	$325	$295	$275	$250

Last MSR was $559.

Add 10% for .38 Super or .40 S&W cal.

* *Bul Commander (M5 Standard)* - similar to M-5 Government, except has 3.8 (disc.), 4 1/3 (new 2004) or 4 1/4 (disc.) in. barrel, 29-30 oz. Imported 1998-2000, reintroduced 2002-2003.

	$525	$450	$375	$325	$295	$275	$250

Last MSR was $559.

Add 10% for .38 Super or .40 S&W cal.
Add $40 for matte chrome finished slide.

* *Bul M5 Stinger* - similar to Bul 1911 Government, except has 10 shot mag., 3 in. barrel, 24 oz. Imported 2002-2003.

	$525	$450	$375	$325	$295	$275	$250

Last MSR was $559.

* *Bul M-5 Standard Street Comp.* - similar to M-5 Standard Commander, except has single port compensated 4 1/4 in. barrel, 32 oz. Imported 1998-99.

	$960	$825	$700	$600	$500	$450	$375

Last MSR was $1,060.

Add $28 for .38 Super or .40 S&W cal.

* *Bul M-5 Multi Caliber* - similar cals. as the M-5 Standard Government, includes 3 upper-ends including Commander length, another with adj. sights, and a third with a single port compensator, cased. Imported 1999-2000.

	$1,575	$1,275	$1,050	$850	$725	$625	$525

Last MSR was $1,768.

BUL M-5 STANDARD IPSC - .38 Super, 9mm Para., .40 S&W, or .45 ACP cal., configured for IPSC competition, with custom slide to frame fit and match grade barrel bushing. Imported 1998-2001, reintroduced 2003.

	$925	$825	$725	$625	$525	$425	$375

Last MSR was $990.

Add $111 for .38 Super or .40 S&W cal. (disc. 2001).
Add $70 for chrome finish (mfg. 2000-2001).

BUL M-5 STANDARD MATCH - IPSC custom race gun, includes multi-port compensator system. Imported 1998-99.

	$1,200	$1,000	$825	$700	$600	$500	$425

Last MSR was $1,655.

Add $24 for .38 Super or .40 S&W cal.

BUL M-5 JET - same cals. as the M-5 Standard IPSC, features Commander length with 4 1/4 in. barrel and 4 port compensator on top of barrel, 31 oz. Imported 1999-2000.

	$875	$725	$625	$525	$475	$400	$350

Last MSR was $1,158.

Add $51 for .38 Super or .40 S&W cal.

BUL M-5 MODIFIED - 9mm Para., .38 Super, .40 S&W, or .45 ACP cal., designed for Modified class competition, features new Optima 2000 optical sight fitted to slide, 5 port compensation on top of barrel, includes carrying case, 38 oz. Imported 1998-2001.

	$1,075	$925	$800	$675	$550	$500	$450

Last MSR was $1,430.

GRADING - PPGS™	100%	98%	95%	90%	80%	70%	60%

BUL M-5 TARGET - same cals. as the M-5 Modified, features 6 in. slide and barrel, choice of sights, and match grade oversize barrel bushing, includes 3 mags and carrying case, 38 oz. Imported 1999-2001.

	$895	$775	$700	$600	$500	$450	$400

Last MSR was $1,196.

Add $315 for Aristocrat Tri-state sights.

BUL M-5 ULTIMATE RACER - top-level IPSC competition gun, includes 3 mags. and carrying case, 38 oz. Imported 1998-2001.

	$1,050	$925	$800	$700	$600	$525	$450

Last MSR was $1,573.

Add $306 for fitted C-more optical sight.

BUSHMASTER FIREARMS INTERNATIONAL LLC

Currently manufactured by Bushmaster Firearms/Quality Parts Company located in Windham, ME. The previous company name was Bushmaster Firearms, and the name changed after the company was sold on April 13, 2006 to Cerberus. Older mfg. was by Gwinn Arms Co. located in Winston-Salem, NC 1972-1974. The Quality Parts Co. gained control in 1986. Distributor, dealer, or consumer direct sales.

During 2003, Bushmaster purchased Professional Ordnance, previous maker of the Carbon 15 Series of semi-auto pistols and rifles/carbines. Carbon 15s are still made in Lake Havasu City, AZ, but are now marked with Bushmaster logo. For pre-2003 Carbon 15 mfg., please refer to the Professional Ordnance section in this text.

PISTOLS: SEMI-AUTO

BUSHMASTER PISTOL - .223 Rem. cal., top bolt (older models with aluminum receivers) or side bolt (most recent mfg.) operation, steel frame on later mfg., 11 1/2 in. barrel, parkerized finish, adj. sights, 5 1/4 lbs.

	$650	$550	$450	$400	$375	$350	$300

Last MSR was $375.

Add $40 for electroless nickel finish (disc. 1988).
Add $200 for matte nickel finish (mfg. circa 1986-1988).

This model uses a 30 shot M-16 mag. and the AK-47 gas system.

During 1985-1986, a procurement officer for the U.S. Air Force ordered 2,100 of this model for pilot use with a matte nickel finish. Eventually, this officer was retired or transferred, and the replacement officer turned down the first batch, saying they were "too reflective". Bushmaster then sold these models commercially circa 1986-1988.

CARBON-15 TYPE 21S/TYPE 21S - .223 Rem cal., ultra lightweight carbon fiber upper and lower receivers, 7 1/4 in. "Profile" stainless steel barrel, quick detachable muzzle compensator, ghost ring sights, 10 or 30 (new late 2004) shot mag., A2 pistol grip, also accepts AR-15 type mags., Stoner type operating sytem, tool steel bolt, extractor and carrier, 40 oz. New 2003 (Bushmaster mfg.).

MSR $1,050	$950	$800	$700	$600	$525	$475	$425

Subtract approx. $200 if without full-length barrel shroud and Picatinny rail (Type 21, disc. 2005).

CARBON-15 TYPE 97/TYPE 97S - similar to Professional Ordnance Carbon 15 Type 20, except has fluted barrel, Hogue overmolded pistol grip and chrome plated bolt carrier, 46 oz. New 2003 (Bushmaster mfg.).

MSR $990	$865	$785	$650	$600	$550	$500	$450

Add $105 for Type 97S with full length barrel shroud, upper and lower Picatinny rail.

CARBON-15 9MM - 9mm Para. cal., blow-back operation, carbon fiber composite receiver, 7 1/2 in. steel barrel with A1 birdcage flash hider, A2 front sight, full-length Picatinny optics rail, Neoprene foam sleeve over buffer tube, 10 or 30 shot mag, 4.6 lbs. New 2006.

MSR $1,025	$925	$850	$775	$700	$650	$600	$550

GRADING - PPGS™	100%	98%	95%	90%	80%	70%	60%

RIFLES: SEMI-AUTO

All currently manufactured Bushmaster rifles are shipped with a hard plastic lockable case. Most Bushmaster barrels are marked "5.56 NATO", and can be used safely with either 5.56 NATO (higher velocity/pressure) or .223 Rem. cal. ammo.

During 2006, Bushmaster began offering a complete gas piston upper receiver/barrel assembly at a $995 MSR (A2 type).

BUSHMASTER RIFLE - .223 Rem. cal., semi-auto, top bolt (older models with aluminum receivers) or side bolt (current mfg.) operation, steel frame (current mfg.), 18 1/2 in. barrel, parkerized finish, adj. sights, wood stock, 6 1/4 lbs., base values are for folding stock model.

	$675	$625	$550	$500	$475	$425	$400

Last MSR was $350.

Add $40 for electroless nickel finish (disc. 1988).
Add $65 for fixed rock maple wood stock.
This model uses a 30 shot M-16 mag. and the AK-47 gas system.

⁎ *Bushmaster Rifle Combination System* - includes rifle with both metal folding stock and wood stock with pistol grip.

	$400	$360	$330	$300	$275	$250	$230

Last MSR was $450.

XM15-E2S/A-2/A-3 TARGET RIFLE - .223 Rem. cal., semi-auto patterned after the Colt AR-15, 20, 24, or 26 in. Govt. spec. match grade chrome lined or stainless steel (new 2002) barrel, 10 or 30 shot mag., manganese phosphate or Realtree Camo (20 in. barrel only, mfg. 2004 - late 2006) barrel finish, rear sight adj. for windage and elevation, cage flash suppressor (disc. 1994), approx. 8.3 lbs. Mfg. began 1989 in U.S.

MSR $1,105	$935	$800	$700	$600	$550	$475	$425

Add $50 for fluted barrel or $40 for stainless steel barrel (new 2002).
Add $10 for 24 in. or $25 for 26 in. (disc. 2002) barrel.
Add $90 for A-3 removable carry handle.
Add $60 for Realtree Camo finish (disc.).

⁎ *XM15-E2S/A-2/A-3 Shorty Carbine* - similar to above, except with fixed or telescoping buttstock and 11 1/2 (disc. 1995), 14 (disc. 1994), or 16 in. barrel with (disc. 1994) or w/o suppressor, approx. 7.4 lbs. Mfg. began 1989.

MSR $1,160	$965	$825	$700	$600	$550	$475	$425

Add $40 for fluted barrel.
Add $10 for dissipator models (features lengthened handguard).
Add $105 for A-3 removable carry handle.
This model does not have the target rear sight system of the XM15-E2S rifle.

⁎ *M4 Post-Ban Carbine (XM15-E2S)* - 16 in. barrel, features fixed or telestock (new late 2004) tubular stock, pistol grip, phosphate or desert camo (stock, pistol grip, and forearm only) finish, M4 carbine configuration with permanently attached Izzy muzzle brake, 30 shot mag. became standard in late 2004. New 2003.

MSR $1,180	$985	$830	$725	$650	$575	$475	$425

Add $35 for desert camo finish (disc. 2005).
Add $85 for A3 removable carrying handle.
Subtract $55 for M4 Patrolman Carbine with A2 birdcage flash supressor, collapsible stock, and 30 round magazine.

⁎ *XM-15 Limited Edition 20th Anniversary Rifle* - 20 in. barrel, features 20th Anniversary engraving on upper and lower receiver, special medallion in buttstock, includes hardwood presentation case. Limited mfg. 1998-99.

	$1,495	$1,300	$1,125	$975	$875	$800	$725

GRADING - PPGS™	100%	98%	95%	90%	80%	70%	60%

* **XM-15 Limited Edition 25th Anniversary Carbine** - features skeletonized tubular stock, pistol grip, A-3 type flatop with flip-up sights, laser engraved 25th anniversary crest on lower magwell, nickel plated ejection port. Limited mfg. of 1,500 during 2003.

			$1,495	$1,300	$1,125	$975	$875	$800	$725

Last MSR was $1,695.

* **E2 Carbine** - .223 Rem. cal., features 16 in. match chrome barrel with new M16A2 handguard and short suppressor, choice of A1 or E2 sights. Mfg. 1994-95.

			$895	$825	$725	$650	$600	$550	$500

    Add approx. $50 for E2 sighting system.

AK CARBINE - .223 Rem. cal., 17 in. barrel featuring AK-47 style muzzle brake, tele-stock standard, choice of A2 or A3 configuration, ribbed oval forearm, approx. 7 1/2 lbs. New 2008.

MSR $1,180			$1,000	$885	$775	$700	$625	$550	$500

    Add $85 for A3 removable carryhandle.

6.8mm SPC (SPECIAL PURPOSE CARTRIDGE) CARBINE - 6.8mm SPC cal., 16 in. M4 profile barrel with Izzy brake, six-position telescoping stock, gas operated, available in A2 or A3 configuration, 26 shot mag., includes black web sling, extra mag. and lockable carrying case, approx. 7 lbs. New late 2006.

MSR $1,195			$995	$850	$750	$675	$600	$550	$500

    Add $100 for A3 configuration.

.450 CARBINE/RIFLE - .450 Bushmaster cal., 16 (carbine) or 20 in. chromemoly steel barrel, 5 shot mag., AR type gas operating system, forged aluminum receiver, A2 pistol grip, solid A2 buttstock with trapdoor, A3 flattop upper receiver with Picatinny rail, 8 1/2 lbs. New 2008.

MSR N/A			$1,100	$925	$825	$725	$650	$575	$500

DISSIPATOR CARBINE - .223 Rem. cal., 16 in. heavy barrel with full length forearm and special gas block placement (gas block system is located behind the front sight base and under the rifle length handguard), A2 or A3 style with choice of solid buttstock or six-position telestock, 30 shot mag., lockable carrying case. New late 2004.

MSR $1,120			$925	$800	$700	$600	$550	$475	$425

    Add $25 for tele-stock.
    Add $50 for fluted barrel (disc. 2005).
    Add $115 for A3 removable carrying handle.

SUPERLIGHT CARBINE - .223 Rem. cal., 16 in. lightweight barrel, choice of fixed, tele-style, or stub stock with finger groove pistol grip, A2 or A3 type configuration, black finish, 5.8 - 6 1/4 lbs. New 2004.

MSR $1,105			$935	$800	$700	$600	$550	$475	$425

    Add $25 for tele-style stock.
    Add $85 for A-3 removable carry handle.

MODULAR CARBINE - .223 Rem. cal., 16 in. barrel with flash suppressor, includes many Bushmaster modular accessories, such as skeleton telestock and four-rail free floating tubular forearm, rear flip up and detachable sight, 10 or 30 (new late 2004) shot mag., 6.3 lbs. New 2004.

MSR $1,745			$1,550	$1,225	$1,025	$900	$800	$725	$650

O.R.C. (OPTICS READY) CARBINE - .223 Rem. cal., 16 in. barrel with A2 birdcage suppressor, receiver length Picatinny rail with risers ready for optical sights, six position telestock, oval M4 type forearm, 6 lbs. New 2008.

MSR $1,085			$925	$800	$700	$600	$550	$475	$425

GRADING - PPGS™	100%	98%	95%	90%	80%	70%	60%

GAS PISTON CARBINE - .223 Rem. cal., features gas piston operating system similar to AK-47 and FAL gas systems, 16 in. M4 profile barrel with flash suppressor, telestock, ribbed oval forearm with flip-up sight. New 2008.

	100%	98%	95%	90%	80%	70%	60%
MSR $1,795	$1,575	$1,225	$1,025	$900	$800	$725	$650

V-MATCH COMPETITION RIFLE - .223 Rem. cal., top-of-the line match/competition rifle, flattop receiver with extended aluminum barrel shroud, choice of 20, 24, or 26 (disc. 2002) in. barrel, 8.3 lbs. New 1994.

	100%	98%	95%	90%	80%	70%	60%
MSR $1,115	$1,025	$900	$750	$650	$575	$515	$465

Add $50 for fluted barrel.
Add $10 for 24 in. or $25 for 26 (disc. 2002) in. barrel.
Add $117 for A-3 removable carry handle.

✷ *V-Match Commando Carbine* - similar to V-Match Competition Rifle, except has 16 in. barrel. New 1997.

	100%	98%	95%	90%	80%	70%	60%
MSR $1,105	$1,025	$900	$750	$650	$575	$515	$465

Add $50 for fluted barrel.
Add $117 for A-3 removable carry handle.

VARMINTER - .223 Rem. cal., includes DCM 24 in. extra heavy fluted or stainless steel varmint barrel, competition trigger, rubberized pistol grip, flattop receiver with mini-risers (add 1/2 in. height for scope mounting), free floating vented tube forearm, 5 shot mag, controlled ejection path. New 2002.

	100%	98%	95%	90%	80%	70%	60%
MSR $1,325	$1,095	$950	$800	$700	$600	$550	$500

The stainless variation includes an adj., ergonomic pistol grip.

PREDATOR - .223 Rem. cal., includes DCM 20 in. extra heavy fluted or stainless steel (disc. 2006) varmint barrel, competition trigger, rubberized pistol grip, flattop receiver with mini-risers (add 1/2 in. height for scope mounting), free floating vented tube forearm, 10 shot mag, controlled ejection path, 8 lbs. New 2006.

	100%	98%	95%	90%	80%	70%	60%
MSR $1,310	$1,075	$950	$800	$700	$600	$550	$500

The stainless variation included an adj., ergonomic pistol grip.

DCM COMPETITION RIFLE - .223 Rem. cal., includes DCM competition features such as modified A2 rear sight, 20 in. extra heavy 1 in. diameter competition barrel, custom trigger job, and free-floating hand guard. Mfg. 1998-2005.

	100%	98%	95%	90%	80%	70%	60%
	$1,375	$1,125	$975	$875	$800	$725	$650

Last MSR was $1,495.

DCM-XR COMPETITION RIFLE - .223 Rem. cal., features redesigned rear sight and specially ground front sight, 20 in. extra heavy competition barrel, free-floating ribbed forearm, competition trigger, choice of A2 solid or A3 removable carry handle, 13.5 lbs. New 2008.

	100%	98%	95%	90%	80%	70%	60%
MSR $1,150	$985	$875	$775	$700	$625	$550	$500

Add $100 for A3 removable carry handle.

M17S BULLPUP - .223 Rem. cal., semi-auto bullpup configuration featuring garotating bolt gas operating system bolt, 10 (C/B 1994) or 30* shot mag., 21 1/2 plain or 22 (disc.) in. barrel with flash-hider (disc.), glass composites and aluminum materials, phosphate coating, 8 1/4 lbs. Mfg. 1992-2005.

	100%	98%	95%	90%	80%	70%	60%
	$700	$650	$525	$475	$425	$400	$385

Last MSR was $765.

CARBON-15 R21 - .223 Rem. cal., ultra lightweight carbon fiber upper and lower receivers, 16 in. "Profile" stainless steel barrel, quick detachable muzzle compensator, Stoner type operating system, tool steel bolt, extractor and carrier, optics mounting base, fixed tube stock, 10 or 30 (new late 2004) shot mag., also accepts AR-15 type mags., 3.9 lbs. New 2003 (Bushmaster mfg.).

	100%	98%	95%	90%	80%	70%	60%
MSR $990	$900	$800	$700	$600	$500	$450	$400

GRADING - PPGS™	100%	98%	95%	90%	80%	70%	60%

✴ *Carbon-15 Lady* - .223 Rem. cal., 16 in. barrel, includes overall tan finish (except for barrel) and webbed tube stock with recoil pad, chrome/nickel plating on small parts, supplied with soft case, 4 lbs. Mfg. 2004-2006.

	100%	98%	95%	90%	80%	70%	60%
	$875	$775	$675	$575	$500	$450	$400

Last MSR was $989.

CARBON-15 R97/97S - .223 Rem. cal., ultra lightweight carbon fiber upper and lower receivers, Stoner type operating system, hard chromed tool steel bolt, extractor and carrier, 16 in. fluted stainless steel barrel, quick detachable muzzle compensator, optics mounting base, 10 or 30 (new late 2004) shot mag., quick detachable stock, also accepts AR-15 type mags., 3.9 or 4.3 (Model 97S) lbs. New 2003 (Bushmaster mfg.).

MSR $1,265	$1,125	$900	$800	$725	$625	$550	$500

Subtract approx. $175 without Picatinny rail and "Scout" extension, double walled heat shield foregrip, ambidextrous safety, and multi-carry silent sling (Model Type 97, disc. 2005).

CARBON-15 .22 LR - .22 LR cal., similar to Carbon-15 R21, 16 in. barrel, Picatinny rail, 10 shot mag., fixed stock, approx. 4.4 lbs.

MSR $790	$685	$575	$485	$415	$350	$300	$265

Bushmaster also makes a Carbon-15 .22 rimfire upper receiver/barrel assembly that is dedicated to Bushmaster lower receivers - current MSR is $387 (new 2005).

CARBON-15 9MM - 9mm Para. cal., blow-back operation, carbon fiber composite receiver, 16 in. steel barrel with A1 birdcage flash hider, A2 front sight and dual aperture rear sight, Picatinny optics rail, collapsible stock, 10 or 30 shot mag, 5.7 lbs. New 2006.

MSR $1,070	$950	$860	$780	$700	$650	$600	$550

CARBON-15 TOP LOADING RIFLE - .223 Rem. cal., blow-back operation, carbon fiber composite receiver, 16 in. M4 profile barrel with Izzy suppressor, A2 front sight and dual aperture rear sight, Picatinny optics rail, collapsible stock, 10 shot top-loading internal mag, 5.8 lbs. New 2006.

MSR $1,050	$940	$860	$780	$700	$650	$600	$550

CARBON-15 MODEL 4 CARBINE - .223 Rem. cal., features carbon composite receiver, collapsible tube stock, 16 in. barrel with compensator, 30 shot mag., semi-auto design styled after the military M4, 5 1/2 lbs. New 2005.

MSR $1,155	$985	$875	$775	$700	$625	$550	$500

CARBON-15 FLAT-TOP CARBINE - .223 Rem. cal., similar to Carbon-15 Model 4 Carbine except has non-extended full-length Picatinny rail with dual aperture flip-up rear sight, 5 1/2 lbs. New 2006.

MSR $1,155	$985	$875	$775	$700	$625	$550	$500

BUSHMASTER .308 SERIES - .308 Win. cal., 16 or 20 in. phosphate coated heavy alloy steel barrel with Izzy compensator, 20 shot mag., solid buttstock or skeletonized stock, available in A2 or A3 style with a variety of configurations, including muzzle brakes, flash suppressors, and sighting options. Mfg. late 2004-2005.

	100%	98%	95%	90%	80%	70%	60%
	$1,495	$1,250	$1,050	$825	$725	$625	$550

Last MSR was $1,750.

Add $25 for A3 removable carry handle.
Add $10 for 20 in. barrel.
Add $50 (16 in. barrel) or $60 (20 in. barrel) for skeletonized stock.
Add approx. $100 for free-floating forearm.

BÜYÜK HUGLU

Current shotgun manufacturer located in Konya, Turkey. No current U.S. importation. Büyük Huglu manufactures good quality semi-auto shotguns in four different grades. Please contact the company directly for more information, including pricing and U.S. availability (see Trademark Index).

C SECTION

CETME

Previous manufacturer located in Madrid, Spain. CETME is an abbreviation for Centro Estudios Technicos de Materiales Especiales.

GRADING - PPGS™	100%	98%	95%	90%	80%	70%	60%

RIFLES: SEMI-AUTO

AUTOLOADING RIFLE - 7.62x51mm NATO cal., 17 3/4 in. barrel, delayed blowback action, utilizing rollers to lock breech, similar to HK-91 in appearance, wood military style stock, aperture rear sight.

$2,950	$2,650	$2,350	$2,000	$1,725	$1,500	$1,350

The H&K G3 is the next generation of this rifle, and many parts are interchangeable between the CETME and the the G3.

CFS GUNS

Previous firearms and airgun manufacturer circa 1997-2006, and located in Istanbul, Turkey.

CFS Guns manufactured a wide variety of O/U, SxS, slide action, and semi-auto shotguns. Some models were imported under the BSA trademark.

C Z (CESKÁ ZBROJOVKA)

Current manufacturer located in Uhersky Brod, Czech Republic, 1936-current. Previous manufacture was in Strakonice, Czechoslovakia circa 1923-late 1950s. Newly manufactured CZ firearms are currently imported exclusively by CZ USA located in Kansas City, KS. Previously imported by Magnum Research, Inc. located in Minneapolis, MN until mid-1994. Previously imported before 1994 by Action Arms Ltd. located in Philadelphia, PA. Dealer and distributor sales.

Ceská Zbrojovka simply means Czech weapons factory. CZ's full name is Ceská Zbrojovka a.s. Uhersky Brod, often abbreviated to CZUB a.s., meaning joint stock company. Uhersky Brod is the town the factory is located in. Zbrojovka Brno means weapons or arms factory located in Brno.

Zbrojovka Brno was built in 1916-1918, as a subsidiary of the Vienna Arsenal. After WWI, this factory was given the responsibility of providing the newly formed Czechoslovakian military with infantry weapons, specifically rifles and light machine guns. Circa 1923, pistol manufacture was transferred from Brno to Ceská Zbrojovka, located in the town of Strakonice, southwest of Bohemia. Since the location change, Zbrojovka Brno has never produced pistols on any great scale (please refer to the Brno section in this text for more information).

Ceská Zbrojovka Strakonice began developing many innovative and revolutionary pistol designs. These models, including the CZ-24, CZ-27, and CZ-52 are certainly well-known throughout the world. During the mid-1950s, CZ's facilities were converted to making motorcycles and precision engineering products.

Ceská Zbrojovka, located in the town of Uhersky Brod, was founded in 1936, as a subsidiary of Ceská Zbrojovka Strakonice, in a government decision designed to move firearms production further away from the German border, and out of the reach of German bombers. Uhersky Brod is located approx. 60 miles east of Brno. Before WWII, the factory produced aircraft machine guns (LK-30), the military pistol (CZ-38 in 9mm Para.), and rifle Models Z242-Z247. During WWII, the factory was taken over by the Germans, and the facilities were used for the production of aircraft machine guns (German designed MG 17s) and related components for other models of military weapons.

Shortly after WWII, Ceská Zbrojovka Uhersky Brod resumed production of firearms for the civilian marketplace, including the CZ 241 semi-auto shotgun, and some O/U shotguns. The production of pistols commenced during the mid-1950s, with the introduction of the Model CZ-

50 and other small pistol models named DUO in 6.35mm cal. Up to this point, the main pistol producer in Czechoslovakia was CZ Strakonice as stated above. The CZ-52 pistol was the last model they produced. Since the end of the 1950s, Ceská Zbrojovka Uhersky Brod has become the sole producer of pistols.

After WWII, the Ceská Zbrojovka Uhersky Brod became massively involved in other types of production besides sporting and hunting firearms. Production reached a high during the 1980s, when hunting/sporting firearms manufacture resulted in approx. 30% of total production. The balance of manufacture was devoted to the production of power hydraulics for tractors, while gears and accessory drive boxes for speed reduction in turbo prop airplane engines made up the rest.

During 1964-1966, the Czech government transferred the production of long guns from Zbrojovka Brno to Ceská Zbrojovka Uhersky Brod. During the 1970s & 1980s, the arms production of Zbrojovka Brno accounted for less than 3% of its total capacity. The activities of this company were diverted into the production of typewriters, diesel motors, and automatic machine tools. While many firearm designs originated in Brno, Zbrojovka Brno was not the manufacturer. Because of this, the long guns manufactured in the mid-1960s, including the ZKK 600-602 series and ZKM rimfires, were manufactured in CZ Uhersky Brod. Because of the Czech government's decision to merge manufacture within both companies, the Brno trademark was also used by Ceská Zbrojovka Uhersky Brod.

This relationship was terminated in 1983, when both companies became part of the Agrozet conglomerate. While confusing, the arms utlizing the Brno trademark were not produced in Brno during this time. All firearms exported from Czechoslovakia at the time carried the Brno logo, and most of them were manufactured by Ceská Zbrojovka Uhersky Brod.

During 1975, Ceská Zbrojovka Uhersky Brod designed and began manufacture of the famous CZ-75 pistol. Production in quantity began in 1977. To date, over 800,000 CZ-75s have been produced. This semi-auto has been made in many variations and/or modifications to suit many military and commercial contracts. During the mid-1980s, the CZ factory released the CZ-85, basically a CZ-75 with ambidextrous safety and slide stop. In the mid-1990s, production of the CZ-100 began - this new model featured a polymer frame. The CZ 550 line of rifles was also introduced at this same time.

For more information and current pricing on both new and used CZ airguns, please refer to the *Blue Book of Airguns* by Dr. Robert Beeman & John Allen (also online).

COMBINATION GUNS

CZ 584 SOLO - 12 ga. over choice of 7x57mm Mauser (importation disc. 1999), 7x57R, 7x65R, .222 Rem. (importation disc. 1999), .223 Rem. (imported 1994-99), .243 Win. (imported 1994-99), .30-06 (new 1994), 7mm Mauser (imported 1994-99), and .308 Win. (importation disc. 1999) cals. also available, 24 1/2 in. barrels, similar action to CZ 581 O/U shotgun, extractors or ejectors, rifle sights, approx. 7.4 lbs. Importation disc. 1986, resumed 1994. Disc. 1995, importation resumed 1999. Disc. 2003.

	$775	$655	$595	$515	$450	$385	$350

Last MSR was $917.

Add 20% for ejectors.

PISTOLS: SEMI-AUTO, DISC.

The models listed below were made in Ceská Zbrojovka Strakonice, with the exception of some models manufactured in Ceská Zbrojovka Prague during the Nazi occupation of Czechoslovakia. The VZ38 was also produced in Uhersky Brod.

"DUO" POCKET AUTOMATIC - .25 ACP cal., 6 shot, 2 1/8 in. barrel, fixed sights, blue or nickel, plastic grips. Mfg. beginning 1926 (current Z pistol by Brno).

	$225	$190	$170	$150	$125	$100	$75

Add 40% for WWII years.

This model was manufactured by Dushek and is similar to the Z pistol equivalent by Brno.

GRADING - PPGS™	100%	98%	95%	90%	80%	70%	60%

CZ 22 - .380 ACP cal., derived from Mauser variation and manufactured under license from Mauser. Mfg. 1923 only.

	100%	98%	95%	90%	80%	70%	60%
	$550	$400	$350	$325	$300	$295	$250

CZ 24 - .380 ACP cal.

* *CZ 24 Standard Frame* - 8 shot mag. Over 175,000 mfg. 1924-38. Over half issued to Czech Army. Same general design as CZ 22 except no gap between trigger and frame. Production continued to 1941.

	100%	98%	95%	90%	80%	70%	60%
Standard mfg.	$425	$375	$325	$300	$275	$235	$200
Kriegsmarine proofed	$1,275	$1,125	$975	$875	$800	$700	$600

Add $50 for Nazi proof.

Beware of counterfeit markings on Kriegsmarine proofed models.

* *CZ 24 Long Frame* - 9 shot mag.

	100%	98%	95%	90%	80%	70%	60%
	$1,750	$1,500	$1,250	$1,000	$900	$800	$700

Add $750 if fit with stock slot (either standard frame or long frame).

CZ 27 - .32 ACP cal.

* *CZ 27 "CESKÁ" Slide Legend Variation* - slanted slide grooves, high polish, available as Prewar Commercial, DR proofed, or Nazi proofed. Ser. no. range 1 - 21,500.

	100%	98%	95%	90%	80%	70%	60%
	$550	$450	$350	$300	$250	$200	$150

* *CZ 27 "BÖHMISCHE" Slide Legend Variation* - vertical slide grooves, high or medium polish, standard or Nazi Police pistols dated 1941, 1942, or 1943 marked with Eagle/K on left trigger guard web, ser. no. range 21,500-261,000.

	100%	98%	95%	90%	80%	70%	60%
Standard mfg.	$350	$300	$250	$200	$150	$135	$100
1941 dated	$775	$675	$550	$450	$325	$275	$225
1942-1943 dated	$700	$600	$500	$400	$300	$275	$200
Kriegsmarine proofed	$1,050	$900	$750	$600	$475	$400	$350

Beware of counterfeit markings on Kriegsmarine proofed models.

* *CZ 27 "fnh" Slide Legend Variation* - medium polish or phosphate. Ser. no. range 261,000-476,000.

	100%	98%	95%	90%	80%	70%	60%
	$300	$250	$200	$175	$150	$125	$100

Add 20% for late phosphate war finish.

* *CZ 27 Sound Suppressor Barrel Variation* - a small number of phosphate pistols were fitted with an extended barrel for suppressor attachment. Usually in 450,000-460,000 ser. no. range.

	100%	98%	95%	90%	80%	70%	60%
	$2,500	$2,000	$1,650	$1,500	$1,350	$1,200	$1,000

* *CZ 27 Post-WWII mfg.* - dated 1945, 1946, 1947, 1948, 1949, 1950, 1951. These models will have the "NARODNI PODNIK" inscription on slide.

Currently, these variations average $250 in 95%+ condition while reworks (very common) average under $200.

VZ 36 - .25 ACP cal., 8 shot, 2 1/2 in. barrel, fixed sights, blue finish, plastic grips, DA, similar to VZ 45, but scarce, some examples mfg. with safety lever on the left frame, some made w/o the lever. Mfg. 1936-1942.

	100%	98%	95%	90%	80%	70%	60%
	$600	$550	$500	$450	$400	$350	$300

VZ 38 DOUBLE ACTION AUTOMATIC - .380 ACP cal., 9 shot, double action only, 4 5/8 in. barrel, fixed sights, blue, plastic grips. Mfg. 1938-39.

	100%	98%	95%	90%	80%	70%	60%
	$550	$450	$350	$300	$250	$200	$150

Add 300% for Waffenampt proofed (E/WaA76 on barrel and left frame), usually phosphate finished and either unnumbered or in B291,000-B293,000 ser. no. range.

Changed to Model 39T after 1939.

VZ 38 "BULGARIAN CONTRACT" - .380 ACP cal., 9 shot, single or double action, prominent safety on left frame. Usually in 420,000-423,000 ser. no. range.

	100%	98%	95%	90%	80%	70%	60%
	$3,250	$2,750	$2,250	$1,500	$1,000	$750	$500

GRADING - PPGS™	100%	98%	95%	90%	80%	70%	60%

VZ 45 - .25 ACP cal., 8 shot, 2 1/2 in. barrel, fixed sights, blue finish, plastic grips, DA, similar to VZ 36, but slightly modified and with no safety lever. Mfg. 1945-1952.

	$300	$275	$250	$225	$200	$175	$150

CZ 28 - .32 ACP cal., blue finish, smooth hardwood grips, four slanted slide serrations on rear of slide, marked "C.S. STRAZ KARLOVY VARY" on right side, "CESKÁ ZBROJOVKA AS v PRAZE" on top of frame, and "CZ 28" on left side below serrations.

	$300	$250	$200	$175	$150	$125	$100

PISTOLS: SEMI-AUTO, RECENT MFG.

The CZ-52 was manufactured in Strakonice.

CZ P-01 - 9mm Para cal., based on CZ-75 design, but with metallurgical improvements, aluminum alloy frame, hammer forged 3.8 in. barrel, 10 or 13 (new 2005) shot mag., decocker, includes M3 rail on bottom of frame, checkered rubber grips, matte black polycoat finish, 27.2 oz. Importation began 2003.

MSR $612	$485	$410	$345	$305	$265	$235	$210

Add $99 for tactical block with bayonet (new 2006).
Add $67 for Crimson Trace laser grips (mfg. 2007).

CZ P-06 - 40 S&W cal., 10 shot mag., otherwise similar to CZ P-01. New 2008.

MSR $612	$485	$410	$345	$305	$265	$235	$210

CZ-40B/CZ-40P -.40 S&W cal. only, CZ-75B operating mechanism in alloy (CZ-40B) or polymer (CZ-40P) M1911 style frame, single/double action, black polycoat finish, 10 shot double column mag., fixed sights, firing pin block safety. Limited importation 2002 only, reintroduced 2007 only.

	$425	$365	$325	$290	$275	$250	$225

Last MSR was $499.

✳ CZ-40 P Compact - .40 S&W cal., 1,500 imported 2004, reimported 2006.

	$325	$285	$265	$245	$225	$200	$175

Last MSR was $370.

CZ-50/70 - .32 ACP cal., double action, blowback action, 3 3/4 in. barrel, loaded chamber indicator, 8 shot mag.

	$150	$125	$110	$100	$90	$80	$70

CZ-52 - 7.62 Tokarev or 9mm Para. cal., single action semi-auto, roller locking breech system, 4.9 in. barrel, 8 shot mag.

	$180	$150	$135	$125	$95	$85	$75

Add $40 for extra 9mm Para. barrel.

Currently imported used CZ-52 models are priced in the $115-$135 range, depending on condition, and will have the current importer's mark visible on the gun.

CZ-70 - 7.65mm/.32 ACP cal., double action, similar to Walther PP, 8 shot mag., 1 lb. 9 oz. Disc.

	$400	$350	$300	$275	$250	$225	$200

A very limited quantity of this model was imported.

CZ-75, CZ-75 B, CZ-75 BD - 9mm Para. or .40 S&W (disc. 1997, reintroduced 1999) cal., Poldi steel, selective double action, double action only, or single action only, frame safety, 4 3/4 in. barrel, 10 (C/B 1994, standard for .40 S&W cal.) or 15* shot mag., currently available in black polycoat/polymer (standard, DA and SA only), matte blue (disc. 1994), high polish (disc. 1994), glossy blue (new 1999), dual tone (new 1998), satin nickel (new 1994), or matte stainless steel (new 2006) finish, black plastic grips, non-suffix early guns did not have a firing pin block safety, reversible mag. release, or ambidextrous safety, and were usually shipped with two mags., B suffix model nomenclature was added 1998, and designated some internal mechanism changes, BD suffix indicates decocker mechanism, 34.3 oz.

MSR $544 $455 $370 $320 $280 $225 $210 $195

Add $16 for .40 S&W cal.
Add $10 for Model CZ-75 BD (decocker).
Add $143 for matte stainless steel (10 shot mag., new 2006).
Add $104 for high capacity stainless steel.
Add $16 for glossy blue, dual tone, or satin nickel finish.
Add $355 for CZ Kadet .22 LR adapter (includes .22 LR upper slide assembly and mag., new 1998).
Add $10 for single action only (Model CZ-75 B SA, black polymer frame).
Add $81 for Crimson Trace laser grips (black poly coat finish only, mfg. 2007).

"First Model" variations, mostly imported by Pragotrade of Canada, are identifiable by short slide rails, no half-cock feature, and were mostly available in high polish blue only. These early pistols sell for $1,200 if NIB condition, chrome engraved $1,650 (NIB), factory competition $1,500 (NIB).

✳ **CZ-75 B Military** - 9mm Para. cal. Importation 2000-2002.

   $365 $315 $270 $250 $225 $210 $195

Last MSR was $429.

✳ **CZ-75 B Tactical** - similar to CZ-75 B, except has OD green frame and matte black polymer slide, includes CZ knife. Limited importation during 2003.

   $425 $355 $305 $270 $225 $210 $195

Last MSR was $499.

✳ **CZ-75 SP-01/SP-01 Tactical** - 9mm Para. cal. only, 4 3/4 in. barrel, includes light rail, ambidextrous thumb safety, adj. tritium sights (Tactical), matte black polycoat finish, decocker, checkered black rubber grips, includes two 19 shot mags, 38 oz. New 2006.

MSR $635 $525 $480 $435 $400 $360 $335 $295

Add $33 for tritium sights (Tactical model).
Add $99 for tactical block with bayonet.

✳ **CZ-75 Semi-Compact** - 9mm Para. cal. only, 13 shot mag., choice of black polymer, matte, or high polish blue finish. Imported 1994 only.

   $350 $300 $275 $250 $230 $250 $200

Last MSR was $519.

Add $20 for matte blue finish.
Add $40 for high polish blue finish.

✳ **CZ-75 Compact** - 9mm Para. or .40 S&W (new 2005) cal. only, otherwise similiar to CZ-75, full-size frame, except has 3.9 in. barrel, 10 (C/B 1994) or 13* shot mag., checkered walnut grips, 33 oz. New 1993.

MSR $575 $465 $385 $350 $295 $255 $230 $210

Add $18 for glossy blue (disc. 2006), dual tone, or satin nickel finish.
Add $37 for .40 S&W cal.
Add $99 for tactical block with bayonet (.40 S&W cal. only, new 2006).
Add $355 for CZ Kadet .22 LR adapter (includes .22 LR upper slide assembly and mag., new 1998).

✳ **CZ-75 D PCR Compact** - 9mm Para. cal., similar to CZ-75 Compact, except has black polymer frame, decocker, 1.7 lbs. Importation began 2000.

MSR $593 $470 $395 $340 $295 $255 $230 $210

✳ **CZ-75 Kadet** - .22 LR cal., black polymer finish, 10 shot mag, 4.88 in. barrel. Mfg. 1999-2004, reintroduced 2006.

MSR $605 $485 $390 $330 $290 $260 $235 $215

✳ **CZ-75 25th Anniversary** - 9mm Para. cal., features include 25th Anniversary markings. Limited mfg. 2000 only.

   $625 $450 $375 $315 $270 $230 $200

Last MSR was $699.

GRADING - PPGS™	100%	98%	95%	90%	80%	70%	60%

✳ CZ-75 Champion - 9mm Para. (new 2000) or .40 S&W cal., dual tone finish, IPSC competition features including 3 port compensator, finger grooved synthetic grips, target trigger and sights, 4 1/2 in. barrel, approx. 2.2 lbs. Imported 1999-2004, reintroduced 2006.

MSR $1,741	$1,425	$1,200	$1,050	$875	$725	$600	$500

✳ CZ-75 Standard IPSC - .40 S&W cal., IPSC features, 5.4 in. barrel, dual tone finish, checkered wood grips, 10 or 16 (new 2005) shot mag., 45 oz. Mfg. 1999-2005.

	$1,000	$900	$750	$625	$550	$450	$350

Last MSR was $1,152.

✳ CZ-75 Tactical Sport - 9mm Para. or .40 S&W cal., dual tone finish, steel frame, 10, 16 (.40 S&W cal.), or 20 (9mm Para. cal.) shot mag., 5.3 in. barrel, ambidextrous safety, checkered wood grips, fixed sights, 45 oz. New 2006.

MSR $1,219	$1,050	$940	$775	$625	$550	$450	$350

✳ CZ-75 Modified - similar to Standard, except has dual port compensator and red dot reflex sight, approx. 2.8 lbs. Imported 2001-2002.

	$1,250	$1,075	$975	$875	$735	$600	$500

Last MSR was $1,567.

✳ CZ-75 Special Editions - 9mm Para. cal., similar to CZ-75, except has optional special edition finishes including all matte nickel, bright nickel frame, matte chrome, all brushed chrome, bright chrome, or gold frame, choice of matching finish slide, master blue slide, gold small parts, or master blue slide with gold small parts, price line refers to all matte nickel finish. Imported 1993-94 by Action Arms only.

	$525	$465	$415	$375	$335	$310	$285

Last MSR was $699.

Add approx. $120 for matte nickel frame with master blue small parts.
Add approx. $180 for matte nickel with gold small parts, matte nickel frame with master blue slide and gold small parts, master blue with gold small parts, or gold frame with master blue slide.

✳ CZ-75 30th Anniversary - 9mm Para. cal., features special 30th anniversary engraving with 24Kt. gold plated controls and accents, 10 or 15 shot mag., high gloss blue finish, birch grips with carved "30." 1,000 mfg. (ser. no. 1-1,000) 2005-2006.

	$875	$750	$625	$500	$450	$395	$350

Last MSR was $999.

CZ-82 - 9x18mm Makarov cal., current Czech military sidearm, most recent exportation was to W. Germany in Makarov chambering.

This model is similar to the CZ-83 except for cal. Prices are similar to the model CZ-83.

CZ-83 - .32 ACP (disc. 1994, reintroduced 1999-2002 and 2006) or .380 ACP (new 1986), or 9mm Makarov (mfg. 1999-2001) cal., modern design, 3-dot sights, 3.8 in. barrel, choice of carry models, blue (disc. 1994), glossy blue (new 1998), satin nickel (new 1999, not available in .32 ACP), or black polymer (disc. 1997) finish, black synthetic grips, 10 (C/B 1994), 12* (.380 ACP) or 15* (.32 ACP) shot mag., 26.2 oz. Mfg. began 1985, but U.S. importation started in 1992.

MSR $451	$355	$280	$235	$195	$180	$170	$160

Add $15 for glossy blue finish.

✳ CZ-83 Special Editions - .380 ACP cal. only, similar to CZ-83, has optional special edition finishes including all matte nickel, master high polish blue, bright nickel frame, matte chrome, all brushed chrome, bright chrome, or gold frame, choice of matching finish slide, master blue slide, gold small parts, or master blue slide with gold small parts, price line refers to all matte nickel or high polish blue finish. Importation disc. 1994.

	$425	$375	$335	$295	$250	$225	$200

Last MSR was $569.

Add approx. $90 for matte nickel frame with master blue small parts.
Add approx. $175 for matte nickel with gold small parts, matte nickel frame with master blue slide and gold small parts, master blue with gold small parts, or gold frame with master blue slide.

GRADING - PPGS™	100%	98%	95%	90%	80%	70%	60%

CZ-85, CZ-85 B - 9mm Para. or 9x21mm (imported 1993-94 only) cal., variation of the CZ-75 with ambidextrous controls, new plastic grip design, sight rib, available in black polymer, matte blue (disc. 1994), glossy blue (mfg. 2001 only), or high-gloss blue (9mm Para. only, disc. 1994) finish, includes firing pin block and finger rest trigger, plastic grips, 15 shot mag. new 2005, B suffix model nomenclature was added during 1998, approx. 2.2 lbs.

MSR $572	$470	$380	$330	$290	$255	$230	$210

Add $291 for CZ Kadet .22 LR adapter (includes .22 LR upper slide assembly and mag., mfg. 1998 only).

* *CZ-85 Combat* - similar to CZ-85B, except has fully adj. rear sight, available in black polymer, matte blue (disc. 1994), glossy blue (new 2001), dual-tone, satin nickel, or high-gloss blue finish, walnut (disc. 1994) or black plastic (new 1994) grips, extended mag. release, drop free 15 shot mag. new 2005. Importation began 1992.

MSR $639	$510	$430	$375	$335	$295	$265	$240

Add $27 for glossy blue, satin nickel, or dual-tone finish.
Add $291 for CZ Kadet .22 LR adapter (includes .22 LR upper slide assembly and mag., mfg. 1998 only).

* *CZ-85 Champion* - .40 S&W or 9x21mm cal., similar to CZ-75 Champion, except has 3 port compensator. Imported 1999 only.

	$1,325	$1,100	$975	$850	$725	$600	$500

Last MSR was $1,484.

* *CZ-85 Special Editions* - 9mm Para. cal., similar to CZ-85, has optional special edition finishes including all matte nickel, bright nickel frame, matte chrome, all brushed chrome, bright chrome, or gold frame, choice of matching finish slide, master blue slide, gold small parts, or master blue slide with gold small parts, price line refers to all matte nickel finish. Imported 1993-94 only.

	$575	$495	$450	$395	$350	$325	$285

Last MSR was $749.

Subtract $60 for matte nickel frame with master blue slide.
Add $130 for matte nickel frame with master blue small parts, matte nickel with gold small parts, matte nickel frame with master blue slide and gold small parts, master blue with gold small parts or gold frame with master blue slide.

* *CZ-85 Combat Special Editions* - 9mm Para. cal., similar finishes to Model CZ-85 Special Editions, price line refers to all matte nickel finish. Limited importation 1994-95.

	$775	$725	$650	$595	$525	$450	$375

Last MSR was $1,049.

Subtract $125 for matte nickel frame with master blue small parts.
Add $245 for matte nickel with gold small parts, matte nickel frame with master blue slide and gold small parts, master blue with gold small parts, or gold frame with master blue slide.

CZ-97 B - .45 ACP cal., single or double action, manual safety with firing pin block safety, 4.84 in. barrel with short recoil system, black polymer or glossy blue finish, checkered wood grips, double column 10 shot mag., last shot hold open slide, 40 oz. New 1998.

MSR $709	$590	$500	$415	$350	$295	$260	$240

Add $18 for glossy blue finish.

CZ-100 - 9mm Para. or .40 S&W cal., double action only with firing pin block and locked breech, w/o external manual safety, black polymer finish, adj. 3-dot sights, high impact plastic frame, 10 or 12 (new 2005, 9mm Para. cal. only) shot mag., 3.9 in. barrel, approx. 24 oz. Mfg. 1996-2007.

	$385	$325	$275	$245	$210	$195	$180

Last MSR was $458.

GRADING - PPGS™	100%	98%	95%	90%	80%	70%	60%

CZ-122 B SPORT - .22 LR cal., semi-auto, single action only, 6 in. solid ribbed barrel with adj. rear sight, manual and firing pin block safety, last shot hold open slide, steel frame and slide with two-tone finish, ribbed black polymer grips, 10 shot mag., 30 oz. Limited mfg. 1998 only.

	$225	$190	$175	$160	$150	$140	$135

Last MSR was $259.

CZ-2075 RAMI - 9mm Para. or .40 S&W cal., SA/DA operation, 3 in. barrel, double stack 8 (.40 S&W cal.), 10 (9mm Para. cal., flush fit) or 14 (9mm Para. cal.) shot mag. with finger extension, snag free sights, black polycoat finish with black checkered grips, alloy or polymer (new 2006) frame, 25 oz. New 2005.

MSR $557	$465	$370	$315	$275	$225	$210	$195

Add $54 for alloy frame with black polycoat finish.

RIFLES: BOLT ACTION, COMMERCIAL MFG.

Ceskị Zbrojovka began manufacturing rifles circa 1936. Long gun production was discontinued between 1948-1964, with the exception of the massive military contracts during that time period.

CZ USA MODEL 3 - .270 WSM, 7mm WSM, or .300 WSM, Mauser style claw extractor, adj. M-70 type trigger, bottom floorplate with three-shot fixed mag., three position safety, blue or stainless matte finished action and 24 in. barrel, right- or left-hand action, drilled and tapped, American black walnut stock with fleur-de-lis, no sights, mfg. in the U.S., 7.9 lbs. Limited mfg. 2005 only.

	$725	$600	$550	$495	$450	$400	$350

Last MSR was $872.

Add $10 for left-hand action.
Add $21 for stainless steel action and barrel.

MODEL CZ 452 STYLE (ZKM-452) - .22 LR or .22 Win. Mag. (disc. 1998) cal., bolt action, 5, 6 (.22 Mag. only), or 10 shot mag., 24.8 in. barrel, choice of black synthetic stock and matte nickel metal finish (new 1999) or uncheckered hardwood stock with Schnabel forend and blue metal finish (disc. 1998), adj. rear sight, 6.6 lbs. Importation began 1995 from CZ, earlier mfg. was by Brno. Reintroduced 2007.

MSR $421	$335	$275	$220	$175	$150	$135	$120

Add $50 for .22 Win. Mag. cal. (disc. 1998).

* *Model CZ 452 Lux/Deluxe (ZKM-452D)* - similar to ZKM-452 only with checkered walnut stock. Importation began 1995.

MSR $421	$335	$280	$225	$175	$150	$135	$120

Add $32 for .22 Win. Mag. cal.
Add $32 for left-hand action (.22 LR cal. only, new 2006).

* *Model CZ 452 Ultra Lux* - .22 LR cal., beechwood stock, 10 shot mag., 28 in. barrel, features gold accents. New 2006.

MSR $368	$295	$260	$215	$180	$160	$135	$120

* *Model CZ 452 American Classic (ZKM-452)* - .17 HMR (new 2003), .17 Mach 2 (new 2005), .22 LR or .22 Win. Mag. cal., 5 shot mag., 16 (new 2007) or 22 1/2 in. barrel w/no sights, American style walnut stock, approx. 6 lbs. Importation began 1999.

MSR $421	$330	$270	$220	$175	$150	$135	$120

Add $32 for .22 Win. Mag. cal.
Add $38 for .17 HMR cal.
Add $40 for left-hand action (.17 HMR or .22 LR cal. only, new 2006).

* *Model CZ 452 FS* - .17 HMR (new 2005), .22 LR or .22 Win. Mag. cal., 5 shot detachable mag., 21 in. barrel, features full length walnut Mannlicher stock, tangent rear adj. sight, 6.4 lbs. New 2004.

MSR $469	$395	$335	$280	$245	$215	$195	$180

Add $9 for .22 Win. Mag. or .17 HMR cal.

GRADING - PPGS™	100%	98%	95%	90%	80%	70%	60%

✳ *Model CZ 452 Silouhette* - .22 LR cal., similar to CZ-452 American Classic, except has black synthetic stock and blue metal, 5.3 lbs. New 2003.

MSR $421	$330	$270	$220	$175	$150	$135	$120

✳ *Model CZ 452 Scout (ZKM-452)* - .22 LR cal. only, youth configuration with shorter 16.2 in. barrel and uncheckered hardwood stock, 5 shot mag., includes single shot adapter, 5 lbs. Importation began 2000.

MSR $273	$215	$170	$140	$115	$95	$75	$65

✳ *Model CZ 452 Training Rifle/Special* - .17 HMR (Special only) or .22 LR cal., similar to CZ-452 Lux, except has beechwood stock and 5 shot mag., 6.4 lbs. New 2002.

MSR $335	$265	$210	$170	$130	$110	$90	$80

   Add $24 for .17 HMR cal. (new 2007).

✳ *Model CZ 452 Varmint (ZKM-452)* - .17 HMR (new 2005), .17 Mach 2 (new 2005), .22 LR or .22 Win. Mag. (new 2004) cal. only, similar to Model ZKM-452D, except has 21 in. heavy barrel and no sights, 6.8 lbs. Importation began 1998.

MSR $453	$365	$295	$245	$190	$170	$150	$140

   Add $26 for .17 HMR or .22 Win. Mag. cal.

CZ 453 - .17 Mach 2 (disc. 2006), .17 HMR (new 2007), or .22 LR cal., 5 fixed (American) or detachable (Varmint) shot mag., 20.9 (Varmint) or 22 1/2 (American) in. barrel, two-position safety, single set trigger, no sights, 6.1 (American) or 7 (Varmint) lbs. New 2006.

MSR $574	$460	$395	$345	$295	$260	$230	$195

   Add $38 for .17 HMR cal.
   Add $50 for fluted barrel (Varmint only, .17 HMR cal., new 2008).

CZ 513 HUNTER - .22 LR cal., entry level bolt action, 5 shot detachable mag., beechwood stock. Imported 1994 only.

	$195	$175	$150	$125	$95	$80	$65

Last MSR was $225.

   Add $30 for Farmer Model.
   This model was imported exclusively by Action Arms.

CZ 513 BASIC - .22 LR cal., 5 shot detachable mag., 20.9 in. barrel, non-adj. trigger, uncheckered beechwood stock, iron sights, 5 3/4 lbs. Mfg. 2004-2005, reintroduced 2007.

MSR $273	$215	$175	$140	$120	$100	$80	$65

CZ 527 LUX - .22 Hornet, .222 Rem., .223 Rem. cal., Mauser style bolt action with silent safety, 21.9 in. barrel with open sights, 5 shot detachable mag., hardwood (disc.) or checkered walnut stock and forend, 6.2 lbs. Importation began 1995.

MSR $654	$540	$445	$400	$345	$300	$275	$250

   Add $76 for left-hand action (.223 Rem. cal. only).

✳ *CZ 527 FS* - similar to Model 527, except has checkered full length Mannlicher walnut stock with steel muzzle cap, vent. recoil pad, 6 1/4 lbs. Importation began 1995.

MSR $753	$610	$530	$450	$395	$355	$335	$295

✳ *CZ 527 American Classic* - similar to CZ 527 Lux, also available in .204 Ruger or .221 Fireball cal. (new 2004), maple (disc.), brown laminate, spring camo laminate, sunset camo laminate, English walnut or fancy American walnut stock, scope rings included, approx. 6 1/2 lbs. New 1999.

MSR $684	$565	$510	$440	$385	$345	$300	$275

   Add $46 for left-hand action.
   Add $122 for English walnut stock or $178 for fancy American walnut stock.
   Subtract $13 for laminated stock.

✳ **CZ 527 M1 American** - .223 Rem. cal., styling similar to U.S. military M1 carbine featuring 3 shot flush detachable mag., walnut or black polymer stock. New 2008.

MSR $624	$525	$450	$395	$350	$300	$275	$250

Add $60 for walnut stock.

✳ **CZ 527 Prestige** - .22 Hornet or .223 Rem. (disc. 2006) cal., similar to CZ 527 Lux, except has deluxe checkered walnut stock and forend, no sights, jewel bolt, SST, scope rings included, 6.3 lbs. Limited mfg. beginning 2001.

MSR $930	$795	$565	$430	$395	$330	$285	$260

✳ **CZ 527 Varmint** - .17 Rem. (mfg. 2005-2006, reintroduced 2007), .204 Ruger (new 2005), or .223 Rem. cal., varmint configuration with heavy barrel and no sights, choice of walnut (.204 Ruger cal. only), maple (.223 Rem. cal., disc. 2006), laminated (new 2002), or H-S Precision Kevlar (new 2002) black stock, approx. 8 lbs. Importation began 2001.

MSR $654	$540	$450	$400	$350	$300	$275	$250

Add $106 for grey laminate stock (.223 Rem. cal. only) or $215 for H-S Precision Kevlar stock (not available in .17 Rem.).

✳ **CZ 527 M Carbine** - .223 Rem. (new 2001) or 7.62x39mm cal., carbine configuration with 18 1/2 barrel with sights, 6 lbs. New 1999.

MSR $662	$555	$455	$400	$350	$300	$275	$250

CZ 537 - .243 Win., .270 Win., .30-06, .308 Win., or 7x57mm cal., detachable 4 shot (.243 Win. and .308 Win. cals. only) or 5 shot fixed mag., choice of regular or Mannlicher (.30-06 or .308 Win. cal. only) stock, hooded ramp front sight, 7 1/4 lbs. Importation 1995 only.

	$495	$425	$370	$330	$300	$275	$250

Last MSR was $649.

Add $100 for Mannlicher style stock.

✳ **CZ 537 Mountain Carbine** - .243 Win. only, 19 in. barrel, 5 shot detachable mag., includes ring mounts, 7.1 lbs. Imported 1994 only.

	$525	$450	$375	$330	$300	$275	$250

Last MSR was $669.

CZ 550 STANDARD - various cals. have been imported to date, 4 shot detachable mag. (.243 Win. or .308 Win. only) or internal 5 shot, 23.6 in. barrel, receiver drilled and tapped for Remington 700 style scope base, no sights, checkered walnut stock and forearm, 7 1/4 lbs. Imported 1995-2000.

	$475	$395	$340	$310	$285	$260	$240

Last MSR was $561.

Add $21 for .243 Win. or .308 Win. cal. with detachable mag.

✳ **CZ 550 Lux** - various cals., similar to CZ 550 Standard, except has deluxe checkered walnut stock with Bavarian style cheekpiece and vent. recoil pad. Mfg. 1998-2004.

	$495	$415	$350	$315	$285	$260	$240

Last MSR was $588.

Add $20 for detachable mag. (.22-250 Rem., .243 Win., or .308 Win. cal., disc.).

❖ **CZ 550 Battue Lux** - similar to CZ 550 Lux, except has 20 1/2 in. barrel with integral barrel fixed rear sight. Limited mfg. 1998 only.

	$450	$375	$330	$300	$280	$260	$240

Last MSR was $519.

Add $30 for .243 Win. or .308 Win. cal. with removable mag.

✳ **CZ 550 Prestige** - .270 Win. or .30-06 cal., similar to CZ 550 Lux, except has deluxe checkered walnut stock and forend, no sights, scope rings included. Imported 2001, reintroduced 2003-2005.

	$740	$510	$405	$380	$325	$285	$260

Last MSR was $854.

✳ CZ 550 American Classic - .22-250 Rem., .243 Win., .270 Win., .30-06, .308 Win., 6.5x55mm (new 2001), 7x57mm (disc. 2004), or 9.3x62mm cal., features American style walnut stock, fixed or detachable mag., scope rings included, no sights, approx. 8 lbs. New mid-1999.

MSR $712	$600	$535	$455	$395	$350	$300	$250

Add $20 for detachable 4-5 shot mag. (.22-250 Rem., .243 Win. and .308 Win. only).

✳ CZ 550 Varmint - .22-250 Rem. (new 2002) or .308 Win. cal., 25.6 in. barrel w/o sights, 4 shot detachable mag., checkered walnut (.308 Win. cal. only), H-S Precision Kevlar (new 2005), or laminated (new 2002) stock with vent. recoil pad, approx. 9 - 10 3/4 lbs. Importation began 2000.

MSR $766	$665	$550	$480	$400	$350	$300	$275

Add $114 for laminated stock (new 2002).
Add $178 for H-S Precision Kevlar stock (new 2005).

✳ CZ 550 FS Mannlicher - similar to CZ 550 American Classic, except has Mannlicher stock and 20 1/2 in. barrel, not available in .22-250 Rem. cal., fixed 5 shot or 4 shot detachable mag. (.243 Win. or .308 Win. cal. only), adj. sights, 7.4 lbs. Imported 1996-98, reintroduced 2001.

MSR $790	$690	$585	$480	$425	$375	$325	$275

Add $25 for 4 shot detachable mag.

✳ CZ 550 Battue FS Mannlicher - similar to CZ 550 FS Mannlicher, except has integral barrel fixed rear sight. Limited mfg. 1998 only.

	$525	$465	$425	$395	$360	$330	$300

Last MSR was $609.

Add $30 for .243 Win. or .308 Win. cal. with removable mag.

✳ CZ 550 Minnesota - similar to CZ 550 Lux, except has select walnut stock w/o cheekpiece, and barrel has no sights. Limited mfg. 1998 only.

	$445	$375	$330	$300	$280	$260	$240

Last MSR was $505.

Add $30 for .243 Win. or .308 Win. cal. with removable mag.

✳ CZ 550 Medium Magnum - .300 Win. Mag. or 7mm Rem. Mag. cal., checkered walnut stock and forearm, open sights, (.300 Win. Mag. has Battue quarter rib., detachable mag. and fiber optic front sight), 23.6 in. barrel, 7 3/4 lbs. New 2007.

MSR $774	$665	$585	$510	$450	$400	$325	$275

✳ CZ 550 Magnum Standard - .300 Win. Mag., .375 H&H, .416 Rem. Mag. (disc. 1998), .416 Rigby, .458 Win. Mag., or 7mm Rem. Mag. (importation disc. 1997) cal., 3-5 shot fixed mag., 25 in. barrel with express rear sight, checkered hardwood stock, 9 1/4 lbs. Limited mfg. 1998 only.

	$525	$475	$440	$400	$375	$350	$335

Last MSR was $595.

Add $40 for .416 Rem. Mag., .416 Rigby, or .458 Win. Mag. cal.

❖ CZ 550 Magnum Standard Lux - similar to CZ 550 Magnum, except has select checkered walnut, last cals. were .300 Win. Mag. and 7mm Rem. Mag., 7.7-9.4 lbs. Mfg. 1998-2005.

	$600	$500	$445	$395	$350	$335	$300

Last MSR was $690.

Add $185 for .375 H&H., .416 Rigby, or .458 Win. Mag. (disc.) cal.

✳ CZ 550 Ultimate Hunting Rifle (UHR) - .300 Win. Mag. cal. only, extra craftsmanship guarantees MOA accuracyto 600 yards, deluxe checkered stock and forend, 23.6 in. barrel, includes scope rings, 4 shot mag., 8 lbs. New 2007.

MSR $1,950	$1,725	$1,525	$1,225	$1,025	$895	$775	$650

Add $1,500 for Nightforce 5.5-22x50 mm scope.

✱ CZ 550 Safari Magnum - .300 Win. Mag. (new 2008), .375 H&H, .416 Rigby, or .458 Win. Mag. cal., express sights, single set trigger, checkered walnut stock with curved cheekpiece, fixed mag., 9.4 lbs. New 2004.

MSR $1,073	$900	$775	$675	$575	$475	$425	$385

✱ CZ 550 American Safari Field Magnum - .375 H&H, .416 Rigby, .458 Win. Mag., or .458 Lott cal., choice of field grade wood or laminate stock, 9.9 lbs. New 2004.

MSR $1,073	$900	$775	$675	$575	$475	$425	$385

  Add $75 for .458 Lott cal.

  Add $244 for brown laminate, spring camo laminate, or sunset camo laminate stock.

✱ CZ 550 American Safari Deluxe Magnum - .375 H&H, .416 Rigby, .458 Win. Mag., or .458 Lott cal., similar to Field Grade, except has deluxe walnut stock. New 2004.

MSR $1,740	$1,475	$1,225	$1,025	$925	$825	$725	$650

  Add $52 for .458 Lott cal.

✱ CZ 550 Safari Classic (Custom Grade Safari Magnum) - .300 H&H (new 2007), .338 Lapua (new 2008), .338 Win. Mag. (new 2008), .375 H&H, .404 Jeffery, .416 Rem. (new 2008), .450 Rigby, .500 Jeffrey (new 2007), or .505 Gibbs cal., custom Magnum action with two-position safety, single set trigger set up for individual requirements, glossy or matte blue metal finish, checkered fancy grade American walnut stock and forend, express sights, built per individual custom order. New 2005.

MSR $2,853	$2,425	$2,075	$1,800	$1,525	$1,250	$1,050	$900

  Add $251 for .338 Lapua, .500 Jeffrey or 505 Gibbs cal. (includes built-in recoil reducer and glass bedded action).

  Subtract $721 for .375 H&H cal. with 20 in. barrel.

ZKK 600 - .270 Win., .30-06, or 7x57mm cal., improved Mauser type action, 23 1/2 in. barrel, checkered walnut stock, 5 shot internal mag., thumb safety, 7.2 lbs. Importation disc. 1995.

$500	$425	$370	$330	$300	$275	$250

Last MSR was $589.

ZKK 601 - .222 Rem., .223 Rem., .243 Win. or .308 Win. cal., otherwise similar to ZKK 600. Importation disc. 1995.

$500	$425	$370	$330	$300	$275	$250

Last MSR was $589.

ZKK 602 - .300 Win. Mag. (disc.), .375 H&H, .416 Rigby (new 1996), .416 Rem. (new 1996), 8x68mm (disc.), or .458 Win. Mag. cal., similar to ZKK 600, except has 25.2 in. barrel and 3 leaf express rear sight, 9.3 lbs. Disc. 1997.

$675	$575	$495	$450	$395	$350	$310

  Last MSR was $799.

CZ 700 SNIPER - .308 Win. cal., sniper design features forged billet receiver with permanently attached Weaver rail, 25.6 in. heavy barrel w/o sights, 10 shot detachable mag., laminated thumbhole stock with adj. cheekpiece and buttplate, large bolt handle, fully adj. trigger, 11.9 lbs. Limited importation 2001 only.

$1,875	$1,575	$1,250	$1,025	$895	$775	$650

Last MSR was $2,097.

CZ 750 SNIPER - .308 Win. cal., sniper design, black synthetic thumbhole stock w/ adj. comb, Weaver rail comes installed for scope mounting, 26 in. barrel w/muzzle brake, includes two 10 shot mags., 11.9 lbs. Limited mfg. beginning 2006.

MSR $1,999	$1,750	$1,525	$1,225	$1,025	$895	$775	$650

GRADING - PPGS™	100%	98%	95%	90%	80%	70%	60%

RIFLES: O/U

CZ-589 STOPPER - .458 Win. Mag. cal. only, Kersten style boxlock action with Blitz type trigger, checkered Turkish walnut stock and forearm, fixed iron sights, includes sling swivels, 9.3 lbs. Approx. 5 mfg. and imported 2001 only.

	$2,695	$2,300	$2,000	$1,750	$1,500	$1,250	$1,050

Last MSR was $2,999.

Add $1,000 for sideplates and special engraving/checkering.

RIFLES: SEMI-AUTO

CZ-M52 (1952) - 7.62x45mm Czech cal., semi-auto, 20 2/3 in. barrel, 10 shot detachable mag., tangent rear sight, this model was also imported briefly by Samco Global Arms, Inc. located in Miami, FL.

	$550	$450	$350	$300	$250	$200	$150

CZ-M52/57 (1957) - 7.62x39mm cal., later variation of the CZ-M52.

	$425	$375	$325	$300	$250	$200	$150

CZ-511 - .22 LR cal., blowback action, 22.2 in. barrel, uncheckered beechwood (disc. 2001) or checkered walnut (new 2006) stock, flip-up rear sight, receiver top slotted for scope mounts, 8 shot mag., approx. 5 1/2 lbs. Previously disc. 1986, importation resumed 1998-2001. Imported 2005-2006.

	$320	$275	$235	$200	$180	$160	$150

Last MSR was $389.

VZ 58 MILITARY/TACTICAL SPORTER - 7.62x39mm cal., gas operated, patterned after the AK-47, milled receiver, 16.14 in. barrel, tilting breech block, choice of Zytel skeletonized (Tactical) or plastic-impregnated wood (Military) stock, alloy 30 shot mag., 7.32 lbs. New 2008.

MSR $970	$850	$750	$650	$575	$500	$425	$350

Add $20 for Tactical model.

SHOTGUNS: O/U

CZ 581 SOLO - 12 ga., 2 3/4 in. chambers, boxlock action with Kersten upper locking mechanism, ejectors, checkered walnut stock and forearm, approx. 7.4 lbs. Importation disc. 1995, resumed 1999-2005.

	$740	$625	$570	$490	$425	$385	$350

Last MSR was $872.

Add 10% for single trigger (disc.).

MALLARD 104A - 12 or 20 ga., DT, extractors, 28 in. VR barrels with multichokes, coin finished alloy receiver, checkered Turkish walnut stock and forearm, 6 1/2 (20 ga.) or 7 1/2 (12 ga.) lbs. New 2005.

MSR $536	$465	$395	$350	$300	$275	$250	$225

CANVASBACK 103D - 12 or 20 ga., 3 in. chambers, 26 or 28 in. VR barrels with choke tubes, extractors, blued frame with light perimeter engraving, SST, stock/forearm similar to Redhead, 6.3 - 7 1/2 lbs. New 2005.

MSR $781	$675	$575	$500	$450	$400	$350	$300

REDHEAD DELUXE 103DE - 12 or 20 ga., boxlock action, SST, ejectors, checkered round knob Turkish walnut pistol grip stock and Schnabel forearm, coin finished frame and triggerguard, 26 or 28 in. VR barrels with screw-in chokes, 6.7 - 7.9 lbs. New 2005.

MSR $921	$800	$725	$650	$575	$525	$475	$425

Subtract $45 for shortened LOP (20 ga. only, 24 in. barrels, and 13 in. LOP - new 2008).

✻ *Redhead 103 D Mini* - 28 ga. or .410 bore, scaled down frame, otherwise similar to Redhead Deluxe, but w/o ejectors, 5.7 (.410 bore) or 6.2 lbs. New 2005.

MSR $954	$825	$750	$675	$600	$550	$500	$450

GRADING - PPGS™	100%	98%	95%	90%	80%	70%	60%

WOODCOCK DELUXE 103FE - 12 or 20 ga., ejectors, SST, 26 or 28 in. barrels with screw-in chokes, color case hardened boxlock frame with sideplates and triggerguard, hand engraving, checkered round knob Turkish walnut stock and Schnabel forearm, 6.8 (20 ga.) or 7.8 (12 ga.) lbs. New 2005.

MSR $1,189		$1,000	$850	$700	$600	$500	$450	$395

∗ *Woodcock 103F Mini* - 28 ga. or .410 bore, scaled down frame, otherwise similar to Woodcock Deluxe, but w/o ejectors, 6-6 1/4 lbs. New 2005.

MSR $1,270		$1,050	$875	$750	$650	$550	$500	$450

WOODCOCK DELUXE CUSTOM GRADE - 20 ga. only, 28 in. barrels, features color case hardened frame, deluxe checkered walnut stock and forearm. New 2006.

MSR $1,999		$1,725	$1,350	$1,100	$925	$825	$725	$650

CZ SPORTING - 12 ga., boxlock action, ejectors, SST, 30 or 32 in. VR backbored barrels with extended forcing cones, Circassian walnut stock and forearm with adj. comb. New 2008.

MSR $2,495		$1,995	$1,750	$1,500	$1,300	$1,100	$900	$775

LIMITED EDITION - 12 ga., 28 in. barrels, Circassian walnut stock and forearm, engraved boxlock action, gold trigger, 50 mfg. beginning 2008.

MSR $2,295		$1,895	$1,650	$1,450	$1,250	$1,025	$825	$675

SHOTGUNS: SxS

DURANGO - 12 or 20 ga., hammerless countroured boxlock action with color case hardened frame, 20 in. barrels, single trigger, multichokes, checkered Turkish walnut round knob stock and splinter forearm, 6 (20 ga.) or 6.7 (12 ga.) lbs. Imported 2005-2006.

		$725	$625	$525	$425	$350	$300	$250

Last MSR was $795.

AMARILLO - similar to Durango, except has double triggers, 5.9 (20 ga.) or 6 1/2 lbs. Imported 2005-2006.

		$625	$550	$475	$375	$300	$250	$200

Last MSR was $695.

BOBWHITE 202B - 12, 16 (new 2006), or 20 ga., 26 or 28 in. barrels with multichokes (N/A in .410 bore), color case hardened engraved boxlock action with sideplates, DT, checkered Turkish walnut straight grip English style stock and semi-beavertail forearm, 6 (20 ga.) or 7 lbs (12 ga.). New 2005.

MSR $765		$675	$625	$550	$475	$375	$300	$250

Add $193 for 16 ga.

∗ *Bobwhite 202B Mini* - 28 ga. or .410 bore, scaled down frame, otherwise similar to Bobwhite, 5.2 (.410 bore) or 5.6 (28 ga.) lbs. New 2005.

MSR $958		$850	$750	$675	$575	$475	$375	$325

RINGNECK 201A - similar to Bobwhite, except has single trigger, approx. 6 (20 ga.) or 7 lbs. New 2005.

MSR $995		$850	$775	$675	$575	$500	$450	$395

∗ *Ringneck 201A Mini* - 28 ga. or .410 bore, proportional frame to gauge, extractors, otherwise similar to Ringneck 201A, 5 1/4 (.410 bore) or 6 (28 ga.) lbs. New 2005.

MSR $1,206		$1,000	$850	$750	$650	$550	$450	$375

RINGNECK DELUXE CUSTOM GRADE - 20 ga. only, features color case hardened frame, deluxe checkered walnut stock and forearm. New 2006.

MSR $1,999		$1,725	$1,350	$1,100	$925	$825	$725	$650

HAMMER COACH MODEL - 12 ga. only, 20 in. barrels with fixed chokes, DT, exposed hammers. New 2006.

MSR $878		$775	$650	$550	$450	$350	$300	$250

GRADING - PPGS™	100%	98%	95%	90%	80%	70%	60%

GROUSE - 12, 20, 28 or .410 bore, 26 (28 ga. or .410 bore) or 28 (12 or 20 ga.) in. barrels, silver receiver, ST, choke tubes. New 2008.

MSR $995	$875	$750	$650	$575	$500	$425	$350

    Add $211 for 28 ga. or .410 bore.

PARTRIDGE - 12, 20, 28 ga., or .410 bore, 26 (28 ga. or .410 bore) or 28 (12 or 20 ga.) or 28 in. barrels, silver receiver, DT, straight grip English stock, choke tubes. New 2008.

MSR $765	$675	$600	$525	$450	$375	$300	$250

    Add $193 for 28 ga. or .410 bore.

SHOTGUNS: SEMI-AUTO

CZ-712/720 - 12 (Model 712) or 20 (Model 720) ga., 3 in. chamber, gas operated, checkered Turkish walnut stock, 26 or 28 in. vent. barrel, matte black chrome, aluminum receiver, Mossy Oak Shadow Grass or Mossy Oak Obsession camo treatment (disc. 2005), multichokes, jeweled bolt, single trigger, 6.3 - 7.3 lbs. Limited mfg. 2005, reintroduced 2008.

MSR $444	$375	$325	$275	$235	$195	$175	$150

    Add $14 for 20 ga.
    Add approx. 10% for 100% camo coverage (disc. 2005).
    Subtract $14 for shortened 13 in. LOP (20 ga., 24 in. barrel, new 2008).

CZ-712 MAGNUM - 12 ga. only, 3 1/2 in. chamber, 24 or 28 in. barrel, matte black chrome, checkered walnut, Mossy Oak Shadowgrass (28 in. barrel) or Mossy Oak Obsession (24 in. barrel) camo treatment, single trigger, vent. rib., 7 1/2 lbs. Limited mfg. 2005.

	$425	$375	$325	$295	$265	$235	$200

Last MSR was $499.

    Add $100 for 100% camo coverage.

CZ (STRAKONICE)

Current manufacturer established in 1919 and located in Strakonice, Czech Republic. No current U.S. importation. Previously imported by Adco Sales, Inc., located in Woburn, MA.

HISTORY OF THE CZ TRADEMARK

An aspect of the post-communist Czech economy is that there are now two rival manufacturing firms bearing the name of CZ (Ceska Zbrojovka). This company was started in Plzen in 1919, and moved to Strakonice in 1921, near the western border of Bohemia. The factory at Straconice remained the primary center for Czech handgun manufacture until the 1960s. Additionally, pistols (and a great many rifles) were made at another CZ - Ceskaslovenska Zbrojovka of Brno. However, the manufacture of pistols was transferred at an early date to the CZ factory at Strakonice.

During the rise of Hitler and the Nazis, the Czechs were justifiably alarmed at having so much of their arms industry within easy reach of the Nazis. Consequently, the two CZs collaborated in opening a joint manufacturing facility in 1936, far from the German border at Uhersky Brod. While Czechoslovakia was united, Uhersky Brod was in the very middle of the country; now it is located only a few kilometers west of the Czech Republic's border with Slovakia.

The CZ facility at Uhersky Brod eventually took over most of Czechoslovakia's firearms manufacturing during the postwar years although handgun manufacture continued on a reduced scale at the plant at Strakonice.

The dismemberment of the state-owned communist economy in the early 1990s has resulted in the existence of the two competitive CZ firms - one based in Uhersky Brod, the other at the older plant at Strakonice. The Brno operation also retains the name "CZ." The CZ based in Uhersky Brod is represented in the U.S. by CZ-USA, based in Kansas City, KS. In recent years, the CZ based in Strakonice has had little or no importation, and the last company was Adco Sales, Inc.

Some information appears courtesy of Jan Libourel and *Gun World* magazine.

GRADING - PPGS™	100%	98%	95%	90%	80%	70%	60%

PISTOLS: SEMI-AUTO

Older Strakonice manufacture can be found in the C Z (Ceska Zbrojovka) section.

CZ-75 - 9mm Para. cal., single/double action, 4 3/4 in. barrel, steel frame, 10 shot mag., blue finish only. Limited importation 2004 only.

	$475	$425	$375	$325	$295	$275	$225

Last MSR was $569.

CZ-TT - 9mm Para., .40 S&W, or .45 ACP cal., single/double action, polymer frame, 3.77 in. ported or unported barrel, matte finish, 10 shot mag., 26.1 oz. Imported 2004-2006.

	$415	$375	$325	$295	$275	$250	$225

Last MSR was $479.

Add $30 for ported barrel (disc.).
Add $40 for ported barrel and slide serrations (disc.).
Add $399 for conversion kit with one mag.

CZ-T POLYMER COMPACT - similar to CZ-TT, except has shorter barrel. Limited importation 2004 only.

	$475	$425	$375	$325	$295	$275	$225

Last MSR was $559.

ADCO/CZ 1911-A1 - .38 Super or .45 ACP cal., standard size government model with 5 in. barrel, black matte finish. Limited importation 2004.

	$475	$425	$375	$325	$295	$275	$225

Last MSR was $559.

Add $10 for .38 Super cal.

CABANAS

Previous trademark manufactured by Industrias Cabanas, S.A. in Aguilas, Mexico 1949-1999. Previously imported and retailed by Mandall Shooting Supplies, Inc. located in Scottsdale, AZ.

Cabanas manufactured a unique single shot bolt action rifle which shot oversized .177 pellets/BBs powered by .22 blanks at 1,150 feet per second. There were at least 8 variations, and secondary market prices today for 95%+ original condition ranges from approx. $65-$120. Transfer requires FFL. This trademark had limited U.S. importation.

CABELA'S INC.

Current sporting goods dealer and catalog company headquartered in Sidney, NE. Consumer direct (store or mail order catalog) sales only.

In addition to the models listed below, Cabela's also imports black powder cartridge Sharps replicas, revolvers, and other reproductions, mostly manufactured in Italy by A. Uberti, Pedersoli, and Pietta (please see individual sections for more info).

Cabela's also has a wide variety of black powder muzzleloading rifles and pistols, in addition to replicas of popular older Colt and Winchester firearms.

Please refer to the *Blue Book of Modern Black Powder Arms* (also online) by John Allen for more information and prices on Cabela's lineup of modern black powder models. *Black Powder Reproductions & Replicas* by Dennis Adler is also an invaluable source for most black powder reproductions and replicas, and includes hundreds of color images on most popular makes/models, provides manufacturer/trademark histories, and up-to-date information on related items/accessories for black powder shooting - www.bluebookinc.com

Cabela's should be contacted directly (see Trademark Index) to receive the most recent information on their complete firearms and black powder line-ups, including related accessories.

GRADING - PPGS™	100%	98%	95%	90%	80%	70%	60%

SHOTGUNS: SxS

HEMINGWAY MODEL - mfg. for Cabela's by V. Bernardelli located in Italy, ST, ejectors. Disc. 1994.

	$925	$775	$700	$640	$575	$525	$465

Last MSR was $975.

AYA GRADE II CUSTOM - mfg. for Cabela's by AYA located in Eibar, Spain, ST, ejectors, similar to AYA Model II with Model 53 engraving and trim. Disc. and sold out.

	$3,650	$3,100	$2,500	$2,000	$1,650	$1,275	$1,000

SHOTGUNS: O/U

VOLO - 12 or 20 ga., 3 in. chambers, 28 in. barrel, five interchangeable chokes, with or w/o gold inlay engraved sideplates (Volo Deluxe). Mfg. in Italy by Fausti. Importation began 2008.

MSR $1,100	$950	$825	$725	$650	$575	$500	$450

Add $200 for gold inlay engraved sideplates.

CAEM, RENATO

Current manufacturer of small gauge, SxS shotguns located in Marcheno Val Trompia, Italy. No current U.S. importation.

Renato Caem manufactures approx. 5 best quality scalloped boxlock SxS shotguns annually, only in 20 ga., 28 ga., or .410 bore. Please contact the factory directly for more information regarding specifications, delivery, and current prices (see Trademark Index).

CAESAR GUERINI, s.r.l.

Current manufacturer located in Marcheno, Italy. Currently imported beginning 2003 by Caesar Guerini USA LLC.

SHOTGUNS: O/U, FIELD

Add $275 for double triggers on 12 ga.
Add $150 for left-hand w/o sideplates.
Add 200 for left-hand with sideplates.

FLYWAY - 12 ga., 3 in. chambers, 28 or 30 in. barrels, beavertail forend, multichokes, blued boxlock receiver with satin finish and gold mallard on bottom, parallel 10mm top rib, shipped with hard case, 7 lbs. 14 oz. - 8 lbs.

	$1,795	$1,495	$1,295	$1,095	$895	$800	$725

Last MSR was $2,295.

WOODLANDER - 12, 20, 28 ga., or .410 bore (new 2006), 2 3/4 or 3 in. chambers, 26 or 28 in. barrels, case hardened boxlock receiver with Bulino style engraved (ruffed grouse in gold on bottom of receiver), Prince of Wales grip and Schnabel forend, 6mm top rib, multichokes, shipped with hard case, 6 lbs. 2 oz.-6 lbs. 14 oz.

MSR $2,850	$2,250	$1,795	$1,495	$1,295	$1,095	$895	$800

Combination packages are available on this model, and are currently priced in the $3,729 - $4,995 range.

TEMPIO - 12, 20, 28 ga., or .410 bore (new 2006), 2 3/4 or 3 in. chambers, 26 or 28 in. barrels, grey "Tinaloy" boxlock receiver featuring gold grouse, quail, and pheasant game scenes surrounded by scroll, Prince of Wales grip and Schnabel forend, oil finished wood, multichokes, factory hard case, 6 lbs. 4 oz.-7 lbs.

MSR $3,125	$2,550	$2,195	$1,895	$1,595	$1,395	$1,195	$995

Add $95 for .410 bore.
Combination packages are available on this model, and are currently priced in the $4,045 - $5,335 range.

GRADING - PPGS™	100%	98%	95%	90%	80%	70%	60%

MAGNUS LIGHT - 12, 20, 28 ga., or .410 bore (new 2006), 2 3/4 or 3 in. chambers, 26 or 28 in. barrels, case hardened sideplate boxlock alloy receiver with gold grouse, pheasant, and quail game scenes, Prince of Wales grip, Schnabel forend, oil finished wood, multichokes, factory hard case, 5 lbs. 4 oz.-6 lbs.

	MSR $3,895		$3,150	$2,495	$2,095	$1,895	$1,495	$1,295	$1,095

Add $95 for .410 bore.

Combination packages are available on this model, and are currently priced in the $4,690 - $5,980 range.

✻ *Magnus* - similar to Magnus Light, except has steel receiver, 6 lbs. 4 oz.-7 lbs.

	MSR $3,895		$3,150	$2,495	$2,095	$1,895	$1,495	$1,295	$1,095

Combination packages are available on this model, and are currently priced in the $4,690 - $5,980 range.

FORUM - 12, 20, 28 ga., or .410 bore (new 2006), 2 3/4 or 3 in. chambers, 26 or 28 in. barrels, coin finished boxlock receiver, blind sideplates with no visible screws, Bulino style engraving with game scenes and floral scroll, Prince of Wales grip, Schnable forend, checkered stock with oil finish, multichokes, factory hard case, 6 lbs. 5 oz.-7 lbs.

	MSR $7,995		$6,250	$4,495	$3,995	$3,200	$2,900	$2,500	$2,100

Combination packages are available on this model, and are currently priced in the $8,800 - $10,250 range.

ESSEX FIELD - 12, 20, 28 ga. or .410 bore, 26 or 28 in. barrels, coin finished sideplates with English rose and scroll engraving, tapered solid rib, round knob pistol grip stock. Less than 100 mfg. for importation during 2006.

	MSR $4,600		$3,995	$3,200	$2,700	$2,300	$1,850	$1,500	$1,250

Combination packages are available on this model, and are currently priced in the $5,590 - $7,175 range.

MAXUM FIELD - 12, 20, 28 ga. or .410 bore, 26 or 28 in. barrels, coin finished sideplates with deep relief floral scroll engraving, deluxe checkered oil finished Turkish walnut stock and forearm. Importation began 2006.

	MSR $5,200		$4,350	$3,995	$3,500	$2,950	$2,300	$1,950	$1,575

Combination packages are available on this model, and are currently priced in the $6,230 - $7,720 range.

SHOTGUNS: O/U, SPORTING CLAYS

Add $275 for double triggers on 12 ga.
Add $150 for left-hand w/o sideplates.
Add 200 for left-hand with sideplates.

SUMMIT SPORTING - 12, 20, 28 ga., or .410 bore (new 2006), 30, 32, or 34 (12 ga. only) in. barrels, grey "Tinaloy" boxlock receiver with neo-modern engraving, 10mm parallel top rib with vent. side ribs, adj. trigger, pistol grip stock, Schnabel forend, right hand palm swell, extended choke tubes, factory case, 7 lbs. 4 oz.-8 lbs. 2 oz.

	MSR $3,200		$2,725	$2,250	$1,995	$1,695	$1,495	$1,295	$1,000

Combination packages are available on this model, and are currently priced in the $4,245 - $5,690 range.
Add $100 for .410 bore.

✻ *Summit Limited Sporting* - similar to Summit Sporting, except has case hardened receiver.

	MSR $3,800		$3,195	$2,295	$2,095	$1,895	$1,495	$1,295	$1,095

Combination packages are available on this model, and are currently priced in the $4,800 - $6,245 range.
Add $100 for .410 bore.

GRADING - PPGS™	100%	98%	95%	90%	80%	70%	60%

MAGNUS SPORTING - 12, 20, 28 ga., or .410 bore (new 2006), 30, 32, or 34 (12 ga. only) in. barrels, sideplate grey "Tinaloy" boxlock receiver featuring gold grouse, quail, and pheasant game scenes, 10mm parallel top rib with vent. side ribs, pistol grip stock and Schnabel forend, adj. trigger, extended choke tubes, factory hard case, 7 lbs. 4 oz.-8 lbs. 2 oz.

MSR $4,350	$3,625	$2,795	$2,495	$2,195	$1,695	$1,495	$1,295

Add $90 for .410 bore.

Combination packages are available on this model, and are currently priced in the $5,200 range.

FORUM SPORTING - 12, 20, 28 ga., or .410 bore (new 2006), 30, 32, or 34 (12 ga. only) in. barrels, coin finished sideplate boxlock receiver, Bulino style game scene engraving, blind sideplates with no visible screws.

MSR $8,200	$6,500	$4,500	$3,750	$3,295	$2,995	$2,495	$2,095

MAXUM SPORTING - 12, 20, 28 ga. or .410 bore, 28, 30, 32, or 34 in. barrels, coin finished sideplates with deep relief floral scroll engraving, deluxe checkered oil finished Turkish walnut stock and forearm, extended sporting chokes. Importation began 2006.

MSR $5,700	$4,950	$4,100	$3,500	$2,950	$2,300	$1,850	$1,575

Combination packages are available on this model, and are currently priced in the $6,670 - $8,240 range.

SHOTGUNS: O/U, TRAP

MAGNUS TRAP - 12 ga., 30, 32, or 34 (unsingle only) barrels, case colored action and sideplates, scroll engraved with gold game scenes, deluxe Turkish walnut. Importation began 2007.

MSR $6,200	$4,800	$4,400	$4,100	$3,750	$3,200	$2,750	$2,175

A combination set of this model is available for $7,395.

SUMMIT TRAP - 12 ga., 30, 32, or 34 (unsingle only) in. barrels, grey alloy receiver with light scroll engraving, adj. comb. New 2007.

MSR $4,950	$3,850	$3,450	$3,100	$2,900	$2,500	$2,000	$1,500

A combination set of this model is available for $6,325.

MAXUM TRAP - 12 ga., 30, 32, or 34 (unsingle only) in. barrels, coin finished hand polished action, deep engraved receiver, extra deluxe Turkish walnut stock. New 2007.

MSR $7,200	$5,750	$5,200	$4,800	$4,500	$3,950	$3,400	$2,800

A combination set of this model is available for $8,400.

CALICO LIGHT WEAPONS SYSTEMS

Previous manufacturer established during 1986, and located in Sparks, NV 1998-2001. Previously located in Bakersfield, CA.

A complete line of accessories was available for all Calico carbines and pistols.

CARBINES

LIBERTY 50-100 - 9mm Para. cal., 16.1 in. barrel, downward ejection, aluminum alloy receiver, synthetic stock with pistol grip (some early post-ban specimens had full wood stocks with thumbhole cutouts), 50 or 100 shot helical feed mag., ambidextrous safety, 7 lbs. Mfg. 1995-2001.

	$850	$725	$650	$600	$500	$450	$400

Last MSR was $860.

Add $125 for 100 shot helical feed mag.

M-100 - .22 LR cal., semi-auto carbine, paramilitary design with folding buttstock, 100 shot helical feed mag., alloy frame, ambidextrous safety, 16.1 in. shrouded barrel with flash suppressor/muzzle brake, 4.2 lbs. empty. Mfg. 1986-94.

	$625	$550	$450	$400	$350	$300	$275

Last MSR was $308.

GRADING - PPGS™	100%	98%	95%	90%	80%	70%	60%

* **M-100 FS** - similar to M-100, except has solid stock and barrel does not have flash suppressor. Mfg. 1996-2001.

| | $550 | $450 | $400 | $360 | $315 | $275 | $250 |

Last MSR was $650.

M-101 - while advertised, this model never went into production.

M-105 SPORTER - similar to M-100, except has walnut distinctively styled buttstock and forend, 4 3/4 lbs. empty. Mfg. 1989-94.

| | $400 | $350 | $280 | $235 | $200 | $175 | $160 |

Last MSR was $335.

M-106 - while advertised, this model never went into production.

M-900 - 9mm Para. cal., retarded blowback action, paramilitary design with collapsible buttstock, cast aluminum receiver with stainless steel bolt, static cocking handle, 16 in. barrel, fixed rear sight with adj. post front, 50 (standard) or 100 shot helical feed mag., ambidextrous safety, black polymer pistol grip and forend, 3.7 lbs. empty. Mfg. 1989-90, reintroduced 1992-93.

| | $875 | $775 | $675 | $575 | $475 | $400 | $350 |

Last MSR was $618.

* **M-900S** - similar to M-900, except has non-collapsible shoulder stock. Disc. 1993.

| | $650 | $550 | $475 | $400 | $350 | $300 | $275 |

Last MSR was $632.

* **M-901 Canada Carbine** - 9mm Para. cal., similar to M-900, except has 18 1/2 in. barrel and sliding stock. Disc. 1992.

| | $675 | $595 | $550 | $475 | $350 | $300 | $285 |

Last MSR was $643.

This model was also available with solid fixed stock (Model 901S).

M-951 TACTICAL CARBINE - 9mm Para. cal., 16.1 in. barrel, similar appearance to M-900 Carbine, except has muzzle brake and extra pistol grip on front of forearm, 4 3/4 lbs. Mfg. 1990-94.

| | $750 | $700 | $675 | $650 | $600 | $475 | $450 |

Last MSR was $556.

* **M-951S** - similar to M-951, except has synthetic buttstock. Mfg. 1991-94.

| | $650 | $595 | $525 | $450 | $400 | $350 | $300 |

Last MSR was $567.

PISTOLS: SEMI-AUTO

M-110 - .22 LR cal., same action as M-100 Carbine, 6 in. barrel with muzzle brake, 100 round helical feed mag., includes notched rear sight and adj. windage front sight, 10 1/2 in. sight radius, ambidextrous safety, pistol grip storage compartment, 2.21 lbs. empty. Mfg. 1989-2001.

| | $475 | $395 | $315 | $260 | $230 | $200 | $180 |

Last MSR was $570.

M-950 - 9mm Para. cal., same operating mechanism as the M-900 Carbine, 6 in. barrel, 50 (standard) or 100 shot helical feed mag., 2 1/4 lbs. empty. Mfg. 1989-94.

| | $450 | $375 | $325 | $285 | $260 | $240 | $225 |

Last MSR was $518.

Many accessories were also available for this model.

CAMEX-BLASER USA, INC.

Previous importer/distributor of Blaser Jagdwaffen Gmbh rifles.

Previously imported Camex-Blaser rifles can be located in the Blaser section in this text.

CAPRINUS

Previous shotgun manufacturer located in Varberg, Sweden.

GRADING - PPGS™	100%	98%	95%	90%	80%	70%	60%

SHOTGUNS: O/U

CAPRINUS SWEDEN - 12 ga., boxlock action, ejectors, ST, stainless steel receiver, unique design breaks down without forearm disassembly, 29 1/2 in. barrels with choke tubes, limited mfg. during early 1980s.

	$3,750	$3,250	$2,850	$2,400	$2,000	$1,600	$1,200

Last MSR was approx. $5,955.

CARBON 15

Please refer to Professional Ordnance (discontinued mfg.) and the Bushmaster (current mfg.) for more information on this trademark.

CARL GUSTAF

Previous manufacturer located in Eskilstuna, Sweden. Previously imported by Hansen & Co. located in Southport, CT during 1994-1995, and by Precision Sales International located in Westfield, MA during 1991-1993.

RIFLES: BOLT ACTION

MODEL CG 2000 STANDARD GRADE - 6.5x55mm, 7x64mm, 9.3x62mm, .243 Win., .270 Win., .30-06, .308 Win., 7mm Rem. Mag., or .300 Win. Mag. cal., bolt action, Monte Carlo walnut stock with checkering and Wundhammer grip, 24 in. barrel, detachable 3 or 4 shot mag., with or without sights, cold-swaged barrel and receiver, 60 degree bolt, 3-way slide safety, 7 1/2 lbs. Imported 1991-95.

	$1,325	$1,050	$875	$725	$575	$475	$375

Last MSR was $1,535.

Add $540 for Mag. cals.

This model was supplied with individual 80 meter signed test targets. This model was also been imported as the Fairfax 2000 series.

✱ *Model 2000 Luxe Grade* - .270 Win., .30-06, .308 Win., or 6.5x55mm cal., features choice of regular or Mannlicher deluxe walnut stock. Imported 1995 only.

	$1,695	$1,400	$1,200	$975	$825	$650	$475

Last MSR was $1,935.

A Model 2000 Super-Luxe was also available in 6.5x55mm or .30-06 cal. - retail was $4,250.

MODEL 3000 - various cals., features Sauer action with non-rotating bolt. Previously imported by Aimpoint.

	$675	$575	$475	$400	$375	$350	$325

STANDARD BOLT ACTION RIFLE - 6.5x55mm, 7x64mm, .270 Win., 7mm Rem. Mag., .308 Win., .30-06, or 9.3x62mm cal., 24 in. barrel, folding rear sight, checkered classic style stock. Mfg. 1970-77.

	$375	$325	$300	$275	$250	$225	$200

✱ *Standard Bolt Action Rifle Monte Carlo stock*

	$450	$395	$350	$300	$275	$250	$225

GRADE II - similar to Monte Carlo Standard, in .22-250 Rem., .25-06 Rem., 6.5x55mm, .270 Win., 7mm Rem. Mag., .308 Win., .30-06, or .300 Win. Mag. cal., select stock and rosewood pistol grip cap, and forearm tip.

	$500	$425	$375	$325	$295	$275	$250

GRADE III - similar to Grade II, except fancy wood, deluxe high gloss finish.

	$575	$475	$425	$350	$325	$300	$275

DELUXE - similar to Grade III, except engraved floorplate and trigger guard, Deluxe French walnut, and jeweled bolt.

	$675	$575	$475	$400	$375	$350	$325

VARMINT TARGET MODEL - .222 Rem., .22-250 Rem., .243 Win., bolt action, fast lock time, or 6.5x55mm cal., 27 in. barrel, no sights, large bakelite bolt knob, target type stock. Mfg. 1970. Disc.

	$550	$495	$440	$385	$360	$320	$290

GRADING - PPGS™	100%	98%	95%	90%	80%	70%	60%

GRAND PRIX SINGLE SHOT TARGET - .22 LR cal., fastest lock time bolt action, 27 in. heavy barrel with adj. weight, no sights, target stock, adj. buttplate. Mfg. 1970. Disc.

$550	$495	$440	$385	$360	$320	$290

CASARTELLI, CARLO

Previous manufacturer located in Brescia, Italy until 2000. Previously imported and distributed until 1999 by New England Arms Corp. located in Kittery Point, ME.

Casartelli rifles and shotguns were available through special order only. Virtually any custom gun configuration could be manufactured to the customer's exact specifications and requirements.

RIFLES

AFRICA MODEL - BOLT ACTION - various heavy and Mag. cals., square bridge Mauser action, full coverage game scene engraving appropriate to caliber, takedown, limited production.

$10,200	$7,500	$5,900	$5,300	$4,700	$4,100	$3,600

Last MSR was $12,000.

SAFARI MODEL - BOLT ACTION - standard cals., regular Mauser action, full coverage game scene engraving, limited production.

$6,250	$5,900	$5,250	$4,950	$4,150	$3,650	$3,150

Last MSR was $8,250.

KENYA - DOUBLE RIFLE - most standard and Mag. cals., sidelock action, elaborate game scene and/or scroll engraving, limited production.

$24,250	$21,500	$17,750	$14,750	$12,000	$9,950	$8,250

Last MSR was $35,000.

SHOTGUNS: SxS

SIDELOCK MODEL - various gauges, elaborate game scene and/or scroll engraving, limited production.

$13,000	$9,750	$7,900	$6,500	$5,200	$4,250	$3,750

Last MSR was $17,000.

CASPIAN ARMS, LTD

Current parts manufacturer located in Wolcott, VT. Dealer direct sales only.

Caspian Arms currently fabricates high quality steel, stainless steel, titanium (new 2002), and alloy (disc. 2006) frames for the Colt Government Model 1911/A1, both in standard and high capacity frames. Frame sizes include the Government, Commander, and Officer's. Caspian Arms Ltd. also manufactures slides, including a damascus variation, and related small parts, in addition to having many special order machine operations available. Please contact them directly for current information on their extensive line of pistol-related components.

PISTOLS: SEMI-AUTO

VIETNAM COMMEMORATIVE - .45 ACP, total production was 1,000, hand engraved by J.J. Adams, nickel plated, branch service medallion installed in grips. Limited mfg. 1986-93.

$1,450	$995	$795	N/A	N/A	N/A	N/A

Last MSR was $1,500.

    Add $350 for gold plating.
    Add $200 for serial numbers below RVN100.

This Vietnam Commemorative was also available in 24Kt. gold hand inlay edition for $14,000 - very limited production.

GRADING - PPGS™	100%	98%	95%	90%	80%	70%	60%

CASULL ARMS CORPORATION

Previous manufacturer and distributor located in Afton, WY 1996-2005.

PISTOLS: SEMI-AUTO

CA-3800 - .38 Casull or .45 ACP cal., single action, 6 in. match barrel, 8 shot mag., blue or stainless finish, checkered exotic wood grips, 2 piece guide rod, fully adj. rear sight and Casull mfg. adj. front sight, hand fitted slide to frame, slide features Dick Casull signature on left side, includes locking aluminum carrying case and 2 mags., 40 oz. Mfg. 2001-2005.

$2,395	$2,150	$1,975	$1,825	$1,675	$1,550	$1,425

Last MSR was $2,495.

Add $300 for 6 in. .45 ACP barrel.
Add $400 for all stainless model.
Add $100 for either stainless steel frame and blue slide or vice versa.
Add $900 for both cals. with custom fitted extra slides.
Add $400 for compensator.

REVOLVERS

CA2000 MINI-FRAME REVOLVER - .22 LR or .32 ACP cal., double action, fold up trigger, hammerless, manual safety, hardwood grips. Mfg. 1997-2005.

$350	$295	$250	$225	$200	$185	$170

Last MSR was $395.

CA3000 SMALL FRAME REVOLVER - while advertised during 1997 (MSR - $1,495), this model never went into production.

CA4000 LARGE FRAME REVOLVER - while advertised during 1997 (MSR - $1,995), this model never went into production.

RIFLES: BOLT ACTION

CAC5000 CONVENTIONAL - standard cals. include .270 Win., .300 Win. Mag., .375 H&H, .458 Win. Mag., or 7mm Rem. Mag. cal., features improved bolt action with conventional extraction, box mag. Limited mfg. 1997-99.

$2,275	$1,950	$1,600	$1,410	$1,160	$980	$800

Last MSR was $2,495.

CRS7000 CASULL RIFLE SYSTEM - .30 Casull or 6.5 Casull cal., patented bolt and extraction system, features new, all-metal bedding system allowing take-down and reassembly without affecting accuracy, box mag., stainless barrel without sights, uncheckered walnut stock, sporter or benchrest configuration. Limited mfg. 1997-99.

$2,700	$2,350	$2,000	$1,740	$1,495	$1,215	$1,000

Last MSR was $2,995.

CAVALRY ARMS CORPORATION

Current manufacturer located in Gilbert, AZ. Previously located in Mesa, AZ.
Cavalry Arms Corporation manufactures the CAV-15 Series rifle, styled after the AR-15. Base price is $850. Additionally, many options and accessories are available. Cavalry Arms also makes paramilitary conversions for select slide action shotguns. Please contact the company directly for more information, including a price quotation (see Trademark Index).

CENTURION ORDNANCE, INC.

Previous importer located in Helotes, TX. Centurion Ordnance imports Aguila ammunition.

GRADING - PPGS™	100%	98%	95%	90%	80%	70%	60%

SHOTGUNS: SLIDE ACTION

POSEIDON - 12 ga., 1 3/4 in. chamber (shoots "mini-shells" and slugs), 18 1/4 in. smoothbore barrel, 13 in. LOP, black synthetic stock and forearm, 6 shot mag., adj. rear sight, 5 lbs., 5 oz. Limited importation 2001.

	$285	$250	$225	$200	$185	$170	$155

While prototypes of this model were imported briefly during 2001, this gun never made it into the consumer marketplace.

Mini-shells retailed for $12.60 for a box of 20 (shot sizes include 7, #4 & #1 buckshot).

CENTURY ARMS

Previous manufacturer circa 1996-1998 located in Balwyn, Victoria, Australia.

RIFLES: SINGLE SHOT

REWA RIFLE - 4 bore ball, break open action, massive single shot with case colored and engraved action, deluxe checkered stock and forearm with ebony tip, iron sights, production limited to a few prototypes only (a convertible shotgun barrel was also planned).

Extreme rarity precludes accurate pricing on this model.

CENTURY INTERNATIONAL ARMS, INC.

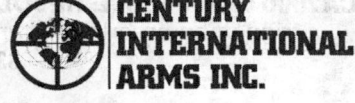

Current importer and distributor with corporate offices located in Delray Beach, FL. Century International Arms, Inc. was previously headquartered in St. Albans, VT until 1997, and Boca Raton, FL from 1997-2004.

Century International Arms, Inc. imports a large variety of used military rifles, shotguns, and pistols. Because inventory is changing daily, please contact the company directly for the most recent offerings and pricing.

Additionally, Century International Arms imports a wide range of accessories, including bayonets, holsters, stocks, magazines, grips, mounts, scopes, misc. parts, new and surplus ammunition, etc., and should be contacted directly (see Trademark Index) for a copy of their most recent catalog, or check their web site for current offerings.

PISTOLS: SEMI-AUTO

Century International Arms Inc. also imports Arcus pistols from Bulgaria and Daewoo pistols from South Korea. Please refer to the individual sections for more information.

M-1911 STYLE PISTOLS - .45 ACP cal., patterned after the Colt Govt. Model 1911, choice of 4 1/4 (Blue Thunder Commodore, Commodore 1911, or GI-Officer's Model) or 5 (SAM Elite/SAM Standard or SAM Chief/Falcon) ported (disc. 2002) or unported barrel, 7 shot mag., various configurations and finishes, many target features are standard on most models. Importation from Phillippines began 2001.

No MSR	$400	$350	$325	$300	$275	$250	$200

Add $35 for Commodore Blue Thunder Model with squared off triggerguard.

RIFLES: SEMI-AUTO

G-3 SPORTER - .308 Win. cal., mfg. from genuine G3 parts, and American made receiver with integrated scope rail, includes 20 shot mag., 19 in. barrel, pistol grip stock, matte black finish, refinished condition only, 9.3 lbs. Imported 1999-2006.

	$585	$500	$450	$425	$395	$375	$350

FAL SPORTER - .308 Win. cal., U.S. mfg., new barrel receiver, synthetic furniture, 20 shot mag. Imported 2004-2006.

	$650	$600	$550	$500	$465	$435	$400

GRADING - PPGS™	100%	98%	95%	90%	80%	70%	60%

CETME SPORTER - .308 Win. cal., new mfg. Cetme action, 19 1/2 in. barrel, 20 shot mag., choice of blue or Mossy Oak Break-Up camo (disc.) metal finish, wood (disc.) or synthetic stock, pistol grip, and vent. forearm, refinished condition only, 9.7 lbs. New 2002.

No MSR	$650	$575	$500	$450	$400	$350	$300

S.A.R. 1 - 7.62x39mm cal., AK-47 styling, 16 1/2 in. barrel, wood stock and forearm, scope rail mounted on receiver, includes one 10 and two 30 shot double stack mags., 7.08 lbs. Mfg. by Romarm of Romania. Importation disc. 2003.

	$450	$395	$350	$325	$285	$250	$225

S.A.R. 2 - 5.45x39mm cal., AK-47 styling, 16 in. barrel, wood stock and forearm, includes one 10 and one 30 shot double stack mags., 8 lbs. Mfg. by Romarm of Romania. Importation disc. 2003.

	$450	$395	$350	$325	$285	$250	$225

S.A.R. 3 - .223 Rem. cal., AK-47 styling, 16 in. barrel, wood stock and forearm, includes one 10 and one 30 shot double stack mags., 8 lbs. Mfg. by Romarm of Romania. Importation disc. 2003.

	$450	$395	$350	$325	$285	$250	$225

WASR-10 LO-CAP - 7.62x39mm cal., AK-47 styling, 16 1/4 in. barrel, wood stock and forearm, includes one 5 and one 10 shot single stack mags., 7 1/2 lbs. Mfg. by Romarm of Romania.

No MSR	$285	$245	$210	$185	$170	$150	$135

WASR-10 HIGH-CAP - 7.62x39mm cal., AK-47 styling, 16 1/4 in. barrel, wood stock and forearm, includes two 30 shot double stack mags., 7 1/2 lbs. Mfg. by Romarm of Romania.

No MSR	$450	$395	$325	$295	$275	$250	$230

Add $130 for 75 shot drum mag.

L1A1 SPORTER - .308 Win. cal., current mfg. receiver patterned after the British L1A1, includes carrying handle, synthetic furniture, 20 shot mag., 22 1/2 in. barrel, fold over aperture rear sight, 9 1/2 lbs. Mfg. in U.S.

No MSR	$485	$395	$350	$325	$295	$275	$250

DRAGUNOV - 7.62x54R cal., new CNC milled receiver, Dragunov configuration, thumbhole stock, 26 1/2 in. barrel, supplied with scope and cleaning kit. Mfg. in Romania.

No MSR	$775	$700	$650	$600	$550	$500	$400

RIFLES: SLIDE ACTION

PAR 1 OR 3 - 7.62x39mm (PAR 1) or .223 Rem. (PAR 3) cal., AK receiver styling, 10 shot mag., accepts double stack AK magazines, wood stock, pistol grip, and forearm, 20.9 in. barrel, 7.6 lbs. Mfg. by PAR, and importation began 2002.

No MSR	$360	$300	$275	$250	$225	$200	$175

SHOTGUNS

ARTHEMIS (SUPER ARTHEMIS) O/U - 12, 20, 28 (new 2004) ga. or .410 bore, 3 in. chambers, 28 in. VR barrels, SST, extractors, checkered walnut stock and forearm, 5.3-7.4 lbs. Mfg. by Khan in Turkey, importation disc.

	$450	$395	$350	$325	$285	$250	$225

Add $25 for 20 ga. or 28 ga.
Add $50 for .410 bore.

PHANTOM SEMI-AUTO - 12 ga. only, 3 in. chamber, 24, 26, or 28 in. VR barrels with 3 choke tubes, black synthetic stock and forearm. Mfg. in Turkey, importation disc.

	$265	$225	$200	$185	$175	$165	$155

GRADING - PPGS™	100%	98%	95%	90%	80%	70%	60%

SAS-12 SEMI-AUTO - 12 ga. only, 2 3/4 in. chamber, detachable 3 (Type II) or 5 shot mag., black synthetic stock and forearm, 22 or 23 1/2 in. barrel. Mfg. by PRC in China.

No MSR	$225	$185	$165	$155	$145	$135	$125

Add approx. $25 for ghost ring rear with blade front or bead sight.

COACH SxS - 12, 20 ga., or .410 bore, exposed hammers, 20 in. barrels, DTs, steel contruction, checkered walnut stock and forearm, includes sling swivels. Mfg. in China.

No MSR	$240	$195	$175	$165	$155	$145	$135

MODEL IJ2 SLIDE ACTION - 12 ga. only, 2 3/4 or 3 in. chamber, 19 in. barrel with ghost ring sights or fiber optic front sights, fixed choke only, 7.2 lbs. Mfg. in China.

No MSR	$199	$170	$150	$125	$100	$90	$80

CENTURY MFG., INC.

Previous manufacturer located in Knightstown, IN, Feb. 2002-late 2004. Previously manufactured in Evansville and Greenfield, IN 1973-circa 1999. Consumer direct and dealer sales.

This revolver design was originally manufactured in 1972 by Russell Wilson, who sandcasted the bronze frame (cloned from the Colt SAA configuration) in Evansville, IN. Gene Phelps purchased the manufacturing rights for this gun and formed a partnership with Earl Keller to produce a redesigned frame, also using sandcast bronze.

The original Century revolver was made in Evansville, IN beginning in 1973 (1973 was the 100th anniversary of the .45-70 Govt. cartridge - hence the term Century) and production was halted in 1976 at ser. no. 524. In late 1976, Phelps and Keller (the two original partners on the venture) dissolved their partnership and each began manufacturing their own version of the .45-70 revolver. Gene Phelps completely redesigned the gun's interior and began manufacturing the Heritage I, with an investment-cast steel frame, and without the Century's novel crossbolt safety. Keller's Century Manufacturing, Inc. continued to produce the original Century, with some design refinements, and in 1985 the company was purchased by Dr. Paul Majors, who died in Dec. of 2001.

The most recent Century revolver featured a manganese bronze frame and other components in addition to having a cross-bolt safety. They were produced in .45-70 and various other cals., in Greenfield, IN. Earl Keller died in 1986. The second series was made in Greenfield, IN with limited production resuming in 1986. Earlier handmade "Evansville" Model 100s (disc.) are currently selling for between $2,500-$3,500, depending on the region.

In Feb., 2002, Century Mfg. was purchased by Dave Lukens & Jeff Yelton and moved to Knightstown, IN. New production guns also included a revolving rifle built on the Model 100 frame. These new production guns carried a limited lifetime guarantee.

REVOLVERS

Less than 3,000 Model 100s were manufactured 1976-2001. The following values below are for .45-70 Govt. cal. Other calibers were priced from $2,000 on up.

MODEL 100 - .30-30 Win. (new 1987), .375 Win. (new 1986), .444 Marlin (new 1986), .45-70 Govt., .50-70 Govt. (new 1987), or .50-110 cal., single action 6 shot, manganese bronze frame, steel cylinder, 6 1/2, 8, 10, or 12 (disc.) in. round or octagon barrel, unique crossbolt safety that locks the hammer, adj. sights, walnut grips, 5 lbs. 14 oz. Disc. 2000, reintroduced 2002-2004.

✱ *Model 100 .45-70 Govt. and other cals.* - includes all cals. except .50-110.

	$1,295	$1,100	$995	$900	$850	$800	$750

Last MSR (2002-2004) was $1,295.
Previous mfg. last MSR was $2,000.

Add $200 for calibers other than .45-70 Govt.
Add $110 for normal octagon barrel.
Add $200 for stainless steel fabrication.

GRADING - PPGS™	100%	98%	95%	90%	80%	70%	60%

✳ *Model 100 .50-110 cal.*

	$2,895	$2,350	$1,950	$1,700	$1,500	$1,250	$1,025

Last MSR was $2,895.

CHAMPLIN FIREARMS, INC.

Current custom manufacturer, gunsmith, and importer located in Enid, OK. Champlin Firearms was established in 1966. Direct sales only.

Champlin Firearms, Inc. manufactures handcrafted rifles built around a patented bolt action of their own design and manufacture. Most guns are built per individual customer order and specifications. Values will vary greatly depending on the configuration, desirability, and special order specifications. All Champlin rifles are built along classic lines with best quality wood and exemplary workmanship. They have been used successfully on safaris and have shot dangerous game throughout the world.

Champlin Firearms, Inc. also inventories a wide selection of high grade, top-quality shotguns and rifles (especially top trademark doubles and bolt actions). Contact George Caswell (owner) directly for a current listing (please refer to Trademark Index). Additional services include a complete gunsmithing service for all grades of English double rifles and shotguns. Custom stocks are also built to individual customer specifications. All double rifles are test fired and checked thoroughly upon completion of manufacture or repair. Again, Champlin Firearms should be contacted for consultation and quotation regarding this additional work.

RIFLES: BOLT ACTION

BOLT ACTION RIFLE - various cals., round or octagon barrel, adj. trigger, each rifle is built to customer specifications. Values below represent base gun with standard wood, no options, and no engraving.

	$8,500	$8,000	$7,000	$6,750	$6,000	$5,250	$4,500

Last MSR was $8,500.

CHAPARRAL ARMS

Current trademark of firearms manufactured in Neustadt, Germany. Currently imported by Charter 2000, located in Shelton, CT.

Chaparral Arms manufactures quality reproductions of the Winchester Model 1866, 1873 and 1876, the Colt 1878, and SAA revolvers. Please contact the importer directly for more information, including pricing and availability (see Trademark Index).

RIFLES: LEVER ACTION, REPRODUCTIONS

MODEL 1866 - .357 Mag./.38 Spl. or .45 LC cal., 19 (round barrel carbine), 20 (octagon rifle) or 24 (octagon rifle) in. barrel. Importation began late 2007.

MSR $800		$695	$625	$550	$475	$425	$375	$325

MODEL 1873 - .357 Mag., .38-40 WCF, .44-40 WCF, or .45 LC cal., patterned after the Model 1873 Winchester, uncheckered straight grip stock, case colored frame, choice of 19 in. round (carbine), 20 or 24 in. octagon barrel. Importation began late 2006.

MSR $1,050		$895	$775	$675	$600	$525	$450	$375

MODEL 1876 - .40-60, .45-60, .45-75, or .50-95 (new 2008) cal., patterned after the Model 1876 Winchester, uncheckered straight grip stock and forearm, case colored frame, 22, 26, or 28 in. octagon barrel. Importation began late 2006.

MSR $1,250		$1,095	$950	$850	$750	$650	$550	$450

Add $100 for NWMP (Northwest Mounted Police) carbine with 22 in. barrel, and full length forearms, .45-75 cal. only.

GRADING - PPGS™	100%	98%	95%	90%	80%	70%	60%

CHAPUIS ARMES

Current manufacturer located in St. Bonnet Le Chateau, France. Currently imported by William Larkin Moore, located in Scottsdale AZ, Evolution USA, located in White Bird, ID, and Heirloom Armes, located in Howard Lake, MN. Previously imported by Chadick's, Ltd. (limited importation) located in Terrell, TX, by GSI, Inc. located in Trussville, AL until 1995 and by Armes De Chasse located in Chadds Ford, PA until 1993.

Chapuis rifles and shotguns are manufactured on a limited basis. Most of their emphasis is on high-quality double rifles and shotguns. For further information regarding this respected French trademark, please contact the importer.

RIFLES: O/U

SUPER ORION C15 MODEL - .300 Win. Mag. or .375 H&H cal., notched boxlock action with ejectors, coin finish only, 23.6 in. barrels with quarter rib, engraved action, approx. 8 lbs. Imported 1995-96.

$8,250	$7,150	$6,250	$5,400	$4,200	$3,500	$3,150

Last MSR was $9,195.

Add $2,900 for .375 H&H cal.

RIFLES: SxS

William Larkin Moore also has The Artisan Express ($13,000 MSR), the Imperial Express ($21,500 MSR), the Safari Express ($10,900 MSR, .300 Win.. Mag. or .375 H&H cal.), Safari Express in .470 NE ($13,500 MSR), and the Safari Deluxe Express (.470 NE cal., $21,500 MSR) Models available. Please contact them directly for more information.

RGEX EXPRESS MODEL - .30-06, .300 Win. Mag., 7x65R, 8x57JRS, or 9.3x74R cal., double rifle, ejectors, boxlock action, 23.6 in. barrels, deluxe checkered walnut stock with cheekpiece, full line of options are available, 7 lbs. 6 oz. Limited importation beginning 1998.

MSR $6,900	$6,375	$5,800	$5,350	$4,900	$4,450	$3,850	$3,250

Add approx. $700 for .300 Win. Mag. cal.
Add approx. 60% for HGEX Express Supreme Model (engraved, not avail. in .300 Win. Mag. cal.).   Add
110% for HGEX Express Imperial Model (scroll engraved, not avail. in .300 Win. Mag. cal.).

UGEX UTILITY GRADE EXPRESS - similar to RGEX, except has select walnut. New 1998.

MSR $5,900	$5,350	$4,600	$3,950	$3,500	$2,950	$2,550	$2,100

Add $500 for .300 Win. Mag. cal.

AFRICAN P.H. (PROFESSIONAL HUNTER) GRADE I - .30-06, .300 Win. Mag., .375 H&H, .416 Rigby, 9.3x74R, or .470 NE cal., notched boxlock action with English scroll border engraving, case colored receiver, selective ejectors, deluxe walnut stock with English cheekpiece.

MSR $10,900	$10,500	$9,350	$8,475	$7,500	$6,500	$5,650	$4,600

Add $3,570 for .470 NE cal.
Add $3,099 for .416 Rigby cal.

Values are for .375 H&H or .300 Win. Mag cal. This model was previously designated Express Agex Brousse.

✱*African PH Grade II* - similar to Grade I, except has master signed scroll engraving with game scene on bottom of coin finished receiver.

MSR N/A	$18,500	$15,250	$12,000	$10,000	$8,000	$7,000	$6,000

Values above assume .470 NE cal. Subtract for smaller cals.

GRADING - PPGS™	100%	98%	95%	90%	80%	70%	60%

BROUSSE MODEL (SAFARI EXPRESS) - .300 Win. Mag., .375 H&H, .416 Rigby, .470 NE , or .500 NE cal., similar to Grade I Professional Hunter, except has full rose and scroll engraving coverage on coin finished receiver. New 1998.

	MSR $8,273	$7,850	$6,600	$5,500	$4,500	$3,500	$3,000	$2,650

Add $3,004 for .416 Rigby cal.
Add $2,877 for .470 NE cal.
Add $5,477 for .500 NE cal.
Add approximately 100% for Safari Deluxe Express in NE cal.

SAVANA MODEL - .30-06, .300 Win. Mag., .375 H&H, .416 R Chapuis (disc.), .416 Rigby, .470 NE, or 9.3x74R cal., deluxe version of the Agex Jungle, except has hand-engraved game scenes on action sides and Cape Buffalo head on floorplate of action, case colored (disc.) or coin finish.

	MSR N/A	$20,250	$17,350	$15,300	$13,000	$10,500	$8,750	$7,500

Add $2,000 for .470 NE cal.
Add $3,000 for .416 Rigby cal.
Subtract $2,500 for .30-06 or 9.3x74R cal.
Subtract $2,000 for .300 Win. Mag. cal.
Values are for .375 H&H cal.

JUNGLE MODEL - .30-06, .300 Win. Mag., .375 H&H, .416 R Chapuis (mfg. 1993-96), .470 NE (new 1992), or 9.3x74R cal., boxlock action, case colored (disc.) or coin finish, special reinforced receiver with double underbites, 25 5/8 in. barrels, fine English scroll engraving with 3 African animals, ejectors, select French walnut with compartment in pistol grip cap.

	MSR N/A	$11,850	$9,950	$8,150	$7,200	$6,250	$5,400	$4,350

Add $2,500 for .470 NE cal.
Add $3,500 for .416 Rigby cal.
Subtract $2,000 for .30-06 or 9.3x74R cal.
Subtract $1,000 for .300 Win. Mag. cal.
Values are for .375 H&H cal.

⁂ *Jungle Second Grade* - features elaborate engraving and best quality wood. Disc. 1996.

	$26,000	$22,500	$19,000	$16,000	$13,000	$10,000	$8,750

Last MSR was $29,395.

Add $3,900 for .470 NE cal.

EXPRESS AGEX AFRICA - same cals. as AGEX Jungle, notched boxlock action, master signed scroll engraving and African game scenes, selective ejectors, cased. Importation disc. 1994.

	$19,250	$17,750	$15,250	$13,500	$11,250	$10,000	$9,000

Last MSR was $20,954.

Add $2,896 for .470 NE cal.
Add $5,626 for .416 R Chapuis cal.

EXPRESS AGEX SAFARI - similar to AGEX Africa, except has top-of-the-line engraving and wood. Importation disc. 1994.

	$29,000	$26,550	$22,350	$19,150	$16,950	$14,000	$12,000

Last MSR was $30,375.

Add $2,040 for .470 NE cal.
Add $5,134 for .416 R Chapuis cal.

RIFLES: SINGLE SHOT

OURAL EXEL MODEL - .270 Win., .300 Win. Mag., 7mm Rem. Mag. cal., notched boxlock action, English scroll engraving, extractors, 23 5/8 in. barrel, fitted and engraved scope mounts. Importation disc. 1994, reintroduced 1999, for current mfg.

	MSR N/A	$4,875	$4,200	$3,775	$3,250	$2,800	$2,400	$1,775

Add approx. 20% for Oural Luxe Model (features better engraving and wood).
Add approx. 58% for Oural Elite Model (features game scene engraving and presentation walnut).

GRADING - PPGS™	100%	98%	95%	90%	80%	70%	60%

SHOTGUNS

SPORTING CLAYS MODEL O/U - 12 or 20 (3 in. Mag.) ga., scalloped boxlock action, 27 1/2 or 30 in. VR barrels, ST, case colored receiver with English scroll engraving. Limited importation 1997-98.

	$3,675	$3,300	$2,900	$2,500	$2,100	$1,675	$1,300

Last MSR was $3,995.

ST. BONNET MODEL SxS - 12, 16, or 20 (3 in. Mag.) ga., boxlock with case colored (disc.) or coin finished sideplates featuring fine English scroll (disc.) or game scene engraving, 27 1/2 in. monobloc barrels, DTs, ejectors, checkered straight grip walnut stock and forearm, hardshell case. Limited importation began 1997.

MSR N/A	$2,675	$2,300	$2,000	$1,675	$1,300	$1,000	$850

RGP/BLE MODEL SxS - 16 or 20 ga., boxlock action, semi-beavertail foream, concave rib, coin finished receiver with fine rose and scroll engraving. Importation began 2005 by William Larkin Moore.

MSR $3,500	$3,250	$2,750	$2,350	$2,050	$1,800	$1,600	$1,400

Add $500 for 20 ga.

CHAPUIS, P. ETS

Previous manufacturer located in Saint-Bonnet le Chateau, France.

P. Chapuis specialized in custom order rifles and shotguns. This company developed a process to color the receiver sideplates while using traditional engraving techniques - resulting in a unique 3-D scene. This is a different company than Chapuis Armes.

CHARLES DALY

See Daly, Charles.

CHARLIN ARMS

Previous manufacturer located in St. Etienne, France.

Charlin Arms previously made shotguns which were patterned after Darne firearms. Typically, they are very high quality and values seem to approximate the Darne guns. Once you have determined the comparable model in Darne, please refer to the Darne section in this book.

CHARTER 2000, INC.

Current manufacturer located in Shelton, CT established during 1998. Currently marketed and distributed beginning mid-2005 by MKS Supply, Inc., located in Dayton, OH.

Charter 2000, Inc. acquired the rights to reproduce the original Charter Arms Undercover Model. Otherwise, it is not affiliated with Charter Arms in any way, nor is it responsible for repair or service on older Charter Arms handguns.

DERRINGERS

DIXIE DERRINGER - .22 LR or .22 Mag. cal., 5 shot, 1 1/8 in. barrel, stainless construction, spur trigger, hardwood grips, 5 oz. New 2002.

MSR $199	$170	$135	$115	$100	$85	$80	$75

REVOLVERS

BULLDOG - .44 Spl. cal., 5 shot, 2 1/2 in. barrel, steel or stainless steel construction, hammer block safety, choice of standard or pocket hammer, round butt with finger groove grips, 21 oz. New late 1999.

MSR $389	$325	$275	$235	$210	$185	$170	$150

Add $10 for stainless steel or DAO (new 2008) in stainless steel.

POLICE BULLDOG - .38 Spl. cal., 5 shot, large frame, 4 in. tapered or bull barrel, exposed ejector rod, full rubber grips, approx. 23 oz. Mfg. 2002-2007.

	$255	$230	$200	$185	$170	$150	$130

Last MSR was $299.

GRADING - PPGS™	100%	98%	95%	90%	80%	70%	60%

UNDERCOVER - .38 Spl. cal., regular double action or DAO, 5 shot, 2 in. barrel, steel or stainless steel construction, checkered compact round butt (standard hammer) or super compact (concealed hammer) synthetic grips (full rubber of boot compact) with finger grooves, 18 oz. New late 1998.

MSR $330	$285	$245	$210	$180	$165	$145	$135

Add $15 for stainless steel.
Add $14 for Undercover Lite Pink Lady with aluminum frame and pink finish.

❋ *Undercover Southpaw* - .38 Spl. cal., reverse configured with cylinder release and loading on the right side, all aluminum one-piece frame with finger groove rubber grips. New 2008.

MSR $375	$315	$270	$230	$200	$185	$160	$140

UNDERCOVERETTE - .32 H&R Mag. cal., 5 shot, stainless, 2 in. barrel, rubber grips, 19 oz. New late 2006.

MSR $345	$290	$240	$210	$180	$150	$125	$100

POLICE UNDERCOVER - .38 Spl. cal., 6 shot, stainless, fixed sights, 2.2 or 4 (disc. 2007) in. barrel, rubber grips, 20 oz. New late 2006.

MSR $370	$300	$245	$200	$175	$160	$145	$130

OFF DUTY - .38 Spl. cal., DAO, 5 shot, 2 in. barrel, aluminum frame, hammerless, combat synthetic grips, 12 oz. New 2002.

MSR $375	$315	$270	$230	$200	$185	$160	$140

MAG. PUG - .357 Mag./.38 Spl., 5 shot, 2.2 in. ported barrel, blue or stainless steel, full rubber grips, 24 oz. New 2001.

MSR $359	$285	$245	$200	$175	$160	$145	$130

PATHFINDER - .22 LR or .22 Mag. cal., 6 shot, 2 or 4 (new 2007) in. barrel, stainless construction, checkered walnut grips, 19 oz. New 2002.

MSR $340	$285	$240	$210	$180	$150	$125	$100

RIFLES: BOLT ACTION

FIELD KING - .243 Win. (disc. 2000), .25-06 Rem., .270 Win., or .30-06 cal., blue or stainless Mauser long action, 4 shot mag., blue or stainless 22 in. E.R. Shaw barrel, checkered black fiberglass reinforced stock with recoil pad, 6 3/4 lbs. Mfg. 2000-2002.

	$300	$250	$215	$165	$130	$125	$100

Last MSR was $345.

Subtract $46 for non-stainless standard blue rifle.

❋ *Field King Carbine* - .308 Win. only, similar to Field King, except is available in 18 in. barrel with compensator only, blue finish or stainless steel. Mfg. 2000-2002.

	$300	$250	$215	$200	$185	$175	$165

Last MSR was $345.

CHARTER ARMS

Previously manufactured by Charco, Inc. located in Ansonia, CT 1992-1996. Previously manufactured by Charter Arms located in Stratford, CT 1964-1991.

The company's first model was the Undercover.

PISTOLS: SEMI-AUTO

MODEL 40 - .22 LR cal. only, double action semi-auto, 3.3 in. barrel, 8 shot mag., 21 1/2 oz., fixed sights, stainless steel. Mfg. 1984-86.

	$265	$240	$220	$170	$135	$125	$105

Last MSR was $319.

GRADING - PPGS™	100%	98%	95%	90%	80%	70%	60%

MODEL 79K - .32 or .380 ACP cal., double action semi-auto, 3.6 in. barrel, 7 shot mag., 24 1/2 oz., fixed sights, stainless steel. Mfg. 1984-86.

	$325	$300	$280	$230	$200	$170	$145

Last MSR was $390.

EXPLORER II & S II PISTOL - .22 LR cal., semi-auto survival pistol, barrel unscrews, 8 shot mag., black, gold (disc.), silvertone, or camouflage finish, 6, 8, or 10 in. barrels, simulated walnut grips. Disc. 1986.

	$90	$80	$70	$60	$55	$50	$45

Last MSR was $109.

This model uses a modified AR-7 action.
Manufacture of this model was by Survival Arms located in Cocoa, FL.

MODEL 42T (COMPETITION II TARGET) - .22 LR cal. only, single action, 5.9 in. barrel, target model with checkered walnut grips, adj. sights, blue finish only. Mfg. 1984-85 only.

	$490	$450	$395	$350	$300	$260	$220

Last MSR was $599.

REVOLVERS: DOUBLE ACTION

All Charter Arms revolvers had a hammer block safety system, 8 groove rifling, unbreakable beryllium copper firing pin, triple safety features, no sideplate, steel frames, and lifetime warranty to the original owner.

BONNIE & CLYDE SET - .32 H&R Mag. (Bonnie) and .38 Spl. (Clyde) cal., matched pair, 6 shot, 2 1/2 in. fully shrouded barrel, wood laminate grips (color coordinated), blue finish, pistols individually marked "Bonnie" or "Clyde" on barrels, supplied with gun rugs. Mfg. 1989-91.

	$425	$365	$335	$295	$260	$240	$220

LADY ON DUTY - .32 S&W or .38 Spl. cal., 5 (.38 Spl.) or 6 shot, 2 in. shrouded barrel, fixed sights, rose neoprene grips, cased. Mfg. 1995-96.

	$195	$165	$145	$130	$115	$100	$85

Last MSR was $219.

PATHFINDER - .22 LR or .22 Mag. (disc. 1989) cal., 6 shot, 2, 3, or 6 (disc. 1985) in. barrels, round butt, adj. sights, walnut grips, wide trigger and spur hammer. Disc. 1990.

	$185	$150	$125	$110	$90	$70	$50

* *Pathfinder - Square Butt* - .22 LR or .22 Mag. (disc. 1989) cal., 6 in. barrel, square butt, otherwise similar to Pathfinder. Disc. 1990.

	$190	$155	$125	$110	$90	$70	$50

* *Pathfinder Stainless* - .22 LR or .22 Mag. (disc. 1989) cal., stainless variation, 3 1/2 in. shrouded barrel. Disc. 1990.

	$185	$150	$130	$105	$90	$75	$70

UNDERCOVER - .32 S&W (disc. 1989) or .38 Spl. cal., 5 shot in .38 Spl., 6 shot in .32 S&W, 2 (.38 Spl.) or 3 in. barrel, wide trigger and spur hammer, fixed sights, .38 Spl. can also be ordered with pocket hammer. Disc. 1991.

	$175	$145	$115	$100	$90	$85	$80

* *Undercover Stainless* - 2 in. shrouded barrel only. Disc. 1994.

	$260	$195	$140	$110	$95	$80	$70

Last MSR was $304.

UNDERCOVERETTE - .32 S&W Long cal., similar to Undercover, 6 shot, 2 in. barrel, blue. Disc.

	$155	$140	$110	$100	$90	$70	$55

GRADING - PPGS™	100%	98%	95%	90%	80%	70%	60%

BULLDOG - .44 Spl. cal., 5 shot, 2 1/2 or 3 (disc. 1988) in. barrels, wide trigger and spur or pocket hammer, checkered bulldog grips (walnut or neoprene), blue or electroless nickel finish. Disc. 1991, reinstated 1994. Disc.1996.

	$225	$195	$155	$125	$110	$90	$70

Last MSR was $268.

Add $22 for electroless nickel finish.

* *Bulldog Stainless* - 2 1/2 in. bull or 3 (disc. 1989) in. regular barrel. Disc. 1991.

	$195	$155	$125	$100	$85	$70	$65

* *Bulldog Target* - .357 Mag. or .44 Spl. cal., 5 shot, 4 in. shrouded barrel, adj. sights, square butt only, blue finish. Mfg. 1980-88.

	$225	$150	$125	$100	$85	$70	$65

Last MSR was $255.

Subtract $10 for .357 Mag. cal.

* *Bulldog Stainless Target* - 9mm Federal, .357 Mag. or .44 Spl. cal., 5 shot, 5 1/2 in. shrouded VR barrel, adj. sights, square butt target grips only, matte finished, 28 oz. Mfg. 1989-91.

	$250	$175	$125	$100	$85	$70	$65

BULLDOG PUG - .44 Spl. cal., 5 shot, 2 1/2 in. shrouded barrel, fixed sights, walnut or neoprene grips. Mfg. 1986-93.

	$240	$195	$160	$130	$110	$100	$90

Last MSR was $279.

* *Bulldog Pug Stainless* - 2 1/2 in. shrouded barrel. Mfg. 1987-93.

	$300	$235	$175	$135	$115	$100	$85

Last MSR was $334.

BULLDOG TRACKER - .357 Mag. (.38 Spl.) cal., 5 shot, 2 1/2, 4 (disc. 1989), and 6 (disc. 1989) in. bull barrels, adj. sights, blue only, checkered bulldog grips, square butt on 4 or 6 in. barrel only. Disc. 1986, reintroduced 1989-91.

	$185	$150	$125	$110	$100	$90	$80

MAGNUM PUG - .357 Mag. cal., 5 shot, fixed sights, 2.2 in. shrouded barrel, blue finish. Mfg. 1995-96.

	$225	$195	$155	$125	$110	$90	$70

Last MSR was $268.

POLICE BULLDOG - .32 H&R Mag., .38 Spl. or .44 Spl. cal., 5 (.44 Spl. only) or 6 shot, fixed sights, blue only, 3 1/2 or 4 in. barrel, Neoprene grips or square butt (.44 Spl. only). Disc. 1991.

	$175	$140	$120	$105	$95	$85	$75

Add $20 for either .44 Spl. cal or 3 1/2 in. shrouded barrel.

* *Bulldog Stainless Police* - .32 Mag., .357 Mag. (new 1989), .38 Spl. (disc. 1988 - reintroduced 1990) or .44 Spl. (new 1989) cal., 5 (.357 Mag. or .44 Spl.) or 6 (.32 Mag. or .38 Spl.) shot, square butt, 3 1/2 or 4 in. shrouded barrel. Mfg. 1987-91.

$195		$160	$150	$140	$115	$95	$80	$70

Add $20 for .357 Mag. or .44 Special cal.

Neoprene grips are standard on these models except for the .357 Mag. (square butt).

POLICE UNDERCOVER - .32 H&R Mag. or .38 Spl. cal., 6 shot, spur or pocket hammer, 2.2 in. shrouded barrel, checkered walnut grips, fixed sights, blue or electroless nickel (new 1994) finish. Disc. 1996.

	$205	$175	$145	$120	$100	$85	$75

Last MSR was $238.

Add $14 for electroless nickel finish.

* *Police Undercover Stainless* - similar to Police Undercover. Disc. 1993.

	$240	$185	$150	$120	$105	$90	$80

Last MSR was $276.

GRADING - PPGS™	100%	98%	95%	90%	80%	70%	60%

OFF DUTY - .22 LR (new 1993), .22 Mag. (new 1994), or .38 Spl. cal., 5 (.38 Spl.) or 6 (.22 LR) shot, 2 in. barrel, fixed sights, conventional or DA only, blue, matte black (disc.), or electroless nickel (new 1994) finish. Disc. 1996.

	$170	$145	$120	$105	$90	$85	$80

Last MSR was $200.

      Add $39 for electroless nickel finish.
      Add $7 for double action only.

＊ *Off Duty Stainless* - similar to Off Duty. Disc. 1993.

	$235	$180	$145	$115	$100	$85	$75

Last MSR was $268.

PIT BULL - 9mm Federal (rare), .357 Mag. (disc. 1989), or .38 Spl. (disc. 1989) cal., 5 shot, 2 1/2, 3 1/2, or 4 (disc. 1989) in. full shrouded barrel, Neoprene grips, approx. 26 oz. Mfg. 1989-91.

	$230	$180	$150	$125	$115	$100	$90

＊ *Pit Bull Stainless* - 2 1/2 or 3 1/2 in. shrouded barrel. Disc. 1991.

	$240	$190	$155	$125	$115	$100	$90

RIFLES: SEMI-AUTO

AR-7 EXPLORER RIFLE - .22 LR cal., takedown, barreled action stores in Cycolac synthetic stock, 8 shot mag., adj. sights, 16 in. barrel, black finish on AR-7, silver-tone on AR-7S. Camouflage finish new 1986 (AR-7C). Mfg. until 1990.

	$125	$100	$85	$75	$65	$55	$50

Last MSR was $146.

In 1990, the manufacturing of this model was taken over by Survival Arms located in Cocoa, FL. Current mfg. AR-7 rifles will be found under the Henry Repeating Arms Company and AR-7 Industries.

CHEYTAC

Current manufacturer located in Arco, ID. Represented by Cheytac Associates, LLC, located in Lansing, NY.

RIFLES: BOLT ACTION

Cheytac currently manufactures an advanced 5 shot bolt action design in .408 Cheyenne Tactical cal. The Intervention Model 200 Military has an MSR of $13,795, weighs 27 lbs., and includes an advanced ballistic computer to help with accuracy. The M-325 model is $3,595 MSR. It also offers an Intervention Model M310 Target Model that is POR. Please contact the company directly for more information, including pricing and commercial availability (see Trademark Index).

CHIPMUNK RIFLES

Previous trademark manufactured by Rogue Rifle Co., Inc., located in Lewiston, ID, 2001-2007. Previously located in Prospect, OR from 1997-2001. Previously manufactured by Oregon Arms, Inc. located in Prospect, OR 1988-1996. Previously manufactured by Chipmunk Manufacturing located in Medford, OR until 1988. Rogue Rifle Co. Inc. was purchased by Keystone Sporting Arms, LLC in Jan., 2007. Keystone is the manufacturer of Crickett rifles.

PISTOLS: SINGLE SHOT

SILHOUETTE PISTOL - .22 LR cal., bolt action design with 14 7/8 in. barrel, iron sights, rear grip walnut stock. Mfg. 1984-88.

	$135	$115	$95	$80	$70	$60	$50

Last MSR was $150.

GRADING - PPGS™	100%	98%	95%	90%	80%	70%	60%

SILHOUETTE/HUNTER - .17 HMR, .17 Mach 2, .22 LR, or .22 Mag. cal., 10 in. barrel, drilled and tapped, left-handed bolt, Truglo sights, choice of poly-coated, walnut or laminate (brown, black, or camo) target style stock with ergonomic grip. Mfg. 2005-2007.

	$155	$130	$110	$95	$80	$70	$60

Last MSR was $190.

Add $10 for walnut stock or $15 for laminate stock.
Add $15 for .22 Mag. cal.
Add $25 for .17 HMR or .17 Mach 2 cal.
Add $28 for stainless steel (new 2006).

RIFLES: BOLT ACTION, SINGLE SHOT

Add approx. $28 for stainless steel action/barrel.

CHIPMUNK STANDARD RIFLE - .17 HMR (new 2002), .17 Mach 2 (new 2005), .22 LR or .22 Mag. (disc. 1987, reintroduced 1999) cal., manually cocked single shot, youth model with 16 1/8 in. barrel and 11 1/2 LOP, choice of black or brown laminate (new 1999), camo (new 2002, various colored woods), synthetic (new 2004), birch (new 2006) or uncheckered Monte Carlo walnut stock, iron sights (adj. aperture rear) or Truglo sights (new 2005), 30 in. overall length, 2 1/2 (standard barrel) or 4 (bull barrel) lbs. Disc. 2007.

	$110	$100	$90	$80	$70	$60	$50

Last MSR was $140.

Add $15 for .22 Mag. cal.
Add $25 for .17 HMR or .17 Mach 2 cal.
Add $10 for birch or $20 for walnut stock.
Add $35 for black/brown laminate or camo stock.
Subtract approx. 10% for black coated wood stock.

✳ *Chipmunk Standard Bull Barrel Model* - similar to Chipmunk Single Shot rifle, features 16 1/8 in. bull barrel, 4 lbs. Mfg. 1999-2007.

	$145	$125	$100	$90	$80	$70	$60

Last MSR was $175.

Add $15 for .22 Mag.
Add $25 for .17 HMR or .17 Mach 2 cal.
Add $15 for laminate or camo stock.

✳ *Chipmunk Standard Deluxe Rifle* - similar to standard rifle, except has upgraded deluxe hand checkered Monte Carlo walnut stock. Mfg. 1987-2007.

	$155	$130	$115	$100	$85	$75	$65

Last MSR was $190.

Add $15 for .22 Mag. cal.
Add $25 for .17 HMR, or .17 Mach 2 cal.

✳ *Chipmunk Standard Target Rifle* - similar to Chipmunk rifle, except has 18 in. heavy barrel, micrometer target sights, target stock with adj. accessory rail and buttplate, 5 lbs. Mfg. mid-2002-2007.

	$295	$255	$215	$185	$165	$150	$135

Last MSR was $350.

✳ *Chipmunk Special Edition* - similar to Deluxe Model, except has hand engraving.
This model was available by custom order only.

BARRACUDA CHIPMUNK - unique design thumbhole stock, pistol grip, floating barrel, also available in bull barrel. Mfg. 2005-2007.

	$180	$155	$125	$100	$85	$75	$65

Last MSR was $220.

Add $15 for .22 Mag.
Add $25 for .17 HMR or .17 Mach 2 cal.

GRADING - PPGS™	100%	98%	95%	90%	80%	70%	60%

SHOTGUNS: SINGLE SHOT

CHIPMUNK .410 SHOTGUN - .410 bore, 18 1/4 in. smoothbore barrel, single shot, manual cocking, blue only, 11 1/2 in. LOP, walnut stock, approx. 3 1/4 lbs. Mfg. mid-2002-2005.

		100%	98%	95%	90%	80%	70%	60%
		$155	$130	$100	$90	$80	$70	$60

Last MSR was $190.

CHRISTENSEN ARMS

Current rifle manufacturer established in 1995, and currently located in Fayette, UT. Previously located in St. George, UT during 1995-99. Direct sales only.

PISTOL

CARBON ONE PISTOL - various cals., graphite barrel lengths up to 14 in., uses Thompson Center Encore or Contender pistol frame, less than 1 in. grouping for 3 shots at 100 yards, satin nickel receiver, approx. 2.5-3 lbs. Limited mfg. beginning 1999.

This model is basically a special order, please contact the company directly.

RIFLES: BOLT ACTION

In addition to the models listed below, Christensen Arms also offers the Carbon One Custom barrel installed on a customer action (any caliber) for $995 ($825 if short chambered by competent gunsmith), as well as providing a Carbon Wrap conversion to an existing steel barrel ($599).

Add $1,200 for Remington titanium action, $195 for titanium muzzle brake, $225 for Jewell trigger, $135 for Teflon coated action, $125 for camo stock (Realtree, Mossy Oak, or Natural Gear), and $75 for lightened action on the models listed below.

CARBON ONE CUSTOM - most popular cals., features Remington 700 BDL short action or Winchester Model 70 action, barrel (up to 28 in. long) features a match grade Shilen/Christensen precision 416R stainless steel barrel liner inside a larger diameter graphite/epoxy barrel casing with crown, black synthetic stock, Shilen trigger, 5 1/2 - 6 1/2 lbs. New 1996.

MSR $3,900		$3,495	$3,000	$2,500	$2,000	$1,650	$1,425	$1,225

Variations include the Carbon Lite (5 lbs.), Carbon King (6-7 lbs., .25-.308 cal.), Carbon Cannon (includes muzzle brake, 6 1/2-7 1/2 lbs., Magnum series), or Carbon Tactical (includes muzzle brake, 6 1/2 lbs., new 1997, or Carbon Conquest (new 1998).

CARBON ONE HUNTER - various popular cals., features Remington M700 (regular or stainless) or Winchester Model 70 stainless action, available with HS Precision or synthetic stock, large diameter graphite barrel with stainless steel barrel liner, 6.5-7 lbs. New 1999.

MSR $1,775		$1,525	$1,275	$975	$850	$700	$600	$500

CARBON RANGER CONQUEST - .50 BMG cal., single shot or repeater (5 shot), McMillan stainless steel bolt action, max barrel length is 32 in. with muzzle brake, Christensen composite stock with bipod, approx. 16 (single shot) - 20 lbs. New 2001.

MSR $6,000		$5,350	$4,600	$3,800	$3,200	$2,625	$2,200	$1,900

Subtract $599 for 5-shot repeater.

CARBON RANGER - .50 BMG cal., large diameter graphite barrel casing (up to 36 in. long), no stock or forearm, twin rails extending from frame sides are attached to recoil pad, Omni Wind Runner action, bipod and choice of scope are included, 25-32 lbs. Limited mfg. 1998-2000 only.

		$9,950	$8,900	$8,000	$7,100	$6,200	$5,300	$4,400

Last MSR was $10,625.

GRADING - PPGS™	100%	98%	95%	90%	80%	70%	60%

CARBON ONE EXTREME - various cals., carbon wrap free floating barrel, Christensen Arms stock, Teflon coated and lightened action, trigger tune, 6-7 lbs. New 2007.

MSR $2,450	$2,175	$1,850	$1,575	$1,275	$1,050	$875	$750

CARBON ONE 10TH ANNIVERSARY MODEL - .270 WSM, .300 WSM, or .325 WSM, Rem. titanium action, graphite stock, titanium muzzle brake, stainless floor plate, SST, laser engraving, individually numbered 1-50. Limited edition beginning mid-2005.

Please contact the company directly for more information on this model, including pricing and availability.

RIFLES: SEMI-AUTO

Christensen Arms also offers a Carbon One Challenge drop-in barrel (16 oz.) for the Ruger Model 10/22. MSR is $499.

CARBON ONE CHALLENGE (CUSTOM) - .17 HMR, .22 LR or .22 Mag. (disc. 2002) cal., features Ruger 10/22 Model 1103 action with modified bolt release, synthetic bull barrel with precision stainless steel liner, 2 lb. Volquartsen trigger, Fajen brown laminated wood (disc.) or black synthetic stock with thumbhole, approx. 3.5-4 lbs. New 1996.

MSR $1,750	$1,500	$1,250	$1,050	$875	$750	$600	$500

Add $350 for .17 HMR or .22 Mag. cal.

The 100% price represents the base model, with no options.

✴ *Carbon One Challenge* - .22 LR cal., non-custom shop variation, 4 lbs. New 1999.

	$550	$495	$440	$400	$365	$330	$295

Last MSR was $599.

CARBON CHALLENGE II - similar to Carbon Challenge I, except has AMT stainless receiver and trigger, black synthetic stock, approx. 4 1/2 lbs. Limited 1997-98 only.

	$1,150	$975	$875	$800	$725	$650	$525

Last MSR was $1,299.

E.J. CHURCHILL GUNMAKERS

Current manufacturer established in 1891, and located in High Wycombe, England since 1996. Previously imported until 2001 by Aspen Outfitters, located in Aspen, CO. Previously manufactured in London, England. This company underwent various trading forms until Churchill, Atkin, Grant & Lang Ltd. closed in 1981. Currently, Churchill Gunmakers' rifles and shotguns are manufactured in High Wycombe, England.

Churchill Guns are very fine quality, and can be ordered with many custom features. We will list both discontinued and current models and approximate values, but strongly urge competent appraisal if purchase or sale is contemplated.

Prices indicated below for manufacturer's suggested retail and 100% condition factors are listed in English pounds. All new prices do not include English VAT. Values for used guns in 98%-60% condition factors are priced in U.S. dollars.

RIFLES: BOLT ACTION

"ONE OF ONE THOUSAND RIFLE" - .270 Win., 7mm Rem. Mag., .308 Win., .30-06, .300 Win. Mag., .375 H&H, or .458 Win. Mag. cal., Mauser type bolt action, 5 shot standard, 3 shot mag. Magnum, 24 in. barrel, classic French walnut stock, swivel recoil pad with trap, trap pistol grip cap. Mfg. 1973 for Interarms 20th Anniversary, only 100 mfg.

	$3,995	$3,500	$2,950	$2,500	$2,000	$1,650	$1,350

Add 50% for .375 H&H or .458 Win. Mag. cal.

GRADING - PPGS™	100%	98%	95%	90%	80%	70%	60%

BARONET RIFLE - various cals. from .30-06 to .375 H&H cal., standard Mauser 98 action with swept bolt handle, fully adj. trigger and 3 position side safety, border engraving, deluxe checkered European walnut stock and forearm, custom order only, allow 8-10 months for delivery, approx. 8.5-9 lbs. New 2001.

MSR £11,500	£11,500	$15,000	$12,500	$10,000	$7,500	$5,000	$3,250

     Add £3,500 for Magnum Mauser action.
     Add £2,535 for detachable scope mounts.

RIFLES: SxS

PREMIERE MODEL - various cals. up to .600 NE, pinless sidelock ejector mechanism with cocking indicators, 24 or 26 in. chopper lump barrels, double triggers, extended top tang, square or rounded body, full traditional fine scroll engraving, color case hardened action, allow 20-24 months for delivery, 9 1/2 - 12 1/2 lbs. Mfg. resumed 1998.

MSR £52,500	£52,500	$65,000	$55,000	$45,000	$35,000	$27,500	$20,000

     Add £650 for hand detachable sidelocks.
     Add £3,000 for .300-.500 NE cals. (cals. over .500 NE are P.O.R.)

SHOTGUNS: O/U

PREMIERE MODEL - 12, 16 (limited mfg.), 20, 28 ga., or .410 bore, 2 3/4 in. chambers, similar barrels and bores as Premiere SxS Model engraved, pinless sidelock ejector with cocking indicators, choice of monobloc (disc.) or chopper lump barrels, mechanical ST, auto ejectors, checkered pistol grip or straight stock, allow 18-24 months for delivery, 6.5 (20 ga.) or 7 (12 ga.) lbs.

MSR £46,500	£46,500	$52,500	$45,000	$37,500	$30,000	$22,500	$16,500

     Add £2,000 for 28 ga. or .410 bore.
     Add £650 for hand detachable sidelocks.
     Add £12,675 for extra set of barrels.
     Add approx. 10% for ordering pair of matched guns.
     Subtract approx. £1,500 for DT. (disc.).

SHOTGUNS: SxS

All models below were built or finished to customer specifications pertaining to choking, chambers, barrel lengths, stock measurements, weight, engraving patterns. Standardized patterns did exist, however, for each model. The "XXV" designation referred to the 25 in. barrel length, which was a Churchill specialty and was also a registered trademark.

PREMIERE MODEL - most gauges, 2 3/4 in. chambers, best quality, easy opening or standard opening, 25 (XXV), 28, 30, or 32 (disc.) in. chopper lump barrels, any choke, sidelock, pinless sidelock ejector with cocking indicators, double triggers standard, engraved, color case hardened action, checkered, straight or pistol grip stock, allow 18-24 months for delivery, 5 lbs. 14 oz. (20 ga.) or 6 lbs. 6 oz. (12 ga.).

MSR £39,500	£39,500	$44,500	$37,500	$31,250	$24,750	$20,750	$16,500

     Add £2,000 for 28 ga.
     Add £8,950 for extra set of barrels.
     Add £3,445 for ST.
     Add approx. 10% for matched guns ordered as a pair.

IMPERIAL MODEL - most gauges, most barrel lengths, second quality sidelock model, ejectors, mostly standard opening, a few made as easy opening. Also mfg. in some double rifles. Disc.

		$13,500	$11,500	$9,500	$7,500	$6,500	$5,250	$4,000

     Add 20% for 20 ga., 40% for 28 ga., and $1,000 for SST, or 35% for double rifle.
     Subtract 10% for 16 ga.

FIELD MODEL - 12 ga. only, most barrel lengths, third quality sidelock model. Disc.

		$9,000	$8,000	$7,000	$6,000	$5,000	$4,500	$3,500

GRADING - PPGS™	100%	98%	95%	90%	80%	70%	60%

HERCULES MODEL - most gauges, 25-30 in. barrels, best quality boxlock model, ejectors, easy opening or standard opening. Also made in some double rifles in .22 Hornet and similar cals.

	$9,000	$8,000	$7,000	$6,000	$5,000	$4,500	$3,500

Add 20% for 20 ga., 40% for 28 ga., $1,000 for SST, and 35% double rifle.
Subtract 10% for 16 ga.

UTILITY MODEL - all gauges (mostly encountered in 12 ga.), 25-30 in. barrels, second quality boxlock model, ejectors, checkered straight or pistol grip stock. Disc.

	$6,250	$4,500	$3,500	$3,000	$2,500	$2,000	$1,800

Add 20% for 20 ga., 40% for 28 ga., 60% for .410 bore, and $500 for SST.
Subtract 10% for 16 ga.

CROWN MODEL - 12, 16, 20 ga., or .410 (rare) bore, third quality boxlock model, various barrel lengths. Disc.

	$4,500	$3,500	$3,000	$2,500	$2,000	$1,600	$1,200

Add 20% for 20 ga., 40% for 28 ga., 60% for .410 bore, and $500 for SST.
Subtract 10% for 16 ga.

REGAL MODEL - 12, 16, 20, 28 ga., or .410 bore, second quality boxlock model introduced after WWII, released after Utility Model was disc. Premium for 28 ga. or .410 bore.

	$6,000	$4,300	$3,750	$3,100	$2,500	$2,000	$1,800

Add 20% for 20 ga., 40% for 28 ga., 60% for .410 bore, and $500 for SST.
Subtract 10% for 16 ga.

* *Regal Grade* - 12, 20, 28 ga., or .410 bore, best quality boxlock model, ejectors, standard opening, limited production.

	$4,800	$4,000	$3,500	$3,000	$2,500	$2,000	$1,800

Last MSR was $5,625.

CHURCHILL

Previous trademark imported and distributed by Ellett Brothers located in Chapin, SC until 1993. Previously imported (until 1988) by Kassnar Imports, Inc. located in Harrisburg, PA. Not affiliated with E.J. Churchill Gunmakers, Ltd.

In late 1988, the Churchill trademark was sold to Ellett Brothers located in Chapin, SC.

RIFLES: BOLT ACTION

HIGHLANDER - .25-06 Rem., .243 Win., .270 Win., .308 Win., .30-06, 7mm Rem. Mag., or .300 Win. Mag. cal., bolt action, 22 in. barrel, thumb safety, no sights, 3 or 4 shot mag., checkered walnut stock, 7 1/2 lbs. Importation disc. 1991.

	$395	$350	$330	$300	$270	$240	$215

Last MSR was $460.

Add $30 for iron sights (disc).

REGENT - same cals. as Highlander, deluxe checkered walnut with Monte Carlo comb and cheekpiece. Last imported by Kassnar in 1988.

	$555	$455	$385	$340	$300	$280	$260

Last MSR was $610.

Add $30 for iron sights.

RIFLES: SEMI-AUTO

ROTARY 22 - .22 LR cal, beginners rifle, bolt hold-open device, adj. rear sight, 10 shot rotary mag. Imported 1989 only.

	$120	$105	$95	$85	$75	$65	$55

Last MSR was $130.

GRADING - PPGS™	100%	98%	95%	90%	80%	70%	60%

SHOTGUNS: O/U

MONARCH - 12, 20, 28 (disc.) ga., or .410 (disc.) bore, 25 (disc.), 26, or 28 in. vent. rib barrels, SST, extractors, boxlock action, DT, silver finish receiver with fine scroll engraving, checkered European walnut stock and forearm, 6 1/2-7 1/2 lbs.

	$460	$370	$340	$300	$250	$230	$210

Last MSR was $520.

> **Add $67 for .410 bore with 26 in. barrels (disc.).**
> **Subtract $40 without SST.**

＊*Monarch Turkey Gun* - 12 ga. only, 24 in. barrels with matte finish. Imported 1990-91 only.

	$460	$370	$340	$300	$250	$230	$210

Last MSR was $529.

SPORTING CLAYS MODEL - 12 ga. only, designed for sporting clays competition with 28 in. VR ported barrels with choke tubes, ejectors, raised target style VR, checkered high gloss finish stock and forearm, 7 lbs. 6 oz. Imported 1992 only.

	$800	$725	$650	$575	$500	$450	$395

Last MSR was $900.

WINDSOR III - 12, 20 ga., or .410 bore (disc.), 27 or 30 in. barrels, double bottom lock, antique silver finish receiver with fine scroll engraving, extractors, SST, vent. rib, checkered pistol grip and forend. Importation disc. 1991.

	$550	$495	$450	$380	$340	$300	$280

Last MSR was $625.

> **Add $140 for Flyweight Model or choke tubes (disc.).**
> **Add $75 for .410 bore.**

NEW WINDSOR IV - 12 or 20 ga., 3 in. chambers, boxlock action, silver receiver with full scroll engraving, 26 or 28 (12 ga. only) VR barrels with choke tubes, ejectors, SST, checkered walnut pistol grip stock with black rubber vent. recoil pad, finger grooved forearm, gloss finish, gold trigger, 5 year warranty. Mfg. 1992 only.

	$625	$525	$450	$375	$325	$295	$275

Last MSR was $690.

WINDSOR IV - DISC. - 12, 20, 28 ga., or .410 bore, 26-30 in. barrels, double bottom lock, antique silver finish receiver with fine scroll engraving, ejectors, SST, vent. rib, checkered pistol grip and forend. Interchangeable chokes became standard in 1989. Importation disc. 1991.

	$725	$640	$530	$470	$430	$395	$360

Last MSR was $852.

> **Subtract $52 for 28 ga. or .410 bore.**
> **Subtract $100 if without choke tubes.**

REGENT V - 12 or 20 ga., 27 in. barrels, double bottom lock, antique silver finish receiver with extra fine scroll engraving, ejectors, single trigger, vent. rib, checkered pistol grip and forend. Interchangeable choke tubes standard. Disc. 1986, reintroduced 1990, disc. 1993.

	$895	$795	$700	$620	$560	$510	$470

Last MSR was $1,100.

This model was previously designated Regent VII until 1989 when it changed to the Regent V.

REGENT TRAP AND SKEET - 12 or 20 ga., 26 or 30 in. barrels, double bottom lock, antique silver finish receiver with sideplates engraved in fine scroll, ejectors, SST, vent. rib, checkered pistol grip and forend. Importation disc. 1991.

	$795	$650	$575	$540	$485	$440	$390

Last MSR was $963.

> **Add $40 for trap variation.**

GRADING - PPGS™	100%	98%	95%	90%	80%	70%	60%

REGENT GRADE SHOTGUN/RIFLE COMBINATION - 12 ga. over either .222 Rem., .223 Rem., .243 Win. (disc.), .270 Win., .30-06, or .308 Win. cal., 25 in. barrels, double bottom lock, antique silver finish receiver with extra fine scroll engraving, ejectors, single trigger, vent. rib, checkered pistol grip and forend. Importation disc. 1991.

	$800	$700	$635	$560	$510	$475	$440

Last MSR was $927.

SHOTGUNS: SxS

WINDSOR I - 10 (disc. 1988), 12, 16, 20, 28 ga., or .410 bore, double barrel, 23-32 in. barrels, Anson and Deeley boxlock, antique silver finish receiver with fine scroll engraving, extractors, double triggers, checkered pistol grip and forend. Importation disc. 1991.

	$550	$465	$450	$385	$300	$250	$230

Last MSR was $653.

Add $150 for 10 ga.
Add $55 for 28 ga. or .410 bore.
Add $30 for Flyweight Models (25 in. barrels - disc. 1988).

WINDSOR II - 12 or 20 ga., 26-30 in. barrels, Anson and Deeley boxlock, antique silver finish receiver with fine scroll engraving, ejectors, double triggers, checkered pistol grip and forend. Add $100 for 10 ga. (disc.). Importation disc. 1987.

	$595	$485	$415	$350	$315	$270	$240

Last MSR was $638.

WINDSOR VI - 12 or 20 (disc.) ga., 25 or 28 in. barrels, sidelock, antique silver finish receiver with fine scroll engraving, ejectors, double triggers, checkered pistol grip and forend. Disc. 1987.

	$840	$700	$600	$550	$510	$460	$420

Last MSR was $900.

ROYAL - 10, 12, 20, 28 ga., or .410 bore, DTs, extractors, checkered walnut stock and forearm, case hardened receiver. Imported late 1988-91.

	$485	$405	$370	$310	$275	$250	$230

Last MSR was $540.

Add $20 for 28 ga.
Add $74 for .410 bore.

SHOTGUNS: SEMI-AUTO

STANDARD MODEL - 12 ga. only, gas operated and shoots different loads interchangeably without alterations, 24, 26, 28 in. VR barrel, magazine cut-off, hand checkered walnut with satin finish, matte metal finish, includes ICT choke tubes. New 1990.

	$495	$415	$375	$310	$275	$250	$230

Last MSR was $550.

✳ *Standard Turkey Model* - similar to Standard Model, except has 24 in. barrel only. New 1990.

	$510	$425	$380	$315	$275	$250	$230

Last MSR was $570.

WINDSOR GRADE - 12 ga. only, 26, 28, or 30 in. barrels, gas operation, anodized alloy receiver, vent. rib, checkered pistol grip and forend, 7 1/2 lbs. Deluxe model includes polished receiver with etching.

	$380	$320	$300	$275	$250	$225	$200

Last MSR was $420.

Add $35 for choke tubes.
Add $55 for Deluxe model.

GRADING - PPGS™	100%	98%	95%	90%	80%	70%	60%

REGENT GRADE - 12 ga. only, 26, 28, or 30 in. barrels, gas operation, anodized alloy receiver, vent. rib, checkered pistol grip and forend, 7 1/2 lbs. Deluxe model includes polished receiver with etching. Disc. 1986.

	$440	$365	$340	$320	$300	$285	$270

Last MSR was $495.

Add $35 for choke tubes.
Add $55 for Deluxe model.

SHOTGUNS: SLIDE ACTION

WINDSOR GRADE - 12 ga. only, 26, 27, 28, or 30 in. barrels, double slides, anodized alloy receiver, vent. rib, checkered pistol grip and forend, 7 1/2 lbs. Disc. 1986.

	$385	$330	$310	$275	$250	$225	$200

Last MSR was $430.

CIMARRON F.A. CO.

Current importer, distributor, and retailer located in Fredricksburg, TX. Cimarron is currently importing A. Uberti, D. Pedersoli, and Armi-Sport firearms and black powder reproductions and replicas. Previous company name was Old-West Co. of Texas. Dealer sales only.

Please refer to the *Blue Book of Modern Black Powder Arms* by John Allen (also online) for more information and prices on Cimarron's lineup of modern black powder models.

Black Powder Reproductions & Replicas by Dennis Adler is also an invaluable source for most black powder reproductions and replicas, and includes hundreds of color images on most popular makes/models, provides manufacturer/trademark histories, and up-to-date information on related items/accessories for black powder shooting - www.bluebookinc.com

REVOLVERS: REPRODUCTIONS, COLT

The Cimarron Arms reproductions of the 1873 Colt Peacemaker, mostly mfg. by Uberti, with the exception of previous limited production by Armi San Marco, are available in two configurations listed below. Beginning in 1984, Cimarron arms reproductions began incorporating many of the features of the 1st Generation Colt SAAs. These SAA revolvers are extremely accurate reproductions of the original Colt pre-war Peacemaker and are marked (and machined) the same as the originals, including serial numbers on frames, backstrap, trigger guard, and cylinder. Barrels are radiused and cylinders are beveled. Frames are color case hardened, stocks are walnut - choice of 4 3/4, 5 1/2, or 7 1/2 in. barrel. All Cimarron SAAs are currently barrel marked "- CIMARRON F.A. MFG. Co. FREDERICKSBURG, TX. U.S.A. -". The "Old Model" configuration has the older style black powder frame, screw-in cylinder pin retainer, and circular "bullseye" ejector head. The Standard Model includes the post-1890 style frame with spring loaded cross-pin cylinder retainer and "half-moon" ejector head. Only the Old Model is available in the authentic old style "charcoal blue" finish (sometimes referred to as fire-bluing).

During 1998, Cimarron introduced an Original Finish (antiqued) that resembles the older, worn finish seen on many of the well-used, original Colt revolvers. This distressed finish is a greyish-brown patina color, and certain areas of these guns (end of barrel, grip straps, frame/cylinder edges, and grips) have been artifically aged to give them an authentic "been carried and used for 100 years" appearance.

Add $40 for Original Finish on SAAs listed below. Add $40 for charcoal blue finish. Add $175 for antique custom nickel or custom nickel finish. Add $350 for silver plating. Add $250 for U.S. Armory finish utilizing bonemeal case coloring. Add $295 for old style color case hardening and Carbona blue finish (disc. 2003). Add $45 for hand checkered walnut grips (disc. 2003). Add $60 for various styles of grips. Add $225 Izit ivory grips (disc. 2006). Add $325 for Izit ivory steer head grips (mfg. 2004-2006). Add $325 for Micarta grips. Add $850 for geniune ivory grips. Add $326 for mother-of-pearl grips (disc. 2006). Add $200 for Tru Ivory grips (new 2007). Add $850 for "A" style engraving (30% coverage) on SAAs listed below (disc 2004). Add $774 for "B" style engraving (50% coverage) on SAAs listed below. Add $1,800 for "C" style engraving (70% coverage) on SAAs listed below (disc. 2004). Add $2,400 for "Texas Cattle Brands" or full (100% coverage) engraving pattern (disc. 2004). Add $1,060 for Patton engraving. Add $1,625 for Teddy Roosevelt engraving. Add $1,365 for Open Top Standard engraving. Add $585 for percussion engraving on Pocket models, or $845 for regular models. Add $2,600 for Judge Roy Bean engraving. Add $2,470 for Wild Bill conversion engraving.

1871-72 OPEN TOP - .38 Long Colt, .38 S&W Spl., .44-40 WCF, .44 Russian, .45 Colt (new 2006) or .45 Schofield cal., 4 3/4 (new 2004, Navy size grips), 5 1/2 (Navy size grips) or 7 1/2 (Army size grips) in. barrel, patterned after the Colt 1871-1872 Open Top, Navy grip frame is available in brass or silver plated. Mfg. by A. Uberti beginning 1999.

MSR $454	$375	$300	$265	$230	$200	$175	$160

Add $52 for charcoal blue finish, or $65 for original or antique finish.
Add $25 for silver plated backstrap and trigger guard on Navy model only.
Add $26 for 7 1/2 in. barrel.

FRONTIER SIX SHOOTER - .22 LR (disc. 1995), .22 Mag. (disc.), .357 Mag., .38 Spl. (disc.), .38-40 WCF, .44 Spl. (new 1998), .44-40 WCF, or .45 LC cal., 4 3/4, 5 1/2, and 7 1/2 in. barrel lengths, steel backstraps and trigger guard. Importation disc. 1999.

✳ *Frontier Six-Shooter (USA Finish)* - .32 WCF, .357 Mag., .38 WCF, .44 Spl., .44 WCF, or .45 LC cal., this variation is disassembled and then refinished in the U.S. in the same type of finish as the original Colt SAA from the late 19th century. New 2008.

MSR $730	$625	$525	$450	$400	$350	$300	$275

✳ *Frontier Six-Shooter Standard or Old Model*

	$395	$300	$250	$220	$195	$175	$160

Last MSR was $469.

Add $30 for convertible .45 ACP cylinder.

✳ *Frontier Six-Shooter Sheriff's Model* - .44-40 WCF or .45 LC cal., w/o ejector, 3 or 4 (disc. 1992) in. barrel, steel backstraps and trigger guard. Disc. 1998, reintroduced 2000-2001.

	$395	$300	$250	$220	$195	$175	$160

Last MSR was $469.

✳ *Frontier Six-Shooter New Sheriff Model* - .357 Mag., .44-40 WCF, .44 Spl., or .45 LC cal., 3 1/2 in. barrel with ejector, Old Model frame only. Importation began 1995.

MSR $480	$400	$325	$265	$225	$195	$175	$160

Add $40 for charcoal blue finish (disc.).
Add $45 for checkered walnut grips.

✳ *Frontier Six-Shooter Target Model* - similar to Standard Model, except has fully adj. target rear sight, brass or steel backstrap. Importation disc. 1991.

	$355	$280	$255	$220	$195	$175	$160

Last MSR was $400.

Add $40 for .357 Mag. cal.
This variation was available in the Standard Model configuration only and with standard finish.

BADLANDS SAA MODEL - .357 Mag. or .45 LC cal., 4 3/4 in. barrel, brass backstrap and trigger guard, flat black receiver and barrel finish, steel frame, smooth wood grips, case colored hammer. Mfg. 2005-2007.

	$275	$245	$220	$200	$185	$160	$150

Last MSR was $325.

MODEL P SAA - .32-20 WCF, .38-40 WCF, .357 Mag., .44-40 WCF, .44 Spl., or .45 LC cal., features pinched frame (.45 LC cal. with 7 1/2 in. barrel only, disc. 2006), Old Model, or pre-war configuration, standard finish or charcoal blue, 4 3/4, 5 1/2, or 7 1/2 in. barrel. Importation began 1996.

MSR $480	$400	$325	$275	$235	$200	$180	$160

Add $50 for convertible .45 ACP cylinder.
Add $52 for charcoal blue finish (Old Model frame).

GRADING - PPGS™	100%	98%	95%	90%	80%	70%	60%

Add $65 for original or antique finish.
Add $5 for pre-war configuration.
Add $50 for target model with adj. sights and flattop frame (7 1/2 in. barrel with .45 LC or .44-40 WCF cal. only, disc. 2006).
Add $130 for stainless steel construction in .357 Mag. or .45 LC cal. only (new 2004).
Add $399 for laser engraving (pre-war frame only).
Add $526 for Teddy Roosevelt model (.45 Colt, 7 1/2 in. barrel, silver backstrap, laser engraving and poly ivory grips).
Add $513 for George Patton model (.45 Colt 5 1/5 in. barrel, silver backstrap, laser engraving, and poly ivory grips).

✳ *Model P Jr. SAA* - .22 LR (new 2007), .38 Colt/S&W Spl., or .41 LC (new 2007) cal., features smaller size frame (20% less) proportioned from the SAA, but with standard single action grip frame, 3 1/2, 4 3/4, or 5 1/2 in. barrel. Mfg. by A. Uberti 2000-2001, reintroduced 2004.

MSR $454	$385	$325	$270	$230	$200	$180	$160

Add $45 for checkered walnut grips.
Add $86 for dual cylinder (.32-20 WCF/.32 H&R Mag. cal., new 2004).
Add $52 for charcoal blue finish.
Subtract $57 for .22 LR or $5 for .41 LC cal.

EVIL ROY SAA - .357 Mag., .44-40 WCF, or .45 LC cal., 4 3/4 or 5 1/2 in. barrel, features wide square notch rear sight and constant with front sight, smooth or checkered slim grips, lightened trigger and hammer springs, color case hardened finish on frame, Evil Roy signature on bottom of grip strap. New 2005.

MSR $644	$525	$460	$410	$375	$330	$310	$275

WYATT EARP LIMITED EDITION BUNTLINE - .45 LC cal., only, 10 in. barrel, sterling silver plaque inlaid into wood grips, case colored receiver. Importation began 2002.

MSR $701	$595	$525	$425	$385	$340	$310	$275

Add $65 for original or antique finish.

BISLEY SAA - .357 Mag., .44 Spl., .44-40 WCF, or .45 LC cal., 4 3/4, 5 1/2, or 7 1/2 in. barrel, Bisley configured grips, case colored receiver, smooth walnut grips, flattop target model available with 7 1/2 in. barrel in .44-40 WCF or .45 LC cal. only. Importation began 2002.

MSR $532	$450	$375	$320	$280	$260	$240	$220

PISTOLERO - .357 Mag. or .45 LC cal., similar to the Model P, except has brass backstrap and trigger guard, 4 3/4, 5 1/2, or 7 1/2 (disc.) in. barrel, case hardened frame with blue barrel and cylinder (disc.) or blue finish, one piece walnut grips. Mfg. 1997 only, reintroduced 2007.

MSR $370	$295	$260	$230	$200	$180	$165	$140

PLINKERTON - .22 LR cal., 4 3/4 in. barrel, matte black metal finish, checkered black plastic grips, 34 oz., mfg. by Chiappa. New 2007.

MSR $155	$125	$115	$95	$85	$80	$75	$70

Add $21 for dual cylinder (.22 Mag.).

BUNTLINE MODEL - .357 Mag., .44-40 WCF, or .45 LC cal., 18 in. barrel, brass or steel backstrap cut for shoulder stock. Disc. 1989.

	$355	$280	$255	$220	$195	$175	$160

Last MSR was $400.

Add $10 for target sights.

BUNTLINE CARBINE - similar cals. to Buntline Model, except also includes .22 LR/.22 Mag. (convertible cylinders, disc.), 18 in. barrel, includes non-detachable shoulder stock with brass hardware and finger extension trigger guard. Importation disc. 1991, reintroduced 2006.

MSR $688	$575	$495	$425	$385	$340	$310	$275

Add 5% for target sights or .22 LR/.22 Mag. combo (disc.).

GRADING - PPGS™	100%	98%	95%	90%	80%	70%	60%

BUCKHORN - .44 Spl. or .44 Mag. cal., reinforced variation of the Cimarron SAA designed for more powerful cartridges, 4 3/4, 6 or 7 1/2 in. barrel, brass or steel backstrap. Disc. 1993.

	$355	$285	$260	$220	$195	$175	$160

Last MSR was $400.

Buckhorn Convertible Model - .44 Mag./.44-40 WCF cylinders are included, 4 3/4, 6 or 7 1/2 in. barrel. Disc. 1989.

	$375	$295	$265	$220	$195	$175	$160

Last MSR was $427.

    Add $12 for target sights.

Buckhorn Target Model - .44 Spl. or .44 Mag. cal., 4 3/4, 6 or 7 1/2 in. barrel, adj. rear sight. Importation disc. 1991.

	$370	$290	$265	$225	$195	$175	$160

Last MSR was $420.

Buckhorn Buntline - .44-40 WCF, .44 Spl., or .44 Mag. cal., 18 in. barrel, fixed or target sights. Disc. 1989.

	$370	$285	$265	$220	$195	$175	$160

Last MSR was $419.

    Add $30 for target sights.

Buckhorn Carbine - .44-40 WCF, .44 Spl., or .44 Mag. cal., 18 in. barrel, includes non-detachable shoulder stock with brass hardware and lanyard ring. Disc. 1990.

	$375	$290	$265	$220	$195	$175	$160

Last MSR was $429.

    Add $30 for target sights.

THUNDERER - .357 Mag., .44 Spl., .44-40 WCF or .45 LC cal., patterned after Colt's Thunderer Model, 3 1/2, 4 3/4, or 5 1/2 (new 2000) in. barrel with full ejector rod housing, birdshead grips, choice of case colored or nickel finish. Importation began 1994.

MSR $508	$425	$325	$265	$220	$195	$175	$160

    Add $45 for checkered walnut grips.
    Add $99 for convertible .45 ACP cylinder (3 1/2 or 4 3/4 in. only).
    Add $123 for stainless steel (available in .357 Mag. or .45 LC in 3 1/2 or 4 3/4 in. barrel only).

Thunderer Long Tom - .357 Mag., .44-40 WCF or .45 LC cal., 7 1/2 in. barrel. New 1997.

MSR $506	$425	$325	$265	$220	$195	$175	$160

    Add $45 for checkered walnut grips.

U.S. 7TH CAVALRY CUSTER MODEL - .45 LC cal., authentic reproduction of original Colt military cavalry contract, 7 1/2 in. barrel, marked "U.S." on lower left frame, one-piece walnut grips with military cartouche.

MSR $520	$450	$385	$335	$285	$265	$240	$220

    Add $52 for charcoal blue finish or $65 for antique finish.

U.S. CAVALRY MODEL P (A.P. CASEY) - .45 LC cal. only, 7 1/2 in. barrel, Old Model frame. Mfg. 1996-97.

	$430	$365	$315	$280	$260	$240	$220

Last MSR was $499.

U.S. ARTILLERY MODEL - Rinaldo A. Carr 1895 U.S. Artillery Model Commemorative, 5 1/2 in. barrel. Limited mfg.

	$430	$365	$315	N/A	N/A	N/A	N/A

Last MSR was $499.

GRADING - PPGS™	100%	98%	95%	90%	80%	70%	60%

U.S. ARTILLERY ROUGH RIDER - .45 LC cal. only, 5 1/2 in. barrel, Old Model frame. New 1996.

MSR $520	$450	$385	$335	$285	$265	$240	$220

Add $52 for charcoal blue finish or $65 for original or antique finish.

7TH CAVALRY CASED SET - U.S. Cavalry Model in case with accessories. Disc. 1990.

	$695	$625	$550	$500	$460	$420	$385

Last MSR was $780.

WILD BILL ELLIOT TEXAS CATTLEBRAND - .45 LC cal. Mfg. 1994-96.

	$1,225	$1,025	$875	$750	$625	$550	$475

Last MSR was $1,395.

JUDGE ROY BEAN COMMEMORATIVE - mfg. to commemorate Judge Roy Bean's Texas cattlebrand. Disc. 1996.

	$1,500	$1,175	$995	N/A	N/A	N/A	N/A

Last MSR was $1,695.

LIGHTNING - .22 LR (new 2007), .38 Colt (disc.), .38 S&W Spl., .41 LC (new 2007) cal., patterned after the original Colt Lightning, 3 1/2, 4 3/4 or 5 1/2 in. barrel, birdshead grips. Mfg. by A. Uberti 1999-2001, reintroduced again in 2003.

MSR $472	$400	$325	$275	$235	$200	$180	$160

Add $86 for dual cylinder (.32-20 WCF/.32 H&R Mag. cal., new 2004).
Add $45 for checkered walnut grips.
Add $52 for charcoal blue finish.
Subtract $31 for .22 LR cal.
Add $15 for .41 LC cal.

REVOLVERS: REPRODUCTIONS, COLT CONVERSIONS

1851 NAVY RICHARDS-MASON - .38 Spl. cal., patterned after the original Richards-Mason 1851 Navy Conversion, 4 3/4, 5 1/2 or 7 1/2 in. barrel, available in standard, charcoal blue, or original finish. Mfg. by Uberti. Importation began 2003.

MSR $469	$400	$325	$275	$235	$200	$180	$160

Add $52 for charcoal blue finish.
Add $65 for antique finish.
Add $25 for silver plated backstrap and triggerguard (disc. 2006).

1851 MAN WITH NO NAME CONVERSION - .38 Colt/S&W Spl. cal., 7 1/2 in. barrel, blue finish, patterned after the original 1851 model used in the 1960s spaghetti westerns. New 2007.

MSR $480	$400	$325	$275	$235	$200	$180	$160

Add $208 for rattlesnake grip inlay.

1860 ARMY RICHARDS-MASON - .38 Spl. (new 2007), .44 WCF and Russian, .45 LC (new 2007) or .45 Schofield cal., patterned after the original Richards-Mason 1860 Conversion, 4 3/4, 5 1/2 or 8 in. barrel, available in standard, charcoal blue or original finish. Mfg. by Uberti. Importation began 2003.

MSR $506	$415	$365	$310	$275	$250	$210	$180

Add $52 for charcoal blue finish.
Add $65 for antique finish.

1868 THUER CONVERSION TO 1860 ARMY - .44-40 WCF cal., Thuer conversion ring and cylinder, cartridge loading tool, all other specifications same as 1860 Army. Disc. 2002.

	$350	$275	$250	$225	$200	$185	$160

Last MSR was $418.

This model requires a special hand-loaded round in .44 cal for the Thuer Conversion.

GRADING - PPGS™	100%	98%	95%	90%	80%	70%	60%

TYPE II RICHARDS TRANSITION MODEL - .38 Spl., .44 Colt, .44 Spl., or .45 LC cal., 5 1/2 or 8 in. barrel, blue finish, case hardened frame, one-piece walnut grips. New 2007.

MSR $519	$425	$365	$310	$275	$250	$210	$180

REVOLVERS: REPRODUCTIONS, REMINGTON

These guns are reproductions of the Models 1875 and 1890.

Add $90 for nickel plating, $10 for charcoal blue finish on models listed below.

MODEL 1875 - .357 Mag., .44-40 WCF, or .45 LC cal., 7 1/2 barrel. Disc. 1993.

	$340	$250	$200	$170	$155	$140	$120

Last MSR was $390.

MODEL 1890 - .357 Mag., .44-40 WCF, or .45 LC cal., 5 1/2 or 7 1/2 in. barrel. Disc. 1993.

	$340	$250	$210	$175	$160	$145	$125

Last MSR was $390.

1871 ROLLING BLOCK TARGET PISTOL - .22 LR, .22 Hornet (new 1990), .22 Mag., or .357 Mag. cal., 9 1/2 in. barrel. Importation disc. 1990.

	$250	$200	$180	$160	$140	$125	$110

Last MSR was $280.

1858 ARMY NEW MODEL CONVERSION - .38 Spl., .44-40 WCF, or .45 LC cal., 5 1/2, 7 3/8, or 8 in. barrel, forged steel frame, blue finish, walnut grips. New 2007.

MSR $493	$415	$315	$265	$225	$195	$175	$150

Add $72 for dual cylinder (.45 LC/.44 cal. Percussion).

REVOLVERS: REPRODUCTIONS, SMITH & WESSON

SCHOFIELD MODEL NO. 3 - .38 Spl. (disc. 1997), .38-40 WCF (disc. 1997), .44 Russian/Spl., .44-40 WCF, .45 Schofield, .45 ACP (disc.), or .45 LC cal., available in 7 (Civilian or Military) or 5 (Wells Fargo only) in. barrel. Mfg. by Armi San Marco 1996-99.

	$730	$640	$570	$515	$450	$400	$360

Last MSR was $849.

Add $100 for nickel finish.
Add $150 for custom nickel finish.

This model was also available as a "Little Big Horn" variation with sub-inspector markings and "SBL" cartouche.

SCHOFIELD MODEL NO. 3 (CURRENT MFG.) - .38 Spl.,.44-40 WCF, or .45 LC cal., 3 1/2, 5, or 7 in. barrel, blue finish, mfg. by Uberti. New 2007.

MSR $930	$800	$725	$650	$550	$450	$350	$300

MODEL NO. 3 RUSSIAN - .44 Russian or .45 LC cal., 6 1/2 in. barrel, blue finish, two-piece walnut grips, blue frame, mfg. by Uberti. New 2007.

MSR $965	$825	$725	$650	$550	$450	$350	$300

RIFLES: REPRODUCTIONS, COLT

LIGHTNING MAGAZINE RIFLE - .357 Mag., .44-40 WCF, or .45 LC cal., 20, 24, or 26 in. round (not available with 26 in. barrel) or octagon barrel, blue or case colored frame, patterned after Colt Lightning rifle. Mfg. by Pedersoli. Importation began 2006.

MSR $1,520	$1,295	$950	$825	$700	$600	$550	$500

Add $78 for octagon barrel.
Add $234 for 24 or 26 in. octagon barrel.

GRADING - PPGS™	100%	98%	95%	90%	80%	70%	60%

RIFLES/CARBINES: REPRODUCTIONS, REMINGTON ROLLING BLOCK

Add $200 for AA select wood, $400 for AAA premium select wood, or $600 for super premium (fine European walnut). Add $150 for fine hand oil finish or $200 for super fine stock finish.

MODEL 1871 ROLLING BLOCK BABY CARBINE - same cals. as Target Pistol, has 22 in. barrel and walnut stock and forearm, brass trigger guard and buttplate. Importation disc. 1990.

	$310	$245	$205	$170	$155	$140	$120

Last MSR was $340.

MODEL 1875 CARBINE - same cals. as Model 1875, 18 in. barrel, includes non-detachable shoulder stock with brass hardware and lanyard ring. Importation disc. 1990.

	$410	$340	$300	$265	$230	$200	$180

Last MSR was $460.

ROLLING BLOCK SPORTING RIFLE - .45-70 cal., 30 in. barrel, walnut stock and forearm. Imported 1989-90 only.

	$625	$565	$430	$395	$350	$320	$300

Last MSR was $620.

* *Deluxe Rolling Block Sporting Rifle* - similar to standard model, except has select wood. Importation disc. 1990.

	$725	$640	$485	$450	$375	$340	$320

Last MSR was $720.

REMINGTON ROLLING BLOCK LONG RANGE CREEDMOOR - .45-70 Govt. cal., 30 in. tapered octagon barrel, deluxe checkered walnut stock. Importation began 1997.

	$1,125	$825	$700	$625	$550	$500	$450

Last MSR was $1,295.

"ADOBE WALLS" ROLLING BLOCK - .45-70 Govt. cal., 30 in. octagon barrel, hand checkered walnut stock, case hardened receiver, German silver nose cap, optional Creedmoor sight. Mfg. by Pedersoli. Importation began 2004.

MSR $1,793	$1,475	$1,225	$950	$850	$750	$650	$550

RIFLES: REPRODUCTIONS, SHARPS

Add $200 for AA select wood, $400 for AAA premium select wood, or $600 for super premium (fine European walnut). Add $150 for fine hand oil finish or $200 for super fine stock finish.

SPORTING #1 RIFLE - .40-65 Win. or .45-70 Govt. cal., 32 in. octagon barrel, pistol grip stock. Mfg. by Pedersoli. Imported 2000-2002.

	$975	$800	$675	$600	$525	$475	$375

Last MSR was $1,095.

SPORTING #1 SILHOUETTE RIFLE - .45-70 Govt. or .50-70 cal., 32 in. octagon barrel with silhouette sights, pistol grip stock. Mfg. by Pedersoli. Importation began 2003.

MSR $1,645	$1,375	$1,175	$950	$775	$650	$550	$475

ARMI-SPORT BILLY DIXON MODEL 1874 SPORTING RIFLE - .38-55 WCF, .45-70 Govt., .45-90 Win., .45-110 (new 2003), or .50-90 (new 2003) cal., 32 in. barrel, nickel silver front blade and forearm cap, checkered deluxe walnut stock, double set triggers. Mfg. by Armi-Sport. Importation began 1997.

MSR $1,247	$1,050	$875	$750	$650	$550	$475	$375

GRADING - PPGS™	100%	98%	95%	90%	80%	70%	60%

PEDERSOLI BILLY DIXON MODEL 1874 SPORTING RIFLE - .45-70 Govt., .45-90 Win., or .50-70 (mfg. 2004-2006) cal., 32 in. barrel, nickel silver front blade and forearm cap, checkered deluxe walnut stock, double set triggers. Mfg. by Pedersoli. Importation began 1997.

MSR $2,157	$1,750	$1,475	$1,200	$875	$775	$675	$575

    Add $26 for .45-90 Win. cal.

ARMI-SPORT QUIGLEY II MODEL 1874 SPORTING RIFLE - .45-70 Govt., .45-90 Win., .45-110 (new 2004), .45-120 Sharps, or .50-90 (new 2002) cal., 34 in. octagon barrel with storage compartment in stock. Mfg. by Armi-Sport. Importation began 2000.

MSR $1,403	$1,200	$875	$750	$650	$550	$500	$450

    Subtract $26 for .45-70 Govt. cal.

PEDERSOLI QUIGLEY MODEL 1874 SPORTING RIFLE - .45-70 Govt., .45-90 Win., .45-110, .45-120 Sharps, .50-70 (mfg. 2004-2006), or .50-90 (new 2002) cal., 34 in. octagon barrel with storage compartment in stock. Mfg. by Pedersoli. Importation began 2000.

MSR $2,230	$1,800	$1,500	$1,225	$875	$775	$675	$575

    Add $47 for .45-90 Win. cal., $108 for .45-110 or .45-120 cal., or $173 for .50-70 or .50-90 cal.

SHARPS BIG 50 LONG RANGE MODEL 1874 SPORTING RIFLE - .50-90 cal., 34 in. barrel, double set triggers, apeture rear sight, checkered stock and forearm. Mfg. by Pedersoli. Importation began 2004.

MSR $2,730	$2,400	$2,050	$1,625	$1,275	$950	$825	$725

SHARPS "PRIDE OF THE PLAINS" MODEL 1874 - .45-70 Govt. cal., 32 in. matte black octagon barrel, hand checkered walnut stock, nickel receiver, Creedmore rear sight. Mfg. by Pedersoli. Importation began 2004.

MSR $2,113	$1,725	$1,475	$1,200	$875	$775	$675	$575

SHARPS PROFESSIONAL HUNTER MODEL 1874 - .45-70 Govt. cal., mfg. by Pedersoli. Importation began 2005.

MSR $1,416	$1,275	$1,050	$825	$675	$550	$475	$400

SHARPS MCNELLY CARBINE MODEL 1874 (TEXAS RANGER) - .45-70 Govt. or .50-70 cal., 22 in. round blue barrel, American black walnut stock, case colored receiver, marked with TS initials with Lone Star in between on barrel. Mfg. by Armi Sport. Importation began 2004.

MSR $1,091	$950	$800	$700	$600	$500	$400	$350

U.S.A. SHOOTING TEAM CREEDMOOR SHARPS - .45-70 Govt. cal., color case hardened frame, blue finish, 34 in. round barrel, walnut stock, mfg. by Armi-Sport.

MSR $1,793	$1,575	$1,250	$975	$850	$725	$625	$525

Cimarron is donating a portion of the sales from this rifle to the U.S.A. shooting team.

RIFLES: REPRODUCTIONS, SPENCER

1865 SPENCER REPEATING RIFLE - .44-40 WCF, .45 Schofield, .45 LC, or .56-60 cal., case colored receiver, 20 or 30 (.56-60 cal. only) in. barrel, blue finish, color case hardened frame, straight grip walnut stock, includes slings, mfg. by Armi-Sport. Importation began 2005.

MSR $1,285	$1,125	$925	$775	$650	$550	$475	$400

    Add $182 for 30 in. barrel.

RIFLES: REPRODUCTIONS, WINCHESTER

The rifles listed below are manufactured by A. Uberti.

    Add $200 for AA select wood, $400 for AAA premium select wood, or $600 for super premium (fine European walnut). Add $150 for fine hand oil finish or $200 for super fine stock finish. Add approx. $78 for charcoal blue finish (new 1997) on most models listed

GRADING - PPGS™	100%	98%	95%	90%	80%	70%	60%

below. Add approx. $110 for original or antique finish on those models listed below where it is an option.

HENRY RIFLE/CARBINE - .44-40 WCF, .44 Spl. (mfg. 1993-95), or .45 LC (new 1993) cal., brass or case colored steel (.44-40 WCF and .45 LC cal. only, new 2002) frame, 24 1/4 in. barrel on rifle, 22 (disc. 1995, .44-40 WCF cal. only) in. barrel on carbine.

MSR $1,260	$1,075	$775	$650	$550	$500	$450	$400

Add for $50 for in-the-white finish (disc.).
Subtract $13 for steel frame model.
Add $975 for standard engraving.
Add $1,235 for steel engraving.
Add $2,145 for Lincoln Presentation engraving.
Previous to 1997, this model could also be special ordered with Grade A engraving ($450 extra), Grade B engraving ($550 extra), and Grade C engraving ($725 extra).

CIVIL WAR HENRY RIFLE - .44-40 WCF or .45 LC (new 1998) cal., 24 1/4 in. barrel, patterned after the U.S. issue original inspected by Chas. G. Chapman (C.G.C.) with military inspector's marks and cartouche, military sling swivels became standard in 1996. Importation began 1993.

MSR $1,364	$1,150	$975	$725	$625	$550	$475	$400

Add $65 for in-the-white finish (disc.).

1866 SPORTING RIFLE (YELLOWBOY) - .22 LR (disc. 1993), .22 Mag. (disc. 1993), .32-20 WCF (new 2002), .38 Spl. (new 1995), .38-40 WCF (new 2002), .44 Spl. (new 2006), .44-40 WCF, or .45 LC (new 1993) cal., brass receiver, 20 (new 2000, Short Rifle) or 24 in. octagon barrel.

MSR $1,039	$865	$650	$525	$425	$350	$300	$250

Add $845 for standard engraving (new 1997).
Add $2,860 for Mexican Eagle engraving (new 1997) or $2,535 for Red Cloud engraving (new 2005).
Add $500 (retail) for A engraving, $650 for B engraving, $1,175 for C engraving. Disc. 1996.

1866 YELLOWBOY CARBINE - .32-20 WCF, .38 Spl., .38-55 WCF, .44 Spl., .44-40 WCF, or .45 LC cal., similar to Model 1866 Sporting Rifle, except has 19 in. round barrel with 2 bands, saddle ring, uncheckered walnut stock and forearm.

MSR $1,039	$865	$650	$525	$425	$350	$300	$250

Add $35 for saddle ring.

* *1866 Trapper Carbine* - .38 Spl. (new 2002), .44-40 WCF, or .45 LC (new 2005) cal., 16 in. round barrel. Importation disc. 1990, reintroduced 2002.

MSR $1,039	$865	$650	$525	$425	$350	$300	$250

Add $35 for saddle ring.

* *1866 Yellowboy Indian Carbine* - .22 LR, .22 Mag., .38 Spl., or .44-40 WCF cal., 19 in. round barrel. Disc. 1989.

	$575	$475	$400	$350	$300	$260	$220

Last MSR was $649.

This model had a photo engraved brass frame and brass tacks in stock and forearm.

* *1886 Red Cloud Commemorative Carbine* - same cals. as Yellowboy Indian Carbine, includes special engraving representing Oglalla Indian tribe symbols, brass tacks in forearm and stock. Disc. 1989.

	$575	$475	$400	N/A	N/A	N/A	N/A

Last MSR was $649.

1873 SPORTING RIFLE - .22 LR (disc. 1993), .22 Mag. (disc. 1993), .32-20 WCF (new 2002), .357 Mag./.38 Spl., .38-40 WCF (new 2002), .44 Spl. (new 2002), .44-40 WCF, or .45 LC cal., 24 1/4 in. octagon barrel, case hardened receiver, full mag., iron sights.

MSR $1,169	$995	$735	$625	$500	$400	$350	$300

Add $425 for old style color case hardening.

GRADING - PPGS™	100%	98%	95%	90%	80%	70%	60%

Add $130 for Deluxe Model with pistol grip.
Add $878 for standard engraving or $1,820 for 1 of 1,000 engraving.
Add $500 (retail) for A engraving, $650 for B engraving, $1,075 for C engraving (disc. 2002).

✻ **1873 Evil Roy Rifle** - .357 Mag. or .45 LC cal., 20 in. barrel, features Evil Roy shooting improvements. Imported 2005-2007.

	$1,500	$1,175	$900	$800	$700	$600	$500

Last MSR was $1,800.

✻ **1873 Larry Crow Signature Series Rifle** - .357 Mag. or .45 LC cal., 20 in. barrel, features Larry Crow shooting improvements and signature. Imported 2005-2007.

	$1,850	$1,525	$1,175	$900	$800	$700	$600

Last MSR was $2,275.

✻ **1873 Short Rifle** - .32-20 WCF (new 2002), .357 Mag./.38 Spl. (new 2000), .38-40 WCF (new 2002), .44 Spl. (new 2002), .44-40 WCF or .45 LC cal., features 20 in. octagon barrel, case hardened receiver, iron sights. Importation began 1990.

MSR $1,169	$995	$735	$625	$500	$400	$350	$300

Add $130 for Deluxe Border Model with pistol grip.

✻ **1873 Long Range Rifle** - .44-40 WCF or .45 LC cal., includes 30 in. octagon barrel with full mag., case hardened receiver, iron sights. New 1990.

MSR $1,231	$1,000	$750	$625	$525	$400	$350	$295

Add $120 for Deluxe Model with pistol grip.
Add $878 for standard engraving or $1,820 for 1 of 1,000 engraving.

✻ **1873 Texas Brush Popper** - .357 Mag./.38 Spl., .44-40 WCF, or .45 LC cal., features 18 in. half-round, half-octagon barrel w/o barrel bands, choice of straight or checkered pistol grip stock.

MSR $1,205	$1,025	$775	$625	$500	$400	$350	$300

1873 SADDLE RING CARBINE - .22 LR (disc. 1993), .22 Mag. (disc. 1993), .32-20 WCF (new 2002), .357 Mag./.38 Spl., .38-40 WCF (new 2002), .44 Spl. (new 2002), .44-40 WCF, or .45 LC cal., blue steel receiver, saddle ring, 19 in. round barrel.

MSR $1,182	$1,000	$735	$625	$500	$400	$350	$300

Add $90 for nickel plating (disc.).

1873 TRAPPER CARBINE - .357 Mag. (new 1990, reintroduced 2004), .44-40 WCF (disc. 1990, reintroduced 2005), or .45 LC (mfg. 1990, reintroduced 2005) cal., 16 in. barrel, blue finish only. Importation disc. 1990, reintroduced 2004.

MSR $1,130	$950	$725	$600	$500	$400	$350	$300

1876 CENTENNIAL SPORTING RIFLE - .40-60 WCF, .45-60 WCF, .45-75 WCF, or .50-95 WCF cal., 22 (Short rifle) or 28 in. octagon barrel, blue finish and case hardened frame, full mag., iron sights, walnut stock and forearm. Importation began 2006.

MSR $1,439	$1,250	$1,075	$875	$750	$650	$575	$500

Add $91 for Short rifle.

1885 HI-WALL RIFLE - .30-40 Krag (new 2004), .348 Win. (new 2004), .38-55 WCF (new 2000), .405 Win. (new 2006), .40-65 WCF, .45-70 Govt., .45-90 WCF (new 2000), .45-120 WCF (mfg. 2002-2004) cal., 28 (disc.) or 30 in. octagon barrel, case hardened finish on frame, iron sights (standard) or optional aperture rear and globe front sight (new 2002). New 1998.

MSR $974	$850	$675	$575	$475	$375	$325	$295

Add $117 for engraved receiver, adj. sights, and pistol grip (new 2002).
Add $878 for standard engraving, $1,625 for deluxe engraving, or $3,575 for deluxe gold line engraving.
Add $136 for double set triggers.
Add $36 for .40-65 WCF, .45-90 WCF, .348 Win., .30-40 Krag, or .405 Win. (Big Medicine) cal.

GRADING - PPGS™	100%	98%	95%	90%	80%	70%	60%

1885 LOW WALL RIFLE - .22 LR, .22 Hornet, .22 Mag., .30-30 Win. (disc. 2007), .32-20 WCF, .357 Mag. (disc. 2007), .38-40 WCF, .44 Mag. (disc. 2007), .38-55 (disc. 2007), .44-40 WCF, or .45 LC cal., 30 in. barrel, hand checkered walnut stock, single or double set trigger. Importation began 2005.

MSR $882	$750	$625	$500	$425	$375	$325	$295

Add $111 for engraved receiver, adj. sights, and pistol grip.
Add $878 for standard engraving, $1,625 for deluxe engraving, or $3,575 for deluxe gold line engraving.
Add $137 for double set triggers.
Add $13 for .32-20, .38-40, .44-40 or .45 LC cals.

1892 RIFLE - .357 Mag., .44 Mag., .44-40 WCF, or .45 LC, 20 or 24 in. barrel, available in either solid or takedown frame, uncheckered walnut stock and forearm, case colored receiver. Importation began 2005.

MSR $948	$795	$650	$550	$450	$400	$350	$300

Add $130 for takedown frame.

1892 CARBINE - .357 Mag., .44-40 WCF, or .45 LC cal., 16 (Trapper), or 20 in. barrel, saddle ring with 20 in. barrel only, solid frame, choice of big loop lever or standard with 20 in. barrel. Importation began 2006.

MSR $948	$815	$675	$550	$450	$400	$350	$300

Add $26 for Trapper model with 16 in. barrel.

SHOTGUNS: REPRODUCTIONS

1878 SxS COACH GUN - 12 ga., 20 in. barrels, 3 in. chambers, blue finish, hammers, DT, uncheckered American walnut stock with pistol grip. Importatin began 2007.

MSR $449	$375	$325	$275	$250	$225	$200	$175

1897 SLIDE ACTION - 12 ga., 2 3/4 in. chamber, 20 in. barrel with choke tubes, patterned after the Model 1897 Winchester, blue finish, uncheckered American walnut stock with pistol grip. Importation began 2007.

MSR $506	$425	$350	$300	$250	$225	$200	$175

CLARIDGE HI-TEC INC.

Previous manufacturer located in Northridge, CA 1990-1993. In 1990, Claridge Hi-Tec, Inc. was created and took over Goncz Armament, Inc.

All Claridge Hi-Tec firearms utilized match barrels mfg. in-house that were button-rifled. The Claridge action is an original design and does not copy other actions. Claridge Hi-Tec models can be altered (Law Enforcement Companion Series) to accept Beretta 92F or Sig Model 226 magazines.

PISTOLS

Add $40 for polished stainless steel frame construction.

L-9 PISTOL - 9mm Para., .40 S&W, or .45 ACP cal., semi-auto paramilitary design, 7 1/2 (new 1992) or 9 1/2 (disc. 1991) in. shrouded barrel, aluminum receiver, choice of black matte, matte silver, or polished silver finish, one-piece grip, safety locks firing pin in place, 10 (disc.), 17, or 30 shot double row mag., adj. sights, 3 3/4 lbs. Mfg. 1991-93.

$595	$525	$375	$300	$265	$225	$200

Last MSR was $598.

Add $395 for a trigger activated laser sighting scope was available in Models M, L, C, and T new mfg.

S-9 PISTOL - similar to L-9, except has 5 in. non-shrouded threaded barrel, 3 lbs. 9 oz. Disc. 1993.

$695	$625	$550	$475	$350	$280	$250

Last MSR was $535.

GRADING - PPGS™	100%	98%	95%	90%	80%	70%	60%

T-9 PISTOL - similar to L-9, except has 9 1/2 in. barrel. Mfg. 1992-93.

	$550	$495	$375	$300	$265	$225	$200

Last MSR was $598.

M PISTOL - similar to L Model, except has 7 1/2 in. barrel, 3 lbs. Disc. 1991.

	$575	$515	$375	$300	$265	$225	$200

Last MSR was $720.

RIFLES: CARBINES

C-9 CARBINE - same cals. as L and S Model pistols, 16.1 in. shrouded barrel, choice of composite or uncheckered walnut stock and forearm, 5 lbs. 12 oz. Mfg. 1991-93.

	$650	$595	$525	$450	$395	$350	$300

Last MSR was $675.

Add $74 for black graphite composite stock.
Add $474 for integral laser model (with graphite stock).

This model was available with either gloss walnut, dull walnut, or black graphite composite stock.

LAW ENFORCEMENT COMPANION (LEC) - 9mm Para., .40 S&W, or .45 ACP cal., 16 1/4 button rifled barrel, black graphite composition buttstock and foregrip, buttstock also provides space for an extra mag., available in either aluminum or stainless steel frame, matte black finish, available with full integral laser sighting system. Limited mfg. 1992-93.

	$750	$650	$575	$495	$425	$375	$325

Last MSR was $749.

Add $400 for integral laser sighting system.

CLARK CUSTOM GUNS, INC.

Current custom gun maker and gunsmith located in Princeton, LA. Clark Custom Guns, Inc. has been customizing various configurations of handguns, rifles, and shotguns since 1950. It would be impossible to list within the confines of this text the many conversions this company has performed. It is recommended to contact this company directly (see Trademark Index) for an up-to-date price sheet and catalog on their extensive line-up of high quality competition pistols and related components. Custom revolvers, rifles, and shotguns are also available in addition to various handgun competition parts, related gunsmithing services, and a firearms training facility called The Shootout.

The legendary James E. Clark, Sr. passed away during 2000. In 1958, he became the first and only full-time civilian to win the National Pistol Championships.

PISTOLS: SEMI-AUTO

Clark Custom Guns currently manufactures a wide variety of M1911 style handguns, including the Bullseye Pistols (MSR $1,420-$2,695), the Custom Combat (MSR $1,925-$2,800), the Meltdown (MSR $1,710-$1,995), Millennium Meltdown (features damascus slide, only 50 mfg. during 2000 - MSR was $3,795), .460 Rowland Hunter LS (MSR $2,295), and the Unlimited (MSR $2,950-3,295). Clark will also build the above configurations on a customer supplied gun - prices are less. Please contact the company directly regarding more information on its wide variety of pistols, including availability and pricing (see Trademark Index).

CLASSIC DOUBLES

Previous trademark manufactured in Tochigi City, Japan until 1987. Previously imported and distributed by Classic Doubles International, Inc. located in St. Louis, MO.

The factory closed in 1987, and all Classic Doubles remaining in inventory were sold to GU Wholesalers located in Omaha, NE in 1990. To date, there has been little collectibility in the Classic Doubles trademark. As a result, values are determined by the shooting value each model has to offer against other competing models in the same configuration. Also, in some regions of the country, 98% condition or less specimens may be priced lower than values shown in this section.

In late 1987, Winchester/Olin discontinued importation of their Japanese shotgun models (Models 101 and 23). At that point, Classic Doubles International, Inc. became the sole importer of these shotguns. There were very few changes made during this changeover of importation. The late manufacture Classic Double shotguns (Models 101 and 201) do not have the Winchester trademark or definitive Winchester proofmark stamped on the barrels. The Model 201 was a new model designation.

SHOTGUNS: O/U, MODEL 101 - FIELD MODELS

The late manufacture Classic Doubles have an interchangeable choke tube system compatible with the older Winchester manufactured models. Prices listed include a luggage style carrying case.

100% values listed below for the Classic Doubles Shotguns assume NIB condition - subtract 10%-15% if without box, warranty card, and original shipping container (with packing materials).

CLASSIC FIELD GRADE I - 12 or 20 ga., 3 in. chambers, vent. rib, 25 1/2 or 28 in. vent. barrels with choke tubes, blue receiver with moderate scroll engraving, ejectors, checkered pistol grip or English stock and forearm, 6 1/4-7 lbs.

$1,400	$1,250	$1,100	$1,000	$900	$825	$750

Last MSR was $1,905.

WATERFOWL MODEL - 12 ga. only, 3 in. chambers, 30 in. barrels with vent. rib and choke tubes, matte blue receiver with moderate engraving, low gloss walnut stock with vent. recoil pad, 7 3/4 lbs.

$1,300	$1,125	$950	$825	$700	$650	$600

Last MSR was $1,520.

CLASSIC SPORTER - 12 ga. only, made for Sporting Clays competition, 28 or 30 in. vent. barrels and rib with choke tubes, quick detachable stock system, border engraved coin finished receiver with non-reflective matte surface on top frame and lever, checkered walnut stock and forearm, 7 3/4 lbs.

$1,995	$1,500	$1,295	$1,150	$1,000	$900	$775

Last MSR was $1,980.

Add $965 for extra barrel.

CLASSIC FIELD GRADE II - 12, 20, 28 ga., or .410 bore, 28 in. VR barrels with choke tubes, deluxe walnut with round knob pistol grip stock and forearm with fine fleur-de-lis checkering, coin finished receiver (different sizes) with game scene engraving featuring hunting motifs on receiver sides and bottom, .410 bore bored M/F only, 6 1/4-7 lbs.

$1,795	$1,475	$1,275	$1,100	$1,000	$900	$795

Last MSR was $2,190.

Add 15% for .410 bore (baby frame).
Add 50% for 28 ga. (baby frame).

The lack of supply of the Winchester/Olin Model 101 28 ga. small frame has caused a significant increase in demand for the .410 bore or 28 ga. The Grade II .410 bore is the only round knob pistol grip produced in both Winchester and Classic Doubles manufacture.

CLASSIC FIELD GRADE II TWO BARREL SET - 12 and 20 ga. barrels, both with Winchokes, 26 in. barrels - 20 ga., 28 in. barrels - 12 ga., coin finished receiver with game scene engraving and borders, 6 1/2 (20 ga.) or 7 (12 ga.) lbs.

$2,695	$2,175	$1,825	$1,550	$1,375	$1,200	$1,075

Last MSR was $3,420.

GRADING - PPGS™	100%	98%	95%	90%	80%	70%	60%

SHOTGUNS: O/U, MODEL 101 - TARGET MODELS

CLASSIC TRAP SINGLE - 12 ga. only, over single 32 or 34 in. VR barrel with choke tubes, blue receiver with light engraving, choice of Monte Carlo or regular stock, recoil pad, 8 1/2 lbs.

	$1,200	$1,100	$1,000	$900	$825	$750	$600

Last MSR was $2,070.

CLASSIC TRAP - 12 ga. only, 30 or 32 in. vent. barrels and rib with choke tubes, finish and engraving similar to Classic Trap Single, choice of Monte Carlo or standard stock with recoil pad, 8 3/4 or 9 lbs.

	$1,300	$1,125	$1,000	$900	$825	$750	$675

Last MSR was $1,905.

CLASSIC TRAP COMBO - includes one set of O/U barrels (30 or 32 in.) and one over single barrel (32 or 34 in.), choke tubes, choice of Monte Carlo or standard stock, 8 3/4 or 9 lbs.

	$2,400	$2,100	$1,875	$1,600	$1,475	$1,300	$1,175

Last MSR was $2,825.

CLASSIC SKEET - 12 or 20 ga., 27 1/2 in. vent. barrels and rib, choke tubes on 12 ga. only, smaller gauges are bored SK/SK, similar metal finish to Classic Trap models, 7 1/4 or 7 3/4 lbs.

	$1,695	$1,375	$1,175	$1,025	$900	$825	$750

Last MSR was $1,905.

* *Classic Skeet 4 ga. Set* - similar to Classic Skeet except has 4 barrels (12, 20, 28 ga., or .410 bore), 12 ga. has choke tubes, smaller gauges are bored SK/SK.

	$4,300	$3,875	$3,500	$3,100	$2,875	$2,600	$2,300

Last MSR was $4,765.

SHOTGUNS: SxS

MODEL 201 CLASSIC - 12 or 20 ga., 3 in. chambers, forged steel monobloc with improved lug design, 26 in. choke tube barrels with vent. rib, high lustre bluing, no engraving, SST, ejectors, premium walnut stock and beavertail forearm with fancy checkering pattern, solid red rubber recoil pad, 6 3/4-7 lbs.

	$2,500	$2,150	$1,875	$1,650	$1,400	$1,200	$995

Last MSR was $2,190.

Add $120 for 20 ga.

The 12 ga. could be ordered with choke tubes at no extra charge. Only 63 were mfg. with choke tubes and slight premiums are being asked.

* *Model 201 Classic Small Bore Set* - 28 ga. and .410 bore two barrel set, similar to Model 201 Classic except has smaller frame and overall dimensions, 28 in. VR barrels only bored IC/M on 28 ga. and M/F on .410 bore, very limited importation, 6 or 6 1/2 lbs.

	$4,250	$3,650	$3,250	$2,800	$2,400	$1,950	$1,475

Last MSR was $3,675.

CLERKE ARMS, LTD.

Previous manufacturer located in Raton, New Mexico 1997-2001.

PISTOLS: SINGLE SHOT

COMPETITOR PISTOL - available in 16 centerfire and 2 rimfire cals., 10, 12, 14, 16, or 20 (.410 bore only) in. barrel, features new uplifting C Breech gun system, Xtender slide can be fitted to all Colt .45 ACPs and replicas with no frame modification, matte finish, checkered wood grips. Mfg. 1998-2001.

	$300	$285	$265	$240	$220	$200	$185

Last MSR was $325.

Add $135-$155 per interchangeable barrel, depending on length.

CLERKE PRODUCTS

Previous manufacturer located in Santa Monica, CA.

REVOLVERS: DOUBLE ACTION

DOUBLE ACTION REVOLVER - .22 S, L, LR, or .32 S&W Long cal., inexpensive double action revolvers that sold to dealers for $15 in 1971.

RIFLES: SINGLE SHOT

HI-WALL - single shot rifle, falling block replica of Winchester 1885 High Wall, lever operated, case hardened receiver, 26 in. barrel, available in most modern calibers, no sights, checkered walnut pistol grip stock, Schnabel forearm. Mfg. 1972-74.

$250	$225	$185	$175	$150	$140	$125

DELUXE HI-WALL - similar to Hi-Wall, except half octagon barrel, select wood and recoil pad.

$300	$275	$235	$210	$180	$160	$145

CLIFTON ARMS

Previous manufacturer of custom rifles from 1992-1997 located in Medina, TX. Clifton Arms specialized in composite stocks (with or without integral, retractable bipod).

Clifton Arms manufactured composite, hand laminated stocks that were patterned after the Dakota 76 stock configuration.

RIFLES: BOLT ACTION

CLIFTON SCOUT RIFLE - .243 Win. (disc. 1993), .30-06, .308 Win., .350 Rem. Mag., .35 Whelen, 7mm-08 Rem. (disc. 1993), or .416 Rem. Mag. cal., choice of Dakota 76, pre-64 Winchester Model 70, or Ruger 77 MK II (standard) stainless action with bolt face altered to controlled round feeding, Shilen stainless premium match grade barrel, Clifton synthetic stock with bipod, many other special orders were available. Mfg. 1992-97.

$3,000	$2,350	$1,650	$$1,455	$1,195	$1,010	$835

This model was available as a Standard Scout (.308 Win. cal. with 19 in. barrel), Pseudo Scout (.30-06 cal. with 19 1/2 in. barrel), Super Scout (.35 Whelen or .350 Rem. Mag. with 20 in. barrel), or African Scout (.416 Rem. Mag. with 22 in. barrel).

COACH GUNS

A coach gun is a SxS shotgun with short barrels, and was used extensively in the American West for the protection of horse-drawn coach passengers, hence the name. They were also called guard guns, as they were used for guard duty and other security purposes.

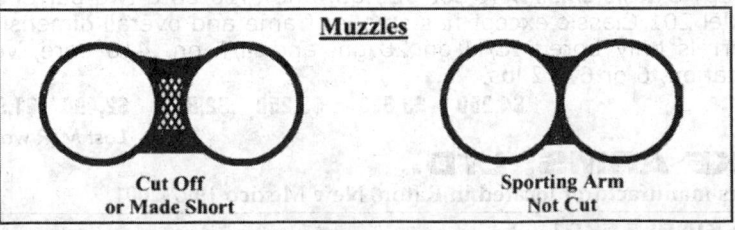

Muzzles

Cut Off or Made Short   Sporting Arm Not Cut

SHOTGUNS: SxS, COACH/GUARD GUNS

The author wishes to express his thanks to Jon Vander Bloomen for compiling much of the following information.

Extensive research indicates that three American gun companies made coach guns in the late 1800s and early 1900s - Colt, Parker, and Ithaca. Remington and Whitney may also have produced some, but there are no factory records to prove it. W.W. Greener of Birmingham, England may have made some short double barrel shotguns for guard use, but no one has seen any factory documentation to support this.

An "original" coach gun, properly called a guard gun, is a double barrel (SxS) shotgun that was made with short barrels, not a long barreled sporting gun that was cut off (see muzzle diagram). However, the muzzles of an original coach gun and a gun whose barrels have been cut off look the same. On both, there is a gap between the muzzles that is filled in with lead. The reason for this is because shotgun barrels are tapered. In order for the muzzles to touch on a 26 inch or shorter gun, the barrel walls would need to be thicker at the muzzle to eliminate the gap.

Some original coach guns may also have original factory markings, identification letters/numerals on the stock and other distinguishing features that indicate that the gun was originally made and marked to identify it as company property. However, don't think that there's "safety in numbers." There are a lot more Wells Fargo marked guns today than there were 85 years ago.

The real question is, how can you tell an original coach gun from a sporting arm whose barrels have been cut down to potentially "enhance" its desirability factor? Hopefully, by obtaining factory documentation. To find out if a coach gun is an original or a "cut" gun, it is recommended that you contact the factory for documentation (if possible), giving the serial number of the gun and asking for the proper barrel length at the time the gun left the factory. Unfortunately, no Remington records exist. Parker records can be found in Vols. I & II of *The Parker Story.* W.W. Greener is still in business, and will look up a serial number, but it will take some time.

Colt records show that several double barrel shotguns left the factory with short barrels. Most of them were the Model 1878 hammer guns with 18 inch barrels. There where only three Model 1883 hammerless, boxlock guns made with short barrels; the lengths are as follows, 18, 22, and 24 inches. All of the Colt Damascus barrels were made in Belgium and shipped to the Colt factory in an unfinished state, so they were just Damascus tubes. Therefore when Colt got an order for a coach/guard gun, the barrels were custom made to length just as the longer barreled guns. These short barreled Colts are "original coach/guard guns." The extreme rarity of a Colt factory coach gun precludes accurate pricing evaluation.

Parker records show that several guns were made with short barrels. Not all short Parkers were made for guard use however, since some hunters preferred short barrels in the field (for fast upland birds). Parker purchased different grades of steel tubes and made their own barrels. When Parker received an order for a guard gun, the barrels were custom made to length. It would have been more costly for Parker to cut a long barreled choked gun, except in the case of used sporting arms that were cut for guard use. It is likely that the lower grade 10 and 12 ga. guns that left the Parker factory with short barrels are "original" coach/guard guns. The extreme rarity factor of a Parker factory coach gun precludes accurate pricing evaluation.

Ithaca records show that 750 hammer doubles were made for Wells Fargo between 1909 and 1917. The first 200 guns had 26 in. barrels, and the remaining 550 had 24 in. barrels. Wells Fargo, as well as other express companies, used various makes of shotguns, mostly used lower grade models that were cut to a shorter length. There is no proof that any company other than Ithaca made guard guns for Wells Fargo. It is recommeded that a buyer get original documentation when considering a purchase of a Wells Fargo coach gun or any other gun that is claimed to have been used by a famous person. Average condition Wells Fargo coach guns are typically priced in the $4,000-$4,500 range, regardless if they are manufactured by Ithaca or are another trademark that had barrels cut. What's important to the buyer is that the gun is a documented Wells Fargo gun, and should have some paperwork specifying that.

What's important to remember is that if there is no original documentation, there's no proof. And if there's no proof, the shotgun may or may not be an original coach gun. It is recommended that when buying, selling, or trading coach guns, the price tag should be proportional to the gun's originality and provenance. Anything less could result in an unwarranted premium for a tired out, "reconfigured" SxS plain Jane shotgun, with some added non-original markings/carvings.

Older sawed-off double barrel shotguns with no documentation as being an express company gun, or a gun used by a famous person are valued in the $200 to $2,000 range, depending on trademark and condition, condition being most important. A good guide for pricing sawed-off doubles is to check the value of the same gun that has not been cut and then deduct 5% to 50%. If no price guide is available for that particular make, then consider availability. For example, tens of thousands of Belgian doubles were made in the 1800s. Because of the increase in collectibility of American western artifacts, original coach guns and all express company guns are highly prized and sought after, but the buyer must always be wary.

GRADING - PPGS™	100%	98%	95%	90%	80%	70%	60%

COBB MANUFACTURING, INC.

Previous rifle manufacturer located in Dallas, GA until 2007.

On Aug. 20, 2007, Cobb Manufacturing was purchased by Bushmaster, and manufacture was moved to Bushmaster's Maine facility. Please refer to the Bushmaster section for current information.

RIFLES: BOLT ACTION

MODEL FA50 (T) - .50 BMG cal., straight pull bolt action, lightweight tactical rifle, standard A2 style stock, ergonomic pistol grip, parkerized finish, Lothar-Walther 22 or 30 in. barrel, recoil reducing Armalite muzzle brake, padded Mil-spec sling, includes two 10 shot mags., detachable M60 bipod, watertight case, 29 lbs. Disc. 2007.

$6,275	$5,300	$4,500	$3,900	$2,700	$2,300	$2,100

Last MSR was $6,995.

Add $300 for 22 in. barrel.
Add $1,000 for Ultra Light model with lightweight 22 or 30 in. barrel.
Add $89 for additonal 10 shot mag.

RIFLES: SEMI-AUTO

MCR (MULTI-CALIBER RIFLE) SERIES - available in a variety of calibers from 9mm Para. to .338 Lapua, offered in MCR 100, MCR 200, MCR 300, and MCR 400 configurations, variety of stock, barrel and finish options. Mfg. 2005-2007.

Prices on this series started at $3,000, and went up according to options chosen by customer.

COBRA

Current trademark imported by Tristar, located in Kansas City, MO. Please refer to the Tristar section.

COBRA ENTERPRISES OF UTAH, INC.

Current pistol manufacturer established in 2001, with headquarters in Salt Lake City, UT. During 2004, the name was changed from Cobra Enterprises to Cobra Enterprises of Utah, Inc.

DERRINGERS

COBRA DERRINGER - .22 LR, .22 Win Mag., .25 ACP, .32 ACP, or .380 ACP cal., 2.4 (Standard Series), 2 3/4 (Big Bore Series) or 3.5 (Long Bore Series) in. barrel, tip-up action, spur trigger, internal hammer block safety, pearl, black, or laminated wood grips, chrome, black powder coat, or satin chrome finish, 9 1/2 oz.

MSR $145	$110	$90	$70	$60	$550	$50	$45

Add $20 for .22 Mag., .32 H&R Mag., .38 Spl., .380 ACP, or 9mm Para cal. with 2 3/4 in. barrel.
Add $20 for .22 Mag., .38 Spl., or 9mm Para cal. with 3 1/2 in. barrel.
Black chrome, royal blue or ruby red finish are available by special order.

PISTOLS: SEMI-AUTO

CA (COBRA) SERIES - .32 ACP (CA32 Model) or 380 ACP (CA380 Model) cal., blowback single action, 2.8 in. barrel, 5 or 6 shot mag., chrome, black powder coat, or satin chrome finish, 22 oz.

MSR $157	$120	$95	$75	$65	$55	$45	$40

Black chrome, royal blue or ruby red finish are available by special order.

FREEDOM SERIES - .32 ACP (FS32 Model) or 380 ACP (FS380 Model) cal., blowback single action, 3 1/2 in. barrel, 7 (.380 ACP) or 8 (.32 ACP) shot mag., bright chrome, black powder coat, or satin nickel finish, 2.1 lbs. New 2004.

MSR $165	$130	$100	$85	$75	$65	$55	$45

Black chrome, royal blue or ruby red finish are available by special order.

GRADING - PPGS™	100%	98%	95%	90%	80%	70%	60%

PATRIOT SERIES - .380 ACP or 9mm Para. cal., DAO, 3.3 in. barrel, polymer frame, 10 shot mag., loaded indicator, stainless steel or optional black melonite coating, 20 1/2 oz.

MSR $315	$250	$220	$195	$170	$150	$125	$110

Add $10 for black finish.

* *Patriot 45* - .45 ACP cal., DAO, black polymer frame with stainless steel slide or black Melonite coating, 3.3 in. barrel, 6 or 7 shot mag., 20 oz.

MSR $380	$290	$240	$200	$175	$150	$135	$120

Add $10 for Melonite coating.

COBRAY INDUSTRIES

See listing under S.W.D. in the S section of this text.

COGSWELL & HARRISON (GUNMAKERS), LTD.

Current manufacturer established durng 1770, and located in London, England. Previously imported by British Game Guns, located in Kent, WA.

In 1993, Cogswell & Harrison came under new management and have concentrated on building best quality guns utilizing Beesley or Purdey type sidelocks, Woodward styled O/Us, and a round action boxlock. The company also provides a serialization service (free of charge), that provides the exact date of manufacture. A Certificate of Origin is also available for a fee, and indicates the original specifications and configuration - weights, dimensions, materials, points of choke, and original owner (including price paid). Cogswell & Harrison also offers a full repair and restoration service.

RIFLES: SxS

Please contact the company directly for an up-to-date quotation on the current models listed below. All new prices do not include VAT. Values for used guns in 98%-60% condition factors are priced in U.S. dollars. Allow 12-14 months for delivery on boxlocks, 18-24 months on sidelocks.

BOXLOCK MODEL - various cals. from .300 H&H - .600 NE, boxlock action, custom order only. New 1999.

Please contact the company directly for an up-to-date quotation on this model.

* *Boxlock Model, Early Ejector Models* - .400 or larger cals., mfg. circa 1900.

These best quality guns should be valued similar to new retail pricing. A Certificate of Origin or individual appraisal is highly recommended.

SIDELOCK MODEL - standard cals. include .300 H&H, .375 H&H, .465, .470 NE, .577, and .600 NE, Beesley or Purdey type action standard, also available with H&H type system, individually made per customer specifications, 8 lbs. 10 oz.- 14 lbs. 6 oz., depending on caliber. New 1999.

MSR N/A	N/A	$50,000	$42,000	$36,000	$30,000	$24,000	$18,000

.375 H&H, .465, and .470 NE cals. will command premiums over values listed above for both used and new guns.

* *Sidelock Model Cals. .577 & .600 NE*

MSR N/A	N/A	$60,000	$50,000	$42,000	$36,000	$30,000	$24,000

SHOTGUNS: O/U, SIDELOCK

WOODWARD TYPE - Woodward style action, finest materials, each gun custom-built for individual specifications, delivery time approx. 18-23 months.

MSR N/A	N/A	$47,250	$41,000	$36,000	$29,500	$22,350	$16,750

Please contact the company directly for an up-to-date quotation on this model.

GRADING - PPGS™	100%	98%	95%	90%	80%	70%	60%

SHOTGUNS: SxS, OLDER MFG.

REGENCY - 12, 16, or 20 ga., 26, 28, or 30 in. barrels, any choke combination, hammerless Anson & Deeley system, boxlock, double triggers, auto ejectors, straight English stock.

	$4,275	$3,750	$3,450	$3,125	$2,750	$2,500	$2,250

Last MSR was $3,200.

AMBASSADOR MODEL - same gauges and barrels as Regency, boxlock with ornamental strengthening sideplates, auto ejectors, double triggers, engraved game scene or scroll rose motif, English stock.

	$5,500	$4,950	$4,450	$3,950	$3,500	$3,100	$2,850

Last MSR was $4,000.

MARKOR - 12, 16, or 20 ga., 27 1/2 or 30 in. barrel and choke, boxlock, double trigger, English stock. Disc.

	$1,675	$1,475	$1,300	$1,050	$975	$825	$700

Add 20% for auto ejectors.

HUNTIC MODEL - 12, 16, or 20 ga., 25, 27, or 30 in. barrels, any choke, sidelock, auto ejectors, English style stock. Disc.

	$3,900	$3,500	$3,200	$3,000	$2,800	$2,500	$2,175

Add $400 for SST.

AVANT TOUT SERIES - 12, 16, or 20 ga., 25, 27 1/2, or 30 in. barrels, boxlock, ornamental strengthening sideplates, straight English stock, auto ejectors, series disc.

	$2,550	$2,250	$1,925	$1,700	$1,495	$1,350	$1,200

REX OR AVANT TOUT III - no sideplates.

	$2,150	$1,800	$1,650	$1,500	$1,350	$1,200	$1,075

SANDHURST OR AVANT TOUT II

	$2,800	$2,500	$2,300	$2,150	$2,000	$1,750	$1,500

KONOR OR AVANT TOUT I

	$3,275	$2,850	$2,500	$2,250	$2,000	$1,750	$1,500

Add $400 for SST.
Add 20% for 20 ga.
Subtract 10% for 16 ga.

BEST QUALITY - 12, 16, or 20 gauges, 25, 26, 28, or 30 in. barrels, any choke, hand detachable sidelock, auto ejectors, double triggers standard, English stock.

✳ *Best Quality Primic Model* - disc.

	$6,200	$5,750	$4,650	$4,150	$3,650	$3,050	$2,500

✳ *Best Quality Victor Model*

	$9,250	$8,500	$7,250	$6,250	$5,000	$4,350	$3,740

Add $400 for SST.
Add 20% for 20 ga.

Note: Degree of engraving and grade of wood are the basic differences among models.

SHOTGUNS: SxS, BOXLOCK & SIDELOCK - CURRENT MFG.

Please contact the company directly for an up-to-date quotation on current models. All new prices do not include VAT. Values for used guns in 98%-60% condition factors are priced in U.S. dollars. Allow 9-12 months for delivery on boxlocks, 18-23 months on sidelocks. All models below are available in 12, 20, or 28 ga.

REGENCY - scalloped boxlock action, DTs, 100% large scroll engraving coverage on receiver and tangs, light barrel engraving, checkered straight grip stock with teardrop. Introduced 1970 to commemmorate C&H's bicentennial.

MSR N/A	N/A	$14,750	$12,250	$10,000	$8,000	$6,500	$4,950

GRADING - PPGS™	100%	98%	95%	90%	80%	70%	60%

VICTORIA - features scalloped round body boxlock action with 100% medium scroll engraving coverage on receiver and tangs, moderate barrel engraving, select checkered stock and forearm.

MSR N/A	N/A	$16,950	$14,500	$12,250	$10,000	$7,800	$6,100

EXTRA QUALITY VICTORIA - similar to Victoria Model, except has better quality wood and more engraving.

MSR £13,180	£13,180	$18,750	$16,250	$14,000	$11,750	$8,900	$7,350

   Add £440 for 20 ga.
   Add £890 for 28 ga.

EXTRA QUALITY (SPECIAL) VICTORIA - top-of-the-line round boxlock action with best quality walnut and chopperlump barrels, removable crosspin, and other refinements.

MSR N/A	N/A	$22,350	$19,450	$16,350	$13,150	$10,250	$8,400

SELF-OPENING SLE SxS - sidelock action, best quality Beesley action and engraving, each gun custom-built per individual specifications, delivery time approx. 18-23 months.

MSR N/A	N/A	$41,000	$36,000	$29,500	$22,350	$16,750	$12,500

COLT'S MANUFACTURING COMPANY, INC.

Current manufacturer with headquarters located in West Hartford, CT.

Manufactured from 1836-1842 in Paterson, NJ; 1847-1848 in Whitneyville, CT; 1854-1864 in London, England; and from 1848-date in Hartford, CT. Colt Firearms became a division of Colt Industries in 1964. In March 1990, the Colt Firearms Division was sold to C.F. Holding Corp. located in Hartford, CT, and the new company is called Colt's Manufacturing Company, Inc. The original Hartford plant was closed during 1994, the same year the company was sold again to a new investor group headed by Zilkha Co., located in New York, NY. During 1999, Colt Archive Properties LLC, the historical research division, became its own entity. In November 2002, Colt was divided into two separate companies, Colt Defense LLC (rifles) and Colt's Manufacturing Company LLC (handguns).

In late 1999, Colt discontinued many of their consumer revolvers, but reintroduced both the Anaconda and Python Elite through the Custom Shop. Production on both models is now suspended. The semi-auto pistols remaining in production are now referred to as Model "O" Series.

For more information and current pricing on both new and used Colt airguns, please refer to the *Blue Book of Airguns* by Dr. Robert Beeman & John Allen (also online). For more information and current pricing on both new and used Colt black powder reproductions and replicas, please refer to the *Blue Book of Modern Black Powder Arms* by John Allen (also online).

Black Powder Reproductions & Replicas by Dennis Adler is also an invaluable source for most black powder reproductions and replicas, and includes hundreds of color images on most popular makes/models, provides manufacturer/trademark histories, and up-to-date information on related items/accessories for black powder shooting - www.bluebookinc.com

REVOLVERS: PERCUSSION

Prices shown for percussion Colts are for guns only. Original cased guns with accessories will bring a healthy premium over non-cased models (200-350% over a gun only is common). Be very careful when buying an "original" cased gun, as many fake cases have shown up in recent years.

If possible, it is advisable to procure a factory letter (available only within the following ser.

100%	98%	95%	90%	80%	70%	60%	50%	40%	30%	20%	10%

no. ranges) before buying, selling, or trading Models 1851 Navy (ser. range 98,000-132,000), 1860 Army (ser. range 1,000-140,000), or 1861 Navy (ser. range 1-12,000). These watermarked letters are available by writing Colt Archive Properties LLC in Hartford, CT, with a charge of $300 or more per serial number (if they can research it). Include your name and address, Colt model name, serial number, and check or credit card information to: COLT ARCHIVE PROPERTIES LLC, P.O. Box 1868, Hartford, CT 06144-1868. Please allow 90-120 days for a response.

Prices shown on the following pages for extremely rare Colt's firearms might not include values in the 90%, 95%, 98%, and 100% condition columns. Prices are very hard to establish since these excellent to mint specimens are seldom seen or sold.

The author wishes to express his thanks to Greg Martin from Greg Martin Auctions for his pricing updates on Colt percussion revolvers, Conversions, Open Tops, Pocket models, and the New Line Series.

Revolvers: Percussion, Paterson Variations

PATERSON NO. 1 POCKET MODEL - also known as "Baby Paterson," .28 cal., 5 shot, 2 1/2 in. to 4 3/4 in. octagon barrels, blue metal, varnished walnut grips. Serial range 1 to approx. 500. Standard bbl. marking "Patent Arms M'g Co. Paterson N.J.-Colt's Pt." Centaur scene with four horse head trademark and "COLT" on 1 1/16 in. cylinder of round or square type. Mfg. 1837-1838.

This and all other Paterson models have 5 shot cylinders and serial numbers are not commonly in evidence externally. Disassembly of the arm is usually necessary to determine the serial number.

The Pocket Model Paterson No. 1 (Baby Paterson) is the first production-made handgun in Colt's Paterson, N.J. facility. It is very small in size, almost appearing as a toy or miniature.

✳ *Paterson No. 1 Pocket Model Standard Production Model* - without attached loading lever.

100%	98%	95%	90%	80%	70%	60%	50%	40%	30%	20%	10%
N/A	N/A	$90,000	$80,000	$72,500	$65,000	$57,500	$55,000	$50,000	$45,000	$40,000	$35,000

✳ *Paterson No. 1 Pocket Model Late Production Ehlers Model* - with attached loading lever, 31/32 round back cylinder and recoil shield milled for ease of capping. Barrel marked "Patent Arms Paterson N.J.-Colt's Pt." Approx. 500 mfg. including the Ehlers Model under Belt Model No. 2 Mfg. 1840-1843.

100%	98%	95%	90%	80%	70%	60%	50%	40%	30%	20%	10%
N/A	N/A	$90,000	$75,000	$67,500	$60,000	$55,000	$50,000	$47,500	$45,000	$40,000	$35,000

PATERSON NO. 2 BELT MODEL - .31 or .34 cal., 5 shot, 2 1/2 in. to 5 1/2 in. octagon barrels, blue metal, varnished walnut grips. Serial range 1-approx. 850 which includes the Belt Model No. 3. All standard production Belt Models No. 2 have straight bottom style grips. Standard bbl. markings "Patent Arms M'g Co. Paterson N-J. Colt's Pt." Centaur scene with four horse head trademark and "COLT" on cylinder of round or square backed type. Mfg 1837-40. Somewhat heavier than the Pocket No. 1 revolver.

✳ *Paterson No. 2 Belt Model Standard Production Model* - without attached loading lever.

100%	98%	95%	90%	80%	70%	60%	50%	40%	30%	20%	10%
N/A	N/A	$80,000	$70,000	$65,000	$60,000	$55,000	$50,000	$47,500	$45,000	$40,000	$35,000

✳ *Paterson No. 2 Belt Model Ehlers* - with attached loading lever, 1 1/16 in. round back cylinder, recoil shield milled for ease of capping. Barrel marked "Patent Arms Paterson N-J. Colt's Pt." Approx. 500 mfg. including the Ehlers Model under Pocket Model No. 1. Mfg. 1840-43.

100%	98%	95%	90%	80%	70%	60%	50%	40%	30%	20%	10%
N/A	N/A	$90,000	$80,000	$77,500	$75,000	$70,000	$65,000	$57,500	$50,000	$45,000	$40,000

PATERSON NO. 3 BELT MODEL - .31 or .34 cal., 5 shot, 3 1/2 in. to 5 1/2 in. octagon barrels, blue metal, a few having case hardened hammers. Varnished walnut grips. Serial range 1-approx. 850 which includes the Belt Model No. 2. All standard production Belt Models No. 3 have the flared bottom style grips. Standard barrel markings "Patent Arms M'g Co. Paterson N-J. Colt's Pt." The square backed cylinder is seen less often than the more common round back,

100%	98%	95%	90%	80%	70%	60%	50%	40%	30%	20%	10%

both bearing the Centaur scene with four horse head trademark and "COLT," with both Belt Models, revolvers exhibiting attached loading levers are less common than those without a lever. Mfg. 1837-40.

✳ *Paterson No. 3 Belt Model Standard w/o Lever* - without attached loading lever.

| N/A | N/A | $95,000 | $85,000 | $80,000 | $75,000 | $67,500 | $60,000 | $57,500 | $55,000 | $50,000 | $45,000 |

✳ *Paterson No. 3 Belt Model Standard With Lever* - with attached loading lever and recoil shield milled for ease of capping (scarce).

| N/A | N/A | $95,000 | $85,000 | $80,000 | $75,000 | $67,500 | $60,000 | $57,500 | $55,000 | $50,000 | $45,000 |

PATERSON NO. 5 HOLSTER MODEL - also known as "Texas Paterson" - .36 cal., 5 shot, 4 in. to 12 in. octagon barrels, blue metal with case hardened frame and hammer. All cylinders bear the stage coach hold-up scene. Varnished walnut grips of flared bottom style. Serial range 1 to approx. 1,000. As with all models of Patersons, the serial number usually cannot be seen without disassembly of the revolver. Very large and heavy compared to the other Paterson models. Enjoys more popularity with collectors because of its military and frontier use. Mfg. 1838-40.

Many specimens encountered in this variation show extreme use. Consequently, fine to mint specimens are quite rare and highly prized by collectors. Values are given for non-military marked specimens. Any specimen bearing an authenticated martial marking is truly a rarity and should be appraised individually. NOTE: Watch for fakes here. There are now many times more faked martial markings, often times on non-original Patersons, than there are originals.

✳ *Paterson No. 5 Holster Model Standard Production Model w/o Lever* - without attached loading lever, round or square backed cylinder.

| N/A | N/A | $150,000 | $125,000 | $115,000 | $100,000 | $87,500 | $75,000 | $72,500 | $70,000 | $65,000 | $60,000 |

✳ *Paterson No. 5 Holster Model Standard Production Model With Lever* - with attached loading lever, round backed cylinder and recoil shield milled for ease of capping.

| N/A | N/A | $175,000 | $125,000 | $110,000 | $90,000 | $85,000 | $80,000 | $77,500 | $75,000 | $70,000 | $65,000 |

Revolvers: Percussion, Walker Model

WALKER MODEL - .44 cal., 6 shot, 9 in. part round, part octagon barrel, blue metal with case hardened frame, lever and hammer. Cylinder left without finish, brass trigger guard. One piece walnut grips. Mfg. 1847; total production approx. 1,100. Ser. numbers beginning with no. 1 were applied for each of five different military companies (A,B,C,D, & E). The total for the military issue Walkers was approx. 1,000 revolvers; the remaining approx. 100 revolvers were produced for civilian distribution. Barrels marked "Address SamL Colt New-York City," found on right side of barrel lug is "US" over "1847," cylinder bears Texas Ranger/Indian fight scene. Various metal parts and walnut grips stamped with Govt. Inspectors' marks.

Because of these arms being subjected to great extremes of use, they will exhibit high degrees of wear, often to the extent that most or all markings will be worn off. Replaced parts are common and many badly worn and damaged specimens have been extensively rebuilt and restored. NOTE: Use great caution when contemplating the purchase of a Walker. A multitude of out-and-out fakes and "antiqued" reproduction Walkers have been fed into the market over the past few decades. Some of these are old enough (and have aged enough naturally) to almost resemble an authentic specimen. Enlist the services of a qualified expert before your dollars are spent. Only 10-12% of the original production of approx. 1,100 specimens have been accounted for. The acquisition of an authenticated Walker revolver is the ultimate goal of serious Colt handgun collectors.

✳ *Walker Standard Military Issue Model*

| N/A | N/A | $600,000+ | $400,000 | $350,000 | $300,000 | $225,000 | $150,000 | $125,000 | $100,000 | $90,000 | $80,000 |

100%	98%	95%	90%	80%	70%	60%	50%	40%	30%	20%	10%

* *Walker Limited Civilian Issue Model* - serial range 1001 to approx. 1100. Similar to military model except Govt. inspectors' marks were not applied. Pricing is difficult on the civilian issue arms. They tend to be in considerably better condition than the much more common military specimens. The factors of scarcity and condition will often bring higher prices from the advanced collector of means, especially in the finer grades of condition. On the other hand, the collector appreciating military usage will pay more for military marked examples. This publication tries to reflect the latest trends on purchase of civilian models.

100%	98%	95%	90%	80%	70%	60%	50%	40%	30%	20%	10%
N/A	N/A	$600,000	$400,000	$300,000	$175,000	$150,000	$125,000	$112,500	$100,000	$90,000	$80,000

Revolvers: Percussion, Dragoon Series

WHITNEYVILLE HARTFORD DRAGOON - .44 cal., 6 shot, 7 1/2 in. part octagon, part round barrel, some of the left-over Walker parts were used in Dragoons, blue metal with case hardened frame, lever, hammer, brass trigger guard and steel cylinder bears Texas Ranger and Indian battle scene. Mfg. 1847. Total production approx. 240. Serial range approx. 1,100 to 1,340 in sequence following civilian Walkers.

* *Whitneyville Hartford Dragoon w/Rear frame cut out for grips*

100%	98%	95%	90%	80%	70%	60%	50%	40%	30%	20%	10%
N/A	N/A	$350,000	$175,000	$140,000	$100,000	$87,500	$75,000	$70,000	$65,000	$57,500	$50,000

* *Whitneyville Hartford Dragoon w/Straight rear frame*

100%	98%	95%	90%	80%	70%	60%	50%	40%	30%	20%	10%
N/A	N/A	$250,000	$150,000	$125,000	$90,000	$77,500	$65,000	$55,000	$45,000	$40,000	$35,000

FIRST MODEL DRAGOON - .44 cal., 6 shot, 7 1/2 in. round and octagon barrel, blue metal with case hardened frame, lever, hammer, brass grip straps, silvered straps for civilian market, serial range numbered after Hartford Dragoon, 1341 to around 8000. Mfg. 1848-50. Total production approx. 7,000. Oval cyl. slots, square back trigger guard, Texas Ranger and Indian fight scene on cylinder.

* *First Model Dragoon Military Model*

100%	98%	95%	90%	80%	70%	60%	50%	40%	30%	20%	10%
N/A	N/A	$125,000	$80,000	$55,000	$30,000	$27,500	$25,000	$20,000	$15,000	$12,500	$10,000

* *First Model Dragoon Civilian Model*

100%	98%	95%	90%	80%	70%	60%	50%	40%	30%	20%	10%
N/A	N/A	$80,000	$60,000	$40,000	$25,000	$22,500	$20,000	$17,500	$15,000	$12,500	$10,000

FLUCK MODEL DRAGOON - basically a First Model Dragoon, with 7 1/2 in. altered Walker barrels and fully martially marked, should be extensively checked over, used to replace defective Walkers. Mfg. 1848. Total production 300. Serial range approx. 2,216 to 2,515.

100%	98%	95%	90%	80%	70%	60%	50%	40%	30%	20%	10%
N/A	N/A	$85,000	$60,000	$55,000	$30,000	$25,000	$20,000	$17,500	$15,000	$13,500	$12,000

SECOND MODEL DRAGOON - .44 cal., 6 shot, 7 1/2 in. round and octagon barrel, serial range following the First Model Dragoon 8,000-10,700. Mfg. 1850-51. Texas Ranger and Indian fight scene on cylinder.

* *Second Model Dragoon Military Model*

100%	98%	95%	90%	80%	70%	60%	50%	40%	30%	20%	10%
N/A	N/A	$85,000	$70,000	$50,000	$30,000	$25,000	$20,000	$16,000	$12,000	$10,000	$7,500

* *Second Model Dragoon Civilian Model*

100%	98%	95%	90%	80%	70%	60%	50%	40%	30%	20%	10%
N/A	N/A	$75,000	$60,000	$40,000	$35,000	$22,500	$20,000	$17,500	$15,000	$11,000	$6,000

* *Second Model Dragoon New Hampshire or Massachusetts* - notice state markings on front portion of trigger guard.

100%	98%	95%	90%	80%	70%	60%	50%	40%	30%	20%	10%
N/A	N/A	$80,000	$65,000	$52,500	$40,000	$37,500	$25,000	$20,000	$15,000	$12,500	$10,000

THIRD MODEL DRAGOON - .44 cal., 6 shot, 7 1/2 in. round or octagon barrel, same basic features as earlier models, but with round trigger guard and rectangular cylinder slots, serial range approx. 10,200-19,600, some overlapping of numbers, with approx. 10,500 mfg. from 1851-61. Texas Ranger and Indian fight scene on cylinder.

* *Third Model Dragoon*

100%	98%	95%	90%	80%	70%	60%	50%	40%	30%	20%	10%
N/A	N/A	$50,000	$35,000	$32,500	$30,000	$25,000	$17,500	$15,000	$12,000	$10,000	$7,500

* *Third Model Dragoon Martially Marked U.S.*

100%	98%	95%	90%	80%	70%	60%	50%	40%	30%	20%	10%
N/A	N/A	$60,000	$40,000	$37,500	$25,000	$22,500	$20,000	$17,500	$15,000	$12,000	$8,500

100%	98%	95%	90%	80%	70%	60%	50%	40%	30%	20%	10%

* *Third Model Dragoon Third Model* - 8 in. barrel.

| N/A | N/A | $65,000 | $45,000 | $35,000 | $27,500 | $25,000 | $22,000 | $21,000 | $19,500 | $14,000 | $9,500 |

* *Third Model Dragoon First and Second Variation* - shoulder stock model.

| N/A | N/A | $60,000 | $45,000 | $35,000 | $25,000 | $22,500 | $20,000 | $17,500 | $15,000 | $12,500 | $9,500 |

* *Third Model Dragoon Third Variation*

| N/A | N/A | $60,000 | $45,000 | $35,000 | $25,000 | $21,000 | $17,500 | $15,000 | $12,000 | $10,000 | $7,500 |

* *Third Model Dragoon C.L. Dragoon*

| N/A | N/A | $65,000 | $50,000 | $40,000 | $30,000 | $26,000 | $22,500 | $19,000 | $15,000 | $12,500 | $10,000 |

ENGLISH HARTFORD DRAGOON - basically a Third Model Dragoon, assembled at Colt's London factory, with unique serial range 1-700, some were assembled from earlier parts inventories, easy to spot with British proofs of crown over V and crown over GP, the blue was of the English type, many were engraved.

| N/A | N/A | $55,000 | $40,000 | $32,000 | $22,500 | $19,000 | $15,000 | $12,500 | $10,000 | $8,750 | $7,500 |

1848 BABY DRAGOONS - .31 cal., 5 shot, 3, 4, 5, or 6 in. octagon barrels, most without loading lever, serial range 1-15,500, a scaled down version of the .44 caliber Dragoons, early ones with Texas Ranger scene and later ones with the holdup scene.

* *1848 Baby Dragoon Type I* - left-hand barrel stamping, Texas Ranger and Indian scene, approx. serial range 1-150.

| N/A | N/A | $25,000 | $15,000 | $11,000 | $7,500 | $7,000 | $6,5000 | $6,000 | $5,500 | $5,000 | $4,500 |

* *1848 Baby Dragoon Type II* - with Texas Ranger and Indian scene, 11,600 serial range, without loading lever.

| N/A | N/A | $17,500 | $12,000 | $9,500 | $6,500 | $6,250 | $6,000 | $5,200 | $4,500 | $4,000 | $3,500 |

* *1848 Baby Dragoon Type III* - with Stagecoach scene and oval cylinder slots, serial range 10,400-12,000.

| N/A | N/A | $17,500 | $12,000 | $9,500 | $6,500 | $6,250 | $6,000 | $5,200 | $4,500 | $4,000 | $3,500 |

* *1848 Baby Dragoon Type IV* - with Stagecoach holdup scene, rectangle cylinder slots, serial range 11,000-12,500.

| N/A | N/A | $17,500 | $12,000 | $9,500 | $6,500 | $6,250 | $6,000 | $5,200 | $4,500 | $4,000 | $3,500 |

* *1848 Baby Dragoon Type V* - with Stagecoach holdup scene, rectangle cylinder slots and loading lever, serial range 11,600-15,500.

| N/A | N/A | $17,500 | $12,000 | $9,500 | $6,500 | $6,250 | $6,000 | $5,200 | $4,500 | $4,000 | $3,500 |

Revolvers: Percussion, Models 1849, 1851, 1855, 1860, 1861, & 1862

1849 POCKET MODEL - .31 cal., 5 or 6 shot, 3, 4, 5, and 6 in. octagon barrels, most with loading levers, blue metal with case hardened frame, lever and hammer, grip straps of brass (silver plated), or steel (silver plated or blue), stagecoach hold-up scene on cylinder, serial range 12,000 to 340,000. Mfg. 1850-73.

* *1849 Pocket Model First Type* - 4, 5, or 6 in. barrel, loading lever and small or large brass trigger guard.

| N/A | N/A | $4,500 | $3,000 | $2,250 | $1,500 | $1,225 | $950 | $850 | $750 | $625 | $500 |

* *1849 Pocket Model Second Type* - 4, 5, or 6 in. barrel, loading lever and steel grip straps.

| N/A | N/A | $4,500 | $3,000 | $2,250 | $1,500 | $1,225 | $950 | $850 | $750 | $625 | $500 |

* *1849 Pocket Model Wells Fargo Model* - 3 in. barrel, without loading lever and with small round trigger guard.

| N/A | N/A | $15,000 | $10,000 | $8,500 | $7,000 | $5,500 | $4,000 | $3,250 | $2,500 | $2,250 | $2,000 |

1849 LONDON POCKET MODEL - London pistols were of the same general configuration, but of better finish, serial range 1-11,000. Mfg. 1853-57.

100%	98%	95%	90%	80%	70%	60%	50%	40%	30%	20%	10%

✳ *1849 London Pocket Model Early Type* - serial numbered under 1500, with small trigger guard and brass grip straps.

| N/A | N/A | $7,500 | $4,500 | $4,000 | $3,500 | $2,900 | $2,250 | $1,750 | $1,200 | $1,075 | $950 |

✳ *1849 London Pocket Model Late Type* - oval trigger guard and steel grip straps.

| N/A | N/A | $4,500 | $3,000 | $2,400 | $1,750 | $1,500 | $1,200 | $1,075 | $950 | $850 | $750 |

1851 NAVY
.36 cal., 6 shot, 7 1/2 in. octagon barrel and loading lever, blue metal with case hardened frame, lever and hammer, one piece walnut finished grips, cylinder scene of Texas Navy battle with Mexico, serial range 1-highest recorded number was 215,348, three barrel addresses 1-74,000 (ADDRESS SAML COLT, NEW YORK CITY), 74,000-101,000 (ADDRESS SAML COLT, HARTFORD, CT.) 101,000-215,348 (ADDRESS COL. SAML COLT, NEW YORK, U.S. AMERICA). Mfg. 1850-73.

✳ *1851 Navy First Model* - square back trigger guard, bottom wedge screw, serial range 1-1,250.

| N/A | N/A | $25,000 | $20,000 | $17,500 | $15,000 | $12,500 | $10,000 | $8,250 | $6,500 | $5,500 | $4,500 |

✳ *1851 Navy Second Model* - square back trigger guard, top wedge screw, serial range 1,250-4,000.

| N/A | N/A | $22,500 | $18,000 | $15,000 | $12,000 | $10,000 | $7,500 | $6,250 | $5,000 | $4,250 | $3,500 |

✳ *1851 Navy Third Model* - small round brass trigger guard, serial range 4,200-85,000.

| N/A | N/A | $7,500 | $6,500 | $5,250 | $4,000 | $3,000 | $2,000 | $1,600 | $1,200 | $1,100 | $1,000 |

✳ *1851 Navy Fourth Model* - large round brass trigger guard, serial range 85,000-215,348.

| N/A | N/A | $7,500 | $6,500 | $5,250 | $4,000 | $3,000 | $2,000 | $1,600 | $1,200 | $1,100 | $1,000 |

✳ *1851 Navy Iron Gripstrap Model* - most often seen in fourth model.

| N/A | N/A | $8,000 | $7,000 | $5,500 | $4,000 | $3,150 | $2,200 | $1,850 | $1,500 | $1,350 | $1,200 |

✳ *1851 Navy Martially Marked U.S. Navys* - brass or iron gripstrap.

| N/A | N/A | $22,500 | $12,000 | $9,750 | $7,500 | $6,000 | $4,500 | $4,000 | $3,500 | $3,000 | $2,500 |

✳ *1851 Navy Cut for shoulder stock* - first and second type (like third model Dragoon).

| N/A | N/A | $15,000 | $10,000 | $9,250 | $8,500 | $6,750 | $5,000 | $3,500 | $2,000 | $1,750 | $1,500 |

✳ *1851 Navy Third Type* - four screw frame.

| N/A | N/A | $9,000 | $4,500 | $3,750 | $3,000 | $2,750 | $2,500 | $2,150 | $1,800 | $1,650 | $1,500 |

51 NAVY LONDON MODEL
basically the same gun as the Hartford piece with London barrel address, with British proof marks in serial range 1-42,000. Mfg. 1853-57.

✳ *51 Navy London Early First Model* - serial range below 2000, brass grip straps and small trigger guard.

| N/A | N/A | $8,500 | $4,500 | $4,000 | $3,500 | $3,000 | $2,500 | $2,250 | $2,000 | $1,750 | $1,500 |

✳ *51 Navy London Late Second Model* - balance of production, large round trigger guard, steel grip straps, all London parts.

| N/A | N/A | $8,000 | $4,500 | $4,000 | $3,5000 | $3,000 | $2,500 | $2,000 | $1,500 | $1,350 | $1,200 |

1855 SIDEHAMMER POCKET MODEL (ROOT MODEL)
.28 cal., had 3 1/2 in. octagon barrel, .31 cal. usually had 3 1/2 in. or 4 1/2 in. round barrel. Blue with case hardened lever and hammer, one piece wraparound style walnut grips.

Commonly called the "Root" Model by collectors, manufactured 1855 through 1870. The .28 cal. model serial numbered 1 through approx. 30,000. The .31 cal. round barrel model serial numbered 1 through approx. 14,000. Total production approx. 44,000.

Easily recognizable by its side mounted hammer and cylinder rotation ratchet at rear of frame.

✳ *1855 Sidehammer Pocket Model 1 and 1A* - .28 cal., 3 7/16 in. octagonal bbl., oct. load lever, Indian/cabin cyl. scene, Hartford barrel address. Serial range 1 to 384.

| N/A | N/A | $12,500 | $8,000 | $6,500 | $5,000 | $4,250 | $3,500 | $3,000 | $2,500 | $2,250 | $2,000 |

100%	98%	95%	90%	80%	70%	60%	50%	40%	30%	20%	10%

✳ *1855 Sidehammer Pocket Model 2* - .28 cal., 3 1/2 in. oct. bbl., Indian/cabin cyl. scene, Hartford barrel address with pointed hand. Serial range 476 to 25,000.

| N/A | N/A | $3,500 | $2,000 | $1,600 | $1,200 | $1,075 | $950 | $850 | $750 | $625 | $500 |

✳ *1855 Sidehammer Pocket Model 3* - .28 cal., 3 1/2 in. oct. bbl., full fluted cylinder, Hartford barrel address with pointed hand. Serial range 25,001 to 30,000.

| N/A | N/A | $3,500 | $2,500 | $1,850 | $1,200 | $1,075 | $950 | $850 | $750 | $625 | $500 |

✳ *1855 Sidehammer Pocket Model 3A* - .31 cal., 3 1/2 in. oct. bbl., full fluted cylinder, Hartford barrel address. Serial range 1 to 1,350.

| N/A | N/A | $3,500 | $2,500 | $1,850 | $1,200 | $1,075 | $950 | $850 | $750 | $625 | $500 |

✳ *1855 Sidehammer Pocket Model 4* - .31 cal., 3 1/2 in. oct. bbl., full fluted cylinder, Hartford barrel address. Serial range 1,351 to 2,400.

| N/A | N/A | $4,000 | $3,000 | $2,400 | $1,750 | $1,500 | $1,200 | $1,075 | $950 | $850 | $750 |

✳ *1855 Sidehammer Pocket Model 5* - .31 cal., 3 1/2 in. round bbl., full fluted cylinder, "COL. COLT NEW-YORK" barrel address. Serial range 2,401 to 8,000.

| N/A | N/A | $4,500 | $3,000 | $2,400 | $1,750 | $1,500 | $1,200 | $1,075 | $950 | $850 | $750 |

✳ *1855 Sidehammer Pocket Model 5A* - .31 cal., 4 1/2 in. round bbl., included in same serial range as Model 5.

| N/A | N/A | $4,500 | $3,500 | $3,000 | $2,250 | $1,875 | $1,500 | $1,350 | $1,200 | $1,075 | $950 |

✳ *1855 Sidehammer Pocket Model 6* - .31 cal., 3 1/2 in. round bbl., stage coach hold-up cylinder scene, "COL. COLT NEW-YORK" barrel address. Serial range 8,001 through 11,074.

| N/A | N/A | $4,500 | $3,500 | $3,000 | $2,250 | $1,875 | $1,500 | $1,350 | $1,200 | $1,075 | $950 |

✳ *1855 Sidehammer Pocket Model 6A* - .31 cal., 4 1/2 in. round bbl., included in same serial range as Model 6.

| N/A | N/A | $4,500 | $3,500 | $3,000 | $2,250 | $1,875 | $1,500 | $1,350 | $1,200 | $1,075 | $950 |

✳ *1855 Sidehammer Pocket Model 7* - .31 cal., 3 1/2 in. round bbl., stage coach hold-up cylinder scene, "COL. COLT NEW-YORK" barrel address. Cylinder pin retained by screw-in cylinder. Serial range 11,075 through 14,000.

| N/A | N/A | $5,500 | $4,000 | $3,500 | $3,000 | $2,750 | $2,500 | $2,000 | $1,500 | $1,350 | $1,200 |

✳ *1855 Sidehammer Pocket Model 7A* - .31 cal., 4 1/2 in. round bbl., including same cylinder scene, barrel address and serial range as Model 7.

| N/A | N/A | $5,000 | $4,000 | $3,500 | $3,000 | $2,625 | $2,250 | $1,750 | $1,200 | $1,100 | $1,000 |

1860 MODEL ARMY - .44 cal., 6 shot, 7 1/2 and 8 in. round barrels with loading lever, blue metal with case hardened frame, lever and hammer, one piece walnut grips, normally blue steel back strap and brass trigger guard, barrel markings were "ADDRESS SAM COLT, HARTFORD, CT." on early productions and "ADDRESS COL. SAM COLT, NEW YORK, U.S. AMERICA" on balance, serial range 1-about 200,500, Texas Navy scene on round cylinder model. Mfg. 1860-73.

✳ *1860 Model Army Fluted Cylinder Model* - Fluted Cylinder Model, full length cylinder flutes and no cylinder scene, 7 1/2 or 8 in. barrel, grips of Navy (very rare) or Army size, usually 4 screw frames.

| N/A | N/A | $22,500 | $15,000 | $11,000 | $7,500 | $6,250 | $5,000 | $4,250 | $3,500 | $3,000 | $2,500 |

✳ *1860 Model Army Round Cylinder Model* - roll engraved Texas Navy scene, some with early Hartford address, Army grips, four screw frame to about 50,000 range, most were sold to the U.S. Government and will be martially marked.

| N/A | N/A | $15,000 | $8,000 | $6,500 | $5,000 | $4,250 | $3,500 | $3,000 | $2,500 | $2,000 | $1,500 |

✳ *1860 Model Army Civilian Model* - same general configurations as Round Cylinder Model, but with 3 screw frame, no shoulder stock cuts and better blue finish than military pieces, late New York barrel address.

| N/A | N/A | $10,000 | $7,500 | $4,250 | $4,000 | $3,250 | $2,500 | $2,000 | $1,500 | $1,350 | $1,200 |

100%	98%	95%	90%	80%	70%	60%	50%	40%	30%	20%	10%

1861 MODEL NAVY - .36 cal., 6 shot, 7 1/2 in. round barrel with loading lever, blue metal with case hardened frame, lever and hammer, silver plated brass grip straps, the barrel address was "ADDRESS COL. SAM COLT, NEW YORK, U.S. AMERICA", serial range 1-38,843, cylinder scene of Texas Navy and Mexico Battle, mfg. 1861-73.

❋ *1861 Model Fluted Cylinder Navy* - in serial range 1-100, with fluted cylinder and without rolled cylinder scene.

N/A	N/A	$40,000	$35,000	$30,000	$25,000	$21,500	$17,500	$15,000	$12,000	$10,000	$7,500

❋ *1861 Model Navy Regular Production model*

N/A	N/A	$20,000	$12,000	$10,000	$7,500	$6,250	$5,000	$4,250	$3,500	$2,750	$2,000

❋ *1861 Model Martially Marked Navys* - will bear the U.S. stamp and inspector's marks, those marked U.S.N. on butt were of a 650 piece order for the Navy.

N/A	N/A	$35,000	$20,000	$12,500	$8,500	$7,250	$6,000	$5,000	$4,000	$3,250	$2,500

❋ *1861 Model London Marked Navy* - with "ADDRESS COL. COLT, LONDON", for barrel address.

N/A	N/A	$22,500	$12,000	$10,000	$7,500	$6,250	$5,000	$4,750	$4,500	$3,250	$2,000

❋ *1861 Model Shoulder Stock Cut Navy* - 4 screw frames in serial range 11,000-14,000, made for third style stock (see Dragoon stocks).

N/A	N/A	$25,000	$15,000	$12,000	$9,000	$7,750	$6,500	$5,500	$4,500	$4,000	$3,500

1862 POLICE MODEL - .36 cal., 5 shot half fluted and rebated cylinder, 4 1/2, 5 1/2, and 6 1/2 in. round barrels (also 3 1/2 in. bbl. but quite rare) and loading lever. Mfg. 1861-73. Serial numbered with Model 1862 Pocket Navy, approx. 28,000 1862 Police Models were produced. Blue with case hardened frame, lever and hammer, grip straps silver plated, one piece walnut grips. Serial range 1 through approx. 47,000. Standard barrel marking "ADDRESS COL. SAML COLT NEW-YORK U.S. AMERICA" "COLTS/PATENT" on left side of frame, "PAT SEPT. 10TH 1850" stamped in cyl. flute.

Many Model 1862 Police and 1862 Pocket Navy revolvers were converted to cartridge with the advent of the metallic cartridge. Consequently these models in their original cap and ball chambering are quite desirable to collectors.

❋ *1862 Police Early Model* - "ADDRESS SAM COLT/HARTFORD CT" barrel address, silvered iron grip straps.

N/A	N/A	$6,000	$4,500	$3,750	$3,000	$2.650	$2,250	$2,000	$1,750	$1,500	$1,200

❋ *1862 Police Early Model* - same but silvered brass grip straps.

N/A	N/A	$6,000	$4,500	$3,750	$3,000	$2.650	$2,250	$2,000	$1,750	$1,500	$1,200

❋ *1862 Police Standard Production Model* - with New York barrel address.

N/A	N/A	$4,500	$3,000	$2,750	$2,500	$2,150	$1,750	$1,500	$1,250	$1,100	$950

❋ *1862 Police Export Production Model* - with "L" below serial numbers (for export to England), steel grip straps. Most often but not always bearing British proofs.

N/A	N/A	$4,500	$3,000	$2,750	$2,500	$2,150	$1,750	$1,500	$1,250	$1,100	$950

❋ *1862 Police London Marked Model* - similar to above, except with "ADDRESS, COL. COLT/LONDON" address on barrel.

N/A	N/A	$17,500	$12,000	$9,000	$6,000	$5,500	$5,000	$4,000	$3,000	$2,500	$2,000

1862 POCKET MODEL NAVY (1865 POCKET PISTOL) - .36 cal., 5 shot rebated cylinder, 4 1/2 in., 5 1/2 in., and 6 1/2 in. octagonal barrels with loading lever. Mfg. 1861-73. Serial numbered with Model 1862 Police Model, approx. 19,000 Model 1862 Pocket Navy Revolvers produced. Blue with case hardened frame, lever and hammer, grip straps silver plated brass, one piece walnut grips. Serial range 1 through approx. 47,000. Standard barrel markings "ADDRESS COL. SAML COLT NEW-YORK U.S. AMERICA" "COLTS/PATENT" on left side of frame, stage coach hold-up scene on cylinder.

This model has been identified for decades to collectors as the Model 1853 or the Model

100%	98%	95%	90%	80%	70%	60%	50%	40%	30%	20%	10%

1862 Pocket Model Navy. Recent research indicates that a more correct model name for this revolver is the 1865 Pocket Pistol.

Because of being produced during the advent of the metallic cartridge, the number remaining in the original cap and ball configuration is rather few; scarce with any serial number, but particularly so in numbers over approx. 19,800.

* *1862 Pocket Model Navy Standard Model* - 4 1/2, 5 1/2 and 6 1/2 in. barrel lengths.

100%	98%	95%	90%	80%	70%	60%	50%	40%	30%	20%	10%
N/A	N/A	$10,000	$7,500	$6,000	$4,500	$3,750	$3,000	$2,750	$2,500	$2,000	$1,500

* *1862 Pocket Model Navy Export Production Model* - with "L" below serial numbers (for export to England), steel grip straps. Often found with British proofs.

N/A	N/A	$10,000	$7,500	$6,000	$4,500	$3,750	$3,000	$2,750	$2,500	$2,000	$1,500

* *1862 Pocket Model Navy London Marked Model* - similar to above but "ADDRESS COL. COLT/LONDON" address on barrel.

N/A	N/A	$17,500	$12,500	$10,000	$7,500	$6,250	$5,000	$4,250	$3,500	$3,250	$3,000

REVOLVERS: PERCUSSION CONVERSIONS

Colt Thuer Conversions

Subtract approx. 50% for factory nickel plating on models listed below.

COLT THUER CONVERSIONS (c. 1868-1872) - .31, .36, and .44 CF cal., less than 5,000 produced in all models. This was Colt's first commercial attempt at converting percussion revolvers to fire fixed ammo. Standard features: usually threaded inside rammer for a Thuer loading tool, a hardened flat face on hammer, deepened loading cutout on right side of lug, Thuer ring and back of cylinder have matching assembly numbers. Beware of fakes! Only non-experimental Colt models are listed. Rarity by barrel length will not be considered here. Serial numbers are often missing on cylinder.

Prices for Colt Conversions reflect values for blue and case hardened examples. Nickel plated specimens are rarely seen, but typically sell for 20%-40% less than blue finish.

Any defects, excessive wear, or dulled blue will affect value. Nickeled conversions that have lost their translucence (become cloudy) should be discounted more than usual 20%-40% from blue and case hardened examples, especially on near-mint to mint specimens.

* *Colt Thuer Conversion 1849 Pocket*

N/A	N/A	$70,000	$40,000	$32,500	$25,000	$21,500	$18,000	$15,000	$12,000	$10,000	$7,500

* *Colt Thuer Conversion 1851 Navy*

N/A	N/A	$30,000	$27,500	$25,000	$22,000	$18,500	$15,000	$11,500	$8,500	$7,250	$6,000

* *Colt Thuer Conversion 1860 Army* - the most common Thuer, but popular because it's a large frame model.

N/A	N/A	$35,000	$27,500	$23,750	$20,000	$18,750	$17,500	$15,500	$12,500	$10,750	$9,000

* *Colt Thuer Conversion 1861 Navy*

N/A	N/A	$35,000	$25,000	$21,000	$17,500	$16,250	$15,000	$12,500	$10,000	$8,750	$7,500

* *Colt Thuer Conversion 1862 Police*

N/A	N/A	$22,500	$18,500	$16,750	$15,000	$13,500	$12,000	$10,250	$8,500	$7,500	$6,500

* *Colt Thuer Conversion 1862 Pocket Navy*

N/A	N/A	$30,000	$27,000	$22,500	$17,500	$16,250	$15,000	$12,500	$10,000	$8,750	$7,500

Richards Conversions: All Variations

Subtract approx. 50% for factory nickel plating on models listed below.

RICHARDS CONVERSION, COLT 1860 ARMY REVOLVER - .44 CF cal., produced circa 1870s, special machining to barrel and breech of cylinder for conversion to a cartridge weapon. Produced in two serial ranges: one numbered under 10,000 and a separate group generally in the 190,000 to 200,000 range.

100%	98%	95%	90%	80%	70%	60%	50%	40%	30%	20%	10%

✻ *1860 Army First Model Richards* - quick ID: integral rear sight on breech plate. Floating firing pin in breechplate. Front edge of barrel lug is same as 1860 percussion Army. Breechplate extends over rear edge of cylinder.

N/A	N/A	$25,000	$15,000	$11,750	$8,500	$7,000	$5,500	$5,000	$4,500	$4,000	$3,500

✻ *1860 Army Second Model Richards* - quick ID: standard Richards type barrel. A space between face of conversion ring and rear of cylinder when viewed from the side. No integral sight on breechplate, cut away at top allowing hammer to directly strike the cartridge.

N/A	N/A	$25,000	$20,000	$14,500	$8,500	$7,750	$7,000	$5,750	$4,500	$4,250	$4,000

✻ *1860 Army Twelve Stop Cylinder Variation Richards* - quick ID: generally the same as standard model Richards except cylinder has extra "safety" notches between the locking notches. This variation was usually produced in the 100-300, 1,000-1,700 and 200,000 serial ranges. Cylinder locking notches over chambers often broken through. Watch for alterations.

N/A	N/A	$35,000	$25,000	$18,500	$12,000	$10,500	$9,000	$8,250	$7,500	$7,000	$6,500

✻ *1860 Army U.S. Marked Richards* - quick ID: generally the same as 1st Model Richards (many minor differences). Has "U.S." stamped on left barrel lug and "A" (Ainsworth) inspector marks in several places. They are converted 1860 percussion Armys, so original numbers are typically in 23,000-144,000 range plus a second set of assembly numbers. Oiled grips, military soft blue finish.

N/A	N/A	$35,000	$25,000	$18,500	$12,000	$10,500	$9,000	$8,250	$7,500	$7,000	$6,500

Richards-Mason Conversions: All Variations

Subtract approx. 50% for factory nickel plating on models listed below.

1860 ARMY RICHARDS-MASON - .44 CF cal., overall, much rarer than Richards Army Conversions, circa 1870s, approximately 2100 produced. A rare variation has an 1860 Army rebated cylinder and a barrel with a lug shaped similar to 1861 Navy Conversion.

✻ *1860 Army Richards-Mason* - quick ID: breechplate without integral rear sight, cutout at top so hammer can strike primer directly. A space can be seen between breechplate and rear of cylinder. Rear of lug is a vertical line instead of the bullet shape cutout seen on Richards models.

N/A	N/A	$30,000	$20,000	$17,500	$15,500	$12,500	$9,500	$8,000	$6,500	$5,750	$5,000

1851 NAVY RICHARDS-MASON - .38 CF and RF cal., circa 1870s. Produced in two different serial ranges. Has improved Richards-Mason breechplate that is flush with diameter of recoil shield. Difficult to locate in prime condition.

✻ *1851 Navy Civilian Model Richards-Mason* - quick ID: Richards-Mason breechplate which is same diameter as recoil shield, octagon barrel, mirrored civilian blue. Nickel finish commonly seen.

N/A	N/A	$17,500	$12,000	$9,500	$6,500	$5,500	$4,500	$4,000	$3,500	$2,500	$2,000

✻ *1851 U.S. Navy Richards-Mason* - quick ID: Richards-Mason breechplate, oiled grips, soft blue military finish, produced in US. percussion range of 40,000-90,000 ranges. Inconsistent "U.S.N." and other inspector markings. Iron straps, "U.S." on frame.

N/A	N/A	$20,000	$15,000	$12,000	$8,500	$7,500	$6,500	$5,500	$4,500	$4,000	$3,500

1861 NAVY RICHARDS-MASON - produced in civilian and military versions, circa 1870s, made in RF and CF cal. in two serial ranges. Round 7 1/2 in. barrel.

✻ *1861 Navy Civilian Model Richards-Mason* - quick ID: Richards-Mason breechplate, round 7 1/2 in. barrel with attached ejector housing, unrebated cylinder. When blue, has a commercial high gloss finish.

N/A	N/A	$25,000	$17,000	$13,750	$10,000	$8,750	$7,000	$6,250	$5,000	$4,000	$3,000

100%	98%	95%	90%	80%	70%	60%	50%	40%	30%	20%	10%

✶ *1861 Navy U.S. Navy Richards-Mason* - soft military blue finish, oiled grips, converted from percussion U.S. Navy revolvers, inconsistent military markings, centerfire, set of extra serial numbers often seen on cylinder.

N/A	N/A	$25,000	$20,000	$16,000	$12,000	$10,500	$8,000	$7,250	$6,000	$4,750	$3,500

COLT 1862 POLICE & POCKET NAVY RICHARDS-MASON CONVERSIONS

(circa 1870s) - .38 RF and CF cal., parts for 1862 Police, 1862 Pocket Navy, as well as 1849 Pockets are often intermixed. As parts bins were depleted, Colt used whatever components that would fit, resulting in a tremendous amount of minor variations. Some barrels were converted from percussion models while others were newly made as cartridge barrels without rammer plugs and loading slots in the lug. There are three different serial ranges (1849, 1862 Police/Pocket Navy, Conversion). 3 1/2 to 6 1/2 in. barrels, again not all features available on all models.

Nickel plated conversions will bring 20%-40% less than blue and case hardened specimens.

✶ *1862 Police & Pocket Navy Richards-Mason Conversion 4 1/2 in. Octagon Barrel Model* - quick ID: 4 1/2 in. octagon barrel without ejector. Rebated Pocket Navy Cylinder.

N/A	N/A	$9,500	$6,500	$5,000	$3,500	$2,600	$1,750	$1,350	$950	$850	$750

✶ *1862 Richards-Mason Conversion Round (Percussion) Barrel Pocket Navy with Ejector* - quick ID: plug in rammer slot; ejector housing, loading cutout in right side of lug, barrel remachined from Pocket Navy percussion barrel, Pocket Navy rebated cylinder. Similar appearance to cartridge barrel variation.

N/A	N/A	$10,000	$8,000	$6,750	$5,000	$4,000	$3,000	$2,250	$1,500	$1,200	$850

1862 POLICE AND POCKET (1865 POCKET MODEL) NAVY CONVERSION

- 4 1/2, 5 1/2, or 6 1/2 in. barrels with 1862 Police percussion profile and added ejector housing. Has rebated Pocket Navy cylinder or rarer half fluted 1862 Police cylinder. 6 1/2 in. barrel will bring a premium.

✶ *1862 Police/Pocket Navy with Rebated Pocket Navy Cylinder* - quick ID: 1862 Police profile barrel with ejector housing and rebated 1862 Pocket Navy cylinder.

N/A	N/A	$9,500	$6,000	$5,250	$4,000	$3,100	$2,250	$1,550	$850	$750	$650

✶ *1862 Police/Pocket Navy with Half Fluted Cylinder* - quick ID: 1862 Police profile barrel with ejector housing and 1/2 fluted Police cylinder.

N/A	N/A	$12,000	$8,500	$6,750	$5,000	$4,000	$3,000	$2,250	$1,500	$1,175	$850

Conversions with Round Cartridge Barrel

Subtract approx. 50% for factory nickel plating on models listed below.

ROUND CARTRIDGE BARREL WITH EJECTOR

- .38 RF and CF cal. 4 1/2, 5 1/2, or 6 1/2 in. barrels produced as a cartridge component without rammer slots and lug cutouts inherent to a percussion barrel.

✶ *1862 Pocket Navy Round Cartridge Barrel* - quick ID: much shorter lug area than similar model converted from percussion barrel. No slots or loading cutouts on barrel. With ejector housing and Pocket Navy rebated cylinder. Often called the "Baby Open Top," very scarce.

N/A	N/A	$10,000	$6,000	$4,750	$3,500	$3,000	$2,500	$2,000	$1,500	$1,350	$1,200

3 1/2 IN. ROUND CARTRIDGE BARREL CONVERSION

- .38 RF or CF cal., sometimes seen with serial numbers that are from 1849 Pocket Model (300,000 range). Barrel newly made for cartridges, not converted from a percussion barrel.

✶ *3 1/2 in. Round Cartridge Barrel* - quick ID: only type conversion with 3 1/2 in. barrel. No ejector, no loading lever slot or loading cutout in lug area. Pocket Navy rebated cylinder.

N/A	N/A	$6,000	$4,000	$3,250	$2,500	$2,000	$1,500	$1,250	$1,000	$875	$750

100%	98%	95%	90%	80%	70%	60%	50%	40%	30%	20%	10%

REVOLVERS: "OPEN TOP" MODELS

If possible, it is advisable to procure a factory letter before buying/selling this Open Top Revolver. These watermarked letters are available by writing Colt Archive Properties LLC in Hartford, CT, with a charge of $200 or more per serial number (if they can research it). Send your name and address, Colt model name, serial number, and check or credit card information to: COLT ARCHIVE PROPERTIES LLC, P.O. Box 1868, Hartford, CT 06144-1868. Please allow 90-120 days for a response.

1871-72 OPEN TOP MODEL RIMFIRE - .44 cal. rimfire, 6 shot, 7 1/2 in. barrel, without frame topstrap, blue metal with casehardened hammer, serial range 1-approx. 7,000, barrel address "ADDRESS COL. SAM COLT, NEW YORK, U.S. AMERICA", forerunner of the single action Army, quite desirable. Mfg. 1871-72.

> **Add 20% for blue finish on models listed below.**

* 1871-72 Open Top Model Rimfire Regular Production Model - 7 1/2 in. barrel, New York address, Navy grips.

100%	98%	95%	90%	80%	70%	60%	50%	40%	30%	20%	10%
N/A	N/A	$45,000	$27,000	$24,000	$20,000	$16,500	$12,000	$10,000	$7,500	$6,250	$5,000

* 1871-72 Open Top Model Rimfire Regular Production - with Army grips.

100%	98%	95%	90%	80%	70%	60%	50%	40%	30%	20%	10%
N/A	N/A	$45,000	$27,000	$24,000	$20,000	$16,500	$12,000	$10,000	$7,500	$6,250	$5,000

* 1871-72 Open Top Model Rimfire Late Production - with address "COLT PT. F. A. MANUFACTURING CO., HARTFORD, CT., U.S.A."

100%	98%	95%	90%	80%	70%	60%	50%	40%	30%	20%	10%
N/A	N/A	$45,000	$25,000	$21,500	$17,500	$13,750	$10,000	$8,250	$6,500	$5,500	$4,000

Add 40% for models with 8 in. barrel or COLTS/PATENT frame markings.

REVOLVERS: PERCUSSION, 2ND & 3RD GENERATION BLACK POWDER SERIES

To learn more about the 2nd & 3rd Generation Percussion Black Powder Series, it is recommended to purchase *Colt Black Powder Reproductions & Replicas - A Collector's & Shooter's Guide* and the *Blue Book of Modern Black Powder Arms* by John Allen. The 2nd Edition contains more information on the Colt 2nd Generation Black Powder Series than anything else previously published. These definitive books are available from Blue Book Publications, Inc. To order, please call, fax, email, or visit www.bluebookinc.com.

DERRINGERS

FIRST MODEL DERRINGER - .41 rimfire cal., single shot, 2 1/2 in. barrel, scroll engraving standard, blue, nickel, or silver plated barrel, downward pivoting barrel, no grips, serial numbered 1-6,500. Mfg. approx. 1870-1890.

100%	98%	95%	90%	80%	70%	60%	50%	40%	30%	20%	10%
$3,325	$2,500	$2,150	$1,925	$1,700	$1,450	$1,275	$1,075	$875	$750	$675	$650

SECOND MODEL DERRINGER - .41 rimfire or centerfire cal., single shot, 2 1/2 in. barrel, scroll engraving standard, blue, nickel, or silver plated barrel, downward pivoting barrel, checkered and varnished walnut grips, "No 2" marked on top of barrel, serial numbered 1-9,000. Mfg. approx. 1870-1890.

100%	98%	95%	90%	80%	70%	60%	50%	40%	30%	20%	10%
$1,775	$1,475	$1,275	$1,100	$950	$850	$750	$650	$585	$535	$500	$475

Add 100% for .41 centerfire cal.

THIRD MODEL DERRINGER (THUER MODEL) - .41 rimfire or centerfire (rare) cal., single shot, side pivoting 2 1/2 in. barrel, varnished walnut grips, blue barrels, bronze frames were either nickel or silver plated, engraving optional, Colt-barrel address, spur trigger, serial numbered approx. 1-45,000. Mfg. approx. 1875-1910.

100%	98%	95%	90%	80%	70%	60%	50%	40%	30%	20%	10%
$1,500	$1,275	$950	$825	$725	$625	$550	$495	$450	$415	$385	$360

Add 30%-50% for .41 centerfire cal. Early models are worth considerably more.

GRADING - PPGS™	100%	98%	95%	90%	80%	70%	60%

FOURTH MODEL DERRINGER (FIRING) - .22 Short cal., single shot similar in appearance to the 3rd Model, 2 1/2 in. barrel, approx. 112,000 mfg. 1959-1963 with either D or N suffix. A few were put in books (sometimes as pairs), picture frames, penholders, bookends, etc. (these will command premiums).

	100%	98%	95%	90%	80%	70%	60%
Gun only	$100	$85	$65	$60	$55	$50	$40
Gun w/accessories	$375	$275	$175	$135	$115	$100	$85

* *Fourth Model Derringer (non-firing)* - this variation was normally used for decoration and is normally encountered in books, picture frames, penholders, bookends, etc. Values below assume all factory materials intact - if not, prices are reduced to $50-$75 for gun only.

100%	98%	95%	90%	80%	70%	60%
$375	$250	$150	$120	$105	$90	$80

Non-firing guns usually do not have the barrel notch, thus preventing the hammer from striking the cartridge.

LORD DERRINGER - .22 Short cal. only, side pivoting Thuer action, gold plated with black chrome barrel and walnut grips. Mfg. 12,000 approx. 1970-73 by Colt, cased.

100%	98%	95%	90%	80%	70%	60%
$175	$140	$100	$90	$80	$75	$70

LADY DERRINGER - .22 Short cal. only, side pivoting Thuer action, full gold plated finish with pearlite grips. Mfg. 3,000 approx. 1970-73 by Colt, cased.

100%	98%	95%	90%	80%	70%	60%
$175	$140	$100	$90	$80	$75	$70

LORD & LADY CASED SET - one each of the Lord & Lady Derringers or combinations, consecutive serial numbers, numbered 1,001-up, with DER suffix.

100%	98%	95%	90%	80%	70%	60%
$495	$375	$275	$225	$195	$165	$140

LADY CASED SET - cased pair of Lady Derringers.

100%	98%	95%	90%	80%	70%	60%
$495	$375	$275	$225	$195	$165	$140

LORD CASED SET - cased pair of Lord Derringers.

100%	98%	95%	90%	80%	70%	60%
$495	$375	$275	$225	$195	$165	$140

BOOKCASE DERRINGER PAIR - .22 Short cal., consecutively numbered Derringers with synthetic ivory grips and nickel finish, cased inside unique hardcover "Colt Derringers" labeled book with red velvet lining, limited mfg. in early 1960s.

100%	98%	95%	90%	80%	70%	60%
$350	$275	$200	$150	$125	$110	$95

100%	98%	95%	90%	80%	70%	60%	50%	40%	30%	20%	10%

REVOLVERS: POCKET MODELS

If possible, it is advisable to procure a factory letter before buying/selling this variation (open top only). These watermarked letters are available by writing Colt Archive Properties LLC in Hartford, CT, with a charge of $200 or more per serial number (if they can research it). Send your name and address, Colt model name, serial number, and check or credit card information to: COLT ARCHIVE PROPERTIES LLC, P.O. Box 1868, Hartford, CT 06144-1868. Please allow 90-120 days for a response.

CLOVERLEAF HOUSE PISTOL - .41 Short or L rimfire cal., cloverleaf configured 4 shot cylinder, spur trigger, 1 1/2 or 3 in. barrel, blue or nickel plated, approx. 7,500 mfg. in ser. no. range 1-8,300 during 1871-76.

100%	98%	95%	90%	80%	70%	60%	50%	40%	30%	20%	10%
$2,550	$2,300	$1,850	$1,600	$1,400	$1,200	$1,100	$925	$825	$725	$650	$600

    Add 30% for blue finish.
    Add 80% for 1 1/2 in. barrel.

This model is sometimes referred to as the Jim Fisk model, as he was murdered by Edward Stokes with a Cloverleaf.

* *5-shot Cloverleaf* - similar to 4-shot model, except has round 5-shot cylinder and 2 5/8 in. barrel only, approx. 2,500 mfg. in ser. no. range 6,160-9,950 during 1871-76.

100%	98%	95%	90%	80%	70%	60%	50%	40%	30%	20%	10%
$2,175	$1,900	$1,600	$1,325	$1,150	$975	$850	$750	$650	$600	$550	$500

100%	98%	95%	90%	80%	70%	60%	50%	40%	30%	20%	10%

OPEN TOP REVOLVER (OLD LINE) - .22 Short or L rimfire cal., 2 3/8 or 2 7/8 in. barrel, without topstrap on frame, with or without integral ejector, blue or nickel plated, varnished walnut grips, approx. 114,200 mfg. 1871-77.

$1,450	$1,250	$1,150	$950	$850	$750	$700	$600	$550	$450	$375	$325

Add 30% for blue finish.
Add 120% for Early Model with ejector and high hammer spur.

REVOLVERS: NEW LINE SERIES & VARIATIONS

If possible, it is advisable to procure a factory letter before buying/selling New Line Revolvers. These watermarked letters are available by writing Colt Archive Properties LLC in Hartford, CT, with a charge of $100 or more per serial number (if they can research it). Send your name and address, Colt model name, serial number, and check or credit card information to: COLT ARCHIVE PROPERTIES LLC, P.O. Box 1868, Hartford, CT 06144-1868. Please allow 90-120 days for a response.

Add 30% for blue finish on models listed below.

1ST MODEL - .22, .30, .32, .38, or .41 cal. rim and centerfire, mfg. 1873-1876, 7 (.22 cal. only) or 5 shot, short cylinder flutes, cylinder stop slots cut on exterior of cylinder, 1 3/4, 2 1/4, or 4 in. barrel, full nickel or blue/case hardened finish, spur trigger. Many thousands mfg. 1873-1884.

$1,250	$1,050	$925	$825	$750	$675	$600	$550	$450	$350	$300	$250

2ND MODEL - similar to 1st Model, except has longer cylinder flutes and cylinder stop slots are on the back of cylinder, may or may not have loading gate. Mfg. 1876-1884.

$1,125	$995	$875	$800	$725	$650	$575	$500	$400	$325	$275	$235

Caliber rarity on both models from highest mfg. to lowest is: .22, .32, .30, .41, and .38.

NEW HOUSE MODEL - .38 or .41 cal. centerfire, 5 shot, 2 1/4 in. barrel, spur trigger, checkered hard rubber grips. Approx. 4,000 mfg. 1880-1886 starting at ser. no. 10,300.

$1,475	$1,150	$1,000	$875	$775	$675	$600	$485	$425	$360	$325	$310

NEW POLICE MODEL - .32, .38, or .41 cal. centerfire, 5 shot, 2 1/4, 4 1/2, 5, or 6 in. barrel, spur trigger, with or without ejector, stamped or etched "NEW POLICE" on barrel. Approx. 4,000 mfg. 1882-1886.

$1,800	$1,525	$1,275	$1,100	$925	$800	$725	$650	$600	$550	$525	$495

REVOLVERS: SAA, 1873-1940 MFG. (SER. NOS. 1-357,000)

The author wishes to express thanks to Charles Layson for making the following information available and reformatting the Colt 1st Generation SAA section.

The Colt SAA was produced in 36 calibers with many special order features or combinations available directly from the Colt factory. These factory special order features can greatly enhance the value of the revolver. The Single Action Colt, or "Peacemaker," as it is often called, is undoubtedly the most collectible handgun in the world, and as such, can command very high prices.   It is prudent to secure several professional opinions as to originality when contemplating an expensive purchase, since many SAAs have been altered or "improved" over the decades. Before he died, Keith Cochran, author of the *Colt Peacemaker Encyclopedia,* Vol. II, guesstimated that over 1/2 of all pre-WWII revolvers were no longer factory original. Because of this, it is advisable to procure a factory letter when buying or selling older or recently manufactured Colt Single Actions (hence guaranteeing original configuration and value credibility). These watermarked letters are based on the original factory handwritten shipping ledgers and are available by contacting Colt Archive Properties LLC in Hartford, CT. While not totally infallible, these letters are normally very accurate. If Colt cannot provide you with proper documentation after conducting research, they will issue a partial refund. No fee will be charged for SAAs serialized over 343,000 that are non-records guns.

Colt's new policy on 1st Generation SAAs is to call Colt Archive Properties, and a charge of $150 or more will be assessed (ser. no. range 354,000 - 357,859 cannot be researched). This service also includes a factory document which will follow in 2-3 weeks. Additionally, historical research premiums exist for factory engraving ($50-$175), unique shipping destination and company executive provenance ($50), and famous Western personalities or Colt family members ($100-$200). For just the date of manufacture, the charge is $25, while identification service providing general information is $50. The phone number is 860-244-1343. Ask for the Archive Dept. between the hours of 1-4 P.M. EST. Once contacted, they will tell you what the historical research charge will be. The address is COLT ARCHIVE PROPERTIES LLC, P.O. Box 1868, Hartford, CT 06144-1868.

Values shown below are for guns without special order features. Factory engraving, ivory grips, very rare special order barrel lengths, and special finishes would add considerably to the values shown below. One final word on single action Colts: Black Powder Colts (pre 165,000 serial range) should be scrutinized carefully for potential problems, including refinishing (including aging), replacement parts, restamped serial numbers, and added, non-factory special order features. This makes a major difference in pricing the SAA, since a genuine, original SAA's price tag will vary immensely from a non-original, made-up "parts gun."

SAA - 1st Generation Civilan/Commercial (Mfg. 1873-1940)

One of the most well known handguns, and certainly the most collected revolver in the world, the Colt Single Action Army has been produced almost continuously since 1873, with only a minor interruption between 1940 and 1955. It is without a doubt, the most copied revolver with over fifteen clones currently in production.

Better known as the "Peacemaker," this firearm has appreciated in value at an accelerated rate over the last fifty years. Spurred by the popularity of television westerns in the 1950's and 60's, a standard pre-war, 1st generation single action in excellent condition has gone from $250 in 1960 to approximately $8000 today, and in some cases much higher.

Not every Colt Peacemaker, however, is worth thousands of dollars. While many factors determine the actual value, the single most important has to be the overall condition of the gun now, compared to the day it left the factory. Because of the demand for Peacemakers in excellent condition many have been reworked and/or reblued, both by private gunsmiths and by the Colt factory itself. Unfortunately only the factory marked its refinished guns, while private individuals normally did not.

The Colt company has used at least three different methods of marking handguns that are to be reworked and/or refinished, and while there is some disagreement among collectors as to exactly what these marks indicate, e.g., refinishing, major parts replacement, or both, it is the opinion of this writer that the first to be used was a six pointed star stamped on the rear right bow of the trigger guard, from approximately 1890 to 1920. The second was a small ampersand placed in the same location, from approximately 1920 to 1945. The third was completely different, and is occasionally found in addition to the ampersand. It was a series of three numbers stamped on most major parts. Called "bin" numbers, they correspond to the numbers on small boxes or "bins" in the custom shop, into which are placed all the parts of a disassembled handgun destined to be reworked and /or refinished. On the Single Action Army, these numbers were placed on the rear flat of the loading gate, visible when it is open (not to be confused with the assembly number stamped on the rear curve of the loading gate), on the front of the cylinder, on the left side of the grip straps, and on the bottom of the barrel, near the frame.

Any reworking or refinishing has a negative effect on the value of a gun to the collector, and the amount varies depending upon the age of the gun, what was actually done and the quality of the workmanship. For example, an early black powder single action that has been expertly refinished by the factory or a qualified restorer is worth only 10 to 20% of what the same gun would be worth in original, mint condition. A late smokeless powder Single Action similarly redone, however, is still worth 40 to 50% of one in near new condition. In many cases, the factory had an irritating habit of adding then current markings to an earlier gun, e.g., a caliber designation added to the barrel of a pre-1890 Single Action, or a rampant Colt to the frame.

SINGLE ACTION ARMY (SAA) - STANDARD MFG. - over 30 cals., six shot single action revolver, three standard barrel lengths. The 4 ¾ barrel had a two line address, while the 5 ½ and 7 ½ had a one line address. Blue with color case-hardened frame or full nickel finish were both available. Of the many (36) calibers offered, 45 Colt was by far the most popular, accounting for 42% of total production, followed by 44/40 (18%), 38/40 (11%), 32/20 (8%) and .41 (4.5%). One piece, varnished walnut grips were standard for the first ten

100%	98%	95%	90%	80%	70%	60%	50%	40%	30%	20%	10%

years, then gradually replaced with two piece hard rubber. When grips are "not listed" on Colt historical letters, you should assume that they were the standard for their time period, either wood or rubber; not the pearl or ivory that someone added at a later date.

* *Pinch Frame SAA (ser. no. range 1-160)* - very rare and seldom found with any original finish, 44 S&W American and 45 Colt calibers, 7 ½ in. barrel, blue and casehardened finish, one piece varnished wood grips, distinctive rear sight situated one-half inch in front of hammer notch, which gives the impression that the top strap has been "pinched." Mfg. 1873.

N/A	N/A	N/A	$150,000	$135,000	$120,000	$105,000	$95,000	$82,000	$75,000	$68,000	$60,000

Add 50% for original .44 S&W American caliber (it is estimated that only 20-25 were produced in this caliber, and most were later converted).

Be aware! There are many counterfeits in this variation.

* *Early Black Powder SAA (Mfg. 1873-1876, ser. no. range 160-22,000)* - .45 LC cal., 7 1/2 in. barrel standard, blue or nickel finish, rear sight changed to standard "V" notch, first few hundred have German silver front sight, distinctive italic script style lettering used in barrel address, two line, two date patent marking on frame, one piece varnished wood grips has more distinctive flair at bottom rear on early guns, serial numbers shared with early martial production, 5 1/2 in. barrels introduced in 1875 in guns for export. Mfg. 1873-76.

❖ **Ser. Nos. 160-999 (Mfg. 1873)**

N/A	N/A	$75,000	$65,000	$55,000	$48,000	$42,000	$38,000	$35,000	$28,000	$22,000	$15,000

❖ **Ser. Nos. 1,000 - 9,999 (Mfg. 1873-1874)**

N/A	N/A	$60,000	$50,000	$42,000	$37,000	$32,000	$27,000	$22,000	$18,000	$14,000	$10,000

❖ **Ser. Nos. 10,000 - 22,0000 (Mfg. 1874 - 1876)**

N/A	$60,000	$52,000	$45,000	$38,000	$31,000	$26,000	$23,000	$19,000	$15,000	$11,000	$7,000

Subtract 50% for nickel finish.

* *Intermediate Black Powder SAA (Mfg. 1876-1890, ser. no. range 22,000-130,000)* - the italic style of lettering in the barrel address is changed to a block letter style in the 22,000 range, the first two piece gutta percha grips with eagle motif appear in 1882 and became the standard by 1888, the 44-40 (44WCF) caliber is introduced in 1878, the round head ejector is changed to oval shape in the 52,000 serial range, 4 ¾" to 5 ½" barrels are becoming more popular, and Colt gradually abandons the practice of placing serial numbers on the cylinders and barrels of civilian revolvers. Nickel plated single actions seldom have numbered barrels and cylinders after the 60,000 serial range. Blue guns normally have numbers on both up to the 110,000 range, and occasionally thereafter up to 125,000. Two line, two date patent markings change to three line, three dates by 1878.

Subtract 50% for nickel finish.
Add 30% for original box.
Add 10% for 4 3/4 in. barrel.
One-piece wood grips are more desirable than two-piece rubber grips.

❖ **Ser. Nos. 22,000 - 54,000 (Mfg. 1876 - 1880)**

N/A	$50,000	$42,000	$32,000	$25,000	$20,000	$15,000	$12,000	$10,000	$8,500	$7,200	$5,500

❖ **Ser. Nos. 54,000 - 130,000 (Mfg. 1880 - 1890)**

N/A	$38,000	$34,000	$28,000	$20,000	$16,000	$12,000	$10,000	$8,700	$7,500	$6,000	$5,000

* *Late Black Powder SAA (Mfg. 1890 - 1896, ser. no. range 130,000-165,000)* - three line patent date format changes to two lines with three dates, circled rampant Colt trademark is added to left side of frame, grips transition from wood and rubber w/eagle to plain two piece rubber by 1892, and caliber designation is added to the barrel and eliminated from triggerguard.

N/A	$32,000	$29,000	$20,000	$16,000	$13,000	$11,000	$9,000	$7,000	$6,000	$5,000	$4,000

Subtract 35% for nickel finish.
Add 25% for original box.
Add 10% for 4 3/4 in. barrel.
Add 20% for wood or rubber w/eagle grips.

100%	98%	95%	90%	80%	70%	60%	50%	40%	30%	20%	10%

* *Early Smokeless Powder SAA (Mfg. 1896 - 1908)* - several important physical characteristics were changed during this transition period. Most notably, in 1896 the vertical screw retaining the cylinder pin was eliminated in favor of the horizontal latch. This was identical to what had already been used on the double action models since 1877. This change coincided with the introduction of ammunition loaded with white or smokeless powder, which was more powerful and less corrosive than black powder. It was necessary for firearms manufacturers, therefore, to modify and strengthen their products to safely use the new ammunition. By adopting the more modern and tool-free horizontal latch to the Single Action at this time, Colt gave it's customers an easy way to tell the new from the old, the stronger from the weaker, and a good excuse to purchase a new Peacemaker! As a result, sales boomed and more Single Actions were sold in the next ten years, than any other ten year period in Colt's history.

The knurling pattern on the hammer spur began a two step revision in 1906. Up until this time, the knurling was enclosed in a border with a line underneath. Beginning in 1906, for approximately two years, the border remained, but the line underneath was eliminated. By late 1908, the border was also eliminated, and thereafter, the knurling ran to the very edges of the hammer spur. Although Colt advertised their improved smokeless powder Single Actions as early as 1897, they did not add the "VP" proof mark (verified proof, Colt's guarantee for smokeless powder use) to the triggerguard until 1904. While the highest production and sales figures were reached during this period, quality did not suffer. Many collectors feel that the fitting, polishing and finishing work performed during this period was superior to any other.

❖ **Ser. Nos. 165,000 - 182,000 (Mfg. 1896 - 1899)** - the first three years of this period, 1896 to 1899, have recently become known as the "blackpowder transition" period, to distinguish Single Actions made with the modern, stronger frame and yet still considered "antique" by federal law that uses January 1st, 1899 as the beginning of the modern gun era.

N/A	$28,000	$20,000	$15,000	$12,000	$9,500	$8,000	$6,500	$5,000	$3,800	$3,000	$2,500

❖ **Ser. Nos. 182,000 - 300,000 (Mfg. 1899 - 1908)**

N/A	$25,000	$18,000	$13,500	$9,000	$7,500	$6,000	$5,000	$4,000	$3,200	$2,500	$2,000

     Add 25% for original box.
     Subtract 25% for nickel finish.

* *Intermediate Smokeless Powder SAA (Mfg. 1908 - 1920, ser. no. range 300,000-339,000)* - physical changes continued to occur during this period. Rampant Colt medallions were inserted into pearl, ivory and checkered walnut grips in 1909, the .44 special caliber was introduced circa 1912, the blueing process was gradually changed, and the circled rampant Colt on the frame began to lose it's circle as the die stamps wore. The company, however, did not quickly give up the use of black powder rifling (wide grooves and narrow lands) completely until 1914, although an experimentation and transition period with narrower grooves and wider lands had begun about 1910. Similarly, the small and low black powder front sight did not change to the larger and higher smokeless profile until 1914. WWI came and went, and SAA sales began to decline. The year 1920 is very significant to Single Action collectors since this was the year that the serial number relocation was completed. Those numbers on the triggerguard and backstrap were moved under the grips beginning the late 338,000 serial range (1919), leaving only the number on the frame visible. This brought to a close a practice which had begun in the 1840's with the percussion revolvers. Many collectors regard this as the end of the "cowboy" period.

     Add 20% for original box.
     Add 10% for smooth, two-piece walnut grips.
     Add 25% for checkered, varnished walnut grips with deep set medallions.
     Subtract 15% for nickel finish.

100%	98%	95%	90%	80%	70%	60%	50%	40%	30%	20%	10%

❖ **Ser. Nos. 300,000 - 328,000 (Mfg. 1908 - 1914)**

100%	98%	95%	90%	80%	70%	60%	50%	40%	30%	20%	10%
N/A	$20,000	$16,000	$10,000	$8,000	$6,000	$5,300	$4,000	$3,500	$3,000	$2,300	$1,900

❖ **Ser. Nos. 328,000 - 339,000 (Mfg. 1914 - 1920)**

100%	98%	95%	90%	80%	70%	60%	50%	40%	30%	20%	10%
N/A	$16,000	$13,000	$9,000	$7,000	$5,500	$4,500	$3,500	$3,000	$2,500	$2,000	$1,700

✳ *Late Smokeless Powder SAA (ser. no. range 339,000-357,000)* - single action sales continued to diminish after 1920, as sales of semi-automatics increased. Only 19,000 SAA's were sold in the twenty year period, with only 100 being produced in 1936. The complete serial number is visible only on the frame, but many cylinders are stamped on the rear with the last two or three digits. In 1928, the caliber marking on the left side of the barrel was changed to read "Colt Single Action Army," followed by the caliber. In 1930, the "V" notch rear sight was replaced with a square groove to match the wider front sight, and in 1935, the finish on the hammer was changed from color casehardened to blue with polished sides. Colt special order grips medallions also made a two step, transitional change in 1923. Since 1909, medallions on pearl, ivory or checkered walnut grips had been recessed into the grips and both horses faced forward. They were first changed to a less expensive, flush mount design, still facing forward and then within the same year to a flush mount, with one facing forward and one backward, a cost cutting measure which required only one die. The finish on the checkered wood grips was also changed from a varnish to an oil finish in 1924.

It is important to remember that while special order grips such as pearl, ivory, or checkered wood may add as much as 25% to an SAA's value, they must be factory original to that particular gun, and be recorded as such in the factory records. Later add-ons enhance a gun's value by much less.

Add 20% for original box in good condition.
Add 25% for original checkered wood, pearl, or ivory grips.
Add 35% for original stag horn grips (very rare!).

❖ **Ser. Nos. 339,000 - 350,000 (Mfg. 1920 - 1928)**

100%	98%	95%	90%	80%	70%	60%	50%	40%	30%	20%	10%
$12,000	$9,500	$8,800	$7,500	$6,200	$5,200	$4,500	$4,000	$3,500	$2,800	$2,300	$2,000

❖ **Ser. Nos. 350,000 - 355,000 (Mfg. 1928 - 1935)**

100%	98%	95%	90%	80%	70%	60%	50%	40%	30%	20%	10%
$10,000	$8,500	$7,800	$6,500	$6,000	$5,000	$4,000	$3,500	$3,000	$2.500	$2,000	$1,800

❖ **Ser. Nos. 355,000 - 357,000 (Mfg. 1935 - 1940)**

100%	98%	95%	90%	80%	70%	60%	50%	40%	30%	20%	10%
$9,000	$7,500	$6,800	$6,000	$5,400	$4,800	$3,500	$3,000	$2,500	$2,000	$1,800	$1,500

> **SAA 1st Generation Commercial, Non-Standard Mfg.**

SINGLE ACTION ARMY (SAA) - NON-STANDARD MFG. - throughout the 1873-1940 period of production, Colt manufactured several distinct types or configurations of SAAs that varied from the standard and therefore, have special significance to the collector.

✳ *.44 Rimfire SAA* .44 Henry rimfire, 7 ½ in. barrel, blue and nickel finishes, most were shipped to the southwest and saw hard use, rare with any original finish remaining, many barrels shortened during their period of use, serial numbered in their own range, 1 - 1,863, mfg. from 1875 to 1880.

100%	98%	95%	90%	80%	70%	60%	50%	40%	30%	20%	10%
N/A	N/A	N/A	N/A	$75,000	$60,000	$47,000	$35,000	$27,000	$22,000	$18,000	$15,000

Beware! Many have been found with cut and/or stretched barrels.

✳ *.22 Rimfire SAA* - blue or nickel finish, 5 ½ in. and 7 ½ in. barrels, manufactured in two distinct runs, slightly less than 100 converted from unsold .44 RF still in inventory in the late 1880s, and approximately 20 mfg. as new in 1891.

100%	98%	95%	90%	80%	70%	60%	50%	40%	30%	20%	10%
N/A	$40,000	$35,000	$32,000	$28,000	$25,000	$22,000	$20,000	$18,000	$15,000	$12,000	$9,000

Add 10% for rare 5 1/2 in. barrel.
Subtract 50% for factory refinished models.
Subtract 10% for those converted from .44 rimfire.

100%	98%	95%	90%	80%	70%	60%	50%	40%	30%	20%	10%

✳ *Buntline Special Model SAA* - .45 LC cal., long barrel model named after Ned Buntline, author of dime novels in the late 19th century. Only 28 believed mfg. with adjustable rear sights and extended hammer screw for attachment of metal skeleton shoulder stock, all in the 28,800 serial range, most with 12 in. or 16 in. barrels. Very rare.

100%	98%	95%	90%	80%	70%	60%	50%	40%	30%	20%	10%
N/A	N/A	$150,000	$135,000	$120,000	$100,000	$80,000	$65,000	$50,000	$40,000	$30,000	$20,000

Add 30% for original factory shoulder stock.

✳ *Etched Panel .44-40 SAA* - refers to Single Actions in .44 W.C.F. caliber with the words "Colt Frontier Six Shooter" acid etched in a panel on the left side of the barrel. This phrase was probably originated by one of Colt's New York distributors or possibly by B. Kittredge & Co. of Cincinnati, OH, who had already advertised the .45 SA as the "Peacemaker" in March 1875, and later had double action Model 1878's etched with the word "OMNIPOTENT" on the barrel. The lowest known etched panel 44/40 is in the 41,000 serial range (1878) and the highest in the 129,000 range circa 1890.

100%	98%	95%	90%	80%	70%	60%	50%	40%	30%	20%	10%
N/A	$45,000	$38,000	$30,000	$22,000	$17,000	$14,000	$12,000	$10,000	$9,000	$8,000	$7,000

Subtract 30% for nickel finish.
Add 10% for 4 ¾ in. barrel.
Add 20% for 5 ½ in. barrel.

✳ *Sheriff's Model SAA* - this term denotes Single Actions without ejectors and ejector housings. Most were produced in .45 and 44-40 caliber, with 3 ½ in. or 4 in. barrels, but 2 1/2 in., 3 in., 4 3/4 in., and 7 1/2 in. were made. According to collector and researcher Wynn Paul, the first ejectorless Sheriff's or Store-keeper's models were shipped from the factory on February 22, 1882 to Hibbard Spencer, Bartlett & Co., Chicago, IL, in two shipments of ten each, one group with 3 ½ in. barrels, one group with 4 in. barrels. Approximately 1,000 were produced, most in the latter part of the 19th century.

Beware of fakes! The *Blue Book of Gun Values* strongly recommends getting a historical letter from Colt, then checking the authenticity of the serial numbers. Many guns have had numbers altered to match records.

Add 20% for 44-40 cal. w/etched panel.
Add 30% for original special order grips.
Add 50% for 2 ½ in. or 7 ½ in. barrel.
Subtract 15% for nickel finish.

❖ **Sheriff's Model SAA Smokeless Powder Frame**

100%	98%	95%	90%	80%	70%	60%	50%	40%	30%	20%	10%
N/A	$75,000	$65,000	$50,000	$38,000	$32,000	$26,000	$22,000	$18,000	$14,000	$10,000	$8,000

❖ **Sheriff's Model SAA Black Powder Frame** - pre-1896 mfg. with old style black powder frame.

100%	98%	95%	90%	80%	70%	60%	50%	40%	30%	20%	10%
N/A	$95,000	$82,000	$67,000	$50,000	$35,000	$22,000	$18,000	$15,000	$12,000	$9,500	$8,500

✳ *Flat-top Target Model SAA* - a target version of the SAA with flat top frame and adj. sights, approximately 925 were manufactured from 1888-1896, both in 5 1/2 in. and 7 1/2 in. barrel and full blue finish, two-piece smooth walnut, two-piece rubber or two-piece checkered walnut grips are known. Many calibers, from .22 RF to .476 Eley were available.

100%	98%	95%	90%	80%	70%	60%	50%	40%	30%	20%	10%
N/A	$25,000	$20,000	$16,000	$13,000	$11,000	$9,000	$8,000	$7,000	$6,000	$5,000	$4,500

Add 30% for 5 1/2 in. barrel.

Beware! Many target models were returned to the factory for refinishing.

✳ *Long Flute Series SAA* - in 1913, Colt decided to make use of approximately 1,500 cylinders left over from the model 1878 double action production. Since it was necessary to add a bolt lock notch and a lead-in groove on these long flute cylinders, a block of serial numbers, 330,000 to 331,480, was set aside to be used for this special production. Manufactured in 1913 and 1914, specimens are known in .32 WCF, .38 WCF, .41 LC, .44 S&W Spl., and .45 Colt.

According to researchers Hull and Rowcliffe, whose survey includes 114 long flute Single Actions, no .44 WCF have been noted. The actual total mfg. possibly may exceed 1,500, and while quite rare, these long flute variations sell for only 5% to 10% more than other Single Actions of this period.

100%	98%	95%	90%	80%	70%	60%	50%	40%	30%	20%	10%

✳ *Pre-war/Post-war Mfg. SAAs* - made from pre WWII parts remaining in inventory after production of the Single Action Army had ended in 1940, many of these post-war guns were given as gifts to dignitaries and retiring Colt employees, known calibers include .30 Carbine, .357 Mag., .38 Spl., .44 Spl., 44-40 WCF and .45 Colt. Most are found with 5 ½ in. barrels and blue and case hardened finish; nickel is rare. Shipping cartons vary from pre-war dark maroon and brown, hinged top, circa 1950, to black 2nd generation style. Approximately 338 were assembled and shipped between 1947-1971.

> **Add 10% for nickel finish.**
> **Add 20% plus for important or well known recipient.**

Most of these guns are found in 95% or better condition, and are valued like the last of the pre-war 1st generation Single Actions.

✳ *Factory Engraved SAAs* - slightly less than 1% (approximately 3,400) Single Actions are thought to have been engraved at the factory or elsewhere by authority from Colt between 1873 and 1940. Colt offered three basic grades of engraving and since many of these guns carried special inscriptions, initials, grips, etc., the value ranges are very wide. Condition also plays a huge role here. Factory engraved black powder SAAs typically sell in the $10,000 to $60,000 range, while factory engraved smokeless powder SAAs usually peak in the $35,000 range. Very special or one of a kind pieces, such as the five known "panel" engraved guns, or one carried by a famous outlaw or lawman may bring upward of $300,000, depending on condition and particulars. Most factory work is documented in the records.

✳ *Non-Factory Engraved SAAs* - value depends on when and where the engraving was done. Early "New York" or "dealer" engraved Single Actions done outside the factory were usually shipped from Colt in the "soft" and w/o finish. The majority of these were done in 1870 or 1880's, and condition being equal, are generally priced at 25% to 50% of factory original specimens. Later guns, well done by a known contemporary artist, are usually priced by adding the value of the gun to the cost of the engraving. Poor execution may actually lower the value of a plain, but original gun, much as refinishing would. The notation of "soft" in the factory records is desirable, since the large wholesalers in the northeast used many of the same engravers as Colt. There are and have been some 20th century engravers who stand out, however, and their work commands higher prices, e.g. Lynton McKenzie, Ben Lane, Cole Agee and Weldon Bledsoe - the two latter being famous for their "cattle brand" style, and Ben Lane for his meticulous duplication of the patterns of Cuno Helfricht, the most famous of all Colt factory engravers.

✳ *Bisley Model SAA* - numbered in the same serial range as the standard Single Action Army, the Bisley model featured a more curved forward and longer grip strap and a smaller, raked back hammer. It was designed with the target shooter in mind and named after Bisley, England, the location of the international shooting matches during the late 19th and early 20th century. It was offered in the same barrel lengths, the same finishes and most all of the more popular Single Action calibers, .32 WCF (32/20) being the most popular. It was advertised from 1894 (approx. ser. no. 156300) to 1915 (approx. ser. no. 331916), and available on special order until 1920, with slightly over 45,000 being produced.

100%	98%	95%	90%	80%	70%	60%	50%	40%	30%	20%	10%
N/A	$10,000	$8,500	$7,500	$6,200	$5,000	$4,200	$3,500	$2,800	$2,200	$1,800	$1,500

> **Add 25% for nickel finish.**
> **Add 20% for original box.**

✳ *Flat-top Target Bisley SAA* - a target version similar to the flat-top target Single Action with adj. sights. Available in all standard calibers with a 7 ½ in. barrel, blue finish and either walnut or rubber grips. Offered from 1894 to 1912, the most popular caliber was .455 Eley followed closely by .32 WCF. Only 976 were manufactured.

100%	98%	95%	90%	80%	70%	60%	50%	40%	30%	20%	10%
N/A	$20,000	$18,000	$15,000	$13,000	$11,000	$9,000	$8,000	$7,000	$6,000	$5,000	$4,000

> **Add 30% for any barrel length other than 7 ½ in.**

100%	98%	95%	90%	80%	70%	60%	50%	40%	30%	20%	10%

* *Battle of Britain SAA* - late 1st generation Single Action Armys purchased by the British government in anticipation of invasion from Germany in 1940. A total of 163, mostly .38 and .45 cal. in both blue and nickel finish were sent to England by Colt. These guns were fully inspected and proofed by the British, in many cases showing the exact specifications of the cartridge on the bottom of the barrel. Most, if not all, were unissued, and remain today in 90% plus condition.

100%	98%	95%	90%	80%	70%	60%	50%	40%	30%	20%	10%
$12,000	$10,000	$8,500	$7,500	$6,500	$5,500	$4,700	$4,200	$3,500	$3,000	$2,500	$2,000

Add 10% for blue and color casehardened finish.

SAA U.S. Military, Mfg. 1873-1903

Since many of the military models listed below are frequently encountered with no original finish remaining, prices for original no condition specimens will be approx. three quarters of the 10% prices listed below. With original specimens getting harder and harder to find, many guns are now observed with major parts replacements, including barrels, cylinders, grips, etc.

Beware of restorations that are purported to be original! One expert believes that as many as 90% of Colt SAA Cavalry & Artillery models currently offered for sale, especially at gun shows, have been intentionally faked, or "enhanced" in some way. Likewise, many "questionable" guns have been consigned to the auction houses for disposal. Many have been altered in the last 40 years in all inspector serial ranges. Some have now been skillfully "aged" to look more original. When making a substantial purchase, a letter of authentication from a reliable source is suggested in addition to a factory historical letter. Also ask for a guarantee of originality in writing from the seller. No factory information is available on U.S. Cavalry revolvers below ser. no. 30,600.

Blue Book Publications, Inc. would be happy to refer you to a credible source for authenticating the military revolvers listed below (very important). While a factory letter (if possible) verifies the configuration, it does not verify originality and/or authenticity. All inquiries are treated confidentially.

SINGLE ACTION ARMY (CAVALRY) - U.S. MILITARY CONTRACT - the Colt SAA was the primary sidearm of the U.S. military forces between 1873 and 1892. While sometimes called the "cavalry" model, this revolver was carried by commissioned officers in the regular army and the state militias, and issued to each man in the mounted units. A total of 37,063 were purchased by the U.S. government at an average cost of $12.50 each. Contract specifications called for 7 ½ in. barrel, .45 Colt caliber, government blue and color casehardened finish (a softer blue color compared to the darker and more brilliant civilian finish, which required a higher polish and was therefore more expensive), and one piece, oil finished walnut grips. Each gun was stamped with the initial(s) of a U.S. ordinance principal sub-inspector and finally, with the letters "U.S." on the frame after being approved for delivery to the National Armory at Springfield, MA.

* *Early U.S. Model SAA (Mfg. 1873 - 1903)* - principal sub-inspectors of this early period used only the first letter of their last name to mark the revolvers which they inspected. Chronologically, they were O.W. Ainsworth (A), S.B. Lewis (L), A.B. Casey(C) and W.W. Johnson (J).

While the lower serial numbers are generally the most desirable, the small number of guns inspected by Lewis, Johnson and Casey make them harder to find and perhaps more valuable than a higher numbered Ainsworth. These guns are in the same number sequence as guns made for the civilian market up to #20,000. There are no known "U.S." marked Single Actions between serial numbers 20,000 and 30,000. According to John Kopec, arguably the most knowledgeable and authoritative U.S. Single Action researcher and co-author of the widely respected work, *A Study of the Single Action Army Revolver*, the earliest known Ainsworth inspected Single Action is serial number "179."

❖ **Ainsworth Serial Range 179 - 999 (1873)**

100%	98%	95%	90%	80%	70%	60%	50%	40%	30%	20%	10%
N/A	N/A	$175,000	$140,000	$100,000	$80,000	$65,000	$55,000	$45,000	$35,000	$25,000	$20,000

❖ **Ainsworth Serial Range 1,000 - 9,999 (1873-1874)**

100%	98%	95%	90%	80%	70%	60%	50%	40%	30%	20%	10%
N/A	N/A	$140,000	$115,000	$90,000	$75,000	$60,000	$50,000	$40,000	$30,000	$20,000	$16,000

Ainsworth inspected guns between serial numbers 4,500 and 6,500 were possibly issued to George Custer's 7th Cavalry, and therefore command a premium. Add 15% to 20% to this range.

100%	98%	95%	90%	80%	70%	60%	50%	40%	30%	20%	10%

❖ **Ainsworth Serial Range 10,000 - 15,000 (1874-1875)**

N/A	N/A	$120,000	$100,000	$80,000	$60,000	$50,000	$40,000	$30,000	$25,000	$18,000	$14,000

❖ **Lewis Serial Range 15,000-16,500 (1875)**

N/A	N/A	$140,000	$115,000	$90,000	$75,000	$60,000	$50,000	$40,000	$30,000	$20,000	$16,000

❖ **Johnson Serial Range 16,8000-18,450 (1875)**

N/A	N/A	$135,000	$110,000	$85,000	$70,000	$58,000	$47,000	$36,000	$25,000	$18,000	$15,000

❖ **Casey Serial Range 16,400 - 19,530 (1875)**

N/A	N/A	$120,000	$100,000	$80,000	$60,000	$50,000	$40,000	$30,000	$25,000	$18,000	$14,000

More than a few Casey range guns are dual inspected, most with a "C" and a "J", but while interesting, this does not add a premium.

✱ *Mid-Range U.S. Model SAA (1876 - 1887)* - when military production resumed in the 30,000 serial range, the principal sub-inspectors during this eleven year period were John T. Cleveland (J.T.C.), Henry Nettleton (H.N.), and David F. Clark (D.F.C.). Starting in 1876, the marking procedure changed from one last name initial to two or all three of the inspector's initials. Also in 1876, the third patent date was added to the left side of the frame in a third line.

❖ **Cleveland Serial Range 30,690 to 35,570 (1876 – 1877)** - these are the very first of the U.S. Cavalry models to be recorded in the Colt records and the first ones that can be lettered by the factory. Slightly more than 2,000 were delivered under government contract, and were inspected by John T. Cleveland. For some reason, a small group of these guns show the initials of Lewis Draper "L.D." stamped on the frames, instead of the normal "J.T.C.", including the cartouche on the right grip. There is also an unusually high ratio of Civilian SAAs in this serial range with the condemned "C" mark on the frame, and there is existing correspondence from Colt and U.S. Ordnance Dept. complaining that Inspector Cleveland was being unduly hard to please. Perhaps Lewis Draper was a temporary replacement during this period. Regardless, this small group of "L.D." marked Single Action Cavalrys are an interesting variation and will command a slight premium.

N/A	N/A	$80,000	$65,000	$50,000	$38,000	$29,000	$20,000	$16,000	$14,000	$12,000	$9,000

Add 10% for "L.D." marked frames.

❖ **Early Henry Nettleton Serial Range 36,800 – 39,880 (1877)** - according to John Kopec's "Cavalry and Artillery Revolvers," there are a small group of known cavalry revolvers which were part of a large surplus of civilian SAAs which were inspected and accepted by the government. While some are Henry Nettleton inspected, most are marked with the "W" of E.C. Wheeler. It is thought that perhaps Wheeler substituted for Nettleton during an illness. Regardless, this is a very small and desirable group of Cavalry SAAs.

N/A	N/A	$87,000	$70,000	$55,000	$42,000	$34,000	$25,000	$18,000	$15,000	$13,000	$10,000

❖ **Early David F. Clark Serial Range 41,000-42,300 (1878) & Later Henry Nettleton Serial Range 47,000-51,100 (1878 – 1879)**

N/A	N/A	$75,000	$50,000	$35,000	$28,000	$22,000	$18,000	$16,000	$14,000	$12,000	$8,000

❖ **Later David F. Clark Serial Range 53,000-121,000 (Mfg. 1880 – 1887)**

N/A	N/A	$55,000	$46,000	$34,000	$26,000	$20,000	$17,000	$15,000	$13,000	$11,000	$7,000

✱ *Late U.S. Model SAA, Serial Range 131,187-140,361 (Mfg. 1890 – 1891)* - this was the last of U.S. Single Action production. Four thousand were inspected by Rinaldo A. Carr during this sixteen month period. As hostilities in the west subsided, demand decreased and many revolvers of this group went to state militias or were left in storage. Consequently, a higher percentage of R.A.C. inspected SAAs are found in excellent condition than those of other inspectors, and this is reflected in their value. The last of this group was shipped from the factory on April 29, 1891.

N/A	$45,000	$41,000	$35,000	$27,000	$21,000	$18,000	$15,000	$13,000	$10,000	$8,000	$5,000

100%	98%	95%	90%	80%	70%	60%	50%	40%	30%	20%	10%

* **Artillery Model SAAs** - refers to U.S. government model SAA revolvers with 5 ½ in. barrels that were reworked and refinished between 1895 and 1903. In response to growing dissatisfaction with the stopping power of the newly adopted M.1892 Colt .38 double action revolvers, the U.S. government directed Springfield Armory to collect all remaining quantities of .45 Colt Cavalry revolves from storage, return them to Colt Manufacturing for refurbishing, and reissue them to troops soon to be involved the Spanish American War. Colt was to shorten all barrels to 5 1/2 inches, replace all worn parts, and refinish. Every effort was made to keep all serial numbers matching, even to the extent of adding the old serial number to new parts. (sometimes using the smaller stamping dies that were customary on the Model 1892 DA). Colt completed this work on approximately 15,000 SAAs in 1895 and 1896. It was only by chance that several "artillery" units received the first ones to be issued. Many of these same revolvers were returned to Colt for refurbishing again between 1900 and 1903, but this time, no regard was given to matching component serial numbers. This shortcut minimized precious time and saved the government $1.50 per gun. A few artillery models are believed to have been redone at various government arsenals, and this could explain the existence of several known artillery revolvers with blue frames. Regardless, the artillery model has become very popular with collectors and one of the most studied and interesting types of Single Action Colts.

N/A	$16,000	$13,000	$9,500	$8,500	$7,500	$6,500	$5,500	$4,700	$4,000	$3,500	$3,000

Add 25% for all matching numbers.
Add 15% for all matching numbers except barrel.
Add 100% for documented "Rough Rider" association.

Only rarely will one be found with all the matching serial numbers, indicating that it escaped the last refinish - these guns will bring a premium price. Inspector's cartouches must be authenticated.

Artillery models with desirable low-numbered frames are currently being re-converted back into all matching Cavalry models with 7 1/2 in. barrels.

* **New York State Militia SAA** - in 1895 before work began on the artillery models, Colt refurbished 800 SAA revolvers supplied by Springfield Armory, and possibly the state of New York, for the New York State Militia. These guns retained their 7 ½ inch barrels and all original parts wherever possible. Replacement parts were serial numbered to match, and strangely, barrels and cylinders were given the first and second digits of the whole serial number which they had never had. In addition to receiving a high polish blue and casehardened civilian finish, their hammers were blued instead of being color casehardened. Since all other Cavalry models in the government's possession were cut to 5 ½ inches shortly thereafter, these 800 are quite possibly the only quantity of original 7 ½ inch SAAs remaining that could actually have seen service on the American frontier against hostiles. All other 7 ½ inch Cavalry revolvers that are seen today were most likely originally issued to state militias rather than the U.S. Army. Some are found with unit markings on grips and with lanyard swivels. These 800 Colt revolvers therefore played a very significant role in the history of the United States.

N/A	$25,000	$22,000	$19,000	$15,000	$13,000	$11,000	$9,000	$8,000	$7,000	$6,000	$5,000

* **Condemned U.S. Cavalry** - throughout military contract production, a small percentage of SAAs did not pass inspection and were condemned, receiving a large "C" stamped on the frame, just over the serial number. These guns, or more often, just the frames, were set aside, and later completed as civilian revolvers. They are often found with the ordinance sub-inspector's initials, such as J.T.C., on the bottom of the frame, but will not have a "U.S." on the left side. This does not have any negative effect on the value of the gun to a collector, and they should be regarded as a normal civilian revolver with an interesting history.

GRADING - PPGS™	100%	98%	95%	90%	80%	70%	60%

REVOLVERS: SAA, 2ND GENERATION: 1956-1975 MFG.

The author wishes to express his thanks to Charles Layson, and Carol and the late Don Wilkerson for their generous contributions and help in reformatting the 2nd & 3rd Generation Colt SAA information. Popular demand brought back the Single Action Army in 1956 with minor modifications, most not detectable except to experts. Serial numbers began at 0001SA, and continued to 73,000SA before the "New Model" was introduced in 1976 (ser. no. 80,000SA). Premiums are paid for rare production variances in NIB condition. It should be noted "premium niches" exist in this model as collectors are establishing premiums paid for rarer production variances (the interrelation of barrel length, caliber, frame type, finish quality, year of manufacture, and other special features). The order of desirability on standard 2nd Generation SAAs is as follows: 4 3/4 in. barrels are the most desirable, followed by 7 1/2 in., and then 5 1/2 in. Caliber desirability is as follows: .45 LC has the most demand, followed by .44 Spl., .38 Spl., and then .357 Mag. It follows that desirable calibers found with desirable barrel lengths will command healthy premiums if production was unusually low for a particular configuration. Reference books specifically on the post-war SAA are a must when determining the rarity factors on these multiple production combinations. Buntlines, Sheriff's Models, and special orders through the Custom Gun Shop are in a class by themselves, and have to be evaluated one at a time.

It is advisable to procure a factory letter when buying or selling older or recently manufactured Colt single actions (hence, guaranteeing authenticity and value credibility). These watermarked letters are based on the original factory handwritten shipping ledgers and are available by contacting Colt Archive Properties LLC in Hartford, CT. While not totally infallible, these letters are normally very accurate. If Colt cannot provide you with proper documentation after conducting research, they will issue a $50 refund. Colt's new policy on 2nd Generation SAAs is to call Colt Archive Properties, and a charge of $200 or more will be assessed. This service also includes a factory document which will follow in 2-3 weeks. Additionally, historical research premiums exist for factory engraving ($50-$175), unique shipping destination, or unique inscription ($50). For just the date of manufacture, the charge is $25, while identification service providing general information is $50. The phone number is 860-244-1343. Ask for the Archive Dept. between the hours of 1-4 P.M. EST. Once contacted, they will tell you what the exact historical research charge will be. The address is COLT ARCHIVE PROPERTIES LLC, P.O. Box 1868, Hartford, CT 06144-1868.

SINGLE ACTION ARMY (SAA, 2ND GENERATION) - .357 Mag., .38 Spl., .44 Spl., or .45 LC cal., denoted by SA suffix, 3 (Sheriff's Model), 4 3/4, 5 1/2, 7 1/2, or 12 (Buntline) in. barrel length-5 1/2, 7 1/2, and 12 in. barrels have the one-line barrel address, all blue, blue/case hardened, or nickel finish. 2nd Generation SAAs have been grouped into the following 3 categories.

* *SAA Early 2nd Generation* - ser. no. range 0001SA to approx. 39,000SA, shipped in one-piece black box similar to pre-war box. Mfg. from 1956-65.

	100%	98%	95%	90%	80%	70%	60%
.45 LC cal.	$2,800	$2,200	$1,800	$1,500	$1,200	$1,000	$900
.44 Spl. cal.	$2,600	$2,000	$1,700	$1,400	$1,100	$900	$800
.38 Spl. cal.	$2,400	$1,900	$1,600	$1,300	$1,000	$850	$750
.357 Mag. cal.	$2,000	$1,800	$1,500	$1,200	$1,000	$850	$750

Add 30% for original black box in good condition.
Add 20% for original nickel finish.
Add 15% for original 4 3/4 in. barrel.

The very earliest models of this group, with serial numbers under 10,000 SA, have become more desirable when found in 100% new condition, with perfect black box, brush and papers - this configuration may bring an additional 20%.

* *SAA Mid-range 2nd Generation* - ser. no. range 39,000SA to 70,055SA, shipped in a red and white, two-piece, stagecoach box. Mfg. 1965-1973.

	100%	98%	95%	90%	80%	70%	60%
.45 LC cal.	$2,000	$1,600	$1,400	$1,200	$1,000	$800	$700
.44 Spl. cal.	$1,900	$1,500	$1,300	$1,100	$900	$700	$600
.357 Mag. cal.	$1,800	$1,400	$1,200	$1,000	$900	$700	$600

Add 30% for original stagecoach box.
Add 10% for original nickel finish.
Add 15% for original 4 3/4 in. barrel.

GRADING - PPGS™	100%	98%	95%	90%	80%	70%	60%

✳ SAA Late 2nd Generation - ser. no. range 70,055SA to 73,205SA, shipped in a brown, wood grain cardboard shell with 2 styrofoam inserts. Mfg. 1973-1976.

	100%	98%	95%	90%	80%	70%	60%
.45 LC cal.	$1,800	$1,500	$1,300	$1,100	$900	$800	$700
.357 Mag. cal.	$1,700	$1,400	$1,200	$1,000	$800	$700	$600

> Add 15% for original brown/styrofoam box.
> Add 10% for original nickel finish.
> Add 10% for original 4 3/4 in. barrel.

2nd Generation SAAs in stagecoach box w/o eagle black grips (ser. numbered under approx. 52,000SA) are more desirable than those with eagle. Also, flat-top hammers are more desirable than round top hammers found between ser. no. range 27,012SA-61,575SA (mfg. mid-1959-1972). Colt manufactured approximately 100 screwless frames during the 1970s, and assembled approximately 50 guns at the time. The other 50 sat in the warehouse for a while until Colt started assembling the screwless frames again during the 1990s. Most of these recent guns are engraved and in .38-40 WCF or .45 LC cal., and have either a 4 3/4 or 5 in. barrel. Typically, the engraver's name is part of the serial number. Bangor's distributed most of these guns, and in today's marketplace they are priced in the $7,500-$10,000+ range.

SHERIFF'S MODEL SAA (1961 MODEL) - .45 LC cal., distinctive configuration with 3 in. barrel and no ejector rod housing, ser. no. followed by SM suffix, 503 were mfg. for Centennial Arms Corp. - 478 had a blue/case hardened finish and 25 were done in nickel.

	$2,000	$1,600	$1,400	$1,200	$1,000	$800	$700

> Add 25% for original two-piece box.
> Add 200% for original nickel finish.
> Add approx. 300% for nickel finish on 100% condition guns.

BUNTLINE SPECIAL SAA (2ND GENERATION) - .45 LC cal. only, 12 in. barrel, blue/case hardened finish, rubber (early mfg.) or walnut grips. Over 3,900 mfg. 1957-1975.

	$1,695	$1,275	$1,000	$900	$850	$800	$750

> Add 100% for original nickel finish (rare, watch for refinishing).
> Add 30% for original black box in good condition.

NEW FRONTIER SAA (2ND GENERATION) - .357 Mag., .38 Spl. (rare), .44 Spl. or .45 LC cal., denoted by flat-top frame, adj. rear sight, and "NF" after the serial number, 4 3/4 (scarce), 5 1/2 (scarce), or 7 1/2 (most common) in. barrel, case hardened frame/blue finish and smooth walnut grips were standard. Approx. 4,200 mfg. 1961-1975.

	$1,250	$950	$900	$850	$800	$750	$700

> Add 15% for later brown/styrofoam box.
> Add 20% for stagecoach or black box (must be in correct ser. no. range).
> Add 35% for early black and gold box.
> Add 50% for 4 3/4 in. barrel.
> Add 25% for 5 1/2 in. barrel.
> Add 200% for .38 Spl. cal. with 5 1/2 in. barrel, 600% for 7 1/2 in. barrel.

NEW FRONTIER BUNTLINE SAA (2ND GENERATION) - .45 LC cal. only, 12 in. barrel, flat-top frame and adj. rear sight. Approx. 72 mfg. 1962-67.

	$2,500	$2,150	$1,650	$1,400	$1,200	$1,100	$1,000

> Add 50% for original black or tan box (must be serial numbered to the gun).

FACTORY ENGRAVED 2ND GENERATION SAAs - approx. 350 revolvers were factory engraved with 90% being in .45 LC cal. Values range from 75%-100% higher than non-engraved specimens, with additional premiums paid for rare styles and configurations and/or for the notoriety of the engraver. Those SAAs done by Albert Herbert, A.A. White, Robert Burt, Leonard Francolini, and Dennis Kiesler are probably the highest-priced examples. Always check authenticity when buying, selling, or trading engraved 2nd Generation SAAs with the Colt Archive Dept. The charge for a factory letter per engraved gun is $150. $50 will be refunded if Colt cannot provide historical documentation.

Factory engraved 2nd Generation SAAs are at least 10 times rarer than engraved 3rd Generation pistols.

GRADING - PPGS™	100%	98%	95%	90%	80%	70%	60%

REVOLVERS: SAA, 3RD GENERATION: 1976-CURRENT MFG.

After a short break in production, Colt Firearms announced the resumption of full-scale production of the Single Action on Feb. 4th, 1976, at the N.S.G.A. (National Sporting Goods Association) Bi-Centennial show in Chicago.

The "New Model Colt Single Action Army" or the "Colt Post-War Single Action Army - New Model," as it was commonly referred to at the time, is known today to collectors as the "3rd Generation Colt Single Action Army." Minor changes include a modified, thin front sight contour, and a return to back to the cylinder pin bushing in late 2002, plus a few other "minor, modern manufacturing techniques that have not changed the appearance, feel, action, or performance of this historic handgun....," according to Colt's press release at the time.

Production began with ser. no. 80,000SA, and reached 99,999SA in 1978. At this point, the SA suffix changed to a prefix beginning with SA01,001. Serialization reached SA99,999 during 1993, and began over, this time separating the letters SA, and starting with S02,001A. As this edition went to press, serial numbers had reached S37,000A (excludes custom serial numbers). For whatever reasons, a few writers have erroneously referred to this current production run as "4th Generation Single Actions." This is an incorrect description, as these revolvers are mechanically identical to those produced since 1976, and should still be considered 3rd Generation guns.

For a listing of Colt's "P-Codes" (referring to the factory's model number designations specifying frame type, caliber, finish, and barrel length), please refer to the Colt Single Action Model Numbers section in the back of this book (located in Colt Serialization).

As with 1st and 2nd Generation Single Actions, a factory letter authenticating configuration and shipping destination can be obtained for $100 by writing to: COLT ARCHIVE PROPERTIES LLC, P.O. Box 1868, Hartford, CT 06144-1868. If Colt cannot provide proper documentation after conducting research, they will issue a refund of $50. Please allow 60-90 days for proper response.

Please contact the Colt Custom Shop for a written quotation ($25) regarding a custom built SAA with special options/features. Their address is: Colt Manufacturing Company, Inc. P.O. Box 1868, Hartford, CT 06101, ATTN: Custom Shop.

POPULAR SAA CUSTOM SHOP SPECIAL ORDER OPTIONS

Add $280 for special barrel length, add $375 for caliber change, add $197 for custom-tuned action, add $268 (available in .45 LC only beginning 2000) for extra regular fluted or unfluted cylinder, add $308 for extra long fluted cylinder, add $155 for beveled front of cylinder, add $200 for mirror brite finish (disc.) or nickel finish, add $425 for gold or silver plating, add $80 for black eagle grips, add $15 for grip medallions, add $155 for smooth walnut grips, add $275 for North American elkhorn grips (disc.), add $400 for red stag grips, add $450 for sandbar stag grips, add $400 for buffalo horn grips, add $375 for mother-of-pearl grips (disc.), add $760 for plain ivory grips, $350 for imitation ivory, approx. 10% for grip checkering, add $250 for scrimshaw engraving (3 initials only), add $65 for consecutive serial numbers, add $310 for individual unique serial number, add $105 to modify and shorten ejector housing, add $180 (per set) for fire blued small parts, add $288 for birdshead and $400 for extended butt frame.

While a few screwless frame SAAs have been mfg. to date (approx. 100), the Custom Shop now lists this option as a standard custom order feature. Price is POR.

STANDARD/CUSTOM SINGLE ACTION ARMY SAA (3RD GENERATION) - .32-20
WCF (new 2005), .357 Mag. (disc. approx. 1983, reintroduced 2005), .38 Spl. (reintroduced 2005), .38-40 WCF (reintroduced 2005), .44 Spl. (disc. approx. 1983), .44-40 WCF, or .45 LC cal., 4 (disc. 1988), 4 3/4, 5 (disc. 1987), 5 1/2, or 7 1/2 (limited production since 1992) in. barrel, 5 1/2 and 7 1/2 in. barrels have the one-line barrel address, standard finishes include color case hardened/blue or nickel, plastic black eagle or walnut grips (used mostly during 1991-92) standard, most recent mfg. has blue shipping box with white slip cover. Mfg. 1976 to date. Original 1976 issue price was approx. $242.

MSR $1,290	$1,290	$995	$825	$725	$650	$600	$550

    Add $200 for nickel finish (current mfg.).
    Add 10% for original .38-40 WCF cal. (disc.)
    Add 25% for original .38 Spl. cal. (disc.)
    Add 10% for black powder frame (disc. 1995).

GRADING - PPGS™	100%	98%	95%	90%	80%	70%	60%

Add $700 for original two-piece ivory grips with screw.
Add $700 for original one-piece ivory grips w/o screw.
Add 5% for original brown box with styrofoam inserts (mfg. 1976-93).

Through 2001, Colt offered the SAA as both Standard and Custom Models. The difference is that single actions that are further customized with engraving, special barrel lengths, stocks, etc., are packaged more eloquently because of the added value of the customizing.

Beginning 2001, all orders for SAA models are processed through the Colt Custom Shop. The 2001 Custom Shop MSR for the Custom SAA was $2,100.

Various custom order barrel lengths have been available on this model for some time.

The .357 Mag. and .44 Spl. cals. were mostly discontinued by 1983.

Colt manufactured approximately 100 screwless frames during the 1970s, and assembled approximately 50 guns at the time. The other 50 sat in the warehouse for a while until Colt started assembling the screwless frames again during the 1990s. Most of these recent guns are engraved and in .38-40 WCF or .45 LC cal., and have either a 4 3/4 or 5 in. barrel. Typically, the engraver's name is part of the serial number. Bangor's distributed most of these guns, and in today's marketplace they are priced in the $8,500-$10,000+ range.

To reference factory coding for the various Standard Model P (SAA) configurations, please refer to the Colt Single Action Model Numbers within the Colt Serialization section in the back of this text.

FRONTIER SIX SHOOTER SAA (3RD GENERATION) -
.44-40 WCF cal., black powder frame, 4 3/4, 5 1/2, or 7 1/2 in. barrel with "Colt Frontier Six Shooter" acid etched in a panel on the left side of barrel, similar to 1st Generation SAAs. New 2008.

MSR $1,350	$1,350	$1,050	$850	$750	$650	$600	$550

BLACK POWDER FRAME SAA (3RD GENERATION) -
.45 LC cal., 4 3/4, 5 1/2, or 7 1/2 in. barrel, features old style blackpowder frame, mfg. disc 1995 reintroduced 2008.

MSR $1,290	$1,290	$995	$825	$725	$650	$600	$550

COLT COWBOY SAA -
.45 LC cal., 4 3/4 (disc. 1999, reintroduced 2002), 5 1/2, or 7 1/2 (disc. 1999) in. barrel marked "COLT COWBOY .45 COLT" on left side, transfer bar safety, all steel construction, frame assembly done in the U.S., charcoal case colors on frame with blue metal parts, rampant Colt black competition grips similar in design to those used on 1st generation SAAs, 40 oz. Not mfg. in U.S. While advertised beginning 1998, this model was not manufactured until 1999-2003.

	$595	$475	$450	$400	$375	$350	$335

Last MSR was $670.

* *Cowboy SAA Collection Set* - includes SAA in .45 LC cal., with 5 1/2 in. barrel, stag (very limited) or imitation ivory (more common) grips, blue/color case hardened finish, accessories include collector's Bowie knife, silver medallion and collector's case, marked "1 of 1,000". Limited mfg. 2000 only.

	$1,250	$750	$625	$500	$425	$400	$400

Last MSR was approx. $1,600.

SHERIFF'S MODEL SAA (3RD GENERATION, MFG 1980-1985) -
.44-40 WCF, .44 Spl., or .45 LC cal., 3 in. barrel w/o ejector rod, blue/case colored, nickel, or royal blue finish. Approx. 4,560 guns mfg. 1980-85.

	100%	98%	95%	90%	80%	70%	60%
.45 LC cal. (blue/CH)	$1,395	$1,150	$900	$850	$800	$750	$700
.44 Spl./.44-40 WCF	$1,075	$975	$850	$750	$675	$600	$525

Add 10% for extra convertible cylinder.
Add 10% for original nickel finish.
Add $550 for original ivory grips.
Subtract 20% for all blue finish.

* *Sheriff's Model SAA (3rd Generation - Current Mfg.)* - .44-40 WCF or .45 LC (most popular) cal., 3 or 4 in. barrel w/o ejector rod, blue/case colored finish, black plastic grips. New 2008.

MSR $1,290	$1,250	$995	$825	$725	$650	$600	$550

GRADING - PPGS™	100%	98%	95%	90%	80%	70%	60%

BUNTLINE MODEL SAA (3RD GENERATION) - .44-40 WCF or .45 LC cal. only, 12 in. barrel, blue/case hardened finish, walnut grips.

	$1,395	$995	$800	$750	$700	$650	$600

Add 10% for original nickel finish.
Add $550 for original ivory grips.

NEW FRONTIER SAA (3RD GENERATION - 1978-1981 MFG.) - .357 Mag., .44-40 WCF (rare), .44 Spl., or .45 LC cal., denoted by "NF" serial suffix, 4 3/4, 5 1/2, or 7 1/2 in. barrel, blue/case hardened finish, flattop frame, adj. rear sight, plain two-piece walnut grips. Mfg. 1978-81.

	100%	98%	95%	90%	80%	70%	60%
.44-40 WCF/.45 LC cal.	$1,050	$900	$800	$750	$700	$650	$600
.44 Spl. cal.	$795	$650	$500	$450	$425	$400	$400
.357 Mag. 7 1/2 in. nickel	$1,050	$900	$800	$750	$700	$650	$600

Subtract 10% for 5 1/2 in. barrel.
Subtract 15% for 7 1/2 in. barrel.
Add 5% for original brown box with styrofoam inserts.

Serial numbers on the New Frontier started at 01001NF, but during 1980 a few New Frontiers with 5 1/2 in. barrels were produced in the 7000NF serial range, where 2nd Generation New Frontiers left off. Therefore, a 3rd Generation New Frontier will either have a ser. no. starting with "0" or will have a higher number than 7288NF with no "O" prefix.

NEW FRONTIER BUNTLINE SPECIAL SAA (3RD GENERATION) - .45 LC cal. only, 12 in. barrel, flat-top frame, adj. rear sight, limited mfg. as the New Buntline Commemorative during 1979. Please refer to the Colt Commemorative section for value information.

STOREKEEPER'S MODEL SAA (3RD GENERATION - 1984-85 MFG.) - .45 LC cal. only, black powder frame, 4 in. barrel w/o ejector rod, full nickel or royal blue/case hardened finish, ivory grips. Approx. 280 mfg. 1984-85.

	$1,700	$1,450	$1,300	$1,100	$900	$800	$750

Add 10% for original nickel finish.

* *Storekeeper's Model SAA (3rd Generation - Current Mfg.)* - .44-40 WCF or .45 LC cal., 4 in. barrel w/o ejector rod, blue/case hardened finish. New 2008.

MSR $1,290	$1,290	$995	$825	$725	$650	$600	$550

CUSTOM & SPECIAL ENGRAVED SAA EDITIONS (3RD GENERATION) - beginning in 1976, with the introduction of the "New Model" SAA (3rd Generation), the Colt Custom Shop produced many custom and special edition engraved Single Army Action revolvers. According to Mr. Don Wilkerson, author of *The Post-War Single Action Revolver 1976-1986*, "the term custom edition is defined as a group of identical revolvers assembled under the direction of the Custom Gun Shop at Colt's and sold through the normal distribution system. A custom edition differs from a special edition in that special editions are a group of revolvers made up to a customer's unique specifications, and sold as a group to one purchaser...." While the exact number is not known, it is thought that approx. 3,500 SAAs have been engraved since 1976. Since each edition is unique, values vary widely, depending upon the notability of the engraver, the amount and type of coverage, and the number produced. Models listed below are recent Colt Custom Editions.

* *SAA Engraved European Model* - 9mm Para. cal., nickel finish only, 4 3/4, 5 1/2, or 7 1/2 in. barrel, rosewood grips with silver medallions, 40-43 oz. Mfg. 1991-92 only.

	$1,650	$1,395	$1,195	$1,065	$855	$750	$610

Last MSR was $1,990.

* *SAA Engraved U.S. Model* - .45 ACP cal., royal blue finish only, 4 3/4, 5 1/2, or 7 1/2 in. barrel, walnut grips, 40-43 oz. Mfg. 1991-92 only.

	$1,850	$1,325	$1,100	$985	$795	$675	$565

Last MSR was $1,960.

GRADING - PPGS™	100%	98%	95%	90%	80%	70%	60%

∗ SAA Old World Engravers Sampler - .45 LC cal., 5 1/2 in. barrel, nickel finish, buffalo horn grips, includes four unique styles of engraving. Mfg. 1997-98, reintroduced 2001-2002.

	$2,975	$2,450	$2,000	$1,740	$1,495	$1,215	$1,000

Last MSR was $3,445.

∗ Legend Rodeo/Legend Rodeo II SAA - disc. 1998.

	$1,950	$1,500	$1,250	$1,100	$895	$785	$630

Last MSR was $2,450.

∗ 125th Anniversary Edition SAA - 2 line patent date, "45 COLT" on left side of barrel, and address on top of barrel, beveled cylinder, fire blue finish. 1,000 mfg. 1997-2002.

	$1,600	$1,150	$825	N/A	N/A	N/A	N/A

Last MSR was $2,070.

∗ Model P w/B Coverage Engraving - choice of cals. and barrel lengths, blue or nickel finish, features unsigned standard American scroll B engraving coverage. Current mfg.

MSR $2,319		$2,250	$2,000	$1,750	$1,500	$1,250	$1,000	$875

Add $231 for nickel finish.

FACTORY ENGRAVED SAAs (3RD GENERATION)

FACTORY ENGRAVED SAAs (3RD GENERATION) - the rarity of the SAA configuration in addition to the notability of the engraver will make the difference on the premiums commanded. 3rd Generation factory engraved SAAs were produced in much greater numbers than were 2nd Generation SAAs. Over 80% of engraved 3rd Generation SAAs are .45 LC caliber, the majority have 7 1/2 in. barrels, and some variation of blue finish. Grade "C" (41% of engraved mfg.) and Grade "D" (24% of engraved mfg.) dominate production.

Use the following add-ons as general guidelines for values on recently manufactured 3rd Generation SAAs.

Add approx. 10% for original nickel finish.
Add 25% for 4 3/4 in. barrel.
Add 15% for 5 1/2 in. barrel.
Add 10% for calibers other than .45 LC.
Add 30% for factory ivory grips.
Add 10% for original blue cardboard or plastic box.

During 1978-79, Colt engraved as many as 300-500 guns on a single factory order. Unfortunately, the quality on many SAAs during this period was substandard, and as a result, these guns usually cap at approx. $2,000. If the level of quality is similar to today's SAAs, the price will also be similar. Today's Custom Shop is once again producing excellent quality engraved SAAs, and Class C engraved revolvers (with ivory grips) are currently priced in the $3,750 range.

SAA CUSTOM SHOP ENGRAVING PRICES - PRE-1997

SAA CUSTOM SHOP ENGRAVING PRICES - PRE-1997 - values below represent 1995 published SAA Custom Shop A-D engraving options before the company started separate Standard, Expert, and Master level pricing during 1997. For current Colt Custom Shop engraving prices, please refer to the "Colt Custom Shop Engraving - Current Mfg." section below.

Add $1,163 for Class "A" engraving (25% metal coverage).
Add $2,324 for Class "B" engraving (50% metal coverage).
Add $3,487 for Class "C" engraving (75% metal coverage).
Add $4,647 for Class "D" engraving (100% metal coverage).
Add an additional 13% (approx.) for buntline engraving.

Standard Engraving was performed mostly by standard level factory engravers and engraving options generally included A-D style coverage. Typically, gold work was not performed by these engravers and specimens are mostly unsigned. Expert Engravers executed classic American style scroll, without gold work, and may have signed their work.

COLT CUSTOM SHOP ENGRAVING, SAA & SEMI-AUTO, CURRENT MFG.

The listings below represent both current and discontinued Custom Shop engraving prices for the various frame sizes, amount of engraving coverage (A = 25% coverage, B = 50% coverage, C = 75% coverage, and D = 100% coverage), and the three levels of engraving execution (i.e., Standard,

GRADING - PPGS™	100%	98%	95%	90%	80%	70%	60%

Expert, and Master levels). SAAs are considered large frame, revolvers and full-size Government Models are considered medium frame, and Government Model 380s are considered small frame. Most buyers of engraved Colt SAAs today are very knowledgeable, and many of them are no longer satisfied with Standard types of patterns and styles. As a result, those engraved guns with the rarest production variances coupled with unique engraving done at an Expert or better level are currently more desireable than their counterparts with Standard engraving patterns. Colt currently employs three full-time engravers at the factory, in addition to several outside sources (at all engraving levels). The name of the engraver is available only when ordering either the Expert or the Master level of engraving.

Large Frame Size

Other Custom Shop options are priced on request, including a wide variety of gold/silver inlays, panel scenes, color enamel inlays, gold/silver frame outlines, etc.

Add 20% to large frame pricing for Buntline Models.
Add $1,139 for A Standard engraving.
Add $1,518 for B Standard, $2,057 for B Expert (signed), or $3,812 for B Master (signed) level engraving.
Add $1,771 for C Standard, $3,025 for C Expert (signed), or $5,542 for C Master (signed) level engraving.
Add $2,024 for D Standard, $4,356 for D Expert (signed), or $7,623 for D Master (signed) level engraving.

Medium Frame Size

Medium frame engraving was discontinued.

Add $900 for Standard A level engraving.
Add $1,200 for B Standard, $1,700 for B Expert, or $3,150 for B Master level engraving.
Add $1,400 for C Standard, $2,500 for C Expert, or $4,538 for C Master level engraving.
Add $1,600 for D Standard, $3,600 for D Expert, or $6,300 for D Master level engraving.

Small Frame Size

Factory small frame engraving was disc. 1998.

Subtract 20% from small frame pricing for Mustang Models.
Add $400 for A Standard, $600 for A Expert, or $800 for A Master level engraving.
Add $600 for B Standard, $800 for B Expert, or $1,000 for B Master level engraving.
Add $800 for C Standard, $1,100 for C Expert, or $1,500 for C Master level engraving.
Add $1,100 for D Standard, $1,300 for D Expert, or $1,900 for D Master level engraving.

REVOLVERS: SAA, SCOUT MODEL

100% values below assume NIB condition. Subtract 10% without box.

FRONTIER SCOUT (Q or F SUFFIX) - .22 LR or .22 Mag. (introduced after 1960) cal., "Q" or "F" suffix, blue with bright alloy frame, all blue, or duotone ("Q" models only) finish (rare), 4 3/4 or 9 1/2 (Buntline) in. barrel, available with interchangeable cylinders after 1964, black composition or walnut grips, approx. 246,000 mfg. 1957-70.

	100%	98%	95%	90%	80%	70%	60%
	$600	$425	$325	$250	$200	$175	$150

Add 10% for extra cylinder.
Add 20% for Buntline model.
Add 25% for "Q" suffix with duo-tone finish (mfg. 1957-58 only).
Add 10% for original box.

FRONTIER SCOUT (K SUFFIX) - Zamac alloy frame version of "Q" Model with "K" suffix, blue or nickel finish with walnut stocks, approx. 44,000 mfg. 1960-70.

	100%	98%	95%	90%	80%	70%	60%
	$600	$425	$325	$250	$200	$175	$150

Add 100% for double cased Scout set.
Add 150% for double cased Scout Buntline set.
Add 10% for original box.

This model used the alloy Zamac for manufacture (as opposed to aluminum in the "Q" and "F" suffix models), and specimens are 6 oz. heavier as a result.

GRADING - PPGS™	100%	98%	95%	90%	80%	70%	60%

FRONTIER SCOUT '62 (P SUFFIX) - blue finish version of "K" Model, except has "P" suffix, staglite grips, approx. 68,000 mfg. 1962-70.

	$600	$450	$375	$275	$225	$175	$160

Add 20% for Buntline.
Add 10% for original box.
Add 50% with extra cylinders.
Add 100% for double cased Scout set.
Add 150% for double cased Scout Buntline set.

PEACEMAKER SCOUT - .22 LR/.22 Mag. cal., color case hardened steel frame, 4.4, 4 3/4, 6, or 7 1/2 (nicknamed Buntline Model but may be marked Peacemaker or Buntline) in. barrel, black composition grips, furnished with interchangeable .22 LR/.22 Mag. cylinders, approx. 190,000 mfg. 1970-77.

	$550	$400	$350	$275	$225	$175	$150

Add 20% for 4.4 in. barrel.
Add 30% for 4 3/4 in. barrel.
Add 10% for original box.
Subtract 10% if without extra cylinder.

This model can be identified by its "G" or "L" serial number prefix.

NEW FRONTIER SCOUT - similar features as Peacemaker Model, except with flat-top frame, ramp front and adj. rear sight, mfg. 1970-1977. Reintroduced in 1982 without convertible .22 Mag. cylinder and added cross bolt safety, available in Coltguard finish, all blue finish became standard in 1985. Mfg. disc. 1986.

	$500	$375	$300	$250	$200	$175	$150

Last MSR was $181.

Add 15% for Buntline model or 4 3/4 in. barrel.

PISTOLS: SEMI-AUTO, DISC.

Most of the semi-auto pistol models listed in the various pistol categories can have their original configuration confirmed with a Colt factory letter. To receive a letter, write: COLT ARCHIVE PROPERTIES, LLC, P.O. Box 1868, Hartford, CT, 06144. The research fee for these pistols is typically either $75 or $100, depending on the model. If they cannot obtain additional information on the variation you request, they will refund $50.

Until several years ago, the Single Action Army revolver commanded the most attention among Colt handgun collectors. Since 1987, Colt Semi-Autos have been in tremendous demand and have out-accelerated many other areas of Colt collecting. Because condition and originality play such a key role in determining Colt Semi-Auto prices, many variations have had their values pushed upward to the point where it is difficult to accurately determine a realistic price, especially on those models in 98% original condition or better. As a result, some of the rarer models seldomly encountered in true 100% original condition have had their values deleted since extreme rarity precludes accurate price evaluation. As always, the hardest prices to ascertain when firearms market conditions are bullish are the 98-100% values.

MODEL 1900 - .38 ACP cal., 6 in. barrel, blue, plain walnut grips - checkered hard rubber grips after S/N 2,450, high spur hammer, sight safety. Mfg. 1900-03.

	N/A	$15,000	$11,000	$7,600	$5,500	$4,000	$3,000

Add 100% for U.S. marked 1st Army contracts (100 guns serial numbered 11-207).
Add 75% for U.S. marked Navy contracts (250 guns serial numbered 1,001-1,250).
Add 60% for U.S. marked 2nd Army contracts (200 guns serial numbered 1,501-1,700).
Subtract 30%-50% for sight safety altered (factory refinished).

This model is serial numbered approx. between 1-4,274.
Somewhere between serial number 2,200 and 2,450, Colt began altering the sights to fixed sights in the production process, shipping both types. By approx. serial number 3,300, most guns shipped were altered during production. Guns altered during production are not refinished. Altered guns below serial number 2,200 were refinished, or at least had the slides refinished.

GRADING - PPGS™	100%	98%	95%	90%	80%	70%	60%

MODEL 1902 SPORTING - .38 ACP, 6 in. barrel, blue, fixed sights, checkered hard rubber grips, no safety, high spur hammer and round hammer. Mfg. 1902-08.

	N/A	$5,750	$4,250	$3,250	$2,500	$1,750	$900

This model is serial numbered approx. 4,275-11,000 and 30,000-30,190.

MODEL 1902 MILITARY - .38 ACP cal., 6 in. barrel, blue, similar to 1902 Sporting, hammer changed to spur type in 1908, checkered black hard rubber grips, lanyard swivel on bottom rear of left grip. Mfg. 1902-29.

	N/A	$5,750	$4,500	$3,500	$2,500	$1,500	$900

Add 30% for front slide checkering.
Add 20% with original box and instructions.
This model is serial numbered approx. 11,000-16,000 and 30,200-43,266.

MODEL 1902 MILITARY-U.S. ARMY MARKED - similar specifications to 1902 Military, only serial number range 15,001-15,200.

	N/A	$18,000	$15,000	$12,500	$10,000	$8,750	$6,000

MODEL 1903 POCKET (.38 ACP) - .38 ACP cal., 3 3/4 or 4 1/2 in. barrel, blue finish standard, checkered black hard rubber grips, similar to 1902 Sporting, but 4 1/2 in. barrel, 7 1/2 in. overall. Mfg. 1903-29.

$5,000	$4,000	$2,750	$2,000	$1,250	$900	$750

Add 30% for early round hammer.
Add 20% with original box and instructions.
This model is serial numbered approx. 16,000-47,226.

MODEL 1903 POCKET (MODEL M .32 ACP) - .32 ACP cal., 4 in. barrel, charcoal blue, checkered hard rubber grips, hammerless, slide lock and grip safeties, barrel bushing. Mfg. 1903-46.

$1,200	$1,000	$650	$500	$400	$325	$275

Add 20% for nickel finish (mostly w/pearl grips).
Add 60% for first model (Type I) mfg. 1903-1911 if in 100%-98% condition. If lower than 98%, add 20%.
Add 30% for Type II if in 100%-98% condition.
Add 50% with original box and instructions.
Type I - 32 ACPs have a 4 in. barrel, barrel bushing, no magazine safety, and are serial numbered 1-71,999.
Type II - 32 ACPs still retain their barrel bushing but have a 3 3/4 in. barrel and were mfg. from 1908-1910. They are serial numbered 72,000-105,050.
Type III - 32 ACPs do not have a barrel bushing and were mfg. from 1910-1926. They are serial numbered 105,051-468,096.
Type IV - 32 ACPs have the added magazine safety (of which there are both the commercial and "U.S. Property" variations). They are serial numbered 468,097-554,446.

✴ *Model 1903 Parkerized* - U.S. Property, 3 1/4 in. barrel, no barrel bushing, magazine safety, serial numbered 554,447-572,214.

$2,000	$1,500	$1,100	$900	$750	$550	$500

Add 50% for blue U.S. Property S/N 554,447 - approx. 562,000.
Add 20% with original box and instructions.
The 100% value on this model assumes NIB condition.

✴ *Model 1903 General Officer's Pistol* - .32 ACP cal., blue (mfg. until 1942) or parkerized (mfg. started 1942) finish.

✴ *Model 1903 Pocket Parkerized*

	N/A	$2,800	$1,800	$1,500	$1,200	$975	$875

✴ *Model 1903 Pocket Blue Finish*

	N/A	$3,200	$2,500	$2,100	$1,750	$1,500	$1,200

Values above assume issue to a General, and there must be paperwork to link the gun to the recipient. Otherwise, these values do not apply - see U.S. Property above for applicable values.

GRADING - PPGS™	100%	98%	95%	90%	80%	70%	60%

MODEL 1905 - .45 ACP cal., 5 in. barrel, blue, fixed sights, checkered walnut stocks, similar to Model 1902 Sporting. Mfg. 1905-11.

	N/A	$7,200	$5,000	$3,800	$3,000	$2,000	$1,500

Add 50% for factory slotted specimens (500 manufactured).
Add 250% for 1907 U.S. Military Contract variation (205 manufactured).
The shoulder stock option for this pistol is exceedingly rare. Depending on the condition, this accessory can add $7,500-$10,000 to the price of the gun.

MODEL 1908 POCKET (MODEL M .380 ACP) - .380 ACP cal., first issue, 3 3/4 in. barrel only, similar to Pocket Model M .32 ACP, except chambered for .380 ACP. Mfg. 1908-40.

	$1,595	$1,425	$1,000	$750	$650	$600	$350

Add 15% for Type I (see explanation below).
Add $100 for nickel finish.
Add 50% for factory pearl grips.
100% values assume NIB condition. Subtract 15% if without cardboard box. Pearl grips are normally encountered with nickel finish on this model.
Type I - 380 ACPs with barrel bushing and were mfg. 1908-1910 (6,251 mfg.). They are serial numbered 1-6,251.
Type II - 380 ACPs do not have a barrel bushing and were mfg. 1910-1926. They are serial numbered 6,252-92,893.
Type III - 380 ACPs have the added magazine safety (of which there are both the commercial and "U.S. Property" variations). They are serial numbered 92,894-134,499.

* *Model 1908 "U.S. Property"* - blue finish only, U.S. Property. Serial numbered 134,500-138,000.

	$3,000	$2,250	$1,750	$1,300	$950	$750	$550

* *Model 1908 General Officer's Pistol* - .380 ACP cal., blue finish only.

	$4,000	$3,250	$2,700	$2,300	$1,950	$1,550	$1,300

Values above assume issue to a General, and there must be paperwork to link the gun to the recipient. Otherwise, these values do not apply - see U.S. Property above for applicable values.

VEST POCKET MODEL 1908-HAMMERLESS - .25 ACP cal., 2 in. barrel, fixed sights, checkered hard rubber grips on early models, walnut on later, magazine disconnect added on guns made after 1916. Mfg. 1908-1946.

* *Vest Pocket Model 1908 Blue finish*

	$800	$700	$550	$425	$350	$275	$200

* *Vest Pocket Model 1908 Nickel finish*

	$1,150	$950	$800	$600	$500	$400	$325

Add 50% for factory pearl grips.
100% values assume NIB condition. Subtract 15% if without cardboard box in 95% or better condition only.
This model was also supplied with a suede purse. Add $150-$200, depending on condition.
Add 200% if "U.S. Property" marked.

MODEL 1909 - .45 ACP cal., straight handle design, 5 in. barrel, checkered walnut grips, approx. 22 mfg., ultra rare.

Extreme rarity factor precludes accurate price evaluation by individual condition factors. Specimens that are original and over 90% have sold for over $35,000 recently.

MODEL 1910 - .45 ACP cal., while not a production model, this gun is probably the most desirable semi-auto Colt pistol.

A nice specimen at a recent auction was gavelled down at $195,000.

PISTOLS: SEMI-AUTO, GOVT. MODEL 1911 COMMERCIAL VARIATIONS

MODEL 1911 COMMERCIAL - .45 ACP cal., 5 in. barrel, fixed sights, 7 shot mag., flat main spring housing, polished blue finish only, checkered walnut grips. Denoted by "C" preceding serial number, approx. ser. no. range C1-C138,532.

GRADING - PPGS™	100%	98%	95%	90%	80%	70%	60%

Watch for fakes. Colt licensed other companies to manufacture under government contracts, 39 oz. Mfg. 1912-1925.

Most M1911 variations listed below are not as collectible if under 60% original condition. However, they are still very desirable as shooters, and values (if in original condition) will approximate the 60% prices if in good mechanical condition.

Colt Model 1911s continue to enjoy high demand as of this writing and prices continue to be strong in the 95%-100% condition factors. Be careful on the 98%+ condition specimens, especially the rarer variations. Some collectors are now requiring a potential high-dollar Model 1911 to pass a metallurgical X-ray examination before purchasing.

✻ *Model 1911 High Polish Blue* - mfg. 1912 through ser. no. 4,500.

	N/A	$15,000	$12,000	$9,000	$6,500	$4,000	$2,000

✻ *Model 1911 Regular Finish* - pistols mfg. after ser. no. 4,500.

	N/A	$3,750	$2,750	$1,850	$1,200	$1,000	$750

Subtract 15% if without cardboard box in 100% condition only.

Approx. 138,532 were mfg. between 1912-25.
100% values assume NIB condition.

PISTOLS: SEMI-AUTO, GOVT. MODEL 1911 MILITARY VARIATIONS

All pistols in this section are .45 ACP (11.25mm) cal., unless otherwise noted. Values for original 98%+ M1911 Military Models have risen considerably in recent years, and as a result, values for original mint guns can double and even sometimes triple the values of 98% condition.

Over 2,550,000 M1911 pistols were ordered for WWI and WWII by the U.S. Government, but approx. 650,000 were mfg. between 1911-1925. Those pistols with a parkerized finish will indicate post-WWI reworking, usually marked with an arsenal code (ie. AA-AUGUSTA ARSENAL, SA-SPRINGFIELD ARSENAL, etc.). These reworks do not have the same values as original, unaltered specimens and prices generally are in the $425-$650 range.

COLT MFG. MODEL 1911 MILITARY - right side of slide marked "MODEL OF 1911 U.S. ARMY", blue finish only (NOT parkerized unless reworked).

Recent sales for original mint examples of the Model 1911 Military are as follows: $14,000 for 1912 mfg., depending on the variation (there are three), $7,000 for 1913-1915 mfg., $7,500 for 1916 mfg., $6,000 for 1917-1918 mfg. and $6,000 for 1918 later mfg. (black Army finish).

✻ *Model 1911 (1912 mfg.)* - includes three variations.

	N/A	$10,000	$7,750	$6,000	$5,000	$4,000	$3,000

✻ *Model 1911 (1913-1915 mfg.)*

	N/A	$5,000	$4,500	$4,000	$3,500	$2,000	$1,500

Add 100% for the first 114 pistols with oversize "United States Property" marking.
Add 75% for pistols in the ser. no. range 115-2,400.

✻ *Model 1911 (1916 mfg.)* - only 4,200 produced.

	N/A	$5,500	$4,750	$4,000	$3,500	$2,000	$1,500

✻ *Model 1911 (1917-1918 early mfg.)* - early blue finish.

	N/A	$4,250	$3,200	$2,050	$1,500	$1,200	$1,000

✻ *Model 1911 (1917-1918 mfg.)* - can be determined by black Army finish.

	N/A	$4,250	$3,200	$2,050	$1,500	$1,200	$1,000

✻ *Model 1911 (1919-1925 mfg.)*

	N/A	$3,500	$3,000	$2,000	$1,500	$1,200	$1,000

NORTH AMERICAN ARMS COMPANY - less than 100 mfg. in Quebec, Canada during 1918 only, blue finish. Be very aware of fakes, as this variation is perhaps the most desirable Colt WWI Govt. semi-auto.

	N/A	N/A	$30,000	$26,000	$22,000	$16,000	$12,000

Note: a characteristic of the North American is the poor finish. The very best condition specimens will be in the 80%-90% range. All mint 100% specimens encountered in this model appear to have been refinished.

98% original condition NAA pistols have recently sold as high as $45,000, w/o auction.

GRADING - PPGS™	100%	98%	95%	90%	80%	70%	60%

REMINGTON - UMC - over 21,500 mfg. (ser. numbered 1-21,676) in 1918-1919 only, blue finish.

	N/A	$5,950	$4,600	$3,500	$3,000	$2,500	$2,000

Most mint 100% specimens encountered in this model have been refinished - be careful. Mint original pistols are currently selling as high as $8,500.

SPRINGFIELD ARMORY - approx. 30,000 mfg. 1914-1915, blue finish.

	N/A	$5,950	$4,600	$3,500	$3,000	$2,500	$2,000

Serialization is 72,751-83,855, 102,597-107,596, 113,497-120,566, and 125,567-133,186. Most mint 100% specimens encountered in this model have been refinished - be careful. Mint original pistols are currently selling in the $7,500 range.

U.S. NAVY - over 31,000 mfg. for U.S. Navy contract between 1911-1914 in defined serial ranges, blue finish. Marked "MODEL OF 1911 U.S. NAVY" on right slide side.

	N/A	$7,500	$5,000	$3,750	$2,750	$1,750	$1,250

Add 100% for specimens under ser. no. 3,500.

U.S. Navy specimens are seldom found in over 80% original condition because of the corrosive factor encountered while at sea.

U.S. MARINE CORPS. - approx. 13,500 mfg. between 1911-13 and 1916-18 in defined serial ranges, blue finish, right side of slide marked "MODEL OF 1911 U.S. ARMY".

	N/A	$7,500	$5,500	$4,500	$3,500	$3,000	$2,250

Mint original specimens are currently selling in the $13,000-$15,000 range.

WWI BRITISH SERIES - .455 cal., serialized W19,000-W110,695, marked "CALIBRE 455", blue finish, proofed with broad arrow British Ordnance punch. Mfg. 1915-19.

	N/A	$4,500	$3,350	$2,600	$2,000	$1,200	$1,000

Subtract 30% if converted to .45 ACP cal.

Many WWI British-series M1911s were exported back to the U.S. following WWI and were converted to .45 ACP. Usually, a "5" has been crossed out of the original cal. designation. Mint original specimens in thismodel have been selling in the $7,500 - $8,500 range.

BRITISH RAF REWORK - this variation is the WWI British series re-issued to RAF officers in the early 1920s, blue finish, differentiated by hand-stamped "RAF" or "R.A.F." on left side of frame.

	N/A	$4,250	$3,250	$2,600	$2,000	$1,200	$1,000

Mint original specimens have been selling in the $5,500 - $6,000 range.

A.J. SAVAGE MUNITIONS CO. - mfg. slides only, blue finish, marked in middle on left side of slide with flaming ordnance bomb with "S" in center.

	N/A	$2,000	$1,750	$1,250	$1,000	$800	$700

Mint original specimens have been selling in the $3,250 - $3,500 range.

NORWEGIAN TRIAL MODEL 1911 COLT - 11.25mm cal., approx. 300 mfg. with "C" prefix in 1913-14 and 1917, usually encountered in 90% or less condition.

	N/A	$4,500	$3,750	$2,750	$2,000	$1,200	$800

These guns were ordered for Norwegian service evaluation and were mfg. by Colt in Hartford, CT.

NORWEGIAN MODEL 1912 11.25MM - 11.25mm cal., mfg. under license from Colt's during 1917, "M1912" slide designation. Approx. 95 mfg.

	N/A	$8,500	$7,500	$6,000	$5,000	$4,000	$3,200

NORWEGIAN 1914 11.25MM - this model has a distinctive extended slide release, all parts should be serial numbered and have numerous matching numbers, approx. 32,750 mfg. 1918-1947, mostly military contract, commercial production was very limited. Most have been refinished.

	N/A	$2,250	$1,650	$1,450	$1,250	$850	$700

Add 250% for Waffenamt Nazi mfg. (mfg. 1945 only).

Serial ranges with corresponding year of manufacture on this model are as follows: 96-600 - 1918, 601-1,150 - 1919, 1,151-1,650 (Naval Artillery) - 1920, 1,651-2,200 - 1921, 2,201- 2,950 -

GRADING - PPGS™	100%	98%	95%	90%	80%	70%	60%

1922, 2,951-4,610 - 1923, 4,611-6,700 - 1924, 6,701-8,940 - 1925, 8,941-11,820 - 1926, 11,821-15,900 - 1927, 15,901-20,100 - 1928, 20,101-21,440 - 1929, 21,441-21,940 - 1932, 21,941-22,040 - 1933, 22,041-22,141 - 1934, 22,142-22,211 - 1936, 22,212-22,311 - 1939, 22,312-22,361 - 1940, 22,362-26,460 - 1941, 26,461-29,614 - 1942, 29,615-32,335 (Waffenamt Nazi proofed) - 1945, 32,336-32,854 - (last original production) 1947.

Nazi production of the M1914 began in 1941. Between 1941-42, approx. 7,000 pistols were mfg. without Waffenamt stampings. Nazi proofed guns (all 1945 dated) began in the mid-29,000 serial range, and 920 were mfg. with the Nazi Eagle.

ARGENTINE CONTRACT MODEL 1916 - identified by the Argentine seal on top of slide, 1,000 mfg. in ser. range C20,001-C21,000, mfg. 1916.

	$2,200	$1,600	$1,450	$1,200	$800	$700	$600

Most specimens of this model have been refinished.

RUSSIAN CONTRACT - approx. 51,000 mfg. in U.S. as commerical guns with random serial numbers approx. C23000-C89000, blue finish, identified by cyrillic inscription on left side of frame (translates to English Order). Mfg. 1916-17.

N/A	$8,750	$4,500	$4,000	$3,250	$2,500	$2,000

This contract is seldolm encountered - beware of fakes.
Mint original specimens have been selling in the $12,500 - $15,000 range.

PISTOLS: SEMI-AUTO, GOVT. MODEL 1911A1 COMMERCIAL VARIATIONS

All pistols in this section are .45 ACP cal., unless otherwise noted.

MODEL 1911A1 - commercial blue finish or parkerized, checkered walnut grips, checkered arched mainspring housing and longer grip safety spur. As in the Model 1911, Colt licensed other companies to produce under govt. contract during WWII. Mfg. 1925-1970.

Most M1911A1 variations listed below are not as collectible if under 60% original condition. However, they are still very desirable as shooters, and values (if in original condition) will approximate the 60% prices if in good mechanical condition.

MODEL 1911A1 PRE-WWII COLT COMMERCIAL - "C" preceding serial number, mfg. 1925-1942. Approx. ser. no. range C138,533-C215,000.

	$5,500	$4,000	$3,200	$2,500	$1,750	$1,300	$900

Add 50% for nickel finish.
Add 20% with original box and instructions.
Add 20% for Swartz safety.

MODEL 1911A1 1946-1970 COLT COMMERCIAL - 5 in. barrel, fixed sights, "C" prefix until 1950 when changed to "C" suffix. Approx. 196,000 mfg. 1946-1970.

❋ *Model 1911A1 1946-1950 Mfg.* - "C" Prefix with serial numbers C221,000-C240,227.

	$2,000	$1,700	$1,500	$1,200	$875	$750	$575

❋ *Model 1911A1 1950-1970 Mfg.* - "C" Suffix with serial numbers 240,228C-336,169C.

	$1,850	$1,500	$1,200	$950	$875	$750	$600

Add 10% for nickel finish.

SUPER .38 AUTOMATIC PISTOL - identical to Govt. Model .45, except chambered for .38 Super cal., blue or nickel finish. Mfg. 1928-70.

❋ *Super .38 Automatic Pistol Pre-War*

	$6,000	$4,750	$3,750	$2,750	$2,000	$1,500	$1,000

❋ *Super .38 Automatic Pistol 2nd Model*

	$2,750	$2,400	$2,000	$1,500	$1,100	$800	$750

❋ *Super .38 Automatic Pistol 3rd Model*

	$2,500	$2,000	$1,800	$1,200	$900	$750	$600

❋ *Super .38 Automatic Pistol 4th Model*

	$2,200	$1,800	$1,600	$1,000	$800	$700	$600

GRADING - PPGS™	100%	98%	95%	90%	80%	70%	60%

* Super .38 Automatic Pistol CS Prefix

	$2,200	$1,800	$1,600	$1,000	$800	$700	$600

Add approx. 50% for nickel finish.

Pre-war variations are serialized below approx. 37,000.

The 2nd Model may be differentiated by noticing the heavier barrel and Rampant Colt on right side. The 3rd Model has a fat barrel with Rampant Colt on left side. The 4th Model has a thin barrel and Rampant Colt on left side.

SUPER MATCH .38 - similar to Super .38, but hand honed action, match grade barrel, recent research indicates that 2,392 had adj. sights, 857 were supplied with fixed sights, and on 557 models the type of sights was not indicated. 4,001 mfg. 1934-1947. Examine carefully for fakes.

Buyer beware - fakes are known to exist!

The first Super Match noted is ser. no. 15550, a fixed sight model, and was shipped on Feb. 9, 1934.

The lowest serial number is 14310, and was shipped on July 10, 1934. However, two serial numbers were much lower than the expected serial number ranges. Ser. no. 2253 was shipped on June 18, 1940 and ser. no. 10312 was shipped on Sept. 25, 1935. It is unknown if these guns were roll marked Super Match, but they were noted in the Colt Records as Super Match models.

The first adj. sight Super Match is ser. no. 17091, and was shipped on Feb. 7, 1935.

The last adj. sight Super Match noted is ser. no. 35731, and was shipped on Jan. 17, 1947.

The highest ser. no. Super Match is ser. no. 35999, a fixed sight model, and was shipped on Oct. 20, 1939.

Approx. 40 were mfg. with match barrels and/or hand fitted actions, w/o mention of the Super Match markings.

Total .38 Super Match pistols recorded in the Colt shipping records is 3,961. 2,250 were noted as having adj. sight, and 831 were noted as having fixed sights.

* Super Match .38 Fixed sights

	$10,000	$8,000	$6,500	$5,250	$4,000	$3,000	$2,000

* Super Match .38 Adj. sights

	$11,500	$9,000	$7,500	$6,250	$5,000	$4,000	$3,000

For adj. sight values to apply, the sight must be an original factory installed Stevens sight. After market adj. sights are not applicable. Be cautious of fixed sight Super Matches converted to adj. sight. A Colt historical letter is available for this model for $100.

There were 3,909 .38 Super Matches manufactured from Feb. 16, 1934 - Jan. 17, 1947. 998 had fixed sights and 2,911 had adj. sights.

MATCH .38 AMU - .38 rimless Spl. cal. (cartridges were mfg. by Win.), this variation was mfg. by Colt from a .38 Super frame (and has .38 Super serialization) with a .38 AMU conversion kit slide, the Army took .45 frames and assembled their guns using .38 AMU kits, blue finish.

* Match .38 AMU Colt mfg. (unmodified)

	$3,500	$2,700	$2,200	$1,900	$1,675	$1,400	$1,100

* Match .38 AMU Army modified

	$2,200	$1,900	$1,500	$1,200	$1,000	$800	$700

* Match .38: AMU kit only

	$850	$750	$500	$400	$350	$325	$295

On this configuration, the barrel, slide, and mag. were marked ".38 AMU".

SUPER MATCH .38 MS - .38 Super cal., 1961 mfg., serial numbered 101MS - 855MS, 754 total mfg, same configuration as the .38 Midrange.

	$5,000	$4,000	$3,000	$2,200	$1,900	$1,500	$1,300

1968-1969 BB TRANSITIONAL - denoted by BB prefix on serial number.

	$1,650	$1,375	$1,100	$945	$875	$750	$600

GRADING - PPGS™	100%	98%	95%	90%	80%	70%	60%

.45 ACP TO .22 LR CONVERSION UNIT - consists of slide assembly, barrel, bushing, floating chamber, ejector, recoil spring and guide, fitted with Stevens adj. rear sight, mfg. 1938 to 1947. Colt Master adj. sight 1947-54.

	$650	$600	$550	$425	$350	$275	$200

> Add 150% for prewar mfg. ("U" prefix S/N on top of slide).
> Add 225% for pre-war documented Marine Corp units.

.22 LR TO .45 ACP CONVERSION UNIT - converted service Ace .22 to .45 ACP cal. Mfg. 1938-1942. Very rare - 112 mfg.

	$4,500	$3,500	$2,500	$1,750	$1,100	$800	$700

> Add 50% for original box and instructions.
> These units have "U" prefixed serial numbers on top of slide.

PISTOLS: SEMI-AUTO, GOVT. MODEL 1911A1 MILITARY VARIATIONS

All pistols in this section are .45 ACP (11.25mm) cal., unless otherwise noted. Values for original 98%+ M1911A1s have risen considerably in recent years, and as a result, values for original mint guns can double and even sometimes triple the values of 98% condition. Inspect carefully for arsenal reworks (so marked by proofing, normally on left side of frame above or behind trigger), and reparkerizing.

COLT MFG. MODEL 1911A1 MILITARY - approx. 1,643,068 mfg. between 1924-1945, ser. nos. 700,000 - on up, right side of frame marked "M1911A1 U.S. ARMY", bright blue finish up to approx. ser. no. 780,000, parkerized finish after that. - standard military finish (WWII mfg.).

	N/A	$3,200	$2,700	$2,200	$2,000	$1,600	$1,000

> Add 200% for 1937 Navy (S/N 710,001 - 712,345) Blue.
> 1937 Navy variations with blue finish are currently selling in the $1,000 - $7,000 range, depending on original condition.
> Add 250% for 1938 Army (S/N 712,350 - 713,645) Blue.
> 1938 Army varitions with blue finish are currently selling in the $1,500 - $9,000 range, depending on original condition.
> Add 200% for 1939 Navy (S/N 713,646 - 717,281) Blue.
> 1939 Navy varitions with blue finish are currently selling in the $1,000 - $7,000 range, depending on original condition.
> Early 1911A1 military models with bright blue finish are currently selling in the $1,000 - $7,000 price range, depending on condition.
> Add 150% for Blue guns outside these serial ranges.
> Add 150% for 1942 Navy (S/N 793,658 - 797,639) Parkerized.

A large grouping of over 7,000 Commercial 1911A1s was transferred to the U.S. government. These pistols had their commercial serial numbers crudely removed (in ser. range 860,000 - 866,000) and renumbered with a new military serial number. Some of these guns are unusual as the frames and slides have been cut for the Schwartz safety. This variation is rare, and a 25%-50% premium exists depending on the condition.

✳ *Model 1911A1 General Officer's Pistol*

	N/A	$4,500	$3,600	$3,000	$2,500	$2,000	$1,500

Values above assume issue to a General, and there must be paperwork to link the gun to the recipient.

DRAKE NATIONAL MATCH - Drake made slides only for use by the U.S. Army Marksmanship Unit to allow assembly of match guns.

	N/A	$2,000	$1,700	$1,400	$1,000	$850	$700

GOVERNMENT NATIONAL MATCH REWORKS - assembled by government armorers, all parts marked "NM". parkerized finish. Most will be "S.A." marked.

	N/A	$2,000	$1,700	$1,400	$1,000	$850	$700

> Add 25% for Air Force pistols marked "AFPG" on slide.
> These pistols were made specifically for the U.S. shooting team at Camp Perry.

GRADING - PPGS™	100%	98%	95%	90%	80%	70%	60%

ITHACA - approx. 369,129 mfg. 1943-1945 in Ithaca, NY, ser. no. ranges 856,405-916,404, 1,208,674-1,279,673, 1,441,431-1,471,430, 1,743,847-1,890,503, 2,075,104-2,134,403, and 2,619,014-2,693,613. Parkerized finish.

	N/A	$2,200	$1,800	$1,500	$1,200	$1,100	$800

Add 20% with original shipping carton.

UNION SWITCH AND SIGNAL - approx. 55,000 mfg. 1943 only in Swissvale, PA, ser. no. range 1,041,405-1,096,404. Sandblast and blue finish.

	N/A	$5,000	$4,250	$3,250	$2,600	$2,000	$1,200

REMINGTON RAND - approx. 1,086,624 mfg. 1943-1945 in Syracuse, NY, ser. no. ranges 916,405-1,041,404, 1,279,649-1,441,430, 1,471,431-1,609,528, 1,743,847-1,816,641, 1,890,504-2,075,103, 2,134,404-2,244,803, and 2,380,014-2,619,013. Parkerized finish.

$2,500	$2,100	$1,900	$1,500	$1,200	$1,000	$900

Add 20% with original shipping carton.

SINGER MFG. CO. - 500 mfg. 1942 in Elizabeth, NJ, ser. no. range S800,001-S800,500. Blue finish with plastic grips.

	N/A	N/A	$37,500	$30,000	$24,000	$18,000	$14,000

The Singer 1911A1 variation is one of the most sought-after Colt models. In recent years, values have increased significantly, and as a result, many fakes have emerged. Therefore, be very cautions when contemplating a purchase. Most specimens are now recognized by ser. no. and be very cautious when contemplating a purchase. Some collectors unsure of authenticity are now requiring X-ray testing to determine originality (slide restampings, ser. no. changes, etc.).

At a recent 2007 Rock Island Auction Co. auction a 90-95% condition, example sold for $80,500.

GENERAL OFFICER'S PISTOL (M15) - standard military finish, issued by Rock Island Arsenal to Generals.

$7,500	$6,500	$5,500	$4,000	$3,200	$2,800	$2,200

MEXICAN CONTRACT - mfg. approx. 1921-27 with "C" prefix ser. nos., frames marked "EJERCITO MEXICANO", most surviving examples show much use.

	N/A	$4,500	$3,500	$2,500	$1,750	$1,200	$1,000

BRAZILIAN CONTRACT

	N/A	$5,500	$4,000	$3,000	$2,250	$1,800	$1,200

ARGENTINE CONTRACT MODEL 1927 - serial numbered 1-10,000 under the mainspring housing and on the top of slide (should be matching), must have Argentine crest and "Model 1927" on right side of slide, external serial number applied to top of slide by the Argentine Arsenal, most have been Arsenal refinished.

$1,500	$1,300	$1,100	$900	$800	$600	$500

Add 75% if original finish.

ARGENTINE MFG. - in 1927, the Argentina Arsenal "DGFM-FMAP" began manufacturing the Model 1911A1. The slide marking is two lines and reads "EJERCITO ARGENTINO SIST.COLT.CAL. 11.25mm MOD.1927".

$1,400	$1,200	$1,000	$800	$700	$600	$500

Add 50% if original finish.
Add 20% for Argentine Navy "ARMADA NACIONAL" (small shipments between 1912-1948). Markings vary on different types.

This variation is not to be confused with the Ballester Molina/Rigaud Models (sold by Hispano Argentino Fábrica de Automóviles S.A., in Buenos Aires, Argentina - also known as the HAFDASA). Please refer to the Hispano Argentino Fábrica de Automóviles S.A. section of this text.

GRADING - PPGS™	100%	98%	95%	90%	80%	70%	60%

ARGENTINE SERVICE MODEL ACE - .22 LR cal., conversion of the 1927 Argentine Contract Model, bottom right side of slide is marked "TRANSE A CAL .22 POR EST. VENTURINI S.A." Originally imported during 1996, this model was arsenal refinished and most pistols were in the 70%-95% condition range.

	$750	$700	$625	$575	$525	$500	$475

PISTOLS: SEMI-AUTO, ACE MODELS, 1931-1947 MFG.

COMMERCIAL ACE - .22 LR cal., similar to Government .45 ACP, but in .22 LR cal., 4 3/4 in. barrel, blue, adj. sights, checkered walnut grips, almost 11,000 mfg. (ser. no. range 1-10,935) 1931-41 and 1947.

	$4,500	$3,500	$2,750	$2,000	$1,500	$1,200	$1,000

Add 20% with original box and instructions.

SERVICE MODEL ACE - .22 LR cal., 5 in. barrel, blue or parkerized finish, similar to .45 ACP National Match except for caliber, has floating chamber to simulate .45 ACP recoil, limited mfg. 1935-1945.

	$7,750	$6,000	$4,500	$3,250	$2,500	$2,000	$1,200

Add 20% with original box and instructions.
Subtract 30% for parkerized finish.

This variation is marked "SERVICE MODEL" on left frame, serial numbers have "SM" prefix and have ranges to approx. 13,800. Other markings such as "U.S. PROP'Y" or "R.S." (inspectors' marks) have also been observed on this model, and can add a premium if original condition is 95% or more.

PISTOLS: SEMI-AUTO, NATIONAL MATCH MODELS - PRE-WWII

NATIONAL MATCH - .45 ACP cal., similar to Government Model, except has hand-honed action, match grade barrel, blue finish. There were a total of 4,813 National Matches manufactured between Feb. 9, 1932 - Sept. 16, 1941, serial numbered C-162997 - C-204640. 3,339 had fixed sights, and 1,474 had adj. sights.

The first National Match and lowest ser. no. C-162997, a fixed sight model, was shipped on Jan. 7, 1932.

The last National Match, ser. no. C-200288, a fixed sight model, was shipped on Feb. 22, 1942.

The highest ser. no. is C-204671, an adj. sight model, and was shipped on Aug. 20, 1941.

Of the total 4,813 National Match pistols, 1,474 were noted as having adj. sights, and 3,339 were noted as having fixed sights.

There were 45 nickel National Match models, four were engraved and two were inscribed.

There were 47 engraved National Match models, four of them nickel and eight with gold inlays.

There were fifteen inscribed National Match models, two of them nickel.

Add 20% with original box and instructions.

* *National Match Fixed sights*

	$8,250	$7,000	$5,000	$4,000	$2,750	$2,000	$1,200

* *National Match Adj. sights*

	$10,000	$8,000	$6,500	$5,000	$3,250	$2,400	$1,300

For adj. sight values to apply, the sight must be an original factory installed Stevens sight. After market adj. sights are not applicable. Be cautious of fixed sight National Match models that have been converted to adj. sight.

A Colt historical letter is available for this model for $100.

PISTOLS: SEMI-AUTO, NATIONAL MATCH MODELS - WWII & POST-WWII

Add 10% for NIB condition on discontinued models listed below.

GRADING - PPGS™	100%	98%	95%	90%	80%	70%	60%

NATIONAL MATCH - .45 ACP cal., match grade barrel, new design bushing, flat or arched (mfg. approx. 1959-64) mainspring housing, long adj. stop trigger, hand fitted slide with enlarged ejection port, adj. target sights, gold medallions in grips, "NM" suffix. Mfg. 1957-70.

	$2,400	$1,800	$1,500	$1,00	$800	$650	$600

Note: This model was the first Gold Cup National Match Model manufactured following WWII.

MKIII NATIONAL MATCH - .38 Spl. cal., similar to National Match, except chambered for .38 Spl., mid-range wadcutter, "NMR" or "MR" suffix. Mfg. 1961-74.

	$2,000	$1,600	$1,200	$1,000	$800	$700	$600

MKIV/SERIES 70 GOLD CUP NATIONAL MATCH - .45 ACP cal., flat mainspring housing, Colt blue finish accurizer barrel and bushing, adj. trigger, target hammer, solid rib, Colt-Elliason sight. Mfg. 1970-83.

	$1,450	$1,200	$1,000	$750	$650	$550	$500

Add 10% for satin nickel.

MKIV/SERIES 70 GOLD CUP 75TH ANNIVERSARY NATIONAL MATCH - similar to Gold Cup, except was mfg. for commemorative aspect of Camp Perry, 1978, 200 mfg. 1978 only.

	$1,450	$1,200	$1,000	$750	$650	$550	$500

GOLD CUP MKIV SERIES 80 NATIONAL MATCH - .45 ACP cal., 5 in. barrel flat mainspring housing, 7 or 8 shot mag., accurizer barrel and bushing, wide grooved adj. target trigger, target hammer, solid rib, Colt-Elliason rear sight, 39 oz. Mfg. 1983-96.

	$1,000	$800	$700	$550	$500	$450	$400

Last MSR was $937.

In 1992, this model was updated to accept an 8 shot mag. During 1997, this updated model was designated the Gold Cup Trophy.

✳ *Gold Cup MKIV Series 80 Stainless Gold Cup National Match* - similar to Gold Cup, only manufactured from stainless steel, matte finish. Mfg. late 1986-96.

	$1,000	$800	$700	$550	$500	$450	$400

Last MSR was $1,003.

Add $70 for "Ultimate" bright stainless steel finish.
Add 10% for NIB condition.

✳ *Gold Cup MKIV Series 80 Elite IX Gold Cup National Match* - 9mm Para. cal., stainless steel and blue, marked "GCNM" on right side, and "ELITE IX - 9mm Luger" on left side, "IX" prefix in ser. no.

	$1,400	$1,100	$900	$700	$675	$550	$400

Add 10% for NIB condition.

✳ *Gold Cup MKIV Series 80 .38 Super Elite National Match* - two-tone gun (stainless slide and blue frame), special edition by Accu-Sports.

	$1,350	$1,100	$900	$700	$675	$550	$400

✳ *Gold Cup MKIV Series 80 Bullseye National Match* - .45 ACP cal., hand-built, tuned, and adjusted by Colt's custom gunsmiths for precise match accuracy, includes factory-installed Bo-Mar sights, equipped with carrying case and 2 extra mags. Mfg. 1991-92.

	$1,450	$1,200	$1,000	$850	$725	$650	$600

Last MSR was $1,500.

✳ *Gold Cup MKIV Series 80 National Match Presentation* - .45 ACP cal., similar to regular Gold Cup Series 80 National Match, except has a deep blue-mirror bright finish accented by custom jeweled hammer, trigger, and barrel hood. Supplied with oak and velvet custom case. Mfg. 1991-92.

	$1,200	$1,000	$900	$825	$750	$650	$550

Last MSR was $1,195.

GRADING - PPGS™	100%	98%	95%	90%	80%	70%	60%

GOLD CUP TROPHY NATIONAL MATCH (MODEL O) - .45 ACP cal., flat main-spring housing, 7- (disc.) or 8-shot mag., accurizer barrel and bushing, flat top slide, adj. aluminum trigger, target hammer, Bo-Mar Elliason style rear sight, checkered black wrap-around rubber grips, shipped with test target, 39 oz. New 1997.

	100%	98%	95%	90%	80%	70%	60%
MSR $1,022	$895	$785	$650	$575	$525	$450	$400

This model replaced the MKIV/Series 80 Gold Cup National Match in 1997, and is only available from the Colt Custom Shop.

PISTOLS: SEMI-AUTO, CUSTOM SHOP ENGRAVING PRICING, PRE-1991

Values below represent pre-1991 factory semi-auto Custom Shop A-D engraving options, before they started separate Standard, Expert, and Master level pricing (1997). It should also be understood that, in most cases, the quality of the engraving and notoriety of the engraver can be as important as the amount of coverage. Small Frame Engraving Options: includes Mustang, .380 ACP Government, Detective Special, and Diamondback models. Medium Frame Engraving Options: includes .45 ACP Gold Cup, Government Model, Officer's ACP, Python, Combat Commander, King Cobra, Trooper MKV, Lawman MKV, and Delta Elite models. Special engraving/options include inlays, seals, custom grips, and lettering. Prices were quoted upon request. Smooth ivory grips were $215 extra (1990 retail). Beginning in 1991, Colt began shipping all models in a distinctive blue plastic carrying case/ shipping container. Please refer to the "Colt Custom Shop Engraving - Current Mfg." listing earlier in this section for current semi-auto engraving options and pricing. Semi-auto custom-order quotations from Colt are available at $25 each (deductible from work order).

Add $776 for Class "A" Engraving (1/4 Metal Coverage).
Add $959 for Class "B" Engraving (1/2 Metal Coverage).
Add $1,426 for Class "C" Engraving (3/4 Metal Coverage).
Add $1,814 for Class "D" Engraving (Full Metal Coverage).
Add $969 for Class "A" Engraving (1/4 Metal Coverage).
Add $1,199 for Class "B" Engraving (1/2 Metal Coverage).
Add $1,783 for Class "C" Engraving (3/4 Metal Coverage).
Add $2,289 for Class "D" Engraving (Full Metal Coverage).
Add 7% for 6 in. barrel, 14% for 8 in. barrel, or 25% for stainless steel construction.

PISTOLS: SEMI-AUTO, SINGLE ACTION, RECENT MFG.

JUNIOR POCKET MODEL - .22 S or .25 ACP cal., 2 1/4 in. barrel, blue, checkered walnut grips, made by Astra in Spain 1958-1968.

	100%	98%	95%	90%	80%	70%	60%
.22 Short	$375	$350	$275	$250	$200	$180	$150
.25 ACP	$350	$325	$250	$225	$175	$160	$140

Add 10% for nickel finish.

A very few conversion kits were offered for this model. They are rare and asking prices are $250-$325 if in mint condition.

COLT AUTOMATIC CALIBER .25 - .25 ACP cal., mfg. by Firearms International for Colt 1970-1973.

	100%	98%	95%	90%	80%	70%	60%
	$325	$300	$250	$210	$175	$150	$130

COMMANDER (PRE-70 SERIES) - 9mm Para, .38 Super, or .45 ACP cal., 4 1/4 in. barrel, full size grips, alloy (Lightweight Model) variations. Mfg. 1950-76.

	100%	98%	95%	90%	80%	70%	60%
9mm Para.	$1,200	$1,000	$950	$800	$650	$550	$450
.38 Super/.45 ACP	$1,400	$1,200	$1,125	$1,000	$900	$700	$600

This model has "LW" suffix.

In early 1950, the government purchased six "protoypes" to try out for possible use as General Officer's pistols, but decided against it. These six guns are serial numbered under 600 LWT, and should be appraised individually for value.

GRADING - PPGS™	100%	98%	95%	90%	80%	70%	60%

GOVERNMENT MODEL MKIV/SERIES 70 - .45 ACP, .38 Super, 9mm Para., or 9mm Steyr cal., 5 in. barrel, checkered walnut grips/medallion. Series 70 models were serial numbered with "SM" prefixes (approx. 3,000 mfg.), "70G" prefixes 1970-76, "70L" and "70S" prefixes also (see Serialization section for more information), "G70" suffixes 1976-80, "B70" suffixes 1979-81, and "70B" prefixes 1981-83. Mfg. 1970-83.

Blue finish	$1,000	$775	$600	$500	$450	$400	$375
Nickel finish	$1,250	$1,000	$800	$675	$450	$400	$375

   Add 10% if in NIB condition, 20% for NIB with early two-piece box.
   Add 10% for .38 Super, 9mm Para., or 9mm Steyr cal. if in 100% condition.
   Add 10% for satin nickel.

9mm Steyr was made for European exportation only. However, a few specimens have found their way into the United States. Prices for NIB specimens are in the $750 range.

✳ *Series 70 Combat Govt.* - .45 ACP cal., bluish-black metal finish, features modifications for combat shooting, forerunner to the Combat Elite.

	$1,250	$1,050	$950	$850	$775	$700	$650

   Add 10% for NIB condition.

✳ *Series 70 Lightweight Commander* - 7.65mm (.30 Luger), 9mm Para, .38 Super, or .45 ACP cal., 4 1/4 in. barrel, full size grips, this model is denoted by a "CLW" prefix. Mfg. 1970-83.

9mm Para.	$1,050	$850	$750	$650	$575	$500	$450
.38 Super/.45 ACP	$1,100	$875	$775	$675	$575	$500	$450
7.65mm	$2,500	$2,000	$1,575	$1,250	$995	$875	$750

   Add 10% for NIB condition.

500 Lightweight Commanders were mfg. in 7.65mm cal. during 1971. While most of these were mfg. for export trade, 5 were sold in the U.S.

✳ *Series 70 Combat Commander*

	$1,000	$850	$750	$650	$575	$500	$450

   Add 10% for NIB condition.
   Add 10% for satin nickel.

This model was also available in satin nickel finish (scarce).

✳ *Government Model MKIV/Series 70 Conversion Unit* - converts .45 ACP to .22 LR, mfg. 1954-84 with either Accro adj. rear sight or fixed sight.

Adj. Sight	$600	$550	$400	$350	$300	$250	$200
Fixed Sight	$700	$600	$450	$375	$300	$250	$200

   Add 50% for conversion units in bright nickel finish (very scarce). Must be accompanied by original box w/nickel label.

GOVERNMENT MODEL SERIES 70 MODEL O - .45 ACP cal., patterned after the original Series 70 pistol, high polish blue finish or stainless steel (new 2005), new release from the Custom Shop beginning 2002.

MSR $919	$825	$750	$650	$575	$495	$425	$375

   Add $31 for stainless steel (new 2005).

POST-WAR ACE SERVICE MODEL - .22 LR cal., similar specifications to previous pre-WWII manufacture, blue (most common) or electroless nickel from Custom Shop finish, "SM" prefix (most common) or "B 70" suffix, approx. 30,000 mfg. between 1978-1982.

	$1,100	$900	$775	$675	$625	$500	$450

   Add 10% for NIB condition.

This model is serial numbered approx. SM14,001-SM43,830.

GRADING - PPGS™	100%	98%	95%	90%	80%	70%	60%

GOVERNMENT MODEL MKIV/SERIES 80 - .38 Super, 9mm Para. (disc. 1992), 9x23 Win. (mfg. 1997 only), or .45 ACP (disc. 1996) cal., single action, 5 in. barrel, 7- or 8- (new 1992) shot mag. in .45 ACP, approx. 38 oz., action has firing pin safety, checkered walnut (pre-1991 mfg.) or rubber combat style grips with medallion (new 1991). Production started in 1983 with ser. no. FG01000.

✳ *Government Model MKIV/Series 80 Blue Finish* - this finish was disc. in 1997.

	$875	$750	$625	$575	$500	$475	$425

Last MSR was $600.

    Add 5% for 9mm Para. (disc. 1992) cal.
    Add 10% for NIB condition.

✳ *Government Model MKIV/Series 80 Nickel Finish* - .45 ACP (disc. 1986) or .38 Super (disc. in 1987) cal.

	$975	$750	$700	$600	$525	$475	$425

Last MSR was $735.

    Add 10% for NIB condition.

✳ *Government Model MKIV/Series 80 Satin Nickel & Blue Finish* - is supplied with Colt-Pachmayr grips. Disc. 1986.

	$1,000	$850	$750	$650	$575	$500	$450

Last MSR was $557.

    Add 10% for NIB condition.

✳ *Government Model MKIV/Series 80 Stainless Steel* - 9mm Para. (mfg. 1991-92), .38 Super (new 1990), .40 S&W (new 1992) or .45 ACP cal. Disc. 1998.

	$900	$800	$675	$600	$525	$475	$425

Last MSR was $813.

    Add 5% for 9mm Para. (disc. 1992) cal.
    Add 10% for NIB condition.

✳ *Government Model MKIV/Series 80 "Ultimate" Bright Stainless Steel* - .38 Super (new 1991) or .45 ACP cal., high polish stainless finish. Mfg. 1986-96.

	$1,000	$850	$750	$650	$575	$500	$450

Last MSR was $863.

    Add 10% for NIB condition.

✳ *Government Model MKIV/Series 80 Limited Class Model .45 ACP* - .45 ACP cal., designed for tactical competition, includes parkerized matte finish, lightweight composite trigger, ambidextrous safety, upswept grip safety, beveled mag. well, accurized, includes signed target. Mfg. 1994-97.

	$1,000	$850	$750	$650	$575	$500	$450

Last MSR was $936.

✳ *Government Model MKIV/Series 80 Custom Compensated Model .45 ACP* - .45 ACP cal., designed for serious competitive shooting, blue slide with full profile BAT Compensator, Bo-Mar rear sight, flared funnel mag. well. Mfg. by Custom Shop 1994-98.

	$2,000	$1,600	$1,350	$1,100	$975	$850	$725

Last MSR was $2,428.

MODEL M1911A1 CUSTOM TACTICAL GOV'T - LEVEL I - .45 ACP cal., designed for tactical competition, Commander style hammer, beveled/contoured mag. well, nylon flat mainspring housing, ambidextrous safety, long nylon trigger with over-travel stop, available in Officer's or Commmander's length. Mfg. 1998-2001.

	$800	$700	$650	$600	$500	$475	$425

Last MSR was $730.

In late 1999, this model was redesignated the Model O Custom Tactical Gov´t.

GRADING - PPGS™	100%	98%	95%	90%	80%	70%	60%

* *Model M1911A1 Custom Tactical Gov't. Model - Level II* - similar to Level I, except has Videcki long aluminum trigger with over-travel stop, Heine fixed combat sights, Colt match grade barrel bushing, high-ride grip safety with palm swell, double diamond stocks. Mfg. 1998-2001.

	$950	$875	$775	$700	$625	$525	$450

Last MSR was $935.

* *Model M1911A1 Custom Tactical Gov't. Model - Level III* - similar to Level II, except has Bo-Mar adj. rear sight, super match hammer. Mfg. 1998-2001.

	$1,150	$1,025	$875	$750	$650	$575	$495

Last MSR was $1,350.

COMBAT GOVERNMENT SERIES 80 - .45 ACP cal., dark matte metal finish, features modifications for combat shooting, successor to the Series 70 Combat Govt. Disc.

	$950	$800	$650	$550	$475	$450	$400

Add 10% for NIB condition.

* *Special Combat Government Competition Model Series 80* - .38 Super (new 2005) or .45 ACP cal., competition model featuring skeletonized trigger, custom tuning, polished ramp, 5 in. throated barrel, flared ejection port, and cut-out hammer. Supplied with two 8 shot mags., two-tone (new 2004) or hard chrome slide and frame, Bo-Mar rear and Clark dovetail front sight, flared mag. well, shipped with certified target. Mfg. by the Custom Shop. New 1992.

MSR $1,676	$1,475	$1,200	$975	$850	$725	$625	$550

* *Special Combat Government (Carry Model) Series 80* - similar to Special Combat Government, except has royal blue finish, bar-dot night sights, and ambidextrous safety. Mfg. 1992-2000.

	$1,125	$925	$750	$650	$575	$495	$400

Last MSR was $1,365.

* *Combat Elite Series 80* - .38 Super or .45 ACP cal., similar to Gold Cup, only with wraparound rubber grips, beveled magazine well, stainless steel frame with carbon steel slide, and Accro adj. sighting system. Disc. 1996.

	$925	$800	$625	$575	$525	$450	$400

Last MSR was $895.

COMBAT GOVERNMENT SERIES 80 CONVERSION UNIT - converts Series 80 Govt. Model only to .22 LR or 9mm Para., mfg. 1984-86, 1995, and 1998, with Accro adj. rear sight.

9mm Para.	$725	$650	$500	$400	$325	$250	$200
.22 LR (mfg. 1984-86)	$750	$650	$500	$400	$325	$250	$200
.22 LR (mfg. 1995, rare)	$775	$675	$525	$425	$325	$250	$200

Last MSR was $305 for .22 LR (mfg. 1984-86).

* *Colt Ace II Conversion Unit* - similar to above, except features an aluminum slide and barrel w/o floating chamber, does not have hold open feature. Mfg. 1998.

	$350	$295	$275	$225	$190	$175	$150

COMBAT TARGET MODEL SERIES 80 - .45 ACP cal. only, 5 in. barrel, adj. sights, matte finish. Mfg. 1997 only.

	$750	$625	$525	$475	$450	$425	$400

Last MSR was $768.

* *Combat Target Model Stainless Series 80* - similar to Combat Target Model, except stainless steel finish. Mfg. 1997 only.

	$800	$675	$550	$500	$450	$425	$400

Last MSR was $820.

GRADING - PPGS™	100%	98%	95%	90%	80%	70%	60%

COMMANDER LIGHTWEIGHT SERIES 80 - 9mm Para, .38 Super, or .45 ACP cal., 4 1/4 in. barrel, similar to Government Model, except shorter and lighter alloy frame, fixed sights, round spur hammer, 27 1/2 oz. Mfg. 1983-97.

	$875	$750	$625	$575	$525	$475	$450

Last MSR was $735.

     Add 10% for .38 Super or 9mm Para. (disc.) cals.

Some pistols are marked "Super Lite Commander - .38 Super - " on left side, and "Lightweight Commander Model" on right side. There may be an "M" on magazine floorplate, with the Colt logo.

COMBAT COMMANDER SERIES 80 - .38 Super (disc.), 9mm Para. (disc. 1992), or .45 ACP cal., similar to Lightweight, except has steel frame.

✳ *Combat Commander Series 80 Blue Finish* - disc. 1996.

	$800	$700	$600	$500	$450	$425	$400

Last MSR was $735.

     Add $20 for 9mm Para. (disc.) or .38 Super (disc.) cal.

✳ *Combat Commander Series 80 Blue Slide/Stainless Steel Receiver* - .45 ACP cal., two-tone matte finish, upswept grip safety, lightweight perforated trigger, black Hogue grips, 8-shot mag., 35 oz. Mfg. 1998 only.

	$750	$600	$500	$475	$450	$425	$400

Last MSR was $813.

✳ *Combat Commander Series 80 Stainless Steel* - .38 Super (mfg. 1992-97) or .45 ACP cal. Mfg. 1990-98.

	$850	$675	$550	$475	$450	$425	$400

Last MSR was $813.

✳ *Combat Commander Series 80 Satin Nickel* - disc. 1986.

	$950	$775	$650	$600	$550	$525	$450

Last MSR was $550.

✳ *Combat Commander Series 80 Gold Cup Commander* - .45 ACP cal., features custom shop alterations including heavy duty adj. target sights, beveled mag. well, serrated front strap, checkered mainspring housing, wide grip safety, and Palo Alto wood grips. Mfg. 1991-93.

	$1,200	$1,050	$925	$875	$825	$700	$600

Last MSR was $936.

✳ *Combat Commander Series 80 Gold Cup Commander Stainless* - stainless variation of the Gold Cup Commander. Mfg. 1992-disc.

	$1,200	$1,050	$925	$875	$825	$700	$600

Last MSR was $949

OFFICER'S MODEL SERIES 80 - .45 ACP cal. only, 3 1/2 in. barrel, 34 oz., 6-shot mag., short version of the Government Model. Mfg. 1985-disc.

✳ *Officer's Model Series 80 Blue Finish* - disc. 1996.

	$850	$700	$600	$500	$400	$350	$300

Last MSR was $735.

✳ *Officer's Model Series 80 Matte Blue Finish* - disc. 1991.

	$850	$750	$650	$550	$450	$425	$400

Last MSR was $625.

✳ *Officer's Model Series 80 Stainless Steel* - matte stainless steel finish. Mfg. 1986-97.

	$850	$750	$650	$550	$450	$425	$400

Last MSR was $813.

     Add $74 for "Ultimate" bright stainless steel finish (mfg. 1987-96).

GRADING - PPGS™	100%	98%	95%	90%	80%	70%	60%

* ***Officer's Model Series 80 Lightweight*** - similar to Officer's ACP, except has alloy frame and weighs 24 oz. Mfg. 1986-97.

		$900	$800	$700	$600	$500	$475	$425

Last MSR was $735.

* ***Officer's Model Series 80 Concealed Carry*** - .45 ACP cal., features matte stainless steel slide with matte blue aluminum alloy receiver, 7-shot mag., black contoured Hogue grips, upswept grip safety, lightweight perforated trigger, 26 oz. Mfg. 1998 only.

		$900	$800	$700	$600	$500	$450	$400

Last MSR was $813.

* ***Officer's Model Series 80 Satin Nickel*** - disc. 1985.

		$950	$850	$750	$650	$550	$500	$450

Last MSR was $513.

* ***General Officer's Model Series 80*** - bright stainless steel with rosewood grips, special edition. Disc. 1996.

		$900	$800	$700	$600	$500	$475	$450

Last MSR was $750.

COLT Z 40 - .40 S&W cal., DAO, alloy frame, double column mag., firing pin safety, 3-dot sights, blue finish with black checkered synthetic grips and silver trigger, straight backstrap, marked "Colt Z40" on top of slide, while approx. 750-800 pieces were mfg. 1998-99 by CZ for a Colt subcontract, they were never shipped, and as a result, very few have made it into the U.S. to date from the Czech Republic.

		$800	$750	$700	$600	$550	$525	$500

DEFENDER MODEL O - .40 S&W (mfg. 1999 only) or .45 ACP cal., 3 in. barrel with 3-dot sights, 7-shot mag., rubber wrap-around grips with finger grooves, lightweight perforated trigger, stainless steel slide and frame - frame finished in matte stainless, firing pin safety, 22 1/2 oz. New 1998.

MSR $885		$785	$675	$600	$495	$430	$365	$315

* ***Defender Plus*** - .45 ACP cal., similar to Defender Model O, except has aluminum receiver and 8-shot mag. Mfg. 2002-2003.

		$850	$750	$675	$600	$550	$525	$450

Last MSR was $876.

DEFENDER NEW AGENT - .45 ACP cal., DAO, 3 in. barrel, Series 80 firing pin system, 7 shot mag., double diamond slim fit grips, black anodized aluminum frame, beveled mag. well, snag free trench style sights, front strap serrations, captive recoil spring system. New 2008.

MSR $885		$785	$675	$600	$495	$430	$365	$315

COLT CONCEALED CARRY - .45 ACP cal., 3 in. barrel, aluminum frame with steel slide, Series 80 firing pin system, checkered double diamond walnut grips, front strap serrations, 25 oz. Mfg. 2007.

		$750	$675	$600	$525	$450	$400	$350

Last MSR was $885.

XSE SERIES MODEL O - .45 ACP cal., 4 or 5 (Govt. Model only) in. barrel, stainless brushed finish, front and rear slide serrations, checkered double diamond rosewood grips, 3-dot sights, new roll marking and enhanced tolerances, extended ambidextrous thumb safeties. New 2000.

* ***XSE Series Model O Government*** - 5 in. barrel, blue (new 2002) or stainless brushed (SS Model) finish, 8-shot mag.

MSR $944		$835	$730	$650	$575	$475	$400	$325

GRADING - PPGS™	100%	98%	95%	90%	80%	70%	60%

✳ *XSE Series Model O Concealed Carry Officers SS* - features lightweight aluminum alloy frame, 4 1/4 in. barrel and 7-shot mag. Limited mfg. 2000 only.

| | $800 | $700 | $600 | $550 | $500 | $450 | $400 |

Last MSR was $750.

✳ *XSE Series Model O Commander SS* - features 4 1/4 in. barrel and 8-shot mag.

| MSR $944 | $835 | $730 | $650 | $575 | $475 | $400 | $325 |

✳ *XSE Series Model O Lightweight Commander SS* - .38 Super or .45 ACP cal., features lightweight aluminum alloy frame, 4 1/4 in. barrel and 8-shot mag.

| MSR $944 | $835 | $730 | $650 | $575 | $475 | $400 | $325 |

GOLD CUP NATIONAL MATCH MKIV/SERIES 80/MODEL O - please refer to the listings for Gold Cup National Match models under Pistols: Semi-Auto, National Match Models - WWII and Post-WWII.

STAINLESS GOLD CUP TROPHY - similar to Gold Cup Trophy National Match, except has round top slide, stainless steel, matte finish, 39 oz. New 1997.

| MSR $1,071 | $950 | $815 | $700 | $600 | $500 | $425 | $350 |

1991 SERIES MODEL O (MKIV SERIES 80) - 9mm Para. (disc. 2001) or .45 ACP cal., similar to original WWII issue pistols with government issue parkerized matte (disc.) or blue finish, fixed sights, checkered rosewood double diamond wood (blue only) or checkered black composite grips, 5 in. barrel, 7-shot mag., 38 oz., includes brown molded case. New 1991.

| MSR $786 | $685 | $600 | $475 | $385 | $325 | $295 | $275 |

This model is serialized consecutively with the last batch of Govt. models manufactured during 1945.

✳ *Model 1991 Stainless Steel* - features matte stainless steel frame and slide, black checkered grips. New 1996.

| MSR $839 | $740 | $635 | $500 | $430 | $375 | $315 | $270 |

✳ *Model 1991 Commander* - .45 ACP cal., 4 1/4 in. barrel, full size grip, 7-shot mag., parkerized finish, 36 oz. Mfg. 1993-2005, reintroduced 2007.

| MSR $786 | $685 | $600 | $475 | $385 | $325 | $295 | $275 |

❖ Model 1991 Commander SS - similar to Model M1991 A1 Commander, except is stainless steel. Mfg. 1999-2005, reintroduced 2007.

| MSR $839 | $740 | $635 | $500 | $430 | $375 | $315 | $270 |

✳ *Model 1991 Officer's Compact* - similar to Model M1991 Commander, except has 3 1/2 in. barrel, 6 shot mag., 34 oz. Mfg. 1992-1999.

| | $600 | $500 | $425 | $400 | $375 | $350 | $325 |

Last MSR was $556.

❖ Model 1991 Officer's Stainless Compact - similar to Model M1991 A1 Officer's Compact, except is stainless steel. Mfg. 1999 only.

| | $650 | $600 | $550 | $500 | $475 | $450 | $400 |

Last MSR was $610.

.38 SUPER MODEL O - .38 Super cal., 5 in. barrel, M1911 (bright stainless only) or M1911A1 style frame, Govt. Model, blue, 3-dot sights, checkered rubber or double diamond walnut (bright stainless only) grips, 9-shot mag., beveled mag. well. New 2003.

| MSR $837 | $750 | $635 | $525 | $450 | $415 | $385 | $350 |

✳ *.38 Super Model O Stainless* - similar to .38 Super Model O, except is available in stainless or bright stainless steel.

| MSR $866 | $775 | $650 | $525 | $450 | $415 | $385 | $350 |

Add $224 for bright stainless steel.

GUNSITE MODEL O - .45 ACP cal., M1911 style frame, Series 70 firing system, 4 1/4 (Commander configuration) or 5 in. barrel, checkered thin rosewood grips, blue or stainless steel, many shooting features are included, such as serrated flat mainspring housing, Gold Cup front strap serrations, Heinie front and Novak rear sights, two 8 shot Wilson mags., McCormick hammer and sear, slide marked with Gunsite logo. Mfg. 2003-2005.

	$1,300	$1,100	$900	$775	$700	$625	$575

Last MSR was $1,400.

M1911 MODEL O SERIES 70 - .45 ACP cal., 5 in. barrel, accurate reproduction of the Model 1911 U.S. military sidearm, original style checkered walnut grips, carbonia blue finish, 7-shot mag., original WWI roll marks, original style packaging (cardboard box with wax paper), 4,400 scheduled for mfg. by the Custom Shop, 38 oz. New 2003.

MSR $990	$875	$775	$675	$575	$475	$425	$375

M1911A1 MODEL O - .45 ACP cal., 5 in. barrel, incorporates pre-Series 70 firing system, accurate reproduction of the Model 1911A1 U.S. military sidearm, original style composite grips, parkerized finish or stainless steel construction, 7-shot mag., original WWII roll marks, lanyard loop on arched serrated mainspring housing, wide spur hammer, safety and slide stop with original serrations, 38 oz., original style packaging (cardboard box with wax paper), approx. 4,000 mfg. by the Custom Shop. Mfg. 2001-2004.

	$995	$875	$775	$675	$575	$475	$400

Last MSR was $940.

M1911 SERIES 70 MODEL 1918 - .45 ACP cal., 5 in. barrel, accurate reproduction of the Model 1911 U.S. military sidearm manufactured during 1918, featuring black finish, original WWI roll marks, limited mfg. by the Custom Shop. New 2008.

MSR $990	$875	$775	$675	$575	$475	$425	$375

DELTA ELITE (1987-1996 MFG.) - 10mm cal., 5 in. barrel, black neoprene grips, high profile 3-dot sights, blue finish, 8-shot mag., 38 oz. Mfg. 1987-96.

	$850	$700	$575	$550	$450	$425	$400

Last MSR was $807.

The first 500 guns of this model (mfg. 1985) were called the Delta Elite First Edition, and featured laser engraving with gold-fill, smooth wood grips, and were furnished with presentation cases. Current pricing is in the $850-$975 range.

✳ *Delta Elite Stainless Steel* - matte stainless steel finish. Mfg. 1989-96.

	$900	$700	$600	$575	$550	$525	$500

Last MSR was $860.

Add $78 for "Ultimate" brite stainless steel finish (disc. 1993).

The first 1,000 guns of this model (mfg. 1988) were called the Delta Elite First Edition, and featured stamped lettering on slide, ebony grips, and did not have display cases. Current pricing is in the $875-$1,000 range.

DELTA ELITE - 10mm cal., 5 in. barrel, stainless steel, features diamond laser cut cocobolo grips with trademark Colt logo on both grips. New 2008.

MSR $983	$875	$775	$675	$575	$475	$425	$375

DELTA GOLD CUP STAINLESS - 10mm cal., target variation, includes Accro adj. rear sight and trigger (serrated also), wraparound combat grips. Mfg. 1989-93, re-released 1995-96.

	$950	$750	$650	$550	$500	$475	$450

Last MSR was $1,027.

✳ *Delta Gold Cup Blue* - similar to Delta Gold Cup Stainless, except has blue finish. Mfg. 1991 only.

	$875	$750	$675	$600	$525	$475	$450

Last MSR was $870.

.380 GOVERNMENT MODEL SERIES 80 - .380 ACP cal. only, single action, 3 1/4 in. barrel, 7-shot mag., fixed sights, composition stocks, 21 3/4 oz. New 1985.

GRADING - PPGS™	100%	98%	95%	90%	80%	70%	60%

✳ *.380 Government Model Series 80 Blue Finish* - finish disc. in 1997.

| | $650 | $550 | $500 | $450 | $400 | $350 | $300 |

Last MSR was $474.

✳ *.380 Government Model Series 80 Nickel Finish* - bright polish nickel finish with white composite grips. Disc. 1994.

| | $700 | $600 | $525 | $450 | $400 | $350 | $300 |

Last MSR was $504.

✳ *.380 Government Model Series 80 Coltguard Finish* - employs a high-strength electroless matte nickel finish. Mfg. 1986-89.

| | $700 | $600 | $525 | $450 | $400 | $350 | $300 |

Last MSR was $406.

✳ *.380 Government Model Series 80 Stainless Steel* - mfg. 1989-97.

| | $650 | $550 | $475 | $425 | $400 | $375 | $350 |

Last MSR was $508.

GOVT. POCKETLITE L.W. - similar to .380 Series 80 Govt. Model, except frame is mfg. with alloy, blue or nickel/stainless (mfg. 1992-93) finish only, black composition grips, 14 3/4 oz. Mfg. 1991-97.

| | $600 | $525 | $450 | $400 | $350 | $325 | $300 |

Last MSR was $462.

     Add $30 for nickel/stainless finish (disc. 1993).

✳ *Govt. Pocketlite Teflon Nickel/Stainless* - similar to Govt. Pocketlite L.W., except has combination of Teflon nickel, stainless steel finish. Mfg. 1997-98.

| | $600 | $500 | $400 | $350 | $300 | $275 | $250 |

Last MSR was $508.

MUSTANG - similar to .380 Series Govt., except has 2 3/4 in. barrel, single action, 5- or 6- (new 1992) shot mag., blue finish only, 18 1/2 oz. Mfg. 1986-97.

| | $600 | $525 | $450 | $400 | $350 | $300 | $275 |

Last MSR was $462.

✳ *Mustang Nickel finish* - bright polish nickel finish with white composite grips. Mfg. 1987-94.

| | $650 | $550 | $475 | $450 | $400 | $350 | $325 |

Last MSR was $504.

✳ *Mustang Stainless Steel* - stainless steel variation of the Mustang. Mfg. 1990-97.

| | $600 | $500 | $425 | $360 | $315 | $260 | $225 |

Last MSR was $508.

✳ *Mustang Coltguard finish* - employs a high-strength electroless matte nickel finish. Mfg. 1987.

| | $650 | $550 | $500 | $425 | $350 | $300 | $275 |

Last MSR was $406.

MUSTANG PLUS II - .380 ACP cal. only, 2 3/4 in. barrel, blue finish, black composition grips, 7-shot mag., 20 oz. Mfg. 1988-96.

| | $600 | $500 | $425 | $350 | $300 | $250 | $225 |

Last MSR was $462.

     This model has the full grip length of the .380 Government Model.

✳ *Mustang Plus II Stainless Steel* - stainless steel variation of the Mustang Plus II. Mfg. 1990-97.

| | $600 | $500 | $425 | $350 | $275 | $235 | $215 |

Last MSR was $508.

GRADING - PPGS™	100%	98%	95%	90%	80%	70%	60%

MUSTANG POCKETLITE L.W. - similar to Mustang, except has aluminum alloy receiver and stainless slide, blue (disc. 1997) or nickel/stainless finish, black composite grips, 12 1/2 oz. Introduced 1987.

	$600	$500	$425	$350	$300	$275	$225

Last MSR was $462.

* *Mustang Pocketlite L.W. Nickel/Stainless Steel Finish* - similar to Mustang Pocketlite, except has nickel finish frame and stainless steel slide. Mfg. 1991-96.

	$600	$500	$425	$350	$300	$275	$225

Last MSR was $493.

* *Mustang Pocketlite Teflon Nickel/Stainless* - similar to Mustang Pocketlite L.W., except has combination of Teflon nickel, stainless steel finish. Mfg. 1997-99.

	$600	$500	$425	$350	$300	$275	$225

Last MSR was $508.

* *Mustang Pocketlite L.W. Lady Elite* - features hard chrome receiver, blue slide with silver painted rollmark, finger extension mag., soft carrying case, limited mfg. 1995-96.

	$600	$500	$425	$350	$300	$275	$225

Last MSR was $612.

* *Mustang Pocketlite L.W. Nite Lite .380* - .380 ACP cal., features bar-dot night sight, Teflon coated alloy receiver with stainless slide, finger extension mag., includes carrying case. Mfg. 1994 only.

	$600	$500	$425	$350	$300	$275	$225

Last MSR was $577.

PISTOLS: SEMI-AUTO, DOUBLE ACTION - RECENT MFG.

DOUBLE EAGLE SERIES 90 I & II - 9mm Para. (mfg. 1991 only), .38 Super (mfg. 1991 only), .45 ACP, or 10mm (disc. 1993) cal., double action semi-auto that operates on the Browning/Colt short recoil, pivoting link locking system used by the Govt. Model, 5 in. barrel, matte stainless steel only, 3 dot sighting system or Accro adj. rear sight (disc. 1994), checkered synthetic Xenoy grips, 8 shot mag. (9 shot in 9mm Para. or .38 Super cal.), decocking lever, squared off combat trigger guard, 39 oz. Mfg. 1990-96.

	$850	$650	$500	$430	$375	$315	$270

Last MSR was $727.

Add $50 for 9mm Para. or .38 Super cal.
Add $20 for 10mm cal.
Add 10% for NIB condition.

The first edition (1,000 mfg. in 1989) on this model did not have a decocking lever - retail was $916.

* *Double Eagle Combat Commander* - .40 S&W (new 1992) or .45 ACP cal., 4 1/4 in. barrel, 8-shot mag., white dot sights, 36 oz. Mfg. 1991-96.

	$850	$650	$500	$430	$375	$315	$270

Last MSR was $727.

* *Double Eagle Officer's Model* - .45 ACP cal., 3 1/2 in. barrel, 8 shot mag., 35 oz. Mfg. 1991-disc.

	$850	$650	$500	$430	$375	$315	$270

Last MSR was $727.

* *Double Eagle Officer's Lightweight Model* - .45 ACP cal. only, 3 1/2 in. barrel, alloy frame with blue finish only, white dot sights, 25 oz. Mfg. 1991-93.

	$900	$700	$500	$400	$365	$330	$295

Last MSR was $696.

GRADING - PPGS™	100%	98%	95%	90%	80%	70%	60%

ALL AMERICAN MODEL 2000 - 9mm Para. cal. only, double action semi-auto, new design features roller-bearing mounted trigger allowing double action only trigger pull every shot, utilizes a recoil operated rotary action featuring integral locking lugs similar to the military M-16 rifle, hammerless, 4 1/2 in. barrel, matte finished steel slide and polymer receiver, 15 shot mag., 3-dot sighting system, ambidextrous mag. release, black synthetic checkered grips, internal striker block safety, checkered trigger guard and front grip strap, 29 oz. Manufacturing difficulty forced discontinuance and design and tooling were returned to Reed Knight. Mfg. 1991-93.

✳ *Model 2000 - Polymer Frame*

	100%	98%	95%	90%	80%	70%	60%
	$750	$650	$525	$450	$375	$325	$275

Last MSR was $575.

    Add 10% for NIB condition.

This model could also be converted to a shorter version using a 3 3/4 in. barrel/bushing kit (no tools or other components were needed - $75 retail during 1993 only).

✳ *Model 2000 - Aluminum Frame* - similar to polymer Model 2000, except frame is aluminum, serial numbered RK00001-RK03000 to commemorate the designer (Reed Knight). Mfg. 1993.

	100%	98%	95%	90%	80%	70%	60%
	$850	$700	$550	$465	$375	$325	$275

Last MSR was $575.

    Add 10% for NIB condition.

PONY SERIES 90 - .380 ACP cal., double action only, 2 3/4 in. barrel, bobbed hammer, 6 shot mag., stainless construction, brushed finish, fixed sights, black composition grips, 19 oz. Mfg. 1997 only.

	100%	98%	95%	90%	80%	70%	60%
	$600	$500	$400	$350	$300	$275	$225

Last MSR was $529.

✳ *Pony Series 90 Pocketlite Lightweight* - .380 ACP cal., similar to Pony Series 90, except utilizes aluminum and stainless steel construction, brushed finish, 13 oz. Mfg. 1997- 99.

	100%	98%	95%	90%	80%	70%	60%
	$600	$500	$400	$350	$300	$275	$225

Last MSR was $529.

POCKET NINE - 9mm Para. cal., double action only, 2 3/4 in. barrel, aluminum frame, ultra slim profile, 6 shot mag., matte/brushed stainless steel, wraparound rubber grips, 3-dot sights, 17 oz. Mfg. 1999 only.

	100%	98%	95%	90%	80%	70%	60%
	$600	$500	$400	$350	$300	$275	$225

Last MSR was $615.

PISTOLS: SEMI-AUTO, .22 CAL. - WOODSMAN SERIES

The publisher wishes to once again express his thanks to Major (ret.) Robert J. Rayburn for his continued generous contributions of information regarding the Colt Woodsman Series.

The Colt Woodsman was made for 62 years, and included a multitude of variations/options in models, sights, barrels, grips, markings, etc. Many of the variations are quite scarce and desirable, but generally known only to specialized collectors. The following price guidelines are for standard production models, and only for those specimens in unmodified, factory original condition.

Over 690,000 Woodsmans with variations were mfg. 1915-1977.

Factory engraved and special order Woodsmans are relatively rare and very desirable. Prices can fluctuate greatly, and auctions can sometimes be the only source of supply for these seldomly encountered pistols.

Note: 100% "as new" 1st Series Colt Woodsmans with box and accessories are almost always locked up in existing collections and are seldom seen for sale except when an entire collection is liquidated. Since the demand exceeds the supply, the price of such pristine items has been rising rapidly. The older or more rare versions in such condition can sell for double or even triple the price of a 98% gun. In the listings in this section, 100% means exactly that - absolutely perfect in every way, without a single blemish, not the slightest trace of blue wear or thinning. Such perfect examples can still be found for some versions. For others, where such condition is rarely, if ever, encountered, market values are too volatile to be listed in the 100% column.

GRADING - PPGS™	100%	98%	95%	90%	80%	70%	60%

PRE-WOODSMAN - .22 LR cal., 6 5/8 in. barrel. 10 shot mag., blue only, bottom mag. release, checkered wood grips, adj. front and rear sights, this model was officially named "Colt Automatic Pistol, Caliber .22 Target Model," magazine base has 2-line legend "CAL .22" "COLT". Standard velocity ammo. only. Approx. 54,000 mfg. 1915-27.

	$2,000	$1,500	$900	$650	$400	$300	$275

Add 10% for pencil barrels (1915-1922 mfg. only, ser. nos. below 31000).

This model was manufactured to use standard velocity ammunition only (not high speed). Colt did offer a conversion kit for high velocity ammo. after the transition to high velocity in 1931.

Woodsmans mfg. between 1915-1922 had a lightweight pencil barrel (approx. serial range 1-31,000). The medium barrel was introduced in 1922 and was retained until the 90,000 serial range (approx. mfg. 1922-1934).

WOODSMAN 1ST SERIES - .22 LR cal., 10 shot mag., blue only, bottom mag. release, checkered wood grips, marked "The Woodsman" on receiver, adj. sights, mfg. from 1927-47, total production was approx. 112,000.

Note: Guns made prior to 1931 were designed for standard velocity .22 LR ammunition only. The new style main spring housing, designed for high velocity ammunition, began appearing at approx. ser. no. 80,000 and was completely phased in by approx. ser. no. 85,000. Later guns, INCLUDING ALL PISTOLS MADE AFTER WWII, were designed for high velocity ammunition.

Between 1934 and 1947 a tapered barrel was standard production (approx. ser. range 90,000-187,423).

✴ *Woodsman Sport Model* - 4 1/2 in. barrel, this model was introduced in 1933.

	$1,850	$1,500	$900	$550	$400	$300	$275

Add 10% for adj. front sight (available beginning 1937).

Add 50% for medium weight barrel (1933-34 mfg. only), and an additional 50% for semi-circular "half moon" front sight (1933 mfg. only).

Approx. serial range on this variation is 86,105-187,423 from 1933 to 1947.

✴ *Woodsman Target Model* - 6 5/8 in. barrel.

	$1,400	$1,100	$650	$450	$325	$300	$275

Note: Colt discontinued the 1st series in 1947. These guns are quite different from the 2nd series started later in 1947. Both the front and rear sights are adjustable.

WOODSMAN 1ST SERIES MATCH TARGET - .22 LR cal. only, 6 5/8 in. heavy barrel, commonly called "Bullseye" Match Target, mfg. 1938-44, production totaled around 16,000. Difficult to find in mint condition. Values listed assume original one- piece extended walnut grips.

	$3,000	$2,500	$1,800	$1,100	$950	$900	$850

In the lower conditions, much of the value derives from the original walnut "Elephant Ear" stocks. The value of the stocks, in excellent original condition, can actually exceed the value of the gun.

The correct magazine on this model has a 3-line legend "COLT WOODSMAN", "CAL. 22 L.R.", and "MATCH TARGET MOD".

✴ *Woodsman 1st Series Match Target "U.S. Property" Marked* - approx. 4,000 Match Target Woodsmans were sold to the U.S. Army and U.S. Navy during WWII. Most have serial numbers above MT12500, although some were shipped out of sequence with lower numbers. The wartime guns had elongated plastic stocks and standard blue finish, although some of them are now parkerized as the result of arsenal refinishing or other non-factory modifications. They are marked with either "US PROPERTY" or the ordnance wheel with crossed cannon, as well as the initials of the govt. inspector. Some also have additional markings.

N/A	$2,800	$1,900	$1,200	$925	$750	$575

Since the military models have two-piece plastic grips, rather than the "Elephant Ear" stocks, the values in the lower condition categories are lower than those for the standard civilian model.

Check parkerized finish carefully for originality on this variation, as some "recent parkerizing" has been observed.

GRADING - PPGS™	100%	98%	95%	90%	80%	70%	60%

WOODSMAN 2ND SERIES - .22 LR cal. only, slide stop and hold open, push button mag. release on this model is located on the left side of frame, Colt Master rear sight was introduced during 1953, Coltwood plastic grips (mfg. 1947-1950) or brown plastic grips (mfg. 1950-55), total production on all 2nd Series was (not including the Challenger) approx. 146,000, serialization has "S" suffix. Mfg. 1947-1955.

* *Woodsman 2nd Series Sport Model* - 4 1/2 in. barrel.

	$950	$795	$550	$395	$350	$295	$250

* *Woodsman 2nd Series Target Model* - 6 in. barrel.

	$850	$695	$495	$350	$325	$275	$225

* *Woodsman 2nd Series Match Target Model* - 4 1/2 in. heavy barrel.

	$1,595	$1,300	$850	$650	$475	$450	$425

* *Woodsman 2nd Series Match Target Model* - 6 in. heavy barrel.

	$1,295	$1,100	$750	$550	$400	$350	$300

WOODSMAN 3RD SERIES - .22 LR cal. only, slide stop and hold open, black plastic grips (mfg. 1955-60) or walnut grips (1960-77), 3rd Models can be differentiated from 2nd Models by their bottom mag. release. Total production of all 3rd series Woodsman models (not including the Huntsman or Targetsman) exceeded 100,000, serialization has "S" suffix. Mfg. 1955-1977.

* *Woodsman 3rd Series Sport Model* - 4 1/2 in. barrel.

	$850	$750	$495	$325	$300	$275	$250

* *Woodsman 3rd Series Target Model* - 6 in. barrel.

	$795	$695	$450	$275	$250	$235	$225

* *Woodsman 3rd Series Match Target Model* - 4 1/2 or 6 in. heavy barrel.

	$1,200	$1,100	$750	$450	$375	$350	$295

Add $200 for a 4 1/2 in. barrel if condition is 95% or better.

CHALLENGER MODEL - similar to Woodsman 2nd Series, only with fixed sights, without hold open, and bottom mag. release, plastic grips, 4 1/2 and 6 in. barrels, mfg. 1950-1955 with total production reaching approx. 77,000.

	$650	$495	$325	$250	$225	$210	$180

HUNTSMAN MODEL - .22 LR cal. only, fixed sights and no hold open, 4 1/2 and 6 in. barrels, black plastic grips to serial number 141094-C - walnut grips after that cutoff. Mfg. 1955-1977 with total production reaching over 100,000.

	$595	$495	$350	$250	$200	$180	$160

The Huntsman is very similar to the Challenger Model, except is built on a 3rd series frame.

* *Huntsman Model S Master Series* - approx. 400 Model S Masters were sold in 1983. This was a parts clean-up by Colt, using Huntsman frames leftover from the last days of production. They were equipped with automatic slide stop and Elliason rear sight, gold etching on the slide, and a French fitted walnut case marked "1 of 400". Approx. 285 had straight, non-tapered Huntsman barrel, while the remainder had the tapered Woodsman Sport barrel with pinned front sight.

	100%	98%	95%	90%	80%	70%	60%
Huntsman barrel	$1,500	$895	$500	$425	$350	$325	$295
Woodsman barrel	$1,600	$800	$600	$500	$425	$350	$325

Above values assume original walnut case included. Values for this model in 98%-60% original condition are hard to compute, as most are mint or new.

TARGETSMAN MODEL - similar to the Huntsman, except has adj. rear sight and thumbrest on left grip, 6 in. barrel only, approx. 65,000 mfg. 1959-77.

	$750	$550	$350	$260	$240	$220	$200

GRADING - PPGS™	100%	98%	95%	90%	80%	70%	60%

CADET - .22 LR cal., 4 1/2 in. barrel, stainless steel, 10 shot mag., predecessor to the Colt 22 Model, originally introduced in 1994, fixed sights, this model was disc. by 1995 because of litigation involving the trademarked model name, 33 1/2 oz.

	$450	$350	$300	$240	$210	$180	$155

COLT 22 - .22 LR cal., 4 1/2 in. VR barrel, stainless steel, fixed sights, 10 shot mag., one-piece black Pachmayr rubber grips, 33 1/2 oz. Mfg. 1994-98.

	$425	$300	$250	$195	$165	$140	$120

Last MSR was $248.

* **Colt 22 Target** - .22 LR cal., 6 in. VR barrel with full length grooved sight rib, adj. rear sight, 40 1/2 oz. Mfg. 1995-99.

	$425	$300	$250	$195	$165	$140	$120

Last MSR was $377.

100%	98%	95%	90%	80%	70%	60%	50%	40%	30%	20%	10%

REVOLVERS: DOUBLE ACTION

Most of the double action revolvers listed can have their original configuration confirmed with a Colt factory letter. To receive a letter, write: COLT ARCHIVE PROPERTIES, LLC, P.O. Box 1868, Hartford, CT, 06144. The research fee for these revolvers is typically either $75 or $100, depending on the model. If they cannot obtain additional information on the variation you request, they will refund $50.

Prices on top condition Colt DAs have continued to remain strong, particularly for correctly boxed/cased guns. Be aware of ill-matched, wrong, or fake vintage boxes or grips being mated to an unmatched gun. Original boxes and grips will enhance the values of all Colt DAs.

MODEL 1877 LIGHTNING - .38 Colt or .32 Colt (very rare) cal., 2, 2 1/2, 3 1/2, 4 1/2, or 6 in. barrels without ejector, 4 1/2, 5, 6, 7, or 7 1/2 in. barrels with ejector, 6 shot double action, long cylinder fluting, blue finish with case hardened frame and hammer, full nickel plating also available. Over 166,000 mfg. from 1877-1910.

$4,000	$3,000	$2,000	$1,700	$1,500	$1,000	$900	$775	$700	$650	$575	$475

Subtract approx. 15% for nickel plating.

Shorter barrel lengths w/o ejector rod will bring a 10%-15% premium, depending on condition (should have a long, knurled cylinder pin).

Also, an etched barrel will command a 10%-15% over a roll marked barrel, depending on condition.

This model has a fragile mechanism - values are for working guns.

MODEL 1877 THUNDERER - .41 Colt cal. only, otherwise same general specifications as Model 1877 Lightning.

$4,000	$3,000	$2,000	$1,800	$1,400	$1,000	$900	$775	$675	$600	$525	$450

MODEL 1878 DA - .22 LR (very rare), .32-20 WCF (scarce), .38 Colt (approx. 40 mfg.), .38-40 WCF (scarce, approx. 1,600 mfg.), .41 LC (scarce), .44 Russian, .44 German, .44 S&W, .44-40 WCF (Colt Frontier Six Shooter), .45 LC, .450 Eley, .455 Eley, or .476 Eley cal., 2 1/2 (scarce), 3 1/2, or 4 in. barrels without ejector, 4 3/4, 5 1/2, 7 1/2, 8, 8 1/2, 9, 10, or 12 in. with ejector. Mfg. 1878-1905. Over 51,000 made.

$5,775	$5,250	$4,750	$3,750	$3,000	$2,500	$1,750	$1,500	$950	$850	$750	$625

This model in .44-40 WCF was called the Colt Frontier Six Shooter, and this inscription is either etched or roll marked on the barrel.

This model had a weak operating mechanism, and should be carefully inspected to make sure the cylinder turns and locks up properly. Since original parts are scarce, at least $500 must be deducted for a non-working action.

Many original 1878 barrels have "found their way" on the front end of a SAA frame since the barrels are interchangable. Because of this, many "original" Model 1878 DAs may have an incorrect and/or later SAA Colt barrel attached. Watch yourself here!

100%	98%	95%	90%	80%	70%	60%	50%	40%	30%	20%	10%

MODEL 1902/1904 (PHILIPPINE CONSTABULARY)

MODEL 1902/1904 (PHILIPPINE CONSTABULARY) - .45 LC cal., similar to Model 1878, except has oversized trigger guard and long trigger, 6 shot standard 1878 type cylinder with long flutes, pinched frame, 6 in. barrel, blue finish, hard rubber grips, many have been arsenal refinished.

✳ 1902 Constabulary - 5,000 mfg., with a smaller number actually issued by the U.S. Army to the Philippine Constabulary (Police) Force (not to be confused with the Philippine Scouts, which were part of the U.S. Army), markings: "R.A.C." on left side of frame, 1902 date on right side of frame near grips, large "U.S." on right side of frame below cylinder, hard rubber grips, but some examples also show period correct wooden grips, perhaps from confirmed arsenal or Colt reworks.

| N/A | N/A | $5,650 | $5,350 | $4,350 | $3,950 | $3,550 | $3,275 | $2,875 | $2,550 | $2,200 | $1,695 |

Subtract 50% for arsenal or Colt refinish.

At a recent 2007 Rock Island Auction Co. auction, a 98% condition example sold for $10,350.

✳ 1904 Model - rare model, approx. 50 more revolvers were delivered to the Army in 1904 within the 51,000 ser. no. range, use unknown, but assumed as Constabulary replacements, same overall configuration as 1902 version, but marked differently w/o R.A.C. or military numbering, the 1904 date and a smaller U.S. appear on right side of frame.

| N/A | N/A | $6,000 | $5,500 | $4,475 | $4,000 | $3,750 | $3,300 | $2,900 | $2,550 | $2,200 | $1,695 |

Subtract 50% for arsenal or Colt refinish.

REVOLVERS: DOUBLE ACTION, SWING OUT CYLINDER

Most of the double action revolvers listed can have their original configuration confirmed with a Colt factory letter. To receive a letter, write: COLT ARCHIVE PROPERTIES, LLC, P.O. Box 1868, Hartford, CT, 06144. The research fee for these revolvers is typically either $75 or $100, depending on the model. If they cannot obtain additional information on the variation you request, they will refund $50.

In Oct. of 1999, Colt announced that all double action revolvers would be discontinued, including any custom shop manufacture. After over 120 years of continuous production, the series of swing out double action revolvers finally ended. As a result, interest and prices for this discontinued revolver configuration have already increased, even on recently discontinued models/configurations. During 2002, Colt announced that the Custom Shop would make both the Anaconda and the Python Elite, and these two double action revolvers are the only ones currently produced by Colt.

Prices on top condition Colt DAs have continued to remain strong, particularly for correctly boxed/cased guns. Be aware of ill-matched or wrong vintage boxes or grips being mated to an unmatched gun. Original boxes and grips will enhance the values of all Colt DAs.

MODEL 1889 "NAVY" (NEW NAVY DA, MODEL OF 1889)

MODEL 1889 "NAVY" (NEW NAVY DA, MODEL OF 1889) - .38 Short and Long Colt, and .41 Short and Long Colt cal., 3, 4 1/2, and 6 in. barrel, blue (military and civilian) or nickel (civilian only) finish, wood (military) or hard rubber (civilian) grips, the first solid frame, swing out cylinder with no visible locking latches (rotates counter-clockwise), sideplate is also on the right-hand side of frame, Colt produced approx. 31,000 mfg. 1889-1894, 1st 5,000 were ordered by U.S. Navy, with some additional orders later in production - hence name.

| $1,850 | $1,650 | $1,350 | $1,150 | $950 | $750 | $650 | $575 | $500 | $425 | $350 | $300 |

Add 40% for 3 in. barrel.

Add 35% for .38 Short or Long Colt cal.

Add 65%-100% for U.S. Navy Contract (ser. no. 1-5,000), U.S.N. on butt (.38 LC cal. only), depending on condition. Beware of fakes.

Note: Nearly all 1889 Navy issues were later converted to 1895 type actions. Uncoverted specimens w/o notch cylinders will bring a premium, but must be authenticated by an expert - fakes are known to exist.

100%	98%	95%	90%	80%	70%	60%	50%	40%	30%	20%	10%

MODEL 1892 "NEW ARMY & NAVY" (2ND ISSUE) - similar to 1889 Navy, but double cylinder notches, double locking bolt, and shorter flutes, square cyl. release thumb catch, hard rubber (commercial models) or plain uncheckered wood (military models) grips, .32-20 WCF cal. (uncommon) added in 1905. Mfg. 1892-1907.

$1,450	$1,200	$950	$800	$500	$400	$300	$250	$225	$210	$195	$180

  Add $100-$750 for U.S.N. markings, depending on condition.
  Add 25% for 3 in. barrel.
  Subtract $100-$200 for broken hard rubber grips or broken action.
  Models made before 1898 will bring a premium.

  ✳ *Models 1892, 1894, 1895, 1896, 1901, 1903* - these were variations of the Model 1892, military model (.38 Long Colt only) values will approximate those shown above, while civilian models will be approx. 10%-25% less, depending on condition.

OFFICER'S MODEL (FIRST ISSUE) - .38 Spl. or .38 Long Colt cal., 6 in. barrel, cylinder rotates counter-clockwise and sideplate is on right-hand side of frame, adj. front - adj. rear type sights, high luster blue, flat-top, last patent date 1901. Mfg. 1904-08.

$1,750	$1,500	$1,250	$950	$775	$625	$550	$495	$395	$295	$275	$250

OFFICER'S MODEL (SECOND ISSUE) - .32 Colt or .38 Spl. cal., 4, 4 1/2, 5, 6, or 7 1/2 in. barrel, cylinder rotates clockwise, high luster blue through 1916, adj. front - adj. rear type sights, checkered walnut grips, deep set medallions in grips were standard from 1913-1923. Mfg. 1908-1926. Last patent date July 4, 1905.

$1,250	$1,100	$850	$515	$450	$395	$330	$290	$250	$225	$210	$195

  Add 75% for .32 Colt cal. or 100% for 7 1/2 in. barrel in .32 Colt cal. (rare).
  Add 60% for 4, 4 1/2, or 5 in. barrel.

OFFICER'S MODEL TARGET (THIRD ISSUE) - similar design to the Second Issue, .22 cal. was added beginning 1930, heavy barrel was introduced in 1935. Mfg. 1927-1949. Last patent date Oct. 5, 1926.

$1,050	$900	$750	$550	$450	$375	$325	$295	$265	$245	$225	$205

  Add 10% for .22 LR cal. (mfg. started 1930).
  Add 50% for .32 Colt cal. (mfg. 1939-1941, and production estimates are 800-1,500 units).
  Add 60% for 4 or 5 in. barrel.

MODEL 1905 MARINE CORPS - .38 Short or Long, similar to New Navy Second Issue, except has a round butt, checkered wood grips w/o medallion, and 6 in. barrel only. Mfg. 1905-1909 in approx. ser. no. range 10,001-10,926, about 926 mfg.

$2,850	$2,550	$2,050	$1,750	$1,625	$1,425	$1,250	$1,000	$895	$795	$695	$595

  Add 30% for Military issue marked "USMC" on butt. Beware of fake USMC markings.

ARMY SPECIAL MODEL - .32-20 WCF, .38 (various), and .41 Colt cals., 4, 4 1/2, 5, and 6 in. barrels, hard rubber grips standard through 1923 - checkered wood with medallions beginning about 1924, blue finish, fixed sights, rounded checkered cylinder release thumb catch, smooth trigger, has heavier frame than New Navy, approx. ser. no. range 291,000-540,000, last patent date on barrel was July 4, 1905. Mfg. 1908-27.

$850	$750	$600	$400	$325	$295	$275	$250	$225	$200	$185	$175

  Add 15% for nickel finish.
  Subtract $50-75 if hard rubber grips are chipped.

NEW SERVICE MODEL - .38 Spl., .357 Mag., .38-40 WCF, .44-40 WCF, .44 Russian, .44 Spl., .45 ACP, .45 LC, .450 Eley, .455 Eley, or .476 Eley cals., 4, 5, or 6 in. barrels in .357 Mag. and .38 Spl., 4 1/2, 5 1/2, and 7 1/2 in. barrel in all others, blue or nickel finish, bright blue finish was used through circa 1916, originally hard rubber (until approx. late '20s), with later guns having walnut grips with medallions. Mfg. 1898-1942.

  Rare cals. (.450 and .476 Eley cals.) and 4 in. barrels will command premiums over values listed below.
  Subtract $150 for broken, damaged or heavily worn grips.

100%	98%	95%	90%	80%	70%	60%	50%	40%	30%	20%	10%

New Service Models marked "NEW SERVICE 45 COLT" in .45 ACP cal. with shorter cylinder for rimmed cartridge are rare. Early models (first type) have flat latches. Later models (second type) have rounded cylinder latches.

Approx. 356,000 Colt New Service revolvers were mfg., but only approx. 122,800 were Commercial variations. 95% were mfg. with blue finish, while 5% were nickel plated (approx. 6,140 revolvers). Colt also mfg. a very limited number (probably less than 10) of New Service revolvers with smooth bores. When encountered, it is important to get a Colt factory letter confirming the smooth bore barrel. Prices can range $6,500-$10,000+, depending on original condition.

✳ *New Service Model Commercial*

100%	98%	95%	90%	80%	70%	60%	50%	40%	30%	20%	10%
$1,975	$1,650	$1,375	$1,250	$995	$875	$775	$650	$500	$425	$375	$295

Add 35% for nickel finish.
Add 50% for factory pearl, ivory or FDL walnut grips.

✳ *New Service Model 1909 Army Model*

100%	98%	95%	90%	80%	70%	60%	50%	40%	30%	20%	10%
$2,100	$1,450	$1,200	$1,000	$925	$850	$775	$680	$590	$510	$435	$375

✳ *New Service Model RNWMP & RCMP Model* - .45 LC or .455 Eley cal., contract for Royal Canadian Northwest Mounted Police.

100%	98%	95%	90%	80%	70%	60%	50%	40%	30%	20%	10%
$1,995	$1,350	$1,175	$1,000	$925	$850	$775	$680	$590	$510	$435	$375

✳ *New Service Model 1909 Navy Model* - shortest production run of the Model 1909 variations.

100%	98%	95%	90%	80%	70%	60%	50%	40%	30%	20%	10%
$3,500	$3,100	$2,600	$2,150	$1,500	$1,150	$1,000	$895	$775	$725	$650	$525

✳ *New Service Model 1909 - USMC*

100%	98%	95%	90%	80%	70%	60%	50%	40%	30%	20%	10%
$4,000	$3,650	$3,200	$2,750	$2,250	$1,875	$1,525	$1,250	$975	$850	$775	$675

✳ *New Service Model 1917 Army*

100%	98%	95%	90%	80%	70%	60%	50%	40%	30%	20%	10%
$1,375	$1,050	$895	$700	$610	$525	$455	$390	$335	$295	$250	$200

✳ *New Service Model 1917 Civilian/Commercial (1917 C/CM)* - .45 ACP cal., 5 1/2 in. barrel only, last patent date is Oct. 5, 1926, checkered walnut grips with medallions, left side of barrel marked "Colt Model 1917 Auto Ctge". Approx. 1,000 mfg. during 1932, serialized 335,000-336,000.

100%	98%	95%	90%	80%	70%	60%	50%	40%	30%	20%	10%
$1,500	$1,275	$1,050	$850	$650	$525	$450	$415	$385	$350	$325	$295

✳ *New Service Model 1917 Civilian/Commercial (Parts Model)* - .38-40 WCF, .44-40 WCF, or .45 LC cal., 4 1/2 or 5 1/2 in. barrel, hard rubber grips, or checkered walnut with medallions, last patent date is July 4, 1905, approx. 1,000 mfg. serialized 336,450- 337,500.

100%	98%	95%	90%	80%	70%	60%	50%	40%	30%	20%	10%
$1,375	$1,050	$925	$800	$625	$495	$415	$380	$360	$330	$300	$275

✳ *New Service Model Target* - similar to New Service Model, flattop frame, handhoned action and adj. front - adj. rear type sights, 6 (scarce) or 7 1/2 in. barrel, square butt, round butt available after 1930, checkered grip straps, checkered walnut grips with medallion after 1913, blue or nickel (scarce) finish. Approx. 3,400 mfg. 1900-1940.

100%	98%	95%	90%	80%	70%	60%	50%	40%	30%	20%	10%
$3,150	$3,000	$2,575	$2,100	$1,750	$1,500	$1,250	$900	$750	$635	$550	$460

Add 40% - 60% for 6 in. barrel, depending on original condition.
Add 25% for flat latch "Old Models" with original high polish finish.

Approx. 1,000 were mfg. in .45 LC cal., 960 in .455 Eley, 700 in .44 Russian, 500 in .44 Spl., and 80 in .45 ACP cal.

✳ *New Service Model Shooting Master* - various cals. from 38 Spl. through .45 LC, 6 in. barrel, checkered walnut grips with Colt Medallion, machined grip straps, trigger, hammer, and ejector rod head, round or square butt, approx. 3,500 mfg. in the ser. no. range 333,000-350,000.

❖ **New Service Model Shooting Master .38 Spl.** - approx. 2,500 mfg.

100%	98%	95%	90%	80%	70%	60%	50%	40%	30%	20%	10%
$1,500	$1,300	$1,025	$900	$825	$755	$665	$575	$500	$435	$395	$375

❖ **New Service Model Shooting Master .357 Mag.** - approx. 500 mfg.

100%	98%	95%	90%	80%	70%	60%	50%	40%	30%	20%	10%
$2,500	$2,300	$2,100	$1,850	$1,600	$1,475	$1,300	$1,100	$995	$825	$750	$650

100%	98%	95%	90%	80%	70%	60%	50%	40%	30%	20%	10%

❖ **New Service Model Shooting Master .45 ACP or .45 LC cals.** - approx. 156 mfg. in .45 LC and 250 mfg. in .45 ACP cal.

100%	98%	95%	90%	80%	70%	60%	50%	40%	30%	20%	10%
N/A	N/A	$3,850	$3,425	$3,050	$2,500	$2,050	$1,675	$1,350	$1,000	$750	$600

❖ **New Service Model Shooting Master .44 Spl. cal.** - approx. 94 mfg.

100%	98%	95%	90%	80%	70%	60%	50%	40%	30%	20%	10%
N/A	N/A	$4,600	$4,050	$3,500	$3,000	$2,500	$2,000	$1,575	$1,250	$1,000	$850

The Shooting Master could be ordered with a square butt after 1933.

OFFICIAL POLICE PRE-WAR - .32-20 WCF (disc. 1942), .38-200 (British), .41 long (disc. 1930), .38 Spl., or .22 LR (introduced 1930 - 4 or 6 in. barrel only, 4 in. scarce) cal., blue finish, 6 shot, round (very scarce) or square butt, 4, 5, or 6 in. barrels, 2 in. barrel (scarce) in .38 Spl., checkered walnut grips, fixed sights, last patent date on barrel was Oct. 5, 1926. Mfg. 1927-46.

100%	98%	95%	90%	80%	70%	60%	50%	40%	30%	20%	10%
$850	$750	$450	$350	$325	$300	$275	$250	$210	$185	$165	$145

Add 100% for round butt with factory verified letter.
Add 15% for nickel finish.
Add 15% for .22 LR cal.

OFFICIAL POLICE POST-WAR - .22 LR or .38 Spl. cal., 2, 4, 5, or 6 in. barrel, Coltwood plastic grips 1947-1954 - checkered walnut thereafter, fixed sights, no patent dates on barrel. Mfg. 1947-69.

100%	98%	95%	90%	80%	70%	60%	50%	40%	30%	20%	10%
$750	$600	$375	$350	$265	$235	$210	$185	$165	$145	$135	$125

Add 15% for nickel finish.
Add 15% for .22 cal.

On this model, the 2 in. barrel in .38 Spl. cal. is scarce. .22 cal. was available with 4 or 6 in. barrel only.

MARSHAL MODEL - .38 Spl. cal., 2 (less common) or 4 in. barrel, round butt, differentiated by "M" suffix and "COLT MARSHAL" on barrel, about 2,500 mfg. 1954-1956 in approx. ser. no. range 833350-M through 845320-M.

100%	98%	95%	90%	80%	70%	60%	50%	40%	30%	20%	10%
$950	$800	$700	$500	$395	$335	$305	$275	$245	$215	$180	$160

Add 60% for 2 in. barrel.
Add 50% for nickel finish.

COMMANDO MODEL - .38 Spl. cal., 2 in. (less common), 4 in. (common), or 6 in. (rare) barrel, should have plastic grips, parkerized finish, about 50,000 mfg. 1942-1945, 32 oz., marked "COLT COMMANDO" on barrel, last patent date on barrel was Oct. 5, 1926.

100%	98%	95%	90%	80%	70%	60%	50%	40%	30%	20%	10%
$850	$750	$600	$375	$350	$315	$280	$260	$240	$220	$195	$180

Add 15% for 2 in. barrel.

OFFICIAL POLICE MKIII - .38 Spl. cal., 4, 5, or 6 in. barrels, no patent dates on barrel. Mfg. 1969-75.

✳ *Official Police MKIII Blue finish*

100%	98%	95%	90%	80%	70%	60%	50%	40%	30%	20%	10%
$400	$325	$250	$150	$135	$125	$115	$105	$100	$95	$90	$85

✳ *Official Police MKIII Nickel finish*

100%	98%	95%	90%	80%	70%	60%	50%	40%	30%	20%	10%
$395	$295	$200	$175	$165	$155	$145	$135	$125	$115	$105	$100

METROPOLITAN MK III - .38 Spl. cal., similar to Official Police, except heavier and 4 in. heavy barrel only, blue finish. Mfg. 1969-72.

100%	98%	95%	90%	80%	70%	60%	50%	40%	30%	20%	10%
$495	$395	$300	$250	$200	$180	$160	$140	$120	$110	$100	$90

OFFICER'S MODEL SPECIAL (FOURTH ISSUE) - .22 LR or .38 Spl. cal., 6 in. barrel, blue, similar to Third Issue, only heavier non-tapered barrel, new style hammer and "Coltmaster Sight," checkered plastic grips, no patent dates on barrel. Mfg. 1949-52.

100%	98%	95%	90%	80%	70%	60%	50%	40%	30%	20%	10%
$825	$725	$600	$425	$325	$295	$265	$245	$225	$205	$190	$175

Add $75 for .22 LR cal.

100%	98%	95%	90%	80%	70%	60%	50%	40%	30%	20%	10%

OFFICER'S MODEL MATCH (FIFTH ISSUE) - .22 LR, .22 Mag, or .38 Spl. cal., 6 in. barrel, single (rare) or double action, tapered heavy barrel, nickel finish is scarce in this model, wide spur hammer, Accro sight, large target grips (walnut). Mfg. 1953-69.

100%	98%	95%	90%	80%	70%	60%	50%	40%	30%	20%	10%
$750	$650	$575	$375	$300	$275	$250	$225	$200	$185	$170	$155

    Add $75 for .22 LR cal.
    Add 100% for .22 Mag. cal. (approx. 850 mfg.).

＊ *Officer's Model Match Single Action only* - limited mfg.

100%	98%	95%	90%	80%	70%	60%	50%	40%	30%	20%	10%
$1,325	$1,200	$995	$925	$850	$775	$700	$650	$600	$550	$475	$425

OFFICER'S MODEL MATCH MK III (SIXTH ISSUE) - .38 Spl. cal. only, 6 in. shrouded VR barrel, wide spur hammer, Accro sights, target grips. 496 mfg. 1969-70 only.

100%	98%	95%	90%	80%	70%	60%	50%	40%	30%	20%	10%
$1,650	$1,375	$1,250	$975	$850	$775	$700	$650	$600	$550	$475	$425

NEW POCKET - .32 Short and LC, or .32 Colt New Police cal., 2 1/2, 3 1/2, 5, or 6 in. barrel, first modern swing out DA, rubber grips, blue or nickel finish, round butt, last patent date on barrel was Nov. 6, 1888. Mfg. 1895-1905.

100%	98%	95%	90%	80%	70%	60%	50%	40%	30%	20%	10%
$900	$795	$595	$495	$375	$300	$250	$215	$190	$170	$150	$140

    Subtract $50-$75 for chipped hard rubber grips (commonly found on this model).

POCKET POSITIVE (FIRST ISSUE) - similar to New Pocket, except has positive lock feature, also chambered for .32 Colt, .32 S&W, and .32 Colt New Police cals., last patent date on barrel was July 4, 1905. Mfg. 1905-27.

100%	98%	95%	90%	80%	70%	60%	50%	40%	30%	20%	10%
$750	$650	$425	$350	$325	$295	$265	$235	$210	$185	$165	$145

    Add 15%-20% for nickel finish.
    Add 15% for 90%+ condition early transitional guns that are double marked with "NEW POCKET" on frame.
    Subtract $50-$75 for chipped hard rubber grips (commonly found on this model).

POCKET POSITIVE (SECOND ISSUE) - similar to Pocket Positive First Issue, except available in 2 in. barrel, stippled and matted top strap, last patent date on barrel was Oct. 5, 1926. Mfg. 1927-1940.

100%	98%	95%	90%	80%	70%	60%	50%	40%	30%	20%	10%
$750	$650	$425	$350	$325	$295	$265	$235	$210	$185	$165	$145

    Add 15%-20% for nickel finish.
    Add 15%-20% for 2 in. barrel.
    Subtract $50-$75 for chipped hard rubber grips (commonly found on this model).

NEW POLICE - .32 Colt and .32 Colt New Police cal., 2 1/2, 4, and 6 in. barrels, fixed sights, same frame as New Pocket, except larger, square butt grips, rubber grips, last patent date on barrel was Nov. 6, 1888. Mfg. 1896-1907.

100%	98%	95%	90%	80%	70%	60%	50%	40%	30%	20%	10%
$850	$750	$550	$375	$325	$275	$215	$185	$170	$160	$150	$145

    Add 25% for nickel finish.
    Subtract $25-$50 for chipped hard rubber grips (commonly found on this model).

NEW POLICE TARGET - .32 Colt cal., 6 in. barrel, blue, late models use New Police frame, but include transistional improvements from later Police Positive Target Model (First Issue), last patent date on barrel was Nov. 6, 1888. Approx. 5,000 mfg. 1897-1907.

100%	98%	95%	90%	80%	70%	60%	50%	40%	30%	20%	10%
$1,650	$1,450	$950	$900	$475	$395	$350	$300	$275	$250	$225	$200

POLICE POSITIVE (FIRST ISSUE) - .32 Colt, .32 New Police, .38 New Police, or .38 S&W cals., 2 1/2 in. (.32 cal., only), 4, 5, or 6 in. barrels, improved "positive lock" version of the New Police, hard rubber grips standard through 1923, checkered walnut grips became standard 1924, denoted by 1905 last patent date and smooth top strap. Mfg. 1907-27.

100%	98%	95%	90%	80%	70%	60%	50%	40%	30%	20%	10%
$700	$550	$375	$295	$275	$250	$225	$205	$185	$170	$160	$150

    Add 15% for nickel finish.
    Add 10% for 90%+ condition early transitional guns that are double marked with "NEW POLICE" on frame.

100%	98%	95%	90%	80%	70%	60%	50%	40%	30%	20%	10%

POLICE POSITIVE (SECOND ISSUE) - similar to Police Positive First Issue, except has 1926 last patent date, serrated top strap, and slightly heavier frame, walnut grips standard. Mfg. 1928-1947.

100%	98%	95%	90%	80%	70%	60%	50%	40%	30%	20%	10%
$700	$550	$375	$295	$275	$250	$225	$205	$185	$170	$160	$150

Add 15% for nickel finish.

POLICE POSITIVE TARGET MODEL (FIRST ISSUE, MODEL "G") - .22 LR, .22 WRF, .32 Colt, or .32 New Police cals., 6 in. barrel, blue, adj. sight, hard rubber grips standard through 1923, checkered walnut grips thereafter, last patent date on barrel was July 4, 1905, 22 oz. Mfg. 1907-1925.

100%	98%	95%	90%	80%	70%	60%	50%	40%	30%	20%	10%
$1,100	$900	$675	$575	$475	$425	$390	$360	$325	$285	$250	$210

Add 40% for .32 cal.

POLICE POSITIVE TARGET MODEL (SECOND ISSUE, MODEL "C") - similar to First Issue, except has slightly heavier frame and a last patent date of Oct. 5, 1926, blue finish, but a few were also mfg. in nickel, 26 oz. Mfg. 1926-41.

100%	98%	95%	90%	80%	70%	60%	50%	40%	30%	20%	10%
$1,100	$900	$675	$575	$475	$425	$390	$360	$325	$285	$250	$210

Add 40% for .32 cal.
Add 100% for nickel - must be verified by factory letter.

POLICE POSITIVE SPECIAL (FIRST ISSUE) - .32-20 WCF, .32 New Police, .38 New Police, or .38 Spl. cals., 4, 5, or 6 in. barrels, fixed sights, frame longer to permit longer cylinder, denoted by 1905 last patent date on top of barrel, longer frame and smooth top strap, rubber grips. Mfg. 1907-27.

100%	98%	95%	90%	80%	70%	60%	50%	40%	30%	20%	10%
$800	$650	$450	$325	$300	$275	$250	$225	$200	$185	$170	$155

POLICE POSITIVE SPECIAL (SECOND ISSUE) - similar to Police Postitive Special (First Issue), except has 1926 last patent date on top of barrel, wood grips only, smooth (early mfg.) or checkered (later mfg.) trigger, and serrated top strap. Mfg. 1928-46.

100%	98%	95%	90%	80%	70%	60%	50%	40%	30%	20%	10%
$800	$650	$450	$325	$300	$275	$250	$225	$200	$185	$170	$155

CAMP PERRY MODEL - .22 LR cal., 8 in. (less common) or 10 in., Officer's Model frame modified to accept a flat single shot chamber. The model name was stamped on the left side of the chamber, the only single shot Colt on a revolver frame, last patent date on barrel was Oct. 5, 1926. 2,488 mfg. 1926-1941.

100%	98%	95%	90%	80%	70%	60%	50%	40%	30%	20%	10%
$2,100	$1,650	$1,450	$950	$875	$775	$715	$645	$575	$495	$425	$365

Add 25% for 8 in. barrel.

BANKER'S SPECIAL - 2 in. barrel, blue, square butt standard through 1933, round butt standard 1934-40, last patent date on barrel was Oct. 5, 1926. Mfg. 1926-40.

  ✳ *Banker's Special .38 cal.* - available in .38 Colt Police Positive (New Police) or .38 S&W cal.

100%	98%	95%	90%	80%	70%	60%	50%	40%	30%	20%	10%
$1,500	$1,100	$900	$700	$550	$425	$375	$275	$235	$205	$185	$165

Add 45% for nickel finish.

  ✳ *Banker's Special .22 LR cal.*

100%	98%	95%	90%	80%	70%	60%	50%	40%	30%	20%	10%
$2,250	$2,000	$1,650	$1,100	$750	$650	$550	$475	$425	$385	$355	$325

Add 30%-50% for nickel finish, depending on original condition.

COURIER - .22 S, L, & LR. or .32 New Police (S&W) cals., double action, 6 shot, 3 in. barrel. Approx. 3,053 mfg. 1953-56.

100%	98%	95%	90%	80%	70%	60%	50%	40%	30%	20%	10%
$950	$850	$750	$550	$475	$425	$395	$350	$325	$295	$260	$230

Add 10% for .22 cal.

Even though fewer .22 cal. Couriers were mfg. than Banker's Specials, the Banker's Specials are still more desirable, as they are of pre-war quality, and are less frequently encountered in 95-100% condition.
Some .32 New Police (S&W) cal. models can be found with alloy or steel cylinders.

100%	98%	95%	90%	80%	70%	60%	50%	40%	30%	20%	10%

AIRCREWMAN - .38 Spl. cal., double action, aluminum frame and cylinder, 2 in. barrel, 11 oz., fixed sights, checkered walnut grips overlapping at top of frame, inset with silver Air Force buttons, mfg. 1951 mostly.

| $4,000 | $3,500 | $2,750 | $2,100 | $1,700 | $1,350 | $1,075 | $950 | $850 | $750 | $675 | $595 |

Approx. 1,200 mfg. within ser. no. range 2,900LW-7,775LW. Most were ordered destroyed. Perhaps less than 25 have survived.

BORDER PATROL (FIRST ISSUE) - .38 Spl. cal., double action, 6 shot, 4 in. heavy barrel, should have plastic grips, 400 mfg. during 1952 only in 823,000 ser. no. range.

| $4,000 | $3,500 | $3,000 | $1,400 | $1,125 | $995 | $875 | $775 | $675 | $595 | $525 | $475 |

This model is built on the Official Police Model frame.

DETECTIVE SPECIAL PRE-WAR (FIRST ISSUE) - .38 Spl. cal., 2 in. barrel, blue, wood grips, square butt standard through 1933, round butt standard thereafter, last patent date on barrel was Oct. 5, 1926. Mfg. 1927-46.

| $1,200 | $1,000 | $725 | $500 | $425 | $325 | $275 | $250 | $225 | $205 | $190 | $175 |

Add 15% for nickel finish.
Add 20% for square butt.

DETECTIVE SPECIAL POST-WAR (SECOND ISSUE) - .32 NP, .38 NP, or .38 Spl. cal., 2 or 3 (scarce) in. barrel, plastic grips 1947-54 - wood grips thereafter, wrap-under wood grips started in 1966. Mfg. 1947-72.

| $750 | $650 | $375 | $275 | $250 | $200 | $185 | $170 | $160 | $150 | $140 | $120 |

Add 15% for nickel finish.
Add 15% for 3 in. barrel.

COBRA (FIRST ISSUE) - .22 LR, .32 Colt NP, .38 Colt NP, or .38 Spl. cal., first issue, 2, 3, or 4 (square butt on early model, later models had round butt) in. barrel, blue or nickel finish, similar to Detective Special, only alloy frame and available in .22 LR, very early guns had plastic grips with silver medallions, changed to plastic w/o medallions, and finally changed to wood grips. Mfg. 1950-72.

| $775 | $700 | $425 | $250 | $225 | $200 | $185 | $170 | $160 | $150 | $140 | $120 |

Add 20% for .22 LR cal.
Add 15% for nickel finish.
Add 15% for .38 cal. with 3 in. barrel.
The .22 LR cal. is available in 3 in. barrel only.

AGENT (FIRST ISSUE) - .38 Spl. cal., similar to Cobra first issue, except shorter grip frame. Mfg. 1955-72.

| $700 | $600 | $375 | $275 | $235 | $180 | $160 | $145 | $130 | $120 | $110 | $100 |

AGENT L.W. (SECOND ISSUE) - .38 Spl. cal., similar to First Issue, except shrouded ejector rod, alloy frame, matte finish since 1982. Mfg. 1973-86.

| $500 | $425 | $350 | $215 | $195 | $175 | $150 | $135 | $125 | $115 | $105 | $100 |

Last MSR was $260.

COBRA (SECOND ISSUE) - .38 Spl. cal., similar to Cobra first issue, except shrouded ejector rod, some were shipped with factory installed hammer shroud. Mfg. 1973-81.

| $500 | $425 | $350 | $250 | $225 | $200 | $190 | $175 | $160 | $150 | $140 | $120 |

DETECTIVE SPECIAL (THIRD ISSUE) - .38 Spl. cal., similar to Second Issue, shrouded ejector rod, 2 or 3 (scarce) in. barrel, fixed sights, wraparound wood grips. Mfg. 1973-86.

| $450 | $425 | $400 | $300 | $260 | $230 | $200 | $185 | $175 | $160 | $150 | $140 |

Last MSR was $429.

Add $50 for nickel.
Add 15% for 3 in. barrel.
Also available with class A engraving - add $590 if in 98% condition or better.

100%	98%	95%	90%	80%	70%	60%	50%	40%	30%	20%	10%

COMMANDO SPECIAL - .38 Spl. cal., similar to Detective Special with steel frame, shrouded ejector rod, 2 in. barrel, matte parkerized finish, rubber grips. Mfg. 1984-86.

100%	98%	95%	90%	80%	70%	60%	50%	40%	30%	20%	10%
$425	$325	$265	$225	$195	$185	$155	$140	$125	$115	$105	$100

Last MSR was $260.

POLICE POSITIVE SPECIAL (THIRD ISSUE) - .38 Spl. cal., similar to Detective Special Second Issue, except 4, 5, or 6 in. barrel. Mfg. 1947-76.

100%	98%	95%	90%	80%	70%	60%	50%	40%	30%	20%	10%
$550	$450	$350	$225	$195	$185	$165	$140	$125	$115	$105	$100

POLICE POSITIVE SPECIAL (FOURTH ISSUE) - .38 Spl. cal., shrouded ejector rod housing only, steel frame, blue or nickel finish. Mfg. 1977-78.

100%	98%	95%	90%	80%	70%	60%	50%	40%	30%	20%	10%
$450	$375	$350	$220	$195	$175	$165	$135	$125	$115	$105	$100

Last MSR was $400.

Add 10% for nickel finish.

POLICE POSITIVE MK V (FIFTH ISSUE) - .38 Spl. cal., full shrouded 4 in. barrel, steel frame, blue finish, rubber grips. Mfg. 1994-95.

100%	98%	95%	90%	80%	70%	60%	50%	40%	30%	20%	10%
					$425	$350	$295	$250	$195	$180	$165

VIPER MODEL - .38 Spl. cal., similar to Police Positive Special (Fourth Issue), alloy frame, 4 in. ejector rod housing only. Mfg. 1977 only.

100%	98%	95%	90%	80%	70%	60%	50%	40%	30%	20%	10%
$500	$450	$375	$250	$225	$200	$190	$175	$160	$150	$140	$120

Add 30% for nickel finish.

DIAMONDBACK - .22 LR, .22 Mag. (rare), or .38 Spl. cal., 2 1/2 (scarce in .22 LR), 4, or 6 in. VR barrel, adj. sights, steel frame, checkered walnut grips. Mfg. 1966-1986.

100%	98%	95%	90%	80%	70%	60%	50%	40%	30%	20%	10%
$950	$800	$575	$425	$350	$285	$260	$230	$210	$190	$175	$160

Last MSR was $461.

Add 20% for nickel finish.
Approx. 2,200 Diamondbacks were made with 6 in. barrels and nickel finish in .22 cal. - made 1979. Add additional $150 for 95+% specimens.
Add 10% for 2 1/2 in. barrel in .38 cal.
Note: .22 Mag. cal. is this model is rare, and values are difficult to price accurately. Buyer beware - fakes are known to exist.

* *Diamondback .22 cal. w/ 2 1/2 In. Barrel* - 2 1/2 in. barrel, blue or nickel finish, rare.

100%	98%	95%	90%	80%	70%	60%	50%	40%	30%	20%	10%
$3,000	$2,700	$2,400	$2,000	$1,750	$1,525	$1,325	$1,100	$875	$700	$575	$450

Add 20% for nickel finish.
A factory letter is now advisable on this configuration.

* *Diamondback .22 cal. w/4 in. Barrel* - blue or nickel finish.

100%	98%	95%	90%	80%	70%	60%	50%	40%	30%	20%	10%
$1,000	$825	$600	$450	$350	$285	$260	$230	$210	$190	$175	$160

Add 100% for nickel finish.

* *Diamondback .22 cal. w/6 in. Barrel* - blue or nickel finish.

100%	98%	95%	90%	80%	70%	60%	50%	40%	30%	20%	10%
$1,250	$1,100	$850	$515	$450	$395	$330	$290	$250	$225	$210	$195

Add 100% for nickel finish.

COLT .357 MAG - 4 in. or 6 in. barrel, heavy frame, Accro sight, blue or nickel finish, checkered walnut grips. Mfg. 1953-61.

* *Colt .357 Mag. Standard hammer*

100%	98%	95%	90%	80%	70%	60%	50%	40%	30%	20%	10%
$700	$650	$450	$300	$275	$265	$255	$245	$230	$220	$210	$200

* *Colt .357 Mag. Wide hammer w/target grips*

100%	98%	95%	90%	80%	70%	60%	50%	40%	30%	20%	10%
$750	$650	$500	$450	$325	$265	$255	$245	$235	$225	$215	$205

Add 15% for nickel finish.
In 1962, this model was absorbed into the Trooper line.

TROOPER - .22 LR (4 in. only, scarce), .357 Mag., or .38 Spl. cal., 4 or 6 in. barrel, blue or nickel finish, quick draw ramp front sight, adj. rear sight, checkered walnut grips. Mfg. 1953-69.

100%	98%	95%	90%	80%	70%	60%	50%	40%	30%	20%	10%

Trooper Standard hammer

| $650 | $500 | $375 | $350 | $275 | $200 | $180 | $170 | $165 | $160 | $155 | $150 |

Trooper Wide hammer and target grips

| $650 | $500 | $375 | $350 | $275 | $200 | $190 | $180 | $170 | $165 | $160 | $155 |

Add $75-$125 for .22 LR cal. (4 in. barrel only), depending on condition.
Add 15% for nickel finish.

GRADING - PPGS™	100%	98%	95%	90%	80%	70%	60%

TROOPER MK III - .22 LR, .22 Mag., .357 Mag., or .38 Spl. cal., 4, 6, or 8 in. solid rib barrel, adj. sights, walnut target grips, redesigned lock work to reduce amount of hand fitting needed on earlier Trooper versions. Mfg. 1969-1983.

	100%	98%	95%	90%	80%	70%	60%
Blue finish	$500	$350	$225	$180	$170	$160	$150
Nickel finish	$550	$375	$250	$200	$185	$170	$160

Add 50% for .22 Mag. cal.

TROOPER MK V - .357 Mag. cal. only, 4, 6, or 8 in. barrel, adj. sights, walnut target grips, improved version of Mark III action, vent. rib barrel, a few made with solid rib, redesigned 1982. Disc. 1986.

	100%	98%	95%	90%	80%	70%	60%
Blue finish	$475	$350	$275	$215	$185	$170	$160
Nickel finish	$495	$400	$300	$235	$200	$185	$170

Last MSR was $362 for Blue finish. Last MSR was $396 for Nickel finish.

LAWMAN SKY MARSHALL - .38 Spl. cal., 2 in. barrel, experimental revolver with a replaceable plastic cylinder preloaded with plastic bullets, blue finish, checkered walnut grips, this model was designed to be carried on airliners by Federal Marshals during the 1970s.

	100%	98%	95%	90%	80%	70%	60%
	$925	$850	$775	$700	$625	$550	$475

LAWMAN MK III - .357 Mag. cal., 2 in. and 4 in. barrel, unshrouded or shrouded ejector rod for 2 in. barrel, fixed sights, checkered walnut grips. Mfg. 1969-83.

	100%	98%	95%	90%	80%	70%	60%
Blue finish	$450	$375	$300	$180	$170	$160	$150
Nickel finish	$500	$400	$325	$250	$200	$180	$170

LAWMAN MK V - .357 Mag. cal., 2 or 4 in. barrel, shrouded ejector rod for 2 in. barrel, fixed sights, checkered walnut grips, improved version of MK III action. Mfg. 1984 and 1985 only.

	100%	98%	95%	90%	80%	70%	60%
Blue finish	$500	$450	$375	$325	$180	$165	$150
Nickel finish	$550	$475	$400	$350	$250	$200	$180

Last MSR was $309 for Blue finish. Last MSR was $328 for Nickel finish.

BORDER PATROL (SECOND ISSUE) - .357 Mag. cal., 4 in. heavy barrel, similar to Trooper Mark III frame, less polishing to frame. Limited mfg. 1970-75.

Border Patrol Blue Finish - 5,356 mfg.

	100%	98%	95%	90%	80%	70%	60%
	$700	$625	$375	$275	$235	$200	$180

Border Patrol Nickel Finish - 1,152 mfg.

	100%	98%	95%	90%	80%	70%	60%
	$750	$675	$500	$400	$325	$275	$235

PEACEKEEPER - .357 Mag. cal. only, similar to Trooper MK V, 4 or 6 in. barrel, matte blue finish, rubber combat grips, adj. rear sight, about 42 oz. Mfg. 1985-87.

	100%	98%	95%	90%	80%	70%	60%
	$500	$425	$325	$225	$195	$180	$165

Last MSR was $330.

BOA - .357 Mag. cal., deep blue polish, full length ejector shroud with Mark V action, 600 each mfg. in 4 and 6 in. barrel lengths. Entire production run was purchased by Lew Horton Distributing Co., Inc. located in Southboro, MA. 1985 retail was $525.

	100%	98%	95%	90%	80%	70%	60%
	$1,350	$1,175	$1,100	$925	$800	$700	$600

✱ *Boa Set* - 100 sets mfg. including 4 and 6 in. barrels with fully shrouded ejector rod housing, consecutive serial numbers, cases were supplied by Lew Horton. 1985 retail was $1,200.

$4,500	$3,850	$3,000	$2,000	$1,740	$1,495	$1,215

DETECTIVE SPECIAL (FOURTH ISSUE) - .38 Spl. cal., 6 shot, 2 in. barrel, steel frame, blue finish, black composition grips with gold medallions, 21 oz. Reintroduced 1993, disc. 1995.

$450	$400	$375	$300	$200	$180	$165

Last MSR was $400.

✱ *Bobbed Detective Special* - .38 Spl. cal., double action only with bobbed hammer, night front sight, honed action, choice of hard chrome or standard blue finish. Mfg. 1994-95.

$595	$500	$375	$300	$250	$200	$175

Last MSR was $599.

Add $30 for hard chrome finish.

COLT .38 SF-VI - .38 Spl. cal., 6 shot, 2 or 4 in. barrel, transfer bar safety, choice of matte (2 in.), bright polished (4 in.), or black (4 in.) finish, stainless steel, regular or bobbed (4 in. barrel only) hammer, fixed sights, black composition combat grips, 21 oz. Mfg. 1995-96.

$475	$350	$295	$235	$205	$175	$155

Last MSR was $408.

✱ *Colt .38 Special Lady* - while advertised during 1996, this model had very limited mfg.

COLT .38 DSII - .357 Mag. (new 1998) or .38 Spl. cal., 6 shot, 2 in. barrel, stainless steel, service hammer, rubber combat style checkered grips, 21 oz. Mfg. 1997-98.

$495	$365	$300	$240	$210	$180	$155

Last MSR was $435.

This model features a redesigned trigger grouping and is capable of shooting .38+P ammo.

COLT MAGNUM CARRY - .357 Mag. cal., 6 shot, 2 in. barrel, transfer bar safety, satin stainless steel, wraparound rubber grips with finger grooves, ramp front sight, 21 oz. Mfg. 1999 only.

$595	$475	$360	$295	$235	$205	$175

Last MSR was $460.

COMBAT COBRA - .357 Mag. cal., 2 1/2 in. barrel, special edition for Lew Horton with "CC" prefix and stainless steel construction.

$575	$475	$400	$335	$290	$245	$215

KING COBRA - .357 Mag. cal., blue metal, black neoprene round butt grips, 2 1/2 (new 1990), 4 or 6 in. solid rib barrel only, outline sights, approx. 42 oz. (4 in. barrel). Mfg. 1986-92.

$495	$350	$300	$250	$210	$200	$185

Last MSR was $410.

KING COBRA STAINLESS - .357 Mag. cal., stainless steel construction, black neoprene round butt grips, 2 (mfg. 1988-94), 4, 6, or 8 (mfg. 1990-94) in. solid rib barrel, white outline sights, approx. 36 oz. (2 1/2 in. barrel). Mfg. late 1987-92, production resumed 1994, disc. 1998.

$550	$425	$325	$265	$230	$195	$170

Last MSR was $485.

✱ *King Cobra "Ultimate" Bright Stainless* - similar to King Cobra, except for bright stainless steel, 2 1/2 (new 1990), 4, 6, or 8 (new 1991) in. barrel. Mfg. 1988-92.

$595	$400	$300	$240	$210	$180	$155

Last MSR was $470.

GRADING - PPGS™	100%	98%	95%	90%	80%	70%	60%

PYTHON - .357 Mag. cal., 2 1/2 (disc. 1994), 3 (a.k.a Combat Python, disc., very scarce), 4, 6, or 8 in. barrel with vent rib, Royal Blue finish, full shrouded ejector rod, adj. rear sight, checkered walnut grips (prior to 1991), rubber Hogue monogrips (2 1/2 or 4 in. barrel), or rubber target (6 or 8 in. barrel) grips, 38-48 oz. Mfg. 1955-96.

✳ *Python Blue or Royal Blue Finish (Mfg. 1955-1969)* - no letter prefix or suffix in ser. no., pre 1968-1969.

	100%	98%	95%	90%	80%	70%	60%
	$1,100	$995	$700	$600	$500	$395	$350

Add 20% for NIB condition.
Add 50% for very early production (circa 1950s) with high polish finish and correct full checkered, non-varnished grips.
Add 40% for 3 in. barrel with factory letter.

✳ *Python Blue or Royal Blue Finish (Mfg. circa 1970-1996)*

	100%	98%	95%	90%	80%	70%	60%
	$1,050	$950	$775	$675	$600	$500	$395

Last MSR was $815.

Add 20% for NIB condition.
Add 35% for 3 in. barrel.
Beware of loose 3 in. barrel models sold by GPC and others during the 1990s.

The standard Python was manufactured 1955-1996, and 1997-recent production is through the Colt Custom Shop by special order only (see Python Elite listing).

During 2001-2002, Colt shipped some Pythons production to dealers with prices in $1,100 - $1,200 retail range. These guns had a slightly different (rougher) line checkering pattern on the cylinder release and hammer parts.

There were also a few Pythons mfg. in .256 Win. Mag. (circa 1961), .38 Spl. (Python Target), .41 Mag., and .44 Spl. cals. While the .22 LR and the .22 WMR (.22 Mag.) were advertised in earlier factory catalogs, they were never mass-produced - only a few prototypes exist. At least one known example of a .22 cal. Python was found at an auction, but it had only a special factory barrel sleeve for photographic purposes, and was not a shootable gun. The amount of premium on these cals. depends on how serious (and deep-pocketed) the Python collector is.

A California distributor special ordered a quantity of the first 3 in. barreled Pythons, which at the time were not available. Colt probably utilized made-up 8 in. guns and either had them modified or re-barreled, with special marking. These guns are an unusual variant (sometimes referred to as a Combat Python), and are priced similarly to later factory 3 in. barrel Pythons.

✳ *Python Nickel finish* - available in nickel, polished or satin nickel, disc. 1985.

	100%	98%	95%	90%	80%	70%	60%
	$1,200	$950	$675	$575	$475	$395	$300
3 in. barrel w/pol. nickel	$2,400	$1,900	$1,200	$1,000	$775	$450	$400
3 in. barrel w/satin nickel	$7,000	$6,000	$5,000	$4,000	$3,250	$2,500	$1,750

Last MSR was $693.

Add 20% for NIB condition (except for 3 in. nickel).
Satin nickel finish is so designated on original boxes as "Royal Coltguard" or "E NICK" (electroless nickel).
Having a Colt factory letter for the 3 in. barrel is recommended.
At a recent 2007 GunBroker.com auction, a 100% condition 3in. BBL, nickel example sold for $13,020.

✳ *Python Stainless Steel* - stainless steel construction, matte or high polish finish, neoprene target or combat stocks, 2 1/2 (disc. 1994), 4, 6, or 8 (new 1989) in. barrel. Mfg. 1983-96.

	100%	98%	95%	90%	80%	70%	60%
	$1,050	$950	$675	$540	$465	$385	$335

Last MSR was $904.

Add 20% for NIB condition.
Later production of the 6 in. barrel includes neoprene target stocks.

✳ *Python "Ultimate" Bright Stainless Steel* - deluxe, highly polished stainless model, 2 1/2 (disc.), 4, 6, or 8 in. VR barrel. Mfg. 1985-disc.

	100%	98%	95%	90%	80%	70%	60%
	$1,200	$950	$675	$565	$480	$400	$350

Last MSR was $935.

Add 20% for NIB condition.

PYTHON ELITE - .357 Mag. cal., 4 or 6 in. VR barrel, choice of Royal Blue or stainless steel, adj. rear sight, rubber service style (disc.) or smooth walnut finger groove grips, current production is roll-marked "Python Elite" on barrel, 38 or 43 1/2 oz. New 1997, disc. 1998, reintroduced 1999, again during 2002-2006.

	$1,395	$1,075	$875	$750	$650	$550	$475

Last MSR was $1,150.

Add 10% for NIB condition.
This model was available by custom order only through the Colt Custom Shop.
Some early production models have Colt-Elliason rear sights, and recent production uses Colt Accro sight. Some guns were shipped with both wood and hard rubber grips until 1999.

∗ *Python Elite Stainless* - similar to Python Elite, except is stainless steel. Mfg. 1997-99, reintroduced 2002-2006.

	$1,395	$1,075	$875	$750	$650	$550	$475

Last MSR was $1,150.

Add 10% for NIB condition.
This model was available by custom order only through the Colt Custom Shop.

ULTIMATE PYTHON - .357 Mag. cal., specially tuned by the custom shop, supplied with both Colt-Elliason target and Accro white outline sighting systems, walnut and rubber grips also included, choice of Colt Royal Blue or Ultimate Stainless finish, 6 in. barrel only. Mfg. 1991-93.

	$1,395	$1,075	$875	$750	$650	$550	$475

Last MSR was $1,140.

Add $120 for Ultimate Stainless Model.
Add 10% for NIB condition.

PYTHON HUNTER - .357 Mag. cal., 8 in. barrel, includes Leupold 2X scope, Halliburton aluminum case and accessories. Mfg. 1981 only.

	$1,800	$1,600	$1,100	$850	$725	$650	$600

Last MSR was $995.

Add 10% for NIB condition.

PYTHON SILHOUETTE - .357 Mag. cal., 8 in. barrel, includes Leupold 2X scope, similar to Python Hunter, except barrel is roll marked with Silhouette name and scope position has been moved rearward, black luggage type case. Mfg. circa 1983.

	$2,100	$1,825	$1,650	$1,100	$850	$700	$650

Add 10% for NIB condition.

PYTHON .38 SPECIAL - 8 in. barrel, blue or nickel finish. Disc.

	$1,050	$900	$675	$550	$500	$400	$350

Add 20% for NIB condition.

PYTHON TEN POINTER - .357 Mag. cal., 8 in. barrel, includes 3X Burris scope, wooden grips, extra set of neoprene composite grips, carrying case. Disc.

	$1,550	$1,450	$1,100	$850	$800	$775	$700

Add 20% for NIB condition.

GRIZZLY - .357 Mag. cal., 6 in. barrel, matte stainless finish, approx. 500 mfg.

	$1,000	$795	$675	$550	$500	$400	$350

Add 20% for NIB condition.
This model was mfg. by the Colt Custom Shop.

WHITETAILER - .357 Mag. cal., 8 in. barrel, matte stainless finish, aluminum hard shell cased with 2X scope.

	$1,195	$950	$750	$640	$535	$450	$390

Add 20% for NIB condition.

∗ *Whitetailer II* - similar to Whitetailer, except has high polish finish, includes Burris 1.5-4x scope and Colt soft case.

	$1,195	$950	$750	$640	$535	$450	$390

Add 20% for NIB condition.

GRADING - PPGS™	100%	98%	95%	90%	80%	70%	60%

KODIAK - .44 Mag. cal., 4 or 6 in. Mag-na-ported barrel with non-fluted cylinder, stainless steel, Pachmayr grips, built on Anaconda frame, "Colt Kodiak .44 Magnum" with outline of bear's footprint on left side of barrel, ser. nos. start with CKA. Approx. 2,000 mfg. in 1993 by Custom Shop.

	100%	98%	95%	90%	80%	70%	60%
	$1,250	$1,050	$875	$700	$575	$475	$375

ANACONDA - .44 Mag. or .45 LC (mfg. 1992-99) cal., double action, 4 (new 1991), 6, or 8 in. VR barrel, transfer bar safety system, 6 shot, choice of matte (disc. 2003), Realtree Grey camo (.44 Mag. with 8 in. barrel only, mfg. 1996 only) finish, or stainless steel, black neoprene combat grips with Colt medallion, red ramp front sight, full length ejector rod housing, white outline rear adj. sight, approx. 47-59 oz. Mfg. 1990-99, reintroduced 2002.

* *Anaconda Recent Mfg.* - from 2002-2006, the Anaconda was only available through the Colt Custom Shop.

	100%	98%	95%	90%	80%	70%	60%
	$950	$650	$425	$335	$290	$245	$215

Last MSR was $1,000.

    Add $50 for 8 in. barrel.

* *Anaconda 1990-99 Mfg.* - standard production, this period of production was not mfg. by the Colt Custom Shop.

	100%	98%	95%	90%	80%	70%	60%
	$850	$700	$500	$430	$375	$315	$270

    Add 10% for .45 LC cal.

* *Anaconda with scope* - .44 Mag. cal. only, 8 in. barrel, Realtree Grey camo finish on gun and scope. Mfg. 1996 only.

	100%	98%	95%	90%	80%	70%	60%
	$1,595	$1,375	$1,075	$850	$575	$480	$410

Last MSR was $999.

* *Anaconda Hunter* - .44 Mag. cal., supplied with Leupold 2X scope, carrying case, cleaning accessories, and both walnut and rubber grips, 8 in. barrel only. Mfg. 1991-93.

	100%	98%	95%	90%	80%	70%	60%
	$1,595	$1,375	$1,075	$850	$575	$480	$410

Last MSR was $1,200.

* *Anaconda Custom Ported* - .44 Mag. cal., features 6 (disc.) or 8 in. Magna-ported barrel and Colt-Elliason rear sight, contoured trigger, and Pachmayr rubber grips, brushed stainless steel. Mfg. 1992-93, re-released 1995-96, again in 2002-2003.

	100%	98%	95%	90%	80%	70%	60%
	$1,050	$800	$625	$500	$425	$375	$325

Last MSR was $1,050.

* *Anaconda 1st Edition* - .44 Mag. cal., Ultimate Stainless finish, special rollmark on left side of barrel reads "Colt Anaconda First Edition", with aluminum carrying case, ser. no. range MM00001-MM01000, 1,000 mfg. 1990 only.

	100%	98%	95%	90%	80%	70%	60%
	$1,750	$1,450	$1,150	$925	$625	$500	$425

100%	98%	95%	90%	80%	70%	60%	50%	40%	30%	20%	10%

RIFLES/CARBINES: PRE-1904

A Colt letter of provenance for the Lightning models listed below is $100 per gun (limited records). Colt-Burgess model factory letters are also available at $100 per gun.

The author wishes to express his thanks to Mr. Wilmer Kellogg and Mr. Michael Kelly for providing much of the information on Colt-Burgess and Lightning rifles in this section.

FIRST MODEL RING LEVER - .34, .36, .38, .40, or .44 cal., 8 or 10 shot revolving cylinder, 32 in. octagon barrel, walnut stock, no forend, 200 mfg., Percussion. Mfg. 1837-1838.

* *First Model Ring Lever Standard Model*

100%	98%	95%	90%	80%	70%	60%	50%	40%	30%	20%	10%
N/A	N/A	N/A	$37,500	$28,000	$21,500	$16,500	$13,500	$11,000	$9,000	$7,500	$6,500

100%	98%	95%	90%	80%	70%	60%	50%	40%	30%	20%	10%

* First Model Ring Lever Improved Model - attached loading lever.

| N/A | N/A | N/A | $41,000 | $29,650 | $22,750 | $17,500 | $14,500 | $12,000 | $10,000 | $8,500 | $7,500 |

SECOND MODEL RING LEVER - similar to First Model, w/o top strap over cylinder, .44 caliber only, Percussion, 5,000 mfg., 1838-1841.

* Second Model Ring Lever Standard Model

| N/A | N/A | N/A | $33,500 | $24,500 | $17,000 | $13,000 | $11,000 | $8,780 | $7,200 | $6,300 | $5,650 |

* Second Model Ring Lever Improved Model

| N/A | N/A | N/A | $34,750 | $26,000 | $17,750 | $13,300 | $11,200 | $8,900 | $7,325 | $6,390 | $5,725 |

MODEL 1839 CARBINE - .52 smooth bore cal., 6 shot cylinder, 24 in. barrel, exposed hammer for cocking, blue, walnut stock, percussion, approx. 950 mfg., 1838-1841.

* Model 1839 Carbine Early Model - no loading lever.

| N/A | N/A | N/A | $40,500 | $38,500 | $29,000 | $22,000 | $17,500 | $14,750 | $11,500 | $9,350 | $7,750 |

* Model 1839 Carbine Standard Model

| N/A | N/A | N/A | $34,000 | $31,000 | $22,500 | $17,000 | $13,500 | $11,250 | $9,000 | $7,500 | $6,600 |

MODEL 1855 REVOLVING - .36, .44, or .56 cal., various barrel lengths and stock styles, 5 or 6 shot cylinder, blue with walnut buttstock, no forend, percussion. Mfg. 1856-1864.

* Model 1855 Revolving 1/2 Stock Sporter - 24, 27, or 30 in. barrel, approx. 1,500 mfg.

| N/A | N/A | N/A | $11,500 | $9,000 | $7,850 | $7,000 | $6,500 | $6,000 | $5,500 | $5,100 | $4,750 |

* Model 1855 Revolving Full Stock Sporter - 21, 24, 27, 30, or 31 in. barrel, approx. 2,000 mfg.

| N/A | N/A | N/A | $13,500 | $11,275 | $9,150 | $8,250 | $7,500 | $6,950 | $6,500 | $6,100 | $5,750 |

* Model 1855 Revolving Military Model, U.S. - marked, 21-37 in. barrel, 9,310 mfg.

| N/A | N/A | N/A | $17,500 | $14,650 | $11,900 | $10,500 | $9,800 | $9,050 | $8,450 | $7,900 | $7,475 |

* Model 1855 Revolving .36 Caliber Carbine Model - 15, 18, or 21 in. barrel, 4,400 mfg.

| N/A | N/A | N/A | $17,150 | $14,350 | $11,660 | $10,525 | $9,600 | $8,875 | $8,275 | $7,750 | $7,300 |

* Model 1855 Revolving .56 Caliber Artillery Carbine - 5 shot, 21 in. barrel with bayonet lug and forestock, approx. 64 mfg.

| N/A | N/A | N/A | $19,000 | $16,500 | $13,500 | $10,875 | $9,850 | $9,100 | $8,400 | $7,950 | $7,500 |

* Model 1855 Revolving Shotgun Model - .60 or .75 cal., smooth bore, 27, 30, 33, or 36 in. barrels, 1,100 mfg.

| N/A | N/A | N/A | $12,750 | $11,000 | $9,000 | $8,000 | $7,250 | $6,750 | $6,300 | $6,000 | $5,600 |

BERDAN - .42 bottle-necked CF cal., breechloading, approx. 30,000 mfg. 1866-circa 1870. Scarce since most were sent to Russia and have Russian barrel markings, approx. 50-100 are Hartford marked.

* Berdan Rifle - .32 1/2 in. barrel, approx. 10 lbs.

| N/A | N/A | N/A | $6,000 | $5,000 | $4,000 | $3,500 | $3,250 | $3,000 | $2,000 | $1,350 | $1,000 |

* Berdan Carbine - half stock, 18 1/4 in. barrel, approx. 50 mfg., both Russian and Hartford marked.

| N/A | N/A | N/A | $8,300 | $7,600 | $6,725 | $6,100 | $5,500 | $4,750 | $3,950 | $3,275 | $2,750 |

MODEL 1861 MUSKET - .58 cal., percussion, muzzle loader, 40 in. barrel, with 3 bands, metal parts, white walnut stock. 75,000 mfg., 1861-65.

| N/A | N/A | N/A | $7,000 | $5,000 | $4,000 | $3,500 | $3,250 | $3,000 | $2,000 | $1,350 | $1,000 |

COLT-BURGESS LEVER ACTION RIFLE - .44-40 cal., 25 1/2 in. barrel, 15 shot tube mag., blue with case hardened lever and hammer, walnut stock, round or octagon barrel. 3,810 rifles mfg. (2556 octagon, 1219 round, and 35 half round and half octagon), 1883-85.

| N/A | N/A | N/A | $15,000 | $9,000 | $6,000 | $5,000 | $4,000 | $3,500 | $3,000 | $2,500 | $1,500 |

100%	98%	95%	90%	80%	70%	60%	50%	40%	30%	20%	10%

COLT-BURGESS LEVER ACTION CARBINE - similar to Rifle, with 20 in. round barrel. 1621 carbines mfg.

| N/A | N/A | N/A | $22,000 | $15,000 | $12,000 | $10,000 | $8,000 | $6,500 | $5,000 | $3,500 | $2,500 |

COLT-BURGESS LEVER ACTION LIGHT CARBINE - lightened version of Carbine, one pound lighter. 972 light carbines mfg.

| N/A | N/A | N/A | $25,000 | $18,000 | $15,000 | $13,000 | $11,000 | $9,000 | $7,000 | $4,000 | $3,000 |

LIGHTNING SLIDE ACTION RIFLE (CLMR) - SMALL FRAME - .22 S or L cal., 24 in. barrel, open sights, walnut straight stock, round or octagon barrel, approx. 90,000 mfg. 1887-1904.

| N/A | N/A | N/A | $5,500 | $4,000 | $3,500 | $3,000 | $2,500 | $2,200 | $1,750 | $1,200 | $500 |

Add 25% for deluxe model.

LIGHTNING SLIDE ACTION RIFLE (CLMR) - MEDIUM FRAME - .32 CLMR, 38 CLMR, or 44 CLMR cal., similar to small frame, except with 26 in. barrel and larger frame. Approx. 90,000 mfg. 1884-1902.

| N/A | N/A | N/A | $7,000 | $5,000 | $4,250 | $3,750 | $3,000 | $2,500 | $2,000 | $1,500 | $1,200 |

Add 25% for deluxe model.

23 factory engraved medium frame rifles were shipped to A.G. Spalding and Brothers during 1897, a major sporting goods supplier located in Chicago. These rifles were probably used for display during the Chicago Exposition. These deluxe rifles represent some of the finest Colt rifles ever manufactured.

LIGHTNING CARBINE MEDIUM FRAME - similar to Medium Frame Rifle, with 20 in. round barrel.

| N/A | N/A | N/A | $9,000 | $7,000 | $6,000 | $5,000 | $4,000 | $3,500 | $3,000 | $2,500 | $2,000 |

LIGHTNING BABY CARBINE MEDIUM FRAME - lightened version of Medium Frame Carbine, one pound lighter.

| N/A | N/A | N/A | $9,000 | $7,000 | $6,000 | $5,000 | $4,000 | $3,500 | $3,000 | $2,500 | $2,000 |

LIGHTNING MILITARY STYLE MUSKET - similar to Medium Frame Rifle, bayonet lug.

| N/A | N/A | N/A | N/A | N/A | N/A | $5,000 | $4,000 | $3,000 | $2,000 | $1,500 | $1,000 |

Approximately 250 of these rifles with 27" round barrels, swivels, and carbine butts, in serial ranges #50,000 and #51,000 were shipped to Costa Rica.

LIGHTNING SAN FRANCISCO POLICE - round barrel Medium Frame Rifle, with S.F. Police #'s 1-401.

| N/A | N/A | N/A | $7,000 | $5,000 | $4,000 | $3,500 | $3,250 | $3,000 | $2,000 | $1,350 | $1,000 |

LIGHTNING SLIDE ACTION RIFLE (CLMR) - LARGE FRAME - .38-56-255, .40-60-260 (most common), .45-60-300 (rarest), .45-85-285, or .50-95 Express (rare) cal., large frame version of previously described Lightnings, approx. 4,600 mfg. 1887-1894.

| N/A | N/A | N/A | $11,000 | $9,000 | $7,500 | $6,500 | $5,000 | $4,000 | $3,000 | $2,000 | $1,500 |

Add 25% for .50-95 Express cal.
Add 25% for deluxe model.

There may be a gap in the serial range of this model from ser. no. 2435 to 4444.

LIGHTNING CARBINE LARGE FRAME - similar to Large Frame Rifle, 22 in. round barrel.

| N/A | N/A | N/A | $13,000 | $10,000 | $8,000 | $6,000 | $5,000 | $4,000 | $3,250 | $3,000 | $2,500 |

Add 25% for .50-95 Express cal.

LIGHTNING BABY CARBINE LARGE FRAME - lightened version of Large Frame Carbine, one pound lighter.

| N/A | N/A | N/A | $13,000 | $10,000 | $8,000 | $6,000 | $5,000 | $4,000 | $3,250 | $3,000 | $2,500 |

Add 50% for .50-95 Express cal.

DOUBLE RIFLE SxS - various cals. in the .45 range, hammers, very limited production between 1878-1880. Most guns were owned by friends of Caldwell Colt - Sam Colt's son, the original designer. Colt Double Rifles are extremely rare and desirable, and should be examined carefully.

Prices typically range between $70,000-$100,000, if all original.

COLTEER 1-22 - .22 LR or .22 Mag. cal., single shot bolt action, 20, 22, or 24 (.22 Mag. only, w/o sights) in. round barrel, adj. rear sight (20 or 22 in. barrel), plain walnut stock. Approx. 50,000 mfg. 1957-66.

	$275	$215	$175	$140	$110	$95	$80

> Add 10% for .22 Mag. cal.
> Subtract 5% if wood and finish are scratched in front of the barrel/forearm band.
> Subtract 5-10% if w/o the front sight hood.

This model has a soft aluminum alloy painted receiver which was very easily scratched. It is quite common to find these guns in 80 to 85% condition with very little market interest. It is becoming common place to find these guns with the receiver repainted. There is a limited market interest in guns that are 98% condition and better. On the models that have the band around the barrel and forearm, it is common to see the wood and finish scratched where the band has been slid forward.

STAGECOACH - .22 LR cal., semi-auto, 16 1/2 in. barrel, 13 shot mag., deluxe walnut, saddle ring w/ leather thong, roll-engraved hold-up scene. Over 25,000 mfg. 1965-mid '70s.

	$325	$275	$215	$175	$140	$110	$90

> Subtract 5% if wood and finish are scratched in front of the barrel/forearm band.
> Subtract 5-10% if w/o the front sight hood.
> Subtract 10% if gold color is missing in stagecoach scene.

This model has a soft aluminum alloy painted receiver which was very easily scratched. It is quite common to find these guns in 80 to 85% condition with very little market interest. It is becoming common place to find these guns with the receiver repainted. There is a limited market interest in guns that are 98% condition and better. On the models that have the band around the barrel and forearm, it is common to see the wood and finish scratched where the band has been slid forward.

COLTEER - .22 LR cal., similar to Stagecoach, except 19 3/8 in. barrel, 15 shot mag., no engraving and plain walnut. Over 25,000 mfg. 1965-mid '70s.

	$275	$215	$175	$140	$110	$95	$80

> Subtract 5% if wood and finish are scratched in front of the barrel/forearm band.
> Subtract 5-10% if w/o the front sight hood.

This model has a soft aluminum alloy painted receiver which was very easily scratched. It is quite common to find these guns in 80 to 85% condition with very little market interest. It is becoming common place to find these guns with the receiver repainted. There is a limited market interest in guns that are 98% condition and better. On the models that have the band around the barrel and forearm, it is common to see the wood and finish scratched where the band has been slid forward.

COURIER - similar to Colteer semi-auto, except pistol-grip stock and enlarged forearm. Mfg. 1970-mid '70s.

	$275	$215	$175	$140	$110	$95	$80

> Subtract 5% if wood and finish are scratched in front of the barrel/forearm band.
> Subtract 5-10% if w/o the front sight hood.

This model has a soft aluminum alloy painted receiver which was very easily scratched. It is quite common to find these guns in 80 to 85% condition with very little market interest. It is becoming common place to find these guns with the receiver repainted. There is a limited market interest in guns that are 98% condition and better. On the models that have the band around the barrel and forearm, it is common to see the wood and finish scratched where the band has been slid forward.

RIFLES: BOLT ACTION, CENTERFIRE

COLT "57" - .243 Win. or .30-06 cal., FN Mauser action, mfg. by Jefferson Mfg. Co. in N. Haven, CT during 1957, approx. 5,000 mfg. starting at ser. no. 1, checkered American Monte Carlo walnut stock, rear aperture and wraparound front sight, drilled and tapped for scope.

	$595	$550	$500	$450	$400	$350	$325

This model was also available in a deluxe version with deluxe hand checkered walnut stock - add 15%.

GRADING - PPGS™	100%	98%	95%	90%	80%	70%	60%

COLTSMAN STANDARD RIFLE - .223 Rem., .243 Win., .264 Win. Mag., .30-06, .300 Win. Mag., or .308 Win. cal., mfg. by Kodiak, Mauser or Sako action, 22 in. or 24 in. (.300 Win. Mag.), 5 or 6 shot mag. Approx. 10,000 (both models) mfg. 1958-66.

	100%	98%	95%	90%	80%	70%	60%
	$495	$450	$425	$400	$350	$325	$300

COLTSMAN CUSTOM RIFLE - deluxe variation including deluxe walnut with ski-pline checkering and rosewood forearm cap.

	$695	$650	$600	$550	$500	$450	$400

COLT SAUER RIFLE (STANDARD ACTION) - .25-06 Rem., .270 Win. or .30-06 cal., non-rotating bolt action, manufactured in Germany by J. P. Sauer & Sohn, 24 in. barrel, 4 shot detachable mag., no sights, checkered walnut stock with rosewood forend tip and pistol grip cap, recoil pad. Mfg. 1974-1985.

	$1,600	$1,400	$1,200	$1,10	$900	$750	$625

Last MSR was $1,257.

Add 15% for .25-06 Rem. cal.

COLT SAUER SHORT ACTION - similar to the standard except in .22-250 Rem., .243 Win. cal. or .308 Win. cal. Mfg. 1976-85.

	$1,700	$1,500	$1,400	$1,100	$1,000	$775	$700

Last MSR was $1,257.

Add 25% for .308 Win. cal.

COLT SAUER MAGNUM - similar to the standard except in 7mm Rem. Mag., 300 Win. Mag., or 300 Weatherby Mag. cal. Mfg. 1974-1985.

	$2,000	$1,750	$1,500	$1,300	$1,000	$900	$800

Last MSR was $1,300.

COLT SAUER GRADE IV - similar to the Magnum except has silver receiver, each caliber features a different engraved animal.

	$3,850	$3,450	$3,000	$2,800	$2,000	$2,400	$2,200

Add 10% for Magnum cals.

COLT SAUER GRAND ALASKAN - heavier version in .375 H&H cal., adj. sights. Mfg. 1978-1985.

	$2,100	$1,800	$1,500	$1,300	$1,200	$1,000	$900

COLT SAUER GRAND AFRICAN - .458 Win. Mag. cal., 4 round capacity, 9 lb. 12 oz. Mfg. 1974-1985.

	$2,100	$1,800	$1,500	$1,300	$1,200	$1,000	$900

Last MSR was $1,400.

COLT LIGHT RIFLE - .243 Win., .260 Rem., .270 Win., .280 Rem., .25-06 Rem., .30-06, .308 Win., 7x57mm, .300 Win. Mag., 7mm-08, or 7mm Rem. Mag. cal., short or long action, matte black synthetic stock, matte metal finish, adj. trigger, 3 position side safety, approx. 5.4 lbs. in short action, manufactured by Saco Defense in the U.S. New 2000.

MSR $779		$675	$550	$500	$450	$400	$350	$295

RIFLES: SINGLE SHOT, CENTERFIRE

COLT-SHARPS RIFLE - .17 Bee, .22-250 Rem., .243 Win., .25-06 Rem., 7mm Rem. Mag., .30-06, or .375 H&H cal., Sharps falling block action, high-gloss bluing, deluxe checkered walnut stock and forearm, includes wood case with accessories. Approx. 500 mfg. 1970-1977.

	$2,295	$1,950	$1,650	$1,200	$1,000	$800	$650

GRADING - PPGS™	100%	98%	95%	90%	80%	70%	60%

DRILLINGS

COLT SAUER DRILLING - 12 ga./.30-06, 16 ga./.30-06 (rare), or .243 Win. cal., 25 in. barrels, engraved receiver, 8 lbs. Disc. 1985.

	100%	98%	95%	90%	80%	70%	60%
	$4,300	$3,600	$3,100	$2,675	$2,200	$1,800	$1,400

Last MSR was $4,228.

RIFLES: SEMI-AUTO, AR-15 & VARIATIONS

The AR-15 rifle and variations are the civilian versions of the U.S. armed forces M-16 model, which was initially ordered by the U.S. Army in 1963. Colt's obtained the exclusive manufacturing and marketing rights to the AR-15 from the Armalite division of the Fairchild Engine and Airplane Corporation in 1961.

Factory Colt AR-15 receivers are stamped with the model names only (Sporter II, Government Model, Colt Carbine, Sporter Match H-Bar, Match Target), but are not stamped with the model numbers (R6500, R6550, R6521, MT6430, CR6724). Because of this, if an AR-15 rifle/carbine does not have its original box, the only way to determine whether the gun is pre-ban or not is to look at the serial number and see if the configuration matches the features listed below within the two pre-ban subcategories.

AR-15 production included transition models, which were made up of obsolete and old stock parts. These transition models include: blue label box models having large front takedown pins, no internal sear block, 20 in. barrel models having bayonet lugs, misstamped nomenclature on receivers, and having green label bolt assemblies.

Rifling twists on the Colt AR-15 have changed throughout the years, and barrel twists are stamped at the end of the barrel on top. They started with a 1:12 in. twist, changed to a 1:7 in. twist (to match with the new, longer .223 Rem./5.56mm SS109-type bullet), and finally changed to a 1:9 in. twist in combination with 1:7 in. twist models as a compromise for bullets in the 50-68 grain range. Current mfg. AR-15s/Match Targets have rifling twists/turns incorporated into the model descriptions.

Colt's never sold pre-ban lower receivers individually. It only sold completely assembled rifles.

A Colt letter of provenance for the following AR-15 models is $100 per gun.

AR-15, Pre-Ban, 1963-1989 Mfg. w/ Green Label Box

Common features of 1963-1989 mfg. AR-15s are bayonet lug, flash hider, large front takedown pin, no internal sear block, and w/o reinforcement around the magazine release button.

AR-15 boxes during this period of mfg. had a green label with serial number affixed on a white sticker. Box is taped in two places with brown masking tape. NIB consists of the rifle with barrel stick down the barrel, plastic muzzle cap on flash hider, factory tag hanging from front sight post, rifle is in plastic bag with ser. no. on white sticker attached to bag, cardboard insert, accessory bag with two 20 round mags., manual, sling, and cleaning brushes. Cleaning rods are in separate bag.

Pre-ban parts rifles are rifles that are not assembled in their proper factory configuration. Counterfeit pre-ban rifles are rifles using post-ban receivers and assembled into a pre-ban configuration (it is a felony to assemble or alter a post-ban rifle into a pre-ban configuration). Unstamped L.E. only rifles are a felony to possess, and can be sold only to sworn law enforcement officers.

Add $100 for NIB condition.

Add $300 for early green label box models with reinforced lower receiver.

SP-1 (R6000) - .223 Rem. cal., original Colt paramilitary configuration without forward bolt assist, 20 in. barrel with 1:12 in. twist, identifiable by the triangular shaped handguards/forearm, no case deflector, A1 sights, finishes included parkerizing and electroless nickel, approx. 6 3/4 lbs. Mfg. 1963-1984.

	100%	98%	95%	90%	80%	70%	60%
	$1,950	$1,825	$1,700	$1,575	$1,450	$1,250	$1,050

Early mfg. will command substantial premiums, especially for very low ser. nos. - ser. range is SP00001 (1963)-SP55301 (1976).

Mint original condition models with early two and three digit serial numbers are selling in the $3,250 - $3,500 range.

Pre-ban serialization is ser. no. SP360,200 and lower.

Early SP-1s were packaged differently than later standard green box label guns.

GRADING - PPGS™	100%	98%	95%	90%	80%	70%	60%

✳ *SP-1 Carbine (R6001)* - similar to SP-1, except has 16 in. barrel, ribbed handguards, and collapsible buttstock with high gloss finish.

	$2,450	$2,250	$1,975	$1,775	$1,625	$1,450	$1,200

Mint original condition models with early two and three digit serial numbers are selling in the $3,250 - $3,500 range.

Pre-ban serialization is ser. no. SP360200 and lower.

Early SP-1s were packaged differently than later standard green box label guns.

SPORTER II (R6500) - .223 Rem. cal., various configurations, receiver stamped "Sporter II", 20 in. barrel, 1:7 twist, A1 sights and forward assist, disc.

	$1,550	$1,325	$1,150	$975	$850	$750	$675

Serial numbers SP360200 and below are pre-ban.

✳ *Sporter II Carbine (R6420)* - similar to Sporter II, except has 16 in. barrel, A1 sights and collapsible buttstock.

	$1,875	$1,650	$1,500	$1,325	$1,175	$1,075	$950

Serial numbers SP360200 and below are pre-ban.

GOVERNMENT MODEL (R6550) - .223 Rem. cal., receiver is stamped Government Model, 20 in. barrel with 1:7 in. twist, A2 sights, forward assist and brass deflector, very desirable because this model has the closest configurations to what the U.S. military is currently using.

	$2,000	$1,850	$1,700	$1,550	$1,400	$1,250	$1,050

In 1987, Colt replaced the AR-15A2 Sporter II Rifle with the AR-15A2 Govt. Model. This new model has the 800 meter rear sighting system housed in the receiver's carrying handle (similar to the M-16 A2).

Serial numbers GS008000 and below are pre-ban.

✳ *Government Model (6550K)* - similar to R6550, except does not have bayonet lug, originally supplied with .22 cal. conversion kit.

	$1,850	$1,700	$1,550	$1,400	$1,250	$1,050	$900

Subtract $300 w/o conversion kit.

Serial numbers GS008000 and below are pre-ban.

✳ *Government Model (R6550CC)* - similar to R6550, except has Z-Cote tiger striped camo finish, very scarce (watch for cheap imitation paint jobs).

	$3,500	$3,350	$3,100	$2,800	$2,600	$2,400	$2,000

Serial numbers GS008000 and below are pre-ban.

H-BAR MODEL (R6600) - H-Bar model with 20 in heavy barrel, 1:7 twist, forward assist, A2 sights, brass deflector, 8 lbs. New 1986.

	$1,800	$1,650	$1,500	$1,350	$1,200	$1,050	$925

Serial numbers SP360200 and below are pre-ban.

✳ *H-Bar (R6600K)* - similar to R6600, except has no bayonet lug, supplied with .22 LR cal. conversion kit.

	$1,800	$1,650	$1,500	$1,350	$1,200	$1,050	$925

Subtract $300 w/o conversion kit.

Serial numbers SP360200 and below are pre-ban.

✳ *Delta H-Bar (R6600DH)* - similar to R6600, except has 3-9X rubber armored variable scope, removable cheekpiece, adj. scope mount, and black leather sling, range selected, aluminum cased. Mfg. 1987-91. - 9mm Para. cal., carbine model with 16 in. barrel and bayonet lug with 1:10 twist, w/o forward bolt assist and brass deflector, two-position collapsible stock, with 20 shot mag., 6 lbs. 5 oz. - 9mm Para. cal., similar to R6450 Carbine, except does not have bayonet lug or collapsible stock. New 1992. - 7.62x39mm cal., 16 in. barrel w/o bayonet lug and 1:12 twist, fixed buttstock. New 1992.

	$2,300	$2,150	$1,925	$1,775	$1,575	$1,375	$1,125

Last MSR was $1,460.

Serial numbers SP360200 and below are pre-ban.

GRADING - PPGS™	100%	98%	95%	90%	80%	70%	60%

AR-15, Pre-Ban,1989-Sept. 11,1994 Mfg. w/Blue Label Box

Common features of 1989-1994 AR-15 production include a small front takedown pin, internal sear block, reinforcement around the mag. release button, flash hider, no bayonet lug on 20 in. models, A2 sights, brass deflector, and forward bolt assist. Models R6430 and 6450 do not have A2 sights, brass deflector, or forward bolt assist.

Blue label boxed AR-15s were mfg. between 1989-Sept. 11, 1994. Please refer to box description under Pre-1989 AR-15 mfg.

Pre-ban parts rifles are rifles that are not assembled in their proper factory configuration. Counterfeit pre-ban rifles are rifles using post-ban receivers and assembled into a pre-ban configuration.

   Add $100 for NIB condition.

AR-15A3 TACTICAL CARBINE (R-6721) - .223 Rem. cal., M4 flattop with 16 in. heavy barrel, 1:9 twist, pre-ban configuration with flash hider, bayonet lug, and 4-position, A2 sights, collapsible stock, removable carry handle, 134 were sold commercially in the U.S., most collectible AR-15. Mfg. 1994 only.

	$2,975	$2,500	$2,275	$2,050	$1,900	$1,775	$1,600

On the R-6721, serial numbers BD000134 and below are pre-ban.
Please note the serial number cutoff on this model, as Colt shipped out a lot of unstamped post-ban law enforcement only "LEO" rifles before finally stamping them as a restricted rifle.

GOVERNMENT CARBINE (R6520) - receiver is stamped Government Carbine, two-position collapsible buttstock, 800 meter adj. rear sight, 16 in. barrel bayonet lug, 1:7 twist, shortened forearm, 5 lbs. 13 oz. Mfg. 1988-94.

	$1,900	$1,750	$1,650	$1,500	$1,375	$1,250	$1,050

Last MSR was $880.

   Add $200 for green label box.
On the R6520, serial numbers GC018500 and below are pre-ban.
Please note the serial number cutoff on this model, as Colt shipped out a lot of unstamped post-ban law enforcement only "LEO" rifles before finally stamping them as a restricted rifle. This model was manufactured in both green and blue label configurations.

COLT CARBINE (R6521) - stamped Colt Carbine, similar to R6520, except has no bayonet lug, 16 in. barrel, 1:7 twist. Disc. 1988.

	$2,050	$1,900	$1,750	$1,600	$1,525	$1,375	$1,200

Last MSR was $770.

Serial numbers CC001616 and below are pre-ban.

SPORTER LIGHTWEIGHT (R6530) - .223 Rem., receiver is stamped Sporter Lightweight, 16 in. barrel, 1:7 twist, similar to R6520, except does not have bayonet lug and collapsible stock.

	$1,500	$1,350	$1,200	$1,050	$900	$800	$700

Last MSR was $740.

Serial numbers SI027246 and below are pre-ban.

9mm CARBINE (R6450)

	$2,050	$1,900	$1,750	$1,600	$1,525	$1,375	$1,200

Last MSR was $696.

On the R6450, serial numbers TA010100 are pre-ban.
Please note the serial number cutoff on this model, as Colt shipped out a lot of unstamped post-ban law enforcement only "LEO" rifles before finally stamping them as a restricted rifle. This model was manufactured with either a green or blue label configurations.

9mm CARBINE (R6430)

	$1,600	$1,450	$1,300	$1,150	$1,025	$925	$825

Serial numbers NL004800 are pre-ban.

7.62x39mm CARBINE (R6830)

	$1,600	$1,450	$1,300	$1,150	$1,025	$925	$825

Serial numbers LH011326 are pre-ban.

GRADING - PPGS™	100%	98%	95%	90%	80%	70%	60%

TARGET COMPETITION H-BAR RIFLE (R6700) - .223 Rem. cal., features flat-top upper receiver for scope mounting, 20 in. H-Bar barrel (1:9 in. twist), quick detachable carry handle which incorporates a 600-meter rear sighting system, dovetailed upper receiver is grooved to accept Weaver style scope rings, 8 1/2 lbs.

	$1,700	$1,550	$1,400	$1,250	$1,050	$875	$725

Serial numbers CH019500 and below are pre-ban.

COMPETITION H-BAR CUSTOM SHOP (R6701) - .223 Rem. cal., similar to the R6700, but is equipped with detachable scope mount, custom shop enhancements added to trigger and barrel, 2,000 mfg. from Colt Custom Shop.

	$1,800	$1,650	$1,500	$1,350	$1,200	$1,050	$900

MATCH H-BAR (R6601) - heavy 20 in. H-Bar barrel with 1:7 twist, fixed buttstock. 8 lbs.

	$1,500	$1,350	$1,200	$1,050	$900	$800	$700

∗ *Delta H-Bar (R6601DH)* - similar to R6601, except has 3-9X rubber armored variable scope, removable cheekpiece, adj. scope mount, and black leather sling, range selected, aluminum cased. Mfg. 1987-91.

	$2,200	$2,050	$1,900	$1,750	$1,600	$1,450	$1,300

Last MSR was $1,460.

Serial numbers MH086020 and below are pre-ban.

SPORTER TARGET (R6551) - similar to R6601, except has 20 in. barrel which tapers down underneath handguard, 7 1/2 lbs.

	$1,500	$1,350	$1,200	$1,050	$900	$800	$700

On the R6551, serial numbers ST038100 and below are pre-ban.

AR-15, Post-Ban, Mfg. Sept. 12, 1994-Present

Due to Colt's current military contracts, the commercial availability of AR-15s and variations listed below has been somewhat limited in recent years.

During 2007, Colt released the M-5 Military Carbine and the LE 10-20, with 11 1/2, 14 1/2, or 16 in. barrel. These guns are only available for military and law enforcement.

Add $368 for Colt Scout C-More Sight on current mfg.
Add $444 for Colt Tactical C-More Sight on current mfg.

MATCH TARGET COMPETITION H-BAR RIFLE (MT6700/MT6700C) - .223 Rem. cal., features flattop upper receiver for scope mounting, 20 in. barrel (1 turn in 9 in.), quick detachable carry handle which incorporates a 600-meter rear sighting system, counterbored muzzle, dovetailed upper receiver is grooved to accept Weaver style scope rings, supplied with two 5, 8, or 9 (new 1999) shot mags., cleaning kit, and sling, matte black finish, 8 1/2 lbs. New 1992.

MSR $1,193			$1,050	$925	$850	$750	$650	$575	$525

Add $57 for compensator (MT6700C, new 1999).

TACTICAL ELITE MODEL (TE6700) - .223 Rem. cal., 20 in. heavy barrel, 1:8 in. barrel rifling twist, Hogue finger groove pistol grip, Choate buttstock, fine tuned for accuracy, includes scope and mount, approx. 1,000 rifles made by the Custom Shop circa 1996-97.

	$1,650	$1,450	$1,250	$1,025	$900	$800	$700

COLT ACCURIZED RIFLE (CR6724) - .223 Rem. cal., 24 in. stainless match barrel, matte finish, accurized AR-15, 8 (disc. 1998) or 9 (new 1999) shot mag., 9.41 lbs. New 1997.

MSR $1,334			$1,150	$1,000	$875	$795	$725	$650	$575

MATCH TARGET COMPETITION H-BAR II (MT6731) - .223 Rem. cal., flattop, 16.1 in. barrel (1:9 in.), matte finish, 7.1 lbs. New 1995.

MSR $1,172			$1,025	$925	$850	$725	$625	$575	$525

GRADING - PPGS™	100%	98%	95%	90%	80%	70%	60%

MATCH TARGET LIGHTWEIGHT (MT6430, MT6530, or MT6830) - .223 Rem. (MT6530, 1:7 in. twist), 7.62x39mm (MT6830, disc. 1996, 1:12 in. twist), or 9mm Para. (MT6430, disc. 1996, 1:10 in. twist) cals., features 16 in. barrel (non-threaded per C/B 1994), initially shorter stock and handguard, adj. rear sight for windage and elevation, includes 2 detachable 5, 8, or 9 (new 1999) shot mags., approx. 7 lbs. Mfg. 1991-2002.

	$925	$795	$725	$665	$600	$550	$495

Last MSR was $1,111.

> **Add $200 for .22 LR conversion kit (disc. 1994).**

TARGET GOVT. MODEL RIFLE (MT6551) - .223 Rem. cal., semi-auto version of the M-16 rifle with forward bolt assist, gas operated, 20 in. barrel (1:7 in.), straight line black nylon stock, aperture rear, post front sight, 5, 8, 9 (new 1999) shot mags., 7 1/2 lbs. Disc. 2002.

	$1,050	$925	$850	$775	$700	$650	$595

Last MSR was $1,144.

> **Add $200 for .22 LR conversion kit (mfg. 1990-94).**

MATCH TARGET M4 CARBINE (MT6400C) - .223 Rem. cal., similar to current U.S. armed forces M4 model, except semi-auto, 10 shot mag., 16.1 in. barrel with 1:7 in. twist, matte black finish, fixed tube buttstock, A3 detachable carrying handle, 7.3 lbs. New 2002.

MSR $1,289		$1,075	$950	$850	$725	$625	$575	$525

MATCH TARGET H-BAR RIFLE (MT6601/MT6601C) - features heavy 20 in. H-Bar barrel, 1:7 in. twist, A2 sights, 8 lbs. New 1986.

MSR $1,182		$1,025	$895	$825	$725	$650	$575	$525

> **Add $200 for .22 LR conversion kit (mfg. 1990-94).**

This model is available with a compensator for $1 (MT6601C, new 1999).

AR-15 SCOPE (3X/4X) AND MOUNT - initially offered with 3X scope, then switched to 4X. Disc.

	$395	$300	$240	$185	$160	$130	$115

Last MSR was $344.

SHOTGUNS: O/U

ARMSMEAR - 12 ga. only, 2 3/4 in. chambers, a few prototypes were mfg. by Worshipful Co. Gunmakers of London, boxlock action with engraved sideplates, checkered high-grade European walnut stock and forearm, 28 (HE) or 30 (LE) in. VR barrels with screw-in chokes, choice of light (Armsmear 12 LE) or heavy (Armsmear 12 HE) engraving, 7 1/2 lbs. This model was originally advertised in 1995.

While advertised, this model was never manufactured.

100%	98%	95%	90%	80%	70%	60%	50%	40%	30%	20%	10%

SHOTGUNS: SxS, DISC.

Strong, original case colors and vivid damascus barrel patterning will make the difference when determining values on the Models 1878 and 1883. Remember, the models listed below were designed to shoot black powder loads only, not smokeless powder.

A Colt letter of provenance for the models listed below is $100 per gun.

MODEL 1878 HAMMER SHOTGUN - 10 or 12 ga., 28-32 in. blue or browned damascus barrels, double triggers, sideplates, case hardened breech, extractors, semi-pistol grip stock, 22,683 mfg. between 1878-89. Many of these guns were ordered with special features - these original guns command premiums above the prices listed below.

$3,750	$3,250	$2,950	$2,675	$2,200	$1,925	$1,650	$1,485	$1,100	$990	$880	$725

100%	98%	95%	90%	80%	70%	60%	50%	40%	30%	20%	10%

MODEL 1883 HAMMERLESS - 8, 10, or 12 ga., 28-32 in. damascus barrels, many deluxe custom orders occur in this model. Mfg. from 1883-95. Approx. serial range is 1-3,050 and 4,055-8,365. Seldom encountered in mint condition.

100%	98%	95%	90%	80%	70%	60%	50%	40%	30%	20%	10%
$4,250	$3,750	$3,350	$2,995	$2,675	$2,200	$1,925	$1,650	$1,485	$1,100	$990	$875

Add 200% for 8 ga.

This model was generally a custom order gun with no standard grades being designated. Quality was extremely high, and the high cost of manufacture is a large reason why the gun never sold in large numbers commercially. The Model 1883 was discontinued after only 12 years of manufacture (it was one of the most expensive shotguns during its day). Values above assume moderate engraving and above average walnut.

GRADING - PPGS™		100%	98%	95%	90%	80%	70%	60%

SxS SHOTGUN MFG. 1961-62 - 12 ga. or 16 ga., various barrel lengths, DTs, checkered stock and forearm, mfg. in France 1961-62 by Fabrication Mechanique, estimated total between 25-50 guns in serial range 467,000-469,000.

100%	98%	95%	90%	80%	70%	60%
$675	$595	$525	$450	$400	$360	$320

SHOTGUNS: SEMI-AUTO

STANDARD AUTO SHOTGUN - 12 or 20 ga. (also available in Mags.), mfg. by Franchi of Italy, aluminum frame, 26, 28, 30, or 32 in. plain or VR barrel almost 5,300 mfg. (both models) 1962-66.

100%	98%	95%	90%	80%	70%	60%
$375	$350	$325	$295	$260	$230	$200

Add $50 for VR barrel.

CUSTOM AUTO SHOTGUN - similar to Standard Model, except deluxe walnut, hand engraved receiver. Mfg. 1962-1966.

100%	98%	95%	90%	80%	70%	60%
$475	$425	$375	$350	$325	$295	$260

SHOTGUNS: SLIDE ACTION

COLTSMAN PUMP SHOTGUN - 12, 16, or 20 ga., Manufrance frame assembled by both Kodiak and Montgomery Wards, 26 or 28 in. plain barrel, aluminum frame. Approx. 2,000 mfg. 1961-1965.

100%	98%	95%	90%	80%	70%	60%
$325	$295	$260	$230	$200	$180	$165

Add 30% for Riot model with extended magazine and 20 in. barrel (not cataloged).

COMMEMORATIVES, SPECIAL EDITIONS, & LIMITED MFG.

During the course of a year, we receive many phone calls and letters on Colt special editions and limited editions that do not appear in this section. It should be noted that a factory commemorative issue is a gun that has been manufactured, marketed, and sold through the auspices of the specific trademark (in this case Colt). There have literally been hundreds of special and limited editions which, although mostly made by Colt (some were subcontracted), were not marketed or retailed by Colt. These guns are NOT Colt commemoratives and, for the most part, do not have the desirability factor that the factory commemoratives have. Your best alternative to find out more information about the multitude of these special/limited editions is to write: COLT ARCHIVE PROPERTIES, LLC, P.O. Box 1868, Hartford, CT, 06144. If anyone could have any information, it will be the factory. Their research fee is $100 per gun, with a premium charge for factory engraving. If they cannot obtain additional information on the variation you request, they will refund $50. Unfortunately, in some cases, a special/limited edition may not be researchable. In situations like this, do not confuse rarity with desirability.

Typically, special and limited editions are made for distributors. These sub-contracts seem to be mostly made to signify/commemorate an organization, state, special event or occasion, personality, etc. These are typically marketed and sold through a distributor to dealers, or a company/ individual to those people who want to purchase them. These special editions may or may not have a retail price and often times, since demand is regional, values decrease rapidly in other

GRADING - PPGS™	100%	Issue Price	Qty. Made

areas of the country. In some cases, if the distributor/wholesaler who ordered the initial special/ limited edition is known (and still in business), you may be able to find more information by contacting them directly. Desirability is the key to determining values on these editions.

Because the commemorative consumer is now more in charge (consumers now own most of the guns since distributor/dealer inventories are depleted) than during the 1980s, commemorative firearms are possibly as strong as they have ever been. When the supply side of commemorative economics has to be purchased from knowledgable collectors or savvy dealers and demand stays the same or increases slightly, prices have no choice but to go up. If and when the manufacturers crank up the commemorative production runs again (and it wont be like the good old days), the old marketplace characteristics may reappear. Until then, however, the commemorative marketplace remains steady, with values having become more predictable.

As a reminder on commemoratives, I would like to repeat a few facts, especially for the beginning collector, but applicable to all manufacturers of commemoratives. Commemoratives are current production guns designed as a reproduction of an historically famous gun model, or as a tie-in with historically famous persons or events. They are generally of very excellent quality and often embellished with select woods and finishes such as silver, nickel, or gold plating. Obviously, they are manufactured to be instant collectibles and to be pleasing to the eye. As with firearms in general, not all commemorative models have achieved collector status, although most enjoy an active market. Consecutive-numbered pairs as well as collections based on the same serial number may bring a premium. Remember that handguns usually are in some type of wood presentation case, and that rifles may be cased or in packaging with graphics styled to the particular theme of the collectible. The original factory packaging and papers should always accompany the firearm, as they are necessary to realize full value at the time of sale, and get more important every year.

NIB commemorative firearms should be absolutely new, unfired, and as issued, since any obvious use or wear removes it from collector status and lowers its value significantly. Many owners have allowed their commemoratives to sit in their boxes while encased in plastic wrappers for years without inspecting them for corrosion or oxidation damage. This is risky, especially if stored inside a plastic wrapper for long periods of time, since any accumulated moisture cannot escape. Periodic inspection should be implemented to ensure no damage occurs - this is important, since even light "freckling" created from touching the metal surfaces can reduce values significantly. A mint or unfired gun without its original packaging can lose as much as 50% of its normal value - many used commemoratives get sold as "fancy shooters" with little, if any, premiums being asked.

A final note on commemoratives: One of the characteristics of commemoratives/special editions is that over the years of ownership, most of the original amount manufactured stays in the same NIB condition. Thus, if supply always is constant and in one condition, demand has to increase before price appreciation can occur. After 47 years of commemorative/special edition production, many models performance records can be accurately analyzed and the appreciation (or depreciation) can be compared against other purchases of equal vintage. You be the judge.

1961 GENESEO, ILLINOIS 125TH ANNIVERSARY DERRINGER - ser. no. range, 87150D-87253D.

	$650	$28	104

1961 SHERIFF'S MODEL - blue and case hardened, 3 in. barrel, "SM" suffix.

	$2,500	$130	478

1961 SHERIFF´S MODEL - nickel, 3 in. barrel, "SM" suffix.

	$6,000	$140	25

1961 125TH ANNIVERSARY MODEL SAA - ser. no. range, 1AM-7390AM.

	$1,495	$150	7,390

1961 KANSAS STATEHOOD CENTENNIAL SCOUT - ser. no. range, 001G-6201G.

	$495	$75	6,201

1961 PONY EXPRESS CENTENNIAL SCOUT - ser. no. range, 1W-550W, 1E-500E.

	$495	$80	1,007

GRADING - PPGS™	100%	Issue Price	Qty. Made

1961 CIVIL WAR CENTENNIAL PISTOL .22 SHORT - ser. no. range, 50W-24189W (numberes 1W-49W and 124W-149W were not mfg.).
| | $175 | $33 | 24,114 |

1962 ROCK ISLAND ARSENAL CENTENNIAL MODEL - ser. no. range, 1RIA-550RIA.
| | $250 | $39 | 550 |

1962 COLUMBUS, OHIO SESQUICENTENNIAL SCOUT - ser. no. range, 001CS-200CS.
| | $550 | $100 | 200 |

1962 FORT FINDLAY, OHIO SESQUICENTENNIAL SCOUT - ser. no. range, FF0001-FF0150, one hundred revolvers shipped as singles, forty shipped as cased pairs.
| | $650 | $90 | 110 |

1962 FORT FINDLAY CASE PAIR - .22 LR and .22 Mag. cals., ser. no. range, FF0001-FF0150, one hundred revolvers shipped as singles, forty shipped as cased pairs.
| | $2,500 | $185 | 20 |

1962 NEW MEXICO GOLDEN ANNIVERSARY SCOUT - ser. no. range, 001NMA-1000NMA.
| | $495 | $80 | 1,000 |

1962 FORT MCPHERSON, NEBRASKA CENTENNIAL DERRINGER - ser. no. range, 001McP-300McP.
| | $395 | $29 | 300 |

1962 WEST VIRGINIA STATEHOOD CENTENNIAL SCOUT - ser. no. range, WV5, WV8, WV9, WV50, and WV100-WV3546, not all shipped.
| | $495 | $75 | 3,452 |

1963 WEST VIRGINIA STATEHOOD CENTENNIAL SAA .45 - ser. no. range, 25WVC-624WVC, not all shipped.
| | $1,495 | $150 | 600 |

1963 ARIZONA TERRITORIAL CENTENNIAL SCOUT - ser. no. range, AT001-AT5355.
| | $495 | $75 | 5,355 |

1963 ARIZONA TERRITORIAL CENTENNIAL SAA .45 - ser. no. range, 100AT-129AT, and 24AC-1273AC.
| | $1,495 | $150 | 1,280 |

1963 CAROLINA CHARTER TERCENTENARY SCOUT - ser. no. range, 001CT-300CT.
| | $495 | $75 | 300 |

1963 CAROLINA CHARTER TERCENTENARY 22/45 COMBO - ser. no. range, Scout: 301CT-550CT and S.A.A.: 301CCT-550CCT.
| | $1,995 | $240 | 251 |

1963 H. COOK "1 TO 100" 22/45 COMBO - ser. no. range, Scout: 001HCK-100HCK and S.A.A.: 001HC-100HC.
| | $1,995 | $275 | 100 |

1963 FORT STEPHENSON, OHIO SESQUICENTENNIAL SCOUT - ser. no. range, 001FS-200FS, records indicate 150 cased singles and 25 cased doubles.
| | $550 | $75 | 200 |

1963 BATTLE OF GETTYSBURG CENTENNIAL SCOUT - ser. no. range, 0001GC-1019GC.
| | $495 | $90 | 1,019 |

1963 IDAHO TERRITORIAL CENTENNIAL SCOUT - ser. no. range, 0001TC-0902TC.
| | $495 | $75 | 902 |

GRADING - PPGS™	100%	Issue Price	Qty. Made

1963 GEN. JOHN HUNT MORGAN INDIANA RAID SCOUT - ser. no. range, 1JHM-100JHM.

	$650	$75	100

1964 CHERRY'S SPORTING GOODS 35TH ANNIVERSARY 22/45 COMBO - ser. no. range, Scout: REC1-REC100 and S.A.A.: EPC1-EPC100.

	$1,995	$275	100

1964 NEVADA STATEHOOD CENTENNIAL SCOUT - ser. no. range, 0001NS-1752NS, 1846NS, 1964NS, and 2001NS-4996NS.

	$495	$75	3,984

1964 NEVADA STATEHOOD CENTENNIAL SAA .45 - ser. no. range, 0001NC-1752NC, 1864NC, 1964NC, and 2001NC-2700NC.

	$1,495	$150	1,688

1964 NEVADA STATEHOOD CENTENNIAL 22/45 COMBO - ser. no. range, Scout: 0001NS-1752NS, 1846NS, 1964NS, and 2001NS-4996NS, S.A.A.: 0001NC-1752NC, 1864NC, 1964NC, and 2001NC-2700NC.

	$1,995	$240	189

1964 NEVADA ST. CENT. 22/45 COMBO W/EXTRA ENGR. CYLS. - ser. no. range, Scout 0001NS-1752NS, 1846NS, 1964NS, and 2001NS-4996NS, S.A.A. 0001NC-1752NC, 1864NC, 1964NC, and 2001NC-2700NC, records do not indicate how revolvers were cased.

	$2,195	$350	577

1964 NEVADA "BATTLE BORN" SCOUT - ser. no. range, 001BB-1001BB.

	$495	$85	981

1964 NEVADA "BATTLE BORN" SAA .45 - ser. no. range, 001NB-100NB, .45 cal., cased singles and cased pairs shipped..

	$1,795	$175	80

1964 NEVADA "BATTLE BORN" 22/45 COMBO - ser. no. range, Scout: 001BB-100BB and S.A.A.: 001NB-100NB.

	$2,595	$265	20

1964 MONTANA TERRITORIAL CENTENNIAL SCOUT - ser. no. range, 0001MF-2300MF.

	$495	$75	2,300

1964 MONTANA TERRITORIAL CENTENNIAL SAA .45 - ser. no. range, 0001MA-0850MA.

	$1,495	$150	851

Approx. 100-200 sets (including the Scout) were sold with matching ser. numbers.

1964 WYOMING DIAMOND JUBILEE SCOUT - ser. no. range, 001DJ-2357DJ.

	$495	$75	2,357

1964 GENERAL HOOD CENTENNIAL SCOUT - ser. no. range, 0001GH-1503GH.

	$495	$75	1,503

1964 NEW JERSEY TERCENTENARY SCOUT - ser. no. range, 0001NJ-1001NJ.

	$495	$75	1,001

1964 NEW JERSEY TERCENTENARY SAA .45 - ser. no. range, 0001JT-0250JT.

	$1,495	$150	250

1964 ST. LOUIS BICENTENNIAL SCOUT - ser. no. range, 0251SL-1051SL.

	$495	$75	802

1964 ST. LOUIS BICENTENNIAL SAA .45 - ser. no. range, 0251SB-0450SB.

	$1,495	$150	200

1964 ST. LOUIS BICENTENNIAL 22/45 COMBO - ser. no. range, Scout: 0001SL-0250SL and S.A.A.: 0001SB-0250SB.

	$1,995	$240	250

1964 CALIFORNIA GOLD RUSH SCOUT - ser. no. range, 0001GR-0500GR.

	$495	$80	500

GRADING - PPGS™	100%	Issue Price	Qty. Made

1964 PONY EXPRESS PRESENTATION SAA .45 - ser. no. range, 1W-500W and 1E-500E also 0E, 00E, 0W, 00W, X1-W, X1-E, and CAL-1.

| | $1,595 | $250 | 1,004 |

1964 CHAMIZAL TREATY SCOUT - ser. no. range, 0001CS-0500CS, 350 singles and 50 cased pairs.

| | $495 | $85 | 450 |

1964 CHAMIZAL TREATY SAA .45 - ser. no. range, 0001CP-0100CP, 50 singles and 1 cased pair.

| | $1,795 | $170 | 50 |

1964 CHAMIZAL TREATY 22/45 COMBO - ser. no. range, Scout: 0001CS-0500CS and S.A.A.: 0001CP-0100CP.

| | $2,295 | $280 | 50 |

1964 COL. SAM COLT SESQUI. PRESENTATION SAA .45 - ser. no. range, 0001SC-5000SC.

| | $1,495 | $225 | 4,750 |

1964 COL. SAM COLT SESQUI. DELUXE PRES. SAA .45 - ser. no. range, 2000SC-2200SC.

| | $2,500 | $500 | 200 |

1964 COL. SAM COLT SESQUI. SPEC. DELUXE PRES. SAA .45 - ser. no. range, 0001SC-5000SC, only numbers ending with 00 or 000.

| | $4,000 | $1,000 | 50 |

1964 WYATT EARP BUNTLINE SAA .45 - ser. no. range, 0001WE-0150WE.

| | $2,750 | $250 | 150 |

1965 OREGON TRAIL SCOUT - ser. no. range, 0001OT-1995OT.

| | $495 | $75 | 1,995 |

1965 JOAQUIN MURIETTA 22/45 COMBO - ser. no. range, Scout: 001JMK-100JMK and S.A.A.: 001JMP-100JMP.

| | $1,995 | $350 | 100 |

1965 FORTY-NINER MINER SCOUT - ser. no. range, 0001FN-0500FN.

| | $495 | $85 | 500 |

1965 OLD FT. DES MOINES RECONSTRUCTION SCOUT - ser. no. range, 0101DM-0800DM.

| | $495 | $90 | 700 |

1965 OLD FT. DES MOINES RECONSTRUCTION SAA .45 - ser. no. range, 0101FD-0200FD.

| | $1,495 | $170 | 100 |

1965 OLD FT. DES MOINES RECONSTRUCTION 22/45 COMBO - ser. no. range, Scout: 0001DM-0100DM and S.A.A.: 0001FD-0100FD.

| | $1,995 | $290 | 100 |

1965 APPOMATTOX CENTENNIAL SCOUT - ser. no. range, 1000AK-2000AK.

| | $495 | $75 | 1,001 |

1965 APPOMATTOX CENTENNIAL SAA .45 - ser. no. range, 1000AP-1249AP.

| | $1,495 | $150 | 250 |

1965 APPOMATTOX CENTENNIAL 22/45 COMBO - ser. no. range, Scout: 0001AK-0250AK and S.A.A.: 0001AP-0250AP.

| | $1,995 | $240 | 250 |

1965 GENERAL MEADE CAMPAIGN SCOUT - ser. no. range, 1GM-1197GM.

| | $495 | $75 | 1,197 |

1965 ST. AUGUSTINE QUADRACENTENNIAL SCOUT - ser. no. range, 1AQ-500AQ.

| | $495 | $85 | 500 |

1965 KANSAS COWTOWN SERIES - Wichita Scout, ser. no. range, 1KW-500KW.

| | $450 | $85 | 500 |

GRADING - PPGS™	100%	Issue Price	Qty. Made

1966 KANSAS COWTOWN SERIES - Dodge City Scout, ser. no. range, 1KD-500KD.

	$450	$85	500

1966 COLORADO GOLD RUSH SCOUT - ser. no. range, 0CG-1350CG.

	$495	$85	1,350

1966 OKLAHOMA DIAMOND JUBILEE - ser. no. range, 1OK-1343OK.

	$495	$85	1,343

1966 DAKOTA TERRITORY SCOUT - ser. no. range, 1DT-1000DT.

	$495	$85	1,000

1966 GENERAL MEADE SAA .45 - ser. no. range, 0001MC-0200MC.

	$1,495	$165	200

1966 ABERCROMBIE & FITCH "TRAILBLAZER" - New York, ser. no. range, 001AF-200AF.

	$1,295	$275	200

1966 KANSAS COWTOWN SERIES - Abilene Scout, ser. no. range, 1KA-500KA.

	$450	$95	500

1966 INDIANA SESQUICENTENNIAL SCOUT - ser. no. range, 1IS-1745IS.

	$495	$85	1,500

1966 PONY EXPRESS .45 SAA 4-SQUARE SET (4 GUNS) - ser. no. range with backstrap marking, PE 001 E-PE 250 E "SACRAMENTO TO FRIDAY'S STATION", PE 251 E-PE 500 E "SALT LAKE CITY TO FORT LARAMIE", PE 001 W-PE 250 W "ST. JOSEPH TO MARYSVILLE"' PE 251 W-PE 500 W "FORT KEARNEY TO JULESBURG".

	$6,500	$1,400	unknown

1966 CALIFORNIA GOLD RUSH SAA .45 - ser. no. range, 0001GP-0500GP, not all shipped.

	$1,495	$175	130

1966 ABERCROMBIE & FITCH "TRAILBLAZER" - Chicago, ser. no. range, 201AF-300AF.

	$1,295	$275	100

1966 ABERCROMBIE & FITCH "TRAILBLAZER" - San Francisco, ser. no. range, 301AF-400AF.

	$1,295	$275	100

1967 LAWMAN SERIES - Bat Masterson Scout, ser. no. range, 1LM-3000LM.

	$495	$90	3,000

1967 LAWMAN SERIES - Bat Masterson SAA .45, ser. no. range, 1LMP-500LMP.

	$1,595	$180	500

1967 ALAMO SCOUT - ser. no. range, cased single 1051A22-4500A22 and cased pairs 251A22-1050A22.

	$495	$85	4,250

1967 ALAMO SAA .45 - ser. no. range, 251A45-1000A45, 450 singles and 300 cased pairs.

	$1,495	$165	750

1967 ALAMO 22/45 COMBO - ser. no. range, 1A22-250A22 and 1A45-250A45.

	$1,995	$265	250

1967 KANSAS COWTOWN SERIES - Coffeyville Scout, ser. no. range, 1KC-500KC.

	$450	$95	500

1967 KANSAS TRAIL SERIES - Chisolm Trail Scout, ser. no. range, 1CH-500CH.

	$450	$100	500

1967 WWI SERIES - .45 ACP cal., Chateau Thierry, ser. no. range, 101CT-7500CT.

	$795	$200	7,400

GRADING - PPGS™	100%	Issue Price	Qty. Made

1967 WWI SERIES - Chateau Thierry Deluxe, ser. no. range, 26CT-100CT.

	$1,350	$500	75

1967 WWI SERIES - Chateau Thierry Spec. Deluxe, ser. no. range, 1CT-25CT.

	$2,750	$1,000	25

1968 NEBRASKA CENTENNIAL SCOUT - ser. no. range, 1NEB-7000NEB.

	$495	$100	7,001

1968 KANSAS TRAIL SERIES - Pawnee Trail Scout, ser. no. range, 1PT-500PT.

	$450	$110	501

1968 WWI SERIES - .45 ACP cal., Belleau Wood, ser. no. range, 1BW-100BW and 201BW-7500BW.

	$795	$200	7,400

1968 WWI SERIES - Belleau Wood Deluxe, ser. no. range, 126BW-200BW.

	$1,350	$500	75

1968 WWI SERIES - Belleau Wood Special Deluxe, ser. no. range, 101BW-125BW.

	$2,750	$1,000	25

1968 LAWMAN SERIES - Pat Garrett Scout, ser. no. range, 1PG-3000PG.

	$495	$110	3,000

1968 LAWMAN SERIES - Pat Garrett .45 SAA, ser. no. range, 1PGP-500PGP.

	$1,595	$220	500

1969 GEN. NATHAN BEDFORD FORREST SCOUT - ser. no. range, 1NBF-3000NBF.

	$450	$110	3,000

1969 KANSAS TRAIL SERIES - Santa Fe Trail Scout, ser. no. range, 1SF-500SF.

	$450	$120	501

1969 WWI SERIES - .45 ACP cal., 2nd Battle of the Marne, 1M2-200M2 and 301M2-7500M2.

	$795	$220	7,400

1969 WWI SERIES - 2nd Battle of the Marne Deluxe, ser. no. range, 226M2-300M2.

	$1,350	$500	75

1969 WWI SERIES - 2nd Battle of the Marne Spec. Deluxe, ser. no. range, 201M2-225M2.

	$2,750	$1,000	25

1969 ALABAMA SESQUICENTENNIAL SCOUT - ser. no. range, 1AS-3098AS, not all shipped.

	$495	$110	3,001

1969 ALABAMA SESQUICENTENNIAL .45 SAA - ser. no. ALA1P.

	$15,000	unknown	1

1969 GOLDEN SPIKE SCOUT - ser. no. range, 1GS-11000GS.

	$495	$135	11,000

1969 KANSAS TRAIL SERIES - Shawnee Trail Scout, ser. no. range, 1ST-500ST.

	$450	$120	501

1969 WWI SERIES - .45 ACP cal., Meuse-Argonne, ser. no. range, 1MA-300MA and 401MA-7500MA.

	$795	$220	7,400

1969 WWI SERIES - Meuse-Argonne Deluxe, ser. no. range, 326MA-400MA.

	$1,350	$500	75

1969 WWI SERIES - Meuse-Argonne Spec. Deluxe, ser. no. range, 301MA-325MA.

	$2,750	$1,000	25

1969 ARKANSAS TERRITORIAL SESQUICENTENNIAL SCOUT - ser. no. range, 1ARK-3500ARK.

	$450	$110	3,500

GRADING - PPGS™	100%	Issue Price	Qty. Made

1969 LAWMAN SERIES - .45 SAA Wild Bill Hickok, ser. no. range, 1WBH-500WBH.

| | $1,595 | $220 | 500 |

1969 LAWMAN SERIES - Wild Bill Hickok Scout, ser. no. range, 1WB-3000WB.

| | $495 | $117 | 3,000 |

1969 CALIFORNIA BICENTENNIAL SCOUT - ser. no. range, 1CBI-5000CBI.

| | $495 | $135 | 5,000 |

1970 KANSAS FORT SERIES - Ft. Larned Scout, ser. no. range, 1FL-500FL.

| | $450 | $120 | 500 |

1970 WWII SERIES - European Theatre, ser. no. range, 0001ETO-9959ETO, not all shipped.

| | $795 | $250 | 11,500 |

1970 WWII SERIES - Pacific Theatre, ser. no. range, 0001PTO-9960PTO, not all shipped.

| | $795 | $250 | 11,500 |

Note: A complete set of the WWI and WWII Series standard grade models (6 guns) with matching serial numbers in NIB condition is currently selling in the $4,750-$5,500 range.

1970 TEXAS RANGER SAA .45 - ser. no. range, N/A.

| | $2,250 | $650 | 1,000 |

1970 TEXAS RANGER GRADE I (95% ENGRAVING COVERAGE) - ser. no. range, N/A.

| | $6,000 | N/A | 90 |

1970 TEXAS RANGER GRADE II (75% ENGRAVING COVERAGE) - ser. no. range, N/A.

| | $5,500 | $2,250 | 80 |

1970 TEXAS RANGER GRADE III (50% ENGRAVING COVERAGE) - ser. no. range, N/A.

| | $5,000 | $2,950 | 90 |

1970 KANSAS FORTS - Ft. Hays Scout, ser. no. range, 1FH-500FH.

| | $450 | $130 | 500 |

1970 MAINE SESQUICENTENNIAL SCOUT - ser. no. range, 1MES-3000MES.

| | $495 | $120 | 3,000 |

1970 MISSOURI SESQUICENTENNIAL SCOUT - ser. no. range, 1MOS-3000MOS.

| | $450 | $125 | 3,000 |

1970 MISSOURI SESQUICENTENNIAL .45 SAA - ser. no. range, P1MOS-P900MOS.

| | $1,495 | $220 | 900 |

1970 KANSAS FORTS - Ft. Riley Scout, ser. no. range, 1FR-500FR.

| | $450 | $130 | 500 |

1970 LAWMAN SERIES - Wyatt Earp Scout, ser. no. range, 1LWE-3000LWE.

| | $575 | $125 | 3,000 |

1970 LAWMAN SERIES - Wyatt Earp .45 SAA, ser. no. range, 1WYE-500WYE.

| | $2,750 | $395 | 500 |

1971 NRA CENTENNIAL .45 SAA - ser. no. range, NRA1-NRA7000, not all shipped.

| | $1,495 | $250 | 5,000 |

1971 NRA CENTENNIAL .357 SAA - ser. no. range, NRA1-NRA7000, not all shipped.

| | $1,395 | $250 | 5,000 |

1971 NRA CENTENNIAL GOLD CUP .45 ACP - ser. no. range, 1NRA-2500NRA, not all shipped.

| | $1,295 | $250 | 2,500 |

GRADING - PPGS™	100%	Issue Price	Qty. Made

1971 1851 NAVY - U.S. Grant, ser. no. range, 251USG-4398USG, not all shipped.
$595 ... $250 ... 4,750

1971 1851 NAVY - Robert E. Lee, ser. no. range, 251REL-4900REL.
$595 ... $250 ... 4,750

1971 1851 NAVY - Lee-Grant Set, ser. no. range, 1LGP-250LGP.
$1,350 ... $500 ... 250

1971 KANSAS SERIES - Ft. Scott Scout, ser. no. range, 1FSC-500FSC.
$450 ... $130 ... 500

1972 FLORIDA TERRITORY SESQUICENTENNIAL SCOUT - ser. no. range, 1FLA-2000FLA.
$495 ... $125 ... 2,001

1972 ARIZONA RANGER SCOUT - ser. no. range, 1AR-3000AR.
$495 ... $135 ... 3,001

1975 PEACEMAKER CENTENNIAL .45 - ser. no. range, PC501-PC2000.
$1,595 ... $300 ... 1,500

1975 PEACEMAKER CENTENNIAL 44.40 - ser. no. range, 501PC-2000PC.
$1,595 ... $300 ... 1,500

1975 PEACEMAKER CENT. CASED PAIR - ser. no. range, .44-40 cal.: 1MPC-500MPC and .45 cal.: MPC1-MPC500.
$3,500 ... $625 ... 500

USS TEXAS BATTLESHIP SPECIAL EDITION (1975) - .45 ACP cal., Model 1911A1 with special embellishments, nickel finish, this model is not a factory commemorative, ser. no. range N/A.
$995 ... unknown ... 500

USS ARIZONA BATTLESHIP SPECIAL EDITION (1975) - .45 ACP cal., Model 1911A1 with special embellishments, nickel finish, this model is not a factory commemorative, ser. no. range N/A.
$995 ... unknown ... 500

1976 U.S. BICENTENNIAL SET - includeD ser. no. range, SAA .45: 0001PM-1776PM, Python .357 Mag.: 0001PY-1776PY, and black powder Dragoon: 0001DG-1776DG, in walnut display case with drawers.
$2,995 ... $1,695 ... 1,776

1976 BICENTENNIAL SAA FREEDOM COLTS - consisted of A, B, and C sets, set As were engraved, Bs had gold work and accessories, Cs were similar to Bs, but had shoulder stock. Set A prices averaged $1,500-$3,000 in 1976, set B prices varied between $3,500-$20,000, and set C prices started at $5,000. Total mfg. was 4 set As, 6 set Bs, and 1 set C. These sets in today's marketplace are too rare to accurately evaluate and pricing is literally "what the market will bear."

These guns were all engraved by Dwain Wright located in Applegate, OR.

1977 2ND AMENDMENT .22 - ser. no. range, G0001RB-G3020RB.
$450 ... $195 ... 3,020

1977 U.S. CAVALRY 200TH ANNIVERSARY SET - ser. no. range, US0001-US3020 and 0001US-3020US, not all shipped.
$1,250 ... $995 ... 3,000

1978 STATEHOOD 3RD MODEL DRAGOON - ser. no. range, N/A.
$6,995 ... $12,500 ... 52

1979 NED BUNTLINE .45 SAA - ser. no. range, NB0001-NB3000.
$1,295 ... $895 ... 3,000

OHIO PRESIDENT'S SPECIAL EDITION (1979) - .45 ACP cal., Model 1911A1 with special Ohio embellishments, this is not a factory commemorative, ser. no. range N/A.
$995 ... unknown ... 250

GRADING - PPGS™	100%	Issue Price	Qty. Made

1979 TOMBSTONE CENTENNIAL .45 SAA - .45 LC cal., 7 1/2 in. barrel, nickel finish, two-piece walnut stocks, P-1876 Model, etched with scroll engraving and Western scenes. 300 mfg. (200 singles and 50 pairs), ser. no. range N/A.

	$1,495	$995	300

This model was not sold retail through the auspices of Colt.

1980 DRUG ENFORCEMENT AGENCY (DEA) .45 AUTO -ser. no. range N/A.

	$1,100	$550	910

This model was not sold retail through the auspices of Colt.

1980 OLYMPICS ACE MODEL SPECIAL EDITION - ser. no. range N/A.

	$1,250	$1,000	200

This model was not sold retail through the auspices of Colt.

1980 HERITAGE-WALKER .44 PERCUSSION - ser. no. range, 0001 C CO-1850 C CO.

	$950	$1,475	1,847

1981 "JOHN M. BROWNING" .45 ACP SEMI-AUTO - ser. no. range, CJMBC0001-CJMBC3000.

	$995	$1,100	3,000

1980-81 .45 ACP GOVT. SIGNATURE SERIES - .45 ACP cal., blue finished Govt. slide with gold auroplated slide or nickel finish. 250 mfg. in both finishes, ser. no. range N/A.

	$995	$833	250

    Add $50 for blue finish.

1980-81 ACE SIGNATURE SERIES - .22 LR cal., featured Cocobolo grips with medallions, blue finish with photo engraving, cased. 1,000 mfg., ser. no. range N/A.

	$1,250	$955	1,000

1981 BUFFALO BILL SPECIAL EDITION - .44-40 WCF cal., 7 1/2 in. barrel, gold and silver plating, Class C engraved, scrimshaw ivory grips featuring Buffalo Bill and his TE Wyoming Ranch brand, leather cased, 250 mfg. serialized 1BB-250BB.

	$4,975	$4,200	250

This model was a special edition (not commemorative) that was made specifically for the Buffalo Bill Historical Center.

1982 JOHN WAYNE SAA STANDARD - ser. no. range, CJWC0001-CJWC3100.

	$2,250	$2,995	3,100

While advertising literature indicated 3,100 were mfg., 3,041 were sold.

1982 JOHN WAYNE SAA DELUXE - ser. no. range, JWD001-JWD500.

	$7,500	$10,000	500

While advertising literature indicated 500 were mfg., only 90 were sold.

1982 JOHN WAYNE SAA PRESENTATION - ser. no. range, JWP001-JWP100.

	$12,000	$20,000	100

While advertising literature indicated 100 were mfg., only 47 were sold.

1983 BUFFALO BILL WILD WEST SHOW CENTENNIAL SAA .45

	$1,595	$1,350	500

1983 CCA LIMITED EDITION SAA - .44-40 WCF cal., 4 3/4 in. barrel, nickel finish, fleur-de-lis checkered walnut grips, two line barrel address and Colt Frontier Six Shooter roll marking. 250 mfg. in 1983 to commemorate Colt Collector's Assn.

	$1,595	$825	250

This model was not sold at retail through the auspices of Colt.

GRADING - PPGS™	100%	Issue Price	Qty. Made

1983 "ARMORY MODEL" SAA .45 ACP - this model had limited production, and should not be confused as being a commemorative. So-called because it was shipped with extra .45 long Colt cylinder and the "Colt Armory Edition" book by E. Grant. Presentation cased.

	$1,795	$1,125	500

20 Armory model commemoratives were available with class A engraving - $2,595, B engraving - $2,995, C engraving - $3,500, D engraving - $3,995.

1983 PYTHON SILVER SNAKE SPECIAL EDITION - .357 Mag. cal., 6 in. barrel, black chrome stainless steel, Pachmayr grips with custom shop pewter medallions, etched engraving, includes custom gun pouch.

	$1,495	$1,150	250

1984 1ST EDITION GOVT. MODEL .380 ACP

	$595	$425	1,000

Serial range RC00000-RC01000.

1984 JOHN WAYNE "DUKE" FRONTIER .22

	$795	$475	5,000

1984 COLT/WINCHESTER SET - 1 ea. of the Model 1894 Winchester carbine and Colt Peacemaker, serial numbered 1WC-4440WC, .44-40 WCF cal., elaborate gold etching, cased. Pistol became available for sale individually in 1986 - see individual listing below for values.

Please refer to 1984 Winchester/Colt Set in the Winchester Commemorative section in this text.

WINCHESTER/COLT SAA - .44-40 WCF cal., 7 1/2 in. barrel, gold etching, this commemorative was originally made as part of the 1984 Winchester/Colt rifle-pistol set, but was later able to be purchased individually. Originally mfg. 1984.

	$1,495	N/A	4,000

1984 USA EDITION SAA - .44-40 WCF cal., 7 1/2 in. barrel, old style black powder frame, bullseye ejector rod head, 3 line patent date, high polished blue with gold line engraving. 100 guns total mfg. - 1 for each state and its capitol.

	$3,500	$4,995	100

1984 KIT CARSON .22 NEW FRONTIER - 6 in. barrel, color case hardened frame, gold artwork, serial numbered KCC0001-KCC1000, cased.

	$495	$550	1,000

1984 SECOND EDITION GOVT. MODEL .380 ACP - serial numbered 00000RC-01000RC.

	$595	$525	1,000

1984 OFFICER'S COMMENCEMENT ISSUE - Officer's ACP with Marine Corps emblem, rosewood grips, silver plated oak leaf scroll, cased.

	$995	$700	1,000

This model was not sold retail through the auspices of Colt.

1984 THEODORE ROOSEVELT COMMEMORATIVE SAA - .44-40 WCF cal., 7 1/2 in. barrel, black powder frame, case colored receiver, factory "B" hand engraving, ivory stocks, cased.

	$1,995	$1,695	500

1984 NORTH AMERICAN OILMEN SAA BUNTLINE - .45 LC cal., 12 in. barrel, non-fluted cylinder, elaborate gold etching, ebony grips with ivory inlays, stand-up glass case, ser. nos. 1-100 mfg. for Canada, 101-200 for the U.S.

	$3,250	$3,900	200

This model was not sold retail through the auspices of Colt.

1985 TEXAS 150th SESQUICENTENNIAL SAA - .45 cal., Sheriff's model, 4 3/4 in. barrel, mirror bright blue, gold etching, 24Kt. gold plated backstrap and trigger guard, smooth ivory grips, French fit oak presentation case. Mfg. 1985 only.

  ✱ *1985 Texas 150th Sesquicentennial SAA Standard Model* - 1,000 mfg.

	$1,495	$1,836	1,000

GRADING - PPGS™	100%	Issue Price	Qty. Made

* 1985 Texas 150th Sesquicentennial SAA Premier Model - elaborate engraving, 75 mfg.

	$4,995	$7,995	75

1986 150th ANNIVERSARY SAA - .45 LC cal., 10 in. barrel, 50% engraved, royal blue finish, Goncalo Alves smooth grips, 150th anniversary logo in stocks, cherrywood case. 490 mfg. 1986 only.

	$1,995	$1,595	490

1986 150th ANNIVERSARY ENGRAVING SAMPLER SAA - various cals., 4 different engraving styles on metal surfaces, 75% coverage, ivory grips, signed by the engraver, available with either blue or nickel finish. New 1986.

	$3,500	$1,613	unknown

1986 150th ANNIVERSARY ENGRAVING SAMPLER .45 M1911A1 - .45 ACP cal., 4 different engraving styles on metal surfaces, 75% coverage, ivory grips, signed by the engraver, available with either blue or nickel finish. New 1986.

	$1,750	$1,155	unknown

Add $60 for nickel.

1986 MUSTANG FIRST EDITION - .380 ACP cal., 1,000 manufactured serialized MU00001-MU01000 (the first thousand of production), rosewood stocks, walnut presentation case. Mfg. 1986 only.

	$595	$475	1,000

OFFICER'S ACP HEIRLOOM EDITION - .45 ACP cal., personalized with individual's choice for serial number (ie. John Smith 1), mirror brite bluing, jeweled barrel, hammer, and trigger, ivory grips, with historical letter and mahogany case. New 1986.

	$1,550	$1,643	open

1986 DOUBLE DIAMOND SET - set is comprised of a Python Ultimate .357 Mag. revolver and Officer's Model .45 ACP, both guns in stainless steel, smooth rosewood grips, presentation cased. 1,000 sets mfg. 1986 only, serial numbered 1-1,000 (matched).

	$3,000	$1,575	1,000

DELTA MATCH H-BAR RIFLE - AR-15 A2 H-Bar rifle selectively chosen and equipped with 3x9 variable power rubber armored scope, leather sling, shoulder stock cheekpiece, cased. Mfg. 1987.

	$1,500	$1,425	open

12TH MAN-'SPIRIT OF AGGIELAND' - .45 ACP cal., mfg. to commemorate Texas A&M University, serial numbered TAM001-TAM999, 24Kt gold plating including wreaths on left frame and inscription on right, cherrywood glass top presentation case, includes personalized class graduation inscription. Available 1987 only.

	$950	$950	999

This model was not sold retail through the auspices of Colt.

KLAY-COLT 1851 NAVY - .36 cal., cased reproduction of the 3rd Model 1851 Navy, special fabrication insuring old world quality, charcoal bluing, heat treated screws and accessories, cased. Introduced 1986.

* Klay-Colt 1851 Navy Standard Edition - no engraving.

	$1,850	$1,850	150

* Klay-Colt 1851 Navy Engraved Edition - choice of engraving.

	$3,150	$3,150	50

Optional engraving patterns with or without gold inlays available at extra cost.

COMBAT ELITE CUSTOM EDITION - .45 ACP cal., with ambidextrous thumb safety, wide grip safety, hand honed action, and carrying case, ser. numbered CG00001-CG00500. Mfg. 1987.

	$1,095	$900	500

GRADING - PPGS™	100%	Issue Price	Qty. Made

1987 SHERIFF'S EDITION - set of 5 SAA Sheriff's configuration revolvers in .45 LC cal., barrel lengths include 2, 2 1/2, 3, 4, and 5 1/2 in., royal blue finish, smooth rosewood grips with medallions, supplied with glass top display case which displays the revolvers in a circle around a brass sheriff's badge. Serialization has 3 numeral prefix (which is the same in each set), followed by the letters "SE," followed by 1 or 2 numerals (indicating barrel length) - i.e. serial number 002SE25 indicates the second set built, Sheriff's Edition (SE), and a barrel length of 2 1/2 inches.

	$6,500	$7,500	200 sets

1989 SNAKE EYES LIMITED EDITION - includes two Python revolvers (2 1/2 in. barrels), one finished in brite stainless steel and the other in Royal Blue finish, grips are ivory-like with scrimshaw "snake eyes" dice on left side and royal flush poker hand on right, includes chips and playing cards, 500 sets only of consecutive serial numbers. New 1989.

	$3,000	$3,500	500

1990 SAA HEIRLOOM II EDITION - .45 LC cal., 7 1/2 in. barrel, color case hardened frame and hammer, balance of metal finished in Colt Royal Blue, one-piece American Walnut grips with cartouche on lower left side, personalized inscription on backstrap, walnut cased. Available 1990 only.

	$1,595	$1,600	open

1990 JOE FOSS LIMITED EDITION .45 ACP GOVT. MODEL - .45 ACP cal., first limited edition in Colt's All American Hero Series, commemorates Joe Foss, famous American WWII Marine Fighter Pilot, gun features gold etched scenes on slide sides, smooth walnut grips. While 2,500 were advertised, only 300+ were mfg. Serial numbered beginning with JF 0001. French fitted walnut presentation case, 38 oz. Mfg. 1990 only.

	$1,850	$1,375	300+

1911A1 50th ANNIVERSARY BATTLE OF THE BULGE - .45 ACP cal., special edition commemorating the Battle of the Bulge, silver plated with gold inlays, 300 mfg. serialized BB001-BB300.

	$1,495	$1,250	300

> Add $150 for deluxe presentation case.

This special edition was sold exclusively by Cherry's located in Greensboro, NC.

1993 CCA LIMITED EDITION SAA - .38-40 WCF cal., 4 3/4 in. barrel, nickel finish, walnut grips, CCA markings on grip strap. 150 mfg. in 1993.

	$1,500	$1,165	150

This model was not sold at retail through the auspices of Colt.

COMANCHE

Current trademark manufactured in Argentina beginning 2001. Currently distributed (master distributor) beginning 2002 by SGS Importers, located in Wanamassa, NJ. Distributor sales.

PISTOLS: SINGLE SHOT

SUPER COMANCHE - .45 LC cal./.410 bore, 10 in. rifled barrel, blue, duo-tone (mfg. 2004-2005), camo (mfg. 2006-2007) or satin nickel finish, black rubber grips and forearm, barrel release lever on front of trigger guard, adj. rear sight, transfer bar and manual safeties, 47 oz. New 2002.

MSR $184	$150	$125	$100	$85	$70	$60	$50

> Add $16 for satin nickel finish or $33 for camo (disc. 2007).

This model is not available for sale in some states.

GRADING - PPGS™	100%	98%	95%	90%	80%	70%	60%

REVOLVERS: SA

COMANCHE I - .22 LR cal., 6 in. full lug barrel, 9 shot, blue, stainless, or alloy, adj. sights, rubber grips, 39 oz. New 2002.

MSR $250	$200	$175	$160	$145	$130	$120	$110

Add $25 for stainless steel construction.
Subtract $66 for alloy.

COMANCHE II - .38 Spl. +P cal., 2 (mfg. 2006), 3 (new 2004) or 4 in. full lug barrel, 6 shot, blue or stainless, adj. sight, approx. 30 oz. New 2002.

MSR $250	$200	$175	$160	$145	$130	$120	$110

Add $17 for stainless steel construction.
Add $9 for 2 in. barrel.

COMANCHE III - .357 Mag. cal., 2 (mfg. 2006), 3, 4, or 6 in. full lug barrel, 6 shot, blue or stainless, adj. sight, 29-39 oz. New 2002.

MSR $267	$225	$185	$165	$150	$140	$130	$100

Add $25 for stainless steel construction.
Add $8 for 2 in. barrel.

COMANCHE IV - .44 Mag. cal., 6 in. barrel only with adj. sights, blue or stainless steel. Mfg. 2004.

	$250	$205	$180	$165	$150	$140	$130

Last MSR was $308.

Add $25 for stainless steel construction.

COMBINATION GUNS

A firearms configuration of either SxS or O/U design, consisting of a rifle and a shotgun barrel. Combination guns originated in Europe.

Many imported combination guns designed for the U.S. have been known as turkey guns in the past, typically with a .22 rimfire/medium cal. centerfire rifle barrel over a 12 ga., 20 ga., or .410 bore shotgun barrel. European guns typically have metric rifle cals., and the shotgun barrel is usually 12 or 16 ga. European combination guns (see configurations below) need to be evaluated individually, since values will depend on the desirability of the gun's configuration in the U.S. (i.e., metric vs. American cals., gauge, type of lock, engraving, quality of wood, etc.). Most non-custom European boxlock combination guns with metric cals. in average condition are currently priced in the $695-$2,250 range. However custom ordered, top quality major trademark European combination guns with profuse engraving and best quality wood can sell for as high as $20,000. Typical American combination guns (the Savage Model 24 and others) are priced in the $375-$625 range.

COMMANDO ARMS

Previous manufacturer located in Knoxville, TN.

Commando Arms became the new name for Volunteer Enterprises in the late 1970s.

RIFLES: CARBINES

MARK 45 - .45 ACP cal., carbine styled after the Thompson sub-machine gun, 16 1/2 in. barrel.

	$495	$425	$350	$315	$280	$225	$195

COMPETITOR CORPORATION

Competitor

Current manufacturer established in 1988 and located in Jaffrey, NH. Previously located in New Ipswich, NH until 2001, and in West Groton, MA from 1988-1995. Dealer direct or distributor sales.

PISTOLS: SINGLE SHOT

COMPETITOR - available in over 400 cals. from .17 LR - .50 AE, ranging from small rimfire to large belted Magnums, 14 in. barrel standard, rotary cannon action, cocks on opening, dual sliding thumb and trigger safety, rotary style ejector, click adj. sights, matte blue or optional electroless nickel finish, choice of synthetic, laminated, or natural wood grips (ambidextrous), extractor or ejector. Approx. 59-73 oz. New 1988.

| MSR $575 | $495 | $435 | $375 | $320 | $290 | $255 | $225 |

- Add $25 for laminated wood stock.
- Add approx. $50 for walnut grips (disc.).
- Add $60 for electroless nickel finish (barreled action only).
- Add $175 for extra 14 in. standard cal. barrel with sights.
- Add $40 for less than 16 in. standard cal. barrel with sights.
- Add $70 for 16-23 in. barrel.
- Add $60 for factory-installed muzzle brake.
- Add $260 for rimfire or centerfire conversion kit.

CONCO ARMS

Current importer of Hambrusch rifles located in Emmaus, PA.

RIFLES: SxS

PRO HUNTER BOXLOCK SxS - various cals. through .700 NE, Anson & Deeley action with double underlocking lugs and scalloped frame, ejectors, standard scroll engraving, H&H style frame reinforcement, checkered Circassian walnut stock and forearm, custom order only, mfg. by Hambrusch in Ferlach, Austria. Importation disc. 2004.

| $23,611 | $18,750 | $15,950 | $12,500 | $10,000 | $8,700 | $7,500 |

Last MSR was $23,611.

Add $673 for .375 H&H, $1,061 for .470 NE cal., $1,987 for .500 NE, $12,816 for .577/.600 NE or $30,318 for .700 NE cal.

PRO HUNTER SIDELOCK SxS - various cals. through .700 NE, full sidelock action with standard scroll engraving, ejectors, hinged DT, checkered Circassian walnut stock and forearm, custom order only, mfg. by Hambrusch in Ferlach, Austria.

| MSR $32,000 | $32,000 | $26,000 | $20,500 | $16,750 | $14,000 | $11,000 | $9,995 |

Premiums exist for .375 H&H cal. and above. PLease contact the importer directly for a price quotation on the larger mag. cals.

CONNECTICUT SHOTGUN MANUFACTURING CO.

Current rifle and shotgun manufacturer established during 1995, and located in New Britain, CT.

Connecticut Shotgun Manufacturing Co. has already established itself as one of America's premier gunmakers, specializing in best quality O/U and SxS shotguns, in addition to a SxS double rifle. Please contact the company directly for more information, including pricing and availability.

RIFLES: SxS

MODEL 21 - .22 LR or .22 Mag. cal., based on a special order small frame, everything is scaled and proportioned exactly, open sights, base price is for Model 21-1 w/light scroll engraving and A fancy wood. New mid-2006.

| MSR $22,500 | $22,500 | $18,750 | $15,250 | $12,000 | $9,000 | $7,500 | $6,250 |

MSR for Grade 21-5 is $28,500, Grade 21-6 is $35,500, and Grand American is $33,500.

GRADING - PPGS™	100%	98%	95%	90%	80%	70%	60%

MODEL 22 - various centerfire calibers, based on the Model 21 action, Grand American styling and features, 4 game animals inlayed in 24Kt. gold, frame scaled proportionately to the caliber, iron sights, SST. Limited mfg. beginning 2002.

Each gun is custom-built to the customer's exact specifications and prices are POR.

SHOTGUNS: O/U, SIDELOCK

A. GALAZAN MODEL - 12, 16, 20, 28 ga., or .410 bore, features strong, low profile sidelock action with Boss-style metal reinforced forearm, top-of-the-line model utilizing best quality materials and U.S. workmanship, wide choice of custom features and engraving options.

Each gun is custom-built to the customer's exact specifications and prices start at $50,000 without engraving.

A. GALAZAN ROUND BODY MODEL - 12, 16, 20, 28 ga., or .410 bore, round body, wide choice of custom features and engraving options.

Each gun is custom-built to the customer's exact specifications and base price is POR.

SHOTGUNS: SxS

MODEL 21 - 12, 16, 20, 28 ga., or .410 bore, 4 frame sizes (12, 16, 20, and 28/.410 bore), various barrel lengths up to 32 in. with either matte solid or vent. rib and fixed chokes, best quality checkered wood, wide choice of custom features and engraving options, new mfg. not associated with Winchester production. Limited mfg. beginning 2002.

Each gun is custom-built to the customer's exact specifications.

* *Model 21-1* - features frame light scroll engraving patterned after Winchester's No. 1 style, A fancy wood. New 2002.

   MSR $12,500 $12,500 $9,995 $8,750 $7,250 $6,500 $5,750 $5,000
   Add $2,000 for 28 ga. or $4,000 for .410 bore.

* *Model 21-5* - features both scroll and three hunting scenes engraving patterned after Winchester's No. 5 style on frame and barrels, AA fancy wood. New 2002.

   MSR $14,500 $14,500 $12,500 $9,950 $8,750 $7,250 $6,500 $5,750
   Add $2,500 for 28 ga. or $4,000 for .410 bore.

* *Model 21-6* - features both tight scroll and dog/game bird engraving patterned after Winchester's No. 6 style on frame and barrels, AAA fancy wood. New 2002.

   MSR $17,500 $17,500 $13,750 $11,250 $9,250 $8,250 $7,000 $6,000
   Add $3,000 for 28 ga. or $6,000 for .410 bore.

* *Model 21 Grand American* - top-of-the-line standard model with 2 sets of barrels, elaborate scroll engraving on barrels and frame, 5 gold inlays, including dogs and birds, B carved stock and forearm, AAA full fancy feather crotch American walnut. New 2002.

   MSR $21,000 $21,000 $17,000 $14,250 $11,650 $9,000 $7,500 $6,250
   Add $3,500 for 28 ga. or $7,000 for .410 bore.

* *Model 21 Royal Exhibition* - top-of-the-line model with 2 sets of barrels, numerous engraving and gold inlay options, best quality wood. New 2002.

   This model is built to customer's specifications and priced on request only.

A. GALAZAN ROUND BODY MODEL - 12, 16, 20, 28 ga., or .410 bore, round body, top-of-the-line model utilizing best quality materials and U.S. workmanship, no visible pins or screws, wide choice of custom features and engraving options.

Each gun is custom-built to the customer's exact specifications and base price is $40,000, w/o engraving.

GRADING - PPGS™	100%	98%	95%	90%	80%	70%	60%

A. GALAZAN RBL - 20 (disc. 2007) or 28 (new 2007) ga., rounded boxlock action, 26, 28, or 30 in. barrels with 5 choke tubes (20 ga. only) or fixed chokes, ejectors, DT or ST, XX walnut, choice of pistol or straight grip stock, launch 20 ga. edition included scroll engraving by Richard Roy, 28 ga. features pointer and setter games scenes designed by James Demunk, hammer sears and triggers are treated in Hard Gold, canvas and leather cased with all accessories, choice of 14 1/4 or 14 3/4 LOP, approx. 5 1/2 (28 ga.) or 6 1/8 lbs. New 2006, limited mfg.

	100%	98%	95%	90%	80%	70%	60%
20 ga.	$2,800	$2,400	$2,100	$1,925	$1,650	$1,400	$1,150
MSR $3,650 (28 ga.)	$3,450	$2,900	$2,500	$2,150	$1,750	$1,500	$1,250

> Add $450 for assisted opening action.
> Add $350 for XXX walnut, $500 for XXXX or $700 for Exhibition wood upgrade.
> Add $175 for beavertail forearm.
> Add $175 for SST.

CONNECTICUT VALLEY CLASSICS, INC.

Previous trademark manufactured by Cooper Arms, located in Stevensville, MT 1996-1998. CVC, Inc. was a division of CVC Sports, Inc. Previous sales and marketing offices were located in Holyoke, MA until 1996 and in Westport, CT 1993-95.

SHOTGUNS: O/U

The models listed below have receiver dimensions built to the exact specifications of the original Classic Doubles Model 101. The only difference is that the tang spacer has been made an integral part of the frame.

> Add $1,350 for each additional barrel set.

CLASSIC 101 SPORTER - 12 ga. only, boxlock action, monoblock, 28, 30, or 32 in. VR barrels with multi-chokes, SST, ejectors, nickel finished receiver with light engraving, checkered American black walnut stock and forearm with low luster finish, approx. 7 3/4 lbs.

			100%	98%	95%	90%	80%	70%	60%
			$1,875	$1,550	$1,225	$1,000	$825	$700	$600

Last MSR was $2,195.

CLASSIC SPORTER SB - 12 ga. only, boxlock action, entry level sporter model. Mfg. 1997-98.

			100%	98%	95%	90%	80%	70%	60%
			$2,250	$1,875	$1,575	$1,175	$950	$775	$650

Last MSR was $2,495.

GRADE I CLASSIC SPORTER - 12 ga. only, boxlock action, monobloc, 28, 30, or 32 in. vented barrels with VR, lengthened forcing cones, and 2 3/8 in. multi-chokes, SST, ejectors, stainless steel receiver with light engraving, checkered 20 LPI AA American black walnut stock and forearm with low luster finish, approx. 7 3/4 lbs. Disc. 1998.

			100%	98%	95%	90%	80%	70%	60%
			$2,695	$2,100	$1,675	$1,250	$1,000	$825	$700

Last MSR was $2,995.

* **Women's Classic Sporter** - similar to Grade I Classic Sporter, except has smaller stock dimensions and 28 in. barrels only, 7 1/2 lbs. Mfg. 1996-98.

			100%	98%	95%	90%	80%	70%	60%
			$2,695	$2,100	$1,675	$1,250	$1,000	$825	$700

Last MSR was $2,995.

> This model was also available in Grade II or Grade III Women's Classic Sporter.

* **Grade II Classic Sporter** - similar to Grade I Classic Sporter, except has AAA American or Claro walnut with 22 LPI hand-checkering, 30 in. barrels only.

			100%	98%	95%	90%	80%	70%	60%
			$3,100	$2,350	$1,800	$1,325	$1,050	$850	$725

Last MSR was $3,595.

* **Grade III Classic Sporter** - similar to Grade II Classic Sporter, except has fleur-de-lis checkering patterns and gold accents. Disc. 1998.

			100%	98%	95%	90%	80%	70%	60%
			$3,600	$2,750	$1,975	$1,450	$1,175	$925	$750

Last MSR was $4,195.

GRADING - PPGS™	100%	98%	95%	90%	80%	70%	60%

GRADE I CLASSIC FIELD - 12 ga. only, similar to Grade I Classic Sporter, except has solid rib and standard flush-mounted choke-tubes, 27 1/2 in. barrels, 7 1/2 lbs. Mfg. 1996-98.

	$2,695	$2,100	$1,675	$1,250	$1,000	$825	$700

Last MSR was $2,995.

✳ *Classic Waterfowler* - 12 ga. only, 30 or 32 (disc. 1995) in. VR barrels, non-reflective surfaces, bird scene engraving, overbored barrels with lengthened forcing cones and four standard CVC chokes, 8 lbs. Mfg. 1993-98.

	$2,495	$2,000	$1,575	$1,175	$950	$775	$650

Last MSR was $2,795.

✳ *Grade II Classic Field* - similar to Grade I Classic Field, except has AAA American or Claro walnut with 22 LPI hand-checkering.

	$3,025	$2,250	$1,750	$1,300	$1,050	$850	$725

Last MSR was $3,495.

✳ *Grade III Classic/English Field* - similar to Grade II Classic Field, except has fleur-de-lis checkering patterns and gold accents, choice of straight English (25 1/2 in. VR barrels only) or pistol grip stock. Disc. 1998.

	$3,575	$2,850	$2,025	$1,500	$1,200	$925	$750

Last MSR was $4,195.

Add $100 for straight English stock.

✳ *Classic Skeet* - 12 ga. only, 29 in. vented barrels with 9mm VR, otherwise similar to Grade I Classic Sporter, 7 1/2 lbs. Mfg. 1996-98.

	$2,695	$2,100	$1,675	$1,250	$1,000	$825	$700

Last MSR was $2,995.

✳ *Classic Flyer* - 12 ga. only, live bird gun featuring AAA walnut and 22 LPI checkering, oil finish, 30 in. vented overbored barrels with 11mm tapered top rib and lengthened forcing cones, scroll engraving with pigeon scene on bottom, 8 lbs. Mfg. 1996-98.

	$3,100	$2,350	$1,800	$1,325	$1,050	$850	$725

Last MSR was $3,595.

CONQUEST

Current trademark of guns manufactured by various companies in Spain, Turkey, Germany, and Italy. No current U.S. importation.

The Conquest trademark currently includes shotguns in O/U, SxS, slide action, and semi-auto configuration. Please contact the company headquarters directly for more information (see Trademark Index).

CONTENTO/VENTURA

Previously imported by Ventura Imports in Seal Beach, CA. Ventura also imported Bertuzzi and Piotti.

SHOTGUNS: O/U

CONTENTO O/U - 12 ga., 32 in. barrels, boxlock, optional screw in choke tubes, high vent. rib, SST, auto ejectors, hand checkered Monte Carlo trap stock.

	$1,045	$990	$935	$880	$770	$690	$635

MK 2 - includes O/U barrels, with extra single barrel.

	$1,375	$1,320	$1,265	$1,210	$1,100	$1,020	$965

MK 2 - leather cased, combination set.

	$1,705	$1,650	$1,595	$1,540	$1,430	$1,350	$1,295

MK 3 - engraved, O/U.

	$1,650	$1,570	$1,485	$1,375	$1,295	$1,185	$1,100

GRADING - PPGS™	100%	98%	95%	90%	80%	70%	60%

MK 3 - includes O/U barrels, with extra single barrel.

	$2,200	$2,035	$1,925	$1,815	$1,650	$1,595	$1,515

MK 3 - leather cased, combination set.

	$2,750	$2,420	$2,200	$2,090	$1,955	$1,815	$1,760

SHOTGUNS: SxS

MODEL 51 - 12, 16, 20, 28 ga., or .410 bore, 26-32 in. barrels, various chokes, extractors, boxlock, double triggers, checkered straight stock.

	$385	$360	$330	$305	$250	$220	$165
Auto ejectors	$495	$440	$385	$360	$305	$275	$220

MODEL 52 - 10 ga., double triggers only, otherwise similar to Model 51.

	$525	$495	$470	$415	$360	$305	$250

MODEL 53 - deluxe version of Model 51, scalloped frame, auto ejectors.

	$470	$440	$415	$385	$330	$275	$220
SST	$605	$550	$525	$495	$440	$385	$330

MODEL 61 - 12 or 20 ga., 26, 27, 28, or 30 in. barrels, H&H sidelocks, various chokes, floral engraved, hand detachable locks, cocking indicators, select walnut pistol grip stock, auto ejectors.

	$880	$825	$770	$745	$690	$605	$550
SST	$1,020	$965	$910	$855	$800	$715	$660

MODEL 65 - similar to Model 61, with elaborate engraving and quality hand finishing.

	$1,100	$1,045	$990	$965	$880	$825	$770

CONTINENTAL ARMS CORPORATION

Previous importer that imported high quality shotguns and rifles (usually Belgian), circa mid-1950s-mid-1970s.

RIFLES

BOLT ACTION - mostly large cals., typically custom Mauser action, makers include Defourney and Dumoulin.

Specimens should be evaluated individually due to the many configurations and embellishments encountered. This model is rarely seen in today's marketplace.

DOUBLE RIFLE - .270 Win., .303 British, .30-40 Krag, .348 Win., .30-06, .375 H&H, .400 Jeffreys, .470, .475, .500, or .600 Nitro Express cal., 24 or 26 in. barrels, Anson & Deeley boxlock system, although some sidelocks were mfg., double triggers, checkered stock.

	$4,950	$4,350	$3,850	$3,300	$2,970	$2,750	$2,500

Add 10% for boxlock with sideplates.
Add 15% for ejectors.
Add 30%-50% for .375 H&H and larger cals., depending on the size of the cal.

SHOTGUNS: O/U

Add 20% for .410 bore.
Add 30% for 28 ga.
Add 10% for Defourney mfg.

CENTAURE BOXLOCK - 12, 20, 28 ga., or .410 bore, ejectors, light engraving, chopper lump barrels with cross-bolt, double underlocks, SST, 3-piece forearm.

	$2,000	$1,675	$1,500	$1,250	$1,025	$875	$750

CENTAURE LIEGE ROYAL CROWN GRADE - similar to Centaure Boxlock, except has game scene engraving, better figured wood and silver crown inlay.

	$3,150	$2,850	$2,600	$2,250	$1,900	$1,600	$1,400

GRADING - PPGS™	100%	98%	95%	90%	80%	70%	60%

CENTAURE IMPERIAL CROWN GRADE - similar to Royal Crown Grade, except has higher grade wood, extensive game scene engraving, oak leaf engraving on barrels, and gold inlay on top lever.

	$4,500	$4,150	$3,750	$3,500	$3,200	$2,900	$2,700

SHOTGUNS: SxS

Add 20% for .410 bore.
Add 30% for 28 ga.
Add 10% for Defourney mfg.

CENTAURE - all gauges, basic boxlock action with double triggers and extractors.

	$1,050	$950	$895	$850	$700	$500	$400

Add 35% for ejectors.

CENTAURE ROYAL CROWN GRADE - all gauges, single trigger, ejectors, checkered stock and forearm, game scene engraving, can be identified by silver crown inlaid on top lever.

	$3,400	$3,150	$2,800	$2,600	$2,325	$2,100	$1,950

CENTAURE IMPERIAL CROWN GRADE - similar to Royal Crown, except gold inlay on top lever, extensive game scene engraving on receiver and barrels.

	$4,275	$3,850	$3,500	$3,150	$2,850	$2,575	$2,300

COOEY, H.W., MACHINE & ARMS CO. LTD.

Previous manufacturer located in Cobourg, Ontario, Canada 1903-1961. During 1961, Cooey was sold to the Olin Corporation and placed under the supervision of the Winchester Western Division. At that point, the manufacture of Winchesters (primarily for Winchester Canada) began and continued through the mid-1970s (see Iver Johnson).

To date, there is limited collector demand for most models in this trademark and values should be based on the shooting utility rather than collector premiums due to rarity. Values for average condition guns will typically range between $75-$150.

RIFLES

Cooey manufactured a wide number of rifles, including bolt actions, single shots, and semi-autos. During the late 1920s-early 1930s, Cooey manufactured the Model X and 2X for Iver Johnson (please refer to Iver Johnson section).
Pre-1961 Cooey mfg. models include: 25, 35, 39, 55, 60, 62, 75, 78, 82, Ace, Ace 1, Ace 2, Ace 3, Ace Repeater, Ace Special, Bisley Sport, Canuck, Canuck 25, Canuck Junior, Canuck Western, Cooey Repeater, HWC, Mohawk, and several unnumbered single shot and repeating sporter rifles. Post-1961 Cooey firearms made by Winchester include: Model 10, Model 39, Model 60, Model 600, Model 64, Model 64 Deluxe, Model 64A, 64B, Model 71, 71 Carbine, Model 75, 750, and 750 Deluxe, Model 710, and Ranger.

SHOTGUNS

Cooey manufactured both double and single barrel shotguns for Iver Johnson (Hercules and Champion) during the late 1920s-early 1930s (see Iver Johnson section). Cooey also manufactured single shot shotguns. Pre-1961 Cooey mfg. models include: .22 rimfire smoothbore, 37A, 410, 84, Canuck 25, and Canuck 410. Post-1961 Cooey firearms made by Winchester include: Models 84 and 840.

COONAN ARMS

Previous manufacture by Dan Coonan, and distributed from November 1994-September 1998 by JS Worldwide Distribution Co. located in Maplewood, MN. Previously located in St. Paul, MN, approx. 1983-1996.

During 1985, Dan Coonan sold Coonan Arms to Bill Davis. In 1990, Dan Coonan left the company, and during July 1994, the company filed for Chapter 11. Coonan Arms was incorporated by JS Worldwide Distribution in November 1994. On Sept. 25, 1998, Coonan Arms and JS Worldwide Distribution was dissolved by the state of MN.

GRADING - PPGS™	100%	98%	95%	90%	80%	70%	60%

PISTOLS: SEMI-AUTO

COONAN .357 MAG. MODEL B - .357 Mag. cal. only, stainless steel and alloy construction, single action, semi-auto, design based on the Colt Model 1911, 7 shot mag., 5 or 6 (new 1989) in. barrel, smooth or checkered (new 1996) walnut grips, Teflon finish options new 1996, 42 oz. Mfg. 1983-99.

$685	$535	$425	$360	$315	$260	$225

Last MSR was $735.

Add $40 for checkered walnut grips.
Add $33 for 6 in. barrel (new 1989).
Add $140 for Millett adj. rear sight.
Add $165 for Bo-Mar sight.
Add $45 for .38 Spl. conversion kit (new 1986).

This model could be differentiated from the Model A in that it had an extended grip safety lever, linkless barrel system, enclosed trigger bar slot, and recontoured rear grip strap. This model became standard in 1985.

* *Coonan .357 Mag. Cadet Model* - similar to .357 Mag. Model B, except is compact variation with 3.9 in. barrel and 6 shot mag., 39 oz. Mfg. 1993-99.

$785	$630	$500	$430	$375	$315	$270

Last MSR was $855.

Options were similar to those listed for the Model B.

* *Coonan .357 Mag. Cadet II* - features standard grip with 7/8 shot mag. Mfg. 1996-99.

$785	$630	$500	$430	$375	$315	$270

Last MSR was $855.

Options were similar to those listed for the Model B.

* *Coonan .357 Mag. Model B Compensated* - 6 in. barrel with compensator. Mfg. 1990-99.

$900	$795	$650	$540	$465	$385	$335

Last MSR was $1,015.

Options were similar to those listed for the Model B.

* *Coonan .357 Mag. Model Classic Compensated* - features 5 in. barrel with integral compensator, Millett white/orange outline sights, checkered black walnut grips, Teflon black and matte stainless two-tone finish, 42 oz. Mfg. 1996-99.

$1,275	$1,025	$825	$675	$595	$525	$450

Last MSR was $1,400.

COONAN .357 MAG. MODEL A - original model without above listed improvements, special order only, inventory depleted in 1991. Serialization is under 2,000 for this model (less than 1,200 were mfg.).

$1,150	$775	$550	$460	$395	$335	$285

Last MSR was $625.

Add approx. $350 for early variations with engraved slide.

This variation will also shoot .38+P loads. The first 25 Model As were engraved on both sides of slide.

COONAN .41 MAGNUM - .41 Mag. cal., 5 in. barrel, smooth or checkered walnut grips. Mfg. 1997-99.

$760	$625	$500	$430	$375	$315	$270

Last MSR was $825.

Options were similar to those listed for the .357 Mag.

GRADING - PPGS™	100%	98%	95%	90%	80%	70%	60%

COOPER FIREARMS OF MONTANA, INC.

Current manufacturer located in Stevensville, MT since 1991. Available through Cooper Arms registered dealers only.

RIFLES: BOLT ACTION

Approx. 15,000 Cooper rifles have been manufactured in over 50 calibers to date.

Add $150 for left-hand action (custom order only) on the models listed below.

MODEL 21 SINGLE SHOT - various medium size cals., 3 front locking lugs.

* *Model 21 Classic* - various cals., single shot, 24 in. chrome moly match grade barrel, stock is AA Claro walnut with 20 LPI hand checkering and hand rubbed oil finish, machined aluminum trigger guard, matte metal finish, approx. 7-7 1/4 lbs. New 1999.

MSR $1,100	$950	$800	$650	$550	$495	$450	$400

* *Model 21 Custom Classic* - Includes Brownell No. 1 checkering pattern, ebony forend tip, and steel grip cap.

MSR $1,995	$1,725	$1,300	$975	$750	$650	$550	$475

* *Model 21 Western Classic* - various cals., features octagon barrel and case hardened action and metal work. New 1997.

MSR $2,595	$2,250	$1,800	$1,550	$1,275	$995	$875	$750

* *Model 21 Varminter* - various cals., 24 in. stainless steel match grade barrel, stock is AA Claro walnut with 20 LPI hand checkering and hand rubbed oil finish, machined aluminum trigger guard, approx. 7-7 1/4 lbs. New 1999.

MSR $995	$875	$750	$625	$550	$495	$450	$400

* *Model 21 Varmint Extreme* - various cals. between .17 Rem.-.223 Rem. (including metric cals.), features stainless barrel, checkered stock. New 1994.

MSR $1,795	$1,650	$1,425	$1,200	$995	$825	$600	$475

Add $465 for Benchrest Model with Jewell trigger (mfg. 1995-96).

* *Model 21 Montana Varminter* - various cals. New 2000.

MSR $1,295	$1,150	$975	$825	$650	$550	$475	$425

* *Model 21 Phoenix* - 24 in. stainless match barrel, flat black or brown spider web synthetic stock, aluminum bedding block, matte metal finish. New 2005.

MSR $1,298	$1,150	$925	$800	$700	$600	$500	$400

MODEL 22 - various mid-action cals., larger scale action of the Model 21.

* *Model 22 Classic* - various mid-action cals., 24 in. chrome moly match grade barrel, stock is AA Claro walnut with 20 LPI hand checkering and hand rubbed oil finish, machined aluminum trigger guard, matte metal finish, approx. 7-7 1/4 lbs. New 1999.

MSR $1,295	$1,150	$975	$825	$650	$550	$475	$425

* *Model 22 Custom Classic* - includes Brownell No. 1 checkering pattern, ebony forend tip, and steel grip cap.

MSR $2,195	$1,900	$1,400	$1,050	$775	$675	$575	$475

* *Model 22 Western Classic* - various cals., features octagon barrel and case hardened action and bolt. New 1997.

MSR $2,795	$2,375	$1,950	$1,675	$1,375	$1,050	$925	$825

* *Model 22 Varminter* - various cals., otherwise similar to the Model 21 Varminter. New 2000.

MSR $1,199	$1,025	$850	$700	$600	$525	$450	$400

* *Model 22 Montana Varminter* - various cals. New 2000.

MSR $1,495	$1,300	$1,075	$900	$700	$600	$500	$425

GRADING - PPGS™	100%	98%	95%	90%	80%	70%	60%

✳ *Model 22 Pro-Varmint Extreme* - .220 Swift, .22 BR (new 1996), .22-250 Rem., .243 Win., .25-06 Rem., .308 Win., 6mm PPC, 6.5x55mm (new 1996) or 7.62x39mm (new 1996) cal., available in either Pro-Varmint, Benchrest, or Black Jack (black synthetic stock) configuration. New 1995.

	100%	98%	95%	90%	80%	70%	60%
MSR $1,995	$1,725	$1,300	$975	$750	$650	$550	$475

Add $400 for Benchrest Model.

✳ *Model 22 Phoenix* - 24 in. stainless match barrel, flat black or brown spider web synthetic stock, aluminum bedding block, matte metal finish. New 2005.

	100%	98%	95%	90%	80%	70%	60%
MSR $1,398	$1,225	$975	$825	$725	$625	$550	$450

MODEL 22 CLASSIC REPEATER - .22-250 Rem., .243 Win., .308 Win., or 7mm-08 Rem. cal., 3 shot mag. While advertised during 1996 only at $2,400 retail, this model was never mfg.

MODEL CUSTOM CLASSIC - .22 LR, .22 Mag., .22 Hornet or .222 Rem. cal., features Anschutz Match 54 action with deluxe walnut stock with American features and smaller trigger guard. Mfg. 1996-99.

		98%	95%	90%	80%	70%	60%
		$1,750	$1,375	$1,075	$900	$725	$600	$500

Last MSR was $1,995.

MODEL CUSTOM MANNLICHER - .22 LR, .22 Mag., .22 Hornet, or .222 Rem. cal., features newest Anschutz Match 54 action with deluxe Mannlicher walnut stock and other special features. Mfg. 1996-99.

		98%	95%	90%	80%	70%	60%
		$1,975	$1,625	$1,425	$1,225	$975	$850	$700

Last MSR was $2,195.

MODEL 36 SPORTSMAN - .22 LR, .17 CCM, or .22 Hornet cal., without Shilen barrel, standard wood with rubber recoil pad. Mfg. 1994 only.

		98%	95%	90%	80%	70%	60%
		$675	$575	$495	$450	$400	$350	$295

Last MSR was $750.

MODEL 36 MARKSMAN - .22 LR, .17 CCM, or .22 Hornet cal., 4 shot mag., 23 in. chrome moly barrel, AA Claro walnut with 22 LPI checkering, 45 degree bolt, sling swivels, hand rubbed oil finish, 7 lbs. Mfg. 1992-94.

		98%	95%	90%	80%	70%	60%
		$975	$750	$625	$550	$495	$450	$400

Last MSR was $1,125.

✳ *Model 36 Montana Trail Blazer* - .22 LR cal. only, lightweight field gun with sporter barrel. Mfg. 1996 only.

		98%	95%	90%	80%	70%	60%
		$1,300	$1,025	$775	$650	$575	$475	$425

Last MSR was $1,475.

✳ *Model 36 Classic* - .22 LR cal. only, features choice of AAA Claro or AA French walnut with Monte Carlo cheekpiece. Disc. 1996.

		98%	95%	90%	80%	70%	60%
		$1,500	$1,175	$875	$700	$625	$525	$450

Last MSR was $1,695.

✳ *Model 36 Varmint Extreme* - various cals., heavy Varmint stainless barrel, checkered stock. Mfg. 1997 only.

		98%	95%	90%	80%	70%	60%
		$1,525	$1,175	$875	$700	$625	$525	$450

Last MSR was $1,695.

✳ *Model 36 Western Classic* - various cals., features octagon barrel and case hardened action and bolt. Mfg. 1997-99.

		98%	95%	90%	80%	70%	60%
		$1,900	$1,400	$1,000	$775	$650	$550	$475

Last MSR was $2,195.

✳ *Model 36 Custom Classic* - includes Brownell No. 1 checkering pattern, ebony forend tip, and steel grip cap. Disc. 1999.

		98%	95%	90%	80%	70%	60%
		$1,625	$1,325	$1,050	$825	$700	$600	$500

Last MSR was $1,850.

GRADING - PPGS™	100%	98%	95%	90%	80%	70%	60%

* **Model 36 TRP-1** - target variation of the Model 36 with ISU synthetic stock and adj. cheekpiece, 23 in. Wiseman/McMillan stainless steel or chrome moly barrel, single shot, fully adj. single stage trigger, vent. forearm. Mfg. 1992-93.

	$950	$795	$625	$525	$475	$425	$375

Last MSR was $1,095.

* **Model MS-36 (TRP-1S)** - silhouette variation of the Model 36 TRP-1, clear epoxy finish, silhouette style stock, Pachmayr buttpad. Mfg. 1992-93.

	$895	$725	$625	$550	$495	$450	$400

Last MSR was $995.

* **Model 36 BR-50** - .22 LR cal., benchrest variation featuring black synthetic stock and heavy stainless barrel. Mfg. 1993-99.

	$1,675	$1,250	$950	$750	$650	$550	$475

Last MSR was $1,950.

* **Model 36 IR-50/50** - .22 LR cal. only, lightweight sporter style competition rifle with heavy 20 in. barrel. Mfg. 1996-99.

	$1,675	$1,250	$950	$750	$650	$550	$475

Last MSR was $1,950.

* **Model 36 Featherweight** - .17 CCM, .22 LR, or .22 Hornet cal., features matte black synthetic stock and metal, Jewell trigger. Mfg. 1994-99.

	$1,600	$1,225	$900	$700	$625	$525	$450

Last MSR was $1,795.

MODEL 38 SPORTER - .17 CCM, or .22 CCM cal., 3 shot mag., 24 in. chrome moly barrel, AA Claro walnut with 22 LPI checkering, 45 degree bolt, sling swivels, hand rubbed oil finish, 8 lbs. Mfg. 1992-93.

	$965	$750	$625	$550	$495	$450	$400

Last MSR was $1,095.

Add $100 for Standard Grade (AA Claro walnut).
Add $200 for Custom Grade.
Add $300 for Custom Classic Grade.

The custom grade includes choice of AAA Claro or AA French walnut with Monte Carlo cheekpiece.

The .17 CCM and .22 CCM cartridges designate Cooper Centerfire Magnum. Basically, the .22 CCM is a centerfire derivative of the .22 Mag. cal., and the .17 CCM is simply a necked down variation.

* **Model 38 Repeater (Deluxe)** - deluxe variation of the Model 38 Sporter. 650 mfg. 1992-1994.

	$1,750	$1,400	$1,000	$775	$650	$550	$475

MODEL 38 SINGLE SHOT - small, mostly rimmed cals., 3 front locking lugs. New 1998.

* **Model 38 Classic** - various cals., single shot, 20 in. chrome moly match grade barrel, stock is AA Claro walnut with 20 LPI hand checkering and hand rubbed oil finish, machined aluminum trigger guard, matte metal finish, approx. 7-7 1/4 lbs. New 1999.

MSR $1,100	$950	$800	$650	$550	$495	$450	$400

* **Model 38 Custom Classic** - includes Brownell No. 1 checkering pattern, ebony forend tip, and steel grip cap.

MSR $1,995	$1,735	$1,325	$975	$750	$650	$550	$475

* **Model 38 Western Classic** - various cals., features octagon barrel and case hardened action and bolt. New 1997.

MSR $2,595	$2,250	$1,800	$1,550	$1,275	$995	$875	$750

GRADING - PPGS™	100%	98%	95%	90%	80%	70%	60%

✳ *Model 38 Varminter* - various cals., single shot, 24 in. stainless steel match grade barrel, stock is AA Claro walnut with 20 LPI hand checkering and hand rubbed oil finish, machined aluminum trigger guard, approx. 7-7 1/4 lbs. New 1999.

MSR $995	$875	$750	$625	$550	$495	$450	$400

✳ *Model 38 Varmint Extreme* - various cals. including the new .19-223, heavy stainless steel barrel w/o sights, checkered stock. New 1997.

MSR $1,795	$1,650	$1,425	$1,200	$995	$825	$600	$475

✳ *Model 38 Montana Varminter* - various cals. New 2000.

MSR $1,295	$1,150	$975	$825	$650	$550	$475	$425

MODEL 40 - .17 CCM (disc. 1995), .17 Ackley Hornet, .22 CCM (disc. 1995), .22 Hornet, or .22 K Hornet cal., 3 lug action, incorporates Anschütz mag., choice of Classic, Custom Classic, or Classic Varminter configuration. Mfg. 1995-96.

	$1,600	$1,200	$950	$750	$650	$550	$475

Last MSR was $1,825.

Add $200 for Custom Classic or Classic Varminter (disc.) Model.

MODEL 57 CLASSIC - .17 HMR (new 2002), .22 LR or .22 Mag. (new 2001) cal., 3 rear locking lugs, various configurations, barrel lengths, and features. New 2000.

MSR $1,149	$965	$815	$675	$550	$495	$450	$400

Add approx. $100 for .17 HMR or .22 Mag. cal. on the following models.

✳ *Model 57 Custom Classic* - new 2000.

MSR $1,895	$1,650	$1,275	$900	$725	$625	$525	$450

✳ *Model 57 Western Classic* - new 2000.

MSR $2,495	$2,250	$1,650	$1,175	$825	$725	$650	$575

✳ *Model 57 LVT* - 24 in. stainless match barrel, oil finished AA select Claro hand checkered walnut, matte metal finish. New mid-2005.

MSR $1,459	$1,275	$1,125	$915	$800	$700	$600	$500

✳ *Model 57 Jackson Squirrel Rifle* - 22 in. stainless match barrel, fluted forearm, oil finished hand checkered AA Claro walnut with roll over cheekpiece, steel grip cap, 6 1/2 lbs. New 2005.

MSR $1,498	$1,325	$1,050	$875	$775	$650	$575	$500

✳ *Model 57 Jackson Hunter* - 22 in. blue match barrel, camo synthetic stock with aluminum bedding block, matte metal finish. New 2005.

MSR $1,298	$1,150	$925	$800	$700	$600	$500	$400

MODEL 72 MONTANA PLAINSMAN - various cals., single shot featuring case colored Win. Model 1885 action with heavy octagon barrel, double set triggers, deluxe checkered straight grip stock and forearm, no sights. While advertised during 1997 at a retail price of $2,195, this model never went into production.

RIFLES: SINGLE SHOT

MODEL 7 PEREGRINE FALLING BLOCK - various cals., falling block action with under lever, choice of varmint extreme or custom sporter configuration, 24 in. barrel, deluxe checkered walnut stock, tang mounted safety, approx. 6 lbs. Limited production 2001 only.

	$1,750	$1,400	$1,100	$925	$800	$675	$550

Last MSR was $1,995.

Add $300 for custom sporter variation.

MODEL 16 - WSSM cals., 24 in. stainless match grade barrel, hand checkered, oil finished walnut stock, available in varmint styles only. New 2005.

MSR $1,395	$1,225	$975	$825	$725	$625	$550	$450

Add $200 for Montana Varminter.
Add $400 for Varmint Extreme.

GRADING - PPGS™	100%	98%	95%	90%	80%	70%	60%

COP

Previous derringer manufacturer located in Torrance, CA.

DERRINGERS

COP DERRINGER - .22 Mag. or .357 Mag. cal., 4 shot, 3 in. barrel, stainless steel mfg., double action, wood grips, 28 oz. COP stands for Compact Off-Duty Police. Disc.

	$350	$325	$285	$250	$220	$195	$175

CORTONA

Current trademark of shotguns manufactured by F.A.I.R. Techni-Mec, located in Marcheno, Italy. Currently imported by Kalispell Case Line, located in Cusick, WA.

SHOTGUNS: O/U

Cortona shotguns utilizes boxlock action with a 3-lug system and Boss style frame in both aluminum and steel. Many variations are possible, and the lineup includes the Legend Series with engraved sideplates (MSR $3,085-$3,285), the Prestige Series with case colored and engraved sideplates and
deluxe Turkish walnut stock and forearm (MSR $3,610-$3,795) (also available in 16 ga.), the Grande Series (MSR $1,785-$1,855), and the Alumino Series (MSR $2,665-$2,800). A GR Series was also available in 12, 20, and 28 ga. MSRs ranged from $1,785 - $2,585 (disc. 2007). Please contact the importer directly for more information, including availability and pricing (see Trademark Index).

COSMI, AMERICO & FIGLIO

Current semi-auto shotgun manufacturer established during 1930, and located in Ancona, Italy. Currently distributed exclusively beginning late 2005 by Dewing's Fly & Gun Shop, located in West Palm Beach, FL. Currently imported by Pacific Sporting Arms, located in Azuza, CA. Previously imported from 2003-2004 by Old Friends Hunting & Shooting Co., from 1985-2003 by New England Arms Co., and from 2001-2002 by Autumn Sales, Inc., located in Fort Worth, TX. Please contact the distributor directly for more information and model availability (see Trademark Index).

Approximately 7,500 Cosmi shotguns have been manufactured since 1930 (the design dates back to 1925). They are known for their unique mechanism and high-quality fabrication techniques. Since each gun's parts are made separately (and individually serial numbered), most components are not interchangeable from one gun to another.

SHOTGUNS: SEMI-AUTO

Add $3,000 for extra barrel, $3,400 for extra barrel with choke tubes.

STANDARD MODEL - 12, 16, or 20 ga., 2 3/4 (16 ga. only) or 3 in. chamber, semi-auto, unique pivoting break open action loads cartridges into stock chamber from inside of receiver, 8 shot mag. with 3 shot option reducer, steel, alloy, or titanium frame, Boehler Antinit steel barrel (moves when shooting) available with or without choke tubes, all internal parts are mfg. from special chrome-nickel steel or titanium (new 1990), custom order gun only with dimensions specified by individual customer (approx. 6 month delivery time on 12 and 20 ga.).

* *Standard Grade* - barrel and attached receiver assembly are blue, frame is chromed-nickel steel, w/o engraving, current importation is with best quality wood only and deluxe case.

MSR $15,000		$14,500	$12,000	$9,000	$7,500	$6,000	$4,500	$3,750

Subtract approx. 25% for older mfg. w/o fancy wood and choke tubes.

❖ **Standard Grade Engraved Models** - The Standard model is available in the following deluxe engraving configurations: Deluxe w/#1 engraving - $19,950 MSR, Deluxe w/#2 engraving - $22,500 MSR, Deluxe w/#3 engraving - $16,500 MSR, Extra Deluxe w/#4 engraving - $24,500 MSR, Extra Deluxe w/#5 engraving - $26,500 MSR, Extra Deluxe w/#6 engraving - $31,500 MSR, Extra Deluxe w/#10 engraving - $31,500 MSR, Prestige "A" engraving - $47,500 MSR, Prestige "B" engraving - $35,500 MSR, and Prestige "C" engraving - $37,500 MSR.

✳ *Standard Aluminum Model* - 12 or 20 ga., receiver made out of machined aluminum, approx. 7 lbs. in 12 ga., approx. 5.9 lbs. in 20 ga., very limited mfg. to date.

MSR N/A		$14,000	$11,000	$9,250	$7,500	$5,000	$4,275 $3,750

Subtract 15% if w/o choke tubes.

✳ *Standard Titanium Model* - 12 or 20 ga., receiver made out of machined titanium, approx. 6.8 lbs. in 12 ga., approx. 5.7 lbs. in 20 ga. New 1990.

MSR $19,500		$18,750	$15,500	$13,000	$11,250	$9,000	$7,000 $5,250

Subtract 15% if w/o choke tubes.

❖ **Standard Titanium Grade Engraved Models** - The Standard Titanium model is available in the following Deluxe engraved editions: Deluxe w/# 1 engraving - $27,500 MSR, Deluxe w/#2 engraving - $29,500 MSR, Deluxe w/# 3 engraving - $25,500 MSR, Extra Deluxe w/# 4 engraving - $32,500 MSR, Extra Deluxe w/# 5 engraving - $34,500 MSR, Extra Deluxe w/# 6 engraving -$38,500 MSR, Extra Deluxe w/#10 engraving - $38,500 MSR, Prestige "A" engraving - $54,500 MSR, Prestige "B" engraving - $39,500, and "Prestige "C" engraving - $44,500 MSR.

COUNTY, S.A.L.

Previous shotgun manufacturer located in Eibar, Spain.

SHOTGUNS: O/U

County manufactured a wide variety of both boxlock and sidelock O/Us, which had very limited U.S. importation.

CRESCENT FIRE ARMS CO. & CRESCENT-DAVIS ARMS CORP.

Previous manufacturers and trademarks manufactured circa 1888-1931 in Norwich, CT.

In 1888, George W. Cilley bought out the defunct Bacon Arms Co. of Norwich, CT. He then formed an alliance with Frank Foster, and borrowed enough money to form the Crescent Fire Arms Company. Cilley and Foster each held several firearms patents, and both were highly qualified in firearms design and manufacture. Production began with single shot tip-up shotguns that had an external side hammer. Double barrel shotgun production was started in 1891. In 1893, they began making bicycle chains, and that same year, H&D Folsom took over the company's financial control. Early in the 1890s, Crescent built a rifle that resembled the Remington No. 4. A very rare Crescent was the .410 bore shotgun pistol, which was introduced in the 1920s. In 1929, N.R. Davis Firearms Co., then owned by Warner Arms Corp., merged with Cresent to become Crescent-Davis Arms Corp. Because of financial crisis, business continued to decline, and they were forced to sell out. Savage Arms Co. acquired Cresent-Davis in 1931, assembled guns from the remaining parts, and these guns were sold under the Crescent name only. In 1932, the city of Norwich, CT, took over the Crescent property for non-payment of back taxes. After the Norwich facility was closed, manufacture was moved to Chicopee Falls.

It is unknown whether or not Crescent did any high grade or custom work. However, a very well engraved SxS, with the Crescent logo, is known to exist in a private collection.

Crescent Fire Arms Company remains best known as a manufacturer of "house brand" shotguns (i.e., Crescent private labeled guns for retailers, distributors, mail-order houses, etc.). Over 100 different trademarks have been observed to date, manufactured by Crescent. Almost all the remaining specimens today are priced as shooters and have no collector value.

GRADING - PPGS™	100%	98%	95%	90%	80%	70%	60%

SHOTGUNS

Certain models may be considered Curios or Relics by the ATF (subject to change). Other models fall under 1934 NFA legislation, and are subject to seizure w/o proper paperwork and registration with the ATF. Please contact your local ATF branch for clarification.

SINGLE SHOT MODEL - 12, 16, 20, 28 ga., or .410 bore, exposed hammer, various barrel lengths, walnut stock and forearm. Disc.

	100%	98%	95%	90%	80%	70%	60%
	$140	$115	$100	$85	$75	$65	$50

Add 15% for 16 or 20 ga., 50% for 28 ga. or .410 bore.

SxS MODEL - values below assume standard models with double triggers, extractors, original finish, and 100% working order. Most shotguns feature sidelock actions. Shotguns with exposed hammers can equal their hammerless counterparts if condition is 80% or better.

	100%	98%	95%	90%	80%	70%	60%
12 ga.	$295	$265	$230	$210	$185	$165	$150
16 ga.	$295	$265	$210	$185	$165	$145	$125
20 ga.	$335	$290	$250	$225	$195	$175	$160
28 ga.	$425	$375	$325	$280	$250	$200	$150
.410 bore	$450	$400	$350	$300	$250	$200	$150

KNICKERBOCKER - 20 ga., 14 in. nickel-plated barrels, case-hardened receiver, pistol grip, mfg. circa 1900s.

Extreme rarity factor precludes accurate pricing information.

VICTOR EJECTOR - .410 bore, 12 in. single barrel, total production unknown, possibly prototype for Crescent Certified Shotgun.

Extreme rarity factor precludes accurate pricing information.

NEW EMPIRE - hammerless .410 smooth bore or 20 ga., 12 1/4 in. barrels, extremely rare firearm whose total production and years of manufacture are unknown at this time (only known documentation is mentioned as an "Auto Burglar Gun" in an advertisement by "Saul Ruben, The Gun Store, 68 E. Long St., Columbus, OH" of the October 1932 issue of *Hunter-Trader-Trapper*, which lists a $14.75 retail price). The receiver is marked "New Empire". At this time, 5 specimens are known in .410 smooth bore, with ser. nos. scattered throughout the S-1 to S-19 range. The ser. no. appears on the metal under the forearm. The Crescent Auto & Burglar Gun may have been distributed by the H. & D. Folsom Arms Co. of New York City through its manufacturing division, the Crescent Firearms Co., Norwich, CT. Crescent's sellers included the Belknap Hardware Co., Louisville, KY and Hibbard-Spencer-Bartlett Co., Chicago, IL.

	100%	98%	95%	90%	80%	70%	60%
	$1,425	$1,200	$1,000	$900	$800	$700	$600

CRESCENT CERTIFIED SHOTGUN - .410 smooth bore, 12 1/2 in. barrel, approx. 4,000 mfg. from approx. 1930-32 by the Crescent-Davis Arms Corp., and possibly thereafter until 1934 by the J. Stevens Arms Co., left receiver side is stamped "Crescent Certified Shotgun/Crescent-Davis Arms Corp./Norwich, Conn. U.S.A." Also termed the "Ever-Ready" Model 200 and advertised with a blue frame, but specimens with "tiger stripe" and regular case coloring have been observed, guns not currently registered with ATF cannot be legally owned and are subject to seizure.

	100%	98%	95%	90%	80%	70%	60%
	$1,425	$1,200	$1,000	$900	$800	$700	$600

Add $100-$300 for original cardboard box.

CRICKET RIFLE

Please refer to the Keystone Sporting Arms, Inc. section in this text.

GRADING - PPGS™	100%	98%	95%	90%	80%	70%	60%

CROSSFIRE LLC

Previous manufacturer located in La Grange, GA 1998-2001.

COMBINATION GUNS

CROSSFIRE MK-I - 12 ga. (3 in. chamber) over .223 Rem. cal., unique slide action O/U design allows stacked shotgun/rifle configuration, 18 3/4 in. shotgun barrel with invector chokes over 16 1/4 in. rifle barrel, detachable 4 (shotgun) and 5 (rifle) shot mags., open sights, Picatinny style rail scope mount, synthetic stock and forearm, choice of black (MK-I) or RealTree 100% camo (MK-1RT) finish, single trigger with ambidextrous fire control lever, 8.6 lbs. Mfg. mid-1998-2001.

	$1,750	$1,550	$1,350	$1,175	$995	$895	$825

Last MSR was $1,895.

Add $100 for camo finish.

CUMBERLAND MOUNTAIN ARMS, INC.

Previous manufacturer located in Winchester, TN early 1993-99.

RIFLES: SINGLE SHOT

PLATEAU RIFLE - .40-65 or .45-70 Govt. cal., patterned after the Browning High Wall single shot, various barrel lengths up to 32 in., manual safety, blue receiver and barrel, Marble's style buckhorn rear sight, receiver drilled for scope mounts. Mfg. 1993-99.

	$1,075	$825	$675	$575	$500	$450	$400

Last MSR was $1,295.

Add approx. $200-$350 for deluxe wood.

CUSTOM GUN GUILD

Previous manufacturer located in Doraville, GA.

FIREARMS

WOOD'S MODEL IV SINGLE SHOT - various cals., custom manufactured, falling block type single shot, lightweight, only 5 1/2 lbs. Mfg. 1984 only.

	$2,975	$2,500	$2,000	$1,850	$1,700	$1,500	$1,250

D SECTION

D'ARCY ECHOLS & CO.

Current manufacturer beginning 1996, and located in Millville, UT.

RIFLES: BOLT ACTION

Models include the Standard Sporter ($13,500 MSR), Classic Light Sporter (disc, $21,000 last MSR), Long Range ($13,700 MSR), Heavy Sporter (scoped or iron sight version, $13,700 MSR). Additionally, many special orders and options are also available. Please contact the company for more information (see Trademark Index).

DGS, INC.

Current custom rifle gunsmith located in Casper, WY.

Custom gunsmith Dale A. Storey manufactures a variety of bolt action rifles built per individual customer order only. They include the Storey Custom and Storey Lightweight, as well as other variations. Please contact the company directly for more information and current prices on these quality custom rifles.

CUSTOM GUNSMITHING

DPMS FIREARMS, LLC

Current manufacturer established in 1986 and located in St. Cloud, MN. Previously located in Becker, MN. Previous company name was DPMS, Inc. (Defense Procurement Manufacturing Services, Inc.). Assembles high quality AR-15 style rifles (including a conversion for .22 cal.), in addition to selling related parts and components. Distributor, dealer, and consumer direct sales.

In December, 2007, Cerberus Capital Management acquired the assets of DPMS. The new company name is DPMS Firearms, LLC.

GRADING - PPGS™	100%	98%	95%	90%	80%	70%	60%

PISTOLS: SEMI-AUTO

DPMS .45 - .45 ACP cal., patterned after the Colt M1911A-1, 7 shot mag., 5 in. barrel, 38 oz. Limited mfg. 2001 only.

$475	$425	$360	$330	$300	$275	$250

Last MSR was $519.

PANTHER .22 LR PISTOL - .22 LR cal., 8 1/2 in. heavy chrome-moly steel barrel, 10 shot mag., black aircraft aluminum flattop upper receiver, black forged aircraft aluminum lower receiver, blowback action, phosphate and hard chrome finished bolt and carrier, aluminum trigger guard, ribbed aluminum free float tube hand guard, no sights, 4 1/4 lbs. Limited mfg. 2006-2007.

$775	$700	$625	$550	$475	$425	$375

Last MSR was $850.

PISTOLS: SLIDE ACTION

PANTHER PUMP PISTOL - .223 Rem. cal., slide action paramilitary design, 10 1/2 in. threaded heavy barrel, aluminum handguard incorporates slide action mechanism, pistol grip only (no stock), carrying handle with sights, 5 lbs.

MSR $1,600		$1,475	$1,200	$1,025	$925	$825	$700	$575

RIFLES: BOLT ACTION

DPMS also distributes Evolution USA bolt action rifles. Please refer to the Evolution USA section for current models and pricing.

GRADING - PPGS™	100%	98%	95%	90%	80%	70%	60%

RIFLES: SEMI-AUTO

Each new DPMS rifle/carbine comes equipped with two mags. (high cap where legal), a nylon web sling, and a cleaning kit. Post-crime bill manufactured DPMS rifles may have pre-ban features, including collapsible stocks, high capacity mags, and a flash hider/compensator. Models with these features are not available in certain states.

The Panther AR-15 Series was introduced in 1993 in various configurations, including semi-auto and slide action, and feature paramilitary design in various barrel lengths and configurations, with a 10 or 30 shot mag.

PANTHER CLASSIC - 5.56x45mm cal., 16 or 20 in. heavy barrel, ribbed barrel shroud, includes carrying handle with sights, 8 lbs.

MSR $804	$730	$625	$550	$475	$425	$375	$335

    Add $76 for left-hand variation (Southpaw Panther).
    Add $10 for 20 in. barrel.

* *Panther Classic Bulldog* - 20 in. stainless fluted bull barrel, flattop, adj. buttstock, vented free float handguard, 11 lbs. Disc. 1999.

	$1,150	$835	$725	$625	$550	$475	$425

Last MSR was $1,219.

PANTHER 7.62x39mm - 7.62x39mm Russian cal., 16 or 20 in. heavy barrel, black Zytel buttstock with trapdoor, 7-9 lbs. New 2000.

MSR $844	$765	$650	$575	$495	$440	$385	$335

    Add $10 for 20 in. barrel.

PANTHER DCM - .223 Rem. cal., 20 in. stainless steel heavy barrel, National Match sights, two-stage trigger, black Zytel composition buttstock, 9 lbs. Mfg. 1998-2003, reintroduced 2006.

MSR $1,104	$995	$795	$675	$595	$525	$460	$415

PANTHER LITE - 5.56x45mm cal., 16 or 20 (new 2007) in. 1x9 twist post-ban chrome-moly barrel, non-collapsible fiberite CAR stock, forged A1 upper with forward bolt assist, black Teflon finish, 5 3/4 lbs. New 2002.

MSR $725	$660	$595	$550	$475	$425	$375	$335

PANTHER CLASSIC SIXTEEN - 5.45x45mm cal., 16 in. heavy barrel, adj. sights, black Zytel composition buttstock, 6 1/2 lbs. New 1998.

MSR $804	$720	$630	$550	$475	$425	$375	$335

    Add $55 for Panther Free Float Sixteen with free floating barrel and vent. handguard.

PANTHER LO-PRO CLASSIC - .223 Rem. cal., 16 in. bull barrel, features flattop lo-pro upper receiver with push pin. New 2002.

MSR $715	$655	$595	$550	$475	$425	$375	$335

PANTHER TUBER - 5.56x45mm cal., features 16 in. post-ban heavy barrel with full length 2 inch aluminum free float handguard, adj. A2 rear sights. New 2002.

MSR $754	$675	$625	$565	$485	$435	$375	$335

PANTHER A2 TACTICAL - 5.56x45mm cal., features 16 in. heavy manganese phosphated barrel, standard A2 handguard, 9 3/4 lbs. New 2004.

MSR $814	$705	$625	$550	$475	$425	$375	$335

PANTHER AP4 CARBINE - 5.56x45mm cal., features 16 in. M4 contour barrel with A2 flash hider, permanently attached Miculek compensator, fixed fiberglass reinforced polymer M4 stock, 7 1/4 lbs. New 2004.

MSR $904	$815	$725	$600	$525	$450	$400	$360

* *Panther AP4 Carbine* - 6.8x43mm SPC or 5.56x45mm cal., 11.5 or 16 in. barrel, collapsible stock, includes carrying handle, 6 1/2 lbs.

MSR $904	$815	$725	$600	$525	$450	$400	$360

The 11.5 in. barrel model is available for law enforcement only.

GRADING - PPGS™	100%	98%	95%	90%	80%	70%	60%

PANTHER AP4 A2 CARBINE - 5.56x45mm cal., 16 in. chrome-moly steel barrel with A2 flash hider, AP4 style contour, standard A2 front sight assembly, A2 fixed carry handle and adj. rear sight, forged aircraft aluminum upper and lower receiver, hard coat anodized teflon coated black AP4 six position telescoping fiber reinforced polymer stock, 7.1 lbs. New 2006.

MSR $804	$725	$650	$575	$500	$450	$400	$375

PANTHER A2 CARBINE "THE AGENCY" - 5.56x45mm cal., 16 in. chrome-moly steel barrel with A2 flash hider, A3 flattop forged receiver, two-stage trigger, tactical charging handle, package includes Surefire quad-rail and flashlight, EO Tech and "Mangonel" rear sights, Ergo Suregrip forearm and collapsible stock, supplied with two 30-shot mags., 7 lbs. New 2007.

MSR $2,001	$1,750	$1,600	$1,475	$1,350	$1,225	$1,100	$875

PANTHER 6.8mm CARBINE/RIFLE - 6.8x43mm Rem. SPC cal., 16 (new 2007) or 20 in. chrome-moly manganese phosphated steel barrel with A2 flash hider, standard A2 front sight assembly, A3 flattop upper receiver with detachable carry handle and adj. rear sight, aluminum aircraft alloy lower receiver, black standard A2 Zytel mil spec stock with trap door assembly, A2 handguard, includes two 25 shot mags., approx. 9 lbs. New 2006.

MSR $994	$895	$775	$650	$550	$475	$425	$375

Add $10 for 20 in. barrel.

PRAIRIE PANTHER - 20 in. heavy fluted barrel, flat-top, vented free float handguard, 8 3/4 lbs. Disc. 1999.

	$875	$750	$635	$550	$475	$425	$375

Last MSR was $959.

PANTHER BULL - .223 Rem. cal., features 16, 20 (standard), or 24 in. stainless free floating bull barrel, flattop, aluminum forearm, 10 lbs.

MSR $920	$835	$725	$600	$525	$450	$400	$360

Subtract $30 for 16 in. barrel (Panther Bull Sweet Sixteen).
Add $30 for 24 in. barrel (Panther Bull Twenty-Four).

* *Panther Bull Classic* - .223 Rem. cal., features 20 in. long, 1 in. bull barrel, adj. sights, 10 lbs. New 1998.

MSR $910	$825	$725	$600	$525	$450	$400	$360

Add $200 for SST lower.

* *Panther Bull Deluxe Twenty-Four Special* - .223 Rem. cal., features 24 in. stainless fluted barrel, adj. A2 buttstock with sniper pistol grip. New 1998.

MSR $1,194	$1,075	$825	$700	$600	$525	$460	$415

* *Panther Bull Super* - .223 Rem. cal., 16, 20, or 24 in. extra heavy bull barrel, flat-top receiver, free float handguard, approx. 11 lbs. Mfg. 1997-98, 24 in. model reintroduced during late 2004, disc. 2006.

	$1,075	$835	$725	$600	$525	$460	$415

Last MSR was $1,199.

* *Panther Bull Extreme Super* - features 24 in. extra heavy stainless steel bull barrel (1 1/8 in. diameter barrel), flat-top, hi-rider upper receiver, skeletonized A2 buttstock, 11 3/4 lbs. Mfg. 1999-2004.

	$1,075	$835	$715	$600	$525	$460	$415

Last MSR was $1,199.

ARTIC PANTHER - .223 Rem. cal., similar to Panther Bull, except has white powder coat finish on receiver and handguard, 10 lbs. New 1997.

MSR $1,104	$995	$795	$675	$595	$525	$460	$415

GRADING - PPGS™	100%	98%	95%	90%	80%	70%	60%

PANTHER PARDUS - 223 Rem. cal., 16 in. stainless steel bull barrel, integrated compensator, titanium nitride plated steel bolt and carrier, three rail extruded upper receiver, aluminum alloy upper and lower receiver, Teflon coated tan or black six position telescoping fiber reinforced polymer stock, curved and serrated buttplate, four-rail aluminum free float handguard, no sights, includes two 30 shot mags., 8.1 lbs. New 2006.

MSR $1,600	$1,395	$1,150	$950	$800	$675	$575	$525

PANTHER MARK 12 - .223 Rem. cal., 18 in. stainless heavy barrel with flash hider, features one-piece four rail free floating tube and six long rail covers, A3 flattop receiver, 5-position collapsible stock with tactical pistol grip, two-stage trigger, two 30 round mags., 8 3/4 lbs. New 2007.

MSR $1,504	$1,275	$1,100	$925	$800	$700	$600	$500

PANTHER SDM-R - .223 Rem. cal., 20 in. heavy stainless barrel with A2 flash hider, features four rail aluminum free float tube, pistol grip stock, National Match front sight, Harris bi-pod with rail adapter, two 30 shot mags., 8.85 lbs. New 2007.

MSR $1,404	$1,250	$1,075	$925	$825	$725	$650	$575

PANTHER 20TH ANNIVERSARY - 223 Rem. cal., 20 in. stainless steel fluted bull barrel, phosphated steel bolt and carrier, hi-rider forged high polished chrome upper and lower receiver with commemorative engraving, chrome plated charging handle, semi-auto trigger group, aluminum trigger guard and mag. release button, A2 black Zytel mil spec stock with trap door assembly and engraved DPMS logo, no sights, vented aluminum handguard, includes two 30 shot mags., approx. 9 1/2 lbs. Limited mfg. 2006.

	$1,995	$1,750	$1,600	$1,475	$1,350	$1,225	$1,100

Last MSR was $1,995.

PANTHER RACE GUN - .223 Rem. cal., 24 in. stainless steel barrel with Hot Rod hand guard, IronStone steel and aluminum stock with rubber buttplate and brass weights, 16 lbs. New 2001.

MSR $1,724	$1,565	$1,250	$1,050	$950	$850	$725	$600

PANTHER SINGLE SHOT - 5.56x45mm cal., 20 in. barrel, A2 black Zytel stock and handguard, single shot only w/o magazine, 9 lbs.

MSR $819	$725	$640	$560	$485	$435	$375	$335

PANTHER .22 RIFLE - .22 LR cal., AR-15 style receiver, 16 in. bull barrel, black Teflon metal finish, Picatinny rail, black Zytel A2 buttstock, 7.8 lbs. New 2003.

MSR $804	$725	$625	$550	$475	$425	$375	$335

PANTHER DCM .22 LR RIFLE - .22 LR cal., features 20 in. fluted stainless steel H-Bar barrel with 1:16 rate of twist, A2 upper receiver with National Match sights, black teflon finish, A2 stock and handguards, also available with optional DCM handguard system. New 2004.

MSR $994	$875	$775	$650	$550	$475	$425	$375

PANTHER AP4 .22 LR RIFLE - .22 LR cal., features 16 in. M4 contoured barrel with 1:16 rate of twist, M4 handguards and pinned carstock, A3 flattop upper receiver, detachable carry handle with A2 sights and black teflon finish, 6 1/2 lbs. New 2004.

MSR $894	$785	$675	$600	$500	$450	$400	$350

This model is also available in a pre-ban configuration for law enforcement.

PANTHER LR-.308 - .308 Win. cal., 24 in. bull barrel with 1:10 rate of twist, ribbed free-floating aluminum forearm tube, aircraft alloy upper/lower, A2 buttstock, black Teflon finish. New mid-2003.

MSR $1,154	$1,025	$850	$750	$650	$575	$500	$450

✳ *Panther LR-.308B* - similar features as the Long Range Rifle, except has 18 in. chrome-moly bull barrel and carbine length aluminum handguard. New late 2003.

MSR $1,154	$1,025	$850	$750	$650	$575	$500	$450

GRADING - PPGS™	100%	98%	95%	90%	80%	70%	60%

✳ *Panther LR-.308T* - similar features as the .308B, except has 16 in. H-Bar barrel. New 2004.

MSR $1,154	$1,025	$850	$750	$650	$575	$500	$450

✳ *Panther LR-.308 AP4* - similar to Panther .308 Long Range, except has AP4 six position telescoping fiber reinforced polymer stock.

MSR $1,255	$1,075	$925	$825	$725	$650	$600	$550

PANTHER LRT-SASS - .308 Win. cal., 18 in. stainless steel contoured barrel with Panther flash hider, A3 style flattop upper receiver solid alumnium lower receiver, AR-15 trigger group, ambi-slector, JP adj. adj. trigger, black waterproof Vltor Clubfoot carbine 5 position stock, vented handguard and Panther tactical pistol grip. New 2006.

MSR $2,104	$1,825	$1,575	$1,325	$1,125	$950	$825	$700

PANTHER MINI-SASS - 5.56x45mm cal., 18 in. stainless steel fluted barrel with Panther flash hider, gas operated rotating bolt, forged A3 flattop upper receiver, aircraft aluminum alloy lower receiver, aluminum trigger guard, tactical pistol grip, includes Harris bipod, 10 1/4 lbs. New 2008.

MSR $1,604	$1,400	$1,150	$950	$800	$675	$575	$525

PANTHER LR-30S - .300 RSUM cal., 20 in. stainless steel fluted bull barrel, aluminum upper and lower receiver, hard coat anodized teflon coated black skeletonized synthetic stock, integral trigger guard, ribbed aluminum free float tube handguard, includes two 4 shot mags., nylon web sling and cleaning kit. New 2004.

MSR $1,255	$1,075	$925	$825	$725	$650	$600	$550

PANTHER LR-204 - .204 Ruger cal., 24 in. stainless steel bull barrel, no sights, A3 flattop forged upper and lower receiver, semi-auto trigger group, standard A2 black Zytel mil spec stock with trap door assembly, includes two 30 shot mags., 10 1/4 lbs. New 2006.

MSR $1,004	$895	$825	$750	$675	$600	$500	$400

PANTHER LR-243 - .243 Win. cal., 20 in. chrome-moly steel heavy barrel, no sights, raised Picatinny rail, aluminum upper and lower receiver, standard AR-15 trigger group, skeletonized black Zytel mil spec stock with trap door assembly, ribbed aluminum free float handguard, includes two 19 shot mags., 10 3/4 lbs. New 2006.

MSR $1,204	$1,050	$900	$800	$725	$650	$600	$550

PANTHER LR-260/LR-260H/LR-260L - .260 Rem. cal., 18 (new 2007, LR-260L), 20 (LR-260H) or 24 (LR-260) in. stainless steel fluted bull barrel, no sights, raised Picatinny rail, thick walled aluminum upper receiver, solid lower receiver, standard AR-15 trigger goup, integral trigger guard, A2 black Zytel stock with trap door assembly, includes two 19 shot mags., 11.3 lbs. New 2006.

MSR $1,204	$1,050	$900	$800	$725	$650	$600	$550

Add $300 for 18 in. barrrel (LR-260L) with skeletonized stock, Miculek compensator and JRD trigger.

PANTHER LR-308C - .308 Win. cal., 20 in. heavy steel barrel, features A3 flattop receiver with detachable carrying handle, standard A2 front sight assembly, four rail standard length free float tube, two 19 shot mags., 11.1 lbs. New 2007.

MSR $1,254	$1,075	$925	$825	$725	$650	$600	$550

RIFLES: SLIDE ACTION

PANTHER PUMP RIFLE - .223 Rem. cal., paramilitary design, 20 in. threaded heavy barrel with flash hider, aluminum handguard incorporates slide action mechanism, carrying handle with sights, bayonet lug, designed by Les Branson, 8 1/2 lbs.

MSR $1,700		$1,525	$1,275	$1,050	$925	$775	$650	$575

DSA INC.

Current manufacturer, importer, and distributor of semi-auto rifles and related components located in Barrington, IL. Previously located in Round Lake and Grayslake, IL.

DSA Inc. is a manufacturer that sells FAL/SA58 rifles for both civilian and law enforcement purposes (L.E. certificates must be filled out for L.E. purchases). Until recently, DSA, Inc. also imported a sporterized Sig 550 rifle.

RIFLES: BOLT ACTION

DS-MP1 - .308 Win. cal., 22 in. match grade barrel, Rem. 700 action with Badger Ordnance precision ground heavy recoil lug, trued bolt face and lugs, hand lapped stainless steel barrel with recessed target crown, black McMillan A5 pillar bedded stock, Picatinny rail, includes test target guaranteeing 1/2 MOA at 100 yards, black or camo Duracoat finish, 11 1/2 lbs. New 2004.

MSR $2,800	$2,500	$2,150	$1,800	$1,550	$1,250	$1,000	$850

RIFLES: SEMI-AUTO

The SA-58 rifles listed are available in either a standard DuraCoat solid (OD Green or GrayWolf), or optional camo pattern finishes - add $250 for camo. Patterns include: Underbrush, Woodland, Winter Twig, Tiger Stripe, Urban Camo, Belgian Camo, Afghan Camo or Mossy Oak Breakup. DSA Inc. makes three types of forged steel receivers, and they are distinguished by the machining cuts on Types I and II, and no cuts on Type III.

SA58 STANDARD RIFLE - .308 Win. cal., FAL design using high precision CNC machinery, 19, 21 (standard or bull) or 24 in. (bull only) steel or stainless steel cyrogenically treated barrel, black synthetic stock, pistol grip (standard 2001) attached to frame, 10 or 20 shot mag., 8.7-11 lbs.

MSR $1,595	$1,400	$1,125	$975	$825	$675	$600	$525

Add $250 for stainless steel barrel.
Add $150 for bull barrel.

✱ *SA58 Standard Rifle Predator* - .243 Win., .260 Rem., or .308 Win. cal., Type 1 or Type 3 receiver, 16 or 19 in. barrel with target crown, green fiberglass furniture, Picatinny scope rail, 5 or 10 shot mag., approx. 9 lbs. New 2003.

MSR $1,650	$1,425	$1,175	$950	$800	$675	$575	$500

Add $100 for .260 Rem. or .243 Win. cal.

✱ *SA58 Standard Rifle Graywolf* - .300 WSM (disc. 2005) or .308 Win. cal., Type 1 or Type 3 receiver, 21 in. bull barrel with target crown, gray aluminum handguard, synthetic stock and adj. pistol grip, Picatinny scope rail, 5 or 10 shot mag., approx. 13 lbs. New 2003.

MSR $2,120	$1,800	$1,550	$1,325	$1,125	$950	$800	$675

✱ *SA58 Standard/Tactical Rifle/Carbine* - similar to SA58 Standard Rifle, except has 16 1/4 in. barrel, 8 1/4 lbs. New 1999.

MSR $1,595	$1,400	$1,125	$975	$825	$675	$600	$525

Add $80 for Tactical Carbine with fluted barrel and w/o muzzle brake (new 2003).
Add $200 for SA58 Lightweight Carbine with aluminum receiver components (disc. 2004).
Add $250 for SA58 Stainless Steel Carbine (included scope mount through 2000).

✱ *SA58 Standard Rifle Collectors Series* - .308 Win. cal., configurations include the Congo ($1,695 - MSR), Para Congo ($1,725 - MSR), and the G1 ($1,695 - MSR). New 2003.

Add $230 for Dura-coat finish.

✱ *SA58 Standard Rifle T48 Replica* - .308 Win. cal., 10 or 20 shot fixed mag., stripper clip top cover, cryogenic barrel, wood furniture, replica Browning flash hider. Importation began 2002.

MSR $1,795	$1,500	$1,275	$1,050	$850	$725	$625	$525

GRADING - PPGS™	100%	98%	95%	90%	80%	70%	60%

STG58 AUSTRIAN FAL - .308 Win. cal., features choice of DSA Type I or Type II upper receiver, carry handle, steel lower receiver, rifle has long flash hider, carbine has Steyr short flash hider, steel handguard with bi-pod cut, metric FAL buttstock and pistol grip, adj. front and rear sight, 10 or 20 shot detachable mag., 10 - 10.4 lbs. Importation began 2006.

MSR $995		$900	$825	$750	$675	$600	$550	$500

Add $50 for carbine.
Add $290 for rifle with folding stock.
Add $340 for carbine with folding stock.

DS-S1 - .223 Win. cal., 16, 20, or 24 in. match chamber stainless steel bull barrel, A2 buttstock with free float aluminum handguard, Picatinny gas block sight base, forged lower receiver, NM two-stage trigger, forged flattop upper receiver, optional fluted barrel, variety of Duracoat solid or camo finishes available, 8-10 lbs. Mfg. 2004-2005.

MSR $950		$850	$775	$675	$600	$525	$450	$400

DS-CV1 CARBINE - 5.56 NATO cal., 16 in. chrome-moly D4 barrel with press on mock flash hider, fixed Shorty buttstock, D4 handguard and heatshield, forged front sight base, forged lower receiver, forged flattop upper receiver, variety of Duracoat solid or camo finishes available, 6 1/4 lbs. Mfg. 2004-2005.

	$775	$700	$625	$550	$500	$450	$400

Last MSR was $850.

DS-LE4 CARBINE - 5.56 NATO cal., 14 1/2 or 16 in. chrome moly D4 barrel with threaded A2 flash hider, collapsible CAR buttstock, D4 handguard with heatshield, forged lower receiver, forged front sight base with bayonet lug, forged flattop upper receiver, Duracoat solid or camo finish, 6.15 or 6 1/4 lbs. New 2004.

The 14 1/2 in. model is for law enforcement only. Please contact the factory directly for pricing on this model.

DS-AR SERIES - .223 Rem cal., available in a variety of configurations including carbine and rifle, standard or bull barrels, various options, stock colors and features. New 2006.

MSR $1,000		$895	$800	$700	$600	$525	$450	$400

Add $243 for SOPMOD Carbine.
Add $30 for 1R Carbine.
Add $150 for 1V Carbine.
Add $130 for S1 Bull rifle.
Add $500 for DCM rifle.
Add $30 for XM Carbine.
Add $1,395 - $1,515 for monolithic rail platform.
Add $675 for Z4 GTC Carbine with corrosion resistant operating system.

DWM

Previous manufacturer located in Berlin, Germany circa 1900-1930. DWM (Deutsche Waffen und Munitions Fabriken) manufactured Lugers are listed in the Luger section.

PISTOLS: SEMI-AUTO

POCKET AUTOMATIC - 7.65mm cal., 3 1/2 in. barrel, blue, hard rubber grips. Mfg. 1921-1931.

	$1,000	$850	$600	$500	$450	$400	$350

DAEWOO

Current manufacturer located in Korea. Current limited importation by Century International Arms, located in Delray Beach, FL. Previous importation included Kimber of America, Inc. until 1997, Daewoo Precision Industries, Ltd., until mid-1996, located in Southampton, PA, and previously distributed by Nationwide Sports Dis-

GRADING - PPGS™	100%	98%	95%	90%	80%	70%	60%

tributors 1993-96. Previously imported by KBI, Inc. and Firstshot, Inc., both located in Harrisburg, PA, and B-West located in Tucson, AZ.

Daewoo makes a variety of firearms, most of which are not imported into the U.S.

PISTOLS: SEMI-AUTO

DH380 - .380 ACP cal., double action design. Imported 1995-96.

		$330	$285	$260	$235	$210	$185	$165

Last MSR was $375.

DH40 - .40 S&W cal., otherwise similar to DP51, 32 oz. Imported beginning 1995.

No MSR	$325	$270	$245	$225	$200	$185	$170

DP51 STANDARD/COMPACT - 9mm Para. cal., double action enabling lowering hammer w/o depressing trigger, 3 1/2 (DP51 C or S, disc.) or 4.1 (DP51) in. barrel, 10 (C/B 1994), 12* (.40 S&W), or 13* (9mm Para.) shot mag., 3-dot sights, tri-action mechanism (SA, DA, or fast action), ambidextrous controls, alloy receiver, polished or sand-blasted black finish, 28 or 32 oz., includes lockable carrying case with accessories. Imported in various configurations beginning in 1991.

No MSR	$315	$265	$240	$220	$200	$185	$170

Add 10% for DP51 Compact (disc.).

DP52 - .22 LR cal., double action, 3.8 in. barrel, alloy receiver, 10 shot mag., blue finish, 23 oz. Imported 1994-96.

	$320	$275	$225	$200	$180	$165	$150

Last MSR was $380.

RIFLES: SEMI-AUTO

MAX II (K2) - .223 Rem. cal., paramilitary design rifle, 18 in. barrel, gas operated rotating bolt, folding fiberglass stock, interchangeable mags. with the Colt M16, 7 lbs. Importation disc. 1986.

	$950	$875	$800	$725	$625	$550	$475

Last MSR was $609.

MAX I (K1A1) - similar to Max II (K2), except has retractable stock. Importation disc. 1986.

	$1,050	$925	$850	$750	$650	$575	$500

Last MSR was $592.

DR200 - .223 Rem. cal., paramilitary configuration with sporterized stock, 10 shot mag. Imported 1995-96.

	$650	$550	$475	$425	$395	$375	$350

Last MSR was $535.

DR300 - 7.62x39mm cal., paramilitary configuration with or w/o thumbhole stock. Importation disc.

	$550	$475	$425	$395	$375	$350	$325

DAISY

Current airgun manufacturer with headquarters located in Rogers, AR. Daisy manufactured firearms 1968-1991.

For more information and current pricing on both new and used Daisy airguns, please refer to the *Blue Book of Airguns* by Dr. Robert Beeman & John Allen (also online).

RIFLES: SINGLE SHOT, DISC.

As the V/L ammunition availability diminishes, the following values may fluctuate.

V/L STANDARD RIFLE - .22 V/L cal. (caseless air ignited cartridge), 1,100 FPS, 18 in. barrel, plastic stock, not particularly accurate. Approx. 19,000 mfg. 1968-69.

	$250	$225	$195	$150	$125	$95	$80

GRADING - PPGS™	100%	98%	95%	90%	80%	70%	60%

V/L PRESENTATION - similar to Collector's Kit, except does not have owner's name inscribed on buttplate, walnut stock. 4,000 mfg. for dealers.

	$325	$295	$265	$235	$195	$160	$130

Last MSR was $125.

V/L COLLECTOR'S KIT - comes with case, gun cradles, 300 rounds of ammo, and a gold plated brass buttplate with owner's name and serial number of gun. Approx. 4,000 mfg., available only by direct factory order.

	$545	$495	$425	$350	$275	$225	$165

Last MSR was $125.

Note: The Daisy .22 V/L was discontinued because the BATF ruled that the gun constituted a firearm, and since Daisy was federally licensed to manufacture air weapons only, the factory decided to discontinue manufacture.

RIFLES: BOLT ACTION, DISC.

All Legacy models have a removable trigger, slings and swivels, takedown barrel, dovetail receiver for scope mounting, rifled inner steel barrel with 12 lands and grooves, and an adj. rear sight. Weight is between 6 1/2-7 lbs.

MODEL 8 - .22 S or LR cal., single shot, 16 in. barrel, black synthetic stock, 30,000 mfg. for Wal-Mart only 1987-88.

	$175	$150	$125	$95	$80	$70	$55

During 1987, Daisy assembled this model using left-over Iver Johnson parts.

LEGACY MODELS 2201/2211 - .22 LR cal., single shot, bolt action, plastic (2201) or walnut finished hardwood (2211) stock, models vary in features, prices range from $150-$175. Mfg. 1988-91.

LEGACY MODELS 2202/2212 - .22 LR cal., bolt action repeater, 10 shot rotary mag., plastic (2202) or walnut finished hardwood (2212) stock, models vary in features, prices range from $150-$175. Mfg. 1988-91.

Model 2202 has copolymer stock with adj. buttplate.

RIFLES: SEMI-AUTO

LEGACY MODELS 2203/2213 - .22 LR cal., 7 shot box mag., models vary in features, prices range from $165-$190. Mfg. 1988-91.

Model 2203 has copolymer stock with adj. buttplate. Model 2213 has American hardwood stock.

DAKIN GUN CO.

Previous importer located in San Francisco, CA circa 1960s.

SHOTGUNS: O/U

MODEL 170 - 12, 16, 20 ga., or .410 bore, boxlock, light engraving, double triggers, vent rib.

	$495	$400	$325	$275	$245	$220	$195

SHOTGUNS: SxS

MODEL 100 - 12 or 20 ga., boxlock, engraved, double trigger.

	$425	$350	$275	$240	$205	$190	$170

MODEL 147 - 12 or 20 ga., boxlock, engraved, vent. rib, double trigger.

	$495	$385	$300	$265	$235	$215	$195

MODEL 160 - 12 or 20 ga., boxlock, single trigger, ejectors, vent. rib.

	$825	$700	$595	$495	$450	$395	$360

MODEL 215 - 12 or 20 ga., sidelock, heavy engraving, special walnut, single trigger, ejectors, vent. rib.

	$2,250	$1,900	$1,675	$1,300	$1,100	$925	$775

GRADING - PPGS™	100%	98%	95%	90%	80%	70%	60%

DAKOTA ARMS, INC.

Current manufacturer and previous importer established in 1987, located in Sturgis, SD. Dealer and direct sales through manufacturer only. This company is not affiliated with Dakota Single Action Revolvers.

Dakota Arms Inc. also owns the rights to Miller Arms and Nesika actions. Please refer to these individual sections for more information.

Dakota Arms models listed below are also available with many custom options - please contact the factory directly for availability and pricing. Left-hand rifles are also available at no extra charge on all models. Actions (barreled or unbarreled) may also be purchased separately. Please contact the manufacturer directly for individual quotations.

RIFLES: BOLT ACTION

DAKOTA .22 RIFLE - .17 HMR (new 2004) .22 LR, .22 Win Mag. (new 2004) or .22 Hornet (disc.) cal., combines features of the Win. Model 52 Sporter and Dakota 76, full sized receiver, trigger and striker block safety similar to Dakota 76, 5 shot mag., 22 in. chrome-moly barrel, checkered XX walnut stock, no sights, 6 1/2 lbs. Mfg. 1992-98, reintroduced 2003-2004.

	$2,650	**$2,250**	**$1,750**	**$1,350**	**$950**	**$750**	**$550**

Last MSR was $3,000.

DAKOTA 76 TRAVELER - various cals. between .25-06 Rem. - .450 Dakota, in addition to Dakota proprietary calibers, almost seamless take down rifle based on the Dakota 76 design, threadless disassembly ensuring scope stability and accuracy, in addition to no possibility of increasing the head space during repeated disassembly, wood stock, right- or left-hand action. New 1999.

MSR $5,095	**$4,625**	**$3,900**	**$3,150**	**$2,625**	**$2,200**	**$1,750**	**$1,450**

Add $900 for Safari Traveler.
Add $1,700 for African Traveler.
Add $1,950 (standard cals.) or $2,150 (Safari cals.) per interchangeable barrel.

DAKOTA 76 CLASSIC GRADE - available in various cals. (short, standard, or long action), custom frame incorporating many Win. Model 70 features, 21 or 23 in. barrel, Mauser type extractor, checkered X English walnut stock, 7 1/2 lbs. Left-hand action available at no extra charge. New 1987.

MSR $4,295	**$3,750**	**$3,100**	**$2,500**	**$2,000**	**$1,650**	**$1,350**	**$1,125**

This Model is also available with a composite stock at no extra charge.

DAKOTA 76 .30-06 100TH ANNIVERSARY - .30-06 cal., 100 year banner on floor plate, Exhibition walnut with limited edition checkering pattern, stainless steel Model 76 Classic action and receiver, custom LOP, only 100 mfg. beginning 2006.

MSR $8,945	**$8,350**	**$7,000**	**$5,750**	**N/A**	**N/A**	**N/A**	**N/A**

DAKOTA 76 VARMINT GRADE - available in 9 cals. between .17 Rem. and 6mm PPC, single shot bolt-action, heavy barrel. Mfg. 1994-97.

	$2,275	**$1,775**	**$1,425**	**$1,175**	**$990**	**$880**	**$770**

Last MSR was $2,500.

DAKOTA 76 SAFARI GRADE - available in various cals., 23 in. barrel, one-piece drop trigger guard assembly with hinged floor plate, checkered XXX English walnut stock with ebony forearm tip. Left-hand action available at no extra charge, 8 1/2 lbs. New 1987.

MSR $5,195	**$4,650**	**$3,925**	**$3,200**	**$2,650**	**$2,200**	**$1,750**	**$1,450**

Subtract $400 (retail) if ordered with composite stock (disc.).

DAKOTA 76 AFRICAN GRADE - .404 Jeffery, .416 Dakota, .416 Rigby, or .450 Dakota cal., 4 shot mag., select wood with cross bolts in the stock, other features similar to Safari Grade Model, 24 in. barrel, "R" prefix on serial number, 9 1/2 lbs. New 1989.

MSR $5,795	**$5,100**	**$4,300**	**$3,600**	**$3,250**	**$2,850**	**$2,400**	**$1,995**

GRADING - PPGS™	100%	98%	95%	90%	80%	70%	60%

DAKOTA 76 ALPINE GRADE - .22-250 Rem., .243 Win., 6mm Rem., .250-3000 Savage, 7mm-08 Rem., .308 Win., or .358 Win. cal., short action variation of the Classic Grade, 21 or 23 in. barrel, lighter weight model featuring a blind 4 shot mag., checkered X English walnut slimmer stock and barrel, serial numbered with a "K" prefix, 6 1/2 lbs. Mfg. 1989-92.

	$1,850	$1,495	$1,300	$1,075	$925	$800	$700

Last MSR was $1,995.

Other calibers were available on a special order basis.

DAKOTA LONGBOW TACTICAL E.R. (T-76) - .300 Dakota Mag., .300 Win. Mag. (new 2006), .330 Dakota Mag., .308 Win. (new 2006), .338 Lapua Mag., or .338 Dakota Mag. cal., 28 in. stainless barrel, long range tactical design, black synthetic stock with adj. comb, includes Picatinny optical rail, Model 70 style trigger, matte finish metal, controlled round feeding, and deployment kit, 13.7 lbs. New 1997.

MSR $4,500	$4,050	$3,475	$2,900	$2,500	$2,050	$1,675	$1,375

DAKOTA MODEL 97 LIGHTWEIGHT HUNTER - available in most popular cals. between .22-250 Rem. and .308 Win., features fiberglass stock with black recoil pad, right hand only, 6 lbs. Mfg. 1998-2004.

	$1,925	$1,625	$1,250	$995	$875	$750	$650

Last MSR was $2,195.

Add $300 for Wood Hunter 97 (includes semi-fancy wood and blind mag.).

✳ *Dakota Model 97 Lightweight Hunter Deluxe* - available in short or long action, matte blue finish, checkered AAA claro stock with cheekpiece, controlled round feed, three position safety, cloverleaf tang, 24 or 26 in. precision match chrome-moly blue or stainless barrel, right or left hand.

MSR $3,295	$2,995	$2,500	$2,150	$1,775	$1,500	$1,250	$1,000

Add $200 for stainless barrel.

✳ *Dakota Model 97 Lightweight Hunter All Weather Outfitter* - available in short or long action, matte blue finish, precision sand-colored composite stock, aluminum pillar bedding, controlled round feed, three position safety, cloverleaf tang, 24 or 26 in. precision match chrome-moly stainless barrel, right or left hand. Limited mfg. 2005.

	$2,650	$2,300	$1,900	$1,625	$1,375	$1,100	$995

Last MSR was $2,995.

DAKOTA MODEL 97 LONG RANGE HUNTER - available in 13 popular cals. between .25-06 Rem. and .375 Dakota Mag., composite black H-S Precision stock, 24 or 26 in. barrel, adj. match trigger, Model 76 ejector system, approx. 7.7 lbs. New 1997.

MSR $2,695	$2,325	$1,925	$1,525	$1,175	$975	$850	$750

Add $300 for Wood Hunter 97 (includes semi-fancy wood and blind mag., disc. 2004).
Add $800 for Deluxe Hunter 97 (includes semi-fancy wood and point panel checkering with floorplate, disc. 2004).

DAKOTA CLASSIC PREDATOR - various cals., special select checkered claro walnut sporter style stock with cheekpiece, 22 in. match grade stainless steel barrel, swivel studs. New 2005.

MSR $4,295	$3,650	$3,200	$2,800	$2,400	$2,000	$1,600	$1,375

✳ *Dakota Classic Predator Serious* - similar to Classic Predator, except has varmint type stock with semi-beavertail forend.

MSR $3,295	$2,850	$2,425	$2,000	$1,750	$1,500	$1,250	$1,075

✳ *Dakota Classic Predator All-Weather* - similar to Serious Predator, except has precision composite varmint stype stock with semi-beavertail forend.

MSR $2,595	$2,275	$1,875	$1,625	$1,275	$1,000	$875	$750

GRADING - PPGS™	100%	98%	95%	90%	80%	70%	60%

RIFLES: SxS

DOUBLE RIFLE - .470 NE, .500 NE, .570 NE, and most rimmed cals., round boxlock action similar to Dakota shotgun, 25 in. chopper lump barrels, selective ejectors, supplied with Americase, limited mfg. by Ferlib beginning 2001.

MSR $28,500	$25,500	$21,250	$17,250	$14,00	$11,250	$9,500	$8,250

RIFLES: SINGLE SHOT

DAKOTA MODEL 10 - available in most rimmed and rimless commercially loaded standard and Mag. cals., standard or enlarged Magnum (new 1994) action, 23 in. round barrel, top tang safety, deluxe checkered XX English walnut stock and forearm, 6 lbs. New 1990.

MSR $4,495	$3,925	$3,350	$2,800	$2,450	$1,800	$1,450	$1,225

MODEL 10 .30-06 100TH ANNIVERSARY - .30-06 cal., 100 year banner on floor plate, Exhibition walnut with limited edition checkering pattern, custom LOP, color case hardened frame, jewelled bolt, only 100 mfg. beginning 2006.

MSR $8,195	$7,600	$6,100	$5,000	N/A	N/A	N/A	N/A

DAKOTA MODEL 97 VARMINT HUNTER - various varmint cals., rounded short action, 24 in. chrome-moly barrel, adj. trigger, black fiberglass stock standard, right-hand only, approx. 8 lbs. New 1998.

		$1,600	$1,375	$1,100	$950	$750	$650	$550

Last MSR was $1,795.

Add $700 for Wood Varmint Hunter 97 (includes semi-fancy wood and blind mag.).
Add $1,200 for Deluxe Varmint Hunter 97 (includes semi-fancy wood and point panel checkering with floorplate).

DAKOTA SHARPS RIFLE - various cals. between .22 LR and .38-55 WCF, features scaled-down frame for smaller cals. (20% smaller than original Sharps), 26 in. octagon barrel, approx. 8 lbs. New 1998.

MSR $3,995		$3,575	$3,150	$2,950	$2,600	$2,250	$1,850	$1,550

Add $500+ for English walnut wood upgrade.
Add $250 for set trigger.

SHOTGUNS: SxS

CLASSIC GRADE - 20 ga. only, case colored round boxlock action, 27 in. barrels with fixed chokes, DTs, straight grip checkered English walnut stock and splinter forearm, no engraving, 6 lbs. Mfg. 1996-98.

		$7,450	$6,750	$6,000	$5,400	$4,800	$4,200	$3,450

Last MSR was $7,950.

PREMIER GRADE - 20, 28 ga. (new 2000), or .410 bore (new 2000), similar to Dakota Classic Field Grade, 27 in. barrels, exhibition grade English walnut, French grey metal finish, 50% engraving coverage, straight grip, splinter forend, DT, hand-rubbed oil finish stock, game rib with gold bead, ejectors, choice of chokes. Mfg. in conjunction with Ferlib.

MSR $14,950	$13,950	$10,250	$8,300	$6,950	$5,650	$4,850	$4,000

Add 10% for 28 ga. or .410 bore.

DAKOTA AMERICAN LEGEND - 20, 28 ga., or .410 bore, fully scroll-engraved coin finish round boxlock action with gold inlays, French grey metal finish, special select English walnut mfg. to customer dimensions, 27 in. barrels with game rib and gold bead, straight grip, DT, round action, ejectors, choice of chokes, oak and leather trunk case, 6 lbs., mfg. by Ferlib. New 1996.

MSR $19,000	$16,000	$13,000	$11,000	$9,250	$7,500	$6,250	$5,000

Add 10% for 28 ga. or .410 bore.

Only 100 guns are scheduled to be mfg. Also offered in a 12 ga. and .410 bore/28 ga. set.

GRADING - PPGS™	100%	98%	95%	90%	80%	70%	60%

DAKOTA CLASSIC FIELD GRADE SUPERLIGHT KNOCKABOUT
- 12, 16, 20, 24 (new 2005), 28, 32 (new 2005) ga., or .410 bore, Anson & Deeley boxlock action, monobloc (12, 20, or 28 ga.) or chopper lump (16 ga. or .410 bore only) 28 or 30 in. barrels, ejectors, DT, custom dimensions, checkered Turkish walnut stock and splinter forearm with oil finish, includes scroll and border engraving. New 2004.

MSR $4,600	$4,200	$3,650	$3,100	$2,600	$2,200	$1,650	$1,350

Add $600 for 16, 32 ga. or .410 bore.

Add $1,501 for Express Gun with rifled 24 1/2 in. barrels with quarter rib and folding leaf express sights (12 or 20 ga. only, disc. 2004).

DAKOTA CLASSIC GRADE II
- similar to Field Grade, except has extra fancy Turkish walnut and game scene engraving. New 2004.

MSR $5,600	$5,100	$4,550	$3,975	$3,500	$3,000	$2,550	$2,200

Add $700 for 16, 32 ga. or .410 bore.

Add $1,501 for Express Gun with rifled 24 1/2 in. barrels with quarter rib and folding leaf express sights (12 or 20 ga. only, disc. 2004).

DAKOTA CLASSIC GRADE III
- similar to Grade II, except has XXX Turkish walnut and scroll and gold game scene engraving. New 2004.

MSR $6,600	$6,100	$5,500	$4,800	$4,150	$3,500	$3,000	$2,500

Add $800 for 16, 32 ga. or .410 bore.

Add $1,501 for Express Gun with rifled 24 1/2 in. barrels with quarter rib and folding leaf express sights (12 or 20 ga. only, disc. 2004).

DAKOTA SINGLE ACTION REVOLVERS

Dakota revolvers are currently manufactured in Italy, and imported and distributed by E.M.F. Co., Inc. located in Santa Ana, CA. Dealer direct sales only.

Other firearms imported by E.M.F. Co., Inc. will be found in the E section of this book.

REVOLVERS: REPRODUCTIONS

Until 2000, most Dakota SAAs were manufactured by Armi San Marco. Beginning 2001, all current SAAs are manufactured by Uberti and Pietta.

Add $125 for combo cylinder on the model listed below (.45 ACP cal. only on Remingtons, .44-40 WCF, .44 Spl., or .45 ACP on Peacemaker SAAs).

1851 CONVERSION - .38 Spl. cal., color case hardened frame, walnut grips, 5 1/2 or 7 1/2 in. barrel. Importation began 2007.

MSR $450	$395	$340	$280	$235	$200	$180	$160

1860 CONVERSION - .38 Spl. cal., 5 1/2 or 8 in. barrel, color case hardened frame, walnut grips. Importation began 2007.

MSR $475	$415	$370	$340	$300	$270	$240	$210

1871 OPEN TOP - .38 Spl. or .45 LC cal., 5 1/2 or 7 1/2 in. barrel, color case hardened frame, walnut grips. Importation began 2007.

MSR $440	$375	$330	$280	$235	$200	$180	$160

OLD MODEL SAA - .22 LR, .32-20 WCF, .357 Mag., .38-40 WCF, .44 Spl., .44-40 WCF, or .45 LC cal., copy of the Colt SAA, 4 5/8, 5 1/2, or 7 1/2 in. barrels, blue finish, case hardened frame, 1-piece walnut grips, solid brass backstrap and trigger guard. Importation disc. 1991.

	$325	$250	$200	$175	$150	$135	$120

Last MSR was $600.

Add $100 for nickel finish (disc.).
Add $110 for convertible cylinders.

GRADING - PPGS™	100%	98%	95%	90%	80%	70%	60%

✳ *Old Model SAA Engraved Old Model* - .32-20 WCF, .357 Mag., .38-40 WCF, .44-40 WCF, or .45 cal., 4 3/4, 5 1/2, or 7 1/2 in. barrel. Disc. 1993, reintroduced 1996, disc. 1998.

	$695	$500	$425	$350	$325	$300	$275

Last MSR was $840.

     Add $160 for nickel finish (disc).

✳ *Old Model SAA Cattlebrand Engraved* - .44-40 WCF or .45 LC cal., 5 1/2, or 7 1/2 in. barrel, patterned after the famous Colt Cattlebrand variation (features various cattlebrands engraved on the barrel, frame and cylinder). Imported 1992-93, reintroduced 1996, disc. 1998.

	$695	$500	$425	$350	$325	$300	$275

Last MSR was $840.

     Add $140 for silver-plating.

NEW DAKOTA SAA - .357 Mag., .44-40 WCF, or .45 LC cal., features forged steel frame, black nickel backstrap and trigger guard, 4 (.45 LC cal. with standard grips), 4 3/4, 5 1/2, or 7 1/2 in. barrel, choice of case hardened or nickel frame, one piece walnut grips, original Colt type hammer (without transfer bar safety). Imported 1991-2004.

	$335	$290	$255	$215	$175	$150	$135

Last MSR was $375.

     Add $85 for combo. cylinder (disc. 2002).
     Add $135 for satin nickel (disc.) or $175 for bright satin nickel finish.

✳ *New Dakota SAA Sheriff Model* - cals. similar to New Model, 3 1/2 in. barrel. Imported 1997-99.

	$340	$285	$230	$175	$150	$135	$120

Last MSR was $435.

DAKOTA PREMIER SAA - .45 LC cal., black powder frame, initial mfg. was with 4 5/8 or 5 1/2 in. barrel, set screw cylinder pin release, steel backstrap and trigger guard, one-piece grips. This model was the predecessor to the New Hartford Model.

	$375	$295	$250	$190	$170	$160	$150

Last MSR was $520.

HARTFORD 1873 SAA (NEW OR OLD STYLE FRAME) - .22 LR (disc. 1992), .32-20 WCF, .357 Mag., .38-40 WCF, .44-40 WCF, .44 Spl., or .45 LC cal., features forged steel frame, backstrap, and trigger guard, exact reproduction of Colt's 1st or 2nd generation SAA, choice of black powder (with base pin frame set screw) or 2nd generation (push button cylinder pin release) frame, case hardened frame, original Colt markings, 4 (.45 LC cal. with standard grips), 4 3/4, 5 1/2, or 7 1/2 in. barrel. Importation began 1991.

MSR $450	$395	$350	$310	$275	$240	$210	$180

     Add $135 for satin nickel (disc.) or $200 for bright satin nickel finish.

     Add $10 for .32.-20 WCF cal.

✳ *Hartford 1873 SAA Old West (Antique) Finish* - .45 LC cal. only, black powder frame, finish has been aged for older appearance. Mfg. 2001-2003, reintroduced 2005-2006.

	$375	$325	$265	$230	$185	$155	$125

Last MSR was $430.

✳ *Hartford 1873 SAA Pinkerton Model* - .357 Mag., .38-40 WCF (disc. 1999), or .45 LC cal., birdshead grips, 4 or 4 3/4 in. barrel. Mfg. 1994-2006.

	$365	$335	$300	$270	$240	$210	$180

Last MSR was $415.

GRADING - PPGS™	100%	98%	95%	90%	80%	70%	60%

✻ *Hartford 1873 SAA Deputy Model* - .45 LC cal., 3 1/2 (new 2003) or 4 (disc. 2000) in. barrel with full length ejector shroud, standard SAA grips. Imported 2000, reimported 2003.

	$415	$335	$300	$265	$225	$175	$150

Last MSR was $480.

✻ *Hartford 1873 SAA Express Model* - .45 LC cal., features "Lightning" grips, 4 or 4 3/4 in. barrel, New Model. Imported 1999-2000.

	$340	$300	$265	$225	$175	$150	$125

Last MSR was $375.

✻ *Hartford 1873 SAA Cavalry Model* - .45 LC cal., 7 1/2 in. barrel, faithful reproduction of the original Colt Cavalry Model, one-piece walnut grips with inspector cartouche, case hardened frame and hammer. Importation began 1991.

MSR $475	$415	$370	$340	$300	$270	$240	$210

✻ *Hartford 1873 SAA Artillery Model* - .45 LC cal., similar to Cavalry Model, except has 5 1/2 in. barrel. Importation began 1991.

MSR $475	$415	$370	$340	$300	$270	$240	$210

✻ *Hartford 1873 SAA Stallion Model* - .38 Spl. cal., 3 1/2 (bird's head grips only) or 4 3/4 in. (walnut grips only) barrel with ejector rod housing, case colored frame, steel backstrap and trigger guard. Importation began 2005.

MSR $400	$355	$320	$290	$255	$220	$195	$160

Add $20 for 3 1/2 in. barrel with bird's head grips.

✻ *Hartford 1873 SAA Texas Sesquicentennial* - .45 LC cal., 4 3/4 in. barrel, 50 mfg. for Texas Sesquicentennial with special engraving, includes numbered belt buckle and presentation case. Disc. 1991.

	$1,200	$925	$725	$610	$515	$425	$375

Original list price was $4,550.

✻ *Hartford 1873 SAA Target Model* - .357 Mag., .44-40 WCF, or .45 LC cal., 5 1/2, or 7 1/2 in. barrel, case hardened frame, brass backstrap. Imported 1987-90.

	$325	$240	$185	$150	$140	$130	$120

Last MSR was $500.

✻ *Hartford 1873 SAA Buntline Model* - .357 Mag. (disc.), .44-40 WCF (disc.), or .45 LC cal., blue only, 10 (mfg. 1997-2002) or 12 in. barrel. Importation disc. 1990, reintroduced 1997.

MSR $490	$430	$380	$350	$310	$275	$240	$210

Add $200 for bright or satin (disc.) nickel finish, $110 for ultra ivory or stag grips (disc.).

✻ *Hartford 1873 SAA Revolver/Carbine* - .357 Mag. or .45 LC cal., features 18 in. barrel and fixed stock with crescent buttplate, finger extension on trigger guard.

MSR $580	$495	$435	$385	$340	$295	$250	$210

✻ *Hartford 1873 SAA Buckhorn Model* - 16 1/4 in. barrel, otherwise similar to Buntline. Importation disc. 1987.

	$295	$250	$180	$170	$160	$150	$140

Last MSR was $495.

HARTFORD PREMIER 1873 SA - .357 Mag., .32-20 WCF, or .45 LC cal., 4 3/4, 5 1/2, or 7 1/2 in. barrel, charcoal bone case colored frame, high polish blue, choice of black Colt style checkered or ultra stag grips, tuned action with light hammer pull. Imported 1999-2004.

	$550	$475	$425	$375	$325	$275	$240

Last MSR was $625.

FRONTIER MARSHAL SA - .357 Mag., .44-40 WCF (disc. 2004), or .45 LC cal., 4 3/4, 5 1/2, or 7 1/2 in. barrel, case colored frame, brass backstrap and triggerguard, blue barrel/cylinder. Importation began 2003.

MSR $390	$350	$310	$275	$245	$210	$180	$160

GRADING - PPGS™	100%	98%	95%	90%	80%	70%	60%

GREAT WESTERN II CUSTOM 1873 SA - .357 Mag., .44-40 WCF, or .45 LC cal., 4 3/4, 5 1/2, or 7 1/2 in. barrel, four metal finishes include all blue, blue w/case colored frame, bright nickel, or satin nickel, ultra ivory grips, mfg. by Pietta. Importation began 2003.

MSR $635	$555	$475	$425	$375	$325	$275	$240

    Add $110 for ultra stag grips (disc.) or $960-$1,300 for engraving options.
    Add $30 for Express birdshead grips (4 3/4 in. barrel only).

✱ *Great Western II Custom 1873 SA Californian* - similar to Great Western II, except has standard charcoal case colored frame and blue finish. Importation began 2003.

MSR $460	$395	$355	$320	$280	$250	$215	$180

    Add $200 for custom bone case coloring or $200 for bright nickel finish.
    Add $110 for ultra ivory or ultra stag fitted grips (disc. 2006).
    Add $30 for Express birdshead grips (4 3/4 in. barrel only).

✱ *Great Western II Custom 1873 Stainless* - .357 Mag. or .45 LC cal., similar to Great Western II, except is stainless steel construction, choice of walnut or ultra-ivory grips. Importation began 2006.

MSR $600	$525	$475	$425	$375	$325	$275	$240

    Add $40 for ultra-ivory grips.
    Add $25 for birdshead Express grips (4 3/4 in. barrel only).

SHERIFF'S OLD/NEW MODEL SAA - .32-20 WCF (disc.), .357 Mag. (disc. 2000), .38-40 WCF (disc.), .44 Spl. (disc.), .44-40 WCF (disc. 2000), or .45 LC cal., 3 1/2 in. barrel only. Importation disc. 1991, resumed 1994-2000, again in 2003.

	$415	$335	$300	$265	$225	$175	$150

Last MSR was $480.

U.S. ARMY SAA - variety of cals., premium quality construction. Disc. 1985.

	$300	$205	$180	$165	$155	$145	$135

Last MSR was $395.

✱ *U.S. Army SAA Commemorative* - .45 LC cal., 7 1/2 in. barrel, serial numbered 1-500, blue finish, case hardened frame, steel backstrap and trigger guard, 1-piece walnut grips. Importation disc. 1987.

	$350	$265	$185	N/A	N/A	N/A	N/A

Last MSR was $495.

CONVERTIBLE MODEL SAA - available with .22 LR/.22 Mag., .32-20 WCF/.32 H&R Mag., .357 Mag./9mm Para., .44-40 WCF/.44 Spl. cal., or .45 LC/.45 ACP double cylinders. Imported 1986-90.

	$380	$310	$260	$220	$195	$170	$150

Last MSR was $580.

FAST DRAW MODEL SAA - .22 LR, .22 Mag., .32-20 WCF, .32 H&R Mag., .357 Mag., .38-40 WCF, 9mm Para., .44 Spl., .44-40 WCF, .45 ACP, or .45 LC cal., case hardened frame, 4 5/8 in. barrel. Importation disc. 1990.

	$340	$295	$225	$165	$150	$135	$125

Last MSR was $480.

BISLEY MODEL SAA - .22 LR (disc.), .22 Mag.(disc.), .32-20 WCF (disc.), .32 H&R Mag. (disc.), .38-40 WCF (disc.), .357 Mag. (disc. 1999), 9mm Para. (disc.), .44 Spl. (disc.), .44-40 WCF (disc.), .45 ACP (disc.), or .45 LC (current mfg.) cal., 4 3/4 (disc. 1994, reintroduced 2001-2003 in .44-40 WCF cal. only), 5 1/2, or 7 1/2 in. barrel lengths. Imported 1986-91, reintroduced 1993-disc. 1995, reintroduced 1997.

MSR $490	$435	$385	$350	$315	$280	$250	$215

    Add $200 for bright or satin (disc.) nickel finish.
    Add $112 for combo. cylinder (.45 ACP - disc.).

GRADING - PPGS™	100%	98%	95%	90%	80%	70%	60%

❋ Bisley Model SAA Engraved - .32-20 WCF, .38-40 WCF, .357 Mag., .44-40 WCF, or .45 LC cal. (disc. 1990), 4 3/4, 5 1/2, or 7 1/2 in. barrel, action engraved throughout. Imported 1987-91.

	$425	$350	$275	$250	$225	$200	$180

Last MSR was $570.

Add $100 for nickel finish.

1873 FRONTIER MODEL SAA - .22 LR cal., 4 3/4 in. barrel, case colored frame, black nickel backstrap and trigger guard. Mfg. by IAR, imported 1999-2002.

	$275	$250	$225	$175	$150	$135	$120

Last MSR was $315.

Add $125 for bright nickel finish.

RUSSIAN TOP-BREAK MODEL 1875 - .44 Russian (3rd Model only), or .45 LC cal., configurations include 2nd Model Hideout (3 1/2 in. barrel), Wells Fargo (5 in. barrel), 3rd Model Russian (6 1/2 in. barrel), or Cavalry (7 in. barrel), blue finish with walnut grips. Importation began 2006.

MSR $900	$795	$675	$600	$525	$450	$400	$350

REMINGTON 1875 SA ARMY/FRONTIER - .357 Mag., .44-40 WCF (disc. 2003, reintroduced 2006) or .45 LC (disc. 2003, reintroduced 2006) cal., available in either 5 1/2 (Frontier) or 7 1/2 (Army, disc. 2003, reintroduced 2006) in. barrel, blue and case colored metal finishes, walnut grips. Mfg. by A. Uberti.

MSR $450	$395	$340	$275	$230	$200	$180	$160

Add $210 for laser engraving with custom patina finish.
Add $15 for steel trigger guard (disc.).
Add $200 for bright or satin (disc. 2000) nickel plating.
Add $250 for engraving (disc.).
Add $85 for convertible cylinder (.45 LC/.45 ACP, disc.).

REMINGTON MODEL 1890 SA POLICE - .45 LC cal., standard blue or engraved frame with custom patina finish, 5 1/2 in. barrel, lanyard ring in buttstock, blue frame, walnut grips, mfg. by A. Uberti. New 1986.

MSR $450	$395	$340	$280	$235	$200	$180	$160

Add $210 for laser engraving with custom patina finish.
Add $10 for steel trigger guard (disc.).
Add $200 for bright or satin (disc. 2000) nickel plating.
Add $85 for convertible cylinder (.45 LC/.45 ACP, disc.).
Add $260 for engraving (disc.).

SCHOFIELD MODEL - .45 LC cal., replica of the original S&W Schofield, choice of 3 1/2 (Hideout), 5 (Wells Fargo) or 7 in. (Civilian/Cavalry) barrel, blue finish. Mfg. by Uberti. Imported 1999-2003.

	$575	$500	$450	$415	$385	$360	$340

Last MSR was $625.

DALVAR OF USA

Current importer of recently manufactured Radom pistols located in Henderson, NV. Please refer to the Radom listing in this text.

DALY, CHARLES: PRUSSIAN MFG.

Previous trademark manufactured in Prussia, England, Belgium, and the U.S. circa 1875-pre-WWII.

Charles Daly was a gentleman (not a company) whose goal was to give the U.S. shotgun consumer a European-manufactured gun of similar quality to the premier American shotguns of the same era. Accordingly, he had various European firms fabricate shotguns with American shooting features and preferences. Many "Prussian" Dalys were built by various firms in Suhl, Germany. Importation ceased prior to WWII. These Prussian Charles Dalys utilized the finest materials and best workmanship of their time.

In 1865, Charles Daly was one of two partners who founded the sporting goods business

GRADING - PPGS™	100%	98%	95%	90%	80%	70%	60%

named Schoverling & Daly. They were importers and dealers located in New York City. In 1873, the company reorganized to include a third partner, and the corporate name was changed to Schoverling, Daly & Gales.

Marking the Charles Daly name on firearms began some time around 1875. Daly's name was chosen because it had an appealing sound and would likely influence potential buyers to choose their firearms. Schoverling, Daly & Gales established their lofty reputation by dealing in top-quality merchandise. Because they were known for their high standard of excellence, the Charles Daly brand garnered much esteem.

Schoverling, Daly & Gales made every effort to select only the finest quality firearms for sale in the United States. Initially, manufacturers in Prussia, such as Schiller and Lindner, and later Heym and Sauer of Germany, were selected for their suberbly constructed shotguns. Early manufacturers also included J&W Tolley of England, Newmann of Belgium, and even Lefever Arms of New York.

Schoverling, Daly & Gales changed ownership several times throughout the years. Eventually, the company's primary asset was the Charles Daly trademark. In 1910, Henry Modell bought the company, and controlled it for several years. In the 1920s, he sold out to the Walzer family, owners of Sloan's Sporting Goods of Ridgefield, CT. The Walzers established a branch of Sloan's in New York known as Charles Daly & Company. Sloan's imported quality shotguns from many companies, including Italian gun makers Beretta and Vincenzo Bernardelli, Miroku of Japan, and Garbi of Spain.

DRILLINGS

DRILLING MODEL - 12, 16, or 20 gauges and .25-20 WCF, .25-35 WCF, or .30-30 WCF cal., 3 barrel combination gun, extractors, double triggers, engraved action, select walnut, mfg. by both Linder and Sauer. Linder mfg. guns are extremely rare - very few specimens are to be found domestically. Sauer guns were not marked for grade, but rather had three levels of engraving which determined the grade. Most Sauer guns had a tang mounted aperture rear sight and a separate rifle cock and were sidelocks. Disc. 1933.

* *Drilling Model Superior Quality* - borderline engraving only.

	100%	98%	95%	90%	80%	70%	60%
Sauer mfg.	$4,500	$3,750	$3,000	$2,600	$2,300	$2,000	$1,700

* *Drilling Model Diamond Quality* - full scroll engraving.

	100%	98%	95%	90%	80%	70%	60%
Sauer mfg.	$7,500	$6,500	$5,500	$4,800	$4,400	$4,000	$3,500

* *Drilling Model Regent Diamond Quality* - top-of-the-line model featuring full game scene coverage.

	100%	98%	95%	90%	80%	70%	60%
Linder mfg.	$15,000	$12,000	$11,000	$10,000	$9,000	$7,000	$6,000
Sauer mfg.	$10,000	$8,000	$7,000	$6,700	$6,000	$5,000	$4,000

Add approx. 25% for gold inlays.

RIFLES

BOLT ACTION GRADE I - .22 Hornet cal., mfg. by F. Jaeger & Co. of Suhl, Germany, 5 shot mag., 24 in. barrel, miniature Mauser bolt action, deluxe walnut. Very limited mfg.

100%	98%	95%	90%	80%	70%	60%
$2,000	$1,750	$1,500	$1,250	$1,025	$825	$650

SHOTGUNS

In the higher grade Prussian Daly variations, there is quite a bit of difference in their manufacture, including engraving options, levels of wood embellishment, and other extra cost features at the time. H.A. Linder produced approx. 2,500 guns (ser. numbered accordingly), and many of the higher grades show a noticeable difference in the amount of engraving (from minimal to considerable game scene engraving). These guns can be either case colored only or have gold inlaid birds and animals (the number of which can also vary) and barrels can have various levels of engraving on both the breech and muzzle ends. All of these factors

GRADING - PPGS™	100%	98%	95%	90%	80%	70%	60%

have considerable impact on the overall value of a particular specimen. It is estimated that it took three craftsmen one year to produce a single Diamond Regent gun.

> **Add 25% - 50% for 20 ga., depending on condition.**
> **Add 200% for 28 ga. on higher grade models (very rare).**
> **Add 100% for .410 bore on higher grade models.**
> **Add approx. 20% for 10 ga. on the following models that apply.**

COMMANDER O/U - 12, 16, 20, 28 ga., or .410 bore, Anson & Deeley boxlock action, single or double triggers, ejectors. Mfg. in Belgium circa 1939.

> **Add 30% for 28 ga. or .410 bore.**
> **Add 10% for single trigger.**

✱ *Commander O/U Model 100*

	100%	98%	95%	90%	80%	70%	60%
	$1,200	$975	$800	$700	$625	$550	$475

> **Add $100 for single trigger.**

✱ *Commander O/U Model 200* - similar to Model 100, except has deluxe walnut.

	$1,500	$1,275	$1,075	$900	$800	$700	$600

EMPIRE O/U - 12, 16, or 20 ga., various barrel lengths, Anson & Deeley boxlock, ejectors and double triggers, fine engraving, deluxe walnut. Disc. 1933.

	$4,000	$3,400	$2,750	$2,375	$2,000	$1,825	$1,625

DIAMOND O/U - similar to Empire model, only finer workmanship and materials.

	$6,000	$5,150	$4,300	$3,475	$3,000	$2,600	$2,300

SUPERIOR SxS - 10, 12, 20, 28 ga., or .410 bore, Anson & Deeley boxlock, various barrel lengths, extractors. Disc. 1933.

	100%	98%	95%	90%	80%	70%	60%
10 ga.	$2,500	$2,150	$1,775	$1,575	$1,350	$1,125	$995
12 ga.	$1,500	$1,300	$1,100	$925	$800	$675	$550
20 ga.	$2,000	$1,775	$1,575	$1,350	$1,125	$995	$825

28 ga. and .410 bore specimens are too rare to accurately evaluated, and should be appraised individually.

EMPIRE SxS - similar to Superior, only more engraving and better wood.

	100%	98%	95%	90%	80%	70%	60%
Linder mfg.	$5,000	$4,400	$3,900	$3,500	$2,800	$2,200	$1,500
Sauer mfg.	$4,200	$3,500	$3,100	$2,800	$2,200	$1,800	$1,400

DIAMOND SxS - similar to Empire model, only more elaborate engraving.

	100%	98%	95%	90%	80%	70%	60%
Linder mfg.	$10,000	$9,000	$8,500	$8,000	$7,000	$6,000	$4,500
Sauer mfg.	$7,000	$6,200	$5,500	$5,000	$4,000	$3,000	$2,000

DIAMOND REGENT SxS - top-of-the-line Prussian side-by-side with or w/o engraving and gold inlays.

	100%	98%	95%	90%	80%	70%	60%
Linder mfg.	$16,000	$13,500	$12,000	$11,000	$8,500	$7,000	$5,000
Sauer mfg.	$12,000	$10,500	$9,150	$8,000	$7,000	$6,000	$5,000

> **Subtract 20% - 25% if w/o gold inlays.**

EMPIRE SINGLE BARREL TRAP - 12 ga., 30-34 in. barrel, Anson & Deeley boxlock, ejector, vent. rib, finely engraved with select walnut, chopper lump extension, top quality. Disc. 1933.

	100%	98%	95%	90%	80%	70%	60%
Linder mfg.	$5,000	$4,500	$4,000	$3,500	$3,100	$2,800	$2,200
Sauer mfg.	$4,000	$3,500	$3,100	$2,750	$2,350	$2,000	$1,700

DIAMOND REGENT SINGLE BARREL TRAP - 12 ga., 30-34 in. barrel, six locking bolts, ejector, vent. rib, elaborately engraved and checkered.

	100%	98%	95%	90%	80%	70%	60%
Linder mfg.	$15,000	$12,750	$10,500	$8,500	$6,500	$5,000	$4,000
Sauer mfg.	$10,500	$9,150	$8,000	$7,000	$6,000	$4,750	$3,750

SEXTUPLE SINGLE BARREL TRAP EMPIRE QUALITY

	100%	98%	95%	90%	80%	70%	60%
Linder mfg.	$6,000	$5,400	$4,600	$4,150	$3,650	$3,100	$2,800

SEXTUPLE SINGLE BARREL TRAP DIAMOND REGENT QUALITY

	100%	98%	95%	90%	80%	70%	60%
Linder mfg.	N/A	$18,000	$15,000	$12,000	$9,250	$7,500	$6,000

GRADING - PPGS™	100%	98%	95%	90%	80%	70%	60%

DALY, CHARLES: JAPANESE MFG.

Previously manufactured by B.C. Miroku, located in Kochi, Japan until 1976.

SHOTGUNS: O/U

In the early sixties, C. Daly guns were manufactured by the firm of B.C. Miroku in Kochi, Japan. This Japanese gun manufacturing company has produced guns for many companies, Browning being the biggest current customer. Miroku guns are high quality with excellent fit and finish. Many of them are highly engraved and are fine examples of the gunmaker's art. Charles Daly Miroku Guns are becoming quite collectible in some areas (smaller gauges with open chokes). Their production ceased in 1976.

O/U MODELS - 12, 20, 28 ga., or .410 bore, 26, 28, or 30 in. vent. rib barrels, various chokes, boxlock, auto ejectors, SST, select walnut checkered pistol grip stock, Superior and Diamond Grade Trap have Monte Carlo stocks, the grades differ in amount of engraving and wood. Mfg. 1963-1976 by Miroku.

Add 20% for 20 ga. on models listed below.
Add 50% for 28 ga. on models listed below.
Add 60% for .410 bore on models listed below.
Add 300% for original 28 ga. Lightweight models in 98%+ condition (rare).

Approx. 1,000 28 ga. Lightweight guns were manufactured. All 28 ga. Lightweights (approx. observed ser. range 230020-230998) have barrel spacing 3/4 in. center to center, while the normal 28 ga. has a measurement of 7/8 in. After the Charles Daly line of O/Us were mechanically redesigned, both the 28 ga. and .410 bore were only made on the new 20 ga. frame. To date, no one has observed a .410 bore Lightweight Charles Daly.

FIELD GRADE - 12 or 20 ga., light engraving.

	100%	98%	95%	90%	80%	70%	60%
	$850	$725	$600	$550	$475	$400	$350

VENTURE GRADE - all gauges, moderate engraving.

	$825	$700	$600	$500	$475	$400	$350

VENTURE SKEET - 26 in. barrels choked skeet and skeet.

	$875	$725	$625	$550	$475	$400	$350

VENTURE TRAP - 30 in. imp. mod. and full.

	$795	$650	$550	$485	$425	$375	$350

SUPERIOR GRADE - all gauges, select checkered walnut stock with round knob, scroll engraving similar to Grade I Browning Superposed.

	$1,225	$1,050	$900	$800	$700	$650	$600

SUPERIOR TRAP

	$1,000	$825	$675	$575	$500	$440	$390

This model has an optional selective ejection system enabling the shooter to deactivate the ejectors.

DIAMOND GRADE - all gauges, extensive engraving with better quality wood.

	$2,000	$1,725	$1,400	$1,125	$995	$895	$775

DIAMOND GRADE SKEET

	$2,100	$1,750	$1,450	$1,150	$1,000	$900	$775

DIAMOND GRADE TRAP

	$1,550	$1,325	$1,035	$850	$775	$700	$625

WIDE RIB DIAMOND GRADE FLATTOP TRAP

	$1,550	$1,325	$1,035	$850	$775	$700	$625

DIAMOND REGENT GRADE - mostly 12 ga., extensive frame engraving with gold inlays, rare.

	$3,995	$3,500	$3,100	$2,500	$2,100	$1,800	$1,500

GRADING - PPGS™	100%	98%	95%	90%	80%	70%	60%

SHOTGUNS: SxS

EMPIRE SHOTGUN - 12, 16, or 20 ga., 26, 28, or 30 in. barrels, various chokes, boxlock, extractors, single trigger, checkered pistol grip stock, early production guns were made by Beretta. Mfg. 1968-1971 in Italy.

	100%	98%	95%	90%	80%	70%	60%
	$675	$585	$525	$475	$415	$360	$300
Vent. rib	$795	$700	$600	$525	$450	$400	$350

Add 25% for 20 ga.

MODEL 500 - 12 or 20 ga., 26 or 28 in. barrels with raised or vent. rib, DT, extractors.

	$450	$400	$350	$315	$285	$260	$230

Add 20% for vent. rib.

1974 WILDLIFE COMMEMORATIVE - duck scene engraved, Diamond Grade, Trap, or Skeet, limited to 500 guns. Mfg. 1974 only.

	$2,000	$1,725	$1,500	N/A	N/A	N/A	N/A

SHOTGUNS: SINGLE BARREL, TRAP

SUPERIOR GRADE SINGLE BARREL TRAP - 12 ga., 32 or 34 in. vent. rib, full choke barrel, auto ejector, Monte Carlo stock with recoil pad. Mfg. 1968-76.

	$625	$575	$525	$495	$440	$385	$330

DALY, CHARLES: 1976 TO PRESENT

Currently manufactured trademark imported since late 1996 by KBI, Inc. located in Harrisburg, PA. Previously imported by Outdoor Sports Headquarters, Inc. located in Dayton, OH until 1995.

In 1976, Sloan's Sporting Goods sold the Daly division to Outdoor Sports Headquarters, Inc., a sporting goods wholesaler located in Dayton, OH. OSHI continued the importation of high-grade Daly shotguns, primarily from Italy and Spain. By the mid-1980s, the Charles Daly brand was transformed into a broad consumer line of excellent firearms and hunting accessories.

In 1996, OSHI was sold to Jerry's Sports Center, Inc. of Forest City, PA, a major wholesaler of firearms and hunting supplies. Within a few months of Jerry's acquisition of OSHI, K.B.I., Inc. of Harrisburg, PA, purchased the Charles Daly trademark from JSC. As it turned out, Michael Kassnar, president of K.B.I., Inc., had produced almost all of the Charles Daly products for OSHI from 1976-1985 in his capacity of president of Kassnar Imports, Inc. K.B.I., Inc. resurrected the complete line of O/U and SxS shotguns in early 1997.

In 1998, the line expanded to include rimfire rifles and the first pistol produced under the Daly name, a Model 1911-A1 in .45 ACP cal. In 1999, semi-auto and slide action shotguns were also reintroduced. In 2000, the additions included 3 1/2 in. slide actions and semi-autos, Country Squire .410 bore shotguns, bolt action centerfire rifles, and the DDA 10-45, the first double action pistol produced under the Charles Daly name.

During 2004, Charles Daly began importing Bul Transmark pistols from Israel. In 2007, the Little Sharps single shot rifles were introduced.

In 2008, a Charles Daly Defense line was established, which includes AR-15 style semi-auto rifles.

COMBINATION GUNS

SUPERIOR COMBINATION MODEL - 12 ga. (multi-chokes became standard in 2001) over choice of .22 Hornet, .22-250 Rem. (disc. 1998), .223 Rem., .243 Win. (disc. 1998), .270 Win. (disc. 1998), .30-06, or .308 Win. (disc. 1998) cal., boxlock action with dovetailed receiver (accepts scope mounts and iron sights), 23 1/2 in. barrels with iron sights, approx. 7 5/8 lbs. Mfg. by Sabatti in Italy. Imported 1997-2005.

	$1,260	$1,000	$825	$700	$575	$475	$375

Last MSR was $1,479.

GRADING - PPGS™	100%	98%	95%	90%	80%	70%	60%

EMPIRE COMBINATION MODEL - 12 ga. (multi-chokes became standard in 2001) over choice of .22 Hornet, .22-250 Rem. (disc. 1998), .223 Rem., .243 Win. (disc. 1998), .270 Win. (disc. 1998), .30-06, or .308 Win. (disc. 1998) cal., boxlock action, 23 1/2 in. barrels, engraved with choice checkered walnut stock and forearm. Mfg. by Sabatti in Italy. Imported 1997-2005.

	$1,800	$1,525	$1,225	$1,000	$850	$725	$600

Last MSR was $2,189.

PISTOLS: SEMI-AUTO

During 2001, the nomenclature on these 1911 models was changed to include a new "E" prefix. The new "E" stands for enhanced, and features include extended high-rise beavertail grip safety, combat trigger, combat hammer, beveled magwell, flared and lowered ejection port, dovetailed front and low profile rear sights, and hand checkered double diamond grips. The Enhanced pistols are manufactured by Armscor of the Philipines. M-5 pistols are manufactured by Bul Transmark in Israel.

GOVERNMENT 1911-A1 FIELD EFS/FS - .38 Super (mfg. 2005-2007), .40 S&W (mfg. 2005-2007), .45 ACP cal., steel frame, single action, skeletonized combat hammer and trigger, ambidextrous safety, 8 or 10 shot mag., extended slide release and beavertail grip safety, oversized and lowered ejection port, 5 in. barrel with solid barrel bushing, matte blue (Field FS), stainless slide/blue frame (Superior FS, mfg. 1999-2002), or all stainless (Empire EFS, new 1999) finish, includes two 8 or 10 shot mags. and lockable carrying case, 39 1/2 oz. New 1998.

MSR $589		$475	$375	$350	$325	$300	$280	$260

Add $50 for Superior EFS Model (disc. 2002).
Add $199 for .22 LR conversion kit with adj. sight (disc. 1999).

✱ *Government 1911A1 Field EFS Stainless Empire* - .45 ACP cal. only, similar to Field FS, except is stainless steel. Disc. 2007.

	$575	$475	$400	$350	$315	$290	$270

Last MSR was $709.

GOVERNMENT 1911-A1 TARGET EFST/FST - similar to Government 1911-A1 Field FS, except has target sights. Imported 2000-2007.

	$550	$475	$400	$360	$325	$295	$275

Last MSR was $679.

Add $40 for Superior FST Model (disc. 2000).
Add $65 for Empire FST Model (disc. 2000).

✱ *Government 1911-A1 Target EFST Stainless Empire* - .45 ACP cal. only, similar to Target EFST, except is stainless steel. Mfg. 2001-2007.

	$650	$550	$450	$400	$350	$300	$250

Last MSR was $789.

✱ *Government 1911-A1 Target Field EFST* - .45 ACP cal., 5 3/4 in. compensated barrel with 3 ports, blue or stainless steel, 44.5 oz. Limited importation 2001 only.

	$550	$450	$395	$360	$330	$300	$265

Last MSR was $679.

Add $100 for stainless steel (Empire EFSTC).

EMPIRE ECMT CUSTOM MATCH - .45 ACP cal., 5 in. barrel, match features, high polish stainless steel, 38 1/2 oz. Imported 2001-2007.

	$750	$650	$575	$500	$425	$350	$275

Last MSR was $895.

COMMANDER 1911-A1 FIELD EMS/MS - similar to Government 1911-A1, except has 4 in. Commander barrel and features, 37 oz. Importation began 1999.

MSR $589		$475	$375	$350	$325	$300	$280	$260

Add $40 for Superior MS Model (includes stainless steel slide and blue frame, disc. 2000).

GRADING - PPGS™	100%	98%	95%	90%	80%	70%	60%

✻ *Commander 1911-A1 Field EMS Stainless Empire* - .45 ACP cal. only, similar to Field EMS/MS, except is stainless steel. Imported 1999-2007.

	$575	$475	$400	$350	$315	$290	$270

Last MSR was $709.

✻ *Commander 1911-A1 Field EMSCC* - carry comp., similar to Commander Field EMS, except has single port compensator, blue or stainless. Imported 2001 only.

	$540	$435	$395	$360	$325	$295	$260

Last MSR was $619.

OFFICER'S 1911-A1 FIELD ECS/CS - similar to Commander, except has 3 1/2 in. barrel and Officer's Model features, 34 1/2 oz. Importation began 1999.

MSR $589		$475	$375	$350	$325	$300	$280	$260

Add $40 for Superior CS Model (includes stainless steel slide and blue frame, disc. 2000).

✻ *Officer's 1911-A1 Field ECS Stainless Empire* - .45 ACP cal. only, similar to Field ECS/CS, except is stainless steel. New 1999.

MSR $709		$575	$475	$400	$350	$315	$290	$270

✻ *Officer's 1911-A1 Field ECSCC* - carry comp., similar to Officer's Field ECS, except has single port compensator, blue or stainless. Importation began 2001.

	$540	$435	$395	$360	$325	$295	$260

Last MSR was $619.

Add $100 for Empire ECS Model (full stainless steel construction).

COMMANDER 1911-A1 POLYMER FRAME PC - .45 ACP only, features polymer frame, 4 in. barrel, available in matte blue (Field PC) or stainless slide/blue frame (Superior PC). Imported 1999-2000.

	$460	$400	$360	$330	$295	$280	$260

Last MSR was $530.

Add $25 for Superior PC Model (includes stainless steel slide and blue frame).

GOVERNMENT 1911-A2 FIELD EFS HC - .40 S&W or .45 ACP cal., 5 in. barrel, similar to Government 1911 A-1 Field EFS, 13 (.45 ACP cal.), or 15 (.40 S&W cal.) shot mag., blue finish only. Imported 2005-2007.

	$595	$485	$400	$350	$315	$290	$270

Last MSR was $725.

Add $124 for Target Model (.45 ACP cal. only, new 2005).

MODEL DDA 10-45 FS (DOUBLE ACTION) - .40 S&W (disc. 2001) or .45 ACP cal., single or double action, 4 3/8 in. barrel, polymer frame with checkering, double stacked 10 shot mag. with interchangeable base plate (allowing for extra grip length), matte black or two-tone (new 2001) finish, 28 1/2 oz. Imported 2000-2002.

	$450	$395	$360	$325	$300	$280	$260

Last MSR was $519.

Add $40 for two-tone finish.

✻ *Model DDA 10-45 CS* - similar to Model DDA 10-45 FS, except has 3 5/8 in. barrel, 26 oz. Imported 2000-2002.

	$450	$395	$360	$325	$300	$280	$260

Last MSR was $519.

Add approx. $10 for colored frame (yellow, OD green, or fuschia, new 2001) and compensated barrel.

FIELD HP HI-POWER - 9mm Para cal., single action, 4 3/4 in. barrel, patterned after the Browning Hi-Power, blue or hard chrome (mfg. 2005) finish, 10 or 13 shot mag., XS Express sight system, mfg. in U.S. Mfg. late 2003 - 2006.

	$385	$350	$310	$270	$240	$210	$175

Last MSR was $458.

Add $120 for hard chrome finish (mfg. 2005).

This model has been produced both by Dan Wesson (2003-2004) and Magnum Research (2005-2006).

GRADING - PPGS™	100%	98%	95%	90%	80%	70%	60%

M-5 FS STANDARD (BUL 1911 GOVERNMENT) - .40 S&W or .45 ACP cal., single action, 5 in. barrel, polymer double column frame, steel slide, aluminum speed trigger, checkered front and rear grip straps, blue or chrome finished slide, 10, 14 (.45 ACP cal.), or 17 (.40 S&W cal.) shot staggered mag., 31-33 oz. Mfg. by Bul Transmark in Israel. Importation began 2004.

MSR $719	$580	$485	$425	$360	$320	$265	$230

* *M-5 MS Standard Commander* - similar to M-5 Standard, except has 4 1/3 in. barrel, 29-30 oz. Importation began 2004.

MSR $719	$580	$485	$425	$360	$320	$265	$230

* *M-5 Ultra-X* - 9mm Para. or .45 ACP cal., 10 or 12 (9mm Para. cal. only) shot mag., compact variation with 3.15 in. barrel. Importation began 2005.

MSR $719	$580	$485	$425	$360	$320	$265	$230

M-5 IPSC - .40 S&W, or .45 ACP cal., configured for IPSC competition, 5 in. barrel, with custom slide to frame fit and match grade barrel bushing. Mfg. by Bul Transmark in Israel. Imported 2004-2007.

	$1,250	$975	$825	$700	$600	$525	$450

Last MSR was $1,439.

ZDA MODEL - 9mm Para. or .40 S&W cal., DA, 4 1/8 in. barrel, 12 (.40 S&W cal.) or 15 (9mm Para. cal.) shot mag., mfg. by Zastava. Limited importation 2005 only.

	$490	$425	$385	$340	$300	$275	$250

Last MSR was $589.

REVOLVERS: DA

S222/S224/S226 SERIES - 22 LR cal., 2 (S222), 4 (S224) or 6 (S226) in. barrel, blue finish, 9 shot, rubber grips, fixed (S222) or adj. (S224 or S226) sights, steel construction. While advertised during 2006, this Series was never imported.

	$265	$230	$200	$180	$160	$140	$120

Last MSR was $321.

S352/S354/S356 SERIES - .357 Mag. cal., 2 (S352), 4 (S354), or 6 (S356) in. barrel, blue finish, 6 shot, fixed (S382) or adj. (S384 or S386) sights, rubber grips, steel construction. While advertised during 2006, this Series was never imported.

	$300	$265	$240	$215	$185	$165	$145

Last MSR was $350.

S382/S384/S386 SERIES - .38 Spl. cal., 2 (S382), 4 (S384), or 6 (S386) in. barrel, blue finish, 6 shot, fixed (S382) or adj. (S384 or S386) sights, rubber grips, steel construction. While advertised during 2006, this Series was never imported.

	$265	$230	$200	$180	$160	$140	$120

Last MSR was $321.

Z222/Z224/Z226 SERIES - 22 LR cal., 2 (Z222), 4 (Z224) or 6 (Z226) in. barrel, blue finish, 9 shot, rubber grips, fixed (Z222) or adj. (Z224 or Z226) sights. While advertised during 2006, this Series was never imported.

	$200	$180	$160	$140	$120	$100	$80

Last MSR was $244.

Z382 - .38 Spl. cal., 2 in. barrel, blue finish, 6 shot, fixed sights, rubber grips. While advertised during 2006, this Series was never imported.

	$210	$185	$160	$140	$125	$110	$95

Last MSR was $249.

GRADING - PPGS™	100%	98%	95%	90%	80%	70%	60%

REVOLVERS: SA

Models were manufactured by Flli. Pietta in Italy.

MODEL 1873 CLASSIC - .357 Mag. or .45 LC cal., 4 3/4, 5 1/2 or 7 1/2 in. barrel, case hardened frame, blue finish, choice of brass (.45 LC only) or steel backstrap and trigger guard. Imported 2004-2007.

	$415	$365	$335	$300	$260	$220	$195

Last MSR was $485.

Add $20 for steel backstrap and trigger guard.

* *Model 1873 Classic Stainless* - similar to Model 1873, except has matte finish, stainless construction with steel backstrap and trigger guard. Imported 2004-2006.

	$515	$475	$425	$375	$325	$285	$250

Last MSR was $587.

MODEL 1873 SONORA - similar to Model 1873 Classic, except has matte blue finish, and not available with steel backstrap and trigger guard. Imported 2006-2007.

	$325	$275	$240	$210	$190	$175	$160

Last MSR was $399.

MODEL 1873 BIRDSHEAD - .45 LC cal. only, 4 3/4 in. barrel, color case hardened finish, steel backstrap and trigger guard. Imported 2006-2007.

	$445	$400	$365	$330	$300	$275	$250

Last MSR was $549.

* *Model 1873 Birdshead Sheriff* - .45 LC cal. only, 3 in. barrel, color case hardened finish, steel backstrap and trigger guard. Imported 2006-2007.

	$445	$400	$365	$330	$300	$275	$250

Last MSR was $549.

MODEL 1873 LIGHTNING - .45 LC cal. only, 4 3/4 in. barrel, color case hardened finish, steel backstrap and trigger guard. Imported 2006-2007.

	$445	$400	$365	$330	$300	$275	$250

Last MSR was $549.

* *Model 1873 Lightning Sheriff* - .45 LC cal. only, 3 in. barrel, color case hardened finish, steel backstrap and trigger guard. Imported 2006-2007.

	$445	$400	$365	$330	$300	$275	$250

Last MSR was $549.

MODEL 1874 RUSSIAN - .44 Russian or .45 LC cal., 6 1/2 in. barrel, blue finish. Limited importation 2006.

	$800	$725	$650	$575	$500	$425	$350

Last MSR was $931.

RIFLES: BOLT ACTION

K.B.I. also imported a wide variety of Mauser and Mini-Mauser actions until 2006. MSRs ranged between $319-$659.

MAUSER 98 - various cals., Mauser 98 action, 22 (new 2001) or 23 (disc.) in. barrel, 3-5 shot, hinged floorplate, fiberglass/graphite composite (Field Grade) or checkered European walnut (Superior Grade) stock, open sights, drilled and tapped receiver, side safety. Mfg. by Zastava. Importation began 1998, and resumed 2001-2005.

* *Mauser 98 Field Grade* - features fiberglass/graphite composite stock, matte blue finish or matte stainless steel.

	$395	$350	$315	$285	$255	$225	$200

Last MSR was $459.

Add $90 for stainless steel.
Add $30 for current Mag. cals. (.300 Win. Mag. or 7mm Rem. Mag.).
Add 50% for .375 H&H or .458 Win. Mag. cal. (disc.).

GRADING - PPGS™	100%	98%	95%	90%	80%	70%	60%

✳ *Mauser 98 Superior Grade* - features checkered European walnut stock and high polish blue finish.

	$525	$450	$395	$350	$325	$295	$275

Last MSR was $599.

> Add $190 for .375 H&H or .458 Win. Mag. cal.
> Add $30 for current Mag. cals. (.300 Win. Mag. or 7mm Rem. Mag.).
> Add $30 for left-hand action (.30-06 cal. only).

MINI-MAUSER 98 - .22 Hornet, .22-250 Rem. (disc.), .223 Rem., or 7.62x39mm cal., similar to Mauser 98, except has 18.1 (new 2001) or 19 1/4 (disc.) in. barrel, 5 shot.

✳ *Mini-Mauser 98 Field Grade* - features fiberglass/graphite composite stock.

	$345	$295	$265	$230	$200	$185	$170

Last MSR was $399.

✳ *Mini-Mauser 98 Superior Grade* - features checkered European walnut stock.

	$525	$450	$395	$350	$325	$295	$275

Last MSR was $599.

> Add $30 for left-hand action (.223 Rem. cal. only).

FIELD HUNTER - .22 Hornet, .223 Rem., .243 Win., .270 Win., .30-06, .308 Win., .300 Rem. Ultra Mag., .300 Win. Mag., .338 Win. Mag., or 7mm Rem. Mag. cal., 22 or 24 (Mag. cals. only) in. barrel w/o sights, detachable mag. on short action cals. (.22 Hornet, .223 Rem., or .243 Win.), high polish bluing, checkered walnut stock and forend, right- or left-hand action, gold trigger, approx. 7 1/3 lbs. Imported 2000 only.

	$475	$425	$375	$350	$325	$280	$240

Last MSR was $565.

> Add approx. $31 for left-hand action (.223 Rem., .243 Win., .270 Win., .30-06, .300 Rem. Ultra Mag., or 7mm Rem. Mag.).

✳ *Field Hunter Stainless/Polymer* - similar to Field Hunter, except has stainless steel barrel and action, black polymer stock with checkering. Imported 2000 only.

	$495	$450	$395	$330	$285	$240	$210

Last MSR was $580.

FIELD GRADE .22 LR CAL. - .22 LR cal., 16 1/4 (True Youth Standard), 17 1/2 (Youth), or 22 5/8 (Standard) in. barrel, single shot (True Youth Standard) or 6 shot mag., all steel shrouded action, grooved receiver, walnut finished hardwood stock. Imported 1998-2002.

	$110	$95	$80	$70	$60	$55	$50

Last MSR was $135.

> Add $14 for repeater Youth Model (6 shot, new 2000).
> Add $20 for single shot True Youth Standard with shortened dimensions.

✳ *Field Grade .22 LR Cal. Polymer/Hardwood* - similar to Field Grade, except has stainless steel action and barrel with black polymer (disc.) or hardwood (new 2001) checkered stock, 6 1/3 lbs. Imported 2000-2002.

	$120	$100	$85	$70	$60	$55	$50

Last MSR was $149.

✳ *Field Grade .22 LR Cal. Superior Grade* - .22 LR (disc. 2001), .22 Mag., or .22 Hornet cal., 22 5/8 in. barrel, 5 or 6 shot mag., features checkered walnut finished stock with adj. rear sight. Imported 1998-2002.

	$175	$135	$105	$90	$80	$70	$60

Last MSR was $209.

> Add $160 for .22 Hornet cal.
> Subtract $20 for .22 LR cal. (disc. 2001).

GRADING - PPGS™	100%	98%	95%	90%	80%	70%	60%

* Field Grade .22 LR Cal. Empire Grade - similar to Superior Grade, except has checkered California walnut stock with rosewood grip and forend caps, high polish bluing and damascened bolt. Imported 1998-2001.

	$290	$260	$230	$215	$195	$180	$170

Last MSR was $349.

Add $20 for .22 Mag. cal.
Add $130 for .22 Hornet cal.

SUPERIOR II RIMFIRE - .17 HMR, .22 LR, or .22 Mag., 22 in. barrel, walnut stock. Limited importation 2005 only.

	$215	$185	$165	$135	$120	$110	$100

Last MSR was $259.

Add $40 for .22 Mag. or $75 for .17 HMR cal.

RIFLES: LEVER ACTION, REPRODUCTIONS

MODEL 1866 - .38 Spl., .357 Mag., or .45 LC cal., brass or case colored blue (rifle, .357 Mag. cal. only) frame, choice of 19 (carbine), 20 (short rifle), or 24 1/4 (rifle) in. barrel, patterened after the Winchester Model 1866, mfg. by Chapparal. Importation began 2008.

MSR $849		$725	$650	$550	$475	$400	$350	$295

MODEL 1873 - .357 Mag. or .45 LC cal., case colored frame, choice of 18 (Trapper), 19 (carbine), 20 (short rifle), or 24 1/4 (rifle) in. barrel, patterened after the Winchester Model 1873, mfg. by Chapparal. Importation began 2008.

MSR $875		$740	$660	$550	$475	$400	$350	$295

Add $40 for half-round, half-octagon rifle or for Triwood stock.

MODEL 1876 - .45-60 WCF or .45-75 WCF cal., case colored or blue (NWMP short rifle) frame, choice of 22 (short rifle or musket), 26, or 28 in. barrel, patterened after the Winchester Model 1876, mfg. by Chapparal. Importation began 2008.

MSR $1,019		$875	$740	$660	$550	$475	$400	$350

Add $250 for NWMP short rifle or musket.
Add $90 for short rifle or $46 for Triwood stock.

1892 RIFLE/CARBINE - .45 LC cal., color case hardened frame, 20 (Carbine) or 24 1/4 (Rifle) in. barrel, patterned after the Winchester Model 1892, mfg. by Armi Sport.

MSR $1,009		$860	$700	$575	$475	$400	$350	$300

* 1892 Rifle/Carbine Takedown - .45 LC cal., color case hardened receiver, 20 (Carbine) or 24 1/4 (Rifle) in. barrel, takedown action.

MSR $1,149		$985	$750	$650	$550	$475	$425	$350

RIFLES: O/U

SUPERIOR EXPRESS - .30-06 cal., 23 1/2 in. barrels with quarter rib and leaf sights, dovetailed receiver for scope mounting, silver finished boxlock receiver, gold SST, checkered walnut stock and forearm, 7 3/4 lbs. Imported 2000-2005.

	$1,900	$1,625	$1,400	$1,225	$1,075	$950	$875

Last MSR was $2,259.

EMPIRE EXPRESS - .30-06, .375 H&H (new 2005), or .416 Rigby (new 2005) cal., 23 1/2 in. barrels with quarter rib and leaf sights, dovetailed receiver for scope mounting, silver finished boxlock receiver with shoulders, gold SST, checkered European style walnut stock with Bavarian cheekpiece and forearm, 7 3/4 lbs. Imported 2000-2005.

	$2,525	$2,000	$1,675	$1,350	$1,100	$950	$875

Last MSR was $2,949.

Add $710 for .375 H&H or .416 Rigby cal.

GRADING - PPGS™	100%	98%	95%	90%	80%	70%	60%

RIFLES: SEMI-AUTO

All currently manufactured semi-auto rifles have forged aluminum alloy receivers which are milspec hard anodized and Teflon coated, manganese phosphate barrel (except stainless), radiused aluminum magazine release button, aluminum trigger guard, safety selector position on right side of receiver, dust cover, brass deflector, forward assist, and include one magazine and hard plastic carrying case. All currently manufactured rifles are covered by a lifetime repair policy.

SEMI-AUTO RIFLE - .22 LR cal., steel receiver, 20 3/4 in. barrel with adj. rear sight, 10 shot mag. Mfg. 1998-2002.

* *Semi-Auto Rifle Field Grade* - features uncheckered walnut finished hardwood stock.

$110	$95	$80	$70	$60	$55	$50

Last MSR was $135.

* *Semi-Auto Rifle Field Grade Polymer/Hardwood* - similar to Field Grade, except has stainless steel action and barrel with black polymer (disc.) or hardwood checkered stock, 6 1/8 lbs. Mfg. 2000-2002.

$120	$100	$85	$75	$65	$60	$55

Last MSR was $149.

* *Semi-Auto Rifle Superior Grade* - features checkered walnut finished stock. Disc. 2001.

$175	$130	$100	$90	$80	$70	$60

Last MSR was $209.

* *Semi-Auto Rifle Empire Grade* - features checkered California walnut stock. Disc. 2001.

$275	$245	$220	$195	$180	$170	$160

Last MSR was $334.

D-M4 CARBINE - 5.56 NATO cal., 16 in. chrome-moly match barrel with M-203 mounting groove, 10, 20, or 30 shot mag., M4 feed ramps, forged "F" front sight base with bayonet lug and rubber coated sling swivel, A3 detachable carry handle, T-Marked flattop upper, six-position telestock, A2 birdcage flash hider, oval double heat shield M4 forend. New 2008.

MSR $1,119	$900	$800	$700	$625	$550	$500	$450

D-M4LE CARBINE - 5.56 NATO cal., similar to D-M4 carbine, except does not have detachable carry handle, has milspec diameter receiver extension with "H" buffer. New 2008.

MSR $1,169	$935	$815	$700	$625	$550	$500	$450

D-M4S CARBINE - similar to D-M4 carbine, except has two Picatinny riser blocks, oval double heat shield M4 forend with QD sling swivel and swivel/bipod stud installed, Magpul enhanced trigger guard. New 2008.

MSR $1,079	$875	$785	$700	$625	$550	$500	$450

D-M4LX CARBINE - 5.56 NATO cal., 16 in. chrome-moly H-bar fluted match barrel, M4 feed ramps, T-Marked flattop upper, flip up rear sight, folding front gas block with bayonet lug, aluminum free floating quad rail forend with swiveling sling stud, nine 5-slot low profile ladder style quad rail covers, Ace M4 SOCOM standard length telestock with half buttpad, Phantom flash suppressor, Ergo Ambi AR grip. New 2008.

MSR $1,619	$1,375	$1,175	$950	$825	$700	$625	$550

DR-15 TARGET - 5.56 NATO cal., 20 in. chrome-moly match H-bar barrel, A2 upper with carry handle, A2 buttstock, A2 birdcage flash hider, forged front sight tower with bayonet lug and rubber coated sling swivel, fixed position stock. New 2008.

MSR $1,089	$895	$785	$700	$625	$550	$500	$450

GRADING - PPGS™	100%	98%	95%	90%	80%	70%	60%

DV-24 MATCH TARGET/VARMINT - 5.56 NATO cal., 24 in. match stainless steel bull barrel, T-Marked flattop upper, two Picatinny half riser blocks, free floating ported aluminum tube forend with swivel/bipod stud installed, Ace skeletonized butt stock, Picatinny rail milled gas block, two-stage match trigger. New 2008.

MSR $1,319	$1,150	$995	$875	$775	$675	$575	$475

RIFLES: SINGLE SHOT

FIELD GRADE - .22 Hornet, .223 Rem., .243 Win., or .270 Win. cal., single shot break open action, 22 in. barrel with mount base, drilled and tapped, adj. or no sights, checkered hardwood stock and forearm. Limited importation 2001 only.

	$165	$140	$110	$95	$80	$70	$60

Last MSR was $189.

Add $10 for adj. sights.

This model was also available in a Youth configuration at no extra charge.

LITTLE SHARPS MODEL - .17 HMR, .218 Bee, .22 LR (new 2008), .22 Hornet, .357 Mag., .30-30 Win., .38-55 WCF (new 2008), .44-40 WCF (new 2008), or .45 LC cal., 24 (rimfire only) or 26 in. tapered octagonal barrel, case colored frame, mfg. by Armi Sport. New 2007.

MSR $1,229	$1,075	$925	$725	$650	$550	$475	$425

SHOTGUNS: O/U

Recent O/U production is from Italy and Turkey.

PRESENTATION MODEL - 12 or 20 ga., with choke tubes, Purdey double underlug locking action with decorative engraved sideplates, French walnut, single trigger, ejectors. Disc. 1986.

	$995	$840	$750	$670	$615	$560	$520

Last MSR was $1,165.

COUNTRY SQUIRE MODEL - .410 bore only, 3 in. chambers, case colored boxlock action, gold DT, 25 1/2 in. vent. barrels with VR and F/F chokes, checkered straight grip stock and Schnabel forearm, approx. 6 lbs. Disc. 2002.

	$640	$575	$525	$475	$425	$375	$350

Last MSR was $715.

FIELD II HUNTER - 12, 16 (new 2001), 20, 28 ga., or .410 bore, similar to DeLuxe Model except has fixed chokes, extractors, machine stock checkering, and blue receiver, 5 1/2 - 7 lbs., depending on ga./barrel lengths. Imported 1989-2005.

	$850	$675	$575	$475	$375	$315	$285

Last MSR was $1,029.

Add $100 for 28 ga. or .410 bore.

* *Field II Hunter with Ejectors* - similar to Field II Hunter, except has ejectors and multi-chokes (not available on 28 ga. or .410 bore), Monte Carlo stock. Imported 1997-2005.

	$1,065	$900	$800	$675	$575	$475	$375

Last MSR was $1,279.

* *Field II Hunter Ultra-Light* - 12 or 20 ga., alloy frame, 26 in. VR barrels only with fixed IC/M (disc. 2000) or multi-chokes (new 2001), thin forearm, approx. 5 1/2 lbs. Imported 1999-2005.

	$965	$840	$725	$625	$525	$425	$325

Last MSR was $1,199.

GRADING - PPGS™	100%	98%	95%	90%	80%	70%	60%

DELUXE MODEL - 12, 20, 28 ga. (disc. 1995), or .410 bore (disc. 1995), boxlock with self adj. crossbolt, 26 or 28 in. chrome lined VR barrels with internal choke tubes, SST, ejectors, antique silver finish on receiver, deluxe hand checkered walnut stock and forearm. Imported 1989-96.

	$650	$525	$475	$425	$400	$375	$350

Last MSR was $770.

SPORTING CLAYS MODEL - 12 ga. only, SST, ejectors, silver engraved receiver, checkered walnut stock and forearm, screw-in chokes, 28 (disc.) or 30 (new 1996) in. VR ported barrels. Imported 1995-96.

	$775	$700	$625	$550	$475	$395	$350

Last MSR was $895.

SUPERIOR II - 12 or 20 ga., various chokes, boxlock action, single trigger, ejectors, engraved. Disc. 1988.

	$675	$575	$475	$425	$395	$375	$350

Last MSR was $875.

Add $35 for 12 ga. Mag. (disc. 1987).

FIELD III - 12 or 20 ga., various chokes, boxlock action, single trigger. Disc. 1989.

	$395	$370	$340	$315	$285	$260	$230

Last MSR was $450.

SUPERIOR II HUNTER - 12, 20, 28 ga. (new 1998), or .410 bore, 3 in. chambers (except 28 ga.), boxlock action, ejectors, 26, 28, or 30 in. VR barrels with multi-chokes (except 28 ga. and .410 bore), barrel porting became standard during 2000, select checkered walnut stock and forearm, 6 1/8-7 lbs. Imported 1997-2005.

	$1,325	$1,075	$900	$800	$675	$575	$475

Last MSR was $1,519.

Subtract $70 for 28 ga. or .410 bore.

* *Superior II Hunter Sporting* - 12 or 20 ga. (disc. 1998), 26 (disc. 1998), 28, or 30 (12 ga. only) in. 10mm VR barrels with multi-chokes and ported barrels. Imported 1997-2005.

	$1,400	$1,150	$950	$825	$725	$625	$525

Last MSR was $1,659.

* *Superior II Hunter Trap* - 12 ga. only, 30 or 32 (disc. 2001) in. VR barrels with choice of fixed chokes or multi-chokes, regular or Monte Carlo stock. Imported 1997-2005.

	$1,450	$1,175	$950	$825	$725	$625	$525

Last MSR was $1,699.

Subtract 10% if w/o multi-chokes with Monte Carlo stock.

* *Superior II Hunter Skeet* - 12 or 20 ga., 26 in. VR barrels with choice of Skeet fixed chokes or multi-chokes, regular or Monte Carlo stock. Imported 1997-98.

	$935	$800	$700	$600	$500	$450	$375

Last MSR was $1,039.

Add $120 for multi-chokes with Monte Carlo stock.

EMPIRE DL HUNTER - 12, 20, 28 ga., or .410 bore, boxlock action, silver receiver with game scene engraving, ejectors, SST, 26 or 28 (12 or 20 ga. only) in. VR barrels with multi-chokes (except 28 ga. and .410 bore). Imported 1997-98.

	$1,025	$875	$750	$650	$550	$475	$395

Last MSR was $1,159.

Add $65 for 28 ga. or $110 for .410 bore.

GRADING - PPGS™	100%	98%	95%	90%	80%	70%	60%

EMPIRE II EDL HUNTER - similar to Empire DL Hunter, except has engraved side-plates featuring game scenes. Imported 1998-2005.

	$1,675	$1,250	$1,000	$875	$775	$675	$575

Last MSR was $2,029.

Subtract $10 for 28 ga. or .410 bore.

＊ *Empire II EDL Hunter Sporting* - 12 or 20 ga. (disc. 1999), 26 (disc. 1999), 28, or 30 (12 ga. only) in. VR barrels with multi-chokes. Imported 1997-2005.

	$1,675	$1,250	$1,100	$875	$775	$675	$575

Last MSR was $2,049.

＊ *Empire II EDL Hunter Trap* - 12 ga. only, 30 or 32 (disc. 2000) in. VR barrels with choice of fixed chokes (32 in. barrel only) or multi-chokes, regular (disc. 1998) or Monte Carlo stock. Imported 1997-2005.

	$1,700	$1,275	$1,050	$925	$800	$700	$600

Last MSR was $2,099.

Subtract 10% if w/o multi-chokes.

＊ *Empire II EDL Hunter Mono Trap* - features 30 or 32 in. single top barrel, standard or adj. Monte Carlo stock. Imported 1999-2005.

	$2,825	$2,400	$2,150	$1,800	$1,425	$1,150	$925

Last MSR was $3,249.

Subtract approx. 20% if w/o adj. Monte Carlo stock.

＊ *Empire II EDL Hunter Trap Combo* - includes mono 32 in. barrel and extra set of 30 in. O/U barrels, standard or adj. Monte Carlo stock. Imported 1999-2005.

	$3,500	$3,150	$2,700	$2,250	$1,925	$1,625	$1,375

Last MSR was $3,919.

Subtract approx. 20% if w/o adj. Monte Carlo stock.

＊ *Empire II EDL Hunter Skeet* - 12 or 20 ga., 26 in. VR barrels with choice of Skeet fixed chokes or multi-chokes, regular or Monte Carlo stock. Imported 1997-98.

	$1,050	$875	$750	$650	$550	$475	$395

Last MSR was $1,189.

Add $125 for multi-chokes with Monte Carlo stock.

DIAMOND FIELD - 12 or 20 ga. (disc. 1986) Mag., with choke tubes. Same action as Presentation Model without sideplates, engraved, select walnut, single trigger, ejectors. Disc. 1986.

	$695	$600	$550	$510	$460	$420	$380

Last MSR was $895.

＊ *Diamond Field Trap or Skeet* - 12 ga. only, 26 or 30 in. barrels only. Disc. 1986.

	$850	$700	$550	$500	$475	$450	$425

Last MSR was $1,050.

Subtract $50 for Skeet Model.

DIAMOND GTX DL HUNTER - 12, 20, 28 ga., or .410 bore, sidelock action, ejectors, SST, elaborate engraving with select checkered walnut stock and forearm, 26, 28 (12 or 20 ga. only), or 30 (12 ga. only) in. VR barrels with multi-chokes (except 28 ga. and .410 bore). Imported 1997 only.

	$11,250	$9,000	$7,000	$5,700	$4,900	$4,200	$3,750

Last MSR was $12,399.

＊ *Diamond GTX EDL Hunter* - more elaborate variation of the Diamond GTX DL Hunter. Imported 1997 only.

	$13,750	$11,250	$9,000	$7,000	$5,700	$4,900	$4,200

Last MSR was $15,999.

DIAMOND GTX SPORTING - 12 or 20 (disc. 1998) ga., boxlock Boss action with light perimeter engraving, 28 or 30 (12 ga. only) in. VR barrels with multi-chokes and porting. Imported 1997-2001.

$5,260	$4,750	$4,275	$3,675	$3,150	$2,750	$2,175

Last MSR was $5,849.

DIAMOND GTX TRAP - 12 ga. only, boxlock Boss action with light perimeter engraving, 30 in. VR barrels with choice of fixed (disc. 1999) or multi-chokes with barrel porting, regular or adj. (new 1999) Monte Carlo stock. Imported 1997-2001.

$5,865	$4,900	$4,400	$3,825	$3,175	$2,750	$2,175

Last MSR was $6,699.

Subtract 10% w/o fixed chokes.

DIAMOND GTX MONO TRAP - features single top barrel, adj. Monte Carlo stock. Imported 1999-2001.

$5,795	$4,850	$4,400	$3,825	$3,150	$2,750	$2,175

Last MSR was $6,619.

✳ *Diamond GTX Mono Trap Combo* - includes 32 in. mono barrel and extra set of 30 in. O/U barrels, adj. Monte Carlo stock. Imported 1999-2001.

$6,775	$5,775	$4,825	$4,325	$3,775	$3,150	$2,750

Last MSR was $7,419.

DIAMOND GTX SKEET - 12 or 20 ga., 26 or 28 (20 ga. only with Monte Carlo stock) in. VR barrels with choice of Skeet fixed chokes or multi-chokes, regular or Monte Carlo stock. Imported 1997-98.

$4,700	$4,100	$3,800	$3,400	$2,975	$2,700	$2,100

Last MSR was $5,149.

Add $140 for multi-chokes with Monte Carlo stock.

DIAMOND REGENT GTX DL HUNTER - 12, 20, 28 ga., or .410 bore, sidelock action, ejectors, SST, best quality engraving with premium checkered walnut stock and forearm, 26, 28 (12 or 20 ga. only), or 30 (12 ga. only) in. VR barrels with multi-chokes (except 28 ga. and .410 bore). Imported 1997 only.

$19,750	$16,250	$13,750	$11,250	$9,000	$7,000	$5,700

Last MSR was $22,299.

✳ *Diamond Regent GTX EDL Hunter* - top-of-the-line model incorporating best quality engraving and premium walnut. Imported 1997 only.

$23,000	$19,500	$16,000	$13,750	$10,500	$8,750	$7,700

Last MSR was $26,429.

MODEL 105 - 12 ga., 26 or 28 in. barrels, fixed chokes, extractors, DT, silver engraved receiver, Turkish walnut stock, mfg. in Turkey. Imported 2006-2007.

$355	$315	$275	$240	$210	$180	$160

Last MSR was $409.

MODEL 106 - 12, 20, 28 ga. or .410 bore, 26 or 28 in. barrels, SST, extractors, fixed (.410 bore) or multi-chokes, inlaid blue receiver, mfg. in Turkey. Imported 2006-2007.

$525	$465	$425	$385	$350	$325	$295

Last MSR was $599.

MODEL 206 - 12 ga., 3 in. chambers, extractors or ejectors, 26 or 28 in. VR barrels with three multichokes, SST, silver receiver, select Turkish Monte Carlo walnut stock, mfg. in Turkey. Importation began 2007.

MSR $649						
	$575	$500	$450	$400	$350	$300	$250

Add $110 for auto ejectors.

GRADING - PPGS™	100%	98%	95%	90%	80%	70%	60%

✳ *Model 206 Sporting* - 12 ga., 28 or 30 in. VR barrels with 5 multichokes, ejectors, SST. Importation began 2007.

MSR $809	$700	$600	$500	$425	$365	$335	$295

✳ *Model 206 Trap* - 12 ga., 30 in. VR barrels with 5 multichokes, ejectors. Importation began 2007.

MSR $875	$745	$625	$525	$450	$400	$350	$300

DALY UL - 12 ga., aluminum receiver, SST, ejectors, 26 in. barrels with five multichokes. Imported 2007 only.

	$525	$465	$425	$385	$350	$325	$295

Last MSR was $599.

MAXI-MAG - 12 ga., 3 1/2 in. chambers, boxlock action, 26 or 28 in. VR barrels with three choke tubes, SST, extractors, checkered walnut stock and forearm. Imported 2007 only.

	$485	$435	$385	$335	$285	$240	$210

Last MSR was $559.

Add $60 for Advantage Max-4 or Realtree HD camo finish.

SHOTGUNS: SxS

FIELD III - 12 or 20 ga., various chokes, boxlock action, single trigger. Disc.

	$350	$315	$285	$260	$230	$210	$195

COUNTRY SQUIRE MODEL - .28 ga. or .410 bore, 3 in. chambers, case colored boxlock action, gold DT, 26 in. barrels with fixed chokes, checkered stock and splinter forearm, approx. 6 lbs. Disc. 2000.

	$600	$550	$500	$450	$400	$360	$330

Last MSR was $680.

FIELD II HUNTER MODEL - 10 (disc. 2002), 12, 16 (new 2005), 20, 28 ga., or .410 bore, boxlock action, 26, 28, 30 (12 ga. only), or 32 (10 ga. only) in. barrels, fixed (disc. 2000) or multi-chokes (12 or 20 ga. only), 6-7 3/8 lbs., or 11 1/4 (10 ga.) lbs. Imported 1997-2005.

	$975	$875	$750	$650	$550	$450	$375

Last MSR was $1,189.

Subtract $90 for 16 ga., 28 ga. or .410 bore (extractors only).
Subtract approx. 15% if w/o ejectors and multi-chokes (not available in 28 ga. or .410 bore).

SUPERIOR - 12 or 20 ga., boxlock action, various chokes, single trigger. Disc. 1985.

	$550	$470	$405	$345	$315	$280	$250

Last MSR was $624.

SUPERIOR HUNTER - 12, 20, or 28 (new 1999) ga. or .410 bore (new 2000), 26 or 28 in. barrels with fixed (disc. 2000) or multi-chokes (new 2001, 12 or 20 ga. only), 5 7/8-6 3/4 lbs. Imported 1997-2005.

	$1,395	$1,150	$975	$850	$725	$625	$525

Last MSR was $1,659.

Subtract $30 for 28 ga. or .410 bore.

LUXE MODEL - 12 (disc. 1991) or 20 ga., boxlock action, SST, ejectors, 26 in. barrels with choke tubes, checkered pistol grip walnut stock with semi-beavertail forearm, recoil pad. Imported 1990-94.

	$575	$450	$395	$350	$315	$285	$260

Last MSR was $650.

This model was manufactured by Hermanos located in Spain.

GRADING - PPGS™	100%	98%	95%	90%	80%	70%	60%

EMPIRE HUNTER - 12, 20, or 28 (disc. 1998) ga., 26 or 28 in. barrels with fixed or multi-chokes (new 2001), 6-6 7/8 lbs. Imported 1997-2005.

| | $1,700 | $1,300 | $1,050 | $925 | $825 | $700 | $600 |

Last MSR was $2,119.

DIAMOND DL - 12, 20, 28 ga., or .410 bore, case colored sidelock action with 3rd lever fastener, scroll engraving, select checkered walnut stock and splinter forearm, 26 or 28 in. barrels with fixed chokes. Importation began 1997.

| | $6,060 | $4,950 | $4,375 | $3,775 | $3,200 | $2,750 | $2,175 |

Last MSR was $6,999.

DIAMOND REGENT DL - 12, 20, 28 ga., or .410 bore, sidelock action with best quality engraving and premium checkered walnut stock and forearm, 26 or 28 in. barrels with fixed chokes. Imported 1997 only.

| | $18,950 | $15,750 | $13,250 | $10,750 | $8,900 | $6,900 | $5,600 |

Last MSR was $21,659.

MODEL 306 - 12 or 20 (new 2007) ga., 3 in. chambers, engraved boxlock action, 26 or 28 in. barrels with three multichokes, gold SST, extractors, checkered Turkish walnut stock and forearm, 6 1/2 - 7 lbs. Importation from Turkey 2006-2007.

| | $580 | $485 | $420 | $350 | $300 | $275 | $250 |

Last MSR was $649.

CLASSIC COACH GUN - 12 ga., 3 in. chambers, engraved boxlock action, 20 in. barrels with three multichokes, gold SST, extractors, checkered Turkish walnut stock and forearm, 6.3 lbs. Imported 2007.

| | $550 | $475 | $425 | $350 | $300 | $275 | $250 |

Last MSR was $635.

SHOTGUNS: LEVER ACTION

MODEL 1887 - 12 ga., patterned after the Winchester Model 1887, case-colored frame, 22 in. barrel. Importation began 2007.

| MSR $1,239 | $1,075 | $925 | $775 | $650 | $550 | $475 | $400 |

SHOTGUNS: SEMI-AUTO

The Charles Daly "Novamatic" shotguns were produced in 1968 by Breda in Italy. The Novamatic series was not imported by Outdoor Sport Headquarters, Inc.

NOVAMATIC LIGHTWEIGHT MODEL - 12 ga., 26 or 28 in. barrel, various chokes, available with quick choke interchangeable tubes, checkered pistol grip stock, similar to the Breda shotgun. Mfg. 1968 only.

| | $305 | $275 | $250 | $220 | $195 | $165 | $140 |

Add $25 for vent. rib.
Add $15 for quick choke.

NOVAMATIC SUPER LIGHTWEIGHT - 12 or 20 ga., similar to Lightweight, except approx. 1/2 lb. lighter.

| | $330 | $305 | $275 | $250 | $220 | $195 | $165 |

Add $25 for vent. rib.
Add $15 for quick choke.

NOVAMATIC MAGNUM - 12 or 20 ga. with 3 in. chambers, similar to Lightweight, 28 or 30 in. vent rib barrel, full choke.

| | $330 | $305 | $275 | $250 | $220 | $195 | $165 |

NOVAMATIC TRAP - similar to Lightweight, with 30 in. full vent. rib barrel, Monte Carlo stock.

| | $360 | $330 | $305 | $275 | $250 | $220 | $195 |

GRADING - PPGS™	100%	98%	95%	90%	80%	70%	60%

MULTI-XII - 12 ga. only, 3 in. chamber, 27 in. VR multichoke barrel, self-adjusting gas operation, deluxe checkered walnut stock with recoil pad and forearm. Imported 1987-88 only.

	$425	$360	$320	$285	$250	$225	$195

Last MSR was $498.

CHARLES DALY AUTOMATIC - 12 ga., 2 3/4 or 3 in. chambers, gas operation, alloy frame, pistol grip (high gloss) or English stock, vent. rib, 5 shot mag. Also available as slug gun with iron sights. Invector chokes became standard in 1986. Disc. 1988.

	$320	$275	$235	$205	$190	$170	$150

Last MSR was $365.

Add $15 for oil finished English stock.

FIELD GRADE ERCT - 12 or 20 ga., 22 in. barrel, adj. sight or cantilever scope mount, blue finish or RealTree Hardwoods camo coverage, extended rifle choke tube, deer variation, mfg. in Turkey. Imported 2006-2007.

	$340	$295	$260	$220	$195	$175	$150

Last MSR was $399.

Add $70 for Youth Model.
Add $10 for cantilever scope mount.
Add $60 for 100% camo coverage.

FIELD GRADE FRB - 12 ga., 22 in. fully rifled barrel with choice of fiber optic sights or cantilever scope mount, blue or camo finish, mfg. in Turkey. Importation began 2007.

MSR $449		$385	$350	$325	$295	$275	$250	$225

Add $70 for 100% camo coverage.
Add $180 for combo variation with cantilever mount barrel and extra 28 in. multi-choke barrel.
Add $16 for cantilever scope mount.

FIELD HUNTER - 12, 20 (new 2002), or 28 (new 2002) ga., 3 in. chamber (12 or 20 ga.), gas operated, aluminum receiver, 22 (Youth or smoothbore slug), 24-30 in. VR barrel with multi-chokes, choice of standard wood/black metal or 100% Advantage (disc. 2001), Advantage Timber HD (new 2002), Realtree (disc. 2001), RealTree Hardwoods HD, Advantage Max-4 HD (12 ga. only, new 2004), Realtree APG (new 2008), Advantage Wetlands (mfg. 2001-2003), or Advantage Classic (disc. 2001) camo coverage, synthetic stock and forearm, 6 7/8-7 1/8 lbs. Importation began 1999.

MSR $415		$345	$300	$265	$220	$195	$180	$160

Add $74 for 100% camo coverage.
Add $24 for 28 ga.
Add $44 for left-hand action (12 ga. only).
Add $20 for Advantage Timber HD camo (20 ga. only).

✱ *Field Hunter Maxi-Mag* - 12 ga. only, 3 1/2 in. chamber, 24, 26 (new 2001), or 28 in. VR barrel with multi-choke, 7mm VR rib, choice of wood/metal or 100% camo coverage similar to Field Hunter, 6 7/8-7 1/8 lbs. Importation began 2000.

MSR $449		$390	$350	$315	$270	$240	$220	$200

Add $66 for 100% camo coverage.

✱ *Field Hunter Maxi-Mag Turkey* - 12 ga. only, includes 24 in. barrel, Hi/TriViz fiber optic sights and XX full ported turkey choke tube, Advantage Timber or Realtree Hardwoods HD camo treatment, Uncle Mike's camo sling and sling swivels. New 2002.

MSR $595		$500	$415	$355	$310	$275	$250	$225

GRADING - PPGS™	100%	98%	95%	90%	80%	70%	60%

✴ *Field Hunter Slug* - 12 ga. only, 22 in. cyl. bore barrel with adj. sights, black synthetic stock and forearm, nickel (disc. 2002) or black chrome finish, adj. open sights. Imported 1999-2003.

	$355	$320	$290	$275	$250	$225	$200

Last MSR was $409.

> Add $20 for satin nickel finish (disc. 2002).
> Add $40 for fully rifled barrel with adj. sights (new 2002).

SUPERIOR II HUNTER - similar to Field Hunter, except has 20 LPI checkered Turkish walnut stock and forearm, gold highlights and trigger. Importation began 1999.

MSR $565	$485	$395	$350	$300	$275	$250	$225

> Add $24 for 28 ga.
> Add $100 for left-hand action (12 ga. only, disc. 2006).

✴ *Superior II Hunter Sporting* - 12 ga. only, similar to Superior Hunter, except has 28 or 30 in. ported 10mm VR barrels. Importation began 1999.

MSR $609	$535	$440	$370	$325	$290	$260	$225

✴ *Superior II Hunter Trap* - 12 ga. only, 30 or 32 (disc. 2007) in. ported barrel with front and mid bead sights. Importation began 1999.

MSR $625	$545	$440	$370	$325	$290	$260	$225

SHOTGUNS: SLIDE ACTION

FIELD ERCT - 12 or 20 ga., 22 in. barrel with rifled choke tubes, blue or RealTree Hardwoods HD camo finish, available with either adj. sights or cantilevered scope mount, also available in Youth Model (20 ga. only), deer variation. Imported 2006-2007.

	$220	$185	$165	$145	$130	$115	$100

Last MSR was $259.

> Add $10 for cantilevered scope mount.
> Add $60 for 100% camo coverage.
> Add $6 for Youth Model (20 ga. only).

FIELD HUNTER - 12 or 20 (new 2001) ga., 3 in. chamber, 22 (Youth, 20 ga. only), 24, 26, 28, or 30 in. VR barrel with multi-choke, synthetic stock and forearm, choice of standard wood/metal or 100% Advantage Timber HD (new 2002), Realtree APG (new 2008), Realtree AP HD (new 2008), Realtree Hardwoods HD 12 ga. only, (new 2002) or Advantage Classic (disc. 2001) camo coverage, 5 5/8-6 7/8 lbs. Importation began 1999.

MSR $275	$225	$190	$165	$145	$125	$110	$100

> Add $14 for Advantage Timber HD or Realtree Hardwoods HD camo.
> Add $64 for Realtree AP HD or APG camo.
> Add $24 for Youth model.

✴ *Field Hunter Maxi-Mag.* - 12 ga. only, 3 1/2 in. chamber, 24, 26 (new 2001), or 28 in. VR barrel with multi-choke, 7mm VR rib, choice of wood/metal or 100% camo coverage similar to Field Hunter, approx. 6 3/4 lbs. Importation began 2000.

MSR $299	$240	$210	$190	$170	$155	$140	$130

> Add $20 for Advantage Timber HD or Realtree Hardwoods HD camo.
> Add $70 for Realtree AP HD or APG camo.
> Add $96 for Advantage Timber HD or Realtree Hardwoods HD camo Turkey Model or $146 for Turkey Model with AP HD or APG camo, Hi/TriViz fiber optic sights and XX full ported turkey choke tube - also includes sling and sling swivels (new 2002).

✴ *Field Hunter Slug* - 12 ga. only, 18 1/2 in. cyl. bore or 22 in. fully rifled (new 2002) barrel with adj. sights, black synthetic stock and forearm, black chrome or dull nickel finish. Imported 1999-2003.

	$210	$190	$180	$165	$150	$135	$125

Last MSR was $229.

> Subtract 15% for 18 1/2 in. barrel.

GRADING - PPGS™	100%	98%	95%	90%	80%	70%	60%

* *Field Hunter Tactical* - 12 ga. only, 18 1/2 in. cyl. bore barrel with front sight, black synthetic stock and forearm, matte blue metal or nickel finish, 6 lbs. Importation began 2000.

	MSR $249	$210	$175	$150	$125	$110	$100	$90

Add $20 for nickel finish and adj. sights.

DAN ARMS OF AMERICA

Previous trademark of shotguns manufactured in Italy by Silma. Previously imported by Dan Arms of America located in Allentown, PA and by Dan Arms of North America (previously called Sportsman's Emporium Ltd.) located in Fort Washington, PA.

All shotguns listed below were discontinued in early 1988.

SHOTGUNS: O/U

LUX GRADE I - 12 or 20 ga., 3 in. Mag. chambers, 26, 28, or 30 in. barrels, vent. rib, extractors, pistol grip, double trigger, European walnut.

	$280	$220	$210	$200	$190	$180	$170

Last MSR was $350.

LUX GRADE II - 12 ga. only, 3 in. Mag. chambers, 26, 28, or 30 in. barrels, vent. rib, extractors, pistol grip, single trigger, European walnut.

	$320	$250	$240	$230	$215	$200	$190

Last MSR was $395.

LUX GRADE III - 12 or 20 ga., 3 in. Mag. chambers, 26, 28, or 30 in. barrels, vent. rib, ejectors, pistol grip, single trigger, checkered European walnut.

	$375	$300	$285	$270	$255	$240	$220

Last MSR was $450.

LUX GRADE IV - 12 ga. only, 3 in. Mag. chambers, 28 in. barrels, vent. rib, ejectors, pistol grip, single trigger, checkered European walnut, multi-chokes with 5 tubes.

	$460	$390	$350	$310	$285	$265	$245

Last MSR was $550.

SKEET MODEL - 12 ga. only, 26 1/2 in. barrels, 10mm vent. rib, anatomical pistol grip.

	$550	$450	$400	$355	$320	$300	$285

Last MSR was $650.

TRAP MODEL - 12 ga. only, 30 in. barrels, 10mm vent. rib, anatomical pistol grip.

	$550	$450	$400	$355	$320	$300	$285

Last MSR was $650.

SILVERSNIPE - 12 or 20 ga., made to customer specifications, sideplates, select high grade walnut, name engraving upon request.

	$1,300	$1,200	$1,050	$900	$800	$700	$600

Last MSR was $1,475.

SHOTGUNS: SxS

FIELD MODEL - 12, 16, 20, 28 ga., or .410 bore, double triggers, extractors, 26 or 28 in. barrels.

	$285	$220	$210	$200	$190	$180	$170

Last MSR was $350.

DELUXE FIELD MODEL - 12 or 20 ga., single triggers, ejectors, 26 or 28 in. barrels.

	$440	$375	$340	$310	$290	$260	$230

Last MSR was $500.

GRADING - PPGS™	100%	98%	95%	90%	80%	70%	60%

DARDICK

Previous manufacturer located in Hamden, CT.

CARBINES

DARDICK CARBINE CONVERSION - .22 or .38 Dardick Tround cal., 23 in. barrel (interchangeable), walnut stock. Limited mfg.

	$1,450	$1,150	$925	$825	$750	$700	$650

PISTOLS: SEMI-AUTO

SERIES 1100 - .38 Dardick Tround cal., double action, 11 shot mag.

	$2,200	$1,900	$1,575	$1,250	$995	$875	$795

Dardick ammunition in itself is collectible - currently, individual "Trounds" are selling in the $5-$10 range.

SERIES 1500 - .22, .30, or .38 Dardick Tround cal., double action, 15 shot mag.

	$1,800	$1,575	$1,125	$975	$850	$700	$600

DARNE S.A.

Current manufacturer producing shotguns 1881-1979 and 1990 to date in Saint Etienne, France. Darne also began making double rifles circa 1996. Currently imported by Geoffroy Gournet, located in PA. Previously imported by The Drumming Stump, Inc. located in Circle Pines, MN circa 1996-2005, and by Wes Gilpin located in Dallas, TX until 1992.

For F. Darne Fils Aîné please refer to the F Section. Also, please refer to the Bruchet section for 1982-1990 mfg. utilizing the Darne action.

RIFLES: DOUBLE

DARNE DAMON PETRIK O/U - 8x57R, 9.3x74R, or .30R Blaser cal.

Base price for this model is $13,500.

MODEL R EXPRESS SxS - 8x57 JRS or 9.3x74R cal., double rifle version of the Darne Model R Series shotgun, many options available, including style of rib, sights, stock configuration, etc. Importation began 1996.

Base price for this model is $17,680.

EXPRESS SUPERPOSEÉ - .30-06, 8x57 JRS, or 9.3.74R cal., double rifle version of the Darne O/U shotgun, boxlock with false sideplates, straight grip stock, many options available. Importation began 1996.

Please contact the importer directly for a price quotation on this model.

MODEL V EXPRESS SxS - 8x57R, 9.3x74R, .30R Blaser or .375 H&H cal., no disks - obturators.

Base price for this model is $27,300.

SHOTGUNS: SxS, PRE-1980 MFG.

DARNE SLIDING BREECH SHOTGUN - 12, 16, 20, or 28 ga., SxS, unique action utilizes sliding breech lock-up, high quality mfg., 27 1/2 in. barrel standard with other lengths available, any choke combination, either straight grip or pistol grip stock, checkered, models differ in amount of engraving and grade of wood.

✱ *Darne Sliding Breech Shotgun Bird Hunter Model R11*

	$1,500	$1,350	$1,100	$950	$825	$700	$600

✱ *Darne Sliding Breech Shotgun Pheasant Hunter Model R15*

	$2,250	$2,000	$1,800	$1,625	$1,500	$1,425	$1,300

✱ *Darne Sliding Breech Shotgun Magnum Model R16*

	$3,500	$3,150	$2,650	$2,300	$2,000	$1,750	$1,500

GRADING - PPGS™	100%	98%	95%	90%	80%	70%	60%

* *Darne Sliding Breech Shotgun Quail Hunter Model V19*

	$4,500	$4,150	$3,700	$3,350	$2,850	$2,400	$1,950

* *Darne Sliding Breech Shotgun Model V22*

	$5,750	$5,300	$4,600	$4,150	$3,650	$3,000	$2,500

* *Darne Sliding Breech Shotgun Hors Series No. 1 Model V*

	$6,350	$5,750	$5,250	$4,500	$3,850	$3,150	$2,600

SHOTGUNS: 1989-CURRENT MFG.

In 1990, Paul Bruchet (the old Darne plant superintendent) obtained permission to once again use the Darne trademark. Hence, all 1990 and later mfg. has been produced by Paul Bruchet.

All new mfg. Darnes can be choked to the customer's choice. All models listed have automatic ejectors, are oil finished by hand, and may be barreled to any length (except for Models R 11, 12, and 13). All prices are subject to change without notice.

O/U Models

SB1 - similar to SB3, traditional European O/U, DT, extractors, straight or semi-pistol grip stock. Importation began 1998.

MSR POR		N/A	N/A	$2,000	$1,650	$1,450	$1,100	$950

SB2 - similar to SB3, except has scroll engraving, wood upgrade, and 28 in. barrels. Importation began 1996.

MSR POR		N/A	N/A	$2,400	$1,975	$1,625	$1,250	$1,000

SB3 - 12 or 20 ga., scalloped boxlock action, extractors, 26 in. barrels, DTs, choice of English straight grip stock or semi-pistol grip. Importation began 1996.

MSR POR		N/A	N/A	$2,900	$2,300	$1,925	$1,800	$1,650

DARNE DAMON PETRIK - 12, 16, 20 ga. or .410 bore (special order only), boxlock action, with or w/o ejectors.

Base price for this model is $12,350 w/o ejectors, $14,300 with ejectors.

SxS Sliding Breech Models

Add $1,100 for single trigger on the following models.

R 11 - 12, 16, 20, 28 ga. or .410 bore, half pistol grip stock, light engraving.
The base price for this model is $6,800.

R 12 - similar to R 11, except with better engraving.
The base price for this model is $11,700.

R 13 - 12, 16, or 20 ga., straight or pistol grip stock, traditional action with bouquet engraving and obturator discs.
The base price for this model is $12,350.

R 14 - 12, 16, or 20 ga., slug gun, choice of forearms, light engraving, and optional cheek rest pistol grip stock was optional. Importation disc. circa 2002.

	N/A	$4,300	$3,400	$2,675	$2,250	$1,950	$1,760

Last MSR was $6,600.

R 15 - 12, 16, 20, 24, 28 ga., or .410 bore, select walnut stock and forearm with fine checkering, large scroll engraving, obturator disks.
The base price for this model is $14,300.

R 16 - same as R 15, except has 3 in. chambers. Importation disc. circa 2002.

	N/A	$4,600	$3,625	$2,900	$2,450	$1,975	$1,825

Last MSR was $7,800.

GRADING - PPGS™	100%	98%	95%	90%	80%	70%	60%

R 17 - 12 (including Mag.), 16, 20, 24, 28 ga., or .410 bore., Magnum model (3 in. chambers), customer's choice engraving patterns, superior quality wood finish. Importation disc. circa 2002.

	N/A	$6,900	$5,900	$4,950	$3,625	$2,950	$2,575

Last MSR was $8,900.

RHS - all gauges, top-of-the-line model incorporating customer's choice of engraving style, type of inlays, and checkering pattern, best quality wood. Due to the unique nature of this model, each specimen must be appraised individually. New guns are priced per individual customer order.

V 19 - all gauges, easy opening large key action, top quality walnut and checkering, full coverage rose and scroll engraving with chiseled fences.

The base price for this model is $20,800.

V 20 - similar to V 19, except has deep relief rosace engraving and chiseled fences. Importation disc. circa 2002.

	N/A	$8,950	$7,600	$6,275	$5,350	$4,200	$3,150

Last MSR was $12,300.

V 21 - similar to V 19, except has 100% coverage English rose and scroll engraving and chiseled fences. Importation disc. circa 2002.

	N/A	$10,250	$8,650	$7,425	$6,150	$5,250	$4,200

Last MSR was $14,400.

V 22 - similar to V 21, except has 100% engraving coverage featuring bouquet patterns and deeply chiseled fences, sculpted shoulders, best quality walnut.

The base price for this model is $29,990.

VHS - all gauges, top-of-the-line model incorporating customer's choice of engraving style, type of inlays, and checkering pattern, best quality wood. Due to the unique nature of this model, each specimen must be appraised individually. New guns are priced per individual customer order.

DAUDSONS ARMOURY

Current manufacturer located in Peshawar, Pakistan. No current U.S. importation.

Daudsons Armoury's orgins stretch back over two centuries dealing in the sporting arms and defense weapons trade. The company provides weapons for the armed forces of Pakistan as well as the Defence Ministry.

Daudsons Armoury manufactures the DSA line of 12 ga. shotguns. There are four basic models: DSA Shooter, DSA Commando, DSA Sure Shot, and the DSA Security. All are manufactured from high grade alloy steel, with black synthetic stocks and forearms, and all parts are completely interchangeable. Daudsons also manufactures double barrel rifles and a semi-auto .22 cal. rifle. For more information on these guns, including pricing and U.S. availability, please contact the company directly (see Trademark Index).

DAVID MILLER CO.

Current custom rifle manufacturer located in Tucson, AZ since 1973.

The David Miller Co., composed of David Miller and Curt Crum, is a custom rifle shop building best quality bolt action rifles only. All guns are built per individual custom order and the company should be contacted directly for more information and price quotations.

All currently crafted rifles from the David Miller Co. are made using highly modified and finished Winchester Model 70 Super Grade actions or, on rare occasion, a Weatherby Mark V action. Two models of rifles are crafted in the Miller shop, the Classic and the Marksmen. The Classic is the top-of-the-line in custom bolt action rifles available today and is priced starting at $48,000. The Marksmen is equally well constructed but without many of the very labor-intensive features and is standard with a laminated wood stock rather than top quality walnut. The Marksmen is intended as a serious hunting rifle and has a starting price of $24,000. The waiting period for either the Classic or the Marksman is about 2 1/2 years. Please contact the David Miller Co. directly for a quotation on a new rifle (see Trademark Index).

GRADING - PPGS™	100%	98%	95%	90%	80%	70%	60%

Used rifles should be individually appraised to ascertain current values. Very few genuine Miller rifles ever appear on the used gun market. At the 2004 Safari Club International annual convention, an early David Miller Co. custom rifle, crafted around a much modified and refined Mauser G33/40 action and chambered for the .30-06 cartridge, equivalent to today's Classic rifle, sold used for $24,000.

DAVIDSON FIREARMS

Previously manufactured by Fábrica de Armas, located in Eibar, Spain.

SHOTGUNS: SxS

MODEL 63B - 12, 16, 20, 28 ga., or .410 bore, 25, 26, 28, or 30 in. barrels, Anson & Deeley boxlock, engraved and nickel plated frame, various chokes, walnut checkered stock. Mfg. 1963-disc.

	$350	$315	$275	$250	$225	$200	$175

Add 30% for 28 ga. or .410 bore.

✳ *Model 63B Magnum* - similar to 63B, except 10 ga. Mag., 12, or 20 ga. Mag., 32 in. barrel.

12 or 20 ga.	$395	$360	$325	$275	$230	$195	$165
10 ga.	$425	$375	$330	$300	$275	$250	$225

MODEL 69SL - 12 or 20 ga., true detachable sidelock action, engraved nickel plated action, 26 in. and 28 in. barrels, imp. cyl. and mod., mod. and full, checkered walnut stock. Mfg. 1963-76.

	$415	$395	$375	$340	$320	$290	$260

MODEL 73 STAGECOACH - 12 or 20 ga., detachable sidelock, exposed hammers, 3 in. chambers, 20 in. mod. and full barrels, checkered walnut stock. Mfg. 1976-disc.

	$275	$260	$220	$200	$175	$165	$155

DAVIDSON'S

Current distributor located in Prescott, AZ.

While Davidson's is not a manufacturer or an importer, this company has been responsible for many special and limited editions that are listed with quantities, but without used values, since they may vary greatly from region to region.

Make/Model	Qty. Made	Year Issue	Retail Price
SPECIAL/LIMITED EDITIONS			
BERETTA			
✳ *Revolvers* ❖ Stampede Ltd. Matched Pair	115	2006	$1,060
BROWNING			
✳ *Handguns*			
❖ BDA Special Limited Edition	N/A	2004	$630
❖ Buck Mark Camper Special Edition	N/A	N/A	$310
❖ Buck Mark Hunter Special Edition	N/A	2006	$340
❖ Buck Mark Grade I John Browning Endowment	2,500	2006	$500
❖ Buck Mark High Grade John Browning Endowment	1,001	2006	$655
COLT ✳ *Pistols* ❖ Colt Tiger Govt. Nickel .38 Super	N/A	1994	$1,000
❖ Colt Panther Govt. .38 Super	250	1995	$1,070
❖ Colt IPSC Standard Tactical Ltd. Ed.	1,500	1995	$1,398
❖ Colt IPSC Superior Tactical Ltd. Ed.	500	1995	$1,802
❖ Colt IPSC Deluxe Tactical Ltd. Ed.	250	1995	$2,660

Make/Model	Qty. Made	Year Issue	Retail Price
FIRESTORM			
✳ *Handguns*			
❖ **Government Special Edition**	N/A	2004	$334
MARLIN ✳ *Rifles* ❖ **Model 336 Ltd. .35 Rem. cal.**	1,001	2000	$515
❖ **Model 1886 Ltd.**	251	2005	$1,450
❖ **Model 1894 Ltd. .41 Mag.**	251	2005	$695
❖ **Model 1894CC41-Ltd. .41 Mag. cal.**	1,001	1999	$715
❖ **Model 1894SC 44/45 Ltd**	1,050	1997	$460
❖ **Model 1894 Cowboy Carbine .44-40 WCF**	325	2000	$715
❖ **Model 1894 Cowboy Carbine Limited .32-20 WCF**	501	2005	$860
❖ **Model 1894SS .357 Ltd.**	351	2006	$660
❖ **Model 1894SS .41 Ltd.**	251	2006	$660
❖ **Model 1894SS .44 Ltd.**	351	2006	$660
❖ **Model 1894SS .45 Ltd.**	251	2006	$660
❖ **Model 1895 Ltd I/II .45-70 Govt.**	2,002	1997	$671
❖ **Model 1895 Ltd. III .45-70 Govt.**	1,001	1999	$715
❖ **Model 1895 Ltd IV .45-70 Govt.**	1,001	2000	$729
❖ **Model 1895GS Ltd. Ed. Guide Gun .45-70**	501	2006	N/A
❖ **Model 917VSFT .17 Mag. Stainless**	250	2007	$450
PUMA			
✳ *Rifles*			
❖ **Model 92 Ltd. Ed. .454 Casull & .480 Ruger**	N/A	2004	$603
SMITH & WESSON			
✳ *Handguns*			
❖ **Model 66 Combat Magnum Special .357 Mag.**	N/A	2003	$641
❖ **Model 629-5 Hunter .44 Mag.**	N/A	2004	$1,059
❖ **Model 657-5 Hunter .41 Mag.**	N/A	2003	N/A
SPRINGFIELD ARMORY			
✳ *Pistols*			
❖ **Leatham Legend Series TGO 1 Service Model**	N/A	2003	$2,999
❖ **Leatham Legend Series TGO 3 Service Model**	N/A	2003	$1,295
❖ **Leatham Legend Series TGO 2 Service Model**	N/A	2003	$1,899
STEYR			
✳ *Handguns*			
❖ **S-Series Special Edition**	N/A	2004	$610
❖ **M-A1 Series Special Edition**	N/A	2004	$610
STURM-RUGER			
✳ *Handguns*			
❖ **WB Ruger NRA Limited Edition Mark II**	N/A	2003	$334
❖ **Mark II Competition Target Special Edition**	N/A	2003	$339
❖ **P90 Special Edition Series**	N/A	2003	$448
❖ **P90 Guns & Ammo 45th Anniversary Special Edition**	45	N/A	$560
❖ **Vaquero 45 Years of Guns & Ammo Special Ltd. Edition**	N/A	2003	$599
❖ **Vaquero Dual Cylinder Special Limited Edition**	N/A	2003	$600
❖ **New Vaquero Limited Edition .32-20 WCF**	N/A	2004	$642
❖ **Bisley Single-Six Vaquero Special Edition**	N/A	2004	$555
❖ **GP-100 Special Limited Edition .357 Mag.**	N/A	2003	$555
❖ **Super Blackhawk Hunter .41 Mag.**	N/A	2004	N/A

Make/Model	Qty. Made	Year Issue	Retail Price
❖ Super Blackhawk Bisley Hunter .41 Mag.	N/A	2004	N/A
❖ New Vaquero Montado	N/A	2007	$714
❖ Mark III 22/45	N/A	2007	$361
❖ Mark III 22/45 Hunter	N/A	2007	$345

TAURUS

✳ Handguns

❖ Model 17 Tracker Ltd. .17 Mag.	N/A	2005	N/A

WALTHER

✳ Pistols

❖ P22 2 Barrel Set	N/A	2006	$450

WINCHESTER

✳ Rifles

❖ Model 1892 Limited Series	500	2004	$1,075
❖ Model 1892 Limited Series Trapper	N/A	2004	$1,075
❖ Model 9417 Limited .17 HMR	N/A	2004	$530
❖ Model 1885 Limited Series	N/A	2003	$1,360
❖ Model 1895 Take-Down Ltd. .405 Win.	1,001	2006	$1,475
❖ Model 1886 Solid Frame .45-70 Govt.	501	2006	$1,370
❖ Model 1886 Solid Frame .45-90 BPCR	501	2006	$1,370
❖ Model 1886 Take-Down .45-90 BPCR	501	2006	$1,450
❖ Model 1885 Ltd. Series .32-20 WCF	N/A	2006	N/A
❖ Model 1885 Ltd. Series .38-55 WCF	N/A	2006	N/A
❖ Model 1885 Ltd. Series .45-70	N/A	2006	N/A
❖ Model 1885 Ltd. Series .45-90	N/A	2006	N/A
❖ Model 1885 Ltd. Series .50-90	N/A	2006	N/A
❖ Model 1885 Ltd. Series Creedmoor .45-90	N/A	2006	N/A
❖ Model 1886 Deluxe Ltd. Series Takedown Octagon	N/A	2007	N/A
❖ Model 1886 Deluxe Ltd. Series Takedown Round	N/A	2007	N/A
❖ 1886 Deluxe Take Down Ltd. .45-70	501	2007	$2,080
❖ 1885 Creedmoor Ltd. .50-90 cal.	126	2007	$2,227
❖ 1885 Creedmoor Ltd. .45-90 cal.	126	2007	$2,227

DAVIS INDUSTRIES

Previous manufacturer located in Chino, CA 1995-2001. Previously located in Mira Loma, CA until 1995. Distributor sales only.

Davis Industries provided a lifetime warranty on all products, which is now void.

GRADING - PPGS™	100%	98%	95%	90%	80%	70%	60%

DERRINGERS

D-SERIES DERRINGER - .22 LR, .22 Mag., .25 ACP, .32 ACP, .32 H&R Mag. (new 1995), .38 Spl. (new 1992), or 9mm Para. cal., O/U steel construction, 2.4 or 2 3/4 (.38 Spl. only) in. vent. rib barrel, 9 1/2 or 11 1/2 oz., black Teflon or chrome finish. Disc. 2001.

$65	$55	$45	$40	$35	$30	$30

Last MSR was $75.

Add $23 for Big-Bore series (larger frame) in .22 Mag., .32 H&R Mag., .38 Spl., or 9mm Para. cal.
Add $29 for Long-Bore cals. (.22 Mag., .32 H&R Mag. - disc., .38 Spl., or 9mm Para.).
In this series, the .25 ACP cal. is the Model D-25 and the .32 ACP cal. is the Model D-32.

GRADING - PPGS™	100%	98%	95%	90%	80%	70%	60%

LONG BORE DERRINGER - .22 Mag., .32 H&R Mag. (disc. 1998), .38 Spl., or 9mm Para. cal., similar to D Series, except has 3 3/4 in. barrel, 13 oz. Mfg. 1995-2001.

	100%	98%	95%	90%	80%	70%	60%
	$90	$75	$65	$55	$45	$40	$35

Last MSR was $104.

PISTOLS: SEMI-AUTO

P-32 - .32 ACP cal., single action, 6 shot mag., 2.8 in. barrel, black Teflon or chrome finish, laminated wood grips, 22 oz. Mfg. 1987-2001.

	100%	98%	95%	90%	80%	70%	60%
	$75	$65	$55	$50	$45	$35	$35

Last MSR was $88.

P-380 - .380 ACP cal., single action, similar to P-32, 5 shot mag., 2.8 in. barrel, bright chrome or black Teflon finish, internal shock resister for recoil, wood (disc.) or black synthetic grips, 22 oz. Mfg. 1989-2001.

	100%	98%	95%	90%	80%	70%	60%
	$85	$75	$65	$55	$45	$35	$35

Last MSR was $98.

DAVIS N.R.

Please refer to the Crescent Fire Arms Co. listing.

DEFOURNEY

Previous long gun manufacturer located in Belgium.

Defourney specialized in both quality sidelock and boxlock (with or w/o sideplates) shotguns in both SxS and O/U configuration. Prices range from $750-$3,250 for boxlock shotguns and start in the $3,500 range for sidelock models, assuming 80% or better original condition.

DEHAAN SHOTGUNS LTD.

Current shotgun manufacturer/importer located in Rigby, ID.

DeHaan shotguns are good quality O/U and SxS models, with a wide variety of engraving and wood options available. Many guns are built per customer order. Please contact the company directly for more information, including availability, pricing and delivery time (see Trademark Index).

DEMAS, ETS

Current manufacturer located in St. Etienne, France since 1967. Currently imported beginning 2004 by Verney-Carron USA, Inc., located in Clay Center, KS. Previously imported by The Drumming Stump, located in Circle Pines, MN.

During 2004, Verney-Carron S.A., located in St. Etienne, France (please refer to separate listing) purchased Demas, which manufactures a full line of quality O/U and SxS rifles and shotguns. Prices vary according to configuration, engraving options, and quality of wood. Please contact Verney-Carron for more information, including current model availability and U.S. pricing (see Trademark Index).

DEMRO

Previous manufacturer located in Manchester, CT.

RIFLES: SEMI-AUTO

T.A.C. MODEL 1 RIFLE - .45 ACP or 9mm Luger cal., blow back operation, 16 7/8 in. barrel, open bolt firing system, lock-in receiver must be set to fire, also available in carbine model.

	100%	98%	95%	90%	80%	70%	60%
	$650	$595	$525	$475	$425	$395	$360

XF-7 WASP CARBINE - .45 ACP or 9mm Luger cal., blow back operation, 16 7/8 in. barrel.

	100%	98%	95%	90%	80%	70%	60%
	$650	$595	$525	$475	$425	$395	$360

Add $45 for case.

GRADING - PPGS™	100%	98%	95%	90%	80%	70%	60%

DEPAR

Previous manufacturer located in Istanbul, Turkey.
Depar manufactured both semi-auto and O/U shotguns.

SHOTGUNS

ATAK O/U - 12 ga. only, 2 3/4 in. chambers, ejectors, SST.

	$350	$295	$250	$225	$200	$185	$170

Last MSR was $350.

Add approx. 30% with scroll engraving and walnut stock and forearm.

ATILGAN SEMI-AUTO - 12 ga. only, 3 in. chamber, gas operated, includes multi-chokes.

	$170	$150	$135	$125	$115	$105	$95

Last MSR was $195.

✳ *Atilgan Semi-Auto De Luxe* - similar to Atilgan Semi-Auto, except has engraved receiver and deluxe walnut stock and forearm.

	$350	$295	$250	$225	$200	$185	$170

Last MSR was $350.

SAFARI SLIDE ACTION - 12 ga. only, 3 in. chamber, synthetic stock standard.

	$170	$150	$135	$125	$115	$105	$95

Last MSR was $170.

Add 10% for walnut stock and forearm.
Add approx. 50% for nickel chrome receiver finish and light scroll engraving.

DESERT INDUSTRIES, INC.

Previous manufacturer located in Las Vegas, NV 1991-1996. See listing under Steel City Arms, Inc. for older models.

In 1990, Desert Industries, Inc. was created - this new company was the same as Steel City Arms, Inc. More recently manufactured guns will have the Las Vegas slide address.

PISTOLS: SEMI-AUTO

THE DOUBLE DEUCE - .22 LR cal., double action, 2 1/2 in. barrel, matte stainless steel construction, 6 shot mag., rosewood grips, 15 oz. Limited mfg. 1991-96.

	$350	$295	$275	$225	$195	$165	$140

Last MSR was $400.

TWO BIT SPECIAL - .25 ACP cal., double action, 2 1/2 in. barrel, similar to Double Deuce, except has 5 shot mag., 15 oz. Approx. 12 protoypes mfg. 1991-96.

	$375	$350	$295	$235	$205	$175	$150

Last MSR was $400.

DETONICS FIREARMS INDUSTRIES

Previous manufacturer located in Bellevue, WA 1976-1988. Detonics was sold in early 1988 to the New Detonics Manufacturing Corporation, a wholly owned subsidiary of "1045 Investors Group Limited."

Please refer to the New Detonics Manufacturing Corporation in the "N" section of this text for complete model listings of both companies.

DETONICS USA

Previous manufacturer located in Pendergrass, GA circa 2004-mid-2007.

PISTOLS: SEMI-AUTO

COMBATMASTER - .45 ACP cal., 3 1/2 in. barrel, 6 shot, available in stainless steel (fixed sights), black bonded, two-tone, or mirror polish finish, 34 oz.

	$1,050	$875	$750	$650	$575	$500	$425

Last MSR was $1,200.

Add $40 for two-tone finish, $100 for black bonded finish, $375 for mirror polish finish, or $550 for mirror polish finish w/stag grips.

GRADING - PPGS™	100%	98%	95%	90%	80%	70%	60%

9-11-01 - .45 ACP cal., 5 in. barrel, 7 shot, logo engraved checkered rosewood grips, low profile fixed combat sights, available in black bonded, two-tone, or mirror polish finish.

	$1,050	$875	$750	$650	$575	$500	$425

Last MSR was $1,200.

Add $40 for two-tone finish, $100 for black bonded finish, or $375 for mirror polish finish.

STREETMASTER - .45 ACP cal., 5 in. barrel, 6 shot, low profile fixed combat sights, stainless steel construction, logo engraved checkered rosewood grips.

	$1,050	$875	$750	$650	$575	$500	$425

Last MSR was $1,200.

SERVICEMASTER - .45 ACP cal., 4 1/4 in. barrel, 7 shot, stainless steel construction, low profile fixed combat sights, logo engraved checkered rosewood grips, choice of Standard or Compact frame, 39 oz.

	$1,050	$875	$750	$650	$575	$500	$425

Last MSR was $1,200.

SCOREMASTER - .45 ACP cal., stainless steel construction, 5 in. barrel, 7 shot, MMC adj. rear sight, logo engraved checkered rosewood grips, available in Tactical (adj. sights and rail) or Target (Bo-Mar adj. sights, ext. slide stop, mag. release, and ambidextrous safety) configuration, 43 oz.

	$1,475	$1,250	$1,050	$925	$800	$775	$625

Last MSR was $1,650.

MILITARY TACTICAL - .45 ACP cal., black bonded finish, adj. sights, includes rail, forward serrations, checkered front strap, and lanyard ring.

	$1,750	$1,525	$1,350	$1,125	$950	$800	$675

Last MSR was $1,975.

DIAMOND SHOTGUNS

Please refer to the Adco Sales Inc. listing.

DIARM S.A.

Previous manufacturing conglomerate (25 companies) located in Deba, Spain 1986-1989. Previously imported and distributed by American Arms, Inc. located in North Kansas City, MO. Older Diarm models can be found under the American Arms, Inc. heading in this publication.

DIAWA

Previous U.S. firearms importer and distributor.

Diawa imported various firearms circa 1960s-early 1970s. Configurations included semi-auto shotguns mfg. by Singer Nikko, Ltd. of Japan, and bolt action rifles. Values are based on the current utilitarian value, since there is little collectibility on these guns.

DICKSON & MACNAUGHTON

Current trading company established in 1996, and located in Edinburgh, Scotland.

During 1999, the directors of James MacNaughton & Sons acquired the whole share capital of John Dickson & Son, from whom they purchased the MacNaughton manufacturing rights in 1996. The two companies now trade under the name of Dickson & MacNaughton, and trademarks currently owned are: John Dickson & Son, Dan'l Fraser, Alex Henry, James MacNaughton & Sons, Alex Martin, and Thomas Mortimer.

JOHN DICKSON & SON

Current trademark purchased during 1999 by James MacNaughton & Sons, located in Edinburgh, Scotland. Both trademarks are currently traded under the name Dickson & MacNaughton.

Please contact the company directly for more information on this trademark (see Trademark Index).

GRADING - PPGS™	100%	98%	95%	90%	80%	70%	60%

DIXIE GUN WORKS

Current importer, distributor, and catalog retailer established 1954, and located in Union City, TN.

In addition to importing a variety of firearms, Dixie Gun Works has also established itself as one of the leaders in black powder reproductions and replicas, related shooting accessories, and acoutrements. For more information regarding black powder reproductions and replicas and related shooting accessories, please contact the company directly and request a catalog. Please refer to the *Blue Book of Modern Black Powder Arms* by John Allen for more information on Dixie Gun Work's black powder reproductions and replicas.

Black Powder Reproductions & Replicas by Dennis Adler is also an invaluable source for most black powder reproductions and replicas, and includes hundreds of color images on most popular makes/models, provides manufacturer/trademark histories, and up-to-date information on related items/accessories for black powder shooting - www.bluebookinc.com

RIFLES: REPRODUCTIONS

The following Pedersoli models are a partial listing of rifles currently available from Dixie Gun Works. PLease contact the company directly for more information, including current offerings and pricing.

REMINGTON ROLLING BLOCK LONG RANGE RIFLE - .40-65 or .45-70 Govt. cal., 30 in. tapered octagon barrel, case colored receiver and buttplate, vernier tang sight.

MSR $900	$775	$695	$595	$500	$400	$350	$325

    Add $150 for .45-70 Govt. cal.

1874 SHARPS LIGHTWEIGHT HUNTER - .45-70 Govt. cal., reproduction of the Sharps No. 3 sporting rifle, 32 in. blued tapered octagon barrel, straight stock, case colored receiver and buttplate, vernier tang sight. Disc. 2004.

	$865	$725	$600	$500	$400	$350	$300

Last MSR was $975.

1874 SHARPS SILHOUETTE RIFLE - .40-65 or 45-70 Govt. cal., reproduction of the Sharps No. 1 sporting rifle, 30 in. blued tapered octagon barrel, pistol grip stock, case colored receiver and buttplate.

MSR $1,100	$950	$800	$650	$550	$475	$400	$325

    Add $900 for engraving with in-the-white receiver and buttplate.

1873 TRAPDOOR CARBINE/RIFLE - .45-70 Govt. cal., blued furniture, oil finished American walnut stock, 7 or 9 lbs.

MSR $875	$765	$675	$600	$500	$425	$350	$275

    Add $225 for Officer's Model, with case colored lock and trigger guard, single set trigger.
    Add $100 for Rifle.

KODIAK MARK IV DOUBLE EXPRESS SxS RIFLE - .45-70 Govt. cal., back action, browned 24 in. barrels with triple leaf express sights, color case hardened frame, trigger guard, and hammers.

MSR $3,250	$2,825	$2,450	$2,150	$1,850	$1,600	$1,400	$1,200

DLASK ARMS CORP.

Current manufacturer located in British Columbia, Canada. Direct sales.

PISTOLS: SEMI-AUTO

Dlask Arms Corp. manufactures custom M-1911 style custom guns for all levels of competition. Current models include the TC Tactical Carry at $1,250 MSR, basic Dlask 1911 at $1,250 MSR, Dlask 1911 "Pro" at $1,560 MSR, and the Dlask 1911 "Pro Plus" at $2,500 MSR. Previous models included the Gold Team at $2,000 last MSR, Silver Team L/S at

GRADING - PPGS™	100%	98%	95%	90%	80%	70%	60%

$1,700 last MSR, and the Master Class at $3,500 last MSR. In addition, Dlask also manufactures a wide variety of custom parts for the M-1911. For more information, please contact the company directly (see Trademark Index).

RIFLES

Current models include the DAR-701 semi rifle in various configurations (AR-15 style) at $1,550 MSR. Please contact the company directly for more information, including pricing and availability (see Trademark Index).

DOMINGO, ACHA

Please refer to Acha section.

DOMINO, IGI

Previous Italian company absorbed during 1990 by FAS (see separate listing in F section). Previously imported by Mandall Shooting Supplies located in Scottsdale, AZ.

PISTOLS: SEMI-AUTO

MODEL OP 601 MATCH PISTOL - .22 Short cal., 5 shot, 5.6 in. barrel, match sights, full target grips, vent. barrel and slide to reduce recoil, adj. and removable trigger.

$1,300	$1,000	$715	$635	$550	$495	$440

Last MSR was $1,495.

MODEL SP 602 MATCH PISTOL - .22 LR cal., 5 1/2 in. barrel, similar to 601, but .22 LR and slightly different trigger.

$1,300	$1,100	$800	$700	$600	$550	$495

Last MSR was $1,495.

DOUBLESTAR CORP.

Current rifle manufacturer located in Winchester, KY. Distributed by JT Distributing. Dealer sales only.

RIFLES/CARBINES: SEMI-AUTO

DSC STARCAR CARBINE - .223 Rem. cal., AR-15 design, fixed post-ban CAR type stock, 16 in. barrel, A2 or flattop upper receiver, 7 lbs.

MSR $775	$695	$625	$550	$485	$440	$400	$365

Add $65 for detachable carrying handle.

DSC STAR M4 CARBINE - .223 Rem. cal., AR-15 M4 carbine design, fixed M4 style post-ban buttstock, 16 in. barrel, M4 handguard, 6.76 lbs.

MSR $875	$795	$715	$640	$565	$500	$465	$430

Add $65 for detachable carrying handle.

DSC STAR DISSIPATOR - .223 Rem. cal., AR-15 design, 16 in. dissipator barrel with full length handguard, A2 or CAR buttstock.

MSR $875	$775	$695	$625	$550	$500	$465	$430

Add $65 for detachable carrying handle.

DSC STAR-15 LIGHTWEIGHT TACTICAL - .223 Rem. cal., AR-15 design, 16 in. fluted H-Bar barrel with attached muzzle brake, shorty A2 buttstock, A2 or flattop upper receiver, 6 1/4 lbs. Disc. 2004.

$775	$695	$625	$550	$500	$465	$430

Last MSR was $880.

Add $70 for detachable carrying handle.

DSC STAR-15 RIFLE - .223 Rem. cal., AR-15 design, 20 in. match barrel, ribbed forearm, A2 or flattop upper receiver, 8 lbs.

MSR $775	$695	$625	$550	$485	$440	$400	$365

Add $80 for flattop with detachable carrying handle.

GRADING - PPGS™	100%	98%	95%	90%	80%	70%	60%

DSC STAR-15 9MM CARBINE - 9mm Para cal., AR-15 design, 16 in. barrel, ribbed forearm, A2 or flattop upper receiver, 7 1/2 lbs. Mfg. 2004 only.

	$875	$775	$675	$575	$525	$475	$425

Last MSR was $995.

DSC CRITTERSLAYER - .223 Rem. cal., AR-15 design, 24 in. fluted Shaw barrel, full length Picatinny rail on receiver and Badger handguard, two-stage match trigger, palmrest, ergonomic pistol grip with finger grooves, includes Harris LMS swivel bipod, flattop or high rise upper receiver, 11 1/2 lbs.

MSR $1,300	$1,185	$1,000	$875	$800	$700	$625	$550

Add $40 for ported barrel.

* *DSC CritterSlayer Jr.* - similar to CritterSlayer, except has 16 in. barrel and fully adj. A-2 style buttstock, DSC flattop or high rise upper receiver.

MSR $1,000	$875	$750	$650	$550	$450	$375	$325

Add $70 for detachable carrying handle or $40 for removable front sight.

DSC EXPEDITION CARBINE/RIFLE - .223 Rem. cal., AR-15 design, 16 or 20 in. lightweight contour barrel, A2 or flattop upper receiver, 8 lbs.

MSR $825	$725	$650	$575	$500	$450	$400	$365

DSC STAR-15 DCM SERVICE RIFLE - 5.56 NATO cal., AR-15 design, 20 in. match barrel, National Match front and rear sights, two-stage match trigger, DCM free-floating handguard, 8 lbs.

MSR $1,000	$895	$825	$725	$650	$550	$485	$440

DSC TARGET CARBINE - .223 Rem. cal., AR-15 design, features 16 in. dissipator barrel with full length round one-piece National Match handguard, flip-up sights, Picatinny rail, flattop upper receiver.

MSR $1,175	$1,000	$875	$775	$695	$625	$550	$485

DSC SUPER MATCH RIFLE - .223 Rem. cal., AR-15 design, 16, 20, 22, or 24 in. stainless steel Super Match barrel, flattop or high rise upper receiver, includes Picatinny rail and one-piece National Match free-floating handguard.

MSR $875	$775	$695	$625	$550	$500	$465	$430

DOWNSIZER CORPORATION

Current pistol manufacturer established in 1994, and located in Santee, CA. Dealer sales only.

DERRINGERS

MODEL WSP (WORLD'S SMALLEST PISTOL) - 9mm Para. (disc. 1999), .357 Mag., .357 Sig. (disc. 1999), .40 S&W (disc. 1999), or .45 ACP cal., single shot pistol, tip-up 2.1 in. barrel with push-button release, internal firing pin block, double action only, synthetic grips, stainless steel, overall size is smaller than a playing card, 11 oz. New 1997.

MSR $499	$415	$300	$235	$185	$150	$135	$110

DREYSE

Previously manufactured by Rheinische Metallwaren and Machinenfabrik, located in Sommerda, Germany.

PISTOLS: SEMI-AUTO

MODEL 1907 AUTOMATIC - 7.65mm/.32 ACP cal., 8 shot, 3 1/2 in. barrel, blue, fixed sights, hard rubber grips. Mfg. 1907-14.

	$250	$185	$150	$120	$95	$75	$50

MODEL 1910 - 9mm Para. cal., mfg. 1912-1915. Production estimated at 1,000 pistols, usually found in the 12xx-13xx ser. no. range. Seldom encountered.

	$6,500	$5,500	$4,500	$3,500	$2,500	$2,000	$1,500

GRADING - PPGS™	100%	98%	95%	90%	80%	70%	60%

VEST POCKET AUTOMATIC - .25 ACP cal., 6 shot, 2 in. barrel, blue, fixed sights, hard rubber grips. Mfg. 1912-15.

		$325	$235	$150	$130	$100	$75	$65

Add 100% for early version with double extractors.

RIFLES: SEMI-AUTO

1907 LIGHT RIFLE - 7.65mm (.32 ACP) cal., 18 3/4 in. barrel, staggered box 6-9 shot mag., used mostly for small game hunting, earlier rifles can be found with full "Rheinmetall" and "Dreyse" markings, and later rifles do not have markings, most have sporter stocks, some have military type stocks with cheekpieces and full forends to near the muzzle, other markings may include European sporting goods dealers and various police agencies, including the South American police. Mfg. 1907-circa 1913.

	$2,500	$2,200	$2,000	$1,800	$1,400	$1,000	$600

Values shown are for the sporter type stock.

DRILLINGS

A Drilling is a three-barrel combination gun (two shotgun barrels and a rifle barrel, vice versa, or three shotgun barrels). Normally, two triggers fire the shotgun barrels and one of them activates the rifle barrel when the barrel selector is moved forward (usually located on the upper tang). Most well-made Drillings in above average condition are surprisingly accurate when using the rifle barrel(s), because of the stiffness gained with three barrels fixed together.

DRILLING CONFIGURATIONS & EXPLANATIONS

Please refer to illustrations below depicting the most commonly encountered Drilling configurations.

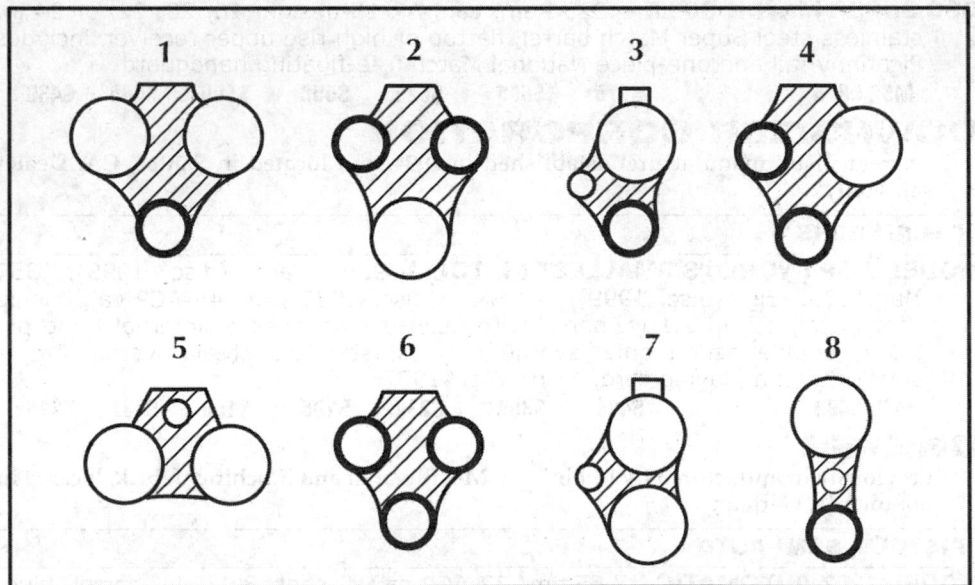

Illustration No. 1 - Normal Drilling configuration with 2 shotgun barrels over a rimmed, centerfire rifle (most are 16 ga. x 16 ga. by either 9.3x72R or 8x57JR cal.).

Illustration No. 2 - Two rifle barrels over a shotgun. This configuration will normally command twice the price as No. 1. German designation is "Doppelbüchsdrilling".

Illustration No. 3 - Three barrels with no two being the same gauge or caliber. This configuration is very collectible, especially if the smallest caliber is .22 LR. Again, price will be double of No. 1.

Illustration No. 4 - Sometimes called a Bock Drilling with one shotgun and two rifle barrels. This variation brings a good premium over No. 1.

Illustration No. 5 - Rib Drilling with rifle caliber generally small (.22 LR or .22 Hornet). German designation is "Schienendrilling".

Illustration No. 6 - Three shotgun barrels with the same gauge or three rifle barrels with different calibers. This configuration is quite rare and healthy premiums are charged over No. 1.

Illustration No. 7 - A variation of No. 3, this configuration features shotgun O/U barrels with a rifle barrel on the side. German designation is "Bock-Doppelpelflinte mit seitlichem Kleinkaliberlauf".

Illustration No. 8 - Very unusual - a 3-barrel drilling in vertical design - 2 rifle barrels under a shotgun barrel. This configuration is seldomly encountered.

The following German nomenclatures apply as follows: single barrel rifle = Büchse; SxS double rifle = Doppelbüchse; O/U double rifle = Bock-Doppelbüchse; SxS double shotgun = Doppelflinte; O/U double shotgun = Bock-Doppelflinte; SxS double shotgun, rifle bbl. under = Drilling; SxS double shotgun, rifle bbl. on top = Schienendrilling; single shotgun, rifle bbl. under = Bock-Büchsflinte; single shotgun, rifle bbl. at side = Büchsflinte; single shotgun, rifle bbl. under and at side = Bock-Drilling; double rifle, shot bbl. under = Doppelbüchsdrilling; O/U double shotgun, rifle bbl. at side = Bock-Doppelflinte mit seitlichem Kleinkaliberlauf; SxS double shotgun, plus two rifle bbls. = Vierling.

DRILLING HISTORY

For over 145 years Drillings have been the classic hunting gun of many European countries, especially Germany and Austria. Because a single hunting trip may require shooting both wildfowl and animals (often times within several hours), Europeans have long favored a single long-arm that could afford both rifle and shotgun shooting, be reliable, and not wear the hunter out while transporting it in the field. In order to save weight, Hubertus Gewehrfabrik of Suhl was the first company to use light alloy metal for receiver construction during 1933. The strength of the SM Spezial-Einsatz Stahl was 55-62 kg./mm2, while the strength of steel was 37-45kg. This weight savings made the drilling even more popular in Europe, becasue it could be carried all day with little fatigue.

Americans, on the other hand, have not placed as much emphasis on this combination gun principle, and more often than not have chosen to buy both a rifle and shotgun for each specific hunting application. Since Drillings are becoming more popular, collectibility has improved in this country for those collectors who see the utility and functionality of these mostly hand-assembled weapons. Very few Drillings manufactured before WWII are alike today in configuration and condition.

DRILLING CALIBERS

Some people may be confused as to how the European metric calibers compare to domestic cartridges in terms of overall performance. This comparison has been added to assist you when contemplating what type of field performance, velocity, and killing power you can expect in these European calibers: 9.3x74 is similar to .375 Win. Mag., 9.3x72R is similar to .44 Mag. or .44-40 WCF, 8x57JRS is similar to .30-06, .30-30 Win. is 7.62x51R, 8x57JR is similar to .30-06, 7x65R is similar to .280 Rem., 7x57R is similar to .257 Roberts, 6.5x57R is similar to .243 Win., 5.6x52R is a .22 Savage Hi-Power, 5.6x34R is similar to .22 Hornet. Drillings can also be encountered in American calibers such as .270 Win., .30-06, .30-30 Win., .38-55 WCF, or .32-20 WCF.

DRILLING VALUES AND CONDITION FACTORS

Rather than list the various manufacturers of Drillings (there are hundreds), it should be noted that guns with major trademarks and established provenances (i.e. Charles Daly, Colt Sauer, Ferlach addressed, Heym, Krieghoff, J.P. Sauer, Berlin [rare] and Suhl addressed, etc.) will usually be more collectible than other, lesser-known brands, even if the quality of workmanship is similar. The overall quality, condition, engraving, wood type/ fanciness, and carving all have to be taken into consideration when evaluating a Drilling. Some Drillings were assembled from manufactured parts by skilled and crafted gunsmiths and are sometimes better quality than factory specimens. Pre-war specimens are generally more desirable to collectors (even though less expensive than post-war variations) and to date, have outperformed post-war specimens in price appreciation. Many older pre-war specimens were designed for rimmed cartridges with lower breech pressures and should not be re-bored or reloaded for the "hotter" cartridges/loads available today. It should be noted that since Drillings are more complex than a typical shotgun, most of the manufacture has been done by hand - some guns have taken individual craftsmen over a year to fabricate! Ordering a new Drilling today would be a very expensive proposition, and buying a good used specimen will save you thousands of dollars (and maybe a year wait). For these reasons, many collectors feel Drillings today are under-priced since they can be purchased at a fraction of the cost for a new one (and may well be better quality also).

Condition is another major consideration. A gun that shows much use and is not operationally intact/correct may bring several thousand dollars less than another similar specimen showing little wear and excellent original finish (including the case colors or coin finish).

Most above average condition boxlock Drillings in the above mentioned trademarks start in the $2,250 range and can go to $10,000 and higher if the configuration, features, and condition are all desirable. Average condition boxlock Drillings w/o a famous trademark usually sell in the $1,850-$3,250 range assuming moderate engraving, metric calibers, and a few features. Sidelock Drillings typically start in the $3,500-$4,000 range, and can go well past $25,000, depending on the trademark, engraving, and desirable features. Also, while not many Drillings are available in the secondary marketplace, they have become increasingly popular due to shooting sports magazines and other gun publications. For these reasons, Drillings have to be evaluated one at a time and a COMPETENT appraisal/evaluation should be procured before buying or selling a specimen.

FEATURES THAT ADD VALUE TO DRILLINGS

Drillings with American calibers and smaller gauges will sometimes be more desirable (depending on engraving, case colors, or coin finish) than the European metric calibers (i.e. a gun configured 20 ga. x 20 ga. by .243 Win. will sell for more than a similar gun in 16 ga. x 16 ga. by 9.3 x 72R cal.). The most commonly encountered gauges and calibers are 16 ga. (most pre-war guns are chambered for 2 9/16 in.). In addition, a sidelock action will be more desirable than a boxlock, and a lot more expensive if the locks are also detachable. Drilling aficionados will mention there are four main things to look for when contemplating a drilling purchase - beauty, condition, quality, and features. Features and embellishments become very critical in ascertaining Drilling values also. A gun with deep relief engraving, carved stock, claw mounts w/ scope, buffalo horn trigger guard and buttplate, cocking indicators, two position front sight (i.e. night sight), middle set of express sights, adj. trigger, concealed upper tang peep sight, a non-Greener safety system, lightweight (under 6 1/2 lbs.), separate rifle cocking, shotgun barrel inserts in .22LR or .22 Mag. cal. (approx. 8 or 11 in. long), cartridge trap, etc. is going to be A LOT more collectible than a plain-Jane hammer model with a loose action.

> **Drillings with original, detachable claw-mounted scopes (rail-mount or swing-off) are worth a 20%-50% premium, depending on overall desirability of the gun. Most original drilling scopes are serial numbered to the gun.**

FEATURES THAT DETRACT VALUE FROM DRILLINGS

If a drilling is worn out and/or needs some service work or parts replaced, in addition to having no eye appeal remaining, values decrease significantly, and can end up in the three digits. Make sure that any drilling is mechanically inspected thoroughly, especially if it shows a lot of use, before contemplating a purchase.

DRULOV
Previous handgun manufacturer located in North Bohemia.

GRADING - PPGS™	100%	98%	95%	90%	80%	70%	60%

PISTOLS: SINGLE SHOT

PAV - .22 LR cal., single shot, 9 3/4 in. barrel, all steel construction. Imported 1986 only.

	$95	$85	$75	$65	$60	$55	$50

Last MSR was $105.

DRULOV 70 - .22 LR cal., single shot. Add $30 for set trigger. Disc. 1986.

	$105	$95	$85	$75	$70	$65	$60

Last MSR was $115.

DRULOV 75 - .22 LR cal., single shot with set trigger & micrometer sights. Also available in left-hand. Importation disc. 1991.

	$300	$250	$215	$185	$155	$140	$120

Last MSR was $349.

DRULOV 78 - .22 LR cal., similar to Drulov 75. Imported 1986 only.

	$275	$240	$200	$175	$150	$130	$110

Last MSR was $180.

DUBIEL ARMS COMPANY

Previous manufacturer located in Sherman, TX. Dubiel Arms made custom bolt action rifles from 1975-approx. 1990.

RIFLES: BOLT ACTION

BOLT ACTION RIFLE - .22-250 Rem.-.458 Win. Mag. cals., custom made bolt action, barrel length and weight to order, no sights, Canjar trigger, all steel parts, custom made rifle stocks available in five styles. Disc.

	$2,000	$1,750	$1,500	$1,275	$1,125	$975	$825

Last MSR was $2,500.

DUCKS UNLIMITED, INC.

National wildlife organization established in 1937, with headquarters located in Memphis, TN.

Model	Manufacturer	Qty.	Year	Issue Price

SHOTGUNS: DINNER GUNS (GUN-OF-THE-YEAR)

The makes and models listed reflect "dinner guns" only. Dinner guns (Gun-of-the-Year) refer to those shotguns sold at the various annual banquets held by Ducks Unlimited chapters. Dinner guns do not have a retail price. Rather, banquet auction prices can vary substantially from chapter to chapter, as can secondary market values. The price ranges listed below are general guidelines for DU dinner guns that are in unfired, NIB condition with all factory materials and boxes.

Model	Manufacturer	Qty.	Year	Issue Price
✳ Model 1100 12 ga.	Remington	500	1973	N/A

Current values for this model in NIB condition range from $4,500 - $5,000.

✳ Model 870 12 ga.	Remington	600	1974	N/A

Current values for this model in NIB condition range from $4,000-$4,500.

✳ Model 12 12 ga.	Winchester	800	1975	N/A

Current values for this model in NIB condition range from $3,500-$4,000.

✳ Model Super X-1 12 ga.	Winchester	900	1976	N/A

Current values for this model in NIB condition range from $3,000-$3,500.

✳ Model 37 12 ga. (40th Ann´y)	Ithaca	1,125	1977	N/A

Current values for this model in NIB condition range from $3,000-$3,500.

Model	Manufacturer	Qty.	Year	Issue Price
✳ *Model 51 12 ga.*	Ithaca	1,250	1978	N/A
Current values for this model in NIB condition range from $2,500-$3,000.				
✳ *Model Patrician 12 ga.*	Weatherby	1,600	1979	N/A
Current values for this model in NIB condition range from $1,500-$1,800.				
✳ *Model Centurion 12 ga.*	Weatherby	2,000	1980	N/A
Current values for this model in NIB condition range from $1,200-$1,500.				
✳ *Model 1100 12 ga. Mag.*	Remington	2,400	1981	N/A
Current values for this model in NIB condition range from $1,000-$1,300.				
✳ *Model 870 12 ga. Mag.*	Remington	3,000	1982	N/A
Current values for this model in NIB condition range from $1,000-$1,300.				
✳ *Model B-80 12 ga.*	Browning	3,400	1983	N/A
Current values for this model in NIB condition range from $800-$1,000.				
✳ *Model BPS 12 ga.*	Browning	3,800	1984	N/A
Current values for this model in NIB condition range from $800-$1,000.				
✳ *Model 1100 12 ga.*	Remington	4,500	1985	N/A
Current values for this model in NIB condition range from $800-$1,000.				
✳ *Model A303 12 ga.*	Beretta	5,500	1986	N/A
Current values for this model in NIB condition range from $1,000-$2,000.				
✳ *Model A303 20 ga.*	Beretta	3,500	1987	N/A
Current values for this model in NIB condition range from $1,200-$1,400.				
✳ *Model A5 12 ga. (50th Ann'y)*	Browning	5,000	1987	N/A
Current values for this model in NIB condition range from $2,000-$2,500.				
✳ *Model A5 16 ga.*	Browning	4,500	1988	N/A
Current values for this model in NIB condition range from $2,500-$3,000.				
✳ *Model A500 12 ga.*	Browning	4,500	1989	N/A
Current values for this model in NIB condition range from $1,800-$2,000.				
✳ *Model A5 20 ga.*	Browning	4,500	1990	N/A
Current values for this model in NIB condition range from $2,000-$2,500.				
✳ *Model A390 12 ga.*	Beretta	4,200	1991	N/A
Current values for this model in NIB condition range from $1,000-$1,200.				
✳ *Model Semi-Auto 12 ga.*	Franchi	4,200	1992	N/A
Current values for this model in NIB condition range from $700-$900.				
✳ *Model 12 20 ga.*	Winchester	3,800	1993	N/A
Current values for this model in NIB condition range from $1,800-$2,000.				
✳ *Model A500R 12 ga.*	Browning	3,300	1994	N/A
Current values for this model in NIB condition range from $800-$1,000.				
✳ *Model 12 Repro. 28 ga.*	Browning	1,000	1995	N/A
Current values for this model in NIB condition range from $2,500-$3,000.				
✳ *Model BPS 12 ga.*	Browning	3,500	1996	N/A
Current values for this model in NIB condition range from $800-$1,000.				
✳ *Model Gold Hunter*	Browning	2,500	1997	N/A
Current values for this model in NIB condition range from $2,500-$3,000.				
This model commemorated DU's 60th anniversary.				
✳ *Model 11-87 12 ga.*	Remington	3,500	1998	N/A
Current values for this model in NIB condition range from $1,700-$1,900.				
✳ *Model BPS 20 ga.*	Browning	3,500	1999	N/A
Current values for this model in NIB condition range from $1,000-$1,200.				
✳ *Model AL390 12 ga.*	Beretta	3,500	2000	N/A
Current values for this model in NIB condition range from $1,400-$1,600.				
This dinner gun is the Gold Mallard variation of the Model AL390.				

Model	Manufacturer	Qty.	Year	Issue Price
✱ *Model Red Lion 12 ga.*	**Fabarm**	**3,600**	**2001**	**N/A**
Current values for this model in NIB condition range from $600-$800.				
✱ *Model BPS 28 ga.*	**Browning**	**3,500**	**2002**	**N/A**
Current values for this model in NIB condition range from $800-$1,000.				
✱ *Model AL391*	**Beretta**	**3,500**	**2003**	**N/A**
Current values for this model in NIB condition range from $1,200-$1,400.				
✱ *SX2*	**Winchester**	**2,800**	**2004**	**N/A**
Current values for this model in NIB condition range from $1,000-$1,200.				
✱ *Model White Onyx*	**Beretta**	**3,200**	**2005**	**N/A**
Current values for this model in NIB condition range from $2,500-$2,700.				
✱ *Model 11-87 Premier Grade*	**Remington**	**3,000**	**2006**	**N/A**
Current values for this model in NIB condition range from $1,000-$1,200.				
✱ *Silver Hunter 70th Anniversary*	**Browning**	**3,300**	**2007**	**N/A**
Current values for this model in NIB condition range from $1,500-$2,000.				
✱ *Viper Semi-Auto*	**TriStar**	**N/A**	**2008**	**N/A**
Current values for this model in NIB condition range from $1,500-$2,000.				
✱ *Model White Onyx 20 ga.*	**Beretta**	**3,3,00**	**2008**	**N/A**

DUMOULIN, ERNEST S.P.R.L.

Current manufacturer located in Herstal, Belgium. No current U.S. importation. Previously imported 1998-2000 by Armes De Chasse LLC, located in Hertford, NC. Previously imported and retailed on a very limited basis by Midwest Gun Sport located in Zebulon, NC until 1990 (formerly from Ellisville, MO). Older importation was by Abercrombie & Fitch located in New York, NY.

Most Ernest Dumoulin (son of Henri) drillings, rifles, and shotguns are essentially custom ordered firearms with a long list of options available which, in some cases, can easily double the values of models shown below. Because of this, these options are not listed individually. Please contact the factory directly for more information regarding current models and pricing.

GRADING - PPGS™	100%	98%	95%	90%	80%	70%	60%

COMBINATION GUNS

EAGLE MODEL - O/U configuration (shotgun barrel on bottom), 12 or 20 ga., .22 Hornet, .222 Rem., .222 Rem. Mag., 6mm Rem., .243 Win., .25-06 Rem., .30-06, 6.5x57R, 7x57R, 8x57JRS, or 9.3x74R cal., boxlock action. 1989-disc.

	100%	98%	95%	90%	80%	70%	60%
	$2,700	$2,400	$2,175	$1,850	$1,595	$1,400	$1,195

Last MSR was $2,700.

RIFLES: BOLT ACTION

E. Dumoulin has had very limited importation since 1989. Beginning in 1998, some bolt action models have been imported into the U.S.

BAVARIA DELUXE - .243 Win. through .458 Win. cals., 21 1/2, 24, or 25 1/2 in. octagonal barrel, French walnut stock with rosewood forend tip and pistol grip cap, no sights, custom made essentially with Sako (disc.) or Mauser action. Disc. 1985.

Series I	$995	$890	$775	$650	$575	$530	$460

Last MSR was $1,080.

Add 15% for .375 H&H or .458 Win. Mag. cal.
Many engraving options were available from $510 to $1,900.

RIFLE MOUSQUETON - .243 Win. through .338 Win. cals., 20 in. barrel, Mannlicher style, French walnut stock and pistol grip cap, no sights, custom made essentially with Sako or Mauser action. Many engraving options available from $510-$1,900. Disc.

	$720	$620	$560	$510	$470	$420	$360

CENTURION MODEL - .270 Win. through .458 Win. cals., 21 1/2, 24, or 25 1/2 in. barrels, French walnut stock with rosewood forearm tip and pistol grip cap, no sights, custom made essentially with Sako or Mauser action. Many engraving options available from $510-$1,900. Importation disc. 1986.

	$660	$590	$535	$480	$425	$390	$360

Last MSR was $740.

CENTURION CLASSIC - standard cals. only, similar to Centurion, Mauser 98 action only and has better wood.

	$1,525	$1,375	$1,175	$975	$800	$700	$600

Last MSR was $1,525.

These models were also available in Mag. cals. that are divided into 4 groups - 1, 2, 3, and 4 Mag. Series. These options retailed in the $50-$300 price range.

✳ *Centurion Classic Diane* - grade up from Centurion Classic, 22 in. barrel, Mauser 98 action, M-70 safety, adj. steel trigger.

	$1,450	$1,250	$1,000	$825	$700	$600	$500

Last MSR was $1,450.

✳ *Centurion Classic Amazone* - grade up from Diane, 20 in. barrel, full stock.

	$1,750	$1,525	$1,325	$1,075	$865	$750	$600

Last MSR was $1,750.

✳ *Centurion Classic Bavaria Deluxe* - .243 Win. through .458 Win. cals., 21 1/2, 24, or 25 1/2 in. octagonal barrel, French walnut stock with rosewood forend tip and pistol grip cap, no sights, custom made essentially with Sako (disc.) or Mauser action.

	$1,900	$1,675	$1,450	$1,200	$995	$775	$650

Last MSR was $1,900.

Many engraving options were available from $510 to $1,900.

✳ *Centurion Classic Safari* - Mag. cals. only.

	$2,350	$1,775	$1,475	$1,200	$995	$775	$650

Last MSR was $2,350.

MANNLICHER MODEL - various cals., Mauser type bolt action, full stocked. Disc. 1985.

	$730	$660	$580	$520	$470	$430	$395

Last MSR was $825.

✳ *Mannlicher Model Classic* - similar to basic Mannlicher, except has better walnut. Disc. 1985.

	$995	$890	$775	$650	$575	$530	$460

Last MSR was $1,065.

MATCH MODEL - match target rifle, adj. sights and stock. Disc. 1985.

	$1,640	$1,490	$1,300	$1,050	$900	$800	$700

Last MSR was $1,860.

✳ *Match Model NATO* - 7.62 cal. match rifle. Disc. 1985.

	$2,640	$2,400	$2,175	$1,850	$1,595	$1,400	$1,195

Last MSR was $3,000.

ST. HUBERT MODEL - Sako action, various cals. and barrel lengths. Disc. 1985.

	$1,900	$1,700	$1,495	$1,300	$1,150	$995	$850

Last MSR was $2,125.

SAFARI SPORTSMAN - .416 Rigby, .375 H&H, .505 Gibbs, or .404 Jeffreys cal., Mauser 98 action, 4 shot mag., limited availability in 1986.

	$5,250	$4,500	$3,550	$3,250	$2,800	$2,400	$2,000

Last MSR was $4,000.

Add 10% for .505 Gibbs cal.
Add approx. $1,200-$1,500 for claw mounts and scope, depending on condition and trademark.

GRADING - PPGS™	100%	98%	95%	90%	80%	70%	60%

SAFARI PROFESSIONAL - various Mag. cals., prices below reflect rifle w/o engraving. Limited importation.

MSR POR	N/A	$9,100	$8,150	$7,400	$6,500	$5,500	$4,500

AFRICAN PRO - similar to Safari Sportsman, except has ebony or buffalo horn forend tip, tilting hood for the front sight, multiple folding rear sight.

	$6,000	$5,350	$4,650	$3,750	$3,250	$2,800	$2,400

Last MSR was $4,800.

GRAND CLASSIC - various cals., prices below reflect rifle w/o engraving. Limited importation.

MSR POR	N/A	$7,300	$6,500	$5,500	$4,500	$3,750	$3,000

RIFLES: SxS

EUROPA I - .22 Hornet, .222 Rem., .222 Rem. Mag., 6mm Rem., .243 Win., .25-06 Rem., .30-06, 6.5x57R, 7x57R, 8x57JRS, or 9.3x74R cal., Anson & Deeley boxlock action, moderate engraving. 1989-disc.

	$4,800	$4,200	$3,800	$3,500	$3,250	$2,995	$2,700

Last MSR was $4,800.

CONTINENTAL I - same calibers as Europa I, sidelock action, 12 engraving options to choose from, many options available on special order. 1989-disc.

	$8,600	$7,700	$6,995	$6,400	$5,600	$4,750	$4,150

Last MSR was $8,600.

"PIONNIER" EXPRESS MODEL - assorted cals. from .22 Hornet through .600 Nitro Express, SxS configuration, heavily engraved, select walnut. Limited production, Anson & Deeley triple lock action, sideplates available at extra charge.

✳ *"Pionnier" Express Model P-I and P-II* - English style scroll or bouquet (P-II) engraving.

	$7,850	$6,500	$5,825	$5,200	$4,650	$4,160	$3,700

Last MSR was $7,850.

    Add $400 for P-II engraving.

✳ *"Pionnier" Express Model P III* - English style lace engraving (tapestry style).

	$8,640	$7,750	$7,000	$6,400	$5,600	$4,750	$4,150

Last MSR was $8,640.

✳ *"Pionnier" Express Model P-IV through P-VIII* - various styles of royal engraving with or without hunting scenes.

	$9,100	$7,995	$7,450	$6,800	$6,000	$5,000	$4,350

Last MSR was $9,100.

    Add $400 for gold inlays.

✳ *"Pionnier" Express Model P-IX through P-XII* - Louis XVI style engraving.

	$9,540	$8,600	$7,800	$7,250	$6,400	$5,250	$4,500

Last MSR was $9,540.

✳ *"Pionnier" Express Model Magnum* - .338 Win. Mag., .375 H&H, .416 Rigby, .416 Hoffman, .458 Win. Mag., .577 Nitro Express, or .600 Nitro Express cal. Boxlock action with Greener crossbolt.

	$10,900	$9,400	$8,650	$7,800	$7,000	$6,450	$5,825

Last MSR was $10,900.

PIONNIER RECENT IMPORTATION - .300 H&H, .300 Win. Mag., .338 Win. Mag., .375 H&H, .416 Rigby, .458 Win. Mag., or .470 NE cal., similar action as described above with or w/o sideplates, prices below reflect rifle w/o engraving. Limited importation.

MSR POR	N/A	$15,000	$12,250	$9,975	$8,500	$7,500	$6,500

    Add $1,800 for sideplates.
    Add $2,800 for .375 H&H, .470 NE, or .500 NE cal.

GRADING - PPGS™	100%	98%	95%	90%	80%	70%	60%

ARISTOCRATE MODEL - available in all cals. up to .375 H&H (also in 20 ga.), single shot action with low profile, exhibition oil finished walnut stock and forearm. Values below assume standard model (12 engraving options available). Imported 1987-88 only.

	100%	98%	95%	90%	80%	70%	60%
	$9,100	$8,450	$7,775	$7,000	$6,450	$5,825	$5,275

Last MSR was $10,400.

PRESTIGE SIDELOCK - similar cals. as the Pionnier Model, best quality sidelock, triple locking, 10 different presentation options available, values below reflect standard model without options. Custom order only, 1 year waiting period. Mfg. began 1986, limited importation.

MSR POR	N/A	$37,500	$31,000	$25,000	$21,750	$19,250	$16,250

FLEURON SIDELOCK - 6.5x57R, 7x57R, 7x65R, .30 Blaser, 8x57 JRS, 8x57 RS, or 9.3x74R cal., made per individual customer specifications. Limited importation.

MSR POR	N/A	$26,000	$21,750	$19,250	$16,750	$14,000	$11,750

SHOTGUNS: O/U

BOSS ROYAL SUPERPOSED - 12, 20 or 28 ga., full sidelock, exhibition grade walnut, double triggers, top-of-the-line quality, built to special order. Values listed assume standard gun (12 engraving options available). 1987-disc.

	$18,500	$16,000	$13,750	$11,000	$9,775	$8,000	$6,950

Last MSR was $18,500.

Add 6% for 28 ga.

SUPERPOSED EXPRESS "INTERNATIONAL" - O/U shotgun, includes extra set of rifle barrels, 20 ga., 7 choices of rifle cals., deluxe walnut. Elaborate engraving patterns available at extra charge, limited production. Disc. 1985.

	$2,400	$2,000	$1,800	$1,575	$1,400	$1,200	$1,050

Last MSR was $2,490.

SHOTGUNS: SxS

EUROPA MODEL - 12, 20, 28 ga., or .410 bore, Anson & Deeley boxlock action, single or double trigger, moderately engraved, oil finished stock and forearm, choice of 6 engraving options. 1989-disc.

	$3,300	$2,750	$2,350	$2,000	$1,800	$1,575	$1,400

Last MSR was $3,300.

LIEGE MODEL - 12, 16 (disc. 1986), 20, or 28 ga., Anson & Deeley locking action, elaborate engraving, deluxe walnut. 1986-disc.

* Liege Model Luxe	$5,300	$4,600	$3,900	$3,300	$2,900	$2,600	$2,300

Last MSR was $5,900 (disc. 1988).

* Liege Model Grand Luxe	$6,900	$6,000	$5,000	$4,300	$3,600	$3,200	$2,875

Last MSR was $6,900.

Add 15% for 28 ga.
Add 15% for sideplates.

Many engraving options and other special order features can be added to the above models.

CONTINENTAL MODEL - 12, 20, 28 ga., or .410 bore, sidelock action, double or single trigger, deluxe oil finished walnut stock, choice of 6 engraving options. 1989-disc.

	$7,400	$6,250	$5,200	$4,400	$3,700	$3,200	$2,875

Last MSR was $7,400.

ETENDARD MODEL - 12, 20, 28 ga., or .410 bore, full sidelock, exhibition grade walnut, double triggers, top-of-the-line quality, built to special order. Values listed assume standard gun (many engraving options available). Mfg. began 1987, limited importation.

MSR POR	N/A	$25,750	$21,750	$19,250	$16,750	$14,000	$11,750

Add $890 for 20, 28 ga. or .410 bore.

DUMOULIN, HENRI & FILS

Current manufacturer located in Herstal, Belgium. No current importation. Previously imported and distributed by New England Arms Corp. located in Kittery Point, ME.

H. Dumoulin has manufactured quality firearms in Liege/Herstal, Belgium since 1947. They specialize in big-bore, high quality bolt action rifles, generally built on Mauser 98 or commercial Mauser actions. The improved double square bridge Imperial Magnum action was developed and introduced in 1987.

RIFLES: BOLT ACTION

GRAND LUXE BOLT ACTION - .300 Wby. Mag., .338 Win. Mag., .375 H&H, .378 Wby. Mag., .404 Jeffrey, .416 Rigby, .460 Wby. Mag., or .505 Gibbs cal., 24, 25.6, or 26 in. barrel, European walnut stock with ebony forend tip and pistol grip cap, folding leaf sights with hooded front, custom made on the Dumoulin Imperial Magnum double square bridge action. Many engraving options available.

MSR POR	N/A	$7,995	$7,525	$6,700	$5,750	$5,100	$4,400

Add $750 for left-hand action.
Add $1,150 for extended top and bottom tang.
Add $1,000 for claw mounts.
Add $1,000 for .505 Gibbs cal.

SOVEREIGN - available in same cals. as Grand Luxe Bolt Action, except with a higher quality finish, knurled bolt handles, gold inlayed lettering. Many engraving options available.

Pricing on this model depends on engraving, wood and other options. Imperial Magnum is also available in various stages of completion, barreled actions, actions in the white, etc. Please contact the factory directly for quotation (see Trademark Index).

RIFLES: SxS CUSTOM

BOXLOCK RIFLE - boxlock action, best quality double rifle, highly figured European walnut, finely hand checkered with standard scroll engraving. Custom ordered to customer's dimensions. Prices start at $15,000.

SIDELOCK RIFLE - sidelock action, best quality hand detachable locks, top quality European walnut, finely hand checkered with standard scroll engraving. Additional engraving or deluxe wood quoted on request. Prices start at $20,000.

SHOTGUNS: SxS, CUSTOM

BOXLOCK MODEL - available in most gauges, individually built per customer special order. The factory should be contacted directly for more information and a price quotation.

SIDELOCK MODEL - available in most gauges, individually built per customer special order. The factory should be contacted directly for more information and a price quotation.

DUMOULIN HERSTAL S.A.

Current manufacturer established in 1997 and located in Herstal, Belgium. This manufacturer's sister company is Ernest Dumoulin S.P.R.L. Currently imported by Empire Rifle Company, LLC, located in Meriden, NH. Previously imported by Arms De Chasse, LLC, located in Hertford, NC.

Dumoulin Herstal manufactures a complete line of quality bolt action and SxS rifles in many configurations and calibers. They also produce their own A2000 LM (Long Magnum) action, based on the 1930s Mauser Oberndorf design, which is available separately. Dumoulin manufactures 100-150 guns annually. Please contact the importer directly regarding current information, including model availability and prices.

RIFLES: BOLT ACTION

The following models employ the A2000 Dumoulin action featuring forged flattop receiver, 3 locking lugs with claw extractors, and one-piece bolt, handle, and knob.

ADVENTURER SERIES - various cals. from .25-06 Rem. - .458 Win. Mag., configurations include Euro 2000 and Euroforest. Limited importation began 1999.

Please contact the importer directly for a price quotation on this model.

GENTLEMAN HUNTER SERIES (LIEGE MODEL) - various cals. from .25-06 Rem. - .458 Win. Mag., including some additional Safari cals., configurations include Liege, Liege Safari, Liege Full Stock (Mannlicher), or Liege Thumbhole. Limited importation began 1999.

Please contact the importer directly for a price quotation on this model.

TRADITIONAL LIEGE CRAFTSMAN SERIES (HERSTAL MODEL) - various cals. from .25-06 Rem. - .458 Win. Mag., including many Safari cals., configurations include Herstal, Herstal Full Stock (Mannlicher), or Herstal Safari (5 shot mag.). Limited importation began 1999.

Depending on caliber and variation, prices on this model range from $7,950 - $10,950.

MODEL WHITE HUNTER SAFARI SPECIAL - .375 H&H, .416 Rigby, .416 Wby. Mag., .500 Jeffery, or .505 Gibbs cal., other cals. available upon request, this model features the proprietary Dumoulin Herstal A2000/LM (Long Magnum) action, hinged floorplate, express sights, deluxe checkered walnut stock with ebony forend. Limited importation began 1999.

Prices for this model start at $14,900.

TONY SANCHEZ-ARINO MAGNUM MAUSER - scroll engraved, animal inlays, extended tang and triggerguard, Tony's signature in gold. Importation began 2007.

Prices for this model start at $18,700.

RIFLES: SxS

PIONNIER BOXLOCK - various dangerous game cals., with or w/o sideplates, ejectors, solid chrome molybdenum forged action, Greener or Purdey treble grip closure, options includes a variety of engraving patterns, sideplates, French grey or case color hardened finish.

Current MSR for the base model is $34,000, or $36,500 if w/sideplates.

PRESTIGE SIDELOCK - various dangerous game cals., sideplates, H&H ejectors with back action mechanism, DT, engraved sidelock action, options includes a variety of engraving patterns, sideplates, French grey or case color hardened finish.

Current MSR for the base model is $62,400.

TONY SANCHEZ-ARINO BOXLOCK - scroll engraved, boxlock action, animal inlays, extended tang and triggerguard, Tony's signature in gold. Importation began 2007.

Prices for this model start at $39,500.

TONY SANCHEZ-ARINO SIDELOCK - scroll engraved, sidelock action, animal inlays, extended tang and triggerguard, Tony's signature in gold. Importation began 2007.

Prices for this model start at $67,400.

E SECTION

E.D.M. ARMS

Current manufacturer established in 1997 and located in Redlands, CA. Dealer and consumer direct sales.

GRADING - PPGS™	100%	98%	95%	90%	80%	70%	60%

RIFLES: BOLT ACTION

WINDRUNNER MODEL 96 (XM107) - .338 Lapua (new 2002) or .50 BMG cal., takedown repeater action, EDM machined receiver, fully adj. stock, match grade 28 in. barrel that removes within seconds, allowing exact head space every time the barrel is reinstalled, includes two 5 (.50 BMG cal.) or 8 (.338 Lapua) shot mags., Picatinny rail, and bipod, 24 (Lightweight Tactical Takedown) or 36 lbs.

MSR $7,600	$7,600	$6,850	$6,200	$5,500	$5,000	$4,500	$4,000

Add $1,000 for left hand action.

* *Windrunner Model 96 SS99* - similar to Windrunner, except is single shot, w/o mag., includes bipod and sling, 32 lbs. New 2002.

MSR $5,850	$5,850	$5,150	$4,450	$3,850	$3,250	$2,850	$2,450

MODEL 06 MINI-WINDRUNNER - .308 Win. cal., 20 in. barrel, 10 shot mag., Picatinny rail, lightweight, tactical, takedown version on the Windrunner Model 96, 11.2 lbs. New 2007.

MSR $4,250	$4,250	$3,750	$3,300	$2,900	$2,550	$2,175	$1,800

MODEL XM04 CHEYENNE TACTICAL - .408 CheyTac cal., takedown repeater, tactical bolt action configuration, 5 shot mag., 30 in. fluted barrel with suppressor, desert camo finish, retractable stock, effective range is 2,500+ yards, 27 lbs. New 2002.

MSR $7,600	$7,600	$6,850	$6,200	$5,500	$5,000	$4,500	$4,000

Subtract $1,400 for single shot action (disc.).

MODEL 50 - .50 BMG cal., bolt action, single shot, twin rail adj. skeletonized stock, Picatinny rail and bipod. Mfg. 2003.

	$4,250	$3,750	$3,250	$2,850	$2,450	$2,050	$1,650

Last MSR was $4,250.

MODEL 98 - .338 Lapua cal., takedown repeating bolt action, single rail adj. stock, pistol grip, 22 lbs. New 2003.

MSR $7,500	$7,500	$6,850	$6,200	$5,500	$5,000	$4,500	$4,000

510 DTC EUROP - .50 DTC Europ cal. (1 in. smaller than .50 BMG), designed for CA shooters and legal in CA. New 2007.

MSR $7,500	$7,500	$6,850	$6,200	$5,500	$5,000	$4,500	$4,000

RIFLES: SEMI-AUTO

WINDRUNNER .50 CAL. - .50 BMG cal., 28 in. Lilja match grade chromemoly barrel, integrated Picatinny rail, removable black stock with cheekrest and adj. buttpad. New 2006.

MSR $9,250	$8,750	$7,500	$6,750	$6,000	$5,250	$4,500	$3,750

E.M.F. CO., INC.

Current importer and distributor established 1956 and located in Santa Ana, CA. Distributor and dealer sales. E.M.F. stands for Early & Modern Firearms Inc.

For information on Dakota Single Action Revolvers imported by E.M.F., please refer to the Dakota Single Action Revolvers section. Please refer

GRADING - PPGS™	100%	98%	95%	90%	80%	70%	60%

to the *Blue Book of Modern Black Powder Arms* by John Allen (also online) for more information and prices on E.M.F.'s lineup of modern black powder models.

Black Powder Reproductions & Replicas by Dennis Adler is also an invaluable source for most black powder reproductions and replicas, and includes hundreds of color images on most popular makes/models, provides manufacturer/trademark histories, and up-to-date information on related items/accessories for black powder shooting - www.bluebookinc.com

DERRINGERS: REPRODUCTIONS

STANDARD MODEL - .22 Short cal., copy of Colt Model Lord or Lady Derringer, blue, nickel, gold (disc.), or silver (disc.) gold finish. Importation disc. 1992.

	100%	98%	95%	90%	80%	70%	60%
	$95	$80	$70	$60	$55	$50	$45

Last MSR was $125.

1872 STANDARD MODEL - .22 Short cal., copy of Colt Model Lord or Lady Derringer, nickel or silver/gold frame finish, hardwood grips, 7 oz. Disc. 2005.

	100%	98%	95%	90%	80%	70%	60%
	$75	$65	$60	$55	$50	$45	$40

Last MSR was $90.

Add $30 for case, $95 for cased set with two Derringers.

PISTOLS: REPRODUCTIONS

REMINGTON ROLLING BLOCK PISTOL - .357 Mag. cal., rolling block design. Disc. 1992.

	100%	98%	95%	90%	80%	70%	60%
	$300	$225	$185	$165	$155	$145	$135

Last MSR was $395.

REVOLVERS: REPRODUCTIONS

Please refer to the Dakota Single Action Revolvers section in this text for a complete listing of reproductions.

RIFLES: SxS

KODIAK MARK IV DOUBLE EXPRESS SXS RIFLE - .45-70 Govt. cal., back action, browned 24 in. barrels with triple leaf express sights, color case hardened frame, trigger guard and hammers.

	100%	98%	95%	90%	80%	70%	60%
MSR $4,000	$3,600	$3,200	$2,750	$2,400	$1,950	$1,700	$1,500

RIFLES: SEMI-AUTO, REPRODUCTIONS

These models are authentic shooting reproductions previously mfg. in Italy.

AP 74 - .22 LR or .32 ACP cal., copy of the Colt AR-15, 15 shot mag., 20 in. barrel, 6 3/4 lbs. Importation disc. 1989.

	100%	98%	95%	90%	80%	70%	60%
	$350	$295	$250	$200	$175	$155	$145

Last MSR was $295.

Add $25 for .32 cal.

✱ *AP74 Sporter Carbine* - .22 LR cal. only, wood sporter stock. Importation disc. 1989.

	100%	98%	95%	90%	80%	70%	60%
	$375	$325	$275	$225	$195	$175	$160

Last MSR was $320.

✱ *AP74 Paramilitary Paratrooper Carbine* - .22 LR cal. only, folding wire stock, black nylon on paramilitary design model. Importation disc. 1987.

	100%	98%	95%	90%	80%	70%	60%
	$395	$350	$300	$260	$215	$175	$165

Last MSR was $325.

Add $10 for wood folding stock.

GRADING - PPGS™	100%	98%	95%	90%	80%	70%	60%

✱ *AP74 "Dressed" Military Model* - with Cyclops scope, Colt bayonet, sling, and bipod. Disc. 1986.

	$395	$350	$300	$265	$240	$220	$200

Last MSR was $450.

GALIL - .22 LR cal. only, reproduction of the Israeli Galil. Importation disc. 1989.

	$350	$295	$250	$200	$175	$155	$145

Last MSR was $295.

KALASHNIKOV AK-47 - .22 LR cal. only, reproduction of the Russian AK-47, semi-auto. Importation disc. 1989.

	$350	$295	$250	$200	$175	$155	$145

Last MSR was $295.

FRENCH M.A.S. - .22 LR cal. only, reproduction of the French Bull-Pup Combat Rifle, with carrying handle, 29 shot mag. Importation disc. 1989.

	$375	$325	$265	$240	$220	$200	$185

Last MSR was $320.

M1 CARBINE - .30 cal. only, copy of the U.S. Military M1 Carbine. Disc. 1985.

	$225	$175	$150	$140	$130	$120	$110

Last MSR was $205.

Add $43 for Paratrooper variation.

RIFLES: REMINGTON REPRODUCTIONS

ROLLING BLOCK CARBINE/RIFLE - .45-70 Govt. cal., authentic reproduction of the Remington Rolling Block Rifle, standard (disc. 2003) or target model, 26 (carbine) or 30 in. octagon barrel. Mfg. by Pedersoli. Imported 1991-2006.

	$775	$675	$600	$550	$500	$450	$395

Last MSR was $880.

Subtract $60 for carbine model (new 2005).
Subtract approx. $100 for standard model.

✱ *Rolling Block Rifle Deluxe* - .45-70 Govt. cal., similar to Rolling Block Rifle, except has 32 in. barrel, checkered pistol grip stock, and German silver forearm cap. Imported 2000-2002.

	$900	$700	$500	$450	$400	$365	$330

Last MSR was $1,125.

BABY ROLLING BLOCK CARBINE/RIFLE - .357 Mag. cal., 22 or 26 in. barrel, color case hardened frame. Mfg. 1992, reintroduced 2006.

	$465	$400	$340	$285	$250	$225	$185

Last MSR was $515.

Add $35 for rifle configuration.

REVOLVING CARBINE - .357 Mag., .44-40 WCF (disc.), or .45 LC cal., 18 in. barrel, case colored frame, walnut grips, Model 1875 Army Single Action design, 5 lbs. Importation disc. 1995, reintroduced 2003.

	$450	$375	$315	$265	$230	$200	$185

Last MSR was $560.

TEXAS CARBINE (1858 REMINGTON) - .22 LR cal., action patterned after Remington revolving carbine, 21 in. octagon barrel, wood stock and forearm, brass frame. Also available with extra .22 Mag. cylinder. Importation disc. 1998.

	$295	$225	$175	$150	$135	$125	$110

Last MSR was $400.

GRADING - PPGS™	100%	98%	95%	90%	80%	70%	60%

RIFLES: SHARPS REPRODUCTIONS

1874 SHARPS HARTFORD SPORTING OR MILITARY RIFLE - .45-70 Govt., .45 LC (mfg. 2004-2006) or .45-120 cal., copy of the Sharps Single Shot, 28 or 30 in. octagonal barrel, case hardened frame, single or double set triggers. Importation disc. 1999, reintroduced 2003.

	100%	98%	95%	90%	80%	70%	60%
MSR $1,025	$900	$800	$700	$625	$550	$475	$395

Add $120 for checkered stock.
Add $180 for in-the-white (no metal finish, disc.).
Add $675 for Billy Dixon variation (new 2007).
Add $120 for brown finish (disc.)
Add $45 for target variation with 1/2 round, 1/2 octagon barrel (disc.)
Add $105 for 1874 Business Rifle configuration in .45-70 Govt. cal. only.

✳ *1874 Sharps Hartford Deluxe Rifle* - .45-70 Govt. or .45-120 (disc.) cal., blue or brown finish, 32 in. tapered octagon barrel, double set triggers, checkered pistol grip and forearm, case hardened frame, silver forend tip.

	100%	98%	95%	90%	80%	70%	60%
MSR $1,500	$1,325	$1,200	$1,025	$875	$775	$695	$625

An engraved version of this model is also available for $2,500, and Super Deluxe with gold inlays is $3,150.

✳ *1874 Sharps Hartford Military Carbine* - saddle ring carbine with 22 in. round barrel, single trigger. Disc. 2005.

	95%	90%	80%	70%	60%		
	$695	$625	$550	$495	$450	$425	$400

Last MSR was $760.

QUIGLEY SHARPS MODEL 1874 SPORTING RIFLE - .45-70 Govt., .45-90 (disc.), .45-110 (new 2007), or .45-120 (disc. 2003, reintroduced 2006) cal., 34 in. heavy octagon barrel with storage compartment in stock. Importation began 2000.

	100%	98%	95%	90%	80%	70%	60%
MSR $1,800	$1,600	$1,400	$1,175	$975	$825	$750	$625

Add $100 for .45-100 or .45-120 cal.

RIFLES: SPENCER REPRODUCTIONS

1865 SPENCER CARBINE -.44-40 WCF or .56-50 cal., 20 in. barrel with barrel band, case colored receiver and hammer, includes sling swivels, 8 lbs. Mfg. by Armi Sport beginning 2006.

	100%	98%	95%	90%	80%	70%	60%
MSR $1,280	$1,095	$950	$825	$700	$600	$500	$400

RIFLES: SPRINGFIELD REPRODUCTIONS

SPRINGFIELD 1873 TRAPDOOR CARBINE/RIFLE - .45-70 Govt. cal., trapdoor single shot action, 22 (carbine), 26 (Officer's Model), or 32 (Rifle) in. barrel, blue action, walnut stock. Mfg. by Pedersoli.

	100%	98%	95%	90%	80%	70%	60%
MSR $1,200	$1,050	$900	$800	$700	$625	$550	$475

Add $190 for Rifle or $300 for Officer's Model.

RIFLES: WINCHESTER REPRODUCTIONS

DELUXE 1860 HENRY RIFLE - .44-40 WCF or .45 LC cal. only, brass or case colored steel frame, deluxe walnut, reproduction of New Haven Arms Co.'s Henry Rifle, 24 in. blue or white barrel. New 1987.

	100%	98%	95%	90%	80%	70%	60%
MSR $1,050	$925	$750	$525	$400	$350	$300	$275

Add $135 for in-the-white barrel or for case colored steel (.45 LC cal. only) frame.

✳ *Deluxe 1860 Henry Rifle Engraved* - similar to deluxe Henry Rifle except has hand engraved receiver. Imported 1987-90.

	100%	98%	95%	90%	80%	70%	60%
	$1,350	$975	$700	$525	$400	$340	$295

Last MSR was $1,598.

GRADING - PPGS™	100%	98%	95%	90%	80%	70%	60%

1866 YELLOWBOY CARBINE - .22 LR (disc. 2002), .22 Mag. (mfg. 2000-2002), .32-20 WCF (mfg. 2000-2002), .38 Spl., .38-40 WCF (mfg. 2000-2002, reintroduced 2005), .44-40 WCF, or .45 LC (new 1993) cal., 19 in. barrel, brass frame, saddle ring carbine. Disc. 2003, reintroduced 2005.

MSR $870	$725	$600	$475	$350	$275	$235	$200

Add $330 for laser engraved Indian model (.45 LC cal. only).

✱ *1866 Yellowboy Rifle* - same cals. as 1866 Yellowboy Carbine, 20 (Border model short rifle, new 1999) or 24 1/4 (Sporting) in. barrel.

MSR $920	$775	$625	$495	$350	$275	$235	$200

Add $50 for in-the-white barrel.

✱ *1866 Yellowboy Carbine Engraved* - .38 Spl. or .44-40 WCF cal. Importation disc. 1990.

	$875	$575	$440	$330	$295	$260	$230

Last MSR was $1,080.

1873 CARBINE - .22 Mag. (disc.), .32-20 WCF (mfg. 1999-2000, reintroduced 2005-2006), .357 Mag. (disc. 2000, reintroduced 2003, and again in 2005), .38-40 WCF (mfg. 2000, reintroduced 2005-2006), .44 Spl. (mfg. 2000, reintroduced 2005-2006), .44-40 WCF (disc. 2000, reintroduced 2005), or .45 LC cal., 16 (Trapper model) or 19 in. round barrel, copy of the Winchester Model 1873 Carbine, blue (disc. 2000) or case hardened steel receiver. Disc. 2003, reintroduced 2005.

MSR $1,040	$875	$700	$525	$425	$325	$275	$235

✱ *1873 Carbine/Rifle* - .32-20 WCF, .357 Mag., .38-40 WCF, .44-40 WCF, or .45 LC cal., 20 (Border model short rifle, new 1999), 24 1/4, or 30 (limited importation 2000, reintroduced 2007) in. barrel, case hardened receiver.

MSR $1,050	$880	$700	$525	$425	$325	$275	$235

Add $30 for 30 in. barrel.
Add $50 for Deluxe Border model.
Add $120 for Deluxe model with checkered pistol grip stock (.357 Mag. or .45 LC cal. only, disc. 2003).

✱ *1873 Carbine/Rifle Youngboy* - .22 LR cal., blue steel, 19 or 24 1/4 in. barrel. Imported 1995-96.

	$800	$600	$450	$330	$295	$260	$230

Last MSR was $1,050.

Add $50 for rifle barrel.

✱ *1873 Carbine Rifle Engraved* - .357 Mag. or .44-40 WCF cal. only. Importation disc. 1987.

	$895	$635	$500	$450	$400	$360	$325

Last MSR was $850.

PREMIER 1873 CARBINE & RIFLE - .45 LC cal., case hardened frame, uncheckered walnut stock and forearm, full mag., rifle has 24 1/4 in. barrel, carbine has 19 in. barrel. Imported 1988-1989 only.

	$850	$595	$450	$330	$295	$260	$230

Last MSR was $1,160.

1876 RIFLE - .40-60 or .45-75 cal., patterned after the Model 1876 Winchester, case hardened frame with 28 in. octagon barrel with open sights. Importation began 2006.

MSR $1,265	$1,050	$875	$750	$625	$500	$450	$400

1885 HIGH WALL RIFLE - .38-55 WCF (new 2000), .40-65 (mfg. 2005-2006), .45-70 Govt., or .45-90 (mfg. 2005-2006) cal., action patterned after the Winchester Model 1885 High Wall, 30 or 32 (mfg. 2003 only) in. barrel, checkered walnut stock. Mfg. by Uberti. Imported 1998-2003, reintroduced 2005.

MSR $900	$795	$675	$550	$450	$375	$325	$295

Add $120 for deluxe model with checkered pistol grip stock.

GRADING - PPGS™	100%	98%	95%	90%	80%	70%	60%

HARTFORD 1892 CARBINE - .357 Mag., .44 Mag. (disc. 2003, reintroduced 2005), .44-40 WCF, .45 LC, or .44-40 WCF (disc. 2003) cal., case hardened, blued, brass, or stainless steel frame, 20 in. round barrel with or w/o saddle ring, buckhorn sights, standard stock with crescent buttplate and forearm, mfg. by Rossi. Importation began 2003.

MSR $430	$375	$325	$295	$265	$235	$200	$185

> Add $20 for case hardened frame or $45 for brass frame.
> Add $45 for stainless steel (.357 Mag. cal. only).

HARTFORD 1892 RIFLE - .357 Mag., .44-40 WCF, .44 Mag., or .45 LC cal., case hardened, blued, brass, or stainless steel frame, 20 (short rifle) or 24 in. octagon barrel with buckhorn sights, standard stock with crescent buttplate and forearm, mfg. by Rossi. Importation began 1998.

MSR $500	$440	$395	$350	$300	$260	$230	$200

> Add $10 for color case hardened frame, $70 for brass frame, or $50 for stainless steel frame.
> Add $20 for Target Model with case hardened receiver, and 1/2 round, 1/2 octagon barrel (disc. 2003).

This model was also packaged with the Great Western II 1873 SA revolver - combination sets range from $950-$1,200 (disc.).

✽ *Model 1892 Takedown Rifle* - .45 LC cal., 20 or 24 in. barrel, takedown action, 6.9 lbs. Mfg. by Armi-Sport.

MSR $1,100	$950	$825	$700	$600	$500	$425	$375

SHOTGUNS

HARTFORD MODEL STAGECOACH SxS SHOTGUN - 12 ga., exposed hammers, 20 in. barrels, checkered walnut stock and forearm, color case hardened frame, mfg. in Spain by Aral. Limited importation 2001-2005.

	$575	$500	$450	$420	$375	$340	$325

> *Last MSR was $650.*

STAGECOACH SxS MODEL - 12 ga. only, features exposed hammers and 20 in. brown barrels, mfg. by S.I.A.C.E. Imported 2000-2002.

	$1,175	$900	$700	$500	$450	$400	$365

> *Last MSR was $1,375.*

MODEL 1878 SxS - 12 ga. only, exposed hammers, 20 in. barrels, patterned after the Colt Model 1878 shotgun. Importation began 2006.

MSR $495	$425	$385	$340	$300	$260	$230	$195

MARK V CONQUEST SEMI-AUTO - 12 ga. only, 28 in. barrel with choke tubes. Limited importation 2003.

	$385	$325	$275	$240	$220	$200	$185

> *Last MSR was $460.*

MODEL 1897 SLIDE ACTION - 12 ga. only, 20 in. barrel, patterned after the Winchester Model 1897, exposed hammer. Importation began 2006.

MSR $515	$440	$395	$350	$300	$260	$230	$195

84 GUN CO.

Previous manufacturer located in Eighty Four, PA. Circa early 1970s.

RIFLES: BOLT ACTION

CLASSIC RIFLE - various calibers. Grades 1-4.

	100%	98%	95%	90%	80%	70%	60%
Grade 1	$420	$315	$275	$235	$210	$190	$170
Grade 2	$780	$585	$512	$430	$390	$355	$315
Grade 3	$860	$645	$560	$475	$430	$390	$345
Grade 4	$1,580	$1,185	$1,030	$870	$790	$715	$640

GRADING - PPGS™	100%	98%	95%	90%	80%	70%	60%
LOBO RIFLE - various calibers. Grades standard, 1-4.							
Standard	$415	$315	$270	$230	$210	$190	$170
Grade 1	$540	$405	$355	$300	$270	$245	$220
Grade 2	$795	$600	$520	$440	$400	$360	$320
Grade 3	$1,600	$1,200	$1,040	$880	$800	$720	$640
Grade 4	$2,350	$1,765	$1,530	$1,295	$1,175	$1,060	$940
PENNSYLVANIA RIFLE - various calibers. Grades standard, 1-4.							
Standard	$420	$315	$275	$235	$210	$190	$170
Grade 1	$540	$405	$355	$300	$270	$245	$220
Grade 2	$795	$600	$520	$440	$400	$360	$320
Grade 3	$1,600	$1,200	$1,040	$880	$800	$720	$640
Grade 4	$2,350	$1,765	$1,530	$1,295	$1,175	$1,060	$940

EAGLE ARMS, INC.

Previous manufacturer located in Geneseo, IL. Previous division of ArmaLite, Inc. 1995-2002, located in Geneseo, IL. Manufacture of pre-1995 Eagle Arms rifles was in Coal Valley, IL.

During 1995, Eagle Arms, Inc. reintroduced the ArmaLite trademark. The new company was organized under the ArmaLite name. In 2003, Eagle Arms became a separate company, and no longer a division of ArmaLite.

Currently, Eagle Arms is making lower receivers only, and no longer manufactures complete rifles.

RIFLES: SEMI-AUTO, RECENT MFG.

On the following M-15 models manufactured 1995 and earlier, A2 accessories included a collapsible carbine type buttstock (disc. per 1994 C/B) and forward bolt assist mechanism. Accessories are similar, except also have National Match sights. The A2 suffix indicates rifle is supplied with carrying handle, A4 designates a flattop receiver, some are equipped with a detachable carrying handle.

AR-10 MATCH RIFLE - .308 Win. cal., very similar to the Armalite AR-10 A4 rifle, 20 or 24 (Match rifle) in. chrome moly barrel, A2 (Service rifle) or A4 style flattop upper receiver (no sights), black stock with pistol grip and forearm, 10 shot mag., 9.6 lbs. Mfg. 2001-2005.

$925 $850 $775 $700 $650 $600 $550

Last MSR was $1,000.

    Add $65 for Service rifle with A2 front/rear sights.
    Add $480 for 24 in. barrel and aluminum free-floating handguard.

MODEL M15 A2/A4 RIFLE (EA-15 E-1) - .223 Rem. or .308 Win. cal., patterned after the Colt AR-15A2, 20 in. barrel, A2 sights or A4 flattop, with (pre 1993) or w/o forward bolt assist, 7 lbs. Mfg. 1990-1993, reintroduced 2002-2005.

$725 $600 $525 $450 $400 $375 $350

Last MSR was $795.

    Add $40 for .223 cal. flattop (Model E15A4B).
    Add $205 for .308 Win. cal. flattop.

✳ *Model M15 A2/A4 Rifle Carbine (EA9025C/EA9027C)* - features collapsible (disc. per C/B 1994) or fixed (new 1994) buttstock and 16 in. barrel, 5 lbs. 14 oz. Mfg. 1990-95, reintroduced 2002-2005.

$725 $600 $525 $450 $400 $375 $350

Last MSR was $795.

    Add $40 for flattop (Model E15A4CB).
    1997 retail for the pre-ban models was $1,100 (EA9396).
    Beginning 1993, the A2 accessory kit became standard on this model.

GRADING - PPGS™	100%	98%	95%	90%	80%	70%	60%

✻ **Model M15 A2 H-BAR Rifle (EA9040C)** - features heavy Target barrel, 8 lbs. 14 oz., includes E-2 accessories. Mfg. 1990-95.

	$825	$725	$600	$525	$450	$400	$375

Last MSR was $895.

1997 retail for this pre-ban model was $1,100 (EA9200).

✻ **Model M15 A4 Rifle Eagle Spirit (EA9055S)** - includes 16 in. premium air gauged National Match barrel, fixed stock, full length tubular aluminum hand guard, designed for IPSC shooting, includes match grade accessories, 8 lbs. 6 oz. Mfg. 1993-95, reintroduced 2002 only.

	$825	$750	$650	$600	$550	$495	$450

Last MSR was $850.

The 1995 pre-ban variation of this model retailed at $1,475 (EA9603).

✻ **Model M15 A2 Rifle Golden Eagle (EA9049S)** - similar to M15 A2 H-BAR, except has National Match accessories and two-stage trigger, 20 in. extra heavy barrel, 12 lbs. 12 oz. Mfg 1991-95, reintroduced 2002 only.

	$995	$850	$725	$650	$550	$500	$450

Last MSR was $1,125.

The 1997 pre-ban variation of this model retailed at $1,300 (EA9500).

✻ **Model M15 A4 Rifle Eagle Eye (EA9901)** - includes 24 in. free floating 1 in. barrel with tubular aluminum hand guard, weighted buttstock, designed for silhouette matches, 14 lbs. Mfg. 1993-95.

	$1,325	$1,075	$875	$725	$600	$525	$450

Last MSR was $1,495.

✻ **Model M15 Rifle Action Master (EA9052S)** - match rifle, flattop, solid aluminum handguard tube that allows for free floating 20 in. barrel with compensator, N.M. accessories, fixed stock, 8 lbs. 5 oz. Mfg. 1992-95, reintroduced 2002 only.

	$725	$650	$550	$500	$450	$395	$350

Last MSR was $850.

The 1995 pre-ban variation of this model retailed at $1,475 (EA5600).

✻ **Model M15 A4 Rifle Special Purpose (EA9042C)** - 20 in. barrel, flattop (A4) or detachable handle receiver. Disc. 1995.

	$850	$725	$600	$525	$450	$400	$375

Last MSR was $955.

The 1995 pre-ban variation of this model retailed at $1,165 (EA9204).

✻ **Model M15 A4 Rifle Predator (EA9902)** - post-ban only, 18 in. barrel, National Match trigger, flattop (A4) or detachable handle receiver. Mfg. 1995 only.

	$1,125	$895	$725	$600	$525	$450	$400

Last MSR was $1,350.

EFFEBI SNC

Current manufacturer located in Concesio, Italy since 1994. No current U.S. importation. Previously imported and distributed 2004-2006 by American Outdoor Adventures, located in Leesburg, GA. Previously named Dr. Franco Beretta until 1994. Also refer to the Dr. Franco Beretta listing.

Effebi manufacturers a variety of good quality shotguns in O/U, SxS, and single barrel configurations, including the top quality SxS sidelock Gemini model. The company should be contacted directly (see Trademark Index) for more information regarding current pricing and shotgun model availability.

EGE SPORTING ARMS

Current shotgun manufacturer located in Izmir, Turkey. Limited U.S. importation.

EGE Sporting Arms manufactures good quality O/U, slide action, and semi-auto shotguns that have had limited importation to date. Please contact the company directly for more information, including U.S. availability (see Trademark Index).

GRADING - PPGS™	100%	98%	95%	90%	80%	70%	60%

EGO ARMAS, S.A.

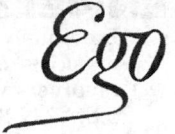

Current manufacturer established circa 1953 and located in Eibar, Spain. No current U.S. importation.

Ego Armas manufactures high quality sidelock double rifles ranging in price from approx. 5,000-8,850 euros in cals. up to .375 H&H, and 13,100 euros for the .416 Rigby or .470 NE., in addition to a boxlock express model for 3,000 euros. Mounted scopes are also available. Boxlock and sidelock shotguns are also available ranging in price from 770-1,050 euros for a boxlock (hammer model also available), and 1,475-2,200 euros for sidelock action with ejectors and English wood finish. More information, including current models and approximate U.S. pricing, can be obtained by contacting this manufacturer directly (see Trademark Index).

EMPIRE RIFLE COMPANY LLC

Current rifle manufacturer located in Meriden, NH.

RIFLES: BOLT ACTION

Empire Rifle Company manufactures a complete line of high quality custom Mauser bolt action rifles, with barrel lengths and caliber specified by the customer.

Values below do not include federal excise tax.

LEGACY MODEL - various cals. from .257 Roberts to .500 Jeffrey, utilizes controlled feed Mauser 98 long double square bridge action, stainless match grade barrel, checkered walnut or Kevlar stock and forearm with cheekpiece, right hand only, integral bolt handle, available in Chrome-Moly or stainless steel receiver, approx. 7 1/2 lbs.

MSR $4,785	$4,350	$3,800	$3,250	$2,850	$2,500	$2,150	$1,850

Add $200 for Guide Model with X walnut stock.
Add $1,360 for Professional Grade with AAA walnut stock.
Add $2,400 for Express Grade with all options included.

LIBERTY MODEL - over 40 various cals., lightweight model, similar action as Legacy Model, scaled down design for smaller shooters, walnut or Kevlar stock, stainless steel match grade barrel, approx. 6 lbs. New 2005.

MSR $4,985	$4,600	$4,150	$3,675	$3,300	$2,950	$2,500	$2,150

Add $200 for Guide model (disc. 2006).
Add $900 for Professional Grade with AAA walnut stock (disc. 2006).
Add $1,800 for Express Grade with all options included (disc. 2006).

STANDARD MODEL - various Magnum cals., features Empire 98S Mauser double square bridge action, stainless match grade barrel, checkered walnut or Kevlar stock and forearm, recoil pad, available in right or left hand, approx. 7 1/2 lbs. New 2005.

MSR $5,585	$5,150	$4,675	$4,225	$3,800	$3,400	$3,000	$2,650

Add $200 for Guide Model with X walnut stock.
Add $1,360 for Professional Grade with AAA walnut stock.
Add $2,400 for Express Grade with all options included.

EAST AFRICA MODEL - various cals. up to .505 Gibbs, Mauser Magnum double square bridge action, right or left hand, checkered walnut or Kevlar pistol grip stock with recoil pad, straight bolt handle, integral box mag.

MSR $9,445	$8,850	$7,475	$6,850	$6,250	$5,400	$4,600	$3,950

Add $1,250 for Professional Grade with AAA walnut stock.
Add $2,540 for Express Grade with all options included.

TITANIUM MODEL - features all titanium receiver, short action only, Kevlar pistol grip stock, 6 lbs., less than 30 mfg. 2005-2006.

	$7,995	$7,200	$6,500	$5,700	$4,950	$4,000	$3,950

Last MSR was $8,495.

GRADING - PPGS™   100%   98%   95%   90%   80%   70%   60%

ENFIELDS

Previously manufactured by the Royal Small Arms Factory located on the northern outskirts of London, in Middlesex, England. Various Enfield rifles, carbines and revolvers were produced and/or converted by other British factories (B.S.A., L.S.A., S.S.A., N.R.F., P. Webley & Son, Webley & Scott Ltd., Albion Motors, W.W. Greener, Westley Richards, Vickers (VSM), ROF Fazakerley, ROF Maltby, BSA Shirley (M47C), as well as Australia (from 1913), in Canada at Long Branch (from 1941), the United States by Stevens-Savage (also from 1941), RFI Ishapore, India (from 1905) and Wah Cantt in Pakistan (from the late 1950s).

The publisher would like to thank Mr. Ian Skennerton for making the following information available.

REVOLVERS

450 ENFIELD REVOLVER Mk I & II - often called the ".476", a commercial ammunition designation. A 6-shot, hinged barrel with exposed knuckle-joint axis at front, a top break action with forward-sliding chamber for extraction. Mk I model (chequered grips) introduced in 1880 with a Mk II variant (plain wooden grips) in 1882. Designed by American Owen Jones and made at Enfield R.S.A.F., it was not liked due to its sliding chamber extraction and cumbersome proportions.

$1,200 $1,050 $900 $750 $650 $500 $395

.455 WEBLEY REVOLVER - purchased privately by officers as well on War Office contracts. Mk I model approved in 1887, Mk II in 1894, Mk III in 1897, Mk IV in 1899, Mk V in 1913, and the Mk VI in 1915. The Mark number is stamped on the revolver frame. Composition grips. Enfield also made the Mk VI Webley during 1921-1926. Earlier Marks can sell at a 30-50% plus premium over the Marks V and VI as well as more scarce Enfield production (1921-1926). Mfg. by Webley & Scott.

$900 $800 $700 $600 $525 $450 $375

.380 WEBLEY REVOLVER - some purchased privately by officers as well by police forces and security, early Marks and RIC (Royal Irish Constabulary) models by P. Webley & Son, the Mark or designation usually stamped on left side of revolver frame, wood or composition grips. Earlier Marks can sell at a 30-50% plus premium over the Mark IV Webley & Scott. Mfg. by Webley & Scott.

$500 $450 $400 $350 $325 $275 $200

NO. 2 MK. I REVOLVER - .380 Enfield (based on .38 S&W with 200 gr. bullet), double action, 6-shot, fixed sights, blued or black finish, wood or composition grips, top break action, introduced in 1932. Essentially an Enfield copy of .380 Webley Mk IV.

$750 $650 $550 $450 $400 $300 $250

NO. 2 MK. I*/MK I REVOLVER** - .380 Enfield with hammer spur removed and other manufacturing concessions applied. Wartime production by Albion in England with very few by Howard Auto Cultivators (H.A.C.) in Australia which bring a huge premium due to a short run of only 355 revolvers. Enfield & Albion production only.

$600 $500 $425 $375 $325 $275 $225

RIFLES

.577 ENFIELD PATTERN 1853 RIFLE/CARBINE/MUSKET - adopted from 1853 as the general service issue, percussion lock marked Tower, Enfield, B.S.A., L.S.A., or Windsor on the lockplate, available in 3-band long rifle, 2-band short rifle, engineer (Lancaster), artillery and cavalry carbine configurations, many were supplied to the Confederacy during America's Civil war.

$1,700 $1,400 $1,200 $950 $825 $750 $625

.577 SNIDER-ENFIELD RIFLE/CARBINE - adopted in 1866 as a breech-loading conversion of the .577 Enfield, single shot, swing-over breech block, modified percussion lock, the Mk III improved locking breech in 1869 was new manufacture.

	$1,200	$1,000	$900	$800	$675	$550	$475

.450 MARTINI-HENRY - Britain's first purpose built breech-loader in 1871, hinged falling block action with internal lock mechanism, early Mk I rifle had a safety catch, Mk II rifle introduced in 1876, Cavalry Carbine in 1877, Artillery Carbine in 1879, Mk III rifle in 1879, and the long lever "humpback" Mk IV in 1887 which was sent to India & Nepal.

	$1,200	$1,000	$850	$750	$650	$500	$425

.303 MARTINI-METFORD - conversion of .450 M.-H. with Metford rifling, converted markings are stamped on left side of receiver. Artillery and Cavalry carbines are more prolific than the rifles; Artillery models are marked "A.C." with Mark number on left side of the receiver, Cavalry models are marked "C.C." followed by the Mark number. Metfords are much rarer than ensuing Martini-Enfield models, only made between 1889 and 1895, with more carbines converted than rifles. A small number of rifles were converted only for the colonies of Natal, South Australia, Western Australia and Canada. Most Martini-Metfords are marked "M.M. 303" on the left side of the action body whereas Martini-Enfields are marked "M.E. .303".

	$1,200	$1,050	$950	$850	$700	$600	$525

Add 50% for Royal Cypher marked M.M. Rifles. Add 25% for commercial pattern.

.303 MARTINI-ENFIELD - conversion of .450 M.-H., the converted markings are stamped on the left side of the receiver. Artillery and Cavalry carbines are more prolific than the rifles, Artillery models are marked "A.C." with the Mark number on the left side of the receiver and cavalry models are marked "C.C.", followed by the Mark number.

	$1,000	$900	$725	$675	$600	$500	$425

Add 50% for Royal Cypher marked M.E. Rifles. Add 10% for commercial pattern.

.303 MAGAZINE LEE-METFORD - introduced in 1888 with 7-groove Metford segmental rifling and 8-round detachable magazine, rifles proceeded through Marks I, I*, II, and II* which is marked on the right side of the action body below the factory and year, underneath the closed bolt handle, rifles have 30.2 in. barrels, carbines have 20 3/4 in. barrels. Mk I and I* rifle have single-row 8 round magazine, carbines are 6 round, Mk II and II* rifles are 10 round staggered box.

	$2,500	$2,100	$1,950	$1,800	$1,750	$1,500	$1,200

Add 50%+ for Mk I and Mk I* models.

.303 MAGAZINE LEE-ENFIELD - introduced in 1895 with 5-groove Enfield rifling for cordite loads, fitted with safety catch on the cocking piece, rifles and carbines went through Marks I and I*, Mk I* has no cleaning rod provision in forend or nosecap.

	$1,800	$1,700	$1,350	$1,250	$1,050	$900	$700

.303 CHARGER LOADING LEE-ENFIELD - M.L.M. and M.L.E. rifles with 30.2 in. barrels, modified for clip charger loading, after 1907 fitted with improved sights and foresight protector, conversions marked on left of receiver butt socket with factory and year.

	$1,650	$1,550	$1,450	$1,300	$1,100	$1,000	$900

.303 S.M.L.E. Mk I (SHORT, MAGAZINE, LEE-ENFIELD) - features a sliding charger guide on the bolthead, bone inserts on the rear sight slide and incurving nosecap foresight protector wings, 10 round staggered row detachable mag. with magazine cut-off provision in the receiver. Introduced 1903, made at Enfield, BSA, and LSA until 1907.

	$1,650	$1,550	$1,400	$1,200	$1,000	$900	$750

.303 S.M.L.E. Mk III (RIFLE No. 1 Mk III) - improved rearsight and rear handguard over the S.M.L.E. Mk I, still retains the magazine cut-off and volley sights of the Mk I S.M.L.E. model., approved in 1907, also made by Lithgow and Ishapore.

	$925	$725	$625	$575	$550	$525	$475

.303 RIFLE No. 1 Mk III* - later model that incorporates production shortcuts, no magazine cut-off, long range volley sights, or backsight windage adjustment. Made by Enfield, BSA, LSA, SSA, Lithgow, and Ishapore, introduced in 1915.

	$550	$500	$450	$400	$325	$250	$200

.303 RIFLE No. 1 Mk III* H.T. SNIPER - factory fitted telescopic sight and heavy barrel, converted at Lithgow, Australia at the end of WWII, special bedding of furniture, some were also fitted with a cheekpiece, British and Lithgow actions.

	$3,500	$3,000	$2,500	$2,000	$1,850	$1,600	$1,250

Buyer beware - check for authentic ser. nos., as there have been some fakes on this model.

.303 S.M.L.E. Mk V - features a folding aperture backsight on upper rear part of action body, reinforcing outer band at the base of the nosecap, full length top handguards, magazine cut-off, "V" marked safety catch with angled thumb grooves, limited production at Enfield in 1922-1924 of 20,000 rifles.

	$950	$900	$850	$800	$750	$650	$575

Many found with damaged rearsight or wanting the upper reinforcing band - check for replacement parts.

.22 PATT 1914 Nos. 1 & 2 - single-shot WW1 conversions by the British gun trade. No. 1 model is from S.M.L.E. Mk I, No. 2 is from S.M.L.E. Mk III.

	$750	$675	$625	$575	$500	$425	$350

The .22 Patt. 1914 No. 1 will bring a 30% premium due to its earlier S.M.L.E. Mk I configuration.

.22 No. 2 Mk IV* - converted No. 1 rifle (S.M.L.E.) to single-loading trainer, modified in Britain, Lithgow (Australia), and Ishapore (India).

	$600	$500	$375	$325	$300	$275	$220

.303 No. 3 (PATTERN 1914 RIFLE) - U.S. manufactured British modified Mauser action during WWI, made by Winchester, Remington and Eddystone, very similar to the U.S. .30 Model 1917, and shares many interchageable component parts.

	$850	$725	$600	$525	$450	$350	$275

Add 40% for Winchester Mk I*(F) with fine adj. backsight.

.303 No. 3 Mk I* (T) (PATTERN 1914 SNIPER) - converted in England by Periscope Prism Co. (1918) & B.S.A. (1938) from Winchester rifles, the Pattern 1918 telescope on crawfoot mounts was fitted.

	$4,500	$4,000	$3,500	$2,750	$2,000	$1,875	$1,625

.303 No. 3 Mk I* (T) A SNIPER - converted in England by Alex Martin in WWII from Winchester MK I* (F) rifles, Great War Aldis & P.P. Co. telescopes (ex-SMLE snipers) were fitted, original SMLE rifle engraved number is usually visible, usually off-set (left).

	$4,000	$3,500	$3,000	$2,750	$2,500	$2,300	$2,100

Add 30% for overhead mount.

.303 No. 4 Mk I & I* - WWII production Lee-Enfield, British R.O.F. Fazakerley, Maltby, and BSA Shirley (M47C) from 1941, Britain only made the Mk I model, wartime U.S. Lend-Lease production marked "US PROPERTY", serial number contains letter "S" while Canadian Long Branch rifles contain an "L", U.S. and Canada made both Mk I and Mk I* models.

	$750	$550	$500	$450	$375	$300	$250

Rare 1933 trials No. 4 rifles made at Enfield will bring a 50%+ premium.

GRADING - PPGS™	100%	98%	95%	90%	80%	70%	60%

.303 No. 4 Mk 2, Mk 1/2 & 1/3 - postwar Fazakerley [ROF(F)] production with the "hung" trigger and better quality fittings than wartime production, Mk 1/2 and 1/3 converted from Mk I and Mk I* rifles respectively, the No. 4 Mk 2 was of new manufacture, also made in the early 1970s at Wah Cantt, Pakistan on ex-Fazakerley machinery.

	$800	$700	$600	$550	$500	$450	$300

Add 30% for Mk II.

.303 No. 4 Mk I (T) - converted by Holland & Holland (S51) during WWII in England, also by Long Branch in Canada from indigenous production, the No. 32 telescopic sight was generally fitted, made in England or by R.E.L. in Canada.

	$4,000	$3,500	$3,000	$2,700	$2,450	$2,250	$1,950

w/o telescope sight
but original mounts

	$1,500	$1,200	$950	$850	$750	$650	$600

Add 25%-30% for issue green painted rifle chest with telescope carrier and case.
Add 30% for matching nos.

.303 No. 5 MK. I JUNGLE CARBINE - 20 1/2 in. barrel with flash hider, lightened action body and shortened furniture. From 1944, for service in the Far East.

	$650	$600	$550	$500	$450	$400	$350

Indian service issues have a transverse wood screw in the forend which is less desirable.

.22 No. 7 - postwar rimfire trainer on No. 4 action, British model has magazine feed, the Long Branch is designated "C No. 7" and is single shot only, but originally issued in chest. Mfg. in England by BSA and in Canada by Long Branch.

	$950	$900	$825	$750	$700	$600	$500

Add $200-$300 for original marked Canadian chest.
Subtract 40% if w/o bolthead.

.22 No. 8 Mk I - postwar rimfire trainer, half-stock target rifle style made by BSA (M47C) and Fazakerley on a modified No. 4 action body.

	$900	$800	$700	$625	$575	$500	$400

.22 No. 9 Mk I - single shot only, full length rifle resembling the No. 4, British conversion of the No. 4 Mk I rifle by Parker Hale for the Royal Navy.

	$750	$650	$600	$550	$500	$450	$400

7.62mm L42A1 SNIPER - Enfield conversion and extensive rebuild of the No. 4 Mk I(T) sniper rifle, fitted with an upgraded No. 32 telescopic sight to L1A1, half-stocked furniture, 7.62mm magazine with integral ejector, with heavy target barrel.

	$5,550	$5,000	$4,500	$4,000	$3,5000	$3,250	$2,750

Add 20% for original green finished chest.

.230 FRANCOTTE CADET MARTINI - turn of the century British empire trainer with Belgian Francotte patent, small size modular Martini action.

	$800	$700	$600	$500	$450	$350	$300

Add 30% for take-down model.

.310 CADET MARTINI - later production small Francotte action on Australian contract by W.W. Greener and BSA, circa 1910.

	$750	$600	$550	$475	$400	$325	$250

RIFLES: U.S. MILITARY

Add 10% for Winchester mfg.
Add 10% for Type I guns.

U.S. MODEL 1917 ENFIELD - .30-06 cal., bolt action, 5 shot, 26 in. barrel, original finish was high polish blue, adj. sights, military stock, derived from English P14 Enfield, over two million mfg. 1917-18, but original guns in 90%+ condition are rare.

GRADING - PPGS™	100%	98%	95%	90%	80%	70%	60%

✳ *U.S. Model 1917 Enfield Rifle Original high polish blue*

	$2,500	$1,800	$1,000	$875	$750	$525	$425

This model was manufactured primarily by Remington at the Eddystone plant in Eddystone, P.A. (Eddystone marked), the Ilion Remington plant, and by Winchester in New Haven, CT.

✳ *U.S. Model 1917 Enfield Rifle matte blue or parkerized reworks* - most frequently encountered variation, many differences in the reworked matte blue and parkerized finishes.

	$700	$600	$500	$400	$350	$315	$265

ENFIELD AMERICA, INC.
Previous manufacturer located in Atlanta, GA.

PISTOLS: SEMI-AUTO

MP-9 - 9mm Para. cal., paramilitary design, similar to MP-45. Mfg. 1985.

	$550	$475	$425	$350	$295	$260	$240

Add $150 for carbine kit.

MP-45 - .45 ACP cal., paramilitary design, 4 1/2, 6, 8, 10, or 18 1/2 in. shrouded barrel, parkerized finish, 10, 30, 40, or 50 shot mag., 6 lbs. Mfg. 1985 only.

	$550	$475	$425	$350	$295	$260	$240

Last MSR was $350.

ENGLISH SHOTGUNS
Shotguns manufactured by various British makers.

Unlike American shotguns such as Parker, L.C. Smith and A.H. Fox, the critical aspect of finish originality is not of premier importance with English shotguns. There are many English gunsmiths in both Britain and the U.S. who are capable of refinishing English guns on a level with the Old World masters. Of course, original guns with 100% original finish have the greatest desirability, but, when done properly, restored guns closely approach the same value of original guns. Do not confuse this with restored American guns, which are only worth a fraction of their "original" finish value.

Percentage of case colors on receivers and blue on barrels is not as critical in determining values, which diminish less drastically than with American guns. Tremendous fluctuations in value do occur in the smaller gauges (20, 28 ga. and .410 bore). The rarity and value of gauges, as they descend, are prodigious in English shotguns. However, the opposite is true in regard to double rifles, where bigger is better. A vintage English double with the original inside labeled trunk style case increases the gun's value $1,000 - $5,000+ depending on style, inclusive tools and accessories, and case materials. Exotic leathers such as crocodile, elephant and ostrich are also very valuable.

A fine old English double, tastefully engraved and stocked with exhibition Turkish walnut by a master craftsman, is a work of art that is highly treasured by collectors, and should be appropriately valued. The same application can apply to American guns, but again, is subject to narrower limitations.

Also unlike most other shotguns, English guns are more delicate and sleek in design, eliminating any excess metal and wood, resulting in minimum weight and balance. Because of this, there is far less margin for error in retaining necessary strength after modification such as chamber lengthening and back boring of barrels. Therefore, the importance of proof or reproofing after modification is a serious consideration. In Britain, it is serious enough to be a matter of law.

After years of hard use and sometimes neglect, rust pits appear in the bores which require back boring to restore them. Barrels can be cut and back bored to simulate chokes which are actually cylinder bore. This back boring must not result in more than a .015 in. increase in bore diameter from that of the original. Barrels more than .015 in. over original are considered "out of proof" and potentially dangerous. In any case, the barrel thickness should always exceed a minimum. Most authorities consider the minimum to be no less than .022 to .025 inch in wall thickness w/o a British reproof. The foregoing only applies to fluid steel barrels. Many consider

GRADING - PPGS™	100%	98%	95%	90%	80%	70%	60%

"nitro proofed" damascus barrels safe to shoot - however, this is a dangerous crapshoot. The above limitations are critical to overall value and must be established to buyer satisfaction prior to purchase. Bore micrometers and barrel thickness gauges are relatively inexpensive compared to the purchase of a $25,000 Purdey that has a true market value of only $10,000 because its aesthetically beautiful barrels are dangerously out of proof. New best English made chopper lump barrels currently cost around $10,000, and original Purdey made barrels are about three times as much. Remember, the most important criteria for purchasing an English shotgun is the barrels.

Somewhat of a paradox is the later serial numbered guns. Albeit generally of lesser quality than early guns, they are generally more valuable on a sliding scale due to the ever increasing cost of currently manufactured guns.

The publisher would like to thank Mr. Larry Baer for providing the above information.

ENTRÉPRISE ARMS INC.

Current manufacturer located in Irwindale, CA, since 1996. Dealer and consumer sales.

PISTOLS: SEMI-AUTO

The models listed are patterned after the Colt M1911, but have "Widebody" frames.

ELITE SERIES - .45 ACP cal., 3 1/4 in. barrel, features steel 1911 Widebody frame, flat mainspring housing, flared ejection port, 10 shot mag., bead blasted black oxide finish, tactical sights, 36 oz. New 1997.

✻ *Elite Series P325*

MSR $700	$625	$565	$500	$450	$400	$360	$330

✻ *Elite Series P425* - similar to Elite P325, except has 4 1/4 in. barrel, 38 oz. New 1997.

MSR $700	$625	$565	$500	$450	$400	$360	$330

✻ *Elite Series P500* - similar to Elite P325, except has 5 in. barrel, 40 oz. New 1997.

MSR $700	$625	$565	$500	$450	$400	$360	$330

TACTICAL SERIES - .45 ACP cal., 3 1/4 in. barrel, features Tactical Widebody with "De-horned" slide and frame allowing snag-free carry, narrow ambidextrous thumb safety, 10 shot mag., low profile Novak or ghost ring sights, squared trigger guard, flat main spring housing, matte black oxide finish, 36 oz. New 1997.

✻ *Tactical Series P325*

MSR $979	$875	$750	$650	$575	$500	$450	$395

✻ *Tactical Series P325 Plus* - similar to P325, except has short officer's length slide/barrel fitted onto a full government frame, designed as concealed carry pistol. New 1998.

MSR $979	$875	$750	$650	$575	$500	$450	$395

✻ *Tactical Series P425* - similar to Tactical P325, except has 4 1/4 in. barrel, 38 oz. New 1997.

MSR $979	$875	$750	$650	$575	$500	$450	$395

✻ *Tactical Series P500* - similar to Tactical P325, except has 5 in. barrel, 40 oz. New 1997.

MSR $979	$875	$750	$650	$575	$500	$450	$395

MEDALIST SERIES (TITLEIST, P500 NATIONAL MATCH) - .40 S&W or .45 ACP cal., 5 in. barrel, features tighter tolerances and numerous custom features, 10 shot mag., front and rear slide serrations, blue slide, includes Bo-Mar low mount rear adj. sight, 40 oz. New 1997.

MSR $979	$875	$750	$675	$575	$525	$475	$425

Add $120 for .40 S&W cal.

During 1999, this model's nomenclature changed from the Titleist Series to the Medalist Series.

GRADING - PPGS™	100%	98%	95%	90%	80%	70%	60%

BOXER SERIES - similar to Titleist Series, except has fully machined "high mass" frame and flattop slide. New 1998.

MSR $1,399	$1,200	$995	$850	$750	$625	$550	$500

    Add $100 for .40 S&W cal.

TOURNAMENT SHOOTER MODEL (TSM I-III) - .40 S&W or .45 ACP cal., 5, 5 1/2 (TSM III only), or 6 (.45 ACP only) in. barrel, blue finish, designed for IPSC competition, 10 shot mag., TSM II is standard, 40-44 oz. New 1997.

MSR $2,000	$1,800	$1,550	$1,325	$1,100	$950	$875	$750

    Add $300 for TSM I.
    Add $700 for TSM III.

CARBINES, SEMI-AUTO

STG58C CARBINE - .308 Win. cal., paramilitary design, 16 1/2 in. barrel with muzzle brake, synthetic pistol grip stock, last shot bolt hold open, adj. gas system, mil-spec black oxide finish, 20 shot mag., 200-600 meter aperture sights, supplied with black nylon sling, various configurations, approx. 9 lbs. New 2000.

* *STG58C Carbine Scout* - Entreprise Type 03 receiver, integral bipod, includes carry handle. New 2000.

MSR $1,199	$1,075	$875	$750	$625	$575	$500	$450

* *STG58C Carbine* - Entreprise Type 01 receiver, machined aluminum free-floating handguards, carry handle. New 2000.

MSR $1,399	$1,200	$995	$850	$750	$625	$550	$500

RIFLES: SEMI-AUTO

STG58C RIFLE - .308 Win. cal., paramilitary design, choice of 16 1/2, 21, or 24 in. barrel with muzzle brake, synthetic pistol grip stock, last shot bolt hold open, adj. gas system, mil-spec black oxide finish, 20 shot mag., 200-600 meter aperture sights, supplied with black nylon sling, various configurations, 8 1/2-13 lbs. New 2000.

* *STG58C Rifle Lightweight Model* - 16 1/2 in. barrel, Entreprise Type 03 receiver, 8 1/2 lbs. New 2000.

MSR $1,199	$1,050	$900	$800	$725	$650	$600	$550

* *STG58C Rifle Standard Model* - 21 in. barrel, Entreprise Type 03 receiver, integral bipod, 9.8 lbs. New 2000.

MSR $899	$795	$700	$625	$525	$475	$425	$375

    Add $100 for CA configuration.

* *STG58C Rifle Government Model* - 21 in. barrel, Entreprise Type 01 receiver, integral bipod, 9 1/2 lbs. New 2000.

MSR $1,199	$1,050	$900	$800	$725	$650	$600	$550

* *STG58C Rifle Target Model* - 21 in. barrel, Entreprise Type 01 receiver, with aluminum free-floating handguards, 11 1/2 lbs. New 2000.

MSR $1,399	$1,200	$995	$850	$750	$625	$550	$500

* *STG58C Rifle Match Target Model* - 24 in. match heavy barrel, Entreprise Type 01 receiver, with aluminum fee-floating handguards, 13 lbs. New 2000.

MSR $1,999	$1,825	$1,650	$1,475	$1,200	$1,000	$850	$750

ERA

Previous manufacturer located in Brazil.

SHOTGUNS

ERA O/U - 12 or 20 ga., 28 in. vent. rib barrel, full and mod., double triggers, extractors, checkered hardwood stock.

	$275	$250	$225	$200	$170	$150	$125

GRADING - PPGS™	100%	98%	95%	90%	80%	70%	60%
Trap version	$300	$275	$250	$225	$200	$175	$150
Skeet version	$300	$275	$250	$225	$200	$175	$150

ERA SxS - 12, 20 ga., or .410 bore, 26, 28, or 30 in. barrels, various chokes, double triggers, extractors, checkered pistol grip stock.

	$165	$150	$135	$125	$110	$100	$85

ERA RIOT SxS - 12 or 20 ga., 18 in. barrels.

	$185	$175	$150	$140	$125	$110	$95

ERA QUAIL SxS - 12 or 20 ga., 20 in. barrels.

	$185	$175	$150	$140	$125	$110	$95

ERHARDT, DENNIS

Current custom manufacturer and gunsmith located in Helena, MT.

Dennis Erhardt is a custom maker specializing in modern classic and European style custom rifles and shotguns. Many options and configurations available. Please contact the company directly for more information and pricing (see Trademark Index).

ERMA SUHL, GmbH

Previous manufacturer located in Suhl, Germany January 1998 - circa 2004. Erma Suhl purchased the remaining assets from Erma-Werke.

RIFLES: BOLT ACTION

SR100 SNIPER RIFLE - .300 Win. Mag., .308 Win., or .338 Lapua Mag. cal., bolt action, tactical rifle featuring brown laminated wood stock with thumbhole, adj. buttplate/cheekpiece, and vent. forend, forged aluminum receiver, 25 1/2 or 29 1/2 in. barrel, muzzle brake, adj. match trigger, approx. 15 lbs. Limited importation 1997-98 only.

	$6,500	$5,750	$5,000	$4,350	$3,750	$3,000	$2,350

Last MSR was $8,600.

This model was imported exclusively by Amtec 2000, Inc., located in Gardner, MA. Most recent importation was in .300 Win. Mag., and included a Steyr scope mount.

ERMA-WERKE

Previous manufacturer located in Dachau, Germany (Erma-Werke production) until bankruptcy occurred in October of 1997. Pistols were previously imported and distributed by Precision Sales International, Inc. located in Westfield, MA, Nygord Precision Products located in Prescott, AZ, and Mandall's Shooting Supplies, Inc. located in Scottsdale, AZ. Previously distributed by Excam located in Hialeah, FL.

Erma-Werke also manufactured private label handguns for American Arms Inc. (refer to their section for listings).

PISTOLS: SEMI-AUTO

MODEL LA 22 - .22 LR cal., action patterned after the Luger. Mfg. 1964-67.

	$395	$335	$275	$240	$200	$175	$140

ERMA KGP68A/BEEMAN MP-08 - .32 ACP or .380 ACP cal., Luger type toggle action, 3 1/2 (Beeman) or 4 in. barrel, 6 shot mag., blue, 1.4 lbs. Mfg. 1968-disc.

	$450	$400	$335	$275	$240	$185	$145

Last MSR was $500.

This model was imported exclusively by Mandall's Shooting Supplies, Inc. located in Scottsdale, AZ. From 1988-90, Beeman took over importation of this model in .380 ACP cal. only with new Luger style checkered walnut grips and 3 1/2 in. barrel. Previous models had plastic grips.

GRADING - PPGS™	100%	98%	95%	90%	80%	70%	60%

ERMA KGP69/BEEMAN P-08 - .22 LR cal., Luger type toggle action, 8 shot mag., 3 3/4 in. barrel, blue, plastic (disc.) or checkered walnut grips. Mfg. 1969-disc.

	$335	$275	$240	$185	$145	$115	$95

Last MSR was $390.

Beeman was the sole importer of this model between 1988-90.

MODEL ESP 85A SPORT/MATCH PISTOL - .22 LR or .32 S&W Long Wadcutter cal., blow back semi-auto, 6 in. barrel, 5 or 8 (.32 S&W only) shot mag., choice of sporting or adj. stippled match grips with thumbrest, fully adj. and interchangeable sights, gun is supplied with 1 extra weight, extra mag., sights, disassembly tools, and attaché style case ($134 option) with foam rubber cut-outs, 2 1/2 lbs. Imported 1989-97.

	$1,225	$925	$800	$650	$550	$495	$450

Last MSR was $1,785.

> Subtract $315 for Junior Model.
> Add $215 for .32 S&W cal.
> Add $110 for Match Model (with anatomical grips).
> Add $980-$1,390 for conversion unit.
> Add approx. $215 for chrome finish.
> Add $24 for left-hand action (Match Model only - disc. 1994).

ESP 85 refers to Junior Model (new 1995). The ESP 85 series was distributed by Precision Sales International, Inc. and Mandall Shooting Supplies, Inc.

✳ *Model ESP 85A Sport/Match Pistol Complete Set* - includes both .22 LR and .32 S&W Long Wadcutter barrels and mags., cased with accessories, complete set was disc. 1991.

	$1,525	$1,350	$1,125	$950	$825	$750	$625

Last MSR was $1,995.

EP-22 - similar to Model LA 22.

	$395	$335	$275	$240	$200	$175	$140

ET-22 LUGER CARBINE - .22 LR cal., 11 3/4 in. barrel, blue rear ramp sight, checkered walnut grips and uncheckered forearm, adj. artillery type rear sight, rarely seen.

	$500	$400	$350	$300	$250	$200	$175

Add 20% for leatherette case.

REVOLVERS: DOUBLE ACTION

These models were distributed by Precision Sales International, Inc. only.

ER-772 STANDARD/MATCH - .22 LR cal., standard or match gun with special adj. contoured grips with stippling, 6 in. barrel, action similar to ER-777, fully adj. and extended rear sight, interchangeable front sight, 3 lbs. Imported 1990-94.

	$1,100	$875	$725	$625	$550	$495	$450

Last MSR was $1,371.

ER-773 STANDARD/MATCH - .32 S&W Long Wadcutter cal., otherwise similar to ER-772 Match, 2.9 lbs. Imported 1990-95.

	$925	$825	$695	$525	$475	$425	$385

Last MSR was $1,068.

ER-777 STANDARD - .357 Mag. cal., 6 shot, 4 or 5 1/2 in. barrel, solid rib and full barrel shroud, adj. target rear sight, blue steel, checkered sport grips, 2 3/4 lbs. Imported 1990-95.

	$875	$775	$650	$475	$425	$385	$350

Last MSR was $1,019.

RIFLES

Models listed were available from Mandall Shooting Supplies, unless otherwise noted.

GRADING - PPGS™	100%	98%	95%	90%	80%	70%	60%

EM-1 .22 CARBINE - .22 LR cal., M1 copy, 10 or 15 shot mag., 18 in. barrel, rear adj. aperture sight, 5.6 lbs. Mfg. 1966-97.

	$365	$295	$250	$215	$190	$175	$160

Last MSR was $400.

EGM-1 - similar to EM-1 except for unslotted buttstock, 5 shot mag.

	$260	$230	$195	$175	$150	$125	$100

Last MSR was $295.

EG-72 PUMP - .22 LR cal., outside hammer, 15 shot mag., 18 1/2 in. barrel. Mfg. 1970-76.

	$125	$95	$90	$75	$70	$65	$60

EG-712 LEVER-ACTION - .22 LR cal., Win. Model 94 copy, tube mag., 18 1/2 in. barrel. Mfg. 1976-97.

	$260	$230	$195	$175	$150	$125	$100

Last MSR was $295.

EG-73 - .22 Mag. cal., similar to EG-712 12 shot mag. Mfg. 1973-97.

	$265	$230	$195	$175	$150	$125	$100

Last MSR was $300.

ERN, MAX

Current custom rifle and shotgun manufacturer located in Leverkusen-Schlebusch, Germany. Currently imported by New England Custom Gun Service, located in Plainfield, NH.

Max Ern builds high quality double (SxS and O/U) rifles, bolt action rifles, and boxlock shotguns. Current base prices are as follows: bolt action Model 98 - €9,880, takedown bolt action Model 98 - €15,760, sidelock single barrel rifle - €37,600, sidelock SxS double rifle - €51,300, O/U sidelock double rifle - €58,200, and SxS boxlock shotgun (20 ga.) - €23,000. A variety of options and special orders are available. Please contact the importer directly for more information, including an individualized price quotation, availability, and delivery time (see Trademark Index).

ESCALADE

Current trademark of slide action shotguns imported by Mitchell's Mausers, located in Fountain Valley, CA.

SHOTGUNS: SLIDE ACTION

ESCALADE MODEL - 12 ga. only, 18 1/2, 22 or 28 in. chrome lined barrel with choke tubes (except Home Defense model), dual action bars, Turkish walnut checkered stock and grooved forearm, available in Home Defense (18 1/2 in.) or Hunting (22 or 28 in.) configurations. Importation from Turkey 2004-2007.

	$360	$295	$260	$220	$175	$150	$125

Last MSR was $395.

ESCORT

Current trademark of shotguns manaufactured by Hatsan Arms Co., located in Izmir, Turkey, and imported beginning 2002 by Legacy Sports International, located in Reno, NV. Previously located in Alexandria, VA.

SHOTGUNS: O/U

ESCORT - 12 ga. only, 3 in. chambers, 28 in. VR barrels with five choke tubes, boxlock action with choice of blue or silver finished receiver, walnut or synthetic stock and forearm, ST, extractors, 7.4 lbs. Importation began 2007.

MSR $564	$485	$425	$375	$325	$275	$225	$185

Add $36 for either walnut stock with silver receiver or synthetic stock with silver receiver.
Add $186 for AAA select walnut stock and silver finished receiver.

GRADING - PPGS™	100%	98%	95%	90%	80%	70%	60%

SHOTGUNS: SEMI-AUTO

Beginning 2004, all models have a round back receiver with 3/8 in. dovetail milled along top for mounting sights.

ESCORT SERIES - 3 IN. - 12 or 20 (new 2005) ga., 3 in. chamber, gas operated action with 2 position adj. screw (disc. 2003), 20, 22 (AS Youth and PS Slug, new 2005), 24, 26 (new 2005), or 28 in. VR barrel with 3 multi-chokes, blue finish, vent recoil pad, gold trigger, checkered walnut (Model AS) or polymer (Model PS) black or 100% camo coverage Mossy Oak Break Up (disc. 2004), Mossy Oak Obsession (new 2005), or Shadowgrass camo stock and forearm, 6.4-7 lbs. Importation began 2002.

MSR $417	$360	$310	$285	$255	$230	$215	$195

Add $23 for walnut stock and forearm.
Add $182 for AS Select Model with select walnut (new 2007).
Add $54 for 100% camo coverage.
Add $45 for Model PS Slug.
Add $175 for Model PS Slug Combo (new 2006).
Add $81 for 24 in. barrel with Model PS TriViz sights and Mossy Oak Break Up camo coverage (disc. 2004).

* *Escort Series - 3 in. - Aimguard* - similar to Escort model, except has black chrome finish, black polymer stock, 18 (new 2006) or 20 (disc. 2005) in. barrel, cylinder bore. Imported 2004-2007.

	$340	$295	$275	$250	$230	$215	$195

Last MSR was $392.

* *Escort Series - 3 in. - Waterfowl/Tukey Combo* - includes camo stock and forearm, 24 in. barrel with HiViz and TriViz sights and 28 in. barrel with HiViz Spark sight, hard case. Importation began 2003.

MSR $599	$490	$415	$375	$335	$300	$280	$260

ESCORT SERIES - 3 1/2 IN. - 12 ga., 3 1/2 in. chamber, polymer stock and forearm, blued steel or Mossy Oak Obsession or Shadowgrass (new 2007) camo coverage, 24 or 28 in. barrel with choke tubes, standard or choice of Spark front sight or TriViz sights, 7.6 lbs. Importation began 2005.

MSR $479	$395	$330	$300	$275	$250	$230	$215

Add $56 for camo and Spark front sight.
Add $64 for 24 in. barrel with Model PS TriViz sights and camo coverage.

SHOTGUNS: SLIDE ACTION

ESCORT SERIES - 12 or 20 (new 2005) ga., 3 in. chamber, matte blue finish or 100% camo coverage with polymer stock and forearm, 18 (Aimguard or MarineGuard Model), 22 (Field Slug, new 2005), 24 (Turkey, includes extra turkey choke tube and FH TriViz sight combo with Mossy Oak Break Up [disc. 2004] or Obsession camo coverage), 26 (new 2005, Field Hunter) or 28 (Field Hunter) in. barrel, alloy receiver with 3/8 in. milled dovetail for sight mounting, trigger guard safety, 4 or 5 shot mag. with cut off button, two stock adj. shims, 6.4-7 lbs. Importation began 2003.

* *Escort Series Aimguard* - 12 ga., 18 in. barrel with black synthetic stock, fixed cyl. bore choke, 6.4 lbs.

MSR $226	$175	$145	$125	$110	$100	$90	$80

* *Escort Series MarineGuard* - 12 ga., 18 in. barrel with black synthetic stock, nickel receiver, fixed cyl. bore choke, 6.4 lbs.

MSR $271	$210	$175	$145	$120	$105	$90	$80

GRADING - PPGS™	100%	98%	95%	90%	80%	70%	60%

* *Escort Series Field Hunter* - 12 or 20 ga., 24 or 28 in. barrel, 100% Mossy Oak Obsession or Shadowgrass camo coverage or matte blue finish, includes 3 choke tubes.

MSR $280	$220	$185	$155	$130	$110	$90	$80

Add $55 for 100% camo coverage.
Add $23 for combo in 12 ga. (disc. 2006).
Add $100 for FH TriViz sights in Obsession camo finish with extra Turkey choke tube.
Add $16 for Slug.
Add $144 for Slug Combo (disc. 2006).

EUROARMS ITALIA Srl

Current black powder replica manufacturer and importer/exporter located in Concesio, Italy.

Euroarms Italia is the new name for Armi San Paolo, and was established during 2002. Euroarms Italia exports its black powder reproductions and accessories through Euroarms of America, Dixie Gun Works, Cabela's, and Navy Arms.

EUROARMS OF AMERICA

Current black powder replica importer and distributor located in Winchester, VA. Manufactured by Euroarms Italia Srl, established 1970, and located in Concesio, Italy. The factory was previously named Armi San Paolo until 2002.

Euroarms imported a variety of firearms, including revolvers and rifles, mfg. by Armi San Paolo between 1970-1996. Values are determined by other similar competitive makes and models, and the condition factor.

Please refer to the *Blue Book of Modern Black Powder Arms* by John Allen (also online) for more information and prices on Euroarms of America's quality lineup of modern black powder reproductions and replicas.

Black Powder Reproductions & Replicas by Dennis Adler is also an invaluable source for most black powder reproductions and replicas, and includes hundreds of color images on most popular makes/models, provides manufacturer/trademark histories, and up-to-date information on related items/accessories for black powder shooting - www.bluebookinc.com

EUROPEAN AMERICAN ARMORY CORP.

Current importer and distributor established in late 1990 and located in Rockledge, FL. Previous located in Sharpes, FL 1990-2006. Distributor and dealer sales.

EAA currently imports its handguns from Tanfoglio, located in Italy, and from H. Weihrauch, located in Germany. All guns are covered by EAA's lifetime limited warranty. EAA has also imported various trademarks of long guns, including Saiga, Weihrauch, and Izhmash. Please refer to these individual sections.

PISTOLS: SEMI-AUTO

The following Witness pistols also have a .22 LR conversion kit available for $229.

WITNESS EA 38 SUPER SERIES - .38 Super cal., action patterned after the CZ-75, selective double action, 4 1/2 in. barrel, steel or polymer frame/steel slide (mfg. 1997-2004), 10 (C/B 1994), 18 (new late 2004) or 19* shot mag., choice of Wonder (heat treated grey satin finish, new 1997), stainless steel (disc. 1996) or blue, blue/chrome (disc. 1994), or brushed chrome (disc. 1996) finish, combat sights, black neoprene grips, 33 oz. Importation began 1994.

MSR $514	$415	$340	$275	$240	$200	$185	$180

Subtract $20 for polymer frame.

* *Model EA 38 Stainless* - similar to EA 38, except is stainless steel. Imported 1994-96.

	$525	$435	$350	$285	$250	$215	$185

Last MSR was $595.

GRADING - PPGS™	100%	98%	95%	90%	80%	70%	60%

✳ *Model EA 38 Compact* - similar to EA 38 Super Series, except has 3 5/8 in. unported or ported barrel, choice of matte blue or Wonder finish, 30 oz. Mfg. 1999-2004.

	$370	$310	$255	$225	$200	$185	$180

Last MSR was $449.

Subtract $20 for polymer frame.
Add $20 for Wonder finish or ported barrel (polymer frame only).

WITNESS EA 9 SERIES - 9mm Para. cal., action patterned after the CZ-75, selective double action, 4 1/2 in. unported or ported (polymer, New Frame only, new 2002) barrel, steel or polymer frame/steel slide (new 1997), 10 (C/B 1994), 16*, or 18 (new late 2004) shot mag., choice of Wonder (new 1997), stainless steel (disc. 1996) or blue, blue/chrome (disc. 1993), or brushed chrome (disc. 1996) finish, combat sights, black neoprene grips, 33 oz. Importation began late 1990.

MSR $514	$415	$340	$275	$240	$200	$185	$180

Subtract $20 for polymer frame (disc.), or $42 for polymer New Frame.

✳ *Model EA 9 Stainless* - similar to EA 9, except is stainless steel. Imported 1992-96.

	$420	$350	$295	$240	$210	$180	$155

Last MSR was $480.

✳ *Model EA 9 (L) Compact* - similar to EA 9, except has 3 5/8 in. unported or ported (polymer frame only, mfg. 2002-2006) barrel and 10 (C/ B 1994), 12 (new late 2004), or 13* shot mag., 27 oz.

MSR $514	$415	$340	$275	$240	$200	$185	$180

Subtract $42 for polymer frame.
Add $10-$20 for ported barrel (polymer frame only, disc. 2006).

WITNESS EA 40 SERIES - .40 S&W cal., action patterned after the CZ-75, selective double action, 4 1/2 in. barrel, steel or polymer frame/steel slide (new 1997), 10 (C/B 1994), 12*, or 15 (new late 2004) shot mag., choice of Wonder (new 1997), stainless steel (disc. 1996) or blue, blue/chrome (disc.), or brushed chrome (disc. 1996) finish, combat sights, black neoprene grips, 33 oz. Importation began late 1990.

MSR $514	$415	$340	$275	$240	$200	$185	$180

Subtract $40 for polymer frame.
Subtract $42 for polymer New Frame.

✳ *Model EA 40 Stainless* - similar to EA 40, except is stainless steel. Imported 1992-96.

	$455	$365	$295	$240	$210	$180	$155

Last MSR was $509.

✳ *Model EA 40 (L) Compact* - similar to EA 40, except has 3 5/8 in. unported or ported barrel, 9 or 12 (new late 2004) shot mag.

MSR $514	$415	$340	$275	$240	$200	$185	$180

Subtract $42 for polymer frame.

Add $10-$20 for ported barrel (polymer frame only, disc. 2005).

WITNESS EA 10 SUPER SERIES - 10mm cal., action patterned after the CZ-75, selective double action, 4 1/2 in. barrel, steel frame, 10, 12*, or 15 (new late 2004) shot mag., choice of stainless steel (disc.), blue, chrome (disc.), or Wonder (new 1999) finish, combat sights, black neoprene grips, 33 oz. Imported 1994 only, resumed 1999.

MSR $514	$415	$340	$275	$240	$200	$185	$180

Add $30 for chrome finish (disc.).
Add $65 for stainless steel (disc.).

GRADING - PPGS™	100%	98%	95%	90%	80%	70%	60%

✳ *Model EA 10 Stainless* - similar to EA 10, except is stainless steel.

	$495	$425	$350	$285	$250	$215	$185

Last MSR was $566.

✳ *Model EA 10 Carry Comp* - similar to EA 10, except has 4 1/2 in. compensated barrel, blue or Wonder (new 2005) finish. Mfg. 1999-2005.

	$415	$350	$285	$240	$215	$190	$180

Last MSR was $489.

Subtract $20 for blue finish.

✳ *Model EA 10 Compact* - similar to EA 10, except has 3 5/8 in. barrel, 8 or 12 (new late 2004) shot mag., 27 oz.

MSR $514	$415	$340	$275	$240	$200	$185	$180

Subtract $42 for polymer frame.

WITNESS EA 41 SERIES - .41 Action Express cal., action patterned after the CZ-75, selective double action, 4 1/2 in. barrel, steel frame, 11 shot mag., blue, blue/chrome, or brushed chrome finish, combat sights, black neoprene grips, 33 oz. Importation disc. 1993.

	$450	$375	$325	$275	$250	$225	$200

Last MSR was $595.

Add $40 for blue/chrome or brushed chrome finish.

✳ *Model EA 41 Compact* - similar to EA 41, except has 3 1/2 in. barrel and 8 shot mag.

	$495	$425	$375	$325	$295	$260	$230

Last MSR was $625.

Add $40 for blue/chrome or brushed chrome finish.

WITNESS EA 45 SERIES - .45 ACP cal., action patterned after the CZ-75, selective double action, 4 1/2 in. standard or compensated (mfg. 1998-2005) barrel, steel frame, polymer full size frame (new 2004), or polymer frame/steel slide (new 1997), 10 (C/ B 1994) or 11* shot mag., choice of Wonder (new 1997), stainless steel (disc. 1996) or blue, blue/chrome (disc. 1993), or brushed chrome (disc. 1996) finish, combat sights, walnut grips, 35 oz. Importation began late 1990.

MSR $514	$415	$340	$275	$240	$200	$185	$180

Add $40 for ported barrel (steel only, with Wonder finish, disc. 2004).
Subtract $42 for polymer frame or blue finish.

✳ *Model EA 45 Stainless* - similar to EA 45, except is stainless steel. Imported 1992-96.

	$510	$430	$350	$285	$250	$215	$185

Last MSR was $595.

✳ *Model EA 45 (L) Compact* - similar to EA 45, except has 3 5/8 in. unported or ported barrel and 8 shot mag., 26 oz.

MSR $514	$415	$340	$275	$240	$200	$185	$180

Add $30 for ported barrel (polymer frame only, disc. 2004).
Add $50 for single port barrel compensator or carry configuration with compensator (disc.).
Subtract $42 for polymer frame.

WITNESS P CARRY - 9mm Para., 10mm, .40 S&W, or .45 ACP cal., SA/DA, 3.6 in. barrel, 10 (.45 ACP), 15 (10mm or .40 S&W), or 18 (9mm Para.) shot mag., full size polymer frame, compact slide, Commander style, Wonder finish, integral M-1913 rail, 27 oz. New 2006.

MSR $545	$425	$350	$285	$240	$210	$185	$180

GRADING - PPGS™	100%	98%	95%	90%	80%	70%	60%

WITNESS CARRY COMP GUN - .38 Super (disc. 1997), 9mm Para. (disc. 1997), .40 S&W cal. (disc. 1997), 10mm (disc. 1994, reintroduced 1999), or .45 ACP cal., full size frame with compact slide and 1 in. compensator, 10 (C/B 1994), 12* (.40 S&W), or 16* (9mm Para.) shot mag., Wonder (new 1997), blue or Duo-Tone (disc. 1994) finish. Imported 1992-2004.

	$425	$360	$310	$270	$235	$210	$195

Last MSR was $479.

Add $10 for Wonder finish.

WITNESS SPORT - .38 Super, 9mm Para., .40 S&W, 10mm (disc. 1994), or .45 ACP cal., 4 1/2 in. barrel, full size frame, standard slide length, Duo-Tone finish, extended safety and high capacity mag., target sights. Imported 1994-95.

	$535	$470	$400	$375	$350	$325	$295

Last MSR was $616.

Add $86 for .38 Super, 10mm, or .45 ACP cal.

WITNESS SPORT LONG SLIDE - .38 Super, 9mm Para., .40 S&W, 10mm (disc. 1994), or .45 ACP cal., long slide variation of the EA Series, except has 4 3/4 in. ported or unported barrel and slide, Duo-Tone finish, extended safety and high capacity mag., competition sights, 34 1/2 oz. Importation disc. 1995.

	$595	$500	$450	$395	$350	$325	$295

Last MSR was $681.

Add $79 for .38 Super, 10mm, or .45 ACP cal.

WITNESS LIMITED CLASS - .38 Super, 9mm Para., .40 S&W, or .45 ACP cal., match frame, competition grips, high capacity mag., single action trigger, long slide with match barrel and super sight, extended safety, blue finish only. Imported 1994-98.

	$855	$715	$610	$500	$450	$400	$375

Last MSR was $967.

* *Witness Limited* - 9mm Para., 10mm, .38 Super, .40 S&W or .45 ACP cal., 4 3/4 in. barrel, competition hard chrome frame, 10 (.45 ACP), 15 (.40 S&W or 10mm) or 18 (9mm Para. or .38 Super) shot mag., square trigger guard, full length dust shroud, cone slide lock up, checkered frame and back strap, skeletonized hammer, low profile checkered walnut grips, 39 oz. Importation began 2005.

MSR $1,102	$950	$800	$675	$550	$500	$450	$425

WITNESS COMBO PACKAGE - includes one built up frame and 9mm Para./.40 S&W complete conversion kits, blue, chrome, or Duo-Tone (disc. 1994) finish, full size variation with 4 1/2 in. barrel. Imported 1992-97.

	$515	$460	$400	$375	$350	$325	$295

Last MSR was $588.

Add $29 for chrome or Duo-Tone finish.

* *Witness Combo Package (L) Compact* - similar to Witness Combo Package, except has 3 5/8 in. barrels, blue only. Imported 1994-97.

	$515	$460	$400	$375	$350	$325	$295

Last MSR was $588.

WITNESS MULTI-CLASS PISTOL PACKAGE - .38 Super, 9mm Para., 9x21mm, .40 S&W, or .45 ACP cal., consists of one Witness Limited Class Pistol and complete Unlimited Class top half (slide and barrel), dual chamber steel compensator, blue finish only. Imported 1994 only.

	$1,450	$1,200	$1,025	$895	$775	$650	$525

Last MSR was $1,638.

GRADING - PPGS™	100%	98%	95%	90%	80%	70%	60%

WITNESS TRI-CALIBER PACKAGE - includes one built up frame and caliber conversions (9mm Para., .40 S&W, and .41 AE) that include slide, barrel, recoil guide, and spring, matte blue or chrome finish, compact or full size variations, includes carry case. Imported 1992-1993 only.

	$975	$825	$700	$575	$495	$425	$375

Last MSR was $1,195.

Add $40 for chrome finish.

WITNESS SILVER TEAM - .38 Super, 9mm Para., 9x21mm, 10mm (disc. 1994), .40 S&W, or .45 ACP cal., dual comp. chambers, SA trigger, super sight and drilled and tapped for scope mount, competition features include hammer, extended safety, paddle mag. release, black rubber grips, double-dip blue finish, high capacity mag. Imported 1992-98.

	$855	$710	$600	$500	$425	$375	$325

Last MSR was $967.

WITNESS GOLD TEAM - .38 Super, 9mm Para., 9x21mm, 10mm (disc. 1994), .40 S&W, or .45 ACP cal., triple comp. chambers, SA trigger, super sight and drilled and tapped for scope mount, top-of-the-line competition model featuring hand-fitted major components and 25 LPI checkering, hard chrome finish. Imported 1992-98.

	$1,875	$1,525	$1,250	$995	$825	$700	$575

Last MSR was $2,150.

This model was also available as a frame only - retail was $389.

✳ *Witness Gold Team* - 9mm Para., .38 Super, .40 S&W or .45 ACP cal., 5 1/4 in. barrel, triple chamber compensator, 15 (.40 S&W or .45 ACP) or 18 (9mm Para. or .38 Super) shot mag., competition hard chrome frame, tapered cone slide lock up, checkered frame and back strap, competition hammer safety, super sight, aluminum grips, 44 oz. Importation began 2005.

MSR $1,879		$1,625	$1,350	$1,100	$975	$850	$700	$575

WITNESS STOCK - 9mm Para., 10mm, .40 S&W or .45 ACP cal., 4 1/2 in. barrel, competition hard chrome frame, 10 (.45 ACP), 15 (.40 S&W or 10mm) or 18 (9mm Para.) shot mag., tapered cone slide lock up, checkered frame and back strap, extended safety, adj. sights, diamond checkered walnut grips, heart shaped hammer, 33 oz. Importation began 2005.

MSR $860		$735	$600	$485	$430	$375	$325	$275

WITNESS MATCH - 9mm Para., 10mm, .38 Super, .40 S&W, or .45 ACP cal., 4 3/4 in. polygonal rifled barrel, competition frame, SA with over travel stop, adj. rear sights, extended mag. release, rubber grips, two-tone finish, 33 oz. Importation began 2006.

MSR $640		$515	$415	$375	$335	$295	$260	$230

WITNESS HUNTER - 10mm or .45 ACP cal., 6 in. barrel, competition hard chrome frame, 10 (.45 ACP) or 15 (10mm) shot mag., checkered frame, blue or camo finish, tapered cone slide lock up, drilled and tapped, single action trigger, extended manual safety, low profile heavy duty adj. front sight, 41 oz. Importation began 2005.

MSR $1,007		$825	$700	$600	$525	$450	$385	$350

WITNESS FCP - .380 ACP, .38 Super, .38 Spl., 9mm Para., .40 S&W, or .45 ACP cal., polymer frame, DAO, blue finish, 6 shot, 4 in. barrel, fast cycle tube chamber, utitlizes simple reusable tubes that encase each round, no detachable mag., 26 oz. Disc. 2007.

	$185	$160	$145	$130	$120	$110	$100

Last MSR was $219.

GRADING - PPGS™	100%	98%	95%	90%	80%	70%	60%

F.A.B. 92 - 9mm Para. or .40 S&W cal., double action featuring hammer drop safety and decocker (Witness style), 4 1/2 in. barrel, 16* (9mm Para.) or 12* (.40 S&W), or 10 (C/B 1994) shot mag., all steel construction, blue, chrome (disc. 1993), or Duo-Tone (disc. 1993) finish, smooth wood grips, 33 oz. Imported 1992-95.

	$335	$280	$235	$210	$190	$170	$155

Last MSR was $386.

Add $40 for chrome or Duo-Tone finish.
Add $29 for .40 S&W cal.

F.A.B. designates Foreign American Brands.

* *F.A.B. 92 Compact* - similar to F.A.B. 92, except has 3 5/8 in. barrel, 13* (9mm Para.), 10 (9mm only, C/B 1994), or 9 (.40 S&W) shot mag., 30 oz. Imported 1992-95.

	$335	$280	$235	$210	$190	$170	$155

Last MSR was $386.

Add $40 for chrome or Duo-Tone finish.
Add $29 for .40 S&W cal.

ZASTAVA EZ - 9mm Para., .40 S&W, or .45 ACP cal., DA/SA, ambidextrous controls, 10 (.45 ACP), 11 (.40 S&W), or 15 (9mm Para.) shot mag., 4 in. barrel, aluminum frame, accessory rail, spur hammer, blue or chrome finish, 33 oz. Importation began 2007.

MSR $499		$450	$395	$350	$300	$275	$250	$225

Add $40 for chrome finish.

* *Zastava EZ Compact* - similar to Zastava EZ Model, except is compact frame, 7 (.45 ACP), 8 (.40 S&W), or 12 shot mag., 3 1/2 in. barrel. Importation began 2007.

MSR $499		$450	$395	$350	$300	$275	$250	$225

Add $40 for chrome finish.

ZASTAVA M88 - 9mm Para. or .40 S&W cal., SA, 8 shot mag. Importation began 2008.

MSR $275		$225	$200	$180	$160	$145	$130	$120

Add $20 for .40 S&W cal.

PISTOLS: SEMI-AUTO, EUROPEAN SERIES

MODEL EA220 - .22 LR cal., 3.88 in. barrel, 10 shot mag., single action, steel frame, 26 oz., blue, chrome or blue/chrome, wood grips. Importation disc. 1992.

	$185	$150	$120	$100	$95	$85	$75

Last MSR was $225.

Add approx. $20 for chrome or blue/chrome finish.

MODEL EA22-T - .22 LR cal., 6 in. barrel, cocking indicator and grip safety, 5 or 12 shot mag., adj. trigger and grip, single action, steel frame, target model, 40 oz. Imported 1991-93.

	$375	$295	$260	$220	$185	$165	$150

Last MSR was $450.

EUROPEAN 32 (320) - .32 ACP cal., 3.88 in. barrel, 7 shot mag., single action, steel frame, 26 oz., blue, chrome or blue/chrome, wood grips. Importation 1991-95.

	$130	$110	$95	$85	$80	$75	$70

Last MSR was $161.

Add $14 for chrome finish.

GRADING - PPGS™	100%	98%	95%	90%	80%	70%	60%

EUROPEAN 380 - .380 ACP cal., single (new 1994) or double (disc. 1994) action, 3 7/8 in. barrel, blue, brushed chrome (disc. 1996), Wonder finish (new 1997), matte blue/chrome (disc. 1993), or blue/gold plated Duo-Tone (European Lady, disc. 1995) finish, 7 shot bottom release mag., steel construction, firing pin safety, external hammer, smooth wood or ivory rose polymer (European Lady) grips, 26 oz. Imported 1992-2001.

	$145	$115	$95	$85	$75	$70	$65

Last MSR was $179.

Add $9 for Wonder finish (new 1997).
Add $67 for European Lady model (disc. 1995).
Add $32 for double action design (disc. 1994).
Add $14 for brushed chrome or matte blue/chrome (disc. 1993) finish.

This model employed a unique patented magazine gun lock system.

PISTOLS: SINGLE SHOT

THOR RAPTOR - .223 Rem., .270 Win., .30-06, .300 Win. Mag., .308 Win., .375 Win., .44 Mag., .45-70 Govt., .500 S&W, 7mm-08 Rem., or 7mm Rem. cal., blue steel frame, 14 in. barrel with polygonal rifling, single action, rubber grips, auto ejector, integral sight base, 5 lbs. Imported 2005 only.

	$895	$775	$700	$625	$550	$475	$395

Last MSR was $1,099.

REVOLVERS: DOUBLE ACTION, WINDICATOR SERIES

STANDARD GRADE - .22 LR (disc.), .22LR/.22 Mag. combo. (disc.), .22 Mag. (disc.), .32 H&R (disc. 1993), .357 Mag. (new 1994), or .38 Spl. (alloy frame only) cal., 2 (.32 H&R, .357 Mag., or .38 Spl. only), 4 (new 1997), or 6 (disc.) in. squared off barrel, blue or chrome (.38 Spl. only, new 1994) finish, steel or alloy frame, 6 (.38 Spl.), 7 (.32 H&R), or 8 (.22 LR/.22 Mag.) shot, finger grooved rubber grips. Importation from Germany began 1992.

MSR $285		$230	$200	$175	$150	$125	$110	$100

Add $10 for steel frame in .357 Mag. cal.
Add $20 for 4 in. barrel.
Add $78 for .22 LR/.22 Mag. combo. (disc.).

TACTICAL GRADE - .38 Spl. cal. only, fixed sights, 6 shot, 2 in. (bobbed hammer) or 4 in. compensated barrel, blue finish only. Imported 1992-93.

	$220	$190	$165	$145	$130	$115	$105

Last MSR was $295.

Add $80 for 4 in. compensated barrel.

TARGET GRADE - .22 LR, .357 Mag., or .38 Spl. cal., 6 or 8 (.22 LR) shot, 6 in. squared off barrel, finger grooved hardwood stocks, adj. trigger pull and rear sight, blue finish only, 3.1 lbs. Imported 1992-1993.

	$425	$325	$260	$220	$200	$185	$170

Last MSR was $550.

REVOLVERS: SAA, BOUNTY HUNTER SERIES

MODEL EASAB - .22 LR cal., single action revolver, 6 shot, 4 3/4 in. barrel, blue or chrome (disc. 1991) finish, wood grips. Importation disc. 1995.

	$70	$55	$50	$45	$40	$35	$30

Last MSR was $85.

Add $20 for chrome finish.

GRADING - PPGS™	100%	98%	95%	90%	80%	70%	60%

MODEL EASAMB COMBO - includes .22 LR and .22 Mag. cal. cylinders, 4 3/4 (standard), 6, or 9 in. barrel, blue finish, wood grips. Importation disc. 1995.

	$85	$75	$65	$55	$50	$45	$40

Last MSR was $100.

Add $14 for 9 in. barrel.
Add $40 for gold backstrap and trigger guard (disc.).

BIG BORE BOUNTY HUNTER - .357 Mag., .44-40 WCF (new 2005, 7 1/2 in. barrel only), .44 Mag., or .45 LC cal., 4 1/2 (new 1994), 5 1/2 (disc. 1993), or 7 1/2 in. barrel, 6 shot, choice of blue, chrome (mfg. 1994-95), nickel (new 1998), or case colored finish, gold trigger guard/backstrap (disc. 1994), or gold (disc.) finish, 32-41 oz. New 1992.

MSR $410	$345	$285	$230	$195	$175	$165	$150

Add $10 for .44 Mag. or .45 LC cal. or $30 for .44-40 WCF cal.
Add $30 for nickel finish.
Add $20 for chrome finish (disc.).
Add $15 for gold-plated grip strap and trigger guard (disc.).
Add approx. $100 for gold plated finish (disc.)

* *Small Bore Bounty Hunter Combo* - includes .22 LR/.22 Mag. cal. cylinders, 4 3/4 or 6 3/4 in. barrel, half cock mechanism and transfer bar safety, choice of 6 or 8 shot, blue or nickel (new 1998) finish. New 1997.

MSR $305	$240	$210	$175	$150	$130	$120	$110

Add $30 for nickel finish.

RIFLES

With the exception of the M-93, EAA rifles were manufactured by Sabatti in Italy (est. 1674), Lu-Mar in Italy, and H. Weihrauch in Germany (see separate listing in the H. Weihrauch section). Imported 1992-96.

SP1822 SEMI-AUTO SPORTER - .22 LR cal., semi-auto, 18 1/2 in. barrel, wood stock and forearm, adj. sights, 10 shot box mag., 5 1/4-6 1/2 lbs. Imported 1994-96.

	$180	$145	$120	$100	$90	$80	$70

Last MSR was $206.

* *SP1822 Semi-Auto Sporter Thumbhole* - similar to Sporter, except has one-piece Bell & Carlson green synthetic thumbhole stock, without sights. Importation disc. 1995.

	$310	$260	$230	$200	$175	$150	$135

Last MSR was $358.

ZASTAVA PAP 762 SEMI-AUTO - 7.62x39mm cal., patterned after the AK-47. Importation began 2008.

MSR $489	$425	$365	$335	$295	$265	$240	$220

ROVER 870 BOLT ACTION - .22-250 Rem., .243 Win., .25-06 Rem., .270 Win., .30-06, .308 Win., 7mm Rem. Mag., .300 Win. Mag., or .338 Win. Mag. cal., bolt action rifle featuring all-steel construction with 22 in. hammer-forged rifled barrel, staggered 5 shot internal mag., open sights. Imported 1993 only.

	$795	$695	$600	$550	$495	$450	$395

Last MSR was $995.

M-93 BLACK ARROW BOLT ACTION - .50 BMG cal., Mauser action, 36 in. fluted heavy barrel with muzzle brake, adj. folding bi-pod, iron sights, detachable 5 shot mag., carry handle, detachable scope mount, wood case, 35 lbs. Mfg. by Zastava, importation began 2007.

MSR $7,035	$6,400	$5,800	$5,000	$4,250	$3,500	$2,900	$2,300

GRADING - PPGS™	100%	98%	95%	90%	80%	70%	60%

SHOTGUNS: O/U

SCIROCCO BASIC - 12 ga. only, single trigger, extractors, 26 or 28 in. fixed choke VR barrels, boxlock action, nickel engraved frame. Imported 1994-95.

	$425	$350	$315	$285	$260	$240	$220

Last MSR was $478.

This model was mfg. by Lu-Mar located in Italy.

SCIROCCO SPORTING CLAYS - 12 ga. only, 28 or 30 in. barrels with 5 choke tubes and wide VR, SST, ejectors, Raybar front sight, nickel engraved frame. Imported 1994-95.

	$650	$550	$495	$450	$400	$350	$315

Last MSR was $734.

This model was mfg. by Lu-Mar located in Italy.

FALCON - 12, 20 ga., or .410 bore, 3 in. chambers, 26, 28, or 30 in. fixed choke VR barrels, boxlock action, single or double trigger, extractors or ejectors, checkered pistol grip and forend. Imported 1993 only.

	$650	$525	$450	$375	$325	$295	$260

Last MSR was $795.

Add $80 for .410 bore.
Add $100 for SST and ejectors.

SPORTING CLAYS PRO GOLD - 12 ga. only, 2 3/4 in. chambers, 28 or 30 in. screw-in choke barrels with wide VR, boxlock action, SST, ejectors, blue frame with engraving, recoil pad with custom carry case. Imported 1993-94.

	$850	$725	$650	$575	$525	$475	$425

Last MSR was $978.

SHOTGUNS: SxS

SABA - 12, 20, 28 ga., or .410 bore, 3 in. chambers, boxlock action with scrolled nickel finish, DT or SST, 26 or 28 in. fixed choke barrels with raised matted rib, ejectors, checkered stock and forearm with sling swivels. Imported 1993 only.

	$950	$825	$700	$575	$495	$425	$375

Last MSR was $1,195.

Add $100 for SST.

SHOTGUNS: SEMI-AUTO

BUNDA SERIES - 12 ga. only, 2 3/4 or 3 in. chamber (depending on barrel) gas operated, 19, 26, 28 or 30 in. barrel with 4 choke tubes, choice of black synthetic or Turkish walnut stock and forearm, aluminum receiver. Limited importation 1998 only.

	$360	$300	$275	$250	$225	$200	$185

Last MSR was $406.

Add $9 for Turkish walnut stock and forearm.

SHOTGUNS: SLIDE ACTION

MODEL PM2 - 12 ga. only, slide action, unique 7 shot detachable mag., 20 in. barrel, black wood stock and composite forearm, dual action bars, cross-bolt safety on triggerguard, available in matte blue or chrome finish, 6.81 lbs. Imported 1992 only.

	$550	$450	$395	$335	$295	$260	$230

Last MSR was $695.

Add $200 for night sights.
Add $75 for matte chrome finish.

GRADING - PPGS™	100%	98%	95%	90%	80%	70%	60%

EVANS, WILLIAM, GUN & RIFLE MAKERS

Please refer to the W section in this text.

EVOLUTION USA

Current rifle manufacturer located in White Bird, ID since 1993.
Distributor and dealer sales.

RIFLES: BOLT ACTION

ARGALI - most short action cals., trued Rem. Model 700 action, Krieger ultra light barrel, synthetic stock, 5 1/2 lbs. Mfg. 2000-2004.

	$2,000	$1,700	$1,450	$1,225	$950	$775	$675

Last MSR was $2,450.

COYOTE - available in various cals., blue printed Rem. Model 700 action, Grand Master (disc. 1999) or Kreiger match barrel with cryogenic treatment, Kevlar/ graphite stock. Mfg. 1996-2004.

	$1,900	$1,600	$1,325	$1,100	$900	$825	$725

Last MSR was $2,296.

COYOTE II - various cals., trued Remington M 700 action and customized trigger, matte black metal parts, HS Precision Kevlar graphite tactical stock with aluminum and fiberglass reinforced bedding. Mfg. 2001-2006.

	$1,900	$1,600	$1,325	$1,100	$900	$825	$725

Last MSR was $2,295.

PHANTOM II - various cals., trued and blue printed custom Evolution (disc.) or Remington repeater action, match stainless steel barrel, super long range, Timney match trigger, McMillan A2 or A3 tactical stock, matte black metal, 11 1/2 lbs. New 1999.

MSR $3,195	$2,995	$2,650	$2,250	$1,900	$1,700	$1,400	$1,100

YELLOW WOLF SPORTER - available in various cals., designed for big game, blue printed Rem. Model 700 action, Kreiger match barrel, Kevlar/graphite stock, available in Standardweight (8.1 lbs.), Lightweight (7 1/2 lbs.), Superlight (6.8 lbs.), and Ultralight (5.8 lbs.). New 1996.

MSR $2,995	$2,850	$2,500	$2,100	$1,800	$1,600	$1,300	$1,000

Add $97 for Lightweight, $180 for Superlight, or $500 for Ultralight configuration.

IMPALA - most popular cals., Rem. Model 700 trued action w/o floor plate, lightweight sporter, Kevlar graphite stock. Mfg. 1998-99.

	$1,275	$1,050	$950	$750	$650	$575	$500

Last MSR was $1,456.

KUDU - most standard length cals., Winchester Pre-64 Model 70 action, stainless steel match barrel, sporter style Kevlar graphite stock. Mfg. 1998-2006.

	$2,150	$1,850	$1,650	$1,350	$1,050	$875	$725

Last MSR was $2,579.

Add $2,500 for presentation walnut stock.

SHI-AWELA - various cals., medium weight sporter, Evolution M1000 stainless action, stainless match barrel, Kevlar/graphite stock. Mfg. 1999-2002.

	$2,600	$2,000	$1,750	N/A	N/A	N/A	N/A

Last MSR Was $3,052.

MBOGO - .375 H&H, .416 Rem., or .458 Win. Mag. cal., choice of Sako (disc.), Dakota (disc.), Rem. Model 700, CZ (new 2007), Win. Pre-64 Model 70 (disc. 2006), or stainless steel Evolution M1000 action, stainless steel match barrel, express style Kevlar graphite stock. New 1998.

This rifle with Evolution action requires 11% federal excise tax.

GRADING - PPGS™	100%	98%	95%	90%	80%	70%	60%

✳ *Mbogo Sako or Remington Action* - disc.

	$1,550	$1,325	$1,100	$925	$750	$650	$575

Last MSR was $1,828.

✳ *Mbogo Win. Pre-64 Model 70, CZ, or Evolution Stainless M-1000 Action*

MSR $3,289		$3,050	$2,700	$2,300	$1,925	$1,700	$1,400	$1,100

Add $71 for CZ action, or $140 for M-1000 Magnum action.
Add $655-$786 for M-1000 action with detachable mag.

✳ *Mbogo Dakota Action*

	$2,775	$2,400	$2,000	$1,750	$1,500	$1,250	$1,000

Last MSR was $3,142.

BOLT ACTION SNIPER/VARMINT SERIES - various cals., 3 different configurations included Sniper, Informal Target Varmint, and Field Grade Varmint, featured match barrel, action, and tuned trigger. Prices for the Sniper rifle started at approx. $3,000 while the Varmint guns started at approx. $2,000. Disc. 2000.

RIFLES: SxS

NYATI - .375 H&H, .416 NE, .470 NE, or .500 NE (disc. 2000) cal., reinforced Anson & Deeley action, choice of color case hardened or coin finished engraved receiver, blue chrome moly barrels, various wood grades available, express sights. New 1999. Custom order only.
Please contact the company directly for pricing on this model.

NYALA - various standard cals., including .300 Win. Mag., 3 grades available, 7 lbs., 9 oz. Mfg. 2001-2006.

	$4,500	$4,000	$3,600	$3,150	$2,750	$2,350	$2,000

Last MSR was $4,895.

RIFLES: SEMI-AUTO

WOLVERINE - .22 LR cal., Grand Master barrel, Kevlar/graphite stock. Mfg. 1996-2000.

	$730	$650	$565	$515	$455	$400	$360

Last MSR was $850.

GRENADA - .223 Rem. cal., paramilitary design based on the AR-15 with flat upper receiver, 17 in. stainless steel match barrel with integral muzzle brake, NM trigger. Disc. 2000.

	$985	$825	$675	$600	$525	$465	$400

Last MSR was $1,195.

DESERT STORM - similar to Grenada, except has 21 in. match barrel. Disc. 2003.

	$975	$825	$665	$560	$500	$450	$400

Last MSR was $1,189.

IWO JIMA - features carrying handle incorporating iron sights, 20 in. stainless steel match barrel, A2 HBAR action, tubular handguard. Limited mfg.

	$1,000	$875	$775	$700	$600	$475	$425

RIFLES : SINGLE SHOT

IMPALA - various standard cals., including .300 Win. Mag., 5 grades available, similar appearance and handling as Nyala. New 2001.
Please contact Evolution USA directly regarding more information and current pricing on this model.

PHANTOM III SINGLE SHOT - .50 BMG or .700 NE cal., Evolution M-2000 stainless single shot action, 28 in. Lilja match barrel with flutes and muzzle brake, approx. 30 lbs. New 2000.

MSR $5,100		$4,950	$4,500	$3,750	$3,250	$2,750	$2,375	$2,000

Add $1,700 for Delta Model (50-80 lbs.) or .700 NE cal. (24-30 lbs.).

GRADING - PPGS™	100%	98%	95%	90%	80%	70%	60%

EXCAM

Previous importer and distributor located in Hialeah, FL that went out of business late 1990. Excam distributed Dart, Erma, Tanarmi, Targa, & Warrior exclusively for the U.S. These trademarks will appear under Excam only in this book. All importation of Excam firearms ceased in 1990.

All Targa and Tanarmi pistols were manufactured in Gardone V.T., Italy. All Erma and Warrior pistols and rifles were manufactured in W. Germany. Senator O/U shotguns were manufactured by A. Zoli located in Brescia, Italy.

HANDGUNS: TANARMI MFG.

TA 38SB O/U DERRINGER - .38 Spl. cal. only, O/U Derringer-copy of Rem. Model 41, 3 in. barrels, 14 oz., with safety, blue finish only, checkered nylon grips. Importation disc. 1985.

	$150	$125	$110	$90	$75	$65	$55

Last MSR was $80.

MODEL TA 22 SAA - .22 LR cal., 6 shot, 4 3/4 in. barrel, brass trigger guard and grip straps, blue finish, wood grips, 34 oz.

	$85	$70	$60	$55	$50	$45	$40

Last MSR was $99.

MODEL TA 76 SAA - .22 LR cal., single action revolver, 4 3/4 in. barrel, 6 shot, blue finish only, wood grips, 32 oz.

	$85	$65	$55	$50	$45	$40	$35

Last MSR was $95.

Add $4 for chrome finish or brass backstrap and trigger guard.

✳ *Model TA 76M SAA Combo* - includes .22 LR and .22 Mag. cal. cylinders, 4 3/4 (standard), 6, or 9 in. barrel, blue finish, wood grips.

	$125	$115	$95	$75	$65	$60	$55

Last MSR was $105.

Add $6 for chrome plated finish (4 3/4 in. barrel only).
Add $10 for 6 (Model TA 766) or 9 (Model TA 769) in. barrel.
Add $16 for brass backstrap and trigger guard (N/A in 9 in. barrel).

TA 41 SERIES SEMI-AUTO - .41 Action Express cal., action similar to TA 90 Series, 11 shot mag., matte blue (Model TA 41B) or matte chrome (Model TA 41C) finish, combat sights, black neoprene grips, 38 oz. Imported 1989-90.

	$450	$390	$360	$330	$295	$265	$240

Last MSR was $490.

Add $70 for adj. target sights (Model TA 41BT).

✳ *TA 41C Series Semi-Auto Model* - matte chrome finish.

	$485	$430	$395	$360	$330	$295	$270

Last MSR was $550.

Add $50 (retail) for adj. target sights (Model TA 41CT).

✳ *TA 41 Series Semi-Auto Model SS* - .41 AE cal., compensated variation of the Model TA 41 except has 5 in. ported barrel and slide, blue/chrome finish, competition sights, 40 oz. Import 1989-90.

	$575	$450	$420	$385	$350	$325	$300

Last MSR was $650.

TA 90 SERIES SEMI-AUTO - 9mm Para. cal., double action, copy of the CZ-75, 4 3/4 in. barrel, steel frame, 15 shot mag., matte blue (Model TA 90B) or matte chrome finish (Model TA 90C), combat sights, wood (disc. 1985) or neoprene grips, 38 oz. New 1985.

	$365	$300	$260	$225	$205	$190	$180

Last MSR was $415.

Add $85 for adj. target sights (TA 90BT).
Earlier models featured a polished blue finish and nickel steel alloy frame (35 oz.).

GRADING - PPGS™	100%	98%	95%	90%	80%	70%	60%

∗ *TA 90C Series Semi-Auto Model* - matte chrome finish.

	100%	98%	95%	90%	80%	70%	60%
	$380	$315	$270	$235	$210	$190	$180

Last MSR was $430.

> **Add $95 for adj. target sights (TA 90CT).**

∗ *BTA 90B and C Series Semi-Auto Model* - 9mm Para. cal., smaller version of TA 90, 3 1/2 in. barrel, 12 shot mag., neoprene grips. Imported 1986-90.

	$380	$315	$270	$235	$210	$190	$180

Last MSR was $430.

> **Add $20 for chrome finish (BTA 90C).**

∗ *TA 90 Series Semi-Auto Model SS* - 9mm Para. cal., compensated variation of the Model TA 90 except has 5 in. ported barrel and slide, blue/chrome finish, competition sights, 40 oz. Imported 1989-90.

	$575	$450	$420	$385	$350	$325	$300

Last MSR was $650.

∗ *TA 90BK Series Semi-Auto Model* - convertible kit including 2 barrels (9mm and .41 AE) and 2 mags.

While advertised, this combination never saw production.

PISTOLS: SEMI-AUTO, ERMA MFG.

RX 22 - .22 LR cal. only, double action-Walther copy, 3 1/4 in. barrel, 8 shot mag., blue only, plastic grips, 17 oz. Assembled in the U.S. Disc. 1986.

	$140	$125	$105	$95	$90	$85	$80

Last MSR was $139.

KGP 22 - .22 LR cal. only, Luger type toggle action, 3.78 in. barrel, 8 shot mag., blue only, plastic grips, 29 oz. Importation disc. 1986.

	$220	$195	$175	$155	$135	$120	$105

Last MSR was $220.

KGP 380 - .380 ACP cal. only, Luger type toggle action, 3 1/2 in. barrel, 5 shot mag., blue only, plastic grips, 23 oz. Disc. 1986.

	$250	$215	$185	$160	$145	$135	$125

Last MSR was $230.

PISTOLS: SEMI-AUTO, TARGA MFG.

GT 22 SERIES - .22 LR cal., 3.88 in. barrel, 10 shot mag., single action 26 oz., steel frame, either satin chrome (GT 22C) or standard blue (GT 22B) finish, wood grips became standard in 1986. GT 22T is 6 in. barrel target version (12 shot mag.).

	$170	$140	$125	$110	$95	$80	$70

Last MSR was $200.

> **Add $15 for chrome finish (Model GT 22C).**

GT 26 and GT 27B OR C - .25 ACP cal., 2 1/2 in. barrel, 6 shot mag., single action, 13 oz., available in standard blue alloy, satin chrome alloy (GT 27B or C), or steel frame (GT 26S), wood grips became standard in 1986.

	$50	$45	$35	$30	$30	$25	$25

Last MSR was $56.

> **Add $59 for steel frame (Model GT 26S).**
> **Add $13 for chrome alloy (Model GT 27C).**

GT 28 SERIES - .25 ACP cal., 2 1/2 in. barrel, 5 shot mag., single action, blue alloy, wood grips. Imported 1990 only.

	$45	$35	$30	$30	$25	$25	$20

Last MSR was $51.

> **Add $18 for chrome finish (Model GT 28C).**

GRADING - PPGS™	100%	98%	95%	90%	80%	70%	60%

GT 32 SERIES - .32 ACP cal., 3.88 in. barrel, 7 shot mag., single action, steel frame, 26 oz., either satin chrome (GT 32C) or standard blue (GT 32B), wood grips became standard in 1986.

	$170	$140	$125	$110	$95	$80	$70

Last MSR was $200.

Add $15 for chrome finish (Model GT 32C).

GT 380 ACP SERIES - .380 ACP cal., 3.88 in. barrel, 6 shot mag., single action, steel frame, 26 oz., either satin chrome (GT 380C) or standard blue (GT 380B), wood grips became standard in 1986.

	$175	$145	$135	$125	$115	$105	$95

Last MSR was $212.

Add $8 for chrome finish (Model GT 380C).

✳ *GT 380 ACP Series LW* - similar to GT 380 Series except has light alloy receiver and 3 1/4 in. barrel.

	$100	$85	$70	$60	$55	$50	$45

Last MSR was $119.

✳ *GT 380 ACP Series BE or CE* - engraved models, either blue (BE) or chrome (CE) finish, wood grips. Importation disc. 1989.

	$180	$155	$145	$135	$125	$115	$105

Last MSR was $220.

Add $25 for chrome finish (Model GT 380 CE).

GT 380 XE - .380 ACP cal., 3.88 in. barrel, 11 shot mag., blue only, wood grips, 28 oz.

	$190	$165	$155	$145	$135	$125	$115

Last MSR was $235.

✳ *GT 32 XEB* - .32 ACP cal., similar to GT 380 XE, 12 shot mag. Disc. 1985.

	$165	$145	$135	$125	$115	$100	$95

Last MSR was $189.

REVOLVERS

RX 38 B - .38 Spl. cal., double action, 6 shot, 2 in. barrel, blue finish only. Imported 1990-disc.

	$150	$125	$100	$85	$65	$55	$50

Last MSR was $95.

ALDO UBERTI CATTLEMAN SA REVOLVER - .357 Mag., .44 Mag., or .45 LC cal., 6 shot, single action, 5 1/2, 6, or 7 1/2 in. barrels, target sights, wood grips, blue finish. Mfg. 1985-86.

	$295	$250	$195	$165	$150	$140	$130

Last MSR was $222.

Add 10% for .44 Mag. or .45 LC cal.

ALDO UBERTI DA INSPECTOR - .38 Spl., double action, 3 or 4 in. barrel, blue finish, wood grips, 6 shot. Disc. 1986.

	$325	$250	$200	$180	$165	$150	$140

Last MSR was $240.

Add $17 for adj. sights.

WARRIOR DOUBLE ACTION MODEL W 722 (B) - .22 LR or .22 Mag. cal. only, double action, 6 in. barrel, 8 shot, blue only, plastic grips, 35 oz. Disc. 1986.

	$100	$80	$70	$65	$60	$55	$50

Last MSR was $98.

Add $50 for .22 Mag. extra cyl.

GRADING - PPGS™	100%	98%	95%	90%	80%	70%	60%

WARRIOR DOUBLE ACTION MODEL W 384 (B) - .38 Spl. cal. only, double action, 4 or 6 in. barrels, 6 shot, blue only, plastic grips, 30 oz. Vent. rib standard. Disc. 1986.

	$135	$110	$100	$90	$80	$70	$65

Last MSR was $125.

Add $5 for 6 in. barrel (W 386 B).

WARRIOR DOUBLE ACTION MODEL W 357 - .357 Mag. cal. only, double action, 4 or 6 in. barrels, 6 shot, blue only, plastic grips, 36 oz. Vent. rib standard. 6 in. barrel (W 3576). Disc. 1986.

	$190	$165	$145	$135	$130	$125	$120

Last MSR was $185.

RIFLES: ERMA MFG.

EG 712 - .22 LR cal. only, lever action copied after the Win. Model 92, 18 1/2 in. barrel, 15 shot, iron sights. Disc. 1985.

	$180	$160	$140	$125	$115	$100	$90

Last MSR was $204.

EG 712L - .22 LR cal. only, lever action copied after the Win. Model 92, 18 1/2 in. octagonal barrel, deluxe walnut silver plated receiver and barrel bands, 15 shot, iron sights. Disc.

	$300	$241	$220	$180	$150	$130	$115

EG 73 - .22 Mag. cal. only, lever action copied after the Win. Model 92, 19 1/4 in. barrel, 12 shot, iron sights, blue only. Disc. 1985.

	$205	$185	$160	$140	$130	$120	$105

Last MSR was $229.

EG 722 - .22 LR cal. only, slide action, 18 1/2 in. barrel, 15 shot, iron sights, blue only. Disc. 1985.

	$180	$160	$140	$125	$115	$100	$90

Last MSR was $204.

EM 1 CARBINE - .22 LR or .22 Mag. cal., gas semi-auto, copy of the original M1 carbine, 19 1/2 in. barrel, 15 shot, iron sights, blue only. ESG 22 is .22 Mag. (12 shot). Disc. 1985.

	$175	$155	$140	$125	$115	$100	$90

Last MSR was $195.

Add $100 for ESG 22, .22 Mag.

SHOTGUNS: O/U

SENATOR MODEL - 12, 20 ga., or .410 bore, 3 in. chambers, 26 or 28 in. F/M barrels, folding action, double triggers, extractors, vent. barrels and rib, checkered walnut stock and forearm, engraved silver finished receiver, mfg. by Antonio Zoli. Imported 1986-87.

	$235	$200	$180	$165	$150	$140	$130

Last MSR was $275.

EXCEL ARMS

Trademark of pistols and rifles manufactured by Excel Industries, Inc., located in Chino, CA.

PISTOLS: SEMI-AUTO

ACCELERATOR MP - .17 HMR (MP-17), .17 Mach 2 (new 2007, SP-17), .22 LR (new 2007, SP-22), or .22 Mag. (MP-22) cal., 6 1/2 (new 2007) or 8 1/2 in. barrel, polymer frame with stainless steel slide, adj. sights, 9 shot mag., 45 or 54 oz. New 2005.

MSR $412		$350	$295	$260	$230	$200	$180	$160

Add $60 for red/green dot optic sight or $83 for 4x32mm scope with illuminated crosshairs.
Add $79 for choice of Realtree Hardwoods HD Green or Digital Desert camo coverage (new 2008).

GRADING - PPGS™	100%	98%	95%	90%	80%	70%	60%

RIFLES: SEMI-AUTO

MR/SR SERIES - .17 HMR (MR17), .17 Mach 2 (SR17, new 2007), .22 LR (SR22, new 2007), or .22 Mag. (MR22) cal., black composite stock with large thumbhole, fluted 18 in. stainless steel barrel and receiver with shroud, black, silver, or camo finish, fully adj. sights, 9 shot mag., standard package is supplied with red dot optics and hard sided case, 8 lbs. New 2004.

MSR $498	$435	$385	$335	$285	$240	$200	$180

Subtract $33 for basic package w/o optics or gun case.
Add $152 for choice of Realtree Hardwoods HD Green or Digital Desert camo coverage (new 2008).

These rifles are also available in various packages (P2-P5) that include sights, scopes, slings, bi-pods, and extra magazines - prices range from $605 - $849.

CR-9 - 9mm Para. cal., stainless steel construction, 18 in. stainless bull barrel, full length Weaver rail and two side rails, adj. and detachable sights, 10 shot mag., nylon sling and detachable swivels. New 2008.

MSR $635	$550	$495	$450	$395	$350	$295	$250

EXEL ARMS OF AMERICA, INC.

Previous importer located in Gardener, MA. Exel Arms previously imported Lanber (Series 100), Ugartechea (Series 200), and Laurona (Series 300) shotguns. Please refer to the appropriate sections for more information on this series.

NOTES

F SECTION

F. DARNE FILS AINÉ

Previous manufacturer located in St. Etienne, France.

Francisque Darne was the eldest son of Regis Darne, who developed the sliding breech gun. In 1910, Francisque left his father's company to form his own, "F. Darne Fils Ainé," producing high quality versions of the original 1894 patent R model Darne. Regis Darne updated most of his designs in 1909 and allowed the older patents to become public domain.

Francisque Darne died in 1917, but his company remained in production until 1955 under at least four different owners. SIFARM, a combination of the manufacturers Berthon Freres, Francisque Darne, Didier-Drevet, Gerest, and Ronchard-Cizeron, was absorbed in 1963 by Verney-Carron, along with the famous Canonnerie (barrel makers) Jean Breuil.

As is usually the case, the earlier production guns are by far the highest quality. Wide variations in quality exist in this marque, depending on the financial health of the owners at the time of production.

GRADING - PPGS™	100%	98%	95%	90%	80%	70%	60%

SHOTGUNS: SxS, PRE-WAR MODELS

CLASSIC MODEL - 12 or 16 ga., an exact copy of the first Darne patent of 1894. Available in four grades.

* *Classic Model Type A* - standard French proof barrels, very light engraving, color case hardened, no quality stamps on barrel flats.

	100%	98%	95%	90%	80%	70%	60%
	$1,200	$1,000	$800	$700	$600	$500	$450

* *Classic Model Type B* - French gray hardened or color case hardened, somewhat more engraving, 1 quality stamp on barrel flats.

	100%	98%	95%	90%	80%	70%	60%
	$1,700	$1,400	$1,200	$900	$700	$600	$500

* *Classic Model Type C* - French gray hardening over modern or old English engraving, double proofed barrels with two quality stamps on barrel flats.

	100%	98%	95%	90%	80%	70%	60%
	$2,000	$1,650	$1,350	$1,000	$800	$650	$550

* *Classic Model Type E* - French gray hardening over elaborate engraving. Better quality wood in either English or semi-pistol grip. Double proof barrels with four quality stamps on barrel flats.

	100%	98%	95%	90%	80%	70%	60%
	$2,400	$2,000	$1,600	$1,300	$1,000	$900	$800

MODEL T - 12 or 16 ga., stylistic improvements to the 1894 patent R model. Two-piece stock, barrels removed by holding a button on forend, 4 grades, all were originally color case hardened, never blue.

Both the T 32 and T 34 were available in 10 ga. with 70mm or 75mm chambers and 72cm or 76cm barrels on special order. The barrels would carry triple proof in 10 ga.

* *Model T 32 Type* - lightly engraved, 3 quality stamps on barrel flats.

	100%	98%	95%	90%	80%	70%	60%
	$1,950	$1,700	$1,250	$950	$700	$600	$500

  Add 30% for 10 ga.

* *Model T 34* - better engraving and wood, 5 quality stamps on barrel flats.

	100%	98%	95%	90%	80%	70%	60%
	$2,100	$1,800	$1,500	$1,100	$850	$675	$575

  Add 30% for 10 ga.

* *Model T 35* - mono bloc barrels of superior French proof steel, better engraving and wood, 6 quality stamps on barrel flats.

	100%	98%	95%	90%	80%	70%	60%
	$2,500	$2,200	$1,800	$1,400	$1,200	$1,000	$800

* *Model T 36* - mono bloc barrels of superior French proof steel, top-of-the-line T model, 7 quality stamps on barrel flats.

	100%	98%	95%	90%	80%	70%	60%
	$2,800	$2,500	$2,100	$1,700	$1,400	$1,200	$850

GRADING - PPGS™	100%	98%	95%	90%	80%	70%	60%

MODEL FIXED - 12 or 16 ga., further tinkering with the 1894 R model, these located the barrels in a rectangular block cut near the flats. Two grades.

  * *Model Fixed Type No. 3* - color case hardened or French gray hardened. Good quality engraving and wood. For pricing, see Type T 34.

  * *Model Fixed Type No. 4* - better wood and engraving. For pricing, see Type T 35.

MODEL PLATINUM - 12 or 16 ga., based on the model Fixed, these were top-of-the-line sliding breech guns. Four grades.

  * *Model Platinum Type No. 5* - mono bloc barrels, English or art nouveau style engraving, chisled fences.

	$3,100	$2,800	$2,500	$2,200	$1,700	$1,400	$1,100

  * *Model Platinum Type No. 6* - mono bloc barrels, English rose and scroll engraving or game scene or art nouveau style, high grade wood.

	$3,400	$2,900	$2,600	$2,350	$1,900	$1,600	$1,200

  * *Model Platinum Type No. 7* - mono bloc barrels of top quality French proof steel, engraved in English rose and scroll or deep chisled art nouveau style, superior wood. Pigeon model.

	$3,800	$3,500	$3,000	$2,800	$2,200	$1,900	$1,500

  * *Model Platinum Type No. 8* - mono bloc barrels of top quality French proof steel. Top-of-the-line model with all details to customer's wishes. Very rare in any condition. Rarity precludes accurate pricing.

SHOTGUNS: SxS, POST-WAR MODELS

Note: the model name of the following post-war guns is usually engraved on the side of the gun in front of the safety lever.

CLASSIC MODEL - 12 or 16 ga. with modified and full choke on 70 cm barrels, simple case colored gun with no engraving and plain wood in semi-pistol grip or straight stock, 2 quality stamps.

	$1,250	$1,000	$850	$700	$600	$525	$400

BARONNET-BROUSSARD - 12, 16, or 20 ga. with 70 cm barrels (two-piece stock on 12 and 16 ga.), lightly engraved with satin chrome receiver finish, Broussard model featured 80 cm barrels but was essentially the same, 3 quality stamps.

	$1,400	$1,200	$1,000	$800	$675	$550	$475

    Add 20% for Broussard model.

GOUVERNEUR MODEL - 12, 16, or 20 ga., better engraving and one-piece stock of select walnut, French gray receiver, choice of barrel lengths in 12 ga. (70 cm, 72 cm, or 74 cm.) classic or modern style engraving, 5 quality stamps.

	$1,800	$1,650	$1,200	$1,000	$750	$600	$550

GOUVERNEUR PLUME AND PLUME MAGNUM - same as above, but with plume (swamped rib) on Plume Model, plume rib and 76mm chambers included on Plume Magnum Model. Prices about 10% higher than previous models due to these having six quality stamps on flats of barrels in spite of being the same basic gun.

RAMBOUILLET MODEL - 12 or 16 ga., double sears in a large key action somewhat similar to the Darne V models stylistically, one-piece stock of select walnut, in semi-pistol grip or straight style, light engraving on color case hardening, choice of rib, 8 quality stamps.

	$1,500	$1,300	$1,100	$900	$700	$650	$575

AMBASSADEUR MODEL - 12 or 16 ga., large key model with double sears. French gray finish on breech with excellent engraving, one-piece stock of good quality walnut, top-of-the-line production model, 10 quality stamps.

	$2,700	$2,400	$2,200	$1,800	$1,500	$1,100	$850

GRADING - PPGS™	100%	98%	95%	90%	80%	70%	60%

PRESTIGE MODEL - top-of-the-line custom gun, mono bloc barrels of Jacob Holtzer steel with plume swamped rib. Large key action with silent operation and double sears, one-piece stock of best quality walnut, in straight style only, 72 cm barrels, excellent full coverage engraving, eight month minimum wait, 12 quality stamps.

    $3,500 $3,100 $2,900 $2,600 $2,200 $1,700 $1,200

F.A.I.R. S.r.l.

Current manufacturer established during 1971 (F.A.I.R. stands for Fabbrica Armi Isidoro Rizzini, owned by Isidoro Rizzini) and located in Marcheno, Italy. Currently, F.A.I.R. manufactures private label shotguns for both Savage Arms (Milano brand), Dewing's Fly & Gun Shop, and Kalispell Case Line (Cortona brand). No current domestic importation under the F.A.I.R. trademark. In 2003, the name changed from F.A.I.R. Tecni-Mec I. Rizzini to F.A.I.R. S.r.l. Previously imported and distributed exclusively by New England Arms Corp. located in Kittery Point, ME.

Please contact the factory directly for more information, including current model availability and pricing.

RIFLES: SINGLE SHOT

KIPPLAUF MODEL 500/500 DELUXE - various cals., single barrel stalking rifle. Mfg. 2002-2005.

    $1,825 $1,650 $1,350 $1,050 $900 $750 $700

Last MSR was $1,995.

SHOTGUNS: O/U

F.A.I.R. manufactures a wide variety of shotguns, rifles, and combination guns, including O/Us and single shots in assorted models. Most models, however, are not being imported into the U.S. at this time under their trademark. Beginning 1999, Models 500, 600, 702, and 900 in 16 ga. have their own size frame (approx. 6 1/4 lbs). A unique, smaller 28 ga. frame was introduced in 2000 (also used for .410 bore), and weighs approx. 5 3/4 lbs. Numerous options are available, including custom dimensions.

MODEL PREMIERE EM DELUXE/SPORTING - 12, 20, 28 ga., or .410 bore, standard model with ST, ejectors, vent. rib barrels, blue frame. Imported 1998-2005.

    $850 $700 $675 $525 $450 $400 $360

Last MSR was $950.

MODEL 500 - 12, 16, 20, 28 ga., or .410 bore, boxlock action with case colored frame and scroll engraving, choke tubes (5) except for .410 bore. Imported 1998-2005.

    $2,000 $1,750 $1,525 $1,275 $1,075 $950 $825

Last MSR was $2,250.

Add $275 for Model 500 Gold (includes gold inlays on receiver).

MODEL 600 GOLD - same gauges as Model 500, features case colored or coin finished receiver with engraved and gold inlaid sideplates. Imported 1998-2005.

    $2,650 $2,225 $1,900 $1,675 $1,400 $1,150 $925

Last MSR was $2,995.

MODEL S 610 - 10 ga., 3 1/2 in. Mag., O/U boxlock action, double underlug locking, 32 in. VR barrels, SST, ejectors, checkered walnut stock and forearm. Imported 1991-97.

    $925 $825 $750 $675 $595 $525 $450

Last MSR was $1,000.

GRADING - PPGS™	100%	98%	95%	90%	80%	70%	60%

MODEL SPL 640 - 12, 16, 20, 28 ga., or .410 bore, folding O/U design, DT, 26 in. VR barrels. Importation disc. 1997.

| | | $465 | $390 | $325 | $260 | $215 | $180 | $160 |

Last MSR was $500.

MODEL 702 - 12, 16, 20, 28 ga., or .410 bore, O/U boxlock with sideplates, standard interchangeable chokes available, case colored receiver with hand inlaid 24Kt. gold wire outlines on sideplates, frame, and triggerguard, SST, ejectors. Imported 1995-2005.

| | $3,500 | $2,450 | $2,000 | $1,750 | $1,500 | $1,350 | $1,225 |

Last MSR was $3,995.

SRL 802 TRAP - 12 or 20 ga., 2 3/4 in. chambers, boxlock action with sideplates, light scroll engraving, checkered pistol stock, choke tubes, various barrel lengths, SST, ejectors.

Domestic U.S. pricing is not available on this model.

MASTER TRAP - 12 or 20 ga., 2 3/4 in. chambers, similar to SRL 802 Trap, except does not have sideplates.

Domestic U.S. pricing is not available on this model.

MODEL 900 - similar to Model 702, except has hand executed Bulino/scroll engraving on coin finished receiver, game scenes vary with each ga., case colored receiver available upon request. Imported 1995-2005.

| | $3,500 | $2,450 | $2,000 | $1,750 | $1,500 | $1,350 | $1,225 |

Last MSR was $3,995.

⁎ **Model 900 EL** - same general specifications as the Model 900, except has full engraving coverage with individually signed Bulino game scene engraving and higher quality wood. Imported 2001-2005.

| | $5,500 | $4,500 | $4,000 | $3,500 | $2,450 | $2,000 | $1,750 |

Last MSR was $5,995.

⁎ **Model 900 EELL** - same general specifications as Model 900 EL, top-of-the-line model with highly figured Turkish walnut, extensive engraving, cased. Imported 2001-2005.

| | $6,875 | $6,000 | $5,500 | $4,500 | $4,000 | $3,500 | $2,450 |

Last MSR was $7,500.

MODEL 902 - similar to Model 900, except has sideplates. Imported 2001-2005.

| | $4,275 | $3,250 | $2,650 | $2,100 | $1,825 | $1,500 | $1,350 |

Last MSR was $4,750.

⁎ **Model 902 EL** - same general specifications as the Model 902, except has full engraving coverage on sideplates and upgraded wood. Imported 2001-2005.

| | $6,275 | $5,300 | $4,500 | $3,900 | $2,700 | $2,300 | $2,100 |

Last MSR was $6,995.

⁎ **Model 902 EELL** - same general specifications as Model 902 EL, top-of-the-line model with highly figured Turkish walnut, extensive Bulino game scene engraving with signature, cased. Imported 2001-2005.

| | $8,350 | $7,500 | $6,500 | $5,600 | $4,600 | $3,600 | $2,750 |

Last MSR was $8,995.

F.A.V.S. di FRANCESCO GUGLIELMINOTTI

Current manufacturer established in 1957, and located in Villar Focchiardo, Italy. No current U.S. importation. F.A.V.S. is an abbreviation for Fabbrica Armi Valle Susa.

RIFLES: SINGLE SHOT

STRADIVARI - various cals., unique "shorty" bullpup configuration utilizing a break open single shot action and pivoting wood buttstock that opens/closes breech, finger grooved pistol grip wood stock with short forend, scope is mounted on front portion of barrel, 19 3/4 in., 24 in., or 29 in. barrel with muzzleweight. Please contact the manufacturer directly regarding U.S. availability and pricing (see Trademark Index).

FAS

Current pistol manufacturer located in Milan, Italy. No current U.S. importation. Previously imported and distributed by Nygord Precision Products located in Prescott, AZ, and Mandall Shooting Supplies, located in Scottsdale, AZ, by Beeman Precision Arms, Inc. located in Santa Rosa, CA and Osborne's located in Cheboygan, MI.

PISTOLS: SEMI-AUTO

MODEL OP601 - .22 Short cal. only, competition pistol, 5.9 in. barrel, 5 shot mag., wraparound match wood grips, 41 1/2 oz.

MSR N/A	$1,025	$875	$695	$640	$565	$500	$450

MODEL 602 - .22 LR cal. only, competition pistol, 5.6 in. barrel, 5 shot mag., ergonomically designed match wood grips, 40 oz. Importation disc. 1994.

	$895	$800	$625	$600	$525	$475	$425

Last MSR was $1,100.

MODEL CF603 - .32 S&W Wadcutter cal. only, competition pistol, 5.3 in. barrel, 5 shot mag., ergonomically designed adj. or non-adj. match wood grips, 40 oz.

MSR N/A	$975	$875	$695	$640	$565	$500	$450

MODEL SP607 (LADY) - .22 LR cal. only, semi-auto competition pistol, similar to Model 602, except has removable barrel weights, 5.6 in. barrel.

MSR N/A	$975	$875	$695	$640	$565	$500	$450

FEG

Current manufacturer located in Hungary (FEG stands for Fegyver es Gepgyar) since circa 1900. Currently imported beginning 2007 by SSME Deutsche Waffen, Inc., located in Plant City, FL. A few models were imported by Century International Arms located in Delray Beach, FL (see additional information under the Century International Arms in this text). Previously imported and distributed by K.B.I., Inc. located in Harrisburg, PA, and distributed until 1998 by Interarms located in Alexandria, VA.

PISTOLS: SEMI-AUTO, INTERARMS IMPORTED

All FEG pistols were supplied with two mags.

MARK II AP22 - .22 LR cal., double action, 3.4 in. barrel, 8 shot mag., blue finish, black plastic grips, 23 oz. Imported 1997-98.

	$235	$200	$175	$160	$145	$130	$115

Last MSR was $269.

MARK II AP - .380 ACP cal., double action, patterned after the Walther PP, 3.9 in. barrel, 7 shot mag., blue finish, black plastic grips, 27 oz. Imported 1997-98.

	$235	$200	$175	$160	$145	$130	$115

Last MSR was $269.

MARK II APK - .380 ACP cal., similar to Mark II AP, except is patterned after the Walther PPK/S, 3.4 in. barrel, 7 shot mag., blue finish, black plastic grips, 25 oz. Imported 1997-98.

	$235	$200	$175	$160	$145	$130	$115

Last MSR was $269.

GRADING - PPGS™	100%	98%	95%	90%	80%	70%	60%

PISTOLS: SEMI-AUTO, RECENT IMPORTATION

In addition to the following imported models, FEG also makes additional models available mostly in Europe. Currently, these pistols include the RL61 (.22 LR cal.), the AP9/APK9 (.380 ACP cal.), P9RZ Compact (9mm Para cal.), and the AC/ACK (.45 ACP cal.).

MODEL PMK-380 - .380 ACP cal., patterned after Walther PP, alloy frame, double action, 4 in. barrel, plastic grips with thumbrest, blue finish, 21 oz. Importation by K.B.I. 1992-2003.

	$205	$180	$160	$135	$120	$110	$100

Last MSR was $239.

MODEL SMC-380 - .380 ACP cal., double action semi-auto, patterned after Walther PPK, alloy frame, 3 1/2 in. barrel, 6 shot mag., plastic grips with thumbrest, blue finish, 18 1/2 oz. Importation by K.B.I. 1993-2003.

	$205	$180	$160	$135	$120	$110	$100

Last MSR was $239.

✱ *Model SMC-22* - .22 LR cal., 8 shot mag., otherwise similar to Model SMC-380. Importation disc. 1997.

	$210	$195	$180	$165	$150	$135	$115

Last MSR was $235.

MODEL SMC-918 - 9x18 Makarov cal., double action, semi-auto, 7 shot mag. Importation disc. 1997.

	$175	$150	$130	$110	$95	$85	$75

Last MSR was $235.

MODEL PA-63 - 9x18 Makarov cal., single or double action, 3.93 in. barrel, blue or bright aluminum anodized frame with blued steel slide, fixed sights, plastic grips, decocking safety. Previously imported by Century International Arms.

	$175	$150	$130	$110	$95	$85	$75

MODEL PPH - .380 ACP cal., patterned after Walther PP, alloy frame, double action, plastic grips with thumbrest, blue finish. Imported 1986-87 only.

	$200	$170	$140	$125	$115	$105	$95

Last MSR was $225.

MODEL B9R - .380 ACP cal., little importation into the U.S., many are encountered with "Turkce Polis" (Turkish Police) on the slide, blue finish. Disc.

	$250	$225	$200	$175	$150	$125	$100

MODEL P9R (MBK-9HP OR R-9) - 9mm Para. cal., patterned after Browning Hi-Power, double action, 4 2/3 in. barrel, 14 shot mag., blue finish, steel construction, checkered wood grips, 36 oz. Imported 1992 only, reimported 2007.

MSR $499	$450	$395	$350	$315	$275	$250	$225

This model is the current Hungarian military/police pistol.

✱ *Model MBK-9HPC* - compact variation of the Model MBK-9HP with 4 in. barrel, 34 oz. Imported 1992 only.

	$325	$275	$250	$225	$200	$185	$170

Last MSR was $359.

MODEL P9M (PJK-9HP) - 9mm Para. cal., patterned after Browning Hi-Power, single action, all steel construction, 4 3/4 in. barrel, thumb safety, 10 (C/B 1994) or 13* shot mag. and cleaning rod, 32 oz. Importation by K.B.I. 1992-2003, reimported 2007.

MSR $475	$425	$375	$335	$300	$275	$250	$225

Add approx. $60 for industrial hard chrome finish (Model PJK-9HPC - includes Uncle Mike's rubber grips, disc. 1999).
Add $175 for .40 cal. conversion kit.

GRADING - PPGS™	100%	98%	95%	90%	80%	70%	60%

* *Model P9L* - similar to P9M, except has 6 in. barrel and resembles the Browning HP. Importation began 2007.

MSR $799	$695	$600	$525	$450	$400	$365	$335

MODEL P9RK (GKK-92C) - 9mm Para. cal., double action semi-auto, 4 in. barrel, 14 shot mag., improved variation of MBK models, includes same accessories as PJK-9H, 34 oz. Importation disc. 1993, reimported 2007.

MSR $499	$450	$395	$350	$315	$275	$250	$225

MODEL GKK-40C - .40 S&W cal., 9 shot mag., otherwise similar to GKK-45. Imported 1995-96.

	$300	$265	$230	$200	$180	$160	$145

Last MSR was $349.

MODEL GKK-45 - .45 ACP cal., double action semi-auto, all steel, 4 1/4 in. barrel, blue (disc. 1994) or chrome (Model GKK-45C) finish checkered walnut grips, 8 shot mag., approx. 37 oz. Imported 1993-96.

	$300	$265	$230	$200	$180	$160	$145

Last MSR was $349.

RIFLES: SEMI-AUTO

MODEL SA-85M - 7.62x39mm cal., sporter rifle utilizing AKM action, 16.3 in. barrel, 6 shot detachable mag., thumbhole stock, 7 lbs. 10 oz. Imported 1991, banned 1998.

	$350	$315	$280	$250	$225	$200	$185

Last MSR was $429.

SA-85 S (SA-2000M) - .223 Rem. (disc. 2000) or 7.62x39mm cal., sporter rifle with skeletonized Choate synthetic stock, 16.3 (new 2007) or 17 3/4 (disc. 2000) in. barrel with muzzle brake, 6, 10, or 30 shot detachable mag. Imported 1999-2000, reimported 2007.

MSR $975	$850	$750	$625	$500	$400	$325	$275

FIAS

Previous long gun and related components manufacturer located in Brescia, Italy. FIAS is an abbreviation for Fabbrica Italiana Armi Sabatti.

FIAS became part of the Sabatti Armi group circa 2002, and is based in Gardone VT, Brescia. Please refer to Sabatti for current information, including any domestic importation.

F.I.E.

Previous importer (F.I.E. is the acronym for Firearms Import & Export) located in Hialeah, FL until 1990.

F.I.E. filed bankruptcy in November of 1990 and all models are discontinued. Some parts or service for these older firearms may be obtained through Numrich Gun Parts Corp. (see Trademark Index), even though all warranties on F.I.E. guns are void.

DERRINGERS

MODEL D38 - .38 Spl. cal., O/U, chrome finish only, no transfer bar. Disc. 1985.

	$70	$60	$55	$45	$40	$35	$30

Last MSR was $82.

Add $17 for walnut grips.

MODEL D86 - .38 Spl. cal., single shot, 3 in. barrel, internal transfer bar safety, ammo storage compartment, blue or Dyna-chrome finish, 11 oz. Mfg. 1986-disc.

	$80	$65	$55	$50	$45	$40	$35

Last MSR was $95.

Add $9 for Dyna-chrome finish.
Add $25 for deluxe model (walnut stocks).
Add $60 for Misty Gold finish (disc.).

GRADING - PPGS™	100%	98%	95%	90%	80%	70%	60%

PISTOLS: SEMI-AUTO, TITAN SERIES

TITAN II (E32 SERIES) - .32 ACP (disc. 1988), or .380 ACP, single action, blue (standard) or chrome finish. Mfg. in U.S. - disc.

$195	$160	$135	$120	$105	$95	$85

Last MSR was $220.

Add $25 for walnut grips.
Add $10 for chrome finish.

This series was redesigned in 1988 to be shorter and more compact. Older series Titans are worth approx. $50 less than values shown above.

SUPER TITAN - .380 ACP cal., proofed AH, otherwise similar to Super Titan II. Mfg in Italy by Tanfoglio.

$215	$185	$155	$135	$120	$105	$95

SUPER TITAN II - .32 ACP (disc. 1988), or .380 ACP cal., single action, 12 shot mag. in .32 ACP, 11 for .380 cal., walnut grips, standard blue only. Mfg. in U.S. - disc.

$215	$185	$155	$135	$120	$105	$95

Last MSR was $260.

.22 TITAN II (E22) - .22 LR cal., single action, 10 shot mag., blue finish only. Walnut grips standard. Mfg. 1990 only.

$130	$105	$90	$80	$70	$65	$60

Last MSR was $161.

  ＊*.22 Titan II Lady* - similar to .22 TITAN II except has combination blue/gold finish with scrimshawed red rose on ivory polymer grips. New 1990.

$185	$155	$130	$120	$105	$95	$85

Last MSR was $208.

THE BEST (A27) - .25 ACP cal., single action, blue only, deluxe finish, walnut grips, steel frame, 6 shot mag. Mfg. in Spain by Astra. Importation disc. 1988.

$125	$105	$90	$80	$70	$65	$60

Last MSR was $155.

.25 TITAN (E27 SERIES) - .25 ACP cal., single action, blue (disc. 1989) or Dyna-chrome finish (standard 1990).

$60	$50	$45	$40	$35	$30	$30

Last MSR was $77.

Subtract $5 for blue finish.
Add $26 for gold trim (new 1986).
Add $62 for Misty Gold finish (1988 only).

  ＊*.25 Titan Tigress* - similar to .25 Titan except is entirely gold plated and cased, ladies pistol. Imported 1989-90 only.

$130	$110	$95	$90	$85	$75	$70

Last MSR was $153.

.25 TITAN (E38 SERIES) - .25 ACP cal., similar to E27 series except has standard blue finish. Mfg. 1990 only.

$50	$45	$40	$35	$30	$30	$25

Last MSR was $59.

Add $9 for Dyna-chrome finish.

SSP SERIES - .32 ACP or .380 ACP cal., single action semi-auto, 3 1/8 in. barrel, 5 shot mag., blue or chrome finish, composition grips, 25 oz. Mfg. in US, 1990 only.

$120	$95	$85	$75	$65	$60	$55

Last MSR was $146.

Add $19 for chrome finish.

* *SSP Series Lady* - similar to SSP except has gold trimmed parts, scrimshawed red rose on ivory polymer grips, and gold case. Mfg. 1990 only.

	$210	$180	$155	$135	$120	$105	$95

Last MSR was $250.

TZ-75 - 9mm Para. cal., double action, 4.72 in. barrel, steel frame and slide, 15 shot mag., patterned after the CZ-75 action, 35 oz. Imported 1982-1989. This model was updated in 1988 (Series 88).

	$375	$325	$290	$270	$250	$235	$220

Last MSR was $440.

Add $20 for satin chrome finish (new 1986).
Add $20 for black rubber grips.

TZ-75 SERIES 88 - 9mm Para. or .41 Action Express cal., improved TZ-75 action, 4.72 in. barrel, steel frame and slide, 11 (.41 AE) or 17 (9mm Para.) shot mag., fixed removable rear sight, choice of matte blue, satin chrome, or blue slide/chrome frame finish, updated CZ-75 action, 35 oz. Mfg. 1988-90.

	$435	$360	$330	$295	$280	$260	$240

Last MSR was $519.

Add $97 for .41 Action Express cal.
Add $20 for satin chrome on 9mm Para., $29 on .41 AE.
Add $14 for black rubber grips.

This model was also available with a blue slide/chrome frame (I.P.S.C. configuration) at no extra charge.

The TZ-75 Series 88 was re-engineered in 1988 to include: frame mounted sear locking safety (cocked and locked), Colt style firing pin safety block, improved recessed slide serrations, muzzle barrel swell, bobbed hammer design, elongated combat style slide stop, new mag. release, and removable rear sight.

* *TZ-75 Series 88 Combo* - includes both .41 Action Express and 9mm Para. barrels. Mfg. 1990 only.

	$615	$535	$475	$430	$395	$370	$350

Last MSR was $709.

Add $29 for satin chrome or blue slide/chrome frame finish.

* *TZ-75 Series 88 Govt. Model* - 9mm Para. cal. only, compact variation of the TZ-75 Series 88, 3 3/5 in. barrel, 12 shot mag., checkered walnut grips, 33 1/2 oz. Mfg. 1990 only.

	$435	$360	$330	$295	$280	$260	$240

Last MSR was $519.

Add $20 for satin chrome or blue slide/chrome frame finish.

* *TZ-75 Series 88 with ported barrel* - similar to the TZ-75 Series 88 except has 5 in. ported barrel and slide. Mfg. 1990 only.

	$615	$535	$475	$430	$395	$370	$350

Last MSR was $709.

* *TZ-75 Series 88 Compensated* - similar to the TZ-75 Series 88 except has 5 3/4 in. compensated barrel, 42 oz. Mfg. 1990 only.

	$700	$615	$535	$475	$430	$395	$370

Last MSR was $804.

MODEL 722 TP SILHOUETTE PISTOL - .22 LR cal., bolt action target pistol, 10 in. free-floating barrel, 4-way adj. trigger, micro adj. rear sight, 6 or 10 shot mag., stippled pistol grip and forearm, supplied with 2-piece scope mount, 3.4 lbs. Mfg. 1990 only.

	$220	$190	$160	$140	$125	$115	$100

Last MSR was $263.

GRADING - PPGS™	100%	98%	95%	90%	80%	70%	60%

SPECTRE PISTOL - 9mm Para. or .45 ACP cal., double action, unique triple action blowback system with two piece bolt, 6 in. barrel, military style configuration, adj. sights, 30 or 50 (optional with unique 4 column configuation) shot mag., 4.8 lbs. Mfg. 1989-90 only.

	$675	$600	$525	$480	$440	$400	$360

Last MSR was $718.

Add $14 for mag. loading tool.

KG-99 - 9mm Para. cal., paramilitary design pistol, 36 shot mag. Mini-99 also available with 20 shot mag. and 3 in. barrel. Disc. 1984.

	$550	$475	$440	$400	$365	$330	$300

This model was not manufactured but sold by F.I.E.

REVOLVERS: DOUBLE ACTION, ARMINIUS SERIES

All pistols under this heading were manufactured in W. Germany under the trademark Arminius. .22 cal. is 8 shot, .32 S&W is 7 shot, all others 6 shot.

MODEL 522TB - .22 LR cal., blue finish, 4 in. barrel, 8 shot.

	$130	$100	$85	$75	$70	$65	$60

Last MSR was $174.

Add $23 for walnut grips.

722 SERIES - .22 LR cal., blue (standard) or chrome finish (disc. 1985), 6 in. barrel, 8 shot.

	$125	$100	$90	$80	$70	$65	$60

Last MSR was $161.

Add $23 for walnut grips.
Add $49 for .22 LR/.22 Mag. combo.
Add $15 for chrome finish.

STANDARD REVOLVER - .22 LR, .22 Mag., .32 Mag. or .38 Spl. cal., 2 or 4 in. barrel, blue finish, fixed sights, without ejector assembly. Mfg in US 1989-90.

	$80	$70	$65	$60	$55	$50	$45

Last MSR was $101.

Add $19 for chrome finish (2 in. barrel only).
Add $38 for gold plated finish (2 in. barrel only).
Add $23 for .22 Combo package (2 cylinders - 4 in. barrel only).
Models with 4 in. barrels were available in blue finish only.

MODEL 532TB - .32 S&W cal., blue (standard) or chrome finish (disc. 1985), adj. sights, 4 in. barrel, 7 shot.

	$145	$120	$100	$80	$75	$70	$65

Last MSR was $183.

Add $23 for walnut grips.
Add $15 for chrome finish.

MODEL 732B - similar to Model 532TB, except has 6 in. barrel and fixed sights. Imported 1988 only.

	$120	$100	$90	$80	$70	$65	$60

Last MSR was $140.

MODEL N-38 (TITAN TIGER) - .38 Spl. cal., blue (standard) or chrome finish (disc. 1985), 2 or 4 in. barrel, fixed sights. Disc. 1990.

	$130	$110	$95	$80	$75	$65	$60

Last MSR was $176.

Add $23 for walnut grips.
Add $15 for chrome finish.

GRADING - PPGS™	100%	98%	95%	90%	80%	70%	60%

ZEPHYR - .38 Spl. cal., 5 shot, aluminum construction, 2 in. barrel, blue finish, checkered grips, 14 oz. Mfg. 1990 only.

	$145	$120	$100	$80	$75	$70	$65

Last MSR was $189.

✳ *Zephyr Lady* - similar to Zephyr, except has gold trimmed parts, scrimshawed red rose on ivory polymer grips, and gold case. Mfg. 1990 only.

	$250	$210	$180	$155	$135	$115	$95

Last MSR was $295.

MODEL 384TB - .38 Spl. cal., blue (standard) or chrome finish (disc. 1985), 6 shot, 4 in. barrel.

	$150	$125	$105	$85	$80	$70	$65

Last MSR was $195.

> Add $23 for walnut grips.
> Add $13 for chrome finish.

MODEL 386TB - .38 Spl. cal., blue (standard) or chrome finish (disc. 1985), 6 shot, 6 in. barrel.

	$150	$125	$105	$85	$80	$70	$65

Last MSR was $195.

> Add $23 for walnut grips.
> Add $13 for chrome finish.

.357 MAG. SERIES - .357 Mag. cal., blue (standard) or chrome finish (disc. 1985), 6 shot, 3 (Model 3573TB), 4 (Model 3574TB), or 6 (Model 3576TB) in. barrels.

	$200	$170	$135	$120	$110	$100	$90

Last MSR was $255.

> Add $23 for walnut grips.
> Add $15 for chrome finish.

Revolvers: Double Action, Snub-Nose

Previously manufactured 2 in. snub-nosed revolvers are listed in the previous category under Standard Revolver, Titan Tiger, and Zephyr.

222 SERIES - .22 LR & .22 Mag. cal., blue (standard) or chrome finish, 2 in. snub-nose barrel. Disc. 1985.

	$135	$115	$90	$85	$75	$65	$60

Last MSR was $120.

> Add $15 for walnut grips.
> Add $45 for .22 LR/.22 Mag. combo.

✳ *222B Series* - .22 LR cal. only 1989, similar to 222 Series. Reintroduced 1987-1989.

	$150	$120	$105	$85	$80	$70	$65

Last MSR was $185.

> Add $45 for .22 LR/.22 Mag. combo (disc. 1988).

232 SERIES - .32 S&W cal., blue (standard) or chrome finish, 2 in. barrel. Disc.

	$120	$90	$85	$75	$65	$60	$55

> Add $15 for walnut grips.
> Add $14 for adj. sights.
> Add $28 for chrome finish.

✳ *232B SERIES* - similar to 232 Series, 2 in. barrel. Reintroduced 1987-1989.

	$150	$125	$110	$95	$85	$75	$70

Last MSR was $185.

> Add $5 for adj. sights.

GRADING - PPGS™	100%	98%	95%	90%	80%	70%	60%

MODEL 382TB - .38 Spl. cal., blue (standard) or chrome finish, 2 in. barrel. Disc. 1985.

	$125	$110	$100	$90	$80	$75	$65

Last MSR was $145.

Add $15 for walnut grips.
Add $16 for chrome finish.

MODEL 3572 - .357 Mag. cal., blue (standard) or chrome finish, 2 in. barrel. Disc. 1984.

	$223	$170	$160	$135	$125	$115	$100

Add $15 for walnut grips.
Add $17 for chrome finish.

REVOLVERS: SINGLE ACTION

Combo designations on the following models indicate 2 cylinders (.22 LR/.22 Mag.).

COWBOY - .22 LR or .22 LR/Mag. cal. combo, 3 1/4 or 6 in. barrel, blue finish, square butt grip, without ejector tube, fixed sights. U.S. mfg. 1989-90.

	$75	$65	$50	$45	$40	$35	$30

Last MSR was $95.

Add $23 for combo.

GOLD RUSH - .22 LR or .22 LR/Mag. cal. combo, 3 1/4, 4 3/4, or 6 1/2 in. barrel, round (3 1/4 in. barrel only) or square butt grip, gold band on barrel and cylinder, ivory-tex grips. Mfg in U.S. 1989-90.

	$155	$125	$110	$95	$85	$75	$70

Last MSR was $189.

Add $47 for combo.

TEXAS RANGER (TEX 22 SERIES) - .22 LR or .22 Mag. cal. (combo only), 3 1/4 (new 1986), 4 3/4, 6 1/2 (new 1989), 7, or 9 in. barrel, 6 shot, blue only. Mfg in U.S. Disc.

	$80	$70	$60	$50	$45	$40	$35

Last MSR was $108.

Add $23 for combo.
Add $6 for 9 in. barrel.
This model with a 3 1/4 in. barrel is called the Little Ranger.

BUFFALO SCOUT (E15 SERIES) - .22 LR or .22 Mag. cal., blue (standard) or chrome finish, 4 3/4 in. barrel. Mfg. in Brescia, Italy. Disc.

	$75	$55	$45	$35	$35	$30	$30

Last MSR was $98.

Add $23 for walnut grips.
Add $23 for combo.
Add $9 for chrome or blue/gold finish.

✳ *Buffalo Scout The Yellow Rose Combo* - all metal parts 24Kt. gold plated, smooth walnut grips. Mfg. 1986-90.

	$130	$110	$95	$90	$85	$80	$75

Last MSR was $161.

Add $151 for scrimshawed ivory polymer grips - walnut cased (new 1989).

LEGEND SAA (PL-22 SERIES) - .22 LR or .22 Mag. cal., blue only. Mfg. in Brescia, Italy. Disc. 1984.

	$120	$90	$85	$75	$65	$60	$55

Add $3 for walnut grips.
Add $17 for combo.

GRADING - PPGS™	100%	98%	95%	90%	80%	70%	60%

HOMBRE MODEL - .357 Mag., .44 Mag., or .45 LC cal., color case hardened receiver, 5 1/2 (disc. 1985), 6, or 7 1/2 in. barrel, 45 oz., smooth walnut grips. Previously mfg. W. Germany.

	$220	$180	$145	$130	$120	$110	$100

Last MSR was $265.

Add $25 for brass back strap and trigger guard (disc.).

✱ *Hombre Model Golden* - same general specifications as Hombre, except all metal surfaces are plated in 24Kt. gold.

	$300	$210	$145	$115	$100	$95	$85

Last MSR was $350.

Add $65 for ivory polymer grips (new 1989).

RIFLES: BOLT-ACTION

MODEL 122 - .22 LR cal., 6 or 10 shot box mag., 21 in. tapered barrel, Monte Carlo walnut stock, adj. sights. Mfg. by Hamilton & Hunter. Mfg. 1986-disc.

	$100	$80	$70	$60	$55	$50	$45

Last MSR was $115.

MODEL 322 - .22 LR cal., competition model, 26.2 in. free floating barrel, adj. trigger, 6 or 10 shot mag., stippled pistol grip, 7 lbs. Mfg. 1990-disc.

	$580	$425	$380	$340	$295	$260	$230

Last MSR was $665.

MODEL 422 - similar to Model 322 except has heavy barrel, 9 lbs. Mfg. 1990-disc.

	$580	$425	$380	$340	$295	$260	$230

Last MSR was $665.

RIFLES: SEMI-AUTO

GR-8 BLACK BEAUTY - .22 LR cal., 14 shot, 19 1/2 in. barrel, 64 oz., tubular feed, black nylon stock, patterned after Rem. Nylon 66. Mfg. by C.B.C. of Brazil. F.I.E. Importation disc. 1988.

	$90	$75	$70	$65	$60	$55	$50

Last MSR was $100.

PARA RIFLE - .22 LR cal., paramilitary designed rifle with tube stock (is also magazine), includes green cloth case with white stenciled letters, takedown, 11 shot mag., matte black receiver finish, approx. 4 lbs. Mfg. by L. Franchi between 1979-84. Imported into the U.S. from 1985-88.

	$325	$275	$225	$195	$155	$130	$110

Last MSR was $225.

8,000 of this model were manufactured by L. Franchi. 5,000 went to the Italian Government and were used as training rifles (with German scopes). The remainder were imported by F.I.E. (without scopes).

SPECTRE CARBINE - 9mm Para. cal., same action as Spectre pistol, paramilitary design carbine, collapsible metal butt stock, 30 or 50 (opt.) shot mag., adj. rear sight, with pistol and forearm grip. Mfg. 1989-disc.

	$550	$450	$375	$300	$275	$250	$225

Last MSR was $700.

SHOTGUNS

All currently manufactured Franchi shotguns can be located in the Franchi section of this text.

S.O.B. - 12, 20 ga., or .410 bore, 18 1/2 in. single barrel, pistol grip only. Disc. 1984.

	$100	$90	$80	$70	$60	$55	$50

GRADING - PPGS™	100%	98%	95%	90%	80%	70%	60%

THE STURDY O/U - 12 or 20 ga., 3 in. chambers, 28 in. barrels, vent. rib and barrels, engraved silver finish receiver, double triggers, extractors, manufactured by Maroccini of Italy. Imported 1985-1988.

	$300	$275	$250	$235	$220	$205	$190

Last MSR was $350.

✳ *The Sturdy O/U Deluxe Priti* - similar to The Sturdy model except has deluxe walnut. Importation disc. 1988.

	$325	$290	$260	$240	$225	$205	$195

Last MSR was $380.

Add $70 for ejectors, SST, and choke tubes.

✳ *The Sturdy O/U Model 12 Deluxe* - 12 ga. only, SST, auto ejectors, multi-choked barrels, select walnut. Imported 1988 only.

	$320	$290	$260	$240	$225	$205	$195

Last MSR was $380.

THE BRUTE - 12, 20 ga, or .410 bore, 19 in. barrels, 30 in. overall length. Side-by-side action, disc. 1984.

	$195	$150	$140	$120	$110	$100	$90

SPAS-12 - this model appears under the Franchi heading in the F section.

SAS-12 - this model appears under the Franchi heading in the F section.

LAW-12 - this model appears under the Franchi heading in the F section.

FMJ

Previous manufacturer located in Copperhill, TN, until circa 1998.

Little information is available regarding FMJ firearms (including short barrel derringers and pistols), except they were inexpensive shooters and have little collectibility, except for some oddball configurations. Their production records were turned in to the BATF during 1998.

FNH USA

Current importer established in 1998, and located in McLean, VA. Dealer and distributor sales.

FNH USA imports a complete line of commercial, law enforcement, and military style firearms, including pistols (mfg. by FN in Belgium), rifles (some models were made by U.S Repeating Arms), and shotguns (mfg. by FN Manufacturing).

CARBINES: SEMI-AUTO

PS90 - 5.7x28mm cal., blowback operation, bullpup configuration, 16 in. barrel, 10 or 30 shot box mag. runs horizontally along the top, empty cases are ejected downward, optic reflex sight, olive drab or black finish, available with three M-1913 rails (PS90TR), 6 1/2 lbs.

MSR $2,075		$1,800	$1,600	$1,400	$1,250	$1,100	$1,000	$900

Add $255 for infrared laser target designator (PS90 USG).

FS2000 TACTICAL - .223 Rem. cal., bullpup configuration, 17.4 in. barrel, gas operated with rotating bolt, 10 or 30 shot AR-15 style mag., empty cases are ejected through a forward port, includes top mounted M-1913 rail, olive drab green or black finish, 7.6 lbs.

MSR $2,699		$2,350	$2,100	$1,875	$1,675	$1,475	$1,325	$1,200

HANDGUNS

In addition to the models listed, FNH USA also imported the HP-SA ($800 last MSR), and the HP-SFS until 2006.

All FNP guns come standard with three magazines and a lockable hard case.

GRADING - PPGS™	100%	98%	95%	90%	80%	70%	60%

FNP-9 - 9mm Para. cal., 4 in. barrel, 10 or 16 shot mag., polymer frame, optional matte finished stainless steel slide, SA/DA or DAO, matte black finish, ambidextrous frame mounted decocker, underframe rail, interchangeable backstrap inserts, 25.2 oz.

MSR $593	$525	$450	$400	$365	$335	$300	$275

Add $118 for night sights.

FNP-9M - 9mm Para. cal., 3.8 in. barrel, 10 or 15 shot mag., polymer frame, similar to the FNP-9, except is smaller frame, 24.8 oz.

MSR $593	$525	$450	$400	$365	$335	$300	$275

Add $118 for night sights.

FNP-40 - .40 S&W cal., 4 in. barrel, 10 or 14 shot mag., SA/DA or DAO, black polymer frame, optional stainless steel slide, underframe rail, interchangeable backstrap, external hammer (except DAO), 25.2 or 26.7 oz.

MSR $593	$525	$450	$400	$365	$335	$300	$275

Add $118 for night sights.

FNP-45 - .45 ACP cal., 4 1/2 in. barrel, SA/DA, 10 or 14 shot mag., polymer frame, matte black finish with optional stainless steel slide, external extractor, underframe rail, interchangeable backstrap, 33.2 oz.

MSR $593	$525	$450	$400	$365	$335	$300	$275

Add $118 for night sights.

FIVE-SEVEN USG - .5.7x28mm cal., 4 3/4 in. barrel, 10 or 20 shot mag., reversible mag. release, textured grip, polymer frame, underframe rail, includes three mags., hard case and cleaning kit, 19 oz.

MSR $1,181	$995	$900	$800	$725	$650	$575	$495

RIFLES: BOLT ACTION

FNH USA currently sells and imports the Patrol Bolt Rifle (PBR) in various configurations (MSRs vary from $1,209 - $1,479), and a series of long range precision special police rifles (SPR) in various configurations (MSRs vary from $1,962 - $3,233 MSR), including the FN A1, FN A1a, FN A2, FN A3 G, FN A4, and the FN A5M. FN A3-A5 shooting systems are also available with MSRs starting at $7,014. Additionally, FNH USA imports a wide range of tactical rifle systems for military and law enforcement only. FNH USA also imported a line of modular system rifles, including the Ultima Ratio Intervention, the Ultima Ratio Commando II, and the .338 Lapua Model. Please contact the company directly for more information, including availability and pricing (see Trademark Index).

SHOTGUNS

FNH USA imports tactical style shotguns, including the FN Police Shotgun ($500 last MSR), FN Self-Loading Police Shotgun ($1,061 MSR) and the FN Tactical Police Shotgun (with or w/o fixed stock, $923 MSR). Please contact the company directly for more information, including availability (see Trademark Index).

FTL

Previously manufactured by Wilkinson Arms located in Covina, CA for the FTL Marketing Corp. located in N. Hollywood, CA.

PISTOLS: SEMI-AUTO

FTL AUTO NINE - .22 LR cal., single action, hammerless, blowback action, 8 shot mag., checkered plastic grips, fixed sights. Disc.

	$200	$160	$125	$105	$95	$85	$75

GRADING - PPGS™	100%	98%	95%	90%	80%	70%	60%

FABARM, S.p.A.

Current manufacturer established in 1900 and located in Brescia, Italy. Currently imported by Tristar, located in Kansas City, MO beginning 2007. Previously imported by SIG Arms during 2005, located in Exeter, NH, and by Heckler & Koch, Inc. 1998-2004. Certain models had limited importation by Ithaca Acquisition Corp. located in King Ferry, NY during 1993-1995. Previously imported and distributed (1988-1990) by St. Lawrence Sales, Inc. located in Lake Orion, MI. Previously imported until 1986 by Beeman Precision Arms, Inc. located in Santa Rosa, CA.

Fabarm currently manufactures approx. 35,000 long guns annually. Firearms which have MSRs with N/A indicate recent importation. Please contact Tristar directly for model availability and current pricing.

SHOTGUNS: O/U

FIELD MODEL - 12 ga. only, 29 1/8 in. VR barrels, single trigger, ejectors, silver finished receiver, also available in Skeet and Trap models. Disc. 1985.

$695	$595	$550	$500	$460	$420	$390

Last MSR was $795.

SKEET/TRAP COMBINATION SET - 12 ga. only, is supplied with both skeet and trap barrel assemblies, cased. Disc. 1986.

$1,050	$900	$840	$780	$720	$670	$600

Last MSR was $1,195.

Add $39 for high gloss wood finish.
Add $30 for auto safety.

The following models have boxlock actions with coin finished receivers and light engraving.

GAMMA FIELD - 12 or 20 (disc.) ga., SST, ejectors, 26, 28, 29, 30, or 32 in. VR barrels, fixed or innerchokes, checkered walnut stock and forearm, 6 1/2 lbs. Imported 1989-95.

$840	$715	$660	$600	$550	$450	$375

Last MSR was $1,044.

Add $28 for 5 innerchokes with wrench (3 in. chambers in 12 ga.).
Add $50 for 20 ga. (3 in. chambers).

✳ *Gamma Field AL Superlight* - 12 ga. only, similar to Gamma Field except receiver is made from Ergal light alloy, 6 lbs. Imported 1989-90.

$875	$760	$695	$625	$550	$450	$375

Last MSR was $970.

Add $41 for 5 innerchokes with wrench.
Add $66 for 20 ga. with 3 in. chambers. New 1990.

This model is chambered for 2 3/4 in. shells only.

GAMMA SPORTING CLAYS COMPETITION - 12 ga. only, designed for sporting clays competition, SST, 28, 29, or 30 in. VR, (10mm) and barrels supplied with 5 innerchokes, special recoil pad, ejectors, checkered walnut stock and forearm. Imported 1989-95.

$950	$825	$725	$650	$575	$495	$400

Last MSR was $1,175.

Add $17 for trap stock and forearm (disc. - includes 28 in. barrels with 5 choke tubes).

GAMMA SKEET - 12 ga. only, 27 1/2 or 28 in. VR barrels, SST, ejectors, supplied with 5 innerchokes, special recoil pad, checkered walnut stock and forearm, reversed Skeet chokes new 1994. Imported 1989-95.

$875	$735	$695	$635	$550	$450	$375

Last MSR was $1,107.

GRADING - PPGS™	100%	98%	95%	90%	80%	70%	60%

GAMMA TRAP - 12 ga. only, 29 or 30 in. VR barrels with special trap chokes and 10mm rib, SST, ejectors, checkered Monte Carlo stock and forearm, 7 1/2 lbs. Imported 1989-95.

	$875	$735	$695	$635	$550	$450	$375

Last MSR was $1,107.

GAMMA PARADOX - 12 ga. only, 25 in. VR barrels with top barrel rifled and lower barrel supplied with 3 innerchokes, SST, ejectors, checkered walnut stock and forearm, 6 lbs. 6 oz. Imported 1989-90.

	$850	$750	$695	$625	$550	$450	$375

Last MSR was $945.

✳ *Gamma Paradox AL Superlight* - similar to Gamma Paradox except receiver is made from Ergal light alloy, 5 lbs. 7 oz. Imported 1989-90.

	$875	$760	$695	$625	$550	$450	$375

Last MSR was $960.

GAMMA 2 FIELD - 12 ga., 3 in. chambers, boxlock action, 26 or 28 in. VR barrels with 5 titanium Innerchokes, ejectors, light grey satin or case colored forged steel receiver with light engraving, gold trigger, checkered walnut stock and Schnabel forearm, approx. 6.6 lbs. Imported 2005.

MSR N/A	$1,395	$1,150	$875	$775	$675	$575	$525

GAMMA 2 SPORTING - 12 ga., 3 in. chambers, boxlock action, similar to Field except has 30 or 32 in. barrels with choke tubes. Imported 2005.

MSR N/A	$1,500	$1,250	$950	$850	$750	$650	$575

WATERFOWLER - 12 ga., 3 1/2 in. chambers, 28 or 30 in. barrels, 100% Max 4 camo coverage on stock and forearm. Imported 2005.

MSR N/A	$1,350	$1,100	$825	$725	$625	$525	$475

STL VS - 12 ga. only, 3 in. chambers, 30 or 32 in. barrels with extended choke tubes, available in Sporting (with HiViz sights) or Trap configuration, adj. comb, checkered deluxe walnut stock and forearm, grey chrome receiver with light engraving, gold trigger, approx. 7.7 lbs. Imported 2005.

MSR N/A	$1,900	$1,675	$1,350	$1,050	$875	$775	$675

EURALFA - 12 ga., 2 3/4 in. chambers, 26 or 28 in. VR barrels with fixed chokes, DT or SNT, extractors, blue receiver with photo engraving, 6 1/2 lbs. Imported 1989-90.

	$495	$460	$420	$390	$350	$310	$275

Last MSR was $571.

✳ *Euralfa AL Superlight* - 12 ga., similar to Euralfa except receiver is made from Ergal light alloy, 6 lbs. Imported 1989-90.

	$515	$475	$430	$400	$360	$320	$285

Last MSR was $603.

✳ *Euralfa Trap* - 12 ga. only, 3 in. chambers, 30 in. barrels bored IM/F. Imported 1990.

	$550	$495	$460	$430	$400	$360	$320

Last MSR was $636.

✳ *Euralfa Magnum* - 12 ga., 3 in. chambers, 26, 28, or 29 in. VR (10mm wide) barrels with fixed chokes, rubber recoil pad. Imported 1989-90.

	$515	$475	$430	$400	$360	$320	$285

Last MSR was $587.

✳ *Euralfa Innerchoke* - 12 ga. only, 3 in. chambers, 28 in. barrels. Imported 1990 only.

	$560	$500	$460	$430	$400	$360	$320

Last MSR was $652.

GRADING - PPGS™	100%	98%	95%	90%	80%	70%	60%

✳ *Euralfa Slug* - 12 ga. only, 24 in. barrels bored cyl./cyl. Imported 1990.

	$500	$475	$430	$400	$360	$320	$285

Last MSR was $571.

EURALFA PARADOX - 12 ga. only, similar to Euralfa except 25 in. VR barrels with top barrel rifled and lower barrel supplied with 3 Innerchokes, 6 lbs. 6 oz. Imported 1989-90.

	$550	$495	$460	$430	$400	$360	$320

Last MSR was $636.

✳ *Euralfa Paradox AL Superlight* - similar to Euralfa Paradox except receiver is made from Ergal light alloy, 5 lbs. 7 oz. Imported 1989-1990.

	$550	$495	$460	$430	$400	$360	$320

Last MSR was $636.

SILVER LION - 12 or 20 ga., similar to Max Lion, except has standard wood and lockable hard plastic case, ported 26 in. TriBore barrels became optional during 1999, standard in 2000, 6.8-7.7 lbs. Imported 1998-2004.

	$1,165	$975	$850	$750	$625	$525	$425

Last MSR was $1,349.

Subtract 10% if w/o TriBore system barrels.

✳ *Silver Lion Cub Model* - similar to Silver Lion, except has youth dimensions (12 1/2 LOP), steel receiver, ported 24 in. TriBore vent. barrels standard, mid rib bead, approx. 6 lbs. Imported 1999-2004.

	$1,135	$950	$850	$750	$625	$525	$425

Last MSR was $1,315.

ULTRA MAG LION - 12 ga. only, 3 1/2 in. chambers, 28 in. standard or ported TriBore (new 1999) barrels, choice of non-glare matte metal finish (disc. 2000) or 100% Advantage Wetlands camo coverage, black colored walnut stock and forearm, non-automatic ejectors, 7.9 lbs., includes lockable plastic case. Imported 1998-2004.

	$1,165	$975	$850	$750	$625	$525	$425

Last MSR was $1,349.

CAMO TURKEY MODEL - 12 ga. only, 3 1/2 in. chambers, 20 in. separated barrels, unique Picatinny rail on top of receiver allows convenient scope mounting, 100% Advantage extra brown camo coverage, includes two ultra-full ported choke tubes, locking fitted luggage case, approx. 7 1/2 lbs. Imported 1999-2000, reintroduced 2002-2004.

	$1,025	$900	$800	$725	$625	$550	$500

Last MSR was $1,235.

SUPER LIGHT LION - 12 ga. only, 3 in. chambers, lightweight alloy receiver, blue finish, 24 in. vent. standard (disc. 1999) or ported TriBore (new 1999, standard 2000) barrels with VR, standard checkered walnut stock and forearm, includes lockable hard plastic case, 6 1/2 lbs. Imported 1998-2000.

	$975	$850	$775	$700	$600	$550	$500

Last MSR was $1,159.

Subtract $100 if w/o ported TriBore barrels (disc. 1999).

✳ *Super Light Lion Cub (Youth) Model* - similar to Silver Lion Youth Model, except has Ergal 55 aluminum receiver, approx. 5 3/4 lbs. Imported 1999-2000.

	$925	$825	$765	$685	$600	$550	$500

Last MSR was $1,099.

SPORTING CLAYS COMPETITION LION - 12 or 20 ga., 3 in. chambers, 28 or 30 (12 ga. only, new 2000) in. vent. ported TriBore barrels with 10mm VR, recoil reducer in buttstock, checkered walnut stock and forearm, adj. SST, includes locking fitted luggage case. Imported 1999-2004.

	$1,185	$1,025	$875	$745	$630	$525	$425

Last MSR was $1,419.

GRADING - PPGS™	100%	98%	95%	90%	80%	70%	60%

✳ *Sporting Clays Competition Lion Extra* - 12 ga. only, 28, 30, or 32 (new 2003) in. unported (mfg. 2001-2004) or ported (mfg. 2000 only) TriBore VR barrels, regular walnut or black competition checkered stock and forearm, adj. cheekpiece, case colored receiver or 100% carbon fiber metal finish, includes 8 choke tubes, locking fitted luggage case, approx. 7.8 lbs. Mfg. 2000-2004.

	$1,700	$1,450	$1,200	$975	$850	$750	$675

Last MSR was $1,925.

Add $74 for case colored receiver with gold inlays and set of 8 choke tubes (mfg. 2004).

BLACK LION COMPETITION - 12 or 20 ga., competition model featuring blue receiver, 26, 28, or 30 (12 ga. only) in. vent. standard or ported TriBore (new 1999) barrels with VR, deluxe checkered wood, 6.8-7.8 lbs. Imported 1998-99.

	$1,300	$1,025	$875	$775	$675	$600	$550

Last MSR was $1,529.

Add $66 for ported TriBore barrels.

MAX LION - 12 or 20 ga., 3 in. chambers, engraved boxlock action with nickel finish, 26, 28, or 30 (12 ga. only) in. vent. standard (disc. 1999) or ported Tri-Bore (new 1999, standard 2000) barrels with VR, rebounding hammers, deluxe checkered stock and forearm, with vent. recoil pad, choke tubes, gold SST, non-automatic safety, includes locking fitted luggage case, 6.8-7.8 lbs. Imported 1998-2003.

	$1,625	$1,350	$1,150	$950	$850	$750	$675

Last MSR was $1,799.

Subtract $100 if w/o ported TriBore barrels (disc. 1999).

✳ *Max Lion Light* - 12 or 20 (new 2001) ga., similar to Max Lion, except has 24 (disc. 2000, reintroduced 2002) or 26 (mfg. 2001 only) in. barrels with Tri-Bore system and gold game birds on satin finished receiver sides, 7-7.2 lbs. Mfg. 2000-2003.

	$1,625	$1,350	$1,150	$950	$850	$750	$675

Last MSR was $1,799.

✳ *Max Lion Sporting Clays* - 12 or 20 ga., includes adj., enhanced walnut competition stock, case hardened receiver, 32 in. Tribore barrels with 8 chokes, 7.9 lbs. Imported 2003.

	$1,625	$1,350	$1,150	$950	$850	$750	$675

Last MSR was $1,799.

✳ *Max Lion Paradox* - 12 or 20 ga., features 24 in. upper smoothbore barrel with Tri-Bore and lower barrel with paradox rifling, VR on 20 ga., case colored receiver, select walnut, sling studs on lower barrel, 7.6 lbs. Mfg. 2002-2003.

	$975	$875	$775	$700	$625	$550	$500

Last MSR was $1,129.

SHOTGUNS: SxS

The following models have boxlock actions with added sideplates.

BETA MODEL - 12 ga. only, 2 3/4 in. chambers, standard model with checkered walnut stock and forearm, ST, ejectors. Imported 1989 only.

	$695	$625	$550	$450	$375	$300	$250

Last MSR was $920.

This model was replaced by the Beta Lux in 1990.

BETA LUX - 12 ga. only, 3 in. chambers, SST, ejectors, boxlock action, 24, 26, 28, or 30 in. barrels bored F/M, 6.6 lbs. Imported 1990-95.

	$1,100	$875	$725	$625	$550	$475	$400

Last MSR was $1,270.

Add $30 for 5 Innerchokes.
Add $114 for competition trap/pigeon model (disc.).

GRADING - PPGS™	100%	98%	95%	90%	80%	70%	60%

BETA EUROPE - 12 ga. only, deluxe model with coin finished game scene engraved sideplates, 26 1/2 or 27 1/2 in. barrels with fixed chokes, ejectors, DT or SST, checkered English stock and splinter forearm, 6 lbs. 6 oz. Imported 1989-90.

	$1,400	$1,100	$850	$700	$575	$495	$450

Last MSR was $1,711.

> Add $33 for semi-beavertail forend.
> Add $130 for competition trap/pigeon model.

CLASSIC LION - 12 ga. only, 3 in. chambers, boxlock action, SST or DT, ejectors, TriBore barrels with 5 choke tubes, approx. 7 lbs. Importation began 1998.

   ✻ *Classic Lion Grade I* - features standard grade wood, 26, 28, or 30 in. VR barrels, English (DT) or pistol grip (disc.) stock, engraved nickel finished receiver, gold SST. Importation disc. 2004.

	$1,375	$1,125	$850	$750	$650	$550	$500

Last MSR was $1,649.

   ✻ *Classic Lion Grade II* - features deluxe wood and removable sideplates with engraving, SST, fitted luggage case.

	$1,875	$1,525	$1,200	$950	$850	$750	$675

Last MSR was $2,325.

   ❖ **Classic Lion Grade II Bill Hanus Birdgun Model** - similar to Grade II, except has best quality wood. Importation disc. 2000.

	$2,275	$1,925	$1,550	$1,225	$995	$875	$800

Last MSR was $2,599.

This model was available through Bill Hanus Birdguns, LLC only.

   ✻ *Classic Lion Elite* - features case colored receiver, DT, select checkered straight grip stock and splinter forearm, 26 or 28 in. fixed choke barrels, 7 3/4 lbs. Importation disc. 2003.

	$1,395	$1,150	$875	$775	$650	$550	$500

Last MSR was $1,689.

SHOTGUNS: SEMI-AUTO

The following models are gas operated, self compensating, have 4 shot mags., aluminum receivers, twin action bars, blue receiver with photo etched game scene engraving, and checkered walnut stock and forearm.

> Add $25 for De Luxe engraving or camouflage wood finish.

DEER GUN - 12 ga. only, 3 in. chamber, 24 in. rifled barrel with front and rear rifle sights, 5 shot mag., 7 lbs. Limited importation 1994-95.

	$695	$475	$425	$375	$325	$300	$285

Last MSR was $775.

ELLEGI STANDARD - 12 ga. only, 28 in. VR barrel with fixed choke, blue receiver, gold trigger, 6 lbs. 9 oz. Imported 1989-90.

	$525	$450	$375	$325	$300	$275	$250

Last MSR was $619.

   ✻ *Ellegi Standard Multichoke* - similar to Ellegi Standard except 5 different choke tubes extend length of barrel up to 6 in., average weight is 6 lbs. 9 oz. Imported 1989-90.

	$540	$475	$395	$350	$325	$300	$265

Last MSR was $644.

The standard barrel length on this model is 24 1/2 in. (30 1/2 in. with full extra-long choke tube).

GRADING - PPGS™	100%	98%	95%	90%	80%	70%	60%

⁕ *Ellegi Standard Innerchoke* - 12 ga. only, 3 in. chamber, 28 in. VR barrel with 5 Innerchokes supplied, 7 lbs. Imported 1989-90.

	$540	$475	$395	$350	$325	$300	$265

Last MSR was $644.

⁕ *Ellegi Standard Magnum* - 12 ga. only, 3 in. chamber, 30 in. VR barrel with fixed choke, recoil pad, 7 1/4 lbs. Imported 1989-90.

	$525	$450	$375	$325	$300	$275	$250

Last MSR was $619.

⁕ *Ellegi Standard Super Goose* - 12 ga. only, 3 in. chamber, 35 1/2 in. VR (12mm wide) barrel with fixed choke, adj. rifle rear sight, supplied with rail for mounting scope rings, rubber recoil pad, designed especially for long range shooting, 7 1/2 lbs. Imported 1989-90.

	$625	$495	$425	$375	$340	$315	$280

Last MSR was $734.

⁕ *Ellegi Standard Slug* - 12 ga. only, 24 1/2 in. barrel, adj. rear sight and bead front, 6 lbs. 9 oz. Imported 1989-90.

	$545	$475	$395	$350	$325	$300	$265

Last MSR was $652.

Add $200 for combo set (includes Innerchoked 28 in. barrel).

⁕ *Ellegi Standard Police* - 12 ga. only, 20 in. cylinder bored barrel, matte black receiver, non-glare stock and forearm. Imported 1989-90.

	$495	$425	$360	$300	$275	$250	$225

Last MSR was $587.

TACTICAL SEMI-AUTO - 12 ga. only, 3 in. chamber, 20 in. barrel with TriBore choke system with cylinder choke, tactical configuration with large cocking handle, oversized safety, black polymer stock and forearm, pistol grip stock design new 2003, choice of Picatinny rail with either integral rear or fixed front and ghost ring (new 2003) sight, 5 shot mag., 6.6 lbs. Imported 2001-2004.

	$875	$775	$650	$575	$515	$450	$400

Last MSR was $1,025.

RED LION MARK II - 12 ga. only, 3 in. chamber, gas operated, alloy receiver, 24, 26, or 28 in. VR standard (disc. 1999) or ported TriBore (standard 2000) barrel, matte finish, reversible safety (oversize beginning 2000), checkered walnut stock and forearm, red receiver logo, lockable plastic case, approx. 7 lbs. Imported 1998-2000.

	$710	$635	$550	$500	$450	$400	$360

Last MSR was $820.

During 2000, the model nomenclature changed to Red Lion Mark II.

GOLD LION MARK II - similar to Red Lion, except has select walnut stock with olive wood pistol grip cap, ported barrel, gold trigger and receiver logo. Imported 1998-2002.

	$750	$675	$595	$550	$500	$450	$400

Last MSR was $849.

During 2000, the model nomenclature changed to Gold Lion Mark II.

GOLD LION MARK III - 12 ga. only, improved Mark II action with Ergal 55 alloy receiver, rubber buffer in gas operating system, 26 or 28 in. VR barrel with TriBore choke system, includes stock shim kit and hardshell case, 7.2 lbs. Imported 2003 only.

	$815	$700	$625	$575	$495	$450	$395

Last MSR was $939.

GRADING - PPGS™	100%	98%	95%	90%	80%	70%	60%

REX LION - 12 ga. only, limited edition of the Gold Lion Mark II, features black and silver finished receiver with gold medallions, checkered Turkish walnut stock, 26 or 28 in. barrel, 7 3/4 lbs. New 2002.

| | $900 | $775 | $700 | $625 | $550 | $500 | $450 |

Last MSR was $1,049.

CAMO LION - 12 ga. only, 3 in. chamber, 20, 24, 26, or 28 in. ported TriBore VR barrel, features 100% Advantage Wetlands camo coverage, approx. 7 lbs. Imported 1999-2002.

| | $850 | $725 | $650 | $575 | $510 | $450 | $400 |

Last MSR was $979.

SPORTING CLAYS LION - 12 ga. only, 28 in. ported TriBore VR barrel, deluxe checkered walnut stock and forearm with olive wood pistol grip cap, matte finish with gold accents on receiver sides, approx. 7.2 lbs. Imported 1999-2000.

| | $865 | $745 | $645 | $565 | $510 | $450 | $400 |

Last MSR was $999.

* *Sporting Clays Lion Extra* - similar to Sporting Clays Lion, 28 or 30 in. barrel, except has carbon fiber metal finish, stock recoil reducer, adj. cheekpiece on checkered walnut or black (new 2002) stock and forearm, includes 6 choke tubes and locking fitted luggage case. Imported 2000-2004.

| | $1,100 | $950 | $825 | $725 | $625 | $550 | $500 |

Last MSR was $1,375.

LION H35 TITAN - 12 ga. only, 26, 28, or 30 in. barrel with choke tubes, 3 or 5 shot mag., sling swivels, interchangeable recoil pad, grey alloy receiver with light engraving, gold trigger, checkered pistol grip walnut stock and forearm with Tri-Wood finish, features titanium protection coating on receiver and new gas system with pulse piston utilizing Zirconium metallurgy. Approx. 6.6 lbs.

| MSR N/A | $1,050 | $950 | $850 | $750 | $650 | $550 | $450 |

LION H368 - 12 ga. only, 3 in. chamber, gas operated, alloy receiver, 24 (Turkey Model, new 2005), 26 (new 2005), 28, or 30 (new 2005) in. VR barrel with TriBore choke system (includes 3 choke tubes), composite synthetic stock with soft touch coating stock and forearm, matte black or 100% Realtree Hardwoods HD (disc. 2004) or Max 4 (new 2005) camo coverage. 7.2 lbs. Imported 2003-2005.

| MSR N/A | $750 | $675 | $600 | $525 | $450 | $375 | $325 |

Add $50 for camo stock and forearm.

SHOTGUNS: SINGLE BARREL

The following models have receivers made out of aluminum alloy, rear trigger guard safety, and matte black finish metal surfaces.

OMEGA STANDARD - 12, 20 ga., or .410 bore, 3 in. chamber, 26 or 28 (12 ga. only) in. barrel, checkered beech stock and forearm, approx. 5 lbs. 5 oz. Imported 1989-90.

| | $120 | $95 | $80 | $70 | $60 | $55 | $50 |

Last MSR was $139.

* *Omega Standard Goose Gun* - 12 ga. only, similar to Omega Standard, except has a 35 1/2 in. barrel, 6 lbs. Imported 1989-90.

| | $135 | $115 | $90 | $80 | $70 | $60 | $55 |

Last MSR was $156.

MONOTRAP SHOTGUN - 12 ga. only, 2 3/4 in. chamber, lightweight 20 ga. frame with nickel finish, 30 (disc. 2001) or 34 (ported, new 2001) in. over single VR barrel with TriBore system and 3 competition choke tubes, adj. trigger, checkered walnut stock and forearm with adj. cheekpiece, recoil system, 6 or 6.9 lbs. Imported 2000-2003.

| | $1,625 | $1,375 | $1,150 | $950 | $825 | $725 | $625 |

Last MSR was $1,799.

GRADING - PPGS™	100%	98%	95%	90%	80%	70%	60%

SHOTGUNS: SLIDE ACTION

The following models are variations of the same action based on a twin bar slide system, alloy receiver with anti-glare finish (including barrel), rear trigger guard safety, and 2 3/4 or 3 in. shell interchangeability.

Add $25 for camouflage wood finish on the following models.

MODEL S.D.A.S.S. - 12 ga. only, 3 in. chamber, originally designed for police and self defense use, 8 shot tube mag., 20 or 24 1/2 in. barrel threaded for external choke tubes, approx. 6 lbs. 6 oz. Imported 1989-90.

	$325	$285	$260	$230	$195	$160	$140

Last MSR was $415.

This model with 24 1/2 in. barrel is threaded for external multi-chokes which can add up to 6 in. to the barrel length - available for a $17 extra charge.

* **Model S.D.A.S.S. Special Police** - similar to Model S.D.A.S.S. except has special heavy 20 in. cylinder bored barrel, VR, cooling jacket, 6 shot mag., rubber recoil pad. Imported 1989-90.

	$340	$295	$265	$230	$195	$160	$140

Last MSR was $440.

* **Model S.D.A.S.S. Martial** - 12 ga. only, 18, 20, 28, 30, or 35 1/2 (disc. 1989) in. barrel, fixed sights and choke, approx. 6 1/4 lbs. Imported 1989-90.

	$330	$290	$260	$225	$190	$160	$140

Last MSR was $424.

Add $41 for VR.
Add $20 for 35 1/2 (disc. 1989) in. barrel.
Add $33 for multi-choke (plain rib with 1 choke and wrench).
Add $65 for innerchoke (includes 1 choke and wrench - VR barrel only).

FP6 - 12 ga. only, 3 in. chamber, 20 or 28 (new 2001) in. shrouded barrel (non-ported TriBore system became standard 2000) with vent. heat shield, with or w/o Picatinny rail, with (new 2003) or w/o ghost ring rear sight, camo (new 2001), matte, or carbon fiber (new 2000) finished metal, 100% Mossy Oak camo (mfg. 2001-2003) or black synthetic stock and forearm, pistol grip stock design new 2003, various security configurations, includes locking plastic case, 6 1/2-7 lbs. Imported 1998-2005.

MSR N/A	$460	$400	$365	$325	$295	$265	$240

Subtract $30 for 100% Mossy Oak Break-up camo coverage (disc. 2003).

FABBRI s.n.c.

Current manufacturer established during 1965, and currently located in Concesio, Italy (previously located in Brescia). Exclusive U.S. dealer is Dewing's, located in West Palm Beach, FL.

Ivo Fabbri and Daniel Perazzi were partners in the shotgun manufacturing business beginning in 1960 - these guns are ser. no. 5001-5339. Circa 1965, Fabbri and Perazzi split up and formed their own individual companies. Fabbri s.n.c. relocated from Brescia to Concesio during 1969 and underwent a name change from Armi Fabbri to Fabbri s.n.c. during 1989. The first CNC machine was installed during 1974. Currently, Fabbri s.n.c. engravers include Creative Art, Pedersoli, Torcoli, and Francassi. Fabbri manufactures perhaps the highest quality shotguns available in today's marketplace - approx. 20-30 guns are mfg. annually. Delivery times range from 2-4 years.

SHOTGUNS: CUSTOM

SxS SHOTGUN - 12 or 20 ga., one of the world's best sidelock SxS shotguns, ejectors, full engraving, "E" prefix ser. no., two types of back action. Disc.

Older Fabbri SxS shotguns manufactured with type II actions and in mint condition are priced in the $65,000 range. Subtract $10,000 for scroll engraving, and/or approx. 50% for type I action.

GRADING - PPGS™	100%	98%	95%	90%	80%	70%	60%

O/U SHOTGUN - 12, 20, or 28 (new 2007) ga., top-of-the-line quality with advanced CNC metal fabrication, steel or stainless steel (new 2002) construction, any combination of engraving, wood, and other options. Both the type/style of engraving and the engraver will make a big difference on the current value of a custom ordered Fabbri O/U shotgun. Because engraving alone can add $50,000+ to the cost of a new shotgun, a qualified appraisal from a reputable dealer/collector is advised when buying or selling recently manufactured Fabbri O/U shotguns.

Current retail starts on the Classic model at approx. $110,000, Full Stainless Steel model is $120,000, and Titanium/Stainless Steel model is $135,000. All prices are FOB Italy, w/o engraving.

Add 25% for matched pair.

Add 15% for 28 ga. on 28 ga. frame.

O/U guns mfg. 1967-1983 (typically marked Ivo Fabbri) are currently priced in the $50,000-$90,000 range, depending on condition and engraving. O/U guns mfg. 1983-1989 (typically marked Ivo Fabbri) are priced in the $95,000-$125,000 range, depending on condition, notoriety of engraver, and amount of engraving coverage. Guns mfg. within the last 10 years are currently priced in the $125,000-$150,000 range, depending on condition, notoriety of engraver, and amount of engraving coverage.

FABRIQUE NATIONALE

Current manufacturer located in Herstal, near Liege, Belgium. The current company name is "Group Herstal," however, the company is better known by "Fabrique Nationale" or "Fabrique Nationale d'Armes de Guerre." FN established their first contract with John M. Browning in 1897 for the manufacture of their first pistol, the FN 1899 Model. Additional contracts were  signed and the relationship further blossomed with the manufacture of the A-5 shotgun. FN was acquired by GIAT of France in 1992. In late 1997, the company was purchased by the Walloon government of Belgium. Additional production facilities are located in Portugal, Japan, and the U.S.

Also See: Browning Arms under Rifles, Shotguns, and Pistols, and FNH USA for current offerings in the U.S.

The author would like to express his sincere thanks to Anthony Vanderlinden from the Browning Collector's Association for making FN contributions to this edition.

PISTOLS: SEMI-AUTO

For FN Models 1899, 1900, 1903, 1905, 1910, 1922 (10/22), Baby Model, Model 10/71, and BAC marked Hi-Powers (post 1954 mfg.), please refer to the Browning Pistol section in this text.

PISTOLS: SEMI-AUTO, HI-POWER VARIATIONS

The F.N. Hi-Power (also known as P-35) was Browning's last pistol design. A 9mm Para., single action, semi-auto pistol, it was the first to incorporate a staggered high capacity magazine. It has a 4 21/32 in. barrel, 13 shot mag., hammer and mag. safeties, a wide variety of finishes and sight options. It's probably the most widely used military pistol in the world.

PRE-WAR COMMERCIAL HP - 9mm Para. cal., single action, blue, wood grips, tangent rear sight, slotted (original) for stock with tangent rear sight, 13 shot mag., Commercial pistols display Liege proofs only, Belgian military pistols display Liege proofs and Belgian military acceptance markings. Mfg. 1935-1940.

Tangent sight & slotted	$2,600	$2,100	$1,700	$1,250	$950	$750	$650

Add $850 for original pre-war commercial flat board stock with attached holster, commercial stocks are most often not numbered.

Add $800 for original prewar Belgian military flat board stock w/o attached holster. Check stock for small Belgian military acceptance marking.

GRADING - PPGS™	100%	98%	95%	90%	80%	70%	60%

PRE-WAR FOREIGN MILITARY CONTRACTS - mfg. under military contract for various countries.

Lithuanian Crest	N/A	$3,300	$2,800	$1,900	$1,350	$1,000	$900
Estonian Contract ("E.V." or "K.L.")	N/A	$3,500	$2,900	$2,500	$1,800	$1,350	$1,000
Finnish Contract ("SA" marked)	N/A	$2,700	$2,200	$1,850	$1,500	$1,000	$800
Paraguayan crest	N/A	$3,750	$3,000	$2,500	$2,250	$1,900	$1,750
Chinese, original finish	N/A	$2,400	$1,850	$1,500	$1,000	$850	$750

Add $850 for original (Finnish contract) pre-war flat board stock with attached holster.
Add $650 for original Finnish contract stock (ser. no. 11,000-15,000) with removed holster.
Add $200 for period Chinese inventory marking on Chinese contract pistols.
Subtract 50% for refinished Chinese contract pistols or reworks with Inglis parts.

Note: Finnish contract guns can be identified by the "SA" marking on frame, and/or slide, and/or mag. 2,400 pistols were shipped to Finland in 1940, all are in ser. no. range: 11,000 - 15,000.
Most Chinese contract pistols were refinished or reworked to include Inglis parts. Chinese contract pistols fall in the 5,000 - 10,000 and 20,000 - 21,000 ser. no. range.
Paraguayan contract guns are rare in the U.S. Numerous counterfeits have surfaced - check crest and slide markings for originality. Check bluing carefully, as most were refinished.

WWII PRODUCTION: WAFFENAMT PROOFED

There is a range of finishes during Nazi production that varies from the excellent pre-war commercial finish on early guns assembled from captured parts to the roughly milled, poorly finished specimens mfg. late in the war. Values listed assume all major parts (slide, barrel, and frame) are matching with original magazine.

In recent years, some Nazi production Hi-Powers have had the rear grip strap milled out and slotted to accept a shoulder stock. Careful observation is advised before purchasing a "rare" (and expensive) slotted and tangent sight specimen. Many HPs have been restored, since the restoration is easily accomplished by professionals.

✳ *WWII Production: Waffenampt Proofed Type I* - Tangent sights, slotted, taken from existing pre-war Belgian production, quality is excellent, correct ser. range is quite limited, approx. 42,000-46,000+. Ser. range for production under German occupation is 50,001-52,500. All are proofed WaA 613.

	N/A	$3,850	$3,600	$3,200	$2,750	$2,450	$1,950

Beware of fakes and restorations. A large percentage of WaA613 pistols iin the U.S. are counterfeits.

✳ *WWII Production: Waffenampt Proofed Type II* - tangent sights, not slotted, approx. 90,000 mfg. with last ser. no. approx. 145,000, generally good quality finish, pistols are proofed WaA613, WaA103, some are WaA140.

	N/A	$1,600	$1,250	$1,000	$800	$700	$600

Add 25% if pistol is marked WaA613.
Add 15% if pistol is marked WaA103.

✳ *WWII Production: Waffenampt Proofed Type III* - standard fixed sights, most common HP pistol produced during the war.

$1,000	$850	$700	$550	$475	$450	$400

Add 15% for late war Bakelite/synthetic grips.
Add 20% for eagle N proof instead of WaA140 proof, or for no WaA140 proof.

POST-OCCUPATION PRODUCTION - commercial assembly began September 1944 from wartime parts. Complete manufacturing from raw materials started in 1946. First imported with BAC markings in 1954 (see Browning HP section). Early (1944-1945) models are identifiable by an "A" serial number prefix and are not fitted with a magazine safety. In 1947, the rear slide bushing became hardened by a new heat treatment process. Other design modifications were added in 1950. Many thousands manufactured for various government contracts.

Add $200-$2,000 for military pistols with crests, depending on condition and variation.

GRADING - PPGS™	100%	98%	95%	90%	80%	70%	60%

✻ *Post-Occupation Production Tangent sight only*

	100%	98%	95%	90%	80%	70%	60%
	$1,300	$1,100	$900	$700	$650	$550	$500

    Add $100 for "T" prefix.

✻ *Post-Occupation Production Tangent sight* - slotted for stock, military or commercial mfg.

	100%	98%	95%	90%	80%	70%	60%
	$1,500	$1,350	$1,100	$900	$750	$600	$500

    Add $150 for "T" prefix.
    Add $50 for internal extractor.

✻ *Post-Occupation Production Fixed sight* - most common variation.

	100%	98%	95%	90%	80%	70%	60%
	$650	$525	$450	$400	$350	$325	$300

    Add $100 for ring hammer.
    Add 40% for "A" prefix, but only in 98%+ condition.

SULTAN OF MUSCAT AND OMAN CONTRACT

✻ *Sultan Of Muscat And Oman Contract First Model* - matte finish, reverse crest, scarce.

	100%	98%	95%	90%	80%	70%	60%
	$4,500	$3,500	$2,500	$2,200	$2,000	$1,600	$1,300

✻ *Sultan Of Muscat And Oman Contract Second Model* - high polish finish, standard crest.

	100%	98%	95%	90%	80%	70%	60%
	$4,000	$2,950	$1,750	$1,540	$1,265	$1,055	$875

INGLIS MANUFACTURED HI-POWERS - SEE INGLIS SECTION.

RIFLES: BOLT ACTION

FN MAUSER SPORTER DELUXE - available in popular American and European calibers, 24 in. barrel, adj. sight, checkered pistol grip stock. Mfg. 1947-63.

	100%	98%	95%	90%	80%	70%	60%
	$900	$750	$500	$450	$400	$350	$300

FN PRESENTATION GRADE - similar to Deluxe, except engraved and select wood.

	100%	98%	95%	90%	80%	70%	60%
	$1,750	$1,500	$1,100	$950	$750	$625	$500

FN SUPREME - .243 Win., .270 Win., 7mm Rem. Mag., .308 Win. cal., or .30-06, 24 in. barrel, peep sight, checkered pistol grip stock. Mfg. 1957-75.

	100%	98%	95%	90%	80%	70%	60%
	$850	$725	$500	$450	$400	$350	$300

FN SUPREME MAGNUM - .264 Win. Mag., 7mm Rem. Mag., .300 Win. Mag., or .375 H&H cal. Mfg. beginning circa 1953.

	100%	98%	95%	90%	80%	70%	60%
	$975	$850	$700	$550	$475	$425	$375

    Add 100% for .375 H&H cal.

FN SNIPER RIFLE (MODEL 30) - .308 Win. cal., this model was a Mauser actioned Sniper Rifle equipped with 20 in. extra heavy barrel, flash hider, separate removable diopter sights, Hensoldt 4X scope, hardcase, bipod, and sling. 51 complete factory sets were imported into the U.S., with additional surplus rifles that were privately imported.

	100%	98%	95%	90%	80%	70%	60%
	$4,750	$4,250	$4,000	$3,500	$3,000	$2,750	$2,500

    Subtract 15% if removable diopter sights or bipod is missing.
    Subtract 10% if scope is not marked with F.N. logo.
Values assume complete factory outfit with all accessories.

RIFLES: SEMI-AUTO

BROWNING PATENT 1900 - .35 Rem. cal. only, usually features matted rib barrel and checkered stock and forearm, similar to Remington Model 8 auto-loading rifle. 4,913 mfg. 1910-1929 by FN, and not officially exported to the U.S.

	100%	98%	95%	90%	80%	70%	60%
	N/A	$1,500	$1,275	$1,050	$900	$800	$700

    Add 15% if rifle has plain barrel with tangent leaf rear sight.

GRADING - PPGS™	100%	98%	95%	90%	80%	70%	60%

MODEL 1949 - 7x57mm Mauser, 7.65mm Mauser, 7.92mm Mauser, or .30-06 cal., (.308 Win. cal. for Argentine conversion rifles), gas operated, 10 shot box mag. (20 round detachable mag. for Argentine conversions), 23 in. barrel, military rifle, tangent rear sight.

	100%	98%	95%	90%	80%	70%	60%
Columbia	$1,500	$1,300	$1,100	$850	$750	$650	$600
Luxemborg	$1,300	$1,100	$900	$750	$650	$550	$500
Venezuela	$900	$775	$750	$700	$600	$500	$450
Argentina	N/A	$825	$775	$750	$650	$600	$500
Egyptian	$1,250	$800	$700	$550	$500	$400	$350

    Add $100 for detachable grenade launcher.
    Subtract 30% for U.S. rebuilt, non-matching rifles with reproduction stocks.
FN-49 contract rifles not listed above are very rare in the U.S. and will demand a premium. Carefully inspect black paint finish for factory originality, as all FN-49s were factory painted. Original sniper rifles are extremely rare and may add $2,000+. Beware of U.S. assembled "sniper" configurations, and Belgian military "ABL" scopes mounted on other contract rifles and sold as original sniper configurations.

RIFLES: SEMI-AUTO, FAL/LAR/CAL/FNC SERIES

After tremendous price increases between 1985-88, Fabrique Nationale decided in 1988 to discontinue this series completely. Not only are these rifles not exported to the U.S. any longer, but all production has ceased in Belgium as well. The only way FN will produce these models again is if they are given a large military contract - in which case a "side order" of commercial guns may be built. 1989 Federal legislation regarding this type of paramilitary design also helped push up prices to their current level. FAL rifles were also mfg. in Israel by I.M.I.

FN FAL - semi-auto, French designation for the F.N. L.A.R. (light automatic rifle), otherwise similar to the L.A.R.

	$2,675	$2,350	$2,100	$1,750	$1,600	$1,450	$1,300

✱ *FN FAL G*

	100%	98%	95%	90%	80%	70%	60%
Standard	$4,800	$4,000	$3,500	$2,950	$2,450	$2,150	$2,000
Paratrooper	$5,200	$4,400	$3,900	$3,350	$2,850	$2,550	$2,400
Heavy Barrel	$6,800	$6,250	$4,950	$4,400	$3,750	$3,250	$2,750
Lightweight	$5,200	$4,250	$3,750	$3,100	$2,600	$2,350	$2,100

    Values listed assume inclusion of factory bipod.
The Standard G Series was supplied with a wooden stock and wood or nylon forearm. The Heavy Barrel variant had all wood furniture and was supplied with a bipod. The Lightweight Model had an aluminum lower receiver, piston tube and magazine.
G Series FALs were imported between 1959-1962 by Browning Arms Co. This rifle was declared illegal by the GCA of 1968, and was exempted 5 years later. Total numbers exempted are: Standard - 1,822, Heavy Barrel - 21, and Paratrooper - 5.

FN L.A.R. COMPETITION (50.00, LIGHT AUTOMATIC RIFLE) - .308 Win. (7.62x51mm) cal., semi-auto, competition rifle with match flash hider, 21 in. barrel, adj. 4 position fire selector on automatic models, wood stock, aperture rear sight adj. from 100-600 meters, 9.4 lbs. Mfg. 1981-83.

	$2,950	$2,700	$2,600	$2,450	$2,300	$2,200	$2,000

This model was designated by the factory as the 50.00 Model.
Mid-1987 retail on this model was $1,258. The last MSR was $3,179 (this price reflected the last exchange rate and special order status of this model).

✱ *FN L.A.R. Competition Heavy barrel rifle (50.41 & 50.42)* - barrel is twice as heavy as standard L.A.R., includes wood or synthetic stock, short wood forearm, and bipod, 12.2 lbs. Importation disc. 1988.

	$3,250	$3,000	$2,850	$2,600	$2,500	$2,300	$2,100

    Add $500 for walnut stock.
There were 2 variations of this model. The Model 50.41 had a synthetic buttstock while the Model 50.42 had a wood buttstock with steel buttplate incorporating a top extension used for either shoulder resting

GRADING - PPGS™	100%	98%	95%	90%	80%	70%	60%

or inverted grenade launching.

Mid-1987 retail on this model was $1,497 (Model 50.41) or $1,654 (Model 50.42). The last MSR was $3,776 (this price reflected the last exchange rate and special order status of this model).

✳ **FN L.A.R. Competition Paratrooper rifle (50.63 & 50.64)** - similar to L.A.R. model, except has folding stock, 8.3 lbs. Mfg. 1950-88.

	$3,875	$3,300	$2,900	$2,700	$2,250	$2,100	$2,000

There were 2 variations of the Paratrooper L.A.R. Model. The Model 50.63 had a stationary aperture rear sight and 18 in. barrel. The Model 50.64 was supplied with a 21 in. barrel and had a rear sight calibrated for either 150 or 200 meters. Both models retailed for the same price.

Mid-1987 retail on this model was $1,310 (both the Model 50.63 and 50.64). The last MSR was $3,239 (this price reflected the last exchange rate and special order status of this model).

CAL - originally imported in 1980, FN's .223 CAL military rifle succeeded the .308 FAL and preceeded the .223 FNC, at first declared illegal but later given amnesty, only 20 imported by Browning.

	$7,800	$7,000	$6,250	$5,500	$4,750	$4,100	$3,600

FNC MODEL - .223 Rem. (5.56mm) cal., lightweight combat carbine, 18 1/2 in. barrel, NATO approved, 30 shot mag., 8.4 lbs. Disc. 1987.

	$2,550	$2,300	$2,150	$1,800	$1,600	$1,450	$1,300

Add $350 for Paratrooper model (16 or 18 1/2 in. barrel).

While rarer, the 16 in. barrel model incorporated a flash hider that did not perform as well as the flash hider used on the standard 18 1/2 in. barrel.

Mid-1987 retail on this model was $749 (Standard Model) and $782 (Paratrooper Model). The last MSR was $2,204 (Standard Model) and $2,322 (Paratrooper Model) - these prices reflected the last exchange rate and special order status of these models.

SHOTGUNS: SxS

FN ANSON SxS STANDARD GRADE - 12 or 16 ga., 26, 28, or 30 (most common) in. barrels, boxlock action, with or w/o ejectors, DT, checkered walnut stock, Greener style crossbolt, FN legend roll engraved on bottom of boxlock, minor engraving on and around screws. Mfg. circa 1910-1940.

	$1,500	$1,300	$950	$625	$550	$375	$325

Add $150 for factory checkered stock options or semi-pistol grip option.
Add $200+ for more elaborate engraving. FN offered six luxury engraving styles.
Subtract $50-$100 if w/o ejectors.

FN NEW ANSON SxS STANDARD GRADE - 12 or 16 ga., 26, 28, or 30 (most common) in. barrels, boxlock action, with or w/o ejectors, DT, checkered walnut stock, FN legend hand engraved on top of the barrels, minor engraving on and around screws. Mfg. circa 1930-1968.

	$1,400	$1,150	$850	$550	$475	$350	$300

Add $150 for factory checkered stock options or semi-pistol grip option.
Add $200+ for more elaborate engraving. FN offered six luxury engraving styles.

FN SIDELOCK STANDARD GRADE - 12 or 16 ga., 26, 28, or 30 (most common) in. barrels, sidelock action, ejectors, DT, checkered walnut stock, minor engraving on sideplates Mfg. 1921-1950. Improved in 1930, and often referred to as the Model 1930.

	$1,500	$1,300	$950	$625	$550	$375	$325

Add $200+ for more elaborate engraving. FN offered six luxury engraving styles.

FALCO, S.R.L.

Current shotgun manufacturer established circa 1960, and located in Marcheno, Italy. No current U.S. importation. Represented in Europe by Effebi, snc. Some models were imported by K.B.I. until 2002.

Falco manufactures a variety of good quality shotgun and rifles in various configurations, including O/U, SxS, combinations, and single shots. Falco is well-known for their folding action design. Please contact the representative directly for information on availability and pricing (see Trademark Index).

GRADING - PPGS™	100%	98%	95%	90%	80%	70%	60%

FALCON FIREARMS

Previous manufacturer located in Northridge, CA from 1986-1990.

PISTOLS: SEMI-AUTO

PORTSIDER - .45 ACP cal., patterned after Colt M 1911 A-1, stainless steel, fixed sights, 5 in. barrel, 7 shot mag., available in left-hand only. Mfg. 1986-90.

$500	$425	$375	$315	$270	$230	$200

Last MSR was $580.

✳ *Portsider Set* - features right- and left-hand models with matching serial numbers. Only 100 sets mfg. 1986-87.

$1,300	$1,100	$895	$785	$655	$550	$465

Last MSR was $1,400.

GOLD FALCON - .45 ACP cal., machined receiver made from solid 17Kt. gold alloy, stainless steel slide, diamond sighting system, choice of grips, standard or personalized engraving options. Only 50 mfg.

$25,000	$17,500	$11,500	N/A	N/A	N/A	N/A

Last MSR was $30,500.

FAMARS di ABBIATICO & SALVINELLI SRL

Current manufacturer established 1967 by Mario Abbiatico and Remo Salvinelli, and located in Gardone, Italy. Distributed and imported by William Larkin Moore, located in Scottsdale, AZ, by Chris Batha, located in Okatie, SC, by Dewing's Fly and Gun, located in West Palm Beach, FL, and by Robin Hollow Outfitters, located in Addieville, RI. Previously distributed by The First National Gun Banque, located in Colorado Springs, CO and by Fieldsport, located in Traverse City, MI. Previously imported by A&S of America, located in Jefferson Boro, PA.

A&S Famars manufactures some of the world's finest rifles and shotguns - approx. 100 are fabricated annually. Most Famars guns include a lifetime warranty. Because every A&S Famars longarm is an individual custom order, each Famars firearm must have its value ascertained on an individual appraisal basis.

All A&S Famars shotguns incorporate a patented A&S Famars mechanism, and many are available in Hunting, Trap, Skeet, Sporting Clays, and Pigeon configurations.

RIFLES: SxS, CUSTOM MFG.

Boxlock and sidelock rifles are all best quality and range in calibers between .22 LR and .600 Nitro Express. Each gun is manufactured per individual customer special order. Further information and price quotations are available by contacting the distributors directly.

A&S Famars models currently manufactured and listed are broken down into three basic grades. The Extra grade is English scroll, Purdey style engraving, with quality 4 wood, and includes leather case. The Prestige grade is game scene or full English scroll engraving, with quality 4 wood and includes leather case. The De Luxe grade includes very detailed, deep ornamental or ornamental and game scene engraving, exhibition quality wood, and leather case.

EXCALIBUR EXPRESS - various cals. up to .375 H&H cal., engraved boxlock action.

MSR $15,600	$14,750	$12,000	$11,000	$9,750	$8,750	$8,000	$7,250

Add $2,350 for Extra.
Add $4,300 for Prestige.
Add $10,100 for De Luxe.

AFRICA EXPRESS STANDARD, EXTRA, PRESTIGE, & DE LUXE - .243 Win., .30-06, 8x57JRS, 9.3x74R, or .375 H&H cal., Anson & Deely boxlock action, chopper lump chrome steel barrels, fixed gold "V" notch front sight, DT, customer selected walnut.

Current MSR on this model is $30,900.
Add $6,000 for Africa Extra.
Add $10,100 for Africa Express Prestige.
Add $19,000 for Africa Express De Luxe.
Add approx. 15% for .500 NE - .600 NE cals.

GRADING - PPGS™	100%	98%	95%	90%	80%	70%	60%

VENUS EXPRESS EXTRA, PRESTIGE, DE LUXE - dangerous game cals., removable sidelock action, ejectors, DT, chopper lump barrels, customer selected walnut.

> Current MSR on this model is $44,600.
> Add $7,000 for Venus Express Prestige.
> Add $19,300 for Venus Express De Luxe.
> Add approx. 10% for .500 NE - .600 NE cals.

VENUS EXPRESS EXTRALUSSO - top-of-the-line model.

> Please contact the importers directly regarding a price quotation on this very limited model.

SHOTGUNS: O/U, CUSTOM MFG.

JOREMA MODEL - 12 or 20 ga., sidelock. Disc. 1999.

	100%	98%	95%	90%	80%	70%	60%
	$25,000	$19,750	$13,500	$10,250	$8,750	$7,500	$6,250

Last MSR was $25,650.

> Add 10% for 20 ga.

SOVEREIGN EXTRA, PRESTIGE, DE LUXE (JOREMA ROYAL, ARIES) - 12, 16, 20, 28 ga. or .410 bore, sidelock action, ejectors, DT or ST, chopper lump barrels, available with optional detachable sidelocks, customer selected walnut.

> Current MSR on this model is $43,900.
> Add $4,000 for Prestige.
> Add $11,100 for De Luxe.
> Add 10% for 28 ga. or .410 bore, depending on the grade.

This model was originally called the Jorema Royal, then renamed the Aries in 2000, and renamed the Sovereign in 2002.

ROYALE SH MODEL - 12, 20, 28 ga., or .410 bore, sidelock, bar action. Disc. 2002.

	100%	98%	95%	90%	80%	70%	60%
	$34,000	$23,750	$17,750	$13,000	$10,000	$8,500	$7,250

Last MSR was $38,875.

> Add 20% for 28 ga. or .410 bore.

CASTORE EXTRA, PRESTIGE, DE LUXE - various gauges, sidelock action, customer selected walnut.

MSR $37,000	98%	95%	90%	80%	70%	60%
	$33,500	$30,250	$26,900	$22,000	$17,000	$13,000 $10,500

> Add $4,000 for Prestige.
> Add $11,000 for De Luxe.
> Add approx. $4,000 for 28 ga. or .410 bore.

PEGASUS EXTRA, PRESTIGE, DE LUXE - features Famars patented sidelocks.

	100%	98%	95%	90%	80%	70%	60%
	$26,750	$21,750	$16,500	$12,500	$10,000	$8,500	$7,250

> Add $2,820 for Prestige.
> Add $10,800 for De Luxe.
> Add 10% for 28 ga. or .410 bore.

EXCALIBUR COMPETITION MODELS - 12, 20, 28 ga. or .410 bore, current models include the BL, BLE (Extra), BLP (Prestige), BLX (sideplate), BLXE, BLXP, SL (sidelock), SLE, and SLP.

> Add approx. 15% for 28 ga. or .410 bore. on the following models.

∗ *Excalibur BL* - 12, 16, 20, 28 ga. or .410 bore, detachable locks, monobloc barrels, ST, ejectors, customer selected walnut.

MSR $14,900	98%	95%	90%	80%	70%	60%
	$13,500	$11,000	$9,750	$8,250	$7,150	$6,000 $4,950

> Subtract approx. $1,500 for Standard BL model (disc. 2005).
> Add $2,300-$4,000 for BL Extra with round action, depending on model.
> Add $1,000 for Prestige.
> Add $8,000 for De Luxe.

GRADING - PPGS™	100%	98%	95%	90%	80%	70%	60%

✳ *Excalibur BL Round Titanium* - titanium round action.

	$21,750	$19,000	$17,000	$14,500	$11,250	$9,750	$8,500

Last MSR was $24,816.

Add $2,376 for Extra.
Add $10,692 for De Luxe.

✳ *Excalibur BLX* -12, 16, 20, 28 ga. or .410 bore, detachable trigger mechanism with sideplates and monobloc barrels, ejectors, ST, customer selected walnut.

MSR $18,900	$17,250	$15,000	$12,750	$10,750	$9,000	$8,750	$7,000

Subtract approx. $1,000 for BLX Standard (disc)..
Add $3,600 for Prestige.
Add $13,100 for De Luxe.

✳ *Excalibur SL* - sidelock action, monobloc barrels. Disc. 2002.

	$21,000	$17,500	$13,250	$9,750	$8,200	$7,500	$6,750

Last MSR was $23,750.

✳ *Excalibur Round Sporting* - 12 or 20 ga., removable trigger mechanism, SST, monobloc barrels with Briley chokes, ejectors, customer selected walnut, color case hardened receiver.

MSR $14,600	$13,250	$11,000	$9,750	$8,250	$7,150	$6,000	$4,950

Add $2,600 for Sporting Extra.

ROMBO VIERLING EXTRA, PRESTIGE, DE LUXE QUATTROCANNE - 28 ga. or .410 bore, Anson & Deeley locking system with sideplates, side opening lever, ST, four chopper lump barrels are arranged in a quad pattern, customer selected walnut, approx. 7 1/2 lbs. Limited mfg.

Current MSR on this model is $70,000.
Add $9,000 for Prestige.
Add $20,000 for De Luxe.

POSEIDON BL - 12, 20, 28 ga. or .410 bore., round action with monobloc or demibloc barrels.

MSR $29,900	$26,500	$22,250	$18,500	$15,000	$13,000	$11,000	$9,250

Add approx. 10% for 28 ga. or .410 bore.
Add approx. 13% for sideplates.

Add $3,000 for Prestige.
Add $11,000 for De Luxe.
Add approx. $5,000 for demibloc barrels (disc.).

✳ *Poseidon BL Round Titanium* - titanium round action with demibloc barrels.

	$27,250	$25,750	$21,000	$17,250	$14,750	$13,000	$11,750

Add $2,160 for BL Extra.
Add $9,720 for De Luxe.

✳ *Poseidon BLX* - monobloc or demibloc barrels.

	$17,250	$16,000	$13,750	$11,500	$9,650	$8,500	$7,250

Add $1,200 for BLX Extra.
Add $3,480 for Prestige.
Add $13,172 for De Luxe.
Add $4,380 for demibloc barrels.

SHOTGUNS: SxS

Add 10% for 28 ga. or .410 bore. on the following models.

CASTORE PRESTIGE/DE LUXE HAMMER GUN - various gauges, double barrel, exposed hammers, double triggers. Limited importation.

MSR N/A	$30,000	$26,250	$23,000	$19,750	$16,750	$14,650	$12,000

Add $3,168 for Prestige.
Add $11,880 for De Luxe.

GRADING - PPGS™	100%	98%	95%	90%	80%	70%	60%

BOXLOCK MODELS - various gauges, available with Anson & Deeley boxlock action, scalloped or rounded frame, various engraving patterns available.

  ✳ *Zeus Extra, Prestige, De Luxe Boxlock* - 12 or 20 ga., features round action, side lever release, DT, limited mfg.

	100%	98%	95%	90%	80%	70%	60%
MSR $29,900	$26,500	$22,250	$18,500	$15,000	$13,000	$11,000	$9,250

    Add $2,000 for Prestige.
    Add $5,800 for De Luxe.

  ✳ *Tribute Extra, Prestige, De Luxe Boxlock* - 12 (disc.), 20 (disc.), 28 ga., or .410 bore (disc.), scalloped back drop lock action, 7 1/4 lbs., limited mfg.

	100%	98%	95%	90%	80%	70%	60%
	$27,750	$24,250	$20,750	$15,250	$12,350	$10,750	$9,250

    Add $3,600 for Prestige.
    Add $11,640 for De Luxe.
    Add approx. 20% for 28 ga. or 10% for .410 bore.

SIDELOCK MODELS

  ✳ *Highline (Veneri) Sidelock Model* - various gauges, round body, back action, very limited mfg. Disc. 1999.

	100%	98%	95%	90%	80%	70%	60%
	$25,500	$20,000	$16,000	$12,250	$10,000	$8,500	$7,250

Last MSR was $30,000.

  ✳ *Venus Extra/Prestige/De Luxe Sidelock Model* - features patented Famars side-locks, back action.

    Add $4,000 for Prestige.
    Add $11,100 for De Luxe.
  Current MSR on this model is $36,900.

AVANTIS - 12, 16, 20, 28 ga. or .410 bore, hand detachable sidelock mechanism is attached to removable trigger group, chopper lump barrels, uncheckered straight grip stock and forearm, customer selected walnut, round frame, 6 - 6 1/2 lbs.

    Current MSR on this model is $33,900.
    Add $2,900 for Prestige.
    Add $6,000 for De Luxe.
  This model is available exclusively in the U.S. through Dewing's Fly & Gun Shop.

FANZOJ, JOHANN

Current long gun manufacturer established in 1790 and located in Ferlach, Austria. Current exclusive U.S. dealer is Dewing's Fly & Gun Shop, located in Palm Beach, FL.

Johann Fanzoj is the 9th generation in his family to manufacture top quality long arms. Today's configurations include double rifles in all possible calibers, double shotguns, bolt action rifles, stalking rifles, combination guns, and the new Tri-Bore three barrel shotgun. Drillings are also available by special order, but typically not imported into the U.S. Fanzoj was also a member of the Ferlach Guild, which was dissolved in 2004. The models listed below are the only ones currently available in the U.S.

RIFLES

Current MSR on the double rifle boxlock in-the-white is €27,000. Current MSR for a double rifle sidelock in-the-white is € 54,000. Current MSR on an underlever stalking rifle in-the-white is €12,000. The Fanzoj bolt action rifle in-the-white starts at €7,500.

SHOTGUNS

Tri-Bore shotguns are available in 12, 16, 20, 28 ga. or .410 bore. Current MSR for a Tri-Bore in-the-white is €47,000 for most gauges, and €51,700 for 28 ga. or .410 bore.

GRADING - PPGS™	100%	98%	95%	90%	80%	70%	60%

FARQUHARSON

Rifle configuration designed by John Farquharson in 1871. The Farquharson was influential during the height of the British Empire, and was popular with sportsmen and soldiers alike.

Currently, Ballard Arms of Cody, Wyoming is building a rifle based on this configuration. Please contact the company directly for more information, including pricing, availability and delivery time (see Trademark Index).

FAUSTI STEFANO SRL

Current manufacturer established in 1948 and located in Marcheno, Italy. Currently imported under private label beginning 2005 by Weatherby, located in Atascadero, CA. Also currently imported on a private label basis by Cabela's. Previously imported 2000-2006 by Traditions, located in Old Saybrook, CT, and until 1999 by American Arms located in N. Kansas City, MO.

FAUSTI® STEFANO s.r.l.

Fausti (Fausti, Cav., Stefano & Figlie snc.). manufactures a variety of excellent quality shotguns in O/U, SxS, and single shot configurations. Fausti is a well established brand name in the European marketplace. Please refer to the Weatherby and Cabela's sections for more information on current Fausti importation. New importation can be determined by the Fausti Stefano SRL markings.

FEATHER INDUSTRIES, INC.

Previous manufacturer located in Boulder, CO until 1995.

DERRINGERS

GUARDIAN ANGEL CENTERFIRE - 9mm Para. or .38 Spl. cal., O/U design, stainless steel, double action backup derringer. Mfg. 1988-89 only.

$130	$95	$75	$70	$60	$55	$50

Last MSR was $140.

This model has interchangeable loading blocks that allow shooting 9mm Para. or .38 Spl. There is no exposed hammer and trigger is totally enclosed.

GUARDIAN ANGEL RIMFIRE - .22 LR or .22 Mag. cal., design is similar to 9mm Para./.38 Spl. model, loading block breech, 2 in. barrel, fixed sights, 12 oz. Mfg. 1990-95.

$100	$75	$60	$55	$50	$45	$40

Last MSR was $120.

Add $30 for individual extra loading blocks.

This model has interchangeable loading blocks that allow shooting .22 LR or .22 Mag. There is no exposed hammer and the trigger is totally enclosed.

PISTOLS: SEMI-AUTO

MINI-AT - .22 LR cal., pistol variation of the AT-22, 5 1/2 in. shrouded barrel, 20 shot mag., approx. 2 lbs. Mfg. 1986-89.

$195	$165	$145	$135	$130	$125	$115

Last MSR was $220.

RIFLES: SEMI-AUTO

AT-22 - .22 LR cal., semi-auto blowback action, 17 in. detachable shrouded barrel, collapsible metal stock, adj. rear sight, with sling and swivels, 20 shot mag., 3 1/4 lbs. Mfg. 1986-95.

$225	$175	$155	$145	$135	$125	$115

Last MSR was $250.

GRADING - PPGS™	100%	98%	95%	90%	80%	70%	60%

F2 - similar to AT-22, except is equipped with a fixed polymer buttstock. Mfg. 1992-95.

| | $245 | $190 | $165 | $150 | $135 | $125 | $115 |

Last MSR was $280.

AT-9 - 9mm Para. cal., semi-auto blowback action, 16 in. barrel, paramilitary design, available with 10 (C/B 1994), 25*, 32 (disc.), or 100 (disc. 1989) shot mag., 5 lbs. Mfg. 1988-95.

| | $700 | $625 | $550 | $495 | $450 | $400 | $350 |

Last MSR was $500.

Add $250 for 100 shot drum mag.

F9 - similar to AT-9, except is equipped with a fixed polymer buttstock. Mfg. 1992-95.

| | $575 | $525 | $450 | $395 | $335 | $295 | $260 |

Last MSR was $535.

SATURN 30 - 7.62x39mm Kalashnikov cal., semi-auto, gas operated, 19 1/2 in. barrel, composite stock with large thumbhole pistol grip, 5 shot detachable mag., drilled and tapped for scope mounts, adj. rear sight, 8 1/2 lbs. Mfg. in 1990 only.

| | $650 | $550 | $475 | $425 | $375 | $325 | $280 |

Last MSR was $695.

KG-9 - 9mm Para. cal., semi-auto blowback action, 25 or 50 shot mag., paramilitary configuration. Mfg. 1989 only.

| | $750 | $675 | $600 | $550 | $500 | $450 | $400 |

Last MSR was $560.

Add $100 for 50 shot mag.

SAR-180 - .22 LR cal., semi-auto blowback action, 17 1/2 in. barrel, 165 shot drum mag., fully adj. rear sight, walnut stock with combat style pistol grip and forend, 6 1/4 lbs. Mfg. 1989 only.

| | $495 | $425 | $375 | $325 | $275 | $240 | $200 |

Last MSR was $500.

Add $250 for 165 shot drum mag.
Add $200 for retractable stock.
Add $395 for laser sight.

This variation was also manufactured for a limited time by ILARCO (Illinois Arms Company), previously located in Itasca, IL.

KG-22 - .22 LR cal., similar to KG-9, 20 shot mag. Mfg. 1989 only.

| | $295 | $250 | $200 | $175 | $155 | $145 | $135 |

Last MSR was $300.

FEATHER USA/AWI LLC

Current rifle manufacturer established 1996 and located in Eaton, CO.

RIFLES: SEMI-AUTO

Feather USA currently manufactures the following paramilitary styled rifles with steel wire stocks: RAV17 (.17 Mach 2 cal., disc., $549 last MSR), RAV22 (.22 LR cal., $249 - $499 MSR, depending on options and accessories), RAV9 (9mm Para. cal. - $499 - $749 MSR), RAV40 (.40 S&W cal. - disc. 2005, $699 last MSR), and the RAV45ACP ($520 - $750 MSR). High accuracy variations (HA suffix) with tapered bull barrels are also available for approx. $100 - $160 extra. Many options are available. Please contact the company directly for more information, including availability (see Trademark Index).

GRADING - PPGS™	100%	98%	95%	90%	80%	70%	60%

FEDERAL ENGINEERING CORPORATION
Previous manufacturer located in Chicago, IL.

RIFLES: SEMI-AUTO

XC-220 - .22 LR cal., semi-auto paramilitary design rifle, 16 5/16 in. barrel, 28 shot mag., machined steel action, 7 1/2 lbs. Mfg. 1984-89.

$495	$450	$400	$350	$320	$295	$275

XC-450 - .45 ACP cal. only, semi-auto paramilitary design carbine, 16 1/2 in. barrel length, 30 shot mag., fires from closed bolt, machined steel action, 8 1/2 lbs. Mfg. 1984-89.

$950	$825	$750	$675	$600	$550	$500

XC-900 - 9mm Para. cal., semi-auto paramilitary design carbine, 16 1/2 in. barrel length, 32 shot mag., fires from closed bolt, machine steel action, 8 lbs. Mfg. 1984-89.

$950	$825	$750	$675	$600	$550	$500

FEDERAL ORDNANCE, INC.
Previous manufacturer, importer, and distributor located in South El Monte, CA from 1966-1992. Brickley Trading Co. bought the remaining assets of Federal Ordnance, Inc. in late 1992, and continued to import various firearms until circa 1998.

Federal Ordnance imported and distributed both foreign and domestic military handguns and rifles until 1992. In addition, they also fabricated firearms using mostly newer parts.

PISTOLS: SEMI-AUTO

In addition to the following Broomhandle models, Federal Ordnance also manufactured other special editions. These models include the British Model, Cut-Away, Cartridge Counter, Para La Guerra, and others. Prices are in the $800-$950 range (retail).

MODEL 714 BROOMHANDLE - 7.63 Mauser or 9mm Para. cal., 5 1/2 in. barrel, new frame, exterior completely refinished, 10 shot detachable mag., "fair" bore, adj. rear sight. Mfg. 1986-91.

$700	$600	$500	$450	$400	$350	$325

Last MSR was $820.

Add $100 for new barrel.

✴ *Model 714 Broomhandle Para La Guerra* - 7.63 Mauser or 9mm Para. cal., remanufactured to duplicate Spanish Civil War configuration Broomhandle, includes 10 in. barrel with "Para La Guerra" engraved on side. Mfg. 1990-91 only.

$750	$650	$550	$450	$400	$350	$325

Last MSR was $890.

✴ *Model 714 Broomhandle Bolo* - similar to Model 714 Broomhandle, except has smaller grips, 3.9 in. barrel, 10 shot mag. standard. Mfg. 1988 only.

$700	$600	$500	$450	$400	$350	$325

Last MSR was $890.

STANDARD BROOMHANDLE - 7.63 Mauser or 9mm Para. cal., refurbished (new barrels, completely refinished, etc.) C-96 pistols, replaced springs, includes original Chinese shoulder/holster stock. Disc. 1991.

$650	$550	$485	$450	$420	$390	$380

Last MSR was $735.

Subtract $150 without shoulder/holster stock.

✴ *Standard Broomhandle Bolo* - similar to Standard Broomhandle, except Bolo configuration (3.9 in. barrel and smaller grips). Includes original Chinese shoulder/holster stock. Mfg. 1990-91 only.

$600	$500	$450	$420	$390	$380	$370

Last MSR was $530.

GRADING - PPGS™	100%	98%	95%	90%	80%	70%	60%

RANGER 1911A1 GI - .45 ACP cal., 5 in. barrel, 7 shot mag., steel construction throughout, checkered walnut grips, 40 oz. Mfg. 1988-92.

| | $450 | $395 | $350 | $310 | $280 | $260 | $240 |

Last MSR was $440.

Add $20 for Ranger Extended Model (40 oz. - new 1990).
Add $40 for Ranger Ambo (ambidextrous safety, 40 oz. - new 1990).
Add $15 for lightweight Ranger Lite Model (32 oz. - new 1990).

These pistols are patterned after the Colt 1911A1 Govt. Model.

* *Ranger 1911A1 GI Ten* - 10mm cal., otherwise similar to regular Ranger 1911A1. Mfg. 1990-91 only.

| | $675 | $525 | $475 | $450 | $420 | $395 | $370 |

Last MSR was $780.

RANGER SUPERCOMP - .45 ACP or 10mm cal., compensated variation of the Ranger 1911A1 with 6 in. compensated barrel, slide, tuned trigger, and other competition features, 42 oz. Mfg. 1990-91 only.

| | $1,250 | $875 | $775 | $675 | $600 | $550 | $495 |

Last MSR was $1,390.

Add $10 for 10mm cal.

THE RANGER ALPHA - .38 Super, 10mm, or .45 ACP cal., 5 or 6 in. barrel, patterned after the Colt Govt. Model. Mfg. 1990-91 only.

| | $895 | $775 | $675 | $575 | $475 | $425 | $380 |

Last MSR was $1,000.

Add $16 for 10mm cal.
Add $16 for 6 in. barrel.
Add $9-$25 for ported 5 or 6 in. barrel depending on cal.

RIFLES/CARBINES

ALL AMERICAN SPORTER BOLT ACTION - .30-06 cal., Springfield M1903 receiver, new sporter stock, drilled and tapped for scope base (included), blue finish. Mfg. late 1991-92.

| | $250 | $220 | $180 | $150 | $120 | $100 | $90 |

MODEL 713 DELUXE MAUSER SEMI-AUTO CARBINE - 7.63 Mauser or 9mm Para. cal., 16 in. barrel, detachable stock, one 10 shot and one 20 shot detachable mag., deluxe walnut, leather case with accessories, adj. sights to 1,000 meters, 5 lbs. 1,500 mfg. 1986-1992.

| | $1,750 | $1,495 | $1,250 | $1,050 | $935 | $755 | $640 |

Last MSR was $1,986.

* *Model 713 Deluxe Mauser Semi-Auto Carbine Field Grade* - 7.63 Mauser or 9mm Para. (new 1989) cal., 16 in. barrel, 10 shot fixed mag., nondetachable walnut stock. Mfg. 1987-92.

| | $900 | $775 | $675 | $600 | $525 | $475 | $425 |

Last MSR was $1,200.

M-14 SEMI-AUTO - .308 Win. cal., legal for private ownership (no selector), 20 shot mag., refinished original M-14 parts, available in either filled fiberglass, G.I. fiberglass, refinished wood, or new walnut stock. Mfg. 1986-91.

| | $975 | $875 | $695 | $640 | $565 | $500 | $450 |

Last MSR was $700.

Add $50 for filled fiberglass stock.
Add $110 for refinished wood stock.
Add $190 for new walnut stock with handguard.

During the end of production, Chinese parts were used on this model. Values are the same.

TANKER GARAND SEMI-AUTO - .30-06 or .308 Win. cal., original U.S. GI parts, 18 in. barrel, new hardwood stock, parkerized finish. Mfg. began late 1991.

| | $825 | $750 | $695 | $650 | $595 | $550 | $475 |

GRADING - PPGS™	100%	98%	95%	90%	80%	70%	60%

CHINESE RPK 86S-7 SEMI-AUTO - 7.62x39mm cal., semi-auto version of the P.R.C.-RPK light machine gun, 75 shot drum mag., 23 3/4 in. barrel, with bipod. Imported 1989 only.

	$1,200	$1,025	$825	$750	$675	$625	$575

Last MSR was $500.

Add $100 for 75 shot drum mag.

FEINWERKBAU

Current manufacturer established circa 1951, and located in Oberndorf, Germany. Currently imported beginning 2005 by Brenzovich Firearms Training Center (B.F.T.C.), located in Fort Hancock, Texas. Previously imported until 2004 by Nygord Precision, located in Prescott, AZ.

Feinwerkbau manufactures some of the world's finest quality target rifles and pistols (.22 LR rimfire and airgun). Target rifles and pistols have had limited importation into the U.S. Feinwerkbau also manufactures world championship winning airguns and a black powder pistol. For more information and current pricing on both new and used Feinwerkbau airguns, please refer to the *Blue Book of Airguns* by Dr. Robert Beeman & John Allen (also online). For more information on the black powder pistol, please refer to the *Blue Book of Modern Black Powder Arms* by John Allen (also online).

PISTOLS: SEMI-AUTO, RIMFIRE

MODEL AW-93 - .22 LR cal., 6 in. barrel, 5 shot mag., ergonomically designed stippled walnut grips with adj. heel, unique damper prevents muzzle jump and recoil, satin nickel/blue receiver finish, bolt burnished, top-of-the-line Target pistol, adj. two-stage trigger, adj. rear sight, right or left hand grip, current mfg. includes plastic case, approx. 2 1/2 lbs. New 1993.

MSR $2,333		$2,200	$1,875	$1,575	$1,375	$1,150	$950	$850

✻ *Model AW-93 Lightweight* - similar to standard Model AW-93, except has lightened frame, blue aluminum damper/weight underneath slide, 2 1/3 lbs. Limited importation began 2004.

MSR $2,333		$2,200	$1,875	$1,575	$1,375	$1,150	$950	$850

RIFLES: BOLT ACTION, RIMFIRE

MODEL 2000 - .22 LR cal. only, single shot, match target bolt action rifle, fully adj. trigger, walnut stocks, four variations featuring different specifications. Importation disc. 1988.

✻ *Model 2000 Universal Model* - 26 3/8 in. barrel, aperture sights, stippled pistol grip and forearm, 9 3/4 lbs.

	$1,150	$925	$850	$735	$650	$595	$550

Last MSR was $1,395.

Add $350 for electronic trigger.
Add $160 for left-hand variation.

✻ *Model 2000 Mini (Junior)* - 22 in. barrel, aperture sights, stippled pistol grip, 9 1/8 lbs.

	$1,025	$875	$825	$700	$625	$575	$525

Last MSR was $1,225.

Add $350 for electronic trigger.
Add $150 for left-hand variation.

✻ *Model 2000 Match Model* - 26 1/4 in. barrel, adj. cheekpiece on stock, stippled pistol grip and forearm, aperture sights.

	$1,075	$895	$825	$700	$625	$575	$525

Last MSR was $1,285.

Add $390 for electronic trigger.
Add $113 for left-hand variation.

GRADING - PPGS™	100%	98%	95%	90%	80%	70%	60%

✱ *Model 2000 Running Target* - adj. cheekpiece on stock, thumbhole stippled pistol grip, no sights, for running boar competition.

	$1,150	$925	$850	$735	$650	$595	$550

Last MSR was $1,398.

Add $142 for left-hand variation.

MODEL 2600 UNIVERSAL - .22 LR cal. only, similar design to Model 600 air rifle, single shot, 26.3 in. barrel, aperture sights, 10.6 lbs. Imported 1986-94.

	$1,425	$1,125	$925	$850	$735	$650	$595

Last MSR was $1,695.

Add $160 for left-hand variation.

MODEL 2600 ULTRA MATCH FREE RIFLE - .22 LR cal., single shot match gun based on Model 2600 action, 26.1 in. barrel, laminated stock with thumbhole, fully adj. aperture sights, 14 lbs. 1 oz. Mfg. 1986-94.

	$2,175	$1,750	$1,400	$1,150	$925	$850	$735

Last MSR was $2,498.

Add $250 for electronic trigger (disc. 1988).
Add $152 for left-hand variation.

MODEL 2602 UNIVERSAL (UIT) RIFLE - .22 LR cal., designed for Match competition, state-of-the-art Target rifle with different color wood laminations possible, adj. cheekpiece, short or long barrel, two-stage trigger. Mfg. 1997-2003.

	$1,450	$1,275	$1,125	$975	$850	$725	$600

Last MSR was $1,615.

Add $125 for left-hand action.

MODEL 2602 FREE RIFLE - .22 LR cal., standard Match rifle with red and blue anodized aluminum stock with adj. cheekpiece and buttplate, and adj. hand rest, 16 3/4 or 26 1/2 in. barrel with unique 13 3/4 in. squared-off barrel sleeve with sight, diopter sights, top-of-the-line competition rifle, approx. 13.86 lbs. Mfg. 1997-2003.

	$2,035	$1,800	$1,575	$1,350	$1,175	$1,000	$850

Last MSR was $2,365.

Add $155 for left-hand action.

MODEL 2602 SUPER MATCH - .22 LR cal., Super Match variation featuring state-of-the-art design, adj. stock, comb, LOP, and trigger pull. Disc. 2003.

	$2,550	$2,175	$1,800	$1,575	$1,350	$1,175	$1,000

Last MSR was $2,995.

Add $130 for left-hand action.
Subtract $130 for Model 2602 Sport RT.

MODEL 2602 SPORT - .22 LR cal., sporter variation of the Model 2602, short or long barrel, right- or left-hand action, two-stage trigger, laminated wood stock with red stripes and thumbhole, adj. cheekpiece and buttplate, approx. 12 3/4 lbs. Mfg. 2000-2003.

	$1,950	$1,750	$1,525	$1,325	$1,175	$1,000	$850

Last MSR was $2,240.

MODEL 2700 UNIVERSAL - .22 LR cal., competition rifle, single action, features laminate stock and adj. cheekpiece, right or left hand action, adj. two-stage trigger, adj. aluminum buttplate, muzzle brake, approx. 12 lbs. New 2004.

MSR $2,329	$2,275	$1,875	$1,575	$1,275	$1,075	$875	$750

MODEL 2700 FREE RIFLE SUPER MATCH - .22 LR cal., current top-of-the-line rifle, 27 in. barrel, single action, right or left hand action, adj. two-stage trigger, features blue or silver aluminum stock, pivoting anatomical grip and interior sliding weight, adj. cheekpiece, ajd. buttplate, sling holder with anatomical handstop, 12 1/4 - 13 1/2 lbs. New 2004.

MSR $3,240	$3,000	$2,750	$2,500	$2,225	$1,875	$1,575	$1,375

GRADING - PPGS™	100%	98%	95%	90%	80%	70%	60%

FEMARU

Previously manufactured by Femaru-Fegyver es Gepgyar R.T. located in Budapest, Hungary.

PISTOLS: SEMI-AUTO

MODEL 1910 - 7.65mm Roth/Steyr cal., rare and only infrequently encountered. Estimated serial range 1-10,000.

$2,750	$2,250	$1,750	$1,250	$975	$850	$725

MODEL 1929 (29M) - .380 ACP cal., 3.93 in. barrel, 8 shot mag., identifiable by squared-off rear slide with vertical serrations, 2 piece walnut grips, approx. 50,000 mfg.

$795	$600	$400	$300	$200	$165	$145

MODEL 1937 (37M) - .32 ACP or .380 ACP cal., 3.93 in. barrel, 8 shot mag., commercial blue finish, left slide marking "FEMARU FEGYVER ES GEPGYAR RT. 37M", vertically grooved 2-piece walnut grips, approx. 200,000 mfg. (.380 ACP cal.) for Hungarian service before Nazi variations began (dubbed "Pistole Modell 37 (ung)," circa 1941), Nazi marked "jhv 41" or "jhv 44", 27 oz.

$500	$400	$300	$250	$225	$200	$175

Add 50% for Waffenamt proofing (.32 ACP only).
Add another 100% if with holster and 2 matching mags.

FROMMER STOP POCKET AUTO - .32 ACP or .380 ACP cal., 6 or 7 shot, 3 7/8 in. barrel, fixed sights, blue, rubber grips, locked breech, outside hammer. Mfg. 1912-1920.

$395	$325	$250	$225	$200	$175	$150

Add 50% for .380 ACP cal.

FROMMER BABY POCKET AUTO - similar to Stop Pocket Auto, except 2 in. barrel, 5 or 6 shot.

$300	$235	$180	$150	$115	$90	$70

FROMMER LILIPUT AUTO - .25 ACP cal., blowback action, 6 shot, 2.14 in. barrel, blue, hard rubber grips. Mfg. in early 1920s.

$400	$300	$200	$145	$115	$90	$75

FERLACH GUNS

Includes those firearms manufactured in Ferlach, Austria from 1558 to present. The Ferlach Guild (Genossenschaft) represented most of Ferlach's gunmakers until it was dissolved in 2004.

Many people mistakenly believe that Ferlach is a trademark - it is not. Rather, it is a small village in Austria where a gun guild was started as early as 1558. At that time, it was absolutely necessary that all the people involved in fabricating a firearm were located together in close proximity. This enabled the barrel maker, the stock maker, and the lock mechanism maker to work together closely to ensure that everyone was performing their task(s) correctly, effectively and efficiently. As the individual skills became better and more refined, more and more firearms were manufactured. Eventually, individual gunsmiths began to put their name on the barrel or frame of those guns which they had either manufactured solely or with the help of their fellow Ferlach craftsmen. Since all Ferlach firearms are essentially hand made per individual special order, very few are exactly alike. In the past, the gunsmiths of Ferlach have produced almost every type of shoulder arm imaginable, including such modern weapons as superposed and juxtaposed rifles and shotguns, hammerless drillings, repeating rifles, 3 barrel rifles, combination guns, 4 barrel rifles/shotguns/combination guns (called Vierlings), hammer guns of every type, etc. Some of these specimens represent the highest refinement in the gunmakers trade. Because of the almost unlimited variety of Ferlach variations, it is recommended that a COMPETENT appraisal is procured before buying or selling a specimen.

As is the case with many other European weapons, those models with desirable American features will generally outperform those with European specifications (i.e. a Ferlach sidelock combination gun that is 20 ga. x .243 Win. will be more valuable than a similar specimen chambered for 16 ga. x 5.6 by 50Rmm with sling swivels). Original condition and overall beauty are the primary factors to consider when contemplating buying or selling a Ferlach longarm. Other considerations include: type of action, difficulty of fabrication (Vierlings are very complicated to construct), caliber/gauge desirability, notoriety of gunsmith on barrel legend, elaborateness of embellishments, condition, rarity, accessories, and any provenance a specimen might have.

Today's master gunsmiths of Ferlach carry on the Old World tradition of quality in every respect. Most guns manufactured today are by individual special order with a wide range of calibers/gauges and other special features and options. As of this writing, these gunsmiths in alphabetical order are: Ludwig Borovnik, Johann Fanzoj, Wilfried Glanznig, Josef Hambrusch, Karl Hauptmann, Gottfried Juch, Josef Just, Jakob Koschat, Peter Michelitsch, Johann & Walter Outschar, Herbert Scheiring, Benedikt Winkler, and Josef Winkler. Anyone wishing to contact these master gunmakers should contact the indivudal gunmaker.

FERLACHER WAFFEN PRÄZISIONSTECHNIK PRODUCTIONS GmbH & CO. KG.

Current organization located in Ferlach, Austria.

When the Ferlach Guild was dissolved in 2004, gunmakers Fanzoj and Schiering bought the remaining assets and reopened the facility. The original function, namely to represent the gunmakers of Ferlach, has not changed.

Please refer to the Ferlach Guild listing for a complete explanation and list of gunmakers.

FERLIB

Current manufacturer established circa late 1940s, and located in Gardone V.T., Italy. During 2005, Ferlib entered into a partnership with B. Rizzini, and the new company is called Rizzini & Tanfoglio srl (see separate listing). SxS rifles were imported and distributed by Dakota Arms, Inc. 1999-2005. Previously distributed until 1999 by Hi-Grade Imports located in Gilroy, CA.

Currently, Ferlib is not manufacturing any guns using the Ferlib trademark.

RIFLES: SxS

Please refer to the Rizzini & Tanfoglio listing for current information on this model.

SHOTGUNS: O/U

BOSS MODEL - features Boss style action, custom order gun, many engraving options.

Please contact the company directly for a price quotation on this model.

SHOTGUNS: SxS

The following models were available in 10, 12, 16, 20, 24, 28, 32 ga., or .410 bore. Also available for an additional charge were extra quality wood and upgraded engraving.

    Add 10% for 24, 28, 32 ga., or .410 bore.
    Add $1,050 for single trigger.
    Add $1,600 for leather case.

MIGNON HAMMER MODEL - back action, exposed hammers, extensive scroll engraving, deluxe checkered walnut stock and forearm.

Please contact the company directly for a price quotation on this model.

MODEL F.VI - 12, 16, 20, 28 ga., or .410 bore, Anson & Deeley scalloped boxlock action, ejectors, double triggers, case hardened frame, select checkered stock and forearm. Disc. 1992.

          $3,500 $2,950 $2,275 $1,975 $1,600 $1,250 $1,000

Last MSR was $3,250.

GRADING - PPGS™	100%	98%	95%	90%	80%	70%	60%

MODEL 7 (F.VII) - 12, 16, 20, 28 ga., or .410 bore, Anson & Deeley scalloped box-lock action, ejectors, double triggers, coin finish, full coverage English scroll or game scene engraving, select checkered stock and forearm.

	$9,950	$8,750	$7,600	$6,500	$5,400	$4,500	$3,400

＊ *Model 7 Rex* - similar to Model 7, except has sideplates with extensive engraving.

	$13,300	$10,650	$9,150	$8,100	$7,000	$6,000	$5,000

＊ *Model 7 Premier* - top-of-the-line boxlock model, similar to Model 7 Rex, except more extensive engraving with gold inlays, best quality walnut.

	$15,000	$12,750	$10,950	$9,250	$8,100	$7,100	$6,100

MODEL F.VII/SC - 12, 16, 20, 28 ga., or .410 bore, Anson & Deeley scalloped box-lock action, ejectors, double triggers, coin finish, game scene with scroll accent engraving with gold inlays, select checkered stock and forearm. Importation disc. 1999.

	$6,200	$5,500	$5,000	$4,500	$3,800	$3,300	$2,750

Last MSR was $7,800.

SIDE PLATE MODEL (F.VII SIDEPLATE) - 12, 16, 20, 28 ga., or .410 bore, Anson & Deeley boxlock action with sideplates, ejectors, single trigger, coin finish, extensive English scroll or game scene and scroll accent engraving, select checkered stock and forearm.

	$12,950	$10,500	$9,000	$8,000	$7,000	$6,000	$5,000

Subtract $400 if English scroll engraved.

＊ *Sideplate Model F.VII/SC Gold* - similar to F.VII Sideplate, except with gold inlays.

	$13,450	$10,950	$9,250	$8,100	$7,100	$6,100	$5,100

PRINCE MODEL - various gauges, contoured Anson & Deeley action with rounded frame, choice of top or side lever opening, DT, deluxe checkered walnut stock and forearm.

	$10,600	$9,250	$8,100	$6,800	$5,550	$4,600	$3,500

Add $2,550 for side lever opening.

FERRELL, ROGER

Current custom rifle manufacturer located in Fayetteville, GA.

Roger Ferrell manufactures custom made to order rifles. Many options and configurations are available. Please contact the company directly for more information (see Trademark Index).

FINNCLASSIC 512S

Current trademark owned by Marocchi. Please refer to the Valmet, Inc. section for current information.

FIALA ARMS AND EQUIPMENT CO.

Previous manufacturer located in New Haven, CT. Fiala Arms and Equipment Co. was founded circa 1920, and went bankrupt shortly thereafter. Fiala Outfits, Inc. of New York City, NY reportedly bought the remaining guns, parts, and inventory and sold them between circa 1922 until approximately 1930. Also see Schall & Co.

The author would like to thank Mr. John Stimson for making the following information available.

PISTOLS: SLIDE ACTION

FIALA REPEATING PISTOL - .22 LR cal., similar to Colt Woodsman, manual operation, blue finish, interchangeable 3, 7 1/2 (fixed or smoothbore) or 20 (smoothbore optional) in. barrel, optional detachable buttstock, smooth or ribbed walnut grips, rear sight is square notched blade that tips up into an elevated adj. aperture sight, marked "Fiala Arms and Equipment Co. Inc./New Haven Conn./Patents Pending" on right side of frame behind the grip, and "MODEL 1920/Made in U.S.A."

GRADING - PPGS™	100%	98%	95%	90%	80%	70%	60%

on the right side of the frame above the triggerguard, left side of frame marked "FIALA ARMS" above the image of a polar bear with "TRADE MARK" below polar bear in area above the triggerguard.

✳ *Fiala Repeating Pistol cased with all 3 barrels and stock*

	$2,850	$2,600	$2,300	$2,000	$1,685	$1,200	$1,050

Add 15% for dovetail vs. screw stock/frame attachment.
Add $100 for smooth bore 20 in. barrel.

✳ *Fiala Repeating Pistol (gun only)*

	$650	$575	$495	$425	$350	$315	$265

This model was available with three different case variations - canvas, black or tan leatherette (velvet lined and fitted with a lock). Some pistols are also marked "Columbia Arms Company" or Botwinik Brothers".

This model has been classified by the ATF as a "Curio" or "Relic" and is collectible when in a complete state with all accoutrements.

FINNISH LION

Previous trademark manufactured by Valmet (now Tikka) located in Sweden. Limited importation into the U.S. by Mandall's Shooting Supplies, Inc. in Scottsdale, AZ.

RIFLES: BOLT ACTION

MATCH MODEL - .22 LR cal., bolt action, single shot, 29 in. barrel, extended aperture sight, globe front sight, thumbhole stock, adj. hook butt. Mfg. 1937-72.

	$495	$415	$360	$305	$250	$210	$195

CHAMPION FREE MODEL - .22 LR cal., bolt action, single shot, 29 in. barrel, double set trigger, full target stock and accessories. Mfg. 1965-72.

	$580	$495	$440	$385	$330	$290	$265

STANDARD ISU TARGET MODEL - .22 LR cal., bolt action, single shot, 27 in. barrel, full target stock and accessories. Mfg. 1966-1977.

	$330	$275	$250	$205	$180	$165	$150

TARGET MODEL - .22 LR cal., target rifle with adj. stock and trigger, bolt action, single shot, aperture sights.

	$725	$595	$495	$440	$385	$340	$295

Last MSR was $795.

FIOCCHI OF AMERICA, INC.

Previous firearms importer and distributor located in Ozark, MO.

Fiocchi of America imported Pardini target pistols until 1990, and continues to manufacture a wide variety of ammunition domestically. Fiocchi also imported Antonio Zoli shotguns until 1988. These trademarks can be found in their respective sections of this text.

FIREARMS INTERNATIONAL (F.I.)

Previous importer and assembler located in Washington, D.C.

F.I. manufactured and imported various pistols, rifles, and shotguns, including AYA, Astra (mostly Star D models), Bronco (.22 LR cal. single shot rifles and .410 bore single shot shotguns), FN Supreme Mauser bolt action rifles, Iver Johnson Pony handguns, Rossi .22 cal. rifles, Sako rifles, Star pistols, and Unique pistols and rifles.

F.I. sold less than 100 Pony .380 ACPs that were marked Colt before the Mustang was introduced - these are rare. While some models are relatively rare, collectability to date has been minimal and most models sell in the $150-$295 range, depending on overall desirability and condition.

Please look under individual manufacturer listings for values on similar models.

FIREARMS INTERNATIONAL, INC.

Current manufacturer established in 1998, and located in Houston, TX. Dealer sales.

In September, 2004, a new company called Crusader Group Gun Company, Inc. was formed, and includes the assets of Firearms International, Inc., High Standard Manufacturing Co., AMT-Auto Mag, and Arsenal Line Products. While IAI (Israel Arms International) was originally established to market firearms manufactured by Israel Arms, Ltd. through Firearms International, Inc., IAI defaulted on this agreement without any sales being made.

PISTOLS: SEMI-AUTO

During 1999, Firearms International, Inc. obtained permission to use older High Standard model nomenclature (Crusader & Supermatic Trophy) for use with their M-1911 pistols. Currently manufactured pistols are marked Firearms International Inc. on the frame, and High Standard on the slide.

Sharpshooter .45 ACP to .22 LR cal. conversion units are also available - fixed sight model retails for $280, adj. rear sight model retails for $340.

MODEL 1911 CRUSADER (CUSTOM SERIES) - 38 Super (mfg. 2002-2005, Two-tone finish only) or .45 ACP cal., 5 in. barrel, 7 (disc.) or 9 (.38 Super cal. only) shot mag., many shooting enhancements are standard, stainless steel (disc.), blue, or Tu-tone (mfg. 2001-2005) finish, adj. sights, 40 oz. Mfg. 2000-2005, reintroduced 2007.

MSR $895	$795	$675	$550	$475	$425	$375	$350

Add $50 for stainless steel (disc.)
Add $30 for Two-tone finish (disc.)
Add $50 for .38 Super cal. (disc.)

* *Model 1911 Crusader Combat* - similar to M-1911 Crusader, except has 4 1/4 (disc.) or 4 1/2 (new 2007) in. barrel and choice of fixed or adj. (disc. 2000) sights, 38 oz. Mfg. 2000-2005, reintroduced 2007.

MSR $895	$795	$675	$550	$475	$425	$375	$350

Add $50 for stainless steel (disc.)
Add $30 for Two-tone finish (disc.)

* *Model 1911 Crusader Compact* - 4 in. barrel, similar to Crusader Combat, except has shorter grip frame, 6 shot mag., 36 oz. Limited mfg. 2000 only.

$715	$600	$500	$475	$425	$375	$325

Last MSR was $775.

STR-5S SUPERMATIC TROPHY MATCH (MATCH MODEL) - similar to M-1911 Crusader, except has National Match 5 or 6 in. barrel and bushing, polished feed ramp and throated barrel, lowered/flared ejection port, 40 oz. New 2000.

MSR $1,095	$950	$800	$700	$600	$525	$450	$375

Subtract approx. 10% for blue finish (disc. 2001).
Subtract approx. 15% f w/o sights and no finish (disc.).
Add $300 for 6 in. barrel.

CAMP PERRY MODEL (TX5870FS/AS) - .45 ACP cal., 5 in. barrel, mil-spec slide, barrel and barrel bushing, blue or Tu-Tone (mfg. 2001 only) finish only, competition tuned, beveled mag. well, 40 oz. New 2000.

MSR $825	$750	$650	$575	$500	$450	$400	$350

Add $70 for adj. sights.

G-MAN - .45 ACP cal., 5 in. barrel, special tolerances, including frame to slide fit, match grade stainless barrel and National Match bushing, polished feed ramp, throated barrel, slotted hammer, lightweight trigger, lowered and flared ejection port, beveled mag. well, checkered American walnut grips, black Teflon finish, includes two 8 shot mag., 39 oz. Mfg. 2001-2005, reintroduced 2007.

MSR $1,395	$1,225	$1,075	$900	$800	$700	$600	$500

GRADING - PPGS™	100%	98%	95%	90%	80%	70%	60%

GI MODEL - .45 ACP cal., 5 in. barrel, parkerized finish, fixed sights, classic WWII style (1911A1 frame), 7 shot mag. Mfg. 2002-2005.

		$475	$425	$375	$335	$300	$285	$270

Last MSR was $549.

ARMY SPECIAL - .45 ACP cal., 5 in. barrel, blue or parkerized finish, 7 shot mag., fixed sights, 39 oz. Limited mfg. 2000.

		$485	$435	$395	$365	$330	$300	$285

Last MSR was $549.

NAVY MODEL - similar to Army Special, except is stainless steel, 39 oz. Limited mfg. 2000.

		$535	$465	$425	$395	$350	$325	$300

Last MSR was $599.

AIR CREW MODEL - similar to Army Special, except is titanium, 26 oz. Introduced 2000.

While advertised, this model never went into production.

UNITED STATES M1911A1 - .45 ACP cal., 5 in. barrel, fixed sights. New 2007.

MSR $539		$475	$425	$360	$330	$300	$260	$220

UNITED STATES M1926A1 - .38 Super cal., 5 in. barrel, fixed sights. New 2007.

MSR $574		$500	$450	$375	$350	$300	$275	$250

RIFLES: SEMI-AUTO

M1 CARBINE - .30 Carbine cal., 18 in. barrel, parkerized finish, wood stock, adj. rear sight, 10 shot mag., mfg. in the U.S., and patterned after the WWII design, 5 1/2 lbs. Limited mfg. 2001-2003.

		$500	$425	$375	$335	$300	$275	$250

Last MSR was $575.

P50 RIFLE/CARBINE - .50 BMG cal., designed by Robert Pauza, gas operation, 24 or 29 in. barrel, MOA accuracy at 1,000 yards, includes two 5 shot mags. and hard case, 25 (carbine) or 30 lbs. Limited mfg. 2001-2003.

		$7,500	$6,750	$5,750	$5,000	$4,500	$4,000	$3,500

Last MSR was $7,950.

FIRESTORM

Current trademark of pistols manufactured by Industria Argentina and Fabrinor, S.A.L. Distributed (master distributor) and imported beginning late 2000 by SGS Imports, International Inc., located in Wanamassa, NJ.

PISTOLS: SEMI-AUTO

Beginning 2004, all Firestorm pistols are available with an integral locking system (ILS).

FIRESTORM SERIES - .22 LR, .32 ACP (disc. 2007), or .380 ACP cal., double action, 3 1/2 or 6 (.22 LR cal. only, Sport Model) in. barrel, matte or duo-tone finish, 7 (.380 ACP) or 10 (.22 LR or .32 ACP) shot mag., 3 dot combat sights, anatomic rubber grips with finger grooves, 23 oz. Importation began 2001.

MSR $310		$260	$220	$180	$155	$145	$135	$125

Add $2 for duo-tone finish in .22 LR or $10 for .380 ACP cal.

MINI-FIRESTORM - 9mm Para., .40 S&W, or .45 ACP (new 2002) cal., double action, 3 1/2 in. barrel, nickel, matte or duo-tone finish, 7 (.45 ACP cal.), 10, or 13 (9mm Para. only) shot mag., 3 dot sights, polymer grips, safeties include manual, firing pin, and decocking, 24 1/2 - 27 oz. Importation began 2001.

MSR $395		$340	$295	$260	$225	$195	$180	$165

Add $7 for duo-tone finish (.40 S&W or .45 ACP cal.).
Add $7 for .45 ACP cal.
Add $15 for nickel finish.

GRADING - PPGS™	100%	98%	95%	90%	80%	70%	60%

FIRESTORM 45 GOVERNMENT - .45 ACP cal., single action, 5 1/8 in. barrel, matte or duo-tone finish, 7 shot mag., anatomic rubber grips with finger grooves, 36 oz. Imported 2001-2005.

	$260	$230	$200	$180	$165	$150	$135

Last MSR was $309.

Add $8 for duo-tone finish.

* *Firestorm 45 Government Compact* - .45 ACP cal., 4 1/4 in. barrel, otherwise similar to Firestorm 45 Government, 34 oz. Imported 2001-2005.

	$260	$230	$200	$180	$165	$150	$135

Last MSR was $309.

Add $8 for duo-tone finish.

* *Firestorm 45 Government Mini Compact* - .45 ACP cal., 3 1/8 in. barrel, chrome or matte or duo- tone finish, 10 shot staggered mag., polymer grips, 31 oz. Imported 2001 only.

	$280	$245	$215	$195	$180	$170	$155

Last MSR was $324.

Add $17 for chrome finish.

FIRESTORM 45 GOVT. 1911 - .45 ACP cal., patterned after the M1911, choice of matte or deluxe blue finish, 7 shot mag., 36 oz. Imported 2006-2007.

	$365	$310	$270	$235	$200	$180	$165

Last MSR was $432.

Add $50 for deluxe blue finish.

FLODMAN GUNS

Current manufacturer established in 1978 and located in Järsta, Sweden. In 1992, Skullman Enterprise AB took over Flodman Guns. No current U.S. importation.

O/U: LONG GUNS

Flodman manufactures a variety of high quality shotguns, combination guns, and double rifles. They offer three designs - hunting, sporting, and luxury. All Flodman O/Us utilize a low profile, boxlock, stainless steel self-opening action, patented ejector (allows dry firing w/o ejector movement), and have no hammer, but a primed firing pin which moves perpendicularly, allowing a .002 seconds lock time. Barrels are available in either titanium from Sandvik steel or stainless steel, and are equipped with choke tubes. Please contact the factory directly for more information regarding an individual price quotation and delivery time (see Trademark Index).

FORT WORTH FIREARMS

Previous manufacturer located in Fort Worth, TX 1995-2000.

PISTOLS: SEMI-AUTO, RIMFIRE

MATCH MASTER STANDARD - .22 LR cal., 3 7/8, 4 1/2, 5 1/2, 7 1/2, or 10 in. bull barrel, double extractors, includes upper push button and standard mag. release, beveled mag. well, angled grip, flared slide, low profile frame. Mfg. 1995-2000.

	$310	$265	$230	$200	$185	$170	$160

Last MSR was $389.

Add $84 for 10 in. bull barrel.

* *Match Master Standard Dovetail* - similar to Match Master Standard, except has 3 7/8, 4 1/2, or 5 1/2 barrel with dovetail rib. Mfg. 1995-2000.

	$385	$325	$285	$240	$215	$190	$170

Last MSR was $473.

GRADING - PPGS™	100%	98%	95%	90%	80%	70%	60%

✳ *Match Master Standard Deluxe* - similar to Match Master Standard, except has Weaver rib on barrel. Mfg. 1995-2000.

	$450	$365	$315	$280	$240	$215	$190

Last MSR was $538.

Add $92 for 10 in. barrel.

SPORT KING - .22 LR cal., 4 1/2 or 5 1/2 in. barrel, blue finish, military grips, drift sight, 10 shot mag. Mfg. 1995-2000.

	$275	$245	$225	$200	$185	$170	$160

Last MSR was $313.

CITATION - .22 LR cal., 5 1/2 in. bull or 7 1/4 in. fluted barrel, military grips, 10 shot mag. Mfg. 1995-2000.

	$310	$265	$230	$200	$185	$170	$160

Last MSR was $389.

TROPHY - .22 LR cal., 5 1/2 or 7 1/4 in. bull barrel, blue finish, military grips, 10 shot mag. Mfg. 1995-2000.

	$330	$285	$240	$200	$185	$170	$160

Last MSR was $411.

Add $41 for left-hand action (5 1/2 in. barrel only).

VICTOR - .22 LR cal., 3 7/8, 4 1/2 (VR or Weaver rib), or 5 1/2 (VR or Weaver rib), 8 (Weaver rib), or 10 (Weaver rib) in. barrel, blue finish, military grips, 10 shot mag. Mfg. 1995-2000.

	$385	$325	$285	$240	$215	$190	$170

Last MSR was $473.

Add $65 for 4 1/2 or 5 1/2 in. Weaver rib barrel.
Add approx. $148 for 8 or 10 in. Weaver rib barrel.

OLYMPIC - .22 LR or Short cal., 6 3/4 in. fluted barrel, blue finish, military grips, 10 shot mag. Mfg. 1995-2000.

	$525	$465	$415	$360	$330	$295	$265

Last MSR was $600.

SHARP SHOOTER - .22 LR cal., 5 1/2 in. bull barrel, blue finish, military grips, 10 shot mag. Mfg. 1995-2000.

	$300	$260	$230	$200	$185	$170	$160

Last MSR was $380.

RIFLES: BOLT ACTION

YOUTH RIFLE - .22 LR cal., bolt action, single shot, shortened stock dimensions. Mfg. 1995-96.

	$120	$105	$90	$80	$70	$60	$50

Last MSR was $138.

SHOTGUNS: SLIDE ACTION

GL 18 - 12 ga. only, security configuration with 18 in. barrel with perforated shroud, thumb operated laser/xenon light built into end of 7 shot mag. tube, ammo storage. Mfg. 1995-96.

	$295	$265	$240	$210	$190	$170	$160

Last MSR was $347.

FOX, A.H.

Current manufacturer located in New Britain, CT. The A.H. Fox trademark was brought to life once again during 1993 when the Connecticut Shotgun Manufacturing Company began producing an A.H. Fox 20 gauge in 5 different grades. Previously manufactured in Philadelphia, PA 1903-1930, and in Utica, NY from 1930-approx. 1946. Manufactured by Savage 1930-1988.

Depending on the remaining A.H. Fox factory data, a factory letter authenticating the configuration of a particular Fox shotgun (not to be confused with the more recent Savage/Stevens designed Fox doubles) may be obtained by contacting John T. Callahan (see Trademark Index for listings and address). If a model number is not known, please include a photo, the ser. no., gauge, barrel length and style, stock and forearm style, markings, patent dates, inspector stamps, etc. The charge for this service is $30.00 for the Sterlingworth Model, and $40.00 for graded models A-F and single barrel trap guns. Please allow 6 weeks for an adequate response.

Mr. Ansley H. Fox first started manufacturing shotguns in circa 1896. This first company was called the Fox Gun Co. and was located in Baltimore, MD. Relatively few guns were made and surviving specimens today are very rare. After this venture, Mr. Fox was employed by the Baltimore Gun Co. for several years (circa 1900-1903). Following this period, he formed the Philadelphia Gun Co. where the predecessors to the A.H. Fox Gun Co. models were manufactured. These Philadelphia Gun Co. models (circa 1904) were the same as the newer Fox shotguns except that the hinge pin was removed. Sources indicate that the lowest grade was an A with the highest being an E (fully engraved and ultra rare). Following this tenure, Mr. Fox went on to form the A.H. Fox Gun Co. that was started approx. 1905. In addition to being an entrepreneur and trend setter, Mr. Fox also had the reputation of being an expert shot in his own right, winning more than a few events on the East Coast around the turn of the century.

The A.H. Fox Gun Company of Philadelphia, Pennsylvania, began production in 1905 and produced high quality double barrel shotguns until 1930. The Savage Arms Company, then of Utica, New York, acquired the Fox Company and produced these guns until 1942, when all but the utilitarian model B series guns were discontinued.

A.H. Fox guns are considered an American classic comparable to L.C. Smith, Parker, and others. Collector interest is high and will undoubtedly grow. The guns do not command quite as high a price as the Smith and Parker guns, but represent a fine investment collectible value.

Savage-made guns from 1930-1942 are usually valued similarly to the early A.H. Fox guns. The recent production B series are just not in the same class and are obviously not intended to be. They are lower priced by today's standards and are designed as a utility grade hunting gun.

FOX COMPANY CHRONOLOGY

1906 - Company formed January 1906, A, B & C Grades introduced in 12 ga. only. D and F Grades introduced in 12 ga. in 1907. Ejector guns introduced in 1908. 1910 saw the introduction of the 12 ga. Sterlingworth - William H. Gough takes over as Chief of Engraving. Ansley Fox resigns in 1911 - first catalog showing Sterlingworth Model (called Model 1911). A-F Grades released in 16 and 20 ga. during 1912, as well as the addition of a 20 ga. Sterlingworth. 16 ga. Sterlingworth introduced in 1913. Fox/Kautsky single trigger introduced in 1914 - engineering transition complete. During 1915, the XE Grade was introduced. The B Grade was dropped in 1918. Single barrel trap guns (J, K, and L Grades) were introduced in 1919. 1920 saw the introduction of the M Grade single barrel trap. In 1922, both the G and HE Grades were released. Beavertail forend and vent. rib were introduced in 1927. 1929 was the Savage buy-out (November), GE Grade dropped. Company moved from Philadelphia, PA to Utica, NY in 1930. Skeeter Grade introduced in 1931 while the 20 ga. HE Grade was disc. 1932 saw the introduction of both the Trap Grade Double and SP Grade. Wildfowl Grade was introduced in 1934. 1935 was the last year of the K and L single barrel trap guns. 1937 was the last year for the J Grade single barrel trap gun. The last 16 and 12 ga. Sterlingworths were built in 1939. The outbreak of the war in 1941 saw the last FE Grade shipped, the Wildfowler Grade dropped, and the introduction of the Model B. 1942 was the last retail catalog. Factory records indicate that the last 12 ga. was shipped in 1945 and the last 20 ga. was shipped during 1946 (SP Grade shipped in December, 1946). However, guns continued to be assembled from left-over parts as late as the 1960s.

GRADING - PPGS™	100%	98%	95%	90%	80%	70%	60%

FOX SERIAL NUMBER ASSIGNMENTS

The publisher wishes to express his thanks to Mr. John Callahan and Mr. Gurney Brown for providing the model serialization and years of mfg. in this section.

Ser. # range 1-35,285 - 12 ga. A-F Grades
Ser. # range 200,000-203,975 - 20 ga., Grades A-F
Ser. # range 300,000-303,875 - 16 ga., Grades A-F
Ser. # range 50,000-161,556 - 12 ga. Sterlingworth
Ser. # range 250,000-271,304 - 20 ga. Sterlingworth
Ser. # range 300,000-378,481 - 16 ga. Sterlingworth
Ser. # range 400,000-450,568 - 12 ga. Single Barrel Traps, Grades J,K,L,M

FOX MODELS BY YEARS IN MFG.

Sterlingworth - 1910-1942 mfg.
Wildfowler - 1934-1940 mfg.
Trap Double - 1932-1936 mfg.
Skeeter - 1931 mfg.
SP - 1932-1946 mfg.
A - 1906-1942 mfg.
B - 1905-1918 mfg.
C - 1905-1942 mfg.
D - 1907-1942 mfg.
F - 1907-1940 mfg.
G - 1922-1929 mfg.
H - 1923-1942 mfg.
J - 1919-1939 mfg.
K - 1919-1934 mfg.
L - 1919-1934 mfg.
M - 1919-1936 mfg.
X - 1915-1942 mfg.

SHOTGUNS: SxS, CURRENT MFG.

Delivery time for custom orders is currently 10-14 months, depending on gauge and grade. The following models are manufactured by the Connecticut Manufacturing Co. located in New Britain, CT. These finely made shotguns have the following standard features: automatic safety, auto ejectors, DTs, Chromox 26, 28, or 30 in. barrels, individual barrel chokings, 2 3/4 in. chambers, scalloped receiver, Turkish Circassian walnut with hand-rubbed oil finish, choice of straight, semi-pistol or full-pistol grip stock with custom dimensions, splinter forearm, ivory bead sights. Special order options are as follows: Krupp steel barrels ($250), Fox SST ($1,800), walnut upgrades ($400-$2,400), custom initials ($350-$900), personalized gold inlays on barrel ($900), skeleton steel buttplate ($800), beavertail forearm ($750), vent. rib ($1,000), wood upgrades ($400-$2,400), and traditional leather trunk case with accessories ($650). Multi-barrel sets (same or multi-gauge) are also available with prices ranging from $5,000-$8,750, depending on the grade.

Add $2,000 for 28 ga. and .410 bore guns on the following models (except Exhibition Grade).

CE GRADE - 16 (new 1995), 20, 28 ga. (new 1995), or .410 bore (new 1995), engraved with fine scroll and game scenes, Grade I Turkish Circassian walnut. New 1993.

MSR $13,500	$13,500	$11,000	$8,500	$6,250	$5,250	$4,500	$3,350

XE GRADE - gauges similar to CE Grade, scroll work and engraved game scenes, Grade II Turkish Circassian walnut. New 1993.

MSR $15,500	$15,500	$12,500	$9,250	$6,500	$5,500	$4,750	$3,500

DE GRADE - gauges similar to CE Grade, intricate and extensive engraving, Grade III highly figured Turkish Circassian walnut. New 1993.

MSR $18,000	$18,000	$15,000	$11,500	$9,500	$7,750	$6,250	$5,000

GRADING - PPGS™	100%	98%	95%	90%	80%	70%	60%

FE GRADE - gauges similar to CE Grade, gold inlays surrounded by different types of scroll work, Grade IV highly figured Turkish Circassian walnut with finest checkering. New 1993.

MSR $23,000		$23,000	$20,000	$16,500	$12,750	$9,750	$8,000	$6,250

EXHIBITION GRADE - gauges similar to CE Grade, individually built per customer specifications on a "cost-no-object" basis, includes best-quality leather trunk case with full accessories, Exhibition Grade Turkish Circassian walnut. New 1993.

This model is a special order only, and the base price is $36,500. Please contact the company directly for an individual price quotation and available options.

100%	98%	95%	90%	80%	70%	60%	50%	40%	30%	20%	10%

SHOTGUNS: SxS, DISC.

STERLINGWORTH - 12, 16, or 20 ga., 26, 28, or 30 in. barrels, various chokes, boxlock, extractors, double trigger, checkered pistol grip stock. Mfg. 1910-1942.

N/A	$1,600	$1,400	$1,100	$875	$750	$575	$500	$450	$395	$350	$300

Add 33% for auto ejectors.
Add 75% for 20 ga. or 50% for 16 ga.
Add 25% for single trigger.
Ser. no. range on 12 ga. Sterlingworths is 50,000-161,556, 16 ga. is 300,000-378,481, and 20 ga. is 250,000-271,304.

STERLINGWORTH DELUXE - similar to Sterlingworth, with recoil pad and ivory bead, 32 in. barrel available.

N/A	$2,100	$1,875	$1,475	$1,100	$950	$850	$750	$650	$550	$475	$425

Add 33% for auto ejectors.
Add 75% for 20 ga. or 50% for 16 ga.
A single trigger was not an option on this model.

STERLINGWORTH SKEET - similar to Sterlingworth, with 26 or 28 in. skeet boring, straight grip stock, beavertail forearm. Mfg. 1935-1945.

This model is very scarce (only several are known) and the extreme rarity factor precludes accurate price evaluation.

SUPER HE GRADE - 12 ga., 2 3/4 (very rare) or 3 in. chambered long range gun, 30 and 32 in. full choke, auto ejectors, otherwise similar to Sterlingworth.

N/A	$5,600	$5,200	$4,800	$4,400	$3,950	$3,400	$2,850	$2,300	$1,900	$1,625	$1,475

Add 10% for SST.

Original 3 in. chambered HE grades are marked "not warranteed, see instruction tag" on barrel flats. The HE grade was also manufactured in 20 ga. but is extremely rare. 2 3/4 in. chambers are rarer than 3 in. guns in this model.

HIGHER GRADE MODELS (A-F) - 12, 16, or 20 ga., the following higher grade Fox shotguns are similar to the Sterlingworth in configuration. The grades differ in engraving and inlays, grade of wood and general workmanship. The E designation means auto ejectors.

Add 50% for 16 ga. (made on same frame as 20 ga.).
Add 75% for 20 ga.
Add $200-$1,000 for SST, depending on grade.
Add $200-$1,000 for beavertail forearm, depending on grade.
Early A and B grades have very little engraving and are much less desirable than later models. The following values are for later guns.
Note: These guns were disc. in 1942 by Savage Arms after they mfg. them for 12 years. Pre-1930 guns were made by A.H. Fox Company.

100%	98%	95%	90%	80%	70%	60%	50%	40%	30%	20%	10%

✳ *Higher Grade Model: A Grade*

| N/A | $2,400 | $2,175 | $1,875 | $1,625 | $1,375 | $1,075 | $900 | $825 | $725 | $650 | $600 |

✳ *Higher Grade Model: AE Grade (ejectors)*

| N/A | $3,000 | $2,700 | $2,400 | $2,075 | $1,675 | $1,400 | $1,150 | $1,000 | $900 | $850 | $825 |

✳ *Higher Grade Model: BE Grade (ejectors)*

| N/A | N/A | $4,800 | $4,450 | $3,950 | $3,475 | $2,950 | $2,500 | $2,250 | $1,975 | $1,800 | $1,675 |

This model is rarely encountered.

✳ *Higher Grade Model: CE Grade (ejectors)*

| N/A | N/A | $5,750 | $5,200 | $4,650 | $4,150 | $3,750 | $3,300 | $3,000 | $2,700 | $2,425 | $2,150 |

✳ *Higher Grade Model: XE Grade (ejectors)*

| N/A | N/A | $8,000 | $7,350 | $6,750 | $5,950 | $5,225 | $4,625 | $4,100 | $3,650 | $3,200 | $2,750 |

✳ *Higher Grade Model: DE Grade (ejectors)*

| N/A | N/A | $13,750 | $11,650 | $9,675 | $8,750 | $7,500 | $6,750 | $6,000 | $5,300 | $4,750 | $4,300 |

✳ *Higher Grade Model: FE Grade (ejectors)* - top-of-the-line model, only infrequently encountered.

| N/A | N/A | $22,000 | $19,500 | $16,450 | $14,150 | $12,000 | $10,500 | $9,750 | $9,150 | $9,000 | $8,750 |

SINGLE BARREL TRAP - 12 ga., 30 or 32 in. vent. rib barrel, full choke, boxlock, auto ejector, checkered trap style stock and recoil pad. The grades differ in wood, engraving, and overall quality. ME grade is custom built and extremely high quality with gold inlays. These models were disc. 1942. 568 single barrel trap guns were mfg. between 1932-42 and have a ser. range of 400,000-400,568, with Monte Carlo stock.

Even though trap guns may be rarer than their SxS counterparts, to date their desirability is less since there are simply fewer collectors.

✳ *Single Barrel Trap JE Grade*

| N/A | $3,860 | $3,550 | $3,200 | $2,800 | $2,500 | $2,100 | $1,800 | $1,600 | $1,500 | $1,425 | $1,325 |

✳ *Single Barrel Trap KE Grade*

| N/A | $5,200 | $4,650 | $4,000 | $3,500 | $3,200 | $2,800 | $2,600 | $2,400 | $2,250 | $2,100 | $1,975 |

✳ *Single Barrel Trap LE Grade*

| N/A | N/A | $6,500 | $5,750 | $5,000 | $4,500 | $4,100 | $3,750 | $3,300 | $3,000 | $2,650 | $2,300 |

✳ *Single Barrel Trap ME Grade*

Extreme rarity factor precludes accurate percentage pricing on this model.

GRADING - PPGS™	100%	98%	95%	90%	80%	70%	60%

MODEL B DOUBLE BARREL - 12, 16, 20 ga., or .410 bore, 24-30 in. barrels, various chokes, vent rib on newer models, boxlock, extractors, double triggers, handcut or pressed checkered pistol grip stock and forearm. Mfg. 1940-86.

	100%	98%	95%	90%	80%	70%	60%
12 or 16 ga.	$450	$395	$350	$295	$265	$235	$200
20 ga.	$650	$575	$500	$450	$400	$365	$335
.410 bore	$1,100	$975	$850	$750	$675	$600	$550

Last MSR was $250.

MODEL B-ST - similar to model B, with single trigger. Mfg. 1955-66.

	100%	98%	95%	90%	80%	70%	60%
12 or 16 ga.	$575	$475	$425	$350	$315	$275	$250
20 ga.	$725	$650	$600	$550	$500	$425	$350
.410 bore	$1,300	$1,075	$925	$800	$700	$600	$500

MODEL B-DL - similar to model B-ST, with satin chrome frame, select wood. Mfg. 1962-65.

	100%	98%	95%	90%	80%	70%	60%
12 or 16 ga.	$600	$475	$425	$350	$315	$275	$250
20 ga.	$750	$675	$600	$550	$500	$425	$350
.410 bore	$1,350	$1,100	$925	$800	$700	$600	$500

GRADING - PPGS™	100%	98%	95%	90%	80%	70%	60%

MODEL B-DE - similar to B-DL, with less checkering. Mfg. 1965-66.

12 or 16 ga.	$575	$475	$425	$350	$315	$275	$250
20 ga.	$725	$650	$600	$550	$500	$425	$350
.410 bore	$1,300	$1,075	$925	$800	$700	$600	$500

MODEL B-SE - 12, 20 ga., or .410 bore, single trigger, selective ejectors, vent. rib, beavertail forearm, select walnut with press checkering. Mfg. 1966-88.

12 ga.	$850	$750	$675	$600	$550	$475	$400
20 ga.	$1,000	$900	$800	$700	$625	$550	$475
.410 bore	$1,550	$1,375	$1,125	$950	$850	$750	$650

Last MSR was $525.

Even though there were multiple series designations assigned to this model, there seems to be little difference in desirability. For that reason, other designations will be priced similarly to values shown above.

FRANCHI, LUIGI

Current manufacturer established during the mid-1860s, and located in Brescia, Italy. This trademark has been imported for approx. the past 50 years. Currently imported exclusively by Benelli USA, located in Accokeek, MD, since 1998. Previously imported and distributed by American Arms, Inc. located in North Kansas City, MO. Some models were previously imported by FIE firearms located in Hialeah, FL.

Also see Sauer/Franchi heading in the S section.

RIFLES: SEMI-AUTO

CENTENNIAL MODEL - .22 LR cal., 21 in. barrel, open sight to commemorate Franchi's 100th anniversary. Mfg. 1968 only.

	$330	$250	$220	$195	$165	$150	$140

✱ *Centennial Model Engraved Deluxe*

	$415	$330	$305	$275	$240	$200	$165

✱ *Centennial Model Gallery*

	$220	$195	$160	$120	$100	$80	$60

SHOTGUNS: O/U

Currently manufactured Franchi O/U shotguns are supplied with a custom-fitted hard case, and use choke tubes that are compatible with both Beretta and Benelli.

DE LUXE MODEL PRITI - 12 or 20 ga., boxlock action, ST, ejectors, 26 or 28 in. VR barrels with fixed chokes. Imported 1988-89 only.

	$395	$350	$315	$285	$240	$215	$185

Last MSR was $460.

This model was imported exclusively by FIE Firearms located in Hialeah, FL.

ALCIONE MODEL - 12 ga., 28 in. barrels, less engraving than Alcione SL, separated barrels. Importation disc. 1989.

	$675	$550	$495	$460	$430	$380	$335

Last MSR was $800.

Previously designated Diamond Model.

This model was imported exclusively by FIE Firearms located in Hialeah, FL.

ALCIONE SL - 12 ga., 27 or 28 in. barrels, 6 lbs. 13 oz., separated barrels, ejectors, single trigger, silver finished frame engraved with luggage case. Importation disc. 1986.

	$1,150	$995	$875	$800	$725	$640	$550

Last MSR was $1,595.

GRADING - PPGS™	100%	98%	95%	90%	80%	70%	60%

ALCIONE 2000 SX (FIELD MODEL) - 12 ga., 3 in. chambers, 28 in. barrels, SST, separated barrels, ejectors, single trigger, engraved silver finished frame with gold accents, with case, 7 lbs. 4 oz. Imported 1997 only.

	$1,675	$1,495	$1,275	$1,025	$875	$750	$650

Last MSR was $1,895.

ALCIONE FIELD - 12 ga. only, 3 in. chambers, blue (Classic Field, new 2004), polished steel (silver) alloy frame with game bird etching, SST, ejectors, 26 or 28 in. interchangeable barrels with choke tubes, checkered satin finished walnut stock and forearm, also available in left-hand, 7.4 lbs. Mfg. 1998-2005.

	$1,125	$960	$825	$725	$600	$500	$425

Last MSR was $1,310.

Add $90 for Classic Field Model with blue receiver, gold trigger, and Schnabel forearm.
This model was previously designated 97-12 IBS.

✳ *Alcione Field LF* - 12 or 20 ga., 3 in. chambers (20 ga. only), lightweight alloy receiver with etching and gold fill, approx. 6.8 lbs. Mfg. 2000-2002.

	$1,150	$975	$875	$775	$650	$550	$425

Last MSR was $1,305.

ALCIONE CLASSIC - 12 ga. only, 3 in. chambers, blue non-engraved reciever, SST, ejectors, 26 or 28 in. VR barrels with choke tubes, checkered satin finished walnut stock and forearm. 7 1/2 lbs. Mfg. 2004-2005.

	$1,125	$960	$825	$725	$600	$500	$425

Last MSR was $1,320.

Add $475 for extra set of 12 or 20 ga. barrels.

ALCIONE SL SPORT - 12 ga. only, 2 3/4 in. chambers (can also be fitted for barrels with 3 in. chambers), polished stainless steel receiver, blue barrels, SST, manual safety, ejectors, 30 in. target rib ported barrels with choke tubes, detachable sideplates, available in left-hand, 7.7 lbs. Disc. 2005.

	$1,435	$1,200	$950	$850	$725	$625	$475

Last MSR was $1,700.

This model was previously designated SL IBS.

ALCIONE SP - 12 ga. only, 3 in. chambers, satin silver finished boxlock action with engraved sideplates including mallard and pheasant gold inlays, gloss finished AA Grade checkered walnut pistol grip stock and Schnabel forearm, 28 in. VR barrels with choke tubes, 20 ga. barrels can be ordered w/o additional gunsmithing, 7 1/2 lbs. Imported 2003-2005.

	$2,325	$2,000	$1,750	$1,500	$1,275	$1,100	$975

Last MSR was $2,780.

Add $490 for extra set of 20 ga. barrels.

ALCIONE SX - 12 ga. only, 3 in. chambers, 26 or 28 in. interchangeable vent. barrels with VR and 3 choke tubes, deluxe walnut, removable sideplates with etched game scenes, gold trigger, approx. 7.4 lbs. Imported 2001-2005.

	$1,535	$1,350	$1,050	$925	$800	$700	$575

Last MSR was $1,855.

Add $490 for extra set of barrels.
Add $125 for Alcione Classic SX with blued receiver (new 2004).

ALCIONE TITANIUM (T) - 12 or 20 ga., 3 in. chambers, features receiver manufactured from aluminum alloy coupled with titanium inserts, 26 or 28 in. interchangeable vent. barrels with VR and 3 choke tubes, deluxe walnut, removable sideplates with etched game scenes, gold trigger with selector switch, approx. 6.8 lbs. Imported 2002-2005.

	$1,260	$1,050	$950	$875	$800	$750	$695

Last MSR was $1,470.

Add $460 for 2 barrel set (includes extra 20 ga. barrels).

GRADING - PPGS™	100%	98%	95%	90%	80%	70%	60%

VELOCE - 20 or 28 ga., 3 in. chambers on 20 ga., 26 or 28 (20 ga. only) in. vent. barrels with 3 choke tubes, aluminum frame with steel reinforcement, etched game scene receiver with gold filled inlays, skeletonized opening lever, deluxe oil finished checkered pistol grip or English (new 2002) stock and forearm, mechanical gold SST, 5.5 (28 ga.) or 5.8 (20 ga.) lbs. Imported 2001-2005.

	$1,260	$1,050	$950	$875	$800	$750	$695

Last MSR was $1,470.

Add $75 for 28 ga.

✳ *Veloce Grade II* - similar to Veloce Model, except has semi-pistol grip deluxe walnut stock. Limited importation 2004 only.

	$1,750	$1,500	$1,250	$1,050	$925	$825	$725

Last MSR was $2,000.

Add $75 for 28 ga.

✳ *Veloce Squire Limited Edition* - includes one set of 26 in. 20 ga. and one set of 26 in. 28 ga. barrels, cased, 5.7 lbs. Imported 2003-2005.

	$2,050	$1,750	$1,450	$1,125	$975	$875	$775

Last MSR was $2,470.

RENAISSANCE FIELD - 12, 20, or 28 ga., 3 in. chambers (2 3/4 in. on 28 ga.), boxlock action with polished blue finish, ejectors, SST, oil finished walnut stock and forearm, Twin Shock absorber recoil pad with gel insert, 5.5 - 6.2 lbs. Importation began 2006.

MSR $1,559	$1,325	$1,125	$950	$850	$725	$600	$500

Add $70 for 28 ga. (disc. 2007).

RENAISSANCE CLASSIC - similar to Renaissance Field, except has gold trigger, A Grade walnut and gold bird inlays. Importation began 2006.

MSR $1,739	$1,495	$1,275	$1,100	$975	$850	$725	$600

Add $60 for 28 ga.

✳ *Renaissance Classic Combo* - includes 26 in. 20 and 28 ga. barrels. New 2008.

MSR $2,599	$2,175	$1,850	$1,650	$1,475	$1,300	$1,150	$1,000

RENAISSANCE ELITE - similar to Renaissance Classic, except has AA Grade walnut, deep relief engraving, gold game scene inlays. Importation began 2006.

MSR $2,279	$1,975	$1,700	$1,425	$1,200	$995	$825	$700

Add $150 for 28 ga.

RENAISSANCE SPORTING - 12 ga., 3 in. chambers, 30 in. VR ported barrels with extended choke tubes, A Grade walnut stock with adj. comb, engraving, approx. 8 lbs. Importation began 2007.

MSR $2,139	$1,850	$1,625	$1,425	$1,225	$995	$825	$700

BLACK MAGIC SPORTING HUNTER - 12 ga. only, 3 in. chambers, 28 in. separated barrels with VR and Franchokes, black frame with gold accents and trigger, SST, ejectors, checkered walnut stock and forearm, 7 lbs. Imported 1989-91.

	$995	$875	$800	$725	$650	$575	$495

Last MSR was $1,249.

The Black Magic Model Series was imported exclusively by American Arms, Inc. located in North Kansas City, MO.

✳ *Black Magic Sporting Hunter Lightweight* - similar to Black Magic Sporting Hunter except 2 3/4 in. chambers only, 26 in. separated barrels with VR and Franchokes, alloy frame, 6 lbs. Imported 1989-91.

	$975	$850	$775	$700	$625	$550	$475

Last MSR was $1,209.

GRADING - PPGS™	100%	98%	95%	90%	80%	70%	60%

SPORTING 2000 - 12 ga. only, design for sporting clays or hunting, 28 in. vent. ported (disc. 1993) or unported (new 1997) barrels with target VR and choke tubes, SST, ejectors, select walnut with checkering, solid pad, hard case, 7 3/4 lbs. Imported 1992-1993, resumed 1997, disc. 1998.

	$1,275	$1,025	$875	$750	$650	$575	$500

Last MSR was $1,495.

ARISTOCRAT FIELD - 12 ga., 26, 28, or 30 in. barrels, various chokes, vent. rib, auto ejectors, boxlock, selective single trigger, checkered pistol grip stock. Mfg. 1960-69.

	$660	$470	$440	$395	$375	$340	$310

ARISTOCRAT MAGNUM - similar to Field, except 32 in. barrel, 3 in. chamber, full choke, pad. Mfg. 1962-65.

	$660	$470	$440	$395	$375	$340	$310

ARISTOCRAT SKEET - similar to Field, but 26 in. vent. rib, bored skeet no. 1 and no. 2. Mfg. 1960-69.

	$715	$525	$495	$450	$430	$395	$365

ARISTOCRAT TRAP - 30 in. vent. rib barrel, bored mod. and full, trap stock Mfg. 1960-69.

	$745	$550	$525	$480	$455	$415	$380

ARISTOCRAT SILVER KING - select wood, engraved coin finished frame. Mfg. 1962-69.

	$750	$560	$535	$485	$470	$430	$400

ARISTOCRAT DELUXE - finer wood, more engraving. Mfg. 1960-66.

	$990	$870	$835	$810	$770	$715	$660

ARISTOCRAT SUPREME - gold inlaid game birds. Mfg. 1960-66.

	$1,430	$1,265	$1,155	$1,075	$990	$935	$880

ARISTOCRAT IMPERIAL - high grade wood, more engraving. Mfg. 1967-69.

	$2,640	$2,200	$2,090	$1,925	$1,815	$1,650	$1,430

ARISTOCRAT MONTE CARLO - highest grade wood, elaborate engraving and inlay, mfg. 1967-69.

	$3,520	$3,080	$2,915	$2,640	$2,420	$2,090	$1,870

FALCONET S - 12 ga., lightweight model of the Alcione SL, 27 or 28 in. barrels, 6 lbs. 1 oz., separated barrels, moderate engraving on silver finish frame. Disc. 1985.

	$895	$765	$660	$560	$510	$460	$410

Last MSR was $1,015.

FALCONET FIELD - 12, 16, 20, 28 ga., or .410 bore, 24-30 in. barrels, various chokes, auto ejectors, select single trigger, engraved alloy frame, checkered walnut stock. Mfg. 1968-75.

	100%	98%	95%	90%	80%	70%	60%
Buckskin (light)	$550	$495	$470	$440	$415	$385	$360
Ebony (black)	$550	$495	$470	$440	$415	$385	$360
Silver	$605	$550	$525	$495	$470	$415	$385

Add 25% for 28 ga. or .410 bore.

FALCONET SKEET - 26 in. barrels, bored skeet no. 1 and no. 2, wide vent. rib, case hardened steel frame. Mfg. 1970-74.

	$935	$855	$825	$770	$715	$690	$650

FALCONET INTERNATIONAL SKEET - higher grade wood, more engraving. Mfg. 1970-74.

	$1,045	$935	$865	$825	$770	$745	$700

GRADING - PPGS™	100%	98%	95%	90%	80%	70%	60%

FALCONET STANDARD TRAP - 12 ga., 30 in. mod. and full, wide vent. rib, trap stock, pad. Mfg. 1970-74.

	$935	$855	$825	$770	$715	$690	$650

FALCONET INTERNATIONAL TRAP - higher grade wood, more engraving. Mfg. 1970-74.

	$1,045	$935	$865	$825	$770	$745	$700

FALCONET 2000 - 12 ga. only, boxlock with alloy frame featuring silver finish with gold plated game scenes, 26 in. separated barrels with VR and choke tubes, SST, ejectors, select checkered walnut stock and forearm, hard case, 6 lbs. Imported 1992-97.

	$1,245	$975	$850	$725	$650	$575	$500

Last MSR was $1,375.

FALCONET 97-12 IBS - 12 ga. only, 2 3/4 in. chambers, ultra light alloy frame with gold inlays, scroll engraving, and nickel finish, SST, ejectors, 26 in. barrels with Franchokes, checkered walnut stock and forearm, includes hard case. Imported 1998-2000.

	$875	$750	$625	$550	$500	$450	$400

Last MSR was $965.

PEREGRINE MODEL 451 - 12 ga., 26-28 in. barrels, various chokes, vent. rib, auto ejectors, alloy frame, selective single trigger, checkered pistol grip stock. Mfg. 1975.

	$605	$550	$525	$495	$440	$415	$360

PEREGRINE MODEL 400 - similar to 451, except steel frame. Mfg. 1975.

	$660	$605	$570	$540	$495	$460	$385

MODEL 2003 TRAP - 12 ga., 30 or 32 in. barrels, imp. mod. and full, or full and full, boxlock, auto ejectors, single selective trigger, high vent. rib, trap style stock, pad, cased. Mfg. 1976. Disc.

	$1,205	$1,090	$1,045	$910	$855	$770	$660

MODEL 2004 TRAP - similar to 2003, except single barrel, cased. Mfg. 1976. Disc.

	$1,205	$1,090	$1,045	$910	$855	$770	$660

MODEL 2005 COMBINATION TRAP - two sets of barrels, one single, one O/U, cased. Mfg. 1976. Disc.

	$1,815	$1,595	$1,515	$1,320	$1,210	$1,075	$935

MODEL 2005/3 COMBINATION TRAP - three sets of barrels, cased. Mfg. 1976. Disc.

	$2,420	$2,090	$1,980	$1,705	$1,515	$1,485	$1,320

UNDERGUN MODEL 3000 - radical competition trap, very high rib separated barrels, under single and O/U, drop in set screw chokes (hex drive), set aluminum cased. Disc.

	$2,750	$2,530	$2,310	$2,090	$1,980	$1,870	$1,760

SHOTGUNS: SxS

AIRONE - 12 ga., choice of barrel length and chokes, box lock, Anson & Deeley, auto ejectors, double triggers, checkered English style stock, engraved. Mfg. 1940-50.

	$1,320	$1,100	$935	$825	$745	$715	$660

ASTORE - similar to Airone, except less engraving, extractors. Mfg. 1937-60.

	$990	$910	$770	$715	$635	$580	$550

ASTORE 5 - similar to Astore, except higher grade wood, more engraving, auto ejectors. Disc.

	$2,200	$1,925	$1,650	$1,540	$1,460	$1,375	$1,320

GRADING - PPGS™	100%	98%	95%	90%	80%	70%	60%

ASTORE II - similar to Astore 5, except less elaborate, currently mfg. in Spain for Franchi.

	$1,210	$1,045	$935	$880	$800	$715	$660

HIGHLANDER - 12, 20, or 28 ga., 3 in. chambers except for 28 ga., English style straight grip walnut stock and splinter forearm, scalloped coin finished boxlock receiver, SST, extractors, 26 in. barrels with fixed chokes, includes fitted hardcase, 5.7-6.4 lbs. Limited importation 2003.

	$1,575	$1,275	$1,075	$950	$825	$700	$600

Last MSR was $1,800.

HIGHLANDER (NEW MFG.) - 12 or 20 ga., 3 in. chambers, scalloped boxlock action, SST, blued or case colored (20 ga. only) frame, 26 in. VR barrels with choke tubes, straight grip A Grade oil finished walnut stock and splinter forearm. Importation began 2007.

MSR $2,799		$2,400	$2,100	$1,800	$1,500	$1,250	$1,000	$850

SIDELOCK DOUBLE BARREL - 12, 16, or 20 ga., barrels and choke custom order, stock to order, hand detachable side lock, self-opening action, auto ejectors, six grades offered, they differ only in overall quality and ornamentation, and grade of wood used.

Condor	$7,700	$6,600	$6,050	$5,720	$5,500	$4,620	$3,960
Imperial	$10,450	$9,350	$8,800	$8,250	$7,480	$6,600	$5,720
Imperiales	$10,670	$9,570	$9,020	$8,470	$7,700	$6,820	$5,940

SIDE-LOCK DOUBLE BARREL - the following models are available through the Beretta Galleries and selected premium dealers only (see Trademark Index).

* *Side-Lock Double Barrel No. 5 Imperial Monte Carlo*

MSR $27,500	N/A	$13,750	$11,000	$9,900	$8,900	$7,750	$6,500

* *Side-Lock Double Barrel No. 17 Imperial Monte Carlo*

MSR $35,000	N/A	$15,250	$12,500	$10,500	$9,350	$8,000	$7,000

* *Side-Lock Double Barrel Imperial Monte Carlo Extra*

Note: Imperial Monte Carlo Extra is currently being mfg. on special order only. Prices range from $53,000-$90,000.

DESTINO - 20 ga., 3 in. chambers, boxlock action with satin nickel finish and game scene engraving with gold inlays, SST, extractors, checkered straight grip AAA English walnut stock, fitted rubber buttpad, limited production of 250 beginning 2007.

MSR $3,495		$3,100	$2,700	$2,300	$1,950	$1,575	$1,375	$1,150

SHOTGUNS: SEMI-AUTO

BLACK MAGIC GAME - 12 ga. only, 3 in. chamber with gas metering system, interchangeable shell handling without adjustments, two-tone black alloy receiver with gold accents and trigger, 24, 26, or 28 in. VR barrel with Franchokes, checkered walnut stock and forearm, 7 lbs. Imported 1989-91.

	$550	$450	$395	$330	$300	$270	$240

Last MSR was $659.

* *Black Magic Game Skeet* - skeet variation of the Black Magic Game, 2 3/4 in. chamber, 26 in. ported VR barrel with fixed Tula skeet choke, skeet dimensioned stock, 7 1/4 lbs. Imported 1989-91.

	$580	$475	$425	$350	$325	$295	$265

Last MSR was $699.

GRADING - PPGS™	100%	98%	95%	90%	80%	70%	60%

✴ *Black Magic Game Trap* - trap variation of the Black Magic Game, 2 3/4 in. chamber, 30 in. VR barrel with Franchoke system, trap dimensioned stock, 7 1/2 lbs. Imported 1989-91.

	$615	$495	$430	$350	$325	$295	$265

Last MSR was $739.

48 AL FIELD MODEL - 12 (disc. 2001), 20, or 28 (new 1996) ga., 2 3/4 in. chamber, 24, 26, 28, or 30 (disc. in 1990) in. VR barrel with (beginning 1989) or w/o choke tubes, long recoil operation, alloy receiver, semi-humpback design, checkered pistol grip walnut stock and forearm, VR standard, standard choke tubes became available in 1989, 12 ga., 6 lbs. 9 oz. and 20 ga., 5 lbs. 6 oz. New 1950.

MSR $819		$675	$585	$475	$400	$350	$300	$275

Add $120 for 28 ga.
Add $30 for 12 ga. 24 in. slug barrel (disc. 1994).
Subtract 10% if without choke tubes.

This model is also available as a Youth Model (12 1/2 LOP, 20 ga. only). Starting in 1990, black receiver, gold accents, and choke tubes became standard.

✴ *48 AL Field Model Deluxe* - 20 or 28 ga., 26 in. barrel, similar to AL 48 Field, except has a high polish blue finish and upgraded walnut pistol grip or English (new 2002) stock and forearm, gold trigger and receiver accents, approx. 5 1/2 lbs. New 2000.

MSR $1,029		$850	$675	$575	$475	$400	$350	$300

Add $100 for 28 ga.

STANDARD MAGNUM (48/AL) - similar to Standard, except has 3 in. chamber with 28 in. (disc. 1988) or 32 in. VR barrel, recoil pad. Mfg. 1954-90.

	$415	$360	$300	$270	$250	$230	$210

Last MSR was $482.

This model was slated to be replaced with the Combo S/T - however, while advertised, the Combo S/T was never mfg.

HUNTER MODEL (48/AL) - similar to Standard, except etched receiver, better wood, VR standard, Franchokes became available in 1989. Mfg. 1950-90.

	$415	$360	$300	$270	$250	$230	$210

Last MSR was $482.

Add $35 for internal Franchokes (3).
This model was imported exclusively by FIE Firearms located in Hialeah, FL.

FENICE - 20 or 28 ga., 26 or 28 in. barrel, checkered oil finished A walnut stock and forearm, 5 shot mag., silver receiver with light scroll and gold game bird inlays, gold trigger, 5.4-5.7 lbs., available from World Class dealers only. Importation began 2007.

MSR $1,199		$1,050	$900	$775	$650	$575	$475	$400

VELOCE SP - 20 ga., 26 in. barrel, checkered oil finished AA walnut stock and forearm, deep relief engraving with gold game bird inlays, gold trigger, 5 1/2 lbs., available from World Class dealers only. Importation began 2007.

MSR $2,499		$2,250	$1,975	$1,750	$1,525	$1,300	$1,100	$900

HUNTER MAGNUM - mfg. 1954-73.

	$430	$380	$370	$340	$315	$290	$275

PRESTIGE MODEL - 12 ga. only, gas operated, vent. rib, various barrel lengths, alloy receiver, Franchokes became available in 1989. Imported 1985-89.

	$575	$475	$395	$325	$310	$295	$275

Last MSR was $720.

Add $40 for internal Franchokes (3).
This model was imported exclusively by FIE Firearms located in Hialeah, FL.

GRADING - PPGS™	100%	98%	95%	90%	80%	70%	60%

✳ *Prestige Model Turkey* - similar to Prestige Model except has dull matte black finish, Franchokes standard. Imported 1989 only.

	$615	$515	$425	$350	$320	$300	$280

Last MSR was $760.

This model was imported exclusively by FIE Firearms located in Hialeah, FL.

ELITE MODEL - same general specifications as the Prestige Model, only etched receiver, Franchokes became available in 1989. Imported 1985-89.

	$595	$500	$425	$350	$320	$300	$280

Last MSR was $740.

Add $45 for internal Franchokes (3).

This model was imported exclusively by FIE Firearms located in Hialeah, FL.

MODEL 610 VS - 12 ga., incorporates gas-operated Variopress System, adjusts for both 2 3/4 and 3 in. shells, 4 lug rotating breech bolt, alloy receiver, non-glare finish, 26 or 28 in. VR barrels with Franchokes, checkered walnut stock and forearm. Imported 1997 only.

	$650	$550	$425	$325	$275	$250	$225

Last MSR was $750.

Add $45 for engraved receiver and bolt (Model 610 VSL).

MODEL 612/620 (VS) - 12 (Model 612) or 20 (Model 620) ga., 3 in. chamber, features VarioSystem/Variomax gas operation utilizing reversible gas adjustment collar on mag. tube, advanced safety system, black receiver with (disc. 2001) or w/o gold borders (new 2002), 24, 26, or 28 in. barrel with choke tubes, last shot hold open, choice of checkered satin walnut, black synthetic (not available in 20 ga.) stock and forearm, 100% Realtree X-tra brown (disc. 1999), Realtree HD Timber (new 2002), Max-4 HD (new 2004, not available in 20 ga.), or Advantage (mfg. 2000-2002) camo coverage, 5.9-7 lbs. New 1998-2004.

	$550	$475	$415	$350	$325	$300	$275

Last MSR was $660.

Add $15 for satin finished walnut stock and forearm.
Add $105 for 100% camo coverage (Models 612/620 VS Camo).
Add $15 for 20 ga. or for Youth Model (20 ga. only, 12 1/2 LOP stock).

This model was previously designated the Variopress 612/620.

✳ *Model 612 Sporting* - 12 ga. only, features blue receiver with gold logo (new 2002), or silver receiver with black border and gold small parts (disc. 1998), matte black receiver with green logo (mfg. 2000-2002), or matte black top/polish sides receiver with gold lettering (new 2003), 28 (disc. 1998) or 30 (new 2000) in. ported target rib barrel with extended 4 in. forcing cone and elongated Franchokes, select checkered walnut stock and forearm, 7.1 lbs. Limited mfg. 1998, reintroduced 2000-2004.

	$825	$750	$625	$525	$450	$375	$325

Last MSR was $975.

This model was previously designated the Variopress 612 Sporting.

MODEL 612 DEFENSE - 12 ga. only, 18 1/2 in. barrel with cyl. bore, matte finish metal with black synthetic stock and forearm, 6 1/2 lbs. Imported 2000-2002.

	$525	$450	$375	$325	$285	$265	$245

Last MSR was $635.

This model was previously designated the Variopress 612 Defense.

MODEL 712 - 12 ga. only, 3 in. chamber, Benelli inertia recoil system with rotating bolt head, aluminum receiver, 24, 26, or 28 in. VR barrel, 5 shot mag., choice of synthetic, Weathercoat walnut, or 100% Advantage Timber HD or Max-4 HD camo coverage, recoil pad, approx. 7 lbs. Limited importation 2004 only.

	$650	$575	$500	$450	$375	$325	$275

Last MSR was $750.

Add $65 for walnut stock and forearm with Weathercoating.
Add $105 for camo finish.

GRADING - PPGS™	100%	98%	95%	90%	80%	70%	60%

✱ *Model 712 Raptor* - features 30 in. ported VR barrel with extended choke tubes, satin nickel receiver with green Franchi logo insert on right side, checkered Weathercoat pistol grip stock with recoil pad, blue finish, 5 shot mag., Benelli rotary bolt design, approx. 7 lbs. Mfg. 2005-2007.

	$845	$700	$575	$500	$440	$395	$350

Last MSR was $999.

MODEL 720 - 20 ga. only, 3 in. chamber, 26 or 28 in. barrel, similar to Model 712, except is not available with synthetic stock, also available with short LOP, blue or 100% Advantage Timber HD (disc. 2007) or Max 4-HD camo coverage, approx. 6 lbs. New 2004.

MSR $949	$795	$675	$575	$475	$400	$350	$300

Subtract $90 for short LOP.

✱ *Model 720 Raptor* - features 28 in. barrel with Weathercoat stock, blue finish, 5 shot mag. Mfg. 2005-2007.

	$845	$700	$575	$500	$440	$395	$350

Last MSR was $999.

✱ *Model 720 Competition* - 20 ga. only, 3 in. chamber, nickel finished receiver, 28 in. VR barrel with extended choke tube, Weathercoat stock and forearm, 6.2 lbs. New 2008.

MSR $1,069	$895	$750	$650	$575	$500	$425	$375

MODEL 912 - 12 ga. only, 3 1/2 chamber, VarioSystem/Variomax gas operation utilizing reversible gas adjustment collar on mag. tube, lightweight alloy receiver, 24, 26, 28, or 30 in. VR barrel with 3 choke tubes, choice of satin walnut stock (new 2002), black synthetic or 100% Advantage Timber HD or Max-4 HD (new 2004) camo coverage, magazine cutoff, includes hard case, 7.5-7.8 lbs. Imported 2001-2005.

	$665	$575	$500	$450	$375	$325	$275

Last MSR was $790.

Add $110 for camo coverage.
Add $60 for satin finished walnut stock and forearm.
Add $60 for Model 912 steady-grip with 24 in. barrel and 100% Timber HD camo coverage.

This model was previously designated the Variopress 912.

I-12 INERTIA - 12 ga. only, 3 in. chamber, 24, 26, or 28 in. VR barrel, inertia operating system with free floating bolt which compresses an inertia spring upon recoil, choice of synthetic or satin walnut stock and forearm, blued, matte blue, Max-4 HD, APG HD (new 2007), or Timber HD (disc. 2007) camo coverage, Twin Shock Absorber recoil pad with gel insert, approx. 7 1/2 lbs. New 2005.

MSR $799	$655	$540	$460	$380	$335	$300	$275

Add $90 for 100% camo coverage.
Add $120 for walnut stock and forearm.

I-12 LIMITED WHITE GOLD - 12 ga. only, similar to I-12 Intertia, except has AA Grade checkered walnut stock and forearm, 28 in. barrel only, blue metal finish, includes hard case. Importation began 2006.

MSR $1,599	$1,350	$1,100	$950	$800	$700	$600	$500

I-12 UPLAND HUNTER - 12 ga. only, 3 in. chamber, 26 in. VR barrel with choke tubes, Weathercoat straight grip stock and forearm. New 2008.

MSR $1,129	$1,050	$900	$750	$650	$550	$475	$400

I-12 SPORTING - 12 ga., 30 in. VR barrel with extended choke tubes, satin finished walnut stock and forearm. New 2008.

MSR $1,369	$1,175	$1,000	$875	$750	$650	$550	$475

GRADING - PPGS™	100%	98%	95%	90%	80%	70%	60%

SPAS-12 - 12 ga., 2 3/4 in. chamber, combat shotgun that offers pump or semi-auto operation, 5 (new 1991) or 8 (disc.) shot tube mag., alloy receiver, synthetic stock with built-in pistol grip (limited quantities were also mfg. with a folding stock or metal fixed stock), one-button switch to change from semi-auto to slide action operation, 21 1/2 in. barrel, 8 3/4 lbs. Importation disc. 1994.

	$675	$575	$475	$400	$350	$300	$280

Last MSR was $769.

This model was imported exclusively by FIE Firearms located in Hialeah, FL until 1990.

SPAS-15 - 12 ga. only, 2 3/4 in. chamber, operates as either semi-auto or slide action that is convertible with a one-button switch, 6 shot detachable box mag., 21 1/2 in. barrel, lateral folding skeleton stock, carrying handle, 10 lbs. Limited importation 1989 only.

This model had very limited importation (less than 200) as the BATF disallowed further importation almost immediately. Even though the retail was in the $700 range, demand and rarity have pushed prices past the $2,000 level.

SAS-12 - 12 ga. only, 3 in. chamber, slide action only, synthetic stock with built-in pistol grip, 8 shot tube mag., 21 1/2 in. barrel, 6.8 lbs. Imported 1988-90 only.

	$415	$360	$300	$270	$250	$230	$210

Last MSR was $473.

This model was imported exclusively by FIE Firearms located in Hialeah, FL.

LAW-12 - 12 ga. only, 2 3/4 in. chamber, gas operated semi-auto, synthetic stock with built-in pistol grip, 5 (new 1991) or 8 (disc.) shot tube mag., 21 1/2 in. barrel, 6 3/4 lbs. Imported 1988-94.

	$570	$485	$400	$360	$320	$300	$280

Last MSR was $719.

TURKEY GUN - 12 ga., similar to Standard Mag., 3 in. chamber only, turkey scene engraved. Mfg. 1963-65.

	$415	$385	$370	$340	$315	$290	$275

SLUG GUN - 22 in. plain barrel, and rifle sights.

	$360	$330	$315	$295	$275	$255	$240

SKEET GUN - 26 in. skeet choke, vent. rib, select wood. Mfg. 1972-74.

	$385	$370	$350	$330	$310	$285	$265

ELDORADO - fancy wood and gold filled engraved receiver. Mfg. 1954-75.

	$450	$420	$395	$380	$360	$340	$320

CROWN GRADE - engraved hunting scene. Mfg. 1954-75.

	$1,540	$1,320	$1,210	$1,045	$965	$910	$855

DIAMOND GRADE SILVER INLAID SCROLL - mfg. 1954-75.

	$1,980	$1,735	$1,540	$1,430	$1,210	$1,045	$965

IMPERIAL GRADE - gold inlaid hunting scene.

	$2,420	$2,090	$1,925	$1,760	$1,595	$1,485	$1,320

Note: Standard, Skeet and Slug with steel frame mfg. 1965-1972, designated "Dynamic" 12 ga., values are the same.

MODEL 500 STANDARD - 12 ga., 26 or 28 in. barrel, various chokes, vent. rib, gas operated, checkered pistol grip stock. Mfg. 1976-disc.

	$330	$310	$305	$265	$230	$195	$165

MODEL 520 DELUXE - engraved receiver.

	$385	$365	$330	$290	$260	$220	$195

MODEL 520 ELDORADO GOLD - fine wood, engraved gold, inlaid receiver. Mfg. 1977-disc.

	$990	$770	$715	$660	$580	$525	$470

GRADING - PPGS™	100%	98%	95%	90%	80%	70%	60%

MODEL 530 AUTO TRAP - similar to 500, except 30 or 32 in. full choke barrels, very high rib, special trap stock, pad.

| | $660 | $550 | $525 | $440 | $415 | $385 | $330 |

FRANCOTTE, AUGUSTE & CIE. S.A.

Previous manufacturer located in Leige, Belgium 1805-2002. Previously imported until 1999 by Armes De Chasse located in Hertford, NC, VL&D between 1900-1930s, and Abercrombie & Fitch until approx. 1962.

It is important to note that original A. Francotte SxS rifles and shotguns should exhibit the "crown over AF" maker's mark amongst the proofmarks.

REVOLVERS

Francotte manufactured Pryse-type revolvers at the end of the 19th century, and these revolvers bore the name of the well-known British retailer. Encountered only infrequently domestically, these specimens found overseas are usually priced in the $150-$650 range.

RIFLES

All recently mfg. rifles in this section were custom made to the purchaser's individual specifications. Francotte took advantage of 5 different frame sizes for its double rifles.

Add 20%-50% for P. Grifnee engraving, depending on coverage and amount of detail.

BOLT ACTION MODEL - many calibers between .18 Bee and .505 Gibbs Mag., select checkered walnut stock, engraved mag. floor plate, gold inlays optional, the following values assume engraving.

❊ *Bolt Action Model Short* - cals. with shorter cartridges.

| | $9,400 | $7,350 | $6,000 | $4,950 | $4,100 | $3,300 | $2,700 |

Subtract $3,250 if without engraving.

❊ *Bolt Action Model Standard* - cals. with medium cartridge lengths.

| | $7,825 | $6,100 | $4,975 | $4,100 | $3,300 | $2,700 | $2,000 |

Subtract $2,675 if without engraving.

❊ *Bolt Action Model Magnum Action* - cals. with longer cartridge lengths.

| | $13,750 | $10,850 | $9,350 | $7,750 | $6,400 | $4,950 | $3,950 |

Subtract $7,850 if without engraving.

SINGLE SHOT MOUNTAIN RIFLE - variety of cals., boxlock or sidelock action, custom order only.

❊ *Single Shot Mountain Rifle Boxlock* - 6.5x50R, 7x57R, or 7x65R cal.

| | $13,900 | $11,000 | $9,450 | $7,850 | $6,500 | $5,000 | $4,000 |

Subtract $4,800 if without engraving.
Add 10% for optional sideplates.

❊ *Single Shot Mountain Rifle Sidelock* - 7x65R or 7mm Rem. Mag. cal.

| | $24,800 | $20,350 | $16,650 | $13,000 | $10,500 | $9,000 | $8,000 |

Subtract $5,725 if without engraving.

BOXLOCK SxS RIFLE - .30-06, .375 H&H, .470 NE, .500-3 in. or 9.3x62mm cal., ejectors, case colored frame with border engraving (including screws), quarter rib on barrel, deluxe checkered pistol grip walnut stock and forearm. Mfg. 1997-disc.

| | $11,850 | $9,700 | $8,500 | $7,250 | $6,000 | $4,950 | $4,100 |

SIDELOCK SxS RIFLE - .30-06, .375 H&H, .470 NE, .500-3 in. or 9.3x62mm cal., ejectors, case colored frame with border engraving (including screws), quarter rib on barrel, deluxe checkered pistol grip walnut stock and forearm. Mfg. 1997-disc.

| | $16,250 | $14,250 | $12,500 | $10,250 | $8,750 | $7,250 | $6,500 |

Add 50% for .375 H&H cal.
Add 100% for .470 NE, .500-3, or 9.3x62mm cal.

GRADING - PPGS™	100%	98%	95%	90%	80%	70%	60%

SHOTGUNS: SxS

All recently manufactured shotguns in this section were custom made to purchaser's individual specifications. Basic types listed were also available in 24 or 32 ga. upon special order. Francotte took advantage of 5 different action sizes, one for each gauge. Auguste Francotte did not manufacture guns by model - all guns were custom order. Original A. Francotte SxS shotguns must have the "Francotte Choke Bore" marking on the water table. Be wary of fake barrel and frame markings, as some guns have recenty surfaced that are not Francotte, but have the Francotte name.

Add 10% for 20 ga. or 15% for 28 ga. or .410 bore.

Add 20%-50% for P. Grifnee engraving, depending on coverage and amount of detail.

BOXLOCK MODEL - 12, 16, 20, 28 ga., or .410 bore, premium grade Belgium side-by-side, double triggers standard, auto ejectors, English scroll engraving, Anson & Deeley boxlock action.

	100%	98%	95%	90%	80%	70%	60%
	$15,450	$11,250	$8,000	$6,250	$5,000	$4,000	$3,250

Subtract $5,925 if without engraving.

Add $1,159 for sideplates with engraving.

✳ *Boxlock Model Deluxe Anson & Deeley* - gold inlaid game scenes, and engraving was by customer's personal preference.

	100%	98%	95%	90%	80%	70%	60%
	$17,500	$14,250	$11,000	$8,750	$7,250	$6,000	$4,750

SIDELOCK MODEL - 12, 16, 20, 28 ga., or .410 bore, true sidelock action, Arabesque scroll engraving, various chokes and barrel lengths, custom order only.

	100%	98%	95%	90%	80%	70%	60%
	$27,300	$22,000	$18,750	$15,150	$12,000	$9,000	$7,750

Subtract $4,850 if without engraving.

✳ *Sidelock Model Deluxe* - gold inlaid game scenes and engraving are by customer's personal preference.

	100%	98%	95%	90%	80%	70%	60%
	$32,500	$27,500	$22,000	$18,750	$15,000	$12,000	$9,500

JUBILEE MODEL - case colored frame with hand engraving, Von Lengerke & Detmold or Abercrombie & Fitch import. Mfg. circa 1920-1970.

	100%	98%	95%	90%	80%	70%	60%
Knockabout	$2,250	$1,875	$1,525	$1,325	$1,100	$975	$850
No. 14	$2,750	$2,250	$1,975	$1,775	$1,600	$1,450	$1,150
No. 18	$2,950	$2,550	$2,250	$1,925	$1,700	$1,550	$1,225
No. 20	$3,450	$2,900	$2,575	$2,275	$1,900	$1,725	$1,375
No. 25	$4,000	$3,500	$3,000	$2,500	$2,150	$1,925	$1,575
No. 30	$5,450	$4,975	$4,500	$4,000	$3,500	$2,500	$2,200
No. 45 Eagle Grade	$7,650	$6,700	$5,850	$4,950	$4,250	$3,800	$3,000

Add 75% for 20 ga.

Add approx. 200%-250% for 28 ga. or .410 bore.

FRASER, DANL. & CO.

Current trademark owned by Dickson & MacNaughton located in Edinburgh, Scotland. Previously imported and distributed by Flying G Ranch, located in Carrizo Springs, TX.

Danl. Fraser & Co. has manufactured rifles since 1873 (originally located in Edinburgh, Scotland).

RIFLES: SINGLE SHOT

HIGHLANDER SINGLE SHOT - .22 LR or .22 Hornet cal., underlever falling block action (color case hardened), 24 in. (1/2 round, 1/2 octagon) barrel, folding express-style sights, pistol grip walnut stock with fine checkering. Disc.

	100%	98%	95%	90%	80%	70%	60%
	$415	$335	$300	$280	$260	$240	$220

Last MSR was $475.

✳ *Highlander Single Shot Royal* - .22 LR or .22 Hornet cal., mfg. in Scotland, rose and scroll engraving with 18Kt. inlays. Special order only.

GRADING - PPGS™	100%	98%	95%	90%	80%	70%	60%

FRASER FIREARMS CORP.

Previously manufactured by R.B. Industries, Ltd. until 1990. Previously distributed by Fraser Firearms Corp. located in Fraser, MI.

PISTOLS: SEMI-AUTO

FRASER 25 CAL. - .25 ACP cal. only, copy of the Bauer semi-auto pocket model, 6 shot mag., 2 1/4 in. barrel, stainless steel construction.

	$120	$100	$90	$85	$80	$75	$70

Last MSR was $133.

Add $17 for Model 2 (black nylon grips).
Add $115 for Model 3 (24 Kt. gold plated).

FREEDOM ARMS

Current manufacturer established during 1983, and located in Freedom, WY. Distributor and dealer sales.

REVOLVERS: MINI, STAINLESS STEEL

Because Freedom Arms' manufacturing capacity has been maximized due to the success of the .454 Casull revolver, the mini-revolver series was discontinued beginning 1989.

FA-S-22LR (PATRIOT) - .22 LR cal., 5 shot, 1, 1 3/4 (disc. 1988), or 3 (disc. 1988) in. barrel, Hi-Gloss finish. Disc. 1989.

	$175	$135	$100	$90	$80	$75	$70

Last MSR was $153.

Add $15 for 3 in. barrel model (FA-BG-22LR, Minute-Man, disc. 1988).

FA-S-22M (IRONSIDES) - .22 Mag. cal., 4 shot, 1, 1 3/4 (disc. 1988), or 3 in. barrel, Hi Gloss finish. Disc. 1989.

	$200	$150	$110	$95	$85	$80	$75

Last MSR was $177.

Add $43 for 3 in. barrel model (Bostonian).

FA-S-22-LR BUCKLE/REVOLVER COMBINATION - .22 LR cal., 1 in. barrel, pistol is housed in belt buckle. Disc. 1989.

	$295	$225	$185	$145	$120	$105	$90

Last MSR was $193.

∗ *FA-S-22-LR Buckle/Revolver Combination .22 Mag. cal.*

	$350	$250	$200	$150	$125	$110	$95

Last MSR was $216.

REVOLVERS: SA, STAINLESS STEEL

Freedom Arms also offers a complete line of accessories and factory installed options. The factory should be contacted directly for an up-to-date listing and prices. Beginning in 1999, all revolvers are equipped with a locking safety device which slides into the muzzle and locks into the chamber under the firing pin, making it impossible to either load the top chamber or turn the cylinder.

Add $272 per interchangeable cylinder in different cals. on most of the following centerfire models.
Add $144 for 4 port Mag-na-ported barrel.
Add $109 for 2 port Mag-na-ported barrel.
Add $468 for octagon barrel.
Add $78 for non-standard barrel length.

MODEL 83 FIELD GRADE - .22 LR, .357 Mag., .41 Mag., .44 Mag., .45 LC (disc. 1990), .454 Casull, .475 Linebaugh, .50 AE (disc. 2004) or .500 Wyoming Express (new 2006) cal., 5 shot, 4 3/4, 6, 7 1/2, 9 (.357 Mag. only), or 10 (not available in .500 Wyoming Express) in. barrel, fixed or aluminum base adj. rear sight with replaceable blade front sight, matte stainless steel construction, manual sliding-bar safety system, Pachmayr presentation grips, 56 oz. (.454 Casull cal. with 7 1/2 in. barrel). New 1988.

MSR $1,623	$1,425	$1,225	$995	$850	$775	$675	$575

Add $68 for .454 Casull, .475 Linebaugh, .50 AE or .500 Wyoming Express cal.
Add $26 for .454 Casull cal. with fixed sight.
Add $237 for .22 LR cal. with match chamber and 10 in. barrel.

MODEL 83 HUNTER PAK FIELD GRADE - .357 Mag., .44 Rem. Mag., or .454 Casull cal., 7 1/2 in. barrel, plastic grips, field grade low profile adj. sight or no front sight base, sling and studs, locking aluminum carrying case with cleaning kit and tool. Mfg. 1990-93.

	$1,150	$975	$875	$775	$700	$625	$550

Last MSR was $1,333.

Add $76 for low profile adj. sight and Pachmayr grips.

✳ *Model 83 Hunter Pak Field Grade Premier* - .357 Mag., .44 Rem. Mag., or .454 Casull cal., 7 1/2 in. barrel, ebony micarta grips, no sights or premier grade adj. sight, sling and studs, locking aluminum carrying case with cleaning kit and tool. Mfg. 1990-93.

	$1,395	$1,125	$925	$825	$750	$675	$500

Last MSR was $1,611.

Add $100 for adj. sights.

MODEL 83 PREMIER GRADE - .357 Mag., .41 Mag., .44 Mag., .454 Casull, .475 Linebaugh, .50 AE (disc.), .500 Wyoming Express (new 2006) cal., 5 shot, 4 3/4, 6, 7 1/2, 9 (.357 Mag. only) or 10 (not available in .500 Wyoming Express) in. barrel, fixed or steel base adj. rear sight and replaceable blade front sight, stainless steel construction, bright brushed finish, manual sliding-bar safety system, and impregnated hardwood grips, 52.8 oz. New 1983.

MSR $2,099	$1,775	$1,475	$1,225	$995	$875	$775	$700

Add $1 for .454 Casull cal. with fixed sight (4 3/4 or 6 in. barrel only).
Add $87 for .454 Casull, .475 Linebaugh, .500 Wyoming Express, or .50 AE cal. with adj. sight.

MODEL 83 VARMINT GRADE - .22 LR cal., 5 shot, dual firing pins, choice of 5 1/8 or 7 1/2 in. barrel, steel base adj. V notch rear sight and replaceable brass bead front sight, stainless steel construction, matte finish, manual sliding bar-safety system, pre-set trigger stop, impregnated hardwood grips, 58 oz. Disc. 2005.

	$1,525	$1,275	$950	$850	$775	$700	$650

Last MSR was $1,828.

Add $264 for extra .22 Mag. cylinder.

MODEL 83 CENTERFIRE SILHOUETTE - .357 Mag., .41 Mag., or .44 Mag. cal., 5 shot, 9 (.357 Mag. only) or 10 in. barrel, Pachmayr presentation grips, Iron Sight Gun Works silhouette rear sight and replaceable adj. front sight blade with hood, stainless steel construction, matte finish, manual sliding-bar safety system.

MSR $1,742	$1,475	$1,250	$1,050	$900	$800	$700	$600

✳ *Model 83 Centerfire Silhouette (.454 Casull Silhouette Model)* - .454 Casull cal., includes 10 in. barrel, Pachmayr grips, field grade finish, silhouette competition sights, and trigger over travel screw.

	$1,600	$1,275	$1,075	$925	$825	$750	$675

Last MSR was $1,958.

GRADING - PPGS™	100%	98%	95%	90%	80%	70%	60%

✻ Model 83 Centerfire Silhouette Pak - .44 Mag. cal., includes 10 in. barrel, silhouette competition sight, honed action with 3 lb. trigger pull, plastic grips, locking aluminum carrying case with cleaning kit and tool. Mfg. 1990 only.

	$1,100	$950	$850	$775	$700	$650	$600

Last MSR was $1,242.

✻ Model 83 Centerfire Silhouette .454 Casull Pak - .454 Casull cal., includes 10 in. barrel, silhouette competition sight, honed action with 3 lb. trigger pull, hardwood grips, locking aluminum carrying case with cleaning kit and tool. Mfg. 1990 only.

	$1,375	$1,175	$995	$850	$775	$700	$650

Last MSR was $1,522.

MODEL 83 .22 CAL. SILHOUETTE CLASS - .22 LR cal., 5 shot, 10 in. barrel, wood (standard), black micarta (standard) or Pachmayr grips, Iron Sight Gun Works silhouette rear sight and replaceable adj. front sight blade with hood, stainless steel construction, matte finish, manual sliding-bar safety system, dual firing pins, lightened hammer for fast lock time, pre-set trigger stop, 63 oz. New 1991.

MSR $1,914	$1,625	$1,185	$875	$765	$635	$530	$455

MODEL 97 PREMIER GRADE - .17 HMR (new 2004), .22 LR (new 2002), .357 Mag., .32 H&R Mag. (new 2004), .41 Rem. Mag. (new 2000), .44 Spl. (new 2003), .45 LC (new 1999) cal., 5 (.41 Mag., .44. Spl., or .45 LC cal.) or 6 (.17 HMR, .22 LR or .357 Mag. cal.) shot, 3 1/2 (mfg. 2004-2005), 4 1/2 (new 2000), 5 1/2, 7 1/2, or 10 in. barrel, fixed or steel base adj. rear sight and replaceable blade front sight, stainless steel construction, bright brushed finish, automatic transfer bar safety system, optional round butt grip, impregnated hardwood grips. New 1997.

MSR $1,772	$1,485	$1,250	$1,050	$925	$800	$700	$600

Add $68 for .17 HMR or .22 LR cal. with sporting chambers.
Add $215 for 3 1/2 in. barrel (disc.).
Add $175 for optional round butt grip.
Subtract $99 for fixed sights (.32 H&R Mag., .357 Mag., .44 Spl. (new 2007), or .45 LC cal. only).

U.S. DEPUTY MARSHAL - 3 in. barrel only with no ejector, fixed or adj. sights, U.S. Marshal medallion in left hardwood grip. Mfg. 1990-93.

	$1,325	$900	$750	$640	$535	$450	$390

Last MSR was $1475 (fixed sights). Last MSR was $1,558 (adj. sights).

Add approx. $80 for adj. sights.

SIGNATURE EDITION - .454 Casull cal., high polish stainless steel, 7 1/2 in. barrel only, rosewood grips, cased with accessories, only 93 of 100 were actually mfg.

	$2,300	$1,750	$1,300	$1,150	$935	$815	$650

Last MSR was $2,684.

PRIMUS INTER PARES - 1 of every 1,000 guns were made in this variation, includes octagonal barrel, ivory grips, 7 1/2 in. barrel, and cased. Disc. 1993.
Rarity factor precludes accurate pricing.

FRENCH MILITARY

Various configurations manufactured in several locations in France.

PISTOLS: SEMI-AUTO

P.38 configurations were manufactured in the French occupied Mauser factory in Oberndorf, Germany, at the end of WWII.

GRADING - PPGS™	100%	98%	95%	90%	80%	70%	60%

svw-45 STANDARD CONFIGURATION - 9mm Para. cal., blue or grey finish, French five pointed star proof located on right side of the slide, some parts may contain E/WaA135 German acceptance stamps, ser. no. range approx. 1g-4,500k. Mfg. by Mauser.

	$750	$675	$600	$525	$475	$450	$425

Add 20% for French assembly with FN manufactured slide (marked ac-43 or ac-44 with E/WaA135 stamps).

svw-46 STANDARD CONFIGURATION - 9mm Para. cal., grey finish, French five pointed star proof located on right side of the slide, some parts may contain E/WaA135 German acceptance stamps, pressed steel grips are common, ser. no. range approx. 4501k-9999k. Mfg. by Mauser.

	$850	$750	$700	$650	$525	$475	$450

svw-46 STANDARD CONFIGURATION (L Serial) - 9mm Para. cal., black/blue finish, French five pointed star proof located on right side of the slide, ser. no. located on left side of slide (early) or under the rear tang of the frame, press steel grips common, ser. no. range 1L-500L. Mfg. by Mauser.

	$950	$875	$800	$750	$675	$600	$550

MODEL 1935A AUTO PISTOL - 7.65mm French Long cal., 8 shot, 4.3 in. barrel, fixed sights, blue, checkered wood grips, French service sidearm. Mfg. 1935-45.

	$275	$225	$180	$135	$110	$100	$90

Add 50% if Nazi proofed.

✳ *MODEL 1935S Auto Pistol* - .32 ACP or .380 ACP cal., 4 1/3 in. barrel, enamel finish, Colt Govt. Model locking system, 26 oz.

	$325	$295	$260	$225	$195	$170	$150

M.A.B. MODEL C - .32 ACP cal., design based on FN Browning Model 1910, 6.1 in. barrel. Introduced 1933.

	$250	$220	$190	$170	$150	$125	$110

M.A.B. MODEL D - .32 ACP cal., 3.96 in. barrel, single action, similar to Model C, mfg. commercially 1933-1940, many thousands mfg. for the German military during WWII (marked "Pistole MAB Kaliber 7.65mm").

	$275	$225	$200	$175	$150	$125	$110

MODEL M.A.B. PA - 15 - 9mm Para. cal., single action, 16 shot, currently used by French military.

	$550	$500	$450	$400	$365	$335	$300

Subtract 10% for phosphate.

MODEL M.A.B. PA - 15 TARGET - rare target variation of PA-15, adj. sight, 6 in. barrel, cased.

	$1,250	$1,000	$750	$675	$600	$550	$500

RIFLES: BOLT ACTION

MODEL 1886 LEBEL - 8mm Lebel cal., 32 in. barrel, adj. sight, military stock. Mfg. 1886-WWII.

	$125	$100	$75	$65	$50	$40	$25

1936 MAS MILITARY RIFLE - 7.5mm MAS cal., 22 in. barrel, adj. sight, military stock, bayonet in forearm. Mfg. 1936-1940.

	$300	$225	$175	$145	$125	$100	$80

MODEL 45 - .22 LR cal., may have Mauser parts, aperture rear sight, post-war mfg.

	$400	$360	$330	$275	$235	$200	$175

GRADING - PPGS™	100%	98%	95%	90%	80%	70%	60%

FRIGON GUNS, INC.

Previously manufactured by Marocchi in Italy. Previously imported by Frigon Guns, Inc. located in Clay Center, KS.

SHOTGUNS

FT-I - 12 ga. only, single barrel trap gun, blue finish, 32 or 34 in. VR barrel, quick-change stock. Mfg. 1986-94.

	$925	$675	$525	$435	$375	$350	$295

Last MSR was $1,100.

FT-C - 12 ga. only, quick-change stock, trap combination gun includes 1 single barrel and 1 set of O/U barrels, cased. Mfg. 1986-94.

	$1,700	$1,325	$1,050	$875	$775	$685	$620

Last MSR was $1,975.

FS-4 - 4-barrel skeet set including 12, 20, 28 ga., or .410 bore, individual forearms, quick-change stock, vent. barrels (except for .410 bore), cased. Mfg. 1986-94.

	$2,575	$1,975	$1,675	$1,475	$1,350	$1,250	$1,150

Last MSR was $2,890.

FROMMER PISTOLS

Previously manufactured by Femaru-Fegyver es Gepgyar R.T., Budapest, Hungary.
Please refer to the Femaru listing in this section.

FURR ARMS

Current manufacturer located in Orem, UT.
Please refer to the Gatling Gun listing in this text.

FULTON ARMORY

Current rifle manufacturer and parts supplier located in Savage, MD. Dealer sales.

RIFLES: SEMI-AUTO

Fulton Armory makes a comprehensive array of the four US Gas Operated Service Rifles: M1 Garand, M1 Carbine, M14 and AR-15-type, including corresponding commercial versions and upper receiver assemblies and related parts and components. Current Fulton Armory FAR-15 models include: Legacy, a '60s semi-auto M16 replication - $900 MSR, Classics, mirroring current military M16A2/A4 and M4 models - $775 MSR, Guardian Carbines - disc., $1,000-$1,100 last MSR, Liberator and Phantom Tactical Carbines and Enhanced Battle Rifles - $1,000-$1,200 MSR, Mirage NRA/DCM National Match Rifles - $l400-$1,800 MSR, Predator Varmint Rifles - $900-$l,800 MSR, Accutron NRA Match Rifles - $1,300-$2,200 MSR, Hornet Lightweight Rifle - $750 MSR, disc. 2003, and the Millennial Lightweight Rifle and Carbine - $750-$850 MSR, disc. 2002.

Current Fulton Armory M14-type rifles using Fulton Armory's semi-auto M14 receiver include: the M14 Service Rifle - $1,800-$2,000 MSR, M14 Competition Rifle (NRA/CMP Service Rifle Match-Legal) - $2,200-$2,500 MSR, M14 JSSW with Sage Stock/Accuracy System - $2,500-$2,900 MSR, and the M14 Peerless Rifle (NRA/CMP Service Rifle Match-Legal) - $2,600-$3,000 MSR.

Additionally, Fulton Armory manufactures U.S. military and enhanced civilian configurations of the M1 Garand and M1 Carbine, using genuine U.S.G.I. receivers. Models include: the M1 Garand Service Rifle - $1,300-$1,500 MSR, M1 Garand Competition Rifle (John C. Garand Match-Legal) - $1,600 MSR, M1 Garand Peerless Rifle (NRA/CMP Service Rifle Match-Legal) - $2,000 MSR, and the M1 Carbine Service Rifle in Cals. .30 Carbine and 5.7 MMJ Spitfire - $1,000-$1,100 MSR.

Please contact the factory directly for more information, including current availability and pricing (see Trademark Index).

NOTES

G SECTION

GALAZAN

Current trademark established in 1995, and manufactured by Connecticut Shotgun Manufacturing Co., located in New Britain, CT. Consumer direct sales.

The Galazan trademark has established itself as one of the premier names in best quality O/U shotguns and double rifles. All guns are custom order. For more information regarding current firearms, please refer to the Connecticut Shotgun Manufacturing Co. listing in this text.

GALEF SHOTGUNS

Previous importer of Zabala Hermanos (Spanish) and Antonio Zoli (Italian) shotguns.

GRADING - PPGS™	100%	98%	95%	90%	80%	70%	60%

SHOTGUNS

COMPANION FOLDING SINGLE BARREL - 12, 16, 20, 28 ga., or .410 bore, 28 in. barrel, full choke, 30 in. full, 12 ga. only, hammerless, underlever, checkered pistol grip stock.

	100%	98%	95%	90%	80%	70%	60%
	$155	$125	$100	$85	$75	$65	$55

MONTE CARLO TRAP SINGLE BARREL - 12 ga., 32 in. full vent. rib, hammerless, underlever, recoil pad, checkered pistol grip Monte Carlo stock. Disc.

	100%	98%	95%	90%	80%	70%	60%
	$225	$185	$175	$150	$135	$125	$100

SILVER SNIPE O/U - 12 or 20 ga., 3 in. chambers, 26, 28, or 30 in. barrels, imp. cyl. and mod. or full and mod. vent. rib, checkered pistol grip stock, boxlock, extractors, single trigger. Mfg. by Angelo Zoli, disc.

	100%	98%	95%	90%	80%	70%	60%
	$525	$500	$475	$400	$375	$325	$275

GOLDEN SNIPE O/U - similar to Silver Snipe, except has auto ejectors.

	100%	98%	95%	90%	80%	70%	60%
	$595	$525	$500	$475	$375	$350	$300

SILVER HAWK SxS - 12 or 20 ga., 3 in. chambers, 26, 28, or 30 in. barrels, imp. cyl. and mod. or mod. and full, boxlock, extractors, checkered pistol grip and beavertail forearm. Mfg. by Angelo Zoli, 1968-72.

	100%	98%	95%	90%	80%	70%	60%
	$450	$400	$375	$350	$300	$275	$250

GALEF ZABALA SxS - 10, 12, 16, or 20 ga., 22, 26, 28, or 30 in. barrels, boxlock, extractors.

	100%	98%	95%	90%	80%	70%	60%
10 gauge	$250	$230	$200	$175	$150	$140	$125
Other gauges	$200	$175	$150	$130	$120	$110	$100

GALENA INDUSTRIES INC.

Please refer to the AMT and Automag listings.

GALIL

Current trademark manufactured by Israel Military Industries (IMI). No current consumer importation. Recent Galil semi-auto sporterized rifles and variations with thumbhole stocks were banned in April, 1998. Beginning late 1996, Galil rifles and pistols were available in selective fire mode only (law enforcement, military only) and are currently imported by UZI America, Inc., a subsidiary of O.F. Mossberg & Sons, Inc. Previously imported by Action Arms, Ltd. located in Philadelphia, PA until 1994. Previously imported by Springfield Armory located in Geneseo, IL and Magnum Research, Inc., located in Minneapolis, MN.

Magnum Research importation can be denoted by a serial number prefix "MR", while Action Arms imported rifles have either "AA" or "AAL" prefixes.

RIFLES: SEMI-AUTO

Models 329, 330 (Hadar II), 331, 332, 339 (sniper system with 6x40 mounted Nimrod scope), 361, 372, 386, and 392 all refer to various configurations of the Galil rifle.

GRADING - PPGS™	100%	98%	95%	90%	80%	70%	60%

MODEL AR - .223 Rem. cal. or .308 Win. cal., semi-auto paramilitary design rifle,
✱ gas operated - rotating bolt, 16.1 in. (.223 Rem. cal. only) or 19 in. (.308 Win. cal. only) barrel, parkerized, folding stock. Flip-up Tritium night sights. 8.6 lbs.

	$2,500	$2,150	$2,000	$1,825	$1,600	$1,495	$1,350

Last MSR was $950.

MODEL ARM - similar to Model AR, except includes folding bipod, vented hardwood handguard, and carrying handle.

	$2,750	$2,500	$2,250	$2,050	$1,850	$1,700	$1,475

Last MSR was $1,050.

GALIL SPORTER - similar to above, except has one-piece thumbhole stock, 4 (.308 Win.) or 5 (.223 Rem.) shot mag., choice of wood (disc.) or polymer hand guard, 8 1/2 lbs. Imported 1991-93.

	$1,200	$1,125	$1,050	$950	$900	$875	$800

Last MSR was $950.

HADAR II - .308 cal., gas operated, paramilitary type configuration, 1 piece walnut thumbhole stock with pistol grip and forearm, 18 1/2 in. barrel, adj. rear sight, recoil pad, 4 shot (standard) or 25 shot mag., 10.3 lbs. Imported 1989 only.

	$1,200	$1,025	$975	$875	$750	$675	$600

Last MSR was $998.

SNIPER OUTFIT - .308 Win. cal., semi-auto, limited production, sniper model built to exact I.D.F. specifications for improved accuracy, 20 in. heavy barrel, hardwood folding stock (adj. recoil pad and adj. cheekpiece) and forearm, includes Tritium night sights, bipod, detachable 6x40mm Nimrod scope, two 25 shot mags., carrying/storage case, 14.1 lbs. Imported 1989 only.

	$6,500	$5,750	$5,000	$4,350	$3,750	$3,250	$2,850

Last MSR was $3,995.

GAMBA, RENATO

RENATO GAMBA

Current trademark established in 1748, and located in Gardone V.T., Italy. Gamba firearms are currently manufactured by Bre-Mec srl beginning 2007, and imported in limited quantities beginning 2005 by Renato Gamba U.S.A., located in Walnut, CA. The U.S. service center is located in Bernardsville, NJ. Gamba of America, a subsidiary of Firing Line, located in Aurora, CO, was the exclusive importer and distributor for Renato Gamba long guns from 1996-2000. Pistols were previously imported and distributed (until 1990) by Armscorp of America, Inc. located in Baltimore, MD. Shotguns were previously (until 1992) imported by Heckler & Koch, Inc. located in Sterling, VA.

Filli Gamba (Gamba Brothers) was founded in 1946. G. Gamba sold his tooling to his brother, Renato, in 1967 when Renato Gamba left his brothers and S.A.B. was formed. Filli Gamba closed in 1989 and the Zanotti firm was also purchsed the same year.

Renato Gamba firearms have had limited importation since 1986. In 1989, several smaller European firearms companies were purchased by R. Gamba and are now part of the Renato Gamba Group - they include Gambarmi and Stefano Zanotti. The importation of R. Gamba guns changed in 1990 to reflect their long term interest in exporting firearms to America. Earlier imported models may be rare but have not enjoyed much collectibility to date.

PISTOLS: SEMI-AUTO

All the following models were discontinued for importation approx. 1990, and importation on certain models began again during 2005.

Please contact the company directly for more information, including current pricing and availability.

MAUSER HSc SUPER - for more information, please refer to the Mauser Pistols: HSc Post-WWII Mfg. section.

GRADING - PPGS™	100%	98%	95%	90%	80%	70%	60%

SAB G90 STANDARD - .30 Luger/7.65 Para. (disc.), 9x18mm Ultra (disc.), 9x21mm (new 2005), or 9mm Para. (disc.) cal., double action, 4.72 in. barrel, 10 (C/B 1994) or 15* shot side release mag., blue or chrome (disc.) finish, hammer drop safety on frame, smooth walnut grips, fixed rear sight, 2.2 lbs.

MSR N/A	$675	$575	$465	$335	$295	$275	$250

Add $145 for chrome finish.

✳ *SAB G90 Standard Competition* - 9mm Para. cal., similar to SAB G90 Standard, except has adj. rear sight, "cocked and locked" operation, and checkered walnut grips. Imported 1990 only.

	$1,175	$425	$375	$325	$300	$275	$250

Last MSR was $1,364.

Add $205 for stainless steel (SAB G90 Service Competition).

SAB G91 COMPACT - similar to SAB G90, except has 3.54 in. barrel, 12 shot mag., 1.87 lbs.

	$625	$375	$325	$295	$275	$250	$225

Last MSR was $736.

Add $65 for chrome finish (disc.).

✳ *SAB G91 Compact Competition* - 9mm Para. cal., similar to SAB G91 Compact, except has adj. rear sight, "cocked and locked" operation, and checkered walnut grips. Imported 1990 only.

	$450	$395	$330	$300	$275	$250	$225

Last MSR was $575.

SAB G2001 - .380 ACP cal., double action, mfg. from forged and milled steel, high polish blue, neoprene grips, slide mounted manual safety with firing pin block, 10 shot mag.

	$615	$395	$325	$295	$275	$250	$225

Last MSR was $699.

REVOLVERS

The following models were discontinued for importation approx. 1990, and certain models were imported again beginning 2005. Please contact the company directly for more information, including current pricing and availability.

TRIDENT FAST ACTION - .32 S&W or .38 Spl. cal., 2 1/2 or 3 in. barrel, double action, blue frame with checkered walnut grips, 6 shot, 23 oz.

	$550	$425	$360	$330	$295	$270	$245

Last MSR was $630.

TRIDENT SUPER - .32 S&W or .38 Spl. cal., 4 in. vent. rib barrel, 6 shot, double action, checkered walnut grips, 25 oz.

	$585	$450	$375	$340	$310	$280	$250

Last MSR was $683.

TRIDENT MATCH 900 - .32 S&W Long W.C. (disc.) or .38 Spl. cal., double action, 6 shot, match gun featuring 6 in. heavy barrel and anatomically compatible checkered walnut (disc.) or rubber (new 2005) grips, adj. sights, 2.2 lbs.

MSR $1,210	$1,050	$800	$700	$600	$500	$450	$400

TRIDENT MATCH 901 - .32 S&W cal., similar to Trident Match 900.

MSR N/A	$1,050	$800	$700	$600	$500	$450	$400

RIFLES

SAFARI EXPRESS SxS - 7x65R, 9.3x74R, or .375 H&H cal., 25 in. barrels with open sights, underlug locking with Greener crossbolt, ejectors except on .375 H&H, coin finished frame with scroll work and game scene engraving, DTs, deluxe checkered walnut stock with cheekpiece and recoil pad, 9.9 lbs.

	$5,685	$4,575	$3,950	$3,575	$3,175	$2,850	$2,500

Last MSR was $6,630.

GRADING - PPGS™	100%	98%	95%	90%	80%	70%	60%

CONCORDE EXPRESS O/U - .30-06, 8x57JRS, or 9.3x74R cal., 23 3/4 in. barrels, monoblock frame, Boss type action, ejectors, cased.

Please contact the company directly for more information, including current pricing and availability.

DAYTONA SL EXPRESS O/U - .30-06, .375 H&H, or 9.3x74R cal., monoblock frame with Boss type improved action, 23 3/4 in. barrels, detachable Gamba trigger assembly, hand engraved sideplates with game scenes and English scroll.

Please contact the company directly for more information, including current pricing and availability.

EXPRESS MAXIM SxS - .375 H&H, .458 Win. Mag., .470 NE, or .458 Lott (new 1995) cal., sidelock action, fine engraving with big game scenes signed by the master engraver, includes leather case.

Please contact the company directly for more information, including current pricing and availability.

MUSTANG EXTRA SINGLE SHOT - 5.6x50mm (disc.), 5.6x57R (disc.), 6.5x57R, 7x65R, .222 Rem. (disc.), .243 Win., .270 Win., or .30-06 cal., single 25 1/2 in. barrel configuration with highly engraved sidelock action featuring triple-bite double Purdey locking system with Greener crossbolt, extra fine vine leaf Renaissance engraving (game scene upon request), double-set triggers, best quality checkered walnut stock and forearm, 6.17 lbs.

Please contact the company directly for more information, including current pricing and availability.

RGZ 1000 BOLT ACTION - 7x64mm, .270 Win., 7mm Rem. Mag., or .300 Win. Mag. cal., modified Mauser K-98 action, 20 1/2 in. barrel, pistol grip stock with cheekpiece, 7 lbs.

	100%	98%	95%	90%	80%	70%	60%
	$1,100	$885	$825	$760	$700	$640	$575

Last MSR was $1,310.

✳ *RGX 1000 Bolt Action Express* - similar to RGZ 1000, except has 23 3/4 in. barrel and double set triggers, 7.7 lbs.

	100%	98%	95%	90%	80%	70%	60%
	$1,255	$960	$875	$795	$725	$650	$575

Last MSR was $1,475.

SHOTGUNS: O/U

Some of the following O/U models were discontinued in 1990 when H&K became the exclusive importer for R. Gamba shotguns.

Add on values for the following models represent the manufacturer's suggested retail on those items, not necessarily the value in the secondary marketplace.

Many of the models in this section with N/As for a MSR indicate little or no importation in recent years. Please contact the company directly for more information, including current pricing and availability.

EUROPA 2000 - 12 ga. only, engraved, silver finished boxlock action with sideplates, vent. rib, single trigger, ejectors, deluxe checkered stock and forearm, 6.84 lbs.

	100%	98%	95%	90%	80%	70%	60%
	$1,075	$925	$895	$835	$775	$715	$650

Last MSR was $1,475.

EDINBURGH SUPER SLUG - 12 ga. only, trap model, SST, ejectors, engraved action, deluxe checkered stock and forearm.

	100%	98%	95%	90%	80%	70%	60%
	$900	$800	$750	$700	$625	$575	$500

Last MSR was $1,425.

GRIFONE SPORTING TRAP - 12 ga. only, trap model, SST, ejectors, moderately engraved action, deluxe checkered stock and forearm.

	100%	98%	95%	90%	80%	70%	60%
	$875	$800	$750	$700	$600	$550	$450

Last MSR was $1,425.

GRINTA TRAP/SKEET - 12 ga. only, trap/skeet model, SST, ejectors, medium engraving coverage.

	100%	98%	95%	90%	80%	70%	60%
	$900	$825	$725	$650	$575	$500	$450

Last MSR was $1,710.

GRADING - PPGS™	100%	98%	95%	90%	80%	70%	60%

VICTORY TRAP/SKEET - similar to Grinta Model, except has better walnut and more engraving.

	$1,200	$1,075	$950	$850	$750	$650	$550

Last MSR was $1,905.

EDINBURG MATCH - similar to Victory Model, except has different style of engraving.

	$1,200	$1,075	$950	$850	$750	$650	$550

Last MSR was $1,930.

MONTREAL MODEL 90/91 - 12 ga. only, boxlock, interchangeable trigger assembly, select walnut, vent. rib. Available in International Trap, American Skeet, Sporting, and Field models.

	$2,350	$2,100	$1,700	$1,400	$1,100	$1,000	$900

Add $200 for single selective trigger.

The Model 90 has a flat-sided receiver, while the Model 91 has a Daytona sculpted receiver.

MONTREAL 90/91 AMERICAN TRAP COMBO - 12 ga. only, 32 in. barrels and adj. impact, single 34 in. barrel, interchangeable trigger assembly.

	$2,425	$2,000	$1,820	$1,540	$1,400	$1,260	$1,120

SINGLE BARREL TRAP-MODEL 496 - 12 ga. only, boxlock, vent. rib.

	$1,150	$865	$750	$635	$575	$520	$460

HUNTER II - 12 ga. only, boxlock action with alloy frame, reinforced barrels including 5 choke tubes, SST, ejectors, 23.5 (Woodcock), 26 or 27 (Game) in. barrels, checkered walnut stock and forearm, approx. 6 lbs. Limited importation beginning 2002.

Please contact the company directly for more information, including current pricing and availability.

LE MANS SPORTING/TRAP - 12 ga. only, boxlock action with steel frame, reinforced barrels including 5 choke tubes, single trigger (Trap) or SST (Sporting), ejectors, checkered walnut stock and forearm, approx. 6 lbs. Limited importation beginning 2002.

Please contact the company directly for more information, including current pricing and availability.

CONCORDE GAME MODEL - 12 or 20 ga., Boss type improved locking system, ejectors, 26 3/4 or 28 in. VR barrels, available in Hunting, Trap, Skeet, and Sporting configurations, 2nd generation Concorde with fixed single trigger group started 2002. Importation began 1995.

MSR N/A	$7,500	$4,500	$3,350	$2,850	$2,350	$2,000	$1,750

Add $500 for SST.
Add $1,129 for Sporting Model.
Add $3,350 for Concorde SL with game scene engraved sideplates (disc.).
Add $2,000 for Trap combo (disc.).

✲ *Concorde Game Model SSLL* - features sideplates, engraved with game scenes, fixed trigger group, ejectors, select walnut stock, 30 in. barrels. Importation began 2005.

Please contact the company directly for more information, including current pricing and availability.

✲ *Concorde Game Model Grade 7* - includes engraving featuring game scenes and English scroll. Disc.

	$12,400	$7,750	$5,950	$5,000	$4,400	$3,850	$3,250

Last MSR was $13,540.

Add $1,070 for Sporting Clays Model.

✲ *Concord Game Model Grade 8* - features top-of-the-line English scroll engraving. Disc.

	$7,525	$6,650	$5,000	$4,250	$3,600	$2,925	$2,400

Last MSR was $10,650.

Add $1,070 for Sporting Clays Model.

GRADING - PPGS™	100%	98%	95%	90%	80%	70%	60%

CARRERA SPORTING MODEL - 12 ga., features similar to Daytona Model, 28, 30, or 32 in. barrels, SST, 5 chokes, upgraded wood, gold woodcock engraved on action. Importation began 2005.

Please contact the company directly for more information, including current pricing and availability.

DAYTONA (2K NEW SERIES) & VARIATIONS - 12 ga. only, monolithic boxlock action, SST, ejectors, detachable trigger group, blue or chrome finish standard, available in either Hunting, Skeet, Pigeon, Sporting Clays, Olympic Trap, or American Trap configuration, deluxe walnut with fine English scroll engraving with game scenes. New Daytona series started in 2000. Importation began 1990.

MSR N/A	$9,100	$8,500	$6,000	$4,300	$3,700	$2,950	$2,400

  Add $1,102 for Sporting Clays Model.
  Add approx. $1,600 for removable trigger group.
  Add $1,530 for New American Trap configuration (disc.).
  Add $2,000 for Daytona combo package (disc.).
  Add $4,160-$4,958 for extra set of O/U barrels.

✳ *Daytona Grade 4 Model* - most elaborately engraved numbered Daytona model, choice of eagle panel scene or fine scroll engraving.

MSR N/A	$22,250	$18,250	$15,000	$11,750	$9,950	$8,900	$7,750

  Add $430 for Luxe game scene and fine English scroll engraving.

✳ *Daytona Grade 5/5E Model* - one grade below Grade 4.

MSR N/A	$21,500	$18,000	$15,000	$11,750	$9,950	$8,900	$7,750

✳ *Daytona Grade 6/6 SCE Model* - one grade below Grade 5, choice of duck game scene or tight scroll engraving.

MSR N/A	$19,250	$17,000	$14,000	$10,450	$8,750	$7,750	$6,750

  Add $3,498 for game scene engraving (Grade 6 SCE).

✳ *Daytona Grade 7 Model* - one grade below Grade 6, oval game scene engraving with English scroll on perimeter.

MSR N/A	$17,250	$15,500	$12,750	$9,750	$7,500	$6,250	$5,000

✳ *Daytona Grade 8 Model* - features English scroll engraving.

MSR N/A	$15,750	$13,750	$11,500	$8,950	$7,250	$6,000	$4,750

DAYTONA SL - deluxe variation of the Daytona Model, except has sideplates with extensive engraving, new mfg. has detachable trigger group, available in the same configurations as the Daytona Model, includes case. Limited importation 1990-94, reintroduced 2000-2005.

	$26,000	$18,000	$11,500	$10,500	$9,000	$7,200	$5,500

Last MSR was $29,310.

✳ *Daytona SL Grade 1* - elaborate engraving with 24Kt. gold game scene engraving.

MSR N/A	$46,250	$40,000	$26,750	$17,500	$14,500	$12,000	$9,750

✳ *Daytona SL Grade 2* - elaborate scroll and game scene engraving, w/o gold inlays.

MSR N/A	$34,000	$28,250	$21,000	$13,500	$11,500	$9,500	$7,750

✳ *Daytona SL Grade 3* - features hand engraved sideplates with English scroll and game scenes. Importation began 1995.

MSR N/A	$29,250	$26,000	$18,750	$11,750	$10,250	$8,250	$7,250

✳ *Daytona SL Grade Royale* - top-of-the-line Daytona Model.

MSR N/A	$33,450	$28,000	$20,000	$12,500	$10,750	$9,150	$7,400

✳ *Daytona SL Grade Purdey* - features Purdey locking system, English scroll engraving.

MSR N/A	$32,500	$27,000	$19,000	$12,000	$10,250	$8,950	$7,300

DAYTONA SLE BEST - features elaborate scroll and 24Kt. gold game scene inlays.

MSR N/A	$53,000	$47,000	$31,000	$20,000	$17,000	$13,500	$10,750

DAYTONA SLE VENUS - features elaborate scroll and game scene engraving.

MSR N/A	$47,750	$42,500	$28,500	$18,750	$15,500	$12,950	$10,250

GRADING - PPGS™	100%	98%	95%	90%	80%	70%	60%

✳ *Daytona SLE Venus Tiger* - features sideplates with African game scenes.

   MSR N/A $45,500 $40,500 $27,500 $17,950 $14,950 $12,950 $10,250

DAYTONA SLHH - 12 or 20 ga., H&H style sidelock action with Boss improved lock-up, top-of-the-line model, game or competition configuration, includes leather case. Importation began in 1990.

Please contact the company directly for more information, including current pricing and availability.

✳ *Daytona SLHH Grade 1* - similar to Grade 2, except has better engraving.

Please contact the company directly for more information, including current pricing and availability.

✳ *Daytona SLHH Grade 2* - available in either Hunting (12 ga. only), Skeet, Trap, Pigeon, or Sporting Clays configuration.

Please contact the company directly for more information, including current pricing and availability.

✳ *Daytona SLHH Grade 3* - features elaborate scroll and game scene engraving.

Current MSR on this model is $66,096.

DAYTONA VENUS SLEHH - boxlock action with engraved sideplates featuring relief scroll and Goddess of the Hunt engraving.

Please contact the company directly for more information, including current pricing and availability.

DAYTONA SLHH "THE BEST" - sidelock action with elaborate engraving and multiple 24Kt. gold game scene inlays.

Renato Gamba also offers a Triptych set of 3 SLHH models (Diamond Collection) in 12, 20, and 28 ga.

Please contact the company directly for more information, including current pricing and availability.

ONE OF THOUSAND - top-of-the-line model with every possible refinement, Boss action, individually special ordered only.

Please contact the company directly for more information, including current pricing and availability.

BAYERN 88 COMBINATION GUN - 12 ga. over same cals. listed for Mustang Model, coin finished boxlock action with game scene engraving, DTs, extractors, deluxe checkered walnut stock with recoil pad, 7 1/2 lbs.

               $1,000 $875 $775 $700 $650 $600 $550

Last MSR was $1,595.

SHOTGUNS: SxS

Many of the models in this section with N/As for a MSR indicate little or no importation in recent years. Please contact the company directly for more information, including current pricing and availability. Previous to 1989, an optional 28 ga. on a 28 ga. frame was available for most of the following models.

   Add 20%+ for 28 ga. on the following models.

HUNTER SUPER - 12 ga. only, Anson & Deeley engraved boxlock action with silver finish, DTs, extractors, 6.84 lbs.

               $1,750 $1,275 $895 $760 $630 $575 $525

Last MSR was $1,506.

PRINCIPESSA - 12 or 20 ga., similar to Hunter Super except has English straight grip stock and better engraving, 6.62 lbs. Importation disc. 1994.

               $2,750 $1,900 $1,525 $1,250 $995 $800 $625

Last MSR was $2,495.

   Add $200 for single trigger.

S. VINCENT 580 EXTRA DELUXE - 12 ga. only, custom made to individual preferences, very high quality, sidelock action, engraving coverage 100%.

               $4,525 $4,250 $3,500 $2,750 $2,125 $1,775 $1,625

GRADING - PPGS™	100%	98%	95%	90%	80%	70%	60%

OXFORD 90 - 12 or 20 ga., boxlock action with Purdey locking system, DTs, ejectors, scroll engraving on sideplates, deluxe checkered straight grip walnut stock with recoil pad or checkered butt, 6.84 lbs. Disc. 1998.

	$2,375	$2,250	$1,925	$1,600	$1,250	$1,025	$875

Last MSR was $4,300.

Add $245 for single trigger.

OXFORD EXTRA - 12 or 20 ga., double Purdey locking system, includes elegantly engraved sideplates, ejectors, and better quality hand checkered stock and forearm. Importation began 1992.

MSR N/A	$6,950	$6,250	$5,750	$3,950	$2,975	$2,475	$2,100

Add $633 for single trigger.

MODEL 624 PRINCE - 12 or 20 ga. (disc.), boxlock action, ejectors, choice of English scroll or with woodcock (Model 624 Prince Beccaccia) on bottom of frame, hand checkered walnut stock and forearm. Importation began 1992.

MSR N/A	$7,250	$6,350	$5,750	$3,950	$2,975	$2,475	$2,100

Add $769 for single trigger.
Add $496 for Model 624 Prince Beccaccia.

MODEL 624 PRINCE EXTRA - similar to Model 624 Prince, except has deep floral hand engraving.

MSR N/A	$12,950	$11,000	$9,995	$6,750	$4,250	$3,150	$2,750

NEW LONDON GOLD - 12 or 20 ga., H&H side-lock system, ejectors, DT or SST, demibloc chopper lump barrels, English scroll engraving, deluxe checkered straight grip stock and forearm, 6.84 lbs.

MSR N/A	$17,250	$15,250	$9,250	$5,750	$3,750	$3,100	$2,500

Add $1,101 for single trigger.

LONDON ROYAL - similar to London Model except has less extensive game scene engraving.

	$9,000	$8,000	$7,000	$5,750	$4,750	$3,950	$3,475

Last MSR was $6,730.

ZANOTTI 1625 MAXIM - 12 or 20 ga., H&H sidelock system, ejectors, demibloc barrels, coin finished action with royal English scroll engraving, cased. New 2002.

Please contact the company directly for more information, including current pricing and availability.

AMBASSADOR MODEL - 12 or 20 ga., H&H sidelock system, available with either gold-line engraving on barrels and frame with blue receiver (Gold and Black Model) or English scroll engraving (English Engraved Model), single trigger, ejectors, deluxe checkered walnut stock and forearm, cased, 6.4 lbs.

Add $1,377 for English scroll engraving.
Subtract 25% for 12 ga. in used condition only.

This model is also available in either Field or Sporting versions upon special request. Please contact the company directly for more information, including current pricing and availability.

AMBASSADOR EXECUTIVE - 12 or 20 ga. only, top-of-the-line model, made to individual order only, every possible refinement.

Subtract 25% for 12 ga. in used condition only.

A matched pair of Ambassador Executive models is also available.
Please contact the company directly for more information, including current pricing and availability.

SHOTGUNS: SLIDE ACTION

MODEL 2100 - 12 ga., 3 in. chamber, 19 1/2 in. barrel, 7 shot mag., law enforcement configuration with matte black metal and wood, 6.62 lbs. Limited importation.

	$450	$375	$325	$295	$275	$250	$225

Last MSR was $715.

GARBI, ARMAS

Current manufacturer located in Eibar, Spain. Imported and distributed exclusively by William Larkin Moore & Co. located in Scottsdale, AZ.

Garbi typically manufactures approx. 100-125 shotguns and rifles annually.

RIFLES: SxS

Garbi also manufactures a deluxe SxS double rifle in 7x65R, 8x57JRS, 9.3x74R, .300 H&H, or .375 H&H cal. This model is POR. Please contact the importer or factory directly for more information (including special orders and prices) on this model.

SHOTGUNS: SxS, DISC.

MODEL 120 - 12, 16, 20, or 28 ga., Holland-pattern sidelock ejector double with chopper lump barrels of nickel-chrome steel, H&H type easy opening mechanism, game scene engraving - 3 patterns available. Well figured walnut stock. Importation disc. 1994.

	100%	98%	95%	90%	80%	70%	60%
	$6,700	$6,000	$4,875	$4,125	$3,375	$2,600	$2,200

Last MSR was $9,400.

SPECIAL WLM - 12, 16, 20, or 28 ga., top-of-the-line Holland-pattern sidelock ejector double with chopper lump barrels, full coverage large scroll engraving, fancy-figured walnut stock. Importation disc. 1994.

$7,125	$6,000	$4,875	$4,125	$3,375	$2,600	$2,200

Last MSR was $9,400.

SPECIAL AG - 12, 16, 20, or 28 ga., top-of-the-line Holland-pattern sidelock ejector double with chopper lump barrels, large scroll engraving patterned after Lebeau-Courally, fancy figured walnut stock. Disc.

$6,975	$6,350	$5,200	$4,300	$3,550	$2,750	$2,300

Last MSR was $9,200.

SHOTGUNS: SxS, RECENT MFG.

On the following models, add $395 for 28 ga., $2,375 for single trigger, $700-$2,500 for English or Turkish walnut wood upgrade, $815 for beavertail forearm, $2,890 - $6,090 per extra set of barrels (depending on grade), and $350 for Churchill style level file-cut rib.

MODEL 100 - 12, 16, or 20 ga., Holland-pattern detachable sidelock ejector double, Purdey style scroll engraving, chopper lump barrels, oil finish, select walnut, articulated trigger.

MSR $9,800	$9,400	$8,750	$7,500	$6,250	$5,150	$4,200	$3,025

MODEL 101 - 12, 16, or 20 ga., round body action and smooth wood now standard, Holland-pattern sidelock ejector double with chopper lump barrels, scroll engraving, selected walnut stock.

MSR $9,800	$9,400	$8,750	$7,500	$6,250	$5,150	$4,200	$3,025

MODEL 103A - 12, 16, 20, or 28 ga., Holland-pattern sidelock ejector double with chopper lump barrels, fine scroll and rosette engraving, selected walnut stock.

MSR $12,800	$11,750	$9,850	$8,400	$6,150	$5,000	$3,575	$2,800

Add $2,890 for Express No. 2 engraving.
Add approx. $3,850 for Purdey style, Prince Albert, or H&H Royal engraving pattern.
Add $4,950 for Prestige engraving.

MODEL 103B - 12, 16, 20, or 28 ga., Holland-pattern sidelock ejector double with chopper lump barrels of nickel-chrome steel, H&H type easy opening mechanism, fine scroll and rosette engraving, well figured walnut stock.

MSR $19,800	$18,750	$16,000	$13,000	$8,950	$7,250	$6,300	$5,150

Add $2,890 for Express No. 2 engraving.
Add approx. $3,695 for Purdey style, Prince Albert, or H&H Royal engraving pattern.
Add $4,900 for Prestige engraving.

GRADING - PPGS™	100%	98%	95%	90%	80%	70%	60%

MODEL 200 - 12, 16, 20, or 28 ga., Holland-pattern sidelock ejector double with chopper lump barrels of nickel-chrome steel, heavy-duty locks, magnum proofed, very fine Continental style floral scroll engraving, well figured walnut stock.

	100%	98%	95%	90%	80%	70%	60%
MSR $15,800	$14,950	$12,500	$9,500	$7,250	$6,000	$4,750	$3,750

GARRAY RIFLES LTD.

Current rifle manufacturer with headquarters located in Kelowna, British Columbia, Canada. Direct sales only.

RIFLES: BOLT ACTION

GARRAY RIFLE - calibers range from .243 to .458, including all standard length cartridges, all other factory and big game calibers available, features exhibition grade walnut stock, Schnabel forend, barrel band, rounded pistol grip, and continental cheekpiece with client's initials in medallion on buttstock, various hand checkering designs available, modern Mauser 98 action, swivel (90 degree) release mounts, all rings and bases included, three point safety and Timney trigger standard.

All GarRay rifles are hand-built with an MSR of $6,995. All rifles are supplied with a custom designed takedown case, including maker's name and customer's name embroidered on the inside.

Please contact the headquarters directly for more information, including options, delivery time, and a price quotation.

GASTINNE RENETTE

Previous manufacturer and retailer 1812-2003, and located in Paris, France.

On Jan. 1, 2003, Gastinne Renette closed its doors at its famous location on Franklin D. Roosevelt Avenue in Paris. Gastinne Renette had limited U.S. importation and distribution, and most guns were subcontracted to other European manufacturers.

RIFLES: BOLT ACTION

Values listed are base prices for each model - since all guns were made to individual order. Wood, level of engraving, and other special features were available at additional cost.

STANDARD MODEL MAUSER ACTION

$5,150	$4,450	$3,850	$3,150	$2,550	$1,900	$1,500

Last MSR was $6,000.

DELUXE MAUSER ACTION

$9,950	$7,850	$6,850	$5,750	$4,750	$3,900	$2,750

Last MSR was $12,000.

RIFLES: SxS, DOUBLE

BOXLOCK MODEL - variety of cals., features Anson & Deeley boxlock mechanism, color case hardened frame. Imported 1993-2002.

$8,950	$7,750	$6,950	$5,850	$4,950	$4,100	$3,200

Last MSR was $10,000.

EUROPEAN SIDELOCK

$31,000	$27,000	$22,500	$18,750	$15,000	$12,500	$10,000

Last MSR was $36,000.

AFRICAN SIDELOCK - various Mag. cals. Imported 1993-2002.

$33,000	$28,750	$23,500	$19,250	$15,500	$12,750	$10,000

Last MSR was $40,000.

STANDARD TYPE G - 9.3x74R, 7.65R, .30-06, or .375 H&H cal., double bolt action, ejectors, reinforced stock, 23 3/4 in. barrels, bouquet style engraving with deluxe walnut stock and forearm, 7 lbs. 6 oz.

$2,995	$2,500	$2,150	$1,700	$1,560	$1,480	$1,340

GRADING - PPGS™	100%	98%	95%	90%	80%	70%	60%

DELUXE TYPE R - 9.3x74R, 7.65R, .30-06, or .375 H&H cal., double bolt action, true sideplates, ejectors, reinforced stock, 23 3/4 in. barrels, animal engraving with deluxe walnut stock and forearm, 7 lbs. 6 oz.

	$3,875	$3,325	$2,700	$2,175	$1,850	$1,700	$1,525

PRESIDENT TYPE PT - 9.3x74R, 7.65R, .30-06, or .375 H&H cal., double bolt action, true sideplates, ejectors, reinforced stock, 23 3/4 in. barrels, light engraving with gold line inlays, best quality walnut, 7 lbs. 6 oz.

	$4,250	$3,725	$3,200	$2,650	$2,250	$1,825	$1,600

RIFLES: SINGLE SHOT

FALLING BLOCK MODEL

	$9,750	$8,250	$6,750	$5,900	$5,000	$4,000	$3,000

Last MSR was $14,000.

SIDELOCK MODEL - features breakdown action. Imported 1993-2002.

	$25,750	$21,250	$18,000	$14,750	$11,350	$9,250	$7,000

Last MSR was $34,000.

SHOTGUNS: SxS

MODEL 105 - 12 or 20 ga., Anson and Deeley type triple bolt action, ejectors, double triggers, case hardened frame, 6 lbs. 8 oz.

	$2,250	$1,800	$1,400	$1,250	$1,125	$1,000	$900

MODEL 98 - 12 and 20 ga., Purdey type triple bolt action, ejectors, double triggers, case hardened frame, 6 lbs. 8 oz.

	$2,995	$2,500	$2,000	$1,850	$1,580	$1,430	$1,260

MODEL 202 - 12 or 20 ga., Purdey type triple bolt action, sidelocks, fine English engraving, first grade French walnut, ejectors, double triggers, coin finished frame, 6 lbs. 10 oz.

	$4,500	$3,950	$3,250	$2,500	$2,175	$1,875	$1,650

Last MSR was $5,250.

MODEL 353 - 12 or 20 ga., Purdey type triple bolt action, hand detachable sidelocks, chopper lump barrels, fine English engraving, first grade French walnut, ejectors, double triggers, case hardened frame, best quality, 6 lbs. 10 oz.

	$17,500	$13,650	$11,000	$8,900	$6,700	$6,250	$5,750

Last MSR was $19,950.

GATEWAY PRECISION ARMS

Current manufacturer located in Affton, MO. Dealer direct sales.

The XL Hunter model was previously manufactured by RPM until 2004.

PISTOLS: SINGLE SHOT

XL HUNTER - over 40 cals., tip-up action, stainless steel frame, 5 1/16 in. underlug, 12 or 14 in. Douglas chrome-moly (new 2004) or stainless steel barrel, ISGW rear and Patridge or hooded front sight, with (became standard 2000) or w/o external positive extractor. New 1995.

MSR $1,500		$1,375	$1,250	$995	$800	$700	$600	$500

Add $250 for stainless steel barrel.
Add $250 for integral muzzle brake.
Add $50 for left-hand action.
Add approx. $400-$550 per extra barrel, depending on length.

GATLING GUNS

Gatling Gun refers to a rifle configuration utilizing multiple barrels and box magazine, which is operated by a rotating hand crank. Original full size Gatling guns were manufactured by Colt and some British manufacturers.

Full size Gatling reproductions are currently manufactured by Battery Gun Company,

GRADING - PPGS™	100%	98%	95%	90%	80%	70%	60%

Thunder Valley Gatling Gun, Schneider Enterprise, Smoke River, and previously by John Anderson. Gatling scale replicas in .22 cal. are currently manufactured by Furr Arms, BWE Firearms, New Zealand Gatling Gun Company, and RG-G Inc. .357 Mag./ .38 Spl. cal. scale replicas are currently being manufactured by Furr Arms.

Furr Arms manufactures high quality 1/6, 1/3, 1/2, 3/4, and full scale brass reproductions of famous, antique Gatling guns and cannons. Model Gatling guns include various models and scales from 1874 to 1893. Model cannons include the British Naval Cannon and the James Six Pounder. Prices vary according to the complexity of each model and are available by contacting Furr Arms.

For space considerations, no indivdual manufacturer/model listings or values are listed, but please check the Trademark Index for more information on currently produced full size and scale replica reproductions.

GAUCHER

Current manufacturer established in 1834, and located in St. Etienne, France. No current U.S. importation. Previously imported and distributed by Mandall Shooting Supplies located in Scottsdale, AZ. Gaucher merged with Bretton in 2000, and the new company name is Bretton-Gaucher (see Trademark Index).

Gaucher **Armes**

During 1997, Gaucher released four shooting rifles with unique sound suppression (approx. 71 dB) in 9mm Para., 12mm cal., or .410 bore. Additionally, Gaucher manufactures rifles (O/U and SxS double, bolt action rimfire, and semi-auto rimfire), shotguns (SxS, single shot), and 22 LR cal. target pistols. To date, there has been little importation of Gaucher firearms. Please contact the Bretton-Gaucher factory directly (see Trademark Index) for more information and up-to-date pricing regarding their current lineup of firearms.

PISTOLS: SINGLE SHOT, TARGET

MODEL GN1 - .22 LR cal., single shot silhouette pistol featuring 10 in. barrel, adj. sights, anatomically shaped grips, monobloc lever cocking, 2.42 lbs. Limited importation.

$360	$325	$290	$260	$230	$200	$185

Last MSR was $380.

MODEL GP - similar to Model GN1, except has forearm integrated into grip. Limited importation.

$300	$275	$250	$225	$200	$185	$160

Last MSR was $323.

GAZELLE ARMS

Current trademark established circa 1970, and manufactured by Hisar Avcilik & Doga Sporlasi San Ve Tic. Ltd. Sti., located in Konak-Izmir, Turkey. Currently imported by EMA Distributors, LLC, located in Pineville, NC.

Gazelle Arms currently manufactures a line of good quality, inexpensive shotguns, including semi-autos, SxSs, single shots, and O/Us. Current MSRs on the semi-auto shotguns range from $345-$390, while the O/U is priced at $500. Please contact the importer directly for more information (see Trademark Index).

GAVAGE

Previous manufacturer located in Liege, Belgium circa 1936-1943.

PISTOLS: SEMI-AUTO

GAVAGE PISTOL - .32 ACP/7.65mm cal., patterned after the Clement, fixed barrel, limited mfg.

$450	$350	$250	$200	$175	$150	$125

Add 250% for Waffenamt proofmarks.

This pistol is very rare if encountered with Waffenamt proofmarks.

GRADING - PPGS™	100%	98%	95%	90%	80%	70%	60%

GENTRY, DAVID - CUSTOM GUNMAKER

Current custom rifle maker located in Belgrade, MT.

David Gentry is a current custom rifle builder who usually fabricates rifles to individual custom order requests. Current models include Gentry's Black Beauty, Mountain "70", Gray Ghost, and the Outfitter's Rifle. The Rough Rider Model was disc. 1994. David Gentry also manufactures top quality muzzle brakes, stainless steel Featherlight scope rings (1 in. and 30mm), and performs custom metalwork. Mr. Gentry should be contacted directly (see Trademark Index) for more information on options/prices.

GERMAN P.38 MILITARY & COMMERCIAL PISTOLS

Please refer to the P.38 entries in the P section.

GEVARM

Previous manufacturer located in Saint Etienne, France.

RIFLES: SEMI-AUTO

E-1 AUTOLOADING RIFLE - .22 LR cal., 19 in. barrel, open sights, walnut pistol grip stock.

	$300	$250	$225	$195	$180	$165	$150

GIANI, VITTORIO

Current manufacturer located in Brescia, Italy.

Vittorio Giani specializes in bolt action rifles, but also manufactures SxS rifles and shotguns, made per special order. Please contact the factory directly for more information, including pricing and availability (see Trademark Index).

GIB

Previous trademark manufactured in Spain.

SHOTGUNS: SxS

10 GAUGE MAGNUM - 10 ga., 3 1/2 in. chambers, 32 in. full choke barrel, case hardened frame, matted rib, rubber pad, checkered pistol grip walnut stock. Disc.

	$275	$250	$235	$220	$200	$175	$150

GIBBS GUNS, INC.

Previously manufactured by Volunteer Enterprises in Knoxville, TN and previously distributed by Gibbs Guns, Inc. located in Greenback, TN.

CARBINES

MARK 45 CARBINE - .45 ACP cal. only, based on M6 Thompson machine gun, 16 1/2 in. barrel, 5, 15, 30, or 90 shot mag. U.S. mfg. Disc. 1988.

	$750	$625	$525	$450	$375	$330	$300

Last MSR was $279.

Add $200 for 90 shot mag.
Add 10% for nickel plating.

GIBBS RIFLE COMPANY, INC.

Previous manufacturer, importer, and distributor located in Martinsburg, WV until 2005. Gibbs manufactured rifles with the Gibbs trademark in Martinsburg, WV 1991-94, in addition to importing Mauser-Werke firearms until 1995. Dealer and distributor sales.

In the past, Gibbs Rifle Company, Inc. imported a variety of older firearms, including British military rifles and handguns (both original and refurbished condition), a good selection of used military contract pistols and rifles, in addition to other shooting products and accessories, including a bipod patterned after the Parker-Hale M-85.

Gibbs Rifle Company, Inc. imported and manufactured military collectibles, historical

GRADING - PPGS™	100%	98%	95%	90%	80%	70%	60%

remakes, and special sporting rifles. All rifles were carefully inspected, commercially cleaned and boxed to ensure their quality, and all had a limited lifetime warranty. Gibbs Rifle Company, Inc. also offered membership in the Gibbs Military Collectors Club, an organization dedicated to military firearms collectors.

RIFLES: BOLT ACTION

M-71/84 MAUSER - 11mm Mauser cal., 31 1/2 in. barrel, available in good original or refurbished condition, 10 lbs. Imported 1999-2004.

$165	$135	$120	$110	$100	$90	$85

Last MSR was $190.

Add $110 for refurbished condition (all parts are historically correct and have been cleaned and hand inspected).

This rifle cannot be safely shot with modern ammunition.

M-1888 MAUSER - 8mm Mauser (7.92x57mm) cal., good original condition, 30 in. barrel, 10 lbs. Imported 1999-2004.

$85	$75	$65	$55	$45	$40	$35

Last MSR was $100.

This rifle cannot be safely shot with modern ammunition.

M-98K ISRAELI MAUSER - .308 Win. cal., rebarreled by the Israeli Arsenal Ha´as, various makers, 23.6 in. barrel, original condition (offered in 3 grades), 9 lbs. Imported 1999-2003.

$150	$125	$115	$105	$95	$90	$85

Last MSR was $170.

Add $10 for Grade 2, or $20 for Grade 1.

M-98 MAUSER SPORTER - .270 Win. or .30-06 cal., Mauser M-98 type action, blue finish, sporterized checkered hardwood stock and forend, 24 in. Wilson barrel. Mfg. in Martinsburg, WV 1998-99.

$295	$265	$245	$225	$210	$195	$180

Last MSR was $330.

2A HUNTER RIFLE/CARBINE - .308 Win. cal., sporterized action features black enamel refinish, synthetic stock, 12 shot mag, and choice of 18 (carbine) or 22 1/2 (rifle) in. barrel with Parker-Hale muzzle brake, approx. 10 lbs. Mfg. 1999 only.

$235	$200	$180	$165	$155	$145	$140

Last MSR was $275.

ENFIELD NO. 5 JUNGLE CARBINE - .303 British cal., older No. 4 Enfield barrel action with newly manufactured stock, bayonet lug and flash hider have been added, 20 in. barrel, 7 3/4 lbs. Imported 1999-2004.

$175	$155	$125	$115	$105	$95	$90

Last MSR was $205.

ENFIELD NO. 7 JUNGLE CARBINE - .308 Win. cal., older 2A action with reconfigured original wood, flash hider and bayonet lug have been added, 20 in. barrel, 8 lbs. Imported 1999-2004.

$170	$150	$125	$115	$105	$95	$90

Last MSR was $200.

QUEST EXTREME CARBINE - .303 British cal., updated No. 5 Enfield action with 20 in. barrel with compensator and flash hider, electroless nickel metal finish, new buttstock with survival kit packaged in butt trap, 7 3/4 lbs. Imported 2000-2004.

$215	$185	$170	$160	$150	$140	$130

Last MSR was $250.

GRADING - PPGS™	100%	98%	95%	90%	80%	70%	60%

QUEST II - .308 Win. cal., modern 2A Enfield barreled action, mfg. from chrome vanadium steel, 20 in. barrel with compensator/flash-hider and adj. rear sight, front sight protector, pre-fitted see-through scope mount accepts all Weaver based optics and accessories, electroless nickel finish, hardwood stock with survial kit included, 12 shot mag., 8 lbs. Imported 2001-2004.

	$235	$200	$185	$170	$160	$155	$150

Last MSR was $280.

QUEST III - .308 Win. cal., similar to Quest II, except has black syntetic stock, w/o survival kit. Imported 2002-2004.

	$250	$220	$200	$185	$170	$160	$155

Last MSR was $300.

SUMMIT FRONTIER .45-70 CARBINE - .45-70 Govt. cal., remanufactured No. 4 Enfield action, new 21 in. button rifled barrel with front sight, blue action and barrel, checkered hardwood sporting stock, 3 shot mag., 8 1/2 lbs. Imported 2000-2005.

	$330	$280	$255	$230	$210	$195	$180

Last MSR was $385.

GIBBS ECONOMY SPORTER - 8mm Mauser cal., sporterized military action with good barrel and sporting sights, walnut finished checkered hardwood stock. Mfg. 1993-94.

	$185	$150	$135	$120	$100	$85	$70

Last MSR was $205.

GIBBS MAUSER SPORTER - .243 Win., .270 Win., .30-06, or .308 Win. cal., features M-98 action, walnut finished checkered hardwood stock, action is drilled and tapped, flip-up rear sight and ramp front. Mfg. 1993-94.

	$250	$220	$195	$175	$150	$135	$120

Last MSR was $295.

MODEL 81 CLASSIC - available in 11 cals. between .22-250 Rem. and 7mm Rem. Mag., 24 in. barrel, open sights, 4 shot mag., select checkered walnut with sling swivels, 7 3/4 lbs.

	$795	$595	$475	$395	$340	$300	$280

Last MSR was $900.

  ✱ *Model 81 Classic African* - .375 H&H or 9.3x62mm cal., similar specifications as Model 81 Classic with quarter rib and express sights, engraved action, Pachmayr recoil pad, 9 lbs.

	$925	$725	$600	$500	$425	$360	$330

Last MSR was $1,050.

MODEL 85 SNIPER RIFLE - .308 Win. cal., bolt action, 24 in. heavy barrel, 10 shot mag., camo green synthetic McMillan stock with stippling, built in adj. bipod and recoil pad, enlarged contoured bolt, adj. sights, 12 lbs. 6 oz.

$1,825	$1,450	$1,275	$1,050	$875	$750	$625

Last MSR was $2,050.

MODEL 87 TARGET - .243 Win., 6.5x55mm, .308 Win., .30-06, or .300 Win. Mag. cal., target stock, aperture sights. Mfg. disc. 1992.

$1,375	$1,100	$900	$775	$650	$550	$495

Last MSR was $1,500.

MODEL 1000 STANDARD - .22-250 Rem., .243 Win., 6mm Rem., 6.5x55mm, 7x57mm, 7x64mm, .270 Win., .30-06, or .308 Win. cal., 22 in. barrel, 4 shot built in mag., checkered walnut stock with cheekpiece, open sights, 7 1/4 lbs.

	$425	$375	$325	$290	$260	$240	$220

Last MSR was $495.

GRADING - PPGS™	100%	98%	95%	90%	80%	70%	60%

✳ *Model 1000 Standard Clip* - similar to Model 1000 Standard, except has detachable 4 shot mag.

	$460	$395	$350	$300	$270	$240	$220

Last MSR was $535.

MODEL 1100 LIGHTWEIGHT - available in 9 cals. between .22-250 Rem. and .308 Win., 22 in. barrel, open sights, 4 shot mag., 6 1/2 lbs.

	$435	$380	$325	$290	$260	$240	$220

Last MSR was $510.

✳ *Model 1100M Lightweight African* - .375 H&H, or .458 Win. Mag. cal., 24 in. barrel, 4 shot mag., 9 1/2 lbs.

	$825	$650	$575	$500	$450	$425	$400

Last MSR was $930.

MODEL 1200 SUPER - .22-250 Rem., .243 Win., 6mm, 6.5x55mm, 7x64mm, .270 Win., .30-06, or .308 Win. cal., bolt action, Mauser type action, 24 in. barrel, folding sight, skip checkered walnut stock, pad swivels, rosewood pistol grip cap and forend tip.

	$495	$400	$350	$325	$285	$270	$255

Last MSR was $595.

✳ *Model 1200 Super Clip* - similar to Model 1200 Super, except has detachable 4 shot box mag.

	$525	$425	$375	$350	$300	$280	$265

Last MSR was $640.

MODEL 1300S SCOUT - .243 Win. or .308 Win. cal., 20 in. barrel with muzzle brake, internal 5 shot or detachable 5/10 shot mag., laminated checkered birchwood stock, sling swivels, 8 1/2 lbs.

	$425	$375	$325	$290	$260	$240	$220

Last MSR was $495.

Add $30 for detachable mag. (Model 1300C).

MODEL 1500S SURVIVOR - .308 Win. cal., bolt action, matte stainless construction, black composite (Kevlar/fiberglass) stock, 22 in. barrel, 4 shot mag., 7 lbs. Mfg. began 1993. Disc.

	$395	$350	$300	$270	$240	$210	$185

Last MSR was $450.

Add $30 for detachable mag. (Model 1500C).

This model was made for the Gibbs Rifle Co. by Bell & Carlson, Inc.

RIFLES: BOLT ACTION, MIDLAND SERIES

MODEL 2100 MIDLAND DELUXE - similar to Model 2600 Midland, except has checkered walnut stock and pistol grip cap.

	$335	$280	$235	$210	$190	$180	$170

Last MSR was $390.

MODEL 2600 MIDLAND - .22-250 Rem., .243 Win., 6mm Rem. (disc. 1994), 6.5x55mm (disc. 1994), 7x57mm (disc. 1994), 7x64mm (disc. 1994), .270 Win., .30- 06, or .308 Win. cal., 22 in. barrel, 4 shot mag., checkered hardwood stock with Monte Carlo cheekpiece, open sights, drilled and tapped action, 7 lbs. Disc. 1997.

	$350	$275	$225	$200	$180	$165	$150

Last MSR was $400.

This model was re-introduced during late 1996, utilizing a 1903 Springfield action with choice of 5 shot fixed mag. with hinged floorplate or 3 shot detachable mag.

GRADING - PPGS™	100%	98%	95%	90%	80%	70%	60%

MIDLAND 2700 LIGHTWEIGHT - lightweight variation of the Model 2100 Midland Deluxe featuring tapered barrel, anodized aluminum trigger housing and lightened stock with full pistol grip and recoil pad, Schnabel forend, 6 1/2 lbs.

	$350	$285	$245	$225	$200	$190	$180

Last MSR was $415.

MIDLAND 2800 - similar to Model 2600 Midland, except has laminated birchwood stock, re-introduced during late 1996, utilizing a 1903 Springfield action, 7 lbs. Disc. 1997.

	$360	$295	$250	$215	$195	$185	$175

Last MSR was $430.

SHOTGUNS: SINGLE SHOT

MIDLAND STALKER - 12 ga., trigger bar safety, unique squeeze break open action and cocking system, 28 1/2 in. barrel bored F, hardwood stock and forearm, 6 lbs.

	$90	$65	$55	$45	$35	$30	$25

Last MSR was $110.

GIL, ANTONIO & CO.

Current manufacturer located in Eibar, Spain. Limited U.S. importation. Previously imported and distributed exclusively late 2000-2004 by New England Arms Corp., located in Kittery Point, ME.

All Antonio Gil shotguns are handmade, and can be built to each customer's exact measurements at no extra cost. All models are equipped with chopper lump barrels as a standard feature. Please contact the company directly for more information, including current U.S. pricing and availability (see Trademark Index).

SHOTGUNS: SxS

All models are sidelock only.

Add 10% for 20, 28 ga. or .410 bore.
Add $500-$1,500 for wood upgrade.
Add $1,000-$1,250 per extra set of barrels.
Add $500 for non-selective trigger.

LAGA - 12, 16, 20, 28 ga. or .410 bore, sidelock action with color case hardened receiver and scroll engraving, demi-bloc barrels, DT, deluxe checkered walnut stock and forearm. Importation began 2001.

MSR N/A	$2,250	$1,750	$1,500	$1,350	$1,200	$1,100	$995

OLIMPIA - 12, 16, 20, 28 ga. or .410 bore, sidelock action, features traditional rose and scroll engraving on coin finished receiver. Importation began 2001.

MSR N/A	$2,575	$2,250	$1,750	$1,500	$1,350	$1,200	$1,050

ALHAMBRA - 12, 16, 20, 28 ga. or .410 bore, sidelock action, features elaborate full coverage floral scroll engraving on coin finished receiver and wood upgrade. Importation began 2001.

MSR N/A	$3,625	$3,150	$2,575	$2,250	$1,750	$1,500	$1,350

DIAMOND - 12, 16, 20, 28 ga. or .410 bore, sidelock action, top-of-the-line model with best engraving and best quality wood. Importation began 2001.

MSR N/A	$5,475	$4,650	$4,125	$3,625	$3,050	$2,500	$2,000

GILA RIVER GUN WORKS

Current custom rifle manufacturer located in Pocatello, ID, and previously located in Yuma, AZ.

RIFLES: CUSTOM

Michael Scherz specializes in high-quality, bolt action rifles in .550 Magnum caliber. Please contact him directly for more information, including pricing and availability (see Trademark Index).

GLISENTI

Please refer to the Italian Military Arms section in this text.

GLOCK

Currently manufactured by Glock GmbH in Austria beginning 1983. Glock also opened a production facility for manufacturing its polymer frames in Smyrna, GA during late 2004. Exclusively imported and distributed by Glock, Inc., located in Smyrna, GA. Distributor and dealer sales.

All Glock pistols have a "safe action" safety system (double action only) which includes trigger safety, firing pin safety, and drop safety. Glock pistols have only 35 parts for reliability and simplicity of operation.

PISTOLS: SEMI-AUTO

Add $18 for adj. rear sight, $22 for steel sight (new 2004), or $47 for Glock night sight (new 2004). Add $80 for fixed Meprolight sight or $105 for fixed Trijicon sight (disc. 2003-2004, depending on model.)
Add $25 for internal locking system (ILS) on most currently manufactured models listed below (new 2004).
Add $95 for tactical light or $284 for tactical light with laser for most currently manufactured pistols listed below.

MODEL 17/17C SPORT/SERVICE - 9mm Para. cal., double action, polymer frame, mag., trigger and other pistol parts, 4.49 in. steel hexagonal rifled barrel with (Model 17C, new 1999) or w/o ports, steel slide and springs, 10 (C/B 1994), 17* (reintroduced late 2004), or 19* (reintroduced late 2004) shot mag., adj. (Sport Model) or fixed (Service Model) rear sight, includes lockable pistol box, cable lock, cleaning rod, and other accessories, extra mag. and spare rear sight, 24.75 oz. Importation began late 1985.

MSR $599	$475	$425	$395	$365	$335	$295	$250

Add $22 for Model 17C with fixed (new 2004) or adj. (disc. 2003) rear sight.
Add $119 for competition model w/ adj. sights (Model 17CC, mfg. 2000-2003).

✳ *Model 17L Sport/Service Competition Model* - 9mm Para. cal., competition version of the Model 17, includes internally compensated 6.02 in. barrel, recalibrated trigger pull (3 1/2 lb. pull), adj. rear sight, 26.3 oz. Mfg. 1988-1999.

	$650	$545	$425	$360	$315	$260	$225

Last MSR was $795.

Add $28 for adj. sight.
Early models with barrel ports matched to relieved slide will command a small premium.

✳ *Model 17 Sport/Service Glock Desert Storm Commemorative* - 9mm Para. cal., features coalition forces listing on top of barrel, inscription on side of slide "NEW WORLD ORDER". 1,000 mfg. in 1991 only.

	$995	$825	$600	N/A	N/A	N/A	N/A

Last MSR was $795.

MODEL 19/19C COMPACT SPORT/SERVICE - 9mm Para. cal., similar to Model 17, except has scaled down dimensions with 4.02 in. ported (Model 19C, new 1999) or unported barrel and serrated grip straps, 10 (C/B 1994), 15* (reintroduced late 2004), or 17* (reintroduced late 2004) shot mag., fixed (Service Model) or adj. (Sport Model) rear sight, 23 1/2 oz. New 1988.

MSR $599	$475	$425	$395	$365	$335	$295	$250

Add $22 for Model 19C with fixed (new 2004) or adj. (disc. 2003) rear sight.
Add $119 for competition model w/ adj. sights (Model 19CC, mfg. 2000-2003).

During 1996, AcuSport Corp. commissioned Glock to make a special production run of matching 9mm Para. cal. sets. Each set consists of a Model 19 and 26 with serialization as follows: Model 19 (ser. range AAA0000-AAA0499) and Model 26 (ser. range AAB0000-AAB0499).

MODEL 20/20C SPORT/SERVICE - 10mm Norma cal., similar action to Model 17, features 4.6 in. ported (Model 20C, new 1999) or unported barrel, 10 (C/B 1994) or 15* (reintroduced late 2004) shot mag., larger slide and receiver, fixed (Service Model) or adj. (Sport Model) rear sight, 30 oz. New 1990.

MSR $637		$500	$440	$410	$375	$350	$325	$295

Add $39 for compensated barrel (Model 20C).
Add $145 for competition model w/ adj. sights (Model 20CC, mfg. 2000-2003).

MODEL 21/21C SPORT/SERVICE - .45 ACP cal., similar to Model 20, except has octagonal profile and rifling, 10 (C/B 1994) or 13* (reintroduced late 2004) shot mag., 29 oz. Introduced May 1991.

MSR $637		$500	$440	$410	$375	$350	$325	$295

Add $39 for compensated barrel (Model 21C).
Add $145 for competition model w/ adj. sights (Model 21CC, mfg. 2000-2003).

MODEL 22/22C SPORT/SERVICE - .40 S&W cal., similar to Model 17, except has locking block pin above trigger guard, 4.49 in. barrel, 10 (C/B 1994) or 15* (reintroduced late 2004) shot mag., 25.5 oz. New 1990.

MSR $599		$475	$425	$395	$365	$335	$295	$250

Add $34 for Model 22C with adj. (disc. 2003) or fixed (new 2004) rear sight.
Add $22 for compensated barrel (Model 22C).
Add $119 for competition model w/ adj. sights (Model 22CC, mfg. 2000-2004).

200 Model 22s were originally shipped with serial numbers beginning with "NY-1." Somehow, they probably were erroneously numbered at the factory (probably thinking that they somehow were part of the New York State Troopers shipment of Model 17s) during 1990. Premiums will occur on this variation.

MODEL 23/23C COMPACT SPORT/SERVICE - .40 S&W cal., compact variation of the Model 22 with 4.02 in. ported (Model 23C, new 1999) or unported barrel and 10 (C/B 1994) or 13* (reintroduced 2004) shot mag., 23 1/2 oz. New 1990.

MSR $599		$475	$425	$395	$365	$335	$295	$250

Add $22 for compensated barrel (Model 23C).
Add $145 for competition model w/ adj. sights (Model 23CC, mfg. 2000-2003).

During 1996, AcuSport Corp. commissioned Glock to make a special production run of matching .40 S&W cal. sets. Each set consists of a Model 23 and 27 with serialization as follows: Model 23 (ser. range AAC0000-AAC1499) and Model 27 (ser. range AAD0000-AAD1499).

MODEL 24/24C - .40 S&W cal., similar to Model 17L Competition, choice of standard or ported (Model 24C) barrel and fixed or adj. rear sight. Mfg. 1994-99.

		$665	$525	$415	$350	$300	$250	$225

Last MSR was $795.

Add $40 for compensated barrel.
Add $28 for adj. rear sight.

MODEL 25 - .380 ACP cal., similar to Model 19 with 4.02 in. barrel, 10 shot mag., 22.5 oz. New 1995.

This model is available for law enforcement only.

MODEL 26 - 9mm Para. cal., sub-compact variation of the Model 19, except has shortened grip, 3 1/2 in. barrel, 10 shot mag., 21 3/4 oz. New 1995.

MSR $599		$475	$425	$395	$365	$335	$295	$250

MODEL 27 - .40 S&W cal., sub-compact variation of the Model 23, except has shortened grip, 3 1/2 in. barrel, 9 shot mag., 21 3/4 oz. New 1995.

MSR $599		$475	$425	$395	$365	$335	$295	$250

MODEL 28 - .380 ACP cal., similar to Model 26/27/33, except has scaled down dimensions with 3.46 in. barrel, approx. 20 oz. New 1999.

This model is available for law enforcement only.

MODEL 29 - 10mm Norma cal., sub-compact model featuring 3.78 in. barrel, 10 shot mag., 27 oz. New 1997.

MSR $637		$500	$440	$410	$375	$350	$325	$295

GRADING - PPGS™	100%	98%	95%	90%	80%	70%	60%

MODEL 30 - .45 ACP cal., compact Model 21, 3 3/4 in. barrel, 10 shot mag., features octagonal profile rifling, and extension on mag., 26 1/2 oz. New 1997.

MSR $637	$500	$440	$410	$375	$350	$325	$295

MODEL 31/31C - .357 SIG cal., similar to Model 17, 4.49 in. ported (Model 31C, new 1999) or unported barrel, fixed sights, 10 shot mag., 26 oz. New 1998.

MSR $599	$475	$425	$395	$365	$335	$295	$250

    Add $22 for compensated barrel (Model 31C).
    Add $119 for competition model w/ adj. sights (Model 31CC, mfg. 2000-2004).

MODEL 32/32C - .357 SIG cal., similar to Model 19, 4.02 in. ported (Model 32C) or unported barrel, 24 oz. New 1998.

MSR $599	$475	$425	$395	$365	$335	$295	$250

    Add $22 for compensated barrel (Model 32C).
    Add $119 for competition model w/adj. sights (Model 32CC, mfg. 2002-2004).

MODEL 33 - .357 SIG cal., compact variation of Models 31 & 32, features 3 1/2 in. barrel with shortened frame and magazine housing, 10 shot mag., 22 oz. New 1998.

MSR $599	$475	$425	$395	$365	$335	$295	$250

MODEL 34 - 9mm Para. cal., similar construction to Model 17, except has 5.32 in. barrel, extended slide stop lever and magazine catch, fixed sights, target grips with finger grooves, thumbrest, receiver has rails for mounting accessories, 10 shot mag., 25.75 oz. New 1998.

MSR $679	$525	$450	$375	$325	$295	$260	$225

MODEL 35 - .40 S&W cal., 27.5 oz., otherwise similar to Model 34. New 1998.

MSR $679	$525	$450	$375	$325	$295	$260	$225

MODEL 36 - .45 ACP cal., similar to Model 30, except has single column 6 shot mag., 22 1/2 oz. New 1999.

MSR $637	$500	$440	$410	$375	$350	$325	$295

MODEL 37 - .45 G.A.P. (Glock Automatic Pistol) cal., 4.6 in. barrel, similar to Model 21, except has extended slide stop lever, wider and heavier slide, changed locking block and ejector, 10 shot double column mag., 26 oz. New 2003.

MSR $614	$535	$450	$375	$325	$295	$260	$225

MODEL 38 - .45 G.A.P. cal., similar to Model 37, 3.46 in. barrel, double action, compact design, 8 shot double column mag., 19.33 oz.

MSR $614	$535	$450	$375	$325	$295	$260	$225

MODEL 39 - .45 G.A.P. cal., 6 shot single column mag., 3.46 in. barrel, subcompact design, 19.33 oz.

MSR $614	$535	$450	$375	$325	$295	$260	$225

PISTOLS: SEMI-AUTO, COMMEMORATIVES

The author wishes to express his thanks to Mr. Shawn McCarver and the Glock Collectors Association for providing the following information.

In 1991, Glock released its first commemorative, the Model 17 Desert Storm Commemorative. Slide markings include "New World Order" and "Operation Desert Storm, Jan. 16-Feb. 24th, 1991". 1,000 were mfg. in serial range UD000US-UD999US. Cases included desert camo material inside.

During 1996, 2,000 "Centennial Georgia Olympic Games" Model 17 pistols were produced in serial range BZE000US-BZE999US and CAE000US-CAE999US. The side of slide was engraved "Atlanta, Georgia, Security Team USA 1996". These guns came with a walnut display case.

Also in 1996, 73 special Glock 23s were made to commemorate the 50th anniversary of the Bell helicopter. Pistols had the Bell 50-year "Ping" logo on the right side of the slide, and the Atlanta 1996 Olympic logo on top of the slide. Serial range was BELL000-BELLL072.

Additionally in 1996, there were 500 matching 9mm Para. cal. sets of the Model 19 and 26 and 1,500 matching .40 S&W cal. sets of the Model 23 and 27 produced. These sets were called "Defense Sets". Approx. 500 total sets exist. It is beleived that some dealers may have broken up the sets for resale.

In 1999, approx. 80 "Alaska Statehood" Model 27 pistols were produced. The side of the slide was engraved with "1959-1999 40 Years of Alaska Statehood". Additionally, a picture outline of Alaska was engraved on the slide. Also in 1999, a one only model, "1 of 1" Ducks Unlimited "Great Outdoors" Model 27 was produced. The side of the slide was engraved with "Ducks Unlimited Great Outdoors" with a high polish blue finish on the slide.

Also during 1999, the "2 Millionth" Glock 17 pistol, ser. no. DAP000US was auctioned off at a Sheriff's Police gun show. This gun bears the engraved signature of Gaston Glock and had an engraved slide. Proceeds were donated to law enforcement. A sister pistol, ser. no. 2,000,001 was auctioned off in Nuremberg, Germany.

During 2000, 725 "NRA" Model 22 pistols were produced. The side of the slide was engraved with "NRA". These guns were made for raffles at various NRA dinners.

In 2001, an unlimited number of Model 17 "GSSF" were produced in serial range GSSF000US to GSSFXXX. The side of the slide was engraved with "GSSF" and "Ten Years of Safe Shooting 1991-2001". There are 55,000 or more members of the GSSF, and these pistols were mfg. for members only.

In 2002, 1,000 pistol runs of the Models 17, 21, and 22 "America's Heroes" were produced in memory of the Sept. 11, 2001 attack on the World Trade Center. Model 17 was serialed USA0000US-USA0999US, Model 21 was serialed USA1000US-USA1999US, and Model 22 was serialed USA2000US-USA2999US. Each gun had a 0, 1, and 2 in front of each serial number to keep the USA prefix on all three pistols. On one side of the slide next to each other was lasered "PD" in a six sided star, "America's Heroes" in scroll, and "FD" in a Maltese cross. Pistols were distributed by Acusport to dealers, and were done to honor the NYPD and NYFD.

Further research is under way for current pricing on Glock commemoratives.

GOLAN
See KSN Industries Ltd. listing.

GOLDEN EAGLE
Previous trademark of rifles/shotguns produced by Nikko Limited located in Tochigi, Japan, circa 1975-1981.

Please refer to the Nikko Firearms Limited listing in this text for a complete chronological history of Nikko - Japan's previous long gun manufacturer.

RIFLES: BOLT ACTION

MODEL 7000 GRADE I - bolt action, all popular American calibers, including .270 Win., and .300 Wby. Mag., 24 or 26 in. barrels, select skipline checkered walnut stock, rosewood forend tip, golden eagle head engraved in pistol grip cap, recoil pad. Mfg. 1976-81.

$600	$550	$525	$450	$375	$340	$290

MODEL 7000 GRADE I AFRICAN - .375 H&H and .458 Win. Mag. cal., similar to 7000, open sights.

$650	$590	$555	$480	$400	$365	$315

MODEL 7000 GRADE II - scroll engraving, better grade wood.

$690	$625	$590	$510	$430	$395	$340

SHOTGUNS: O/U

MODEL 5000 GRADE I (FIELD) - 12 or 20 ga., 26, 28, or 30 in. barrels, various chokes, vent. rib, engraved frame, gold eagle head inlay, auto ejectors, SST, checkered pistol grip beavertail stock. Mfg. 1975-81.

$850	$775	$700	$625	$560	$510	$440

MODEL 5000 GRADE I SKEET - similar to 5000 Field, except 26 or 28 in. skeet bored, wide rib.

$875	$800	$725	$650	$580	$510	$440

GRADING - PPGS™	100%	98%	95%	90%	80%	70%	60%

MODEL 5000 GRADE I TRAP - similar to 5000 Field, except 30 or 32 in. barrel, mod. and full, imp. mod. and full, or full and full choke, wide rib, trap stock with pad.

	100%	98%	95%	90%	80%	70%	60%
	$875	$800	$725	$650	$580	$510	$440

MODEL 5000 GRADE II - available in Field, Trap, and Skeet, more engraving, better grade wood, with screaming eagle on frame in gold.

	100%	98%	95%	90%	80%	70%	60%
	$950	$875	$790	$710	$630	$540	$460
Skeet	$975	$895	$810	$725	$640	$540	$460
Trap	$975	$895	$810	$725	$640	$540	$460

GRANDEE GRADE III - similar to 5000 Grade II, except elaborate engraving, inlays, and better grade wood.

	$2,500	$2,200	$1,900	$1,575	$1,250	$1,000	$850

GOLDEN STATE ARMS

Previous importer located in Pasadena, CA. Golden State Arms imported and subcontracted various firearms constructed by European and Japanese manufacturers - achieving private label status on some guns.

Most firearms previously imported by Golden State Arms (including private labels) are not that collectible. In many cases, the shooting value will determine the price of a specimen. In some models or configurations which are currently desirable, however, premiums may exist.

GONCZ ARMAMENT, INC.

Previous manufacturer located in North Hollywood, CA circa 1984-1990.

While advertised, BATF records indicate very few Goncz pistols or carbines were actually produced. All of these guns were prototypes or individually hand-built and none were ever mass produced through normal fabrication techniques. In 1990, Claridge Hi-Tec, Inc. purchased Goncz Armament, Inc.

GRAND POWER s.r.o.

Current manufacturer located in the Slovak Republic. Currently imported beginning 2007 by STI International, located in Georgetown, TX.

Grand Power s.r.o. manufactures a lightweight semi-auto polymer pistol in 9mm Para. cal. Please contact the importer directly for more information, including availability and pricing (see Trademark Index).

GRANGER, G.

Current manufacturer established during 1902, and located in Saint Etienne, France. Current U.S. agent is Jean-Jacques Perodeau, located in Enid, OK.

All guns are made on a custom order basis. Please contact the U.S. agent directly for more information (please refer to Trademark Index).

SHOTGUNS: SxS, SIDELOCK

GRANGER SxS - 12, 16, 20, or 28 ga., case hardened receiver, Granger sidelock mechanism and plates, DT or SNT, choice of pistol or straight grip, deluxe French walnut stock and forearm, prices will vary per older customer specifications and appointments, delivery time is 12-36 months. Limited mfg.

Add $4,767 for fine English engraving.
Add $1,783 for Aiglon fastening action.

Please contact the importer directly for pricing and availability.

GRANITE MOUNTAIN ARMS, INC.

Current rifle and action manufacturer located in Phoenix, AZ. Previously located in Prescott, AZ. Consumer and dealer sales.

Granite Mountain Arms, Inc. manufactures a double square bridge Mauser magnum rifle and action, available in four sizes, in both left and right hand. Sizes range from Short Magnum, Standard Magnum, Express Magnum, and the African Express Magnum for the largest of calibers such as the .505 Gibbs and the .585 cal. Rifles start at $8,500 and go up accordingly, depending on features, caliber and other specifications. Please contact the company directly for more information, including availability and pricing (see Trademark Index).

GRADING - PPGS™	100%	98%	95%	90%	80%	70%	60%

GRANT, STEPHEN

Current trademark manufactured by Atkin, Grant & Lang, established in 1867, and located in Hertfordshire, England.

The Stephen Grant trademark is responsible for mostly custom order SxS rifles and shotguns. Shotguns can be top or side lever and are equipped with sidelocks and a self-opening mechanism. Please contact the company directly for current information, availability, delivery time, and custom order pricing.

Atkin, Grant & Lang provide a useful historical research service on older Stephen Grant shotguns and rifles. The charge for this service is £25 per gun, and the company will give you all pertinent factory information regarding the history.

RIFLES: SxS

Prices on current custom order rifles and shotguns do not include VAT or importation costs.

SIDELOCK MODEL - various cals. between .300 H&H - .577 NE, best quality sidelock, individually made per customer specifications.

MSR N/A	N/A	$39,250	$35,000	$31,000	$27,000	$24,000	$20,500

SHOTGUNS: O/U

Prices on current custom order rifles and shotguns do not include VAT or importation costs.

SIDELOCK MODEL - 12, 16, 20, 28 ga., or 410 bore, best quality sidelock ejector, individually made per customer specifications.

MSR N/A	N/A	$18,500	$15,000	$12,000	$10,000	$8,850	$7,500

Add 20% for 20 ga.
Add 30% for 28 ga. and .410 bore.

SHOTGUNS: SxS

Prices on current custom order rifles and shotguns do not include VAT or importation costs.

SIDELOCK MODEL - 12, 16, 20, 28 ga., or .410 bore, best quality sidelock ejector, top or side lever opening, individually made per customer specifications.

MSR N/A	N/A	$12,000	$9,900	$8,700	$7,500	$6,250	$5,000

Add 20% for 20 ga.
Add 30% for 28 ga. and .410 bore.

GREAT WESTERN ARMS COMPANY

Previous manufacturer located in Los Angeles, CA circa 1954-1964.

Most firearms enthusiasts are more or less familiar with Great Western Arms Co., an enterprise initially organized in Los Angeles through the efforts of Hy Hunter and established by three partners; Dr. Hassam, a prominent surgeon, Dan Reeves, owner of the L.A. Rams and Dan Fortmann. Bill Wilson, a former production engineer at North American Aviation, served as president.

Wilson established his shop in a tin covered building on Minor Street in Southgate, CA and staffed it with a small group of employees, some taken from Weatherby. As time went by, as many as fifty workers were busy producing guns.

Hy Hunter's American Weapons Corp. in Burbank was chosen by the partners to be the exclusive distributor. Hunter so aggressively marketed the Frontier Six Shooter that his name became synonymous with Great Western and many believed that he was the owner of the company.

With Bob Green as financial officer and Bill Hensley as plant superintendent, machining of parts to manufacture exact copies of the original Colt Model P began in early 1954. Fitting, de-burring, polishing, finishing and assembly began slowly in the spring, eventually gaining notoriety with the proprietary .357 Atomic cartridge.

Great Western Arms Co. operated for approximately ten years, during which time they were reorganized by at least five different owners. Albeit the company was well funded with $250,000 initially, it was never stable, lacking in manufacturing expertise and management skills. But they made up for it with enthusiasm and a genuine desire to

GRADING - PPGS™	100%	98%	95%	90%	80%	70%	60%

accommodate their customers.

Appearing in early Great Western brochures and catalogues were spokesmen John Wayne and Audie Murphy. Exhibition shooters Dee Woolem and Sam Toole represented the company with their fast draw talents.

The Great Western revolver line-up offered a well-rounded out variety of models with sub-variants. A good selection of barrel lengths, finishes, decoration and calibers were available. They offered interchangeable auxiliary cylinders and a variety of other special and innovative accessories.

The author would like to thank Mr. John Dougan for providing information and values for this section.

ADDITIONAL HISTORY

Examination and survey of approximately four hundred Great Western revolvers and derringers revealed the following.

- A small, quantity of smooth bore guns were shipped.
- Single-actions with a through the frame firing pin hole feature a full radius to the front of the cylinder frame, indicating it to be of Colt origin. Many of the earliest revolvers were made with the Colt cylinder frame; serial number 73, 95, 111, 245, 332, 348 and 367.
- Serial number GW5543 is roll marked on the side of the cylinder frame "GREAT WESTERN LOS ANGELES"
- Occasionally an example will be found that has a letter T stamped on the cylinder frame. Assembler Toni Rimerez hand stamped the guns that she assembled until she was instructed to stop.
- Some revolvers feature chrome lined barrels.
- Standard finishes were cyanide case colored, blued, chrome, nickel, silver, gold and bead blasted and blued.
- A specially fabricated Great Western revolver was built to be used by Don Knotts in the Disney production, *The Shakiest Gun in the West*, it was designed to fall apart upon cocking.

DERRINGERS

GREAT WESTERN DERRINGER - .38 S&W or .38 S&W Spl. cal. (not interchangeable). Basically an improved version of the Remington Double Derringer frame.

	$800	$750	$700	$600	$550	$500	$450

Add a premium for engraving, plating and presentation case.

One verified .22 WRM prototype is known.

Some derringers were shipped with plated finishes and several are known to have been engraved. One cased salesman sample, serial number 1838 was engraved by Carl Courts, it is gold & silver plated and fitted with pearl grip panels.

Derringer serial number 25 was given to Elvis.

There were two distinct frame configurations specific to the hinge, at first the hinge was in identical proportion to the original Remington, and like the originals many failed. A more robust hinge was introduced and is visually discernable. The original configuration was referred to in Great Western catalogues and parts lists as the Old Model and the guns with the larger hinge lug were of course referred to as the New Model. The change occurred at approximately serial number 1800.

REVOLVERS: SINGLE ACTION

FRONTIER SIX SHOOTER - chambered for .22 rimfire and a variety of centerfire calibers, 4 3/4, 5 1/2, 7 1/2, or 12 in. barrel, plastic faux stag (standard), walnut, stag, pearl or ivory grips, cyanide case colored, blue, chrome or nickel plated finish, Christy Gun Works firing pin mounted in recoil shield.

	$650	$600	$550	$450	$400	$350	$300

Add a premium for plating or presentation case.
Add $100 for 12 in. Buntline model.

A .22 LR/.22 Mag. convertible model was listed in the catalog.

GRADING - PPGS™	100%	98%	95%	90%	80%	70%	60%

SHERIFF'S MODEL - .45 LC cal., nickel, blue, cyanide case colored finish, plastic faux stag grips standard.

	$750	$700	$650	$550	$500	$450	$400

Add a premium for plating or presentation case.

Aside from the definitive short barrel, Sheriffs Models were made with three features which distinguished them from the rest of the guns. Oral history is that Great Western purchased Colt's existing inventory of single-action parts, cylinder frames and some tools when they began operations.

When viewed from the bottom, the Sheriffs Model offers strong evidence of this, all Sheriffs Models examined feature a full radius to the front of the cylinder frame, whereas the Great Western frames exhibit a pinched and elliptical appearance. Further, all of the Sheriffs Models examined feature a Colt hammer with the firing pin and a hole through the recoil shield. It is believed that these cylinder frames were actually made by Colt.

To make a Sheriffs Model, the ejector rod housing lug was simply removed. It has been noted that Sheriffs Models are serial numbered below 400.

The words "GREAT WESTERN" were roll marked on the side of the barrel, there was not space enough on top of the barrels.

FAST DRAW MODEL - solid brass backstrap and triggerguard, 4 3/4 in. barrel, blue finish, plastic faux stag grips.

	$675	$625	$575	$475	$425	$375	$325

Dee Woolem initiated the Fast Draw project and personally fitted and set-up each gun. Based on the Frontier Six Shooter, these revolvers came from the factory fitted with a solid brass back-strap and trigger-guard. The hammer spur was slightly longer and turned upward. The action was smoothed-up.

TARGET MODEL - most .22 LR cal., blue or case colored finish.

	$700	$650	$600	$500	$450	$400	$350

Again, based on the Frontier Six Shooter, this model was fitted with a MICRO front blade and adjustable rear sights. The top strap was planed or milled flat and the rear sight mounted with two screws. Various calibers and barrel lengths were shipped, most were .22 LR cal. Blue or case colored examples are known.

DEPUTY MODEL - .22 LR, .38 Spl., or .357 Mag. cal., 4 in. barrel, deluxe blue finish, walnut grips.

	$800	$750	$700	$600	$550	$500	$450

Announced in 1956, the first of these special revolvers were designated for Great Western Arms Co. distributors and dealers. The accepted quantity is sixty guns. They all feature a 4" barrel with a full length sight rib with adjustable rear sight. These are the rarest of the cataloged Great Western revolvers, according to Great Western's service manager John McCormick, they number less than 100 and until recent years, many believed that only prototype Deputy Models were made. They appear in the 17XXX - 19XXX serial number range.

ENGRAVED MODEL

Values will vary depending on the configuration, engraver, case, provenance, and verification of authenticity.

Offered from the beginning, this model could be ordered with any amount of coverage in any style of engraving or inlay. Cattle brand engraving was popular. Finishes were gold, silver, nickel and blue.

Carl Courts was Great Western's primary artist and engraved most of the verifiable revolvers, including the following cased presentation pairs - serial numbers GW1 & GW2 for Bill Wilson, serial numbers GW3 & GW4 for Dan Fortmann and serial numbers GW9828 & GW9737 for Mel Torme, a brace with 4 3/4 in. barrels for John Wayne which were later used in The Shootist, his last movie in 1976.

Special engraved single examples were serial numbers, GW73 factory sales sample, GW5000 for President Eisenhower, A.A. White engraved serial number 17694. Carl Courts engraved another for the Duke. George Montgomery received GW5571 & GW5572 and 17856 & 17857, the officers and crew of the USS Taluga presented Capt. R.H. Caldwell with serial numbers 12250 & 12251. Nickel plated serial number 12838 for film actor Arvo Ojala. Exhibition shooters Sam Toole and Dee Woolem were presented with cased pairs. Dozens of other notable personalities were presented revolvers and Derringers.

Ruger engraver Charles H. Jerred completed at least one gun, serial number 11390 in November 1955 and the correspondence between Wilson and Jerred suggest that he may have engraved others.

Cole Agee was a well known and popular engraver at the time and according to John McCormick engraved the pair of 5 ½ in. Frontier Models that John Wayne is pictured holding in the photograph on the back of Great Western catalogs. Agee is also credited with engraving a Derringer for the Duke.

KIT GUNS

Unassembled in box - $650.
Unassembled with no box - $400.
Assembled - depending on quality of fit and finish - $200 - $300.

Unthinkable in today's climate of litigation, Great Western sold guns that could be assembled and completed at the kitchen table with a few basic tools and average skills. The kit guns came with all machining complete, all holes were drilled and tapped and the final contours roughed out. To finish the gun, the customer would de-burr and final polish all surfaces. Of course the lock-work had to be cleaned-up and honed and the preferred finish applied.

According to service manager John McCormick there could have been as many as 1000 Kit Guns shipped.

Typically, the first digit of the serial number on Kit Guns is zero, followed by five numbers, i.e. 020173. The Kit Guns first made their debut in the 1956 catalog and were priced at $59.95. Unassembled Kit Guns in the original box with assembly instructions are extremely rare.

THE MYTHS OF GREAT WESTERN ARMS COMPANY

Very often, either one or two of the prevailing misconceptions will be raised at the mention of Great Western Arms Co., depending upon the respondents' knowledge of firearms. One is that Hy Hunter was the founder and owner of Great Western. The second myth is Great Western revolvers and derringers were manufactured in Italy, Spain or Germany.

Hy Hunter, *arms dealer to the stars*, aggressively promoted Great Western through his American Weapons Corp., retail store and his catalog. Hunter fostered the Frontier Six Shooter to a degree that his name became a synonym for Great Western. In the beginning Hunter served in the capacity as sole West Coast distributor and was never an equity partner or corporately involved with any of the four companies that bore the Great Western marquee. Further, the back page of the 1956 GW Arms Sales Company, Inc. catalogue makes the following statement.

Note: Great Western Arms Company is the manufacturer, GW Arms Sales Co. is the distributor and there are no agreements expressed or implied between these companies and Hy Hunter, American Weapons and/or Crown International of Burbank, California, and these companies have not been purchasers of Great Western products since about the middle of 1955.

Eventually, in the early 1960s, Hunter imported and marketed a line of lower quality European made single-action revolvers and derringers that were roll-marked with his name. Hy Hunter marked guns are relatively scarce today and there is not much collector interest in the single-action revolvers or derringers.

Secondly, no Great Western components were fabricated offshore. Castings, barrels and other parts were provided by outside contractors. An exception can be the stag, pearl and ivory grip panels traditionally produced overseas and imported by grip distributors. Final fitting, polishing, finishing and assembly were accomplished in-house. All Great Western facilities and correspondent shops were located in and around Los Angeles, Burbank and Long Beach, which were the West Coast equivalent to Bridgeport and New Haven.

During WW II, Southern California developed the same capabilities for manufacturing as New England and was the greatest producer of war material on the Pacific Rim.

Following is an annual production schedule. At this juncture, it is an educated guess based on surviving documents, letters, and invoices, and should be used as a general guide only.

1953	GW1 - GW150
1954	GW150 - GW4500
1955	GW4500 - GW11000
1956	GW11000 - GW11500
1957	11500 - 15000
1958	15000 - 17000
1959	17000 - 18500
1960	18500 - 20500
1961	GW20500 - GW21500
1963	GW21500 - GW22000

Regrettably, from a collector perspective, interest in the Great Western guns has remained an esoteric subject, however, at the time of this writing, a dedicated following seems to be rallying. Along with other short lived modern manufacturers, Great Western Arms Co. should some day be afforded the same status as some obscure pre-Victorian makers now enjoy.

GRADING - PPGS™	100%	98%	95%	90%	80%	70%	60%

GREEN, ROGER

Current custom gun maker located in Evansville, WY.

Roger Green builds high quality custom made rifles and shotguns to order per customer's specifications. A variety of gunsmithing services are also available. Please contact him directy for more information, including pricing, availability, and custom order options (see Trademark Index).

GREENER, W.W., LIMITED

Current manufacturer established in 1829 and located in Hagley, England, with sales and administration offices located in Wiltshire, England. No current U.S. importation. Until 1994, Gibbs Rifle Co. located in Martinsburg, WV was the U.S. agent.

RIFLES: SxS, CURRENT MFG.

Boxlock and sidelock rifle quotations may be obtained by writing the company directly (see Trademark Index). A complete choice of calibers, engraving options, and walnut selection are available on a special order basis only.

SHOTGUNS: SINGLE SHOT

GENERAL PURPOSE - 12 ga., improved Martini action, single shot, 26, 30, or 32 in. barrel, full or mod., auto ejectors, straight checkered stock.

	100%	98%	95%	90%	80%	70%	60%
	$330	$305	$275	$220	$195	$165	$160

GP MK II - 12 ga. only, famed general purpose (GP) English shotgun configuration featuring Greener Martini action, 28 or 30 in. barrel, walnut stock and forearm. Mfg. resumed in 1991.

MSR N/A	$522	$450	$400	$350	$300	$250	$195

Older, used military contract variations of this model have been imported recently - typically seen in the $165-$200 range.

SHOTGUNS: SxS, DISC.

FARKILLER GRADE F35 - 12 ga., 28, 30, or 32 in. barrels, hammerless boxlock, checkered straight or semi-pistol grip stock.

	$2,420	$2,200	$2,090	$1,870	$1,760	$1,650	$1,540
Auto ejectors	$3,300	$3,025	$2,750	$2,475	$2,035	$1,925	$1,650

FARKILLER GRADE F35 LARGE BORE - 8 or 10 ga., similar to F35.

	$2,750	$2,585	$2,310	$2,090	$1,980	$1,815	$1,650
Auto ejectors	$3,575	$3,300	$3,080	$2,860	$2,640	$2,090	$1,925

HAMMERLESS EJECTOR MODELS - 12, 16, 20, 28 ga., or .410 bore, 26, 28, or 30 in. barrels supplied with any choke combination, auto ejectors, single or double triggers, straight or semi-pistol grip stock, grades differ as follows:

✳ *Hammerless Ejector Model Jubilee Grade DH35*

	$2,420	$2,255	$2,090	$1,925	$1,650	$1,540	$1,375

✳ *Hammerless Ejector Model Sovereign Grade DH40*

	$2,860	$2,695	$2,420	$2,200	$1,980	$1,815	$1,595

✳ *Hammerless Ejector Model Crown Grade DH55*

	$3,300	$3,080	$2,915	$2,750	$2,420	$2,035	$1,760

✳ *Hammerless Ejector Model Royal Grade DH75*

	$4,400	$4,180	$3,850	$3,300	$3,080	$2,915	$2,640

Add $400 for SST.

Note: Degree of engraving and grade of wood are the basic differences between models.

EMPIRE - 12 ga. only, 2 3/4 or 3 in., any choke, 28, 30, or 32 in. barrel, hammerless, boxlock, straight stock or semi pistol grip.

	$1,760	$1,540	$1,320	$1,100	$935	$825	$770
Auto ejectors	$1,980	$1,760	$1,540	$1,320	$1,155	$1,045	$990

GRADING - PPGS™	100%	98%	95%	90%	80%	70%	60%

EMPIRE DELUXE - similar to Empire, only better grade wood.

	100%	98%	95%	90%	80%	70%	60%
	$1,980	$1,760	$1,540	$1,320	$1,155	$1,045	$990
Auto ejectors	$2,200	$1,980	$1,760	$1,540	$1,375	$1,265	$1,100

SHOTGUNS: SxS, CURRENT MFG.

Various hard and soft cases are available for the following models with prices ranging from $500 up to $3,200.

NO. 5 NEEDHAM EJECTOR - 12, 16, 20 ga., or .410 bore, scalloped boxlock action, DT, any barrel length.

MSR N/A	$4,470	$3,750	$3,175	$2,750	$2,250	$1,825	$1,475

This model has been re-introduced to commemorate the takeover of J. V. Needham by W.W. Greener in 1874.

DH 40 - similar to No. 5 Needham Ejector, except has better engraving and deluxe walnut stock and forearm.

MSR N/A	$6,705	$5,900	$5,000	$4,250	$3,500	$2,850	$2,100

DH 75 - 12 ga. only, 2 3/4 in. chambers, Greener "Facile Princeps" scalloped boxlock action 27, 28, or 30 in. barrels, case hardened receiver, choice of engraving (game scene or fine scroll work).

MSR N/A	$11,175	$9,950	$8,450	$7,250	$6,000	$4,950	$3,875

DOH 90 - 12, 16, 20 ga., or .410 bore, 2 1/2, 2 3/4 or 3 in. Mag. chambers, best boxlock featuring Anson & Deeley scalloped boxlock action with Greener easy-opening device, French walnut stock, DT.

MSR N/A	$14,900	$12,500	$9,750	$8,250	$7,000	$5,850	$4,675

L 120 - 12, 16, 20 ga., or .410 bore, best sidelock ejector model with dovetail lump barrels, fine scroll engraving with choice of bright or color case hardened frame finish.

MSR N/A	$22,350	$19,500	$16,000	$13,000	$10,000	$7,850	$6,000

L 150 - 12, 16, 20 ga., or .410 bore, 2 1/2 or 3 in. chambers, very best sidelock ejector model with chopper lump barrels and easy-opening device, bright or color case hardened frame finish.

MSR N/A	$29,800	$24,000	$21,000	$17,000	$14,000	$11,000	$8,500

L 500 - 12, 16, 20 ga., or .410 bore, new St. George sidelock ejector model incorporating top-of-the-line carved engraving, walnut, and workmanship.

Because this model is entirely custom ordered per individual choice, a price quotation is necessary on every order.

GREIFELT AND COMPANY

Previous manufacturer located in Suhl, Germany (formerly East Germany).

COMBINATION GUNS

COMBINATION MODEL - 12, 16, 20, 28 ga., or .410 bore, shotgun barrel, rifle in any rimmed caliber, 24 or 26 in. solid rib barrel, pre-WWII.

	$5,200	$4,800	$4,400	$4,000	$3,600	$3,150	$2,800

Add $700 for auto ejectors.
Subtract 10% for 16 ga.
Add 20% for 28 ga. or .410 bore.
Subtract 40-50% for obsolete rifle caliber.
Above values for 12 or 20 ga. over obtainable rifle cartridge.

GRADING - PPGS™	100%	98%	95%	90%	80%	70%	60%

DRILLINGS

DRILLING MODEL - 12, 16, or 20 ga., SxS shotgun over rimmed rifle caliber, 26 in. barrels, boxlock, extractors, double triggers, rifle sight activated by barrel selector, pre-WWII.

		$3,500	$3,000	$2,750	$2,550	$2,300	$2,000	$1,750

Subtract 10% for 16 ga.
Subtract 40-50% for obsolete cals.
Above values for 12 or 20 ga. over obtainable rifle cartridge.

SHOTGUNS: O/U

GRADE NO. 1 - 12, 16, 20, 28 ga., or .410 bore, O/U, any barrel 26-32 in., choke, vent. or solid rib, Anson & Deeley boxlock, auto ejectors, checkered pistol grip or English stock, pre-war.

12 or 20 ga.

	$3,600	$3,200	$2,850	$2,500	$2,100	$1,750	$1,500

Subtract 10% for 16 ga.
Add 30% for 28 ga. or .410 bore.
Add $300 for vent. rib.
Add $400 for SST.

GRADE NO. 3 - similar to No. 1, except less elaborate engraving, pre-WWII.

12 or 20 ga.

	$2,850	$2,500	$2,200	$2,000	$1,650	$1,350	$1,200

Subtract 10% for 16 ga.
Add 20% for 28 ga. or .410 bore.
Add $300 for vent. rib.
Add $400 for SST.

MODEL 143E - similar to No. 1, except not as high quality as pre-war model, not available in 28 ga. or .410 bore. Mfg. post-WWII.

		$2,400	$2,150	$1,850	$1,550	$1,350	$1,175	$1,000

Add 10% for vent. rib and SST.

SHOTGUNS: SxS

MODEL 22 - 12 or 20 ga., 28 or 30 in. mod. and full, hammerless, boxlock, false side-plates, extractors, checkered pistol grip or English style stock, post-WWII.

		$2,200	$1,760	$1,595	$1,320	$1,100	$990	$825

MODEL 22E - similar to Model 22, except has auto ejectors.

		$2,750	$2,200	$1,980	$1,760	$1,540	$1,430	$1,265

MODEL 103 - 12 or 16 ga., 28 or 30 in. mod. and full, extractors, double triggers, checkered pistol grip or English stock, post-war.

		$1,980	$1,650	$1,485	$1,210	$990	$880	$715

MODEL 103E - similar to Model 103, except has auto ejectors.

		$2,200	$1,760	$1,595	$1,320	$1,100	$990	$825

GRENDEL, INC.

Previous manufacturer located in Rockledge, FL, circa 1990-95.

PISTOLS: SEMI-AUTO

MODEL P-10 SERIES - .380 ACP cal., blowback double action, 10 shot mag., small dimensions, hammerless, matte blue finish, 15 oz. Mfg. disc. 1991.

		$140	$125	$115	$105	$95	$90	$85

Last MSR was $155.

Add $15 for electroless nickel finish.
Add $15 for nickel green finish.
Green finish was available at no extra charge.

GRADING - PPGS™	100%	98%	95%	90%	80%	70%	60%

MODEL P-12 - .380 ACP cal., double action only, 3 in. barrel, steel construction with polymer grip area, no external safety, 11 shot Zytel mag., blue or electroless nickel finish, 11 lb. trigger pull, 13 oz. Mfg. 1992-95.

	$155	$135	$120	$110	$100	$90	$80

Last MSR was $175.

      Add $20 for nickel finish.
      Add $50 for threaded barrel with muzzle brake parts option.

MODEL P-30 - .22 Mag. cal., blowback similar action to P-12, 5 in. barrel, hammerless, matte black finish, 10 (C/B 1994) or 30* shot mag., 21 oz. Mfg. 1990-95.

	$240	$200	$175	$155	$140	$125	$115

Last MSR was $225.

      Add $25 for electroless nickel finish (disc. 1991).
      Add $35 for scope mount (Weaver base).

   ✳ *Model P-30M* - similar to Model P-30, except has 5.6 in. barrel with removable muzzle brake. Mfg. 1990-95.

	$250	$210	$180	$160	$140	$125	$115

Last MSR was $235.

      Add $25 for electroless nickel finish (disc. 1991).

MODEL P-30L - similar to Model P-30, except has 8 in. barrel with removable muzzle brake, 22 oz. Mfg. 1991-92.

	$275	$235	$200	$180	$160	$140	$125

Last MSR was $280.

      Add $15 for Model P-30LM that allows for fitting various accessories.

MODEL P-31 - .22 Mag. cal., same action as P-30, except has 11 in. barrel, enclosed synthetic barrel shroud and flash hider, 48 oz. Mfg. 1990-95.

	$350	$315	$275	$240	$215	$185	$160

Last MSR was $345.

RIFLES & CARBINES

MODEL R-31 - similar design to Model P-31, except has 16 in. barrel and telescoping stock, 64 oz. Mfg. 1991-95.

	$365	$325	$275	$235	$210	$185	$165

Last MSR was $385.

SRT-20F COMPACT - .243 Win. or .308 Win. cal., bolt action based on the Sako A-2 action, 20 in. match grade finned barrel with muzzle brake, folding synthetic stock, integrated bipod rest, no sights, 9 shot mag., 6.7 lbs. Disc. 1989.

	$575	$525	$475	$395	$365	$340	$320

Last MSR was $525.

    Grendel previously manufactured the SRT-16F, SRT-20L, and SRT-24 - all were disc. 1988. Values are approx. the same as the SRT-20F.

GRIFFIN & HOWE

Griffin & Howe

Current custom gunsmith, rifle manufacturer, and importer established 1923, with store locations in Bernardsville, NJ (gunsmithing also), and Greenwich, CT. Griffin & Howe also had a NY City store location until April, 2003.

    Founded in 1923 by Seymour Griffin and James Howe, Griffin & Howe continues to build its custom rifles as well as providing the full spectrum of gunsmithing services and importation of fine English guns.

    Griffin & Howe has been building custom rifles since 1923. They also perform a variety of custom gunsmithing services. Prices may vary greatly depending on configuration, desirability, condition and special features. Most used Griffin & Howe Custom Rifles in

GRADING - PPGS™	100%	98%	95%	90%	80%	70%	60%

average condition and without special engraving start at $3,150+ and rise according to condition and nature of the individual gun. Since 1923, fewer than 2,800 have been made. In 1930, Griffin & Howe became a subsidiary of Abercrombie & Fitch and remained with them until 1976, when it became a privately held company. Because all Griffin & Howe rifles are essentially special ordered, accurate pricing can be ascertained only by examining each individual gun. Elaborate specimens by this maker trademark will command over $10,000. Engraving by Joseph Fugger, Winston Churchill, Robert Swartley or Rudolph Kornbrath will add considerably to the value. Pricing on new custom rifles, with a wide selection of options, is available directly from Griffin & Howe.

RIFLES: BOLT ACTION

Values represent a standard gun with no upgrades or options.

G&H CLASSIC FRENCH WALNUT STOCK - most popular cals., custom honed action with lapped lugs, Douglas premium barrel, hand engraving, French walnut sporter stock with ebony forend tip, G&H pistol grip cap, "Griffin & Howe, New York" barrel address, custom order.

Current MSR on this model is $15,000.

WIN M70 STANDARD ACTION - for .243 Win., .270 Win., .30-06, or .308 Win. cal.

	$5,750	$5,000	$4,500	$4,250	$3,750	$3,300	$2,750

WIN M70 MEDIUM - .300 Win. Mag., 7mm Rem. Mag., or .338 Win. Mag. cal.

	$6,750	$6,250	$5,500	$4,750	$4,000	$3,450	$2,950

WIN M70 MAGNUM - .375 H&H or .416 Rigby cal.

	$7,000	$6,500	$5,650	$4,850	$4,100	$3,550	$3,000

WIN M52 - .22 LR cal.

	$5,000	$4,500	$4,000	$3,400	$3,100	$2,700	$2,400

WIN HIGHWALL

	$3,800	$3,500	$3,150	$2,850	$2,500	$2,100	$1,850

SPRINGFIELD 1903

	$4,950	$4,400	$3,750	$3,450	$3,150	$2,800	$2,550

SPRINGFIELD 1922

	$4,500	$4,100	$3,650	$3,350	$3,000	$2,750	$2,500

MAUSER STANDARD

	$5,750	$5,000	$4,500	$4,250	$3,750	$3,300	$2,750

MAUSER MAGNUM

	$9,850	$9,000	$8,500	$7,850	$6,850	$5,950	$4,950

SAVAGE 99

	$2,850	$2,550	$2,250	$2,000	$1,850	$1,600	$1,350

G&H PRE-'64 MODEL 70 CLASSIC SYNTHETIC STOCK - most popular cals., features glass bedded synthetic classic sporter stock in black or woodgrain finish, Douglas premium barrel, "Griffin & Howe, New York" barrel address, custom order. Disc. 2002.

	$4,750	$4,450	$4,000	$3,700	$3,500	$3,300	$3,100

Last MSR was $2,250.

SHOTGUNS: O/U

MADISON - 12, 20, 28 ga., or .410 bore, case hardened frame, 26 1/2, 28, or 30 in. VR barrels, scroll engraved with gold accents. Mfg. by the Belgian Browning custom shop using a B25 action 1999-2006.

	$9,000	$8,250	$7,750	$7,150	$6,450	$5,500	$4,500

Last MSR was $9,750.

GRADING - PPGS™	100%	98%	95%	90%	80%	70%	60%

CLAREMONT - 12 ga. only, case hardened frame, shallow frame BOSS style lock-up, 30 in. VR barrels standard length, scroll engraving with gold accents. Mfg. by Gamba beginning 1999.

MSR $8,750		$8,000	$7,500	$7,100	$6,250	$5,750	$5,000	$4,300

EXTRA FINISH CLAREMONT - similiar to Claremont, except has coin finished frame with full coverage acanthus scroll engraving and drop out trigger group. Importation began 1999.

MSR $11,500		$10,800	$9,950	$8,500	$7,300	$6,500	$5,700	$5,200

CLAREMONT LUSSO - similar to Extra Finish Claremont, except has fully engraved sideplates. Importation began 2000.

MSR $18,000		$17,250	$16,750	$14,800	$12,000	$10,250	$9,000	$8,000

BROADWAY - 12 or 20 ga., case hardened frame, 26, 28, or 30 in. VR barrels, scroll engraving with gold accents. Mfg. by the Belgian Browning custom shop using a B125 action 1999-2003.

	$5,750	$5,250	$4,600	$4,150	$3,650	$2,950	$2,550

Last MSR was $5,750.

SUPERBRITTE - 12 or 16 ga., unique side opening design, built by Britte company in Liege, Belgium before WWII, purchased by G&H in 2001.

	$23,500	$21,250	$18,500	$16,750	$14,950	$12,750	$11,500

Last MSR was $25,000.

BLACK RAM - 12 or 20 ga., boxlock action, inertial cocking system, single bolt locking system, SST, 30 or 32 in. barrels with Briley chokes, traditional check-ered Turkish walnut stock with pistol grip and recoil pad, 8 1/4 lbs. Mfg. by Zoli, importation began 2007.

MSR $5,450		$4,950	$4,500	$4,000	$3,500	$3,000	$2,500	$2,000

SILVER RAM - 12 or 20 ga., boxlock action, inertial cocking system, single bolt locking system, SST, 30 or 32 in. barrels with Briley chokes, traditional check-ered Turkish walnut stock with pistol grip and recoil pad, game scene engrav-ing, 8 1/4 lbs. Mfg. by Zoli, importation began 2007.

MSR $8,450		$7,750	$6,700	$5,900	$5,100	$4,300	$3,600	$2,950

SHOTGUNS: SxS

ROUND BODY GAME GUN - 12, 16, 20, 28 ga., or .410 bore, features case col-ored round frame with sidelock action, "SAFE" in gold, H&H style selective ejectors, 25-30 in. barrels, double triggers, checkered straight grip stock and splinter forearm, G&H name gold inlaid, cased (optional 2004). Mfg. by Arri-eta, importation began 1989.

MSR $5,950		$5,500	$5,100	$4,750	$4,150	$3,600	$3,100	$2,500

Add $500 for 20 ga., $900 for 28 ga. or .410 bore.
Add $1,150 for single trigger.

✳ *Round Body Game Guns Pair* - 12, 16, 20, 28 ga. or .410 bore, scroll engraved with case colored hardened finish, "SAFE" in gold, round sidelock action, H&H style selective ejectors, 25-30 in. barrels, double triggers, checkered straight grip and splinter forearm, G&H name inlaid in gold, built as a pair, and gold numbered 1 & 2 on barrels, forend, and top lever. Mfg. by Arrieta.

MSR $12,950		$11,950	$10,500	$9,500	$8,500	$7,650	$6,850	$6,000

Add $1,000 for pair of 20 ga.
Add $3,000 for assisted opening.

EXTRA FINISH ROUND BODY GAME GUN - same action as Round Body Game Gun, except has coin finished frame and game scene engraving with gold accents, upgraded wood. Importation began 1999.

MSR $8,950		$8,300	$7,850	$7,200	$6,400	$5,600	$4,900	$4,000

Add $800 for 20 ga. or $1,000 for 28 ga. or .410 bore.
Add $1,150 for single trigger.

GRADING - PPGS™	100%	98%	95%	90%	80%	70%	60%

❋ *Extra Finish Round Body Game Guns Pair* - built as a pair, gold numbered 1 & 2 on barrels, forend, and top lever.

MSR $19,750	$18,500	$16,500	$14,750	$13,500	$11,500	$9,750	$8,500

Add $1,250 for pair of 20 ga.
Add $3,000 for assisted opening.

BRITTE - 12 ga. only, best quality sidelock ejector, built by Britte company in Liege, Belgium before WWII, purchased by G&H in 2001.

	$13,750	$12,900	$11,700	$10,500	$9,250	$8,400	$7,500

Last MSR was $15,000.

CONTINENTAL SIDELOCK - 12 ga. only, best quality Britte action, finished by current Belgium gunmakers such as Lebeau-Courally, various scroll patterns, case colored or bright finish, finest European walnut stock. Disc. 2006.

	$17,000	$15,000	$13,100	$11,000	$9,250	$8,300	$6,900

Last MSR was $18,500.

❋ *Continental Sidelocks Pair* - 12 ga. only, built as a pair, gold numbered 1 & 2 on barrels, forend, and top lever. Disc. 2006.

	$35,500	$31,400	$28,750	$26,750	$23,500	$19,500	$17,750

Last MSR was $38,500.

TRADITIONAL GAME GUN - 12, 16, 20, 24, 28 ga., or .410 bore, square body action, color case hardened with bright brush finish, DT, seven pin lock assemblies, 29 in. barrels with IC/Mod. chokes, English style straight checkered Turkish walnut stock, available with optional game scene engraving, 6 3/4 lbs. Importation began 2007.

MSR $7,500	$6,750	$5,900	$5,100	$4,300	$3,600	$3,100	$2,650

Add $750 for 20 ga.
Add $825 for 28 ga. or .410 bore.
Add $3,000 for game scene engraving.

❋ *Traditional Game Gun Pair* - 12 and 16 ga.

MSR $16,000	$14,500	$13,250	$12,000	$10,000	$8,950	$7,750	$7,000

Add $3,000 for assisted opening.
Add $1,500 for 20 ga.
Add $6,000 for game scene engraving.

GRIFFON

Currently manufactured by Continental Weapons (Pty) Ltd. established in 1996, and located in Midrand, Johannesburg, South Africa. No current U.S. importation. Previously imported and distributed by Griffon USA, Inc., a subsidiary of 21st Century Technologies, Inc., located in Ft. Worth, TX, and by First Defense International located in San Clemente, CA. Values represent the most recent U.S. pricing.

PISTOLS: SEMI-AUTO

GRIFFON 1911 A1 COMBAT - .45 ACP cal., patterned after the Colt M1911, single action, 4.13 in. barrel, 7 shot mag., ported barrel/slide, black Teflon finish, Commander hammer, Tritium sights, 36.5 oz. New 1997.

MSR N/A	$445	$375	$335	$300	$275	$250	$225

GRIFFON CW 11 - 9mm Para. cal., 8 shot mag., 4 in. barrel without porting, combo blue/chrome finish, perforated trigger, 3 dot sighting system. New 1997.

MSR N/A	$445	$375	$335	$300	$275	$250	$225

GRADING - PPGS™	100%	98%	95%	90%	80%	70%	60%

GRULLA ARMAS

Current manufacturer located in Eibar, Spain since 1932. Currently imported and distributed by Merkel USA, located in Trussville, AL, Hi-Grade Imports, located in Gilroy, CA, Fieldsport, located in Traverse City, MI, Lion Country Supply, located in Port Matilda, PA, and by Dale's Decoy Den, located in Nelsonville, OH.

Grulla Armas manufactures a complete line of quality SxS shotguns in addition to both SxS and double rifles.

RIFLES

C-95 BOLT ACTION - .338 Win. Mag. or .375 H&H cal., deluxe bolt action featuring extensively scroll engraved square bridge receiver with elongated upper tang, octagon barrel with quarter rib and express sights, deluxe checkered wood with ebony forend tip, custom made per individual order. New 1996.

This model is POR. Please contact the importer directly for an individualized quotation.

E-95 SxS DOUBLE RIFLE - 9.3x74R or .375 H&H cal., top-of-the-line double rifle utilizing H&H type sidelocks with scroll engraving, skeleton steel buttplate, regulated barrels, beavertail forend, custom-made per individual order. New 1996.

This model is POR. Please contact the importer directly for an individualized quotation.

SHOTGUNS: SxS, SIDELOCK

The following models are currently available in 12, 16, 20, 28 ga., or .410 bore. All guns have double triggers with hinged front, selective auto-ejectors, and straight grip stock with splinter forearm. Values represent standard models with no options.

MODEL 209 - HOLLAND - choice of case colored, antique silver, or coin finished receiver, scroll engraving with hand rubbed oil finish, 27 or 28 in. chopper lump barrels, gas escape valves. Disc. 2008.

	$5,995	$5,200	$4,500	$3,850	$3,250	$2,500	$2,150

Last MSR was $6,595.

Add $400 for 28 ga.or .410 bore.

MODEL 215 - similar to Model 209, except has rose and scroll engraving and nicer wood.

MSR N/A	$4,250	$3,600	$3,000	$2,500	$2,100	$1,800	$1,500

Add $200 for Model 215 Home.

MODEL 216 - similar to Model 215, except features Purdey style scroll hand engraving.

MSR N/A	$4,750	$4,100	$3,550	$2,975	$2,475	$2,100	$1,800

MODEL 216RB - round body version of the Model 216, features Purdey style scroll hand engraving, drop points absent, upgraded wood, deluxe finish.

MSR N/A	$4,975	$4,250	$3,725	$3,050	$2,500	$2,000	$1,800

MODEL 216RL - 12, 20, or 28 ga., round body, H&H style sidelocks, deluxe checkered straight grip walnut stock and forearm, 28 in. chopper lump barrels, 6-7.1 lbs. Importation began 2004.

MSR $8,895	$7,775	$7,125	$6,300	$5,400	$4,600	$3,800	$3,000

Add $400 for 28 ga. or .410 bore.
Add $2,100 for Elite Model.

This model is imported exclusively by Merkel USA.

MODEL 216SL - 12, 16, 20 ga., or .410 bore, 28 in. barrels, H&H style sidelock, DT, ejectors, straight grip English stock, luxury grade wood, coin finished receiver with hand engraved Purdey style rose and scroll.

MSR $8,295	$7,495	$6,850	$6,400	$5,500	$4,750	$4,000	$3,250

Add $400 for 28 ga. or .410 bore.

GRADING - PPGS™	100%	98%	95%	90%	80%	70%	60%

MODEL 217RB - various gas., game gun, 3 in. chambers, flat file rib, 10 in. semi-beavertail forearm and select wood.

MSR $7,995	$7,200	$6,200	$5,200	$4,350	$3,650	$3,150	$2,600

Add $300 for 28 ga. or .410 bore.

MODEL 219 - features more elaborate engraving and better wood.

	$5,325	$4,950	$4,000	$3,550	$2,950	$2,475	$1,995

Last MSR was $6,050.

MODEL 219-P

	$7,050	$6,225	$5,600	$4,850	$4,100	$3,200	$2,600

Last MSR was $7,750.

CONSORT - features easy-opening H&H style action, upgraded wood, approx. 50% floral pattern engraving, deluxe finish, 27 or 28 in. chopper lump barrels, gas escape valves.

MSR N/A	$6,250	$5,350	$4,700	$3,850	$3,275	$2,650	$2,200

WINDSOR - similar to Consort Model, except has approx. 70% engraving, round action, drop points absent, deep relief engraving with upgraded wood, deluxe finish, 27 or 28 in. chopper lump barrel.

MSR N/A	$6,950	$6,225	$5,600	$4,975	$4,350	$3,750	$3,000

Add $3,100 for Windsor Woodcock model.

SUPER MH - best quality sidelock with Purdey style engraving, seven pin H&H lock, H&H style assisted opening, chrome nickel steel barrels, fitted leather case, select XXX walnut stock, deluxe hand rubbed oil finish.

	$11,400	$9,500	$8,475	$7,425	$6,200	$5,000	$4,150

Last MSR was $12,395.

NUMBER 1 - next to the top-of-the-line gun with best quality features.

	$13,175	$10,625	$8,800	$7,575	$6,350	$5,150	$4,200

Last MSR was $15,550.

SUPREME - 12, 16, 20, 28 ga. or .410 bore, features drop forged round body steel frame, disc strikers, H&H style assisted self-opening action, ejectors, case colored receiver, chopper lump barrels, articulated DT, seven-pin sidelock mechanisms with intercepting sears and cocking indicators, best quality Exhibition oil finished walnut stock and forearm, includes leather covered trunk style fitted case. New 2008.

MSR $17,995	$16,500	$13,500	$10,750	$8,750	$7,500	$6,500	$5,750

ROYAL - 12 (disc.), 20 , 28 ga. or .410 bore, top-of-the-line model with H&H style scroll engraving, seven pin H&H lock, H&H style assisted opening, chrome nickel steel barrels, fitted leather case, select XXX walnut stock, deluxe hand rubbed oil finish.

MSR $24,995	$22,000	$18,000	$15,000	$12,500	$10,00	$8,500	$7,250

GRUND, KARL

Current rifle manufacturer located in Ferlach, Austria. No current U.S. importation. Karl Grund manufactures high quality custom double rifles in a variety of configurations, including drillings and express rifles. Please contact him for more information, including pricing, U.S. availability and a price quotation (see Trademark Index).

GRÜNIG & ELMIGER AG

Current rifle manufacturer located in Malters, Switzerland. Currently represented in the U.S. by Gunsmithing, Inc., located in Colorado Springs, CO, Champion's Choice, located in Lavergne, TN, and by Brenzovich Firearms Training Center, located in Ft. Hancock, TX.

Grünig & Elmiger AG manufacture both rimfire and centerfire high quality competition and sporter rifles. Please contact the U.S. representatives directly for current U.S. availability and pricing (see Trademark Index).

GRADING - PPGS™	100%	98%	95%	90%	80%	70%	60%

GUN 1

Current trademark owned by Savage Arms, Inc.

RIFLES

GUN 1 SERIES - .22 LR cal., 16 (Junior) or 19 (Youth) in. barrel, short LOP, Acutrigger. New 2008.

MSR $213	$180	$165	$150	$140	$130	$120	$110

Add $9 for 19 in. barrel.

✻ *Gun 1 Series Youth Centerfire* - .243 Win. cal., 22 in. barrel, Acutrigger, similar to Gun 1 Series, short LOP. New 2008.

MSR $605	$550	$495	$450	$400	$350	$300	$250

GUN WORKS, LTD.

Previous manufacturer and distributor located in Buffalo, NY. Early guns were made in Tonawanda, NY.

HANDGUNS

X-CALIBER - .44 Mag. cal., single shot, tip up pistol, 8 in. barrel, matte type blue finish, ergonomic hardwood grips, probably used older Sterling Arms parts and restamped the barrel address. Limited mfg.

$350	$300	$260	$230	$200	$175	$150

MODEL 9 - .357 Mag., 9mm Para., .38 Super, or .38 Spl. cal., O/U derringer, electroless nickel finish, 2 1/2 in. barrel, wood grips, Millett sights, 15 oz. Disc. 1986.

$135	$120	$105	$95	$65	$55	$50

Last MSR was $149.

GUNCRAFTER INDUSTRIES

Current pistol manufacturer located in Huntsville, AR.

PISTOLS: SEMI-AUTO

Guncrafter Industries manufactures two base semi-auto pistol models patterned after the M1911. The Model No. 1 and the Model No. 2 ("The Beast") are both available in .50 GI or .45 ACP cal., with a wide variety of custom options and accessories. Prices begin at $2,895 MSR. Please contact the company directly for more information on these custom-made pistols (see Trademark Index).

GUSTAF, CARL

See listing under Carl Gustaf.

GYROJET

See MBA Gyrojet listing in the M Section of this text.

H SECTION

HHF
Please refer to the Huglu section.

H.J.S. INDUSTRIES, INC.
Previous manufacturer located in Brownsville, TX.

GRADING - PPGS™	100%	98%	95%	90%	80%	70%	60%

DERRINGERS

FRONTIER FOUR - .22 LR cal., 4 shot derringer, stainless steel construction, 5 1/2 oz.

	100%	98%	95%	90%	80%	70%	60%
	$115	$90	$80	$75	$70	$60	$50

LONE STAR - .38 S&W cal., single shot derringer, stainless steel construction, 6 oz.

	100%	98%	95%	90%	80%	70%	60%
	$137	$105	$95	$80	$75	$65	$50

H & R 1871, LLC. (HARRINGTON & RICHARDSON)

Current manufacturer and holding company located in Gardner, MA since 1991. During 2000, Marlin Firearms Co. purchased the assets of H&R 1871, Inc., and the name was changed to H&R 1871, LLC. Production of H&R products continues at the factory located in Gardner, MA.

H & R 1871 LLC utilizes the original H & R trademark and does not accept warranty work for older (pre-1986 mfg.) Harrington & Richardson, Inc. firearms. Distributor sales only. The use of the original Harrington & Richardson trademark was permitted during 1991. All new manufacture will use this trademark, but older H & Rs manufactured by Harrington & Richardson, Inc. are not the responsibility of H & R 1871, LLC.

REVOLVERS

Additional revolvers using the New England Firearms trademark may be located in the N section of this text. During 1997-99, all H & R 1871, Inc. revolvers were supplied with a lockable plastic case.

929 SIDEKICK - .22 LR cal., 9 shot, blue metal, swing-out cylinder, 4 in. heavy barrel, square butt with brown laminate grips, fixed sights, 30 oz. Mfg. 1996-99.

	100%	98%	95%	90%	80%	70%	60%
	$150	$120	$100	$85	$75	$65	$55

Last MSR was $173.

✳ *929 Sidekick Trapper Edition* - similar to 929 Sidekick, except has grey laminate grips and special barrel markings, limited mfg. 1996 only, distributed through 1996.

	100%	98%	95%	90%	80%	70%	60%
	$150	$115	$95	$85	$75	$65	$55

Last MSR was $175.

939 PREMIER WESTERN TARGET - .22 LR cal., 9 shot, blue metal, swing-out cylinder, target model with ribbed 6 in. heavy barrel and adj. rear sight, hardwood grips, 36 oz. Mfg. 1995-99.

	100%	98%	95%	90%	80%	70%	60%
	$150	$125	$105	$90	$75	$65	$55

Last MSR was $190.

FOURTY-NINER (WESTERN 949) - .22 LR cal., 9 shot fixed cylinder, case colored frame, 5 1/2 or 7 1/2 in. barrel, hardwood grips, fixed sights, approx. 37 oz. Mfg. 1995-99.

	100%	98%	95%	90%	80%	70%	60%
	$150	$125	$105	$90	$75	$65	$55

Last MSR was $190.

SPORTSMAN 999 - .22 LR cal., single or double action, top break action with auto shell ejection, 9 shot, 4 or 6 in. barrel with fluted solid rib, smooth hardwood stocks, transfer bar safety, blue finish, adj. sights, 30-34 oz. Mfg. 1991-99.

	100%	98%	95%	90%	80%	70%	60%
	$230	$180	$145	$125	$115	$100	$90

Last MSR was $285.

GRADING - PPGS™	100%	98%	95%	90%	80%	70%	60%

RIFLES: SINGLE SHOT

H&R 1871 began providing the Trigger Guardian trigger locking system beginning Dec. 1, 1999 at no extra charge. During 2008, H&R 1871 reintroduced its Ultragon rifling on its rifled slug barrels, which feature six oval lands and grooves w/o sharp corners. All H&R models are built in the U.S.A.

ULTRA HUNTER MODEL - .22 Mag. (mfg. 2002-2007), .22-250 Rem. (disc. 1994), .223 Rem. (disc. 1997, reintroduced 2002), .25-06 Rem. (new 1995), .243 Win., .270 Win. (mfg. 2005-2006), .30-06 (mfg. 2005-2007), .308 Win. (new 1995), .357 Rem. Max. (mfg. 1996-98), .450 Marlin (mfg. 2001-2004), .45-70 Govt. (new 2008), 7x57mm (mfg. 1997 only), or 7x64mm (mfg. 1997 only) cal., single shot break-open action with ejector, side-lever release, 22 in. heavy (.22-250 Rem. or .223 Rem.), 22 in. normal (.22 Mag., .308 Win. or .450 Marlin), 24 in. bull (.223 Rem. or .243 WIn. cal., new 2006) or 26 in. (.25-06 Rem.) steel or stainless (new 2008) barrel with scope mount rail, checkered curly maple (disc. 1994), laminated cinammon hardwood Monte Carlo stock with black line recoil pad, or thumbhole stock (new 2008), sling swivel studs, 7-8 lbs. New 1993.

MSR $328	$270	$225	$160	$120	$110	$95	$85

  Subtract $30 for metric cals. (disc.).
  Add $64 for thumbhole laminate stock (new 2008).
  Add $117 for .45-70 Govt. cal. with thumbhole laminate stock and polished stainless barrel and frame (new 2008).

This model features a scope rail on .25-06 Rem. and .308 Win. cals.

✳ *Ultra Model .22 Mag.* - .22 Mag. cal. only, 22 standard or 24 in. heavy (disc.) in. barrel. Disc. 2008.

	$150	$125	$105	$90	$85	$80	$75

Last MSR was $183.

✳ *Ultra Model Varmint* - .204 Ruger (new 2005), .22-250 Rem. (new 2005), .223 Rem. or .243 Win. (disc. 2004, reintroduced 2006) cal., features heavy 24 in. fluted (new 2005) or unfluted barrel, blue finish, natural finish cinnamon laminate Monte Carlo stock with (new 2008) or w/o thumbhole, or skeletonized black synthetic stock (new 2005, fluted barrel only), includes scope mount rail, 7 lbs. New 1998.

MSR $374	$290	$225	$165	$120	$110	$95	$85

  Subtract approx. 15% if w/o fluted barrel.

✳ *Ultra Model Comp.* - .270 Win. or .30-06 cal., features 23 in. barrel with integral compensator, blue finish, multi-color checkered laminate wood stock and forearm. Approx. 7-8 lbs. Mfg. 1997-2003.

	$310	$240	$195	$150	$125	$105	$95

Last MSR was $376.

✳ *Ultra Model Rocky Mountain Elk Foundation Commemorative 1st Ed.* - .280 Rem. cal., 26 in. blue barrel, features RMEF medallion in stock, high gloss bluing, 7-8 lbs. Mfg. 1995-96.

	$220	$175	$135	N/A	N/A	N/A	N/A

Last MSR was $270.

✳ *Ultra Model Rocky Mountain Elk Foundation Commemorative 2nd Ed.* - .35 Whelen cal., 26 in. blue barrel, features RMEF medallion in multi-color laminate stock and forearm, high gloss bluing, 7-8 lbs. Mfg. 1996-97.

	$260	$215	$160	N/A	N/A	N/A	N/A

Last MSR was $300.

HANDI-MAG - 7mm Rem. Mag. or .300 Win. Mag. cal., blued receiver, 26 in. stainless barrel w/o sights, black polymer synthetic Monte Carlo stock, includes scope mount rail, approx. 7 1/2 lbs. New 2008.

MSR $319	$265	$225	$165	$135	$120	$110	$100

GRADING - PPGS™	100%	98%	95%	90%	80%	70%	60%

WHITETAILS UNLIMITED COMMEMORATIVE RIFLE - .30-30 (new 1998) or .45-70 Govt. cal., Topper style break-open action, 22 in. barrel, blue frame with special etching, checkered American walnut stock (with medallion) and forearm. 7 lbs. Mfg. 1997-98.

	$250	$210	$170	N/A	N/A	N/A	N/A

Last MSR was $290.

HARRINGTON & RICHARDSON BUFFALO CLASSIC - .45 LC (new 2007) or .45-70 Govt. cal., top lever break open action, 20 (.45 LC cal.) or 32 in. barrel, case hardened frame, checkered walnut stock and forearm, 8 lbs. New 1995.

MSR $413	$355	$285	$230	$180	$145	$125	$105

This model was also produced under the Wesson & Harrington trademark.

HARRINGTON & RICHARDSON TARGET RIFLE - .38-55 WCF cal., 28 in. heavy barrel, target sights, blue finish 7 1/2 lbs. Mfg. 1998-2007.

	$345	$280	$230	$180	$145	$125	$105

Last MSR was $395.

This model was also produced under the Wesson & Harrington trademark.

SHOTGUNS: O/U

PINNACLE - 12 or 20 ga., 3 in. chambers, boxlock action, 26 (12 ga.) or 28 (20 ga.) in. vent. rib barrels with choke tubes, SST, ejectors, checkered walnut pistol grip stock with fluted comb, vent. recoil pad, bead front sight, 6 3/4 lbs. Limited importation 2005 only.

	$675	$525	$450	$400	$365	$335	$295

Last MSR was $886.

SHOTGUNS: SEMI-AUTO

EXCELL AUTO 5 - 12 ga., 3 in. chamber, 28 in. VR barrel with choke tubes, 5 shot mag., black synthetic, walnut, or Realtree Advantage Wetlands 100% camo covered pistol grip stock with fluted comb, vent. recoil pad, bead front sight, approx. 7 lbs. New 2005.

MSR $374	$300	$250	$210	$180	$160	$140	$120

Add $29 for walnut stock or $82 for 100% camo coverage (Waterfowl model).

✳ *Excell Auto 5 Turkey* - 12 ga., 3 in. chamber, 5 shot mag., 22 in. vent. rib barrel with choke tubes and fiber optic sights, Realtree Advantage Hardwoods camo covered pistol grip stock and barrel, 7 lbs. New 2005.

MSR $456	$395	$345	$300	$265	$230	$195	$170

✳ *Excell Auto 5 Combo* - includes 24 in. rifled slug barrel and 28 in. regular barrel, synthetic stock only. New 2005.

MSR $512	$425	$380	$330	$290	$260	$230	$200

SHOTGUNS: SINGLE SHOT

H&R 1871 began providing the Trigger Guardian trigger locking system beginning Dec. 1, 1999 at no extra charge.

TOPPER (098) - 12, 16 (mfg. 1992-2007), 20, 28 (mfg. 1992-95, reintroduced 1998-2005) ga., or .410 bore, 2 3/4 (16 and 28 ga.) or 3 in. chamber, 26 or 28 in. barrel, break open side lever release action, transfer bar safety, ejector, satin nickel frame with blue barrel, black finish hardwood stock with full pistol grip and forearm, 5-6 lbs. New 1991.

MSR $140	$110	$95	$80	$70	$60	$50	$40

✳ *Topper 3 1/2 in.* - 12 ga. only, 3 1/2 in. chamber, satin nickel frame with blue barrel, 28 in. barrel with 1 choke tube, black finish hardwood stock (with recoil pad) and forearm, 5-6 lbs. New 1991.

MSR $164	$125	$110	$90	$75	$60	$50	$40

GRADING - PPGS™	100%	98%	95%	90%	80%	70%	60%

* Topper Deluxe Classic - 12 or 20 (new 2005) ga., 3 in. chamber, 26 (20 ga. only, new 2005) or 28 (12 ga. only) in. VR barrel with choke tube, matte nickel plated receiver, checkered American walnut pistol grip stock and forearm with recoil pad. New 2004.

MSR $207	$170	$145	$120	$95	$80	$70	$60

* Topper Deluxe Rifled Slug Gun - 12 ga. only, 3 in. chamber, 24 in. compensated barrel, rifle sights, dark American hardwood stock and forearm, satin nickel frame, approx. 5 1/2 lbs. Mfg. 1996-99.

	$150	$115	$95	$85	$75	$65	$55

Last MSR was $170.

* Topper Jr. - 20 ga. or .410 bore, smaller variation of the Topper 098 with youth dimensions including 22 in. barrel and shortened hardwood stock with recoil pad, satin nickel frame with blue barrel, 12 1/2 in. LOP, 5-6 lbs. Mfg. began 1991.

MSR $148	$115	$95	$80	$70	$60	$50	$40

* Topper Jr. Classic - 20, 28 (disc. 2004) ga., or .410 bore, 22 in. barrel, checkered American black walnut stock and forearm, recoil pad, 12 1/2 in. LOP. Mfg. began 1991.

MSR $181	$150	$115	$90	$80	$70	$65	$60

* Topper Trap - 12 ga., 3 in. chamber, 30 in. VR barrel with IM extended choke tube, checkered walnut stock and forearm with decelerator recoil pad, nickel finished receiver with blue barrel, 7 lbs. New 2008.

MSR $362	$295	$250	$210	$185	$170	$160	$150

* Topper NWTF Turkey Mag. - 10 (mfg. 1996 only) or 12 (mfg. 1991-95) ga., 3 1/2 in. chamber, 24 in. drilled and tapped barrel with 1 choke tube, entire gun is covered in Mossy Oak camo, includes sling and swivels, 6 lbs. Mfg. 1991-96.

	$145	$120	$100	$85	$75	$65	$55

Last MSR was $180.

This model was part of the National Wild Turkey Federation (NWTF) sponsorship program.

* Topper 1994 NWTF Youth Turkey Gun - 20 ga., 3 in. chamber, 22 in. full choke barrel, features Realtree camo finish and sling, limited mfg. 1994-95.

	$140	$110	$95	$85	$75	$65	$55

Last MSR was $160.

* Topper 2000 NWTF/Youth Edition - 12 or 20 ga., 3 in. chamber, 20 ga. is NWTF Youth Edition with 22 in. barrel, camo finished laminate stock and forend with NWTF laser engraved frame, includes sling and swivels. Mfg. 2000-2004.

	$175	$130	$115	$95	$80	$70	$60

Last MSR was $207.

Add $9 for NWTF Edition - 12 ga. with 24 in. barrel.

THE TAMER - 20 ga. (new 2007) or .410 bore, 3 in. chamber, synthetic thumbhole stock is designed to hold 4 shells, transfer bar system, 19 or 20 (20 ga. only) in. full choke barrel, electroless nickel finish, 6 lbs. New 1994.

MSR $158	$120	$100	$80	$70	$60	$50	$40

SB1-920 ULTRA SLUG HUNTER - .20 ga. only, utilizes 12 ga. action and barrel that has been under-bored to 20 ga. and fully rifled, hardwood Monte Carlo stock and forearm, matte black frame. Mfg. 1996-disc.

	$190	$155	$125	$100	$85	$75	$65

Last MSR was $225.

ULTRA SLUG HUNTER - 12 or 20 ga., 3 in. chamber, 22 (20 ga., Youth Model) or 24 in. fully rifled heavy barrel, side-release lever, black Monte Carlo hardwood stock with recoil pad, matte finished frame, 8-9 lbs. New 1995.

MSR $248	$200	$170	$135	$105	$90	$75	$65

Add $39 for 3-9x32mm scope (new 2007).

GRADING - PPGS™	100%	98%	95%	90%	80%	70%	60%

✳ *Ultra Slug Hunter Deluxe* - similar to Ultra Slug Hunter, except has checkered camo laminate wood and scope mount rail, adj. rear sight. New 1997.

MSR $306		$255	$215	$170	$130	$105	$90	$80

✳ *Ultra Light Slug* - 12 or 20 ga., 3 in. chamber, 24 in. rifled barrel w/o sights, blue finish, walnut stained hardwood stock and forearm, 5 1/4 lbs. New 2008.

MSR $194		$165	$145	$120	$100	$85	$75	$65

✳ *Ultra Slug Hunter Thumbhole* - 12 or 20 ga., 3 in. chamber, features colored laminate thumbhole stock and forearm, 24 in. rifled barrel w/Weaver rail type scope base, blue finish, 8 1/2 lbs. New 2008.

MSR $342		$295	$265	$230	$200	$180	$160	$150

WHITETAILS UNLIMITED RIFLED SLUG GUN - 12 ga., 3 in. chamber, 24 in. fully rifled heavy barrel, hand checkered Monte Carlo black laminate stock and forend, Whitetails medallion, hammer extension, swivels and sling. Mfg. 1998-99.

	$220	$185	$145	$120	$100	$85	$75

Last MSR was $255.

H-S PRECISION, INC.

Current custom pistol and rifle manufacturer established 1990 and located in Rapid City, SD. H-S Precision, Inc. also manufactures synthetic stocks and custom machine barrels as well. Dealer and consumer direct sales.

H-S Precision introduced the aluminum bedding block for rifle stocks in 1981, and has been making advanced composite synthetic stocks and custom ballistic test barrels for more than two decades.

In addition to the following models, H-S Precision, Inc. also built rifles using a customer's action (mostly Remington 700 or Winchester Post 64 Model 70). 2004 MSRs ranged from $1,520-$1,830.

PISTOLS: SINGLE SHOT

PRO-SERIES 2000 VP/SP - various cals., stainless steel receiver, 15 in. fluted stainless steel barrel, 3 position safety, laminated composite Pro-Series stock, Teflon coated receiver and barrel, choice of varmint (VP, no sights) or silhouette (SP, drilled and tapped for sights) configuration, choice of stock colors. New late 1997.

MSR $2,210		$1,875	$1,575	$1,300	$1,100	$995	$875	$750

RIFLES: BOLT ACTION, PRO-SERIES 2000

All H-S Precision rifles feature Kevlar/graphite laminate stocks, cut rifle barrels, and other high tech innovations including a molded aluminum bedding block system. Beginning in 1999, H-S Precision began utilizing their H-S 2000 action, and model nomenclature was changed to begin with Pro-Series 2000.

Add approx. $200 for left-hand action.

PRO-SERIES 2000 VARMINT TAKEDOWN (VTD) - .22-250 Rem., .270 Win., .308 Win., or .300 Win. Mag. cal., accurized Remington Model 700 receiver (disc. 1999) or H-S 2000 action (new 2000), H-S stainless steel cut rifled and fluted barrel, 5 or 10 shot detachable mag, Teflon coated metal finish. New 1997.

MSR $4,500		$4,200	$3,600	$3,200	$2,750	$2,250	$1,750	$1,500

Add $100 for extended barrel port (Model VTD EP, disc.).
Add $2,500 - $3,000 for extra take-down barrel, depending on cartridge case head size.

PRO-SERIES 2000 SPORTER/VARMINT (VAR/SPR/SPL) - various short and long action cals., Remington ADL action only, each rifle is built per individual specifications, fluted barrel became standard 2006. New 1990.

MSR $2,680		$2,450	$2,100	$1,750	$1,350	$975	$825	$725

Add $120 for 2000 Varmint VAR model.
Add $145 for 2000 SPL model (lightweight, 7 lbs.).
Add $100 for extended barrel port (Model VAR/SPR EP, disc.).
Add $880 for extra stainless barrel (disc.).

PRO-SERIES 2000 PRO-HUNTER RIFLE (PHR) - available in 10 Safari cals., 24 or 26 in. fluted stainless steel barrel with cut rifling, Teflon finish, Pro-Series sporter stock, long action only.

MSR $2,925	$2,675	$2,275	$1,900	$1,600	$1,300	$1,100	$950

Add $1,575 for Pro-Hunter takedown rifle (PTD).
Add $2,500 - $3,000 for extra take-down barrel, depending on head size.

PRO-SERIES 2000 PRO-HUNTER LIGHTWEIGHT (PHL) - short action only, various cals. including WSM, 20 or 22 in. fluted barrel, Teflon coated action and barrel, green/tan camo stock, 5 1/2 lbs. New 2004.

MSR $3,050	$2,800	$2,375	$2,000	$1,650	$1,350	$1,050	$950

PRO-SERIES 2000 LONG RANGE (HEAVY TACTICAL MARKSMAN, HTR) - various cals., stainless fluted barrel standard, Remington BDL (disc. 1999) or Pro-Series 2000 (new 2000) action. New 1990.

MSR $2,950	$2,675	$2,275	$1,900	$1,600	$1,300	$1,100	$950

Add $100 for extended barrel port (Model HTR EP, disc.).

PRO-SERIES 2000 SHORT TACTICAL (STR) - .308 Win. cal., 20 in. fluted barrel, matte Teflon finished action and barrel, 20 in. fluted barrel with standard porting, Pro Series Tactical stock. New 2004.

MSR $2,925	$2,675	$2,275	$1,900	$1,600	$1,300	$1,100	$950

PRO-SERIES 2000 TAKEDOWN TACTICAL LONG RANGE (TTD) - various short and long action cals., stainless steel barrel, Remington BDL takedown action, matte blue finish. Mfg. 1990-2005, reintroduced 2008.

MSR $5,000	$4,650	$4,200	$3,750	$3,250	$2,750	$2,250	$1,650

Add $100 for extended barrel port (Model TTD EP, disc.).
Add $2,500 - $3,000 for extra take-down barrel, depending on cartridge case head size.

PRO SERIES 2000 RAPID DEPLOYMENT RIFLE (RDR) - .308 Win. cal., Pro-Series 2000 stainless steel short action only, 20 in. fluted barrel, black synthetic stock with or w/o thumbhole, black teflon metal finish, approx. 7 1/2 lbs. New 2000.

MSR $2,800	$2,575	$2,200	$1,875	$1,600	$1,300	$1,100	$950

Add $125 for PST60A Long Range stock (disc.).
Add $150 for RDT model (new 2006).

TAKEDOWN LONG RANGE (TACTICAL MARKSMAN) - .223 Rem., .243 Win., .30-06, .308 Win., 7mm Rem. Mag., .300 Win. Mag., or .338 Win. Mag. cal., includes "kwik klip" and stainless fluted barrel. Mfg. 1990-97.

	$2,895	$2,225	$1,675	$1,350	$995	$850	$750

Last MSR was $2,895.

A complete rifle package consisting of 2 calibers (.308 Win. and .300 Win. Mag.), scope and fitted case was available for $5,200 retail.

HWP INDUSTRIES

Previous manufacturer located in Milwaukee, WI circa 1989.

REVOLVERS

THE SLEDGEHAMMER - .500 HWP Mag. cal., 5 shot revolver, double action, stainless steel, full shrouded 4 in. barrel (quick change), Pachmayr grips. Limited mfg. 1989 only.

	$1,150	$895	$750	$640	$535	$450	$390

Last MSR was $1,295.

HAENEL, C.G.

Previous manufacturer located in Suhl, Germany. Haenel mfg. many varieties of firearms between 1925-circa 1940. Currently, Haenel trademarked airguns are manufactured mostly for Europe. Presently not imported into the U.S.

During 1925-WWII, C.G. Haenel manufactured a variety of sporting longarms, mostly concentrating on bolt action rifles, drillings, and SxS shotguns. Some of these guns are extremely well executed, and must be appraised individually. If quality, condition, and overall desirability are at a level similar to pre-war Sauers, Krieghoffs, etc., Haenel values could be similar to the trademarks just mentioned. However, a standard grade Haenel rifle/shotgun/drilling, in an obscure metric caliber with no engraving in 70% or less original condition, gets priced for its utilitarian shooting value as opposed to adding a collector premium.

For more information and current pricing on both new and used Haenel, C.G., airguns, please refer to the *Blue Book of Airguns* by Dr. Robert Beeman & John Allen (also online).

PISTOLS: SEMI-AUTO

SCHMEISSER MODEL 1 & 2 - .25 ACP cal., similar to Baby Browning.

	100%	98%	95%	90%	80%	70%	60%
	$500	$400	$300	$275	$230	$200	$180

MODELS 200-205 - see Hämmerli-Walther.

RIFLES: BOLT ACTION

MAUSER-MANNLICHER SPORTING RIFLE - 7x57mm, 8x57R, or 9x57R cal., M/88 Mauser type action, 22 or 24 in. octagon barrel, Mannlicher box mag., double set triggers, raised rib on barrel, leaf sight, sporter stock.

	100%	98%	95%	90%	80%	70%	60%
	$775	$700	$625	$575	$525	$475	$425

MODEL 1900 - metric cals., features round receiver, mag. guide reinforcement, separate ejector housing, latch release on floorplate.

	100%	98%	95%	90%	80%	70%	60%
	$900	$800	$700	$625	$575	$525	$475

MODEL 1909 - metric cals., round receiver bridge, bolt does not have a guide rib, two-piece ejector/bolt stop housing, push button mag. release on left side of trigger guard, no dovetail guiding on cocking piece.

	100%	98%	95%	90%	80%	70%	60%
	$1,100	$925	$800	$700	$625	$575	$525

HAKIM

Trademark of rifle adopted by the Egyptian army during the early 1950s.

RIFLES: SEMI-AUTO

HAKIM - 7.92x57mm cal., gas operated, 25.1 in. barrel with muzzle brake, cocking the bolt is done by sliding the top cover foreword, then pulling it back, manual safety is located in rear of receiver, 10 shot detachable box mag., can also be reloaded using stripper clips, adj. rear sight, hardwood stock, 9.7 lbs. Approx. 70,000 mfg. circa 1950s-1960s, with Swedish machinery.

	100%	98%	95%	90%	80%	70%	60%
	$495	$450	$400	$360	$320	$285	$245

A scaled down variation of the Hakim rifle was manufactured later, and called the Rasheed - it was produced in small numbers.

HALO ARMS, LLC

Current rifle manufacturer established in 2003, and located in Phoenixville, PA.

RIFLES

Halo Arms, LLC manufactures good quality AR-15 style rifles in military, law enforcement, and civilian configurations. Current models include the single shot HA 50 FTR (Field Tactical Rifle, MSR $4,350), the single shot HA 50 LRR (Long Range Rifle, MSR $4,500), and the 5-shot HA .308 (MSR - POR). Many accessories and options are available.

Please contact the company for more information, including delivery time and availability (see Trademark Index).

GRADING - PPGS™	100%	98%	95%	90%	80%	70%	60%

HAMBRUSCH JAGDWAFFEN GmbH

Current manufacturer established in 1752, and located in Ferlach, Austria. Currently imported and distributed exclusively by CONCO Arms, located in Emmaus, PA.

Hambrusch Jagdwaffen was a member of the Ferlach Gun Guild until it was dissolved in 2004. This company manufactures many types of high-grade long arms, including SxS shotguns, combination guns, drillings, double rifles, and single shot rifles. The combinations of these configurations are almost endless. During 2002, Hambrusch introduced a new proprietary big game cartridge, the .600/538 MM (Mega Magnum with 722 grain bullet). Please refer to the Conco Arms section for more information on select Hambrusch models, or contact Conco Arms directly for more information, availability, and current pricing.

HÄMMERLI AG

Current trademark purchased during 2006 by Walther, located in Ulm/Donau, Germany. As this edition goes to press, Walther has yet to produced new Hämmerlis in its new facility in Ulm.

Previous manufacturer located in Lenzburg, Switzerland until late 2005. Currently imported and distributed by Larry's Guns, located in Portland, ME, Brenzovich Firearms, located in Fort Hancock, TX, Champion's Choice, located in LaVergne, TN. Previously imported by SIG Arms Inc. located in Exeter, NH, Gunsmithing Inc., located in Colorado Springs, CO, Hämmerli Pistols USA, located in Groveland, CA, and by Beeman Precision Arms located in Santa Rosa, CA.

For more information and current pricing on both new and used Hämmerli airguns, please refer to the *Blue Book of Airguns* by Dr. Robert Beeman & John Allen (also online).

PISTOLS: SINGLE SHOT, RIMFIRE

Values listed below for recently manufactured pistols reflect older mfg. by Hämmerli in Lenzburg, Switzerland.

FP-10 FREE PISTOL - .22 LR cal., top-of-the-line Hämmerli pistol. Imported 2000-2004.

$1,525	$1,200	$950	$850	$750	$650	$575

Last MSR was $1,749.

MODEL 33MP - .22 LR cal., similar to the Model 100, except not available in a deluxe model. Mfg. 1933-49.

$925	$725	$650	$550	$470	$440	$385

MODEL FP 60 - .22 LR cal., refined ergonomic design from the FP-10, 12 3/4 in. barrel, increased stability, adj. rear sight with integral front sight, many accessories available, approx. 2 1/2 lbs. Importation began 2005.

MSR N/A						
	$2,050	$1,675	$1,450	$1,275	$1,050	$875	$750

MODEL 100 FREE PISTOL - .22 LR cal., 11 1/2 in. octagon barrel, blue, martini action single shot, set trigger, micro rear sight, walnut stock and forearm. Mfg. 1950-56.

$880	$660	$605	$550	$470	$440	$385

Add 15%-20% for Olympic rings, "London," and "1948" markings (indicative of Swiss shooting team).

✳ *Model 100 Free Pistol Deluxe Model* - carved stock.

$990	$770	$715	$660	$580	$550	$495

MODEL 101 - similar to Model 100, but heavy round barrel, improved action and sights, matte finish. Mfg. 1956-60.

$880	$660	$605	$550	$470	$440	$385

MODEL 102 - similar to Model 101, except high polished finish. Mfg. 1956-60.

$880	$660	$605	$550	$470	$440	$385

GRADING - PPGS™	100%	98%	95%	90%	80%	70%	60%

* *Model 102 Deluxe Model*

	$990	$770	$715	$660	$580	$550	$495

MODEL 103 FREE PISTOL - similar to Model 101, except lighter octagon polished barrel. Mfg. 1956-60.

	$935	$715	$660	$605	$580	$550	$495

MODEL 104 MATCH PISTOL - similar to Model 103, except lighter round barrel, redesigned stock, mfg. 1961-65.

	$760	$660	$550	$495	$470	$440	$385

MODEL 105 MATCH PISTOL - similar to Model 103, except redesigned action and stock, octagon barrel. Mfg. 1962-65.

	$935	$715	$660	$605	$580	$550	$495

MODEL 106 MATCH PISTOL - similar to Model 105, except improved trigger.

	$910	$690	$580	$525	$495	$470	$415

MODEL 107 MATCH PISTOL - similar to Model 105, except improved trigger.

	$990	$770	$660	$550	$525	$495	$440

* *Model 107 Match Pistol Deluxe model* - engraved and carved wood.

	$1,320	$990	$880	$660	$635	$605	$550

MODEL 120-1 SINGLE SHOT FREE PISTOL - .22 LR cal., bolt action, 9.9 in. barrel, blue barrel and receiver, side lever operated, anodized aluminum lever and frame, walnut checkered grips.

	$625	$550	$475	$425	$375	$325	$295

MODEL 120-2 - similar to 120-1, except stocks hand contoured.

	$700	$600	$550	$475	$425	$375	$325

MODEL 120 HEAVY BARREL - similar to 120-1, with 5.7 in. bull barrel, 1,000 mfg.

	$800	$700	$600	$550	$475	$425	$375

This model was cased with test target and tools.

MODEL 150 FREE PISTOL - .22 LR cal., 11.3 in. barrel, improved Martini-type action, set trigger, innovative design incorporating many unusual features. Disc. 1989.

	$1,850	$1,495	$1,275	$1,120	$980	$900	$850

Last MSR was $1,980.

Add $113 for left-hand variation.
The Model 150 was replaced by the Model 151.

MODEL 151 FREE PISTOL - replacement for the Model 150 Free Pistol. Imported 1990-93.

	$1,850	$1,495	$1,275	$1,120	$995	$900	$800

Last MSR was $1,980.

MODEL 152 FREE PISTOL - .22 LR cal., 11.3 in. barrel. improved Martini-type action, electronic trigger release, innovative design incorporating many unusual features. State-of-the-art target pistol. Disc. 1992.

	$1,995	$1,600	$1,350	$1,195	$1,090	$990	$895

Last MSR was $2,105.

Add $57 for left-hand variation.

MODEL 160 FREE PISTOL - .22 LR cal., similar to Model 150, except has poly-carbon fiber forend, includes carrying case. Mfg. 1993-2002.

	$1,725	$1,475	$1,175	$900	$800	$700	$595

Last MSR was $1,850.

Add $290 for smaller adj. grips.

MODEL 162 FREE PISTOL - .22 LR cal., replacement for the Model 152 Free Pistol, includes poly-carbon fiber forend, includes carrying case. Imported 1993-2000.

	$2,150	$1,700	$1,375	$1,125	$900	$800	$700

Last MSR was $2,410.

Add $290 for smaller adj. grips.

GRADING - PPGS™	100%	98%	95%	90%	80%	70%	60%

PISTOLS: SEMI-AUTO

Values listed below for recently manufactured pistols reflect older mfg. by Hämmerli in Lenzburg, Switzerland.

MODELS 200-205 - see Hämmerli-Walther.

INTERNATIONAL MODEL 206 - .22 Short or .22 LR cal., semi-auto, 7 1/16 in. barrel with muzzle brake, adj. sights, walnut grips, blue. Mfg. 1962-69.

	$675	$625	$525	$450	$395	$365	$330

INTERNATIONAL MODEL 207 - similar to 206, except adj. grip heel.

	$725	$650	$550	$475	$425	$375	$350

INTERNATIONAL MODEL 208 - .22 LR cal., 9 shot, 6 in. barrel, blue, adj. sights, checkered walnut grips with adj. heel. Mfg. 1966-88.

	$2,000	$1,700	$1,450	$1,150	$925	$825	$725

Last MSR was $1,755.

This model was replaced by the Model 208S.

* *International Model 208S* - similar to Model 208, except has redesigned triggerguard and safety with interchangeable rear sight element. Imported 1988-2000.

	$2,450	$2,150	$1,750	$1,450	$1,150	$925	$825

Last MSR was $2,021.

> Add $125 for factory scope mount.
> Add $180 for smaller adj. grips.

* *International Model 208 Deluxe* - similar to Model 208, except has carved grips and elaborate engraving. Importation disc. 1988.

	$2,995	$2,500	$1,995	$1,735	$1,495	$1,215	$1,000

Last MSR was $3,250.

* *International Model 208C (Commemorative)* - limited edition commemorative. Disc. 1987.

	$2,100	$1,750	$1,400	N/A	N/A	N/A	N/A

Last MSR was $2,225.

INTERNATIONAL MODEL 209 - .22 Short cal., semi-auto, 5 shot, 4 3/4 in. barrel, muzzle brake, adj. sights, blue, walnut stock. Mfg. 1966-70.

	$800	$690	$635	$550	$525	$485	$440

INTERNATIONAL MODEL 210 - similar to 209, but grips have adj. heel. Mfg. 1966-70.

	$800	$715	$660	$590	$540	$525	$495

MODEL 211 - .22 LR cal., semi-auto, 9 shot, 6 in. barrel, adj. sights, blue, similar to Model 208 except non-adj. walnut stocks. Importation disc. 1990.

	$1,550	$1,275	$1,050	$950	$880	$835	$770

Last MSR was $1,669.

MODEL 212 HUNTER - .22 LR cal., semi-auto, hunter's pistol, 9 shot, 5 in. barrel, adj. sights, blue, walnut stocks. Importation disc. 1993.

	$2,000	$1,800	$1,650	$1,400	$1,200	$850	$675

Last MSR was $1,395.

MODEL 215 - .22 LR cal., semi-auto, commercial target version with Model 208 specifications, 9 shot, 5 in. barrel, adj. sights, blue, walnut stocks. Importation disc. 1990.

	$2,300	$1,950	$1,775	$1,550	$1,300	$1,150	$995

Last MSR was $1,505.

> Add $300 for Model 215S.

MODEL 230 RAPID FIRE PISTOL - .22 S cal., semi-auto, 5 shot, 6.3 in. barrel, blue, adj. sights, smooth walnut grips. Mfg. 1970-83.

	$705	$635	$580	$530	$485	$450	$415

MODEL 230-2 - similar to 230, except checkered grips with adj. heel. Mfg. 1970-83.

$735	$655	$605	$570	$515	$485	$470

MODEL 232-1 RAPID FIRE PISTOL - .22 S cal., semi-auto, 6 shot, 5.1 in. barrel, blue, adj. sights, contoured walnut grips. Importation disc. 1993.

$1,395	$1,125	$950	$850	$750	$700	$650

Last MSR was $1,505.

Add $25 for wraparound grips sizes S-M-LG (Model 232-2).

MODEL 280 - .22 LR or .32 S&W Wadcutter cal., new modular pistol design utilizing carbon fiber synthetic material to replace frame and other critical parts, adj. grips, trigger, and rear sight, 4.6 in. barrel, 5 or 6 shot mag., approx. 2.2 lbs. Imported 1988-2000.

$1,450	$1,125	$900	$800	$675	$575	$475

Last MSR was $1,643.

Add $200 for .32 S&W Wadcutter cal.
Add $765 (.22 LR) or $965 (.32 S&W Wadcutter) for conversion kit.
Add $200 for smaller adj. grips.
A package was also available with both calibers, magazines, and hard case for $2,595.

MODEL SP 20 - .22 LR or .32 S&W Wadcutter cal., replacement for Model 280, features low-level sight line, colored alloy receiver (blue, red, gold, violet, or black), adj. "JPS" buffer system that varies recoil characteristics per individual preference, black Hi-Grip anatomical grips. Mfg. 1998-2002.

$1,325	$1,075	$925	$800	$700	$600	$500

Last MSR was $1,450.

Add $110 for .32 S&W Wadcutter cal.
Add $499 for .22 LR conversion, $599 for .32 S&W Wadcutter conversion.

MODEL SP 20 RRS - .22 LR or .32 S&W Wadcutter cal., state-of-the-art target pistol featuring composite frame with redesigned ergonomic grips, RRS designates recoil reducing system, fully hand adj. rear sight, various slide colors available. New 2002.

MSR N/A						
$1,430	$1,250	$1,125	$1,025	$925	$825	$725

Add $113 for .32 S&W Wadcutter cal.
Add $795 for .22 LR conversion, or $850 for .32 Wadcutter conversion.

MODEL P-240 - see SIG-Hämmerli for this model.

TRAILSIDE - .22 LR cal., single action, 4 1/2 or 6 in. barrel, two-tone finish, choice of ultralight polymer composite grips or target variation which includes wood grips and adj. rear sight, 10 shot mag., cased with trigger lock, 28 or 30 oz. Mfg. 1999-2005.

$395	$350	$300	$275	$250	$225	$200

Last MSR was $455.

Add $79 for 4 1/2 in. barrel with target sights, or $95 for 6 in. barrel with target sights.
This model was also available as one of SIG Arms' limited editions in Jan. 2004 - it included a BSA 30mm red dot optical sight with integrated mount and 6 in. barrel. Last MSR was $709.

* *Trailside Competition* - includes 6 in. barrel with blue anatomical stippled grips and adj. bottom rest, cased with trigger lock, 37.2 oz. Limited importation 2000-2005.

$580	$500	$400	$350	$300	$265	$225

Last MSR was $710.

X-ESSE - .22 LR cal., European variation of the Trailside, available in Sport, Long, and Short configurations, 4 1/2 or 6 in. barrel, polymer or anatomic stippled polymer target grips, adj. hand rest, 10 shot mag. Not imported into the U.S. until 2007.

MSR $577						
$550	$495	$450	$400	$365	$335	$300

Add approx. $33 for 6 1/2 in. target barrel.
Add approx. $254 for Competition (Sport) Model.

GRADING - PPGS™	100%	98%	95%	90%	80%	70%	60%

RIFLES: BOLT ACTION, TARGET

OLYMPIC 300 METER - .30-06 cal., bolt action, single shot free rifle, U.S.A. import, 7x57mm overseas, 20 1/2 in. heavy barrel, double set trigger, aperture rear sight, globe front, free rifle stock with thumbhole pistol grip, beavertail forearm, Swiss style target butt. Mfg. 1945-59.

	$880	$745	$605	$550	$470	$440	$415

HÄMMERLI-TANNER 300 METER FREE RIFLE - similar to Olympic 300, except 7.5mm standard, also was available in other calibers. Mfg. 1962-disc.

	$895	$825	$770	$715	$660	$580	$520

Last MSR was $935.

MODEL 45 SMALLBORE MATCH RIFLE - .22 LR cal., bolt action, single shot, 27 1/2 in. heavy barrel, same sights and stock type as Hämmerli-Tanner. Mfg. 1945-57.

	$660	$550	$470	$440	$385	$360	$330

MODEL 54 SMALLBORE MATCH RIFLE - similar to 45 Smallbore, except adj. butt. Mfg. 1954-57.

	$670	$560	$480	$450	$395	$370	$340

MODEL S 205 - 6mm BR, 7.5x55mm, or .308 Win. cal., designed for 300 meter competition, adj. blue aluminum or wood stock, 5 shot mag., Hammerli apeture rear sight, Sauer produced 205 action with 26 in. heavy free floating barrel, 12 lbs. New 2004.

MSR N/A	$3,995	$3,650	$3,300	$3,000	$2,650	$2,300	$1,850

Add $723 for adj. aluminum stock.

This model is not currently being manufactured.

MODEL 503 SMALLBORE FREE RIFLE - similar to 54 Smallbore, except free style stock.

	$660	$550	$470	$440	$385	$360	$330

MODEL 505 MATCH RIFLE - match stock with aperture sights.

	$690	$580	$495	$470	$415	$385	$360

MODEL 506 SMALLBORE MATCH RIFLE - similar to 503 Smallbore. Mfg. 1963-66.

	$690	$580	$495	$470	$415	$385	$360

SPORTING RIFLE - various calibers, set triggers, Mauser repeating action.

	$725	$650	$490	$425	$360	$325	$300

HÄMMERLI-WALTHER

Previously manufactured semi-auto target pistols made under joint effort from Hämmerli and Walther.

PISTOLS: SEMI-AUTO, RIMFIRE

MODEL 200 OLYMPIA - .22 Short or LR cal., 7 1/2 in. barrel, 1952 type, adj. sights, barrel weight, blue, checkered walnut grips. Mfg. 1952-58.

	$660	$605	$550	$440	$415	$385	$360

MODEL 200 OLYMPIA - 1958 type, similar to 1952 type, except has muzzle brake. Mfg. 1958-63.

	$715	$605	$550	$495	$470	$415	$385

MODEL 201 - similar to 200, 1952 type, except 9 1/2 in. barrel. Mfg. 1955-57.

	$660	$605	$550	$440	$415	$385	$360

MODEL 202 - similar to 201, except adj. heel grips. Mfg. 1955-57.

	$715	$605	$550	$495	$470	$415	$385

MODEL 203 - similar to 200, except has adj. heel grip.

✳ *Model 203 1955 Type* - no muzzle brake.

	$715	$605	$550	$495	$470	$415	$385

GRADING - PPGS™	100%	98%	95%	90%	80%	70%	60%

✳ *Model 203 1958 Type* - muzzle brake.

	$770	$660	$605	$550	$525	$470	$440

MODEL 204 - similar to 200, except .22 LR cal. only.

✳ *Model 204 1956 Type* - no muzzle brake.

	$745	$635	$580	$525	$495	$470	$440

✳ *Model 204 1958 Type* - muzzle brake.

	$800	$690	$635	$550	$525	$495	$470

MODEL 205 - .22 LR cal., similar to 204, except adj. heel grips.

✳ *Model 205 1956 Type* - no muzzle brake.

	$800	$690	$635	$550	$525	$495	$470

✳ *Model 205 1958 Type* - muzzle brake.

	$855	$745	$715	$635	$580	$525	$495

HARRINGTON & RICHARDSON, INC.

Previous manufacturer located in Gardner, MA - formerly from Worcester, MA. Successors to Wesson & Harrington, manufactured from 1871 until January 24, 1986. H & R 1871, LLC was formed during 1991 (an entirely different company, see listing in the front of this section). H & R 1871, LLC is not responsible for the warranties or safety of older pre-1986 H & R firearms.

A manufacturer of utilitarian firearms for over 115 years, H & R ceased operation on January 24, 1986. Even though new manufacture (under H & R 1871, LLC) is utilizing the H & R trademark, the discontinuance of older models in either NIB or mint condition may command slight asking premiums, but probably will not affect values on those handguns only recently discontinued. Most H & R firearms are still purchased for their shooting value rather than collecting potential.

Please refer to H & R listing in the Serialization section for alphabetical suffix information on how to determine year of manufacture for most H & R firearms between 1940-1982.

The author would like to thank Mr. W.E. "Bill" Goforth and Mr. Jim Hauff for providing pricing and information on many of the H&R models.

COMBINATION GUNS: SINGLE SHOT

MODEL 058 - 20 ga./.30-30, .22 Rem. Jet, .22 Hornet, .357 Mag., or .44 Mag. cal. combination, 2 separate barrels supplied, blue only. Disc. 1985.

	$175	$150	$125	$100	$85	$75	$65

Last MSR was $145.

MODEL 258 COMBINATION HANDY GUN II - supplied with 20 ga., 22 in. barrel and 22 in. rifle barrel in .22 Hornet, .30-30 Win., or .357 Mag. cal., electroless, matte nickel finish, side lever action release, cased, 6 1/2 lbs. Disc. 1985.

	$195	$175	$150	$130	$120	$100	$95

Last MSR was $195.

HANDGUNS 1871-1986

HAMMERLESS SMALL FRAME - .22 LR, 7 shot, or .32 S&W, 5 shot cal., double action, 2, 3, 4, 5, or 6 in. barrels, top break, blue or nickel, black rubber grips.

	$250	$200	$150	$120	$75	$55	$50

HAMMERLESS LARGE FRAME - .32 S&W, 6 shot, or .38 S&W, 5 shot cal., double action, 3 1/4, 4, 5, or 6 in. barrels, break open.

	$350	$300	$200	$150	$100	$75	$50

.22 SPECIAL - .22 LR, or .22 WRF cal., 9 shot, double action, 6 in. barrel, break open, large frame, blue only, gold plated front sight, walnut grips.

	$300	$250	$200	$150	$100	$75	$50

GRADING - PPGS™	100%	98%	95%	90%	80%	70%	60%

MATCH TARGET PISTOL (MODEL 195) - .22 LR cal., many configurations, including 14 different stocks (including variations by Walter Roper), 5 trigger guards, 3 triggers, 2 hammers, 2 extractors, 3 barrel lengths (7, 8, or 10 inch), and 3 barrel rib designs, approx. 3,500 mfg. by H&R 1928-1941.

✳ *Match Target Pistol Variation 1 Pre-U.S.R.A.* - not marked "U.S.R.A.", known as the H&R Single Shot Pistol, no finger rest between the trigger guard and the front gripstrap, advertised with a "sawhandle" shape grip copied from the Model 1 or 2 smoothbore H&R Handy Gun, mfg. with a 10 in. barrel with deeply undercut rib. First 500 pistols mfg. 1928-1930.

	$550	$500	$375	$300	$275	$250	$200

✳ *Match Target Pistol Variation 2 U.S.R.A. Keyhole Barrel* - standard early model marked "U.S.R.A.", finger rest, non-sawhandle grips, optional grip shapes, grip screw goes from rear of grip into threaded hole in back grip strap. Mfg. 1930-31.

	$550	$500	$400	$350	$300	$250	$200

✳ *Match Target Pistol Variation 3 Modified Keyhole Barrel* - modification of Variation 2 to improve rear sight, barrel catch changed, reduced spent cartridge force by replacing cylindrical extractor with less powerful hinged type, hammer cocking spur and finger rest were wider, 8 in. optional or 10 in. standard barrel, optional grip shapes, transition model between early Variation 2 and final Variation 4 designs. Mfg. 1931.

	$550	$500	$400	$350	$300	$250	$200

✳ *Match Target Pistol Variation 4 Tapered Slabside Barrel* - new "truncated teardrop" barrel cross section shape, 7 in. standard or 10 in. optional barrel, adj. trigger, new sear, grips screw location was changed to front of grip, front sight was adj for elevation, trigger design changed from curved to straight beveled type with relocated cocking surfaces, 13 optional grip shapes, front sight protector standard, optional luggage style case. Mfg. 1931-1941.

	$600	$500	$450	$400	$350	$200	$250

This model was introduced circa 1931, the 1932 advertisements describe a fully redesigned gun, but pictured the Variation 2, indicating that H&R probably did not rephotograph the new design. The final variation had a special, tight bore .217 inches in diameter, with bullet seating .03125 in (1-32 in.) into rifling, and is among the most accurate single shot .22 cal. pistols. The Model 195 U.S.R.A. was expensive, costing approx. $30 in 1932, and increased to more than $36 by the time production had ended in 1941, yet was the least expensive of all single shot quality .22 cal. target pistols during this time.

SINGLE ACTION SPUR TRIGGER REVOLVERS: 1871-1883

WESSON & HARRINGTON MARKED SINGLE ACTION SPUR TRIGGER - .22 Short, .32 rimfire, .38 rimfire, or .41 rimfire cal., 5 or 7 shot, 2 1/2 (Third type), 3 3/16 (First type, No. 3) or 3 1/2 in. octagon barrel, First type has brass frame silver-plated, patented cartridge ejector, birds-head grip frame, rosewood grips, Second type has iron frame nickel-plated patented cartridge ejector, birds-head grip frame, rosewood grips, Third type has iron frame nickel-plated birds-head grip frame, no cartridge ejector pull pin cylinder release. No. 2 is 7 shot, .22 Short, small frame, 3 3/16 in. octagon barrel, No. 3 is 5 shot, .32 rimfire cal., medium frame, 3 3/16 octagon barrel, No. 4 is 5 shot, .38 rimfire cal., large frame, 3 1/2 in. octagon barrel. Both First and Second type will be marked with Feb.7 and June 13 1871 patent dates. Mfg. 1871-1876.

	100%	98%	95%	90%	80%	70%	60%
First Type (rare)	$1,200	$1,000	$865	$765	$660	$575	$495
Second Type No. 2, 3, & 4	$600	$520	$440	$390	$340	$285	$245
Third Type	$400	$350	$300	$265	$225	$190	$165

Add 50% for late production with Harrington & Richardson barrel markings.

GRADING - PPGS™	100%	98%	95%	90%	80%	70%	60%

H&R MODEL 1 SPUR TRIGGER SINGLE ACTION - .32 or .38 rimfire cal., 5 or 7 shot, pull pin cylinder release, 3 inch octagon barrel, birds-head grip frame, hard rubber grip panels, only slightly changed version of the Wesson & Harrington Third Type marked with patent date May 23, 1876. Mfg. 1876-1883.

	$500	$440	$375	$325	$275	$235	$200

H&R SPUR TRIGGER SINGLE ACTION - pull pin cylinder release, nickel finish only, most will be marked with patent date May 23, 1876 and company name and address on left side of barrel, sometimes called 'New Design of 1878", saw handle, grip shape. Mfg. 1878-1883.

Subtract 50%-70% for models not marked H&R.

The above model as well as modified Wesson & Harrington Models can be found marked with the following Brand Names: AETNA, VICTOR, BANGUP, CROWN, EAGLE, ELY & WRAY, GREAT WESTERN, PANTHER, SMOKY CITY and maybe more names.

✳ *Model 1 1/2* - .32 rimfire cal. 5 shot, 2½ inch octagon barrel (actual barrel length may vary slightly), medium frame.

	$400	$350	$300	$265	$225	$190	$165

✳ *Model 2 1/2* - .32 rimfire cal., 7 shot, 3¼ inch octagon barrel (actual barrel length may vary slightly), large frame.

	$400	$350	$300	$265	$225	$190	$165

✳ *Model 3 1/2* - .38 rimfire cal., 5 shot, 3½ inch octagon barrel (actual barrel length may vary slightly), large frame.

	$400	$350	$300	$265	$225	$190	$165

✳ *Model 4 1/2* - .41 rimfire cal., 5 shot, 3½ inch octagon barrel (actual barrel length may vary slightly), large frame, rare.

	$700	$600	$525	$450	$385	$340	$285

SOLID FRAME REVOLVERS: 1880-1952

MODEL 1880 MEDIUM DOUBLE ACTION, (BLACK POWDER ONLY) - .32 or .38 centerfire cal., 5 or 6 shot, 2 ½ in round barrel, nickel finish, pull pin cylinder release, side plate on left side of frame, hard rubber grip panels with floral design, marked with patent date January 20, 1880 and company name and address on left side of barrel. Mfg. 1880-1883.

	$550	$475	$415	$360	$315	$265	$230

AMERICAN DOUBLE ACTION FIRST MODEL, (BLACK POWDER MODEL) - .32, .38, or .44 cal., 5 (.38 or .44) or 6 (.32 cal.) shot, 2½, 4½ or 6 in. barrel, nickel finish standard, blue finish considered rare, pull pin cylinder release, marked on top strap "AMERICAN DOUBLE ACTION", first variation has round barrel and nickel trigger guard (1884-1887), second variation has octagon barrel and nickel trigger guard (1888-1897), third variation has octagon barrel, blue trigger guard and company name and address on left side of barrel (1898-1904). Mfg. 1884-1904.

	$225	$195	$170	$140	$125	$110	$95

Add 50% for first variation (rare).
Add 15% for blue finish.
Add 10% for 4 1/2 or 6 in. barrel.
Add 5%-10% for nickel trigger guard (pre-1898 mfg.).

BULLDOG FIRST MODEL LARGE FRAME - .32 or .38 rimfire cal., 5 (.38 cal.) or 6 (.32 cal.) shot, variation of American Double Action First Model marked on top strap "H&R BULL DOG". Mfg. 1888-1904.

	$235	$200	$180	$150	$125	$110	$95

SAFETY HAMMER DOUBLE ACTION FIRST MODEL - same as American Double Action First Model except has patented spurless hammer, patent date will be marked on hammer, marked on top strap "SAFETY HAMMER DOUBLE ACTION". Mfg. 1888-1904.

	$235	$200	$180	$150	$125	$110	$95

GRADING - PPGS™	100%	98%	95%	90%	80%	70%	60%

AMERICAN DOUBLE ACTION SECOND MODEL (SMOKELESS POWDER) - .32, .38, or .44 Webley (disc. 1921) cal., 5 (.38 or .44 cal.) or 6 (.32 cal.) shot, pull pin cylinder release, calibers and barrel lengths are the same as first model, nickel or blue finish, difference between First Model and Second Model is the caliber, markings on the left side of the barrel, after 1930 this model was listed in catalogs as: AMERICAN DOUBLE ACTION No. 60 .32 Caliber 6 shot, and AMERICAN DOUBLE ACTION No. 65 .38 Caliber 5 shot. Mfg. 1905-1941.

	$225	$195	$170	$140	$125	$110	$95

Add 15% for blue finish or 10% for 4 1/2 or 6 in. barrel.

BULLDOG SECOND MODEL LARGE FRAME - .32 or .38 rimfire cal., 5 (.38 cal.) or 6 (.32 cal.) shot, variation of American Double Action Second Model, marked on top strap "H&R BULL DOG". Mfg. 1905-1923.

	$235	$200	$180	$150	$125	$110	$95

SAFETY HAMMER DOUBLE ACTION SECOND MODEL - same as American Double Action Second Model except has patented spurless hammer, patent date may be marked on hammer, marked on top strap "SAFETY HAMMER DOUBLE ACTION". Mfg. 1904-1940.

	$235	$200	$180	$150	$125	$110	$95

VEST POCKET FIRST MODEL MEDIUM FRAME (BLACK POWDER) - .32 S&W cal., 5 shot, 1¼ in. round or 2 in. octagon barrel (rare), double action, pull pin cylinder release, spurless hammer, blue (rare) or nickel finish, markings are on top strap "VEST POCKET SELF COCKER" "VEST POCKET SAFETY HAMMER" or "VEST POCKET", First Variation has 1¼ in. round or 2 in. octagon barrel, nickel finish and nickel trigger guard (1891-1897), Second Variation has 1¼ in. round or 2 in. octagon barrel, nickel finish, blue trigger guard (1897-1904). Mfg. 1891-1904.

	$215	$195	$165	$135	$120	$100	$90

Add 50% for 2 in. octagon barrel or 15% for blue finish.

VEST POCKET SECOND MODEL SMALL FRAME (SMOKELESS POWDER), - .22 rimfire cal., 7 shot, 1¼ in. round barrel, spurless hammer, nickel or blue finish, pull pin cylinder release, markings are on top strap "VEST POCKET SAFETY HAMMER" or "VEST POCKET" company name and address marked on bottom of butt, after 1930 catalog listing is: VEST POCKET No. 77 22 rimfire caliber 7 shots. Mfg. 1905-1941.

	$220	$190	$165	$140	$125	$110	$95

Add 5% for blue finish.

VEST POCKET SECOND MODEL MEDIUM FRAME (SMOKELESS POWDER) - similar to Small Frame model, except is .32 S&W cal., 5 shot and medium frame. Mfg. 1905-1941.

	$195	$175	$155	$125	$110	$95	$85

Add 15% for blue finish.

YOUNG AMERICA DOUBLE ACTION FIRST MODEL (BLACK POWDER) - .22 rimfire or .32 S&W cal., 2, 4 1/2, or 6 in. round or octagon barrel, small (.22 cal.) or medium (.32 cal.) frame, pull pin cylinder release, nickel or blue (rare) finish, marking on top strap only "YOUNG AMERICA DOUBLE ACTION" or "YOUNG AMERICAN DOUBLE ACTION", First Variation has round barrel and nickel trigger guard (1884-1887), Second Variation has octagon barrel and nickel trigger guard (1888-1897), Third Variation has octagon barrel, blue trigger guard and company name and address on left side of barrel (1897-1904). Mfg. 1884-1904.

First Variation	$275	$245	$210	$170	$145	$120	$110
	$225	$195	$170	$140	$125	$110	$95

Add 15% for blue finish or 10% for 4 1/2 or 6 in. barrel.

YOUNG AMERICA SAFETY HAMMER FIRST MODEL - spurless hammer variation of Young American First Model. Mfg. 1884-1904.

	$235	$200	$180	$150	$125	$110	$95

YOUNG AMERICA BULLDOG FIRST MODEL MEDIUM FRAME - .32 Short cal., 5 shot. Mfg. 1888-1904.

	$235	$200	$180	$150	$125	$110	$95

YOUNG AMERICA DOUBLE ACTION SECOND MODEL SMALL FRAME - .22 Short cal., 7 shot, 2, 4½, or 6 in. barrel, pull pin cylinder release, nickel or blue finish, caliber and company name and address marked on side of barrel, top strap will be marked "YOUNG AMERICA DOUBLE ACTION" or "YOUNG AMERICAN DOUBLE ACTION", after 1930 listed in catalogs as: YOUNG AMERICA No. 70 DOUBLE ACTION. Mfg. 1905-1941.

	$235	$200	$180	$150	$125	$110	$95

Add 15% for blue finish or 10% for 4 1/2 or 6 in. barrel.

YOUNG AMERICA DOUBLE ACTION SECOND MODEL MEDIUM FRAME - .32 S&W cal., 5 shot, pull pin cylinder release, nickel or blue finish, 2, 4½ or 6 in. barrel, caliber and company name and address marked on side of barrel, top strap will be marked "YOUNG AMERICA DOUBLE ACTION" or "YOUNG AMERICAN DOUBLE ACTION", after 1930 listed in catalogs as: YOUNG AMERICA No. 73 DOUBLE ACTION .32 Rimfire short 5 shot and YOUNG AMERICA No. 74 DOUBLE ACTION .32 S&W 5 shot. Mfg. 1905-1941.

	$225	$195	$170	$140	$125	$110	$95

Add 15% for blue finish or 10% for 4 1/2 or 6 in. barrel.

YOUNG AMERICA BULLDOG MEDIUM FRAME SECOND MODEL - only advertised as a separate model until 1923. Mfg. 1905-1923.

	$225	$195	$170	$140	$125	$110	$95

YOUNG AMERICA SAFETY HAMMER MEDIUM FRAME SECOND MODEL - only advertised as a separate model until 1939. Mfg. 1905-1939.

	$205	$185	$165	$130	$120	$100	$90

VICTOR (BRAND NAME VERSION OF AMERICAN DOUBLE ACTION AND YOUNG AMERICA DOUBLE ACTION SERIES) - .32 S&W Long or .38 S&W cal., 5 (.32 cal.) or 6 (.38 cal.) shot, 2½ or 4½ in. barrel (Large Solid Frame), .32 S&W cal., 5 shot, 2 or 4 in. barrel (Medium Sold Frame Double Action), or .22 rimfire cal., 7 shot, 2 or 4 in. barrel (Small Solid Frame Double Action), marked "VICTOR DOUBLE ACTION" and have a round barrel and unfluted cylinder, pull pin cylinder release, may have company name and address marked on frame or bottom of the butt (not listed in any H&R catalogs). Mfg. 1913-1936.

	$195	$175	$155	$125	$110	$95	$85

MODEL 1904 LARGE SOLID FRAME DOUBLE ACTION - .38 S&W cal., 5 shot, 2½, 4½ or 6 in. barrel, hard rubber target logo grips, pull pin cylinder release, blue or nickel finish, marked with company name and address on left side of barrel and on top strap in two lines "H&R DOUBLE ACTION MODEL 1904 .38 CAL.", after 1930 listed in catalogs as: H&R MODEL 4 DOUBLE ACTION No. 83 .38 S&W CALIBER 5 shot. Mfg. 1905-1941.

	$230	$195	$175	$150	$125	$110	$95

MODEL 04 LARGE SOLID FRAME DOUBLE ACTION - .32 S&W cal., 6 shot, 2½, 4½ or 6 in. barrel, pull pin cylinder release, blue or nickel finish, hard rubber target logo grips, marked with company name and address on left side of barrel and on top strap in two lines "H&R DOUBLE ACTION MODEL 04 .32 6 SHOT", after 1930 listed in catalogs as: H&R MODEL 4 DOUBLE ACTION No. 80 .32 S&W Long Caliber 6 shot. Mfg. 1905-1941.

	$220	$190	$165	$140	$125	$110	$95

MODEL 1905 MEDIUM SOLID FRAME DOUBLE ACTION - .32 S&W cal., similar to Model 1904, marked with company name and address on left side of barrel and on top strap in two lines "H&R DOUBLE ACTION MODEL 1905 .32 CAL.", after 1930 listed in catalogs as: H&R MODEL 5 DOUBLE ACTION No. 90 .32 S&W CALIBER 5 shot. Mfg. 1905-1941.

	$225	$195	$170	$140	$125	$110	$95

MODEL 1906 SMALL SOLID FRAME DOUBLE ACTION - .22 rimfire cal., 7 shot, similar to Model 1905, marked with company name and address on left side of barrel and on top strap in two lines "H&R MODEL 1906 22 CAL. R.F.", after 1930 listed in catalogs as: H&R MODEL 6 DOUBLE ACTION No. 96 .22 RF CALIBER 7 shot. Mfg. 1905-1941.

	$185	$165	$140	$120	$100	$90	$80

TRAPPER SMALL SOLID FRAME DOUBLE ACTION - .22 rimfire cal., 7 shot, 6 in. octagon barrel, two-piece oversize walnut grips, pull pin cylinder release, blue finish only, marked "H&R TRAPPER" on top strap, after 1930 listed in catalogs as: TRAPPER MODEL 722 SMALL SOLID FRAME DOUBLE ACTION .22 RIMFIRE 7 shot. Mfg. 1924-1941.

	$365	$315	$275	$225	$200	$165	$140

HUNTER SMALL SOLID FRAME DOUBLE ACTION - .22 rimfire cal., 7 shot, 10 in. octagon barrel, two piece oversize walnut grips, pull pin cylinder release, blue finish only, marked "H&R HUNTER" on the top strap, some with the "HUNTER" marking were assembled late in production with short 2 1/2 inch barrel and the small two piece Target Logo hard rubber grips. Mfg. 1926-1929.

	$475	$425	$355	$300	$260	$220	$195

HUNTER LARGE SOLID FRAME DOUBLE ACTION - .22 rimfire cal., 9 shot, (built on the M922 frame), 10 inch octagon barrel only, pull pin cylinder release, blue finish only, two-piece oversize walnut grips, marked on top strap "H&R HUNTER" of just "HUNTER", after 1930 catalogs listed as: MODEL 933 DOUBLE ACTION. Mfg. 1929-1939.

	$565	$$485	$415	$360	$310	$260	$225

MODEL 922 DOUBLE ACTION FIRST MODEL LARGE SOLID FRAME - .22 rimfire cal., 9 shot, 6 in. octagon barrel, pull pin cylinder release, blue finish, two piece over size walnut grips saw handle shaped, marked with company name and address on top of barrel, right side of barrel H&R 922 and caliber on left side of barrel. Mfg. 1927-1952.

	$195	$175	$150	$125	$110	$95	$85

Add 40% for First Variation, or 20% for Second, Third, Fourth, or Fifth Variations.

First Variation 1927-1930, serial number range 125270*-144000*(estimate).

Second Variation 1931, Difference: new grip shape (saw handle shape eliminated) serial number range 144000*-160000*(estimate).

Third Variation 1932-1937, Difference: new safety cylinder, serial number range 160000*-171000*(estimate).

Fourth Variation 1938-1939, Difference: new grip frame and round barrel, serial number range 171000*-192000*(estimate).

Fifth Variation 1940-1947, Difference: same as 4th variation except letter code prefix to serial number A thru H.

Sixth Variation 1948-1949, Difference: a new barrel length, serial number letter codes I and J.

Seventh Variation 1949-1952, Difference: all-in-one cartridge extraction system, serial number letter codes J thru M.

Eighth Variation 1952, models for M922 Camper and M922 Bantam weight (REVOLVERS: RECENT MFG.).

MODEL 923 DOUBLE ACTION LARGE SOLID FRAME - .22 rimfire cal., similar to Model 922 Sixth and Seventh Variations, except has chrome finish. Mfg. 1949-1952.

	$205	$185	$165	$135	$120	$100	$90

GRADING - PPGS™	100%	98%	95%	90%	80%	70%	60%

TOP BREAK REVOLVERS 1885-1952

MANUAL EJECTING MODEL (MANUAL SHELL EXTRACTOR, BLACK POWDER) - .32 S&W or .38 S&W cal., 5 (.32 cal.) or 6 (.38 cal.) shot, manual ejecting rod under barrel, hard rubber grip panels with Floral design, nickel finish, marked on top of barrel with company name and address only, 3¼ inch barrel length, modified American Double Action mechanism and frame. Mfg. 1885-1889.

$525	$465	$395	$340	$295	$250	$220

AUTOMATIC EJECTING FIRST MODEL (BLACK POWDER) - .32 S&W or .38 S&W cal., 5 (.38 cal.) or 6 shot cylinder, hard rubber grip panels with floral design, 3 1/4 in. barrel, modified American Double Action mechanism and frame, nickel finish, First Variation marked on top of barrel with company name and address only and two guide rods for ejector (1885-1886), Second Variation patent date 10-4-87 marked on top of barrel along with company name and address, extractor does not have extra guide rods (1887-1889). Mfg. 1885-1889.

$325	$285	$250	$200	$175	$150	$125

Add 30% for First Variation.

AUTOMATIC EJECTING SECOND MODEL (BLACK POWDER) - 32 S&W or .38 S&W cal., 5 (.32 cal.) or 6 (.38 cal.) shot, new frame shape and new hard rubber grip panels with target logo, nickel or blue finish, 2 1/2 (rare), 3 1/4 (standard), 4, 5, or 6 in. barrel, if there is no caliber marking on the left side of the barrel, then it was manufactured for black powder, top of barrel markings include company name and address and patent dates. Mfg. 1890-1904.

$225	$195	$170	$140	$125	$110	$95

Add 75% for 2 1/2 in. barrel or 25% for 4, 5, or 6 in. barrels.
Add 15% for blue finish.
Add 10% for First, Second, Third, or Fourth Variations with nickel trigger guard and nickel finish.
First Variation; one patent date OCT-4-87 only (1890-1892).
Second Variation one patent date marked OCT-4-1887 (year marked in full) (1890-1892*).
Third Variation three patent dates, Oct-4-1887, May 14 & Aug-6-89 (1893-Only*).
Fourth Variation three patent dates Oct-4-87, May-14 & Aug-6-89 (note 87 date des not have full year markings) (1894-1896*).
Fifth Variation five patent dates Oct-4-87, May 14 & Aug-6-89, April-2-95, April-7-96 (1897-1904*).
*Serial numbers found on the bottom side of the top strap will have letter codes with them.

AUTO-EJECTING POLICE SECOND MODEL (BLACK POWDER) - similar to Auto-Ejecting Second model except has a patented Spurless Hammer, the Police Model will be found in all variations of and calibers the Second Model. Mfg. 1890-1904.

$235	$200	$180	$150	$125	$110	$95

AUTOMATIC EJECTING THIRD MODEL (SMOKELESS POWDER) - .32 S&W Long or .38 S&W cal., 5 (.32 cal.) or 6 (.38 cal.) shot, hard rubber grip panels with target logo, blue or nickel finish, 2½ (rare), 3¼ (standard), 4, 5 or 6 in. barrel, top of barrel markings include company name and address and early production has patent dates, the one recognizable difference in the Second and Third Models is the caliber is marked on the left side of the barrel on the Third Model, if it has a calliber marked on the left side of the barrel, then it was manufactured for smokeless powder. Mfg. 1905-1940.

$235	$200	$180	$150	$125	$110	$95

Add 75% for 2 1/2 in. barrel, or 25% for 4, 5, or 6 in. barrel.
Add 15% for blue finish.
First Variation 4 patent dates (5-14 & 8-6-89, 4-2-95, 4-7-97) model name and caliber on left side of barrel (1905-1908).
Second Variation 2 patent dates (8-6-89 and 10-8-95) model name and caliber on left side of barrel (1909-1912).

Third Variation no patent dates the name of the state is marked as MASS (1913-1915).
Fourth Variation no patent dates the state name of Massachusetts is spelled (1916-1924).
Fifth Variation new grip frame, it is now the same size as the rest of the frame with no step down for the grip panel (1925-1941).
After 1931 listed in Catalogs as: AUTOMATIC EJECTING No.10 .32 S&W LONG CALIBER 6 shots.
After 1931 listed in Catalogs as: AUTOMATIC EJECTING No. 25 .38 S&W CALIBER 5 shots.
After 1932 listed in Catalogs as: AUTOMATIC EJECTING No. 20.38 S&W CALIBER 5 shots.

AUTO-EJECTING POLICE THIRD MODEL (SMOKELESS POWDER)
- similar to Auto-Ejecting Third Model except has a patented spurless hammer, Police Model will be found in all variations and calibers of the Third Model until 1939. Mfg. 1905-1939.

	100%	98%	95%	90%	80%	70%	60%
	$245	$215	$185	$150	$125	$110	$95

AUTO-EJECTING KNIFE MODEL
- similar to regular Auto-Ejector Model except 4 in. barrel with a 2¼ inch double edge knife attached under the barrel, only finish listed in catalogs was nickel but some blue finish examples have turned up, Second Model Black Powder mfg. 1901-1904, Third Model Smokeless Powder mfg. 1905-1917.

	100%	98%	95%	90%	80%	70%	60%
	$2,000	$1,700	$1,500	$1,150	$850	$700	$625

Add 10% for blue finish.
Subtract 60% if knife is missing.

LARGE FRAME TOP BREAK
- .22 rimfire or .22 WRF cal., 6 in. barrel, 7 or 9 shot, blue finish, two-piece walnut grips (after 1932 one-piece grips). Mfg. 1925-1941.

	100%	98%	95%	90%	80%	70%	60%
	$330	$290	$255	$200	$175	$150	$125

Add 50% for .22 WRF cal., 15% for First Variation, or 10% for Fourth and Fifth Variation.
First Variation, 7 shot, .22 rimfire only, oversized 2 piece saw handle shaped walnut grips (serial number range above 490000*) (1926-1928).
Second Variation, 9 shot, .22 rimfire and 7 shot, 22WRF, (serial number range 497000-559100*) (1928-1930).
Third Variation, new rounded two-piece grip (saw handle shape eliminated) (serial number range unknown) (1931-1932).
Fourth Variation, safety cylinder and new grip frame (RICE FRAME) (serial number range 559100-590000*) (1933-1938).
Fifth Variation, automatic cylinder stop (serial number range above 590000*) (1939-1942).
After 1930 listed in catalogs as: MODEL 944 LARGE FRAME TOP BREAK .22 RIMFIRE CALIBER 9 shots.
After 1930 listed in catalogs as: MODEL 945 LARGE FRAME TOP BREAK .22 Winchester Rim Fire CALIBER 7 shot.

22 EXPERT LARGE FRAME TOP BREAK
- similar as Large Frame Top Break, except has 10 in. barrel. Mfg. 1927-1941.

	100%	98%	95%	90%	80%	70%	60%
	$430	$370	$320	$275	$235	$195	$175

Add 50% for .22 WRF cal.
After 1930 listed in catalogs as: MODEL 955 LARGE FRAME TOP BREAK .22 RIMFIRE CALIBER 9 shot, or MODEL 956 LARGE FRAME TOP BREAK .22WRF CALIBER 7 shot.

H&R BOBBY LARGE FRAME TOP BREAK
- .32 or .38 centerfire cal., double action, 5 or 6 shot, round ribbed 4 inch barrel, fixed sights, blue finish, one piece oversize checkered walnut grips (some furnished with one piece plastic grips), free wheeling cylinder, only the 32 caliber seems to have been purchased by London's Metropolitan Police, these will be marked MK-II, on the top strap as well as having the company name and address on the top of the barrel rib, No. 15 model is .32 cal. 6 shot, No. 25 model is .38 cal. 5 shot, own serial number range, overall length 9 inches, 23 oz. Mfg. 1939-1942.

	100%	98%	95%	90%	80%	70%	60%
	$285	$255	$220	$175	$150	$125	$115

Add 100% for Metropolitan Police marked model (MK-II on top strap, M.P. P on front of grip frame.
Subtract $25 for plastic grips.

H&R HAMMERLESS FIRST MODEL LARGE FRAME TOP BREAK (BLACK POWDER) - .38 S&W cal., 5 shot, double action, double top post barrel latch, nickel or blue finish, hard rubber grips with a target logo at the top, 3¼ (standard), 4, 5 or 6 in. barrel, rebounding hammer; automatic cylinder stop, top of barrel is marked with the same 5 patent dates as the Auto-Ejector Second Model 5th Variation, no caliber markings on left side of barrel means designed for black powder cartridge pressures only. Mfg. 1899-1904.

	$295	$260	$220	$180	$160	$140	$120

Add 10% for blue finish or 20% for 4, 5, or 6 in. barrel.

Serial number range is approximately 01* to 45000* (No letter codes): Highest known 43308 (* Estimate).

H&R HAMMERLESS SECOND MODEL LARGE FRAME TOP BREAK (SMOKELESS POWDER) - .38 S&W cal., 5 shot, double top post barrel latch, nickel or blue finish, grips are hard rubber with a target logo at the top; 3¼ (standard), 4, 5, or 6 in. barrel, rebounding hammer, automatic cylinder stop, cylinder was lengthen to take the 32 S&W long cartridge and the catalogs now listed the calibers as: 6 shot 32 S&W, 32 S&W Long, 32 Colt New Police cartridges, also offered in 5 shot 38 S&W and 38 Colt New Police, caliber marked on left side of barrel, designed for smokeless powder cartridge. Mfg. 1905-1941.

	$325	$285	$250	$200	$175	$150	$125

Add 10% for blue finish. Add 20% for 4, 5, or 6 in. barrel.

First variation, 5 patent dates same as First model with caliber marked on left side of barrel, serial number range 45000*-55000* (estimate) - 1905.

Second Variation, patent dates, 5-14 & 8-6-89, 4-2-95, 4-7-96, serial number range: 55000*-100000*(estimate) - 1906-1908.

Third Variation, patent dates 8-6-1889, 10-8-1895, serial number range: 100000*-120000*(estimate) - 1909-1912.

Fourth Variation, no patent dates, state In address not spelled out (MASS.), serial number range: 120000*-160000*(estimate) - 1913-1915.

Fifth Variation, no patent dates, state name in address is spelled out (MASSACHUETTS), serial number range: 160000*-190000*(estimate) - 1916-1924.

Sixth Variation, new grip frame same as Auto-Ejector, serial number range: unknown - 1925-1940.

There is some indication production of the hammerless model stopped somewhere In the early 1920's but it was carried in catalogs until 1941.

After 1930 listed in Catalogs as: H&R HAMMERLESS No. 50 TOP BREAK .32 S&W LONG 6 shot.

After 1930 listed in Catalogs as: H&R HAMMERLESS No. 55 TOP BREAK .38 S&W 5 shot.

H&R HAMMERLESS FIRST MODEL SMALL FRAME TOP BREAK (BLACK POWDER) - .32 S&W cal., 5 shot, double top post barrel latch, nickel or blue finish, hard rubber grips with a target logo at the top, 3¼ (standard), 4, 5 or 6 in. barrel, rebounding hammer, automatic cylinder stop, no caliber markings on left side of barrel, designed for black powder cartridge pressures. Mfg. 1899-1904.

	$255	$225	$195	$155	$130	$115	$100

Add 10% for blue finish. Add 20% for 4, 5, or 6 in. barrel.

First Variation, patent dates 10-4-87, 4-2-95, 4-7-96, serial number range: 01*-82000* (Estimate) - 1899-1903.

Second Variation, patent dates 5-14-89,4-2-95, 4-6-96, serial number range: 82000*-90000* (Estimate) - 1904.

H&R HAMMERLESS BICYCLE FIRST MODEL - .32 S&W cal., 5 shot, similar to H&R Hammerless First Model, except has 2 in. barrel only. Mfg. 1895-1904.

	$275	$245	$210	$170	$145	$120	$110

Add 10% for blue finish.

GRADING - PPGS™	100%	98%	95%	90%	80%	70%	60%

H&R HAMMERLESS SECOND MODEL SMALL FRAME TOP BREAK (SMOKELESS POWDER) - .22 rimfire or .32 S&W cal., 5 (.32 cal.) or 7 (.22 cal.) shot, double top post barrel latch, nickel or blue finish, hard rubber grips with target logo at the top, 3¼ (standard), 4, 5, or 6 in. barrel, rebounding hammer, automatic cylinder stop, caliber marking on left side of barrel, designed for smokeless powder cartridge pressures only. Mfg. 1905-1941.

$265 $235 $200 $160 $135 $110 $100

Add 10% for blue finish. Add 20% for 4, 5, or 6 in. barrel, or 20% for .22 rimfire cal.

First Variation, patent dates 5-14-89, 4-2-95, 4-7-96, serial number range: 90000*-100000* (estimate) - 1905-1906.

Second Variation, patent dates 4-2-95, 4-7-96, serial number range: 100000*-120000* (estimate) - 1907-1909.

Third Variation, patent date 10-8-95, serial number range: 120000*-180000* (estimate) - 1910-1913.

Fourth Variation, no patent dates small font use for company name, serial number range: 180000*-190000* (estimate) - 1914.

Fifth variation, large font used in company name and state not spelled out (MASS), serial number range: 190000*-200000* (estimate) - 1915.

Sixth Variation, state name in address spelled out (MASSACHUSETTS), serial number range: 200000*-220000* (estimate) - 1916-1924.

Seventh Variation, new grip frame, it is now same width as rest of frame, no step down for grips, serial number range: unknown - 1925-1942.

After 1930 listed in catalogs as: HAMMERLESS No. 40 TOP BREAK 22 Rimfire 7 shot.

After 1930 listed in catalogs as: HAMMERLESS No. 45 TOP BREAK 32 S&W 5 shot.

H&R HAMMERLESS BICYCLE SECOND MODEL - .22 rimfire or .32 S&W cal., 5 or 7 shot, similar to H&R Hammerless First Model, except has 2 in. barrel only, not listed as a separate model after 1920 but 2 inch barrel was still available. Mfg. 1905-1920.

$295 $260 $225 $185 $160 $140 $120

Add 10% for blue finish or 20% for .22 rimfire cal.

H&R PREMIER FIRST MODEL SMALL FRAME TOP BREAK (BLACK POWDER) - .22 rimfire or .32 centerfire cal., 5 or 7 shot, double top post barrel latch, free wheeling cylinder (no automatic cylinder stop), nickel with case harden hammer and barrel latch, 3 (standard), 4, 5, or 6 in. barrel, features a scaled down version of the new frame and double action mechanism introduced in 1890 on the Auto-Ejecting Second Model, does not have caliber marking on left, manufactured for black powder cartridge pressures. Mfg. 1895-1904.

$285 $255 $220 $175 $150 $125 $115

Add 10% for blue finish, 20% for 4, 5, or 6 in. barrel, or 20% for .22 rimfire cal.

First Variation, patent dates 10-4-87, 5-14-89, 2-23-92, serial number range 01*-15,000 (estimate) - 1895-April 1896.

Second Variation, patent dates 10-4-87, 5-14-89, 4-2-95, 4-7-96, serial number range 15,000*-20,000* (estimate) - May 1896.

Third Variation, patent dates 10-4-87, 4-2-95, 4-7-96, serial number range 20,000* to 100,000* (estimate) - 1897-1898.

Fourth Variation, automatic cylinder stop, same patent dates as 3rd variation several different serial number series that may have letter codes - 1899-1903.

Fifth Variation, use different font in barrel markings and may have an A letter code in the serial number - 1904.

H&R PREMIER BICYCLE MODEL FIRST MODEL TOP BREAK (BLACK POWDER) - similar to Premier First Model, except has 2 in. barrel only. Mfg. 1895-1904.

$295 $260 $220 $180 $160 $140 $120

Add 10% for blue finish or 20% for .22 rimfire caliber.

H&R PREMIER POLICE SPURLESS HAMMER BLACK POWDER - similar to Premier First Model, except has patented spurless hammer. Mfg. 1895-1904.

$300 $265 $225 $185 $160 $140 $120

Add 10% for blue finish, 20% for .22 rimfire caliber, or 20% for 4, 5, or 6 in. barrel.

GRADING - PPGS™	100%	98%	95%	90%	80%	70%	60%

H&R PREMIER POLICE BICYCLE FIRST MODEL (BLACK POWDER) - similar to Premier First Model, except has 2 in. barrel and patented spurless hammer. Mfg. 1895-1904.

	$315	$280	$235	$190	$165	$145	$125

Add 10% for blue finish or 20% for .22 rimfire caliber.

H&R PREMIER SECOND MODEL SMALL FRAME TOP BREAK R.F. & C.F. - .22 rimfire or .32 S&W cal., double top post barrel latch, 5 or 7 shot, automatic cylinder stop, nickel finish with case harden hammer and barrel latch, 2, 3 (standard), 4, 5 and 6 in. barrel, caliber markings on left side of barrel, manufactured for smokeless powder cartridge pressures. Mfg. 1905-1941.

	$265	$235	$200	$160	$135	$110	$100

Add 10% for blue finish, 20% for 4, 5, or 6 in. barrel, 20% for .22 rimfire cal., or 10% for Seventh Variation.

There has not been enough data gathered on serial number to try to come up with a serial number range for the different variations.

First Variation, model name & caliber marked on left side of barrel, patent dates 5-14-89, 4-2-95, 4-7-96 - 1905.

Second Variation, model name & caliber marked on left side of barrel, patent dates 4-2-95, 4-7-96 - 1906-1908.

Third Variation, caliber only marked on left side of barrel, patent date 10-8-95 - 1909-1913.

Fourth Variation, caliber only marked on left side of barrel, no patent date, state not spelled out in address (MASS) - 1904-1915.

Fifth Variation, caliber only marked on left side of barrel, same as 4th except different font used in barrel markings - 1914-1915.

Sixth Variation, caliber only marked on left side of barrel. State name in barrel marking spelled out (MASSACHUSETTS) - 1916-1924.

Seventh Variation, new grip frame, there is no step down for the grip panels to fit into - 1925-1942.

After 1930 listed in catalogs as: PREMIER No. 30 .22 Rimfire 7 shot or PREMIER No. 35 .32 S&W 5 shot.

H&R PREMIER BICYCLE SECOND MODEL (SMOKELESS POWDER) - similar to Premier Second Model, except has 2 in. barrel, not listed as a separate model after 1919. Mfg. 1905-1920.

	$285	$255	$220	$175	$150	$125	$115

Add 10% for blue finish or 20% for .22 rimfire caliber.

H&R PREMIER POLICE SECOND MODEL (SMOKELESS POWDER) - similar to Premier Second Model, except has spurless hammer, not listed as a separate model after 1938. Mfg. 1905-1939.

	$275	$245	$210	$170	$145	$120	$110

Add 10% for blue finish, 20% for .22 rimfire caliber, or 20% for 4, 5, or 6 in. barrel.

H&R PREMIER POLICE BICYCLE SECOND MODEL (SMOKELESS POWDER) - similar to Premier Second Model, except has 2 in. barrel and patented spurless hammer, not listed as a separate model after 1919. Mfg. 1905-1920.

	$285	$255	$220	$175	$150	$125	$115

Add 10% for blue finish or 20% for .22 rimfire caliber.

H&R TARGET SMALL FRAME TOP BREAK - .22 rimfire cal., 7 shot, blue finish, 6 in. barrel, double action, oversized two-piece walnut grips, marked on left side of barrel "H&R TARGET" 22 rimfire on the right side of the barrel, company name and address on the top of the barrel rib. Mfg. 1925-1934.

	$325	$285	$250	$200	$175	$150	$125

After 1930 listed in the catalogs as: MODEL 766 TARGET SMALL FRAME TOP BREAK REVOLVER 7 SHOT.

GRADING - PPGS™	100%	98%	95%	90%	80%	70%	60%

MODEL 299 NEW DEFENDER - .22 rimfire cal., 9 shot, 2 in. barrel, large frame top break revolver, adj. sights, one piece walnut grips, pocket size, marked on right side of barrel with model name and caliber, modified "Rice Frame", automatic cylinder stop, finger rest trigger guard, overall length only 6¼ inches, serial number range unknown believed to be in the same series as the Model 999 Sportsman. Mfg. 1935-1939.

	$525	$465	$395	$340	$295	$250	$220

H&R DEFENDER SPECIAL MODEL 299 - .38 S&W cal., 5 shot, 2 in. flat sided barrel, large frame double action top break revolver, adj. front and rear sight, blue finish, finger rest trigger guard, birds-head grip frame shortened for special one-piece pocket size checkered walnut grips, automatic cylinder stop, overall length 6 ¼ in., serial number range unknown. Mfg. 1935-1939.

	$600	$520	$440	$390	$340	$285	$245

DEFENDER NO MODEL NUMBER TOP BREAK - .38 S&W cal., 5 shot, large frame double action top break revolver, 4, 5 or 6 inch flat sided barrel, fixed sights, blue finish, no finger rest on trigger guard, birds-head grip frame, one-piece oversized checkered walnut grips, automatic cylinder stop, hammer mounted firing pin, top of barrel marked with company name and address, left side of barrel is marked "DEFENDER 38" and right side is marked "38 S&W CTGE". Mfg. 1940-1942.

	$325	$285	$250	$200	$175	$150	$125

    Add 20% for 5 or 6 (scarce) in. barrel.

Most likely this is the beginning of the Defender 38 Model 25, but the literature for the Model 25 shows a slightly different revolver. The literature for this revolver refers to it as the Defender 38. Believed to be in a separate serial number range and possibly have letter code prefixes.

DEFENDER NO. 25 LARGE FRAME TOP BREAK - .38 S&W cal., 5 shot, 4 in. flat sided barrel, double action, adj. front and rear sights, blue finish, no finger rest on trigger guard, birds-head grip frame, one-piece oversized checkered black plastic grips, automatic cylinder stop, cylinder release via push button on left side of barrel lug, right side of barrel is marked with company name and address and caliber, left side of barrel marked "DEFENDER 38", serial number series is believed to be a separate series. Mfg. 1943-1945.

	$325	$285	$250	$200	$175	$150	$125

DEFENDER MODEL 925 LARGE FRAME TOP BREAK - .38 S&W cal., 5 shot, 4 in. flat sided barrel, adj. front and rear sights, blue finish, no finger rest on trigger guard, birds-head grip frame, one-piece oversized checkered black plastic grips, automatic cylinder stop, cylinder release via push button on left side of barrel lug, overall length 9 inches, 25 oz. Mfg. 1946-1947.

	$325	$285	$250	$200	$175	$150	$125

    Add 50% for manual ejecting model.

There has been one model 925 that is a factory manual ejection revolver with a serial number low enough that it actually may be a Model 25. It has company name and address on top of the barrel, "DEFENDER" on right side of barrel and the caliber on the left side of the barrel.

ULTRA SPORTSMAN MODEL 777 - .22 rimfire cal., 9 shot, large frame single action top break, 6 in. flat top oval shaped barrel (same as the Model 199) adj. front and rear sight, elevation screw on front of barrel just above muzzle, oversized one-piece checkered walnut grips (eleven different styles available), straight trigger, arched hammer spur, cylinder release is a vertical lever on the right side of barrel lug, rear of cylinder has the patented H&R safety rim, finger rest trigger guard, trigger pull factory set 2 ½ to 3 pounds, hammer mounted firing pin, serial numbered in its own series U01 to at least U900, markings on top of barrel rib: "HARRINGTON & RICHARDSON ARMS CO.", left side of barrel: "ULTRA, WORCHESTER, MASS. U.S.A. H & R No. 777", right side of barrel "22 Long Rifle CTGE. SPORTSMAN". Mfg. 1938-1939.

	$675	$585	$500	$435	$375	$325	$275

EUREKA SPORTSMAN MODEL 196 - .22 rimfire cal., 6 shot, large frame single action top break, cylinder chambers individually recessed, 6 in. flat top oval (same as late production Sportsman) barrel, adj. front and rear sight (has a different configuration than found on any other H&R adj. rear sight), oversized one-piece checkered walnut grips (eleven different styles available), trigger guard is heaver and wider than Model 777, trigger pull factory set 2 ½ to 3 pounds, with over travel adjustment, curved trigger and heavy straight hammer spur, frame mounted firing pin, birds-head shaped grip frame, markings on top of barrel rib: "HARRINGTON & RICHARDSON ARMS CO.", left side of barrel three lines: "EUREKA, WORCESTER, MASS. U.S.A. H & R No. 196 SPORTSMAN", right side of barrel: "22 Long Rifle CTGE", overall length approx. 10 ¾ inches, 30-32 oz. Mfg. 1940 only.

	$895	$760	$670	$580	$525	$450	$395

Add $250 for fitted case (rare).

SPORTSMAN SINGLE ACTION MODEL 199 LARGE FRAME TOP BREAK - .22 rimfire cal., 9 shot, safety rim cylinder, blue finish, 6 in. round heavy rib barrel, automatic cylinder stop, adj. front and rear sights, finger rest trigger guard, one-piece oversized checkered walnut grips, birds-head grip frame, top of barrel marked with company name and ddress, left side of barrel marked in two lines: "H & R SPORTSMAN SINGLE ACTION", right side of barrel marked: "22 LONG RIFLE CTGE", eerial numbered in series from 01 up and early production will have S letter code denoting single action. Mfg. 1932-1951.

	$495	$435	$370	$325	$275	$235	$200

Add 15% for First Variation or 10% for Fifth Variation.

First Variation; heavy ribbed barrel with non-adjustable front sight - Oct. 1932-April 1933.
Second Variation; oval shaped barrel with flat top, fully adjustable sights - May 1933-disc.
Third Variation; very small lettering on cylinder patent date - unknown-1936.
Fourth Variation; firing pin moved to the hammer - 1937-1941.
Fifth Variation; limited production 1949=J101-J148, 1950=K101-K265, 1951=L111-L112 - 1949-1951.

SPORTSMAN DOUBLE ACTION MODEL 999 LARGE FRAME TOP BREAK - .22 rimfire cal., 7 shot, blue finish, 6 in. ribbed barrel, safety rim cylinder, automatic cylinder stop, adj. rear sight, three different front sights - fixed full blade, Partridge type and Partridge type pinned to barrel top rib, finger rest trigger guard, one-piece oversized checkered walnut grips, birds-head grip frame (Rice frame), frame mounted firing pin, hammer face is flat, cylinder release is long pivoting lever on right side of frame (there are two different version of this), serial numbered in its own series from 01 up to at least 89761 by the end of 1939, starting in 1940 letter codes were used. Mfg. 1932-1952.

	$425	$365	$315	$275	$235	$195	$175

Add 15% for First Variation, 50% for .22 WRF cal., or 30% for 3 in. barrel (scarce).

Early production until about 1933 the letter code "D" was used to denote double action.
First Variation; round heavy weight ribbed barrel with Blade non-adjustable front sight - 1932- to before April 18,1933.
Second Variation; adjustable front sight - 1933 (after 4-18-1933).
Third Variation; firing pin moved to hammer - 1934.
Fourth Variation; three inch barrel was offered - 1935.
Fifth Variation; two patent dates marked on cylinder (before there was only one) - 1936 (after 3-17)-1937.
Sixth Variation; top of barrel markings moved to right side of barrel - 1937-1939.
Seventh Variation; 22 WFR caliber dropped, 3 inch barrel dropped - 1940-1941.
Eighth Variation; one piece over size plastic grips are standard, limited production during WWII years - 1942-1952.

GRADING - PPGS™	100%	98%	95%	90%	80%	70%	60%

SINGLE SHOT PISTOLS

HANDY GUN SMOOTH BORE - 28 ga. or .410 bore, smooth bore pistol with shotgun type break open action, blue finish, color case hardened frame, built on H&R's small frame Model 1915 Single Barrel Shotgun action, 28 ga. standard factory loads (early production 2 ½ inch and late production 2 ¾ inch chamber), black and smokeless powder, round ball loads are obtainable, 410 gauge chambered for 2 ½ inch shells, barrel length 8 and 12¼ inches, oversized unchecked one-piece checkered walnut grips saw handle shaped, detachable wire stock offered after 1932. Serial number in a separate series from 01 up to about 54,000 with both gauges in the same series classified by the government as NFA Curio & Relic. Mfg. 1924-1934.

    These guns are high level, specialized collector pieces and values are estimated at $550 - $900+.

    After 1930 listed in catalogs as HANDY GUN No. 141 SINGLE SHOT SMOOTH BORE .410 BORE.
    After 1930 listed in catalogs as HANDY GUN No. 128 SINGLE SHOT SMOOTH BORE .28 GAUGE.

HANDY GUN RIFLED BARREL - .22 rimfire or .32-20 WCF cal., blue finish with color case hardened frame, with shotgun type break open action, built on H&R's small frame Model 1915 Single Barrel Shotgun action, 12 ¼ in. barrel, oversized one-piece checkered rounded walnut grips, short unchecked walnut forend, .22 rimfire is serial numbered in a separate series 1 (or 101) to approx 300, and 32-20 in same series as smooth bores. Mfg. 1931-1934.

    These models are rarely seen. A refinished nickel .22 cal. model recently brought $1,400+ at auction.

    HANDY GUN No. 122 SINGLE SHOT RIFLED BARREL .22 RF CALIBER.
    HANDY GUN No. 132 SINGLE SHOT RIFLED BARREL .32-20 WCF CALIBER.

H&R SINGLE SHOT PISTOL TOP BREAK - .22 LR cal., large frame, blue finish, oversized checkered walnut grips, adj. sights, automatic ejector, serial number location is on the front of the grip strap or on the left side of the grip frame under the grips and on the bottom of the breach block, original production has a 10 inch barrel only, later production could be ordered with a 7 or 8 inch barrel, birds-head grip frame (called by collectors "Rice Frame"), serial numbered in its own series from o1 up to about o40,000, after 1930 this model is known as the U.S.R.A. Model. Mfg. 1928-1942.

	N/A	N/A	$1,500	$1,050	$825	$650	$550

    Add 25% for rare square plate type ejector.
    Add $300 for fitted case and accessories.

There are many combinations of this model due to special orders and factory reworks.
First Variation; two piece walnut grips, round ribbed barrel with non-adj. front sight, 10 inch barrel only - 1928.
Second variation; features a plunger type (round head) ejector, one-piece walnut grips - 1928-1929.
Third Variation; grooved trigger, name and model markings changed to U.S.R.A. Model 195 -1930.
Fourth Variation; 7 inch barrel length added, new front & rear sight and different shaped rib - 1931-1932.
Fifth Variation; grooved trigger, new barrel shape - 1933-1934.
Sixth variation; lever type automatic ejector - 1935-1942.

SEMI-AUTO PISTOLS

SELF LOADING .25 ACP - .25 ACP cal., 6 shot mag., 2 in. barrel, blue, nickel or in the white finish, flat panel hard rubber grips, magazine follower: flat and straight on early production and curved and stepped at rear on late production, 12 slide serrations on early production and 16 on late production, two different types of slide markings. Mfg. 1912-1920.

First Variation	$565	$485	$415	$355	$300	$250	$225
Second Variation	$525	$465	$395	$340	$295	$250	$220

The serial numbers may be in a separate series. One source lists only 16,500 manufactured between 1912 and 1916, however it was carried in the catalogs until 1920. First Variation markings Early (1-10,000); slide right side: "HARRINGTON & RICHARDSON ARMS CO.", slide left side: "H & R SELF-LOADING WORCESTER, MASS. U.S.A. CALIBER 25 PAT. AUG.20.'07. APRIL 13, 1909", frame left side at rear: serial number, Second Variation markings late 10,000-up, slide right side: "HARRINGTON & RICHARDSON ARMS CO.", slide right side: "H & R SELF-LOADING WORCESTER, MASSACHUSETTS, U.S.A. CALIBER 25 PAT. AUG.20, 1907 APRIL 13, 1909", frame left side at rear: serial number.

SELF LOADING .32 ACP - .32 ACP cal., 8 shot mag., 3½ in. barrel, grip safety, blue finish (some nickel versions have been reported but catalogs only listed a blue finish), magazine follower: flat and straight on early production and curved and stepped at rear on late production 12 slide serrations on early production and 16 on late production, slide marking are the same type as the 25 ACP Model, 22 oz. Mfg. 1914-1924.

	100%	98%	95%	90%	80%	70%	60%
Type 1	$525	$465	$395	$340	$295	$250	$220
Type 2	$495	$435	$370	$320	$275	$235	$200

The serial number series may be different from the 25 ACP Model. One source list 34,500 were manufactured between 1914 and 1924. TYPE 1 1914 serial numbers up to approx. 2000, markings; slide right side: "HARRINGTON & RICHARDSON ARMS CO.", slide left side: "H & R SELF-LOADING WORCESTER, MASS. U.S.A. CALIBER 32 PAT. AUG.20.'07. APRIL 13, 1909", slide right side: "H & R SELF-LOADING CALIBER 32", TYPE 2 1918 serial Numbers after approx. 2000, slide right side: "HARRINGTON & RICHARDSON ARMS CO.", slide right side: "H & R SELF-LOADING WORCESTER, MASSACHUSETTS, U.S.A. CALIBER 32 PAT. AUG.20, 1907 APRIL 13, 1909".

SELF LOADING .32 ACP SECOND OFFERING - no new production, sold as remaining inventory and appeared in 1939-1940 catalog.

	100%	98%	95%	90%	80%	70%	60%
Type 2	$495	$435	$370	$320	$275	$235	$200

REVOLVERS: RECENT MFG.

MODEL 504 SQUARE BUTT - .32 H&R Mag. cal., 5 shot, blue finish, 3, 4, or 6 in. barrel, transfer bar ignition, solid frame, DA, swing out cylinder, pull pin cylinder release, square butt. Mfg. 1984-1986.

			100%	98%	95%	90%	80%	70%	60%
			$235	$200	$175	$140	$125	$110	$95

Last MSR was $185.

Add 10% for 3 in. barrel, or 15% for 6 in. barrel.

✳ *Model 504 Round Butt* - compact design available with 3 or 4 in. barrel only. Disc. 1985. - similar to Model 925, except with nickel finish.

		100%	98%	95%	90%	80%	70%	60%
		$165	$145	$135	$120	$110	$100	$90

Last MSR was $185.

MODEL 532 - .32 H&R Mag. cal., blue finish, 2 1/2 or 4 in. barrel, case colored hardened frame, 5 shot, DA, solid frame, transfer bar ignition, rod ejection, Western syle grips, adj. sights. Mfg. 1983-1986.

		100%	98%	95%	90%	80%	70%	60%
		$165	$145	$125	$110	$90	$80	$70

Last MSR was $115.

MODEL 586 - .32 H&R Mag. cal., 5 shot, similar to Model 686, Western-style revolver, double action, 4 1/2, 5 1/2, 7 1/2, or 10 in. barrels, adj. rear sight, fixed cylinder, antique finish, black plastic or walnut grips. Mfg. 1983-1985.

		100%	98%	95%	90%	80%	70%	60%
		$275	$245	$210	$170	$145	$120	$110

Last MSR was $195.

Add 30% for 10 in. barrel.

MODEL 600 FORTY-NINER - .22 LR cal., 9 shot, 5 1/2 in. barrel, DA, solid frame, rod ejection, blue finish, Western style grips. Mfg. 1960 only.

		100%	98%	95%	90%	80%	70%	60%
		$200	$180	$160	$130	$120	$100	$90

MODEL 603 - .22 Mag. cal., similar to Model 903 but is 6 shot, 6 in. full round bull barrel, DA, transfer bar ignition, swing out cylinder. Mfg. 1980-83.

		100%	98%	95%	90%	80%	70%	60%
		$210	$190	$165	$135	$120	$100	$90

GRADING - PPGS™	100%	98%	95%	90%	80%	70%	60%

MODEL 604 - .22 Mag. cal., 6 shot, blue finish, 6 in. flat sided bull barrel, DA, solid frame, swing out cylinder, square butt. Mfg. 1980-1983.

| | $210 | $190 | $165 | $135 | $120 | $100 | $90 |

MODEL 622 - .22 S-L-LR cal., solid frame, DA, 6 shot, 2 1/2, 4, 6 or 10 in. barrels, blue finish, round or square butt, plastic grips, pull pin cylinder release. Mfg. 1957-1973.

| | $155 | $135 | $120 | $100 | $85 | $75 | $65 |

Last MSR was $104.

✳ *Model 622 Second Model* - similar to Model 622, except round butt only, 2 1/2 or 4 in. barrel, transfer bar ignition system. Mfg. 1974-1986.

| | $165 | $145 | $125 | $110 | $90 | $80 | $70 |

MODEL 623 - similar to Model 622, chrome/nickel finish only. Mfg. 1957-1964.

| | $165 | $145 | $125 | $110 | $90 | $80 | $70 |

✳ *Model 623 Second Model* - similar to Model 622 Second Model, except electroless nickel finish. Mfg. 1977-1979.

| | $175 | $155 | $130 | $115 | $95 | $85 | $75 |

MODEL 632 - .32 S&W cal., 6 shot, blue finish, large solid frame, DA, round or square butt, 2 1/2 or 4 in. barrel, pull pin cylinder release. Mfg. 1952-1959.

| | $165 | $145 | $125 | $110 | $90 | $80 | $70 |

✳ *Model 632 Second Model* - .32 S&W Long cal., 2 1/2 or 4 in. barrel, blue finish, 6 shot, transfer bar ignition system, DA, solid frame, pull pin cylinder, round or square butt. Mfg. 1973-1986.

| | $175 | $155 | $130 | $115 | $95 | $85 | $75 |

MODEL 633 - similar to the Model 632, except chrome/nickel finish, 2 1/2 in. barrel only, round butt. Mfg. 1953-1959.

| | $185 | $165 | $140 | $120 | $100 | $90 | $80 |

✳ *Model 633 Second Model* - similar to Model 632 Second Model, 2 1/2 in. barrel only. Mfg. 1977-1979.

| | $195 | $175 | $150 | $125 | $110 | $95 | $85 |

MODEL 642 - .22 Mag cal., 2 1/2 or 4 in. barrel, 6 shot, blue finish, DA, solid frame, pull pin cylinder release, round butt, transfer bar ignition. Mfg. 1980-1983.

| | $195 | $175 | $150 | $125 | $110 | $95 | $85 |

MODEL 649 CONVERTIBLE - .22 LR/.22 Mag. cal., furnished with extra cylinder, similar to Model 949, Western style, double action, side loading, 5 1/2 or 7 1/2 in. barrel, 6 shot, walnut grips, blue finish. Mfg. 1976-1985.

| | $250 | $225 | $175 | $150 | $125 | $100 | $90 |

Last MSR was $160.

MODEL 650 CONVERTIBLE - similar to Model 649, except with nickel finish and only available with 5 1/2 in. barrel. Mfg. 1975-1986.

| | $250 | $235 | $200 | $160 | $135 | $110 | $100 |

Last MSR was $175.

MODEL 660 GUNFIGHTER - .22 LR cal., 6 shot, blue finish, 6 in. barrel, DA, solid frame, Western style grip. Mfg. 1960-1961.

| | $325 | $285 | $250 | $200 | $175 | $150 | $125 |

MODEL 666 CONVERTIBLE - .22 LR/.22 Mag. cal., 6 shot, 6 in. barrel, blue finish, plastic grips, square butt, extra cylinder. Mfg. 1975-1979.

| | $145 | $125 | $110 | $90 | $80 | $75 | $70 |

MODEL 676 CONVERTIBLE - .22 LR/.22 Mag. cal., similar the Model 649, except has finger spur on trigger guard, blue/case colored finish, 6 shot, 4 1/2, 5 1/2, 7 1/2, or 12 in. barrel, side load and eject, one piece walnut stock, fixed sights. Mfg. 1975-1980.

$275 $245 $210 $170 $145 $120 $110

Add 20% for 12 in. barrel.
Subtract $35 if with only one cylinder.

MODEL 686 CONVERTIBLE - .22 LR/.22 Mag. cal., similar to Model 676 except with adj. target sights, larger frame, 4 1/2, 5 1/2, 7 1/2, or 12 in. barrel, transfer bar ignition. Mfg. 1980-1986.

$285 $255 $215 $175 $150 $125 $110

Add 20% for 12 in. barrel.
Subtract $35 if with only one cylinder.

MODEL 732 GUARDSMAN - .32 S&W or .32 H&R Mag. cal., similar to Model 929, 6 shot, 2 1/2 and 4 in. barrels, DA, fixed sights, swing out cylinder, blue finish, round or square butt, black plastic grips. Mfg. 1959-1973.

$185 $165 $140 $120 $100 $90 $80

✳ *Model 732 Guardsman Second Model* - similar to Model 732 Guardsman, except with transfer bar ignition. Mfg. 1974-1986.

$195 $175 $150 $125 $110 $95 $85

MODEL 733 GUARDSMAN - similiar to the Model 732, except chrome/nickel finish, 2 1/2 in. barrel, round butt. Mfg. 1957-1986.

$195 $175 $150 $125 $110 $95 $85

Add $15 for .32 H&R Mag. cal.

✳ *Model 733 Guardsman Second Model* - .32 S&W Long cal., 6 shot, nickel finish, 2 1/2 or 4 (rare) in. barrel, transfer bar ignition, solid frame, DA, swing out cylinder, rount butt. Mfg. 1973-1986.

$195 $175 $150 $125 $110 $95 $85

Add 10% for 4 in. barrel.

MODEL 826 - .22 Mag. cal., 6 shot, 3 in. barrel, adj. rear sight, solid frame, DA,swing out cylinder, transfer bar ignition. Mfg. 1981-1983.

$190 $175 $150 $125 $110 $95 $85

MODEL 829 - .22 LR cal., 9 shot, blue finish, 3 in. barrel, adj. rear sight, solid frame, DA, swing out cylinder, transfer bar ignition. Mfg. 1981-1983.

$190 $175 $150 $125 $110 $95 $85

MODEL 830 - similar to Model 829, but with nickel finish. Mfg. 1982-1983.

$195 $175 $150 $125 $110 $95 $85

MODEL 832 - .32 S&W Long cal., similar to Model 830. Mfg. 1981-1983.

$190 $175 $150 $125 $110 $95 $85

MODEL 833 - similar to Model 832, but with nickel finish. Mfg. 1982-1983.

$195 $175 $150 $125 $110 $95 $85

MODEL 900 - .22 S, L, or LR cal., 9 shot, 2 1/2, 4, or 6 in. barrels, snap out cylinder, DA, blue finish, black plastic grips, solid frame. Mfg. 1962-1973.

$145 $125 $110 $90 $85 $70 $65

MODEL 901 - similar to Model 900, but chrome finish with white tenite grips. Mfg. 1962-1964.

$170 $150 $125 $110 $90 $80 $70

MODEL 903 - .22 LR cal., successor to the Model 939, 6 in. heavy barrel with raised rib, 9 shot, blue finish, adj. sights, DA, solid frame, swing out cylinder, transfer bar ignition. Mfg. 1980-1983.

$225 $195 $170 $140 $125 $110 $95

GRADING - PPGS™	100%	98%	95%	90%	80%	70%	60%

MODEL 904 - .22 S, L, LR cal., SA, similar to Model 903 except has 4 or 6 in. round bull barrel, target grade, 9 shot, adj. sights. Mfg. 1980-1985.

	$245	$215	$185	$150	$125	$110	$100

Last MSR was $168.

MODEL 905 - similar to Model 904, except with nickel finish and 4 in. round bull barrel only. Mfg. 1980-1986.

	$255	$225	$195	$160	$135	$120	$100

Last MSR was $185.

MODEL 922 BANTAM WEIGHT - .22 LR cal., blue finish, 2 1/2 in. barrel, 9 shot, DA, solid frame, pull pin cylinder release, round butt. Mfg. 1952-1961.

	$215	$195	$165	$135	$120	$100	$90

MODEL 922 CAMPER - .22 LR cal., similar to Model 922 Bantam Weight, except has 4 in. barrel. Mfg. 1952-1955.

	$215	$195	$165	$135	$120	$100	$90

MODEL 922 SECOND MODEL - .22 LR cal., features new frame, 2 1/2, 4 or 6 in. barrel, 9 shot, blue finish, solid frame, DA, pull pin cylinder release, round or square butt. Mfg. 1953-1961.

	$195	$175	$150	$125	$110	$95	$85

MODEL 922 THIRD MODEL - .22 LR cal., similar to Model 922 Second Model, except has transfer bar ignition. Mfg. 1973-1979.

	$200	$180	$160	$130	$120	$100	$90

MODEL 923 BANTAM WEIGHT - .22 LR cal., 9 shot, chrome finish, 2 1/2 in. barrel, DA, solid frame, pull pin cylinder release, round butt. Mfg. 1953-1961.

	$215	$195	$170	$135	$120	$100	$90

MODEL 923 SECOND MODEL - .22 LR cal., similar to Model 922 Second Model, features new frame. Mfg. 1953-1961.

	$205	$185	$165	$135	$125	$100	$90

MODEL 923 CAMPER - .22 LR cal., similar to Model 923 Bantam Weight, except has 4 in. barrel. Mfg. 1952-1955.

	$215	$195	$165	$135	$120	$100	$90

MODEL 923 THIRD MODEL - .22 LR cal., similar to 922 Third Model. Mfg. 1977-1979.

	$210	$190	$165	$135	$120	$100	$90

MODEL 925 DEFENDER SECOND MODEL - .22 LR or .38 S&W cal., new frame version or pre-1953 Model 925, blue or matte black finish, 2 1/2 or 4 (disc. 1969) in. barrel, top break, DA, 5 (.38 cal.) or 9 (.22 cal.) shot, birds-head grip, square butt (4 in. barrel 1968-69). Mfg. 1964-1972.

	$235	$200	$175	$140	$125	$110	$95

    Add 10% for 4 in. barrel.
    Add 75% for 4 in. barrel (.22 cal.).
    Add 15% for matte black finish.

MODEL 925 DEFENDER THIRD MODEL - .38 S&W cal., similar to Second Model, except 2 1/2 in. barrel only, 5 shot, transfer bar ignition. Mfg. 1973-1978.

	$235	$200	$175	$140	$125	$110	$95

MODEL 926 MANUAL EJECTOR - .22 LR or .38 S&W cal., 5 (.38 S&W) or 9 (.22 LR) shot, 4 in. barrel, blue finish, DA, square butt, manual ejection, adj. rear sight, top break, walnut grips. Mfg. 1968-1972.

	$225	$195	$170	$140	$125	$110	$95

MODEL 926 MANUAL EJECTOR SECOND MODEL - .22 LR or .38 S&W cal., 5 (.38 S&W) or 9 (.22 LR) shot, 4 in. barrel, blue finish, DA, square butt, manual ejection, adj. rear sight, top break, walnut grips, transfer bar ignition. Mfg. 1973-1978.

	$245	$215	$185	$150	$125	$110	$95

GRADING - PPGS™	100%	98%	95%	90%	80%	70%	60%

MODEL 929 SIDEKICK - .22 LR cal., 9 shot, 2 1/2, 4, or 6 in. barrels, swing out cylinder, plastic grips, blue finish, DA, round or square butt. Mfg. 1957-1973.

	$175	$155	$130	$115	$95	$85	$75

Last MSR was $127.

MODEL 929 SIDEKICK SECOND MODEL - .22 LR cal., 9 shot, 2 1/2, 4, or 6 in. barrels, swing out cylinder, plastic grips, blue finish, DA, round or square butt, transfer bar ignition. Mfg. 1974-1986.

	$195	$175	$150	$125	$110	$95	$85

Last MSR was $127.

MODEL 930 SIDEKICK - similar to 929 Sidekick Second Model, except chrome/nickel finish and not available with 6 in. barrel. Mfg. 1957-1986.

	$215	$195	$170	$135	$120	$100	$90

Last MSR was $140.

MODEL 930 SIDEKICK SECOND MODEL - similar to Model 930 Sidekick, except has transfer bar ignition, nickel finish. Mfg. 1957-1986.

	$220	$190	$165	$135	$120	$95	$80

MODEL 935 DEFENDER - similar to Model 925 Third Model, top break, DA, nickel finish, transfer bar ignition. Mfg. 1977-1978.

	$275	$245	$210	$170	$145	$120	$110

MODEL 939 ULTRA SIDEKICK - .22 S, L, or LR cal., 9 shot, 6 in. flat sided bull barrel, swing out cylinder, vent rib, adj. sights, blue finish, solid frame, DA, square butt. Mfg. 1957-1972.

	$295	$260	$220	$180	$155	$135	$115

In 1962, the hammer mounted cylinder release button was discontinued. A key lock for safety was added in 1962, and discontinued in 1972. This model was H&R's second most expensive revolver.

MODEL 939 ULTRA SIDEKICK SECOND MODEL - similar to Model 939 Ultra Sidekick, except has transfer bar ignition. Mfg. 1973-1980.

	$275	$245	$210	$170	$145	$120	$110

MODEL 940 ULTRA SIDEKICK - similar to Model 939, except has 6 in. full round bull barrel. Mfg. 1970-1972.

	$300	$265	$225	$185	$160	$140	$120

MODEL 940 ULTRA SIDEKICK SECOND MODEL - similar to Model 940 Ultra Sidekick, except has transfer bar ignition. Mfg. 1973-1980.

	$305	$270	$230	$185	$160	$140	$120

MODEL 949 "FORTY NINER" - .22 S, L, or LR cal., 5 1/2 in. barrel, DA, solid frame, 9 shot, side load and Western style ejection, adj. rear sight, walnut grips. Mfg. 1961-1972.

	$250	$225	$175	$150	$125	$100	$90

Last MSR was $127.

MODEL 949 "FORTY NINER" SECOND MODEL - .22 S, L, or LR cal., similar to Model 949 Forty Niner, except has transfer bar ignition. Mfg. 1973-1986.

	$265	$230	$200	$160	$140	$115	$100

MODEL 950 - similar to Model 949, except with nickel finish. Mfg. 1974-1986.

	$275	$245	$210	$170	$145	$120	$110

Last MSR was $145.

MODEL 976 CONVERTIBLE - .22 LR/.22 Mag. cal., 6 shot, 7 1/2 in. barrel, solid frame, DA, Western style grips, blue finish, case colored hardened frame, fixed sights, transfer bar ignition. Mfg. 1977-1981.

	$295	$260	$220	$180	$155	$135	$115

Subtract $35 if with only one cylinder.

GRADING - PPGS™	100%	98%	95%	90%	80%	70%	60%

MODEL 976 CONVERTIBLE DELUXE - .22 LR/.22 Mag. cal., 6 shot, 7 1/2 in. barrel, solid frame, DA, Western style grips, blue finish, case colored hardened frame, fixed sights, transfer bar ignition. Mfg. 1977-1981.

	$305	$270	$230	$185	$160	$140	$120

Subtract $35 if with only one cylinder.

MODEL 999 ENGRAVED - similar to 999, only engraved throughout, 6 in. barrel only. Disc. 1985.

	$425	$375	$300	$260	$225	$190	$175

Last MSR was $525.

MODEL 999 SPORTSMAN SECOND MODEL (NEW FRAME) - .22 LR cal., 9 shot, 6 in. barrel, adj. sights, top break, DA, blue finish. Mfg. 1953-1972.

	$425	$375	$300	$260	$225	$190	$175

MODEL 999 SILVER SPORTSMAN - .22 LR cal., 9 shot, 6 in. barrel, top break, DA, chrome finish, serial number letter codes Z, AA, AB only, scarce. Mfg. 1963-1966.

	$450	$395	$335	$285	$245	$210	$180

MODEL 999 SPORTSMAN THIRD MODEL - .22 LR cal., 9 shot, 4 (new 1979) or 6 in. barrel, adj. sights, top break, DA, blue finish, adj. sights. Mfg. 1973-1986.

	$425	$375	$300	$260	$225	$190	$175

In 1979, this model was advertised as the Model 999 Automatic Ejecting and was offered as a 6 shot in .32 S&W Long cal.

MODEL 999 SPORTSMAN 1 of 999 - .22 LR cal., top break, DA, 9 shot, 6 in. barrel, adj. sights, engraved with fitted wood case. Mfg. 1979-1986.

	$700	$600	$525	$450	$385	$340	$285

Values are only for unfired models with all original tags, manuals, commemorative medallion, wooden presentation case and cardboard box. Use Model 999 Third Model values if not intact.

RIFLES

M1 GARAND - please refer to M1 Garand listing under U.S. Military.

REISING MODEL 60 - .45 ACP cal., semi-auto, 12 or 20 shot detachable mag., 18 1/4 in. barrel, plain wood stock with sling swivels. Approx. 3,500 mfg. 1944-46.

	N/A	N/A	$2,750	$2,350	$2,150	$1,950	$1,775

Add 15% for finned barrel with blue finish.

USMC MODEL 65 MILITARY - .22 LR cal., 10 shot mag., 23 in. barrel, Redfield aperture rear sight. Mfg. 1944-46 for USMC.

	$1,000	$900	$850	$750	$650	$550	$500

STANDARD CIVILIAN MODEL - .22 LR cal., similar to USMC Model 65 Military model.

	$250	$230	$200	$165	$145	$130	$110

MODEL 150 LEATHERNECK - .22 LR cal., semi-auto, 22 in. barrel, 5 shot. Mfg. 1949-1953.

	$250	$225	$200	$150	$125	$100	$85

MODEL 155 - .44 Mag. or .45-70 Govt. cal., single shot, break open. Mfg. 1972-disc.

	$150	$130	$115	$95	$75	$55	$45

MODEL 157 - .22 Mag., .22 Hornet, or .30-30 cal., single shot, break open, Mannlicher stock. Mfg. 1976-84.

	$165	$150	$135	$100	$80	$65	$45

MODEL 158 - .22 Jet, .22 Hornet, .30-30, .357 Mag., or .44 Mag. cal., single shot break open, 22 in. barrel, side or top lever action release, ejector, case hardened frame. Disc. 1985.

	$150	$135	$125	$90	$80	$60	$50

Last MSR was $115.

GRADING - PPGS™	100%	98%	95%	90%	80%	70%	60%

✱ *Model 158 Combination* - supplied with rifle barrel and 20 ga., 26 in. barrel. Disc. 1985.

	$195	$175	$150	$135	$115	$100	$90

Last MSR was $145.

MODEL 165 - .22 LR cal., 10 shot. Mfg. 1945-61.

	$120	$110	$95	$85	$70	$55	$50

MODEL 171 - .45-70 Govt. cal., Model 1873 Trapdoor copy, 22 in. barrel, Model 174 is the deluxe model. Disc.

	$350	$300	$270	$250	$230	$210	$195

MODEL 171-DL - .45-70 Govt. cal., single shot, Springfield copy, 22 in. barrel. Mfg. 1984-85.

	$400	$350	$295	$250	$225	$200	$185

Last MSR was $385.

MODEL 174

	$400	$375	$325	$300	$250	$210	$195

MODEL 300 ULTRA - .22-250 Rem., .243 Win., .270 Win., .30-06, .308 Win., 7mm Mag., or .300 Win. Mag. cal., bolt action, 22 or 24 in. barrel. Mfg. 1965-78.

	$495	$450	$425	$400	$350	$325	$295

MODEL 301 CARBINE - similar to 300, but 18 in. barrel, full length Mannlicher stock, N/A .22-250 Rem. cal.

	$440	$415	$360	$305	$250	$220	$195

MODEL 317 ULTRA WILDCAT - .17 Rem., .17 223, .222 Rem., or .223 Rem. cal., short action Sako, 20 in. barrel, no sights. Mfg. 1968-76.

	$1,000	$925	$825	$725	$650	$600	$550

MODEL 317P PRESENTATION - similar to Model 317, but deluxe wood basketweave checkering. Mfg. 1968-76.

	$1,300	$1,150	$995	$875	$775	$675	$575

MODEL 322 - .222 Rem. cal., short throw bolt action, 6 shot mag., 24 in. barrel, checkered hardwood Monte Carlo stock with cheekpiece, drilled and tapped, approx. 6 3/4 lbs. Mfg. circa 1973-80.

	$395	$350	$325	$300	$250	$225	$200

MODEL 333 - 7mm Mag. cal., similar to Model 300, plainer version. Mfg. 1974 only.

	$395	$350	$325	$300	$250	$225	$200

MODEL 340 - .243 Win., .270 Win., .30-06, .308 Win., or 7mm Mauser cal., bolt action, 5 shot, 22 in. barrel, checkered walnut. Mfg. 1982-84.

	$395	$300	$275	$240	$220	$200	$180

MODEL 360 ULTRA AUTOMATIC - .243 Win. or .308 Win. cal., 3 shot, 22 in. barrel. Mfg. 1965-78.

	$395	$350	$325	$300	$275	$250	$225

MODEL 370 ULTRA MEDALIST TARGET - .22-250 Rem., .243 Win., or 6mm Rem. cal., Varmint Rifle, 5 shot mag., 24 in. varmint weight barrel, uncheckered target stock with rollover cheekpiece and semi-beavertail forearm, 9 1/2 lbs. Mfg. 1968-73.

	$475	$425	$385	$360	$340	$325	$295

MODEL 422 - .22 S, L, or LR cal., slide action. Mfg. 1956-58.

	$300	$250	$200	$150	$100	$75	$50

✱ *Model 450* - similar to Model 451 Medalist, only has no sights.

	$350	$300	$250	$175	$125	$100	$75

MODEL 451 MEDALIST - .22 LR cal., bolt action, 5 shot, 26 in. barrel. Mfg. 1948-61.

	$165	$150	$140	$110	$100	$85	$55

GRADING - PPGS™	100%	98%	95%	90%	80%	70%	60%

MODEL 700 - .22 Mag. cal., semi-auto, 5 shot, clip mag., 22 in. barrel. Mfg. 1977-85.

	$275	$250	$225	$200	$175	$150	$125

Last MSR was $210.

MODEL 700DL - similar to Model 700 except deluxe checkered walnut. 4-power scope is standard, recoil pad. Disc. 1985.

	$395	$350	$325	$300	$275	$250	$200

Last MSR was $360.

MODEL 750 - .22 LR cal. single shot bolt action, 22 in. barrel, open sights, youth stock dimensions. Disc. 1985.

	$85	$75	$60	$50	$45	$40	$35

Last MSR was $95.

MODEL 865 PIONEER - .22 LR cal. bolt action, 5 shot mag., 22 in. barrel. Disc. 1985.

	$90	$80	$65	$55	$50	$45	$40

Last MSR was $105.

MODEL 5200 TARGET - .22 LR cal. target rifle, heavy 28 in. barrel, adj. trigger, no sights, single shot. 11 lbs. Disc. 1985.

	$500	$450	$400	$350	$300	$275	$250

Last MSR was $450.

MODEL 5200 SPORTER - .22 LR cal., bolt action, 5 shot, 24 in. barrel, adj. sights, checkered walnut. Disc. 1983.

	$650	$600	$550	$475	$450	$400	$350

SHOTGUNS

HARRICH NO. 1 - 12 ga., single barrel Trap Gun, 32 or 34 in. full choke, high quality, engraved, vent. rib. Mfg. in Ferlach, Austria from 1971-75.

	$1,650	$1,595	$1,485	$1,320	$1,100	$880	$770

MODEL 3 HAMMERLESS - similar to Model 8, but no visible external hammer. Mfg. 1908-42.

	$250	$225	$200	$150	$100	$80	$60

MODEL 5 LIGHTWEIGHT - 24, 28 ga., or .410 bore only. Mfg. 1908-42.

	$350	$315	$260	$220	$160	$120	$95

MODEL 6 HEAVY BREECH - similar to Model 8, only 10 ga. - 20 ga., heavier barrels. Mfg. 1908-42.

	$150	$125	$100	$80	$60	$50	$40

MODEL 7 OR 9 BAY STATE - similar to Model 8, only 12, 16, 20 ga., or .410 bore, rounded pistol grip. Mfg. 1908-42.

	$200	$175	$140	$110	$80	$65	$50

MODEL 8 STANDARD - 12, 16, 20, 24, 28 ga., or .410 bore, single shot, 26-32 in. barrel, plain pistol grip stock, auto ejector, break open. Mfg. 1908-42.

	$150	$125	$95	$75	$65	$60	$55

Add 100% for 28 ga. or .410 bore.

FOLDING GUN - 12, 16, 20, 28 ga., or .410 bore, single shot, hinged frame (two sizes), barrel folds against stock. Mfg. 1908-42.

	$225	$195	$160	$125	$100	$85	$60

Add 75% for 28 ga. or .410 bore.

TOPPER - 12, 16, 20 ga., or .410 bore, single shot, top or side lever break open action, 10 different variations of this shotgun, all are very similar and values run too close to differentiate, with ejector. Mfg. 1946-disc.

	$145	$125	$100	$85	$70	$55	$45

Add 15% for Topper Deluxe (Model 488, chrome finish).

This model was also designated the Model 48, Model 158 (not in 28 ga.), Model 162 Buck gun with open sights, and Model 198 (28 ga. or .410 bore only).

GRADING - PPGS™	100%	98%	95%	90%	80%	70%	60%

MODEL 088 - 12, 16, 20, 28 ga., or .410 bore, single shot, hammer model, ejector, top or side lever break open action, blue barrel finish with case hardened frame. Disc. 1985.

	$85	$75	$55	$50	$45	$40	$35

Last MSR was $95.

MODEL 099 - 12, 16, 20 ga., or .410 bore, similar to Model 088, only electroless nickel finish, ejector, top or side lever break open action. Disc. 1984.

	$95	$80	$60	$55	$50	$45	$40

MODEL 162 - 12 or 20 ga., single shot, 24 in. slug barrel with rifle sights, case hardened frame, top or side lever break open action. Disc. 1984.

	$115	$105	$90	$80	$65	$55	$45

MODEL 176 - 10 (3 1/2 in.), 12, or 20 ga., Mag., single shot, 32-36 in. heavy barrel, top or side lever break open action. Mfg. 1977-85.

	$110	$95	$80	$70	$60	$50	$45

Last MSR was $125.

MODELS 348/349 BOLT ACTION - 12 or 16 ga., 3 shot tube mag., 28 in. barrel (Model 349 has adj. vari-choke), walnut stock, 7 1/2 lbs. Disc.

	$115	$90	$75	$60	$50	$45	$40

MODEL 400 PUMP ACTION - 12, 16, or 20 ga., 28 in. full choke. Mfg. 1955-67.

	$155	$145	$125	$110	$90	$75	$55

MODEL 401 PUMP - similar to 400, but H&R variable choke. Mfg. 1956-63.

	$165	$155	$140	$120	$100	$90	$65

MODEL 402 PUMP - .410 bore, similar to 400, lightweight. Mfg. 1959-67.

	$175	$165	$150	$140	$110	$100	$85

MODEL 403 AUTOLOADER - .410 bore, 26 in. full choke, takedown. Mfg. 1964 only.

	$195	$180	$165	$155	$120	$100	$85

MODEL 404 - 12, 20 ga., or .410 bore, double barrel, SxS, 26 or 28 in. barrel, boxlock, extractors, double triggers. Mfg. by Rossi of Brazil 1969-72.

	$185	$175	$165	$145	$110	$90	$70

MODEL 404C - similar to 404, only checkered stock.

	$200	$185	$175	$155	$120	$100	$85

MODEL 440 - 12, 16, or 20 ga., pump action, 26, 28, or 30 in. barrels, available in various chokes, plain pistol grip and slide. Mfg. 1968-73.

	$145	$130	$110	$100	$85	$70	$55

MODEL 442 - pump action, similar to 440, only vent. rib, checkered stock. Mfg. 1969-73.

	$175	$165	$155	$140	$100	$85	$65

MODEL 490 - 20 ga. or .410 bore, made for junior shooters, Greenwing finish - add $10. Disc. 1984.

	$85	$65	$60	$50	$45	$40	$40

MODEL 1212 - 12 ga., O/U, Field, 2 3/4 in., 28 in. vent. rib barrels, various chokes, checkered walnut stocks. Mfg. by Lanber Arms, Spain, from 1976-disc.

	$310	$295	$275	$250	$200	$175	$155

MODEL 1212 WATERFOWL - 12 ga., 3 in. chamber, similar to Model 1212, 30 in. barrel.

	$320	$310	$285	$260	$210	$185	$165

COMMEMORATIVES

CHISHOLM TRAIL MODEL 999 - 300 mfg., not listed in catalogs. Mfg. 1967.

	$495	$435	$370	$320	$270	$230	$195

GRADING - PPGS™	100%	98%	95%	90%	80%	70%	60%

NEBRASKA CENTENNIAL - serial numbered letter codes NE, presentation case, unknown number mfg. 1967.

	$1,000	$865	$765	$660	$575	$495	$450

A 100% NIB model with presentation case recently sold at auction for $1,250.

MODEL 926 ABILENE KANSAS CENTENNIAL - .22 LR cal., barrel is marked "Abilene Kansas" and "1869 Centennial 1969", not listed in catalogs, 300 mfg. 1969 only.

	$350	$320	$275	$225	$200	$165	$140

MODEL 999 1 of 999 - similar to previous Model 999 1 of 999, except listed in 1981 catalog, values are for complete set. Mfg. 1981-1986.

	$700	$600	$525	$450	$385	$340	$285

H&R 100TH ANNIVERSARY OFFICER'S MODEL - 1871-1971, Commemorative Officer's Model, Springfield 1873 Replica, Trapdoor, .45-70 Govt. cal., engraved metal work, 26 in. barrel, anniversary plaque on stock, 10,000 mfg. in 1971.

	$595	$550	$500	N/A	N/A	N/A	N/A

Last MSR was $250.

MODEL 171 AND 171 DELUXE - please refer to listings under Rifles section.

MODEL 172 SILVER CARBINE - .45-70 Govt. cal., 22 in. barrel, Trapdoor action, walnut stock, all metal silver plated, with pistol grip cap, tang sight, shipped in wood case with blue lining. Mfg. 1978-82.

	$1,500	$1,250	$1,000	$750	$640	$535	$450

MODEL 173 RIFLE - .45-70 Govt. cal., similar to Officer's Model, no plaque on stock. Mfg. 1972-83.

	$495	$425	$325	$265	$230	$195	$170

MODEL 174 CARBINE (LITTLE BIG HORN) - .45-70 Govt. cal., Little Big Horn Commercial Carbine. Quantity unknown.

	$495	$450	$400	$350	$275	$225	$200

Last MSR was $220 (1972).

MODEL 178 - .45-70 Govt. cal., Infantry Musket Replica, 32 in. barrel. Mfg. 1973-84.

	$550	$325	$250	$195	$165	$140	$120

1873 SPRINGFIELD TRAPDOOR - .45-70 Govt. cal., unknown quantities mfg. 1973.

	$450	$350	$275	$225	$195	$165	$140

Last MSR was $250.

CUSTER MEMORIAL ISSUE - .45-70 Govt. cal., limited production, deluxe walnut stock, highly engraved, gold inlaid, mahogany display case and two volumes on Custer history. Each weapon bears the name of one who fell at Little Big Horn.

＊ *Custer Memorial Issue Officer's Model* - 25 mfg., must be NIB w/original box and accessories.

	$3,995	$3,150	$2,400	$2,100	$1,900	$1,500	$1,200

Last MSR was $3,000 (1973).

＊ *Custer Memorial Issue Enlisted Men's Model* - 243 mfg., must be NIB w/original box and accessories.

	$1,995	$1,400	$900	$785	$655	$550	$465

Last MSR was $2,000 (1973).

HARRIS GUNWORKS

Previous firearms manufacturer located in Phoenix, AZ 1995-March 31, 2000. Previously named Harris-McMillan Gunworks and G. McMillan and Co., Inc. (please refer to the M section for more information on these two trademarks).

GRADING - PPGS™	100%	98%	95%	90%	80%	70%	60%

RIFLES: BOLT ACTION

BENCHREST COMPETITOR - .222 Rem. (disc.), .243 Win., 6mm Rem., 6mm PPC, 6mm BR, or .308 Win. cal., benchrest configuration. Mfg. 1993-2000.

	$2,675	$2,425	$1,950	$1,675	$1,425	$1,200	$1,025

Last MSR was $3,050.

NATIONAL MATCH COMPETITOR - .308 Win., or 7mm-08 Rem. cal. Mfg. 1993-2000.

	$3,125	$2,675	$2,300	$1,875	$1,650	$1,325	$1,100

Last MSR was $3,500.

LONG RANGE TARGET MODEL - .300 Win. Mag., .300 Phoenix, .30-378 Wby. Mag., .30-416 Rigby, .338 Lapua, or 7mm Rem. Mag. cal., black synthetic fully adj. stock, w/o sights, grey barrel finish. Mfg. 1996-2000.

	$3,225	$2,700	$2,325	$1,900	$1,650	$1,325	$1,100

Last MSR was $3,620.

TALON SPORTER - available in various cals. between .22-250 Rem. and .416 Rem., receiver available in either 4340 chrome molybdenum or 17-4 stainless steel, drilled and tapped, match grade barrel. Mfg. 1992-2000.

	$2,600	$2,075	$1,725	$1,375	$1,050	$895	$800

Last MSR was $2,900.

The Talon action was patterned after the Winchester pre-64 Model 70. It featured a cone breech, controlled feed, claw extractor, and 3 position safety.

SIGNATURE CLASSIC SPORTER - various cals. available between .22-250 Rem. and .416 Rem., premium wood stock, matte metal finish, buttoning used on rifling for 22 or 24 in. stainless steel barrel, McMillan action made from 4340 chrome moly steel (either left- or right-handed), 3 or 4 shot mag. supplied with 5 shot test target. Mfg. 1988-2000.

	$2,450	$2,000	$1,675	$1,325	$1,000	$895	$800

Last MSR was $2,700.

SIGNATURE VARMINTER - similar to Signature Model, except is available in 12 cals. between .22-250 Rem. and .350 Rem. Mag., hand bedded fiberglass stock, adj. trigger, 26 in. heavily contoured barrel. Mfg. 1988-2000.

	$2,450	$2,000	$1,675	$1,325	$1,000	$895	$800

Last MSR was $2,700.

SIGNATURE TITANIUM MOUNTAIN RIFLE - .270 Win., .280 Rem., .30-06, .300 Win. Mag., .338 Win. Mag., or 7mm Rem. Mag. cal., lighter weight variation with shorter stainless steel or graphite/steel composite barrel, 5 3/4 (w/graphite barrel), or 6 1/2 lbs. Mfg. 1990-2000.

	$2,950	$2,575	$2,300	$1,925	$1,650	$1,325	$1,100

Last MSR was $3,300.

Add $400 with graphite barrel.

SIGNATURE ALASKAN - available in many cals. between .270 Win. and .458 Win. Mag. Mfg. 1990-2000.

	$3,425	$2,725	$2,275	$1,650	$1,250	$1,125	$900

Last MSR was $3,800.

TALON SAFARI - available in many cals. between .300 Win. Mag. and .460 Wby. Mag., hand bedded fiberglass stock, 4 shot mag., 24 in. stainless steel barrel, matte black finish, 9 1/2 lbs. Mfg. 1988-2000.

	$3,650	$2,850	$2,500	$2,150	$2,000	$1,850	$1,700

Last MSR was $3,900.

Add $300 for .300 Phoenix, .30-416 Rigby, .30-378 Wby. Mag., .338 Lapua, .335-378, .338-378, .378 Wby. Mag., .416 Wby. Mag. or Rigby, or .460 Wby. Mag. cal.

The Talon action was patterned after the Winchester pre-64 Model 70. It featured a cone breech, controlled feed, claw extractor, and 3 position safety. Older Signature action rifles do not have this new Talon action.

M-40 SNIPER RIFLE - .308 Win. cal., Remington action with McMillan match grade heavy contour barrel, fiberglass stock with recoil pad, 4 shot mag., 9 lbs. Mfg. 1990-2000.

	100%	98%	95%	90%	80%	70%	60%
	$1,825	$1,450	$1,125	$925	$800	$700	$600

Last MSR was $2,000.

M-86 SNIPER RIFLE - .300 Phoenix (disc. 1996), .30-06 (new 1989), .300 Win. Mag. or .308 Win. cal., fiberglass stock, variety of optical sights. Mfg. 1988-2000.

	100%	98%	95%	90%	80%	70%	60%
	$2,450	$2,000	$1,675	$1,325	$1,000	$895	$800

Last MSR was $2,700.

> Add $300 for .300 Phoenix cal. with Harris action (disc. 1996).
> Add $200 for takedown feature (mfg. 1993-96).

.300 PHOENIX - available in most popular .30 cals., special fiberglass stock with adj. cheekpiece and buttplate, right- or left-hand action, 12 1/2 lbs. Mfg. 1997-2000.

	100%	98%	95%	90%	80%	70%	60%
	$3,025	$2,650	$2,325	$1,925	$1,675	$1,325	$1,100

Last MSR was $3,380.

M-87 LONG RANGE SNIPER RIFLE - .50 BMG cal., stainless steel bolt action, 29 in. barrel with muzzle brake, single shot, camo synthetic stock, accurate to 1500 meters, 21 lbs. Mfg. 1988-2000.

	100%	98%	95%	90%	80%	70%	60%
	$3,450	$2,800	$2,375	$2,000	$1,850	$1,700	$1,575

Last MSR was $3,885.

✳ *M-87R Long Range Sniper Rifle* - similiar specs. as Model 87, except has 5 shot fixed box mag. Mfg. 1990-2000.

	100%	98%	95%	90%	80%	70%	60%
	$3,725	$2,950	$2,550	$2,200	$2,000	$1,850	$1,700

Last MSR was $4,000.

M-88 U.S. NAVY - .50 BMG cal., reintroduced U.S. Navy Seal Team shell holder single shot action with thumb hole stock (one-piece or breakdown two-piece), 24 lbs. Mfg. 1997-2000.

	100%	98%	95%	90%	80%	70%	60%
	$3,250	$2,600	$2,200	$1,625	$1,250	$1,125	$900

Last MSR was $3,600.

> Add $300 for two-piece breakdown stock.

M-89 SNIPER RIFLE - .308 Win. cal., 28 in. barrel with suppressor (also available without), fiberglass stock adj. for length and recoil pad, 15 1/4 lbs. Mfg. 1990-2000.

	100%	98%	95%	90%	80%	70%	60%
	$2,875	$2,525	$2,250	$1,875	$1,650	$1,325	$1,100

Last MSR was $3,200.

> Add $425 for muzzle suppressor (disc. 1996).

M-92 BULL PUP - .50 BMG cal., bullpup configuration with shorter barrel. Mfg. 1993-2000.

	100%	98%	95%	90%	80%	70%	60%
	$4,300	$3,250	$2,750	$2,300	$2,050	$1,850	$1,700

Last MSR was $4,770.

M-93 - .50 BMG cal., similar to M-87, except has folding stock and detachable 5 or 10 shot box mag. Mfg. 1993-2000.

	100%	98%	95%	90%	80%	70%	60%
	$3,800	$3,250	$2,750	$2,300	$2,000	$1,850	$1,700

Last MSR was $4,150.

> Add $300 for two-piece folding stock or dovetail combo. quick disassembly fixture.

M-95 TITANIUM/GRAPHITE - .50 BMG cal., features titanium alloy M-87 receiver with graphite barrel and steel liner, single shot or repeater, approx. 18 lbs. Mfg. 1997-2000.

	100%	98%	95%	90%	80%	70%	60%
	$4,650	$4,175	$3,475	$2,875	$2,300	$2,050	$1,850

Last MSR was $5,085.

> Add $165 for fixed mag.
> Add $315 for detachable mag.

GRADING - PPGS™	100%	98%	95%	90%	80%	70%	60%

M-96 SEMI-AUTO - .50 BMG cal., gas-operated with 5 shot detachable mag., carry handle scope mount, steel receiver, 30 lbs. Mfg. 1997-2000.

	$6,200	$5,625	$5,075	$4,650	$4,175	$3,475	$2,875

Last MSR was $6,800.

RIFLES SxS

BOXLOCK MODEL - various cals. from .270 Win. - .500 NE, engraved boxlock action, 3 leaf express rear sights, AAA wood, high polish barrel blue, equipped with aluminum case and chain, custom order. Mfg. 1998-2000.

	$12,000	$10,000	$8,500	$7,000	$6,000	$5,000	$4,000

Last MSR was $12,000.

Add $1,000 for quick detachable claw scope mounts.
Add $6,000 for additional set of rifle barrels.
Add $5,000 for additional set of shotgun barrels.

SIDELOCK MODEL - various cals. from .375 H&H - .577 NE, engraved sidelock action, 3 leaf express rear sights, AAA wood, high polish barrel blue, equipped with aluminum case and chain, custom order. Mfg. 1998-2000.

	$18,200	$15,750	$12,000	$10,000	$8,500	$7,000	$6,000

Last MSR was $18,200.

Add $1,000 for quick detachable claw scope mounts.
Add $6,000 for additional set of rifle barrels.
Add $5,000 for additional set of shotgun barrels.

HARRISON & HUSSEY LTD.

Current trademark founded in 1919 and currently owned by Cogswell & Harrison, located in Slough, England.

Harrison & Hussey Ltd. was founded in 1919 and purchased by Stephen Grant & Joseph Lang Ltd. in 1930. Boss & Co. took over Harrison & Hussey's original 41 Albermarle Street location and remained there until 1961.

Harrison & Hussey guns are best quality English longarms. It is recommended that an appraisal be obtained before purchase. Harrison & Hussey records have remained intact, and Cogswell & Harrison can provide owners with a date of manufacture free of charge, providing there is a serial number. A full repair and restoration service is also offered. Please contact Cogswell & Harrison for more information about these services (see Trademark Index).

HARTFORD ARMORY

Previous manufacturer located in Collinsville, CT circa 2003-2006.

REVOLVERS: REPRODUCTIONS

MODEL 1875 - .357 Mag., .44 Mag., .44-40 WCF, or .45 LC cal., reproduction of original Remington Model 1875 with reinforced barrel, 5 3/4 or 7 1/2 in. barrel, blue metal finish standard (optional frame case colors by Doug Turnbull), or stainless steel construction, includes wooden presentation box with six brass snap caps. Limited mfg. 2004-2005.

	$1,325	$1,100	$875	$700	$600	$500	$450

Last MSR was $1,495.

Add $325 for stainless steel.
Add $325 for case colored frame.

MODEL 1890 - .357 Mag., .44 Mag., .44-40 WCF, or .45 LC cal., reproduction of original Remington Model 1890, 5 3/4 or 7 1/2 in. barrel, blue metal or stainless steel, includes wooden presentation box with six brass snap caps. Limited mfg. 2004-2005.

	$1,325	$1,100	$875	$700	$600	$500	$450

Last MSR was $1,495.

Add $325 for stainless steel.
Add $325 for case colored frame.

GRADING - PPGS™	100%	98%	95%	90%	80%	70%	60%

HARTFORD ARMS & EQUIPMENT COMPANY

Previous manufacturer located in Harford, CT 1925-1932. Established in 1925, this firm was bankrupt when purchased by the High Standard Company in 1932.

PISTOLS: SEMI-AUTO, RIMFIRE

HARTFORD AUTOMATIC TARGET MODEL 1925 - .22 LR cal., 6 3/4 in. round barrel, checkered black hard rubber or ribbed walnut grips, 10 shot, frame marked "Manfd. by/the Hartford Arms and Equip. Co./Hartford, Conn./Patented/.22 cal./Long Rifle" on left side in front of breech. Approx. 5,000 mfg. 1925-1930.

$565	$515	$465	$405	$325	$300	$280

Add $150 for guns in original Hartford Arms box numbered to gun.

HARTFORD REPEATING PISTOL - The existence of this pistol is in doubt. If encountered, please have the gun checked for authenticity by an expert. The interrelationship of Fiala, Hartford, and Schall through the common gun designer suggests that if this gun exists, then it is probably a Hartford marked repeater like the Fiala and Schall models. Numerous examples of unmarked Schall pistols exist, and some have confused the Schall as a Hartford repeater.

PISTOLS: SINGLE SHOT

HARTFORD SINGLE SHOT TARGET - .22 LR cal., single shot, manual operation, 6 3/4 in. round barrel, fixed sights, ribbed walnut or composition grips, frame marked "Manfd. by/the Hartford Arms and Equip. Co./Hartford, Conn./Patented/.22 cal./Long Rifle" on the left side in front of the breech, resembles a semi-auto, no mag.

$675	$600	$550	$500	$425	$350	$310

Add $150 for guns in original Hartford Arms box numbered to gun.
Add $250 for guns in original High Standard box numbered to gun.

High Standard produced a number of these models in 1933. These guns were mfg. from Hartford parts and carried the Hartford markings. Boxes for High Standard manufactured guns carry the High Standard and Hartford names. Hartford production is unknown, but probably less than 800. High Standard production less than 900 pistols.

HARTMANN & WEISS GmbH

Current manufacturer established during 1965 and located in Hamburg, Germany.

Hartmann and Weiss, previously employed by James Purdey & Sons, Ltd., manufactures only top quality longarms, including sidelock SxS shotguns and rifles, O/U shotguns and rifles, falling block single shot rifles (including the Heeren and Hagn action), and bolt action rifles with three lengths of action. Please contact the manufacturer directly for more information and/or a price quotation (see Trademark Index).

HASKELL MANUFACTURING

Previous manufacturer of .45 ACP cal. semi-auto pistols located in Lima, OH. Previously distributed by MKS Supply located in Mansfield, OH.

Refer to listing under Hi-Point Firearms.

HATFIELD GUN CO., INC.

Previous manufacturer located in St. Joseph, MO. The following shotguns were previously manufactured until 1996 by the Hatfield Gun Co., Inc. (designated Hatfield Rifle Works until 1986).

SHOTGUNS: O/U

BOXLOCK - 20 ga. only, boxlock action with satin grey finished receiver, maple stock. Mfg. 1995-96.

$3,350	$2,950	$2,550	$2,175	$1,725	$1,450	$1,100

Last MSR was $3,749.

Add $1,425 for extra 28 ga. barrels.

GRADING - PPGS™	100%	98%	95%	90%	80%	70%	60%

SHOTGUNS: SxS

In addition to Grades I and II, Hatfield also offered custom order shotguns built per individual special order - prices started at $3,000.

GRADE I UPLANDER - 20 or 28 ga., 3 in. chambers, 26 in. IC/M, matted rib barrels, case hardened boxlock action, single trigger, ejectors, deluxe checkered straight grip maple stock and forearm, 5 3/4 lbs, cased. Mfg. 1987-96.

	$1,975	$1,700	$1,500	$1,325	$1,150	$900	$725

Last MSR was $2,249.

Add $800 for extra 28 ga. barrels.

✻ *Grade I Uplander Collector's* - mfg. 1990-92.

	$1,475	$1,200	$1,000	$875	$700	$550	$475

Last MSR was $1,625.

Add $400 for extra 28 ga. barrels.

GRADE II PIGEON - similar to Grade I, except has scroll engraving on top lever, sides, floor plate, and triggerguard, cased. Mfg. 1987-96.

	$2,650	$2,250	$1,825	$1,475	$1,100	$900	$775

Last MSR was $2,995.

Add $995 for extra 28 ga. barrels.

✻ *Grade II Pigeon Collector's* - mfg. 1990-92.

	$2,675	$2,000	$1,600	$1,250	$1,050	$875	$775

Last MSR was $3,025.

Add $400 for extra 28 ga. barrels.

GRADE III SUPER PIGEON - includes heavy relief scroll engraving (total coverage) on frame, top lever, floor plate, and triggerguard, leather cased. Mfg. 1987-disc.

	$2,350	$1,900	$1,495	$1,200	$1,025	$900	$775

Last MSR was $3,500.

Add $900 for extra 28 ga. barrels.

✻ *Grade III Super Pigeon Collector's* - mfg. 1990-disc.

	$3,000	$2,500	$2,000	$1,750	$1,400	$1,175	$995

Last MSR was $4,375.

Add $900 for extra 28 ga. barrels.

GRADE IV GOLDEN QUAIL - more extensive engraving including six 24Kt. gold inlays on frame and floor plate, 2 gold barrel bands, leather cased. Mfg. 1987-disc.

	$3,995	$3,575	$2,900	$2,350	$1,900	$1,600	$1,300

Last MSR was $5,500.

Add $900 for extra 28 ga. barrels.

✻ *Grade IV Golden Quail Collector's* - mfg. 1990-disc.

	$4,475	$3,900	$3,300	$2,650	$2,175	$1,800	$1,500

Last MSR was $6,625.

Add $1,350 for extra 28 ga. barrels.

GRADE V WOODCOCK - previous top-of-the-line model with best quality engraving and multiple gold inlays, leather cased. Mfg. 1987-disc.

	$4,600	$4,400	$3,350	$2,700	$2,175	$1,800	$1,500

Last MSR was $6,900.

Add $1,500 for extra 28 ga. barrels.

✻ *Grade V Woodcock Collector's* - mfg. 1990-disc.

	$6,200	$5,700	$4,475	$3,900	$3,300	$2,650	$2,200

Last MSR was $8,500.

Add $2,000 for extra 28 ga. barrels.

GRADING - PPGS™	100%	98%	95%	90%	80%	70%	60%

GRADE VI BLACK WIDOW - mfg. 1990-disc.

	100%	98%	95%	90%	80%	70%	60%
	$5,200	$4,875	$3,700	$3,000	$2,500	$2,100	$1,800

Last MSR was $7,900.

GRADE VII ROYALE - mfg. 1990-disc.

	$5,200	$4,875	$3,700	$3,000	$2,500	$2,100	$1,800

Last MSR was $7,900.

GRADE VIII TOP HAT - top-of-the-line model with best quality wood and extensive engraving with gold inlays. Built to individual customer specifications. Mfg. 1990-disc.

	$12,000	$9,750	$8,750	$7,500	$6,500	$5,500	$4,500

Last MSR was $17,500.

SIDELOCK MODEL - 20 ga. only, satin grey finished receiver, full engraving. Mfg. 1995-96.

	$10,750	$8,750	$7,500	$6,250	$5,000	$4,850	$3,600

Last MSR was $12,000.

✳ *Sidelock Model Grade II* - features high relief full coverage engraving, color case hardened receiver, multiple gold and silver inlays.

	$15,000	$12,000	$10,750	$8,750	$7,000	$5,750	$4,650

Last MSR was $17,500.

HATFIELD GUN COMPANY LLC

Current importer of sidelock O/U and SxS shotguns manufactured in Turkey, established 2005 and located in Des Plains, IL. Previously located in Sagle, ID.

Hatfield Gun Company LLC represents the Hatfield trademark on shotguns manufactured in Turkey. Current models include the Mayfair sidelock O/U and London sidelock SxS. These shotguns feature the Hatfield seven pin jeweled lock plate, and semi-chopper lump barrels with double locking underlugs. Many options are available, including wood upgrades. Please contact the company directly for more information, including availability and pricing. If you can't get ahold of Ted, he's probably fishing!

Shotguns imported into North America by Kimber can be found in the Kimber section.

HATFIELD'S

Current manufacturer established during 2003, and located in St. Joseph, MO.

SHOTGUNS: O/U

HATFIELD 1 OF 100 - 28 ga., small frame O/U, 28 in. barrels with five choke tubes, vent. rib, chrome lined bores, SST, extractors, matte blue finish, checkered Circassian pistol grip stock and forend. New 2007.

MSR $1,695	$1,550	$1,375	$1,175	$975	$825	$700	$600

SHOTGUNS: SxS

UPLANDER 28 - 28 ga., small scalloped boxlock frame, extractors, SST or DT, 26 in. monobloc barrels with matte rib, checkered Circassian walnut straight grip stock and splinter forearm, case colored frame, 4 lbs. New 2004.

MSR $1,499	$1,350	$1,200	$1,000	$875	$700	$550	$475

Add $100 for single trigger.

HATSAN ARMS COMPANY

Current shotgun manufacturer established in 1976, and located in Izmir, Turkey. Currently imported by Legacy Sports International LLC, located in Reno, NV. Previously located in Alexandria, VA.

Hatsan Arms Company manufactures the Escort line of shotguns imported by Legacy. Please refer to the Escort section for current model availability and pricing.

KARL HAUPTMANN JAGDWAFFEN

Current manufacturer located in Ferlach, Austria. Consumer direct sales.

Karl Hauptmann was a member of the Ferlach Guild until it was dissolved in 2004. His son Gerd Hauptmann is currently the managing director of the company. Hauptmann Jagdwaffen manufactures high quality shotguns, combination guns, and double rifles, and a very unique, three barrel SxSxS rifle. Since every gun is custom made according to each customer's specifications, please contact the factory directly for an individual price quotation and delivery time (see Trademark Index).

HAWES FIREARMS

Previously manufactured by J.P. Sauer & Sohn in Eckernforde, Germany. Previously imported by Hawes Firearms in Van Nuys, CA.

Hawes Firearms was created after Hy Hunter discontinued their gun line in the early 1960s.

Rather than give an individual listing of the various single action and double action (including Medallion models) revolvers that have been imported, a generalized price range is as follows: centerfire single actions usually are in the $200-$395 range, centerfire double actions are $175-$295, while .22 rimfire models are typically valued between $100-$200.

HECKLER & KOCH

Current manufacturer established in 1949, and located in Oberndorf/Neckar, Germany. Currently imported and distributed by Merkel USA, located in Trussville, AL. Previously imported and distributed by Heckler & Koch, Inc. located in Sterling, VA (previously located in Chantilly, VA). During 2004, H & K built a new plant in Columbus, GA, primarily to manufacture guns for American military and law enforcement. In early 1991, H & K was absorbed by Royal Ordnance, a division of British Aerospace (BAE Systems) located in England. During December 2002, BAE Systems sold Heckler & Koch to a group of European investors. Heckler & Koch, Inc. and HKJS GmbH are wholly owned subsidiaries of Suhler Jag- und Sportwaffen Holding GmbH and the sole licensees of Heckler & Koch commercial firearms technology.

PISTOLS: SEMI-AUTO, RECENT MFG.

USP and USP Compact (with bobbed hammer) Models are divided into 9 variations. They include: USP Variant 1 (DA/SA with control safety decocking lever on left), USP Variant 2 (DA/SA with control safety decocking lever on right), USP Variant 3 (DA/SA with control safety decocking lever on left), USP Variant 4 (DA/SA with control safety decocking lever on right), USP Variant 5 (DAO with control safety decocking lever on left), USP Variant 6 (DAO with control safety decocking lever on right), USP Variant 7 (DAO with no control lever), USP Variant 9 (DA/SA with safety control lever on left), and USP Variant 10 (DA/SA with safety control lever on right).

Add $66 for ambidextrous control lever (safety/decocking lever on right side), and $387 for laser sighting device BA-6 (mfg. 2002-2005) on currently manufactured USP and USP Compact models. Also add $25 for any USP/USP Compact variant other than Variant 1.

HK4 - .380 ACP, .32 ACP, .25 ACP, and .22 LR cals., double action auto, available with all caliber conversion units, 3 1/3 in. barrel, blue, plastic grips. Disc. 1984.

	100%	98%	95%	90%	80%	70%	60%
.25 ACP or .32 ACP cal.	$295	$260	$230	$215	$180	$150	$130
.22 LR or .380 ACP cal.	$375	$325	$300	$250	$195	$160	$140

This model was also available as a H & K commemorative model with gold tone plaque on slide and came in a plastic presentation box. Add approx. 25% to .22 LR or .380 ACP cal. prices if NIB.

* *HK4 .380 ACP with .22 LR conversion*

	100%	98%	95%	90%	80%	70%	60%
	$480	$385	$350	$325	$310	$290	$280

* *HK4 .380 ACP with all conversions*

	100%	98%	95%	90%	80%	70%	60%
	$650	$550	$450	$420	$390	$375	$360

This model was also mfg. in a French model in .22 LR and/or .32 ACP (about 500 imported).

GRADING - PPGS™	100%	98%	95%	90%	80%	70%	60%

✳ *HK-4 Commemorative Combo* - includes one .22 cal. and one .380 cal. barrel. Mfg. 1971.

	$650	$565	$485	$425	$360	$310	$265

HK45 - .45 ACP cal., SA/DA and variants (10), 4.53 in. barrel, features black polymer frame with finger groove grips, integrated Picatinny rail, low profile 3-dot sights, interchangable grip panels, twin slide serrations, 10 shot mag., internal mechanical recoil reduction system reduces recoil 30%, 27.7 oz. New 2008.

MSR $1,099	$950	$850	$750	$625	$500	$450	$400

✳ *HK45 Compact* - similar to HK45, except has 8 shot mag. and small grip frame. New 2008.

MSR $1,099	$950	$850	$750	$625	$500	$450	$400

P9S - .45 ACP or 9mm Para. cal., double action combat model, 4 in. barrel, phosphate finish, sculptured plastic grips, fixed sights. Although production ceased in 1984, limited quantities were available until 1989.

	$850	$775	$650	$525	$450	$375	$300

Last MSR was $1,299.

Add 25% for .45 ACP.

P9S TARGET - .45 ACP or 9mm Para. cal., 4 in. barrel, phosphate finish, adj. sights and trigger. Although production ceased in 1984, limited quantities were available until 1989.

	$1,000	$800	$600	$540	$500	$465	$430

Last MSR was $1,382.

P9S COMPETITION KIT - 9mm Para. or .45 ACP (rare) cal., similar to P9S Target, except extra 5 1/2 in. barrel and weight, competition walnut grip, 2 slides. Disc. 1984.

	$1,150	$950	$875	$800	$720	$640	$550

Last MSR was $2,250.

P7 PSP - 9mm Para. cal., older variation of the P7 M8, without extended trigger guard, ambidextrous mag. release (European style), or heat shield. Standard production ceased 1986. A reissue of this model was mfg. in 1990, with approx. 150 produced. Limited quantities remained through 1999.

	$850	$750	$650	$550	$460	$410	$390

Last MSR was $1,111.

Add $200 for European Model with larger frame.

P7 M8 - 9mm Para. cal., unique squeeze cocking single action, extended square combat type trigger guard with heat shield, 4.13 in. fixed barrel with polygonal rifling, 8 shot mag., ambidextrous mag. release, fixed 3-dot sighting system, stippled black plastic grips, black phosphate or nickel (mfg. 1992-2000) finish, includes 2 mags., 28 oz. Disc. 2005.

	$1,125	$950	$775	$650	$550	$500	$450

Last MSR was $1,515.

Add $102 for Tritium sights (various colors, new 1993).
Add $566 for .22 LR conversion kit (barrel, slide, and two mags., disc. 1999).

P7 M13 - similar to P7 M8, only with staggered 13 shot mag., 30 oz. Disc. 1994.

	$1,575	$1,250	$1,050	$825	$700	$575	$525

Last MSR was $1,330.

Add $85 for Tritium sights (various colors, new 1993).
Add 10% for factory wood grips.

P7 M10 - .40 S&W cal., similar specifications as P7 M13, except has 10 shot mag., 39 oz. Mfg. 1991-94.

	$1,125	$950	$775	$650	$550	$500	$450

Last MSR was $1,315.

Add $85 for Tritium sights (various colors, new 1993).

GRADING - PPGS™	100%	98%	95%	90%	80%	70%	60%

P7 K3 - .22 LR or .380 ACP cal., uses unique oil-filled buffer to decrease recoil, 3.8 in. barrel, matte black or nickel (less common) finish, 8 shot mag. (includes 2), 26 1/2 oz. Mfg. 1988-94.

	$1,295	$850	$715	$600	$525	$450	$410

Last MSR was $1,100.

Add $525 for .22 LR conversion kit.
Add $228 for .32 ACP conversion kit.
Add $85 for Tritium sights (various colors, new 1993).

P30 - 9mm Para. cal., 3.86 in. barrel, 15 shot mag., 3-dot sights, lower accessory rail, interchangeable backstraps, self decocking DA hammer, firing pin block safety, loaded chamber indicator, ergonomic grips with interchangeable side panels and backstraps, double slide serrations, internal recoil reduction system, approx. 23 oz. Importation began mid-2007.

MSR $939		$825	$725	$575	$475	$400	$350	$300

P2000 - 9mm Para., .357 SIG (new 2005), or .40 S&W cal., SA/DA or LEM (Law Enforcement Modification) DAO (w/o control lever), compact design, patterned after USP Compact Model, features pre-cocked hammer system with very short trigger rest distance, lockout safety device, 3-dot sights, 3.62 in. barrel with polygon rifling, 10 or 12 shot mag. with finger extension, or optional 13 shot mag. (new late 2004), with or w/o decocker, interchangeable rear grip panels, black finish, approx. 22 oz.

MSR $879		$775	$675	$550	$475	$400	$350	$300

Add $33 for magazine disconnect.

✴ *P2000 SK SubCompact* - similar to P2000, features LEM (Law Enforcement Modification) trigger system, 2.48 in. barrel, 9 (.357 SIG or .40 S&W cal.) or 10 (9mm Para.) shot mag., approx. 27 oz. Importation began 2005.

MSR $919		$785	$695	$550	$475	$400	$350	$300

USP COMBAT COMPETITION - 9mm Para. or .40 S&W cal., 4 1/4 in. barrel, includes jet funnel kit with two 16 (.40 S&W) or 18 (9mm Para) mags., Novak combat sight system, match trigger, lower accessory rail on frame, 26 1/2 oz. Importation began 2007.

MSR $1,199		$1,075	$940	$835	$725	$600	$500	$450

USP COMPETITION - similar to USP Combat Competition, except features LEM match trigger system. Importation began 2007.

MSR $1,279		$1,125	$975	$850	$750	$625	$500	$450

USP 9 - 9mm Para. cal., available in regular DA/SA mode or DA only (10 variants), 4.13 in. barrel with polygonal rifling, Browning-type action with H & K recoil reduction system, polymer frame, all metal surfaces specially treated, can be carried cocked and locked, stippled synthetic grips, bobbed hammer, 3-dot sighting system, multiple safeties, 10 (C/B 1994), 15 (new late 2004), or 16* shot polymer mag., 26.5 oz. New 1993.

MSR $859		$750	$675	$550	$500	$450	$395	$350

Add $102 for Tritium sights (various colors, new 1993).

✴ *USP 9 SD* - similar to USP 9, except has target sights and 4.56 threaded barrel, approx. 27 oz. Imported 2004-2006.

	$825	$700	$625	$550	$500	$450	$400

Last MSR was $939.

✴ *USP 9 Stainless* - similar to USP 9, except has satin finished stainless steel slide. Mfg. 1996-2001.

	$700	$565	$475	$415	$360	$300	$255

Last MSR was $817.

GRADING - PPGS™	100%	98%	95%	90%	80%	70%	60%

USP 9 COMPACT - 9mm Para. cal., compact variation of the USP 9 featuring 3.58 in. barrel, 10 or 13 (new late 2004) shot mag., 25.5 oz. New 1997.

MSR $879	$765	$685	$550	$500	$450	$395	$350

✳ *USP 9 Compact Stainless* - similar to USP 9 Compact, except has satin finished stainless steel slide. Mfg. 1997-2004.

	$735	$595	$500	$430	$375	$315	$270

Last MSR was $849.

✳ *USP 9 Compact LEM* - LEM designates law enforcement modification, DAO, unique trigger mechanism decreases trigger pull to 7 1/2 - 8 1/2 lbs, blue only, approx. 24 1/2 oz. Imported 2003-2004.

	$695	$575	$495	$450	$400	$350	$315

Last MSR was $799.

USP 9x19 TACTICAL - 9mm Para cal. enhanced variation of the USP 9, 4.92 in. threaded barrel with rubber o-ring, 10 or 15 shot mag., adj. target type sights and trigger, approx. 28 1/2 oz. New 2007.

MSR $1,039	$925	$825	$725	$600	$500	$450	$400

USP 357 - .357 SIG cal., available in 4.25 (Standard, disc. 2004) or 3.58 (Compact) configuration, 10 or 12 (optional beginning 2004) shot mag., black finish, approx. 24.5 oz. Imported 2001-2005.

	$695	$560	$500	$450	$395	$350	$300

Last MSR was $799.

Subtract $30 for Standard Model (disc. 2004).

USP 40 - .40 S&W cal., similar to USP 9, 9 variants of DA/SA/DAO, 10 (C/B1994), 13* (reintroduced late 2004), or 16 (optional, new 2005, needs jet funnel modification) shot mag., 27.75 oz. New 1993.

MSR $859	$750	$675	$550	$500	$450	$395	$350

Add $102 for Tritium sights (various colors, new 1993).

A desert tan or finish became available during 2005 at no extra charge (includes matching nylon carrying case).

✳ *USP 40 Stainless* - similar to USP 40, except has satin finished stainless steel slide. Mfg. 1996-2003.

	$700	$565	$470	$415	$360	$300	$255

Last MSR was $817.

USP 40 COMPACT - .40 S&W cal., compact variation of the USP 40 featuring 3.58 in. barrel, 10 or 12 (new late 2004) shot mag., 27 oz. New 1997.

MSR $879	$765	$685	$550	$500	$450	$395	$350

A desert tan finish became available during 2005 at no extra charge(includes matching nylon carrying case). Grey was also available in limited quantites during 2005 only.

✳ *USP 40 Compact Stainless* - similar to USP 40 Compact, except has satin finished stainless steel slide. Mfg. 1997-2004.

	$735	$595	$500	$430	$375	$315	$270

Last MSR was $849.

✳ *USP 40 Compact LEM* - LEM designates law enforcement modification, DAO, unique trigger mechanism decreases trigger pull to 7 1/2 - 8 1/2 lbs, blue only, approx. 24 1/2 oz. Imported 2002-2005.

	$695	$575	$495	$450	$400	$350	$315

Last MSR was $799.

USP 40 TACTICAL - .40 S&W cal., enhanced variation of the USP 40, 4.92 in. threaded barrel with rubber o-ring, 10 (standard) or 13 shot mag., adj. target type sights and trigger, 30 1/2 oz. New 2005.

MSR $1,179	$1,050	$925	$825	$725	$600	$500	$450

GRADING - PPGS™	100%	98%	95%	90%	80%	70%	60%

USP 45 - .45 ACP cal., similar to USP 9, 9 variants of DA/SA/DAO, 10 (C/B 1994), 12 (new late 2004) or 13* shot mag., 27 3/4 oz. New 1995.

MSR $919		$795	$650	$550	$475	$425	$350	$315

Add $102 for Tritium sights (various colors, new 1993).

A desert tan or green finish became available during 2005 at no extra charge (includes matching nylon carrying case). Grey was also available in limited quantites during 2005 only.

✳ *USP 45 Stainless* - similar to USP 45, except has satin finished stainless steel slide. Mfg. 1996-2003.

	$760	$600	$500	$430	$375	$315	$270

Last MSR was $888.

✳ *USP 45 Match Pistol* - .45 ACP cal., features 6.02 in. barrel with polygonal rifling, micrometer adj. high relief and raised rear sight, raised target front sight, 10 shot mag., barrel weight, fluted, and ambidextrous safety, choice of matte black or stainless steel slide, supplied with additional o-rings and setup tools, 38 oz. Mfg. 1997-98.

	$1,275	$1,025	$825	$750	$675	$550	$500

Last MSR was $1,369.

Add $72 for stainless steel slide model.

USP 45 COMPACT - .45 ACP cal., compact variation of the USP 45, featuring 3.8 in. barrel, 8 shot mag., 28 oz. New 1998.

MSR $959		$835	$750	$625	$525	$450	$400	$350

✳ *USP 45 Compact Stainless* - similar to USP 45 Compact, except has satin finished stainless steel slide. Mfg. 1998-2004.

	$775	$615	$510	$440	$385	$325	$275

Last MSR was $894.

✳ *USP 45 Compact 50th Anniversary* - commemorates the 50th year of H & K (1950-2000), 1 of 1,000 special edition featuring high polish blue slide with 50th Anniversary logo engraved in gold and silver, supplied with presentation wood case and commemorative coin. Limited mfg. 2000 only.

	$1,150	$895	$795	N/A	N/A	N/A	N/A

Last MSR was $999.

USP 45 TACTICAL PISTOL - .45 ACP cal., enhanced variation of the USP 45, 4.92 in. threaded barrel with rubber o-ring, 10 or 12 (optional beginning late 2004) shot mag., adj. target type sights and trigger, limited availability, 36 oz. New 1998.

MSR $1,239		$1,075	$950	$850	$750	$625	$525	$475

A desert tan finish became available during 2005 at no extra charge (includes matching nylon carrying case).

✳ *USP 45 Tactical Pistol Compact* - .45 ACP cal., compact variation of the USP 45 Tactical, 8 shot mag. Importation began 2006.

MSR $1,179		$1,050	$925	$825	$725	$600	$500	$450

USP EXPERT - 9mm Para. (mfg. 2003-2005), .40 S&W (new 2002) or .45 ACP cal., features new slide design with 5.2 in. barrel, 10 (standard), 12 (.45 ACP), 13 (.40 S&W), or 15 (9mm Para.) shot mag., match grade SA or DA trigger pull, recoil reduction system, reinforced polymer frame, adj. rear sight, approx. 30 oz. Importation began 1999.

MSR $1,339		$1,200	$1,025	$900	$800	$700	$625	$525

USP ELITE - 9mm Para. (disc. 2005) or .45 ACP cal, long slide variation of the USP Expert, 6.2 in. barrel, match trigger parts, target sights, ambidextrous control levers, blue finish, includes two 10 shot mags. or 12 (.45 ACP) or 15 (9mm Para.) shot mag. Importation began 2003.

MSR $1,339		$1,200	$1,025	$900	$800	$700	$625	$525

GRADING - PPGS™	100%	98%	95%	90%	80%	70%	60%

MARK 23 SPECIAL OPERATIONS PISTOL - .45 ACP cal., 5.87 in. threaded barrel, polymer frame and integral grips, 3-dot sighting, 10 or 12 (optional beginning late 2004) shot mag., squared off trigger guard, 2.6 lbs., limited availability. New 1996.

MSR $2,139	$1,925	$1,700	$1,475	$1,200	$895	$750	$650

"MK23" is the official military design. Not available to civilians.

A desert tan finish became available during 2005 at no extra charge (includes matching nylon carrying case).

SP 89 - 9mm Para. cal., recoil operated delayed roller-locked bolt system, 4 1/2 in. barrel, 15 shot mag., adj. aperture rear sight (accepts HK claw-lock scope mounts), 4.4 lbs. Mfg. 1990-93.

$3,750	$3,500	$3,000	$2,900	$2,750	$2,650	$2,400

Last MSR was $1,325.

VP 70Z - 9mm Para. cal., 18 shot, double action only, 4 1/2 in. barrel, parkerized finish, plastic receiver/grip assembly. Disc. 1984.

$650	$575	$500	$450	$400	$350	$300

Add 125% if frame cut for shoulder stock (Model VP 70M, NFA Class III).

The majority of pistols that were cut for shoulder stock are the Model VP 70M, and are subject to NFA Class III regulation.

RIFLES: BOLT ACTION

BASR - .22 LR, .22-250 Rem., 6mm PPC, .300 Win. Mag., .30-06, or .308 Win. cal., Kevlar stock, stainless steel barrel, limited production. Special order only. Mfg. 1986 only.

$5,750	$5,000	$4,500	$4,000	$3,650	$3,300	$2,600

Last MSR was $2,199.

Less than 135 of this variation were manufactured and they are extremely rare. Contractual disputes with the U.S. supplier stopped H & K from receiving any BASR models.

RIFLES: SEMI-AUTO

Most of the models listed, being of a paramilitary design, were disc. in 1989 due to Federal legislation. Sporterized variations mfg. after 1994 with thumbhole stocks were banned in April, 1998.

In 1991, the HK-91, HK-93, and HK-94 were discontinued. Last published retail prices (1991) were $999 for fixed stock models and $1,199 for retractable stock models.

In the early '70s, S.A.C.O. importers located in Virginia sold the Models 41 and 43 which were the predecessors to the Model 91 and 93, respectively. Values for these earlier variations will be higher than values listed.

SR-9 - .308 Win. cal., semi-auto sporting rifle, 19.7 in. barrel, Kevlar reinforced fiberglass thumbhole stock and forearm, 5 shot mag., diopter adj. rear sight, accepts H & K claw-lock scope mounts. Mfg. 1990-93.

$1,875	$1,525	$1,200	$1,025	$875	$750	$650

Last MSR was $1,199.

While advertised again during 1998, this model was finally banned in April, 1998.

SR-9T - .308 Win. cal., precision target rifle with adj. MSG 90 buttstock and PSG-1 trigger group, 5 shot mag. Mfg. 1992-93.

$2,595	$2,175	$1,850	$1,575	$1,175	$995	$850

Last MSR was $1,725.

While advertised again during 1998, this model was finally banned in April, 1998.

SR-9TC - .308 Win. cal., similar to SR-9T except has PSG-1 adj. buttstock. Mfg. 1993 only.

$3,150	$2,725	$2,400	$2,075	$1,725	$1,275	$1,050

Last MSR was $1,995.

While advertised again during 1998, this model was finally banned in April, 1998.

GRADING - PPGS™	100%	98%	95%	90%	80%	70%	60%

PSG-1 - .308 Win. cal. only, high precision marksman's rifle, 5 shot mag., adj. buttstock, includes accessories (Hensholdt illuminated 6x42mm scope) and case, 17.8 lbs. Importation disc. 1998.

	$12,500	$10,950	$9,500	$8,500	$7,500	$7,000	$6,500

Last MSR was $10,811.

MODEL 41 A-2 - .308 Win. cal., predecessor to the Model 91 A-2, originally imported by Golden State Arms.

	$3,500	$3,250	$3,000	$2,850	$2,400	$2,200	$2,000

MODEL 43 A-2 - predecesor to the Model 93 A-2. Disc.

	$3,750	$3,500	$3,250	$3,000	$2,500	$2,300	$2,100

MODEL 91 A-2 - .308 Win. cal., semi-auto paramilitary design rifle, delayed blow-back roller locking bolt system, attenuated recoil, black cycolac stock, 17.7 in. barrel, 20 shot mag., 9.7 lbs. Importation disc. 1989.

* *Model 91 A-2 Fixed stock model*

	$2,950	$2,750	$2,500	$2,350	$2,000	$1,900	$1,725

Last MSR was $999.

Add $200 for desert camo finish.
Add $275 for NATO black finish.

* *Model 91 A-2 SBF (Semi-Beltfed)* - supplied with bipod and M60 link (200 shot with starter tab) and MG42 modified belt (49 shot with fixed starter tab), limited mfg. Disc.

	$10,500	$9,500	$8,500	N/A	N/A	N/A	N/A

* *Model 91 A-3* - with retractable metal stock.

	$3,100	$2,900	$2,700	$2,500	$2,150	$2,000	$1,895

Last MSR was $1,114.

Add $775 for .22 LR conversion kit.

* *Model 91 A-2 Package* - includes A.R.M.S. mount, B-Square rings, Leupold 3x9 compact scope with matte finish. Importation disc. 1988.

	$3,150	$2,750	$2,400	$2,150	$1,900	$1,700	$1,475

Last MSR was $1,285.

Add 30% for retractable stock.

MODEL 93 A-2 - .223 Rem. cal., smaller version of the H & K 91, 25 shot mag., 16.14 in. barrel, 8 lbs.

* *Model 93 A-2 Fixed stock model*

	$3,150	$2,950	$2,700	$2,550	$2,400	$2,300	$2,000

Last MSR was $946.

Add 10% for desert camo finish.
Add 15% for NATO black finish.

* *Model 93 A-3* - with retractable metal stock.

	$3,400	$3,250	$3,000	$2,800	$2,650	$2,500	$2,250

Last MSR was $1,114.

* *Model 93 A-2 Package* - includes A.R.M.S. mount, B-Square rings, Leupold 3x9 compact scope with matte finish. Importation disc. 1988.

	$3,500	$3,100	$2,850	$2,550	$2,400	$2,100	$1,895

Last MSR was $1,285.

Add 10% for retractable stock.

MODEL 94 CARBINE A-2 - 9mm Para. cal., semi-auto carbine, 16.54 in. barrel, aperture rear sight, 15 shot mag. New 1983.

* *Model 94 Carbine A-2 Fixed stock model*

	$3,950	$3,750	$3,500	$3,400	$3,000	$2,600	$2,500

Last MSR was $946.

* *Model 94 Carbine A-3* - retractable metal stock.

	100%	98%	95%	90%	80%	70%	60%
	$4,150	$3,900	$3,700	$3,550	$3,200	$2,800	$2,700

Last MSR was $1,114.

* *Model 94 Carbine A-2 Package* - includes A.R.M.S. mount, B-Square rings, Leupold 3x9 compact scope with matte finish. Importation disc. 1988.

	$4,300	$3,875	$3,650	$3,300	$3,000	$2,800	$2,500

Last MSR was $1,285.

Add 10% for retractable stock.

* *Model 94 Carbine A-2 SGI* - 9mm Para. cal., target rifle, aluminum alloy bi-pod, Leupold 6X scope, 15 or 30 shot mag. Imported 1986 only.

	$3,950	$3,750	$3,500	$3,000	$2,750	$2,500	$2,150

Last MSR was $1,340.

MODEL 270 - .22 LR cal., sporting rifle, 19.7 in. barrel with standard or polygonal rifling, 5 or 20 shot mag., high luster blue, plain walnut stock, approx. 5.7 lbs. Disc. 1985.

	$875	$795	$625	$575	$425	$350	$300

Last MSR was $200.

MODEL 300 - .22 Mag. cal., 5 or 15 shot, polygonal rifling standard, otherwise similar to H & K 270 with checkered walnut stock. Importation disc. 1989.

	$1,200	$900	$775	$675	$600	$550	$500

Last MSR was $608.

Add $350-$400 for factory H & K scope mount system.

* *Model 300 Package* - includes A.R.M.S. mount, B-Square rings, Leupold 3x9 compact scope with matte finish. Importation disc. 1988.

	$1,475	$1,125	$925	$800	$700	$650	$600

Last MSR was $689.

MODEL 630 - .223 Rem. cal., delayed roller lock bolt system, 17.7 in. barrel with or w/o muzzle brake (early mfg.), reduced recoil, checkered walnut, 4 or 10 shot mag., 7.04 lbs. Importation disc. 1986.

	$1,450	$1,200	$1,000	$950	$850	$750	$650

Last MSR was $784.

Add $350-$400 for factory H & K scope mount system.
The .222 Rem. cal. was also available in this model. Most were French contracts.

MODEL 770 - .308 Win. cal., 3 or 10 shot mag., 19.7 in. barrel with or w/o muzzle brake (early mfg.), otherwise similar to Model 630, 7.92 lbs. Importation disc. 1986.

	$2,000	$1,750	$1,500	$1,275	$1,050	$950	$850

Last MSR was $797.

Add $350-$400 for factory H & K scope mount system.
Significant price increases stopped the importation of this model.
Approx. 6 Model 770s were imported in .243 Win. cal. during 1984. Values for the .243 Win. cal. will be considerably higher than listed for the .308 Win. cal.

MODEL 911 - .308 Win. cal., earlier importation. Disc.

	$1,750	$1,550	$1,350	$1,175	$950	$850	$725

MODEL 940 - .30-06 cal., 21.6 in. barrel with or w/o muzzle brake (early mfg.), otherwise same as Model 770, 8.62 lbs. Importation disc. 1986.

	$1,950	$1,750	$1,500	$1,250	$995	$875	$750

Last MSR was $917.

Add $350-$400 for factory H & K scope mount system.
Cals. 7x64mm and 9.3x62mm were also available in this model.
Significant price increases stopped the importation of this model.

* *Model 940K* - similar to Model 940, except has 16 in. barrel and higher cheekpiece. Two imported 1984 only.
Rarity precludes accurate price evaluation.

SLB 2000 - .30-06 or .308 Win. (new 2003) cal. (same bolt system allows cartridge changeability), short stroke piston actuated gas operating system, alloy receiver with black weather resistant coating, gold accents on receiver, 19.69 in. barrel (interchangeable), checkered walnut stock and specially angled pistol grip, tang mounted safety blocks hammer and trigger, 2, 5, or 10 shot mag., iron sights, 7.28 lbs. Imported 2001-2003.

$1,150 $995 $895 $825 $775 $700 $650

Last MSR was $1,299.

MODELS SL6 & SL7 CARBINE - .223 Rem. or .308 Win. cal., 17.71 in. barrel, delayed roller lock bolt system, reduced recoil, vent. wood hand guard, 3 or 4 shot mag., 8.36 lbs., matte black metal finish, HK-SL6 is .223 Rem. cal., HK-SL7 is .308 Win. cal. Importation disc. in 1986.

$1,400 $1,200 $1,000 $900 $775 $700 $550

Add $250-$300 for factory H & K scope mount system.

These models were the last sporter variations H & K imported into the U.S. - no U.S. importation since 1986.

MODEL SL8-1 - .223 Rem. cal., short stroke piston actuated gas operating system, advanced grey carbon fiber polymer construction based on the German Army G36 rifle, thumbhole stock with adj. cheekpiece and buttstock, 10 shot mag., modular and removable Picatinny rail sight, removable sights from rail, 20.8 cold hammer forged heavy barrel, adj. sights, 8.6 lbs. Imported 2000-2003, reimported beginning 2007.

MSR $2,449 $1,950 $1,650 $1,500 $1,350 $1,200 $1,000 $900

Add $338 for carrying handle with 1.5X-3X optical sights.
Add $624 for carrying handle with 1.5X-3X optical sights and red dot reflex sight.

MODEL USC .45 ACP CARBINE - .45 ACP cal., similar design/construction as the Model SL8-1, except is blowback action, and has 16 in. barrel and grey skeletonized buttstock, 10 shot mag., 6 lbs. Imported 2000-2003, reimported beginning 2007.

MSR $1,729 $1,425 $1,250 $1,000 $900 $800 $700 $600

SHOTGUNS: SEMI-AUTO

Previously imported H & K Benelli shotguns can be found under their own heading.

MODEL 512 - 12 ga. only, mfg. by Franchi for German military contract, rifle sights, matte finished metal, walnut stock, fixed choke pattern diverter giving rectangular shot pattern. Importation disc. 1991.

$1,500 $1,300 $1,100 $925 $800 $700 $600

Last Mfg.'s Wholesale was $1,895.

SLS 2002 - 12 ga. only, 3 in. chamber, IQ-port gas operation (excess gas is vented forward through forearm cap), various barrel lengths, including slug barrel, double slide rails, deluxe checkered walnut stock and forearm, phosphate black finish, approx. 6 3/4 lbs. European introduction 2002.

While advertised during 2002, this gun has not been imported into the U.S.

N.L. HEINEKE, INC.

Current custom bolt action rifle manufacturer located in Laramie, WY.

RIFLES: BOLT ACTION, CUSTOM

Nathan Heinke manufactures high quality bolt action rifles on a custom order basis only. The base price is $15,000, and many options and accessories are available, including engraving. Please contact the company directly for more information, including delivery time (approx. 12 months), custom options, and availability (see Trademark Index).

GRADING - PPGS™	100%	98%	95%	90%	80%	70%	60%

HEINIE SPECIALTY PRODUCTS

Current pistol and related components manufacturer established in 1973, and located in Quincy, IL.

Heinie manufactures both scratch built personal defense and tactical/carry 1911 packages in a wide variety of chamberings. Please contact the factory directly for information regarding current pricing and availability (see Trademark Index).

HELLIS, CHARLES

Current trademark of shotguns established in 1884 and located in London, England.

SHOTGUNS: CUSTOM

Charles Hellis manufactures high quality traditional SxS and O/U shotguns with a unique spring assisted opening mechanism. All guns are entirely hand made to custom order. SxS prices begin at £32,500, and O/U prices begin at £39,950. Please contact the company directly for more information, including pricing, availability and delivery time (see Trademark Index).

HELWAN

Previous trademark imported by Navy Arms Co. and Interarms until 1995.

PISTOLS: SEMI-AUTO

BRIGADIER - 9mm Para. cal., single action, 4 1/2 in. barrel, all steel construction, 8 shot mag. with finger extension, black plastic grips, 32.6 oz. Imported 1988-94.

	$195	$150	$125	$115	$105	$95	$85

Last MSR was $260.

This model is patterned after the Beretta Model 951 Brigadier. They were manufactured at the Helwan arsenal in Egypt.

HENDRY, RAMSAY & WILCOX

Previous manufacturer located in Perth, Scotland.

Hendry, Ramsay & Wilcox manufactured top quality shotguns and rifles which were priced per individual quotation. The company, now called Hendry, Ramsay & Waters, Ltd., is a hunting and sporting outfitter.

HENRY, ALEX

Current trademark owned and manufactured by Dickson & MacNaughton, located in Edinburgh, Scotland.

Please contact Dickson & MacNaughton directly for more information regarding this trademark, including current availability and pricing (see Trademark Index).

HENRY REPEATING ARMS COMPANY

Current rifle manufacturer established during 1997, and located in Brooklyn, NY. Distributor and dealer sales.

RIFLES

HENRY MINI-BOLT - .22 S & LR cal., single shot, 16 1/4 in. barrel, stainless steel receiver and barrel, Williams fire sights, manual safety, 11 1/2 in. LOP, black synthetic stock, 3 1/4 lbs. New 2002.

MSR $240		$195	$160	$130	$110	$95	$90	$85

HENRY ACU-BOLT - .17 HMR, .22 LR or .22 Mag. cal., scaled down action, 20 in. stainless steel barrel and receiver, checkered black fiberglass stock, includes 4X scope with cantilever mount, 4 1/4 lbs. New 2004.

MSR $400		$335	$285	$225	$185	$160	$140	$120

GRADING - PPGS™	100%	98%	95%	90%	80%	70%	60%

HENRY LEVER ACTION - .22 S-L-LR or .22 Mag. (new 2000) cal., side ejection, blue steel receiver, 18 1/4 (.22 LR only), 19 1/4 (.22 Mag. only, disc. 2005) in. round or 20 in. octagon (new 2006) barrel, 11 (.22 Mag.) or 15 (.22 LR) shot mag., deluxe American walnut stock and forearm, adj. rear sight and hooded front, 5 1/2 lbs. New 1997.

MSR $320	$265	$220	$185	$165	$150	$130	$120

Add $150 for .22 Mag. cal.
Add $100 for octagon barrel.

This model is also available as a Youth Model, with 13 in. LOP and shorter barrel.

* *Henry Lever Action Carbine* - similar to Henry Lever Action, except has 16 1/8 in. barrel and large loop lever, 4 1/2 lbs. New 1998.

MSR $330	$270	$220	$185	$165	$150	$130	$120

* *Henry Lever Action Varmint Express* - .17 HMR cal., similar to Henry Lever Action, except has 20 in. barrel, includes cantilever scope mount, Williams Fire Sights, 11 shot tube mag., Monte Carlo stock, 5 3/4 lbs. New 2003.

MSR $540	$460	$375	$315	$250	$200	$175	$150

* *Henry Lever Action BSA Venturing Edition* - .22 S-L-LR cal., 18 1/4 in. round blue barrel, 15 (.22 LR), 16 (.22 Long), or 21 (.22 Short) shot mag., straight grip American walnut stock, "10th Anniversary Venturing" logo on receiver, adj. rear sight, hooded front sight, 5 1/4 lbs. New 2008.

MSR $430	$385	$340	$300	$265	$235	$200	$175

* *Henry Lever Action Golden Boy* - .17 HMR, .22 S-L-LR, or .22 Mag. cal., features brasslite receiver, buttplate, and buckhorn sight, 20 in. blue octagon barrel, 16 shot mag., approx. 6 3/4 lbs. New mid-1999.

MSR $500	$425	$335	$260	$200	$175	$160	$140

Add $80 for .22 Mag. cal. (new 2002).
Add $100 for .17 HMR cal. (new 2005).

* *Henry Lever Action Golden Boy Deluxe* - .17 HMR (new 2006) or .22 S-L-LR cal., features hand engraved gold and silver brasslite receiver, deluxe uncheckered walnut stock and forearm. New 2004.

MSR $1,577	$1,395	$1,225	$1,035	$900	$750	$600	$525

Add $29 for .17 HMR cal.

* *Henry Golden Boy BSA Venturing Edition* - .22 S-L-LR cal., 20 in. octagon blue barrel, 16 or 21 shot mag., straight grip American walnut stock, "10th Anniversary Venturing" logo in buttstock, Marbles adj. semi-buckhorn rear sight with reversible diamond insert, brass bead front sight, brasslite receiver, buttplate, and barrel band. New 2008.

MSR $650	$575	$500	$425	$350	$300	$265	$235

HENRY "BIG BOY" LEVER ACTION - .38 Spl./.357 Mag. (new 2008), .44 Mag./.44 Spl. or .45 LC (new 2004) cal., brass receiver, buttplate, and barrel band, 20 in. octagon barrel with 10 shot tube mag., buckhorn rear sight, straight grip walnut stock and forearm, 8.68 lbs. New 2003.

MSR $900	$785	$650	$550	$450	$400	$350	$300

Add $420 for Wildlife Edition or Cowboy Edition (mfg. 2006-2007).

* *Henry Big Boy Deluxe* - .38 Spl./.357 mag. (new 2008), .44 Mag. or .45 LC cal., features hand engraved brass frame and barrel band, deluxe uncheckered walnut stock and forearm, 1,000 mfg. beginning 2007.

MSR $1,995	$1,725	$1,500	$1,225	$995	$850	$700	$575

* *Henry Big Boy BSA Venturing Edition* - .44 Mag. cal., 20 in. octagon blue barrel, 10 shot mag., straight grip American walnut stock, Marbles adj. semi-buckhorn rear sight with reversible diamond insert, brass bead front sight, solid brass receiver, buttplate, and barrel band. New 2008.

MSR $1,000	$875	$750	$675	$600	$525	$475	$400

GRADING - PPGS™	100%	98%	95%	90%	80%	70%	60%

HENRY PUMP ACTION - .22 S-L-LR or .22 Mag. (new 2006) cal., blue grooved receiver, 18 1/4 in. round (disc. 2005) or 20 1/2 octagon (new 2006) barrel, walnut straight grip stock and forearm, 12 (.22 Mag.) or 16 (.22 LR) shot mag., adj. buckhorn rear sight, approx. 5 1/2 lbs. New 1999.

MSR $500	$435	$340	$255	$200	$175	$160	$140

    Add $80 for .22 Mag. cal.

HENRY U.S. SURVIVAL .22 SEMI-AUTO - .22 LR cal., patterned after the Armalite AR-7 with improvements, takedown design enables receiver, 2 mags., and barrel to stow in ABS plastic stock, 100% Mossy Oak Break-Up camo (new 2000) or weather resistant silver or black (new 1999) stock/metal finish, two 8 shot mags., adj. sights, 16 1/2 in. long when disassembled and stowed in stock, includes plastic carrying case, approx. 2 1/2 lbs. New 1997.

MSR $237	$195	$170	$150	$135	$120	$110	$100

    Add $60 for 100% camo finish (new 2000).

HENRY .30-30 LEVER ACTION - .30-30 Win. cal., lever action, 6 shot mag., 20 in. round or octagon barrel, straight grip American walnut stock with buttplate, fully adj. Marbles semi-buckhorn rear sight with reversible white diamond insert, brass bead front sight, blue steel or brass receiver, barrel band, drilled and tapped, 8.3 lbs. New 2008.

MSR $750	$675	$600	$525	$450	$395	$335	$275

    Add $220 for octagon barrel with brass receiver.

HENRY RIFLE

Please refer to the Winchester section in this text for this model.

HERITAGE MANUFACTURING, INC.

Current manufacturer located in Opa Locka, FL since 1992.

PISTOLS: SEMI-AUTO

H-25/25S - .25 ACP cal., 6 shot mag. with finger extension, single action, exposed hammer, choice of blue or blue/gold finish, 13 1/2 oz. Mfg. 1995-99.

$125	$95	$80	$65	$55	$50	$45

Last MSR was $150.

    Add $10 for nickel steel.
    Add $10 for Model H-25G (blue/gold finish with checkered grips).

STEALTH SHADOW COMPACT - 9mm Para. or .40 S&W cal., striker firing mechanism, stainless steel slide and 3.9 in. barrel, black all polymer frame, manual safety, 10 shot mag. with finger extension, fixed sights, choice of stainless slide, two-tone stainless slide, or all black (Shadow) finish, 20.5 oz. Mfg. 1996-2000.

$255	$220	$190	$165	$150	$135	$110

Last MSR was $300.

    Add $30 for .40 S&W cal.

REVOLVERS

Rough Rider SAA models are made in the U.S.A.

ROUGH RIDER SAA RIMFIRE SERIES - .17 HMR (new 2003), .22 LR or .22 LR/.22 Mag. cal. combo, SAA design with choice of alloy (33.4 oz.) or steel (35 oz., new 2000) frame, hammer block safety, blue, nickel (disc. 2001), black satin (new 2002), satin (new 2001), or silver satin (new 2005) finish, 4 3/4, 6 1/2, or 9 (combo only) in. barrel, fixed or adj. (new 2001) rear sight, smooth or camo (new 2003) wood grips, approx. 33 1/2 oz. New 1993.

GRADING - PPGS™	100%	98%	95%	90%	80%	70%	60%

✳ *Rough Rider SAA Series Steel Frame* - available in blue, black satin (mfg. 2003), or case hardened (mfg. 2003) finish, includes extra .22 Mag. cylinder, choice of regular or bird's head grips.

MSR $230		$185	$150	$130	$110	$90	$80	$70

Add $51 for nickel finish (combo package only, disc. 2001).
Add $50 for .17 HMR cal. with adj. sights (new 2003, not available in 4 3/4 in. barrel).
Add $20 for 9 in. barrel (available with combo package only).
Subtract $50 for alloy frame with combo package (disc. 2002).

✳ *Rough Rider SAA Series Fixed Sight* - .22 LR/.22 Mag. cal. combo only, 4 3/4, 6 1/2, or 9 in. barrel.

MSR $170		$135	$110	$95	$80	$70	$60	$50

Add $40 for satin or black satin finish.
Add $30 for faux mother-of-pearl grips.
Add $15 for 9 in. barrel.
Add $25 for case colored frame (new 2006).
Subtract $15 if with .22 LR cylinder only.

✳ *Rough Rider SAA Series Adjustable Sight* - .17 HMR (new 2006) or .22 LR/.22 Mag. cal. combo, 4 3/4, 6 1/2, or 9 in. barrel.

MSR $210		$165	$140	$110	$95	$80	$70	$60

Add $50 for satin or black satin finish.
Add $30 for .17 HMR cal.
Add $30 for steel frame (disc. 2002).

During 2004, a Williams red ramp front sight and Millett adj. microclick rear sight became available on the 6 1/2 in. barrel.

✳ *Rough Rider SAA Series Illuminator* - .22 LR/.22 Mag. cal. combo only, features Adco Hot Shot Red Dot frame mounted sight, 6 1/2 in. barrel only. Disc. 2007.

		$160	$135	$110	$95	$80	$70	$60

Last MSR was $200.

✳ *Rough Rider SAA Series with Birds Head Grip* - .22 LR/.22 Mag. cal. combo only, choice of 2 3/4 (disc. 1997), 3 (disc. 1994), 3 1/2, or 4 3/4 in. barrel. New 1993.

MSR $170		$140	$115	$95	$85	$75	$65	$60

Add $45 for black satin finish or $30 for faux mother-of-pearl grips.
Add $30 for nickel finish (disc. 2001).

ROUGH RIDER SAA CENTERFIRE SERIES - .32 H&R Mag. (blue finish only), .357 Mag., .44-40 WCF or .45 ACP cal., 3 1/2 (.32 H&R cal. only, with birdshead grips), 4 3/4, 5 1/2, 6 1/2 (.32 H&R cal. only), or 7 1/2 in. barrel, blue, nickel, stainless steel or case harded frame, one piece cocobolo grips, 6 shot, fixed open sight, approx. 36 oz. Mfg. by Pietta.

MSR $390		$345	$300	$265	$235	$200	$180	$160

Add $20 for case hardened frame.
Add $60 for nickel finish.
Add $110 for stainless steel.
Subtract $150 for .32 H&R cal.

SENTRY DA SERIES - .22 Mag. (disc. 1996), .32 Mag. (disc. 1996), .38 Spl., or 9mm Para. (disc. 1996) cal., snubnose design, with 2 or 4 (.22 LR or .38 Spl.) in. barrel, 6 (centerfire) or 8 (rimfire) shot, transfer bar safety, blue or nickel finish, black polymer grips, ramp front sight. Mfg. 1993-97.

		$110	$85	$70	$55	$50	$45	$40

Last MSR was $130.

Add $10 for nickel finish.

HEROLD RIFLE

Previously manufactured by Franz Jaeger, located in Suhl, Germany.

GRADING - PPGS™	100%	98%	95%	90%	80%	70%	60%

RIFLES: BOLT ACTION

SPORTING RIFLE - .22 Hornet cal., miniature Mauser action, 24 in. barrel, leaf sight, double set trigger, select checkered stock, imported by Daly & Stoeger, pre-WWII.

	100%	98%	95%	90%	80%	70%	60%
	$990	$880	$825	$770	$660	$550	$495

HERTERS

Previous importer, distributor, and retailer headquartered in Waseca, MN from early 1960s - 1979. Herters also had additional retail stores scattered throughout the upper Midwest.

Herters subcontracted various manufacturers (mostly European) to fabricate Powermag revolvers, U-9/J-9 rifles, and shotguns which were mostly patterned after more famous original models. Most of these copies were designed to undersell the competition at the time and while quality in most cases was quite good, consumer sales were not strong enough to continue production. While many Herters models are relatively rare, collectibility to date has been minimal. Herters model values are usually under the original trademarks from which they were derived and to date have been based more on the shooting utility than the collector potential.

HESSE ARMS

Previous manufacturer located in Inver Grove Heights, MN.

Hesse Arms manufactured very limited quantities of semi-auto pistols, bolt action and semi-auto rifles. Because of this and due to space considerations, individual models have not been individually listed and priced as in previous editions.

HEYM AG

Current manufacturer established in 1865 and located in Gleichamberg, Germany since 1995. Currently imported beginning 2006 by Double Gun Imports LLC, located in Dallas, TX. Limited importation 1999-2005 by New England Custom Gun Service, Ltd., located in Plainfield, NH. During 1998, Heym underwent a management change. The company name was changed from Heym Waffenfabrik AG to Heym AG during mid-2007. Previously manufactured in Muennerstadt, Germany circa 1952-1995 and Suhl, Germany between 1865-1945. Originally founded in 1865 by F.W. Heym. Previously imported by JagerSport, Ltd. located in Cranston, RI 1993-94 only, Heckler & Koch, Inc. (until 1993) located in Sterling, VA, Heym America, Inc. (subsidiary of F.W. Heym of W. Germany) located in Fort Wayne, IN, and originally by Paul Jaeger, Inc. 1970-1986.

Please contact the importer for more information, current pricing and domestic model availability (see Trademark Index).

Pre-war guns in 95%+ original condition will bring a premium over values listed.

COMBINATION GUNS

MODEL 22 S2 O/U - rifle/shotgun combination, 12, 16, or 20 ga. (3 in.), under rifle (17 cals. available), single set trigger, takedown feature (standard 1990), coin finish with engraving, 5 1/2 lbs.

	$3,675	$3,000	$2,450	$1,875	$1,575	$1,325	$1,100

Last MSR was $4,125.

Subtract $380 without engraving.

This model featured a dampened rifle barrel which prevents the "climbing" of groups, thereby enhancing accuracy.

MODEL 25 O/U - rifle/shotgun combination, 12, 16, or 20 ga. over various rifle cals., 23 3/4 in. barrels with iron sights, checkered walnut stock and forearm, 5.9 lbs.

MSR N/A	$2,425	$1,725	$1,350	$1,125	$950	$800	$700

Add $800 for deluxe game scene engraving.

GRADING - PPGS™	100%	98%	95%	90%	80%	70%	60%

MODEL 55 BF O/U - rifle/shotgun combination, popular U.S. and European cals., shotgun barrels interchangeable in 12 (disc.), 16, or 20 ga., 25 or 28 in. barrels, boxlock, auto ejectors, silver finish, fine German engraving, folding leaf sight, checkered pistol grip stock.

	$6,500	$5,400	$4,950	$4,525	$3,950	$3,615	$3,210

Last MSR was $7,485.

Add $3,250 for O/U rifle and $2,250 for O/U shotgun or shotgun/rifle combination extra barrels.

MODEL 88 BF SxS - 2 barrel set with 20 ga. barrels and an extra set of rifle barrels available in cals. .375 H&H Mag., .458 Win. Mag., .470 N.E., or .500 N.E.

	$13,100	$10,750	$9,600	$8,150	$6,900	$5,850	$4,850

Last MSR was $15,060.

This model is a larger frame variation of the Model 88 B.

✱ *Model 88B/F SxS Safari* - includes set of rifle and shotgun barrels, choice of .375 H&H, .458 Win. Mag., .470 NE, or .500 NE cal. and extra set of 20 ga. 3 in. chamber barrels.

	$16,150	$14,100	$11,950	$10,250	$8,950	$6,750	$5,250

Last MSR was $18,530.

MODEL 88 F SxS - available in various cals. and 20 ga. with 2 3/4 or 3 in. chambers.

	$13,300	$11,250	$10,100	$9,400	$8,000	$6,950	$5,800

Last MSR was $14,650.

DRILLINGS

MODEL 33 BOXLOCK STANDARD - 16 or 20 ga., boxlock, Arabesque engraving, shotgun barrels over popular European cals., and .222 Rem., .243 Win., .270 Win., .308 Win., and .30-06 cal. rifle barrel, 25 in. full and mod. barrels, set trigger on rifle, checkered pistol grip stock.

MSR N/A	$6,075	$5,300	$4,525	$3,950	$3,350	$2,750	$2,150

✱ *Model 33 Boxlock Standard Deluxe* - similiar specifications as Standard Model, only hunting scene engraved.

MSR N/A	$6,450	$5,425	$4,650	$4,025	$3,400	$2,750	$2,150

MODEL 35 STANDARD - 3 barrels, (two rifle and one shotgun), choice of cals. with top barrel either 16 or 20 ga., light border engraving, 8 1/4 lbs.

	$13,650	$11,000	$9,250	$8,000	$6,850	$5,700	$4,600

Last MSR was $15,100.

Add $2,430 for hunting scene engraving.

MODEL 37 SIDELOCK STANDARD - shotgun barrels (12, 16, or 20 ga.) over rifle, detachable sidelocks, select French walnut, border engraving, 8 lbs.

MSR N/A	$8,650	$7,850	$6,950	$6,000	$5,000	$4,000	$2,950

✱ *Model 37 Sidelock Standard Deluxe* - similar to Model 37 Standard, except has large engraved hunting scenes.

MSR N/A	$9,650	$8,700	$7,600	$6,500	$5,400	$4,300	$3,200

MODEL 37 B STANDARD - rifle barrels over shotgun (20 ga.), sidelock, border engraved, about 8.6 lbs.

	$13,250	$10,875	$9,500	$8,400	$7,550	$6,500	$5,650

Last MSR was $15,065.

✱ *Model 37 B Standard Deluxe* - similar to Model 37 B Standard, except has large hunting scene engraving.

	$15,600	$12,750	$10,700	$9,450	$8,200	$7,050	$5,750

Last MSR was $17,620.

GRADING - PPGS™	100%	98%	95%	90%	80%	70%	60%

RIFLES: BOLT ACTION

On most of the models listed, the "N" suffix in the model denotes standard calibers, whereas "G" refers to Mag. cals.

MODEL SR 10 SPORTER - various cals., originally mfg. by H & K. Limited mfg.

	100%	98%	95%	90%	80%	70%	60%
	$1,325	$1,100	$950	$850	$750	$650	$550

MODEL SR 20N & CLASSIC - available in 18 cals., Mauser type bolt action, single trigger, French walnut, 24 in. Krupp steel barrel except Mag. (25 in.). Importation disc. 2001.

	100%	98%	95%	90%	80%	70%	60%
	$1,825	$1,425	$1,100	$900	$800	$700	$600

Last MSR was $2,100.

> Subtract $70 without iron sights.
> Add $430 for left-hand variation.
> Add $300 for Mag. cals. (G suffix).
> Add $1,140 for .375 H&H cal. (Model SR20 G Etoscha).
> Add $260 for Classic Model.
> Add $300 for carbine Classic Model.

✳ *Model SR 20 Hunter* - similar to Model SR 20N, except has classic style fiberglass stock with either matte blue or parkerized metal finish. Imported 1988-90.

	100%	98%	95%	90%	80%	70%	60%
	$1,500	$1,225	$1,050	$900	$800	$700	$600

Last MSR was $1,750.

✳ *Model SR 20L* - Mannlicher style stock, European configuration, 18 in. barrel, 7 lbs.

	100%	98%	95%	90%	80%	70%	60%
	$1,475	$1,225	$985	$895	$785	$720	$650

Last MSR was $1,700.

SR 20 TROPHY - available in all SR 20 cals., bolt action, 22 or 24 (Mag. cals. only) in. octagonal barrel, classic stock configuration with cheekpiece and recoil pad. Importation began 1989.

	100%	98%	95%	90%	80%	70%	60%
	$2,550	$2,100	$1,800	$1,500	$1,250	$985	$895

Last MSR was $2,815.

> Add $120 for Mag. cals.

This model was also available in either right-hand or left-hand action.

SR 20G CLASSIC SPORTER - available in various cals., bolt action, 22 or 24 in. round barrel, steel grip cap. Importation began 1989.

	100%	98%	95%	90%	80%	70%	60%
	$1,875	$1,600	$1,300	$1,050	$900	$785	$720

Last MSR was $2,235.

> Subtract $70 without iron sights.

This model was also available in either right-hand or left-hand action.

SR 20 ALPINE - available in standard cals. between .243 Win. and 9.3x62mm, mountain style rifle with Mannlicher forend and classic buttstock, supplied with mounted open sights. Importation began 1989.

	100%	98%	95%	90%	80%	70%	60%
	$1,900	$1,650	$1,325	$1,075	$925	$800	$750

Last MSR was $2,165.

This model was also available in either right-hand or left-hand action.

SR 20 MATCH - .308 Win. cal., 24 in. heavy barrel, target stock with accessory rail, large bolt handle, supplied without sights, 9 lbs. Imported 1991-94.

	100%	98%	95%	90%	80%	70%	60%
	$1,860	$1,600	$1,300	$1,050	$900	$785	$720

Last MSR was $2,200.

SR 20 CLASSIC SAFARI - .375 H&H, .404 Jeffery (disc.), .425 Express, or .458 Win. Mag. cal., 24 in. barrel only, express rear sight and large front post sights, tight grained walnut. Imported 1989-94.

	100%	98%	95%	90%	80%	70%	60%
	$2,150	$1,650	$1,250	$1,050	$875	$800	$700

Last MSR was $2,530.

This model was also available in either right-hand or left-hand action.

SR 21 N - 26 standard and metric cals., traditional bolt action that is bascially a Mauser M90 design with modern extractor recessed in the bolt face, single set trigger, unique interchangeable barrel/receiver, detachable mag., 3 position side safety, right- or left-hand action, iron sights, approx. 7 lbs. New 2001.

MSR N/A	$1,950	$1,500	$1,175	$950	$825	$725	$625

Add $325 for carbine (Model SR 21 N Classic).
Add $1,325 for Model SR 21 N Concorde.
Add $110 for Model SR 21 N Keiler.

SR 30 N - various cals., straight pull bolt with lock in the receiver head, iron sights, deluxe checkered walnut stock with rosewood pistol grip cap and forend tip, sling swivels, available in various configurations, 7-7 1/2 lbs.

MSR N/A	$2,350	$1,950	$1,500	$1,225	$950	$850	$750

Add $264 for SR 30 N Classic Model (carbine).
Add $1,505 for SR 30 N Concorde Model.
Add $155 for SR 30 N Wild Boar Model.

EXPRESS SERIES RIFLE - .338 Lapua Mag., .375 H&H, .378 Wby. Mag., .404 rimless Jeffery (disc. 1992), .416 Rigby, .450 Ackley, .460 Wby. Mag., .500 NE (new 1994), .500 A-Square, or .505 Gibbs cal., express sights, Timney single trigger. New 1989.

MSR N/A	$5,500	$4,800	$4,050	$3,150	$2,500	$2,150	$1,875

Add $525 for .460 Wby. Mag. - .505 Gibbs cal.
Add $375 for muzzle brake (includes installation).
Add $555 for left-hand action (disc. 1992).

✳ *Express Series Rifle .577 NE & .600 NE Cals.* - .577 NE or .600 NE cal., 24 in. barrel, reinforced action, 2 shot mag. New 1991.

MSR N/A	$9,550	$8,350	$7,250	$6,100	$5,000	$3,750	$2,950

Add $1,125 for .600 NE cal.

RIFLES: O/U

MODEL 26 B - .30 R Blaser, 8x57JRS, or 9.3x74R cal., double lock system, manual cocking, ST, buttstock with slightly curved stock comb and Bavarian cheekpiece, border engraving. New 2006.

MSR $4,175	$3,700	$3,250	$2,875	$2,450	$2,100	$1,800	$1,600

Add $550 for Luxus model.

This model is also available in Luxus variation, with higher grain wood, wild boar sights, and hunting scene engraving.

MODEL 55 BOXLOCK - various cals., engraving similar to Model 55 BF.

MSR N/A	$6,350	$5,400	$4,500	$3,750	$3,250	$2,750	$2,450

Add $500 for deluxe game scene engraving.

MODEL 55 SIDELOCK - O/U rifle only with different caliber for each barrel, double set triggers, "Bergstutzen" design.

MSR N/A	$9,350	$8,000	$6,850	$5,950	$5,125	$4,500	$3,975

Add $1,000 for Deluxe Model.

RIFLES: SxS

MODEL 80 B - various cals., modified boxlock action with top sear bars, regular or manual cocking, 23 3/4 in. barrels with quarter rib and iron sights, DT or ST, deluxe checkered walnut stock and forearm, 6.6 lbs.

MSR N/A	$6,025	$5,300	$4,550	$3,950	$3,350	$2,750	$2,150

Add $600 for ST with hand cocking, $700 for DT with hand cocking.

MODEL 88 B SAFARI CLASSIC - available in most safari cals. between .300 Win. Mag. - .458 Win. Mag. boxlock action, Krupp steel barrels, double underlocking lugs with Greener crossbolt, ejectors, checkered circassian walnut, built to customer specifications, 7 1/2 lbs.

MSR N/A	$11,650	$9,750	$8,600	$7,100	$6,125	$5,420	$4,575

Add $550 for .416 Rigby - .500 NE cal.

GRADING - PPGS™	100%	98%	95%	90%	80%	70%	60%

* *Model 88 B Safari Classic Sidelock (BSS)* - sidelock model with interceptor sears.

MSR N/A	$15,500	$13,000	$10,250	$8,750	$7,425	$6,300	$5,175

This model is also available in both .577 NE and .600 NE cal. Prices start at $28,575 for the .577 NE, and $32,500 for .600 NE.

* *Model 88 B Safari Classic Boxlock* - available in various safari cals., double safety bar, 24 in. barrels, 9.9 lbs.

MSR N/A	$9,850	$8,600	$7,400	$6,300	$5,175	$4,500	$3,750

Add $1,150 for .300 Win. Mag. - .500 NE cal.

* *Model 88 B Safari Classic Sidelock* - sidelock model with interceptor sears.

MSR N/A	$12,250	$10,250	$8,850	$7,500	$6,300	$5,175	$4,250

IVORY HUNTER - large dangerous game cals. only, sidelock model, Purdey locking system, custom engraving, steel pistol grip cap, steel trigger guard, Classic stock with German cheekpiece, rubber recoil pad, custom order only, 12.8 lbs.

Please contact the importer for pricing on this model (see Trademark Index).

RIFLES: SINGLE SHOT

MODEL HR 30N - available in many cals., Ruger No. 1 falling block action, 24 in. barrel, French walnut with Bavarian cheekpiece, round barrel, Sporter or full length carbine style French walnut stock, engraved coin finished receiver, 6.6 lbs.

	$3,500	$2,975	$2,350	$1,950	$1,675	$1,350	$1,175

Last MSR was $4,040.

Add $440 for Mag. cals.
Add $1,710 for Mannlicher stocked Carbine Model.
Add $850 for hunting scene engraving (minimum extra charge).

MODEL HR 38 N - available in many cals., Ruger No. 1 falling block action 24 in. barrel, octagon barrel, French walnut with Bavarian cheekpiece, Sporter or full length carbine style French walnut stock, engraved coin finished receiver, 6.6 lbs.

	$4,150	$3,450	$2,875	$2,300	$1,950	$1,675	$1,350

Last MSR was $4,835.

Add $235 for Mag. cals.
Add $2,400 for sideplates with engraved large game hunting scenes.

MODEL 44 B - various standard and metric cals., single lock action with thumbpiece and sideplates, open sights with barrel quarter rib, deluxe checkered stock and forearm, 6.6 lbs.

MSR N/A	$4,900	$4,350	$3,550	$3,025	$2,350	$2,000	$1,750

Add $1,100 for Deluxe Model.

SHOTGUNS: O/U

MODEL 55 F - 16 or 20 ga., ejectors, engraved, 6.6 lbs. Importation disc. 1992.

	$5,100	$4,525	$3,950	$3,615	$3,200	$2,775	$2,300

Last MSR was $5,500.

MODEL 55 SS - sidelock version of Model 55 F, large engraved hunting scenes.

	$4,500	$3,825	$3,300	$2,850	$2,400	$2,000	$1,700

Last MSR was $4,890.

MODEL 200 - 20 ga., 3 in. chambers, boxlock action, DTs, 28 in. VR barrels, light engraving, previous importation.

	$895	$795	$700	$650	$600	$550	$500

VIERLINGS

MODEL 37 V - 4 barrel configuration, various cals. and gauges, special order only. Limited mfg.

MSR N/A	$14,500	$11,000	$9,000	$7,750	$6,500	$5,500	$4,500

Add $1,700 for Deluxe Model.

GRADING - PPGS™	100%	98%	95%	90%	80%	70%	60%

HIENDLMAYER, KLAUS

Current manufacturer located in Eggenfelden, Germany. No current U.S. importation. Klaus Hiendlmayer specializes in custom guns and engraving, and manufactures a version of the SIG 550 sniper rifle. Please contact the company directly for more information, including pricing, and domestic availability (see Trademark Index).

HI-POINT FIREARMS

HI-POINT FIREARMS

Current trademark marketed by MKS Supply, Inc. located in Dayton, Ohio. Hi-Point firearms have been manufactured since 1988. Dealer and distributor sales.

Prior to 1993, trademarks sold by MKS Supply, Inc. (including Beemiller, Haskell Manufacturing, Inc., Iberia Firearms, Inc., and Stallard Arms, Inc.) had their own separate manufacturers' markings. Beginning in 1993, Hi-Point Firearms eliminated these individualized markings and chose instead to have currently manufactured guns labeled "Hi-Point Firearms". All injection molding for Hi-Point Firearms is done in Mansfield, OH.

CARBINES

MODEL 995/4095 - 9mm Para. or .40 S&W (Model 4095, new late 2003) cal., 16 1/2 or 17 1/2 (.40 S&W cal. only) in. barrel, one-piece camo or black polymer stock features pistol grip, 10 shot mag., aperture rear sight, parkerized or chrome (disc. 2007) finish. New 1996.

MSR $220	$180	$140	$120	$100	$85	$75	$70

Add $22 for .40 S&W cal.
Add $10 for chrome finish (disc. 2007).
Add $15 for camo stock (new 2002).
Add $75 for detachable compensator, laser, and mount (new 1999).
Add $25 for 4x scope or $55 for red dot scope.

This model is manufactured by Beemiller, located in Mansfield, OH.

PISTOLS: SEMI-AUTO

Beginning 2000, all compact models feature magazine disconnect safety and last shot hold open, and all pistols are shipped with a rear adj. aperture sight (which can replace the standard rear adj. sight).

MODEL CF-380 POLYMER - .380 ACP cal., single action, 3.5 or 4 (new 2002) in. barrel, polymer frame, 3-dot adj. sights, 8 shot mag. with thumb activated release, chrome slide (disc.) or two-tone black satin finish, 29 oz. New 1995.

MSR $135	$110	$90	$80	$65	$55	$50	$45

Add $15 for 4 in. barrel with compensator and two mags. (Model 380 Comp, disc. 2007).

This model is manufactured by Beemiller, located in Mansfield, OH.

JS-9 - 9mm Para. cal., single action, 4 1/2 in. barrel, thumb safety, fixed (disc. 1999) or adj. (new 2000) sights, 8 shot mag., non-glare military blue finish (early mfg.) or black satin finish (new 1991), copolymer synthetic grips, 39 oz. Mfg. 1990-2000.

	$140	$110	$95	$80	$70	$65	$60

Last MSR was $159.

Add 10% for nickel finish (disc.).

This model was manufactured by Beemiller, Inc. located in Mansfield, OH.

✱ JS-9 Compact (Model C-9) - compact variation of the Model JS-9 with 3 1/2 in. barrel and 8 shot mag., choice of alloy or polymer (new 1994, various slide/frame finishes) frame, 3-dot adj. sights became standard in 2000, 32 (polymer) or 29 oz. New 1993.

MSR $115	$120	$95	$85	$70	$65	$60	$55

This model is manufactured by Beemiller, Inc. located in Mansfield, OH.

GRADING - PPGS™	100%	98%	95%	90%	80%	70%	60%

✱ *JS-9 Comp* - features 4 in. barrel with compensator, with (new 1999) or w/o laser sight package, adj. sights, 10 shot mag. Mfg. 1998-2006.

	$135	$115	$100	$90	$80	$75	$70

Last MSR was $159.

Add $61 for laser sights and mount.

JS-40 - .40 S&W cal., single action, steel frame, black finish, 4 1/2 in. barrel, 3-dot adj. sights, 8 shot mag., 39 oz. Mfg. 1992-2002.

	$135	$110	$100	$90	$80	$75	$70

Last MSR was $159.

Add $7 for nickel finish (disc. 1994).

This model was manufactured by Iberia Firearms, Inc. located in Iberia, OH.

JC-40 - .40 S&W cal., single action, polymer frame, black finish, 4 1/2 in. barrel, 3-dot adj. sights, accessory rail (new 2004), 10 shot mag., 32 oz. New 2002.

MSR $187	$150	$125	$100	$90	$80	$75	$70

This model is manufactured by Iberia Firearms, Inc. located in Iberia, OH.

JS-45 - .45 ACP cal., single action, steel frame, similar to JS-9, except has 7 shot mag. and 4 1/2 in. barrel, adj. sights, 39 oz. Mfg. 1991-2002.

	$135	$110	$100	$90	$80	$75	$70

Last MSR was $159.

Add $10 for nickel finish (disc. 1994).

This model was manufactured by Haskell Mfg., Inc. located in Lima, OH.

JH-45 - .45 ACP cal., single action, polymer frame, similar to JS-9, except has 9 shot mag. and 4 1/2 in. barrel, accessory rail (new 2004), adj. sights, 32 oz. New 2003.

MSR $186	$150	$125	$100	$90	$80	$75	$70

This model is manufactured by Haskell Mfg., Inc. located in Lima, OH.

HIGGINS, J.C.

Previous trademark used on Sears & Roebuck rifles and shotguns manufactured between 1946-1962.

The J.C. Higgins trademark has appeared literally on hundreds of various models (shotguns and rifles) sold through the Sears & Roebuck retail network. Most of these models were manufactured through subcontracts with both domestic and international firearms manufacturers. Typically, they were "spec." guns made to sell at a specific price to undersell the competition. Most of these models were derivatives of existing factory models (i.e., Browning, High Standard, Marlin, Mossberg, Savage, Stevens, Winchester, etc.) with less expensive wood and perhaps missing the features found on those models from which they were derived.

To date, there has been minimal interest in collecting J.C. Higgins guns, regardless of rarity. Rather than list J.C. Higgins models, a general guideline is that values generally are under the models of their "1st generation relatives" (listed above). The Ranger trademark was also used by Sears & Roebuck - it is not any more desirable than those guns marked "J.C. Higgins". As a result, prices are ascertained by the shooting value of the gun, rather than its collector value.

For converting J.C. Higgins models to the subcontracted manufacturers, please refer to the Store Brand Crossover List.

HIGH STANDARD

Previous manufacturer located in New Haven, Hamden, and East Hartford, CT. High Standard Mfg. Co. was founded in 1926. They entered the firearms business when they purchased Hartford Arms and Equipment Co. in 1932. The original plant was located in New Haven, CT. During WWII High Standard operated plants in New Haven and Hamden. After the war, the operations were consoli-

GRADING - PPGS™	100%	98%	95%	90%	80%	70%	60%

dated in Hamden. In 1968, the company was sold to the Leisure Group, Inc. A final move was made to East Hartford, CT in 1977 where they remained until the doors were closed in late 1984. In early 1978, the Leisure Group sold the company to the management and the company became High Standard, Inc.

Many collectors have realized the rarity and quality factors this trademark has earned. 13 different variations (Models C, A, D, E, H-D, H-E, H-A, H-B First Model, G-380, GB, GD, GE, and Olympic, commonly called the GO) had a total production of less than 48,000 pistols. For these reasons, top condition High Standard pistols are getting more difficult to find each year.

As a final note on High Standard pistols, they are listed under the following category names: Letter Series, Letter Series w/ Hammer, Lever Letter Series, Lever Name Series, 100 Series, 101 Series, 102 Series, 103 Series, 104 Series, 105 Series, 106 Series - Military Models, 107 Series, Conversion Kits, and SH Series.

Note: catalog numbers were not always consistent with design series, and in 1966-1967 changed with accessories offered, but not design series.

The approx. ser. number cut-off for New Haven, CT marked guns is 442,XXX.

The approx. ser. number range for Hamden, CT marked guns is 431,XXX-2,500,811, G 1,001-G 13,757 (Shipped) or G15,650 (Packed) or ML 1,001-ML 23,065. One exception is a 9211 Victor serial number 3,000,000 shipped 1 March, 1974.

The first gun shipped 16 June, 1977 from E. Hartford was a Victor 9217 serial number EH0001.

The approx. ser. number ranges for E. Hartford, CT manufacture is ML 25,000-ML 86,641 and SH 10,001-SH 34,034. One exception is a single gun numbered ML90,000.

Original factory boxes have become very desirable. Prices can range from $50-$100 for a good condition Model 106 or 107 factory box to over $150 for an older box of a desirable model.

DERRINGERS

DERRINGER MODELS - .22 or .22 Mag. cal., double action only O/U, 2 shot, 3 1/2 in. barrels.

The first derringer was mfg. about 1962, at the approximate serial number 1,261,903 in Hamden, CT. The serial numbers continued in the handgun serial number series until serial number 2,500,464 in 1975, when the derringers were put into a separate serial number group with a D prefix, D 1,001 through D 96,098 V. Serial number D 12,047 was the last Hamden made gun, with E. Hartford production beginning with D 13,000. After 1976, the guns were made in East Hartford. Three different styles of roll marking methods were used during production.

The First style is marked with the caliber and "D-100" or "DM-101" on left side of frame, "Hi-Standard Derringer" with eagle logo on left side of barrel.

The Second style is marked with the caliber and "D-100", "D-101", or "DM-101" on left side of frame, "Hi-Standard Derringer" with trigger logo on left side of barrel. Both the first and second types were marked "HIGH STANDARD MFG. CORP./-HAMDEN, CONN. U.S.A.-"

The Third style is marked with the caliber and "D-101" or "DM-101" on left side of frame, "Derringer" on left side of barrel. The third style was marked with different addresses and company names on the right side of the barrel. Style 3A is marked on the right side of the barrel the same as types one and two. Type 3B is marked with "HIGH STANDARD MFG. CORP./-E. HARTFORD, CONN. US.A.-" and type 3C is marked "HIGH STANDARD INC./-E. HARTFORD, CONN. U.S.A.-" Later third style is not marked with the "D-101" or "DM-101". The early derringers had a grooved back grip strap, which changed to a smooth grip strap just before the move to E. Hartford.

Near the end of production, a "V" suffix was added to some visually impaired guns, which were sold at discount. These guns were guaranteed to function properly, but the company would not allow them to be returned for appearance reasons. Numerous guns' earlier serial numbers, held back because of visual flaws, were also marked with the "V" and were shipped in 1984. The earliest V suffix gun found to date is D 25,945V.

✱ ***Derringer Model Blue Finish*** - .22 LR or .22 Mag. cal ., blue, white or black grips.

	100%	98%	95%	90%	80%	70%	60%
	$270	$225	$200	$165	$135	$105	$95

Add $25 for hinged maroon case.

.22 LR D-100 First series, catalog #9193, mfg. 1962-67, ser. no. 1,261,903.

GRADING - PPGS™	100%	98%	95%	90%	80%	70%	60%

.22 LR D-100 Second series, catalog #9193, mfg. 1967-1969, ser. no. 1,6XX,XXX.
.22 LR D-101 Second series, catalog #9193, mfg. 1969-1970, ser. no. 2,1XX,XXX.
.22 LR D-101 Third series, catalog #9193, mfg. 1970-75, ser. no. 2,497,125.
.22 LR Third series, catalog #9193, mfg. 1975-77, ser. no. D 02,809-D 13,319.
.22 LR Third series, catalog #9193, mfg. 1982-84, ser. no. D 73,100-D 96,098 V.
.22 Mag. DM-101 First series, catalog #9194, mfg. 1963-67, ser. no. 1,301,611.
.22 Mag. DM-101 Second series, catalog #9194, mfg. 1967-1970, ser. no. 1,6XX,XXX.
.22 Mag. DM-101 Third series, catalog #9193, mfg. 1970-1975, ser. no. 2,500,464.
.22 Mag. Third series, catalog #9193, mfg. 1975-1982, ser. no. D 01,001.
.22 Mag. Third series, catalog #9193, mfg. 1982-84, ser. no. D95,217 V.

✳ *Derringer Model Nickel Finish* - .22 LR or .22 Mag. cal., nickel, black grips, ivory grips were used on some early models, introduced 1970.

	$285	$240	$205	$170	$140	$110	$100

.22 LR D-101 Third series, catalog #9305, mfg. 1970-75, ser. no. 2,182,780-2,476,0XX.
.22 LR Third series, catalog #9305, mfg. 1975-77, ser. no. D05,543-D 13,426.
.22 Mag. DM-101 Third series, catalog #9306, mfg. 1970-75, ser. no. 2,182,380-2,500,464.
.22 Mag. Third series, catalog #9306, mfg. 1975-1984, ser. no. D 01,001-D 95,217 V.

✳ *Derringer Model Gold plated* - .22 LR or .22 Mag. cal., with black grips, includes presentation case, introduced 1964.

	$570	$450	$350	$265	$230	$195	$170

Add $85 for derringers with 1-3 digit serial numbers.
Subtract $75 if w/o presentation case.
#9195 derringers found in the regular serial number series around 1,339,002-1,339,080 beginning the end of 1963. #9196 found in regular serial number series around 2,366,556-2,366,561, 2,398,810-2,397,819 in 1973, and D 81,122 in 1982. Others are in a separate serial number series running from 1 through 123 which contains about 25 #9195 and 30 #9196 derringers.
.22 LR D-100 First Series, catalog #9195, mfg. 1963-1973.
.22 Mag. DM-101 First Series, catalog #9196, mfg. 1964-1973.
.22 LR D-100 First Series, cased pair, catalog #9197 .
.22 Mag. DM-101 First Series, cased pair, catalog #9198.
While matched sets did have factory catalog numbers, rarity and lack of known sales preclude accurate valuation.

✳ *Derringer Model Electroless Nickel Finish* - . 22 LR or .22 Mag. cal., checkered walnut grips.

	$305	$265	$230	$180	$145	$125	$105

.22 LR Third series, catalog #9421, mfg. 1981-83, ser. no. D 74,351 - D 87,705.
.22 Mag Third series, catalog #9420, mfg. 1981-83, ser. no. D 63.390 - D 93,632.

PRESIDENTIAL DERRINGER - .22 Mag. cal., gold plated, smooth walnut grips, includes walnut case marked "PRESIDENTIAL DERRINGER".

	$540	$465	$400	$335	$290	$245	$215

Subtract $100 if w/o presentation case.
Third series, catalog #9196, mfg. 1974-78. Serial numbers DM1 through DM 416 (353 guns) and HDM153 through HDM160 (7 guns) and a few special prefixes on about 10 guns.

PRESENTATION DERRINGER

✳ *Presentation Derringer Gold Plated* - .22 Mag. cal., smooth walnut grips, includes presentation case marked "PRESENTATION DERRINGER", ser. no GP0 through GP1000, approx. 917 produced in 1980 in E. Hartford.

	$500	$450	$375	$285	$250	$215	$185

Subtract $75 if w/o presentation case.
Third series, catalog #9196, mfg. 1980 only.

✳ *Presentation Derringer Silver Plated* -.22 Mag. cal., faux mother-of-pearl grips, includes presentation case marked "PRESENTATION DERRINGER", ser. nos. SP0 through SP500, 501 were mfg. 1981.

	$550	$495	$390	$325	$280	$235	$200

Subtract $100 if w/o presentation case.
Third series, catalog #9341.

PISTOLS: SEMI-AUTO, LETTER SERIES

These were the first models made and used letters to designate the various models. A few guns from this series were sold after WWII. Catalog numbers for this series were assigned after the war in order to utilize the record keeping system of that time. This design series utilized three different takedowns. Types I-A and I-B takedowns have the takedown lever on the left side of the frame. Type I-A takedown has a round retracting rod protruding through the rear of the slide off center to the left side. Type I-B takedown is an improved, more durable design with a rectangular retracting rod. Type II takedown has the takedown lever in the right side of the frame with a round pick-up button on the top of the slide. Type I-A takedown was utilized from 1932 to February 1938 and the type I-B takedown was utilized from that time until August 1939. Models B and C are the only models with the Type I-A takedown. The Model B and other Letter Models utilized type I-B and II takedowns. Guns with original boxes and original papers can add significant premiums but, like the guns, the condition is very important as is the requirement that the box be numbered to the gun. Those guns listed as a Curio or Relic by BATF are noted in this text with a C-R abbreviation at the end of the model description. Serial number ranges are best estimates as of this printing and may change with further research. All serial numbers are located on the front gripstrap.

Add approx. 15% for original box with papers in the same condition as gun on the following models.

MODEL B - .22 LR cal., original High Standard pistol, basically the same gun as Hartford Arms 1925 Automatic, small frame, 4 1/2 or 6 3/4 in. lightweight barrel (approx .63" diameter at frame), fixed Patridge type front and rear sights, checkered hard rubber grips (later production versions have checkered grips impressed with the High Standard monogram), 10 shot mag. Beginning ser. no. 5,000. Approx. 65,000, early production utilized Hartford front sight, safety and takedown levers. Post War models have the frame contour of the B-US. C-R.

$595	$465	$375	$275	$175	$140	$100

Add $75 for I-B Type takedown.
Add $75 for early models with Hartford Arms parts.
Add $50 for post-war versions (ser. nos. greater than 146,000).

4 1/2 in. barrel #9000 1932 - 1942 & 1946
6 3/4 in. barrel #9001 1932 - 1942 & 1946
Most guns found in serial number ranges from 5,000 to about 95,894 and from about 148,198 to about 151,021.

MODEL B-US - a version of the Model B with slight contour modification to the back of the frame. 4 1/2 in. barrel only. 14,000 made for the US government during 1942-1943. Most are marked "PROPERTY OF U.S." on the top of the barrel and on the right side of the frame above trigger guard. Crossed cannon ordnance stamp usually found on the right side of the frame. Monogrammed hard rubber grips. Type II takedown only. Note the early Model Bs shipped to the government and marked "PROPERTY OF U.S." had the original frame contour with transition to the B-US contour between ser. no. 99,261 and 100,972, .22 LR cal., 10 shot mag.

$825	$695	$570	$470	$370	$270	$195

Most guns found in serial number range from about 92,344 to about 111,631.

MODEL S - .22 LR cal., chambered for .22 LR shot shell cartridge, essentially a Model B with a 6 3/4 in. smooth bore barrel only without choke, ivory bead front sight, left side of slide is stamped "HI-STANDARD MODEL S .22 LR SHOT ONLY", this variation was never a production model, ten are registered as Model S. Additional five with Model C slides are registered, Model C/S. Others may exist but only 15 are registered with BATF (see serial numbers below). Manufactured in 1939 and 1940. Values for both variations are equal. 6 3/4 in. barrels. C-R.

$4,750	$4,320	$3,900	$3,325	$2,850	$2,450	$2,100

Serial numbers: Model S - 48,142, 48,143, 48,144, 48,145, 48,146, 59,474 , 59,496, 59,458, 59,459, 59,493, Model C/S: 59,279, 59,460, 59,469, 59,473, 59,478. S/N 59,484 is listed as a Model S in the factory records but is not currently registered with the BATF.

GRADING - PPGS™	100%	98%	95%	90%	80%	70%	60%

MODEL C - .22 Short cal. only, identical to Model B in appearance, small frame, 4 1/2 or 6 3/4 in. light weight barrel, fixed rear sight, checkered hard rubber grips with or without H.S. monogram, this action was adapted for the decreased power of the .22 Short cartridge. Early production in separate serial number series beginning with 500 and continuing through 3,116. Joined regular serial number series at 42,806. There are numerous Model Cs in the regular serial number series earlier than 42,806 around 25,600 which shipped a date later than the Model Bs in the same serial number range. C-R.

		$880	$715	$510	$405	$305	$215	$175

   Add $75 for I-A takedown.
   Add $175 for I-B takedown.
Most guns found in serial number ranges from 500 to 3,116 and from about 42,806 to about 86,249.
This model was used primarily for plinking and gallery shooting. The Model C was made in all 3 variations of takedowns - I-A, I-B, and Type II.
4 1/2 in. barrel #9061 1936 -1942
6 3/4 in. barrel #9062 1936 -1942

MODEL A - .22 LR cal., similar to Model B, except grip part of frame is lengthened with a squared-off butt, 4 1/2 or 6 3/4 in. light weight barrel, adj. rear sight, checkered walnut grips, checkered thumb rest walnut grips optionally available separately, automatic slide lock, 10 shot mag. Approx. 7,300 mfg. C-R.

	$750	$650	$525	$430	$310	$230	$180

   Add $175 for I-B takedown.
Most guns found in serial number range from about 33,209 to about 97,734.
A very few guns found in serial number range between 500 and 555.
4 1/2 in. barrel #9005 1938 - 1942
6 3/4 in. barrel #9006 1938 - 1942

MODEL D - .22 LR cal., identical to Model A except 4 1/2 or 6 3/4 in. medium weight barrel (approx .79" diameter at frame), adj. sights, walnut grips, checkered thumb rest walnut grips optionally available separately, slide lock, trigger stop, 10 shot mag. Approx. 2,500 mfg. C-R.

	$950	$755	$570	$455	$330	$230	$190

   Add $175 for I-B takedown.
4 1/2 in. barrel #9063 1938 - 1942
6 3/4 in. barrel #9064 1938 - 1942
Most guns found in serial number range from about 33,216 to about 95,206.
A very few guns found in serial number range between 500 and 555.

MODEL E - .22 LR cal., high quality, deluxe model of the hammerless series, adj. sight, 4 1/2 or 6 3/4 in. heavy bull barrel (approx .90" diameter at frame), checkered walnut target grips with thumb rest, automatic slide lock, trigger stop, 10 shot mag. Approx. 2,600 mfg. C-R.

	$1,150	$950	$780	$655	$505	$370	$245

   Add $175 for I-B takedown.
4 1/2 in. barrel #9067 1938 - 1942
6 3/4 in. barrel #9068 1938 - 1942
Most guns found in serial number range from about 34,419 to about 98,306.

PISTOLS: SEMI-AUTO, LETTER SERIES W/HAMMER

Second series of models made, like the letter models with external hammers. Letters were still used to designate the various models. Most were produced before the war, but a few models were produced after the war. Catalog numbers for this series were assigned after the war in order to utilize the record keeping system of that time. Type II takedown only. Guns with original boxes and original papers can add significant premiums but, like the guns, condition is very important, as is the requirement that the box be numbered to the gun. Those

GRADING - PPGS™	100%	98%	95%	90%	80%	70%	60%

guns listed as a Curio or Relic by BATF are noted - C-R. Serial number ranges are best esti-mates as of this printing and may change with further research. All ser. numbers are located on forestrap of frame.

> **Add approx. 15% for original box with papers in the same condition as the gun on the following models.**

MODEL H-D - .22 LR cal., first exposed hammer model, similar to Model D, 4 1/2 or 6 3/4 in. medium weight barrel, adj. sight, trigger stop, slide lock, checkered walnut grips, (checkered thumb rest walnut grips optionally available sepa-rately), no external safety, 10 shot mag, pistols in the 135,990 to 145,439 range have a safety and are marked "Model HD" but do not have the adjustable sight or trigger overtravel screw. Approx. 6,900 mfg. C-R.

	$1,175	$995	$700	$505	$415	$320	$235

Most guns found in serial number ranges from about 45,463 to about 93,164 and from about 135,990 to about 145,439.
4 1/2 in. barrel #9065 1940 - 1941 & 1945
6 3/4 in. barrel #9066 1940 - 1941

USA-MODEL-HD - .22 LR cal., this model was developed because the government needed a training pistol similar to the Colt Model 1911 .45 ACP, the result was a Model HD with external safety and fixed sight, 4 1/2 in. medium weight barrel, the barrel is marked "Property of USA", black checkered hard rubber grips, first models mfg. had high gloss blue finish, changed to a parkerized finish near ser. no. 130XXX. Approx. 34,000 mfg. 1943-45. C-R.

	$1,000	$850	$705	$615	$520	$405	$315

> **Add 20% for early blue finish.**
> **Add $150 for box.**

Most guns found in serial number range from about 103,863 to about 145,700.

MODEL USA-HD-MS - .22 LR cal., variation of the USA-Model-HD with integral silencer, mfg. for U.S. Government for the OSS during 1944 and 1945, owner-ship requires NFA transfer, approx. 2,000 mfg. Only a few registered with BATF for civilian ownership.

	$6,000	$5,600	$5,250	$4,875	$4,540	$4,250	$3,750

Most guns found in serial number range from about 110,074 to about 130,040.

MODEL H-D MILITARY -.22 LR cal., though called H-D Military, this model was not mfg. for the government, essentially a Model H-D with an external safety, 4 1/2 or 6 3/4 in. barrel, plastic (early mfg.) or checkered walnut grips (later mfg,) trigger stop (later manufacture), 10 shot mag. Approx. 150,000 mfg. C-R.

	$585	$480	$405	$330	$230	$150	$125

4 1/2 in. barrel #9050 1945 - 1950
6 3/4 in. barrel #9051 1945 - 1950
Most guns found in serial number range from about 145,196 to about 334,751.

MODEL H-E - .22 LR cal., deluxe model of exposed hammer series, 4 1/2 or 6 3/4 in. heavy barrel, adj. sight, trigger stop, slide lock, deluxe hand checkered wal-nut grips with thumb rests, no external safety, 10 shot mag. Rare - approx 1,000 mfg. 1941-42. C-R.

	$2,100	$1,800	$1,500	$975	$700	$575	$450

4 1/2 in. barrel #9026 1940 - 1942
6 3/4 in. barrel #9027 1940 - 1942
Most guns found in serial number range from about 51,802 to about 90,588.

MODEL H-A - .22 LR cal., similar to Model A, 4 1/2 or 6 3/4 in. lightweight barrel, adj. sight, slide lock, plain checkered walnut grips, no external safety, 10 shot mag. Rare - approx. 1,000 mfg. C-R.

	$1,275	$1,090	$910	$715	$505	$350	$225

4 1/2 in. barrel #9007 1940 - 1942
6 3/4 in. barrel #9008 1940 - 1942
Most guns found in serial number range from about 53,176 to about 92,816.

GRADING - PPGS™	100%	98%	95%	90%	80%	70%	60%

MODEL H-B - .22 LR cal., duplicate of Model B with external hammer, 4 1/2 or 6 3/4 in. lightweight barrel, fixed sight, checkered hard rubber grips with or w/o H.S. monogram, no external safety, 10 shot mag. Approx. 2,100 mfg. C-R.

	$775	$650	$510	$385	$275	$225	$175

4 1/2 in. barrel 1940 - 1941
6 3/4 in. barrel 1940 - 1941
Most guns found in serial number range from about 52,405 to about 86,155.

✳ *Model H-B Second Model* - reintroduced as the H-B second model similar to first model, except with external safety. C-R.

	$600	$525	$425	$325	$225	$185	$150

4 1/2 in. barrel #9003 1948 - 1949 274,197 - 311,535
6 3/4 in. barrel #9004 1948 - 1949 274,996 - 311,520

PISTOLS: SEMI-AUTO, LEVER LETTER SERIES

These were the third design models made, which incorporate interchangeable barrels with a lever takedown. The .22 caliber guns evolved from the Model G-380, High Standard's first production removable barrel gun which is included in this section. Like the letter models with external hammers, these .22 caliber models still use letters to designate the various models. New to this series was the adjustable Davis sight. Also introduced in this series was a breech face shrouded by the slide. Significant premiums can be asked for guns with the combination of both barrels, if verified by factory records that the gun shipped as a combination. (Buyer beware - many "combinations" have been created after leaving the factory). Non-factory combinations should have additional value equal to the value of an extra barrel. Guns with original boxes and papers can add significant premiums but, like the guns, the condition is very important, as is the requirement that the box be numbered to the gun. Those guns listed as a Curio or Relic by BATF are noted - C-R. Serial number ranges are best estimates, and may change with further research. Ser. numbers are on the right side of slide and rear right side of frame. Mfg. 1949-50.

Add approx. 15% for original box with papers in the same condition as gun on the following models.

MODEL G-380 CENTERFIRE - .380 ACP cal., only in-house production of a centerfire pistol, transition model to the G-series using a lever takedown, exposed hammer, fixed sights, checkered black plastic grips, external safety, 5 in. barrel only, 6 shot mag. Approx. 7,400 mfg. in a serial number series of its own but a few examples exist in the regular serial number range around 329,337. C-R.

	$600	$500	$400	$325	$245	$210	$180

5.00" barrel #9060 1947 - 1950 123 - 7,551

MODEL GB - .22 LR cal., similar to Model B with light barrel, small frame, external safety, fixed sight, monogrammed checkered brown plastic grips, interchangeable 4 1/2 or 6 3/4 in. barrel with lever takedown, 10 shot mag., last short frame model produced. Approx. 4,900 mfg. C-R.

	$600	$450	$375	$300	$225	$175	$150

Add $225 for factory combination.
4 1/2 in. barrel #9110 1949 - 1950 310,449 - 335,278
6 3/4 in. barrel #9111 1949 - 1950 309,578 - 335,095
Combination with both barrels #9112 1949 - 1950 311,001 - 335,066

MODEL GD - .22 LR cal., large frame, medium weight, interchangeable 4 1/2 or 6 3/4 in. barrel with lever takedown, adj. Davis sight (named for designer G.F. Davis), sight is adj. for both windage and elevation, trigger stop, slide lock, grips avail. in plain checkered walnut or deluxe with thumb rest, 10 shot mag. Approx. 3,300 mfg. C-R.

	$995	$900	$750	$535	$400	$300	$225

Add $325 for factory combination.
Add $75 for factory target grips.
4 1/2 in. barrel standard walnut grips #9020 1949 - 1950 315,445 - 335,279

GRADING - PPGS™	100%	98%	95%	90%	80%	70%	60%

6 3/4 in. barrel standard walnut grips #9021 1949 - 1950 311,804 - 335,300
Combination with both barrels and standard walnut grips #9022 1949 - 1950 312,001 - 335,247
4 1/2 in. barrel thumb rest walnut grips #9023 1949 - 1950 316,623 - 326,850
6 3/4 in. barrel thumb rest walnut grips #9024 1949 - 1950 311,804 - 335,222
Combination with both barrels and thumb rest walnut grips #9025 1949 - 1950 317,914 - 335,278.

MODEL GE - .22 LR cal., deluxe top-of-the-line model, large frame, interchangeable 4 1/2 or 6 3/4 in. heavy bull barrel with lever takedown, Davis adj. sight, deluxe walnut hand checkered grips with thumb rest, trigger stop, slide lock, 10 shot mag. Approx. 2,900 mfg. C-R.

	$1,360	$1,185	$840	$740	$465	$350	$250

Add $375 for factory combination.
4 1/2 in. barrel #9030 1949 - 1950 314,050 - 335,275
6 3/4 in. barrel #9031 1949 - 1950 314,027 - 335,198
Combination with both barrels #9032 1949 - 1950 312,002 - 335,200.

OLYMPIC (G-O) - .22 Short cal., adaptation of Model GE in .22 Short cal., also known as First Model Olympic, first fired in Olympic competition in 1948, deluxe top-of-the-line quality, interchangeable 4 1/2 or 6 3/4 in. heavy bull barrel with lever takedown, Davis adj. sight, deluxe hand checkered walnut grips with thumb rests, trigger stop, slide lock, grooved fore and rear strap, first High Standard large production gun with aluminum slide, special curved magazine, a few guns exist which will utilize a magazine with a straight back, the majority of these Olympics use the curved magazine with a humped back, grooved surface on top of barrel and slide. Rare - approx. 1,200 mfg. C-R.

	$1,650	$1,380	$1,115	$825	$550	$525	$425

Add $375 for factory combination.
Add $300 for the straight back magazine variation.
4 1/2 in. barrel #9040 1949 - 1950 325,929 - 334-735
6 3/4 in. barrel #9041 1949 - 1950 307,734 - 334,979
Combination with both barrels #9042 1949 - 1950 329,590 - 334,399.

PISTOLS: SEMI-AUTO, LEVER NAME SERIES

These models were the fourth design evolving from the lever letter series with slight changes. This series followed the precedent of naming the models instead of utilizing letters set by the Olympic (G-O). The upscale models, the Supermatic and Olympic, incorporated a rib dovetailed to the top of the barrel and a dovetail slot on the bottom of the barrel for mounting balance weights. This series continued the breech face shrouded by the slide. Significant premiums can be asked for guns with the combination of both barrels, if verified by factory records that the gun shipped as a combination. (Buyer beware - many "combinations" have been created after leaving the factory). Non-factory combinations should have additional value equal to the value of the extra barrel. Adjustable sight models continued to use the Davis sight. No guns in this series were offered with barrels incorporating the integral stabilizer but stabilizer barrels were offered in 1954 after the series ended. Most guns in this series utilized a single screw to retain the grips. However, the earliest Olympics used a screw for each side before changing to a single screw. Guns with original boxes and original papers can add significant premiums but, like the guns, the condition is very important, as is the requirement that the box be numbered to the gun. Serial number ranges are best estimates, and may change with further research. Those guns which have Curio or Relic status by virtue of being over 50 years old are noted C-R.

Add approx. 15% for original box with papers in the same condition as gun on the following models.

GRADING - PPGS™	100%	98%	95%	90%	80%	70%	60%

SPORT-KING (FIRST MODEL) - .22 LR cal., 10 shot mag., similar to Field-King except has fixed sight and lightweight interchangeable 4 1/2 or 6 3/4 in. barrel featuring lever takedown, early models did not have a slide hold back when the magazine became empty, early variation w/o hold back was produced in about twice the quantity as the later models incorporating this feature. C-R.

	$425	$350	$300	$250	$200	$150	$100

    Add $25 for guns with hold back.
    Add $200 for factory combination.
4 1/2 in. barrel #9080 1950 - 1954 335,001 - 442,605
6 3/4 in. barrel #9081 1950 - 1954 335,012 - 442,572
Combination with both barrels #9082 1951 - 1953 337,699 - 442,574

FIELD-KING (FIRST MODEL) - .22 LR cal., plain version of Supermatic, 10 shot mag., interchangeable 4 1/2 or 6 3/4 in. barrels with lever takedown, Davis adj. sight, trigger stop, slide lock, 10 shot mag., no rib on barrels or provisions for weights. C-R.

	$625	$550	$450	$340	$275	$225	$175

    Add $225 for factory combination.
4 1/2 in. barrel #9090 1951 - 1953 342,703 - 439,658
6 3/4 in. barrel #9091 1951 - 1953 341,751 - 439,665
Combination with both barrels #9092 1951 - 1953 348,762 - 439,660

SUPERMATIC (FIRST MODEL) - .22 LR cal., 4 1/2 or 6 3/4 in. interchangeable barrel with lever takedown, Davis adj. sight, trigger stop, 10 shot mag., slide lock, front and back straps grooved, brown plastic thumb rest grips, serrated rib between front and rear sight, adj. 2 oz. and 3 oz. weights which dovetail into and beneath barrel, a filler strip was provided for when the weights were not used. C-R.

	$775	$650	$525	$415	$320	$225	$175

    Add $250 for factory combination.
    Add $30 for each weight and $25 for filler strip if present with gun.
Price is for pistol without both weights and filler strip.
4 1/2 in. barrel with provisions for weights #9070 1951 - 1953 340,103 - 438,698
6 3/4 in. barrel with provisions for weights #9071 1951 - 1953 338,210 - 438,726
Combination with both barrels #9072 1951 - 1953 340,101 - 438,714

OLYMPIC (SECOND MODEL) - .22 Short cal., identical in all respects to the Supermatic, except has aluminum slide for rapid recoil, 10 shot mag., interchangeable 4 1/2 or 6 3/4 in. barrel with lever takedown, also available as combination with both barrels, Davis adj. sight, ribbed barrels and provisions for weights, 2 oz. and a 3 oz. weight were provided with this model, as was a filler strip for when the weights were not used, grooved front and back straps on frame. A few guns exist which utilize the hump back curved magazine from the previous series, but the majority of these Olympics use a newly developed straight magazine. C-R.

	$1,150	$950	$775	$600	$500	$400	$300

    Add $250 for factory combination.
    Add a slight premium for curved magazine version.
    Add $30 for each weight and $25 for filler strip if present with gun.
Price is for pistol without both weights and filler strip.
Note: Conversion kits for converting from .22 LR to .22 Short became available in 1956 (see the information at the end of the 101 section).
4 1/2 in. barrel with provisions for weights #9043 1951 - 1953 341,795 - 428,989
6 3/4 in. barrel with provisions for weights #9044 1951 - 1953 341,788 - 428,982
Combination with both barrels #9045 1951 - 1953 348,505 - 428,990

PISTOLS: SEMI-AUTO, 100 SERIES

The 100 Series firearms were the fifth design models evolving from the Lever Name Series designs. This series introduced the small, push button barrel release takedown, and deleted the shrouded breech. This series featured slanted plastic grips as standard issue. The upscale models continued with the ribbed barrel and a dovetail slot on the bottom of the barrel for mounting balance weights. Adjustable sight models continued to use the Davis sight. New to this series was the introduction of an aluminum frame on the Flite King and the Sport King Lightweight. Significant premiums can be asked for guns with the combination of both barrels, if verified by factory records that the gun shipped as a combination. Buyer beware - many "combinations" have been created after leaving the factory. Non-factory combinations should have additional value equal to the value of the extra barrel. Guns with original boxes and original papers can add significant premiums but, like the guns, the condition is very important, as is the requirement that the box be numbered to the gun. There are some pistols that represent a transition between the 100 Series in the Field King, Supermatic, and Olympic models where the slides are marked with the 100 Series, but the barrels are from the 101 Series. These transistion pistols are generally listed as 101 Series pistols and only the factory records will tell the tale. Serial number ranges starting points are best estimates, and may change with further research. Those guns which have Curio or Relic status by virtue of being over 50 years old are noted C-R.

> **Add approx. 13% for original box with papers in the same condition as gun on the following models.**

SPORT-KING (SECOND MODEL) - .22 LR cal., similar to Flite-King but with steel slide and frame, SK 100 stamped on right side of slide, front and rear grip straps on this model are smooth, slide lock, fixed rear sight.

	100%	98%	95%	90%	80%	70%	60%
	$400	$350	$275	$200	$175	$150	$100

> **Add $200 for factory combination.**
> **Add $350 for ARMAMEX version.**

In late 1958, Col. Rex Applegate imported about three hundred into Mexico. These guns are marked with his company's name, ARMAMEX. Marked "ARMAMEX, MEXICO" on the right side of the barrel and "SPORT KING / CAL. 22 L.R." on the left side of the barrel. Customary "HI-STANDARD" marking on the left side of the slide. Serial numbers around 870,084-870,383. Note that the Applegate guns were made after the 102 series was in production. Armamex catalog number 1910.

4 1/2 in. barrel #9100 1954 - 1957 436,311 - 804,081
6 3/4 in. barrel #9101 1954 - 1957 436,308 - 804,080
Combination with both barrels #9102 1954 - 1957 443,651 - 804,075

SPORT-KING LIGHTWEIGHT - .22 LR cal., similar to standard Sport-King, except has forged aluminum alloy frame, "Lightweight" is inscribed in script on the left side of frame, also available in nickel.

	100%	98%	95%	90%	80%	70%	60%
	$500	$400	$325	$250	$175	$150	$100

> **Add $150 for nickel finish.**
> **Add $200 for factory combination.**

4 1/2 in. barrel blue #9156 1955 - 1964 506,248 - 1,333,056
6 3/4 in. barrel blue #9157 1955 - 1964 506,243 - 1,333,043
Combination with both barrels blue #9158 1956 - 1959 506,320 - 1,030,619
4 1/2 in. barrel nickel #9167 1957 - 1960 726,752 - 1,136,533
6 3/4 in. barrel nickel #9168 1957 - 1960 726,745 - 1,136,534
Combination with both barrels nickel #9169 1957 - 1959 726,909 - 1,025,505

FLITE-KING (FIRST MODEL) - .22 Short cal., 10 shot mag., blued finish with black anodized aluminum frame and slide, 4 1/2, 6 3/4 in. barrel, or a combination with both barrel lengths, brown plastic checkered thumb rest grips, fixed sights.

	100%	98%	95%	90%	80%	70%	60%
	$575	$475	$400	$340	$260	$180	$135

> **Add $200 for factory combination.**

4 1/2 in. barrel #9103 1953 - 1957 431,297- 1,090,206
6 3/4 in. barrel #9104 1953 - 1957 431,286 - 1,131,844
Combination with both barrels #9105 1954 - 1957 431,532 - 1,039,917

GRADING - PPGS™	100%	98%	95%	90%	80%	70%	60%

FIELD-KING (SECOND MODEL) - .22 LR cal., 4 1/2 or 6 3/4 in. interchangeable barrel with push-button takedown, FK 100 stamped on right side of slide, 10 shot mag., front and rear grip straps on this model are smooth, slide lock, trigger stop, adj. rear sight. Mfg. briefly in 1954. C-R.

	$750	$625	$525	$425	$350	$250	$150

Add $225 for factory combination.

4 1/2 in. barrel #9106 1954 - 1954 446,645
6 3/4 in. barrel #9107 1954 - 1954 446,595
Combination with both barrels #9108 1954 - 1954 446,601

SUPERMATIC (SECOND MODEL) - .22 LR cal., 4 1/2 or 6 3/4 in. interchangeable barrel with push-button takedown, "S-100" stamped on right side of slide, 10 shot mag., adj. 2 oz. or 3 oz. weights, slide lock, trigger stop, adj. rear sight, grooved front and back straps on frame, a 2 oz. and a 3 oz. weight were provided with this model as was a filler strip for when the weights were not used. Mfg. briefly in 1954. C-R.

	$825	$725	$625	$500	$350	$250	$150

Add $250 for factory combination.
Add $30 for each weight and $25 for filler strip if present with gun.
Price is for pistol without both weights and filler strip.

4 1/2 in. barrel with provisions for weights #9109 1954 - 1954 446,516 -
6 3/4 in. barrel with provisions for weights #9110 1954 - 1954 446,445 -
Combination with both barrels #9111 1954 - 1954 446,705 -

OLYMPIC (THIRD MODEL) - .22 Short cal., 4 1/2 or 6 3/4 in. interchangeable barrel with push-button takedown, 10 shot mag., "O-100" stamped on right side of alloy slide, adj. 2 oz. or 3 oz. weights, adj. rear sight, slide lock, trigger stop, grooved front and back straps on frame, a 2 oz. and a 3 oz. weight were provided with this model as was a filler strip for when the weights were not used. Mfg. briefly in 1954. C-R.

	$1,175	$925	$750	$575	$425	$300	$200

Add $250 for factory combination.
Add $30 for each weight and $25 for filler strip if present with gun.
Price is for pistol without both weights and filler strip.
Note: Conversion kits for converting from .22 LR to .22 Short became available in 1956 - see the information at the end of the 101 section.

4 1/2 in. barrel with provisions for weights #9112 1954 - 1954 447,209
6 3/4 in. barrel with provisionsfor weights #9113 1954 - 1954 447,210
Combination with both barrels #9114 1954 - 1954 447,205

PISTOLS: SEMI-AUTO, 101 SERIES

The 101 Series were the sixth design models evolving from the 100 Series. This series continued the small push button barrel release takedown. The ribbed barrel was dropped from the upscale models, but the dovetail slot on the bottom of the barrel for mounting balance weights continued. Adjustable sight models continued to use the Davis sight (Note: the Flight King, Sport King, and Sport King Lightweight did not upgrade to this series). Significant premiums can be asked for guns with the combination of both barrels, if verified by factory records that the gun shipped as a combination. Buyer beware - many "combinations" have been created after leaving the factory. Non-factory combinations should have additional value equal to the value of the extra barrel. Guns with original boxes and papers can add significant premiums, but like the guns, the condition is very important, as is the requirement that the box be numbered to the gun. Serial number ranges are best estimates and may change with further research.

Add approx. 13% for original box with papers in same condition as gun on the following models.

FIELD-KING (THIRD MODEL) - .22 LR cal., 4 1/2 or 6 3/4 in. interchangeable barrel with push-button takedown, FK 101 stamped on right side of slide, 10 shot mag., front and rear grip straps on this model are smooth, adj. rear sight, slide lock, trigger stop, brown plastic thumb rest grips, 6 3/4 in. barrel incorporates a muzzle brake with one slot either side of the front sight. A few shipped in 1959 around ser. no. 1,039,1XX.

$650	$550	$475	$425	$350	$235	$175

Add $225 for factory combination.

4 1/2 in. barrel #9115 1954 - 1957 447,149
6 3/4 in. barrel #9116 1954 - 1957 447,146 - 799,260
Combination with both barrels #9117 1954 - 1957 - 799,259

SUPERMATIC (THIRD MODEL) - .22 LR cal, 4 1/2 or 6 3/4 in. interchangeable barrel with push-button takedown, "S 101" stamped on right side of slide, 10 shot mag., adj. 2 oz. or 3 oz. weights and a filler strip for when the weights were not used, 6 3/4 in. barrel incorporates a muzzle brake with one slot either side of the front sight, slide lock, trigger stop, adj. rear sight, brown plastic thumb rest grips, grooved front and back straps on frame, also produced with U.S. marking for the military.

$750	$675	$550	$475	$350	$235	$175

Add $250 for factory combination.
Add $30 for each weight and $25 for filler strip if present with gun.
Price is for pistol without both weights and filler strip.
4 1/2 in. barrel with provisions for weights #9118 1954 - 1957 447,586 -
6 3/4 in. barrel with provisions for weights and integral stabilizer #9119 1954 - 1957 446,511 -
Combination with both barrels #9120 1954 - 1957 447,595 -

OLYMPIC (FOURTH MODEL) - .22 Short cal., 4 1/2 or 6 3/4 in. interchangeable barrel with push-button takedown, "O-101" stamped on right side of alloy slide, 10 shot mag., adj. 2 oz. or 3 oz. weights and a filler strip for when the weights were not used, 6 3/4 in. barrel incorporates a muzzle brake with one slot either side of the front sight, adj. rear sight, slide lock, trigger stop, brown plastic thumb rest grips, grooved front and back straps on frame.

$1,060	$818	$725	$595	$450	$325	$200

Add $250 for factory combination.
Add $30 for each weight and $25 for filler strip if present with gun.
Price is for pistol without both weights and filler strip.
4 1/2 in. barrel with provisions for weights #9121 1954 - 1957 447,230 -
6 3/4 in. barrel with provisions for weights and integral stabilizer #9122 1954 - 1957 447,214 -
Combination with both barrels #9123 1954 - 1957 447,227 -

✳ *Olympic (Fourth Model) Conversion kits* - kits for converting .22 LR guns to .22 Short were announced in both the 1956 catalog and in a 1956 brochure. Kits include a barrel, an aluminum slide, and magazine (.22 short to .22 LR conversion had a steel slide).

$525	$435	$375	$315	$270	$230	$200

Values are for kits in original boxes - subtract 20% if w/o box.

Cat.# 9150 Supermatic/Field King to 22 short, 4 1/2 Bbl.
Cat.# 9151 Supermatic/Field King to 22 short, 6 3/4 Bbl.
Cat.# 9152 Olympic to Supermatic 22 L.R., 4 1/2 Bbl.
Cat.# 9153 Olympic to Supermatic 22 L.R., 6 3/4 Bbl.
Cat.# 9154 Olympic to Field King 22 L.R., 4 1/2 Bbl.
Cat.# 9155 Olympic to Field King 22 L.R., 6 3/4 Bbl.
Kits were also offered for the earlier lever name series and the 100 Series guns. Catalog numbers are unknown for conversion kits for lever name series or the the 100 series guns.

GRADING - PPGS™	100%	98%	95%	90%	80%	70%	60%

PISTOLS: SEMI-AUTO, DURA-MATIC SERIES

The Dura-Matic pistols are a striker fired design that was designed and patented by O.O. Sunderland, a former designer for High Standard. The design was shopped around, and High Standard became the producer of this low cost plinker. The basics of this design can also be found in the Colt Cadet, Colt 22 and the Beretta U22 Neos.

Add approx. 10% for original box with papers in same condition as gun on the following models.

DURA-MATIC M-101 - .22 LR cal., 4 1/2 or 6 1/2 in. barrel, fixed sight, oversized plastic grips, "M-101" stamped on right side of slide (mfg. 1954 to 1970), later appeared renamed "Plinker" M-101 during 1971 to 1973.

	100%	98%	95%	90%	80%	70%	60%
	$300	$235	$200	$160	$125	$100	$80

Add $150 for factory combination.
Add $80 for Plinker with case in original box.

The Plinker was not available with both barrel combination. During the first year, the Plinker came with a zippered carrying case. The Dura-matic was sold by Sears Roebuck & Co. as the J.C. Higgins Model 80. This Sears variation had some minor exterior differences but, mechanically it was the same - including a unique thumb screw takedown, push-button mag. release and oversized trigger guard.

A slightly modified version was sold by Sears Roebuck & Co. as the J. C. Higgins M-80.

* *Dura-Matic M-101*
  4 1/2 in. barrel #9124 1955 - 1970 47X,XXX
  6.50" barrel #9125 1955 - 1970 47X,XXX
  Combination with both barrels #9126 1955 - 1959 47X,XXX - 1,030,956

* *Dura-Matic Sears M-80*
  4 1/2 in. barrel #9133 1955-1962 477,292
  6.50" barrel #9134 1955-1962 477,649
  Combination with both barrels #9135 1955-1962 477,303

* *Dura-Matic M-101 Plinker*
  4 1/2 in. barrel #9214 1971 - 1973
  6 3/4 in. barrel #9215 1971 - 1973

DURA-MATIC M-100 - .22 LR cal., 4 1/2 or 6 1/2 in. barrels, fixed sight, striker fired, oversized plastic grips, M-100 stamped on right side of slide, unique thumb screw takedown, pushbutton release for the thumb screw, push-button mag. release and oversized trigger guard. Mfg. 1954.

	100%	98%	95%	90%	80%	70%	60%
	$325	$275	$225	$175	$150	$125	$100

Add $150 for factory combination.
4 1/2 in. barrel #9124 1954 - 1954 458,801 - 47X,XXX
6 1/2 in. barrel #9125 1954 - 1954 458,802 - 47X,XXX
Combination with both barrels #9126 1954 - 1954 459,675 - 47X,XXX

PISTOLS: SEMI-AUTO, 102 SERIES

The 102 Series was a major design change, incorporating a new frame with a large push button takedown release, and a superb adjustable sight. There is little difference between the two series. Pistols in this series are marked Model 102 on right side of the slide. Three variations of ejectors were utilized during the 102 Series. No premiums exist for these variations. Significant premiums can be asked for guns with the combination of both barrels, if verified by factory records that the gun shipped as a combination. Buyer beware - many "combinations" have been created after leaving the factory. Non-factory combinations should have additional value equal to the value of the extra barrel. The 102 Series was produced from 1958 to 1960, ending at approx. ser. no. 1,12X,XXX. Guns with original boxes and papers can add significant premiums but, like the guns, the condition is very important as is the requirement that the box be numbered to the gun.

Original cased 102 Series Trophy, Olympic Citation models, and Special Presentation combinations in 98%+ condition are currently in great demand and are bringing asking prices in the $1,700-$2,600 range.

Add approx. 15% for original box with papers in same condition as gun on the following models.

SPORT-KING - .22 LR cal., 10 shot mag., 4 1/2 or 6 3/4 in. lightweight, round and tapered barrels, blued finish, fixed sights, checkered plastic grips, smooth grip straps, also available as a combination with both barrel lengths.

	$365	$300	$250	$215	$160	$120	$90

Add $200 for factory combination.

4 1/2 in. tapered barrel blued #9200 1958 - 1960 778,028
6 3/4 in. tapered barrel blued #9201 1958 - 1960 778,021
Combination with both barrels #9202 1958 - 1959 778,026

FLITE-KING - .22 Short cal., otherwise similar to the Sport King Models 102 and 103, steel frames with an alloy slide.

	$500	$415	$360	$310	$240	$170	$120

Add $200 for factory combination.

4 1/2 in. tapered barrel blued #9220 1958 - 1960 791,149
6 3/4 in. tapered barrel bluled #9221 1958 - 1960 791,150
Combination with both barrels #9222 1958 - 1959 791,169

SUPERMATIC TOURNAMENT - .22 LR cal., 10 shot, 4 1/2 or 6 3/4 in. tapered barrel, brown diamond checkered plastic slant grips, adj. sight, push button takedown, smooth front and back grip straps.

	$660	$580	$475	$375	$300	$220	$150

Add $200 for factory combination.
Add $50 for factory guns marked U.S.

4 1/2 in. tapered barrel #9270 1958 - 1960 796,555
6 3/4 in. tapered barrel #9271 1958 - 1960 796,536
Combination with both barrels #9272 1958 - 1959
The U.S. Govt. ordered the Model 102 Tournaments to use for training. These models were marked "U.S." on left side of frame.

SUPERMATIC CITATION - .22 LR cal., 10 shot, 6 3/4, 8, and 10 in. tapered barrels, diamond checkered plastic slant grips, adj. sight, push-button takedown, one grade above Tournament, grooved front and back grip straps, trigger stop, trigger pull adjustment, adj. sight located on 8 and 10 in. barrel, detachable stablizer and 2 or 3 oz. barrel weights available.

	$775	$650	$515	$430	$340	$250	$180

Add $150 for 8 in. barrel.
Add $200 premium for 10 in. barrel.
Add $50 for each weight and $90 for muzzle brake if present with gun.
Add $50 for factory guns marked U.S.

Price is for pistol without both weights and muzzle brake.
6 3/4 in. tapered barrel with provisions for weights and stabilizer #9260 1958 - 1960 803,303
8 in. tapered barrel with provisions for weights and stabilizer #9261 1958 - 1960 795,726
10 in. tapered barrel with provisions for weights and stabilizer #9262 1958 - 1960 771,275
The U.S. Govt. ordered a quantity of Model 102 Citations to be used for training, marked "U.S." on left side of frame.

SUPERMATIC TROPHY - .22 LR cal., 10 shot, 6 3/4 in., 8 in. and 10 in. tapered barrels, high gloss "Trophy" finish, detachable barrel weights and stabilizer also available, walnut checkered thumb rest grips, grooved front and back grip straps, trigger stop, trigger pull adjustment, gold trigger, gold safety button and gold inlaid lettering, adj. sight and push-button takedown.

	$1,150	$925	$775	$615	$445	$325	$215

Add $175 for 8 in. barrel.
Add $225 for 10 in. barrel.
Add $60 for each weight and $120 for muzzle brake if present with gun.

Price is for pistol without both weights and muzzle brake.
6 3/4 in. tapered barrel with provisions for weights and stabilizer #9250 1958 - 1960 812,641
8 in. tapered barrel with provisions for weights and stabilizer #9251 1958 - 1960 791,247
10 in. tapered barrel with provisions for weights and stabilizer #9252 1958 - 1960 791,246

GRADING - PPGS™	100%	98%	95%	90%	80%	70%	60%

OLYMPIC - .22 Short cal., similar to Citation, adj. sight located on 8 and 10 in. barrel and on the slide of the 6 3/4 in barrel, early models marked "Olympic Citation", then changed to "Olympic" only about 1960, grooved front and back straps on frame, checkered plastic grips, trigger stop, trigger pull adjustment.

	100%	98%	95%	90%	80%	70%	60%
	$1,150	$925	$775	$615	$445	$325	$215

Add $175 for 8 in. barrel.
Add $225 for 10 in. barrel.
Add $300 for "Olympic Citation" marked guns.
Add $50 for each weight and $90 for muzzle brake if present with gun.

6 3/4 in. tapered barrel with provisions for weights and stabilizer #9280 1958 - 1960 812,365
8 in. tapered barrel with provisions for weights and stabilizer #9281 1958 - 1960 796,924
10 in. tapered barrel with provisions for weights and stabilizer #9282 1958 - 1960 796,930

PISTOLS: SEMI-AUTO, 103 SERIES

The 103 Series is much the same as the later 102 Series pistols. There is little difference between the two Series. This Series is marked Model 103 on right side of the slide. Significant premiums can be asked for guns with the combination of both barrels, if verified by factory records that the gun shipped as a combination. Buyer beware - many "combinations" have been created after leaving the factory. Non-factory combinations should have additional value equal to the value of the extra barrel. The 103 Series was produced 1960 to 1963, except for the Sport King, the Flite King, the Supermatic Tournament, and the Sharpshooter - see date ranges of the individual models below. After mid-1975, the Sport King and the Sharpshooter appeared in the "G" prefix serial numbered series - see serial number chart. Guns with original boxes and papers can add significant premiums but, like the guns, the condition is very important as is the requirement that the box be numbered to the gun.

Original cased 103 Series Trophy, Olympic Trophy, Olympic Citation models, and Special Presentation combinations in 98%+ condition are currently in great demand, with asking prices in the $1,700-$2,600 range.

Add approx. 15% for original box with papers in the same condition as gun on the following models.

SPORT-KING - .22 LR cal., 4 1/2 or 6 3/4 in. lightweight, round and tapered barrel, 10 shot mag., blue finish, fixed sights, checkered plastic grips, smooth grip straps, available as a combination with both barrel lengths.

	100%	98%	95%	90%	80%	70%	60%
	$355	$300	$250	$200	$150	$120	$90

Add $100 for nickel finish.

4 1/2 in. tapered barrel blued #9200 1960 - 1970 & 1973 - 1977
6 3/4 in. tapered barrel blued #9201 1960 - 1970 & 1973 - 1978
4 1/2 in. tapered barrel nickel #9220 1973 - 1977
6 3/4 in. tapered barrel nickel #9221 1973 - 1977
Note that later production models were not marked 103. 254 Sport Kings (#9200 & #9201) shipped in May, 1977 with serial numbers between G160,000 - G162,590. 116 guns, #9201 Sport Kings, shipped April and May 1978 serial numbers G20,106 - G20,223.

FLITE-KING - .22 Short cal., similar to Sport King Model 103, steel frame with an alloy slide.

	100%	98%	95%	90%	80%	70%	60%
	$500	$415	$360	$310	$240	$170	$120

Add $200 for factory combination.

4 1/2 in. bull tapered barrel #9220 1960 - 1965
6 3/4 in. fluted tapered barrel #9221 1960 - 1965

SUPERMATIC TOURNAMENT - .22 LR cal., 4 1/2, 5 1/2 bull (avail. 1963), or 6 3/4 in. tapered barrel, 10 shot mag., brown diamond checkered plastic slant grips, adj. sight, push button takedown, this model featured smooth front and back grip straps.

	100%	98%	95%	90%	80%	70%	60%
	$645	$550	$475	$375	$300	$220	$150

Add $50 for factory guns marked U.S.

4 1/2 in. tapered barrel #9270 1960 - 1962
6 3/4 in. tapered barrel #9271 1960 - 1965
5 1/2 in. bull barrel with provisions for weights and stabilizer #9275 1962 - 1965

SHARPSHOOTER - .22 LR cal., 5 1/2 in. bull barrel, 10 shot mag., blue finish, adj. sights, checkered plastic grips, smooth grip straps, some mfg. with Model 103 marked slides.

	$550	$450	$350	$240	$200	$160	$125

Add $25 for "SPORT KING" marked guns.

5 1/2 in. bull barrel #9205 1971 - 1977
Although the Model 103 marked guns have 1969 and later serial numbers, they were shipped after the introduction of the Sharpshooter in 1971, and were probably converted from unsold Sport Kings. Some early Sharpshooters have "Sport King" on the left side of the frame.

SUPERMATIC CITATION - .22 LR cal., 6 3/4, 8, or 10 in. tapered barrels, 10 shot, diamond checkered plastic slant grips, adj. sight, push-button takedown, one grade above Tournament, grooved front and back grip straps, trigger stop, trigger pull adjustment, adj. sight located on 8 and 10 in. barrel (a 5 1/2 in. target bull barrel became avail. in 1962), detachable stabilizer and 2 or 3 oz. barrel weights available.

	$760	$625	$510	$430	$340	$250	$180

Add $150 for 8 in. barrel.
Add $200 for 10 in. barrel.
Add $50 for each weight and $90 for muzzle brake if present with gun.
Add $50 for factory guns marked U.S.
Add $125 for extra magazine (#9263 only).

6 3/4 in. tapered barrel with provisions for weights and stabilizer #9260 1960 - 1964
8 in. tapered barrel with provisions for weights and stabilizer #9261 1960 - 1964
10 in. tapered barrel with provisions for weights and stabilizer #9262 1960 - 1963
5 1/2 in. bull barrel #9263 1962 - 1963
The U.S. Govt. ordered a quantity of Model 103 Citations to be used for training, marked "U.S." on left side of frame.
Price is for pistol without weights and muzzle brake.

SUPERMATIC TROPHY - .22 LR cal., 6 3/4 in., 8 or 10 in. tapered barrels, 5 1/2 bull and 7 1/4 in. fluted barrels became avail. in 1962, high gloss "Trophy" finish, 10 shot, detachable barrel weights and stabilizer were also available, walnut checkered thumbrest grips, grooved front and back grip straps, trigger stop, trigger pull adjustment, gold trigger, gold safety button and gold inlaid lettering, adj. sight and push-button takedown.

	$1,100	$925	$815	$650	$475	$350	$225

Add $175 for 8 in. barrel.
Add $225 for 10 in. barrel.
Add $60 for each tapered barrel weight, $30 for each fluted or bull barrel weight, and $120 for muzzle brake if present with gun.

Values are for pistol w/o weights and muzzle brake.
6 3/4 in. tapered barrel with provisions for weights and stabilizer #9250 1960 - 1962
8 in. tapered barrel with provisions for weights and stabilizer #9251 1960 - 1962
10 in. tapered barrel with provisions for weights and stabilizer #9252 1960 - 1962
5 1/2 in. bull barrel #9253 4/62 - 1962
5 1/2 in. bull barrel with provisions for weights and stabilizer #9254 1963 - 1963
7 1/4 in. fluted barrel with provisions for weights and stabilizer #9255 4/63 - 1963

ISU OLYMPIC - .22 Short cal., 6 3/4 in. barrel with integral stabilizer, 10 shot, grooved grip straps, checkered walnut thumbrest grips, trigger stop, trigger pull adjustment, alloy slide.

	$1,125	$925	$700	$475	$330	$260	$180

Add $1,000 for Model 9289 marked "Olympic Trophy" if in 98% or better condition.
Add $50 for each weight if present with gun.

6 3/4 in. tapered barrel with integral stabilizer - with accessories #9299 1961 - 1963
6 3/4 in. tapered barrel with integral stabilizer - with accessories #9289 1961 - 1962
5 1/2 in. bull barrel #9294 1963 - 1963
There was also an Olympic ISU with a Supermatic Trophy finish (catalog number 9289) - fewer than 500 were produced.
Price is for pistol without weights and muzzle brake.

GRADING - PPGS™	100%	98%	95%	90%	80%	70%	60%

OLYMPIC - .22 Short cal., similar to Citation, adj. sight located on 8 in and 10 in. barrel and on the slide of the 6 3/4 in barrel, grooved front and back straps on frame, checkered plastic grips, trigger stop, trigger pull adjustment.

	$1,135	$935	$685	$475	$335	$275	$220

> Add $175 for 8 in. barrel.
> Add $225 for 10 in. barrel.
> Add $50 for each weight and $90 for muzzle brake if present with gun.

6 3/4 in. tapered barrel with provisions for weights and stabilizer #9280 1960 - 1963
8 in. tapered barrel with provisions for weights and stabilizer #9281 1960 - 1963
10 in. tapered barrel with provisions for weights and stabilizer #9282 1960 - 1963
Values are for pistol w/o weights and muzzle brake.

PISTOLS: SEMI-AUTO, 104 SERIES

The 104 Series is the last of the slant grip gun designs. Early production marked "Model 104". Later production is unmarked. The trigger stop screw moved from the right side of the frame to the trigger on the up scale models with that feature. During the production of this series, the accessories were deleted in lieu of a price increase. The serial numbers of later guns produced after mid-1975 utilized a new serial numbering system with the slant grip models utilizing a "G" prefix on the serial number. This series was produced from 1963 to 1978. Guns with original boxes and papers can add significant premiums but, like the guns, the condition is very important as is the requirement that the box be numbered to the gun.

Add approx. 12% for original box with papers in same condition as gun on the following models.

SUPERMATIC CITATION - .22 LR cal., similar to Model 102/103 Series, 10 shot mag., blue finish, adj. sights, brown plastic grips were standard on the 6 3/4, 8, and 10 in. guns, or thumbrest walnut checkered grips standard on the 5 1/2 in. model, grooved front and back straps.

	$725	$625	$500	$430	$340	$250	$180

> Add $150 for 8 in. barrel.
> Add $250 for 10 in. barrel.
> Add $50 for each tapered barrel weight, $30 for each bull barrel weight, and $90 for muzzle brake if present with gun.
> Add $125 for extra magazine (#9263 only).

103 guns, #9244 Citations, shipped March-May, 1978 serial numbers G20,000-G-20,105.
6 3/4 in. tapered barrel with provisions for weights and stabilizer #9260 1963 - 1965
8 in. tapered barrel with provisions for weights and stabilizer #9261 1963 - 1965
10 in. tapered barrel with provisions for weights and stabilizer #9262 1963 - 1963
5 1/2 in. bull barrel with extra magazine #9263 1963 - 1966
5 1/2 in. bull barrel w/o extra magazine #9244 1967 - 1978
Values are for pistol w/o weights and muzzle brake.

SUPERMATIC TROPHY - .22 LR cal., similar to Model 102/103 Series, top-of-the-line target model, 5 1/2 in. bull, or 7 1/4 in. fluted barrel, extra mag., muzzle brake and weights were supplied with gun, grooved front and back straps, checkered walnut grips, super polished blue finish, adjustable sights, 2 and 3 oz. adjustable weights, checkered walnut thumb rest grips, grooved front and back straps on frame. Mfg. 1964-65.

	$1,060	$885	$655	$375	$325	$240	$170

> Add $150 for high polish blue finish.
> Add $40 for each weight and $120 for muzzle brake if present with gun.

5 1/2 in. bull barrel with accessories #9254 1963 - 1965
7.25" fluted barrel with accessories #9255 1963 - 1965
Price is for pistol without weights and muzzle brake.

OLYMPIC - .22 LR cal., similar to Model 102, grooved front and back straps, checkered plastic grips.

	$1,030	$890	$690	$465	$300	$225	$150

> Add $50 for each weight and $90 for muzzle brake if present with gun.

8 in. barrel #9281 1963 - 1963
Price is for pistol without weights and muzzle brake.

GRADING - PPGS™	100%	98%	95%	90%	80%	70%	60%

ISU OLYMPIC - .22 Short cal., similar to Model 102, grooved front and back straps, 6 3/4 in. barrel with integral muzzle brake, the 5 1/2 in. bull barrel was supplied with muzzle brake and weights, wts. avail., walnut checkered thumbrest grips standard, 5 1/2 in. barrel introduced 1964.

	100%	98%	95%	90%	80%	70%	60%
	$1,050	$900	$725	$500	$350	$225	$150

> **Add $50 for each weight and $90 for muzzle brake on bull barrel if present with gun.**
> **Add $125 for extra magazine (#9299 only).**

5 1/2 in. barrel w/accessories #9295 1964 - 1965
6 3/4 in. tapered barrel with integral stabilizer - with accessories #9299 1963 - 1966
6 3/4 in. tapered barrel with integral stabilizer - w/o accessories #9237 1967 - 1977
Catalog and price lists refer to #9295 as both the Olympic and Olympic ISU. This model met ISU regulations and included a removable muzzlebrake and weights.
Values are for pistol w/o weights and muzzle brake.

THE VICTOR (SLANT GRIP) - .22 LR cal., 10 shot mag. 4 1/2 in. or 5 1/2 in. slab sided barrels with either ventilated or solid ribs, adj. sights are integral with the rib, blue finish, barrel tapped for weight, checkered walnut thumb rest grips, grooved front and back straps on frame, trigger is adj. for both pull force and over travel, probably fewer that 700 of these slant grip Victors were mfg. in all configurations, and probably fewer than 40 each of the 4 1/2 in. guns. Most guns are in the ser. no. range above 2,401,XXX, with a few in the ML serial number series.

	100%	98%	95%	90%	80%	70%	60%
	3,000	$2,500	$1,850	$850	$550	$250	$200

> **Add $75 for steel rib.**
> **Add $200 for solid rib.**
> **Add $300 for 4 1/2 in. barrel.**
> **Add $30 for original weight if present with gun.**

4 1/2 in. slabbed barrel with ventilated steel rib #9218 1973 - 1973
5 1/2 in. slabbed barrel with ventilated steel rib #9219 1973 - 1973
4 1/2 in. slabbed barrel with solid aluminum rib #9226 1974 - 1974
5 1/2 in. slabbed barrel with solid aluminum rib #9229 1974 - 1974
4 1/2 in. slabbed barrel with ventilated aluminum rib #9218 1973 - 1974
5 1/2 in. slabbed barrel with ventilated aluminum rib #9219 1973 - 1974
Note the early vent. rib. barrels were steel, and the later ones were aluminum - w/o a change in the catalog numbers. Buyer beware - fakes exist.

CONVERSION KITS MODEL 102/103/104

	100%	98%	95%	90%	80%	70%	60%
	$500	$450	$400	$325	$275	$200	$150

> **Add $250 for Trophy Conversions.**
> **Add $125 for 8 in. barrel.**
> **Add $225 for 10 in. barrel.**

Cat. # 9266 Olympic to Supermatic Citation, 6 3/4 Bbl.,
Cat. # 9264 Olympic to Supermatic Citation, 8 Bbl.,
Cat. # 9265 Olympic to Supermatic Citation, 10 Bbl.,
Cat. # 9283 Supermatic Citation to Olympic, 6 3/4 Bbl.,
Cat. # 9284 Supermatic Citation to Olympic, 8 Bbl.,
Cat. # 9285 Supermatic Citation to Olympic, 10 Bbl.,
Cat. # 9286 Supermatic Trophy to Olympic, 6 3/4 Bbl.,
Cat. # 9287 Supermatic Trophy to Olympic, 8 Bbl.,
Cat. # 9288 Supermatic Trophy to Olympic, 10 Bbl.

PISTOLS: SEMI-AUTO, 105 SERIES

Note: High Standard designed the Model 105 but did not produce it. The 105 Series was to have been a 104 Series gun with the bridge style sight that appeared on the 106 series.

PISTOLS: SEMI-AUTO, 106 SERIES, MILITARY MODELS

Referred to as military models, this series was designed to provide same grip angle and feel of the Colt Military Model 1911. This design was introduced in 1965, and continued through most of 1968. The design utilized the tooling of the 104 Series guns, which resulted in the occasional appearance of a bullet shaped brass design in the rear grip strap when the spring hole was not properly plugged. This design appears as both a full bullet shape or only the outline. There is no premium for this feature. The magazines in this series have a red plastic bottom. The right side of the frame is marked "MODEL 106"/"MILITARY". During the production of this series, the accessories were deleted in lieu of a price increase. This resulted in two catalog numbers for each model. Guns with original boxes and papers can add significant premiums but, like the guns, the condition is very important as is the requirement that the box be numbered to the gun.

Add approx. 12% for original box with papers in same condition as gun on the following models.

SUPERMATIC TOURNAMENT MILITARY - .22 LR cal., entry level target pistol, early guns had smooth front and back straps and no trigger stop, later models had stippled grip straps and a trigger stop, slide mounted rear sight instead of bridge sight, 5 1/2 in. bull or 6 3/4 in. tapered barrel with military grips.

	100%	98%	95%	90%	80%	70%	60%
	$625	$475	$375	$250	$200	$150	$125

Add $125 for guns with boxes and accessories if factory records verify model numbers.

5 1/2 in. bull barrel with accessories #9230 1965 - 1966 1,484,801 - 1,602,XXX
6 3/4 in. barrel with accessories #9231 1965 - 1966 1,484,817 - 1,599,XXX
5 1/2 in. bull barrel w/o accessories #9232 1966 - 1968 1,594,XXX - 1,93X,XXX
6 3/4 in. barrel w/o accessories #9233 1966 - 1968 1,598,XXX - 1,94X,XXX

SUPERMATIC CITATION MILITARY - .22 LR cal., 5 1/2 in. bull or 7 1/4 in. fluted barrel, mid-level target pistol, trigger stop, trigger pull adjustment, stippled front and back straps, new rear bridge type sight.

	100%	98%	95%	90%	80%	70%	60%
	$700	$600	$495	$375	$275	$200	$175

Add $150 for guns with boxes and accessories if factory records verify model numbers.
Add $30 for each weight and $90 for muzzle brake if present with gun.

5 1/2 in. bull barrel with accessories #9240 1965 - 1966 1,465,195 - 1,595,XXX
7.25" fluted barrel with accessories #9241 1965 - 1966 1,467,353 - 1,595,XXX
5 1/2 in. bull barrel w/o accessories #9242 1966 - 1968 1,595,XXX - 1,98X,XXX
7.25" fluted barrel w/o accessories #9243 1966 - 1968 1,592,XXX - 1,98X,XXX

SUPERMATIC TROPHY MILITARY - .22 LR cal., 5 1/2 bull or 7 1/4 in. fluted barrel, high gloss "Trophy" finish on early guns, top-of-the-line target pistol, trigger stop, trigger pull adjustment, stippled front and back straps, gold plated trigger, safety and magazine release, gold filled lettering, new rear bridge type sight.

	100%	98%	95%	90%	80%	70%	60%
	$1,000	$850	$650	$500	$375	$225	$175

Add $100 for high polish blue finish.
Add $200 premium for guns with boxes and accessories if factory records verify model numbers.
Add $30 for each weight and $90 for muzzle brake if present with gun.
Add $10 per weight or $20 for muzzle brake with high gloss Trophy finish.

5 1/2 in. bull barrel with accessories #9245 1965 - 1966 1,436,172 - 1,595,XXX
7.25" fluted barrel with accessories #9246 1965 - 1966 1,436,170 - 1,595,XXX
5 1/2 in. bull barrel w/o accessories #9247 1966 - 1968 1,595,XXX - 1,97X.XXX
7.25" fluted barrel w/o accessories #9248 1966 - 1968 1,595,XXX - 1,97X,XXX

OLYMPIC MILITARY - listed in catalog but not in shipping records.

Catalog number #9235 for 5 1/2 in. barrel.

OLYMPIC ISU MILITARY - .22 Short cal., target pistol, 6 3/4 in. tapered barrel with integral stabilizer, trigger stop, trigger pull adjustment, stippled front and back straps, rear bridge type sight, military grips, supplied with extra mag. and weights.

	100%	98%	95%	90%	80%	70%	60%
	$1,075	$850	$675	$475	$350	$250	$175

Add $50 for each weight if present with gun.
Add $200 if w/box and accessories and factory records can verify model.

6 3/4 in. tapered barrel with integral stabilizer - with accessories #9238 1965 - 1966
6 3/4 in. tapered barrel with integral stabilizer - w/o accessories #9236 1966 - 1968 1,511,284

GRADING - PPGS™	100%	98%	95%	90%	80%	70%	60%

PISTOLS: SEMI-AUTO, 107 SERIES

The 107 Series was the evolutionary successor to the 106 Series. This Series had the frame redesigned to eliminate the plugging of the spring hole produced with the old tooling. During the time of this series' production, the "MODEL 107" and the "MILITARY" marking on the frame was removed at about serial number 2,330,000. Then later the "MILITARY" marking reappeared at about serial number 2,4XX,XXX and remained until the end of the traditional serial number series. The "MILITARY" marking is absent from the guns with the "ML" prefixed serial numbers. There is no premium associated with these variations. These marking changes were not a change in design series, but rather only a change in markings. The traditional serial number series ran until August of 1975. The serial numbers on guns produced beginning July 1975 utilized a new serial numbering system. The Military models utilized an "ML" prefix on the serial number. Early production utilized the red bottomed magazines. Later guns had magazines with blued steel bottoms. The 107 Series was produced from 1968 until Sept 1981. Production was at Hamden, CT from 1968 to 1976 (S/N ML23,065), and at East Hartford 1977 (S/N ML25,000) to 1981 (S/N ML 86,641). Note that early E. Hartford pistols used up old stock of Hamden marked barrels.

The desirability factor for Hamden guns is higher than for East Hartford guns. Guns with original boxes and papers can add significant premiums, but like the guns, the condition is very important as is the requirement that the box be numbered to the gun.

Add approx. 12% for original box with papers in same condition as gun on the following models.

Subtract about 10% for East Hartford mfg.

Use 106 Series pricing for weights and muzzle brakes if present with gun.

SPORT KING - .22 LR cal., similar to previous Sport Kings, except has military grips, labeled "SPORT KING-M." Mfg. in East Hartford only.

$325	$250	$200	$175	$150	$125	$100

4 1/2 in. barrel #9258 1978 - 1981 ML35,454 - ML86,493
6 3/4 in. barrel #9259 1978 - 1981 ML35,453 - ML86,488
6 3/4 in. barrel (123 guns) #9259 1980 - 1980 MLG20,224 - MLG20,408

SHARPSHOOTER - .22 LR cal., early models were marked "SHARPSHOOTER", later models were labeled "SHARPSHOOTER-M." Mfg. in East Hartford only.

$425	$365	$300	$250	$200	$150	$125

5 1/2 in. bull barrel #9210 1977 - 1981 ML29,215 - ML86,641

✳ *Sharpshooter Survival Pack* - introduced 1981, includes Sharpshooter-M pistol, electroless nickel, 5 1/2 in. bull barrel, push-button takedown, packaged in canvas carrying case with extra nickel magazine.

$625	$550	$450	$350	$250	$200	$150

Subtract $100 for guns without the case.

Subtract $65 for guns without the extra magazine for guns in exc. condition.

5 1/2 in. bull barrel #9424 1981 - 1981 ML 85,635 - ML86,044

SUPERMATIC TOURNAMENT MILITARY - .22 LR cal., similar to Model 106 Series, last of the Tournament pistols, adj. sight mounted on slide, smooth front and back straps on frame.

$550	$475	$375	$300	$250	$150	$125

5 1/2 in. bull barrel #9232 1968 - 1971
6 3/4 in. barrel #9233 1968 - 1971

SUPERMATIC CITATION MILITARY - .22 LR cal., similar to Model 106 Series, 7 1/4 fluted and 5 1/2 in. bull barrel available, mid-level target pistol.

$675	$575	$460	$340	$280	$230	$175

5 1/2 in. bull barrel #9242 1968 - 1981
7.25" fluted barrel #9243 1968 - 1981

GRADING - PPGS™	100%	98%	95%	90%	80%	70%	60%

SUPERMATIC TROPHY MILITARY - .22 LR cal., similar to Model 106 Series, top-of-the-line target pistol.

	$900	$750	$575	$450	$325	$250	$175

5 1/2 in. bull barrel #9247 1968 - 1981
7.25" fluted barrel #9248 1968 - 1981

1972 OLYMPIC COMMEMORATIVE - .22 LR cal., highly engraved version of a Supermatic Trophy Military Model 107, high polish blue finish, 5 1/2 in. bull barrel, has 5 Olympic gold rings on right side of receiver, ser. no. has a "T" prefix, came with a lined presentation case, early models were marked "MODEL 107", and were not high polished. C-R.

	$6,500	$5,000	$4,000	N/A	N/A	N/A	N/A

Last MSR was $605.

Values assume guns in original presentation cases.
5 1/2 in. bull barrel #9207 1972 - 1975 T0,000,000 - T0,000,999
This model was a limited edition with 1,000 guns planned, but only 108 guns were listed in the shipping records, plus one frame manufactured due to their high price. A couple of prototypes are believed to exist in the regular serial number series. The original Issue price was $550. One fully engraved gun is known. Buyer beware - fakes may exist.

OLYMPIC ISU MILITARY - .22 Short cal., target pistol for Olympic Style Rapid Fire Events, 6 3/4 in. fluted barrel with integral stabilizer and two detachable weights.

	$1,050	$875	$675	$575	$475	$325	$250

Add $50 for each weight if present with gun.
6 3/4 in. barrel #9238 1968 - 1977

1980 OLYMPIC COMMEMORATIVE - engraved, right side of slide has the five gold ring Olympic logo, "USA" prefix on serial numbers from 0001 to 1000, lined presentation case, a limited edition of the Model 107 Olympic ISU with 1000 being produced. C-R.

	$1,350	$1,000	$875	N/A	N/A	N/A	N/A

Values assume complete guns with box, papers, and presentation case - subtract $250 for guns in exc. condition w/o box, papers and presentation case. Subtract $100 for guns with presentation case but w/o box and papers.
6 3/4 in. barrel #9239 1980 - 1980 USA 0001 - USA 1000

THE VICTOR - .22 LR cal., 4 1/2 or 5 1/2 in. slab sided barrels with either ventilated or solid ribs, 10 shot mag., adjustable sights are integral with the rib, blue finish, barrel tapped for weight, checkered walnut thumb rest grips, stippled front and back straps on frame, earliest ventilated steel ribs (1971) were smooth on top, later steel ventilated ribs were grooved, aluminum replaced the steel on later ventilated ribs, still later a clearance groove was added for spent shell ejection behind the barrel, solid aluminum ribs introduced 1973, early models marked "THE VICTOR" on the left side of the barrel, later guns marked simply "VICTOR" on the left side of the frame, a few transition guns are marked in both locations, early wts. are rectangular with round bottoms, later weights were flat bottomed with three grooves.

	$750	$600	$525	$400	$300	$200	$150

Add $150 for smooth topped vent. steel rib from first year of production.
Add $125 for steel ribs.
Add $150 for solid rib guns.
Add $100 for 4 1/2 in. barrel.
Add $140 for Hamden guns (7digit serial numbers and ML prefix serial numbers below ML 23,066).
Add $35 if weight is present with gun.
4 1/2 in. slabbed barrel with ventilated steel rib #9216 1971 - 1973
5 1/2 in. slabbed barrel with ventilated steel rib #9217 1971 - 1973
4 1/2 in. slabbed barrel with solid aluminum rib #9206 1973 - 1977
5 1/2 in. slabbed barrel with solid aluminum rib #9211 1973 - 1977
4 1/2 in. slabbed barrel with ventilated aluminum rib #9216 1973 - 1979
5 1/2 in. slabbed barrel with ventilated aluminum rib #9217 1973 - 1981

GRADING - PPGS™	100%	98%	95%	90%	80%	70%	60%

10X - .22 LR cal., 5 1/2 in. bull barrel, push-button takedown. Specifically designed for top flight shooting, hand-picked parts and precisely assembled by one of only five High Standard Master Gunsmiths (with his initials under the left grip of each gun), black matte finish, black painted checkered walnut grips, stippled front and back straps. Mfg. in East Hartford.

		$2,675	$2,200	$1,895	$1,300	$950	$725	$575

Values are for guns with box and papers including test target - subtract $150 if missing.

5 1/2 in. bull barrel #9372 1980 - 1981 ML71,116 - ML86,123

PISTOLS: SEMI-AUTO, CONVERSION KITS

These kits for the conversion of .22 LR cal. to .22 Short cal. contained an aluminum slide, the barrel and accessory listed below, and two Short mags., and comes in "gun size box" set in styrofoam. Manufactured in E. Hartford 1979-1982

VICTOR KIT - includes 5 1/2 in. barrel with aluminum vent rib and barrel weight, designated #9370 when mfg.

	$550	$450	$350	$285	$250	$215	$185

TROPHY/CITATION KIT - includes a 5 1/2 in. bull barrel and a stabilizer, designated #9371 when mfg.

	$550	$450	$350	$285	$250	$215	$185

SILHOUETTE KIT - includes a .22 LR cal., 10 in. bull barrel with front sight and rear sight adapter for adj. rear sights, barrel will work with either large push button takedown or socket head screw takedown.

	$550	$450	$350	$285	$250	$215	$185

PISTOLS: SEMI-AUTO, SH SERIES

This was the final series of High Standard pistols and can be differentiated from the 107 Series by the new barrel release in place of the push button takedown. An allen head screw attached the frame to the barrel. This was a cost reduction design change. Shipped from late May 1981- October 1984. Serial No. range was SH10,001-SH34,034. Near the end of production, a "V" suffix was added to some visually impaired guns which were sold at discount. These guns were guaranteed to function properly, but the company would not allow them to be returned for appearance reasons. A few guns were made in this Series with an "SH" prefix serial number with the Model 107 pushbutton takedown. Serial number ranges are best estimates, and may change with further research.

Add approx. 10% for original box with papers in same condition as gun on the following models.

Use 106 Series pricing for weights or muzzle brakes if present with gun.

SPORT KING - M - .22 LR cal., similar to ML series, except has allen screw takedown, 4 1/2 or 6 3/4 in. barrel, electroless nickel finish also available, also called the "SPORT KING-M."

	$275	$235	$215	$185	$150	$125	$100

Add 15% for the electroless nickel guns.

Values are for the blued guns.

4 1/2 in. barrel blued #9258 1981 - 1984 SH10,889 - SH33,964
6 3/4 in. barrel blued #9259 1981 - 1983 SH10,001 - SH28,232
4 1/2 in. barrel electroless nickel #9450 1983 - 1983 SH27,003 - SH31,436
6 3/4 in. barrel electroless nickel #9451 1983 - 1983 SH27,004 - SH31,054

SHARPSHOOTER - M - .22 LR cal., "SH" prefix serial no. with allen screw takedown, military grips, electroless nickel version utilized in some survival kits.

	$350	$285	$240	$200	$175	$150	$125

5 1/2 in. bull barrel #9210 1981 - 1982 SH10,8XX - SH25,074

GRADING - PPGS™	100%	98%	95%	90%	80%	70%	60%

SUPERMATIC CITATION MILITARY - .22 LR cal., similar to previous Citation model, except with allen screw takedown and military grips.

	$500	$435	$350	$275	$225	$175	$150

5 1/2 in. bull barrel #9242 1981 - 1982 SH10,550 - SH25,166
7.25" fluted barrel #9243 1981 - 1982 SH10,513 - SH25,167

CITATION II - .22 LR cal., 10 shot, new variation of the Supermatic Citation, 5 1/2 or 7 1/4 in. slab sided barrel, checkered military-type wood grips, allen screw takedown, SH prefix serial no., slab sided barrel, rear sight mounted on slide, electroless nickel model also available in the survival pack, this model replaced the Sharpshooter and the Supermatic Citation.

	$475	$400	$325	$275	$225	$175	$150

5 1/2 in. slab sided barrel #9348 1982 - 1984 SH25,326 - SH31,495
7.25" slab sided barrel #9349 1982 - 1984 SH25,575 - SH31,496

SUPERMATIC TROPHY MILITARY - .22 LR cal., similar to previous Trophy Model with "SH" prefix, except has allen screw takedown, military grips.

	$650	$525	$375	$300	$250	$200	$150

5 1/2 in. bull barrel #9247 1981 - 1984 SH10,865 - SH32,630
7.25" fluted barrel #9248 1981 - 1984 SH10,492 - SH33,828

VICTOR - .22 LR cal., similar to previous Victor, new allen screw takedown, "SH" prefix, military grips, 5 1/2 in. vent. barrel only mfg. in this Victor Series, some Victor ser. numbers had a "V" suffix.

	$525	$465	$375	$275	$180	$140	$120

Add $35 if weight is present with gun.
5 1/2 in. slabbed barrel with vent. aluminum rib 9217 1984 - 1984 SH10,321 - SH34,034

10X - .22 LR cal., top-of-the-line model similar to previous 10X, but with allen screw takedown, also available with 7 1/4 in. fluted barrel and a 5 1/2 in. ribbed barrel like a Victor.

	$2,125	$1,795	$1,450	$1,025	$795	$675	$575

Add $1000-$900 for ribbed barrel model.
Add $500-$600 for fluted barrel.
Values are for guns with box and papers including test target - subtract $150 if missing.
5 1/2 in. bull barrel #9372 1981 - 1983 SH10,200 - SH29,640
7.25" fluted barrel #9249 1983 - 1983 SH27,536 - SH29,641
5 1/2 in. Slabbed barrel w/vent. rib #9434 1983 - 1983 SH26,657 - SH29,601
Buyer beware - fakes are known to exist.

SURVIVAL PACK - .22 LR cal., Sharpshooter "M" or Citation II electroless nickel, allen screw takedown, packaged in canvas carrying case with extra nickel magazine (two different fabrics utilized during production).

	$550	$500	$375	$300	$250	$200	$175

Subtract $100 for guns without the case and $65 for guns without the extra magazine for guns in exc. condition.
Sharpshooter version #9424 1981 - 1982 SH10,048 - SH25,XXX
Citation II version #9424 1982 - 1984 SH25,XXX - SH31,312

REVOLVERS: POLICE STYLE

The Sentinel revolvers begin with the R-100 design series, and continue through the R-109 design series. Later steel framed Sentinels carry no design series markings. A change of design series designation indicates design changes to the guns. The R-105 has the fewest known survivors. The design series designations and the associated catalog numbers which follow are best estimates, and may require further research. Earliest Sentinels in 1955 were in a separate serial number series from 1 through approximately 45,000. Then they were included in a serial number series common to all handguns. In 1974, they were again put in a

GRADING - PPGS™	100%	98%	95%	90%	80%	70%	60%

separate serial number series with a prefix - S101 through S79946. Many of the later guns had a "V" suffix which indicates it was visually impaired, but guaranteed to work properly. High Standard private labeled the aluminum framed Sentinels for both Sears and Western Auto. A few were also provided to Col. Rex Applegate for his ARMAMEX company in Mexico.

Add 20% for extra convertible cylinder (.22 LR/.22 Mag.) on those models listed that apply.

Add $30 for box and papers unles otherwise specified.

SENTINEL - .22 S, L, or LR cal., aluminum frame, nine shot, SA or DA, swing out cylinder, 2 3/8, 3, 4, 5, or 6 in. barrel, fixed sights, return spring on ejector beginning with R-102 Series, until 1960 the 2 3/8 in. barrel model had a bobbed hammer, beginning in 1961 this changed to a standard spur hammer with no change in Cat. No.

✳ *Sentinel Blue finish*

	100%	98%	95%	90%	80%	70%	60%
	$225	$200	$140	$100	$85	$70	$55

✳ *Sentinel Nickel Finish*

	100%	98%	95%	90%	80%	70%	60%
	$250	$225	$200	$115	$95	$85	$65

Subtract $15 for early models without spring return ejector.
Add $25 for 5 in. barrel.

R-100, R-101, R-102 Series 3 in. bbl., brown sq. butt, plastic grips, blue, #9127, mfg. 1955-1960.
R-100, R-101, R-102 Series 3 in. bbl., brown sq. butt, plastic grips, nickel #9136, mfg. 1956-1960.
R-100 Series 5 in. bbl., brown sq. butt, plastic grips, blue, #9128, mfg. 1955 only.

✳ *Sentinel R-100, R-101, R-102 Series 6 in. bbl.*

Brown sq. butt, plastic grips, blue, #9128 mfg. 1956-1964.
White sq. butt, plastic grips, nickel #9137 mfg. 1956-1964.

✳ *Sentinel R-102, R-103 Series 4 in. bbl.*

Brown sq. butt, plastic grips, blue #9159 mfg. 1957-1964.
White sq. butt, plastic grips, nickel #9160 mfg. 1957-1964.

✳ *Sentinel R-102, R-103 Series 2 3/8 in. barrel* - faux ivory round butt, plastic grips.

Blue #9144 mfg. 1957-1966.
Nickel #9145 mfg. 1957-1966.

✳ *Sentinel w/Dura-Tone colors* - 2 3/8 in. barrel, offered in three different color anodized frames, featured nickel plated cylinders, triggers, and hammers, round butt ivory colored plastic grips, mahogany finished case.

Add $40 for R-102 models.
Subtract $50 if w/o wood presentation case.

✳ *Sentinel Turquoise Finish*

	100%	98%	95%	90%	80%	70%	60%
	$525	$495	$395	$220	$170	$140	$110

✳ *Sentinel Pink Finish*

	100%	98%	95%	90%	80%	70%	60%
	$525	$495	$395	$220	$170	$140	$110

✳ *Sentinel Gold Finish*

	100%	98%	95%	90%	80%	70%	60%
	$500	$400	$350	$225	$175	$125	$110

Gold R-101, R-102 Series #9161 mfg. 1957-1962 710,397 - 1,221,102
Turquoise R-101, R-102 Series #9162 mfg. 1957-1962 710,463 - 1,221,101
Pink R-101, R-102 Series #9163 mfg. 1957-1962 710,393 - 1,160,442

SENTINEL IMPERIAL - similar to Sentinel, except has adj. sights, two piece walnut grips, mfg. 1962-64.

✳ *Sentinel Imperial Blue Finish*

	100%	98%	95%	90%	80%	70%	60%
	$240	$225	$200	$125	$110	$95	$85

✳ *Sentinel Imperial Nickel Finish*

	100%	98%	95%	90%	80%	70%	60%
	$250	$225	$200	$135	$110	$100	$90

R-104 Series 4 in. bbl., blue #9187 mfg. 1962-1964.
R-104 Series 6 in. bbl., blue #9188 mfg. 1962-1964.
R-104 Series 4 in. bbl., nickel #9191 mfg. 1962-1964.
R-104 Series 6 in. bbl., nickel #9192 mfg. 1962-1964.

GRADING - PPGS™	100%	98%	95%	90%	80%	70%	60%

SENTINEL DELUXE - similar to Sentinel, except has two piece walnut square butt grips and fixed sights, wide trigger, 24 or 26 oz.

✳ *Sentinel Deluxe Blue finish*							
	$225	$200	$175	$115	$95	$85	$75
✳ *Sentinel Deluxe Nickel Finish*							
	$250	$225	$200	$115	$100	$90	$80

R-106, R-107 Series 4 in. bbl., blue #9146 mfg. 1965-69, 1972-73.
R-106, R-107 Series 4 in. bbl., nickel #9148 mfg. 1965-1973.
R-106, R-107 Series 6 in. bbl., blue #9147 mfg. 1965-69, 1972-73.
R-106, R-107 Series 6 in. bbl., nickel #9149 mfg. 1965-1973.

SENTINEL SNUB - similar to Sentinel Deluxe, except has checkered bird's-head grip, blue or nickel finish, 2 3/8 in. barrel, 20 oz.

✳ *Sentinel Snub Blue Finish*							
	$225	$200	$160	$110	$100	$90	$80
✳ *Sentinel Snub Nickel Finish*							
	$250	$225	$200	$120	$110	$95	$85

R-108 Series, brown round butt, plastic grip
Blue #9344 mfg. 1967-69, 1972-73.
Nickel #9345 mfg. 1967-69, 1972-73.

KIT GUN - 22 LR cal., swing out cylinder, 9 shot, 4 in. barrel, adj. sights, blue finish, aluminum frame, round butt walnut grips.

	$250	$200	$175	$120	$110	$100	$90

R-109 Series #9304 mfg. 1971-1973.

CAMP GUN - 22 LR or .22 Mag. cal., 6 in. barrel, blue, adj. rear sight, checkered walnut grips, also available as a combination with both cylinders.

	$250	$225	$200	$155	$120	$110	$100

Add $50 for combination with both cylinders.
R-109 Series, .22 S/L/LR #9342 mfg. 1976-77.
R-109 Series, .22 Mag. #9343 mfg. 1976-77.
R-109 Series, Combination #9393 mfg. 1977-1984.

SENTINEL MARK I - .22 S, L, or LR cal., SA or DA, swing out cylinder, 2, 3, or 4 in barrel, steel frame, fixed sights, blue or nickel finish, adj. sights on 3 or 4 in. barrel, smooth wood, square butt grips.

✳ *Sentinel Mark I Blue Finish*							
	$245	$220	$200	$155	$120	$105	$95
✳ *Sentinel Mark I Nickel Finish*							
	$275	$250	$200	$155	$130	$110	$100

$25 premium for adj. sights.
2 in. bbl., fixed sights, blue #9350 mfg. 1974-77.
2 in. bbl., fixed sights ,nickel #9351 mfg. 1974-77.
3 in. bbl., fixed sights, blue #9352 mfg. 1974 only.
3 in. bbl., fixed sights, nickel #9354 mfg. 1974 only.
3 in. bbl., adj. sights, blue #9353 mfg. 1974 only.
3 in. bbl., adj. sights, nickel #9355 mfg. 1974 only.
4 in. bbl., fixed sights, blue #9356 mfg. 1974-77.
4 in. bbl., fixed sights, nickel #9358 mfg. 1974-77.
4 in. bbl., adj. sights, blue #9357 mfg. 1974-77.
4 in. bbl., adj. sights, nickel #9359 mfg. 1974-77.

SENTINEL MARK IV - similar to Sentinel Mark I, except .22 Mag. cal.

✳ *Sentinel Mark IV Blue Finish*							
	$265	$225	$200	$165	$130	$110	$100
✳ *Sentinel Mark IV Nickel Finish*							
	$295	$250	$200	$185	$150	$130	$110

Add $25 for adj. sights.

GRADING - PPGS™	100%	98%	95%	90%	80%	70%	60%

2 in. bbl., fixed sights, blue #9360 mfg. 1974-77.
2 in. bbl., fixed sights, nickel #9361 mfg. 1974-77.
3 in. bbl., fixed sights, blue #9362 mfg. 1974-77.
3 in. bbl., fixed sights, nickel #9363 mfg. 1974-77.
3 in. bbl., adj. sights, blue #9364 mfg. 1974-77.
3 in. bbl., adj. sights, nickel #9365 mfg. 1974-77.
4 in. bbl., fixed sights, blue #9366 mfg. 1974-77.
4 in. bbl., fixed sights, nickel #9367 mfg. 1974-77.
4 in. bbl., adj. sights, blue #9368 mfg. 1974-77.
4 in. bbl., adj. sights, nickel #9369 mfg. 1974-77.

POWER PLUS - .38 Spl. cal., 5 shot, SA or DA, swing out cylinder, blue finish, steel frame, serial numbers between PG 1010 and PG1273, only 177 mfg. 1983-84.

	100%	98%	95%	90%	80%	70%	60%
	$550	$500	$425	$360	$250	$200	$150

Catalog number 9438 .

SENTINEL - similar to Mark I Sentinel, except without the Mark I markings, steel frame, blue finish, offered as a combination with cylinders for .22 LR and .22 Mag.

	100%	98%	95%	90%	80%	70%	60%
	$265	$250	$240	$215	$205	$195	$185

Add $25 for adj. sights.
Subtract $50 for guns with only one cylinder.
Values are for guns with both cylinders.
2 in. bbl., fixed sights #9390 mfg. 1978-1984.
4 in. bbl., adj. sights #9392 mfg. 1978-1984.

SENTINEL MARK II - .357 Mag. cal., SA or DA, 6 shot, swing out cylinder, blue finish, steel frame, fixed sights, produced by Dan Wesson for High Standard from 1974-75.

	100%	98%	95%	90%	80%	70%	60%
	$270	$235	$200	$180	$150	$140	$130

Serial numbers had an "H" prefix H10001 to H35100. A few preproduction guns were sold to employees (H1 to about H28).
2 1/2 In. bbl., #9401, 4 in. bbl., #9402.
6 in. bbl., #9403.

SENTINEL MARK III - similar to Mark II, except adj. sights, mfg. by Dan Wesson.

	100%	98%	95%	90%	80%	70%	60%
	$300	$260	$230	$200	$165	$150	$140

2 1/2 in. and 6 in. bbl. #9407
4 in. bbl. #9408
6 in. bbl. #9409

CRUSADER - planned production only in .357 Mag., .44 Mag. or .45 Colt cal., swing-out cylinder, unique geared action, adj. sights.
.357 Mag., 4 1/4 in. barrel, medium frame, catalog #9458 advertised 1979-1980.
.357 Mag., 6 1/2 in. barrel, medium frame, catalog #9459 advertised 1979-1980.
.357 Mag., 4 1/4 in. barrel, large frame, catalog #9471 advertised 1979-1980.
.357 Mag., 6 1/2 in. barrel, large frame, catalog #9472 advertised 1979-1980.
.44 Mag., 4 1/4 in. barrel, large frame, catalog #9452 advertised 1979-1980.
.44 Mag., 6 1/2 in. barrel, large frame, catalog #9453 advertised 1979-1980.
.44 Mag., 8 3/4 in. barrel, large frame, catalog #9454 advertised 1979-1980.
.45 Colt, 4 1/4 in. barrel, large frame, catalog #9455 advertised 1979-1980.
.45 Colt, 6 1/2 in. barrel, large frame, catalog #9456 advertised 1979-1980.
.45 Colt, 8 3/4 in. barrel, large frame, catalog #9457 advertised 1979-1980.
Only a few prototypes with "EX" prefix serial numbers of this model exist, and pre-production Crusaders with serial numbers C1001 and C1002 exist.

CRUSADER 50TH ANNIVERSARY - .44 Mag. or .45 LC cal., 51 mfg. for each cal. in 8 3/8 in. barrel with 1/3 coverage engraving (ser. no. 0-50), double action employing gear assembly, blue with a gold crusader figure on the side plate, and an anniversary rollmark to commemorate High Standard's 50th anniversary, cased.

✳ *Crusader 50th Anniversary Standard Model w/o engraving*

	100%	98%	95%	90%	80%	70%	60%
	$775	$700	$650	$475	$400	$325	$275

GRADING - PPGS™	100%	98%	95%	90%	80%	70%	60%

✳ *Crusader 50th Anniversary 8 3/8 in. barrel*

	100%	98%	95%	90%	80%	70%	60%
	$1,475	$1,250	$1,100	$900	$750	$625	$500

    Add 25% for single digit serial number.

Limited availability might affect asking prices considerably. Two gun sets with matching serial numbers were also available - current asking prices are over $3,250.

Advertising materials at the time listed 450 revolvers of each cal. in a 6 1/2 in. barrel (ser. no. 51-500). Serial numbers for the 8 3/4 in. barrels are 44M0 through 44M50 (shipped 1979 through 1981) and 45C0 through 45C50 (shipped in 1981). Serial numbers 44M51 through 44M500 (approx 425 guns shipped 1978 through 1983). Serial numbers 45C51 through 45C487 (approx 339 guns shipped 1981 through 1983).

.44 Mag., 8 3/4 in. bbl., first 51 of 501 commemoratives #9601 mfg. 1979-981.
.44 Mag., 6 1/2 in. bbl., balance of 501 commemoratives #9603 mfg. 1978-983.
.45 Colt, 8 3/4 in. bbl., first 51 of 501 commemoratives #9600 mfg. 1981 only.
.45 Colt, 6 1/2 in. bbl., balance of 501 commemoratives #9602 mfg. 1981-1983.

REVOLVERS: WESTERN STYLE

The Western style revolvers begin with the W-100 design series and continue through the W-106 design series. The changes of design series designations indicate design changes to the guns. The design series designations and the associated catalog numbers which follow are best estimates. Early western revolvers were in the serial number series common to all handguns. In 1972, they were put in a separate serial number series with an "M" prefix - M 1001 through M90916. Many of the later guns had a "V" suffix which indicated the gun signified visually impaired but guaranteed to work properly. High Standard private labeled the aluminum frame Western style revolvers for both Sears and Western Auto.

DURANGO - .22 S, L, or LR cal., single/double action, 9 shot, blue or nickel finish, aluminum or steel frame, 4 1/2 or 5 1/2 in. barrel, fixed or adj. sights, square butt walnut grips, two models have their grip straps and trigger guard nickel plated.

✳ *Durango Blue Finish*

	100%	98%	95%	90%	80%	70%	60%
	$250	$200	$175	$120	$85	$70	$55

✳ *Durango Nickel Finish*

	100%	98%	95%	90%	80%	70%	60%
	$275	$225	$185	$130	$95	$85	$65

    Add $25 for steel frame.
    Add $25 for adj. sights.
Values assume aluminum frames.

✳ *Durango W-105 Series, aluminum frame*
    4 1/2 in. bbl., blue with brass trim #9302 mfg. 1970-73.

✳ *Durango W-105 Series, aluminum frame*
    5 1/2 in. bbl., blue #9307 mfg. 1971-73.

✳ *Durango W-105 Series, aluminum frame*
    5 1/2 in. bbl., nickel #9308 mfg. 1971-73.

✳ *Durango W-106 Series, steel frame*
    5 1/2 in. bbl., blue with nickel trim, #9316 mfg. 1974 only.

✳ *Durango W-106 Series, steel frame*
    5 1/2 in. bbl., nickel #9317 mfg. 1974 only.

✳ *Durango W-106 Series, steel frame*
    5 1/2 in. bbl., adj. sights, blue/nickel #9318 mfg. 1974 only.

HOMBRE - similar to Double Nine aluminum frame, but no ejector rod housing, 4 1/2 in. barrel, fixed sights and square butt walnut grips.

✳ *Hombre Blue finish*

	100%	98%	95%	90%	80%	70%	60%
	$250	$200	$175	$120	$85	$70	$65

✳ *Hombre Nickel Finish*

	100%	98%	95%	90%	80%	70%	60%
	$250	$225	$200	$130	$95	$85	$65

    W-105 Series, blue #9300 mfg. 1970-1972.
    W-105 Series, nickel #9301 mfg. 1970-1972.

GRADING - PPGS™	100%	98%	95%	90%	80%	70%	60%

LONGHORN - .22 LR or .22 Mag. cal., DA, 4 1/2, 5 1/2, or 9 1/2 in. barrel, 9 shot, swing out cylinder, fixed sights except for one model.

✱ *Longhorn 1958-1970 Mfg.* - .22 S, L, or LR cal., SA or DA, aluminum frame guns, blue finish, fixed sights, square butt grips, one model has grip straps and trigger guard with gold plating contrasting with the blue frame.

	$325	$300	$275	$200	$150	$100	$80

Subtract $15 for early models w/o spring return ejector.

These guns are found in the W-100, W-101, W-102, W-103, and W-104 design series.

✱ *Longhorn Aluminum Frame*

4 1/2 in. bbl., faux ivory plastic grips #9175 mfg. 1961 only.
5 1/2 in. bbl., faux ivory plastic grips #9176 mfg. 1961 only.
9 1/2 in. bbl., ivory colored plastic grips #9177 mfg. 1961 only.
4 1/2 in. bbl., pearl style plastic grips #9178 mfg. 1961-65.
5 1/2 in. bbl., stag style plastic grips #9179 mfg. 1961-65.
9 1/2 in. bbl., walnut grips #9180 mfg. 1961-65.
Sears version #9184
9 1/2 in. bbl., walnut grips,gold colored trim #9199 mfg. 1966 only.
9 1/2 in. bbl., walnut grips #9399 mfg. 1967-1970.

✱ *Longhorn Steel Frame 1971-1984 Mfg.* - .22 S, L, LR, or .22 Mag. cal., steel frame, or a combination with both cylinders.

	$320	$280	$255	$200	$140	$105	$90

Add $45 for combination models.
Add $25 for adj. sights

✱ *Longhorn Steel Frame W-106 SERIES*

9 1/2 in. bbl., .22 S/L/LR #9397 mfg. 1984 only.
9 1/2 in. bbl., .22 Mag. #9327 mfg. 1971-74.
9 1/2 in. bbl., combination #9326 mfg. 1971-76.
9 1/2 in. bbl., combination, adj. sights #9328, mfg. 1976-1984.

DOUBLE NINE

✱ *Double Nine 1958-1970 Mfg* - .22 S, L, or LR cal., SA or DA, aluminum frame, one model has grip straps and trigger guard with gold plating contrasting with the blue frame, return spring on ejector beginning with W-102 Series.

❖ **Double Nine 1958-1970 Mfg Blue finish**

	$235	$200	$175	$125	$100	$80	$70

Subtract $15 for early models without spring return ejector.

❖ **Double Nine 1958-1970 Mfg Nickel finish**

	$250	$215	$190	$140	$95	$80	$70

Subtract $15 for early models without spring return ejector.

These guns are found in the W-100, W-101, W-102, W-103, and W-104 design series.
Catalog Nos.
Blue with faux ivory plastic grip #9169 mfg. 1958-1965.
Nickel with black plastic grips #9170 mfg. 1958-1970.
Sears version, Blue, "Ranger" #9171.
Sears version, Nickel, "Ranger" #9174
Blue/gold colored trim, stag style grips #9129, mfg. 1966 only.
Blue, stag style grips #9329 mfg. 1967-1970.

✱ *Double Nine 1971-1984 Mfg.* - steel frame, walnut grips.

❖ **Double Nine 1971-1984 Mfg. Blue finish**

	$265	$235	$210	$165	$130	$100	$90

❖ **Double Nine 1971-1984 Mfg. Nickel finish**

	$285	$240	$215	$165	$135	$100	$90

Add $45 for combination models.
W-106 Series, blue, combination #9320 mfg. 1971-79.
W-106 Series, blue, .22 Mag. #9321 mfg. 1971-73.
W-106 Series, nickel, combination #9322 mfg. 1971-73.

W-106 Series, nickel, .22 Mag. #9323 mfg. 1971-76.
W-106 Series, blue, combination, adj. sights #9324 mfg. 1971-1984.
W-106 Series, blue, .22 Mag., adj. sights #9325 mfg. 1971-73.

THE GUN/HIGH SIERRA - .22 S, L, LR cal., single/double action, 9 shot, available as a combination model with a second cylinder in .22 Mag., blue finish with gold plated grip straps and trigger guard, steel frame, 7 in. octagon barrel, fixed or adj. sights and square butt walnut grips, gold plated grip frame.

$315	$275	$250	$200	$150	$120	$100

> **Add $40 for presentation case.**
> **Add $45 for combination models.**
> **Add $25 for adj. sights.**

This gun was introduced as "The Gun" in the February 1973 price list and the name changed to "High Sierra" by the November 1973 price list. Note that the early production had neither "High Sierra" markings nor any other name. The name High Sierra was the result of a "name the gun" contest after the gun was introduced.
.22 S, L, LR, in a case #9313 mfg. 1973-74.
Combination, in a case #9314 mfg. 1973-74.
Combination, in a case, adj. sights #9315 mfg. 1973-74.
Combination, without a case #9374 mfg. 1975 only.
Combination, without a case, adj. sights #9375 mfg. 1975-1984.
.22 S, L, LR, without a case #9379 mfg. 1984 only.

POSSE - similar to Double Nine aluminum, except has 3 1/2 in. barrel, blue, brass grip frame, fixed sights, walnut grips.

$250	$225	$200	$125	$90	$80	$70

W-104 and W-105 Series #9181 mfg. 1961-1965.
Sears version #9183

NATCHEZ - .22 S, L, LR cal., SA or DA, 9 shot, blue finish, aluminum frame, 4 1/2 in. barrel, fixed sights, faux ivory bird's head grips.

$375	$325	$300	$225	$150	$125	$95

> **Add $50 for box and papers.**

W-104 and W-105 Series #9182 mfg. 1961-1965.
Sears version #9186

MARSHAL - .22 S, L, LR cal., SA or DA, 9 shot, blue finish, aluminum frame, fixed sights, 5 1/2 in. long barrel, square butt stag style plastic grips.

$235	$200	$175	$120	$110	$90	$80

> **Values are for gun alone. Add $50 if box, papers and accessories are present and in excellent condition.**

Catalog number 9330 , mfg. 1971-73.
Offered in a special promotion package with a holster, trigger lock, and spray can of G-96 gun scrubber.

RIFLES/CARBINES

SPORT KING FIELD SEMI-AUTO RIFLE - .22 S, L, or LR cal., 22 1/4 in. barrel, walnut stock, open sights, 15, 17, or 21 shot tube mag.

$165	$145	$120	$90	$70	$60	$50

A-100, A-103. Catalog number #8000 mfg. 1960-1965.

SPORT KING SPECIAL - similar to Field Model, except has beavertail forearm and Monte Carlo stock.

$185	$165	$145	$125	$100	$80	$60

A-100, A-103. Catalog number #8001 mfg. 1960-1965.

SPORT KING SEMI-AUTO CARBINE - .22 S, L, or LR cal., 18 1/4 in. barrel, straight grip walnut stock with barrel band and sling, open sights, 12, 14, or 17 shot tube mag.

$195	$175	$155	$140	$110	$80	$60

A-101, A-102. Catalog number #8002 mfg. 1962-1971.

SPORT KING DELUXE / SPORT KING SEMI-AUTO RIFLE
revised nomenclature for the Sport King Special, catalog number 6005 is also the same gun but called Sport King, a special promotional package (catalog number 8007) was offered which included the Sport King rifle, a zippered gun case, a plastic trigger lock, and G-96 gun lubricant.

	100%	98%	95%	90%	80%	70%	60%
	$215	$180	$160	$140	$110	$80	$60

Add 10% for complete 8007 package in original box.
A-1041 Sport King Deluxe Catalog number #8005 mfg. 1966-1971.
Sport King Catalog number #8007 mfg. 1971 only.
Sport King Catalog number #6005 mfg. 1973-1976.

HI-POWER FIELD CENTERFIRE BOLT ACTION
.270 Win. or .30-06 cal., Mauser type action, 4 shot mag., 22 in. barrel, folding rear sight, plain stock.

	100%	98%	95%	90%	80%	70%	60%
	$350	$325	$295	$250	$225	$175	$150

H-100 .30-06 Catalog number #8507 mfg. 1962-1965.
H-100 .270 Catalog number #8509 mfg. 1962-1965.

HI-POWER DELUXE
similar to Field, except has checkered Monte Carlo stock and sling swivels.

	100%	98%	95%	90%	80%	70%	60%
	$405	$380	$355	$320	$275	$225	$175

H-100 .30-06 Catalog number #8506 mfg. 1962-1965.
H-100 .270 Catalog number #8508 mfg. 1962-1965.
H-100 .308 Catalog number #8511 mfg. 1965-1965.
H-100 .243 Catalog number #8513 mfg. 1965-1965.

SPORT KING/FLITE KING SLIDE ACTION RIFLE
.22 S, L, or LR cal., 24 in. barrel, tube mag., hammerless, Patridge sight, Monte Carlo stock with pistol grip, semi beavertail forearm.

	100%	98%	95%	90%	80%	70%	60%
	$175	$150	$120	$100	$80	$65	$50

P-100 Sport King Catalog number #8004 mfg. 1963-1965.
P-1011 Sport King Catalog number #8006 mfg. 1966-1971.
Flite King Catalog number #6006 mfg. 1973-1976.

SHOTGUNS: BOLT ACTION

MODEL 514
some of the Sears versions of this shotgun were recalled for safety considerations in the late 1990s.

	100%	98%	95%	90%	80%	70%	60%
	$135	$120	$90	$70	$60	$50	$40

CATALOG NUMBERS
Series Barrel Full Choke Adj Choke Single Shot Full Choke Date Range
12 Ga 514 Plain 8370 8373 8376 Unknown
16 Ga 514 Plain 8371 8374 8377 Unknown
20 Ga 514 Plain 8372 8375 8378 Unknown
The catalog numbers shown are from a parts book which does not provide production dates.

SHOTGUNS: SEMI-AUTO

High Standard began making shotguns for Sears Roebuck in the late 1940s. In 1960, High Standard began marketing shotguns under their own name and the approximately 200 models in the following listing is derived from the High Standard catalogs and price lists of that time. A redesign of the shotgun line occurred with new models introduced in 1966. In 1973, High Standard introduced their new "Trophy Line" of shotguns and this marked a change in catalog numbers from the number beginning with the numeral 8 to the number beginning with the numeral 6. At this time the previous catalog numbers were referred to as the "Regular Line". Some regular line guns were cataloged in 1973, but this was the last year for them except the Police models. The 12 gauge pumps in the Trophy line were the guns which had interchangeable barrels. Serial numbers began appearing on the High Standard shotguns during mid to late 1967. Beginning about 1958, many of the shotguns had a two letter date code.
Additionally, there are over 150 catalog numbers for both semi-auto and slide action shotguns not listed here which represent models with High Standard markings but with special roll mark-

ing or other features which High Standard produced for several large distributors. Many of these distributor specials had their own model names which included Point Right, Pointer, Birdwing, NATO Pintail Field Classic Mallard Model 200 (J.C. Penney 20 ga. semi-auto), Model 220, and Sport Deluxe. These distributor label guns are not listed in the following data.

The choke markings used by High Standard are: * Full, ** Modified, *** Improved Cylinder, and **** Skeet Bore. Cylinder Bore has no mark.

SUPERMATIC FIELD - 12 or 20 ga., 2 3/4 (12 ga.) or 3 (20 ga.) chambers, 28 or 30 in. barrel, full or modified choke, improved cylinder, gas operated, blue finish, plain pistol grip walnut stock and forearm, 4 shot mag. capacity.

	100%	98%	95%	90%	80%	70%	60%
	$225	$210	$185	$170	$150	$140	$120

Add 10% for 20 gauge.

Supermatic Field models were superceded by models in the Supermatic Deluxe group beginning in 1966.

SUPERMATIC FIELD CATALOG NUMBERS
Series Barrel 30 in. Full 28 in. Modified 26 in. Imp. Cyl. 27 in. Adj.Date Range
12 ga. C-100 Plain 8203 8200 8201 8202 1960-1965
20 ga. C-200 Plain 8270 8271 8273 1963-1965

SUPERMATIC SPECIAL - 12 or 20 ga., similar to the Supermatic Field except has 27 in. barrel with 6 position click stop adjustable choke, 2 3/4 (12 ga.) or 3 in. (20 ga.) chambers.

	100%	98%	95%	90%	80%	70%	60%
	$230	$210	$195	$175	$150	$140	$120

Add 10% for 20 ga.

Supermatic Special models were superceded by models in the Supermatic Deluxe group beginning in 1966.
C-100 catalog #8250 mfg. 1961-65.
C-200 catalog #8272 mfg. 1963-65.

SUPERMATIC DELUXE - 12 or 20 ga., 2 3/4 (12 ga.) or 3 (20 ga.) in. chambers, gas operated, blue finish, 26, 27, 28, or 30 in. barrel, checkered pistol grip, walnut stock and forearm, 4 shot mag., recoil pad (new 1966).

	100%	98%	95%	90%	80%	70%	60%
	$270	$245	$205	$175	$150	$140	$130

Add $20 for vent rib versions.
Add 10% for 20 ga.

SUPERMATIC DELUXE CATALOG NUMBERS
12 Ga Series Barrel 30" Full 28" Full 28" Modified 26" Imp Cyl 27" adj. Date Range
C-100 Plain 8213 8210 8211 8212 1960-1965
C-100 Vent Rib 8214 8215 8216 1960-1965
C-1200 Plain 8207 8204 8205 8206 8251 1966-1972
C-1200 Vent Rib 8224 8225 8226 8227 1966-1973
Late Plain 6207 6205 1973-1975
Late Vent Rib 6224 6225 6226 6232 1973-1976
20 Ga Series Barrel 28" Full 28" Modified 26" Imp Cyl 27" adj. Date Range
C-200 Plain 8274 8276 8279 8275 1963-1965
C-2011 Plain 8280 8283 8279 8275 1966-1973
C-2011 Vent Rib 8284 8285 8282 1966-1974
Late Plain 6280 6283 6279 1973-1975
Late Vent Rib 6284 6285 - 6282 1973-1976

SUPERMATIC CITATION - similar to Supermatic Trophy model except w/o vent. rib, 2 3/4 in. chambers, 6 click stop adjustable choke.

	100%	98%	95%	90%	80%	70%	60%
	$245	$230	$210	$190	$160	$140	$115

Catalog #8220 has a compensator integral with the adjustable choke.
12 ga., 27 in. barrel, adjustable catalog #8220 mfg. 1960.
C-100, 12 ga., 27 in. barrel, adjustable catalog #8221 mfg. 1961-62.

SUPERMATIC TROPHY - 12 or 20 ga., 2 3/4 (12 ga.) or 3 (20 ga.) in. chamber, gas operated, blue finish, checkered walnut stock and forend, 4 shot mag., 6 click stop adjustable choke.

	$255	$235	$210	$190	$165	$145	$120

Add 10% for 20 ga.
Catalog #8230 has a compensator integral with the adjustable choke.
12 ga., 27 in. barrel, Adjustable Vent Rib, catalog #8230 mfg. 1960.
C-100, 12 ga., 27 in. barrel, Adjustable Vent Rib, catalog #8231 mfg. 1961-65.
C-200, 20 ga., 27 in. barrel, Adjustable Vent Rib, catalog #8281 mfg. 1963-65.

SUPERMATIC DUCK - 12 ga., 3 in. magnum chamber, (also fits 2 3/4 in. shells), blue finish, checkered pistol grip walnut stock and forearm, 5 (2 3/4 in. shells) or 4 (3 in. shells) shot mag.

	$285	$255	$205	$175	$145	$125	$110

Add $20 for vent rib.
C-101, 12 ga., 3 in., 30 in. barrel, Full Choke Vent Rib, catalog #8240 mfg. 1960 only.
C-101, 12 ga., 3 in., 30 in. barrel, Full Choke, catalog #8241 mfg. 1961-62.
12 ga., 3 in., 30 in. barrel, Full Choke Vent Rib, catalog #8242 mfg. 1961-65.
12 ga., 3 in., 30 in. barrel, Full Choke, catalog #8243 mfg. 1963-65.
C-1211, 12 ga., 3 in., 30 in. barrel, Full Choke, catalog #8244 mfg. 1966-1973.
C-1211, 12 ga., 3 in., 30 in. barrel, Full Choke Vent Rib, catalog #8247 mfg. 1966-1973.
12 ga., 3 in., 30 in. barrel, Full Choke Vent Rib, catalog #6247 mfg. 1973-75.

SUPERMATIC DEER GUN - similar to Supermatic Deluxe, except has 22 in. cylinder bore barrel, rifle sights, checkered stock and forearm, recoil pad.

	$250	$225	$195	$175	$150	$125	$115

Receiver tapped for aperture sight on cat no. 8246.
12 ga., 22 in. barrel, Cylinder Bore, catalog #8245 mfg. 1965 only.
C-1200, 12 ga. , 22 in. barrel, Cylinder Bore, catalog #8246 mfg. 1966-1972.

SUPERMATIC SKEET - similar to Supermatic Deluxe, except has select American walnut stock and forearm, 2 3/4 (12 ga.) or 3 (20 ga.) in. chamber.

	$290	$270	$240	$210	$180	$160	$140

Add 10% for 20 ga.
C-100, 12 ga., 26 in. barrel, Skeet Choke, Vent Rib, catalog #8260 mfg. 1962-63.
12 ga., 26 in. barrel, Skeet Choke, Vent Rib, catalog #8262 mfg. 1964-65.
C-1200, 12 ga., 26 in. barrel, Skeet Choke, Vent Rib, catalog #8264 mfg. 1966-72.
12 ga., 26 in. barrel, Skeet Choke, Vent Rib, catalog #6264 mfg. 1973-75.
20 ga. , 26 in. barrel, Skeet Choke, Vent Rib, catalog #8277 mfg. 1964-65.
C-2011, 20 ga., 26 in. barrel, Skeet Choke, Vent Rib, catalog #8287 mfg. 1964-1972.
20 ga., 26 in. barrel, Skeet Choke Vent Rib, catalog #6287 mfg. 1973-75.

SUPERMATIC TRAP - similar to Supermatic Deluxe, except has select American walnut stock and forearm and recoil pad.

	$275	$250	$230	$200	$180	$160	$140

Catalog number 8266 is the Executive Trap model with Fajen Monte Carlo stock and 2 3/4 in. chamber.
C-100, 12 ga., 30 in. barrel, Full Choke, Vent Rib, catalog #8261 mfg. 1962-63.
12 ga., 30 in. barrel, Full Choke, Vent Rib, catalog #8263 mfg. 1964-65.
C-1200, 12 ga., 30 in. barrel, Full Choke, Vent Rib, catalog #8265 mfg. 1966-1972.
12 ga., 30 in. barrel, Full Choke, Vent Rib, catalog #8266 mfg.1970-72.
12 ga., 30 in. barrel, Full Choke, Vent Rib, catalog #6265 mfg. 1973-75.

SHOTGUNS: SLIDE ACTION

FLITE KING FIELD - 12, 16, 20 ga. or .410 bore, 2 3/4 (12 or 16 ga.) or 3 (20 ga. or .410 bore) in. chamber, blued finish, 4 or 5 shot mag., plain pistol grip walnut stock and forend.

	$200	$175	$150	$130	$115	$105	$95

Add 50% for .410 bore, add 5% for 16 ga., and 10% for 20 ga.
FLITE KING FIELD CATALOG NUMBERS

Series Barrel 30" Full 28" Full 28" Modified 26" Imp Cyl Date Range
12 Ga K-100 Plain 8103 8100 8101 8102 1960-1965
16 Ga K-160 Plain - 8300 8301 8302 1960-1965
20 Ga K-200 Plain - 8400 8401 8402 1960-1965
.410 bore Plain - - - 8450 1962-1965

FLITE KING SPECIAL - 12, 16, or 20 ga., 2 3/4 (12 or 16 ga.) or 3 (20 ga.) in. chamber, 5 shot mag., blued finish, 27 in. barrel, 6 click adj. choke, walnut stock and forend.

	$200	$175	$150	$130	$115	$105	$95

Add 5% for 16 ga., or 10% for 20 ga.
K-100, K-10, 12 ga., catalog #8110 mfg. 1961-65.
K-160, 16 ga., catalog #8310 mfg. 1961-64.
K-200, 20 ga., catalog #8410 mfg. 1961-65.

FLITE KING DELUXE - 12, 16, 20, 28 ga., or .410 bore, 2 3/4 (12, 16, 28 ga.) or 3 (20 ga. or .410 bore) chamber, blued finish, checkered walnut pistol grip stock and forearm, 5 shot mag., 6 click adj. choke, available with and without a vent rib, recoil pad beginning 1966 except .410 models.

	$205	$185	$160	$140	$120	$100	$90

Add 5% for 16 ga. or 10% for 20 ga.
Add $20 for vent rib.
Add 50% for plain barrel in 28 ga. or .410 bore.
Add 70% for ribbed barrel in 28 ga. or .410 bore.
Add $25 for catalog numbers 6135-6142 with interchangeable barrels capability.

Catalog nos. 8411 and 6411 were the Converta Pump sold with two stocks - one youth sized and one adult size. The 12 ga. models with catalog nos. 6115 through 6142 are models with provisions for interchangeable barrels.

12 Ga Series Barrel 30" Full 28" Full Modified 26" Imp Cyl 27" Adj Date Range
K-100 Plain 8123 8120 8121 8122 1961-1962
K-100 Vent Rib 8127 8124 8125 8126 1961-1965
K-121/1221 Plain 8135 8132 8133 8134 8115 1966-1972
K-121/1221 Vent Rib 8136 8137 8138 6142 1973-1975
Late Plain 6135 6132 6133 6134 6115 1973-1975
Late Vent Rib 6136 6137 6138 6142 1973-1975
16 Ga Series Barrel 28" Full 28" Modified 26" Imp Cyl Date Range
K-160 Plain 8320 8321 8322 1961-1962
K-160 Vent Rib 8324 8325 8326 1961-1965
20 Ga Series Barrel 28" Full 28" Modified 26" Imp Cyl 27" Adj Date Range
K-200 Plain 8400 8401 8402 1961-1962
K-200 Vent Rib 8425 8426 8427 1961-1965
K-2011 Plain 8403 8404 8405 1966-1972
K-2011 Vent Rib 8429 8430 8443 8442 1966-1972
Late Plain 6403 6404 1973-1975
Late Vent 6429 6430 6443 6442 1973-1975
28 Ga Series Barrel 26" Full 26" Modified Date Range
K-2800 Plain 8332 8333 1966-1972
K-2800 Vent Rib 8334 8335 1966-1972
Late Plain 6332 6333 1973-1975
Late Vent Rib 6334 6335 1973-1975
.410 Bore Series Barrel 26" Full 26" Skeet Date Range
K-4111 Vent Rib 8451 8452 1963-1965
Plain Vent Rib
K-4111 Plain 8453 8454 1966-1972
Late 26" Full 6453 6454 1973-1975

MODEL 200 - 12 ga., also sold as part of a promotional package beginning in 1971, which included the Model 200, a zippered gun case, a plastic trigger lock, and G-96 gun lubricant.

	$175	$160	$140	$120	$105	$95	$90

Add $20 premium for entire promotional package in original box.

FLITE KING CITATION - 12 or 16 ga., 2 3/4 in. chamber, similar to Flite King Trophy, except does not have vent rib.

	$210	$195	$175	$150	$120	$100	$90

> **Add 5% for 16 ga.**

Catalog #8130 has a compensator integral with the adjustable choke.
K-100, 12 ga., 26 1/2 in. barrel, 6 click stop adjustable, catalog #8130 mfg. 1960.
K-10, 12 ga., 27 in. barrel, 6 click stop adjustable, catalog #8131 mfg. 1961-62.
K-160, 16 ga., 27 in. barrel, 6 click stop adjustable, catalog #8331 mfg. 1961-62.

FLITE KING TROPHY - 12, 16, or 20 ga., 2 3/4 (12 or 16 ga.) or 3 (20 ga.) in. chamber, blued finish, walnut stock and forend, 5 shot mag, vent. rib.

	$220	$210	$180	$160	$130	$110	$100

> **Add 5% for 16 ga. or 10% for 20 ga.**

Catalog #8140 has a compensator integral with the adjustable choke.
K-100, 12 ga., 26 1/2 in. barrel, 6 click stop adjustable, vent rib, catalog #8140, mfg. 1960.
K-10, 12 ga., 27 in. barrel, 6 click stop adjustable, vent rib, catalog #8141, mfg. 1961-65.
K-160, 16 ga., 27 in. barrel, 6 click stop adjustable, vent rib, catalog #8341, mfg. 1961-64.
K-200, 20 ga., 27 in. barrel, 6 click stop adjustable, vent rib., catalog #8441, mfg. 1962-65.

FLITE KING BRUSH - 12, ga., 2 3/4 in. chamber, similar to the Flite King Field, except has adjustable rifle sights, receiver is tapped for the Williams sight and provisions exist for sling swivels, deluxe models have Williams receiver sight, a leather sling and a recoil pad.

	$225	$200	$175	$150	$120	$100	$90

> **Add $10 for deluxe model.**
> **Add $25 for catalog no. 6166 with interchangeable barrel capability.**

K-102, K-101, 12 ga., 20 in. barrel, cylinder bore, catalog #8105 mfg. 1962-65.
K-102, 12 ga., 20 in. barrel, Cylinder Bore Deluxe, catalog #8106 mfg. 1964-65.
K-101, 12 ga., 26 in. barrel, Cylinder Bore, catalog #8107 mfg. 1962-63.
K-102, 12 ga., 26 in. barrel, Cylinder Bore Deluxe, catalog #8108 mfg. 1964-65.
K-102, 12 ga., 18 in. barrel, Cylinder Bore, catalog #8109 mfg. 1964-65.
K-120, K-1200, 12 ga., 20 in. barrel, Cylinder Bore, catalog #8116 mfg. 1966 - 1972.
K-120, K-1200, 12 ga., 20 in. barrel, Cylinder Bore Deluxe, catalog #8117 mfg. 1966 - 1972.
12 ga., 20 in. barrel, Improved Cylinder, catalog #6116 mfg. 1973-75.

FLITE KING SKEET - 12, 20, 28 ga. or .410 bore, 2 3/4 (12 or 28 ga.) or 3 (20 ga. or .410 bore) in. chamber, similar to Flite King Deluxe except has select American walnut stock and forearm and no recoil pad.

	$290	$260	$230	$185	$150	$120	$100

> **Add 50% for 28 ga. or .410 bore.**
> **Add 10% for 20 ga.**

Cat #6164 is a model with provisions for interchangeable barrels - add $25.
K-10, 12 ga., 26 in. barrel, Skeet Bore, Vent Rib, catalog #8160, mfg. 1962-63.
12 ga., 26 in. barrel, Skeet Bore, Vent Rib, catalog #8162, mfg. 1964-65.
K-121, K-1211, 12 ga., 26 in. barrel, Skeet Bore, Vent Rib, catalog # 8164, mfg. 1966 - 1972.
12 ga., 26 in. barrel, Skeet Bore, catalog #6164, mfg. 1973-75,
K-200, 20 ga., 26 in. barrel, Skeet Bore, catalog #8428, mfg. 1964-65.
K-2011, 20 ga., 26 in. barrel, Skeet Bore, catalog #8431, mfg. 1966 -1972.
20 ga., 26 in. barrel, Skeet Bore, catalog #6431, mfg. 1973-75.
K-2800, 28 ga., 26 in. barrel, Skeet Bore, catalog #8336, mfg. 1968 - 1972.
28 ga., 26 in. barrel, Skeet Bore, catalog #6336, mfg. 1973.
.410 bore , 26 in. barrel, Skeet Bore, catalog #8452, mfg. 1964 -65.
K-4111, .410 bore, 26 in. barrel, Skeet Bore, catalog #8455, mfg. 1968 - 1972.
.410 bore, 26 in. barrel, Skeet Bore, catalog #6455, mfg. 1973.

FLITE KING TRAP - 12 ga., 2 3/4 in. chamber, similar to Flite King Deluxe, except has select American Walnut stock and forearm and recoil pad, 30 in. barrel.

	$275	$225	$195	$175	$150	$130	$110

> **Add $25 for Fajen Monte Carlo stock.**

Cat. #8166 is the Executive trap model with Fajen Monte Carlo stock. Add $25 for Cat. #6165 - a model with provisions for interchangeable barrels.

GRADING - PPGS™	100%	98%	95%	90%	80%	70%	60%

K-10, 12 ga., 30 in. barrel, Full Choke, Vent Rib, catalog #8161, mfg. 1962-63.
12 ga., 30 in. barrel, Full Choke, Vent Rib, catalog #8163, mfg. 1964-65.
K-121, K-1211, 12 ga. 30 in. barrel, Full Choke, Vent Rib, catalog #8165, mfg. 1966 - 1972.
12 ga. , 30 in. barrel, Full Choke, Vent Rib, catalog #8166, mfg. 1970-71.
12 ga., 30 in. barrel, Full Choke, Vent Rib, catalog #6165, mfg. 1973-75.

SHOTGUNS: IMPORTED

SUPERMATIC SHADOW INDY O/U - 12 ga., boxlock, selective auto ejectors, single trigger, fully engraved receiver, skipline checkered walnut stock with pistol grip, vent. forearm, recoil pad, special "Airflow" rib. Imported from Nikko in Japan.

	100%	98%	95%	90%	80%	70%	60%
	$860	$820	$770	$720	$625	$550	$500

12 ga., 2 3/4 in., 271/2 in. barrel, Skeet / Skeet Choke, catalog #54230, imported 1974-75.
12 ga., 2 3/4 in., 29 3/4 in. barrel, Full / Full Choke, catalog #54231, imported 1974-75.
12 ga., 2 3/4 in., 29 3/4 in. barrel, Imp.Mod / Full Choke, catalog #54232, imported 1974-75.

SUPERMATIC SHADOW SEVEN - similar to Shadow Indy, except has a standard size vent. rib, conventional forearm, no recoil pad, standard checkering, and less engraving. Imported from Nikko in Japan.

	100%	98%	95%	90%	80%	70%	60%
	$695	$660	$620	$575	$480	$430	$390

12 ga., 2 3/4 in., 27 1/2 in. barrel, Skeet / Skeet Choke, catalog #54220, imported 1974-75.
12 ga., 2 3/4 in., 27 1/2 in. barrel, Mod./ Imp. Choke, catalog #54221, imported 1974-75.
12 ga., 2 3/4 in., 27 1/2 in. barrel, Full / Mod. Choke, catalog #54222, imported 1974-75.
12 ga., 2 3/4 in., 29 3/4 in. barrel, Full / Full Choke, catalog #54223, imported 1974-75.
12 ga., 2 3/4 in., 29 3/4 in. barrel, Imp. Mod./ Full Choke, catalog #54224, imported 1974-75.

SUPERMATIC SHADOW AUTOMATIC - 12 or 20 ga., semi-auto, gas operated, interchangeable barrels, checkered walnut stock and forearm, special "Airflow" rib. Imported from Nikko in Japan.

	100%	98%	95%	90%	80%	70%	60%
	$400	$370	$345	$270	$200	$175	$150

12 ga., 2 3/4 in., 28 in. barrel, Imp. Mod. Choke, catalog #54200, imported 1974-75.
12 ga., 2 3/4 in., 28 in. barrel, Mod. Choke, catalog #54201, imported 1974-75.
12 ga., 2 3/4 in., 26 in. barrel, Skeet Choke, catalog #54203, imported 1974-75.
12 ga., 2 3/4 in., 28 in. barrel, Full Choke, catalog #54204, imported 1974-75.
12 ga., 2 3/4 in., 30 in. barrel, Full Choke, catalog #54205, imported 1974-75.
12 ga., 2 3/4 in., 30 in. barrel, Trap Choke, catalog #54206, imported 1974-75.
12 ga., 2 3/4 in., 30 in. barrel, Imp. Mod. Choke, catalog #54207, imported 1974-75.
20 ga., 3 in., 28 in. barrel, Imp. Mod. Choke, catalog #54210 , imported 1974-75.
20 ga., 3 in., 28 in. barrel, Mod. Choke, catalog #54211, imported 1974-75.
20 ga., 3 in., 26 in. barrel, Imp. Choke, catalog #54212, imported 1974-75.
20 ga., 3 in., 26 in. barrel, Skeet Choke, catalog #54213, imported 1974-75.
20 ga., 3 in., 28 in., barrel, Full Choke, catalog #54214 , imported 1974-75.

SHOTGUNS: DEFENSE & LAW ENFORCEMENT

SEMI AUTOMATIC MODEL - 12 ga., 20 in. cylinder bore barrel, 4 shot mag., recoil pad walnut stock and forearm.

	100%	98%	95%	90%	80%	70%	60%
	$250	$205	$180	$160	$130	$110	$100

C-1200, 12 ga., 20 in. barrel, cylinder bore, Riot 20-5, catalog #8294, mfg. 1969.
C-1200, 12 ga., 20 in. barrel, cylinder bore, rifle sights, Riot 20-5, catalog #8295, mfg. 1969.

MODELS 10A/10B SEMI-AUTO - 12 ga., combat model, 18 in. barrel, semi-auto, unique bullpup design incorporates raked pistol grip in front of receiver and metal shoulder pad attached directly to rear of receiver, black cycolac plastic shroud and pistol grip, very compact size (28 in. overall). Disc. - 12 ga., folding carrying handle, provisions made for attaching a Kel-lite flashlight to receiver top, extended blade front sight, 4 shot mag., carrying case.

✳ *Model 10-A Semi-Auto* - 4 shot mag., fixed carrying handle and integral flashlight.

	100%	98%	95%	90%	80%	70%	60%
	$775	$725	$665	$600	$475	$400	$350

12 ga., 18 in. barrel, cylinder bore, catalog #8290, mfg. 1967-69.

GRADING - PPGS™	100%	98%	95%	90%	80%	70%	60%

✳ *Model 10-B Semi-Auto*

	$700	$655	$600	$575	$450	$375	$325

Add 15% for flashlight.

Cat. No. 50284 optional carrying case and attachable flashlight; Cat. No. 50285 sold optionally. 12 ga., 18.13 in. barrel, cylinder bore, catalog #8291, mfg. 1970-77.

SLIDE ACTION RIOT SHOTGUN - 12 ga. only on the Flite King Action, 18 or 20 in. barrel, police riot gun, available with or w/o rifle sights, plain pistol grip oiled walnut stock & forearm forearm, changed to walnut stained and lacquered birch in the mid-1970s.

	$230	$200	$175	$150	$125	$115	$105

Catalog #8111/#8113 magazine capacity 6. # 8104/#8129 magazine capacity 5. A 1963 flyer mentions the #8105 Flite King Brush 20 in. and the #8107 Flite King Deluxe 20 in. as riot guns. The data on the #8105 and #8107 is listed under the Flite King Brush.

K-101, K-120, K-1200, 12 ga., 20 in. barrel, cylinder bore, Riot 20-6, catalog #8104, mfg. 1963-1977.

K-120, K-1200, 12 ga., 18 1/8 in. barrel, cylinder bore, Riot 18-7, catalog #8111, mfg. 1964-1978.

K-120, K-1200, 12 ga., 18 in. barrel, cylinder bore, rifle sights, Riot 18-7, catalog #8113, mfg. 1965-1978.

K-120, 12 ga., 18 1/8 in. barrel, cylinder bore, rifle sights, Riot 18-6, catalog #8118, mfg. 1968.

12 ga., 20 in. barrel, cylinder bore, rifle sights, catalog #8129, mfg. 1976-77.

K-102, 12 ga., 20 in. barrel, cylinder bore, catalog #8112, 1964-65.

12 ga., 18 in. barrel, cylinder bore, rifle sights, catalog #8128, mfg. 1976-77.

HIGH STANDARD MANUFACTURING CO.

High Standard is a current trademark of firearms manufactured by Firearms International Inc., established in 1993 and located in Houston, TX.

This company was formed during 1993, utilizing many of the same employees and original material vendors which the original High Standard company used during their period of manufacture (1926-1984). During 2004, Crusader Group Gun Company, Inc. was formed, and this new company includes the assets of High Standard Manufacturing Co, Firearms International Inc., AMT-Auto Mag, Interarms, and Arsenal Line Products.

PISTOLS: SEMI-AUTO, RIMFIRE

SPORT KING - .22 LR cal., 4 1/2 or 6 3/4 in. barrel, blue finish, military grips, 10 shot mag. Limited edition produced in small quantities.

MSR $695		$625	$550	$495	$450	$395	$325	$250

PLINKER - .17 High Standard or .22 LR cal., same design as former Ram-Line pistol, 4, 6, or 8 in. barrel with adj. rear sight, uses many plastic materials, interchangeable barrels, 10 shot mag., 14 1/4 oz.

While advertised during late 2003, this model has yet to be manufactured.

SUPERMATIC CITATION - .22 LR cal., 5 1/2 or 7 1/4 (disc. 1995) in. barrel, matte blue (disc. 1996) or parkerized finish, military grips, open sights (disc. 2001) or universal scope base, 9 shot mag., 44 oz. Mfg. 1994-2003.

	$415	$325	$260	$225	$200	$185	$170

Last MSR was $490.

Add $317 for .22 Short conversion kit (includes barrel, slide, and 2 mags.).

SUPERMATIC CITATION MS - .17 High Standard (new 2003) or .22 LR cal., features 10 in. barrel, mounting bracket with scope base, designed for the Metallic Silhouette shooter, 54 oz. New 1997.

MSR $845		$725	$625	$525	$425	$375	$300	$265

Add approx. $119 for RPM sights (scope base only, disc).

GRADING - PPGS™	100%	98%	95%	90%	80%	70%	60%

SUPERMATIC CITATION 10X - .22 LR cal., 5 1/2 in. barrel, blue finish, military grips, High Standard's most accurate pistol, choice of either factory or Shea custom tuning, 10 shot mag., approx. 45 oz., custom shop only. New 1994.

✳ *Supermatic Citation 10X Factory Tuned*

MSR $1,095	$950	$875	$775	$675	$575	$475	$375

✳ *Supermatic Citation 10X Custom Shea* - limited mfg. (approx. 150 pistols annually), hand-built by Bob Shea. New 1995.

MSR $1,295	$1,100	$975	$850	$750	$650	$550	$450

SUPERMATIC TOURNAMENT - .22 LR cal., choice of 4 1/2 (disc. 1995), 5 1/2, or 6 3/4 (disc. 1995) in. barrel, matte blue, non-adj. trigger, approx. 44 oz. Mfg. 1995-97, reintroduced 2004 through the custom shop.

MSR $795	$675	$595	$550	$475	$375	$300	$250

SUPERMATIC TROPHY - .17 High Standard (new 2003) or .22 LR cal., 5 1/2 or 7 1/4 in. barrel, blue finish, scope base became standard on 5 1/2 in. barrel in 2000, 2002 for 7 1/4 in. barrel, with or w/o iron sights, military grips, 10 shot mag., 44 or 46 oz. New 1994.

MSR $745	$650	$575	$525	$450	$350	$275	$225

    Add $50 for adj. sights.
    Add $50 for 7 1/4 in. barrel.
    Add $317 for .22 Short conversion kit (includes barrel, slide, and 2 mags.).

VICTOR - .17 High Standard (new 2003) or .22 LR cal., 4 1/2 or 5 1/2 in. barrel, blue or parkerized (new 1995, 5 1/2 in. barrel only) finish, military grips, with open sight rib or universal mount (HSUM, blue only, new 1996), 10 shot mag., approx. 45 oz., custom shop only. New 1994.

MSR $745	$650	$575	$525	$450	$350	$275	$225

    Add $50 for open sights (5 1/2 in. barrel only, disc.).
    Add $50 for iron sights.
    Add $317 for .22 Short conversion kit (includes VR barrel, slide, and 2 mags.).

✳ *Victor 10X* - factory tuned and individually tested, includes test target signed by the gunsmith, 46 oz. New 1997.

MSR $1,195	$1,050	$900	$800	$725	$625	$525	$425

✳ *Victor 10X Shea* - parkerized finish, 5 1/2 in. barrel only, 150 built by Bob Shea annually, 46 oz. New 1996.

MSR $1,395	$1,125	$975	$850	$750	$650	$550	$425

LIMITED EDITIONS - during 1996, High Standard offered several limited editions. They included the Victor (fully engraved, 6 mfg., $1,862 MSR), the Tournament (non-engraved, 26 mfg., $608 MSR), and the engraved Tournament (50% engraved, 6 mfg. $1,062 MSR). Additionally, only 5 sets were mfg. with 4 guns included - the Olympic 8 in. Space Gun, Tournament, Flite King, and Victor. Retail was $3,200 (non-engraved) or $7,200 (engraved). A 3 gun set was also available (w/o Olympic) for $2,150 (non-engraved) or $5,150 (engraved). Extreme rarity of these guns precludes accurate pricing.

OLYMPIC I.S.U. - .22 Short cal., 6 3/4 in. fluted barrel with integral muzzle brake, blue finish, military grips, 10 shot mag. Mfg. 1994-95 only.

	$550	$450	$385	$315	$250	$200	$185

Last MSR was $625.

OLYMPIC MILITARY - .22 Short cal., 5 1/2 in. fluted bull barrel with removable stabilizer, aluminum alloy slide with steel frame, scope base or open sights. New 1995.

MSR $795	$675	$575	$475	$400	$350	$300	$250

    Subtract approx. $60 if w/o open sights.

GRADING - PPGS™	100%	98%	95%	90%	80%	70%	60%

OLYMPIC RAPID FIRE - .22 Short cal., 4 in. VR barrel with integral muzzle brake and forward mounted compensator, gold-plated small parts, matte finish, special grips with rear support, adj. trigger, 46 oz., custom shop only. New 1996-2003.

	100%	98%	95%	90%	80%	70%	60%
	$925	$725	$625	$525	$425	$375	$325

Last MSR was $1,027.

RIFLES/CARBINES: SEMI-AUTO

High Standard manufactures the Model HSA-15 line of AR-15 and M4 style carbines and rifles. Current AR-15 and M4 rifles and carbines are $890-$990, and are available exclusively through Lipsey's Inc. Please contact the company directly for more information (see Trademark Index).

AR-15 - .223 Rem. cal., available with either 20 in. (National Match) or 24 in. (Long Range Rifle) fluted barrel, includes Knight's military two-stage trigger. New 2006.

MSR $1,250			$1,075	$925	$800	$675	$575	$500	$425

M-4 POLICE MODEL - .223 Rem. cal., 16 in. chrome lined barrel, A2 sights, six-position collapsible stock, quad rails, match two-stage trigger, Hogue grip, and other accessories. New 2006.

MSR $2,300			$2,050	$1,775	$1,525	$1,300	$1,125	$900	$775

HIGH TECH CUSTOM RIFLES

Current manufacturer of bolt action rifles located in Colorado Springs, CO.

RIFLES: BOLT ACTION, CUSTOM

High Tech Custom Rifles manufactures a complete line of custom built, high quality bolt action rifles, including the Shadow (base price $2,200), Shadow II, Falcon Series (base price $2,450), Varmint Hunter (base price $2,200), Alaskan Pro Hunter (base price $2,800) and Mountain Hunter (base price $2,200). They also manufacture and install their own proprietary muzzle brake (60%-80% recoil reduction). Please contact the company directly for more information, including pricing, availability and a custom quotation (see Trademark Index).

HILL COUNTRY RIFLE COMPANY

Current manufacturer of bolt action rifles established in 1996, and located in New Braunfels, TX. Consumer direct sales.

RIFLES: BOLT ACTION

Hill Country Rifles currently manufactures a complete line of custom built, high quality bolt action rifles, including the Custom Hunter (MSR - $2,495), Custom Sheep, (MSR - $2,495) Custom Varmint (MSR - $2,895), Hill Country Classic (MSR - $2,895), Dangerous Game (disc. 2006, last MSR - $5,400), Semi-Custom (disc. 2006, last MSR - $1,595), Safari Synthetic (MSR - $4,500), American Classic (POR), and American Classic Dangerous Game (POR). All synthetic custom rifles are built on a customer provided Rem. 700 or Win. Model 70 Classic action. Hill Country Rifles also accurizes rifles and performs complete gunsmithing services. For current model availability, features, special orders, and pricing information (including a custom quotation and delivery time), please contact the factory directly (see Trademark Index).

HISPANO ARGENTINO FABRICADE AUTO-MOVILES SA (HAFDASA)

Previous car manufacturer located in Buenos Aires, Argentina.

This company accepted and sold both commercial and military pistols manufactured by Ballester-Rigaud initially, followed by Ballester-Molina. Please refer to the Ballester-Molina listing.

GRADING - PPGS™	100%	98%	95%	90%	80%	70%	60%

GEORGE HOENIG, INC.

Current custom rifle builder located in Emmett, ID. Previously located in Boise, ID.

LONG GUNS

George Hoenig builds a unique patented rotary round action O/U rifle, shotgun, or combination gun. Opening is achieved by rotating barrels quarter turn to the right, then sliding barrel assembly forward. Because of this, there is no top opening lever. Standard features include double triggers, extractors, rotary safety on stock, and coin finished scroll engraved frame. Prices for a 28 or 20 ga. game gun start at $19,980 (approx. 6-6 1/4 lbs., 12 month delivery time), while the double rifle (approx. 7 1/3 - 8 1/3 lbs.) and combination guns have a base price of $24,975. For more information, delivery time, and current pricing, please contact George Hoenig directly (see Trademark Index).

HOFER-JAGDWAFFEN, PETER

Current master gunsmith located in Ferlach, Austria. Custom order only, best quality rifles (most configurations), combination guns, drillings, and shotguns (O/U and SxS) made per individual order. Prices usually start in the $20,000 range, and can go up to over $600,000! Information (including an individualized quotation) can be obtained by contacting Mr. Hofer directly (see Trademark Index).

P.L. HOLEHAN, INC.

Current custom rifle manufacturer located in Tucson, AZ. Consumer direct sales.

P.L. Holehan, Inc. is a custom rifle maker fabricating best quality bolt action rifles only. The company is also known for its integral return to zero scope mounting system. All guns are essentially built per individual custom order and the company should be contacted directly for more information, including special order options/features (see Trademark Index).

RIFLES: BOLT ACTION

On the following models with walnut stocks, the price of the wood is not included. Wood blank prices can range from $1,600-$2,000.

SAFARI HUNTER - various Safari cals., features Win. M-70 controlled feed claw extractor, double square bridge action, premium grade barrel, satin blue metal finish, fiberglass (disc. 2005) or oil finished premium walnut stock with ebony forend tip, Pachmayr decelerator pad, hinged floor plate, 9 1/2 lbs.

MSR $13,300	$13,300	$11,000	$9,000	$7,000	$6,000	$5,000	$4,500

AFRICAN HUNTER - various Safari cals., similar to Safari Hunter, except features Dakota Magnum action, 10 1/4 lbs. New 2002.

MSR $14,400	$14,400	$11,750	$9,500	$7,500	$6,500	$5,500	$5,000

CLASSIC HUNTER - available in most popular non-Safari cals., walnut stock, hinged floor plate, standard or blind box mag., 7 1/2 - 8 lbs.

MSR $11,900	$11,900	$9,750	$8,750	$7,750	$6,750	$5,500	$4,500

LONG RANGE HUNTER - various cals., choice of short or long action, 26 in. fluted barrel, satin blue or matte Teflon metal finish, laminated stock, 8 3/4 lbs.

MSR $11,700	$11,700	$9,650	$8,650	$7,750	$6,750	$5,500	$4,500

LIGHTWEIGHT CLASSIC HUNTER - various cals., features short action, Win. M-70 controlled feed claw extractor, checkered walnut stock, customer choice of barrel weight and length, standard or blind box mag., 6 1/2 - 7 lbs.

MSR $11,650	$11,650	$9,600	$8,600	$7,750	$6,750	$5,500	$4,500

Add $1,500 for left hand.

GRADING - PPGS™	100%	98%	95%	90%	80%	70%	60%

ALPINE HUNTER - various cals., Win. M-70 short or standard length action with controlled feeding, blind box mag., fiberglass (disc.), Kevlar, or McMillian (new 2005) stock, approx. 6-6 3/4 lbs. New 2000.

MSR $5,900		$5,900	$5,250	$4,500	$3,900	$3,300	$2,800	$2,300

HOLLAND & HOLLAND LTD.

Current manufacturer established in 1835 and located in London, England since 1835, with gun showrooms currently located in New York City, NY, and London, England. The Paris, France location closed during 2007.

Holland & Holland over the years has justly earned the reputation of producing some of the finest firearms ever manufactured, exhibiting out-standing quality and superior craftsmanship. Most of these fine arms were made to order for the famous, wealthy, or royalty of their day. Because of the individual nature of each firearm, these early guns, as with any high grade item, must be individually appraised.

HOLLAND & HOLLAND
— *Established 1835* —

All H&H long guns are built per individual special order. Orders may be placed directly with the office in England or through their Paris showroom. Please refer to these listings in the Trademark Index for address, telephone, or fax information

The early double rifles were proofed and regulated with the black powder ammunition of their day. These exposed hammer rifles were almost exclusively sold cased with accessories by Holland & Holland, and are seldom encountered today. Purchase of these as well as any high grade firearm should include trusted appraisal.

RIFLES: MODERN

During 2003, H&H released two new large proprietary cartridges. They are: .400 H&H Mag. Belted Rimless (400 grain bullet with 400 H&H headstamp), and .465 H&H Belted Rimless (480 grain bullet with 465 H&H headstamp).

All currently manufactured H&H rifles are priced in English pounds, and 98%-60% values are not included. All older and recently manufactured used rifles are priced in dollars.

ROOK RIFLE - .250, .295/.300, .360, .380 black powder cals., single shot, break-open action, various levels of embellishment - Royal Models were made but most Rook rifles were base models with few extra features. Disc.

Values today range from $1,000 (average condition, small cal.) to $3,000 (larger cal., engraving, better wood, perhaps cased).

BEST QUALITY MAGAZINE RIFLE - Mauser 98 (current mfg.) or Enfield (disc.) action, various cals., built per individual customer specifications, checkered French walnut stock available in traditional configuration or with Monte Carlo pattern.

✴ *Best Quality Magazine Rifle Current Mfg.*

The current MSR on this model is £18,165.
Add £1,575 for calibers .375 H&H and greater.
Add £2,670 for full length carbine stock.
Add £1,210+ for deluxe grade walnut.
Add £675 for takedown.
The values listed represent the standard model without additional options or engraving (of which there are a wide array).

✴ *Best Quality Magazine Rifle Older & Recent Mfg.*

	N/A	$17,750	$15,250	$11,750	$9,000	$7,750	$6,500

Subtract 25% for Enfield action.

DE LUXE MAGAZINE RIFLE - similar to Best Quality, except with deluxe grade walnut and various engraving options, very limited mfg.

There is no standard base price on this model - rather, individual options are custom ordered and are individually priced.

GRADING - PPGS™	100%	98%	95%	90%	80%	70%	60%

DOMINION GRADE NO. 2 MODEL DOUBLE RIFLE SxS - various British and American cals., 24-28 in. barrels, sidelock, folding leaf sight, checkered French walnut stock, auto ejectors.

	100%	98%	95%	90%	80%	70%	60%
	$22,500	$19,000	$16,000	$14,000	$12,000	$10,000	$8,750

Add 50% for .400-.500 cals.
Add 100% for .500 or larger cals.
Subtract 25% for extractors.

ROYAL DOUBLE SxS RIFLE - OLDER & RECENT MFG. - similar to No. 2, except has deluxe finish and more engraving.

	100%	98%	95%	90%	80%	70%	60%
.300 H&H cal. or less	N/A	N/A	$52,250	$44,000	$39,600	$33,000	$27,500
Up to .375 H&H cal.	N/A	N/A	$65,000	$55,000	$48,000	$40,000	$36,000
Up to .470 NE cal.	N/A	N/A	$92,500	$82,500	$72,500	$60,000	$55,000
Up to .600 NE cal.	N/A	N/A	$100,000	$89,000	$76,000	$68,000	$60,000

Add 50% for self-opening action.
Subtract 25% if w/o ejectors.
Subtract 25% if w/o reinforced action.

ROYAL DE LUXE SxS RIFLE - CURRENT MFG. - same cals. as the Royal Double SxS, except also available in .700 H&H cal., top-of-the-line model, every refinement, 22-26 in. chopper lump barrels, traditional royal scroll engraving, color case hardened frame or bright finish, built to individual order only with almost any option possible, includes aluminum travel case, 8 3/4 - 15 lbs.

∗ *Royal De Luxe - .240 H&H, 7mm or 8mm cal.*
Current MSR on this model is £75,075.

∗ *Royal De Luxe - .275 H&H (disc.), .300 H&H, or 9.3mm cal.*
Current MSR on this model is £77,700.

∗ *Royal De Luxe - .375 H&H or .500/.465 H&H cal.*
Current MSR on this model is £83,475.

∗ *Royal De Luxe - .577 NE or .600 NE cal.*
Current MSR on this model is £91,350.

H&H .700 BORE SxS DOUBLE RIFLE - .700 H&H cal., 1,000 grain jacketed bullet, approx. 19 lbs. with 26 in. barrels chambered 3 1/2 in. This is the largest caliber rifle available in the world today.

∗ *SxS Double Rifle Royal Model* - this model is not currently mfg. 1997 retail was $115,920.

∗ *SxS Double Rifle Royal De Luxe Model*
Current MSR on this model is £131,250.

ROUND ACTION SIDELOCK SxS DOUBLE RIFLE - available in standard flanged cals., rounded back action sidelock with DT, 24 in. chopper lump barrels, English rose and fine scroll and border engraving, color case hardened or bright finish frame, 8-10 3/4 lbs. New 2004.
Current MSR on this model is £40,165.

SHOTGUNS: O/U

All currently manufactured H&H shotguns are priced in English pounds, and 98%-60% values are not included. All older and recently manufactured used rifles are priced in dollars.

ROYAL OLD MODEL - 12 ga., customer specifications as to barrel length and choke, hand detachable sidelocks, auto ejectors, checkered straight grip stock. Mfg. until 1951. Very rare, very few mfg., but not nearly as desirable as newer model.

	100%	98%	95%	90%	80%	70%	60%
	$37,500	$32,000	$28,000	$23,500	$20,000	$18,000	$16,500

Add 5% for single trigger.

ROYAL NEW MODEL - similar to Old Model, with improved narrow action. Mfg. until 1960, fewer than 30 mfg.

	100%	98%	95%	90%	80%	70%	60%
	$36,000	$31,000	$27,000	$22,500	$19,000	$17,000	$15,500

GRADING - PPGS™	100%	98%	95%	90%	80%	70%	60%

ROYAL SIDELOCK GAME GUN - 12, 20, 28 (new 1997) ga., or .410 bore (new 1997), somewhat similar to New Model, with improved cocking, striking and ejection, slimmer action body, DT, 25 to 30 in. game or VR barrels, 2 3/4 in. chambers, finest checkered walnut straight hand or pistol grip stock, scroll engraved receiver with color case hardened or bright finish, prototype testing has finished and guns are available for demonstration, includes aluminum case, 5 lbs. 1 oz - 7 lbs. 8 oz. Written quotations on this re-released model are available by contacting H&H directly (see Trademark Index). Values listed are for base models only and reflect the most recent factory information.

  ✳ *Royal Sidelock Game Gun 12 or 20 ga.*
      Current MSR on this model is £60,375.
      Add £3,150 for 28 ga. or .410 bore.
      Add £1,425 for single trigger.
      Add £12,075 per extra set of barrels.

ROYAL DE LUXE MODEL - similar to Royal Sidelock Game Gun, except choice of more elaborate engraving and exhibition wood.
      This model is quoted per individual special order only.

SPORTING MODEL - 12, 16, 20, or 28 ga., 2 3/4 or 3 in. chambers, designed with a trigger plate action, Game or Sporting Clays configuration featuring detachable SST mechanism, 25 to 32 in. game or VR barrels, medium scroll engraving, bright finish only. Options on specifications to include screw-in chokes, 12 ga. - 7 1/4-8 lbs., 28 ga. - 6 lbs. New 1993. Values listed reflect most recent factory information.
      Current MSR on this model is £36,490.
      Add £1,250 for color case hardened action with gold name inlay.
      Add £9,135 per extra set of barrels.

SPORTING DE LUXE MODEL - similar to Sporting O/U Model, except with choice of more elaborate engraving and exhibition wood. New 1993.
      This model is quoted per individual special order only.

SHOTGUNS: SxS

Holland & Holland currently manufactures the Royal De Luxe Game Gun and Royal Game Gun (limited mfg.) models in sidelock configuration. In addition to the sidelock models, H&H also manufactured the boxlock models Cavalier, Cavalier De Luxe, Northwood, and Northwood De Luxe until recently. The following values assume standard model with double triggers, game rib, standard walnut, or casing. Additional special order features will add considerable value to the price of a new custom order.

In 1988, Holland & Holland absorbed W & C Scott and manufactured the Chatsworth, Bowood, and Kinmount boxlock models until they were discontinued in late 1990. H&H has phased this trademark out, and more information can be found in the W & C Scott section of this text.

All currently manufactured H&H shotguns are priced in English pounds, and 98%-60% values are not included. All older and recently manufactured used rifles are priced in dollars.

NORTHWOOD SxS BOXLOCK - 12, 16 (disc. 1992), 20, or 28 (disc. 1992) ga., 28 or 30 in. barrels, scalloped-case colored receiver, boxlock, auto ejectors, double triggers, border engraving, checkered pistol grip or straight stock. The values shown are for standard model. Disc. 1993.

	100%	98%	95%	90%	80%	70%	60%
	$5,950	$5,200	$4,450	$3,850	$3,300	$2,800	$2,300

Last MSR was $6,705.

      Add approx. 10% for 20 ga.
      Add approx. 20% for 28 ga.

  ✳ *Northwood SxS Boxlock De Luxe* - 12, 16, 20, or 28 ga., scalloped-case colored receiver with moderate engraving and select walnut, double triggers. Disc. 1993.

	100%	98%	95%	90%	80%	70%	60%
	$6,950	$5,950	$5,000	$4,250	$3,500	$3,000	$2,500

Last MSR was $7,450.

      Add approx. 10% for 20 ga.
      Add approx. 20% for 28 ga.

GRADING - PPGS™	100%	98%	95%	90%	80%	70%	60%

CAVALIER SxS BOXLOCK - 12, 20, or 28 (disc. 1992) ga., best quality model boxlock with scalloped frame, double triggers, ejectors, and case colored receiver. Disc.

	$9,500	$7,750	$6,350	$5,500	$4,850	$4,100	$3,500

Last MSR was $11,175.

> Add approx. 10% for 20 ga.
> Add approx. 20% for 28 ga.

✳ *Cavalier SxS Boxlock De Luxe* - similar to Cavalier Model, except has deluxe walnut and better engraving. Disc. 1993.

	$9,950	$8,000	$6,500	$5,600	$4,950	$4,200	$3,600

Last MSR was $11,920.

> Add approx. 10% for 20 ga.
> Add approx. 20% for 28 ga.

DOMINION GAME GUN - 12, 16, or 20 ga., 25-30 in. barrels, any choke, sidelock, auto ejectors, double triggers, checkered straight grip stock. Disc. 1990.

	$6,750	$6,150	$5,650	$4,750	$4,150	$3,650	$3,250

> Add 50% for 20 gauge.
> Add 100% ejector sidelock model with 2 in. chamber.

ROUND ACTION SIDELOCK - 12 or 20 ga., 2 3/4 in. chambers, rounded frame with back action sidelock, DT, 25-30 in. chopper lump barrels with game rib, scroll and border engraving, color case hardened or bright finish. New 2004.

> Current MSR on this model is £28,615.
> Add £5,200 for traditional English rose and fine scroll engraving pattern.

ROUND ACTION SIDELOCK PARADOX - 12 ga., 2 3/4 or 3 in. chambers, rounded back action sidelock design, DT, 28 in. chopper lump barrels with paradox rifled chokes, two-leaf folding rear sight regulated for 50 and 100 yards, bright or case colored finish, approx. 7 1/4 or 8 lbs. New 2005.

> Current MSR on this model is £35,175.
> Add £5,200 for traditional English rose and fine scroll engraving pattern.

ROYAL HAMMERLESS EJECTOR SIDELOCK (OLDER & RECENT MFG.) - 12, 16, 20, 28 ga., or .410 bore, non-self (disc.) or self-opening (recent mfg.), customer specifications as to barrel length and chokes, hand detachable sidelocks, stocked in pistol grip or straight style to specifications. Mfg. 1885-disc.

12 ga.	N/A	$32,500	$27,750	$25,000	$23,000	$21,000	$19,500
20 ga.	N/A	$40,000	$36,000	$33,000	$30,000	$27,500	$25,000
28 ga.	N/A	$55,000	$50,000	$45,000	$41,000	$36,000	$31,000
.410 bore	N/A	$65,000	$57,500	$51,000	$45,000	$39,500	$35,000

> Add 15% for self-opening action.
> Add 10%-15% if cased with accessories.
> Subtract approx. 10%-15% on 12 ga. with 2 1/2 in. chambers.

Values listed are for older, previously manufactured specimens.

ROYAL GAME GUN (CURRENT MFG.) - 12, 16, 20, 28 ga., or .410 bore, best quality sidelock self-opening game gun. Mfg. per individual customer specifications, includes aluminum travel case, 4 3/4 - 10 3/4 (12 ga.) lbs. The following values reflect most recent factory information. Mfg. 1922 to date.

✳ *Royal Game Gun (Current Mfg.) 12, 16, or 20 ga.*
> Current MSR on this model is £49,530.
> Add £2,970 for 28 ga. or .410 bore.
> Add £1,420 (inertia type) or £3,920 (mechanical type) for ST.
> Add £10,290 per extra set of barrels.
> Add $3,100 for VR (disc.).

ROYAL DE LUXE GAME GUN - 12, 16, 20, 28 ga., or .410 bore, top-of-the-line sidelock self-opening shotgun. Mfg. per individual customer specifications. Current production.

> This model is quoted per individual special order only.
> Older mfg. is sometimes referred to as the De Luxe Model.

GRADING - PPGS™	100%	98%	95%	90%	80%	70%	60%

BADMINTON SIDELOCK - 12, 16, or 20 ga., similar to Royal model, except has traditional rose and scroll engraving and does not have self-opening action. Disc.

	100%	98%	95%	90%	80%	70%	60%
12 or 16 ga.	N/A	$25,000	$22,000	$20,000	$18,000	$16,000	$14,000
20 ga.	N/A	$28,500	$24,000	$22,000	$20,000	$18,000	$16,000

Add $1,000 for SST.

❋ *Badminton Sidelock Game Gun* - 12 or 20 ga., double or single trigger. Disc. 1988.

	100%	98%	95%	90%	80%	70%	60%
	N/A	$31,000	$27,000	$24,000	$21,000	$18,000	$16,000

Last MSR was $28,000.

RIVIERA SIDELOCK - similar to Badminton model, with two sets of barrels. Mfg. until 1967.

	100%	98%	95%	90%	80%	70%	60%
12 or 16 ga.	N/A	$31,000	$28,000	$25,000	$22,000	$19,000	$17,000
20 ga.	N/A	$33,000	$29,500	$26,000	$23,000	$20,000	$18,000

CENTENARY SIDELOCK - 12 ga., 2 in. chambers, lightened version of Royal, Badminton, and Dominion grades. The values would be the same as for the standard models, mfg. until 1962.

SHOTGUNS: SINGLE SHOT

SINGLE BARREL TRAP GUN - 12 ga., 30 or 32 in. full choke barrel, vent. rib, boxlock, auto ejector, Monte Carlo pistol grip stock, pad. Disc.

	100%	98%	95%	90%	80%	70%	60%
	N/A	$9,250	$8,000	$6,750	$5,800	$4,750	$3,950

Last MSR was $28,420.

❋ *Single Barrel Trap Guns - Older Mfg.*

	100%	98%	95%	90%	80%	70%	60%
Standard Grade	N/A	$4,500	$4,000	$3,250	$2,500	$2,250	$2,000
De Luxe Grade	N/A	$7,000	$6,250	$5,000	$4,500	$3,750	$3,000
Exhibition Grade	N/A	$8,950	$7,500	$6,000	$5,500	$5,000	$4,250

HOLLENBECK GUN COMPANY

Previous manufacturer located in Whelling, WV circa 1901-1903, Moundsville, WV circa 1903-1910.

The Hollenbeck Gun Company began circa 1901, moved to Moundsville, WV in 1903 and stayed until they went out of business in 1910. The company name changed in 1905 to The Three Barrel Gun Company (circa 1905-1909), and then to The Royal Gun Company (circa 1909-1910). The company made a total of 1,500 three barrel guns. After going out of business, an unknown Florida man bought the name and all the assets. He assembled and sold some three barrel guns as late as 1930.

Pricing on these three-barrel shotguns with unique, sculpted recoil shields in average original condition typically ranges from $950 - $1,500 for both damascus (most common) and steel barrels. There were two basic grades - 0 and 1, but there are also shotguns with more elaborate engraving which will command a premium.

Information appears courtesy of AntiqueGuns.com and the Gurnmeister.

HOLLOWAY & NAUGHTON

Current trade name of long guns manufactured since 1909 in Leicestershire, England. No current U.S. importation.

Founded by Thomas Naughton and G. O'Connor Holloway, Holloway & Co. manufactured traditional sidelock and boxlock shotguns, double and bolt action rifles in Birmingham. Naughton managed the company for approx. 15 years, when it was sold to H. Ludlow England, owner of Midland Gun Co. Naughton stayed on as manager, eventually buying back the company in early 1909, and changing the name to Holloway & Naughton. In 1911, the firm bought the name J.W. Tolley. Naughton died in 1921, and his son T.J. continued the business until the early 1950s.

Holloway & Naughton currently produces very high quality long guns, with many options, and a delivery time between 6 - 24 months. Please contact the factory directly (see Trademark Index) for more information including individual quotations. Holloway & Naughton makes 7-10 best quality, custom order only guns annually. They also perform all services, including engraving, in-house.

GRADING - PPGS™	100%	98%	95%	90%	80%	70%	60%

RIFLES: CUSTOM

O/U DOUBLE RIFLE - custom order, Boss style, best quality. New 2005.

Entry price for an O/U double rifle starts at £75,000, and increases according to customer's specifications.

SxS DOUBLE RIFLE - custom order, Boss style, best quality. New 2005.

Entry price for a SxS double rifle starts at £65,000, and increases according to customer's specifications.

SHOTGUNS: CUSTOM

SIDELOCK O/U MODEL - 12, 16, 20, 28 ga. or .410 bore (special order only), various configurations including field and sporting clays, features lightweight true Boss case colored action (semi-bright or muted colors) with reinforced forearm, exhibition grade wood is standard, choice of engraving - medium scroll, traditional bouquet and scroll, or per individual customer specifications, chopper lump barrels range from 25 to 34 in., choice of fixed or multi-chokes, game or sporting clays ribs, inicludes hand made fitted leather case with accessories and tools, 6 - 7 3/4 lbs. Special delivery only, approx. 12 months (20 ga. occasionally in stock).

  ✱ *Sidelock Game/Field O/U* - traditional Boss style design, customer package made to order.

Prices for this model start at £65,000.

  ✱ *Sidelock De Luxe Sporting Clays O/U* - almost any specification made to custom order, hand built.

Prices for this model start at £35,000

BOXLOCK SxS MODEL - 12 or 20 ga., Anson & Deeley boxlock action, moderate engraving, special order only. Disc. 2004.

Last MSR was $18,000.

BOXLOCK O/U MODEL - 12 or 20 ga., Anson & Deeley boxlock action, moderate engraving, special order only. Disc. 2003.

Last MSR was approx. $14,000.

TRIGGER PLATE O/U - 12 or 20 ga., 2 3/4 in. chambers, designed for game or sporting clays, H&N trigger plate with inertia single or double triggers, rose and scroll or English scroll engraving, 28 to 34 in. barrels, fixed or multi-chokes, deluxe high grade Turkish walnut stock with choice of pistol. semi-pistol, or Prince of Wales grip, slim game or Schnabel forend, includes tools and leather case.

Prices for this model begin at £37,000.

HOLLOWAY ARMS CO.

  Previous manufacturer located in Fort Worth, TX.

  Holloway firearms did not make many rifles or carbines before operations ceased.

RIFLES: SEMI-AUTO

HAC MODEL 7 RIFLE - .308 Win. cal., gas operated semi-auto paramilitary design rifle, 20 in. barrel, adj. front and rear sights, 20 shot mag., side folding stock, right or left-hand action. Mfg. 1984-85 only.

	$3,500	$3,150	$2,900	$2,650	$2,495	$2,250	$1,950

Last MSR was $675.

  ✱ *HAC Model 7C Rifle Carbine* - 16 in. carbine, same general specifications as Model 7. Disc. 1985.

	$2,150	$1,865	$1,715	$1,550	$1,400	$1,300	$1,200

Last MSR was $675.

Also available from the manufacturer were the Models 7S and 7M (Sniper and Match models).

GRADING - PPGS™	100%	98%	95%	90%	80%	70%	60%

HOLMES FIREARMS

Previous manufacturer located in Wheeler, AR. Previously distributed by D.B. Distributing, Fayetteville, AR.

PISTOLS: SEMI-AUTO

These pistols were mfg. in very limited numbers, most were in prototype configuration and exhibit changes from gun to gun. These models were open bolt and subject to 1988 federal legislation regulations.

MP-83 - 9mm Para. or .45 ACP cal., paramilitary design pistol, 6 in. barrel, walnut stock and forearm, blue finish, 3 1/2 lbs.

$700	$600	$500	$450	$400	$375	$350

Last MSR was $450.

Add 10% for deluxe package.
Add 40% for conversion kit (mfg. 1985 only).

MP-22 - .22 LR cal., 2 1/2 lbs., steel and aluminum construction, 6 in. barrel, similar appearance to MP-83. Mfg. 1985 only.

$395	$360	$320	$285	$250	$230	$210

Last MSR was $400.

SHOTGUNS

COMBAT 12 - 12 ga., riot configuration, cylinder bore barrel. Disc. 1983.

$795	$720	$650	$595	$550	$500	$450

Last MSR was $750.

HOPKINS & ALLEN ARMS COMPANY, 1902-1914

Previous manufacturer located in Norwich, CT. H&A started their firearms business in 1867, manufacturing percussion revolvers.

Before 1870, they were producing rimfire cartridge guns and eventually centerfire handguns and long guns. Prior to 1896, H&A guns were marked "HOPKINS & ALLEN MANUFG. CO. NORWICH CONN." or other private trade names, including Merwin, Hulbert & Company. Hopkins & Allen guns are about equally priced with Stevens, N.R. Davis, Crescent Firearms Co., etc. There are many exceptions due to the numerous limited production guns, examples of which are the AA GRADE double shotgun and the "PARROT BEAK" Derringer. Hopkins & Allen also manufactured firearms which were not described in their catalogs. Compiled from Hopkins & Allen catalogs by Charles E. Carder.

HANDGUNS

Most H&A handguns were nickel plated, with blue finish originally costing $.50 extra, grips were hard rubber, wood or pearl. Some had engraving from low to very good quality. Revolver barrel lengths varied from 1 3/4-6 in. Calibers were .22 rimfire (.22 S, L, or LR) up to .38-40 WCF. Specific calibers have not been listed in this section.

FOREHAND MODEL - .32 cal., top break, double action, five shot.

$190	$160	$140	$120	$100	$85	$75

FOREHAND MODEL - similar to above except hammerless. (This model was offered in large and small frame).

$190	$160	$140	$120	$100	$85	$75

FOREHAND MODEL - large frame as above in .32 and .38 centerfire cal. with full hammer or "bobbed" hammer.

$190	$160	$140	$120	$100	$85	$75

FOREHAND MODEL - solid frame and hard rubber grips, otherwise as above in small frame.

$170	$140	$120	$100	$85	$75	$65

GRADING - PPGS™	100%	98%	95%	90%	80%	70%	60%

FOREHAND MODEL - similar to above models, with "folding hammer." .22 rimfires were seven shot, while .32 and .38 centerfires were five shot. By 1909, the Forehand logo was dropped from these revolvers.

	100%	98%	95%	90%	80%	70%	60%
	$210	$180	$150	$125	$100	$85	$75

H&A NEW MODEL AUTOMATIC HAMMER REVOLVER - similar to top break with hammer, produced in small and large frame, in .22 rimfire, .32 and .38 centerfire cal.

	$170	$140	$120	$100	$85	$75	$65

H&A SOLID FRAME - .32 and .38 centerfire cal., five shot, double action, hammer or "bobbed" hammer.

	$175	$140	$120	$100	$85	$70	$55

H&A XL MODEL - similar to above in .22, .32 and .38 cal.

	$160	$140	$120	$100	$85	$70	$55

H&A RANGE MODEL - .22, .32 and .38 cal., solid frame, loading gate on right side, wood target style grips, single or double action (two models, large and small frames).

	$200	$175	$140	$120	$100	$85	$70

H&A TRIPLE ACTION SAFETY POLICE REVOLVER - .22, .32 and .38 cal., top break with newly designed locking mechanism, hard rubber or pearl grips (considered to be one of the best designed breaktops in its time). Other options for this model included hammerless, engraved, and wood target or pearl grips.

	$375	$340	$310	$275	$235	$200	$185

H&A NEW VEST POCKET DERRINGER - .22 Short rimfire cal., single shot, tip up, single action, 3 1/2 in. overall length, folding trigger, blue or nickel finish, wood or pearl grips with golden monograms. This model was first listed about 1910 and known as the "Parrot Beak." It is estimated that less than one thousand were produced, and they are very rare.

	$2,375	$2,100	$1,800	$1,550	$1,250	$950	$650

H&A NEW MODEL TARGET PISTOL - .22 rimfire cal., single shot top break with the same new locking mechanism as the Safety Police Revolver, wood target grips with golden monograms, blue finish and 6, 8, or 10 in. barrels.

	$565	$495	$440	$375	$325	$285	$250

H&A NEW MODEL SKELETON STOCK TARGET PISTOL - similar to above, with rounded hard rubber grips with logo, detachable "skeleton metal stock," 18 in. barrel, and blue finish.

	$850	$775	$675	$600	$550	$500	$465

RIFLES

Hopkins & Allen started building "falling block" rifles circa 1887-1914 with the buy-out of the Baystate Arms Company. Most commonly seen is the "Junior" model, known after 1902 as 922, 925, and 932. These numbers were in reference to the catalog numbers, not model numbers. In the very late 1890s or early 1900s, the Number 722, 822, and 832 rifles were added. In 1906, a "bolt action" repeater was added to their line, followed in 1909 by a "bolt action" single shot "military." Specific calibers have not been listed in this section.

Add $60-$75 for Lyman tang sights on the following models.

NUMBER 922 - .22 cal. rimfire, falling block, lever operated, with round bbl.

	$310	$245	$195	$195	$165	$125	$110

NUMBER 925 - similar to above in .25 cal. rimfire.

	$390	$310	$245	$195	$150	$110	$95

NUMBER 932 - similar to above in .32 cal. rimfire.

	$310	$245	$195	$150	$110	$95	$80

NUMBER 938 - similar to above in .38 S&W centerfire.

	$440	$350	$285	$225	$200	$175	$150

NUMBER 1922 - similar to above in .22 cal. rimfire with octagon bbl.

	$310	$250	$200	$180	$165	$150	$125

GRADING - PPGS™	100%	98%	95%	90%	80%	70%	60%

NUMBER 1932 - similar to above in .32 cal. rimfire.

	$310	$250	$200	$165	$125	$110	$90

NUMBER 2922 - similar to above in .22 cal. rimfire, with checkering.

	$420	$335	$265	$225	$195	$175	$150

NUMBER 2932 - similar to above in .32 cal. rimfire.

	$420	$335	$265	$225	$195	$175	$150

NUMBER 3922 - similar to above in .22 cal. rimfire, "SCHUETZEN RIFLE," nickeled Swiss buttplate, octagon barrel (Schuetzen rifles in good cond. are somewhat rare).

	$775	$620	$495	$450	$400	$365	$325

NUMBER 3925 - similar to above in .25-20 WCF (this caliber rifle is more rare than the .22 cal. rimfire).

	$1,010	$810	$650	$600	$550	$500	$450

NUMBER 44XL - chambered for the 44XL shotshell, similar to Number 922, except has smooth bore (referred to as "TAXIDERMIST'S" or "LADIES GUN").

	$530	$430	$350	$325	$275	$235	$200

NUMBER 722 - .22 cal. rimfire, rolling block, thumb operated.

	$300	$240	$195	$165	$125	$110	$90

SCOUT MILITARY RIFLE - similar to above with military style stock and with a "Bonneted Indian" stamped on the left side of frame (these are somewhat rare).

	$505	$405	$325	$285	$250	$200	$175

NUMBER 822 - .22 cal. rimfire, rolling block, lever operated.

	$300	$240	$195	$175	$150	$125	$100

NUMBER 832 - .32 cal. rimfire, otherwise similar to Model 822 (this model was offered first with "pig tail" type levers and later with "loop" type levers. The "loop" levers are somewhat rare).

	$350	$280	$225	$200	$175	$150	$125

NUMBER 4922 - .22 rimfire cal., bolt action, repeater.

	$260	$205	$165	$135	$120	$100	$80

NUMBER 5022 - similar to above with deluxe checkering.

	$340	$270	$215	$175	$150	$135	$100

MILITARY RIFLE - similar to above, except single shot with military style stock and sling (in good condition, these are somewhat rare).

	$490	$395	$315	$250	$225	$200	$185

NOISELESS - .22 rimfire, similar to the Number 922, except for checkered wood and the addition of a noise suppressor attached to the muzzle, by means of mating threads inside of suppressor and outside of barrel. The machining/threading is so precise, that it is difficult to recognize the suppressor. The front sight is attached to a dovetail slot in the suppressor. These rifles are listed under the National Firearms Act of 1934 and must have proper licensing. Very rare.

	$690	$625	$575	$500	$450	$395	$325

SHOTGUNS: SxS

Hopkins & Allen purchased Forehand Arms Co. and W.H. Davenport and continued to produce their line of firearms, and after a few years dropped the Forehand name. In 1902, they offered the Forehand double boxlocks with or without outside hammers. Most models were offered in 12, 16 & 20 gauge. Sidelocks were added 1906-09. In 1902, the AA GRADE, a very high quality boxlock, was offered for $100 to $125. It had fine damascus barrels, straight grip, plain or automatic ejectors, fine wood, and engraving, and was competitive with some Remingtons, L.C. Smiths, Bakers and other fine guns of that era. This gun was very short lived and today is rare. One feature found on all H&A double barrel guns is the "rib extension" or "doll's head."

GRADING - PPGS™	100%	98%	95%	90%	80%	70%	60%

BOXLOCK - Anson & Deeley type frame, damascus, twist, and steel barrels.

	$315	$275	$235	$195	$160	$130	$95

BOXLOCK - similar to above, except with outside hammers.

	$315	$275	$235	$195	$160	$130	$95

SIDELOCK - hammerless, damascus, twist, and steel barrels.

	$315	$275	$235	$195	$160	$130	$115

SIDELOCK - similar to above, except with outside hammers.

	$315	$275	$235	$195	$160	$130	$95

SHOTGUNS: SINGLE SHOT

H&A produced a "falling block" shotgun in most gauges circa 1887-early 1900s. Falling Blocks (FBs) in 12 ga. were built on heavy frames with the 20 and 16 gauges sharing a medium frame. Prior to 1902, some FBs were chambered for .45-70 shotshells and, today, these are rare if in good condition. From the 1890s through 1914, 38XL, 44XL shotshell guns were periodically offered in the Junior frame. After 1902, "tip-over" single shotguns were offered in Forehand designs and, later, the Davenport designs.

FALLING BLOCK - lever operated, outside hammer.

	$275	$235	$210	$180	$160	$145	$125

BOXLOCK - with outside hammer, damascus, twist, and steel barrels.

	$190	$170	$150	$130	$110	$95	$80

BOXLOCK - hammerless, top safety.

	$190	$170	$150	$130	$110	$95	$80

GOOSE GUNS - outside hammer, 8, 10, or 12 ga., were offered with barrels up to 40 inches long.

	$250	$225	$190	$170	$150	$135	$115

"SAFETY SINGLE GUN" - engraved with outside hammer and top safety. Was offered in 1911 and recommended for trap shooting for $15.00.

	$250	$225	$195	$175	$155	$140	$125

HORTON, LEW, DIST. CO.

See Lew Horton Dist. Co. listing.

HOWA

Current manufacturer established in 1967, and located in Tokyo, Japan. Howa sporting rifles are currently imported beginning Oct., 1999 by Legacy Sports International, LLC, located in Reno, NV. Previously located in Alexandria, VA. Previously imported until 1999 by Interarms/Howa, located in Alexandria, VA, Weatherby (Vanguard Series only), Smith & Wesson (pre-1985), and Mossberg (1986-1987).

RIFLES: BOLT ACTION

Howa also manufactures barreled actions in various configurations. MSRs range from $405-$560.

MODEL 1500 HUNTER - various cals., 3 (Mag. or WSM cals. only) or 5 shot, 22 or 24 in. barrel, adj. rear sight and trigger, checkered walnut stock, blue metal finish or stainless steel (new 1999) construction, approx. 7.6 lbs. Imported by Interarms 1988 only, reintroduced by Legacy 1999-2006.

	$460	$345	$295	$250	$215	$175	$160

Last MSR was $574.

Add $21 for Mag. cals.
Add $108 for stainless steel.

GRADING - PPGS™	100%	98%	95%	90%	80%	70%	60%

MODEL 1500+/1500 LIGHTNING - various cals., lightweight variation of the Model 1500 Hunter featuring heavy (new 2007) or lightweight regular or Carbolite (disc.) black synthetic stock with cheekpiece and pressed checkering or Realtree camo (new 2005), 22 or 24 in. barrel, no sights, 3 or 5 shot mag., blue or stainless steel, approx. 7-7.6 lbs. Imported 1988-1991, reimportation began 1993.

MSR $506	$435	$385	$325	$275	$235	$210	$175

Last MSR was $539 when disc. in 1991.

> Add $21 for standard Mag. cals. or $27 for WSM cals.
> Add $187 for camo stock and stainless steel barrel.
> Add $77 for camo stock (scope not included).
> Add $99 for heavy blue barrel w/camo stock.
> Add $223 for heavy stainless barrel w/camo stock.
> Add $156 for scope package with Leupold VX-I scope.

The Model 1500+ was introduced during 2005, and features a three position safety.
During 2007, this model is supplied with a Nikko Sterling scope with rings and bases (black polymer stock only).

MODEL 1500+/1500 ULTRALIGHT - .22-250 Rem., .223 Rem., .243 Win., .308 Win. (new 2003), or 7mm-08 Rem. (new 2003) cal., 20 in. barrel, short bolt throw, non-glare blue, blue/black metal, or stainless steel finish, laminated hardwood stock with black textured coating, 5 shot mag., w/o sights, Youth model with 12 5/8 in. LOP introduced 2003, 6.4 lbs. Importation began 2002.

MSR $599	$485	$385	$335	$295	$250	$225	$200

> Add $149 for stainless steel (.308 Win. or 7mm-08 cals. only).
> Subtract $16 for Nikko scope package.

The Model 1500+ was introduced during 2005, and features a three position safety.

MODEL 1500 VARMINT - .204 Ruger (new 2006), .22-250 Rem., .223 Rem., .243 Win. (new 2005), or .308 Win. (mfg. 1990-92, reintroduced 2001) cal., 24 in. heavy barrel without sights, 5 shot mag., blue steel or stainless steel (new 1999) construction, black polymer (new 1999), 100% Realtree camo (new 2005), or walnut stock, approx. 9.3 lbs. Imported 1988-92, and from 2001-2006.

MSR $546	$450	$365	$310	$245	$210	$175	$160

> Add $64 for wood stock.
> Add $36 for camo.
> Add $118 for stainless steel.

MODEL 1500 AXIOM VARMINTER - various cals., 20 or 24 in. heavy blue barrel, 4 or 5 shot mag., choice of black aluminum, black synthetic, or camo synthetic Knoxx Industries stock (with patented recoil reduction). New 2007.

MSR $911	$795	$700	$625	$550	$500	$400	$300

> Add $147 for camo stock.
> Add $360 for black aluminum stock.
> Add approx. $130 for rifle package with Nikko Platinum scope, rings and bases.

MODEL 1500+/1500 SUPREME - available in various standard and Mag. cals. between .22-250 Rem. - .338 Win. Mag., 22 or 24 in. barrel, 3 or 5 shot mag., choice of JRS Classic, black (Varminter only), Thumbhole Sporter, Varminter, or Thumbhole Varminter stock configuration available in either pepper or nutmeg finish, blue metal finish or stainless steel, 8-9.9 lbs. Importation began 2003.

The Model 1500+ was introduced during 2005, and features a three position safety.

* *Model 1500+/1500 Supreme JRS Classic* - standard stock configuration, w/o sights, 8 lbs. Imported 2003-2006.

	$515	$395	$340	$300	$265	$240	$220

Last MSR was $646.

> Add $109 for stainless steel.
> Add $29 for Mag. cals.

GRADING - PPGS™	100%	98%	95%	90%	80%	70%	60%

❋ *Model 1500+/1500 Supreme Varminter* - .204 Ruger (new 2006), .22-250 Rem., .223 Rem., .243 Win. (new 2005) or .308 Win. cal., nutmeg, pepper, or black synthetic stock, 9.3 lbs. Importation began 2003.

	100%	98%	95%	90%	80%	70%	60%
MSR $756	$600	$450	$375	$335	$300	$275	$250

Add $108 for stainless steel.

❋ *Model 1500+/1500 Supreme Varminter Thumbhole* - similar to Supreme Varminter, except has thumbhole stock configuration. Importation began 2003.

MSR $774	$615	$450	$395	$350	$315	$285	$225

Add $113 for stainless steel.

❋ *Model 1500+/1500 Supreme Thumbhole Sporter* - similar to Thumbhole Varminter, except has 22 in. barrel, nutmeg and pepper colored stock only, 8 lbs. Importation began 2003.

MSR $721	$575	$410	$355	$310	$275	$250	$225

Add $113 for stainless steel.
Add $29 for standard Mag. cals. or $60 for WSM cals.

MODEL 1500 CUSTOM - .300 Win. Mag. or .300 WSM cal., 22 or 24 (.300 Win. Mag. cal. only) in. barrel, black polymer or laminate wood in either the Classic JRS or thumbhole configuration, 3 shot mag., blue (.300 Win. Mag. cal. only) or stainless steel barrel and action, 7.6-8.1 lbs. Imported 2002-2004.

	$775	$695	$625	$550	$500	$465	$435

Last MSR was $858.

Add $30 for JRS nutmeg finish stock and blued finish.
Add $102 for JRS laminate stock.
Add $131 for thumbhole laminate stock in pepper finish.

MODEL 1500 TEXAS SAFARI - .270 Win. or .300 Win. Mag. cal., features Howa M-1500 barreled action with Bill Wiseman recontoured bolt sleeve and receiver, bolt release, and 3-position safety, 3 or 5 shot mag., non-glare blue Teflon metal finish, brown laminate glass bedded stock, individually test fired, approx. 7.8 lbs. Imported 2002-2003.

	$1,350	$1,150	$950	$825	$675	$575	$500

Last MSR was $1,580.

Add $240 for .300 Win. Mag. cal.

This model was also available as a complete custom rifle with many options and special orders.

MODEL 1500 PCS - .308 Win. cal., police counter sniper rifle featuring 24 in. barrel, choice of blue metal or stainless steel, black synthetic or checkered walnut stock, no sights, approx. 9.3 lbs. Imported 1999-2000.

	$385	$315	$265	$225	$195	$175	$160

Last MSR was $465.

Add $20 for wood stock.
Add $60 for stainless steel.

MODEL 1500 TROPHY - .22-250 Rem., .223 Rem., .243 Win., .270 Win., .308 Win., .30-06, .300 Win. Mag., .338 Win. Mag. or 7mm Rem. Mag. cal., 3 (Mag. cals. only) or 5 shot, 22 or 24 in. barrel, adj. rear sight and trigger, select Monte Carlo stock with skipline checkering. Imported 1988-92.

	$528	$410	$335	$290	$260	$240	$225

Last MSR was $528.

Add $20 for Mag. cals.

MODEL 1500 HOGUE - .204 Ruger, .223 Rem., .22-250 Rem., .243 Win., .25-06, .270 Win., .30-06, .308 Win., .300 Win. Mag., .338 Win. Mag., 7mm Rem. Mag., .300 WSM, .270 WSM, or 7mm WSM cal., 22 or 24 in. blue or stainless regular or heavy varmint barrel, 3, 4, or 5 shot mag., choice of black or green Hogue overmolded stock, 7.6 - 9.3 (heavy barrel) lbs. New 2007.

MSR $546	$450	$365	$310	$245	$210	$175	$160

Add $31 for standard Mag. cals. or $57 for WSM cals. w/blue barrel.

GRADING - PPGS™	100%	98%	95%	90%	80%	70%	60%

Add $28 for Mag. cals. or $58 for WSM cals. w/stainless steel barrel.
Add $122 for stainless steel.
Add $61 for varmint configuration w/heavy barrel.
Add $53 for Nikko Stirling Platinum night eater scope package.

LIGHTNING WOODGRAIN - .243 Win., .270 Win., .30-06, .308 Win., or 7mm Rem. Mag. cal., features lightweight Carbolite synthetic stock with simulated wood grain and checkering, 22 in. barrel, 5 shot mag., no sights, 7 1/2 lbs. Imported 1994 only.

	$450	$395	$365	$320	$275	$250	$225

Last MSR was $537.

Add $19 for 7mm Rem. Mag. cal.

REALTREE CAMO RIFLE - .270 Win. or .30-06 (disc. 1993) cal., 22 in. barrel, 5 shot mag., monobloc receiver, drilled and tapped, thumb safety, entire rifle is coated with a Realtree brown leaf camo pattern, no sights, 8 lbs. Imported 1993-94.

	$495	$400	$350	$325	$300	$280	$260

Last MSR was $620.

HOWA/CHRISTENSEN CARBON FIBER RIFLE - .204 Ruger, .223 Rem., .22-250 Rem., .243 Win., or .308 Win. cal., 24 in. Christensen carbon fiber barrel, 4 or 5 shot mag., pepper colored TH Varminter stock, includes green Howa soft case, 8 lbs. Limited production beginning 2007.

MSR $1,923	$1,675	$1,425	$1,250	$1,000	$875	$750	$625

Add $153 for Nikko Stirling Night Eater scope package.

HUG-SAN

Previous shotgun manufacturer located in Huglu, Turkey until 2000.

Hug-San manufactured slide action, semi-auto, and O/U shotguns, in various configurations and gauges.

HUGLU

Current shotgun manufacturer established in 1962, and located in Huglu, Turkey. Currently imported beginning 2005 by CZ-USA, located in Kansas City, KS. Previously imported 2002-2004 by Armsco Firearms Corp., located in Des Plaines, IL, and from 1999-2002 by Huglu USA, located in Rigby, ID.

Huglu makes a wide variety of quality O/U, semi-auto, and SxS shotguns available in all gauges, and are now imported exclusively by CZ-USA. Please refer to the CZ section for current models and pricing. Some Huglu models were imported 1999-2002 by Huglu USA, and are stamped "Huglu USA, Rigby, ID" on the barrel. Huglu USA Ltd. Co. was reorganized in January 2003 as H-Legacy Shotguns Ltd. Co., and is now a Huglu dealer. For more information, including current models, prices, and U.S. availability, please contact CZ-USA directly (see Trademark Index).

SHOTGUNS: O/U

Armsco previously imported the 103 Series. Models with last MSRs included: 103D - $679 MSR, 103D Mini (28 ga. or .410 bore) - $849 MSR, 103DE (ejectors) - $849 MSR, 103C (case colored receiver) - $799 MSR, 103C Mini - MSR $999, 103CE - $949 MSR, 103F - $949, 103F Mini - $1,199 MSR, 103FE - $1,099 MSR, 103FEC - $1,199 MSR, 103FC Mini - $1,299 MSR., 104A $499 - MSR, and 104A Mini - $699 MSR.

SHOTGUNS: SxS

Armsco's previous lineup of Huglu SxS shotguns through 2003 with last MSRs included: 201A - $899 MSR, 201AC (choke tubes) - $999 MSR, 201A Mini - $1,099, 201AC Mini - $1,199, 202B - $599 MSR, 202B Mini - $799 MSR, 202BCB - $599 MSR, and the 200ACB - $799 MSR.

Current SxS models include: the Bobwhite - $699 MSR, Bobwhite Silver - $899 MSR, Ringneck - $999 MSR, Ringneck Small Gauge - $1,199 MSR, Woodcock - disc. 2004, last MSR was $1,049, Woodcock Small Gauge - disc. 2004, last MSR was $1,299, Woodcock Deluxe - disc. 2004, last MSR was $1,199, Amarillo - $699 MSR, and the Durango - $849 MSR.

GRADING - PPGS™	100%	98%	95%	90%	80%	70%	60%

SHOTGUNS: SEMI-AUTO

Armsco previous lineup of Huglu's semi-auto shotguns through 2003 with last MSRs included: 501GA - $499 MSR, 501GB - $499 MSR, 601GA - $499 MSR, 601GB - $499 MSR, 601GM (3 1/2 in. chamber) - $599 MSR, 701GA - $499 MSR, and the 701GB - $499 MSR.

SHOTGUNS: SINGLE SHOT

Armsco imported the Model 301A. MSR was $199.

HUNTER ARMS COMPANY

Previous manufacturer located in Fulton, NY circa 1891-1945.

The Hunter Arms Company was formed to manufacture L.C. Smith shotguns circa 1891. During 1915, Hunter Arms began producing its own line of shotguns. Please refer to the L.C. Smith section in this text for further information regarding this manufacturer (including Fulton, Fulton Special, and Hunter Special models).

HUSQVARNA

Previous manufacturer located in Husqvarna, Sweden.

Also see: Lahti Pistols.

RIFLES: BOLT ACTION

HI-POWER - .220 Swift, .270 Win., or .30-06 cal., Mauser type action, open sight, checkered beech wood. Mfg. 1946-51, early models found in 6.5x55mm, 8x57R, 9.3x57mm cals.

	100%	98%	95%	90%	80%	70%	60%
	$625	$550	$500	$450	$400	$365	$335

MODEL 1951 - similar to Hi-Power, except high profile stock.

	$500	$465	$425	$385	$340	$300	$270

SERIES 1100 DELUXE - similar to Model 1951, except has European walnut and jeweled bolt. Mfg. 1952-56.

	$520	$480	$440	$360	$330	$310	$290

SERIES 1000 SUPER GRADE - similar to Model 1951, has walnut Monte Carlo stock. Mfg. 1952-56.

	$520	$480	$440	$360	$330	$310	$290

SERIES 3100 CROWN GRADE - .243 Win., .270 Win., .30-06, 7x57mm, or .308 Win. cal., improved HVA Mauser action, 24 in. barrel, walnut stock, black forend tip and pistol grip cap. Mfg. 1954-72.

	$575	$525	$475	$400	$360	$330	$315

SERIES 3000 CROWN GRADE - similar to 3100, except has Monte Carlo stock.

	$660	$595	$525	$475	$400	$360	$330

SERIES 4100 LIGHTWEIGHT - HVA Mauser action, calibers same as 3100, 20 1/2 in. barrel, open sights, lightweight walnut stock, pistol grip, Schnabel forend. Mfg. 1954-72.

	$575	$525	$475	$400	$360	$330	$315

SERIES 4000 LIGHTWEIGHT - similar to 4100, except has Monte Carlo stock, no sights.

	$660	$595	$525	$475	$400	$360	$330

MODEL 456 LIGHTWEIGHT - similar to 4000/4100, except full length stock. Mfg. 1959-70.

	$600	$550	$495	$415	$385	$360	$330

SERIES 6000 IMPERIAL GRADE - similar to 3100, except has select wood, 3 leaf folding sight. Mfg. 1968-70.

	$695	$625	$575	$495	$470	$440	$395

GRADING - PPGS™	100%	98%	95%	90%	80%	70%	60%

SERIES 7000 IMPERIAL LIGHTWEIGHT - similar to 6000 Imperial, except 20 1/2 in. barrel, lightweight stock.

	$775	$695	$625	$575	$495	$470	$440

SERIES P-3000 PRESENTATION - similar to Crown, except engraved action, special wood. Mfg. 1968-70.

	$925	$850	$775	$675	$575	$500	$450

MODEL 9000 CROWN GRADE - cals. similar to Model 3100 Crown Grade, except also available in .300 Win. Mag. cal., Husqvarna action, 23 1/2 in. barrel, adj. trigger, adj. sight, walnut stock. Mfg. 1971-72.

	$575	$525	$475	$400	$360	$330	$315

MODEL 8000 IMPERIAL - similar to 9000, but jeweled bolt, engraved floor plate, no sights and deluxe stock. Mfg. 1971-1972.

	$750	$675	$595	$525	$495	$470	$415

SHOTGUNS: SxS

Husqvarna also manufactured limited quantities of SxS shotguns in various configurations. Most of these shotguns are currently selling in the $375-$1,200 range, depending on the desirability of the configuration and original condition.

HY-HUNTER INC. FIREARMS MANUFACTURING CO.

Previous trademark imported by Hy-Hunter Inc., located in Hollywood, CA.

Hy-Hunter Inc. imported single action revolvers in various calibers and O/U derringers manufactured in West Germany. Typically, prices are determined by their shooting value rather than their collector value. Prices generally range from $100-$175 depending on caliber and finish.

HYPER

Previous manufacturer located in Jenks, OK.

RIFLES: SINGLE SHOT

SINGLE SHOT RIFLE - all calibers, all standard lengths and contours, falling block trigger guard lever activated, adj. trigger, no sights, stocked to customer specifications, in AA grade walnut. Disc. 1984.

	$2,200	$1,980	$1,925	$1,870	$1,650	$1,540	$1,375

Add $75 for stainless barrel.
Add $85 for octagon barrel.

NOTES

I SECTION

I.A.B. srl

Current manufacturer (Industria Armi Bresciane) of modern firearms, black powder replicas and historical Sharps rifles located in Gardone, Valtrompia, Brescia, Italy. Currently imported by E.M.F., located in Santa Ana, CA, Dixie Gun Works, located in Union City, TN, Kiesler's, located in Jeffersonville, IN, and Tristar Sporting Arms, located in Kansas City, MO. Previously imported by American Arms, located in Kansas City, MO. Previously distributed by Sporting Arms International, Inc. located in Indianola, MS.

Please refer to indiviual importers for model information and pricing.

I.A.B. also manufactures shotguns (O/U and single barrel trap or skeet) in various styles and configurations including combo sets. These guns employ a boxlock action, have ejectors, and various amounts of engraving. Prices for 100% condition usually start in the $650-$1,000 price range. I.A.B. shotguns are not being imported currently - values for older models will be determined by the prices shooters, not collectors, are willing to pay for them.

IAC

Please refer to Interstate Arms corp. listing.

IAI

Please refer to Intrac Arms International LLC listing.

IAI INC. - AMERICAN LEGEND

Previous manufacturer, importer, and distributor located in Houston, TX. Firearms were manufactured by Israel Arms International, Inc., located in Houston, TX. IAI designates Israel Arms International, and should not be confused with Irwindale Arms, Inc. (also IAI).

The models listed were part of an American Legend Series that are patterned after famous American and Belgian military carbines/rifles and semi-auto pistols.

GRADING - PPGS™	100%	98%	95%	90%	80%	70%	60%

CARBINES/RIFLES

MODEL 888 M1 CARBINE - .22 LR or .30 Carbine cal., 18 in. barrel, mfg. from new original M1 parts and stock by IAI (barrel bolt and receiver) and unused GI parts, 10 shot mag., choice of birch or walnut stock, parkerized finish, metal or wood handguard, 5 1/2 lbs. Mfg. by IAI in Houston, TX 1998-2004.

	100%	98%	95%	90%	80%	70%	60%
	$475	$395	$365	$335	$295	$260	$240

Last MSR was $556.

Add $11 for .22 LR cal.
Add $31 for walnut/metal forearm or $47 for walnut/wood forearm.

MODEL 333 M1 GARAND - .30-06 cal., patterned after the WWII M1 Garand, 24 in. barrel, 8 shot en-bloc mag., parkerized finish, 9 1/2 lbs. Mfg. 2003-2004.

	100%	98%	95%	90%	80%	70%	60%
	$850	$775	$675	$575	$475	$375	$325

Last MSR was $972.

PISTOLS: SEMI-AUTO

MODEL 2000 - .45 ACP cal., patterned after the Colt Govt. 1911, 5 or 4 1/4 (Commander configuration, Model 2000-C) in. barrel, parkerized finish, plastic or rubber finger groove grips, 36-38 oz. Mfg. in South Africa 2002-2004.

	100%	98%	95%	90%	80%	70%	60%
	$415	$365	$325	$295	$275	$250	$225

Last MSR was $465.

GRADING - PPGS™	100%	98%	95%	90%	80%	70%	60%

I A I

Please refer to the Irwindale Arms, Inc. heading in this section.

IAR, Inc.

Current importer and distributor since 1995 located in San Juan Capistrano, CA.

IAR, Inc. (International Antique Reproductions, Inc.) imports and distributes a wide variety of firearms, including SA revolvers, rolling block pistols, rolling block target rifles, Henry rifle reproductions, baby rolling block carbines, exposed hammer shotguns, and reproduction rifles and carbines. IAR, Inc. also imports black powder reproductions and replicas, plus a complete lineup of blank firing arms and ammunition, including pistols, revolvers, and rifles. Please contact the company directly regarding their current product lineup and consumer pricing (see Trademark Index).

Black Powder Reproductions & Replicas by Dennis Adler is also an invaluable source for most black powder reproductions and replicas, and includes hundreds of color images on most popular makes/models, provides manufacturer/trademark histories, and up-to-date information on related items/accessories for black powder shooting - www.bluebookinc.com

I G A/STOEGER SHOTGUNS

Current trademark with manufacturing facilities located in Vera-nopolis, Brazil (O/U and SxS shotguns only), and by Vursan Man-ufacturing (semi-auto shotguns only) beginning in 2000, located in Istanbul, Turkey. Currently imported by Stoeger Industries, Inc. located in Accokeek, MD. Previously located in Wayne, NJ.

During 2000, Stoeger Industries was purchased by Beretta USA Corp., located in Accokeek, MD. Currently manufactured shotguns have Stoeger markings, but earlier guns were marked I G A.

SHOTGUNS: O/U

CONDOR MODEL - 12 ga. only, single trigger, ejectors, presentation walnut, chrome lined bores. Disc. 1985.

	$580	$500	$450	$410	$375	$350	$325

Last MSR was $667.

CONDOR I SINGLE TRIGGER - 12, 16 (new 2006), 20 ga. or .410 bore (new 2005), 3 in. chambers, boxlock action, deluxe checkered walnut, extractors, 26 or 28 in. VR separated barrels with chokes tubes (standard beginning 1992), 7.7 lbs.

MSR $399	$350	$315	$265	$230	$210	$195	$180

Add $150 for Condor combo, including set of 12 ga. and 20 ga. barrels (new 2004).

This model is also available in a Youth model with 22 in. barrels and 13 in. LOP stock in 20 ga. or .410 bore.

CONDOR II DOUBLE TRIGGER - 12 or 20 (disc.) ga., boxlock action, VR, check-ered walnut, separated barrels. Disc. 1997.

	$350	$295	$260	$230	$195	$170	$150

Last MSR was $459.

CONDOR I SPECIAL - similar to Condor I, except features matte stainless steel receiver, oil finished hardwood stock and forearm. Imported 2002-2006.

	$365	$325	$275	$235	$215	$195	$180

Last MSR was $415.

Add $135 for Condor combo, including set of 12 ga. and 20 ga. barrels (new 2004).

CONDOR SUPREME - 12 or 20 ga., boxlock action, single trigger, ejectors, 26 or 28 in. VR barrels with choke tubes, deluxe checkered walnut stock and fore-arm. Imported 1995-2000.

	$500	$450	$395	$360	$320	$280	$240

Last MSR was $629.

GRADING - PPGS™	100%	98%	95%	90%	80%	70%	60%

CONDOR SUPREME DELUXE - 12 or 20 ga., 3 in. chambers, 24 (20 ga. only), 26, or 30 (disc. 2001) in. VR barrels with choke tubes, high polish blue, gold SST, AE, checkered AA grade high gloss American walnut stock and forearm, approx. 7.7 lbs. Importation began 2000.

MSR $599	$525	$440	$385	$345	$300	$285	$265

Add $120 for Condor combo, including set of 12 ga. and 20 ga. barrels (new 2004).

CONDOR OUTBACK - 12 or 20 ga., 3 in. chambers, 20 in. barrels with screw-in chokes, ST, extractors, choice of checkered walnut or black painted walnut stock and forearm, rifle sights, separated barrels, blue or polished nickel finish, 6 1/2 - 7 lbs. New 2007.

MSR $369	$325	$270	$230	$210	$195	$180	$160

Add $80 for polished nickel metal.

CONDOR COMPETITION - 12 or 20 ga., 3 in. chambers, 30 in. ported barrels with choke tubes, SST, AE, checkered AA grade select American walnut stock and forearm. New 2005.

MSR $599	$525	$440	$385	$345	$300	$285	$265

Add $230 for Condor combo with 12 and 20 ga. barrels (new 2007).

TURKEY SERIES - 12 ga. only, 3 in. chambers, 26 in. VR barrels with choke tubes, ST, ejectors, Advantage camo on wood and metal (except receiver). Mfg. 1997-2000.

	$615	$525	$450	$380	$335	$300	$270

Last MSR was $729.

HUNTER CLAYS MODEL - 12 ga. only, ST, ejectors, 28 in. barrels with choke tubes, deluxe checkered stock and forearm, gold trigger. Mfg. 1997-99.

	$595	$515	$435	$375	$335	$300	$270

Last MSR was $699.

WATERFOWL SERIES - 12 ga. only, 3 in. chambers, similar to Turkey Series, except has 30 in. barrels. Mfg. 1998-2000.

	$615	$525	$450	$380	$335	$300	$270

Last MSR was $729.

TRAP SERIES - 12 ga., features SST, ejectors, 30 in. VR barrels with choke tubes, deluxe checkered Monte Carlo stock and forearm. Mfg. 1998-99.

	$595	$515	$435	$375	$335	$300	$270

Last MSR was $699.

ERA 2000 MODELS - 12 ga. only, 26 or 28 in. VR barrels with choke tubes, single trigger. Imported 1992-94.

	$585	$375	$315	$250	$215	$195	$180

Last MSR was $710.

SHOTGUNS: SxS

UPLANDER MODEL - 12, 16 (new 1996), 20, 28 ga., or .410 bore, 3 in. chambers, 24 (English style stock only), 26, or 28 in. barrels with extractors, DT, underlug lockup, checkered satin finished grade A pistol grip or straight English (20 ga. or .410 bore only) stock.

MSR $369	$325	$250	$200	$160	$140	$125	$110

Subtract approx. 10% if w/o choke tubes.

This model is also available in a Youth variation in 20 ga. or .410 bore with 22 in. barrels and shortened LOP.

UPLANDER SPECIAL - 12, 20, or 28 ga., 3 in. chambers (not available in 28 ga.), 24 or 26 in. barrels, fixed chokes on 28 ga., features straight grip Brazilian hardwood checkered English stock and forearm, DT, approx. 7.3 lbs. Mfg. 2002-2005.

	$340	$300	$260	$230	$200	$165	$125

Last MSR was $375.

GRADING - PPGS™	100%	98%	95%	90%	80%	70%	60%

UPLANDER SUPREME - 12 or 20 ga., 3 in. chambers, 24 (20 ga. only), 26, or 28 in. barrels with choke tubes, extractors, gold ST, high gloss AA grade checkered walnut stock and forearm. Importation began 2000.

MSR $489	$425	$375	$325	$285	$235	$200	$175

Add $160 for combo package (includes 12 and 20 ga. or 20 and 28 ga. barrels, new 2005).

DELUXE MODEL - 12, 20, 28 ga., or .410 bore, features better quality checkered walnut stock and forearm, gold triggers, 12 and 20 ga. have choke tubes, 28 ga. and .410 bore have fixed chokes. Mfg. 1997-99.

	$425	$365	$310	$270	$230	$195	$170

Last MSR was $559.

Subtract $40 for 28 ga. or .410 bore (fixed chokes only).

COACH GUN MODEL - 12, 20 ga., or .410 (new 1991) bore, hammerless, choice of blue or nickel (new 1996) finish, 20 in. barrels with choke tubes or fixed chokes (.410 bore, IC/M), choice of dark (nickel finish only) or light hardwood stock, 6 1/2 lbs.

MSR $369	$315	$260	$210	$165	$135	$110	$100

Add $100 for polished or matte nickel finish.
Add $64 for carved stagecoach scene on stock (mfg. 1996-99).

✳ Coach Gun Model Deluxe - similar to Coach Gun Model, includes deluxe checkered walnut stock and forearm, fixed (IC/M) or choke tubes (new 1998), gold triggers. Mfg. 1997-99.

	$385	$325	$290	$260	$230	$195	$170

Last MSR was $499.

COACH GUN SILVERADO - similar to Coach Gun, except features a matte nickel metal finish and oil finished hardwood pistol grip or straight English (not available in .410 bore) stock and forearm. Imported 2002-2004.

	$320	$270	$215	$180	$150	$130	$110

Last MSR was $375.

COACH GUN SUPREME - 12, 20 ga. or .410 bore (disc. 2005), blue, polished nickel, or stainless steel receiver, blue or polished nickel 20 or 24 (disc. 2005) in. barrels with choke tubes (except for .410 bore), checkered AA grade walnut stock with recoil pad and beavertail forearm, DT, extractors. Importation began 2004.

MSR $469	$400	$325	$250	$200	$160	$130	$110

TURKEY SERIES MODEL - 12 ga. only, 3 in. chambers, 24 in. barrels, DT, choke tubes. Mfg. 1997-2000.

	$425	$365	$310	$270	$230	$195	$170

Last MSR was $559.

SHOTGUNS : SEMI-AUTO

MODEL 2000 - 12 ga. only, 3 in. chamber, Benelli licensed inertia recoil operating system, 26, 28, or 30 in. VR barrel with 5 choke tubes, checkered walnut or black synthetic (new 2002) stock and forearm, matte metal, 100% Advantage Timber HD camo (new 2002), AP GHD (new 2007), or Max-4 camo (new 2004) finish, approx. 7.1 lbs. Mfg. by Vursan Manufacturing located in Istanbul, Turkey, with importation beginning 2001.

MSR $479	$395	$345	$295	$260	$230	$195	$175

Add $70 for 100% camo coverage.
Add $20 for checkered walnut stock and forearm.
Add $56 for Turkey configuration with Timber HD steady grip and 24 in. barrel.
Add $75 for 13 oz. recoil reducer (synthetic or camo only).
Add $121 for Model 2000 Deluxe with upgraded wood and floral etched receiver trim (disc. 2003).

GRADING - PPGS™	100%	98%	95%	90%	80%	70%	60%

This model is also available as a combo package which includes a smoothbore slug barrel with screw-in IC choke and rifle sights - MSR is $645 in synthetic, $725 with camo, and $580 with walnut (disc. 2002).

✳ *Model 2000 Slug* - 12 ga. only, 3 in. chamber, available with walnut or synthetic with 100% Advantage Timber HD finish, 24 in. smoothbore barrel with adj. rifle sights, 6.7 lbs. Imported 2003-2004.

	100%	98%	95%	90%	80%	70%	60%
	$365	$320	$285	$250	$225	$195	$175

Last MSR was $430.

Add $15 for walnut stock and forearm.
Add $75 for 100% camo coverage.

SHOTGUNS : SINGLE BARREL

REUNA SINGLE BARREL - 12, 20 ga., or .410 bore, exposed hammer with half-cock, extractor. Disc. 1998.

	100%	98%	95%	90%	80%	70%	60%
	$95	$70	$60	$50	$45	$40	$35

Last MSR was $120.

Add $22 for choke tubes (12 ga. new 1992, 20 ga. new 1993).

✳ *Reuna Single Barrel Youth* - 20 ga. or .410 bore, 22 in. barrel, features rubber recoil pad. Imported 1993-98.

	100%	98%	95%	90%	80%	70%	60%
	$100	$75	$60	$50	$45	$40	$35

Last MSR was $132.

SINGLE BARREL CLASSIC - 12, 20 ga., or .410 bore, 3 in. chamber, break open action activated by moving triggerguard rearward, exposed hammer or hammerless (new 2003), 26 or 28 in. barrel with (new 2003) or w/o VR (disc. 2003), hardwood stock and forend, matte metal finish, Youth Model also available in 20 ga. or .410 bore (13 in. LOP), approx. 5 1/2 lbs. Mfg. 2002-2005.

	100%	98%	95%	90%	80%	70%	60%
	$95	$80	$65	$55	$45	$40	$35

Last MSR was $119.

Add $6 for Special Model with matte finished stainless steel receiver (new 2004).

SHOTGUNS : SLIDE ACTION

MODEL P350 - 12 ga. only, 3 1/2 in. chamber, 18 1/2 (Home Security, cyl. fixed choke), 24, 26, or 28 in. barrel, includes 5 screw-in chokes, choice of black synthetic, Timber HD, AP HGD or Max-4 HD camo coverage, approx. 6.9 lbs. New 2005.

	100%	98%	95%	90%	80%	70%	60%
MSR $309		$260	$220	$190	$165	$145	$120	$100

Add $80 for 100% camo coverage.
Add $75 for 13 oz. recoil reducer.
Add $10 for black synthetic pistol grip stock.
Add $76 for Turkey configuration with Timber HD steady grip and 24 in barrel or $110 for Turkey configuration with AP HD steady grip and 24 in. barrel.

I.O., INC.

Current importer located in Monroe, NC.

I.O. Inc. imports a wide variety of rifles and handguns, mostly from former Soviet bloc countries. One of their more popular models is the STG-2000C, based on a modified AK-74 platform. MSR is $469.

Please contact the company directly for more information on their current lineup of firearms and pricing (see Trademark Index).

IBERIA FIREARMS

Current manufacturer of .40 S&W cal. pistols located in Iberia, OH. Distributed by MKS Supply located in Dayton, OH. Distributor sales only.

Please refer to the Hi-Point section in this text.

GRADING - PPGS™	100%	98%	95%	90%	80%	70%	60%

IMPERIAL GUN CO. LTD

Previous manufacturer located in Surrey, Great Britain circa 1992-1995. The Imperial Gun Co. Ltd. had limited importation into the U.S.

Imperial Gun secondary marketplace values must be based realistically on their competitive shooting value, not collectibility.

INDIAN ARMS

Previous trademark manufactured by Indian Arms Corporation located in Detroit, MI.

PISTOLS: SEMI-AUTO

INDIAN ARMS .380 - .380 ACP cal., patterned after Walther PPK, stainless steel, 3 1/4 in. barrel, 6 shot mag., natural or blue finish, with (early specimens) or without key lock safety, with or without VR barrel, walnut grips, 20 oz. Mfg. 1975-77.

	$395	$285	$230	$180	$140	$125	$105

This model had limited manufacture with approx. 1,000 guns being made.

INDUSTRIA ARMI GALESI

Previous manufacturer located in Brescia, Italy.

PISTOLS: SEMI-AUTO

GALESI MODEL 6 POCKET AUTO - .22 LR or .25 ACP cal., 6 shot, 2 1/4 in. barrel blue, fixed sights, plastic grips. Mfg. 1930-disc.

	$165	$135	$120	$105	$90	$75	$65

Add 100% if chrome engraved.

GALESI MODEL 9 POCKET AUTO - .22 LR, .32 ACP, or .380 ACP cal., 8 shot, 3 1/4 in. barrel, blue, fixed sights, plastic grips. Mfg. 1930-disc.

	$195	$165	$130	$110	$100	$85	$65

Add 100% if chrome engraved.

INFALLIBLE

Previous trademark manufactured by Warner Arms Corp. located in Norwich, CT, and Davis-Warner Arms Corp. located in Assonet, MA.

PISTOLS: SEMI-AUTO

INFALLIBLE PISTOL - .32 ACP cal., 3.2 in. barrel, 7 shot mag., 24.7 oz.

✳ *Infallible Pistol Type I* - mfg. and marked "Warner Arms Corp., Norwich, Conn.", serial range is 501-2,299.

	$450	$325	$295	$270	$250	$225	$200

✳ *Infallible Pistol Type II* - marked "Davis-Warner Arms Corporation, Assonet, Massachusetts", serial range is 2,300-5,299.

	$400	$300	$250	$225	$195	$170	$150

✳ *Infallible Pistol Type III* - marked "Warner Arms Corporation, Norwich, Connecticut", serial range is 5,300-7,400.

	$400	$300	$250	$225	$195	$170	$150

INFINITY FIREARMS

Current trademark manufactured by Strayer-Voight Inc. since 1994 and located in Grand Prairie, TX. Currently distributed by JP Enterprises, located in White Bear Lake, MN. Distributor and dealer sales.

GRADING - PPGS™	100%	98%	95%	90%	80%	70%	60%

PISTOLS: SEMI-AUTO

Strayer-Voight manufactures a complete line of custom high quality M1911-based semi-auto pistols in a wide variety of finishes, materials (including titanium), options, and special orders. Some models have included the Tiki, Titanium Model, Bushing, Comp. Gun, Hybri-comp, IED 1911, Duotone 1911, PPC Masterpiece, and Competition Gun. Please contact JP Enterprises directly for more information on pricing and availability regarding Infinity firearms (see Trademark Index).

INGLIS HI-POWERS

Previously manufactured by John Inglis Co. Limited of Toronto, Canada. Over 151,000 Inglis Hi-Powers were manufactured between February 1944 and September 1945 under military contractual agreements.

PISTOLS: SEMI-AUTO

CHINESE CONTRACT PATTERN 35

✱ *Chinese Contract Pattern 35 No. 1* - 9mm Para. cal., large Chinese characters (6) on left slide, slotted for stock and tangent sights, can be denoted by no numerical prefix before the "CH" in serial number.

$3,500	$3,000	$2,350	$1,500	$1,000	$750	$600

Add approx. $350 for original wood holster stock (beware of reproductions).
Add $350-$450 for early front sight (approx. first 100 pistols only).

CH SERIES MILITARY

✱ *CH Series Military MK 1-No. 1 Inglis* - 9mm Para. cal., tangent sight, slotted, contracts included Canadian, Chinese, and other countries.

$1,325	$1,050	$875	$725	$650	$550	$450

Add 10%-20% for decal on front strap.
Add approx. $350 for original wood holster stock. Beware of reproductions.
This model has been recently imported again. Most recent imports have been painted black or refinished, and are priced in the $350-$575 range.

T SERIES CANADIAN MILITARY

✱ *T Series Canadian Military MK 1-No. 2 Inglis* - 9mm Para. cal., fixed sight, without slot, numerical prefix references (0-10) the number of guns in increments of 10,000. Scarcer variations include: 0, 9, and 10.

$1,000	$750	$600	$400	$350	$295	$275

Add 10%-20% for original decal on front strap.
Add 15% for 0 variation prefix.
Add 10% for 9 variation prefix.
Add 30% for 10 variation (ser. no.) prefix.
Since the original decals are very fragile, most are observed with approx. 10%-90% of the decal remaining.
This model has been recently imported again. Most recent imports are priced $350-$650.

✱ *T Series Canadian Military Inglis "DIAMOND" logo* - refers to Inglis trademark in diamond shaped logo on left side of slide, only a few prototypes were mfg. 1946-47.

$3,000	$2,750	$2,000	$1,500	$1,200	$800	$600

Add 50% for polished steel (parkerized finish is more common).
Add 50% for 5 CH Series.
All Inglis diamond variations are in the 5CH or 9T ser. no. range.
Be careful of fakes!

✱ *T Series Canadian Military MK 1-No. 2 Inglis* - fixed sight, slotted. Inspect slot very carefully, and provenance verification is advised.

$1,950	$1,250	$1,100	$900	$800	$650	$500

INGRAM

Previously manufactured until late 1982 by Military Armament Corp. (MAC) located in Atlanta, GA.

PISTOLS: SEMI-AUTO

MAC 10 - .45 ACP or 9mm Para. cal., open bolt, semi-auto version of the sub machine gun, 10 (.45 ACP cal.), 16 (9mm Para cal.), 30 (.45 ACP cal.), or 32 (9mm Para cal.) shot mag., compact all metal welded construction, rear aperture and front blade sight. Disc. 1982.

$850	$775	$700	$650	$600	$550	$495

Add approx. $160 for accessories (barrel extension, case, and extra mag.).

MAC 10A1 - similar to MAC 10 except fires from a closed bolt.

$295	$275	$250	$230	$215	$200	$190

MAC 11 - similar to MAC 10 except in .380 ACP cal.

$650	$595	$550	$525	$500	$480	$460

INLAND

Previous WWII subcontractor of M1 carbines. Former division of General Motors, located in Dayton, OH.

Please refer to U.S. M1 Carbines/Rifles listings under U.S. Military.

INTERARMS

Previous importer and distributor located in Alexandria, VA, from circa 1962-1999.

Interarms imported a multitude of trademarks and models since the early 1960s. Most of the models listed were recent imports. The FEG, Howa, Rossi, and Walther trademarks will be found in their own sections listed alphabetically in this text.

PISTOLS: SEMI-AUTO, FEG & HELWAN MFG.

Please refer to the FEG & HELWAN sections in this text.

REVOLVERS: SA, VIRGINIAN SERIES

Virginian Revolvers were previously manufactured in Europe by various manufacturers (including Hämmerli of Switzerland). They were also manufactured in Midland, VA from 1976-1984. Older models with exceptional quality (including Hämmerli guns) are worth a premium over values listed.

VIRGINIAN DRAGOON STANDARD - .41 Mag., .44 Mag., or .45 LC (mfg. 1982-84) cal., improved action patterned after Colt SAA design, 6 shot, 6, 7 1/2, 8 3/8, or 12 (Buntline) in. barrel, blue finish, smooth walnut grips, adj. rear sight, 51 oz. with 7 1/2 in. barrel.

$255	$225	$205	$190	$180	$170	$160

Last MSR was $315.

Add 15% for Buntline Model.

* *Virginian Dragoon Standard Stainless* - .41 Mag., .44 Mag., or .45 LC cal., 6 (disc.), 7 1/2 (disc.), or 8 3/8 in. barrel, same general specifications as Standard Dragoon.

$265	$230	$210	$160	$135	$120	$100

Last MSR was $315.

DRAGOON SILHOUETTE - .357 Mag. or .44 Mag. cal., stainless steel, 7 1/2, 8 3/8, or 10 1/2 in. (standard on .357 Mag.) barrel, special sights and grips.

$365	$320	$275	$225	$195	$165	$140

Last MSR was $425.

GRADING - PPGS™	100%	98%	95%	90%	80%	70%	60%

DRAGOON ENGRAVED - .44 Mag. cal. only, choice of stainless steel or blue finish, 6 or 7 1/2 in. barrel., "Sic Semper Tyrannis" inscription on butt with a 5 point star.

	$545	$470	$430	$395	$360	$320	$285

Last MSR was $625.

Add $75 for presentation case.

DRAGOON "DEPUTY" - .357 Mag. or .44 Mag. cal., blue barrel, case hardened frame, 5 in. barrel only.

	$250	$215	$195	$180	$165	$155	$145

Last MSR was $295.

✳ *Dragoon "Deputy" Stainless* - similar to above, except .44 Mag. available in 6 in. barrel only, stainless steel.

	$255	$225	$205	$150	$125	$110	$95

Last MSR was $295.

VIRGINIAN .22 CONVERTIBLE - .22 LR/.22 Mag. cal. cylinders, 5 1/2 in. barrel only, adj. rear sight, 38 oz.

	$185	$155	$145	$135	$125	$115	$105

Last MSR was $219.

✳ *Virginian .22 Convertible Stainless* - stainless steel fabrication, otherwise similar to above.

	$200	$170	$155	$125	$110	$95	$85

Last MSR was $239.

RIFLES: BOLT ACTION, DISC.

MODEL JW-15 - .22 LR cal., 5 shot detachable mag., 23.8 in. barrel, open sights, blue finish, Model 70 style safety, patterned after the Brno Model ZKM, 5 1/2 lbs. Mfg. by Norinco. Imported 1990-96.

	$85	$70	$60	$50	$40	$35	$30

Last MSR was $109.

ENFIELD NO. 4 - .303 British cal., genuine British Commonwealth issue, 25 1/4 in. barrel, 10 shot box mag., 9 lbs. Importation disc. 1996.

	$75	$60	$50	$40	$35	$35	$35

Last MSR was $86.

RIFLES: BOLT ACTION, HOWA MFG.

Please refer to the Howa section in this text.

RIFLES: BOLT ACTION, MAUSER ACTIONS

Whitworth rifles were mfg. in England. Mark X rifles were mfg. in Yugoslavia by Zastava Arms until late 1997.

MARK X VISCOUNT - .22-250 Rem. (disc. 1993), .243 Win. (disc. 1993), .25-06 Rem. (disc. 1993), .270 Win. (disc. 1993), 7x57mm (disc. 1993), 7mm Rem. Mag. (disc. 1994), .308 Win. (disc. 1994), .30-06, or .300 Win. Mag. (disc. 1994) cal., 5 shot, 3 shot mag., 24 in. barrel, adj. rear sight and trigger, classic style Monte Carlo stock. Disc. 1983, re-introduced 1985, disc. 1996.

	$375	$300	$265	$240	$225	$205	$190

Last MSR was $471.

Add $15 for 7mm Rem. Mag. or .300 Win. Mag. cal.

This model is often referred to as the Viscount. Early manufacture was done in Manchester, England. Recent manufacture is in Yugoslavia. Earlier Manchester guns (before approx. 1980) will bring a slight premium over the values listed.

GRADING - PPGS™	100%	98%	95%	90%	80%	70%	60%

✴ *Mark X Viscount Mini* - .223 Rem. or 7.62x39mm (new in 1990) cal., miniature M98 Mauser System action, 20 in. barrel with iron sights, checkered hardwood stock, 5 shot mag., adj. trigger, 6.35 lbs. Imported 1987-94.

	$360	$295	$265	$240	$225	$205	$190

Last MSR was $455.

✴ *Mark X Viscount Lightweight* - .22-250 Rem. (new 1994), .270 Win. (disc.), .30-06 (disc. 1994), or 7mm Rem. Mag. (disc.) cal., similar to Mark X Viscount, except has Carbolite (synthetic) stock and 20 in. barrel, 7 lbs. Imported 1988-90, reintroduced 1994-97.

	$350	$290	$265	$240	$225	$205	$190

Last MSR was $438.

CAVALIER - similar to Viscount, except modern style stock, roll-over cheekpiece, rosewood pistol grip cap and forend tip, recoil pad. Disc.

	$365	$330	$305	$290	$265	$230	$195

MANNLICHER STYLE CARBINE - similar to Cavalier, except 20 in. barrel, full length stock, no Magnum or varmint calibers. Disc.

	$365	$330	$305	$290	$265	$230	$195

CONTINENTAL CARBINE - similar to Mannlicher Style, except with double set trigger. Disc.

	$395	$365	$330	$310	$285	$255	$220

THE MARQUIS - .243 Win., .270 Win., .308 Win., 7x57mm, or .30-06 cal., 20 in. barrel, adj. trigger. Mannlicher style carbine. Disc. 1984.

	$430	$325	$300	$275	$250	$230	$215

ALASKAN - similar to Mark X, except .375 H&H or .458 Win. Mag. cal., recoil pad and extra stock crossbolt. Disc. 1984.

	$460	$350	$330	$310	$290	$250	$210

MARK X REALTREE - .270 Win. or .30-06 cal., features Realtree Camo finish. Imported 1994-96.

	$460	$390	$365	$320	$275	$250	$225

Last MSR was $549.

MARK X WHITWORTH - .270 Win., .30-06, and .300 Win. Mag. cals, Mauser action, 24 in. barrel, open sights, 5 shot mag. (.300 Win. Mag. is only 3), checkered deluxe walnut with ebony forearm tip, thumb safety with sling swivels, adj. trigger, rubber recoil buttplate, 7 lbs. Imported 1984-96.

	$475	$400	$365	$320	$275	$250	$225

Last MSR was $565.

Add $19 for 7mm Rem. Mag. (disc.) or .300 Win. Mag. cal.

This model was the Whitworth American Field Series until 1987. Early manufacture was done in Manchester, England. Later manufacture was by Zastava located in Yugoslavia. Earlier Manchester guns (before approx. 1980) will bring a slight premium over the values listed.

WHITWORTH MANNLICHER STYLE CARBINE - .243 Win., .270 Win., .308 Win., 7x57mm, or .30-06 cal., bolt action with full length walnut Mannlicher style stock, open sights, sling swivels, thumb safety, 20 in. barrel, 5 shot mag., 7 lbs. Imported 1984-87.

	$570	$495	$455	$410	$375	$340	$310

Last MSR was $675.

WHITWORTH EXPRESS RIFLE - .375 H&H (disc. 1993) or .458 Win. Mag. cal., 3 shot, 24 in. barrel, 3 leaf express sight, English style walnut stock, checkered pistol grip and forend, 8 1/2 lbs. Imported 1974-96.

	$600	$540	$465	$425	$395	$375	$350

Last MSR was $703.

GRADING - PPGS™	100%	98%	95%	90%	80%	70%	60%

RIFLES: SEMI-AUTO

22-ATD - .22 LR cal. only, patterned after the Browning Semi-Auto, 19.4 in. barrel, 11 shot mag. in stock, blue finish, checkered hardwood stock, take-down design, adj. rear sight, 4.6 lbs. Mfg. by Norinco 1987-96.

	$110	$95	$90	$80	$75	$70	$65

Last MSR was $121.

Add $16 for camo case (disc.).

INTERARMS ARSENAL

Current trademark of firearms imported and distributed by High Standard Manufacturing Company, located in Houston, TX.

Interarms Arsenal's line of firearms includes the M1911A1 and M1911 Crusader pistol (Lipsey's exclusive), the Model 200 Enforcer shotgun (MSR $226), Power Plus revolver (Lipsey's exclusive), AK74 Tantal rifle ($599 MSR), M1 Carbine (TBA MSR), and the Sharpshooter rifle (MSR $149-$169).

Please contact the importer directly for more information, including availability (see Trademark Index).

INTERCONTINENTAL ARMS INC.

Previous importer located in Los Angeles, CA circa 1970s.

Intercontinental Arms Inc. imported a variety of SA revolvers, an AR-15 type semi-auto rifle, a derringer, a rolling block single shot rifle, and a line of black powder pistol reproductions and replicas. While these firearms were good, utilitarian shooters, they have limited desirability in today's marketplace. The single action revolvers manufactured by Hämmerli are typically priced in the $200-$395 range, the derringer is priced in the $115-$175 range, the AR-15 copy is priced in the $425-$675 range, and the single shot rolling block rifle is priced in the $150-$200 range, depending on original condition.

INTERDYNAMIC OF AMERICA, INC.

Previous distributor located in Miami, FL 1981-84.

PISTOLS: SEMI-AUTO

KG-9 - 9mm Para. cal., 3 in. barrel, open bolt, paramilitary design pistol. Disc. approx. 1982.

	$750	$700	$650	$600	$575	$550	$525

KG-99 - 9mm Para. cal., 3 in. barrel, semi-auto paramilitary design pistol, closed bolt, 36 shot mag., 5 in. vent. shroud barrel, blue only, a stainless steel version of the KG-9. Mfg. by Interdynamic 1984 only.

	$375	$325	$275	$230	$200	$180	$160
KG-99M, mini pistol	$450	$400	$350	$285	$235	$200	$180

INTERNATIONAL BUSINESS MACHINE CORP. (IBM)

Previous WWII subcontractor of M1 carbines located in Poughkeepsie, NY.

Please refer to U.S. M1 Carbines/Rifles listings under U.S. Military.

INTERNATIONAL HARVESTER CORP.

Previous WWII subcontractor of M1 Garand rifles.

Please refer to U.S. M1 Carbines/Rifles listings under U.S. Military.

INTERSTATE ARMS CORP.

Current importer located in Billerica, MA.

Interstate Arms Corp. imports a variety of Chinese made cowboy action shotguns and reproductions.

GRADING - PPGS™	100%	98%	95%	90%	80%	70%	60%

SHOTGUNS: SxS

MODEL 99 COACH GUN - 12 or 20 ga., 3 in. chambers, exposed hammers, 20 in. barrels with cyl./cyl. fixed chokes, blue finish with checkered stock and forearm, 7.2 lbs. Importation began 1999, currently manufactured by SD2 Linyi.

MSR $299	$245	$215	$190	$175	$155	$145	$130

SHOTGUNS: LEVER ACTION

MODEL 87W - 12 ga. only, 2 3/4 in. chamber, patterned after the Winchester Model 1887, 20 in. barrel, walnut stock and forearm, mfg. by SD1 Rizhou. Importation began mid-2003.

MSR $529	$445	$375	$335	$275	$235	$200	$180

SHOTGUNS: SLIDE ACTION

MODEL 97W HAMMER - 12 ga. only, patterned after the Win. Model 97, hammer, 20 in. plain barrel with cylinder bore fixed choke, solid frame, oil finish American walnut (new 2005) or hardwood (disc. 2004) stock with grooved "corn cob" forearm, mfg. by SD1 Rizhou. Importation began 2001.

MSR $399	$325	$295	$260	$220	$190	$175	$160

MODEL 97T WWI TRENCH GUN - 12 ga. only, authentic reproduction of the original Winchester WWI Trench Gun, complete with shrouded barrel, proper markings, finish, and wood. Imported mid-2002-2006.

	$345	$295	$265	$225	$195	$175	$160

Last MSR was $425.

MODEL 372 - 12 ga., 3 in. chamber, 18 1/2 in. barrel with heat shield and ghost ring sights, bottom ejection port, cylinder choke, black synthetic stock and forearm. Limited importation 2007.

While advertised, this model had limited mfg. with no established pricing.

MODEL 982T (981) - 12 ga. only, 3 in. chamber, defense configuration with 18 1/2 in. cylinder bore barrel with fixed choke, black synthetic stock and forearm, matte black metal finish, current mfg. uses ghost ring sights. Importation began 2001.

MSR $235	$200	$170	$150	$125	$115	$95	$85

MODEL 1893/97 - similar to Model 97, except built on receiver patterned after Winchester Model 1893, mfg. by SD1 Rizhou. Limited importation mid-2006-2007.

	$325	$285	$250	$220	$190	$175	$160

Last MSR was $399.

INTRAC ARMS INTERNATIONAL INC.

Previous importer located in Knoxville, TN. Intrac imported trademarks manufactured by Arsenal Bulgaria, and by IM Metal Production facility in Croatia late 2000-2004. Previously imported by HS America, located in Knoxville, TN.

PISTOLS: SEMI-AUTO

HS 2000 - 9mm Para., .357 SIG, or .40 S&W cal., short recoil locked breech mechanism, polymer frame, trigger and grip safety, 3 dot low profile sights, loaded chamber indicator, black finish, 23 oz. Imported from Croatia 2000-2004.

	$350	$295	$250	$225	$200	$185	$175

Last MSR was $419.

GRADING - PPGS™	100%	98%	95%	90%	80%	70%	60%

MAKAROV - .380 ACP or 9x18mm cal., double action, black phosphate finish, black grips, supplied with two 8 shot mags. and holster. Imported 2002-2004.

	$145	$125	$110	$95	$85	$80	$75

Last MSR was $159.

RIFLES: SEMI-AUTO

ROMAK 1 & 2 - 7.62x39mm (Romak 1) or 5.45x39mm (Romak 2) cal., AK-47 copy with 16 1/2 in. barrel and scope mount on left side of receiver, wood thumbhole stock, includes 5 and 10 shot mags., and accessories. Imported 2002-2004.

	$395	$350	$300	$295	$275	$250	$200

Last MSR was $329.

SLR-101 - similar to Romak, except has 17 1/4 in. cold hammer forged barrel and black polymer stock and forearm, includes 2 mags. and accessories. Imported 2002-2004.

	$450	$395	$350	$325	$300	$295	$250

Last MSR was $359.

ROMAK 3 - 7.62x54R cal., based on current issue PSL/FPK sniper configuration, 5 or 10 shot mag., last shot bolt hold open, 26 1/2 in. barrel with muzzle brake, mil-spec scope with range finder, bullet drop compensator and illuminated recticle. Imported 2002-2004.

	$800	$725	$650	$600	$550	$500	$450

Last MSR was $899.

INTRATEC

Previous manufacturer circa 1985-2000 located in Miami, FL.   ⊞⊟INTRATEC

PISTOLS: SEMI-AUTO

PROTEC-25 - .25 ACP. cal., double action only, 2 1/2 in. barrel, 8 shot mag., 13 oz. Disc. 2000.

	$110	$80	$65	$45	$35	$30	$25

Last MSR was $137.

Add $5 for Tec-Kote finish or black slide/frame finish (disc.).

TEC-DC9 - 9mm Para. cal., paramilitary design pistol, 5 in. shrouded barrel, matte black finish, 10 (C/B 1994) or 32* shot mag. Mfg. 1985-94.

	$375	$325	$275	$230	$200	$180	$160

Last MSR was $269.

* *TEC-9DCK* - similar to TEC-9, except has new durable Tec-Kote finish with better protection than hard chrome. Mfg. 1991-94.

	$395	$365	$330	$295	$265	$235	$210

Last MSR was $297.

* *TEC-DC9S* - matte stainless version of the TEC-9. Disc. 1994.

	$450	$400	$350	$315	$275	$235	$195

Last MSR was $362.

Add $203 for TEC-9 with accessory package (deluxe case, 3-32 shot mags., paramilitary design grip, and recoil compensator).

TEC-DC9M - mini version of the Model TEC-9, including 3 in. barrel and 20 shot mag. Disc. 1994.

	$395	$365	$330	$295	$265	$235	$210

Last MSR was $245.

* *TEC-DC9MK* - similar to TEC-9M, except has Tec-Kote rust resistant finish. Mfg. 1991-94.

	$425	$345	$295	$265	$225	$195	$160

Last MSR was $277.

GRADING - PPGS™	100%	98%	95%	90%	80%	70%	60%

✴ *TEC-DC9MS* - matte stainless version of the TEC-9M. Disc. 1994.

	$475	$400	$365	$320	$275	$250	$225

Last MSR was $339.

TEC-22 "SCORPION" - .22 LR cal., paramilitary design, 4 in. barrel, ambidextrous safety, military matte finish, or electroless nickel, 30 shot mag., adj. sights, 30 oz. Mfg. 1988-94.

	$275	$230	$175	$155	$140	$130	$120

Last MSR was $202.

Add $20 for TEC-Kote finish.

✴ *TEC-22N* - similar to TEC-22, except has nickel finish. Mfg. 1990 only.

	$240	$200	$175	$160	$140	$125	$105

Last MSR was $226.

Add $16 for threaded barrel (Model TEC-22TN).

TEC-22T - threaded barrel variation of the TEC-22 "Scorpion." Mfg 1991-94.

	$275	$230	$175	$155	$140	$130	$120

Last MSR was $161.

Add $23 for Tec-Kote finish.

SPORT-22 - .22 LR cal., 4 in. non-threaded barrel, 10 shot Ruger styled rotary mag., matte finish, adj. rear sight, 29 1/2 oz. New 1995.

	$140	$110	$95	$80	$65	$55	$45

Last MSR was $170.

Add $15 for stainless steel barrel.

CAT-9, CAT-45, CAT-380 - .380 ACP (new 1995), 9mm Para., or .45 ACP (new 1995) cal., double action only, black finish, polymer frame with top sight channel, only 27 parts, blowback action on 9mm Para., locked breech on .45 ACP, 6 (.45 ACP cal.) or 7 (.380 ACP or 9mm Para.) shot mag., 3 or 3 1/4 (.45 ACP only) in. barrel, 18-21 oz. Mfg. 1993-2000.

	$215	$180	$155	$135	$120	$100	$90

Last MSR was $260.

Subtract $25 for .380 ACP cal.
Add $20 for .45 ACP cal.
Add $15 for Fire Sights.
This series was designed by N. Sirkis of Israel.

AB-10 - 9mm Para. cal., design similar to Luger, 2 3/4 in. non-threaded barrel, choice of 32* (limited supply) or 10 shot mag., black synthetic frame, firing pin safety block, black or stainless steel finish, 45 oz. Mfg. 1997-2000.

	$235	$200	$180	$160	$150	$135	$120

Last MSR was $225.

Add $20 for stainless steel (new 2000).
Add $75 for 32 shot mag.

INTRATEC U.S.A.
Previous manufacturer located in Miami, FL.

CARBINES

TEC-9C - 9mm Para. cal., carbine variation with 16 1/2 in. barrel, 36 shot mag.
Only 1 gun mfg. 1987 - extreme rarity precludes pricing.

DERRINGERS

TEC-38 DERRINGER - .22 Mag., .32 H&R Mag., or .38 Spl. cal., O/U, 3 in. barrel, blue frame, double action, 13 oz. Mfg. 1986-88.

	$110	$95	$85	$75	$65	$60	$55

Last MSR was $125.

GRADING - PPGS™	100%	98%	95%	90%	80%	70%	60%

PISTOLS: SEMI-AUTO

PROTEC-22 - while advertised for $112 MSR during 1993, this model never went into production.

TEC-9 - 9mm Para. cal., paramilitary design, 5 in. shrouded barrel, 32 shot mag. Disc.

	$450	$400	$350	$315	$275	$235	$195

INVESTARM, s.p.a.

Current trademark of Armi Salvinelli, a manufacturer established in 1975, and located in Marcheno, Italy. Previously distributed by Kimber until 2005, located in Yonkers, NY.

Investarm manufactures a wide variety of shotguns in various configurations, including folding single shots, folding O/Us, which are not currently distributed in the U.S., in addition to muzzle loading black powder rifles and pistols. Please contact the company directly for more information, including pricing and availability (see Trademark Index). The high quality competition and hunting models are sold under the name Armi Salvinelli - please refer to this listing for more information.

INVESTMENT ARMS INC.

Previous company specializing in limited/special editions located in Fort Collins, CO. Investment Arms Inc. subcontracted various gun manufactures to produce their own limited editions/special editions. These guns are typically limited by county or state, and feature various engraving motifs, configurations, and other embellishments. Secondary marketplace liquidity is difficult to determine, based on relative desirability and limited collectibility.

IRWIN PEDERSON ARMS CO.

Previous WWII subcontractor of M1 carbines located in Grand Rapids, MI.

Please refer to U.S. M1 Carbines/Rifles listings under U.S. Military.

IRWINDALE ARMS, INC. (IAI)

Previous manufacturer located in Irwindale, CA 1988-1991.

PISTOLS: SEMI-AUTO

In June, 1991, AMT reacquired the manufacturing rights to all IAI models. Please refer to the AMT section for recent models.

AUTOMAG III - .30 Carbine or 9mm Win. Mag. (mfg. 1990-92) cal., stainless steel only, 6 3/8 in. barrel, patterned after Colt Govt. Model, Millett adj. sights with white outline, grooved Lexan grips, 8 shot mag., 43 oz. Mfg. 1989-91.

	$550	$475	$395	$330	$285	$240	$210

Last MSR was $606.

AUTOMAG IV - .45 Win. Mag., or 10mm cal., semi-auto, 6 1/2 or 8 5/8 (mfg. 1991) in. barrel, 7 shot mag., Millett adj. sights, stainless steel only, 46 oz. Mfg. 1990-91.

	$565	$485	$500	$430	$375	$315	$270

Last MSR was $630.

JAVELINA - 10mm cal., semi-auto, 5 (disc. 1991) or 7 in. barrel, 8 shot mag., Millett adj. sights, wraparound Neoprene grips, stainless steel, wide adj. trigger, long grip safety, 48 oz. Mfg. 1990-91.

	$525	$450	$375	$315	$270	$230	$200

Last MSR was $570.

BACKUP PISTOL - .380 ACP cal., semi-auto action, 2 1/2 in. barrel, stainless steel, Lexan grips, 5 shot mag., 18 oz. Older disc. walnut grip models are worth a slight premium. Disc. 1989.

	$200	$165	$135	$110	$95	$75	$65

Last MSR was $243.

GRADING - PPGS™	100%	98%	95%	90%	80%	70%	60%

ISRAEL ARMS INTERNATIONAL, INC.

Previous importer (please refer to IAI listing) and manufacturer located in Houston, TX, 1997-2004.

ISRAEL ARMS LTD.

Previous manufacturer located in Kfar Saba, Israel. Imported and distributed exclusively by Israel Arms International, Inc. located in Houston, TX 1997-2001.

PISTOLS: SEMI-AUTO

MODEL 1500 HI POWER - 9mm Para. cal., single action, 3.85 (Compact) or 4.64 (Standard, disc. 1998) in. barrel, two-tone finish, rubberized grips, regular or Meprolite sights, 10 shot mag., 33.6 oz. Imported 1997-98 only.

	$360	$305	$255	$225	$200	$185	$170

Last MSR was $413.

Add approx. $160 for two-tone finish with Meprolite sights.

✳ *Model 1500/1501 Hi-Power Compact* - 9mm Para. or .40 S&W cal., compact variation with 3.85 in. barrel, choice of two-tone (Model 1500) or blue (Model 1501) finish, 32.2 oz. Imported late 1999-2000.

	$360	$305	$255	$225	$200	$185	$170

Last MSR was $412.

MODEL 2500 - 9mm Para. or .40 S&W cal., single or double action, ambidextrous safety with decocking feature, steel slide with alloy frame, 3 7/8 in. barrel, 10 shot mag., matte black finish, 34 oz.

While advertised during 1999, this model had very limited importation.

MODEL 3000 - 9mm Para cal., double action. Limited importation 2000-2001.

	$335	$295	$260	$230	$200	$175	$150

Last MSR was $374.

MODEL 4000 - .40 S&W cal., double action. Limited importation 2000-2001.

	$335	$295	$260	$230	$200	$175	$150

Last MSR was $374.

MODEL 5000/5001 COMBAT - .45 ACP cal., single action, 4 1/4 in barrel, combat configuration with ambidextrous safety, competition trigger, hammer, and slide stop, front and rear slide serrations, blue (Model 5001) or two-tone (Model 5000) finish, wraparound rubber grips, 42 oz., mfg. in Philipines. Imported 1999-2001.

	$395	$365	$330	$295	$265	$235	$210

Last MSR was $448.

MODEL 6000/6001 STANDARD - .45 ACP cal., single action, 5 in. stainless steel barrel, features beveled feed ramp, extended slide stop, safety and magazine release, ambidextrous safety, beavertail grip safety and combat style hammer, blue (Model 6001) or two-tone (Model 6000, disc. 2000) finish, 38 oz., mfg. in Philipines. Imported 1999-2001.

	$395	$365	$330	$295	$265	$235	$210

Last MSR was $448.

MODEL 7000/7001 WIDE FRAME - .45 ACP cal., single action, similar to Model 6000/6001, except has double stack mag., blue (Model 7001) or two-tone (Model 7000) finish, 40 oz. Imported 1999-2000.

	$445	$395	$350	$300	$255	$225	$200

Last MSR was $490.

GRADING - PPGS™	100%	98%	95%	90%	80%	70%	60%

RIFLES

MODEL 333 M1 GARAND - .30-06 cal., 24 in. barrel, parts remanufactured to meet GI and mil specs, parkerized finish, 8 shot en-bloc mag., 9 1/2 lbs. Mfg. 2000-2001.

	$750	$700	$650	$550	$450	$350	$300

Last MSR was $852.

MODEL 444 FAL - .308 Win. cal., patterned after the FN FAL model. Mfg. by Imbel, located in Brazil, 2000-2001.

	$825	$745	$685	$625	$575	$525	$500

Last MSR was $897.

ISRAELI MILITARY INDUSTRIES (IMI)

Current manufacturer established during 1933, and located in Israel. Limited importation currently.

IMI manufactured guns (both new and disc. models) include Galil, Jericho, Magnum Research, Timberwolf, Uzi, and others, and can be located in their respective sections.

ITALIAN MILITARY ARMS

Previous Italian popular military models mfg. since 1891.

PISTOLS: SEMI-AUTO

GLISENTI MODEL 1910 - 9mm Glisenti cal., 4 in. barrel, 7 shot mag., checkered wood grips, official Italian service pistol of both WWI and WWII, 32 oz.

	$1,350	$1,000	$800	$600	$500	$400	$300

Warning: 9mm Para. ammunition (9x19mm) cannot be used in this pistol - only 9mm Glisenti, as it is approx. 25% less powerful than the 9mm Para.

BRIXIA - similar to Glisenti Model 1910, except utilizes simplified mfg. techniques, mostly sold to civilians.

	$1,500	$1,200	$900	$850	$500	$400	$300

SOSSO - 9mm Para. cal., large experimental semi-auto, early pistols were double action and marked "Sosso", late guns were single action and built by FNA. All Sosso pistols feature a unique continuous "chain link" 19 or 21 shot mag. Approx. 5 guns mfg.

Extreme rarity factor precludes accurate price evaluation.

RIFLES: BOLT ACTION

MODEL 1891 MANNLICHER-CARCANO - 6.5x52mm Carcano cal., integrated 6 shot mag. that forms front part of trigger guard housing, 31 in. barrel, straight handle, adj. sight, military stock, mfg. in Italian Govt. Arsenals, located in Terni, Brescia, Torre Annuziata, and Torino circa 1891-1918. Approx. 3.5-4 million mfg.

	$175	$150	$125	$100	$85	$70	$55

MODEL 38 TERNI MILITARY RIFLE - 7.35x52mm Carcano cal., similar to 1891, except turned down bolt handle, 21 in. barrel and folding bayonet.

	$175	$150	$125	$100	$85	$70	$55

ITHACA CLASSIC DOUBLES

Previous importer and SxS shotgun manufacturer 1998-2003, and located in Victor, NY from 1999-2003 and Mendon, NY until 1999.

Ithaca
CLASSIC DOUBLES
The Legend Returns

RIFLES: SxS

DOUBLE RIFLE - many popular cals., including .45-70 Govt., also available in 20 ga. with 26 in. fully rifled barrels, express sights, German claw type scope mounts, DT, ejectors, exhibition walnut standard, many options were available. Limited importation only.

Advertised MSR was $8,500, w/o engraving or other special orders/features.

GRADING - PPGS™	100%	98%	95%	90%	80%	70%	60%

SHOTGUNS: SxS

All Ithaca Classic Doubles shotguns were handmade to order in the U.S. Frames were made from the traditional forgings and internal parts from solid steel. Barrels were hammer forged from geniune Krupp steel. Metal finishing, checkering, oil finish, and engraving were done completely by hand. All guns were fitted to customer's specifications and wood selection. Guns were available in .410 bore through 12 ga., with full rifle barrels available in 12 or 20 ga and .45-70 Govt. cal. Each gauge has its own frame size, and serial numbers were continued from the last gun Ithaca manufactured in 1948 (ser. no. 469,999).

The Ithaca custom shop manufactured custom orders, including special options and features.

> **For Special Combination Sets - add $3,000 (4E, 5E, 6E) and $3,750 (Grades 7E & Sousa) for extra set of 16 (20 ga. frame) or 28 (.410 bore frame) ga. barrels.**
> **Add $600-$2,150 for canvas, canvas and leather, leather, or oak and leather cases.**
> **Add $1,125 for SST and vent. rib.**
> **Add $950 for VR.**

SKEET GRADE (SPECIAL FIELD) - 16 (new 2001), 20, 28 ga., or .410 bore, designed for field and clay shooting, DT, ejectors, 26, 28, or 30 in. barrels with fixed chokes, light perimeter hand engraving with metal stippling on shoulders and in front of top opening lever, Turnbull bone and charcoal case colors, checkered pistol grip or English feather crotch walnut stock and forearm, 5lbs. 5 oz.-6 lbs. 6 oz. Mfg. late 1998-2002.

	$5,500	$4,750	$3,750	$3,250	$2,650	$2,175	$1,775

Last MSR was $5,999.

> **Add 20% for SST or vent. rib option.**

CLASSIC COMPETITION GRADE - all gauges, competition features. Mfg. 2002-2003.

	$5,500	$4,750	$3,750	$3,250	$2,650	$2,175	$1,775

Last MSR was $5,995.

GRADE 4E CLASSIC - 16 (new 2001), 20, 28 ga., or .410 bore, features gold plated triggers, jewelled barrel flats, hand tuned locks, hand engraved three game scenes with floral scroll, deluxe walnut stock and forearm with fleur-de-lis pattern and 22 LPI checkering, other specifications similar to Special Field/Skeet Grade. Mfg. 1998-2003.

	$6,750	$5,750	$4,900	$4,100	$3,300	$2,500	$1,850

Last MSR was $7,500.

STAR MODEL COMPETITION - competition model. Limited mfg. 2003.

	$6,750	$5,750	$4,900	$4,100	$3,300	$2,500	$1,850

Last MSR was $7,500.

GRADE 5E CLASSIC - step up from Grade 4E, with more elaborate frame engraving and gold inlays on frame sides, upgraded walnut. Mfg. 2002-2003.

	$7,500	$6,500	$5,750	$4,850	$4,100	$3,500	$2,500

Last MSR was $8,500.

GRADE 6E CLASSIC - step up from Grade 5E, with fine scroll engraving and gold dog inlays on frame sides, upgraded walnut. Mfg. 2002-2003.

	$8,500	$7,500	$6,500	$5,750	$4,950	$4,150	$3,250

Last MSR was $9,999.

GRADE 7E CLASSIC - 16 (new 2001), 20, 28 ga., or .410 bore, features hand engraved oak leaf scroll on frame and barrels, and 24Kt. flat gold game scene inlays, including a bald eagle on floor plate, exhibition grade American walnut with 12 checkered panels in fleur-de-lis pattern, other specifications similar to Special Field/Skeet Grade. Mfg. 1998-2003.

	$9,250	$8,250	$7,250	$6,150	$5,350	$4,450	$3,500

Last MSR was $11,000.

GRADING - PPGS™	100%	98%	95%	90%	80%	70%	60%

SOUSA SPECIAL - 16 (new 2001), 20, 28 ga., or .410 bore, top-of-the-line model with every possible refinement, each gun individually hand fitted, jewelled, and polished, includes famous 24Kt. Sousa mermaid on trigger guard, other specifications similar to Special Field/Skeet Grade. Special order only, limited mfg. 1998-2003.

	$16,750	$14,000	$12,000	$10,000	$8,250	$7,000	$5,750

Last MSR was $18,000.

SUPERLATIVE CLASS - custom order, best quality model with a wide choice of engraving options and inlays, exhibition grade walnut, approx. 10-15 guns were mfg. annually. Limited mfg. 2002-2003.

Prices for this model started at $20,000.

SHOTGUNS: SINGLE SHOT

KNICKERBOCKER SINGLE BARREL TRAP - limited mfg. of 100 guns during 2003.

Prices for this model started at $9,000, w/o engraving.

ITHACA GUN COMPANY LLC

Previous manufacturer located in Ithaca, NY from 1883-1986, King Ferry, NY circa 1989-2005, and Auburn, NY right before it closed in June, 2005.

Ithaca Gun Company, LLC had resumed production on the Model 37 slide action shotgun and variations during 1989, and then relocated to King Ferry, NY shortly thereafter. In the past, Ithaca also absorbed companies including Syracuse Arms Co., Lefever Arms Co., Union Fire Arms Co., Wilkes-Barre Gun Co., as well as others.

COMBINATION GUNS

LSA-55 TURKEY GUN - O/U shotgun-rifle combo, 12 ga., .222 Rem., 24 1/2 in. ribbed barrel, exposed hammer, folding rear sight, checkered Monte Carlo stock. Mfg. by Tikka, Finland 1970-81.

	$650	$575	$475	$450	$425	$385	$330

HANDGUNS

ITHACA WWII MILITARY MFG. - .45 ACP cal., mfg. for WWII military M1911A1 contracts, 7 shot mag. 5 in. barrel, ser. no. ranges 856,405-916,404, 1,208,674-1,279,673, 1,441,431-1,471,430, 1,743,847-1,890,503, 2,075,104-2,134,403, and 2,619,014-2,693,613. Parkerized finish.

N/A	$1,700	$1,350	$1,125	$1,000	$950	$800

Add 20% with original shipping carton.

For more information on other WWI and WWII M1911/A1 military contracts, please refer to the Colt's Manufacturing section Pistols: Semi-Auto, Govt. M1911/1911A1 Military Variations in this text.

ITHACA 50TH SEMI-AUTO ANNIVERSARY MODEL - .45 ACP cal., 5 in. match barrel with bushing, blue polished or tactical matte finish, checkered diamond pattern walnut grips, extended beavertail grip safety, includes plastic case and certificate, only 125 mfg. with special serialization 1995-97. Disc.

$695	$625	$550	$500	$450	$400	$360

Last MSR was $795.

This model was offered exclusively by All American Sales, Inc. located in Memphis, TN.

X-CALIBER SINGLE SHOT - .22 LR or .44 Mag. (advertised only) cal., break open action with contoured wood grip and forearm, 8, 10 or 15 in. barrel, unique dual firing pin detonates both rimfire and centerfire cartridges. While advertised in 1988, the Models 20 & 30 were never retailed. Approx. 300 units were mfg. in 22 cal. only.

Currently the price range on this model is $175-$350.

GRADING - PPGS™	100%	98%	95%	90%	80%	70%	60%

RIFLES: BOLT ACTION

LSA-55 STANDARD - .222 Rem., .22-250 Rem., 6mm Rem., .243 Win., or .308 Win. cal., Mauser type action, 22 in. barrel, leaf sight, 3 shot mag., checkered Monte Carlo stock. Mfg. in Finland by Tikka from 1969-77.

	$400	$375	$350	$310	$275	$250	$230

The LSA Model designation stands for Light, Strong, Accurate.

LSA-55 DELUXE - similar to Standard, except rollover cheekpiece, rosewood pistol grip cap and forend tip, skipline checkering, no sights, scope mounts furnished.

	$495	$450	$425	$400	$365	$345	$325

LSA-55 HEAVY BARREL - similar to LSA-55, except .222 Rem. or .22-250 Rem. cal. only, target heavy barrel, special beavertail stock, 8 1/2 lbs.

	$450	$425	$400	$375	$350	$325	$300

LSA-65 - similar to LSA-55, except long action for calibers .25-06 Rem., .270 Win., or .30-06. Mfg. 1969-77.

	$400	$375	$350	$310	$275	$250	$230

LSA-65 DELUXE - similar to LSA-55, except has deluxe checkered walnut stock, .25-06 Rem., .270 Win., or .30-06.

	$495	$450	$425	$400	$365	$345	$325

RIFLES: LEVER ACTION

MODEL 49 SADDLEGUN - .22 LR or .22 Mag. cal., lever action, single shot. Mfg. 1961-78. Martini-style action.

	$145	$130	$110	$80	$65	$50	$40

Add 15% for .22 Mag. cal.
Add 20% for Deluxe Model.

MODEL 49R - similar to Model 49 Saddlegun, except is slide action repeater. Mfg. 1965-1971.

	$265	$250	$235	$200	$175	$150	$125

Add 15% for .22 Mag. cal.

MODEL 49 PRESENTATION - similar to Model 49 Saddlegun, except gold-plated trigger, hammer, engraved receiver, fancy walnut. Mfg. 1962-1974.

	$295	$275	$250	$235	$200	$165	$135

MODEL 49 ST. LOUIS BICENTENNIAL - like Deluxe Model 49, except inscription on receiver. 200 mfg. 1964.

	$325	$255	$215	$165	$130	$115	$95

Last MSR was $35.

MODEL 72 SADDLEGUN - .22 or .22 Mag. cal., lever action, 18 1/2 in. barrel, hooded front sight. Mfg. 1973-78 by Erma Werke, W. Germany.

	$375	$325	$275	$200	$175	$145	$125

MODEL 72 DELUXE - similar to Model 72, except has silver finished engraved receiver, deluxe walnut, octagon barrel. Mfg. 1974-76.

	$450	$400	$300	$250	$225	$175	$145

RIFLES: SEMI-AUTO

MODEL X5-C - .22 LR cal., 7 shot mag., grooved forearm, Model X5-T has tube mag. Mfg. 1958-64.

	$195	$165	$125	$100	$80	$70	$60

MODEL X-15 - .22 LR cal., similar to X5-C, except forearm is not grooved. Mfg. 1964-67.

	$195	$165	$125	$100	$80	$70	$60

GRADING - PPGS™	100%	98%	95%	90%	80%	70%	60%

RIFLES: SINGLE SHOT

MODEL 89 - .243 Win., .30-06, .375 H&H, .416 Rigby, or 7x57mm cal., falling block action, 26 or 28 in. Shilen barrel, full-length uncheckered walnut stock.
While advertised at $658 MSR during 1994, this model never went into production.

SHOTGUNS: O/U, PREVIOUS IMPORTATION

Note: Ithaca was the sole importer for Perazzi in the '70s. All new and used models will be in the P section under Perazzi. Perazzi currently distributes their own firearms.
Note: Please refer to the Fabarm section in this text for those models previously imported by Ithaca (imported 1994-95).
Note: Previously imported SKB O/U shotguns can be found under the SKB heading.

SHOTGUNS: SxS, PREVIOUS IMPORTATION

Note: Previously imported SKB SxS shotguns can be found under the SKB heading.

SHOTGUNS: SxS, 1880-1948 MFG.

AUTO & BURGLAR SxS - 20 ga. smooth bore with 10 in. double barrels, case hardened finish, pistol grip, Model A (approx. 2,500 mfg.) has grip spur, Model B (approx. 2,000 mfg.) has squared grip; both were mfg. in lots of about 100 according to demand, and serial numbers are mixed with those of regular Ithaca shotguns. Guns not currently registered with BATF cannot be legally owned and are subject to seizure. Mfg. 1922-34.

* *Auto & Burglar SxS Model A* - serial no. range is 343,336-398,365.

	$1,850	$1,450	$1,200	$975	$775	$675	$575

* *Auto & Burglar SxS Model B* - serial no. range is 425,000-464,699.

	$1,450	$1,200	$975	$775	$675	$575	$465

Add $300-$500 for original holster (very rare). Prototype or special order guns (in 16, 28 ga., or .410 bore) are extremely rare and command premiums of 100%+.

ITHACA HAMMERLESS - 12, 16, 20, 28 ga., or .410 bore, 26-32 in. fluid steel or damascus barrels, boxlock, extractors, double triggers, any standard choke, checkered pistol grip stock and forearm, grades shown differ in overall quality, ornamentation, grade of wood, and style of checkering. In 1925, the rotary bolt and stronger frame were adapted (ser. numbers after 400,000 - commonly referred to as NID or New Ithaca Double). Values are the same as for pre-400,000 serial range shotguns. Ithaca doubles incorporated a number of design changes made on the action - they are referred to as the Lewis, Crass, Flues, and Minier frame variations.

Add $200 for SST.
Add $150 for SNT.
Add $350 for VR on Grades 4, 5, 7, and $2,000 Grade.
Add $200 for VR - lower grades.
Add $175 for beavertail forearm.
Add 33% for auto ejectors on Grades No. 1, 2, and 3.
Subtract 33% if without ejectors on Grades 4E-7E.
Early hammer doubles in average condition are approx. valued between $175-$450. However, if 60%+ condition remains (including original case colors), values can approximate those listed.

Values below are for guns mfg. between 1925-1948.

100%	98%	95%	90%	80%	70%	60%	50%	40%	30%	20%	10%

FIELD GRADE

* Field Grade 10 ga. Mag.

100%	98%	95%	90%	80%	70%	60%	50%	40%	30%	20%	10%
N/A	N/A	$1,500	$1,400	$1,300	$1,200	$1,100	$950	$825	$775	$675	$630

3 1/2 in. chambered 10 ga. Mags. are serial numbered over 500,000. Total mfg. was approx. 850 guns for all grades. 2 7/8 in. chambered 10 gauges are priced the same as a 12 ga. A 12 ga., 3 in. model was also made on the 10 ga. frame - only 87 were mfg. and specimens are noted in the 500,000 serial range.

* Field Grade 12 ga.

100%	98%	95%	90%	80%	70%	60%	50%	40%	30%	20%	10%
$1,000	$800	$600	$550	$500	$450	$415	$380	$350	$325	$300	$280

* Field Grade 16 ga.

100%	98%	95%	90%	80%	70%	60%	50%	40%	30%	20%	10%
$1,500	$1,200	$1,000	$800	$700	$650	$600	$550	$500	$425	$375	$340

* Field Grade 20 ga.

100%	98%	95%	90%	80%	70%	60%	50%	40%	30%	20%	10%
$1,600	$1,300	$1,100	$1,000	$850	$800	$750	$700	$600	$550	$500	$440

* Field Grade 28 ga.

100%	98%	95%	90%	80%	70%	60%	50%	40%	30%	20%	10%
N/A	N/A	$3,000	$2,700	$2,400	$2,300	$2,250	$2,200	$2,100	$2,050	$2,025	$2,000

* Field Grade .410 bore

100%	98%	95%	90%	80%	70%	60%	50%	40%	30%	20%	10%
N/A	N/A	$3,500	$3,000	$2,500	$2,300	$2,250	$2,200	$2,100	$2,050	$2,025	$2,000

GRADE NO. 1 - manufactured in both Flues and NID models, similar to Field Grade.

* Grade No. 1 12 ga.

100%	98%	95%	90%	80%	70%	60%	50%	40%	30%	20%	10%
$1,225	$1,000	$800	$600	$550	$500	$450	$415	$380	$350	$325	$315

* Grade No. 1 16 ga.

100%	98%	95%	90%	80%	70%	60%	50%	40%	30%	20%	10%
$1,700	$1,550	$1,275	$1,150	$925	$825	$750	$700	$650	$600	$550	$500

* Grade No. 1 20 ga.

100%	98%	95%	90%	80%	70%	60%	50%	40%	30%	20%	10%
$1,950	$1,700	$1,400	$1,200	$1,000	$900	$850	$800	$750	$700	$600	$550

* Grade No. 1 28 ga.

100%	98%	95%	90%	80%	70%	60%	50%	40%	30%	20%	10%
N/A	N/A	$2,750	$2,200	$2,000	$1,800	$1,700	$1,600	$1,500	$1,400	$1,200	$1,125

* Grade No. 1 .410 bore

100%	98%	95%	90%	80%	70%	60%	50%	40%	30%	20%	10%
N/A	N/A	$2,850	$2,250	$2,000	$1,800	$1,700	$1,600	$1,500	$1,400	$1,200	$1,125

GRADE NO. 2

* Grade No. 2 10 ga. Mag.

100%	98%	95%	90%	80%	70%	60%	50%	40%	30%	20%	10%
$2,400	$2,000	$1,800	$1,600	$1,400	$1,300	$1,200	$1,100	$950	$900	$800	$735

3 1/2 in. chambered 10 ga. Mags. are serial numbered over 500,000. Total mfg. was approx. 850 guns for all grades. 2 7/8 in. chambered 10 gauges are priced the same as a 12 ga.

* Grade No. 2 12 ga.

100%	98%	95%	90%	80%	70%	60%	50%	40%	30%	20%	10%
$1,950	$1,700	$1,550	$1,275	$1,150	$925	$825	$750	$700	$650	$600	$550

* Grade No. 2 16 ga.

100%	98%	95%	90%	80%	70%	60%	50%	40%	30%	20%	10%
$1,500	$1,200	$1,000	$900	$800	$750	$700	$650	$600	$550	$500	$475

* Grade No. 2 20 ga.

100%	98%	95%	90%	80%	70%	60%	50%	40%	30%	20%	10%
$2,150	$1,950	$1,700	$1,400	$1,200	$1,000	$900	$850	$800	$750	$700	$600

* Grade No. 2 28 ga.

100%	98%	95%	90%	80%	70%	60%	50%	40%	30%	20%	10%
N/A	N/A	$3,650	$3,250	$2,500	$2,000	$1,950	$1,850	$1,750	$1,650	$1,550	$1,450

* Grade No. 2 .410 bore

100%	98%	95%	90%	80%	70%	60%	50%	40%	30%	20%	10%
N/A	N/A	$3,750	$3,250	$2,500	$2,000	$1,950	$1,850	$1,750	$1,650	$1,550	$1,450

GRADE NO. 3

* Grade No. 3 10 ga. Mag.

100%	98%	95%	90%	80%	70%	60%	50%	40%	30%	20%	10%
$3,500	$2,900	$2,300	$1,850	$1,600	$1,400	$1,300	$1,200	$1,100	$950	$825	$735

3 1/2 in. chambered 10 ga. Mags. are serial numbered over 500,000. Total mfg. was approx. 850 guns for all grades. 2 7/8 in. chambered 10 gauges are priced the same as a 12 ga.

* Grade No. 3 12 ga.

100%	98%	95%	90%	80%	70%	60%	50%	40%	30%	20%	10%
$2,300	$2,075	$1,850	$1,500	$1,200	$1,000	$800	$750	$700	$650	$600	$550

* Grade No. 3 16 ga.

100%	98%	95%	90%	80%	70%	60%	50%	40%	30%	20%	10%
N/A	N/A	$1,950	$1,700	$1,400	$1,200	$1,000	$900	$850	$800	$750	$700

100%	98%	95%	90%	80%	70%	60%	50%	40%	30%	20%	10%

✱ Grade No. 3 20 ga.

100%	98%	95%	90%	80%	70%	60%	50%	40%	30%	20%	10%
N/A	N/A	$2,150	$1,950	$1,700	$1,400	$1,200	$1,000	$900	$850	$800	$750

✱ Grade No. 3 28 ga. - only 5 mfg.

Extreme rarity factor precludes accurate pricing evaluation.

✱ Grade No. 3 .410 bore - only 7 mfg.

Extreme rarity factor precludes accurate pricing evaluation.

GRADE NO. 4E - auto ejectors.

✱ Grade No. 4E 10 ga. Mag.

100%	98%	95%	90%	80%	70%	60%	50%	40%	30%	20%	10%
$5,800	$5,350	$4,650	$4,100	$3,350	$2,650	$2,100	$1,975	$1,875	$1,750	$1,650	$1,550

3 1/2 in. chambered 10 ga. Mags. are serial numbered over 500,000. Total mfg. was approx. 850 guns for all grades. 2 7/8 in. chambered 10 gauges are priced the same as a 12 ga.

✱ Grade No. 4E 12 ga.

100%	98%	95%	90%	80%	70%	60%	50%	40%	30%	20%	10%
N/A	$3,750	$3,325	$3,000	$2,500	$2,100	$1,700	$1,550	$1,325	$1,200	$1,100	$995

✱ Grade No. 4E 16 ga.

100%	98%	95%	90%	80%	70%	60%	50%	40%	30%	20%	10%
N/A	N/A	$4,100	$3,750	$3,325	$3,000	$2,400	$2,000	$1,875	$1,650	$1,550	$1,450

✱ Grade No. 4E 20 ga.

100%	98%	95%	90%	80%	70%	60%	50%	40%	30%	20%	10%
N/A	N/A	$5,000	$4,625	$4,250	$3,725	$3,525	$3,300	$3,100	$2,950	$2,700	$2,300

✱ Grade No. 4E 28 ga.

Extreme rarity factor precludes accurate pricing evaluation.

✱ Grade No. 4E .410 bore

Extreme rarity factor precludes accurate pricing evaluation.

GRADE NO. 5E - auto ejectors.

✱ Grade No. 5E 10 ga. - only 9 mfg.

Extreme rarity factor precludes accurate pricing evaluation.

✱ Grade No. 5E 12 ga.

100%	98%	95%	90%	80%	70%	60%	50%	40%	30%	20%	10%
N/A	N/A	$4,750	$4,200	$3,750	$3,325	$3,000	$2,700	$2,200	$1,875	$1,650	$1,325

✱ Grade No. 5E 16 ga.

100%	98%	95%	90%	80%	70%	60%	50%	40%	30%	20%	10%
N/A	N/A	$5,400	$4,750	$4,200	$3,750	$3,325	$3,000	$2,700	$2,200	$1,875	$1,650

✱ Grade No. 5E 20 ga.

100%	98%	95%	90%	80%	70%	60%	50%	40%	30%	20%	10%
N/A	N/A	$6,000	$5,400	$4,750	$4,200	$3,750	$3,325	$3,000	$2,700	$2,200	$1,875

✱ Grade No. 5E 28 ga.

Extreme rarity factor precludes accurate pricing evaluation.

✱ Grade No. 5E .410 bore

Extreme rarity factor precludes accurate pricing evaluation.

GRADE NO. 7E - auto ejectors, only 22 mfg. in all gauges.

Extreme rarity factor precludes accurate pricing evaluation on this model.

$2,000 GRADE - 12 ga., top-of-the-line model, auto ejectors, single selective trigger.

100%	98%	95%	90%	80%	70%	60%	50%	40%	30%	20%	10%
N/A	N/A	$8,450	$7,400	$6,500	$5,650	$4,750	$4,000	$3,250	$2,600	$2,100	$1,700

Rarity on 16 or 20 ga. precludes accurate pricing.

PRE-WAR $1,000 GRADE - 12 ga., top-of-the-line models, auto ejectors, single selective trigger.

100%	98%	95%	90%	80%	70%	60%	50%	40%	30%	20%	10%
N/A	N/A	$9,500	$8,450	$7,400	$6,500	$5,650	$4,750	$4,000	$3,250	$2,600	$2,250

Rarity on 16 or 20 ga. precludes accurate pricing.

SOUSA GRADE - has mermaids on trigger guard in gold, only 11 manufactured (including one .410 bore). This model is very rare and prices are hard to establish. Recently, the price range has been approx. $15,000-$40,000, depending on gauge and original condition.

The famous band director and composer, John Phillip Sousa, assisted in the development of this model.

SHOTGUNS: SEMI-AUTO

MODEL 51A FEATHERLIGHT STANDARD - 12 or 20 ga., 30 in. full, 28 in. full or mod., 26 in. imp. cyl., gas operated, autoloading, checkered pistol grip stock. Vent. rib became standard during late production. Mfg. 1970-1985.

	100%	98%	95%	90%	80%	70%	60%
Older models w/o VR	$250	$230	$200	$180	$165	$150	$130
Recent production (w/VR)	$295	$265	$235	$210	$190	$175	$165

Last MSR with VR was $477.

MODEL 51A MAGNUM - similar to 51 Standard, except 3 in. shells only, blue finish, recoil pad, VR became standard in 1984. Disc. 1985.

	100%	98%	95%	90%	80%	70%	60%
Older models w/o VR	$265	$235	$220	$205	$180	$165	$150
Vent. rib	$325	$275	$250	$225	$200	$185	$170

MODEL 51A MAGNUM WATERFOWLER - similar to 51 Standard, except 3 in. shells only, matte finished metal & flat finished walnut, recoil pad. Vent. rib standard. Mfg. 1984-86.

100%	98%	95%	90%	80%	70%	60%
$325	$295	$275	$250	$230	$200	$180

Last MSR was $625.

Add $40 for camouflaged exterior finish (mfg. 1986 only).

MODEL 51A SUPREME TRAP - similar to 51 Standard, except 12 ga. only, 30 in. barrel, 7 post rib, full choke, select wood, pad, trap style stock. Add $36 for Monte Carlo. Mfg. 1970-86.

100%	98%	95%	90%	80%	70%	60%
$450	$375	$325	$295	$270	$250	$230

Last MSR was $869.

MODEL 51A SUPREME SKEET - similar to 51 Standard, except 26 in. VR barrel, skeet choke, select wood, 20 ga. was available 1983. Mfg. 1970-1986.

100%	98%	95%	90%	80%	70%	60%
$465	$395	$340	$300	$280	$260	$240

Last MSR was $858.

MODEL 51A DEERSLAYER - similar to 51 Standard, with 24 in. slug barrel, rifle sights, recoil pad, no rib. Mfg. 1972-83.

100%	98%	95%	90%	80%	70%	60%
$350	$300	$260	$230	$195	$180	$165

Last MSR was $477.

MODEL 51A TURKEY GUN - 12 ga. Mag. only, 26 in. barrel, matte finish, sling and swivels included. Mfg. 1984-86.

100%	98%	95%	90%	80%	70%	60%
$360	$305	$275	$265	$250	$230	$210

Last MSR was $625.

MODEL 51 DUCKS UNLIMITED - similar to 51 Deluxe, with D/U emblem on receiver.

100%	98%	95%	90%	80%	70%	60%
$425	$375	$335	$300	$280	$260	$230

MODEL 51 PRESENTATION - 12 ga., blue, engraved, gold engraved receiver with deluxe walnut. Mfg. 1984-86.

100%	98%	95%	90%	80%	70%	60%
$1,325	$1,050	$875	$700	$575	$450	$325

Last MSR was $1,658.

MODEL XL 300 - 12 or 20 ga., gas operated, various barrel lengths with or w/o VR. Mfg. 1973-76.

100%	98%	95%	90%	80%	70%	60%
$250	$230	$200	$180	$165	$150	$130

Add 15% for VR barrel.

MODEL XL 900 - 12 or 20 ga., gas operated, various barrel lengths with VR. Mfg. 1973-78.

100%	98%	95%	90%	80%	70%	60%
$295	$275	$245	$210	$185	$170	$150

Add 10% for skeet, trap, or slug variations.

GRADING - PPGS™	100%	98%	95%	90%	80%	70%	60%

Shotguns: Semi-Auto, Mag-10 Series

All Ithaca Mag-10s were disc. 1986.

MAG-10 - 10 ga., 3 1/2 in. Mag., various barrel lengths, stainless steel breech block assembly, gas operated, various chokes, plain barrel, 11 lb. Mfg. 1975-86.

> **100% values assume NIB condition - if without, subtract 10%.**

✳ *Mag-10 Standard Grade* - no checkering, ribless barrel, dull finished wood.

	$675	$600	$550	$500	$460	$430	$395

> *Last MSR was $726.*

✳ *Mag-10 Standard Grade with VR* - available in 22, 26, 28, or 32 in. barrel lengths - otherwise similar to Standard Grade.

	$750	$650	$550	$495	$450	$400	$360

> *Last MSR was $781.*

> **Add $60 for camouflaged exterior finish.**
> **Add $60 for interchangeable choke tubes (3) - became available in 1986.**

✳ *Mag-10 Deluxe Vent* - select checkered walnut stock and forearm, 22, 26, 28, or 32 in. barrels, high lustre wood finish.

	$800	$700	$600	$550	$495	$450	$400

> *Last MSR was $924.*

✳ *Mag-10 Supreme Grade* - extra-select checkered walnut stock and forearm, otherwise similar to Deluxe Vent.

	$995	$800	$725	$675	$595	$550	$495

> *Last MSR was $1,124.*

✳ *Mag-10 Mag. 10 Roadblocker* - 22 in. cylinder bored ribless barrel, parkerized finish.

	$750	$625	$575	$500	$460	$430	$400

> *Last MSR was $741.*

✳ *Mag-10 National Wild Turkey Fed. Special Edition* - mfg. in 1985 only.

	$950	$795	$625	N/A	N/A	N/A	N/A

MAG-10 PRESENTATION OR CENTENNIAL - 10 ga. Mag., blue, engraved, gold inlaid receiver, extra fancy walnut. Limited production. Approx. 200 mfg. in Presentation Grade 1983-86.

	$1,875	$1,550	$1,300	$1,050	$915	$830	$745

> *Last MSR was $1,727.*

This configuration was also offered as a 3 gun set - a NIB set is currently selling in the $4,750 range.

SHOTGUNS: SINGLE SHOT, LEVER ACTION

MODEL 66 - 12, 20 ga., or .410 bore single shot lever action, field gun only. Mfg. 1963-78.

	$150	$125	$100	$75	$70	$65	$55

> **Add 33% to .410 bore.**
> **Add 25% for VRs that were also available on special order.**

✳ *Model 66 RS* - 20 ga. slug gun with 22 in. barrel and rifle type sights, recoil pad.

	$195	$165	$135	$115	$90	$80	$70

> **Add 25% for special order VR.**

SHOTGUNS: SINGLE BARREL TRAP

CENTURY TRAP - please refer to the SKB section.

CENTURY II TRAP - please refer to the SKB section.

GRADING - PPGS™	100%	98%	95%	90%	80%	70%	60%

SINGLE BARREL TRAP - 12 ga., 30, 32, or 34 in. barrels, VR, boxlock, auto ejector, checkered pistol grip and forearm, grades differ in engraving, overall workmanship, and grade or wood and checkering. Values on these models sometimes vary greatly depending on originality of finish, customer alterations, and other variations trap shooters might use to alter dimensions for their particular shooting requirements. Values represent trap guns in original, unaltered condition.

Note: Flues model mfg. prior to 1921 with serial numbers under 400,000 generally have better engraving than NID (New Ithaca Double) models over serial number 400,000 (also referred to as Knick models).

Trap guns under 60% original condition will be within 25% of the value shown in the 60% column.

* *Single Barrel Trap Victory Grade* - disc. 1938.

	100%	98%	95%	90%	80%	70%	60%
	$1,250	$995	$850	$775	$675	$575	$495

* *Single Barrel Trap No. 4E* - disc. 1976.

	100%	98%	95%	90%	80%	70%	60%
	$2,950	$2,675	$2,450	$2,200	$2,000	$1,825	$1,625

* *Single Barrel Trap No. 5E* - 12 ga., 32 or 34 in. barrel, custom order only, elaborate engraving, quality worksmanship throughout. Originally mfg. 1925-86, mfg. resumed 1988-91.

	100%	98%	95%	90%	80%	70%	60%
	$4,000	$3,500	$3,000	$2,550	$2,175	$1,900	$1,725

Last MSR was $7,500.

* *Single Barrel Trap No. 6E* - this model was available by special order only. Rarity factor precludes accurate pricing.

* *Single Barrel Trap No. 7E* - disc. 1964.

	100%	98%	95%	90%	80%	70%	60%
	$6,500	$5,500	$4,700	$4,000	$3,500	$3,000	$2,500

* *Single Barrel Trap Dollar Grade* - 12 ga., 32 or 34 in. barrel. Top-of-the-line model custom built to customer specifications. Original mfg. was stopped 1986 and resumed 1988-91.

	100%	98%	95%	90%	80%	70%	60%
	$6,750	$5,950	$5,200	$4,600	$3,850	$3,250	$2,775

Last MSR was $10,000.

* *Single Barrel Trap $5,000 Grade* - similar to Pre-War $1,000 grade.

	100%	98%	95%	90%	80%	70%	60%
	$9,500	$8,900	$8,175	$7,650	$6,725	$5,825	$4,950

* *Single Barrel Trap Sousa Grade* - extremely rare.

Extreme rarity factor precludes accurate pricing evaluation. Prices will be higher than the $5,000 Grade.

SHOTGUNS: SLIDE ACTION

During late 1996, Ithaca Gun Co., LLC resumed manufacture of the Model 37, while discontinuing the Model 87. In 1987, Ithaca Acquisition Corp. reintroduced the Model 37 as the Model 87. Recently manufactured Model 87s are listed in addition to both new and older Model 37s (produced pre-1986).

Over 2 million Model 37s have been produced.

Model 37s with ser. nos. above 855,000 will accept both 2 3/4 and 3 in. chambered barrels interchangeably. Earlier guns have incompatible threading for the magnum barrels.

MODEL 37 TRENCH AND RIOT GUNS - see separate listing under Trench Guns in the T Section.

MODEL 37 DS POLICE SPECIAL - 12 ga. only, 18 1/2 in. barrel with rifle sights, Parkerized finish on metal, oil finished stock, typically subcontracted by police departments or law enforcement agencies, with or without unit code markings.

	100%	98%	95%	90%	80%	70%	60%
	$325	$275	$235	$200	$185	$170	$160

GRADING - PPGS™	100%	98%	95%	90%	80%	70%	60%

MODEL 37 FEATHERLIGHT STANDARD - 12, 16, or 20 ga., bottom ejection, 4 shot mag., 26, 28, or 30 in. barrel, hammerless, take down, any standard choke, checkered walnut stock and forearm. Mfg. 1937-disc.

	$600	$550	$475	$400	$325	$250	$200

Add 25% for 16 or 20 ga.

MODEL 37 $1000 GRADE - all gauges, deluxe engraving and checkering, gold inlaid, select figured walnut, hand-finished parts. Mfg. 1937-40.

	$5,750	$5,200	$4,750	$4,250	$3,750	$3,250	$2,650

MODEL 37 $5000 GRADE - similar to $1000 Grade, post-war designation. Mfg. 1947-67.

	$5,250	$4,850	$4,250	$3,850	$3,250	$2,850	$2,250

MODEL 37V - similar to 37, except VR. Mfg. 1962-disc.

	$315	$260	$240	$195	$180	$170	$165

All recently manufactured Model 37s have the Featherlight designation. Prices are for older manufactured Model 37s.

MODEL 37D - similar to 37, except recoil pad, beavertail forearm, checkered wood. Mfg. 1954-1981.

	$295	$275	$235	$200	$185	$175	$160

MODEL 37DV - similar to 37D, except VR. Mfg. 1962-81.

	$375	$325	$265	$225	$200	$185	$170

MODEL 37 ULTRA FEATHERLIGHT - 20 ga. only, bottom ejection, 4 shot mag., 26 or 28 in. VR barrel, standard choke, approx. 4 3/4 lbs. Disc.

	$395	$340	$275	$235	$210	$190	$175

MODEL 37 ULTRA FEATHERLIGHT RUFFED GROUSE SOCIETY SPECIAL EDITION - 20 ga. only, bottom ejection, aluminum receiver, 22 or 24 in. barrel, English style American walnut stock. Limited mfg. 2003-2004.

	$715	$565	$435	$375	$300	$260	$230

Last MSR was $840.

MODEL 37 FIELD GRADE MAGNUM - 12 or 20 ga., 3 in. chambers, VR, walnut stock and corncob forearm, supplied with three choke tubes. Mfg. 1984-86.

	$300	$240	$195	$180	$170	$165	$150

Last MSR was $428.

MODEL 37 FIELD GRADE STANDARD - 12 or 20 ga., economy model, corncob style forearm, 26, 28, or 30 in. barrel. Mfg. 1983-1985 only.

	$245	$225	$195	$175	$160	$140	$120

Last MSR was $298.

MODEL 37 ULTRALIGHT - 12 (disc.) or 20 ga., new manufacture features checkered pistol grip (with Sid Bell red grip cap) and forearm, most recent mfg. was in deer configuration, 20 ga. only with 20 or 25 in. smooth bore barrel. Mfg. 1996-2002.

	$475	$380	$340	$300	$275	$250	$225

Last MSR was $600.

MODEL 37 ENGLISH ULTRALIGHT DELUXE - 12 (disc.), 16 or 20 ga., 24, 25 (disc.), 26 or 28 in. barrels, choice of English straight grip stock with checkered forearm or pistol grip stock and grooved forearm, aluminum receiver, world's lightest pump, 20 ga. weighs 4 3/4 lb., 12 ga. weighs 5 1/2 lbs., checkered straight stock. Mfg. 1983-1986, reintroduced 1999-2005.

	$520	$410	$300	$250	$225	$200	$185

Last MSR was $659.

GRADING - PPGS™	100%	98%	95%	90%	80%	70%	60%

✳ *Model 37 English Ultralight Deluxe Classic* - 16 or 20 ga., choice of pistol grip or English straight grip deluxe checkered walnut stock and forearm, 24, 26, or 28 in. VR barrel with three choke tubes, 5 1/4 lbs.

	$700	$555	$425	$375	$300	$260	$230

Last MSR was $834.

MODEL 37R - 12, 16, or 20 ga., solid rib. Mfg. 1937-67.

	100%	98%	95%	90%	80%	70%	60%
Plain stock	$295	$200	$175	$145	$130	$110	$90
Checkered stock	$335	$245	$200	$175	$165	$145	$120

Add 20% for 16 or 20 ga.

MODEL 37R DELUXE - similar to 37R, except fancy wood. Mfg. 1937-1955.

	$600	$550	$475	$400	$325	$250	$200

MODEL 37 PROTECTION SERIES - 12 ga. only, 18.5 or 20 in. smoothbore barrel w/o chokes, 5 or 8 shot tube mag., approx. 6 3/4 lbs. Limited mfg. 2005.

	$425	$375	$325	$275	$250	$225	$195

Last MSR was $482.

Add $27 for 20 in. barrel.

TURKEYSLAYER - 12 (Storm) or 20 (new 2000, Storm Light)) ga., 3 in. chamber, choice of matte blue or 100% camo coverage in Realtree Hardwoods (disc. 2002), Realtree Hardwoods HD (new 2003), Realtree Timber (disc. 2002), or Advantage (disc. 2001) pattern, 22 (disc. 2002) or 24 in. barrel with extended choke tube, Truglo fiber optic sights standard beginning 2003, 7 lbs. Mfg. 1996-2004.

	$375	$335	$300	$275	$250	$225	$200

Last MSR was $459.

Add $20 for ported choke tube (disc.).

✳ *Turkeyslayer Youth* - 20 ga. only, features 22 in. barrel and shortened youth dimension stock. Mfg. 1998-2003.

	$500	$375	$295	$225	$175	$160	$145

Last MSR was $615.

TURKEYSLAYER II GUIDE SERIES - 12 ga. only, 3 in. chamber, 20 in. interchangeable barrel with turkey choke, choice of Realtree Hardwoods Green or 100% Mossy Oak Break Up camo coverage, pistol grip stock, includes 30mm red dot scope and sling, fiber optic sights. Limited production 2005 only.

	$500	$425	$365	$330	$300	$275	$250

Last MSR was $599.

WATERFOWLER - 12 (Storm) or 20 (Storm Light) ga., features black finish or Wetlands (disc.), Realtree Hardwoods HD Green, or Realtree Max 4 camo treatment, 24, 26, 28 (standard) or 30 in. barrel designed for shooting steel shot. Mfg. 1998-2004.

	$425	$375	$335	$300	$275	$250	$225

Last MSR was $499.

Add $50 for Realtree Max 4 camo.

MODEL 37 DELUXE W/VR - 12, 16 (Featherlight, new 1999), or 20 ga., similar to Model 87 Field Grade except has cut checkering, 26, 28, or 30 (disc. 2002) in. VR barrel, high gloss lacquer finish, and gold trigger, newer mfg. includes 3 choke tubes. Mfg. 1996-2005.

	$500	$380	$285	$230	$175	$160	$145

Last MSR was $627.

Add $30 for 20 ga. Youth Model.

GRADING - PPGS™	100%	98%	95%	90%	80%	70%	60%

✳ *Model 37 Deluxe W/VR English* - 12 (new 2000) or 20 ga., features 24, 26, or 28 in. English style vent. rib barrel, approx. 7 lbs. Mfg. 1998-2003.

		$485	$365	$275	$225	$175	$160	$145

Last MSR was $600.

Add $30 for 20 ga.

MODEL 37 CLASSIC - 12, 16 (Featherlight, new 1999), or 20 ga., features knuckle cut receiver, corncob style forearm, hand checkering, and sunburst recoil pad, 26 or 28 in. VR barrel with choke tubes, choice of pistol grip or English straight grip deluxe checkered walnut stock and forearm, 6 1/2 - 7 lbs . Limited production 1998-2005.

$680	$540	$425	$375	$300	$260	$230

Last MSR was $812.

✳ *Model 37 Classic NRA Women's* - 16 or 20 ga., 24 in. VR barrel with three choke tubes, 5 1/4 or 6 1/2 lbs. Mfg. 2003-2004.

$715	$565	$435	$375	$300	$260	$230

Last MSR was $840.

MODEL 37 SUPREME - 12, 16, or 20 ga., deluxe checkered walnut stock and forearm, 28 or 30 in. VR barrel, engraved receiver, approx. 7 3/4 lbs. Originally mfg. 1967-1986, reintroduced late 1996, disc. 1997, reintroduced 2003-2004.

	$895	$650	$550	$450	$400	$350	$425
1967-1997 Mfg.	$675	$575	$495	$425	$375	$325	$295

Last MSR was $1,185.

MODEL 37S SKEET GRADE - similar to 37, except Knicker VR, large forearm, fancy wood. Mfg. 1937-55.

$495	$445	$375	$335	$300	$275	$250

Add 20% for 16 or 20 ga.

MODEL 37 SPORTING CLAYS - 12 ga. only, 24 (disc.), 26 (disc.), 28, or 30 (disc.) in. VR ported (standard 2001) or unported (disc. 2000) barrel with 3 Briley choke tubes, similar in appearances and features to Model 37 Trap. New 2000-2004.

$1,275	$1,075	$925	$800	$650	$525	$450

Last MSR was $1,495.

MODEL 37T TRAP GRADE - similar to 37S, except trap stock, select walnut, recoil pad. Mfg. 1937-55.

$475	$425	$375	$325	$295	$275	$250

Add 20% for early models with fleur-de-lis checkering.

MODEL 37 TRAP - 12 ga. only, 30 in. VR ported (standard 2001) or unported (disc. 2000) barrel with 3 Briley choke tubes, antique silver finished receiver with scroll style engraving and gold inlays on receiver sides, optional adj. cheekpiece stock. Mfg. 2000-2004.

$1,275	$1,075	$925	$800	$650	$525	$450

Last MSR was $1,495.

MODEL 37T TARGET GRADE - replaced 37S and 37T. Mfg. from 1955-61.

$475	$425	$375	$325	$295	$275	$250

MODEL 37 DEERSLAYER - 12, 16, or 20 ga., original Deerslayer, smooth bore with fixed choke only, rifle sights. Mfg. circa 1959-1986.

$300	$240	$195	$180	$170	$165	$150

MODEL 37 SUPER DELUXE DEERSLAYER - similar to Model 37 (87) Deerslayer, except Williams aperture rear sight and fancy wood. Mfg.1962-1985.

$375	$335	$300	$270	$235	$210	$185

Last MSR was $447.

GRADING - PPGS™	100%	98%	95%	90%	80%	70%	60%

MODEL 37 DEERSLAYER DELUXE - 12, 16 (new 1999 - smooth bore only, rifled beginning 2000) or 20 ga., 20, 24, or 25 (disc.) in. smooth bore (disc.) or rifled barrel, 100% Realtree Hardwoods 20/200 camo (mfg. 2000-2002, 12 ga. only) or walnut stock and forearm with cut checkering, light receiver engraving. Mfg. 1959-2005.

	$495	$410	$330	$285	$240	$210	$185

Last MSR was $591.

Add $50 for Hardwoods camo (disc.).

DEERSLAYER II - 12, 16 (new 2001), or 20 ga., 20, 24 (new 2003) or 25 (disc.) in. barrel with 1:34 rifling (also available with fast twist 1:25 rifling, 12 ga. only, disc.), Monte Carlo stock and forearm with cut checkering, receiver is drilled and tapped for scope mounting, 6.25-7 lbs. Mfg 1996-2005.

	$520	$390	$310	$230	$175	$160	$145

Last MSR was $642.

✳ *Deerslayer II Model 37 Storm* - 12 or 20 (Storm Light) ga., 24 in. smooth bore barrel with choke tube and open rifle sights, 100% DSS treatment on stock, approx. 6 1/2 lbs. Mfg. 2003-2004.

	$350	$300	$275	$250	$225	$200	$185

Last MSR was $399.

DEERSLAYER II GUIDE SERIES - 12 or 20 ga., 20 or 24 in. rifled barrel with fiber optic sights, 3 in. chamber, blued metal, grey camo laminate pistol grip stock and forearm. Limited production 2005.

	$500	$415	$330	$285	$240	$210	$185

Last MSR was $599.

DEERSLAYER III - 12 ga., 26 in. smooth bore barrel with DSR-1 choke tube, 11 lbs. Mfg. 2003-2004.

	$750	$675	$600	$525	$450	$375	$300

Last MSR was $900.

MODEL 37 BICENTENNIAL - 12 ga., engraved, fancy wood, cased with pewter buckle, 1,776 mfg. 1976, 100% value assumes NIB condition with case and belt buckle.

	$595	$450	$325	$265	$230	$195	$170

MODEL 37 2500 SERIES CENTENNIAL - 12 ga., customized version of the Model 37 commemorating Ithaca's 100th year anniversary, silver plated, etched antique finish receiver, deluxe walnut. Mfg. 1980-84.

	$775	$625	$450	$385	$335	$280	$235

Last MSR was $919.

MODEL 37 60TH ANNIVERSARY LIMITED EDITION - 20 ga., scroll engraving by A&A Engraving on both sides of nickel receiver with dog game scene/eagle motif, supreme grade wood, includes case. 200 mfg. 1997 only.

	$1,450	$850	$475	$415	$360	$300	$255

Last MSR was $2,000.

MODEL 37 PRESENTATION - 12 ga., blue, engraved, gold mounted receiver with extra-fancy walnut, cased, limited production. Mfg. 1981-86.

	$1,500	$1,245	$1,080	$915	$830	$745	$665

Last MSR was $1,658.

A 3 gun set was also available - an NIB set is currently priced in the $4,500 range.

MODEL 37 DUCKS UNLIMITED - 12 ga., VR.

	$385	$305	$275	$225	$195	$165	$140

MODEL 37 60TH ANNIVERSARY - 20 ga., 3 in. chamber, 26 in. VR barrel, checkered Supreme wood, engraved, cased. 200 mfg. 1997 only.

	$1,750	$1,250	$850	$740	$620	$515	$440

GRADING - PPGS™	100%	98%	95%	90%	80%	70%	60%

MODEL 87 FIELD (BASIC) - 12 or 20 ga., 3 in. chamber, economy model, walnut stock and forearm with pressed checkering, 26, 28, or 30 (disc.) in. barrel with 3 choke tubes standard. Reintroduced 1987-96.

	$360	$290	$240	$195	$170	$160	$145

Last MSR was $477.

✱ *Model 87 Field Basic Combo* - 12 or 20 ga., includes 20/25 in. deer barrel with special bore and 28 in. VR multi-choke field barrel, uncheckered walnut stock and corncob forearm, 7 lbs. Mfg. 1989-92.

	$400	$315	$275	$235	$210	$190	$170

Last MSR was $459.

> **Add $32 for rifled bore barrel.**
> **Add $104 for laminated wood (includes rifle bored barrel).**

✱ *Model 87 Field Camo* - 12 ga. only, 3 in. chamber, 24, 26, or 28 in. VR barrel, camo-seal rust resistant finish on exterior parts. Available in either green or brown camo finish. Mfg. began 1986, resumed 1988, disc. 1996.

	$425	$315	$260	$200	$175	$160	$145

Last MSR was $542.

✱ *Model 87 Field Turkey* - 12 ga. only, 24 in. VR barrel with choice of fixed full choke or full choke tube, camo or matte blue finish. Mfg. 1989-96.

	$365	$285	$235	$190	$170	$160	$145

Last MSR was $466.

> **Add $85 for camo finish. Add $43 for full choke tube.**

MODEL 87 ULTRALITE FIELD - 12 or 20 ga., 3 in. chamber, aluminum receiver, 20 (disc. 1988), 24, 25 (disc. 1988), or 26 in. barrel. 20 ga. weighs 5 lbs., 12 ga. weighs 5 3/4 lbs, multi-chokes (3) became standard in 1989. Originally mfg. 1985-86, reintroduced 1988-90.

	$445	$375	$295	$240	$210	$190	$170

Last MSR was $481.

> **Add $50 for slim grip model (12 1/2 in. stock - disc. 1985).**
> **Subtract $42 if without multiple choke feature.**
> The 20 and 25 in. barrels were disc. when mfg. was resumed 1988.

✱ *Model 87 Ultralite Field Deluxe* - similar to Model 87 Ultralite Field except has cut checkering, high gloss lacquer finish, and gold trigger. Mfg 1989-1991.

	$425	$360	$300	$250	$220	$190	$170

Last MSR was $514.

MODEL 87 ENGLISH - 20 ga. only, 3 in. chamber, 24 or 26 in. VR barrel with 3 choke tubes, steel receiver, checkered walnut stock and forearm, recoil pad, 6 3/4 lbs. Mfg. 1991-96.

	$425	$315	$260	$200	$175	$160	$145

Last MSR was $545.

MODEL 87 DELUXE - similar to Model 87 Field Grade except has cut checkering, 26, 28, or 30 in. VR barrel, high gloss lacquer finish, and gold trigger, newer mfg. includes 3 choke tubes. Mfg. 1989-96.

	$415	$310	$255	$200	$175	$160	$145

Last MSR was $533.

> **Add $54 for combo package (includes 20 in. special bore deer barrel, disc. 1992).**
> **Add $87 for combo package with 20 or 25 in. rifled bore deer barrel, disc. 1992.**

✱ *Model 87 Deluxe Magnum* - 12 or 20 ga., 3 in. chambers, VR, deluxe wood with checkered forearm. Mfg. 1981-86, production resumed 1988 only.

	$320	$270	$230	$210	$200	$185	$165

Last MSR was $395.

> **Add $77 for Combo package (extra 28 in. barrel).**
> Recent mfg. 20 ga. shotguns were available with a 25 in. barrel only (with choke tubes).

GRADING - PPGS™	100%	98%	95%	90%	80%	70%	60%

MODEL 87 SUPREME GRADE - 12 or 20 ga., presentation walnut, high luster blue, limited production, previously available in either trap, skeet, or field models, fixed chokes. Mfg. 1988-96.

	$640	$475	$395	$325	$295	$270	$250

Last MSR was $809.

BASIC DEERSLAYER - 12 ga. only, 20 or 25 in. special bore or rifled barrel, oil finished stock and corncob style forearm with no checkering, iron sights, matte metal finish, 7 lbs. Mfg. 1989-1996.

	$345	$280	$240	$195	$175	$160	$145

Last MSR was $425.

Add $40 for rifled barrel.

MODEL 87 FIELD DEERSLAYER - 12 or 20 ga., rifle slug barrel, 20 or 25 in. special smooth bore barrel with open sights. Mfg. 1959-86, reintroduced 1988-93.

	$300	$250	$210	$180	$160	$150	$140

Last MSR was $364.

MODEL 87 DELUXE DEERSLAYER - similar to Field Deerslayer except has cut checkering, high gloss lacquer finish, and gold trigger. Mfg. 1989-96.

	$365	$285	$235	$190	$170	$160	$145

Last MSR was $465.

Add $34 for rifled bore.
Add $120 for combo package (28 in. multi-choke barrel).

 * *Model 87 Deluxe Deerslayer Ultra* - similar to Deluxe Deerslayer except has aluminum frame. Mfg. 1989-90 only.

	$350	$285	$245	$200	$175	$160	$145

Last MSR was $444.

MONTE CARLO DEERSLAYER II - 12 ga. only, 20 or 25 in. barrel with rifling, Monte Carlo stock and forearm with cut checkering, receiver is drilled and tapped for scope mounting, 7 lbs. Mfg. 1989-96.

	$445	$335	$270	$210	$175	$160	$145

Last MSR was $567.

DEERSLAYER II FAST TWIST - 12 ga. only, 25 in. rifled permanently fixed barrel, Monte Carlo stock with checkering, receiver is drilled and tapped. Mfg. 1992-93.

	$440	$385	$325	$275	$235	$200	$180

Last MSR was $550.

MODEL 87 MILITARY & POLICE - 12 (3 in.) or 20 (new 1989) ga., short barrel Model 37 w/ normal stock or pistol grip only, 18 1/2, 20, or 24 3/4 (scarce) in. barrel, choice of front bead or rifle sights, front blade was usually a flourescent orange plastic, 5, 8, or 10 shot. Originally disc. 1983, reintroduced 1989-95.

	$265	$230	$200	$180	$170	$160	$150

Last MSR was $323.

Add $104 for nickel finish (mfg. 1991-92 only).

ITHACA GUNS USA, LLC

Current manufacturer established in 2006 and located in Upper Sandusky, OH.

During December of 2005, Ithaca Guns USA, LLC bought out the remaining assets and equipment of Ithaca Gun Company LLC and moved production to Upper Sandusky, OH.

SHOTGUNS

Currently, the company is offering the Model 37 in various 12 ga. configurations - Featherlight and Ultralight, Deerslayer II, Deerslayer III, Law Enforcement, Riot Gun, and a Turkeyslayer. Please contact the company directly for more information, including pricing and availability (see Trademark Index).

GRADING - PPGS™	100%	98%	95%	90%	80%	70%	60%

IVER JOHNSON ARMS, INC. (NEW MFG.)

Current manufacturer established during 2004 and located in Rockledge, FL.

The new Iver Johnson Arms, Inc. company was formed during 2004, and currently manfactures the Raven Series, based on the M1911 design, in both .22 LR (MSR $550) and .45 ACP cals. (MSR is $500), the Target Eagle Series (MSR $625), the Frontier Four Derringer (MSR is TBA), and the Model PM 30G M1 Carbine (MSR is N/A). Please contact the company directly for more information, including availability and pricing (see Trademark Index).

IVER JOHNSON ARMS, INC.

Previously manufactured in Fitchburg, MA, 1883-1984 and Jacksonville, AR 1984-1993. Formerly Johnson Bye & Co. 1871-1883. Renamed Iver Johnson & Co. in 1871 until 1891. Renamed Iver Johnson's Arms & Cycle Works in 1891 with manufacturing moving to Fitchburg, MA. In 1975 the name changed to Iver Johnson's Arms, Inc., and two years later, company facilities were moved to Middlesex, NJ. In 1982, production was moved to Jacksonville, AR under the trade name Iver Johnson Arms, Inc. In 1983, Universal Firearms, Inc. was acquired by Iver Johnson Arms, Inc.

Iver Johnson Arms was sold in March of 1987 and was acquired by American Military Arms Corporation (AMAC). AMAC ceased operations in early 1993.

PISTOLS: SEMI-AUTO

AMAC also manufactured Delta 786 9mm Para. (disc. 1989), the Super Enforcer .30 Carbine, and the M-2 machine gun in .30 Carbine which are not listed in this text.

TRAILSMEN PISTOL - .22 LR cal. only, all steel construction, 4 1/2 or 6 in. barrel, blue finish, black checkered composition grips, 10 shot mag., approx. 30 oz. Mfg. 1985-86 and reintroduced 1990 only.

$200	$165	$145	$130	$120	$110	$100

Last MSR was $230.

Add $20 for hardwood stocks and high polish blue (disc. 1990).

PONY PISTOL (PO380 SERIES) - .380 ACP cal. only, semi-auto single action, 3 in. barrel, 6 shot mag., all steel construction, blue or matte blue finish, 20 oz. Mfg. 1985-1986 (by Firearms International) and reintroduced 1990 only.

$290	$245	$210	$185	$170	$155	$140

Last MSR was $330.

✳ *Pony Pistol .380 Stainless* - similar to Pony Pistol, except is stainless steel construction. New 1990 only.

$315	$280	$240	$185	$155	$130	$110

Last MSR was $365.

✳ *Pony Pistol Nickel* - with nickel finish. Mfg. 1985 only.

$260	$230	$215	$200	$185	$170	$160

Last MSR was $290 for nickel finish.

POCKET PISTOL (TP SERIES) - .22 LR or .25 ACP cal., semi-auto, double action, 3 in. barrel, 7 shot finger tip extension mag., black plastic grips, fixed sights, blue or matte finish, 15 oz. Previously mfg. 1985-86, reintroduced 1988-90.

$145	$125	$110	$100	$90	$80	$70

Last MSR was $165.

Add $15 for nickel finish (disc. 1989).

AMAC-22/25 COMPACT - .22 Short (disc.) or .25 ACP cal., semi-auto, single action, 5 shot mag., 2 in. barrel, all steel construction, plastic grips, 9.3 oz. Disc. 1993.

$165	$135	$115	$100	$90	$80	$70

Last MSR was $200.

Add $10 for nickel finish (disc. 1990).

GRADING - PPGS™	100%	98%	95%	90%	80%	70%	60%

✱ *AMAC-22/25 Compact Elite Engraved* - similar to .25 ACP Compact, except has extensive engraving. Mfg. 1991-93.

	$850	$600	$475	$415	$360	$300	$255

Last MSR was $1,000.

SILVER HAWK - .22 LR or .25 ACP cal., double action semi-auto, similar to TP-22 Series, except is stainless steel. Mfg. 1990-93.

	$215	$185	$160	$130	$115	$95	$85

Last MSR was $250.

SUPER ENFORCER (MODEL 3000) - .30 Carbine cal. only, pistol version of the Carbine with 11 in. shrouded barrel. Mfg. 1985-1986 only.

	$400	$350	$325	$300	$200	$175	$160

Last MSR was $255.

Add $40 for stainless steel (disc. for 1986).

✱ *Super Enforcer* - similar to Super Enforcer Model 3000, except has 10 1/2 in. barrel. Mfg. 1988-1993.

	$450	$400	$300	$275	$225	$200	$175

Last MSR was $417.

REVOLVERS

CATTLEMAN MAGNUM - .357 Mag., .44 Mag., or .45 LC cal., single action, 6 shot, Colt replica, 4 3/4, 5 1/2, or 7 1/2 in. barrel, case color frame, blue barrel, and brass grip frame, smooth walnut grips, fixed sights. Mfg. in Italy. Disc. 1984.

	$250	$200	$190	$150	$140	$130	$125
.44 Mag.	$275	$240	$200	$175	$165	$145	$135

BUCKHORN MAGNUM - similar to Cattleman, except flattop, adj. sights.

	$275	$225	$200	$175	$165	$145	$140

BUNTLINE BUCKHORN MAGNUM - similar to Buckhorn, only 18 in. barrel, detachable stock.

	$375	$335	$310	$275	$260	$250	$225
.44 Mag.	$400	$350	$325	$295	$280	$275	$250

TRAIL BLAZER - .22 LR, or .22 Mag. cal., interchangeable cylinder, 5 1/2 or 6 1/2 in. barrel, blue.

	$175	$145	$130	$120	$110	$100	$80

MODEL 1900 - .22 L, S, LR, .32 S&W, or .38 S&W cal., double action, 2 1/2, 4 1/2, or 6 in. barrel, fixed sights, blue or nickel, rubber grips. Mfg. 1900-47.

	$200	$165	$145	$130	$120	$110	$100

MODEL 1900 TARGET - .22 LR cal., 6 shot, 6 or 9 1/2 in. barrel, blue, fixed sights. Mfg. 1925-42.

	$225	$200	$165	$145	$130	$120	$110

TARGET SEALED 8 - .22 LR cal., 8 shot, 6 or 10 in. barrel, blue, fixed sights, rubber grips. Mfg. 1931-57.

	$150	$100	$95	$80	$75	$65	$60

Add 50% for 10 in. barrel.

TARGET 9 SHOT - similar to Target Sealed 8, except 9 shot. Mfg. 1929-46.

	$145	$90	$80	$70	$65	$55	$50

SAFETY HAMMER MODEL - .22 LR, .32 S&W, or .38 S&W cal., 2 or 3 in. barrel standard, 4, 5, or 6 in. available at extra cost, fixed sights, blue (standard) or nickel, break open. Mfg. 1892-50.

	$125	$80	$70	$60	$55	$45	$40

GRADING - PPGS™	100%	98%	95%	90%	80%	70%	60%

SAFETY HAMMERLESS - .32 S&W or .38 S&W cal., 2, 3 (.32 only), 3 1/4, 4, 5, or 6 in. barrel, double action only, break open, fixed sights, rubber grips, blue or nickel. Mfg. 1895-50.

	$125	$100	$95	$80	$75	$65	$60

.22 SUPERSHOT - .22 LR cal., 6 in. barrel, blue, fixed sights, checkered wood grips, break open, no counterbore. Mfg. 1929-49.

	$200	$165	$145	$130	$120	$110	$100

TRIGGER COCKING SINGLE ACTION - .22 LR cal., 8 shot, 6 in. barrel, break open, counterbored, blue, checkered wood grips, first pull on trigger cocks, second fires. Mfg. 1940-47. Rare in 100% condition.

	$350	$300	$250	$175	$100	$85	$75

.22 TARGET SINGLE ACTION - .22 LR cal., 8 shot, 6 in. barrel, break open, counterbored, checkered wood, adj. grips and sights. Mfg. 1938-48.

	$300	$250	$225	$200	$150	$125	$100

SUPERSHOT SEALED 8 - .22 LR cal., 8 shot, break open, blue, adj. sights, checkered wood grips. Mfg. 1931-57.

	$250	$225	$200	$165	$145	$130	$120

SUPERSHOT 9 - similar to Sealed 8, only 9 shot, not counterbored. Mfg. 1929-49.

	$135	$90	$80	$75	$60	$50	$40

PROTECTOR SEALED 8 - .22 LR cal., 8 shot, 2 1/2 in. barrel, break open, fixed sights, blue, wood grips. Mfg. 1933-49.

	$175	$135	$125	$110	$90	$80	$75

SUPERSHOT MODEL 844 - .22 LR cal., 8 shot, 4 1/2 or 6 in. barrel, adj. sights, break open, blue, wood grips. Mfg. 1955-56.

	$100	$90	$85	$80	$75	$60	$50

ARMSWORTH MODEL 855 - .22 LR cal., single action, 8 shot, 6 in. barrel, break open, blue, adj. sights, wood grips, adj. finger rest. Mfg. 1955-57.

	$300	$250	$225	$200	$150	$125	$100

MODEL 55A TARGET - .22 LR cal., 8 shot, 4 1/2 or 6 in. barrel, solid frame, blue, fixed sights, wood grips, loading gate. Mfg. 1955-84.

	$100	$75	$65	$50	$40	$35	$25

CADET - .22 LR, .22 WRM, .32 S&W, .38 S&W, or .38 Spl. cal., 2 1/2 in. barrel, blue, fixed sights, plastic grips. Mfg. 1955-84.

	$110	$90	$80	$75	$65	$55	$50

MODEL 57A TARGET - .22 LR cal., 8 shot, 4 1/2 or 6 in. barrel, solid frame, blue, adj. sights, wood grips. Mfg. 1955-75.

	$100	$80	$75	$65	$55	$45	$40

MODEL 66 TRAILSMAN - .22 LR cal., 6 in. barrel, break open, blue, adj. sights, rebounding hammer, wood grips. Mfg. 1958-75.

	$110	$90	$85	$75	$65	$55	$50

SIDEWINDER - .22 LR cal., 6 or 8 shot, 4 3/4 or 6 in. barrel, solid frame, blue, nickel, or case hardened finish, plastic grips, wood on case color model. Mfg. 1961-disc. 8 shot pre-1975.

	$110	$90	$85	$75	$65	$55	$50

SIDEWINDER S - similar to Sidewinder, except .22 WMR, interchangeable cylinder.

	$125	$100	$95	$85	$75	$65	$60

MODEL 67 VIKING - .22 LR cal., 8 shot, 4 1/2 or 6 in. barrel, break open, blue, adj. sights, wood grips with thumbrest. Mfg. 1964-75.

	$135	$110	$100	$95	$85	$75	$65

GRADING - PPGS™	100%	98%	95%	90%	80%	70%	60%

MODEL 67S VIKING - .22 LR, .32 S&W, or .38 S&W cal., 8 shot in .22, 5 shot in .32 or .38, 2 3/4 in. barrel, break open, adj. sights, plastic grips. Mfg. 1964-75.

	100%	98%	95%	90%	80%	70%	60%
	$130	$100	$95	$85	$75	$60	$50

AMERICAN BULLDOG - .22 LR, .22 WRM, or .38 Spl. cal., 6 shot in .22, 5 shot in .38, 2 1/2 or 4 in. barrel, blue or nickel, adj. sights, plastic grips. Mfg. 1974-76.

	$135	$110	$100	$90	$80	$65	$60

ROOKIE - .38 Spl. cal., 5 shot, 4 in. barrel, solid frame, blue or nickel, plastic grips. Mfg. 1975-84.

	$135	$110	$100	$90	$80	$65	$60

SPORTSMAN - .22 LR cal., 6 shot, 4 3/4 or 6 in. barrel, solid frame, blue, fixed sights, plastic grips. Mfg. 1974-76.

	$100	$80	$75	$65	$55	$45	$35

DELUXE TARGET - similar to Sportsman, adj. sights. Mfg. 1975-76 only.

	$110	$90	$85	$75	$65	$55	$40

SWING OUT - .22 LR, .22 WRM, .32 S&W, or .38 S&W cal., 6 shot in .22, 5 shot in .32 or .38, 2, 3, or 4 in. barrel, VR, 4 or 6 in., blue or nickel, fixed or adj. sights. Mfg. 1977-84.

	$130	$110	$100	$90	$80	$75	$65

✳ *Swing Out VR Barrel* - 4 or 6 in. VR barrel, adj. sights.

	$170	$150	$140	$130	$125	$120	$100

RIFLES

MODEL X - .22 Short, Long, or LR cal., bolt action, single shot, 22 in. barrel, open sight, pistol grip with knob forend. Mfg. 1928-32.

	$250	$225	$200	$165	$145	$130	$120

This model was mfg. both in the U.S. and Canada (by Cooey). Canadian models generally have birch stocks.

✳ *Model XA* - same as Model X, except equipped with Lyman No. 55J receiver peep sight, ivory bead, swivels and leather sling strap, scarce. Mfg. 1928-32.

	$350	$300	$250	$200	$175	$150	$100

MODEL 2X - improved Model X, 24 in. heavy barrel, larger stock, adj. sights. Mfg. 1932-55.

	$250	$225	$200	$165	$145	$130	$120

✳ *Model 2XA* - same as the Model 2X, except equipped with Lyman No. 55J receiver peep sight, ivory bead, swivels and leather sling, scarce. Mfg. 1932-1945.

	$300	$250	$225	$175	$120	$125	$100

Add 25% for factory checkered stock.

LI´L CHAMP - .22 LR cal. only, single shot bolt action, 16 1/4 in. barrel, black molded stock, nickel plated bolt, youth dimensions, (32 1/2 in. overall length), 3 lbs. Introduced 1986, reintroduced 1988 only.

	$75	$60	$50	$45	$40	$35	$35

Last MSR was $92.

LONG RANGE RIFLE - .308 Win. (new 1991) or .50 BMG cal., bolt action design, single shot, 29 in. stainless steel fluted barrel with muzzle brake, adj. trigger pull, built-in bipod, adj. rail stock, includes Leupold M-1 Ultra 20X scope, 36 lbs. Limited mfg. between 1988-93.

	$3,150	$2,750	$2,400	$2,100	$1,800	$1,600	$1,400

Last MSR was $5,000.

GRADING - PPGS™	100%	98%	95%	90%	80%	70%	60%

9MM PARA. CARBINE (JJ9MM SERIES) - 9mm Para. cal. only, copy of U.S. military M1, 16 in. barrel, blue finish only, 20 shot mag. Mfg. 1985-86 only.

✳ *9mm Para. Carbine (JJ9MM Series) Hardwood Stock Model* - disc. 1986.

	$230	$200	$180	$170	$160	$150	$140

Last MSR was $255.

✳ *9mm Para. Carbine (JJ9MM Series) Standard Model* - with plastic stock. Disc. 1985.

	$225	$200	$180	$170	$160	$150	$140

Last MSR was $250.

✳ *9mm Para. Carbine (JJ9MM Series) Folding Plastic Stock Model* - disc. 1985.

	$350	$300	$265	$230	$200	$180	$170

Last MSR was $281.

DELTA-786 CARBINE - 9mm Para. cal., semi-auto, patterned after the U.S. military M1 Carbine, 16 in. barrel, matte black finish. Mfg. 1989 only.

	$575	$425	$360	$325	$295	$260	$230

Last MSR was $665.

.30 CARBINE - .30 Carbine or 9mm Para. (new 1991) cal., semi-auto, 18 or 20 (new 1991) in. barrel, available in various stock configurations, hardwood stock. Mfg. 1985-1986, reintroduced 1988-1993.

	$285	$215	$190	$165	$150	$140	$130

Last MSR was $350.

Add $16 for 9mm Para. cal.
Add $35 for walnut stock, Parkerized finish (disc. 1990), or 20 in. barrel (new 1991).

✳ *.30 Carbine Paratrooper Model* - similar to standard model, except has folding synthetic stock. Disc. 1993.

	$400	$345	$270	$225	$195	$165	$150

Last MSR was $433.

✳ *.30 Carbine Stainless Steel Variation* - disc. 1985.

	$230	$200	$180	$140	$120	$100	$85

Last MSR was $250.

✳ *5.7mm Johnson (Spitfire) Cal.* - 5.7mm Johnson Spitfire cal., remilled.

	$195	$175	$165	$155	$145	$135	$125

Last MSR was $219.

Add $30 for stainless steel.

.22 CAL. U.S. CARBINE - .22 LR or .22 Mag. cal., 18 1/2 or 19.3 (.22 Mag.) in. barrel, 5.8 lbs., 15 shot mag., sling swivels. Mfg. in Germany by Erma 1985-1986, reintroduced 1988 only.

	$150	$120	$110	$100	$90	$85	$80

Last MSR was $166 for .22 LR cal. Last MSR was $183 for .22 Mag. cal.

Add $120 for .22 Mag. model (gas operated - disc. 1986).

TARGETMASTER SLIDE ACTION - .22 LR or .22 Mag. (disc. 1986) cal., 18 1/2 in. barrel, 12 shot (LR) tube mag., 5 3/4 lbs. Mfg. in Germany by Erma 1985 only, reintroduced 1988-90.

	$175	$140	$125	$115	$100	$90	$80

Last MSR was $209.

This model was designated EW.22 HBP previously.

GRADING - PPGS™	100%	98%	95%	90%	80%	70%	60%

MODEL EW.22 HBL LEVER ACTION (WAGONMASTER) - .22 S, L, and LR or .22 Mag. cal., 18 1/2 in. barrel, walnut finish, hardwood stock, blue finish, 5 3/4 lbs., grooved for scope mounts. Mfg. in Germany by Erma 1985-1986, reintroduced 1988-90.

	$175	$140	$125	$115	$100	$90	$80

Last MSR was $209.

     Add $23 for .22 Mag. cal. (19 in. barrel).

This model was also available in a Junior variation with smaller dimensions; values same as listed.

TRAIL BLAZER SEMI-AUTO (MODEL IJ.22 HB) - .22 LR cal. only, 10 shot mag., 18 1/2 in. barrel, 5.8 lbs. Mfg. 1985 only.

	$115	$100	$90	$85	$80	$75	$70

Last MSR was $125.

SHOTGUNS

CHAMPION SINGLE BARREL - 10, 12, 16, 20, 24, 28, 32 ga., or .410 bore, also available in .44, .45, 12mm, or 14mm rifle cal., single barrel shotgun or rifle, 26-32 in. full barrel, exposed hammer, auto ejector, plain pistol grip stock. Mfg. 1909-56.

	$250	$225	$200	$175	$150	$100	$75

     Subtract 25% for birch stock (12 ga. only, 1970s mfg.).
     Add 20% for 16 ga.
     Add 30% for 20 ga.
     Add 100% for 28 ga.
     Add 300% for 24 or 32 ga.
     Add 50% for .410 bore.
     Add approx. 50% for rifle.

Iver Johnson Champion models were mfg. for Montgomery Ward during the 1930s-1940s under the "Western-Field" name. These models were also manufactured in Canada by Cooey during the late 1920s-early 1930s. Values are similar to above.

MATTED RIB GRADE SINGLE SHOT - similar to Champion, except not available in 10 or 24 ga., solid rib, checkered stock. Mfg. 1909-48.

	$300	$250	$225	$200	$175	$125	$100

     Add 50% for .410 bore, 28 ga., or 32 ga.

This model has either a semi-octagon (with top matted) or jacketed breech.

TRAP GRADE SINGLE SHOT - similar to Matted Rib Grade, except 30 or 32 in. full barrel, super select wood, 12 ga., vent rib. Mfg. 1926-1942.

	$450	$400	$350	$300	$250	$200	$150

HERCULES SxS GRADE - 12, 16, 20, 28 ga., or .410 bore, 26-32 in. barrels, hammerless, boxlock, various chokes, extractors and double triggers standard, checkered pistol grip or straight stock. Mfg. 1918-43.

	$1,050	$850	$650	$600	$525	$375	$325

     Add $300 for auto ejectors.
     Add $350 for Miller SST.
     Add 20% for 16 ga.
     Add 30% for 20 ga.
     Add 200% for 28 ga.
     Add 100% for .410 bore.
     Add 200%+ for rare factory engraved specimens.

The Hercules Model was mfg. in both USA and Canada by Cooey. The Hercules name was dropped in 1936 and became known as the "Iver Johnson Hammerless" until the end of production. Case colored frames were standard until 1936, blue frames were standard 1937-1943. A special run of Hercules Doubles was built in the 1930s for Montgomery Ward under the "Western Field" Model 53 nomenclature. All Western Field guns had a beavertail forearm, twin ivory sights, and recoil pad. Hercules 28 ga. SxSs are extremely rare.

GRADING - PPGS™	100%	98%	95%	90%	80%	70%	60%

SKEET-ER SxS MODEL - 12, 16, 20, 28 ga., or .410 bore, similar to Hercules Grade, except has blue receiver, super select wood and beavertail forearm, many Skeeters were special order guns with options including selective or non-selective Miller trigger, custom stock, barrel chokes, chamber lengths, checkering and wood finishes, sling swivels, extra barrels, recoil pad, checkered butt, VR, and various engraving patterns. Approx. 1,200 mfg. 1933-1942.

	$1,995	$1,695	$1,400	$1,100	$1,000	$800	$700

> Add 30% for auto ejectors.
> Add 50% for SST.
> Add 20% for non-selective trigger.
> Add 100% for factory VR.
> Add 30% for 20 ga.
> Add 100% for 16 ga.
> Add 200% for 28 ga. or .410 bore.
> Add 200% for rare factory engraving (be wary of upgrades).
> Add 50% for scarce factory case colors (be wary of new colors).

.410 bore is the most commonly encountered gun and was made on a special small frame. This model was probably responsible for more Skeet records than any other American .410 bore SxS shotgun.

✱ *Skeet-er SxS Model (Italian Mfg.)* - .410 bore, straight grip, DT, Arkansas address, extractors, figured wood, a few were imported during the late 1970s-early 1980s as a possible reintroduction of the Skeet-er Model, not cataloged, rare.

Values are approx. 25% less than U.S. mfg. models.

SUPER SxS TRAP - 12 ga. only, 32 in. full VR, boxlock, extractors, checkered pistol grip stock, beavertail forend and recoil pad. Mfg. 1928-42. Scarce.

	$1,595	$1,295	$850	$650	$550	$475	$450

> Add $200 for auto ejectors.
> Add $300 for Miller SST.

SILVER SHADOW - O/U, 12 ga., 26 or 28 in. barrels, various chokes, extractors, vent rib, checkered pistol grip stock, Italian mfg. Disc.

	$375	$325	$300	$275	$225	$185	$175

IZHMASH

Current manufacturer located in Izhevsk, Russia. Currently imported by Russian American Armory, located in Scottsburg, IN. Previously imported and distributed until 2004 by European American Armory (certain models only), located in Sharpes, FL. Other models were also imported by Kalashnikov USA, located in Port St. Lucie, FL. Previously distributed by Interstate Arms Corp., located in Billerica, MA, and by L.A. Austin International, Inc., located in Surprise, AZ.

Other Izhmash trademarks include Legion, Saiga, Hesse-Saiga, Krebs-Saiga, Romak, Sobol (not imported) , Korshun (not imported), LOS, Maral (not imported), and Dragunov.

RIFLES: BOLT ACTION

URAL 5.1 MATCH RIFLE - .22 LR cal., single shot, competition model with eccentric bolt, adj. cheekpiece, trigger, and buttplate, 26 1/2 in. barrel with aperture sights, 11.3 lbs. Imported 2000.

	$1,075	$950	$825	$700	$600	$500	$425

URAL 6-1 MATCH RIFLE - .22 LR cal., U.I.T. configuration with adj. buttplate and 26 3/4 in. barrel, aperture sights, various accessories included, 10 2/3 lbs. Imported 2000-2002.

	$550	$500	$450	$400	$360	$330	$300

Last MSR was $625.

GRADING - PPGS™	100%	98%	95%	90%	80%	70%	60%

URAL 6-2 MATCH RIFLE - .22 LR cal., features laminated stock. Imported 2000-2002.

	$1,000	$875	$750	$650	$550	$450	$350

Last MSR was $1,125.

BIATHLON BASIC - .17 HMR (new 2003), 22 LR, or .22 Win. Mag. (new 2003) cal., entry level biathlon model, beech stock, heavy barrel with Weaver rail, 6.1 lbs. Imported 2002-2004.

	$315	$275	$240	$195	$175	$160	$145

Add $10 for .22 Mag. or $20 for .17 HMR cal.
Add $50 for adj. sights.

BIATHLON 7-4 - .22 LR cal., features pivoting crank action, extra mags. that can be stored on the stock, 19.7 in. barrel with aperture sights, includes biathlon harness, spare mags., and counter weights, 9.1 lbs. Imported 2000-2004.

	$895	$725	$650	$550	$450	$350	$300

CM-2 - .22 LR cal., light match rifle, similar overall to Ural 6-1, 19.8 in. (Youth) or 26.7 in. barrel. Imported 2000-2002, reintroduced 2003.

	$365	$325	$285	$250	$225	$200	$180

LOS 7-1 SPORTER - .223 Rem., .308 Win., or 7.62x39mm cal., 21.8 in. hammer forged barrel with two lug bolt lockup, detachable 5 shot mag., adj. trigger, checkered hardwood stock with vent. recoil pad, includes scope, 7.3 lbs. Imported 2000-2002.

	$360	$330	$300	$270	$240	$210	$190

Last MSR was $395.

Subtract 10% if w/o scope.

SHOTGUNS

Please refer to the Saiga section for more information about these models.

J SECTION

J.B. CUSTOM INC.

Current manufacturer and restorer located in Fort Wayne, IN. Consumer direct sales.
J.B. Custom also offers service parts and restoration services for Winchester commemorative lever action rifles and carbines.

GRADING - PPGS™	100%	98%	95%	90%	80%	70%	60%

PISTOLS: LEVER ACTION

MODEL 1892 MARES LEG - .357 Mag., .44-40 WCF, .45 LC or .454 Casull (new mid-2007) cal., blue finish, 12 in. barrel, 6 shot, adj. rear sight, dovetail front sight, big loop lever, saddle ring, straight grip walnut stock.

MSR $1,495	$1,395	$1,125	$975	$875	$800	$725	$650

Add $200 for .454 Casull cal.

Custom engraved models are available beginning at $15,000.

J.C. HIGGINS

Please refer to listing in the H section.

J.O. ARMS

Previous importer of KSN Industries, Ltd. pistols until 1997.

J.L.D. ENTERPRISES, INC.

Previous rifle manufacturer located in Farmington, CT. In 2006, the company name was acquired by PTR 91, Inc.
Please refer to PTR 91, Inc. listing for current information.

JMC FABRICATION & MACHINE, INC.

Previous manufacturer located in Rockledge, FL 1997-99.

RIFLES: BOLT ACTION

MODEL 2000 M/P - .50 BMG cal., rapid takedown, 30 in. barrel, matte black finish, cast aluminum stock with Pachmayr pad, fully adj. bipod, 10 shot staggered mag., two-stage trigger, includes 24X U.S. Optics scope, prices assume all options included, 29 1/2 lbs. Limited mfg. 1998-99.

$7,950	$7,400	$6,800	$6,150	$5,500	$4,900	$4,200

Last MSR was $8,500.

Subtract $2,800 if w/o options.

JP ENTERPRISES, INC.

Current manufacturer and customizer established in 1978, and located in White Bear Lake, MN since 2000, Vadnais Heights, MN 1998-2000, and in Shoreview, MN 1995-98. Distributor, dealer, and consumer sales.
JP Enterprises is a distributor for Infinity pistols, and also customizes Remington shotgun models 11-87, 1100, and 870, the Remington bolt action Model 700 series, Glock pistols, and the Armalite AR-10 series. Please contact the company directly or refer to their website (www.jprifles.com) for more information regarding these customizing services.

PISTOLS: SEMI-AUTO

Level I & Level II custom pistols were manufactured 1995-97 using Springfield Armory slides and frames. Only a few were made, and retail prices were $599 (Level I) and $950 (Level II).

GRADING - PPGS™	100%	98%	95%	90%	80%	70%	60%

RIFLES: BOLT ACTION

MODEL MOR-07 - .260 Rem. or .308 Win. cal., 24 in. stainless steel cryo-treated bull barrel, benchrest quality bolt action, Picatinny rail, Magpul Precision butt stock, Jewel trigger, benchrest or tactical style forend, Magpul MIAD grip system, matte black hard coat anodizing, 10 shot, includes hard case.

MSR $3,899	$3,700	$3,300	$2,900	$2,500	$2,000	$1,600	$1,275

RIFLES: SEMI-AUTO

BARRACUDA 10/22 - .22 LR cal., features customized Ruger 10/22 action with reworked fire control system, choice of stainless bull or carbon fiber superlight barrel, 3 lb. trigger, color laminated "Barracuda" skeletonized stock. Mfg. 1997-2003.

	$1,075	$950	$775	$650	$575	$475	$400

Last MSR was $1,195.

A-2 MATCH - .223 Rem. cal., JP-15 lower receiver with JP fire control system, 20 in. JP Supermatch cryo-treated stainless barrel, standard A-2 stock and pistol grip, DCM type free float tube, Mil-Spec A-2 upper assembly with Smith National Match rear sight. Mfg. 1995-2003.

	$1,525	$1,300	$1,100	$925	$825	$700	$600

Last MSR was $1,695.

JP15 (GRADE I A-3 FLAT TOP) - .223 Rem. cal., features Eagle Arms (disc. 1999), DPMS (disc. 1999) or JP15 lower assembly with JP fire control system, Mil-spec A-3 type upper receiver with 18 or 24 in. JP Supermatch cryo-treated stainless barrel, synthetic modified thumbhole or laminated wood thumbhole (disc. 2002) stock, JP vent. two-piece free float tube, JP adj. gas system and recoil eliminator. New 1995.

MSR $1,899		$1,700	$1,425	$1,150	$925	$825	$700	$600

Add $400 for NRA Hi-Power version with 24 in. bull barrel and sight package (disc. 2002).

Add $200 for laminated wood thumbhole stock (disc. 2002).

✳ *JP15 Grade I IPSC Limited Class* - similar to Grade I, except has quick detachable match grade iron sights, Versa-pod bipod. Mfg. 1999-2004.

	$1,675	$1,400	$1,150	$995	$775	$625	$550

Last MSR was $1,795.

✳ *JP15 Grade I Tactical/SOF* - similar to Grade I, all matte black non-glare finish, 18, 20, or 24 in. Supermatch barrel. Mfg. 1999-2003.

	$1,425	$1,225	$1,050	$925	$800	$700	$600

Last MSR was $1,595.

Add $798 for Trijicon A-COG sight with A-3 adapter.

GRADE II - .223 Rem. cal., features Mil-spec JP lower receiver with upper assembly finished in a special two-tone color anodizing process, JP fire control and gas system, 18-24 in. cryo treated stainless barrel, composite skeletonized stock, Harris bipod, choice of multi-color or black receiver and handguard, includes hard case. Mfg. 1998-2002.

	$1,750	$1,450	$1,200	$1,025	$825	$700	$600

Last MSR was $1,895.

Add $200 for laminated wood thumbhole stock.

GRADING - PPGS™	100%	98%	95%	90%	80%	70%	60%

GRADE III (THE EDGE) - .223 Rem. cal., RND machined match upper/lower receiver system, 2-piece free floating forend, standard or laminated thumbhole wood stock, 18 to 24 in. barrel (cryo treated beginning 1998) with recoil eliminator, includes Harris bipod, top-of-the-line model, includes hard case. Mfg. 1996-2002.

	$2,550	$2,125	$1,750	$1,450	$1,150	$875	$750

Last MSR was $2,795.

Add $250 for laminated thumbhole stock.

MODEL AR-10T - .243 Win. or .308 Win. cal., features Armalite receiver system with JP fire control, flat-top receiver, vent. free floating tube, 24 in. cryo treated stainless barrel, black finish. Mfg. 1998-2004.

	$2,175	$1,825	$1,600	$1,450	$1,150	$875	$750

Last MSR was $2,399.

Add $150 for anodized upper assembly in custom color.
Add $350 for laminated wood thumbhole stock.

✱ *Model AR-10LW* - lightweight variation of the Model AR-10T, includes 16-20 in. cryo treated stainless barrel, composite fiber tube, black finish only, 7-8 lbs. Mfg. 1998-2004.

	$2,175	$1,825	$1,600	$1,450	$1,150	$875	$750

Last MSR was $2,399.

Add $200 for detachable sights.

CTR-02 COMPETITION TACTICAL RIFLE - .223 Rem. cal., state-of-the-art advanced AR design with many improvements, integral ACOG interface, various stock configurations, available with two different types of operating systems, depending on use, JP recoil eliminator and fire control system, 1/4 MOA possible, Trijicon advanced combat optical sight, also available in NRA Hi-Power version with competition features. New 2002.

MSR $2,499	$2,250	$1,800	$1,350	$1,050	$825	$750	$650

Add $599 for presentation grade finish.

MODEL LRP-07 - .260 Rem. or .308 Win. cal., 18 or 22 in. stainless steel cryo-treated barrel, tactical compensator, A2 or JPBRS stock with Hogue pistol grip, JP adj. gas system, matte black hard coat anodizing, aluminum components, 19 shot mag.

MSR $2,899	$2,750	$2,500	$2,150	$1,850	$1,500	$1,250	$1,000

J R DISTRIBUTING

Current manufacturer located in Moorpark, CA. J R Distributing is a division of J R Sports Distribution Corporation. Dealer and consumer sales.

RIFLES: SEMI-AUTO

.22 MAG. CUSTOM RIFLE - .22 Mag. cal., choice of Ruger 10/22 or AMT action, 20 in. bull barrel with laminate or synthetic stock, 9 shot rotary mag., supplied with hard case. New 1998.

MSR $795	$725	$650	$550	$500	$450	$400	$360

JSL (HEREFORD)

Previous manufacturer located in Hereford, England. Imported until 1994 by Specialty Shooters Supply, Inc. located in Fort Lauderdale, FL.

PISTOLS: SEMI-AUTO

SPITFIRE (G1) - 9mm Para. or 9x21mm cal., patterned after the Czech CZ-75/85, 3.7 in. barrel, ambidextrous safety, commander style hammer, black non-slip rubberized grip panels, investment cast stainless steel fabrication, 10 (C/B 1994) or 15* shot mag., 2.2 lbs. Imported 1992-94.

GRADING - PPGS™	100%	98%	95%	90%	80%	70%	60%

* Spitfire Standard - includes fixed rear sight, 2 mags., presentation case, and allen key.

	$1,332	$1,100	$925	$810	$670	$565	$475

Last MSR was $1,332.

Add $81 for adj. rear sight (Sterling Model).

JACKSON HOLE FIREARMS

Previous manufacturer located in Jackson Hole, WY circa mid-70s.

RIFLES: BOLT ACTION

STANDARD RIFLE - various cals., Mauser 98 action utilizing patented system for interchangeable barrels, checkered walnut stock.

	$1,050	$875	$800	$725	$650	$575	$495

Jackson Hole Firearms manufactured a limited quantity of their unique interchangeable barrel bolt action rifles. Collectibility to date has been minimal, and values are affected by the J.P. Sauer Models 90 and 200 which also feature the interchangeable barrel design.

JACKSON RIFLES

Current rifle manufacturer located in Castle Douglas, Scotland. No current U.S. importation.

Jackson Rifles manufacturers high quality long-range competition rifles, including the J5-P (single shot) and the J5-T (bolt action repeater), available in both right and left-hand actions. Please contact the company directly for more information, including pricing, U.S. availability, and delivery time (see Trademark Index).

JAEGER, FRANZ

Previous manufacturer located in Suhl, Germany circa 1900-1945. Franz Jaeger firearms included pistols, rifles, and shotguns.

Franz Jaeger, the founder, obtained many firearms patents and many Jaeger firearms were manufactured in a wide variety of configurations. Perhaps the company's most famous gun was an auto-loading pistol manufactured between 1914-1918 that featured sheet metal stampings (approx. 13,000 were manufactured). Values for Jaeger firearms today depend on the overall desirability factor and original condition.

HISTORY OF FRANZ JAEGER

Franz Jaeger's inventions still play an important role in the guns of today. He was born in 1876 in Rampitz, Merseburg County. Jaeger apprenticed as an actioner in Zella Mehlis, opened his own gunshop in Halle, then moved to America. He found employment as a gunsmith in New York, met and married Fanny Strauss, also from Germany. Their first son, Paul was born, and he began to develop his own ideas and he took out his first patent for a single trigger mechanism. Franz opened his own business with a partner (Bittner & Jaeger) on Broadway in New York.

Around the turn of the century, the family returned to Germany and settled in Suhl. Franz installed single triggers for other manufacturers and gun owners. Between 1901-1914, Franz Jaeger obtained eight patents. The catalogs of that period showed a wide variety of guns, most of them with Jaeger patents.

Franz Jaeger designed the "Jaeger Pistol" in a period of 3 months. It used steel stampings and castings, something unheard of at the time. The army rejected it for official use with one word: "Blech" (sheet metal). Nevertheless, the Jaeger factory produced about 15,000 of the pistols.

The following year Franz Jaeger was drafted into the army. Finally the "Hindenburg Proclamation" discharged skilled craftsmen and brought him home for the rest of the war, but fortunes soon declined into the Great Depression.

An order from abroad for good but reasonably priced stalking rifles brought the Magnus brothers together with Franz Jaeger to establish the Magnus-Jaeger Company. They set up manufacturing facilities in Maebendorf near Suhl, but soon barely escaped a bankruptcy.

The Hitler years brought an improvement of the economy and work for Suhl's gunmakers. However, the extermination of Jews in Europe became a reality, and Fanny Jaeger was Jewish. She was transported to the concentration camp in Theresienstadt but survived.

GRADING - PPGS™	100%	98%	95%	90%	80%	70%	60%

During this time, Franz Jaeger and 2 to 3 loyal employees continued to make hunting guns, and the family was reunited after the war. But then the Americans left and the Russian troops arrived. Under a communist government, private initiative was not tolerated. Younger members of the family slipped to West Germany illegally, but Franz Jaeger and his wife turned down the offer to immigrate to America.

Two of his important patents are still used by major gun companies today.

JAGD-UND SPORTWAFFEN SUHL GmbH

Previous company name of Merkel, located in Suhl, Germany since 1535.

Currently, the famous Merkel trademark (mfg. by Merkel Jagd-Und Sportwaffen Suhl GmbH) is imported by Merkel USA, located in Trussville, AL. Previously imported by Heckler & Koch, located in Sterling, VA. Please refer to the Merkel listing in this text for current information regarding this older European trademark. See the Trademark Index in this text for current factory information.

JANZ GmbH

Current revolver manufacturer established in 2000, and located in Malente, Germany. Currently imported beginning 2007 by Brenzovich, located in Fort Hancock, TX. Previously imported 2003-2004 by Rocky Mountain Armoury, located in Silverthorne, CO.

REVOLVERS

Plpease contact the imported directly for current pricing and availability.

JTL-E - .22 LR, .357 Mag./.38 Spl., .44 Mag., .45 Win. Mag., .454 Casull/.45 LC cal., or .500 S&W (new 2005) cal., DA, 5 (.500 S&W cal.), 6, or 7 (.357 Mag.) shot, 4-10 in. barrel with full lug, ergonomic stippled wood grips, target sights, quick change cylinder. New 2000.

Prices on this model are POR and will increase according to caliber and barrel length.

JTL-S - .22 LR, .357 Mag./.38 Spl., .44 Mag., .45 Win. Mag., .454 Casull/.45 LC cal., DA, 6 or 7 (.357 Mag.) shot, unique interchangeable barrels and cylinders allow cals. to be changed rapidly, 4-10 in. barrel with full lug, ergonomic stippled wood grips, target sights. New 2003.

Prices on this model are POR.

This model is also available as a package with .357 Mag., .44 Mag., and .454 Casull barrels.

JAPANESE MILITARY

Previously manufactured prior to and during WWII in Japan by various manufacturers.

PISTOLS: SEMI-AUTO

Please refer to the Nambu section for further information on Nambus and variations.

HAMADA VARIATIONS

* *Hamada Variations Type I* - .32 ACP cal., similar to FN Model 1910, except has 9 shot mag., early production pistols have chrysanthemum and Japanese characters on left slide, salt blue. Mfg. estimated at 5,000, but examples are scarce and usually in the 2,000-3,000 ser. range.

$4,500	$4,000	$3,500	$3,000	$2,500	$2,000	$1,500

Add 10% for early variation.

* *Hamada Variations Type II* - 8mm cal., designed to replace the Type 94 Nambu, larger than Type I and with a more squared profile, essentially a pre-production gun, all known examples are roughly finished in the white and are serial numbered 1-50.

$6,000	$5,000	$4,000	$3,000	$2,500	$2,200	$1,900

GRADING - PPGS™	100%	98%	95%	90%	80%	70%	60%

REVOLVERS

1893 REVOLVER (MODEL 26) - 9mm Japanese cal., double action only, 4.7 in. barrel, blue, wood grips. Approx. 59,000 mfg. 1893-1925.

	$1,250	$1,000	$750	$500	$400	$325	$250

Subtract 25% for arsenal rework.
Add 100% for early mfg. with internal numbers (approx. first 300 revolvers), or final Kokura assembled pistols in 58,971-59,183 serial range.

RIFLES: MILITARY

Subtract 20% if National Crest (chrysanthemum flower) has been ground off front receiver ring.
Subtract 20% if serial numbers are not matching (does not apply to sniper rifles, as they are only rarely found with matching scopes and mounts).
Subtract 10%-40% for training rifles of each type.

MODEL 38 ARISAKA RIFLE - 6.5X51R Arisaka cal., Jap. Mauser type bolt action, 31 in. barrel, adj. sight, adopted 1905.

	$625	$525	$400	$300	$225	$125	$75

MODEL 38 A & B CAVALRY CARBINE - 6.5x51R Arisaka cal., similar to Model 38 Arisaka Rifle, except has 19 in. barrel. Mfg. 1911.

	$625	$550	$450	$325	$225	$125	$75

Add 300% for paratrooper variation with hinged stock (often referenced as Type I, has crude construction and cast iron hinge).

MODEL 44 CAVALRY ARISAKA CARBINE - 6.5x51R Arisaka cal., similar to Model T38 Carbine, features 19 in. barrel and folding bayonet.

	$1,150	$950	$800	$650	$500	$400	$325

MODEL 97 SNIPER RIFLE - based on Model 38 Arisaka Rifle.

	$3,500	$2,750	$2,200	$1,950	$1,650	$1,375	$1,100

Add $1,000 if complete with scope.

MODEL 99 SERVICE RIFLE - 7.7x58mm Arisaka cal., WWII version of Model 38 Arisaka Rifle, mostly encountered with shorter barrels than the Model 38 Arisaka Rifle.

	100%	98%	95%	90%	80%	70%	60%
	$375	$275	$225	$195	$150	$90	$65
Sniper rifle w/4Xscope	$3,800	$3,450	$3,000	$2,600	$2,200	$1,800	$1,400

Add 20% for monopod (non-Sniper).
Add 75% for long barrel (non-Sniper).
Add 50% for externally adjustable scope.

MODEL 99 PARATROOPER TAKEDOWN VERSION - 7.7x58mm Arisaka cal., adopted 1940, crossbolt barrel lock.

Type 2	$2,500	$2,200	$1,850	$1,425	$1,125	$850	$700

JARRETT RIFLES, INC.

Current manufacturer established in 1979, and located in Jackson, SC. Direct custom order sales only.

HANDGUNS

CUSTOM XP-100 HUNTER - various cals., re-machined Remington XP-100 action, Jarrett match grade stainless steel barrel, McMillan fiberglass stock, various options. Limited mfg.

	$3,450	$2,650	$2,150	$1,750	$1,350	$1,050	$995

ULTIMATE REDHAWK - .44 Mag. cal., features Hogue grips and muzzle brake. Mfg. 1995-2000.

	$1,150	$1,025	$850	$675	$575	$500	$450

Last MSR was $1,150.

GRADING - PPGS™	100%	98%	95%	90%	80%	70%	60%

RIFLES: BOLT ACTION

Jarrett rifles are justifiably famous for their well-known Beanfield rifles (refers to shooting over a beanfield at long range targets). A Jarrett innovation is the Tri-Lock receiver, which has 3 locking lugs, and a semi-integral recoil lug. Jarrett blueprints every action for proper dimensioning and rigid tolerances, and this explains why their rifles have set rigid accuracy standards.

A wide variety of options are available for Jarrett custom rifles (holders of 16 world records in rifle accuracy). The factory should be contacted directly (see Trademark Index) for pricing and availability regarding these special order options. Custom gunsmithing services for Jarrett rifles are also available and the manufacturer should be contacted directly for gunsmith quotations.

Prices on current models do not include federal excise tax.

STANDARD HUNTING RIFLE - various cals., Remington Model 700 right-hand or left-hand action, McMillan fiberglass stock, blue receiver, Jarrett satin finish match grade barrel, sling studs and leather sling, rings and base, weights vary. Disc. 2003.

$4,625	$4,150	$3,650	$3,150	$2,750	$2,150	$1,750

Last MSR was $4,625.

WALK ABOUT - various cals. in short action only, features Remington Model 7 action (left-hand utilizes Rem. Model 700 short action), weights vary. Mfg. 1995-2003.

$4,625	$4,150	$3,650	$3,150	$2,750	$2,150	$1,750

Last MSR was $4,625.

TRUCK GUN - various small bore cals., 19-20 in. barrel, black synthetic stock. Mfg. 1999-2003.

$4,625	$4,150	$3,650	$3,150	$2,750	$2,150	$1,750

Last MSR was $4,625.

BENCHREST/YOUTH/TACTICAL - various cals., various configurations depending on application. New 1999.

$4,625	$4,150	$3,650	$3,150	$2,750	$2,150	$1,750

Last MSR was $4,625.

SERIES RIFLE - various cals., various configurations, only 100 made of each series. Mfg. 1993-2003.

✳ *Series Rifle Standard* - various cals.

$5,025	$4,450	$3,850	$3,250	$2,850	$2,250	$1,850

Last MSR was $5,025.

✳ *Series Rifle Coup de Grace* - various cals. Mfg. 1996-99.

$3,295	$2,750	$2,300	$1,800	$1,500	$1,250	$995

Last MSR was $3,495.

✳ *Series Rifle Nombre Unique* - various cals., 100 mfg. 1999 only.

$3,495	$2,900	$2,400	$1,850	$1,550	$1,250	$995

Last MSR was $3,695.

SIGNATURE SERIES - various cals., Jarrett tri-lock stainless steel receiver, fiberglass, wood laminate, or deluxe walnut stock, helical fluted bolt with three lugs, built to special order only. New 2004.

MSR $7,640						
$7,640	$6,900	$5,700	$4,850	$4,000	$3,325	$2,850

WIND WALKER SERIES - various cals. up to .30 cal., Rem. M-700 ADL action only, lightweight design, 24 in. tapered barrel with muzzle brake, Brown Precision stock, 7 1/4 lbs. New 1999.

MSR $7,380						
$7,380	$6,650	$5,375	$4,700	$4,000	$3,300	$2,850

GRADING - PPGS™	100%	98%	95%	90%	80%	70%	60%

ORIGINAL BEANFIELD RIFLE - built on customer supplied action, choice of caliber, stock style, color, barrel length and finish, with or w/o muzzle brake, supplied with 20 rounds of ammo and test target. New 2005.

MSR $5,380	$5,380	$4,850	$4,250	$3,825	$3,400	$3,000	$2,600

PROFESSIONAL HUNTER - Mag. cals. to customer's specifications, starting with .375 H&H, features Winchester controlled round feed Model 70 action with claw extractor and 3 position bolt shroud safety, Jarrett match grade stainless steel barrel, McMillan stock, quarter rib with iron sights, includes 2 sets of detachable rings and two 1.75-6x32mm Leupold scopes, takedown action, includes custom built Americase.

MSR $10,400	$10,400	$8,850	$7,200	$6,000	$4,600	$4,200	$3,700

.50 CAL. - .50 BMG cal., McMillan custom receiver, choice of repeater or single shot, 30 or 34 in. barrel with muzzle brake, 28-45 lbs. Mfg. 1999-2003.

	$8,050	$6,500	$5,300	$4,350	$3,650	$3,000	$2,500

Last MSR was $8,050.

Add $300 for repeater action.

CLASSIC SERIES - various cals., 100 mfg. 1989 only.

	$3,195	$2,650	$2,100	$1,650	$1,375	$1,150	$875

INVESTOR SERIES - various cals., 100 mfg. 1989 only.

	$3,195	$2,650	$2,100	$1,650	$1,375	$1,150	$875

ACCURACY LEGEND SERIES - various cals., similar to Jarrett Custom Rifle, except has many accuracy tune-ups incorporated as well as muzzle brake. 100 mfg. 1993 only.

	$3,495	$2,850	$2,300	$1,850	$1,500	$1,250	$995

Last MSR was $3,495.

COUP de MAIM - various cals., similar to the Jarrett Custom Rifle, includes muzzle brake, matte black or olive drab finish, Model 70 style bolt release. 100 mfg. 1995 only.

	$2,750	$2,300	$1,800	$1,500	$1,250	$995	$775

Last MSR was $3,495.

PRIVATE COLLECTION - various cals., similar quality as the Jarrett Custom Rifle, except many extra cost special order options are included, ser. numbered 1-100. Mfg. 1994 only.

	$3,495	$2,850	$2,300	$1,850	$1,500	$1,250	$995

Last MSR was $3,495.

SILENT PARTNER SERIES - various cals., only 10 mfg. 1994 only.

	$3,495	$2,850	$2,300	$1,850	$1,500	$1,250	$995

ULTIMATE HUNTER SERIES - various cals., 100 mfg. 1989 only.

	$3,495	$2,850	$2,300	$1,850	$1,500	$1,250	$995

RIFLES: RIMFIRE, SEMI-AUTO

SQUIRREL KING - .22 LR cal., reworked Ruger 10/22 action, 18 in. barrel, McMillan or Brown Precision synthetic stock. Mfg. 1999-2003.

	$1,650	$1,300	$1,050	$900	$700	$575	$475

Last MSR was $1,800.

Add $195 for Target King variation.

SHOTGUNS: SLIDE ACTION

JARRETT ULTIMATE SHOTGUN - 12 ga., Remington Model 870 action with 21 in. hand lapped barrel with interchangeable chokes, 8 shot mag. extension, matte black or olive drab green finish. Disc. 1999.

	$900	$825	$675	$550	$450	$350	$295

Last MSR was $1,000.

JEFFERY, W.J. & CO. LTD

Current trademark established in 1888, and manufactured by J. Roberts & Son (Gunmakers) Ltd., located in London, England. Previous manufacture was also in London, England.

J. Roberts & Son (Gunmakers) Ltd. currently manufactures W.J. Jeffery shotguns, bolt action and double rifles. Many options are available, including calibers, special engraving, etc. Please contact the company directly for more information, including pricing, delivery time and availability (see Trademark Index). In addition to making a complete line of their own shotguns and rifles, W.J. Jeffery also was subcontracted by many other exporters, distributors, and retailers, including London's famous Army & Navy department store (see separate listing). Many models were produced and, rather than list them individually, a generalized format has been adopted for determining values on both discontinued rifles and shotguns. Current MSRs do not include English VAT.

RIFLES, CURRENT MFG.

BOLT ACTION RIFLE - various cals. between .243 Win. - .500 Jeffery, manufactured with both original Mauser actions and recent production (non-Mauser mfg.) actions, other commercial actions are available upon request.

> Current MSR range from £7,000 - £15,000, depending on configuration, features, accessories, engraving, and grade of wood. Delivery time is approx. 6-15 months.

SxS MODEL - standard cals are 9.3x74R, .375 H&H, .470 NE, or .500 Jeffrey, choice of boxlock or sidelock action, ejectors, includes deep scroll engraving and case.

> Current MSR for the boxlock ejector model starts at £30,000, depending on caliber, configuration, features, and grade of wood. The sidelock ejector rifle MSR starts at £40,000 (£30,000 for 9.3x74R cal.), depending on caliber, features, configuration, and grade of wood.

RIFLES, DISC.

SINGLE SHOT - various cals., falling block action, checkered walnut stock and forearm, usually multiple folding leaves rear sight (also tangent), excellent quality.

> Prices start in the $750 range for poor condition specimens in obsolete or undesirable cals. and can go up to $6,500 for 100% condition in .600 Nitro Express.
> Subtract substantially for the Martini action variation.

BOXLOCK DOUBLE RIFLE - many cals., various engraving patterns, top or under (usually large cals.) lever opening, multiple folding leaves rear sight, checkered walnut stock and forearm.

> Prices usually start in the $1,750 range for poor condition in undesirable cals. and can exceed $10,000 if encountered with elaborate engraving in .475 Express or larger cals.
> Subtract approx. 40% if with hammers, over 50% if with damascus barrels.

SIDELOCK DOUBLE RIFLE - various cals., available in No. 1 or No. 2 grade, top-lever opening, best quality engraving, deluxe checkered walnut stock and forearm, almost any custom order could be filled.

> Prices start in the $7,500 range for 60% condition in smaller cals. and can easily go to $25,000+ when found in excellent condition in the larger cals.
> Subtract approx. 40% if with hammers, over 50% if with damascus barrels.

SHOTGUNS, CURRENT MFG.

Please contact the company directly (see Trademark Index) for more information on currently manufactured W.J. Jeffery shotguns, including the sidelock ejector models, and the London finished SxS and O/U Italian and Spanish shotguns manufactured under J. Roberts & Son patterns.

SXS SIDELOCK MODEL - 12 or 20 ga., choice of H&H self-opening style or Beesley/Purdey action, deep scroll engraving is standard.

> Current MSR on this model starts at £35,000 for H&H action, or £38,000 for Beesley/Purdey action.

GRADING - PPGS™	100%	98%	95%	90%	80%	70%	60%

SHOTGUNS: SxS, DISC.

BOXLOCK SHOTGUN - most ga., many combinations of options available, top-lever opening, many ranges of engraving, high quality and worksmanship.
> Values usually start in the $950 range if in poor condition and can go to $5,500+ if in a small ga. in near new condition.
> Subtract approx. 40% if with hammers, over 50% if with damascus barrels.

SIDELOCK SHOTGUN - most ga., many combinations of options available, top-lever opening, many ranges of engraving, high quality and worksmanship.
> Values usually start in the $2,250 range if in poor condition and can go to $20,000+ if in a small ga. in near new condition.

JEFFERY SHARPS

Current rifle configuration manufactured by Ballard Arms, located in Cody, WY.

The original Jeffery Sharps was crafted during the late 1880s by W.J. Jeffery of London, and was based on the Winchester Model 1885.

New guns built in Cody are based on the original design and will come in calibers from .400 Jeffery to .577 NE. Please contact Ballard Arms directly for more information, including a price quotation and delivery time (see Trademark Index).

JENNINGS FIREARMS

Previous trademark and distributor established 1978 and located in City of Industry, CA until 1985. Jennings was a brand name for Bryco Arms, and was also the exclusive distributor for Bryco. Jennings also distributed Sundance and Accu-Tek.

PISTOLS: SEMI-AUTO

MODEL J-22 - .22 LR cal., 6 shot, single action, 2 1/2 in. barrel, positive safety locks sear, satin nickel, bright chrome or black teflon finish, 13 oz. Disc. 1985.

	$65	$50	$40	$35	$30	$30	$30

Last MSR was $79.

JERICHO

Previous trademark of Israeli Military Industries (I.M.I.). Previously imported by K.B.I., Inc. located in Harrisburg, PA.

PISTOLS: SEMI-AUTO

JERICHO 941 - 9mm Para. cal. or .41 Action Express (by conversion only) cal., semi-auto double action or single action, 4.72 in. barrel with polygonal rifling, all steel fabrication, 3 dot Tritium sights, 11 or 16 (9mm Para.) shot mag., ambidextrous safety, polymer grips, decocking lever, 38 1/2 oz. Imported 1990-92.

	$550	$475	$425	$375	$325	$295	$260

Last MSR was $649.

> **Add $299 for .41 AE conversion kit.**
> Industrial hard chrome or nickel finishes were also available for all Jericho pistols.

✳ *Jericho 941 Pistol Package* - includes 9mm Para. and .41 AE conversion kit, cased with accessories. Mfg. 1990-91 only.

	$850	$775	$700	$625	$575	$495	$450

Last MSR was $775.

JIMENEZ ARMS

Current manufacturer located in Henderson, NV. Previously located in Costa Mesa, CA until 2005. Distributed by Shining Star Investments, LLC, located in Lewisville, TX.

Paul Jimenez, former plant manager of Bryco Arms, bought the remaining assets of Bryco in 2004. Currently, the company manufactures semi-auto pistols - the JA-Nine, JA-380, the JA-22 and the JA-25 Auto. Please contact the distributor directly for pricing and availability (see Trademark Index).

GRADING - PPGS™	100%	98%	95%	90%	80%	70%	60%

JOHANNSEN RIFLES

Currently manufactured by Reimer Johannsen GmbH, located in Germany. Currently imported by New England Custom Gun Service, located in Plainfield, NH. Previously imported until 2003 by Johannsen, Inc.

RIFLES: BOLT ACTION

Johannsen rifles feature high quality short, medium, and Magnum Mauser actions in many calibers. Actions are manufactured by Orth, using sophisticated CAD and CNC technology, in addition to Old World gunsmithing techniques.

Johannsen take down express rifles are unique in that the bolt locks into the barrel with the same precision every time. This design ensures that point of impact remains identical after each assembly/disassembly. Please contact the importer directly for more information, including current pricing and domestic availability.

Add approx. $6,450 for take down action on some of the models listed. Extra barrels start at $2,760. Prices do not include duty or VAT, FOB Hamburg.

PROFESSIONAL MODEL - .500 Jeffrey or .505 Gibbs cal., double square bridge, adj. trigger, flag safety, English stock, various options available.

MSR $12,625 $12,625 $10,000 $8,425 $7,000 $6,000 $5,000 $4,200

Add $1,475 for .505 Gibbs cal.

CLASSIC SAFARI - various cals., single square bridge action with thumbcut, express sight with two leaves, safari English style stock, open sights, 8 lbs. 3 oz.

MSR $10,830 $10,830 $9,000 $7,500 $6,500 $5,500 $4,500 $3,750

SAFARI RIFLE - various cals. between .25-06 to .500 Jeffrey, features medium or Magnum double square bridge action, adj. trigger, three position safety, express sight with two leaves, safari English stock with satin oil finish.

MSR $11,100 $11,100 $9,200 $7,600 $6,500 $5,500 $4,500 $3,750

Add $800 for .375 H&H, .404 Jeffrey, .416 Rigby, .450 Rigby, .458 Lott, or .500 Jeffrey cal.

TRADITION RIFLE - various cals. between .17 Rem. to .458 Lott, available in mini, short, medium, or Magnum action, adj. trigger, three position safety, low bolt handle, pivot insert in front square bridge, express sight with one leaf, straight grip stock with satin oil finish.

MSR $11,350 $11,350 $9,375 $7,700 $6,550 $5,500 $4,500 $3,750

Add $1,950 for mini-action, $450 for short action, or $1,220 for Magnum action.

MOUNTAIN RIFLE - various cals. between .243 Win. to 9.3x62mm, short or medium action, double square bridge, adj. trigger, three-position safety, low bolt handle, integral mount in rear square bridge, express sight with one leaf, satin oil finished high gloss stock, lightweight. New 2007.

MSR $11,350 $11,350 $9,375 $7,700 $6,550 $5,500 $4,500 $3,750

Add $1,950 for short action.

JOHNSON AUTOMATICS, INC.

Previous manufacturer located in Providence, RI. Johnson Automatics, Inc. moved many times during its history, often with slight name changes. M.M. Johnson, Jr. died in 1965, and the company continued production at 104 Audubon Street in New Haven, CT as Johnson Arms, Inc. mostly specializing in sporter semi-auto rifles with Monte Carlo stocks in .270 Win. or 30-06 cal.

RIFLES: SEMI-AUTO

MODEL 1941 - .30-06 or 7x57mm cal., 22 in. removable air cooled barrel, recoil operated, perforated metal handguard, aperture sight, military stock. Most were made for Dutch military, some used by U.S. Marine Paratroopers, during WWII all .30-06 and 7x57mm were ordered by South American governments.

$7,350 $6,750 $6,000 $5,250 $4,500 $3,950 $3,250

MilTech offers a restored version of this model, and inspect this model carefully for originality before considering a possible purchase. Values are somewhat lower for restored guns.

GRADING - PPGS™	100%	98%	95%	90%	80%	70%	60%

JUCH-GRUND JAGDWAFFEN INH. KARL GRUND

Current rifle manufacturer located in Ferlach, Austria.

Karl Grund manufactures high quality double rifles in a variety of configurations. Eazch gun is made per individual customer specifications. Please contact the company directly for more information, including pricing, delivery time, and availability (see Trademark Index).

JUNG, WAFFEN, GMBH

Please refer to Waffen Jung GmbH.

JURRAS, LEE E.

Custom pistolsmith previously located in Hagerman, New Mexico. Howdah pistols were distributed by J & G Sales located in Prescott, AZ.

Ammunition for Jurras pistols was manufactured by Robert Davis, Jr. located in Athens, TN.

Lee Jurras was the founder and president of Super Vel Cartridge Corporation. Mr. Jurras also made custom AutoMags (see AutoMag section). He established the Outstanding American Handgunner Awards, and was a pioneer of the first metallic silhouette shooting matches.

PISTOLS

100 LEJ Howdah pistols were custom built in the late 1970s. The action was based on the Thompson/Center Contender receiver. Almost any caliber, barrel length, finish, and stock was available by special order. Original MSR was approx. $800.

HOWDAH - most common in .375, .416, .460, .475, .500, or .577 Jurras cals., action based on Thompson/Center Contender receiver, 12 in. bull barrel, satin nickel, nickel, or blue finish, adj. rear sights, ebony, mesquite, or walnut stocks, special order serial number range from 001-100, limited mfg. (100).

* *Howdah Custom Grade*

$1,150	$925	$800	$725	$650	$575	$500

* *Howdah Presentation Grade* - .375 Jurras or .460 Jurras cals. standard, deluxe Claro walnut stock and forearm.

$2,000	$1,750	$1,500	$1,250	$1,050	$950	$825

Special order .416, .475, .500, or .577 Jurras calibers command a premium on this model.

JUST, JOSEF

Current custom long gun manufacturer and gunsmith established in 1790, and located in Ferlach, Austria.

Josef Just was a member of the Ferlach Guild until it was dissolved in 2004, and manufactures a variety of high quality long gun configurations (including SxSs, O/Us, drillings, vierlings, combination guns, and single shot), all to custom order. Please contact Mr. Just directly for more information and an individual price quotation (see Trademark Index).

K SECTION

K.B.I., INC.

Current importer and distributor located in Harrisburg, PA. Distributor sales.

K.B.I., Inc. currently imports Charles Daly semi-auto pistols, Bul Transmark semi-auto pistols, SA revolvers, AR-15 style rifles, and shotguns in many configurations, including O/U, SxS, semi-auto, lever action, and slide action. K.B.I. has imported Armscor (Arms Corp. of the Philippines), FEG pistols, and Liberty revolvers and SxS coach shotguns. These models may be found within their respective alphabetical sections. K.B.I. previously imported the Jericho pistol manufactured by I.M.I. from Israel. The Jericho pistol may be found under its own heading in this text.

GRADING - PPGS™	100%	98%	95%	90%	80%	70%	60%

RIFLES: BOLT ACTION

KASSNAR GRADE I - available in 9 cals., thumb safety that locks trigger, with or w/o deluxe sights, 22 in. barrel, 3 or 4 shot mag., includes swivel posts and oil finished standard grade European walnut with recoil pad, 7 1/2 lbs. Imported 1989-93.

	100%	98%	95%	90%	80%	70%	60%
	$445	$385	$325	$275	$225	$195	$175

Last MSR was $499.

NYLON 66 - .22 LR cal., patterned after the Remington Nylon 66. Imported until 1990 from C.B.C. in Brazil, South America.

	100%	98%	95%	90%	80%	70%	60%
	$125	$110	$95	$85	$75	$70	$65

Last MSR was $134.

MODEL 122 - .22 LR cal., bolt action design with mag. Imported from South America until 1990.

	100%	98%	95%	90%	80%	70%	60%
	$125	$110	$95	$85	$75	$70	$65

Last MSR was $136.

MODEL 522 - .22 LR cal., bolt action design with tube mag. Imported from South America until 1990.

	100%	98%	95%	90%	80%	70%	60%
	$130	$115	$100	$85	$75	$70	$65

Last MSR was $142.

BANTAM SINGLE SHOT - .22 LR cal., youth dimensions. Imported 1989-90 only.

	100%	98%	95%	90%	80%	70%	60%
	$110	$90	$85	$75	$70	$65	$60

Last MSR was $120.

SHOTGUNS

GRADE I O/U - 12, 20, 28 ga., or .410 bore, gold plated SST, extractors, vent. rib, checkered walnut stock and forearm. Imported 1989-93.

	100%	98%	95%	90%	80%	70%	60%
	$525	$425	$350	$295	$265	$240	$220

Last MSR was $599.

Add $70 for 28 ga. or .410 bore.
Add $50 for choke tubes (12 and 20 ga. only).
Add $150 for automatic ejectors (with choke tubes only).

GRADE II SxS - 10, 12, 16, 20, 28 ga., or .410 bore, boxlock action, case hardened receiver, English style checkered European walnut stock with splinter forearm, chrome barrels with concave rib, extractors, double hinged triggers. Imported 1989-90 only.

	100%	98%	95%	90%	80%	70%	60%
	$515	$435	$375	$325	$275	$250	$225

Last MSR was $575.

Add $95 for 28 ga. or .410 bore.
Add $85 for 10 ga.

GRADING - PPGS™	100%	98%	95%	90%	80%	70%	60%

KDF, INC.

Current manufacturer and custom riflesmith specializing in restocking and installing muzzle brakes, in addition to supplying specialized rifle parts.

Located in Seguin, TX. KDF utilized Mauser K-15 actions imported from Oberndorf, Germany for many rifle models. Previously, KDF rifles were manufactured by Voere (until 1987) in Vöhrenbach, W. Germany.

Older KDF rifles were private labeled by Voere and marked KDF. Since Voere was absorbed by Mauser-Werke in 1987, model designations changed. Mauser-Werke does not private label (i.e. newer guns are marked Mauser-Werke), and these rifles can be found under the Mauser-Werke heading in this text.

RIFLES: BOLT ACTION, U.S. MFG.

KDF also builds custom rifles on Remington & Winchester actions, in addition to converting Rem. M700 and Winchester M70 rifles into custom rifles. Please contact the company directly for more information and pricing.

In 1989, KDF announced the release of a new American built redesigned Model K15 with many improvements. While advertised, approximately only 25 were manufactured in various cals.

K15 - .22-250 Rem. (disc. 1992), .243 Win., 6mm Rem., .25-06 Rem., .270 Win., .280 Rem., .30-06 cal. or .308 Win. cal., 60 degree short lift bolt action with 3 lugs, Kevlar composite or laminate walnut stock, adj. single stage competition trigger, box magazine, thumb activated slide safety, satin blue finish, 24 in. match grade barrel, deluxe checkered walnut stock with ebony accents and Pachmayr Decelerator recoil pad, approx. 8 lbs. Limited mfg. in U.S. starting 1989.

$1,750	$1,375	$1,150	$950	$750	$650	$575

Last MSR was $1,950.

* *K15 Magnum* - .270 Wby. Mag., .300 Win. Mag. (disc.), .300 Wby. Mag., 7mm Rem. Mag., .338 Win. Mag., .340 Wby. Mag. (disc.), .375 H&H, .411 KDF, .416 Rem. Mag. (disc.), or .458 Win. Mag. cal., similar to K15, except has 26 in. barrel. Mfg. in U.S. starting in 1989. Disc.

$1,795	$1,400	$1,175	$975	$775	$675	$600

Last MSR was $2,000.

KDF CLASSIC - cals. similar to K15, custom tuned Remington 700 action, bench rest barrel, Brown Precision stock, KDF accurizing, Arnold jewell custom trigger, matte blue finish, Pachmayr Decelerator pad, includes rings and bases.

$1,750	$1,375	$1,150	$950	$750	$650	$575

Last MSR was $1,950.

Add $50 for Mag. cals.

KDF FRONTIER - cals. similar to KDF Classic, custom tuned Winchester Model 70 action, bench rest barrel, Brown Precision stock, KDF accurizing, Arnold jewell custom trigger, matte blue finish, Pachmayr Decelerator pad, includes rings and bases.

$1,750	$1,375	$1,150	$950	$750	$650	$575

Last MSR was $1,950.

Add $50 for Mag. cals.
Add $150 for action with positive feeding claw extractor.

KDF VARMINT - varmint cals., custom tuned Remington Model 700 or XP action, bench rest heavy contour barrel, Brown Precision stock, KDF accurizing, Arnold jewell custom trigger, matte blue finish, Pachmayr Decelerator pad, includes rings and bases.

$2,000	$1,725	$1,425	$1,200	$950	$750	$650

Last MSR was $2,250.

Add $250 for Rem. XP action.

GRADING - PPGS™	100%	98%	95%	90%	80%	70%	60%

KDF MAUSER 98 - .22-250 Rem. (new 2000), .243 Win. (new 2000), .25-06 Rem. (new 2000), .270 Win., .30-06, .308 Win. (new 2000), or 6.5x55mm (new 2000) cal., sporterized action, Wilson (disc.), Adams, or Bennett barrel, Butler Creek black synthetic stock, 7 1/2 lbs. New 1998.

MSR $379	$325	$275	$250	$225	$200	$185	$170

> Add $90 for adj. trigger.
> Add $160 for adj. trigger with thumb safety and custom bolt shroud.
> Add $89 for walnut stock with Schnabel forend.
> Subtract $40 for 6.5x55mm cal.

KDF CUSTOM MAUSER PACKAGE - various cals., features custom bolt shroud, adj. trigger, glass bedding, 1 in. rings, and KDF Slimline muzzle brake. Mfg. 1998-1999.

	$675	$550	$500	$450	$400	$360	$330

Last MSR was $750.

RIFLES: OLDER VOERE MFG. (PRE-1988)

TITAN SPORTER SERIES - various cals., 24 or 26 in. barrel, select walnut, pistol grip stock.

This series was available with either European Monte Carlo high-luster stock or in classic featherweight configuration with Schnabel forend - add $50-$200.

✱ *Titan Sporter Series Menor* - .222 Rem. or .223 Rem. cal. Importation disc. 1987.

	$675	$615	$560	$495	$450	$395	$350

Last MSR was $765.

> Add $100 for Match or Competition model (.223 Rem. cal.).

✱ *Titan Sporter Series II Standard* - many cals., between .243 Win. and .30-06. Disc. 1988.

	$950	$825	$725	$625	$550	$500	$450

Last MSR was $1,075.

> Add $100 for Match or Competition model (.308 Win. cal.).

✱ *Titan Sporter Series II Magnum* - available in cals. between 7mm Rem. Mag. and .375 H&H. Disc. 1988.

	$995	$875	$750	$650	$575	$520	$475

Last MSR was $1,125.

✱ *Titan Sporter Series .411 KDF Mag.* - .411 KDF cal., 26 in. barrel with recoil arrestor, 3 shot mag., blue or electroless nickel finish, 9 1/4 lbs. Imported 1986-88.

	$1,175	$965	$810	$725	$650	$575	$520

Last MSR was $1,300.

MODEL 2005 - .22 LR cal. only, semi-auto, 19 1/2 in. barrel, Monte Carlo stock, 5 shot mag., iron sights, 6 lbs. Imported 1986 only.

	$235	$215	$195	$175	$160	$145	$135

Last MSR was $165.

This model was ruled no longer importable by the BATF.

✱ *Model 2005 Deluxe* - similar to Model 2005, except has deluxe checkered walnut. Mfg. 1986-87 only.

	$260	$230	$210	$185	$165	$145	$135

Last MSR was $185.

MODEL 2107 - .22 LR or .22 Mag. cal., bolt action, 19 1/2 in. barrel, 5 shot mag., adj. iron sights, 6 lbs. Imported 1986-87 only.

	$175	$150	$125	$105	$95	$85	$80

Last MSR was $197.

> Add $42 for .22 Mag. cal.

GRADING - PPGS™	100%	98%	95%	90%	80%	70%	60%

* *Model 2107 Deluxe (Mauser 107)* - similar to Model 2107, except has deluxe checkered walnut. Imported 1986-88.

	$185	$165	$140	$125	$110	$105	$100

Last MSR was $219.

Add $50 for .22 Mag. cal.

This model was redesignated KDF-Mauser Model 107 when Voere distributor/dealer inventories were depleted.

MODEL 2112 - .22 LR or .22 Mag. cal., similar to Model 2107, except has extra select walnut. Imported 1988 only.

	$235	$200	$180	$160	$145	$135	$125

Last MSR was $279.

Add $50 for .22 Mag. cal.

K-14 INSTA FIRE RIFLE - .22-250 Rem., .270 Win., .300 Wby. Mag., or .458 Win. Mag. cal., 24 or 26 in. barrel, no sights, ultra fast lock time, hidden detachable mag., checkered Monte Carlo stock, recoil pad. Imported 1971-78.

	$725	$650	$575	$525	$475	$425	$375
K15 (.22 cal.)	$235	$205	$175	$150	$135	$120	$105

K-15 (MODEL 225) - available in 13 cals. between .243 Win. and .300 Wby. Mag., bolt action, 60 degree bolt lift with 3 locking lugs, ultra fast lock time, adj. trigger, 24 or 26 (Mag. only) in. barrel, 3 or 5 shot mag., no sights, guaranteed 1/2 in. accuracy at 100 yards, many stock options available at extra cost. Left-handed action available in certain cals. at a $50 charge.

* *K-15 Deluxe Standard Sporter* - standard model available in 6 regular cals. and 9 Mag. cals. Disc. 1988.

	$1,075	$950	$810	$700	$625	$550	$495

Last MSR was $1,275.

Add $50 for Magnum action.
Add $525 for .411 KDF cal.

In addition to the 15 regular cals., it was also possible to order various other factory cals. as a $200 option.

This model was redesignated KDF-Mauser Model 225 when Voere distributor/dealer inventories were depleted.

* *K-15 Fiberstock Pro-Hunter* - similar to the K-15, except is supplied with fiberglass stock (various colors), choice of parkerized, matte blue, or electroless nickel metal finish, and recoil arrestor installed. Imported 1986-88.

	$1,420	$1,200	$950	$835	$685	$585	$485

Last MSR was $1,680.

Add $50 for Magnum action.

This model was redesignated KDF-Mauser Model 225 when Voere distributor/dealer inventories were depleted.

* *K-15 Dangerous Game* - .411 KDF Mag. (new cartridge 1985) cal., choice of finishes, oil finished deluxe American walnut stock. Imported 1986-88.

	$1,895	$1,500	$1,150	$1,025	$830	$710	$590

Last MSR was $2,100.

This model was redesignated KDF-Mauser Model 225 when Voere distributor/dealer inventories were depleted.

* *K-15 Swat Rifle* - .308 Win. cal. standard, 24 or 26 in. barrel, parkerized metal, oil finished target walnut stock, 3 or 4 shot detachable mag., 10 lbs. Importation disc. 1988.

	$1,475	$1,250	$1,000	$850	$725	$650	$575

Last MSR was $1,725.

GRADING - PPGS™	100%	98%	95%	90%	80%	70%	60%

K-16 - available in 6 standard cals. between .243 Win. and .300 Win. Mag. in addition to optional cals., modified Remington Model 700 action, standard features include KDF accurizing and Insta Fire ignition, single stage adj. trigger, Dupont Rynite stock (camel or grey), choice of finishes (high-gloss blue standard), recoil pad and quick detachable sling swivels, many options available. Imported 1988 only.

	$765	$675	$615	$560	$495	$450	$395

Last MSR was $876.

Add $120 for KDF muzzle brake.
Add $250 for optional cals.
Add $350 for .411 KDF Mag. cal.

K-22 (MAUSER 201) - .22 LR or .22 Mag. cal., bolt action, free floating 21 in. barrel, 5 shot mag., adj. trigger, scaled down version of the K-15, unusual action incorporates two front-located locking lugs on bolt face that engage Stellite inserts on the front receiver portion, guaranteed 1 in. groupings at 100 yards, blue only, no sights, select walnut stock with cheekpiece, standard model disc. 1987.

	$310	$285	$260	$240	$225	$210	$195

Last MSR was $345.

Add $50 for .22 Mag. cal.

✻ *K-22 Deluxe (Mauser 201)* - better walnut and stock options. Model notation changed in 1988.

	$410	$360	$295	$275	$250	$235	$210

Last MSR was $495.

Add $50 for .22 Mag. cal.

This model was redesignated KDF-Mauser Model 201 when Voere distributor/dealer inventories were depleted.

✻ *K-22 Deluxe Custom* - richly layered walnut and stock options. Importation disc. 1987.

	$655	$595	$550	$495	$450	$395	$350

Last MSR was $725.

Add $50 for .22 Mag. cal.

✻ *K-22 Deluxe Special Select* - top-of-the-line bolt action, double set triggers. Importation disc. 1987.

	$1,060	$950	$850	$750	$695	$650	$595

Last MSR was $1,225.

Add $50 for .22 Mag. cal.

SHOTGUNS

CONDOR O/U - 12 ga., 28 in. barrel, various chokes, selective single trigger, auto ejectors, wide VR, boxlock, checkered pistol grip stock, Italian made.

	$660	$635	$605	$580	$525	$470	$415

BRESCIA SxS - 12 ga., 28 in. barrel, full and mod., double triggers, engraved, checkered pistol grip stock.

	$330	$305	$275	$250	$195	$165	$140

K.F.C.

Previously manufactured by Kawaguchiya Firearms Co., Ltd. Previously imported and distributed by La Paloma Marketing, Inc. located in Tucson, AZ.

SHOTGUNS

MODEL 250 SEMI-AUTO - 12 ga. only, semi-auto incorporating a patented, cushioned piston assembly, 26, 28, or 30 in. barrel, matte blue finish, vent. rib standard, checkered premium walnut, 7 lbs. Manufactured 1980-86.

	$360	$290	$270	$250	$235	$220	$205

Last MSR was $485.

Add $60 for multi-chokes.

GRADING - PPGS™	100%	98%	95%	90%	80%	70%	60%

✴ *Model 250 Semi-Auto Deluxe* - same specifications as Model 250, except has scrolled acid etching panels on both sides of normally black receiver. Disc. 1986.

| | $395 | $310 | $290 | $270 | $250 | $225 | $210 |

Last MSR was $520.

FIELD GUN O/U - 12 ga. only, VR, premium grade walnut, semi pistol grip stock, F&IC chokes. Disc. 1986.

| | $645 | $565 | $530 | $495 | $470 | $445 | $410 |

Last MSR was $748.

E-1 TRAP OR SKEET O/U - 12 ga. only, VR, oil finished premium grade walnut, semi pistol grip stock, engraved. Disc. 1986.

| | $935 | $800 | $750 | $700 | $625 | $550 | $495 |

Last MSR was $1,070.

E-2 TRAP OR SKEET O/U - 12 ga. only, VR, oil finished premium grade walnut, semi pistol grip stock, detailed engraving. Disc. 1986.

| | $1,450 | $1,250 | $1,075 | $950 | $850 | $750 | $650 |

Last MSR was $1,660.

KSN INDUSTRIES LTD.

Previous distributor (1952-1996) located in Houston, TX. Previously imported until 1996 exclusively by J.O. Arms, Inc. located in Houston, TX. Currently mfg. Israel Arms, Ltd. pistols may be found under their individual listing.

PISTOLS: SEMI-AUTO

The pistols listed below were mfg. by Israel Arms, Ltd.

KAREEN MK II - 9mm Para. or .40 S&W (new late 1994) cal., single action, 3.85 (Compact) or 4.64 (Standard) in. barrel, two-tone finish, rubberized grips, regular or Meprolite sights, 10 (C/B 1994), 13*, or 15* shot mag., 33 oz. Imported 1993-96.

| | $360 | $305 | $255 | $225 | $200 | $185 | $170 |

Last MSR was $411.

Add approx. $160 for two-tone finish with Meprolite sights.

✴ *Kareen Mk II Compact* - compact variation with 3.85 in. barrel. Imported 1993-96.

| | $415 | $360 | $315 | $255 | $225 | $200 | $185 |

Last MSR was $497.

GOLAN MODEL - 9mm Para. or .40 S&W cal., single or double action, ambidextrous safety with decocking feature, steel slide with alloy frame, 3 7/8 in. barrel, matte black finish, 29 oz. Imported 1994-96.

| | $565 | $515 | $460 | $410 | $360 | $330 | $295 |

Last MSR was $650.

Add $35 for .40 S&W cal.

KAHR ARMS

Current manufacturer established 1993, with headquarters located in Blauvelt, NY, and manufacturing in Worchester, MA. Distributor and dealer sales.

PISTOLS: SEMI-AUTO

All Kahr pistols are supplied with two mags., hard polymer case, trigger lock, and lifetime warranty.

CW9 - 9mm Para. cal., black polymer frame, matte stainless steel slide, 7 shot mag., DAO, 3 1/2 in. barrel, textured polymer grips, adj. rear sight, pinned in polymer front sight, white dot combat sights, 15.8 oz. New 2005.

| MSR $533 | $450 | $410 | $375 | $325 | $295 | $275 | $250 |

GRADING - PPGS™	100%	98%	95%	90%	80%	70%	60%

CW40 - .40 S&W cal., black polymer frame, matte stainless steel slide, 6 shot mag., DAO, 3.6 in. barrel, textured polymer grips, adj. rear sight, pinned in polymer front sight, white dot combat sights, 16.8 oz. New 2008.

	MSR $533	$450	$410	$375	$325	$295	$275	$250

CW45 - .45 ACP cal., otherwise similar to CW40, 19.7 oz. New 2008.

	MSR $566	$475	$425	$395	$335	$300	$275	$250

E9 - 9mm Para. cal., economized version of the K9 Compact, matte black finish or duo-tone (new 2003), supplied with one mag. Mfg. 1997 only, reintroduced 2003 only.

$425	$365	$335	$300	$280	$265	$250

Last MSR was $490.

K9 COMPACT - 9mm Para. cal., trigger cocking, double action only with passive striker block, locked breech with Browning type recoil lug, steel construction, 3 1/2 in. barrel with polygonal rifling, 7 shot mag., wraparound black polymer grips, matte black, black titanium (Black-T, mfg. 1997-98), or electroless nickel (mfg. 1996-99) finish, 25 oz. Mfg. 1993-2003.

$560	$485	$435	$385	$340	$315	$285

Last MSR was $648.

Add $74 for electroless nickel finish (disc.).
Add $126 for black titanium finish (Black-T, disc.).
Add $103 for tritium night sights (new 1996).

✳ *K9 Compact Economy* - features black matte finish, shipped with one mag. only. Limited mfg. 1999 only.

$350	$300	$275	$250	$230	$210	$190

Last MSR was $399.

✳ *K9 Compact Stainless* - similar to K9 Compact, except is matte finished stainless steel, NYCPD specs became standard 2006 (trigger LOP is 1/2 in. compared to 3/8 in.). New 1998.

	MSR $855	$750	$665	$550	$450	$385	$335	$280

Add $130 for tritium night sights.
Add $46 for matte black finish (new 2004).

✳ *K9 Compact Elite 98 Stainless* - similar to K9 Compact, except has high polish slide and specially designed combat trigger utilizing shorter trigger stroke. New 1998.

	MSR $932	$785	$700	$600	$500	$425	$375	$300

Add $122 for tritium night sights.

✳ *K9 Compact Wilson Custom Package* - includes Wilson customizing with Metalloy hard chrome frame, black slide, checkered front strap and beveled mag. well. Limited quantities mfg. 1998.

$1,175	$995	$875	$775	$700	$625	$550

Last MSR was $1,310.

✳ *K9 Compact Kahr Lady* - similar to K9 Compact, except has lightened recoil spring, not available in black titanium finish, 25 oz. Mfg. 1997-99.

$480	$435	$395	$365	$315	$285	$250

Last MSR was $545.

Add $74 for electroless nickel finish.
Add $85 for tritium night sights (new 1996).

P9 POLYMER COMPACT - 9mm Para cal., similar to K9 Compact, except has 3.6 in. barrel, lightweight polymer frame, 7 shot mag., matte stainless slide, 17.9 oz. New 1999.

	MSR $739	$630	$525	$450	$375	$325	$285	$250

Add $118 for tritium night sights (new 2000).
Add $47 for matte black stainless slide (new 2004).

GRADING - PPGS™	100%	98%	95%	90%	80%	70%	60%

✴ *P9 Polymer Compact Covert* - similar to K9 Polymer Compact, except has 1/2 in. shorter frame, supplied with one 6 and one 7 (with grip extension) shot mag., 16.9 oz. Limited mfg. 1999, reintroduced 2002 - 2006.

		$595	$495	$430	$365	$325	$285	$250

Last MSR was $697.

     Add $111 for tritium night sights (new 2000).

MK9 MICRO SERIES - 9mm Para. cal., micro compact variation of the K9 Compact featuring 3 in. barrel, double action only with passive striker block, overall size is 4 in. H x 5 1/2 in. L, duo-tone finish with stainless frame and black titanium slide, includes two 6 shot flush floor plate mags. Mfg. 1998-99.

		$650	$575	$515	$465	$425	$395	$375

Last MSR was $749.

     Add $85 for tritium night sights.

✴ *MK9 Micro Series Box* - similar to MK9 Micro, except has matte stainless steel frame with steel matte black slide, duo-tone finish. Limited mfg. 2003, reintroduced 2004-2005.

		$400	$325	$285	$235	$200	$170	$145

Last MSR was $475.

     Add $100 for tritium night sights (disc.).

✴ *MK9 Micro Series Stainless* - similar to MK9 Micro, except is stainless steel, supplied with 6 and 7 shot mag., 24 oz. New 1998.

MSR $855		$695	$575	$475	$375	$325	$260	$225

     Add $103 for tritium night sights.

✴ *MK9 Micro Series Elite 98 Stainless* - similar to MK9 Micro, except has high polish slide and specially designed combat trigger utilizing shorter trigger stroke, 24 oz. New 1998.

MSR $932		$795	$675	$595	$475	$415	$360	$300

     Add $122 for tritium night sights.

✴ *MK9 Micro Series Elite 2000 Stainless* - similar to MK9 Elite 98 Stainless, except features black stainless frame and slide, black Roguard finish. Mfg. 2001-2002.

		$575	$485	$425	$360	$315	$260	$225

Last MSR was $694.

PM9 MICRO POLYMER COMPACT - 9mm Para cal., 3 in. barrel with polygonal rifling, black polymer frame, trigger cocking DAO, blackened stainless steel slide, 6 or 7 (with mag. grip extension, disc.) shot mag., 16 oz. New 2003.

MSR $771		$650	$535	$450	$395	$350	$300	$275

     Add $119 for tritium night sights.
     Add $49 for matte black stainless slide (new 2004).

MP9 COMPACT POLYMER - 9mm Para cal., features lightweight polymer frame and matte stainless steel slide, 3 in. barrel, DAO with passive striker block, supplied with 6 and 7 shot mag with grip extension, includes hard case and trigger lock, 15.9 oz. Mfg. 2002-2003.

		$565	$485	$415	$380	$340	$300	$275

Last MSR was $660.

     Add $101 for tritium night sights.

T9 - 9mm Para cal., 4 in. barrel with polygonal rifling, matte stainless steel construction, checkered Hogue Pau Ferro wood grips, 8 shot mag., Elite 98 trigger, MMC (disc.), white bar-dot (new 2006) or optional Novak low profile night sights, 28 oz. New 2002.

MSR $831		$695	$565	$460	$395	$345	$285	$240

     Add $137 for Novak night sights.

GRADING - PPGS™	100%	98%	95%	90%	80%	70%	60%

TP9 - 9mm Para cal., similar to T9, except has black polymer frame and standard sights, 20 oz. New 2004.

MSR $697	$600	$500	$425	$360	$315	$260	$225

Add $141 for Novak night sights.

K40 COMPACT - .40 S&W cal., similar to K9, except has 6 shot mag., matte black or electroless nickel finish (disc. 1999), 26 oz. Mfg. 1997-2003.

	$560	$485	$435	$385	$340	$315	$285

Last MSR was $648.

Add $103 for tritium night sights (new 1997).
Add $74 for electroless nickel finish (disc. 1999).
Add $126 for black titanium finish (Black-T, disc. 1998).

* *K40 Compact Stainless* - similar to K40 Compact, except is stainless steel. New 1997.

MSR $855	$695	$575	$475	$375	$325	$260	$225

Add $130 for tritium night sights.
Add $36 for matte black stainless steel (new 2004).

* *K40 Compact Elite 98 Stainless* - similar to K40 Compact, except has high polish slide and specially designed combat trigger utilizing shorter trigger stroke. New 1998.

MSR $932	$785	$700	$600	$500	$425	$375	$300

Add $122 for tritium night sights.

* *K40 Compact Wilson Custom Package* - includes Wilson customizing with Metalloy hard chrome frame, black slide, checkered front strap, and beveled mag. well. Limited quantities mfg. 1998.

	$1,175	$995	$875	$775	$700	$625	$550

Last MSR was $1,310.

* *K40 Compact Covert Stainless (KS40 Small Frame)* - .40 S&W cal., similar to Kahr Compact K40, except grip is 1/2 in. shorter, supplied with 5 and 6 shot mags., 25 oz. Mfg. 1998-2000.

	$500	$440	$400	$335	$290	$245	$215

Last MSR was $580.

Add $88 for tritium night sights.

P40 COMPACT POLYMER - .40 S&W cal., similar to P9 Compact, 6 shot mag., 18.9 oz. New 2001.

MSR $739	$630	$525	$450	$375	$325	$285	$250

Add $113 for tritium night sights.
Add $47 for matte black stainless slide (new 2004).

* *P40 Compact Polymer Covert* - similar to P40 Compact Polymer, except has 1/2 in. shorter frame, matte stainless slide, supplied with one 6 and one 7 (with grip extension) shot mag., 16.9 oz. Mfg. 2002-2006.

	$600	$500	$425	$370	$325	$285	$250

Last MSR was $697.

Add $111 for tritium night sights.

MK40 MICRO - .40 S&W cal., micro compact variation of the Compact K40, featuring 3 in. barrel, matte stainless frame and slide, supplied with one 5 shot and one 6 shot (with grip extension) mag., 25 oz. New 1999.

MSR $855	$750	$665	$550	$450	$385	$335	$280

Add $103 for tritium night sights.

* *MK40 Micro Elite Stainless* - similar to MK40 Micro, except has high polish slide and specially designed combat trigger utilizing shorter trigger stroke. New 2000.

MSR $932	$785	$700	$600	$500	$425	$375	$300

Add $122 for tritium night sights.

GRADING - PPGS™	100%	98%	95%	90%	80%	70%	60%

PM40 COMPACT POLYMER - .40 S&W cal., black polymer frame, 3 in. barrel, supplied with one 5 shot and one 6 shot (with grip extension) mag., matte finished stainless slide, 17 oz. New 2004.

MSR $771	$650	$535	$450	$395	$350	$300	$275

Add $119 for tritium night sights.
Add $49 for matte black stainless slide (new 2005).

T40 - .40 S&W cal., 4 in. barrel with polygonal rifling, matte stainless steel construction, checkered Hogue Pau Ferro wood grips, 7 shot mag., Elite 98 trigger, MMC (disc. 2005), white bar dot (standard, new 2006), or optional Novak low profile night sights, 29 oz. New 2004.

MSR $831	$695	$565	$460	$395	$345	$285	$240

Add $137 for Novak night sights (T40 Tactical).

TP40 - .40 S&W cal., similar to T40, except has polymer frame. New 2006.

MSR $697	$600	$500	$425	$370	$325	$285	$250

Add $141 for Novak night sights (TP40 Tactical).

P45 POLYMER - .45 ACP cal., DAO, black polymer frame with matte or black stainless steel slide, 3.54 in. barrel, 6 shot mag., ribbed grip straps, low profile, white dot combat sights, 18 1/2 oz. New 2005.

MSR $805	$685	$560	$460	$410	$340	$290	$250

Add $116 for Novak night sights.
Add $50 for black stainless slide (new 2006).

PM45 POLYMER - similar to TP45, except has 3.14 in. barrel and 5 shot mag., approx. 19 oz. New 2007.

MSR $838	$745	$660	$550	$450	$385	$335	$280

Add $117 for Novak night sights.

TP45 POLYMER - .45 ACP cal., DAO, 4.04 in. barrel, 7 shot mag., matte stainless slide only, otherwise similar to P45, approx. 23 oz. New 2007.

MSR $697	$595	$495	$430	$365	$325	$285	$250

Add $142 for Novak sights.

KASSNAR IMPORTS, INC.

Previous importer and distributor located in Harrisburg, PA. Kassnar Imports operations ceased April, 1989.

Kassnar also imported Churchill and Omega shotguns which can be found in their individual section.

PISTOLS: SEMI-AUTO

PJK-9HP - 9mm Para. cal., single action, patterned after the Browning Hi-Power, 4 3/4 in. barrel, 13 shot mag., cone hammer, checkered walnut grips, 32 oz.

	$225	$200	$185	$175	$165	$155	$145

Add $15 for VR barrel.

This pistol was imported from Hungary. Approx. 18,000 (including the MBK-9HP) were imported until importation was disc. because of Federal ramifications.

MBK-9HP - 9mm Para. cal., double action, patterned after the Browning Hi-Power, 4 2/3 in. barrel, spur hammer, blue metal, checkered walnut grips, 14 shot mag., 36 oz. Limited importation was stopped in late 1985.

	$295	$260	$230	$190	$175	$165	$155

PMK-380 - .380 ACP cal., double action, patterned after the Walther PP, plastic grips with thumbrest, 4 in. barrel, 7 shot mag., 21 oz. Limited importation.

	$275	$235	$200	$185	$175	$165	$155

This model was imported in very limited quantities before Interarms began exclusive importation.

KEBERST INTERNATIONAL

Previously manufactured and distributed by Kendall International located in Paris, KY.

GRADING - PPGS™	100%	98%	95%	90%	80%	70%	60%

RIFLES: BOLT ACTION

KEBERST MODEL 1A - .338 Lapua Mag., .338-416 Rigby, or .338-06 cal., muzzle brake and unique recoil pad, camouflaged synthetic stock, package includes 3-9 power Leupold scope, stainless steel cleaning rod, custom designed case, built to special order only. Mfg. 1987-88 only.

	$3,475	$2,850	$2,475	$2,100	$1,750	$1,400	$1,150

Last MSR was $3,750.

Add $275 for 10X Ultra scope.

KEL-TEC CNC INDUSTRIES, INC.

Current manufacturer established in 1991, and located in Cocoa, FL. Dealer sales.

CARBINES/RIFLES: SEMI-AUTO

SUB-9/SUB-40 CARBINE - 9mm Para. or .40 S&W cal., unique pivoting 16.1 in. barrel rotates upwards and back, allowing overall size reduction and portability (16 in. x 7 in.), interchangable grip assembly will accept most popular, double column, high capacity handgun mags., including Glock, S&W, Beretta, SIG, or Kel-Tec, tube stock with polymer buttplate, matte black finish, 4.6 lbs. Mfg. 1997-2000.

	$325	$295	$265	$240	$215	$195	$180

Last MSR was $700.

Add $25 for .40 S&W cal.

SUB-2000 CARBINE - 9mm Para or .40 S&W (new 2004) cal., similar to Sub-9/Sub-40, choice of blue, parkerized (mfg. 2003-2006) or hard chrome (mfg. 2003-2006), 4 lbs. New 2001.

MSR $406		$340	$310	$265	$240	$215	$195	$180

Add $28 for parkerized finish or $38 for hard chrome finish (disc. 2006).

SU-16 RIFLE/CARBINE - .223 Rem. cal., unique downward folding stock, forearm folds down to become a bipod, 16 (new 2005) or 18 1/2 in. barrel, Picatinny receiver rail, M16 breech locking and feeding system, black synthetic stock (stores extra mags.) and forearm, approx. 4.7 lbs. New 2003.

MSR $665		$595	$515	$460	$400	$350	$300	$265

Add $53 for lightweight variation.
Add $105 for carbine.

PISTOLS: SEMI-AUTO

P-3AT - .380 ACP cal., developed from the P-32, 2.76 in. barrel, 6 shot mag., black composite frame with parkerized steel slide, 8.3 oz. New 2003.

MSR $324		$270	$215	$180	$160	$150	$135	$125

Add $42 for parkerized finish.
Add $58 for hard chrome finish.

P-11 - 9mm Para. cal., double action only, locked breech design, 3.1 in. barrel, composite frame with steel slide, transfer bar safety, matte blue, parkerized (new 1997), hard chrome (new 1999), or electroless nickel (disc. 1995) finish, black, grey, or green (disc. 1998) synthetic grips, 10 shot double column mag., 14.4 oz. New 1995.

MSR $333		$275	$220	$185	$165	$150	$135	$125

Add $85 for night sights (mfg. 1997-2003, reintroduced 2007).
Add $44 for parkerized finish (choice of grips).
Add $57 for hard chrome finish (new 1999).
Add $30 for electroless nickel finish (disc. 1995).
Add $175 for 9mm Para. to .40 S&W cal. conversion kit (disc. 2002).

GRADING - PPGS™	100%	98%	95%	90%	80%	70%	60%

* *P-11 Stainless* - similar to P-11, except is stainless steel, available with black (P- 11SB), grey (P-11SGY), or green (P-11SGN) grips. Mfg. 1996-98.

	$350	$275	$230	$180	$140	$125	$105

Last MSR was $408.

P-32 - .32 ACP cal., double action only with internal hammer block safety, 7 shot mag., composite frame with steel slide, 2.68 in. barrel, choice of parkerized, blue, or hard chrome finish, choice of light blue, dark blue, grey, green or full ivory grips, 6.6 oz. New 1999.

MSR $318	$265	$210	$180	$160	$150	$135	$125

Add $43 for parkerized finish.
Add $59 for hard chrome finish.

P-40 - .40 S&W cal., double action only with internal hammer block safety, composite frame with steel slide, 3.3 in. barrel, choice of parkerized, blue, or hard chrome finish, 9 or 10 shot mag., 15.8 oz. Mfg. 1999-2001.

	$275	$225	$190	$175	$160	$140	$130

Last MSR was $331.

Add $41 for parkerized finish.
Add $58 for hard chrome finish.

PLR-16 - .223 Rem. cal., M16 type gas operation, 9.2 in. threaded barrel, upper frame has integrated Picatinny rail, detachable mag., black composite frame, 3.2 lbs. New 2006.

MSR $665	$590	$510	$430	$375	$325	$295	$275

PF-9 - 9mm Para. cal., similar operating system as P-11, 3.1 in. barrel, single stack 7 shot mag., includes lower accessory rail, black finish, 12.7 oz. Limited mfg. 2006.

	$270	$215	$180	$165	$150	$135	$125

Last MSR was $320.

KEMEN

Current competition shotgun manufacturer established in 1990, and located in Elgoibar, Spain. Currently imported exclusively by Fieldsport (all models), located in Traverse City, MI. Previously imported by Target Shotguns, located in Arden, NC, American Shooting Centers, located in Houston, TX, by Fly and Field, located in Bend, OR, and by New England Custom Gun Service (Model KM-4 only), located in Plainfield, NH. Gun service is available through Briley.

SHOTGUNS: O/U

Kemen shotguns are built to individual customer specifications. 250-300 special order guns are made annually - delivery time is 4-6 months. Their unique metal finish makes them almost impervious to any type of oxidation or rust.

Add 7% for 20 ga. or 28 ga. on models listed below.

KM-4 STANDARD - 12 or 20 ga., boxlock action, competition shotgun various length vent. or separated barrels with VR and Briley choke tubes, detachable trigger group, blue receiver with gold accents, checkered walnut stock and forearm, wood upgrades available, cased, 8-8 1/2 lbs.

MSR N/A	$7,450	$5,900	$5,000	$4,425	$3,800	$3,400	$2,850

* *KM-4 Standard Combo* - includes 20 and 28 ga. barrels. New 2004.

MSR N/A	$11,250	$9,450	$8,550	$6,650	$5,950	$4,950	$4,000

KM-4 SPORTING - 12 or 20 ga., 32 or 34 in. barrels with choke tubes, black receiver with no engraving, checkered walnut stock with pistol grip, SST, recoil pad, includes hard case, 8 1/4 lbs.

MSR N/A	$7,450	$5,900	$5,000	$4,425	$3,800	$3,400	$2,850

GRADING - PPGS™	100%	98%	95%	90%	80%	70%	60%

KM-4 LUXE A/B - similar to KM-4 Standard, except has nickel finished frame with choice of fine scroll or game scene engraving. Limited importation.

MSR N/A	$13,500	$9,950	$8,250	$7,300	$6,200	$5,300	$4,475

Subtract $1,000 for KM-4 Luxe B.

KM-4 SUPER LUXE A/B/C - similar to KM-4 Luxe A/B, except has nickel finished frame with more elaborate game scene engraving, "A" suffix features game scene engraving, "B" suffix includes gold line engraving, "C" suffix has high relief scroll work and gold trigger. Limited importation.

MSR N/A	$14,000	$10,250	$8,450	$7,550	$6,450	$5,500	$4,600

Add $700 for Super Luxe A variation.
Add $2,200 for Super Luxe B variation.

KM-4 EXTRA LUXE A/B/C - similar to KM-4 Super Luxe, except has nickel finished frame with sideplates and choice of Purdey style fine scroll (Extra Luxe A), extra fine game scene (Extra Luxe B), or gargoyle motif (Extra Luxe C) engraving. Limited importation.

MSR N/A	$14,850	$11,000	$9,000	$8,000	$7,000	$6,000	$5,000

Add $3,000 for Extra Luxe B variation.
Add $8,000 for Extra Luxe C variation.

KM-4 EXTRA GOLD A/B - 12 or 20 ga., features engraved sideplate action with multiple gold inlays, select wood. Limited importation.

MSR N/A	$22,750	$18,250	$15,000	$12,000	$9,950	$8,750	$7,500

Add $1,000 for Extra Gold B variation.

SUPREMA AX/BX/CX - 12 or 20 ga., top-of-the-line model, sidelock action, Suprema AX features English fine scroll engraving, custom ordered to individual specifications. Limited importation.

MSR N/A	$35,000	$29,500	$25,000	$22,000	$18,000	$14,500	$11,000

Add $1,000 for BX Model or $3,000 for AX Model.

SHOTGUNS: SxS

KM-4 PARALELAS FIELD - sidelock action with blued frame, fixed chokes, checkered buttstock.

MSR N/A	$13,000	$9,750	$8,250	$7,300	$6,200	$5,100	$4,300

IMPERIAL AX/BX - best quality sidelock model, many options available.

MSR N/A	$16,750	$13,000	$10,000	$9,000	$7,500	$6,500	$5,750

Add $4,200 for Imperial BX Model.

SHOTGUNS: SINGLE BARREL

KM-4 TRAP - 12 ga., 34 in. single barrel with 20mm tapered step VR. Limited importation began 2004.

MSR N/A	$8,650	$7,450	$5,900	$5,000	$4,425	$3,800	$3,200

Add $2,500 for set of 32 in. O/U barrels with 20mm tapered step rib VR.

KENDALL INTERNATIONAL

Previous importer and distributor located in Paris, KY. Kendall International also imported Australian Automatic Arms, and the Keberst Rifle, Air rifles can be found in the *Blue Book of Airguns* by Dr. Robert Beeman & John Allen (also online).

KENTUCKY RIFLES

U.S. flintlock/percussion long rifle configuration originating in Pennsylvania. Kentucky rifles are a field unto themselves, and should be evaluated by an experienced and known source for accurate identification and/or price evaluation.

KENTUCKY RIFLES INDENTIFICATION & PRICING

The author wishes to express his thanks once again to Mr. James Buelow for updating the following information.

GRADING - PPGS™	100%	98%	95%	90%	80%	70%	60%

The Kentucky rifle was the creation of early settlers from Europe. This new American configuration combined the architectural elements of the English Fowler with the ornamental features of the German Jaeger.

The earliest recorded use of the term "Kentucky rifle" was in a ballad written after the battle of New Orleans. The battle was won by the American Long Rifle, in the hands of 2,000 frontiersmen. During that period, the area west of the 13 colonies was known as Kentucky; hence the name Kentucky rifle.

Kentucky rifles began appearing around the middle of the 18th century and disappeared by the middle of the 19th century. Their origin is credited to eastern Pennsylvania, but soon spread to many other states, including Maryland, Virginia, Tennessee, North Carolina, and areas where the rifle maker found a market for his skills.

The styles vary, but they have two things in common: they are long, and most had curly maple stocks. The bores are found both rifled and smooth. The rifles most prized by the collector are the ones that have relief or incised carving. Carved Kentucky rifles are considered one of America's earliest art forms and are now considered Americana personified. Present values may range from as low as $1,000 all the way up to $50,000+! Non-carved or plain Kentuckys are most often encountered.

The present value of an uncarved, original flintlock Kentucky rifle in average condition is approx. $3,000. An uncarved percussion specimen in average original condition is approx. $2,000. These prices diminish when the Kentucky rifle lacks a maker's name, usually found on the top of the barrel, or if it does not have a patch box. Kentucky rifle values vary greatly, due to maker popularity, quality of carving, condition, rifle style, and a multitude of other factors.

During the past several decades, many fine contemporary Kentucky rifles have been built by craftsmen who understand the trade. Many of these guns are now available in the secondary marketplace. A large percentage have outstanding craftsmanship, and are highly sought after. These specimens sell in the $2,000-$10,000 range, depending on the notoriety of the builder and the sophistication of the work. Because of this, these guns have to be evaluated one at a time.

The best way to find out the value of a Kentucky rifle is to seek out a knowledgeable Kentucky rifle collector. To find such a person in your area, contact the Kentucky Rifle Association's Administrative Assistant: Ruth Collis, 2319 Sue Ann Dr., Lancaster, PA, 17602. For information regarding contemporary Kentucky rifles makers (with some contact information), visit the Contemporary Longrifle Association at www.longrifle.ws, or see their listing under Firearms Associations.

KEPPELER - TECHNISCHEEN-TWICKLUNGEN GmbH

Current rifle manufacturer located in Fichtenberg, Germany. No current U.S. importation.

Keppeler manufactures a wide variety of top quality rifles, in many target configurations (including UIT-CISM, Prone, Free, and Sniper Bullpup). Both metric and domestic calibers are available as well as a variety of special order options. Keppeler also manufactures precision caliber conversion tubes for the shotgun barrel(s) on combination guns and drillings. Please contact the factory directly for more information and current pricing (see Trademark Index).

KEPPLINGER, ING. HANNES

Please refer to the Kufsteiner Waffenstube section.

KESSLER ARMS CORPORATION

Previous manufacturer located in Silver Creek, NY.

SHOTGUNS

LEVERMATIC MODEL - 12, 16, or 20 ga., lever action, 26 or 28 in. full choke, takedown, plain pistol grip stock. Disc. 1953.

$175	$150	$125	$100	$85	$65	$55

GRADING - PPGS™	100%	98%	95%	90%	80%	70%	60%

BOLT ACTION MODEL - 12, 16, or 20 ga., 26 or 28 in. full, takedown, plain stock. Mfg. 1951-53.

	$90	$65	$50	$45	$35	$35	$35

KEYSTONE SPORTING ARMS, INC.

Current rifle manufacturer established 1996, and located in Milton, PA. Distributor and dealer sales.

In January, 2007, Keystone purchased the remaining assets of Rogue Rifle Co., manufacturers of Chipmunk rifles.

RIFLES: BOLT ACTION

CRICKETT SPORTER - .22 Short, .22 LR or .22 Mag. (mfg. 2001-2004) cal., manually cocked single shot, 16 1/8 in. barrel with adj. rear aperture sight, steel or stainless steel (new 1999) construction, 11 1/2 in. LOP (youth dimension), choice of walnut, colored laminate, camo synthetic, or molded black synthetic stock, stainless or blue barrel and receiver, 30 in. overall length, 2 1/2 lbs. New 1997.

MSR $165		$150	$135	$120	$105	$95	$85	$75

Add $20 for solid walnut stock.
Add $45-$60 for color laminated stock (various colors).
Add $35 for stainless steel, and $20 for bull barrel.
Add $25 for .22 Mag. cal. (disc. 2004).

✴ *Crickett Sporter Custom/Deluxe* - features deluxe hand checkered stock. Mfg. 1998-2000.

	$225	$195	$175	$150	$135	$120	$105

Last MSR was $250.

Add $10 for deluxe configuration.

KHAN

Current trademark of shotguns established in 1985, and manufactured in Istanbul, Turkey. Currently imported on a private label basis by Mossberg. Previously imported late 2004-2005 by Legacy Sports International, LLC, located in Alexandria, VA.

SHOTGUNS: O/U

ARTHEMIS ELITE FIELD/DELUXE - 12, 20, 28 ga. or .410 bore, 3 in. chambers (except for 28 ga.), 26 or 28 in. VR barrels with multichokes (fixed chokes on .410 bore), extractors, SST, matte blue (Field) or bright blue (Deluxe) metal finish, light engraving, choice of satin finish (Field) or polished select finish (Deluxe) walnut stock, 5.7-7.9 lbs.

	$500	$450	$400	$350	$300	$265	$235

Last MSR was $617.

Add $15 for 20 ga.
Add $22 for 28 ga. or .410 bore.
Add $174 for Deluxe Model with bright blue metal and polished select wood stock (12 or 20 ga. only).

✴ *Arthemis Elite Field/Deluxe Sporting Clays* - 12 ga., 2 3/4 in. chambers, ejectors, 28 in. barrels, ST, otherwise similar to Arthemis Field, 8 lbs.

	$925	$825	$725	$650	$575	$495	$425

Last MSR was $1,104.

SHOTGUNS: SxS

COACH GUN - 12 ga., 2 3/4 in. chamber, bright blue metal, hammerless boxlock action, extractors, polished select wood stock and forearm, 20 in. barrels with fixed cyl. bore chokes, 6.9 lbs.

	$675	$595	$525	$450	$375	$300	$225

Last MSR was $784.

KIMAR srl

Current division of Armi Sport Chiappa Silvia e. C. S.N.C., located in, Brescia, Italy. Currently imported by Valor Corporation, located in Sunrise, FL, Traditions, located in Old Saybrook, CT, Taylor's, located in Winchester, VA, and by IAR, located in San Juan Capistrano, CA.

Kimar is well known for its starter/signal revolvers and pistols in many popular configurations. Additionally, the company also manufactures a single shot, folding barrel shotgun in small hunting calibers. Please contact the importers directly for more information and U.S. availability (see Trademark Index).

J. KIMBALL ARMS CO.

Previous manufacturer located in Detroit, MI circa 1958.

PISTOLS: SEMI-AUTO

AUTOMATIC PISTOL - .30 Carbine or .22 Hornet (very rare) cal., 7 shot, 3 in. (Combat Model) or 5 in. (Target Model) barrel, approx. 32 oz. Less than 300 mfg. in 1958 only.

$1,700	$1,450	$1,250	$1,000	$850	$725	$550

Add 50% for .22 Hornet cal.

Functional weaknesses of this pistol caused discontinuance. Surviving specimens should be checked carefully for slide failures and other potential problems. Values assume no operational damage to the pistol.

KIMBER

Current trademark manufactured by Kimber Mfg., Inc., established during 1997, with company headquarters and manufacturing located in Yonkers, NY. Previous rifle manufacture was by Kimber of America, Inc., located in Clackamas, OR circa 1993-97. Dealer sales.

PISTOLS: SEMI-AUTO

Kimber pistols, including the very early models marked "Clackamas, Oregon", have all been manufactured in the current plant in Yonkers, NY. Prior to the 1998 production year, the "Classic" model pistols were alternately roll-scrolled "Classic", "Classic Custom" or "Custom Classic". During 1997-98, the "Classic" moniker was dropped from Kimber pistol nomenclature as a specific model.

All Kimber pistols are shipped with lockable high impact synthetic case with cable lock and one mag., beginning 1999.

Beginning in 2001, the "Series II" pistol, incorporating the Kimber Firing Pin Safety System, was, again, phased into almost all centerfire models. All pistols incorporating the firing pin block have the Roman Numeral "II" following the name of the pistol presented on the slide directly under the ejection port. This conversion was completed by February, 2002, and almost all subsequent Kimber centerfire pistols were Series II. There was no "Series I" pistol per se, but pre-series II models are often referred to in that manner.

During 2003, external extractors were phased into almost all .45 ACP models. Due to consumer demans, most models were phased back to traditional (internal) extractors during 2006.

All three changes (disuse of the term "Classic" for pistols, Series II safety system, and external extractor) were "phased in" throughout normal production cycles. Therefore, no distinctive cut-off dates or serial numbering series were established to identify specific product runs or identify when these features were incorporated.

Add $314 for .22 LR cal. or $344-$379 for .17 Mach 2 cal. (mfg. 2005-2006) conversion kit for all mil-spec 1911 pistols (includes complete upper assembly, lightweight aluminum slide, premium bull barrel, and 10 shot mag.). Available in satin black and satin silver. Kimber began manufacture of these kits in early 2003. Prior to that, they were mfg. by a vendor.

GRADING - PPGS™	100%	98%	95%	90%	80%	70%	60%

CUSTOM II - .45 ACP cal., patterned after the Colt Government Model 1911, 5 in. barrel, various finishes, 7 shot mag., forged steel frame, match grade barrel, bushing and trigger group, dovetail mounted sights, frame machined from steel forging, high ride beavertail grip safety, choice of rubber, laminated wood (disc.), walnut or rosewood (disc.) grips, 38 oz. New 1995.

	MSR $795	$645	$535	$445	$375	$335	$300	$275

> Add $24 for walnut or rosewood (disc.) grips.
> Add $150 for night sights.
> Add $148 for Royal II finish (polished blue and checkered rosewood grips).

This series' nomenclature added the Roman numeral "II" during 2001.

✳ *Custom Target II* - similar to Custom II, except features Kimber adj. rear sight. New 1998.

	MSR $901	$760	$620	$530	$455	$395	$340	$300

✳ *Stainless II* - .38 Super (advertised in 1999, mfg. began late 2005), 9mm Para (advertised in 1999, new 2008), .40 S&W (mfg. 1999-2007), or .45 ACP cal., similar to Custom II, except has stainless steel slide and frame.

	MSR $913	$755	$620	$485	$420	$395	$340	$300

> Add $153 for night sights.
> Add $10 for 9mm Para. or $11 for .40 S&W (disc. 2007) cal.
> Add $143 for high polish stainless in .38 Super cal. only (new late 2005).
> Subtract $27 for Stainless Limited Edition marked "Stainless LE" (disc. 1998).

✳ *Stainless Target II* - similar to Stainless II, except is available in .38 Super (new 2002), 9mm Para., or 10mm (new 2003) cal., features Kimber adj. rear sight. New 1998.

	MSR $1,025	$845	$675	$565	$465	$400	$350	$285

> Add $30 for .40 S&W cal. (disc. 2002).
> Add $34 for .38 Super cal. or $88 for 10mm or 9mm Para. cal.
> Add $130 for high polish stainless in .38 Super cal. only (new late 2005).

GOLD MATCH II - .45 ACP cal., features Kimber adj. sight, stainless steel match barrel and bushing, premium aluminum match grade trigger, ambidextrous thumb safety became standard in 1998, 8 shot mag., fancy checkered rosewood grips in double diamond pattern, high polish blue, hand fitted barrel by Kimber Custom Shop, 38 oz.

	MSR $1,256	$1,095	$915	$765	$640	$525	$450	$400

This series' nomenclature added the Roman numeral "II" during 2001.

✳ *Gold Match Stainless II* - .38 Super (advertised in 1999, never mfg.), 9mm Para (advertised in 1999, new 2008), .40 S&W (mfg. 1999-2007), or .45 ACP cal., similar to Gold Match, except is stainless steel, 38 oz.

	MSR $1,427	$1,225	$1,025	$815	$700	$575	$475	$400

> Add $31 for 9mm Para. or .40 S&W cal.

TEAM MATCH II - .45 ACP or .38 Super (limited mfg. 2003-2004, reintroduced 2006) cal., same pistol developed for USA Shooting Team (2004 Olympics Rapid Fire Pistol Team) competition, satin finish stainless steel frame and slide, 5 in. match grade barrel, 30 LPI front strap checkering, match grade trigger, Tactical Extractor system, extended magazine well, 8 shot mag., laminated red/white/blue grips, 38 oz. New 2003.

	MSR $1,403	$1,175	$1,050	$800	$675	$575	$465	$410

> Add $48 for .38 Super cal.

A donation is made to the U.S.A. Shooting Team for every Team Match II sold.

GOLD COMBAT II - .45 ACP cal. only, 5 in. barrel, full size carry pistol based on the Gold Match, steel frame and slide, stainless steel match grade barrel and bushing, KimPro finish, tritium night sights, checkered walnut grips, 38 oz, mfg. by Custom Shop. New 1999.

	MSR $1,825	$1,575	$1,175	$995	$825	$675	$575	$400

This series' nomenclature added the Roman numeral "II" during 2001.

GRADING - PPGS™	100%	98%	95%	90%	80%	70%	60%

✳ *Gold Combat Stainless II* - similar to Gold Combat, except is all stainless steel. New 1999.

MSR $1,761	$1,500	$1,125	$935	$825	$675	$575	$475

✳ *Gold Combat RL II* - similar to Gold Combat, except is has Picatinny rail machined into the frame to accept optics and other tactical accessories. New 2003.

MSR $1,869	$1,575	$1,200	$1,025	$900	$775	$675	$575

SUPER MATCH II - .45 ACP cal. only, 5 in. barrel, top-of-the-line model, two-tone stainless steel construction, KimPro finish on slide, match grade trigger, custom shop markings, 38 oz. New 1999.

MSR $2,089	$1,625	$1,200	$1,000	$875	$775	$675	$575

This series' nomenclature added the Roman numeral "II" during 2001.

LTP II - .45 ACP cal., designed for Limited Ten competition, Tactical Extractor, steel frame and slide, KimPro finish, 20 LPI front strap checkering, 30 LPI checkering under trigger guard, tungsten guide rod, flattop serrated slide, beveled mag. well, ambidextrous thumb safety, adj. sight. Mfg. by Custom Shop 2002-2006.

	$1,850	$1,610	$1,300	$1,000	$875	$750	$625

Last MSR was $2,106.

RIMFIRE TARGET - .17 Mach 2 (mfg. 2004-2005) or .22 LR cal., aluminum frame in silver or black anodized finish (disc. 2006), black oxide steel or satin stainless slide, 5 in. barrel, black synthetic grips, Kimber adj. rear sight, 28 oz. Mfg. 2003-2006, reintroduced 2008.

MSR $782	$650	$640	$460	$375	$335	$300	$275

Add $39 for .17 Mach 2 cal.

✳ *Rimfire Target Super* - .22 LR cal., similar to Rimfire Target, except has flattop slide with agressive fluting on upper sides, premium aluminum trigger, ambidextrous safety, rosewood grips with logo inserts, guaranteed to fire a sub-1.5 in. 5 shot group at 25 yards, test target included, 23 oz., mfg. by Kimber Custom Shop. New 2004.

MSR $1,102	$935	$825	$735	$650	$575	$500	$450

POLYMER MODEL - .45 ACP cal., features widened black polymer frame offering larger mag. capacity, choice of fixed (Polymer Model) or adj. Kimber target (Polymer Target Model, disc. 1999) rear sight, matte black slide, 10 shot mag., 34 oz. Mfg. 1997-2001.

	$675	$575	$525	$475	$425	$375	$330

Last MSR was $795.

Add $88 for Polymer Target Model.

All Polymer Models were disc. in 2002 in favor of the new "Ten" Series with improved Kimber made frame. Magazines are interchangeable.

✳ *Polymer Model Stainless* - .38 Super (advertised in 1999, never mfg.), 9mm Para (advertised in 1999, never mfg.), .40 S&W (mfg. 1999 only), or .45 ACP cal., similar to Polymer Model, except has satin finish stainless steel slide. Mfg. 1998-2001.

	$745	$625	$550	$460	$395	$335	$285

Last MSR was $856.

Add $88 for Polymer Stainless Target Model (disc. 1999).

✳ *Polymer Model Gold Match* - .45 ACP cal. only, similar to Gold Match, except has polymer frame, supplied with 10 shot double stack mag., 34 oz. Mfg. 1999-2001.

	$925	$850	$725	$650	$550	$450	$400

Last MSR was $1,041.

❖ **Polymer Model Gold Match Stainless** - similar to Gold Match, except has polymer frame and stainless steel slide, 34 oz. Mfg. 1999-2001.

	$1,025	$900	$750	$640	$535	$450	$390

Last MSR was $1,177.

GRADING - PPGS™	100%	98%	95%	90%	80%	70%	60%

❋ *Polymer Model Pro Carry* - .45 ACP cal. only, 4 in. bushingless bull barrel, steel slide, 32 oz. Mfg. 1999-2001.

	$725	$650	$575	$485	$435	$375	$330

Last MSR was $814.

❖ **Polymer Model Pro Carry Stainless** - similar to Polymer Pro Carry, except has stainless steel slide. Mfg. 1999-2001.

	$755	$625	$550	$460	$395	$335	$285

Last MSR was $874.

❋ *Polymer Model Ultra Ten* - .45 ACP cal., black polymer frame with aluminum frame insert, stainless slide, 3 in. barrel, 10 shot staggered mag., low profile sights, lighter version of the Polymer Series frame, Kimber Firing Pin Safety, 24 oz.

While advertised during 2001 with an MSR of $896, this model never went into production.

COMPACT II - .45 ACP cal., features 4 in. barrel, .4 in. shorter aluminum or steel frame, 7 shot mag., Commander style hammer, single recoil spring, low profile combat sights, checkered black synthetic grips, 28 (aluminum) or 34 (steel) oz. Mfg. 1998-2001.

	$635	$535	$455	$395	$365	$325	$295

Last MSR was $764.

❋ *Compact Stainless II* - .40 S&W (mfg. 1999-2001) or .45 ACP cal., features stainless steel slide, 4 in. bull barrel, 4 in. shorter aluminum (disc.) or stainless (new 2002) frame, 7 shot mag., Commander style hammer, single recoil spring, low profile combat sights, black synthetic grips, 34 oz. New 1998.

MSR $947	$775	$615	$495	$425	$365	$300	$255

Add $32 for .40 S&W cal. (disc. 2001).

This model's nomenclature added the Roman numeral "II" during 2001.

❋ *Compact II Aluminum Stainless* - .40 S&W or .45 ACP cal., features aluminum frame and stainless steel slide, 28 oz. Mfg. 1999-2001.

	$700	$575	$475	$415	$360	$300	$255

Last MSR was $837.

Add $36 for .40 S&W cal.

COMBAT CARRY - .40 S&W or .45 ACP cal., 4 in. barrel, carry model featuring aluminum frame and trigger, stainless steel slide, tritium night sights, and ambidextrous thumb safety, 28 oz. Limited mfg. 1999 only.

	$940	$815	$675	$600	$500	$450	$400

Last MSR was $1,044.

Add $30 for .40 S&W cal.

PRO CARRY II - 9mm Para. (new mid-2005), .40 S&W (disc. 2001) or .45 ACP cal., 4 in. barrel, features full length grip similar to Custom Model, aluminum frame (except Pro Carry HD), steel slide, 7 or 8 shot mag., 28 oz. New 1999.

MSR $834	$685	$575	$455	$395	$355	$325	$295

Add $35 for .40 S&W cal. (disc.).
Add $108 for night sights (.45 ACP cal. only).
Add $34 for 9mm Para. cal.

This series' nomenclature added the Roman numeral "II" during 2001.

❋ *Stainless Pro Carry II* - similar to Pro Carry, except has stainless steel slide, not available in 9mm Para. cal. New 1999.

MSR $920	$775	$650	$495	$425	$365	$300	$255

Add $37 for 9mm Para (new 2008) or $38 for .40 S&W (disc. 2007) cal.
Add $108 for night sights (.45 ACP cal. only).
Add $277 for Crimson Trace grips (.45 ACP cal. only).

❋ *Pro Carry II HD* - .38 Super (new 2002) or .45 ACP cal., similar to Pro Carry Stainless, except has heavier stainless steel frame, 35 oz. New 2001.

MSR $947	$775	$625	$495	$425	$365	$300	$255

Add $40 for .38 Super cal.

GRADING - PPGS™	100%	98%	95%	90%	80%	70%	60%

ULTRA CARRY II - .40 S&W (disc. 2001) or .45 ACP cal., 3 in. barrel, aluminum frame, 7 shot mag., 25 oz. New 1999.

MSR $828	$695	$575	$510	$445	$395	$350	$325

    Add $39 for .40 S&W cal. (disc. 2001).
    Add $109 for night sights.
    Add $383 for Crimson Trace grips.

This series' nomenclature added the Roman numeral "II" during 2001.

＊*Stainless Ultra Carry II* - 9mm Para. (new 2008), .40 S&W (disc. 2007), and .45 ACP cal., similar to Ultra Carry, except has stainless steel slide. New 1999.

MSR $916	$775	$645	$495	$425	$365	$300	$255

    Add $44 for 9mm Para. (new 2008) or $45 for .40 S&W cal. (disc. 2007).
    Add $108 for night sights (.45 ACP cal. only).

ECLIPSE II SERIES - 10mm (Eclipse Custom II, new 2004) or .45 ACP cal., stainless steel slide and frame, black matte finish with brush polished flat surfaces for elegant two-tone finish, Tritium night sights, target models have adj. bar/dot sights, silver/grey laminated double diamond grips, black small parts, 30 LPI front strap checkering, include Eclipse Ultra II (3 in. barrel, short grip), Eclipse Pro II and Eclipse Pro-Target II (4 in. barrel, standard grip), Eclipse Custom II, and Eclipse Target II (full size). New 2002.

MSR $1,152	$1,050	$885	$750	$650	$525	$450	$400

    Add $20 for Eclipse Custom II.
    Add $109 for Eclipse Target II or Eclipse Pro-Target II.
    Add $57 for Eclipse Custom II in 10mm cal.

The initial Custom Shop version of these pistols was mfg. during late 2001, featuring an ambidextrous thumb safety, and "Custom Shop" markings on left side of slide, 7,931 were mfg.

CUSTOM TLE II SERIES - .45 ACP cal., tactical law enforcement pistol with exactly the same features as the Kimber pistols carried by LAPD SWAT, black oxide coated frame and slide, same features as Custom II, except has 30 LPI front strap checkering and night sights. New 2003.

MSR $980	$865	$750	$645	$530	$460	$375	$325

    Add $274 for Crimson Trace laser grips.

＊*Stainless Custom TLE II* - similar to Custom TLE II, except has stainless steel slide and frame. New 2004.

MSR $1,131	$995	$850	$675	$550	$475	$385	$335

＊*Custom TLE/RL II Series* - similar to Custom TLE II, except has Picatinny rail machined into the frame to accept optics and other tactical accessories. New 2003.

MSR $1,113	$975	$835	$665	$545	$465	$385	$335

＊*Stainless Custom TLE/RL II* - similar to Custom TLE/RL II, except is stainless. New 2004.

MSR $1,262	$1,095	$915	$685	$575	$480	$400	$350

＊*Pro Custom TLE/RL II* - similar to Custom TLE/RL II, except has 4 in. bushingless barrel. New 2004.

MSR $1,117	$985	$825	$660	$540	$465	$385	$335

＊*Pro TLE II (LG)* - similar to Custom TLE/RL II, except has 4 in. bushingless barrel and Crimson Trace laser grips. New 2006.

MSR $1,275	$1,125	$975	$800	$750	$650	$525	$475

    Subtract $240 if w/o Crimson Trace laser grips (new 2008).

＊*Stainless Pro Custom TLE/RL II* - similar to Stainless TLE/RL II, except has 4 in. bushingless barrel. New 2004.

MSR $1,242	$1,080	$895	$685	$575	$480	$400	$350

TACTICAL II SERIES - 9mm Para (Tactical Pro II, new 2004) or .45 ACP cal., lightweight tactical pistol, grey anodized frame with black carbon steel slide, external extrator, fixed tritium Meprolight 3-dot night sights, extended magazine well, 30 LPI front strap checkering, black/grey laminated logo grips, 7 shot mag. with bumper pad, available in Tactical Ultra II (3 in. barrel, short grip, 25 oz.), Tactical Pro II (4 in. barrel, standard grip, 28 oz.), and Tactical Custom II (5 in. barrel, standard grip, 31 oz.). New 2003.

MSR $1,158		$1,035	$875	$735	$615	$515	$425	$375

Add $36 for Tactical Pro II in 9mm Para. cal.

A Custom Shop version of the Pro Tactical II was manufactured in 2002, but w/o checkering and night sights.

STAINLESS TEN II SERIES - .45 ACP cal., high capacity polymer frame, stainless steel slide with satin finish, impressed front grip strap checkering and serrations under trigger guard, textured finish, polymer grip safety and mainspring housing, 10 or 13 (new 2005) round double stack mag., includes Ultra Ten II (3 in. barrel, short grip, disc. 2003), Pro Carry Ten II (4 in. barrel, standard grip), Stainless Ten II (full size), and Gold Match Ten II (stainless steel barrel, polished stainless steel slide flats, hand fitted barrel/bushing to slide, adj. sight), 14 (pre-ban) round mags. also available, accepts magazines from older Kimber mfg. Polymer pistols. Mfg. 2002-2007.

$715	$625	$525	$450	$395	$360	$320

Last MSR was $812.

Add $9 for Pro-Carry Ten II, $35 for Ultra Ten II (disc. 2003), or $294 for Gold Match Ten II.

✳ *BP Ten II* - similar to Stainless Ten II, except has black oxide carbon steel slide, and aluminum subframe for lighter weight. Mfg. 2003-2007.

$570	$475	$385	$325	$300	$275	$250

Last MSR was $652.

✳ *Pro BP Ten II* - similar to Pro Carry Ten II, except has black oxide carbon steel slide, and aluminum subframe for lighter weight. Mfg. 2003-2007.

$570	$470	$385	$335	$300	$275	$250

Last MSR was $666.

CDP II (CUSTOM DEFENSE PACKAGE) - 9mm Para. (new 2008), .40 S&W (disc. 2007), or .45 ACP cal., Custom Shop pistol featuring tritium night sights, stainless steel slide with black anodized aluminum frame, 3 in. (Ultra CDP II, 25 oz.), 4 in. (Pro CDP II and Compact CDP II, 28 oz.), or 5 in. (Custom CDP II, 31 oz.) barrel, carry bevel treatment, ambidextrous thumb safety, double diamond pattern checkered rosewood grips, 30 LPI checkered front strap and under trigger guard (new 2003), two-tone finish. New 2000.

MSR $1,255		$1,075	$895	$750	$660	$525	$450	$400

Add $40 for .40 S&W cal., available in either Ultra CDP II or Pro CDP II configuration.
Add $40 for 9mm Para cal. (new 2008).

The Pro CDP II has a full length grip frame.

This series' nomenclature added the Roman numeral "II" during 2001.

ULTRA TEN II CDP - .45 ACP cal., tritium night sights, stainless steel slide with black polymer frame, 3 in. barrel, carry bevel treatment, standard manual safety, 10 shot mag., 24 oz. Mfg. 2003 only.

$825	$725	$635	$525	$450	$400	$365

Last MSR was $926.

RAPTOR II - .45 ACP cal., full size carbon steel or stainless steel (new 2008) frame with "scales" on front strap, continuing on slide in lieu of standard serrations, black oxide finish, back cut flattop, 5 in. stainless barrel with engraved "Raptor II" and "Custom Shop", black anodized trigger, ambidextrous safety, scaled Zebra wood grip panels with Kimber logo, fixed slant night sights, 38 oz. New mid-2004.

MSR $1,295		$1,100	$900	$700	$575	$475	$400	$325

Add $122 for stainless steel frame (new 2008).

GRADING - PPGS™	100%	98%	95%	90%	80%	70%	60%

PRO RAPTOR II - .45 ACP cal., full size stainless steel frame with "scales" on front strap, continuing on carbon steel slide in lieu of standard serrations, black oxide finish, back cut flattop, 4 in. stainless barrel with engraved "Pro Raptor II" and "Custom Shop", black anodized trigger, ambidextrous safety, scaled Zebra wood grip panels with Kimber logo, fixed slant night sights, 38 oz. New mid-2004.

MSR $1,171	$995	$835	$665	$550	$450	$375	$300

ULTRA RAPTOR II - .45 ACP cal., all-matte black finish, 3 in. ramped bushingless barrel, lightweight aluminum frame, lizard scale serrations on flat-top slide and frontstrap, feathered logo wood grips, night sights, mfg. by Custom Shop. New 2006.

MSR $1,171	$995	$835	$665	$550	$450	$375	$300

GRAND RAPTOR II - .45 ACP cal., full-size stainless steel frame, two-tone finish, lizard scale rosewood grips with Kimber logo, extended ambidextrous thumb safety, bumped beavertail grip safety, night sights, mfg. by Custom Shop. New 2006.

MSR $1,490	$1,265	$1,050	$900	$800	$700	$600	$500

WARRIOR - .45 ACP cal., production began following adoption of this pistol by the Marine Expeditionary Unit (MEU) Special Operations Capable (SOC), Detachment 1 (Det. 1), civilian version with 5 in. barrel, Series I (no firing pin block), carbon steel slide and frame, integral Picatinny light rail, internal extractor, lanyard loop, bumped grip safety, G-10 material grip (coyote brown), wedge night sights, ambidextrous safety, GI length guide rod finished in black KimPro, 38 oz. New mid-2004.

MSR $1,353	$1,125	$965	$825	$700	$600	$500	$400

DESERT WARRIOR - similar to Warrior, except has Dark Earth metal finish and light tan G-10 grips. New mid-2005.

MSR $1,369	$1,135	$965	$825	$710	$600	$500	$400

COVERT SERIES - .45 ACP cal., 3 (Ultra Covert II) or 4 (Pro Covert II) in. bushingless barrel, Custom Covert II has Kimber logo and digital camo pattern, carry bevel treatment, 30 LPI front strap checkering, night sights, Desert Tan finish, matte black oxide slide, approx. 25-30 oz. New 2007.

MSR $1,500	$1,275	$1,075	$850	$715	$600	$500	$400

KPD - .40 S&W cal., 12 shot mag., reinforced black polymer frame, 4.1 in. steel barrel, stainless steel slide, interchangable back straps, Picatinny rail, ambidextrous mag. release, front and rear slide serrations, black KimPro II finish, fixed three dot sights, 25 oz. New 2007.

MSR $545	$495	$450	$395	$365	$335	$295	$250

SIS SERIES - .45 ACP cal., stainless steel slide, frame, and serrated mainspring housing, 7 or 8 shot mag., 3 (Ultra), 4 (Pro), or 5 (Custom or Custom RL) in. barrel, SIS Night Sight, cocking shoulder for one-hand cocking, lightweight hammer, solid trigger, slide serrations, grey KimPro II finish, beavertail grip safety, stippled black laminate logo grips, ambidextrous thumb safety, choice of rounded frame and mainspring housing (SIS Ultra), Picatinny rail (SIS Pro & Custom RL), standard length guide rod (Custom & Custom RL), 31-39 oz. New 2008.

MSR $1,316	$1,125	$925	$725	$600	$500	$425	$350

Add $105 for SIS Custom RL model with standard length guide rod and Picatinny rail.

Pistols: Kimber Non-Cataloged Models

Kimber has over the past several years, manufactured a number of pistols that did not appear in their catalog. To help identify non-cataloged models, pistols are listed in three categories: Custom Shop/Special Edition Pistols, Limited Edition Pistols, and Mid-Year Introduction Pistols.

Pistols: Kimber Custom Shop/Special Editions

Beginning in 1998, the Kimber Custom Shop began producing special edition pistols. Special edition models have been issued in either fixed numbers, or time limited. Where available, time limited models show the actual number produced. All models are .45 ACP caliber unless otherwise specified.

ROYAL CARRY - compact aluminum frame, 4 in. bushingless barrel, highly polished blue, night sights, ambidextrous safety, hand checkered rosewood grips, 28 oz. 600 mfg. 1998.

Last MSR was $903.

GOLD GUARDIAN - highly polished stainless steel slide and frame, hand fitted 5 in. match barrel and bushing, tritium night sights, ambidextrous safety, extended magazine well, skeletonized match trigger, hand checkered rosewood grips, 38 oz. 300 mfg. 1998.

Last MSR was $1,350.

ELITE CARRY - black anodized compact aluminum frame, stainless slide, 4 in. barrel, meltdown treatment on slide and frame, tritium night sights, 20 LPI checkered front strap, ambidextrous safety, aluminum match trigger, hand checkered rosewood grips, 28 oz. 1,200 mfg. 1998.

Last MSR was $1,019.

STAINLESS COVERT - meltdown stainless slide and frame finished in silver Kim-Pro, 4 in. barrel, 30 LPI front strap checkering, 3-dot tritium night sights, hand checkered rosewood grips, 34 oz. 1,000 mfg. 1999.

Last MSR was $1,135.

PRO ELITE - aluminum frame with silver KimPro finish, stainless slide with black KimPro finish, full meltdown treatment on slide and frame, 4 in. barrel, 30 LPI front strap checkering, 3-dot tritium night sights, hand checkered rosewood grips, 28 oz. 2,500 mfg. 1999.

Last MSR was $1,140.

ULTRA ELITE - aluminum frame with black KimPro finish, satin stainless slide, full meltdown treatment on slide and frame, 3 in. barrel, 30 LPI front strap checkering, 3-dot tritium night sights, hand checkered rosewood grips, 25 oz. 2,750 mfg. 1999.

Last MSR was $1,085.

HERITAGE EDITION - black oxide steel frame and slide, 30 LPI front strap checkering, ambidextrous safety, premium aluminum trigger, NSSF Heritage medallion and special markings on slide, ser. no. begins with KHE, 38 oz. 1,041 mfg. 2000.

Last MSR was $1,065.

STAINLESS GOLD MATCH SE II - .38 Super or .45 ACP cal., stainless steel frame and slide, 5 in. barrel, serrated flat-top slide, 30 LPI front strap checkering, hand checkered rosewood grips, ambidextrous safety, polished flats, ser. no. begins with KSO, 38 oz. 260 (.38 Super) and 294 (.45 ACP) mfg. 2001.

Last MSR was $1,487.

> **Add $88 for .38 Super cal.**

ULTRA SHADOW II - black steel slide and anodized aluminum frame, 3 in. barrel, fixed tritium night sights, 30 LPI front strap checkering, grey laminate grips, silver grip and thumb safeties and mainspring housing, ser. no. begins with KUSLE, 25 oz.

Last MSR was $949.

PRO SHADOW II - black steel slide and anodized aluminum frame, 4 in. barrel, fixed tritium night sights, 30 LPI front strap checkering, grey laminate grips, silver grip and thumb safeties and mainspring housing, ser. no. begins with KPSLE, 28 oz.

Last MSR was $949.

ULTRA CDP ELITE II - .45 ACP cal., first Kimber .45 pistols with ramped match grade barrels, black anodized aluminum frame, black oxide carbon steel slide, 3 in. barrel, carry melt treatment for rounded and blended edges, Meprolight 3-dot tritium night sights, 30 LPI checkering on front strap and under trigger guard, ambidextrous thumb safety and charcoal/ruby laminated logo grips, 25 oz. Mfg. 2002-Jan., 2003.

Last MSR was $1,216.

ULTRA CDP ELITE STS II - .45 ACP cal., first Kimber .45 pistols with ramped match grade barrels, silver anodized aluminum frame, satin stainless steel slide, 3 in. barrel, carry melt treatment for rounded and blended edges, Meprolight 3-dot tritium night sights, 30 LPI checkering on front strap and under trigger guard, ambidextrous thumb safety and charcoal/ruby laminated logo grips, 25 oz. Mfg. 2002-Jan., 2003.

Last MSR was $1,155.

ULTRA RCP II - .45 ACP cal., refined carry pistol, black annodized frame, melt-down treatment with bobbed heel, 3 line ball milled front strap and bobbed grip safety, Kimpro finished, melted 3 in. trench cut slide (no sights), carbon steel barrel, bobbed spur hammer, black micarta call milled slim grips, bobbed magazine catch, 25 oz. Mfg. 2003-2005.

$1,075 $950 $825 $750 $675 $600 $525

Last MSR was $1,228.

✳ *Ultra SP II* - special anodized frame colors (black/blue, black/red, and black/silver) with black oxide slide, 7 shot mag., 3 in. bushingless barrel, 3-dot sights, carry melt, ball milled micarta grips, standard fixed sights, 25 oz. Mfg. 2003-2005.

$1,025 $900 $800 $725 $625 $575 $495

Last MSR was $1,175.

25th ANNIVERSARY CUSTOM LIMITED EDITION - .45 ACP cal., black oxide frame and slide, 5 in. barrel, premium aluminum trigger, fancy walnut anniversary logo grips, "1979-2004" engraving on slide, Series I safeties and traditional extractor, ser. no. range is KAPC0001-KAPC1911. Limited production of 1,911 during 2004-2005.

$825 $725 $650 $575 $500 $425 $350

Last MSR was $923.

✳ *25th Anniversary Custom Limited Edition Gold Match* - blued frame and slide, deep polish on flats, 5 in. stainless barrel, premium aluminum trigger, ambidextrous safety, adj. sights, fancy walnut anniversary logo grips, "1979-2004" engraving in slide, Series I safeties and traditional extractor, ser. no. range KAPG0001-KAPG0500, 38 oz. Limited production of 500 during 2004-2005.

$1,175 $995 $875 $775 $700 $625 $550

Last MSR was $1,357.

✳ *25th Anniversary Custom Limited Edition Pistol Set* - includes one Custom (ser. no. range KMSC0001-KMSC250) and one Gold Match (ser. no. range KMSG0001 - KMSG250), matched ser. nos., wood presentation case. Limited production of 250 during 2004-2005.

MSR $2,620 $2,250 $2,000 $1,775 $1,525 $1,300 $1,100 $900

Pistols: Kimber Limited Editions

Kimber has produced limited runs of pistols for dealer groups, NRA Events, sporting goods stores, law enforcement agencies, special requests, etc. Limited run pistols can be as small as 25 mfg.

PRO CARRY SLE - all stainless steel slide and frame, 4 in. barrel, identicial to Stainless Pro Carry Model, except has stainless frame, mfg. for Kimber Master Dealers, cataloged in 2001, later production known as Pro Carry HD II, 1,329 mfg. during 2000.

Last MSR was $815.

PRO COMBAT - black oxide stainless steel frame and slide, 4 in. barrel, ambidextrous safety, tritium 3-dot night sights, match grade aluminum trigger, 30 LPI front strap checkering, hand checkered rosewood grips, 35 oz. Marketed by RGuns. 52 mfg. 2000.

Last MSR was $860.

TARGET ELITE II - two-tone stainless frame and slide, black oxide coating on frame, slide natural stainless, adj. rear sight, rosewood double diamond grips, sold through stores affiliated with Sports Inc. buying group, 38 oz. 220 mfg. 2001.

Last MSR was $950.

CUSTOM DEFENDER II - two-tone stainless frame and slide, black oxide coating on frame, slide natural stainless, fixed low profile rear sight, double diamond rosewood grips, sold only through stores affiliated with National Buying Service, 38 oz. 290 mfg. 2001.

Last MSR was $839.

CUSTOM ECLIPSE II - stainless slide and frame, 5 in. barrel, black oxide finish brush polished on the flats, 30 LPI front strap checkering, adj. night sights, laminated grey grips, ser. no. begins with KEL, 38 oz. 4,522 mfg. 2001.

Last MSR was $1,121.

PRO ECLIPSE II - stainless steel frame and slide, 4 in. barrel, black oxide finish brush polished on the flats, 30 LPI front strap checkering, fixed 3-dot night sights, laminated grey grips, ambidextrous safety, ser. no. begins with KRE, 35 oz. 2,207 mfg. 2001.

Last MSR was $1,065.

ULTRA ECLIPSE II - stainless steel frame and slide, 3 in. barrel, black oxide finish brush polished on the flats, 30 LPI front strap checkering, fixed 3-dot night sights, laminated grey grips, ambidextrous safety, 34 oz. 1,202 mfg. 2001.

Last MSR was $1,054.

STRYKER TEN II - Ultra Ten II with black polymer frame and frame insert and small parts, natural stainless slide, 25 oz. 200 mfg. 2002.

Last MSR was $850.

LAPD SWAT - black oxide coated stainless frame and slide, 5 in. barrel, low profile Meprolight 3-dot night sights, 30 LPI front strap checkering, black rubber double diamond grips, 38 oz. 300 mfg. 2002.

Following extensive testing to select a duty pistol, LAPD SWAT chose a Kimber Stainless Custom II and had it enhanced to their specifications. This model was made strictly for law enforcement and not sold to the public. A civilian version called the Tactical law Enforcement (TLE) Series went into production in 2003.

NRA EPOCH II - stainless slide and frame, 5 in. barrel, black oxide finish brush polished on flats, 30 LPI front strap checkering, standard safety, fixed tritium night sights, laminated grey grips, ser. no. begins with KNRAE, Friends of NRA pistol available only at NRA banquets, 38 oz. 58 mfg. 2002.

This model had no established MSR.

THE BOSS II - limited edition to commemotate Blythe Sports 50th anniversary, stainless steel slide and frame, carry melt treatment, fixed white dot sights, premium aluminum 2 hole trigger, 5 in. carbin barrel, engraved "The BOSS II" on ejection port side, and "SPECIAL EDITION", black and sliver laminate grips with Blythe 50th anniversary logo in center on white insert, ser. no. KBSS000-KBSS024, 25 mfg.

This model had no established MSR.

ECLIPSE CLE II - 5 in. barrel, Eclipse Custom II finish on slide with black over stainless frame (no front strap checkering), charcoal/ruby Kimber logo grips, sold only through stores affiliated with National Buying Service, 38 oz. 271 mfg. 2003.

Last MSR was $917.

GRADING - PPGS™	100%	98%	95%	90%	80%	70%	60%

✳ *Eclipse PLE II* - similar to Eclipse CLE II, except has 4 in. bushingless barrel, sold only through stores affiliated with Sports Inc. buying group, 35 oz. 232 mfg. 2003.

Last MSR was $877.

✳ *Eclipse ULE II* - Eclipse Ultra II finish on slide with black over stainless frame (no front strap checkering), 3 in. bushingless barrel, charcoal/ruby Kimber logo grips, sold only through stores affiliated with National Buying Service, 34 oz. 227 mfg. 2003.

Last MSR was $890.

TEAM MATCH II - .38 Super cal., identical to original Team Match II, with .38 Super ramped barrel, match grade chamber, bushing and trigger group, special Team Match features, including 30 LPI checkered front strap, adj. sight, extended magazine well, premium aluminum trigger and red, white, and blue USA Shooting Team logo grips, 38 oz. Mfg. 2003-2004.

	$1,150	$995	$875	$775	$675	$575	$475

Last MSR was $1,352.

MCSOCOM ICQB (2004) - .45 ACP cal., at the request of the Marine Corps Special Operations Command (MCSOCOM) Detachment 1 (Det. 1), Kimber produced Interim Close Quarters Battle (ICQB) 1911 patterned pistols in accordance with very high specific requirements: steel frame and slide finished in matte black, internal extractor, GI length, guide rod and plug, light rail, bumped grip safety and ambidextrous manual safety, lanyard loop, Simonich G-10 "Gunner" grips, and Novak low mount night sights.

There was no MSR on this model, as it was not available for sale to the general public. The civilian version of this pistol is called the Warrior.

TARGET MATCH - .45 ACP cal., oversized 5 in. stainless steel barrel, matte black frame and slide with brush polished flats, high relief cut under triggerguard, wide cocking serrations, solid match trigger, engraved bullseye inlaid burl walnut logo grips, 30 LPI checkering on froont strap and under trigger guard, special ser. no. starting with "KTM", 38 oz. 1,000 mfg. beginning 2006.

MSR $1,427		$1,215	$1,025	$875	$775	$700	$600	$500

CLASSIC TARGET II - .45 ACP cal., two-tone stainless steel frame, matte black oxide slide, no cocking serrations, adj. sights, premium match grade trigger, smooth/stippled logo grips, match grade chamber, barrel, and barrel bushing, 38 oz. Sold exclusively through Gander Mountain. New 2006.

MSR $999		$825	$675	$555	$460	$395	$350	$300

FRANKLIN CUSTOM II - similar to Custom II, silver finished slide stop, bushing, mag. release, grip safety and mainspring housing, red, white and blue laminate grips with Franklin's Gun Shop logo, commemorates 44th anniversary of Franklin's Gun Shop, ser. no. KFGS01 - KFGS50, 50 mfg. 2006.

This model had no established MSR.

Pistols: Kimber Mid-Year Introductions

Kimber occasionally chooses to introduce new pistols at times other than at the beginning of each model year in order to respond to customer demand. Models introduced normally transfer to successive model years with major features intact, but minor changes may be made to improve aesthetics or the function of the pistol.

ULTRA CDP - black anodized aluminum frame, satin stainless slide, full meltdown treatment, 3 in. barrel, 30 LPI front strap checkering, 3-dot tritium night sights, ambidextrous safety, hand checkered rosewood grips, 25 oz. Introductory run 2000, became part of standard Kimber lineup during 2001.

Last MSR was $1,086.

PRO CDP - similar to Ultra CDP, except has 4 in. barrel and full sized frame, 28 oz. Introductory run 2000, became part of standard Kimber lineup during 2001.

Last MSR was $1,086.

GRADING - PPGS™	100%	98%	95%	90%	80%	70%	60%

COMPACT CDP - similar to Pro CDP, except grip frame is .400 inches shorter, 28 oz. Introductory run 2000, became part of standard Kimber lineup during 2001.

Last MSR was $1,086.

PRO TACTICAL II - grey anodized aluminum frame, black carbon steel slide, 4 in. barrel, fixed white dot sights, extended steel magazine well, black/grey laminated logo grips, 7 shot mag. with bumper pad, 25 oz. 335 mfg. 2002-Jan., 2003.

Last MSR was $917.

ULTRA TACTICAL II - grey anodized frame, black carbon steel slide, 3 in. barrel, fixed white dot sights, extended aluminum mag. well, black/grey laminated logo grips, 7 shot mag. with bumper pad, 25 oz. 335 mfg. 2002.

Last MSR was $917.

CUSTOM TLE II - tactical law enforcement pistol similar to LAPD SWAT, black oxide coated stainless frame and slide, 5 in. barrel, low profile Meprolight 3-dot night sights, 30 LPI front strap checkering, black rubber double diamond grips, 38 oz. Mfg. 2002-Jan., 2003.

Last MSR was $910.

TEAM MATCH II - exact replica of USA Shooting Team (2004 Olympic Rapid Fire Pistol Team) training .45 ACP cal. pistol, satin finish stainless steel frame and slide, 5 in. barrel, 30 LPI front strap checkering match grade trigger and stainless barrel, external extractor, extended magazine well, 8 shot mag., laminated red/white/blue USA Shooting Team grips, 38 oz. Mfg. 2002.

Last MSR was $1,420.

BP TEN II - full size polymer pistol with black anodized aluminum rail insert, 5 in. carbin slide and barrel, external extractor, standard fixed sights, 10 shot mag., 34 oz. Mfg. 2003.

Last MSR was $619.

❋ *BP Ten II Pro* - similar to BP Ten II, except has 4 in. bushing less barrel, 32 oz. Mfg. 2003.

Last MSR was $633.

STAINLESS TARGET 10MM - first Kimber chambered for 10mm, ramped 5 in. match grade barrel, match grade chamber and bushing, 8 shot mag., dovetail mounted adj. sight, 38 oz. Mfg. 2003.

	100%	98%	95%	90%	80%	70%	60%
	$925	$800	$650	$540	$465	$385	$335

Last MSR was $1,026.

❋ *Stainless Target II 9mm* - similar to 10mm model, except is 9mm Para. cal., 9 shot mag., beavertail grip safety, extended thumb safety, slightly extended magazine release button standard, 38 oz. Mfg. 2003.

	100%	98%	95%	90%	80%	70%	60%
	$925	$800	$650	$540	$465	$385	$335

Last MSR was $1,026.

GOLD COMBAT RL II - carbon steel slide and frame, integral Picatinny light rail, 5 in. barrelm 30 LPI front strap and under triggerguard checkering, black KimPro finish, extended mag. well, ambidextrous safety, fixed 3 dot sights, premium aluminum trigger and double diamond rosewood grips, 38 oz. Mfg. 2003.

Last MSR was $1,749.

CUSTOM TLE/RL II - carbon steel slide and frame with integral Picatinny light rail, 5 in. barrel, 30 LPI front checkering and all black oxide finish, fixed 3 dot sights, standard aluminum trigger, black rubber grips, 38 oz. Mfg. 2003.

Last MSR was $1,033.

AEGIS II SERIES - 9mm Para. cal., 3 (Ultra), 4 (Pro), or 5 (Custom) in. barrel, 8 or 9 shot mag., compact aluminum frame w/satin silver premium KimPro II finish, matte black slide, thin rosewood grips, 30 LPI front strap checkering, high relief cut under triggerguard, tactical Wedge night sights, bumped and grooved grip safety, hammer, thumb safety and mag. release button are bobbed, carry melt treatment on both frame and slide, 25 oz. New 2006.

	100%	98%	95%	90%	80%	70%	60%
MSR $1,195	$1,050	$895	$750	$635	$525	$450	$400

GRADING - PPGS™	100%	98%	95%	90%	80%	70%	60%

ULTRA RCP II - .45 ACP cal., refined carry pistol, black annodized frame, carry melt treatment, matte black slide with premium KimPro II finish, no sights, bobbed mag. release, hammer, beavertail grip safety and thumb safety, round mainspring housing and rear of frame, thin black micarta grip panels, older mfg. had distinctive "hook" on hammer, new mfg. has straight hammer, 25 oz. Mfg. 2003-2005 by Custom Shop, reintroduced 2007.

MSR $1,217	$1,065	$895	$750	$635	$525	$450	$400

RIFLES: BOLT ACTION

Rimfire Models, Repeating and Single Shot

A three position Win. Model 70 type safety became a standard feature on all Kimber .22 LR and .17 Mach 2 cal. rifles in early 2004.

HUNTER - .17 Mach 2 (new 2007) or .22 LR cal., similar to Classic, except has grade A walnut, clear stock finish, straight barrel contour, 6.7 lbs. Mfg. 2002-2007.

	$715	$595	$515	$455	$400	$350	$300

Last MSR was $863.

Add $40 for .17 Mach 2 cal.

YOUTH - .22 LR cal., similar to Hunter, except has 12 1/4 in. LOP.
While this model was cataloged during 2002-2003 with an MSR of $746, it never went into production.

CLASSIC - .22 LR cal., Mauser claw extractor with 2 position Model 70 type safety, unique eccentric bolt that allows a "centerfire-type" firing pin for faster lock time and greater strength, AA walnut sporter stock with 20 LPI 4-point panel checkering and hand rubbed oil finish, 22 in. match grade sporter barrel with match chamber and Custom Sporter contour, 5 shot mag., steel grip cap, pillar bedding, bead blasted blue finish, adj. trigger, approx. 6 1/2 lbs. Mfg. 1999-2007.

	$1,025	$875	$765	$655	$550	$450	$350

Last MSR was $1,223.

Through 2002, all Kimber .22 cal. Classic rifles had an A grade claro walnut stock, 2-point checkering pattern, urethane finish, and straight barrel taper contour.

✳ *Classic Varmint* - .17 Mach 2 (new mid-2004) or .22 LR cal., similar to Classic, except has A walnut and 20 in. stainless fluted barrel in a heavy sporter contour. Mfg. 2003-2007.

	$975	$825	$725	$600	$500	$425	$375

Last MSR was $1,125.

✳ *Classic Pro Varmint* - .17 Mach 2 (new mid-2004) or .22 LR cal., similar to Classic Varmint, except has grey laminate uncheckered stock, brush polished stainless 20 in. barrel with black flutes. Mfg. 2004-2007.

	$995	$850	$760	$655	$550	$450	$350

Last MSR was $1,182.

Add $46 for .17 Mach 2 cal.

✳ *Custom Classic* - .22 LR cal., similar to Classic, except has 24 LPI wrap checkering, ebony forend tip and AAA walnut stock, 6 1/2 lbs. Mfg. 2003-2007.

	$1,375	$1,150	$900	$765	$650	$550	$475

Last MSR was $1,607.

SUPERAMERICA MODEL - .22 LR cal., top-of-the-line model with AAA claro walnut with 24 LPI full wrap checkering, highly polished blue finish, hand rubbed oil finish, Custom Sporter barrel contour, ebony forend tip, cheekpiece and black recoil pad, 5 shot mag., 6 1/2 lbs. Limited mfg. 2001-2007.

	$1,675	$1,375	$1,100	$925	$825	$700	$600

Last MSR was $1,988.

Through 2001, all Superamerica rifles had urethane finish and straight taper barrel contour.

GRADING - PPGS™	100%	98%	95%	90%	80%	70%	60%

✳ *SuperAmerica Model Custom Match 25th Anniversary Ltd. Ed.* - .22 LR cal., similar to SuperAmerica model, except has AAA French walnut stock, black oxide matte finish barrel and receiver, steel buttplate, engraved grip cap, specially marked barrel and jeweled bolt. Limited production of 300 sequentially numbered rifles during 2004-2005.

	$2,325	$2,000	$1,700	$1,400	$1,100	$900	$750

Last MSR was $2,852.

SVT (SHORT VARMINT/TARGET) MODEL - .17 Mach 2 (new mid-2004) or .22 LR cal., 18 in. fluted stainless steel bull barrel, uncheckered grey laminate wood stock with high comb target design, matte blue action and satin stainless steel barrel, 5 shot mag., no sights, 7 1/2 lbs. Mfg. 1999-2007.

	$945	$800	$700	$575	$475	$375	$300

Last MSR was $1,073.

Add $52 for .17 Mach 2 cal.

HS (HUNTER SILHOUETTE) MODEL - .22 LR cal., features 24 in. half-fluted medium sporter match grade barrel w/o sights, checkered walnut high comb Monte Carlo stock with clear stock finish, adj. trigger, matte blue finish, 7 lbs. Mfg. 1999-2007.

	$850	$700	$585	$515	$425	$350	$275

Last MSR was $976.

Through 2001, all HS Models had urethane finish.

MODEL 82C CLASSIC - .22 LR cal., 22 in. drilled and tapped receiver, repeater with 4 shot mag., checkered A claro walnut stock, polished and blue metal, 6 1/2 lbs. Mfg. 1995-99.

	$775	$625	$550	$475	$400	$360	$330

Last MSR was $917.

The C suffix on this model designates manufacture by Kimber of America.

✳ *Model 82C Classic Stainless* - .22 LR cal., features stainless steel barrel with matte blue action. Approx. 600 mfg. 1997-98.

	$800	$650	$565	$470	$400	$345	$295

Last MSR was $968.

✳ *Model 82C Classic Stainless Varmint* - .22 LR cal., features 20 in. fluted stainless steel barrel, A claro walnut with 18 LPI side panel checkering. Approx. 1,000 mfg. 1995-98.

	$825	$675	$575	$500	$425	$350	$275

Last MSR was $1,002.

MODEL 82C SVT - .22 LR cal., single shot, features 18 in. fluted heavy stainless barrel with uncheckered high comb target style walnut stock, matte blue action, 7 1/2 lbs. Mfg. 1997 only.

	$675	$550	$495	$425	$375	$315	$270

Last MSR was $825.

SVT designates Short Varmint/Target.

MODEL 82C HS - while advertised during 1997, this model never went into production.

MODEL 82C SUPERAMERICA - .22 LR cal., 22 in. drilled and tapped barrel, 4 shot mag., AAA claro checkered walnut stock with steel pistol grip cap, polished and blue metal, 6 1/2 lbs. Mfg. 1993-99.

	$1,275	$995	$875	$750	$650	$575	$400

Last MSR was $1,488.

GRADING - PPGS™	100%	98%	95%	90%	80%	70%	60%

MODEL 82C CUSTOM MATCH - .22 LR cal., features AA French walnut with 22 LPI wraparound checkering, steel Neidner-style buttplate, matte rust blue finish. Mfg. 1995-99.

$1,900	$1,525	$1,225	$975	$775	$650	$525

Last MSR was $2,158.

MODEL 82C SUPER CLASSIC - .22 LR cal., features AAA claro walnut with 18 LPI side panel checkering, polished and blue metal. Mfg. 1995-96.

$975	$875	$775	$675	$600	$550	$450

Last MSR was $1,090.

Centerfire Models

The models below feature a Mauser style action with controlled round feeding and extraction.

MODEL 84C SINGLE SHOT CLASSIC - while advertised during 1996-97, this model never went into production.

MODEL 84C SINGLE SHOT SUPERAMERICA - while advertised during 1996-97, this model never went into production.

MODEL 84C SINGLE SHOT VARMINT STAINLESS - while advertised during 1997, this model never went into production.

MODEL 84C SINGLE SHOT VARMINT - .17 Rem. or .223 Rem. cal., features 24 (first 200 rifles only), or 25 in. stainless match grade fluted barrel with recess crown, matte blue receiver finish, checkered A claro walnut stock with beavertail forend, 7 1/2 lbs. Mfg. 1997-99.

$895	$765	$625	$515	$450	$375	$325

Last MSR was $1,032.

Add $150 for .17 Rem. cal. (less than 100 mfg.).

MODEL 84M - .22-250 Rem., .204 Ruger (new 2004), .223 Rem. (new 2004), .243 Win. (new 2004), .260 Rem., .308 Win., or 7mm-08 Rem. cal., true Mauser action, much improved version of the Model 84C, longer and stronger receiver, 2 position Model 70 type safety, 22 in. light sporter (Classic), 24 in. heavy stainless steel fluted (.308 Win. cal., LongMaster Classic, new 2002), 26 in. heavy stainless steel fluted sporter (Varmint), or 26 in. stainless bull (.22-250 Rem. cal., LongMaster VT) match grade barrel, match grade trigger, 5 shot mag. with sculpted steel floorplate), grey/black laminate target stock with high comb and extended pistol grip (LongMaster VT) or checkered walnut stock and forend, 5 lbs., 10 oz. (Sporter), 7 lbs., 5 oz. (Varmint and LongMaster Classic), or 10 lbs (LongMaster VT). New 2001.

A three position Win. Model 70 type safety became a standard feature on all Kimber 84M rifles in early 2004.

✳ *Model 84M Classic* - .22-250 Rem., .243 Win., .257 Roberts (Select Grade only), .260 Rem., .308 Win., 7mm-08 Rem., or .338 Federal (new 2007) cal.

MSR $1,114	$950	$800	$675	$575	$500	$450	$395

Add $159 for Classic Select Grade with Claro walnut (new 2006).
Add $164 for Classic Select Grade with French walnut (mfg. 2006-2007).

✳ *Model 84M Longmaster Classic* - .223 Rem., .243 Win. (disc. 2007), or .308 Win. cal.

MSR $1,224	$1,075	$875	$725	$600	$525	$450	$400

✳ *Model 84M Longmaster VT* - .22-250 Rem. cal. only.

MSR $1,357	$1,125	$950	$775	$675	$550	$475	$425

✳ *Model 84M SVT* - .223 Rem cal., short barrel variation of the Model 84M Longmaster VT.

MSR $1,357	$1,125	$950	$775	$675	$550	$475	$425

✳ *Model 84M Varmint* - .204 Ruger or .22-250 Rem. cal., features 26 in. heavy stainless steel fluted barrel.

MSR $1,224	$1,075	$875	$725	$600	$525	$450	$400

GRADING - PPGS™	100%	98%	95%	90%	80%	70%	60%

✳ *Model 84M Pro Varmint* - .204 Ruger, .22-250 Rem., or .223 Rem. cal., grey laminate uncheckered stock, brush polished 24 in. stainless steel barrel with black flutes. New 2004.

MSR $1,302	$1,075	$925	$800	$700	$575	$475	$400

MODEL 84M SUPERAMERICA - .223 Rem., .243 Win., .260 Rem., 7mm-08 Rem., .308 Win., or .338 Federal cal., similar to Model 84M Repeater, except has 24 LPI wrap checkering, ebony forend tip, AAA walnut, highly polished blue action and barrel. New 2003.

MSR $2,124	$1,800	$1,525	$1,250	$995	$875	$750	$675

MODEL 84M MONTANA - .243 Win., .257 Roberts (new 2008), .260 Rem., 7mm-08 Rem., .308 Win., or .338 Federal (new 2007) cal., synthetic stock and satin stainless steel barreled action, 5 lbs. 2 oz. New 2003.

MSR $1,276	$1,100	$950	$725	$625	$525	$450	$400

Add $248 for Montana Black KimPro in .308 Win. cal. only (disc.).

MODEL 84M LONGMASTER PRO - .22-250 Rem. or .308 Win. cal., similar to Longmaster VT, except has synthetic stock, 24 (.308 Win. cal.) or 26 (.22-250 Rem. cal.) in. brush polished stainless bull barrel with black flutes.

While this model was cataloged during 2003 with an MSR of $1,189, it never went into production.

MODEL 8400 CLASSIC - .25-06 Rem. (new 2006), .270 WSM, .270 Win. (new 2006), 7mm WSM, .300 WSM, .300 Win. Mag. (new 2006), .30-06 (new 2006), .325 WSM (new 2005), or .338 Win. Mag. (new 2006) cal., A walnut stock, 20 LPI panel checkering, 3-position Model 70 type safety, 24 in. sporter match grade blue barrel, match grade adj. trigger. New 2003.

MSR $1,172	$995	$800	$675	$575	$475	$425	$375

Add $187 for Classic Select Grade with Claro walnut (new 2006, .270 WSM, .300 WSM, or .325 WSM cals. only).

Add $171 for Classic Select Grade with French walnut (mfg. 2006-2007, .270 WSM, .300 WSM, or .325 WSM cals. only).

While a left-hand version of this model was cataloged during 2003, they were never produced.

✳ *Model 8400 Classic SuperAmerica* - .270 WSM, 7mm WSM, .300 WSM, .300 Win. Mag. (new 2006), .325 WSM (new 2005), or .338 Win. Mag. (new 2006) cal., similar to Model 8400 Classic, except has AAA walnut stock, 24 LPI panel checkering, ebony forend tip, highly polished blue action, and 24 in. custom sporter barrel. New 2003.

MSR $2,240	$1,850	$1,575	$1,275	$975	$850	$725	$625

✳ *Model 8400 Montana* - .25-06 Rem. (new 2006), .270 Win. (new 2006), .270 WSM, 7mm WSM, .300 WSM, .300 Win. Mag. (new 2006), .30-06 (new 2006), .325 WSM (new 2005) or .338 Win. Mag. (new 2006) cal., similar to Model 8400 Classic, except has synthetic stock and 24 in. satin stainless steel custom sporter barrel, 6 lbs., 2 oz. New 2003.

MSR $1,312	$1,075	$900	$750	$625	$525	$425	$375

✳ *Model 8400 Tactical Series* - .308 Win. cal., matte blue (Tactical) or KimPro II Dark Earth (Advanced Tactical) finish, grey (Tactical) or Desert Camo (Advanced Tactical) McMillan synthetic stock, 24 in. fluted bull barrel, 5 shot mag., 9 lbs., 4 oz. New 2007.

MSR $1,937	$1,650	$1,375	$1,100	$950	$825	$725	$625

Add $697 for Advanced Tactical.

MODEL 8400 CAPRIVI - .375 H&H or .458 Lott cal., 24 in, contoured blue barrel, 4 shot mag., Mauser claw extractor, 3-position Model 70 style safety, adj. trigger, oil finished checkered pistol grip stock, pancake cheekpiece, ebony forend tip, swivel studs, three leaf express sight, double cross bolts, recoil pad, 8 lbs., 7 oz. New 2008.

MSR $3,196	$2,775	$2,400	$2,100	$1,800	$1,500	$1,275	$1,075

GRADING - PPGS™	100%	98%	95%	90%	80%	70%	60%

MODEL 8400 TALKEETNA - .375 H&H cal. New 2008.

MSR $2,108	$1,775	$1,525	$1,250	$975	$875	$750	$650

MODEL 8400 SONORA - .25-06 Rem., .30-06, .300 Win. Mag., or .308 Win. cal. New 2008.

MSR $1,359	$1,100	$900	$775	$650	$550	$500	$400

MODEL K770 CLASSIC - while advertised during 1997, this model never went into production. Prototypes only.

MODEL K770 SUPER AMERICA - while advertised during 1997, this model never went into production. Prototypes only.

MODEL 84M LPT (LIGHT POLICE TACTICAL) - .223 Rem. or .308 Win. cal., 24 in. matte blue heavy sporter contour fluted barrel, 5 shot mag., black laminate stock with panel stippling, Picatinny rail, oversize bolt handle, sling swivels, recoil pad, full length Mauser claw extractor, 3-position Model 70 style safety, adj. trigger, 8 lbs., 7 oz. New 2008.

MSR $1,315	$1,075	$925	$775	$650	$550	$475	$425

Mauser 96 Sporters

MODEL 96 SPORTER - .308 Win. cal., features M-96 action with stainless steel fluted heavy barrel. Mfg. 1995-97.

	$450	$415	$365	$300	$260	$225	$200

Last MSR was $520.

During 1995-96, Kimber began sporterizing the Swedish Mauser Model 96 military surplus rifles. They featured stainless steel fluted barrels and a black synthetic Ramline stock, receivers were drilled and tapped to accept Weaver scope mounts, bead blasted bluing, and original reprofiled military bolt. The Sporter configuration included .243 Win., 6.5x55mm, or .308 Win. cal., while the heavy fluted barrel models were available in .22-250 Rem. or .308 Win. (Varmint or Heavy Barrel). Retail prices ranged from $340-$415 for the Standard Sporter, while the Varmint/Heavy barrel variation was priced at approx. $510. Sporter variations were also available as a combo package with scope and hardshell case - add approx. $30.

Mauser 98 Sporters

MODEL 98 SPORTER - .220 Swift (100 mfg.), .257 Roberts (100 mfg.), .270 Win., .280 Rem. (100 mfg.), .30-06, .300 Win. Mag., .338 Win. Mag., or 7mm Rem. Mag. cal., features Mauser M-98 action with stainless match grade fluted barrel, choice of synthetic or claro walnut stock, and Warne bases, matte black finish receiver. Mfg. 1996-98.

	$465	$425	$375	$315	$270	$230	N/A

Last MSR was $535.

Add $25 for Mag. cals.
Add $100 for Claro walnut stock.

* *Mauser 98 Sporter Matte* - .300 Win. Mag., .338 Win. Mag., or 7mm Rem. Mag. cal., features 25 in. non-fluted sporter barrel, synthetic stock, and Weaver style bases. Disc. 1998.

	$275	$250	$225	$200	$185	$170	$155

Last MSR was $339.

SHOTGUNS: O/U

AUGUSTA SERIES - 12 ga., 2 3/4 (Trap & Skeet) or 3 (Sporting & Field) in. chambers, Boss type boxlock action with shallow frame, blue (Trap & Skeet) or polished metal (Field & Sporting) frame, ejectors, SST, tang safety with ejector, 26-34 in. vent. barrel lengths with VR backbored to .736 in., available in Field,

GRADING - PPGS™	100%	98%	95%	90%	80%	70%	60%

Sporting, Skeet, and Trap variations, beavertail or Schnabel forend, Pachmayr Decelerator recoil pad, 7 lbs., 2 oz-7 lbs., 13 oz. Mfg. in Italy by Investarm 2002-2005, limited delivery 2003-2005.

	$4,750	$4,250	$3,750	$3,250	$2,750	$2,250	$1,850

Last MSR was $5,676.

MARIAS SERIES - 12 or 20 ga., 3 in. chambers, 26, 28, or 30 in. VR barrels with 5 choke tubes, ejectors, charcoal case colored detachable sidelock action with engraving, deluxe checkered walnut English or pistol grip stock and forearm, available in Grade I with Grade III Turkish walnut or Grade II with Grade IV Turkish walnut, imported from Turkey. New 2006.

MSR $5,799	$4,995	$4,375	$3,750	$3,250	$2,700	$2,200	$1,825

SHOTGUNS: SxS

VALIER SERIES - 16 (new 2006) or 20 ga., 26 or 28 in. barrels, hand engraved sidelock action with seven pins, hand checkered Turkish walnut straight grip English stock, DT, fixed chokes, hand engraved blue (20 ga. only), case colored, or optional bone charcoal case colored action, extractors, approx. 6 1/2 lbs., mfg. in Turkey 2005-2007.

	$3,525	$3,050	$2,675	$2,200	$1,850	$1,450	$1,100

Last MSR was $3,999.

✳ *Valier Grade II* - similar to Grade I, except has ejectors, with or w/o (disc. 2007) charcoal case colored frame, mfg. in Turkey. New 2005.

MSR $4,999	$4,495	$3,995	$3,050	$2,675	$2,200	$1,850	$1,450

Subtract approx. $600 if w/o bone charcoal case colors.

KIMBER OF OREGON, INC.

Previous manufacturer located in Clackamas, OR circa 1980-1991. Kimber of Oregon went out of business with its final sale in 1991. In some models, magazines for these fine quality rifles are getting extremely hard to find with healthy premiums being asked. Once "B" suffix models were introduced, older manufacture started being referred to as "A" models.

PISTOLS: BOLT ACTION

PREDATOR MODEL - .221 Fireball, .223 Rem., 6mm TCU (disc. 1987), 7mm TCU, or 6x45mm (disc. 1987) cal., single shot Model 84 action with shortened 14 7/8 in. barrel, scope use only, one piece deluxe walnut stock with contoured pistol grip, 5 1/4 lbs., rare cals. will command a premium. Approx. 200 mfg. 1987-88 only.

✳ *Predator Model Hunter Grade* - AA Claro walnut without checkering. Disc. 1988.

	$1,995	$1,750	$1,500	$1,250	$950	$800	$700

Last MSR was $995.

✳ *Predator Model Super Grade* - similar to Hunter Grade, except has select French walnut with ebony forend tip and 22 lines/in. checkering. Disc. 1988.

	$3,000	$2,650	$2,250	$2,000	$1,750	$1,400	$1,250

Last MSR was $1,195.

RIFLES: BOLT ACTION

Note: No suffix in Kimber models denotes pre-1986 action design, "B" suffix models incorporate the new action with improved cocking system, faster lock time, swept-back bolt design, improved recoil lug, and are right-handed. Pre '83 rifles had no bolt release.

Add $175 for skeleton grip cap on models listed below.
Add $275 for skeleton buttplate on models listed below.
Add $100 for checkered bolt handle on models listed below.

GRADING - PPGS™	100%	98%	95%	90%	80%	70%	60%

Add $300 for raised quarter rib.
Add $100 for forend tip.
Extra fancy walnut on any Kimber will always command a premium.

Model 82, .22 Cal. Series

Add $200-$500 for .22 Hornet or .22 Mag. cal. on the models listed below, depending on the variation.

STANDARD MODEL 82 - .22 LR, .22 Mag., or .22 Hornet cal., Mauser type rear locking bolt action, 3 (.22 Hornet), 4 (.22 Mag.), or 5 (.22 LR) shot mag., 22 in. (Sporter) or 24 in. (Varmint) barrel, deluxe claro walnut, steel buttplate, rocker style safety, right or left-hand action, 6 1/2 lbs.

* *Standard Model 82 Classic* - disc. 1988.

	100%	98%	95%	90%	80%	70%	60%
	$885	$745	$650	$525	$450	$375	$335

Last MSR was $750.

* *Standard Model 82 Cascade* - Monte Carlo cheekpiece, disc. 1988.

	100%	98%	95%	90%	80%	70%	60%
	$885	$745	$650	$525	$450	$375	$335

Add $350 for Custom Cascade Model, with higher grade walnut, ebony forend tip, and Niedner style buttplate (34 mfg).

* *Standard Model 82 Custom Classic* - higher grade claro walnut, ebony forearm tip, Niedner style steel buttplate. Disc. 1988.

	100%	98%	95%	90%	80%	70%	60%
	$1,050	$900	$750	$675	$500	$475	$425

Last MSR was $995.

Add 25% for .218 Bee cal. (approx. 130 standard mfg.).
Add 10% for .22 Mag. cal.
Add 100% for .218 Mashburn mfg.

Also available in .25-20 (approx. 200 mfg. single shot only) cals. Mfg. 1985 only (retail price was $695).

* *Standard Model 82 Deluxe Grade* - .22 LR cal. only, similar to Custom Classic Model, AA walnut, 5 or 10 (optional) shot mag., 6 1/2 lbs. Mfg. 1989-90 only.

	100%	98%	95%	90%	80%	70%	60%
	$1,050	$925	$725	$625	$525	$450	$395

Last MSR was $1,195.

A left-hand variation was also available at no extra charge, but had limited mfg. in 1990.

SPORTER MODEL - .17 Ackley Hornet (approx. 9 mfg.), .17 K. Hornet (approx. 88 mfg.), or .22 LR cal., includes Model 82A action, 22 in. sporter weight barrel, 4 shot mag., round top receiver with bases, checkered stock and forend, 6 1/2 lbs. Mfg. 1991 only.

	100%	98%	95%	90%	80%	70%	60%
	$940	$785	$675	$575	$500	$450	$395

Last MSR was $995.

Add approx. 100% for .17 K Hornet or .17 Ackley Hornet cals.

RIMFIRE VARMINTER - .22 LR cal. only, Model 82A action, free floating 25 in. medium heavy barrel, laminated stock, 5 or optional 10 shot mag., rubber buttpad, 8 1/4 lbs. Mfg. 1990-91 only.

	100%	98%	95%	90%	80%	70%	60%
	$895	$775	$650	$575	$500	$450	$400

Last MSR was $795.

HUNTER GRADE - .22 LR cal. only, similar to Rimfire Varminter with Super America configured barrel and action with low glare metal finish. Mfg. 1990 only.

	100%	98%	95%	90%	80%	70%	60%
	$785	$625	$535	$455	$395	$340	$295

Last MSR was $895.

MINI CLASSIC - .22 LR cal. only, Model 82 action, 18 in. barrel, steel buttplate, sling swivels. Mfg. 1988 only.

	100%	98%	95%	90%	80%	70%	60%
	$700	$550	$500	$450	$400	$500	$300

Last MSR was $795.

GRADING - PPGS™	100%	98%	95%	90%	80%	70%	60%

GOVERNMENT MODEL 82A TARGET - .22 LR cal. only, specifically designed for U.S. Army training, 25 in. heavy target barrel including scope blocks, over-sized stock, some rifles are "star" marked indicating an accuracy guarantee, 10 3/4 lbs. Mfg. 1987-91.

	$735	$600	$515	$460	$410	$350	$325

Last MSR was $595.

20,000 rifles were mfg. 1987-1989 to fill the initial U.S. government contract. U.S. property marked guns do exist in private hands - all within a low serial number range (watch markings carefully). Commercial guns were manufactured for the private sector with values listed.

ALL AMERICAN MATCH - .22 LR cal. only, precision rifled 25 in. free floating target grade barrel, stock is adj. both vertically and for length of pull, fully adj. single stage trigger, approx. 9 lbs. Mfg. 1990-91 only.

	$790	$625	$540	$465	$400	$340	$295

Last MSR was $895.

CONTINENTAL - .22 LR, .22 Mag., or .22 Hornet cal., Sporter action only, full length Mannlicher stock, open sights, deluxe walnut. Add $200 for .22 Mag. or .22 Hornet cal. New 1987.

This model was only available as a special order with prices on request from the factory.

✳ *Continental Super* - similar to Continental, except has AAA claro walnut with 22 lines/in. checkering. Mfg. 1987-88.

	$1,695	$1,500	$1,375	$1,250	$1,000	$875	$750

Last MSR was $1,465.

Add 100% if model is one of three known laminated stock variations with cheekpieces that were mfg., all in .22 LR cal.

S SERIES - .22 LR (535 mfg.), .22 Hornet (354 mfg.) or .22 Mag. (88 mfg.) cal., top-of-the-line limited production model, grooved for scope mounting, Neidner checkered steel buttplate, best quality walnut, continental cheekpiece, ebony forend tip, Sporter configuration only. Mfg. early 1980s.

	$1,400	$1,200	$1,000	$825	$675	$550	$450

SUPER AMERICA - top-of-the-line model, includes detachable scope mounts, Niedner checkered steel buttplate and best quality walnut, cheekpiece and ebony forend tip added after 1983, available in Sporter configuration only. This model was disc. 1988, and reintroduced 1990-91.

	$1,400	$1,200	$1,000	$825	$675	$550	$450

Last MSR was $1,295.

✳ *Super America Super Grade* - similar to Super America, AAA walnut, beaded cheekpiece, 5 or 10 (optional) shot mag., 6 1/2 lbs. Mfg. 1989 only.

	$1,250	$1,000	$900	$750	$675	$550	$500

Last MSR was $1,295.

Add a small premium for 10 shot mag.

CUSTOM MATCH - .22 LR or .22 Mag. cal., limited edition of 217 rifles, match dimension chamber, French walnut stock with 22 L.P.I. checkering, rust blue finish, other custom rifle features. Introduced 1984.

	$2,500	$2,000	$1,500	$1,250	$1,000	$850	$750

Add $500 for .22 Mag. cal.

BROWNELL - .22 LR cal., only 500 mfg. to commemorate the late Leonard Brownell, Mannlicher style extra deluxe claro walnut stock. Mfg. 1986 only.

	$2,000	$1,800	$1,500	$1,325	$1,085	$930	$750

Last MSR was $1,500.

GRADING - PPGS™	100%	98%	95%	90%	80%	70%	60%

CENTENNIAL - .22 LR cal. only, limited edition (100 rifles) to commemorate centennial of .22 LR cal., includes hand-picked checkered walnut, moderate engraving, special Wilson Arms match barrel, skeleton buttplate and other refinements, serial numbered C1-C100. Mfg. 1987 only.

$2,875	$2,500	$1,875	$1,645	$1,400	$1,130	$940

Last MSR was $2,950.

TENTH ANNIVERSARY ISSUE - .22 LR cal., limited edition, French walnut stock featuring slim forend design with shadowed cheekpiece, Neidner steel buttplate and other refinements. Mfg. 1989 only.

$1,800	$1,600	$1,400	$1,235	$1,000	$870	$700

Add $100 for matte finish.

Model 84 Centerfire Series

Model 84 caliber rarity is as follows: .222 Rem. and .223 Rem. are common. 6x45mm or 47mm, .221 Fireball, .17 Rem., and .17 Mach IV are less common and more desirable. .222 Rem. Mag. is rare, while 5.6x50mm is extremely rare.

Add $200-$375 for rare calibers.

Add $75 for forend tip - option A. Add $300 for iron sights - option B. Add $100 for checkered bolt handle - option C. Add $200 for skeleton grip cap - option D. Add $300 for skeleton buttplate - option G. Add $250-$300 for 3-position safety in this series.

STANDARD MODEL 84 - .17 Rem., .17 Mach IV (disc. 1987), 6x45 or 47mm (disc. 1987), 5.6x50mm (disc. 1987), .221 Fireball, .222 Rem., .222 Rem. Mag. (disc. 1987), or .223 Rem. cal., "Mini-Mauser" type head locking bolt action, 5 shot mag., 22 (Sporter) or 24 (Varmint) in. barrel, deluxe Claro walnut, steel buttplate, rocker style safety, 6 1/2 lbs.

* *Standard Model 84 Classic* - disc. 1988.

$1,095	$1,000	$875	$750	$600	$500	$400

Last MSR was $885.

Add $55 for disc. Cascade Model (Monte Carlo cheekpiece).
Add 20% for left-hand action.

Also available in left hand action in .22 Hornet, .222 Rem., .223 Rem., 6x45mm, 6x47mm, .17 Rem., and .17 Mach IV (very limited mfg.).

CUSTOM CLASSIC MODEL - higher grade Claro walnut, ebony forearm tip, Niedner style steel buttplate. Disc. 1988.

$1,400	$1,200	$1,000	$825	$675	$550	$450

Last MSR was $1,130.

* *Custom Classic Model Deluxe Grade Sporter* - .17 Rem., .221 Rem., or .223 Rem. cal., Mauser action, AA walnut, similar to Custom Classic Model, 6 1/4 lbs. Mfg. 1989-90.

$1,400	$1,200	$1,000	$825	$675	$550	$450

Last MSR was $1,295.

Also available in left-hand action (.223 Rem. cal. only), limited mfg.

CONTINENTAL - .221 Fireball (extremely rare, mfg. 1988 only) .222 Rem. or .223 Rem. cal., Sporter action only, full length Mannlicher stock, open sights, deluxe walnut. New 1987.

Extreme rarity precludes accurate price evaluation on this model.

* *Continental Super* - similar to Continental (same cals.), except has AAA Claro walnut with 22 lines/in. checkering. Mfg. 1987-88.

$2,100	$1,850	$1,500	$1,250	$1,000	$800	$700

Last MSR was $1,600.

Add 100% if model is one of three known laminated stocks that were mfg. in .223 Rem. cal.

GRADING - PPGS™	100%	98%	95%	90%	80%	70%	60%

HUNTER GRADE - .17 Rem., .222 Rem., or .223 Rem. cal., laminated stock, Super America configured action and barrel with low glare metal finish. Mfg. 1990 only.

	$995	$875	$750	$650	$550	$475	$400

Last MSR was $995.

SPORTER - .17 Rem., .22 Hornet, .222 Rem., .22-250 Rem., or .223 Rem. cal., 22 in. sporter weight barrel, A grade Claro walnut, round top receiver with bases, 4 shot mag., hand checkering. Mfg. 1991 only.

	$1,020	$850	$725	$625	$550	$500	$495

Last MSR was $1,095.

This model was available in either right or left-hand action.

* ***Sporter Big Bore*** - .250 Savage or .35 Rem. cal., similar action to Sporter Model, except has 3/4 in. red Pachmayr Decelerator recoil pad. Mfg. 1991 only.

Last MSR was $1,095.

Extreme rarity precludes accurate price evaluation on this model - consult an expert when buying/selling this model. This model was available in either right or left-hand action.

SUPER AMERICA/SUPER GRADE - .17 Rem., .17 MK IV, .221 Fireball, .22 Hornet, .222 Rem., .222 Rem. Mag., .22-250 Rem., .223 Rem., 5.6x56mm, or 6x47mm cal., 22 in. sporter weight barrel, top-of-the-line, with detachable scope mounts, available in Sporter configuration only, cheekpiece and ebony forend tip added after 1983, 4 shot mag., right or left hand action. Disc. 1988, reintroduced 1990-91.

	$1,695	$1,500	$1,250	$1,000	$850	$725	$675

Last MSR was $1,495.

Be careful when buying rare cals. and/or options on this model.

* ***Super America/Super Grade Big Bore*** - .250 Savage or .35 Rem. cal., similar action to Super America Model, except has 3/4 in. red Pachmayr Decelerator recoil pad. Mfg. 1991 only.

	$2,100	$1,775	$1,425	$1,125	$925	$800	$700

Last MSR was $1,495.

CUSTOM MATCH - .222 Rem. or .223 Rem. cal., limited edition of 200 rifles, match dimension chamber, French walnut stock with 22 L.P.I. checkering, rust blue finish, other custom rifle features. Introduced 1986.

	$2,500	$2,000	$1,800	$1,500	$1,100	$1,000	$750

TENTH ANNIVERSARY ISSUE - .223 Rem. cal., limited edition, French walnut stock featuring slim forend design with shadowed cheekpiece, 22 in. barrel, roundtop receiver with mounts, Neidner steel buttplate and other refinements. Mfg. 1989 only.

	$1,995	$1,650	$1,250	$1,100	$895	$785	$630

Add $100 for matte finish.

ULTRA VARMINTER - .17 Rem., .22 Hornet (rare, new 1991), .221 Rem. (disc. 1990), .222 Rem., .22-250 Rem. (rare), or .223 Rem. cal., 24 in. medium weight stainless steel barrel, laminated birch stock, plain buttstock, right- or left-hand action, 7 3/4 lbs. Mfg. 1989-91 only.

	$1,600	$1,300	$1,175	$1,000	$850	$750	$675

Last MSR was $1,295.

* ***Ultra Varminter Super*** - similar to Ultra Varminter except has steel barrel, AAA walnut stock with beaded cheekpiece, 7 1/4 lbs. Mfg. 1989-91 only.

	$2,000	$1,850	$1,500	$1,200	$975	$775	$675

Last MSR was $1,495.

GRADING - PPGS™	100%	98%	95%	90%	80%	70%	60%

Model 89 Centerfire, Big Game Series

Fewer than 5,000 Model 89 BGRs were mfg. Note: fancy wood is harder to find in Model 89s.

MODEL 89 BGR - .270 Win., .280 Rem., 7mm Rem. Mag., .30-06, .300 Win. Mag., .338 Win. Mag., or .375 H&H cal., new action incorporates features from both Mauser 98 and Win. pre-64 Model 70, three position safety, 22 or 24 in. barrel, matte blue finish will command a premium. Introduced late 1988.

* *Model 89 BGR Classic Model* - deluxe Claro walnut checkered 18 lines/in. with steel buttplate. Disc. 1988.

	100%	98%	95%	90%	80%	70%	60%
	$875	$725	$600	$500	$415	$350	$300

Last MSR was $985.

Add $200 for .375 H&H cal.
Add $100 for matte finish.

* *Model 89 BGR Custom Classic Model* - higher grade Claro walnut, ebony forearm tip, Niedner style steel buttplate. Disc. 1988.

	100%	98%	95%	90%	80%	70%	60%
	$1,125	$950	$775	$650	$525	$450	$375

Last MSR was $1,230.

Add $200 for .375 H&H cal.

DELUXE GRADE - similar to Custom Classic Model, round top receiver with Model 70 scope mount hole configuration, AA walnut stock with ebony forend tip and rubber recoil pad (no cheekpiece), 22 or 24 in. barrel, 7 1/2-8 1/2 lbs. New 1989.

* *Deluxe Grade Featherweight Barrel Model* - .257 Roberts (rare), .25-06 Rem., 7x57mm (rare, disc. 1990), .270 Win., .280 Rem., or .30-06 cal., 5 shot mag., 22 in. Featherweight barrel, right-hand action only, 7 1/2 lbs. Disc. 1990.

	100%	98%	95%	90%	80%	70%	60%
	$1,600	$1,225	$1,000	$850	$700	$600	$525

Last MSR was $1,795.

Add 25% for 7x57mm cal.
Add $470 for Super America Grade with square bridge, dovetail receiver.
Add $100 for matte finish.

The Super America Grade will accept Kimber double lever scope mounts and has one grade better wood than the Deluxe Grade with beaded cheekpiece.

* *Deluxe Grade Medium-weight Barrel Model* - .300 Win. Mag., .300 H&H (rare, disc. 1990), .300 Wby. Mag. (very rare, new 1991), .338 Win. Mag., .35 Whelen (rare, disc. 1990), or 7mm Rem. Mag. cal., 3 shot mag., 24 in. medium-weight barrel, right-hand action only, 7 3/4-8 1/2 lbs. Disc. 1990.

	100%	98%	95%	90%	80%	70%	60%
	$1,675	$1,250	$1,025	$875	$725	$625	$550

Last MSR was $1,895.

Add a premium for rare cals.
Add $495 for Super America Grade with square bridge, dovetail receiver.
Add $100 for matte finish.

The Super America Grade will accept Kimber double lever scope mounts and has one grade better wood than the Deluxe Grade with beaded cheekpiece.

* *Deluxe Grade Heavy-weight Barrel Model* - .375 H&H Mag. cal., 3 shot mag., 24 in. heavy weight barrel, right-hand action only, 9 lbs. Disc. 1990.

	100%	98%	95%	90%	80%	70%	60%
	$2,000	$1,750	$1,500	$1,250	$1,000	$800	$700

Last MSR was $1,995.

Add $495 for Super America Grade with square bridge, dovetail receiver.
Add $100 for matte finish.

The Super America Grade will accept Kimber double lever scope mounts and has one grade better wood than the Deluxe Grade with beaded cheekpiece.

GRADING - PPGS™	100%	98%	95%	90%	80%	70%	60%

SPORTER MODEL - same cals. as Deluxe/Super America Models, 22 in. feather-weight or 24 in. medium or heavy barrel, double square bridge dovetail receiver, A grade Claro walnut stock with 3/4 in. red Pachmayr Decelerator recoil pad (Mag. cals. only with 24 in. barrel). Mfg. 1991 only.

	$1,395	$1,050	$900	$775	$650	$500	$450

Last MSR was $1,595.

> Add $100 for medium Magnum action.
> Add $200 for heavy Magnum action (.375 H&H and .458 Win. Mag. cals.).

HUNTER GRADE - .270 Win., .30-06, .300 Win. Mag., .338 Win. Mag., or 7mm Rem. Mag. cal., laminated stock, Super America configured action and barrel with low glare metal finish. Mfg. 1990-91 only.

	$1,325	$1,025	$895	$750	$625	$525	$450

Last MSR was $1,495.

> Add $100 for Mag. cals.

SUPER GRADE - similar to Super America Model, square top frame, AAA walnut, 22 or 24 in. barrel, plain buttstock, 7 1/2-8 1/2 lbs. Mfg. 1989 only.

	$1,575	$1,325	$995	$825	$695	$550	$500

Last MSR was $1,495.

> Add $100 for .375 H&H cal.
> Add $100 for matte blue metal finish.
> The 24 in. barrel was available in Mag. cals. only.

LIMITED WILDLIFE EDITION SERIES - series of 5 guns, includes .257 Roberts (Whitetail Deer Edition), .270 Win. (Mule Deer Edition), .338 Win. Mag. (Rocky Mt. Elk Edition), 7mm Rem. Mag. (Big Horn Sheep Edition), and .375 H&H (Grizzly Bear Edition) cals. included, hand select walnut, special Shilen Rifle barrel, gold plated trigger, receivers are stamped "Wildlife Edition", special prefix serialization, only 25 sets were to be manufactured in 1991 only, includes rings, swivels, and hard case.

> While advertised, only one .270 Win. Mule Deer model was mfg. Retail price was scheduled to be $3,595.

MODEL 89 AFRICAN - .375 H&H (rare), .416 Rigby (most common) cal., or .505 Gibbs (rare) cal., Magnum action, 24 in. heavy barrel, AA English walnut stock with beaded cheekpiece and rubber recoil pad, includes twin recoil cross bolts, express sights on quarter rib, drop box magazine, 10-10 1/2 lbs. Mfg. 1990-91 only.

	$5,500	$4,500	$4,000	$3,500	$2,750	$2,250	$1,650

Last MSR was $3,595.

> .375 H&H or .505 Gibbs cal. will command a premium.

KIMEL INDUSTRIES, INC.

Previously manufactured until late 1994 by A.A. Arms located in Monroe, NC. Previously distributed by Kimel Industries, Inc. located in Matthews, NC.

CARBINES

AR-9 CARBINE - 9mm Para. cal., carbine variation of the AP-9 with 16 1/2 in. barrel, 20 shot mag., and steel rod folding stock. Mfg. 1991-94.

	$550	$475	$425	$365	$315	$275	$220

Last MSR was $384.

PISTOLS: SEMI-AUTO

AP-9 PISTOL - 9mm Para. cal., paramilitary design, blowback action with bolt knob on left side of receiver, 5 in. barrel with vent. shroud, front mounted 10 (C/B 1994) or 20* shot detachable mag., black matte finish, adj. front sight, 3 lbs. 7 oz. Mfg. 1989-94.

	$425	$365	$325	$275	$250	$225	$200

Last MSR was $279.

GRADING - PPGS™	100%	98%	95%	90%	80%	70%	60%

✳ *AP-9 Pistol Mini* - compact variation of the AP-9 Model with 3 in. barrel, blue or nickel finish. Mfg. 1991-94.

	$475	$425	$350	$295	$275	$250	$225

Last MSR was $273.

✳ *AP-9 Pistol Target* - target variation of the AP-9 with 12 in. match barrel with shroud, blue finish only. Mfg. 1991-94.

	$495	$462	$375	$325	$295	$275	$250

Last MSR was $294.

✳ *P-95 Pistol* - similar to AP-9, except without barrel shroud and is supplied with 5 shot mag., parts are interchangeable with AP-9. Mfg. 1990-91 only.

	$350	$295	$265	$235	$195	$165	$13

Last MSR was $250.

KING'S GUN WORKS, INC.

Current custom handgun and accessories manufacturer established during 1949 and currently located in Glendale, CA. Dealer and consumer direct sales.

King's Gun Works manufactures a complete line of custom pistols patterned after Colt M-1911, in addition to many related accessories and/or after-market parts. Please contact the company directly for current information and prices (see Trademark Index listing).

KINTREK, INC.

Previous rifle manufacturer located in Owensboro, KY.

RIFLES: SEMI-AUTO

BULLPUP MODEL - .22 LR cal., bullpup configuration, hinged dust cover, clear Ram-Line type coil spring mag., black synthetic thumbhole stock, A-2 type front/rear sight. Disc.

	$275	$225	$200	$180	$160	$140	$120

KLEINGUENTHER FIREARMS CO.

KLEINGUENTHER®

Previous custom rifle manufacturer located in Seguin, TX until circa 2001. The original KDF Co. was started by Mr. Robert Kleinguenther and sold in the early 1980s. Mr. Kleinguenther then started a new company called Kleinguenther Firearms Co.

RIFLES: BOLT ACTION

Values listed below are for base model only with no additional customer special order options. Mr. Keinguenther also custom built rifles utilizing customer actions.

BOLT ACTION RIFLE - various cals., individual customer special order rifle with a variety of options, guns are guaranteed to shoot 1/2 M.O.A., choice of actions, various weights.

✳ *Bolt Action Rifle Winchester Model 70 Custom*

	$975	$800	$675	$575	$500	$450	$400

Last MSR was $975.

✳ *Bolt Action Rifle Sako Action* - various cals., newer guns feature the ballistic recoil muzzle brake system (60-70% recoil reduction), most newer stocks are mfg. out of high tech laminated wood with 28-32 resin coated panels.

	$1,550	$1,325	$1,100	$950	$825	$725	$625

Last MSR was $1,750.

Add $155 for ballistic recoil muzzle brake system.

✳ *Bolt Action Rifle K-15*

	$1,375	$1,100	$950	$800	$675	$575	$500

Last MSR was $1,375.

GRADING - PPGS™	100%	98%	95%	90%	80%	70%	60%

KNIGHT'S MANUFACTURING COMPANY

Current manufacturer established in 1993, and located in Titusville, FL. Previously located in Vero Beach, FL. Dealer and consumer direct sales.

RIFLES: SEMI-AUTO

Some of the models listed below were also available in pre-ban configurations. Current mfg. is shipped with 9 shot (.308 Win. cal.) or 10 shot (.223 Rem. cal.) mag.

STONER SR-15 M-5 RIFLE - .223 Rem. cal., 20 in. standard weight barrel, flip-up low profile rear sight, two-stage target trigger, 7.6 lbs. New 1997.

MSR $1,837	$1,675	$1,475	$1,225	$1,025	$900	$825	$725

✳ *Stoner SR-15 M-4 Carbine* - similar to SR-15 rifle, except has 16 in. barrel, choice of fixed synthetic or non-collapsible buttstock. Mfg. 1997-2005.

	$1,400	$1,175	$950	$850	$775	$700	$650

Last MSR was $1,575.

Add $100 for non-collapsible buttstock (SR-15 M-4 K-Carbine, disc. 2001).

✳ *Stoner SR-15 URX E3 Carbine* - features 16 in. free floating barrel with URX forearm, E3 type rounded lug improved bolt. New 2004.

MSR $2,063	$1,875	$1,600	$1,300	$1,050	$900	$775	$675

STONER SR-15 MATCH RIFLE - .223 Rem. cal., features flattop upper receiver with 20 in. match grade stainless steel free floating barrel with RAS forend, two-stage match trigger, 7.9 lbs. New 1997.

MSR $1,972	$1,795	$1,525	$1,200	$975	$850	$750	$700

STONER SR-25 SPORTER - .308 Win. cal., 20 in. lightweight barrel, AR-15 configuration with carrying handle, 5, 10, or 20 (disc. per C/B 1994) shot detachable mag., less than 2 MOA guaranteed, non-glare finish, 8.8 lbs. Mfg. 1993-97.

	$2,650	$2,250	$1,900	$1,600	$1,300	$1,000	$850

Last MSR was $2,995.

✳ *Stoner RAS Sporter Carbine (SR-25 Carbine)* - 16 in. free floating barrel, grooved non-slip handguard, removable carrying handle, 7 3/4 lbs. Mfg. 1995-2005.

	$3,025	$2,550	$2,125	$1,750	$1,500	$1,250	$1,000

Last MSR was $3,495.

Subtract 15% if w/o RAS.

In 2003, the Rail Adapter System (RAS) became standard on this model.

SR-25 STANDARD MATCH - .308 Win. cal., free-floating 24 in. match barrel, fiberglass stock, inlcudes commercial gun case and 10 shot mag.

MSR $3,918	$3,600	$3,300	$2,950	$2,600	$2,300	$2,000	$1,600

SR-25 RAS MATCH - similar to SR-25 Standard, except has 24 in. free floating match barrel and flat-top receiver, less than 1 MOA guaranteed, RAS became standard 2004, 10 3/4 lbs. New 1993.

MSR $3,789	$3,350	$2,800	$2,300	$1,800	$1,500	$1,250	$1,000

Subtract approx. 15% if w/o Rail Adapter System (RAS).

Over 3,000 SR-25s have been made to date.

✳ *SR-25 RAS Match Lightweight* - features 20 in. medium contour free floating barrel, 9 1/2 lbs. Mfg. 1995-2004.

	$2,875	$2,450	$2,125	$1,750	$1,500	$1,250	$1,000

Last MSR was $3,244.

Add approx. 15% for Rail Adapter System.

GRADING - PPGS™	100%	98%	95%	90%	80%	70%	60%

SR-25 MK11 MOD O CIVILIAN DELUXE SYSTEM PACKAGE - .308 Win. cal., consumer variation of the Navy Model Mark Eleven, Mod O, w/o sound supressor, includes Leupold 3.5-10X scope, 20 in. military grade match barrel, backup sights, cell-foam case and other accessories. New 2003.

MSR $8,534	$7,950	$7,250	$6,350	$5,850	$5,100	$4,500	$4,000

SR-25 MK11 MATCH RIFLE - .308 Win. cal., includes MK11 Mod O features and 20 in. heavy barrel. New 2004.

MSR $6,325	$5,675	$5,200	$4,775	$4,400	$3,750	$3,150	$2,700

SR-25 MK11 CARBINE - .308 Win. cal., includes MK11 Mod O features and 16 in. match grade stainless steel barrel with muzzle brake, URX 4x4 rail forend, 4-position buttstock. New 2005.

MSR $6,636	$6,000	$5,500	$4,950	$4,550	$3,875	$3,250	$2,800

SR-25 BR CARBINE - .308 Win. cal., similar to SR-25 MK11 Carbine, except has chrome lined steel barrel. New 2005.

MSR $6,307	$5,675	$5,200	$4,775	$4,400	$3,750	$3,150	$2,700

SR-M110 SASS - 7.62x51mm cal., 20 in. military match grade barrel, full RAS treatment on barrel, civilian variation of the Army's new semi-auto sniper rifle system, includes Leupold long-range tactical power scope, 600 meter back up iron sights, system case and other accessories. New 2006.

MSR $14,436	$13,000	$11,000	$9,500	$8,000	$7,000	$6,000	$5,000

"DAVID TUBB" COMPETITION MATCH RIFLE - .260 Rem. or .308 Win. cal., incorporates refinements by David Tubb, top-of-the-line competition match rifle, including adj. and rotating buttstock pad. Mfg. 1998 only.

	$5,200	$4,000	$3,600	$3,150	$2,700	$2,300	$1,995

Last MSR was $5,995.

STONER SR-50 - .50 BMG cal., features high strength materials and lightweight design, fully locked breech and two lug rotary breech bolt, horizontal 5 shot box mag., tubular receiver supports a removable barrel, approx. 31 lbs. Limited mfg. 2000, non-commercial sales only.

Last MSR was $6,995.

KODIAK CO.

Previous manufacturer located in North Haven, CT circa 1963-66.

Kodiak Co. was in business for only a short time. They produced the first .22 Mag. semi-auto rifle (Model 260), as well as a centerfire bolt action (Model 158 Deluxe), and a slide action shotgun (Model 458). While Kodiak long guns are rare and extremely well made, collectability to date has been minimal with most specimens selling at a slight premium over similar quality trade name counterparts of that era. Prior to 1963, Kodiak firearms were marketed under the trade name of Jefferson.

KOLAR ARMS

Current manufacturer located in Racine, WI. Dealer direct sales.

SHOTGUNS

Kolar Arms manufactures fine quality O/U and single barrel boxlock shotguns in Skeet, Sporting Clays, and Trap configurations. Many options are available, including custom orders and engraving. Please contact the company directly for more information, including model availability, delivery time, and pricing.

KOLIBRI

Previous trademark manufactured 1914-1925 by Georg Grabner located in Rehberg, Austria.

GRADING - PPGS™	100%	98%	95%	90%	80%	70%	60%

PISTOLS: SEMI-AUTO

KOLIBRI PISTOL - 2.7 or 3mm centerfire cal., unrifled barrel, 5 shot box mag., world's smallest semi-auto centerfire pistol.

| | $2,250 | $1,950 | $1,750 | $1,500 | $1,350 | $1,175 | $1,000 |

Add approx. $300 for original case.
Add approx. 20% for nickel finish (rare).

Individual rounds of 2.7 or 3mm (more rare) ammunition are currently trading in the $75 range as it has the distinction of being the world's smallest centerfire shell (shooting a 3 grain bullet at approx. 475 fps and generating 1.75 ft./lbs. of muzzle energy!).

KONGSBERG

Previous manufacturer circa 1814-1998 located in Kongsberg, Norway. Previously imported and distributed 1996-98, by Kongsberg America L.L.C. located in Fairfield, CT, and by Lew Horton Distributing Co., Inc. until 1996, located in Westboro, MA.

RIFLES: BOLT ACTION

Add $50 for iron sights on models listed below.

393 SERIES - .22-250 Rem., .243 Win., .270 Win., .30-06, .308 Win., 6.5x55 Swedish, 7mm Rem. Mag., .300 Win. Mag., or .338 Win. Mag. cal., available in either Classic, De Luxe, Thumbhole (.22-250 Rem. or 308 Win. only), or Select (Standard) configuration, checkered pistol grip, forend mounted recoil lug which connects to stock, 3-position rear safety, fixed rotary mag., fully adj. trigger. Imported 1994-98.

✳ *393 Series Classic Model*

| | $875 | $750 | $675 | $575 | $495 | $440 | $385 |

Last MSR was $995.

Add $114 for Mag. cals.
Add $138 for left-hand action.

✳ *393 Series Select Model (Standard Model in Europe)*

| | $860 | $735 | $660 | $560 | $495 | $440 | $385 |

Last MSR was $980.

Add $113 for Mag. cals.
Add $138 for left-hand action.

✳ *393 Series De Luxe Model*

| | $940 | $795 | $700 | $595 | $515 | $450 | $395 |

Last MSR was $1,124.

Add $112 for Mag. cals.
Add $137 for left-hand action.

✳ *393 Series Thumbhole Model* - .22-250 Rem. or .308 Win. cal., features thumbhole stock. Mfg. 1996-98.

| | $1,350 | $1,175 | $1,000 | $875 | $750 | $625 | $500 |

Last MSR was $1,580.

Add $138 for left-hand action.

KORA BRNO

Current revolver trademark manufactured by Kroko a.s., located in Brno, Czech Republic. No current U.S. importation.

To date, the Kora Brno revolver/revolver carbine line has had little or no importation into the U.S. Models include many configurations of both .22 LR, .22 Mag., and .38 Spl. cals. Please contact the factory directly for more information (see Trademark Index).

KORRIPHILA

Previous trademark manufacturered until 2004 by Intertex, located in Eislingen, Germany. Previously imported 1999-2004 by Korriphila, Inc., located in Pineville, NC, and by Osborne's located in Cheboygan, MI until 1988.

GRADING - PPGS™	100%	98%	95%	90%	80%	70%	60%

PISTOLS: SEMI-AUTO

Less than 30 Korriphila pistols were made annually.

HSP 701 - 7.65 Luger (disc.), .38 Spl. (disc.), 9mm Para., 9mm Police (disc.), 9mm Steyr (disc.), .45 ACP, or 10mm Norma (disc.) cal., double action, Budischowsky delayed roller block locking system assists in recoil reduction, 40% stainless steel parts, 4 or 5 in. barrel, blue or satin finish, walnut grips, 7 or 9 shot mag., approx. 2.6 lbs, very limited production.

	$6,500	$5,500	$3,750	$2,950	$2,150	$1,850	$1,675

✱ *HSP 701 Odin's Eye (Damascus)* - similar to HSP 701, except is completely made from one block of Damascus stainless steel, rosewood grips with Manta skin inlays, custom order only.

	$12,250	$10,250	$8,500	N/A	N/A	N/A	N/A

KORTH

Current manufacturer established 1954, and located in Ratzeburg, Germany. No current importation. Previously imported 2000-2005 by Korth USA, a division of Earl's Repair Service, Inc., located in Tewksbury, MA. Previously imported 1997-99 by Keng's Firearms Specialty, Inc. located in Atlanta, GA. Previously imported by Mandall Shooting Supplies, Inc. located in Scottsdale, AZ, Beeman Precision Arms, located in Santa Rosa, CA and by Osborne's in Cheboygan, MI.

Korth handguns are very high quality and are literally manufactured one-at-a-time, resulting in limited mfg. (less than 100 annually) and importation. 7,140 revolvers in 10 different configurations were manufactured between 1964-1981.

Retail values listed below reflect the most recent U.S. pricing from Korth USA.

PISTOLS: SEMI-AUTO

KORTH SEMI-AUTO - 9mm Para., .357 SIG (disc. 2002), .40 S&W (disc. 2004), .45 ACP (Tactical Model, mfg. 2003-2004) or 9x21mm IMI (disc.) cal., double action, 4, 4 1/2 threaded, or 5 (disc.) in. barrel, all steel construction, 8 (.45 ACP cal.), 9 (.40 S&W and .357 SIG) or 10 (9mm Para. or 9x21mm IMI) shot mag., adj. sights, checkered walnut grips, top quality manufacture throughout. Introduced 1986 with first guns shipped 1988, very limited mfg.

The most recent MSR on this model is $6,495.

Add $587 for .45 ACP Tactical Model. Add $2,000 for Model Schalldampfer (9mm Para cal. only, threaded barrel, new 2003). Add $285 for silver matte plasma finish. Add $740 for silver polished plasma finish. Add $845 for polish blue plasma finish. Add $1,440 per interchangeable barrels. Add $180 for extra mag.

Base values are for high polish blue finish.

JAEGER MODEL - 9mm Para. cal., 4 in. barrel, ivory grips with hunting scene, left side has hunter and dog, right side has deer in forest, gold inlaid, grey "pickled" finish, fully engraved in Arabesque style.

The most recent MSR on this model is $19,200.

WILLIE KORTH "JUBILEE" 50th ANNIVERSARY MODEL - 9mm Para cal., 4 in. barrel, combat trigger guard, gold inlaid with head of Willie Korth and dates (1954-2004), 50 Jahre oak leaf, and acorn engraving in high polish blue, deluxe hand engraved wood grips. Only 5 to be mfg. beginning 2004.

The most recent MSR on this model is $18,000.

A special case which holds both the anniversary pistol and the revolver, as well as a matching commemorative knife is also available.

REVOLVERS

The crane of the main cylinder and of the extra cylinder (.22 LR/.22 Mag. or .357 Mag./9mm Para.) are cut from the same billet of steel, and for reasons of smallest tolerance that Korth guarantees, once a gun is made with a single cylinder, the extra convertible cylinder cannot be ordered at a later date. Korth currently produces the world's most expensive revolver.

Add $255 for silver matte plasma finish. Add $520 for silver polished plasma finish. Add $620 for bright blue polished plasma finish.

Subtract approx. $550-$700 if w/o interchangeable different cal. cylinder on Combat, Sport, and Target Models.

TROJA MODEL - .22 LR, .22 Mag., or .357 Mag. cal., 4 or 6 in. barrel, matte finish, smooth oversized walnut finger groove grips. New 2003.

The most recent MSR on this model is $4,500.

COMBAT MODEL - .22 LR, .22 Mag., .38 Spl., or .357 Mag. cal., 3 (solid only), 4 VR, 5 1/4 VR, 6 VR, or 8 in. barrel, steel or stainless steel (disc., limited mfg.) construction, 6 shot, combat sights fully adj., full length shrouded ejector rod, adj. trigger, checkered and oil finished walnut grips, 2.6 lbs. Introduced 1967.

The most recent MSR on this model is $6,880.

Used specimens of this model are infrequently encountered, and secondary values are difficult to determine.

SPORT MODEL - .22 LR, .32 S&W Long, .38 Spl., or .357 Mag. cal., 2 1/2 (disc., scarce), 4, 5 1/4, 6 VR, or 8 in. barrel, 5 (early mfg.) or 6 shot, micro adj. sights, full length shrouded ejector rod, adj. trigger, checkered and oil finished walnut grips, 2.6 lbs. Introduced 1967.

The most recent MSR on this model is $7,000.

Subtract approx. 50% for 5 shot, depending on condition.

Used specimens of this model are infrequently encountered, and secondary values are difficult to determine.

TARGET MODEL - .22 LR, .32 S&W Long, .38 Spl., or .357 Mag. cal., 5 1/4 or 6 VR in. barrel, 6 shot, micro adj. sights, adj. trigger, stippled oversized target walnut grips, 2.6 lbs.

The most recent MSR on this model is $7,240.

Used specimens of this model are infrequently encountered, and secondary values are difficult to determine.

WECHSEL MODEL - centerfire and .22 LR/.22 Mag. cals., both cylinder and barrel can be changed. Mfg. 2003-2004.

Last MSR was $10,000.

Revolvers: Special/Limited Editions

MODEL EVEREST 40 YEARS KORTH SPECIAL EDITION - .357 Mag., 5 1/4 in. barrel only, deeply engraved frame and barrel with gold inlays, smooth select walnut grips, cased, only 25 mfg. 1994 only.

$8,950	$6,350	$4,500	N/A	N/A	N/A	N/A

Last MSR was $8,500.

WILLIE KORTH "JUBILEE" 50th ANNIVERSARY MODEL - .357 Mag., 4 in. barrel, gold inlaid with head of Willie Korth and dates (1954-2004), 50 Jahre oak leaf, and acorn engraving in high polish blue, deluxe hand engraved wood grips. Only 5 to be mfg. beginning 2004.

The most recent MSR on this model is $18,000.

A special case which holds both the anniversary pistol and the revolver, as well as a matching commemorative knife is also available.

ANNO DOMINI 2000 - 357 Mag., 4 in. combat model, PVD gold plasma coating, deep relief engraving featuring thorns, includes black leather briefcase, only 10 mfg. during 2000.

Extreme rarity precludes accurate pricing on this model - manufacturer's suggested retail was $10,000.

GRADING - PPGS™	100%	98%	95%	90%	80%	70%	60%

PLATINUM MODEL - .357 Mag. cal., 6 shot, 4 in. barrel, platinum engraved model with deluxe grips, includes black leather briefcase. New 2002.
> The most recent MSR on this model is $9,600.

ARABESQUE MODEL - .357 Mag. cal., 6 shot, 4 in. barrel, arabesque engraved model with deluxe grips, includes black leather briefcase. New 2003.
> The most recent MSR on this model is $9,600.

EICHENLAUB MODEL - .357 Mag. cal., 6 shot, 4 in. barrel, oak leaf engraved model with deluxe grips, includes black leather briefcase. New 2003.
> The most recent MSR on this model is $12,000.

JAEGER MODEL - .357 Mag. cal., 4 in. barrel, ivory grips with hunting scene, left side has hunter and dog, right side has deer in forest, gold inalid, grey "pickled" finish, fully engraved in Arabesque style.
> The most recent MSR on this model is $19,200.

MODEL BELLEZZA - .357 Mag. cal., 6 in. barrel, ruby and diamonds with palladium finish, special female figured grips, Arabesque engraving, includes case, very limited mfg.
> The most recent MSR on this model is $150,000.

"Bellezza" comes from a Handel opera, and means "the triumph over sorrow and disappointment."

CUSTOM PRESENTATION MODEL - deluxe variation of Sport/Combat model.
> This variation is available with engraving and other special options that are priced per individual quotation from the factory.

KOSCHAT, JAKOB

Current longarm manufacturer located in Ferlach, Austria. No current U.S. importation. Jakob Koschat manufactures high quality shotguns and double rifles in a variety of sporting configurations. Many options are available. Please contact him directly for more information, including pricing, availability, and delivery time (see Trademark Index).

KRAG-JORGENSEN (30/40 KRAG)

Previous U.S. magazine fed military rifle. Official government designation is United State Magazine Rifle and Carbine, Caliber 30. First U.S. (.30-40 Krag) military repeating rifle to shoot smokeless powder ammunition. Approx. 475,000 mfg. by Springfield Armory 1894-1904.

There have been many alterations and conversions of Krag-Jorgensen rifles - some of which are hard to identify. As a rule, these alterations and conversions almost remove any collectibility, and pricing is determined mostly by its competitive shooter value. Since prices for upper condition (95%+), original Krag-Jorgensens have increased significantly in recent years, beware of non-original guns, conversions, and in some cases, fakes.

RIFLES: BOLT ACTION

MODEL OF 1892 RIFLE (DATED 1894) - traditionally, these models have been categorized as either Type I (solid upper band) or Type II (double strap upper band), but this is too simple a definition - there were many variations. Ordnance documents list approx. 14 changes that were made during the production run, and examination of original rifles have found many more. 24,562 mfg.

$12,000 $10,000 $7,500 $5,000 $3,000 $2,000 $1,200

> Early rifles in original condition will have numbered bolt parts (below S/N 500) and magazine parts (below S/N 1,500) - they will command a premium.

It is essential that anyone considering purchasing this model thoroughly research the sequence and scope of the changes.

Only one rifle that has all the appropriate bolt and magazine parts numbered to the receiver is known.

✻ *Model of 1892 Rifle Carbine* - rare, only 2 known - one in a government museum, and the other in a private collection.

Extreme rarity precludes accurate pricing on this model.

MODEL 1892/1896 RIFLE (ARSENAL ALTERED) - numerous variations of Model 1892 rifles arsenal altered to Model 1896. 21,264 altered.

	$1,000	$875	$775	$675	$600	$525	$375

Add a small premium for models upgraded in 1897 by being restocked but retaining the Model 1892 extractor, and a receiver with no notch.

MODEL 1892 CADET RIFLE - rare, 2 variations - 400 in the 18-19,000 serial number range, with 1894 dated receiver, 4 in the 35,XXX serial number range with 1896 receiver, both have 1896 dated cartouches, three of the 400 were surveyed or condemned, and the remainder were converted to service rifle configuration. 3 of the group of 4 are known - 2 are in private collections and one is at West Point. 404 mfg.
Extreme rarity precludes accurate pricing on this model.

MODEL 1895/1896 TRANSISTION RIFLE - these rifles were produced prior to the official introduction of the Model 1896, receiver dates 1895 or 1896 with the MODEL prefix, cartouche dates will be 1896. 1,368 mfg.

	$4,000	$3,000	$1,750	$950	$650	$500	$400

MODEL OF 1896 RIFLE - receivers marked Model 1896, cartouche dates are 1896, 1897, and 1898. 60,528 mfg. - receivers stamped "MODEL 1896", with 1896, 1897, 1898, or 1901 dated cartouches (rare), rear leaf sight is calibrated to 20 and will be stamped at the top right with a "C" and the base will have a "C" on the right side. 14,942 mfg.

	$4,000	$3,000	$1,750	$950	$650	$500	$400

Add a premium for rifles with 1897 dated cartouches impressed sideways.
Add a premium for rifles with 1901 dated cartouches.

✱ *Model 1895/1896 Rifle Transition Carbine* - a "crash" program was started in the spring of 1895 and completed in May, 1896 to arm the regular cavalry, receivers dated 1894 (rare) 1895, or 1896 with no MODEL prefix, 1896 cartouche date. 7,111 mfg.

	$5,000	$4,500	$2,750	$1,850	$1,150	$825	$600

Add a premium for rare early version with two cleaning rod holes in the butt, stacked one above the other.

✱ *Model of 1896 Rifle Carbine*

	$5,000	$4,500	$2,750	$1,850	$1,150	$825	$600

Buyer beware - some models may have fake sights.

MODEL OF 1898 RIFLE - some 25 variations exist in this model. 342,526 mfg.

	$3,000	$2,500	$1,000	$700	$600	$500	$400

Subtract 20%-40% for "as modified" guns.
Collectors must be aware of the correct combination of serial number, sight variation, and cartouche date of a rifle in original "as made" condition.

✱ *Model of 1898 Rifle Carbine* - scarce and rare in authentic original condition. 5,002 mfg.

	$5,000	$4,500	$3,500	$1,800	$1,500	$1,200	$1,000

Beware of fakes.

✱ *Model of 1898 Rifles with Parkhurst Device* - scarce/rare, most were destroyed. 100 modified.
Extreme rarity precludes accurate pricing on this model.

MODEL OF 1899 CARBINE - numerous variations, sight and hand guard changes. 36,052 mfg.

	$5,000	$4,000	$2,350	$1,450	$1,100	$850	$600

Subtract 20% - 40% for "as modified" or parts guns.
Collectors must be aware of the correct combination of serial number, sight variation, hand guard, and stock cartouche date.

✱ *Model of 1899 Carbine with Parkhurst Device* - scarce/rare, most were destroyed. 100 modified.
Extreme rarity precludes accurate pricing on this model.

GRADING - PPGS™	100%	98%	95%	90%	80%	70%	60%

BOARD OF ORDNANCE RIFLE - 26 in. barrel, rare. 100 mfg.
Extreme rarity precludes accurate pricing on this model.

PHILIPPINE CONSTABULARY RIFLE - records from the Bureau of Insular Affairs show that the civil government of the Philippines purchased Model of 1899 carbines, and had them modified by the U.S. military at the Manila Ordnance Facility. 4,980 converted.
The absence of an authenticated example of this model precludes accurate pricing.

SCHOOL GUN - officially known as the United States Magazine Carbine, Model of 1899, Modified for Use with Knife Bayonet and Gun Sling, these were carbines and stocks modified between 1906-1916 at both Springfield and Rock Island, examples of Springfield modification have been observed with a block J.F.C. cartouche. 3,371 carbines and 6,118 stocks converted.

	$4,500	$3,800	$1,800	$1,200	$1,000	$800	$600

DCM/NRA CARBINE - original carbines and cut down rifles were sold by the DCM to NRA members and others during the 1930s-40s, widely imitated by commercial vendors.

	$1,500	$1,200	$1,000	$800	$600	$500	$400

Buyer beware - this gun should have original documentation before considering a purchase.

KRICO

Current trademark manufactured by Kriegeskorte Handels GmbH, located in Pyrbaum, Germany. Currently imported exclusively beginning mid-2005 by Northeast Arms LLC, located in Fort Fairfield, ME. Previously distributed by Precision Sales, Int'l, located in Westfield, MA 1999-2002. Previously manufactured in Vohburg-Irsching, Germany 1996-1999, and in Fürth-Stadeln, Germany by Sportwaffenfabrik Kriegeskorte GmbH pre-1996.

During 2000, Krico was purchased by Marocchi. Krico has been imported/distributed by over ten U.S. companies/individuals. Krico manufactures high quality rifles, and to date, has mostly sold their guns in Europe. Many of the discontinued models listed below may still be current within the European marketplace. Please contact the importer directly for more information, including availability and pricing (see Trademark Index).

RIFLES: BOLT ACTION

Values and information below reflect the most current information available to the publisher. Please contact the factory directly for current pricing and model availability.

SPORTING RIFLE - .22 Hornet or .222 Rem. cal., miniature Mauser action, 4 shot, 22, 24, or 26 in. barrel, single or double set triggers, open sights, checkered walnut stock, pistol grip. Mfg. 1956-62.

	$605	$550	$495	$440	$400	$360	$305

CARBINE - similar to Sporting Rifle, except 20 or 22 in. barrel, full length stock.

	$635	$580	$415	$470	$420	$375	$320

SPECIAL VARMINT RIFLE - similar to Sporting Rifle, except heavy barrel, no sights.

	$605	$550	$495	$440	$400	$360	$300

MODEL 300 SPORTER - .22 LR, .22 Mag., or .22 Hornet cal., select walnut with straight, checkered stock and fuller forearm, 23 1/2 in. barrel, 5 shot mag., grooved receiver, 6 1/2 lbs. Importation disc. 1999.

	$550	$495	$450	$410	$380	$350	$320

Last MSR was $595.

Add $30 for .22 Mag. cal.
Add $155 for .22 Hornet cal.
This model was designated Model 302 Sporter until 1986.

GRADING - PPGS™	100%	98%	95%	90%	80%	70%	60%

* Model 300 Sporter Deluxe - similar to Model 300 Standard, except has deluxe wood and checkering. Imported 1991-99.

	$625	$550	$480	$430	$385	$350	$320

Last MSR was $695.

Add $25 for .22 Mag. cal.
Add $200 for .22 Hornet cal.

MODEL 311 SMALL BORE RIFLE - .22 LR cal. only, bolt action, 5 or 10 shot, 22 in. barrel, single or double set trigger, open sights, checkered stock. Disc.

	$330	$275	$250	$220	$195	$165	$155

Add 30% for Kahles 2 1/2 power scope.

MODEL 320 MANNLICHER SPORTER - .22 LR, .22 Mag., or .22 Hornet cal., full stock sporter, 19 1/2 in. barrel, 5 shot mag., double set triggers, 6 lbs. Importation disc. 1999.

	$650	$575	$500	$460	$430	$395	$370

Last MSR was $750.

Add $25 for .22 Mag. cal.
Add $150 for .22 Hornet cal.

This model was designated Model 304 Mannlicher Sporter until 1986. In 1991, it was redesignated the Model 320 Stutzen.

MODEL 340 S ST - .22 LR cal. only, silhouette model, 21 in. bull barrel, match trigger, no sights, 5 shot mag., stippled pistol grip and forearm, 7 1/2 lbs. Importation disc. 1999.

	$750	$625	$550	$500	$450	$375	$325

Last MSR was $795.

* Model 340 S ST Kricotronic - similar to above, except with Krico electronic trigger. Importation disc. 1988.

	$1,295	$995	$900	$800	$690	$600	$550

Last MSR was $1,450.

* Model 340 S ST Mini-Sniper - non-glare wood and metal finish, military style barrel with muzzle brake, vent. forearm, no sights, match trigger (interchangeable), 5 shot, raised cheekpiece. Importation disc. 1988.

	$1,050	$825	$725	$600	$550	$500	$450

Last MSR was $1,200.

BIATHLON MODEL 360 S - .22 LR cal., standard biathlon configuration with conventional straight pull bolt. Importation disc. 1999.

	$1,375	$1,075	$925	$750	$625	$550	$500

Last MSR was $1,695.

BIATHLON MODEL 360 S2 - .22 LR cal., biathlon competition rifle featuring unique pistol grip operated rapid fire action, includes 5 mags., aperture sights, snow guards, and black stock. Importation disc. 1999.

	$1,300	$1,050	$900	$750	$625	$550	$500

Last MSR was $1,595.

MODEL 400 SPORTER - .22 LR or .22 Hornet cal., 23 1/2 in. barrel, select checkered walnut with European style curved cheekpiece, 5 shot mag., open sights, 6.8 lbs. Importation disc. 1999.

	$840	$750	$625	$550	$500	$450	$375

Last MSR was $895.

Add $55 for .22 Hornet cal.

* Model 400 Sporter Match Single Shot - .22 LR only, match rifle configuration. Importation disc. 1999.

	$875	$750	$625	$550	$500	$450	$375

Last MSR was $950.

GRADING - PPGS™	100%	98%	95%	90%	80%	70%	60%

✱ *Model 400 Sporter Silhouette* - .22 LR only, designed for silhouette shooting, no sights. Importation disc. 1999.

	$725	$615	$550	$500	$450	$375	$325

Last MSR was $775.

MODEL 420 L ST MANNLICHER SPORTER - .22 Hornet only, full stock sporter, 19 1/2 in. barrel, double set triggers, 5 shot, 6 1/2 lbs.

	$875	$750	$625	$550	$500	$450	$375

MODEL 440 - .22 Hornet, otherwise similar to Model 340. Importation disc. 1988.

	$900	$725	$575	$525	$450	$400	$360

Last MSR was $1,025.

MODEL 600 HUNTING - .222 Rem., .223 Rem., .22-250 Rem., .243 Win., .308 Win., or 5.6x50 Mag. cal., 23 1/2 in. barrel, select checkered walnut with curved European style cheekpiece and vent. forend, 3 or 4 shot mag., open sights, single set trigger, 7 lbs. Importation disc. 1999.

	$1,100	$975	$850	$750	$625	$550	$500

Last MSR was $1,295.

Add $55 for Model 600 SC.
Add $300 for Model 600 Benchrest.
Add $355 for Model 600 in sniper configuration.

This model was also available in single shot configuration at no extra charge as well as in a Match Model Group I & II - add $100 for Group II.

MODEL 620 MANNLICHER SPORTER - same cals. as Model 600, full stock sporter, 20 3/4 in. barrel, double set triggers, 3 shot mag., 6.8 lbs. Importation disc. 1988.

	$1,165	$965	$875	$760	$695	$650	$590

Last MSR was $1,300.

MODEL 640 S ST VARMINT - .22-250 Rem., .222 Rem., or .223 Rem. cal., 23 3/4 in. heavy barrel, high Monte Carlo comb and full cheekpiece, rosewood forearm tip and grip cap, Wundhammer hand swell, double set triggers, 4 shot mag., 9.6 lbs. Importation disc. 1990.

	$875	$750	$625	$550	$500	$450	$375

Last MSR was $950.

✱ *Model 640 S ST Varmint Sniper* - similar to Model 640, except has non-adj. cheekpiece. Importation disc. 1988.

	$1,325	$1,075	$965	$875	$760	$695	$650

Last MSR was $1,500.

MODEL 640 DELUXE/SUPER SNIPER - .223 Rem. or .308 Win. cal., 23 in. barrel, select walnut stock has stippled hand grip, adj. cheekpiece and vent. forearm, engine turned bolt assembly, 3 shot mag., match trigger, 10 lbs. Importation disc. 1988.

	$1,495	$1,175	$1,025	$875	$760	$695	$650

Last MSR was $1,725.

This model was known as the 650 Sniper/Match until 1986.

MODEL 700A ECONOMY - .222 Rem., .243 Win., or .308 Win. cal. (Group I) or 6.5x55mm, 7x64mm, .270 Win., or .30-06 cal. (Group II), without sights, single trigger. Imported 1991-99.

	$900	$775	$650	$550	$500	$450	$375

Last MSR was $995.

Add $70 for Group II cals.

GRADING - PPGS™	100%	98%	95%	90%	80%	70%	60%

MODEL 700 SERIES - .17 Rem., .22-250 Rem., .222 Rem., .222 Rem. Mag., .223 Rem., 5.6x50mm Mag., .243 Win., .308 Win., or 5.6x57 RWS cal. (Group I), 6.5x55mm, 7x57mm, .270 Win., 7x64mm, .30-06, or 9.3x72 cal. (Group II), or 6.5x68mm, 7mm Rem. Mag., .300 Win. Mag., 8x68S, 7.5mm Swiss, or 6x62mm Freres (Group III) cal., matte black metal finish, open sights, approx. 7 lbs. Imported 1991-99.

∗ *Model 700 Series Hunting* - available in Group I or II cals. only, walnut hunting stock with Bavarian cheekpiece, recoil pad, and palm swell grip. Importation disc. 1999.

	$1,075	$950	$850	$750	$625	$550	$500

Last MSR was $1,249.

Add $50 for Group II cals.

∗ *Model 700 Series DeLuxe* - similar to Model 700 Hunting, except has better grade walnut and is available in Group III cals. also. Importation disc. 1999.

	$1,150	$1,000	$875	$750	$625	$550	$500

Last MSR was $1,379.

Add $20 for Group II cals.
Add $71 for Group III cals.
Add $150 for left-hand action.
Add $346-$516 for repeating variation in Groups I-III.

∗ *Model 700 Series Stutzen* - full stock variation (Mannlicher) of the Model 700 DeLuxe. Importation disc. 1999.

	$1,200	$1,025	$895	$750	$625	$550	$500

Last MSR was $1,450.

Add $39 for Group II cals.
Add $160 for Group III cals.
Add $275 for DeLuxe variation (includes better wood and finish).

MODEL 700 DL R SPORTER - .270 Win. or .30-06 cal., 23 1/2 in. barrel, curved European cheekpiece, select walnut, 3 shot Mag., single set trigger, open sights, 7 lbs. Importation disc. 1990.

	$925	$800	$650	$575	$500	$450	$375

Last MSR was $1,025.

Subtract $30 for Model 700 DM ST.
Add $470 for Model 700 DLM.

MODEL 720 MANNLICHER SPORTER - similar to Model 700, only has 20 3/4 in. barrel, double set triggers, 6.8 lbs. Importation disc. 1990.

	$1,100	$975	$850	$750	$625	$550	$500

Last MSR was $1,295.

∗ *Model 720 Mannlicher Sporter Limited Edition* - .270 Win. cal. only, 24Kt. gold scroll work on bolt handle, receiver, barrel, and mounts. Trigger and front sight are gold plated. Serial numbered in gold. Disc. 1986.

	$2,310	$1,990	$1,700	$1,450	$1,200	$1,050	$950

Last MSR was $2,659.

MODEL 902 DELUX GRADE I - .222 Rem., .243 Win., .270 Win., .30-06, 6.5x55mm, 7x64mm, 8x68mm, 9.3x64mm, or 7mm Rem. Mag. cal., 22 1/4 or 24 1/4 in. barrel, Oxidal deep black or satin finish, various grades, checkered walnut stock and forend. Importation began late 1999, mfg. by CD Europe, srl.

MSR N/A	$1,650	$1,400	$1,200	$995	$875	$750	$625

∗ *Model 902 Delux Grade II*

MSR N/A	$3,100	$2,750	$2,375	$2,050	$1,750	$1,450	$1,150

∗ *Model 902 Delux Grade III*

MSR N/A	$3,950	$3,500	$3,100	$2,750	$2,375	$2,050	$1,750

GRADING - PPGS™	100%	98%	95%	90%	80%	70%	60%

❋ *Model 902 Delux Grade IV*

    MSR N/A $4,950 $4,450 $3,800 $3,200 $2,600 $2,250 $1,875

❋ *Model 902 Delux Grade V* - custom model, individually built per customer specifications, POR.

RIFLES: SEMI-AUTO

MODEL 260 SPORTER - .22 LR cal. only, standard features. Importation began 1991.

    MSR N/A $550 $495 $450 $410 $380 $350 $320

H. KRIEGHOFF GUN CO. (SHOTGUNS OF ULM)

Current manufacturer located in Ulm, Germany since circa 1954. Previous manufacture was in Suhl, Germany 1886-1947. Currently imported and distributed by Krieghoff International, Inc. located in Ottsville, PA. Dealer direct sales only.

KRIEGHOFF

    Currently, Krieghoff manufacturers 2,000 guns annually, in all configurations.

DRILLINGS

H. Krieghoff drillings can be ordered with a variety of cals. (.222 Rem., .243 Win., .270 Win., or .30-06) and special order features. The universal trigger system (UAS) and Combicocking device are standard on all Plus, Steingass, and Quadro drillings. Prices shown below are for standard guns with no options. Better models will have a finer grade walnut and exhibit more elaborate deep relief engraving.

    Add $450 for free floating rifle barrels on Trumpf and Neptun Models listed below (both regular steel frame and Dural variations).

    Add $1,290 for 3-claw scope mount system (disc.).

PLUS MODEL - 12, 16, or 20 ga. over rifle barrel (.222 Rem., .243 Win., .270 Win., or .30-06 cal.), boxlock action, includes universal trigger system (UAS) as standard, light engraving, choice of soldered or free floating rifle barrel with adj. point of impact (Thermo TS Stabil - Model Plus TS). Mfg. 1988-2004.

     $5,125 $3,650 $2,800 $2,200 $1,825 $1,525 $1,200

    Last MSR was $6,275.

    Add $1,700 for full length stock (Model Steingass, 20 ga. only).

QUADRO TS MODEL - 12 or 20 ga. over 21 1/2 in. rifle barrel (various rifle cals.), features Thermo Stabil barrels, standard engraving is small arabesque, includes soft case. New 2003.

    MSR $10,950 $9,350 $8,200 $7,100 $6,500 $5,500 $4,500 $3,500

    Add $2,800 for Quadro 20 Model with double rifle and 20 ga. shotgun barrel configuration.

    Add $2,295 - $2,595 for KS full length rifled barrel insert, depending on caliber (up to 9.3x74R).

    Add $1,975 for pivot mount for installed and sighted in pivot mount.

    Add $975 for single trigger, or $1,295 for single/double trigger.

❋ *Quadro African Drilling* - .20 ga. under rifle barrels (.375 flanged mag. NE, .500/.416 NE or .470 NE), 20 ga. drilling frame with reinforced sidewalls, hinged front trigger, similar sights as the Classic Big 5 double rifle. New 2003.

    This gun is available by custom order only - pricing starts at $22,500.

TRUMPF MODEL - 12, 16, or 20 ga. O/U, or rifle shotgun combo., various cals., boxlock, 25 in. barrels, 7 1/2 lbs. Disc. 2003.

     $8,300 $6,300 $5,350 $4,250 $3,300 $2,750 $2,200

    Last MSR was $9,950.

    Add $1,850 for single trigger.

GRADING - PPGS™	100%	98%	95%	90%	80%	70%	60%

✻ *Trumpf Model Dural* - Dural aluminum frame variation of the Trumpf, 6.8 lbs., cased. Disc. 2003.

	$8,300	$6,300	$5,350	$4,250	$3,300	$2,750	$2,200

Last MSR was $9,950.

NEPTUN MODEL - 12, 16, or 20 ga., variety of cals., elaborate engraving, side-locks. Pre-WWII-disc. 2003.

	$13,250	$10,400	$9,000	$7,550	$6,200	$5,100	$4,150

Last MSR was $16,500.

✻ *Neptun Model Dural* - Dural aluminum frame variation of the Neptun, cased. Disc. 2003.

	$13,250	$10,400	$9,000	$7,550	$6,200	$5,100	$4,150

Last MSR was $16,500.

NEPTUN PRIMUS MODEL - similar to Neptun Model, only hand detachable side-locks and elaborate deep relief engraving. Disc. 2003.

	$18,500	$13,650	$10,450	$8,400	$7,100	$5,850	$4,950

Last MSR was $24,500.

✻ *Neptun Primus Model Dural* - Dural aluminum frame variation available at no extra charge. Disc. 2003.

	$18,500	$13,650	$10,450	$8,400	$7,100	$5,850	$4,950

Last MSR was $24,500.

PISTOLS: SEMI-AUTO

WWII Krieghoff Lugers will appear in the Luger section of this text.

KRIEGHOFF LUGER - 9mm Para. cal., 8 shot mag., toggle lock action, based on the WWII production with checkered walnut grips, 4 in. barrel, and special ser. no. range. Only 200 mfg. beginning 2006, serial numbered 18001-18200.

MSR $15,950		$14,500	$12,000	$9,000	$7,000	$5,000	$4,000	$3,500

RIFLES: DOUBLE, O/U & SxS

Various grades differ in style and amount of engraving, choice of walnut and various options that can be special ordered.

Add $1,950 for 4-claw scope mount (standard or European).

TECK O/U - .30-06, .300 Win. Mag. (disc. 1994), .308 Win., 7x56R (disc. 1994), 7x65R (new 1995), 8x57JRS, 8x75RS (new 1995), 9.3x74R, .375 H&H (disc. 1988), or .458 Win. Mag. cal., 25 in. barrels, boxlock action, cocking indicators, hard case included.

	$8,725	$6,475	$5,200	$4,300	$3,650	$3,300	$3,000

Last MSR was $10,500.

Add $1,400 for .375 H&H or .458 Win. Mag. cal.
Add $990 for DTs with front set trigger.

✻ *Teck-Handspanner O/U* - 7x65R, .30-06, or .308 Win. cal. on 16 ga. receiver frame, manual cocking.

	$10,200	$7,950	$6,675	$5,175	$4,375	$3,950	$3,200

Last MSR was $12,495.

ULTRA TS O/U - various cals. up to 9.3x74R, features unique manual cocking/self cocking device and interchangeable muzzle wedge for adjustable point of impact. New 1993.

MSR $8,980		$7,950	$6,950	$5,900	$5,000	$4,275	$3,500	$2,950

Add $975 for single trigger.

GRADING - PPGS™	100%	98%	95%	90%	80%	70%	60%

CLASSIC O/U - same standard cals. as Teck O/U, boxlock action, light engraving. Mfg. 1995-2004.

	$6,975	$5,900	$5,150	$4,300	$3,500	$2,950	$2,250

Last MSR was $7,850.

✳ *Classic O/U Big Five (Big Bore)* - .375 H&H, .375 Flanged Mag. NE, .500/.416 NE, .458 Win. Mag., .470 NE, or .500 NE/3 in. cal. Mfg. 1995-2004.

	$8,250	$6,925	$5,950	$5,000	$4,150	$3,350	$3,150

Last MSR was $9,450.

ULM O/U - similar to Teck Double Rifle, except has any combination of cals., with sidelocks and more elaborate engraving.

	$14,300	$10,350	$8,550	$6,900	$6,100	$5,500	$4,950

Last MSR was $17,900.

Add $695 for hand detachable sidelocks.
Add $1,775 with single/double trigger.

✳ *Ulm O/U Dekor* - sidelock with light scroll engraving. Importation disc. 1991.

	$10,450	$9,150	$8,000	$6,750	$5,600	$5,000	$4,400

Last MSR was $12,500.

✳ *Ulm O/U Primus* - deluxe sidelock. Disc. 2004.

	$19,750	$13,000	$10,250	$8,100	$6,550	$5,700	$5,300

Last MSR was $26,000.

TRUMPF SxS - boxlock action, similar to Teck model, except in .30-06, 8x57JRS, or 9.3x74R cal. Disc. 1994.

	$13,200	$9,700	$8,350	$6,900	$6,100	$5,500	$4,950

Last MSR was $16,150.

CLASSIC SxS STANDARD - current cals. include .30-06, 7x57R, 7x65R, .30R Blaser, 8x57JRS, 8x75RS, and 9.3x74R, boxlock action, 21 1/2 (optional) or 23 1/2 in. regulated barrels, DTs, Combi cocking device, removable wedge and integrated front sight in cals. up to .375 H&H, extractors, choice of standard or Bavarian style stock, light engraving, with or w/o sideplates, various engraving options, 7 1/2 - 11 lbs. New 1995.

MSR $9,795	$8,950	$7,725	$6,500	$5,400	$4,500	$3,550	$2,950

Add $3,995 for a set of 20 ga., 3 in. chambered barrels.
Add $5,750 per set of interchangeable rifle barrels.
Add $3,950 for sideplates with standard scroll engraving or $1,725 for boxlock standard engraving.

✳ *Classic SxS Standard Big Five (Big Bore)* - .375 H&H, .375 Flanged Mag. NE (new 1996), .416 Rigby, .458 Win. Mag., .470 NE, .500/.416 NE (new 1996) or .500 NE cal., hinged front trigger, non-removable muzzle wedge, 23 1/2 in. barrels with express style quarter rib, 9 1/2 - 10 1/2 lbs. New 1995.

MSR $12,795	$10,950	$8,600	$7,500	$6,500	$5,500	$5,000	$4,500

Add $3,995 for a set of 20 ga./3 in. barrels.
Add $7,950 per set of interchangeable rifle barrels.
Add $3,950 for sideplates with standard scroll engraving or $1,725 for boxlock standard engraving.

NEPTUN SxS - sidelock double rifle, same features as the Ulm model. Importation disc. 1991.

	$12,750	$10,400	$8,700	$7,350	$6,000	$5,450	$4,995

Last MSR was $15,500.

RIFLES: SINGLE SHOT

HUBERTUS RIFLE - available in .22-250 Rem., .222 Rem., .243 Win., .270 Win., .30-06, .308 Win., .270 Wby. Mag. (disc.), .300 Win. Mag., 7mm Rem. Mag., and in 12 metric cals. between 5.6x50R Mag. - 9.3x74R, single shot stalking rifle with Kickspanner (unique manual cocking device), engraved boxlock

GRADING - PPGS™	100%	98%	95%	90%	80%	70%	60%

action, 23 1/2 in. barrel with quarter rib, fast lock time, double underlugs, approx. 6 1/2 lbs. Importation began circa 1997.

MSR $5,995	$5,500	$4,725	$4,000	$3,450	$2,950	$2,575	$1,850

Add $1,000 for Mag. cals.
Add $3,950 for sideplates with standard scroll engraving.

RIFLES: SLIDE ACTION

SEMPRIO - .243 Win., .270 Win., 7x64, .30-06,.308 Win., 8x57IS, 9.3x62mm, 7mm Rem. Mag., or .300 Win. Mag. cal., unique in-line action is operating by using the forearm to slide the barrel assembly forward (not backward), fluted bolt, full take-down capability, 3 shot detachable mag., 21.7 or 25 (Mag. cals.) in. barrel, open sights, checkered pistol grip stock, universal trigger system, drilled and tapped, black or nickel anodized finish, combi cocking device, sling swivels, rubber recoil pad, approx. 7 1/2 lbs. New 2007.

MSR $4,990	$4,500	$3,950	$3,500	$3,000	$2,500	$2,000	$1,650

Add $400 for Mag. cals.
Add $1,890 - $2,300 per extra barrel, depending on configuration.

SHOTGUNS: O/U

Subtract 15% for 26 in. barrels on used models.
Subtract 25% for 26 in. barrels on used higher grade models.
Add $1,850 - $2,100 for "KS" full length rifle insert barrel, depending on caliber - available in 12, 16, or 20 ga. (new 2006).

MODEL 32 STANDARD - 12, 20, 28 ga., or .410 bore, O/U, 28-32 in. high rib barrels, ejectors, boxlock, single trigger, select wood. Disc. 1983.

Standard	$2,500	$2,250	$2,000	$1,900	$1,700	$1,500	$1,250
San Remo	$5,250	$4,500	$3,750	$3,000	$2,250	$1,950	$1,650
Monte Carlo	$6,750	$5,625	$4,875	$4,125	$3,000	$2,250	$1,875
Crown	$7,500	$6,000	$5,250	$4,500	$3,375	$2,625	$2,250
Super Crown	$9,000	$7,500	$6,000	$5,250	$3,750	$3,000	$2,625

✻ *Model 32 Standard Low Rib* - 28 ga. or .410 bore.

	$3,950	$3,575	$2,875	$2,650	$2,200	$1,900	$1,600

Add approx. 20% for two-barrel set.

MODEL 32 4-BARREL SKEET SET - 12, 20, 28 ga., or .410 bore, O/U, matched barrels in case, grades differ in engraving and wood quality. Disc. 1983.

Standard	$8,450	$7,450	$6,500	$5,600	$4,650	$3,725	$2,775
München Grade	$9,950	$8,450	$7,450	$6,500	$5,600	$4,650	$3,725
San Remo Grade (unmarked)	$12,750	$10,350	$8,250	$6,750	$5,850	$4,950	$4,750
Monte Carlo (Silver Crown, 50 mfg.)	$18,750	$16,000	$13,750	$11,000	$9,000	$7,800	$6,600
Crown Grade (400 mfg.)	$24,995	$21,000	$17,750	$14,750	$12,100	$10,350	$9,650
Super Crown Grade (48 mfg.)	$29,995	$25,750	$20,750	$16,750	$14,775	$12,650	$10,350

K-20 SPORTING AND FIELD - 20, 28 ga., or .410 bore, compact 20 ga. frame, incorporates all of the technical refinements of the K-80, nickel plated receiver with satin grey finish and classic scroll engraving, 28 or 30 in. separated barrels (28 ga. and .410 bore barrels can be purchased separately but must be fitted) with tapered flat rib, SST, AE, checkered walnut stock and Schnabel forearm, includes 5 choke tubes, approx. 7 1/4 lbs., includes fitted aluminum case. Importation began 2000.

MSR $10,695	$8,000	$7,000	$6,000	$5,500	$4,750	$4,000	$3,200

Add $155 for 28 ga. or .410 bore.
Add $3,995 for extra set of 20 ga. barrels, or $4,150 for 28 ga. or .410 bore.
Add $850-$3,500 for wood upgrades, depending on quality.
Add $4,150 for 20/28 ga. set or $8,320 for 3 gauge set.
A 20/28 ga. set with 10 choke tubes and hard case is also available for $13,945. A 3 gauge set (20,

GRADING - PPGS™	100%	98%	95%	90%	80%	70%	60%

28 ga. and .410 bore) with 15 choke tubes and hard case is also available for $18,115

Additional options for the K-20 include case colors ($2,250), and K-20 models with engraving options include Super Standard ($13,495 MSR), Super Scroll ($15,495 MSR), Suhl Scroll ($17,195 MSR), Parcours Special ($16,445 MSR), Gold Super Scroll (coin or blue finish, $18,795 MSR), Bavaria (disc. 2004) Bavaria Royale (new 2005, $18,690 MSR), Gold Uplander (coin or blue finish, $22,295 MSR), Gold Plantation Scroll (coin or blue finish, $20,595 MSR), Plantation Scroll/Uplander (nickel or blue finish, $17,445 MSR), Millennium ($28,695 MSR, new 2005), Waterfowl Medallion Nitride ($25,595, new 2005), and Bavaria Suhl ($25,145 MSR).

K-80 TRAP - 12 ga. only, available in O/U, Unsingle, Top Single (single top barrel, disc. 2005 w/fixed rib), and Combo (O/U with extra trap barrel) configurations, standard model has silver finished receiver, adj. rib allowing variable points of impact (new 1993). In O/U configuration the barrels are separated, about 8 1/2 lbs. A wide variety of custom order options can be ordered on this model.

> Add $750 for O/U barrel screw-in chokes capability (5 tubes).
> Add $475 for 3 screw-in chokes capability (single barrel guns only).
> Add $3,195 (O/U) or $4,425 (unsingle) per extra barrel(s), w/o choke tubes.
> Add $550 for single release trigger or $895 for double release trigger.
> Subtract 20% for old style receiver with "K-80" on side.

Beginning 2000, options for the K-80 Trap include case colors ($2,250), and K-80 models with engraving options include: Super Standard (new 2005, $2,100 MSR), Super Scroll ($4,100 MSR), Suhl Scroll ($5,700 MSR), Parcours Special ($5,200 MSR), Gold Super Scroll (coin or blue finish, $6,950 MSR), Gold Uplander (coin or blue finish, $10,400 MSR), Gold Plantation Scroll (coin or blue finish, $9,200 MSR), Plantation Scroll/Uplander (nickel or blue finish, $5,800 MSR), and Bavaria Suhl ($13,000 MSR).

Additonal custom engraving options (must be added to the Standard Grade price) include: Bavaria/Bavaria Royale ($7,300), Millenium ($10,800), Waterfowl Medallion ($12,500), Gold Bavarian Royale ($14,900), Danube ($28,000), and Gold Target ($31,500).

* **K-80 Trap Standard Unsingle** - 32 or 34 in. lower barrel with either fixed choke or choke tubes.

MSR $11,700	$8,725	$7,350	$6,000	$4,550	$3,550	$3,200	$2,850

> Add $1,300 for Trap Special Unsingle (new 2007).
> Add approx. 30% for Combo (includes unsingle and O/U barrels), or approx. 35%-75% for Trap Special Combo CTIII (new 2005), depending on grade.
> Add $475 for choke tubes.

* **K-80 Trap Standard O/U** - 30 or 32 in. barrels with either fixed chokes or choke tubes.

MSR $9,945	$7,675	$6,350	$5,275	$4,250	$3,325	$2,900	$2,600

> Add $825 for Trap Special Model (new 2007).
> Add approx. 50% for Combo Standard K-80 variations.
> Subtract 20% for top single variation (very limited mfg.).
> Add $750 for choke tubes.

* **K-80 Trap Centennial Model** - 12 ga. only, available in combo configuration only, 100 only mfg. 1986 to commemorate Krieghoff's centennial year, ser. no. 14501-14600, H. Krieghoff's signature inlaid in gold on frame sides.

	$6,000	$5,000	$4,400	$3,825	$3,400	$2,950	$2,600

Last MSR was $5,995.

K-80 SKEET/SKEET SPECIAL - 12 ga. only, available in Standardweight (8mm rib) or International (12mm rib) configuration, 28 or 30 in. barrels, approx. 8 3/4 lbs.

Beginning 2000, options for the K-80 Skeet include case colors ($2,250),and K-80 models with engraving options include: Super Standard (new 2005, $2,800 MSR), Super Scroll ($4,800 MSR), Suhl Scroll ($6,500 MSR), Parcours Special ($5,750 MSR), Gold Super Scroll (coin or blue finish, $8,100 MSR), Gold Uplander (coin or blue finish, $11,600 MSR), Gold Plantation Scroll (coin or blue finish, $9,900 MSR), Plantation Scroll/Uplander (nickel or blue finish, $6,750 MSR), and Bavaria Suhl ($14,450 MSR).

Additonally, custom engraving options (added to the Standard Grade price) are also available. Add $7,995 for Bavaria Royale, $10,800 for Millenium (disc. 2007), $15,900 for Waterfowl Medallion, $19,200 for Gold Bavaria, $20,900 for Monarch, and $11,900 for Schilling Scroll.Gold Target, Danube, Crown, Majestic, and San Remo Bulino engraving are POR.

GRADING - PPGS™	100%	98%	95%	90%	80%	70%	60%

✳ **K-80 Skeet/Skeet Special Standard Model** - available in Standardweight frame, hard case optional.

MSR $9,470	$7,000	$6,000	$4,800	$3,625	$2,950	$2,450	$2,150

Add $3,245 per extra set of barrels with fixed chokes, $3,995 with choke tubes (Skeet Special), or $3,550 for heavy Skeet barrels.
Subtract 20% for receivers with "K-80" on side.
Add $750 for choke tubes.

✳ **K-80 Skeet Special Model** - similar to Standard Model, except includes 5 choke tubes and tapered flat rib.

MSR $10,220	$7,500	$6,500	$5,000	$4,100	$3,350	$2,850	$2,500

Subtract 20% for receivers with "K-80" on side.

✳ **K-80 Special Centennial Skeet** - available in skeet configuration - special features as noted above on Centennial Model description listed under K-80 Trap. Mfg. 1986 only.

$3,675	$3,150	$2,700	$2,425	$2,100	$1,800	$1,650

Last MSR was $3,980.

K-80 2-BARREL LIGHTWEIGHT SKEET SET - 12 ga., includes one set of 28 in. barrels with Tula chokes and one set of carrier barrels allowing use of sub-gauge tubes (carrier barrels cannot be used for 12 ga.), 8mm rib, hard case standard. Mfg. 1988-99.

✳ *K-80 2-Barrel Lightweight Skeet Set Standard Grade*

$8,750	$7,000	$5,150	$4,300	$3,875	$3,300	$3,000

Last MSR was $11,840.

Subtract $1,845 for heavy barrel variation, which does not include sub-gauge tubes.
Retail price for 2 barrel heavy set with choke tubes was $9,995.

✳ *K-80 2-Barrel Lightweight Skeet Set Bavaria Model* - game scene engraved silver receiver with light perimeter scroll work, select walnut. Imported 1988-99.

$12,950	$10,000	$8,000	$7,200	$6,200	$5,250	$4,800

Last MSR was $16,990.

Subtract $1,845 for heavy barrel variation, which does not include sub-gauge tubes.
Retail price for 2 barrel heavy set with choke tubes was $15,145.

✳ *K-80 2-Barrel Lightweight Skeet Set Danube Model* - fine English scroll work on receiver sides and floor plate. Imported 1988-99.

$22,945	$15,250	$17,750	$9,400	$7,750	$7,000	$6,650

Last MSR was $28,090.

Subtract $1,845 for heavy barrel variation, which does not include sub-gauge tubes.
Retail price for 2 barrel heavy set with choke tubes was $26,245.

✳ *K-80 2-Barrel Lightweight Skeet Set Gold Target Model* - deep chiseled scroll engraving with gold line accents, 100% coverage finest quality walnut. Importation disc. 1999.

$25,975	$20,500	$15,950	$12,375	$9,950	$8,700	$7,500

Last MSR was $31,635.

Subtract $1,845 for heavy barrel variation.
Retail price for heavy 2 barrel set with choke tubes was $29,790.

K-80 4-BARREL SKEET SET - 1 barrel each of 12, 20, 28 ga., and .410 bore, 12 ga. is Tula choked (even patterning), 8mm tapered flat or standard VR, includes hard case. Since most shooters prefer different gauge insert tubes (Briley, etc.) rather than barrel sets, values have gone down considerably recently for these 4 gauge sets.

✳ *K-80 4-Barrel Skeet Set Standard Grade* - satin finished receiver with skeet scroll engraving. Importation disc. 1999.

$10,000	$8,000	$6,500	$5,350	$4,500	$4,000	$3,650

Last MSR was $16,950.

GRADING - PPGS™	100%	98%	95%	90%	80%	70%	60%

✴ *K-80 4-Barrel Skeet Set Bavaria Model* - game scene engraved silver receiver with light perimeter scrollwork, select walnut. Importation disc. 1999.

	$14,000	$12,000	$9,500	$8,250	$6,900	$5,400	$4,350

Last MSR was $22,100.

✴ *K-80 4-Barrel Skeet Set Danube Model* - fine English scroll work on receiver sides and floor plate. Importation disc. 1999.

	$22,500	$17,000	$13,000	$10,500	$8,700	$7,500	$6,250

Last MSR was $33,200.

✴ *K-80 4-Barrel Skeet Set Gold Target Model* - deep chiseled scroll engraving with gold line accents, 100% coverage finest quality walnut. Importation disc. 1999.

	$29,650	$17,350	$13,000	$10,500	$8,700	$7,500	$6,250

Last MSR was $36,745.

K-80 PIGEON - 12 ga. only, available with 28 or 30 in. barrels, standard tapered step rib, IM/F choking, available in Standardweight configuration.

Beginning 1992, the K-80 Pigeon Model is available by special order only. Rather than list the various Pigeon models separately, their current values will be approximately the same as the corresponding K-80 Trap/Skeet Models listed.

ULM-P LIVE PIGEON - 12 ga. only, live pigeon gun with hand detachable sidelocks, 28 or 30 in. VR barrels, standard grade has light scrollwork engraving.

	$17,500	$12,000	$9,175	$7,700	$6,000	$5,450	$4,995

Last MSR was $22,500.

✴ *ULM-P Live Pigeon Bavaria Grade* - similar to Ulm-P, only with elaborate game scene engraving.

	$22,000	$16,000	$12,000	$9,000	$7,250	$6,000	$5,500

Last MSR was $29,500.

K-80 SPORTING CLAYS - 12 ga. only, 28, 30 (new 1991), 32 (new 1993), or 34 (new 2003) in. barrels with 5 choke tubes, choice of 8mm VR skeet, tapered flat (broadway) or step rib (special order), sporting clay stock dimensions. New 1988.

For options on the Model K-80 Sporting, please refer to the options on the K-80 Skeet, as they are similar in price.

✴ *K-80 Sporting Clays Standard Grade* - satin finished receiver with sporting scroll engraving.

MSR $10,695			$8,000	$7,000	$6,000	$5,650	$5,050	$4,300	$3,450

Add $3,995 for extra set of O/U barrels with 5 choke tubes or $3,595 w/o choke tubes.

Subtract 10% for 28 in. barrels.

KS-2 SERIES - any ga., full H&H type sidelocks, priced by individual special order. Prices started at $24,000. Disc. 1988.

SHOTGUNS: O/U OR COMBINATION GUNS

Add $695 for hand detachable sidelocks (Ulm only).
Add $1,290 for 4-claw scope mount system (disc.).
Add $1,150 for pivot mount system.

TECK MODEL - 12 and 16 ga., O/U shotgun or rifle/shotgun combo., various cals. (7x57R, 7x64mm, 7x65R, .30-06, or .308 Win.), boxlock action, Kersten double crossbolt, auto ejectors, 7 1/2 lbs. Importation disc. 2004.

	$6,650	$5,100	$4,400	$3,550	$3,000	$2,600	$2,295

Last MSR was $7,750.

✴ *Teck Model Dural* - dural aluminum frame variation of the Teck, 6.8 lbs. Importation disc. 2004.

	$6,625	$5,100	$4,400	$3,550	$3,000	$2,600	$2,295

Last MSR was $7,750.

GRADING - PPGS™	100%	98%	95%	90%	80%	70%	60%

ULM - similar to Teck, except sidelock and fully engraved with leaf arabesques. Importation disc. 2004.

	$12,325	$9,250	$7,950	$6,350	$5,250	$4,400	$3,500

Last MSR was $14,500.

* *Ulm Dural* - dural aluminum frame variation of the Ulm. Importation disc. 2004.

	$12,325	$9,250	$7,950	$6,350	$5,250	$4,400	$3,500

Last MSR was $14,500.

ULM PRIMUS - similar to Ulm, except game scene engraved with English arabesques. Importation disc. 2004.

	$19,000	$13,750	$10,000	$8,750	$7,500	$6,250	$5,500

Last MSR was $22,850.

* *Ulm Primus Dural* - dural aluminum frame variation of the Ulm Primus. Importation disc. 2004.

	$19,000	$13,750	$10,000	$8,750	$7,500	$6,250	$5,500

Last MSR was $22,850.

ULTRA TS COMBINATION GUN - 12 (disc. 2007) or 20 ga., combination O/U, various calibers (lower barrel), 25 in. barrels, "Kickspanner" mechanism allows manual cocking from thumb safety, satin finish receiver, VR, 6 lbs. New 1985.

MSR $7,890	$6,650	$5,650	$4,950	$4,250	$3,600	$2,950	$2,300

* *Ultra-B TS Combination Gun* - similar to Ultra, except features a selector to switch the front set trigger to the top shotgun barrel. Disc. 1995.

	$4,050	$2,675	$1,925	$1,550	$1,350	$1,150	$1,000

Last MSR was $4,990.

SHOTGUNS: SxS

ESSENCIA - 12, 16, 20 , 28 ga. or .410 bore (sidelock only), 2 3/4 or 3 (20 ga.) in. chambers, round body boxlock or back action sidelock, 26 1/2, 28, or 30 in. barrels choked IC/Mod., four frame sizes, ejectors, DTs, color case hardened receiver with fine English scroll engraving, gold plated cocking indicators and Krieghoff engraved in gold on receiver sides, Turkish walnut straight grip stock with semi-beavertail forearm, Americase (disc.) or Krieghoff leather case, 6 3/4 - 7 lbs. New 2003.

MSR $29,895	$22,950	$18,750	$15,750	$13,250	$11,000	$9,500	$8,250

Subtract $3,945 for boxlock action (not available in .410 bore).
Add $1,000 for 28 ga.
Add $4,055 for 28 ga. on small frame (sidelock only).
Add $5,055 for .410 bore on 28 ga. frame (sidelock only).
Add $1,500 for Briley thin wall choke tubes.
Add $1,450 for single non-selective trigger. Add $2,000 for wood upgrade. Add $1,500 for oak and leather case.
Add $10,450 - $12,750 for extra set of interchangable barrels, depending on ga./bore.

Krieghoff also manufactures special editions of this gun on a private label basis for LeArmes, featuring a North American Game Bird Series (including Woodland Grade, Upland Grade, and Sierra Nevada Grade).

SHOTGUNS: SINGLE BARREL TRAP

MODEL 32 - 12 ga., same action as Model 32 O/U, 32-34 in. barrel, VR, mod., imp. mod., or full choke.

	$1,800	$1,700	$1,600	$1,500	$1,400	$1,300	$1,200

KS-5 - 12 ga. only, 32 or 34 in. barrel, adj. point of impact, innovative trigger configuration, optional choke tubes, redesigned streamlined receiver (new 1993). Mfg. 1985-99.

	$2,500	$2,250	$2,100	$2,000	$1,875	$1,625	$1,400

Last MSR was $3,675.

Add $2,100 per additional barrel.

GRADING - PPGS™	100%	98%	95%	90%	80%	70%	60%

Add $200 for screw-in choke option.
Add $200 for factory adj. comb stock.
Subtract $250 if w/o factory aluminum case.
Subtract 20% for blued receiver.
Subtract 15% for receiver with "KS-5" engraved on sides.
Subtract 10% for 32 in. barrel.

Adj. point of impact on this model is achieved by means of different, optional front hangers.

* **KS-5 Special** - 12 ga. only, 32 or 34 in. barrel, features adj. rib and comb stock, cased. Mfg. 1990-99.

	$3,700	**$3,250**	**$2,975**	**$2,475**	**$2,050**	**$1,750**	**$1,500**

Last MSR was $4,695.

Add $2,750 per additional barrel.
Add $200 for screw-in choke option.
Subtract 10% for 32 in. barrel.

KX-5 - 12 ga. only, 2 3/4 in. chamber, 32 (disc. 2005) or 34 in. barrel, adj. point of impact, innovative adj. trigger (pull or release type), adj. stock comb, light scroll engraving, includes choke tubes and aluminum case. New 2002.

MSR $5,995		**$4,695**	**$4,200**	**$3,400**	**$3,000**	**$2,650**	**$2,400**	**$2,150**

Add $425 for factory release trigger.
Subtract 10% for 32 in. barrel.

KRISS

Current manufacturer of civilian and law enforcement firearms established in 2007 and located in Washington, D.C.

Kriss offers semi-automatic paramilitary rifles and carbines under the Vector trademark, in addition to a Kriss-based semi-auto shotgun. Please contact the company directly for more information, including configurations, availability, and pricing (see Trademark Index).

KUFSTEINER WAFFENSTUBE

Previous rifle manufacturer located in Kufstein, Austria.

RIFLES

Kufsteiner rifles were essentially built per individual order, and should be appraised by a knowledgeable person for an accurate price evaluation based on condition, quality of materials/construction and special features.

In addition to his unique bolt action, he also made other bolt action designs and O/U rifles as well.

Additionally, Kepplinger also manufactured an entire range of set triggers for many popular domestic rifles - these were distributed through Brownell's, located in Montezuma, IA. The company also made double stage triggers for Mauser M-98 rifles.

KAISERBUCHSE 3-S SYSTEM BOLT ACTION RIFLE - various cals. inlcuding Magnum calibers, unique short action allows for straight on cartridge loading, high strength alloy main parts, grip safety on lower pistol grip, unique uncocking device allowing manual cocking/decocking of the firing pin spring, 23.6 in. standard barrel, 3 shot detachable mag., iron sights, receiver drilled for scope mounts, best quality wood, available in either Schnabel forearm or Mannlicher configuration, many styles of engraving are optional, 7.14 lbs.

JAGERBUCHSE REPEATING RIFLE - various cals., bolt action, 3 front locking lugs, firing pin safety, ST, removable 5 shot mag., European walnut stock with Bavarian cheekpiece and Schnabel forearm, 5.8-10 lbs.

KUPEC, PAVEL

Current longarm manufacturer located in the Czech Republic. No current U.S. importation.

Pavel Kupec manufactures high quality hunting and sporting longarms made to custom order. For more information, including pricing and availability, please contact the factory directly (see Trademark Index).

L SECTION

L.A.R. MANUFACTURING, INC.

Current rifle manufacturer located in West Jordan, UT. Dealer sales.

GRADING - PPGS™	100%	98%	95%	90%	80%	70%	60%

PISTOLS: SEMI-AUTO

GRIZZLY WIN. MAG. MARK I - .357 Mag., .357/.45 Grizzly Win. Mag. (new 1990), .45 ACP, 10mm, or .45 Win. Mag. cal., single action, based on the Colt 1911 design, 5.4 in. (new 1986), 6 1/2 in., 8 in. (new 1987), or 10 in. (new 1987) barrel, parkerized finish, 7 shot mag., ambidextrous safeties, checkered rubber grips, adj. sights, 48 oz. Also can be converted to .45 ACP, 10mm (new 1988), .357 Mag., or .30 Mauser (disc.). Mfg. 1984-1999.

* *Grizzly Win. Mag. Mark I Short Barrel Lengths* - 5.4 or 6 1/2 in. barrel.

$875	$675	$625	$525	$495	$475	$450

Last MSR was $1,000.

Add $14 for .357 Mag. cal.
Add $150 for hard chrome or nickel frame.
Add $260 for full hard chrome or nickel frame.
Add $233-$248 for cal. conversion units.

Conversion units include .357 Mag., 10mm, .40 S&W (1991-1993 only), and .45 ACP cals.

* *Grizzly Win. Mag. Mark I Long Barrel Lengths* - .357 Mag., .45 Win. Mag., or .357/.45 Grizzly Win. Mag. (new 1990) cal., 8 or 10 in. barrel, extended slides. Disc. 1995.

$1,195	$975	$895	$800	$725	$650	$575

Last MSR was $1,313.

Add $62 for 10 in. barrel.
Add $24 for .357 Mag.
Add $143 for scope mounts (disc.).
Add $110 for muzzle compensator.

* *Grizzly Win. Mag. Mark I State Special Edition* - .45 Grizzly Win. Mag., 50 mfg. beginning 1998 to commemorate each state (ser. numbers match the order each state was admitted to the union), features gold etchings on frame, gold small parts, faux mother-of-pearl grips, cased. Limited mfg. 1998-99.

Regional demand/interest preclude accurate pricing on this model.

GRIZZLY .44 MAG. MARK 4 - .44 Mag. cal., choice of lusterless blue, parkerized, chrome, or nickel finish, 5.4 or 6 1/2 in. barrel, adj. sights. Mfg. 1991-99.

$875	$715	$635	$550	$495	$475	$450

Last MSR was $1,014.

GRIZZLY .50 MARK 5 - .50 Action Express cal., single action semi-auto, 5.4 or 6 1/2 in. barrel, 6 shot mag., checkered walnut grips, 56 oz. Mfg. 1993-99.

$1,025	$865	$720	$615	$525	$495	$475

Last MSR was $1,152.

Add $178-$189 per coversion unit (new 1996).

GRIZZLY WIN. MAG. MARK II - similar to Mark I, except has fixed sights, standard safeties, and different metal finish. Mfg. 1986 only.

$625	$550	$525	$495	$475	$450	$425

Last MSR was $550.

Add $25 for .357 Mag.

GRADING - PPGS™	100%	98%	95%	90%	80%	70%	60%

RIFLES: BOLT ACTION

GRIZZLY BIG BOAR COMPETITOR RIFLE - .50 BMG cal., single shot, bolt action design in bullpup configuration, alloy steel receiver and bolt, 36 in. heavy barrel with compensator, thumb safety, match or field grade, includes bipod, scope mount, leather cheek pad and hard carry case, 30.4 lbs. New 1994.

	100%	98%	95%	90%	80%	70%	60%
MSR $2,350	$2,150	$1,725	$1,450	$1,300	$1,125	$995	$895

Add $100 for parkerizing.
Add $250 for nickel trigger housing finish.
Add $350 for full nickel frame.
Add $250 for stainless steel Lothar Walther barrel.
Add $522 for redesigned (2002) tripod and pintle mount.

RIFLES: SEMI-AUTO

GRIZZLY 15 - .223 Rem. cal., patterned after the AR-15, available in either A2 or A3 configuration, limited mfg. 2004-2005.

	100%	98%	95%	90%	80%	70%	60%
	$725	$650	$575	$525	$475	$425	$375

Last MSR was $795.

Add $85 for detachable carry handle.

L E S INCORPORATED

Previous manufacturer located in Morton Grove, IL.

PISTOLS: SEMI-AUTO

P-18 ROGAK - 9mm Para. cal., double action, 18 shot, 5 1/2 in. barrel, stainless steel, black plastic grips with partial thumb rest. Disc.

	100%	98%	95%	90%	80%	70%	60%
	$350	$295	$265	N/A	N/A	N/A	N/A
High Polish Finish	$395	$330	$295	N/A	N/A	N/A	N/A

This pistol was patterned after the Steyr Model GB. Approx. 2,300 P-18s were mfg. before being disc.

LABANU INCORPORATED

Labanu, Inc. SKSs were manufactured by Norinco in China, and imported exclusively until 1998 by Labanu, Inc., located in Ronkonkoma, NY.

RIFLES: SEMI-AUTO

MAK 90 SKS SPORTER RIFLE - 7.62x39mm cal., sporterized variation of the SKS with thumbhole stock, 16 1/2 in. barrel, includes accessories, 5 lbs. Importation began 1995, banned 1998.

	100%	98%	95%	90%	80%	70%	60%
	$375	$325	$300	$285	$270	$250	$200

Last MSR was $189.

LAHTI PISTOL

Previous manufacturer located in Husqvarna, Sweden. Also mfg. by Vkt (state rifle factory) in Jyvaskyla, Finland.

PISTOLS: SEMI-AUTO

SWEDISH MODEL 40 - 9mm Para. cal., 4 3/4 in. barrel, blue finish, fixed sights, plastic grips, mfg. 1940-44.

	100%	98%	95%	90%	80%	70%	60%
	$600	$500	$400	$300	$260	$250	$240

Add 10% for Holster-Rig.

Note: It is important to note that there are diversely marked variations of this pistol, such as RPLT (Danish State Police); such police markings reduce value by about 10%.

FINNISH L-35 - 9mm Para., 4 basic variations - only the first 2 types have the more desirable shoulder stock lug. Military pistols are usually "SA" marked, approx. 9,100 mfg. 1938-1954.

GRADING - PPGS™	100%	98%	95%	90%	80%	70%	60%

✳ *Finnish L-35 1st Variation* - can be identified by "hump" for yoke locking piece and loaded indicator, ser. no. range 1001-3700.

	$3,000	$2,500	$2,000	$1,650	$1,400	$1,100	$800

✳ *Finnish L-35 2nd Variation* - does not have the "hump" for yoke locking piece, scarcer than 1st Variation, ser. no. 3701-4700.

	$3,000	$2,500	$2,000	$1,650	$1,400	$1,100	$800

✳ *Finnish L-35 3rd Variation* - can be identified by small changes in loaded indicator, most are marked "Valmet", ser. no. range 4701-6800.

	$1,750	$1,350	$850	$750	$700	$650	$600

✳ *Finnish L-35 4th Variation* - w/o loaded indicator, marked "Valmet," and sold commercially, ser. no. range 6801-9100.

	$1,500	$1,250	$850	$750	$700	$650	$600

✳ *Finnish L-35 Shoulder Stocks* - the shoulder stock for this model (w/o serial numbers) features a sheet metal compartment which contains a cleaning rod and extra magazine. Original stocks (only 50 mfg.) are currently selling in the $3,000-$3,500 range, while more recently manufactured stocks utilizing original hardware are currently priced in the $1,800-$2,250 range.

LAKE FIELD ARMS LTD.

Previous manufacturer located in Ontario, Canada. Lake Field Arms Ltd. was acquired by Savage Arms, Inc. during late 1994. Distributor sales only through most major U.S. distributors.

Lake Field rifles manufactured after the Savage acquisition are marked Savage - please refer to the Savage section for current mfg.

RIFLES: .22 RIMFIRE

MARK I - .22 LR cal., single shot bolt action, 20 3/4 in. rifled or smooth bore barrel, adj. rear sight, thumb rotary safety, walnut finish hardwood stock, 5 1/2 lbs. Disc.

	$110	$75	$65	$55	$50	$40	$30

Last MSR was $135.

Add $14 for left-hand variation.

This model was also available in youth dimensions (19 in. barrel) at no extra charge (Model Mark I-Y).

MARK II - .22 LR cal., bolt action, 10 shot mag., 20 3/4 in. barrel, adj. rear sight, thumb rotary safety, walnut finish hardwood stock, 5 1/2 lbs. Disc.

	$120	$80	$70	$60	$50	$40	$30

Last MSR was $140.

Add $15 for left-hand variation (mfg. 1993-95).

This model was also available in youth dimensions (19 in. barrel) at no extra charge (Model Mark II-Y).

MODEL 64B - .22 LR cal., semi-auto, side ejection, 10 shot mag., 20 1/4 in. barrel, adj. rear sight, thumb rotary safety, walnut finish hardwood stock, 5 1/2 lbs. Disc.

	$120	$85	$75	$65	$55	$45	$40

Last MSR was $143.

MODEL 90B (BIATHLON) - .22 LR cal., biathlon rifle, includes five 5-shot mags., 21 in. barrel, aperture sights, one-piece natural finish hardwood stock, 8 1/4 lbs. Mfg. 1991-95.

	$430	$300	$225	$195	$170	$150	$130

Last MSR was $570.

Add $55 for left-hand variation (new 1993).

GRADING - PPGS™	100%	98%	95%	90%	80%	70%	60%

MODEL 91T - .22 LR cal., target rifle, single shot, 25 in. barrel with aperture sights, dark hardwood finished stock, 8 lbs. Mfg. 1991-95.

	$340	$255	$215	$175	$150	$135	$115

Last MSR was $455.

Add $45 for left-hand variation (mfg. 1993-95).

✳ *Model 91TR* - repeater version of the Model 91T, 5 shot mag. Mfg. 1993-95.

	$360	$265	$215	$175	$150	$135	$115

Last MSR was $485.

Add $45 for left-hand variation (mfg. 1993-95).

MODEL 92S - .22 LR cal., 5 shot detachable mag., 21 in. barrel, hardwood stock with Monte Carlo cheekpiece, 8 lbs. Mfg. 1993-95.

	$300	$240	$200	$175	$160	$150	$135

Last MSR was $388.

Add $37 for left-hand variation.

MODEL 93M - .22 Mag. cal., 5 shot mag., thumb operated rotary safety, 20 3/4 in. barrel, hardwood stock, 5 3/4 lbs. Mfg. 1995 only.

	$140	$120	$100	$85	$75	$65	$55

Last MSR was $168.

LAKELANDER

Previous trademark circa 1976-1999. Manufacture was by MIPRO AB (c. 1946-1999) in Sweden. Previously imported and distributed 1996-98 by Lakelander U.S.A., Inc. located in Gulfport, MS.

RIFLES: BOLT ACTION

LAKELANDER 389 - .270 Win., .30-06, or .308 Win. cal., unique design with many shooter enhancements, 4 shot integrated mag. with rotary swing plate, 3 configurations including Premium (22 in. barrel with skip-line checkering and Monte Carlo stock), Classic (22 in. barrel, standard stock with checkering), Match-Maker (target model with 21.7 in. barrel and competition stock and adj. cheekpiece, .308 Win. only), 7.3-8.4 lbs. Mfg. 1996-98.

	$1,425	$1,225	$995	$850	$700	$600	$500

Last MSR was $1,599.

Add $500 for Match-Maker Model.

LAMBOY, S.R. & CO. INC.

Previous importer located in Victor, NY until 2003. S.R. Lamboy manufactured Ithaca Classic Doubles and imported Renato Caem and other high quality, low production long guns from Italy. Please check indivdual listings for more information.

LAMES

Previous manufacturer located in Italy.

SHOTGUNS: O/U

FIELD MODEL - 12 ga., 26, 28, or 30 in. barrels, various chokes, VR, engraving, SST, auto ejectors, checkered pistol grip stock with pad.

	$400	$380	$365	$350	$325	$300	$275

Add 25% for separated barrels.

STANDARD TRAP - similar to Field, 30 or 32 in. various trap bore barrels, with wide VR, trap style Monte Carlo stock.

	$600	$575	$550	$525	$425	$400	$450

CALIFORNIA TRAP - similar to Standard Trap, with separated barrels.

	$700	$675	$650	$625	$525	$500	$450

GRADING - PPGS™	100%	98%	95%	90%	80%	70%	60%

SKEET MODEL - similar to Field, with 26 in. skeet bore barrels, skeet stock and separated barrels.

	$600	$575	$550	$525	$425	$400	$350

LANBER

Current shotgun (O/U and semi-auto only) trademark manufactured by ComLanber, S.A., located in Zaldibar, Spain, and established in 1973. Currently imported beginning late 2006 by Lanber USA, located in Westfield, MA. Previously located in Blakely, GA. Previously imported 1999-2006, O/U shotguns by Wingshooting Adventures, located in Coopersville, MI, 1996-99 by ITC International, Inc. located in Marietta, GA, until 1994, by Eagle Imports, Inc. located in Wanamassa, NJ, by Exel Arms of America, Inc., located in Gardener, MA, and by Lanber Arms of America located in Adrian, MI.

Lanber makes a wide range of quality O/U and semi-auto shotguns.

SHOTGUNS: O/U, DISC.

The last MSR on all models listed below reflects 1987 pricing. Please contact Wingshooting Adventures directly (see listing in Trademark Index) for more information on current Lanber model availability and pricing. The following models were imported by Lanber Arms of America, Inc. located in Adrian, MI until business ceased in late 1986.

EXEL SERIES 100: MODELS 101-104 - 12 ga., boxlock action, vent. rib, extractors, single trigger.

	$400	$350	$310	$270	$240	$225	$200

Last MSR was $451.

Add $16 for 103 Mag., $92 for ejectors (Model 104 only).
These models were previously designated the 844ST Series.

EXEL MODEL 105 - 12 ga., boxlock action, single trigger, ejectors, Lanber screw-in chokes, deluxe wood, engraved satin finish action.

	$575	$495	$440	$405	$370	$345	$310

Last MSR was $644.

This model was previously designated the Model 2004LCH.

EXEL MODELS 106 & 107 - 12 ga., similar to 105, only more deluxe version with vent. barrels and rib, blued receiver only, interchangeable Lanber screw-in chokes. Trap model is Model 107.

	$725	$625	$550	$500	$475	$450	$425

Last MSR was $845.

These models were previously designated 2008LCH and 2009LCH respectively.

844 ST - 12 ga. only, boxlock, 26 or 28 in. barrels, choked IC/IM, extractors, SST, automatic safety, VR, European walnut with hand checkering, blued finish with engraved receiver, 7 1/8 lbs. Importation disc. 1986.

	$395	$340	$320	$300	$285	$270	$255

Last MSR was $450.

✷ *844 MST* - 12 ga. only, 3 in. chambers, 30 in. F & M barrels, otherwise similar to 844 ST. Importation disc. 1986.

	$405	$350	$335	$320	$310	$300	$295

Last MSR was $470.

2004 LCH - 12 ga. only, boxlock action, 28 in. barrels, SST, ejectors, supplied with 5 screw-in choke tubes, engraved satin finish receiver, checkered European walnut, 7 3/8 lbs. Importation disc. 1986.

	$575	$485	$460	$440	$420	$395	$380

Last MSR was $650.

GRADING - PPGS™	100%	98%	95%	90%	80%	70%	60%

2004 LCH SKEET - 12 ga. only, 28 in. barrels supplied with 5 choke tubes, blued finish, moderately engraved, select checkered walnut, 7 3/8 lbs. Importation disc. 1986.

	$740	$635	$585	$560	$540	$520	$495

Last MSR was $845.

2004 LCH TRAP - 12 ga. only, 30 in. barrels supplied with 3 choke tubes, European walnut has trap dimensions, blued finish. Importation disc. 1986.

	$675	$625	$585	$560	$540	$520	$495

Last MSR was $845.

MODEL 82 FIELD GRADE - 12 or 20 ga., 3 in. chambers, boxlock action, SST, ejectors, 26 or 28 in. VR barrels with fixed chokes, checkered walnut stock and forearm. Limited importation 1994 only.

	$500	$425	$395	$360	$330	$295	$275

Last MSR was $585.

MODEL 87 DELUXE FIELD GRADE - 12 or 20 ga., better quality walnut stock and forearm, 26 (20 ga. only) or 28 in. VR barrels with choke tubes. Limited importation 1994 only.

	$800	$675	$575	$500	$425	$350	$295

Last MSR was $915.

MODEL 97 SPORTING CLAYS - 12 ga. only, Sporting Clays configuration featuring 28 in. barrels with choke tubes. Limited importation 1994 only.

	$835	$695	$585	$500	$425	$350	$295

Last MSR was $965.

SHOTGUNS: O/U, CURRENT IMPORTATION

MODEL 2077 - 12 ga. only, 2 3/4 in. chambers, boxlock action, SST, black receiver finish, 26 in. VR barrels with 5 choke tubes, ejectors, checkered walnut stock and forearm, 6.2 lbs. Importation began 2000.

MSR N/A	$750	$650	$575	$525	$475	$400	$350

MODEL 2087 - similar to Model 2077, except has 3 in. chambers, engraved receiver and 28 in. barrels, 7 lbs. Importation began 2000.

MSR N/A	$725	$625	$550	$495	$450	$375	$325

MODEL 2088 - 12 ga. only, 2 3/4 in. chambers, sporting clays configuration, 28 in. VR barrels with 5 choke tubes, oil finished top quality European walnut, 7 1/2 lbs. Importation began 2000.

MSR N/A	$1,350	$1,175	$950	$825	$750	$625	$500

MODEL 2097 - 12 ga. only, 3 in. chambers, sporting clays configuration, engraved receiver, 28 or 30 in. VR barrels with 5 choke tubes, 7 3/4 lbs. Importation began 2000.

MSR N/A	$800	$700	$600	$525	$465	$415	$365

MODEL 2098 - 12 ga. only, 2 3/4 in. chambers, top-of-the-line sporting clays model with engraved coin finished sideplates, 7 lbs., 10 oz. Importation began 2000.

MSR N/A	$1,650	$1,325	$1,075	$950	$825	$750	$625

LANG, JOSEPH

Current trademark established in 1821 and manufactured by Atkin, Grant & Lang, located in Hertfordshire, England. No current U.S. importation.

During 1925, the company of Joseph Lang & Son amalgamated with Steven Grant & Son, forming the new company of Grant & Lang, Ltd. The company achieved notoriety for its unique thumbnail and key lock hand detachable sidelocks.

Prices indicated are for manufacturer's suggested retail and 100% condition factors are listed in English pounds. All new prices do not include VAT. Values for used guns in 98%-60% condition factors are priced in U.S. dollars.

Please contact the factory directly for more information and model availability (see Trademark Index). Atkin, Grant & Lang provide a useful historical research service on older Joseph Lang shotguns and rifles. The charge for this service is £25 per gun, and the company will give you all pertinent factory information regarding the history.

RIFLES: SxS

JOSEPH LANG DOUBLE RIFLE - available in cals. between .300 H&H - .577 NE, best quality double rifle, individually made per customer specifications.

MSR N/A	N/A	$30,000	$26,000	$21,000	$19,000	$16,250	$14,750

Add 25% for .450 NE - .577 NE cals.

SHOTGUNS: SxS

IMPERIAL SIDELOCK EJECTOR - 12, 16, 20, 28 ga., or .410 bore, best quality sidelock ejector model, individually made per customer specifications.

MSR N/A	N/A	$28,875	$24,750	$20,750	$17,250	$15,000	$13,250

Add 50% for 20 ga., 75% for 28 ga. or 100% for .410 bore.
Add 15% for key hand detachable locks, or 25% for thumbnail hand detachable locks.

LAPORTE HOLDING

Current shotgun manufacturer located in Biot, France. No current U.S. importation. Laporte Holding manufactures a unique reduced recoil 12 ga. O/U shotgun called the SwingTrap/Pro II, reducing recoil by 50% and noise by 75%. Please contact the company directly, including pricing and availability (see Trademark Index).

LASERAIM ARMS, INC.

Previous distributor located in Little Rock, AR. Previously manufactured until 1999 in Thermopolis, WY. Laseraim Arms, Inc. was a division of Emerging Technologies, Inc.

PISTOLS: SEMI-AUTO

SERIES I - .40 S&W, .400 Cor-Bon (new 1998), .45 ACP, or 10mm cal., single action, 3 3/8 (Compact Model), 5, or 6 in. barrel with compensator, ambidextrous safety, all stainless steel metal parts are Teflon coated, beveled mag. well, integral accessory mounts, 7 (.45 ACP) or 8 (10mm or .40 S&W) shot mag., 46 or 52 oz. Mfg. 1993-99.

		$325	$295	$265	$215	$185	$150	$125

Last MSR was $349.

Add $120 for wireless laser combo (new 1997).

* *Series I Compact* - .40 S&W or .45 ACP cal., features 3 3/8 in. non-ported slide and fixed sights. Mfg. 1993-99.

		$325	$295	$265	$215	$185	$150	$125

Last MSR was $349.

Series I Illusion and Dream Team variations were made during 1993-94. Retail prices respectively were $650 and $695.

SERIES II - .40 S&W (disc. 1994), .45 ACP, or 10mm cal., similar technical specs. as the Series I, except has non-reflective stainless steel finish, fixed or adj. sights, and 3 3/8 (Compact Model, .45 ACP only), 5, or 7 (.45 ACP only) in. non-compensated barrel, 37 or 43 oz. Mfg. 1993-96.

		$485	$385	$300	$240	$210	$180	$155

Last MSR was $550.

Series II Illusion and Dream Team variations were made during 1993-94. Retail prices respectively were $500 and $545.

GRADING - PPGS™	100%	98%	95%	90%	80%	70%	60%

SERIES III - .45 ACP cal., 5 in. ported barrel, serrated slide, Hogue grips. Mfg. 1994-disc.

	$595	$465	$415	$375	$345	$310	$275

Last MSR was $675.

SERIES IV - .45 ACP cal., 3 3/8 (Compact Model) or 5 in. ported barrel, serrated slide, diamond checkered wood grips. Mfg. 1994-disc.

	$550	$450	$400	$360	$330	$300	$265

Last MSR was $625.

LASALLE

Previous manufacturer located in France.

SHOTGUNS

SLIDE ACTION SHOTGUN - 12 or 20 ga., 26, 28, or 30 in. barrels, various chokes, alloy frame, checkered pistol grip stock.

	$250	$225	$200	$175	$150	$125	$100

SEMI-AUTO SHOTGUN - 12 ga., 26, 28, or 30 in. barrels, various chokes, gas operated, checkered pistol grip stock.

	$300	$275	$250	$225	$200	$175	$150

LAURONA

Current trademark established in 1941, and manufactured by Armas Eibar, S.A.L., located in Eibar, Spain. No current U.S. importation. Previously imported until 1993 by Galaxy Imports located in Victoria, TX.

Laurona was founded in Eibar during 1941 by four craftsmen (hence the name Laurona, which in Basque means "of the four"), each a specialist in a discipline of shotgun mfg. Laurona made SxS guns until 1978, at which time they discontinued SxS models in order to concentrate on the O/U marketplace.

Laurona manufactures good quality O/U shotguns and O/U express rifles/combination guns. Beginning 1992, Laurona switched from a one-piece, demi-block type of fabrication to a monobloc system which has improved strength characteristics while reducing weight in their X-Series line of shotguns and express rifles.

Laurona long guns come standard with a black chrome metal finish that is extremely resistant to oxidation. Left hand stocks are available for the 83 MG Super Game, 85 MS Super Game, Trap, and Super Skeet, Silhouette Trap models, and Silhouette Sporting Clays.

Suffix designations on Laurona shotguns refer to the following: G - twin non-selective triggers, S - selective single trigger, M - multi-chokes, T - Tulip, BV - beavertail, U - single non-selected triggers.

All Super Game Models were available with a deluxe package which includes a recoil pad, mid-bead sight, and select wood for an additional $250. Special order dull matte finished barrels (with multi-chokes) were available for an additional $200 - extra barrels were priced between $635 (20 ga.) or $800 (12 ga.) per set.

RIFLES: O/U CURRENT MFG.

MODEL 2000X EXPRESS RIFLE - .30-06, 8x57JRS, 8x57RS, 9.3x74R, or .375 H&H cal., monobloc construction, 24 in. separated barrels featuring quarter rib sight and convergence adjustment at muzzle, matte black chrome finish, open sights, ejectors or extractors, SST or DT, approx. 8.1 lbs. New 1992.

This model must be custom ordered - please contact the factory for more information.
This model accepts Leupold or European styled ring mounts.

✳ *Model 2000X Express Rifle Combo* - includes choice of cals. listed, except for .375 H&H cal. with 12 ga. under-barrel. New 1992.

This model must be custom ordered.

GRADING - PPGS™	100%	98%	95%	90%	80%	70%	60%

SHOTGUNS: O/U, RECENT MFG.

The author wishes to express his thanks to Thomas E. Barker for making the following information available.

1967 Series (Earliest O/U Model)

MODEL 67 (VERSIONS G & U) - 12 ga., first O/U model mfg. with manual extractors, G designation stands for Gemini for twin select trigger system (triggers will function as single or double), front trigger is non-selective firing in bottom to top sequence, and back trigger in top to bottom sequence, U designation stands for non-selective single triggers, boxlock action and barrel bluing, light walnut stock, skip diamond checkering.

$500	$400	$350	$300	$250	$200	$150

1971 Series

MODEL 71 (VERSIONS G & U) - similar to Model 67 with minor improvements, bright chrome receiver with rolled engraved game scene, earlier models had traditional solid center ribbed blue barrels, later models had solid ribbed barrels with Black Chrome finish. G & U designations are the same as Model 67.

$500	$400	$350	$300	$250	$200	$150

This model was imported and sold by Sears & Roebuck in 1973-74.

1982 Series

12 ga. only, similar to Model 71 with auto-ejectors. (Manual extractors were disc.) Firing pins changed to traditional round type, many internal parts were improved for better reliability. Skip diamond and standard checkering. All SUPER Series barrels separated (w/o center rib) with Black Chrome finish and hard chrome bores with long forcing cones in chambers. In most respects, the 82 Models are comparable to present day Laurona O/U shotguns and will share most internal parts. G & U designations are the same as Model 67.

MODEL 82 GAME (VERSIONS G & U) - 12 ga, 28 in. black chromed barrels, 2 3/4 or 3 in. chambers, long forcing cones, solid side ribs, hard chrome bores, 5mm vent. rib, chokes ****/** or ***/* (IC/IM/M/F), Imperial nickel receiver with Louis XVI style engraving, tulip forend, field stock drop 35/65mm with plastic buttplate, 7 lbs.

$550	$475	$400	$350	$300	$250	$200

MODEL 82 TRAP COMBO (VERSIONS G & U) - 12 ga., similar to 82 Game, except has 28 (chokes ***/*) or 29 (chokes **/*) in. barrels, steel rib, 8mm trap buttstock drop 35/55mm with rubber special trap recoil pad, 8 lbs.

$550	$475	$400	$350	$300	$250	$200

82 TRAP COMPETITION (VERSION U) - 12 ga., similar to 82 Trap Combo, except has 13mm aluminum rib with long white sight, engraved motif on receiver, beavertail fluted forend, Monte Carlo trap stock drop 35/55mm with black rubber special trap recoil pad, 8 lbs.

$600	$550	$475	$400	$350	$300	$250

82 PIGEON COMPETION (VERSION U) - 12 ga., similar to 82 Trap Competition, except has 28 in. barrels choked ****/** or ***/*, special competiton Pachmayr recoil pad with imitation leather face, 7 lbs, 13 oz.

$650	$600	$550	$475	$400	$350	$300

Model 82 Super Series

The Super Models listed have nickel finished receivers with full coverage, delicate scroll engraving with Black Chrome relief, and forend iron. All barrels are split (w/o side ribs), and have very durable rust resistance Black Chrome finish.

GRADING - PPGS™	100%	98%	95%	90%	80%	70%	60%

82 SUPER GAME (VERSIONS G & U) - 12 ga., similar to 82 Game, except has more elaborate fine scroll engraving.

	$575	$475	$400	$350	$300	$250	$200

82 SUPER TRAP (VERSION U) - 12 ga., similar to 82 Trap Competition, except has special trap Pachmayr recoil pad with imitation leather face and fine scroll engraving.

	$675	$600	$550	$475	$400	$350	$300

82 SUPER SKEET - 12 ga., similar to 82 Super Trap, except has 28 in. barrels choked Skeet/Skeet, buttstock drop 35/65mm with plastic buttplate, 7 lbs.

	$600	$550	$475	$400	$350	$300	$250

82 SUPER PIGEON - 12 ga., similar to 82 Super Trap, except has 28 in. barrels choked ****/** or ***/*, 7 lbs, 9 oz.

	$675	$600	$550	$475	$400	$350	$300

Model 83 Super Series

83MG SUPER GAME - 12 or 20 ga., 3 in. chambers, 26 (20 ga. only) or 28 in. barrels, 8mm rib, similar to 82 Super Game, except had Laurona's new multi-choke, not compatible with any other brand of screw in chokes because of the black chrome plating of the metric threads, 7 lbs.

	$995	$675	$600	$550	$475	$400	$350

Model 84 Super Series

The Super Game Models listed were available with an extra set of 26 or 28 in. 20 ga. multi-choke barrels and cast-on stocks for left-handed shooters.

> **Add $400 for multi-choke barrels.**
> **Add $50 for left-hand stock.**

84S SUPER GAME - 3 in. chambers, similar to 82 Super Game, except for new single selective trigger, ejectors, 28 in. barrels choked IC/IM or M/F, 8mm rib, 7 lbs.

	$750	$675	$600	$550	$475	$400	$350

> **Add $400 for extra set of 20 ga. multi-choke barrels.**

84S SUPER SKEET - 12 ga. only, 2 3/4 in. chambers, with elongated forcing cones, 28 in. separated barrels choked Skeet/Skeet, 13mm aluminum rib, extensive fine scroll engraving, rust resistant black chrome finish, 7 lbs. Imported 1988-1990.

	$995	$675	$600	$550	$475	$400	$350

84S SUPER TRAP - 12 ga., 29 in. barrels with 2 3/4 in. chambers and long forcing cones, chokes IM and full, 13mm aluminum rib, auto ejectors, nickel plated receiver with fine scroll engraving, Black Chrome relief, beavertail forearm, MC or standard trap stock, 7 lbs., 12 oz.

	$1,250	$975	$875	$750	$625	$550	$475

Model 85 Super Series

85MS SUPER GAME - 12 or 20 ga., 3 in. chambers, similar to 83MG Super Game, except for single selective trigger, 7 lbs.

	$995	$675	$600	$550	$475	$400	$350

85MS SUPER TRAP - similar to 84S Super Trap, except for multi-choke in bottom barrel with fixed full on top, 7 lbs., 12 oz.

	$1,250	$975	$875	$750	$625	$550	$475

85MS SUPER PIGEON - similar to 85MS Super Trap, except for 28 in. barrels with fixed IM choke on top with multi-choke on bottom, intended for live bird competition, 7 lbs., 4 oz.

	$1,250	$975	$875	$750	$625	$550	$475

GRADING - PPGS™	100%	98%	95%	90%	80%	70%	60%

85MS SPECIAL SPORTING - similar to 85MS Super Pigeon, except field buttstock with plastic buttplate, intended for upland game, 7 lbs., 4 oz.

	$1,250	$975	$875	$750	$625	$550	$475

Excel 300 Series

EXEL 300 SERIES - 12 or 20 ga. The Model 301 was a basic field gun, and the Model 310 was the highest grade.

✳ *Exel 300 Series Models 301 and 302* - 12 ga., double selective trigger system, ejectors, pistol grip, vent. rib, lightly engraved chrome finish receiver, various chokes and barrel lengths. Importation disc. 1986.

	$485	$415	$380	$340	$300	$275	$250

Last MSR was $553.

✳ *Exel 300 Series Models 303 and 304* - 12 ga., similar to Models 301/302, except has better engraving on coin finish receiver, vent. barrels. Importation disc. 1987.

	$545	$470	$430	$385	$340	$315	$270

Last MSR was $623.

Previously designated Model 82G Super.

✳ *Exel 300 Series Models 305(A) and 306(A)* - 12 or 20 ga., similar to Models 303/304, except has better engraving on coin finish receiver, screw-in choke tubes. Importation disc. 1987.

	$625	$535	$470	$430	$390	$350	$315

Last MSR was $711.

Previously designated Models 83MG and 85MS.

✳ *Exel 300 Series Models 307 and 308* - 12 ga., trap model, 29 in. barrels, extensive engraving, Monte Carlo stock. Importation disc. 1987.

	$580	$500	$460	$420	$380	$340	$300

Last MSR was $668.

Previously designated Model 82U Trap.

✳ *Exel 300 Series Models 309 and 310* - super trap model, 29 in. vent. barrels, more extensive engraving than Models 307/308. Importation disc. 1987.

	$630	$545	$495	$460	$415	$385	$340

Last MSR was $726.

Previously designated Model 82 S. Trap.

Silhouette 300 Series

These shotguns are basically the same as the Super Series, with the following exceptions; this series was readily indentifiable by their white and black chrome striped receiver, with the model name engraved on the receiver side. Both barrels were multi-choked and had an 11mm steel rib. Two types of chokes were used. Some guns came with knurl head type as in the Super Models, and others were made with flush Invector style. A later option for ease of changing chokes was the knurl long choke, which is a flush type with the knurl head added. Both later type chokes (flush and knurl long), can be used in the early multi-choke models with some extension showing.

SILHOUETTE 300 TRAP - 12 ga., 2 3/4 in. chambers, 29 in. 11mm VR barrels with long forcing cones and hard chrome bores, beavertail forearm and straight comb trap stock with vent. black rubber recoil pad, 8 lbs.

	$1,250	$975	$875	$775	$700	$650	$595

SILHOUETTE 300 SPORTING CLAYS - 12 ga., 3 in. chambers, similar to 300 Trap, except has 28 in. barrels and field type butt stock with plastic buttplate or hard rubber sporting clays pad, 7 1/2 lbs.

	$1,250	$975	$875	$775	$700	$650	$595

GRADING - PPGS™	100%	98%	95%	90%	80%	70%	60%

SILHOUETTE 300 ULTRA MAGNUM - 12 ga. 3 1/2 in. chambers, similar to 300 Sporting Clays, Black Chrome finish, 7 1/2 lbs.

	100%	98%	95%	90%	80%	70%	60%
	$1,300	$1,025	$875	$775	$700	$650	$595

SHOTGUNS: SxS, BOXLOCK

Shotguns mfg. after 1975 with "X" after the model number featured Black Chrome barrels and actions with hard chrome bores. 28 ga. and .410 bore could be special ordered. SxS shotguns were disc. by Laurona during 1978 in an effort to concentrate on the O/U marketplace.

MODEL 11 - 12, 16, or 20 ga., triple Greener type round crossbolt with independent firing pins bushed into the face of the action, Bellota steel barrels.

| $400 | $350 | $315 | $260 | $210 | $175 | $140 |

MODEL 13 - 12, 16, or 20 ga., similar to Model 11, except utilizes Purdey type bolt system, extractors are of double radius, sold through Sears & Roebuck.

| $400 | $350 | $315 | $260 | $210 | $175 | $140 |

* *Model 13 E* - similar to Model 13, except has ejectors.

| $500 | $450 | $395 | $350 | $315 | $260 | $210 |

* *Model 13 X* - similar to Model 13, except has black chrome finished barrels and action with hard chrome bores.

| $500 | $450 | $395 | $350 | $315 | $260 | $210 |

* *Model 13 XE* - similar to Model 13 E, except has black chrome finish and hard chrome bores.

| $600 | $525 | $450 | $395 | $350 | $315 | $260 |

MODEL 15 ECONOMIC PLUMA - 12, 16, or 20 ga., similar to Model 13, except was first model to have hard chrome bores.

| $450 | $395 | $350 | $315 | $260 | $210 | $175 |

* *Model 15 E Economic Pluma* - similar to Model 15 Economic Pluma, except has ejectors.

| $550 | $475 | $400 | $350 | $315 | $260 | $210 |

* *Model 15 X Economic Pluma* - similar to Model 15 Economic Pluma, except has Black Chrome finish and hard chrome bores.

| $500 | $450 | $395 | $350 | $315 | $260 | $210 |

* *Model 15 XE Economic Pluma* - similar to Model 15 E, except has ejectors.

| $600 | $525 | $450 | $395 | $350 | $315 | $260 |

MODEL 52 PLUMA - 12, 16, or 20 ga., back of actions scalloped and engraved in fine English scroll, Churchill rib and double radius extractors, hard chrome bores, 6 lbs.

| $750 | $675 | $600 | $525 | $450 | $395 | $350 |

* *Model 52 E Pluma* - similar to Model 52 Pluma, except has ejectors, 6 lbs., 2 oz.

| $850 | $750 | $675 | $600 | $525 | $450 | $395 |

SHOTGUNS: SxS, SIDELOCK

Models listed were available in 12, 16, or 20 ga. 28 ga. and .410 bore were available by special order.

MODEL 103 - 12, 16, or 20 ga., blue sidelocks with light border engraving, triple Purdey type bolt system, double radius extractors, Bellota steel barrels with hard chrome bores.

| $895 | $800 | $675 | $575 | $525 | $475 | $425 |

* *Model 103-E* - similar to Model 103 except with ejectors.

| $995 | $895 | $800 | $675 | $575 | $525 | $475 |

GRADING - PPGS™	100%	98%	95%	90%	80%	70%	60%

MODEL 104 X - 12, 16, or 20 ga., case colored sidelock with Purdey type bolting system, double radius extractors, fine double safety sidelocks, gas relief vents, articulated trigger, hard chromed bores, demi-block barrels of special Bellota steel, black chrome barrels.

	$1,200	$1,075	$925	$825	$700	$600	$525

✳ *Model 104 XE* - same as Model 104 X, but with H&H style automatic selective ejectors.

	$1,350	$1,200	$1,075	$925	$825	$700	$575

MODEL 105 X FEATHER - 12, 16, or 20 ga., similar to Model 104 X, except has concave rib, approx. 6 lbs. 2 oz. (12 ga.).

	$1,250	$1,100	$950	$875	$800	$725	$650

✳ *Model 105 XE Feather* - similar to Model 105 X, except has H&H automatic selective ejectors.

	$1,400	$1,225	$1,075	$925	$850	$775	$700

MODEL 502 FEATHER - 12, 16, or 20 ga., Purdey type bolting system, hand detachable sidelocks, gas relief vents, H&H style automatic selective ejectors, articulated trigger, inside hard chromed demi-block barrels of special Bellota steel, black chrome finish, fine English scroll engraving, marble grey or Laurona Imperial finish, Churchill or concave type rib, 6.4 lbs. (12 ga.).

	$2,200	$2,050	$1,875	$1,650	$1,525	$1,400	$1,275

MODEL 801 DELUXE - 12, 16, or 20 ga., similar to Model 502 Feather, except engraving is true deluxe Renaissance style, fully handmade with Laurona Imperial finish, best quality checkered walnut stock and forearm.

	$4,400	$4,150	$3,650	$3,250	$2,900	$2,600	$2,250

MODEL 802 EAGLE - 12, 16, or 20 ga., similar to Model 801 Deluxe, except features highly artistic bas-relief engraving of hunting scenes, hand engraved with burin and chisel.

	$5,000	$4,400	$3,900	$3,375	$2,825	$2,375	$1,875

LAW ENFORCEMENT ORDNANCE CORPORATION

Previous manufacturer located in Ridgway, PA until 1990.

SHOTGUNS: SEMI-AUTO

STRIKER-12 - 12 ga. Mag., paramilitary design shotgun featuring 12 shot rotary mag., 18 1/4 in. barrel, semi-auto, alloy shrouded barrel with PG extension, folding or fixed paramilitary design stock, 9.2 lbs., limited mfg. 1986-90.

	$1,000	$875	$750	$675	$600	$550	$500

Last MSR was $725.

Add $200 for folding stock.
Add $100 for Marine variation ("Metal Life" finish).

Earlier variations were imported and available to law enforcement agencies only. In 1987, manufacture was started in PA and these firearms could be sold to individuals (18 in. barrel only). This design was originally developed in South Rhodesia.

HARRY LAWSON LLC

Current custom gun manufacturer and customizer established during 1965 and currently located in Tucson, AZ. Consumer direct sales.

Harry Lawson is well-known for custom stock work. This company also manufactures their own line of sporting rifles, most feature an innovative thumbhole stock design. Please contact the factory directly for more information regarding custom model availability/configuration and current pricing (see Trademark Index).

GRADING - PPGS™	100%	98%	95%	90%	80%	70%	60%

RIFLES: BOLT ACTION

Harry Lawson manufactures the 650 Series in both Mountaineer and Ultralite configurations. These bolt action rifles are custom order, and can be built on a customer supplied Remington 700 barreled action or the action can be purchased separately from $550 - $750. With a customer supplied action, prices start at $2,385 for Grade II XX wood. Additionally, the company customizes a customer supplied Weatherby Mark V barreled action. Prices start at $2,070 for Grade II XX wood.

LAZZERONI ARMS COMPANY

Current manufacturer located in Tucson, AZ since 1995. Direct/ dealer sales.

RIFLES: BOLT ACTION

Lazzeroni ammunition is precision loaded in Lazzeroni's Tucson facility under rigid tolerances. All ammunition is sealed for absolute weatherproofing. Lazzeroni proprietary calibers are already established as being extremely effective at long distances.

SAKO MODEL TRG-S - 7.21 Firebird (.284, new 2002) or 7.82 Warbird (.308) cal., features Sako TRG action with free floating 26 in. barrel, 3 shot detachable mag., fully adj. trigger, and scope rings, 7.9 lbs. Mfg. 1999-2004.

	$825	$700	$600	$495	$430	$365	$315

Last MSR was $900.

Add $400 for metal finish upgrade or $1,200 for metal finish upgrade with Burris 4-16x50mm mil-dot scope.

SAVAGE 16LZ - 7.21 Tomahawk (.284, disc. 2001) or 7.82 Patriot (.308) cal., stainless steel action with 2 locking lugs, 24 in. stainless barrel, detachable box mag., injection molded composite stock, 6.8 lbs. Mfg. 2001-2004.

	$475	$400	$350	$285	$250	$215	$185

Last MSR was $550.

Add $100 for left-hand action.
Add $400 for Cabela's 4.5-14x42mm scope.

MODEL 700ST - various Lazzeroni cals., Rem. M-700 action, features remachined bolt face, squared recoil lug and receiver, mag. and follower are replaced with Lazzeroni style units, steel (disc.) or stainless steel (new 1999) action, blue steel or stainless steel 24 in. barrel. Mfg. 1998-99.

	$2,150	$1,750	$1,425	$1,255	$1,020	$885	$715

Last MSR was $2,395.

MODEL 2000 SERIES - available in either Lazzeroni short magnum (6.17 Spitfire - .243 cal., 6.71 Phantom - .264 cal., 7.21 Tomahawk - .284 cal., 7.82 Patriot - .308 cal., 8.59 Galaxy - .338 cal., or 10.57 Maverick - .416 cal.) or Lazzeroni long magnums (6.53 Scramjet - .257 cal., 7.21 Firebird - .284 cal., 7.82 Warbird - .308 cal., 8.59 Titan - .338 cal., or 10.57 Meteor - .416 cal.), features precision machined steel (disc.) or stainless steel (new 1999) receiver, helically fluted bolt with heavy duty extractor, stainless steel match barrel with integral muzzle brake, adj. benchrest trigger, matte finish metal, 3 position firing pin safety on most models (new 1999), 2 or 3 (new 1999) shot internal mag., various stock configurations. Mfg. 1996-2005.

 ✳ *Model L2000ST* - features 27 in. barrel with conventional fiberglass stock, 8.1 lbs.

	$5,250	$4,100	$3,175	$2,650	$2,300	$1,950	$1,650

Last MSR was $5,899.

GRADING - PPGS™	100%	98%	95%	90%	80%	70%	60%

✳ *Model L2000ST-28* - .308 Warbird cal., shoots 130 grain BarnesX boattail at 4,000 fps, 28 in. stainless steel fluted barrel, includes Schmidt & Bender 4-16x50mm scope, stainless action, black synthetic stock, approx. 8.3 lbs. Mfg. 1999-2001.

	$5,875	$5,250	$4,750	$4,250	$3,600	$3,100	$2,650

Last MSR was $6,310.

This model was advertised as the flattest shooting hunting rifle then manufactured, and was at zero in at 100, 200, and 300 yards.

✳ *Model L2000ST-W* - features 27 in. barrel with conventional black wood laminate stock. Mfg. 1996 only.

	$4,400	$4,050	$3,600	$2,550	$2,200	$1,925	$1,625

Last MSR was $4,795.

✳ *Model L2000ST-WF Package* - features 27 in. barrel with one conventional fiberglass and one black wood laminate stock. Disc. 1997.

	$4,875	$4,450	$4,050	$2,650	$2,400	$2,100	$1,750

Last MSR was $5,295.

✳ *Model L2000DG* - .375 Saturn or .416 Meteor cal. only, features Fibergrain stock finish, removable muzzle brake, 3 shot mag., 24 in. barrel, includes sling swivels, 10.1 lbs. Mfg. 1998-2005.

	$5,575	$4,850	$4,350	$3,275	$2,800	$2,500	$2,000

Last MSR was $6,199.

✳ *Model L2000LLT* - .257 Scramjet, .284 Firebird, .308 Warbird, or .338 Titan cal., lightweight variation with 26 in. barrel and detachable muzzle brake, 4 shot mag., right- or left-hand action, 7.4 lbs. Mfg. 2004-2005.

	$5,400	$4,750	$4,250	$3,175	$2,750	$2,450	$1,950

Last MSR was $5,899.

✳ *Model L2000SA* - .243 Spitfire, .264 Phantom, .284 Tomahawk, .308 Patriot, .338 Galaxy, .358 Eagle, .375 Hellcat, or .416 Maverick cal., short action cals. only, lightweight mountain configuration with 24 in. fluted barrel, 6.8 lbs. Mfg. 1998-2004.

	$4,750	$4,350	$3,800	$2,600	$2,350	$2,050	$1,750

Last MSR was $5,499.

✳ *Model L2000SLR* - features 28 in. extra heavy fluted barrel and conventional fiberglass stock, not chambered in .338 Titan. Disc. 1999.

	$3,775	$3,400	$2,975	$2,600	$2,300	$2,000	$1,800

Last MSR was $4,195.

✳ *Model L2000SP* - 25 in. fluted barrel, thumbhole fiberglass stock, 7.8 lbs. Disc. 2004.

	$4,750	$4,350	$3,800	$2,600	$2,350	$2,050	$1,750

Last MSR was $5,499.

✳ *Model L2000SP-W* - 23 in. barrel, thumbhole black wood laminate stock.

	$4,400	$4,050	$3,600	$2,550	$2,200	$1,925	$1,625

Last MSR was $4,795.

✳ *Model L2000SP-FW Package* - features 23 in. barrel with one thumbhole fiberglass and one black wood laminate thumbhole stock. Disc. 1997.

	$4,875	$4,450	$4,050	$2,650	$2,400	$2,100	$1,750

Last MSR was $5,295.

MODEL 2005 GLOBAL HUNTER SERIES - available in various Lazzeroni proprietary cals., various configurations including Short Magnum Lite, Long Magnum Lite, Long Magnum Thumbhole, Long Magnum Special Long Range, Short Magnum Dangerous Game and Long Magnum Dangerous Game, features stainless steel receiver, match grade fluted or unfluted barrel with muzzle brake, Jewell competition trigger, diamond fluted or helical cut bolt shaft, titanium firing pin, Limbsavr recoil pad, slim line graphite composite stock, approx. 6.1-7 lbs. New 2005.

MSR $6,999		$6,250	$5,400	$4,750	$4,250	$3,250	$2,750	$2,300

Add $1,100 for Mag. cals.

LEBEAU-COURALLY

Current manufacturer established during 1865 and located in Liege, Belgium. Currently imported by William Larkin Moore, located in Scottsdale, AZ, by Griffin & Howe, located in Bernardsville, NJ, and by Heirloom Armes, located in Howard Lake, MN. Previously imported until 1998 by New England Arms Co. located in Kittery Point, ME.

Lebeau-Courally manufactures only best quality rifles and shotguns. Approximately 50 are manufactured annually. Prices do not include engraving. Please contact the importer directly for a firm quotation on a Lebeau-Courally rifle or shotgun (see Trademark Index).

RIFLES: SxS

BOXLOCK EJECTOR - 8x57JRS or 9.3x74R cal., Anson & Deeley boxlock, ejectors, select French walnut stock, quarter rib with ramp front sight, about 8 lbs. Importation disc. 1988, resumed 1993.

The importers should be contacted directly for current information and prices regarding this model (see Trademark Index).

SIDELOCK EJECTOR EXPRESS RIFLE - 7x65R, 8x57JRS, 9.3x74R, .30-06, .375 H&H, .458 Win. Mag., .470 NE (new 1991), or .577 NE (new 1992) cal., chopper lump barrels, reinforced action, select French walnut stock, quarter rib with ramp front sight, engraving not included, approx. 8 lbs.
Currently, this model is POR.

The importers should be contacted directly for current information and availability regarding this model (see Trademark Index).

RIFLES: SINGLE SHOT

SINGLE SHOT - 6.5x57R, 7x65R, .30R Blaser, 6.5x65, or 7mm Rem. Mag. cal., best quality, boxlock or sidelock action.
Currently, this model is POR.

The importers should be contacted directly for current information and availability regarding this model (see Trademark Index).

SHOTGUNS: O/U

SIDELOCK - 12, 20, or 28 ga., Greener locking system.
Currently, this model is POR.

The importers should be contacted directly for current information and availability regarding this model (see Trademark Index).

BOSS SLE-VEREES - 12 or 20 ga., Boss pattern sidelock with low profile action, prices include Edinbough engraving, top-of-the-line O/U individually made to customer specifications.
Current MSR on this model is approx. $180,000, depending on the exchange rate.

The importers should be contacted directly for current information and availability regarding this model (see Trademark Index).

SHOTGUNS: SxS

For currently manufactured shotguns - add $2,500 for single trigger. Older mfg. Lebeau-Courally shotguns have a completely different action and locking system than the newer models.

SOLOGNE - 12, 16, or 20 ga., Anson & Deeley boxlock action, various chokes and barrel lengths, select walnut, no engraving.

MSR N/A	$13,250	$11,250	$9,350	$7,500	$6,250	$5,150	$4,350

GRAND RUSSE MODEL - grade up from Sologne Model.

MSR N/A	$16,480	$13,000	$10,750	$8,475	$7,375	$5,250	$4,450

GRADING - PPGS™	100%	98%	95%	90%	80%	70%	60%

BOXLOCK EJECTOR - 12, 16, or 20 ga., choice of classic or rounded action, with or without sideplates, select French walnut stock, choice of numerous engraving patterns (optional), 26, 28, or 30 in. barrels, double trigger.

MSR N/A	$23,250	$14,000	$11,500	$9,950	$8,500	$7,250	$6,000

Subtract approx. 15%-20% w/sideplates.

SIDELOCK SLE EJECTOR - 12, 16, 20, 28 ga., or .410 bore, choice of classic or rounded action, chopper lump barrels, select French walnut stock, base price include Prince Koudacheff engraving, choice of numerous engraving patterns (optional), 26, 28, or 30 in. barrels, double triggers.

Current MSR on this model is approx. $138,000, depending on the exchange rate.

The importers should be contacted directly for current information and availability regarding this model (see Trademark Index).

LEFEVER ARMS COMPANY

Previous shotgun manufacturer located in Syracuse, NY circa 1885-1948.

SHOTGUNS: SxS

The Lefever was the first commercially successful hammerless double barrel shotgun made in America. They were made in Syracuse, NY from 1885-1916, at which time the company was acquired by Ithaca Gun Company. Ithaca made the Lefever after 1916. In 1921, the Box Lock Nitro Special was introduced and in 1934, the Lefever Grade A was introduced. Production of Lefever guns ceased in 1948.

The practice of assigning new serial numbers to guns returned to the factory for alterations absorbed approximately 5,000 numbers. Also, the serial number series started with 5,000, so approx. 62,000 guns were built.

The following is a percentage breakdown of gauges made between 1885-1916 (totaling 100%): 8 ga.-1/2%, 10 ga.-25%, 12 ga.-60%, 14 ga.-1/2%, 16 ga.-8%, 20 ga.-6%. Total serial numbers used was approx. 72,000 during this period. Damascus specimens of this trademark are worth approximately the same if in 60% or better original condition as their fluid steel barrel counterparts because of the rarity and desirability factors. Hammer guns are valued the same as damascus hammerless guns (grade for grade). Subtract 10%-30% on values with respective condition factors 50%-10%. Prices shown for 90% and up condition are very difficult to evaluate and are meant as a guide only - any Lefever shotgun in over 95% is rare and hard to evaluate.

100%	98%	95%	90%	80%	70%	60%	50%	40%	30%	20%	10%

SIDEPLATE MODELS - 10, 12, 16, or 20 ga., 26-32 in. barrels, any choke, boxlock action (even though model nomenclature referred to sidelock model), cocking indicators on all but DS and DSE grades, double triggers standard, checkered straight or pistol grip stock, auto ejectors designated by letter E after grade, most lower grades marked at water table near serial number. Mfg. 1885-1919.

Add 50% for 16 ga.
Add 100% for 20 ga.
Add 10% for SST.

✱ *Model I Grade*

N/A	$1,525	$1,375	$1,250	$1,025	$925	$850	$775	$700	$630	$565	$500

✱ *Model DS Grade*

N/A	$1,525	$1,375	$1,250	$1,025	$925	$850	$775	$700	$630	$565	$500

✱ *Model DSE Grade*

N/A	$2,000	$1,800	$1,575	$1,275	$1,100	$950	$850	$775	$715	$650	$600

✱ *Model H Grade*

N/A	$2,175	$1,975	$1,700	$1,375	$1,200	$1,100	$1,000	$950	$900	$800	$750

✱ *Model HE Grade*

N/A	$3,000	$2,750	$2,350	$1,800	$1,600	$1,400	$1,250	$1,100	$1,000	$900	$850

	100%	98%	95%	90%	80%	70%	60%	50%	40%	30%	20%	10%
* *Model G Grade*												
	N/A	$2,175	$1,975	$1,700	$1,500	$1,400	$1,300	$1,200	$1,100	$1,000	$900	$800
* *Model GE Grade*												
	N/A	$3,125	$2,850	$2,200	$1,800	$1,700	$1,500	$1,400	$1,300	$1,200	$1,100	$1,000
* *Model F Grade*												
	N/A	N/A	$2,375	$2,150	$1,700	$1,600	$1,500	$1,400	$1,100	$1,000	$900	$800
* *Model FE Grade*												
	N/A	N/A	$3,250	$2,950	$2,400	$2,000	$1,800	$1,600	$1,400	$1,300	$1,100	$1,000
* *Model E Grade*												
	N/A	N/A	$3,600	$3,000	$2,500	$2,100	$1,900	$1,800	$1,600	$1,400	$1,200	$1,100
* *Model EE Grade*												
	N/A	N/A	$5,400	$4,750	$3,750	$3,150	$2,700	$2,500	$2,300	$2,100	$1,900	$1,800
* *Model D Grade*												
	N/A	N/A	$4,550	$4,150	$3,250	$2,750	$2,150	$1,800	$1,600	$1,500	$1,400	$1,200
* *Model DE Grade*												
	N/A	N/A	$6,600	$5,700	$4,800	$3,700	$3,200	$2,700	$2,200	$2,000	$1,800	$1,600
* *Model C Grade*												
	N/A	N/A	$6,350	$5,500	$4,850	$4,000	$3,200	$2,700	$2,400	$2,200	$2,000	$1,900
* *Model CE Grade*												
	N/A	N/A	$8,400	$7,500	$6,500	$5,500	$4,800	$4,400	$3,600	$3,200	$2,800	$2,400
* *Model B Grade*												
	N/A	N/A	$9,300	$8,100	$7,500	$6,000	$5,250	$4,800	$4,000	$3,400	$3,000	$2,500
* *Model BE Grade*												
	N/A	N/A	$9,900	$8,750	$7,900	$6,600	$5,700	$5,100	$4,400	$3,800	$3,400	$3,150
* *Model A Grade* - auto ejectors standard.												
	N/A	N/A	$18,500	$15,500	$13,750	$11,250	$9,250	$8,150	$7,200	$6,300	$5,400	$4,700
* *Model AA Grade* - auto ejectors standard.												
	N/A	N/A	$26,000	$23,000	$19,000	$16,000	$13,000	$10,250	$8,250	$7,150	$6,500	$6,000

* *Model Optimus Grade* - auto ejectors standard.
Prices typically range from $30,000-$60,000, depending on original condition.

* *Model Thousand Dollar Grade* - auto ejectors standard.
Prices range from $35,000 - $100,000, depending on condition.

GRADING - PPGS™	100%	98%	95%	90%	80%	70%	60%

NITRO SPECIAL - 12, 16, 20 ga., or .410 bore, 26-32 in. barrels, various chokes, boxlock, extractors, checkered pistol grip stock. Mfg. 1921-48.

	100%	98%	95%	90%	80%	70%	60%
12 ga.	$650	$575	$450	$395	$350	$300	$250
16 ga.	$825	$725	$650	$575	$475	$400	$350
20 ga.	$1,100	$975	$875	$775	$675	$575	$450
.410 bore	$3,150	$2,800	$2,450	$2,150	$1,725	$1,400	$1,175

Add 10% for ST.

GRADE A FIELD MODEL - 12, 16, 20 ga., or .410 bore, 26-32 in. barrels, various chokes, boxlock, checkered pistol grip stock. Mfg. 1934-42.

	100%	98%	95%	90%	80%	70%	60%
12 ga.	$1,100	$975	$875	$800	$725	$650	$575
16 ga.	$1,275	$1,125	$950	$875	$775	$675	$600
20 ga.	$1,650	$1,450	$1,250	$995	$875	$775	$675
.410 bore	$3,995	$3,550	$3,100	$2,750	$2,450	$2,150	$1,725

Add 33% for auto ejectors.
Add 10% for ST.

GRADING - PPGS™	100%	98%	95%	90%	80%	70%	60%

GRADE A SKEET MODEL - similar to Grade A, with 26 in. skeet bore barrels, auto ejector, single trigger and beavertail forearm standard.

	100%	98%	95%	90%	80%	70%	60%
12 ga.	$1,650	$1,450	$1,275	$1,075	$925	$800	$675
16 ga.	$2,000	$1,750	$1,475	$1,250	$1,075	$950	$800
20 ga.	$2,575	$2,300	$1,975	$1,700	$1,500	$1,250	$995
.410 bore	$4,500	$4,000	$3,500	$2,750	$2,450	$2,150	$1,725

SHOTGUNS: SINGLE BARREL

TRAP GUN - 12 ga. only, 30 or 32 in. VR barrel, full choke, boxlock, auto ejector, checkered pistol grip stock. Disc. 1942.

	$600	$550	$440	$385	$330	$275	$250

LONG RANGE FIELD - 12, 16, 20 ga., or .410 bore, 26-32 in. barrel, boxlock, extractor, checkered pistol grip stock. Disc. 1942.

	$395	$350	$295	$265	$225	$170	$140

LEFEVER, D.M.

Previous manufacturer circa 1901-1906. Company names and locations have been D.M. Lefever & Sons, Syracuse, NY (1901), D.M. Lefever, Sons & Co., Syracuse, NY (1901-1902), D.M. Lefever Gun Mfg., Defiance OH (1903-1904), and D.M. Lefever Co., Bowling Green, OH (1905-1906).

"Uncle Dan Lefever" founded the Lefever Arms Co. in 1884. He left the company in 1901 to found the above listed companies. While all were short-lived, the last was dissolved in 1906 the year of his death. Lefever Arms Co. continued manufacturing shotguns until sold to Ithaca Gun Co. in 1916. Ithaca assembled the Lefever gun until circa 1921, when they started building the "Nitro Special".

SHOTGUNS

"Uncle Dan" Lefever, founder of Lefever Arms, designed and manufactured the first breech loading double hammerless shotgun made in the U.S. Production started in 1872 and continued in the Syracuse, NY plant until he sold his interest in the Lefever Arms Company during the early 1900s. He then moved to Ohio and started another factory under the name D.M. Lefever & Son. After his death a few years later the Ohio factory was closed, while his old company (Lefever Arms Co.) continued manufacturing Lefevers until being sold to Ithaca Gun Company in 1916. From that point, Lefever Arms Co. was a branch of Ithaca and continued to make shotguns until shortly after WWII.

Total production on D.M. Lefever shotguns between 1901-1904 totaled less than 1,200. Because of their inherent rarity, values listed show only 10%-80% condition specimens. D.M. Lefever specimens are so rare in 80%+ condition that prices cannot be accurately ascertained.

100%	98%	95%	90%	80%	70%	60%	50%	40%	30%	20%	10%

SHOTGUNS: SxS

NEW LEFEVER MODEL - 12, 16, or 20 ga., boxlock action, any length barrel and choke on order, auto ejectors standard on all grades except O Excelsior, double triggers standard on all except Uncle Dan grade, optional single triggers available, checkered walnut pistol grip or straight stock, grades differ as to engraving, wood, checkering and overall quality. Mfg. 1901-1906.

Add 50% for 16 ga. or 20 ga.
Add 10% for SST.

* *New Lefever Model O Excelsior Grade*

100%	98%	95%	90%	80%	70%	60%	50%	40%	30%	20%	10%
N/A	N/A	N/A	N/A	$2,800	$2,425	$1,925	$1,650	$1,475	$1,350	$1,175	$950

* *New Lefever Model Excelsior Grade w/ejectors*

100%	98%	95%	90%	80%	70%	60%	50%	40%	30%	20%	10%
N/A	N/A	N/A	N/A	$3,150	$2,725	$2,300	$1,925	$1,595	$1,450	$1,300	$1,045

100%	98%	95%	90%	80%	70%	60%	50%	40%	30%	20%	10%

* New Lefever Model F Grade, No. 9

| N/A | N/A | N/A | N/A | $3,150 | $2,725 | $2,300 | $1,925 | $1,595 | $1,450 | $1,300 | $1,045 |

* New Lefever Model E Grade, No. 8

| N/A | N/A | N/A | N/A | N/A | $4,000 | $3,600 | $3,100 | $2,700 | $2,300 | $1,900 | $1,600 |

* New Lefever Model D Grade, No. 7

| N/A | N/A | N/A | N/A | N/A | $4,950 | $4,500 | $4,125 | $3,850 | $3,375 | $2,975 | $2,750 |

* New Lefever Model C Grade, No. 6

| N/A | N/A | N/A | N/A | N/A | $6,250 | $5,600 | $4,800 | $4,300 | $3,900 | $3,575 | $3,175 |

* New Lefever Model B Grade, No. 5

| N/A | N/A | N/A | N/A | N/A | $6,600 | $5,850 | $5,000 | $4,500 | $4,000 | $3,650 | $3,250 |

* New Lefever Model AA Grade, No. 4

| N/A | N/A | N/A | N/A | N/A | $9,250 | $8,500 | $7,700 | $6,600 | $5,500 | $4,850 | $4,400 |

UNCLE DAN GRADE - extremely rare, original specimens are selling for $150,000+

SHOTGUNS: SINGLE BARREL TRAP

TRAP GUN - 12 ga., 26-32 in. full choke, auto ejector, boxlock, checkered pistol grip stock. Mfg. 1904-06.

Extreme rarity factor precludes accurate pricing.

LE FORGERON

Previous manufacturer located in Belgium. Previously imported and distributed by Midwest Gun Sport in Zebulon, NC.

GRADING - PPGS™	100%	98%	95%	90%	80%	70%	60%

RIFLES: SxS

MODEL 6020 - 9.3x74R cal., boxlock action, beavertail forearm, pistol grip stock.

| | | | $4,450 | $4,025 | $3,750 | $3,475 | $3,100 | $2,800 | $2,550 |

Last MSR was $4,900.

Add $700 for sideplates (Model 6040).

MODEL 6030 - sidelock action, engraved action with deluxe French walnut stock and forearm.

| | | | $8,475 | $7,900 | $7,100 | $6,300 | $5,500 | $4,700 | $4,000 |

Last MSR was $8,950.

SHOTGUNS: SxS

Prices represent the importer's last information available (1989).

BOXLOCK EJECTOR - 20 or 28 ga. only, with or without sideplates, select French walnut stock, choice of engraving patterns (optional), single trigger.

| | | | $3,975 | $3,650 | $3,325 | $2,995 | $2,600 | $2,250 | $1,900 |

Last MSR was $4,400.

Add $1,000 for sideplates.

SIDELOCK EJECTOR - 20 or 28 ga. only, select French walnut stock, choice of engraving patterns (optional), rounded action, single trigger.

| | | | $10,200 | $9,250 | $8,500 | $7,900 | $7,100 | $6,300 | $5,500 |

Last MSR was $11,600.

LE FRANCAIS PISTOLS

Previous trademark manufactured by Manufacture Francaise d´Armes et Cycles de Saint-Etienne, located in Saint Etienne, France. Trade name was MANUFRANCE.

GRADING - PPGS™	100%	98%	95%	90%	80%	70%	60%

PISTOLS: SEMI-AUTO

POCKET MODEL AUTOMATIC - .25 ACP cal., double action, 7 shot, 2 3/8 in. hinged barrel, blue, fixed sights, hard rubber grips. Mfg. 1914-1966.

	$300	$250	$210	$180	$150	$125	$100

Add 50%-100% for engraved models, depending on amount of coverage.

TYPE POLICEMAN MODEL AUTOMATIC - .25 ACP cal., similar to Pocket Model, except has 3 1/2 in. hinged barrel, some are marked "FRANCO". Mfg. 1922-1968.

	$400	$300	$250	$210	$180	$150	$125

Add 50%-100% for engraved models, depending on amount of coverage.

.32 AUTOMATIC MODEL - .32 ACP cal., double action, 8 shot, 3 1/4 in. hinged finned barrel, blue, fixed sights, rubber grips. 10,000 mfg. 1950-1969, very few imported into the U.S.

	$1,250	$1,000	$850	$750	$600	$500	$400

TYPE ARMY MODEL AUTOMATIC - 9mm Browning Long cal., double action, 8 shot, 5 in. hinged barrel, blue, fixed sights, checkered walnut grips, some are marked "FRANCO". 4,000 mfg. 1928-1938. Early model with plain tapered barrel (1928), later model with finned barrel (1931).

	$1,950	$1,600	$1,250	$800	$650	$500	$400

Add 10% for later model with finned barrel (1931).
Add 50%-100% for engraved models, depending on amount of coverage.

LEGACY SPORTS INTERNATIONAL

Current importer located in Reno, NV. Previously located in Alexandria, VA.

Legacy Sports International imports a wide variety of shotgun and rifle trademarks, including Breda, Escort, Howa, Puma, and Pointer. Please refer to these individual listings. Legacy also imports Howa actions, with current MSRs ranging from $273-$345.

LEGEND

Previous rifle trademark manufactured circa 1996-2006 by D´Arcy Echols & Co. and located in Millville, UT.

RIFLES: BOLT ACTION

Previous Legend rifles utilized an extensively modified and refined Winchester Model 70 claw extractor action. Synthetic stocks were built by special order. Current rifles may be found under the D'Arcy Echols & Co. listing in the D section.

LEGION

Current trademark manufactured by Izhmash, located in Izhevask, Russia. No current importation.

LEITNER-WISE RIFLE CO. INC.

Current manufacturer located in Springfield, VA beginning 2006. Previously located in Alexandria, VA 1999-2005. Dealer sales.

RIFLES: SEMI-AUTO

LW 15.22 - .22 LR or .22 Mag. cal., paramilitary configuration patterned after the AR-15, forged upper and lower receivers, choice of carry handle or flattop upper receiver, forward bolt assist, last shot hold open, 16 1/2 or 20 in. barrel, 10 or 25 shot mag. Mfg. 2000-2005.

	$775	$675	$600	$550	$500	$450	$425

Last MSR was $850.

Add $50 for A2 carrying handle.

GRADING - PPGS™	100%	98%	95%	90%	80%	70%	60%

LW 15.499 - .499 (12.5x40mm) cal., receiver and action patterned after the AR-15, mil spec standards, 16 1/2 in. steel or stainless steel barrel, flattop receiver, 5 (disc.), 10, or 14 (new 2006) shot mag., approx. 6 1/2 lbs. New 2000.

	MSR N/A	$1,350	$1,150	$995	$875	$750	$675	$600

    Add $92 for stainless steel barrel.

LW 6.8/5.56 S.R.T. - 5.56x45mm NATO or 6.8x43mm SPC cal., 16.1 in. barrel, hard chrome lined bore, gas operated, locking bolt, Troy front and rear sights, forged T7075 aluminum flattop upper receiver, six position collapsible stock, Picatinny rail, removable carry handle, A2 flash hider, LW forged lower receiver, 28 or 30 shot mag., 5.38 lbs. New 2006.

	MSR N/A	$2,050	$1,800	$1,600	$1,400	$1,200	$1,000	$850

    Add $100 for 6.8x43mm SPC cal.

LES BAER CUSTOM, INC.

Current manufacturer and customizer established in 1993, and located in Hillsdale, IL. Dealer sales only.

PISTOLS: SEMI-AUTO

Les Baer has been customizing and manufacturing M1911 type pistols for decades. The company should be contacted directly (see Trademark Index) for an up-to-date price sheet and catalog on their extensive line-up of high quality competition/combat pistols that range in price from $1,666-$3,230. Additionally, specialty models, including Presentation Grades ($6,095-$6,595 MSR) are available in various configurations and calibers. A wide range of competition parts and related gunsmithing services are also available. Early guns with low ser. nos. have become collectible.

RIFLES: SEMI-AUTO

CUSTOM ULTIMATE AR MODEL - .204 Ruger (new 2004), .223 Rem., or 6.5 Grendel (new 2007) cal., individual rifles are custom built with no expense spared, everything made in-house ensuring top quality and tolerances, all models are guaranteed to shoot 1/2-3/4 MOA groups, various configurations include Varmint Model (disc.), Super Varmint Model, NRA Match Rifle, Super Match Model (new 2002), M4 Flattop Model, and IPSC Action Model. New 2001.

	MSR $1,989		$1,850	$1,650	$1,450	$1,250	$1,050	$925	$800

    Add $800-$1,100 for scope package (includes Leupold Vari-X III 4.5-14x40mm scope).
    Add $271 for 6.5 Grendel cal. in M4 variation or $146 in Super Varmint Model.

The $1,989 MSR represents the base price on the Super Varmint Model. Other variations are typically priced $100-$500 more, depending on the configuration.

LEW HORTON DIST. CO.

Current firearms distributor located in Westboro, MA. While Lew Horton is not a manufacturer or an importer, this company has been responsible for many special and limited editions which are listed with

quanities, but without prices, since they may vary greatly from region to region. Special/Limited Editions began in 1983.

SPECIAL/LIMITED EDITIONS

In addition to the special/limited editions listed, Lew Horton also subcontracted special editions that were sold from company flyers and other promotional materials. They include the following Smith & Wesson Models - Classic Hunter M29 (500 mfg. 1989), Model 63 2 in. (500 mfg. 1989), Model 36 2nd Amendment (200 mfg. 1989), Model 60 25th Anniversary (100 mfg. 1989), Model 629 Classic Hunter (mfg. 1986), Model 5967 (500 mfg. 1990), and the Model 3914 (200 mfg. 1990). There are two Remington models - the M1100 Special Field (200 mfg. 1987-88) and the M700 BDL .257 Roberts cal. (500 mfg. 1990). There are

Make/Model	Qty. Made	Year Issue	Retail Price

three Colt models - the Combat Python (750 mfg. 1987-88), the Pocketlite (350 mfg. 1989), and the Custom Cobra Stainless Sets (2 sets, mfg. 1989).

BERETTA

Make/Model	Qty. Made	Year Issue	Retail Price
✳ Lady Beretta	100	1985	$285

COLT MODELS

Make/Model	Qty. Made	Year Issue	Retail Price
✳ SAA Horse Pistol	100	1983	$1,100
✳ Presidential - Gold SAA & Det. Spec. w/Gold Eye	600	1985	$525
✳ Colt Boa (includes both 4 and 6 in. barrel)	600	1985	$525
✳ Ultimate Officer´s .45 ACP	500	1989	$777
✳ Lt. Commander .45 ACP	800	1985	$590
✳ Combat Cobra 2 1/2 in.	1,000	1987	$500
✳ Lady Colt (MK IV .380 ACP)	1,000	1989	$547
✳ Night Commander .45 ACP	250	1989	$725
✳ El Presidente .38 Super Govt.	350	1990	$800
✳ El Comandante .38 Super Govt.	500	1991	$800
✳ El General .38 Super Govt.	500	1991	$850
✳ El Capitan .38 Super	500	1991	$875
✳ Detective Special	100	1992	$430
✳ Elite Ten/Forty	100	1992	$900
✳ El Patron	500	1992	$850
✳ El Jefe	500	1992	$849
✳ El Dorado	750	1992	$1,099
✳ El Teniente	400	1992	$1,037
✳ El Teniente	300	2001	N/A
✳ El Coronel	750	1993	$900
✳ Classic Gold Cup	300	1993	$1,285
✳ Classic Single Action	180	1993	$680
✳ Night Officer	350	1993	$680
✳ El Presidente Premier Edition	10	1993	$3,000
✳ Classic Government	300	1993	$965
✳ Night Government	300	1993	$705
✳ El Caballero	500	1994	$986
✳ El Potro	500	1994	$1,025
✳ Frontier Six Shooter	100	1994	$1,849
✳ McCormick Factory Racer	500	1994	$1,149
✳ Springfield Armory Bicentennial Edition	400	1994	$1,000
✳ Springfield Armory Premier Bicentennial	200	1994	$1,213
✳ Classic 45 Special Edition	500	1995	$960
✳ Comp Commander .45 ACP Ported	350	1998	$889
✳ Defender Custom .45 ACP 3 in. w/4 Ports	100	1998	$900
✳ Delta 98 10mm 5 in. Matte SS	100	1998	$800
✳ El Aquila Supreme .38 Sup. Engraved	20	1999	$3,000
✳ El Aquila .38 Sup. 5 in. RB	350	1999	$1,000
✳ El Cabo .38 Sup. 5 in. Bright SS	350	1999	$1,200
✳ El Campecon .38 Super Blue	550	1997	$870

Make/Model	Qty. Made	Year Issue	Retail Price
✱ El Centauro .38 Sup. BTS	350	1997	$798
✱ El Embajador .38 Sup. BTS/Gold	350	1998	$1,000
✱ El General 5 Star Deluxe 38 Sup. Engr.	10	1997	$2,000
✱ El Jefe Supremo Supreme 38 Sup. Engr.	20	1999	$3,000
✱ El Jefe Supremo 38 Sup BSTS/Fire Bl.	350	1999	$1,410
✱ El Oficial .38 Sup R/Blue w/gold	450	1998	$1,003
✱ El Sargento .38 Super 5 in. RB/SS	350	1999	$1,000
✱ El Soldado 38 Super 5 in. Ryl Blue/Pearlite grips	350	2000	$1,020
✱ El Soldado Supreme 38 Super A Engraved	20	2000	$2,996
✱ El Soldado Supreme	20	2001	N/A
✱ El Soldado Supreme Proposed	20	2001	N/A
✱ El Senador	350	2001	N/A
✱ El Senador Supreme	20	2001	N/A
✱ El Toro 38 Super Bl w/jeweled parts	350	2000	$1,020
✱ El Toro	350	2001	N/A
✱ El Toro Supreme	20	2001	N/A
✱ El Obra Maestra .38 Super Royal Blue/Gold	350	2001	$1,130
✱ El Matadore .38 Super 5 in. Bright Stainless w/Gold	350	2001	$1,425
✱ El Rey Hi Polish Stainless S teel Blue .38 Super	350	2001	$1,050
✱ McCormick Combat Cmdr 45 Engr.	50	1995	$1,213
✱ McCormick Combat Cmdr 45 Chrome	500	1995	$1,073
✱ McCormick Officer Cmdr 45 Chrome	300	1995	$1,073
✱ Night Officer II Chrm 45 Night Sight	100	1994	$829
✱ Night Officer III SS/Matte 45	200	1996	$810
✱ Officers Ultimate .45 ACP Bl/SS	500	1995	$900
✱ Officers Ultimate .45 ACP Engr.	10	1995	$1,995
✱ SAA CC/B Mop. Std. Eng.	15	1999	$5,345
✱ SAA .45 LC Nickel Bird´s Head Mother-of-Pearl, Std. C	30	2001	$5,715
✱ U.S. Shooting Team .45 ACP	750	1995	$1,150
✱ Govt. Model XSE w/gold scroll	20	2006	$1,170
✱ M1991A1 w/scroll & gold detail	20	2006	$1,000
EUROPEAN AMERICAN ARMORY			
✱ Witness Competitor 45 Ported	100	1998	$460
✱ Witness Competitor Polymer 45 Ported	100	1998	$460
✱ Witness Defender II 45 Ported	100	1998	$460
✱ Witness Defender Polymer 45 Ported	100	1998	$496
✱ Witness Tactical .40 S&W 12rd	300	1997	$400
✱ Witness Tactical .45 ACP 10rd	300	1997	$400
H&R 1871, INC.			
✱ 999 Premier Edition	100pr.	1993	$345
MOSSBERG			
✱ Night Persuader Special Edition	300	1990	N/A

Make/Model	Qty. Made	Year Issue	Retail Price
REMINGTON			
✳ *Model 541J Curly Maple*	500	1994	$500
✳ *Model 700 Police .308 Win., 26 in. fluted*	500	2004	$1,000
✳ *Model 700 Police .308 Win. w/spruce green stock*	500	2004	$930
SIGARMS			
✳ *P220 Premium Edition .45 ACP*	200	1994	$850

SMITH & WESSON - Lew Horton is a major distributor of S&W's Heritage Series and Performance Center models. Please contact Lew Horton directly to find out more information on this wide variety of handguns, including current availability and pricing.

Make/Model	Qty. Made	Year Issue	Retail Price
✳ *Model 25-3 Lew Horton Special*	100	1977	$500
✳ *Model 29-3 Lew Horton Special*	5,000	1984	$425
✳ *Model 629-3 Lew Horton Special*	5,000	N/A	$400
✳ *Model 24-3 Lew Horton Special*	5,000	1983-84	$380
✳ *Model 686 Lew Horton Special*	N/A	1984	$450
✳ *Model 657-3 Lew Horton Special*	5,000	1986	$410
✳ *Model 624-2 Lew Horton Special*	7,000	1986-87	$395
✳ *Model 640 Carry Comp*	250	1991	$750
✳ *.40 Compensated*	150	1992	$1,699
✳ *.40 Tactical*	200	1992	$1,499
✳ *Shorty Forty*	N/A	1992	$950
✳ *Model 629 Hunter*	200	1992	$1,234
✳ *Model 629 Carry Comp*	300	1992	$1,000
✳ *Model 686 Carry Comp 4 in.*	300	1992	$1,000
✳ *Model 657 Classic Hunter*	350	1993	$545
✳ *Model 356 Shorty*	N/A	1993	$999
✳ *Model 356 Tactical*	N/A	1993	$1,350
✳ *Model 629 Hunter II*	200	1993	$1,234
✳ *Model 629 Carry Comp II*	100	1993	$1,000
✳ *Model 686 Carry Comp 3 in.*	300	1993	$1,000
✳ *Model 686 Competitor*	400	1993	$1,100
✳ *Model 686 Hunter*	200	1993	$1,153
✳ *Model 5906 Shorty Nine*	200	1993	$999
✳ *Model 60 Carry Comp*	300	1993	$800
✳ *Model 629 Unfluted*	300	1993	$1,234
✳ *Model 629 Hunter III*	300	1994	$1,234
✳ *Model 640 Paxton Quigley*	250	1994	$800
✳ *Model 625 Classic Snub*	300	1994	$603
✳ *Model 629 Classic Hunter*	500	1994	$1,234
✳ *Model 629 Quad-magnaported .44 Mag.*	150	1994	$900
✳ *Shorty Forty Mark II*	150	1995	$999
✳ *Shorty .40 Mark III*	500	1997	$1,025
✳ *Shorty .45*	225	1997	$1,096
✳ *Shorty .45 Mark II*	N/A	1997	N/A
✳ *Model 625 Hunter .45 LC Fluted*	150	1997	$1,234
✳ *Model 629 Hunter .44 Mag. Unfluted*	500	1997	$1,234
✳ *Model 686 Hunter 7 Shot Unfluted*	300	1997	$1,234

Make/Model	Qty. Made	Year Issue	Retail Price
✳ Model 640 Quadport .357 Mag. 2 in. Brl	500	1997	$836
✳ Model 681 Quadport .357 Mag. 7 Shot	300	1997	$700
✳ PC M627 357 2 5/8 in. 8 shot RRWO Unfluted	450	2000	$1,025
✳ Model 686 7 Shot Night Sight	300	1997	$1,000
✳ F Comp. 3 in. Comp. Barrel	500	1997	$800
✳ Model 629 Classic Carry 3 in. Unfluted	300	1997	$590
✳ M625 .45 LC 3 in. Rosewood Red ramp WO	400	1998	$755
✳ M625 45 Colt 3 FL Rosewood RRWO	150	2000	$755
✳ M627 Classic Hunter 41 Mg 6.5 in. wood flt.	150	1997	$614
✳ M627 Classic Hunter 41 Mg 6.5 in. wood unfl	400	1997	$614
✳ PC M629 44 6 in. Hunter w/barrel cut out, unfluted	350	2000	$1,300
✳ PC M629 44 12 in. barrel FL w/sling, Bomar sights	400	2000	$1,059
✳ PC M1006 Classic Ser 10mm 5 in. 9 shot	28	1998	$550
✳ PC M27 .357 Mag. 5 in. fluted cyl. SB	16	1999	$670
✳ PC M29 Classic Ser .44 Mag. 7.5 wood c/s	19	1998	$1,060
✳ PC M41 Classic Ser .22 LR 7 in. S&W sights	14	1998	$801
✳ PC M4516 Classic Ser .45 ACP 3 3/4 in.	7	1998	$866
✳ PC M4563 CQB .45 ACP 4 Alloy Frame	100	1998	$1,235
✳ PC M4563 CQB .45 ACP 4 in. two-tone	200	1998	$1,235
✳ PC M4566 CQB .45 ACP 4 in. SS frame	100	1998	$1,235
✳ PC M4567 Classic Ser .45 4.5 in. two-tone	14	1998	$1,010
✳ PC M627 Htr .357 6 in. 8 shot unf. wood	200	1997	$1,060
✳ PC M627 .357 Mg. 5 in. 8 shot ported	100	1997	$1,050
✳ PC M627 .357 2 5/8 in. 8 shot RRWO unflt.	300	1999	$1,025
✳ PC M627 .357 5 in. 8 shot unf. wood cmbt	1,200	1997	$1,000
✳ PC M627 .357 5 in. 8 shot unf. rosewood	200	1998	$1,000
✳ PC M627 .357 6.5 in. 8 shot fluted rosewood	200	1998	$1,025
✳ PC M629 .44 Mg. 6 1/2 in. flt. 6 sht RMB	200	1998	$1,020
✳ PC M629 .44 Mg. 2 5/8 in. 6 sht rosewood	300	1999	$1,026
✳ PC M629 6 in. Htr w/bbl CO Unf port	100	1999	$1,060
✳ PC M657 Classic Ser .41 Mg. 3 in.	7	1994	$550
✳ PC M657 Classic Ser .41 Mg. 4 in.	25	1998	$550
✳ PC M657 41 Mg. 6 1/2 in. FL 6 sht	200	1998	$1,020

Make/Model	Qty. Made	Year Issue	Retail Price
✳ PC M686 .357 3 in. 7 sht ss night sights	500	1996	$1,000
✳ PC M686 .357 6 in. 7 sht Hntr w/port	175	1996	$1,024
✳ PC M686 .357 Mg. 7 sht profile bbl	125	1998	$1,025
✳ PC M9 Shorty 9 MKII 9mm Compact	150	1995	$1,050
✳ PC M625 3 in.	N/A	2004	$1,110
✳ PC M329 .44 cal., Clear Scandium frame, 3 in. Stainless bbl	100	2004	$1,200
✳ PC M329 .44 cal., Black Scandium frame, 3 in. bl. bbl.	500	2004	$1,200
✳ PC M629 .44 Mag. cal., 7.5 in. bbl Compted Hunter TDA	500	2004	$1,171
✳ M15 .38 Spl. 4 in. color case blue	200	2001	$770
✳ M15 .38 Spl. 4 in. nickel	200	2001	$750
✳ M15 .38 Spl. 5 in. nickel McGivern	150	2001	$1,070
✳ M15 .38 Spl. 6 in. blue McGivern	150	2001	$1,040
✳ M15 .38 Spl. 6 in. color case blue	100	2001	$1,070
✳ M17 .22 LR 6 in. AS blue	200	2001	$1,040
✳ M17 .22 LR 6 1/2 in. color case blue	150	2001	$1,070
✳ M24 .44 Spl. 6 1/2 in. color case frame	300	2001	$1,110
✳ M24 .44 Spl. 6 1/2 in. fluted blue	150	2001	$1,050
✳ M25 (1917) .45 ACP 5 1/2 in. 6 shot	200	2001	$1,047
✳ M25 .45 Colt 6 1/2 in. color case blue frame	150	2001	$1,111
✳ M25 .45 Colt 6 1/2 in. fluted blue	150	2001	$1,050
✳ M25 (1917) .45 ACP 5 1/2 in. color case blue	100	2001	$1,110
✳ M25 (1917) .45 ACP 5 1/2 in. Military	150	2001	$1,050
✳ M27 5 1/2 in. Nickel	100	2007	$1,510
✳ M27 3 1/2 In. Nickel	100	2007	$1,500
✳ M29 .44 Mag. 6 1/2 in. blue	250	2001	$1,045
✳ M29 .44 Mag. 6 1/2 in. nickel	200	2001	$1,070
✳ Schofield M3 .45 S&W	100	2001	$1,520
✳ Schofield 7 in. bright nickel	100	2001	$1,520
✳ Model SW1911 "United We Stand"	250	2005	$1,127
✳ PC Model 625 .45 LC Scandium SS 2 in.	100	2005	$1,291
✳ SW 1911 SS .45 ACP Engraved	50	2006	$1,005
✳ PC Model 500 SS .500 Mag.	1,000	2004	$1,350
✳ PC Model 625-10 Scandium SS .45 ACP	800	2003	$1,110
✳ Model 36 .38 Spl, nickel/blue	250	2006	$857
✳ SW1911 Land of the Free w/gold	150	2004	$1,137
✳ SW1911 Gold Eagle Ltd.	60	2005	$2,000
✳ PC M460 Spl. Ed. .460 S&W Mag. SS 3 1/2 in.	500	2005	$1,600
✳ PC M460 Spl. Ed. .460 S&W Mag. SS 6 1/2 in.	750	2005	$1,500
✳ SW1911 SS Long May It Wave w/gold	100	2004	$1,137
✳ SW1911 SS Rebel Flag Ltd. Ed.	100	2005	$1,137
✳ SW1911 SS Mexican Eagle Ltd. Ed.	100	2004	$1,147
✳ PC M460 .460 S&W Mag. Two-tone 3 1/2 in.	100	2006	$1,600

Make/Model	Qty. Made	Year Issue	Retail Price
SPRINGFIELD			
* *Night Light Compact 1911-A1 Lightweight*	500	1997	$749
* *Night Light Standard 1911-A1 Lightweight*	300	1997	$749
* *M1911 Ltw Compact .45 ACP bi-tone 7rd*	125	1998	$675
* *M1911 Ltw Std. .45 ACP bi-tone 8rd*	300	1998	$675
* *Springfield Armory Bicentennial Edition*	500	1994	$775
SAVAGE			
* *10FP Tactical .223 Rem. Short Action*	200	1999	$492
* *10FP Tactical .308 Win. HB 20*	550	1999	$500
* *30 Joshua Stevens .22 LR*	250	2001	$400
TAURUS			
* *Model PT-92AF*	250	1990	$454
* *Model 85 3 in. Ported Blue*	500	1995	$229
* *Model 85 3 in. Ported Stainless*	500	1995	$349

LEWIS MACHINE & TOOL COMPANY

Current paramilitary rifle and accessories manufacturer located in Milan, IL.

Lewis Machine & Tool Company manufactures both commercial and military AR-15 style rifles, including the Defender/Guardian. Please contact the company directly for more information, including availability and pricing (see Trademark Index).

LIBERATOR

Previously manufactured by the Guide Lamp Corporation (division of General Motors) circa 1942.

100%	98%	95%	90%	80%	70%	60%	50%	40%	30%	20%	10%

PISTOLS: SINGLE SHOT

LIBERATOR PISTOL - .45 ACP cal., simplistic design and action utilizing nonstrategic WWII materials, mfg. for European resistance movement during WWII, very limited number used in Europe, most used in Philipines and China, each gun was individually packaged in a paraffin-coated cardboard box with wood ejector rod, wood spacer, and a smaller box containing 10 rounds of .45 ACP ammo with a graphics only instruction sheet on top, 4 in. smooth bore barrel, sheet steel stamping mfg. with welds, no ser. no., 1 million mfg. 1942 only.

N/A	N/A	$3,950	$3,500	$3,250	$3,000	$2,750	$2,500	$2,300	$2,100	$1,900	$1,750

Add $600-$800 for original box.

Add $400-$600 for original B&W instruction sheet.

Auction prices on this model have topped $7,000 for a nice original specimen.

An authentic instruction sheet will have a watermark reading "WHITING MUTUAL BOND RAG CONTENT," and all ammo will have a headstamp of "FA 42". This is the only pistol that could be mfg. (6.6 sec.) faster than it could be loaded (10 sec.). While the Liberator's appearance is crude, remember that the entire production run (1 million) was mfg. and ready for overseas shipment in 10-11 weeks.

Even though 1 million of these pistols were mfg., remaining specimens brought into the U.S. are rare. Complete pistols in original box are extremely rare.

GRADING - PPGS™	100%	98%	95%	90%	80%	70%	60%

LIBERTY

Previous trademark imported 1997-2003 by K.B.I., Inc. located in Harrisburg, PA.

REVOLVERS: SAA

FRONTIER MODEL - .38-40 Win. (disc. 1998), .357 Mag. (disc. 1998, reintroduced 2000 only), .44- 40 WCF (disc. 2000), or .45 LC cal., 4 3/4, 5 1/2, or 7 1/2 in. barrel, case hardened, bright nickel, or antique silver (new 1999) frame, choice of brass or steel backstrap and trigger guard, mfg. by Uberti. Imported 1997-2001.

$295	$250	$235	$210	$195	$175	$160

Last MSR was $339.

Add $45 for steel backstrap and trigger guard.
Add $80 for antique silver finish (new 1999).
Add $25 for bright nickel finish (.44-40 WCF or .45 LC only).

TARGET MODEL - similar to Frontier Model, except is not available in .357 Mag. cal., and has adj. rear sight. Imported 1997-98.

$300	$265	$240	$220	$200	$180	$165

Last MSR was $319.

BISLEY MODEL - .44-40 WCF or .45 LC cal., features Bisley grip configuration, 4 3/4, 5 1/2, or 7 1/2 in. barrel, case hardened or bright nickel finish, steel backstrap and trigger guard. Limited importation 1999 only.

$415	$365	$325	$295	$260	$230	$200

Last MSR was $459.

Add $60 for bright nickel finish.

LIBERTY I/II - .357 Mag., .44-40 WCF, or .45 LC cal., 4 3/4, 5 1/2, or 7 1/2 in. barrel, case hardened frame, blue finish, choice of brass or steel backstrap and trigger guard.

$275	$250	$235	$210	$195	$175	$160

Last MSR was $319.

Add $70 for steel backstrap and trigger guard.

This model changed nomenclature to Charles Daly Model 1873 during 2004 - please refer to the Charles Daly 1976-present section for current information on this model.

RIFLES: LEVER ACTION

MODEL 1892 CARBINE - .357 Mag. or .45 LC cal., choice of case hardened or brass plated receiver, 20 in. round barrel. Limited importation 2000 only.

$595	$525	$475	$425	$395	$360	$330

Last MSR was $665.

Add $15 for brass plated receiver.

MODEL 1892 RIFLE - .357 Mag., .44-40 WCF, or .45 LC cal., choice of case hardened, brass plated, or antique silver finished receiver, 24 in. octagon barrel. Limited importation 2000 only.

$610	$535	$485	$430	$400	$360	$330

Last MSR was $680.

RIFLES: REPRODUCTIONS

SHARPS TRAPDOOR CARBINE/RIFLE/BUSINESS - .45-70 Govt. cal., case hardened receiver finish, choice of 22 (Carbine), 28 (Rifle), or 32 (Business, limited importation 2000 only) in. round barrel, single or double set triggers. Imported from Pedersoli 2000-2001.

$675	$575	$500	$450	$400	$350	$300

Last MSR was $769.

Add $20 for Hunter rifle.
Add $60 for Business Model (limited importation 2000 only).

GRADING - PPGS™	100%	98%	95%	90%	80%	70%	60%

ROLLING BLOCK CARBINE/RIFLE - .357 Mag., .45 LC, or .45-70 Govt. cal., case hardened receiver finish, 22 in. round (Carbine) or 28 in. octagon (Rifle) barrel. Imported from Pedersoli 2000-2001.

	$615	$550	$475	$425	$375	$325	$275

Last MSR was $689.

Add $10 for Rifle.

SPRINGFIELD TRAPDOOR CARBINE/RIFLE - .45-70 Govt. cal., case hardened receiver finish, 22 (Carbine) or 26 (Rifle) in. round barrel. Imported from Pedersoli 2000-2001.

	$725	$650	$600	$550	$475	$425	$375

Last MSR was $815.

Add $34 for rifle with 26 in. barrel.

RIFLES: SxS

LIGHTNING EXPRESS DOUBLE RIFLE - .44-40 WCF, .45 LC, or .45-70 Govt. cal., exposed hammers, 22 in. barrels, choice of case hardened, bright nickel (disc.), or antique silver (new 2000) finish. Limited importation 1999-2000.

	$750	$650	$550	$475	$425	$375	$325

Last MSR was $840.

Add $40 for antique silver finish.

SHOTGUNS: SxS

LIBERTY I/II COACH GUN - 12 ga. only, exposed hammers, 20 or 24 (disc. 2000, reintroduced 2002) in. barrels, choice of case hardened or antique silver finish, fixed chokes (cyl./cyl., 20 in. barrels only, or IC/M, 24 in. barrels only). Imported 1999-2003.

	$475	$435	$375	$345	$315	$285	$250

Last MSR was $559.

∗ *Liberty I/II Coach Gun/Express Rifle Combination Set* - includes 20 in. 12 ga. barrels, and choice of 22 in. rifle barrels in any Lightning Express cal., blue finish only. Limited importation 1999 only.

	$1,025	$875	$750	$625	$550	$475	$425

Last MSR was $1,159.

LIBERTY ARMS WORKS, INC.

Previous manufacturer located in West Chester, PA circa 1991-1996.

PISTOLS: SEMI-AUTO

L.A.W. ENFORCER - .22 LR, 9mm Para., 10mm, .40 S&W (new 1994), or .45 ACP cal., patterned after the Ingram MAC 10, single action, 6 1/4 in. threaded barrel, closed bolt operation, manual safety, 10 (C/B 1994) or 30∗ shot mag., 5 lbs. 1 oz. Mfg. 1991-96.

	$575	$500	$450	$415	$385	$335	$295

Last MSR was $545.

LIEGEOISE D´ARMES

Previous manufacturer located in Belgium.

Small manufacturer that specialized in boxlock shotguns, normally engraved and with ejectors. Prices usually range from $600-$1,200, depending on condition and engraving.

GRADING - PPGS™	100%	98%	95%	90%	80%	70%	60%

LIGNOSE (BERGMAN)

Previous manufacturer located in Suhl, Germany.

PISTOLS: SEMI-AUTO

EINHAND MODEL 2A POCKET AUTOMATIC - 6.35mm/.25 ACP cal., 6 shot, 2 in. barrel, blue, rubber grips, can be cocked by rearward pressure on triggerguard.

	$395	$325	$225	$165	$140	$110	$85

MODEL 3 POCKET AUTOMATIC - similar to 3A, except without one hand cocking trigger guard.

	$300	$250	$200	$165	$140	$110	$85

MODEL 3A POCKET AUTOMATIC - similar to 2A, except longer grip, 9 shot capacity.

	$450	$350	$250	$200	$140	$110	$85

MODEL 2 POCKET AUTOMATIC - similar to 2A, without one hand cocking triggerguard.

	$325	$265	$215	$165	$90	$75	$55

LILIPUT

Previous trademark manufactured by August Menz, located in Suhl, Germany.

PISTOLS: SEMI-AUTO

4.25mm cal. - 4.25mm centerfire Liliput cal. (shoots 12 grain bullet), blue or nickel finish, limited 1920s mfg.

	$700	$550	$425	$385	$340	$300	$280

Ammunition for this caliber is very rare, and is currently selling for approx. $200 per round.

6.35mm cal. - .25 ACP cal., mfg. in large quantities pre-WWII.

	$250	$200	$140	$110	$90	$75	$55

LINDNER GUN COMPANY

Current manufacturer located in Sandornville, NH.

Lindner Gun Company manufactures fine quality long arms per individual custom order. Please contact the company directly for more information, including model availability and pricing (see Trademark Index).

LINEBAUGH, JOHN

Current pistolsmith located in Cody, WY.

Mr. John Linebaugh has been making specialized, custom sixguns since 1980. He is the inventor of the .475 Linebaugh cartridge (introduced 1988), and the .500 Linebaugh caliber (the first successful .50 caliber revolver and cartridge introduced in 1986). Current pricing for a customer supplied Ruger Bisley model is $2,000-$3,500. Please contact him directly for more information, including a price quotation (see Trademark Index).

LITTLE SHARPS RIFLE MFG.

Current rifle manufacturer established in 1996, and located in Big Sandy, MT. Consumer direct sales.

RIFLES: SINGLE SHOT

LITTLE SHARPS RIFLE - various rimmed cals. between .22 LR and .375 LSR, features scaled down frame for smaller cals. (20% smaller than original Sharps), octagon barrel. New 1998.

MSR $3,250	$2,900	$2,600	$2,250	$1,850	$1,550	$1,275	$1,050

Add $250 for set trigger.

GRADING - PPGS™	100%	98%	95%	90%	80%	70%	60%

LJUNGMAN

Previously manufactured by Carl Gustaf, located in Eskilstuna, Sweden.

RIFLES: SEMI-AUTO

AG 42 - 6.5x55mm Swedish cal., 10 shot mag., wood stock, tangent rear and hooked front sight, bayonet lug, designed in 1941. This was the first mass produced, direct gas operated rifle. This weapon was also used by the Egyptian armed forces and was known as the Hakim, and chambered in 8x57mm Mauser.

$850	$700	$600	$495	$450	$400	$365

LJUTIC LLC

Current shotgun manufacturer established circa 1955 and located in Yakima, WA. Dealer direct and retail sales.

Prior to 1960, Ljutic Industries, Inc. did business as Ljutic Gun Co. The name changed again in 2006 to Ljutic LLC.

SHOTGUNS: O/U

LM 6 - 12 ga. only, supplied with one set of O/U barrels, deluxe wood and checkering, separated barrels on O/U.

$19,995	$15,750	$11,000	$9,250	$8,400	$7,500	$6,600

Last MSR was $19,995.

Add $7,000 for extra set of O/U barrels.
Add $9,000 for top single barrel (includes 2 pull trigger groups, and 2 forearms).

DYNA BICENTENNIAL - 12 ga. only, includes one set of O/U barrels, steel or stainless steel frame, deluxe wood and checkered stock and forearm. Mfg. 2000-2007.

$18,995	$16,000	$12,000	$9,250	$8,400	$7,500	$6,600

Last MSR was $18,995.

Subtract $2,000 for steel frame.

SHOTGUNS: SEMI-AUTO

BI MATIC AUTO LOADER - 12 ga., 2 shot, 26-32 in. barrels, low recoil, trap or skeet models available, stock and choking to customer specifications. Limited mfg. until 1999.

$5,995	$4,450	$2,500	$2,100	$1,750	$1,250	$900

Last MSR was $5,995.

Add $2,000 for extra barrel.
Add $750 for extra release trigger.

SHOTGUNS: SINGLE BARREL TRAP

To date approx. 15,000 target shotguns have been manufactured total (all models).

DYNATRAP MODEL - 12 ga., 33 in. barrel, full choke, push button opening, extractor, trap stock.

$2,500	$2,150	$1,600	$1,475	$1,300	$1,200	$1,100

Add $300 for release trigger.
Add $400 for extra release trigger.
Add $250 for extra pull trigger.

MODEL X-73 MODEL - 12 ga., 33 in. barrel. full choke, push button opening, high rib fancy Monte Carlo stock.

$2,500	$2,250	$2,000	$1,850	$1,700	$1,600	$1,500

Add $300 for extra pull trigger.
Add $500 for extra release trigger.

GRADING - PPGS™	100%	98%	95%	90%	80%	70%	60%

DYNOKIC MODEL - 12 ga., 32 (disc.) or 33 in. barrel with 2 choke tubes, patented recoil reduction system reduces felt recoil by 50%, checkered walnut stock, many options available. Mfg. 1997-2003.

	$4,795	$4,000	$3,450	$2,900	$2,500	$2,000	$1,650

Last MSR was $4,795.

Add $1,000 for stainless steel construction.

✳ *Dynokic Model Supreme* - similar to Dynokic Model, except has deluxe walnut stock with checkering. Mfg. 2000-2004.

	$5,595	$4,250	$3,400	$3,000	$2,650	$2,300	$1,900

Last MSR was $5,595.

✳ *Dynokic Model Centennial Pro Stainless* - 12 ga., high grade walnut stock and forearm, 33 in. stainless steel barrel with 2 chokes, recoil reduction system reduces recoil by 50%.

	$7,995	$6,250	$4,875	N/A	N/A	N/A	N/A

Last MSR was $7,995.

MONO GUN - 12 ga., 34 in. barrel, custom choked, custom stocked, pull or release trigger, a "built to customers specifications" trap gun. Also known as Standard Rib or Medium Rib.

✳ *Mono Gun Standard, Medium, or Olympic Rib Model*

MSR $6,995	$6,995	$5,300	$3,850	$3,400	$2,700	$2,300	$1,900

Add $400 for stainless choke tubes.
Add $1,000 for stainless steel construction.
Add $1,500 for stainless steel SLE Pro Model.
Add $1,000 for SLE Pro Package (includes Laib adj. comb, adj. alum. base plate with 2 pads, and Pro barrel with special bore).
Approximately 3,100 Mono Guns have been manufactured to date.

✳ *Mono Gun LTX (Deluxe Mono Trap)* - similar to Mono Gun except has 33 (disc.) or 34 in. medium rib barrel and exhibition wood and checkering. Disc. 2006.

	$7,995	$6,800	$5,725	$4,750	$3,800	$2,900	$2,350

Last MSR was $7,995.

Add $500 for extra pull trigger.
Add $650 if with release trigger.
Add $300 for choke tube barrel with 2 chokes.
Add $850 for extra release trigger.
Add $2,499 for extra barrel.
Add $1,200 for stainless steel package.

✳ *Mono Gun Pro 3 (Deluxe Mono Trap)* - similar to Mono Gun except is lighter weight, 34 in. medium rib ported barrel, exhibition wood and checkering, Briley Series 12 choke tubes, pull trigger. New 2000.

MSR $8,495	$8,495	$7,150	$5,950	$4,850	$3,800	$2,900	$2,350

Add $1,000 for adj. comb.
Add $499 for adj. rib.
Add $750 for extra pull trigger.
Add $650 if with release trigger.
Add $850 for extra release trigger assembly.
Add $2,599 for extra barrel with fixed chokes or $2,995 with SIC.
Add $1,000 for stainless steel Pro 3 Package.

SPACE GUN - 12 ga. only, single barrel, unusual design permits in-line round stock with recoil pad, circular forearm wraps around barrel, high post rib on muzzle half of barrel, patented recoil reduction system reduces recoil by 50%. Disc. 1999.

	$5,995	$4,150	$3,375	$2,825	$2,300	$2,000	$1,750

Last MSR was $5,995.

GRADING - PPGS™	100%	98%	95%	90%	80%	70%	60%

LLAMA - Fabrinor S.A.L.

Previous manufacturer established during 1904, and located in Alava, Spain from 1992-2005. Previously located in Vitoria, Spain until 1992. Previously distributed until 2005 by Import Sports, Inc. located in Wanamassa, NJ. Previously imported and distributed by Stoeger Industries, Inc. located in South Hackensack, NJ until 1993, and by R.S.A. Ent., Inc., located in Ocean, NJ. Previous company name was Llama - Gabilondo y Cia S.A.

During 1992, Llama Gabilondo/Vitoria went bankrupt. In January 2000, after arranging new financing, manufacture was taken over by approx. 60 employees of Gabilondo under the name Fabrinor S.A.L. - a cooperative.

PISTOLS: SEMI-AUTO

Most of the pistols listed below were imported by Stoeger, long time exclusive U.S. importer, and are so marked on the guns.

MODEL IIIA - .380 ACP cal., 7 shot, 3 in. barrel, adj. sights, blue, plastic grips., vent. rib slide. Mfg. 1951-disc.

$295	$225	$180	$160	$140	$120	$110

MODEL XA - similar to Model IIIA, except .32 ACP.

$295	$225	$180	$160	$140	$120	$110

MODEL XV - similar to Model XA, except .22 LR.

$295	$225	$180	$160	$140	$120	$110

Add 50% for airweight.

MODEL XVII - .22 S cal.

$295	$225	$180	$160	$140	$120	$110

Add 15%-30% for Deluxe Executive Model with choices of chrome or gold finish and engraving.
Add $1,500 if gold damascened.

MODEL XVIII - .25 ACP cal., blue finish standard, available with optional chrome or gold finish and stag grips.

$325	$250	$200	$160	$140	$120	$110

Add 15%-30% for Deluxe Executive Model with choices of chrome or gold finish and engraving.
Add $1,500 if gold damascened.

MODELS C-IIIA, C-XA, C-XV - similar to Model C, except engraved chrome.

$450	$375	$275	$225	$180	$155	$140

MODELS BE-IIIA, BE-XA, BE-XV - similar to Model CE, except engraved, blue.

$450	$375	$275	$225	$180	$155	$140

Deluxe Models, all blue or chrome engraved with simulated pearl grips, add $20.

MODEL G-IIIA - similar to IIIA, except gold damascened, simulated pearl grips.

$2,250	$1,950	$1,650	$1,225	$800	$700	$600

MODEL VIII - .38 Super cal., 9 shot, 5 in. barrel, fixed sights, wood grips. Mfg. 1952-disc.

$350	$295	$235	$195	$180	$165	$140

MODEL IXA - similar to Model VIII, except .45 ACP, vent. rib slide.

$350	$295	$235	$195	$180	$165	$140

MODEL XI - similar to Model IXA, except 9mm Para.

$350	$295	$235	$195	$180	$165	$140

MODELS C-VIII, C-IXA, C-XI - similar to Model VIII, except satin chrome.

$375	$325	$285	$260	$220	$195	$165

GRADING - PPGS™	100%	98%	95%	90%	80%	70%	60%

MODELS CE-VIII, CE-IXA, CE-XI

	100%	98%	95%	90%	80%	70%	60%
	$425	$350	$310	$285	$265	$220	$195

MODELS BE-VIII, BE-IXA, BE-XI - similar to Model CE, except blue, engraving.

	100%	98%	95%	90%	80%	70%	60%
	$495	$395	$295	$275	$250	$210	$180

Add $20 for Deluxe Models (simulated pearl grips).

OMNI - .45 ACP or 9mm Para. cal., double action, all steel construction, 2 sear bars, 3 safeties, 4 1/4 in. barrel, 7 shot mag. in .45 ACP, 13 shot mag. in 9mm Para., blue finish. Importation disc. 1986.

	100%	98%	95%	90%	80%	70%	60%
9mm Para.	$440	$380	$330	$295	$260	$225	$200
.45 ACP	$395	$360	$320	$285	$250	$220	$195

Last MSR was $546 for 9mm Para. Last MSR was $500 for .45 ACP.

SMALL FRAME MODEL - .22 LR (disc. 1994), .32 ACP (disc. 1993), or .380 ACP cal., Colt 1911A1 design, single action, 3 11/16 in. barrel, 7 shot mag., 23 oz. Also available in satin chrome, optional engraving patterns. Disc. 1997.

	100%	98%	95%	90%	80%	70%	60%
	$220	$180	$155	$135	$120	$110	$100

Last MSR was $259.

Add $60 for duo-tone finish (.380 ACP only, mfg. 1991-1993).
Add $33 for satin chrome finish (not avail. in .32 ACP cal.).

COMPACT FRAME MODEL (IX-B) - 9mm Para. (disc.) or .45 ACP cal., scaled down variation of the Large Frame Model, 4 1/4 in. barrel, 7 or 9 shot mag., 34 or 37 oz. Mfg. 1986-97.

	100%	98%	95%	90%	80%	70%	60%
	$325	$255	$200	$180	$160	$155	$150

Last MSR was $409.

Add $16 for satin chrome finish.
Add $90 for duo-tone finish (mfg. 1990-1993).

GOVERNMENT MODEL (IX-C) - 9mm Para. (disc.), .38 Super (mfg. 1988-1996), or .45 ACP cal., similar to Small Frame Model, 5 1/8 in. barrel, 36 oz., 9 shot mag. in 9mm Para., 10 shot mag. in .45 ACP. Engraved and deluxe models available also. Disc. 1997.

	100%	98%	95%	90%	80%	70%	60%
	$325	$255	$200	$180	$160	$150	$140

Last MSR was $409.

Add $16 for satin chrome finish (.45 ACP only).
Add $90 for duo-tone finish (.45 ACP only, mfg. 1991-1993).

MAX I MODEL - 9mm Para. or .45 ACP cal., patterned after the Colt Govt. Model, 4 1/4 (Compact Model) or 5 1/2 in. barrel, 3-dot combat sights, 7 (.45 ACP) or 9 (9mm Para.) shot mag., matte blue, satin chrome, or duo-tone finish, rubber grips, 34 or 36 oz. Mfg. 1995-99.

	100%	98%	95%	90%	80%	70%	60%
	$265	$225	$200	$180	$160	$150	$140

Last MSR was $299.

Add $10 for duo-tone finish (.45 ACP cal. only).
Add $16 for satin chrome finish (new 1996).

✳ *Max-I Model Compensated* - .45 ACP only, 7 or 10 shot mag., features compensated barrel. Disc. 1997.

	100%	98%	95%	90%	80%	70%	60%
	$445	$385	$330	$250	$200	$180	$160

Last MSR was $492.

Add $25 for 10 shot model.

MINI-MAX - 9mm Para. (disc. 1999), .40 S&W (disc. 2004), or .45 ACP cal., mini-compact variation featuring 6 or 8 shot mag., choice of matte, satin chrome, duo-tone (.45 ACP only), or stainless steel finish/construction, 34 oz. Mfg. 1996-2005.

	100%	98%	95%	90%	80%	70%	60%
	$265	$230	$190	$170	$150	$140	$130

Last MSR was $309.

Add $25 for satin chrome finish.
Add $7 for duo-tone finish (.45 ACP only).
Add $66 for stainless steel construction (disc.).

GRADING - PPGS™	100%	98%	95%	90%	80%	70%	60%

✱ *Mini-Max Sub Compact* - 9mm Para. (disc. 2000), .40 S&W (disc. 2000), or .45 ACP cal., 3.14 in. barrel, all steel construction, 3-dot combat sights, 10 shot mag., polymer grips, choice of matte, satin chrome, or duo-tone finish, 31 oz. Mfg. 1999-2005.

	$270	$235	$195	$175	$150	$140	$130

Last MSR was $316.

Add $26 for satin chrome finish.
Add $9 for duo-tone finish (.45 ACP cal. only).

MICRO-MAX - .32 ACP (mfg. 1999-2004, matte finish only) or .380 ACP cal., features standard or lightweight steel design, polymer grips, 7 or 8 shot mag., 3 dot combat sights, slimline slide and frame, non-glare matte or satin chrome finish, 23 oz. Mfg. 1998-2005.

	$250	$220	$200	$170	$160	$150	$140

Last MSR was $282.

Subtract $15 for Ultra Lite Model (disc.).
Add $18 for satin chrome finish (.380 ACP cal. only, beginning 1999).

MAX II - 9mm Para. or .45 ACP cal., 4.25 (Compact) or 5 1/8 (Government) in. barrel, 3-dot combat sights, anatomically designed polymer grips, 13 (.45 ACP) or 17 (9mm Para.) shot mag., 39-41 oz. Limited mfg. 2005.

	$275	$240	$200	$180	$155	$140	$130

Last MSR was $325.

MODEL 82 - 9mm Para. cal., double action, 4 1/4 in. barrel, blue finish, 3-dot sighting system, 15 shot mag., ambidextrous safety, loaded chamber indicator, black polymer grips, 39 oz. Imported 1988-93.

	$550	$500	$450	$400	$350	$300	$275

Last MSR was $975.

MODEL 87 COMPETITION - 9mm Para. cal., competition variation of the Model 82, includes built in ported compensator, oversize magazine and safety release, fixed barrel bushing, beveled rapid load magazine well, 14 shot mag., extended and serrated triggerguard, and adj. trigger. Imported 1989-93.

	$995	$850	$750	$700	$625	$575	$500

Last MSR was $1,450.

REVOLVERS: DOUBLE ACTION

MARTIAL MODEL - .22 LR or .38 Spl. cal., 6 shot, 4 and 6 in. barrels, target sights, blue, checkered wood grips. Mfg. 1969-76.

	$220	$200	$180	$165	$140	$120	$100

DELUXE MARTIAL - similar to Martial, except finish as follows:

Satin chrome	$275	$250	$220	$195	$165	$140	$120
Chrome, engraved	$450	$395	$350	$300	$250	$200	$150
Blue, engraved	$450	$395	$350	$300	$250	$200	$150
Gold, damascened	$2,250	$1,950	$1,650	$1,225	$800	$700	$600

COMANCHE I - .22 LR cal., similar to Martial DA, mfg. 1977-82.

	$255	$220	$195	$165	$155	$140	$110

COMANCHE II - .38 Spl. cal., similar to Martial DA, mfg. 1977-82 and 1986 in .22 LR and .22 Mag. only.

	$240	$220	$195	$165	$155	$140	$110

Last MSR was $272.

GRADING - PPGS™	100%	98%	95%	90%	80%	70%	60%

COMANCHE III - .22 LR (disc.) or .357 Mag. cal., 6 shot, 4, 6, or 8 1/2 (disc. 1986) in. barrel, blue, adj. sights, checkered walnut grips. Mfg. 1975-95. Before 1977, it was called "Comanche."

	$280	$245	$200	$165	$155	$140	$130

Last MSR was $339.

* *Comanche III Satin Chrome Finish (disc.)*

	$330	$270	$230	$205	$185	$170	$160

Last MSR was $395.

* *Comanche III Gold Damascene Finish (disc.)*

	$2,250	$1,950	$1,650	$1,225	$800	$700	$600

SUPER COMANCHE IV - .44 Mag. cal., 6 or 8 1/2 in. VR barrel, adj. sights, blue only. Disc. 1998.

	$350	$285	$235	$220	$205	$185	$175

Last MSR was $440.

SUPER COMANCHE V - .357 Mag. cal., 6 shot, 4, 6, or 8 1/2 in. VR barrel, adj. sights, blue only. Importation disc. 1988.

	$335	$275	$230	$210	$200	$190	$180

Last MSR was $414.

LONE STAR ARMAMENT, INC.

Previous pistol manufacturer circa 1970-2004, and located in Stephenville, TX. During 2003, Lone Star Armament was absorbed by STI, located in Georgetown, TX.

PISTOLS: SEMI-AUTO

Lone Star Armament manufactured a lineup of M1911 style pistols. Models included: Ranger Match ($1,595 last MSR), Lawman Match ($1,595 last MSR), Lawman Series ($1,475 last MSR), Ranger Series ($1,475 last MSR), and the Guardian Series ($895 last MSR).

LONE STAR RIFLE CO., INC.

Current rifle manufacturer established 1992 and located in Conroe, TX, specializing in Remington Rolling Block rifle reproductions. Dealer and consumer direct sales.

RIFLES: REPRODUCTIONS

REMINGTON ROLLING BLOCK SERIES - various black powder cartridge cals., configurations, and options, case colored or nickel plated receiver, rust or nitre blue barrel, extra select checkered walnut, single or double set triggers.

* *Remington Rolling Block Creedmoor* - features competition long range 34 in. full octagon or half octagon/half round barrel with pistol grip and shotgun butt, single trigger set at 3 lbs., per Creedmoor rules, 10 lbs.

MSR $1,995	$1,850	$1,550	$1,250	$995	$875	$725	$600

* *Remington Rolling Block Silhouette (Target)* - designed for silhouette competition, with 30, 32, or 34 in. full octagon or half octagon/half round barrel with pistol grip and shotgun butt.

MSR $1,995	$1,850	$1,550	$1,250	$995	$875	$725	$600

* *Remington Rolling Block Silhouette Standard Rifle* - .40-65 or .45-70 Govt. cal., similar to #5 Sporting Standard Rifle, except has 32 or 34 in. barrel, steel shotgun butt plate, pistol grip stock, 11 lbs. Mfg. 1999-2006.

	$1,400	$1,150	$900	$750	$600	$550	$475

Last MSR was $1,595.

* *Remington Rolling Block Cowboy Action Rifle* - .32-40 WCF, .38-55 WCF, .40-65 WCF, .44-77, .45 LC (disc. 2002), .45-70 Govt., or .50-70 cal., heavy 28 in. barrel, 8 1/2 lbs. Mfg. 1999-2006.

	$1,400	$1,150	$900	$750	$600	$550	$475

Last MSR was $1,595.

GRADING - PPGS™	100%	98%	95%	90%	80%	70%	60%

* *Remington Rolling Block #5 Sporting Standard Rifle* - .25-35 WCF (new 2002), .30-30 Win. (new 2000) or .30-40 Krag cal., 26 in. round barrel, single trigger, case colored frame, standard American walnut stock and forearm, 6 lbs. Mfg. 1999-2006.

		$1,400	$1,150	$900	$750	$600	$550	$475

Last MSR was $1,595.

* *Remington Rolling Block Classic #5* - .22 Hornet, .25-35 WCF, .30-30 Win., .30-40 Krag, or .33 WCF cal., rapid taper octagon barrel, approx. 6 lbs. New 2007.

MSR $2,500	$2,500	$2,000	$1,750	$1,550	$1,250	$995	$875

* *Remington Rolling Block #7 Sporting Rifle* - .25-20 WCF, .32-20 WCF, or .22 Hornet cal. Mfg. 2002-2007.

	$3,000	$2,650	$2,350	$1,950	$1,725	$1,500	$1,200

Last MSR was $3,500.

* *Remington Rolling Block Sporting Rifle* - various cals., standard sporting rifle designed for accuracy, 28, 30, or 32 in. barrel, straight grip stock.

MSR $1,995	$1,850	$1,550	$1,250	$975	$850	$725	$600

* *Remington Rolling Block Deluxe Sporting Rifle* - deluxe variation of the Sporting Rifle with 28, 30, or 32 in. full octagon or half octagon/half round barrel with pistol grip and shotgun butt, buckhorn rear sight and choice of front sight.

MSR $1,995	$1,850	$1,550	$1,250	$975	$850	$725	$600

* *Remington Rolling Block Custer Rifle* - .50-70 cal., an exact reproduction of Gen. G.A. Custer's original Remington Rolling Block, 28 in. octagon barrel with SST, straight grip, crescent buttplate, and Schnabel forearm tip.

MSR $3,500	$3,000	$2,650	$2,350	$1,950	$1,725	$1,500	$1,200

* *Remington Rolling Block Buffalo Rifle* - various cal., features relic finish enabling a new gun to appear somewhat worn, double set triggers, exact copy of the original, 16 lbs.

MSR $3,200	$2,900	$2,575	$2,225	$1,875	$1,625	$1,400	$1,200

* *Remington Rolling Block Take Down Model* - features take down action. Mfg. 2001-2002.

	$3,600	$3,150	$2,750	$2,300	$1,995	$1,700	$1,375

Last MSR was $4,000.

GOVE ROLLING BLOCK - various cals., new rolling block with underlever design by Carlos Gove. Mfg. 1998-2002.

	$2,650	$2,250	$1,875	$1,625	$1,400	$1,200	$1,000

Last MSR was $2,995.

LORCIN ENGINEERING CO., INC.

Previous handgun manufacturer located in Mira Loma, CA, 1989-1999.

DERRINGERS: O/U

STAINLESS MODEL - .357 Mag. or .45 LC cal., 3 1/2 in. barrel, synthetic grips, tip-up action, rebounding hammer, fixed sights. Mfg. 1996-98.

	$95	$80	$65	N/A	N/A	N/A	N/A

Last MSR was $110.

PISTOLS: SEMI-AUTO

During the height of production in the mid-90s, Lorcin was making 40,000 semi-auto pistols a month. One year, their production totalled 400,000 units.

L-22 MODEL - .22 LR cal., similar to L-25 Model, except 2.55 in. barrel and 9 shot mag., black or chrome finish, 16 oz. Mfg. 1992-99.

	$75	$60	$50	$45	$40	$35	$35

Last MSR was $89.

GRADING - PPGS™	100%	98%	95%	90%	80%	70%	60%

L-25 MODEL - .25 ACP cal., single action, 6 shot mag., 2.4 in. barrel, anatomically designed grips to fit hand better, choice of black and gold, chrome and pearl, satin chrome and pearl, Teflon camo finish (new 1992), or black and pearl finish, 13.5 oz. Mfg. 1989-99.

	$65	$50	$45	$40	$35	$35	$35

Last MSR was $79.

Add $20 for lightweight frame (Model LT 25, new in 1990).

✳ *L-25 Model Lady Lorcin* - same specifications as the L-25 Model, except is available in chrome, satin chrome, or black exterior finish with pink grips. Mfg. 1990-99.

	$70	$60	$50	$45	$40	$35	$35

Last MSR was $79.

L-32 - .32 ACP cal., single action, 7 shot mag., 3 1/2 in. barrel, available in black or chrome finish, 23 oz. Mfg. 1992-99.

	$80	$70	$60	$50	$45	$40	$35

Last MSR was $89.

L-380 - .380 ACP cal., single action, 7 shot mag., 3 1/2 in. barrel, available in black or chrome finish, 23 oz. Mfg. 1992-99.

	$85	$75	$65	$55	$50	$45	$40

Last MSR was $100.

LH-380 - .380 ACP cal., similar to L9MM, 36 oz. Mfg. 1995-99.

	$125	$115	$100	$90	$85	$80	$75

Last MSR was $149.

L9MM - 9mm Para. cal., single action, 10 (C/B 1994) or 13* shot mag., 4 1/2 in. barrel, grip safety, black finish, 3-dot sights, 36 oz. Mfg. 1994-99.

	$125	$115	$100	$90	$85	$80	$75

Last MSR was $149.

Add $20 for disc. 13 shot mag. variation.

LORENZO, CRESS

Current rifle manufacturer located in Minersville, UT.

Custom gunmaker Cress Lorenzo specializes in custom express rifles built to customer specifications. Many options are available, in addition to general gunsmithing services. Please contact Mr. Lorenzo directly for more information, including models, options, availability and pricing (see Trademark Index).

LUCCHINI, SANDRO

Current manufacturer located in Sarezzo (Brescia), Italy.

Lucchini manufactures high quality, made to order, double rifles and SxS shotguns (approx. 10-12 guns annually). Starting prices for shotguns are as follows (not including engraving) - Purdey style rose and scroll is approx. $2,000, while elaborate work by a master engraver can exceed $20,000): $8,000 for Anson action without sideplates (add $1,500 for sideplates), $18,000 for standard sidelock, manual cocking extractor hammer guns start at $9,000, self cocking ejectors are $20,000. Add 10% for 28 ga. or .410 bore, and $500 for single trigger. All shotgun barrels are demi-bloc construction. New O/U scaled frame 20 and 28 ga. shotguns begin at $8,000, including fine line gold inlay and case colors. Double rifles started at $30,000 for calibers under .375 H&H, and were available up to .600 NE. All double rifles feature Ferlach barrels. Add $6,000 for extra set of barrels.

LUGERS WITH VARIATIONS

Semi-auto pistol design originated by Georg Luger, circa 1899. Many previous manufacturers - see main text for more information. Previous post-WWII manufacture (through 1997) was by Mauser-Werke Oberndorf Waffensysteme, located in Oberndorf, Germany.

Note: The Luger section in this book is arranged chronologically by year of manufacture under individual manufacturer headings.

Often times, year of production can be hard to nail down, especially on commercial models. An easier way to initially identify your Luger is to categorize by toggle marking first - then by chamber marking within groups (chronologically for dated chambers). Once you know period of manufacture, simply refer to the appropriate subheading in this section. While some rare variations will be excluded in this generalized overview, it will be very helpful to establish correct, basic knowledge about your particular Luger.

While many recently imported Lugers would make workable shooters, they have in no way lowered prices on 90%+ condition specimens due to normal collector activity in original condition only pistols. Recently imported Lugers should have the importer's name visibly stamped on an exterior surface. Most of these recent imports are in the 9mm Para. - 4 in. barrel configuration. Recently imported Lugers with the importer's markings visible are typically priced in the $450-$700 range.

Every year more and more reblued, restrawed, regripped, reframed, rebarreled Lugers are sold to unknowing military handgun collectors as rare variations. On any expensive contract variation, careful inspection on all parts must be made before potentially purchasing. If in doubt, secure 2 or 3 additional appraisals/observations from qualified individuals. Lugers are a field in themselves and an experienced Winchester dealer would not be qualified to guesstimate the originality of these German handguns.

A final note on Lugers: Original pistols in 90%-100% condition have not been affected by the influx of recent imports as these newly imported guns are usually in 80% and lower condition or have been reblued.

It seems that every year the prices of top quality (98%+ condition) original Lugers get more expensive and less predictable. For this reason, the 100% values on many Lugers have been omitted intentionally, since rarity precludes accurate price evaluation in this condition factor. In many cases, the value for a mint original military Luger can double the 98% price listed.

For Borchardt models, please refer to Borchardt listing.

REFERENCE GUIDE BY TOGGLE MARKING

DWM TOGGLE IDENTIFICATION

DWM MODELS

* *DWM MODELS* - mfg. from 1900 to 1930 in Berlin, Germany.
* *DWM Models 1900* - grip safety and "Dished" Toggles, ser. nos. 1-24,999.
* *DWM Models 1906* - grip safety, many chamber markings, ser. nos. 25,000-74,000.
* *DWM Models 1908 Commercial* - no grip safety, 9mm Para., ser. nos. 39,000-74,000.
* *DWM Models 1908 Military* - no stock lug.
* *DWM Models 1914 Military* - stock lug, dated 1913-18.
* *DWM Models 1920 Commercial* - no grip safety, usually 3 7/8 in. barrel. Most common Luger, undated chamber, 7.65mm Para. or 9mm Para.

Note: Lugers with 4 inch barrels are most frequently encountered in military and commercial models. 6 in. barrels usually denote "Navy" models. 8 in. barrels usually denote "Artillery" models. Guns with barrels over 8 inches are rare and should be checked carefully for originality.

DWM COMMERCIAL LUGERS

DWM MEANS DEUTSCHE WAFFEN & MUNITIONS FABRIKEN. These are models manufactured from 1900-1923 found in the five digit serial range.

MODEL 1900 - ser. range 1-20,000. Configuration: 4 3/4 in. x .30 Commercial, American Eagle, Swiss.

MODEL 1900 - ser. range 20,001-21,000. Configuration: 4 3/4 in. x .30 Bulgarian.

MODEL 1902 - ser. range 21,001-25,000. Configuration: 9mm Para. x 4 in. "Fat Barrels" and 11 3/4 in. x 7.65mm Para. Carbine models, intermixed with 4 3/4 x 7.65mm Para. American Eagles and Commercials.

MODEL 1906 - ser. range 25,001-39,000. Configuration: Commercial American Eagle, Navy Commercial and Swiss, both 4 3/4 in. x 7.65mm Para. and 9mm Para. x 4 in. grip safety models.

MODEL 1908 - ser. range 39,001-71,000. Configuration: First 9mm Para. x 4 in. without grip safety, M1908 Commercials were interspersed with 7.65mm Para. and 9mm Para. Eagles, Commercials, Navy Commercials, and a few Carbines and Swiss.

MODEL 1914 - ser. range 71,001-74,000. Configuration: Last pre-WWI Commercial Lugers, made with stock lug, with a few 9mm Para. Commercials mixed in.

MODEL 1920 - ser. range 2,000i-9,999u. Configuration: Post-WWI Commercials, mostly 3 7/8 in. x 7.65mm Para. cal.

MODEL 1923 - ser. range 89,001-91,000. Configuration: The last thousand or so made have "safe" on lever and "loaded" on the extractor, 3 7/8 in. x 7.65mm Para. barrels.

ERFURT TOGGLE IDENTIFICATION

ERFURT MODELS - produced from 1911-1914 and 1916-1918 in Erfurt, Germany. Military Model - Chamber dated 1911-1914 and 1916-1918. Erfurt models exhibit the most proof marks and individual parts numbering. Walnut grips.

SIMSON & CO. TOGGLE IDENTIFICATION

SIMSON & CO. - manufactured 1922 to 1934 in Suhl, Germany. Most Simson Lugers are military models (9mm - 4 in. barrels). During this 12 year period, Simson supplied the German Army Lugers exclusively. Can be dated 1925-1928 or not dated at all. Many reworks of WWI DWM Military Lugers were refurbished by Simson, and can be detected by the Simson "Eagle-over-6" proof on repaired parts. A very few Simsons made in 1934 have just an "S" on the toggle (very rare).

SWISS TOGGLE IDENTIFICATION

SWISS BERN MODELS - Manufactured 1918 to 1947 by WAFFENFABRIK Bern, Switzerland. Relatively rare - these Swiss models have "improved" changes (flat and curved front grip strap), 4 3/4 in. barrels, walnut or plastic grips, grip safety. 1929 model (flat front grip strap) has Swiss Cross in shield on front link.

MAUSER TOGGLE IDENTIFICATION

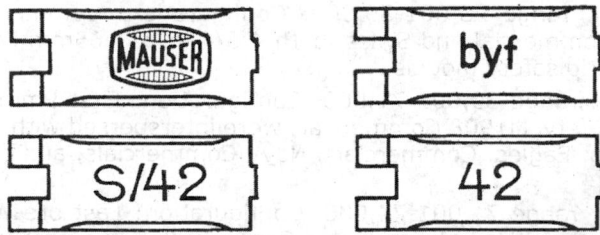

MAUSER VARIATIONS - Manufactured 1934-1942 in Oberndorf, Germany. Between 1930 and 1934 Mauser Werke was primarily engaged in reworking older Lugers, since transfer of machinery and personnel to the DWM plant in Berlin was completed in 1931. Mauser "Banner" models were made from 1934 to 1942, many are dated from 1939-1942 on the chamber. S/42 models are MOSTLY MILITARY contract guns manufactured between 1934 and 1940, usually chamber marked. "42" toggle marked guns (Mauser code) were mfg. 1939 and 1940 and are dated. "byf" marked toggles indicate guns made for German military use after 1940 and are more common than other military models. The Mauser Werke trademark also appears on those Lugers made in the 1970s.

KRIEGHOFF TOGGLE IDENTIFICATION

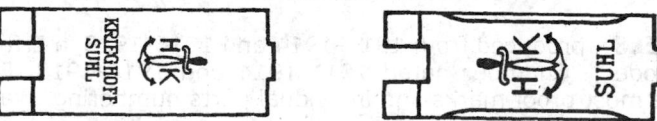

KRIEGHOFF MODELS - Manufactured between 1934-1946 in Suhl, Germany. Early Krieghoffs are side frame inscribed. The German Luftwaffe contracted with Krieghoff for military guns in 1935. Early military Krieghoffs have "S" marked chambers, most are chamber dated between 1936 and 1945. Krieghoff Lugers are prized for their quality fit and finish and command higher prices because of their rarity factor. The vast majority of commercial Krieghoff Lugers have the letter P before the serial number.

VICKERS TOGGLE IDENTIFICATION

VICKERS - Manufactured by Vickers, Ltd., circa 1921, in England from DWM parts for military contract sale to the Netherlands. Added barrel date is a date of arsenal refinish or refurbishing. Distinguishable by Vickers toggle and "rust"

marked safety. Serial range is 1-10,100. Grips can be finely checkered with shallow contour or very coarsely checkered. Configuration is 9mm Para., 4 in. barrel, and grip safety.

LUGERS: MATCHING MAGAZINE(S) & MILITARY HOLSTER ADD ONS

Values for all variations of Lugers listed assume a proper original magazine and matching parts.

Add approx. 50% for one original matching magazines on all Lugers listed below that were originally manufactured with numbered magazines.

Add approx. 75%-100% for two original matching magazines on all Lugers listed in the following sections that were originally manufactured with numbered magazines, depending on condition.

Add approx. $250-$375 for original military holster, depending on condition.

PISTOLS: SEMI-AUTO, LUGERS & VARIATIONS

Lugers: Pre-1900 & 1900 DWM Mfg.

Values on most 100% Lugers have been omitted intentionally since rarity precludes accurate price evaluation in this condition factor.

1898/99 BORCHARDT LUGER TRANSITIONAL - 7.65mm Para. cal., 5 in. barrel, this is perhaps one of the most desirable Lugers, only few mfg. Examples scarce, no reported sales, an original example would command a price in the 5-figure range.

1899/1900 SWISS TEST MODEL - 7.65mm Para. cal., 4 3/4 in. barrel, 100 or less mfg., the very first true Luger. Engraved "Swiss Cross" chamber marking.

	N/A	$39,000	$33,500	$37,250	$20,500	$15,500	$11,000

Approx. 50 pistols serial numbered in the 1-50 range.

Buyers should be very cautious when considering a purchase of this rare model, as good fakes do exist.

1900 COMMERCIAL DWM - 7.65mm Para. cal., 4 3/4 in. barrel, 5,500 mfg.

	N/A	$5,500	$4,900	$4,100	$2,950	$2,400	$1,850

1900 SWISS COMMERCIAL DWM - 7.65mm Para. cal., 4 3/4 in. barrel, 2,000 commercially mfg.

	N/A	$6,000	$5,100	$4,300	$3,200	$2,650	$2,000

Add 15% for wide trigger (found only in ser. no. range 4,000).

1900 SWISS MILITARY DWM - 7.65mm Para. cal., 4 3/4 in. barrel, 3,000 military mfg.

	N/A	$6,000	$5,100	$4,300	$3,200	$2,650	$2,000

Add 15% for wide trigger (found only in ser. no. range 4,000).

1900 AMERICAN EAGLE DWM - 7.65mm Para. cal., 4 3/4 in. barrel, approx. 12,000 mfg.

	N/A	$6,250	$5,000	$4,250	$2,950	$2,400	$1,900

Add 40% for U.S. Test Model (approx. ser. no. range 6,009 - 7,500) - not marked Germany, has no proofmarks, has last two digits of ser. no. on right side of locking bolt.

1900 BULGARIAN DWM - 7.65mm Para. cal., 4 3/4 in. barrel, 1,000 mfg., very rare in U.S., most often seen in the 60% and lower condition.

	N/A	$10,750	$9,000	$7,000	$5,100	$4,200	$3,500

Subtract 30% if rebarreled.

Lugers: 1902-DWM Mfg.

1902 COMMERCIAL - 9mm Para. cal., 4 in. barrel, serial number range 22,300-22,400 and 22,900-23,500 (500-600 mfg.). Commonly called "Fat Barrel" model.

	N/A	$11,250	$9,250	$7,750	$5,950	$4,850	$3,750

GRADING - PPGS™	100%	98%	95%	90%	80%	70%	60%

1902 AMERICAN EAGLE - 9mm Para. cal., 4 in. barrel, 600-700 mfg., commonly called the "Fat Barrel." Same ser. range as 1902 Commercial Model.

	N/A	$15,000	$13,000	$11,000	$9,000	$7,500	$5,900

1902 CARTRIDGE COUNTER AMERICAN EAGLE - 9mm Para. cal., only 50 mfg. with the Powell Indication Device; be extremely wary of fakes. Ser. no. range 22,401- 22,450.

	N/A	$41,000	$35,000	$27,500	$18,750	$13,500	$11,750

1902 DANZIG TEST - 7.65mm Para. or 9mm Para. cal., blank toggle, 4 in. barrel, Crown D proofs.

	N/A	$7,850	$6,500	$5,500	$4,500	$3,700	$2,950

1902 CARBINE - 7.65mm Para. cal., 11 3/4 in. barrel, approx. 2500 mfg.

Gun w/matching stock	N/A	$18,000	$15,500	$13,000	$10,250	$7,500	$6,500
Gun only	N/A	$11,000	$9,250	$7,500	$5,750	$5,250	$3,500

Add approx. 40% for American Eagle variation.
Subtract 20% for non-matching stock.

1902/06 TRANSITIONAL CARBINE - 11 3/4 in. barrel, 50-100 mfg., may have new model frame. Ser. nos. start at 50,000.

	N/A	$11,500	$9,000	$6,850	$4,850	$4,500	$4,250

Subtract 30% if without matching stock.

1903 COMMERCIAL - 7.65mm Para. cal., 4 in. barrel, 50 mfg., extractor marked "charge," ser. range 25,000-25,050, with 90 degree toggle checkering.

	N/A	$8,250	$7,450	$6,000	$5,600	$4,850	$3,500

Lugers: 1904-DWM Mfg.

1904 NAVY DWM - 9mm Para. cal., 6 in. barrel, limited mfg., a Transitional Navy, "Fat Barrel" with 90 degree toggle checkering and toggle lock, should have 2-digit ser. no.

Extreme rarity precludes pricing for individual condition factors. Good condition (70%-95%), no problem, original specimens are currently selling in the $30,000 - $50,000 range. Most of these pistols available for sale are fakes - buyer beware!

Lugers: 1906-DWM Mfg.

1906 COMMERCIAL 7.65mm Para. W/"GESICHERT" MARKED SAFETY - 7.65mm Para. cal., 4 3/4 in. barrel, "GESICHERT" marked safety, long frame. Approx. 750 mfg.

	N/A	$3,400	$2,950	$2,550	$1,875	$1,350	$1,000

1906 COMMERCIAL 9mm Para. - 9mm Para. cal., 4 in. barrel, 3,500-4,000 mfg. Scarcer than 7.65mm Para.

	N/A	$3,400	$2,950	$2,550	$1,875	$1,350	$1,000

1906 COMMERCIAL 7.65mm Para. - 7.65mm Para. cal., 4 3/4 in. barrel, area under safety polished bright, 5,000 mfg.

	N/A	$2,950	$2,600	$2,200	$1,650	$1,100	$900

1906 AMERICAN EAGLE - 9mm Para. cal., 4 in. barrel, American Eagle stamped in front of breech, 3,000 mfg.

	N/A	$4,150	$3,550	$2,950	$2,100	$1,500	$1,200

1906 AMERICAN EAGLE - 7.65mm Para. cal., 4 3/4 in. barrel, 7,500-8,000 mfg.

	N/A	$3,600	$3,000	$2,600	$1,875	$1,350	$1,000

Add 40% for long frame.

1906 NAVY COMMERCIAL - 9mm Para. cal., 6 in. barrel, approx. 2,500 mfg.

	N/A	$5,100	$4,350	$3,575	$2,800	$2,150	$1,350

Add 50% for 7.65mm Para. cal. with 6 in. barrel.

GRADING - PPGS™	100%	98%	95%	90%	80%	70%	60%

1906 NAVY MILITARY FIRST ISSUE - 9mm Para. cal., 6 in. barrel, first issue, 19,000 mfg., mostly altered safety marking - "GESICHERT" in upper position. Ser. no. range 1-9,000a.

	N/A	$6,500	$4,850	$3,575	$2,800	$2,150	$1,350

Add 10% for Navy unit markings.
Add 25% for unaltered safety variation.

1906 NAVY MILITARY SECOND ISSUE - 9mm Para. cal., 6 in. barrel, second issue, 2,000 mfg. Ser. range 9,000a-1,000b.

	N/A	$6,500	$4,850	$3,575	$2,800	$2,150	$1,350

Add 10% for Navy unit markings.

Lugers: 1906-1918 DWM & Erfurt Mfg.

Most common variations in good supply within this section in 50% or less condition will approximate the 60% value. This reflects its value as a representative shooter rather than a higher priced collector's gun.

1906 SWISS COMMERCIAL - 7.65mm Para. or 9mm Para. cal., 4 3/4 in. barrel, less than 1,000 mfg., Swiss "Cross in Sunburst", short frame.

	N/A	$2,950	$2,575	$2,100	$1,875	$1,350	$1,025

Add 20% for "Cross in Shield".

1906 SWISS MILITARY - 7.65mm Para. cal., 4 3/4 in. barrel, long frame, Swiss Police has "Cross in Shield". Either "Cross in Shield" or "Cross in Sunburst."

	N/A	$2,950	$2,575	$2,100	$1,875	$1,350	$1,025

1906/23 DUTCH - 9mm Para. cal., 4 in. barrel, approx. 4,000 mfg., often seen as arsenal rework.

	N/A	$3,550	$3.000	$2,550	$1,875	$1,350	$1,025

Add 200% for original finish and barrel.

1906 BRAZILIAN - 7.65mm Para. cal., 4 3/4 in. barrel, 5,000 mfg., extremely rare in fine condition.

	N/A	$3,250	$2,750	$2,350	$1,700	$1,250	$900

1906 BULGARIAN - 7.65mm Para. cal., 4 3/4 in. barrel, 1,500 mfg., most rebarrelled to 9mm Para.

	N/A	$6,300	$5,100	$4,300	$3,1000	$2,650	$1,875

Subtract 60% for versions rebarreled to 9mm Para. cal.
This is the rarest Bulgarian - most are fakes or have been restored.

1908 BULGARIAN - 9mm Para. cal., 4 in. barrel, "DWM" on chamber, 10,000 mfg., extremely rare in mint condition.

	N/A	$3,850	$3,300	$2,750	$1,925	$1,350	$1,025

1906 PORTUGUESE ARMY - 7.65mm Para. cal., 4 3/4 in. barrel, "Manuel II" crest on chamber. Approx. 5,000 mfg.

	N/A	$3,200	$2,800	$2,200	$1,600	$1,100	$950

1906 ROYAL PORTUGUESE NAVY - 9mm Para. cal., 4 in. barrel, "Anchor & Crown" on chamber, very rare. Most are fakes.

	N/A	$10,750	$8,000	$6,250	$4,000	$3,000	$2,000

1906 REPUBLIC OF PORTUGAL NAVY - 7.65mm Para. cal., "Anchor R.P." on chamber, very rare. Most are fakes.

	N/A	$10,750	$8,000	$6,250	$4,000	$3,000	$2,000

1906 RUSSIAN - 9mm Para. cal., 4 in. barrel, approx. 1,000 mfg., only 7 reported.

	N/A	$17,500	$15,000	$12,000	$9,500	$8,000	$6,000

1906 VICKERS DUTCH - 9mm Para., 4 in. barrel, approx. 10,000 assembled by Vickers Ltd. from DWM supplied parts.

	N/A	$4,125	$3,525	$2,850	$1,975	$1,350	$1,025

GRADING - PPGS™	100%	98%	95%	90%	80%	70%	60%

1906 FRENCH COMMERCIAL - 7.65mm Para. cal., 4 3/4 in. barrel.

	N/A	$3,200	$2,800	$2,200	$1,600	$1,200	$995

Add 100% if cased with accessories.

1908 DWM COMMERCIAL AND MILITARY - 9mm Para. cal., 4 in. barrel, Test/Acceptance Model, approx. 500 mfg. Ser. no. range 69,000-71,200.

	N/A	$2,200	$1,925	$1,525	$1,100	$925	$800

1908 NAVY COMMERCIAL - 9mm Para. cal., 6 in. barrel.

	N/A	$6,850	$5,800	$4,600	$2,900	$2,400	$1,875

Add 50% for 7.65mm Para. with 6 in. barrel.

1908 DWM MILITARY - 9mm Para. cal., 4 in. barrel, undated 1st issue or dated 1910-1913, no stock lug, except for a few late 1913 mfg. guns.

	N/A	$1,950	$1,750	$1,400	$1,100	$925	$800

Add 20%+ for Imperial unit markings (depends on history of unit).
Add 20% for undated or for 1913 date w/stock lug.

Approx. 25,000 1st issue pistols were mfg., 20,000 dated 1910, 15,000 dated 1911, 10,000 dated 1912, 25,000 dated 1913.

1908 DWM COMMERCIAL - 9mm Para. cal., 4 in. barrel, no stock lug or hold open, blank chamber.

	N/A	$2,200	$1,925	$1,525	$1,100	$925	$800

1911-1914 DATED 1908 ERFURT MILITARY - 9mm Para. cal., 4 in. barrel (dated 1911-14), 1911, 1912, and most 1913 chamber dates do not have stock lugs.

	N/A	$2,200	$1,925	$1,525	$1,100	$925	$800

Add 20%+ for Imperial unit markings (depends on history of unit).
Add 20% for 1913 chamber date with stock lug.
Add 20% for 1914 date.

WWI ERFURT MILITARY SERIAL RANGES

CHAMBER DATE	OBSERVED LOW SERIAL	OBSERVED HIGH SERIAL	APPROXIMATE QTY. MADE
1911	575	9548	10,000
1912	255	866b	22,000
1913	575	2563b	25,000
1914	2137	539A	25,000
1915	none observed		
1916	13	5764b	80,000
1917	844	2854n	150,000
1918	304	5816s	180,000

Production data appears courtesy of Jan C. Still.

1908 NAVY - 9mm Para. cal., 6 in. barrel, scarce. Ser. no. range 1,000B-10,000B, 9,000 mfg.

	N/A	$8,000	$7,200	$5,750	$5,100	$4,100	$2,950

1908 BOLIVIAN CONTRACT - 9mm Para. cal., 4 in. barrel.

	N/A	$4,000	$3,550	$2,750	$1,850	$1,350	$1,100

1913 COMMERCIAL DWM - 9mm Para. cal., 4 in. barrel, grip safety and stock lug, horizontal "N" proof mark, 71,000 ser. no. range, rare.

	N/A	$3,550	$3,000	$2,550	$1,800	$1,350	$1,025

GRADING - PPGS™	100%	98%	95%	90%	80%	70%	60%

1914 COMMERCIAL DWM - 9mm Para. cal., 4 in. barrel, undated, stock lug, horizontal crown-N proofed.

	N/A	$2,400	$1,950	$1,550	$1,150	$975	$750

1914 NAVY - 9mm Para. cal., 6 in. barrel, scarce. Dated 1916 and 1917.

	N/A	$4,950	$4,350	$3,600	$2,700	$2,200	$1,900

Add 20% for 16 date.

Watch for fakes made from 1920 Commercials with new barrels and rear toggles added. Crown M proofs and date will look "fresh" (1917 date usually encountered).

1916-1918 DATED ERFURT MILITARY - 9mm Para. cal., 4 in. barrel, dated 1916-18, there are no known 1915 chamber dated Erfurts.

	N/A	$1,750	$1,400	$1,100	$900	$800	$700

Add 20% for 1914 date.
Add 20%+ for Imperial unit markings (depends on history of unit).

Note: Date stamped on top frame is date of production; thus dates could be 1914, 1916, 1917, or 1918. All are Military P.08s, however, 99%-100% Erfurts are rare.

1914 ERFURT ARTILLERY - 9mm Para. cal., 1914 date is only one seen, 8 in. barrel.

	N/A	$4,400	$3,750	$3,000	$2,050	$1,350	$1,100

Add 20%+ for Imperial unit markings (depends on history of unit).

1910-1918 DATED WWI DWM MILITARY 1908 PRODUCTION NOT DATED - 9mm Para. cal., 4 in. barrel. 1910-1918 dated. Most frequently encountered WWI military Luger, w/stock lug mid-1913-1918.

	N/A	$1,750	$1,400	$1,100	$900	$800	$700

Add approx. 20% for 1910-1913 chamber dated mfg.
Add 20%+ for Imperial unit markings (depends on history of unit).

Note: Date stamped on top frame is date of production; thus, dates could be 1914, 1915, 1916, 1917, or 1918, but all are military P. 08s.

WWI DWM MILITARY SERIAL RANGES

CHAMBER DATE	OBSERVED LOW SERIAL	OBSERVED HIGH SERIAL	APPROXIMATE QTY. MADE
1908	(undated) 34	2636b	25,000
1910	5095b	5358d	20,000
1911	1524c	4825e	13,000
1912	599	9974	10,000
1913	2617	3850d	25,000
1914	282	6212c	40,000
1915	1398	2557d	100,000
1916	287	5438q	180,000
1917	587	3521m	60,000
1918	3690	9018n	190,000

Production data appears courtesy of Jan C. Still.

1914-1918 DATED DWM ARTILLERY - 9mm Para. cal., 8 in. barrel. Dated 1914-18.

	N/A	$4,150	$3,500	$2,900	$1,950	$1,350	$1,100

Add $750-$1,000 for matching stock, depending on condition.
Add $350 for proper non-matching stock.
Add $550 for original leather holster with shoulder strap.
Add 200% for rare 1914 chamber date.
Add 20% for 1915 chamber date.
Add 20%+ for Imperial unit markings (depends on history of unit).

GRADING - PPGS™	100%	98%	95%	90%	80%	70%	60%

Lugers: 1920-1930 DWM

Most common variations in good supply within this section in 50% or less condition will approximate the 60% value. This reflects its value as a representative shooter rather than a higher priced collector's gun.

1920 DWM OR ERFURT - 9mm Para. cal., 4 in. barrel, military and police, reworked and issued to police units, many thousand reworked, double date also, 1920 and 1921 dated.

	N/A	$1,250	$1,050	$875	$725	$600	$500

1920 COMMERCIAL - 7.65mm Para. or 9mm Para. cal., 3 7/8-4 in. barrel, available in many configurations, since these guns were assembled using the parts of previously manufactured Lugers, including 1900-06 mfg. with the grip safety on the frame.

	N/A	$1,250	$1,050	$875	$725	$600	$500

Add 25% for 9mm Para. cal.

These prices reflect original condition, and are not to be confused with recent imports (with import markings).

1920 NAVY COMMERCIAL - 9mm Para. cal., 6 in. barrel, very rare rework, Navy rear sight.

	N/A	$3,300	$2,900	$2,250	$1,650	$1,100	$950

Add 20% for 7.65mm Para. with 6 in. barrel.

1920 COMMERCIAL ARTILLERY - 9mm Para. cal., 8 in. barrel, very rare rework.

	N/A	$4,000	$3,500	$2,900	$1,950	$1,400	$1,100

1920 "LONG BARREL" COMMERCIAL - 7.65mm Para. or 9mm Para. cal., 10-20 in. barrel, extremely rare.

	N/A	$4,000	$3,500	$2,900	$1,950	$1,400	$1,100

Watch for fakes - these guns have to be evaluated one at a time. Barrel should have matching nos. and Crown N proof.

1920 NAVY CARBINE - 7.65mm Para. cal., 11 3/4 in. barrel, long frame (if short frame, be wary of fakes, very few produced). Navy rear sight, no forearm under barrel.

	N/A	$4,400	$3,750	$3,000	$2,200	$1,450	$1,100

1920 CARBINE - 7.65mm Para. cal., 11 3/4 in. barrel, very rare.

		N/A	$6,800	$5,800	$4,600	$3,650	$2,850	$2,150
Gun only		N/A	$6,800	$5,800	$4,600	$3,650	$2,850	$2,150
Gun with stock		N/A	$10,000	$8,500	$6,500	$5,500	$4,650	$3,650

1920 SWISS REWORK - 7.65mm Para. cal., 3 5/8-6 in. barrel, several hundred produced.

	N/A	$2,200	$1,850	$1,450	$1,000	$875	$800

ABERCROMBIE & FITCH COMMERCIAL - 7.65mm Para. or 9mm Para. cal., long frame, 4 3/4 in. barrel, 100 mfg., total for both cals.

	N/A	$5,200	$4,400	$3,700	$2,900	$2,500	$2,150

Add 30% for 6 in. barrels (rare).

Inspect barrel legend very carefully (as in beware of fakes) - must have reinforced frame (look for rib in rear frame well).

1920/21-DWM - 9mm Para. cal., 4 in. barrel.

	N/A	$1,200	$1,050	$925	$725	$575	$450

Subtract 20% if arsenal reworked.

1920/23 STOEGER AMERICAN EAGLE - 7.65mm Para. or 9mm Para. cal., 3 5/8-24 in. barrels, less than 1,000 mfg., made by DWM for Stoeger, sold in USA, longer barrel models have higher value.

		N/A						
3 7/8 - 6 in. barrels		N/A	$5,200	$4,400	$3,700	$2,900	$2,500	$2,150
8 in. barrel		N/A	$6,000	$5,000	$4,150	$2,950	$2,500	$2,200

Add 50% for Mauser mfg., safe and loaded extractor, or V ser. no. suffix.

GRADING - PPGS™	100%	98%	95%	90%	80%	70%	60%

Be extremely careful when examining the frame markings on this variation as there are many fakes in the marketplace.

1923 DWM COMMERCIAL - 7.65mm Para. cal., 3 5/8 in. barrel, 14,000 mfg. ser. range 74,000-89,000.

	N/A	$1,400	$1,200	$1,000	$775	$575	$500

1923 DWM "SAFE AND LOADED" COMMERCIAL - 7.65mm Para. cal., "safe and loaded" marked on frame and extractor, 7.65mm Para. cal., 3 7/8 in. barrel, safety and extractor marked in English, 2,000 mfg. ser. range 89,000-91,000.

	N/A	$2,200	$1,850	$1,450	$1,000	$875	$800

1923 FINNISH LUGER - 7.65mm Para. cal., approx. 5,000-7,000 units made for Finnish military contract (Army and Navy), marked "SA" surrounded by a rectangle, most have been recently imported into the U.S.

	N/A	$1,200	$1,050	$925	$725	$575	$450

Lugers: Krieghoff Mfg.

Please refer to the Krieghoff section for recently manufactured Krieghoff Lugers.

1923 DWM/KRIEGHOFF COMMERCIAL - 7.65mm Para. (3 7/8 in. barrel only) or 9mm Para. (4 in. barrel only), few mfg., reworked by Krieghoff, chamber dated 1921 or unmarked, most in "i" range, Krieghoff stamped on back of frame. Be wary of fakes.

	N/A	$2,200	$1,850	$1,450	$1,000	$875	$800

DWM/KRIEGHOFF COMMERCIAL - 7.65mm Para. or 9mm Para. cal., 4 in. barrel, a few hundred made, side frame marked Krieghoff. Most are fake.

	N/A	$3,450	$2,900	$2,500	$1,800	$1,500	$1,200

KRIEGHOFF COMMERCIAL SIDE FRAME - 7.65mm Para. or 9mm Para. cal., 4 or 6 in. barrel, approx. 1500 mfg., 1,000 with side frame marking, and 500 without side frame marking.

	N/A	$6,000	$5,200	$4,400	$3,250	$2,750	$2,200

Add 30% for side frame marked 7.65mm Para.
Add approx. 30% if w/o side frame marking.

Almost all Krieghoff Commercial Lugers have the letter P before the serial number.

KRIEGHOFF S CODE EARLY - 9mm Para. cal., 4 in. barrel, 1,800 mfg., German Luftwaffe. Has fat walnut grips, "H-K Suhl" toggle.

	N/A	$4,300	$3,650	$3,000	$2,300	$1,400	$1,250

KRIEGHOFF S CODE MID SERIES - 9mm Para. cal., 4 in. barrel, 500-700 mfg., Luftwaffe, ser. no. range 1600-2500, finely checkered plastic grips.

	N/A	$4,650	$3,900	$3,300	$2,900	$1,500	$1,350

KRIEGHOFF S CODE LATE - 9mm Para. cal., 4 in. barrel, 1,800 mfg., Luftwaffe, ser. no. range 2300-4200.

	N/A	$4,100	$3,500	$2,900	$2,100	$1,350	$1,200

KRIEGHOFF 36 DATE - 9mm Para. cal., 4 in. barrel, 500-700 made, Luftwaffe military, 2 digit date, coarsely checkered plastic grips.

	N/A	$4,200	$3,600	$3,000	$2,000	$1,400	$1,250

KRIEGHOFF 1936-1945 DATED - 9mm Para. cal., 4 in. barrel, approx. 9,000 mfg., 4 digit chamber date, 1936, 1937, and 1940 most common.

	100%	98%	95%	90%	80%	70%	60%
1936-37 & 1940	N/A	$4,100	$3,500	$2,900	$2,100	$1,350	$1,200
1938	N/A	$4,500	$3,750	$3,150	$2,400	$1,500	$1,350
1941	N/A	$5,400	$4,600	$3,800	$3,000	$2,550	$1,600
1942-43	N/A	$7,500	$6,500	$5,400	$4,500	$2,750	$2,150
1944	N/A	$10,000	$7,600	$6,100	$5,200	$3,300	$2,700
1945	N/A	$11,000	$8,500	$6,500	$6,000	$3,500	$2,700

The 1941 "large date" is very rare - watch for fakes (re-dated frames) on this model in general.

GRADING - PPGS™	100%	98%	95%	90%	80%	70%	60%

POST-WAR KRIEGHOFF TYPE I - 9mm Para. cal., 4 in. barrel, 150 mfg. for occupation forces, H-K marked toggle link.

	N/A	$3,500	$3,000	$2,600	$1,900	$1,550	$1,250

POST-WAR KRIEGHOFF TYPE II - 9mm Para. cal., 4 in. barrel, 150 mfg., unmarked toggle link, many parts proofed "Eagle-over-2."

	N/A	$3,500	$3,000	$2,600	$1,900	$1,550	$1,250

POST-WAR KRIEGHOFF COMMERCIAL - 7.65mm Para. cal., 4 in. barrel, 100-200 mfg., unmarked toggle, many parts proofed "Eagle-over-2".

	N/A	$3,100	$2,750	$1,950	$1,500	$1,100	$900

Lugers: Mauser Mfg.

Most common variations in good supply within this section in 50% or less condition will approximate the 60% value. This reflects its value as a representative shooter rather than a higher priced collector's gun.

1935-06 PORTUGUESE GNR - 7.65mm Para. cal., 4 3/4 in. barrel, 564 mfg., "GNR" on chamber, Portuguese marked safety and extractor.

	N/A	$3,350	$2,850	$2,500	$1,850	$1,550	$1,250

1934/06 MAUSER SWISS COMMERCIAL - 7.65mm Para. cal., 4 3/4 in. barrel, a few hundred produced, "Cross in Sunburst" or blank chamber, grip safety.

	N/A	$3,950	$3,400	$2,800	$1,900	$1,500	$1,200

1934 MAUSER BANNER COMMERCIAL - 7.65mm Para. or 9mm Para. cal., 4 in. barrel, hundreds produced, unmarked chamber, "v" suffix to ser. no.

	N/A	$3,950	$3,400	$2,800	$1,900	$1,500	$1,200

Add 15% for "Kal. 7.65" barrel marking.

S/42 K DATE - 9mm Para. cal., 4 in. barrel, approx. 10,000 mfg. during 1934 only for military.

	N/A	$6,600	$5,850	$4,850	$3,800	$2,950	$2,350

Add 100% for "large eagle over M Navy" proofmark.

S/42 G DATE - 9mm Para. cal., 4 in. barrel, many thousand produced 1935 only.

	N/A	$2,575	$2,100	$1,650	$1,250	$1,100	$900

Add 20% for Navy markings.

S/42 DATED CHAMBER - 9mm Para. cal., 4 in. barrel, many thousands produced, "S/42" stamped rear toggle, chamber dated 1936-1940. One of the most frequently encountered WWII military Lugers.

	N/A	$2,050	$1,850	$1,450	$1,050	$950	$825

Add 100% for Navy markings.
Add 20% for 1936 date.
Add 30% for "strawed" 1937 date.

The last regular production S/42 Models were mfg. approx. April of 1939.

MAUSER PERSIAN (IRANIAN) CONTRACT - 9mm Para. cal., 4 and 8 in. barrels, approx. 1,000 mfg. with 8 in. barrel, and 2,000-3,000 mfg. in 4 in. barrel, Farsi numerals.

		100%	98%	95%	90%	80%	70%	60%
4 in. barrel		N/A	$4,350	$3,900	$3,250	$2,950	$1,950	$1,750
Artillery (8 in.)		N/A	$4,750	$4,250	$3,600	$3,200	$2,100	$1,900
Cutaway		N/A	$7,500	$7,000	$6,000	$5,250	$3,500	$3,000

Add 50% for Artillery with matching rig.

Mauser produced fifty 4 in. barrel cutaways with the Persian contract for training purposes.

1936-1942 DATED MAUSER BANNER - 9mm Para. cal., 4 in. barrel, over 1,000 mfg., commercial and contract sales, wood grips, no sear safety, often have strawed small parts.

	N/A	$3,575	$2,950	$2,650	$1,900	$1,575	$1,250

GRADING - PPGS™	100%	98%	95%	90%	80%	70%	60%

MAUSER BANNER DUTCH CONTRACT - 9mm Para. cal., 4 in. barrel, 1,000 mfg., safety marked "Rust". Dated 1936-40.

| | N/A | $3,575 | $2,950 | $2,650 | $1,900 | $1,575 | $1,250 |

Add 25% for 1936, 1937, 1938, or 1939 chamber date.

MAUSER BANNER SWEDISH CONTRACT - 275 mfg. in 9mm Para. cal., 4 3/4 in. barrels, dated 1938, 25 mfg. in 9mm Para. cal., dated 1939, 30 mfg. in 7.65mm Para. cal., dated 1939, very rare in 7.65mm Para. dated 1940.

| | N/A | $3,850 | $3,250 | $2,700 | $2,050 | $1,800 | $1,650 |

Add 15% for 7.65mm Para. cal. (4 3/4 in. barrel).

CODE "S/42" COMMERCIAL CONTRACT - 9mm Para. cal., 4 in. barrel, a few hundred produced, dated 1938. Commercial proof marks only.

| | N/A | $2,950 | $2,475 | $2,100 | $1,650 | $1,425 | $1,200 |

CODE "42" - 9mm Para. cal., 4 in. barrels, dated 1939-1940, rear toggle marked "42." One of the most frequently encountered WWII military Lugers.

| | N/A | $1,950 | $1,700 | $1,400 | $1,150 | $1,025 | $975 |

Add 100% for Navy markings.

MAUSER BANNER POLICE - 9mm Para. cal., approx. 30,000 mfg., dated 1939-1942, police contract, have sear safeties, blue small parts. A few observed dated 1938.

| | N/A | $2,900 | $2,475 | $2,050 | $1,650 | $1,425 | $1,300 |

Add 30% with 1938 chamber date (rare).

CODE "41-42" - 9mm Para. cal., 4 in. barrel, 2-digit date, approx. 7,000 mfg. in January of 1941, "41" dated chamber, "42" code, most 42 dates are reworks.

| | N/A | $4,250 | $3,200 | $2,750 | $2,200 | $1,875 | $1,650 |

CODE "byf" - 9mm Para. cal., 4 in. barrel, thousands made, chamber dated 41 and 42. Rear toggle is stamped "byf," standard magazine was "fxo" marked and had an un-numbered plastic bottom. One of the most frequently encountered WWII military Lugers.

| | N/A | $1,950 | $1,700 | $1,400 | $1,150 | $1,025 | $925 |

Add 30% for original black bakelite grips.
Code "byf" Lugers with black bakelite grips are referred to as the "Black Widow" variation.

AUSTRIAN BUNDES HEER - 9mm Para. cal., 4 in. barrel, several hundred produced, Austrian Federal Army, no serial letter suffix-same ser. placement as Mauser 42 KU. Rarely encountered in mint condition.

| | N/A | $2,650 | $2,200 | $1,850 | $1,425 | $1,325 | $900 |

MAUSER 1934 CODE BYF, S/42 AND 42 KU - 9mm Para. cal., 3,500 mfg. Post-1942 Luftwaffe subcontract.

| | N/A | $3,200 | $2,750 | $2,200 | $1,875 | $1,650 | $1,200 |

Lugers: Reworks

DEATH'S HEAD REWORK - 9mm Para. cal., 4 in. barrel, very rare, possible early SS unit issue. Most are fakes.

| | N/A | $2,500 | $1,800 | $1,500 | $1,400 | $1,200 | $1,000 |

SIMSON REWORK - 9mm Para. cal., 4 in. barrel, DWM toggles, Simpson Eagle proofs on reworked parts.

| | N/A | $1,250 | $1,075 | $895 | $725 | $625 | $575 |

DOUBLE DATED DWM/ERFURT - 9mm Para. cal., 4 or 8 in. barrel, very scarce. 1920 over 1910-18 chamber dates. Often with sear safety and mag. safety remnant.

| | N/A | $1,375 | $1,200 | $995 | $800 | $700 | $650 |

Add 100% for intact mag. safety.
Add 40% for 8 in. barrel.

GRADING - PPGS™	100%	98%	95%	90%	80%	70%	60%

KONZENTRATION LUGER REWORK - 9mm Para. cal., 4 in. barrel, 200-300 marked "KI 1933" and issued to guards working in the first concentration camps - most went to Dachau. Most are fakes.

	N/A	$1,925	$1,575	$1,200	$1,000	$700	$600

Lugers: Simson Mfg.

SIMSON & COMPANY - 7.65mm Para. or 9mm Para. cal., 3 7/8 or 4 in. barrel, military and limited commercial sales, many thousands produced, but rarely found.

	N/A	$4,250	$3,600	$2,950	$2,300	$2,000	$1,300

SIMSON MILITARY DATED - 9mm Para. cal., 4 in. barrel, 2,000 mfg., dated 1925.

	N/A	$5,500	$4,600	$3,800	$3,000	$2,600	$1,650

This model is most commonly encountered with a 1925 chamber date.

SIMSON S CODE - 9mm Para. cal., 4 in. barrel, less than 1,000 mfg. Rare.

	N/A	$4,250	$3,600	$2,950	$2,300	$2,000	$1,300

Lugers: Swiss Bern

1906 BERN - 7.65mm Para. cal., 4 3/4 in. barrel, "Waffenfabrik Bern" on toggle, Swiss military, bordered checkered walnut grips, exactly 17,874 mfg.

	N/A	$3,100	$2,600	$2,200	$1,900	$1,700	$1,200

1929 SWISS BERN - 7.65mm Para. cal., 4 3/4 in. barrel, 29,857 mfg., many machining changes to simplify production, straight front grip strap, "P" prefix designates commercial model, brown or black plastic grips.

	N/A	$2,450	$2,000	$1,750	$1,500	$1,350	$1,000

Add 20% for red plastic grips and mag. bottom.

Lugers: KDF, Interarms, Stoeger, & Recent Import

Note: Post-WWII Lugers have been manufactured by Mauser Werke in Oberndorf, W. Germany during the 1970s, and by both Stoeger Industries and Mitchell Arms (see separate listing under Mitchell Arms) in recent years. Earlier Mauser importation was by Precision Imports, Inc. located in San Antonio, TX and Interarms of Alexandria, VA (and so marked on these guns).

Prices for 100% condition Lugers assume NIB status. If without box and accessories, deduct 25%.

INTERARMS MAUSER P.08 - 7.65mm Para. or 9mm Para. cal., 4 or 6 in. barrel, fully-contoured front grip strap.

	$1,500	$850	$650	$450	$375	$350	$300

INTERARMS "SWISS-STYLE" MAUSER EAGLE - 7.65mm Para. or 9mm Para. cal., "straight" front grip strap, American eagle logo on top of frame.

	$800	$650	$425	$375	$350	$325	$300

Add 10% for 6 in. barrel in 9mm Para.

STOEGER .22 CAL. LUGER - .22 LR cal., toggle action, all steel or aluminum construction, 4 1/2 or 5 1/2 in. barrel, right or left-hand safety, 10 shot mag. capacity, previously mfg. in the U.S. until 1985.

	$225	$190	$145	$120	$100	$70	$60

Last MSR was $200.

✳ *Stoeger .22 Cal. Luger "1 of 1,000"* - .22 LR cal., 1,000 mfg. in 1984-85, includes wooden box and extra mag.

	$295	$225	$175	N/A	N/A	N/A	N/A

GRADING - PPGS™	100%	98%	95%	90%	80%	70%	60%

STOEGER LUGER - 9mm Para. cal., choice of 4 or 6 (Navy) in. barrel, stainless steel construction, choice of polished stainless or matte black (new 1996) upper frame finish, American eagle engraved on top of frame, curved front grip strap, 7 shot mag., plastic mag. bottom, approx. 30 oz. Mfg. 1994-disc.

	$675	$475	$325	N/A	N/A	N/A	N/A

Last MSR was $720.

Add $79 for matte black finish.

NEW MODEL CARBINE WITH STOCK - 9mm Para. cal., authentic reproduction of the original Luger Carbine complete with matching stock, accessories, and case. Inventory was depleted during 1998.

	$6,500	$5,500	$4,000	N/A	N/A	N/A	N/A

Last MSR was $7,431.

CARTRIDGE COUNTER - 9mm Para. cal., left grip is slotted and contains a numbered metal strip. Manufacture began 1983, and inventory was depleted during 1998.

	$2,650	$1,550	$950	N/A	N/A	N/A	N/A

Last MSR was $3,865.

COMMEMORATIVE BULGARIAN - 9mm Para. cal., 100 available on U.S. market.

	$1,800	$1,200	$800	N/A	N/A	N/A	N/A

COMMEMORATIVE RUSSIAN - 9mm Para. cal., 100 available on U.S. market.

	$1,800	$1,200	$800	N/A	N/A	N/A	N/A

* *Commemorative Russian Matched pair of each*

	$4,000	$2,550	$1,850	N/A	N/A	N/A	N/A

MAUSER SPORT PARABELLUM - 7.65mm Para. or 9mm Para. cal., imported target barrel and adj. sights. 10 mfg. of each cal.

	$2,500	$2,000	$1,250	N/A	N/A	N/A	N/A

* *Mauser Sport Parabellum Consecutive Pair* - 7.65mm Para. or 9mm Para. cal.

	$4,250	$3,175	$1,950	N/A	N/A	N/A	N/A

Lugers: Special Interest

SPANDAU LUGER - be wary of originality on this model.

MO4/05 G.L. BABY LUGER - 7.65mm Para. or 9mm Para. cal., 3 1/4 in. barrel, G.L. proofed, hand made under Georg Luger's supervision, two known to exist. Made with shortened barrel, mag., and grip frame.

BABY LUGER 1925/26 - .380 ACP/.32 ACP cal., prototype, 4 mfg., only one known is .380. Only Luger documented by the manufacturer.

VONO REWORK - 7.65mm Para. or 9mm Para. cal., 4 in. barrel, commercial, rework by W.P. Von Nordheim, extremely rare variation.

	$1,500	$1,275	$1,050	$900	$800	$700	$600

1900 DWM CARBINE - 7.65mm Para. cal., 11 3/4 in. barrel, 100 mfg., only one known to exist. Characterized by "Ski slope" sight on rear toggle.

Extreme rarity precludes accurate pricing on this model.

1907 U.S. ARMY TEST TRIAL - .45 ACP cal., at least four originally mfg., serial numbered 1-4, plus an un-numbered prototype.

Extreme rarity precludes accurate pricing on this model. Undoubtedly, this is the most desirable semi-auto pistol ever manufactured, and is priced accordingly.

CONVERSIONS: JOHN MARTZ - John Martz of Lincoln, CA has converted WWII P.38s (please refer to P.38 section) and WWI or WWII Lugers into various configurations since 1968. These conversions are known for their quality workmanship and functional accuracy. Below is a generalized listing of variations he has fabricated and their values to date with production totals.

* *Conversions: John Martz .380 ACP Baby Luger* - 6 fabricated, disc.

	$6,000	$3,200	$2,400	N/A	N/A	N/A	N/A

GRADING - PPGS™	100%	98%	95%	90%	80%	70%	60%

✱ *Conversions: John Martz 7.65mm Para. Baby Luger (Grip Safety)* - 192 mfg. total, includes 9mm Baby Luger also.

	$3,000	$2,500	$1,900	N/A	N/A	N/A	N/A

✱ *Conversions: John Martz 9mm Para. Baby Luger* - 2 1/4 (disc.), 2 1/2 (disc.), or 2 5/8 in. barrel.

	$3,000	$2,500	$2,000	N/A	N/A	N/A	N/A

✱ *Conversions: John Martz Big-Bore .45 ACP Luger* - 79 fabricated (5 are babies), .45 ACP cal., fixed sights, 2 3/4, 4, 6, or 8 in. barrel. Disc.

	$5,500	$3,350	$2,400	N/A	N/A	N/A	N/A

✱ *Conversions: John Martz .45 ACP Luger Reproduction* - made to original 1907 U.S. Army test trial specifications by Mike Krause (limited mfg.).

This variation typically sells in the $8,500-$12,500 range, depending on condition.

✱ *Conversions: John Martz Navy Model* - .45 ACP cal., 6 or 8 in. barrel, adj. rear Navy sight, estimated mfg. is 25 pistols, disc.

	$6,000	$4,450	$3,300	N/A	N/A	N/A	N/A

Add 10% for Navy Model with 100-200 meter rear sight.

✱ *Conversions: John Martz Navy Model Ltd. Edition* - .38 Super cal., 6 in. barrel, adj. rear Navy sight, 10 fabricated, disc.

	$5,000	$3,950	$3,100	N/A	N/A	N/A	N/A

Subtract 10% for fixed rear sight (standard model with 4 in. barrel).

✱ *Conversions: John Martz Standard Model* - .38 Super cal., 4 to 8 in. barrel, fixed sight, 3 fabricated.

	$4,500	$3,150	$2,400	N/A	N/A	N/A	N/A

✱ *Conversions: John Martz Target Luger* - .22 Mag. cal., 6 or 9 in. barrel, fixed sight, 11 fabricated, disc.

	$7,500	$5,400	$3,400	N/A	N/A	N/A	N/A

✱ *Conversions: John Martz Luger Carbines (with shoulder stock)* - .22 Mag. (disc.), 7.65mm Para., 9mm Para., or .38 Super cal., 11-18 in. barrel with adj. rear sights. Disc.

	$7,900	$5,650	$3,600	N/A	N/A	N/A	N/A

Add 20% for .22 Mag. cal. (2 fabricated).

83 Luger carbines with 16 in. barrels were fabricated with shoulder stocks.
42 Luger carbines with 12 in. barrels were fabricated w/o shoulder stocks.

✱ *Conversions: John Martz Experimental Lugers* - experimental pistols have been made in .40 S&W (disc.), .41 AE (disc.), .357 SIG (11 mfg., 7, 8, or 9 in. barrel) and .357 Mag. Most have 8 in. barrels (except for .40 S&W cal., disc.). Extreme rarity (and not for sale status) precludes accurate price evaluation.

The .357 SIG model had a retail price of $3,500.

LUGERS: ACCESSORIES

Conversion Units - .22 cal.

ERMA - postwar-green cardboard box.

	$675	$600	$525	$450	$375	$325	$300

ERMA-PREWAR IN WOODEN BOX - Pre-war in wooden box.

	$2,000	$1,750	$1,500	$1,300	$1,100	$900	$700

Add 50% for Nazi Navy property numbered.
Subtract 20% for mismatched.

Detachable Stocks

ARTILLERY TYPE FLAT BOARD

	$625	$550	$500	$400	$300	$250	$225

GRADING - PPGS™	100%	98%	95%	90%	80%	70%	60%
ARTILLERY HOLSTER RIG, COMPLETE							
	$3,200	$2,850	$2,100	$1,750	$1,400	$1,150	$950
Subtract 20% if shoulder strap is missing.							
NAVAL-TYPE FLAT BOARD							
	$2,750	$2,450	$1,925	$1,650	$1,395	$1,150	$950
NAVAL HOLSTER RIG, COMPLETE							
	$5,450	$4,650	$4,125	$3,575	$2,750	$1,925	$1,525
Subtract 20% if shoulder strap is missing.							
CARBINE CONTOURED (ORIGINAL)							
	$4,650	$4,000	$3,400	$2,750	$1,875	$1,325	$1,100
IDEAL TELESCOPING WITH GRIPS - mfg. U.S. by Ideal Corp.							
	$3,000	$2,800	$2,300	$1,600	$1,200	$850	$650

"Snail" Drum Magazines

	100%	98%	95%	90%	80%	70%	60%
1ST ISSUE	$1,950	$1,625	$1,375	$1,200	$975	$875	$695
2ND ISSUE	$1,650	$1,425	$1,225	$1,100	$875	$750	$625
LOADING TOOL	$1,225	$1,050	$875	$775	$650	$550	$475

SHOTGUNS: O/U

CLASSIC MODEL - 12 ga., 3 1/2 in. chambers, engraved boxlock action, 26, 28, or 30 in. vent. barrels with VR and 3 choke tubes, gold SST, AE, checkered walnut stock and forearm, approx. 7 1/2 lbs.

While advertised for $919 by Stoeger Industies during 2000, this model was never imported. However, it has had limited importation to date from domestic distributors.

SHOTGUNS: SEMI-AUTO

ULTRA-LIGHT MODEL - 12 ga. only, 3 in. chamber, gas operated, 26 or 28 in. VR barrel with 3 choke tubes, checkered walnut stock and forearm, approx. 6 1/2 lbs.

	100%	98%	95%	90%	80%	70%	60%
	$295	$260	$230	$210	$195	$180	$165

While advertised by Stoeger Industies during 2000, this model was never imported by Stoeger Industries. However, it has had limited importation to date from domestic distributors.

LU-MAR s.r.l.

Previous shotgun manufacturer located in Gardone, Italy. Limited U.S. importation. Lu-Mar made a wide variety of O/U shotguns. In addition to their fine O/U lineup, Lu-Mar also manufactured SxS shotguns. These guns had little or no importation into the U.S.

LUNA

Previous manufacturer located in Germany.

PISTOLS: SINGLE SHOT

MODEL 200 FREE PISTOL - .22 LR cal., 11 in. barrel, blue, target sights, checkered target grips, pre-WWII.

	100%	98%	95%	90%	80%	70%	60%
	$1,100	$990	$855	$770	$660	$605	$525

RIFLES: SINGLE SHOT

TARGET RIFLE - falling block action, .22 LR or .22 Hornet cal., 20 in. barrel, adj. sights, target type stocks, pre-WWII.

	100%	98%	95%	90%	80%	70%	60%
	$990	$880	$800	$690	$605	$550	$495

NOTES

M SECTION

MAB

Please refer to listings under the French Military heading.

MAC (MILITARY ARMAMENT CORP.)

Please refer to FMJ and Ingram sections in this text. MAC was located in Ducktown, TN.

MAS

Previously manufactured by D´Armes St. Etienne (MAS) located in France.
Please refer to the French Military heading in this text.

MBA GYROJET

Previous manufacturer circa 1966-1969 located in San Ramon, CA.

GRADING - PPGS™	100%	98%	95%	90%	80%	70%	60%

PISTOLS: SEMI-AUTO

MARK I GYROJET PISTOL - 12mm or 13mm (no cartridge case) cal., uses spin-stabilized rocket projectiles that accelerate to 1,250 FPS in .12 seconds, 2 in. (rare) or 5 in. barrel, 6 shot semi-auto action drives rocket projectile (primer activated) into fixed firing pin, smooth walnut grips, black, antique nickel, or gold-plated finish, 13 or 16 oz., "A" prefix until ser. no. 49, "B" prefixes followed, there are also other variations and experimental models in addition to the production models listed. Not particularly accurate.

The rocket ammunition for this model is rare and typically sells in the $30-$35/round range per shell.

* *Mark I Gyrojet Pistol Model A Cased* - 13mm, black finish, smooth walnut grips, walnut cased with 10 rounds and medal.

	100%	98%	95%	90%	80%	70%	60%
	$2,395	$2,100	$1,800	$1,400	$1,125	$950	$875

* *Mark I Gyrojet Pistol Model B Cased* - 13mm, black, nickel, satin, or green finish, many variations with different grips, casings, and barrel lengths, wood cased, includes 10 dummy rounds and bronze medal honoring rocket pioneers Robert H. Goddard and Joseph J. Stubbs.

	100%	98%	95%	90%	80%	70%	60%
	$2,195	$1,825	$1,500	$1,250	$975	$850	$725

    Add approx. 25% for satin finish.

* *Mark I Gyrojet Pistol Model B Uncased or Cardboard* - either with cardboard case or no case, black finish.

	100%	98%	95%	90%	80%	70%	60%
	$1,200	$1,000	$850	$750	$625	$500	$400

* *Mark II Gyrojet Pistol Model C Uncased or Cardboard* - 12mm, black finish, walnut grips.

	100%	98%	95%	90%	80%	70%	60%
	$1,200	$1,000	$850	$750	$625	$500	$400

This variation was manufactured in 12mm to conform with the 1968 GCA, since any caliber over .50 was classified as a destructive device (i.e., 12mm = .49 cal. and 13mm =.51 cal.). In 1982, the 13mm guns were reclassified as curios and relics.

RIFLES: SEMI-AUTO, CARBINES

MARK I MODEL A or B CARBINE - 13mm cal., same action as Mark I pistol, black (Model A) or satin (Model B) finish, full stock with pistol grip extension, 18 in. barrel, nickel finish, 4 1/2 lbs. Limited mfg.

	100%	98%	95%	90%	80%	70%	60%
Model A	$3,000	$2,650	$2,250	$1,850	$1,700	$1,475	$1,350
Model B	$2,000	$1,700	$1,425	$1,150	$950	$850	$750

GRADING - PPGS™	100%	98%	95%	90%	80%	70%	60%

MG ARMS INCORPORATED

Current manufacturer established in 1980, and located in Spring, TX. MG Arms Incorporated was previously named Match Grade Arms & Ammunition. Consumer direct sales.

REVOLVERS

MGA CUSTOM BIG 5 - .45 LC+P, .454 Casull, .475 Linebaugh, .50 AE, or .500 Linebaugh cal., Ruger frame, stainless 5 shot cylinder, custom barrels, standard finish or optional camo coverage. Mfg. 2000-2007.

	$1,175	$975	$875	$775	$700	$625	$525

Last MSR was $1,295.

MG Arms also offered a conversion package for $795 (customer supplies Ruger revolver).

MGA DRAGON SLAYER - .44 Mag., .44 Colt, .454 Casull, .50 AE, .475 Linebaugh, .500 Linebaugh, .445 Super Mag., .450 Marlin, .460 S&W Mag., or .500 S&W Mag. cal., single action, 5 shot, stainless steel construction, choice of grips, includes of 20 rounds of custom loaded ammo. New 2008.

MSR $1,695	$1,595	$1,275	$1,025	$875	$750	$625	$550

RIFLES: BOLT ACTION

ULTRA-LIGHT MODEL - various cals., lightened and skeletonized Wby. Vanguard (disc. 2004) or Rem. 700 (new 2005) action, MGA button rifled barrel, Teflon metal finish, epoxy stock with Pachmayr decelerator pad, Super Eliminator muzzle brake, variety of camo finishes on stock, 5 1/2 lbs.

MSR $3,295	$3,150	$2,850	$2,450	$2,075	$1,750	$1,425	$1,125

Add $200 for Win. M70 action (disc. 2006).

MGA VARMINTER - various cals., squared and lapped Rem. M700 action, stainless steel National Match barrel with Super Eliminator muzzle brake, black Teflon metal finish, camo epoxy stock.

MSR $2,595	$2,300	$2,000	$1,650	$1,325	$1,050	$925	$750

SIGNATURE CLASSIC - various cals., Nesika Hunter action, Hart stainless steel barrel with Super Eliminator muzzle break, Jewell trigger, fiberglass or claro walnut stock. Limited mfg. (approx. 10 guns per year) beginning 2000.

MSR $5,400	$5,150	$4,600	$4,100	$3,650	$3,000	$2,450	$1,800

M-K SPECIALTIES INC.

Previous rifle manufacturer circa 2000-2002 located in Grafton, WV.

RIFLES: SEMI-AUTO

M-14 A1 - .308 Win. cal., forged M-14 steel receiver using CNC machinery to original government specifications, available as Rack Grade, Premier Match, or Tanker Model, variety of National Match upgrades were available at extra cost, base price is for Rack Grade. Mfg. 2000-2002.

	$1,400	$1,200	$995	$875	$750	$625	$500

Last MSR was $1,595.

National Match upgrades ranged from $345-$955.

MK ARMS INC.

Previous manufacturer located in Irvine, CA circa 1992.

CARBINES

MK 760 - 9mm Para. cal., paramilitary design carbine configuration, steel frame, 16 in. shrouded barrel, fires from closed bolt, 14, 24, or 36 shot mag., parkerized finish, folding metal stock, fixed sights. Mfg. 1983-approx. 1992.

	$675	$625	$575	$525	$475	$415	$375

Last MSR was $575.

GRADING - PPGS™	100%	98%	95%	90%	80%	70%	60%

MKE

Current manufacturer located in Ankara, Turkey. No current U.S. importation. Previously distributed by Mandall Shooting Supplies, Inc., located in Scottsdale, AZ.

MKE also manufactures a wide variety of military and law enforcement models, in addition to the consumer semi-auto rifles. Please contact the company directly for more information, including pricing and availability (see Trademark Index).

PISTOLS: SEMI-AUTO

KIRIKKALE AUTOMATIC - 7.65mm Para. (disc.) or .380 ACP cal., double action, 7 shot, blue, fixed sights, checkered plastic grips, this is a close copy of Walther's PP and the Turkish Army's standard service pistol. Disc. 1987.

$365	$295	$240	$215	$185	$170	$155

Last MSR was $395.

RIFLES: SEMI-AUTO

MKE currently manufactures both semi-auto sporting and hunting rifles in 9mm Para. and .308 Win. cals.

M.O.A. CORPORATION

Current manufacturer located in Sundance, WY since 2005. Previous located in Eaton, OH. Dealer direct sales only.

PISTOLS: SINGLE SHOT

Approx. 500-600 Maximum pistols are produced annually. Allow 4-6 months for delivery.

MAXIMUM - available in 30 standard chamberings between .22 Rimfire and .454 Casull cal., additional custom calibers are also available upon special order, single shot lever action pistol, falling block action, Chromoly receiver (disc. 1991), Armoloy coated Chromoly (disc. late 1992), or stainless steel (new 1991, standard 1992) receiver, 8 3/4 (new 1989), 10 1/2, or 14 in. interchangeable barrel, transfer bar safety, adj. open sights, walnut grips and forearm. New 1986.

MSR $823	$715	$585	$500	$450	$400	$375	$350

Subtract 10% for older steel receiver.
Add $60 for scope mounts.
Add $96 for stainless steel barrel on either receiver.
Add $125 for muzzle brake.
Add $269 per extra steel barrel.
Add $336 per extra stainless steel barrel.

Barrels must be fitted to individual receivers at the factory initially. Afterwards, they can be changed by the customer with the spanner wrench (included with extra barrels).

* *Maximum Carbine Model* - cals. up to .250 Sav., stainless receiver, otherwise similar to Maximum, except has 18 in. blue barrel. Mfg. began 1986, and production has been disc. several times.

MSR $1,023	$925	$850	$750	$650	$575	$525	$475

M.R. NEW SYSTEM ARMS

Current designer and handgun manufacturer located in Cerrione, Italy. No current U.S. importation.

Inventor and designer Marco Rigido mostly manufactures the largest caliber handguns on a limited, custom order basis - models include a 5 shot SA model Cucciolo in .728 MR cal. and a single shot Devastator in .728 MR cal. M.R. New System Arms also manufactures boxlock and sidelock O/U shotguns, express rifles (O/U and SxS), and bolt action rifles. Please contact the company directly for more information, including U.S. availability and pricing (see Trademark Index).

GRADING - PPGS™	100%	98%	95%	90%	80%	70%	60%

MTs ARMS

Current trademark manufactured by Sporting and Hunting Guns Central Design and Research Bureau, a subsidiary of the State Unitary Enterprise, Instrument Design Bureau, (GUP "KBP" - "TsKIB SOO"), located in Tula, Russia. No current U.S. importation.

MTs Arms manufactures a variety of firearms, including SxS and O/U shotguns, combination guns, self-loading shotguns, slide action shotguns, bolt action rifles, drillings, competition guns, and semi-auto rifles. TsKIB SOO is the only manufacturer of quality hunting guns in Russia and the countries of the CIS (Commonwealth of Independent States). Please contact the company directly for more information regarding this trademark and current domestic availability (see Trademark Index).

JAMES MacNAUGHTON & SONS

Current trademark owned and manufactured by Dickson & MacNaughton, located in Edinburgh, Scotland.

The firm of James MacNaughton was founded in Edinburgh, Scotland in 1864. During 1947, the company was acquired by John Dickson and during 1996, the ownership of the company changed again, having purchased the manufacturing rights from Dickson. In 1999, the directors of James MacNaughton & Sons acquired the whole share capital of John Dickson & Son, and the two companies now trade as one under the name of Dickson & MacNaughton. Please contact Dickson & MacNaughton directly for more information regarding this trademark, including current availability and pricing (see Trademark Index).

RIFLES: SxS

SIDELOCK RIFLE - .375 H&H or .470 NE cal., specifications per individual customer order.

Please contact the manufacturer directly regarding domestic availability and pricing.

SHOTGUNS

SxS SIDELOCK MODEL - 20 or 28 ga., lightweight construction.

Please contact the manufacturer directly regarding domestic availability and pricing.

MAADI-GRIFFIN CO.

Previous rifle manufacturer located in Mesa, AZ until 2003. Consumer direct sales.

RIFLES: SEMI-AUTO

MODEL MG-6 - .50 BMG cal., gas operated, bullpup configuration, one piece cast lower receiver, 5, 10, or 15 shot side mounted mag., 26-30 in. barrel, includes bipod, hard carrying case, and 3 mags. 23 lbs. Mfg. 2000-2003.

$5,500	$4,750	$3,850	$3,250	$2,600	$2,200	$1,800

Last MSR was $5,950.

Add $450 for MK-IV tripod.

RIFLES: SINGLE SHOT

MODEL 89 - .50 BMG cal., one piece cast lower receiver, 36 in. barrel, felt recoil is less than 12 ga., tig-welded interlocking assembly, no screws, tripod optional, 22 lbs. Mfg. 1990-2003.

$2,900	$2,600	$2,300	$2,000	$1,750	$1,500	$1,250

Last MSR was $3,150.

Add $600 for stainless steel.

MODEL 92 CARBINE - .50 BMG cal., 20 in. barrel, 5 lbs. trigger pull, 18 1/2 lbs. Mfg. 1990-2003.

$2,800	$2,500	$2,200	$1,850	$1,650	$1,400	$1,200

Last MSR was $2,990.

Add $650 for stainless steel.

GRADING - PPGS™	100%	98%	95%	90%	80%	70%	60%

MODEL 99 - .50 BMG cal., similar to Model 89, except has 44 in. barrel, 28 lbs. Mfg. 1999-2003.

	$3,150	$2,725	$2,450	$2,050	$1,775	$1,500	$1,250

Last MSR was $3,350.

Add $650 for stainless steel.

MAGNUM RESEARCH, INC.

Current trademark of pistols and rifles with company headquarters located in Minneapolis, MN. Centerfire pistols (Desert Eagle Series) are manufactured beginning 1998 by IMI, located in Israel. Previously mfg. by Saco Defense located in Saco, ME during 1995-1998, and by TAAS/IMI (Israeli Military Industries) 1986-1995. .22 Rimfire semi-auto pistols (Mountain Eagle) were previously manufactured by Ram-Line. Single shot pistols (Lone Eagle) were manufactured by Magnum Research sub-contractors. Distributed by Magnum Research, Inc., in Minneapolis, MN. Dealer and distributor sales.

MRI CUSTOM SHOP

In addition to the standard models listed, Magnum Research can also provide a variety of special order options through their custom shop, including many choices of Desert Eagle finishes, in addition to various sight systems and grips.

MRI's current custom shop Desert Eagle (not Baby Eagle) finish options with MSRs with 6 in. barrels are as follows: Polished hard chrome (PC) - MSR is $1,730, matte chrome (MC) - MSR - $1,730, brushed hard chrome (BC) - MSR - $1,730, black chrome - disc. 2007, MSR was $1,949, bright nickel (BN) - MSR is $1,730, satin nickel (SN) - MSR is $1,730, polished blue (PB) - MSR is $1,730, or gold accents (add $290). 24Kt. gold (GO) finish, titanium gold finish (TG, new 2000), titanium gold with tiger stripes (new 2005, .50 AE cal. only), or titanium carbon nitride (TCN, new 2002) - MSR is $2,020.

PISTOLS: SEMI-AUTO, RIMFIRE

THE MOUNTAIN EAGLE - .22 LR cal., single action, 6 (new 1995) or 6 1/2 (disc. 1994) in. polymer and steel barrel, features alloy receiver and polymer technology, matte black finish, adj. rear sight, 15 or 20 shot mag. 21 oz. Mfg. 1992-96.

	$185	$155	$135	$115	$100	$85	$75

Last MSR was $239.

∗ *The Mountain Eagle Compact Edition* - similar to Mountain Eagle, except has 4 1/2 in. barrel with shortened grips, adj. rear sight, 10 or 15 shot mag., plastic case, 19.3 oz. Mfg. 1996 only.

	$165	$135	$120	$105	$95	$80	$70

Last MSR was $199.

∗ *The Mountain Eagle Target Edition* - .22 LR cal., Target variation of the Mountain Eagle, featuring 8 in. accurized barrel, 2-stage target trigger, jeweled bolt, adj. sights with interchangeable blades, 23 oz. Mfg. 1994-96.

	$235	$185	$150	$135	$120	$105	$95

Last MSR was $279.

PICUDA MLP-1722 - .17 Mach 2 or .22 LR cal., 10 in. graphite barrel, no sights, features MLR-22 frame, choice of laminated nutmeg, forest camo, or pepper colored Barracuda stock, integral scope base, target trigger, 10 shot mag., approx. 3 lbs. New 2007.

MSR $699	$595	$525	$450	$400	$350	$300	$250

GRADING - PPGS™	100%	98%	95%	90%	80%	70%	60%

PISTOLS: SEMI-AUTO, CENTERFIRE

IMI SP-21 - 9mm Para., .40 S&W, or .45 ACP cal., DA or SA, traditional Browning operating system, polymer frame with ergonomic design, 3.9 in. barrel with polygonal rifling, 10 shot mag., finger groove grips, 3 dot adj. sights, reversible mag. release, multiple safeties, matte black finish, decocking feature, approx. 29 oz. Limited importation from IMI late 2002-2005.

$425	$375	$335	$300	$280	$260	$240

Last MSR was $499.

The IMI SP-21 uses the same magazines as the Baby Eagle pistols. This model is referred to the Barak SP-21 in Israel.

PISTOLS: SEMI-AUTO, CENTERFIRE - EAGLE SERIES

Magnum Research also offers a Collector's Edition Presentation Series. Special models include a Gold Edition (serial numbered 1-100), a Silver Edition (serial numbered 101-500), and a Bronze Edition (serial numbered 501-1,000). Each pistol from this series is supplied with a walnut presentation case, 2 sided medallion, and certificate of authenticity. Prices are available upon request by contacting Magnum Research directly.

Alloy frames on the Desert Eagle Series of pistols were discontinued in 1992. However, if sufficient demand warrants, these models will once again be available to consumers at the same price as the steel frames.

Beginning late 1995, the Desert Eagle frame assembly for the .357 Mag., .44 Mag., and .50 AE cals. is based on the .50 caliber frame. Externally, all three pistols are now identical in size. This new platform, called the Desert Eagle Pistol Mark XIX Component System, enables .44 Mag. and .50 AE conversions to consist of simply a barrel and a magazine - conversions to or from the .357 Mag. also include a bolt.

The slide assembly on the Mark I and Mark VII is physically smaller than the one on a Mark XIX. Also, the barrel dovetail on top is 3/8 in. on a Mark I or Mark VII, while on a Mark XIX, it is 7/8 in., and includes cross slots for scopes.

> **Individual Desert Eagle Mark XIX 6 in. barrels are $389-$564, depending on finish, and 10 in. barrels are $459-$634, depending on finish. Add $129 for Trijicon night sights (new 2006). Add $49-$89 for Hogue Pau Ferro wooden grips (new 2007) or $49 for Hogue soft rubber grips with finger grooves.**

THE BABY EAGLE - 9mm Para., .40 S&W, .41 AE (disc.), or .45 ACP (3.7 in. barrel only, new 2000) cal., double action, all steel or polymer (3.5 or 3.7 in. barrel, 9mm Para. or .40 S&W only) frame construction, 3.5 (new 2000), 3.62 (mfg. 1993-99), 3.7 (new 2000), or 4.52 in. barrel, short recoil operation, polygonal rifling, combat styled trigger guard, decocking slide safety or frame mounted safety (Model 9mmF), blued (disc. 1995), standard black (new 1996), or chrome (disc. 1999) finish, 10 (C/B 1994), 13 (.40 S&W only, new 2005), 16* (9mm Para., disc.), 11* (.41 AE), or 15 (9mm Para. only, new 2005) shot mag., shipped with two magazines beginning 2006, 38 1/2 oz. Imported 1991-96. Reintroduced mid-1999-2007.

* *The Baby Eagle Full Size* - 9mm Para. or .40 S&W cal., 4.52 in. barrel, steel frame only. Disc. 2007.

$465	$385	$320	$275	$235	$210	$190

Last MSR was $569.

> **Add $239 for conversion kit (9mm Para. to .41 AE or .41 AE to 9mm Para., includes barrel, spring, and mag.), disc. 1996.**

This model was also available in various optional finishes, including brushed or polished chrome - MSR was $804, titanium gold - MSR was $1,069, or titanium carbon nitride - MSR was $1,069.

GRADING - PPGS™	100%	98%	95%	90%	80%	70%	60%

✳ *The Baby Eagle Semi-Compact* - 9mm Para., .40 S&W, or .45 ACP cal., same general specifications as Baby Eagle, except has 3.7 in. barrel, .45 ACP not available in polymer, 36 oz. (steel) or 29 oz. (polymer). Disc. 2007.

	$465	$385	$320	$275	$235	$210	$190

Last MSR was $569.

This model was also available in brushed or polished chrome finish - MSR was $804, titanium gold or titanium nitride - MSR was $1,069.

✳ *The Baby Eagle Compact* - 9mm Para. or .40 S&W cal., same general specifications as Baby Eagle, except has 3 1/2 in. barrel, 10 or 12 (9mm Para. only) shot mag., 27 oz. (polymer) or 34 oz (steel). Disc. 2007.

	$465	$385	$320	$275	$235	$210	$190

Last MSR was $569.

This model was also available in brushed chrome finish - MSR was $804.

THE BABY EAGLE II - 9mm Para., .40 S&W, or .45 ACP cal., similar specs as the Baby Eagle, except has improved rear sight and Picatinny rail, choice of black polymer or steel frame, black, brushed chrome, or custom finishes. New 2008.

✳ *The Baby Eagle II Full Size* - 4.52 in. barrel with ergonomic rear sight and lower Picatinny rail. New 2008.

MSR $619	$550	$495	$450	$415	$375	$335	$295

Add $235 for brushed or polished chrome.
Add $500 for titanium gold.

✳ *The Baby Eagle II Semi-Compact* - 9mm Para., .40 S&W, or .45 ACP cal., similar to Baby Eagle II Full Size, except has 3.7 in. barrel with ergonomic rear sight and lower Picatinny rail. New 2008.

MSR $619	$550	$495	$450	$415	$375	$335	$295

Add $235 for brushed or polished chrome.

✳ *The Baby Eagle II Compact* - similar to Baby Eagle II Semi-Compact, except has 3 1/2 in. barrel w/o Picatinny rail. New 2008.

MSR $619	$550	$495	$450	$415	$375	$335	$295

Add $235 for brushed chrome.

MARK I DESERT EAGLE .357 MAG - .357 Mag. cal., similar to Mark VII, except has standard trigger and safety lever is teardrop shaped, and slide catch release has single serration. Disc.

	$925	$825	$725	$625	$525	$450	$400

MARK XIX .357 MAG. DESERT EAGLE - features .50 cal. frame and slide, standard black finish, 6 or 10 in. barrel, 4 lbs., 6 oz. Mfg. by Saco 1995-98, and IMI again beginning 1998.

MSR $1,440	$1,200	$1,025	$850	$750	$625	$550	$475

Add $100 for 10 in. barrel.

MARK VII .357 MAG. DESERT EAGLE - .357 Mag. cal., gas operated, 6 (standard barrel length), 10, or 14 in. barrel length with 3/8 in. dovetail rib, steel (58.3 oz.) or alloy (47.8 oz.) frame, adj. trigger, safety lever is hook shaped, slide catch/release lever has three steps, adaptable to .44 Mag. with optional kit, 9 shot mag. (8 for .44 Mag.). Mfg. 1983-95, limited quantities were made available again during 1998 and 2001.

	$995	$875	$750	$650	$550	$475	$425

Last MSR was $929.

Add approx. $150 for 10 or 14 in. barrel (disc. 1995).
Add $495 for .357 Mag. to .41 Mag./.44 Mag. conversion kit (6 in. barrel). Disc. 1995.
Add approx. $685 for .357 Mag. to .44 Mag. conversion kit (10 or 14 in. barrel). Disc. 1995.

GRADING - PPGS™	100%	98%	95%	90%	80%	70%	60%

✶ *Mark VII .357 Mag. Desert Eagle Whitetail Special* - 14 in. barrel, includes scope mount, target walnut grips, and Desert Eagle premiums. Mfg. 1990-92.

	$925	$750	$650	$550	$450	$400	$375

Last MSR was $1,088.

Add $50 for stainless steel frame.

✶ *Mark VII .357 Mag. Desert Eagle Stainless Steel* - similar to .357 Mag. Desert Eagle, except has stainless steel frame, 58.3 oz. Mfg. 1987-95.

	$750	$650	$550	$460	$395	$335	$285

Last MSR was $839.

Add approx. $150 for 10 or 14 in. barrel.

MARK VII .41 MAG. DESERT EAGLE - .41 Mag. cal., similar to .357 Desert Eagle, 6 in. barrel only, 8 shot mag., steel (62.8 oz.) or alloy (52.3 oz.) frame. Mfg. 1988-95, limited quantities available during 2001.

	$785	$675	$565	$500	$465	$420	$390

Last MSR was $899.

Add $395 for .41 Mag. to .44 Mag. conversion kit (6 in. barrel only).

✶ *Mark VII .41 Mag. Desert Eagle Stainless Steel* - similar to .41 Mag. Desert Eagle, except has stainless steel frame, 58.3 oz. Mfg. 1988-95.

	$825	$700	$550	$460	$395	$335	$285

Last MSR was $949.

MARK I DESERT EAGLE .44 MAG - .44 Mag. cal., similar to Mark VII, except has standard trigger and safety lever is teardrop shaped, and slide catch release has single serration. Disc.

	$975	$850	$750	$650	$550	$475	$425

MARK XIX .44 MAG. DESERT EAGLE - features .50 cal. frame and slide, standard black finish, 6 or 10 in. barrel, 4 lbs., 6 oz. Mfg. by Saco 1995-98, and by IMI again beginning 1998.

MSR $1,440		$1,200	$1,025	$850	$750	$625	$550	$475

Add $100 for 10 in. barrel.

MARK VII .44 MAG. DESERT EAGLE - .44 Mag. cal., similar to .357 Desert Eagle, 8 shot mag., steel (62.8 oz.) or alloy (52.3 oz.) frame. Originally mfg. 1986-95, re-released 1998-2000.

	$975	$850	$750	$650	$550	$475	$425

Last MSR was $1,049.

Add $100 for 10 (current) or 14 (disc. 1995) in. barrel.
Add $475 for .44 Mag. to .357 Mag. conversion kit (6 in. barrel). Disc. 1995.
Add $675 for .44 Mag. to .357 Mag. conversion kit (10 or 14 in. barrel). Disc. 1995.
Add $395 for .44 Mag. to .41 Mag. conversion kit (6 in. barrel). Disc. 1995.

✶ *Mark VII .44 Mag. Desert Eagle Stainless Steel* - similar to .44 Mag. Desert Eagle, except has stainless steel frame, 58.3 oz. Mfg. 1987-95.

	$900	$800	$700	$600	$500	$450	$400

Last MSR was $949.

Add approx. $210 for 10 or 14 in. barrel.

HUNTER EDITION MARK VII - .357 or .44 Mag. cal., 6 in. barrel with extra 14 in. hunting barrel, includes Leupold 2X EER scope, scope mount. Mfg. late 1987-93.

	$1,200	$975	$825	$675	$550	$475	$425

Last MSR was $1,350.

Add $110 for .44 Mag. cal.

GRADING - PPGS™	100%	98%	95%	90%	80%	70%	60%

MARK VII .50 MAG. DESERT EAGLE - .50 AE cal., 6 in. barrel with 7/8 in. rib with cross slots for Weaver style rings, steel only, black standard finish, frame slightly taller than the Mark VII .357 Mag./.44 Mag., 7 shot mag., 72.4 oz. Mfg. 1991-95 by IMI, limited quantities were made available again during 1998 only.

	$1,175	$950	$825	$700	$575	$500	$450

Last MSR was $1,099.

This cartridge utilized the same rim dimensions as the .44 Mag. and was available with a 300 grain bullet. The .50 Action Express cal. has 60% more stopping power than the .44 Mag., with a minimal increase in felt recoil.

MARK XIX CUSTOM 440 - .440 Cor-Bon cal., similar to Mark XIX .44 Mag. Desert Eagle, 6 or 10 in. barrel, standard black finish, rechambered by MRI Custom Shop, limited mfg. 1999-2001.

	$1,175	$995	$850	$725	$575	$500	$450

Last MSR was $1,389.

Add $40 for 10 in. barrel.

MARK XIX .50 MAG. DESERT EAGLE - features .50 AE cal., larger frame, standard black finish, 6 or 10 in. barrel, 4 lbs., 6 oz. Mfg. by Saco 1995-98, and by IMI again beginning 1998.

MSR $1,440		$1,200	$1,025	$850	$750	$625	$550	$475

Add $100 for 10 in. barrel.

MARK XIX 3 CAL. COMPONENT SYSTEM - includes Mark XIX .44 Mag. Desert Eagle and 5 barrels including .357 Mag. (6 and 10 in.), .44 Mag., and .50 AE (6 and 10 in.) cals., .357 bolt assembly and ICC aluminum carrying case. Also available in custom finishes at extra charge. New 1998.

MSR $4,182		$3,700	$3,100	$2,600	$2,300	$2,000	$1,750	$1,500

✱ *Mark XIX 3 Cal. Component System* - Includes component Mark XIX system in 6 or 10 in. barrel only. New 1998.

MSR $2,766		$2,350	$2,050	$1,750	$1,500	$1,250	$1,000	$850

Add $240 for 10 in. barrel.

PISTOLS: SINGLE SHOT

LONE EAGLE (SSP-91) - .22 LR (disc. 1992), .22 Mag. (disc. 1992), .22 Hornet, .22-250 Rem., .223 Rem., .243 Win., .260 Rem. (new 1997), .30-30 Win., .30-06, .300 Win. Mag. (Ltd. ed., mfg. 1997-99), .308 Win., 6mmBR (disc. 1992), 7mm-08 Rem., 7mmBR, .35 Rem., .357 Max. (disc. 1997, reintroduced 2001), .358 Win., .44 Mag., .440 Cor-Bon (new 1999), .444 Marlin, or 7.62x39mm (new 1996) cal., circular rear breech action, quick change 14 in. barrels (drilled and tapped), black or chrome (new 1997) finish, black synthetic Valox ambidextrous pistol grip, 4 lbs. 3 oz.-4 lbs. 7 oz. Mfg. 1991-2001.

	$380	$315	$275	$230	$200	$185	$170

Last MSR was $438.

Add $40 for chrome finish.
Add $35 for adj. hunting sights.
Add $129 for adj. silhouette sights by RPM.
Add $319 for standard black finish barrel, $418 for standard barrel with muzzle brake, $359 for chrome barrel, and $469 for chrome barrel with muzzle brake.

The grip assembly ($119) and barreled actions were available individually on this model.

GRADING - PPGS™	100%	98%	95%	90%	80%	70%	60%

REVOLVERS

BFR LONG CYLINDER - .30-30 Win. (new 2004), .444 Marlin, .45 LC/.410 bore, .450 Marlin (new 2002, 10 in. barrel only), .45-70 Govt., .460 S&W Mag. (new 2006), or .500 S&W Mag. (new 2003) cal., single action, 5 shot, stainless steel, 7 1/2 (.45 LC/.410 bore and .45-70 Govt.) or 10 (.444 Marlin, .450 Marlin, or .45-70 Govt.) in. barrel, checkered rubber grips, 4 lbs.-4.36 lbs. New 1999.

MSR $899		$775	$650	$525	$440	$385	$325	$280

This model was originally advertised as the BFR Maxine, then was changed to BFR (Biggest Finest Revolver).

BFR SHORT CYLINDER - .22 Hornet, .45 LC+P (disc. 2001), .454 Casull, .475 Linebaugh/.480 Ruger (new 2002), or .50 AE (disc. 2001, reintroduced 2004) cal., similar to BFR Model, 6 1/2 (.45 LC+P, .454 Casull, .475 Linebaugh, or .480 Ruger cal.), 7 1/2, or 10 (not available in .50 AE or .45 LC+P cal.) barrel, 3.2-4.36 lbs. New 1999.

MSR $899		$775	$650	$525	$440	$385	$325	$280

This model was originally advertised as the BFR Little Max, then was changed to BFR (Biggest Finest Revolver).

RIFLES: BOLT-ACTION

MOUNTAIN EAGLE RIFLE - .223 Rem. (new 2000), 270 Win., .280 Rem., .30-06, 7mm STW (mfg. 1998-99), .300 Win. Mag., .300 Wby. Mag., .338 Win. Mag., .340 Wby. Mag. (disc. 1997), 7mm Rem. Mag., .375 H&H, or .416 Rem. Mag. cal., Sako action, adj. trigger, 4 or 5 shot mag., match grade Krieger barrel with cut rifling, H-S Precision composite stock with aluminum bedding block, includes carrying case. Mfg. 1994-2000.

		$1,325	$1,075	$900	$775	$625	$550	$495

Last MSR was $1,499.

Add $200 for muzzle brake.
Add $50 for left-hand action.
Add $300 for .375 H&H or .416 Rem. Mag. cal.

✳ *Mountain Eagle Rifle Varmint* - .222 Rem. or .223 Rem. cal., 26 in. stainless steel heavy fluted barrel, w/o sights, approx. 9 3/4 lbs. Mfg. 1996-2000.

		$1,425	$1,100	$925	N/A	N/A	N/A	N/A

Last MSR was $1,629.

MOUNTAIN EAGLE MAGNUM LITE - .223 Rem. (varmint only), .22-250 Rem. (varmint only), .280 Rem., .30-06, .300 Win. Mag., .300 WSM (new 2003), 7mm WSM (new 2003), or 7mm Rem. Mag. cal., custom-built Rem. short action or Sako (disc.) action with one-piece forged bolt, adj. trigger, 24 in. sport tapered or 26 in. varmint bull graphite barrel with stainless steel liner, no sights, black swirl H-S Precision Kevlar graphite or Hogue overmolded (7mm WSM or .300 WSM only) stock, 4 or 5 shot mag, approx. 7 1/4 lbs. New 2001.

MSR $2,295		$1,995	$1,700	$1,400	$1,100	$825	$700	$575

Magnum Lite graphite barrels are available in 3 configurations for $599.

MOUNTAIN EAGLE TACTICAL RIFLE - .223 Rem. (new 2002), .22-250 Rem. (new 2002), .308 Win., .300 Win. Mag., or .300 WSM (new 2002) cal., accurized Rem. M-700 action, 26 in. Magnum Lite barrel, H-S Precision tactical stock, adj. stock and trigger, 9 lbs., 4 oz. New 2001.

MSR $2,400		$2,075	$1,750	$1,425	$1,125	$850	$700	$575

Add $150 for .300 WSM cal.

MAGNUM LITE 77 - .17 HMR cal., features 22 in. graphite barrel. New 2006.

MSR $999		$875	$750	$625	$500	$400	$325	$250

GRADING - PPGS™	100%	98%	95%	90%	80%	70%	60%

RIFLES: SEMI-AUTO

Magnum Lite .22 graphite barrels are also available individually starting at $269. For the .17 Mach 2 barrel a bolt kit is also included. MLR 17/22 barrels will also fit Ruger 10/22 rifles.

Add $140 for Clark custom upgrade (includes Clark deluxe trigger kit, tuned extractor, and bolt release) on the models listed (not available in .17 HMR cal., disc. 2006).

MAGNUM LITE RIFLE - .17 HMR (new 2004), .17 Mach 2 (new 2005), .22 LR or .22 Mag. (new 2000) cal., features Ruger 10/22 WMR (.17 HMR or .22 Mag. only beginning 2006) or one-piece Model 17/22 MLR receiver featuring large bolt handle machined from solid billet of aluminum (available in .22 LR or .17 Mach 2 cal.), with Acculite (disc.) or graphite (new 1999) barrel utilizing unidirectional graphite carbon fiber with stainless steel liner, barrel weighs 13 oz. New 1997.

✳ *Magnum Lite Rifle* - choice of walnut (new 2006), black Hogue Overmolded or Fajen high stock (disc. 1999) in either midnight or coffee color, 4.3 (.22 LR cal.) or 5.4 (.22 Mag. cal.) lbs. with Hogue stock. New 1997.

MSR $629	$545	$465	$400	$360	$330	$275	$250

Add $90 for .22 Mag. or .17 HMR cal.
Add $170 for walnut stock (only available in .17 Mach 2 or .22 LR cal., Model 17/22).

✳ *Magnum Lite Rifle w/ Fajen Thumbhole Stock* - features choice of Fajen thumbhole sporter or thumbhole silhouette in midnight or coffee color. Mfg. 1997-99.

	$625	$525	$450	$395	$360	$330	$275

Last MSR was $699.

Add $100 for thumbhole silhouette stock configuration.

✳ *Magnum Lite Rifle w/ Barracuda Stock* - features skeletonized sporter stock with thumbhole, choice of green (disc.), nutmeg (new 2006), forest camo (new 2006), pepper (new 2006) or coffee (disc.) laminate, choice of blued, red, or blue anodized receiver, 4.4 (.22 LR cal.) or 5.4 (.22 Mag.) lbs. New 1997.

MSR $759	$665	$575	$500	$440	$395	$350	$325

Add $60 for .17 HMR or .22 Mag. cal. (Model 10/22 only).
Add $40 for red or blue anodized receiver (.17 Mach 2 or .22 LR cal. only).

MAGNUM HEAVY VARMINT - .17 HMR or .22 Mag. cal., choice of blued steel or stainless steel barrel, choice of Hogue overmolded stock or Barracuda with skeletonized sporter stock. New 2008.

MSR $719	$625	$550	$475	$425	$375	$325	$275

Add $100 for Barracuda forest camo, nutmeg, or pepper colored laminate skeletonized stock.

MAGTECH

Current importer and distributor of CBC (Companhia Brasileria de Cartuchos) ammunition located in Centerville, MN. Previously located in Madison, CT 1999-2001 and in Las Vegas, NV until 1999. Magtech previously imported firearms manufactured by CBC located in Brazil.

RIFLES

MODEL 7022 SEMI-AUTO - .22 LR cal., Ruger 10/22 style action, 10 shot, 18 in. barrel, choice of hardwood or synthetic stock. New 2001.

	$120	$100	$85	$75	$70	$65	$60

MODEL 122 BOLT ACTION - .22 LR cal., 6 shot detachable mag., safety lever disconnects trigger from firing mechanism, uncheckered hardwood stock, 5.7 lbs. Imported 1992 only.

	$115	$95	$80	$70	$60	$50	$40

Last MSR was $131.

GRADING - PPGS™	100%	98%	95%	90%	80%	70%	60%

SHOTGUNS

MODEL 151 SINGLE SHOT - 12, 16, 20 ga., or .410 bore, 26, 28, or 30 in. barrel, exposed hammer, ejector, front triggerguard opening mechanism, some plastic used for buttons, levers, and bushings, 5-6 1/2 lbs. Imported 1992 only.

	$95	$80	$70	$60	$50	$40	$35

Last MSR was $109.

MODEL 199 - 12, 16, 20, 28 ga., or .410 bore, all steel construction, exposed hammer with underlever opening, unique hammer/firing pin safety, 24 or 28 in. barrel, uncheckered Brazilian stock and forearm, recoil pad supplied on Youth Models (20 ga. or .410 bore only), New 2001.

	$100	$85	$75	$70	$65	$60	$55

MODEL MT-586-2 SLIDE ACTION - 12 ga. only, 3 in. chamber, standard Field model shotgun, 28 in. barrel with fixed chokes, hardwood stock and forearm, double slide bars. Imported 1993-95.

	$190	$175	$160	$140	$130	$120	$110

Last MSR was $229.

The Model MT-586 preceded the MT-586-2. The MT-586 was disc. 1994.

＊ *Model MT-586-2-VR Slide Action* - similar to Model MT-586, except has choice of 26 or 28 in. VR barrel with interchangeable chokes. Imported 1993-95.

	$220	$185	$170	$155	$140	$130	$120

Last MSR was $259.

MODEL MT-586 SLIDE ACTION SLUG - 12 ga. only, slug gun featuring 24 in. cylinder bore barrel with rifle sights, matte finished metal parts, and special Monte Carlo stock. Imported 1993-95.

	$195	$180	$165	$145	$130	$120	$110

Last MSR was $239.

MODEL MT-586-2P - 12 ga. only, 3 in. chamber, slide action, 19 in. cylinder bore barrel, 7 shot mag., double slide bars, steel construction, hardwood stock, 7.3 lbs. Imported 1992-96.

	$185	$170	$155	$140	$130	$120	$110

Last MSR was $219.

MAJESTIC ARMS, LTD.

Current manufacturer established during 2000, and located on Staten Island, NY. Dealer sales only.

CARBINES: SEMI-AUTO

MA 2000 - .22 LR cal., Henry Repeating Arms Co. AR-7 takedown action, fiberoptic sights, American walnut forearm, pistol grip, and buttplate, fixed tubular stock with butt bag, 16 1/4 in. Lothar Walther barrel with crown, black teflon or silver bead blast finish, 4 lbs. New 2000.

MSR $389	$350	$295	$250	$225	$195	$175	$150

MA 4 - .17 HMR, .17 Mach 2 (new 2005), .22 LR (new 2005), or .22 Mag. cal., takedown action, traditional stock or wire frame, interchangeable barrel/bolt assembly. While intially advertised during 2004 with a MSR of $399, this model has yet to go into production.

SHOTGUNS: SLIDE ACTION

BASE-TAC - 12 or 20 ga., 3 in. chamber, based on M870 Remington action, approx. 18 in. barrel with ghost ring sights, black synthetic (12 ga.) or hardwood stock and forearm, extended 6 shot tube mag., 6-7 lbs. New 2004.

MSR $729	$650	$575	$500	$450	$400	$350	$300

Add $40 for 20 ga.

GRADING - PPGS™	100%	98%	95%	90%	80%	70%	60%

MAKAROV

Pistol design originating from the former Soviet Union. Russian mfg. Makarovs may be found under the "Russian Service Pistol and Rifle" heading in this text. Pistols listed have recently been imported by various companies, including Century International Arms, Inc. located in St. Albans, VT.

PISTOLS: SEMI-AUTO

MAKAROV COPIES - 9mm Makarov cal., patterned after the Soviet PM pistol, mfg. in eastern Germany, Bulgaria, and China, double action, blowback design, all steel, slide mounted safety that doubles as a decocking lever, 3.6 in. barrel, 8 shot mag., 25 oz.

No MSR	$185	$145	$125	$105	$95	$85	$75

Add approx. $35-$40 for polished blue or silver matte finish (Bulgarian mfg. only).
The importation of this type of pistol increased beginning 1992.

MALIN, F.E.

Previous manufacturer located in England. Previously imported by Saxon Arms, Inc. located in Clearwater, FL. Charles Boswell purchased Malin shortly before manufacture stopped.

SHOTGUNS: SxS, CUSTOM

BOXLOCK - made to individual order, choice of game scene engraving, Anson & Deeley boxlock actions, select European hybrid walnut, double triggers, leather cased. Prices started at $3,750 and each shotgun was priced per individual special order.

SIDELOCK - made to individual order, choice of game scene engraving, H&H sidelock action, select European hybrid walnut, double triggers, leather cased. Prices started at $5,000 and each shotgun was priced per individual special order.

MAMBA

Previously manufactured by Viper Mfg. Co. (a division of Sandock Austral Boksburg) located in South Africa.

PISTOLS: SEMI-AUTO

AUTO PISTOL - 9mm Para. cal., double action, 5 in. barrel, 14 shot mag., designed in Rhodesia, manufacture was not successful due to the non-hardened steel used in the investment cast construction process, poor exterior finish, less than 80 imported into the U.S., and 25 prototypes were built for Navy Arms.

Rarity factor precludes accurate pricing and values vary greatly in different regions.

MANCHESTER ARMS INC.

Previous manufacturer located in Lenoir, TN.

PISTOLS: SEMI-AUTO

COMMANDO MARK 45 - .45 ACP cal., paramilitary type design with detachable mag., wood pistol grip, 5 in. barrel with muzzle brake. Disc.

$525	$450	$395	$350	$300	$265	$235

MANDALL SHOOTING SUPPLIES, INC.

Current importer, distributor, and retailer located in Scottsdale, AZ.

Mandall Shooting Supplies distributes/imports various firearms including pistols, revolvers, rifles, and shotguns, as well as other models. Mandall Shooting Supplies, Inc. should be contacted directly for current pricing and special order questions (see Trademark Index).

GRADING - PPGS™	100%	98%	95%	90%	80%	70%	60%

MANNLICHER PISTOLS

Previously manufactured in Austria and Switzerland starting circa 1894.

PISTOLS: SEMI-AUTO

MODEL 1894 - 6.5mm or 7.6mm cal., unique blow forward design, fewer than 100 mfg. by Fabrique d´Armes in Neuhauson, Switzerland, and OWGS, Austria.

$15,000	$12,500	$9,500	$8,500	$7,500	$6,000	$5,000

Add 30% for 7.6mm cal.

MODEL 1897 - 7.63mm Mannlicher cal., first Mannlicher pistol with detachable mag. (matching), unique cocking lever on right frame, approx. 1,000 mfg.

$9,500	$8,000	$6,500	$5,000	$4,000	$3,500	$3,000

Add 100% for extended barrel version with adj. sight and detachable shoulder stock.
Add 150% for Model 1896 prototype in similar configuration, but with fixed mag.
Subtract 15% for rifle (carbine).

MODEL 1899 - 7.63 Mannlicher cal., rear sight mounted on barrel, large safety lever on left frame, approx. 300 mfg.

$8,500	$7,000	$5,500	$4,500	$4,000	$3,500	$3,000

MODEL 1901 - 7.63 Mannlicher cal., rear sight mounted on barrel, safety on rear of right slide, approx. 1,000 mfg.

$4,500	$3,000	$2,000	$1,250	$800	$700	$600

MODEL 1905 - 7.63 Mannlicher cal., final and most common variation.

$2,500	$1,950	$1,250	$750	$600	$500	$400

ARGENTINE MODEL 1905 - 7.65mm cal., Argentine crest on right panel is usually machined off. Values assume matching numbers but removed crest.

$700	$600	$500	$400	$300	$275	$250

✳ *Argentine Model 1905* - with Original Military Crest.

$3,500	$2,750	$2,000	$1,500	$1,000	$750	$500

MANNLICHER SCHOENAUER SPORTING RIFLES

Originally manufactured by Oesterreich Waffenfabrik Gesellschaft Steyr in Steyr, Austria from the 1850s until 1971. The current manufacturer is Steyr-Mannlicher, also of Steyr, Austria. Products made from 1968 to date are listed under Steyr-Mannlicher current production. Please refer to the Steyr-Mannlicher section.

The first of these "true" Mannlicher-Schoenauers were made in 1900, with serial production starting in 1903 or 1905 (depending upon the source).

RIFLES: BOLT ACTIONS, PRE-WWII

Add approx. 25% for all takedown pre-war models.

MODEL 1903 CARBINE - 6.5x54mm Mannlicher Schoenauer cal., 5 shot, 17.7 in. barrel, rotary mag., two leaf rear sight, double set trigger, full length stock.

N/A	$2,500	$2,200	$1,975	$1,750	$1,500	$1,225

This caliber may also be referred to as 6.5x53mm. This model is normally encountered in poor condition.

The Greek government ordered over 100,000 M1903 rifles, and many of these have been modified to a sporting configuration. These converted guns can be difficult to differentiate from true commercial Model 1903s, and values above are for original sporting carbines.

MODEL 1903 RIFLE - 6.5x54mm Mannlicher Schoenauer cal., 5 shot, various barrel lengths up to 23 inches, otherwise similar to Carbine.

N/A	$2,500	$2,200	$1,950	$1,750	$1,500	$1,225

Full stocked rifles may be encountered.

The Greek government ordered over 100,000 M1903 rifles, and many of these have been modified to a sporting configuration. These converted rifles can be difficult to differentiate from true commercial Model 1903s, and values above are for original sporting rifles.

MODEL 1905 CARBINE - similar to Model 1903, except 9x56mm Mannlicher Schoenauer cal., 19.7 in. barrel.

	N/A	$1,900	$1,625	$1,275	$975	$850	$725

This model is normally encountered in poor condition. It is perhaps the least desirable of pre-war models because of the wide variation in bore diameters.

MODEL 1905 RIFLE - similar to Model 1905 Carbine, except available in various barrel lengths up to 25 inches.

	N/A	$1,900	$1,625	$1,275	$975	$850	$725

MODEL 1908 CARBINE - 8x56mm Mannlicher Schoenauer cal., 5 shot rotary mag., 19.7 in. barrel, two leaf rear sight, double set or single trigger, full length stock.

	N/A	$1,900	$1,625	$1,275	$975	$850	$725

This model is frequently noticed in better condition factors. Some exceptional takedown variations also exist within this model.

MODEL 1908 RIFLE - similar to Model 1908 Carbine, except available in various barrel lengths up to 24 inches.

	N/A	$1,575	$1,300	$1,025	$875	$725	$600

MODEL 1910 CARBINE - 9.5x56mm Mannlicher-Schoenauer (.375 Rimless Nitro Express or 9.5x57mm Mauser cal.), 7x57mm, 8x57mm, and other custom calibers, 19.7 in. barrel, 5 shot rotary magazine, two leaf rear sight, double set trigger, full length stock.

	N/A	$1,800	$1,575	$1,225	$950	$850	$725

MODEL 1910 RIFLE - 9.5x56mm Mannlicher-Schoenauer (standard cal.), may also be found in 7x57mm, 8x57mm, and other custom cals., similar to 1910 Carbine, except available in various barrel lengths up to 26 inches.

	N/A	$1,575	$1,300	$1,025	$875	$725	$600

Fully stocked rifles may be encountered.

MODEL 1924 (HIGH VELOCITY SPORTING RIFLE) - .30-06, 7x64mm, 8x60mm, 9.3x62mm, or 10.75x68mm cal., 23.6 in. barrel, three leaf rear sight, half stock, double set or single trigger.

	N/A	$2,200	$1,850	$1,625	$1,350	$1,195	$975
10.75x68mm cal.	N/A	$4,500	$4,000	$3,600	$3,200	$2,750	$2,000

Fully stocked rifles may be encountered.

This model was referred to as the Model 1925 in Europe. The difference is that the Model 1925 has the caliber engraved on the receiver ring, and the Model 1924 does not.

RIFLES: BOLT ACTION, POST-WWII-1971 MFG.

Values below represent standard models with no engraving. Original engraving will add at least $500-$1,500 to prices listed with some heavily engraved Premier & Alpine models selling for large premiums. A variation of the 1950-1952 Series is called the "GK" because of its traditionally styled European stock, which is a variant of the pre-war style and approaches the design of the Model 1951 MCA. Of the calibers listed for post-WWII models, the 6.5x54mm is considered one of the most desirable, as well as the 9.3x62mm.

In 1951, Steyr (at Stoeger's request) made the following changes to the Model 1950 (named Improved Model 1950). These include: an ebony tip and fuller forend, left-side dummy plate cuts for side mount, left side of receiver was flattened to facilitate side scope mount, and flatter bolt handle requiring slot inside of stock.

In 1952, changes included a carved cheekpiece, change from 3/4 in. sling swivels to 1 in., swept back bolt handle, wood on left-side of stock over the dummy sideplate cutout thickened to strengthen the stock with a side mount in place, and removal of loading ears and clip guides, thereby streamlining the receiver and enabling lower scope mounting.

At one time Stoeger listed 18 versions of the M1950-52 family, defined as #S-1 through #S-18, with three major differences existing within each block of Model 1950, Improved Model

1950, and Model 1952. The differences were: single and double set triggers (DST), rifle or carbine style, 6.5mm Carbine, single trigger, or DST.

From the M1950 through the improved M1952, these rifles were in continuous change and parallel production, thus rifles can be found with 1950 characteristics and proofmarks as late as 1954. Some examples are found with "nonstandard" markings such as "Model 1952" and no reference to the "Improved" standard. After mid-1965, U.S. market rifles were drilled and tapped for the Redfield scope mount. Some rifles were chambered for 8x57mm and 7x64mm.

During 1952-55, a small amount of Deluxe and Super Deluxe Mannlicher-Schoenauer were manufactured. These are typically encountered with better grade wood and model nomenclature is the same as the standard guns.

Add approx. 35% for 6.5x54mm, 9.3x62mm, .257 Roberts, or 6mm cal.

MANNLICHER-SCHOENAUER MAGNUM RIFLE - .257 Wby. Mag., 6.5x68mm, .264 Win. Mag., 8x68mm, .338 Win. Mag., or .458 Win. Mag., similar to Model 1956 MC, except has straight bolt handle, 5 shot rotary mag., 22 in. barrel with half stock, double set or single trigger.

	N/A	$4,000	$3,500	$2,700	$2,250	$1,800	$1,600

MODEL 1950 RIFLE - .270 Win., .30-06, 6.5x54mm, or 9.3x62mm Mauser, bolt action, 5 shot rotary mag., 24 in. barrel, straight style bolt handle, double or single set trigger, half stock.

$1,750	$1,500	$1,250	$1,000	$850	$725	$600

MODEL 1950 CARBINE - 6.5x54mm cal., similar to Model 1950, except has 18 1/4 in. barrel and full length stock.

$1,875	$1,650	$1,300	$1,050	$900	$750	$600

IMPROVED MODEL 1952 RIFLE - .257 Roberts, .270 Win., .30-06, 9.3x62mm cal., 24 in. barrel, 5 shot rotary mag., rear angled bolt handle, double set or single trigger, half stock.

$1,650	$1,350	$1,100	$925	$750	$650	$550

IMPROVED MODEL 1952 CARBINE - .257 Roberts, 6.5x54mm, .270 Win., 7x57mm, .308 Win. (new 1953), or .30-06 cal., 18.25 (6.5x54mm cal. only) or 20 in. barrel, rear angled bolt handle, double or single trigger.

$1,875	$1,650	$1,300	$1,050	$900	$750	$600

MODEL 1956 MC RIFLE - .243 Win., 6.5x55mm, 6.5x57mm, 7x57mm, 7x64mm, 8x57mm, 8x60mm, 9.3x62mm, .244 Rem, .257 Rob, .270, .280, .308, .30-06, .358 WCF, or .30-06 cal., similar to Model 1952, high comb stock design, 5 shot rotary mag., 22 in. barrel, half length stock, double set or single trigger. Mfg. 1956-1961.

$1,875	$1,650	$1,300	$1,050	$900	$750	$600

MODEL 1956 MC CARBINE - .243 Win., 6.5x54mm, .257 Roberts, 6.5x55mm, 6.5x57mm, 7x64mm, 8x57mm, 8x60mm, .244 Rem., .280 Rem., 7x57mm, .270 Win., .30-06, .308 Win., or .358 Win. cal., similar to Model 1956 MC Rifle, except has 20 in. barrel with half stock, double set or single trigger. Mfg. 1956-1961.

$1,875	$1,650	$1,300	$1,050	$900	$750	$600

During 1956, Steyr began to advertise "special order" calibers such as 8x57mm, 7x64mm, and 9.3x64mm.

MODEL 1961 MCA RIFLE - .243 Win., .270 Win., or .30-06 cal., similar to Model 1956 Rifle, except has Monte Carlo stock, 5 shot rotary mag., 22 in. barrel with half stock, double set or single trigger. Mfg. 1961-1971.

$1,650	$1,350	$1,100	$925	$750	$650	$550

Subtract $250 for models with plastic tang safety.

GRADING - PPGS™	100%	98%	95%	90%	80%	70%	60%

MODEL 1961 MCA CARBINE - .243 Win., 6.5x54mm, .270 Win., .30-06, 7x57mm, .308 Win., or .358 Win. (rare) cal., 20 in. barrel with half stock, similar to Model 1956 Carbine, except has Monte Carlo stock. Mfg. 1961-1971.

$1,875	$1,650	$1,300	$1,050	$900	$750	$600

Subtract $250 for models with plastic tang safety.

During production, the European market included the Model NO (Model MC/MCA) with GK stock and a straight pre-war bolt handle, produced in metric calibers such as 6.5x55mm Swedish, 7x64mm, and 8x57mm.

RIFLES: BOLT ACTION, CURRENT PRODUCTION 1972-PRESENT

Current production guns are now called Steyr-Mannlicher models and can be located under this trademark in the S section.

MANU-ARM

Current rifle and airgun manufacturer located in Veauche, France. No current U.S. importation.

Manu-Arm manufactures good quality utilitarian .22 cal. bolt action and semi-auto rifles, in addition to an O/U in 9mm Para., .410 bore, and 32 ga. Please contact the factory directly for more information, including U.S. availability and pricing.

MANUFRANCE

Current manufacturer established circa 1887 and located in St. Etienne, France. No current U.S. importation.

Manufrance currently manufactures both SxS rifle and shotgun variations (the Robust Models being the most popular) that are not being currently imported into the U.S. Please contact the factory directly for more information, including model availability, parts, and domestic prices.

SHOTGUNS: DISC.

SEMI-AUTO MODEL - 12 ga., 26, 28, or 30 in. imp. cyl., mod. and full, 2 3/4 or 3 in. chamber, gas operated, walnut stock, black matte receiver, VR.

$330	$305	$290	$275	$255	$240	$220

FALCOR O/U - 12 ga., VR, 26 in. imp. cyl. and mod., 28 in. mod. and full, SST, auto ejector, chrome lined barrel, walnut checkered stock.

$715	$665	$635	$605	$550	$495	$470

MANURHIN

Current trademark manufactured by Manufacture d. Armes de tir Chapuis beginning in 1998, and located in Saint Bonnet Le Chateau, France. No current U.S. importation. During 1998, Chapuis Armes purchased Manurhin, and new revolvers are currently being manufactured in the new Manufacture d. Armes de tir Chapuis facility located in Saint Bonnet Le Chateau, France, utilizing the original production machinery. Previously manufactured by Manurhin Equipment 1972-1998, located in Mulhouse, France. Currently available by contacting the factory directly. Previously owned by Matra Manurhin Defense. Previously imported and distributed by Sphinx U.S.A. located in Meriden, CT. Previously imported (1984-86) directly by Matra-Manurhin International, Inc., located in Fort Lauderdale, FL.

Manurhin in France has been manufacturing models PP, PPK, and PPK/S since 1952. Previously, they were imported by Interarms out of Alexandria, VA. In 1984, Manurhin imported their new models directly and they were marked Manurhin on the left front slide assembly. This differs from the previous Walther stamped guns. Also, no Interarms logo appears on the right side.

PISTOLS: SEMI-AUTO, DISC.

P-1 - 9mm Para. cal., similar to W. German P-38, double action, 5 in. barrel.

$350	$325	$300	$275	$230	$215	$200

GRADING - PPGS™	100%	98%	95%	90%	80%	70%	60%

MODEL P4 - 9mm Para. cal., P.38 variation issued to the French Police when in Berlin during post-WWII.

	$375	$340	$300	$245	$230	$215	$200

MODEL PP - .22 LR, .32 ACP, or .380 ACP cal., 3 7/8 in. barrel, 10 shot mag.-.22 LR, 8 shot mag.-.32 ACP, 7 shot mag.-.380 ACP, blue only, all steel construction, double action with positive steel hammer block safety, 24 oz. Add $10 for .22 LR cal., $46 for Durgarde finish. Imported 1984-86.

	$360	$320	$275	$230	$205	$185	$170

Last MSR was $419.

✳ *Model PP Collector Model* - blue finish, special engraving. Imported 1986 only.

	$465	$415	$350	$285	$250	$215	$185

Last MSR was $529.

✳ *Model PP Presentation Model* - blue finish, special ornamentation. Imported 1986 only.

	$720	$650	$500	$430	$375	$315	$270

Last MSR was $819.

Also available with various engraving options in either blue, nickel, or gold finish - prices range from $222-$540.

MODEL PPK/S - .22 LR, .32 ACP, or .380 ACP cal., 3 1/4 in. barrel, 10 shot mag.-.22 LR, 8 shot mag.-.32 ACP, 7 shot mag.-.380 ACP, blue only, all steel construction, double action with positive steel hammer block safety, 23 oz. Imported 1984-86.

	$360	$320	$275	$230	$205	$185	$170

Last MSR was $419.

Add $10 for .22 LR cal.

✳ *Model PPK/S Durgarde* - similar to PPK/S, only with bonded brushed chrome finish.

	$410	$365	$325	$290	$265	$250	$240

Last MSR was $465.

Add $14 for .22 LR cal.

✳ *Model PPK/S Collector Model* - blue finish, special engraving. Imported 1986 only.

	$465	$415	$350	$285	$250	$215	$185

Last MSR was $529.

✳ *Model PPK/S Presentation Model* - blue finish, special ornamentation. Imported 1986 only.

	$720	$650	$500	$430	$375	$315	$270

Last MSR was $819.

Also available with various engraving options in either blue, nickel, or gold finish - prices range from $222-$540.

PP SPORT - .22 LR cal. only, double action, 6.1 or 8.1 in. barrel, blue finish only, precision adj. sights, contoured plastic grips with thumbrest, 25 oz. New Manurhin design for 1985. Imported 1984-86.

	$675	$525	$430	$385	$325	$290	$270

Last MSR was $635.

Add 10% for 8.1 in. barrel.

✳ *PP Sport-C* - similar to PP Sport, except has single action with lightened trigger pull.

	$650	$500	$415	$370	$310	$280	$260

Last MSR was $635.

REVOLVERS

MODEL 73 DEFENSE - .357 Mag./.38 Spl. cal., 6 shot, 2 1/2, 3, or 4 in. barrel, checkered wood stocks, mfg. to precise tolerances, 31-33 1/2 oz. Importation began 1988.

MSR N/A	$1,200	$1,000	$850	$725	$600	$500	$425

MODEL 73 GENDARMERIE - .357 Mag./.38 Spl. cal., 6 shot, similar to Model 73 Defense except has adj. sighting components and also is offered in 5 1/4, 6, or 8 in. barrel lengths. Manufactured for police requirements. Importation began 1988.

MSR N/A		$1,675	$1,125	$900	$750	$625	$525	$450

MODEL 73 SPORT - .357 Mag./.38 Spl. cal., 6 shot, sport shooting features include minimized hammer stroke, micrometer rear sight, and free release trigger with fitted adj. sights. Importation began 1988.

MSR N/A		$1,675	$1,125	$900	$750	$625	$525	$450

MODEL 73 CONVERTIBLE - includes choice of .22 LR/.38 Spl. or .22 LR/.32 Long cal. cylinders and barrels (5 3/4 in. for .38 Spl. and 6 in. for .22 LR/.32 Long). Imported 1988-95.

		$1,925	$1,675	$1,325	$1,125	$950	$800	$700

Last MSR was $2,200.

✻ *Model 73 Convertible 3 Cylinder* - similar to Model 73 Convertible except includes 3 calibers (.22 LR, .32 Long, and .38 Spl.). Imported 1988-95.

		$2,375	$1,950	$1,700	$1,375	$1,150	$975	$850

Last MSR was $2,690.

MODEL 73 SILHOUETTE - .22 LR or .357 Mag. cal., Silhouette variation with fully adj. rear sight and either 10 (.22 LR) or 10 3/4 (.357 Mag.) in. heavy barrel with full shroud, contoured wooden target grips, approx. 4 lbs. Importation began 1988.

MSR N/A		$1,750	$1,175	$925	$750	$625	$525	$450

Add $13 for .357 Mag. cal.

MODEL MR 88 - .357 Mag. cal., stainless steel, 4, 5, or 6 in. barrel, fixed sights, rubber grips. Importation began 1996.

MSR N/A		$775	$625	$450	$385	$335	$280	$235

MODEL MR 96 - .357 Mag. cal., black finish, 3, 4, 5, or 6 in. VR barrel, adj. rear sight, ergonomic rubber grips. Importation began 1996.

MSR N/A		$750	$615	$425	$375	$350	$325	$295

This model allows the user to unlock, swing the cylinder out, and eject the cases with one movement of the hand.

MARATHON PRODUCTS, INC.

Previously manufactured by Santa Barbara Armaments exclusively for Marathon Products, Inc. Most of the models listed were also available in kit form, but are not shown in this book.

PISTOLS: SINGLE SHOT

HOT SHOT MODEL - .22 LR cal., single shot, fixed sights, 14 3/4 in. barrel, hardwood stock with target grip configuration. Mfg. 1986-87.

		$55	$45	$40	$35	$35	$30	$30

Last MSR was $60.

RIFLES: BOLT ACTION

.22 FIRST SHOT - .22 LR cal., single shot, 16 1/2 in. barrel, hardwood stock, open sights, 31 in. total length, 3.8 lbs. Mfg. 1985-87.

		$55	$45	$40	$35	$35	$30	$30

Last MSR was $60.

✻ *.22 First Shot Super* - similar to First Shot, except with 24 in. barrel and regular dimension stock. Mfg. 1985-87.

		$55	$45	$40	$35	$35	$30	$30

Last MSR was $60.

GRADING - PPGS™	100%	98%	95%	90%	80%	70%	60%

CENTERFIRE MODEL - .243 Win., .270 Win., 7x57mm, 7mm Rem. Mag., .30-06, .300 Win. Mag., or .308 Win. cal., Mauser type action, 5 shot fixed box mag., 24 in. barrel, select walnut with recoil pad, adj. trigger, open sights, 7.9 lbs. Available 1985-86 only.

	$295	$240	$215	$195	$180	$170	$160

Last MSR was $320.

MARBLE ARMS & MFG. CO.

Previous firearms manufacturer circa 1907-late 1950s, located in Gladstone, MI. Marble Arms is still in business, manufacturing sights, knives, and compasses.

In addition to axes and compasses, Marble Arms & Mfg. Co. also manufactured their Game Getter O/U combination gun from approx. 1907 to the early 1950s. During this period of production, the gun underwent quite a few changes including sights (an aperture sight mounted on the rear backstrap was optional in 1908), different configuration folding metal stock, and other changes.

FIREARMS

GAME GETTER MODELS - starting manufacture in 1908, 2 variations of the Model 1908 Game Getter were offered, the 1908A featured a flexible rear sight mounted behind the hammer and the 1908B had a filler blank in that space. The 1908s featured a .22 cal. rifled top barrel, and in standard configuration, a smooth bored bottom barrel chambered for the .44 round ball or .44 shot. Very late in production, chambering for the 2 in. .410 could be ordered. Standard barrel lengths were 12 in., 15 in., and 18 in., but Marbles was ready to please their customers, and on special order, 8 in., 10 in., 17 in., and 22 in. barrels were made, some were even shipped from the factory fitted with silencers, and a very few guns were ordered without the milling for the round tubular folding stock. A pivoting striker on the hammer was used to select the barrel to be fired, and the tip-up barrels were opened by pressing the trigger guard to the rear. The top frame featured a folding leaf sight, and the front barrel band incorporated the front sight, the grips were checkered black hard rubber with fleur-de-lis design. On very early 1908 guns, the buttplate was a separate piece secured to the tubing with 2 screws and later stocks were all one piece. A few guns were built with bottom barrels chambered for .25-20 & .32-20, but these are very rare. The gun was shipped in a dovetailed wooden box with sliding lid, and included a shoulder holster, cleaning rod, and directions for use. The first 1908 was shipped from the factory June 21, 1909, and serial letters A-M were used. Then, starting with serial number 1, they continued through 9981, and the last gun was shipped from the factory May 22, 1918.

	$2,300	$2,100	$1,700	$1,400	$1,400	$1,200	$1,050

Add $400 for Model 1908A with original flexible tang sight.
Add $100-$200 for original holster, depending on condition of leather.
Add $600-$900 for correct original box, depending on condition.

* *Game Getter Model 1921* - the 1921 was an entirely new gun, with similar barrel lengths (12, 15, or 18 in.), not nearly as pleasing in appearance as the 1908. The same barrel lengths were standard, but the bottom barrel was chambered for the 2 in. .410. In 1924, the standard chamber was changed to 2 1/2 in. .410. It featured a bag style, oiled walnut grip, and a unique "Triple Combination Rear Sight," which was developed and made only for this model. A number of guns in the 14,000 to 16,000 serial number range can be found with brown plastic grips, and a coventional "v" notch rear sight adjustable for elevation. The 1921 featured a folding hinged 3 piece stock with an improved lock which eliminated wobble, but had no adjustment for drop. It also had a shorter action than the 1908, which was a faster action, and the hammer rebounded to a safety notch after firing. As with the 1908 Model, Marbles would accomodate the wishes of the customer, and barrels as short as 8 in.

can be found. Some guns were ordered choke bored, and some were chambered just for .44 Game Getter on the bottom barrel. A few had no provision for stock, at least 2 were shipped in .32-20, and as records are not complete, .38-40 cal. models are known to exist and calibers like the .25-20 are thought to exist. Supplied with a heavy cardboard box, shoulder holster, cleaning rod and instructions. First shipment was serial number 10,001 - shipped to William L. Marble, the west coast representative, on Oct. 4, 1921. Serial range 10,000-20,076.

$2,000 $1,800 $1,600 $1,400 $1,200 $1,100 $1,000

Add $150-$200 for original holster if in good condition.
Add $600-$900 for correct original box, depending on wood condition.
Add $300-$500 for cardboard box, depending on condition (just cardboard lift-off lid).

The first 200-300 of this model were shipped in 1908 boxes with 1921 yellow end label on the box.

Values assume legal 18 in. barrels or correct registration. If not legal configuration, the gun is basically a black market item subject to BATF confiscation. The U.S. government and foreign countries continued to purchase 15 in. guns after the 1934 law was passed, and the last gun was shipped during the mid 1950s. 200 M1921 models with 15 in. barrels were assembled from parts and sold by Marbles as collector's items in 1960.

MARCEL THYS & SONS

Current SxS rifle and shotgun manufacturer established in 1960 and located in Crisnée, Belgium. The U.S. agent is currently Jean-Jacques Perodeau, located in Enid, OK.

Marcel Thys & Sons manufactures fine quality double rifles and shotguns, with many engraving options and special orders. Since these guns are custom-made per individual order, please contact the U.S. agent or the factory directly (see Trademark Index) for current information, availability, and a firm price quotation.

MARGOLIN

Original pistol design by M.V. Margolin developed after WWII as a training firearm for members of the Russian shooting team. The Margolin is currently manufactured at the Izhevsk mechanical plant located in Izhevsk, Russia, and known as the "MTsN" sporting pistol. Limited importation.

PISTOLS: SEMI-AUTO

TARGET MODEL - .22 LR cal., originally developed from the TT (Tula Tokarev), manufactured to precise tolerances, many specimens are made to individual shooters' specifications, seldom encountered in the U.S., while rare, desirability to date has been limited, current mfg. - limited importation.

Margolin pistols are typically priced in the $475-$850 range, depending on features and assuming 95%+ original condition. While currently imported Chinese copies are considerably less expensive, they do not have the quality (or accuracy) of the Russian Margolins.

MARLIN FIREARMS COMPANY

Current manufacturer located in North Haven, CT. Marlin has been manufacturing firearms since 1870. Recent manufacture (1969-present) is in North Haven, CT. Previously, Marlin was manufactured (1870-1969) in New Haven, CT. Distributor sales only.

On Nov. 10th, 2000, Marlin Firearms Company purchased H&R 1871, Inc. This includes the brand names Harrington & Richardson, New England Firearms, and Wesson & Harrington (please refer to individual sections in this text).

During 2005, Marlin Firearms Company once again started manufacturing a L.C. Smith line of both SxS and O/U shotguns.

In late Jan. of 2008, Remington acquired the Marlin Firearms Company, including the H&R, New England Firearms (NEF), and L.C. Smith brands, and plans to continue with production of these trademarks.

Marlin Firearms Company had been a family-owned and operated business from 1921 until 2007.

100%	98%	95%	90%	80%	70%	60%	50%	40%	30%	20%	10%

PISTOLS: DERRINGERS AND REVOLVERS

Many of the more common variations in average condition sell in the $150-$250 range, while rarer specimens with 90%+ original condition will be priced in the $450-$1,750 range, depending on rarity and condition.

RIFLES: LEVER ACTION, ANTIQUE

Factory information by individual serial number may be available from the Cody Firearms Museum in Cody, WY on the following models with serial numbers 4001-355,504: Models 1881, 1888, 1889, 1892, 1893, 1894, 1895, and 1897. Marlin had only one series of serial numbers for all lever action repeating rifles from 1883-1906: therefore serial numbers do not reflect the place in production or sequence number of a gun within a model. Sometimes, a record shows two or even three guns with the same serial number from the same time period.

Values below are for standard models only without special order features. 98% and 100% prices have been intentionally replaced with N/As (not applicable), since these conditio[n] factors are seldom encountered and hard to accurately price, as their values have drama[ti]cally increased during the past 3-5 years.

Add a premium for all mint condition guns with vibrant case coloring on receivers.

MODEL 1881 - .32-40 WCF, .38-55 WCF, .40-60 WCF, .45-70 Govt., or .45-85 Marlin cal., tube mag., 28 in. octagonal barrel standard, top ejection, blued finish with case hardened hammer, lever, and buttplate. Approx. 20,000 mfg. 1881-1892.

N/A	N/A	$3,000	$2,600	$2,250	$1,850	$1,600	$1,375	$1,150	$1,000	$825	$675

Add approx. 15% for .45-70 or .45-85 cal.
Add 200-300% premium for rare First models (pre-ser. no. 600).
Add a premium for very early First models with hand engraved script barrel markings - approx. first 60 rifles mfg.

This model came in 3 frame styles for various calibers.

MODEL 1888 - .32-20 WCF, .38-40 WCF, or .44-40 WCF cal., 24 in. octagonal barrel most frequently encountered, top ejection, blued finish with case hardened hammer, lever, and buttplate, short throw lever action principle. Approx. 4,800 mfg. 1888-1889. Ser. range approx. 19,560-27,850.

N/A	N/A	$2,600	$2,300	$2,000	$1,700	$1,475	$1,250	$1,000	$875	$750	$625

Add 40% for half-round, half-octagon barrel (23 mfg.).
Add 20% for round barrel (266 mfg.).
Add 25% for half magazine (78 mfg.).

MODEL 1889 - .25-20 WCF (very rare), .32-20 WCF, .38-40 WCF, or .44-40 WCF cal., 24 (approx. 39,300 mfg.) or 28 (approx. 2,260 mfg.) in. octagonal barrel most frequently encountered, side ejection with solid top frame, blued finish with case hardened hammer, lever, and buttplate, short throw lever action principle. Approx. 55,000 mfg. 1889-1899. Ser. range approx. 25,000-100,000.

N/A	N/A	$1,325	$1,125	$800	$600	$500	$400	$340	$295	$260	$230

Add 300-500% for Musket.
Add 25% for carbine.
Add 15% for .44-40 WCF cal.
Factory special orders/features will add premiums, depending on the desirability of each option and the gun's original condition factor.

Also available as Carbine with either a 15 in. (only 367 mfg.) or 20 in. (approx. 10,000 mfg.) barrel or Musket (30 in. barrel - very rare).

100%	98%	95%	90%	80%	70%	60%	50%	40%	30%	20%	10%

MODEL 1891 - .22 Rimfire and .32 Rimfire/Centerfire cal., 24 in. octagonal barrel most often encountered, choice of side loading (1st variation) or tube loading (2nd variation), blued finish with case hardened hammer, lever, and buttplate, sear safety system on lever action. Approx. 18,650 mfg. between 1891-1897. Ser. no. range is approx. 37,500-118,000.

| N/A | N/A | $1,950 | $1,700 | $1,350 | $1,125 | $950 | $875 | $775 | $695 | $625 | $550 |

Add 50% for deluxe, pistol grip checkered model.
Subtract 40% for tube loading model (.32 Centerfire).
Add $100 each for special sights (including correct Lyman, Marbles, Beeches combo, etc.).
Factory special orders/features will add premiums, depending on the desirability of each option and the gun's original condition factor.

MODEL 1892 - .22 S, L, or LR, .32 S or L cal., 16, 24, 26, or 28 in. barrel, tubular mag., open sight, plain straight stock. Mfg. 1892-1916.

| N/A | N/A | $1,500 | $1,275 | $1,000 | $825 | $700 | $600 | $525 | $475 | $425 | $385 |

Add 10% for .22 cal.
Subtract 10% for .32 cal.
Add $100 each for special sights (including correct Lyman, Marbles, Beeches combo, etc.).
Factory special orders/features will add premiums, depending on the desirability of each option and the gun's original condition factor.
.22 cals. will bring a premium in this model.

MODEL 1893 RIFLE - .25-36 Marlin, .30-30 Win., .32 Spl., .32-40 WCF, or .38-55 WCF cal., 20-32 in. round or octagonal barrels, blue (Model B) or case colored receiver, 10 shot tube mag., straight grip stock. Musket model also mfg. - 30 in. barrel and military style forearm. Mfg. 1893-1936.

| N/A | N/A | $2,750 | $2,300 | $1,800 | $1,275 | $1,000 | $725 | $550 | $450 | $375 | $350 |

Add 100% for Musket.
Add 1%5-20% for calibers other than .30-30 Win. or .32 Spl.
Add 15%-20% for takedown model, depending on condition.
Add approx. 20% for special Lightweight Model.
Subtract 10%-20% for the Model B with blue receiver.
Factory special orders/features will add premiums, depending on the desirability of each option and the gun's original condition factor.
Strong, original case colors over 95% condition can result in $2,500 asking prices.
Although incorrect, more than a few people refer to all 20 in. barrels as "Lightweight" models. Technically, the Lightweight variation has a 7 1/2 in. forearm rather than the standard 9 in. Later production guns were marked "Model '93" and have less value. This model had two barrel variations - one was marked "special smokeless steel" while the other was marked "for Black Powder". The latter (also known as Model B) are 1st Models only and have blue receivers rather than case colored.

MODEL 1893 CARBINE - .30-30 Win., .32 Spl., .32-40 WCF cal., or .38-55 WCF cal., 15 (only 61 mfg.) or 20 in. round barrel, case colored receiver, 7 shot tube mag., straight or pistol grip stock. Mfg. 1893-1935.

Add 15%-20% for calibers other than .30-30 Win. or .32 Spl.
Factory special orders/features will add premiums, depending on the desirability of each option and the gun's original condition factor.

✳ *Model 1893 Carbine 1st Model* - with saddle ring. Mfg. 1893-1915.

| N/A | N/A | $1,600 | $1,300 | $1,100 | $900 | $750 | $600 | $500 | $400 | $375 | $350 |

Strong, original case colors over 95% condition can result in $2,500 asking prices.

✳ *Model 1893 Carbine 2nd Model* - .30-30 Win. or .32 HPS (High Power Special) cal., has "Bull's-eye" in stock, no saddle rings. Mfg. 1922-35.

| N/A | N/A | $850 | $725 | $600 | $475 | $425 | $385 | $350 | $325 | $300 | $285 |

✳ *Model 1893 Carbine Sporting* - .30-30 Win. or .32 Spl. cal., 20 in. round barrel, 2/3 mag., 5 shot, carbine style front sight, Rocky Mountain rear, straight stock, hard rubber buttplate, bull's-eye in stock. Mfg. 1923-35.

| N/A | N/A | $1,375 | $1,100 | $900 | $750 | $700 | $550 | $475 | $400 | $375 | $350 |

Subtract 40% for 2nd Model made in 1935 with "S" steel buttplate and ivory bead front sight.

100%	98%	95%	90%	80%	70%	60%	50%	40%	30%	20%	10%

MODEL 1894 - .25-20 WCF, .32-20 WCF, .38-40 WCF, or .44-40 WCF cal., case colored receiver, 10 shot tube mag., 24 in. round or octagon barrel, straight or pistol grip stock. Mfg. 1894-1934.

N/A	N/A	$2,500	$1,995	$1,650	$1,250	$875	$625	$450	$400	$375	$350

Add 25% for saddle ring carbine.
Add 10% for .44-40 WCF cal.
Add 40% for Baby Carbine with 18 in. barrel and 1/2 mag.
Add 15%-20% for takedown model, depending on condition.
Add 100% for Musket.
Factory special orders/features will add premiums, depending on the desirability of each option and the gun's original condition factor.
Strong, original case colors over 95% condition can result in $2,500 asking prices.
Later production guns were marked "Model '94" and have less value. This model was also available in both a Carbine and Musket variation.

MODEL 1895 - .33 WCF, .38-56 WCF, .40-65 WCF, .40-70 WCF, .40-82 WCF, .45-70 Govt., or .45-90 cal., case colored receiver, 9 shot tube mag., 24 or 26 in. round or octagon barrel standard, other lengths were available, open sights, plain straight or pistol grip stock. Mfg. 1895-1915.

N/A	N/A	$3,500	$3,000	$2,500	$2,000	$1,500	$1,200	$1,000	$750	$600	$550

Add 15%-25% for takedown model, depending on condition.
Premiums exist for .40-70 WCF (approx. 60 mfg.), .45-70 Govt., and .45-90 WCF cal.
Factory special orders/features will add premiums, depending on the desirability of each option and the gun's original condition factor.
Strong, original case colors over 95% condition can result in $3,500 asking prices.
In 1912, a lightweight variation was introduced with hard rubber buttplate and half-magazine, cals. were .33 WCF and .45-70 Govt. (commands a premium), and round barrels were either 22 or 24 in. A Carbine variation was also offered with approx. 200 mfg. - premiums may run as high as 150% over rifle values listed.

MODEL 1897 - .22 S, L, or LR cal., tube mag., 16, 24, 26, or 28 in. barrel, case colored receiver, takedown, open sights, plain straight or pistol grip stock. Mfg. 1897-1922.

N/A	N/A	$2,500	$1,750	$1,475	$1,250	$1,000	$850	$625	$450	$400	$375

Add 100% for 16 in. barrel "Bicycle Rifle."
Add 15%-20% for takedown model, depending on condition.
Add $100 each for special sights (including correct Lyman, Marbles, Beeches combo, etc.).
Factory special orders/features will add premiums, depending on the desirability of each option and the gun's original condition factor.
Strong, original case colors over 95% condition can result in $2,500 asking prices.

RIFLES: MODERN PRODUCTION

Year of manufacture can be determined from 1946-1968 by the following letter/numeral prefixes: 1946-C, 1947-D, 1948-E, 1949-F, 1950-G, 1951-H, 1952-J, 1953-K, 1954-L, 1955-M, 1956-N, 1957-P, 1958-R, 1959-S, 1960-T, 1961-U, 1962-V, 1963-W, 1964-Y,Z, 1965-AA, 1966-AB, 1967-AC, 1968-AD, 1969-69, 1970-70, 1971-71, 1972-72. Starting in 1973, the year can be determined by subtracting the first 2 numbers of the serial number from 100.

The models below are listed in alphabetical sequence first, followed by numerical sequence for easy reference.

Machine cut checkering became standard on many Marlins beginning 1995. Safety locks have been shipped with every new rifle/shotgun beginning 1999. In 2004, the T-900 fire control system became standard on all Marlin 900 Series rifles, except the Papoose and the Model 717M2. This improved trigger has a pull of 3-5 lbs., features a new safety mechanism with positive click positions for fire and safe, and a crisp let-off.

In 2007, Marlin changed its bolt action rimfire synthetic stocks to a new classic design featuring a fluted comb, deep molded checkering, and sling swivel studs.

GRADING - PPGS™	100%	98%	95%	90%	80%	70%	60%

MODEL MR-7 BOLT ACTION - .22-250 Rem. (advertised in 1998, but never mfg.), .243 Win. (advertised in 1998, but never mfg.), .25-06 Rem. (new 1997), .270 Win., .280 Rem. (new 1998), .30-06, or .308 Win. (advertised in 1998, but never mfg.) cal., 4 shot box mag. with removable hinged floorplate, 3 position safety, adj. 3-6 lb. trigger, 22 in. barrel, checkered American walnut stock, cocking indicator, forged receiver, damascened bolt, includes sling swivels, with or without sights, approx. 7 1/2 lbs. Mfg. 1996-99.

	$495	$440	$375	$315	$275	$240	$215

Last MSR was $603.

Add $40 for open sights (.270 Win., .280 Rem., or .30-06).

✳ *Model MR-7B Bolt Action* - .270 Win. or .30-06 only, similar to Model MR-7, except has birch stock and forearm with cut checkering. Mfg. 1998-99.

	$380	$250	$185	$165	$150	$130	$125

Last MSR was $483.

Add $40 for open sights (mfg. 1998 only).

MODEL XL7 BOLT ACTION - .25-06 Rem., .270 Win., or 30-06 cal., 22 in. blue barrel joined to receiver by barrel nut, no sights, 4 shot internal mag., black synthetic or Realtree APG HD camo treated pillar bedded stock, Pro-Fire adj. trigger system, two-position safety, recoil pad, fluted bolt, fully enclosed bolt shroud with cocking indicator, recessed target style muzzle crown, steel sling swivel studs, approx. 6 1/2 lbs. New 2008.

MSR $326	$280	$240	$210	$190	$175	$165	$155

Add $30 for camo (Model XL7C).

MODEL 9 CAMP CARBINE SEMI-AUTO - 9mm Para. cal. only, 16 1/2 in. barrel, 12 or 20 shot mag. (disc. 1989), 4 shot mag. became standard in 1990, sand blasted steel receiver, open sights, last shot automatic hold-open, 6 3/4 lbs. Mfg. 1985-99.

	$340	$230	$170	$150	$140	$130	$125

Last MSR was $443.

Add 10% for nickel plating (mfg. 1991-94, Model 9N).
A new high visibility orange front sight post with cutaway hood was added in 1989.

MODEL 15YN "LITTLE BUCKAROO" SINGLE SHOT - .22 S, L, or LR cal., single shot, 16 1/4 in. barrel, youth dimensions with 12 LOP, adj. rear sight, grooved receiver, pressed checkering, 4 1/4 lbs. Disc. 2003.

	$155	$135	$105	$80	$75	$70	$65

Last MSR was $209.

✳ *Model 15YS "Little Buckaroo" Single Shot Stainless Steel* - similar to Model 15YN, except is stainless steel and has Fire Sights. Mfg. 2002-2003.

	$175	$150	$115	$90	$75	$70	$65

Last MSR was $233.

MODEL 17V BOLT ACTION - .17 HMR cal., 7 shot detachable mag., 22 in. heavy barrel, walnut finished checkered hardwood Monte Carlo stock and forend, red cocking indicator, grooved receiver, includes scope mounts, 6 lbs. Mfg. 2002-2003.

	$220	$200	$180	$170	$160	$145	$130

Last MSR was $269.

✳ *Model 17VS Bolt Action* - similar to Model 17V, except has bead blasted stainless steel barrel and receiver, laminated black/grey hardwood Monte Carlo stock, 7 lbs. Mfg. 2002-2004.

	$330	$270	$225	$175	$140	$125	$105

Last MSR was $402.

MODEL 18 SLIDE ACTION - .22 S, L, or LR cal., tube mag., 20 in. round or octagon barrel, open sight, exposed hammer, plain straight grip stock. Mfg. 1906-09.

	$650	$550	$450	$325	$225	$175	$135

GRADING - PPGS™	100%	98%	95%	90%	80%	70%	60%

MODEL 20 SLIDE ACTION - .22 S, L, or LR cal., 24 in. octagon barrel, open sight, exposed hammer, takedown, plain straight grip stock. Mfg. 1907-22.

	$625	$525	$400	$295	$200	$165	$125

MODEL 25 SLIDE ACTION - .22 Short cal. and CB cap., tube mag., 23 in. barrel, open sight, exposed hammer, takedown, plain straight grip stock. Mfg. 1909-10.

	$775	$650	$550	$475	$400	$350	$300

MODEL 25MB BOLT ACTION - .22 Mag. cal., bolt action, 16 1/4 in. micro-groove barrel, 7 shot mag., hardwood stock, takedown action, 6 lbs. Mfg. 1987-88 only.

	$145	$115	$95	$85	$75	$70	$65

Last MSR was $173.

This model included both a scope and gun case.

MODEL 25MG GARDEN GUN - please refer to the Marlin bolt action shotgun section for information on this model.

MODEL 25MN BOLT ACTION - .22 Mag. cal., bolt action, 7 shot mag., 22 in. barrel, choice of walnut finished hardwood or Mossy Oak Breakup camo (new 2001) stock (pressed checkering became standard 1994), grooved receiver, adj. rear sight (new 1995), 6 lbs. Mfg. 1989-2003.

	$185	$140	$105	$85	$75	$70	$65

Last MSR was $241.

Add $6 for 4X scope (disc. 2000).
Add $37 for Mossy Oak Breakup camo stock.

MODEL 25N BOLT ACTION - .22 LR cal., 7 shot mag., 22 in. barrel, press checkered Monte Carlo stock, 5 1/2 lbs. Disc. 2003.

	$155	$135	$110	$80	$75	$70	$65

Last MSR was $212.

Add $8 for 4X scope.

✱ *Model 25NC Bolt Action* - similar to Model 25N, except has Mossy Oak Breakup camo stock. Disc. 2003.

	$190	$145	$105	$85	$75	$70	$65

Last MSR was $248.

MODEL 27 SLIDE ACTION - .25-20 WCF, or .32-20 WCF cal., 2/3 tube mag., 7 shot, 24 in. octagon barrel, open sight, plain straight grip stock. Mfg. 1910-11.

	$425	$350	$250	$200	$165	$140	$125

Subtract 15% for .25RF cal.

MODEL 27S - .25RF, .25-20 WCF, or .32-20 WCF cal., similar to Model 27, except has safety button on right side of receiver, round or octagonal barrel added in 1913.

	$400	$350	$300	$250	$200	$150	$100

MODEL 29 SLIDE ACTION - similar to Model 20, with 23 in. round barrel, 1/2 tube mag. Mfg. 1913-16.

	$400	$325	$250	$200	$165	$140	$125

MODEL 30/30A LEVER ACTION - .30-30 Win. cal., 20 in. barrel, promotional Glenfield model with birch stock and pressed checkering. Mfg. 1964-83.

	$220	$185	$160	$135	$120	$110	$100

This model was replaced by the Model 30AS in 1983.

MODEL 336A/336AS (30AS) LEVER ACTION - .30-30 Win. cal. only, 20 in. barrel, 6 shot tube mag, walnut finished birch stock (pressed checkering became standard 1995, cut checkering became standard 1998), open sights (adj. rear sight became standard 1995), no frills version of the 336CS, 7 lbs. Mfg. 1983-2007.

	$325	$255	$175	$145	$125	$120	$115

Last MSR was $423.

Add $50 for 4X scope (disc. 2006) or $41 for 3-9x32mm bore sighted scope.
Prior to 2000, this was designated the Model 30AS. The Model 30AS was formerly part of the Glenfield line. During 2001, this model's nomenclature was changed from 336AS to 336A.

GRADING - PPGS™	100%	98%	95%	90%	80%	70%	60%

✳ *Model 336W (30AW) Lever Action* - similar to Model 30AS, except has carbine style barrel band and gold trigger.

MSR $452	$350	$290	$190	$150	$130	$120	$115

Add $53 for 4X scope (disc. 2006), or $43 for 3-9x32mm bore sighted scope (new 2007). This model was previously sold by Wal-Mart only. Model nomenclature was changed during 1998.

✳ *Model 336CC Lever Action* - similar to Model 336W, except has Mossy Oak Breakup camo stock and forearm, 7 lbs. Mfg. 2001-2004.

$365	$285	$190	$155	$135	$125	$115

Last MSR was $503.

✳ *Model 336Y Lever Action SpikeHorn* - similar to Model 336W, 5 shot tube mag, 16 1/2 in. barrel, shorter stock (12 1/2 in. LOP) with vent. recoil pad, 6 1/2 lbs. Mfg. 2003-2005.

$410	$320	$210	$165	$135	$125	$115

Last MSR was $566.

MODEL 32 SLIDE ACTION - .22 S, L, or LR cal., 2/3 tube mag., 24 in. octagon barrel, open sight, plain pistol grip stock, hammerless. Mfg. 1914-15.

$600	$525	$425	$350	$300	$225	$150

MODEL 1936 - .30-30 Win. or .32 HPS (High Power Special) cal., 6 shot, 20 or 24 in. barrel, tubular mag., open sights, pistol grip stock, barrel band, leaf mainspring, thinner "perch belly" forearm, case colored receiver, upper tang, buttstock has a fluted comb and flat hard rubber buttplate. Mfg. 1936-37.

$750	$650	$500	$350	$275	$200	$150

Add 10% for vivid case colors with strong greens, reds, and yellows.
Add 10% for rifles and sporting carbines.

Rifles have "A" suffix, sporting carbine has "SC" suffix, and regular and carbine has "RC" suffix. The Model 1936 has an upper tang inscription "Model 1936" and a case colored receiver. Also, the Model 1936 did not have a letter prefix in the ser. no.

MODEL 36 - 1ST VARIATION - same as Model 1936 - called Model 36 in catalog only. Mfg. 1937-40.

$725	$650	$500	$350	$250	$200	$150

Add 10% for rifles and sporting carbines.

The Model 36 - 1st Variation has an upper tang inscription "Model 1936" and a case colored receiver. Also, the Model 36 - 1st variation did not have a letter prefix in the ser. no.

MODEL 36 - 2ND VARIATION - similar to Model 1936, still has case colored receiver with "Model 1936" on upper tang, coiled main spring, buttstock is heavier style and no longer has fluted comb, buttplate is a thicker, slightly curved style - hard rubber, forearm is a heavier beaver-tailed style, "B" prefix in ser. no. Mfg. 1941.

$750	$500	$400	$300	$250	$200	$165

Add 10% for rifles and sporting carbines.

MODEL 36 ADL DELUXE RIFLE - similar to Model 1936, case colored receiver, checkered pistol grip buttstock and forearm, pistol grip cap, Winchester quick detachable swivels with 1 in. sling, "B" prefix in ser. no., has "Model 1936" on upper tang. Less than 50 mfg. in 1945 only.

$1,150	$1,000	$800	$600	$400	$275	$250

Both the rear and front swivel bases are attached with two wood screws and are not inletted into the wood.

GRADING - PPGS™	100%	98%	95%	90%	80%	70%	60%

MODEL 36 - 3RD VARIATION - .30-30 Win. or .32 SPEC cal., blued receiver, no upper tang markings, model no. and cal. marked on barrel, rifles have "A" suffix, Sporting Carbine has "SC" suffix, and regular carbine has "RC" suffix, small case "c" prefix in 1946, and large "D" prefix in 1947. Mfg. 1946-47.

		$500	$425	$350	$225	$165	$150	$125

Add 10% for rifles and sporting carbines.

Some standard rifles may have the "ADL" barrel markings in 1946-47. 1946 mfg. has a lower-case "c" prefix and 1947 mfg. has a capital "D" prefix in ser. no.

✻ *Model 36 3rd Variation ADL Deluxe* - similar to Model 36 3rd Variation, has checkered pistol grip stock and forearm, forearm has checkering on sides and underneath, round swivel stud in buttstock and on forearm cap, deluxe quick detachable swivels and 1 in. leather sling, does not have model designation on upper tang or pistol grip cap, hooded front ramp screw on front sight, Rocky Mountain rear, letter prefix in ser. no. is "C" or "D."

	$850	$700	$550	$450	$400	$375	$350

MODEL 37 SLIDE ACTION - similar to Model 29, with 24 in. barrel, full length tube mag. Mfg. 1913-16.

	$500	$450	$400	$300	$200	$150	$125

MODEL 38 SLIDE ACTION - .22 S, L, or LR cal., 2/3 tube mag., 24 in. octagon barrel, open sights, hammerless, takedown, plain pistol grip stock. Mfg. 1920-30.

	$700	$600	$500	$400	$350	$200	$150

MODEL 39 LEVER ACTION - .22 S, L, or LR cal., 24 in. octagon barrel with tube mag., open sights, takedown, case hardened receiver and lever, S-shaped pistol grip stock, bluing on barrel, forend tip, mag. tube, bolt, hammer, and screws, various qualities of walnut (X, 2X, or 3X), hard rubber buttplate. Approx. 40-50,000 mfg. 1922-38.

	N/A	N/A	$3,000	$2,500	$2,100	$1,600	$1,300

Early models with fancy 2X-3X wood will bring a considerable premium.

Excellent original condition in this model is extremely hard to find since most specimens were well used due to the 16/25 shell mag. capacity, reliability, and the fact that the balance point of the gun (the receiver) normally wore first due to carrying wear. Earlier guns without a prefix or with an "S" prefix are noted for their superior workmanship and fine finish. Later "HS" prefix (High Speed) are not quite as valuable as these earlier guns.

MODEL 39A - similar to Model 39, with case hardened receiver (mfg. 1939-1945), includes 1st and 2nd Models with round barrel. 3rd Model 1st Variation was introduced in 1946 and has blue receiver, 3rd Model 2nd Variation has flutes in buttstock comb and was introduced in 1951, and 3rd Model 3rd Variation has Micro-Groove rifling, no pistol grip cap, and was introduced in 1954.

✻ *Model 39A 1st Model* - case colored frame, no prefix. Mfg. 1939 only.

	N/A	$1,400	$1,100	$900	$775	$650	$500

The first variation of the Model 39A mfg. in 1939 is distinguishable by a buttstock and lever similar to those on earlier Model 39s.

✻ *Model 39A 2nd Model* - case colored frame, "B" prefix. Mfg. 1941.

	N/A	$1,100	$825	$675	$575	$450	$395

The second variation had a rounded lever like current production and no "S" shape to bottom of pistol grip.

✻ *Model 39A 3rd Model 1st Variation* - features blued receiver, new ramp front sight, hard rubber buttplate, and Ballard rifling. Mfg. 1946-50.

	N/A	$550	$500	$450	$400	$350	$300

✻ *Model 39A 3rd Model 2nd Variation* - similar to 3rd Model 1st Variation, except has flutes in buttstock comb, white plastic spacer next to buttplate, and pistol grip cap with white spacer and brass insert. Mfg. 1951-53.

	N/A	$400	$350	$300	$275	$250	$225

GRADING - PPGS™	100%	98%	95%	90%	80%	70%	60%

✳ *Model 39A 3rd Model 3rd Variation* - similar to 3rd Model 2nd Variation, except has Micro-Groove rifling, and no pistol grip cap. Mfg. 1954-57.

	N/A	$375	$325	$300	$250	$200	$175

GOLDEN 39A - similar to Model 39A, with gold-plated trigger, sling swivels. Mfg. 1957-87.

	$395	$350	$300	$250	$200	$175	$150

Add 30% to pre-1970 (oil finished stock) models.

GOLDEN 39M - similar to Golden 39A, except is carbine variation.

$395	$350	$300	$250	$150	$125	$100

MODEL 39A "MOUNTIE" - straight grip stock, slim forearm, otherwise similar to 39A. Mfg. 1953-72.

$450	$400	$350	$300	$250	$200	$175

✳ *Model 39A "MOUNTIE" with K prefix* - 24 in. barrel and slender forearm. 4,335 mfg. 1953 only.

$750	$650	$550	$475	$425	$350	$300

90TH ANNIVERSARY 39A RIFLE - 24 in. chrome barrel and action, select checkered walnut stock, carved squirrel on side of buttstock. 500 mfg. in 1960.

$1,200	$1,000	$750	$500	$425	$350	$250

Last MSR was $100.

90TH ANNIVERSARY MODEL 39M MOUNTIE CARBINE - similar to 90th Anniversary Model 39A, except 20 in. barrel, straight stock. 500 mfg. in 1960.

$1,200	$1,000	$750	$600	$400	$350	$250

Last MSR was $100.

Add $50-$75 for original box and papers.

MODEL 39AWL - special model made exclusively for Wal-Mart, supporting the Wildlife Management Institution and Wildlife Forever, features similar to Marlin 1897CL CLassic, 24 in. half-round, half-octagon barrel, half mag., checkered black American walnut pistol grip stock, adj. semi-buckhorn rear sight, engraved receiver with scroll and "Wildlife for Tomorrow" and "Sportsmen Supporting Conservation". 2,000 mfg. 1997 only.

$850	$750	$550	$500	$450	$400	$350

Last MSR was $729.

MODEL 39A-DL - similar to 90th Anniversary, with blue barrel and action, regular production. Mfg. 1961-1963.

$900	$800	$750	$500	$400	$300	$200

This model is also known as the "Marlin 39A Squirrel Gun."

MODEL 39 PRESENTATION - .22 cal., one of the pair in the "Brace of 1,000," engraved receiver, 20 in. tapered octagon barrel, select fancy walnut straight grip stock and forend. Mfg. 1970 only.

$750	$600	$500	$430	$375	$315	$270

MODEL 39A OCTAGON - similar to Golden 39A, with octagon barrel, no pistol grip cap, 2,551 rifles and 2,140 carbines were produced. Mfg. 1973.

$595	$550	$475	$425	$360	$295	$250

MODEL 39 CARBINE - similar to 39M, with light barrel, 3/4 tube mag. 9,695 mfg. 1963-67.

$500	$450	$400	$325	$275	$200	$150

MODEL 39D - similar to 39M, with pistol grip stock. Mfg. 1971-73.

$395	$350	$300	$250	$150	$125	$100

GRADING - PPGS™	100%	98%	95%	90%	80%	70%	60%

MODEL 39A/AS - .22 LR cal., current production model, lever action, 19-26 shot tube mag., 24 in. barrel, walnut stock (cut checkering became standard 1994), open sights, gold trigger, takedown, 6 1/2 lbs.

MSR $593	$445	$350	$265	$195	$150	$125	$100

This model was previously designated the Model 39A. In 1988, the Model 39AS became the standard production model and included a rebounding hammer and hammer block safety. In 2001, the model nomenclature was changed back to the Model 39A.

MODEL 39TDS - .22 LR cal., carbine variation of the Model 39AS, 16 1/2 in. barrel with open sights, 5 1/4 lbs. Mfg. 1988-95.

	$500	$450	$350	$200	$175	$150	$125

Last MSR was $443.

MODEL 39M - carbine version of Model 39A, 20 in. lightweight barrel, 16 shot tube mag., squared finger lever, 6 lbs. Disc. 1987.

	$395	$350	$300	$275	$225	$175	$150

Last MSR was $304.

MODEL 39M OCTAGON - similar to Model 39M, with octagon barrel. 2,140 mfg. 1973.

	$550	$495	$475	$425	$360	$295	$250

MODEL 39 CENTURY LTD - Marlin Centennial 1870-1970 Commemorative, 20 in. octagon barrel, select walnut straight stock, brass forearm cap and buttplate, name plate in butt. 35,388 mfg. 1970.

	$625	$500	$400	N/A	N/A	N/A	N/A

This model should have the original box for 100% values.

MODEL 39A ARTICLE II - NRA Centennial Commemorative 1871-1971, "Right to Bear Arms" medallion in receiver, 24 in. octagon barrel, fancy pistol grip stock, brass buttplate and forearm cap. 6,244 mfg. 1971.

	$450	$395	$375	N/A	N/A	N/A	N/A

MODEL 39M ARTICLE II CARBINE - similar to 39A Article II, with 20 in. barrel, straight grip stock. Mfg. 3,824.

	$450	$395	$375	$350	$295	$250	$195

MODEL 45 CARBINE - .45 ACP cal. only, 7 shot mag., sandblasted steel receiver, 16 1/2 in. barrel, last shot hold open device, pressed checkering, adj. rear sight, 6 3/4 lbs. Mfg. 1986-99.

	$340	$230	$175	$150	$140	$130	$125

Last MSR was $443.

A new high visibility orange front sight post with cutaway hood was added in 1989.

MODEL 56 - similar to Model 57 Levermatic, 22 or 24 in. barrel, with mag. Mfg. 1955-64.

	$300	$250	$200	$150	$125	$100	$85

MODEL 57 LEVERMATIC - .22 S, L, or LR cal., tube mag., 22 in. barrel, open sight, Monte Carlo pistol grip stock. Mfg. 1959-65.

	$375	$350	$300	$250	$200	$150	$125

MODEL 57M - .22 Mag. cal., similar to Model 57 Levermatic, except has 24 in. barrel.

	$400	$350	$300	$250	$200	$150	$110

MODEL 60 SEMI-AUTO - .22 LR cal., 14 shot (LR) tube mag., entry level rifle with 19 or 22 (disc. 2002) in. Micro-Groove barrel, blue finish, aluminum receiver, walnut finished laminated hardwood stock (laminated now standard) with pressed checkering, adj. rear sight, crossbolt safety, last shot hold open, approx. 5 1/2 lbs. New 1960.

MSR $179	$145	$115	$95	$80	$75	$65	$60

Add $8 for 4X scope (disc. 2006).

GRADING - PPGS™	100%	98%	95%	90%	80%	70%	60%

✳ *Model 60C Semi-Auto* - similar to Model 60, except has full coverage Mossy Oak Breakup camo stock, 5 1/2 lbs. New 2000.

MSR $211	$160	$130	$110	$85	$75	$65	$60

✳ *Model 60DL Semi-Auto* - similar to Model 60, except has Walnutone walnut patterned finish. Mfg. 2004-2006.

	$175	$140	$110	$85	$75	$65	$60

Last MSR was $236.

✳ *Model 60SN* - features black synthetic stock, blue finish, includes sling swivel studs. New 2007.

MSR $173	$145	$120	$100	$80	$75	$65	$60

Add $13 for 4x20mm bore sighted scope.

MODEL 60SS SEMI-AUTO STAINLESS - .22 LR cal., 14 shot tube mag., nickel plated aluminum receiver and other parts, laminated black/grey birch stock with Monte Carlo cheekpiece, Mar-Shield finish, 19 or 22 (disc. 2002) in. stainless barrel, most recent mfg. has adj. semi-buckhorn folding rear with high visibility post and removable cutaway Wide-scan hood front sight, 5 1/2 lbs. New 1993.

MSR $283	$220	$175	$150	$120	$105	$90	$80

✳ *Model 60SB Semi-Auto Stainless* - similar to Model 60SS, except has uncheckered (mfg. 1998 only) or press-checkered (new 1999) birch Monte Carlo stock, laminated hardwood became standard 2004. New 1998.

MSR $226	$165	$145	$120	$100	$85	$70	$65

Add $17 for 4X scope (disc. 2006).

This model was previously sold to Wal-Mart only.

✳ *Model 60SSK Semi-Auto Stainless* - similar to Model 60SS, except has black fiberglass stock with Monte Carlo cheekpiece. Mfg. 1998-2006.

	$215	$180	$140	$110	$95	$80	$70

Last MSR was $269.

Add $15 for 4X scope (disc. 2001).

✳ *Model 60S-CF* - similar to Model 60SN, except features synthetic stock with carbon fiber pattern, includes sling studs. New 2007.

MSR $273	$195	$160	$130	$100	$85	$75	$65

MODEL 62 LEVERMATIC - .256 Mag. or .30 Carbine cal., 4 shot mag., 23 in. barrel, open sight, pistol grip Monte Carlo stock. Mfg. 1963-69.

.256 Mag.	$500	$450	$400	$325	$300	$195	$175
.30 Carbine	$400	$350	$300	$250	$225	$175	$150

MODEL 70P (PAPOOSE) SEMI-AUTO - .22 LR cal. only, semi-auto, takedown carbine with 16 1/4 in. barrel, 7 shot mag., rustproof receiver, bolt hold open, is supplied with floating nylon carrying case. Mfg. 1986-94.

	$170	$125	$90	$75	$65	$60	$55

Last MSR was $225.

Subtract $25 if without 4X scope (became standard 1993).

✳ *Model 70PSS Semi-Auto* - similar to Model 70P, except has stainless steel construction with black checkered synthetic stock with swing swivels, last shot hold-open became standard in 1996, includes blue nylon floatable case, 3 1/4 lbs. New 1995.

MSR $284	$220	$175	$150	$120	$105	$90	$80

✳ *Model 70HC Semi-Auto* - .22 LR cal., semi-auto, carbine with 18 in. barrel. Mfg. 1988-95.

	$185	$155	$130	$120	$110	$100	$90

GRADING - PPGS™	100%	98%	95%	90%	80%	70%	60%

MODEL 81TS BOLT ACTION - .22 S, L, or LR cal., 22 in. barrel with 17-25 shot tube mag., black synthetic stock with molded checkering, adj. rear sight, 6 lbs. Disc. 2003.

	$165	$130	$100	$80	$75	$65	$60

Last MSR was $213.

MODEL 83TS BOLT ACTION - .22 Mag. cal., 22 in. barrel, 12 shot mag., otherwise similar to Model 81TS, 6 lbs. Disc. 2003.

	$195	$150	$125	$95	$85	$75	$70

Last MSR was $259.

MODEL 308MX LEVER ACTION - .308 Marlin Express cal., 22 in. barrel, walnut pistol grip stock and forearm, blue finish, 5 shot tube mag. New 2007.

MSR $619	$475	$400	$355	$300	$265	$235	$200

This model was developed to take advantage of the new Hornady LEVERevolution ammunition, which greatly improves range, energy, and accuracy.

✳ *Model 308MXLR* - similar to Model 308MX, except has 24 in. stainless steel barrel and laminated stock, fluted bolt. New 2007.

MSR $816	$640	$540	$430	$360	$315	$260	$225

This model was developed to take advantage of the new Hornady LEVERevolution ammunition, which greatly improves range, energy, and accuracy.

MODEL 322 BOLT ACTION VARMINT - .222 Rem. cal., Sako Mauser type action, 3 shot mag., 24 in. medium weight barrel, 2 position aperture sight, checkered stock. Approx. 5,850 mfg. 1954-57.

	$550	$500	$475	$400	$325	$300	$250

MODEL 336A LEVER ACTION RIFLE (DISC.) - improved 36A, .30-30 Win., .35 Rem., or .32 Spl. cal., round breech bolt, 24 in. barrel with 2/3 mag. Mfg. 1948-1962, re-introduced 1973-1980.

	$500	$450	$400	$350	$300	$195	$175

Add 20% for 1st Model mfg. 1948-52.
Add 10% for 1953-62 mfg.

The .35 Rem. cal. was added in 1950, .32 Spl. was disc. in 1962.

✳ *Model 336ADL Rifle* - similar to Model 336A Rifle, except has deluxe checkered walnut stock and forearm, quick detachable swivels and 1 in. sling. Mfg. 1948-62.

	$625	$550	$500	$450	$375	$325	$275

Add 20% for 2nd Model (1957-1962).
Add 20% for .32 Spl. or .35 Rem. cal.

The 336ADL 1st Model (mfg. 1948-56) did not have a raised comb or cheekpiece. The 2nd Model (mfg. 1957-62) is identifiable by a Monte Carlo buttstock with raised comb and cheekpiece. Wood was supplied by Bishop.

MODELS 336A/336AS/336CC/336W - these models are listed previously under the Model 30AS.

MODEL 336RC CARBINE - .30-30 Win., .32 Spl., or .35 Rem. cal., standard model carbine. Mfg. 1948-68.

	$495	$425	$350	$315	$275	$200	$175

Add 10% for 1st Model mfg. 1948-52.

MODEL 336C CARBINE (DISC.) - .30-30 Win., .32 Spl., or .35 Rem. cal., standard model carbine with 20 in. barrel. Mfg. 1969-83.

	$450	$375	$300	$250	$220	$200	$175

Add 10% for .35 Rem. cal.

MODEL 336SC SPORTING CARBINE - similar to Model 336C, with 20 in. barrel and 2/3 length mag. tube, raised comb buttstock (1957-63). Mfg. 1948-63.

	$625	$550	$475	$400	$350	$300	$250

Add 10% for 1st Model mfg. 1948-52.

GRADING - PPGS™	100%	98%	95%	90%	80%	70%	60%

MODEL 336SC .219 ZIPPER - similar to Model 336SC, in .219 Zipper cal., 5 shot mag. 3,230 mfg. 1955-60.

	$800	$700	$600	$550	$500	$450	$400

MODEL 336SD CARBINE (SPORTING DELUXE) - .30-30 Win., .32 Spl., or .35 Rem. cal., deluxe sporting carbine with 20 in. barrel, checkered stock and forearm, raised comb, no cheekpiece, quick detachable swivels and 1 in. sling. Mfg. 1954-62.

	$800	$700	$600	$425	$275	$200	$185

MODEL 336C (336CS) CARBINE - .30-30 Win. or .35 Rem. cal., 6 shot tube mag., 20 in. barrel, hammer block safety, American black walnut pistol grip stock (cut checkering became standard 1994), 7 lbs. Introduced 1984.

MSR $530	$385	$310	$230	$195	$175	$165	$150

During 2001, this model's nomenclature was changed from 336CS to 336C.

MODEL 336SS (336M) - .30-30 Win. cal. only, similar to Model 336W/30AW, except is stainless steel, 6 shot tube mag., 7 lbs. New 2000.

MSR $650	$485	$395	$330	$275	$235	$200	$185

During 2001, this model's nomenclature was changed from 336M to 336SS.

MODEL 336XLR - .30-30 Win. or .35 Rem. (new 2007) cal., features stainless steel construction with 24 in. barrel, broached rifling, fluted bolt, 5 shot mag., black/grey laminate stock with deluxe recoil pad, adj. folding semi-buckhorn rear sight, hammer block safety, 7 1/2 lbs. New 2006.

MSR $816	$640	$535	$430	$360	$315	$260	$225

This model was developed to take advantage of the new Hornady LEVERevolution ammunition, which greatly improves range, energy, and accuracy.

MODEL 336LTS CARBINE - .30-30 Win. cal. only, 16 1/4 in. barrel, 5 shot tube mag., 6 1/2 lbs. 2,671 mfg. 1988-89 only.

	$450	$400	$350	$200	$175	$165	$150

Last MSR was $346.

MODEL 336 COWBOY - .30-30 Win. (disc. 2001) or .38-55 WCF cal., 8 shot tube mag., squared off finger lever, 24 in. tapered octagon barrel with deep cut Ballard-type rifling (6 grooves), cut checkered (disc. 2001) straight grip walnut stock and forearm, adj. Marbles semi-buckhorn rear and carbine front sight, ser. no. is on left side of receiver, instead of on tang, 7 1/2 lbs. Mfg. 1999-2004.

	$550	$475	$385	$310	$275	$250	$225

Last MSR was $735.

Add 10% for .30-30 Win. cal.

MODEL 336ER (EXTRA RANGE) - .356 Win. cal., 5 shot tube mag., 20 in. barrel, walnut pistol grip stock, open sights, 7 lbs. 2,441 mfg. 1983-86.

	$550	$475	$325	$225	$200	$175	$150

Last MSR was $350.

Although advertised, this model was never manufactured in .307 cal.

MODEL 336T CARBINE "TEXAN" - .30-30 Win., .35 Rem., or .44 Mag. (1965-1967 only) cal., similar to 336C, with straight stock, 18 1/2 (1983 only) or 20 in. barrel, saddle ring (1965-1971 only). Mfg. 1954-83.

	$450	$400	$350	$300	$250	$200	$150

MODEL 336DT CARBINE (DELUXE TEXAN) - .30-30 Win. or .35 Rem. cal., select stock version of 336T, longhorn and map of Texas carved on buttstock. Mfg. 1962-63.

	$750	$625	$450	$300	$200	$150	$135

Add 10% for .35 Rem. cal.

GRADING - PPGS™	100%	98%	95%	90%	80%	70%	60%

MODEL 336TS TEXAN - similar to 336 CS, except is .30-30 Win. cal., 18 1/2 in. barrel, straight grip stock and squared finger lever, crossbolt safety. Mfg. 1984-87.

	100%	98%	95%	90%	80%	70%	60%
	$325	$275	$225	$175	$150	$130	$120

Last MSR was $314.

MODEL 336 OCTAGON RIFLE - .30-30 Win. cal. only, with 22 in. octagon barrel, standard model. 2,414 mfg. 1973 only.

	$500	$425	$300	$250	$200	$175	$150

MODEL 336 MARAUDER CARBINE - .30-30 Win. or .35 Rem. cal., 16 1/4 in. barrel. 5,856 mfg. 1963-64.

	$550	$475	$425	$350	$275	$235	$210

Add 10% for .35 cal.

Approx. 65% were mfg. in .30-30 Win. cal., and 35% were mfg. in .35 Rem. cal.
Be careful of re-barreled examples of this model.

MODEL 336 MAGNUM CARBINE - .44 Mag. cal., 20 in. standard carbine configuration, w/o saddle ring. 2,823 mfg. 1963-64 only.

	$450	$400	$350	$300	$250	$200	$175

MODEL 336T - .44 Mag. cal., with saddle ring, 13,895 mfg. 1965-67.

	$375	$325	$295	$250	$200	$170	$160

MODEL 336 ZANE GREY CENTURY CARBINE - .30-30 Win. cal., similar to 336 Octagon, 22 in. octagon barrel, Zane Grey medallion inlaid in receiver, select walnut stock, pistol grip, brass buttplate and forearm cap. 7,871 mfg. in 1971.

	$450	$350	$300	$240	$210	$180	$155

This model was mfg. to commemorate the 100th anniversary of the birth of Zane Grey.

MODEL 336 PRESENTATION RIFLE - .30-30 Win. cal., one of the pair in the "Brace of 1,000," 22 in. octagon barrel, engraved receiver, sold with Model 39 Presentation. Mfg. 1970 only.

	$600	$450	$375	$315	$270	$230	$200

Add a premium for serial numbers under 100.

CENTENNIAL MATCHED PAIR "BRACE OF 1,000" - Model 336 and Model 39 serial numbered the same, .30-30 Win. or .22 LR cal., engraved by Robert Kain and Winston Churchill, deluxe wood, inlaid medallions, cased. 1,000 mfg. sets in 1970.

	$1,500	$1,350	$900	$785	$655	$550	$465

Last MSR was $750.

MODEL 375 - similar to Model 336 CS, except is .375 Win. cal. 16,315 mfg. 1980-83.

	$450	$400	$350	$300	$250	$200	$150

MODEL 444 LEVER ACTION - .444 Marlin cal., 4 shot tube mag., 24 in. barrel, open sights, straight grip, Monte Carlo stock, recoil pad, swivels, sling, 1st Model. Mfg. 1965-71.

	$425	$375	$275	$225	$200	$185	$160

✳ *Model 444S Lever Action* - similar to Model 444, except has pistol grip stock. Mfg. 1972-83.

	$325	$265	$225	$200	$185	$165	$150

MODEL 444P OUTFITTER - .444 Marlin cal., 5 shot tube mag., 18 1/2 in. ported barrel with deep cut Ballard-type rifling (6 grooves), adj. semi-buckhorn folding rear sight with ramp front, checkered straight grip walnut stock and forearm, tapped for scope mount, approx. 7 lbs. Mfg. 1999-2002.

	$495	$395	$315	$245	$195	$180	$170

Last MSR was $631.

GRADING - PPGS™	100%	98%	95%	90%	80%	70%	60%

MODEL 444 (444SS) SPORTER - .444 Marlin cal., similar to Model 444, with 22 in. barrel and hammer block safety, pistol grip stock without Monte Carlo configuration (cut checkering became standard 1994), 7 1/2 lbs. New 1984.

MSR $619	$470	$335	$295	$235	$195	$180	$170

During 2001, this model's nomenclature was changed from 444SS to 444.

MODEL 444XLR - .444 Marlin cal., features stainless steel construction with 24 in. barrel, broached rifling, fluted bolt, 5 shot mag., black/grey laminate stock with deluxe recoil pad, adj. folding semi-buckhorn rear sight, hammer block safety, 7 1/2 lbs. New 2006.

MSR $816	$640	$535	$430	$360	$315	$260	$225

This model was developed to take advantage of the new Hornady LEVERevolution ammunition, which greatly improves range, energy, and accuracy.

MODEL 455 BOLT ACTION SPORTER - .30-06, or .308 Win. cal., FN Mauser action with Sako trigger, 24 in. barrel, stainless steel barrel, Lyman aperture sight, checkered Monte Carlo pistol grip stock. 1,079 were mfg. in 30.06 cal., 59 in .308 Win. cal. Mfg. 1957-59.

	$650	$525	$375	$250	$220	$195	$165

Add 20% for .308 Win. cal.

MODEL 717M2 SEMI-AUTO - .17 Mach 2 cal., 7 shot detachable mag., 18 in. sporter barrel with open sights, walnut finished hardwood stock, last shot bolt hold open, crossbolt safety, 5 1/2 lbs. Mfg. 2005-2007.

	$180	$160	$140	$120	$110	$100	$90

Last MSR was $222.

MODELS 780, 781, 782, and 783 BOLT ACTION - .22 LR or .22 Mag. (Models 782 and 783) cal., tube or mag., 22 in. barrel. Disc. 1988.

	$110	$85	$75	$70	$65	$55	$50

Last MSR was $162.

Add $17-$25 for Models 782 and 783.

MODEL 795 SEMI-AUTO - .22 LR cal., 10 shot detachable mag., 18 in. barrel, black synthetic Monte Carlo stock, grooved receiver, last shot bolt hold open, approx. 5 lbs.

MSR $157	$125	$95	$80	$75	$65	$60	$55

✳ *Model 795SS Semi-Auto* - similar to Model 795, except has stainless steel barrel and nickel plated parts. New 2002.

MSR $227	$180	$150	$120	$100	$85	$70	$65

MODELS 880/881 BOLT ACTION - .22 LR or .22 Mag. cal., replacement for Models 780, 781, Model 880 is .22 LR with 7 shot detachable mag. and 22 in. barrel, (cut checkering became standard 1994), Model 881 is .22 LR with 17 shot tube mag. and 22 in. barrel, 6 lbs. Mfg. 1989-97.

	$185	$145	$100	$85	$75	$70	$65

Last MSR was $251.

Add $10 for Model 881.

✳ *Model 880SS Bolt-Action* - similar to Model 880, except is stainless steel, black fiberglass synthetic stock, approx. 6 lbs. Mfg. 1994-2003.

	$240	$175	$115	$90	$75	$60	$40

Last MSR was $316.

✳ *Model 880SQ (Squirrel Rifle) Bolt-Action* - similar to Model 880, except has black fiberglass filled synthetic stock with checkering and heavy 22 in. barrel, without sights and grooved receiver, matte finish, 7 lbs. Mfg. 1996-2003.

	$245	$190	$135	$100	$80	$70	$65

Last MSR was $330.

GRADING - PPGS™	100%	98%	95%	90%	80%	70%	60%

MODELS 882/883 BOLT ACTION - .22 Win. Mag. cal., 7 shot detachable (Model 882) or 12 shot tube mag. (Model 883), 22 in. barrel, checkered (cut checkering became standard 1994), black walnut Monte Carlo stock with Mar-Shield finish, adj. semi-buckhorn rear sight and hooded front, thumb safety, 6 lbs. Mfg. 1989-2003.

	$240	$185	$130	$95	$85	$75	$70

Last MSR was $324.

> **Add $13 for Model 883.**
> **Add $35 for nickel finish on Model 883N (disc. 1993).**
> The Models 882 and 883 are the replacements for Models 782 and 783.

✳ *Model 882SS Bolt Action* - .22 Win. Mag. cal., similar to Model 882, except is stainless steel and stock is black synthetic with molded-in checkering, fire sights (red fiberoptic inserts with cutaway hood) became standard 1998, approx. 6 lbs. Mfg. 1995-2003.

	$250	$190	$130	$100	$85	$70	$65

Last MSR was $345.

✳ *Model 882SSV Bolt Action* - .22 Win. Mag. cal., features 22 in. bead blasted stainless barrel and receiver with black fiberglass reinforced synthetic stock, 7 shot mag., grooved receiver, w/o sights, ring mounts included, 7 lbs. Mfg. 1997-2003.

	$245	$185	$125	$100	$85	$70	$65

Last MSR was $338.

✳ *Model 882L Bolt Action* - similar to Model 882, except has two-tone brown laminated hardwood stock, 6 1/4 lbs. Mfg. 1992-2003.

	$250	$200	$140	$100	$85	$75	$70

Last MSR was $342.

✳ *Model 883SS Bolt Action* - .22 Win. Mag. cal., 12 shot tube mag., similar to Model 883, except barrel is stainless steel and stock is laminated two-tone brown birch with Monte Carlo cheekpiece. Mfg. 1993-2003.

	$265	$205	$145	$115	$100	$85	$75

Last MSR was $358.

MODEL 915Y "LITTLE BUCKAROO" SINGLE SHOT - .22 S, L, or LR cal., 16 1/4 in. barrel, features T-900 fire control system, cocks on opening, youth dimensions, adj. rear sight, thumb safety, grooved receiver, walnut finished hardwood stock, 4 1/4 lbs. New 2004.

MSR $203		$165	$140	$110	$80	$75	$70	$65

> Add $24 for front fiber optic fire sight (Model 915YS, new 2004).

MODEL 917M2 BOLT ACTION - .17 Mach 2 cal., otherwise similar to Model 917V, 6 lbs. Mfg. 2005-2007.

	$185	$160	$145	$130	$100	$90	$80

Last MSR was $232.

✳ *Model 917M2S Bolt Action* - similar to Model 917M2, except has laminated grey/black hardwood Monte Carlo stock and stainless steel barrel, 7 lbs. Mfg. 2005-2006.

	$300	$225	$175	$150	$125	$110	$100

Last MSR was $410.

MODEL 917 - .17 HMR cal., black synthetic stock, 4 and 7 shot mags. supplied standard beginning 2007, T-900 fire control system, 22 in. barrel with sights, thumb safety, cocking indicator, adj. rear sight, 6 lbs. New 2006.

MSR $240		$195	$165	$145	$120	$110	$100	$90

> Add $47 for stainless steel (Model 917S, new 2007).

GRADING - PPGS™	100%	98%	95%	90%	80%	70%	60%

MODEL 917V SERIES BOLT ACTION - .17 HMR cal., 4 and 7 shot detachable mags. supplied standard beginning 2007, 22 in. heavy barrel, features T-900 fire control system, walnut finished checkered hardwood Monte Carlo stock, thumb safety, no sights, scope base included, 6 lbs. New 2004.

	MSR $262	$215	$180	$155	$135	$115	$100	$90

Add $38 for 3-9x32mm bore sighted scope (new 2007).

✳ *Model 917VR Bolt Action* - similar to Model 917, except has 22 in. heavy barrel, 7 lbs. New 2006.

	MSR $252	$200	$170	$155	$135	$115	$100	$90

✳ *Model 917VS Bolt Action* - similar to Model 917V, except has laminated grey/black hardwood Monte Carlo or synthetic carbon fiber pattern (new 2007) stock and stainless steel barrel. New 2004.

	MSR $376	$295	$235	$180	$150	$125	$110	$100

Add $23 for fluted barrel (Model 917VSF, new 2005).
Subtract $17 for synthetic stock (new 2007).

✳ *Model 917VT* - .17 HMR cal., features 22 in. heavy blue bull barrel, 4 or 7 shot mag., two-tone brown laminated stock with thumbhole pistol grip, swivel studs, rubber butt pad, no sights, drilled and tapped, 7 lbs. New 2008.

	MSR $382	$310	$245	$190	$160	$135	$120	$110

✳ *Model 917VST* - .17 HMR cal., similar to Model 917VT, except has stainless steel barrel, grey laminated thumbhole stock. New 2008.

	MSR $427	$345	$265	$210	$175	$150	$125	$110

MODEL 922M SEMI-AUTO - .22 Win. Mag. cal., 7 shot detachable mag., 20 1/2 in. barrel, Garand style safety, alloy receiver, hold-open device, uncheckered or checkered (became standard 1994) walnut stock with solid pad, blue steel (hard coated on receiver), 6 1/2 lbs. Mfg. 1993-2001.

		$360	$295	$240	$200	$185	$175	$165

Last MSR was $454.

MODEL 925 SERIES BOLT ACTION - .22 LR cal., 7 shot detachable mag., features T-900 fire control system, 22 in. barrel, thumb safety, adj. rear sight, grooved receiver, walnut finished hardwood stock with swivel studs, 5 1/2 lbs. New 2004.

	MSR $206	$165	$135	$110	$80	$75	$70	$65

Add $10 for 4x scope (disc. 2006).

✳ *Model 925C Bolt Action* - similar to Model 925, except has Mossy Oak Break Up camo stock. New 2004.

	MSR $239	$190	$150	$125	$95	$80	$70	$65

✳ *Model 925R Bolt Action* - similar to Model 925, except has Monte Carlo black synthetic stock, 5 1/2 lbs. New 2006.

	MSR $199	$165	$135	$110	$80	$75	$70	$65

Add $38 for 3-9x32mm bore sighted scope (new 2007).

MODEL 925M BOLT ACTION - .22 Mag. cal., 4 and 7 shot detachable mags. supplied standard beginning 2007, features T-900 fire control system, 22 in. barrel, thumb safety, adj. rear sight, grooved receiver, walnut finished hardwood stock with swivel studs, 6 lbs. New 2004.

	MSR $234	$185	$155	$130	$95	$85	$80	$75

Add $40 for Model 925MC with Monte Carlo stock and Mossy Oak Break-Up camo finish (disc. 2006).

MODEL 980S BOLT ACTION - .22 LR cal., 7 shot detachable mag., 22 in. stainless steel barrel, other metal parts stainless steel/nickel plated, T-900 fire control system, black fiberglass synthetic stock with molded checkering, thumb safety, adj. buckhorn rear sight, approx. 6 lbs. New 2004.

	MSR $298	$235	$190	$155	$125	$110	$95	$85

Add $30 for black synthetic stock with carbon fiber pattern (Model 980S/CF).

GRADING - PPGS™	100%	98%	95%	90%	80%	70%	60%

✳ *Model 980V Bolt Action* - similar to Model 980S, except has 22 in. heavy steel barrel with recessed muzzle, double bedding screws, swivel studs, no sights, grooved receiver with scope bases, drilled and tapped, 7 lbs. Mfg. 2004-2006.

	$265	$210	$170	$145	$120	$100	$80

Last MSR was $349.

MODEL 981T BOLT ACTION - .22 S, L, or LR cal., 17-25 shot tube mag., 22 in. barrel, black fiberglass synthetic stock, features T-900 fire control system, thumb safety, adj. rear sight, approx. 6 lbs. New 2004.

MSR $205		$165	$135	$105	$85	$75	$65	$60

MODEL 982 BOLT ACTION - .22 Mag. cal., 7 shot detachable mag., 22 in. regular barrel, T-900 fire control system, checkered American Monte Carlo stock, adj. buckhorn rear sight, thumb safety, rubber buttplate, 6 lbs. Mfg. 2004-2006.

	$255	$210	$170	$145	$120	$100	$80

Last MSR was $341.

Add $20 for Model 982L with two-tone brown laminated stock (new 2004).
Add $23 for Model 982S with stainless steel barrel and nickel/stainless steel small parts (mfg. 2004-2005).

✳ *Model 982VS* - similar to Model 980, except has black synthetic stock and 22 in. heavy stainless barrel, 4 and 7 shot mags. supplied standard beginning 2007. New 2004.

MSR $309		$250	$195	$165	$145	$120	$110	$90

Add $41 for synthetic stock with carbon fiber pattern (new 2007).

MODEL 983 SERIES BOLT ACTION - .22 Mag. cal., 12 shot tube mag., 22 in. barrel, features T-900 fire control system, checkered walnut Monte Carlo stock, adj. folding buckhorn sight, 6 lbs. New 2004.

MSR $308		$250	$200	$170	$150	$125	$105	$85

✳ *Model 983T Bolt Action* - .22 Mag. cal., 12 shot tube mag., 22 in. barrel, features T-900 fire control system, black fiberglass synthetic stock with molded-in checkering, adj. rear sight, 6 lbs. New 2004.

MSR $245		$205	$170	$150	$130	$110	$90	$75

✳ *Model 983S Bolt Action* .- similar to Model 983T, except has stainless steel barrel and nickel plated/stainless steel parts, two-tone brown hardwood laminate stock, 6 lbs. New 2004.

MSR $337		$265	$220	$185	$145	$125	$105	$90

MODEL 990 SEMI-AUTO - .22 LR cal. only, 18 shot tube mag., 22 in. barrel, last shot automatic bolt hold-open, Monte Carlo American black walnut stock with pistol grip, 5 1/2 lbs. Disc. 1987.

	$115	$90	$75	$65	$60	$55	$50

Last MSR was $159.

MODEL 990L SEMI-AUTO - .22 LR cal., 14 shot tube mag., 22 in. barrel, laminated two-tone brown Monte Carlo stock, gold trigger, adj. rear sight, grooved receiver, 5 3/4 lbs. Mfg. 1993-94.

	$180	$160	$145	$130	$120	$110	$100

Last MSR was $223.

MODEL 995 SEMI-AUTO - .22 LR cal., 7 shot mag., 18 in. barrel, Monte Carlo walnut stock, 5 lbs. Disc. 1994.

	$160	$125	$85	$70	$65	$60	$55

Last MSR was $206.

✳ *Model 995SS Semi-Auto* - .22 LR cal., stainless steel barrel and nickel-plated small parts, black fiberglass stock with molded-in checkering, adj. rear sight, last shot hold-open new 1996, 5 lbs. Mfg. 1995-99.

	$195	$145	$110	$90	$75	$60	$50

Last MSR was $255.

GRADING - PPGS™	100%	98%	95%	90%	80%	70%	60%

MODEL 1894 (1969-1984 MFG.) - .44 Spl. or .44 Mag. cal., 20 in. bbl., 10 shot tube mag., adj. sights, straight grip walnut stock and forearm, 6 lbs. Mfg. 1969-84.

	$375	$300	$250	$195	$165	$145	$130

MODEL 1894 (1894S) - .41 Mag. (disc. 1991), .44 Mag./.44 Spl., or .45 LC (mfg. 1988-91, reintroduced 2005 only) cal., Model 1894 with addition of cross bolt ("S" suffix) and hammer block safety, 20 in. barrel, 10 shot tube mag., adj. sights, straight grip walnut stock and forearm (cut checkering became standard 1994), 6 lbs. Disc. 2002, reintroduced 2005.

MSR $576	$455	$360	$255	$185	$150	$140	$130

During 2001, this model's nomenclature was changed from 1894S to 1894.

MODEL 1894C CARBINE - .357 Mag. cal., 18 1/2 in. barrel, w/o hammer block safety, 6 lbs. Mfg. 1979-84.

	$350	$275	$225	$180	$160	$145	$130

MODEL 1894 SPORTER - .44 Mag. cal. only, 6 shot half mag. tube, crescent shaped hard rubber buttplate, 1,398 mfg. 1973 only.

	$500	$425	$360	$300	$250	$200	$175

MODEL 1894C SERIES CARBINE (1894CS) - copy of original Model 1894, .357 Mag./.38 Spl. cal., 9 shot mag., 18 1/2 in. round barrel, open sights (hooded front became standard 1999), straight grip stock (cut checkering became standard 1994), squared finger lever, 6 lbs. New 1984.

MSR $576	$455	$360	$255	$185	$150	$140	$130

During 2001, this model's nomenclature was changed from 1894CS to 1894C.

✳ *Model 1894CP Carbine* - similar to Model 1894C, except has 16 1/4 in. ported round barrel, 8 shot mag., approx. 5 3/4 lbs. Mfg. 2001-2002.

	$440	$320	$235	$185	$150	$140	$130

Last MSR was $566.

✳ *Model 1894CL Carbine* - .32-20 Win. cal., 6 shot tube mag., 22 in. barrel with button rifling and barrel band, Marble sights, American walnut stock and forearm with cut checkering, 6 lbs. New 2005-2007.

	$595	$515	$425	$350	$300	$250	$225

Last MSR was $755.

MODEL 1894P CARBINE - .44 Mag./.44 Spl. cal., 16 1/4 in. ported barrel with deep-cut Ballard type 6 groove rifling, 8 shot tube mag., checkered straight grip walnut stock with vent. recoil pad, 5 3/4 lbs. Mfg. 2000-2002.

	$440	$320	$235	$185	$150	$140	$130

Last MSR was $566.

✳ *Model 1894S Carbine Limited* - .44 Mag./.44 Spl. cal., features 16 1/4 in. barrel with "The Marlin Limited" roll stamped on barrel, approx. 1,500 mfg. 1996 only.

	$450	$400	$350	$285	$250	$215	$185

MODEL 1894FG - .41 Mag. cal., similar to Model 1894, except has pistol grip stock with cut checkering and 10 shot mag., 6 1/2 lbs. Mfg. 2003-2007.

	$495	$375	$275	$195	$160	$145	$130

Last MSR was $588.

MODEL 1894PG - .44 Mag. cal., similar to Model 1894FG. Mfg. 2003-2004.

	$490	$340	$255	$190	$160	$145	$130

Last MSR was $622.

MODEL 1894SS - .44 Mag./.44 Spl. cal., stainless steel, 20 in. barrel, 10 shot tube mag., straight grip, checkered black walnut stock and forearm, offset hammer spur, approx. 6 lbs. New 2002.

MSR $704	$560	$440	$325	$265	$225	$185	$160

MODEL 1894 COWBOY (COWBOY II) - .32 H&R Mag. (mfg. mid-2004-2006), .357 Mag. (new 1997), .44-40 WCF (mfg. 1997-99), .44 Mag. (new 1997), or .45 LC cal., 10 shot tube mag., incorporates "cowboy action shooting" features, straight grip stock w/o or with checkering (disc. 2001), adj. Marbles-type rear sight, blued finish, 20 (new 2003, n/a in .45 LC cal.) or 24 in. tapered octagon barrel, 7 1/2 lbs. New 1996.

MSR $822	$600	$515	$440	$330	$275	$225	$195

The Model 1894 Cowboy II refers to the three new cals. introduced 1997. This model in .32 H&R Mag. cal. (new 2004) loads through a port in the front of the mag. tube, not a receiver port like the other cals.

* *Model 1894 Cowboy Competition* - .38 Spl. or .45 LC (new 2003) cal., 10 shot tube mag., 20 in. tapered octagon barrel with deep cut Ballard type rifling, hammer block safety, Marbles sights, case colored receiver, lever, and bolt, 6 1/2 lbs. Mfg. 2002-2005.

	$765	$660	$505	$425	$375	$325	$295

Last MSR was $986.

MODEL 1894M (.22 MAG.) - .22 Mag. cal., with 20 in. barrel, 11 shot tube mag., straight grip walnut stock and forearm, 6 1/4 lbs. Disc. 1989.

	$450	$395	$350	$250	$200	$175	$150

Last MSR was $358.

MODEL 1894CL - .218 Bee (new 1990), .25-20 WCF or .32-20 WCF cal., 6 shot (two-thirds length) tube mag., 22 in. barrel, 6 1/4 lbs. Mfg. 1988-94.

	$450	$395	$350	$250	$200	$175	$150

Last MSR was $502.

  Add 10% for .218 Bee cal.

MODEL 1894 CENTURY LIMITED - .44-40 WCF cal., limited edition commemorative mfg. to celebrate the Model 1894's 100th Anniversary, 24 in. tapered octagon barrel with full 12 shot tube mag., features Giovanelli engraved receiver, bolt, and lever, receiver is case colored using traditional methods, checkered straight grip stock and forearm, crescent buttplate, 6 1/2 lbs. 2,500 mfg. 1994 only.

	$1,000	$850	$600	N/A	N/A	N/A	N/A

Last MSR was $1,088.

MODEL 1894 CENTURY LIMITED (EMPLOYEE SPECIAL EDITION) - employee special edition featuring gold inlaid Marlin horse and rider logo. 100 mfg. 1994-95 in ser. no. range 1-100.

	$3,650	$2,750	$1,800	N/A	N/A	N/A	N/A

MODEL 1894 OCTAGON - similar to 1894 Carbine, with octagon barrel. Mfg. 1973.

	$475	$425	$350	$275	$225	$200	$185

MODEL 1895 LEVER ACTION - .45-70 Govt. cal., 4 shot tube mag., 22 in. barrel, open sights, straight grip stock with curved buttplate, forearm cap, sling and swivels. Mfg. 1972-1984.

	$395	$350	$300	$250	$200	$175	$160

  Add 10% for guns mfg. 1972-1978.
  Add 10% for pre-micro-groove.

Early new Model 1895 Marlins had cut rifling suitable for cast bullets, while later mfg. was switched to Marlin's "Micro Groove" shallow rifling. Changes were also made from a straight stock to a pistol grip stock and from a traditional receiver to one with the newer hammer-block, push-button safety. Early guns with a straight grip stock, traditional receiver, and cut rifling command premiums over later mfg. Cut rifling occured during the first year of production only - these guns have a ser. no. prefix of "B.O." More recently mfg. models have pistol grip, Micro Groove rifling, and hammer-block safety - these newer guns are the least desirable from a collector's standpoint.

GRADING - PPGS™	100%	98%	95%	90%	80%	70%	60%

✳ *Model 1895S Lever Action* - similar to Model 1895, except has pistol grip stock and straight buttpad.

	$325	$300	$275	$200	$175	$150	$140

MODEL 1895 (1895SS) - .45-70 Govt. cal., similar to Model 1895, checkered pistol grip stock, hammer block safety, cut checkering became standard 1994, 7 1/2 lbs. New 1983.

MSR $619	$520	$390	$275	$195	$155	$140	$130

During 2001, this model's nomenclature was changed from 1895SS to 1895.

✳ *Model 1895SS Cody Stampede 75th Anniversary* - .45-70 cal., includes semi-fancy checkered walnut stock with medallion, serial numbered CS-001-CS-200, 200 mfg. 1994 only.

	$750	$500	$400	$335	$290	$245	$215

Last MSR was $695.

✳ *Model 1895 LTD V* -45-70 Gov't. cal., 24 in. half round/half octagon barrel, full length 8 shot mag. tube, checkered walnut stock and forearm. Mfg. 2001.

	$595	$495	$415	$365	$310	$280	$260

MODEL 1895XLR - .45-70 Govt. cal., features stainless steel construction with 24 in. barrel, broached rifling, fluted bolt, 4 shot mag., black/grey laminate stock with deluxe recoil pad, adj. folding semi-buckhorn rear sight, hammer block safety, 7 1/2 lbs. New 2006.

MSR $816	$675	$525	$435	$365	$315	$260	$225

This model was developed to take advantage of the new Hornady LEVERevolution ammunition, which greatly improves range, energy, and accuracy.

MODEL 1895M - .450 Marlin Mag. cal. (belted), 4 shot tube mag., 18 1/2 in. ported barrel, checkered straight grip walnut stock and forearm, vent. recoil pad, adj. folding buckhorn rear sight, 7 lbs. New 2000.

MSR $678	$555	$485	$390	$320	$275	$250	$225

MODEL 1895MR - similar to Model 1895M, except has 22 in. barrel, 7 1/2 lbs. Mfg. 2003-2004.

	$610	$485	$395	$325	$285	$255	$225

Last MSR was $761.

MODEL 1895M XLR - .450 Marlin cal., features stainless steel construction with 24 in. barrel, broached rifling, fluted bolt, 4 shot mag., black/grey laminate stock with deluxe recoil pad, adj. folding semi-buckhorn rear sight, hammer block safety, 7 1/2 lbs. New 2006.

MSR $816	$675	$525	$435	$365	$315	$260	$225

This model was developed to take advantage of the new Hornady LEVERevolution ammunition, which greatly improves range, energy, and accuracy.

MODEL 1895 COWBOY - .45-70 Govt., features 26 in. tapered octagon barrel and 9 shot tube mag., uncheckered straight grip walnut stock and forearm, Marble front and rear (adj.) sights, 8 lbs. New 2001.

MSR $785	$625	$525	$435	$365	$315	$260	$225

MODEL 1895G GUIDE GUN - .45-70 Govt. cal., features 18 1/2 in. ported barrel with Ballard style cut rifling, cut checkered American stock and forearm, adj. folding buckhorn rear sight, 4 shot tube mag., vent. recoil pad, approx. 7 lbs. 2,500 to be mfg. beginning 1998.

MSR $630	$520	$415	$310	$200	$155	$140	$130

✳ *Model 1895GS Guide Gun* - similar to Model 1895G, except is stainless steel. New 2001.

MSR $752	$615	$465	$335	$260	$210	$175	$150

GRADING - PPGS™	100%	98%	95%	90%	80%	70%	60%

MODEL 1895RL - .480 Ruger/.475 Linebaugh cal., 6 (.480 Ruger) or 5 (.475 Linebaugh) shot tube mag., 18 1/2 in. barrel, walnut pistol grip stock, otherwise similar to Model 1895, 7 lbs. Limited mfg. 2004 only.

	$565	$455	$380	$315	$275	$250	$225

Last MSR was $695.

MODEL 1895 CENTURY LIMITED (CLTD) - .45-70 cal., commemorates Marlin's 125th Anniversary, engraving includes grizzly bear on left side, Marlin horse and rider logo on right, 24 in. half-round half-octagonal barrel, crescent buttplate, satin finished receiver, checkered walnut stock and forearm. Approx. 2,500 mfg. 1995 only.

	$1,100	$850	$550	$460	$395	$335	$285

Last MSR was $1,104.

A Marlin Collector's Association Edition was also mfg. and was the same as the Model 1895 Century Limited.

✳ *Model 1895 Century Limited (CLTD) Employee Edition* - features 3 elk on left side and gold inlaid Marlin horse and rider logo on right. 100 mfg. 1995-96 in ser. no. range 1-100.

	$2,600	$1,950	$1,300	N/A	N/A	N/A	N/A

MODEL 1897 COWBOY - .22 S, L, or LR cal., takedown action, 19 shot (.22 LR cal.), tube mag., rebounding hammer with block safety, 24 in. tapered octagon barrel with Micro-Groove (16 grooves) rifling, cut checkered walnut stock and forearm, adj. Marble semi-buckhorn rear and carbine front sight with brass bead, high polish blue, 6 1/2 lbs. Mfg. 1999-2001.

	$575	$495	$400	$350	$295	$265	$235

Last MSR was $708.

MODEL 1897T - .22 S, L, or LR cal., 14-21 shot mag., 20 in. tapered octagon barrel, hammer block safety, Marble front and rear sights, 6 lbs. Mfg. 2002-2003.

	$585	$430	$365	$330	$285	$240	$195

Last MSR was $748.

MODEL 1897 CENTURY LIMITED LEVER ACTION - .22 LR cal., 100th anniversary of the Model 1897, features extensive receiver engraving and gold accenting, 24 in. half round/half octagon barrel with open sights, checkered fancy walnut stock and forearm. Limited mfg. 1997 only, limited quantities remained through 1999.

	$850	$700	$625	$540	$465	$385	$335

Last MSR was $1,055.

✳ *Model 1897 Century Limited Lever Action Employee Edition* - .22 LR, features gold scroll work on lever, less than 100 mfg. 1997 only in ser. no. range 1-100.

	$1,200	$1,000	$850	N/A	N/A	N/A	N/A

MODEL 1897 ANNIE OAKLEY - .22 LR cal., features 18 1/2 in. tapered octagon barrel with marble sights, blue receiver with rolled scroll engraving featuring gold Annie Oakley etched name on bolt, deluxe checkered walnut stock and forearm. Mfg. 1998 only.

	$700	$600	$500	$430	$375	$315	$270

Last MSR was $1,054.

Add $100 for employee variation.

An employee variation of this model was made with gold inlays on finger lever, 100 mfg. total.

MODEL 2000 TARGET BOLT ACTION - .22 LR cal., single shot (can be converted), 22 in. heavy barrel with match chamber and Lyman adj. sights, 2 stage target trigger, molded synthetic stock made from fiberglass and Kevlar with twice baked blue enamel, adj. buttplate, aluminum forearm rail, 8 lbs. Mfg. 1991-95.

	$525	$410	$350	$300	$275	$250	$225

Last MSR was $602.

Add $34 for 5-shot conversion unit (for summer biathlon competition).

GRADING - PPGS™	100%	98%	95%	90%	80%	70%	60%

✳ *Model 2000A Target Bolt Action* - similar to Model 2000 Target, except has adj. comb, ambidextrous pistol grip, and molded-in logo. Mfg. 1994 only.

	$550	$425	$365	$315	$290	$260	$230

Last MSR was $625.

✳ *Model 2000L Target Bolt Action* - .22 LR cal., updated version of the Model 2000, featuring grey/black laminated stock, adj. aperture rear and aperture insert front sight, double bedding screws, factory test target supplied with each gun, 8 lbs. Mfg. 1996-2002.

	$600	$475	$380	$320	$280	$250	$225

Last MSR was $745.

MODEL 7000 SEMI-AUTO - .22 LR cal., 10 shot detachable mag., 18 in. heavy barrel without sights and recessed muzzle, black fiberglass synthetic stock with molded-in checkering, grooved receiver, no sights, last shot hold open, scope mounts provided, 5 1/2 lbs. Mfg. 1997-2006.

	$210	$190	$165	$140	$130	$120	$110

Last MSR was $263.

✳ *Model 7000T Semi-Auto* - .22 LR cal., target model with 18 in. heavy barrel, red, white and blue laminated hardwood stock with adj. pad, two stage target trigger with stop, aluminum forend rail with adj. stop, grooved receiver w/o sights, 7 1/2 lbs. Mfg. 1999-2001.

	$365	$300	$240	$200	$185	$175	$165

Last MSR was $465.

MARLIN PROMOTIONAL MODELS - Models 15 (disc.), 15Y (disc.), 15N (mfg. 1998- 99, last MSR $188), 15YN (refer to individual listing), 25 (disc.), 25M (disc.), 25N (refer to individual listing), 25NC (refer to individual listing), 70 (disc.), 70HC (mfg. 1989-95, last 1995 MSR was $167), 75C (disc.), 81TS (refer to individual listing), and 795 Semi-Auto (refer to individual listing), are inexpensive, utilitarian .22 LR or .22 Mag. cal. (Model 25M only), rifles designed for inexpensive shooting.

Series 15 and 25 Models designate bolt action, Series 60 and 70 designate semi-auto design.

RIFLES: .22 CAL.

From 1930 to date, Marlin has made a number of .22 cal. rimfire rifles, bolt action single shots, bolt action repeaters and auto loaders. These have normally been good quality, inexpensive weapons. In 1960, the name Glenfield was also used in connection with these guns. We will list these models for reference purposes with price ranges appearing at the end of each listing.

BOLT ACTION, SINGLE SHOT
Model 65 - 1932-1938. Price Range $40- $75.
Model 65E - 1932-1938. Price Range $50 - $85.
Model 100 - 1936-1941. Price Range $50 - $85.
Model 100S Tom Mix Special - disc. Price Range $140 - $275.
Model 100SB - 1936-1941. Price Range $55 - $95.
Model 101 - 1941-1977. Price Range $50 - $85.
Model 101 DL - disc. Price Range $65 - $100.
Model 101 Crown Prince - 1959. Price Range $85 - $165.
Model 101G - 1960-1965, Marlin Glenfield. Price Range $45 - $80.
Model 10 - 1966-disc., Marlin Glenfield. Price Range $45 - $75.
Model 122 - 1966-disc. Price Range $45 - $70.

BOLT ACTION: REPEATING RIFLES
Model 80 - 1934-1939. Price Range $50 - $95.
Model 80E - 1934-1940. Price Range $55 - $100.
Model 80C - 1940-1970. Price Range $55 - $100.
Model 80DL - 1940-1965. Price Range $70 - $105.
Model 80G - 1960-1965, Marlin Glenfield. Price Range $45 - $80.

GRADING - PPGS™	100%	98%	95%	90%	80%	70%	60%

Model 20 - 1966-disc., Marlin Glenfield. Price Range $45 - $80.
Model 780 - 1971-1988. Price Range $50 - $85.
Model 781 - 1971-1988. Price Range $50 - $85.
Model 782 - 1971-1988, .22 WRM. Price Range $75 - $135.
Model 783 - 1971-1988, .22 WRM. Price Range $75 - $135.
Model 980 - 1962-1970, .22 WRM. Price Range $75 - $135.
Model 81 - 1937-1940. Price Range $50 - $95.
Model 81E - 1937-1940. Price Range $65 - $110.
Model 81C - 1940-1970. Price Range $65 - $110.
Model 81DL - 1940-1965. Price Range $65 - $100.
Model 81G - 1960-1965 Marlin Glenfield. Price Range $55 - $85.

AUTOLOADING RIFLES

Model 50 - 1931-1935. Price Range $85 - $150.
Model 50E - 1931-1934. Price Range $85 - $165.
Model A-1 - 1936-1940. Price Range $85 - $155.
Model A-1E - 1935-1946. Price Range $85 - $160.
Model A-1C - 1941-1946. Price Range $75 - $155.
Model A-1DL - 1941-1946. Price Range $75 - $155.
Model 88-C - 1948-1956. Price Range $75 - $150.
Model 88-DL - 1953-1956. Price Range $75 - $150.
Model 89-C - 1948-1961. Price Range $75 - $150.
Model 89-DL - 1950-1961. Price Range $75 - $150.
Model 98 - 1957-1959. Price Range $75 - $150.
Model 99 - 1959-1960. Price Range $75 - $150.
Model 99C - 1961-1978. Price Range $75 - $150.
Model 99G - 1960-1965, Marlin Glenfield. Price Range $75 - $150.
Model 60 - 1960-present, Marlin Glenfield (2000 MSR $200).
Model 99DL - 1960-1964. Price Range $75 - $150.
Model 49 - 1968-1970. Price Range $75 - $150
Model 49DL - 1971-1978. Price Range $75 - $150.
Model 99M1 - 1964-1978. Price Range $75 - $150.
Model 989M2 - 1966-disc. Price Range $75 - $150.
Model 989 - 1962-1965. Price Range $75 - $150.
Model 70 (HC) - 1966-1995, Marlin Glenfield. Price Range $85 - $160.
Model 989G - 1962-1964, Marlin Glenfield. Price Range $75 - $150.
Model 990 - disc. Price Range $75 - $150.

SHOTGUNS: BOLT ACTION

MODEL 25MG GARDEN GUN - .22 Mag. shot shell, features 22 in. smooth bore barrel with high visibility bead front sight only, 7 shot detachable mag., black synthetic stock, thumb safety, 6 lbs. Mfg. 1999-2002.

	$190	$155	$130	$110	$100	$90	$80

Last MSR was $245.

MODEL 50 DL - 12 ga. only, upland game model, 28 in. barrel bored M, black Rynite stock with molded-in checkering, 2 shot mag., 7 1/2 lbs. Mfg. 1997-99.

	$255	$195	$150	$125	$115	$100	$90

Last MSR was $330.

MODEL 55 - 12, 16, or 20 ga., 2 shot detachable mag., 26 and 28 in. full choke barrel, plain pistol grip stock. Mfg. 1950-65.

	$90	$70	$55	$40	$35	$30	$25
With adj. choke	$100	$85	$65	$50	$45	$40	$30

MODEL 55 GOOSE GUN - similar to Model 55, except 12 ga. only, 36 in. full choke barrel, 3 in. chamber, 2 shot mag., leather carrying strap and detachable swivels, walnut stock with rubber recoil pad, 8 lbs. Mfg. 1962-96.

	$235	$185	$145	$125	$115	$100	$90

Last MSR was $308.

GRADING - PPGS™	100%	98%	95%	90%	80%	70%	60%

* **Model 55 Goose Gun GDL** - similar to Model 55 Goose Gun, except has black Rynite synthetic stock. Mfg. 1997-2000.

	$330	$240	$200	$180	$160	$145	$130

Last MSR was $396.

MODEL 55 SWAMP GUN - similar to Model 55, 12 ga., 20 in. adj. choke barrel, 3 in. mag. Mfg. 1963-65.

	$105	$90	$70	$55	$50	$45	$35

MODEL 55S SLUG GUN - 24 in. barrel, cylinder bore, rifle sights. Mfg. 1974-83.

	$140	$120	$110	$95	$85	$55	$40

MODEL 59 SINGLE SHOT - .410 bore, 2 1/2 or 3 in. chamber, 24 in. barrel bored F, walnut pistol grip stock and forearm, 48,447 mfg. 1956-1965.

	$150	$125	$110	$95	$85	$55	$40

MODEL 512 SLUGMASTER - 12 ga., 3 in. chamber, bolt action, 2 shot box mag., 21 in. rifled barrel, adj. rear sight, receiver is drilled and tapped for scope mount (included), walnut finished birch stock with pressed checkering and vent. recoil pad, 8 lbs. Mfg. 1994-99.

	$295	$220	$195	$175	$160	$145	$130

Last MSR was $361.

* **Model 512DL Slugmaster** - similar to Model 512 Slugmaster, except has black Rynite stock, Fire Sights (with red fiberoptic inserts) became standard 1998. Disc. 1998.

	$310	$230	$200	$180	$160	$145	$130

Last MSR was $372.

* **Model 512P Slugmaster** - 12 ga., 3 in. chamber, features 21 in. ported fully rifled barrel with front and rear Fire Sights (high visibility red and green fiberoptic inserts), 2 shot detachable box mag., black fiberglass synthetic stock with molded-in checkering, receiver is drilled and tapped, 8 lbs. Mfg. 1999-2001.

	$315	$235	$200	$180	$165	$155	$145

Last MSR was $388.

MODEL 5510 - 10 ga., 3 1/2 in. mag., 2 shot mag., 34 in. barrel, leather carrying strap and detachable swivels, rubber recoil pad, 10 1/2 lbs. Mfg. 1976-85.

	$220	$170	$160	$150	$140	$130	$120

Last MSR was $282.

SHOTGUNS: LEVER ACTION

MODEL .410 LEVER ACTION (1929-1932 MFG.) - .410 bore, 22 or 26 in. barrel, full choke, lever action, similar to 1893, exposed hammer, plain pistol grip stock. Mfg. 1929-32 as a stockholders' promotional firearm.

	$1,400	$1,200	$950	$750	$600	$550	$475

Add 20% for 22 in. barrel.

* **Model .410 Deluxe Lever Action** - includes deluxe checkered walnut stock and forearm.

	$1,800	$1,600	$1,350	$1,100	$900	$800	$700

Deluxe forearm does not have flute in it.

NEW MODEL .410 LEVER ACTION - .410 bore, 2 1/2 in. chamber, 4-5 shot tube mag., 22 in. cylinder bore barrel, hammer block safety, checkered black American walnut stock and forend, folding rear with green fiberoptic front sight, 9 1/2lbs. Mfg. 2004-2005.

	$475	$400	$360	$320	$285	$255	$225

Last MSR was $614.

GRADING - PPGS™	100%	98%	95%	90%	80%	70%	60%

SHOTGUNS: O/U

Please refer to the L.C. Smith section for currently manufactured L.C. Smith O/U shotguns.

MODEL 90 SHOTGUN - 12, 16, 20 ga., or .410 bore shotgun or combination gun configuration (12 ga. over .30/30 barrels), 26, 28, or 30 in. barrels, boxlock, extractors, checkered pistol grip stock. Mfg. 1937-1958. Guns made from 1937-49 had vent. separated barrels, after 1949, solid barrels.

✳ *Model 90 Shotgun w/ double triggers*

	100%	98%	95%	90%	80%	70%	60%
	$475	$425	$375	$330	$290	$265	$230
.410 bore	$1,175	$1,000	$875	$775	$675	$600	$525

    Add 15% for 16 or 20 ga.

✳ *Model 90 Shotgun w/ single trigger*

	100%	98%	95%	90%	80%	70%	60%
	$625	$575	$525	$475	$440	$400	$375
.410 bore	$2,950	$2,600	$2,300	$2,000	$1,700	$1,500	$1,350

✳ *Model 90 Shotgun Combination Gun* - shotgun over .22 LR, .22 Hornet, .218 Bee, or .30-30 Win. cal., very rare, approx. 500 mfg. Mfg. 1937-1959.

100%	98%	95%	90%	80%	70%	60%
$1,350	$1,125	$950	$825	$725	$625	$550

SHOTGUNS: SxS

Please refer to the L.C. Smith section for both older and newly manufactured L.C. Smith SxS shotguns.

SHOTGUNS: SINGLE SHOT

MODEL 60 - 12 ga., 30 or 32 in. barrel, full choke, top lever, break open, exposed hammer, pistol grip stock. Approx. 3,000 mfg. 1923.

100%	98%	95%	90%	80%	70%	60%
$150	$135	$110	$90	$80	$70	$60

SHOTGUNS: SLIDE ACTION, 1898-1963 PRODUCTION

During 1998, Marlin issued a service bulletin recommending that slide action exposed hammer Models 1898, 16, 17, 19, 19S, 19G, 19N, 21, 24, 24G, 26, 30, 42, 49, and 49N, in addition to hammerless Models 28, 31, 43, 44, 53, and 63 should not be fired, as many of these guns are 70-100 years old, and system failures can and do happen.

MODEL 1898 - 12 ga., 5 shot tube mag., 26-32 in. barrels, various chokes, exposed hammer, pistol grip stock, grades differ in quality of wood and engraving on C and D. Mfg. 1898-1905.

	100%	98%	95%	90%	80%	70%	60%
Grade A	$325	$275	$225	$200	$165	$150	$140
Grade B	$580	$495	$440	$415	$360	$305	$275
Grade C	$880	$715	$635	$580	$525	$495	$440
Grade D	$1,760	$1,540	$1,320	$1,210	$1,045	$965	$880

Factory information by individual ser. no. from the Cody Firearms Museum may be available for this model in the ser. range 19,601-67,000.

MODEL 16 - 16 ga. only, 26 or 28 in. barrel, various chokes, takedown, pistol grip stock. Mfg. 1904-10.

	100%	98%	95%	90%	80%	70%	60%
Grade A	$325	$275	$225	$200	$165	$150	$140
Grade B	$495	$415	$360	$330	$305	$275	$250
Grade C	$635	$525	$495	$440	$415	$385	$330
Grade D	$1,320	$1,100	$990	$825	$715	$635	$550

MODEL 17 - 12 ga., 30 or 32 in. full choke barrel, solid frame, straight stock. Mfg. 1906-08.

100%	98%	95%	90%	80%	70%	60%
$335	$275	$235	$200	$165	$150	$140

GRADING - PPGS™	100%	98%	95%	90%	80%	70%	60%

MODEL 17 BRUSH GUN - similar to Model 17, with 26 in. cylinder bore barrel. Mfg. 1906-08.

	$325	$275	$235	$200	$165	$150	$140

MODEL 17 RIOT GUN - similar to Model 17, with 20 in. barrel. Mfg. 1906-08.

	$325	$275	$235	$200	$165	$150	$140

MODEL 19 - improved lightened version of Model 1898, matte top surface on barrel. Mfg. 1906-07.

	100%	98%	95%	90%	80%	70%	60%
Grade A	$325	$275	$235	$200	$165	$150	$140
Grade B	$495	$415	$360	$330	$305	$275	$250
Grade C	$635	$525	$495	$440	$415	$385	$330
Grade D	$1,320	$1,100	$990	$825	$715	$635	$550

MODEL 21 - straight grip version of Model 19.

	100%	98%	95%	90%	80%	70%	60%
Grade A	$325	$275	$235	$200	$165	$150	$140
Grade B	$495	$415	$360	$330	$305	$275	$250
Grade C	$635	$525	$495	$440	$415	$385	$330
Grade D	$1,320	$1,100	$990	$825	$715	$635	$550

MODEL 24 - improved 21, takedown, automatic recoil lock on slide, solid matte rib. Mfg. 1908-15.

	100%	98%	95%	90%	80%	70%	60%
Grade G	$295	$265	$225	$195	$165	$150	$140
Grade A	$325	$275	$235	$200	$165	$150	$140
Grade B	$525	$440	$385	$360	$330	$305	$275
Grade C	$660	$550	$525	$470	$440	$415	$360
Grade D	$1,375	$1,155	$1,045	$880	$770	$660	$580

MODEL 26 - similar to Model 24 Grade A, with solid frame, 30 or 32 in. full choke barrel. Mfg. 1909-15.

	$275	$230	$210	$195	$165	$150	$140

MODEL 26 BRUSH GUN - 26 in. cylinder bore barrel. Mfg. 1909-15.

	$275	$230	$210	$195	$165	$150	$140

MODEL 26 RIOT GUN - 20 in. cylinder bore barrel. Mfg. 1909-15.

	$250	$195	$180	$165	$150	$140	$120

MODEL 28 HAMMERLESS - 12 ga., 26-32 in. barrels, various chokes, takedown, matte top barrel, pistol grip stock. Mfg. 1913-22.

	100%	98%	95%	90%	80%	70%	60%
Grade A	$295	$265	$235	$200	$165	$150	$140
Grade B	$495	$415	$360	$330	$305	$275	$250
Grade C	$635	$525	$495	$440	$415	$385	$330
Grade D	$1,320	$1,100	$990	$825	$715	$635	$550

MODEL 28TS TRAP GUN - similar to Model 28, with 30 in. matte rib barrel, full choke, high comb straight grip stock. Mfg. 1915.

	$415	$330	$275	$250	$220	$195	$165

MODEL 28T - similar to Model 28TS, with fancy wood, checkering, better finish. Mfg. 1915.

	$605	$525	$495	$470	$415	$360	$305

MODEL 30 - similar to Model 16, with automatic recoil lock on slide, also mfg. in 20 ga. 1915-1917 (Model 30-20). Mfg. 1910-14.

	100%	98%	95%	90%	80%	70%	60%
Grade A	$325	$275	$235	$200	$165	$150	$140
Grade B	$495	$415	$360	$330	$305	$275	$250
Grade C	$635	$525	$495	$440	$415	$385	$330
Grade D	$1,320	$1,100	$990	$825	$715	$635	$550

GRADING - PPGS™	100%	98%	95%	90%	80%	70%	60%

MODEL 30 FIELD GRADE - similar to Model 30 Grade B, with 25 in. mod. barrel, straight stock. Mfg. 1913-17.

	100%	98%	95%	90%	80%	70%	60%
	$335	$275	$220	$180	$160	$130	$115

MODEL 31 - scaled down small ga. (16 and 20 ga.) version of the Model 28, has 26 and 28 in. barrels, various chokes, Model 31-16 was mfg. 1914-17, Model 31-20 was mfg. 1911-23.

	100%	98%	95%	90%	80%	70%	60%
Grade A	$385	$305	$250	$220	$195	$165	$140
Grade B	$495	$415	$360	$330	$305	$275	$250
Grade C	$636	$525	$495	$440	$415	$385	$330
Grade D	$1,320	$1,100	$990	$825	$715	$635	$550

MODEL 31F FIELD GUN - 25 in. mod. barrel. Mfg. 1915-17.

	100%	98%	95%	90%	80%	70%	60%
	$395	$350	$325	$295	$265	$225	$200

MODEL 42A - similar to Model 24, but lesser quality finishing. Mfg. 1922-34.

	100%	98%	95%	90%	80%	70%	60%
	$250	$220	$195	$165	$140	$120	$100

MODEL 43 HAMMERLESS - similar to Model 28, with lesser quality finish. Mfg. 1923-30.

	100%	98%	95%	90%	80%	70%	60%
	$275	$225	$200	$175	$150	$125	$100

MODEL 43TS - similar to Model 28T, lower quality.

	100%	98%	95%	90%	80%	70%	60%
	$525	$440	$415	$385	$360	$305	$275

MODEL 44A - similar to Model 31 Grade A, 20 ga. only. Mfg. 1923-35.

	100%	98%	95%	90%	80%	70%	60%
	$360	$275	$250	$220	$195	$165	$140

MODEL 44S - select checkered stock.

	100%	98%	95%	90%	80%	70%	60%
	$470	$385	$360	$330	$195	$165	$140

MODEL 49 - lower priced version of Model 42A. They were given to purchasers of 4 shares of Marlin stock. 3,000 mfg. in 1925-28.

	100%	98%	95%	90%	80%	70%	60%
	$440	$360	$305	$275	$220	$195	$165

MODEL 53 - similar to Model 43 Hammerless. Mfg. 1929-30.

	100%	98%	95%	90%	80%	70%	60%
	$330	$275	$250	$220	$195	$165	$140

MODEL 63 - similar to Model 43 Hammerless, later model. Mfg. 1931-35.

	100%	98%	95%	90%	80%	70%	60%
	$330	$250	$220	$195	$165	$140	$110

MODEL 63TS - similar to Model 43TS, with trap style stock.

	100%	98%	95%	90%	80%	70%	60%
	$385	$305	$250	$220	$195	$165	$140

MODEL 120 MAGNUM - slide action, 12 ga., 3 in. chamber, 26-40 in. barrel, takedown, various chokes, checkered pistol grip stock. Mfg. 1971-85.

	100%	98%	95%	90%	80%	70%	60%
	$290	$225	$215	$205	$195	$180	$165

Last MSR was $370.

Add 10%-15% for Model 120 MXR with 40 in. barrel (mfg. 1974-75).
Subtract $35 if without VR.

MODEL 778 - 12 ga. Mag. slide action, 20-38 in. barrels, 7 3/4 lbs. Disc. 1984.

	100%	98%	95%	90%	80%	70%	60%
	$225	$190	$175	$155	$140	$125	$110

PREMIER MARK I - 12 ga. only, aluminum receiver, takedown, manufactured in France for Marlin.

	100%	98%	95%	90%	80%	70%	60%
	$200	$180	$160	$150	$140	$120	$95

PREMIER MARK II - similar to Mark I, except with engraved receiver and checkering. Mfg. 1960-63 in France.

	100%	98%	95%	90%	80%	70%	60%
	$275	$235	$200	$175	$150	$125	$100

PREMIER MARK IV - similar to Mark II, only deluxe grade with better wood, more engraving. Mfg. 1960-63 in France.

	100%	98%	95%	90%	80%	70%	60%
	$305	$250	$220	$195	$165	$140	$110
With VR	$330	$275	$250	$220	$195	$165	$140

MAROCCHI

Current trademark established in 1922, and currently manufactured by CD Europe SRL, located in Sarezzo, Italy. No current U.S. importation. Previously imported 2005-2007 by Glenn Rea Sport Guns located in Granbury, TX, by GSI, located in Trussville, AL. Previously distributed by Precision Sales International, Inc. located in Westfield, MA.

Marocchi O/U shotguns are high quality, and currently have limited U.S. importation. Discontinued Frigon guns (manufactured by Marocchi) appear under the F section in this text.

COMBINATION GUNS

VALLEY COMBO - 12 ga. over .222 Rem. cal., 23 1/2 in. separated barrels with VR, 3 in. chamber, fold down rear sight and will accept claw scope mounts, fixed cylinder choke, DTs, engraved silver receiver, satin finish walnut Monte Carlo stock with checkering and recoil pad, 8 1/4 lbs. Disc. 1994.

$585	$480	$415	$375	$325	$295	$275

Last MSR was $700.

SHOTGUNS: O/U, 1995 & EARLIER

FIELD MASTER I - 12 ga. only, 26 or 28 in. VR barrels and rib with choke tubes, engraved coin finished receiver, extractors, SNT, checkered walnut stock and forearm. Disc. 1994.

$455	$350	$295	$260	$225	$210	$190

Last MSR was $530.

This model was imported exclusively by Sile Distributors.

* *Field Master II* - similar to Field Master I except has SST and choke tubes. Disc. 1994.

$475	$395	$325	$275	$240	$215	$200

Last MSR was $550.

SKEET MODEL - 12 ga. only, 26 in. barrels bored SK/SK. Disc. 1994.

$445	$395	$325	$275	$240	$215	$200

Last MSR was $520.

This model was imported exclusively by Sile Distributors.

TRAP MODEL - 12 ga. only, 30 in. barrels bored M/F, ejectors. Disc. 1994.

$560	$485	$415	$360	$300	$260	$230

Last MSR was $630.

This model was imported exclusively by Sile Distributors.

AVANZA - 12 or 20 (disc. 1993) ga., 3 in. chambers, monobloc boxlock action, 26 or 28 in. vent. barrels with VR (with or without choke tubes), SST, ejectors, deluxe checkered walnut stock and forearm with vent. recoil pad, high polish bluing with gold accents, all steel lightweight mfg., 6 lbs. 5 oz.-6 lbs. 13 oz. Imported 1990-95.

$775	$675	$575	$525	$475	$425	$375

Last MSR was $829.

Add $45 for 20 ga. (disc. 1993).
Subtract 10% if without choke tubes (3).

This model was imported exclusively by Precision Sales International, Inc.

* *Avanza Sporting Clays* - 12 ga. only, 3 in. chambers, built on 20 ga. frame, 28 in. vent. barrels with VR and choke tubes, select checkered walnut stock with deluxe recoil pad and forearm, gold-plated trigger, 7 lbs. Mfg. 1991-95.

$825	$725	$600	$550	$495	$450	$400

Last MSR was $889.

Add $99 for Premier Grade (disc., included select walnut and gold etched triggerguard).
This model features a trigger that is adjustable for length and pull without special tools.

GRADING - PPGS™	100%	98%	95%	90%	80%	70%	60%

SHOTGUNS: O/U, RECENT PRODUCTION

In the U.S., Conquista shotguns are identical in specifications and features to the Marocchi Classic Doubles sold in Europe, with the exception of Classic Doubles U.S.A.

GOLDEN SNIPE III FIELD - 12 ga. only, 3 in. chambers, field configuration with 28 in. VR barrels and choke tubes. Mfg. 1998-2003.

	$725	$675	$625	$575	$525	$475	$425

Last MSR was $800.

GOLDEN SNIPE III SPORTING - 12 ga. only, entry level sporting clays model with 28 or 30 in. VR barrels with choke tubes, checkered walnut stock and forearm. Imported 1999-2003.

	$850	$750	$675	$625	$575	$525	$450

Last MSR was $950.

CONQUISTA FIELD MAGNUM GRADE I - 12 ga. only, 3 in. chambers, features 28 in. 8mm VR barrels with choke tubes, nickel finished receiver, SST, checkered walnut stock and forearm with smooth rosewood buttplate, approx. 7 1/4 lbs. Imported 1999-2001.

	$1,275	$1,025	$900	$800	$700	$625	$550

Last MSR was $1,490.

CONQUISTA USA SPORTING - 12 ga. only, 3 in. chambers, features 30 in. vent. barrels with 10mm VR, muzzle porting, back boring, and lengthened forcing cones, blued barrels and receiver with gold accents, checkered standard or adj. walnut stock and forearm, approx. 8 lbs. Mfg. 1999-2003.

	$1,275	$1,025	$900	$800	$700	$625	$550

Last MSR was $1,490.

Add $100 for adj. stock.

CONQUISTA SPORTING CLAYS - 12 ga. only, boxlock action with brushed coin finish, SST, ejectors, adj. trigger, choice of 28, 30, or 32 in. 10mm VR barrels with choke tubes, right- or left-hand (Grade I only) action, checkered walnut stock and forearm with recoil pad, 7 7/8 lbs. Imported 1994-2000.

* *Conquista Sporting Clays Grade I* - features coin finished receiver with perimeter line engraving.

	$1,725	$1,450	$1,200	$1,000	$850	$700	$550

Last MSR was $1,995.

Add $125 for left-hand variation.
Add $151 for adj. stock (new 1999).

* *Conquista Sporting Clays Lady Sport* - 12 ga. only, features lighter weight specialized stock designed to fit women, cased, 7 1/2 lbs. Mfg. 1995-99.

	$1,800	$1,525	$1,250	$1,000	$850	$700	$550

Last MSR was $2,120.

Add $180 for left-hand variation (Sport Spectrum only).
Add $79 for Lady Sport Spectrum (partially colored receiver).

* *Conquista Sporting Clays Grade II* - features better walnut and game scene engraving on receiver.

	$1,995	$1,675	$1,425	$1,200	$1,000	$850	$700

Last MSR was $2,330.

Add $355 for left-hand variation.

* *Conquista Sporting Clays Grade III* - features more elaborate game scene engraving on receiver sides and fine scrollwork throughout rest of action, includes hard gun case and stock wrench.

	$3,225	$2,650	$2,250	$1,875	$1,650	$1,400	$1,175

Last MSR was $3,599.

Add $396 for left-hand variation.

GRADING - PPGS™	100%	98%	95%	90%	80%	70%	60%

✳ *Conquista Sporting Clays Grade IV* - top-of-the-line Sporting Clays model. Importation began 1997. Price available by request only.

CONQUISTA TRAP MODEL - 12 ga. only, Trap configuration, 30 or 32 (disc. 1997, reintroduced 2000) in. 10mm VR barrels with fixed chokes, 8 1/4 lbs. Imported 1994-2000.

✳ *Conquista Trap Model Grade I* - features coin finished receiver with perimeter line engraving.

	$1,725	$1,475	$1,225	$1,000	$850	$700	$550

Last MSR was $1,995.

Add $151 for adj. stock (new 1999).

✳ *Conquista Trap Model Grade II* - features better walnut and game scene engraving on receiver.

	$1,995	$1,675	$1,450	$1,200	$1,000	$850	$700

Last MSR was $2,330.

✳ *Conquista Trap Model Grade III* - features more elaborate game scene engraving on receiver sides and fine scrollwork throughout rest of action, includes hard gun case and stock wrench.

	$3,225	$2,650	$2,250	$1,875	$1,650	$1,400	$1,175

Last MSR was $3,599.

✳ *Conquista Trap Model Grade IV* - top-of-the-line Trap model. Importation began 1997. Price available by request only.

CONQUISTA SKEET MODEL - 12 ga. only, Skeet configuration, 28 in. 10mm VR barrels with fixed Skeet chokes, 7 3/4 lbs. Imported 1994-2000.

✳ *Conquista Skeet Model Grade I* - features coin finished receiver with perimeter line engraving.

	$1,725	$1,475	$1,225	$1,000	$850	$700	$550

Last MSR was $1,995.

✳ *Conquista Skeet Model Grade II* - features better walnut and game scene engraving on receiver.

	$1,995	$1,675	$1,450	$1,200	$1,000	$850	$700

Last MSR was $2,330.

✳ *Conquista Skeet Model Grade III* - features more elaborate game scene engraving on receiver sides and fine scrollwork throughout rest of action, includes hard gun case and stock wrench.

	$3,225	$2,650	$2,250	$1,875	$1,650	$1,400	$1,175

Last MSR was $3,599.

✳ *Conquista Skeet Model Grade IV* - top-of-the-line Skeet model. Importation began 1997. Price available by request only.

CLASSIC DOUBLES MODEL 92 - 12 ga. only, 3 in. chambers, sporting clays configuration featuring 30 in. vented barrels with VR, back-boring, elongated forcing cones, and three screw-in chokes, low profile blued receiver, checkered walnut stock, and Schnabel forearm, adj. trigger, gold receiver accents and trigger. Imported 1996-98.

	$1,450	$1,175	$950	$850	$775	$700	$650

Last MSR was $1,598.

MODEL 99 - 12 ga. only, 2 3/4 in. chambers, boxlock action with Boss locking system, silver grey receiver finish, SST, ejectors, adj. trigger, choice of 28 (Sporting or Skeet), 30, or 32 in. 10mm VR barrels with 5 extended choke tubes, choice of Sporting, Trap, or Skeet configuration, right-hand action only, deluxe checkered walnut stock and Schnabel forearm with recoil pad, approx. 7 1/2-8 lbs. New 2000.

GRADING - PPGS™	100%	98%	95%	90%	80%	70%	60%

∗ Model 99 Grade I

MSR N/A $2,700 $2,475 $2,050 $1,750 $1,500 $1,250 $1,000

Add $1,600 per extra set of barrels.

∗ Model 99 Grade II - features better walnut and engraving on receiver. Disc. 2003.

$2,475 $2,125 $1,725 $1,400 $1,100 $925 $800

Last MSR was $2,870.

Add $155 for gold inlays.

∗ Model 99 Grade III - features more elaborate engraving with gold inlays and wood upgrade, flush choke tubes.

MSR N/A $3,950 $3,500 $3,000 $2,500 $2,100 $1,700 $1,525

Subtract approx. $250 if w/o gold inlays.

MODEL 99 CUSTOM GRADES - 12 ga. only, 2 3/4 in. chambers, available in either Sporting, Trap, or Skeet configuration, deluxe Model 99 with best quality walnut and elaborate engraving options per model - base model is the Blackgold (non-engraved with gold line frame accents), 28, 30, or 32 in. barrels. Importation began 2000.

Please contact the company directly for more information regarding available options and pricing for the Maroccchi custom shop.

SHOTGUNS: SINGLE SHOT

MODEL 2000 - 12 ga. only, 3 in. chamber, hammer, 28 in. barrel, ejector, lightly engraved receiver. Importation disc. 1991.

$80 $70 $60 $50 $45 $40 $35

Last MSR was $94.

MARTIN, ALEX

Current trademark owned and manufactured by Dickson & MacNaughton, located in Edinburgh, Scotland.

Please contact Dickson & MacNaughton directly for more information regarding this trademark, including current availability and pricing.

MARTINI

Please refer to individual listings in the BSA Guns, Limited section.

MASTERPIECE ARMS, INC.

Previous manufacturer of derringers located in Carrollton, GA from 2000-2004.

Masterpiece Arms manufactured derringers in both steel and stainless steel configuration.

MASQUELIER S.A.

Previous manufacturer located in Belgium. Previously distributed (until 1986) by Ambel Ltd., Inc. located in Sugarland, TX.

RIFLES: SxS

CARPATHE - .243 Win., .270 Win., .30-06, 7x57R, or 7x65R cal., single shot, hair trigger, push-down cocking system. Importation disc. 1986.

$3,500 $3,200 $2,900 $2,600 $2,300 $2,100 $1,850

Last MSR was $3,850.

EXPRESS - .270 Win., .30-06, 8x57JRS, or 9.3x74R cal., O/U configuration, SST, ejectors. Add $800 for extra set of 20 ga. barrels. Importation disc. 1986.

$3,300 $3,000 $2,800 $2,600 $2,300 $2,100 $1,850

Last MSR was $3,600.

ARDENNES MODEL - top-of-the-line model, custom order only. Importation disc. 1986.

$6,600 $6,000 $5,400 $4,800 $4,300 $3,900 $3,450

Last MSR was $7,250.

GRADING - PPGS™	100%	98%	95%	90%	80%	70%	60%

SHOTGUNS: SxS

BOXLOCK - 12 ga. only, 2 3/4 in. chambers, Anson & Deeley boxlock action, ejectors, fine scroll engraving with French walnut stock. Importation disc. 1986.

	$4,400	$4,000	$3,650	$3,300	$2,995	$2,600	$2,200

Last MSR was $4,780.

SIDELOCK - 12 ga. only, 2 3/4 in. chambers, H&H style sidelocks, auto ejectors, English style fine scroll engraving with French walnut. Importation disc. 1986.

	$12,500	$10,000	$8,750	$7,600	$6,700	$5,800	$5,000

Last MSR was $15,850.

MATCHGUNS srl

Current manufacturer established during 2001, and located in Parma, Italy. Distributed in Europe by Gehmann, located in Karlsruhe, Germany. No current U.S. importation.

During 2001, Cesare Morini left Morini Competition Arm S.A. of Switzerland and started a new company, Matchguns srl, with headquarters in Parma, Italy. For more information and current pricing on both new and used Matchguns airguns, please refer to the *Blue Book of Airguns* by Dr. Robert Beeman & John Allen (also on CD-ROM and online).

PISTOLS

MG2 - .22 LR cal., innovative new semi-auto action with patented compact mechanism allowing recoil reduction of up to 50% w/o the use of counterweights or muzzle brakes, 6 in. barrel, fully adj. rear sight, fully adj. anatomical walnut grips, 5 shot mag., blue only, adj. trigger from 60 grams - 950 grams, includes case and tools, approx. 2 lbs. New mid-2002.

MSR N/A	$1,295	$1,125	$975	$850	$725	$650	$575

MG3 - .22 Short cal., otherwise similar to MG2. New 2004.

MSR N/A	$1,295	$1,125	$975	$850	$725	$650	$575

MG5 - .22 LR cal., free pistol, single shot, carbon fiber stabilizer rods with steel adjustable weights, 11 1/2 in. barrel length, adj. sights, adj. anatomical grip, importation began 2004.

Please contact the company directly for current pricing on this model.

MATCH GRADE ARMS & AMMUNITION

Please refer to MG Arms, Inc. listing.

MATEBA

Current trademark manufactured in Italy. Currently distributed by AWA USA, located in Hialeah, FL. Previously located in Pavia, Italy. Limited U.S. importation and distribution until 2004 by American Western Arms, located in Delray Beach, FL. Previously imported 2000-2001 by Keisler's Wholesale, located in Jeffersonville, IN, and by American Arms, Inc. until late 1999. Previously manufactured by Macchine Termo Balistiche located in Italy. Older mfg. has had little domestic importation.

PISTOLS: SEMI-AUTO

MATEBA M1911 - .45 ACP cal., choice of dual tone blue or hard chrome, 8 shot mag. New 2003.

MSR N/A	$1,375	$1,150	$895	$800	$675	$525	$450

GRADING - PPGS™	100%	98%	95%	90%	80%	70%	60%

REVOLVERS

MATEBA REVOLVER - various cals. (older mfg.), most recent mfg is .357 Mag./ .38 Spl., .44 Mag., or .454 Casull cal., combination semi-auto pistol and revolver, action allows cylinder and slide assembly to move back when fired, causing the cylinder to rotate, unique design permits barrel to fire lowest shell in cylinder (6 o´clock position), mechanism to rear of cylinder, single or double action, 6, 7 (older mfg.), or 8 (older mfg.) shot, 3, 4, 6, or 8 in. barrel, steel/alloy frame, blue finish, flared ergonomic walnut grips, interchangeable barrels, 2 3/4 lbs.

MSR $1,300		$1,175	$1,000	$875	$775	$675	$525	$450

    Add $100 for frame mounted scope mount
    Add $200 for .454 Casull cal.
    Add $170 for polished nickel finish.
    Add $100 for carbine variation with 18 in. barrel.

MATHELON ARMES

Current SxS rifle and drilling manufacturer located in Rumilly, France. No current U.S. importation. Previously imported by Rocky Mountain Armoury, located in Silverthorne, CO.

Mathelon Armes manufactures high quality drillings, double rifles, and stalking rifles. Current models include the MX and MX Express double rifles, the MD, MXD, MXDL, and MXT drillings, and the MXDK Kipplauf stalking rifle. Please contact the company directly for more information and current pricing (see Trademark Index).

MATRA MANURHIN DEFENSE

Please refer to the Manurhin heading in this section.

MAUNZ

Previous manufacturer located in Maumee, OH until 1987.

RIFLES: SEMI-AUTO

MATCH SERVICE RIFLE - .308 Win. cal., 22 in. barrel, M1A configuration with M1 and M14 G.I. parts, fiberglass stock, NM sights, M1 trigger assembly, 10 lbs., approx. 200 mfg.

		$2,000	$1,800	$1,500	$1,250	$1,050	$925	$800

MODEL 77 - .308 Win. cal., utilized M1A Springfield receiver initially, followed by Valley Ordnance mfg., receiver has removable lug under the barrel, red, white and blue laminated stock, ser. no. 000011-005040.

		$1,800	$1,500	$1,250	$1,050	$925	$800	$600

MODEL 87 - various cals., 26 in. medium weight barrel, synthetic stock, G.I. parts with TRW bolts, satin black finish, open sights, ser. nos. 00001-03030, 11 lbs. Mfg. 1985-89.

		$2,000	$1,800	$1,500	$1,250	$1,050	$925	$800

MAUSER JAGDWAFFEN GmbH

Current trademark established during 1871, and currently owned by San Swiss Arms AG beginning late 2000. Mauser Model 98 Magnum bolt action rifles are currently manufactured by Mauser Jagdwaffen GmbH, located in Isny, Germany. Beginning late March, 2006, Models 98 and 03 are distributed exclusively by Briley Manufacturing, located in Houston, TX. The former transition name was Mauser Jagd-und Sportwaffen GmbH. On January 1, 1999, Mauser transferred all production and distribution rights of both hunting and sporting weapons to SIG-Blaser. SIG Arms AG was purchased by San Swiss Arms AG in 2000. Mauser-Werke Oberndorf Waffensysteme GmbH continues to manufacture military defense contracts (including making small bore barrel liners for tanks), in addition to other industrial machinery.

GRADING - PPGS™	100%	98%	95%	90%	80%	70%	60%

Previously imported exclusively by Brolin Arms, located in Pomona, CA during 1997-98 only. During 1998, the company name was changed from Mauser-Werke Oberndorf Waffensysteme GmbH. During 1994, the name was changed from Mauser-Werke to Mauser-Werke Oberndorf Waffensysteme GmbH. Previously imported by GSI located in Trussville, AL, until 1997, Gibb's Rifle Co., Inc. until 1995, Precision Imports, Inc. located in San Antonio, TX until 1993, and KDF located in Seguin, TX (1987-89).

HANDGUNS: EARLY PRODUCTION

MODEL 1877 SINGLE SHOT - 9mm cal., single shot, barrel release in usual hammer position and safety on left side, examples are rare.

	100%	98%	95%	90%	80%	70%	60%
	N/A	$12,500	$9,500	$7,000	$6,000	$5,000	$4,000

MODEL 1878 "ZIG-ZAG" REVOLVER - 7.6mm, 9mm (most common) or 10.6mm cal., Zig-Zag refers to Z-pattern grooves cut into cylinder, earliest revolvers were solid frame, gate loaded, and chambered in 9mm, most were designed with a hinged frame, third and last version had an "improved" sliding release on the forward frame, most revolvers had a rust blue frame and barrel complementing a fire blue cylinder, grips were checkered or hard rubber with a floral pattern.

	100%	98%	95%	90%	80%	70%	60%
7.6mm	N/A	$5,500	$4,500	$3,000	$2,000	$1,850	$1,700
9mm	N/A	$6,500	$5,000	$4,000	$3,000	$2,250	$1,900
10.6mm	N/A	$7,500	$6,500	$5,000	$4,000	$3,000	$2,000

Add 10% for earliest pistols with "midnight blue" finish. Premiums exist for solid frame, late improved model, and factory cased guns.

PISTOLS: SEMI-AUTO, DISC.

The Models 1906-08, 1912-14, and HSv are very rare and only infrequently encountered. A competent appraisal is advisable before buying or selling these models.

MODEL 1906-08 - 9mm Export (9x25mm) cal., detachable mag., incorporates features of both the pocket pistols and Model 1896 Broomhandle. Ser. range 1-100 (est.).

	100%	98%	95%	90%	80%	70%	60%
	N/A	$45,000	$35,000	$30,000	$25,000	$20,000	$15,000

MODEL 1912-14 - generally chambered for 9mm Para. cal., similar to pocket pistol configuration, but considerably larger, earliest specimens have inscribed slide legend. Those under serial number 100 (approx.) are not slotted for shoulder stock while those over 100 are generally slotted. Ser. range 1-175 (est.).

	100%	98%	95%	90%	80%	70%	60%
	N/A	$30,000	$25,000	$22,500	$20,000	$15,000	$10,000

Add 50% if slotted with matching shoulder stock.

This variation is very rare in .45 ACP cal. or with a tangent rear sight.

WTP MODEL I VEST POCKET AUTOMATIC - 6.35mm cal., 6 shot, 2 1/2 in. barrel, blue, rubber grips. Mfg. 1922-37.

	100%	98%	95%	90%	80%	70%	60%
	N/A	$550	$425	$300	$275	$250	$225

WTP MODEL II - similar to Model I, but 2 in. barrel. Mfg. 1938-40.

	100%	98%	95%	90%	80%	70%	60%
	N/A	$950	$750	$550	$400	$300	$250

POCKET MODEL 1910 - 6.35mm or 7.65mm cal., 9 shot, 3 in. barrel, blue fixed sights, checkered walnut or hard rubber grips. Mfg. 1910-34.

	100%	98%	95%	90%	80%	70%	60%
	N/A	$550	$350	$225	$175	$150	$140

Add 30% for sidelatch variation.

POCKET MODEL 1914 - similar to Model 1910, but 7.65mm cal., 3.4 in. barrel. Mfg. 1914-34.

	100%	98%	95%	90%	80%	70%	60%
	N/A	$500	$350	$225	$175	$150	$140
Humpback Model	N/A	$3,000	$2,350	$1,800	$1,600	$1,350	$1,100

Add 10% for military acceptance proof by rear sight (Prussian eagle WWI proofs and/or crown D).

GRADING - PPGS™	100%	98%	95%	90%	80%	70%	60%

POCKET MODEL 1934 - similar to Model 1914, but reshaped grip. Mfg. 1934-39.

	N/A	$550	$350	$225	$195	$150	$140

Add 100% for Waffenamt or 50% for Nazi Police.
Add 150% for Nazi Navy marked.

MODEL HSv - 9mm Para. cal., only 2 or 3 known, similar features to Model HSc, except has larger dimensions.

Extreme rarity precludes accurate pricing on this model.

Mauser Pistols: HSc Models

MODEL HSc DOUBLE ACTION - 7.65mm (8 shot) or .380 ACP (7 shot) cal., 3.4 in. barrel, blue or nickel, fixed sights, checkered walnut grips. Mfg. 1938-disc. (most recent mfg. was by R. Gamba in Italy circa 1996).

Mauser Pistols: HSc WWII Military Mfg.

✳ *HSc WWII Military Mfg. Low Grip Screw* - very rare, first variation with ser. numbers starting at 700,000, less than 2,000 mfg.

	N/A	$5,000	$4,000	$3,250	$2,500	$1,750	$1,200

Add 20% if Navy marked.

✳ *HSc WWII Military Mfg. Early Nazi Army* - proofed 655 and 135.

	N/A	$750	$550	$350	$300	$250	$200

Add 50% for small 655 additionally test-proofed on left tang.

✳ *HSc WWII Military Mfg. Early Nazi Navy* - marked on front grip strap.

	N/A	$1,200	$900	$650	$500	$400	$350

✳ *HSc WWII Military Mfg. Early Nazi Police* - Eagle L proof only.

	N/A	$650	$500	$400	$350	$300	$250

✳ *HSc WWII Military Mfg. Wartime Nazi Army* - proof 135 and WaA 135. Eagle N proofed also.

	N/A	$600	$475	$350	$275	$250	$200

✳ *HSc WWII Military Mfg. Wartime Nazi Navy* - proofed on left side of triggerguard.

	N/A	$1,000	$850	$700	$600	$500	$400

✳ *HSc WWII Military Mfg. Wartime Nazi Police* - proofed Eagle L.

	N/A	$550	$450	$350	$325	$285	$245

Add 10% if Eagle F.

✳ *HSc WWII Military Mfg. Wartime Commercial* - standard WWII Commercial Model.

	N/A	$450	$350	$300	$275	$250	$225

✳ *HSc WWII Military Mfg. Swiss Commercial* - ser. range 800,000-900,000. Very rare.

	N/A	$1,400	$1,250	$1,125	$995	$900	$850

✳ *HSc WWII Military Mfg. Cutaways* - mfg. to visibly show mechanism. Should not be proofed.

	N/A	$1,495	$1,000	$900	$850	$800	$750

Mauser Pistols: HSc Post-WWII Mfg.

✳ *HSc Post-WWII Mfg. French Manufacture* - frequently encountered in poor condition - post-WWII production.

	N/A	$400	$350	$300	$250	$200	$175

✳ *HSc Post-WWII Mfg. Mauser Production* - .32 or .380 cal., 15 shot, mfg. 1968-81.

	N/A	$400	$350	$300	$250	$200	$175

Deduct 20% if not boxed or in .32 cal.

GRADING - PPGS™	100%	98%	95%	90%	80%	70%	60%

* *HSc Post-WWII Mfg. Interarms Import* - imported by Interarms from 1983-1985 (Mauser and Italian mfg. by Gamba).

	$350	$300	$250	$220	$180	$150	$125

Last MSR was $415.

* *HSc Post-WWII Mfg. One of Five Thousand Edition* - American Eagle edition (marked on gun), 5,000 total mfg. (serial numbered 1-5000).

	N/A	$450	$350	$300	$240	$210	$180

* *HSc Post-WWII Mfg. Armes De Chasse Import* - previously imported by Armes De Chasse located in Chadds Ford, PA on a limited basis.

	$475	$425	$330	$300	$260	$240	$220

Last MSR was $695.

Add $195 for Limited Series.
Add $58 For G15 variation (9 shot).

* *HSc Post-WWII Mfg. E.A.A. Import* - imported by European American Armory, distributed by RSR Wholesale.

	$265	$225	$195	$175	$150	$125	$110

* *HSc Post-WWII Mfg. Recent Gamba Mfg.* - .32 ACP or .380 ACP cal., steel construction, double action, double safety, stippled walnut grips, recently imported by Gamba, USA until approx. 1996, and reintroduced during 2005.

MSR N/A	$675	$375	$315	$265	$240	$220	$200

Mauser Pistols: Luger Mfg.

Both pre-war and post-war Mauser manufactured Lugers will be found in the Luger section of this book.

Mauser Pistols: P.38 Mfg.

Please refer to the P.38 entries under the P alphabetical heading.

PISTOLS: SEMI-AUTO, RECENT IMPORTATION

MODEL 80 SA - .380 ACP or 9mm Para. cal., semi-auto single action patterned after the Browning Hi-power, 4 2/3 in. barrel, blue finish with checkered walnut grips, round hammer, steel construction, 10 (C/B 1994) or 13* shot mag., 1.95 lbs. Mfg. by FEG in Hungary, imported 1992-96.

	$450	$325	$275	$240	$215	$185	$165

Last MSR was $520.

MODEL 90 DA - similar to Model 80 SA, except is double action, spur hammer, and has 10 (C/B 1994) or 14* shot mag., 2.15 lbs. Mfg. by FEG, imported 1992-96.

	$445	$325	$275	$240	$215	$185	$165

Last MSR was $516.

* *Model 90 DAC* - similar to Model 90 DA, except is compact model with 4 1/8 in. barrel, 2.05 lbs. Imported 1992-96.

	$450	$325	$275	$240	$215	$185	$165

Last MSR was $520.

M-2 - .357 SIG (disc. 2001), .40 S&W, or .45 ACP cal., short recoil operation, striker fired operating system, rotating 3.54 in. barrel lockup, manual safety, 8 (.45 ACP) or 10 shot, DAO, hammerless, aluminum alloy frame with nickel chromium steel slide, black finish, includes case and trigger lock, approx. 29 or 32 1/2 oz. Mfg. by SIG in Europe, limited importation 2000-04.

	$450	$400	$350	$300	$275	$250	$225

GRADING - PPGS™	100%	98%	95%	90%	80%	70%	60%

PISTOLS: SEMI-AUTO, MODEL 1896 BROOMHANDLES

Note: Manufactured in Oberndorf, Germany between 1897 & 1938.

While many variations of the famous 1896 Broomhandle exist, most common Broomhandles are pre-war Commercials, Model 1930 Commercials, Red 9s, and Bolos. They can be found in chronological order in this section. Holster stocks are a very popular accessory in this model. Commercial stocks may be matching or may not be serial numbered to gun (proper stock).

In 1984, Federal legislation once again allowed importation of non-domestic WWI and WWII military handguns. While many of these newer imports would make workable shooters, they have in no way lowered prices on 90%+ condition specimens due to normal collector activity in top quality only pistols. Recently imported Broomhandles should have the importer's name visibly stamped on an exterior surface.

Mauser Broomhandles: Conehammer Variations

STANDARD CONEHAMMER - 7.63 Mauser cal., distinguishable by circular machined upper hammer with concentric rings. 5 1/2 in. barrel, 23 groove wooden grips, rear adjustable sight available in 1-10, 50-500, 100-300, 50-300, 50-700 meter configurations, 10 shot mag.

N/A	$3,500	$2,750	$2,000	$1,500	$1,250	$1,000

Add 40% for matching stock.

FIXED SIGHT CONEHAMMER - 7.63 Mauser cal., similar to Standard Conehammer, except has fixed rear sight.

N/A	$4,500	$3,000	$2,500	$2,000	$1,500	$1,000

6 SHOT CONEHAMMER - FIXED SIGHT - 7.63 Mauser cal., 4 3/4 in. barrel, 6 shot mag., rare.

N/A	$8,500	$6,500	$4,500	$3,250	$2,750	$2,250

✱ *6 Shot Conehammer - Adjustable Sight* - 7.63 Mauser cal., 5 1/2 in. barrel, very rare.

N/A	$12,500	$10,000	$7,500	$5,000	$3,500	$2,500

Sales of this variation are extremely limited.

TURKISH CONEHAMMER - 7.63 Mauser cal., 5 1/2 in. barrel, 10 shot mag. Approx. 1,000 mfg. for Turkey in 1898, Farsi serial numbers.

N/A	$8,500	$6,500	$4,500	$3,500	$2,750	$2,250

"SYSTEM MAUSER" CONEHAMMER - 7.63 Mauser cal., "SYSTEM MAUSER" marked on top of chamber, improved 5 1/2 in. tapered barrel, 10 shot mag.

N/A	$15,000	$12,500	$10,000	$7,500	$5,000	$3,000

✱ *System Mauser Conehammer Stepped barrel variation* - similar to System Mauser variation, except has older 5 1/2 in. stepped barrel with no taper.

N/A	$25,000	$22,500	$15,000	$10,000	$9,000	$8,000

Add 40% for "SYSTEM MAUSER" stock.

20 SHOT CONEHAMMER - 7.63 Mauser cal., 20 shot non-detachable mag., frame can either be flatside or have milled panels, 5 1/2 in. tapered barrel, extremely rare.

N/A	$35,000	$28,500	$17,500	$12,000	$9,000	$8,000

Add 20% for milled panel variation.

Add 40% for matching stock cut for 20 shot mag.

Several restored guns have recently sold in the $10,000 range.

Many fake 20 shot pistols (especially flat side with fake stocks) have surfaced over the last few years. Use extreme caution when considering purchase.

EARLY TRANSITIONAL LARGE RING HAMMER - 7.63 Mauser cal., distinguishable by large, open centered ring, 10 shot mag., 5 1/2 in. barrel.

N/A	$3,000	$2,500	$2,000	$1,500	$1,250	$1,000

This variation is normally found in the 12,000-15,000 serial range only.

GRADING - PPGS™	100%	98%	95%	90%	80%	70%	60%

Mauser Broomhandles: Flatside Variations

Add approx. $500-$750 for matching shoulder stock, $350-$500 for non-matching stock.

ITALIAN CONTRACT FLATSIDE - 7.63 Mauser cal., distinguishable by flatside frame and DV/AV proofmarks, 10 shot mag., 5 1/2 in. barrel.

	N/A	$4,500	$2,500	$2,000	$1,500	$1,000	$700

This variation is found in the 1-5,000 serial range only.

FLATSIDE COMMERCIAL - 7.63 Mauser cal., 5 1/2 in. barrel, 23 groove walnut grips, adj. rear sight typically marked 1-10 or 50-1,000.

	N/A	$2,700	$2,000	$1,500	$1,000	$750	$500

Early specimens may have pinned rear sights. Found in serial range 20,000-30,000.

Mauser Broomhandles: Post-1900 Variations

Add approximately $1,000-$1,500 for a matching shoulder stock on the following models, $400-$550 for non-matching, depending on the original condition. Some exceptions are noted.

PRE-WAR LARGE RING BOLO - 7.63 Mauser cal., 3.9 in. barrel, floral grips, usually found in 29,000 and 40,000 serial range.

	N/A	$3,500	$2,500	$2,000	$1,500	$1,250	$1,000

Add $850 for short pre-war bolo stock, $1,500 if stock matches pistol.

LARGE RING SHALLOW MILLING - 7.63 Mauser cal., 5 1/2 in. barrel, 23 groove walnut or hard rubber grips, normally found in the 30,000-33,000 ser. range.

	N/A	$2,000	$1,500	$1,000	$950	$600	$425

LARGE RING DEEP MILLING - 7.63 Mauser cal., 5 1/2 in. barrel, 35 groove walnut or hard rubber grips, normally found in the 34,000 ser. range.

	N/A	$2,250	$1,500	$1,000	$750	$500	$400

PRE-WAR SMALL RING BOLO - 7.63 Mauser cal., 3.9 in. barrel, floral/checkered rubber or 31-36 groove walnut grips, usually found in 40,000-44,000 serial range.

	N/A	$3,000	$2,250	$1,500	$1,000	$750	$500

Add $850 for short pre-war bolo stock, $1,500 if stock matches pistol.

6-SHOT BOLO - 7.63 Mauser cal., distinctive 6 shot mag., 3.9 in. barrel, either fixed rear sight (more common) or adjustable, could have either large ring or small ring hammer.

	N/A	$6,500	$5,000	$4,000	$3,000	$2,500	$2,000

Add $850-$1,000 for short pre-war bolo stock, $1,500-$2,000 if stock matches pistol, depending on original condition.

STANDARD PRE-WAR COMMERCIAL - 7.63 Mauser cal., 5 1/2 in. barrel, 10 shot mag., 34 groove walnut or checkered black rubber grips, typically 50-1,000 meter adj. rear sight.

	N/A	$2,250	$1,850	$1,500	$1,000	$775	$650

This variation is the most commonly encountered of all M1896 broomhandles. It can be encountered in the 39,000-274,000 serial range. Early guns below serial no. 100,000 are often Von Lengerke and Detmold marked and can be encountered with hard rubber grips. Rifling changed from 4 groove to 6 groove at approx. serial no. 100,000.

Note: This model is once again being imported by domestic distributors/dealers. Condition is somewhat poor, and prices usually start in the $250 range. These specimens usually have been reblued in addition to other reworking because the original condition has generally been very poor.

MAUSER BANNER CHAMBER MARKED - 7.63 Mauser or 9mm Export/9mm Mauser (rare) cal., 5 1/2 in. barrel, distinguishable by Mauser banner trademark on top of chamber, 32 groove walnut grips. Approx. 10,000 mfg. in serial range 84,000-94,000.

	N/A	$3,500	$2,250	$1,750	$1,250	$750	$500

This model is very similar in appearance to the Pre-War Commercial.

GRADING - PPGS™	100%	98%	95%	90%	80%	70%	60%

PERSIAN CONTRACT - 7.63 Mauser cal., 5 1/2 in. barrel, distinguished by Persian lion crest in left rear frame panel, must be in the 154,000 serial range, 50-1,000 meter adj. rear sight.

	N/A	$4,500	$3,500	$2,500	$2,000	$1,500	$1,000

This variation is frequently faked - pay close attention to serial no. and Persian crest.

STANDARD WARTIME COMMERCIAL - 7.63 Mauser cal., 5 1/2 in. barrel, 10 shot mag., 30 groove walnut grips, adj. 50-1,000 meter rear sight.

	N/A	$1,875	$1,550	$1,250	$875	$700	$600

This variation is encountered almost as frequently as the Standard Pre-War Commercial. It is usually found in the 290,000-440,000 serial range. It was the first model to utilize the "new safety" design, and can be noticed by the "NS" marking on the back of hammer. Similar features as the Pre-War Commercial, except finish and polishing exhibit more machine and tooling marks.
Note: This model is once again being imported by domestic distributors/dealers. Condition is somewhat poor, and prices usually start in the $250 range. These specimens usually have been reblued in addition to other reworking because the original condition has generally been very poor.

RED-9 ADJ. SIGHT - 9mm Para. cal., 5 1/2 in. barrel, 10 shot mag., 24 groove walnut grips usually marked with large red no. 9, adj. 50-500 meter rear sight, standard WWI military contract model with separate serial range 1-150,000, generally poorly finished. Mfg. 1916-1918.

	N/A	$3,250	$2,750	$2,250	$1,750	$1,250	$850

    Add $350 for original leather.
    Add 10% if Prussian Eagle proofed on front of magazine well.
The Red-9 may be the most popular Commercial Broomhandle whose value far outstrips its rarity.
Note: Be cautious for originality since metal refinishing is prevalent in this model. The last 10,000 guns of this German military contract are not military proofed, are better polished, and will command a slight premium.

RED-9 FIXED SIGHT - 9mm Para. cal., 3.9 in. barrel, this is a 1920 commercial rework of the Red-9 military, may be dated 1920 and/or have police markings on front grip strap.

	N/A	$1,750	$1,500	$1,250	$1,000	$750	$500

Because of the Treaty of Versailles following WWI, barrels had to be shortened to less than 4 inches and the adj. rear sight removed.

FRENCH GENDARME - 7.63 Mauser cal., 3.9 in. barrel, distinguished by Bolo barrel length on large frame, hard rubber or walnut (rare) grips, found in the serial range 431,000-434,000, adj. 50-500 meter rear sight.

	N/A	$3,000	$2,250	$1,750	$1,250	$750	$500

EARLY POST-WAR BOLO - 7.63 Mauser cal., 3.9 in. barrel, short extractor, small ring hammer, usually found in the 440,000-500,000 serial range. Fit with full-size stock.

	N/A	$2,250	$1,750	$1,100	$725	$600	$500

    Add 50% for long barrel Bolos in approx. the 475,000 serial range.

LATE POST-WAR BOLO - 7.63 Mauser cal., 3.9 in. barrel, similar features of Early Post-War Bolo except has Mauser banner trademark on left rear frame panel, usually encountered in the 500,000-700,000+ serial range. Fit with full-size stock.

	N/A	$2,750	$2,000	$1,500	$1,000	$800	$600

    Add 10% for late pistols with high polish salt blue finish.

Mauser Broomhandles: Post-1930 Variations

Add approximately $1,000-$1,500 for Mauser banner marked stock, depending on original condition (should match the gun). These late stocks were not marked with a serial number.

GRADING - PPGS™	100%	98%	95%	90%	80%	70%	60%

EARLY MODEL 1930 COMMERCIAL - 7.63 Mauser cal., 5.2 (common) or 5 1/2 in. stepped barrel, 12 groove walnut grips, adj. 50-1,000 meter rear sight, usually found in the 800,000-890,000 serial range.

	N/A	$2,850	$2,300	$1,750	$1,450	$1,050	$850

This broomhandle variation had a high polish, salt blue finish. Small parts are still fire blue and milling grooves were machined in receiver rails.

LATE MODEL 1930 COMMERCIAL - 7.63 Mauser cal., 5 1/2 in. stepped barrel, similar appearance to early 1930 Commercial except has solid receiver rails and various small parts are salt blued. Ser. range 890,000-921,000 with production ending in late 1930s.

	N/A	$2,850	$2,300	$1,750	$1,450	$1,050	$850

This model is serial numbered on rear top of barrel extension assembly.

MODEL 1930 REMOVABLE MAG. - 7.63 Mauser cal., 5 1/2 in. stepped barrel, 12 groove walnut grips, adj. 50-1,000 meter rear sight, very rare.

	N/A	$18,000	$15,000	$9,000	$5,000	$4,000	$3,200

Original specimens of this variation have frames without the extra cuts required for the selector switch. Fakes are usually welded up Schnellfeuers made to look original. Only a very few are known in the 84,000-88,000 serial range.

SCHNELLFEUER (MODEL 712) - 7.63 Mauser cal., 5 1/2 in. stepped barrel, 12 groove walnut grips, adj. 50-1,000 meter rear sight, switchable full auto variation generally with selector switch, separate serial range 1-100,000, 10 or 20 shot detachable mag. 712 stock is internally grooved for selector switch.

	N/A	$6,500	$4,500	$3,250	$2,300	$1,500	$1,200

Add $750-$1,200 for correct stock.

The Model 712 is classified as a machine gun and is subject to registration and payment of a $200 transfer tax.

Broomhandle Carbines

FLUTED BARREL MODEL - marked "July 1897".

	N/A	$16,000	$12,000	$8,000	$6,000	$5,000	$4,000

FLATSIDE CONE HAMMER - 7.63mm cal., 11 3/4 in. barrel, experimental variation.

	N/A	$20,000	$15,000	$9,500	$7,500	$6,000	$5,000

FLATSIDE TRANSITIONAL - 7.63mm cal., 11 3/4 in. barrel.

	N/A	$16,500	$13,500	$10,000	$7,000	$6,000	$5,000

LARGE RING HAMMER TRANSITIONAL - 7.63mm cal., 11 3/4 in. barrel.

	N/A	$15,000	$12,500	$10,000	$8,500	$7,500	$6,500

LARGE RING HAMMER - 7.63mm cal., 14 1/2 in. barrel.

	N/A	$15,000	$12,500	$10,000	$8,500	$7,500	$6,500

SMALL RING HAMMER - 7.63mm cal., 14 1/2 in. barrel.

	N/A	$13,000	$11,000	$9,000	$7,000	$6,000	$4,500

Broomhandles: Copies from Other Countries

These pistols are Chinese manufactured copies of the original German design.

HAND-MADE MAUSER CHINESE MARKED AND OTHERS - 9mm Para. or .45 ACP cal., copies of the Mauser Broomhandle, many thousands made, fixed (.45 ACP cal.) or detachable (9mm Para.) mag., quality can vary significantly, recent imports will have import markings. IAR, Inc. imported these recently.

9mm Para.	N/A	$750	$600	$500	$400	$325	$275
.45 ACP	N/A	$1,200	$950	$740	$680	$600	$500

Add $100 for reproduction shoulder stock holster (with or w/o leather).

Subtract 25% for poor quality (QC with slave labor only goes so far).

GRADING - PPGS™	100%	98%	95%	90%	80%	70%	60%

HAND-MADE UNMARKED - poor quality.

	N/A	$750	$600	$500	$400	$300	$250

ASIATIC FLATSIDE UNMARKED - better quality, not exceedingly rare.

	N/A	$2,000	$1,750	$1,500	$1,250	$750	$500

TAKU-NAVAL DOCKYARD FLATSIDE - machine-made, better quality, not exceedingly rare, approx. 6,000 mfg.

	N/A	$2,500	$2,000	$1,500	$1,250	$750	$500

Add 30% with correct stock.
Add 5% if with holster.

SHANSEI ARSENAL .45 CAL. - .45 ACP cal., approx. 8,500 mfg., scarce and desirable in excellent condition, as most remaining original pistols are in rough condition, original stripper clips for this model are rare.

	N/A	$6,500	$5,000	$3,500	$2,500	$2,000	$1,500

Recently, a small number of currently manufactured pistols have been marketed as "restorations." Buyer beware! These newly made guns are currently priced in the $1,000-$1,500 range. Also, fake stocks have recently surfaced.

Broomhandles: Spanish Copies

VERY EARLY ASTRA-900 - Bolo grips, frame has single-line address, approx. 1,200 mfg.

	N/A	$2,750	$2,200	$2,000	$1,750	$1,600	$1,475

EARLY ASTRA-900 - single-line address, approx. ser. range 1,200-12,000.

	N/A	$2,200	$1,500	$1,100	$800	$625	$500

LATE ASTRA-900 - two and three-line address, two-line address ser. range is approx. 12,000-20,000, three-line address ser. range is approx. 20,000-34,400.

	N/A	$2,000	$1,500	$1,000	$750	$700	$525

Add 20% for Japanese character variation in the 27,000 serial range or if in Nazi procurement range.

ROYAL SEMI-AUTO - early Royals are mostly seen in semi-auto with round bolts.

	N/A	$2,750	$2,000	$1,500	$1,000	$700	$600

There were many variations of the Royals and values assume standard variation.

ROYAL SELECTIVE FIRE - 7.63mm cal., most of approx. 25,000 Royals manufactured were selective fire, several variations, Class III transferable only.

Class III	N/A	$2,500	$2,200	$2,000	$1,800	$1,700	$1,600

Add 20% if detachable mag.
Add 400% if MM34 with pneumatic rate retarder (production under 1,000 pistols).
This model had either a fixed mag. or detachable mag. May have been fit with pneumatic rate retarder.

RIFLES: MILITARY PRODUCTION

Add 20%-25% if with matching bayonet.
Subtract 50%-60% if bolt is not matching or contract crests have been removed, depending on remaining condition.

ARGENTINA

	100%	98%	95%	90%	80%	70%	60%
Model 1891 Rifle							
Argentine pattern	$800	$775	$750	$550	$500	$400	$275
Model 1891 Carbine	$750	$725	$700	$550	$450	$300	$200
Model 1909 Rifle	$900	$850	$750	$675	$550	$400	$300
Model 1909 Sniper							
Rifle w/scope	$2,300	$2,100	$1,800	$1,600	$1,525	$1,200	$1,000

GRADING - PPGS™	100%	98%	95%	90%	80%	70%	60%
Model 1909							
Cavalry Carbine	$800	$700	$600	$550	$475	$400	$300
Model 1909							
Mountain Carbine	$800	$700	$600	$550	$475	$400	$300
Model 1933 Mauser Banner	$700	$650	$550	$450	$400	$300	$250
Model 1935 Mauser Banner	$700	$650	$550	$450	$400	$300	$250
AUSTRIA							
Model 1914 Rifle	N/A	N/A	$2,000	$1,750	$1,500	$1,000	$600
BELGIUM							
Model 1889 Rifle FN mfg.	N/A	$1,750	$1,300	$950	$800	$750	$650
Model 1889 Rifle							
Hopkins & Allen	$1,750	$1,350	$950	$800	$750	$650	$575
Model 1889 Carbine							
(pre-WWI)	$850	$800	$775	$650	$575	$500	$450
Model 1889 Carbine							
(lightened)	$900	$850	$775	$650	$575	$500	$450
Model 1916 Carbine							
(all WWI makes)	$700	$650	$600	$475	$400	$350	$300
Model 1935 Short Rifle							
(FN receiver)	$700	$650	$550	$475	$425	$375	$350
Model 1935 Short Rifle							
(other receiver)	$650	$600	$500	$425	$375	$350	$300
Model 1889/36 Short rifle	$600	$500	$425	$375	$300	$250	$200
Model 50 "L" Crest	$600	$525	$475	$425	$350	$300	$225
Model 50 "B" Crest	$575	$500	$450	$400	$325	$275	$200
Model 50 Belgian							
Congo "FP" Crest	$950	$850	$750	$650	$500	$450	$375
Model 50 .22 cal.							
single shot trainer	$950	$900	$850	$750	$600	$500	$450

Add 25% for WWI German captured Belgian Mausers (rifles & carbines) converted by the Germans to 7.92mm cal. and marked with Imperial German proofs.

BOLIVIA

	100%	98%	95%	90%	80%	70%	60%
Model 1895 Rifle							
(Argentine M1891 Rifle)	$600	$550	$450	$350	$250	$200	$125
Model 1907 Rifle	$800	$750	$700	$600	$500	$400	$275
Model 1907 Short Rifle	$800	$750	$700	$600	$500	$400	$275
Czech marked Model							
VZ24 Short Rifle	$800	$750	$700	$600	$500	$400	$275
Standard Model Mauser							
Banner Short Rifle	$700	$650	$550	$425	$350	$275	$150
Model 1950 Rifle							
Series B-50	$700	$650	$550	$425	$350	$275	$150

BRAZIL

	100%	98%	95%	90%	80%	70%	60%
Model 1894 Rifle,							
Loewe mfg.	$800	$650	$550	$450	$400	$300	$250
Model 1894 Rifle, FN mfg.	$1,000	$850	$650	$550	$450	$400	$350
Model 1894 Carbine	$1,000	$850	$650	$550	$450	$400	$350

GRADING - PPGS™	100%	98%	95%	90%	80%	70%	60%
Model 1904 Mauser Vergueiro Rifle	$600	$500	$400	$300	$225	$175	$100
Model 1907 Rifle	$600	$500	$400	$300	$225	$175	$100
Model 1907 Carbine	$600	$500	$400	$300	$200	$175	$100
Model 1908 Rifle	$1,100	$1,000	$900	$800	$600	$400	$200
Model 1908 Short Rifle	$825	$775	$650	$500	$375	$250	$100
FN Mle. 1922 Carbine	$750	$650	$550	$400	$300	$225	$125
Model 1924 VZ 24 Carbine	$800	$675	$575	$450	$300	$225	$100
Model 1924/34 Czech Carbine	$800	$675	$575	$450	$300	$225	$100
Model 1908/34 Rifle .30-06 cal.	$800	$675	$575	$450	$300	$225	$100
Model 1935 Mauser Banner Rifle	$1,100	$1,000	$900	$800	$600	$400	$200
Model 1935 Mauser Banner Carbine	$1,100	$1,000	$900	$800	$600	$400	$200
Model M954 Rifle .30-06 cal.	$800	$650	$500	$375	$200	$150	$100

CHILE

	100%	98%	95%	90%	80%	70%	60%
Model 1893 Rifle - Bent bolt handle	$700	$650	$575	$475	$375	$300	$175
Model 1895 Rifle - Army	$700	$650	$590	$475	$325	$225	$100
Model 1895 Rifle - Anchor crest	$700	$650	$590	$475	$325	$225	$100
Model 1895 Short Rifle	$650	$600	$550	$425	$275	$175	$80
Model 1895 Carbine	$600	$550	$450	$325	$250	$195	$100
Model 1912 Rifle	$700	$650	$575	$495	$375	$250	$125
Model 1912 Rifle (7.62 NATO)	$700	$650	$575	$495	$375	$250	$125
Model 1912 Short Rifle	$700	$650	$575	$495	$375	$250	$125
Model 1912 Short Rifle (7.62 NATO)	$700	$650	$575	$495	$375	$250	$125
Model 1935 Carbine (7.62 NATO)	$650	$600	$550	$425	$275	$175	$80
Mauser Banner	$900	$850	$775	$650	$550	$375	$250

CHINA

	100%	98%	95%	90%	80%	70%	60%
Gew 1871 Rifle - Chinese marked	$1,100	$1,050	$925	$850	$700	$550	$300
Kar 1871 Rifle - Chinese marked	$1,100	$1,050	$925	$850	$700	$550	$300
Kar 98a Carbine	$800	$750	$700	$550	$400	$275	$225
Model 1907 Rifle - China contract	$1,000	$950	$900	$750	$500	$400	$300
Model 1907 Carbine	$1,000	$950	$900	$750	$500	$400	$300
Model 98/22 Rifle	$700	$650	$600	$475	$325	$250	$150
FN Mle. 1924 or 1930 Short rifles	$700	$650	$600	$475	$325	$250	$150

GRADING - PPGS™	100%	98%	95%	90%	80%	70%	60%
Model 21 Chinese-made VZ 24	$700	$650	$500	$400	$350	$250	$125
Std. Model 1933 Mauser Banner Rifle	$900	$850	$800	$675	$550	$425	$300
Std. Model 1933 Mauser Banner Carbine	$950	$875	$800	$675	$525	$350	$275
Chiang Kai-Shek Rifle - Chinese copy	$800	$750	$675	$550	$400	$300	$175
Chinese VZ 24 P prefix - "1937" SH. Rifle	$650	$550	$495	$350	$275	$175	$100
Chinese copy VZ 24 w/Jap. folding byt.	$1,000	$925	$800	$700	$550	$400	$300

COLOMBIA

	100%	98%	95%	90%	80%	70%	60%
Model 1891 Rifle - Argentine pattern	$800	$750	$700	$600	$450	$300	$195
Model 1912 Rifle - Steyr	$700	$600	$400	$250	$185	$150	$100
Model 1912 Short Rifle - Steyr	$700	$600	$400	$250	$185	$150	$100
Model VZ 24 Short Rifle	$700	$600	$400	$250	$185	$150	$100
Model 29 Short Rifle - Steyr	$800	$700	$550	$425	$325	$225	$175
FN Mle. 1930 Carbine	$850	$750	$700	$600	$500	$400	$350
FN Mle. 1930 Short Rifle	$600	$500	$400	$300	$275	$225	$175
FN Mle. 1950 Short Rifle (.30-06 cal.)	$600	$500	$400	$300	$275	$225	$150

COSTA RICA

	100%	98%	95%	90%	80%	70%	60%
Model 1895 Rifle	$800	$700	$575	$425	$350	$250	$125
Model 1910 Rifle	$700	$600	$495	$375	$295	$175	$100
FN Mle. 1924/1930 Short Rifle	$750	$700	$600	$500	$450	$400	$375

CZECHOSLOVAKIA

	100%	98%	95%	90%	80%	70%	60%
Model 1919 Mauser - Jelen Rifle	N/A	N/A	$4,000	$3,500	$2,800	$1,900	$1,700
Model 1921 Mauser - Jelen Rifle	N/A	N/A	$3,500	$3,000	$2,400	$1,800	$1,500
Model 98/22 Rifle	$600	$500	$400	$295	$200	$150	$90
Model VZ 23 Short Rifle	$600	$500	$400	$290	$200	$150	$100
Model VZ 23A Short Rifle	$600	$500	$400	$290	$200	$150	$100
Model VZ 24 Short Rifle	$600	$575	$500	$450	$325	$200	$100
Model 98/29 Rifle	$600	$500	$400	$275	$200	$125	$90
Model VZ 08/33 Carbine	$600	$550	$500	$450	$350	$250	$150
Model VZ 12/33 Carbine - light VZ 24	$700	$600	$500	$400	$290	$190	$125

GRADING - PPGS™	100%	98%	95%	90%	80%	70%	60%
Model VZ 16/33	$800	$700	$550	$450	$325	$250	$175
Model "JC" Short Rifle	$800	$700	$500	$400	$350	$300	$250
Model "L" SH. Rifle cal., .303, Lithuania	N/A	$1,600	$1,300	$1,000	$800	$700	$600

DOMINICAN REPUBLIC

	100%	98%	95%	90%	80%	70%	60%
M1953 Rifle - Ex-Brazil M1908	$600	$475	$275	$175	$150	$100	$75
M1953 SH. Rifle - Ex-Brazil M1908 SHR.	$600	$475	$275	$175	$150	$100	$75

ECUADOR

	100%	98%	95%	90%	80%	70%	60%
Model 71/84 Rifle	$600	$550	$350	$200	$150	$125	$900
Model 1891 Rifle - Argentine pattern	$550	$495	$400	$275	$190	$125	$85
Model 1907 Rifle	$600	$500	$400	$325	$250	$190	$150
Model VZ 23 Short Rifle	$500	$425	$325	$275	$190	$150	$90
Model VZ 24 Short Rifle	$500	$425	$325	$275	$190	$150	$90
Model VZ 12/33 Short Rifle	$500	$425	$325	$275	$190	$150	$90
FN Mle. 1930 Short Rifle	$750	$700	$600	$500	$450	$400	$375

EL SALVADOR

	100%	98%	95%	90%	80%	70%	60%
Model 1895 Rifle - Chilean pattern	$600	$550	$500	$400	$300	$180	$90
Model VZ 12/33 Carbine	$500	$450	$400	$300	$200	$125	$90
Standard Model 1935 Export	$500	$450	$350	$290	$250	$150	$90
FN M50 Israeli Short Rifle	$500	$450	$320	$260	$200	$125	$90

ESTONIA

	100%	98%	95%	90%	80%	70%	60%
Czech Model "L"Short Rifle - .303 cal.	N/A	N/A	$1,000	$825	$700	$595	$475

ETHIOPIA

	100%	98%	95%	90%	80%	70%	60%
FN Mle. 1930 Short Rifle	N/A	N/A	$1,250	$1,100	$900	$800	$650
FN Mle. 1930 Carbine	N/A	N/A	$1,350	$1,100	$950	$850	$700
Model 1933 Standard Model Rifle	$1,300	$1,200	$1,000	$800	$650	$550	$450

svw MB | ☆ FRANCE

	100%	98%	95%	90%	80%	70%	60%
Modified 98K Carbine - Hex. stacking rod	$600	$500	$400	$325	$250	$200	$150

GERMANY

	100%	98%	95%	90%	80%	70%	60%
Model 1871 Rifle - Gew 71	$1,200	$1,100	$1,000	$800	$600	$400	$300
Model 1871 Carbine - Kar 71	$1,200	$1,100	$1,000	$800	$600	$400	$300
Model 1871 Short Rifle - Jaeger 71	$1,400	$1,300	$1,200	$950	$700	$550	$400
Model 1871/84 Rifle	$1,200	$1,100	$1,000	$800	$600	$400	$175
Model 1888 Commission Rifle	$900	$850	$750	$600	$400	$275	$150
Model 1888/05 Commission Rifle	$900	$850	$750	$600	$400	$275	$150
Model 1888/14 Commission Rifle	$900	$850	$750	$600	$400	$275	$150

GRADING - PPGS™	100%	98%	95%	90%	80%	70%	60%
Model 1888							
Commission Carbine	$900	$850	$750	$600	$400	$300	$200
Model 1891 Comm. Carbine							
w/stacking hook	$900	$850	$750	$600	$400	$300	$200
Model 1888/97 Rifle	N/A	N/A	N/A	$6,000	$5,000	$3,800	$3,000
Model 1898 Rifle - Gew 98	$900	$800	$700	$600	$375	$250	$150
Model 1898 Carbine -							
Kar. 98, 16.9 in. bbl.	N/A	$6,000	$5,000	$4,200	$3,700	$3,200	$2,500
Model 1898/17 Rifle Exp.	N/A	N/A	N/A	$5,000	$4,200	$3,200	$2,500
Model 1898/18 Rifle Exp.	N/A	N/A	N/A	$5,000	$4,200	$3,200	$2,500
Model 1909 Self							
Loading Carbine	N/A	$7,500	$5,500	$4,500	$4,000	$3,500	$2,800
Model 1898A Carbine	$800	$725	$700	$600	$450	$250	$195
Model 1898AZ							
Carbine (also Model 98a)	$800	$725	$700	$600	$450	$250	$195
Model 1898b Carbine	$1,000	$950	$800	$600	$500	$350	$250
Model Gew. 98 (Trans.)	$700	$625	$550	$450	$325	$200	$150
Model K98k Carbine							
(1936-45, coded mfg.)	$895	$800	$725	$600	$400	$300	$200
Model K98k,							
Para-troop Model	$3,500	$3,200	$2,800	$2,000	$1,600	$1,200	$900
Model K98k "Kriegsmodell"	$600	$550	$500	$300	$195	$150	$100
Model 33/40							
Carbine ("945" 1940)	$1,300	$1,200	$1,100	$800	$600	$450	$300
Model 33/40							
Carbine ("DOT" 1941-43)	$1,300	$1,200	$1,100	$800	$600	$450	$300
Model 24 (T) Rifle	$875	$800	$725	$600	$450	$300	$195
Model 98/40	$775	$700	$625	$500	$350	$250	$195
Model 29 (O)							
Rifle L/W issue	$1,000	$900	$800	$875	$550	$400	$350
Model VG-1	N/A	N/A	N/A	$1,200	$900	$775	$600
G 43 Semi-Auto Rifle	$2,500	$2,200	$2,000	$1,700	$1,400	$1,100	$900
G 43 Sniper Rifle	$5,500	$4,900	$4,400	$3,800	$3,200	$2,750	$2,200
G 41M Semi-Auto Rifle	$6,000	$5,000	$4,000	$3,500	$2,600	$2,300	$2,000
G 41W Semi-Auto Rifle	$6,000	$5,000	$4,000	$2,750	$2,100	$1,800	$1,500

GREECE

	100%	98%	95%	90%	80%	70%	60%
FN Mle. 1930 Short Rifle	$750	$700	$600	$500	$400	$300	$200

GUATEMALA

	100%	98%	95%	90%	80%	70%	60%
Czech VZ 24 Short Rifle	$700	$675	$600	$425	$350	$275	$75
M1895 Rifle	$500	$450	$400	$275	$200	$125	$75

HAITI

	100%	98%	95%	90%	80%	70%	60%
FN Mle. 1950 Short Rifle	$700	$650	$575	$450	$300	$175	$100

IRAN (PERSIA)

	100%	98%	95%	90%	80%	70%	60%
Model 1895 Rifle	$600	$550	$500	$300	$200	$175	$125
Model 98/29 Rifle	$900	$850	$800	$650	$500	$300	$195
Model 98/29 Short Rifle	$875	$825	$775	$475	$360	$295	$175

GRADING - PPGS™	100%	98%	95%	90%	80%	70%	60%
Model 49 Carbine	$800	$700	$550	$400	$300	$250	$195
FN Mle. 1924 Short Rifle	$1,200	$1,100	$950	$800	$700	$600	$500
MVZ 24 Short Rifle	$900	$800	$700	$500	$375	$275	$200

IRAQ

	100%	98%	95%	90%	80%	70%	60%
Model 1948 98k Carbine	$600	$500	$400	$300	$250	$195	$100

ISRAEL

	100%	98%	95%	90%	80%	70%	60%
German 98k with Israeli marks	$600	$500	$400	$300	$200	$150	$90
Czech 98k w/ large triggerguard	$600	$550	$450	$275	$200	$120	$80
FN Mle. 1950 Short Rifle	$600	$550	$450	$425	$375	$325	$275
FN Mle. 1950 .22 single shot trainer	$850	$750	$650	$550	$500	$450	$400
Model 1954 Short Rifle	$625	$575	$450	$350	$250	$180	$125

LATVIA

	100%	98%	95%	90%	80%	70%	60%
Czech VZ 24 Short Rifle	$800	$750	$650	$500	$275	$225	$150

LIBERIA

	100%	98%	95%	90%	80%	70%	60%
FN Mle. 1930 Short Rifle	N/A	N/A	$850	$750	$650	$500	$400

LITHUANIA

	100%	98%	95%	90%	80%	70%	60%
Czech "L" Model Short Rifle (.303)	N/A	N/A	$900	$700	$600	$500	$425
Model VZ 24 Short Rifle	N/A	N/A	$900	$800	$600	$450	$325
FN Mle. 1930 Short Rifle	N/A	$1,250	$1,150	$975	$850	$750	$675
Model 1900 Rifle	$800	$700	$600	$400	$325	$275	$190

MANCHURIA

	100%	98%	95%	90%	80%	70%	60%
Mukden Arsenal Rifle	$1,500	$1,400	$1,200	$950	$800	$650	$400

MEXICO

	100%	98%	95%	90%	80%	70%	60%
Model 1895 Rifle	$550	$475	$400	$250	$190	$125	$80
Model 1895 Carbine	$550	$475	$400	$250	$190	$125	$80
Model 1902 Rifle	$1,500	$1,400	$1,300	$1,050	$925	$800	$500
Model 1907 Rifle	$600	$500	$450	$375	$300	$250	$125
Model 1910 Rifle	$500	$400	$300	$200	$175	$125	$90
Model 1910 Carbine	$500	$400	$300	$200	$175	$125	$90
Model 1912 Rifle	$700	$600	$500	$325	$275	$225	$175
Model 1912 Short Rifle	$700	$600	$500	$325	$275	$225	$175
Model 1924 Short Rifle	$700	$650	$600	$475	$300	$250	$175
Model 1924 Carbine	$700	$600	$500	$325	$275	$225	$175
Model 1936 Short Rifle	$700	$675	$600	$475	$400	$275	$195
Model 1954 Short Rifle	$675	$650	$600	$475	$425	$300	$225

GRADING - PPGS™	100%	98%	95%	90%	80%	70%	60%
MOROCCO							
FN Mle. 1950 Carbine	$650	$550	$475	$400	$350	$300	$250
w/threaded barrel for grenade launcher	$700	$650	$600	$500	$450	$375	$300
NETHERLANDS							
FN Mle. 1950 Carbine "W" crest	$900	$800	$700	$600	$500	$450	$375
FN Mle. 1950 Carbine "J" crest	$850	$750	$650	$550	$450	$400	$350
NICARAGUA							
Model VZ 12/33 Short Rifle	$700	$675	$625	$500	$400	$300	$195
Model VZ 24 Short Rifle	$600	$550	$500	$400	$300	$195	$125
ORANGE FREE STATE							
Model 1896 Rifle (OVS marked), DWM	$1,100	$1,000	$950	$825	$675	$525	$400
Model 1896 Rifle (OVS marked), Loewe & Sons	$1,000	$900	$800	$650	$525	$400	$250
Model 1896 Rifle, Chile overmark	$700	$625	$550	$425	$375	$300	$200
Model 1895 Short Rifle	$700	$650	$550	$425	$350	$275	$195
Model 1895 Carbine	$700	$650	$550	$425	$350	$275	$195
PARAGUAY							
Model 1895 Rifle	$500	$425	$295	$200	$150	$110	$75
Model 1907 Rifle (DWM)	$600	$425	$295	$200	$150	$110	$75
Model 1907 Carbine (Full-stocked)	$600	$425	$295	$200	$150	$110	$75
Model 1927 Rifle (Oviedo)	$495	$400	$275	$200	$150	$100	$80
Model 1927 Short Rifle	$495	$400	$275	$200	$150	$100	$80
Model 1927 Carbine (Full-stocked)	$495	$400	$275	$200	$150	$125	$90
FN Mle. 1930 Short Rifle	$850	$750	$650	$550	$450	$400	$350
Model 1933 Standard Model Rifle	$550	$450	$380	$320	$260	$190	$120
PERU							
Model 1891 Rifle (Lange sight)	$495	$450	$400	$300	$225	$150	$90
Model 1891 Carbine (Lange sight)	$495	$450	$400	$300	$225	$150	$90
Model 1909 Rifle	$1,200	$1,100	$1,000	$850	$725	$675	$500
Model VZ 24 Short Rifle (Model 32)	$600	$550	$500	$395	$350	$295	$195
Model VZ 32 Short Rifle (Model 32)	$700	$650	$600	$495	$375	$325	$225

GRADING - PPGS™	100%	98%	95%	90%	80%	70%	60%
FN Short Rifle Modelo 1935	$700	$650	$600	$495	$375	$325	$225
FN Carbine Modelo 1935	$900	$850	$775	$700	$550	$400	$295

POLAND
	100%	98%	95%	90%	80%	70%	60%
Model 1898 Rifle	$600	$550	$500	$395	$325	$275	$195
Model 1898 Carbine (Kar 98a)	$600	$550	$500	$395	$325	$275	$195
Model 1929 Short Rifle (Wz 29)	$800	$750	$700	$495	$425	$280	$175

PORTUGAL
	100%	98%	95%	90%	80%	70%	60%
Model 1904 Mauser-Verguiero Rifle	$700	$675	$600	$500	$425	$275	$180
Model 1937 Short Rifle	$700	$675	$600	$475	$375	$250	$175
Model 1937a Short Rifle	$700	$650	$600	$475	$375	$250	$180
Model 1941 Short Rifle	$900	$850	$800	$650	$525	$300	$200

ROMANIA
	100%	98%	95%	90%	80%	70%	60%
Model VZ 24 Short Rifle, "M" or "C" Crest	$800	$750	$650	$550	$400	$250	$125

SAUDI ARABIA
	100%	98%	95%	90%	80%	70%	60%
FN Mle. 1950 Short Rifle	N/A	N/A	$1,100	$950	$800	$700	$600

SERBIA
	100%	98%	95%	90%	80%	70%	60%
Model 1878/80 Rifle	$1,400	$1,300	$1,150	$900	$750	$600	$300
Model 1885 Cavalry Carbine	$1,250	$1,175	$1,050	$900	$750	$600	$350
Models 1886/6C and 1880/7C	$1,200	$1,100	$1,000	$850	$750	$600	$300
Model 1899 Rifle	$650	$575	$500	$400	$275	$200	$110
Model 1889/07 Rifle	$600	$525	$430	$325	$250	$125	$90
Model 1899/08 Rifle	$600	$525	$430	$325	$250	$125	$90
Model 1899C Short Rifle	$600	$525	$430	$325	$250	$125	$80
Model 1899/08 Carbine	$900	$800	$700	$600	$400	$300	$195
Model 1910 Rifle	$525	$450	$390	$300	$225	$160	$125
Model 1924 Short Rifle	$575	$500	$450	$400	$350	$300	$250
Model 1924 Carbine	$850	$700	$650	$550	$450	$400	$350

SIAM (THAILAND)
	100%	98%	95%	90%	80%	70%	60%
Model 1902 Rifle (Type 45)	$550	$450	$400	$390	$270	$195	$100
Model 1923 Short Rifle (Type 66)	$550	$450	$400	$390	$270	$195	$100

SLOVAK REPUBLIC
	100%	98%	95%	90%	80%	70%	60%
Model VZ 24 Short Rifle	$800	$700	$600	$500	$375	$300	$180

GRADING - PPGS™	100%	98%	95%	90%	80%	70%	60%
SOUTH AFRICAN REPUBLIC							
Model 1896 Rifle							
"ZAR" marked $1,100	$1,025	$950	$775	$600	$400	$195	
SPAIN							
Model 1891 Rifle	$800	$750	$700	$550	$400	$300	$250
Model 1892 Rifle	$1,300	$1,225	$1,100	$950	$800	$650	$500
Model 1892 Carbine	$750	$700	$600	$500	$375	$295	$195
Model 1893 Rifle	$750	$700	$600	$500	$375	$295	$195
Model 1895 Carbine (Full-stocked)	$700	$625	$575	$495	$375	$295	$195
Model 1916 Short Rifle	$600	$525	$475	$400	$325	$225	$180
Model 1916 Experimental 8mm	$750	$700	$625	$450	$375	$295	$190
Model 1943 Short Rifle	$500	$425	$350	$275	$195	$125	$75
SWEDEN							
Model 1894 Carbine	$750	$700	$650	$600	$480	$390	$275
Model 1896 Rifle	$600	$500	$400	$300	$220	$185	$120
Model 1938 Short Rifle	$600	$500	$400	$300	$200	$125	$80
Model 1940 Short Rifle (8mm)	$800	$700	$650	$500	$375	$295	$225
SYRIA							
Model 1948 Carbine	$500	$400	$325	$275	$200	$120	$80
TURKEY							
Model 1887 Rifle	$1,500	$1,400	$1,300	$1,100	$900	$700	$500
Model 1887 Carbine	$1,500	$1,400	$1,300	$1,100	$900	$700	$500
Model 1890 Rifle	$1,200	$1,150	$1,000	$900	$775	$625	$500
Model 1893 Rifle	$1,300	$1,225	$1,050	$900	$775	$675	$500
Model 1903 Rifle 7.65mm	$1,200	$1,150	$1,000	$900	$700	$550	$400
Model 1905 Carbine	$1,200	$1,150	$1,000	$900	$700	$500	$350
Model VZ 98/22 Rifle	$600	$500	$400	$250	$190	$125	$90
Model 1888 Rifle (Turkish marked)	$500	$400	$250	$200	$140	$90	$70
Model 1888/38 Rifle (improved)	$500	$400	$250	$200	$140	$90	$70
Model 1938 Rifle 8mm	$500	$400	$250	$200	$140	$90	$60
Model 1938 Short Rifle	$500	$400	$250	$200	$140	$90	$60
URUGUAY							
FN Mle. 1895 Rifle	$900	$850	$775	$600	$400	$250	$125
Model 1904 Rifle	$700	$625	$550	$400	$325	$260	$200

GRADING - PPGS™	100%	98%	95%	90%	80%	70%	60%
Model 1908 Rifle	$800	$700	$600	$450	$400	$300	$200
Model 1980 Short Rifle	$700	$600	$500	$450	$400	$300	$200
Czech VZ 32 Short Rifle (Model 1934)	$800	$700	$600	$500	$290	$200	$120
Czech VZ 24 Short Rifle (Model 1934)	$800	$700	$600	$500	$390	$275	$195
FN Mle. 1930 Short Rifle	$675	$575	$500	$450	$400	$350	$300
VENEZUELA							
Model 1910 Rifle	$500	$425	$350	$290	$240	$130	$90
Czech VZ 24/26 Short Rifle	$600	$500	$450	$375	$300	$225	$160
FN Mle. 1930 or 1950 Short Rifle	$800	$700	$600	$500	$400	$300	$150
FN Mle. 1930 or 1950 Carbine	$800	$700	$600	$500	$400	$300	$150
YEMEN							
FN Mle 1930 Short Rifle	N/A	N/A	$900	$800	$650	$550	$450
YUGOSLAVIA							
FN Mle 1924 Short Rifle	$600	$550	$450	$375	$295	$225	$160
FN Mle. 1924 Carbine	$700	$650	$600	$475	$395	$295	$195
Czech VZ 24 Short Rifle	$600	$550	$450	$375	$250	$175	$115
Model 1924 Short Rifle (Kragujevac)	$600	$550	$450	$375	$250	$175	$115
M90T Short Rifle (ex-Turkish M1890)	N/A	$800	$700	$500	$400	$250	$150
Model M24B Rifle (ex-Mexican M1912)	N/A	$800	$700	$500	$400	$250	$150

RIFLES: BOLT ACTION, 1898-1946 COMMERCIAL MFG.

Approx. 125,000 commercial sporting Mausers were built between 1898 and 1946. Three action lengths; overall measurements: Short (Kurz) 8 1/4 in., Standard 8 3/4 in., and Magnum 9 1/4 in. Optional squarebridge receiver rings for custom sight mounting. Innumerable variations of triggers, barrels, sights and checkering.

    Add $350-$550 for conversion unit.
    Add 50% for single square bridge action.
    Add 100% for double square bridge action.
    Add 100% for Short (Kurz) action, except on Type K below.
    Add 100% for Magnum action, except on African Type below.

SPECIAL RIFLE, TYPE A - expressly made for English market, superior finish, with round tapered barrel, silver-bead front sight on sleeved-on block with matted surface, hinged floorplate, pear shaped bolt knob, horn forend tip and PG cap, sling eyes.

    $5,500 $5,000 $4,000 $3,000 $2,000 $1,500 $1,200

NORMAL RIFLE, TYPE B - 24 in. barrel, steel-capped PG, Schnabel forend, sling swivels, pear shaped bolt knob, hinged floorplate.

    $4,750 $4,250 $3,500 $2,650 $1,750 $1,250 $1,000

GRADING - PPGS™	100%	98%	95%	90%	80%	70%	60%

LIGHT SHORT RIFLE, TYPE K - 6.5x54 Mauser, 8x51mm, or .250-3000 Savage cal., short action, 22 in. barrel, steel PG cap, sling swivels, pear shaped bolt knob, hinged floorplate, hard rubber buttplate.

$6,000	$5,000	$4,000	$3,000	$2,500	$2,000	$1,650

CARBINE, TYPE S - 20 or 24 in. barrel stocked to muzzle, steel PG cap, horn buttplate, sling swivels, pear shaped bolt knob, hinged floorplate.

$4,250	$3,675	$3,100	$2,500	$2,000	$1,500	$1,250

CARBINE, TYPE M - 20 in. barrel stocked to muzzle with steel forend cap, steel PG cap, trapdoor steel buttplate holding sectional cleaning rod, butterknife bolt handle, hinged floorplate.

$5,500	$5,000	$4,500	$4,000	$3,500	$3,000	$2,500

MILITARY SPORTING RIFLE, TYPE C - stepped round barrel, spherical bolt knob, half grip, banner Mauser imprint in side of buttstock.

$1,750	$1,550	$1,325	$1,100	$900	$750	$600

AFRICAN TYPE - 28 in. round barrel, stocked to 4 in. from muzzle, Magnum action, pear shaped bolt knob.

$8,000	$7,000	$6,000	$4,000	$3,000	$2,500	$2,000

RIFLES: BOLT ACTION, RECENT PRODUCTION

During April, 2001, SIG-Blaser completed the purchase of the production and distribution rights for Mauser sporting and hunting weapons.

Add $150 for double set triggers on all current models.

MODEL 03 - various cals. between .222 Rem. - .375 H&H, Mauser square bridge action with safety/cocking lever on rear of breech bolt, interchangeable barrels, manual cocking, Combi-trigger can be used as single stage or set trigger, synthetic or wood stock (Grades 2-11, 2 is standard), 60 degree bolt lift, detachable mag., open sights standard (elevated rear sight at mid-barrel), Mauser double square bridge scope mount, approx. 7 3/4 lbs. New 2005. Mfg. by Blaser in Isny, Germany.

MSR $3,395	$2,995	$2,600	$2,250	$1,850	$1,500	$1,275	$1,050

Add $225 for Mag. cals. Add $500 for left hand action. Add $1,100 for Arabesque grade with Grade 4 wood and engraving. Add $2,800 for Deluxe grade with Grade 5 wood, elaborate engraving with animal motifs. Add $450 or $675 (.300 Win. Mag. cal.) for match grade rifle. Add $1,350 for Africa rifle. Add $1,350 for Africa rifle. Add $900 per interchangeable standard cal. barrel. Add $1,130 per standard Mag. cal. barrel. Add $695 per bolt assembly, and/or $225 per bolt head. Current MSR for Old Classic Grade with Old World metal finishing and Grade 6 wood is $7,095.

Beginning late 2006, Mauser began grading wood between grades 2-11. Grade 2 is standard wood, and the following additional charges apply to the additional wood upgrades: Grade 3 - $300, Grade 4 - $500, Grade 5 - $1,130, Grade 6 - $2,060, Grade 7 - $3,090, Grade 8 - $4,520, Grade 9 - $6,215, Grade 10 - $7,910, Grade 11 - approx. $9,000.

MODEL 66A - similar to Model 66S except has American configured laminate stock (wood grain), cals., action, and features are the same as the Model 66S. Imported 1988-89 only.

✳ *Model 66A Standard Calibers*

$1,900	$1,425	$1,150	$925	$800	$700	$650

Last MSR was $2,100.

Add $630 per interchangeable barrel.
The "A" suffix on this model denotes American.

✳ *Model 66A Magnum Calibers* - includes Weatherby Mag. cals. also.

$2,050	$1,500	$1,200	$975	$825	$700	$650

Last MSR was $2,270.

Add $670 per interchangeable barrel.

GRADING - PPGS™	100%	98%	95%	90%	80%	70%	60%

✳ *Model 66A Big Game Calibers* - includes most popular Mag. cals. up to .458 Win. Mag.

	100%	98%	95%	90%	80%	70%	60%
	$2,350	$1,900	$1,425	$1,150	$950	$825	$750

Last MSR was $2,700.

MODEL 66S STANDARD - telescoping short action, 5.6x57mm, 6.5x57mm, 7x57mm Mauser (disc. 1992), 7x64mm, 9.3x62mm, .243 Win., .270 Win., .30-06, or .308 Win. cal., 24 in. barrel, standard interchangeable barrels, single or double set triggers, adj. and detachable sights, Monte Carlo walnut stock with checkering, swivels, new safety, rosewood tipped forearm and pistol grip, rubber recoil pad, 7 1/2 lbs. Mfg. 1974-95.

	100%	98%	95%	90%	80%	70%	60%
	$2,350	$1,275	$995	$875	$775	$695	$625

Last MSR was $2,722.

✳ *Model 66 Standard Magnum* - 28 in. barrel, 6.5x68mm, 8x68S, 9.3x64mm, 7mm Rem. Mag., .300 Win. Mag., or .300 Wby. Mag. cal., 7.9 lbs. Disc. 1995.

	100%	98%	95%	90%	80%	70%	60%
	$2,500	$1,325	$1,050	$900	$795	$695	$625

Last MSR was $2,925.

✳ *Model 66 Standard Carbine (Stutzen-Mannlicher)* - .243 Win., .270 Win., .30-06, 7x64mm, or 9.3x62mm cal., 21 in. barrel, full-stock (Mannlicher only) and half-stock (disc. in 1989), double or single triggers, 7 1/2 lbs. Disc. 1995.

	100%	98%	95%	90%	80%	70%	60%
	$2,500	$1,325	$1,050	$900	$795	$695	$625

Last MSR was $2,925.

This model was available in a half-stock "Ultra" variation until 1989. Values are similar to those listed.

✳ *Model 66S Standard Diplomat* - similar cals. as the Model 66S Standard, except not available in 5.6x57mm, similar features, except includes selected walnut and special engraving including deer and wild boar game scenes. Disc. 1995.

	100%	98%	95%	90%	80%	70%	60%
	$4,650	$3,850	$3,350	$2,750	$2,250	$1,850	$1,400

Last MSR was $5,317.

Add $390 for Mag. cals. (similar to Model 66S Magnum).

✳ *Model 66 Standard Safari/Big Game* - .375 H&H or .458 Win. Mag. cal., single trigger, 9.3 lbs. Disc. 1995.

	100%	98%	95%	90%	80%	70%	60%
	$2,950	$1,850	$1,350	$1,025	$875	$775	$650

Last MSR was $3,487.

MODEL 66SM - telescoping short action, .243 Win. (disc.), .270 Win., 7x57mm Mauser (disc.), 7x64mm, .308 Win., .30-06, or 6.5x57mm cal. (disc.), 24 in. barrel, standard interchangeable barrels, set trigger, adj. and detachable sights, Monte Carlo walnut stock with checkering, swivels, new safety, anatomical gripped select walnut stock with Mauser-nose, cocking lever on tang, rubber recoil pad, 7 1/4 lbs. Importation 1981-95.

	100%	98%	95%	90%	80%	70%	60%
	$2,875	$1,800	$1,325	$1,025	$875	$775	$650

Last MSR was $3,398.

✳ *Model 66SM Ultra* - all standard cals., 21 in. barrel, 7 1/4 lbs.

	100%	98%	95%	90%	80%	70%	60%
	$1,625	$1,325	$1,140	$920	$760	$650	$550

Last MSR was $1,903.

✳ *Model 66SM Magnum* - cals. similar to Model 66S Magnum, except not available in 9.3x64mm cal., 26 in. barrel, 8.4 lbs. Disc. 1995.

	100%	98%	95%	90%	80%	70%	60%
	$3,025	$1,925	$1,375	$1,025	$875	$775	$650

Last MSR was $3,578.

✳ *Model 66SM Diplomat* - similar cals. as the Model 66SM Standard, similar features, except includes selected walnut and special engraving including deer and wild boar game scenes. Disc. 1995.

	100%	98%	95%	90%	80%	70%	60%
	$5,075	$3,975	$3,450	$2,775	$2,250	$1,850	$1,400

Last MSR was $5,943.

Add $382 for Mag. cals. (similar to Model 66SM Magnum).

GRADING - PPGS™	100%	98%	95%	90%	80%	70%	60%

✳ *Model 66SM Carbine (Mannlicher type full stock)* - .30-06 cal., 21 in. barrel, 7 lbs. Disc. 1995.

	$3,025	$1,925	$1,375	$1,025	$875	$775	$650

Last MSR was $3,578.

These models were previously available on a custom order only basis through KDF, Inc. located in Seguin, TX.

MODEL 66SL - similar to Model 66SM, except features extra select walnut with special graining, 7 1/4 lbs. Disc. 1985.

	$1,370	$1,275	$890	$720	$580	$475	$420

Last MSR was $1,470.

✳ *Model 66SL Ultra* - 7x64mm or .30-06 cal., 21 in. barrel, 7 1/4 lbs. Disc. 1985.

	$1,475	$1,325	$940	$750	$600	$450	$400

Last MSR was $1,520.

✳ *Model 66SL Magnum Calibers* - similar to Model 66 S, 8.4 lbs. Disc. 1985.

	$1,475	$1,325	$940	$750	$600	$450	$400

Last MSR was $1,520.

✳ *Model 66SL Mannlicher Type Full Stock* - 21 in. barrel, 7 lbs. Disc. 1985.

	$1,475	$1,325	$940	$750	$600	$450	$400

Last MSR was $1,520.

MODEL 66SL DIPLOMAT - same specifications as Model 66SM, except includes selected walnut and special engraving including deer and wild boar game scenes.

Add $93 for Mannlicher full-stock (21 in. barrel).

Add $387 for Mag. cals.

This model was available on an individual custom order basis only. The last published retail price (1988) for a standard model without options was $3,167.

MODEL 660 - U.S. designation of 66S. Imported 1971-73.

	$925	$820	$720	$600	$500	$450	$400

MODEL 66S DELUXE - special order engraved and inlaid, select wood. Priced per individual customer order. All guns are custom made only.

MODEL 66P - imported 1995 only.

	$4,250	$3,575	$3,075	$2,600	$2,075	$1,700	$1,375

Last MSR was $4,888.

MODEL 66SP SUPER MATCH - .300 Win. Mag. or .308 Win. cal., telescoping short action, 27 1/2 in. heavy barrel with muzzle brake, no sights, match trigger, 3 shot mag., select European walnut stock with stippling and thumbhole, adj. cheekpiece and buttplate, includes premium scope, 12 lbs. Never imported domestically.

	$4,150	$3,500	$3,050	$2,600	$2,075	$1,700	$1,375

Last MSR was $4,737.

MODEL 77 - .243 Win., .270 Win., 6.5x57mm, 7x64mm, .308 Win., or .30-06 cal., 24 in. barrel, set trigger on tang, adj. and detachable sights, walnut stock with European cheekpiece and hand checkering, swivels, new safety, steel detachable box mag., rubber recoil pad, 7 1/4 lbs. Disc.

	$1,130	$950	$875	$810	$750	$675	$595

Last MSR was $1,331.

✳ *Model 77 Ultra* - 6.5x57mm, 7x64mm or .30-06 cal., 20 in. barrel, 7.7 lbs. Disc.

	$1,175	$975	$895	$835	$760	$675	$595

Last MSR was $1,394.

✳ *Model 77 Magnum Calibers* - similar to Model 66S, 8 1/8 lbs. Disc.

	$1,175	$975	$895	$835	$760	$675	$595

Last MSR was $1,394.

GRADING - PPGS™	100%	98%	95%	90%	80%	70%	60%

✳ *Model 77 Mannlicher type full stock* - 20 in. barrel, Mauser-set trigger, 7.7 lbs. Disc.

	$1,175	$975	$895	$835	$760	$675	$595

Last MSR was $1,394.

✳ *Model 77 Big Game Model* - .375 H&H cal., 26 in. barrel, 8 1/8 lbs. Disc.

	$1,075	$1,000	$900	$795	$675	$575	$475

Last MSR was $1,150.

MODEL 77 SPORTSMAN - .243 Win. or .308 Win. cal., sports version of the Model 77, set trigger on tang, no sights, 24 in. barrel, 9 lbs. Disc.

	$1,495	$1,230	$1,075	$985	$895	$820	$740

Last MSR was $1,754.

Add $430 for Zeiss 2 1/2-10X scope and mounts.

MODEL 83 MATCH SINGLE SHOT - .308 Win. cal. only, cylinder locking action with 3 locking lugs in rear, match trigger, anatomical match stock with select walnut, adj. comb and buttplate. Disc.

	$2,170	$1,815	$1,660	$1,545	$1,400	$1,195	$925

Last MSR was $2,594.

This model is a UIT standard rifle for 300-meter competition.

MODEL 83 MATCH UIT FREE RIFLE - .308 Win. cal. only, cylinder locking action with 3 locking lugs in rear, match trigger, anatomical match stock with select walnut, adj. comb and buttplate. Disc.

	$2,320	$1,940	$1,760	$1,600	$1,430	$1,195	$925

Last MSR was $2,771.

MODEL 83 STANDARD RIFLE - similar to Model 83 Match, except has removable 10 shot steel mag., 26 in. barrel. Disc.

	$2,320	$1,950	$1,800	$1,625	$1,460	$1,250	$1,000

Last MSR was $2,766.

MODEL 86 LAMINATED/FIBERGLASS (SR) - .308 Win. cal., updated version of the Model 83 action, 25.6 (disc.) or 28 3/4 (new 1997) in. fluted barrel with muzzle brake, black laminate wood (with thumbhole) or fiberglass (disc.) stock with rail in forearm, adj. trigger, 9 shot detachable mag., cased, 10.8 lbs. Imported 1989-1996, recent mfg. included a 2 1/2-10X power Zeiss tactical scope with detachable mount.

	$10,750	$8,900	$7,700	$6,500	$5,500	$4,500	$3,500

Last MSR was $11,795.

MODEL SR 93 - .300 Win. Mag. cal., precision rifle employing skeletonized cast magnesium/aluminum stock, combination right-hand/left-hand bolt, adj. ergonomics, 27 in. fluted barrel with muzzle brake, integrated bipod, 4 or 5 shot mag., approx. 13 lbs. without accessories. Disc. 1996.

	$20,000	$17,250	$14,750	$11,950	$8,700	$6,500	$5,000

Last MSR was $21,995.

MODEL 94 - .243 Win., .270 Win., .30-06, .308 Win., .300 Win. Mag., 7x64mm, 7mm Rem. Mag., 8x68S (disc. 1996), or 9.3x62 Mag. cal., 22 or 24 in. interchangeable barrel, aluminum block in stock bedding system, 60 degree bolt, 6 lug locking system, checkered walnut stock and forearm, 3 or 4 shot mag., lateral slide safety, approx. 7 1/4 lbs. Mfg. began 1994, U.S. importation was disc. 1995, resumed 1997 only.

	$1,925	$1,550	$1,325	$1,100	$925	$850	$775

Last MSR was $2,295.

Add $799 per interchangeable barrel assembly.

MODEL 96 - .25-06 Rem. (new 1997), .270 Win., .30-06, .308 Win. (new 1997), 7x64mm (new 1997), .300 Win. Mag. (new 1997), or 7mm Rem. Mag. (new 1997) cal., 16 lug bolt slides straight back allowing for low scope mounts, 22 or 24 (Mag. cals., new 1997) in. barrel, safety mechanism in bolt in addition to rear 3-position tang safety, checkered walnut stock, 4 (Mag. cals., new 1997) or 5 shot top loading mag., w/o sights, 6 1/4 lbs. Imported 1996-97.

	$625	$550	$500	$450	$400	$360	$330

Last MSR was $699.

MODEL 98 COMMERCIAL - various cals., features original breech mechanisms refurbished to new condition, barrel, trigger system, and stock are new from factory.

This model was mostly distributed in Europe with no domestic MSR.

MODEL 1898 COMMEMORATIVE - 8x57mm Mauser cal., special limited edition model mfg. to commemorate the 100th anniversary of the original M-98, bright royal blue on most major metal parts, bolt and receiver have silver satin finish, checkered select European walnut. 1,998 mfg. 1998 only.

	$2,175	$1,775	$1,500	N/A	N/A	N/A	N/A

Last MSR was $2,300.

MODEL 98 STANDARD/MAGNUM SAFARI - various cals. from .22-250 Rem-9.3x64mm, Safari cals include .375 H&H (disc. 2002, reintroduced 2004), .338 Lapua (new 2004), .416 Rigby, .450 Dakota (new 2001), .458 Lott (new 2001), or .500 Jeffrey (new 2001) cal., 3-5 shot mag., original M-98 Magnum square bridge action with 3 lugs, Model 70 style wing safety, folding express sights (Safari model only), 24 in. barrel, features custom workmanship, extra select checkered walnut stock, 8.8 lbs., delivery time is approx. 8-12 months. Limited mfg. beginning 1998.

MSR $12,400		$10,800	$9,000	$7,750	$5,850	$4,500	$3,750	$3,000

Add $1,400 for Magnum Safari, or $2,400 for Magnum Safari in .500 Jeffrey cal.

MODEL 99 - 5.6x57mm, 6.5x57mm, 7x57mm, 7x64mm, .243 Win., .25-06 Rem., .270 Win., .30- 06 or .308 Win. cal., bolt action with 60 degree throw, 24 in. free-floating barrel, jeweled bolt, available in either hand-rubbed oil or high-luster lacquer finish for stock, mini-claw extractor, adj. single stage trigger, 4 shot detachable mag., no sights, 8 lbs. Imported 1989-disc.

✻ *Model 99 Classic Lacquer Finish* - high-luster lacquer finish for stock.

	$1,110	$925	$850	$775	$700	$625	$550

Last MSR was $1,272.

This model was available with either a Schnabel forearm with regular stock or rosewood capped forearm with American Monte Carlo stock.

✻ *Model 99 Classic Oil Finish* - hand rubbed oil finish for stock. Disc.

	$1,130	$995	$875	$775	$700	$625	$550

Last MSR was $1,130.

This model was available with either a Schnabel forearm with regular stock or rosewood capped forearm with American Monte Carlo stock.

MODEL 99 MAGNUM - 8x68S, 9.3x64mm, 7mm Rem. Mag., .257 Wby. Mag., .270 Wby. Mag., .300 Wby. Mag., .300 Win. Mag., .338 Win. Mag., or .375 H&H cal., similar specifications as Model 99, except has 26 in. barrel and 3 shot mag. Imported 1989-disc.

✻ *Model 99 Magnum Classic Lacquer Finish* - high-luster lacquer finish for stock.

	$1,135	$950	$875	$775	$700	$625	$550

Last MSR was $1,322.

This model was available with either a Schnabel forearm with regular stock or rosewood capped forearm with American Monte Carlo stock.

GRADING - PPGS™	100%	98%	95%	90%	80%	70%	60%

✱ *Model 99 Magnum Classic Oil Finish* - hand-rubbed oil finish for stock.

	$1,025	$895	$795	$725	$625	$550	$495

Last MSR was $1,180.

This model is available with either a Schnabel forearm with regular stock or rosewood capped forearm with American Monte Carlo stock.

MODEL 225 - available in 13 cals. between .243 Win. and .300 Wby. Mag., bolt action, 60 degree bolt lift with 3 locking lugs, ultra fast lock time, adj. trigger, 24 or 26 (Mag. only) in. barrel, 3 or 5 shot mag., no sights, guaranteed 1/2 in. accuracy at 100 yards, many stock options available at extra cost.

✱ *Model 225 Deluxe Standard Sporter* - standard model available in 6 regular cals. and 9 Mag. cals. Importation disc. 1989.

	$1,275	$1,000	$875	$750	$625	$550	$495

Last MSR was $1,400.

Add $90 for Mag. cals.

This model was formerly the KDF Model K-15.

MODEL 226 - left-handed variation of the Model 225 with slight changes. Disc. 1989.

	$1,275	$1,000	$875	$750	$625	$550	$495

Last MSR was $1,400.

MODEL 2000 (DISC.) - .270 Win., .308 Win., or .30-06 cal., 5 shot mag., 24 in. barrel, leaf rear sight, checkered walnut stock. Mfg. by F.W. Heym for Mauser, 1969-71.

	$495	$475	$450	$400	$375	$350	$325

MODEL 2000 CLASSIC - .270 Win., .30-06, .308 Win., .300 Win. Mag., or 7mm Rem. Mag. cal., features new design allowing interchangeable calibers from standard to standard and Magnum to Magnum models, bolt locks directly into barrel, detachable mag., deluxe walnut stock with checkering and rosewood forend, double function set trigger, high polish blue, includes studs. Limited importation 1998 only.

	$1,595	$1,375	$1,125	$950	$825	$700	$575

Last MSR was $1,800.

✱ *Model 2000 Classic Varmint* - .22-250 Rem. or .243 Win. cal., choice of black synthetic or special varmint wood stock with accessory rail, heavy fluted barrel. Limited importation 1998 only.

	$1,900	$1,550	$1,350	$1,100	$900	$775	$650

Last MSR was $2,200.

✱ *Model 2000 Classic Sniper* - .300 Win. Mag. or .308 Win. cal., features heavy fluted barrel, special set trigger system, bipod rail, and other special shooting performance features, satin blue metal finish, custom built with individual certificate. Limited importation 1998 only.

	$1,900	$1,550	$1,350	$1,100	$900	$775	$650

Last MSR was $2,200.

✱ *Model 2000 Classic Professional* - .300 Win. Mag. or .308 Win. cal., features recoil reduction compensator, camo all-weather special pistol grip stock, satin blue metal finish, custom built with individual certificate. Limited importation 1998 only.

	$3,175	$2,725	$2,400	$2,100	$1,800	$1,500	$1,250

Last MSR was $3,500.

MODEL 3000 - .243 Win., .270 Win., .308 Win., or .30-06 cal., 5 shot mag., 22 in. barrel, no sights, walnut Monte Carlo style stock, rosewood forearm and pistol grip, skipline checkering, recoil pad and swivels. Mfg. 1971-74.

	$525	$475	$450	$425	$395	$335	$285

GRADING - PPGS™	100%	98%	95%	90%	80%	70%	60%

MODEL 3000 MAGNUM - similar to 3000, except 7mm Rem. Mag., .300 Win. Mag., or .375 H&H cal., 3 shot mag., 26 in. barrel.

	$575	$525	$475	$450	$415	$350	$295

This model was mfg. by Heym for Mauser.

MODEL 4000 VARMINT RIFLE - similar to 3000, except smaller action, .222 Rem. or .223 Rem. cal., folding leaf rear sight, rubber buttplate.

	$425	$400	$375	$350	$300	$260	$225

This model was mfg. by Heym for Mauser.

LIGHTNING MODEL - .308 Win. or 7.62x39mm cal., slide-bolt action, locking bolt similar to M-16 enabling locking directly onto free floating short barrel, fixed internal mag., specially bedded receiver, satin blue finish or stainless steel, open sights, synthetic stock available in black, light grey, blue, or NATO green. Limited importation 1998 only.

	$495	$425	$375	$325	$295	$275	$250

Last MSR was $550.

LIGHTNING HUNTER MODEL - .243 Win., .270 Win., .30-06, .308 Win., .300 Win. Mag., or 7mm Rem. Mag. cal., slide-bolt mechanism, detachable mag., choice of satin blue or bright blue metal finish, checkered satin or high gloss walnut stock, with or w/o sights, free floating barrel, bedded receiver. Limited importation 1998 only.

	$650	$575	$500	$450	$400	$360	$330

Last MSR was $730.

Add $50 for open sights.
Add $20 for bright blue metal finish with high gloss stock.

＊ *Lightning Hunter Model Stainless Steel* - similar to Lightning Hunter Model, except has satin finish stainless steel receiver and barrel, checkered satin finished walnut stock. Limited importation 1998 only.

	$665	$585	$500	$430	$375	$315	$270

Last MSR was $750.

Add $50 for open sights.

LIGHTNING HUNTER ALL-WEATHER MODEL - similar to Lightning Hunter, except has black synthetic stock, satin blue metal finish, scope mounts included, with or w/o sights. Limited importation 1998 only.

	$625	$550	$475	$400	$350	$325	$295

Last MSR was $700.

Add $50 for open sights.

＊ *Lightning Hunter All-Weather Model Stainless Steel* - similar to Lightning Hunter All-Weather Model, except is satin stainless steel. Limited importation 1998 only.

	$650	$575	$500	$425	$375	$325	$295

Last MSR was $730.

Add $50 for open sights.

LIGHTNING VARMINT MODEL - .22-250 Rem. or .243 Win., features slide-bolt action, free floating heavy fluted barrel, satin blue metal finish, choice of special varmint wood or synthetic stock. Limited importation 1998 only.

	$895	$775	$675	$600	$525	$475	$425

Last MSR was $1,000.

＊ *Lightning Varmint Model Stainless* - similar to Lightning Varmint Model, except is satin stainless steel. Limited importation 1998 only.

	$895	$775	$675	$600	$525	$475	$425

Last MSR was $1,000.

GRADING - PPGS™	100%	98%	95%	90%	80%	70%	60%

LIGHTNING SNIPER MODEL - .300 Win. Mag. or .308 Win. cal., slide-bolt action, features free floating heavy fluted barrel w/o sights, special wood or synthetic stock with built-in bipod rail, detachable mag., satin blue metal finish. Limited importation 1998 only.

	$895	$775	$675	$600	$525	$475	$425

Last MSR was $1,000.

* *Lightning Sniper Model Stainless* - similar to Lightning Sniper Model, except is satin stainless steel. Limited importation 1998 only.

	$895	$775	$675	$600	$525	$475	$425

Last MSR was $1,000.

LIGHTNING PROFESSIONAL MODEL - .300 Win. Mag. or .308 Win. cal., slide-bolt action, features special black or camo synthetic adj. stock with pistol grip, special tuned trigger system, free floating heavy fluted barrel, recoil reduction compensator. Limited importation 1998 only.

	$1,595	$1,375	$1,125	$950	$825	$700	$575

Last MSR was $1,800.

RIFLES: BOLT ACTION, .22 CAL.

MODEL 20/22 - .22 LR or .22 Mag. cal., bolt action, features free floating barrel, precision trigger, standard or deluxe checkered walnut stock. Limited importation 1998 only.

	$625	$550	$475	$400	$350	$325	$295

Last MSR was $700.

Add $100 for Deluxe Model.

MODEL 107 STANDARD - .22 LR cal. only, bolt action, 19 1/2 in. barrel, 5 shot mag., adj. iron sights, 6 lbs. Imported 1988-89, reintroduced 1993 only.

	$300	$260	$215	$185	$170	$155	$140

Last MSR was $356.

This model is the same as KDF's previous Model 2107 mfg. by Voere.

* *Model 107 Standard Deluxe* - .22 LR or .22 Mag. cal., similar to Model 107, except has deluxe checkered walnut. Imported 1988-89 only.

	$290	$240	$210	$175	$150	$135	$120

Last MSR was $320.

Add $90 for .22 Mag. cal.

This model is the same as KDF's previous Model 2107 Deluxe mfg. by Voere.

MODEL 201 - .22 LR or .22 Mag. cal., bolt action, free-floating 21 in. barrel, 5 shot mag., adj. trigger, scaled-down version of the K-15, unusual action incorporates two front-located locking lugs on bolt face that engage Stellite inserts on the front receiver portion, blue only, no sights, beechwood stock with cheekpiece, 6 1/2 lbs. Disc. 1997.

	$635	$515	$465	$415	$365	$315	$260

Last MSR was $716.

Add $19 for sights (disc.).
Add $77 for .22 Mag. cal. (Model 201-SM).

This model is the same as KDF's disc. Model K-22 mfg. by Voere. Before 1989, this model came standard with a walnut stock.

* *Model 201 Luxus* - similar to the Model 201 except has walnut stock with rosewood forend. Disc. 1997.

	$710	$650	$550	$475	$425	$375	$295

Last MSR was $809.

Add $27 for sights (disc.).
Add $67 for .22 Mag. cal.

This model is the same as KDF's previous Model K-22 Deluxe mfg. by Voere.

GRADING - PPGS™	100%	98%	95%	90%	80%	70%	60%

MODEL DSM34 - .22 LR cal., bolt action, 25.98 in. barrel. "Deutsches Sportmodell" lightweight trainer, side sling, no bayonet lug.

	$625	$375	$325	$300	$260	$225	$200

MODEL MS 420B - .22 LR Sporter cal., bolt action, pre-war, 5 shot mag.

	$1,425	$875	$725	$625	$525	$450	$395

Add 15%-25% for double set triggers (rare).

MODEL ES340 - .22 LR cal., single shot, bolt action, 25 1/2 in. barrel, adj. sights, checkered pistol grip, grooved forearm, pre-1935.

	$725	$425	$350	$325	$295	$260	$230

MODEL ES350 - .22 LR cal., single shot, bolt action, 27 1/2 in. barrel, championship rifle, micrometer rear sight, ramp front sight, checkered full target stock, swivels, pre-1935.

	$925	$550	$500	$460	$430	$400	$375

Add 15%-25% for double set triggers (rare).

MODEL EN310 - .22 LR cal., single shot, bolt action, 19 3/4 in. barrel, fixed sights, plain pistol grip stock, pre-1935.

	$625	$365	$315	$280	$260	$225	$200

MODEL EL320 - .22 LR cal., single shot, bolt action, 23 1/2 in. barrel, fixed sights, checkered pistol grip stock.

	$695	$395	$330	$295	$275	$250	$225

MODEL KKW - .22 LR cal., single shot, bolt action, target, 26 in. barrel, tangent rear sight, military style stock with bayonet lug. This weapon was also produced by Walther, Gustloff, and Anschütz. It was used as a training rifle in addition to commercial sales. Deduct 15% for 4mm KKW Models.

	$900	$800	$700	$600	$500	$400	$300

MODEL MS350B - .22 LR cal., bolt action, repeating, 5 shot mag., 26 3/4 in. barrel, grooved receiver for scope or sight, micrometer rear sight, ramp front sight, target stock, checkered pistol grip and forearm, swivels.

	$1,200	$725	$650	$550	$495	$450	$395

MODEL ES350B - .22 LR cal., bolt action, single shot, 5 shot mag., 26 3/4 in. barrel, grooved receiver for scope or sight, micrometer rear sight, ramp front sight, target stock, checkered pistol grip and forearm, swivels.

	$750	$425	$350	$325	$295	$260	$230

MODEL ES340B - .22 LR cal., bolt action, single shot, 26 3/4 in. barrel, adj. sight, plain pistol grip stock.

	$650	$375	$325	$300	$260	$225	$200

MODEL MM410B - .22 LR cal., bolt action sporter, 5 shot mag., 23 1/2 in. barrel, adj. sights, lightweight stock, checkered pistol grip, swivels.

	$2,000	$1,750	$1,500	$1,250	$1,000	$750	$500

MODEL MS420B - .22 LR cal., bolt action target, 5 shot mag., 26 3/4 in. barrel, adj. sights, target style stock, checkered pistol grip, swivels.

	$1,100	$650	$575	$500	$450	$400	$365

RIFLES: SEMI-AUTO, .22 LR

MODEL 105 STANDARD - .22 LR cal. only, 10 shot mag., approx. 5 lbs. Imported 1995-97.

	$285	$250	$205	$180	$170	$155	$140

Last MSR was $330.

GRADING - PPGS™	100%	98%	95%	90%	80%	70%	60%

SHOTGUNS

Mauser shotguns were sub-contracted to various European firms and were made in various O/U (including field and target), SxS (both boxlock and sidelock), and single shot configurations. While they are relatively rare (these shotguns had limited importation into the U.S. by Bauer located in Michigan - models included the 496 single shot, 496 SxS, 580 SxS, 610 O/U, 620 O/U, 71E O/U, and others), collectability to date has been minimal. Values will depend on the grade, configuration, features, engraving, and overall desirability. Pricing guidelines are as follows: $95 - $175 for the Model 496 single shot, $300 - $650 for the Model 496, $995 - $3,500 for the 580 SxS (mfg. by R. Gamba - same as Ambassador model), and $475 - $1,350 for the boxlock O/U models, depending on configuration, features, and original condition.

MAVERICK ARMS, INC.

Currently manufactured by Maverick Arms, Inc. located in Eagle Pass, TX. Administrative offices are at O.F. Mossberg & Sons, located in North Haven, CT. Distributor sales only.

SHOTGUNS

Beginning 1992, all Maverick slide action shotguns incorporate twin slide rails in the operating mechanism.

MODEL 60 SEMI-AUTO - while advertised, this model was never manufactured.

MODEL 88 FIELD SLIDE ACTION - 12 ga. only, 3 in. chamber, slide-action, 24 (Deer Model with iron sights), 28, or 30 in. plain or VR barrel, wood (disc.) or black synthetic stock and forearm with recoil pad, fixed or Accu-chokes (disc. 1997, reintroduced 2002), 6 shot (w/ two 3/4 in. shot shells), aluminum alloy receiver, crossbolt safety, approx. 7 1/4 lbs. New 1989.

MSR $249	$195	$160	$140	$125	$115	$105	$100

Add $14 for Deer Model (24 in. cyl. bore barrel, disc. 1996).
Subtract 10% if w/o Accu-choke barrel.

Maverick 88 barrels are interchangeable with Mossberg Model 500 barrels within gauge and capacity.

✳ *Model 88 Field Slide Action Slug* - 12 ga., 3 in. chamber, 24 in. fully rifled or cylinder bore barrel with adj. rifle sights, blue finish, black synthetic stock and forearm.

MSR $206		$165	$135	$115	$110	$105	$100	$95

Add $20 for fully rifled barrel.

✳ *Model 88 Field Slide Action Deer Combos* - includes various combinations of extra Deer barrels with rifle sights, 28 in. plain or VR barrel, or extra 18 1/2 in. cyl. bore barrel. Mfg. 1990-95.

	$245	$190	$160	$130	$120	$110	$105

Last MSR was $294.

Add $10 for VR barrel.
Add $17 for Accu-choke barrel.
Add $29 for wood stock and forearm (mfg. 1992 only).

✳ *Model 88 Field Slide Action Security* - 12 ga., 18 1/2 (6 shot) or 20 (8 shot) in. barrel with cyl. bore fixed choke, regular or pistol grip (disc. 1997) synthetic stock, 6 or 8 shot, plain synthetic forearm. New 1993.

MSR $199		$165	$135	$115	$110	$105	$100	$95

Add $7 for 8 shot model with 20 in. barrel.
Add $98 for Bullpup configuration (6 or 9 shot) (disc. 1994).
Add $47-$65 for combo package (disc.).

GRADING - PPGS™	100%	98%	95%	90%	80%	70%	60%

✳ *Model 88 Field Slide Action Combat* - 12 ga. only, combat design featuring pistol grip stock and forearm, black synthetic stock is extension of receiver, 18 1/2 in. cyl. bore barrel with vented shroud with built-in carrying handle, open sights. Mfg. 1990-92.

	$375	$335	$285	$250	$225	$200	$185

Last MSR was $282.

MODEL 91 SLIDE ACTION - 12 ga. only, 3 1/2 in. chamber, 18 1/2 cyl. bore or 28 in. VR barrel with 1 choke tube, otherwise similar to Model 88. Mfg. 1991-95.

	$230	$190	$170	$160	$150	$140	$130

Last MSR was $269.

Add $2 for VR barrel.

MODEL 95 BOLT ACTION - 12 ga. only, 3 in. chamber, synthetic stock with recoil pad, 25 in. barrel bored mod., cross-bolt triggerguard safety. Mfg. 1995-97.

	$155	$135	$115	$100	$90	$80	$70

Last MSR was $184.

McCANN INDUSTRIES

Current rifle and accessories manufacturer located in Spanaway, WA.

McCann Industries manufactures new Garand semi-auto rifles with design improvements that utilize a .338 or .458 Mag cal. cartridge (not Win. Mag.), in addition to a .300 Win. Mag. bolt action pistol. For more information, including pricing and availability, contact the company directly (see Trademark Index).

McMILLAN BROS. RIFLE CO.

Current division of McMillan Group International, located in Phoenix, AZ. Dealer and consumer direct sales. During 1998, the company name changed from McBros Rifles to McMillan Bros. Rifle Co. The company name changed again during 2007 to McBros Rifle Company. Please refer to McBros Rifle Company listing.

McMillan Group International is the corporate parent for the following companies: McMillan Fiberglass Stocks, McMillan Tactical Products, McMillan Operator Development, McMillan Hunting Products, McBros Rifle Company, McMillan Firearms Manufacturing LLC, and the McMillan Machine Company.

Please refer to McMillan Tactical Products and McMillan Hunting Products for currently manufactured rifles.

RIFLES: BOLT ACTION

AMERICAN HUNTER - available in 16 cals. between .22-250 Rem. and .416 Rem. Mag. (disc. 1997), camoflauged fiberglass stock, match grade stainless steel barrel, choice of MCRT (Rem. Model 700 custom type action mfg. to aerospace standards) or MCR (disc., Rem. Model 700 BDL action that has been trued). Mfg. 1993-2007

	$3,050	$2,550	$2,100	$1,825	$1,550	$1,375	$1,100

Last MSR was $3,500.

✳ *American Hunter Yukon Hunter* - available in 6 Mag. cals. between .300 Wby. Mag. and .458 Win. Mag., built to aerospace tolerances for any hunting situation, barrel band sling swivel, folding leaf sight, black synthetic stock. Mfg. 1993-2005.

	$3,350	$2,800	$2,400	$2,050	$1,775	$1,500	$1,350

Last MSR was $3,700.

✳ *American Hunter Outdoorsman* - .30-378 Wby. Mag., .338 Lapua (new 2004), or .338-378 Wby. Mag. (disc. 1997) cal., RT action only. New 1996.

MSR $3,700	$3,350	$2,800	$2,400	$2,050	$1,775	$1,500	$1,350

GRADING - PPGS™	100%	98%	95%	90%	80%	70%	60%

MCR TACTICAL - .308 Win. or .300 Win. Mag. cal. Mfg. 1993-2007.

	$2,950	$2,400	$1,900	$1,500	$1,250	$1,050	$925

Last MSR was $3,300.

This model was formerly designated the MCR Sniper Model.

✳ *MCRT Tactical* - .300 Win. Mag. or .338 Lapua (new 1998), similar to MCR Tactical. Mfg. 1993-2007.

	$3,050	$2,550	$2,100	$1,825	$1,550	$1,375	$1,100

Last MSR was $3,500.

Add $500 for .338 Lapua Mag (muzzle brake is standard).
This model was formerly designated the MCRT Sniper Model.

BENCHREST COMPETITOR - .222 Rem., 6mm PPC, 6mm BR, 7mm BR, or .308 Win. cal., benchrest configuration. Mfg. 1993-99.

	$2,400	$1,925	$1,575	$1,275	$1,050	$900	$775

Last MSR was $2,800.

1000 YARD BENCHREST (NATIONAL MATCH COMPETITOR) - .300 Win. Mag. (new 1996), .30-378 Wby. Mag. (new 1996), 7.82 Warbird (new 1996), .308 Win. (disc. 1995) or .338-378 Wby. Mag. (mfg. 1996-97) cal. Mfg. 1993-99.

	$2,450	$1,950	$1,575	$1,275	$1,050	$900	$775

Last MSR was $2,875.

TUBB 2000 - .243 Win., .260 Rem., 7mm-08 Rem., 6mm, or .308 Win. cal., target rifle featuring metal 4 way adj. stock, Picatinny rail, hand lapped Schneider match barrel, Anschütz 2 stage trigger, state-of-the-art action, vent. handguard, 12 lbs. Mfg. 2000-2007.

	$2,875	$2,475	$2,000	$1,550	$1,250	$1,025	$875

Last MSR was $3,150.

Add $400 for Tubb 2000 C (includes four 10 shot mags., cleaning rod guide, etc.).
Add $550 for Schneider custom stainless steel match barrel.

BIG MAC/BOOMER - .50 BMG cal., available as either single shot sporter, repeater sporter, light benchrest, or heavy benchrest variation. Mfg. 1993-2007.

	$4,450	$3,850	$3,250	$2,700	$2,225	$1,825	$1,525

Last MSR was $4,900.

Add $300 for repeating action.
Add $500 for Tactical 50 variation.
Add $100 for Tactical single shot.
Add $100 for heavy benchrest variation.

McMILLAN, G. & CO., INC.

Previous trademark established circa 1988, located in Phoenix, AZ.
   G. McMillan & Co., Inc. had various barrel markings from 1988-1995 including G. McMillan, Harris - McMillan, and Harris Gunworks.

HANDGUNS

WOLVERINE - available in 9mm Para., 10mm, .38 Super, .38 Wad Cutter, .40 S&W, .45 ACP, or .45 Italian cal., interchangeable barrels, competition ready handgun patterned after the Colt 1911. Imported 1992-95.

✳ *Wolverine Combat* - combat features including 5 1/2 in. compensated barrel.

	$1,600	$1,350	$1,025	$875	$750	$625	$550

Last MSR was $1,700.

✳ *Wolverine Competition Match* - competition features including 6 in. non-compensated barrel.

	$1,600	$1,350	$1,025	$875	$750	$625	$550

Last MSR was $1,700.

GRADING - PPGS™	100%	98%	95%	90%	80%	70%	60%

COMPETITION MODELS - available in Metallic Silhouette (.308 Win. or 7mm-08 Rem. cal. - disc. 1989), National Match (.308 Win. cal. only), Long Range (.300 Win. Mag. only), or Bench Rest (shooter's choice). Each model made specifically for individual competition events. Mfg. 1988-95.

	$2,325	$1,775	$1,450	$1,100	$895	$800	$700

Last MSR was $2,600.

Add $200 for Benchrest Model.
Subtract $300 for Metallic Silhouette model (disc. 1989).

MCBROS RIFLE COMPANY

McMILLAN GROUP INTERNATIONAL

Currently manufactured by McMillan Firearms Manufacturing, LLC, located in Phoenix, AZ beginning 2007.

McMillan Group International is the corporate parent for the following companies: McMillan Fiberglass Stocks, McMillan Tactical Products, McMillan Operator Development, McMillan Hunting Products, McBros Rifle Company, McMillan Firearms Manufacturing LLC, and the McMillan Machine Company.

Rifles are currently marketed by McMillan Tactical Products and McMillan Hunting Products.

RIFLES: HUNTING

Current models include the Legacy ($3,790 MSR), the Prodigy ($3,790 - $4,050 MSR), the Dynasty ($3,910 MSR), the Heritage ($4,490 MSR), the Outdoorsman ($4,190 MSR), and Tactical Hunter ($3,840 MSR).

Please contact the company directly for more information (see Trademark Index).

RIFLES: TACTICAL

Current models include the TAC bolt action Series in various centerfire calibers - MSRs range from $4,599 - $4,999. A TAC 50 in .50 BMG cal. is also available with a current MSR of $6,999. McMillan also has a M1A Series patterned after the popular M1A rifle, with either a folding or collapsible stock. MSRs are currently $2,599 - $2,799. The R79 Series is a line of AR-15 style rifles in either .223 Rem. or .308 Win. cal. Various configurations are available, and MSRs are as follows - R79A - $999, R79S - $1,549, and the R79L - $2,099.

Please contact the company directly for more information (see Trademark Index).

MEDWELL & PERRETT LIMITED

Current long gun manufacturer located in Suffolk, England. Consumer direct sales.

Medwell & Perrett manufactures best quality bolt action and double rifles, in addition to O/U shotguns. Delivery time is approx. 6-18 months, depending on caliber and configuration.

RIFLES

MEDWELL & PERRETT BOLT ACTION - various cals. up to .505 Gibbs, Medwell & Perrett action, Timney adj. trigger, select checkered walnut stock and forend, custom order only.

MSR N/A		$9,480	$8,600	$7,500	$6,500	$5,500	$4,500	$3,500

Add $820 for Mag. length action.
Add $2,340 for .500 Jeffrey or .505 Gibbs cal.
Add $1,770 for takedown action.

MEDWELL & PERRETT SQUARE BRIDGE BOLT ACTION - various cals. up to .505 Gibbs, square bridge action, integral telescopic mount system, barrel quarter rib, adj. trigger, deluxe checkered walnut stock and forend.

MSR N/A		$15,320	$12,950	$9,950	$8,500	$7,250	$6,000	$5,500

Add $815 for Mag. length action.
Add $1,530 for .500 Jeffrey or .505 Gibbs cal.

GRADING - PPGS™	100%	98%	95%	90%	80%	70%	60%

DOUBLE RIFLE SxS - most cals. up to .600 NE, back action, sidelock, ejectors, reinforced bolsters, DT, 22-26 in. chopper lump barrels with folding express sights, oil finished checkered walnut stock and forearm, 8 lbs., 14 oz.-14 lbs., 4 oz.

MSR N/A	$42,000	$38,000	$32,000	$26,500	$21,000	$16,000	$12,000

Add $525 for detachable sidelocks.
Add $3,750 for cals over .375 H&H - .470 NE.
Add $9,180 for cals. over .470 NE - .577 NE.
Add $12,500 for .600 NE cal.

SHOTGUNS

O/U SIDELOCK - 12, 16, 20, 28 ga. or .410 bore, back action, sidelock, ejectors, ST, 25-30 in. barrels, oil finished deluxe walnut stock and forearm, house engraving pattern is standard, 5 lbs., 6 oz.-7 lbs., 4 oz.

MSR N/A	$39,420	$35,000	$30,000	$25,000	$20,000	$16,000	$13,500

Add $4,560 for 28 ga. or .410 bore.
Add $7,200 for an extra set of interchangeable barrels (if ordered with new gun).
Add $630 for Teague choke tubes.

SxS SIDELOCK - 12, 16, 20, 28 ga. or .410 bore, ejectors, best quality SxS. New 2001.

MSR N/A	$34,750	$31,000	$26,000	$22,000	$18,000	$14,000	$11,000

Add $4,440 for 28 ga. or .410 bore.

MENZ, AUGUST

Previous manufacturer located in Suhl, Germany.
Please refer to listings in the Liliput section of this text.

MERCURY (PISTOLS)

Previous manufacturer located in Belgium. Previously imported 1962-68 by Tradewinds, Inc. located in Tacoma, WA.

PISTOLS: SEMI-AUTO

MERCURY MODEL - .22 LR cal., 7 shot mag., steel frame, fixed sights.

	$400	$375	$325	$300	$275	$225	$200

MERCURY (SHOTGUNS)

Previous importer of Spanish manufactured shotguns.

SHOTGUNS: SxS

MAGNUM MODEL - 10, 12, or 20 ga. Mag., 28 and 32 in. barrels, full and mod., boxlock, extractors, double triggers, engraved frame, checkered pistol grip stock.

12 or 20 ga.	$300	$275	$250	$225	$200	$180	$150
10 ga.	$400	$375	$325	$300	$275	$225	$200

MERKEL

Current trademark manufactured by Suhler Jagd-und Sportwaffen GmbH located in Suhl, Germany since circa 1898. Currently imported and distributed exclusively beginning mid-2005 by Merkel USA (previously GSI), located in Trussville, AL. Previously imported during 2004 by Heckler & Koch, located in Sterling, VA, and by GSI located in Trussville, AL circa 1992-2003. Previously imported until 1992 by Armes De Chasse located in Chadds Ford, PA.

MERKEL HISTORY

During the course of its existence, Merkel has been traded under a variety of names, including E.A. Merkel, Merco, Abesser & Merkel, B. Merkel, and Gebrüder Merkel. Most of these names were used by descendants of the family patriarch, Friedrich Ernst Ferdinand Merkel.

GRADING - PPGS™	100%	98%	95%	90%	80%	70%	60%

At the end of WWII, the Merkel company was initially taken over by American troops, but then after approx. 3 months, it was turned over to the Russians for the duration of their occupation. Once the communist German government was established, the factory was owned by the government until Germany was reunited. The East German economy, like that of most former Soviet bloc countries, suffered due to lack of capitalization and from very restrictive gun laws.

Merkel was first managed by the "Treuhand", the government trustee that tried to find new owners for all East German commerce and industry. Among the applicants who had an interest in acquiring the remaining Suhl gun industry was Sturm, Ruger & Co., together with members of the Simson family, who owned the biggest gun factory in Suhl before the Nazis came to power. Their offer was rejected in favor of a group of investors who enriched themselves, and went out of business after only one year.

The "Treuhand" then turned the company over to a bank and the Austrian Steyr-Mannlicher Company circa 2001. A few years later, H&K took over the company and expanded it. They had 126 employees in 2003, and are now at 171 employees. Because of H&K's engineering and marketing, Merkel became profitable again and expanded into the Eastern Europe and US marketplaces. The company went back to the original name Merkel, and bought the business and facilities of GSI, located in Trussville, AL.

During 2007, Merkel was sold to Caracal International LLC, located in the United Arab Emirates.

For many years Merkel shotguns were unfairly disadvantaged in this country because of the politics of importing firearms from communist bloc countries (goods were subject to a 65% non-favored nation tax). With the reunification of Germany in 1991, this trademark became more competitive domestically. Merkel continues to manufacture high quality guns in Suhl, Germany.

Beginning in 1995, Merkel serialization employed an alphanumeric date code for year of manufacture, making it difficult to determine year of manufacture by serial number. Higher grade models (including the 300 Series) continue to be manufactured one at a time by hand, with less than 30 being mfg. annually.

Many Merkel collectors are now categorizing older production guns into three different categories. The first is guns made before 1962, when the Berlin Wall was created. The second is the GDR guns (German Democratic Republic). The last is after the Berlin wall came down (post-1991). Premiums are paid on pre-WWII manufacture and some GDR guns. All pre-war guns may have different actions such as square, half round, and square reinforced, etc. These older production models should be appraised by a knowledgeable person, since there are a lot of things to consider when evaluating these earlier Merkels. Some guns made up for the Nürnberg and Leipzig trade shows have top quality workmanship, especially the engraving.

The engraver's signature will appear on all factory engraved Merkels manufactured since 1992.

COMBINATION GUNS

O/U MODEL - 12, 16, or 20 ga. (2 3/4 in. chamber) over 5.6x50R, 5.6x52R, 6.5x55mm, 6.5x57R, 7x57R, 7x65R, 8x57JRS, 9.3x74R, .22 Hornet (disc. 1997), .222 Rem., .243 Win., .30-06, .308 Win., or .375 H&H (disc. 1994) cal., 25.6 in. barrels, various chokes. Disc. 1999.

* *Model 210E*

	100%	98%	95%	90%	80%	70%	60%
	$5,700	$4,600	$3,700	$3,150	$2,600	$2,100	$1,800

Last MSR was $6,195.

* *Model 211E*

	$6,650	$4,750	$3,900	$3,300	$2,775	$2,275	$1,925

Last MSR was $7,495.

* *Model 213E* - disc. 1997.

	$13,000	$10,750	$8,250	$6,975	$5,825	$4,600	$3,550

Last MSR was $14,795.

* *Model 240E-1* - 20 ga. over .22 Rem., 7x57R, or .30-06 cal. Imported 2003-2005.

	$6,175	$5,150	$3,900	$3,400	$2,900	$2,400	$2,125

Last MSR was $7,195.

GRADING - PPGS™	100%	98%	95%	90%	80%	70%	60%

* *Model 313E* - disc. 1997.

	$19,350	$14,950	$12,500	$9,950	$8,350	$7,100	$5,900

Last MSR was $22,795.

MODEL 314 - 12 ga. over 7mm-.470 NE cal., detachable H&H sidelock system, elaborate scroll engraving. Disc. pre-WWII.

	$21,250	$15,750	$13,000	$10,000	$8,500	$7,200	$6,200

SxS MODEL - similar gauges and cals. to O/U Combination Gun, boxlock models included 8EI and 9EI, 10EI is a sidelock, boxlock models ranged in MSRs from $5,500-$7,000 and the Model 10EI MSR was $9,500. Importation disc. 1990.

DRILLINGS

Previously, the Drilling Models 90 (disc. 1994), 90S (disc. 1997), 90K (disc. 1997), 95 (disc. 1994), 95K (disc. 1998), and 95S (disc. 1997) were also imported. Models differ in the amount of engraving, cocking systems, and quality of wood.

MODEL 96K - choice of 12, 16 (disc. 2005), or 20 ga., with the rifle barrel being bored in most popular U.S. and metric cals. between .22 Hornet and 9.3x74R (disc., current standard cals. are .243 Win. or .30-06), 23.6 in. barrels, current models are boxlocks with Greener crossbolt and double under barrel locking lugs, extractors, tang mounted cocking for rifle, case hardened receiver with arabesque scroll engraving, DT, fitted leather case.

MSR $8,095	$7,325	$5,900	$4,750	$3,650	$3,000	$2,500	$1,995

Add $1,200 for hunting scene engraving (Model 96K Engraved).

MERKEL ANSON - 12, 16, or 20 ga., calibers 7x57R, 8x57JR, and 9.3x74R cals. most common, others noted, usually 2 shotguns over rifle, although 2 rifles over shotgun have been noted, 25.6 in. or 21.6 in. barrels, boxlock, Anson & Deeley system, double triggers, extractors, checkered pistol grip stock, pre-WWII.

Engraved Model 142	$5,000	$4,000	$3,000	$2,750	$2,500	$2,200	$2,000
Less Engraved Model 142	$4,000	$3,500	$3,000	$2,500	$2,250	$2,100	$2,000
Model 145 (least engraving)	$3,000	$2,800	$2,700	$2,600	$2,500	$2,100	$1,900

MODEL 961L - 20 ga. only over .30-06 or 9.3x74R cal., similar to Model 96K, except does not have tang mounted cocking slide, 21.6 in. barrels, standard engraving is Arabesque scroll. Importation began 2008.

MSR $8,995	$7,775	$6,500	$5,250	$4,500	$3,750	$3,000	$2,750

Add $2,000 for silver finished receiver with fine hunting scenes.

* *Model 961LS* - similar to Model 961L, except has elaborately engraved sideplates.

MSR $12,995	$11,250	$9,000	$7,750	$6,750	$5,750	$5,000	$4,250

RIFLES: BOLT ACTION

MODEL 190 - various cals., Mauser M-98 system, checkered walnut stock and extended forend, values depend on caliber and action size. Disc. pre-WWII.

	$7,500	$6,500	$5,275	$4,200	$3,200	$2,350	$1,500

Premiums exist for Magnum or Kurz (short) action.

MODEL KR1 PREMIUM - .243 Win., .270 Win., .30-06, 7mm-08, .308 Win., 7mm Rem. Mag., .300 Win. Mag., .270 WSM, or .300 WSM cal., modular design allows changing a different cal. barrel, short lock and bolt movement, three position safety, two or three shot detachable mag., fine trigger with set feature, six locking lugs, quick release mount system, pistol grip stock with cheekpiece and swivels, approx. 6.4 lbs. Importation began 2006.

MSR $1,995	$1,750	$1,500	$1,300	$1,100	$900	$800	$700

Add $500 for left-hand action.

Add $695 per interchangable barrel, $295 for scope mounts or $225 per individual bolt group.

GRADING - PPGS™	100%	98%	95%	90%	80%	70%	60%

✳ *Model KR1 Premium Stutzen Antique Carbine* - .243 Win., .270 Win., .30-06, 7mm-08, .308 Win., or 9.3x62mm (new 2007) cal., similar to KR1 Premium, except has 20 1/4 in. barrel and full Mannlicher stock with fishscale carving. Importation began 2006.

MSR $3,395		$2,950	$2,600	$2,250	$1,850	$1,500	$1,250	$1,075

Add $500 for left-hand action.

✳ *Model KR1 Premium Weimar Luxury* - .243 Win., .270 Win., .30-06, 7mm-08, .308 Win., 7mm Rem. Mag., .300 Win. Mag., .270 WSM, or .300 WSM cal., similar to KR1 Premium, except has deep relief hand engraved hunting scenes on silver-grey receiver, high grade stock with rosewood forearm tip, double fold Bavarian cheekpiece with modified Kaiser grip, gold plated trigger and bolt head. Limited importation 2006.

	$8,850	$7,500	$6,250	$5,000	$4,000	$3,250	$2,500

Last MSR was $9,995.

Add $200 for Mag. cals.

RIFLES: DOUBLE

O/U MODEL - same cals. as the O/U Combination Gun, various actions, engraving options, and other special orders.

✳ *Model 220E Boxlock* - boxlock Blitz action, scroll engraved case hardened receiver, DTs, pistol grip with cheekpiece. Importation disc. 1994.

$9,575	$8,250	$7,150	$6,100	$5,100	$4,250	$3,500

Last MSR was $10,795.

✳ *Model 221E Boxlock* - similar to 220E, except has silver-grey receiver with hunting scene engraving. Disc. 1998.

$12,500	$10,500	$8,650	$7,450	$6,300	$5,100	$4,250

Last MSR was $10,895.

✳ *Model 223E Sidelock* - sidelock action with scroll or game scenes, removed without tools. Disc. 1997.

$22,500	$19,000	$16,750	$13,650	$11,000	$9,750	$8,500

Last MSR was $17,895.

✳ *Model 323E Sidelock* - similar to 223E Sidelock, except has scrollwork or game scene engraving, top-of-the-line O/U double rifle. Disc. 1997.

$29,500	$26,750	$23,300	$20,000	$17,500	$13,500	$11,250

Last MSR was $27,195.

MODEL 324 O/U - 6.5x55mm - .470 NE cal., premium quality pre-WWII double rifle, elaborate scroll engraving and best quality walnut. Disc. pre-WWII.

$26,500	$23,000	$20,000	$17,500	$13,500	$11,250	$9,750

B3 O/U BOXLOCK - .30-06 or 9.3x74R cal., boxlock action, 21.6 in. barrels, checkered walnut pistol grip stock and forearm, single trigger, standard Jagd configuration or deluxe with extra engraving. Importation began 2007.

MSR $5,495		$4,750	$3,950	$3,300	$2,750	$2,350	$1,900	$1,600

Add $1,000 for B3 Deluxe with fishscale wood carving and better engraving.

SxS MODELS - same cals. as listed for the O/U Combination Gun.

✳ *Model 128* - various cals., scalloped Anson & Deeley action featuring engine turned removable locks and hinged floorplate, elaborate scroll and game scene engraving (on barrels), deluxe checkered walnut stock and forearm, pre-WWII mfg.

N/A	$25,000	$21,000	$18,000	$15,500	$13,250	$11,000

GRADING - PPGS™	100%	98%	95%	90%	80%	70%	60%

✳ *Model 132* - various cals., boxlock action with triple Greener cross bolt system, barrels, mfg. from Bohler steel, extractors (Model 132) or H&H system ejectors (Model 132E), DT, elaborate engraving and premium checkered walnut stock and forearm, pre-WWII mfg.

| | $12,000 | $10,500 | $8,500 | $6,500 | $5,750 | $4,900 | $4,150 |

Add 20% for ejectors (Model 132E).

✳ *Model 140-1* - Anson & Deeley boxlock action with cocking indicators, double triggers, engraved case hardened receiver. Imported 1994-2005.

| | $6,100 | $4,450 | $3,300 | $2,625 | $2,100 | $1,825 | $1,675 |

Last MSR was $7,195.

Subtract approx. $400 if w/o H&H ejectors (pre-2002).
Add approx. $200 for set front trigger.
Add $1,100 for engraved hunting scenes on silver/grey receiver (Model 140-1.1).

✳ *Model 140-2* - .375 H&H, .416 Rigby, .470 NE, or .500 NE (new 2006) cal., similar to Model 140-1, except has scroll engraved silver grey receiver and positive extractors or ejectors, includes fitted leather luggage case. Importation began 2000.

| MSR $11,495 | $9,650 | $7,850 | $6,100 | $4,800 | $3,800 | $3,100 | $2,600 |

Add $500 for ejectors.

❖ Model 140-2.1 - similar to Model 140-2, except has Africa game scene engraving. Importation began 2000.

| MSR $12,695 | $10,750 | $8,250 | $6,100 | $4,850 | $3,850 | $3,350 | $2,850 |

Add $500 for ejectors.

❖ Model 140-2.2 - .375 H&H, .470 NE or .500 NE cal., similar to Model 140 2.1, except has more engraving. Importation began 2007.

| MSR $17,995 | $15,350 | $12,000 | $9,750 | $8,000 | $6,500 | $5,500 | $5,000 |

✳ *Model 141-1* - .30-06, .308 Win. (disc.), 7x57R (new 2007), or 9.3x74R cal., Greener crossbolt Anson & Deeley boxlock action with double underbarrel locking lugs, petite frame, scroll engraved silver grey finish, ejectors, DT, deluxe checkered pistol grip walnut stock with cheekpiece and forearm, includes fitted leather case, 6.6 lbs. Importation began 2004.

| MSR $7,795 | $6,650 | $5,100 | $4,100 | $3,350 | $2,750 | $2,250 | $1,950 |

❖ Model 141-1.1 - similar to Model 141-1, except has hunting scene engraving and single non-selective trigger. Importation began 2004.

| MSR $8,995 | $7,375 | $5,400 | $4,550 | $3,750 | $3,000 | $2,500 | $2,175 |

Add $1,700 for Leupold scope combo (mfg. 2005-2007).

✳ *Model 150-1* - Anson & Deeley boxlock action with cocking indicators and sideplates, double triggers, silver grayed receiver with arabesque engraving. Imported 1994-98.

| | $6,500 | $5,275 | $4,375 | $3,750 | $3,250 | $2,675 | $2,100 |

Last MSR was $7,495.

Add $385 for H&H ejectors.
Add approx. $200 for set front trigger.

❖ Model 150-1.1 - similiar to Model 150-1, except has elaborate hunting scene engraving. Importation disc. 2000.

| | $7,750 | $5,350 | $4,250 | $3,550 | $2,900 | $2,400 | $2,000 |

Last MSR was $8,995.

✳ *Model 160S-1* - sidelock action with Greener crossbolt featuring fine arabesque engraving, H&H ejectors, DTs, pistol grip stock with cheekpiece. Disc. 1998.

| | $11,400 | $9,350 | $7,675 | $6,500 | $5,300 | $4,400 | $3,550 |

Last MSR was $13,295.

Add $415 for H&H ejectors.
Add approx. $500 for set front trigger.
Add approx. $1,000 for single non-selective trigger.

GRADING - PPGS™	100%	98%	95%	90%	80%	70%	60%

❖ **Model 160-1.1** - similiar to Model 150-1, except has elaborate hunting scene engraving on silver-grey receiver. Importation disc. 2000.

	$13,250	$11,000	$9,000	$7,775	$6,600	$5,400	$4,750

Last MSR was $14,995.

❖ **Model 160-2.1** - .375 H&H, .416 Rigby, .470 NE, or .500 NE (new 2006) cal., features octagon barrels, African game scene engraving with gold wire inlays on silver receiver, includes fitted leather luggage case, special order only. Imported 2002-2006.

	$20,400	$17,500	$14,750	$12,250	$10,000	$8,950	$7,750

Last MSR was $23,995.

✳ *Model 161-1.1* - 7x57R, .30-06, or 9.3x74R cal., sidelock action built on 28 ga. frame, 21.65 in. barrels, Greener crossbolt with double barrel locking lugs, fine engraved hunting scenes with silver grey sidelocks, H&H ejectors, DT, high grade Turkish walnut pistol grip stock with cheekpiece and semi-beaver-tail forend, 6.6 lbs. Imported 2006.

	$13,850	$11,000	$9,000	$7,500	$6,000	$5,250	$4,500

Last MSR was $15,995.

RIFLES: SEMI-AUTO

SR1 - .30-06, .308 Win., .300 Win. Mag., 9.3x62, 7x64 (European only), or 8x57 (European only) cal., 19.7 or 20.8 (.300 Win. Mag. cal. only) in. free-floating precision barrel, gas operated, 2 or 5 shot mag., solid rotary bolt head with 2x3 locking lugs, trigger safety, checkered walnut stock and forearm, rubber recoil pad, Battue rib sight with contrast line, adj. front sight, approx. 7 lbs. Importation began 2007.

MSR $1,595		$1,350	$1,175	$1,000	$875	$750	$625	$525

RIFLES: SINGLE SHOT

MODEL K1 JAGD STALKING RIFLE - available in 11 cals. between .243 Win. - 9.3x74R, Franz Jaeger break open action, cocking/uncocking slide type safety, matte silver receiver, adj. trigger pull, 23.6 or 25.6 (Wby. Mag. cals. only) in. barrel, pistol grip, includes 1 in. or 30mm quick detachable mounts, silver border engraving is standard, 5 lbs. 5 oz. Importation began 2002.

MSR $3,795		$3,350	$2,900	$2,375	$1,925	$1,600	$1,300	$1,100

Add $300 for Premium Model with light arabesque scroll engraving (disc.).
Add $1,195 per extra barrel.
Add $944 for Swarovski scope combo (mfg. 2005-2007).

✳ *Model K1 Jagd Stalking Rifle Stutzen Carbine* - .243 Win., .270 Win., 7x57R, .308 Win., 7mm-08 or .30-06 cal., similar to K1 Jagd Stalking Rifle, except has 19.7 in. barrel with Mannlicher full stock. Importation began 2006.

MSR $4,195		$3,675	$3,000	$2,475	$2,050	$1,650	$1,325	$1,100

MODEL K-2 STALKING RIFLE - .243 Win., .270 Win., 7x57R, .308 Win., .30-06 cal., 7mm Rem. Mag., .300 Win. Mag., or 9.3x74R cal., Franz Jager single shot break open action, cocking/uncocking slide safety, octagon barrel, submodels vary in type and amount of engraving, includes best quality wood with stock carving. Importation began 2005.

✳ *Model K-2 Weimar Stalking Rifle* - .30-06, .308 Win., .300 Win. Mag. or 7mm Rem. Mag. cal., features deep relief hand engraved hunting scenes.

MSR $15,995		$13,750	$11,250	$9,000	$7,500	$6,250	$5,000	$4,150

✳ *Model K-2 Erfurt Stalking Rifle* - features deep relief engraving on ornamental sideplates and silver pistol grip monogram. Limited importation 2005-2006.

	$18,350	$14,995	$12,500	$10,000	$8,250	$7,000	$5,750

Last MSR was $20,995.

GRADING - PPGS™	100%	98%	95%	90%	80%	70%	60%

✳ *Model K-2 Suhl Luxury Stalking Rifle* - features deep relief engraving on ornamental sideplates, gold inlays, gold gilded trigger, and silver pistol grip monogram. Limited importation 2005-2006.

| | $24,000 | $20,000 | $16,000 | $13,000 | $10,000 | $8,500 | $7,700 |

Last MSR was $26,995.

MODEL 180 - various cals., with (Model 180E) or w/o ejector, double triggers, checkered walnut stock and extended forend, values depend on caliber and action size. Disc. pre-WWII.

| | $8,500 | $7,250 | $5,775 | $4,600 | $3,750 | $3,000 | $2,500 |

MODEL 183E - various cals., sidelock, top-of-the-line rifle with elaborate engraving. Disc. pre-WWII.

| | $12,500 | $10,750 | $8,250 | $6,975 | $5,825 | $4,600 | $3,550 |

SHOTGUNS: O/U, DISC.

MODEL 100 - 12, 16, or 20 ga., various barrel lengths and chokes, boxlock, Greener cross bolt, double triggers, extractors, checkered pistol grip or English style stock, pre-WWII.

	100%	98%	95%	90%	80%	70%	60%
Plain	$1,850	$1,675	$1,450	$1,250	$1,000	$925	$850
Ribbed	$1,950	$1,775	$1,550	$1,300	$1,050	$950	$875

MODEL 101 - similar to 100, except selective extractors, rib barrel, some English style scroll engraving, pre-WWII.

| | $2,050 | $1,850 | $1,600 | $1,325 | $1,100 | $1,000 | $900 |

MODEL 101E - similar to 100, except auto ejectors, pre-WWII.

| | $2,200 | $2,000 | $1,750 | $1,425 | $1,250 | $1,150 | $1,000 |

MODEL 400 - similar to 101, except arabesque engraving and Kersten double cross bolt, pre-WWII.

| | $2,075 | $1,875 | $1,650 | $1,350 | $1,200 | $1,100 | $975 |

MODEL 400E - similar to 400, except auto ejector, pre-WWII.

| | $2,250 | $2,050 | $1,800 | $1,450 | $1,325 | $1,175 | $1,025 |

MODEL 410 - similar to 400, except more engraving and fancier wood, pre-WWII.

| | $2,200 | $2,000 | $1,750 | $1,425 | $1,250 | $1,150 | $1,000 |

MODEL 410E - similar to 410, except auto ejectors, pre-WWII.

| | $2,325 | $2,175 | $1,900 | $1,600 | $1,450 | $1,225 | $1,100 |

MODEL 200 - 12, 16, 20, 24, 28, or 32 ga., ribbed barrels in various lengths, Kersten double cross bolt, scalloped frame, boxlock, double triggers, extractors, cocking indicators, either pistol grip or English style checkered stock.

| | $2,750 | $2,475 | $2,225 | $2,000 | $1,750 | $1,400 | $1,175 |

Add 10%-15% for 28 ga., depending on condition.

MODEL 210 - similar to 200, except engraved and better grade wood, pre-WWII.

| | $3,000 | $2,750 | $2,475 | $2,250 | $2,000 | $1,650 | $1,325 |

Add 10%-15% for 28 ga., depending on condition.

MODEL 201 - 12, 16, or 20 ga., Greener crossbolt, hunting engraving or fine arabesque, dark walnut.

| | $3,250 | $3,000 | $2,625 | $2,400 | $2,200 | $1,825 | $1,500 |

MODEL 201E (PRE-WAR) - similar to 201, except with auto ejectors, pre-WWII.

| | $,700 | $4,350 | $3,750 | $3,375 | $3,050 | $2,650 | $2,400 |

MODEL 202 (PRE-WAR) - similar to 201, except with false sideplates, higher quality wood, more profuse engraving, pre-WWII.

| | $5,750 | $5,100 | $4,500 | $3,900 | $3,500 | $2,950 | $2,600 |

GRADING - PPGS™	100%	98%	95%	90%	80%	70%	60%

MODEL 202E (PRE-WAR) - similar to 202, with auto ejectors, pre-WWII.

	$4,650	$4,100	$3,675	$3,200	$2,800	$2,485	$2,050

MODEL 203E (PRE-WAR) - sideloc, similar to 202E, except better engraving and wood.

	$6,000	$5,500	$4,900	$4,300	$3,800	$3,250	$2,650

MODEL 204E - similar to 203E, but fine English scroll engraving and Merkel side-locks, ejectors, pre-WWII.

	$6,950	$6,500	$5,650	$4,900	$4,300	$3,850	$3,300

MODEL 300 - 12, 16, 20, 24, 28, 32 ga. or .410 bore, various lengths and choke ribbed barrels, Merkel-Anson boxlock, Kersten double cross bolt, two underlugs, scalloped frame, either English or pistol grip style stock, cocking indicators, pre-WWII.

	$5,150	$4,600	$4,100	$3,600	$3,100	$2,650	$2,400

Add 10%-15% for 28 ga.

MODEL 300E - similar to Model 300, with auto ejectors, pre-WWII.

	$5,750	$5,150	$4,600	$4,100	$3,600	$3,100	$2,650

This model is usually encountered without engraving and has standard wood.

MODEL 301 - similar to Model 300, but more profusely engraved and better grade wood, pre-WWII.

	$6,750	$6,100	$5,250	$4,250	$3,995	$3,500	$3,000

MODEL 310E - similar to Model 300, with auto ejectors, pre-WWII.

	$7,950	$7,200	$6,250	$5,300	$4,450	$3,900	$3,400

MODEL 302 - similar to Model 301, but has auto ejectors and more elaborate ornamentation, false sideplates and better grade wood.

	$14,000	$12,000	$10,500	$8,500	$6,500	$5,750	$4,900

MODEL 304E - special order version of Model 303E, higher quality and more ornamentation, very fine scroll engraving similar to Model 303 EL Luxus, top of Merkel O/U line.

	$22,500	$18,750	$15,750	$12,000	$10,500	$8,750	$7,500

SHOTGUNS: O/U, RECENT PRODUCTION

MODEL 200E BOXLOCK - 12, 16, or 20 ga., case hardened scalloped boxlock action with minor scroll engraving, 26 (disc.), 26 3/4, or 28 in. barrels, checkered European walnut stock and forearm, ejectors, SST or DT, pistol grip or English style stock, solid rib, 6-7 lbs. Importation disc. 1994, quantities remained until 1998.

	$3,600	$2,750	$2,150	$1,900	$1,600	$1,300	$1,100

Last MSR was $3,995.

* *Model 200ES Boxlock Skeet* - 12 ga. only, 26 3/4 in. VR barrels bored skeet/skeet. Imported 1993-94.

	$4,550	$3,950	$3,500	$3,000	$2,500	$2,100	$1,625

Last MSR was $4,995.

* *Model 200ET Boxlock Trap* - 12 ga. only, 30 in. VR barrels bored full/full (other choke configurations available upon request). Importation disc. 1994.

	$4,400	$3,750	$3,300	$2,800	$2,300	$2,000	$1,550

Last MSR was $5,195.

MODEL 2000CL - 12, 20, or 28 ga., 28 in. barrels with fixed IC/M chokes, Kersten double crossbolt lock, scroll engraved case hardened receiver, scalloped boxlock frame, modified Anson & Deely boxlock action, selectable ejectors, round knob, SST, high grade wood stock with semi-pistol grip or straight English style, three piece forearm, approx. 6.8 lbs. Importation began 2006.

MSR $7,995	$6,950	$5,750	$5,100	$4,300	$3,600	$3,000	$2,500

GRADING - PPGS™	100%	98%	95%	90%	80%	70%	60%

* **Model 2000CL Sporter** - 12, 20, or 28 ga., similar to Model 2000CL, except chokes are SK/IC only. Limited importation 2006.

	$6,350	$5,400	$4,800	$4,200	$3,600	$3,000	$2,500

Last MSR was $7,195.

MODEL 2000EL - 12, 20, 28 (new 1999) ga. or .410 bore (new 2004), Kersten double cross-bolt lock, scroll engraved, silver receiver, modified Anson & Deeley boxlock action, 26 or 28 in. fixed choke barrels, ejectors, ST or DT, select checkered walnut with pistol grip or English style stock, 3 piece forearm, 6.4-7 lbs. Imported 1998-2005.

	$5,700	$4,450	$3,750	$2,975	$2,400	$1,775	$1,600

Last MSR was $6,495.

* **Model 2000EL Sporter** - 12, 20, or 28 ga., similar to Model 2000EL, except chokes are SK/IC only. Imported 1999-2005.

	$5,700	$4,450	$3,750	$2,975	$2,400	$1,775	$1,600

Last MSR was $6,495.

MODEL 2001EL (201E) - 12, 16 (disc. 1997), 20, 28 (new 1995) ga. or .410 bore (mfg. 2004-2005), similar to Model 200E, except has coin finished action with light game scene engraving, fixed IC/MOD chokes, three piece forearm, current mfg. includes fitted luggage case.

MSR $9,395	$8,100	$6,250	$4,600	$3,800	$3,200	$2,500	$2,250

This model's nomenclature was changed from 201E to 2001EL during 1998.

* **Model 2001EL Sporter** - 12, 20, or 28 ga., similar to Model 2001EL, except chokes are SK/IC only. Importation began 1999.

MSR $9,395	$8,100	$6,250	$4,600	$3,800	$3,200	$2,500	$2,250

* **Model 201ES Skeet** - 12 ga. only, 26 3/4 in. VR barrels bored skeet/skeet. Imported 1993-97.

	$7,850	$6,675	$5,400	$4,300	$3,450	$2,900	$2,250

Last MSR was $8,495.

* **Model 201ET Trap** - 12 ga. only, 30 in. VR barrels bored full/full (other choke configurations available upon request). Importation disc. 1997.

	$7,850	$6,675	$5,400	$4,300	$3,450	$2,900	$2,250

Last MSR was $8,495.

MODEL 2002EL (202E) - similar to Model 201E/2001EL, except has fine hunting scenes with arabesque engraving on silver false sideplates, 3 piece forearm, choice of pistol grip or English straight grip stock, includes fitted luggage case. Imported 1993-2003.

	$10,625	$8,000	$6,000	$5,000	$4,000	$3,500	$3,150

Last MSR was $12,395.

This model's nomenclature was changed from 202E to 2002EL during 1998.

MODEL 203E SIDELOCK - 12, 16 (disc. 1997), or 20 ga. (24, 28, and 32 gauges were once available but are now disc.), 26 (disc.), 26 3/4, or 28 in. barrels, VR, H&H ejectors, SST (current) or DT, elaborate scroll engraving on coin finished receiver, sidelock screws are H&H style but the removable sidelocks are not, choice of English or pistol grip stock, 6-7 lbs. Disc. 1998.

	$9,750	$6,450	$4,950	$3,900	$3,400	$2,550	$2,150

Last MSR was $11,995.

* **Model 203ES Sidelock Skeet** - 12 ga. only, 26 3/4 in. VR barrels bored sk/sk. Imported 1993-97.

	$12,050	$9,100	$7,300	$5,975	$4,950	$3,950	$3,500

Last MSR was $14,595.

GRADING - PPGS™	100%	98%	95%	90%	80%	70%	60%

❊ *Model 203ET Sidelock Trap* - 12 ga. only, 30 in. VR barrels bored full/full (other choke configurations available upon request). Importation disc. 1997.

	$12,050	$9,100	$7,300	$5,975	$4,950	$3,950	$3,500

Last MSR was $14,595.

MODEL 2016CL - similar to 2000CL, except is 16 ga., 28 in. barrels with fixed IC/Mod. chokes, approx. 6.8 lbs. Importation began 2006.

MSR $7,995	$6,950	$5,750	$5,100	$4,300	$3,600	$3,000	$2,500

Add $4,300 for two barrel set (16 and 20 ga., bored IC/Mod.).

MODEL 2016EL SIDELOCK - 16 ga., scroll engraved case hardened receiver, action similar to Model 2001EL, three piece forearm. Imported 2004-2005.

	$5,700	$4,450	$3,750	$2,975	$2,400	$1,775	$1,600

Last MSR was $6,495.

Add $3,200 for 2 barrel set (16 and 20 ga. bored IC/Mod.).

MODEL 2116EL SIDELOCK - 16 ga., similar to Model 2016EL, except has upgraded wood and more engraving. Importation began 2004.

MSR $9,395	$8,100	$6,250	$4,600	$3,800	$3,200	$2,500	$2,250

Add $4,100 for 2 barrel set (16 and 20 ga. bored IC/Mod.).

MODEL 303EL (LUXUS) - 12, 20, or 28 (new 1998) ga., similar to Model 203EL, except has H&H type sidelock action with hidden thumbnail detachable sidelocks, double underlugs, more ornamentation and better wood, DT with articulated front. Importation disc. 2006.

	$21,000	$17,000	$13,500	$10,500	$9,250	$7,750	$7,000

Last MSR was $23,995.

Luxus variations are also encountered in the 201 and 203 series in addition to older pre-war models.

SHOTGUNS: SxS, PRE-WWII PRODUCTION

Merkel began manufacturing SxS shotguns during 1914.

MODEL 126E - 12, 16, or 20 ga., similar action as the Model 127, except features game scene and other engraving patterns, H&H style system ejectors, pre-WWII mfg.

	N/A	$24,725	$21,500	$16,500	$12,500	$10,000	$8,800

MODEL 127E - 12, 16, or 20 ga., various barrel lengths and chokes, H&H style hand detachable sidelocks, auto ejectors, double triggers, pistol or English style stock, elaborate scroll engraving only, this is a best grade gun, pre-WWII mfg.

	N/A	$24,725	$21,500	$16,500	$12,500	$10,000	$8,800

MODEL 128E - 12, 16, or 20 ga., scalloped Anson & Deeley action featuring engine turned removable locks and hinged floorplate, DT, H&H system ejectors, elaborate scroll and game scene engraving (including scroll work on barrels), deluxe checkered walnut stock and forearm, pre-WWII mfg.

	N/A	$20,000	$16,500	$14,000	$12,000	$10,000	$8,000

MODEL 130 - 12, 16, or 20 ga., various barrel lengths and chokes, Anson & Deeley action with false side plates, boxlock, auto ejectors, English style or pistol grip stock, elaborate game scenes and arabesque engraving, pre-WWII mfg.

	N/A	$13,800	$12,000	$9,500	$7,500	$6,350	$5,400

SHOTGUNS: SxS, RECENT PRODUCTION

Left-hand stocks are also available on some of the models in this category. Please contact Merkel USA directly for a price quotation.

GRADING - PPGS™	100%	98%	95%	90%	80%	70%	60%

MODEL 8 - 12, 16 (disc.), or 20 ga., case hardened scalloped boxlock action with light engraving, Greener crossbolt with chopper lump extension, extractors, SST (current) or DT, standard walnut with checkering, pistol grip or English style stock, sling swivels (disc. 1992). Disc. 1994.

	$1,150	$950	$795	$700	$625	$550	$475

Last MSR was $1,695.

MODEL 47E - 12, 16 (disc. 2001), or 20 ga., case hardened scalloped boxlock action with chopper lump extension and Greener crossbolt, 26 (disc.), 26 3/4, or 28 in. barrels with fixed chokes, SST (current) or DT, ejectors, deluxe checkered walnut, pistol grip or English style stock, sling swivels (disc. 1992), 5.9-6.8 lbs.

MSR $4,395		$3,475	$2,400	$1,625	$1,250	$900	$800	$700

✳ *Model 47EL Custom Ltd. Ed.* - 20 ga. only, 28 in. VR barrels with IC/Mod. fixed chokes, features luxury grade wood with English straight grip stock with medallion and DTs. Importation began 2008.

MSR $5,495		$4,650	$3,550	$2,775	$2,200	$1,725	$1,400	$1,150

MODEL 47SL - 12, 16 (disc. 2001), 20, 28 (disc.) ga., or .410 (disc.) bore, coin finished sidelock action with scroll engraving, Greener crossbolt, ST (current) or DT, deluxe walnut stock (with cheekpiece) and forearm, sling swivels (disc. 1992).

MSR $8,495		$7,300	$5,475	$4,450	$3,350	$2,650	$2,000	$1,625

Add approx. $600 for 28 ga. or .410 bore (mfg. 1992 only).

MODEL 76E - top-of-the-line boxlock shotgun. Importation disc. 1992.

	$2,600	$2,100	$1,850	$1,600	$1,325	$995	$775

Last MSR was $3,500.

MODEL 122 - 12, 16, or 20 ga., Anson & Deeley boxlock action with silver greyed false sideplates, H&H ejectors, SST or DT, fine hunting scenes with arabesque engraving, pistol grip or English style stock. Imported 1993-99.

	$3,750	$3,375	$3,000	$2,600	$2,300	$2,000	$1,600

Last MSR was $4,495.

MODEL 122E - 12, 16, or 20 ga., coin finished boxlock action with Greener crossbolt and chopper lump extension, cocking indicators, ejectors, DTs, deluxe game scene engraving. Importation disc. 1991.

	$4,100	$3,650	$3,200	$2,800	$2,250	$1,950	$1,650

Last MSR was $3,500.

MODEL 147 - 12, 16, 20, or 28 (new 1995, 147E only) ga., 26 3/4 or 28 in. barrels, Anson & Deeley boxlock, any choke, SST (current) or DT, extractors, straight or pistol grip stock, hunting scene engraved. Disc. 1998, some inventory remained until 1999.

	$2,400	$1,875	$1,425	$1,100	$875	$750	$650

Last MSR was $2,995.

Add $200 for H&H style auto ejectors (Model 147E).

✳ *Model 147E* - 12 or 20 ga., similar to Model 147, except has ejectors, fixed choke barrels, 5.8-6.8 lbs.

MSR $5,495		$4,650	$3,550	$2,775	$2,200	$1,725	$1,400	$1,150

✳ *Model 147EL* - similar to Model 147E, except has luxury grade wood upgrade, fixed choke barrels. Importation began 1999.

MSR $6,795		$5,825	$4,450	$3,500	$3,000	$2,400	$1,875	$1,500

Add $500 for Model 147EL Custom Ltd. Ed. with English straight grip stock medallion and DTs (new 2008).

GRADING - PPGS™	100%	98%	95%	90%	80%	70%	60%

❖ **Model 147EL Sporter** - similar to Model 147EL, except available in 30 in. barrels with skeet chokes. Limited importation 2006, reintroduced 2008.

MSR $6,795	$5,825	$4,450	$3,500	$3,000	$2,400	$1,875	$1,500

MODEL 147SL - 12, 16 (disc. 2001), 20, 28 ga. (disc. 2003), or .410 (mfg. 1992 only) bore, coin finished sidelock action with Greener crossbolt and chopper lump extension, 25 1/2 (disc.), 26 (disc.), 26 3/4, or 28 in. fixed choke barrels, ejectors, ST (current) or DT, deluxe game scene engraving, 6-7 lbs.

MSR $10,495	$8,975	$6,600	$5,500	$4,400	$3,550	$2,850	$2,200

Add $750 for .410 bore (mfg. 1992 only).

✳ *Model 147SSL* - similar to Model 147SL, except has luxury wood upgrade. Imported 1999-2003.

	$8,600	$7,000	$6,000	$5,000	$4,450	$3,650	$3,150

Last MSR was $9,995.

28 ga. had limited availability during 2001.

MODEL 247SL - 12, 16 (disc. 2001), 20, or 28 ga., similar to Model 147SL, except has deluxe scroll engraving. Importation disc. 1991, resumed 1993-2003.

	$7,700	$5,300	$4,250	$3,425	$2,900	$2,500	$2,150

Last MSR was $8,995.

MODEL 280 PETITE FRAME - 28 ga. only, Anson & Deeley boxlock action with Greener crossbolt and double under barrel locking lugs, scroll engraving, case hardened receiver, H&H ejectors, DT, English style stock, 28 in. barrels bored IC/M, includes fitted luggage case. Importation began 2002.

MSR $4,695	$3,925	$2,600	$1,775	$1,325	$950	$875	$750

✳ *Model 280/360 2 Barrel Set* - includes 28 in. 28 ga. and .410 bore barrels bored IC/M. Importation began 2002.

MSR $7,295	$6,250	$5,400	$4,550	$3,900	$3,200	$2,650	$2,250

MODEL 280E PETITE FRAME - similar to Model 280 Petite Frame, except has fine hunting scenes engraved on silver receiver. Importation began 2002.

MSR $5,695	$4,900	$4,200	$3,400	$2,900	$2,400	$1,950	$1,500

MODEL 280EL PETITE FRAME - 28 ga. only, Anson & Deeley boxlock action with Greener crossbolt and double underbarrel locking lugs, fine hunting scene engraving, ejectors, DT, pistol grip or English style stock, 28 in. barrels bored IC/M, includes fitted luggage case, 5.2 lbs. Importation began 2000.

MSR $7,295	$6,350	$5,000	$4,100	$3,250	$2,650	$2,200	$1,750

Add $700 for Model 280EL Custom Ltd. Ed. with luxury wood Enlish style stock and DTs (new 2008).

✳ *Model 280EL/360EL 2 Barrel Set* - consists of both 28 ga. and .410 bore barrels with fitted luggage case. Importation began 2000.

MSR $10,595	$9,200	$7,600	$6,500	$5,850	$5,000	$4,200	$3,500

The Model 360EL was discontinued during 2005.

MODEL 280SL PETITE FRAME - 28 ga. only, H&H style sidelock action with Greener crossbolt and double under barrel locking lugs, English style arabesque engraving featuring small scrolls, ejectors, DT, pistol grip or English style stock, 28 in. barrels bored IC/M, includes fitted luggage case, 5.2 lbs. Importation began 2000.

MSR $10,995	$9,475	$7,600	$6,600	$5,800	$5,000	$4,150	$3,500

✳ *Model 280SSL Petite Frame* - similar to Model 280SL Petite Frame, except has quick detachable sideplates. Imported 2002-2003.

	$8,900	$7,450	$6,250	$5,100	$4,300	$3,600	$3,200

Last MSR was $10,495.

GRADING - PPGS™	100%	98%	95%	90%	80%	70%	60%

MODEL 347SL - 12, 16, or 20 ga., similar to Model 247S, except has more elaborate engraving and better walnut. Importation disc. 1991, resumed 1993-97.

	$7,000	$4,850	$3,950	$3,350	$2,775	$2,275	$1,925

Last MSR was $7,895.

MODEL 360 PETITE FRAME - .410 bore, 28 in. barrels bored IC/F, otherwise similar to Model 280 Petite Frame. Importation began 2002.

MSR $4,695	$4,100	$2,650	$2,000	$1,600	$1,150	$875	$750

MODEL 360E PETITE FRAME - similar to Model 360 Petite Frame, except has fine hunting scenes engraved on silver receiver. Imported 2002-2006.

	$4,750	$3,950	$3,300	$2,750	$2,350	$1,900	$1,600

Last MSR was $5,495.

MODEL 360EL PETITE FRAME - .410 bore, otherwise similar to Model 280EL, 5 1/2 lbs. Importation began 2000.

MSR $7,295	$6,450	$5,150	$4,250	$3,500	$2,775	$2,250	$1,850

MODEL 360SL PETITE FRAME - .410 bore, otherwise similar to Model 280SL, 5 1/2 lbs. Importation began 2000.

MSR $10,995	$9,475	$7,600	$6,600	$5,800	$5,000	$4,150	$3,500

✳ *Model 360SSL Petite Frame* - similar to Model 360SL Petite Frame, except has quick detachable sideplates. Imported 2002-2003.

	$8,950	$7,500	$6,350	$5,400	$4,700	$4,200	$3,500

Last MSR was $10,495.

MODEL 280SL/360SL 2 BARREL SET - consists of both 28 ga. and .410 bore barrels with fitted luggage case. Importation began 2000.

MSR $14,995	$13,000	$11,250	$9,850	$8,800	$7,300	$6,000	$4,900

The Model 360SL was discontinued during 2005.

MODEL 280SSL/360SSL 2 BARREL SET - similar to 280SL/360SL 2 barrel set, except has quick detachable sideplates. Imported 2002-2003.

	$12,450	$11,000	$9,950	$8,950	$7,500	$6,250	$5,000

Last MSR was $14,395.

MODEL 447SL - similar to Model 347S, except is also available in 28 ga. and has more delicate scroll engraving. Importation disc. 1991, resumed 1993-2003.

	$9,250	$8,350	$7,500	$6,500	$5,500	$4,500	$3,500

Last MSR was $10,995.

MODEL 1620 - 16 ga. only, Anson & Deely boxlock action, Greener crossbolt with double underbarrel locking lugs, 28 in. barrels with IC/Mod. fixed chokes, case hardened receiver with scroll engraving, H&H style ejectors, DT, English straight grip stock, includes fitted luggage case. Importation began 2002.

MSR $4,695	$4,100	$3,250	$2,650	$2,200	$1,850	$1,500	$1,275

✳ *Model 1620 2 Barrel Set* - includes 28 in. 16 and 20 ga. barrels bored IC/M. Importation began 2002.

MSR $7,295	$6,325	$5,250	$4,500	$3,750	$3,100	$2,650	$2,150

MODEL 1620E - 16 ga., similar to Model 1620, except has fine engraved hunting scenes on silver receiver. Importation began 2006.

MSR $5,695	$5,000	$4,200	$3,700	$3,225	$2,850	$2,300	$1,800

MODEL 1620EL - similar to Model 1620, except has finely engraved hunting scenes on silver receiver and luxury wood upgrade. Importation began 2002.

MSR $7,295	$6,225	$5,100	$4,375	$3,740	$3,150	$2,650	$2,150

✳ *Model 1620EL 2 Barrel Set* - includes 28 in. 16 and 20 ga. barrels bored IC/M. Importation began 2002.

MSR $10,595	$9,400	$8,000	$7,100	$6,200	$5,150	$4,250	$3,500

GRADING - PPGS™	100%	98%	95%	90%	80%	70%	60%

MODEL 1620SL - similar to Model 1620EL, except has sidelock action. Importation began 2002.

MSR $10,995	$9,475	$7,600	$6,600	$5,800	$5,000	$4,150	$3,500

✳ *Model 1620SL 2 Barrel Set* - includes 28 in. 16 and 20 ga. barrels bored IC/M. Importation began 2002.

MSR $14,995	$13,000	$11,250	$9,850	$8,800	$7,300	$6,000	$4,900

MODEL 1622 - 16 ga., 28 in. barrels, Greener crossbolt, double barrel under-barrel locking lugs, case hardened receiver with cocking indicators, Anson & Deely boxlock action with full sideplates, H&H ejectors, SST or DT, pistol grip or English style stock, 6.3 lbs. Imported 2006-2007.

	$4,750	$4,100	$3,650	$3,300	$2,950	$2,400	$1,875

Last MSR was $5,495.

✳ *Model 1622 2 Barrel Set* - includes 28 in. 16 and 20 ga. barrels bored IC/M. Imported 2006-2007.

	$7,375	$6,100	$5,500	$4,900	$4,250	$3,450	$2,750

Last MSR was $8,295.

✳ *Model 1622E* - similar to Model 1622, except had hand engraved game scenes on silver finished receiver. Imported 2006-2007.

	$5,975	$4,950	$4,400	$3,875	$3,400	$2,950	$2,300

Last MSR was $6,895.

✳ *Model 1622EL* - similar to Model 1622E, except has luxury grade wood. Imported 2006-2007.

	$8,000	$6,400	$5,850	$5,200	$4,750	$3,950	$3,150

Last MSR was $9,195.

✳ *Model 1622EL 2 Barrel Set* - includes 28 in. 16 and 20 ga. barrels bored IC/M. Imported 2006-2007.

	$10,400	$8,750	$7,950	$7,100	$6,300	$5,200	$4,000

Last MSR was $11,995.

SHOTGUNS: SPORTING CLAYS

MODEL 47LSC SxS SPORTING CLAYS - 12 ga. only, features Anson & Deeley boxlock action with scroll engraved case hardened receiver, 28 in. barrels with Briley screw-in chokes, H&H style ejectors, SST adj. for length of pull, select grade checkered walnut stock with pistol grip and beavertail forearm, competition recoil pad. Disc. 1994.

	$2,725	$2,400	$2,050	$1,725	$1,450	$1,125	$925

Last MSR was $2,995.

MODEL 200SC O/U SPORTING CLAYS - 12 ga. only, 3 in. chambers, 30 in. VR fixed choke barrels with lengthened forcing cones, Kersten double cross-bolt lock, color case hardened receiver, Blitz action, SST, fitted luggage case. Imported 1995-96.

	$6,750	$4,600	$3,750	$3,200	$2,625	$2,175	$1,850

Last MSR was $7,495.

Add $500 for Briley choke tubes (5 total).

MERRILL

Previous manufacturer located in Tucson, AZ. This original pistol design was by Jim Rock, who then joined R.P.M.

A newer variation of the Sportsman, now designated the XL and Hunter Model XL was offered by R.P.M. Please refer to the R.P.M. listing for more information.

GRADING - PPGS™	100%	98%	95%	90%	80%	70%	60%

PISTOLS: SINGLE SHOT

SPORTSMAN MODEL - .22 S, L, or LR, .22 Mag., .22 Rem. Jet., .22 Hornet, .30 Herrett, .30 Merrill, .38 Spl., .357 Mag., .357 Herrett, 7mm Merrill, 7mm Rocket, .256 Win. Mag., .45 LC, .44 Mag., or .30-30 Win. cal., 9, 10 3/4, or 14 in. barrel, hinged break open action, smooth walnut grips.

	$650	$575	$525	$450	$395	$350	$300

    Add $70 for interchangeable barrels.
    Add $25 for wrist support.

MERWIN HULBERT & CO.

Previous company with headquarters located in New York, NY circa 1874-1891.

Merwin Hulbert offered very high quality revolvers which were serious competitors with the Colt, Smith & Wesson, and Remington large frame single actions during this era. Their guns are believed to have been manufactured in a separate section of the Hopkins & Allen plant. Most will have both Merwin Hulbert and Hopkins & Allen markings on the barrel.

Merwin revolvers have a unique twist-open mechanism. The latch on the bottom of the frame is pushed towards the rear, while barrel & cylinder are twisted clockwise and pulled forward. This design was intended to allow selective ejection of empty cases while leaving unfired cartridges in the cylinder.

Merwins will often be found with a distinctive, and unusual "punch dot" style engraving, often with some sort of simple panel scene (an animal, bird, flowers, etc.) on one or (rare) both sides of the frame. These will usually bring perhaps a 50% premium in lower grades, while in higher condition may bring double or triple what an undecorated gun will bring.

100%	98%	95%	90%	80%	70%	60%	50%	40%	30%	20%	10%

REVOLVERS: LARGE FRAME

All chambered for either .44 Merwin Hulbert (usually no caliber markings), .44 Russian (usually marked "Russian Model"), or .44-40 (marked "Calibre Winchester 1873"). Blue finish is rare and will being a premium.

The Merwin Hulbert system was copied by various Spanish and possibly other makers. These foreign copies will bring significantly less than original Merwins.

FIRST MODEL FRONTIER ARMY SA - .44 cal., square butt, open-top, scoop flutes on cylinder, 7 1/2 in. barrel, 1 screw above triggerguard.

$8,000	$6,000	$3,500	$2,750	$1,800	$1,600	$1,400	$1,200	$1,050	$950	$875	$750

SECOND MODEL FRONTIER ARMY SA - similar to First Model, except has only one screw above triggerguard.

$7,500	$5,500	$3,250	$2,500	$1,700	$1,500	$1,250	$1,100	$995	$900	$800	$700

SECOND MODEL POCKET ARMY SA - similar to Second Model Frontier Army, except has birdshead butt instead of square butt, 3 1/2 in. or 7 (scarce) in. barrel, may be marked "POCKET ARMY".

$7,000	$5,000	$3,000	$2,500	$1,250	$1,100	$1,000	$900	$800	$700	$600	$500

    Add 10% for 7 in. barrel.
There are no First Model Pocket Army models.

THIRD MODEL FRONTIER ARMY SA - .44 cal., square butt, top strap, usually has conventional fluting on cylinder, but some have scoop flutes, 7 in. round barrel with no rib.

$6,000	$4,250	$3,000	$2,500	$1,250	$1,100	$1,000	$900	$800	$700	$600	$500

THIRD MODEL FRONTIER ARMY DA - similar to Third Model Frontier Army SA, except is double action.

$6,000	$3,950	$2,750	$2,250	$1,150	$1,000	$900	$800	$700	$625	$550	$450

There are no First or Second Model Army double action models.

100%	98%	95%	90%	80%	70%	60%	50%	40%	30%	20%	10%

THIRD MODEL POCKET ARMY SA - .44 cal., single action, birdshead butt, top strap, 3 1/2 in. or 7 in. round barrel with no rib.

100%	98%	95%	90%	80%	70%	60%	50%	40%	30%	20%	10%
$6,000	$3,950	$2,750	$2,250	$1,150	$1,000	$900	$800	$700	$625	$550	$450

THIRD MODEL POCKET ARMY DA - similar to Third Model Pocket Army SA, except is double action.

$4,750	$3,950	$2,750	$2,250	$1,150	$1,000	$900	$800	$700	$625	$550	$450

FOURTH MODEL FRONTIER ARMY SA - .44 cal., 3 1/2, 5 (most common), or 7 in. unique ribbed barrel, square butt, top strap, conventional flutes.

$7,000	$5,750	$5,000	$4,250	$3,500	$2,500	$1,750	$1,250	$1,050	$925	$850	$750

FOURTH MODEL FRONTIER ARMY DA - similar to Fourth Model Frontier Army SA, except is double action.

$7,000	$5,250	$4,750	$3,500	$2,750	$2,150	$1,650	$1,150	$975	$875	$725	$625

FOREIGN COPIES OF LARGE FRAME REVOLVERS - .44 cal.

> These models may be based on any configuration, but 2nd & 3rd Frontier Army styles are probably the most commonly found. The words "Merwin Hulbert" (such as "Sistema Merwin Hulbert") may appear somewhere on the revolver, but are rarely, if ever, found with the Hopkins & Allen marking. These will usually bring half or less what a comparable genuine Merwin will bring.

REVOLVERS: MEDIUM & SMALL FRAME

Medium frame revolvers were usually 5 shot in .38 cal., or 7 shot in .32 cal. The small frame was a 5 shot in .32 cal. Models chambered for .38 MH or .32 MH cal. are very similar to the black powder loadings of the .38 S&W and .32 S&W cal.

FIRST POCKET MODEL SA - .38 cal., 5-shot, spur-trigger, w/ cyl. pin exposed at the front of the frame, distinguishing feature is round loading hole in recoil shield, with no loading gate.

$1,600	$1,200	$825	$750	$625	$550	$495	$450	$375	$325	$275	$225

SECOND POCKET MODEL SA - .38 cal., 5-shot, similar to First Model, except has sliding loading gate.

$1,500	$1,100	$750	$675	$600	$500	$460	$425	$360	$315	$260	$215

THIRD POCKET MODEL SA - .38 cal., 5-shot, similar to First Model, except has enclosed cylinder pin.

$1,350	$1,000	$700	$650	$575	$475	$440	$415	$350	$300	$255	$210

THIRD POCKET MODEL SA WITH TRIGGERGUARD - .38 cal., 5-shot, similar to Third Pocket Model, except has conventional triggerguard.

$1,350	$1,000	$700	$650	$575	$475	$440	$415	$350	$300	$255	$210

MEDIUM FRAME DA POCKET MODEL - .38 cal., 5 shot, double action, may have folding hammer spur.

$950	$775	$500	$450	$415	$365	$335	$300	$275	$250	$225	$200

Add 10% for folding hammer spur.

MEDIUM FRAME DA POCKET MODEL - .32 cal., 7 shot, double action.

$1,200	$875	$675	$625	$550	$450	$425	$395	$340	$295	$250	$210

SMALL FRAME DA POCKET MODEL - .32 cal., 5 shot, double action.

$1,000	$775	$500	$450	$415	$365	$335	$300	$275	$250	$225	$200

TIP-UP .22 MODEL - .22 rimfire cal., 7 shot, spur trigger, closely patterned after the S&W Model One. Very scarce.

$1,200	$875	$675	$625	$550	$450	$425	$395	$340	$295	$250	$210

RIFLES: SINGLE SHOT

These rifles were generally patterned after the Hopkins & Allen single shots. The Merwin Hulbert name marking may bring a 25%-50% over models that do not have this marking.

MICHIGAN ARMS

Previous manufacturer located in Michigan until circa 1981.

PISTOLS: SEMI-AUTO

GUARDIAN - SS - .380 ACP cal., patterned after the Walther PPK, bears close resemblance to the Indian Arms .380 semi-auto, 3 1/4 in. barrel, checkered walnut grips with medallion, 6 shot finger extension mag., fixed sights. Limited mfg.

$375	$295	$225	$210	$190	$170	$150

This model was mfg. by using Indian Arms tooling.

M1911 A1 - .45 ACP cal., patterned after the Colt M1911 A1, fixed sights, 7 shot mag. Disc.

$450	$395	$350	$275	$225	$210	$190

MIDLAND RIFLES

Previous trademark of rifles manufactured by Gibbs Rifle Co. (please refer to the G section for previous models and pricing) and older models mfg. by Parker-Hale, Ltd. (please refer to the P section).

MIIDA

Previously manufactured by Nikko Firearms, Ltd. in Tochigi, Japan. Previously imported by Marubeni America Corp. located in New York, NY circa 1972-1974.

SHOTGUNS: O/U

MODEL 612 FIELD - 12 ga., 26 or 28 in. barrels, VR, various chokes, boxlock, auto ejectors, single selective trigger, checkered pistol grip stock. Mfg. 1972-1974.

$800	$725	$650	$575	$510	$440	$400

MODEL 2100 SKEET GUN - similar to Model 612, with 27 in. VR, skeet bore barrels, more elaborate engraving. Mfg. 1972-1974.

$875	$775	$700	$615	$550	$465	$425

MODEL 2200T TRAP GUN - similar to Model 2100, except with 29 3/4 in. imp. mod. and full choke barrels, wide VR, 60% engraved coverage and select wood. Mfg. 1972-1974.

$925	$825	$750	$665	$595	$500	$450

MODEL 2200S SKEET GUN - similar to Model 2200T, except with 27 in. skeet bore barrels.

$925	$825	$750	$665	$595	$500	$450

MODEL 2300 SERIES TRAP OR SKEET - similar to Model 2200 Trap/Skeet but with more engraving. Mfg. 1972-1974.

$975	$875	$800	$715	$630	$550	$500

MODEL GRT GRANDEE TRAP GUN - 12 ga., 29 3/4 in. full choke barrels, single selective trigger, auto ejector, boxlock with side plates, receiver fully engraved as well as breech ends of barrel, triggerguard and locking lever, gold inlaid, extensive silver line inlays, high grade select walnut stock. Mfg. 1972-1974.

$2,500	$2,200	$1,900	$1,575	$1,250	$1,000	$850

MODEL GRS GRANDEE SKEET GUN - similar to Model GRT, with 27 in. skeet bored barrels.

$2,500	$2,200	$1,900	$1,575	$1,250	$1,000	$850

MILLER ARMS

Current trademark owned by Dakota Arms, and located in Sturgis, SD.

GRADING - PPGS™	100%	98%	95%	90%	80%	70%	60%

RIFLES: LEVER ACTION

SINGLE SHOT RIFLE - various cals. between .17 Dakota - .416 Rem. Mag., XXX English style checkered walnut stock and Schnabel forend, falling block action. New 2004.

✳ *Single Shot Classic* - various centerfire cals. up to .375 H&H, 24 in. round barrel, Hi-Wall falling block action with curved Farquharson lever, plain matte receiver, 7 1/2 lbs.

MSR $4,595	$4,350	$3,700	$3,175	$2,725	$2,350	$1,975	$1,500

✳ *Single Shot Low Boy* - various centerfire cals., 24 in. half round, half octagon barrel, falling block action, case colored receiver with gold Miller banner, jeweled block, 7 lbs.

MSR $5,195	$4,800	$4,200	$3,625	$3,125	$2,600	$2,300	$1,800

✳ *Single Shot Model F* - various centerfire cals. up to .45-110, 26 in. octagon barrel, lever style falling block action, perch belly buttstock, Queen Anne grip, cheekpiece, stainless steel receiver, tang sight with front globe, checkered steel buttplate or black recoil pad, 6 lbs.

MSR $6,095	$5,650	$4,900	$4,100	$3,550	$3,100	$2,750	$2,250

MILLER, DAVID CO.

See David Miller Co. listing.

MIL-SPEC INDUSTRIES CORP.

Previous pistol manufacturer and current components supplier located in Roslyn Heights, NY since 1996.

PISTOLS: SEMI-AUTO

MIL-SPEC 1911 A1 - 9mm Para., 9x21mm, 9x22mm, .40 S&W, .45 HP, or .45 ACP cal., high tech polymer and stainless steel frame, beavertail grip safety, aluminum trigger, 10 shot mag., 3 15/16 (Compact), 5 5/16 (Combat with compensator), or 5 (Government) in. barrel, choice of wood, plastic, or rubber grips, 39 1/2-46 oz. Mfg. late 1996-2006.

	$625	$550	$500	$450	$400	$360	$330

Last MSR was $690.

Add $5 for parkerized finish.
Add $45 for electroless nickel finish.
Add $50 for hard chrome finish.

MILTEX, INC.

Previous handgun importer located in La Plata, MD. Miltex imported commercial Makarovs until approx. 2000.

MIROKU FIREARMS MFG. CO.

Current manufacturer established during 1893 and located in Kochi, Japan. Miroku currently manufactures long arms for Browning and Winchester (please refer to individual sections), in addition to their own line of firearms mostly distributed in Europe.

Shotguns marked Miroku only without another trademark listing represent that period of manufacture before Miroku began manufacturing shotguns for other companies (i.e. Charles Daly, Browning, and others). Most guns marked Miroku only were made on a limited basis and although somewhat rare, collector desirability to date has been minimal. Since model notations were not specified in most instances (many shotguns were made to test market demand), a model rundown is virtually impossible. Values can be approx. ascertained by comparing a Miroku shotgun of similar gauge, features, engraving/wood, and condition to an equivalent Japanese Charles Daly model. Miroku also manufactured revolvers up until approx. 1964 which may be designated Liberty Chief - limited importation into the U.S.

GRADING - PPGS™	100%	98%	95%	90%	80%	70%	60%

MITCHELL ARMS, INC.

Previous manufacturer, importer, and distributor located in Fountain Valley, CA.

DERRINGERS: O/U

GUARDIAN ANGEL - .22 LR or .22 Mag. cal., double action, hammerless, choice of blue, satin, nickel, or gold finish. Mfg. 1996-97.

$125	$105	$95	$85	$80	$75	$70

Last MSR was $150.

Add $10 for .22 Mag. cal.
Add $20 for blue or nickel finish.
Add $40 for gold finish.
Add $10 for Deluxe Model with case and angel charm.

PISTOLS: SEMI-AUTO

AMERICAN EAGLE LUGER - 9mm Para. cal., 4 in. barrel, stainless steel with toggle action, checkered American walnut grips, American Eagle version, contoured front grip strap. Disc. 1994.

$590	$475	$400	$335	$290	$245	$215

Last MSR was $695.

ROLLING BLOCK PISTOL - .22 LR, .22 Mag., .223 Rem., .357 Mag., or .45 LC cal., reproduction of the Remington Rolling Block design, 10 in. barrel. Mfg. 1991-92 only.

$340	$285	$240	$210	$185	$170	$150

Last MSR was $395.

Mitchell .22 Cal. Target Pistols

Mitchell Arms manufactured High Standard marked pistols during 1993-94. Due to litigation, the High Standard logo was dropped in 1994, and High Standard model nomenclature was dropped in 1996. These guns feature push button barrel takedown and usually, a choice between stainless steel or royal blue steel construction. Mitchell Arms is not responsible for the older High Standard pistols manufactured in New Haven and East Hartford, CT, even though Mitchell parts are interchangeable with original High Standard pistols.

MONARCH (CITATION II) - .22 LR cal., 5 1/2 bull or 7 1/4 in. fluted barrel, frame mounted bridge rear sight, checkered walnut grips with thumbrest, push button takedown, stippled front and rear grip straps, adj. trigger, travel, and weight, stainless steel or royal blue finish. Mfg. 1993-2000.

$395	$295	$245	$215	$190	$170	$150

Last MSR was $490.

MEDALIST (OLYMPIC I.S.U.) - .22 S or LR (new 1994) cal., military grip style, 6 3/4 in. special barrel with internal stabilizer, adj. barrel weights, other features similar to Citation II, stainless steel or blue finish. Mfg. 1993-2000.

$625	$550	$425	$375	$325	$275	$22

Last MSR was $700.

BARON (SHARPSHOOTER II) - .22 LR cal., 5 1/2 in. bull barrel, standard trigger, adj. rear sight, smooth grip frame, stainless steel or blue (disc.) finish. Mfg. 1993-2000.

$320	$280	$240	$210	$185	$160	$135

Last MSR was $400.

SPORTSTER (SPORT KING II) - .22 LR cal., 4 1/2 or 6 3/4 in. tapered barrel, military black checkered plastic grips, stainless steel only, adj. rear sight. Mfg. 1993-2000.

$270	$220	$185	$160	$135	$120	$110

Last MSR was $330.

GRADING - PPGS™	100%	98%	95%	90%	80%	70%	60%

MEDALLION (TROPHY II) - .22 LR cal., 5 1/2 in. bull or 7 1/4 in. fluted barrel, military grips with full checkering and thumbrest, bridge rear sight, gold-plated trigger safety and mag. release, stippled front and rear grip straps, stainless steel or royal blue (disc. 1997) finish. Mfg. 1993-2000.

	$425	$350	$275	$225	$190	$170	$150

Last MSR was $500.

SOVEREIGN (VICTOR II) - .22 LR cal., 4 1/2 or 5 1/2 in. full length VR or black rib barrel, checkered walnut grips with thumbrest, stainless steel became standard 1998, gold-plated trigger, safety, mag. release, and slide lock, rib mounted sights. Mfg. 1993-2000.

	$500	$425	$375	$325	$275	$225	$195

Last MSR was $600.

Add $80 for Weaver style base built into VR.

HIGH STANDARD COLLECTORS ASSOCIATION SPECIAL EDITIONS

* **HSCA-SE Trophy II** - .22 LR cal., 100 mfg. 1993 only, cased.

	$450	$375	$300	$240	$210	$180	$155

* **HSCA-SE Victor II**

	$495	$400	$325	$265	$230	$195	$170

* **HSCA-SE Citation II**

	$435	$365	$285	$225	$195	$165	$140

* **HSCA-SE Three Gun Set** - includes Trophy II, Olympic II, and Victor II.

	$1,495	$1,295	$1,050	$935	$755	$640	$535

* **HSCA-SE Six Gun Set** - includes 6 3/4 in. I.S.U. Olympic (.22 Short), 4 1/2 in. Victor, 7 1/4 in. Citation, 5 1/2 in. Sharpshooter, 4 1/2 in. Sport King, and Trophy Model. Special engraving, cased, HSCA prefix with 2-digit serial number, 19 sets total mfg. 1994 only.

	$2,650	$2,100	$1,675	$1,475	$1,210	$1,015	$845

Last MSR was $2,995.

Mitchell Centerfire Pistols

MODEL 57A (TOKAREV DESIGN) - .30 Mauser cal., single action semi-auto, 9 shot mag., hammer block and mag. safety, all steel construction. Imported from Yugoslavia 1990 only.

	$240	$215	$180	$160	$145	$135	$120

Last MSR was $280.

MODEL 70A (TOKAREV DESIGN) - 9mm Para. cal., otherwise similar to Model 57A. Imported from Yugoslavia 1990 only.

	$240	$215	$180	$160	$145	$135	$120

Last MSR was $280.

88A OFFICERS MODEL (TOKAREV DESIGN) - 9mm Para. cal., newer slenderized variation issued to the Officers Corps., short slide and frame, finger extension mag. Imported from Yugoslavia 1990 only.

	$255	$225	$190	$165	$145	$135	$120

Last MSR was $300.

SKORPION - while advertised during 1987, this model never went into production.

SPECTRE - while advertised during 1987, this model never went into production.

1911 GOLD/SIGNATURE SERIES (STANDARD) - .45 ACP cal., features new tapered barrel slide lock-up, wide body accepts staggered mag., full length guide rod recoil buffer assembly, beveled mag. well, blue (disc. 1995) or stainless steel, 8 shot mag., walnut checkered grips, fixed or adj. sights. New 1994-disc.

GRADING - PPGS™	100%	98%	95%	90%	80%	70%	60%

✳ *1911 Gold/Signature Series (Standard) Blue Finish*

	$465	$395	$350	$325	$295	$270	$250

Last MSR was $535.

✳ *1911 Gold/Signature Series (Standard) Stainless Steel* - disc. 1997.

	$675	$585	$525	$440	$385	$325	$280

Last MSR was $675.

✳ *1911 Gold/Signature Series (Standard) Tactical Model* - stainless steel, features elongated grip safety and serrated front slide, fixed or adj. rear sight. Mfg. 1996-97.

	$640	$550	$500	$430	$375	$315	$270

Last MSR was $735.

Add $40 for adj. rear sight.

✳ *1911 Gold/Signature Series (Standard) Bullseye Model* - similar to Tactical Model, except has fully adj. rear sight. Mfg. 1996-97.

	$850	$700	$575	$480	$410	$350	$295

Last MSR was $950.

✳ *1911 Gold/Signature Series (Standard) IPSC Limited Model* - choice of ghost ring or adj. rear sight. Mfg. 1996-97.

	$1,075	$875	$675	$565	$480	$400	$350

Last MSR was $1,195.

Add $45 for ghost ring sight.

1911 GOLD/SIGNATURE SERIES (WIDE BODY) - .45 ACP cal., features new tapered barrel slide lock-up, full length guide rod recoil buffer assembly, beveled mag. well, blue (disc. 1995) or stainless steel, 10 (C/B 1994) or 13* shot mag., walnut checkered grips, fixed or adj. sights. Mfg. 1994-97.

✳ *1911 Gold/Signature Series (Wide Body) Blue Finish*

	$595	$525	$475	$425	$375	$335	$295

Last MSR was $685.

✳ *1911 Gold/Signature Series (Wide Body) Standard Model* - stainless steel, fixed sights, smooth grips. Mfg. 1996-97.

	$765	$650	$550	$460	$395	$335	$285

Last MSR was $840.

✳ *1911 Gold/Signature Series (Wide Body) Tactical Model* - stainless steel, features elongated grip safety and serrated front slide, adj. rear sight. Mfg. 1996-97.

	$795	$675	$575	$480	$410	$350	$295

Last MSR was $895.

MITCHELL .44 - .44 Mag. cal., 5 1/2 in. barrel, blue finish, 7 shot mag., checkered walnut grips, adj. rear sight. Mfg. 1996-97.

	$1,050	$900	$800	$725	$650	$575	$495

Last MSR was $1,190.

JEFF COOPER SIGNATURE/COMMEMORATIVE MODEL - .45 ACP cal., blue finish. Mfg. 1996-97.

✳ *Jeff Cooper Signature Model*

	$725	$625	$560	N/A	N/A	N/A	N/A

Last MSR was $795.

✳ *Jeff Cooper Commemorative Model* - 1,000 mfg. 1996-97.

	$1,650	$1,400	$1,200	N/A	N/A	N/A	N/A

Last MSR was $1,895.

ALPHA SERIES - while advertised in 1995, this model never went into production.

GRADING - PPGS™	100%	98%	95%	90%	80%	70%	60%

REVOLVERS: SINGLE ACTION

SINGLE ACTION ARMY - .22 LR (disc.), .357 Mag., .44-40 WCF (new 1998), .44 Mag. (disc.), .45 ACP (disc.), or .45 LC cal., 4 3/4, 5 1/2, 6 (disc. 1993), or 7 1/2 in. barrel lengths, hammer block safety mechanism, steel construction, case hardened frame, one-piece walnut stock. Imported 1986-94, re-introduced 1997. Disc.

❋ *SAA Cowboy Model* - .357 Mag., .44-40 WCF, .45 ACP (disc.), or .45 LC cal., 4 3/4 in. barrel.

$395	$350	$315	$275	$260	$245	$230

Last MSR was $450.

Add $50 for nickel finish.
Add $50 for adj. rear sight (disc.).
Add $150 for dual cylinder (.357 Mag./9mm Para., .45 LC/.45 ACP, or .44-40 WCF/.44 Spl.).
Add $95 for steel back strap and triggerguard (disc.).
This model is also available in a Bat Masterson variation.

❋ *SAA U.S. Army Model* - similar to Cowboy Model, except has 5 1/2 in. barrel.

$395	$350	$315	$275	$260	$245	$230

Last MSR was $450.

Add $50 for nickel finish.
Add $150 for dual cylinder (.357 Mag./9mm Para., .45 LC/.45 ACP, or .44-40 WCF/.44 Spl.).

❋ *SAA U.S. Cavalry Model* - similar to Cowboy Model, except has 7 1/2 in. barrel.

$395	$350	$315	$275	$260	$245	$230

Last MSR was $450.

Add $150 for dual cylinder (.357 Mag./9mm Para., .45 LC/.45 ACP, or .44-40 WCF/.44 Spl.).
Add $50 for nickel finish.

❋ *SAA .44 Mag.* - .44 Mag. cal., fully adj. target sights. Disc. 1992.

$425	$350	$295	$250	$200	$180	$165

Last MSR was $495.

❋ *SAA Rimfire Model* - .22 LR cal. Importation disc. 1989.

$230	$200	$180	$160	$145	$130	$120

Last MSR was $280.

Add $30 for adj. rear sight.

❋ *SAA Silhouette Model* - available with 10, 12, or 18 in. barrel in .44 Mag. or .45 LC cal. Importation disc. 1991.

$395	$325	$260	$220	$195	$170	$155

Last MSR was $450.

Add $175 for shoulder stock (available with 18 in. barrel only).
The shoulder stock was available with .44 Mag./.44-40 WCF cals. only.

❋ *SAA Dual Cylinder* - available in either .22 LR/.22 Mag. (disc.), .22 LR/.22 Mag. stainless (disc. 1988), .357 Mag./9mm Para. (disc. 1993), .44 Mag./.44-40 WCF (disc. 1991), or .45 LC/.45 ACP (new 1990) cal. Imported 1986-94.

$475	$415	$365	$335	$300	$275	$250

Last MSR was $549.

Add $50 for adj. rear sight (disc.).
Add $39 for nickel finish.
Add $93 for for steel backstrap.

❋ *SAA Stainless Model* - available in .22 LR or .357 Mag. (disc. 1987) cal. only, adj. sights. Imported 1986-88 only.

$260	$225	$195	$145	$120	$105	$90

Last MSR was $301.

Add $25 for .357 Mag.

GRADING - PPGS™	100%	98%	95%	90%	80%	70%	60%

BAT MASTERSON MODEL - .45 LC cal., 4 3/4 , 5 1/2, or 7 1/2 in. barrel with full ejector rod housing, nickel-plated, one-piece walnut stocks, hammer-block safety, rear sight is square notch in frame, two-piece backstrap. Imported 1989-94.

	$375	$285	$240	$210	$185	$170	$150

Last MSR was $450.

Add $156 for extra .45 ACP cylinder.

MODEL 1875 REMINGTON - .357 Mag. or .45 LC cal., royal blue finish with color case hardened frame, walnut grips. Imported 1990-91.

	$345	$285	$245	$210	$185	$170	$150

Last MSR was $399.

Add $76 for nickel finish.
Add $51 for extra convertible .45 ACP cylinder.

REVOLVERS: DOUBLE ACTION

TITAN II - .357 Mag. cal., 6 shot, 2, 4, or 6 in. barrel, blue or stainless, fixed sights, shrouded ejector rod, target hammer. Mfg. 1995 only.

	$285	$250	$220	$190	$170	$150	$135

Last MSR was $339.

TITAN III - similar to Titan II, except has adj. rear sight. Mfg. 1995 only.

	$340	$285	$245	$200	$175	$150	$135

Last MSR was $429.

GUARDIAN II - .38 Spl. cal., 6 shot, 3 or 4 in. barrel, fixed sights, blue only, target or combat grips. Mfg. 1995 only.

	$240	$215	$185	$165	$145	$130	$120

Last MSR was $275.

GUARDIAN III - similar to Guardian II, except has adj. rear sight, and 6 in. barrel. Mfg. 1995 only.

	$260	$230	$195	$175	$155	$140	$130

Last MSR was $305.

RIFLES: BOLT ACTION, RECENT MAUSER IMPORT

Beginning 1999, Mitchell Arms imported a sizeable quantity of WWII Mauser 98Ks manufactured in Yugoslavia during/after WWII. These guns are basically in new condition, having been only test fired over the past 50 years. They are supplied with bayonet and scabbard, military leather sling, original field cleaning kit, and leather ammo pouch. Caliber is 8mm Mauser (7.9x57mm), and all parts numbers match on these rifles. Basic retail on the Standard Grade is $225, w/o accessories. Additionally, a Collector Grade is $395, and a premium grade rifle is available for $495 (both include accessories).

RIFLES: DISC.

MODEL 15/22 OR 20/22 SEMI-AUTO CARBINE - .22 LR cal., American walnut stock, high polish blue, detachable 10 shot mag. Mfg. 1994-95.

	$155	$125	$105	$95	$85	$75	$65

Last MSR was $179.

Subtract $40 for 20/22 Special.
Add $20 for Deluxe model (includes deluxe walnut, rosewood accents, and fine line checkering).

LW22 SEMI-AUTO - .22 LR cal., 10 shot mag., composite or skeleton stock, patterned after Feather Industries semi-auto. Limited mfg. 1996-97.

	$240	$220	$195	$175	$160	$145	$130

Last MSR was $275.

Add $30 for composite stock.

GRADING - PPGS™	100%	98%	95%	90%	80%	70%	60%

LW9 SEMI-AUTO - 9mm Para. cal., semi-auto, blowback action, composite or skeleton stock, patterned after Feather Industries 9mm Para. semi-auto. Limited mfg. 1996-97.

	$450	$395	$360	$330	$300	$270	$240

Last MSR was $500.

Add $35 for composite stock.

MODEL 9303/9304/9305 STANDARD BOLT ACTION - .22 LR (9303) or .22 Mag. (9304, new 1995) cal., standard or deluxe variation, 10 shot mag. Mfg. 1994-95.

	$240	$195	$180	$160	$145	$130	$120

Last MSR was $275.

Add $14 for .22 Mag. cal.
Subtract $76 for special bolt action (9305).

MODEL 9301/9302 DELUXE BOLT ACTION - similar to 9304/9305, except includes deluxe walnut, rosewood accents, and fine line checkering. Mfg. 1994-95.

	$265	$220	$190	$170	$150	$135	$125

Last MSR was $313.

Add $12 for .22 Mag. cal.

M-16A3 - .22 LR, .22 Mag. (disc. 1987), or .32 ACP cal., patterned after Colt's AR-15. Mfg. 1987-94.

	$335	$295	$275	$260	$245	$230	$220

Last MSR was $266.

Add $100 for .22 Mag. cal. or .32 ACP (disc. 1988).

CAR-15/22 - .22 LR cal., carbine variation of M-16 with shorter barrel and collapsible stock. Mfg. 1990-94.

	$335	$295	$275	$260	$245	$230	$220

Last MSR was $266.

GALIL - .22 LR or .22 Mag. cal., patterned after Galil semi-auto paramilitary design rifle, choice of wood stock or folding stock (new 1992). Mfg. 1987-93.

	$285	$240	$195	$160	$150	$140	$130

Last MSR was $359.

MAS - .22 LR or .22 Mag. cal., patterned after French MAS rifle. Mfg. 1987-93.

	$285	$240	$195	$160	$150	$140	$130

Last MSR was $359.

Add $75 for .22 Mag. cal. (disc. 1988).

PPS-30/50 - .22 LR cal., patterned after the Russian WWII PPS military rifle, full length barrel shroud, 20 shot banana mag., adj. rear sight, walnut stock. Mfg. 1989-94.

	$235	$195	$175	$160	$145	$130	$120

Last MSR was $266.

Add $100 for 50 shot drum magazine.

SPECTRE CARBINE - while advertised during 1987, this model never went into production.

AK-22 - .22 LR or .22 Mag. (new 1988) cal., copy of the famous Russian AK-47, fully adj. sights, built-in cleaning rod, high quality European walnut or folding stock, 20 shot mag. Mfg. 1985-94.

	$235	$195	$175	$160	$145	$130	$120

Last MSR was $266.

Add $40 for folding stock.

GRADING - PPGS™	100%	98%	95%	90%	80%	70%	60%

AK-47 - 7.62x39 cal., copy of the original Kalashnikov AK-47, semi-auto, teak stock and forend, 30 shot steel mag., last shot hold open. Mfg. in Yugoslavia. Imported 1986-89.

               $1,795 $1,650 $1,600 $1,500 $1,350 $1,200 $1,000

Last MSR was $675.

     Add $23 for steel folding buttstock.
     Add $150 for 75 shot steel drum mag.

.308 WIN. NATO AK-47 (M77B1) - .308 Win. cal., milled receiver, adj. gas port, otherwise similar to AK-47 except has scope rail, day/night Tritium sights, and 20 shot mag. Imported 1989 only.

               $1,350 $1,225 $1,100 $975 $875 $800 $750

Last MSR was $775.

     Add $600 for military issue sniper scope and rings.

M76 - similar to AK-47, except is 7.92mm cal. and has longer barrel and frame set up for scope mount, counter sniper design, 10 shot mag., mfg. to mil. specs. Imported 1986-89.

               $1,875 $1,650 $1,475 $1,200 $950 $850 $760

Last MSR was $1,995.

SKS-M59 - 7.62x39 cal., copy of the SKS-M59 standard rifle, full walnut stock, fully adj. sights, gas operated. Mfg. in Yugoslavia. Imported 1986-89.

               $725 $600 $525 $450 $400 $350 $300

Last MSR was $699.

R.P.K. - 7.62x39mm or .308 Win. cal., forged heavy barrel with cooling fins, teak stock, detachable bipod, mil. specs. Importation disc. 1992.

               $1,100 $975 $850 $750 $650 $550 $500

Last MSR was $1,150.

     Add $845 for .308 Win. cal.

MODEL M-90 - 7.62x39mm or .308 Win. cal., AK-47 type action, in various configurations (heavy barrel, folding or fixed stock, finned barrel, etc.), plastic thumbhole stock, 5 shot mag., limited importation from Yugoslavia 1991-92.

               $900 $800 $700 $650 $600 $550 $500

Last MSR was $829.

     Add 20% for folding stock.
     Add 10% for .308 Win. cal. (wood stock only).

This model was subjected to modification due to ATF regulations after arrival in the U.S.

RIFLES: REPRODUCTIONS

HENRY RIFLE - .44-40 WCF cal., polished brass frame, octagonal barrel, original loading system. Imported 1990.

               $840 $650 $585 $520 $465 $415 $375

Last MSR was $999.

Iron frame also available at extra charge.

MODEL 1866 - .22 LR (disc.), .38 Spl. (disc.), or .44-40 WCF cal., patterned after the Winchester Model 1866 rifle, solid brass frame, octagon barrel. Imported 1990-93.

               $715 $535 $465 $415 $375 $335 $295

Last MSR was $829.

This model was also available in a carbine variation.

GRADING - PPGS™	100%	98%	95%	90%	80%	70%	60%

MODEL 1873 - .22 LR (disc.), .38 Spl.(disc), .357 Mag. (disc.), .44-40 WCF (disc.), or .45 LC cal., patterned after the Winchester 1873 rifle, octagon barrel, solid steel frame. Imported 1990-93.

	$810	$640	$550	$515	$465	$415	$375

Last MSR was $950.

This model was also available in a carbine variation until 1992.

SHOTGUNS: SLIDE ACTION

MODEL 9104/9105 - 12 ga. only, features 20 in. barrel with bead sights, 5 shot mag. tube, uncheckered walnut stock and forearm. Mfg. 1994-96.

	$240	$195	$175	$160	$145	$130	$120

Last MSR was $279.

Add $20 for adj. rear rifle sight (Model 9105).
Add $20 for interchangeable choke tube (Model 9104 only).

MODEL 9108/9109 - 12 ga. only, all-purpose self-defense model featuring 20 in. barrel with 7 shot mag., choice of military green (special order), brown walnut, or black regular or pistol grip stock and forearm. Mfg. 1994-96.

	$240	$195	$175	$160	$145	$130	$120

Last MSR was $279.

Add $20 for adj. rear rifle sight (Model 9109).
Add $20 for interchangeable choke tube (Model 9108 only).

MODEL 9111/9113 - 12 ga. only, 18 1/2 in. barrel with bead sights, 6 shot mag., choice of brown or green synthetic (special order), brown walnut or black regular or pistol grip stock and forearm. Mfg. 1994-96.

	$240	$195	$175	$160	$145	$130	$120

Last MSR was $279.

Add $20 for adj. rear rifle sight (Model 9113).
Add $20 for interchangeable choke tube (Model 9111 only).

MODEL 9114 - 12 ga. only, designed for police and riot control, choice of synthetic pistol grip or top folding (disc. 1994) buttstock, 20 in. barrel with iron sights, 6 shot mag. Mfg. 1994-96.

	$295	$255	$210	$180	$160	$145	$130

Last MSR was $349.

MODEL 9115 - 12 ga. only, design based on Special Air Services riot gun, 18 1/2 in. barrel with vent. heat shield, parkerized finish, 6 shot mag., stealth grey stock featuring 4 shell storage. Mfg. 1994-96.

	$295	$255	$210	$180	$160	$145	$130

Last MSR was $349.

Add $20 for interchangeable choke tube.

MITCHELL'S MAUSERS

Current importer located in Fountain Valley, CA.

Additionally, Mitchell's Mausers imports centerfire ammunition, including the .50 BMG cal. Please refer to the Escalade and Sabre sections for currently imported semi-auto and slide action shotguns.

PISTOLS: SEMI-AUTO

Mitchell's Mausers also imports older Luger pistols in many variations. Current MSR for a P08 WWI 4 in. is $4,995, P08 WWII 4 in. is $4,495, $6,495 for 6 in. Navy Model, $7,995 for 8 in. Artillery Model, P08 Treaty of Versailles is $5,995, and $9,995 for Carbine w/stock. All have been restored and are cased with accessories. Additionally, the company also imports a restored WWII P.38, cased with accessories - current MSR is $1,295.

GRADING - PPGS™	100%	98%	95%	90%	80%	70%	60%

GOLD SERIES - 9mm Para., .40 S&W, or .45 ACP cal., M1911 design, blue finish or stainless steel construction, front and rear slide serrations, extended thumb and grip safeties, adj. rear sight, checkered walnut grips. Disc. 2006.

	$875	$725	$650	$550	$495	$450	$400

Last MSR was $995.

WHITE LIGHTNING - .17 Mach 2, .17 HMR, .22 LR, or .22 Mag cal., black synthetic frame with stainless steel barrel/slide, 8 1/2 in. barrel with Picatinny black synthetic rail and barrel rib, 9 shot mag. Mfg. 2006-2007.

	$535	$465	$435	$395	$360	$330	$295

Last MSR was $595.

REVOLVERS

CENTURION - .357 Mag. cal., blue finish or stainless steel construction, 6 shot, target trigger, hammer and grips, adj. rear sight, laminated one piece wood grip with medallion. Limited importation.

	$625	$550	$500	$450	$400	$350	$300

Last MSR was $695.

VALKYRIE - .44 Mag. cal., red ramp front sight, laminated one piece wood grip with medallion. Limited importation.

	$775	$650	$575	$500	$450	$400	$350

Last MSR was $895.

RIFLES: BOLT ACTION

Mitchell's Mausers imports Mauser K98 WWII rifles in many variations. Current MSRs range from $2,500-$10,000. All have been restored and are cased with accessories.

MODEL M48 - 8mm Mauser cal., original Mauser 98K rifle manufactured with German technology in Serbia, various grades, matching serial numbers on all parts. Limited importation 2006.

	$450	$395	$375	$345	$295	$265	$235

Last MSR was $499.

The above price is for the Premium grade rifle without accessories. A special Museum Grade with bayonet, scabbard, belt hanger, and other accessories for $1,000. The Collector Grade was also available for $299 MSR.

TANKER MAUSER M63 (MODEL M48) - .243 Win., .270 Win., .30-06, 8mm Mauser, or .308 Win. cal., similar to Model 48, except the barrel length is 17.4 in., 5 shot internal mag., 1400m adj. rear sight, hardwood stock with semi-gloss finish, 7.4 lbs. Importation began 2006.

MSR $495		$450	$395	$375	$345	$295	$265	$235

MAUSER SPORTERS (K98/M98) - 8mm Mauser cal., sporterized military Mauser action with choice of black laminate, brown laminate or American walnut stock with rollover cheekpiece and recoil pad, adj. rear sight, adj. trigger, controlled round feeding. Imported 2003-05.

	$440	$395	$375	$345	$295	$265	$235

Last MSR was $495.

The above price is for the Premium rifle, with bayonet, scabbard, belt hanger and other accessories. Other grades included the Collector Grade - $295 MSR (includes bayonet and accessories), Service Grade - $175 MSR, Trucker Grade - $149 MSR.

MODEL K98 - 8mm Mauser cal., original WWII Mauser mfg., all matching parts, various configurations available, including Collector Grade and Premium Grade.

MSR $499		$450	$395	$375	$345	$295	$265	$235

GRADING - PPGS™	100%	98%	95%	90%	80%	70%	60%

MODEL 98 NORTH AMERICAN - .270 Win., .270 WSM, .30-06, .308 Win., .300 Rem. Ultra Mag., .300 Win. Mag., or 7mm Rem. Mag. cal., Mauser 98 double square bridge receiver. Importation began 2003.

MSR $7,900	$7,400	$6,500	$5,500	$4,500	$3,500	$3,000	$2,500

MODEL 98 VARMINTER - .220 Swift, .22-250 Rem., .223 Rem., or .223 WSM cal., features double square bridge receiver, varmint stock with Turkish walnut and fluted barrel, fully adj. trigger, 3 position side safety. Imported 2003-2006.

	$5,950	$5,250	$4,500	$3,750	$3,000	$2,250	$1,500

Last MSR was $6,500.

MAUSER MAGNUM M98 - various big game cals. from .375 H&H - .500 Jeffery, double square bridge, magnum receiver, deluxe checkered walnut stock with forend cap, folding iron sights. Importation began 2003.

MSR $8,900	$8,200	$7,400	$6,500	$5,500	$4,500	$3,500	$3,000

Add $2,000 for .500 Jeffery cal.

BLACK ARROW - 50 BMG cal., Mauser action, 5 shot detachable box mag., fluted and compensated barrel, includes bipod and quick detachable scope mount, shock absorbing buttstock. Imported 2003-2006.

	$5,750	$4,950	$4,275	$3,600	$3,000	$2,400	$2,150

Last MSR was $6,500.

RIFLES: SEMI-AUTO

BLACK LIGHTNING - .17 Mach 2, .17 HMR, .22 LR, or .22 Mag cal., black synthetic thumbhole stock with full length aluminum shroud and Picatinny rail, 18 in. stainless steel barrel/action, 9 shot mag. New 2006.

MSR $495	$450	$400	$360	$330	$300	$260	$230

MODULO MASTERPIECE

Current manufacturer located in Torino, Italy. No current U.S. importation.

Modulo Masterpiece manufactures high quality pistols and rifles. Please contact the company directly for more information, including pricing and availability (see Trademark Index).

MOLL, M.F.

Current custom rifle manufacturer and gunsmith located in Moenchengladbach, Germany. Consumer direct sales.

M.F. Moll manufactures high quality reproductions of the Sharps Model 1874 rifle. He also provides many gunsmithing services, including his own proprietary color case hardening process. Please contact him directly for more information, including an individual price quotation and U.S. availability.

MOLOT

Current manufacturer established during 1941, and located in Vyatskie Polyany, Kirov region, Russia.

Currently manufactured trademarks include: Vepr. rifles and shotguns, a SKS semi-auto rifle line, several models of bolt action rifles, including target models, in addition to Becas slide action and semi-auto shotguns. Please refer to these sections for more information.

MONTANA ARMORY, INC.

Current distributor of C. Sharps Arms Co., Inc. rifles located in Big Timber, MT. Please refer to the C. Sharps Arms Co. listing in the S section for more information.

MONTGOMERY WARD & CO.

Catalog sales/retailer that has subcontracted various domestic and international manufacturers to private label various brand names under the Montgomery Ward conglomerate.

Montgomery Ward shotguns and rifles have appeared under various labels and endorsers, including Western Field and others. There have literally been hundreds of various models (shotguns and rifles) sold through the Montgomery Ward retail network. Most of these models were manufactured through subcontracts with both domestic and international firearms manufacturers. Typically, they were "spec." guns made to sell at a specific price to undersell the competition. Most of these models were derivatives of existing factory models with less expensive wood and perhaps missing the features found on those models from which they were derived. Please refer to the Store Brand Crossover Section in the back of this book under Western Field for converting Montgomery Ward models to the respective manufacturer.

To date, there has been very little interest in collecting Montgomery Ward guns, regardless of rarity. Rather than list Montgomery Ward models, a general guideline is that values generally are under those of their "1st generation relatives." As a result, prices are ascertained by the shooting value of the gun, rather than its collector value.

MORINI COMPETITION ARM SA

Current target pistol manufacturer located in Bedano, Switzerland. Currently imported by Pilkington Competition Equipment, LLC, located in Monteagle, TN. Previously imported and distributed by Nygord Precision Products located in Prescott, AZ, and by Osborne's, located in Cheboygan, MI.

For more information and current pricing on both new and used Morini airguns, please refer to the *Blue Book of Airguns* by Dr. Robert Beeman & John Allen (also online).

PISTOLS: TARGET

Morini was one of the first companies to develop a sophisticated anatomical grip for handgun target shooting, and continues to be a leader in grip design.

CM-22 SEMI-AUTO - .22 LR cal., design for NRA or ISSF "standard pistol" competition, split trigger guard, direct bullet feed, fully adj. rear sight and trigger, 6 shot mag., 5.1 in. barrel, alloy and steel construction, adj. anatomical wood grips. New 2000.

MSR N/A	$1,525	$1,325	$1,150	$925	$825	$725	$625

CM-32 SEMI-AUTO - .32 S&W Wadcutter cal., otherwise similar to CM-22. New 2000.

MSR N/A	$1,550	$1,395	$1,225	$995	$875	$775	$675

CM-80 STANDARD SINGLE SHOT - .22 LR cal. only, adj. grips, frame, and sights. Importation disc. 1989.

$925	$825	$725	$650	$585	$520	$465

Last MSR was $1,015.

Add $50 for left-hand model.

✳ *CM-80 Standard Single Shot Super Competition* - similar to CM-80 Standard, except has deluxe finish, and unique plexiglass front sighting system. Importation disc. 1989.

$1,085	$920	$800	$690	$590	$520	$450

Last MSR was $1,196.

Add $50 for left-hand model.

CM-84E FREE PISTOL - .22 LR cal., single shot, anatomical grips, unique electronic trigger features optic beam safety, cased.

MSR N/A	$1,650	$1,325	$1,100	$925	$800	$675	$575

GRADING - PPGS™	100%	98%	95%	90%	80%	70%	60%

MODEL CM-102E SEMI-AUTO - .22 LR cal., advanced rapid fire competition pistol featuring updated ergonomic grips and flared trigger guard, first target pistol to utilize an electronic trigger. Mfg. 1992-97.

	$1,525	$1,250	$995	$895	$795	$695	$595

Last MSR was $1,695.

MORTIMER, THOMAS

Current trademark owned and manufactured by Dickson & MacNaughton, located in Edinburgh, Scotland.

Please contact Dickson & MacNaughton directly for more information regarding this trademark, including current availability and pricing.

MOSSBERG, O.F. & SONS, INC.

Current manufacturer located in North Haven, CT, 1962-present and New Haven, CT, 1919-1962.

Oscar Mossberg developed an early reputation as a designer and inventor for the Iver Johnson, Marlin-Rockwell, Stevens, and Shattuck Arms companies. In 1915, he began producing a 4-shot, .22 palm pistol known as the "Novelty," with revolving firing pin. After producing approx. 600 of these pistols, he sold the patent to C.S. Shattuck, which continued to manufacture guns under the name "Unique." The first 600 had no markings except serial numbers, and were destined for export to South America. Very few of these original "Novelty" pistols survived in this country, and they are extremely rare specimens. Mossberg acquired Advanced Ordnance Corp. during 1996, a high quality manufacturer utilizing state-of-the-art CNC machinery.

DERRINGERS

BROWNIE - .22 LR cal., top break action, rotating firing pin, 4-bbl. derringer, double action, 4-shot, approx. 32,000 mfg. 1919-32.

	$500	$400	$300	$275	$250	$205	$175

RIFLES: DISC.

The models listed appear alphabetically first, followed by numerical models in sequence. Mossberg also has made several .22 bolt action and semi-auto sporters that are in the $115-$130 price range. While they are good shooting models, they are not covered in this section, as they are not collectible.

MODEL K - .22 S, L, or LR cal., tube mag., hammerless, 22 in. bbl., takedown, open sights, plain straight stock. Mfg. 1922-31.

	$400	$350	$300	$200	$150	$100	$85

MODEL M - similar to Model K, except has 24 in. octagonal bbl. Mfg. 1928-31.

	$400	$350	$300	$200	$150	$100	$85

MODEL S - similar to Model K, except has shorter mag. tube and 19 3/4 in. bbl., very rare. Mfg. 1927-31.

	$600	$450	$400	$300	$200	$150	$135

MODEL L - .22 S, L, or LR cal., falling block action, single shot, 24 in. takedown bbl., open sights, pistol grip stock. Mfg. 1929-32.

	$600	$450	$400	$350	$300	$185	$165

MODEL L-1 - rare target version of Model L with Lyman 2A tang sight and factory sling.

Add $100 to Model L values.

MODEL R - .22 S, L ,and LR cal., bolt action, 24 in. round bbl., first tube feed, ivory bead front sight, open sporting bbl. sight. Mfg. 1930-32.

	$350	$300	$250	$200	$150	$100	$85

GRADING - PPGS™	100%	98%	95%	90%	80%	70%	60%

MODEL RM-7 - .30-06 or 7mm Rem. Mag. cal., bolt action, 22 inch (.30-06) or 24 inch (7mm Rem. Mag.) round barrel, three-position safety, folding leaf rear sight, gold bead front sight, hand-checkered American walnut with grip cap, built on imported Swedish rotary magazine action, cartridge release lever for unloading magazine from top. 3 (7mm Rem. Mag.) or 4 (.30-06) shot mag. Mfg. approx. 1979-80.

	$400	$325	$265	$245	$230	$215	$200

MODEL B - .22 S, L, or LR cal., single shot, bolt action, 22 in. round tapered bbl. Mfg. 1930-32.

	$200	$175	$150	$100	$80	$50	$35

MODEL C - .22 S, L and LR cal., single shot, 24 in. bbl., ivory bead front sight, open sporting rear sight. Mfg. 1931-32.

	$200	$175	$150	$100	$80	$50	$35

MODEL C-1 - target version of Model C, Lyman front and rear sights, leather sling and swivels, special walnut stock, rare.
   Add $100 to Model C values.

MODELS 10, 14, 20, 21, 25, 25A, 125 - .22 S, L, or LR cal., single shot models. Mfg. 1933-38.

	$250	$200	$150	$100	$60	$50	$35

   Add 25% to prices for models equipped with aperture sights.

MODEL 26B - .22 S, L, or LR cal., entirely new design in single shot rifles, easily identified by bolt handle at extreme rear of bolt, 26 in. tapered bbl., hooded ramp front sight, No. 4 rear peep, open bbl. sight, swivels. Mfg. 1938-41.

	$250	$200	$150	$100	$60	$50	$35

MODEL 26-C - similar to Model 26B with less expensive sights. Mfg. 1938-41.

	$250	$200	$150	$100	$60	$50	$35

MODEL 26M (OR B26M) - rare version of 26 series model with two-piece Mannlicher-style stock. Mfg. 1938.

	$450	$400	$300	$250	$200	$150	$100

MODEL 30 - .22 S, L, or LR cal., single shot, 24 in. bbl., rear peep and ramp front sights, swivels. Mfg. 1933-35.

	$250	$200	$150	$100	$65	$55	$45

MODEL 34 - similar to Model 30, except with heavy stock, target style. Mfg. 1934-35.

	$275	$225	$150	$100	$70	$55	$45

MODEL 35 - .22 S, L, LR cal., single shot, first full target model, 26 in. heavy target bbl., walnut stock, hooded front ramp, No. 4 rear peep with adj. aperture, approx. 9 1/2 lbs. Mfg. 1935-37.

	$325	$275	$250	$225	$200	$150	$110

MODEL 35A - revised version of Model 35, with all-new "master action," approx. 8 1/4 lbs. Mfg. 1937.

	$325	$275	$250	$225	$200	$150	$110

   Add 50% for Model 35A-LS with Lyman sights.

MODEL 40 - .22 S, L, or LR cal., repeater with tube mag., 16 shot, 24 in. bbl., No. 3 Mossberg aperture sight, hooded ramp front sight, swivels, approx. 5 lbs. Mfg. 1933-35.

	$250	$200	$150	$90	$70	$65	$60

MODEL 44 - similar to Model 40, but with heavier target stock, approx. 6 lbs. Mfg. 1934-35.

	$300	$250	$200	$150	$90	$80	$75

GRADING - PPGS™	100%	98%	95%	90%	80%	70%	60%

MODEL 42 - .22 S, L, or LR cal., first model with 7 rd. magazine, 24 in. bbl., front ramp, sporting bbl., rear aperture sights, 42 in. overall length, approx. 5 lbs. Mfg. 1935-37.

	$250	$200	$125	$100	$70	$65	$60

MODEL 42A - redesign of Model 42, new master action with shorter bolt and receiver. Mfg. 1937-38.

	$200	$150	$100	$90	$80	$70	$65

MODEL 42B - same basic specs. as Model 42A, approx. 6 lbs. Mfg. 1938-41.

	$200	$150	$100	$90	$80	$70	$65

MODEL 42C - similar to Model 42B, with open bbl. and bead front sights. Mfg. 1938-41.

	$200	$150	$100	$90	$80	$70	$65

MODEL 42M - .22 S, L, or LR cal., 7-shot magazine, bolt action, two-piece Mannlicher-style stock, 23 in. bbl., 40 in. overall length, 6 3/4 lb., front ramp, open bbl., receiver aperture sights, trapdoor buttplate for extra mag. in buttstock. Mfg. 1940-44.

	$250	$200	$150	$120	$100	$75	$50

Add $40 for extra magazine in buttstock.

MODELS 42M(a), 42M(b), 42M(c) - similar to Model 42M with minor changes in extractors and sights. Mfg. 1944-50.

	$250	$200	$150	$110	$100	$75	$50

MODEL 42MB - military version of the Model 42M, approx. 50,000 mfg. for U.S. and British troops as a training rifle. "US Property" marked with serial number, usually found w/o bbl. sight. Mfg. 1942-43.

	$300	$250	$200	$150	$110	$100	$75

Add $50 for Lend-Lease models with British proofs.

MODEL L42A - left-handed version of Model 42A with true left-handed aperture sight, walnut stock, 1 1/4 in. swivels. Mfg. 1937-38.

	$500	$400	$350	$300	$250	$200	$175

MODEL 43 - .22 S, L, or LR cal., target rifle, 7-round magazine, external trigger adjustment, 13/16 in. diameter barrel, 26 in. long walnut stock with four-position 1 1/4 in. swivels in front, Lyman 17A front sight, Lyman 57 MS receiver peep sight, rare. Mfg. 1937-38.

	$350	$300	$250	$200	$175	$150	$135

Add $100 for 43S Model and $100 for 43SS Model.

MODEL L43 - left-handed version of Model 43 target rifle with left-handed Lyman 57 MS rear aperture sight, rare. Mfg. 1937-38.

	$600	$400	$350	$300	$250	$225	$200

Add $100 for models with true left-handed Mossberg scope.

MODEL 43B - similar to Model 44B.

	$350	$300	$250	$200	$175	$150	$135

MODEL 44B - .22 S, L, LR cal. target model, mag. fed, 26 in. heavy bbl., 43 in. overall length, approx. 8 lbs., front ramp and No. 4 receiver aperture sights, four-position front swivels, walnut stock. Mfg. 1938-41.

	$300	$250	$200	$185	$175	$150	$135

MODEL 44US - .22 S, L, or LR cal. target model, 7 round magazine, bolt action, 26 in. heavy bbl., overall length 43 in., approx. 8 1/2 lbs., ramp front sight with hood, rear aperture sight, detachable swivels. Mfg. 1943-45.

	$300	$275	$200	$165	$150	$135	$125

GRADING - PPGS™	100%	98%	95%	90%	80%	70%	60%

MODEL 44US (US PROPERTY MARKED) - used by all branches of military for target training, approx. 53,000 mfg. 1943-44.

	$350	$300	$250	$175	$150	$125	$100

MODELS 44US(a), 44US(b), 44US(c), 44US(d) - same rifle as 44US with minor changes in sights and extractors. Mfg. 1944-49.

	$300	$250	$200	$175	$150	$135	$125

MODEL 45 - .22 S, L, or LR cal., tube fed, bolt action, 24 in. heavy target bbl., overall length 42 1/2 in., approx. 6 3/4 lbs., hooded front sight, sporting bbl. sight, receiver aperture sight. Mfg. 1935-37.

	$250	$200	$150	$125	$100	$85	$65

MODEL 45-A - similar to Model 45 with newer, master action. Mfg. 1937-38.

	$200	$150	$135	$125	$100	$85	$65

MODEL L45-A - similar to Model 45-A, true left-handed version. Mfg. 1937-38.

	$600	$400	$300	$250	$200	$150	$100

MODEL 46 - .22 S, L, or LR cal., tube fed, bolt action, 26 in. heavy bbl., overall 44 1/2 in., beavertail walnut stock, hooded ramp front, rear aperture sight, 7 1/2 lbs. Mfg. 1935-37.

	$250	$200	$150	$135	$125	$100	$85

MODEL 46T - similar to Model 46 with heavier bbl. and stock. Mfg. 1936-37.

	$300	$250	$200	$150	$125	$100	$75

MODEL 46A - similar to Model 46 with master action. Mfg. 1937-38.

	$250	$200	$150	$135	$125	$100	$85

MODEL 46-ALS - similar to Model 46-A with Lyman 17A front sight and 57 MS rear aperture, rare. Mfg. 1937-38.

	$275	$250	$225	$200	$175	$150	$125

MODEL L46-ALS - similar to Model 46-ALS with true left-handed action and left-handed Lyman rear sight, very rare. Mfg. 1937-38.

	$600	$450	$400	$300	$225	$200	$175

MODEL 46B - .22 S, L, or LR cal., tube fed, new streamlined design, 43 1/3 in. overall, walnut stock, 7 lbs. Mfg. 1938-45.

	$250	$200	$150	$110	$100	$85	$75

MODEL 46B-T - heavy barrel and stock, target version of Model 46-B, rare. Mfg. 1938.

	$300	$250	$200	$175	$150	$110	$95

MODEL 46M - .22 S, L, or LR cal., bolt action, tube fed, with two-piece Mannlicher-style walnut stock, 23 in. bbl., overall 40 in., hooded front, sporting bbl., rear aperture sight, 7 lbs. Mfg. 1940-45.

	$250	$225	$200	$175	$150	$110	$95

MODELS 46M(a), 46M(b) - similar to Model 46M with minor changes in sights. Mfg. 1945-52.

	$250	$225	$200	$175	$150	$110	$95

MODEL 50 - .22 S, L, or LR cal., semi-auto, tube fed through buttstock, 24 in. bbl., overall 43 3/4 in., hooded front sight, open bbl. sight, no swivels, 6 3/4 lbs. Mfg. 1939-42.

	$225	$200	$150	$135	$125	$110	$85

MODEL 51 - similar to Model 50 with receiver aperture sight, heavier, beavertail stock, QD swivels, 7 1/4 lbs. Mfg. 1939.

	$225	$200	$150	$125	$110	$85	$65

GRADING - PPGS™	100%	98%	95%	90%	80%	70%	60%

MODEL 51M - similar to Model 51 with two-piece Mannlicher style walnut stock, 20 in. bbl, 40 in. overall, front ramp, rear aperture, sporting bbl. sights, 7 lbs. Mfg. 1939-46.

	$250	$225	$175	$150	$125	$110	$95

MODEL 140B - .22 S, L, or LR cal., bolt action, mag. fed, 24 1/2 in. bbl., 42 in. overall, walnut stock, front ramp, sporting bbl., rear aperture sight, 5 3/4 lbs. Mfg. 1957-58.

	$200	$150	$135	$125	$110	$85	$65

MODEL 140K - similar to Model 140B with post front and no aperture sight. Mfg. 1955-58.

	$175	$125	$100	$80	$70	$60	$50

MODEL 142A - .22 S, L, or LR cal., bolt action, 7 round mag., carbine model with fold down forearm, walnut stock with sling, 18 in. bbl., 27 in. overall length, rear aperture sight and military front sight, no bbl. sight, early models had "T" shaped bolt handles and wood forearms, later models had round knob bolt handle and black plastic forearm, 5 lbs. Mfg. 1949-57.

	$225	$160	$140	$125	$110	$85	$65

MODEL 142K - similar to Model 142A with less expensive sights, sporting barrel and post front type. No aperture sight. Mfg. 1953-57.

	$200	$150	$125	$100	$80	$75	$55

MODEL 144 - .22 S, L, or LR cal., full target rifle, heavy 26 in. bbl., 43 in. overall length, 8 lbs., QD swivels, four-position front swivels, rear aperture, front ramp sights, "T" shaped bolt handle. Mfg. 1949-1954.

	$300	$250	$200	$165	$150	$135	$125

MODEL 144LS - similar to Model 144, with round knob handle, Lyman 57 MS rear aperture and 17A front sight. Mfg. 1954-60.

	$325	$300	$275	$250	$200	$185	$165

MODEL 144LS-A - similar to Model 144LS, with Mossberg S 130 rear aperture in place of Lyman 57 MS. Mfg. 1960-79.

	$300	$275	$250	$225	$185	$165	$150

MODEL 144LS-B - last generation of 144 series, 27 in. bbl., 15/16 in. diameter, 44 in. overall length, new Mossberg S 331 aperture, Lyman 17A front sight, 8 1/2 lbs. Mfg. 1979-85.

	$325	$275	$250	$210	$190	$175	$165

MODEL 146-B - .22 S, L, or LR cal., bolt action, tube fed, capacity of 30S, 23L, 20LR, 26 in. bbl., overall length 43 1/4 in., ramp front sight, leaf bbl. and rear aperture sight, walnut Monte Carlo stock with cheekpiece, QD swivels, adj. trigger, Schnabel forend, 7 lbs. Mfg. 1949-54.

	$225	$150	$135	$125	$100	$85	$65

MODEL 146B-A - similar to Model 146-B, with different bbl. sight. Mfg. 1954-58.

	$200	$150	$135	$125	$100	$85	$65

MODEL 151-K - .22 S, L, or LR cal., semi-auto, butt fed, 24 in. bbl., overall 44 in., open sights, walnut Monte Carlo stock with cheekpiece and Schnabel forend, 6 lbs. Mfg. 1950-51.

	$200	$150	$135	$100	$80	$70	$60

MODEL 151(M) - .22 S, L, or LR cal., semi-auto butt fed, capacity 15LR, 20 in. bbl., overall 40 in., two-piece Mannlicher-style walnut stock, QD swivels, steel buttplate, hooded ramp front, sporting rear, micro-click aperture sights, 7 lbs. Mfg. 1946-47.

	$250	$200	$150	$135	$125	$100	$85

GRADING - PPGS™	100%	98%	95%	90%	80%	70%	60%

MODELS 151M(a), 151M(b), 151M(c) - similar to Model 151M with minor changes in buttplate and sights. Mfg. 1947-58.

	$250	$200	$150	$135	$125	$100	$85

MODEL 152 - .22 S, L, or LR cal., semi-auto, mag. fed with 7 round capacity, carbine model with hinged, fold-down forend, Monte Carlo stock with adj. sling, 18 in. bbl., 27 in. overall, receiver aperture and military post front sights, 5 lbs. Mfg. 1948-52.

	$225	$175	$135	$125	$100	$85	$65

MODEL 152K - similar to Model 152 with open sights. Mfg. 1950-57.

	$200	$150	$110	$100	$90	$75	$50

MODEL 320B - .22 S, L, or LR cal., single shot, junior target model, bolt action, new closed breech design, 24 in. bbl., overall 43 1/2 in., 5 3/4 lbs., walnut finish Monte Carlo stock with swivels and pistol grip, front ramp, rear aperture and sporting bbl. sights. Mfg. 1960-71.

	$200	$150	$125	$110	$85	$75	$55

MODELS 320K, 320K-A - similar to Model 320B with open sights, no swivels, later models marked 321, 321K. Mfg. 1960-80.

	$200	$150	$100	$70	$60	$55	$50

MODEL 333 - .22 LR cal., semi-auto, 20 in. barrel with full mag., checkered Monte Carlo pistol grip stock and forearm with sling swivels, blue finish, gold trigger, 6 1/4 lbs. Mfg. 1972 - disc.

	$225	$175	$145	$125	$100	$85	$65

MODELS 340B, 340B-A - .22 S, L, or LR cal., bolt action, 7 round magazine, 24 in. bbl., 43 1/2 in. overall length, walnut, Monte Carlo stock with cheekpiece and pistol grip, front ramp, sporting bbl., rear aperture sights, 6 1/2 lbs. Mfg. 1958-80.

	$200	$150	$125	$110	$85	$75	$55

At least one example of a Model 340B smoothbore gun is known. This particular specimen was factory fitted with a stock that lacked a magazine cut-out, so the gun could only be fired as a single shot. The muzzle was not threaded to accept any sort of barrel adaptor.

MODELS 340K, 340K-A - similar to Model 340B with open sights, later models marked 341. Mfg. 1958-80.

	$150	$100	$80	$70	$60	$55	$50

MODEL 340M - .22 S, L, or LR cal. bolt action, mag. fed, same operating design as other 340 series, with one-piece, walnut Mannlicher-style Monte Carlo stock with pistol grip and swivels, 18 1/2 in. bbl., 38 1/2 in. overall, open rear and bead front sights, rare, 5 1/4 lbs. Mfg. 1970-72.

	$400	$350	$300	$250	$185	$175	$165

MODEL 342 - .22 S, L, or LR cal., bolt action, mag. fed, carbine model with hinged, black plastic, fold-down forend, walnut Monte Carlo stock with swivels and sling, 18 in. bbl., 38 in. overall length, military post front and rear aperture sight, 5 lbs. Mfg. 1957-59.

	$225	$175	$125	$110	$85	$75	$55

MODELS 342K, 342K-A - similar to Model 342 with open sights. Mfg. 1958-71.

	$200	$175	$150	$100	$75	$55	$50

MODELS 344, 344K - .22 S, L, or LR cal., bolt action, mag. fed, walnut finish, checkered stock, 344K is carbine length. Mfg. 1985.

	$200	$175	$150	$125	$85	$75	$55

GRADING - PPGS™	100%	98%	95%	90%	80%	70%	60%

MODEL 346B - .22 S, L, or LR cal., bolt action tube feed, closed-breech design, walnut Monte Carlo stock with cheekpiece, QD swivels, capacity 25S, 20L, 18LR, 24 in. bbl., 42 1/2 in. overall length, rear aperture, sporting bbl., hooded front ramp sights, 6 1/2 lbs. Mfg. 1958-60.

	$200	$175	$150	$125	$85	$75	$55

MODELS 346K, 346K-A - similar to Model 346B w/ open sights. Mfg. 1958-68.

	$200	$175	$150	$125	$80	$70	$55

MODEL 350K - .22 LR cal., semi-auto, LR only, mag. fed, walnut Monte Carlo stock with pistol grip and cheekpiece, 23 1/2 in. bbl., overall length 43 1/2 in., open sights, 6 lbs. Mfg. 1958-60.

	$200	$175	$150	$125	$60	$50	$40

MODEL 350 K-A - similar to Model 350K with dovetail bbl. sight. Mfg. 1960-68.

	$200	$175	$150	$100	$60	$50	$40

MODEL 351K - .22 LR cal., semi-auto, tube fed through stock, walnut Monte Carlo stock with pistol grip, 24 in. bbl., 43 in. overall length, 6 lbs. Mfg. 1958-60.

	$200	$175	$150	$100	$60	$50	$40

MODEL 351K-A - similar to Model 351K with dovetail bbl. sight. Mfg. 1960-68.

	$200	$175	$150	$100	$60	$50	$40

MODEL 352 - .22 LR cal., mag. fed, carbine model with fold-down black plastic forend, walnut Monte Carlo stock, pistol grip, swivels, web strap, 18 in. bbl., overall length 38 in., rear peep, post front sights, 5 lbs. Mfg. 1957-59.

	$200	$175	$150	$100	$75	$65	$55

MODELS 352K, 352 K-A, 352K-B - similar to Model 352 with open sights. Mfg. 1960-71.

	$200	$175	$150	$100	$70	$65	$55

MODEL 353 - similar to Model 352K-A, except has front ramp and open rear sights, w/o swivels, 5 lbs. Mfg. 1972-1985.

	$200	$175	$150	$100	$70	$65	$55

MODEL 354 - similar to Model 353, except stock configuration was altered. Mfg. 1985 - disc.

	$200	$175	$150	$100	$70	$65	$55

MODEL 377, "PLINKSTER" - .22 LR cal., semi-auto, tube fed, synthetic stock with thumbhole, capacity 15 rds., 20 in. bbl., overall length 40 in., 6 1/4 lbs., equipped with 4X scope. Mfg. 1977-79.

	$250	$200	$150	$135	$100	$85	$75

MODELS 380, 380S - same basic design as Model 377, only with solid wood stock, open sights. Model 480 same in 1985. Mfg. 1980-85.

	$175	$150	$100	$85	$75	$65	$55

MODEL 400 "PALAMINO" - .22 S, L, and LR cal., lever action, tube fed, walnut, beavertail stock and forearm, crossbolt safety, 24 in. bbl., overall length, 41 in., bead front, open rear sights, 5 1/2 lbs. Mfg. 1959-64.

	$300	$250	$200	$150	$135	$100	$85

Model 400-A similar to in specs and value, dovetail.

MODEL 402 - carbine version of Model 400, 20 in. barrel. Mfg. 1961-71.

	$300	$250	$200	$150	$135	$100	$85

MODEL 430 - .22 LR cal., semi-auto, tubular mag. under bbl. with capacity of 18 LR, walnut checkered Monte Carlo stock and checkered forend, 24 in. bbl., overall length 43 1/2 in., open sights, 6 1/4 lbs. Mfg. 1970-1971.

	$200	$150	$100	$85	$75	$65	$55

GRADING - PPGS™	100%	98%	95%	90%	80%	70%	60%

MODEL 432 - similar to Model 430 with 20 in. bbl., straight grip, smooth stock and forend, walnut finish. Mfg. 1970-71.

	$300	$250	$175	$100	$65	$60	$50

MODEL 472 CARBINE - .30-30 Win. or .35 Rem. cal., lever action carbine, 20 in. barrel, open sights, pistol grip or straight stock, saddle ring on straight model. Mfg. 1972-disc.

	$250	$200	$145	$130	$120	$110	$90

MODEL 472 RIFLE - similar to Carbine, except 24 in. barrel, pistol grip stock. Mfg. 1974-76.

	$250	$200	$155	$145	$130	$120	$100

MODEL 472 BRUSH GUN - similar to Carbine, except 18 in. barrel, straight stock only. Mfg. 1974-76.

	$275	$225	$175	$145	$130	$120	$100

MODEL 472 ONE IN FIVE THOUSAND - similar to Brush Gun, except Indian scene etched on receiver, brass buttplate, saddle ring and barrel bands, select stock, only 5,000 mfg., 1974.

	$500	$350	$225	$175	$165	$145	$120

MODEL 479 PCA - .30-30 Win. cal., lever action, 20 in. barrel, 6 shot capacity.

	$250	$200	$150	$110	$95	$85	$75

MODEL 479 RR - limited edition "Roy Rogers" signature model, gold trigger, barrel bands, 5,000 total mfg. New 1983.

	$500	$350	$300	$195	$165	$140	$120

MODEL 479 - .30-30 Win. cal. only, lever action, 6 shot tube mag., 20 in. barrel with adj. sights, 7 lbs. Mfg. 1985 only.

	$250	$200	$160	$150	$145	$140	$135

Last MSR was $232.

MODEL 480 - similar to Models 380 and 380S.

	$175	$150	$125	$100	$75	$65	$55

MODEL 620K - .22 Mag. cal., single shot, bolt action, walnut Monte Carlo stock, pistol grip, cheekpiece, sling swivels, 24 in. bbl., overall 44 3/4 in., open rear, post front sights, 6 lbs. Mfg. 1959-60.

	$200	$150	$115	$100	$85	$75	$65

MODEL 620K-A - similar to Model 620K with change in bbl. sight. Mfg. 1960-68.

	$250	$200	$150	$115	$100	$85	$75

MODELS 640K, 640K-S - similar to 620 series, but 5 shot mag. repeater. Mfg. 1959-84.

	$300	$250	$200	$135	$125	$105	$90

MODEL 640KS - similar to Model 640K with deluxe checkered stock and gold trigger. Mfg. 1960-68.

	$260	$200	$185	$150	$135	$120	$110

MODEL 640M - full length, Mannlicher-styled stock, version of 640, checkered Monte Carlo cheekpiece, pistol grip, swivels and leather strap, heavy receiver, jeweled bolt, 20 in. bbl., overall 40 3/4 in., open rear sights, bead front, 6 lbs. Mfg. 1971.

	$500	$400	$350	$300	$200	$165	$150

MODEL 642K - .22 Mag. cal., carbine style, bolt action, 5 rd. mag., fold-down forend, walnut stock with web sling, 18 in. bbl., overall 38 1/4 in., open bbl. and bead front sights, 5 lbs. Mfg. 1960-68.

	$300	$250	$200	$150	$135	$120	$110

GRADING - PPGS™	100%	98%	95%	90%	80%	70%	60%

MODEL 800 - .222 Rem., .22-250 Rem., .243 Win., or .308 Win. cal., bolt action, 22 in. barrel, folding sight, checkered pistol grip stock. Mfg. 1967-disc.

| | $350 | $275 | $225 | $150 | $100 | $75 | $50 |

MODEL 800VT - similar to 800, except .222 Rem., .22-250 Rem., or .243 Win. cal., 24 in. heavy barrel, no sights. Mfg. 1968-disc.

| | $350 | $300 | $250 | $150 | $100 | $75 | $50 |

MODEL 800M - similar to 800, except 20 in. barrel, full length stock, spoon bolt handle. Mfg. 1969-72.

| | $450 | $325 | $300 | $275 | $200 | $160 | $145 |

MODEL 800D - similar to 800, with roll-over combination and cheekpiece, checkered stock with rosewood forearm tip and pistol cap, no .222 Rem. available. Mfg. 1970-73.

| | $400 | $325 | $300 | $275 | $225 | $200 | $165 |

MODEL 810 - .270 Win., .30-06, 6.5mm Rem. Mag., or .338 Win. Mag. cal., bolt action, 22 or 24 in. barrel, rear leaf sight, checkered Monte Carlo stock. Mfg. 1970-disc.

| | $350 | $275 | $250 | $225 | $200 | $175 | $150 |

MODEL 1500 MOUNTAINEER GRADE I - .223 Rem., .243 Win., .270 Win., .30-06, or 7mm Rem. Mag. cal., bolt action, 22 or 24 (7mm Rem. Mag. only) in. barrel, 5 or 6 shot mag., available with or without sights, hardwood stock is satin finished, blued finish, about / lbs. 10 oz. Imported 1986-87 only.

| | $325 | $275 | $240 | $195 | $180 | $165 | $150 |

Last MSR was $335.

Add $15 for 7mm Rem. Mag. cal., $25 for iron sights.

In 1985, Mossberg purchased the parts inventory and importing rights for those Model 1500 rifles that Smith & Wesson imported from Howa of Japan. These models were identical to those models which S&W disc.

✱ *Model 1500 Mountaineer Grade I Varmint* - .22-250 Rem., .223 Rem., or .308 Win. cal., similar to Model 1500 Grade I, except has 24 in. heavy barrel only, Monte Carlo stock. Imported 1986-87 only.

| | $385 | $325 | $300 | $250 | $205 | $190 | $175 |

Last MSR was $457.

Add $10 for parkerized finish (oil finished stock with swivels - not available in .22-250 Rem. cal.).

Blue finish and high gloss wood finish available with .22-250 Rem. or .223 Rem. cal. only. Parkerized variation is available in .223 Rem. or .308 Win. cal. only (matte wood finish, includes swivels).

MODEL 1500 MOUNTAINEER GRADE II - similar to Grade I Mountaineer, except has select checkered American walnut stock. Also available in .300 Win. Mag. or .338 Win. Mag. cal. Imported 1986-87 only.

| | $350 | $295 | $260 | $205 | $190 | $175 | $160 |

Last MSR was $368.

Add $15 for Mag. cals.
Add $25 for iron sights.

MODEL 1550 - similar to Model 1500, except has detachable mag. and available in standard cals. (.243 Win., .270 Win., or .30-06), with or without sights. Imported 1986-87 only.

| | $365 | $305 | $275 | $225 | $190 | $175 | $160 |

Last MSR was $391.

Add $24 for iron sights.

GRADING - PPGS™	100%	98%	95%	90%	80%	70%	60%

MODEL 1700 LS - .243 Win., .270 Win., or .30-06 cal., no sights, jeweled bolt body and knurled bolt handle, detachable mag., Schnabel forend, deluxe checkering, 7 lbs. Imported 1986-87 only.

	$450	$400	$350	$275	$225	$200	$190

Last MSR was $492.

Mossberg "Targo" Smoothbore Models

These dual-purpose smoothbore rifles were designed to fire both .22 RF bullets and shot-shell ammunition. Targo barrels are threaded either externally (Models 26T, 42TR, 42T, B42T) or internally (Models 320TR, 340TR) at the muzzle for attachment of rifled and smoothbore adapters which enable the shooter to use the gun as a standard rifle, or (with the smoothbore adapter installed) as a miniature shotgun. Mossberg produced a line of Targo accessories including a barrel-mounted miniature clay target launcher, a pistol grip hand trap frame, a hand thrower (three known variations), a target carrier, clay targets, hard rubber "practice" targets, and a target catching net. The presence of one or more of these accessories augments the value of any model Targo gun. Prices quoted below are for guns with all listed features exclusive of Targo accessories.

MODEL 26-T SINGLE SHOT - .22 RF/shotshell cal., bolt action, thumb lever safety located at rear of bolt, black plastic buttplate and contoured black plastic trig-gerguard (#R413), rifle-style open rear sight with screw adjustments for windage and elevation, shotgun style elevated front bead sight with remov-able sight hood, smoothbore and rifled screw-on barrel adapters and spanner wrench for adapter removal and installation, stock generally provided with sling swivels, forend necks down toward muzzle, takedown screw has retain-ing bail to facilitate removal by hand. Mfg. 1940-42 (only 873 mfg.).

	$600	$450	$375	$335	$280	$245	$220

100% price is estimated since an example would be extremely rare.

MODEL 42T BOLT ACTION REPEATER - .22 RF/shotshell cal., box magazine (7-round) fitted with adapter screw to enable firing of .22 Short cartridges, same safety, buttplate, optional stock swivels, and shotgun style front sight as Model 26T, #R145 contoured black plastic triggerguard, supplied with the smoothbore barrel adapter only (rifled adapter, open rear sight, and front sight hood were not provided), produced 1940-42 (906 guns made), exam-ples in 95% or better condition are uncommon.

	$440	$325	$310	$295	$260	$235	$200

MODEL 42TR BOLT ACTION REPEATER - .22 RF/shotshell cal., produced before and after WWII until roughly 1949. Pre-war (1940-42) guns identical to Model 42T except rifled adapter, open rear sight, and front sight hood were pro-vided, and no stock swivels. The earliest pre-war 42TRs were marked using a 42T barrel stamp and a separate "R" (stamped to the right of the "T"). Post-war (1946-49) guns have slotted takedown screw, magazine plate, shorter unnecked forend, and (frequently) a blue bolt knob. The most common of all Targo guns. A total of 6,577 guns were produced during the period 1940-42 (post-war production figures are not available). Both early and late versions of this model are comparably priced.

	$415	$345	$295	$280	$245	$190	$175

Add $250 for cased gun with clay targets and Targo accessories.
Cased Targo guns with all accessories have been seen for $1,000+.

Note: A very small number of 42TRs were supplied with fitted cases and Targo accessories and may have been used as dealer displays. Several variations in the internal compartmental-ization of these cases have been noted. The pre-war 42TR display guns came in a hard (ply-wood) luggage case. The post-war guns were supplied in a semi-hard (fiberboard) luggage case.

GRADING - PPGS™	100%	98%	95%	90%	80%	70%	60%

MODEL B42T BOLT ACTION REPEATER - .22 RF/shotshell cal., identical to the Model 42TR, except stock has sling swivels and metal buttplate with trapdoor for magazine storage. Gun was supplied with extended 15-round box magazine in addition to the standard 7-round mag. A comparatively scarce model marketed exclusively through mail order stores (e.g., Spiegel) in the early 1940s. According to factory records, only 250 guns were made, all in 1940.

	$465	$385	$350	$325	$285	$250	$210

The 15 round magazine originally supplied with this model is scarce - good specimens are currently selling for approx. $85-$120 (may exceed legal capacity limits, depending on state).

MODEL 320TR SINGLE SHOT BOLT ACTION - .22 RF/shotshell, automatic safety with thumb lever located on right side of receiver, black plastic buttplate and contoured black plastic triggerguard. Rifle-style ("U" notch) rear sight adjustable for elevation (via sliding wedge) and windage (by deflecting sight arm laterally by hand). Sporting type vertical blade front sight. Gun supplied with rifled and smoothbore screw-in barrel adapters. A wire target carrier and a hand thrower for launching miniature clay targets were included with each gun. Limited mfg. 1961-62.

	$350	$300	$275	$190	$150	$135	$115

Factory records indicate that only 962 guns were sold during the production period.

MODEL 340TR BOLT ACTION REPEATER - .22 RF/shotshell cal., 7-round box magazine featuring adjustable top bar to accommodate feeding of .22 S, L, or LR cartridges. Two known variations of thumb lever safety markings (words "OFF"/"ON" and red dot). Other features identical to Model 320TR. Limited mfg. 1961-62.

	$350	$300	$275	$215	$165	$145	$125

Factory records indicate that only 2,026 guns were sold during the production period.

RIFLES: BOLT ACTION, CURRENT PRODUCTION

4x4 RIFLE - .25-06 Rem., .270 Win., .30-06, 7mm Rem. Mag., .300 Win. Mag., or .338 Win. Mag. cal., 24 in. barrel, 4 or 5 shot detachable box mag., matte blue or Marinecote finish, walnut, sculpted Monte Carlo grey or brown laminate (Marinecote only) or black skeletonized synthetic stock, vent. forearm, Weaver style scope base, rifle sights (.30-06, .300 Win. Mag., or .338 Win. Mag. only), 6.7 - 7.1 lbs. new 2007.

MSR $437	$350	$315	$280	$250	$225	$200	$180

Add $129 for walnut or grey laminate stock.
Add $44 for Marinecote finish.
Add $154 for rifle sights with walnut stock.
Add $53 for scope package (3-9x40mm, not available in .25-06 or .338 Win. mag. cal).

MODEL 100 ATR (ALL TERRAIN RIFLE) - .243 Win. (new 2006), .270 Win., .30-06, or .308 Win. (new 2006) cal., 22 in. free floating barrel, short or long action, matte blue or Marinecote (.270 Win. or .30-06), walnut (new 2006), black synthetic, Dura-Wood synthetic or 100% camo coverage stock with recoil pad, 3 shot top loading magazine, approx. 7 lbs. New 2005.

MSR $361	$285	$230	$190	$150	$135	$125	$115

Add $36 for Dura-Wood synthetic stock (long action only).
Add $45 for Marinecote (long action only).
Add $36 for camo.
Add $25 for rifle sights (new 2007).
Add $53 for 3-9x40mm scope (new 2006).
Add $45 for walnut stock.

＊ *Model 100 ATR Bantam/Super Bantam* - .243 Win. or .308 Win. cal., short action, 20 in. barrel, 5 shot, Weaver type base, matte blue metal, choice of black synthetic (Super Bantam) or walnut (Bantam) stock and forearm, Super Bantam has adj. 12-13 in. LOP, Bantam has fixed 12 in. LOP, 6 1/2 - 7 3/4 lbs. New 2007.

MSR $361	$285	$230	$190	$150	$135	$125	$115

    Add $53 for 3-9x40mm scope (Super Bantam only).
    Add $45 for walnut stock.

MODEL 802 PLINKSTER - .22 LR cal., 18 or 21 (brushed chrome finish only, new 2007) in. barrel with adj. iron sights, aluminum alloy receiver, blue or brushed chrome (new 2007) finish, black synthetic stock, 10 shot mag., approx. 4 lbs. New 2006.

MSR $138	$115	$100	$90	$80	$70	$60	$50

    Add $8 for scope.
    Add $13 for brushed chrome finish (new 2007).

MODEL 817 - .17 HMR cal., similar to 802 Plinkster, except not available in 18 in. barrel, and 5 shot mag. New 2007.

MSR $161	$135	$120	$100	$90	$80	$70	$60

    Add $14 for brushed chrome finish (new 2007).

RIFLES: LEVER ACTION

MODEL SSi-ONE INTERCHANGEABLE RIFLE/SHOTGUN - .22-250 Rem., .223 Rem., .243 Win., .270 Win., .30-06, or .308 Win. cal., also available in 12 ga., design allows interchangeable rifle/shotgun barrels, single shot, satin finished or Mossy Oak Breakup camo (new 2003, available in shotgun configuration only) checkered walnut stock and forearm, matte blue metal, 24 in. regular or heavy (.22-250 Rem. or .223 Rem. cal.) rifle barrel with ejector or 12 ga. (3 in. chamber with rifled bore for Slug, 3 1/2 in. chamber for Turkey) ported barrel, break open action, cocking indicator, drilled and tapped intergral scope base, automatic safety, approx. 8 (regular) or 10 (heavy) lbs. Mfg. 2001-2004.

	$400	$315	$255	$225	$200	$180	$160

Last MSR was $483.

    Add $240 per interchangeable rifle barrel and $298 for SSi-One Slug Model barrel.
    Add $55 for Mossy Oak Breakup stock and forearm (Turkey Model) or $77 for Mossy Oak Breakup stock and forearm (Slug Model).
    Add $22 for heavy bull barrel or 12 ga. Slug (fully rifled bore) variation.

MODEL 464 - .30-30 Win. cal., 18 or 20 in. blue barrel, uncheckered straight grip walnut stock, drilled and tapped, 5.6 - 6.7 lbs. New 2008.

MSR $473	$395	$350	$300	$260	$230	$200	$175

RIFLES: SEMI-AUTO

MODEL 702 PLINKSTER - .22 LR cal., 18 or 21 (chrome finish only) in. barrel with open sights, blue or brushed chrome metal finish, choice of synthetic, Mossy Oak New Break-Up camo with walnut Dura-Wood, tiger maple Dura-Wood, or carbon fiber synthetic stock, 10 shot mag., aluminum alloy receiver, crossbolt safety, approx. 4 lbs. New 2006.

MSR $138	$115	$95	$80	$70	$60	$55	$50

    Add $9 for scope (available in Bantam configuration also).
    Add $28 for any stock except synthetic.
    Add $14 for chrome finish (21 in. barrel only).

GRADING - PPGS™	100%	98%	95%	90%	80%	70%	60%

SHOTGUNS: BOLT ACTION - DISC.

MODELS G-4, 70, 73, 73B - .410 bore, single shot, mfg. 1932-40.

	$150	$100	$85	$70	$60	$50	$40

MODELS 80, 83, 83B, 83D - .410 bore, 3 or 4 shot, internal top-loading mag., mfg. 1933-46.

	$150	$110	$95	$75	$60	$50	$40

MODELS 75, 75A, 75B - 20 ga., bolt action, single shot, mfg. 1933-40.

	$150	$100	$85	$70	$60	$50	$40

MODELS 85, 85A, 85B, 85D - 20 ga., 2 or 3 shot mag., mfg. 1934-40.

	$150	$100	$85	$70	$60	$50	$40

MODELS 173, 173A, 173Y - .410 bore, single shot, "Y" designates youth model, mfg. 1957-73.

	$150	$100	$85	$70	$60	$50	$40

MODELS 183, 183D, 283D(a), 183D-B, 183D-C, 183D-D, 183D-E, 183D-F, 183K, 183K-B, 183K-C, 183T, 184T, 184TY, 283T, 284T, 284TY - .410 bore, bolt action shotgun, 2 or 3 shot mag., various screw-on or C-Lect choke on some models, mfg. 1948-1985.

	$150	$110	$95	$75	$60	$55	$50

MODELS 185, 185D, 185D-A, 185D-B, 185D-C, 185K, 185K-A, 185K-B - 20 ga., 2 shot 2 3/4 in. mag., various screw-on or C-Lect chokes, mfg. 1947-59.

	$150	$110	$95	$75	$60	$55	$50

MODELS 190, 190D, 190D-A, 190K-A, 190K-B - 16 ga., bolt action, 2 shot 2 3/4 in. mag., various screw-on or C-Lect choke, mfg. 1955-58.

	$150	$110	$95	$75	$60	$55	$50

MODELS 195, 195A, 195K-A, 195D - same as model 185 Series, only 12 ga. version, mfg. 1954-68.

	$150	$110	$95	$75	$60	$55	$50

MODELS 385, 385K, 385KA, 385T, 485A, 485B - 20 ga., bolt action, 3 in. chamber, detachable box mag., mfg. 1960-86.

	$150	$110	$95	$75	$60	$55	$50

MODELS 390, 390K-A, 390K-B, 490A - 16 ga., 3 in. chamber, detachable box mag., mfg. 1971-76.

	$150	$110	$95	$75	$60	$55	$50

MODELS 395, 395K, 395KA, 395S, 395 SPL., 495A, 495B - 12 ga., 3 in. chamber, detachable box mag., mfg. 1963-83.

	$150	$110	$95	$75	$60	$55	$50

Add $40 for slug barrel ("S" designation) or 38 in. barrel (Spl.).

MODELS 595, 595K - 12 ga., bolt action, special police stock, 4 shot mag., mfg. 1983-85.

	$175	$150	$135	$110	$95	$85	$75

Add $40 for 38 in. barrel (Spl.).

SHOTGUNS: RECENT PRODUCTION

In 1985, Mossberg purchased the parts inventory and manufacturing rights for the shotguns that Smith & Wesson discontinued in 1984. These 1000 and 3000 Series models (manufactured in Japan) are identical to those models which S&W discontinued. Parts and warranties are not interchangeable.

Beginning 1989, all Mossbergs sold in the U.S. and Canada have been provided with a Cablelock which goes through the ejection port, making the gun's action inoperable.

To celebrate its 75th anniversary, Mossberg released a new Crown Grade variation within

GRADING - PPGS™	100%	98%	95%	90%	80%	70%	60%

most models during 1994, including the slide action 500 and 835 Series. These can be differentiated from previous manufacture by cut checkering, redesigned walnut or American hardwood stocks and forearms, screw-in choke tubes, and 4 different camo patterns. The Crown Grade was discontinued in 2000.

MODEL 200K SLIDE ACTION - slide action shotgun, 12 ga., 28 in., select choke, plain pistol grip stock, black nylon slide handle. Mfg. 1955-59.

	$250	$200	$150	$125	$100	$55	$40

MODEL 200D - similar to 200K, except interchangeable choke tubes (2). Mfg. 1955-59.

	$250	$200	$150	$125	$100	$55	$40

MODEL 500 SLIDE ACTION FIELD (1962-1998 MFG.) - 12, 20 ga., or .410 bore, slide action, 24 in. (with rifle sights) or 20-28 in. barrel (with various chokes), upper receiver slide safety, C-Lect (disc.) & Accu-choke (became standard 1994) choke system, checkered hardwood pistol grip stock after 1973. Mfg. 1962-98.

	$250	$200	$165	$135	$120	$110	$100

Last MSR was $309.

Subtract 10% if without VR (disc.).
Subtract 10% for fixed choke barrel in 12 or 20 ga.

For recent Model 500 information and values, please refer to Model 500 Field - Current Mfg. later in this section.

✱ *Model 500 Slide Action Field Slugster* - 12, 16, or 20 (disc. 1997) ga., 24 in. cyl. (disc. 1997) or rifled bore (became standard 1998) barrel, barrel porting became standard in 1998, choice of sights, walnut finished hardwood stock and forearm. Disc. 1998.

	$270	$220	$175	$145	$125	$110	$100

Last MSR was $336.

Subtract $75 if w/o barrel porting or rifled bore.

✱ *Model 500 Slide Action Field Bantam* - 20 ga. or .410 bore (new 1991) only, 22 in. (20 ga.), 24 in. fixed choke barrel (.410 bore), or 26 in. VR barrel with Accu-choke(s), blue or blue matte (disc.), Bantam Jake with Realtree Camo finish in 20 ga./22 in. VR barrel only (disc.), 20 ga. has walnut finish stock and .410 bore has synthetic stock (both stocks are tailored for youth dimensions), 6.9 lbs. Mfg. 1990-96, reintroduced 1998 only.

	$200	$195	$165	$135	$120	$110	$100

Last MSR was $312.

Subtract $12 for .410 bore.
Add $45 for Bantam Jake configuration (disc. 1993).

✱ *Model 500 Slide Action Field Turkey* - 12 or 20 (new 1995) ga., 22 (20 ga. only), or 24 in. barrel, Woodlands metal/wood camo finish. Disc. 1997.

	$265	$195	$150	$120	$105	$90	$80

Last MSR was $324.

Subtract $15 for 20 ga.
Add $60 for 24 in. VR barrel with Ghost Ring Sight (12 ga. only).

✱ *Model 500 Slide Action Field Muzzleloader Combo* - 12 ga. only, includes 24 in. (rifled bore only, new 1993) or 28 in. VR Accu-choke barrel and additional 24 in. .50 cal. muzzleloader conversion barrel with rifled bore and iron sights, walnut finished hardwood stock and forearm, 7.2 lbs. Mfg. 1991-96.

	$335	$280	$240	$200	$180	$160	$145

Last MSR was $385.

GRADING - PPGS™	100%	98%	95%	90%	80%	70%	60%

✱ *Model 500 Slide Action Field Quail Unlimited* - 20 ga. only, 26 in. VR barrel with Accu-II chokes (3), engraved receiver and hand selected stock and forearm, 3,500 mfg. in 1991 to commemorate the 10th anniversary of Quail Unlimited.

	$350	$275	$225	$145	$125	$105	$90

Last MSR was $359..

✱ *Model 500 Slide Action Field Sporting Steel Shot* - 12 ga. only, 3 in. chamber, 28 in. VR Accu-choke barrel with special Accu-steel tube for shooting steel shot. Mfg. 1987-90.

	$250	$200	$175	$165	$155	$145	$135

Last MSR was $295.

Add $29 for camo stock (disc. 1989).

This model was phased out of production in 1990 since all Mossberg shotguns currently manufactured are capable of shooting steel shot safely.

MODEL 500 REGAL SERIES - 12 or 20 ga., slide action, 26 or 28 in. barrel, select checkered walnut, VR. Disc. 1987.

	$240	$195	$175	$165	$155	$145	$135

Last MSR was $286.

Add $39 for Combo pack (includes 1 extra 24 in. slugster barrel).
Add $19 for Accu-choke.

MODEL 500 CAMPER - 12, 20 ga., or .410 bore only, 18 1/2 in. barrel, synthetic pistol grip (no stock), camo carrying case optional, blued finish. Mfg. 1986-90 only.

	$250	$190	$175	$165	$155	$145	$135

Last MSR was $276.

Add $25 for .410 bore.
Add $30 for camo case.

MODEL 500 HI-RIB TRAP - 12 ga. only, high post trap rib, 28 or 30 in. barrel. Disc. 1986.

	$375	$340	$270	$225	$175	$155	$140

Last MSR was $334.

Add $20 for Accu-choke.

MODEL 500 SUPER GRADE - similar to Model 500 Field, except VR and checkered, no 16 ga. Mfg. 1965-76.

	$250	$215	$180	$170	$160	$140	$130

MODEL 500 ATR SUPER GRADE - similar to Model 500 Field, except 12 ga., VR, 30 in. full, checkered Monte Carlo. Mfg. 1968-71.

	$350	$300	$250	$200	$175	$155	$140

MODEL 500 PIGEON GRADE - similar to 500 Super Grade, except etched and scroll engraving, select wood, floating VR. Mfg. 1971-75.

	$385	$330	$305	$250	$210	$185	$165

MODEL 500 APTR PIGEON GRADE TRAP - similar to 500 ATR, except trap style stock. Mfg. 1971-75.

	$440	$415	$330	$250	$220	$200	$175

MODEL 500 DSPR DUCK STAMP COMMEMORATIVE - similar to Pigeon Grade, except wood duck etching. 1,000 mfg. 1975.

	$525	$330	$310	$285	$260	$220	$195

MODEL 500AA 50th ANNIVERSARY - 12 ga., Pigeon grade, trap, field, and skeet configuration, hand checkered walnut stock, red bead front and middle sights, left side of receiver engraved with 50th Anniversary emblem in gold, 50th Anniversary on pistol grip cap, limited mfg. 1969 only.

	$500	$425	$400	N/A	N/A	N/A	N/A

GRADING - PPGS™	100%	98%	95%	90%	80%	70%	60%

MODEL 500L SERIES - similar to 500 Field Grade, except no 16 ga., etched receiver, new style stock and slide. Mfg. 1977-83.

	100%	98%	95%	90%	80%	70%	60%
	$250	$220	$210	$200	$175	$165	$140

MODEL 500 BULLPUP - 12 ga., 18 1/2 (6 shot) or 20 (9 shot) in. barrel, bullpup configuration, 6 or 9 shot mag., includes shrouded barrel, carrying handle, ejection port in stock, employs high impact materials. Mfg. 1986-90.

	100%	98%	95%	90%	80%	70%	60%
	$500	$425	$385	$350	$300	$225	$200

Last MSR was $425.

Add $15 for 8 shot mag. (disc.).

MODEL 500 SPECIAL HUNTER - 12 or 20 ga., 3 in. chamber, 26 or 28 in. VR barrel with or w/o porting and Accu-chokes set, parkerized metal finish, black synthetic stock and forearm. Mfg. 1999-2002.

	100%	98%	95%	90%	80%	70%	60%
	$260	$210	$170	$140	$120	$110	$100

Last MSR was $327.

MODEL 500 VIKING - 12 or 20 ga., 24 (12 ga. only, with rifled barrel and sights, porting became standard in 1997), 26 (20 ga. only) or 28 (12 ga. only, porting became standard in 1997) in. ported (new 1997, 12 ga. only) or unported VR barrel with one Accu-choke and twin bead sights, matte finish with green synthetic stock and forearm, approx. 7 lbs. Mfg. 1996-98.

	100%	98%	95%	90%	80%	70%	60%
	$230	$190	$155	$135	$120	$110	$100

Last MSR was $287.

Add $40 for 12 ga. rifled barrel.
Add $108 for Slug Shooting System with ported barrel.

* *Model 500 Viking Turkey* - 12 ga. only, 24 in. ported VR barrel, green synthetic stock, matte finish, Accu-choke. Mfg. 1997-98.

	100%	98%	95%	90%	80%	70%	60%
	$230	$190	$155	$135	$120	$110	$100

Last MSR was $286.

MODEL 500 FIELD - CURRENT MFG. - 12, 20 ga., or .410 bore, 3 in. chamber, 24, 26, or 28 in. ported (new 1997, 12 ga. only, 26 or 28 in. barrel) or unported VR (unless with rifle sights) barrel, Slug model offers choice of 12 ga. with 24 in. ported barrel and rifle sights (mfg. 2001-2004) or .410 bore (new 2003) with adj. fiberoptic sights and vent. rib, matte (12 or 20 ga. only, new 2005) or blue finish, walnut finished or synthetic (.410 bore only) stock, safety on back of receiver top, Accu-chokes except for Slug Model and .410 bore, supplied with 1 Accu-choke, 6-7 1/2 lbs.

MSR $327	100%	98%	95%	90%	80%	70%	60%
	$260	$215	$180	$155	$145	$140	$135

Add $14 for Slug Model in .410 bore with adj. fiber optic sights and VR barrel (disc. 2004).
Add approx. $34-$93 for various combo packages, depending on configuration.
This model also includes the Crown Grade, manufactured 1994-2000.

* *Model 500 Field Bantam* - 12 (new 2001), 20 ga. or .410 bore, 3 in. chamber, similar to Model 500 Field, except has shortened, specially contoured stock and forearm (13 in. LOP), and 22 (20 ga. only) or 24 in. ported (12 ga. only, with VR) or unported barrel.

MSR $327	100%	98%	95%	90%	80%	70%	60%
	$260	$215	$180	$155	$145	$140	$135

Add $43 for Field combo w/fully rifled deer barrel.

* *Model 500 Field Super Bantam* - 20 ga. only, 22 (Accu-Set or X-full chokes) or 24 (fully rifled bore with porting) in. barrel, adj. 12-13 in. LOP synthetic stock and forearm, matte blue finish or 100% Mossy Oak New Break-Up (Slug model only) or Realtree Hardwoods HD Green camo coverage. New 2005.

MSR $327	100%	98%	95%	90%	80%	70%	60%
	$260	$215	$180	$155	$145	$140	$135

Add $51 for Turkey model or Slug model with Mossy Oak New Break-Up finish.
Add $93 for Super Bantam combo w/Field and rifled deer barrel.

GRADING - PPGS™	100%	98%	95%	90%	80%	70%	60%

✴ *Model 500 Field Slugster* - 12 or 20 ga., 24 in. ported (standard 1997) or unported (disc. 1996) barrel with choice of cyl. (disc. 2000) or rifled (standard 2001) bore, blue or Marinecote (mfg. 1995-97) finish, choice of rifle (Bantam Model in 20 ga.), Truglo fiberoptic sights (12 ga. only, disc. 2004), or Trophy Slugster integral scope base, press checkered hardwood stock and forearm or 100% camo coverage (new 2004), 6 1/2 -7 1/4 lbs.

MSR $327	$260	$215	$180	$155	$145	$140	$135

   Add $23 for Truglo fiberoptic sights (mfg. 1998-2004).
   Add $24 for dual comb stock and integral scope base (new 2003, includes extra synthetic cheekpiece).
   Add $51 for 100% camo coverage (new 2004).
   Add $125 for Marinecote finish (with synthetic stock, disc.).
This model also includes the Crown Grade Slugster, manufactured 1994-2000.

✴ *Model 500 Field Synthetic* - 12, 20 ga. or .410 bore, 3 in. chamber, 24 (slug model with ported barrel with cylinder bore choke and adj. rifle sights, new 2001), 26 (20 ga. only), or 28 (12 ga. ported only) in. VR barrel, black parkerized metal finish, black synthetic stock and forearm, 7-7 1/2 lbs. Disc. 2004.

	$255	$205	$175	$150	$145	$140	$135

Last MSR was $316.

   Add $14 for .410 bore Bantam Slug Model.

✴ *Model 500 Turkey Synthetic Thumbhole* - 12 ga. only, matte blue finish, features synthetic thumbhole stock and 20 in. barrel with X-factor turkey tube, 7 lbs. New 2007.

MSR $381	$295	$240	$185	$145	$120	$100	$90

MODEL 500 CAMO - 12 or 20 ga., 100% camo includes parkerized camo (disc.), OFM Camo (standard, mfg. 1991-96), Woodlands (mfg. 1995-2003), and various other camo finishes, metal and synthetic stock coverage, 24 (disc.), 26 (disc.), 28, or 30 (disc.) in. ported (standard 1997) or unported (disc. 2000) VR barrel (choice of cylinder bore with rifle sights or Accu-II chokes), front fiberoptic sight, includes swivels, camo sling, and drilled and tapped receiver, older Speedfeed stock (disc. 1990) holds 4 extra shells, 7 1/2 lbs. New 1986.

   Subtract 10% if without Accu-II choke system.
   Add $30 for Speedfeed in synthetic stock (disc. 1990).
Accu-chokes became standard in 1991. Current models are supplied with 2 choke tubes.

✴ *Model 500 Camo All Purpose* - 12 or 20 ga. (disc. 2004), 26 in. barrel, fiber optic sights, 100% Mossy Oak New Break Up (12 ga. only) or Mossy Oak Shadowgrass (20 ga. only) camo coverage.

MSR $378	$295	$240	$185	$145	$120	$100	$90

✴ *Model 500 Camo Waterfowl* - 12 ga. only, 28 in. VR ported barrel with Accu-Set choke tubes, synthetic stock and forearm, 100% Woodlands (disc.), Mossy Oak Duck Blind (new 2007), Advantage Max-4 (new 2004), or Mossy Oak Shadowgrass (new 2004) camo coverage.

MSR $378	$295	$240	$185	$145	$120	$100	$90

✴ *Model 500 Camo Flyway Series Waterfowl* - 12 ga. only, 3 in. chamber, 28 in. VR barrel with X-factor ported barrel and choke tube, fiber optic sights, synthetic stock and forearm with Advantage Max-4 camo, includes padded sling and embossed logo. New 2005.

MSR $435	$350	$290	$235	$195	$165	$145	$125

✴ *Model 500 Camo Turkey* - 12 or 20 ga., 20 (features ported turkey tube, new 2004) or 24 in. ported barrel with fiber optic sights and XX-full choke tube only, choice of thumbhole, adj. tactical synthetic (new 2006) or synthetic stock and forearm with Woodlands (disc. 2003), Realtree Hardwoods HD Green (new 2004),

GRADING - PPGS™	100%	98%	95%	90%	80%	70%	60%

Mossy Oak New Break Up (new 2004), or Mossy Oak Obsession (mfg. 2004, reintroduced 2007) camo treatment, 7 1/4 - 7 1/2 lbs. New 1999.

MSR $378	$295	$245	$190	$150	$120	$100	$90

Add $11 for Grand Slam Turkey model with X-factor ported turkey tube.
Add $107 for tactical synthetic stock and X-factor choke tube (new 2006).
Add $51 for thumbhole stock.

❖ **Model 500 Camo Turkey Bantam** - 20 ga. only, 22 in. VR barrel with fiberoptic sights and Accu-II X-full choke only, available in Woodlands (100% coverage), Mossy Oak Realtree Hardwoods HD Green (new 2004) or Mossy Oak Treestand camo (mfg. 2003 only) stock and forearm only, 6 1/2 lbs. Mfg. 1997-2004.

	$290	$235	$185	$145	$120	$100	$90

Last MSR was $364.

✳ *Model 500 Camo Combo* - 12 or 20 ga., includes a wide variety of extra barrel combinations including slug barrel options, prices vary slightly depending on the configuration (gauge/barrel/choke set-up). Rifled bores, VR barrels, and Accu-chokes became standard in the combo package late 1994. Disc. 1998.

	$375	$295	$250	$200	$180	$160	$145

Last MSR was $434.

MODEL 500 HOME SECURITY - 20 (1996 only) ga. or .410 bore, 3 in. chamber, 18 1/2 in. barrel with spreader choke, Model 500 slide-action, 5 shot mag., blue metal finish, synthetic field stock with pistol grip forearm, 6 1/4 lbs. New 1990.

MSR $373	$290	$240	$210	$175	$150	$125	$110

✳ *Model 500 Home Security Laser .410* - includes laser sighting device in right front of forearm. Mfg. 1990-93.

	$400	$350	$315	$280	$250	$225	$195

Last MSR was $451.

MODEL 500 PERSUADER - 12 or 20 (new 1995) ga., 6 or 8 shot, 18 1/2 in. plain barrel, cyl. bore or Accu-chokes (new 1995), optional rifle (12 ga./20 in. cyl. bore barrel only) or ghost ring (new 1999) sights, blue, matte (new 2006, 12 ga. only), or parkerized (12 ga. with ghost ring sights only) finish, Speedfeed stock was disc. 1990, optional bayonet lug, plain pistol grip wood (disc. 2004) or synthetic stock, approx. 6 3/4 lbs.

MSR $364	$290	$220	$175	$155	$120	$100	$90

Add $12 for pistol grip stock kit.

Add $127 for parkerized finish and ghost ring sights (disc. 2004).
Add $40 for combo with pistol grip (disc.).
Add $23 for rifle sights (disc., 12 ga. only).

✳ *Model 500 Persuader Night Special Edition* - 12 ga. only, includes synthetic stock and factory installed Mepro-Light night sight bead sight, only 300 mfg. for Lew Horton Distributing in 1990 only.

	$295	$250	$200	$175	$150	$130	$115

Last MSR was $296.

MODEL 500 TACTICAL - 12 ga. only, 3 in. chamber, 18 1/2 in. cylinder bore barrel, 6 shot, adj. tactical synthetic stock, choice of matte blue or Marinecoate finish. New 2006.

MSR $471	$400	$320	$265	$230	$200	$180	$160

Add $120 for Marinecote finish.

GRADING - PPGS™	100%	98%	95%	90%	80%	70%	60%

MODEL 500 SPECIAL PURPOSE - 12 ga. only, 18 in. cylinder bored barrel, choice of blue or parkerized finish, synthetic stock with or without Speedfeed. Disc. 1996.

	$330	$270	$240	$220	$200	$175	$160

Last MSR was $378.

Add $21 for Speedfeed stock.
Add $76 for ghost ring sight (parkerized finish only).

MODEL 500 CRUISER - 12, 20, or .410 (new 1993) ga., 14 (12 ga. only, Law Enforcement Model, disc. 1995), 18 1/2, 20, or 21 (20 ga. only - mfg. 1995-2002) in. cylinder bore barrel, shroud is available in 12 ga. only, 6 or 8 (12 ga. only) shot mag., pistol grip forearm only, 5 3/4 - 7 lbs. New 1989.

MSR $364	$285	$215	$180	$150	$145	$135	$120

Add $12 for heat shield around barrel (12 ga. only).
Add $96 for 14 in. barrel (disc.).
Add approx. $34 for camper case (1993-96).

✳ *Model 500 Cruiser Mil-Spec* - 12 ga. only, 20 in. cylinder bored barrel with bead sights, built to Mil-Specs., parkerized finish. Mfg. 1997 only.

	$395	$350	$325	$295	$275	$250	$225

Last MSR was $478.

MODEL 500 GHOST RING SIGHT - 12 ga. only, 3 in. chamber, 18 1/2 or 20 in. cyl. bore or Accu-choke (20 in. only - new 1995) barrel, 6 or 9 shot tube mag., blue or parkerized finish, synthetic field stock, includes ghost ring sighting device. Mfg. 1990-97.

	$270	$225	$180	$160	$150	$140	$130

Last MSR was $332.

Add $53 for parkerized finish.
Add $49 for 9 shot mag. (20 in. barrel only).
Add $123 for Accu-choke barrel (parkerized finish only).
Add $134 for Speedfeed stock (new 1994 - 9 shot, 20 in. barrel only).

MODEL 500 MARINER - 12 ga. only, 3 in. chamber, 18 1/2 or 20 in. cyl. bore barrel, 6 or 9 shot, Marinecote finish on all metal parts (more rust-resistant than stainless steel), pistol grip black synthetic stock and forearm, fixed or ghost ring (mfg. 1995-99) sights, approx. 6 3/4 lbs.

MSR $497	$420	$315	$235	$180	$140	$125	$105

Add $49 for 9 shot model with 20 in. barrel.

Add $68 for ghost ring sights (disc. 1999).
Add $23 for Speedfeed stock (mini-combo only - disc.).

MODEL 500 J.I.C. (JUST IN CASE) - 12 ga., 3 in. chamber, comes with pistol grip, impact resistant tube and strap, available in three configurations: Crusier (survival kit in a can, blue metal, OD Green tube), Mariner (multi-tool and knife, Orange tube, Marinecote finish), or Sandstorm (Desert camo tube and finish), 5 1/2 lbs. New 2007.

As this edition went to press, retail pricing was not available on this model.

MODEL 505 YOUTH ALL PURPOSE FIELD SLIDE ACTION - 20 ga. or .410 bore, 3 in. chamber, 20 in. barrel with Accu-Set or fixed Mod. choke, vent. rib, brass mid-bead and white front bead sights, wood stock, blue metal finish, short 12 in. LOP. New 2005.

MSR $327	$260	$210	$175	$150	$145	$140	$135

Model 505 Youth barrels are not interchangeble with any Mossberg slide action shotgun.

MODEL 535 SLIDE ACTION - ATS (ALL TERRAIN SHOTGUN) - 12 ga. only, 3 in. chamber, features safety on rear of receiver, various configurations, 6 1/2 - 7 lbs. New 2005.

✱ *Model 535 Slide Action ATS All Purpose Field* - 12 ga. only, 28 in. barrel with Accu-set chokes, vent. rib, blue metal, walnut stock, white bead front sight. New 2005.

MSR $345		$280	$220	$185	$150	$145	$140	$135

✱ *Model 535 Slide Action ATS Turkey* - 12 ga. only, 20 (includes X-factor ported choke tube, new 2006) or 22 in. barrel with XX-Full choke, vent. rib, fiber optic sights, matte blue, Mossy Oak New Break-Up, Mossy Oak Obsession (new 2007), or Realtree Hardwoods HD Green finish, standard or tactical (new 2006) synthetic stock. New 2005.

MSR $345		$280	$220	$185	$150	$145	$140	$135

Add $59 for camo.
Add $165 for tactical synthetic stock with X-factor ported choke tube (new 2006).

✱ *Model 535 Slide Action ATS Thumbhole Turkey* - similar to Turkey model, except has synthetic thumbhole stock and 20 in. barrel with X-factor ported choke tube, not available in Mossy Oak Obsession. New 2007.

MSR $397		$325	$295	$265	$235	$200	$185	$165

Add $59 for 100% camo coverage.

✱ *Model 535 Slide Action ATS Waterfowl* - 12 ga. only, 28 in. barrel with Accu-set choke, vent. rib, synthetic stock, matte blue, Mossy Oak New Break-Up, Mossy Oak Duck Blind (new 2007), or Advantage Max-4 camo, fiber optic sights. New 2005.

MSR $345		$280	$220	$185	$150	$145	$140	$135

Add $59 for camo.
Add $100 for Turkey/Waterfowl combo package.

✱ *Model 535 Slide Action ATS Slugster* - 12 ga. only, 24 in. fully rifled bore barrel, synthetic stock, rifle sights or integral scope base, matte blue metal, Realtree AP (new 2007), or Mossy Oak New Break-Up camo. New 2005.

MSR $345		$280	$220	$180	$150	$145	$140	$135

Add $59 for camo and $27 for integral scope base (Realtree AP camo only).

MODEL 500/590 INTIMIDATOR LASER - 12 ga. only, 3 in. chamber, 18 1/2 (Model 500) or 20 (Model 590) in. cyl. bore barrel, 6 (Model 500) or 9 (Model 590) shot tube mag., blue or parkerized finish, synthetic field stock, includes laser sighting device. Mfg. 1990-93.

✱ *Model 500 Intimidator*

		$440	$375	$340	$295	$260	$230	$195

Last MSR was $505.

Add $22 for parkerized finish.

✱ *Model 590 Intimidator*

		$495	$440	$375	$340	$295	$260	$230

Last MSR was $556.

Add $45 for parkerized finish.

MODEL 590 SPECIAL PURPOSE SLIDE ACTION - 12 ga., 3 in. chamber, similar to Model 500, except has 9 shot mag., 20 in. cyl. bore barrel with or w/o 3/4 shroud, and bayonet lug, blue or parkerized finish, regular black synthetic stock, with or w/o Speedfeed, 7 1/4 lbs. New 1987.

MSR $435		$355	$290	$235	$195	$165	$145	$125

Add $47 for parkerized finish.
Add $140 for heavy barrel with ghost ring sights, metal triggerguard and safety.
Add $81 for ghost ring sights.
Add $33 for Speedfeed (blue, disc. 1999) or $90 for Speedfeed (parkerized) stock.

❊ *Model 590 Special Purpose Slide Action Mariner* - similar to Model 500 Mariner except is 9 shot and has 20 in. barrel. Mfg. 1989-93.

	$310	$250	$200	$185	$165	$145	$125

Last MSR was $353.

Add $17 for Speedfeed stock (disc. 1990).
Add $15 for pistol grip adapter (mini combo - disc.).

❊ *Model 590 Special Purpose Slide Action Bullpup* - similar to Model 500 Bullpup except is 9 shot and has 20 in. barrel. Mfg. 1989-90 only.

	$500	$475	$400	$350	$300	$225	$200

Last MSR was $497.

❊ *Model 590A1 Special Purpose Slide Action* - 12 ga., marked 590A1 on receiver, parkerized, ghost ring rear sight, synthetic stock and forend, ramp front sight. Disc. 1997.

	$450	$395	$360	$330	$295	$260	$230

❊ *Model 590 Special Purpose Slide Action Double Action* - 12 ga. only, 3 in. chamber, world's first double action shotgun (long trigger pull), 18 1/2 or 20 in. barrel, 6 or 9 shot, bead or ghost ring sights, black synthetic stock and forearm, top tang safety, parkerized metal finish, 7-7 1/4 lbs. Mfg. 2000-2003.

	$450	$415	$360	$330	$295	$260	$230

Last MSR was $510.

Add $31 for 9 shot capacity.
Add $48 for ghost ring sights.
Add $124 for Speedfeed stock (20 in. barrel with ghost ring sights only).

❊ *Model 590 Special Purpose Slide Action Line Launcher* - special purpose Marine and rescue shotgun with blaze orange synthetic stock, line dispensing canister, floating and distance heads, nylon and spectra line refills, includes case and two boxes of launching loads.

	$850	$800	$700	$650	$540	$465	$385

Last MSR was $927.

MODEL 695 BOLT ACTION - 12 ga. only, with detachable 2 shot mag., 3 in. chamber, 22 in. barrel with fully rifled and ported (new 1999) or Accu-choke (disc. 1998) barrel, black synthetic or Woodlands camo (with bead sights, disc. 2001) on stock and forearm, rifle or Truglo fiberoptic sights, 7 1/2 lbs. Mfg. 1996-2002.

	$275	$220	$185	$150	$135	$120	$115

Last MSR was $345.

Subtract approx. $50 for Accu-choke barrel.
Add $22 for Truglo fiberoptic sights (new 1998).
Add $52 for Truglo fiberoptic sights and Woodlands camo finish (disc. 2001).

MODEL 712 SEMI-AUTO - 12 ga. only, gas operated, shoots 2 3/4 and 3 in. shells interchangeably, plain barrel or VR, top of receiver safety, checkered hardwood stock, rubber recoil pad, fixed or Accu-choke II choking. Mfg. 1986-88 only.

	$285	$250	$220	$200	$190	$175	$160

Last MSR was $345.

Subtract $25 without Accu-II choking.
Add $90 for combo pack (includes 1 extra 24 in. slugster barrel).

❊ *Model 712 Semi-Auto Steel Shot* - similar to Model 712, except has Accu-steel choking system for steel shot, 28 in. VR barrel. Mfg. 1988 only.

	$290	$250	$220	$200	$190	$175	$160

Last MSR was $349.

GRADING - PPGS™	100%	98%	95%	90%	80%	70%	60%

✻ *Model 712 Semi-Auto Camo/Speedfeed* - 12 ga. only, similar to Model 712, except has camo finished metal parts, stock, and forearm, 24 or 28 in. barrel. Mfg. 1986-87 only.

	$340	$295	$240	$185	$155	$130	$110

Last MSR was $390.

Add $20 for Accu-II choke.

MODEL 712 REGAL SEMI-AUTO - 12 or 20 ga., action same as Model 712, special bright bluing, VR only, deluxe checkered walnut stock and forearm, gold trigger, inlaid medallion on receiver, top of receiver safety. Mfg. 1986-87 only.

	$310	$280	$250	$225	$200	$185	$170

Last MSR was $366.

Add $20 for Accu-II choke.

NEW HAVEN BRAND - trademark used on previous models, plainer finish. Disc.
Values are 20% less per similar model.

MODEL 835 ULTI-MAG SLIDE ACTION - 12 ga. with 3 1/2 in. chamber (new 1988), slide action, 24 (Turkey Model - new 1990) or 28 in. VR barrel with Accu-mag choke tubes, 6 shot mag., safety on top rear of receiver, choice of camo synthetic or checkered hardwood stock. Introduced late 1988, disc. 1991.

	$375	$310	$265	$220	$190	$165	$150

Last MSR was $430.

Add $30 for synthetic camo field stock.

Various Combo packages were available in this model with prices ranging from $469-$534 depending on barrel chokings and scope base options.

This model was followed by the 835 Regal Series introduced in late 1991.

MODEL 835 ULTI-MAG FIELD GRADE SLIDE ACTION - 12 ga. only, 3 1/2 in. chamber, 24 in. cyl. bore (disc.), 24 in. VR (Turkey Special, disc. 1993), or 28 in. ported (new 1997) or unported VR barrel with 1 Accu-mag choke, walnut finish stock and forearm (pressed checkering became standard 1994), blue finish, approx. 7 1/2 lbs. Disc. 1998.

	$270	$230	$200	$185	$165	$145	$125

Last MSR was $331.

Add $40 for combo package (disc. 1993).

MODEL 835 ULTI-MAG SYNTHETIC (SPECIAL HUNTER) - 12 ga. only, 3 1/2 in. chamber, 26 (disc. 1999, reintroduced 2004) or 28 in. VR ported barrel with mod. Accu-mag choke, parkerized finish, black synthetic stock, 7 3/4 lbs. Mfg. 1998-2005.

	$315	$260	$220	$185	$165	$145	$125

Last MSR was $394.

MODEL 835 ULTI-MAG FIELD (CROWN GRADE) - similar to Field Grade, except has gold trigger and cut checkering on walnut finished hardwood stock, blue or OFM Woodland camo (24 in. Turkey only) finish, ported (standard 1997) or unported (disc.) VR barrel, 7 3/4 lbs. Mfg. 1994-2005.

	$315	$260	$220	$185	$165	$145	$125

Last MSR was $394.

✻ *Model 835 Ulti-Mag Field Turkey* - 12 ga. only, 24 in. ported VR barrel, parkerized finish, walnut finished stock and forearm. Mfg. 1997-2000.

	$320	$255	$215	$190	$165	$145	$125

Last MSR was $378.

✴ *Model 835 Ulti-Mag Field New Turkey* - 12 ga. only, 24 in. ported barrel with Ulti-full choke only, choice of Realtree Advantage Timber (new 2001), Realtree Hardwoods (mfg. 2000 only), Realtree Xtra brown (disc. 1999) or Woodlands (disc. 1999) 100% camo finish, fiberoptic sights, 7 1/2 lbs. Mfg. 1999-2001.

	$450	$380	$345	$300	$270	$235	$210

Last MSR was $525.

✴ *Model 835 Ulti-Mag Field Crown Grade* - 12 ga. only, 3 1/2 in. chamber, 28 in. VR ported (standard 1997) or unported barrel, walnut stock and forearm, Accu-mag choke. Disc. 1998.

	$365	$300	$260	$230	$200	$180	$160

Last MSR was $421.

Add $7 for duo-comb stock.

MODEL 835 VIKING - 12 ga. only, 28 in. VR ported (standard 1997) or unported (1996 only) barrel with one Accu-Choke and twin bead sights, matte blue finish with green synthetic stock and forearm, 7.7 lbs. Mfg. 1996-98.

	$260	$225	$200	$185	$165	$145	$125

Last MSR was $316.

MODEL 835 ULTIMAG CAMO TURKEY & WATERFOWL - 12 ga. only, 3 1/2 in. chamber, OFM Woodland Camo (all-purpose camo, combo. only mfg. 1997-99), Realtree (mfg. 1993-99), Realtree AP (all purpose grey, mfg. 1996-99), Realtree X-tra Brown (mfg. 2000-2002), Brown Leaf (disc. 1999), Woodlands (new 2000), Mossy Oak Shadow Grass (new 2000, Waterfowl only), Realtree Hardwoods (mfg. 2002, Turkey only), Mossy Oak New Break-up (new 2003), Mossy Oak Forest Floor (mfg. 2003 only), Mossy Oak Obsession (mfg. 2004, reintroduced 2007), Mossy Oak Duck Blind (new 2007, Waterfowl only), Advantage Max-4 (Waterfowl only, new 2004), Realtree Hardwoods HD Green (new 2003), Advantage Timber (mfg. 2001-2002), or Mossy Oak (mfg. 1994-99) finish, 20 (Grand Slam Turkey Model with X-factor ported turkey tube, new 2004), 24 (Turkey Special), 26 (Waterfowl, new 2004) or 28 (Waterfowl only) in. VR ported (new 1997) or unported (disc. 2000) barrel with 6 choke tubes, dual comb wood (Turkey/Deer combo only) or synthetic stock, approx. 7 1/2 lbs. New 1991.

MSR $450		$385	$355	$300	$270	$235	$210	$190

Add $56 for Turkey/Deer or Turkey/Waterfowl combo.
Add $22 for any camo finish other than Woodlands.
Add $6 for synthetic thumbhole stock with matte blue or $74 for synthetic thumbhole stock with camo coverage (new 2007).
Add $139 for Specialty Turkey Model with laminated thumbole or tactical synthetic stock with X-factor ported choke tube and fiber optic sights (new 2006).
Add $32 for Grand Slam Turkey Model with 20 in. barrel and X-factor ported turkey tube (new 2004).
Add $65 for 28 in. barrel with Mossy Oak Shadow Grass and hunter set of chokes (Waterfowl Model, disc.).
Subtract $46 for Waterfowl model w/o camo finish.
OFM Woodland camo finish on this model included a dual comb stock.

MODEL 835 SLUGSTER - 12 ga. only, 3 1/2 in. chamber, 6 shot mag., 24 in. ported rifled slug barrel, integral scope base or rifle sights, choice of wood dual comb or synthetic stock, Realtree AP camo coverage, 7 3/4 lbs. New 2007.

MSR $472		$400	$360	$310	$270	$235	$210	$190

GRADING - PPGS™	100%	98%	95%	90%	80%	70%	60%

MODEL 835 WALNUT ULTI-MAG (REGAL) - 12 ga., 3 1/2 in. chamber, 28 in. VR barrel with Accu-Mag chokes (disc. 1996) or 24 in. rifled slug barrel, single (new 1993) or dual comb (2 comb inserts are provided for the stock affording different shooting positions), aluminum receiver, back-bored barrel, double slide bars, high gloss walnut stock with recoil pad, approx. 7 1/2 lbs. Mfg. 1991-96.

	$350	$290	$260	$230	$200	$175	$160

Last MSR was $404.

Add $8 for dual comb stock.
Add $30 for 24 in. slug barrel with trophy scope base and dual comb stock.
Add $72-$83 for combo package (includes extra slug barrel with choice of sights).

MODEL 835 WILD TURKEY FED. LIMITED EDITION - 12 ga. with 3 1/2 in. chamber, 24 in. VR barrel with Accu-mag. chokes, camo finish, includes camo sling, medallion in stock, and 10-pack of Federal Turkey loads. Mfg. 1989 only.

	$425	$360	$295	$240	$210	$180	$155

Last MSR was $477.

MODEL 835 NWTF SPECIAL EDITION - 12 ga. only, 24 in. VR barrel with Accu-mag chokes, features Realtree camo finish, drilled and tapped receiver, 7 1/2 lbs. Mfg. 1991 only to commemorate the National Wild Turkey Federation.

	$380	$300	$225	$175	$140	$125	$105

Last MSR was $436.

MODEL 835 WATERFOWL LIMITED EDITION - 12 ga. with 3 1/2 in. chamber, 28 in. VR barrel with Accu-mag. chokes, camo finish, synthetic stock, camo sling. Mfg. 1990 only.

	$425	$360	$295	$240	$210	$180	$155

Last MSR was $480.

MODEL 835 FLYWAY SERIES WATERFOWL - 12 ga. only, 3 1/2 in. chamber, 28 in. VR with X-factor porting barrel and choke tubes, fiber optic sights, synthetic stock and forearm with Advantage Max-4 camo, includes padded sling and embossed logo. New 2005.

MSR $521	$420	$330	$270	$230	$200	$180	$160

MODEL 930 SEMI-AUTO - 12 ga. only, 3 in. chamber, various configurations, approx. 7 3/4 lbs. New 2005.

* *Model 930 Semi-Auto All Purpose Field* - 12 ga. only, 26 or 28 in. ported barrel with Accu-set chokes, vent. rib, blue metal, walnut stock, white bead front sight. New 2005.

MSR $525	$430	$335	$275	$230	$200	$180	$160

* *Model 930 Semi-Auto Turkey* - 12 ga. only, 24 in. ported barrel with XX-Full choke, vent. rib, fiberoptic sights, matte blue, Mossy Oak New Break-Up, Mossy Oak Obsession (new 2007), or Realtree Hardwoods HD Green finish, synthetic stock. New 2005.

MSR $503	$410	$320	$260	$230	$200	$180	$160

Add $108 for camo.

* *Model 930 Semi-Auto Waterfowl* - 12 ga. only, 26 or 28 in. ported barrel with Accu-set choke, vent. rib, walnut or synthetic stock, matte or matte blue (wood stock only), Mossy Oak Duck Blind (new 2007), Mossy Oak New Break-Up or Advantage Max-4 camo, fiber optic sights. New 2005.

MSR $503	$410	$320	$260	$230	$200	$180	$160

Add $22 for walnut stock and foream with matte blue metal finish.
Add $108 for camo.

GRADING - PPGS™	100%	98%	95%	90%	80%	70%	60%

❋ *Model 930 Semi-Auto Slugster* - 12 ga. only, 24 in. fully rifled bore barrel, choice of walnut, synthetic, or Monte Carlo synthetic, rifle sights or integral scope base, matte blue metal, Realtree AP (new 2007), or Mossy Oak New Break-Up camo. New 2005.

MSR $503	$410	$320	$260	$230	$200	$180	$160

Add $22 for walnut stock and forearm.
Add $108 for camo.
Add $77 for All-Purpose Combo or $55 for Waterfowl Combo (new 2006).

❋ *Model 930 Home Security* - 12 ga., 3 in. chamber, 18 1/2 cylinder bore barrel, bead sights, blue finish, black synthetic stock, 7 1/2 lbs. New 2007.

MSR $503	$410	$320	$260	$230	$200	$180	$160

MODEL 935 MAGNUM SEMI-AUTO - 12 ga. only, 3 1/2 in. chamber, choice of turkey or waterfowl configuration, 22 (Grand Slam Turkey model with X-factor ported turkey tube), 24 (turkey only), 26, or 28 VR barrel with choke tube(s) and fiber optic front sight, matte or camo metal finish, wood (disc.) or synthetic stock and forearm, choice of full coverage Mossy Oak New Break Up, Advantage Max-4, Mossy Oak Duck Blind (new 2007), Mossy Oak Shadowgrass, Mossy Oak Obsession (new 2007), or Realtree Hardwoods HD Green camo, approx. 7 3/4 lbs. New 2004.

MSR $568	$465	$410	$370	$340	$300	$280	$260

Add $109 for 100% camo coverage.
Add $122 for Grand Slam Turkey model with 22 in. barrel and X-factor ported turkey tube.
Add $179 for Turkey/Deer or Turkey/Waterfowl combo (new 2005).

MODEL 935 MAGNUM SLUGSTER - 12 ga. only, 24 in. fully rifled barrel, choice of Monte Carlo or regular synthetic stock and foream, choice of rifle sights or intergral scope base, Realtree AP camo, 7 1/2 lbs. New 2007.

MSR $677	$575	$500	$425	$350	$300	$265	$235

MODEL 935 FLYWAY SERIES WATERFOWL - 12 ga. only, 3 1/2 in. chamber, 28 in. VR with X-factor ported barrel and choke tubes, fiber optic sights, synthetic stock and forearm with Advantage Max-4 camo, includes padded sling and embossed logo. New 2005.

MSR $721	$595	$485	$435	$375	$325	$300	$275

MODEL 1000 SEMI-AUTO - 12 or 20 ga., gas semi-auto, 2 3/4 in. chamber, scroll engraved aluminum alloy receiver, plain or VR barrel, also available in trap and skeet configuration, checkered walnut stock and forearm. Imported 1986-87 only. VR became standard in 1987.

	$410	$345	$300	$270	$245	$220	$200

Last MSR was $472.

Add $28 for Multi-Choke II.
Deduct $50 if without VR.

Model 1000 barrels are not interchangeable with Model 1000 Super barrels.
Manufactured by Howa, Mossberg took over this series after Smith & Wesson decided to drop the line.

❋ *Model 1000 Semi-Auto Junior* - similar to Model 1000, except 20 ga. only, shortened stock, and 22 in. VR Multi-Choke barrel. Imported 1986-87 only.

	$425	$355	$310	$275	$250	$220	$200

Last MSR was $499.

❋ *Model 1000 Semi-Auto Slug* - 12 or 20 ga., 22 in. barrel with rifle sights, recoil pad. Imported 1986-87 only.

	$405	$340	$295	$270	$245	$220	$200

Last MSR was $464.

GRADING - PPGS™	100%	98%	95%	90%	80%	70%	60%

✳ *Model 1000 Semi-Auto Skeet* - 12 or 20 ga., steel receiver, 26 in. VR barrel bored skeet. Mfg. 1986 only.

	$395	$335	$295	$270	$245	$220	$200

Last MSR was $439.

MODEL 1000 SUPER SEMI-AUTO - 12 or 20 (Super 20) ga., gas semi-auto, 3 in. chambers, shoots 2 3/4 and 3 in. shells interchangeably, steel receiver, vent. recoil pad, select checkered walnut stock and forearm, Multi-Choke II is standard (except on slug barrel). Slug models are approx. the same price as values listed directly below. Imported 1986-87 only.

	$495	$405	$365	$330	$295	$270	$245

Last MSR was $577.

Model 1000 Super barrels are not interchangeable with Model 1000 barrels.
Manufactured by Howa, Mossberg took over this series after Smith & Wesson decided to drop the line.

✳ *Model 1000 Super Semi-Auto Waterfowler* - 12 ga. only, matte finished wood and metal, includes swivels and camouflaged sling, 28 in. Multi-Choke barrel. Imported 1986-87 only.

	$510	$430	$370	$315	$270	$230	$200

Last MSR was $605.

✳ *Model 1000 Super Semi-Auto Skeet* - 12 or 20 ga., 25 in. barrel, jug choking. Imported 1986-87 only.

	$575	$495	$450	$410	$375	$330	$295

Last MSR was $658.

✳ *Model 1000 Super Semi-Auto Trap* - 12 ga. only, 30 in. Multi-Choke II barrel with high VR, Monte Carlo stock, recoil pad. Mfg. 1986 only.

	$470	$380	$345	$320	$285	$270	$250

Last MSR was $560.

MODEL 3000 SLIDE ACTION - 12 or 20 ga. only, 3 in. chamber, slide action, steel receiver, double action bars, various chokes and VR barrel lengths, checkered walnut stock and forearm, vent. recoil pad. This model was introduced in 1986 and the field version was disc. in 1987.

	$325	$275	$250	$220	$200	$185	$170

Last MSR was $360.

   Add $25 for Multi-Choke II.

✳ *Model 3000 Slide Action Waterfowler* - 12 ga. only, similar to Model 3000, except has dull matte finish on wood and metal, includes swivels and camouflaged sling, VR only. Mfg. 1986 only.

	$340	$295	$265	$215	$185	$150	$120

Last MSR was $386.

   Add $30 for Multi-choke II option, $70 for camo/speedfeed stock.

✳ *Model 3000 Slide Action Law Enforcement* - 12 or 20 ga. only, 18 1/2 or 20 in. cylinder bore only, rifle or bead sights. Mfg. 1986-87 only.

	$325	$275	$250	$220	$200	$185	$170

Last MSR was $362.

   Add $25 for rifle sights.
   Add $33 for black speedfeed stock.

MODEL 5500 SEMI-AUTO - 12 ga., 2 3/4 or 3 in. mag., gas operated, 18 1/2 - 30 in. barrels. Disc. 1985.

	$250	$235	$205	$185	$170	$155	$140

Last MSR was $307.

   Add $20 for VR.

GRADING - PPGS™	100%	98%	95%	90%	80%	70%	60%

❊ *Model 5500 Semi-Auto Mag.* - 12 ga. only, 3 in. chamber, 30 in. VR barrel. Disc. 1985.

	$275	$250	$225	$205	$190	$175	$160

Last MSR was $325.

MODEL 5500 MKII SEMI-AUTO - 12 ga. only, supplied with 2 VR barrels - 26 in./2 3/4 in. chamber and 28 in./3 in. chamber VR barrels, includes choice of Accu-II choke tubes (lead shot only) or Accu-Steel choke tubes, blue or camo finish (new 1990), checkered hardwood stock and forearm, top receiver safety, recoil pad, 7 1/2 lbs. Mfg. 1989-92.

	$260	$225	$200	$180	$160	$140	$125

Last MSR was $294.

> Add $10 for 24 in. rifled slug barrel.
> Add $43 for camo metal finish and synthetic stock.
> Add $30 for Turkey Model (24 in. barrel, camo finish, and synthetic stock).
> This model was also available with different Combo options. Prices varied between $463-$484, depending on configuration of barrel choking.

❊ *Model 5500 Mk II Semi-Auto U.S. Shooting Team* - 2 3/4 in. chamber, 26 in. non-Mag. barrel with VR and Accu-II chokes, blue finish, checkered walnut stock and forearm, 7 1/2 lbs. Mfg. 1991-92.

	$325	$250	$225	$200	$185	$170	$160

Last MSR was $376.

❊ *Model 5500 Mk II Semi-Auto NWTF Special Edition* - 12 ga. only, 3 in. chamber, 24 in. VR barrel with 1 choke tube, Mossy Oak Camo finish with synthetic stock and forearm, 7.3 lbs. Mfg. 1991-92.

	$365	$300	$265	$235	$200	$175	$160

Last MSR was $428.

MODEL 6000 SEMI-AUTO - 12 ga. only, 2 3/4 or 3 in. chamber 28 in. VR barrel with Accu-choke, economical model with walnut finish stock, blue finish, 7.7 lbs. Mfg. 1993 only.

	$280	$240	$215	$200	$185	$165	$145

Last MSR was $321.

MODEL 9200 CROWN SEMI-AUTO - 12 ga. only, 3 in. chamber, gas operated, shoots any shell interchangeably, 18 1/2 (SP only), 22 (Bantam only), 24 in. rifled, 24 (Turkey), 26 (U.S. Shooting Team variation, new 1993), or 28 in. VR barrel with 3 Accu-chokes, engraved aluminum receiver, synthetic (18 1/2 in. barrel only) or walnut stained hardwood stock (1 in. shorter on Bantam Model) and forearm, top receiver safety, approx. 7 1/2 lbs. Mfg. 1992-2001.

	$460	$335	$275	$225	$190	$170	$160

Last MSR was $574.

> Add approx. $73-$95 for combo package.
> Add $33 for Truglo fiberoptic sights (mfg. 1998 only).
> Add $23 for 24 in. rifled slug barrel with trophy scope base.
> Subtract $90 for synthetic stock (Special Purpose with matte blue finish, 18 1/2 in. barrel).

❊ *Model 9200 Crown Semi-Auto Viking* - 12 ga. only, 28 in. VR barrel with one Accu-Choke and twin bead sights, matte finish with green synthetic stock and forearm, 7.7 lbs. Mfg. 1996-98.

	$365	$310	$270	$230	$200	$175	$160

Last MSR was $429.

❊ *Model 9200 Crown Semi-Auto Special Hunter* - 12 ga. only, 28 in. VR barrel with Accu-II choke set, parkerized finish, black synthetic stock. Mfg. 1998-2001.

	$425	$345	$285	$245	$200	$175	$160

Last MSR was $491.

GRADING - PPGS™	100%	98%	95%	90%	80%	70%	60%

✳ *Model 9200 Crown Semi-Auto Camo* - 12 ga. only, similar to Model 9200, except is supplied with OFM (disc. 1996), Mossy Oak (disc. 1999), Realtree (mfg. 1994-95), Realtree AP (mfg. 1996-99) or Woodlands (new 1995) camo finish, 24 (Turkey) or 28 in. VR barrel. Mfg. 1992-99.

	$445	$320	$265	$230	$195	$170	$160

Last MSR was $556.

Subtract approx. $40 for Turkey Model with Woodlands camo and one choke tube.

❖ **Model 9200 Crown Semi-Auto Camo New Turkey** - 12 ga. only, 24 in. VR barrel with XX-full choke tube only and fiberoptic sights, choice of 100% Woodlands or Mossy Oak Shadow Branch camo treatment. Mfg. 1999-2001.

	$415	$300	$250	$225	$195	$170	$160

Last MSR was $517.

Add approx. $95 for Mossy Oak Shadow Branch camo coverage.

✳ *Model 9200 Crown Semi-Auto Jungle Gun* - 12 ga. only, 18 1/2 in. plain barrel with cyl. bore, parkerized metal, synthetic stock. Mfg. 1998-2001.

	$610	$500	$360	$300	$250	$225	$200

Last MSR was $704.

SILVER/ONYX RESERVE O/U - 12, 20, 28 ga., or .410 bore, boxlock action with dual locking lugs, 26 or 28 in. barrels, Silver Reserve Field models feature detailed game scenes engraved on silver receiver, Onyx has blue receiver with scroll engraving, checkered walnut stock and forearm, SST, extractors, five interchangeable choke tubes on 12, 20 or 28 ga., Sporting models (12 ga. only) have ported barrels, wide rib, scroll engraving on silver or blue receiver, Bantam model has 26 in. barrels and short LOP, 6 - 7.7 lbs. New 2005.

MSR $560	$475	$425	$375	$330	$300	$275	$250

Add $122 for Sporting Models.
Add $283 for 12/20 ga. combo (new 2007).

MOUNTAIN RIFLERY, INC.

Current custom rifle builder located in Pocatello, ID. Consumer direct sales.

John Bolliger has been producing top quality, custom made bolt action rifles for over 30 years. Currently, Mountain Riflery is concentrating on 3 series of rifles: the Signature Series, the Excalibur Series, and the Crown Series. Since almost all rifles are special ordered per customer specifications (with many options also available), please contact Mountain Riflery directly for more information, including pricing and options.

MOUNTAIN RIFLES INC.

Previous rifle manufacturer located in Palmer, AK 1995-98.

RIFLES: BOLT ACTION

MOUNTAINEER - various cals., choice of M-700 Rem. or M-70 Win. action, Chrome Moly barrel with ultra muzzle brake, Timney trigger, parkerized finish, fiberglass stock with decelerator pad, 5 1/2 lbs. Limited mfg. 1995-98.

	$1,825	$1,475	$1,100	$900	$750	$675	$550

Last MSR was $1,995.

SUPER MOUNTAINEER - similar to the Mountaineer, except has Kevlar epoxy bedded stock with steel crossbolts on Mag. cals., 4 1/4 lbs. Limited 1995-98.

	$2,575	$2,025	$1,475	$1,100	$900	$750	$675

Last MSR was $2,895.

PRO MOUNTAINEER K.S. - various cals., Winchester M-70 controlled feed action, choice of fiberglass pillar epoxy bedded, Kevlar, or KSDB (Kevlar Stock Drop Box mag.) stock with decelerator pad, parkerized finish. 6 lbs. Limited mfg. 1995-98.

	$2,395	$1,950	$1,425	$1,050	$875	$725	$650

Last MSR was $2,695.

Add $500 for KSDB stock with drop mag.

GRADING - PPGS™	100%	98%	95%	90%	80%	70%	60%

PRO SAFARI - various cals., Winchester M-70 controlled feed action, high gloss bluing, exhibition grade English walnut with decelerator pad, 4 shot detachable mag. 7-9 lbs. Limited mfg. 1995-98.

	$3,795	$3,350	$2,875	$2,350	$1,775	$1,450	$1,200

Last MSR was $3,995.

ULTRA MOUNTAINEER - various cals., features stainless steel match grade barrel with black Kevlar/Graphite thumbhole stock, approx. 5 lbs. New 1997.

	$2,650	$2,075	$1,500	$1,100	$900	$750	$675

Last MSR was $2,995.

Add $500 for Rigby length.

MUSGRAVE

Previous manufacturer located in the Republic of South Africa. Musgrave had very limited importation into the U.S. Newer models manufactured by Musgrave (imported into Austria and Switzerland) included the Model 90 (features Musgrave action) Standard Rifle, Model 90 Light Rifle, Mini-90, Model 90 Varmint, Model 90 De Luxe Rifle, and Magnum Rifle, in addition to the same series in the Mauser 98 action.

RIFLES: BOLT ACTION

VALIANT BOLT ACTION RIFLE - .243 Win., .270 Win., .30-06, .308 Win., or 7mm Rem. Mag. cal., 24 in. barrel, leaf sight, skip line checkered straight stock, pistol grip. Mfg. 1971-1976.

	$375	$325	$275	$250	$220	$195	$175

PREMIER - similar to Valiant, with 26 in. barrel, select Monte Carlo stock, rosewood pistol grip cap and forearm tip.

	$425	$365	$315	$275	$250	$225	$200

RSA SINGLE SHOT TARGET RIFLE - .308 Win. cal. only, 26 in. heavy barrel, target sights and stock. Mfg. 1971-1976.

	$425	$365	$315	$275	$250	$225	$200

MUSKETEER RIFLES

Previous trademark of rifles previously imported by Firearms International Company (FIC), located in Washington, D.C.

RIFLES: BOLT ACTION

SPORTER - .243 Win., .25-06 Rem., .270 Win., .264 Win. Mag., .308 Win., .30-06, 7mm Rem. Mag., or .300 Win. Mag. cal., bolt action, FN Mauser action, 24 in. barrel, no sights, checkered Monte Carlo stock. Mfg. 1963-1972.

	$375	$325	$275	$250	$220	$195	$175

SPORTER DELUXE - adj. trigger, select wood, tear drop pistol grip, skipline checkering.

	$425	$365	$315	$275	$250	$225	$200

CARBINE - similar to Sporter, except 20 in. barrel and full length stock.

	$375	$325	$275	$250	$220	$195	$175

NOTES

N SECTION

NS FIREARMS CORP.

Previous importer located in Atlanta, GA until 1994. NS Firearms was a division of KFS, Inc. located in Atlanta, GA. Previously manufactured in China.

GRADING - PPGS™	100%	98%	95%	90%	80%	70%	60%

RIFLES: SEMI-AUTO

MODEL 522 SPORTER - .22 LR cal., 21 in. cold hammer forged barrel, 5 shot detachable mag., grooved receiver, checkered walnut stock, 7 3/4 lbs. Imported 1994 only.

	100%	98%	95%	90%	80%	70%	60%
	$250	$215	$185	$165	$145	$125	$110

Last MSR was $299.

NAMBU PISTOLS

Previously manufactured in Japan for the Japanese military between 1902-1945.

PISTOLS: SEMI-AUTO

Please refer to Japanese Military Pistols for the Hamada variations and the 1893 revolver.

TYPE 14 - 8mm Nambu cal., recoil operated, 4.7 in. barrel, blue, wood grips, 8 shot mag., a simply designed pistol used by Japanese armed forces from 1925-45.

Add 25% for 3.X date Tokyo.
Add 50% for 2.X date Nagoya.
Add 400% for early Taisho era pistols dated 15.11 or 15.12 from Nagoya arsenal.
Add 10% for matching mag. on models listed.

Type 14 Nambus have a 3 or 4 digit number just forward of the lanyard ring on the right side of frame (on back of grip). Earliest Taisho era pistols are dated 15.11 or 15.12 from the Nagoya arsenal - can be identified by small trigger guard and other early features. Fewer than 100 mfg. To determine year and month of manufacture for most type 14 pistols, add "1925" to the first two digits and the last number will indicate the month (i.e. code 13.3 indicates a gun built in March of 1938).

✳ *Type 14 1925-1930 Mfg.*

	100%	98%	95%	90%	80%	70%	60%
	$1,300	$1,150	$900	$750	$500	$400	$300

✳ *Type 14 1930-1939 Mfg.* - small trigger guard.

	$1,100	$850	$700	$550	$400	$350	$300

✳ *Type 14 1939-1945 Mfg.* - large trigger guard.

	$700	$550	$400	$325	$250	$220	$200

Add 10% for strawed trigger and safety.

TYPE 94 - 8mm Nambu cal., recoil operated, 3.8 in. barrel, blue, and bakelite wood grips, 6 shot mag. Mfg. 1935-45.

	$525	$400	$350	$300	$250	$225	$200

Add 400% for 10.X date, 200% for 11.X date, 100% for 12.X date, 30% if pre-WWII, and 20% if late square back.

HAMADA NAMBU Please refer to Japanese Military section.

BABY NAMBU - 7mm Nambu cal., 3 1/4 in. barrel, blue, wood grips, grip safety, one of the most desirable Japanese handguns.

	$4,500	$3,500	$3,000	$2,500	$2,250	$2,000	$1,750

Add 10% for matching mag.
Add 50% for chamber marked "TGE" (Tokyo Gas & Electric).

PAPA NAMBU (MODEL 1904) - 8mm Nambu cal., 4.7 in. barrel, wood grips, grip safety, 8 shot mag., essentially the same action as the Baby, but a larger version. Mfg. 1904-25.

	100%	98%	95%	90%	80%	70%	60%
	$3,000	$2,500	$2,000	$1,750	$1,500	$1,100	$995

Add 10% for matching mag.
Add 50% for chamber marked "TGE" (Tokyo Gas & Electric).

GRANDPA NAMBU - 8mm Nambu cal., similar to Papa Nambu, except has smaller trigger guard and fixed lanyard ring, cherry wood based mag., issued with 2 matching mags. Early Tokyo arsenal or later Thai issue, all Grandpa frames are slotted.

	100%	98%	95%	90%	80%	70%	60%
	$8,500	$7,000	$6,000	$5,000	$4,000	$3,000	$2,000

Add 100% for matching shoulder stock.
Add $5,000 for original stock.
Add 10% for second matching mag.
Original stocks are rare and expensive.

NATIONAL POSTAL METER
Previous WWII subcontractor of M1 carbines located in Rochester, NY.
Please refer to U.S. M1 Carbines/Rifles listings under U.S. Military.

NATIONAL WILD TURKEY FEDERATION
Current national conservation organization located in Edgefield, SC.

Although the National Wild Turkey Federation is not a manufacturer or importer, this organization has been responsible for many special and limited editions that are listed with quanities but with issue prices only as current market values, which may vary greatly from region to region. Also, many are sold at auction, making pricing difficult to determine. "NWTF" suffix after model name indicates National Wild Turkey Federation gun of the year. Some of the models (and current values) may be listed under manufacturer listings in this text.

Model	Manufacturer	Qty.	Year	Issue Price
RIFLES: AUCTION/TRADE EDITIONS				
✳ *Vanguard Deluxe .300 Wby. Mag. Auction*	Weatherby	2,500	2008	N/A
SHOTGUNS: AUCTION/TRADE EDITIONS				
✳ *Black Powder 12 ga. NWTF*	Navy Arms	500	1983	$350
✳ *Model 101*	Winchester	300	1985	$1,895
✳ *BPS 12 ga. NWTF*	Browning	500	1986	$495
✳ *SxS 10 ga. 3 1/2 in.*	American Arms	150	1985/86	$695
✳ *Model 1300 Win-Cam 12 ga.*	Winchester	500	1987/88	$449
✳ *Model 1300 12 ga. Trade Gun*	Winchester	N/A	N/A	$458
✳ *Model A-303 12 ga. NWTF*	Beretta	500	1988/89	$695
✳ *Model 1300 12 ga. Win-Cam NWTF*	Winchester	500	1989	$479
✳ *Model 1300 12 ga. Trade Gun*	Winchester	N/A	N/A	$458
✳ *Model A5 12 ga. NWTF*	Browning	500	1990	$925
✳ *Model 835 12 ga. Auction*	Mossberg	500	1991	$567
✳ *Model 835 12 ga. Trade Gun*	Mossberg	N/A	N/A	$436
✳ *Model 11-87 12 ga. Auction*	Remington	N/A	1992	N/A
✳ *Model 11-87 12 ga. Trade Gun*	Remington	N/A	N/A	$698
✳ *Model 1300 12 ga. Auction*	Winchester	500	1993	$671
✳ *SxS 20 ga. Auction*	New England Firearms	N/A	N/A	$167

Model	Manufacturer	Qty.	Year	Issue Price
✳ SxS 12 ga. Trade Gun	New England Firearms	N/A	N/A	$200
✳ SxS 10 ga. Trade Gun	New England Firearms	N/A	N/A	$240
✳ Model Turkey 12 ga. Auction	American Arms	300	1993	N/A
✳ Model 9200 12 ga. Auction	Mossberg	600	1994	$690
✳ Model 9200 12 ga. Trade	Mossberg	N/A	1994	N/A
✳ Model 610 12 ga. Auction	Luigi Franchi	600	1995	N/A
✳ O/U 12 ga. Auction	Fausti	720	1996	N/A
✳ Topper Jr. 20 ga. Auction	New England Firearms	N/A	1996	N/A
✳ O/U 12 ga. Auction	Fausti	900	1997	N/A
✳ Jakes Topper Jr. 20 ga. Auction	New England Firearms	N/A	1997	N/A
✳ Model 870 12 ga. Auction	Remington	1200	1998	N/A
✳ Model AL390 12ga.	Beretta	1400	1999	N/A
✳ Model 37 12ga.	Ithaca	1700	2000	N/A
✳ BPS 12 ga.	Browning	1900	2001	N/A
✳ Super X2	Winchester	2100	2002	N/A
✳ Model 9410 .410 bore	Winchester	2200	2003	N/A
✳ Model 1100 20 ga.	Remington	2400	2004	N/A
✳ BPS 12 ga.	Browning	2400	2005	N/A
✳ Model 700 .270 WSM	Remington	N/A	2006	N/A
✳ BPS 12 ga.	Browning	1,000	2007	N/A

NAVY ARMS COMPANY

Current importer established during 1958, and located in Union City, NJ, beginning 2001. Previously located in Ridgefield, NJ. Navy Arms imports are fabricated by various manufacturers including the Italian companies Davide Pedersoli & Co., Pietta & Co., and A. Uberti & C. Distributor and dealer sales.

Navy Arms imports a number of original British military rifles (antique and modern). Models include British P-1842 percussion musket, British Model 1864, Nepalese Gahendra Martini rifle, British P-1871 short lever Martini, and the British M1853 Enfield musket. Prices range from $525-$835.

Navy Arms has also sold a wide variety of original military firearms in used condition. Handguns included the Mauser Broomhandle, Japanese Nambu, Colt 1911 Government Model, Tokarev, Browning Hi-Power, S&W Model 1917, and others. Rifles included Mauser contract models, Japanese Type 38s, Enfields, FNs, Nagants, M1 Carbines, M1 Garands, Chinese SKSs, Egyptian Rashids, French MAS Model 1936s, among others. Most of these firearms are priced in the $75-$500 price range depending on desirability of model and condition.

For more information and up-to-date pricing regarding recent Navy Arms black powder models, please refer to *Blackpowder Reproductions and Replicas* by Dennis Adler and the *Blue Book of Modern Black Powder Arms* by John Allen (also online). These books feature hundreds of color photographs and support text of the most recent black powder models available, as well as complete pricing and a reference guide.

PISTOLS

TU-711 MAUSER - 9mm Para. cal., patterned after Mauser 711 (semi-auto version of the Model 712 Schnellfeuer), 5 1/4 in. barrel, 712 upper receiver that has been converted to 9mm Para. and mounted on new lower receiver, supplied with 10 and 20 shot detachable mag., mfg. in China, 2 lbs. 11 oz. Imported 1992 only.

$575 $475 $425 $375 $325 $295 $275

Last MSR was $650.

GRADING - PPGS™	100%	98%	95%	90%	80%	70%	60%

TT-OLYMPIA - .22 LR cal., patterned after the Walther Olympia that won 1936 Olympics, 4 5/8 in. barrel, checkered walnut grips, mfg. in China, 27 oz. Imported 1992-98.

		$255	$225	$195	$175	$160	$150	$140

Last MSR was $290.

TU-90 PISTOL - .30 Tokarev or 9mm Para. cal., patterned after the rare Tokagypt variation (improved TT-33 Tokarev), 4 1/2 in. barrel, single action, wrap-around synthetic grips, unique forward motion safety, mfg. in China, 30 oz. Imported 1992-98.

		$115	$100	$90	$80	$70	$60	$50

Last MSR was $130.

    Add $15 for 9mm Para. cal.
    Add $40 for pistol combo (includes both cals.).

LUGER MODEL - .22 LR cal. only, 10 shot mag., Luger toggle type action, available in blue or matte finish, 4, 6, or 8 in. barrel, checkered walnut stocks. Mfg. in U.S. 1986-87 only.

		$140	$120	$95	$85	$75	$70	$65

Last MSR was $165.

GRAND PRIX SILHOUETTE - .30-30 Win., 7mm Spl., .44 Mag., or .45-70 Govt. cal., 13 3/4 in. barrel, non-glare matte blue finish, walnut forearm and grips, adj. heat dispersing aluminum rib, adj. target sights, 4 lbs. Mfg. 1985 only.

		$320	$280	$240	$220	$195	$175	$150

Last MSR was $375.

REVOLVERS: REPRODUCTIONS

1872 OPEN TOP - .38 Spl. cal., 5 1/2 or 7 1/2 in. round barrel, case colored frame with blue cylinder and barrel, silver plated brass trigger guard and backstrap, 2 1/2-2 3/4 lbs. Limited importation 2000-2001 only.

		$335	$275	$220	$185	$165	$150	$135

Last MSR was $400.

1873 SAA - GUNFIGHTER SERIES & VARIATIONS - .32-20 WCF (mfg. 2002, reintroduced 2007), .357 Mag. (new 1998), .44-40 WCF or .45 LC cal., reproduction of the Colt SAA, case hardened frame with blue or nickel (disc. 1998) finish, 3 (Sheriff's Model - mfg. 1992-98), 4 3/4, 5 1/2, or 7 1/2 in. barrel, the Gunfighter Series was introduced during 2003, approx. 36 oz.

MSR $511		$415	$335	$295	$230	$180	$160	$145

    Add $65 for nickel finish (disc.).
    Add $30 for Pinched Frame Model (7 1/2 in. barrel, .45 LC, disc. 2002).
    Subtract $20 for brass trigger guard and backstrap (disc.).

The Gunfighter Series, introduced in 2003, is different than previous production in that it features a U.S. mfg. Wolff spring kit, German silver plated backstrap and trigger guard, and black checkered gunfighter grips.

✱ *1873 SAA Gunfighter Series Stainless Steel Model* - .357 Mag. or .45 LC cal., 4 3/4, 5 1/2, or 7 1/2 in. barrel, stainless steel construction. Importation began 2003.

MSR $608		$485	$375	$315	$250	$215	$185	$155

✱ *1873 SAA Gunfighter Series Deluxe Model* - .32-20 WCF cal., deluxe model with color case hardened and charcoal blue finishes, high polish walnut grips, includes Wolff springs. Limited importation 2003.

		$365	$295	$230	$200	$180	$165	$140

Last MSR was $435.

This model is sold exclusively through AcuSport.

GRADING - PPGS™	100%	98%	95%	90%	80%	70%	60%

✳ *1873 SAA Gunfighter Series Economy Model* - .44-40 WCF or .45 LC cal., 3, 4 3/4, 5 1/2, or 7 1/2 in. barrel, brass trigger guard and backstrap, 2-piece walnut grips. Imported 1993-96.

	$295	$230	$185	$160	$145	$130	$120

Last MSR was $345.

✳ *1873 SAA Gunfighter Series Deputy Model* - .44-40 WCF or .45 LC cal., patterned after the Colt 1877 Thunderer double action, birdshead grips, 3, 3 1/2, 4, or 4 3/4 in. barrel, case colored frame. Imported 1997-98 only.

	$350	$275	$210	$180	$160	$145	$130

Last MSR was $405.

✳ *1873 SAA Gunfighter Series Flattop Target Model* - .45 LC cal. only, features flat-top frame, 7 1/2 in. barrel only, adj. spring loaded front sight and dovetailed rear sight, 30 oz. Imported 1999-2006.

	$425	$350	$285	$240	$205	$175	$150

Last MSR was $514.

✳ *1873 SAA Gunfighter Series Shootist Model* - .357 Mag., .44-40 WCF, or .45 LC cal., interchangeable parts with original Colt 1st and 2nd Generation SAAs, designed for Cowboy Action Shooting, 4 3/4, 5 1/2, or 7 1/2 in. barrel, case colored frame and hammer, blue cylinder barrel, trigger guard and backstrap. Limited importation 2000 only.

	$350	$275	$210	$180	$160	$145	$130

Last MSR was $385.

✳ *1873 SAA Gunfighter Series Bisley Model* - .44-40 WCF or .45 LC cal., patterned after the Colt Bisley, 4 3/4, 5 1/2, or 7 1/2 in. barrel, case colored frame, spur hammer, walnut grips. Importation began 1997.

MSR $511	$415	$335	$295	$230	$180	$160	$145

❖ 1873 SAA Gunfighter Series Bisley Model Flattop Target - .44-40 WCF or .45 LC (disc. 2006) cal., features flattop frame, adj. front sight, and dovetailed rear sight, 40 oz. Importation began 1999.

MSR $608	$485	$375	$315	$250	$215	$185	$155

✳ *1873 SAA Gunfighter Series Cavalry Model* - .45 LC cal. only, exact replica of the original U.S. Government issue SAA, 7 1/2 in. barrel, arsenal stampings, inspector's cartouche on walnut stocks.

MSR $594	$515	$385	$335	$280	$230	$200	$175

✳ *1873 SAA Gunfighter Series Artillery Model* - similar specifications to the Cavalry Model, except has 5 1/2 in barrel.

MSR $594	$515	$385	$335	$280	$230	$200	$175

✳ *1873 SAA Gunfighter Series Scout Small Frame Model* - .38 Spl. cal., scaled down variation of the SAA, 4 3/4 or 5 1/2 in. barrel only. Importation began 2003.

MSR $511	$415	$335	$295	$230	$180	$160	$145

1875 REMINGTON REVOLVER - .44-40 WCF or .45 LC cal., reproduction of the 1875 Remington revolver, 7 1/2 in. barrel, case colored frame, 41 oz. Importation disc. 1991, resumed 1994-2000.

	$360	$295	$260	$230	$200	$175	$150

Last MSR was $435.

1890 REMINGTON REVOLVER - .44-40 WCF or .45 LC cal., reproduction of the 1890 Remington revolver, 5 1/2 in. barrel, brass trigger guard and lanyard loop, 39 oz. Importation disc. 1991, resumed 1994-2000.

	$370	$295	$260	$230	$200	$175	$150

Last MSR was $445.

GRADING - PPGS™	100%	98%	95%	90%	80%	70%	60%

1875 SCHOFIELD SERIES - various cals., patterned after the original S&W Schofield Model, blued finish, smooth wood grips, case colored hammer, trigger guard and opening lever. Imported 1994-2003. - .44-40 WCF or .45 LC cal., similar to Wells Fargo Model, except has 3 1/2 in. barrel, 34 oz. New 1999. - .45 LC cal., charcoal blue barrel and cylinder, case colored receiver, backstrap, trigger guard, and trigger, 7 1/2 in. barrel, white ivory tex grips. Importation began 2003. - .44-40 WCF or .45 LC cal., similar to Deluxe Schofield, except does not have gold inlays, extensive B or C coverage scroll engraving on both frame, cylinder, and barrel. Special order only beginning 1999. - .44-40 WCF or .45 LC cal., available in Cavalry, Wells Fargo, or Hideout configurations, with light scroll engraving on frame and cylinder with extensive frame, barrel, and cylinder gold line inlays and scroll motifs. Special order only beginning 1999.

	$615	$535	$455	$375	$325	$250	$195

Last MSR was $716.

✳ *1875 Schofield Series Cavalry Model* - .38 Spl. (new 2003), .44-40 WCF, or .45 LC cal., patterned after the original Schofield Cavalry Model, 7 1/2 in. barrel, 37 oz. New 1994.

MSR $849	$715	$600	$485	$395	$335	$250	$195

✳ *1875 Schofield Series Wells Fargo Model* - .38 Spl. (new 2003), .44-40 WCF, or .45 LC cal., 5 1/2 in. barrel, 35 oz. New 1994.

MSR $849	$715	$600	$485	$395	$335	$250	$195

✳ *1875 Schofield Series Hideout Model* - 3 1/2 in. barrel.

MSR $849	$715	$600	$485	$395	$335	$250	$195

✳ *1875 Schofield Series Founders Model* - .38 Spl. or .45 LC cal., 7 in. barrel, features charcoal blue barrel and cylinder, case colored frame, backstrap, trigger and trigger guard, "VF" serial number prefix.

MSR $946	$800	$665	$515	$400	$350	$250	$195

✳ *1875 Schofield Series Engraved Model*

	$1,425	$1,225	$1,000	$875	$750	$625	$525

Add $215 for C engraving.

✳ *1875 Schofield Series Deluxe Model*

	$1,675	$1,450	$1,250	$995	$875	$750	$625

NEW MODEL RUSSIAN - .44 Russian cal., patterned after the S&W Model 3 Russian Third Model Single Action, 6 1/2 in. barrel, blue metal with case colored trigger, trigger guard, and hammer, smooth walnut grips, 40 oz. Importation began 1999.

MSR $908	$765	$635	$500	$400	$350	$250	$195

REVOLVERS: REPRODUCTIONS, COLT CARTRIDGE CONVERSIONS

1851 NAVY RICHARDS-TYPE CONVERSION - .38 Spl. or .38 LC cal., patterned after the Colt 1851 Navy Conversion, 5 1/2 or 7 1/2 in. barrel, case colored frame and hammer, blue cylinder and barrel, brass back strap and trigger guard, 40 or 44 oz. Imported 1999-2001.

	$320	$255	$200	$175	$160	$145	$130

Last MSR was $375.

1860 ARMY RICHARDS-TYPE CONVERSION - .38 Spl. or .38 LC cal., patterned after the Colt 1860 Army Conversion, other specifications similar to 1851 Navy Conversion. Imported 1999-2001.

	$320	$255	$200	$175	$160	$145	$130

Last MSR was $375.

GRADING - PPGS™	100%	98%	95%	90%	80%	70%	60%

1861 NAVY RICHARDS-TYPE CONVERSION - .38 Spl. or .38 LC cal., patterned after the Colt 1861 Navy Conversion, other specifications similar to 1851 Navy Conversion. Imported 1999-2001.

	$320	$255	$200	$175	$160	$145	$130

Last MSR was $375.

REVOLVERS: PREMIUM BLUE REPRODUCTIONS, CARTRIDGE CONVERSIONS

During 2003, Navy Arms planned to introduce its line of Premium Blue custom guns. However, these guns were never manufactured, except for a few prototypes. Models included were: 1860 Army Richards Type I ($1,995 MSR), Richards-Mason Colt Pocket Navy Model ($2,995 MSR), Richards-Mason Colt Police Model ($2,695 MSR), 1842 Paterson Conversion Model ($2,100 MSR), Remington Navy .38 Colt Cartridge Conversion, Remington Army 5 Shot Cartridge Conversion ($1,295 MSR), and the Remington 6 Shot Cartridge Conversion ($1,495 MSR).

RIFLES: REPRODUCTIONS

REVOLVING CARBINE - .357 Mag., .44-40 WCF, or .45 LC cal., 6 shot cylinder, 20 in. barrel, case hardened frame, straight stock. Mfg. 1968-1984.

	$575	$475	$425	$375	$325	$275	$225

REMINGTON ROLLING BLOCK BUFFALO RIFLE - .444 Marlin (disc.), .45-70 Govt., or .50-70 (disc.) cal., replica of Remington Rolling Block, 26 or 30 in. heavy octagon or 1/2 round/ 1/2 octagon barrel (disc. 2000), open sight, straight grip stock. Mfg. 1971-2003.

	$655	$465	$350	$260	$195	$160	$140

Last MSR was $850.

Brass fittings were disc. during 1998, and replaced with steel fittings.

* *Remington Rolling Block Buffalo Carbine* - similar to Rifle, with 18 in. barrel. Disc. 1985.

	$385	$325	$280	$230	$180	$160	$140

Last MSR was $375.

* *Remington Rolling Block Buffalo Baby Rifle* - .22 LR, .22 Hornet, .357 Mag., or .44-40 WCF cal., replica of small frame Remington, 20 in. octagon or 22 in. round barrel, open sight, straight stock. Mfg. 1968-84.

	$215	$175	$140	$110	$90	$65	$55

REMINGTON ROLLING BLOCK BODINE RIFLE - single or double set triggers, 30 in. heavy matte finished octagon barrel, "Soule" target rear tang sight, and split level globe front sight, No. 2 configuration became available during 2003, 12 lbs.

MSR $1,856	$1,625	$1,375	$1,100	$950	$800	$650	$500

ROLLING BLOCK PLAINS RIFLE - .45-70 Govt. cal., features 30 in. tapered octagon barrel with straight grip stock, bright polished receiver with steel furniture, 9 lbs. Imported 1997-98 only.

	$650	$500	$400	$285	$195	$175	$150

Last MSR was $800.

* *Rolling Block Plains Rifle Deluxe* - similar to Plains Rifle, except has hand engraved coin finished receiver and trigger guard, rust blue barrel with German silver forearm tip. Imported 1997-98.

	$1,475	$1,250	$1,050	$850	$725	$600	$525

Last MSR was $1,625.

ROLLING BLOCK NO. 2 CREEDMOOR TARGET - similar to Buffalo Rifle, in .45-70 Govt. or .50-70 (disc.) cal., with Creedmoor tang sight, color case hardened receiver, checkered walnut.

MSR $1,754	$1,450	$1,175	$975	$800	$650	$500	$400

GRADING - PPGS™	100%	98%	95%	90%	80%	70%	60%

* Rolling Block No. 2 Creedmoor Target Deluxe - featured hand engraved coin finished receiver and trigger guard, rust blue barrel and German silver forearm tip. Imported 1997-98.

	$1,625	$1,400	$1,200	$1,000	$850	$725	$600

Last MSR was $1,875.

SHARPS NO. 2 SILHOUETTE - .45-70 Govt. cal., 30 in. octagon barrel, 10 3/4 lbs. Importation began 2003.

MSR $1,739	$1,450	$1,150	$995	$850	$750	$650	$575

SHARPS NO. 2 HUNTER - limited importation 2003 only.

	$750	$650	$575	$525	$475	$425	$375

Last MSR was $815.

1874 SHARPS PLAINS RIFLE - .45-70 Govt. cal., 32 in. octagon barrel, case hardened receiver, checkered stock and forearm, double set triggers, 9 1/2 lbs. Mfg. 1996-2002.

	$1,020	$900	$800	$725	$625	$575	$525

Last MSR was $1,175.

Add $75 for vernier rear tang or $55 for globe sight.

* 1874 Sharps Plains Rifle Engraved - .45-70 Govt. cal., features hand engraved coin finished receiver. Imported 1997-98.

	$2,325	$2,000	$1,800	$1,600	$1,400	$1,200	$995

Last MSR was $2,500.

Add $700 for gold inlays (Deluxe Model).

1874 SHARPS BUFFALO RIFLE - .45-70 Govt. or .45-90 (disc. 2000) cal., 28 in. octagon heavy barrel, case colored receiver, checkered stock, 10 lbs. 10 oz. Mfg. 1996-2002.

	$1,035	$925	$825	$725	$625	$575	$525

Last MSR was $1,200.

Add $75 for vernier rear tang or $55 for globe sight.

* 1874 Sharps Buffalo Rifle Engraved - .45-70 Govt. or .45-90 cal., features hand engraved coin finished receiver. Imported 1997-98.

	$2,325	$2,000	$1,800	$1,600	$1,400	$1,200	$995

Last MSR was $2,515.

Add $700 for gold inlays (Deluxe Model).

SHARPS SPORTING RIFLE - .45-70 Govt. cal., similar to Plains Rifle, except has pistol grip stock, No. 2 configuration became available during 2003. Importation began 1997.

MSR $1,739	$1,450	$1,150	$995	$850	$750	$650	$575

1874 SHARPS QUIGLEY - .45-70 Govt. cal., 34 in. octagon barrel, exact reproduction of rifle used in "Quigley Down Under" movie, with patchbox. Importation began 2002.

MSR $1,826	$1,525	$1,250	$1,025	$875	$725	$625	$550

1874 SHARPS NO. 2 CREEDMOOR - .45-70 Govt. cal., 30 in. thin tapered round barel, polished nickel frame and action, "Soule" rear tang sight with front globe, 9 lbs. Importation began 2002.

MSR $1,739	$1,450	$1,150	$995	$850	$750	$650	$575

1874 SHARPS NO. 3 LONG RANGE - .45-70 Govt. cal., 34 in. medium weight octagon barrel with globe front target sight, shotgun buttplate, double set triggers, German silver forearm cap, 10 lbs. 14 oz. Importation began 2000.

MSR $2,194	$1,825	$1,500	$1,250	$1,075	$925	$725	$600

GRADING - PPGS™	100%	98%	95%	90%	80%	70%	60%

1874 SHARPS SNIPER/INFANTRY RIFLE - .45-70 Govt. cal., patterned after the 3-band military sniper rifle, 30 in. barrel, color case hardened frame, hammer, and furniture, ST or DST (Sniper rifle, disc. 1995). Mfg. 1994-2000.

	$895	$780	$650	$475	$395	$350	$325

Last MSR was $1,060.

Add $55 for DST (Sniper).

1874 SHARPS SNIPER/INFANTRY CAVALRY CARBINE - .45-70 Govt. cal., patterned after Sharps Cavalry carbine, 22 in. barrel, color case hardened frame, hammer, patchbox, and furniture. New 1994.

MSR $1,246	$975	$800	$665	$475	$395	$350	$325

1873 SPRINGFIELD INFANTRY RIFLE - .45-70 Govt. cal., 32 1/2 in. barrel, 8 lbs, 4 oz. Imported 1997-2000.

	$840	$750	$650	$475	$395	$350	$325

Last MSR was $995.

1873 SPRINGFIELD INFANTRY CAVALRY CARBINE - similar to the 1873 Springfield Rifle, except has 22 in. barrel, 1 barrel band, 7 lbs. Importation began 1997.

MSR $1,519	$1,325	$1,050	$900	$775	$650	$550	$450

Add $324 for Springfield Officer's Model.

KODIAK MARK IV DOUBLE RIFLE - .45-70 Govt. cal., patterned after the Colt Double rifle, semi-regulated barrels, hammers, folding leaf rear sight, 24 in. barrels, color cased hardened receiver, 10 lbs. 3 oz. Mfg. 1996-2000.

	$2,450	$2,250	$2,000	$1,800	$1,600	$1,400	$1,200

Last MSR was $2,815.

* *Kodiak Mark IV Double Rifle Deluxe* - similar to Kodiak Mark IV Double rifle, except has brown barrels and hand engraved satin finished receiver. Mfg. 1996-2000.

	$3,300	$2,900	$2,600	$2,375	$2,000	$1,750	$1,500

Last MSR was $3,690.

HENRY RIFLE - .44-40 WCF, .44 Rimfire (disc. 1989), or .45 LC (new 1998) cal., reproduction of Winchester's famous Henry Rifle, brass or iron frame. New 1985.

* *Henry Rifle Military* - 24 in. barrel, brass frame, blue barrel, walnut stock, original style sling swivels, 9 1/4 lbs. New 1985.

MSR $1,199	$925	$725	$575	$450	$325	$250	$225

* *Henry Rifle Union Pacific Railroad Commemorative* - .44-40 WCF cal., only 100 mfg.

	$795	$575	$475	N/A	N/A	N/A	N/A

Last MSR was $695.

* *Henry Rifle Engraved* - limited mfg., extensive engraving on brass frame. Disc. 1988.

	$1,510	$1,275	$1,100	$900	$750	$650	$550

Last MSR was $1,850.

Add $100 for steel frame.

* *Henry Carbine* - 24 in. barrel, limited edition of 1,000 units including 50 engraved specimens, no swivels, 8 1/4 lbs. Importation disc. 2002.

	$685	$540	$450	$350	$275	$225	$195

Last MSR was $875.

* *Henry Engraved Carbine* - limited production, only 50 mfg. Disc. 1988.

	$1,450	$1,225	$1,075	$900	$750	$650	$550

Last MSR was $1,750.

* *Henry Rifle Trapper Model* - 16 1/2 in. barrel, 7 1/4 lbs., 34 1/4 in. overall length. Disc. 2000.

	$685	$540	$450	$350	$275	$225	$195

Last MSR was $875.

GRADING - PPGS™	100%	98%	95%	90%	80%	70%	60%

* *Henry Rifle Iron Frame Model* - with steel frame and buttplate, 24 in. blue barrel, select walnut, 9 1/4 lbs.

MSR $1,258	**$1,000**	**$825**	**$650**	**$550**	**$450**	**$375**	**$325**

Add $17 for color case hardened frame.

This model is available with either blue (.44-40 WCF cal. only) or color case hardened receiver.

MODEL 1866 YELLOWBOY CARBINE/RIFLE - .22 LR (disc.), .357 Mag. (disc.), .38 Spl. (new 1998), .44-40 WCF, or .45 LC (new 1998) cal., choice of rifle (24 1/4 in. octagon barrel), short rifle (20 in. octagon barrel), or carbine (19 in. round barrel), brass (disc.) or case hardened receiver, replica of the Winchester Model 1866. Mfg. 1972-84, reintroduced.

MSR $908	**$745**	**$600**	**$450**	**$350**	**$250**	**$225**	**$200**

Add $34 for rifle.

* *Model 1866 Yellowboy 100th Anniversary Indian Victory in Little Big Horn*

	$725	**$625**	**$525**	**$440**	**$385**	**$325**	**$280**

YELLOWBOY TRAPPER - .44-40 WCF cal., 16 1/2 in. barrel. Disc.

	$675	**$575**	**$475**	**$425**	**$375**	**$325**	**$275**

MODEL 1873 CARBINE/RIFLE - .357 Mag. (new 1998), .44-40 WCF or .45 LC cal., choice of rifle (24 in. octagon barrel) or carbine (19 in. round barrel), replica of the Winchester Model 1873.

MSR $1,054	**$885**	**$715**	**$575**	**$450**	**$350**	**$295**	**$250**

Add $25 for rifle variation.

* *Model 1873 Carbine Trapper* - .44-40 WCF cal., similar to Carbine, with 16 1/2 in. barrel. Disc.

	$700	**$600**	**$500**	**$425**	**$375**	**$325**	**$275**

* *Model 1873 Border Model Rifle* - .357 Mag., .44-40 WCF, or .45 LC cal., features 20 in. short octagon rifle barrel, case hardened receiver with blue barrel, 7 lbs. 6 oz. Importation began 1999.

MSR $1,079	**$915**	**$725**	**$685**	**$450**	**$350**	**$295**	**$250**

* *Model 1873 Deluxe Border Model Rifle* - similar to Model 1873 Deluxe Sporting Rifle, except has 20 in. barrel. Importation began 2001.

MSR $1,218	**$1,000**	**$825**	**$625**	**$500**	**$400**	**$300**	**$225**

* *Model 1873 Deluxe Sporting Rifle* - deluxe variation of the Model 1873 featuring case hardened receiver, lever, and hammer, checkered pistol grip stock, and choice of 24 1/4 or 30 (not available in .357 Mag. cal., disc. 2002) in. barrel, 8 lbs. 4 oz. or 8 lbs., 14 oz. New 1992.

MSR $1,218	**$1,000**	**$825**	**$625**	**$500**	**$400**	**$300**	**$225**

Add $30 for 30 in. barrel (disc. 2002).

* *Model 1873 Deluxe Sporting Rifle Long Range* - .44-40 WCF cal., 30 in. barrel with rear tang sight. Imported 2003 only.

	$995	**$800**	**$625**	**$475**	**$350**	**$300**	**$250**

Last MSR was $1,140.

* *Model 1873 1 of 1,000* - only 1,000 mfg., deluxe wood, special engraving.

	$1,000	**$775**	**$550**	**$460**	**$395**	**$335**	**$285**

MODEL 1892 CARBINE/RIFLE - .357 Mag., .44-40 WCF, or .45 LC cal., features 20 (carbine, w/o forearm cap, disc. 2001) or 24 (rifle) in. octagon barrel, choice of brass (disc.), blue, or case hardened receiver and crescent buttplate, uncheckered straight grip walnut stock and forearm, 5 lbs. 14 oz. or 7 lbs. Imported 1999-2003.

	$465	**$385**	**$335**	**$280**	**$240**	**$210**	**$185**

Last MSR was $561.

Subtract approx. $65 for carbine configuration (disc. 2001).

GRADING - PPGS™	100%	98%	95%	90%	80%	70%	60%

✳ *Model 1892 Carbine/Rifle Stainless* - similar to Standard Model 1892, except is stainless steel, not available in .44-40 WCF cal. Imported 2000-2003.

	$435	$360	$300	$240	$210	$180	$155

Last MSR was $530.

Add $73 for rifle configuration.

✳ *Model 1892 Short Rifle* - also available in .32-20 WCF cal. (new 2002), similar to Model 1892 Standard Rifle, except has 20 in. short barrel, not available with brass frame, approx. 6 1/4 lbs. Imported 1999-2003.

	$465	$385	$335	$280	$240	$210	$185

Last MSR was $561.

✳ *Model 1892 Stainless Short Rifle* - similar to Model 1892 Short Rifle, except is stainless steel. Imported 2000 only.

	$485	$360	$300	$240	$210	$180	$155

Last MSR was $603.

MODEL 1885 HIGH WALL RIFLE - .45-70 Govt. cal., available with 30 in. medium heavy octagon barrel with crescent buttplate or 28 in. round barrel with shotgun style buttplate, standard or open target sights, case hardened frame and lever, uncheckered European walnut stock and forearm, 9 1/4 or 10 lbs. Importation began 1999.

MSR $1,168	$875	$750	$625	$500	$400	$300	$275

Add $117 for rear tang sight.

RIFLES: MODERN PRODUCTION

In addition to the models listed, Navy Arms in late 1990 purchased the manufacturing rights of the English firm Parker-Hale. In 1991, Navy Arms built a manufacturing facility, Gibbs Rifle Co., located in Martinsburg, WV and produced these rifles domestically 1991-1994 (see Gibbs Rifle Co. listing for more info on models the company currently imports).

TU-KKW TRAINING RIFLE - .22 LR cal., replica of the German "KKW" Gewehr training rifle, full sized Mauser 98K action with military sights, 26 in. barrel, detachable 5 shot mag., mfg. in China, 8 lbs. Imported 1992-94.

	$240	$210	$180	$150	$135	$120	$105

Last MSR was $310.

Add $125 for 2 3/4 power Type 89 quick mount scope (Sniper Trainer).

TU-33/40 CARBINE - .22 LR or 7.62x39mm cal., based on WWII Mauser G33/40 mountain carbine, 20 3/4 in. barrel, includes sling, adj. rear sight, mfg. in China, 7 lbs. 7 oz. Imported 1992-94.

	$210	$180	$150	$135	$120	$105	$90

Last MSR was $210.

JW-15 RIFLE - .22 LR cal., sporter bolt action based on Brno Model 5 action, 24 in. barrel, detachable 5 shot mag., receiver top is dove-tailed, mfg. in China, 5 lbs. 12 oz. Imported 1992-94.

	$85	$70	$60	$50	$40	$35	$30

Last MSR was $100.

MARTINI TARGET RIFLE - .444 Marlin or .45-70 Govt. cal., single shot, 26 or 30 in. octagon barrel, tang sight, pistol grip stock. Mfg. 1972-84.

	$480	$420	$350	$250	$195	$175	$150

RPKS-74 - .223 Rem. or 7.62x39mm (new 1989) cal., semi-auto version of the Chinese RPK Squad Automatic Weapon, Kalashnikov action, 19 in. barrel, integral folding bipod, 9 1/2 lbs. Imported 1988-89 only.

	$525	$445	$350	$250	$195	$175	$150

Last MSR was $649.

GRADING - PPGS™	100%	98%	95%	90%	80%	70%	60%

MODEL 1 CARBINE/RIFLE - .45-70 Govt. cal., action is sporterized No. 1 MKIII Enfield, choice of 18 (carbine) or 22 (rifle) in. barrel with iron sights, black Zytel Monte Carlo (rifle) or straight grip walnut (carbine) stock, 7 (carbine) or 8 1/2 (rifle) lbs. Limited importation 1999 only.

	$325	$255	$200	$175	$160	$145	$130

Last MSR was $375.

MODEL 4 CARBINE/RIFLE - .45-70 Govt. cal., action is sporterized No. 4 MKI Enfield, choice of 18 (carbine) or 22 (rifle) in. barrel, blue metal, choice of checkered walnut Monte Carlo (rifle) or uncheckered straight grip (carbine, disc. 1999) stock, 7 or 8 lbs. Mfg. 1999-2001.

	$325	$255	$200	$175	$160	$145	$130

Last MSR was $375.

✱ *Model No. 4 Carbine/Rifle Enfield Sporter Deluxe* - .303 British cal., synthetic Zytel Monte Carlo stock, 25 in. barrel with original military sights, approx. 8 1/2 lbs. Mfg. 1999-2001.

	$115	$95	$85	$75	$65	$55	$50

Last MSR was $125.

2A HUNTER CARBINE/RIFLE - .308 Win. cal., action is sporterized 2A Enfield, 18 (carbine) or 22 (rifle) in. barrel with Parker-Hale style muzzle brake, includes scope mount, 12 shot mag., black enamel synthetic Zytel stock, 6 3/4 or 10 1/4 lbs. Mfg. 1999-2001.

	$240	$210	$190	$175	$160	$145	$130

Last MSR was $275.

Add $50 for rifle variation.

✱ *2A Hunter Carbine/Rifle Enfield Sporter Deluxe* - .308 Win. cal., 25 in. barrel, black Zytel Monte Carlo stock, original 2A Enfield military sights, approx. 8 1/2 lbs. Mfg. 1999-2001.

	$130	$110	$95	$85	$75	$65	$55

Last MSR was $150.

SHOTGUNS: O/U, RECENT IMPORTATION

Importation of the models listed was disc. in 1990.

MODEL 83 - 12 or 20 ga., manufactured in Italy by R. Luciano, 3 in. chambers, extractors, double triggers, engraved chrome receiver, vent. barrels (bored M/F or IC/M) and rib. Introduced 1985.

	$280	$240	$215	$195	$170	$160	$150

Last MSR was $320.

MODEL 93 - 12 or 20 ga., manufactured in Italy by R. Luciano, 3 in. chambers, ejectors, double triggers, engraved chrome receiver, vent. barrels (bored M/F or IC/M) and rib. Introduced 1985.

	$325	$285	$250	$220	$200	$185	$160

Last MSR was $380.

MODEL 95 - similar to Model 93, except with single trigger and multi-chokes (includes 5 tubes), extractors.

	$375	$330	$295	$265	$235	$210	$190

Last MSR was $420.

MODEL 96 SPORTSMAN - 12 ga. only, 3 in. chambers, vent. barrels and rib, engraved chrome receiver, gold-plated receiver, multi-choked with 5 choke tubes, ejectors. Introduced 1985.

	$470	$425	$375	$330	$295	$260	$230

Last MSR was $530.

GRADING - PPGS™	100%	98%	95%	90%	80%	70%	60%

MODEL 100 - 12, 20, 28 ga., or .410 bore, 3 in. chambers, 26 in. VR barrels, photo engraved hard chrome receiver, single trigger, extractors, checkered walnut stock and forearm, approx. 6 1/4 lbs. Introduced 1985.

	$225	$205	$190	$170	$160	$150	$140

Last MSR was $250.

SHOTGUNS: SxS, RECENT IMPORTATION

MODEL 100 - 12 or 20 ga., 3 in. chambers, 27 1/2 in. barrels, checkered European walnut, double triggers, extractors, 6 1/2 or 7 lbs. Imported 1985-87 only.

	$380	$330	$290	$260	$230	$200	$170

Last MSR was $475.

MODEL 150 - similar to Model 100, except with ejectors. Imported 1985-87 only.

	$455	$395	$350	$310	$280	$250	$220

Last MSR was $574.

SHOTGUNS: SINGLE SHOT

MODEL 105 SINGLE BARREL - 12, 20 ga., or .410 bore, 26 or 28 in. full choke barrel only, folding action, engraved chrome receiver, checkered hardwood stock and forearm. New 1985.

	$80	$70	$65	$60	$55	$50	$45

Last MSR was $90.

This model was designated the Model 600 before 1988.

✱ *Model 105 Single Barrel Deluxe* - similar to Model 105, except has European walnut stock and VR.

	$95	$85	$75	$65	$60	$55	$50

Last MSR was $105.

This model was designated the Model 600 Deluxe before 1988.

P.V. NELSON, (GUNMAKERS)

Current manufacturer located in Bucks, England.

P.V. Nelson manufactures best quality shotguns and double rifles per individual customer order. Double rifles feature back action locks, and bolsters for extra strength. Side-by-side and over/under shotguns are available in most gauges, with a choice of rounded or regular action. Please contact the company directly (see Trademark Index) to find out more information about this quality English manufacturer.

NESIKA

Current trademark of rifles and actions manufactured by Nesika Bay Precision, Inc., located in Sturgis, SD. Actions are currently distributed by Dakota Arms. Previously located in Poulsbo, WA until 2003. Dealer and consumer sales.

RIFLES: BOLT ACTION

Nesika also sells its proprietary rifle actions in Classic ($1,275 - $1,475 MSR), Round ($1,000 - $1,350 MSR), Hunter ($1,050 - $1,450 MSR), and Tactical ($1,400 - $1,700 MSR) configurations and in a variety of cals. A Model NXP bolt action single shot pistol model is also available for $1,100 MSR.

CLASSIC HUNTER - various cals., stainless Nesika action and barrel, adj. trigger, composite, laminated, or Turkish walnut stock, hinged floorplate, various options. Mfg. 2004-2005.

	$3,450	$2,950	$2,650	$2,325	$2,000	$1,600	$1,250

Last MSR was $3,710.

Add $60 for Model V or $450 for Model M.

GRADING - PPGS™	100%	98%	95%	90%	80%	70%	60%

NESIKA VARMINT - various varmint cals., single shot or repeater, stainless Nesika action and helical fluted bolt, stainless barrel, composite or wood laminated stock, various options. Mfg. 2004-2005.

	$3,050	$2,650	$2,375	$2,000	$1,750	$1,500	$1,250

Last MSR was $3,440.

Add $60 for Model K.

URBAN TACTICAL - various tactical cals., heavy duty receiver with Picatinny rail and fluted 24 or 28 in. barrel, detachable box mag., black synthetic stock with adj. recoil pad. Mfg. 2004-2005.

	$4,500	$4,000	$3,500	$3,000	$2,500	$2,000	$1,650

Last MSR was $5,040.

Add $160 for heavy .308 Win. cal. or $520 for Lapua or Lazzeroni Warbird or Patriot cals.

NEW ADVANTAGE ARMS, INC.

Previous handgun manufacturer located in Tucson, AZ, circa mid-1990s.

DERRINGERS

4 BARREL DERRINGER - .22 LR or .22 Mag. cal., 4 barrel, double action with rotating hammer, 4 shot mag., high grade alloy, 2 1/2 in. barrel, blue steel alloy or stainless steel, fixed sights, walnut grips, 15 oz. Disc.

	$175	$150	$120	$110	$100	$90	$80

NEW DETONICS MANUFACTURING CORPORATION

Previous manufacturer located in Phoenix, AZ 1989-1992. Formerly named Detonics Firearms Industries (previous manufacturer located in Bellevue, WA 1976-1988). Detonics was sold in early 1988 to the New Detonics Manufacturing Corporation, a wholly owned subsidiary of "1045 Investors Group Limited."

PISTOLS: SEMI-AUTO, STAINLESS

MARK I - .45 ACP cal., matte blue. Disc. 1981.

	$550	$450	$395	$335	$290	$245	$215

MARK II - .45 ACP cal., satin nickel finish. Disc. 1979.

	$495	$375	$300	$240	$210	$180	$155

MARK III - .45 ACP cal., hard chrome finish. Disc. 1979.

	$520	$390	$325	$265	$230	$195	$170

MARK IV - .45 ACP cal., polished blue. Disc. 1981.

	$539	$410	$360	$295	$255	$220	$185

COMBATMASTER MC1 (FORMERLY MARK I) - .45 ACP, 9mm Para., or .38 Super cal., 3 1/2 in. barrel, two-tone (slide is non-glare blue and frame is matte stainless) finish, 6 shot mag., fixed sights, 28 oz. Disc. 1992.

	$775	$575	$450	$385	$335	$280	$235

Last MSR was $920.

Add $15 for OM-3 model (polished slide - disc. 1983).
Add $100 for 9mm Para. or .38 Super cal. (disc. 1990).
This model was originally the MC1, then changed to the Mark I, then changed back to the MC1.

COMBATMASTER MARK V - .45 ACP, 9mm Para., or .38 Super cal., matte stainless finish, fixed sights, 6 shot mag. in .45 ACP, 7 shot in 9mm Para. and .38 Super, 3 1/2 in. barrel, 29 oz. empty. This model was disc. 1985.

	$620	$550	$495	$430	$375	$315	$270

Last MSR was $689.

Add $100 for 9mm Para. or .38 Super cal.

GRADING - PPGS™	100%	98%	95%	90%	80%	70%	60%

COMBATMASTER MARK VI - .45 ACP, 9mm Para., or .38 Super cal., 3 1/2 in. barrel, 6 shot mag., adj. sights and polished stainless slide sides. Disc. 1989. - limited mfg. 1,000. Disc. 1985.

		$685	$575	$450	$385	$335	$280	$235

Last MSR was $795.

> Add $100 for 9mm Para. or .38 Super cal.

✳ *Combatmaster Mark VI .451 Detonics Mag. Cal.*

		$1,000	$900	$775	$665	$560	$465	$410

Last MSR was $1,165.

COMBATMASTER MARK VII - similar to Mark VI, only no sights, special order only, 25 oz.

		$895	$775	$600	$495	$430	$365	$315

> Add $100 for 9mm Para. or .38 Super cal.
> Add $350 for .451 Detonics Mag., (disc. 1982).

MILITARY COMBAT MC2 - .45 ACP, 9mm Para., or .38 Super cal., dull, non-glare combat finish, fixed sights. Comes with camouflaged pile-lined wallet, and Pachmayr grips. Disc. 1984.

		$621	$560	$500	$430	$375	$315	$270

> Add $55 for 9mm Para. or .38 Super.

O.S. MODEL - .45 ACP cal. only, emergency backup pistol, similar to Combatmaster, 6 shot mag., choice of satin stainless or all black finish. 2 mfg. 1991 only. Extreme rarity precludes accurate price evaluation.

SCOREMASTER - .45 ACP or .451 Mag. cal., match gun with closer tolerances, 5 or 6 in. barrel. Millett adj. sights, grip safety, 7 or 8 shot mag., 42 oz. Disc. 1992.

		$995	$850	$695	$585	$500	$415	$365

Last MSR was $1,178.

> Add $40 for 6 in. barrel.

COMPMASTER - .45 ACP cal. only, similar to Scoremaster, except is fully compensated. Mfg. 1988-92.

		$1,995	$1,575	$1,250	$1,100	$895	$785	$630

Last MSR was $1,550.

This model was called the Janus Competition Scoremaster in 1988-1989.

COMPETITION MASTER T.F. - .45 ACP cal., competition model with dual port compensator, rotational torque compensating vents, patented coned barrel system, hand tuned trigger, includes all competition modifications. Disc. 1992.

		$1,995	$1,575	$1,250	$1,100	$895	$785	$630

Last MSR was $1,550.

SERVICEMASTER - .45 ACP cal. only, shortened version of the Scoremaster, non-glare combat finish, 4 1/4 in. barrel, coned barrel system, 8 shot mag., interchangeable front and adj. rear sights, 39 oz. Disc. 1986.

		$825	$675	$575	$480	$410	$350	$295

Last MSR was $686.

✳ *Servicemaster II* - similar to Servicemaster, except has polished stainless steel finish. Mfg. 1986-92.

		$925	$750	$625	$515	$450	$375	$325

Last MSR was $998.

POCKET 9 - 9mm Para. cal., double action, 3 in. barrel, 6 shot mag., soft matte sheen finish, 26 oz. Limited mfg. 1985-86 only.

		$495	$400	$335	$275	$235	$200	$175

Last MSR was $458.

The entire Pocket 9 series was disc. 1986.

GRADING - PPGS™	100%	98%	95%	90%	80%	70%	60%

* *Pocket 9 LS* - similar to Pocket 9, except has 4 in. barrel. Limited mfg. 1986 only.

	$575	$450	$375	$315	$270	$230	$200

Last MSR was $458.

* *Pocket .380* - similar to Pocket 9, except is .380 ACP cal., 23 oz. Limited mfg. 1986 only.

	$575	$450	$375	$315	$270	$230	$200

Last MSR was $458.

POWER 9 - 9mm Para. cal., similar to Pocket 9, except has polished slide sides and is supplied with 2 mags. Disc. 1986.

	$575	$450	$375	$315	$270	$230	$200

Last MSR was $509.

New Detonics Ladies Escort Series

This series was designed specifically to suit a woman's shooting requirements.

ROYAL ESCORT - .45 ACP cal., action similar to Combatmaster, 3 1/2 in. barrel, 6 shot mag., black frame, slide and grips are iridescent purple, hammer and trigger are 24Kt. gold-plated. Less than 25 were mfg. 1990-92.

	$1,000	$850	$650	$540	$465	$385	$335

Last MSR was $990.

MIDNIGHT ESCORT - similar to Royal Escort, except is stainless with a black slide and smooth black grips. Less than 30 were mfg. 1990-92.

	$1,150	$925	$750	$640	$535	$450	$390

Last MSR was $1,090.

JADE ESCORT - similar to Midnight Escort, except has stainless frame, jade colored slide and grips. Less than 10 were mfg. 1990 only.

	$1,200	$950	$600	$495	$430	$365	$315

Last MSR was $918.

NEW ENGLAND ARMS CORP.

Previous importer, distributor, and retailer from 1975-2004, and located in Kittery Point, ME.

New England Arms Corp. imported, distributed, or retailed the following trademarks: Arrieta, P. Arrizabalaga, Bertuzzi, Luciano Bosis, Cosmi, Henri Dumoulin, Fair Techni-Mec (I. Rizzini), Antonio Gil, Lebeau-Courally, F.lli Rizzini, B. Rizzini, Luciano Rota, S.I.A.C.E., and Fabio Zanotti. These trademarks may be found under their own headings in this text.

New England Arms Corp. should not be confused with New England Firearms.

NEW ENGLAND CUSTOM GUN SERVICE, LTD.

Current importer of various firearms trademarks located in Plainfield, NH. The company also represents custom-made guns from small makers in Germany, including Johannsen, Max Ern, and Adamy-Jagdwaffen.

NECG, Ltd. specializes in custom gun services including checkering, stock fitting/alterations, claw mount scope installation and repair, detachable rifle scope mounts, and other gunsmithing services. Please contact the company directly regarding more information on their extensive line of products and services.

NEW ENGLAND FIREARMS

Current trademark established during 1987, located and previously manufactured in Gardner, MA until Nov. 1, 2007. Beginning Nov. 1, 2007, the NEF trademark applies to imported guns only. Distributor sales.

During late Jan. of 2008, Remington acquired the Marlin Firearms Company, which purchased the H&R, New England Firearms (NEF), and L.C. Smith brands during 2000. On May 31st, 2007, Remington Arms Co. was acquired by Cerebrus Capital.

New England Firearms should not be confused with New England Arms Corp.

GRADING - PPGS™	100%	98%	95%	90%	80%	70%	60%

REVOLVERS: DOUBLE ACTION

Ultra Models listed were available in blue finish only. All Ultras were supplied with a lockable storage case beginning 1993.

STANDARD REVOLVER .22 (MODEL R92) - .22 S, L, and LR cal., 9 shot, swing out cylinder, 2 1/2 (disc. 1997), 3 (new 1998) or 4 in. barrel, blue or nickel finish, hardwood stocks, fixed rear sight, 25-28 oz. Mfg. 1988-99.

	$125	$95	$85	$70	$60	$55	$40

Last MSR was $144.

Add $10 for nickel finish.

✳ *Standard Revolver .32 H&R Mag. (Model R73)* - .32 H&R Mag. cal. similar to Standard Revolver .22, except has 5 shot cylinder, 2 1/2 (disc.), 3, or 4 in. barrel, choice of blue or nickel finish (not available with 4 in. barrel), 23-26 oz. Mfg. 1988-99.

	$125	$95	$85	$70	$60	$55	$40

Last MSR was $144.

Add $10 for nickel finish (2 1/2 or 3 in. barrel only).

ULTRA MODEL - .22 S, L, and LR cal., 9 shot, swing-out cylinder, 4 or 6 in. solid rib target-grade barrel with rebated muzzle and fully adj. rear sight, blue finish, smooth hardwood grips, 36 oz. Disc. 1999.

	$150	$115	$95	$80	$70	$60	$55

Last MSR was $180.

ULTRA MAG (MODEL R22) - .22 Mag. cal., 6 shot, 4 (disc. 1997) or 6 in. solid rib barrel, adj. rear sight, swing-out cylinder, blue finish, 36 oz. Mfg. 1988-99.

	$150	$115	$95	$80	$70	$60	$55

Last MSR was $180.

LADY ULTRA - .32 H&R Mag. cal., swing-out cylinder, 5 shot, blue finish, 3 (disc. 1997, reintroduced 1999) or 4 (mfg. 1998 only) in. barrel with rib, adj. sights, thinner contoured grips, 31 oz. Mfg. 1991-99.

	$150	$115	$95	$80	$70	$60	$55

Last MSR was $180.

RIFLES: SEMI-AUTO

SPORTSTER SL - .22 LR cal., 19 in. barrel, 10 shot mag., uncheckered hardwood stock, grooved steel receiver, 5 1/2 lbs. Mfg. 2004 only.

	$125	$105	$90	$80	$70	$60	$55

Last MSR was $157.

RIFLES: SINGLE SHOT

Beginning Nov. 1, 2007, H&R 1871 decided that all products built in the USA will carry the H&R brand name, and all imported products will be sold under the NEF brand name. The Handi-Rifle, Super Light Handi-Rifle, Sportster, and Survivor are now under the H&R brand name, but remain in this section for this edition.

HANDI-RIFLE - .204 Ruger (new 2005), .22 Hornet, .22-250 Rem. (mfg. 1992-94, reintroduced 2004), .223 Rem., .243 Win. (new 1992), .25-06 Rem. (new 2004), .270 Win. (new 1993), .280 Rem. (new 1996), .30-30 Win., .30-06 (new 1992), .308 Win. (new 1998), .35 Whelen (new 2006), .357 Mag. (mfg. 1999-2003), .44 Rem. Mag. (new 1996), .444 Marlin (new 2007), .45-70 Govt., 7mm-08 Rem. (new 2003), .500 S&W (new 2005), 7x57mm Mauser (mfg. 1998-2003), 7.62x39mm (new 2006), or 7x64mm Brenneke (mfg. 1998-2003) cal., break open single shot action, 22 or 26 (.280 Rem. only) in. regular or bull (.223 Rem., .243 Win., or .22-250 Rem.) barrel, blue receiver, regular or Monte Carlo walnut stained hardwood stock, scope mount rail or ramp front and adj. rear sights, sling swivels, 7 lbs. New 1989.

MSR $270		$220	$180	$145	$110	$80	$70	$60

Add $20 for Handi-Rifle .243 Win./Huntsman .50 cal. black powder muzzleloader rifle combo (disc. 2002).

GRADING - PPGS™	100%	98%	95%	90%	80%	70%	60%

Add $39 for 3-9x32mm mounted and bore sighted scope (.223 Rem. or .243 Win. cal. only). This model in .22-250 Rem., .223 Rem., 7.62x39mm, or .243 Win. cal. is supplied with heavy barrel, scope mount, and no sights.

✴ **Handi-Rifle Synthetic** - .22 Hornet, .223 Rem., .243 Win., .270 Win., .280 Rem., .30-30 Win. (disc. 2003), .30-06, .357 Mag. (mfg. 2002-200, reintroduced 2008), .44 Rem. Mag. (disc. 2003, reintroduced 2008), .444 Marlin (new 2008), or .45-70 Govt. cal., 22 or 26 (.280 Rem. only) in. barrel, blue finish, features black synthetic stock and forearm, adj. sights on some cals., scope base mount only on others, 7 lbs. New 1998.

MSR $278	$220	$180	$140	$110	$80	$70	$60

Add $23 for Handi-Rifle combo with 20 ga. Pardner barrel (not available in all cals., disc. 2006). Subtract $42 for .357 Mag. or .44 Mag. cal.

✴ **Handi-Rifle Synthetic Stainless** - .22-250 Rem. (new 2004), .223 Rem., .243 Win., .270 Win., or .30-06 (new 2004) cal., similar to Handi-Rifle Synthetic, features 22 in. matte stainless steel barrel with matte nickel finished receiver, 7 lbs. New 2003.

MSR $319	$255	$200	$160	$120	$80	$70	$60

✴ **Handi-Rifle Youth** - .223 Rem., .243 Win., or 7mm-08 Rem. (new 2005) cal, features 22 in. barrel and shortened stock dimensions (13 1/2 in. LOP), blue finish, supplied with scope rail mount and hammer extension, no iron sights, approx. 7 lbs. Mfg. 1998-2006.

	$235	$185	$140	$110	$85	$70	$60

Last MSR was $292.

✴ **Handi-Rifle 10th Anniversary** - same cals. as Handi-Rifle, limited edition features scroll engraving by Ken Hurst, deep bluing on receiver, steel trigger guard and forearm spacer, select hand checkered walnut, less than 100 mfg. 1997 only.

	$695	$475	$350	$285	$250	$215	$185

Last MSR was $750.

✴ **Handi-Rifle NTA Anniversary Edition** - .223 Rem. only, 24 in. heavy barrel w/o sights, features checkered black/grey laminate stock and forearm with NTA (National Trapper's Association) medallion in stock. Limited production 1999 only.

	$225	$200	$175	$160	$145	$135	$125

Last MSR was $272.

SUPER LIGHT HANDI-RIFLE - .22 Hornet, .223 Rem., or .243 Win. cal., break open single shot, black synthetic stock and forearm, recoil pad, 20 in. special contour barrel with rebated muzzle, .22 Hornet has sights (Model SB2-SL4), .223 Rem. has scope base and hammer extension (Model SB2-SL3), approx. 5 1/2 lbs. New 1997.

MSR $278	$220	$180	$140	$110	$80	$70	$60

Add $23 for Handi-Rifle combo with 20 ga. Pardner barrel (not available in all cals., disc. 2006). Add $31 for 3-9x32mm mounted and bore sighted scope (.243 Win. cal., Youth only, new 2007). This model is also available as a Youth Model with shorter stock dimensions (11 3/4 in. LOP).

SPORTSTER - .17 HMR (new 2002), .17 Mach 2 (mfg. 2005-2007), .22 LR, or .22 Mag. (new 2001) cal., 20 (mid-weight) or 22 (.17 HMR cal. only, heavy) in. barrel with Weaver style scope rail, no iron sights, available in either adult or youth (.22 LR cal. only) dimensions, black polymer stock and forearm. New 1999.

MSR $148	$120	$100	$85	$75	$65	$55	$50

Add $13 for .17 Mach 2 (disc.) or $29 for .17 HMR cal.

GRADING - PPGS™	100%	98%	95%	90%	80%	70%	60%

SURVIVOR - .223 Rem., .308 Win. (new 1999), .357 Mag. (disc. 1998) or .410/45 LC (new 2007) cal., similar in design to the Survivor Series shotgun, removable forearm for ammo storage, thumbhole design with storage compartment, no iron sights, 20 (.410/45 LC cal. only) or 22 in. barrel, blue or nickel finish, .357 Mag. cal. has open sights, .223 Rem. and .308 Win. cal. have heavy barrels and scope mount rail, 6 lbs. New 1996.

	100%	98%	95%	90%	80%	70%	60%
MSR $281	$230	$180	$145	$110	$80	$70	$60

Add approx. $15 for nickel finish (disc. 1998, reintroduced 2007 for .410/45 LC cal. only).
Subtract $76 for .410/45 LC cal. (new 2007).

SHOTGUNS: SEMI-AUTO

EXCELL AUTO - 12 ga., 3 in. chamber, 28 in. VR barrel with screw-in choke tubes, 5 shot mag., black synthetic or walnut pistol grip stock with fluted comb, vent. recoil pad, bead front sight, approx. 7 lbs. New 2008.

	100%	98%	95%	90%	80%	70%	60%
MSR $374	$300	$250	$210	$180	$160	$140	$120

Add $29 for walnut stock.

＊*Excell Auto Turkey* - 12 ga., 3 in. chamber, 5 shot mag., 22 in. vent. rib barrel with choke tubes and fiber optic sights, Realtree Advantage Hardwoods camo covered pistol grip stock and barrel, 7 lbs. New 2008.

	100%	98%	95%	90%	80%	70%	60%
MSR $456	$395	$345	$300	$265	$230	$195	$170

＊*Excell Auto Waterfowl* - 12 ga., 28 in. VR barrel, 5 shot, 100% Advantage Wetlands camo coverage, 7 lbs. New 2008.

	100%	98%	95%	90%	80%	70%	60%
MSR $456	$395	$345	$300	$265	$230	$195	$170

＊*Excell Auto Combo* - includes 24 in. rifled slug barrel and 28 in. regular barrel, synthetic stock only. New 2008.

	100%	98%	95%	90%	80%	70%	60%
MSR $512	$425	$380	$330	$290	$260	$230	$200

SHOTGUNS: SINGLE SHOT

Beginning Nov. 1, 2007, H&R 1871 decided that all products built in the USA will carry the H&R brand name, and all imported products will be sold under the NEF brand name. The Pardner Series and Tracker Slug are now under the H&R brand name, but remain in this section for this edition.

PARDNER - 12, 16 (new 1989), 20, 28 ga. (new 1991), or .410 bore, 2 3/4 or 3 in. chamber (12, 20 ga., and .410 bore), single shot, break open action, safety transfer bar mechanism on hammer, side lever release, color case hardened receiver, 14 in. LOP, 24 (disc.), 26, 28, or 32 in. barrel, fixed or mod. choke tube (12 or 20 ga. only, with black synthetic stock and forearm), extractor, walnut stained hardwood or black synthetic (12 or 20 ga. only) stock and forearm, 5-6 lbs. New 1987.

	100%	98%	95%	90%	80%	70%	60%
MSR $129	$100	$85	$75	$65	$55	$45	$40

Add $15 for 32 in. barrel (12 ga. only).
Add $22 for modified choke tube (12 or 20 ga. only).
Add $65 for Pardner 12 ga. Shotgun/Huntsman .50 cal. black powder muzzleloader combo (disc. 2002).

＊*Pardner Compact (Youth)* - 12 (new 1998), 20, 28 ga., or .410 bore, similar to Pardner, except has 22 in. barrel and straight grip stock with recoil pad, 12 1/2 in. LOP.

	100%	98%	95%	90%	80%	70%	60%
MSR $137	$115	$95	$75	$65	$55	$45	$40

Add $21 for Pardner Youth .22 cal. barrel/.410 bore Versa-Pack combo (disc. 2007).
Add $14 for modified choke tube (20 ga. only with black synthetic stock and forearm).

GRADING - PPGS™	100%	98%	95%	90%	80%	70%	60%

✳ **Pardner Turkey Gun** - 10 or 12 ga. only, 3 (disc.) or 3 1/2 in. chamber, 24 in. barrel with fixed or full choke tube, camo or matte black wood finish, 6 or 9 (10 ga.) lbs. New 1999.

MSR $176	$135	$115	$90	$80	$70	$60	$50

Add $10 for Mossy Oak Break-Up camo in 12 ga. with full choke bore.
Add $58 for 10 ga. in black matte wood finish (disc. 2007).
Add $88 for 10 ga. with camo wood finish.

✳ **Pardner Youth Turkey** - 20 ga. only, features 22 in. full choke barrel and camo painted wood. New 1999.

MSR $186	$135	$110	$90	$80	$70	$60	$50

✳ **Pardner Waterfowl (Special Purpose)** - 10 or 12 (mfg. 2002-2006) ga., 3 1/2 in. chamber, 28 or 32 (10 ga. only, new 1996) in. barrel, blue barrel and receiver, walnut or Mossy Oak Break Up camo (new 2002) finish on stock and forearm, recoil pad, 9 1/2 lbs. New 1988.

MSR $228	$185	$150	$125	$100	$85	$65	$55

Add $36 for camo.
Subtract 15% for 12 ga.

✳ **Pardner NRA Foundation Youth** - 20, 28 (disc. 2001) ga. or .410 bore, 22 in. barrel, high luster bluing, features "NRA Foundation Youth Endowment Edition" laser etched in black on stock, approx. 5 1/2 lbs. Mfg. 1999-2002.

	$130	$105	$90	$75	$65	$55	$45

Last MSR was $161.

✳ **Pardner National Wild Turkey Federation (NWTF)** - 10 or 20 (new 1993) ga., 22 (20 ga. only) or 24 in. barrel with full screw-in choke, full Mossy Oak camo treatment, includes swivels and sling. Mfg. 1992-96.

	$190	$160	$135	$110	$95	$80	$70

Last MSR was $230.

Subtract $80 for 20 ga.
This model was drilled and tapped for scope mounts.

SURVIVOR SERIES - 12 (disc. 2003), 20 ga. (disc. 2003), or .410/.45 LC (new 1995) bore, 3 in. chamber, 20 (.410/.45 LC) or 22 in. barrel with Mod. choke, blue or electroless nickel finish, synthetic thumbhole designed hollow stock with pistol grip, removable forend holds additional ammo, sling swivels, and black nylon sling, 13 1/4 in. LOP, 6 lbs. Mfg. 1992-93, reintroduced 1995-2006.

	$175	$150	$120	$100	$85	$75	$65

Last MSR was $219.

Add $18 for electroless nickel finish.
Subtract 20% for 12 or 20 ga.

TRACKER SLUG MODEL - 10 ga. (mfg. 1994 only), 12, or 20 ga., 3 (12 or 20 ga.) or 3 1/2 (10 ga. only) in. chamber, 24 in. cylinder bore barrel, case colored receiver, includes recoil pad and adj. sights, 6 lbs. Mfg. 1992-2001.

	$120	$90	$75	$60	$50	$45	$40

Last MSR was $143.

✳ **Tracker Slug Model II** - 12 or 20 ga., 3 in. chamber, similar to Tracker Slug Model except has 24 in. rifled slug barrel, 14 in. LOP, 5 1/4 lbs. New 1995.

MSR $194	$150	$120	$90	$75	$60	$50	$45

Add $44 for Tracker II 12 ga. Slug Gun/Huntsman .50 cal. black powder muzzleloader (disc. 2002).

GRADING - PPGS™	100%	98%	95%	90%	80%	70%	60%

SHOTGUNS: SLIDE ACTION

PARDNER PUMP - 12 or 20 (new 2006) ga., 3 or 3 1/2 (mfg. 2006) in. chamber, steel reciever, crossbolt safety, double action bars, 28 in. VR barrel with choke tube, black synthetic (new 2005), synthetic with carbon fiber dip, or uncheckered walnut stock with or w/o camo coverage, recoil pad, matte black metal finish, 7 1/2 lbs. New 2004.

MSR $203	$160	$130	$115	$100	$90	$80	$70

Add $18 for walnut stock and forearm.
Add $20 for synthetic stock with carbon fiber dip (new 2008).
Add $68 for synthetic stock with 100% Realtree APG/HD camo coverage.
Add $65 for 12 ga. with 3 1/2 in. chamber (disc. 2007).

✴ *Pardner Pump Turkey* - includes 100% Mossy Oak Breakup (disc.) or Realtree (new 2006) camo coverage, 22 in. barrel with Truglo front and rear sights, one Turkey choke tube. New 2005.

MSR $265	$215	$185	$160	$145	$130	$115	$100

Add $24 for 100% Realtree APG/HD camo coverage.

✴ *Pardner Pump Combo* - 12 ga. only, 3 in. chamber, includes 22 in. rifled slug and 28 in. barrel with modified choke tube. New 2005.

MSR $303	$240	$215	$180	$150	$125	$115	$100

✴ *Pardner Pump Protector* - .12 ga., black synthetic stock, 18 1/2 in. barrel, bead front sight, matte finished metal, swivel studs, vent. recoil pad, 5 shot tube mag., crossbolt safety. Mfg. 2006-2007.

		$155	$135	$115	$100	$85	$75	$65

Last MSR was $186.

✴ *Pardner Pump Compact (Youth)* - 20 ga., take-down action, 21 in. barrel, black American walnut or black synthetic pistol grip stock with or w/o camo, fluted comb, vent. recoil pad, bead front sight, drilled and tapped, 5 shot mag., 13 in. LOP, approx. 6 1/2 lbs. New 2006.

MSR $203	$185	$145	$115	$100	$85	$75	$65

Add $18 for black walnut stock and forearm.
Add $68 for 100% Realtree APG/HD camo coverage (new 2008).

✴ *Pardner Pump Slug* - 12 or 20 ga., take-down action, 21 (20 ga.) or 22 (12 ga.) in. rifled barrel, matte metal finish, black synthetic (12 ga.) or walnut (20 ga.) pistol grip stock with fluted comb, swivel studs, vent. recoil pad, ramp front sight, adj. rear sight, drilled and tapped, 5 shot mag., crossbolt safety, approx. 6 1/2 lbs. New 2006.

MSR $259	$210	$185	$155	$140	$115	$100	$90

NEW ULTRA LIGHT ARMS LLC

Current rifle manufacturer located in Granville, WV. Dealer sales.

RIFLES: BOLT ACTION

Add approx. $100 for left-hand action.

ULTRA LIGHT RIFLE - caliber to customer specs., various actions, 2-position 3-function safety in top of stock, Timney trigger, Douglas barrel, no sights, Kevlar stock reinforced with graphite, recoil pad, Dupont Imron epoxy finish, designed to customer specifications, includes hard case, 5 1/4-5 3/4 lbs.

Please contact the company directly for a price quote on this model.

MODEL 20 SERIES - various short action centerfire cals. available between .17 Rem. and .358 Win, 5 1/4 lbs.

MSR $3,000	$2,650	$2,200	$1,700	$1,300	$1,050	$925	$850

✴ *Model 20 RF* - .22 LR cal., single shot or repeater, 5 1/4 lbs.

MSR $1,300	$1,125	$975	$825	$650	$425	$300	$250

Add $50 for repeater action.

GRADING - PPGS™	100%	98%	95%	90%	80%	70%	60%

MODEL 24 - various cals. between .25-06 Rem. - .338-06 cal., long action, 5 1/4 lbs.

	100%	98%	95%	90%	80%	70%	60%
MSR $3,100	$2,700	$2,000	$1,450	$1,050	$875	$775	$675

MODEL 28 MAGNUM - various Mag. cals. between .264 Win. Mag. - .338 Win. Mag., 5 3/4 lbs.

MSR $3,400	$3,000	$2,225	$1,650	$1,250	$975	$800	$700

MODEL 32 MAGNUM - 7mm STW, .300 Wby. Mag., or .340 Wby. Mag. cal., other calibers available by request, dangerous game rifle. New 2005.

MSR $3,400	$3,000	$2,225	$1,650	$1,250	$975	$800	$700

MODEL 40 MAGNUM - .416 Rigby cal., other calibers available by request, otherwise similar to Model 28 Magnum.

MSR $3,400	$3,000	$2,225	$1,650	$1,250	$975	$800	$700

NEWTON ARMS CO.

Previous manufacturer located in Buffalo, NY circa 1913-1932.

RIFLES: BOLT ACTION

NEWTON-MAUSER - .256 Newton - .30 Adolph Express cals., Oberndorf 98 bolt action, 24 in. barrel, sporting style stock, various grades and variations, some with double set triggers. A small number of these commercial rifles were built in Germany in 1914, and shipped to the U.S.

	$2,000	$1,500	$1,250	$1,000	$900	$800	$700

1922 NEWTON MAUSER - .256 Newton cal., commercial Mauser 98 action, double set triggers opposed in guard, stock and/or barrels marked "Made in Germany", some barrels marked "Chas. Newton Rifle Corp., Buffalo, NY", leaf type rear sight. Approx. 100 rifles imported.

	N/A	$1,750	$1,250	$1,050	$875	$775	$675

This model can can vary quite a bit from specimen to specimen.

FIRST TYPE STANDARD - .22 Newton, .256 Newton, .30 Newton, .33 Newton, .35 Newton, or .30-06 cal., 24 in. standard barrel, open barrel sight, bolt peep sight was optional, checkered pistol grip stock, segmentally rifled barrels are marked "Newton Arms Co., Buffalo, NY", double set triggers. Approx. 4,000 mfg. 1917-19.

	$3,500	$2,800	$2,500	$1,800	$1,500	$1,000	$750

Add $100 for optional bolt aperture sight.
Add $100 for figured wood or cheekpiece.

SECOND TYPE STANDARD - prototype only, this model never went into production.

BUFFALO NEWTON - .256 Newton, .30-06, .30 Newton, or .35 Newton cal., checkered sporting stock, reversed double set triggers, Enfield style bolt handle, open sights, 24 in. parabolically rifled barrel marked "Buffalo Newton Rifle Corp., New Haven Conn". Approx. 1,000 mfg. 1923-29 in New Haven, CT.

	$2,500	$2,200	$2,000	$1,500	$1,000	$650	$500

NEWTON SPRINGFIELD - kit consisting of a Marlin-made sporting stock and .256 Newton barrel, customer supplied Springfield 1903 action and sights, original kit guns will have conventional square cut rifled barrels marked "Newton Arms Co. Buffalo, NY". Mfg. 1914-17.

	$1,200	$1,100	$1,000	$900	$800	$700	$650

Due to the low numbered Springfield receivers and the fact that many of these barrels were customer fitted, it is not advisable to fire these rifles until a competent gunsmith has performed an inspection.

GRADING - PPGS™	100%	98%	95%	90%	80%	70%	60%

NIGHTHAWK CUSTOM

Current manufacturer located in Berryville, AR. since 2004. Consumer custom order sales.

PISTOLS: SEMI-AUTO

Nighthawk Custom offers a complete line of high quality 1911 style semi-auto pistols. Please contact the company directly for more information on custom pistols, a wide variety of options, gunsmithing services and availability.

GRP (GLOBAL RESPONSE PISTOL) - .45 ACP cal., black Perma Kote ceramic based finish, 5 in. match grade barrel, match grade trigger, front and rear cocking serrations, Novak Extreme Duty adj. night sights, Gator Back grips.

MSR $2,320	$2,150	$1,825	$1,550	$1,275	$1,000	$850	$725

    Add $100 for GRP II with 4 1/4 in. barrel.
    Add $200 for GRP Recon Model with integrated lower rail with Surefire X200 weapon light.
    Add $400 for GRP Recon Model with Crimson Trace laser grips and Surefire X200 weapon light.

TALON - .45 ACP cal., blue finish, 5 in. match grade or bull barrel, lightweight aluminum match trigger, hand checkering on rear of slide with serrated top slide, Novak night sights.

MSR $2,420	$2,225	$1,950	$1,600	$1,300	$1,050	$875	$750

    Add $54 for Talon II with green lower frame.
    Add $105 for Talon III with 4 1/4 in. barrel.

* *Talon IV* - similar to Talon, except compact model with 3.6 in. barrel, gray frame and black slide, rear slide serrations, and black grips.

MSR $2,425	$2,225	$1,950	$1,600	$1,300	$1,050	$875	$750

PREDATOR - .45 ACP cal., 5 in. barrel, grey finish with black slide, black checkered grips, top-of-the-line model.

MSR $2,824	$2,575	$2,175	$1,850	$1,525	$1,200	$1,000	$850

    Add $51 for Predator II with 4 1/4 in. barrel.
    Add $101 for Predator III model with Officer frame and 4 1/4 in. barrel.

DOMINATOR - .45 ACP cal., 5 in. match grade barrel hard chrome frame with black PermaKote slide, front and rear slide serrations, 25 LPI checkering on front strap, cocobolo grips with laser engraved Nighthawk Custom logo, adj. sights.

MSR $2,795	$2,550	$2,150	$1,850	$1,525	$1,200	$1,000	$850

NIKKO FIREARMS CO., LTD.

Previous manufacturer located in Tochigi, Japan circa 1958-1989.

NIKKO HISTORY AND GENERAL INFORMATION

The publisher wishes to thank the Golden Eagle Collectors Association located at 11144 Slate Creek Road, Grass Valley, CA 95945 for providing this publication with the information listed. Please refer to the Golden Eagle heading in this text for information on Nikko manufactured Golden Eagle firearms.

Both Nikko Firearms Co., Ltd. and Nikko Arms Co., Ltd. were trade names used by the Kodensha Co., Ltd. of Tochigi, Japan on products they manufactured and distributed worldwide. Nikko is the name of the Prefecture, or district, in which Tochigi City is located, about 50 miles north of Tokyo. The word Nikko translates to English as "sunshine." Kodensha first manufactured or distributed under the Nikko name in April 1955, and exported out of Japan beginning in August 1958. Nothing is known of the origin of the Kodensha Co.

Kodensha first approached the American shotgun market in about 1958 or 1959 using the Japanese export marketing firm of Kyowa-Boeki-Bussan. They contacted various U.S. distributors, and in about 1959 or 1960, Continental Arms Co. of New York City began importing the Nikko "Grade 5." Continental imported these Nikko over/unders, in various models and configurations, until about 1972.

In 1962, the Kodensha Co., Ltd. formed a joint venture with Olin/Winchester of New Haven, CT to produce the Winchester Model 101 over/under shotgun. This venture was known as the Olin-

Kodensha Co. Ltd. Added a little later was the side-by-side Model 23, and the Model 96 Xpert (a budget priced 101). The "pre-Olin" Kodensha factory was considerably outdated, and the joint venture began a complete modernization process, with the financial and technical assistance of Olin. Millions of dollars of machinery and technology were brought in, and the entire manufacturing process was upgraded to the then current standards.

One of the conditions of the joint venture was that Kodensha restrict their own products (made in the same factory, but recorded separately from the joint venture) to sale in Japan only. At the outset of the 25 years that the joint venture existed, Kodensha was probably amenable to this, as they were reaping huge financial and technical benefits from Olin. But, by the mid 1960s, when the factory was in place and running smoothly, Kodensha essentially ignored that condition of the agreement, leaving Olin at somewhat of a disadvantage, not wanting to jeopardize their investment or production source. Additionally, Olin/Winchester was allowed only two permanent personnel, hardly enough to monitor the activities of a factory which employed up to 400 people. As an example, when walnut stock blanks arrived from France, Kodensha took first pick, and Olin got what was left over.

Kodensha converted an existing building near the manufacturing plant into an assembly area for Nikko, and other brands of guns. This building was probably the "true" Nikko Firearms Co., Ltd. Manufactured components from the Olin-Kodensha factory were carted to the Nikko plant for final assembly and fitting. This "dual-factory" arrangement continued until the mid 1980s. In 1981, for an unknown reason, the Olin-Kodensha name was changed to OK Firearms Co. Ltd. In October 1987, Olin/Winchester sold their interest in OK Firearms to Classic Doubles International, which continued making the 101 style shotgun under their own name. For reasons unknown, Classic Doubles went out of business in December 1988. Shortly thereafter, the entire factory was torn down, and all that remains today is a vacant lot.

During the "dual-factory" days, Nikko produced firearms for the following distributors or retailers: 1) Kanematsu Gosho of Arlington Heights, IL approx. 1974-1982 - distributed Nikko brand shotguns, Golden Eagle brand shotguns and rifles (1975 through March 1977 only); 2) Golden Eagle Firearms, Houston, TX March 1977 through early 1981 - Golden Eagle shotguns and rifles; 3) Tradewinds, Inc. of Tacoma, WA exported from Japan by Caspoll International, Tokyo January 1971 through December 1972 - Shadow Seven; Shadow Indy (Model 707); Gold, Silver, and Black Shadow over/ under shotguns; 4) Marubeni America, Inc. of New York City 1972-1974 - Miida brand over/under shotguns; 5) Winchester GMBH of West Germany, manufactured by Olin-Kodensha (dates unknown - early 1980s) - Winchester Model 777 rifle (Golden Eagle look-alike); 6) Parker Reproduction shotguns, distributed in the US by Reagent Chemical & Research, Inc. 1984-1988; 7) International Star Commerce Corp. (ISCC) of Salt Lake City, Utah approx. 1982 - distributor of Nikko brand shotguns; 8) Moore Supply Co. of Salt Lake City, UT beginning mid-1981 - distributor of Nikko brand shotguns; 9) USA Nikko, Inc. of Los Angeles, CA (factory reps and distributors of Nikko shotguns), initial date unknown, through December 1981; 10) Weatherby, Inc. of Los Angeles, CA May 1972 to 1981. Centurion semi-auto and Patrician pump shotguns, some Mark 22 rifles. Olympian O/U shotgun and possibly other O/Us from 1978-81. Model 82 semi-auto and Model 92 pump shotguns; 11) Savage Industries of Hamden, CT 1981-1982 - Savage/Fox FA-1 and FP-1 shotguns; 12) Charles Daly. "Automatic" distributed by Sloans (Japanese made only) mid-1980s; 13) Sears, Roebuck Co. Ted Williams Model 400 and possibly others; 14) Churchill semi-auto, imported by Kassnar mid-1980s; 15) High Standard of Hamden, CT 1974-75 - Supermatic Shadow Indy (Model 707, an O/U), Supermatic Shadow Seven (also O/U), and Supermatic Shadow semi-auto.

NOTE: ALL of the semi-auto shotguns used essentially the same design. Each distributor may have made a few cosmetic or dimensional embellishments to differentiate their gun. Differences exist in barrel/breech fit, magazine caps, pistol grip caps, checkering pattern, piston size, ejector location, fluted bolt. Use caution if interchanging parts. Generally, the same statement can be made about the pump versions also.

NOBLE MFG. CO.

Previous manufacturer and importer of Spanish SxS shotguns located in Haydenville, MA 1953-1971.

Noble manufactured semi-auto, lever, and slide action rifles and slide action shotguns, in addition to importing Spanish SxS shotguns. Shotgun models included the Model

GRADING - PPGS™	100%	98%	95%	90%	80%	70%	60%

420, 420 EK, and 450 E. While most models were relatively inexpensive, good working, utilitarian guns, there has been little collectibility to date and most rifles are seen priced in the $45-$150 price range while the shotguns are priced in the $75-$300 range, depending on gauge and features.

NOR-CAL PRECISION

Current manufacturer and riflesmith established in 1989 and located in American Canyon, CA.

Nor-Cal Precision manufacutures custom rifles based on the Rem. M700 action, in addition to a variety of gunsmithing services. Please contact the company directly for more information, including availability and pricing (see Trademark Index).

NORINCO

Current Chinese conglomerate (China North Industries Corp.) located in China which manufactures small arms and military weapons. Previously imported and distributed exclusively by Interstate Arms Corp., located in Billerica, MA. Previous importers have included: Norinco Sports U.S.A., located in Diamond Bar, CA, Century International Arms, Inc. located in St. Albans, VT; China Sports, Inc. located in Ontario, CA; Interarms located in Alexandria, VA; KBI, Inc. located in Harrisburg, PA; and others. Dealer and distributor sales only.

Norinco pistols, rifles, and shotguns are manufactured in the People's Republic of China by China North Industries Corp. (Norinco has over 100 factories). Currently, due to the 1994 Crime bill and recent presidential orders, Norinco cannot legally sell weapons in the U.S.

PISTOLS: SEMI-AUTO

MODEL 213 - 9mm Para. cal., single action, satin blue finish. Imported 1988 only.

	$185	$150	$135	$125	$115	$105	$100

Last MSR was $200.

TYPE 54-1 TOKAREV STANDARD - 7.62x25mm Tokarev or .38 Super cal., single action semi-auto, 4 1/2 in. barrel, 8 shot mag., fixed sights, blue finish, 29 oz. Imported 1989-95.

	$125	$100	$80	$70	$65	$60	$55

Last MSR was $145.

* *Type 54-1 Tokarev Standard Double Column* - similar to Standard Model, except is also available in 9mm Para. cal. and has 10 (C/B 1994) or 13* shot mag., 35 oz. Imported 1991-95.

	$155	$135	$120	$110	$100	$90	$80

Last MSR was $185.

* *Type 54-1 Tokarev Standard Compact* - .38 Super, 9mm Para., or 7.62x25mm Tokarev cal., 3.8 in. barrel, 8 shot mag., 27 oz. Imported 1991-95.

	$155	$135	$120	$110	$100	$90	$80

Last MSR was $185.

TYPE 59 MAKAROV - 9x18mm Makarov or .380 ACP cal., double action semi-auto, 3 1/2 in. barrel, 8 shot bottom release mag., checkered plastic grips, PPK design with additional features, adj. rear sight, 24 oz. Imported 1989-95.

	$150	$135	$125	$115	$95	$85	$75

Last MSR was $185.

TYPE 77B - 9mm Para. cal., semi-auto single action, action patterned after the older German Lignose (unique design permits one handed operation utilizing "trigger guard cocking" enabling the slide to be moved backward cocking the hammer), 5 in. barrel, 8 shot mag., adj. rear sight, 34 oz. Limited importation 1991-95.

	$350	$295	$250	$225	$195	$165	$135

Last MSR was $285.

GRADING - PPGS™	100%	98%	95%	90%	80%	70%	60%

MODEL 1911 A1 - .45 ACP cal. only, patterned after the Colt 1911 A1, 5 in. barrel, 7 shot mag., fixed sights, blue or parkerized finish, wood grips, 39 oz. Imported 1991-95.

		$525	$475	$450	$400	$350	$300	$275

Last MSR was $320.

RIFLES: SEMI-AUTO

TYPE 84S AKS RIFLE - .223 Rem. cal., semi-auto Kalashnikov action, 16.34 in. barrel, hardwood stock and pistol grip, 30 shot mag., 1,000 meter adj. rear sight, includes bayonet and sheath, 8.87 lbs. Imported 1988-89 only.

$1,450	$1,250	$1,150	$1,000	$925	$875	$795

Last MSR was $350.

＊ *Type 84S-1 AKS Rifle* - similar to Type 84S AKS except has under-folding metal stock. Imported 1989 only.

$1,600	$1,500	$1,400	$1,250	$1,100	$1,000	$900

Last MSR was $350.

＊ *Type 84S-3 AKS Rifle* - similar to Type 84S AKS except has composite fiber stock (1 1/2 in. longer than wood stock). Imported 1989 only.

$1,295	$1,100	$1,000	$950	$900	$800	$750

Last MSR was $365.

＊ *Type 84S-5 AKS Rifle* - similar to Type 84S AKS except has side-folding metal stock. Imported 1989 only.

$1,600	$1,500	$1,450	$1,350	$1,200	$1,100	$1,000

Last MSR was $350.

NHM-90/91 (AK-47 THUMBHOLE) - .223 Rem. or 7.62x39mm cal., features new thumbhole stock for legalized import, 5 shot mag. Imported 1991-1993, configuration was restyled and renamed NHM-90/91 in 1994.

$750	$675	$575	$500	$450	$350	$300

Last MSR was $375.

NHM-90/91 SPORT - 7.62x39mm cal., choice of 16.34 (NHM-90) or 23.27 (NHM-91) in. barrel, hardwood thumbhole stock, NHM-91 has bipod, 5 shot mag., 9-11 lbs. Imported 1994-95.

$550	$500	$450	$425	$385	$350	$325

The .223 Rem. cal. was also available for the Model NHM-90. Each Model NHM-90/91 was supplied with three 5 shot mags., sling, and cleaning kit.

MODEL B THUMBHOLE - 9mm Para. cal., patterned after the Uzi, features sporterized thumbhole wood stock, 10 shot mag. Importation 1995 only.

$795	$695	$600	$550	$500	$450	$400

Last MSR was $625.

R.P.K. RIFLE - 7.62x39mm cal., includes bipod. Importation disc. 1993.

$1,200	$1,000	$900	$800	$725	$650	$600

Last MSR was $600.

TYPE SKS - .223 Rem. or 7.62x39mm cal., SKS action, 20.47 in. barrel, 10 (C/B 1994) or 30* shot mag., 1,000 meter adj. rear sight, hardwood stock, new design accepts standard AK mag., with or w/o folding bayonet, 8.8 lbs. Imported 1988-1989, reintroduced 1992-95 with Sporter configuration stock.

$475	$400	$350	$325	$300	$250	$225

Last MSR was $150.

Add $100 for synthetic stock and bayonet.
Subtract 15% if refinished.

GRADING - PPGS™	100%	98%	95%	90%	80%	70%	60%

TYPE 81S AKS RIFLE - 7.62x39mm cal., semi-auto Kalashnikov action, 17 1/2 in. barrel, 5, 30, or 40 shot mag., 500 meter adj. rear sight, fixed wood stock, hold open device after last shot, 8 lbs. Imported 1988-1989.

	$1,200	$1,000	$900	$800	$725	$650	$600

Last MSR was $385.

* *Type 81S-1 AKS Rifle* - similar to Type 81S AKS except has under-folding metal stock. Imported 1988-89.

	$1,300	$1,075	$950	$850	$750	$625	$575

Last MSR was $385.

TYPE 56S-2 - 7.62x39mm cal., older Kalashnikov design with side-folding metal stock. Importation disc. 1989.

	$1,500	$1,350	$1,200	$1,100	$1,000	$900	$800

Last MSR was $350.

TYPE 86S-7 RPK RIFLE - 7.62x39mm cal., AK action, 23.27 in. heavy barrel with built-in bipod, in-line buttstock, 11.02 lbs. Imported 1988-1989.

	$1,500	$1,275	$1,075	$950	$850	$750	$650

Last MSR was $425.

TYPE 86S BULLPUP RIFLE - 7.62x39mm cal., bullpup configuration with AK action, under-folding metal stock, 17 1/4 in. barrel, ambidextrous cocking design, folding front handle, 7 lbs. Imported 1989 only.

	$1,850	$1,650	$1,500	$1,250	$1,100	$1,000	$900

Last MSR was $400.

DRAGUNOV (MODEL 350 NDM-86) - 7.62x54mm Russian, sniper variation of the AK-47, features 24 in. barrel with muzzle brake, special laminated skeletonized wood stock with vent. forearm, detachable 10 shot mag., 8 lbs. 9 oz. Importation disc. 1995.

	$2,650	$2,400	$2,250	$2,000	$1,850	$1,650	$1,500

Last MSR was $3,080.

This model was also imported by Gibbs Rifle Co. located in Martinsburg, WV.

* *Dragunov Carbine* - similar to Dragunov rifle, except shorter barrel, various accessories including a lighted scope were also offered, plastic furniture.

	$1,200	$1,000	$875	$775	$675	$600	$550

OFFICERS NINE - 9mm Para. cal., 16.1 in. barrel, action patterned after the IMI Uzi, 32 shot mag., black military finish, 8.4 lbs. Limited 1988-89.

	$1,100	$995	$850	$725	$650	$575	$500

Last MSR was $450.

RIFLES: .22 CAL.

MODEL EM-321 - .22 LR cal., slide action, 19 1/2 in. barrel, 10 shot tube mag., hardwood stock and forearm, fixed sights, 6 lbs. Importation began 1989-90, resumed 1994-disc.

	$135	$115	$95	$85	$75	$65	$55

TYPE EM-332 - .22 LR cal., bolt action, 18 1/2 in. barrel with adj. rear sight, mag. holder on stock holds two extra 5 shot mags., Monte Carlo stock with cheekpiece and recoil pad, 4 1/2 lbs. Imported 1991-93.

	$225	$195	$165	$140	$120	$95	$80

SHOTGUNS: O/U

TYPE HL12-203 - 12 ga. only, 2 3/4 in. chambers, boxlock action, ejectors, 30 in. vent. barrels and rib, single trigger, multi-chokes, checkered stock and forearm, 7 1/2 lbs. Imported 1989-1993.

	$400	$350	$300	$265	$225	$200	$185

GRADING - PPGS™	100%	98%	95%	90%	80%	70%	60%

SHOTGUNS: SEMI-AUTO

MODEL 2000 FIELD - 12 ga. only, 2 3/4 in. chamber, steel receiver and aluminum alloy trigger guard, 26 or 28 in. VR barrel with M choke tube, choice of black synthetic or checkered hardwood stock and forearm, approx. 7 1/2 lbs. Limited importation 1999 only.

	100%	98%	95%	90%	80%	70%	60%
	$260	$230	$200	$185	$170	$160	$150

Last MSR was $299.

Add $8 for wood stock and forearm.
Choke tubes are interchangeable with the WinChoke system.

✴ *Model 2000 Field Defense* - 12 ga. only, 2 3/4 in. chamber, 18 1/2 in. barrel with cyl. choke tube and choice of bead, rifle, or ghost ring sights, matte black metal finish, black synthetic stock and forearm with recoil pad. Limited importation 1999 only.

	100%	98%	95%	90%	80%	70%	60%
	$245	$225	$190	$175	$160	$155	$145

Last MSR was $282.

Add $5 for rifle sights.
Add $17 for ghost ring sights.

SHOTGUNS: SLIDE ACTION

TYPE HL12-102 - 12 ga. only, 2 3/4 in. chamber, 28.4 in. barrel, 3 shot mag., crossbolt safety on rear trigger guard, fixed chokes, 9.3 lbs. Imported 1989-93.

	100%	98%	95%	90%	80%	70%	60%
	$230	$200	$175	$165	$150	$135	$120

MODEL 98 FIELD - 12 ga. only, 3 in. chamber, 26 or 28 in. VR barrel with M choke tube, choice of black synthetic or uncheckered hardwood stock and forearm with recoil pad, approx. 7 lbs. Limited importation 1999 only.

	100%	98%	95%	90%	80%	70%	60%
	$185	$160	$140	$125	$110	$100	$90

Last MSR was $205.

Add $8 for wood stock and forearm.
Add $55 for Field Combo (includes extra 18 1/2 in. barrel) or $82 for Field Combo with 22 in. slug or turkey barrel.

✴ *Model 98 Field Turkey* - similar to Model 98 Field, except has 22 in. VR barrel with extra full choke tube, black synthetic stock and forearm only. Limited importation 1999 only.

	100%	98%	95%	90%	80%	70%	60%
	$190	$165	$140	$125	$110	$100	$90

Last MSR was $216.

✴ *Model 98 Field Defense* - 12 ga. only, 3 in. chamber, 18 1/2 in. barrel with cyl. choke tube and choice of bead, rifle, or ghost ring sights, matte black metal finish, black synthetic stock and forearm with recoil pad. Limited importation 1999 only.

	100%	98%	95%	90%	80%	70%	60%
	$170	$150	$130	$115	$100	$90	$80

Last MSR was $190.

Add $15 for ghost ring sights.

MODEL 983 - 12 ga. only, 22 in. barrel with external rifled choke tube and adj. rifle sights, synthetic black stock. Limited importation 2002 only.

	100%	98%	95%	90%	80%	70%	60%
	$215	$170	$155	$135	$125	$105	$95

Last MSR was $230.

MODEL 984/985/987 - 12 ga. only, 3 in. chamber, field series with 26 or 28 in. VR barrel and M choke tube, black synthetic or uncheckered hardwood stock and forearm, matte black metal finish. Limited importation 2001-2002.

	100%	98%	95%	90%	80%	70%	60%
	$200	$170	$155	$135	$125	$105	$95

Last MSR was $235.

Add $10 for hardwood stock (Models 985 & 987).

GRADING - PPGS™	100%	98%	95%	90%	80%	70%	60%

NORINCO USA

Current manufacturer located in Jefferson City, MO.

Retired Marine Jon Morgan recently applied for the Norinco trademark to be used for weapons manufactured in the U.S. Currently, he is only in the planning stages and does not have any completed firearms yet with the Norinco name. Please contact the company directly for more information as it becomes available (see Trademark Index).

NORSMAN SPORTING ARMS & OUTFITTERS LLC

Current rifle manufacturer/customizer located in Havre, MT since 1999. Previously located in Bismarck, ND until 1999. Consumer direct sales.

Norsman specializes in both wood and synthetic take-down rifles and multiple barrel/caliber configurations, along with a complete line of built-to-order custom double rifles. Please contact the factory directly (see Trademark Index) for additional information and prices.

RIFLES: BOLT ACTION

VIKING GRADE - most standard cals., unique NSA takedown action, many options, including left-hand models, custom orders also available.

MSR N/A	$6,615	$5,750	$5,250	$4,500	$3,750	$3,000	$2,500

Add $1,500 per interchangeable barrel.

VIKING GRADE MAGNUM - most standard Mag. cals., unique NSA takedown action, many options and custom orders available, including left-hand.

MSR N/A	$9,890	$8,900	$8,000	$7,000	$6,000	$5,000	$4,000

Add $2,000 per interchangeable barrel.

FIELD GRADE SYNTHETIC - most standard cals., unique NSA takedown action, many options and custom orders available.

MSR N/A	$3,735	$3,350	$2,850	$2,500	$2,100	$1,850	$1,500

Add $1,200 per interchangeable barrel.

ODIN GRADE - .223 Rem. - .505 Gibbs cal., available in right- or left-hand Mauser style action, presentation grade walnut stock, match grade barrel, competition trigger, three position wing safety, quarter rib with banded ramped front sights, barrel band swivel, gold monogram stock oval, metal pistol grip cap, leather covered recoil pad, hand cut checkering, quick detachable scope bases and rings, engraving with gold inlays. New 2003.

MSR N/A	$11,500	$10,000	$8,500	$7,750	$6,500	$5,500	$4,150

THOR GRADE - .223 Rem. - .416 Rem. cal., right- or left-hand Mauser style action, extra fancy grade walnut stock, premium match grade barrel, competition trigger, three position wing safety, quarter rib with banded ramped front sights, barrel band swivel, metal pistol grip cap, rubber recoil pad, hand cut checkering, quick detachable scope bases and rings. New 2003.

MSR N/A	$9,200	$8,400	$7,400	$6,400	$5,500	$4,500	$3,500

TYR GRADE - .223 Rem. - .416 Rem. cal., right- or left-hand Mauser style action, fiber core or kevlar wrapped composite stock, premium match grade barrel, competition trigger, teflon all-weather coating on metal and stock, adj. rear and banded ramped front sights, three position wing safety, swivel studs, rubber recoil pad, quick detachable scope bases and rings. New 2003.

MSR N/A	$6,900	$6,200	$5,500	$4,750	$3,950	$3,250	$2,400

VOYAGER GRADE - .223 Rem. - .416 Rem. cal., Mauser style titanium action, fiber core or kevlar wrapped composite stock, premium match grade barrel, competition trigger, teflon all-weather coating on metal and stock, adj. rear and banded ramped front sights, three position wing safety, swivel studs, rubber recoil pad, quick detachable scope bases and rings. New 2003.

MSR N/A	$11,500	$10,000	$8,500	$7,750	$6,500	$5,500	$4,150

GRADING - PPGS™	100%	98%	95%	90%	80%	70%	60%

RIFLES: SxS

VIKING GRADE - most standard cals. including .30-30 WCF, .30-40 Krag, .375 Win., .444 Marlin, .45-70 Govt., as well as traditional European NE cals. up to .600 NE, built per individual custom order. New 2000.

MSR N/A	$22,550	$19,750	$16,400	$14,000	$12,000	$10,000	$8,500

NORTH AMERICAN ARMS, INC.

Current manufacturer established circa 1976, and currently located in Provo, UT. Distributor and dealer sales.

North American Arms was originally founded under the name Rocky Mountain Arms circa 1974-1975 by noted handgun entrepreneur Dick Casull. During 1976-1977, the company's name was changed to North American Arms, and it became part of the Tally Corp. of Newbury Park, CA. North American Arms was relocated from Salt Lake City to Provo, UT in 1978, and moved again in 1984 to Spanish Fork, UT. During 1986-1987, Teleflex Corp., an aerospace company, bought North American Arms' parent company, the Tally Corp. In 1992, Teleflex decided to sell off the gunmaking company, and North American Arms was purchased by Sandy Chisholm, a Teleflex employee. The company relocated again in 1994 to Provo, UT.

PISTOLS: SEMI-AUTO

In addition to many accessories being available for the Guardian Pistol Series, there is also a Guardian Custom Shop that offers consumers a customized Guardian model, with a wide variety of finish, slide, sight, grips, and serialization options. Please contact the company directly for more information on these custom shop special orders and options.

NAA .25 GUARDIAN - .25 ACP cal., similar to NAA .32 Guardian, except is smaller size, 15 oz. New 2006.

MSR $402		$355	$285	$245	$195	$165	$140	$120

NAA .32 GUARDIAN - .32 ACP cal., double action only, hammerless, stainless steel construction, 6 shot mag., 2 1/8 in. barrel, fixed low profile sights, dimpled black synthetic grips, 13 1/2 oz. New 1999.

MSR $402		$355	$285	$245	$195	$165	$140	$120

Add $28 for ILS option.

NAA .32 NAA GUARDIAN - .32 NAA cal. (.380 ACP casing necked down to .32 cal.), double action only, larger version of the NAA .32 Guardian, 2.49 in. barrel, 6 shot mag., dimpled black grips, 18.7 oz. New 2002.

MSR $449		$385	$300	$250	$195	$165	$140	$120

NAA .380 GUARDIAN - .380 ACP cal., double action only, larger version of the NAA .32 Guardian, 2.49 in. barrel, 6 shot mag., dimpled black grips, mfg. in partnership with Kahr Arms, 18.7 oz. New 2001.

MSR $449		$385	$300	$250	$195	$165	$140	$120

Add $30 for ILS option.

REVOLVERS: MINI SERIES

All NAA mini revolvers are manufactured to highest quality control standards and have halfway notches cut on the front cylinder face allowing the hammer to lock up the cylinder between cartridges. This allows the gun to be carried fully loaded without the danger of accidental discharge.

NAA .17 - .17 HMR or .17 Mach 2 cal., otherwise similar to NAA .22 Model. New 2005.

MSR $193		$155	$120	$95	$85	$75	$70	$65

Add $22 for holster grip accessory.
Add $15 for .17 HMR cal.
Add $43 for .17 HMR cal. with extra .17 Mach 2 conversion cylinder.

GRADING - PPGS™	100%	98%	95%	90%	80%	70%	60%

NAA .22 S/LR - .22 Short (new 1994) or .22 LR cal., 5 shot, single action, spur trigger, 1 1/8, 1 5/8, or 2 1/2 (disc.) in. barrel, stainless steel, plastic (disc.) or laminated rosewood grips, approx. 4 1/2 oz. New 1975.

	MSR $193	$155	$120	$95	$85	$75	$70	$65

Add $15 for 2 1/2 in. barrel (disc.).
Add $22 for holster grip accessory.
Add $39 for quick-release belt buckle option.

The optional holster grip allows the pistol to fold forward allowing concealability, safety, and has a clip which allows it to be attached to a belt.

NAA .22 MAGNUM - similar to .22 LR, except in .22 Mag. cal.

	MSR $208	$170	$130	$110	$95	$90	$85	$75

Add $18 for 2 1/2 in. barrel (disc.).
Add $21 for holster grip accessory.
Add $34 for quick-release belt buckle option.

NAA .22 MAGNUM CONVERTIBLE - similar to NAA .22 Mag., except has extra LR cylinder in pouch.

	MSR $236	$200	$170	$120	$100	$90	$85	$75

Add $18 for 2 1/2 in. barrel (disc.).
Add $22 for holster grip accessory.

NAA PUG - .22 Mag. cal., 1 in. barrel, tritium or white dot XS sight system, oversized pebble textured rubber grips, 6.4 oz. New mid-2007.

	MSR $292	$250	$215	$185	$160	$135	$120	$100

Add $20 for tritium sights.

MINI-MASTER TARGET REVOLVER - .17 HMR (new 2003), .17 Mach 2 (new 2005), .22 LR, or .22 Mag. cal., 5 shot, 4 in. heavy vent. barrel, unfluted bull cylinder, spur trigger, fixed or adj. white outline rear sight, oversize black rubber Mini-master grip, 10.7 oz. New 1990.

	MSR $272	$235	$200	$170	$135	$115	$100	$85

Add $29 for extra combo cylinder.
Add $29 for adj. rear sight (elevation only).

This model was also available in hot fuschia colored oversized grips.

MINI-MASTER BLACK WIDOW - .17 HMR (new 2003), 17 Mach 2 (new 2005), .22 LR or .22 Mag. cal., 2 in. heavy VR barrel, full size black rubber grip, fixed or adj. rear sight, unfluted cylinder, 8.8 oz. New 1991.

	MSR $258	$215	$170	$130	$105	$85	$70	$65

Add $29 for extra combo cylinder.
Add $29 for adj. rear sight (elevation only).

This model was also available in hot fuschia colored oversized grips.

NAA STANDARD SET - 3 gun set (.22 Short, .22 LR, and .22 Mag. cals.) in walnut display case with matching serial numbers, high polish finish with matte contours.

	MSR $719	$525	$455	$365	$310	$265	$225	$200

NAA DELUXE SET - 3 gun set (.22 Short, .22 LR, and .22 Mag. cals.) in walnut display case with matching serial numbers, high polish finish on entire gun.

	MSR $863	$725	$575	$425	$360	$315	$260	$225

CASED .22 MAG. - includes .22 Mag. cal. model in walnut display case with high polish finish with matte contours.

	MSR $330	$275	$200	$160	$130	$115	$95	$85

NAA SINGLE ACTION REVOLVER - .45 Win. Mag. or .450 Mag. Express cal., polished stainless steel, transfer bar safety inside the hammer, 5 shot, 7 1/2 in. barrel, walnut grips, includes presentation case. Disc. 1984.

	100%	98%	95%	90%	80%	70%	60%
Matte finish	$1,200	$950	$700	$585	$500	$415	$365
High polish finish	$1,400	$1,100	$850	$740	$620	$515	$440

GRADING - PPGS™	100%	98%	95%	90%	80%	70%	60%
Both cylinders	$1,650	$1,275	$975	$860	$700	$600	$500

Last MSR was $650.

This model was also available by special order with 10 1/2 in. barrel and optional scope. Extra cylinders were also available at $75-$100 and were fitted to the gun. A set including 2 cylinders could also be ordered. North American Arms cannot perform any repair work on .450 Mag. Express revolvers.

NORTH AMERICAN SAFARI EXPRESS

Previous trademark for those rifles (SxS) assembled by A. Francotte of Belgium for exclusive importation by Armes De Chasse located in Chadds Ford, PA.

NORTHWEST ARMS

Please refer to Wilkinson Arms listing.

NOSLER, INC.

Current rifle, ammunition, and bullet manufacturer located in Bend, OR.

John Nosler founded Nosler, Inc. in 1948, and is responsible for the development of numerous ammunition lines specializing in accuracy and dangerous game calibers.

RIFLES: BOLT ACTION

Rifle packages include scope, ltd. ed. Nosler sling, aluminum Kalispel case and two boxes of custom ammo. The serial number of the rifle matches the serial number of the scope and the case.

MODEL 48 SPORTER - .260 Rem., .270 WSM, 7mm-08 Rem., .300 WSM, .308 Win., or .325 WSM cal., features Nosler Custom push feed action, 24 in. barrel w/o sights, 3 position safety, Timney adj. trigger, ultralightweight Kevlar composite stock with Ceracote sniper grey metal coating, guaranteed 3/4 in. group at 100 yards, 6 3/4 lbs. New 2005.

MSR $2,595	$2,595	$2,325	$2,000	$1,750	$1,500	$1,250	$1,000

LIMITED EDITION SERIES - .280 Ackley Improved (Series II) or .300 WSM (Series I, limited quantities) cal., features Nosler Custom barreled action with double square bridge and integral scope mount bases, blue finish, Timney 3-position trigger, 24 in. barrel w/o sights, fancy checkered walnut stock with forend, and pistol grip, Pachmayr Decelerator recoil pad, only 500 of each series mfg. (ser. no. range 001-500), 9 lbs. New 2005.

MSR $3,995	$3,995	$3,795	$3,400	$3,100	$2,700	$2,200	$1,900

Add $200 for Series I in .300 WSM cal. (limited quantities).

The Series I rifle comes with a Leupold VXIII 2.5-8x36 scope calibrated for the Nosler ammo sold with the gun.

The Series II rifles comes with a Leupold VXIII 2.5-8x36, VXIII 3.5-10x40, or VXIII 4.5-14x40 scope, calibrated for the Nosler ammo sold with the gun.

NOWLIN MFG., INC.

Current custom handgun and components manufacturer established in 1982, and located in Claremore, OK. Dealer or consumer direct sales.

PISTOLS: SEMI-AUTO

Nowlin Mfg., Inc. manufactures a complete line of high quality M1911 A1 styled competition and defense pistols, available in 9mm Para., 9x23mm, .38 Super, .40 S&W, or .45 ACP cal. Various frame types are available, including a variety of Nowlin choices. Recent models (available in blue or nickel finish) include the NRA Bianchi Cup (approx. 1997 retail was $2,750 - disc.), 007 Compact ($1,395 - disc.), Compact X2 ($1,436 - disc.), Match Classic ($1,695), Crusader ($1,999), Avenger w/ STI frame ($2,279), Challenger ($2,049), World Cup PPC ($2,219), STI High Cap. Frame ($1,595 - disc. 1999), Mickey Fowler Signature Series ($2,187), Compact Carry ($1,695 - disc. 1999), Compact 4 1/4 in. ($1,750, .45 ACP, disc. 2002), Gladiator ($1,447 in .45 ACP cal., disc. 2002), Match Master ($2,795), Bianchi Cup Master Grade ($5,019 MSR, .38 Super cal.) and the Custom Shop Excaliber Series ($3,029). Please contact the factory directly for more information, including specific pricing (see Trademark Index).

O SECTION

O'BRIEN RIFLE CO.

Previous bolt action rifle manufacturer located in Las Vegas, NV circa 1966-1971.

Vern O'Brien manufactured high quality bolt action rifles, many of which were chambered for proprietary calibers, including the .17 Mach 4, .17 Javelina, .17-222, .17-222 Mag., and .17-223. There were basically two grades - a Field Grade with rosewood forend tip and pistol grip, and a Presentation Grade with basket weave checkering, Javelina inlaid in the stock opposite the cheekpiece, and a diamond inlaid below the action. All rifles were based on the Sako L-461 action. Circa 1971, Vern O'Brien sold his company to H&R, which produced a rifle similar to his called the 317 Ultra Wildcat. Values are hard to predict in today's marketplace because so few are encountered. A starting price range for the Field Grade is $750-$1,400, and $1,150-$2,500 for the Presentation Grade.

O.D.I. (OMEGA DEFENSIVE INDUSTRIES)

Previous manufacturer located in Midland Park, NJ circa 1981-82.

Essex Arms, located in Island Pond, VT, acquired the remaining O.D.I. Viking inventory of parts for the Viking pistol, in addition to being a components supplier (slides and receivers) for M-1911 styled pistols. Previously, Randco Manufacturing, located in Monrovia, CA, was providing service (and had parts) for these older O.D.I. pistols.

GRADING - PPGS™	100%	98%	95%	90%	80%	70%	60%

PISTOLS: SEMI-AUTO

VIKING & VIKING COMBAT - .45 ACP or 9mm Para. (advertised, but never mfg.) cal., Viking Model is Government size and the Combat Model is Commander size. All stainless steel construction, the design utilizes the Seecamp double action, teakwood grips. 5 in. barrel on the Viking Model and 4 1/4 in. barrel on the Viking Combat Model, 7 shot mag., 39 oz. Approx. 200-300 Viking Combat Models were made from kits.

	100%	98%	95%	90%	80%	70%	60%
	$495	$385	$295	$240	$210	$180	$155

Last MSR was $579.

Add $100 for slide with crossbolt safety.

OBERLAND ARMS

Current manufacturer of paramilitary style firearms located in Habach, Germany. No current U.S. importation.

Oberland Arms manufactures a wide variety of high quality paramilitary style rifles and pistols. Many options and configurations are available. Please contact the company directly for more information, including pricing, options, and U.S. availability (see Trademark Index).

OBREGON

Previously manufactured by Fabrica de Armas Mexico located in Mexico City, Mexico.

PISTOLS: SEMI-AUTO

OBREGON - 11.43mm cal., patterned somewhat after the Colt Model 1911A1, features tubular slide and Savage/Steyr type action, 1,000 pistols mfg. in Mexico for commercial sale during and after WWII, slide marked "Sistema Obregon Cal 11.43mm".

100%	98%	95%	90%	80%	70%	60%
$4,750	$4,250	$3,750	$3,250	$2,750	$2,250	$1,750

OHIO ORDNANCE WORKS, INC.

Current rifle manufacturer established in 1981, and located in Chardon, OH. Consumer direct sales.

GRADING - PPGS™	100%	98%	95%	90%	80%	70%	60%

RIFLES: SEMI-AUTO

MODEL BAR 1918A3 - .30-06 cal., patterned after the original Browning BAR (M1918A2) used during WWI, all steel construction utilizing original parts except for lower receiver, 24 in. barrel, original folding type rear sight, includes two 20 shot mags., matte metal and wood finish, Bakelite or American walnut stock and forearm, carrying handle, web sling, bipod, flash hider, bolt open hold device, 20 lbs.

MSR $3,500	$3,500	$3,150	$2,600	$2,350	$1,975	$1,650	$1,425

Add $300 for American black walnut stock and forearm.

MODEL BAR A1918 SLR - .30-06 cal., similar to Model BAR 1918A3, except does not have A3 carry handle, mfg. by Ohio Ordnance Works, Inc. 2005-2007.

	$3,100	$2,800	$2,450	$2,100	$1,800	$1,575	$1,300

Last MSR was $3,350.

Add $200 for walnut stock.

MODEL 1928 BROWNING - .30-06, 7.65mm, .308 Win., or 8mm (disc.) cal., semi-auto action patterned after the 1928 Browning watercooled machine gun, blue (disc.) or parkerized finish, includes tripod, water hose, ammo can, 3 belts, and belt loader. Limited production late 2001-2007.

	$3,750	$3,400	$3,000	$2,650	$2,300	$2,100	$1,900

Last MSR was $4,000.

Add $200 for .308 Win. or 8mm (disc.) cal.
Add approx. $2,000 for blue finish (limited mfg.).

MODEL M-240 SLR - 7.62mm cal., belt fed, gas operated, air cooled, fires from closed bolt, sling, cleaning kit, ruptured case extractor, gas regulator cleaning tool, disassembly tools, 2500 M-13 links, custom fit hard case. New 2007.

MSR $13,500	$13,500	$11,750	$9,750	$8,250	$7,500	$6,750	$6,000

MODEL VZ2000/VZ2000 SBR - 7.62x39mm cal., Czech VZ 58 copy, new milled receiver, original barrels, bakelite stocks, heat cured paint finish (matches original Czech finish), folding stock, includes four 30 shot mags., pouch, sling, cleaning kit, original bayonet.

MSR $1,125	$1,125	$950	$825	$700	$600	$500	$400

Add $125 for VZ2000 SBR.

OLD-WEST GUN CO.

Previous importer and distributor that took over the inventory of Allen Firearms after they went out of business in early 1987.

Old-West Gun Co. changed their name to Cimarron Arms in late 1987. Please refer to Cimarron Arms in this text for approximate prices on similar models from Old-West Gun Co.

OLLENDORFF, PHILIPP

Current manufacturer established during 1986, and located in Scharnitz, Austria.

Philipp Ollendorff manufactures best quality double rifles, O/U shotguns, stalking rifles, and other configurations. All guns are made to custom order, and there are many options available. Please contact the manufacturer directly for more information, including model availability and a price quotation (see Trademark Index).

OLYMPIC ARMS, INC.

Current manufacturer established during 1976, and located in Olympia, WA. Dealer direct sales.

In late 1987, Olympic Arms, Inc. acquired Safari Arms of Phoenix, AZ. As of Jan., 2004, the Safari Arms product name was discontinued, and all 1911 style products are now being manufactured in the Olympic Arms facility in Olympia, WA. Schuetzen Pistol Works is the in-house custom shop of Olympic Arms.

GRADING - PPGS™	100%	98%	95%	90%	80%	70%	60%

PISTOLS: SEMI-AUTO

Please refer to the Safari Arms section for previously manufactured pistols made under the Safari Arms trademark.

WHITNEY WOLVERINE - .22 LR cal., patterned after original Whitney Wolverine, 4 5/8 in. barrel, features lightweight polymer frame and vent. rib, marked "Olympic Arms" on side of frame, 10 shot mag., black checkered grips, 19.2 oz.

MSR $294	$260	$230	$200	$185	$170	$165	$155

ENFORCER - .45 ACP cal., 3.8 (disc.) or 4 in. bushingless bull barrel, 6 shot mag., shortened grip, available with max hard finish aluminum frame, parkerized, electroless nickel, or lightweight (disc.) anodized finishes, Triplex counter-wound self-contained spring recoil system, flat or arched mainspring housing, adj. sights, ambidextrous safety, neoprene or checkered walnut grips, 27 (lightweight model) or 35 oz.

MSR $1,039	$925	$825	$675	$575	$475	$400	$350

This model was originally called the Black Widow. After Safari Arms became Schuetzen Pistol Works, this model was changed extensively to include stainless construction, beavertail grip safety, and combat style hammer.

MATCHMASTER - similar to the Enforcer, except has 5 or 6 in. barrel and 7 shot mag. rounded (R/S) or squared off trigger guard, finer slide serrations, approx. 40 oz.

MSR $899	$775	$675	$575	$475	$425	$395	$375

Add $60 for 6 in. barrel.

BLAK-TAC MATCHMASTER - .45 ACP cal., 5 in. National Match barrel, 7 shot mag., widened and lowered ejection port, Blak-Tac treated frame and slide, low profile combat sights, adj. trigger, approx. 40 oz. New 2003.

MSR $995	$875	$775	$675	$575	$500	$450	$400

BIG DEUCE - .45 ACP cal., 6 in. longslide version of the MatchMaster, matte black slide with satin stainless steel frame, smooth walnut grips, 40.3 oz. Mfg. 1995-2004, reintroduced 2006.

MSR $1,039	$925	$825	$675	$575	$475	$400	$350

COHORT PISTOL - .45 ACP cal., features Enforcer slide and MatchMaster frame, 3.8 in. stainless steel barrel, beavertail grip safety, extended thumb safety and slide release, commander style hammer, smooth walnut grips with laser etched Black Widow logo, 37 oz. New 1995.

MSR $975	$850	$750	$650	$550	$450	$400	$350

STREET DEUCE - .45 ACP cal., M1911A1 styled frame, 5.2 in. stainless steel National Match bushingless barrel, stainless frame, steel slide, lowered and widened ejection port, 7 shot mag., diamond pattern checkered rosewood grips, 38 oz. New 2001 from Custom Shop.

MSR $1,299	$1,150	$1,000	$875	$775	$675	$575	$475

JOURNEYMAN - similar to Street Deuce, except has 4.2 in. bull barrel and 6 shot mag., 35 oz. New 2001.

MSR $1,299	$1,150	$1,000	$875	$775	$675	$575	$475

WESTERNER - .45 ACP cal., 5 in. barrel, 7 shot mag., 100% case colored finish on frame and slide, fitted barrel bushing, wide beavertail grip safety, shaped and tensioned extractor, fully adj. LPA rear sight, dovetail front blade sight, custom made laser etched smooth holly grips, 39 oz. New 2003.

MSR $1,039	$925	$825	$675	$575	$475	$400	$350

* *Westerner Trail Boss* - similar to Westerner, except has 6 in. bull barrel, 7 shot mag., laser engraved grips, 43 oz. New 2005.

MSR $1,099	$965	$850	$700	$600	$500	$400	$350

GRADING - PPGS™	100%	98%	95%	90%	80%	70%	60%

* Westerner Constable - similar to Trail Boss, except has 4 in. bull barrel, compact frame, 35 oz. New 2005.

MSR $1,159	$1,000	$875	$750	$650	$550	$450	$350

K23P - .223 Rem. cal., 6 1/2 in. steel barrel, A2 upper w/aluminum handguard, flash supressor, recoil buffer in back of frame. New 2007.

MSR $869	$785	$685	$575	$475	$400	$350	$300

Add $95 for A3 upper receiver or $144 for A3 upper w/Picatinny rail and Firsh handguard.

OA-93 PISTOL - .223 Rem. (most common, current mfg.) or 7.62x39mm (very limited mfg., disc.) cal., semi-auto, gas operated without buffer tube stock, or charging handle, 6 (most common, disc.), 6 1/2 (new 2005), 9 (disc.), or 14 (disc.) in. free-floated match threaded barrel with flash suppressor, upper receiver utilizes integral scope mount base, 30 shot mag., 4 lbs. 3 oz., approx. 500 mfg. 1993-94 before Crime Bill discontinued production, reintroduced late 2004.

MSR $1,079	$995	$875	$800	$750	$700	$650	$600

Last MSR in 1994 was $2,700.

Add $800 for 7.62x39mm cal.

OA-96 AR PISTOL - .223 Rem. cal., 6 in. barrel only, similar to OA-93 Pistol, except has pinned (fixed) 30 shot mag. and rear takedown button for rapid reloading, 5 lbs. Mfg. 1996-2000.

	$860	$775	$650	$575	$495	$450	$395

Last MSR was $860.

OA-98 PISTOL - .223 Rem. cal., skeletonized, lightweight version of the OA-93/OA-96, 6 1/2 in. non-threaded barrel, 10 shot fixed (disc.) or detachable (new 2006) mag., denoted by perforated appearance, 3 lbs. Mfg. 1998-2003, reintroduced 2005-2007.

	$995	$875	$800	$750	$700	$650	$600

Last MSR was $1,080.

RIFLES: BOLT ACTION

In 1993, Olympic Arms purchased the rights, jigs, fixtures, and machining templates for the Bauska Big Bore Magnum Mauser action. Please contact Olympic Arms (see Trademark Index) for more information regarding Bauska actions both with or without fluted barrels.

ULTRA MAG BBK-01 - various cals. between .300 Win. Mag.-.505 Gibbs, custom order rifle available with many barrel options and other special order features, price on request from the factory.

This model was formerly the Bauska BBK-02.

BOLT ACTION SAKO - various cals. between .17 Rem.-.416 Rem. Mag., 26 in. fluted barrel, various stock configurations, values represent base price with no options. Disc. 2000.

	$660	$575	$500	$450	$400	$360	$330

Last MSR was $660.

ULTRA CSR TACTICAL RIFLE - .308 Win. cal., Sako action, 26 in. broach cut heavy barrel, Bell & Carlson black or synthetic stock with aluminum bedding, Harris bipod, carrying case. Mfg. 1996-2000.

$1,450	$1,250	$1,100	$1,000	$800	$700	$600

Last MSR was $1,140.

COUNTER SNIPER RIFLE - .308 Win. cal., bolt action utilizing M-14 mags., 26 in. heavy barrel, camo-fiberglass stock, 10 1/2 lbs. Disc. 1987.

$1,300	$1,100	$975	$895	$750	$650	$600

Last MSR was $1,225.

GRADING - PPGS™	100%	98%	95%	90%	80%	70%	60%

SURVIVOR I CONVERSION UNIT - .223 Rem. or .45 ACP cal., converts M1911 variations into carbine, bolt action, collapsible stock, 16 1/4 in. barrel, 5 lbs.

	$275	$225	$195	$150	$125	$110	$95

This kit was also available for S&W and Browning Hi-Power models.

RIFLES: SEMI-AUTO

Olympic Arms is currently shipping high capacity mags. with its rifles/carbines to those states where legal.

The PCR (Politically Correct Rifle) variations listed below refer to those guns manufactured after the Crime Bill was implemented in September 1994 and through 2004. PCR rifles have smooth barrels (no flash suppressor), a 10 shot mag., and fixed stocks. Named models refer to the original, pre-ban model nomenclature.

COMPETITOR RIFLE - .22 LR cal., Ruger 10/22 action with 20 in. barrel featuring button cut rifling, Bell & Carlson thumbhole fiberglass stock, black finish and matte stainless fluted barrel, includes bipod, 6.9 lbs. Mfg. 1996-99.

	$575	$500	$450	$400	$360	$330	$300

Last MSR was $575.

ULTRAMATCH/PCR-1 - .223 Rem. cal., AR-15 action with modifications, 20 or 24 in. match stainless steel barrel, Picatinny flattop upper receiver, Williams set trigger optional, scope mounts, 10 lbs. 3 oz. New 1985.

✳ *Ultramatch PCR-1* - disc. 2004.

	$800	$725	$675	$625	$575	$525	$475

Last MSR was $1,074.

✳ *Ultramatch PCR-1P* - .223 Rem. cal., premium grade ultramatch rifle with many shooting enhancements, including Maxhard treated upper and lower receiver, 20 or 24 in. broach cut Ultramatch bull barrel, 1x10 in. or 1x8 in. rate of twist. Mfg. 2001-2004.

	$1,050	$900	$800	$700	$600	$550	$500

Last MSR was $1,299.

✳ *Ultramatch UM-1* - 20 in. stainless Ultramatch barrel with non-chromed bore, approx. 8 1/2 lbs. Disc. 1994, reintroduced late 2004.

MSR $1,150	$975	$875	$775	$700	$650	$600	$550

Last MSR in 1994 was $1,515.

✳ *Ultramatch UM-1P* - similar to UM-1 Ultramatch, except has 20 (disc. 2006) or 24 in. Ultramatch bull barrel, premium grade ultramatch rifle with many shooting enhancements, 9 1/2 lbs. New 2005.

MSR $1,559	$1,425	$1,150	$950	$825	$700	$600	$550

INTERCONTINENTAL - .223 Rem. cal., features synthetic wood-grained thumbhole buttstock and aluminum handguard, 20 in. ultramatch barrel (free floating). Mfg. 1992-93.

	$1,650	$1,350	$1,050	$875	$750	$600	$550

Last MSR was $1,371.

INTERNATIONAL MATCH - .223 Rem. cal., similar to Ultramatch, except has custom aperture sights. Mfg. 1991-93.

	$1,475	$1,150	$950	$800	$675	$575	$525

Last MSR was $1,240.

SERVICE MATCH/PCR SERVICE MATCH - .223 Rem. cal., AR-15 action with modifications, 20 in. SS Ultramatch barrel, carrying handle, standard trigger, choice of A1 or A2 flash suppressor (Service Match only), 8 3/4 lbs.

✳ *Service Match SM-1* - 9.7 lbs., disc. 1994, reintroduced late 2004.

MSR $1,099	$995	$875	$775	$700	$625	$550	$500

Last MSR in 1994 was $1,200.

GRADING - PPGS™	100%	98%	95%	90%	80%	70%	60%

✳ *Service Match SM-1P Premium Grade* - .223 Rem. cal., Maxhard upper and lower receiver, 20 in. broach cut Ultramatch super heavy threaded barrel (1 turn in 8 in. is standard), flash suppressor, 2-stage CMP trigger, Blak-Tak Armour bolt carrier assembly, Bob Jones NM interchangable rear sight system, AC4 pneumatic recoil buffer, Turner Saddlery competition sling, GI style pistol grip. New 2005.

MSR $1,493	$1,375	$1,150	$975	$850	$725	$625	$500

✳ *Service Match PCR* - disc. late 2004.

	$825	$750	$675	$625	$550	$500	$450

Last MSR was $1,062.

✳ *Service Match PCR-SMP Premium Grade* - .223 Rem. cal., Maxhard upper and lower receiver, 20 in. broach cut Ultramatch super heavy barrel (1 turn in 8 in. is standard), 2-stage CMP trigger, Blak-Tak Armour bolt carrier assembly, Bob Jones NM interchangable rear sight system, AC4 pneumatic recoil buffer, Turner Saddlery competition sling, GI style pistol grip. Mfg. 2004 only.

	$1,100	$950	$800	$700	$600	$550	$475

Last MSR was $1,613.

MULTIMATCH ML-1/PCR-2 - .223 Rem. cal., tactical short range rifle, 16 in. Ultramatch barrel with A2 upper receiver, aluminum collapsible (Multimatch ML-1) or fixed (PCR-2) stock, carrying handle, stealth vortex flash suppressor (Multimatch ML-1 only). New 1991.

✳ *Multimatch ML-1* - 7.35 lbs.

MSR $1,026	$925	$800	$725	$650	$600	$550	$500

Last MSR in 1994 was $1,200.

✳ *Multimatch PCR-2* - disc. late 2004.

	$750	$675	$600	$525	$450	$425	$400

Last MSR was $958.

MULTIMATCH ML-2/PCR-3 - .223 Rem. cal., features Picatinny flattop upper receiver with stainless steel 16 in. Ultramatch bull (new 2005) barrel, carrying handle (disc.), 5 lbs. 14 oz. New 1991.

✳ *Multimatch ML-2* - 7 1/2 lbs., disc. 1994, reintroduced late 2004.

MSR $1,026	$925	$800	$725	$650	$600	$550	$500

Last MSR in 1994 was $1,200.

✳ *Multimatch PCR-3* - disc. late 2004.

	$700	$625	$550	$500	$450	$350	$300

Last MSR was $958.

AR-15 MATCH/PCR-4 - .223 Rem. cal., patterned after the AR-15 with 20 in. barrel and solid synthetic stock, 8 lbs. 5 oz. Mfg. 1975-2004.

✳ *PCR-4*

	$730	$650	$575	$525	$475	$425	$395

Last MSR was $803.

✳ *AR-15 Match*

	$995	$875	$775	$650	$575	$495	$450

Last MSR was $1,075.

CAR-15/PCR-5 - modified AR-15 with choice of 11 1/2 (disc. 1993) or 16 in. barrel, stow-away pistol grip and collapsible stock (CAR-15 only), 7 lbs. Mfg. 1975-1998, PCR-5 reintroduced 2000-2004.

✳ *PCR-5* - .223 Rem., 9mm Para. (new 1996), .40 S&W (new 1996), or .45 ACP (new 1996) cal. Disc. 1998, reintroduced 2000-2004.

	$850	$800	$725	$650	$600	$550	$500

Last MSR was $755.

Add $45 for 9mm Para., .40 S&W, or .45 ACP cal.

GRADING - PPGS™	100%	98%	95%	90%	80%	70%	60%

* **CAR-15** - .223 Rem., 9mm Para., .40 S&W, .45 ACP, or 7.62x39mm cal.

	$960	$860	$775	$650	$575	$495	$450

Last MSR was $1,030.

Add $170 for pistol cals.

PCR-6 - 7.62x39mm cal., 16 in. barrel, post-ban only, A-2 stowaway stock, carrying handle, 7 lbs. Mfg. 1995-2002.

	$795	$725	$650	$500	$475	$425	$375

Last MSR was $870.

PCR-7 ELIMINATOR - .223 Rem. cal., similar to PCR-4, except has 16 in. barrel, 7 lbs. 10 oz. Mfg. 1999-2004.

	$750	$675	$625	$585	$540	$510	$480

Last MSR was $844.

PCR-8 - .223 Rem. cal., same configuration as the PCR-1, except has standard 20 in. stainless steel heavy bull barrel with button rifling. Mfg. 2001-2004.

	$725	$675	$640	$600	$550	$525	$500

Last MSR was $834.

* **PCR-8 Mag.** - .223 WSSM or .243 WSSM cal., otherwise similar to PCR-8. Mfg. 2004.

	$825	$750	$675	$600	$550	$500	$450

Last MSR was $1,074.

This model was also scheduled to be available in .308 Olympic Mag. and 7mm Olympic Mag. cals.

PCR-9/10/40/45 - 9mm Para., 10mm, .40 S&W, or .45 ACP cal., similar to PCR-5 Carbine except for pistol cal., A2 upper standard, 16 in. barrel, A2 buttstock, mil spec lower receiver. Mfg. 2001-2004.

	$650	$585	$535	$485	$435	$400	$375

Last MSR was $835.

PCR-16 - .223 Rem. cal., 16 in. match grade bull barrel, two-piece aluminum free-floating handguard, Picatinny receiver rail, 7 1/2 lbs. Mfg. 2003-2004.

	$650	$600	$565	$535	$500	$475	$450

Last MSR was $714.

PCR-30 - .30 Carbine cal., forged aluminum receiver with matte black anodizing, parkerized steel parts, A-2 adj. rear sight, accepts standard GI M1 .30 Carbine mags., 16 in. barrel with 1 turn in 12 in. twist, 7.15 lbs. Mfg. 2004.

	$825	$775	$725	$675	$625	$595	$550

Last MSR was $899.

PLINKER - .223 Rem. cal., similar to PCR-5, except has 16 in. button rifled barrel standard, A1 sights, cast upper/lower receiver, 100% standard mil spec parts, 7 lbs. Mfg. 2001-2004.

	$650	$595	$550	$500	$495	$450	$425

Last MSR was $598.

PLINKER PLUS - .223 Rem. cal., similar to Plinker, except has 16 or 20 in. button rifled threaded barrel with flash suppressor, A1 sights, cast upper/lower receiver, 100% standard mil spec parts, 7-8.4 lbs. New 2005.

MSR $629		$560	$515	$475	$425	$400	$385	$370

Add $150 for 20 in. barrel.

CAR-97 - .223 Rem., 9mm Para., 10mm, .40 S&W, or .45 ACP cal., similar to PCR-5, except has 16 in. button rifled barrel, A2 sights, fixed CAR stock, post-ban muzzle brake, approx. 7 lbs. Mfg. 1997-2004.

	$695	$650	$585	$530	$490	$460	$430

Last MSR was $780.

Add approx. $65 for 9mm Para., .40 S&W, or .45 ACP cal.

GRADING - PPGS™	100%	98%	95%	90%	80%	70%	60%

* *CAR-97 M4* - .223 Rem. cal., M4 configuration with contoured barrel, fixed carbine tube stock, factory installed muzzle brake, oversized shortened handguard. Mfg. 2003-2004.

	$695	$650	$600	$550	$500	$450	$400

Last MSR was $839.

Add $95 for detachable carrying handle (new 2004).

FAR-15 - .223 Rem. cal., featherweight model with lightweight 16 in. barrel, fixed collapsible stock, A1 contour lightweight button rifled barrel, 9.92 lbs. Mfg. 2001-2004.

	$625	$575	$525	$475	$425	$395	$375

Last MSR was $822.

GI-16 - .223 Rem. cal., forged aluminum receiver with black matte finish, A1 type upper receiver, parkerized steel parts, A1 adj. rear sights, 16 in. button rifled match grade barrel, collapsible stock, 6.6 - 7 lbs. Mfg. 2004, reintroduced 2006.

MSR $743		$665	$560	$500	$450	$400	$375	$350

GI-20 - .223 Rem. cal., similar to GI-16, except has 20 in. heavy barrel and A-2 lower receiver, 8.4 lbs. Mfg. 2004.

	$595	$540	$495	$450	$425	$400	$375

Last MSR was $749.

OA-93 CARBINE - .223 Rem. cal., 16 in. threaded barrel, design based on OA-93 pistol, aluminum side folding stock, flattop receiver, round aluminum handguard, Vortex flash suppressor, 7 1/2 lbs. Mfg. 1995 - civilian sales disc. 1998, reintroduced 2004-2007.

	$985	$875	$825	$750	$675	$600	$550

Last MSR in 1994 was $1,550. Last MSR in 2007 was $1,074.

* *OA-93PT Carbine* - .223 Rem. cal., aluminum forged receiver, black matte hard anodized finish, no sights, integral flattop upper receiver rail system, match grade 16 in. chromemoly steel barrel with removable muzzle brake, push button removable stock, vertical pistol grip, 7.6 lbs. Mfg. 2004 only, reintroduced 2006-2007.

	$985	$875	$825	$750	$675	$600	$550

Last MSR was $1,074.

LTF/LT-MIL4 LIGHTWEIGHT TACTICAL RIFLE - .223 Rem. cal., available in LTF (fluted) or LT-MIL4 configuration, black matte anodized receiver, Firsh type forearms with Picatinny rails, parkerized steel parts, adj. flip-up sight system, 16 in. non-chromed fluted or MIL4 threaded barrel with flash suppressor, tube style Ace FX buttstock, 6.4 lbs. New 2005.

MSR $1,097		$995	$900	$825	$750	$675	$600	$525

Add $82 for fluted barrel (LTF).

K3B CARBINE - .223 Rem. cal., 16 in. match grade chromemoly steel threaded barrel with flash suppressor, adj. A2 rear sight, A2 buttstock, adj. front post sight, optional A3 flattop receiver.

MSR $815		$750	$635	$560	$500	$465	$435	$400

Add $95 for A3 flattop receiver.

* *K3B-CAR Carbine* - similar to K3B Carbine, except has carbine length handguard and collapsible stock, approx. 6 lbs. New 2005.

MSR $839		$775	$685	$615	$550	$500	$450	$425

Add $95 for A3 upper receiver.

* *K3B-FAR Carbine* - similar to K3B Carbine, except has smaller diameter barrel and is lightweight, 5.8 lbs. New 2005.

MSR $880		$800	$715	$625	$550	$500	$450	$425

Add $95 for A3 upper receiver.

GRADING - PPGS™	100%	98%	95%	90%	80%	70%	60%

✱ *K3B-M4 Carbine* - similar to K3B Carbine, except has M4 handguard, collapsible stock, and M4 barrel, 6.3 lbs. New 2005.

MSR $899	$795	$725	$625	$550	$500	$465	$435

Add $154 for A3 upper receiver.

✱ *K3B-M4-A3-TC Carbine* - similar to K3B-M4, except is tactical carbine version with Firsh handguard, flattop upper receiver and Picatinny rail, 6.7 lbs. New 2005.

MSR $1,079	$965	$850	$750	$700	$650	$600	$550

K4B - .223 Rem. cal., 20 in. match grade chromemoly steel button rifled threaded barrel with flash supressor, adj. A2 rear sight, A2 buttstock, adj. front post sight, A2 upper receiver and handguard, 8 1/2 lbs.

MSR $839	$775	$665	$600	$550	$500	$450	$425

Add $95 for Picatinny flattop receiver and A3 detachable carry handle.

K4B-A4 - .223 Rem. cal., features 20 in. barrel with A2 flash suppressor, elevation adj. post front sight, bayonet lug, Firsh rifle length handguard with Picatinny rails, flattop receiver, 9 lbs. New 2006.

MSR $941	$850	$760	$675	$600	$550	$500	$450

K7 ELIMINATOR - .223 Rem. cal., 16 in. stainless steel threaded barrel with flash suppressor, adj. A2 rear sight, A2 buttstock, adj. front post sight, 7.8 lbs. New 2005.

MSR $844	$775	$675	$600	$550	$500	$450	$425

Add $141 for A3 upper flattop receiver and detachable carry handle.

K8 - .223 Rem. cal., 20 in stainless steel button rifled bull barrel, A2 buttstock, Picatinny flattop upper receiver, 8 1/2 lbs. New 2005.

MSR $839	$765	$650	$600	$540	$500	$450	$425

This model is marked "Target Match" on mag. well.

✱ *K8-MAG* - similar to K8, except available in .223 Rem., .243 Win., .25 WSSM, or .300 WSM (mfg. 2006) cals., and has 24 in. barrel, 9.4 lbs. New 2005.

MSR $1,186	$1,050	$875	$775	$675	$600	$550	$500

K9/K10/K40/K45 - 9mm Para. (K9), 10mm Norma (K10), .40 S&W (K40), or .45 ACP (K45) cal., blow back action, adj. A2 rear sight, 10 shot converted Uzi (10mm, .40 S&W or .45 ACP cal.) or 32 (9mm Para.) shot converted Sten detachable mag., 16 in. threaded barrel with flash suppressor, collapsible buttstock, bayonet lug, 6.7 lbs. New 2005.

MSR $869	$795	$675	$600	$535	$485	$435	$400

Add $95 for A3 upper receiver.

✱ *K9GL/K40GL* - similar to K9 Series, except available only in 9mm Para. or .40 S&W cal., lower receiver designed to accept Glock magazines, 16 in. barrel with flash suppressor, collapsible stock, does not include magazine. New 2005.

MSR $959	$875	$765	$675	$600	$550	$500	$465

Add $95 for A3 upper receiver.

K16 - .223 Rem. cal., 16 in. free floating button rifled barrel, A2 buttstock, Picatinny flattop upper receiver, 7 1/2 lbs. New 2005.

MSR $714	$650	$550	$500	$465	$435	$400	$375

K30 - .30 Carbine cal., similar to K16, except has A2 upper receiver, collapsible stock, and threaded barrel with flash suppressor, 6.6 lbs. Mfg. 2005-2006.

	$825	$700	$625	$550	$500	$450	$400

Last MSR was $905.

Add $95 for A3 upper receiver.

K30R - 7.62x39mm cal., 16 in. rifled stainless steel barrel, M4 six-point collapsible stock, A2 flash supressor, pistol grip, matte black anodized receiver, parkerized steel parts, A2 upper with adj. rear sight, 7.9 lbs. New 2007.

MSR $846	$775	$675	$600	$550	$500	$450	$425

Add $95 for A3 upper receiver.

GRADING - PPGS™	100%	98%	95%	90%	80%	70%	60%

K68 - 6.8 Rem. SPC cal., 16 in. stainless steel barrel, M4 six-point collapsible stock, A2 upper with adj. rear sight, matte black anodized receiver, parkerized steel parts, pistol grip, A2 flash supressor, 6.62 lbs. New 2007.

	MSR $905	$825	$750	$675	$600	$550	$500	$450

Add $95 for A3 upper receiver.

OMEGA

Previous trademark manufactured by Armero Specialistas Reunidas, located in Eibar, Spain, circa 1920s.

PISTOLS: SEMI-AUTO

SEMI AUTOMATIC PISTOL - 6.35mm or 7.65mm cal., "Eibar" type action, marked "Omega" on slide, 6 shot mag.

6.35 cal.	$225	$180	$130	$110	$70	$55	$40
7.65 cal.	$250	$195	$135	$115	$80	$70	$55

OMEGA FIREARMS

Previous manufacturer located in Flower Mound, TX circa 1965-1969.

RIFLES: BOLT ACTION

OMEGA III SINGLE SHOT - various cals., rotary mag., premium walnut or laminated stock. Disc. late 1960s.

$775	$650	$575	$495	$425	$360	$295

OMEGA PISTOL

Previously manufactured and distributed by Springfield Armory located in Geneseo, IL. Omega conversion kits only were available until 1996 from Safari Arms located in Olympia, WA under license from Peters-Stahl in Germany.

PISTOLS: SEMI-AUTO

OMEGA - .38 Super, 10mm Norma, or .45 ACP cal., single action, ported slide, 5 or 6 in. interchangeable ported or unported barrel with polygon rifling, special lock-up system eliminates normal barrel link and bushing, Pachmayr grips, dual extractors, adj. rear sight. Mfg. 1987-90.

$625	$560	$495	$425	$360	$295	$265

Last MSR was $849.

Add $663 for interchangeable conversion units.
Add $336 for interchangeable 5 or 6 in. barrel (including factory installation).
Each conversion unit includes an entire slide assembly, one mag., 5 or 6 in barrel, recoil spring guide mechanism assembly, and factory fitting.

OMEGA RIFLES/SHOTGUNS

Previous trademark of select rifles/shotguns imported by K.B.I., Inc. located in Harrisburg, PA, until 1994.

RIFLES

To date, there has been little collector interest for Omega rifles. Values are mostly determined by the shooting value rather than collector value.

SHOTGUNS

STANDARD O/U - 12, 20 (disc.), 28 (disc.) ga., or .410 (disc) bore, boxlock action, folding design, SNT, 26 or 28 in. VR barrels, extractors, checkered walnut stock and forearm, 5 1/2-7 lbs. Disc. 1994.

$425	$330	$295	$260	$230	$200	$180

GRADING - PPGS™	100%	98%	95%	90%	80%	70%	60%

✳ *Deluxe O/U* - 12 ga. only, similar to Standard Model except has better walnut. Importation disc. 1990.

	$335	$290	$255	$220	$185	$160	$140

Last MSR was $379.

STANDARD SxS - 20, 28 ga., or .410 bore, boxlock action, folding design, double triggers, hardwood stock and forearm, 26 in. barrels, extractors, 5 1/2 lbs. Disc. 1989.

	$190	$165	$140	$120	$110	$100	$90

Last MSR was $229.

> Add $40 for 28 ga. or .410 bore.

✳ *Deluxe SxS* - .410 bore only, similar to Standard Model except has better walnut. Disc. 1989.

	$200	$185	$170	$155	$140	$130	$120

Last MSR was $249.

SINGLE BARREL - 12, 20 ga., or .410 bore, various barrel lengths, matte blue finish, extractor. Importation disc. 1987.

	$85	$75	$65	$55	$45	$40	$35

Last MSR was $95.

STANDARD FOLDING SINGLE BARREL - 12, 16, 20, 28 ga., or .410 bore, 28 or 30 in. barrel, checkered hardwood stock, matte chrome receiver, approx. 5 1/2 lbs. Importation disc. 1987.

	$160	$135	$115	$100	$85	$70	$65

Last MSR was $180.

DELUXE FOLDING SINGLE BARREL - 12, 16, 20, 28 ga., or .410 bore, similar to Standard Model, except has checkered walnut stock and forearm, blue receiver. Importation disc. 1987.

	$195	$160	$135	$115	$100	$85	$70

Last MSR was $220.

OMEGA WEAPONS SYSTEMS INC.

Current shotgun manufacturer established circa 1998, and located in Tucson, AZ. Distributed by Defense Technology, Inc., located in Lake Forest, CA.

SHOTGUNS: SEMI-AUTO

OMEGA SPS-12 - 12 ga. only, 2 3/4 in. chamber, features gas operation and 5 shot detachable mag., 20 in. barrel, protected ghost ring sights, synthetic stock (with or w/o pistol grip) and forearm, 9 lbs. New 1998.

MSR $225	$195	$180	$165	$150	$135	$125	$115

OMNI

Previous manufacturer located in Riverside, CA 1992-1998. During 1998, Omni changed its name to E.D.M. Arms. Previously distributed by First Defense International located in CA.

RIFLES: BOLT ACTION

LONG ACTION SINGLE SHOT - .50 BMG cal., competition single shot, chromemoly black finished receiver, 32-34 in. steel or stainless steel barrel with round muzzle brake, benchrest fiberglass stock, designed for FCSA competition shooting, 32 lbs. Mfg. 1996-98.

	$3,200	$2,800	$2,500	$2,150	$1,800	$1,500	$1,250

Last MSR was $3,500.

> Add $400 for painted stock (disc. 1996).

GRADING - PPGS™	100%	98%	95%	90%	80%	70%	60%

SHELL HOLDER SINGLE SHOT - similar to Long Action Single Shot, except has fiberglass field stock with bipod, 28 lbs. Mfg. 1997-98.

	$2,525	$2,150	$1,800	$1,500	$1,250	$1,100	$925

Last MSR was $2,750.

MODEL WINDRUNNER - .50 BMG cal., long action, single shot or 3 shot mag., 1-piece I-beam, chromemoly black finished receiver, 36 in. barrel with round muzzle brake, fiberglass tactical stock, 35 lbs. Mfg. 1997-98.

	$6,950	$6,425	$5,875	$5,325	$4,750	$4,175	$3,500

Last MSR was $7,500.

Add $750 for 3 shot repeater.

MODEL WARLOCK - .50 BMG or 20mm cal., single, 3 (20mm), or 5 (.50 BMG) shot fixed mag., fiberglass field stock, massive design chromemoly black finished receiver, muzzle brake, 50 lbs. Mfg. 1997-98.

	$10,750	$8,950	$7,750	$6,750	$5,500	$4,750	$3,950

Last MSR was $12,000.

E.D.M. ARMS MODEL 97 - available in most cals. up to .308 Win., single shot or repeater (cals. .17 Rem. through .223 Rem. only), wire-cut one-piece design, black tactical stock with pillar-bedded chromemoly barrel, black finished receiver, unique trigger with safety, 9 lbs. Mfg. 1997-98.

	$2,525	$2,150	$1,800	$1,500	$1,250	$1,100	$925

Last MSR was $2,750.

E.D.M. ARMS WINDRUNNER WR50 - .50 BMG cal., sniper rifle, 5 shot mag., removable tactical adj. stock, take-down action w/ removable barrel, wire-cut one-piece receiver, titanium muzzle brake, blackened chromemoly barrel, approx. 29 lbs. Mfg. 1998 only.

	$11,750	$10,250	$9,500	$8,250	$7,000	$5,750	$4,500

Last MSR was $12,900.

OPTIMA

Current trademark of O/U shotguns manufactured by Hatsan Arms Company, located in Izmir, Turkey. No current U.S. importation.

OPUS SPORTING ARMS, INC.

Previous manufacturer located in Long Beach, CA.

RIFLES: BOLT ACTION

OPUS ONE - .243 Win., .270 Win., or .30-06 cal., U.S.R.A. Co. Model 70 action, 24 in. barrel, deluxe checkered walnut stock with ebony forend cap, 6 3/4 lbs., Halliburton cased. Mfg. 1987-88 only.

	$2,350	$1,995	$1,675	$1,250	$1,000	$875	$795

Last MSR was $2,700.

OPUS TWO - similar to Opus One, except in 7mm Rem. Mag. or .300 Win. Mag. cal., 7 1/4 lbs., cased. Mfg. 1987-88 only.

	$2,350	$2,050	$1,705	$1,300	$1,000	$875	$795

Last MSR was $2,700.

OPUS THREE - similar to Opus Two, except in .375 H&H or .458 Win. Mag. cal., 10 1/4 lbs., cased. Mfg. 1987-88 only.

	$2,600	$2,275	$1,800	$1,375	$1,050	$900	$825

Last MSR was $2,850.

OREGON ARMS

Please refer to the Chipmunk Rifles, Inc. section.

GRADING - PPGS™	100%	98%	95%	90%	80%	70%	60%

ORTGIES PISTOLS

Previous trademark of pistols manufactured by Deutsche Werke A.G. located in Erfurt, Germany.

PISTOLS: SEMI-AUTO

VEST POCKET AUTOMATIC - .25 ACP cal., 6 shot, 2 3/4 in. barrel, blue or nickel finish, fixed sights, wood grips. Mfg. 1921-28.

	$325	$225	$175	$150	$130	$115	$100

POCKET AUTOMATIC - .32 ACP cal. (8 shot) mfg. 1920-1928 or .380 ACP cal. (7 shot) mfg. 1922-1926, 3 1/4 in. barrel, blue or nickel finish, fixed sights, wood grips.

	$300	$225	$175	$150	$130	$115	$100

Add 20% for .380 ACP cal. or double safety variation.

ORVIS

Current catalog retailer and importer of private label subcontracted shotguns located in Manchester, VT and many other locations.

Orvis imports various shotguns under subcontract with various international manufacturers, including Arrieta and Caesar Guerini. Typical custom order delivery time is 2-8 months. Most of these private label models will approximate the values of the equivalent model manufactured by the subcontractor unless there are additional features and/or options which will add to the value.

SHOTGUNS: O/U

SKB GREEN MOUNTAIN UPLANDER (MODEL 555) - 12, 20, 28 ga., or .410 bore, 25-27 in. barrels, blue frame, straight stock with leather covered recoil pad. Disc.

	$750	$675	$600	$550	$500	$450	$400

Last MSR was $995.

Add 15% for 28 ga. or .410 bore.

UPLANDER SERIES - 12 (disc. 1998), 20, or 28 ga., boxlock action, 26 in. barrels with choke tubes (except 28 ga.), SST, straight grip, select American black walnut with 24 LPI checkering, leather covered recoil pad since 1992, 6-7 lbs. Mfg. by P. Beretta of Italy.

MSR N/A	N/A	$2,450	$2,000	$1,550	$1,200	$995	$875

Add $1,250 for 28/20 ga. combo with case.

WATERFOWLER - 12 ga. only, 3 in. chambers, matte metal finish, 28 in. barrels with choke tubes, steel shot compatible, 7 1/2 lbs. Mfg. by P. Beretta of Italy.

MSR N/A	N/A	$2,650	$2,150	$1,650	$1,250	$1,025	$900

SPORTING CLAYS - 12 ga. only, 30 in. vented barrels with VR and choke tubes, adj. trigger, oil finished checkered walnut stock and forearm. New 1994.

MSR N/A	N/A	$2,550	$2,000	$1,550	$1,175	$995	$875

This model is also available in a women's configuration in 20 ga. with lightweight frame - includes carrying case.

SUPER FIELD - 12 or 20 ga., 26 (Uplander 20 ga. only), 28 (All Rounder), or 30 (Sporting Clays) in. VR barrels, configurations include Uplander 20 ga. with straight grip stock, All Rounder 12 ga. with 28 in. barrels and pistol grip stock, and Sporting Clays 12 ga. with 30 in. barrels, wide rib, and pistol grip stock, blue receiver, choke tubes, mfg. in Italy. Limited importation 1995 only.

	$1,495	$1,250	$1,000	$875	$750	$625	$500

Last MSR was $2,150.

GRADING - PPGS™	100%	98%	95%	90%	80%	70%	60%

PREMIER GRADE - 12 or 20 ga., 3 in. chambers, 20 ga. features 28 in. barrels with straight grip stock, 12 ga. features pistol grip stock, select oil-finished European stock and forearm, choke tubes, blue frame with scrolled engraving, adj. trigger, cased, mfg. in Belgium 1995-98.

	$6,450	$5,875	$5,250	$4,675	$4,000	$3,450	$2,675

Last MSR was $6,450.

Add $100 for Premier Grade Sporting.
This model is also available as a 20 ga. Superlight with straight grip stock and 26 in. barrels.

ORVIS DELUXE GRADE - similar to Uplander and Waterfowler, except has engraved bird scenes and scroll work on antique coin-finished receiver, deluxe checkered walnut stock and forearm, case. Imported 1993-94 only.

	$4,250	$3,575	$2,950	$2,300	$1,900	$1,500	$1,275

Last MSR was $4,950.

RUGER/ORVIS MODEL - 12 or 20 ga., 3 in. chambers, Red Label Ruger action with customized Orvis features including blue receiver and straight grip English checkered stock. Disc. 1993.

	$1,295	$975	$850	$725	$600	$495	$450

Last MSR was $1,295.

SHOTGUNS: SxS

WATERFOWLER - 12 ga. only, 3 in. chambers, matte metal finish, 28 in. barrels with choke tubes, 7 3/4 lbs. Mfg. by P. Beretta of Italy until 1993.

	$1,950	$1,725	$1,475	$1,125	$950	$825	$700

Last MSR was $1,950.

CUSTOM UPLANDER - 12, 16, 20, 28 ga., or .410 bore, traditional frame, 25 or 27 in. barrels only, case colored or blue sidelock action with light engraving, DT, custom ordered gun, mfg. by Arrieta located in Spain.

MSR N/A	N/A	$2,525	$2,250	$1,950	$1,650	$1,450	$1,025

Add $950 for SNT.
Add $1,200 for extra set of barrels (same ga.).

FINE GRADE - 12, 16, 20, 28 ga., or .410 bore, custom ordered gun, custom order barrel lengths, sidelock action, DT, mfg. by Arrieta located in Spain. Disc. 1999.

	$4,650	$3,775	$3,150	$2,500	$1,995	$1,500	$1,150

Last MSR was $4,650.

Add $950 for SNT.
Add $1,950 for extra set of barrels (same ga.).

ROUNDED ACTION - similar to Fine Grade, except sidelock action has rounded corners and finer engraving (100% coverage) and wood upgrade, leather cased, mfg. by Arrieta located in Spain.

MSR N/A	N/A	$5,550	$4,250	$3,775	$3,300	$2,550	$1,995

* *Rounded Action Uplander* - similar to Rounded Action, except has less engraving, blue or case hardened frame. New 2000.

MSR N/A	N/A	$4,450	$3,950	$3,500	$3,000	$2,500	$2,000

P SECTION

P.A.F.

Previous manufacturer located in S. Africa. P.A.F. stands for Pretoria Arms Factory.

GRADING - PPGS™	100%	98%	95%	90%	80%	70%	60%

PISTOLS: SEMI-AUTO

.25 ACP PISTOL - .25 ACP cal., patterned after the Baby Browning, blue finish. Approx. 10,000 mfg.

	100%	98%	95%	90%	80%	70%	60%
	$300	$275	$250	$235	$225	$200	$180

P.A.W.S., INC.

Previous manufacturer located in Salem, OR. Distributor and dealer sales. Previously distributed by Sile Distributors, Inc. located in New York, NY.

CARBINES

ZX6/ZX8 CARBINE - 9mm Para. or .45 ACP cal., semi-auto paramilitary design carbine, 16 in. barrel, 10 or 32* shot mag., folding metal stock, matte black finish, aperture rear sight, partial barrel shroud, 7 1/2 lbs. Mfg. 1989-2004.

	100%	98%	95%	90%	80%	70%	60%
	$715	$635	$550	$475	$375	$300	$250

The ZX6 is chambered for 9mm Para., while the ZX8 is chambered for .45 ACP.

PGW DEFENCE TECHNOLOGIES, INC.

Current manufacturer established in 1992, and located in Winnipeg, Manitoba, Canada. Previous company name was Prairie Gun Works until 2003. Currently imported by LBVG, located in Glasgow, MT.

RIFLES: BOLT ACTION

PGW manufactures approx. 50-60 guns annually. They also sell their actions separately for $400-$2,300, depending on caliber and configuration.

M-15 Ti ULTRA LITE - various cals., titanium (denoted by "Ti" model suffix) or re-machined Rem. 700 (disc.) short action, 20 in. barrel, Kevlar stock with glass bedding, matte metal finish, approx. 4 1/2-6 1/4 lbs. New 1996.

MSR N/A	$2,650	$2,300	$2,000	$1,750	$1,750	$1,525	$1,375

Subtract $300 for benchrest or varmint single shot.
Add $100 for tactical stainless.
Add $200 for stainless steel (disc.).
Add $120 for Ultra Lite muzzle brake (disc.).
Add $200 for teflon black finish.
Add $100 for electroless nickel plating (disc.).

This model is also available in a hunter tactical configuration (Model M-15 Ti/HT) at no extra charge.

M-18 Ti ULTRA LIGHT - most long action cals. to .340 Wby. Mag., titanium or re-machined Rem. Model 700 long (disc.) action, 22 in. barrel, matte metal finish, approx. 4 3/4 lbs. New 1996.

MSR N/A	$2,650	$2,300	$2,000	$1,750	$1,750	$1,525	$1,375

Subtract $300 for single shot.
Add $100 for stainless steel.
Add $200 for teflon black finish.
Add $120 for Ultra Lite muzzle brake (disc.).
Add $100 for electroless nickel plating (disc.).

TIMBERWOLF - .338 Win. or .408 Cheyenne cal., titanium or stainless steel construction, adj. trigger, 5 shot mag., custom teflon finish, single shot or repeater, various barrel lengths and stock configurations.

MSR N/A	$5,200	$4,700	$4,250	$3,650	$3,000	$2,400	$1,800

GRADING - PPGS™	100%	98%	95%	90%	80%	70%	60%

COYOTE - .308 Win. cal., titanium or stainless steel construction, adj. trigger, 5 shot mag., custom teflon finish, single shot or repeater, match grade fluted barrel, various barrel lengths and stock configurations.

MSR N/A	$3,450	$3,100	$2,800	$2,500	$2,250	$1,950	$1,750

LRT-2 (PGW/GIBBS) - various large cals. starting with .378, designed for dangerous game, 4 1/2 in. mag. box, one piece bolt, Sako type extraction, choice of Safari style or A-2 stock, 10-18 lbs. New 1999.

MSR N/A	$2,625	$2,350	$1,950	$1,750	$1,500	$1,250	$1,000

Add $100 for A-2 stock.
Add $725 for .408 Cheyenne cal.

LRT-3 (PGW/GIBBS) - .50 BMG cal., single shot action, Big Mac stock. New 1999.

MSR N/A	$4,150	$3,700	$3,400	$3,100	$2,800	$2,500	$2,250

PKP, INC.

Previous manufacturer and distributor located in Tempe, AZ. Dealer or consumer direct sales.

PISTOLS

POWELL KNIFE PISTOL MR-38 - .38 Spl., unique knife-pistol design allows barrel to be incorporated into the upper rear portion of the break-action blade assembly, 1 3/4 in. barrel, stainless steel with wood handles, 17 oz. Limited mfg. 1997-98.

	$415	$350	$275	$225	$195	$165	$140

Last MSR was $450.

P.S.M.G. GUN COMPANY

Previous manufacturer located in Arlington, MA.

PISTOLS: SEMI-AUTO

SIX IN ONE SUPREME - .22 LR, 7.65mm Luger, .38 Super, .38 Spl., 9mm Para., or .45 ACP cal., single action, 3 1/4, 5, or 7 1/2 in. barrel with solid cooling rib, adj. rear sight, limited mfg. Mfg. 1988-89.

	$700	$600	$500	$450	$400	$365	$330

Last MSR was $895.

Add $20-$55 for caliber options.
Add $25 for 7 1/2 in. barrel.
Add $35 for satin nickel plating.
Add $225 per extra barrel.
Add $450 per individual conversion unit.

P.V. NELSON, (GUNMAKERS)

Please refer to the N section for this manufacturer.

PTK INTERNATIONAL, INC.

Previous distributor located in Atlanta, GA.

Please refer to listing under Poly-Technologies in this section.

P.38 MILITARY & COMMERCIAL PISTOLS

Previously manufactured P.38s from various German companies circa 1938-1946, including Mauser (byf code), Spreewerke (cyq code), and Walther (AC code). See French military section for late war/post-war French mfg. (svw code and star proof). Also includes Walther post-war mfg. and recent conversions fabricated by John Martz.

Also See: CZ, Fabrique Nationale, Luger, Mauser, and Walther for other German military pistols.

GRADING - PPGS™	100%	98%	95%	90%	80%	70%	60%

PISTOLS: SEMI-AUTO, CIRCA 1938-1946

Subtract 40%-50% on most common P.38s if recently imported and/or refinished by importer. Add 75% for two Walther matching magazines where applicable. Beware of fakes or post-war re-numbering.

AP "ARMEE PISTOLE" - 9mm Para. cal., concealed hammer prototype from 1936, approx. 50 handmade examples, each one different in some details, walnut checkered grips.

Extreme rarity precludes accurate pricing on this model. However, examples seen at auctions have been priced at $35K-$45K.
Add 30% for dural finish.
Add 30% for matching mag.
Add 30% for slotted milling for stock.

PROTOTYPE HP "HEERES PISTOLE" & FIRST MODEL P.38 - 7.65mm or 9mm Para. cal., first experimental production, ser. numbered 1010-1050, many different configurations, some have acid etched "PRIVAT" markings on receiver, checkered takedown lever, thick safety lever, rectangular firing pin, thin rear sight.

Extreme rarity precludes accurate pricing. Auction pricing indicates $10,000 - $15,000.
Add 30% for 7.65mm cal.
Add 30% for matching mag. (rare).
Add 100% for factory short barrel (sleeved but not proofed).
Add 50% for Mod. P.38 designation.

This production range has only the short barrel variation to be authenticated (1029, 7.65mm, Mod. P.38). Most surviving prototypes are in poor condition due to GI use as a shooter after the war, and most mint examples are fakes.

HP "HEERES PISTOLE" - 9mm Para. cal., early Walther commercial production begins at 1050, high polish until approx. 13000 ser. no. range beginning at 1050, approx. 24000 mfg. 1938-1944.

It is recommended that early variations are evaluated and priced by an expert. Watch for fakes.

✱ *HP "Heeres Pistole" Experimental "Concealed Extractor"* - 7.65mm or 9mm Para., first experimental production ser. range 1050 - approx. 1080, handmade high polish finish, approx. 20 mfg. Rarely seen in U.S. market.

N/A	$12,000	$10,000	$8,000	$7,000	$6,000	$5,000

Add 20% for 7.65mm Para. cal.
Add 30% for dural aluminum frame.

✱ *HP "Heeres Pistole" "Swedish" HP* - experimental first production HP for Swedish trials, ser. range H1001-H2065, "H" prefix, rectangular firing pin and crown/N proofs, thin sight, thick safety lever, high polish, handmade craftsmanship.

$3,300	$3,000	$2,500	$2,100	$1,700	$1,500	$1,100

Add 30% for rare matched magazines.
Subtract 20% for 2nd variation (without "H" prefix) ser. range 2065-2600.

✱ *HP "Heeres Pistole" Standard HP Production* - ser. range 2080-approx. 24000, high polish finish until approx. ser. no. 13000 - then changed to military blue (1942).

$2,500	$2,100	$1,900	$1,400	$1,200	$1,100	$995

Add 20% for Nazi eagle over 359 (E/359) military proof.
Add 20% for high polish finish.
Add 300% for alloy frame, ser. range 6850-6950.

✱ *HP "Heeres Pistole" 7.65mm Para HP Production* - 7.65mm Para cal., single or double action, very limited mfg., rarest collector category for standard production P.38s, ser. no. range 3000-3200.

N/A	$14,000	$11,500	$10,000	$8,500	$7,000	$6,000

Add 100% for single action with long tang and target sights.

GRADING - PPGS™	100%	98%	95%	90%	80%	70%	60%

✳ *HP "Heeres Pistole" Late War Mod. P.38 Production* - marked "MOD P38" on left slide, rough military blue finish, some frames show heavy tool marks, ser. range 24150-25990.

	$2,800	$2,600	$2,100	$1,700	$1,500	$1,200	$1,050

ZERO-SERIES - 9mm Para. cal., features Walther banner, high polish finish, black checkered grips, up to 5-digit number w/o suffix. Mfg. 1940, ser. no. range 01-013714.

✳ *Zero Series - 1st Issue* - internal extractor, square firing pin, ser. range 01-01000.

	N/A	$9,000	$7,000	$5,000	$4,000	$2,500	$2,000

  Add 30% for matching mag.

✳ *Zero Series - 2nd Issue* - external extractor, thin slide, square firing pin, ser. range 02005-03478, more difficult to find than 1st Issue.

	N/A	$7,500	$5,000	$4,500	$3,200	$1,800	$1,500

  Add 30% for matching mag.

✳ *Zero Series - 3rd Issue* - external extractor, round firing pin, ser. no. range 03520-013714, after ser. no. 10000, some models had brown military style grips, baseline for military P.38s to follow.

	N/A	$3,000	$2,600	$2,200	$1,600	$1,400	$1,000

  Add 20% for matching mag.

P.38 - 9mm Para. cal., double action, 5 in. barrel, 8 shot mag., fixed sights, brown or black composite grips, blue finish. Many variations exhibiting a variety of metal finishes and codings, 34 oz. Over 1,000,000 manufactured during WWII.

Based on the prototype "Armee Pistol" from 1936, this model was adopted as the standard service pistol of the German Military in 1938 and refined in the "Zero Series". The P.38 was manufactured by Walther - code "480" and "ac" (mfg. April 1940-1945), Mauser - code "byf" and "svw" (mfg. late 1942-1945), and Spreewerke - "cyq" and "cvq" (mfg. 1942-1945). The finish on most WWII 1942 and Later P.38s is not of the same quality as the pre-war and early war Walther guns with the Spreewerke models being the poorest.

✳ *480 Code First Military Contract* - 9mm Para. cal. "480" code replaces Walther banner on slide, approx. 7,200 mfg. with ser. range 1-7374, rare in any condition above 90%. Production started April 1940. "480" code changed to "ac" approx. October 1940.

	N/A	$6,000	$5,200	$4,200	$2,800	$2,100	$1,500

  Add 20% for matching mag.

ac-NO DATE (UNDATED) - 9mm Para. cal., "ac" (Walther code) appears on slide without date, "ac" on left triggerguard, 2,620 mfg. with ser. range 7,384-9,912, rarest military coded P.38, rarely encountered in 90% or better original condition.

	N/A	$7,000	$6,000	$5,000	$4,000	$3,000	$2,500

  Add 20% for matching mag.

✳ *ac-40 Surcharge* - 9mm Para. cal., hand pantographed or stamped "40" date added underneath "ac" code after the slide was blued, ser. range. 9988-5942a, 6,000 mfg., high polish, rare in any condition above 90%.

	N/A	$3,600	$3,200	$2,500	$2,000	$1,500	$1,000

  Add 20% for matching mag.

✳ *ac-40 Standard* - 9mm Para. cal., machined stamped, "40" indicates 1940 mfg., approx. 10,000 mfg., ser. range 5942a-9965b.

	$2,600	$2,400	$2,100	$1,700	$1,350	$1,100	$850

  Add 20% for matching mag.

GRADING - PPGS™	100%	98%	95%	90%	80%	70%	60%

* *ac-41 1st and 2nd Variation* - 9mm Para. cal., last military high polish P.38s, only 1st var. has "ac" on left trigger guard (ser. range 1-4833b), 2nd var. continues to serial no. 4527i.

	$2,300	$1,800	$1,400	$1,100	$750	$550	$500

Add 20% for matching mag.

* *ac-41 3rd Variation* - 9mm Para. cal., standard (dull) military blue finish over un-polished metal surface begins, ser. range. approx. 5015i-9973j.

	$1,450	$1,200	$950	$700	$600	$500	$450

Add 20% for matching mag.

* *ac-42 1st and 2nd Variations* - 9mm Para. cal., dull military finish, serial range 1-9197k, ac-42 1st var. last P.38 to have E/359 stamped small parts and serialized magazine. Serialized mag. stop at approx. 9500c.

	$1,075	$975	$800	$575	$475	$425	$400

Add 25% for 1st variation.
Add 20% for matching mag.

* *ac-43, ac-44 and ac-45 Standard Issue* - 9mm Para. cal., dull military finish, letters are followed by two digit code corresponding to year of mfg. 1943, 44 and 45. Early two-line "stacked" codes are more desirable than later single line models, except for ac-43 3rd var. Highest P.38 production occurred in 1943 and 1944.

	$850	$750	$650	$575	$500	$450	$425

Add 15% for ac-43 single line code.
Add 20% for fnh marked barrel.
Add 30% for FN frame (marked with "MI" or E/140).
Add 20% for ac-45 all matching "c" block.
Deduct 20% for ac-45 "c" block mismatch (one E/359 slide stamp).
FN slide (ac-43 or ac-44). Extreme rarity precludes accurate pricing. Approx. 200-250 assembled.

* *ac-45 0-Series* - 9mm Para. cal., late war 0-Series with rough milled finish, ser. range 025960-027659. Serialized in commercial manner.

	$2,500	$2,200	$1,800	$1,250	$1,000	$800	$650

byf-42 STANDARD ISSUE - 9mm Para. cal., "byf" (Mauser code) appears on slide, 9mm Para cal., dull military finish, ser. range 1-4783a. Some very early pistols have eagle 135 (E/135) stamped on five small parts (trigger, hammer, etc.)

	$1,800	$1,500	$1,2000	$1,000	$800	$600	$500

Add 30% for early E/135 proofed parts.

byf-43 & byf-44 STANDARD ISSUE - 9mm Para. cal., dull military finish, byf-43 ser. range 1-approx. 6500q, byf-44 9000p-10000z and 1-approx. 5000e (overlap with svw-45)

	$850	$750	$650	$575	$500	$450	$425

Add 10% for mixed E/135 and E/WaA135 acceptance stamps.
Add 100% for mixed blue and phosphate finish major components, also known as "Dual Tone".
Add 150% for Mauser assembly with FN slide (marked ac-43 or ac-44 with E/WaA135 stamps).
Add 25% for byf-44 with all E/135 acceptance stamps.

byf-43 & byf-44 POLICE ISSUE - 9mm Para. cal., dull military finish, eagle over "L" (E/L) or eagle over "F" (E/F) acceptance and commercial eagle over "N" (E/N) proof stamps, unique ser. range 1-7600.

	$2,400	$2,200	$1,800	$1,500	$1,000	$800	$600

Add 20% for byf-43 E/L.
Add 50% for FN slide (ac-43 or ac44 marked).
Add 20% for byf-44 E/F.

GRADING - PPGS™	100%	98%	95%	90%	80%	70%	60%

svw-45 STANDARD ISSUE - 9mm Para. cal., "svw" (Mauser code) appears on slide, 9mm Para. cal., Nazi proofed only, most with dual tone finish, few all blue (rare) or all gray.

	$2,400	$2,150	$1,700	$1,300	$950	$750	$650

> Add 20% for all blue or all gray phosphate finish.

* **svw-45 Police Issue** - 9mm Para. cal., dull military finish, E/F acceptance and E/N proof stamps.

> Extreme rarity precludes accurate pricing. It is recommended that this variation is evaluated and priced by an expert. Watch for fakes.

cyq STANDARD ISSUE - 9mm Para. cal., "cyq" (Spreewerke code) appears on slide, 9mm Para. cal., dull military finish, eagle over "88" (E/88) acceptance, variation typically exhibits rough machining with visible circular milling marks, ser. range 1-approx. 9500z, no year dates are used by Spreewerke.

	$750	$675	$600	$525	$475	$450	$425

> Add 100% for E/359 small parts (very few noted during initial production).
> Add 15% for early features (early frame and secondary extractor cut), ser. range 1 - approx. 1000d.
> Add 100% for FN frame (marked with "MI" or E/140).

* **cvq Standard Issue Later Production** - 9mm Para. cal., dull military finish, E/88 acceptance, ser. range approx. 9500z-10000z and a1-approx. b5000

	$750	$675	$600	$550	$475	$450	$425

> Add 30% for "A" or "B" serial prefix.

* **cyq Zero Series** - 9mm Para. cal., dull military finish, E/88 acceptance, ser. range 01-approx. 08000.

	$1,400	$1,200	$900	$650	$525	$475	$425

> Add 50% for Spreewerke assembly with FN slide (marked ac-43 or ac-44 with E/88 stamps).

PISTOLS: SEMI-AUTO, WALTHER POST-WAR MFG.

MODEL P38 - post-war version of P38 Military, .22 LR, .7.65mm Luger, or 9mm Para. cal., 5 in. barrel, 8 shot, alloy frame, matte black finish, 28 oz. W. German manufacture. Mfg. began 1956, currently imported into the U.S. by Earl's Repair Service. See German WWII Military Pistols for wartime listings.

	$800	$600	$500	$375	$325	$275	$225

> Add approx. $400 for .22 LR conversion kit.

Note: Due to the release of large numbers of W. German Police and Army trade-ins of P.38 9mm Para. and PP .32 ACP cal. models, the actual value of original models in 90% or less condition has decreased somewhat. The two models most affected are the P-1 variation of the P.38, and the German PP in .32 ACP cal.

* **Model P38 Long Barrel Special Edition** - 9mm Para. cal., steel frame, 6, 7, or 8, in. barrel, wood grips, 50 mfg. 1988.

	$3,950	$3,400	$2,800	N/A	N/A	N/A	N/A

* **Model P38 Steel Frame** - .22 LR, 7.65mm Luger or 9mm Para. cal., similar to regular P.38, except has steel frame, 34 oz. Imported 1987-89 only, and in limited quantities.

	$1,350	$975	$700	$575	$465	$385	$335

> *Last MSR was $1,400.*

> Add 30% for 7.65mm Luger cal.
> Add 40% for German-marked frame with high polish finish.

* **Model P38 in .22 LR Cal.** - disc. 1989.

	$1,050	$700	$550	$475	$375	$325	$225

> *Last MSR was $1,050.*

MODEL P38 II - similar to the Standard P.38, except has reinforced slide.

	$750	$575	$450	$375	$325	$275	$225

GRADING - PPGS™	100%	98%	95%	90%	80%	70%	60%

MODEL P38K - 7.65mm Luger or 9mm Para. cal., shortened 2.8 in. barrel variation of P.38, front sight on slide, adj. rear sight, 27.9 oz. 3,000 mfg. 1974-81.

	100%	98%	95%	90%	80%	70%	60%
	$875	$750	$625	$500	$425	$350	$275

Add 30% for 7.65mm Luger cal.

MODEL P38 SPECIAL EDITIONS/ENGRAVED

✳ *Model P38 50th Year Commemorative* - 9mm Para. cal., steel frame, carved grips, presentation engraved with deluxe walnut presentation case. Introduced 1987, inventory depleted 1992.

	100%	98%	95%	90%	80%	70%	60%
	$2,450	$1,825	$1,300	N/A	N/A	N/A	N/A

Last MSR was $950.

✳ *Model P38 HP 60th Year Commemorative* - 9mm Para. or 7.65mm (.30 Luger) cal., special production, steel frame, high polish, wood grips, includes wood presentation case. Approx. 100 mfg. in each caliber. Mfg. 1998.

	100%	98%	95%	90%	80%	70%	60%
	$2,425	$1,800	$1,300	N/A	N/A	N/A	N/A

Add 10% for 7.65mm cal.

✳ *Model P38 100th Year Commemorative* - 9mm Para. cal., alloy or steel frame with slide engraving "100 Jahre Walther 1886-1986." Imported by Interarms.

	100%	98%	95%	90%	80%	70%	60%
	$950	$750	$525	N/A	N/A	N/A	N/A

Add 75% for steel frame.

✳ *Model P38 Blue Engraved* - .22 LR, 7.65mm Luger, or 9mm Para. cal.

	100%	98%	95%	90%	80%	70%	60%
9mm Para.	$2,250	$1,750	$1,500	N/A	N/A	N/A	N/A
7.65mm Luger	$2,500	$2,000	$1,500	N/A	N/A	N/A	N/A
.22 LR	$2,500	$2,000	$1,500	N/A	N/A	N/A	N/A

Last MSR was $1,850.

✳ *Model P38 Chrome Engraved* - .22 LR, 7.65mm Luger, or 9mm Para. cal.

	100%	98%	95%	90%	80%	70%	60%
	$1,950	$1,500	$1,000	N/A	N/A	N/A	N/A

Last MSR was $2,125.

✳ *Model P38 Silver Engraved* - .22 LR, 7.65mm Luger, or 9mm Para. cal.

	100%	98%	95%	90%	80%	70%	60%
	$1,950	$1,500	$1,000	N/A	N/A	N/A	N/A

Last MSR was $2,100.

✳ *Model P38 Gold Engraved* - .22 LR, 7.65mm Luger, or 9mm Para. cal.

	100%	98%	95%	90%	80%	70%	60%
	$2,500	$2,000	$1,500	N/A	N/A	N/A	N/A

Last MSR was $2,050.

MODEL P1 - 9mm Para. cal., post-war commercial variation of the P.38 with steel slide and alloy frame, 5 in. barrel, 8 shot mag., blue or phosphate finish, black plastic grips. Disc.

	100%	98%	95%	90%	80%	70%	60%
	$675	$550	$400	$300	$250	$215	$165
Imp. Police Trade-Ins	$450	$350	$300	$225	$200	$170	$135

MODEL P4 - 9mm Para. cal., modernized variation of the original P.38, 4 1/2 in. barrel, 8 shot mag., updates include reinforced steel slide and alloy frame, includes decocking lever and automatic safeties, rear sight, 29 oz. Mfg. 1975-81, importation disc. 1982.

	100%	98%	95%	90%	80%	70%	60%
	$725	$600	$525	$425	$300	$250	$200

Add 30% for commercial variation.

PISTOLS: SEMI-AUTO, JOHN MARTZ CONVERSIONS

P.38 - JOHN MARTZ CONVERSIONS BABY - 9mm Para. cal., shortened barrel (3 in.) grip, and two 7 shot mags., 62 fabricated.

	100%	98%	95%	90%	80%	70%	60%
	$2,750	$2,200	$1,650	$1,450	$1,200	$1,025	$825

P.38 - JOHN MARTZ CONVERSIONS - .38 Super (4 or 6 in. barrel, 9 fabricated) or .45 ACP (4 or 7 1/2 in. barrel, 24 fabricated) cal. Disc.

	100%	98%	95%	90%	80%	70%	60%
	$4,950	$3,025	$2,150	$1,875	$1,600	$1,200	$1,075

GRADING - PPGS™	100%	98%	95%	90%	80%	70%	60%

P.38 - JOHN MARTZ CONVERSIONS CARBINE - 9mm Para. cal., 16 in. barrel, adj. rear sight, 30 fabricated w/ shoulder stocks. Disc.

	$8,700	$6,550	$4,325	$3,750	$3,250	$2,750	$2,300

M. PADRÓNE

Current shotgun manufacturer located in Marcheno, Italy. Currently imported by Padrone USA, located in San Antonio, TX.

M. Padróne manufactures high quality round body boxlock O/U shotguns on a small action – 12 ga. is not available. Current MSR is $6,795, w/o special orders. Please contact the importer for more information regarding availability and pricing (see Trademark Index).

PALMETTO ARMS CO.

Current manufacturer located in Brescia, Italy. No current importation.

Palmetto Arms Co. manufactures black powder reproductions and replicas, but they have produced only a small number of firearms, including the Outlaw SA revolver, and the Lightning slide action rifle/carbine. Please contact the company directly for more information about their current model lineup and U.S. availability (see Trademark Index).

PARAMOUNT

Previous trademark manufactured by Imperial Gun Co., Ltd. located in Surrey, England. Actions were previously imported by O.K. Weber, Inc. located in Eugene, OR and Olympic Arms, Inc. located in Olympia, WA.

RIFLES: SINGLE SHOT

THE IMPERIAL - .308 Win. cal., single shot target rifle featuring thumbhole stock and CPE aperture rear sight, fully adj. trigger, vent. forearm. Disc. 1994.

	$3,250	$2,700	$2,250	$1,850	$1,400	$1,000	$795

Last MSR was $3,400.

RANGEMASTER - various cals., single shot design, steel frame, contoured walnut grips, satin chrome finish, 8 1/2 lbs. Limited importation 1992-94.

	$1,600	$1,400	$1,200	$995	$895	$795	$695

Last MSR was $1,800.

PARA-ORDNANCE MFG. INC.

Current manufacturer established in 1988, and located in Scarborough, Ontario, Canada. Distributed in the U.S. by Para USA, located in Ft. Lauderdale, FL. Dealer and distributor sales.

PISTOLS: SEMI-AUTO

In 1999, Para-Ordnance introduced their LDA trigger system, originally standing for Lightning Double Action. During 2002, all alloy frame pistols were discontinued, and the abbreviation LDA became Light Double Action. Beginning 2003, all Para-Ordnance models are shipped with two magazines. Beginning Jan. 1, 2004, all Para-Ordnance models were replaced for the general market (except California) with the introduction of the new Power Extractor (PXT) models. The Griptor system, featuring front grip strap grasping grooves, became available during 2005, and the light rail frame option became available during 2006.

Previous Para-Ordnance model nomenclature typically listed the alphabetical letter of the series, followed by a one or two digit number indicating magazine capacity, followed by the number(s) of the caliber. Hence, a Model P14.45 is a P Series model with a 14 shot mag. in .45 ACP cal., and a 7.45LDA indicates a .45 ACP cal. in Light Double Action with a 7 shot mag.

Current Para-Ordnance nomenclature typically features the configuration type on the left side of the slide. The model designation is located on the right side of the slide and underneath it on the frame the product code (new 2006)/order number (changed to product code during 2006), which is alpha-numeric, may also appear. For current product codes for the various Para-Ordnance models, please visit www.paraord.com.

GRADING - PPGS™	100%	98%	95%	90%	80%	70%	60%

Para-Ordnance offers the following finishes on its pistols: Regal (black slide, black frame w/ stainless fire controls), Midnight Blue (blue slide, blue frame w/blue fire controls), Coyote Brown, Covert Black (black slide, black frame, and black fire controls), Black Watch (black slide, green frame, green (double stack) or black (single stack) fire controls), Spec Ops (green slide, green frame w/black fire controls), or Sterling (all stainless, black slide w/polished sides), in addition to stainless steel construction.

6.45 LDA/LLDA - Models 6.45 LDA (changed to Para-Companion, marked Para-Companion on left side of slide and C7.45LDA on right side of slide) and 6.45 LLDA were advertised in the 2001 Para-Ordnance catalog (became the Para-Carry, marked Para-Carry on left side of slide and 6.45 LLDA on right side of frame), the 6.46 LLDA was never mfg., prototype only. Mfg. 2001-2003.

C SERIES MODELS - .45 ACP cal., DAO, 3 (Carry), 3 1/2 (Companion or Companion Carry), 4 1/2 (CCW or Tac-Four), or 5 in. barrel, stainless steel only, single or double (Tac-Four only) stack mag., 6 (Carry), 7, or 10 (Tac-Four only) shot mag., approx. 30-34 oz. Mfg. 2003.

	$775	$595	$495	$430	$375	$315	$270

Last MSR was $939.

Add $70 for Companion Carry Model.

D SERIES MODELS - 9mm Para., .40 S&W, or .45 ACP cal., DAO, 3 1/2 or 5 in. barrel, 7 or 10 shot single stack mag., steel receiver, matte black finish or stainless steel. Mfg. 2003.

	$715	$575	$475	$425	$350	$325	$295

Last MSR was $859.

Add $80 for stainless steel.

P SERIES MODELS - 9mm Para. or .45 ACP cal., single action, 3 1/2, 4 1/4, or 5 in. barrel, 10 shot mag., matte black (5 in. barrel only) or stainless steel finish.

＊*P Series Model P10* - 9mm Para. (new 1998), .40 S&W, .45 ACP, 10mm (mfg. 1998 only, stainless steel) cal., single action, super compact variation featuring 3 in. barrel and shortened grip, 10 shot double column mag., 3-dot sights, choice of alloy (matte black), steel (matte black), or stainless (duo-tone - disc. 2000, or bright finish) frame, 31 oz. with steel frame or 24 oz. with alloy frame. Mfg. 1997-2002.

	$625	$500	$435	$390	$350	$325	$295

Last MSR was $740.

Add $10 for steel frame.
Add $49 for stainless steel.
Add $45 for stainless steel with duo-tone finish (disc. 2000).

＊*P Series Model P12* - .40 S&W (disc. 2002) or .45 ACP cal., compact variation of the P14 featuring 10 (C/B 1994) or 11* shot mag. and 3 1/2 in. barrel, 33 oz. with steel frame (disc. 2002) or 24 oz. with alloy frame (disc. 2002) or stainless steel (standard beginning 2003, duo-tone stainless was disc. 2000). Mfg. 1990-2003.

	$750	$575	$475	$425	$375	$325	$295

Last MSR was $899.

Subtract 10% for steel frame (disc. 2002).

＊*P Series Model P13* - .40 S&W (disc. 2000) or .45 ACP cal., similar to P14, except has 10 (C/B 1994) or 12* shot mag., 4 1/4 in. barrel, 35 oz. with steel frame (disc. 2002) or 25 oz. with alloy frame (disc. 2002), stainless steel became standard 2003 (duo-tone stainless was disc. 2000). Mfg. 1993-2003.

	$750	$575	$475	$425	$375	$325	$295

Last MSR was $899.

＊*P Series Model P14* - .40 S&W (mfg. 1996-2000) or .45 ACP cal., patterned after the Colt Model 1911A1 except has choice of alloy (matte black, disc. 2002), steel (matte black), or stainless steel (stainless or duo-tone finish) frame that has been widened slightly for extra shot capacity (13* shot), 10

GRADING - PPGS™	100%	98%	95%	90%	80%	70%	60%

shot (C/B 1994) mag., single action, 3-dot sight system, rounded combat hammer, 5 in. ramped barrel, 38 oz. with steel frame or 28 oz. with alloy frame (disc. 2002), duo-tone stainless steel was disc. 2000. Mfg. 1990-2003.

	$685	$550	$475	$425	$375	$325	$295

Last MSR was $829.

Add $70 for stainless steel.

* P Series Model P15 - .40 S&W cal., otherwise similar to P13, 36 oz. with steel frame or 28 oz. with alloy frame. Mfg. 1996-99.

	$625	$500	$435	$390	$350	$325	$295

Last MSR was $740.

Add $10 for steel frame.
Add $59 for stainless steel.
Add $45 for stainless steel with duo-tone finish.

* P Series Model P16 - .40 S&W cal., otherwise similar to P14, steel or stainless steel (new 1997) frame only. New 1995-2002.

	$640	$515	$435	$385	$350	$325	$295

Last MSR was $750.

Add $49 for stainless steel.
Add $35 for duo-tone stainless steel (disc. 2000).

* P Series Model P18 - 9mm Para. cal., 5 in. ramped barrel, stainless steel, solid barrel bushing, flared ejection port, quadruple safety, adj. rear sight, 40 oz. Mfg. 1998-2003.

	$800	$625	$495	$430	$375	$315	$270

Last MSR was $960.

PXT 1911 SINGLE STACK SERIES - .38 Super or .45 ACP cal., features new power extractor design with larger claw (PXT), left slide is marked "Para 1911", right side marked with individual model names, various configurations, barrel lengths, and finishes, single action, single stack mag., spurred or spurless (light rail models only) hammer. New 2004.

* Slim Hawg - .45 ACP cal. only, 3 in. barrel, 6 shot mag., 3-dot sights, choice of stainless steel or Covert Black (new 2006) finish, 24 or 30 (stainless) oz.

MSR $959		$825	$700	$600	$500	$450	$400	$350

Add $140 for stainless steel.

* Super Hawg Single Stack - .45 ACP cal., similar to S14.45 Ltd., except has 6 in. barrel and stainless finish, 8 shot mag. New 2008.

MSR $1,349		$1,175	$1,000	$850	$725	$600	$525	$450

* 1911 OPS - .45 ACP cal. only, 3 1/2 in. barrel, 7 shot mag., 3-dot sights, stainless steel construction, 32 oz.

MSR $1,099		$975	$845	$735	$625	$525	$450	$400

* 1911 LTC - 9mm Para. (new 2008) or .45 ACP cal., 4 1/4 in. barrel, 8 or 9 (9mm Para) shot mag., 3-dot sights, steel alloy or stainless steel construction, Covert black (9mm Para.) or Regal finish, 28 (alloy) or 35 oz.

MSR $929		$795	$675	$575	$500	$450	$400	$350

Add $20 for steel, or $150 for stainless steel.

* 1911 SSP Series - .38 Super or .45 ACP cal., 5 in. barrel, 8 or 9 (.38 Super cal. only) shot mag., 3-dot or Novak adj. (Tactical Duty Model only) sights, steel or stainless steel (new 2006) construction, Black Covert (new 2008) or Regal finish, stainless, or bright stainless (.38 Super cal. only), checkered wood or pearl (.38 Super cal.) grips, 39 oz.

MSR $899		$775	$665	$575	$500	$450	$400	$350

Add $230 for stainless steel.
Add $250 for .38 Super cal., or $280 for .38 Super with pearl grips.
Add $250 for Tactical Duty SSP with Novak adj. sights (disc. 2008).

GRADING - PPGS™	100%	98%	95%	90%	80%	70%	60%

* **1911 Limited** - .45 ACP cal., 5 in. barrel, 8 shot mag., fiber optic front and adj. rear sight, stainless steel with Sterling finish, gold Para emblem on checkered wood grips, 39 oz.

| MSR $1,249 | | $1,095 | $900 | $775 | $650 | $550 | $450 | $375 |

* **1911 Nite-Tac** - .45 ACP cal. only, 5 in. barrel, 8 shot mag., 3-dot sights, stainless steel construction, Covert Black finish or stainless, features light rail on frame, flush spurless hammer, 40 oz.

| MSR $1,149 | | $1,025 | $875 | $750 | $650 | $550 | $450 | $375 |

* **Todd Jarrett USPSA Limited Edition** - .45 ACP cal., 5 in. barrel, 8 shot mag., features Novak adj. sights, steel construction, Covert Black/Sterling finish, 39 oz.

| MSR $1,729 | | $1,550 | $1,325 | $1,175 | $1,000 | $925 | $825 | $750 |

PXT HIGH CAPACITY SERIES - 9mm Para., 40 S&W, or .45 ACP cal., single action, 10 shot or high capacity mag., various barrel lengths, construction, and finishes.

* **Hawg 9** - 9mm Para. cal., compact frame, 12 shot mag., 3 in. ramped barrel with guide rod, dovetailed, low mount, 3-dot fixed sights, alloy receiver, steel slide, spurred competition hammer, match grade trigger, balck polymer grips, Regal black finish, three safeties, 24 oz. New 2005.

| MSR $929 | | $795 | $665 | $575 | $520 | $450 | $375 | $325 |

* **Lite Hawg 9** - similar to Hawg 9, except is steel and has light rail, flush spurless hammer, Covert Black finish.

| MSR $1,099 | | $990 | $865 | $760 | $675 | $600 | $525 | $450 |

* **Lite Hawg .45** - .45 ACP cal., similar to Lite Hawg 9, except has 10 shot mag., flush spurless hammer, Covert Black finish.

| MSR $1,099 | | $990 | $865 | $760 | $675 | $600 | $525 | $450 |

* **Warthog** - .45 ACP cal., lightweight, compact design, 3 in. ramped barrel, alloy or stainless frame, 10 shot mag., tritium night (disc.) or 3-dot sights, spur competition hammer, match grade trigger, extended slide lock, beavertail grip and firing pin safeties, black polymer grips, Covert Black (Para-Kote, disc.), or Regal finish, or stainless steel construction, 24 or 31 oz. New 2004.

| MSR $929 | | $795 | $665 | $575 | $520 | $450 | $375 | $325 |

Add $120 for stainless steel.

* **Nite Hawg** .45 ACP cal., 3 in. barrel, 10 shot mag., tritium night sights, compact alloy frame, Covert Black finish, black plastic grips, 24 oz.

| MSR $1,059 | | $950 | $825 | $715 | $600 | $500 | $425 | $350 |

* **Big Hawg** .45 ACP cal., 5 in. barrel, 14 shot mag., 3-dot sights, alloy frame, Regal finish with chrome accents, black plastic grips, 28 oz.

| MSR $929 | | $795 | $665 | $575 | $520 | $450 | $375 | $325 |

* **Super Hawg High Capacity** - .45 ACP cal., similar to S14.45 Ltd., except has 6 in. barrel and stainless finish. New 2008.

| MSR $1,349 | | $1,175 | $1,000 | $850 | $725 | $600 | $525 | $450 |

* **P14.45** .45 ACP cal., 5 in. barrel, 14 shot mag., 3-dot sights, Covert Black finish steel (new 2008) or stainless steel construction, black synthetic grips, brushed stainless steel, 40 oz.

| MSR $899 | | $785 | $675 | $600 | $525 | $450 | $375 | $325 |

Add $130 for stainless steel.

* **P18.9** 9mm Para. cal., 5 in. barrel, 18 shot mag., adj. sights, stainless steel construction, black synthetic grips, brushed stainless steel, 40 oz.

| MSR $1,109 | | $925 | $785 | $675 | $575 | $500 | $425 | $375 |

* **S14.45 Limited (PXT High Capacity Limited)** - .45 ACP cal., single action, 10 (disc.) or 14 shot mag., adj. sights, 3 1/2 (stainless steel, disc. 2005), 4 1/4 (stainless steel, disc. 2005), or 5 (steel, disc. 2005, or stainless steel) in. barrel, Covert (disc. 2005) or Sterling finish, black synthetic grips, 40 oz.

| MSR $1,229 | | $1,085 | $925 | $815 | $700 | $600 | $500 | $400 |

Add $75 for 3 1/2 or 4 1/4 in. barrel or stainless steel (disc. 2006).

GRADING - PPGS™	100%	98%	95%	90%	80%	70%	60%

✳ **S16.40 Limited (PXT High Capacity Limited)** - .40 S&W cal., single action, 10 (disc.) or 16 shot mag., adj. sights, 3 1/2 (stainless steel, disc. 2005), 4 1/4 (stainless steel, disc. 2005), or 5 (steel, disc. 2005, or stainless steel) in. barrel, Covert (disc. 2005) or Sterling finish, black synthetic grips, 40 oz.

MSR $1,229	$1,085	$925	$815	$700	$600	$500	$400

  Add $75 for 3 1/2 or 4 1/4 in. barrel or stainless steel (disc. 2006).

✳ **S12-45 Limited** - .45 ACP cal., 3 1/2 in. ramped barrel, 10 or 12 shot mag., stainless steel frame with black slide, Novak adj. rear sight, spur competition hammer, checkered cocobolo grips with gold medallions, 34 oz. Mfg. 2005-2006.

	$995	$850	$725	$610	$515	$425	$375

  Last MSR was $1,105.

✳ **Todd Jarrett USPSA .40 Limited Edition** - .40 S&W cal., single action, 16 shot mag., 5 in. barrel, Novak adj. sights, steel construction, Covert Black/Sterling finish, flared magwell, black synthetic grips, 40 oz.

MSR $1,729	$1,495	$1,250	$1,050	$875	$750	$675	$575

PXT LDA SINGLE STACK (CARRY OPTION SERIES) - 9mm Para. (new mid-2006), .45 GAP (new mid-2006) or .45 ACP cal., DAO, single stack mag., various barrel lengths and finishes, features Griptor grips (grooved front grip strap), spurless flush hammer and rounded grip safety.

✳ **Carry Gap** - .45 GAP cal., 3 in. barrel, 6 shot mag., 3-dot sights, steel frame, Covert Black finish, 30 oz.

MSR $1,079	$975	$850	$750	$675	$600	$525	$450

✳ **CCO Gap** - similar to Carry Gap, except has 7 shot mag. and 3 1/2 in. barrel, 31 oz. New 2006.

MSR $1,079	$975	$850	$750	$675	$600	$525	$450

✳ **Covert Black Carry** - .45 ACP cal., 6 shot mag., 3 in. barrel, Novak adj. sights, stainless steel construction, Covert Black finish, 30 oz.

MSR $1,199	$1,055	$925	$815	$700	$600	$525	$450

✳ **Carry** - similar to Covert Black Carry, except has 3-dot sights and is brushed stainless steel.

MSR $1,129	$1,000	$865	$775	$700	$600	$525	$450

✳ **Carry 9** - 9mm Para. cal., 8 shot mag., 3 in. barrel, 3-dot sights, alloy frame, Covert Black finish, 24 oz. New mid-2006.

MSR $979	$855	$735	$630	$525	$450	$375	$325

✳ **PDA** - 9mm Para cal., 3 in. barrel with fiber optic front and two-dot rear sights, alloy frame with Sterling/Covert Black finish. New 2008.

MSR $1,059	$930	$825	$725	$625	$525	$425	$350

✳ **PDA .45** - .45 ACP cal., 3 in. barrel with three dot sights, 6 shot mag., alloy frame with stainless/Covert Black finish. New 2008.

MSR $1,139	$1,000	$865	$775	$700	$600	$525	$450

✳ **CCO** - .45 ACP cal., 7 shot mag., 3 1/2 in. barrel, 3-dot sights, stainless steel construction, brushed stainless finish, 32 oz.

MSR $1,129	$1,000	$865	$775	$700	$600	$525	$450

✳ **CCW** - similar to CCO model, except has 4 1/4 in. barrel, 34 oz.

MSR $1,129	$1,000	$865	$775	$700	$600	$525	$450

PXT LDA SINGLE STACK - .45 ACP cal., DAO, non-carry option models, spurless flush hammer, various configurations and barrel lengths.

✳ **CCO Companion Black Watch** - .45 ACP cal., 7 shot mag., 3 1/2 in. barrel, 3-dot sights, stainless steel construction, Black Watch finish, 32 oz.

MSR $1,099	$975	$865	$760	$675	$600	$525	$450

GRADING - PPGS™	100%	98%	95%	90%	80%	70%	60%

* **Tac-S** - .45 ACP cal., 8 shot mag., 4 1/4 in. barrel, 3-dot sights, steel frame, Spec Ops finish, 35 oz.

MSR $999	$865	$735	$630	$525	$425	$375	$325

* **LDA SSP** - .45 ACP cal., 8 shot mag., 5 in. barrel, 3-dot sights, stainless steel construction, brushed stainless finish, 39 oz.

MSR $1,079	$945	$835	$725	$625	$525	$425	$350

* **Covert Black Nite-Tac SS** - .45 ACP cal., 8 shot mag., 5 in. barrel, 3-dot sights, stainless steel construction, Covert Black finish, includes light rail, checkered wood grips, 40 oz. Mfg. 2006-2007.

	$1,000	$875	$750	$650	$550	$450	$375

Last MSR was $1,125.

* **Nite-Tac SS** - .45 ACP cal., 8 shot mag., 5 in. barrel, 3-dot sights, stainless steel construction, brushed stainless finish, includes light rail, checkered wood grips, 40 oz. Mfg. 2006-2007.

	$1,000	$875	$750	$650	$550	$450	$375

Last MSR was $1,125.

* **PXT LDA Limited** - .45 ACP cal., DAO, single stack 7 shot mag., steel or stainless steel, 5 in. barrel.

	$935	$800	$700	$600	$500	$400	$350

Last MSR was $1,035.

Add $75 for stainless steel.

PXT LDA HIGH CAPACITY (CARRY OPTION SERIES) - 9mm Para., .40 S&W, or .45 ACP cal., spurless flush hammer, rounded grip safety, various options, barrel lengths and magazine capacity.

* **Carry 12** - .45 ACP cal., 12 shot mag., 3 1/2 in. barrel, low mount 3-dot tritium night sights, stainless steel construction, black synthetic grips, brushed stainless finish, 34 oz.

MSR $1,199	$1,050	$915	$800	$700	$600	$500	$425

* **Tac-Four** - .45 ACP cal., 13 shot mag., 4 1/4 in. barrel, 3-dot sights, stainless steel construction, black synthetic grips, brushed stainless finish, 36 oz.

MSR $1,099	$960	$840	$735	$625	$525	$425	$350

* **Tac-Forty** - .40 S&W cal., 15 shot mag., 4 1/4 in. barrel, 3-dot sights, stainless steel construction, black synthetic grips, brushed stainless finish, 36 oz. Mfg. 2007.

	$925	$825	$725	$625	$525	$425	$350

Last MSR was $1,049.

* **Tac-Five** - 9mm Para cal., 18 shot mag., 5 in. barrel, Novak adj. sights, stainless steel construction, black synthetic grips, Covert Black finish, 37 1/2 oz. Mfg. 2007.

	$1,050	$875	$750	$625	$525	$450	$375

Last MSR was $1,185.

PXT LDA HIGH CAPACITY SERIES - .45 ACP cal., DAO, 14 shot mag., 5 in. barrel, 3-dot sights, steel or stainless steel construction, spurless flush hammer, Covert Black finish or stainless steel.

* **Covert Black Hi-Cap .45** - steel frame, Covert Black finish.

MSR $1,099	$950	$775	$650	$525	$425	$375	$325

* **Hi-Cap .45** - stainless steel construction, brushed stainless finish.

MSR $1,099	$955	$840	$730	$625	$525	$425	$350

* **Covert Black Nite-Tac .45** - steel frame, Covert Black finish, includes light rail. New 2006.

MSR $1,099	$955	$840	$730	$625	$525	$425	$350

GRADING - PPGS™	100%	98%	95%	90%	80%	70%	60%

* *Coyote Brown Nite-Tac .45* - .45 ACP cal., similar to Covert Black Nite-Tac, except has adj. fiber optic sights and Coyote Brown finish.

MSR $1,349		$1,175	$1,000	$850	$725	$600	$525	$450

* *Nite-Tac .45* - stainless steel construction, brushed stainless finish, includes light rail. New 2006.

MSR $1,199		$1,025	$900	$775	$650	$550	$450	$350

* *Hi-Cap Limited .45* - adj. sights, stainless steel construction, Sterling finish.

MSR $1,279		$1,075	$925	$775	$675	$575	$475	$375

* *Colonel* - .45 ACP cal., 4 1/4 in. ramped barrel, white low mount 3-dot fixed sights, steel frame, 10 or 14 shot mag., spur competition hammer, LDA trigger, black polymer grips with medallions, green spec. ops. finish, 37 oz. Mfg. 2005-2006.

	$795	$700	$600	$500	$450	$375	$325

Last MSR was $899.

PXT LDA HIGH CAPACITY LIMITED - 9mm Para., .40 S&W, or .45 ACP cal., DAO, 10, 14, 16, or 18 shot mag., steel or stainless steel, 5 in. barrel. Disc. 2006.

	$935	$800	$700	$600	$500	$400	$350

Last MSR was $1,035.

Add $75 for stainless steel.

PXT LTC HIGH CAPACITY - .45 ACP cal., 4 1/4 in. barrel, 10 or 14 shot mag., 3-dot fixed sights, stainless steel frame, match grade trigger, black polymer grips with medallions, green spec. ops. finish, three safeties, 37 oz. Mfg. 2005-2006.

	$750	$650	$550	$460	$395	$335	$285

Last MSR was $855.

S SERIES MODELS - .40 S&W or .45 ACP cal., single action, 3 1/2, 4 1/4, or 5 in. barrel, 10 shot mag., matte black (5 in. barrel only) or stainless steel finish.

* *S Series Model S10 Limited* - similar to P10, except has competition shooting features, including beavertail grip safety, competition hammer, tuned trigger, match grade barrel, front slide serrations, choice of steel or alloy frame with matte black finish or stainless steel, 40 oz. Mfg. 1999-2002.

	$765	$650	$525	$450	$395	$350	$325

Last MSR was $865.

Add $10 for steel receiver.
Add $24 for stainless steel.

* *S Series Model S12 Limited* - .40 S&W (disc. 2002) or .45 ACP cal., similar to P12, except has competition shooting features, including beavertail grip safety, competition hammer, tuned trigger, match grade barrel, front slide serrations, choice of steel or alloy (disc. 2002) frame, matte black (disc. 2002) or stainless steel finish, 40 oz. Mfg. 1999-2003.

	$895	$750	$650	$525	$450	$395	$350

Last MSR was $1,049.

Subtract 10% for steel frame (disc. 2002).

* *S Series Model S13 Limited* - .40 S&W (disc. 2002) or .45 ACP cal., similar to P13, except has competition shooting features, including beavertail grip safety, competition hammer, tuned trigger, match grade barrel, front slide serrations, choice of steel or alloy (disc. 2002) frame, matte black (disc. 2002) or stainless steel finish, 40 oz. Mfg. 1999-2003.

	$895	$750	$650	$525	$450	$395	$350

Last MSR was $1,049.

GRADING - PPGS™	100%	98%	95%	90%	80%	70%	60%

✳ *S Series Model S14 Limited* - .40 S&W (disc. 2002) or .45 ACP cal., similar to P14, except has competition shooting features, including beavertail grip safety, competition hammer, tuned trigger, match grade barrel, front slide serrations, matte black or stainless steel, 40 oz. Mfg. 1998-2003.

	$850	$725	$625	$525	$450	$395	$350

Last MSR was $989.

Add $60 for stainless steel.

✳ *S Series Model S16 Limited* - .40 S&W cal., similar to P16, except has 5 in. barrel and competition shooting features, including beavertail grip safety, competition hammer, tuned trigger, match grade barrel, front slide serrations, matte black steel or stainless steel, 40 oz. Mfg. 1998-2003.

	$850	$725	$625	$525	$450	$395	$350

Last MSR was $989.

Add $60 for stainless steel.

T SERIES MODELS - 9mm Para., .40 S&W (stainless steel only), or .45 ACP cal., DAO, 5 in. barrel, 7 (.45 ACP cal. only, single stack mag.) or 10 shot mag., steel or stainless steel, matte black finish or stainless steel. Mfg. 2003.

	$825	$615	$500	$450	$385	$335	$295

Last MSR was $1,009.

Add $80 for stainless steel.

PARDINI, ARMI S.r.l.

Current manufacturer located in Lido di Camaiore, Italy. Currently imported by Larry's Guns, located in Portland, ME. Previously imported until 2004 by Nygord Precision Products located in Prescott, AZ, and distributed until 1996 by Mo's Competitor Supplies & Range, Inc. located in Brookfield, CT, and until 1990 by Fiocchi of America, Inc., located in Ozark, MO.

For more information and current pricing on both new and used Pardini airguns, please refer to the *Blue Book of Airguns* by Dr. Robert Beeman & John Allen (also online).

PISTOLS: SEMI-AUTO

PC45 - .40 S&W, .45 ACP, or 9x21mm cal., single action mechanism designed for stock competition category, adj. trigger pull. Limited importation by Nygord 2000-2004.

	$1,295	$1,050	$840	$715	$575	$500	$440

Add $75 for 6 in. barrel and slide.

✳ *PC45S* - similar to PC, except has compensator and optic sight with scope mount.

	$1,500	$1,250	$1,100	$950	$850	$725	$600

✳ *PCS-Open* - similar to PCS, except w/o scope and frame mount, top-of-the-line semi-auto.

	$1,650	$1,400	$1,250	$1,100	$950	$850	$725

GT9/40/45 - 9x21mm IMI, .40 S&W, or .45 ACP cal. 5 or 6 in. barrel, single action, diamond wood grips, matte silver, 13 or 17 (9x21mm) shot mag., black or two-tone finish. Importation began late 2004.

MSR $1,639	$1,529	$1,275	$1,000	$875	$775	$650	$550

Add $95 for 6 in. barrel and slide (disc.).
Add $40 for silver finish.
Add $20 for .45 ACP cal.
Add $230 for GT45S Model with compensator in silver finish.
Add $90 for 6 in. barrel.

GRADING - PPGS™	100%	98%	95%	90%	80%	70%	60%

PISTOLS: TARGET

Pardini pistols have always been known for their technological improvements developed from ongoing design research. During 1991, the entire Pardini pistol line was modified both internally and externally to improve function and reliability - these changes included the addition of grooves on the barrel shroud to accept scope mounts directly.

MODEL SP/MODEL SP NEW (STANDARD PISTOL) - .22 LR cal. only, semi-auto, target grips, adj. sights, 4.92 in. barrel, interchangeable grips, 5 shot detachable mag., SP features mechanical trigger, SP New features second generation electronic trigger, approx. 2.4 lbs. New 1991.

    MSR $1,639   **$1,529**   **$1,275**   **$1,000**   **$875**   **$775**   **$650**   **$550**

    Add $145 for SP Master Model (disc.).

    Subtract approx. 10% for SP model with mechanical trigger.

MODEL SP1 - .22 LR cal., semi-auto, features electronic trigger, blue/silver two-tone finish, adj. anatomic target wood grips, includes six Tungsten weights. New 2005.

    MSR N/A   **$1,525**   **$1,325**   **$1,150**   **$1,000**   **$900**   **$800**   **$675**

MODEL SP1/SP1 NEW RAPID FIRE - .22 LR cal., semi-auto, similar to Model SP1, SP1 has second generation electronic trigger, SP1 New has mechanical trigger, developed for rapid fire discipline, includes six Tungsten weights. New 2005.

    MSR N/A   **$1,675**   **$1,425**   **$1,200**   **$1,000**   **$850**   **$775**   **$700**

LADIES PISTOL - similar to Model SP, except grips are suitable for smaller hands. Importation disc. 1999.

        $850   **$700**   **$600**   **$520**   **$460**   **$410**   **$380**

        Last MSR was $995.

MODEL GP/GP E (RAPID FIRE PISTOL) - .22 Short cal., semi-auto, features enclosed style grip assembly, adj. sights, choice of electronic (GP E, new 2004) or mechanical (GP) trigger, 5.12 in. barrel. Imported 1991-2004.

        $1,425   **$1,250**   **$1,050**   **$875**   **$775**   **$675**   **$575**

    Add $500 for "Schumann" Model (wraparound grip, special muzzle ports, sights, weights, etc.).

MODEL HP/HP E/HP NEW (CENTERFIRE PISTOL) - .32 S&W Wadcutter cal., semi-auto, similar to Model SP Pistol, 4.92 in. barrel, beginning 2004, HP has second generation electronic trigger, HP E has electronic trigger, HP New has mechanical trigger, 5 shot mag., includes 4 (HP) or 6 (HP E & HP New) weights. New 1991.

    MSR $1,869   **$1,736**   **$1,450**   **$1,250**   **$1,050**   **$875**   **$775**   **$675**

    Add $290 for HP E model with electronic trigger.

MODEL K22 - .22 LR cal., top-of-the-line single shot target pistol, 11.8 in. barrel, mechanical trigger, toggle bolt pushes cartridge into chamber, unique ventilated front sight assembly that also supports counterweights, cocking lever action, 38 1/2 oz. Importation began 2000.

    MSR $1,899   **$1,770**   **$1,475**   **$1,250**   **$1,050**   **$875**   **$775**   **$675**

MODEL K50 (FREE PISTOL) - .22 LR cal., single shot, sliding rotating bolt, 9.06 in. barrel, tilted anatomical grip, top-of-the-line match pistol. Mfg. 1991-99.

        $925   **$750**   **$600**   **$500**   **$450**   **$420**   **$395**

        Last MSR was $1,050.

PARDINI/NYGORD MASTER - .22 LR cal., designed for NRA bullseye shooting, micrometer rear sight and red-dot sight, includes small Adco sight, anatomical target grips. Imported 2000-2004.

        $1,325   **$1,145**   **$875**   **$750**   **$650**   **$550**   **$450**

PARKER BROS. GUNMAKERS

Current manufacturer established 1999 and located in Meriden, CT.

SHOTGUNS: O/U

Currently, Parker Bros. Gunmakers manufactures an O/U in 12 ga., based on the original Parker specifications. Six grades are offered, including the Invincible ($125,000), A-1 Special ($90,000), AA ($65,000), B ($37,500), C ($24,500), and PA ($18,500). Prices do not include engraving. Please contact the company directly for more information, including engraving options, special features, and availability (see Trademark Index).

PARKER BROTHERS

Previously manufactured in Meriden, CT from 1866-1934. Remington took over production in 1934, and in 1938, the plant was moved to Ilion, NY. Over 4,500 "Transition Guns" (exhibiting Meriden and Ilion characteristics) were produced in Meriden between 1934-1937 and about 1,600 Parkers were manufactured at the Ilion location before production stopped circa 1942. Total production reached approx. 242,487.

During 2006, Remington Arms Co. announced the release of a new AAHE 28 ga. Parker, manufactured in the U.S. by Connecticut Shotgun Co.

95% of the original Parkers bought and sold each year are in 30% or less condition (referring to original case colors). Percentages on following pages refer to the amount of original case colors remaining on frame.

Parker Gun Identification & Serialization was published in late 2002, and has been reprinted due to popular demand. Compiled by using records from *The Parker Story, Vols. I & II*, this title features more than 100 detailed images allowing easy visual identification on the grades, frame sizes, and other important information. Additionally, listings on over 155,000 serial numbers are provided, specifying the original configuration, including grade, action type, extra features, stock configuration, gauge, and barrel length - an invaluable asset when determining original configuration on most Parker Brothers Shotguns. The author wishes to thank Mssrs. Charles Price, William Mullins, Roy Gunther, Louis C. Parker III, and Daniel Cote for sharing the following Parker production statistics with this publication.

SHOTGUNS, SxS, DAMASCUS BARRELS

Parker damascus barreled shotguns (hammer or hammerless) are very collectible if original condition is over 40%. Specimens in 80% or better condition with strong case colors can approximate values of the steel barrel models if the bores are in excellent condition (no pitting). Values for under 40% specimens fall off rapidly and are no longer comparable to steel barrel guns. As an example, a 12 ga. steel "D" Grade (without ejectors) has a price range from $2,250 to $8,000 (10%-100%) with a rather even downward progression of values in between the high and low ranges. A 100% damascus hammer "D" Grade could have a $12,000-$15,000 price tag hanging from the trigger guard, while a 5%-15% condition specimen is typically seen priced in the $1,500-$2,500 range. A truly 95%-100% original damascus barreled, hammer Parker is more rare and desirable than a similar grade damascus hammerless Parker or a steel barreled hammerless Parker. Remember, the guns are not rare but their condition is.

Due to recent articles in a national firearms quarterly publication discussing the "shootability" of damascus barreled guns (Parker and other major manufacturers), and the positive results obtained, there has been a renewed interest in these guns. Prices have increased accordingly, and in some instances values for high condition guns have exceeded their steel barreled counterparts.

SHOTGUNS: MISC. FACTS

Values listed in the 95%-100% condition columns can vary a lot as there is very little supply and strong demand for these high condition "cream puffs."

Note: Values below are for guns without ejectors, unless otherwise indicated. An "E" suffix indicates ejectors. Skeet models with ejectors, beavertail forearm, and single selective trigger are valued at approx. 50%-75% higher than values shown. Higher grade Parkers typically had ejectors, and ejectors typically add 25%-50% value to a Parker in all grades. Also, lower condition, high grade models sometimes have their values established by the potential gain in refurbishing these specimens. Remember, it only cost a few hundred dollars more to refinish an A1 Special compared a VH Grade.

Due to the extremely high value of Parker Guns, extreme care should be taken in their purchase. There are many upgraded and refinished guns represented as original; expert advice should always be sought. Many collectors would rather own a specimen with 30% original case colors than a refinished gun that is 100% (regardless who did the work). Many advanced collectors will discount a refinished Parker's value 40%-60% off the price for an original gun. Misrepresentation of refinished or upgraded Parkers is rampant today - especially case colors. Also, beware of fake boxes and hanging tags - if the box and Parker shotgun are an original "pair," the value is enhanced tremendously. If the box/hanging tag is fake, you could pay as much as $1,500 to learn this lesson! In other words, do your homework, be careful, shop carefully, and above all, get a receipt for exactly what it is that you are purchasing.

Frame size on Parker shotguns is determined by the number on the bottom of the rear barrel lug on breech. Frame sizes (from largest to smallest) include 7, 6, 5, 4, 3, 2, 1 1/2, 1, 1/2, 0, 00, and 000. 8 ga. guns typically are framed 6 or 7. 10 ga. guns typically are 3 or 4. 12 ga. guns typically range from 2 through 1 (more desirable). "1/2" frame 12 ga. guns are very rare and desirable. 20 and 16 gauges range from 2 through 0 (more desirable, rare in 16 ga.). 28 ga. guns are either 0 or 00 (more desirable and approx. 50% more). .410 bore shotguns are 00 or 000 (most common and most desirable). 8 and 10 ga. steel barreled shotguns are very rare, and prices can equal .410 bore values if the original condition is there. Factory original 10 ga., 3 1/2 in. Mag. guns command premium prices, as very few were made and they are extremely rare. These guns are stamped "For 3 1/2 shells" on the barrel lug and are late serial numbered (240,000 range).

The grade on Parker shotguns is a number or initials located on the water table of the frame. An alphabetical designation would indicate the grade immediately. For numerals, a "2" would indicate a GH, while an "8" would specify an A-1 Special - interpolate for the others (numbers 3 through 7). Parker shotguns manufactured by Remington will have date codes stamped on left barrel flat that correspond to the month and the year (see Remington serialization in the Serialization Section). Also, if a Parker gun was returned to Remington for repair, alteration, or refinishing, it will usually have the date code stamped with a suffix of 3 (i.e., OK3 represents some type of rework completed in either July of 1941 or 1963). There is some ambiguity with the year as the year codes repeat.

Skeleton buttplates were furnished as standard on Parker guns starting with Grade 3 or on D and higher grades over most of the years of production. They were perhaps an option on the lower grades at times, and no doubt a customer could have ordered one as a special option on a lower grade for additional cost. Since skeleton buttplates were standard on the D Grades and above, they should be not considered an added value on these grades. And even if present on lower grades, if you cannot prove factory originality, a skeleton buttplate will not add any value.

A note about Parker condition: Percentages of condition indicate the amount of original case colors remaining on the frame, but sometimes these colors are faded and the rest of the gun is excellent - hence, all the separate condition factors must be considered when determining overall condition.

A Parker IS NOT 60% if the barrel bluing and stock/forearm varnish are 60% but case colors are only 10%. Typically, a 60% case color Parker shotgun will have 90%+ blue and varnish, yet this does not mean the gun is 90% overall. Similarly, a 20% case color Parker will probably have 90% barrel bluing remaining. Strong, original case colors are the key in determining Parker condition and subsequent values. However, for shotguns under 30% condition, the overall condition of the gun should determine value.

Collectors also place value on the screws on the receiver being aligned as they left the factory and not tampered with.

The Parker Story, Vol. I was published in late 1998. This book has production statistics derived from factory records, and the quantities manufactured listed in this text for steel-barreled hammerless Parker guns are taken from this book. This new publication also has

100%	98%	95%	90%	80%	70%	60%	50%	40%	30%	20%	10%

more detailed production statistics on Parker guns produced from 1869-1942, including a breakdown by action type (lifter, top lever, and hammerless), grade, barrel steel, gauge, and barrel length. Some grades, gauges, etc., are fewer in number than previously estimated. All the grades are pictured in color, including the Invincible. Parker Reproductions are also covered in detail, including production statistics. *Vol. II* was published in late 2000. The Parker Gun Collectors Association can also provide research letters on certain Parkers. Please refer to their listing under Firearms Organizations in the back of this text for contact information.

SHOTGUNS, PARKER MODELS & PRICING

The desirability of older Parker shotguns in today's marketplace can be greatly enhanced if the stock dimensions fit today's potential owner (typically 13 1/2 in. - 14 1/2 in. LOP), adding value due to the shootability.

Add 20% for SST.
Add 20% for beavertail forearm.
Add 40%-50% for VR (rare on smaller gauges).
Add 20% for straight English stock.
Add 20% for original skeleton steel buttplate (standard on Grade D/3 and higher).
Add 20% for short barrels (26 in. with open chokes) on 12 ga.
Add 20% for 30 or 32 in. barrels on 28 ga. or .410 bore shotguns.

TROJAN - Parker's lowest-priced gun, single or double triggers, but no auto ejectors available, very rarely found in mint condition because they were used a lot, a genuine utility gun, introduced 1912-13 with approx. 33,000 total mfg.

✳ *Trojan 12 ga.*

100%	98%	95%	90%	80%	70%	60%	50%	40%	30%	20%	10%
N/A	$4,000	$3,500	$3,000	$2,750	$2,500	$2,000	$1,750	$1,500	$1,250	$1,000	$750

✳ *Trojan 16 ga.*

N/A	$4,500	$4,000	$3,500	$3,000	$2,750	$2,500	$2,000	$1,800	$1,500	$1,200	$995

✳ *Trojan 20 ga.*

N/A	$5,000	$4,500	$4,250	$4,000	$3,500	$3,000	$2,750	$2,400	$2,000	$1,800	$1,350

VH - Parker's biggest selling model, offered with all options, the most commonly found Parker. Approx. 79,000 mfg. 10 ga. is very rare in this model.

Add 25%-50% for ejectors, depending on original condition (VHE Model).

✳ *VH 12 ga.*

N/A	$4,500	$4,000	$3,500	$3,000	$2,750	$2,500	$2,250	$2,000	$1,750	$1,500	$1,000

✳ *VH 16 ga.*

N/A	$5,000	$4,500	$4,250	$3,500	$3,2250	$3,000	$2,750	$2,500	$2,250	$2,000	$1,750

✳ *VH 20 ga.*

N/A	$8,000	$7,500	$7,000	$6,500	$6,000	$5,000	$4,500	$4,000	$3,500	$3,000	$2,250

✳ *VH 28 ga.*

N/A	N/A	$25,000	$22,000	$18,000	$15,000	$12,250	$10,000	$8,000	$7,000	$6,500	$6,000

✳ *VH .410 bore.*

N/A	N/A	$30,000	$25,000	$20,000	$17,500	$15,000	$13,500	$12,000	$10,250	$9,000	$7,100

PH - offered for a very short time, most had twist barrels, prices here are for fluid steel barrels only. Approx. 1,400 mfg. A very few .410 bores were mfg. 10 ga. with fluid steel barrels is very rare in this model.

Add 25%-50% for ejectors, depending on original condition (PHE Model).

✳ *PH 12 ga.*

N/A	$5,000	$4,500	$4,000	$3,250	$3,000	$2,750	$2,500	$2,250	$2,000	$1,500

✳ *PH 16 ga.*

N/A	$5,500	$5,000	$4,500	$4,000	$3,750	$3,500	$3,250	$3,000	$2,750	$2,000	$1,500

✳ *PH 20 ga.*

N/A	$9,000	$8,500	$7,950	$7,000	$6,500	$6,000	$5,500	$5,000	$4,500	$4,000	$3,250

100%	98%	95%	90%	80%	70%	60%	50%	40%	30%	20%	10%

✳ *PH 28 ga. & .410 bore*
Extreme rarity precludes accurate pricing on this model.

GH - very popular model, barrels marked "Parker Special Steel", engraved moderately with all options available. 10 ga. with fluid steel barrels is very rare in this model, approx. 4,300 mfg.
    Add 25%-50% for ejectors, depending on original condition (GHE Model).

✳ *GH 12 ga.*

100%	98%	95%	90%	80%	70%	60%	50%	40%	30%	20%	10%
N/A	$6,500	$6,000	$5,500	$5,000	$4,500	$4,000	$3,500	$3,000	$2,750	$2,500	$1,950

✳ *GH 16 ga.*

N/A	$7,000	$6,500	$6,000	$5,500	$5,000	$4,500	$4,000	$3,500	$3,250	$3,000	$2,250

✳ *GH 20 ga.*

N/A	$10,000	$9,500	$8,950	$8,000	$7,250	$6,500	$6,000	$5,500	$5,000	$4,500	$4,000

✳ *GH 28 ga.*

N/A	N/A	$30,000	$25,000	$20,000	$18,250	$15,000	$12,250	$10,000	$8,750	$7,500	$6,950

✳ *GH .410 bore*

N/A	N/A	$40,000	$35,000	$30,000	$25,000	$20,000	$17,250	$15,000	$13,500	$12,000	$10,000

DH - the most popular higher grade gun, very tastefully engraved and flawlessly finished, approx. 9,400 mfg.
    Add 25%-50% for ejectors, depending on original condition (DHE Model).

✳ *DH 12 ga.*

N/A	$8,000	$7,500	$7,000	$6,000	$5,500	$5,000	$4,500	$4,000	$3,500	$3,000	$2,250

✳ *DH 16 ga.*

N/A	$8,500	$8,000	$7,000	$6,500	$6,000	$5,500	$5,000	$4,500	$4,000	$3,500	$2,950

✳ *DH 20 ga.*

N/A	$12,000	$11,500	$10,950	$10,000	$9,000	$8,500	$7,950	$7,000	$6,000	$5,500	$5,000

✳ *DH 28 ga.*

N/A	N/A	$40,000	$35,750	$30,000	$25,250	$21,000	$18,000	$16,500	$14,500	$12,750	$10,500

✳ *DH .410 bore*

N/A	N/A	$60,000	$55,000	$45,000	$40,000	$35,000	$30,000	$25,000	$20,000	$18,000	$15,000

CH - scarce because they were only slightly more decorative than the DH, Acme steel barrels. Approx. 1,100 mfg. 10 ga. is very rare in this model.
    Add 25%-50% for ejectors, depending on original condition (CHE Model).

✳ *CH 12 ga.*

N/A	N/A	$12,000	$11,500	$10,750	$9,000	$8,500	$8,000	$7,500	$7,000	$6,500	$6,000

✳ *CH 16 ga.*

N/A	N/A	$15,000	$14,500	$12,000	$11,500	$11,000	$9,950	$8,500	$7,750	$7,000	$6,000

✳ *CH 20 ga.*

N/A	N/A	$18,000	$17,500	$15,000	$14,500	$14,000	$12,000	$10,000	$9,000	$8,500	$7,950

✳ *CH 28 ga.*

N/A	N/A	$60,000	$55,000	$45,000	$40,000	$35,000	$30,000	$25,000	$20,000	$18,000	$15,000

✳ *CH .410 bore* - very rare, approx. 6 are known to exist.
This model/gauge is very rare, and prices typically start in the $45,000-$80,000 range, depending on original condition.

BH - quite popular and decorative, 4 styles of engraving available, Acme steel barrels. Approx. 700 mfg. 10 ga. is very rare in this model.
    Add 25%-50% for ejectors, depending on original condition (BHE Model).

✳ *BH 12 ga.*

N/A	N/A	$15,000	$14,500	$12,000	$11,500	$11,000	$10,000	$8,500	$8,000	$7,000	$6,000

✳ *BH 16 ga.*

N/A	N/A	$18,000	$17,500	$15,000	$14,500	$14,000	$12,000	$10,000	$9,000	$8,500	$7,950

✳ *BH 20 ga.*

N/A	N/A	$24,000	$21,500	$18,000	$17,000	$16,000	$14,000	$12,000	$11,000	$10,000	$8,000

100%	98%	95%	90%	80%	70%	60%	50%	40%	30%	20%	10%

✳ *BH 28 ga.*

| N/A | N/A | N/A | $80,000 | $70,000 | $60,000 | $50,000 | $42,000 | $40,000 | $35,000 | $30,000 | $25,000 |

✳ *BH .410 bore* - only 2 guns are known in this grade. Extreme rarity precludes accurate price evaluation, but will be VERY expensive.

AH - a scarce gun, extremely decorative and flawlessly executed, Acme steel barrels. Approx. 300 mfg. 10 ga. is very rare in this model.

Add 25%-50% for ejectors, depending on original condition (AHE Model).

✳ *AH 12 ga.*

| N/A | N/A | $25,000 | $23,000 | $20,000 | $19,000 | $18,000 | $16,950 | $15,500 | $14,950 | $14,000 | $12,000 |

✳ *AH 16 ga.*

| N/A | N/A | $30,000 | $28,000 | $25,000 | $24,000 | $23,000 | $21,250 | $20,000 | $18,250 | $17,000 | $15,000 |

✳ *AH 20 ga.*

| N/A | N/A | $40,000 | $38,000 | $35,000 | $34,000 | $33,000 | $31,250 | $30,000 | $28,000 | $27,000 | $25,000 |

✳ *AH 28 ga.*

| N/A | N/A | N/A | $80,000 | $75,000 | $65,000 | $50,000 | $45,000 | $40,000 | $35,000 | $30,000 | $25,000 |

✳ *AH .410 bore* - it is believed that only one gun was manufactured.
Rarity precludes accurate pricing.

AAH - very elaborate model, early AAs have Whitworth barrels, late ones have Peerless. Approx. 240 mfg.

Add 25%-50% for ejectors, depending on original condition (AAHE Model).

✳ *AAH 12 ga.*

| N/A | N/A | $40,000 | $38,000 | $35,000 | $33,250 | $32,000 | $31,000 | $30,000 | $28,250 | $27,000 | $25,000 |

✳ *AAH 16 ga.*

| N/A | N/A | $45,000 | $43,000 | $40,000 | $38,250 | $37,000 | $36,000 | $35,000 | $33,500 | $32,000 | $30,000 |

✳ *AAH 20 ga.*

| N/A | N/A | $60,000 | $58,000 | $55,000 | $52,250 | $50,000 | $47,500 | $45,000 | $42,500 | $40,000 | $35,000 |

✳ *AAH 28 ga.*

| N/A | N/A | N/A | $100,000 | $98,000 | $92,000 | $85,000 | $80,000 | $75,000 | $70,000 | $65,000 | $60,000 |

AAHE (NEW MFG.) - 28 ga., available through Remington Arms Co., and made by Connecticut Shotgun, serialization continues from the last of the Parker Bros. production, limited availability beginning 2006.

The current MSR on this model is $49,000.

A-1 SPECIAL GRADE - 100% engraved, all were special ordered, each one inspected by the company president before being shipped. Approx. 80 mfg.

✳ *A-1 Special Grade 12 ga.*

| N/A | N/A | $80,000 | $75,000 | $70,000 | $65,000 | $60,000 | $55,000 | $50,000 | $45,000 | $40,000 | $35,000 |

✳ *A-1 Special Grade 16 ga.*

| N/A | N/A | $90,000 | $85,000 | $80,000 | $75,000 | $70,000 | $65,000 | $60,000 | $55,000 | $50,000 | $45,000 |

✳ *A-1 Special Grade 20 ga.*

| N/A | N/A | N/A | $120,000 | $115,000 | $110,000 | $100,000 | $95,000 | $90,000 | $85,000 | $80,000 | $75,000 |

✳ *A-1 Special Grade 28 ga.* - extreme rarity and desirability factors preclude accurate price evaluation by condition factors. 70% original condition A-1 Specials HAVE sold for up to $200,000.

INVINCIBLE GRADE - only 3 documented mfg. $1,250 MSR circa 1930, extreme rarity and desirability factors preclude accurate price evaluation on this model. Currently, all three guns are owned by the same collector.

SHOTGUNS: SINGLE BARREL TRAP

12 or 20 (rare) ga., 26 (20 ga. only, rare), 28 (very rare), 30 (rare), 32, or 34 (rare) in. barrels, any boring was available, as was stock configuration, boxlock, auto ejector. The grades differ only in engraving, checkering and wood finish.

It should be noted that single barrel trap guns cannot be compared to the SxS models, as they

100%	98%	95%	90%	80%	70%	60%	50%	40%	30%	20%	10%

are not as desirable, even though they are more rare. Approximately 1,900 Parker single barrel trap guns were manufactured, mostly in SC Grade. Most SxS collectors are not that interested in single barrel trap models and very few collectors specialize in single barrels.

Add 15% for 30 or 34 in. barrel.

S.C. GRADE

N/A	$8,000	$7,500	$7,000	$6,000	$5,000	$4,000	$3,250	$2,500	$2,250	$2,000	$1,800

S.B. GRADE

N/A	$9,000	$8,500	$8,000	$7,000	$6,000	$5,000	$4,000	$3,500	$3,250	$3,000	$2,000

S.A. GRADE

N/A	$12,000	$11,500	$11,000	$10,000	$9,000	$8,000	$7,000	$6,500	$6,250	$6,000	$5,500

S.A.A. GRADE

Extreme rarity (research indicates only one manufactured) precludes accurate pricing.

S.A.-1 SPECIAL GRADE

Extreme rarity (research indicates only four manufactured) precludes accurate pricing. One known 100% example recently sold in the $30,000 - $40,000 range.

PARKER PISTOLS

Refer to the Wyoming Arms section in this text.

PARKER REPRODUCTIONS

Previously imported by the Parker Reproduction Division of Reagent Chemical & Research, Inc., located in Middlesex, NJ. Previously distributed by Parker Reproductions located in Webb City, MO. These shotguns were manufactured in Japan to original Parker specifications by Winchester until the factory closed in January, 1989.

In 1984, Winchester was contracted by Reagent Chemical & Research, Inc. to manufacture a new Parker shotgun. The new SxS was a DHE model, available in 20 and 28 ga. initially. These models were fabricated in Japan to original Parker specifications, and the reproduction was so authentic that most parts are interchangeable with the late Parkers made by Remington in Ilion, NY. In 1993, a 16/20 ga. combo was introduced in some models. On Sept. 17, 1999, a flood destroyed all remaining inventory including parts.

During 2004, Connecticut Shotgun Manufacturing Company offered a limited quantity of A1 Specials in-the-white w/o metal finish and engraving in 12 or 20 ga. only, without cases or accessories. MSRs were $5,850 for one set of barrels and $6,750 for a 2 barrel set.

GRADING - PPGS™	100%	98%	95%	90%	80%	70%	60%

SHOTGUNS: SxS

Because of the high quality and limited mfg. of these reproductions, they have become very collectible, as they offer the shooter the only realistic alternative to using an original Parker Bros. shotgun. Currently, higher grade Parker Reproductions in smaller gauges are very desirable, and 95%-100% values are getting harder to accurately determine.

DHE GRADE - 12 (new 1986), 20, or 28 (new 1984) ga., 26 or 28 in. barrels, boxlock action, ejectors, single selective or double triggers, beavertail or splinter forend, straight or pistol grip stock, skeleton steel buttplate, engraving in original DH style, case hardened frame, rust blue barrels. Supplied with leather trunk case, canvas and leather cover, and snap caps. Disc.

	100%	98%	95%	90%	80%	70%	60%
12 ga.	$3,495	$3,150	$2,750	$2,500	$2,250	$2,000	$1,850
20 ga.	$4,000	$3,750	$3,450	$3,050	$2,750	$2,500	$2,250
28 ga.	$5,000	$4,500	$3,900	$3,300	$2,850	$2,600	$2,350

Add approx. 10% for SST.
Add $150 for beavertail forend.
Add $650 for Sporting Clays Model w/ choke tubes.
Add $700-$1,150 per extra set of barrels, depending on gauge, configuration, and condition.
Quantities mfg. for this model are as follows: 12 ga. - 2,137 mfg., 20 ga. - 6,050 mfg., 28 ga. - 4,203 mfg.

GRADING - PPGS™	100%	98%	95%	90%	80%	70%	60%

✳ *DHE Grade Steel Shot Special* - similar to 12 ga. D Grade, except has strengthened No. 1 1/2 barrels, 3 in. chambers, and 28 in. chrome lined barrels, 7 1/4-7 1/2 lbs. Approx. 350 mfg. 1987-89.

	$4,350	$3,650	$3,100	$2,675	$2,250	$1,850	$1,700

Last MSR was $3,370.

 Add $100 for beavertail forend.

✳ *DHE Grade Small Gauge Combo* - available in either 28 ga./.410 bore (disc.) or 16/20 ga. (mfg. 1993-97) combo with 2 barrels and 2 forends. Less than 160 mfg. of the 28 ga./.410 bore combo. Disc.

❖ **DHE Grade Small Gauge Combo 28 ga./.410 bore**

	$7,000	$5,750	$4,500	$4,000	$3,625	$3,150	$2,900

Last MSR was $4,970.

❖ **DHE Grade Small Gauge Combo 16/20 ga.** - new 1994 - disc.

	$6,250	$4,750	$4,000	$3,600	$3,300	$2,950	$2,600

Last MSR was $4,870.

✳ *DHE Grade 3-Barrel Set* - includes two 28 ga. and one .410 bore barrels, cased. Disc.

	$9,000	$7,500	$6,500	$5,500	$4,750	$4,000	$3,600

Last MSR was $5,630.

BHE GRADE LIMITED EDITION - 12, 20, 28 ga. or 410 bore, original Parker BH specifications, single selective or double trigger(s), 26 or 28 in. barrels, straight or pistol grip stock, engraved skeleton buttplate, bank note scroll engraving around game scenes, cased. Only 100 manufactured in each gauge during late 1987-89. Disc.

	$5,850	$5,000	$4,650	$4,150	$3,750	$2,750	$2,150

Last MSR was $3,970.

 Add $1,000 for 20 ga.
 Add $4,000 for 28 ga. or .410 bore.
 Add $1,750 per extra set of barrels, if in mint condition.
 Add $150 for beavertail forend.
 A 28 ga./.410 bore combo was also available with 2 forends. Only seven 28 gauges were mfg. in this model.

A-1 SPECIAL - 12, 16/20 ga. combo (introduced 1993), 20, or 28 ga., original Parker A-1 specifications, 26 or 28 in. barrels, single selective or double trigger(s), fine scroll engraving with game scenes, 32 lines/in. checkering, cased with accessories. Limited mfg. 1988-89.

	$10,500	$8,500	$7,250	$6,000	$5,475	$4,800	$4,350

Last MSR was $11,200.

 Add $3,000+ for 28 ga.
 Add $2,000 for 20 ga.
 Add $1,750 for extra set of barrels.
 Add $200 for beavertail forend.
 Add $1,700 for 16 ga. barrel (splinter model only).
 Fourteen 3 barrel sets were mfg. in this grade, which included two 28 ga. barrels (26 and 28 in.) and one .410 bore barrel (26 in.). Rarity factor precludes accurate pricing.

✳ *A-1 Special Custom Engraved* - custom (per individual special order) engraving, available with two sets of barrels only, cased with accessories. Limited mfg. 1988-89. Prices started at $11,000 and go up according to individualized special features.

✳ *A-1 Special Federal Duck Stamp Collector's Series* - available in 12 or 20 ga., A-1 Special specifications, authorized by U.S. Department of Interior. Mfg. was limited to 10 per year in 1988-89 only.

	$13,500	$10,000	$8,000	$7,000	$6,250	$5,500	$4,750

Last MSR was $14,000.

This model included special case and 2 barrels per buyer's specifications.

GRADING - PPGS™	100%	98%	95%	90%	80%	70%	60%

PARKER-HALE LIMITED

Previous gun manufacturer located in Birmingham, England. Rifles were manufactured in England until 1991 when Navy Arms purchased the manufacturing rights and built a plant in West Virginia for fabrication. This new company was called Gibbs Rifle Company, Inc. and they manufactured models very similar to older Parker-Hale rifles during 1992-94. Shotguns were manufactured in Spain and imported by Precision Sports, a division of Cortland Line Company, Inc. located in Cortland, NY until 1993.

Parker was the previous trade name of the A.G. Parker Company, located in Birmingham, England, which was formed from a gun making business founded in 1890 by Alfred Gray Parker. The company became the Parker-Hale company in 1936. The company was purchased by John Rothery Wholesale circa 2000.

Parker-Hale Ltd. continues to make a wide variety of high quality firearms cleaning accessories for both rifles and shotguns, including their famous bipod.

RIFLES: BOLT ACTION

All Parker-Hale rifle importation was discontinued in 1991. Parker-Hale bolt action rifles utilize the Mauser K-98 action and were offered in a variety of configurations. A single set trigger option was introduced in 1984 on most models, which allows either "hair trigger" or conventional single stage operation - add $85.

MODEL 81 CLASSIC - available in 11 cals. between .22-250 Rem., and 7mm Rem. Mag., 24 in. barrel, open sights, 4 shot mag., select checkered walnut with sling swivels, 7 3/4 lbs. New 1985.

$715	$565	$475	$395	$340	$300	$280

Last MSR was $860.

✱ *Model 81 Classic African* - .375 H&H or 9.3x62mm Mauser cal., similar specifications as Model 81 Classic and has engraved action. New 1986.

$875	$700	$600	$500	$425	$360	$330

Last MSR was $1,110.

MODEL 84 TARGET - .308 Win. cal., match rifle with special sights, adj. cheekpiece on stock. Importation disc. 1990.

$1,080	$875	$760	$680	$610	$530	$465

Last MSR was $1,300.

MODEL 85 SNIPER RIFLE - .308 Win. cal., bolt action, extended heavy barrel, 10 shot mag., camo green synthetic stock with stippling, built in adj. bipod, enlarged contoured bolt, adj. recoil pad. Importation began 1989.

$2,650	$2,250	$1,700	$1,475	$1,250	$1,050	$875

Last MSR was $1,975.

MODEL 86 TARGET - .308 Win. cal., 27 1/2 in. barrel, 5 shot mag., stippled stock and forend, aperture front and rear sights, 11 1/4 lbs. Distributed 1986 only by North American Precision.

$980	$830	$760	$690	$610	$530	$465

Last MSR was $1,149.

MODEL 87 TARGET - .243 Win., 6.5x55mm Swedish, .308 Win., .30-06, or .300 Win. Mag. cal., target stock, aperture sights. Importation began 1987.

$1,375	$1,100	$900	$775	$650	$550	$495

Last MSR was $1,525.

MODEL 1000 STANDARD - available in 9 cals. between .22-250 Rem. and .308 Win., 22 in. barrel, 4 shot mag., walnut stock with cheekpiece, 7 1/4 lbs. Disc. 1988.

$400	$330	$285	$255	$230	$215	$195

Last MSR was $500.

GRADING - PPGS™	100%	98%	95%	90%	80%	70%	60%

MODEL 1100 LIGHTWEIGHT - available in 9 cals. between .22-250 Rem. and .30-06, 22 in. barrel, open sights, 4 shot mag., 6 1/2 lbs. New 1985.

	$495	$400	$350	$325	$285	$270	$255

Last MSR was $595.

* *Model 1100M Lightweight African* - .375 H&H, .404 Jeffery, or .458 Win. Mag. cal., 24 in. barrel, 4 shot mag., 9 1/2 lbs.

	$800	$650	$575	$500	$450	$425	$400

Last MSR was $960.

MODEL 1200 SUPER - bolt action, Mauser type action, .22-250 Rem., .243 Win., 6mm Rem., .25-06 Rem., .270 Win., .30-06, .300 Win. Mag., 7mm Rem. Mag., or .308 Win. cal., 24 in. barrel, folding sight, skip checkered walnut stock, sling swivels, rosewood pistol grip cap and forend tip. New 1968-disc.

	$540	$450	$375	$330	$295	$275	$260

Last MSR was $680.

This model in Magnum cals. was called the 1200 M Super Magnum.

* *Model 1200 C (Super Clip)* - similar to Model 1200 Super, except has detachable 4 shot box mag.

	$590	$500	$400	$350	$300	$280	$265

Last MSR was $740.

MODEL 1200P PRESENTATION - similar to 1200, except .243 Win. or .30-06 cal., scroll engraved, no sights. Mfg. 1969-75.

	$495	$425	$395	$340	$315	$305	$275

MODEL 1200 SUPER VARMINT - similar to 1200, except .22-250 Rem., 6mm Rem., .25-06 Rem., or .243 Win. cal., 24 in. heavy barrel, no sights. Disc. 1988.

	$525	$425	$365	$325	$285	$270	$255

Last MSR was $660.

MODEL 1300 C SCOUT - shorter barrel variation.

	$695	$550	$450	$385	$330	$300	$275

Last MSR was $785.

MODEL 2100 MIDLAND (HYBRID ACTION) - available in 11 cals. between .22-250 Rem. - .300 Win. Mag. cal., 22 in. barrel, 4 shot mag., open sights, 7 lbs.

	$325	$270	$230	$200	$190	$180	$170

Last MSR was $365.

* *Model 2100 Midland Magnum* - .300 Win. Mag., or 7mm Rem. Mag. cal., 24 in. barrel, 4 shot mag., 9 1/2 lbs. Imported 1989-90 only.

	$380	$325	$295	$270	$260	$250	$240

Last MSR was $430.

MODEL 2600 MIDLAND SPECIAL - .243 Win., .270 Win., .308 Win., or .30-06 cal., Midland Gun Co. action, iron sights. New 1989.

	$295	$250	$225	$200	$190	$180	$170

Last MSR was $330.

MIDLAND 2700 LIGHTWEIGHT - lightweight variation of the Model 2600.

	$340	$285	$240	$200	$190	$180	$170

Last MSR was $390.

SHOTGUNS: SxS

Parker-Hale shotguns were manufactured by Ugartechea in Eibar, Spain and imported as Parker-Hale models by Precision Sports located in Cortland, NY until 1994.

GRADING - PPGS™	100%	98%	95%	90%	80%	70%	60%

PATRIOT ORDNANCE FACTORY

Current rifle manufacturer located in Glendale, AZ.

Patriot Ordnance Factory manufactures AR-15 style paramilitary rifles, as well as upper and lower receivers and various parts. Current models include the P-415 rifle with 16 or 18 in. barrel (MSR starts at $1,595), and the P308 with a 16 1/2 or 20 in. barrel (MSR is $2,400). Please contact the company directly for more information, including options and availability (see Trademark Index).

PASTUSEK INDUSTRIES

Previous manufacturer located in Fort Worth, TX 1993-2000.

PISTOLS: SEMI-AUTO

HSK (SPORT KING) - .22 LR cal., 4 1/2 or 5 1/2 in. barrel. Mfg. 1995-2000.

$275	$250	$225	$195	$175	$150	$135

Last MSR was $312.

HSS (SHARPSHOOTER) - .22 LR cal., 5 1/2 in. bull barrel. Mfg. 1995-2000.

$315	$275	$240	$210	$190	$165	$150

Last MSR was $379.

HSC (SUPERMATIC CITATION) - .22 LR cal., 5 1/2 bull or 7 1/4 in. fluted barrel. Mfg. 1995-2000.

$340	$295	$265	$230	$210	$180	$165

Last MSR was $388.

Add $22 for 7 1/4 in. fluted barrel.

This model was also available with an 8, 10, or 12 in. bull barrel.

HST (SUPERMATIC TROPHY) - .22 LR cal., 5 1/2 bull or 7 1/4 in. fluted barrel. Mfg. 1995-2000.

$400	$340	$275	$240	$220	$180	$165

Last MSR was $494.

This model was also available with an 8, 10, or 12 in. bull barrel. Left-hand ejection is also an option on this model.

HSV (VICTOR) - .22 LR cal., 3 7/8, 4 1/2, 5 1/2, 8 (optional), or 10 (optional) in. VR barrel. Mfg. 1995-2000.

$475	$375	$300	$250	$230	$185	$165

Last MSR was $569.

Add $30 for dove tail rib on 5 1/2 in. barrel only.
Add $79 for Weaver rib on 5 1/2 in. barrel only.

HSO (OLYMPIC) - .22 S or .22 LR cal., 6 3/4 in. barrel only. Mfg. 1995-2000.

$495	$395	$325	$265	$245	$195	$170

Last MSR was $599.

PAUZA SPECIALTIES

Previously manufactured by Pauza Specialties circa 1991-96, and located in Baytown, TX. Previously distributed by U.S. General Technologies, Inc. located in South San Francisco, CA.

Pauza currently manufactures the P50 semi-auto rifle for Firearms International, Inc. - please refer to that section for current information.

RIFLES

P50 SEMI-AUTO - .50 BMG cal., semi-auto, 24 (carbine) or 29 (rifle) in. match grade barrel, 5 shot detachable mag., one-piece receiver, 3-stage gas system, takedown action, all exterior parts Teflon coated, with aluminum bipod, 25 or 30 lbs. Mfg. 1992-96.

$5,950	$5,250	$4,600	$4,100	$3,650	$3,200	$2,800

Last MSR was $6,495.

GRADING - PPGS™	100%	98%	95%	90%	80%	70%	60%

PEACE RIVER CLASSICS

Previous manufacturer located in Bartow, FL until 2001. Peace River Classics was a division of Tim's Guns.

RIFLES: SEMI-AUTO

PEACE RIVER CLASSICS SEMI-AUTO - .223 Rem. or .308 Win. (new 1998) cal., available in 3 configurations including the Shadowood, the Glenwood, and the Royale, hand-built utilizing Armalite action, patterned after the AR-15, matched parts throughout, special serialization, laminate thumbhole stock. Mfg. 1997-2001.

$2,575	$2,275	$2,000	$1,775	$1,525	$1,250	$995

Last MSR was $2,695.

Add $300 for .308 Win. cal.

PEDERSEN CUSTOM GUNS

Previously manufactured circa 1973-1975 by O.F. Mossberg located in North Haven, CT. Pedersen Custom Guns was a division of O.F. Mossberg.

RIFLES: BOLT ACTION

MODEL 3000 - .270 Win., .30-06, 7mm Rem. Mag., or .338 Win. Mag. cal., Mossberg Model 810 action, 22 or 24 in. barrel, open sights, checkered Monte Carlo stock.

* *Model 3000 Grade III* - no engraving.

$550	$495	$470	$440	$420	$385	$330

* *Model 3000 Grade II* - moderately engraved.

$660	$580	$525	$495	$440	$420	$385

* *Model 3000 Grade I* - heavily engraved and inlaid, with select wood.

$990	$770	$745	$690	$635	$560	$495

* *Model 3000 Presentation* - top-of-the-line model.

$1,250	$1,000	$895	$800	$745	$690	$635

MODEL 4700 - .30-30 Win. or .35 Rem. cal., custom deluxe lever action, (Model 472 Mossberg), 5 shot, tube mag., 24 in. barrel, open sight, black walnut stock.

$250	$195	$165	$155	$145	$130	$120

SHOTGUNS: O/U

MODEL 1500 HUNTING GUN - 12 ga., 2 3/4 or 3 in. chambers, 26 in. imp. cyl. and mod., 28 in. mod. and full, 30 in. mod. and full barrels, boxlock, auto ejectors, selective or non-selective single trigger, checkered pistol grip stock. Mfg. 1973-75.

$700	$575	$500	$440	$415	$385	$365

MODEL 1500 SKEET - similar to Hunting Gun, except 27 in. skeet barrel, skeet stock. Mfg. 1973-75.

$725	$600	$525	$450	$425	$400	$385

MODEL 1500 TRAP - similar to Hunting Gun, except 30 and 32 in. full barrels, trap Monte Carlo stock. Mfg. 1973-75.

$650	$550	$475	$435	$410	$375	$350

MODEL 1000 HUNTING GUN - 12 or 20 ga., 26, 28, or 30 in. barrels, various chokes, boxlock, auto ejectors, SST, checkered select walnut stock, silver inlays, more engraving. Mfg. 1973-75.

Grade I	$2,200	$1,980	$1,870	$1,700	$1,540	$1,460	$1,375
Grade II	$1,815	$1,540	$1,430	$1,265	$1,185	$1,100	$1,045

GRADING - PPGS™	100%	98%	95%	90%	80%	70%	60%

MODEL 1000 TRAP GUN - similar to Hunting Gun, but 12 ga., 30 or 32 in. mod. and full barrels, Monte Carlo trap stock. Mfg. 1973-75.

	100%	98%	95%	90%	80%	70%	60%
Grade I	$2,100	$1,800	$1,650	$1,500	$1,350	$1,200	$995
Grade II	$1,650	$1,500	$1,375	$1,200	$1,050	$900	$725

MODEL 1000 SKEET - similar to Hunting Gun, except 26 or 28 in. barrels, bored skeet. Mfg. 1973-75.

	100%	98%	95%	90%	80%	70%	60%
Grade I	$2,255	$2,145	$2,035	$1,870	$1,705	$1,625	$1,540
Grade II	$1,980	$1,705	$1,595	$1,430	$1,350	$1,265	$1,210

SHOTGUNS: SxS

MODEL 200 - 12 or 20 ga., 26 in. imp. cyl. and mod., 28 in. mod. and full, 30 in. mod. and full barrels, boxlock, auto ejectors, SST. Mfg. 1973-74.

	100%	98%	95%	90%	80%	70%	60%
Grade I	$2,420	$2,175	$2,090	$1,955	$1,790	$1,705	$1,625
Grade II	$2,200	$1,955	$1,815	$1,735	$1,625	$1,540	$1,485

MODEL 2500 - 12 or 20 ga., 26 in. imp. cyl. and mod., 28 in. mod. and full barrels, auto ejectors, boxlock, checkered pistol grip stock and forearm.

100%	98%	95%	90%	80%	70%	60%
$470	$385	$360	$305	$275	$260	$240

SHOTGUNS: SLIDE ACTION

MODEL 4000 - custom Mossberg Model 500, 12, 20 ga., or .410 bore, 3 in. chamber, 26 in. imp. cyl. or skeet, 28 in. full or mod. barrel, 30 in. full, vent. rib, floral engraved, checkered select walnut stock. Mfg. 1975.

100%	98%	95%	90%	80%	70%	60%
$460	$375	$330	$305	$265	$230	$220

MODEL 4000 TRAP - similar to 4000, except 12 ga., 30 in. full barrel, Monte Carlo trap stock and pad. Mfg. 1975.

100%	98%	95%	90%	80%	70%	60%
$485	$395	$350	$325	$285	$255	$240

MODEL 4500 - similar to 4000, less engraving.

100%	98%	95%	90%	80%	70%	60%
$420	$330	$305	$275	$240	$200	$175

MODEL 4500 TRAP - similar to 4000 Trap, less engraving.

100%	98%	95%	90%	80%	70%	60%
$440	$350	$310	$280	$240	$210	$200

PEDERSOLI, DAVIDE & C. Snc.

Current manufacturer of modern, black powder, and older historically significant firearms located in Brescia, Italy. Currently, full-line distributors include Cherry's Fine Guns, located in Greensboro, NC, and Dixie Gun Works, Inc., located in Union City, TN. Current importers include Cabela's, located in Sidney, NE, Cimarron, FA Co., located in Fredricksburg, TX, and Navy Arms, located in Martinsburg, WV. Previously imported by E.M.F., located in Santa Ana, CA.

D. Pedersoli manufactures top quality black powder replicas and other high quality firearms reproductions.

For more information and up-to-date pricing regarding current Pedersoli black powder models, please refer to the *Blue Book of Modern Black Powder Arms* by John Allen. These books feature hundreds of color photographs and support text of the most recent black powder models available, as well as complete pricing and a reference guide.

Black Powder Reproductions & Replicas by Dennis Adler is also an invaluable source for most black powder reproductions and replicas, and includes hundreds of color images on most popular makes/models, provides manufacturer/trademark histories, and up-to-date information on related items/accessories for black powder shooting - www.bluebookinc.com

RIFLES: REPRODUCTIONS

Pedersoli reproduction rifles are listed separately under Dixie Gun Works and the importers listed above (except Cabela's) - please refer to the individual listings. Current models include: Remington Rolling Block (various configurations), 1859 Sharps (various configura-

GRADING - PPGS™	100%	98%	95%	90%	80%	70%	60%

tions), 1863 Sharps, 1874 Sharps (many variations), Springfield Trapdoor Rifle/Carbine (many variations), Lightning slide action rifle (including an engraved model, 300 mfg. beginning 2007 with $2,995 MSR, available from Cherry's only), and the Kodiak SxS double rifle (many variations). For current pricing on older Pedersoli marked reproductions, please refer to similar model/configurations under the importer's listings.

SHOTGUNS: REPRODUCTIONS

Pedersoli also manufactured a limited number of O/U and SxS shotguns between 1957-1973. These guns have had little importation into the U.S. Current values for these guns would be $650-$1,250, depending on features and configurations.

PENTHENY de PENTHENY

Current manufacturer and gunsmith established in 1987, and located in Santa Rosa, CA.

RIFLES: BOLT ACTION

The rifles listed include ebony forend tips, old English style black recoil pads, steel skeleton grip caps, four panels of 22 LPI checkering, and other custom features. These models are built on a U.S.R.A. Model 70 action.

THE INVADER - small and medium bore cals., classic styled Claro walnut stock, blue finish.

MSR $5,400	$5,400	$4,500	$3,850	$2,975	$2,400	$1,975	$1,500

THE NORMAN - Mag. cals., classic styled English walnut stock, blue finish.

MSR $5,400	$5,400	$4,500	$3,850	$2,975	$2,400	$1,975	$1,500

THE CONQUEROR - large bore cals., classic styled English walnut stock, blue finish, rifle has secondary recoil lug, dual steel reinforcing bolts, and express sights including fixed and folding leaves.

MSR $6,300	$6,300	$5,500	$4,750	$3,650	$3,000	$2,400	$1,975

PERAZZI

Current manufacturer established in 1957, and located in Brescia, Italy. Imported and distributed by Perazzi USA, Inc. located in Azusa, CA. Previously located in Monrovia, CA until 2002, and in Rome, NY.

Ivo Fabbri and Daniel Perazzi were partners in the shotgun manufacturing business beginning in 1960 - these guns are ser. no. 5001-5339.

Note: Previously, Perazzi shotguns were imported by both Winchester and Ithaca during the 1960s and 1970s. The company now has its own distribution network and its current model line-up is extensive. Perazzi shotguns are well known for their quality control standards and reliability in clay target championships and in-field conditions.

SHOTGUNS

Perazzi shotguns have incorporated many improvements during their manufacture. One of the most important changes has been the modification of the forearm design. Basically, there have been 4 different types: Type 1 has a serial range of 30,000-33,250, Type 2 is serial numbered 33,251- 35,450, Type 3 has a range of 35,451-51,242, Type 4 started at 51,243 and is still current as of this writing. Differences include changes in the forearm iron and barrel lug attachment. Because of these forearm changes (and other parts modifications), the desirability factor on a Type 4 forearm shotgun as opposed to a Type 1 is much greater. Competition shooters prefer Type 4 as they are the current design. If a Type 1 or 2 competition gun develops problems, they are automatically retrofitted to the Type 4 design - and these modifications are expensive. For these reasons, the serial number of a Perazzi competition gun will determine its type. Since Types 1 through 3 are discontinued, Types 1 and 2 will be less desirable (and less expensive) than the values listed for Type 4.

As a final note on older Perazzi shotguns, the most collectible models will be those specimens which exhibit the highest quality and are equally rare. Older SCO grades on small frames with older style "V" springs are at the top for desirability. Also, any older SPECIAL GUNS were all custom made - usually engraved by master engravers with Angelo Galeazzi being considered the best.

Perazzi Shotguns Information

Not until 1988 did most single barrel trap guns have a "Special" option package which includes an adjustable trigger group (designated P4).

Models listed in the following sections assume a Type 4 forearm attachment design and are serial numbered 51,243 and above. Models that are serial numbered below 51,243 are an older design and will be priced less than the newer Type 4 models.

Rather than describe all the following models individually, descriptions will appear only once and are listed. The various grades have similar features and engraving (i.e., an SCO Grade Sideplate in American Skeet would appear similar to an American Trap SCO Grade Sideplate, except for stock dimensions of course).

Older SHO (Type 3s) and DHO models with rebounding hammers (disc.) are perhaps the most collectible Perazzi shotguns currently.

SC3 and other higher grade models have not been listed due to space consideration. The 14th edition does include all pertinent information (including 1993 pricing) pertaining to Perazzi higher grade models.

Recently, some Model MX8s have been modified by adding sideplates and other markings of the Extra Gold and SCO Models. These forgeries usually have the original markings polished off and have not been reproofed. Perazzi will verify any gun suspected of upgrading. Perazzi discontinued "Mirage" model nomenclature during 1998.

Perazzi Grades and Descriptions

Due to space considerations and relative low manufacture, the higher grade Perazzis have been described but not individually priced. Please contact Perazzi, USA for more information and prices on these higher grades (see Trademark Index).

GRADES AND DESCRIPTIONS

✱ *Special Model* - introductory level model with high polished blue on barrels and receiver, normally listing model name on lower frame sides in gold letters and numerals. Checkered walnut stock (interchangeable) and forearm, all have adjustable trigger assembly.

✱ *Gold Outline Model* - similar to Standard Model, except has gold line engraving around perimeter of frame, also features better grade of walnut. This configuration is very rare.

✱ *SC3 Model* - features coin finished receiver with different styles of scroll engraving and different patterns of game scene engraving (snipe, grouse, pointing bird dog, or woodcock). Better grade of walnut than the Gold Outline Model.

✱ *SCO Model* - more elaborate than SC3 Model in that it features different styles of scroll engraving (deep relief "gargoyles" or fine English scroll) and different game scene engraving patterns. Again, a better grade of walnut (in addition to finer checkering) is utilized.

✱ *SCO Gold Grade Model* - differentiated from SCO Model in that it has engraving patterns featuring multiple gold inlays on receiver sides (including different duck scenes, separate grouse scenes, woodcock, and deep relief "gargoyle").

✱ *SCO Grade Sideplate Model* - includes coin finished receiver with game scene engraved sideplates (with boxlock action). Game scene engraving choices include different duck scenes, grouse, "Chisel" relief scroll, and Diana Goddess of the Hunt pattern.

✱ *SCO Gold Grade Sideplate Model* - similar to SCO Grade Sideplate Model, except has game figures on sideplates in relief gold. Patterns include different grouse scenes, separate ducks patterns, and dogs flushing upland game. This model can also be ordered with detachment lever for sideplates.

✳ *Extra Grade Model* - denoted by top-of-the-line fine bank note style game scene engraving with elaborate scroll and relief work on metal perimeters. Game scene choices include different dog scenes, grouse, and duck. Top quality Circassian walnut finely checkered.

✳ *Extra Gold Grade Model* - top-of-the-line boxlock model that differs from Extra Grade Model in that birds/dogs are in gold relief. This model can also be ordered with detachment lever for sideplates.

✳ *SHO Over & Under Model* - features sidelock action with coin finished receiver and intricate bank note game scene engraving with choices including different duck patterns and pheasant. Top quality walnut and checkering. Type One SHOs have non-rebounding firing pins, while Type Two guns have rebounding firing pins (since 1985).

This model is individually handmade per customer's specifications. Currently, no orders are being taken for this series.

✳ *SHO Gold Over & Under Model* - similar to SHO Over & Under Model, except features game scene of wildlife in relief gold. This model is the best sidelock special order grade that Perazzi currently offers for sale.

This model is individually handmade per customer's specifications. Currently, no orders are being taken for this series.

✳ *DHO SxS Models* - top-of-the-line sidelock model in 12 ga. only for DHO and DHO Gold grades. DHO Extra and DHO Gold Extra grades have similar engraving to Extra Grade and Extra Gold Grade models and are available in all gauges. The DHO Gold Extra is the most elaborate, highly finished SxS shotgun that an individual can currently special order from any company. The DHO model is exceedingly rare, and specimens should be appraised individually.

This model is entirely handmade per customer's specifications. Currently, no orders are being taken for this series.

SHOTGUNS: RECENT MFG.

Perazzi manufactures approx. 2,000 O/U and single barrel shotguns annually, yet there are nearly 200 models! Because of this, and due to space considerations, only the Standard Grade models are listed and priced separately below, with discipline(s) listed in either O/U or single barrel configurations. Current models listed below have a removable trigger group, fixed ribs, chokes, and stocks unless otherwise noted.

Higher grade Perazzi models, including the SC3 Grade, SCO Grade, SCO Gold Grade, SCO Grade w/ sideplates, and SCO Gold w/sideplates have current MSRs only, and are listed under the individual discipline category names.

The MX-3, MX-3 Special, MX-5, MX-6, MX-7, MX-11, MX-14, MX-15, and the MX-16 models all have plain receivers, not sea shell scalloped. The MX-3, MX-5, MX-6, and the MX-7 models all have rounded monobloc barrels.

In recent years, some grey market Perazzis have been imported to the U.S. from the England. These guns may not have the same warranty as the shotguns imported by Perazzi USA.

All values are for O/U models, unless otherwise stated.

Add $300 for detachable trigger group with barrel selector.
Add $200 for guns with older generation factory choke tube set.
Add $400 for guns with fourth generation or newer factory choke tube set.
Subtract 20% for models with only one single barrel w/o adj. rib, unless originally priced as a single barrel gun.
Subtract 20% for fixed SK/SK choke.
Subtract 10% for all fixed choke Trap guns with non-selective trigger group, unless originally priced as a Trap model.

MIRAGE - similar features as the MX-8, in all configurations.

	$6,000	$5,000	$4,000	$3,500	$3,000	$2,750	$2,500

Subtract 20% for older Ithaca and Winchester imports.

MT-6 - introduced for the 1976 Montreal Olympics, silver strips on receiver, fixed trigger group.

$3,200	$2,500	$2,200	$2,000	$1,800	$1,600	$1,400

Add 5% for later production blue receiver.

MS 80 - introduced for the 1980 Moscow Olympics, fixed trigger group.

$3,700	$3,000	$2,400	$2,100	$1,900	$1,700	$1,500

MX-1 - same type of receiver as the MX-8, live pigeon gun, top firing, removable trigger group.

MSR $11,731

$6,500	$5,500	$4,500	$3,500	$3,000	$2,700	$2,400

Currently, live pigeon guns that fire the top barrel first are not as desirable as bottom first, since chokes are reversed.

MX-3 - plain receiver, detachable trigger group, top firing, rounded monobloc, econo model. Disc.

$4,000	$3,200	$2,700	$2,400	$2,100	$1,800	$1,600

Add 5% for "Special" model with adj. trigger group and square monobloc.

MX-5 - plain side receiver, fixed trigger group, rounded monobloc, entry level model introduced in 1985.

$3,900	$3,200	$2,600	$2,200	$2,000	$1,700	$1,500

Add 10% for 20 ga. Field.

MX-6 - plain side receiver, same removable trigger group as the MX-8, rounded monobloc, entry level model.

$4,200	$3,400	$2,800	$2,500	$2,200	$1,900	$1,700

MX-7 - plain side receiver, fixed trigger group, rounded monobloc, entry level model introduced in 1992.

$4,100	$3,300	$2,700	$2,300	$2,100	$1,800	$1,600

MX-8 - 12, 20, 28 ga. or .410 bore, single or O/U barrels, standard of all current Perazzi models, removable trigger group with flat or coil spring, made in all configurations and disciplines, introduced in 1968 as the model for the Mexico City Olympics.

MSR $11,731

$7,800	$6,800	$5,800	$4,800	$4,000	$3,500	$3,000

Subtract 20%-25% for older Ithaca and Winchester imports.

✴ *MX-8B* - similar to MX-8, detachable coil spring trigger group, promotional model, limited configuration.

$6,800	$5,800	$4,800	$3,800	$3,000	$2,750	$2,500

✴ *MX-8L* - similar to MX-8, except has engraved action, this model is not available as a pigeon gun.

MSR $13,804

$9,150	$7,775	$6,250	$5,500	$4,850	$4,250	$3,750

Add $1,501 for seven choke tubes and engraving (Model MX-8LC, Sporting configuration only).

✴ *MX-8 Special* - similar to MX-8, except has ramped rib and adj. trigger. New 2004.

MSR $12,155

$8,200	$6,200	$5,500	$5,000	$4,400	$3,800	$3,250

MX-9 - similar to MX-8, except has changeable sight and adj. comb.

$6,500	$5,500	$4,900	$4,400	$3,800	$3,300	$2,800

MX-10/MX-10RS - similar to MX-8, except has adj. rib and comb, motly in Trap configuration, RS model has higher adj. rib for American Trap.

MSR $11,914

$8,000	$7,000	$5,800	$4,700	$4,000	$3,500	$3,000

MX-11 - plain side receiver with square monobloc, removable trigger group, entry level model.

$5,000	$4,200	$3,500	$3,100	$2,800	$2,600	$2,200

GRADING - PPGS™	100%	98%	95%	90%	80%	70%	60%

MX-12/MX-20 - 12 or 20 ga., non-removable trigger group, available in only Sporting or Field configuration, seashell sculpted receiver, engraving on frame border, trigger guard and forend.

MSR $11,731	$7,800	$6,500	$5,500	$4,500	$3,800	$3,300	$3,000

Add approx. $400 ($834 MSR) for seven choke tubes (Model MX-12C - MX-20C, Sporting configuration only).

MX-14 TRAP - unsingle combo with fixed rib, adj. comb, same receiver as the MX-15, entry level model.

Combo	$6,800	$5,900	$5,200	$4,600	$4,000	$3,500	$3,000

MX-15 SINGLE BARREL TRAP - unsingle only, with adj. rib, adj. comb, plain side receiver with removable trigger group.

MSR $9,987	$5,800	$4,800	$4,000	$3,600	$3,200	$2,700	$2,200

* *MX-15L Single Barrel Trap* - similar to MX-15, except has engraved action.

MSR $12,060	$6,500	$5,700	$5,100	$4,600	$4,000	$3,500	$3,000

MX-16 - limited production entry level model, plain side receiver, non-detachable, selective trigger with flat spring.

	$5,800	$4,800	$4,000	$3,600	$3,200	$2,800	$2,400

MX-28 - 28 ga., Field Grade only, otherwise similar to MX-12.

MSR $23,462	$14,000	$8,500	$7,500	$6,600	$5,800	$5,200	$4,600

Add approx. $400 for choke tubes.

MX-410 - .410 bore, Field Grade only, otherwise similar to MX-28.

MSR $23,462	$14,000	$8,500	$7,500	$6,600	$5,800	$5,200	$4,600

MX-2000 - 12, 20, 28 ga. or .410 bore, single or O/U barrels, all disciplines and configurations, similar features as the MX-8, including removable trigger group, but with MX-2000 style engraving and gold letter on receiver, fixed or adj. (Trap Model only) rib.

MSR $13,166	$8,800	$7,600	$6,800	$5,800	$4,800	$3,800	$3,300

Add $1,501 for multi-choke barrel with seven chokes.
Add $600 for adj. rib.
Subtract 20% for single barrel models.
Subtract 20% for fixed SK/SK choke Skeet models.
Subtract 10% for fixed choke Trap models with non-selective trigger group.

* *MX-2000S* - similar to MX-2000, except has non-detachable trigger group and barrel selector on safety lever like the MX-12.

	$8,800	$7,600	$6,800	$5,800	$4,800	$3,800	$3,300

MX-2005 - American Trap model with extra high adj. rib, unsingle or combo.

Unsingle	$7,800	$6,800	$5,800	$4,800	$4,000	$3,500	$3,000
Combo	$10,000	$8,800	$8,000	$7,000	$6,000	$5,000	$4,000

TM1 SINGLE BARREL TRAP - low rib barrel, American Trap model, single barrel receiver, detachable trigger.

	$2,900	$2,500	$2,100	$1,800	$1,500	$1,200	$1,100

Add $150-$200 for Special model with adj. trigger.

TMX SINGLE BARREL TRAP - newer production, similar features as TM1, except has high rib.

	$3,600	$3,000	$2,500	$2,100	$1,800	$1,500	$1,200

SHOTGUNS: O/U, AMERICAN COMBO SETS (TRAP, SKEET, AND SPORTING)

Perazzi offers a wide variety of combination sets in Trap, Skeet, and Sporting configurations. These combination sets include a choice of either 29 1/2 or 31 1/2 in. O/U VR barrels with or w/o choke tubes and one VR barrel (chooice of top single or bottom single) with or w/o choke tubes. There are numerous configurations available, including many engraving, rib, and stock options. All shotguns, except the MX12, are equipped with a removable trigger group and flat springs.

Currently, Perazzi offers the following Trap, Skeet, and Sporting combination sets:

Standard Grade Combo Models: MX8 Trap ($16,408 MSR), MX10 Trap ($18,238 MSR), MX10RS Trap ($18,238 MSR), MX2000/8 Trap ($17,565 MSR), MX2000/10 Trap ($19,755 MSR), MX2000/RS ($19,755 MSR), MX8 Skeet ($13,139 MSR), MX8L Skeet ($15,171 MSR), MX2000/8 Skeet ($14,617 MSR), MX14 Trap ($13,702 MSR), MX12 Sporting ($14,195 MSR), MX2000S Sporting ($15,616 MSR), MX2000/8 Sporting ($15,616 MSR), MX14L Trap ($15,734 MSR), MX-2005 ($19,755 MSR), DB81 Trap ($16,023 MSR), MX2000/8 Gold Trap ($26,467 MSR), MX2000 Gold Trap ($24,4000 MSR), MX2000/8 Gold Skeet ($23,701 MSR), and the MX2000S Gold Sporting ($21,296 MSR).

SC3 Grade Models: MX8 SC3 Trap ($23,043 MSR), SC3 Trap ($25,935 MSR), MX8 SC3 Skeet ($20,299 MSR), and the MX12 SC3 Sporting ($18,780 MSR).

SCO Grade Models: MX8 SCO Trap ($38,057 MSR), SCO Gold Trap ($40,937 MSR), MX8 SCO Skeet ($39,452 MSR), and the MX12 SCO Sporting ($40,450 MSR).

SCO Gold Grade: MX8 SCO Gold Trap ($42,196 MSR), SCO Gold Trap ($45,088 MSR), MX8 SCO Gold Skeet ($34,790 MSR), and the MX12 SCO Gold Sporting ($35,670 MSR).

SCO Grade Models w/sideplates: MX8 SCO Trap ($54,659 MSR), SCO Trap ($57,550 MSR), MX8 SCO Skeet ($51,914 MSR), and the MX12 Gold Sporting ($52,913 MSR).

SCO Gold Grade Models w/sideplates: MX8 SCO Gold Trap ($60,624 MSR), SCO Gold Trap ($63,424 MSR), MX8 SCO Gold Skeet ($57,879 MSR), and the MX12 SCO Gold Sporting ($58,878 MSR).

SHOTGUNS: O/U, COMPETITON - OLYMPIC & DOUBLE TRAP

12 or 20 ga. Current barrel lengths include 29 1/2, 30 3/4, or 31 1/2 in.

The MX2/MX2L configuration is available mainly for the European marketplace. Values for this model represent recent pricing - Perazzi U.S.A. should be contacted directly for an up-to-date price quotation.

Perazzi offers a wide variety of competition style shotguns. Current Olympic Trap and Double Trap models include: Standard Trap w/ adj. rib ($23,100 MSR), and the MX2000S/20S Gold Sporting ($21,659-$22,430 MSR).

SC3 Grade: MX8 SC3 ($18,394 MSR), MX8/20 SC3 ($18,394 MSR), SC3/12 ($19,833 MSR), SC3/20 ($19,833 MSR), MX8/20 SC3 ($18,394 MSR), MX8/20C Sporting ($18,394-$19,800 MSR), MX12C SC3 and MX20C SC3 Sporting ($18,394-$19,165 MSR).

SCO Grade: MX8 SCO ($31,275 MSR, w/ adj. rib $32,716 MSR), and the MX8/20 SCO ($31,275 MSR, w/adj. rib $32,716 MSR).

SCO Gold Grade: MX8 SCO Gold ($31,160 MSR), MX8/20 Gold ($31,160 MSR), SCO Gold/12 ($32,220 MSR), and the SCO Gold/20 ($32,220 MSR).

SCO Grade w/sideplates: MX8 SCO ($42,300 MSR), MX8/20 SCO ($42,300 MSR), SCO/12 ($43,360 MSR), and the SCO/20 ($43,360 MSR).

SCO Gold Grade w/sideplates: MX8 SCO Gold ($47,740 MSR), MX8/20 SCO Gold ($47,740 MSR), SCO Gold/12 ($48,800 MSR), and the SCO Gold/20 ($48,800 MSR).

O/U SIDELOCK MODELS - older models without rebounding hammers are not as desirable. The most desirable configurations in this model are the Skeet, Pigeon, and Sporting variations (pricing follows new SHO Gold values). All SHO sidelock models were disc. 1992.

✻ *Sidelock Model SHO Older Mfg.*

	100%	98%	95%	90%	80%	70%	60%
	$12,000	$11,000	$10,000	$9,000	$8,500	$7,600	$6,800

Add $6,000 for game scene engraving.

✻ *Sidelock Model SHO Newer Mfg.*

	100%	98%	95%	90%	80%	70%	60%
	$28,500	$25,000	$21,500	$18,000	$16,500	$14,000	$12,000

Last MSR was $43,000.

✻ *Sidelock Model SHO Gold Older Mfg.*

	100%	98%	95%	90%	80%	70%	60%
	$17,000	$15,000	$13,000	$11,000	$9,950	$8,750	$7,000

GRADING - PPGS™	100%	98%	95%	90%	80%	70%	60%

* *Sidelock Model SHO Gold Newer Mfg.*

	$34,000	$29,500	$25,000	$21,250	$17,750	$14,000	$12,000

Last MSR was $48,000.

* *Sidelock Model SHO Extra* - while advertised, none were sold.

Last MSR was $80,000.

* *Sidelock Model SHO Gold Extra* - while advertised, none were sold.

Last MSR was $86,000.

SHOTGUNS: O/U, COMPETITION SKEET

12 or 20 ga., 26 3/4, 27 9/16, 28 3/8, 29 1/2, or 34 in. barrels.
Perazzi offers a wide variety of competition style shotguns. Current Skeet models include:
SC3 Grade: MX8 SC3 ($16,220 MSR), MX8/20 SC3 ($16,220 MSR), SC3/12 ($17,490 MSR), and the SC3/20 ($17,490 MSR).
SCO Grade: MX8 SCO ($31,275 MSR), MX8/20 SCO ($31,275 MSR), SCO/12 ($28,850 MSR), and the SCO/20 ($28,850 MSR).
SCO Gold Grade: MX8 SCO Gold ($31,160 MSR), MX8/20 Gold ($31,160 MSR), SCO Gold/12 ($32,220 MSR), and the SCO Gold/20 ($32,220 MSR).
SCO Grade w/sideplates: MX8 SCO ($42,300 MSR), MX8/20 SCO ($42,300 MSR), SCO/12 ($43,360 MSR), and the SCO/20 ($43,360 MSR).
SCO Gold Grade w/sideplates: MX8 SCO Gold ($47,740 MSR), MX8/20 SCO Gold ($47,740 MSR), SCO Gold/12 ($48,800 MSR), and the SCO Gold/20 ($48,800 MSR).

> **Subtract $250-$500 on older Mirage Models (without the "Special" designation) that do not have the adjustable 4 position trigger.**

O/U SIDELOCK MODELS - older models without rebounding hammers are not as desirable.

* *Sidelock Model SHO Older Mfg.*

	$15,000	$12,000	$9,500	$8,500	$7,600	$6,800	$5,900

* *Sidelock Model SHO Newer Mfg.*

	$35,850	$30,000	$25,000	$20,000	$17,000	$14,500	$12,750

Last MSR was $43,000.

* *Sidelock Model SHO Gold Older Mfg.*

	$18,000	$15,750	$12,000	$9,500	$8,500	$7,600	$6,800

* *Sidelock Model SHO Gold Newer Mfg.*

	$45,000	$34,500	$27,250	$22,000	$18,500	$15,950	$13,750

Last MSR was $48,000.

* *Sidelock Model SHO Extra* - imported 1985-92.

	$68,750	$54,700	$38,100	$32,000	$26,500	$21,250	$18,000

Last MSR was $80,000.

* *Sidelock Model SHO Gold Extra* - similar to SHO Extra, except has gold inlays. Imported 1992 only.

	$72,750	$56,500	$39,500	$33,000	$27,000	$22,000	$18,500

Last MSR was $86,000.

> **Subtract $20,000 if not signed by a known engraver.**

SHOTGUNS: O/U, 4-GAUGE SKEET SETS

STANDARD GRADE MODELS

* *Standard Grade Model MX3 Special*

	$5,200	$4,875	$4,650	$4,500	$4,150	$3,650	$3,150

Last MSR was $15,400.

* *Standard Grade Model Mirage Special* - disc. 1994.

	$5,850	$5,500	$4,850	$4,600	$4,200	$3,700	$3,200

Last MSR was $17,500.

SHOTGUNS: O/U, COMPETITION SPORTING

12 or 20 ga.

Perazzi offers a wide variety of competition style shotguns. Current Sporting models include:

SC3 Grade: MX8 SC3 ($16,220 MSR), MX8/20 SC3 ($16,220 MSR), SC3/12 ($17,490 MSR), SC3/20 ($17,490 MSR), MX8C SC3 and MX8/20C SC 3 ($17,460 MSR), MX12 SC3 and MX20 SC3 ($16,220 MSR), and the MX12C SC3 and MX20C SC3 ($16,900 MSR).

SCO Grade: MX8 SCO ($27,580 MSR), MX8/20 SCO ($27,580 MSR), SCO/12 ($28,850 MSR), SCO/20 ($28,850 MSR), MX8C SCO and MX8/20C SCO $28,820 MSR), MX12 and MX20 SCO (27,580 MSR), and the MX12C and MX20C SCO ($28,260 MSR).

SCO Gold Grade: MX8 SCO Gold ($35,336 MSR), MX8/20 Gold ($35,336 MSR), SCO Gold/12 ($36,742 MSR), SCO Gold/20 ($32,220 MSR), MX8C SCO Gold and MX8/20 C Gold ($31,160 MSR), MX12 SCO Gold and MX20 SCO Gold ($31,160 MSR), MX12C SCO and MX20 SCO Gold ($31, 840 MSR), and the MX8 SCO Gold ($31,160 MSR).

SCO Grade w/sideplates: MX8 SCO ($47,968 MSR), MX8/20 SCO ($47,968 MSR), SCO/12 ($43,360 MSR), SCO/20 ($48,739 MSR), MX8C SCO and MX8/20 C SCO ($42,980 MSR), MX12 SCO and MX20 SCO ($42,300 MSR) and the MX12C SCO and MX20C SCO ($42,980 MSR).

SCO Gold Grade w/sideplates: MX8 SCO Gold ($54,137 MSR), MX8/20 SCO Gold ($55,543 MSR), SCO Gold/12 ($54,137 MSR), SCO Gold/20 ($54,908 MSR), MX8C SCO Gold and MX8/20 C SCO Gold ($48,980 MSR), MX12 SCO Gold and MX20 SCO Gold ($48,980 MSR), and the MX12C SCO Gold and the MX20C SCO Gold ($48,420 MSR).

SHOTGUNS: O/U, PIGEON-ELECTROCIBLES

Perazzi offers a wide variety of Pigeon shotguns.
Current models include:
SC3 Grade: MX8 SC3 ($18,393 MSR).
SCO Grade: MX8 SCO ($31,275 MSR).
SCO Gold Grade: MX8 SCO Gold ($35,336 MSR).
SCO Grade w/sideplates: MX8 SCO ($47968,300 MSR).
SCO Gold Grade w/sideplates: MX8 SCO Gold ($54,137 MSR).

SHOTGUNS: O/U, GAME/HUNTING - BOXLOCK ACTION

Available in 12, 20, 28 ga., or .410 bore, 26 (disc. on MX8/12 ga. and MX12 1994), 26 3/4, 27 9/16, 28 3/8, or 29 1/2 in. barrels. Perazzi offers a wide variety of game/hunting configurations. Current models include: SC3 Grade Models: MX8 SC3 and MX8/20 SC3 ($18,394 MSR), MX12 SC3 and MX20 SC3 ($18,394 MSR), MX28 SC3 and MX410 SC3 ($29,189 MSR).

SCO Grade Models: MX8 SCO and MX/820 SCO ($31,275 MSR), MX12 SCO and MX20 SCO ($31,275 MSR), MX28 SCO and MX410 SCO ($42,196 MSR).

SCO Gold Grade: MX8 SCO Gold and MX8/20 Gold ($35,336 MSR), MX12 SCO Gold and MX20 SCO Gold ($35,336 MSR), MX28 SCO Gold and MX410 SCO Gold ($46,142 MSR).

SCO Grade w/sideplates: MX8 SCO and MX8/20 SCO ($47,968 MSR), MX12 SCO and MX20 SCO ($47,968 MSR), and the MX28 and MX410 SCO ($58,888 MSR).

SCO Gold Grade w/sideplates: MX8 SCO Gold and MX8/20 SCO ($54,137 MSR), MX12 SCO Gold and MX20 SCO Gold ($54,137 MSR), MX12 SCO and MX20 SCO Gold ($54,137 MSR), MX28 SCO and MX410 SCO Gold ($64,683 MSR).

SHOTGUNS: O/U, HUNTING - SIDELOCK MODELS

All SHO models were disc. in 1992 (they were available through special order only).

SHO MODELS - all SHO Hunting models should be evaluated and possibly appraised by someone who has a great deal of knowledge of both newer and older higher grade Perazzi shotguns. There are many variables that can come into play for price consideration, therefore an expert opinion is encouraged before buying, selling or trading the following models.

GRADING - PPGS™	100%	98%	95%	90%	80%	70%	60%

∗ *SHO Model Older Mfg.* - older models without rebounding hammers are not as desirable.

	$12,000	$9,500	$8,500	$7,600	$6,800	$5,950	$5,150

∗ *SHO Model Newer Mfg.* - 12 ga. only, introductory sidelock O/U model with bank note game scene engraving on coin finished receiver.

	$29,950	$25,000	$20,000	$17,000	$14,500	$12,750	$10,250

Last MSR was $43,000.

∗ *SHO Model Gold Older Mfg.* - older models without rebounding hammers are not as desirable.

	$18,000	$15,750	$12,000	$9,500	$8,500	$7,600	$6,800

∗ *SHO Model Gold Newer Mfg.* - similar to SHO, except has game scenes in gold relief.

	$38,650	$31,500	$26,500	$21,250	$18,000	$15,500	$13,750

Last MSR was $48,000.

∗ *SHO Model Extra* - importation began 1992.

	$68,750	$54,700	$38,100	$32,000	$26,500	$21,250	$18,000

Last MSR was $80,000.

∗ *SHO Model Gold Extra* - similar to SHO Extra, except has gold inlays. Importation began 1992.

	$72,750	$56,500	$39,500	$33,000	$27,000	$22,000	$18,500

Last MSR was $86,000.

SHOTGUNS: SxS, HUNTING - SIDELOCK MODELS

DHO Models have not been included within the scope of this text due to the extreme rarity factor. Please contact Perazzi, USA for more information on these models and current pricing.

Subtract 40% without rebounding hammers on older DHO models.

PEREGRINE INDUSTRIES, INC.

Previous company located in Huntington Beach, CA circa 1991.
While advertised, Peregrine Industries, Inc. never manufactured the Falcon Model.

PERUGINI-VISINI

Current manufacturer established during 1968 and located in Nuvolera, Brescia, Italy. No current U.S. distribution. Previously imported 2002-2004 by Old Friends Hunting & Shooting Co., located in Livingston, MT. Rifles were previously imported and distributed until 1992 by William Larkin Moore & Co., previously located in Westlake Village, CA. All other models listed were previously imported and distributed by Armes De Chasse located in Chadds Ford, PA until 1988.

Perugini-Visini makes best quality boxlock and sidelock rifles and shotguns, including bolt action and single shot rifles. Annual production is approx. 60 guns on a custom order basis only. All pricing is FOB Italy, and subject to change.

Please contact the factory directly for more information, including pricing and availability (see listing in Trademark Index).

RIFLES

STANDARD MODEL: BOLT ACTION - available in most U.S. and metric cals., Mauser 98K action, 24 or 26 in. barrel, 3 shot mag.(non-detachable), matte finished European walnut, high polish bluing, no sights. Importation disc. 1987.

	$4,250	$3,800	$3,400	$2,950	$2,500	$2,000	$1,800

Last MSR was $4,250.

GRADING - PPGS™	100%	98%	95%	90%	80%	70%	60%

DELUXE MODEL: BOLT ACTION - similar to Standard Model, except has finely checkered oil finished walnut stock, sights, knurled bolt handle, and is cased. Importation disc. 1987.

	$4,250	$3,800	$3,400	$2,950	$2,500	$2,000	$1,800

Last MSR was $4,250.

MODEL EAGLE SINGLE SHOT - available in most U.S. and metric cals., Anson & Deeley type action, ejector, sights, adj. trigger, oil finished finely checkered European walnut stock, 24 or 26 in. Hämmerli barrel. Importation disc. 1987.

	$5,255	$4,500	$3,800	$3,400	$2,950	$2,500	$2,000

Last MSR was $5,255.

EAGLE MODEL SINGLE SHOT (CURRENT MFG.) - available in many traditional U.S. and European cals., best quality single shot, built on patented Perugini-Visini action with optional sideplated versions available, supplied with Perugini-Visini claw mounts and set trigger. Engraving is optional.

This model has a current MSR of $19,500 for the Standard Model. Many options available, including multi-barrels sets, scope mounts, cases and engraving options.

"PROFESSIONAL" BOLT ACTION MAGAZINE RIFLE - dedicated Perugini & Visini Mauser action for cals. up to .375 H&H, includes express sights, sling swivels, and quarter rib. Claw mounts, optics, and engraving are optional.

MSR $21,300		$18,250	$15,250	$12,650	$10,250	$8,750	$7,500	$6,250

"PROFESSIONAL" BOLT ACTION MAGNUM RIFLE - available in calibers from .375 H&H to .505 Gibbs, dedicated Perugini-Visini magnum Mauser action, includes quarter rib, express sights and sling swivels, unique takedown feature. Claw mounts, optics, and engraving are optional.

MSR $24,600		$22,000	$18,000	$15,250	$13,000	$11,000	$9,000	$7,500

"SELOUS" EXPRESS SxS DOUBLE RIFLE - available in cals. up to .600 NE, best quality H&H back action SxS sidelock with Perugini-Visini patented ejectors for rimless cartridges, chopper lump barrels, Purdey style locking action, hand detachable locks, ejectors, best quality Turkish walnut stock, English rose and scroll engraving is standard, ornamental engraving is optional.

The Standard Model with scroll engraving, leather case and game scene engraved vignette on trigger plate starts at $54,000 for .375 H&H cal. Add $14,000 for .470 NE - .500 NE cals., and $23,000 for .577 NE to .600 NE cals.

The Deluxe Model with full game scene Big 5 engraving starts at $60,000 for .375 H&H cal. Add $10,000 for .470 NE - .500 NE cals., and $29,000 for .577 NE - .600 NE cals.

Additional custom engraving is available by request.

* *"Selous" Express SxS Double Rifle* - 9.3x74R, .375 H&H, .458 Win. Mag., .470 NE, or .500 3 in. NE cal., H&H style detachable sidelock action, ejectors, folding leaf rear sight, border engraving with best quality checkered walnut, top-of-the-line model, leather cased. Importation disc. 1992.

	$23,000	$18,500	$15,000	$12,000	$10,000	$9,000	$8,150

Last MSR was $26,000.

* *"Selous" Express SxS Double Rifle Sidelock Super Express* - choice of 9 different cals. including .470 Nitro Express, H&H patterned sidelocks, chopper lump barrels, third lever fastener, multi-leaf express sights, coin finished or case hardened receiver, engraving patterns optional. Importation disc. 1989.

	$9,500	$8,400	$7,400	$6,850	$6,100	$5,600	$5,000

Last MSR was $10,500.

VICTORIA MODEL D EXPRESS SxS DOUBLE RIFLE - available in calibers up to .500 NE, best quality A&D boxlock action with Perugini-Visini patented ejectors, chopper lump barrels with quarter rib and express sights, claw mounts are optional.

This model has a current MSR of $34,500.

GRADING - PPGS™	100%	98%	95%	90%	80%	70%	60%

Victoria Model D Express SxS Double Rifle Mag. - similar to Model Victoria, except in .375 H&H, .458 Win., .470 NE, or .500-3 in. NE cal., demi-bloc barrels, and has elaborate engraving. Importation disc. 1992.

	$10,950	$9,150	$8,200	$7,400	$6,600	$5,800	$5,100

Last MSR was $13,750.

VICTORIA MODEL M EXPRESS SxS DOUBLE RIFLE - available in cals. up to 9.3x74R cal., similar to Victoria Model D, except has monobloc barrel construction.

This model has a current MSR of $25,900.

Victoria Model M Express SxS Double Rifle - .30-06, 7x57R, 7x65R or 9.3x74R cal., Anson & Deeley boxlock action, border engraving, ejectors, folding leaf rear sight, DT, 24 or 26 in. monobloc barrels with chopper lumps, leather cased. Importation disc. 1992.

	$7,000	$5,700	$4,600	$3,500	$2,950	$2,500	$2,000

PRINCESS MODEL D EXPRESS O/U DOUBLE RIFLE - available in all cals. up to traditional express calibers, best quality Boss style boxlock action with automatic ejectors, chopper lump barrels with quarter rib and express sights, optional claw mounts.

MSR $35,600	$32,000	$27,000	$23,000	$18,500	$15,000	$12,500	$11,250

PRINCESS MODEL M EXPRESS O/U DOUBLE RIFLE - available in cals. up to 9.3x74R cal., similar to Princess Model D, except has monobloc barrel construction.

MSR $26,900	$24,000	$20,500	$17,000	$14,000	$11,000	$9,000	$7,000

RENAISSANCE DOUBLE RIFLE .375 H&H cal., demi-block barrels, Anson & Deeley boxlock action, includes scroll engraving with game scene on trigger plate.

This model has a current MSR of $24,950.

BOXLOCK EXPRESS SxS - .444 Marlin or 9.3x74R cal., Anson & Deeley boxlock action, ejectors, color case hardened frame, iron sights. Importation disc. 1989.

	$3,150	$2,800	$2,500	$2,200	$1,950	$1,700	$1,475

Last MSR was $3,500.

BOXLOCK MAGNUM O/U - .270 Win., .375 H&H, or .458 Win. Mag. cal., Anson & Deeley boxlock action, ejectors, monobloc barrels, select walnut. Importation disc. 1989.

	$5,500	$4,900	$4,300	$3,750	$3,100	$2,600	$2,200

Last MSR was $6,100.

MODEL CARBINE - available in many calibers, dexlue gun with game scene engraved floor plate, case hardened engraved receiver, Mauser action, quick detachable claw mounts, includes Swarovski or Zeiss scope and case.

The Standard Model has a MSR of $15,000.
The Deluxe Model has a MSR of $30,000.

SHOTGUNS

AUSONIA SxS - 12 or 20 ga., exposed hammers with double Purdey type sidelock action, various engraving options, demibloc barrels. Disc.

	$7,140	$6,500	$5,750	$4,950	$4,200	$3,500	$2,550

Last MSR was $7,140.

LIBERTY MODEL SxS - 12, 16, 20, 28 ga., or .410 bore, scalloped Anson & Deeley boxlock ejector with chopper lump barrels, Purdey lock, light rose and scroll engraving, oval for initials and factory gold crest on forearm, leather cased.

MSR $14,900	$13,500	$11,000	$9,000	$8,000	$7,000	$5,500	$4,500

GRADING - PPGS™	100%	98%	95%	90%	80%	70%	60%

CLASSIC MODEL SxS - 12, 16, 20, 28 ga. or .410 bore, best quality H&H style sidelock action with chopper lump barrels, exhibition wood stock with gold crest in forearm and stock oval, every refinement incorporated, supplied with Nizzoli leather case, engraving by master engraver in traditional style, ornamental engraving optional.

	MSR $31,800		$28,000	$24,000	$19,250	$16,250	$14,000	$12,500	$10,000

REGINA MODEL SxS - 12 ga., heavy frame competition and hunting model, features removable trigger group with chopper lump barrel construction, border engraving is standard, supplied with extra trigger group and Nasco case, engraving upgrade and sideplates optional.

	MSR N/A		N/A	$11,500	$9,950	$8,700	$7,600	$6,500	$5,150

ROMAGNA HAMMER GUN - 12,16, 20, 28 ga. or .410 bore, best quality bar action hammer gun, includes every refinement, engraved by master engraver in traditional style, available in heavy frame pigeon configuration for competition, ornamental engraving optional.

	MSR $27,600		$25,000	$20,500	$15,000	$10,000	$7,500	$5,000	$3,750

Add $2,900 for ejectors and self-cocking mechanism.

MAESTRO O/U - Boss style scalloped receiver with removable trigger group, monobloc barrels are standard, with chopper lump barrels optional, sideplated versions available in various competition and hunting style models.

Perugini-Visini uses advanced CNC fabrication and hand finishing with all Maestro models. Maestro models are also available with a 20 ga. receiver, and in 28 ga. and .410 bore barrel sets.

✷ *Maestro O/U Traveling Hunter Model* - coin finished receiver with mirror polished internal parts, custom Briley chokes and Nasco case, best finish with exhibition wood stock, entry level engraving and adj. trigger standard.

	MSR $12,000		$10,950	$9,750	$8,600	$7,600	$6,700	$5,800	$4,350

✷ *Maestro O/U Lusso Model* - sideplated version with exhibition wood stock, adj. trigger group, English rose and scroll engraving standard, best quality, gold oval and factory gold crest, ornamental engraving optional.

	MSR $26,500		$23,750	$19,000	$16,500	$13,750	$11,000	$9,000	$8,250

✷ *Maestro O/U Reale Piccione Model* - ultimate competition O/U, designed with particular MOI for Flyer and Helice shooting, adj. trigger and English rose and scroll engraving standard, Boss side ribs and Anson plunger forearm, gold oval and factory gold crest, ornamental engraving optional.

	MSR $33,750		$29,500	$25,000	$21,000	$17,000	$13,750	$11,750	$9,475

NOVA O/U - best quality Boss pattern sidelock with back action locks, Boss style forend iron and side ribs, best quality English rose and scroll engraving is standard, ornamental engraving is optional.

Current MSR is $62,900.

PETERS STAHL GmbH

Current pistol manufacturer located in Paderborn, Germany. Currently imported by Euro-Imports, located in Yoakum, TX. Previously distributed by Swiss Trading GmbH, located in Bozeman, MT. Previously imported 1998-1999 by Peters Stahl, U.S.A. located in Delta, UT, and by Franzen International Inc. located in Oakland, NJ until 1998. Dealer direct sales only.

PISTOLS: SEMI-AUTO

Peters Stahl manufactures high quality semi-auto pistols based on the Model 1911 design, but to date, has had limited U.S. importation. Current models include the Multicaliber, 92-Sport, O7-Sport, HC-Champion and variations, 1911-Tactical/Classic, PLS, and a .22 LR. Peters-Stahl also manufactures multicaliber conversion kits of the highest quality. Recent models previously imported (until 2000) included the Model Millennium (MSR was $2,195),

GRADING - PPGS™	100%	98%	95%	90%	80%	70%	60%

Match 22 LR (MSR was $1,995), Trophy Master (MSR was $1,995), Omega Match (MSR was $1,995), High Capacity Trophy Master (MSR was $1,695), O7 Multicaliber (MSR was $1,995), and the 92 Multicaliber (MSR was $2,610-$2,720). In the past, Peters Stahl has manufactured guns for Federal Ordnance, Omega, Schuetzen Pistol Works, and Springfield Armory. The importer should be contacted directly (see Trademark Index) for current model information, U.S. availability, and pricing.

PFEIFER-WAFFEN

Current manufacturer located in Feldkirch, Austria. No current U.S. importation.
Pfeifer-Waffen manufactures the unique "safety-rifle" in two configurations, the SR2 and the SR2-Sport, a Liliput youth rifle in .22 Hornet, a repeating rifle, and a Zeliska revolver in .458 Win. Mag. or .600 NE cal. Please contact the company directly for more information, including pricing and availability (see Trademark Index).

PHELPS MFG. CO.

Previous manufacturer located in Evansville, IN circa 1978-1996.
Phelps Manufacturing Company began shipping guns in early 1978. Phelps guns were investment cast in 4140 steel, with basic single action simplicity, using a transfer bar in the action.

REVOLVERS

HERITAGE I - .45-70 cal., single action revolver, incorporates transfer bar hammer safety, blue finish (standard), nickel (optional), adj. rear sight, 8 in. barrel standard, other barrel lengths up to 20 in. available, 6 lbs. Disc. 1996.

	100%	98%	95%	90%	80%	70%	60%
	$2,500	$2,000	$1,675	$1,425	$1,255	$1,020	$885

Last MSR was $2,250.

Add $20 for each additional in. of barrel.

EAGLE I - .444 Marlin cal., single action revolver, blue finish, adj. rear sight, barrel options same as Heritage I, 6 lbs. Disc. 1996.

	$2,050	$1,675	$1,425	$1,255	$1,020	$885	$715

Last MSR was $2,250.

PATRIOT - .375 Win. cal., single action revolver, blue finish, adj. rear sight, barrel options are the same as Heritage I. Limited mfg. 1993-94.

	$1,925	$1,550	$1,350	$1,185	$965	$840	$670

Last MSR was $2,225.

GRIZZLY .50-70 - .50-70 cal., otherwise similar to Heritage I. Mfg. 1992-96.

	$2,300	$1,875	$1,500	$1,325	$1,085	$930	$750

Last MSR was $2,580.

Add $20 for each additional in. of barrel.

PHILLIPS & ROGERS, INC.

Previous manufacturer 1992-2003, and located in Huntsville, TX since 1997. Previously located in Conroe, TX circa 1992-1997.
In addition to manufacturing the firearms listed, Phillips & Rogers also made a multi-caliber conversion cylinder for all Ruger .357 Mag., new model Blackhawk revolvers (disc. 1996) - the retail price was $145. Multi-caliber conversion cylinders are also available for the Ruger new Model Blackhawk (allows shooting .45 LC, .45 Win. Mag., or .45 ACP - retail price was $185) and the Ruger Super Blackhawk (converts .44 Mag. to .50 AE - $550). A new version of the Ruger .50 AE conversion was also available for $995.

GRADING - PPGS™	100%	98%	95%	90%	80%	70%	60%

REVOLVERS

MEDUSA MODEL 47 REVOLVER - multi-caliber, over 25 cals. in the .355 - .380 diameter range (including .357 Mag., .38 Super, .38 Spl., 9mm Para., etc.), unique design does not utilize half-moon clips or cylinder/barrel changes, 2 1/2, 4, 5, 6, or 8 in. barrel, 6 shot, double action, matte blue finish, rubber or wood grips. Mfg. 1993-2003.

	$525	$475	$435	$400	$375	$350	$325

Last MSR was $599.

Add $95 for 8 in. barrel.

RIFLES: BOLT ACTION

WILDERNESS EXPLORER - .218 Bee, .22 Hornet, .44 Mag., or .50 AE cal., bolt action, features 18 in. match grade barrel, quick change bolt face and barrel allowing interchangeable calibers, white speckled black synthetic stock, side safety, 5 1/2 lbs. Mfg. 1997 only.

	$925	$825	$725	$650	$575	$500	$425

Last MSR was $995.

PHOENIX ARMS

Current manufacturer located in Ontario, CA since 1992. Distributor sales only.

PISTOLS: SEMI-AUTO

RAVEN - .25 ACP cal., single action, 2 7/16 in. barrel, 6 shot mag., alloy frame, choice of finishes and grips. Disc. 1998.

	$69	$50	$45	$40	$35	$30	$25

Last MSR was $79.

This model was supplied with a magazine disconnect lock.

HP MODEL - .22 LR or .25 ACP cal., single action, 3 in. VR barrel, 10 (.25 ACP), 10 (C/B 1994), or 11* (.22 LR) shot staggered mag., alloy frame, firing pin block safety, adj. rear sight, choice of polished blue or satin nickel finish, keyed mag. lock and safety cable lanyard, 20 oz. New 1994.

MSR N/A	$100	$80	$70	$60	$50	$45	$40

Add $99 for laser sight and mount (new 1998).
Add $45 for 2-in-1 target barrel and magazine conversion kit.

* *HP Model Range Kit* - includes HP Model in .22 LR with 5 in. extended barrel, extended mag., locking plastic storage case (compartmentalized during 2000), and cleaning kit. New 1998.

MSR N/A	$140	$115	$100	$90	$75	$65	$55

* *HP Model Deluxe Range Kit* - similar to HP Range Kit, except has 3 and 5 in. barrels and extended mag. New 1999.

MSR N/A	$185	$165	$135	$110	$100	$90	$80

PHOENIX ARMS CO.

Previous importer located in Lowell, MA.

PISTOLS: SEMI-AUTO

PHOENIX - .25 ACP cal., Belgian semi-auto, previously manufactured by Robar et DeKerkhove located in Liege, Belgium.

	$495	$450	$400	$350	$300	$250	$200

GRADING - PPGS™	100%	98%	95%	90%	80%	70%	60%

PIETTA, F.LLI

Current black powder and firearms manufacturer established in 1960, and located in Gussago, Italy. Both firearms and black powder reproductions and replicas are distributed in the U.S. by E.M.F. Co., Inc., Cabela's, Cimarron, Dixie Gun Works, Navy Arms Company, Taylor's & Co., Inc.,and Traditions, Inc.

Pietta manufactures good quality black powder and modern firearms reproductions in many configurations for various American companies. During 2000-2001, Pietta developed its own proprietary centerfire bottleneck cartridge - the .30-357 AeT, which never went into production. The company also completed a modern SAA revolver during 2003, in cals. .357 Mag., .44-40 WCF, and .45 LC. During 2005, Pietta introduced the Challenge semi-auto shotgun line with two models, the Mistral 2 and the Zephyrus 3, with production occuring in 2006. These shotguns are not currently imported into the U.S. Please visit their web site for current information or to request a comprehensive catalog listing of the wide assortment of firearms this company manufactures (see Trademark Index).

For more information and up-to-date regarding current Pietta black powder models, please refer to the *Blue Book of Modern Black Powder Arms*, by John Allen. These books feature hundreds of color photographs and supporting text of the most recent black powder models available, as well as a complete pricing and reference guide.

Black Powder Reproductions & Replicas by Dennis Adler is also an invaluable source for most black powder reproductions and replicas, and includes hundreds of color images on most popular makes/models, provides manufacturer/trademark histories, and up-to-date information on related items/accessories for black powder shooting - www.bluebookinc.com

Pietta firearms are listed separately under the importers - please refer to the individual listings.

PIOTTI

Current manufacturer established circa 1955, and located in Brescia, Italy. Currently imported and distributed exclusively by William Larkin Moore & Co. located in Scottsdale, AZ.

Fratelli Piotti is one of the world's premier gunmakers. These shotguns meet the highest standards of craftsmanship and are made to customer specifications. Variety of gauges, engraving, styles, chokes, etc. are available. Fratelli Piotti manufactures approx. 65-70 guns per year.

RIFLES: CUSTOM

Piotti also manufactures a custom SxS double rifle on a very limited basis. Please contact the company directly for an individualized quotation.

During the 2007 SCI banquet, a .470 NE cal. sidelock ejector with special engraving by G.S. Pedretti sold for $125,000.

SHOTGUNS: O/U

PIOTTI BOSS - 12, 16, 20, or 28 ga., 26-32 in. barrels, single or double triggers, standard with King 2 engraving, Turkish Circassian walnut, various engraving patterns available, 6 - 7 1/2 lbs. New 1995.

MSR $59,900	$55,000	$50,000	$35,000	$28,750	$23,650	$18,950	$15,450

Add $3,820 for single trigger.
Add $4,250 for 16 or 20 ga.
Add $10,600 for 28 ga.

GRADING - PPGS™	100%	98%	95%	90%	80%	70%	60%

SHOTGUNS: SxS

For the following models - add $3,200 for single trigger, $12,100 for H&H type self-opening mechanism, $1,320 - $2,150 for hand-detachable locks, $1,100 for pinless action or $755 for rounded action, approx. $1,725 - $2,450 for leather case, $7,125 for 10 ga., $1,185 for 16 or 20 ga., $1,650 for 28 ga. or .410 bore boxlock, and $3,150 for 28 ga. or .410 bore sidelock.

HAMMER GUN - 12 ga. only, self cocking ejector model, DT, exposed hammers, back action with fine scroll engraving. Importation began 2001.

MSR $38,600		$35,000	$31,000	$24,000	$19,250	$12,250	$10,000	$8,700

Add $2,000 for ejectors and self-cocking mechanism.

PIUMA (BSEE) - 10, 12, 16, 20, 28 ga., or .410 bore, Anson & Deeley boxlock ejector double with chopper lump barrels, level file-cut rib, light scroll and rosette engraving, scalloped frame.

MSR $18,500		$16,750	$12,250	$10,000	$8,500	$7,000	$5,750	$4,500

WESTLAKE - 12, 16, 20, 28 ga., or .410 bore, H&H sidelock action, moderate scroll engraving. Mfg. disc. 1989.

	$8,500	$7,500	$6,050	$5,300	$4,700	$4,200	$3,750

Last MSR was $8,400.

MONTE CARLO - 12, 16, 20, 28 ga., or .410 bore, best-quality H&H pattern sidelock ejector double with chopper lump barrels, Purdey style scroll and rosette engraving. Importation disc. 1990.

	$10,500	$9,250	$8,200	$7,100	$6,000	$5,000	$4,500

Last MSR was $11,400.

KING NUMBER 1 - 12, 16, 20, 28 ga., or .410 bore, best-quality H&H pattern sidelock ejector double with chopper lump barrels, level file-cut rib, very fine full coverage scroll engraving with small floral bouquets, gold crest in forearm, gold crown in top lever, name in gold, and finely figured wood.

MSR $36,600		$33,750	$24,000	$19,500	$14,250	$10,050	$7,750	$6,600

KING EXTRA - 12, 16, 20, 28 ga., or .410 bore, best-quality H&H pattern sidelock ejector double with chopper lump barrels, level file-cut rib, choice of either Bulino game scene engraving or standard cameo game scene engraving with gold inlays, engraved and signed by a master engraver, exhibition grade wood.

Please contact the importer directly for a price quotation on this model.

LUNIK - 12, 16, 20, 28 ga., or .410 bore, best-quality H&H pattern sidelock ejector double with lump (demi-bloc) barrels, level file-cut rib, Renaissance style large scroll engraving in relief, gold crown in top lever, gold name, gold crest in forearm, finely figured wood.

MSR $38,000		$34,000	$23,500	$19,750	$15,000	$11,500	$8,700	$6,950

MONACO NUMBER 1 OR 2 - 12, 16, 20, 28 ga., or .410 bore, best-quality H&H pattern sidelock ejector double with lump (demi-bloc) barrels, level file-cut rib, Renaissance style large scroll engraving in relief, gold crown in top lever, gold name, gold crest in forearm, finely figured wood.

MSR $46,500		$43,000	$35,000	$29,500	$23,500	$20,000	$18,000	$16,000

MONACO NUMBER 3 - next to top-of-the-line model.

Current MSR on this model is $49,600.

MONACO NUMBER 4 - top-of-the-line model with every refinement incorporated. Custom order only and extremely rare.

Current MSR on this model is $60,400.

PIRANHA

Previous trademark of pistols manufactured by R.T.I. (Recoilless Technologies, Inc.), located in Glendale, AZ. While advertised, were never manufactured (except a few prototypes). Previous trademark of a recoilless semi-auto 9mm Para. cal. pistol that was advertised circa 1996, but never manufactured by Recoilless Tech, Inc. located in Phoenix, AZ.

R.T.I. tried to develop its manufacturing capability for the semi-auto Piranha Recoilless Pistol, utilizing hesition lock bi-angular springs to reduce 85% of the recoil, and which also allowed changing calibers by changing the barrel.

PLAINS RIFLE

A Plains rifle is a modification of the Kentucky rifle. Its original purpose was for use on the western frontier.

The Plains rifle is often referred to as a half stock, and first appeared around the end of the first quarter of the 19th century, with production ending by 1880. There was a demand for shorter rifles to be carried on horseback and larger bores for bigger game. Bores ranged from .50 to .60 caliber, and barrel lengths were 36 to 40 inches. Plains rifles are generally found with percussion ignition systems.

Like the Kentucky rifle, Plains rifles were all handmade. Jacob and Samuel Hawken are considered the originators of the Plains rifle. They were the sons of Christian Hawken, Kentucky rifle maker of Hagerstown, MD. The popularity of Jacob and Samuel's guns spread rapidly. Gunmakers from across the country began to copy the Plains style rifle. In addition to the Hawken brothers, other well-known makers were Horace Dimick, J.P. Gemmer, James Henry, and Henry Leman. Like Kentucky rifles, values for Plains rifles differ greatly, depending on the maker, condition, and style. Values can range anywhere from $350-$25,000! Flintlock Plains rifles are scarce.

The publisher would like to thank Mr. Jim Buelow for making the above information available to the *Blue Book of Gun Values*.

POINTER

Current trademark of shotguns imported by Legacy Sports International, located in Reno, NV. Previously located in Alexandria, VA.

SHOTGUNS: O/U

POINTER TURKISH SPORTING/FIELD - 12 ga., 3 in. chambers, 28 in. barrels, blue (disc.) or electroless nickel finish with floral engraving, five multi-chokes, select walnut stock and forearm, Kickeez buttpad, Truglo sight, extractors, gold trigger, 7.7 lbs. Mfg. by Zafer Arms Co. in Turkey. Limited importation 2006-2007.

	$525	$460	$415	$350	$300	$260	$220

Last MSR was $599.

POINTER ITALIAN SPORTING/FIELD - 12, 20, 28 ga., or .410 bore, 3 in. chambers, 28 in. barrels, blue/nickel finish, fixed or multi-chokes, select walnut stock and forearm, ejectors, 6.1-7.4 lbs. Importation began 2007.

MSR $1,299	$1,150	$995	$875	$750	$625	$525	$450

Add $200 for 28 ga. or .410 bore.

POINTER ITALIAN SPORTING CLAYS - 12 ga., 3 in. chambers, 28 in. barrels, blue/nickel finish, multi-chokes, select walnut stock and forearm, ejectors, 7.6 lbs. Importation began 2007.

MSR $1,299	$1,150	$995	$875	$750	$625	$525	$450

GRADING - PPGS™	100%	98%	95%	90%	80%	70%	60%

POLI, ARMI F.LLI

Current manufacturer established in 1966, and located in Gardone, Italy. Currently imported by Anglo American Sporting Agency, located in Corona Del Mar, CA, Deep River Sporting Clays, located in Sanford, NC. Previously imported by Cole Gunsmithing, located in Harpswell, ME.

Armi F.lli Poli manufactures high quality, SxS and single barrel hammer shotguns in 12, 16, 20, 28 ga., or .410 bore. Current models include the Ivory (hammerless, boxlock action), Opal (hammerless, boxlock action with sideplates), Lapis (lightweight, scalloped boxlock action, hammerless), Onix (scalloped boxlock action, hammerless), Coral (sidelock back action w/hammers), Ruby (petite sidelock back action w/hammers), Emerald (sidelock back action w/hammers), Amethist (sidelock, hammerless), Sapphire, Kristal, Zircon, and Zircon Deluxe. Please contact the importer for more information, including pricing and availability (see Trademark Index).

POLI NICOLETTO & C. snc.

Current manufacturer established in 1975, and located in Brescia, Italy. No current U.S. importation.

Poli Nicoletto manufactures good quality lightweight hunting rifles and shotguns, in addition to choke tubes, scope mounts, and .22 LR pistol conversion kits. Plese contact the company directly for more information, including pricing and availability (see Trademark Index).

POLY TECHNOLOGIES, INC.

Previously distributed by PTK International, Inc. located in Atlanta, GA. Previously imported by Keng's Firearms Specialty, Inc., located in Riverdale, GA. Manufactured in China by Poly Technologies, Inc.

Poly Technologies commercial firearms are made to Chinese military specifications and have excellent quality control.

These models were banned from domestic importation due to 1989 Federal legislation.

RIFLES: SEMI-AUTO

Add 10% for NIB.

POLY TECH AKS-762 - 7.62x39mm or .223 Rem. cal., 16 1/4 in. barrel, semi-auto version of the Chinese AKM (Type 56) paramilitary design rifle, 8.4 lbs., wood stock. Imported 1988-89.

$1,350	$1,200	$1,050	$950	$850	$795	$750

Last MSR was $400.

Add $100 for side-fold plastic stock.

This model was also available with a downward folding stock at no extra charge.

CHINESE SKS - 7.62x39mm cal., 20 9/20 in. barrel, full wood stock, machine steel parts to Chinese military specifications, 7.9 lbs. Imported 1988-89.

$475	$400	$350	$300	$275	$250	$225

Last MSR was $200.

RUSSIAN AK-47/S (LEGEND) - 7.62x39mm cal., 16 3/8 in. barrel, semi-auto configuration of the original AK-47, fixed, side-folding, or under-folding stock, with or w/o spike bayonet, 8.2 lbs. Imported 1988-89.

$1,950	$1,750	$1,500	$1,350	$1,200	$1,000	$925

Last MSR was $550.

Add $50 for folding stock.

The "S" suffix in this variation designates third model specifications.

✱ *Russian AK-47/S National Match Legend* - utilizes match parts in fabrication.

$1,750	$1,550	$1,275	$1,050	$975	$900	$825

GRADING - PPGS™	100%	98%	95%	90%	80%	70%	60%

RPK - 7.62x39mm cal. Disc.

	$1,300	$1,150	$1,025	$925	$850	$775	$700

U.S. M-14/S - .308 Win. cal., 22 in. barrel, forged receiver, patterned after the famous M-14, 9.2 lbs. Imported 1988-89.

	$950	$850	$775	$725	$650	$575	$500

Last MSR was $700.

POWELL, WILLIAM & SON (GUNMAKERS) LTD.

Please refer to the W Section for this trademark.

PRAIRIE GUN WORKS

Please refer to PGW Defence Technologies listing.

PRANDELLI-GASPERINI

Previous manufacturer located in Brescia, Italy. Previously imported by Richland Arms located in Blissfield, MI.

Prandelli-Gasperini made both O/U and SxS shotguns in either sidelock or boxlock. Currently, values for the older boxlock models are in the $475-$675 range (assuming 80% or better original condition). Sidelock models in similar condition are usually valued in the $1,350 - $2,100 range, depending on gauge, embellishments, and condition. Approx. 250 specimens of this trademark were imported during Richland Arms importation.

PRECHTL, WAFFEN

Current rifle manufacturer specializing in Mauser actions located in Birkenau, Germany. Currently imported by Mitchell's Mausers, located in Fountain Valley, CA.

Waffen Prechtl specializes in manufacturing a Mauser 98 short, standard, or Magnum length bolt action rifle patterned after the Mauser drawings from the 1930s. A wide variety of calibers and options are available. Please contact the importer for more information, including pricing and U.S. importation (see Trademark Index).

PRECISION SMALL ARMS, INC. (PSA)

Current manufacturer established in 1979, and made under F.N. license in Aspen, CO, beginning 2006. Previously manufactured in Montrose, CO during 2005, in Irvine, CA until 2002, and in Charlottesville, VA until 1999.

PISTOLS: SEMI-AUTO

The PSP pistol was not in full scale production from 1995-2005, but approx. 1,000 nickel plated units were sold to various dealers between 1996-97. The new model manufactured previously in Montrose, CO is now called the PSA-25, and will be produced in Apsen on a limited run basis.

(PSP) PSA-25 TRADITIONAL - .25 ACP, single action, Baby Browning design mfg. in the U.S., 2 1/8 in. barrel, 6 shot mag., checkered black polymer grips, all steel construction with choice of polished blue (new 1999), black oxide (disc. 1999), brushed satin white nickel (Nouveau satin), or highly polished white nickel finish (Nouveau mirror), dual safety system, 7 1/4-9 1/2 oz. Mfg. 1989-2002, reintroduced 2005.

MSR $498		$425	$365	$325	$295	$250	$200	$175

Add $28 for Nouveau-Satin finish or $37 for Nouveau-Mirror finish.

This pistol is mfg. in the U.S. under license from Fabrique Nationale.

* *PSP-25 Stainless Steel* - features stainless steel construction. Mfg. 1996 only.

	$285	$230	$195	$145	$120	$105	$90

Last MSR was $327.

* *PSP-25 Featherweight* - features aircraft aluminum frame with high polish nickel slide and mag., gold-plated trigger, smooth pearlescent polymer grips. Mfg. 1996-2002, reintroduced 2005.

MSR N/A		$475	$425	$375	$335	$300	$275	$250

GRADING - PPGS™	100%	98%	95%	90%	80%	70%	60%

✳ **PSP-25 Diplomat** - features blue, high polish frame and slide, 24Kt. gold plated external components, ivory grips. Mfg. 1999-2002, reintroduced 2005.

MSR N/A	$750	$675	$575	$475	$400	$325	$275

✳ **PSP-25 Montreux** - high polish 24Kt. gold plated frame, slide, and external components, ivory grips. Mfg. 1999-2002, reintroduced 2005.

MSR N/A	$850	$750	$625	$525	$425	$350	$300

✳ **PSP-25 Presidential** - features highly polished 24Kt. gold plated slide, frame, magazine, and trigger, Dendrite ivory grips. Disc. 1999.

	$600	$475	$375	$315	$270	$230	$200

Last MSR was $725.

✳ **PSP-25 Renaissance** - features chrome receiver with full coverage scroll engraving. Mfg. 1996-2002, reintroduced 2005.

MSR N/A	$1,350	$1,175	$995	$875	$775	$675	$575

✳ **PSP-25 Imperiale** - features hand inlaid 24Kt. gold scroll pattern on frame and slide by Angelo Bee, black oxide finish, ivory grips. Limited mfg.

MSR N/A	$4,400	$3,950	$3,500	$2,950	$2,500	$2,000	$1,650

✳ **PSP-25 Signature Editions** - similar to Imperiale, except has "Michael B. Kassnar" signature on left slide top in gold. Mfg. 1989-91.

	$325	$295	$260	$230	$200	$175	$160

Last MSR was $385.

There were also two Limited Signature Editions (less than 10 mfg.) which retailed for $1,458 and approx. $2,150.

PREMIER

Previous trademark manufactured in Italy and Spain by various companies.

SHOTGUNS: SxS

Note: Premier is a trade name for guns that have been produced in both Spain and Italy for various importers.

REGENT MODEL - 12, 16, 20, 28 ga., or .410 bore, 26, 28, or 30 in. barrels, various chokes, checkered pistol grip stock and beavertail forearm. Mfg. 1955-disc.

	$275	$250	$220	$195	$140	$110	$100

REGENT MAGNUM EXPRESS - 12 ga., 3 in. chambers only, 30 in. full barrel, recoil pad. Mfg. 1957-disc.

	$305	$275	$250	$220	$165	$140	$110

REGENT 10 GAUGE MAGNUM - similar to 12 ga. Mag., but 10 ga., 3 1/2 in. chamber, 32 in. full and full barrel. Mfg. 1975-disc.

	$330	$305	$275	$250	$195	$165	$140

BRUSH KING - 12 or 20 ga., 22 in. imp. cyl. and mod. barrels, straight grip stock. Mfg. 1959-disc.

	$275	$250	$220	$195	$140	$110	$100

MONARCH SUPREME GRADE - 12 or 20 ga., 26 or 28 in. barrels, various chokes, boxlock, auto ejectors, select stock. Mfg. 1959-disc.

	$440	$385	$360	$330	$275	$250	$200

PRESENTATION CUSTOM GRADE - custom-made, gold and silver game scene. Mfg. 1959-disc.

	$1,100	$990	$880	$825	$715	$605	$495

AMBASSADOR MODEL - 12, 16, 20 ga., or .410 bore, 26 or 28 in. barrels, mod. and full choke, checkered pistol grip stock. Mfg. 1957-disc.

	$385	$360	$330	$305	$250	$220	$195

GRADING - PPGS™	100%	98%	95%	90%	80%	70%	60%

PRINZ

Previous manufacturer of bolt action rifles, single shot rifles, and combination guns. Previously imported and distributed by Helmut Hofmann Inc. located in Placitas, NM.

RIFLES

GRADE 1 BOLT ACTION - .243 Win., .30-06, .308 Win., .300 Win. Mag., or 7mm Rem. Mag. cal., single or double set trigger(s), oil finished walnut stock.

$495	$440	$385	$360	$330	$275	$250

* *Grade 1 Bolt Action Carbine* - similar to Grade 1 except has carbine barrel.

$570	$495	$435	$390	$360	$330	$275

GRADE 2 BOLT ACTION - similar to Grade 1 except has rosewood forend cap.

$545	$485	$425	$385	$360	$330	$275

TIP-UP RIFLE - available in 8 cals. between .222 Rem. and .30-06, high quality and limited mfg. Importation began 1989.

$2,175	$1,900	$1,675	$1,375	$1,100	$950	$775

PRINCESS MODEL 85 - combination gun available in 12 ga. (2 3/4 in. chamber) and choice of 8 cals. between .222 Rem. and .30-06.

$1,450	$1,275	$1,100	$925	$800	$775	$650

This model came standard with a leather case.

PROFESSIONAL ORDNANCE, INC.

Previous manufacturer located in Lake Havasu City, AZ 1998-2003. Previously manufactured in Ontario, CA circa 1996-1997. Distributor sales only.

During 2003, Bushmaster bought Professional Ordnance and the Carbon 15 trademark. Please refer to the Bushmaster section for currently manufactured Carbon 15 rifles and pistols (still manufactured in Lake Havasu City).

PISTOLS: SEMI-AUTO

CARBON-15 TYPE 20 - .223 Rem. cal., Stoner type operating system with recoil reducing buffer assembly, carbon fiber upper and lower receiver, hard chromed bolt carrier, 7 1/4 in. unfluted stainless steel barrel with ghost ring sights, 30 shot mag. (supplies were limited), also accepts AR-15 type mags., 40 oz. Mfg. 1999-2000.

$800	$725	$650	$575	$525	$475	$425

Last MSR was $1,500.

CARBON-15 TYPE 21 - .223 Rem cal., ultra lightweight carbon fiber upper and lower receivers, 7 1/4 in. "Profile" stainless steel barrel, quick detachable muzzle compensator, ghost ring sights, 10 shot mag., also accepts AR-15 type mags., Stoner type operating sytem, tool steel bolt, extractor and carrier, 40 oz. Mfg. 2001-2003.

$750	$675	$600	$550	$500	$450	$395

Last MSR was $899.

CARBON-15 TYPE 97 - similar to Carbon 15 Type 20, except has fluted barrel and quick detachable compensator, 46 oz. Mfg. 1996-2003.

$795	$725	$625	$575	$525	$475	$425

Last MSR was $964.

RIFLES: SEMI-AUTO

CARBON-15 TYPE 20 - .223 Rem. cal., same operating system as the Carbon-15 pistol, 16 in. unfluted stainless steel barrel, carbon fiber buttstock and forearm, includes mil spec optics mounting base, 3.9 lbs. Mfg. 1998-2000.

$850	$795	$725	$650	$550	$475	$425

Last MSR was $1,550.

GRADING - PPGS™	100%	98%	95%	90%	80%	70%	60%

CARBON-15 TYPE 21 - .223 Rem. cal., ultra light weight carbon fiber upper and lower receivers, 16 in. "Profile" stainless steel barrel, quick detachable muzzle compensator, Stoner type operating system, tool steel bolt, extractor and carrier, optics mounting base, quick detachable stock, 10 shot mag., also accepts AR-15 type mags., 3.9 lbs. Mfg. 2001-2003.

		$850	$775	$675	$575	$500	$450	$400

Last MSR was $988.

CARBON-15 TYPE 97/97S - .223 Rem. cal., ultra lighweight carbon fiber upper and lower receivers, Stoner type operating system, hard chromed tool steel bolt, extractor and carrier, 16 in. fluted stainless steel barrel, quick detachable muzzle compensator, optics mounting base, quick detachable stock, 30 shot mag., also accepts AR-15 type mags., 3.9 lbs. Mfg. 2001-2003.

		$900	$825	$750	$675	$600	$550	$500

Last MSR was $1,120.

Add $165 for Model 97S (includes Picatinny rail and "Scout" extension, double walled heat shield foregrip, ambidextrous safety, and multi-carry silent sling).

PTR 91, INC.

Current rifle manufacturer located in Farmington, CT. Represented by Vincent A. Pestilli & Associates, located in Brownfield, ME. Previous company name was J.L.D. Enterprises.

RIFLES: SEMI-AUTO

All models include polymer case, trigger lock, and one 20 shot mag.

MODEL PTR-91 - .308 Win. cal., CNC machined scope mounts, front sight blade, German style rear sight, 18 in. barrel with 1:12 twist, black furniture, with (PTR-91 C) or w/o muzzle brake (PTR-91 F), H&K Navy type polymer trigger group, 20 shot mag., one piece forged cocking handle, parkerized finish, matte black coated.

MSR $1,140		$1,025	$900	$800	$700	$600	$500	$450

Add $200 for tactical handguard, side folding stock and pre-ban flash hider (PTR-91R).
Add $200 for tactical handguard, side folding stock and muzzle brake (PTR-91 RC).

✳ *Model PTR-91T* - .308 Win. cal., similar to Model PTR-91, except has green furniture and original H&K flash hider. Limited mfg. 2005.

		$895	$800	$700	$600	$500	$450	$400

Last MSR was $995.

MODEL PTR-91 AI - .308 Win. cal., match grade rifle with polymer trigger group, front sight blade, German style rear sight with 4-position aperture diopter, 20 shot mag., steel bipod, handguard bipod recesses into original H&K flash hider, with (PTR-91 AIC) or w/o (PTR-91 AI F) muzzle brake with match grade barrel. New 2005.

MSR $1,295		$1,150	$925	$825	$725	$600	$500	$425

MODEL PTR-91 KC - .308 Win. cal., "Kurz" law enforcement carbine with 16 in. barrel, front sight blade, German style rear sight with 4-position aperture diopter, 20 shot mag., tropical green (disc.) or black furniture, wide handguard with bipod recesses, includes flash hider or muzzle brake. New 2005.

MSR $1,322		$1,200	$1,050	$925	$825	$725	$600	$500

Add $100 for PTR-91 KFO with side folding stock and pre-ban flash hider (disc. 2006).

MODEL PTR-91 KFM4 - .308 Win. cal., "Kurz" paratrooper carbine, 16 in. barrel, front sight blade, German style rear sight with 4-position aperture diopter, 20 shot mag., tropical green (disc.) or black furniture, wide handguard with bipod recesses, includes three complete rails, H&K Navy type polymer trigger group, M4 type 6 position telescoping stock and flash hider. New 2005.

MSR $1,320		$1,200	$1,050	$925	$825	$725	$600	$500

GRADING - PPGS™	100%	98%	95%	90%	80%	70%	60%

PUMA RIFLES

Current trademark of rifles imported by Legacy Sports International LLC, located in Reno, NV. Previously located in Alexandria, VA.

RIFLES: LEVER ACTION

MODEL 92 - .357 Mag./.38 Spl., .44 Mag., .45 LC, .454 Casull (new 2002, carbine only), or .480 Ruger (new 2004) cal., 9 (.454 Casull) or 10 shot tube mag., 20 in. round or 24 in. octagon barrel, choice of blue, brass, case colored frame, or stainless steel receiver and barrel, regular or large loop (.357 Mag. or .45 LC cal. only, new 2005), uncheckered walnut stock and forearm. Importation began 2001.

   * *Model 92 Round Barrel Carbine* - .357 Mag./.38 Spl., .44 Mag., .45 LC, .454 Casull (new 2002), or .480 Ruger (new 2004) cal., blue, brass, case colored (disc.) or stainless steel, 16, 18, or 20 in. ported (.44 Mag. or .454 Casull cal. only, new 2005) or unported barrel, 8 or 10 shot mag., 6.1 lbs.

MSR $613	$500	$400	$325	$275	$225	$200	$175

   Add $87 for stainless steel construction.
   Add $30 for HiViz sights and ported barrel (not available on .357 Mag. or .45 LC cal.).
   Add $31 for .454 Casull or $47 for .480 Ruger cal.
   Add $7 for large loop lever (.357 Mag. or .45 LC cal. only).

   * *Model 92 Octagon Barrel Rifle* - .357 Mag./.38 Spl., .44 Mag., or .45 LC cal., choice of blue/case colored, stainless steel, or stainless steel/brass (not available in .44 Mag. cal.), 20 (new 2007) or 24 in. octagon barrel, 10 or 12 shot mag., 7.7 lbs.

MSR $731	$575	$475	$425	$350	$300	$275	$250

   Add $16 for blue/case colored finish.
   Add $41 for brass.
   Add $93 for buckhorn sights and saddle ring (new 2002).
   Add $55 for stainless steel construction.

PURDEY, JAMES & SONS, LTD.

Current manufacturer established in 1814, and located in London, England. Annual production is approximately 75 guns.

Purdey guns have long been regarded as among the finest in the world. They have typically been made to customer specifications, and as such, should be appraised individually for purposes of evaluation. Values vary with gauge, barrel length, chamber length and age. Listed are the modern models and approximate values for reference purposes.

Prices indicated are for manufacturer's suggested retail and 100% condition factors are listed in English pounds. All new prices do not include VAT. Values for used guns in 98%-60% condition factors are priced in U.S. dollars.

RIFLES: CUSTOM ORDER & OLDER PRODUCTION

New rifle prices represent the base price with standard fine scroll and bouquet engraving.

PURDEY DOUBLE RIFLE CURRENT MFG. - various English Nitro Express cals., 25 1/2 in. barrels, folding leaf sight, checkered pistol grip stock, recoil pad, sidelock, auto ejectors.

   * *Purdey Double Rifle Smaller Calibers* - .300 H&H or .375 H&H cal.

MSR £77,500	£77,500	$75,000	$62,000	$50,000	$45,000	$40,000	$35,000

   * *Purdey Double Rifle .416 Rigby - .500 NE*

MSR £85,200	£85,200	$86,000	$72,000	$65,000	$60,000	$55,000	$50,000

   * *Purdey Double Rifle 577 NE & .600 NE*

MSR £94,000	£94,000	$105,500	$89,500	$80,000	$75,000	$70,000	$65,000

   The values represent base price only. Since each Purdey is basically a special order, new gun pricing is calculated per individual customer work order.

GRADING - PPGS™	100%	98%	95%	90%	80%	70%	60%

PURDEY DOUBLE RIFLE OLDER MFG.

.300 H&H cal. or less	N/A	$52,250	$46,000	$42,000	$37,000	$32,000	$28,500
Up to .375 H&H cal.	N/A	$59,500	$51,000	$45,000	$40,000	$35,000	$30,000
Up to .470 NE cal.	N/A	$80,000	$72,500	$65,000	$57,500	$50,000	$45,000
Up to .600 NE cal.	N/A	$87,500	$80,000	$70,000	$60,000	$55,000	$50,000

Add 30% for self-opening action.
Subtract 15% if w/o ejectors.

MAGAZINE RIFLE - cals. up to .375 H&H are built on Mauser action, 24 in. barrel, folding leaf sight, checkered best quality walnut pistol grip stock, individually built per customer specifications.

MSR £18,250	£18,250	£20,000	$16,000	$13,500	$9,750	$8,500	$7,000

MAGNUM MAGAZINE RIFLE - .375 H&H, .416/450, and .500 cal., built on modern Magnum action, individually built per customer's specifications.

MSR £19,500	£19,500	£24,500	$18,000	$14,500	$11,250	$9,650	$8,500

SHOTGUNS: CUSTOM ORDER & OLDER PRODUCTION

New shotgun prices represent the base price with standard fine scroll and bouquet engraving.

BEST QUALITY GAME GUN SxS - 10, 12, 16, 20, 28 ga., or .410 bore, best quality sidelock action. 26-30 in. barrels, any choke and style of rib, checkered straight or pistol grip stock, auto ejector gun, best quality only, includes leather case. Mfg. since 1880.

MSR £53,000	£53,000	$55,000	$43,000	$35,000	$25,000	$20,000	$16,500

Add £1,195 for 28 ga., or £3,400 for .410 bore or 10 ga. on new mfg.
Add £9,900 for extra set of barrels.

* *Best Quality Game Gun Older Mfg.*

	$25,795	$21,725	$18,425	$14,300	$11,825	$10,175	$8,745

* *Best Quality Heavy Duck Gun*

	$20,500	$17,000	$14,000	$11,000	$9,500	$8,750	$7,500

Add 50% for 20 ga.
Add 35%-50% for 28 ga. or .410 bore, depending on condition.
Subtract 10%-15% if not cased with accessories.
Add $1,000 for SST.

O/U GUN - 12, 16, 20, 28 ga., or .410 bore best quality sidelock action. 26-30 in. barrels, any choke, auto ejectors, ST, checkered straight or pistol grip stock, includes leather case. Since WWII, Purdey has taken over the Woodward Company, and later guns have the Woodward O/U action. Very few early actions.

MSR £62,500	£62,500	$65,000	$48,000	$35,000	$32,000	$28,000	$25,000

Add £3,400 for 28 ga. or £4,700 for .410 bore.
Add £14,300 (same ga.) or £16,975 (different ga.) for extra set of barrels.

* *O/U Gun Older mfg.*

	$43,000	$38,000	$34,000	$30,000	$27,500	$25,000	$22,500

Add $3,000 for Woodward action.
Add 50% for 20 ga.
Add 100% for 28 ga.
Add 10% for SST.

PURDEY SPORTER O/U - 12 or 20 ga., 28 - 32 in. barrels, trigger plate action, solid or vent. rib, detachable single or double trigger, includes Sporter pattern large scroll engraving, major parts mfg. by Purdey and sent to Italy for assembly by Perugini & Visini. New 2008.

MSR £25,000	£25,000	$30,000	$26,000	$22,000	$18,000	$15,000	$12,500

GRADING - PPGS™	100%	98%	95%	90%	80%	70%	60%

HAMMER EJECTOR GAME GUN - 12 or 20 ga., ejectors, top tang safety, special order only, case colored receiver, traditional fine scroll engraving, checkered straight grip English stock and splinter forearm. First U.S. importation during 2008. New 2002.

	100%	98%	95%	90%	80%	70%	60%
MSR £54,250	£54,250	$50,000	$42,000	$36,000	$32,000	$26,000	$22,000

Griffin & Howe is the exclusive U.S. agent for this model.

SINGLE BARREL TRAP GUN - 12 ga. Purdey action only, similar to O/U specifications. Mfg. prior to WWII.

100%	98%	95%	90%	80%	70%	60%
$11,250	$10,000	$8,750	$7,900	$7,200	$6,750	$5,950

NOTES

Q SECTION

Q.S. PROGETTO MECCANICA s.a.s.

Current pistol and ammunition manufacturer located in Lecco, Italy. No current U.S. importation.

Q.S. Progetto Meccanica s.a.s. manufacturers a M1911-A1 style pistol with its proprietary 7penna centerfire ammunition (7x23mm). For more information regarding this model and ammunition, please contact the company directly (see Trademark Index).

QFI (QUALITY FIREARMS INC.)

Previous manufacturer located in Opa Locka, FL circa December 1990-1992.

GRADING - PPGS™	100%	98%	95%	90%	80%	70%	60%

PISTOLS: SEMI-AUTO

MODEL LA380 - .380 ACP cal., single action, 6-shot, magazine disconnect, hammer, trigger, and firing pin block safety, 3 1/4 in. barrel, blue or chrome finish. Mfg. 1991-92.

	100%	98%	95%	90%	80%	70%	60%
	$125	$100	$90	$80	$70	$60	$55

Last MSR was $147.

Add $23 for chrome finish.

✳ *Model LA380SS* - stainless steel variation of the Model LA380. Mfg. 1992 only.

	100%	98%	95%	90%	80%	70%	60%
	$195	$165	$135	$110	$95	$75	$70

Last MSR was $220.

MODEL SA 25 - .25 ACP cal., single action, 2 1/2 in. barrel, 6-shot, includes inertial firing pin, external exposed hammer with half cock, and trigger blocking thumb safety, blue, Dynachrome, or blue/gold finish, smooth walnut grips. Mfg. 1991 only.

	100%	98%	95%	90%	80%	70%	60%
	$55	$45	$40	$35	$30	$25	$25

Last MSR was $55.

Add $50 for blue/gold finish.
Add $10 for chrome finish with pearlite plastic grips.

TIGRESS MODEL - .25 ACP or .380 ACP cal., single action, 2 1/2 (.25 ACP) or 3 1/4 (.380 ACP) in. barrel, blue frame with gold-plated slide, 6-shot with finger extension on mag., white polymer grips with a red rose scrimshawed on both sides, designed for women, supplied with zippered gold pouch, 14 or 25 oz. Mfg. 1991 only.

	100%	98%	95%	90%	80%	70%	60%
	$130	$100	$90	$80	$70	$60	$55

Last MSR was $155.

Add $85 for .380 ACP cal.

REVOLVERS: DOUBLE ACTION

All revolvers under this heading are 6-shot.

RP SERIES STANDARD REVOLVER - .22 LR, .22 Mag., .32 S&W Long, .32 H&R Mag or .38 Spl. cal., 2 or 4 in. barrel, blue or chrome finish, fixed sights, hammer block safety, without ejector assembly, composition grips. Mfg. in U.S. 1990-disc.

	100%	98%	95%	90%	80%	70%	60%
	$85	$70	$65	$60	$55	$50	$45

Last MSR was $105.

Add $15-20 for chrome finish.
Add approx. $5 for 4 in. barrel.

MODEL SO 38 - .38 Spl. cal., swing out cylinder, 6-shot, 2 in. SR or 4 in. VR barrel, hammer block safety, composition grips. Mfg. 1991 only.

	100%	98%	95%	90%	80%	70%	60%
	$175	$135	$115	$95	$80	$75	$65

Last MSR was $175.

GRADING - PPGS™	100%	98%	95%	90%	80%	70%	60%

REVOLVERS: SINGLE ACTION

SAA WESTERN RANGER - .22 LR cal., 6-shot, 3, 4 (disc. 1991), 4 3/4 (new 1992), 6 (disc. 1991), 6 1/2 (new 1992), 7 (disc. 1991), or 9 in. barrel, blue finish with gold accenting, walnut grips. Mfg. 1991-92.

	$85	$70	$65	$60	$55	$50	$45

Last MSR was $105.

> Add approx. $5 for 7 (disc.) or $7 for 9 in. barrel.
> Add approx. $15-$35 for .22 Mag. extra cylinder (combo).

SAA PLAINS RIDER - similar to Western Ranger, except has black composition grips and no gold accenting. Mfg. 1991-92.

	$80	$65	$55	$50	$45	$40	$35

Last MSR was $100.

> Add $11 for 9 in. barrel.
> Add approx. $26 for .22 Mag. extra cylinder (combo).

SAA HORSEMAN SERIES - .357 Mag., .44 Mag., or .45 LC cal., 6-shot, 6 1/2 or 7 1/2 in. barrel, color case hardened or blue (Dark Horseman only) finish, walnut or black composition grips, hammer block safety. Mfg. 1991 only.

	$250	$220	$190	$170	$150	$130	$115

Last MSR was $250.

The Dark Horseman had an extended grip frame with black composition grips and an adj. rear sight.

QIQIHAR HAWK INDUSTRIES CO., LTD.

Current manufacturer located in Heilongjiang Province, China.

Qiqihar manufactures good quality SxS, slide action, and semi-auto shotguns. Please contact the company directly for more information, including pricing and domestic availability (see Trademark Index).

QUACKENBUSH, H.M.

Previous rifle manufacturer circa 1886-1922, and located in Herkimer, NY. Quackenbush also manufactured airguns 1871-1943.

For more information on Quackenbush airguns, including the combination rimfire/airgun, please refer to the *Blue Book of Airguns,* by Dr. Robert Beeman & John Allen (also online).

RIFLES: .22 CAL., RIMFIRE

Only one breech mechanism was used on all H.M. Quackenbush .22 cal. rimfire rifles, the company's only rifle configuration, a swinging breech single shot. These models were supplied in several different boxes, and often came with a cleaning rod. These and other accessories will significantly add to the value of the firearms prices listed. No serial numbers were applied to Quackenbush guns. Many variations of these models are encountered, which can also add premiums to the values listed, and can be used to estimate date of manufacture. Quackenbush also manufactured heavy metal targets for these rifles, 1884-1931.

SAFETY RIFLE - single shot, swinging breech, walnut stock, 18 or 22 in. barrel. Mfg. 1886-1922.

	$800	$700	$600	$400	$350	$325	$275

> Add 10% for each of the following with heavy cast iron buttplate, original factory blue finish, optional Town & Country combination rear and front sights, or for barrel and optional sights where rear sight is approx. 1 in. forward of the breech end of the barrel, and for factory walnut forearm.

JUNIOR SAFETY RIFLE - similar to Safety Model, except smaller and has tubular receiver, wire stocked, swinging breech, 18 in. barrel only. Mfg. 1890-1920.

	$900	$800	$700	$500	$400	$375	$350

> Add 10% for original factory blue finish.

BYCYCLE RIFLE - similar to Safety Model, retractable wire stock, smaller, and has a wire pistol grip, fixed rear sight, nickel finish, 12 in. barrel. Mfg. 1896-1919.

$1,800 $1,750 $1,550 $1,300 $1,150 $1,000 $700

Add 10% for original factory blue finish.
Subtract 50% if retractable shoulder stock is missing.

QUAIL UNLIMITED, INC.

Current national conservation organization with national headquarters located in Edgefield, SC.

Although Quail Unlimited, Inc. is not a manufacturer or importer, this organization has been responsible for many special and limited editions. These are listed below with quantities, but without secondary market prices, since they may vary greatly from region to region. Some of the models (and current values) may be listed under manufacturer listings in this text. Because of the relatively low quantities involved with these special editions, most of the models listed below have premiums currently being asked over issue prices, and the amount will vary with the region and acceptance by Quail Unlimited members. Quail Unlimited designated their special editions as follows: 1986 - Grand Slam I - Bobwhite Edition, 1987 - Grand Slam II - California Edition, 1988 - Grand Slam III - Gambel Edition, 1989 - Grand Slam IV - Mountain Quail Edition, 1990 - Grand Slam V - Scaled Quail Edition, 1992 - Gun Dog I - Pointer Edition, 1993 - Gun Dog II - Setter Edition, 1994 - Gun Dog III - Brittany Edition, 1995 - Gun Dog IV - German Shorthair Edition, 1996 - Gun Dog V - Belgian Edition. 1994 - Golden Covey I - Full Covey Edition, 1995 - Golden Covey II - Bobwhite Edition, 1997 - Upland I - Ruffed Grouse Edition.

Model	Manufacturer	Qty.	Year	Issue Price
SPECIAL/LIMITED EDITIONS				
✳ *Superposed 20 ga.*	Browning	100	1986	$2,850
✳ *Model 101 28 ga.*	Winchester	100	1987	$2,195
✳ *Sweet 16 16 ga.*	Browning	100	1988	$1,895
✳ *Model 23 12 ga.*	Winchester	100	1989	$2,885
✳ *Citori Lightning .410 bore*	Browning	100	1990	$2,295
Add $500 to issue price for silver finish (standard finish was nickel).				
Add $700 to issue price for gold finish (standard finish was nickel).				
✳ *Model A-5 20 ga.*	Browning	100	1992	$1,795
✳ *Citori Lightning 28 ga.*	Browning	100	1993	$2,395
✳ *Model A-5 20 ga.*	Browning	100	1993	$1,795
✳ *Citori Lightning .410 bore*	Browning	100	1994	$2,395
✳ *Citori Lightning German Shorthair 20 ga.*	Browning	100	1995	$2,395
✳ *Model A-5 20 ga. 3 in. GRIII (15th Anniv.)*	Belgian Browning	75	1996	$2,195
✳ *Model A-5 20 ga. 3 in. GRV (15th Anniv.)*	Belgian Browning	25	1996	$3,995
✳ *SxS 20 ga. (15th Anniv.)*	Rizzini	34	1996	$2,850
✳ *SxS 20 ga. (Gold) (15th Anniv.)*	Rizzini	15	1996	$4,250
✳ *Citori Superlight 20 ga.*	Browning	100	1997	$2,495
✳ *Model 12 20 ga.*	Winchester	100	1997	$995
✳ *Model 12 20 ga. Chevy/QU Exclusive*	Winchester	298	1997	$995
✳ *Citori Superlight 28 ga.*	Browning	100	1998	$2,495
✳ *Model A-5 Chevrolet*	Browning	299	1998	$1,495
✳ *620 VS 20 ga.*	Franchi	100	1999	$1,195
✳ *Citori Upland 12 ga.*	Browning	100	1999	$2,495

Model	Manufacturer	Qty.	Year	Issue Price
* Whitewing TWRA Executive Ed. 12 or 20	Beretta	72	1999	$1,595
* AL390 TWRA Reg. Ed. 12 or 20 ga.	Beretta	40	1999	$995
* AL390 TWRA Youth Ed. 12 or 20 ga.	Beretta	25	1999	$995
* Citori Superlight 20 ga.	Browning	100	2000	$2,495
* Red Label 28 ga. Chevrolet	Sturm Ruger	259	2000	$1,995
* Feniche 28 ga. 20th Anniversary	Franchi	125	2000	$1,195
* Model 37 16 ga. 20th Anniversary	Ithaca Gun	150	2000	$995
* 620 VS 20 ga. Chevrolet	Franchi	400	2001	$1,395
* Citori Superlight .410 bore	Browning	100	2001	$2,495
* Feniche 28 ga. Encore	Franchi	100	2001	$1,295
* 620VS 20 ga. Chevrolet	Franchi	252	2001	$1,395
* Triton Upland Special 20 ga.	Browning	50	2002	$1,695
* Citori Feather 20 ga.	Browning	100	2002	$2,595
* Gold Auto 20 ga. Heritage I Ed. (GR2)	Browning	75	2002	$1,895
* Gold Auto 20 ga., Heritage I Ed. (GR3)	Browning	25	2002	$2,195
* Superior Hunter 20 ga. 20th Anniversary	Charles Daly	100	2002	$789
* Gold Auto 12 ga. Heritage I Ed. (GR2)	Browning	75	2003	$1,895
* Gold Auto 12 ga., Heritage I Ed. (GR3)	Browning	25	2003	$2,195
* 620VS 20 ga. Dinner Gun	Franchi	150	2003	$1,295
* Superior Hunter II 28 ga.	Charles Daly	50	2003	$799
* Superior Hunter II 12 ga.	Charles Daly	50	2004	$789
* Citori Feather 16 ga. Heritage III (GR2)	Browning	75	2004	$2,695
* Citori Feather 16 ga. Heritage III (GR3)	Browning	25	2004	$2,995
* 48AL Dlx 28 ga. Dinner Gun	Franchi	150	2005	$1,395
* 525 Citori 28 ga. Heritage IV (GR2)	Browning	75	2005	$2,699
* 525 Citori 28 ga. Heritage IV (GR3)	Browning	25	2005	$2,899
* 11-87 20 ga. 25th Anniversary	Remington	150	2006	$1,395
* 525 Citori 410 ga. Bore Heritage V (GR2)	Browning	75	2006	$2,599
* 525 Citori 410 ga. Bore Heritage V (GR3)	Browning	25	2006	$2,999
* Gold 25th Anniversary 20 ga.	Browning	25	2006	$1,595
* Citroi Gran Lightning ga.	Browning	1	2007	$6,000
* 525 Citori .410 Bore Heritage V (GR2)	Browning	75	2008	$2,599
* 525 Citori .410 Bore Heritage V (GR3)	Browning	25	2008	$2,899

QUALITY PARTS CO./BUSHMASTER

Quality Parts Co. was a division of Bushmaster Firearms, Inc. located in Windham, ME that manufactured AR-15 type paramilitary rifles and various components and accessories for Bushmaster. Please refer to the Bushmaster section in this text for current model listings and values.

R SECTION

RAF

Previous manufacturer of shotguns and rifles located in St. Etienne, France circa 1994-96. RAF manufactured superposed rifles, shotguns, combination guns, and semi-auto rimfire rifles.

RBA

Current competition pistol manufacturer located in Granarolo Emilia, Italy. No current U.S. importation.

PISTOLS: SEMI-AUTO

Renzo Bonora Armi (RBA) currently manufactures high quality competition pistols in both .22 LR and .32 S&W Wadcutter. Please contact the factory directly for more information, including pricing and U.S. availablility (see Trademark Index).

RND MANUFACTURING

Current manufacturer located in Longmont, CO. Previously distributed by Mesa Sportsmen's Association, L.L.C. located in Delta, CO. Dealer or consumer direct sales.

GRADING - PPGS™	100%	98%	95%	90%	80%	70%	60%

RIFLES: SEMI-AUTO

RND EDGE SERIES - .223 Rem. (RND 400), .300 WSM (new 2003), .300 RSM (new 2003), .338 Lapua Mag. (RND 2000, new 1999) or 7.62x39mm cal., patterned after the AR-15, CNC machined, 18, 20, or 24 in. barrel, choice of synthetic (Grade I), built to individual custom order, handmade laminated thumbhole (Grade II, disc. 1998), or custom laminated thumbhole stock with fluted barrel (Grade III, disc. 1998), vented aluminum shroud, approx. 11 1/2-16 lbs., custom order only, values represent base model. New 1996.

	100%	98%	95%	90%	80%	70%	60%
MSR $2,195	$2,195	$1,950	$1,725	$1,300	$1,050	$850	$725

Add $355 for Grade II.
Add $605 for Grade III or .308 Win. cal.
Add $1,855 for .338 Lapua Mag. cal.

R.F.M.

Please refer to Rota, Luciano listing.

R.G. INDUSTRIES

Previous importer located in Miami, FL. Operations ceased in January of 1986.

HANDGUNS

R.G. Industries manufactured and imported plain utilitarian revolvers and semi-auto pistols. Unfortunately, because of a product liability situation, R.G. Industries was litigated out of business during 1986. Although their models represent good values, they are not collectible, and so a generalized listing is provided.

RG 14 S, RG 23, RG 31

	100%	98%	95%	90%	80%	70%	60%
	$95	$80	$70	$60	$55	$50	$45

RG 40, RG 74, & HIGHNOON S.A.

	100%	98%	95%	90%	80%	70%	60%
	$125	$115	$95	$80	$70	$60	$55

RG 26 SEMI-AUTO - .25 ACP cal., 6 shot mag., 2 1/4 in. barrel, plastic grips, single action, 12 oz.

	100%	98%	95%	90%	80%	70%	60%
	$65	$55	$50	$40	$35	$30	$25

Last MSR was $66.

RPA INTERNATIONAL LTD.

Current rifle manufacturer located in Kent, England. No current U.S. importation.

RIFLES

RPA International Ltd. manufactures high quality bolt action rifles, including a long range sniper model (Rangemaster), in addition to target rifles (Ranger and Elite), sporting rifles with or w/o a thumbhole stock (Hunter), and the Interceptor sporting model. Additionally, the company makes custom rifles and actions. Please contact the company directly for pricing, availability and options (see Trademark Index).

RPB INDUSTRIES

Previous company located in Avondale, GA. RPB Industries' guns were made by Masterpiece Arms.

CARBINES: SEMI-AUTO

RPB CARBINE - .45 ACP cal., closed bolt blowback action, 16 1/4 in. barrel, fixed skeletonized stock and forearm pistol grip, accepts M-3 mags., black finish, 9 1/2 lbs. Mfg. 2000-2004.

| | $450 | $375 | $325 | $285 | $260 | $235 | $210 |

Add $75 for Deluxe Model with EZ cocker and installed scope mount.

RPM

Previous manufacturer located in Afton, MO 2002-2003. Previously located in Tuscon, AZ.

During 2004, RPM changed the name of the company to Gateway Precision Arms. Please refer to this listing for current information.

PISTOLS: SINGLE SHOT

XL PISTOL - many cals. available, tip-up action, 8, 10 3/4, 12, or 14 in. barrel, positive thumb safety, steel frame, cocking indicator, right- or left-hand action. Disc.

| | $785 | $675 | $600 | $550 | $500 | $450 | $395 |

Last MSR was $858.

XL HUNTER - please refer to Gateway Precision Arms for current information on this model.

RWS

Current trademark of Dynamit Nobel GmbH which has been manufacturing firearms and airguns in Nuremberg, Stadeln, and Troisdorf, Germany since 1865. Dynamit Nobel is now a division of RUAG AmmoTec GmbH, located in Furth, Germany. RWS firearms were imported until 1995 by Dynamit Nobel of America, Inc. located in Closter, NJ. Other trademarks (including Rottweil) by Dynamit Nobel can be located under individual heading names in this text.

For more information and current pricing on both new and used RWS airguns produced by Dianawerk, Mayer, and Grammelspacher, please refer to the *Blue Book of Airguns* by Dr. Robert Beeman & John Allen (also online).

RIFLES: BOLT ACTION, TARGET

MODEL 820 L - .22 LR cal. only, 24 (disc.) or 26 in. barrel, no. 100 aperture sight, oil polished stock for 3 position match, stippled pistol grip and forearm, recoil pad, adj. trigger, 10.6 lbs. Disc. 1994.

| | $1,275 | $1,000 | $850 | $700 | $575 | $475 | $400 |

Last MSR was $1,500.

Previous to 1986 this model was designated the 820 S and was supplied with a no. 75 aperture rear sight.

GRADING - PPGS™	100%	98%	95%	90%	80%	70%	60%

✳ *Model 820 S* - with Model 82 aperture sight.

| | $1,100 | $895 | $795 | $650 | $560 | $480 | $420 |

Last MSR was $995.

MODEL 820 F MATCH - similar to Model 820 L, except has heavy match barrel, 15.4 lbs. Disc. 1994.

| | $1,750 | $1,400 | $1,275 | $1,000 | $850 | $700 | $575 |

Last MSR was $2,000.

✳ *Model 820 SF Match* - with Model 820 L aperture sight. Disc.

| | $1,125 | $900 | $795 | $650 | $560 | $480 | $420 |

Last MSR was $1,010.

MODEL 820 K - .22 LR cal. only, made for running boar competition, 24 in. barrel, stock similar to Model 820 SF, no sights, 9 1/2 lbs. without barrel weight or scope. Importation disc. 1986.

| | $900 | $775 | $695 | $615 | $540 | $470 | $420 |

Last MSR was $870.

RADOM

Trademark manufactured 1931-1945 by the Polish Arsenal located in Radom, Poland & Steyr, Austria. Post WWII also manufactured by Z.M.Lucznik (Radom Factory) in Radom, Poland. Currently imported to Dalvar of U.S.A., located in Seligman, AZ. Previously located in Richardson, TX and Henderson, NV.

REVOLVERS

RADOM REVOLVER - Nagant design, dated 1931-36.

| | $2,200 | $1,500 | $1,150 | $900 | $700 | $550 | $450 |

PISTOLS: SEMI-AUTO, 1935-1939 PRODUCTION

Serial number ranges use #### for the no alphabetical prefix series, 1#### for the first alphabetical prefix series, and 2#### for the second alphabetical prefix series. Mill marks are more prominent as the war progressed.

P-35 AUTOMATIC - 9mm Para. cal., 8 shot, blue finish, 4 3/4 in. barrel, blue, fixed sights, black VIS/FB plastic grips. Mfg. 1935 through WWII.

✳ *wz.35 VIS Polish Eagle* - eagle logo, unblued barrel, rust blue, lanyard loop, ser. no. 01-49,000, dated 1936, 1937 (rarest date), 1938, or 1939.

| | $2,700 | $2,300 | $1,925 | $1,400 | $1,100 | $825 | $675 |

Add 50% for 1937 mfg. if in 95%+ condition, otherwise, add 15%.
Add 25% for 1936 mfg. if in 95%+ condition, otherwise, add 10%.

PISTOLS: SEMI-AUTO, LATE 1939-1945 PRODUCTION

Serial number ranges use #### for the no alphabetical prefix series, 1#### for the first alphabetical prefix series, and 2#### for the second alphabetical prefix series. Mill marks are more prominent as the war progressed.

P.35 VIS POLISH EAGLE NAZI CAPTURE - eagle log and WaA marks, rust blue, all 3 levers, lanyard loop, many small parts serial numbered, ser. no. range 49,400-52,500.

| | N/A | $3,150 | $2,500 | $2,000 | $1,600 | $1,200 | $850 |

Beware of fakes!

P.35 NAZI RADOM TYPE 1 - 3 LEVER & SLOT - rust blue, unblued barrel, lanyard loop, black VIS/FB plastic grips, many small parts ser. numbered, ser. nos. 01-12,500 & 1/A0001-1/E8000 (1st Series) prefix.

| | $1,375 | $1,075 | $900 | $725 | $575 | $500 | $425 |

Add 100% for Navy characteristics: Kriegs Eagle/M marked, blued barrel, may/may not be "N"/"O" grip strap marked.
Add 50% for S/N Range 01-12,500, early characteristics: blued barrel, early slide/logo position, no P.35(p), no lanyard loop.
Beware of fakes!

P.35 NAZI RADOM TYPE II - 3 LEVER & NO. SLOT - salt blue, lanyard loop, early e/WaA77 on left frame and slide changes to later e/77, some brown VIS/FB plastic grips, a few with pressed VIS/FB wood grips, serial numbered 1/E8001-1/Z1000 (1st Series) prefix.

	$775	$650	$550	$475	$400	$350	$300

Add 30% if P.35(p) marked if in 95%+ condition, otherwise add 15%.

P.35 NAZI RADOM TYPE III - 2 LEVER & NO. SLOT - lanyard loop, salt blue, e/77 on left side of slide and frame, brown plastic VIS/FBN grips common, pressed VIS/FB wood grips rarely seen, serial numbered 1/Z1001-2/H8900.

	$675	$550	$475	$400	$325	$300	$275

Certain Radoms w/ German acceptance marks will bring a premium.

✴ *P.35 Nazi Steyr Type III - 2 Lever & No. Slot* - salt blued or phosphate exterior with blued small parts also on phosphate models, serial numbered in late 2/A or 2/B with e/77 on left side of slide and frame and 2/H8901 through 2/K w/o e/77 on left side of slide and frame, e/623 on front left side of trigger guard, many with grooved wood grips, mostly all Steyr mfg.

	$1,625	$1,400	$1,300	$1,000	$775	$625	$550

✴ *P.35 Nazi Steyr Type III - 2 Lever & No. Slot "bnz" Slide* - rough milled phosphate exterior, some "blank" slides noted, wood grips, serial numbered 2/K1440-2/K2400, mostly all Steyr mfg.

	$2,850	$2,500	$2,200	$1,800	$1,400	$1,100	$850

PISTOLS: SEMI-AUTO, RECENT PRODUCTION

VIS P-35 - 9mm Para. cal., patterned after the 1937 P-35, large Polish eagle stamped on left side of slide, with or w/o slotted rear grip strap for shoulder stock, 4 1/2 in. barrel, 36 oz. Limited mfg. 1997 only.

	$2,600	$1,425	$1,215	$1,015	$925	$825	$750

Last MSR was $2,999.

MODEL 64 - PPK sized pistol chambered for the 9x18mm Makarov cartridge. Rare.

	$250	$150	$125	$100	$95	$85	$80

TOKAREV (PISTOLET TT) - Polish copy w/manual safety, well made.

	$500	$400	$350	$325	$300	$250	$200

✴ *TT-33 (FB Radom)* - 7.62x25 cal., includes two mags. and cleaning rod, mfg. FB Radom, Poland 1947-1950.

	$275	$230	$200	$180	$165	$150	$140

✴ *TT-33 (Radom)* - 7.62x25 cal., inlcudes two mags. and cleaning rod, mfg. by Radom in Poland 1950-1954.

	$275	$230	$200	$180	$165	$150	$140

VANAD P-83 - 9x18mm Makarov cal., 8 shot mag., available in Standard Military Issue or Special Eagle Limited Edition, loaded chamber indicator, firing pin block safety, steel receiver with external hammer, 3 1/2 in. barrel, drift adj. target sights, checkered composition grips, 26 oz. Importation began 1994 (Standard Military Issue) or 1997.

MSR N/A	$350	$290	$265	$235	$210	$190	$170

Add $46 for Standard Military Issue.

✴ *Vanad P-93 9mm* - 9mm Makarov cal., similar to the Vanad P-83, except decocking lever is on the frame instead of the slide, black oxide finish, 3.9 in. barrel.

	$350	$250	$225	$200	$175	$150	$125

MAG 95 - 9mm Para. cal., single or double action with firing pin block, external hammer, ambidextrous hammer drop safety, 4 1/2 in. barrel, 37 oz. Limited importation 1997 only.

	$650	$550	$450	$400	$350	$300	$275

Last MSR was $749.

GRADING - PPGS™	100%	98%	95%	90%	80%	70%	60%

RAM-LINE, INC.

Previous manufacturer located in Grand Junction, CO until 1995.

In addition to the Ram-Tech pistol, Ram-Line, Inc. also manufactured a complete line of synthetic and wood stocks for a variety of firearms. Ram-Line continues to manufacture a complete line of magazines for most popular pistols and rifles.

PISTOLS: SEMI-AUTO

EXACTOR PISTOL - .22 LR cal., single action, aircraft alloy receiver with 5 1/2 in. polymer VR barrel and steel liner, unique two-motion safety featuring blocks on hammer, trigger, and sear, 15 shot mag., matte finish, easy disassembly, injected molded grip, fixed sight, 20.3 oz., supplied with case. Mfg. 1990-93.

$195	$165	$135	$110	$95	$75	$70

Last MSR was $225.

✳ *Exactor Pistol Target* - similar to above, except has 7 1/2 in. barrel, 23 oz. Disc. 1993.

$265	$230	$195	$150	$125	$110	$95

Last MSR was $300.

RAM-TECH PISTOL - similar to Exactor pistol, except 4 1/2 in. barrel w/o VR. Mfg. 1994-95.

$175	$145	$125	$100	$85	$70	$65

Last MSR was $200.

RAMO DEFENSE SYSTEMS

Previous rifle manufacturer 1999-2003 and located in Nashville, TN.

RIFLES: BOLT ACTION

TACTICAL .308 - .308 Win. cal., Rem. M-700 long action, match grade stainless steel barrel, skeletonized black synthetic stock with cheekpad, matte black metal finish, 4 shot mag., 16 lbs. Mfg. 1999-2003.

$2,495	$2,100	$1,850	$1,600	$1,400	$1,200	$995

Last MSR was $2,495.

M91/M91A2 - .308 Win. or .300 Win. Mag. cal., Rem. M-700 long action, black Kevlar and fiberglass stock, matte black metal finish, 4 shot mag., 14 lbs. Mfg. 1999-2003.

$2,695	$2,250	$1,950	$1,675	$1,475	$1,250	$995

Last MSR was $2,695.

Add $200 for .300 Win. Mag. cal.

M600 SINGLE SHOT - .50 BMG cal., single shot, twin tube skeletonized stock with pistol grip and cheekpiece, 32 in. barrel with fins at breech and muzzle brake, 23 lbs. Mfg. 1999-2003.

$4,195	$3,700	$3,200	$2,750	$2,250	$1,950	$1,675

Last MSR was $4,195.

M650 REPEATER - .50 BMG cal., repeater action with 6 shot detachable rotary mag., stock and barrel (30 in.) similar to M600, approx. 30 lbs. Mfg. 1999-2003.

$6,395	$5,750	$5,150	$4,500	$3,750	$3,000	$2,250

Last MSR was $6,395.

RANDALL FIREARMS COMPANY

Previously manufactured in Sun Valley, CA. Manufactured between June 7, 1983 and December 15, 1984 - final plant closing was June 15, 1985.

Before manufacturing ceased in May of 1985, 24 models with 12 variations in 3 different calibers had been produced. In some instances, production on certain models was very limited and premiums for these low volume niches are starting to develop. Between June of 1983 and May of 1984, 9,968

GRADING - PPGS™	100%	98%	95%	90%	80%	70%	60%

handguns were manufactured with 75% of all 9mm Para. pistols being exported to Europe and 35% of 9mm Para. production employing a 10 groove barrel. Models manufactured after 1984 came equipped with an extended slide stop, long trigger, and beavertail grip safety. Production ser. nos. started at 02000 for right-hand models and 02100 for left-hand models. All but the first 200 (approx.) serial numbers started with "RF" and ended with "C" or "W." A few rare mis-marks are in circulation. Total mfg. for all models and variations was 9,968. Randall prototype serialization starts with a "T" - less than 45 were manufactured and these specimens command up to a 50% premium. In addition, 78 serial numbers under 2,000 were manufactured by special order.

Models listed are generally described with values per specific variations listed afterward.

PISTOLS: SEMI-AUTO

The following is a complete listing for Randall Firearms variations including production statistics. Values shown represent recent aftermarket prices, but it should be noted that regional interest can change these prices significantly. All original Randall pistols had no blue parts. Only the front and rear sights were finished in black oxide.

100% Randall prices assume NIB condition with paperwork.
Add 50% for prototypes with "T" serial numbers.

COMBAT MODEL - same size as Service Model, ribbed top fixed sight slide, Pachmayr grips on right-hand model only, left-hand models had Herrett walnut grips. While this model was advertised as having a flat mainspring housing, it never went into production.

Last MSR was $549.

RAIDER/SERVICE MODEL-C - 9mm Para. or .45 ACP cal., Colt Commander Model design, 4 1/4 in. barrel, 36 oz., total stainless steel construction, roll-marked Service Model-C in 1983 and Raider in 1984.

Last MSR was $460.

Add $130 for adj. sights/ribbed slide, available in either right-hand or left-hand (only 2 mfg.) model.

＊ *Raider/Service Model-C Featherweight* - .45 ACP cal. only, alloy receiver, stainless steel slide, roll-marked Service Model-C, T-type serial numbers, 29 oz. Disc. 1984, only 4 mfg.

FULL SIZE SERVICE MODEL - .38 Super, 9mm Para., or .45 ACP cal., Colt Model 1911 A1 design, 5 in. barrel, total stainless steel construction, 38 oz. Available in either right-hand or left-hand model.

Last MSR was $460.

CURTIS E. LEMAY 4-STAR MODEL - 9mm Para. or .45 ACP cal., Gen. Curtis E. LeMay design, 4 1/4 in. barrel, 6 (.45 ACP) or 7 (9mm Para.) shot mag., total stainless steel construction, 35 oz. Available in either right-hand or left-hand model, left-hand models are a true mirror image with over 17 major parts changes.

Last MSR was $533.

This model was 1/2 in. shorter in magazine well and had a cast, squared-off triggerguard compared to the Colt 1911A1 design.

＊ *Curtis E. LeMay 4-Star Model Featherweight* - .45 ACP cal. only, alloy receiver, stainless steel slide, T-type serial numbers, 28 oz. Disc. 1984 (only one mfg.).

RANDALL MATCHED SETS - .45 ACP cal. only, each set consisted of a right-hand and a left-hand Service Model with matching serial numbers. Only 4 sets were mfg. on a special order basis. A111/B111 model configuration.

Last MSR was $1,250.

Randall Variations & Identification

Randall pistols are denoted by a four-character model notation, starting with an alphabetical prefix followed by three digits. The alphabetical prefix will be either A, B, or C. A designates right-hand configuration only, B designates left-hand configuration only, and C

GRADING - PPGS™	100%	98%	95%	90%	80%	70%	60%

designates right-hand lightweight model. The first numerical digit will be 1, 2, or 3. 1 denotes Service Model, 2 denotes Service Model - C or Raider, and 3 represents the C.E. LeMay Model. The second numerical digit will be either 1, 2, or 3. 1 designates round top and fixed sight slide, 2 denotes flattop fixed sight slide, and 3 represents adj. sights, flattop frame. The third numerical digit will also be either 1, 2, or 3. 1 denotes .45 ACP cal., 2 designates 9mm Para., and 3 represents .38 Super. Hence, if you had a left-hand Randall in the service model size with a flattop adj. sight slide, and in .45 ACP cal., your model would be a B131. These model codes are not marked on the pistols.

A111 - 3,421 mfg.

	$680	$595	$510	$465	$400	$350	$295

Five A111s were mfg. with Austrian proofmarks with premiums existing.

A112 - 301 mfg.

	$895	$795	$650	$525	$440	$385	$325

A121 - 1,067 mfg.

	$700	$625	$510	$465	$400	$350	$295

A122 - 19 mfg.

	$1,325	$1,125	$940	$795	$695	$585	$485

A131 - 2,083 mfg.

	$725	$640	$535	$495	$430	$375	$315

A211 - 992 mfg.

	$750	$660	$535	$480	$415	$360	$300

A212 - 76 mfg.

	$925	$815	$600	$500	$430	$375	$315

A231 - 574 mfg.

	$850	$750	$535	$505	$430	$375	$315

A232 - 5 mfg.

	$1,500	$1,075	$990	$775	$665	$560	$465

A311 - 361 mfg.

	$1,100	$950	$725	$575	$480	$410	$350

Most LeMay models (4 1/4 in. barrel) were shipped in gun rugs without a factory box. Original factory LeMay boxes are rare - add 10% premium. Beware of Randall LeMay and service model pistols made from parts kits. There were 226 LeMay receivers and 322 service model receivers (all right-hand) sold that could be parts guns.

A312 - 1 mfg.
Rarity precludes accurate price evalution.

A331 - 293 mfg.

	$1,200	$1,075	$700	$595	$495	$430	$365

The note that appears for the Model A311 also applies to this variation.

A332 - 9 mfg.

	$1,450	$1,275	$975	$825	$720	$600	$500

B111 - 297 mfg.

	$1,250	$1,100	$850	$750	$640	$535	$450

B121 - 110 mfg.

	$1,500	$1,325	$1,075	$895	$785	$655	$550

B122 - 2 mfg.
Rarity precludes accurate price evaluation.

B123 - 2 mfg.
Rarity precludes accurate price evaluation.

B131 - 225 mfg.

	$1,450	$1,250	$925	$775	$665	$560	$465

GRADING - PPGS™	100%	98%	95%	90%	80%	70%	60%

B311 - 52 mfg.

	$1,575	$1,325	$895	$750	$640	$535	$450

B312 w/ .45 ACP FACTORY CONVERSION - 1 mfg.

Rarity precludes accurate price evaluation.

B312 - 9 mfg.

	$2,750	$2,300	$1,800	$1,550	$1,365	$1,125	$950

B321 - 1 mfg.

Rarity precludes accurate price evaluation. The B321 was the only factory 3-slide set. It was fitted with the 3 different LH LeMay slides available (B311, B321, & B331). This model was mirror polished, engraved, and had ivory grips with the Randall logo.

B331 - 45 mfg.

	$1,775	$1,495	$1,050	$875	$765	$635	$530

B2/321 - 1 mfg.

Rarity precludes accurate price evaluation. This was the only factory model variation to leave Randall Firearms. This was a left-hand Raider with the C.E. LeMay slide.

C211 - 5 mfg.

Rarity precludes accurate price evaluation.

C331 - 1 mfg.

Rarity precludes accurate price evaluation.

C332 - 4 mfg.

Rarity precludes accurate price evaluation.

＊ *C332 Matched Sets* - large premiums exist for different models with the same serial number if NIB condition. Only 4 were mfg.

RANGER ARMS INC.

Previous manufacturer located in Gainesville, TX until the early 1970s.

Ranger Arms Inc. manufactured good quality, bolt action rifles in various calibers and configurations. Although somewhat rare in that there were not a large number manufactured, collectibility to date has been limited with specimens in 90%+ condition, typically priced in the $375-$500 range.

RAPTOR ARMS CO., INC.

Previous rifle manufacturer located in Shelton, CT, approx. 1997-mid 1999. Previously distributed by Davidson's and Jerry's Sport Centers.

RIFLES: BOLT ACTION

RAPTOR SPORTING RIFLE - .243 Win., .25-06 Rem., .270 Rem., .30-06, or .308 Win. cal., features "Taloncote" or blue (mfg. 1998 only) finished barreled action, black checkered fiberglass reinforced synthetic stock, adj. trigger, with or w/o sights. Mfg. 1997-99.

	$230	$195	$175	$160	$150	$140	$130

Last MSR was $259.

Add $30 for sights (disc.).
Add $15 for blue finish (disc.).
Add $36 for heavy barrel.
Add $50 for stainless steel barreled action with sights (new 1999).

＊ *Raptor Sporting Rifle Peregrine Deluxe* - similar to Raptor Sporting Rifle, except has deluxe checkered or plain hardwood stock. Mfg. 1998 only.

	$265	$225	$195	$175	$160	$150	$140

Last MSR was $309.

Subtract $10 for plain hardwood stock and no sights (blue finish only).

GRADING - PPGS™	100%	98%	95%	90%	80%	70%	60%

RASHEED (RASHID)
Previous Egyptian military rifle mfg. circa mid-1960s.

RIFLES: SEMI-AUTO

RASHEED - 7.62x39mm cal., gas operated mechanism with tilting bolt, 20 1/2 in. barrel with folding bayonet, bolt cocking is by separate bolt handle installed on right side of receiver, detachable 10 shot mag., open type sights, hardwood stock with vent. forend, approx. 8,000 mfg. circa mid-1960s.

	$600	$550	$475	$425	$350	$275	$200

RAVELL
Previous manufacturer located in Barcelona, Spain.

RAVELL LTD.

RIFLES: SxS

MAXIM DOUBLE RIFLE - .375 H&H or 9.3x74R cal., H&H type sidelock action with automatic ejectors, Purdey scroll engraving, 23 in. barrels, deluxe walnut with full pistol grip and rubber buttplate, double articulated triggers. Importation disc. circa 1998.

	$6,600	$6,100	$5,000	$4,000	$3,500	$2,950	$2,600

Last MSR was $7,000.

Add 10% for .375 H&H cal.

RAVEN ARMS
Previous manufacturer located in Industry, CA circa 1970-1991. Approximately 2 million were mfg.

PISTOLS: SEMI-AUTO

P-25 - .25 ACP cal., single action, 2 7/16 in. barrel, 6 shot mag., walnut grips, available in nickel, blue, or chrome finish, 15 oz. Disc. 1984.

	$70	$60	$50	$40	$30	$25	$25

MP-25 - similar to Model P-25, except die-cast slide serrations are slightly different. Disc. 1992.

	$60	$50	$45	$40	$35	$30	$25

Last MSR was $70.

Walnut, slotted plastic, or ivory colored grips were available for this model. In 1987, a new sear - block safety was incorporated into manufacture.

RECORD-MATCH
Previously manufactured by Anschütz, located in Zella-Mehlis, Germany circa pre-WWII.

PISTOLS: SINGLE SHOT, TARGET

MODEL 210 FREE PISTOL - .22 LR cal., Martini action, 11 in. barrel, single shot, blue, carved and checkered walnut grips and forearm, set trigger (button release), micrometer rear sight, deluxe target pistol, pre-WWII.

	$1,320	$1,265	$1,210	$1,100	$880	$745	$550

MODEL 210A - similar to Model 210, except alloy frame.

	$1,265	$1,210	$1,155	$1,045	$825	$690	$495

MODEL 200 FREE PISTOL - similar to Model 210, except less deluxe features and spur trigger guard, pre-WWII.

	$990	$935	$770	$660	$525	$440	$360

GRADING - PPGS™	100%	98%	95%	90%	80%	70%	60%

RED ROCK ARMS

Current manufacturer established April 2003 and located in Mesa, AZ. During late 2006, the company name was changed from Bobcat Weapons, Inc. to Red Rock Arms.

PISTOLS: SEMI-AUTO

BWA5 FSA - 9mm Para cal., paramilitary design, delayed blowback, 8.9 in. stainless steel barrel, black duracoat finished stock, pistol grip, and forearm, 10, 30, or 40 shot mag., approx. 5.3 lbs. New 2007.

MSR $1,700	$1,525	$1,350	$1,125	$900	$775	$650	$550

RIFLES: SEMI-AUTO

BW-5 FSA - 9mm Para cal., paramilitary design, stamped steel lower receiver, roller lock bolt system with delayed blowback, 16 1/2 in. stainless steel barrel (3-lug barrel and 9 in. fake supressor), black duracoat finished stock, pistol grip, and forearm, 10, 30, or 40 shot mag., approx. 6.7 lbs. New 2006.

MSR $1,700	$1,525	$1,350	$1,125	$900	$775	$650	$550

ATR-1 CARBINE - .223 Rem. cal., 16 1/4 in. barrel, adj. front and rear sight, black furniture, 30 shot AR-15 style mag., available with or w/o flash supressor, 8 lbs. New 2007.

MSR $1,400	$1,250	$1,075	$925	$825	$750	$650	$575

REDOLFI F.LLI S.N.C.

Current long gun manufacturer located in Brescia, Italy. No current U.S. importation. Redolfi F.lli manufactures high quality rifles and shotguns. Many custom options are available. Please contact the company directly for more information, including pricing, U.S. availability and delivery time (see Trademark Index).

GARY REEDER CUSTOM GUNS

Current custom manufacturer located in Flagstaff, AZ. Consumer direct sales.

For over 25 years, Gary Reeder has specialized in customizing revolvers from various manufacturers, and is now building several series of custom revolvers on his own frames. Gary's son Kase also manufacturers several series of 1911's built to customers specifications in 45 ACP and 10mm. Reeder currently produces well over 60 different series of custom hunting handguns, cowboy guns, custom 1911s, and large caliber hunting rifles. For more information on his extensive range of custom guns, please contact the factory directly (see Trademark Index).

REISING ARMS COMPANY

Previous manufacturer originally located in Hartford, CT and later in New York, NY.

PISTOLS: SEMI-AUTO

TARGET AUTOMATIC PISTOL - .22 LR cal., 12 shot, 6 3/4 in. barrel, blue, brown hard rubber grips, hinged frame, outside hammer. Mfg. 1921-24.

$1,000	$900	$800	$675	$575	$475	$375

This model was mfg. in Hartford, CT from serial number 1,001-4,000. The New York, NY address occurs in the serial range 10,000-12,000.

Warning: This pistol's slide may crack if modern high speed .22 LR ammo is used extensively.

REMINGTON ARMS COMPANY, INC.

Remington®

Current manufacturer and trademark established in 1816, with factories currently located in Ilion, NY, and Mayfield, KY.

Founded by Eliphalet Remington II and originally located in Litchfield, Herkimer County, NY circa 1816-1828. Remington established a factory in Ilion, NY next to the Erie Canal in 1828, and together with his sons Philo, Samuel, and Eliphalet III pioneered many improvements in firearms manufacture. Corporate offices were moved to

100%	98%	95%	90%	80%	70%	60%	50%	40%	30%	20%	10%

Madison, NC in 1996. DuPont owned a controlling interest in Remington from 1933-1993, when the company was sold to Clayton, Dubilier & Rice, a New York City based finance company. The Mayfield, KY plant opened in 1997. On May 31st, 2007, a controlling interest in the company was sold to Cerebrus Capital. Currently, Remington employs 2,500 workers in the U.S., including 1,000 in its Ilion, NY plant alone.

For current information on long guns imported by Spartan Gun Works, a Remington subsidiary, please refer to the Spartan Gun Works section in this text.

REMINGTON TRADEMARKS - 1816-PRESENT

1816-1847 - Remington (mostly barrel and lock markings)
1847-1856 - E. Remington & Son
1856-1888 - E. Remington & Sons
1888-1911 - Remington Arms Company
1911-1916 - Remington Arms & Ammunition Company, Inc.
1916-1920 - Remington Arms - Union Metallic Cartridge Co., Inc.
1920 to date - Remington Arms Company, Inc.

HANDGUNS: 1857-1945 PRODUCTION

BEALS' FIRST MODEL POCKET REVOLVER - percussion .31 cal., 5 shot, smooth cylinder, 3 in. octagon barrel, blue finish, 1-piece hard rubber grip, brass or iron trigger guard. Approx. 3,000 produced, 1857-58.

N/A	$5,000	$4,000	$3,500	$2,500	$2,000	$1,500	$1,000	$800	$600	$500	$400

Add 75% for original pasteboard box and accessories.

BEALS' SECOND MODEL POCKET REVOLVER - percussion .31 cal., 5 shot, smooth cylinder, 3 in. octagon barrel, blue finish, 2-piece hard rubber grips, spur trigger. Less than 1,000 produced 1858-61. Quite rare.

N/A	$10,000	$9,000	$7,500	$6,000	$5,000	$4,750	$4,000	$3,000	$2,500	$2,000	$1,750

BEALS' THIRD MODEL POCKET REVOLVER - percussion .31 cal., 5 shot, smooth cylinder, 4 in. octagon barrel, blue finish, 2-piece hard rubber grips, spur trigger, first Remington revolver with loading lever. Less than 1,000 mfg. 1859-1861.

N/A	$5,000	$4,000	$3,500	$2,500	$2,000	$1,500	$1,000	$800	$600	$500	$400

BEALS' NAVY REVOLVER - percussion .36 cal., 6 shot, smooth cylinder, 7 1/2 in. octagon barrel, blue finish, 2-piece walnut grips, some martially marked with inspector's initials and cartouche on grips. Approx. 15,000 produced, 1861-62. Barrel address is "Beals' Patent, Sept. 14, 1858 - Manufactured by Remingtons', Ilion, N.Y."

   ٭ Beals' Navy Revolver Commercial Model - single wing base pin (very rare), less than 400 mfg. Serial range under 400, very desirable.

N/A	$7,000	$6,000	$5,500	$5,000	$4,250	$3,500	$3,000	$2,500	$2,000	$1,500	$1,250

   ٭ Beals' Navy Revolver Commercial Model - several variations with approx. serialization 1-15,500, most were purchased by military but were not inspected.

N/A	$6,500	$5,750	$5,250	$4,500	$4,000	$3,000	$2,500	$2,250	$1,750	$1,250	$1,000

Subtract 20% for cartridge conversion.

   ٭ Beals' Navy Revolver Martially marked - serial range 13,500 to approx. 16,000, approx. 500 mfg.

N/A	$7,500	$6,750	$6,000	$5,250	$4,500	$3,750	$3,250	$2,750	$2,250	$1,750	$1,500

BEALS' ARMY REVOLVER - percussion .44 cal., 6 shot, smooth cylinder, 8 in. octagon barrel, blue finish, 2-piece walnut grips. Barrel address is "Beals' Patent, Sept. 14, 1858 - Manufactured by Remingtons', Ilion, N.Y."

N/A	$6,500	$5,750	$5,250	$4,500	$4,000	$3,000	$2,500	$2,250	$1,750	$1,250	$1,000

Subtract 20% for cartridge conversions.

   ٭ Beals' Army Revolver Martially marked - serial range is approx. 850-1,900 inspected by "WAT" or "CGC", very desirable, approx. 1,000 mfg.

N/A	$7,500	$6,750	$6,000	$5,250	$4,500	$3,750	$3,250	$2,750	$2,250	$1,750	$1,500

100%	98%	95%	90%	80%	70%	60%	50%	40%	30%	20%	10%

RIDER'S DOUBLE-ACTION POCKET REVOLVER - percussion .31 cal., 5 shot, unusual "mushroom-shaped" cylinder, 3 in. octagon barrel, blue finish, 2-piece hard rubber grips, brass triggerguard, no loading lever. One of the earliest double action handguns produced. Approx. 20,000 produced, 1860-70.

| N/A | $2,750 | $2,500 | $2,000 | $1,500 | $1,250 | $1,000 | $800 | $700 | $600 | $500 | $400 |

Subtract 20% for cartridge conversion.

RIDER'S SINGLE-SHOT PARLOR PISTOL - percussion .17 cal., all brass construction, grips included. Fewer than 1,000 produced, 1859-1860. MANY FAKES, caveat emptor.

| N/A | $10,000 | $9,000 | $8,000 | $7,000 | $5,000 | $4,500 | $4,000 | $3,500 | $3,000 | $2,500 | $2,000 |

MODEL 1861 NAVY REVOLVER - percussion .36 cal., 6 shot, unfluted cylinder, 7 1/2 in. octagon barrel, blue finish, 2-piece walnut grips. Loading lever has slot allowing cylinder pin to be pulled forward without lowering lever. Approx. 6,000 produced 1862-63 in serial range approx. 15,000-21,000. Barrel address "Patented Dec. 17, 1861, 1858 - Manufactured by Remingtons', Ilion, N.Y."

* *Model 1861 Navy Revolver Commercial Model*

| N/A | $6,500 | $5,750 | $5,250 | $4,500 | $4,000 | $3,000 | $2,500 | $2,250 | $1,750 | $1,250 | $1,000 |

Subtract 20% for cartridge conversion.

* *Model 1861 Navy Revolver Martially marked* - over 4,000 martially inspected "CGC".

| N/A | $7,500 | $6,750 | $6,000 | $5,250 | $4,500 | $3,750 | $3,250 | $2,750 | $2,250 | $1,750 | $1,500 |

MODEL 1861 ARMY REVOLVER - percussion .44 cal., 6 shot, unfluted cylinder, 8 in. octagon barrel, blue finish, 2-piece walnut grips. Majority are martially inspected "CGC". Loading lever has slot allowing cylinder pin to be pulled forward without lowering lever. Approx. 10,000 produced 1862-63 in approx. serial range 1,900-12,000. Barrel address "Patented Dec. 17, 1861, 1858 - Manufactured by Remingtons', Ilion, N.Y."

| N/A | $7,500 | $7,000 | $5,000 | $4,000 | $2,500 | $2,000 | $1,800 | $1,500 | $1,250 | $1,000 | $750 |

Subtract 20% for cartridge conversion.

NEW MODEL ARMY REVOLVER - percussion .44 cal., 6 shot, unfluted cylinder, 8 in. octagon barrel, blue finish, 2-piece walnut grips. Approx. 135,000 produced 1863-1888 in serial range 12,000-148,000. Barrel address "Patented Sept. 14, 1858 - Manufactured by Remingtons', Ilion, N.Y. - New Model." Early models lack "New Model" markings on barrel and have transition features from "1861" model. Erroneously called the "Remington Model 1858 Revolver."

| N/A | $7,500 | $7,000 | $5,000 | $4,000 | $2,500 | $2,000 | $1,800 | $1,500 | $1,250 | $1,000 | $750 |

Subtract 20% for cartridge conversion (most are in .46 rimfire).
Add 15% for martially inspected.

NEW MODEL NAVY REVOLVER - percussion .36 cal., 6 shot, unfluted cylinder, 7 1/2 in. octagon barrel, blue finish, 2-piece walnut grips. Approx. 18,000 produced in percussion from 1863-1878 with serial range 21,000-48,000. None were martially marked at time of mfg. Approx. 4,000 were purchased by U.S. Navy during 1863-65 in serial range 21,000-32,000. Barrel address "Patented Sept. 14, 1858 - Manufactured by Remingtons', Ilion, N.Y. - New Model." Early specimens lack "New Model" markings on barrel and have transition features from "1861" model.

| N/A | $7,000 | $6,750 | $4,750 | $3,750 | $2,250 | $1,800 | $1,500 | $1,400 | $1,200 | $900 | $750 |

Subtract 20% for cartridge conversion (most are in .38 rimfire).
Add 15% for martial markings.

NEW MODEL BELT REVOLVER, SINGLE ACTION - percussion .36 cal., 6 shot, unfluted or fluted cylinder, 6 1/2 in. octagon barrel, blue or nickel finish, 2-piece walnut grips. Approx. 5,000 produced 1863-72.

| N/A | $5,000 | $4,500 | $4,000 | $3,000 | $2,250 | $1,900 | $1,500 | $1,300 | $1,100 | $900 | $800 |

Add 30% for fluted cylinder (cylinder numbered to the gun).
Subtract 20% for cartridge conversion (mfg. 1870-1886).

100%	98%	95%	90%	80%	70%	60%	50%	40%	30%	20%	10%

NEW MODEL BELT REVOLVER, DOUBLE ACTION - percussion .36 cal., 6 shot, smooth or fluted cylinder, 6 1/2 in. octagon barrel, blue or nickel finish, 2-piece walnut grips. Approx. 2,500 produced 1863-72.

| N/A | $5,000 | $4,500 | $4,000 | $3,000 | $2,250 | $1,900 | $1,500 | $1,300 | $1,100 | $900 | $800 |

Add 30% for fluted cylinder (most not numbered to the gun).
Subtract 20% for cartridge conversion.

NEW MODEL POLICE REVOLVER - percussion .36 cal., 5 shot, smooth cylinder, 3 to 6 1/2 in. octagon barrels, blue or nickel finish, 2-piece walnut grips. Approx. 18,000 produced 1863-72.

| N/A | $4,800 | $4,400 | $3,750 | $2,750 | $2,000 | $1,750 | $1,400 | $1,200 | $1,000 | $850 | $750 |

Add 10% for 6 1/2 in. barrel.
Subtract 20% for cartridge conversion.

NEW MODEL POCKET REVOLVER - percussion .31 cal., 5 shot, smooth cylinder, spur trigger, 3 to 4 1/2 in. octagon barrel, blue or nickel finish, 2-piece walnut grips. Approx. 25,000 produced, 1863-88.

| N/A | $4,800 | $4,400 | $3,750 | $2,750 | $2,000 | $1,750 | $1,400 | $1,200 | $1,000 | $850 | $750 |

Add 25% for brass frame.
Subtract 20% for cartridge conversion.

ELLIOT'S ZIG-ZAG DERRINGER - .22 short rimfire cartridge, 6 shot, 6 barrel cluster (rotating), ring trigger, 3 in. barrel cluster, blue finish, 2-piece hard rubber grips. Fewer than 1,000 produced, 1861-63. Reputed to be Remington's first cartridge handgun. William Elliot's patent, desirable.

| N/A | $6,000 | $5,000 | $4,000 | $3,000 | $2,400 | $2,200 | $2,000 | $1,800 | $1,500 | $1,250 | $1,000 |

ELLIOT'S FIVE SHOT "RING TRIGGER" DERRINGER - .22 short rimfire cartridge, 5 shot, 5 barrel cluster (fixed), 3 in. barrel cluster, blue finish, 2-piece hard rubber, walnut, ivory or pearl grips, ring trigger. Approx. 25,000 produced (combined production total with .32 cal.).

| N/A | $5,000 | $4,750 | $3,500 | $2,500 | $2,250 | $2,000 | $1,750 | $1,500 | $1,400 | $1,200 | $950 |

ELLIOT'S FOUR SHOT "RING TRIGGER" DERRINGER - cartridge .32 rimfire cal., 4 shot, 4 barrel cluster (fixed), ring trigger, 3 3/8 in. barrel cluster, blue finish, 2-piece hard rubber, walnut, ivory or pearl grips. Approx. 25,000 produced (combined production with .22 cal.).

| N/A | $5,000 | $4,750 | $3,500 | $2,500 | $2,250 | $2,000 | $1,750 | $1,500 | $1,400 | $1,200 | $950 |

VEST POCKET DERRINGER - rimfire cartridge .22, .30, .32, or .41 cal., single shot, various barrel lengths, blue or nickel (post 1870) finish, 2-piece walnut grips, spur trigger. Rider's patent.

✳ *Vest Pocket Derringer .22 Rimfire* - approx. 25,000 produced, 1865-1888.

| N/A | $3,000 | $2,750 | $2,000 | $1,500 | $1,000 | $900 | $800 | $600 | $500 | $400 | $300 |

Subtract 25% for guns lacking company name.

✳ *Vest Pocket Derringer .30 or .32 Rimfire* - number produced unknown, 1865-1888.

| N/A | $3,100 | $2,800 | $2,100 | $1,600 | $1,100 | $1,000 | $900 | $700 | $600 | $500 | $400 |

✳ *Vest Pocket Derringer .41 Rimfire* - approx. 25,000 produced, 1865-88.

| N/A | $3,100 | $2,800 | $2,100 | $1,600 | $1,100 | $1,000 | $900 | $700 | $600 | $500 | $400 |

ELLIOT'S OVER AND UNDER DERRINGER (MODEL 95 OR NO. 95) - cartridge .41 Rimfire cal., 2 shot, 3 in. superimposed barrels, oscillating firing pin, spur trigger, blue and/or nickel finish, hard rubber, walnut, ivory or pearl 2-piece grips. Approx. 150,000 produced, 1866-1934. William Elliot's patent.

✳ *Over And Under Derringer Type One, Early Variation* - maker's name and patent data stamped between the barrels, made without extractor. 1866-88.

| N/A | N/A | $2,750 | $2,500 | $2,000 | $1,500 | $1,200 | $1,000 | $900 | $750 | $600 | $500 |

✳ *Over And Under Derringer Type One, Late Variation* - maker's name and patent data stamped between the barrels, made with extractor. 1866-88.

| N/A | N/A | $2,400 | $2,200 | $2,150 | $1,750 | $1,400 | $1,100 | $975 | $775 | $650 | $550 |

100%	98%	95%	90%	80%	70%	60%	50%	40%	30%	20%	10%

❋ *Over And Under Derringer Type Two* - two line markings atop barrels, maker's name and patent data. 1866-88.

N/A	N/A	$1,500	$1,400	$1,250	$1,100	$1,000	$900	$800	$700	$600	$500

❋ *Over And Under Derringer Type Three* - marked on top of barrel, single line, "REMINGTON ARMS CO., ILION, N.Y." 1888-1911.

N/A	N/A	$1,500	$1,400	$1,250	$1,100	$1,000	$900	$800	$700	$600	$500

❋ *Over And Under Derringer Type Four* - marked on top of barrel, single line, "REMINGTON ARMS-U.M.C. CO. ILION, N.Y."

N/A	N/A	$2,000	$1,500	$1,250	$1,100	$1,000	$900	$800	$700	$600	$500

MODEL 1866 NAVY ROLLING BLOCK PISTOL - cartridge .50 rimfire cal., single shot, 8 1/2 in. round barrel, spur trigger, walnut grip and forearm, blue finish. Approx. 6,500 produced, 1866-67. Erroneously designated as "Model of 1865 Navy".

❋ *Model 1866 Navy Rolling Block Pistol Martially Marked*

N/A	N/A	$6,000	$5,250	$4,500	$4,000	$3,500	$3,000	$2,500	$2,000	$1,750	$1,500

    Subtract 30% if not martially marked (Commercial Model mfg. 1866-1868).
    Subtract 25% for centerfire breech block.
    Fewer than 150 remain in original condition.

COMBINATION PISTOL-SHOTGUN - 20 ga., 11 3/4 in. single barrel with smooth bore, rolling block action, designed as a pistol or shotgun (with detachable shoulder stock). Mfg. circa mid-1920s by an unknown manufacturer (possibly Bannerman's). Rolling block receivers appear to have been from foreign made military rifles.

    Extreme rarity factor precludes accurate pricing information.
    In either configuration, this model is an NFA firearm that cannot be legally owned unless registered with the BATF.

MODEL 1870 NAVY ROLLING BLOCK PISTOL - cartridge .50 centerfire cal., single shot, 7 in. round barrel, standard trigger with triggerguard, walnut grip and forearm, blue finish. Approx. 6,400 produced 1870-75. Modified by Remington for the Navy from Model 1866 pistols.

N/A	N/A	$3,150	$2,550	$2,050	$1,800	$1,500	$1,300	$1,200	$1,100	$1,000	$900

    Add approx. 20% for 8 in. commercial version (approx. 200-400 mfg.) without inspector's marks.

MODEL 1871 ARMY ROLLING BLOCK PISTOL - cartridge .50 centerfire cal., single shot, 8 in. round barrel, standard trigger with triggerguard, walnut grip and forearm, blue finish. Approx. 5,000 produced, 1871-72.

N/A	$4,000	$3,500	$3,000	$2,500	$2,000	$1,750	$1,500	$1,400	$1,100	$1,000	$900

    Subtract 10% for Commercial Model.

MODEL OF 1887 PLINKER ROLLING BLOCK PISTOL - cartridge .22, .25 rimfire and .32, .50 centerfire cals., single shot, utilizing surplus M-1871 Army rolling block frames, 8 in. round barrel, standard trigger with triggerguard, walnut grip and forearm, blue finish. Approx. 800 mfg. 1887-91.

N/A	$2,500	$2,250	$2,000	$1,750	$1,500	$1,250	$1,000	$900	$800	$700	$600

    Add 10% for Navy rolling block framed.
    Navy framed 1887s are discernible by military proofs on right side of frame, Remington altered from original Navy Model 1870. Estimated mfg. of 100.

MODEL 1891 TARGET MODEL ROLLING BLOCK PISTOL - cartridge .22, .25 rimfire and .32 centerfire cals., single shot, 10 in. part octagon, part round barrel, standard trigger with triggerguard, smooth walnut grip and forearm, blue finish. Limited mfg. of 116 between 1891-1900.

N/A	$2,500	$2,250	$2,000	$1,750	$1,500	$1,250	$1,000	$900	$800	$700	$600

    Removing the grips on this model may reveal a 4-digit number, indicating the refurbished military action.

100%	98%	95%	90%	80%	70%	60%	50%	40%	30%	20%	10%

MODEL 1901 TARGET ROLLING BLOCK PISTOL - cartridge .22 S and L, .25 rimfire, .32 centerfire, or .44 S&W Russian cal., single shot, 10 in. part octagon, part round barrel, standard trigger with trigger guard, checkered walnut grip and forearm, blue finish. Limited mfg. of only 734 sold between 1901-1909.

| N/A | $2,750 | $2,500 | $2,000 | $1,750 | $1,500 | $1,250 | $1,000 | $900 | $800 | $700 | $600 |

Add $200 for .44 S&W Russian cal.

Removing the grips on this model may reveal a 4-digit number, indicating the refurbished military action.

RIDER'S MAGAZINE PISTOL - .32 rimfire cal., 5 shot, 3 in. octagonal barrel, spur trigger, walnut, rosewood, ivory or pearl grips. Limited mfg. 1871-1888.

| N/A | $3,500 | $3,000 | $2,500 | $1,750 | $1,400 | $1,200 | $1,000 | $850 | $750 | $650 | $500 |

Add 75% for original case hardened receiver and blued barrel.

Most of this model were engraved, and a non-engraved specimen, while rare, is not necessarily more desirable.

ELLIOT'S SINGLE SHOT DERRINGER - .41 rimfire cartridge cal., single shot, 2 1/2 in. round barrel, spur trigger, walnut 2-piece grips, blue and/or nickel finish. Approx. 10,000 produced, 1867-1888. Also known as the "Mississippi Derringer."

| N/A | $3,300 | $3,000 | $2,500 | $2,000 | $1,500 | $1,400 | $1,200 | $1,000 | $900 | $750 | $650 |

NO. 1 (SMOOT PATENT) REVOLVER - cartridge .30 Rimfire cal., 5 shot, 2 3/4 in. octagon barrel, spur trigger, walnut, hard rubber, pearl or ivory 2-piece grips. Number produced debatable, 1873-1888.

| N/A | $2,500 | $2,300 | $2,000 | $1,750 | $1,500 | $1,200 | $900 | $750 | $600 | $500 | $400 |

Add 50% on early No. 1s with revolving recoil shield.
Add 75% for original pasteboard box with label.

On Number 1 through Number 4 Revolvers, ivory grips refer to Remington Celluloid, not genuine ivory. Only in rare instances does ivory appear.

NO. 2 (SMOOT PATENT) REVOLVER - cartridge .30 or .32 Rimfire cal., 5 shot, 2 3/4 in. octagon barrel, spur trigger, hard rubber, pearl or ivory 2-piece grips. Number produced debatable, 1873-88.

| N/A | $2,500 | $2,300 | $2,000 | $1,750 | $1,500 | $1,200 | $900 | $750 | $600 | $500 | $400 |

Add 75% for original pasteboard box with label.

NO. 3 (SMOOT PATENT) REVOLVER - cartridge .38 Rimfire or Centerfire cal., 3 3/4 in. octagon barrel with or without barrel rib, spur trigger, hard rubber, ivory or pearl 2-piece grips, "Bird-Head and SawHandle" grip frame with Remington logo "R" on the "SawHandle" hard rubber grips, Bird-Head referred to models with or without a barrel rib. Number produced debatable, 1875-88.

| N/A | $2,500 | $2,300 | $2,000 | $1,750 | $1,500 | $1,200 | $900 | $750 | $600 | $500 | $400 |

Add a small premium for centerfire calibers.
Add 75% for original pasteboard box with label.

NO. 4 REVOLVER - cartridge .38 and .41 Rimfire or Centerfire cals., 5 shot, 2 1/2 in. round barrel, hard rubber, pearl or ivory 2-piece grips. Number produced debatable, 1877-88.

| N/A | $2,500 | $2,300 | $2,000 | $1,750 | $1,500 | $1,200 | $900 | $750 | $600 | $500 | $400 |

Add a small premium for centerfire calibers.
Add 25% for original pasteboard box with label.

IROQUOIS REVOLVER - .22 rimfire cartridge cal., 7 shot, 2 1/4 in. round barrel, spur trigger hard rubber, pearl or ivory 2-piece grips, nickel finish, fluted or non-fluted cylinder. Approx. 10,000 produced 1878-1888.

| N/A | $2,200 | $2,000 | $1,800 | $1,500 | $1,300 | $1,000 | $850 | $750 | $600 | $450 | $375 |

Subtract 25% if unmarked.
Add 25% for fluted cylinder.
Add 75% for original pasteboard box with label.

100%	98%	95%	90%	80%	70%	60%	50%	40%	30%	20%	10%

MODEL 1875 SINGLE ACTION REVOLVER - .44 Rem., .44-40 Win., or .45 Colt centerfire cal., 6 shot, 7 1/2 or 5 3/4 (scarce) in. round barrel, standard trigger with triggerguard, blue or nickel finish, walnut, ivory, or pearl 2-piece grips, serial numbered in at least two batches. Approx. 30,000-40,000 produced, 1875-1888.

| N/A | $12,000 | $11,000 | $9,000 | $5,000 | $3,500 | $3,000 | $2,400 | $2,200 | $2,000 | $1,750 | $1,500 |

> Add 25% for blue finish.
> Add 50% for U.S.I.D. "Indian Police" markings (beware of fakes).
> Add 10% for .45 cal.

There is some debate over originality of the 5 3/4 in. barrel - some are known, but many were altered post-factory.

MODEL 1888 SINGLE ACTION REVOLVER - cartridge .44 Centerfire cal., resembles 1890 SA, has "E. Remington & Sons" barrel address, 5 3/4 in. barrel, nickel finish with walnut grips, very desirable and little known.

| N/A | $12,000 | $11,000 | $9,000 | $5,000 | $3,500 | $3,000 | $2,400 | $2,200 | $2,000 | $1,750 | $1,500 |

This model was never listed in a Remington catalog nor price list. Rather, it first appeared in a Hartly Graham ad in late 1888. This revolver was made from parts of Models 1875 & 1890 pistols. Model nomenclature has been created by collectors, not the factory.

MODEL 1890 SINGLE ACTION REVOLVER - .44-40 WCF cal., 6 shot, 7 1/2 or 5 3/4 in. round barrel, standard trigger with trigger guard, hard rubber 2-piece grips with Remington monogram, ivory or pearl grips on special order, blue or nickel finish. Approx. 2,000 produced, 1891-94.

| N/A | $11,000 | $10,000 | $8,000 | $5,000 | $4,000 | $3,000 | $2,000 | $1,500 | $1,000 | $900 | $700 |

> Add 25% for blue finish.
> Add 50% for original pasteboard box.

MODEL 51 SEMI-AUTO - .32 ACP or .380 ACP cal., 8 shot (7 in mag., 1 in chamber), hard rubber 2-piece grips with company's name, black finish. Approx. 65,000 mfg. 1918-1926.

| $800 | $750 | $650 | $500 | $375 | $350 | $300 | $250 | $225 | $200 | $175 | $160 |

> Add 40% for original box, brochure, oiler, and cleaning rod.

Note: .380 ACP cal. much more common than .32 ACP cal., but commands a slight premium.

MODEL 1911 REMINGTON - UMC - .45 ACP cal., WWI M1911 military contract, over 21,500 mfg. (ser. numbered 1-21,676) in 1918-19 only, blue finish.

| N/A | $5,000 | $4,500 | $3,500 | $3,000 | $2,500 | $2,000 | $1,900 | $1,600 | $1,400 | $1,200 | $1,000 |

Most 98%-100% specimens encountered in this model have been refinished - be careful. Mint original pistols are currently selling as high as $6,000.

MODEL 1911A1 REMINGTON RAND - approx. 1,086,624 mfg. 1943-1945 in Syracuse, NY, ser. no. ranges 916,405-1,041,404, 1,279,649-1,441,430, 1,471,431-1,609,528, 1,743,847-1,816,641, 1,890,504-2,075,103, 2,134,404-2,244,803, and 2,380,014-2,619,013, parkerized finish. Mfg. by Remington Rand Corp, and not a true Remington Arms Company product.

| $2,500 | $2,100 | $1,900 | $1,500 | $1,200 | $1,000 | $900 | $750 | $650 | $550 | $450 | $375 |

> Add 20% with original shipping carton (watch for fakes).

MARK III SIGNAL PISTOL - 10 ga., single shot, brass frame, 9 in. round steel barrel, spur trigger, walnut 2-piece grips. Approx. 25,000 produced, 1915-18.

| N/A | $600 | $525 | $400 | $325 | $275 | $250 | $225 | $200 | $180 | $160 | $150 |

HANDGUNS: POST-WWII PRODUCTION

Model XP-100 & Variations

Manufacture stopped on the XP-100 at the end of 1994, and resumed briefly during 1998-99 (Model XP-100R).

MODEL XP-100 - .221 Rem. Fireball cal., single shot bolt action pistol, one-piece Dupont Zytel (nylon) pistol grip stock, adj. sights, drilled and tapped for

GRADING - PPGS™	100%	98%	95%	90%	80%	70%	60%

receiver sight and scope, 4-digit ser. no., 3 3/4 lbs. Mfg. 1963-85.

	$900	$850	$750	$600	$400	$300	$250

MODEL XP-100 VARMINT SPECIAL - single shot bolt action pistol, .223 Rem. (new 1986) cal., 14 1/2 in. barrel, drilled and tapped for receiver sights and scope, one-piece pistol grip nylon stock, 4 1/8 lbs. Mfg. 1986-92.

	$900	$850	$750	$600	$400	$300	$250

Last MSR was $419.

Add $100 for original hard zipper case.

XP-SILHOUETTE - .35 Rem. (mfg. 1987-92) or 7mm BR Rem. (mfg. 1980-92) cal., bench rest model, 14 1/2 in. barrel, drilled and tapped, nylon (disc. 1992) or walnut (new 1992) stock, 3 7/8 lbs. Disc. 1992.

	$900	$850	$750	$600	$400	$300	$250

Last MSR was $427.

Add $15 for .35 Rem. cal.

MODEL XP-100 HUNTER - .223 Rem., 7mm BR Rem., 7mm-.08 Rem., or .35 Rem. cal., 14 1/2 in. barrel, drilled and tapped for sights, laminated wood stock, 4 3/8 lbs. New 1993-94.

	$900	$850	$750	$600	$400	$300	$250

Last MSR was $548.

MODEL XP-100 WALNUT - 7mm BR Rem. cal., 10 1/2 in. barrel, solid American walnut stock and target sights, 3 7/8 lbs. Mfg. 1993-94.

	$900	$850	$750	$600	$400	$300	$250

Last MSR was $625.

XP-100R KS - .22-250 Rem. (new 1992), .223 Rem., .250 Savage (new 1991), 7mm-08 Rem., .308 Win. (new 1992), .35 Rem., or .350 Rem. Mag. (new 1991) cal., repeater variation, Kevlar synthetic stock, right-hand action only, open sights (except for .223 Rem. and .250 Savage) 4 1/8 lbs. Mfg. 1990-94.

	$950	$875	$775	$675	$595	$495	$400

Last MSR was $840.

This model was available through Remington's Custom Shop only.

MODEL XP-100R - .22-250 Rem., .223 Rem., .260 Rem., or .35 Rem. cal., right-hand repeater with 4 or 5 shot blind mag., fiberglass composite stock, 14 1/2 in. barrel, drilled and tapped receiver, approx. 4 1/2 lbs. Mfg. 1998-99.

	$900	$850	$750	$600	$400	$300	$250

Last MSR was $665.

XP-100 CUSTOM - .22-250 Rem. (new 1992), .223 Rem., .250 Savage, 6mm BR Rem., 7mm BR Rem., .308 Win. (new 1992), .35 Rem., or 7mm-08 Rem. cal., choice of standard or heavy barrel, available through custom gun shop only, choice of right- or left-hand action, wood stock with contoured pistol grip, without sights. Mfg. by Custom Shop 1986-94.

	$1,000	$925	$800	$700	$600	$500	$400

Last MSR was $945.

100%	98%	95%	90%	80%	70%	60%	50%	40%	30%	20%	10%

RIFLES: DISC.

REVOLVING PERCUSSION RIFLE - .36 or .44 (rare) cal., 6 shot unfluted cylinder, 24 or 28 in. octagon barrel, walnut stock with crescent butt, scroll triggerguard, blue with case hardened frame. Fewer than 1,000 mfg. 1866-72.

N/A	N/A	$18,000	$12,000	$6,000	$5,000	$4,000	$3,500	$3,000	$2,500	$2,250	$2,000

Receivers were made especially for this model, and are not altered New Model revolvers. .38 R.F. factory conversions will be serial numbered on the recoil plate and cylinder. The ultimate in rarity in Remington Revolving Rifles is the .46 rimfire cal. Only three of this model are presently known.

100%	98%	95%	90%	80%	70%	60%	50%	40%	30%	20%	10%

MODEL 1862 "ZOUAVE RIFLE" - .58 cal., muzzle loading percussion, 33 in. round barrel, two barrel bands, blue barrel, case hardened lock, brass furniture. Mfg. 12,501, 1862-65.

N/A	$5,500	$4,500	$4,000	$2,750	$2,500	$2,100	$2,000	$1,750	$1,500	$1,250	$1,000

Add $450 for correct sword type bayonet in excellent condition.

Most models are in excellent condition, as few, if any, were distributed to the troops during the Civil War.

U.S. NAVY M1867 ROLLING BLOCK CARBINE - .50-45 centerfire cal., 23 1/4 in. barrel, open sight, blue with case hardened frame, bar and ring on frame, walnut straight grip stock. 5,000 mfg. 1868-69 by Springfield Armory from receivers made by E. Remington & Sons in Ilion, NY.

N/A	N/A	$4,500	$4,000	$2,500	$2,000	$1,750	$1,500	$1,250	$1,000	$750	$500

U.S. NAVY "ANNAPOLIS CADET" MILITARY RIFLE - .50-45 centerfire cal., Mfg. by Springfield Armory utilizing rolling block receivers supplied by E. Remington & Sons in Ilion, NY. Mfg. 1868.

N/A	N/A	$4,000	$3,000	$2,500	$2,000	$1,750	$1,500	$1,250	$1,000	$750	$500

Add $150 for correct angular bayonet in excellent condition.

U.S. ARMY MODEL 1870 "EXPERIMENTAL" TRIALS CARBINE - .50-70 Govt. cal., single shot, rolling block action with sling ring on left side of receiver, mfg. by Springfield Armory under license from E. Remington & Sons. 331 mfg. 1870.

N/A	N/A	$16,000	$14,000	$12,000	$10,000	$9,000	$8,000	$7,000	$6,000	$5,000	$4,000

This model is extremely rare, and fewer than six are known to be in private hands.

U.S. ARMY MODEL 1870 "EXPERIMENTAL" TRIALS MILITARY RIFLE - .50-70 Govt. cal., single shot, rolling block action, mfg. by Springfield Armory under license from E. Remington & Sons. Mfg. 1870.

N/A	N/A	$6,000	$5,500	$5,000	$4,500	$4,000	$2,750	$2,250	$1,750	$1,250	$1,000

Approx. 1,041 were mfg. 1870 and issued to infantry troops on the frontier for trial. This is a rarely encountered Springfield firearm.

U.S. NAVY MODEL 1870 (TYPES 1 & 2) MILITARY RIFLE - mfg. by Springfield Armory under license from E. Remington & Sons. Mfg. 1870.

N/A	$5,000	$4,500	$4,000	$3,000	$2,000	$1,500	$1,250	$1,000	$800	$1,000	$600

Add $300-$600 for correct Ames sword bayonet.

10,000 of these models were mfg. in 1870, but were not accepted by the U.S. Navy, reputedly because of the "unsafe" location of the rear sight (too close to the chamber). These "Type 1" Navy rifles were sold to Poultney & Trimble, who sold them to France. Springfield Armory subsequently manufactured 14,000 "Type 2" rifles with the rear sight moved up the barrel, and these models were accepted by the U.S. Navy. Values are the same for both types.

U.S. ARMY MODEL 1871 MILITARY RIFLE - .50-70 Govt. cal., single shot, rolling block action, mfg. by Springfield Armory under license from E. Remington & Sons. Mfg. 1872.

N/A	$3,500	$3,250	$2,750	$2,000	$1,750	$1,500	$1,200	$900	$700	$500	$400

10,101 of these models were mfg., but there is no evidence to suggest that they were ever issued to the troops. As a result, many of these models can be found in excellent or above average condition.

NO. 1 LONG RANGE "CREEDMOOR" - .44-77, .44-90, or .44-100 cal., rolling block, barrel 1/3 octagon, case hardened receiver, long range tang sight, globe front sight, checkered pistol grip stock, blue. Approx. 500 mfg., 1873-1878.

N/A	$12,000	$10,000	$8,500	$6,250	$4,475	$3,875	$3,175	$2,700	$2,475	$2,150	$1,800

Add premiums for higher grade guns with select wood, additional checkering, and other deluxe features.

Add 25% for factory cased guns.

Factory cased guns are rarely encounted.

100%	98%	95%	90%	80%	70%	60%	50%	40%	30%	20%	10%

NO. 1 SPORTING RIFLE - rolling block, .40-50, .40-70, .44-70, .44-77, .45-70, .50-45, or .50-70 centerfire, .38 or .46 rimfire cal., 28 or 30 in. octagon barrels, folding leaf sight, straight grip stock. Approx. 10,000 mfg., 1868-86.

N/A	$6,000	$5,000	$3,500	$3,000	$2,500	$2,000	$1,500	$1,000	$750	$500	$300

Subtract 25% for rimfire cals.
Add 20% for .44-77, .45-70, or .50-70 cal. (primary buffalo hunting cals.).

NO. 1 1/2 SPORTING RIFLE - .22, .25 Stevens, .25 Long, .32, and .38 Long & Extra Long rimfire cal., also in .32-20 WCF, .38-40 WCF, and .44-40 WCF, 24-28 in. octagon medium weight barrel, straight grip walnut stock, somewhat lighter than the No. 1 Sporting. Several thousand mfg., 1888-97.

N/A	$3,500	$3,000	$2,500	$1,750	$1,250	$900	$800	$650	$550	$450	$300

Add 20% for centerfire cals.

NO. 2 SPORTING RIFLE - available in many rimfire cals. between .22 and .38 as well as several centerfire cals. between .22 and .38-40 WCF, blue barrel finish with case hardened frame, perch belly style walnut stock, many special orders available, smaller size action than the No. 1 and rear of frame is curved, mfg. 1873-1909.

N/A	$3,000	$2,750	$2,000	$1,000	$750	$700	$600	$400	$300	$200	$150

LIGHT BABY CARBINE - rolling block, .44-40 WCF cal., 20 in. lightweight round blue barrel with band, straight stock, nickel or case colored receiver. Several thousand mfg., 1892-1902, a few are known to exist in .44 Long rimfire cal.

N/A	$7,000	$6,000	$5,000	$3,500	$2,750	$2,250	$1,750	$1,500	$1,000	$750	$600

Add 25% for blue barrel with color case hardened receiver.

REMINGTON - HEPBURN NO. 3 - falling block, single shot, side lever actuated, blue barrel, case hardened actions, patented 1879, first introduced 1880, many custom features were offered, variations as follows:

✳ *Remington - Hepburn No. 3 Sporting & Target* - various cals. from .22 rimfire to .50-90 Sharps, 26, 28, or 30 in. round or octagon barrel, open sight, semi-pistol grip stock. Mfg. 1880-1907.

N/A	$7,000	$6,500	$5,000	$4,000	$2,500	$2,250	$2,000	$1,500	$1,250	$1,000	$800

.22 rimfire caliber version of this model are rare.

✳ *Remington - Hepburn No. 3 Match Rifle A Quality* - similar to Sporting and Target, with target match sights (tang), and Schuetzen stock. Fewer than 1,000 mfg., 1883-1907.

N/A	$8,000	$7,500	$6,000	$4,000	$2,500	$2,250	$2,000	$1,500	$1,250	$1,000	$800

❖ **Remington - Hepburn No. 3 Match Rifle B Quality** - select grade wood and vernier rear tang sight.

N/A	$9,000	$8,500	$7,000	$5,000	$3,000	$2,500	$2,000	$1,500	$1,250	$1,000	$800

✳ *Remington - Hepburn No. 3 Long Range Creedmoor* - .44-77, .44-90, or .44-105 centerfire cal., 32 or 34 in. octagon barrel, tang sight, otherwise similar to Target Model. A few hundred mfg., 1880-1907.

N/A	$10,500	$9,500	$8,825	$6,250	$4,475	$3,875	$3,175	$2,700	$2,475	$2,150	$1,800

✳ *Remington - Hepburn No. 3 Mid Range Creedmoor* - similar to Long Range, in .40-65 WCF and other cals., 28 in. barrel.

N/A	$9,000	$8,500	$7,000	$5,000	$3,500	$2,750	$2,500	$2,000	$1,750	$1,500	$1,000

✳ *Remington - Hepburn No. 3 Long Range Military* - similar to Creedmoor, with 34 in. full musket stock, in .44-75-520 Rem. cal., military sights, rarely encountered. Mfg. circa 1880s.

N/A	$11,000	$9,800	$8,825	$6,250	$4,475	$3,875	$3,175	$2,700	$2,475	$2,150	$1,800

✳ *Remington - Hepburn No. 3 Walker-Hepburn Schuetzen Match* - under-lever action, 30 or 32 in. barrel, tang sight, palm rest, target stock, approx. 23 mfg. in 1903-1904, perhaps the rarest single shot American rifle.

Extreme rarity factor precludes accurate price evaluation but a few have been observed with price tags in the $20,000 - $75,000+ range, depending on condition.

100%	98%	95%	90%	80%	70%	60%	50%	40%	30%	20%	10%

✻ *Remington - Hepburn No. 3 Walker-Hepburn Schuetzen Match With False Muzzle*
Add a premium according to condition - very rare.

NO. 4 ROLLING BLOCK RIFLE - .22 S-L-LR, .25 Stevens (barrels marked "25-10"), or .32 Short or Long cal. rimfire, 22 1/2 octagon barrel standard with round barrels available late in the series, smooth bore barrel was introduced approx. 1911, blue finish with case hardened frame, solid frame initially followed by takedown in 2 different types (lever release introduced approx. 1901, screw in approx. 1924), this model was Remington's smallest rolling block. Approx. 350,000 mfg. 1890-1933.

N/A	$1,500	$1,300	$1,000	$700	$600	$500	$450	$400	$375	$300	$250

Solid frame variations will command a premium, especially if over 90% original condition.

✻ *No. 4 Rolling Block Rifle Cadet Model* - similar to Boy Scout, 28 in. barrel, lever takedown, tapered forend, no handguard, no barrel band or bayonet lug, frame unmarked, pre-dates the Boy Scout Model. Mfg. 1911-1912, rare.

N/A	$3,000	$2,500	$2,000	$1,900	$1,750	$1,500	$1,200	$1,110	$1,000	$900	$800

The existence of this No. 4 variation has only recently been discovered.

✻ *No. 4-S Rolling Block Rifle "Boy Scout"*

N/A	$3,500	$3,000	$2,500	$2,000	$1,600	$1,300	$1,000	$900	$800	$700	$600

✻ *No. 4-S Rolling Block Rifle Military* - .22 S-L-LR cal., either marked "MILITARY MODEL" (most common) or "AMERICAN BOY SCOUT" (rare), 28 in. round barrel with musket type forend (1 barrel band), thought to have been used by military academies to train their young cadets.

N/A	$2,500	$2,250	$1,800	$1,700	$1,500	$1,200	$1,000	$900	$800	$700	$600

Original pot-metal bayonets for No. 4-S rifles are exceedingly rare and one in excellent condition may bring $1,250+. A correct leather scabbard can bring an additional $500.

NO. 6 FALLING BLOCK RIFLE - .22 S-L-LR or .32 short or long rimfire cal., 20 in. round barrel, boy's gun with small dimensions, takedown action, case hardened (early mfg.) or blue finish, also available in smooth bore, 497,000 mfg. 1901-33.

N/A	$650	$600	$500	$350	$300	$250	$225	$200	$180	$170	$150

Add 10% for smooth bore barrel.

Original case colors will bring a premium on this model.
Improved Model 6 became available circa 1905, and featured a blue frame in 24 in. barrel.

NO. 7 ROLLING BLOCK RIFLE - .22 S, .22 LR, or .25-10 Stev. rimfire cal., constructed on Rem. Model 1871 SS pistol action frame, 24, 26, or 28 in. 1/2 round, 1/2 octagon tapered barrels, marked "REMINGTON ARMS CO. ILION, NY USA" on barrel top flat, dinstictive long tang pistol grip stock, checkered pistol grip and forearm, hard rubber buttplate, available in Target or Sporting configurations, with or w/o special Lyman tang mounted sight, ser. no. range 300,000. Last of the Rolling Block Rifles. Approx. 350 mfg. 1903-10.

N/A	$9,000	$8,000	$7,000	$5,500	$4,900	$4,300	$3,700	$3,100	$2,650	$2,250	$1,750

REMINGTON KEENE MAGAZINE BOLT RIFLE - .45-70 Govt., .40, or .43 cal. Approx. 5,000 mfg. 1880-1888.

✻ *Remington Keene Magazine Bolt Rifle Frontier Model* - those made for U.S. Dept. of Interior (Indian Police), marked U.S.I.D. will command a 75% premium.

N/A	N/A	$5,000	$4,000	$3,000	$2,225	$1,750	$1,500	$1,000	$900	$800	$700

✻ *Remington Keene Magazine Bolt Rifle Full Stock Carbine Model* - 22 in. barrel, full stock.

N/A	N/A	$5,000	$4,000	$3,000	$2,225	$1,750	$1,500	$1,000	$900	$800	$700

✻ *Remington Keene Magazine Bolt Rifle Carbine Model* - 20 in. barrel, half stock, very limited mfg.

✻ *Remington Keene Magazine Bolt Rifle Army Rifle* - 32 1/2 in. barrel, full stock.

N/A	N/A	$5,000	$4,000	$3,000	$2,225	$1,750	$1,500	$1,000	$900	$800	$700

100%	98%	95%	90%	80%	70%	60%	50%	40%	30%	20%	10%

✳ *Remington Keene Magazine Bolt Rifle Sporter Rifle* - 1/2 oct. barrel, full or "BUT-TON" mag. Add for pistol grip and select wood variations.

N/A	N/A	$5,000	$4,000	$3,000	$2,225	$1,750	$1,500	$1,000	$900	$800	$700

✳ *Remington Keene Magazine Bolt Rifle Navy Rifle* - 29 1/2 in. barrel, full stock.

N/A	N/A	$5,000	$4,000	$3,000	$2,225	$1,750	$1,500	$1,000	$900	$800	$700

REMINGTON-LEE MAGAZINE BOLT ACTION RIFLE (MODEL 1879) -

marked "Lee Arms Co., Bridgeport, Conn, USA, patented Nov. 4th, 1879" on upper left flat of receiver but all rifles were made at E. Remington & Sons, Ilion, NY. Remington, on April 1, 1881, acquired all the materials, fixtures and tooling from Sharps to complete the US Navy contract, uses the Lee-Borchardt projected nose magazine or the Lee-Cook magazine with the sliding detent on the side.

✳ *U.S. Navy First Contract* - .45-70 Govt. cal., 29 in. barrel, one piece bolt with the bolt handle forward and part of the right locking lug, serial numbers 1-300, US Navy Insp. WWK & HN, 300 delivered January 1882.

N/A	N/A	$3,000	$2,000	$1,000	$600	$500	$450	$400	$350	$300	$250

✳ *U.S. Navy Non-Contract* - .45-70 Govt. cal., 29 in. barrel, Remington Rolling Block front and rear sights, bolt handle is forward and part of the right locking lug, serial number range 301 - 1300, US Navy Insp. WMF, 700 delivered late 1884.

N/A	N/A	$2,200	$1,200	$1,000	$600	$500	$450	$400	$350	$300	$250

✳ *Military Non-Contract* - .43 Spanish cal., 29 or 32 in. barrel, one piece bolt with the bolt handle moved to the classic Lee bent down position behind the right receiver wall, serial numbers 1301 - 7000, over 3,900 were sold to the Chinese Govt. in June 1884.

N/A	N/A	$2,000	$1,200	$1,000	$600	$500	$450	$400	$350	$300	$250

REMINGTON LEE MAGAZINE RIFLE (MODEL 1882) -

Marked "Lee Arms Co., Bridgeport, Conn, USA, Patented Nov. 4th, 1879 on upper left flat of receiver and E. Remington & Sons, Ilion, NY, USA, Sole Manufacturers and Agents" on the left receiver side wall, uses the Lee-Diss box magazine with two grooves on the side, one-piece bolt with the bolt handle bent down and back of the right receiver wall.

✳ *U.S. Army Trials* - .45-70 Govt. cal., 32 1/2 in. barrel, serial number range 8800 - 9800, 750 were delivered September 1884 to the US Army, US Army Insp. DFC stamped on receiver, barrel and in a boxed script on the buttstock, field tested in 1885, withdrawn, declared surplus and about 400 were sold to a Boston arms dealer, these were later sold to the Massachusetts Naval Brigade and stamped or painted unit markings applied to the buttstock. Front and rear sights are of the US Springfield pattern.

N/A	N/A	$3,000	$2,000	$1,000	$600	$500	$450	$400	$350	$300	$250

✳ *Chinese Contract* - .45-70 Govt. or .43 Spanish cal., 20 1/2 (carbine), 28, 29, or 32 in. barrel, serial number range est. 11000 - 25000, over 14,000 produced starting in late 1884, around serial number 14000 the Lee Arms Co. markings were discontinued and the E. Remington & Sons markings moved to the upper left flat on the receiver, Chinese ideograms stamped on receiver ring, the Chinese defaulted on the contract in mid 1885, Remington resold the rifles after removing the Chinese markings, some rifles were fitted with a bayonet lug on the side of the barrel for a saber bayonet, front and rear sights are of the rolling block pattern.

N/A	N/A	$2,000	$1,200	$1,000	$600	$500	$450	$400	$350	$300	$250

Add 25% for carbine. Add 50% for conversion Model 1882 or 1885 (120 rifles and 100 carbines were inventoried with "altered bolts" in 1888). Subtract 10% for .43 Spanish cal.

100%	98%	95%	90%	80%	70%	60%	50%	40%	30%	20%	10%

REMINGTON LEE MAGAZINE RIFLE (MODEL 1885)

REMINGTON LEE MAGAZINE RIFLE (MODEL 1885) - 32 in. barrel, marked "E. Remington & Sons, Ilion, NY, USA, Sole Manufacturers and Agents, Patented Nov. 4th, 1879", serial number range 41000 - 47000, action revised to accept the new two piece bolt with separate bolt head, uses the Lee-Diss box magazine with two grooves on the side. Mfg. after the 1886 bankruptcy and 1888 reorganization of E. Remington & Sons.

| N/A | N/A | $2,000 | $1,200 | $1,000 | $600 | $500 | $450 | $400 | $350 | $300 | $250 |

Add 100% for New Zealand purchase, marked N^Z over 87 on receiver ring. 500 sold to New Zealand in 1887.

Add 200% for British Trials rifle, 300 purchased January 1887, marked "W^D" on buttstock and fitted with cutoff on right side of action.

✳ *U.S. Navy Contract* - .45-70 Govt. cal., 32 1/2 in. barrel, serial number range 50001 - 54000, front and rear sights are of the US Springfield pattern, over 3,400 were accepted by the US Navy from 1888 to 1894, marked on the receiver ring - USN over anchor over Navy serial number over US Navy inspector, the Naval serial numbers range from 1001 to over 4000, the Navy inspectors are: WWK, HHE, ACD, CEC, HE, and SWV, a few rifles were issued without being inspected.

| N/A | $3,000 | $2,200 | $1,500 | $1,000 | $600 | $500 | $450 | $400 | $350 | $300 | $250 |

Add 50% for documented Hawaiian National Guard Purchase, "NGH" stamped on buttstock, no USN proofs. 350+ purchased in 1893 by Provisional Government of Hawaii.

REMINGTON LEE SMALL BORE MAGAZINE RIFLE (MODEL 1899)

REMINGTON LEE SMALL BORE MAGAZINE RIFLE (MODEL 1899) - marked "Remington Arms Company, Ilion, NY, USA, Patented Aug, 26th, 1884, Sept. 9th, 1884, March 17th, 1885, Jan. 18th 1887", two-piece bolt with two locking lugs on the bolt head, uses the Lee-Diss box magazine with three grooves on the side.

✳ *Michigan National Guard Contract* - .30-40 Govt. cal., 29 1/2 in. barrel, serial number range 100001 - 102200. 1,001 shipped in 1898 and 1,000 in 1899.

| N/A | $3,000 | $2,200 | $1,500 | $1,000 | $600 | $500 | $450 | $400 | $350 | $300 | $250 |

✳ *Cuban Contract* - .30-40 Govt. cal., 20 (carbine) or 29 1/2 (rifle) in. barrel, serial number range 1 - 3000. 2,600 carbines and 400 rifles shipped to Cuba in 1905, the Cuban Coat of Arms and serial number are stamped on the receiver ring, in 1914 a number of the carbines and rifles were returned to Remington, the Cuban crest polished off, reblued and, in 1915, 1,153 carbines sold to the French Army for their Automobile Corps.

| N/A | $3,000 | $2,200 | $1,500 | $1,000 | $600 | $500 | $450 | $400 | $350 | $300 | $250 |

Add 25% for carbine.

REMINGTON LEE SPORTING & TARGET RIFLES

REMINGTON LEE SPORTING & TARGET RIFLES - The original 1879 Lee Arms catalog advertised a sporting rifle "to be made in the ensuing season". Only a few handmade, tool room model sporters were made at Sharps and at least one of these has the turned down bolt handle, a search of period E. Remington & Sons advertising from 1881 to 1888 has not turned up any mention of Remington Lee sporters, the Keene sporter apparently met the need for a bolt action sporter and any factory Remington Lee sporter from this period should be considered a tool room model.

✳ *Remington Lee M1885* - .43 Spanish, .44-77, .45-70 Govt., or .45-90 cal., 26 in. round barrel, the 1904-05 Remington Arms catalog advertised Remington Lee sporters, based on the US Navy M1885 action, checkered half pistol grip stock with rifle buttplate and two points facing the action, serial number range 54000.

| N/A | N/A | $3,000 | $2,200 | $1,500 | $1,000 | $600 | $500 | $450 | $400 | $350 | $300 |

100%	98%	95%	90%	80%	70%	60%	50%	40%	30%	20%	10%

✳ *Remington Lee M1899* - 6mm USN, 7mm Spanish Mauser, 7.65 Belgian Mauser, .30-30 Win., .30-40 Krag, .303 British, .32 Win. Spl., .32-40 Ballard & Winschester High Power, .35 Win., .38-55 High Power, .38-72 or .405 Win. cal., the Standard Grade sporter has 24, 26 (standard), or 28 in. round barrel, checkered half pistol grip stock with rifle buttplate and two points facing the action, Standard Grade, Heavy Weight sporter has 24 and 26 in. heavy barrel, express sights, checkered half pistol grip stock with shotgun buttplate and three points facing the action, Special Remington Lee Sporter is high grade, 26 in. half round, half octagon barrel, select extra fine checkered English walnut stock, shotgun butt with center grain exposed and heel and toe steel tips and five points facing the action, wind gauge front Lyman sight and aperture rear sight, the standard three groove on the side Lee-Diss magazine was used, to accommodate the shorter cartridges the .30-30, .32 Win. and .32-40 Ballard & Winschester magazines have a rear spacer while the .38-55 magazine has a front spacer. Serial number range 75001-76446. A total of 1,446 factory sporters were shipped from 1899 to 1909.

N/A	$3,000	$2,200	$1,500	$1,000	$600	$500	$450	$400	$350	$300	$250

Add 100% for Special Remington Lee Sporter.

Add 200-300% for documented Military or Sporting Target Rifle.

Original retail price for the Standard Grade Sporter was $25 in 1905. Original retail price for the Special Remington Lee Sporter was $60 in 1905.

MODEL 1903-A3 MAGAZINE BOLT RIFLE - please refer to listing under Springfield Armory.

MODEL 1917 ENFIELD (REMINGTON MFG.) - mostly mfg. by the Remington plants in Eddystone, PA and Ilion, NY. Please refer to listings under Enfield.

GRADING - PPGS™	100%	98%	95%	90%	80%	70%	60%

RIFLES: ROLLING BLOCK, RECENT MFG.

The following models are manufactured in limited quantities by the Remington Custom Shop.

NO. 1 ROLLING BLOCK CREEDMOOR - .45-70 Govt. cal., rolling block action, patterned after the original Remington No. 1 mid-range Creedmoor-style configuration, 30 in. half-round half-octagon tapered 30 in. barrel, includes rear tang aperture and front globe sight with four interchangeable inserts, checkered walnut stock and forearm, SST, case colored receiver, cased, 9 7/8 lbs. Mfg. 1997-98.

		$2,800	$2,500	$1,900	$1,665	$1,415	$1,140	$950

Last MSR was $2,799.

NO. 1 ROLLING BLOCK MID-RANGE SPORTER .30-30 Win. (disc. 1998), .444 Marlin (disc. 1998), or .45-70 Govt. cal., 30 in. round barrel, checkered pistol grip sporter stock and forearm, blue barrel end and receiver, adj. buckhorn rear sight, 8 3/4 lbs. New 1998.

MSR $2,927		$2,495	$2,250	$1,850	$1,600	$1,375	$1,100	$900

NO. 1 ROLLING BLOCK SILHOUETTE - .45-70 Govt. cal., meets BPCR silhouette requirements, similar to No. 1 Rolling Block Mid-Range Sporter, except has 30 in. round heavy barrel w/o sights and single set or double triggers, blue or case colored receiver. New 2000.

MSR $3,366		$2,850	$2,400	$1,950	$1,700	$1,425	$1,125	$925

Add $200 for case colored receiver.

Add $167 for single set trigger.

GRADING - PPGS™	100%	98%	95%	90%	80%	70%	60%

RIFLES: SEMI-AUTO - CENTERFIRE

The models have been listed in numerical sequence for quick reference.

MODEL FOUR - 6mm Rem., .243 Win., .270 Win., .280 Rem. (mfg. 1984-87), .30-06, .308 Win. (disc. 1984), or 7mm Express (mfg. 1981-83) cal., cartridge "head" imbedded in bottom of receiver, gas operation with metering system, 22 in. barrel, 4 shot detachable mag., deluxe Monte Carlo stock and forend, detachable sights. Mfg. 1981-87.

	$600	$525	$450	$375	$275	$225	$200

Last MSR was $475.

✳ *Model Four Special Diamond Anniversary* - .30-06 cal. only, commemorates the 75th anniversary of the Model 8, laser engraved with gold and premium checkered walnut stock and forearm. One grade only, approx. 1,400 shipped from 1982-1988, final 100 shipped in 1994 using Model 7400 stocks.

	$1,300	$1,200	$1,000	N/A	N/A	N/A	N/A

✳ *Model Four High Grades* - only two mfg.
Extreme rarity precludes accurate pricing.

MODEL 8 - .25 Rem., .30 Rem., .32 Rem., or .35 Rem. cal., 22 in. barrel, open sights, 5 shot non-detachable box mag., plain stock. Approx. 60,000 mfg. 1906-36.

	$700	$600	$500	$400	$300	$200	$150

Add 15% for .25 Rem. cal.
Add substantial premiums for higher grades C through F.

MODEL 74 SPORTSMAN - .280 Rem. (European special order only) or .30-06 cal., 22 in. barrel, 4 shot mag., uncheckered hardwood stock and forearm, open sights, 7 1/2 lbs. Mfg. 1984-87.

	$350	$325	$300	$250	$225	$200	$150

Last MSR was $353.

MODEL 81 WOODSMASTER - .30 Rem., .32 Rem., .35 Rem., or .300 Savage cal., semi-auto, takedown action, 5 shot, non-detachable box mag., 22 in. round barrel, notched elevator rear sight. An improvement of the Model 8; was available in 5 grades. Better grades bring higher prices. 56,091 mfg. 1936-50.

	$600	$500	$400	$300	$200	$175	$150

The .32 Rem. cal. was dropped after WWII and the .300 Savage was added in 1940. A few specimens have been observed in .25 Rem. cal., but this was not a production caliber.

MODEL 740 WOODMASTER - .244 Rem. (mfg. 1957-59), .280 Rem. (mfg. 1957-59), .30-06 (first caliber, introduced 1955) or .308 Win. (introduced 1956) cal., 22 in. barrel, open sight, box mag., gas operated, plain pistol grip stock. Mfg. 1955-59.

	100%	98%	95%	90%	80%	70%	60%
.244 Rem. or .30-06 cal.	$325	$275	$225	$210	$200	$190	$180
.280 Rem. or .308 Win. cal.	$325	$275	$225	$210	$200	$190	$180

MODEL 740ADL - similar to 740A, with checkered stock, grip cap and sling swivels. Mfg. 1955-1959.

.244 Rem. or .30-06 cal.	$375	$325	$280	$250	$225	$200	$180
.280 Rem. or .308 Win. cal.	$415	$350	$300	$275	$250	$225	$200

MODEL 740BDL - similar to 740ADL, with select wood. Mfg. 1955-1957.

.244 Rem. or .30-06 cal.	$395	$340	$295	$250	$225	$200	$180
.308 Win. cal.	$425	$375	$350	$325	$275	$225	$200

BDLs were not listed in the 1958 or 1959 Remington price list.

MODEL 740D PEERLESS GRADE - similar to Model 740, with scroll engraving and fancy wood. Mfg. 1955-1960.

	$2,500	$1,800	$1,200	N/A	N/A	N/A	N/A

GRADING - PPGS™	100%	98%	95%	90%	80%	70%	60%

MODEL 740F PREMIER GRADE - similar to Model 740, with extensive hand engraved game scenes and scroll work, best grade wood.

	$4,500	$3,850	$2,600	N/A	N/A	N/A	N/A

✳ *Model 740F Premier Grade w/Inlays* - similar to Model 740F Premier Grade, except has game scenes inlayed with gold.

	$6,500	$5,700	$4,100	N/A	N/A	N/A	N/A

MODEL 742 WOODSMASTER - 6mm Rem. (mfg. 1963), .243 Win. (mfg. 1968), .280 Rem. (marked 7mm Express 1979-1980), .30-06, or .308 Win. cal., 22 in. barrel, open sights, 4 shot box mag., gas operated, checkered pistol grip stock. Mfg. 1960-80.

	$325	$290	$275	$250	$235	$210	$185

Add 10% for .280 Rem. cal.

MODEL 742ADL DELUXE - similar to the Model 742, except has fine checkering, sling swivels and roll engraved game scenes on receiver.

	$350	$300	$275	$260	$235	$215	$195

MODEL 742BDL DELUXE - similar to Model 742, except .30-06 or .308 Win. cal., step receiver, right-hand action with choice of right-hand or left-hand cheek-piece, Monte Carlo basket weave stock and forend, black pistol grip cap and forend tip. Mfg. 1966-80.

	$400	$350	$300	$260	$235	$215	$195

MODEL 742C CARBINE - similar to 742, except .280 Rem., .30-06, or .308 Win. cal. only, 18 1/2 in. barrel. Mfg. 1961-80.

	$450	$400	$350	$300	$275	$260	$235

✳ *Model 742CDL Deluxe Carbine* - similar to Model 742C carbine, except has fine checkering, sling swivels and roll engraved game scenes on receiver. Mfg. 1961-1963.

	$475	$425	$375	$325	$300	$275	$250

MODEL 742D PEERLESS GRADE - similar to Model 742, with scroll engraving and fancy wood. Mfg. 1961-1980.

	$2,500	$1,870	$1,200	N/A	N/A	N/A	N/A

MODEL 742F PREMIER GRADE - similar to Model 742, with extensive hand engraved game scenes and scroll work, best grade wood.

	$4,500	$3,850	$2,650	N/A	N/A	N/A	N/A

✳ *Model 742F Premier Grade w/Inlays* - similar to Model 742F Premier Grade, except has game scenes inlayed in gold.

	$6,500	$5,785	$4,180	N/A	N/A	N/A	N/A

MODEL 742 150TH YEAR ANNIVERSARY - .30-06 cal. only. 11,412 Mfg. 1966 only.

	$425	$325	$300	N/A	N/A	N/A	N/A

MODEL 742 CANADIAN CENTENNIAL - 1,968 mfg. in 1967. Issue price was $200.

	$450	$350	$300	N/A	N/A	N/A	N/A

REMINGTON/RUGER CANADIAN CENTENNIAL SET - please refer to the Sturm Ruger section of this text.

MODEL 742 BICENTENNIAL - similar to 742, with inscription on receiver. 10,108 Mfg. 1976 only.

	$425	$325	$300	$275	$225	$200	$185

MODEL 750 WOODMASTER RIFLE/CARBINE - .243 Win., .270 Win., .30-06, .308 Win., or .35 Whelen cal., 18 1/2 (carbine) or 22 in. barrel with iron sights, replaces the wood stocked Model 7400, and features improved gas system, lower profile, rotary bolt lockup, redesigned black synthetic or checkered walnut stock and forearm, sling swivels became standard 2007, R3 recoil pad, 7 1/2 lbs. New 2006.

MSR $751	$630	$500	$440	$380	$340	$295	$265

Add $101 for wood stock.

Carbine variation is available in .30-06, .308 Win., or .35 Whelen cal. Synthetic stock is not available in .35 Whelen cal.

GRADING - PPGS™	100%	98%	95%	90%	80%	70%	60%

MODEL 7400 - 6mm Rem. (disc. 1987), .243 Win., .270 Win., 7mm Express (mfg. 1981-83), .280 Rem. (introduced 1984, disc. 2000), .30-06, .308 Win., or .35 Whelen (mfg. 1993-95) cal., modified Model 742 action, gas operation, 22 in. barrel, 4 shot detachable mag., pressed checkered Monte Carlo walnut stock, 7 1/2 lbs. Mfg. 1981-2005.

	$515	$410	$325	$260	$230	$210	$185

Last MSR was $651.

> **Add 15% for .35 Whelen cal.**
>
> Beginning in 1991, a high gloss wood finish became available in cals. .270 Win. and .30-06 (Model 7400 High Gloss). From 1998-2003, receiver panels had fine line rolled game scene engraving.

✳ *Model 7400 Carbine* - .30-06 cal. only, similar to Model 7400 Rifle, except has 18 1/2 in. barrel, 7 1/4 lbs. Mfg. 1988-2005.

	$515	$410	$325	$260	$230	$210	$185

Last MSR was $651.

✳ *Model 7400 SP (Special Purpose)* - .270 Win. or .30-06 cal., similar to Model 7400, except has non-reflective matte finish on both wood and metalwork. Mfg. 1993-94.

	$435	$370	$300	$255	$230	$210	$185

Last MSR was $524.

✳ *Model 7400 Weathermaster* - .270 Win. or .30-06 cal., features matte nickel plated receiver, barrel, and magazine, black synthetic stock and forearm, 22 in. barrel with open sights, 7 1/2 lbs. Mfg. 2003-2004.

	$495	$400	$315	$255	$230	$210	$185

Last MSR was $624.

✳ *Model 7400 Synthetic* - same cals. as Model 7400, features black fiberglass reinforced synthetic stock and forend, matte black metal finish, 22 in. barrel only. Mfg. 1998-2006.

	$465	$385	$330	$285	$265	$240	$220

Last MSR was $589.

❖ **Model 7400 Synthetic Carbine** - .30-06 cal., similar to Model 7400 Synthetic, except has 18 1/2 in. barrel. 7 1/4 lbs. Mfg. 1998-2006.

	$465	$385	$330	$285	$265	$240	$220

Last MSR was $589.

✳ *Model 7400 175th Anniversary* - .30-06 cal. only, Anniversary Model with roll engraving and high gloss finish. 5,000 mfg. in 1991 only.

	$475	$400	$300	N/A	N/A	N/A	N/A

Last MSR was $515.

> A limited quantity of .270 Win. cal. were specially made in this 175th Anniversary Model for distributor Bill Hicks in MN. Pricing varies, since these rifles are a special edition.

✳ *Model 7400 ADF Limited Edition* - .30-06 cal. only, special edition 1997 only featuring Buckmaster's American Deer Foundation, special ADF engraving. Approx. 800 mfg. 1997 only.

	$495	$400	$315	N/A	N/A	N/A	N/A

Last MSR was $600.

MODEL 7400 ENGRAVED - the engraved Model 7400s were introduced 1988.

✳ *Model 7400 D Grade (Peerless)* - scroll engraving and fancy wood.

	N/A	$2,900	$2,075	N/A	N/A	N/A	N/A

Last MSR was $4,532.

GRADING - PPGS™	100%	98%	95%	90%	80%	70%	60%

* Model 7400 F Grade (Premier) - extensive hand engraved game scenes and scroll work, best grade wood.

	N/A	$6,000	$4,400	N/A	N/A	N/A	N/A

Last MSR was $8,799.

* Model 7400 F Grade with gold inlays (Premier Gold) - with game scenes inlayed in gold.

	N/A	$5,550	$3,600	N/A	N/A	N/A	N/A

Last MSR was $11,999.

R-15 VTR PREDATOR - .204 Ruger or .223 Rem. cal., 18 (carbine) or 22 in. free floating chromemoly fluted barrel, fixed or tele (Carbine CS) stock with pistol grip, 5 shot detachable mag., single stage trigger, flattop receiver with Picatinny rail, no sights, round vent. forearm, 100% Advantage Max-1 HD camo coverage, includes lockable hard case, mfg. by Bushmaster. New 2008.

MSR $999		$895	$775	$700	$625	$550	$495	$450

RIFLES: SLIDE ACTION, CENTERFIRE

MODEL SIX - 6mm Rem. (disc. 1985), .243 Win., .270 Win., .30-06, or .308 Win. (disc. 1984) cal., cartridge "head" imbedded in bottom of receiver, 4 shot mag. Mfg. 1981-1987.

	$600	$525	$450	$375	$275	$225	$200

Last MSR was $439.

* Model Six High Grades

Only three high grade Model Sixes were manufactured. Extreme rarity precludes accurate pricing.

MODEL 14/14A RIFLE - .25 Rem., .30 Rem., .32 Rem., or .35 Rem. cal., 22 in. barrel, 5 shot mag., open sight, plain pistol grip stock, 22 in. steel barrel, 6 lbs. Mfg. 1912-35.

	$800	$700	$600	$500	$400	$300	$200

Add 30% for "thumbnail" safety (introduced in 1918).
Add 15% for .25 Rem.

This model was also manufactured in higher grades, including A, C, and F. Premiums vary according to originality and condition.

MODEL 14R CARBINE - similar to 14A, with 18 in. barrel, straight grip stock.

	$900	$800	$700	$600	$500	$400	$350

Add 25% for .25 Rem. cal.
Add 10% for .35 Rem. cal.

MODEL 14 1/2 RIFLE - .38-40 WCF or .44-40 WCF cal., similar to 14A, with 10 shot mag., 22 1/2 in. barrel. Mfg. began Dec. 5, 1913-34.

	$1,200	$1,075	$950	$875	$800	$725	$650

Add 10% for .44-40 WCF cal.

Quantities mfg. of this model are unknown, as serial numbers were intermixed with the Model 14.

This model was also manufactured in higher grades, including A, C, and F. Premiums vary according to originality and condition.

MODEL 14 1/2 R CARBINE - similar to 14 1/2 Rifle, with 8 shot mag. and 18 in. barrel.

	$3,500	$3,000	$2,750	$2,500	$2,000	$1,750	$1,500

Add 30% for "fingernail" safety (introduced in 1918).

MODEL 25/25A - .25-20 WCF or .32-20 WCF cal., 24 in. barrel, open sight, tube mag., plain pistol grip stock. Mfg. 1923-35.

	$800	$700	$625	$550	$450	$350	$275

MODEL 25R CARBINE - similar to 25A, with 18 in. barrel and straight stock.

	$1,100	$1,050	$925	$825	$750	$650	$525

GRADING - PPGS™	100%	98%	95%	90%	80%	70%	60%

MODEL 76 SPORTSMAN - .30-06 cal. only, 22 in. barrel, 4 shot mag., unchecked-ered hardwood stock and forearm, open sights, 7 1/2 lbs. Mfg. 1984-87.

	$300	$275	$250	$200	$170	$160	$150

Last MSR was $319.

MODEL 141/141A - .25 Rem. (very few mfg. during 1936 only), .30 Rem., .32 Rem., or .35 Rem. cal., 24 in. barrel, takedown, open sight, plain pistol grip stock. Mfg. 1936-50.

	$465	$425	$350	$295	$240	$195	$165

Add 60% for .25 Rem. cal.
Add 10% for .35 Rem. cal.

MODEL 141 CARBINE - mfg. 1936-42.

	$825	$750	$700	$650	$600	$550	$500

MODEL 760 GAMEMASTER RIFLE - .222 Rem. (mfg. 1958-61), .223 Rem. (limited mfg. 1964-69), 6mm Rem. (introduced 1969), .243 Win. (introduced 1968), .244 (mfg. 1956-59), .257 Roberts (mfg. 1955-58), .270 Win., .280 Rem. (mfg. 1958-1967), .30-06, .300 Sav. (disc. 1958), .308 Win., or .35 Rem. (mfg. 1952-67, and 1980) cal., 22 in. barrel, detachable mag., uncheckered or checkered (new 1964) pistol grip stock. Mfg. 1952-1980.

	100%	98%	95%	90%	80%	70%	60%
	$375	$325	$275	$250	$225	$200	$175
.222 Rem. cal.	$1,150	$900	$800	$725	$650	$575	$500
.223 Rem. cal.	$1,350	$995	$850	$775	$700	$625	$575
.257 Roberts cal.	$850	$695	$575	$450	$400	$350	$300

Add 10% for .300 Savage or .35 Rem. cal.

The Model 760 seems to have regional pricing differences in the rare calibers. Values in the Eastern U.S. seem to be quite a bit higher than prices encountered in the Midwest and West. Hence, values on the .222 Rem., .223 Rem., and .257 Roberts cals. reflect a nationalized average rather than one region's high or another's low. A few Model 760s were also mfg. in .244 cal. (before going to 6mm Rem.) - very rare with pricing unpredictable.

MODEL 760C CARBINE - .270 Win., .280 Win., .30-06, .308 Win., or .35 Rem. cal., 18 1/2 in. barrel.

	$450	$400	$375	$325	$300	$275	$250

Subtract 10% for .30-06 cal.

MODEL 760 (CDL) CARBINE - similar to Model 760C Carbine, except has checkered stock, pistol grip cap and sling swivels. Mfg. 1961-1963.

	$475	$425	$400	$375	$325	$300	$275

Add 20% for .280 Rem. cal.

MODEL 760D PEERLESS GRADE - similar to 760, with scroll engraving and fancy wood. Mfg. 1953-1980.

	$2,500	$1,800	$1,200	N/A	N/A	N/A	N/A

MODEL 760F PREMIER GRADE - similar to Model 760 Peerless, with extensive hand engraved game scenes, and scroll work, best grade wood.

	$4,500	$3,850	$2,600	N/A	N/A	N/A	N/A

✳ *Model 760F Premier w/Inlays* - similar to Model 760F Premier Grade, except has game scenes inlaid in gold.

	$6,500	$5,700	$4,100	N/A	N/A	N/A	N/A

MODEL 760 150 YEAR ANNIVERSARY - .30-06 cal. only, similar to Model 760, except has commemorative inscription roll engraved on receiver. 4,610 mfg. 1966 only.

	$450	$325	$300	N/A	N/A	N/A	N/A

MODEL 760 BICENTENNIAL - .30-06 cal. only, similar to Model 760, with commemorative inscription, roll engraved on receiver. 3,804 mfg. 1976 only.

	$450	$325	$300	$275	$225	$200	$185

GRADING - PPGS™	100%	98%	95%	90%	80%	70%	60%

MODEL 760ADL - similar to Model 760, except with checkered stock, grip cap, sling swivels. Mfg. 1953-1963.

	$425	$375	$350	$300	$275	$250	$225

MODEL 760BDL - similar to Model 760ADL, except has select grade wood. Mfg. 1953-1957.

	$475	$425	$400	$375	$325	$300	$275

Only a few BDL grade rifles have been observed with the grade marked on the receiver. Flawed BDL grade stocks were downgraded and fitted to ADL grade rifles.

MODEL 760BDL DELUXE - similar to Model 760, except .270 Win., .30-06, or .308 Win. cal. only, step receiver, available with right- or left-hand cheekpiece on Monte Carlo stock, basket weave checkering pattern, black pistol grip and forend tip. Mfg. 1966-1980.

	$425	$375	$350	$300	$275	$250	$225

Add 20% for .308 Win. cal.

MODEL 7600 - 6mm Rem. (disc. 1984), .243 Win., .270 Win., .280 Rem. (mfg. 1988-2000), .30-06, .308 Win., or .35 Whelen (mfg. 1988-96) cal., modified 760 action, 22 in. barrel, 4 shot detachable mag., pressed checkered pistol grip stock and forearm, 7 1/2 lbs. New 1981.

MSR $768	$610	$455	$340	$265	$215	$185	$165

Add 10% for .35 Whelen cal.

Depending on overall desirability, typical NIB asking prices for Grice Wholesale guns listed below will be 10%-15% higher than standard production.

In addition, walnut stocked rifles in .35 Whelan and carbines in .35 Rem. cal. were offered.

Beginning in 1990, a high gloss wood finish became available in cals. .270 Win. and .30-06 (Model 7600 High Gloss). From 1996-2003 receiver panels have fine line rolled game scene engraving.

A Pennsylvania distributor, Grice Wholesale, has offered a wide variety of special order, non-cataloged Model 7600s since 1990. The initial 1990 order was for 500 Model 7600s in 7mm-08 cal., followed by 1,000 7mm-08 cal. 175th Anniversary roll marked rifles in 1991. In 1992, the Door Hunter Special, with a roll marked, gold filled deer scene was offered. This model was repeated in 1993 with a cabin and game scene engraving - 500 in .270 Win., 500 in .30-06, and 1,000 in 7mm-08 cal. were offered each year.

Over the years, Grice has also offered non-cataloged calibers such as 6mm Rem., .257 Roberts, .25-06 Rem., .260 Rem., .35 Rem. and .35 Whelan. Black and brown laminate stocks have also been offered.

The 2005 special orders were Model 7600s with maple stocks in 6mm Rem., .25-06 Rem., and 7mm-08 cal. 500 rifles were offered in .30-06 with a special roll marking commemorating the 100th anniversary of the .30-06, also with maple stocks.

In late 2006, Grice offered several Model 7600s with black laminated stocks - 7mm-08 cal., .30-06 w/a laser engraved "ONE OF 250 .30-06 100TH ANNIVERSARY 1906-2006" logo on the buttstock and a Model 7615 in .223 Rem. cal. with a 22 in. barrel. Additionally, 300 walnut stocked Model 7600s in .300 Sav. cal. were also offered.

✳ *Model 7600 Carbine* - .30-06 cal. only, similar to Model 7600 Rifle, except has 18 1/2 in. barrel, 7 1/4 lbs.

MSR $768	$610	$455	$340	$265	$215	$185	$165

A total of 170 Larry Benoit Commemorative carbines were manufactured in 1999 and 2000 for Wilderness Trading and Supply Co. in VT. MSR was $995. Pricing varies on these models, since these guns were a limited special order.

✳ *Model 7600P Patrol Rifle* - .308 Win. cal., 16 1/2 in. barrel, synthetic stock, parkerized finish, Wilson Combat ghost ring sights, designed for police/law enforcement only.

Remington does not publish consumer retail pricing for this police/law enforcement model. Secondary prices for this model will be slightly higher than for current pricing on the Model 7600 Synthetic.

GRADING - PPGS™	100%	98%	95%	90%	80%	70%	60%

✳ *Model 7600 SP (Special Purpose)* - .270 Win. or .30-06 cal., similar to Model 7600, except has non-reflective matte finish on wood and metalwork. Mfg. 1993-94.

	100%	98%	95%	90%	80%	70%	60%
	$420	$360	$280	$230	$205	$185	$165

Last MSR was $496.

✳ *Model 7600 Synthetic* - same cals. as Model 7600, features black fiberglass reinforced synthetic stock and forend, matte black metal finish, 22 in. barrel only, 7 1/2 lbs. New 1998.

MSR $643	$495	$400	$335	$300	$265	$240	$225

❖ **Model 7600 Synthetic Carbine** - .30-06 cal., similar to Model 7600 Synthetic, except has 18 1/2 in. barrel. 7 1/4 lbs. New 1998.

MSR $643	$495	$400	$335	$300	$265	$240	$225

✳ *Model 7600 175th Anniversary* - also available in 7mm-08 Rem. cal., 1,000 mfg. 1991 only.

	$625	$525	$375	N/A	N/A	N/A	N/A

✳ *Model 7600 ADF Limited Edition* - .30-06 cal. only, special edition 1997 only featuring Buckmaster's American Deer Foundation, special ADF engraving. Approx. 800 mfg. 1997 only.

	$500	$425	$325	N/A	N/A	N/A	N/A

Last MSR was $567.

MODEL 7600 ENGRAVED - hand engraved Model 7600s were introduced 1988.

✳ *Model 7600 D Grade (Peerless)* - features scroll engraving and fancy wood.

MSR POR	N/A	$2,900	$2,075	N/A	N/A	N/A	N/A

The last published MSR on this model was $4,532.

✳ *Model 7600 F Grade (Premier)* - features extensive hand engraved game scenes and scroll work and best grade wood.

MSR POR	N/A	$6,000	$4,400	N/A	N/A	N/A	N/A

The last published MSR on this model was $8,799.

✳ *Model 7600 F Premier Grade w/Inlays* - top-of-the-line custom shop model with game scenes inlaid in gold.

MSR POR	N/A	$5,550	$3,600	N/A	N/A	N/A	N/A

The last published MSR on this model was $11,999 (2007).

MODEL 7615 - .223 Rem., 10 shot AR-15 compatible detachable box mag., 16 1/2 (tactical model with pistol grip and non-collapsible tube stock and Knoxx Special Ops NRS recoil suppressor), 18 1/2 (ranch rifle, walnut stock and forearm), or 22 (camo hunter, 100% Mossy Oak Brush camo coverage) in. barrel w/o sights, synthetic or walnut (ranch carbine) stock and forearm, drilled and tapped, approx. 7 lbs. New 2007, mfg. in Ilion, NY.

MSR $955	$790	$685	$575	$500	$450	$400	$350

Add $54 for Camo Hunter with 100% camo coverage.

MODEL 7615P PATROL RIFLE - .223 Rem. cal., 16 1/2 in. barrel, 10 shot mag., synthetic stock, parkerized finish, extended mag., accepts AR-15 and M16 style magazines, Wilson Combat ghost ring sights, designed for police/law enforcement, 7 lbs.

Remington does not publish consumer retail pricing for this police/law enforcement model. Secondary prices for this model will be slightly higher than for current pricing on the Model 7600 Carbine.

MODEL 7615 SPS - .223 Rem. cal., 16 1/2 in. blue barrel, Picatinny rail, action, slide release and safety based on the Model 870, 10 shot mag, accepts aftermarket AR-15 style mags., black pistol grip synthetic stock. New 2008.

MSR $805	$695	$625	$550	$500	$450	$400	$350

This model is available through Remington Premier dealers only.

GRADING - PPGS™	100%	98%	95%	90%	80%	70%	60%

RIFLES: RIMFIRE

From 1930-1960 Remington produced a number of bolt action .22 cal. Rimfire rifles, both single shot and repeaters. They were good quality, serviceable weapons with many slight variations upon a basic design. Whenever possible, models have been listed in numerical sequence.

On factory engraved E & F grade rifles, the ser. no. is usually engraved instead of stamped, and there is no standard factory engraving pattern on these grades.

	100%	98%	95%	90%	80%	70%	60%
✳ MODEL 33	$225	$175	$125	$100	$85	$75	$60
✳ MODEL 33 NRA	$500	$350	$250	$200	$150	$125	$100
✳ MODEL 33-P	$250	$200	$175	$150	$125	$100	$75
✳ MODEL 33 SB	$350	$325	$300	$290	$280	$260	$250

263,557 of the Model 33 were mfg. 1932-35.

	100%	98%	95%	90%	80%	70%	60%
✳ MODEL 34	$250	$200	$125	$100	$85	$75	$60
✳ MODEL 34-P	$300	$225	$200	$175	$150	$125	$100
✳ MODEL 34 NRA	$450	$400	$350	$300	$275	$250	$200

162,941 of the Model 34 were mfg. 1932-36.

	100%	98%	95%	90%	80%	70%	60%
✳ MODEL 341 A	$200	$150	$100	$90	$85	$80	$75
✳ MODEL 341 P	$225	$175	$125	$100	$85	$75	$70
✳ MODEL 341 SB	$450	$350	$300	$290	$280	$260	$250

131,604 of the Model 341 "Sportsmaster" were mfg. 1936-40.

	100%	98%	95%	90%	80%	70%	60%
✳ MODEL 41 A	$175	$150	$100	$75	$65	$60	$55
✳ MODEL 41 AS (.22 REM. SPEC. CAL.)	$325	$250	$175	$150	$140	$125	$110
✳ MODEL 41 P	$200	$150	$100	$85	$65	$60	$55
✳ MODEL 41 SB	$325	$275	$250	$240	$230	$220	$210

306,880 of the Model 41 "Targetmaster" were produced 1936-39.

	100%	98%	95%	90%	80%	70%	60%
✳ MODEL 411	$600	$450	$350	$300	$250	$225	$200

Add 50% premium for .22 Short.

The Model 411 is similar to the Model 41 single shot, but in CB Cap or .22 Short and without safety on rear of bolt. Eye screw for gallery use. 1,316 mfg. 1937-39 (although never cataloged).

	100%	98%	95%	90%	80%	70%	60%
✳ MODEL 510 A	$185	$150	$90	$75	$65	$60	$55
✳ MODEL 510 C (CARBINE)	$300	$225	$125	$100	$75	$65	$60
✳ MODEL 510 P	$225	$200	$95	$85	$75	$65	$60
✳ MODEL 510 ROUTLEDGE/SMOOTHBORE	$275	$260	$250	$240	$230	$220	$210

Add 15% for Mo-Skeet-O Bore.

These models were mfg. 1939-62. Approx. 545,000 were mfg.

	100%	98%	95%	90%	80%	70%	60%
✳ MODEL 511 A	$200	$175	$145	$100	$85	$80	$75
✳ MODEL 511 P	$225	$200	$150	$110	$100	$90	$85

These models were mfg. 1939-62. Approx. 375,000 mfg.

	100%	98%	95%	90%	80%	70%	60%
✳ MODEL 512 A	$200	$175	$145	$100	$85	$80	$75
✳ MODEL 512 P	$215	$190	$125	$110	$100	$90	$85

These models were mfg. 1940-62. Approx. 395,000 mfg.

	100%	98%	95%	90%	80%	70%	60%
✳ MODEL 510-X	$185	$150	$125	$100	$90	$80	$70
✳ MODEL 510-X SB	$275	$260	$250	$240	$225	$210	$200
✳ MODEL 511-X (29,120 MFG.)	$200	$175	$150	$125	$100	$85	$75
✳ MODEL 512-X (30,670 MFG.)	$200	$175	$150	$125	$100	$85	$75

These models were mfg. 1964-66. 19,901 Model 510-Xs were mfg. and mixed with the Model 511-X and 512-X.

GRADING - PPGS™	100%	98%	95%	90%	80%	70%	60%
* MODEL 514 (1948-1970)	$140	$110	$90	$75	$65	$55	$40
* MODEL 514 P (1952-1971)	$180	$170	$150	$120	$85	$75	$65
* MODEL 514 BOY'S RIFLE (1961-1970)	$160	$150	$130	$100	$85	$75	$65
* MODEL 514 ROUTLEDGE/ SMOOTHBORE	$250	$230	$220	$210	$200	$195	$190

The Routledge/Smoothbore was mfg. 1951-1969 - 5,557 were mfg. Serialization began in 1968, approx. 780,000 mfg.

MODEL FIVE BOLT ACTION - .17 HMR (new 2008), .22 LR or .22 Mag. cal., 22 in. barrel with adj. flip-up rear sight, blued finish, 5 shot detachable mag., checkered satin finished brown laminated or European walnut (.22 LR only, new 2008) stock and forend, grooved steel receiver, safety located next to bolt, 6 3/4 lbs., mfg. in Serbia. New 2006.

MSR $349	$295	$265	$230	$200	$175	$160	$145

Add $14 for .22 Mag. or .17 HMR cal.
Subtract $70 for European walnut stock.

* *Model Five Bolt Action Youth* - .22 LR cal., 16 1/2 in. barrel with open sights, shortened LOP, hardwood stock. New 2008.

MSR $237	$195	$170	$150	$135	$120	$100	$90

MODEL 12A SLIDE ACTION RIFLE - .22 S, L, and LR cal., hammerless, 22 in. round or octagon barrel, open sights, tube mag., plain grip stock, approx. 840,000 (all variations) were mfg. 1909-1936.

	$925	$825	$700	$600	$400	$325	$300

Originally this model was designated "The New .22 Repeater," and did not have a model number. It was also available in Grades 1-6.

MODEL 12B (GALLERY SPECIAL) - similar to Model 12C, except in .22 Short cal., all had octagon barrels.

	$1,250	$1,000	$750	$650	$525	$425	$375

Add 15% for extended mag. tube.

MODEL 12C - similar to Model 12A, except 24 in. octagon barrel.

	$1,100	$995	$800	$700	$600	$500	$400

Add premiums for grades D, E, and F.

MODEL 12C NRA TARGET - limited manufacture.

	$1,600	$1,400	$1,200	$1,100	$1,000	$900	$800

MODEL 12CS - similar to Model 12C, chambered for .22 Rem. Spl. (.22 WRF) cal.

	$1,100	$995	$800	$700	$600	$500	$400

MODEL 16/16A AUTOLOADING RIFLE - .22 Rem. Autoloading cal., 22 in. barrel, open sight, tube mag. in buttstock, straight stock. 17,738 mfg. 1914-28.

	$700	$600	$450	$325	$300	$275	$250

Add premiums for higher grades C, D, E, and F.

MODEL 24/24A AUTOLOADING RIFLE - .22 S or LR cal., 19 in. barrel, open sights, Browning semi-auto design, bottom ejection, tube mag. through buttstock, takedown, plain pistol grip stock. Approx. 131,000 mfg. 1922-35.

	$450	$350	$250	$175	$150	$125	$115

Add premiums for higher grades C Special, D Peerless, E Expert, and F Premier.

MODEL 37 "RANGEMASTER" BOLT ACTION TARGET RIFLE - .22 LR cal., 5 shot with single shot adapter, 28 in. barrel, target sight and scope bases, target stock, 12 1/2 lbs. Mfg. 1937-40.

	$1,100	$900	$700	$600	$525	$475	$450

Add 100% for stock with original barrel band.

GRADING - PPGS™	100%	98%	95%	90%	80%	70%	60%

MODEL 37 - 1940 - improved trigger and stock design. Mfg. 1940-54.

	$1,100	$900	$700	$600	$525	$475	$450

Total manufacture of the Model 37 was 12,198.

MODEL 121A SLIDE ACTION RIFLE - hammerless, .22 S, L, or LR cal., 24 in. round barrel, tube mag., plain pistol grip stock. 201,000 were mfg. 1936-54.

	$600	$500	$400	$250	$225	$215	$200

Originally designated Model 121.

MODEL 121S - similar to Model 121A, except chambered for .22 Rem. Spl. (rare) cal.

	$1,000	$800	$550	$350	$325	$300	$275

MODEL 121SB/ROUTLEDGE - similar to Model 121A, except smooth bore for .22 shot, at least 5 different chamberings and barrel markings. Approx. 3,000 were mfg. pre-WWII-1952.

	$1,100	$900	$700	$600	$575	$550	$525

MODEL 241A SPEEDMASTER SEMI-AUTO - .22 S or LR cal., 24 in. barrel, replaced the Model 24, open sights, takedown, tube mag. in buttstock, non-checkered walnut stock and forearm. Approx. 132,000 mfg. 1935-49.

	$475	$400	$300	$200	$150	$125	$115

Add premiums for Special, Peerless, Expert, and Premier Grade models. Add a premium for .22 Short cal.

MODEL 412 YOUTH BOLT ACTION - .22 LR cal., single shot with second shot holder, 19 3/4 in. barrel with adj. sights, automatic safety, uncheckered hardwood stock, blue finish, 4 1/2 lbs. Limited mfg. 2006.

While advertised with a MSR of $136, these rifles were mfg. in Mexico, but were not shipped to Remington.

MODEL 504 BOLT ACTION - .17 Mach 2 (new 2005) or .22 LR cal., bolt action, drilled and tapped solid steel receiver, 20 in. barrel w/o sights, matte metal finish, features 5-R button rifling (same as the Model 40-XR), dual bedding points, fully adj. trigger group, dual extractors, 6 shot detachable mag., checkered American walnut stock, cocking indicator, approx. 6 lbs. Mfg. 2004-2006 in Ilion, NY.

	$615	$485	$430	$365	$335	$295	$265

Last MSR was $738.

✳ *Model 504-T Bolt Action* - .17 HMR or .22 LR cal., similar to Model 504, except has 20 in. heavy free floating barrel, Eley match chamber, 5 (.17 HMR) or 6 shot mag., brown laminate Monte Carlo stock with palm swell and beavertail forend, satin blue metal, approx. 6 1/2 lbs. Mfg. 2005-2006.

	$695	$545	$475	$400	$350	$315	$285

Last MSR was $839.

Add $26 for .17 HMR cal.

MODEL 504 CUSTOM C GRADE - .22 LR cal., bolt action, 24 in. carbon steel blue barrel, "C" grade fancy semi-gloss American walnut stock with rosewood pistol grip and forend caps, 6 1/2 lbs., limited mfg. 2006-2008.

	$1,495	$1,300	$1,025	$875	$750	$650	$575

Last MSR was $1,836.

MODEL 513T (TARGET) "MATCHMASTER" BOLT ACTION - .22 LR cal., 27 in. barrel, Redfield aperture sight, target stock, 6 shot, sling swivels, approx. 166,000 were mfg. 1940-68.

	$450	$400	$350	$325	$300	$250	$200

A "TR" suffix on this gun indicated with sights, a "TX" indicated w/o sights, a "TS" indicated sporter. Most 513s are marked either 513T (Target) or 513S (Sporter).

GRADING - PPGS™	100%	98%	95%	90%	80%	70%	60%

MODEL 513S (SPORTER) - similar to Model 513T, with Marbles open sight and checkered sporter stock. 13,677 were mfg. 1941-56.

	$750	$650	$600	$550	$475	$400	$350

MODEL 521T/TL JR. BOLT ACTION - .22 LR cal., 25 in. barrel, Lyman target sights, takedown, 6 shot mag., target stock, approx. 67,000 were mfg. 1947-68.

	$395	$350	$300	$250	$200	$175	$150

These models had no ser. no. until 1954. This model's nomenclature changed to the 521T in 1959.

MODEL 522 VIPER SEMI-AUTO - .22 LR cal., semi-auto blowback action, 20 in. barrel, full-length black synthetic resin stock with beavertail forend, 10 shot mag., cocking indicator, adj. rear sight, grooved synthetic receiver, 4 5/8 lbs. Mfg. 1993-97.

	$150	$125	$110	$100	$90	$80	$70

Last MSR was $152.

MODEL 540X RIMFIRE - .22 LR cal., single shot bolt action, 26 in. heavy barrel, no sights, target stock, adj. butt, approx. 5,115. Mfg. 1969-74.

	$425	$400	$300	$250	$200	$185	$175

MODEL 540XR - similar to Model 540X, with large position style stock with adj. buttplate. Mfg. 1974-83.

	$350	$325	$300	$250	$200	$185	$175

✳ *Model 540XR JR* - similar to Model 540X, except 1 1/2 in. shorter stock. Mfg. 1974-83.

	$350	$325	$300	$250	$200	$185	$175

MODEL 541S CUSTOM BOLT ACTION - .22 S, L, or LR cal., bolt action, 24 in. barrel, drilled and tapped, 5 shot mag., adj. match trigger, scroll engraved receiver and triggerguard, checkered walnut stock with rosewood pistol grip cap, buttplate, and forend tip. Mfg. 1972-1984.

	$695	$600	$500	$425	$375	$325	$275

MODEL 541T BOLT ACTION - .22 LR cal. only, 5 shot mag., 24 in. standard or heavy (new 1993) barrel, checkered American walnut stock with satin finish, barrel is drilled and tapped, 5 7/8 lbs. Mfg. 1986-1999.

	$450	$375	$250	$200	$180	$165	$150

Last MSR was $465.

Add $50 for heavy barrel.

MODEL 541X - .22 LR cal. only, bolt action, U.S. military training rifle, 27 in. barrel, 5 shot mag., ser. no. inscribed by hand on bolt, 9,077 mfg. 1984-86.

	$550	$450	$400	$375	$350	$325	$300

MODEL 547 BOLT ACTION CUSTOM CLASSIC - 17 HMR or .22 LR cal., Model 700 style action and bolt handle, high polished 22 in. Shilen custom barrel w/o sights, classic walnut stock with rosewood forend tip, 3 lbs. trigger pull, guaranteed 1/2 in. 5 shot groups at 50 yards, mfg. by custom shop. New 2008.

MSR $1,284	$1,050	$900	$800	$700	$600	$500	$400

MODEL 550A SEMI-AUTO - .22 S, L, or LR cal., 24 in. barrel, open sight, shell deflector, 2 extractors, tube mag., plain one piece pistol stock. 34,577 Mfg. 1941-46.

	$275	$225	$150	$100	$80	$70	$60

Add 100% if w/o shell deflector (not tapped).

MODEL 550-1 - similar to Model 550A, except has single extractor. Approx. 730,000 mfg. 1946-1970.

	$250	$200	$110	$90	$75	$65	$55

MODEL 550P - similar to Model 550-1, with aperture (peep) sight.

	$275	$225	$175	$150	$135	$120	$100

GRADING - PPGS™	100%	98%	95%	90%	80%	70%	60%

MODEL 550-2G - .22 Short cal., similar to Model 550-1, except 22 in. barrel and eye screw for counter chain in shooting gallery.

	$275	$225	$175	$150	$135	$120	$100

MODEL 552A SPEEDMASTER SEMI-AUTO - .22 S, L, or LR cal., 23 in. barrel, semi-auto open sight, tube mag., pistol grip stock. Mfg. 1957-disc.

	$175	$150	$120	$100	$85	$75	$65

This model was also mfg. in a 150th Anniversary Model (1966 only, approx. 6,565 mfg.) and a 175th Anniversary (1991 only). Slight premiums are being asked if condition is 98% or better.

MODEL 552C - similar to Model 552A, with 21 in. barrel. Mfg. 1961-77.

	$175	$150	$130	$110	$95	$85	$75

✳ *Model 552 BDL Deluxe Speedmaster* - similar to Model 552C, except checkered gloss finished walnut Monte Carlo stock and forearm, 21 in. barrel, approx. 5 1/2 lbs. New 1966.

MSR $572	$425	$325	$265	$225	$195	$165	$145

✳ *Model 552 BDL Deluxe Fieldmaster NRA Edition* - features laser etched NRA on both sides of receiver. Limited mfg. 2006-2007.

	$400	$300	$250	$215	$185	$150	$130

Last MSR was $532.

MODEL 552 175th ANNIVERSARY - 1,000 mfg. 1991 only.

	$395	$275	$200	N/A	N/A	N/A	N/A

MODEL 572 LIGHTWEIGHT SLIDE ACTION - .22 S, L, LR cal., slide action, anodized alloy receiver and barrel, steel sleeved, checkered "Sun-Grain" stock and forend, 4 lbs. Offered in 3 colors. Approx. 34,785 mfg., 1958-62.

Buckskin Tan	$325	$275	$200	$150	$120	$110	$100
Crow-Wing Black	$425	$375	$345	$295	$195	$150	$125
Teal-Wing Blue	$800	$700	$600	$425	$300	$250	$225

MODEL 572SB/ROUTLEDGE - similar to Model 572A, except smooth bore.

	$450	$400	$350	$325	$300	$275	$250

MODEL 572 FIELDMASTER SLIDE ACTION - .22 S, L, or LR cal., slide action, 21 in. barrel, walnut stock and forearm, tube mag., 5 1/2 lbs. Mfg. 1955-88.

	$225	$195	$125	$105	$90	$75	$65

Last MSR was $176.

This model was also mfg. in a 150th Anniversary Model (1966 only). 20% premiums if condition is 98% or better.

✳ *Model 572 BDL Deluxe Fieldmaster* - similar to Model 572, except is also available in .22 Smoothbore (new 2007), checkered gloss finished walnut Monte Carlo stock and forearm. New 1966.

MSR $585	$440	$315	$240	$195	$165	$140	$120

Add $27 for .22 Smoothbore (Model 572 SB).

This model has also been available in several limited production runs. Prices are usually slightly higher than the standard pricing listed above.

MODEL 572 175th ANNIVERSARY - 300 mfg. 1991 only.

	$425	$295	$225	N/A	N/A	N/A	N/A

MODEL 580 SINGLE SHOT - .22 S, L, or LR cal., bolt action, 24 in. barrel, open sights, Monte Carlo stock. Mfg. 1967-78.

	$175	$165	$125	$110	$100	$95	$90

Add 50% for smooth bore (Model 580SB).

MODEL 580BR - Boy's Model, 1 in. shorter stock. Mfg. 1971-78.

	$185	$170	$135	$110	$100	$95	$90

GRADING - PPGS™	100%	98%	95%	90%	80%	70%	60%

MODEL 581 BOLT ACTION - .22 LR cal., bolt action, 6 shot mag., converts to single shot. Mfg. 1967-83.

	$195	$175	$150	$115	$100	$90	$80

MODEL 581 SPORTSMAN - .22 LR cal., bolt action, 5 shot mag., 24 in. barrel, hardwood uncheckered stock, 4 3/4 lbs. Mfg. 1986-99.

	$175	$160	$135	$115	$100	$95	$90

Last MSR was $239.

MODEL 582 BOLT ACTION - similar to 581, with tube mag. Mfg. 1967-83.

	$195	$175	$150	$120	$100	$95	$90

MODEL 591 BOLT ACTION - 5mm Rimfire Mag. cal., 24 in. barrel, open sight, 5 shot mag., Monte Carlo stock. Approx. 27,000 mfg. 1970-74.

	$175	$125	$100	$95	$90	$85	$75

5mm rimfire ammo has been disc. for some time, and as a result, collectibility on this model is mostly for 95% or better condition. There is little shooter utility in lower conditions, so the discontinued ammo has become too expensive. Original 5mm ammo is selling for $50 or more per box.

MODEL 592 BOLT ACTION - similar to 591, with tube mag. Approx. 25,000 mfg. 1970-74.

	$175	$125	$100	$95	$90	$85	$75

MODEL 597 SEMI-AUTO - .22 LR cal., alloy receiver with nickel plated bolt, matte black metal finish, one-piece dark grey smooth synthetic stock, 20 in. free-floating barrel, 10 shot staggered detachable mag., adj. iron sights, new trigger design, 5 1/2 lbs. New 1997, mfg. in Mayfield, KY.

MSR $188	$150	$125	$110	$95	$85	$75	$65

Add $41 for 3-9x32mm scope combo (new 2007).

This model has also been available in several limited production runs. Prices are usually slightly higher than the standard pricing listed above.

✳ *Model 597 Semi-Auto Sporter* - similar to Model 597, except has hardwood stock, includes sling swivel studs. Mfg. 1998-2000.

	$160	$135	$115	$100	$90	$80	$70

Last MSR was $199.

✳ *Model 597 Semi-Auto Stainless Sporter* - similar to Model 597 Sporter, except has stainless steel barrel and hardwood stock. Mfg. 2000 only.

	$190	$155	$130	$105	$90	$75	$70

Last MSR was $239.

✳ *Model 597 Semi-Auto SS* - similar to Model 597, except is stainless synthetic with satin finished receiver and barrel, beavertail style forend. Mfg. 1998-2007.

	$220	$170	$135	$110	$90	$80	$70

Last MSR was $283.

✳ *Model 597 Semi-Auto LSS* - similar to Model 597, except has stainless steel barrel with matching alloy receiver, and satin finished brown wood laminate stock, 5 1/2 lbs. Mfg. 1997-2007.

	$285	$220	$170	$135	$110	$95	$85

Last MSR was $348.

✳ *Model 597 Semi-Auto HB LS* - similar to Model 597 LSS, except has 20 in. heavy steel barrel. Mfg. 2001-2007.

	$275	$210	$170	$130	$110	$95	$85

Last MSR was $337.

✳ *Model 597 Semi-Auto Camo* - features Truglo fiber optic sights and Mossy Oak Blaze orange or pink camo stock. New 2008.

MSR $252	$210	$180	$165	$145	$125	$115	$100

GRADING - PPGS™	100%	98%	95%	90%	80%	70%	60%

✳ *Model 597 Semi-Auto TVP (Target Varmint Plinker)* - .22 LR cal., bolt guidance system with twin steel guide rails, stainless action and barrel, non-glare matte finish, ambidextrous laminated thumbhole stock with scalloped forend, 10 shot mag., includes scope mounting rail. New 2008.

MSR $532	$425	$345	$280	$225	$195	$165	$140

MODEL 597 CUSTOM TARGET - .22 LR cal., 20 in. custom contoured satin finish heavy stainless free floating barrel w/o sights, match chamber, special green laminated stock with Monte Carlo profile and beavertail forend. Mfg. 1998-2000.

	$495	$400	$300	$240	$210	$180	$155

Last MSR was $599.

✳ *Model 597 Custom Target* - .22 Mag. cal. Disc. 2000.

	$600	$450	$350	$285	$250	$215	$185

Last MSR was $745.

MODEL 597 MAGNUM SYNTHETIC - .17 HMR (mfg. 2003-2007) or .22 Mag. cal., similar in appearance to Model 597, 8 shot mag., 20 in. barrel, black synthetic stock with sling swivel studs, 6 lbs. New 1997.

MSR $476	$365	$280	$215	$190	$170	$150	$130

Add $29 for .17 HMR cal.

✳ *Model 597 Magnum Synthetic LS* - .17 HMR (mfg. 2002-2003 only) or .22 Mag. (disc. 2003) cal., features brown laminate stock with sling swivel studs and steel barrel. Mfg. 1998-2003.

	$315	$265	$230	$190	$160	$140	$125

Last MSR was $377.

✳ *Model 597 Magnum Synthetic LS Heavy Barrel* - .17 HMR (disc. 2007) or .22 Mag. cal., similar to Model 597 Magnum LS, except has 20 in. heavy barrel, 6 lbs. New 2001.

MSR $569	$440	$365	$300	$250	$200	$165	$140

Add $32 for .17 HMR cal.

MODEL 597 SEMI-AUTO TARGET RIFLE - .22 LR cal., heavy barrel, black, grey and yellow ShurShot target laminated skeletonized stock, scope rail, 10 shot detachable mag., last shot hold open, twin steel guide rails. New 2008.

MSR $505	$425	$375	$325	$285	$250	$225	$195

This model is available through Remington Premier dealers only.

RIFLES: RIMFIRE - "NYLON SERIES"

These models can be identified by the markings on the grip cap.

NYLON 10 SINGLE SHOT - .22 S, L, or LR cal., bolt action. 8,606 were mfg. 1962-64.

	$350	$300	$200	$175	$150	$125	$100

✳ *Nylon 10-SB Single Shot* - similar to Nylon 10, except smooth bore barrel used for .22 shot cartridges. 2,064 mfg.

	$1,000	$800	$500	$300	$175	$155	$135

This model is infrequently encountered.

MOHAWK 10-C - similar to Model 77, renamed after changing to a 10 shot mag., approx. 129,000 were mfg. 1971-78.

	$200	$175	$125	$115	$110	$105	$100

MODEL 11 NYLON - .22 S, L, or LR cal., bolt action repeater, 6 or 10 shot mag., 4 1/2 lbs. 22,423 were mfg. 1962-64.

	$400	$350	$275	$250	$200	$150	$100

MODEL 12 NYLON - similar to 11, with tube mag. 27,551 were mfg. 1962-64.

	$450	$350	$275	$250	$200	$150	$100

GRADING - PPGS™	100%	98%	95%	90%	80%	70%	60%

NYLON 66 AUTOLOADER - .22 LR cal., 19 5/8 in. barrel, open sights, buttstock tube mag. holds 14 shells, 4 lbs. Stock made from Zytel plastic in black, brown, or green. 1,050,336 were mfg. 1959-90.

	$200	$175	$125	$115	$110	$105	$100

Last MSR was $124.

Add 25% for Black Diamond (56,000 mfg.).
Add 40% for Apache black or chrome finish (221,000 mfg.).
Add 50% for Seneca green (45,000 mfg.).
Add 100% for Gallery Special (.22 Short cal. only).

NYLON 66 150TH ANNIVERSARY - 3,792 mfg. in 1966 only with 150th Anniversary Remington logo on receiver.

	$500	$475	$350	$250	$175	$165	$150

NYLON 66 BICENTENNIAL - inscription on receiver, 10,268 mfg. 1976 only, brown nylon stock only.

	$450	$400	$300	$250	$225	$200	$150

NYLON 76 LEVER ACTION - similar appearance to Nylon 66 with brown or black stock, short throw lever action, 25,312 mfg. in standard finish, 1,615 mfg. in black chrome finish 1962-64 only.

	100%	98%	95%	90%	80%	70%	60%
Standard finish (25,312 mfg.)	$500	$450	$300	$275	$250	$225	$200
Apache Black/chrome finish (1,615 mfg.)	$900	$850	$750	$600	$500	$450	$400

The Nylon 76 "Trail Rider" is the only lever action repeating rifle ever mfg. by Remington.

NYLON 77 - similar to Nylon 10-C, except with 5 shot mag. 15,327 were mfg. 1970-71 only.

	$300	$250	$200	$150	$125	$115	$100

NYLON APACHE 77 - similar to Model 10-C, but bright green stock. Mfg. for K-Mart in 1987-89.

	$165	$150	$100	$90	$80	$70	$60

RIFLES: BOLT ACTION, CENTERFIRE

The models in this section have been listed in numerical sequence for quick reference. Remington has manufactured many limited production runs for various distributors and wholesalers over the years. These rifles are usually built to a specific configuration (caliber, stock, barrel length, finish, etc.), and are usually available until supplies run out. While these models are not included in this section, pricing in most cases will be similar to the base models from which they were derived.

MODEL SEVEN LIGHTWEIGHT - .17 Rem. (mfg. 1993-95), .222 Rem. (disc. 1984), .223 Rem. (new 1984), .243 Win., .260 Rem. (new 1997), 6mm Rem. (disc. 1994), 7mm-08 Rem., or .308 Win. cal., short action, 18 1/2 in. barrel, 4 or 5 shot mag., individually test fired, shortened LOP, oil finished American walnut stock, adj. rear and ramp front sight (w/o sights on .17 Rem.), 6 1/4 lbs. Mfg. 1983-1999.

	$475	$370	$275	$225	$205	$180	$165

Last MSR was $585.

Add 5%-10% for .17 Rem. cal.
Add 10% for .222 Rem. cal.

All steel Model Sevens (including floor plate and triggerguard) are currently commanding a small premium.

✳ *Model Seven Lightweight LS* - .223 Rem., .243 Win., .260 Rem. (disc. 2001), .308 Win., or 7mm-08 Rem. cal., features brown laminated stock, 20 in. steel barrel, matte barrel and satin wood finish, 6 1/2 lbs. Mfg. 2000-2005.

	$590	$455	$325	$260	$225	$200	$180

Last MSR was $735.

* **Model Seven Lightweight LS Magnum** - .300 Rem. SAUM or 7mm Rem. SAUM cal., short action, 22 in. barrel, blue action and barrel, 3 shot mag. with detachable floor plate, brown laminated stock, sling swivel studs, 7 1/8 lbs. Mfg. 2002-2005.

	$615	$455	$350	$285	$250	$215	$185

Last MSR was $775.

* **Model Seven Lightweight LSS** - .22-250 Rem., .243 Win. (disc. 2001), or 7mm-08 Rem. cal., similar to Model Seven LS, except has stainless steel barrel w/o sights. Mfg. 2000-2003.

	$610	$445	$325	$265	$230	$195	$170

Last MSR was $770.

* **Model Seven Lightweight SS** - .223 Rem. (mfg. 1997-2002), .243 Win., .260 Rem. (new 1997), .308 Win., 6.8mm Rem. SPC (new 2006) or 7mm-08 Rem. cal., features stainless steel construction, 20 in. barrel w/o sights, and synthetic stock, 6 1/4 lbs. Mfg. 1994-2006.

	$650	$475	$350	$260	$225	$195	$170

Last MSR was $825.

* **Model Seven Lightweight SS Magnum** - .300 Rem. SAUM or 7mm Rem. SAUM cal., short action, satin finished stainless steel action and 22 in. barrel, 3 shot mag. with detachable floor plate, black synthetic stock, sling swivel studs, 7 1/8 lbs. Mfg. 2002-2006.

	$675	$500	$375	$295	$255	$220	$185

Last MSR was $852.

* **Model Seven Lightweight Youth** - .204 Ruger (limited mfg. 2004 only), .223 Rem. (new 2000), .243 Win., 6mm Rem. (disc. 1994), .260 Rem. (new 1998), .308 Win. (disc.), 6.8mm Rem. SPC (mfg. 2006), or 7mm-08 Rem. (new 1994) cal., also available in 20 in. barrel beginning 2000, uncheckered hardwood (.260 Rem. cal.) or synthetic (new 2004) stock shortened 1 in., 6 lbs. Mfg. 1993-2007.

	$525	$425	$335	$275	$230	$200	$185

Last MSR was $684.

Subtract $33 for limited edition synthetic model in .204 Ruger cal.

* **Model Seven Lightweight FS** - .243 Win., 7mm-08 Rem., or .308 Win. cal., 18 1/2 in. parkerized blue barrel, grey or grey camo Kevlar fiberglass stock, adj. rear sight, 5 1/4 lbs. Mfg. 1987-89 only.

	$525	$455	$415	$375	$335	$310	$285

Last MSR was $600.

* **Model Seven XCR Camo** - .243 Rem., .270 WSM, .300 WSM, .308 Win., or 7mm-08 Rem. cal., 20 in. fluted stainless barrel, stainless action utilizing TriNyte corrosion protection, Realtree AP HD camo stock with R3 recoil pad, 3-4 shot non-detachable mag., approx. 7 lbs. Mfg. 2007 only.

MSR $1,080	$925	$825	$725	$625	$550	$475	$400

Add $67 for WSM cals.

* **Model Seven Predator** - .17 Rem. Fireball, .204 Ruger, .223 Rem., .22-250 Rem., or .243 Win. cal., 22 in. barrel, 100% Mossy Oak Brush camo coverage, 2 3/4 in. shorter than normal Model 700, designed for smaller shooters, Model 700 BDL action, 7 lbs. New 2008.

MSR $799	$695	$625	$550	$475	$400	$350	$295

* **Model Seven Lightweight CDL (Classic Deluxe)** - .17 Rem. Fireball (new 2007), .204 Ruger (disc. 2007), .223 Rem. (disc. 2007), .22-250 Rem. (disc. 2007), .243 Win., .260 Rem., 6.8mm Rem. SPC (mfg. 2006), 7mm-08 Rem., or .308 Win. cal., 20 or 22 in. barrel, no sights, checkered deluxe walnut stock and forearm with R3 recoil pad, 6 1/2 lbs. New 2006.

MSR $929	$730	$585	$475	$375	$330	$285	$260

GRADING - PPGS™	100%	98%	95%	90%	80%	70%	60%

❊ *Model Seven Lightweight CDL Magnum* - .270 WSM, 7mm RSAUM (disc. 2007), .300 RSAUM (disc. 2007), .300 WSM, or .350 Rem. Mag. cal., 22 in. barrel, no sights except for .350 Rem. Mag., checkered deluxe walnut stock and forearm with R3 recoil pad, 7 3/8 lbs. New 2006.

	MSR $997	$795	$665	$535	$425	$350	$300	$275

Subtract $40 for .350 Rem. Mag. cal.

❊ *Model Seven Lightweight Custom MS (Mannlicher Stock)* - .222 Rem., .22-250 Rem., .223 Rem., .243 Win., .250 Savage, .257 Roberts, .260 Rem. (new 1997), .308 Win., .35 Rem., .350 Rem. Mag., 6mm Rem., or 7mm-08 Rem. cal., features 20 in. custom shop barrel with Model 7 action bedded to a Mannlicher style laminate full stock, 6 1/2 lbs. New 1993.

MSR $2,927	$2,495	$2,150	$1,850	$1,550	$1,250	$1,000	$775

This model is available from the Custom Shop only (special order).

❊ *Model Seven Lightweight Custom KS* - .223 Rem. (new 1989), .260 Rem. (new 1998), 7mm BR Rem. (mfg. 1989-1990), 7mm-08 Rem. (new 1989), .308 Win. (new 1991), .35 Rem., or .350 Rem. Mag. cal., 20 in. barrel with (.35 Rem. or .350 Rem. Mag.) or w/o sights, Aramid/Kevlar fiberglass synthetic stock with solid recoil pad, 5 3/4 lbs. New 1987.

MSR $2,487	$2,150	$1,850	$1,600	$1,375	$1,150	$925	$775

This model is available from the Custom Shop only (special order).

❊ *Model Seven Lightweight AWR (Alaskan Wilderness Rifle)* - 6.8mm SPC (mfg. 2005-2007), .300 Rem. SAUM, or 7mm Rem. SAUM cal., short action, stainless steel action and 22 in. barrel with matte black Teflon satin finish, 3 shot mag. with detachable floor plate, fiberglass matte black stock, sling swivel studs, 6 1/8 lbs. New 2002.

MSR $2,927	$2,495	$2,150	$1,850	$1,550	$1,250	$1,000	$775

This model is available from the Custom Shop only (special order).

❊ *Model Seven 25th Anniversary Ltd. Ed.* - 7mm-08 Rem. cal., 20 in. barrel, Classic Deluxe style American walnut stock laser engraved with "Model Seven 25th Anniversary" 25th Anniversary medallion inledded in pistol grip cap, high lustre blue with jeweled bolt, X-Mark Pro trigger, 6 1/2 lbs. New 2008.

	MSR $969	$775	$650	$550	$450	$395	$350	$295

MODEL 30A RIFLE - .25 Rem., .30 Rem., .30-06 (original cal.), .32 Rem., .35 Rem., or 7x57mm Mauser (introduced 1931), Enfield M/1917 type action, 22 in. barrel, checkered pistol grip stock. Mfg. 1921-40.

		$600	$550	$475	$400	$350	$300	$260

MODEL 30R CARBINE - .25 Rem., .30 Rem., .32 Rem., .35 Rem., or .30-06 cal., similar to Model 30A, with 20 in. barrel. Introduced 1927.

		$625	$575	$500	$450	$375	$325	$275

MODEL 30 EXPRESS - .25 Rem., .30 Rem., .32 Rem., .35 Rem., or .30-06 cal. Introduced 1926.

		$600	$550	$475	$400	$350	$300	$260

MODEL 30S (SPECIAL GRADE) - .25 Rem. rimless (introduced 1931), .257 Roberts (new 1934), 7x57mm Mauser (introduced 1931), or .30-06 (original cal.) cal., deluxe version of Model 30A, 22 or 24 in. barrel, Lyman receiver sight, special stock, 7 1/2 lbs. Mfg. 1930-40.

		$740	$675	$550	$500	$450	$375	$300

The Model 30S Express Rifle was introduced in 1934 in .257 Roberts cal.

MODEL 78 SPORTSMAN - .223 Rem., .243 Win., .270 Win., .30-06, or .308 Win. cal., 22 in. barrel, 4 shot mag., uncheckered hardwood stock, open sights, 7 lbs. Mfg. 1984-89.

		$300	$250	$210	$190	$170	$160	$150

Last MSR was $333.

GRADING - PPGS™	100%	98%	95%	90%	80%	70%	60%

MODEL XR-100 RANGEMASTER - .204 Ruger, .22-250 Rem., or .223 Rem., features XP-100 single shot target pistol action with Model 40-XP target adj. trigger, 26 in. barrel, laminate thumbhole stock with vent. beavertail forend, 9 1/8 lbs. Mfg. 2005-2007.

	$875	$725	$625	$525	$450	$400	$375

Last MSR was $1,057.

MODEL 600 - .222 Rem., .223 Rem. (very rare), 6mm Rem., .243 Win., .308 Win., or .35 Rem. cal., 18 1/2 in. VR barrel, dog leg bolt handle, checkered pistol grip stock. 94,086 were mfg. 1964-68.

Reg. cals.	$475	$365	$290	$220	$200	$180	$160
.35 Rem.	$610	$525	$370	$335	$310	$280	$260
.222 Rem.	$525	$490	$440	$400	$365	$340	$300
.223 Rem.	$1,050	$865	$735	$525	$420	$370	$340

315 Model 600s in .223 Rem. cal. were mfg.

✳ *Model 600 Montana Centennial* - 6mm Rem., 1,020 mfg. in 1964 only.

	$900	$700	$600	N/A	N/A	N/A	N/A

Last MSR was $125.

MODEL 600 MAGNUM - 6.5mm Rem. Mag. or .350 Rem. Mag. cal., laminated walnut/beech stock with or without recoil pad (early mfg. walnut stocks did not have recoil pad). Mfg. 1965-68.

	$975	$875	$775	$675	$575	$475	$425

MODEL 600 MOHAWK - .222 Rem., 6mm Rem., .243 Win., or .308 Win. cal., this variation was a promotional model, 18 1/2 in. barrel with no rib. 94,920 were mfg. 1971-79.

	$420	$340	$300	$285	$255	$235	$210

MODEL 660 STANDARD - .222 Rem., 6mm Rem., .243 Win., or .308 Win. cal., 20 in. barrel, open sight, dog leg bolt handle, checkered pistol grip stock, black pistol grip cap and forend tip. 50,536 were mfg. 1968-71.

	$525	$485	$445	$400	$365	$340	$310

Add 10% for .222 Rem. cal.

✳ *Model 660 Standard .223 Rem. cal.* - 227 total mfg. This cal. was never listed in a Remington catalog.

	$1,100	$875	$725	$600	$500	$400	$350

MODEL 660 MAGNUM - 6.5mm Rem. Mag. or .350 Rem. Mag. cal., laminated stock and recoil pad.

	$925	$735	$630	$475	$420	$365	$315

MODEL 673 GUIDE RIFLE - .300 Rem. Ultra Mag., .350 Rem. Mag., 6.5mm Rem. Mag. (new 2004) or .308 Win. (new 2004) cal., patterned after the Model 600 Magnum and features the Model Seven action, 22 in. contoured barrel with VR and iron sights, drilled and tapped, two-tone tan wide striped checkered laminate stock with solid recoil pad, 3 shot hidden mag., polished blue metal, 7 1/2 lbs. Mfg. 2003-2006.

	$745	$625	$550	$495	$440	$395	$365

Last MSR was $893.

MODEL 710 SPORTSMAN - .270 Win., .243 Win. (new 2006), .30-06, 7mm Rem. Mag. (new 2004) or .300 Win. Mag. (new 2004) cal., unique bolt to barrel lockup design utilizing 3 locking lugs on bolt face that lock directly in an integrated rear barrel design (as opposed to locking into the receiver), long action, steel (became standard 2005) or polymer receiver sleeve (disc. 2004), adj. trigger, detachable 4 shot box mag, 60 degree bolt throw, 22 in. ordnance grade steel barrel with matte

GRADING - PPGS™	100%	98%	95%	90%	80%	70%	60%

finish, grey synthetic stock with solid pad, supplied with bore sighted 3-9x40mm Bushnell Sharpshooter scope and mounts, ISS (Integrated Security System) locking bolt safety, 7 1/8 lbs. Mfg. 2001-2006.

	$360	$320	$295	$265	$250	$240	$230

Last MSR was $439.

Add $39 for limited edition Skyline Excel camo (mfg. 2004 only).

This model was also available in a Youth Model (.243 Win. cal. only, shortened LOP - includes scope, new 2006) at no extra charge.

MODEL 715 SPORTSMAN - .243 Win., .270 Win., .30-06, 7mm-08 Rem., 7mm Rem. Mag., or .300 Win. mag. cal., 22 or 24 in. blue ordnance grade barrel, black synthetic stock with molded sling swivel studs, 60 degree bolt, updated magazine latch, detachable 3-4 shot mag., no sights, Picatinny rail. New 2008.

MSR $349	$295	$265	$235	$215	$190	$170	$150

This model is available through Remington Premier dealers only.

MODEL 720A - Enfield type action, .257 Roberts, .270 Win., or .30 - 06 cal., 22 in. barrel, open sights, 5 shot, checkered pistol grip stock, 2,500 mfg. 1941-44.

	$1,325	$1,200	$995	$800	$650	$550	$450

Add 50%+ for .270 Win. cal.

Add 100%+ for .257 Roberts cal.

Most of this model was chambered for .30-06 cal.

MODEL 720 MILITARY - .257 Roberts, .270 Win., or .30-06 cal., purchased by the Dept. of Navy during 1942 and used for trophies, discernible by crossed cannon proofs on wood, approx. 100 were chambered for .270 Win. and 20 or less were chambered for the .257 Roberts. 920-1,000 mfg. 1942 only.

	100%	98%	95%	90%	80%	70%	60%
.30-06	$2,400	$2,150	$1,800	$1,575	$1,225	$1,000	$850
.270 Win.	$2,800	$2,400	$2,150	$1,800	$1,575	$1,225	$1,000
.257 Roberts	$3,650	$3,300	$2,875	$2,450	$2,150	$1,800	$1,575

MODEL 720R - similar to 720A, except with 20 in. barrel.

	$1,475	$1,150	$950	$785	$675	$570	$470

This is the rarest variation in the Model 720 Series.

MODEL 720S - similar to 720A, except with 24 in. barrel.

	$1,575	$1,175	$950	$785	$630	$525	$420

MODEL 721 - .264 Win. Mag., .270 Win., .280 Rem. (new 1960), or .30-06 cal., 24 in. barrel, open sights, 4 shot, plain pistol grip stock. Mfg. 1948-1962.

	$450	$400	$350	$300	$250	$200	$175

.280 Rem. (688 mfg.) and .264 Win. Mag. (1,115 mfg.) are rare in this model. 100% condition on these calibers could bring $700+.

MODEL 721ADL - similar to Model 721A, except has deluxe checkered stock.

	$495	$440	$395	$350	$295	$255	$210

This model's suffix does not appear on the gun. ADL features will determine the model.

MODEL 721BDL - similar to 721ADL, except has extra select wood.

	$575	$495	$450	$395	$350	$315	$290

This model's suffix does not appear on the gun. BDL features will determine the model.

MODEL 721A MAGNUM - .264 Win. Mag. or .300 H&H cal., 26 in. heavy barrel, recoil pad, 3 shot mag., 8 1/4 lbs.

	$650	$600	$550	$500	$450	$400	$350

Add 15% for .264 Win. Mag. cal.

MODEL 721ADL MAGNUM - 264 Win. Mag., similar to 721A Mag., checkered. 1,115 mfg. 1961-62, not cataloged.

	$700	$650	$600	$550	$500	$450	$400

MODEL 721BDL MAGNUM - similar to 721ADL Mag., select wood.

	$795	$750	$700	$600	$500	$450	$400

GRADING - PPGS™	100%	98%	95%	90%	80%	70%	60%

MODEL 722(A) - short action version of 721A, .222 Rem. (mfg. 1950-62), .222 Rem. Mag. (mfg. 1958-62), .243 Win. (mfg. 1960-62), .244 Rem. (mfg. 1957-62), .257 Roberts (disc. 1960), .300 Savage (disc. 1959), or .308 Win. (mfg. 1956-62) cal., 7 lbs. Mfg. 1948-62.

	$450	$400	$350	$300	$250	$200	$180

Subtract 10% for .300 Savage cal.
Add 20% for .257 Roberts or .308 Win. cal.
.222 Rem. Mag. (3,803 mfg.) and .243 Win. (2,186 mfg.) are rare in this model. Add approx. 25% to values for these cals.

MODEL 722ADL - similar to Model 722(A), except with deluxe checkered wood.

	$525	$445	$315	$290	$240	$210	$190

This model's suffix does not appear on the gun. ADL features will determine the model.

MODEL 722BDL - similar to Model 722ADL, except features extra select wood.

	$795	$750	$700	$600	$500	$450	$400

This model's suffix does not appear on the gun. BDL features will determine the model.

MODEL 725ADL - .222 Rem., .243 Win., .244 Rem., .270 Win., .280 Rem., or .30-06 cal., 22 in. barrel, open sights, 4 shot, checkered Monte Carlo stock. 16,635 mfg. 1958 - 61.

	100%	98%	95%	90%	80%	70%	60%
.30-06 cal.	$650	$600	$550	$450	$400	$375	$350
.270 Win.	$700	$575	$450	$400	$375	$350	$325
.280 Rem.	$900	$700	$525	$450	$400	$350	$325
.222 Rem.	$750	$625	$500	$450	$400	$350	$325
.244 Rem.	$800	$675	$500	$450	$400	$350	$325
.243 Win.	$800	$675	$500	$450	$400	$350	$325

Caliber mfg. breakdown is as follows: 7,657 in .30-06; 2,784 in .280 Rem.; 2,818 in .270 Win.; 840 in .244 Rem.; 1,478 in .222 Rem.; 998 in .243 Win.

MODEL 725 KODIAK - .375 H&H Mag. or .458 Win. Mag. cal., 26 in. barrel, 3 shot, recoil reducer in muzzle, deluxe checkered Monte Carlo stock, black pistol grip cap and forend tip. 52 mfg. 1961 only.

	$4,000	$3,200	$2,700	$2,250	$2,000	$1,800	$1,650

Only 24 rifles in .458 Win. Mag. were mfg. and 28 rifles in .375 H&H Mag.

MODEL 770 - .243 Win., .270 Win., .30-06, .308 Win., .300 Win. Mag., 7mm-08 Rem., or 7mm Rem. Mag. cal., matte black metal finish, Picatinny rail, 3 or 4 shot detachable mag., black synthetic stock with raised cheekpiece, includes factory mounted and bore sighted 3-9x40mm Bushnell scope, 22 or 24 in. barrel, Model 700 based action with 60 degree bolt, "R" on pistol grip cap, also available in Youth model with short LOP (.243 Win. cal. only), 8 1/2 lbs. New 2007, mfg. in Mayfield, KY.

MSR $452	$395	$340	$295	$260	$230	$200	$185

* *Model 770 Stainless* - .270 Win., .30-06, 7mm Rem. Mag., or .300 Win. Mag. cal., similar to Model 770, except has 22 or 24 in. stainless steel barrel and Realtree AP HD camo stock. New 2008.

MSR $532	$450	$395	$350	$315	$275	$250	$225

MODEL 788 - .222 Rem. (disc. 1979, reintroduced 1982-83), .22-250 Rem., .223 Rem. (new 1975), 6mm Rem. (mfg. 1969-1979), .243 Win. (new 1969), .308 Win. (new 1969), .30-30 Win. (disc. 1972), 7mm-08 Rem. (new 1980), or .44 Mag. (disc. 1970) cal., 18 1/2 (Carbine, .243 Win., .308 Win., or 7mm-08 Rem. cal.), 22 (6mm Rem., .243 Win., and .308 Win. cal.), or 24 (.222 Rem., .22-250 Rem., .223 Rem. cal. 1967-1979), .223 Rem. and .22-250 Rem. cal. 1980-83) in. barrel, short action, open sight, plain pistol grip Monte Carlo stock. Mfg. 1967-1983.

	$450	$415	$365	$325	$275	$250	$225

Add 10% for .30-30 Win. cal.
Add 15% for 7mm-08 Rem. cal.

GRADING - PPGS™	100%	98%	95%	90%	80%	70%	60%

Add 30% for .44 Mag. cal.

Add 10% for left-hand action (6mm Rem. and .308 Win. cal. only, mfg. 1969-1979).

In 1970, this gun was also manufactured with a 4X scope as a promotion, but was a non-Remington catalog item.

MODEL 798 - various cals. between .243 Win. - .458 Win. Mag., features square bridge Mauser 98 long action, 22 or 24 in. steel or stainless steel (green laminate stock only) barrel w/o sights, polished blue finish, hinged floorplate, black synthetic (Model 798 SPS, new 2008), satin walnut, Realwood walnut (Safari Grade only, new 2008), or brown or green (mfg. 2007) laminate stock, controlled round feeding with claw extractor, sporter style two position safety, 7 lbs. Importation from Zastava began 2006.

MSR $527	$450	$415	$375	$350	$325	$300	$285

Add $43 for .300 Win. Mag. or 7mm Rem. Mag. cal.

Add $443 for .375 H&H or $513 for .458 Win. Mag. cal. (26 in. barrel only).

Add $121 for satin walnut stock.

✳ *Model 798 Safari Grade* - .375 H&H or .458 Win. Mag., 22 in. heavy barrel with adj. open sights, Realwood laminated stock, front barrel band with sling swivel, drilled and tapped, 8 1/4 lbs. New 2008.

MSR $1,141	$950	$850	$750	$650	$575	$500	$450

Add $72 for .458 Win. Mag. cal.

MODEL 799 - .22 Hornet (detachable mag.), .22-250 Rem., .222 Rem., .223 Rem., or 7.62x39mm cal., features Mauser 98 short action, brown laminate stock, 20 in. barrel w/o sights, otherwise similar to Model 798. Importation began 2006.

MSR $648	$550	$475	$425	$375	$335	$295	$275

RIFLES: BOLT ACTION, MODEL 700 & VARIATIONS

MODEL 700 TITANIUM ULTIMATE LIGHTWEIGHT - .260 Rem., .270 Win., .30-06, .300 Rem. SAUM (new 2004), .308 Win. (new 2002), 7mm Rem. SAUM (new 2004), or 7mm-08 Rem cal., titanium receiver (drilled and tapped), spiral cut breech bolt with flutes and skeleton handle, 22 in. stainless steel barrel, satin stainless finish on receiver and barrel, ultra lightweight carbon-fiber matte finished Kevlar reinforced stock, 3-4 shot fixed mag., sling swivel studs, 5 1/4 - 5 1/2 lbs. Mfg. 2001-2006.

	$1,095	$925	$775	$700	$600	$500	$450

Last MSR was $1,412.

Add $40 for Rem. SAUM cals.

MODEL 700 AS - .22-250 Rem., .243 Win., .270 Win., .280 Rem., .30-06, .308 Win., 7mm Rem. Mag., or .300 Wby. Mag. cal., synthetic stock is made from Arylon resin, matte black finished stock and metal, 22 or 24 in. barrel, 6 1/2 lbs. Mfg. 1989-91 only.

	$475	$370	$310	$275	$250	$220	$195

Last MSR was $528.

Add $21 for 7mm Rem. Mag. or .300 Wby. Mag. cal.

MODEL 700 FS - .243 Win., .270 Win., .30-06, .308 Win., or 7mm Rem. Mag. cal., 22 in. polished blue barrel, grey or grey camo Kevlar fiberglass stock with solid recoil pad, iron sights, 6 1/4 lbs. Mfg. 1987-88 only.

	$530	$460	$415	$375	$335	$310	$285

Last MSR was $613.

Add $20 for 7mm Rem. Mag. cal. (24 in. barrel).

MODEL 700 TACTICAL - 6.8mm SPC cal., 20 in. parkerized barrel, synthetic stock, approx. 9 lbs. Limited availability 2005-2006.

	$795	$625	$500	$375	$335	$300	$275

Last MSR was $990.

MODEL 700 XCR TACTICAL - .223 Rem., .308 Win. or .300 Win. Mag. cal., 3-5 shot mag., features 26 in. stainless steel receiver/barrel with black TriNyte PVD coating, tactical Bell & Carlson OD Green stock with full length aluminum bedding, X-Mark Pro trigger, 9 1/8 lbs. New 2007.

	MSR $1,365	$1,145	$975	$875	$750	$650	$550	$500

* *Model 700 XCR Compact Tactical* - .223 Rem. or .308 Win. cal., similar to Model 700 XCR, except has 20 in. fluted varmint contour barrel, compact dimensions, 7 1/2 lbs. New 2008.

	MSR $1,434	$1,200	$995	$875	$775	$650	$550	$500

MODEL 700P & VARIATIONS - various cals., long or short action, various barrel lengths, designed for police/law enforcement and military, current configurations include: 700P, 700P TWS (Tactical Weapons System, includes scope, bipod and case), 700P LTR (Light Tactical Rifle), 700P LTR TWS (Light Tactical Rifle/Tactical Weapons System, includes scope, bipod, and case), and the Model M-24 (combination of Model 700 and Model 40-XB design, sniper weapon system with scope, case, and bipod).

Remington does not publish consumer retail pricing for these police/law enforcement models. Secondary prices for base models w/o scopes and other options will be slightly higher than for current pricing on the Model 700BDL Custom Deluxe. Prices for rifles with scopes and other features will be determined by how much the individual options and accessories add to the base value.

MODEL 700 RS - .270 Win., .280 Rem., or .30-06 cal., 22 in. matte finished barrel and action, grey or grey camo DuPont Rynite synthetic stock with smooth cheekpiece and solid recoil pad, iron sights, 7 1/4 lbs. Mfg. 1987-88 only.

	$550	$475	$425	$385	$350	$310	$285

Last MSR was $547.

Add 30% for .280 Rem. cal.

In 1987 less than 500 rifles were dual barrel marked - 7mm EXP REM .280 REM. These specimens will command a 40% premium.

MODEL 700 CAMO SYNTHETIC - .22-250 Rem. (disc. 1993), .243 Win., .270 Win. (disc. 1993), .280 Rem. (disc. 1993), 7mm-08 Rem. (disc. 1993), 7mm Rem. Mag., .30-06, .308 Win. (disc. 1993), or .300 Wby. Mag. (disc. 1993) cal., 22 or 24 (Mag. only) in. barrel, features synthetic stock and is fully camouflaged in Mossy Oak Bottomland pattern, iron sights, approx. 7 1/4 lbs. Mfg. 1992-94.

	$490	$425	$350	$315	$285	$265	$250

Last MSR was $581.

Add $27 for Mag. cals.

MODEL 700ADL DELUXE RIFLE - .22-250 Rem. (disc. 1991), .222 Rem. (disc.), .222 Rem. Mag. (disc.), .25-06 Rem. (disc. 1991), 6mm Rem. (disc.), .243 Win. (disc. 1997), .270 Win., .280 Rem. (disc. 1997 - marked 7mm Express 1979-82), .30-06, .308 Win. (disc. 2001), or 7mm Rem. Mag. (disc. 2002) cal., 20 (disc.), 22, or 24 in. barrel, open sights, 4 shot mag., checkered Monte Carlo stock or brown laminated stock (new 1988). Mfg. 1962-2005.

	$475	$375	$295	$250	$215	$185	$165

Last MSR was $580.

Add 5% for 7mm Rem. Mag. cal. (disc. 2002).
Add 20% for 20 in. barrel (mfg. 1962-63).
Add 50% for .222 Rem. Mag. or .280 Rem. cal. 20 in barrel.
Add 15% for 7mm Rem. Mag., .264 Win. Mag., or .300 Win. Mag. cal. with stainless steel barrel (mfg. 1962-1970).

During 1962-63, the 20 in. barrel was standard on .222 Rem., .222 Rem. Mag., .243 Win., .270 Win., .280 Rem., .30-06, or .308 Win. cal. In 1964, these cals. had a standard barrel length of 22 in.; 24 in. barrels were standard on 7mm Rem. Mag. and .264 Win. Mag. cal.

Remington, in 1987-89, introduced a Model 700 Gun Kit that enabled the owner to assemble the stock to the barreled action. All metal work is completely finished and wood finishing is all that is required. This kit was available in most popular cals. - last MSR price was $333 (1989).

GRADING - PPGS™	100%	98%	95%	90%	80%	70%	60%

✴ *Model 700ADL Deluxe Rifle Synthetic* -.22-250 Rem. (new 1999), .223 Rem., .243 Win., .270 Win., .30-06, .308 Win., .300 Win. Mag. (new 1999), or 7mm Rem. Mag., features fiberglass reinforced synthetic stock with positive checkering, black matte finish on metal, open sights, approx. 7 3/8 lbs. Mfg. 1996-2005.

	$395	$315	$260	$215	$185	$170	$155

Last MSR was $500.

     Add $27 for .300 Win. Mag. or 7mm Rem. Mag. cal.

✴ *Model 700ADL Deluxe Rifle Synthetic Youth* - .243 Win., .270 Win. (new 2004), .30-06 (new 2004), or .308 Win. cal., similar to Model 700ADL Synthetic, except has 20 in. barrel and 1 in. shorter LOP. Disc. 2005.

	$395	$315	$260	$215	$185	$170	$155

Last MSR was $500.

✴ *Model 700ADL/LS Deluxe Rifle* - .243 Win. (mfg. 1989-1993), .270 Win. (new 1989), .30-06, or 7mm Rem. Mag. (mfg. 1988-1993) cal., brown laminate stock with checkering. Mfg. 1988-1993, reintroduced 2002-2004. - .30-06 cal., features curly maple stock with ebony forend cap and pistol grip, 200th Anniversary and Remington cameo/caption laser etched on floorplate. Limited mfg. 1993 only.

	$460	$360	$280	$230	$175	$165	$155

Last MSR was $580.

     Add $27 for 7mm Rem. Mag. cal. (disc.).
This model was available through selective distributors only.

MODEL 700BDL CUSTOM DELUXE - .17 Rem. (disc. 2007), .22-250 Rem. (disc. 2007), .222 Rem. (disc. 2007), .223 Rem. (disc. 2007), .243 Win., .25-06 Rem. (disc. 2007), .264 Win. Mag. (disc.), .270 Win., .280 Rem. (mfg. 1992-95, resumed 2000-2002), .300 Savage (mfg. 1992 only), .30-06, .308 Win. (disc. 1995), .35 Whelen (mfg. 1989-94), 6mm Rem. (disc. 1994), 7mm-08 Rem. (disc. 1994, reintroduced 2000-2002), 7mm Rem. Mag., .308 Win. (left-hand only, disc. 2004), .300 Win. Mag. (disc. 2007), .300 Rem. Ultra Mag (new 1999), .338 Win. Mag. (mfg. 1988-94, resumed 1997-2002), .338 Rem. Ultra Mag. (mfg. 2000-2002, mfg. 2004 in left-hand only), .375 Rem. Ultra Mag. (mfg. 2001-2002), 7mm Rem. Ultra Mag. (mfg. 2001-2007), or 8mm Mag. (disc.) cal., 22, 24 (Magnum), or 26 (SAUM cals.) in. barrel, similar to 700ADL Deluxe, except with hinged floorplate, cut skipline checkering, black pistol grip cap and forend tip, receiver and floorplate fine line engraving was standard 1997-2001, non-embellished beginning 2002, supplied with iron sights first year, hooded ramp front sight and adj. rear sight then became standard, R3 recoil pad supplied on Mag. cals., X-Mark Pro trigger became standard 2008, approx. 7 1/4-7 5/8 lbs.

	100%	98%	95%	90%	80%	70%	60%
MSR $900	$725	$550	$425	$340	$295	$250	$225
.222 Rem. Mag.	$600	$500	$425	$340	$300	$280	$260
.350 Rem. Mag.	$800	$575	$450	$350	$325	$300	$275
6.5mm Rem. Mag.	$800	$575	$450	$350	$325	$300	$275

     Add $27 for .17 Rem., 7mm Rem. Mag., .300 Win. Mag., .338 Win. Mag., .300 Rem. Ultra Mag. or 7mm Rem. Ultra Mag. cal.
     Add $27-$67 for left-hand model (available in certain cals. only, short action .22-250 Rem. and .243 Win. cals. are scarce in left-hand, disc. 2004).
     Add 15% for 7mm Rem. Mag., .264 Win. Mag., or .300 Win. Mag. cal. with stainless steel barrel (mfg. 1962-1970).

In 1962, the 20 in. barrel was standard on .222 Rem., .222 Rem. Mag., .243 Win., .270 Win., .280 Rem., .30-06, or .308 Win. cal. In 1964, these cals. had a standard barrel length of 22 in. 24 in. barrels were standard on 7mm Rem. Mag. and .264 Win. Mag. cals.
Remington mfg. the Model 700BDL in .350 Rem. Mag. and 6.5mm Rem. Mag. (1,584 mfg. between 1969-75). 1,558 were assembled in 1969, and sold through 1975. The .350 Rem. Mag. mfg. in 1969 is 3 times rarer than the 1985 Model 700 Classic chambered for .350 Rem. Mag.

MODEL 700BDL 200th ANNIVERSARY SPECIAL EDITION

	100%	98%	95%	90%	80%	70%	60%
	$725	$650	$575	$500	$400	$300	$200

MODEL 700BDL CLASSIC (LTD EDITION) - similar to 700BDL, except has classic straight stock, high polish bluing, has been offered in .17 Rem., .220 Swift, .221 Fireball (new 2002), .222 Rem., .22-250 Rem. (Classic only), .223 Rem., .250 Savage (250/3000), 6.5x55mm Swedish, 6mm Rem. (Classic only), 7x57mm Mauser, 8mm Rem. Mag., 8mm Mauser, .243 Win. (Classic only), .25-06 Rem., .257 Roberts, .264 Win. Mag., .270 Win. (Classic only), .280 Rem., .300 Savage (new 2003), .300 Win. Mag., .300 Wby. Mag., .30-06 (Classic only), .308 Win. (new 2005), 7mm-08 Rem., 7mm Wby. Mag., .338 Win. Mag., .350 Rem. Mag., .35 Whelen, .300 H&H, or .375 H&H cal. The original Model 700 Classic was mfg. 1978-1985. Limited edition calibers were introduced during 1981 (see listings), and continued to be produced annually until 2005.

	$600	$500	$400	$325	$275	$250	$225

Last MSR was $716.

Add 10% for 7x57mm Mauser, .220 Swift, .338 Win. Mag., or .350 Rem. Mag. cal.
Add 25% for .250 Savage, .257 Roberts, .300 H&H, or .35 Whelen cal.

The Model 700 Classic was originally introduced in 1978 in .22-250 Rem., 6mm Rem., .243 Win., .270 Win., .30-06, and 7mm Rem. Mag., and was part of the standard Remington product lineup until 1985. Limited editions were introduced during 1981, and are still being produced today.

This model is produced in limited quantities of a different caliber each year. Add premiums for several calibers in NIB condition only (including 7x57mm Mauser, .257 Roberts, .300 H&H, and .375 H&H).

The following is a list of annual Limited Classic calibers offered previously with year of manufacture: 7x57mm Mauser (1981), .257 Roberts (1982), .300 H&H (1983), .250 Savage (1984), .350 Rem. Mag. (1985), .264 Win. Mag. (1986), .338 Win. Mag. (1987), .35 Whelen (1988), .300 Wby. Mag. (1989), .25-06 Rem. (1990), 7mm Wby. Mag. (1991), .220 Swift (1992), .222 Rem. (1993), 6.5x55mm Swedish (new 1994), .300 Win. Mag. (1995), .375 H&H Mag. (1996), .280 Rem. (1997), 8mm Rem. Mag. (1998), .17 Rem. (1999), .223 Rem. (2000), 7mm-08 Rem. (2001), .221 Fireball (2002), .300 Savage (2003), 8mm Mauser (2004), and .308 Win. (2005).

MODEL 700BDL DM (DETACHABLE MAG.) - .243 Win. (disc. 1999), .25-06 Rem. (disc. 1997), .260 Rem., .270 Win., .280 Rem. (disc. 1999), 6mm Rem. (disc. 1996), 7mm Rem. Mag., 7mm-08 Rem. (disc. 1999), .30-06, .308 Win. (disc. 1996), .300 Win. Mag. (disc. 2002), or .338 Win. Mag. (disc. 1996) cal., 22 or 24 in. barrel, Monte Carlo walnut stock with 20 LPI skip-line checkering, high polish bluing, black forend cap, receiver and floorplate fine line engraving was standard 1997-2001, open sights, 3-4 shot detachable mag. Mfg. 1995-2004.

	$600	$480	$390	$330	$285	$265	$250

Last MSR was $749.

Add $27 for .300 Win. Mag. and 7mm Rem. Mag. cals.
Left-hand actions on this model were disc. in 1999. Their last retail prices ranged from $665 - $692, depending on caliber.

✱ *Model 700BDL Lew Horton Special Edition* - .257 Roberts cal., 500 mfg. in 1990 only, first time the 700BDL has been offered in .257 Roberts cal.

	$575	$525	$450	$395	$360	$325	$280

Last MSR was $580.

MODEL 700BDL SS (STAINLESS SYNTHETIC) - .223 Rem. (mfg. 1993-94), .243 Win. (mfg. 1993-94), .25-06 Rem. (disc. 1994), .270 Win., .280 Rem. (disc. 1995), .30-06, .308 Win. (disc. 1994), 7mm Rem. (mfg. 1993-94), 7mm-08 Rem. (mfg. 1993-94), .300 Win. Mag. (new 1993), .300 Rem. Ultra Mag. (new 1999), .300 Rem. SA Ultra Mag. (new 2003), .300 Wby. Mag. (mfg. 1993-94), .338 Win. Mag. (mfg. 1993-94, resumed 1997-2002), .338 Rem. Ultra Mag. (new 2000), 7mm Rem. Mag., 7mm Rem. Ultra Mag. (new 2001), 7mm Rem.

GRADING - PPGS™	100%	98%	95%	90%	80%	70%	60%

SA Ultra Mag. (new 2003), 7mm Wby. Mag. (scarce, disc. 1994), .375 Rem. Ultra Mag. (mfg. 2001-2002), or .375 H&H (mfg. 1997-2002) cal., features matte finished 416 stainless steel barrel, receiver, and bolt, black synthetic stock with checkering, R3 recoil pad became standard during 2004, drilled and tapped, hinged floorplate mag., 24 or 26 (Rem. Ultra Mag. cals.) in. barrel, no sights, 6.25-7 lbs. Mfg. 1992-2004.

	$585	$470	$355	$285	$250	$215	$185

Last MSR was $735.

Add $26 for Mag. cals., except 7mm Rem. Mag.
Add $40 for Ultra Mag. or SA Ultra Mag. cals.
Add approx. $100 for .223 Rem. cal., $150 for 7mm Wby. Mag. cal.

✳ *Model 700BDL LSS* - .270 Win. (left-hand only, disc. 2000), .300 Win. Mag., .300 Rem. Ultra Mag. (new 1999), .338 Rem. Ultra Mag. (new 2000), .30-06 (left-hand only, disc. 2000), 7mm Rem. Ultra Mag., 7mm Rem. Mag., or .375 Rem. Ultra Mag. cal., stainless steel barreled action, grey tinted laminate Monte Carlo wood stock, 24 or 26 (Rem. Ultra Mag. cals.) in. barrel, w/o sights, 7 1/2 lbs. Mfg. 1996-2004.

	$660	$510	$390	$325	$280	$240	$215

Last MSR was $827.

Add $13 for Rem. Ultra Mag. cal.
Add $40 for Mag. cals. in left-hand action.

✳ *Model 700BDL SS DM (Detachable Mag.)* - .243 Win. (disc. 1997), .25-06 Rem. (disc. 2002), .260 Rem. (mfg. 1997-2000), .270 Win., .280 Rem. (disc. 2002), 6mm Rem. (disc. 1995), 7mm Rem. Mag., 7mm-08 Rem. (disc. 1998, resumed 2000-2001), .30-06, .308 Win. (disc. 1999), .300 Win. Mag., .300 Wby. Mag. (disc. 2000), or .338 Win. Mag. (disc. 1996) cal., features 3-4 shot detachable mag., stainless steel, 24 in. barrel, satin finish metalwork, R3 recoil pad became standard during 2004, black non-reflective stock with checkering, receiver and floorplate fine line engraving was standard in 1997-2001, w/o sights, 7 3/8 lbs. Mfg. 1995-2004.

	$670	$560	$460	$395	$340	$285	$240

Last MSR was $801.

Add $27 for Mag. cals.
Add $89 for muzzle brake (Model 700BDL SS DM-B, mfg. 1996-2001, available in 7mm STW, 7mm Rem. Mag. [disc. 1999] or .300 Win. Mag. cals. only).

MODEL 700BDL VARMINT SPECIAL - .22-250 Rem., .222 Rem., .223 Rem., .25-06 Rem.(disc.), 6mm Rem., .243 Win., .308 Win., or 7mm-08 Rem. cal., 24 in. heavy barrel, checkered walnut stock, no sights. Mfg. 1967-94.

	$480	$420	$350	$315	$285	$265	$250

Last MSR was $565.

✳ *Model 700VS (Varmint Synthetic)* - .220 Swift (disc. 1996), .22-250 Rem., .223 Rem., .243 Win. (mfg. 1997-98), or .308 Win. cal., short action, composite, textured black and grey synthetic stock features Kevlar, fiberglass, and graphite, matte metal finish, 26 in. heavy barrel w/o sights, 9 1/8 lbs. Mfg. 1992-2004.

	$650	$470	$410	$330	$295	$265	$250

Last MSR was $811.

Add $26 for left-hand action.
The right-hand model was disc. 1998, but resumed in 2000.

✳ *Model 700VSF Varmint Special* - .17 Rem. Fireball (new 2007), .22-250 Rem., .223 Rem., or .308 Win. cal., updated Model 700VS with VS SFII stock design in desert tan with black webbing and R3 recoil pad, 26 in. fluted heavy blue barrel, blue receiver, available in right- or left-hand action, 9 lbs. Mfg. 2005-2007.

	$925	$825	$700	$600	$525	$450	$400

Last MSR was $1,159.

Add $26 for left-hand action.

GRADING - PPGS™	100%	98%	95%	90%	80%	70%	60%

✴ *Model 700VS SF/SF-P (Varmint Synthetic Stainless Fluted/Ported)* - .220 Swift (ported barrel only until 2000), .22-250 Rem., .223 Rem. (w/o porting), .308 Win. (ported barrel only, disc. 1999) or .338 Rem. Ultra Mag. (mfg. 2000 only) cal., stainless steel action with 26 in. barrel with flutes, 2 barrel ports became an option in some cals. during 1998-99 only (Model SF-P), 8 1/2 lbs. Mfg. 1994-2004.

	$820	$600	$475	$415	$360	$300	$255

Last MSR was $976.

Add 5% for ported barrel (Model 700VS SF-P, disc. 1999).

✴ *Model 700VS SF-II Varmint Special (Varmint Synthetic Stainless Fluted)* - .17 Rem. Fireball (new 2008), .204 Ruger, .220 Swift, .22-250 Rem., or .223 Rem. cal., updated Model 700 VS SF with reconfigured H-S Precision composite stock, palm swell and contoured beavertail forend, 26 in. heavy barrel with black fluting, black synthetic stock with spruce green webbing, X-Mark Pro trigger became standard 2007, 8 1/2 lbs. New 2005.

MSR $1,284	$1,050	$915	$775	$650	$575	$500	$425

✴ *Model 700VLS (Varmint Laminated Stock)* - .204 Ruger (new 2005), .222 Rem. (mfg. 1995 only), .22-250 Rem., .223 Rem., .243 Win., 6mm Rem. (mfg. 1998-2007), .260 Rem. (disc. 1999), .308 Win., or 7mm-08 Rem. (mfg. 1997-99) cal., 26 in. heavy barrel, blue metalwork, w/o sights, brown laminated stock with (disc. 2001) or w/o skip line checkering, beavertail shaped forend became standard 1998, X-Mark Pro trigger became standard 2007, 9 3/8 lbs. New 1995.

MSR $951	$765	$650	$575	$500	$425	$375	$325

✴ *Model 700LV SF (Light Varmint Stainless Fluted)* - .204 Ruger (new 2005), .17 Rem., .221 Rem. Fireball, .223 Rem., or .22-250 Rem. cal., short action, 22 in. fluted barrel w/o sights, black composite stock with R3 recoil pad, stainless action and barrel, jeweled bolt, blind box mag., 6 3/4 lbs. Mfg. 2004-2007.

	$835	$650	$525	$425	$365	$335	$295

Last MSR was $1,040.

✴ *Model 700VL SS Thumbhole* - .204 Ruger, .22-250 Rem., or .223 Rem. cal., stainless action with 26 in. heavy stainless barrel w/o sights, 4 or 5 shot mag., X-Mark Pro trigger, brown laminated thumbhole stock with vent. beavertail forend, X-Mark Pro trigger became standard 2007, 9 1/b lbs. New 2007.

MSR $1,053	$895	$765	$650	$575	$500	$425	$375

MODEL 700 VTR - .204 Ruger, .223 Rem., .22-250 Rem., or .308 Win. cal., 22 in. barrel, OD Green overmolded stock, integrated muzzle brake design, triangular barrel fluting, X-Mark Pro trigger. New 2008.

MSR $805	$650	$550	$475	$400	$350	$300	$275

MODEL 700VS COMPOSITE - .22-250 Rem., .223 Rem., or .308 Win. cal., similar to Model 700 Sendero Composite, except is available in short action only. Mfg. by Custom Shop 1999-2000.

	$1,550	$1,225	$825	$700	$600	$550	$500

Last MSR was $1,912.

MODEL 700BDL SS CAMO RMEF - .300 Rem SA Ultra Mag. (mfg. 2003), .300 Rem. Ultra Mag. (mfg. 2001), .300 Win. Mag. (new 2004), or 7mm Rem. Ultra Mag. (mfg. 2002) cal., Realtree Hardwoods camo stock treatment, satin finished receiver and round barrel, laser engraved floorplate including RMEF logo, limited special edition for the Rocky Mountain Elk Foundation, approx. 7 1/2 lbs. New 2001-2004.

	$680	$525	$405	N/A	N/A	N/A	N/A

Last MSR was $835.

GRADING - PPGS™	100%	98%	95%	90%	80%	70%	60%

MODEL 700BDL DALE EARNHARDT JR. - .30-06 cal., 22 in. blue barrel, 4 shot mag., synthetic stock with Dale Earnhardt Jr. signature #8 logo, special ser. no. (DEJ8xxx), R3 recoil pad, no sights, drilled and tapped. Limited mfg. 2004 only.

	$675	$525	$425	N/A	N/A	N/A	N/A

Last MSR was $735.

MODEL 700 MOUNTAIN RIFLE DM (DETACHABLE MAG.) - .243 Win. (disc. 1997), .260 Rem. (new 1998), .25-06 Rem. (disc. 2002), .270 Win., .280 Rem., 7mm-08 Rem., or .30-06 cal., detachable mag., 22 in. barrel, satin finished American walnut stock, R3 recoil pad became standard on Mag. cals. during 2004, satin bluing, without sights, approx. 6 1/2 lbs. Mfg. 1995-2006.

	$685	$550	$425	$350	$300	$265	$250

Last MSR was $841.

* *Model 700 Mountain Rifle LSS (Laminated Stock Stainless)* - .260 Rem. (disc. 2007), .270 Win., .280 Rem. (new 2007), .30-06, or 7mm-08 Rem. cal., features stainless action and 22 in. barrel w/o sights, brown laminate stock, X-Mark Pro trigger became standard 2008, approx. 6 1/2 lbs. New 1999.

MSR $1,040	$875	$765	$650	$525	$450	$400	$325

MODEL 700BDL MOUNTAIN RIFLE (FIXED MAG.) - .243 Win. (new 1988), .25-06 Rem. (new 1992), .257 Roberts (new 1991), .270 Win., 7mm-08 Rem. (new 1988), .280 Rem., .30-06, .308 Win. (new 1988), or 7x57mm Mauser (new 1990) cal., 22 in. tapered barrel, checkered satin finished American walnut stock with cheekpiece and ebony forend, 4 shot mag., without sights, 6 3/4 lbs. Mfg. 1986-94.

	$445	$380	$315	$275	$250	$220	$195

Last MSR was $532.

* *Model 700BDL Mountain Rifle Stainless* - .25-06 Rem., .270 Win., .280 Rem., or .30-06 cal., 22 in. barrel, black synthetic stock with pressed checkering, blind mag., 7 1/4 lbs. Mfg. 1993 only.

	$450	$385	$315	$275	$250	$220	$195

Last MSR was $532.

MODEL 700BDL EUROPEAN - .243 Win., .270 Win., .280 Rem., 7mm-08 Rem., 7mm Rem. Mag., .30-06, or .308 Win. cal., Monte Carlo stock with hand-rubbed oil finish, 22 or 24 (Mag. cals. only) in. barrel, hinged floorplate, iron sights, approx. 7 1/4 lbs. Disc. 1994.

	$445	$375	$325	$280	$250	$220	$195

Last MSR was $532.

Add $27 for 7mm Rem. Mag. cal.

MODEL 700CDL - various cals. between .223 Rem. - .35 Whelen, classic style checkered walnut stock with satin finish, black forend tip and pistol grip cap, satin blue or high polish (new 2008, select cals. only) metal finish, Supercell (high polish only) or R3 recoil pad standard, 24 or 26 (Mag. cals.) in. barrel w/o sights, integral extractor, hinged floorplate, X-Mark Pro trigger, approx. 7 1/2 lbs. New 2004.

MSR $931		$795	$665	$565	$475	$425	$335	$300

Add $26 for Mag. cals.
Add $26 for left-hand action (select cals. only, new 2005).

This model was also manufactured in .204 Ruger cal. as part of a Friends of NRA limited edition - 1,050 were manufactured. Values can vary significantly depending on locality and perceived desirability.

GRADING - PPGS™	100%	98%	95%	90%	80%	70%	60%

✴ *Model 700CDL SF Limited* - .17 Rem. Fireball (mfg. 2007), .260 Rem. (new 2008) or .30-06 (mfg. 2006) cal., 24 in. stainless fluted barrel, checked satin finished walnut stock, black forend tip and pistol grip cap, engraved floorplate, commemorates the 100th anniversary of the .30-06 (disc.) or the new .17 Rem. Fireball (new 2007), drilled and tapped, X-Mark Pro trigger became standard 2007. Limited mfg. by caliber beginning 2006.

MSR $1,100	$895	$765	$660	$575	$500	$425	$350

✴ *Model 700CDL SF (Stainless Fluted)* - .17 Rem. Fireball (disc.), .257 Wby. Mag. (new 2008), .270 Win., .270 WSM, .7mm-08 Rem., 7mm Rem. Mag., .30-06, or .300 WSM cal., 3-4 shot mag., 24 or 26 (.30-06 cal. only) in. stainless fluted barrel, satin finished checkered walnut stock and forearm, R3 recoil pad, X-Mark Pro trigger, approx. 7 1/2 lbs. New 2007.

MSR $1,065	$875	$750	$650	$575	$500	$425	$350

Add $27 for Mag. cals. or $47 for WSM cals.

✴ *Model 700 CDL "Boone & Crockett" Series* - .243 Win., .270 Win., .270 WSM, .30-06, 7mm-08 Rem., 7mm Rem. Mag., .300 WSM, or .300 Win. Mag. cal., 24 or 26 in. fluted blue barrel, brown laminate stock, "Boone & Crockett" medallion insert on grip cap, "Boone & Crockett" laser engraved on barrel, X-Mark Pro trigger. New 2008.

MSR $959	$800	$725	$650	$575	$525	$450	$375

Add $26 for regular Mag. cals. or $66 for WSM cals.

This model is offered through Remington Premier dealers only.

MODEL 700 SENDERO - .25-06 Rem., .270 Win. (disc. 2001), .300 Win. Mag., or 7mm Rem. Mag. cal., similar to Model 700 VS, except has long action for Mag. cals., 24 (non-cataloged) or 26 in. barrel, 9 lbs. Mfg. 1994-2002.

	$635	$510	$420	$335	$295	$265	$250

Last MSR was $788.

Add $27 for Mag. cals.
Add approx. $100 for fluted barrel (not cataloged).

✴ *Model 700 Sendero Special SF (Stainless Fluted)* - .25-06 Rem. (disc. 2002), .300 Win. Mag., .300 Wby. Mag. (mfg. 1997-2001), .300 Rem. Ultra Mag. (new 1999), .300 Rem SA Ultra Mag. (new 2003), .338 Rem. Ultra Mag. (new 2000), 7mm STW (mfg. 1997-2002), 7mm Rem. Mag., 7mm Rem. Ultra Mag. (new 2001), or 7mm Rem. SA Ultra Mag. (new 2003) cal., 26 in. varmint type fluted barrel, approx. 8 1/2 lbs. Mfg. 1996-2004.

	$835	$640	$475	$415	$360	$300	$255

Last MSR was $1,003.

✴ *Model 700 Sendero Special SF-II* - .264 Win. Mag., .300 Win. Mag., .300 Rem. Ultra Mag., 7mm Rem. Mag., or 7mm Rem. Ultra Mag. cal., 3-4 shot mag., stainless steel action and 24 or 26 in. fluted heavy barrel, black H-S-Precision synthetic stock with grey webbing and full length aluminum bedding, X-Mark Pro trigger became standard 2007, 8 1/2 lbs. New 2006.

MSR $1,311	$1,050	$925	$825	$725	$625	$525	$425

MODEL 700 SENDERO COMPOSITE - .25-06 Rem., .300 Win. Mag., or 7mm STW cal., features 26 in. composite barrel, matte black finished steel action, Kevlar reinforced black synthetic stock, 7 7/8 lbs. Mfg. 1999 only.

	$1,395	$1,125	$750	$650	$575	$525	$475

Last MSR was $1,665.

MODEL 700 LSS - .257 Wby. Mag. cal., 26 in. stainless steel barrel, black laminate stock, adj. X-Mark Pro trigger, SuperCell recoil pad. New 2008.

MSR $972	$840	$735	$650	$575	$525	$450	$375

This model is available through Remington Premier dealers only.

GRADING - PPGS™	100%	98%	95%	90%	80%	70%	60%

MODEL 700 ALASKAN Ti - .25-06 Rem., .270 Win., .270 WSM, .280 Rem., 7mm-08 Rem., 7mm Rem. Mag., .30-06, .300 WSM, .300 Win. Mag., or .308 Win. (disc. 2007) cal., titanium receiver with spiral cut flutes, lightweight fluted stainless 24 in. barrel w/o sights, black pillar bedded Bell & Carlson synthetic stock with MaxxGuard finish and R3 recoil, X-Mark Pro trigger, 3-4 shot mag., hinged floorplate, approx. 6 1/4 lbs. New 2007.

MSR $2,159	$1,725	$1,475	$1,225	$1,000	$875	$800	$725

    Add $26 for 7mm Rem. Mag. and .300 Win. Mag., or $122 for WSM cals.

MODEL 700 ETRONX VS SF - .220 Swift (electronic primer), .22-250 Rem. (electronic primer), or .243 Win. (electronic primer) cal., features patented Etronx technology utilizing an electronic discharge for virtually instant cartridge ignition, CPU located in stock incorporates standard 9V battery, and allows electric signal to be passed through a ceramic coated firing pin, which in turn activates the specially designed electronic primer. There are no moving parts in this system, and therefore, nothing to delay ignition. Electronic trigger mechanism enables almost zero lock time. LED on top of grip indicates system status (fire or safe mode), chamber status (loaded or not loaded), low battery indicator, and any possible system malfunction. 26 in. heavy stainless steel barrel with black flutes, alumiunum bedding, Kevlar reinforced composite stock with matte black finish, 8 7/8 lbs. Mfg. late 1999-2003.

	$1,150	$950	$750	$640	$535	$450	$390

    Last MSR was $1,332.

This model can fire only Etronx ammunition which used an electronic primer. Remington still manufactures Etronx ammunition in .22-250 Rem. and .220 Swift only.

Because the Etronx ignition system used an electronic primer the same size as a standard rifle primer, reloading was no different than using standard cases, powder, and bullets. The only thing that changed was the electronic primer. Ammunition is now scarce, but Etronx primers are still available from Remington.

MODEL 700 SPS (SPECIAL PURPOSE SYNTHETIC) - various cals., standard or Youth synthetic stock with Supercell or R3 recoil pad, X-Mark Pro trigger on Youth model, approx. 7 3/8 lbs. New 2005, mfg. in Ilion, NY.

MSR $620	$495	$445	$390	$340	$310	$270	$230

    Add $33 for .270 or .300 WSM cals.

This model is available in a Youth variation in cals. .243 Win., .270 Win., 7mm-08 Rem., .30-06 or .308 Win. at no extra charge.

✳ *Model 700 SPS DM* - .243 Win., .270 Win., .30-06, 7mm-08 Rem., 7mm Rem. Mag. or .300 Win. Mag. cal., features detachable mag., X-Mark Pro trigger, otherwise similar to Model SPS. New 2005.

MSR $649	$515	$460	$400	$350	$315	$270	$235

✳ *Model 700 SPS Stainless* - various cals., features stainless steel barreled action, synthetic stock with R3 (disc. 2007) or Supercell (new 2008) recoil pad, X-Mark Pro trigger standard 2008, approx. 7 1/4 lbs. New 2005.

MSR $729	$585	$500	$440	$385	$325	$275	$235

    Add $35 for WSM cals.

✳ *Model 700 SPS Varmint* - .17 Rem. Fireball, .204 Ruger, .22-250 Rem., .223 Rem., .243 Win. or .308 Win. cal., features 26 in. heavy barrel, matte metal finish, black synthetic stock with vent. beavertail forend, X-Mark Pro trigger, approx. 8 1/2 lbs. New 2007.

MSR $663	$525	$460	$400	$350	$315	$270	$235

    Add $26 for left-hand action (new 2008, not available in .204 Ruger).

✳ *Model 700 SPS Buckmasters Edition* - .243 Win., .270 Win., .30-06, .300 Win. Mag., 7mm-08 Rem., or 7mm Rem. Mag. cal., 3 or 4 shot mag., 20-26 in. barrel, engraved floorplate with Buckmasters logo, Realtree Hardwoods camo stock, also available in Youth, R3 recoil pad, approx. 7 1/8 lbs. New 2007.

MSR $687	$540	$465	$400	$350	$315	$270	$235

GRADING - PPGS™	100%	98%	95%	90%	80%	70%	60%

❋ *Model 700 SPS Tactical* - .223 Rem. or .308 Win. cal., 20 in. heavy contour barrel, black oxide finish, black synthetic overmolded Hogue stock, laser engraved "Tactical" on barrel, X-Mark Pro trigger. New 2008.

MSR $681	$575	$525	$450	$415	$380	$330	$295

This model is available through Remington Premier dealers only.

MODEL 700 XCR (XTREME CONDITIONS RIFLE) -

- .25-06 Rem. (new 2007), .270 Win., .270 WSM, .30-06, 7mm Rem. Mag., .300 WSM, .300 Win. Mag., 7mm Rem. Ultra Mag., 7mm-08 Rem. (new 2007), .300 Rem. Ultra Mag., .338 Rem. Ultra Mag., .338 Win. Mag., .375 H&H, or .375 Rem. Ultra Mag., 24 or 26 in. stainless steel barrel with TriNyte corrosion control, patented black Hogue overmolded stock with R3 recoil pad, X-Mark Pro trigger, approx. 7 1/2 lbs. New 2005.

MSR $1,065	$865	$665	$560	$500	$450	$400	$350

Add $27 for Mag. cals. or $76 for WSM cals.

Add $27 for left-hand action (available in .270 Win., .30-06, .300 Rem. Mag., or .300 Rem. Ultra Mag., new 2008).

❋ *Model 700 XCR RMEF* - 7mm Rem. Mag. (disc.), 7mm Rem. Ultra Mag. (new 2008), .300 Rem. Ultra Mag. (mfg. 2007), or .300 WSM (mfg. 2006) cal., features RMEF camo Realtree Hardwood HD (disc. 2006) or AP (new 2007) camo overmolded stock with R3 recoil pad, X-Mark Pro trigger became standard 2007. New 2005.

MSR $1,199	$950	$825	$675	$575	$500	$425	$375

Subtract approx. 10% for 7mm Rem. Mag. cal.

MODEL 700 CUSTOM KS MOUNTAIN RIFLE -

.270 Win., .280 Rem., .300 Win. Mag., .300 Wby. Mag. (new 1989), .300 Rem. Ultra Mag. (new 1999), .30-06, .338 Win. Mag. (new 1986), .338 Rem. Ultra Mag. (new 2000), .35 Whelen (new 1989), 7mm STW (new 1999), 7mm Rem. Mag., 7mm Rem. Ultra Mag. (new 2001), 8mm Rem. Mag. (new 1986), .375 Rem. Ultra Mag. (new 2001), or .375 H&H cal., 22 (disc.), 24 or 26 (Ultra Mag. cal.s only) in. carbon steel barrel, no sights, features extra lightweight Kevlar fiber-reinforced stock, available in either right- or left-hand action, 6 3/8 - 7 lbs. Mfg. 1986-2004, reintroduced 2006.

MSR $1,453	$1,175	$925	$800	$700	$600	$500	$450

Add $80 for left-hand action.

This model is available from the Custom Shop only (special order).

❋ *Model 700 Custom KS Mountain Rifle Stainless* - similar to Model 700 Custom KS Mountain Rifle, except has stainless steel action and barrel. Mfg. 1995-2004, reintroduced 2006.

MSR $1,657	$1,300	$1,075	$875	$750	$675	$600	$525

Add $80 for left-hand action.

❋ *Model 700 Custom KS Mountain Rifle Wood Grained Kevlar* - similar to Model 700 Custom KS Safari Grade, except has wood grained Kevlar stock. Mfg. 1992-93.

	$1,000	$875	$750	$650	$550	$485	$430

Last MSR was $1,109.

Add $63 for left-hand action.

MODEL 700 SAFARI GRADE -

.375 H&H, 8mm Rem. Mag. (new 1986), .416 Rem. Mag. (new 1989), or .458 Win. Mag. cal., heavier 700BDL barrel, 3 shot mag., 24 in. barrel, available with either Classic or Monte Carlo stock configuration, custom shop special order only, 9 lbs. Mfg. 1962-2000.

	$1,015	$800	$595	$440	$415	$385	$330

Last MSR was $1,225.

Add $73 for left-hand model (Classic stock only).

GRADING - PPGS™	100%	98%	95%	90%	80%	70%	60%

✱ *Model 700 Safari Grade Custom KS* - 8mm Rem. Mag., .375 H&H, .416 Rem. Mag., or .458 Win. Mag. cal., stock made from Aramid fiber or Kevlar (disc.) and fiberglass, 24 in. barrel with barrel band, including sling swivel, adj. safari sights, blind floorplate, 9 lbs. Mfg. 1989-2004, reintroduced 2006.

MSR $2,780	$2,325	$2,000	$1,750	$1,500	$1,250	$1,050	$900

   Add $80 for left-hand model (disc.).

✱ *Model 700 Safari Grade Custom KS Stainless* - .375 H&H, .416 Rem. Mag., or .458 Win. Mag. cal., features fiberglass and Aramid or Kevlar (disc.) stock and stainless steel action. Mfg. 1993-2004, reintroduced 2006.

MSR $3,000	$2,500	$2,125	$1,850	$1,550	$1,300	$1,050	$900

MODEL 700 ABG (AFRICAN BIG GAME) - .375 H&H, .375 Rem. Ultra Mag., .416 Rem. Mag., or .458 Win. Mag. cal., straight line 3 shot detachable box mag., checkered brown laminate stock with right-hand cheekpiece, open sights, matte blue finished steel receiver, 26 in. barrel with barrel band and safari sights, custom shop special order only, 9 1/2 lbs. Mfg. 2001-2004, reintroduced 2006.

MSR $3,147	$2,625	$2,175	$1,850	$1,550	$1,325	$1,100	$975

MODEL 700 APR (AFRICAN PLAINS RIFLE) - .300 Win. Mag., .300 Wby. Mag., .300 Rem. Ultra Mag. (new 1999), .338 Win. Mag., .338 Rem. Ultra Mag. (new 2000), .375 H&H, 7mm Rem. Mag, 7mm STW (by request only, ltd. mfg.), 7mm Rem. Ultra Mag. (new 2001), or .375 Rem. Ultra Mag. (new 2001) cal., 3 shot, custom shop variation with 26 in. custom shop barrel, satin finish metal and brown, pressure laminated, checkered wood stock with satin finish and buttpad, machined steel triggerguard and floor plate, 7 3/4 lbs. Mfg. 1994-2004, reintroduced 2006.

MSR $2,780	$2,325	$2,000	$1,750	$1,500	$1,250	$1,050	$900

MODEL 700 AWR (ALASKAN WILDERNESS RIFLE) - .300 Win. Mag., .300 Wby. Mag., .300 Rem. Ultra Mag. (new 1999), .338 Win. Mag., .338 Rem. Ultra Mag. (new 2000), .375 H&H, 7mm STW (new 1998), 7mm Rem. Mag., 7mm Rem. Ultra Mag. (new 2001), or .375 Rem. Ultra Mag. (new 2001) cal., black synthetic fiberglass with Kevlar stock, black stainless steel action with Teflon coating, approx. 7 lbs. Mfg. 1994-2004, reintroduced 2006-2007.

	$1,475	$1,250	$1,000	$875	$750	$650	$550

Last MSR was $1,761.

   Add $80 for left-hand action.

MODEL 700 AWR II (ALASKAN WILDERNESS RIFLE) - varous cals., black TriNyte full length stock with aluminum bedding block, adj. Model 40-X trigger, machined stainless steel trigger guard and floorplate, fluted barrel. New 2008.

MSR $3,427	$2,850	$2,400	$1,995	$1,650	$1,450	$1,225	$1,050

MODEL 700 NORTH AMERICAN CUSTOM - various cals., short or long action, blue steel or stainless steel fluted barrel, composite stock with full length aluminum bedding block, Model 40-X adj. trigger, machined steel trigger guard and floorplate. New 2008.

MSR $2,856	$2,375	$2,050	$1,775	$1,500	$1,250	$1,050	$900

   Add $214 for stainless steel action and barrel.

MODEL 700C GRADE (CUSTOM SHOP) - various standard and Mag. cals., from custom shop, no engraving, deluxe checkered Monte Carlo C grade wood stock with rosewood forearm cap, high polish finish, BDL style trigger guard and hinged floorplate, 24 or 26 in. steel barrel, blued high polished action, 7 1/2 lbs. Mfg 1964-1983, 2003-2004, reintroduced 2006.

MSR $3,141	$2,625	$2,175	$1,850	$1,550	$1,325	$1,100	$975

GRADING - PPGS™	100%	98%	95%	90%	80%	70%	60%

MODEL 700D PEERLESS GRADE (CUSTOM SHOP) - scroll engraving, best wood. Mfg. 1962-83.

	$2,000	$1,625	$1,400	$1,175	$900	$800	$700

MODEL 700F PREMIER GRADE (CUSTOM SHOP) - elaborate engraving, best wood. Mfg. 1962-83.

	$3,450	$2,850	$2,500	$2,200	$2,035	$1,870	$1,760

MODEL 700 CUSTOM GRADE - special order only, grades differ in amount of engraving and type of walnut. Available as a custom order only through Remington. Values reflect 1991 information. The Remington Custom Shop should be contacted for a current price quotation and the availability of options.

Special order Model 700s mfg. between early ´60s-1982 were designated C Grade, D Grade, or F Grade. Values will approximate Custom Grade Models I-III listed. In 1991, Remington discontinued Custom Grade Model designations.

⁎ *Model 700 Custom Grade Model I* - mfg. 1983-91.

	$1,200	$1,000	$795	$690	$585	$485	$415

Last MSR was $1,314.

⁎ *Model 700 Custom Grade Model II* - mfg. 1983-91.

	$1,995	$1,675	$1,295	$1,145	$935	$815	$650

Last MSR was $2,335.

⁎ *Model 700 Custom Grade Model III* - mfg. 1983-91.

	$2,900	$2,150	$1,750	$1,540	$1,265	$1,055	$875

Last MSR was $3,650.

⁎ *Model 700 Custom Grade Model IV* - mfg. 1983-91.

	$4,875	$4,100	$2,950	N/A	N/A	N/A	N/A

Last MSR was $5,695.

MODEL 700 CUSTOM RIFLE - the Remington Custom Shop should be contacted directly (see Trademark Index) for current information regarding this model. New 1992.

MSR POR	N/A	$3,000	$2,500	$1,500	$1,000	$850	$725

Beginning 1992, Remington stopped Custom Grade Model designations in favor of individualized quotations per work order.

The Custom Shop should be contacted directly regarding special order pricing for this model (see Trademark Index). The last published MSR on this model was $3,999 (2007).

RIFLES: BOLT ACTION, MODEL 40X & VARIATIONS

MODEL 40X SPORTER - .22 LR cal. only, sporterized version of the 40X Target Rifle, 5 shot mag., custom 700 stock, a special order only gun from the factory. Rare, less than 700 mfg. 1969-77, parts clean-up to 1980.

	$3,000	$2,300	$1,800	$1,700	$1,600	$1,475	$1,300

Add 10% if NIB.

This model was last listed in the 1977 Remington catalog - retail was $525.

MODEL 40X TARGET RIFLE (RANGEMASTER) - .22 LR cal., 28 in. heavy barrel, Redfield Olympic sights, scope bases, target stock, rubber butt, first production rifle with built in bedding device and adjustment screws, 12 3/4 lbs. Mfg. 1956-64.

	$800	$700	$600	$525	$450	$375	$325
No sights	$750	$650	$550	$475	$400	$350	$300

MODEL 40X STANDARD BARREL (RANGEMASTER) - similar to 40X Target Rifle, with lighter barrel, 10 3/4 lbs.

	$550	$475	$380	$310	$250	$220	$190
No sights	$495	$450	$360	$295	$240	$200	$180

GRADING - PPGS™	100%	98%	95%	90%	80%	70%	60%

MODEL 40X CENTERFIRE (RANGEMASTER) - similar to Model 40X Rim Fire, except in .222 Rem., .222 Rem. Mag., .30-06, or .308 Win. cal. Mfg. 1961-64.

		$550	$475	$380	$310	$250	$220	$190
No sights		$495	$450	$360	$295	$240	$200	$180

MODEL 40-XB RANGEMASTER RIMFIRE - .22 LR cal., bolt action single shot, 28 in. light or heavy barrel, no sights, target stock with guide rail, rubber butt. Mfg. 1964-74.

	$575	$525	$420	$335	$275	$220	$195

MODEL 40-XB RANGEMASTER CENTERFIRE - available in 18 cals. between .22 BR Rem. and .300 Rem. Ultra Mag., custom made, 27 1/4 in. barrel (current production is stainless steel action and barrel), single shot or repeater (5 shot mag.), walnut stock, test fired, right- or left-hand action, 10 1/2 -11 1/4 lbs. Mfg. by Custom Shop. New 1964.

MSR $2,487	$2,050	$1,750	$1,500	$1,250	$995	$750	$600

Add $197 for repeater model.

An International Free Rifle was also offered - only 107 were mfg. with premiums being paid.

MODEL 40-XBBR - similar to Model 40-XB Rangemaster Centerfire, except single shot only, 20 or 24 in. barrel.

	$1,300	$1,150	$975	$800	$650	$500	$450

Add $125 for 2 oz. trigger.

MODEL 40-XB KS (KEVLAR STOCK) - 18 short action cals. between .22 BR Rem. - .300 Rem. Ultra Mag., 27 1/4 in. bright finished stainless steel barrel w/o sights, drilled and tapped, single shot or repeater, black finish Aramid fiber/Kevlar stock w/cheekpiece, right- or left-hand action, no sights, 9 3/4 - 10 1/4 lbs. Mfg. by Custom Shop. Mfg. 1987-2005, reintroduced 2007.

MSR $2,780	$2,350	$1,995	$1,700	$1,475	$1,200	$975	$775

Add $147 for repeater model.

Add approx. $200 for 2 oz. trigger.

MODEL 40-XBBR KS - similar to Model 40-XB KS, except is bench rest model and single shot, 10 1/2 lbs. Mfg. by Custom Shop. New 1987.

MSR $3,806	$3,300	$2,900	$2,200	$1,800	$1,400	$1,100	$900

MODEL 40-XC KS - .223 Rem. (mfg. 1995-99) or .308 Win. cal., 24 in. stainless steel barrel w/o sights, National Match Course 5 shot repeater rifle, adj. trigger pull, adj. comb, drilled and tapped, wood (disc. 1989) or fiberglass with Kevlar (standard 1990) stock, 11 lbs. Disc. 2004, reintroduced 2006.

MSR $3,000	$2,550	$2,175	$1,775	$1,425	$1,150	$925	$800

Subtract approx. $120 for wood stock.

MODEL 40-XB TACTICAL - .308 Win. cal., repeater action with adj. 40-X trigger, aluminum bedding block, 27 1/4 in. button rifled fluted stainless barrel, Teflon coated metal, matte black H-S Precision synthetic tactical stock with vertical pistol grip, 10 1/4 lbs. New 2004.

MSR $2,927	$2,500	$2,150	$1,775	$1,425	$1,150	$925	$800

MODEL 40-XB/XS - .308 Win. cal., 27 1/4 in. stainless steel barrel, repeater action, Teflon coated synthetic H-S Precision stock, XS Model includes Leuplod scope, Harris bipod, and case, mfg. by the Custom Shop.

Remington does not publish consumer retail pricing for this police/law enforcement model. Secondary prices for base models w/o scopes and other options will be similar to the Model 40-XB Tactical listed above. Prices for rifles with scopes and other features will be determined by how much the individual options and accessories add to the base value.

GRADING - PPGS™	100%	98%	95%	90%	80%	70%	60%

MODEL 40-XRBR KS RIMFIRE SINGLE SHOT - .22 LR cal., 24 in. heavy stainless barrel, no sights, adj. buttplate and palm stop, target wood (disc. 1989) or fiberglass with Kevlar (became standard 1990, and was available only in benchrest configuration) stock, Remington green standard beginning 2007, approx. 9 3/4 lbs. Mfg. 1974-2004, reintroduced 2007.

MSR $2,927	$2,500	$2,150	$1,775	$1,425	$1,150	$925	$800

Subtract 20% for wood stock.

MODEL 40-XR KS SPORTER - .22 LR or .22 Mag. cal., Model 40-XR action, match chambered, custom sporter contoured 24 in. barrel, fiberglass with Kevlar stock, drilled and tapped receiver, w/o sights, special order. Mfg. 1994-99.

	$1,375	$1,100	$750	$625	$550	$500	$450

Last MSR was $1,638.

MODEL 40-XB THUMBHOLE - available in 18 centerfire cals. between .22 BR Rem. - .300 Rem. Ultra Mag, 27 1/4 in. heavy stainless barrel w/o sights, single shot or repeater action, drilled and tapped, two-tone laminated satin finished thumbhole stock with rollover cheekpiece, 11 3/4 lbs. New 1999.

MSR $2,780	$2,350	$1,995	$1,700	$1,475	$1,200	$975	$775

Add $147 for repeater action (new 2000).

MODEL 40-XR CUSTOM SPORTER - .22 LR or .22 Win. Mag. (new 2000) cal., repeater action, top-of-the-line sporter from the custom shop, individually made per customer's specifications. Disc. 2006, reintroduced 2008.

MSR $4,391	$3,750	$3,075	$2,500	$1,975	$1,625	$1,325	$1,100

MODEL 40-XR CUSTOM SPORTER HIGH GRADES - .22 LR cal. only, single shot, available on special order from Remington's Custom Shop only, Grades I-IV (disc. 1991) increase by amount of engraving, quality of wood, and other special order options and features. Mfg. 1986-1991.

Values for Custom Grades listed reflect 1991 (the year of discontinuance) price information. The Remington Custom Shop should be contacted directly regarding current values and options.

✳ *Model 40-XR Custom Sporter High Grade Model I* - mfg. 1986-91.

	$1,100	$925	$795	$690	$580	$485	$415

Last MSR was $1,314.

✳ *Model 40-XR Custom Sporter High Grade Model II* - mfg. 1986-91.

	$1,995	$1,675	$1,295	$1,150	$935	$815	$650

Last MSR was $2,335.

✳ *Model 40-XR Custom Sporter High Grade Model III* - mfg. 1986-91.

	$2,900	$2,150	$1,750	$1,540	$1,265	$1,055	$875

Last MSR was $3,650.

✳ *Model 40-XR Custom Sporter High Grade Model IV* - mfg. 1986-91.

	$4,875	$4,100	$2,950	$2,650	$2,350	$2,000	$1,750

Last MSR was $5,695.

SHOTGUNS: O/U

100% values listed for Model 3200s assume NIB condition - subtract 10%-15% if without box, warranty card, and original shipping container (with packing materials).

MODEL 32 - 12 ga., double lock action, DT (early mfg.) or SST (standard 1938), separated barrels, 26, 28, or 30 in. barrels without rib, SR, or VR. Approx. 6,050 mfg. (ser. range approx. 0001-6,053) 1931-1947. There is a discrepancy as to when serialization started on this model.

	N/A	$2,000	$1,800	$1,500	$1,000	$800	$700

Add 10% for SST.
Add 10% for vent. or solid rib.
Add 20% for VR on 28 in. barrels.

Model 32 serialization is as follows: 1932 - 1-903; 1933 - 904-948; 1934 - 949-1,727; 1935 - 1,728-2,610; 1936 - 2,611-3,259; 1937 - 3,260 - 3,755; 1938 - 3,756-3,958; 1939 - 3,959-4,202; 1940 - 4,203-4,425; 1941 - 4,426-4,741; 1942 - 4,742 - 5,020; 1943 - 5,021-5,031; 1944 - 5,032-5,049; 1945 to 1947 - 5,050-6,053.

GRADING - PPGS™	100%	98%	95%	90%	80%	70%	60%

MODEL 32D TOURNAMENT

	100%	98%	95%	90%	80%	70%	60%
	$3,750	$3,000	$2,500	$2,000	$1,750	$1,400	$1,175

MODEL 32E EXPERT - less than 35 mfg.

	$4,500	$3,950	$3,500	$2,975	$2,650	$2,200	$1,875

MODEL 32F PREMIER

	$6,500	$5,500	$5,000	$4,500	$3,520	$2,750	$2,300

Note: Grades differ in quality, grade of wood, and amount of engraving.

MODEL 32 SKEET - similar to 32A, with 26 or 28 in. (more desirable) skeet bored barrels, SST. Mfg. 1932-42.

	N/A	$2,000	$1,800	$1,500	$1,000	$800	$700

Add 10% for VR.
Add 10%-15% for 28 in. barrels.

MODEL 32TC TARGET - similar to 32A, with 30 or 32 in. VR full choke barrels, trap style stock. Mfg. 1932-42.

	$3,000	$2,300	$1,800	$1,700	$1,600	$1,475	$1,300

Add 10% for 30 in. VR barrels.

MODEL 300 IDEAL - 12 ga. only, 3 in. chambers, boxlock action, features unique forearm latching system that incorporates barrel selector switch, 26, 28, or 30 in. 8mm VR barrels with twin beads and Rem Chokes (3), engraved receiver sides, gold SST, high polish blue, checkered satin finished American walnut stock and forearm with English style solid recoil pad, 7 3/8 - 7 7/8 lbs. Mfg. 2000-2001.

	$1,150	$995	$875	$800	$750	$700	$650

Last MSR was $1,332.

MODEL 332 - 12 ga. only, 3 in. chambers, new modified boxlock action with underlock custom shop design, low profile receiver with Model 32 type styling, engraved frame panels, 26, 28, or 30 in. 8mm VR light contour monobloc barrels with Rem Chokes, glass-bead blasted black oxide metal finish with resembles Model 32 rust bluing, high gloss finished checkered walnut stock and slim forearm with solid rubber recoil pad, mechanical SST, ejectors, 7 1/2 - 8 lbs. Mfg. in Ilion late 2001-2006.

	$1,425	$1,075	$925	$775	$625	$550	$475

Last MSR was $1,759.

* *Model 332 Engraved* - introduced 2004.

  ❖ **Model 332 D Grade (Peerless)**

	$3,150	$2,200	$1,500	N/A	N/A	N/A	N/A

Last MSR was $4,184.

  ❖ **Model 332 F Grade (Premier)**

	$6,300	$4,550	$2,975	N/A	N/A	N/A	N/A

Last MSR was $7,706.

  ❖ **Model 332 F Grade w/gold inlays (Premier Gold)** - top-of-the-line Custom Shop model.

	$9,375	$5,300	$3,575	N/A	N/A	N/A	N/A

Last MSR was $11,122.

MODEL 396 SKEET/SPORTING CLAYS - 12 ga. only, satin finished boxlock action with engraved sideplates, 28 or 30 in. barrels with 10mm VR and Rem Chokes, select checkered walnut stock and target style forend, Sporting Clays Model has ported barrels, SST, ejectors, approx. 7 1/2 lbs. Mfg. 1996-98.

* *Model 396 Skeet*

	$1,750	$1,475	$1,250	$1,075	$925	$800	$700

Last MSR was $1,993.

GRADING - PPGS™	100%	98%	95%	90%	80%	70%	60%

* Model 396 Sporting Clays

	$1,875	$1,575	$1,300	$1,100	$950	$825	$725

Last MSR was $2,126.

MODEL 3200 FIELD - 12 ga., 26, 28, or 30 in. barrels, VR, various chokes, box-lock, auto ejectors, single selective trigger, checkered pistol grip stock, separated barrels. Mfg. 1973-77.

	$1,100	$1,000	$950	$900	$850	$800	$750

During 1998-2000, the custom shop once again manufactured a limited amount of the Model 3200 from existing parts (parts cleanup).

Model 3200s with shorter barrels (26 or 28 in.) and open choking are more desirable than 30 in. tubes bored F/M.

MODEL 3200 serialization is as follows: 1973 - 4,200-16,667; 1974 - 16,668-27,393; 1975 - 27,394-35,303; 1976 - 35,304-39,216; 1977 - 39,217-41,432; 1978 - 41,433-42,813; 1979 - 42,814-44,278; 1980 - 44,279-45,504; 1981 - 45,505-45,974; 1982 - 45,975-47,200; 1983 - 47,201-47,308.

MODEL 3200 MAGNUM - 12 ga., 3 in. chambers, 30 in. heavy wall barrels (steel shot compatible), less than 1,000 mfg. 1975-77.

	$1,695	$1,575	$1,475	$1,200	$1,050	$950	$850

MODEL 3200 SKEET - similar to 3200 Field, with 26 or 28 in. skeet bored barrels, skeet style stock. Mfg. 1973-80.

	$1,295	$1,050	$950	$850	$750	$650	$575

28 in. barrels will command a premium on this model.

This model was also mfg. in a 28 in. IM/F configuration with gold pigeon on bottom for live pigeon shooting. Since less than 300 were mfg., prices in the $2,700 range are being asked if NIB condition. This model generally had a trap style rib, but there have been some field ribs as well. Originally, it was called the "Competition Live Pigeon" and was mfg. with a competition receiver and trap grade style wood.

* Model 3200 Skeet Competition Four Ga. Set - includes 12, 20, 28 ga., or .410 bore, cased. Mfg. 1980-83.

	$5,500	$5,000	$4,600	$4,200	$4,000	$3,800	$3,500

Add 10%-15% for 28 in. barrels.

28 in. barrels will command a premium on this model.

MODEL 3200 COMPETITION SKEET - similar to 3200 Skeet, with scroll engraved frame and trigger guard, select wood. Mfg. 1976-83.

	$1,700	$1,450	$1,250	$995	$950	$850	$750

Add 10%-15% for 28 in. VR barrels.

MODEL 3200 TRAP - similar as 3200 Field, with 30 or 32 in. barrels choked IM/F or F/F, stock and rib. Mfg. 1973-77.

	$1,375	$1,100	$950	$875	$800	$750	$700

30 in. barrels are more desirable than 32 in.

MODEL 3200 SPECIAL TRAP - similar to 3200 Trap, except fancy wood. Mfg. 1973-80.

	$1,450	$1,300	$1,200	$1,000	$875	$800	$750

MODEL 3200 COMPETITION TRAP - similar to 3200 Trap, with scroll engraving. Mfg. 1976-83.

	$1,950	$1,800	$1,675	$1,450	$1,200	$950	$875
Pigeon Grade	$2,450	$2,150	$1,850	$1,500	$1,250	$995	$900

The Pigeon Grade featured a gold pigeon on receiver bottom - approx. 250 mfg. 1979-83. There was a special production of this model during 1991-92 which was limited to approx. 100 guns.

GRADING - PPGS™	100%	98%	95%	90%	80%	70%	60%

MODEL 3200 PREMIER - 12 ga., sold through Remington's International Division, 500 mfg. 1975 only, patterned after "One of 1000" series, regular or Monte Carlo stock.

	100%	98%	95%	90%	80%	70%	60%
	$2,900	$2,500	$2,150	$1,800	$1,500	$1,200	$1,025

Add 125% for engraving (only 116 mfg., engraving was done in Belgium).

MODEL 3200 "ONE OF 1000" - limited edition, elaborate engraving, fancy wood, supplied with hard case, made in both skeet and trap models. Mfg. 1,000 each model: 1973 (Trap) and 1974 (Skeet).

	100%	98%	95%	90%	80%	70%	60%
Trap (30 IM/F or F/F)	$2,150	$1,750	$1,475	$1,325	$1,200	$1,075	$875
Skeet (26 or 28 in. SK/SK)	$1,925	$1,675	$1,475	$1,325	$1,200	$1,075	$875

Add 10% for 28 in. barrels on the Skeet Model.

PEERLESS FIELD GRADE - 12 ga. only, 3 in. chambers, 26, 28, or 30 in. VR barrels with Rem Chokes, boxlock with engraved sideplates, SST, ejectors, high-gloss checkered walnut stock and forearm with vent. recoil pad, 3.28 milliseconds lock time, blue metal, approx. 7 1/2 lbs. Mfg. 1993-98.

	100%	98%	95%	90%	80%	70%	60%
	$1,000	$900	$850	$800	$750	$700	$650

Last MSR was $1,172.

This model is an entirely new design not sharing any parts with either the Models 32 or 3200.

PREMIER FIELD MODEL - 12, 20, or 28 ga., 3 in. chambers, 26 or 28 in. 7mm VR barrels, nickel finished receiver with game scene engraving, boxlock action, gold trigger, satin finished deluxe walnut stock with Schnabel forearm, solid recoil pad, SST, ejectors, includes hard case, 6 1/2 - 7 3/4 lbs. New 2006, imported from Italy.

	100%	98%	95%	90%	80%	70%	60%
MSR $2,086	$1,850	$1,575	$1,325	$1,125	$975	$850	$725

Add $42 for 28 ga.

* *Premier Model Competition STS* - 12 ga., similar to Premier Model, 28, 30, or 32 (new 2008) in. VR barrels, titanium PVD finished receiver, 10mm target type VR with five extended choke tubes, high gloss wood finish, barrel selector on tang safety, approx. 7 1/2 lbs. New 2006.

	100%	98%	95%	90%	80%	70%	60%
MSR $2,540	$2,200	$1,925	$1,650	$1,450	$1,275	$1,050	$850

Add $350 for adj. comb (new 2007).

* *Premier Model Upland Special* - similar to Premier Field Model, except has color case hardened receiver with gold game scene engraving and oil finished wood. New 2006.

	100%	98%	95%	90%	80%	70%	60%
MSR $2,226	$1,950	$1,650	$1,375	$1,125	$975	$850	$725

Add $42 for 28 ga.

* *Premier Ruffed Grouse* - 20 ga., 3 in. chambers, 26 in. vent. rib blue barrels, features two 14 Kt. ruffed grouse gold inlays on each side of frame, oil finished straight grip walnut stock, 6 3/4 lbs.

	100%	98%	95%	90%	80%	70%	60%
MSR $2,380	$2,050	$1,700	$1,400	$1,125	$975	$850	$725

SHOTGUNS: SxS

The author wishes to express thanks to Charles Semmer for once again updating the following section on older Remington SxS Shotguns.

Because E. Remington & Sons shotguns are classified as antique, it may be helpful to consult the "NRA Antique Condition Standards" section in the front of this text to convert to the Percentage Grading System listed.

For Remington serialization, please refer to the Serialization section.

MODEL 1873 "HAMMER LIFTER" - 10 or 12 ga., also known as Whitmore Hammer Lifter, 28 or 30 in. decarbonized, twist, or damascus barrels, top "thumb lever" action activated by pushing upward to open, rib top marked "E. REMINGTON & SONS, ILION, N.Y.", patented "AUG. 8, 1871, APRIL 16, 1872", steel buttplate, pistol grip was optional, grades above 3 were made to order. Approx. 5,000 mfg. from 1873-78, starting with ser. no. 1.

100%	98%	95%	90%	80%	70%	60%	50%	40%	30%	20%	10%

✻ *Model 1873 "Hammer Lifter" Grade 1* - decarbonized steel barrels, no checkering or engraving.

| $2,200 | $1,900 | $1,500 | $1,200 | $1,100 | $900 | $700 | $575 | $425 | $300 | $250 | $225 |

✻ *Model 1873 "Hammer Lifter" Grade 2* - twist steel barrels, checkering, no engraving.

| $3,100 | $2,700 | $2,400 | $1,800 | $1,500 | $1,200 | $1,075 | $875 | $750 | $550 | $350 | $275 |

✻ *Model 1873 "Hammer Lifter" Grade 3* - twist or damascus steel barrels, checkering and engraving.

| $4,600 | $4,400 | $3,800 | $2,800 | $1,800 | $1,500 | $1,375 | $1,200 | $875 | $650 | $450 | $350 |

Add 10%-20% to Grade 3 prices for higher grades (extra fine engraving).

MODEL 1875 AND 1876 "LIFTER" (WHITMORE LIFTER) - 10 or 12 ga., 28 or 30 in. decarbonized, twist, or damascus barrels, top "thumb lever" action activated by pushing upward to open, rib top marked "E. REMINGTON & SONS, ILION, N.Y.", patented "AUG. 8, 1871, APRIL 16, 1872", steel buttplate, pistol grip was optional, the Model 1875 started with ser. no. 1, and went to approx. 3,350, the Model 1876 started with ser. no. 3,350 and went to approx. 5,900. Approx. 5,900 Model 1875s and 1876s were mfg. 1875-1882.

✻ *Model 1875/1876 "Lifter" Grade 1* - decarbonized steel barrels, no checkering or engraving.

| $2,200 | $1,900 | $1,500 | $1,200 | $1,100 | $900 | $700 | $575 | $425 | $300 | $250 | $225 |

✻ *Model 1875/1876 "Lifter" Grade 2* - twist steel barrels, checkering, no engraving.

| $2,500 | $2,300 | $1,800 | $1,500 | $1,200 | $1,100 | $900 | $750 | $650 | $500 | $350 | $275 |

✻ *Model 1875/1876 "Lifter" Grade 3* - twist or damascus steel barrels, checkered and engraving.

| $4,300 | $4,000 | $3,500 | $3,000 | $1,600 | $1,400 | $1,100 | $1,000 | $750 | $600 | $500 | $400 |

✻ *Model 1875/1876 "Lifter" Grade 4* - twist or damascus steel barrels, checkered and extra fine engraving.

| $5,000 | $4,600 | $3,800 | $2,900 | $2,400 | $1,900 | $1,500 | $1,200 | $1,000 | $700 | $600 | $450 |

✻ *Model 1875/1876 "Lifter" Grade 5* - damascus steel barrels, checkered and superior engraving.

| $5,500 | $5,000 | $4,200 | $3,600 | $3,000 | $2,400 | $1,800 | $1,400 | $1,150 | $900 | $700 | $500 |

Add 100% to the few Model 1873s and 1875s that are rib marked "NEW YORK & LONDON".

Add 100% for double rifles and combination guns in Models 1873, 1875, and 1876.
There were very few double rifles and combination guns made in Models 1873, 1875, and 1876 - they are very rare, and be aware of fake double rifles.

MODEL 1878 HAMMER (HEAVY DUCK GUN) - 10 ga., called the Heavy Duck Gun, 30-32 in., 9 3/4 and 10 lbs., "thumb-lever" action, thick bolsters, top extension rib, no flash fences, steel buttplate. Approx. 2,500 mfg. from 1878-82, starting with ser. no. 1.

✻ *Model 1878 Hammer Grade 1* - decarbonized steel barrels, no checkering, no engraving.

| $2,200 | $1,900 | $1,500 | $1,200 | $1,100 | $900 | $700 | $575 | $425 | $300 | $250 | $250 |

✻ *Model 1878 Hammer Grade 2* - twist steel barrels, checkered, no engraving.

| $2,500 | $2,300 | $1,800 | $1,500 | $1,200 | $1,100 | $900 | $750 | $650 | $500 | $375 | $300 |

✻ *Model 1878 Hammer Grade 3* - laminated steel barrels, checkered, engraved.

| $5,000 | $4,600 | $3,800 | $2,900 | $2,400 | $1,900 | $1,500 | $1,200 | $1,000 | $700 | $600 | $450 |

✻ *Model 1878 Hammer Grade 4* - damascus steel barrels, checkered, extra fine engraving.

| $5,500 | $4,500 | $4,200 | $3,600 | $3,000 | $2,400 | $1,800 | $1,400 | $1,150 | $900 | $650 | $600 |

MODEL 1879 SxS HAMMER - some 10 ga., usually 12 ga., top extension rib, no flash fences, steel buttplate, only Whitmore model with Deeley & Edge forend catch. Ser. nos. within the Model 1878.

Add 40% for this scarce variation to Model 1878 listed prices.

100%	98%	95%	90%	80%	70%	60%	50%	40%	30%	20%	10%

MODEL 1882 SxS HAMMER - (includes the unique Model 1883), 10 or 12 ga., 30 or 32 in. decarbonized, twist or damascus steel barrels, rib marked "E. REMINGTON & SONS, ILION, N.Y.", typical top lever, all grades have checkered pistol grip and forend with various designs according to grade. All contain Deeley & Edge forend catch. Approx. 16,000 Model 1882s, possibly 1,000 Model 1883s were mfg. from 1882-88. Started with ser. no. 1,000.

* *Model 1882 SxS Hammer Grade 1* - decarbonized steel barrels, no enraving, steel buttplate.

$1,800	$1,500	$1,300	$1,100	$1,000	$800	$700	$600	$450	$300	$250	$200

* *Model 1882 SxS Hammer Grade 2* - twist steel barrels, no engraving, steel buttplate.

$1,900	$1,650	$1,500	$1,200	$1,100	$900	$800	$675	$550	$375	$275	$225

* *Model 1882 SxS Hammer Grade 3* - laminated steel barrels, engraved, steel buttplate.

$2,200	$2,000	$1,700	$1,500	$1,200	$1,100	$900	$750	$650	$450	$350	$250

* *Model 1882 SxS Hammer Grade 4* - damascus steel barrels, engraved, steel buttplate.

$3,200	$2,600	$2,200	$1,700	$1,500	$1,200	$1,000	$850	$700	$550	$400	$300

* *Model 1882 SxS Hammer Grade 5* - fine damascus steel, finely engraved, superior rubber buttplate.

$4,300	$3,800	$3,200	$2,700	$2,500	$2,100	$1,700	$1,400	$1,100	$900	$650	$500

* *Model 1882 SxS Hammer Grade 6* - extra fine damascus, fine scroll engraved, superior rubber buttplate.

$6,900	$6,300	$5,500	$4,500	$3,900	$3,300	$3,100	$2,700	$2,000	$1,300	$1.100	$900

Add 25% for optional auxiliary rifle barrel insert.

MODEL 1883 - identified by its hammer shape which is different that the Model 1882.

Add 50% to the values for this model.

MODEL 1885/1887 SxS HAMMER - 10, 12, or 16 ga., different hammer style variation of the Model 1882, 28, 30, or 32 in. decarbonized, twist or damascus steel barrels, rib marked "E. REMINGTON & SONS, ILION, N.Y.", top lever, all grades are checkered pistol grip and forend with various designs according to grade, Deeley & Edge forend catch, rubber buttplate with ERS logo. Approx. 7,000 mfg. from 1885-88. Ser. nos. started at 16,700. Guns before ser. no. 20,200 are considered Model 1885s, ser. nos. after are Model 1887s.

* *Model 1885/1887 SxS Hammer Grade 1* - decarbonized steel barrels, no engraving.

$1,800	$1,500	$1,300	$1,100	$1,000	$800	$700	$600	$450	$300	$250	$200

* *Model 1885/1887 SxS Hammer Grade 2* - twist steel barrels, no engraving.

$1,900	$1,650	$1,500	$1,200	$1,100	$900	$800	$675	$550	$375	$300	$225

* *Model 1885/1887 SxS Hammer Grade 3* - damascus steel barrels, no engraving.

$2,300	$2,000	$1,700	$1,500	$1,200	$1,100	$900	$750	$650	$450	$350	$250

* *Model 1885/1887 Hammer Grade 4* - damascus steel barrels, engraved.

$3,200	$2,600	$2,200	$1,800	$1,500	$1,300	$1,100	$900	$800	$675	$500	$400

* *Model 1885/1887 SxS Hammer Grade 5* - fine damascus steel barrels, finely engraved.

$4,400	$3,800	$3,300	$2,900	$2,600	$2,400	$2,000	$1,600	$1,300	$1,000	$900	$500

* *Model 1885/1887 SxS Hammer Grade 6* - extra fine damascus barrels, fine scroll engraved.

$6,900	$6,300	$5,800	$5,000	$4,500	$4,000	$3,500	$2,800	$2,000	$1,500	$1,200	$900

* *Model 1885/1887 SxS Hammer Grade 7* - superior damascus barrels, extra fine scroll engraved, game scene.

$10,000	$9,500	$8,800	$8,000	$7,500	$6,800	$6,000	$4,800	$4,200	$3,400	$2,200	$1,100

Add 25% for optional auxiliary rifle barrel insert.
Add 30% for 16 ga.

100%	98%	95%	90%	80%	70%	60%	50%	40%	30%	20%	10%

MODEL 1889 SxS HAMMER - 10, 12, or 16 ga., 28, 30, or 32 in., a few 26 in. are known. Decarbonized, twist, or damascus barrels, exposed "circular" hammers, rib marked "REMINGTON ARMS CO. ILION, N.Y. U.S.A.", top lever, all grades have checkered pistol grip and forend with various designs according to grade, Deeley & Edge forend catch. Grade number is stamped on water table left of the ser. no. Rubber buttplate with RACo logo. 134,200 mfg. 1889-1908. Ser. range from 30,000 to 100,000. After the year 1900, ser. nos. are in the 200,000 range.

✳ *Model 1889 SxS Hammer Grade 1* - decarbonized steel barrels, no engraving.

100%	98%	95%	90%	80%	70%	60%	50%	40%	30%	20%	10%
$1,900	$1,650	$1,500	$1,200	$1,100	$900	$800	$675	$550	$375	$275	$225

✳ *Model 1889 SxS Hammer Grade 2* - twist steel barrels, no engraving.

$2,200	$2,000	$1,700	$1,500	$1,200	$1,100	$900	$750	$650	$450	$350	$250

✳ *Model 1889 SxS Hammer Grade 3* - damascus steel barrels, no engraving.

$2,400	$2,200	$1,900	$1,700	$1,400	$1,200	$1,000	$850	$750	$550	$400	$300

✳ *Model 1889 SxS Hammer Grade 4* - damascus steel barrels, engraved.

$4,400	$3,800	$3,200	$2,700	$2,500	$2,100	$1,700	$1,400	$1,100	$900	$650	$500

✳ *Model 1889 SxS Hammer Grade 5* - damascus steel barrels, finely engraved.

$6,900	$6,300	$5,500	$4,500	$3,900	$3,300	$3,100	$2,700	$2,000	$1,300	$1,100	$875

✳ *Model 1889 SxS Hammer Grade 6* - extra fine damascus barrels, fine scroll engraved.

$10,000	$9,500	$8,800	$8,000	$7,500	$6,800	$6,000	$4,800	$4,200	$3,400	$2,200	$1,100

✳ *Model 1889 SxS Hammer Grade 7* - superior damascus barrels, extra fine scroll engraved, game scene.

$20,000	$18,750	$15,000	$11,000	$9,800	$8,500	$7,300	$6,000	$4,800	$3,850	$2,750	$1,600

Add 20% for 16 ga.

Grades 4 through 7 may command higher values. To date, there are only 22 examples known of these engraved Model 1889 hammer guns - nine Grade 4s, five Grade 5s, four Grade 6s, and four Grade 7s.

MODEL 1894 SxS HAMMERLESS - 10, 12, or 16 ga., 26 to 32 in. "Remington", "Ordnance", or Damascus steel barrels, auto ejectors, boxlock, double triggers, checkered pistol grip or straight stock, Purdey forend snap. Grades A, B, F, and C have RACo hard rubber butt, Grade D, horn butt, Grade E, horn or heel and toe plates. Grade is usually stamped on the water table. 16 and especially 10 ga., are considered scarce and will command a higher value. 41,194 mfg. between 1894-1910 in the 100,000 block serial range.

✳ *Model 1894 SxS Hammerless Grade AE* - no engraving.

$1,900	$1,650	$1,500	$1,200	$1,100	$900	$800	$675	$550	$400	$300	$250

✳ *Model 1894 SxS Hammerless Grade BE* - scroll and line engraving.

$3,800	$3,500	$3,000	$2,700	$2,400	$2,000	$1,700	$1,200	$900	$600	$500	$375

✳ *Model 1894 SxS Hammerless Grade FE Trap* - scroll and line engraving.

$3,800	$3,500	$3,000	$2,700	$2,400	$2,000	$1,700	$1,200	$900	$600	$500	$375

✳ *Model 1894 SxS Hammerless Grade CE* - extra scroll engraving, silver name plate.

$5,600	$5,400	$5,000	$4,500	$4,000	$3,600	$3,000	$2,400	$1,800	$1,100	$700	$600

✳ *Model 1894 SxS Hammerless Grade DE* - fine scroll and game engraving, silver name plate.

$12,000	$11,000	$9,000	$8,400	$7,800	$7,200	$6,000	$4,800	$3,600	$2,200	$1,800	$1,100

✳ *Model 1894 SxS Hammerless Grade EE* - finest quality scroll, bird and game engraving, gold name plate.

$23,000	$21,500	$18,000	$14,500	$12,000	$9,600	$8,400	$7,800	$6,000	$3,850	$2,750	$2,300

Add 15% to CE and BE guns that are extractor only.
Add 25% for "Ordnance" barrels.

A few Remington SPECIAL grade guns were produced; they are so rare, it is not practical to attempt a value.

100%	98%	95%	90%	80%	70%	60%	50%	40%	30%	20%	10%

MODEL 1900 SxS HAMMERLESS - 12 or 16 ga., 28 or 30 in. "Remington" or damascus steel barrels, lower priced gun to meet market competition, quality a cut below the Model 1894, but mechanically the same, snap forend. No engraving was offered on this model. 98,475 mfg. between 1900-10 in the 300,000 block serial range.

   * *Model 1900 SxS Hammerless Grade K and KD* - Remington or Damascus steel barrels, non-ejector.

100%	98%	95%	90%	80%	70%	60%	50%	40%	30%	20%	10%
$1,500	$1,375	$1,250	$1,150	$1,000	$875	$750	$650	$500	$375	$250	$200

   * *Model 1900 SxS Hammerless Grade KE and KED* - Remington or damascus steel barrels, ejectors.

100%	98%	95%	90%	80%	70%	60%	50%	40%	30%	20%	10%
$1,650	$1,500	$1,375	$1,250	$1,150	$1,000	$875	$750	$650	$500	$350	$250

PARKER AHE - while advertised, the Remington re-issue of the original Parker AHE Model was never mfg. due to product liability considerations. Older Remington manufactured Parkers may be found in the Parker section.

PARKER AAHE - please refer to the Parker Brothers section.

GRADING - PPGS™	100%	98%	95%	90%	80%	70%	60%

PREMIER - 12, 20, 28 ga. or .410 bore, 2 3/4 (28 ga.) or 3 in. chambers, Anson & Deeley boxlock action, ejectors, gold SST, 27 (28 ga. or .410 bore) or 28 in. polished blue barrels with choke tubes, single bead sights, case colored receiver, oil finished walnut stock, semi beavertail forend, Remington "R" logo in gold on bottom of frame, gold woodcock inlaid on each side of receiver, three different frame sizes, 6 1/2 - 7 1/2 lbs. Limited mfg. 2007, imported from Spain.

			100%	98%	95%	90%	80%	70%	60%
			$1,850	$1,575	$1,325	$1,125	$975	$850	$725

Last MSR was $2,086.

     Subtract $56 for 12 or 20 ga.

   * *Premier Upland Special* - 28 ga. or .410 bore, features 27 in. polished blue barrels with Rem Chokes, similar to Premier, except has straight grip English style stock, 6 1/2 lbs. Limited mfg. 2007.

			100%	98%	95%	90%	80%	70%	60%
			$1,850	$1,575	$1,325	$1,125	$975	$850	$725

Last MSR was $2,086.

SHOTGUNS: SEMI-AUTO, DISC.

REMINGTON AUTOLOADING SHOTGUN (PRE-MODEL 11) - 12 ga. only, original Remington mfg. of the Browning A-5, 5 shot, magazine cutoff, left side of the receiver has BROWNING trademark with a portrait of John Browning engraved on it, barrels were marked "Browning Arms Company St. Louis, MO (choke) Special Steel" and "Gauge 2 3/4 in. or 3 in." on three lines, various grades, 20 (riot), 26, or 28 in. plain or matted rib barrel. Mfg. 1905-1910.

			$395	$350	$275	$225	$175	$160	$135

     Add 20% for matted rib.

MODEL 11A AUTOLOADER 5-SHOT - 12, 16 (introduced 1931), or 20 (introduced 1930) ga., 26-32 in. barrels, takedown, various chokes, Browning type, checkered pistol stock. Approx. 300,000 mfg., 1911-48.

	100%	98%	95%	90%	80%	70%	60%
Plain barrel	$295	$240	$215	$185	$165	$150	$120
Solid rib	$395	$315	$235	$200	$185	$165	$140
Vent. rib	$440	$360	$335	$305	$275	$220	$165

     Add 35% for barrels marked "Long Range" - beware of fakes.

This model was mfg. under patent agreement with John Browning.

MODEL 11B SPECIAL - higher grade wood with hand checkered stock and forearm.

			$1,200	$1,075	$950	$825	$700	$650	$600

GRADING - PPGS™	100%	98%	95%	90%	80%	70%	60%

MODEL 11D TOURNAMENT

| | $1,500 | $1,300 | $1,100 | $950 | $825 | $700 | $650 |

MODEL 11E EXPERT

| | $3,000 | $2,750 | $2,500 | $2,250 | $2,000 | $1,800 | $1,600 |

MODEL 11F PREMIER

| | $3,950 | $3,550 | $3,100 | $2,750 | $2,500 | $2,150 | $1,850 |

Note: Grades differ in quality, grade of wood, and amount of engraving.

MODEL 11R - 12 ga. only, similar to Model 11A, except has 20 in. cylinder bore barrel, 4 shot mag. Mfg. circa 1920s.

| | $325 | $265 | $235 | $200 | $150 | $120 | $100 |

SPORTSMAN MODEL SEMI-AUTO - 12, 16, or 20 ga., 26 (3 shot only) in. barrel, skeet choke, beavertail forend. Mfg. 1931-49.

	100%	98%	95%	90%	80%	70%	60%
Plain barrel	$325	$275	$250	$195	$165	$140	$120
Solid rib	$400	$350	$300	$250	$200	$180	$150
Vent. rib	$470	$415	$360	$330	$275	$250	$220

This model was manufactured in Field, Riot, and Skeet configurations.

MODEL 48 MOHAWK (SPORTSMAN) - 12, 16, or 20 ga., 26, 28, or 32 in. barrels, 3 shot, mechanical (solid breech) ejection system, various chokes, rounded receiver, checkered pistol grip stock with cap. Approx. 275,000 mfg., 1949-60.

	100%	98%	95%	90%	80%	70%	60%
	$300	$225	$200	$185	$175	$165	$140
VR barrel	$325	$275	$250	$200	$175	$165	$140

MODEL 48B SELECT

| | $420 | $360 | $310 | $290 | $245 | $220 | $195 |

MODEL 48D TOURNAMENT

| | $1,500 | $1,300 | $1,100 | $950 | $825 | $700 | $650 |

MODEL 48F PREMIER

| | $3,950 | $3,550 | $3,100 | $2,750 | $2,500 | $2,150 | $1,850 |

MODEL 48A RIOT GUN - 12 ga. only, 20 in. plain barrel.

| | $275 | $220 | $195 | $165 | $150 | $140 | $110 |

MODEL 48SA SKEET - 26 in. barrel, skeet bore, ivory bead. Mfg. 1949-60.

	100%	98%	95%	90%	80%	70%	60%
	$305	$275	$255	$230	$210	$195	$165
With VR barrel	$395	$350	$300	$260	$230	$210	$195

MODEL 48SC SKEET - "C" suffix designates C-grade wood.

| | $495 | $450 | $375 | $325 | $285 | $250 | $225 |

MODEL 48SD TOURNAMENT - custom shop engraved.

| | $1,500 | $1,300 | $1,100 | $950 | $825 | $700 | $650 |

MODEL 48SF PREMIER - custom shop engraved.

| | $3,950 | $3,550 | $3,100 | $2,750 | $2,500 | $2,150 | $1,850 |

MODEL 11-48 SEMI-AUTO - 12, 16, 20, 28 (introduced 1952) ga., or .410 (introduced 1954) bore, recoil operated action, walnut stock. Approx. 429,000 mfg., 1949-68.

	100%	98%	95%	90%	80%	70%	60%
Plain barrel	$300	$225	$200	$185	$175	$165	$140
VR barrel	$325	$275	$250	$200	$175	$165	$140

Add 25%-60% for 28 ga. or .410 bore, depending on condition.

MODEL 58ADL "SPORTSMAN - 58" SEMI-AUTO - 12, 16, or 20 ga., 26, 28, or 30 in. barrel, gas operation, various chokes, 3 shot, checkered pistol grip stock, scroll game scene engraved. Approx. 271,000 mfg., 1956-63.

	100%	98%	95%	90%	80%	70%	60%
Plain barrel	$275	$250	$220	$195	$140	$120	$110
VR barrel	$360	$305	$275	$250	$220	$165	$140

Add 5% for Magnum in 12 ga.

GRADING - PPGS™	100%	98%	95%	90%	80%	70%	60%

MODEL 58 X-SERIES (SUNGRAIN) - similar to Model 58ADL semi-auto, except has blonde stock, available in Field (special order only), Skeet, or Trap configuration.

	$395	$350	$300	$250	$175	$160	$140

MODEL 58BDL - similar to 58ADL, with select wood.

	100%	98%	95%	90%	80%	70%	60%
Plain barrel	$295	$275	$250	$225	$210	$195	$165
VR barrel	$375	$335	$300	$275	$250	$200	$175

MODEL 58SA SKEET GUN - similar to 58ADL, with 26 in. skeet bore VR barrel, skeet stock.

	$450	$400	$350	$300	$275	$250	$200

MODEL 58SC SKEET - "C" suffix designates C-grade wood.

	$550	$500	$440	$415	$385	$330	$305

MODEL 58D TOURNAMENT - custom shop engraved.

	$1,500	$1,300	$1,100	$950	$825	$700	$650

MODEL 58F PREMIER - custom shop engraved.

	$3,950	$3,550	$3,100	$2,750	$2,500	$2,150	$1,850

Note: Models differ in grade of wood, amount of engraving, and gold inlays.

MODEL 878A "AUTOMASTER" - 12 ga. gas operated semi-auto, 26, 28, or 30 in. barrels, action similar to Model 58. Approx. 62,000 mfg., 1959-1962.

	$265	$235	$200	$185	$170	$160	$150

Add 10% for VR.

Barrels on this model are interchangeable with those on the Model 58.

SHOTGUNS: SEMI-AUTO, CURRENT/RECENT PRODUCTION

MODEL SP-10 - 10 ga., 3 1/2 in. chamber, semi-auto stainless steel gas system operation, lighter recoil than most 12 ga. Mags., 30 in. barrel with 3/8 in. VR and Rem Chokes (2), checkered stock and forearm with low gloss satin finish, matte metal finish, crossbolt safety, R3 recoil pad became standard 2004, supplied with camo sling, approx. 11 lbs. Introduced 1989.

MSR $1,727	$1,375	$1,150	$975	$875	$775	$675	$575

Add $365 (factory MSR) per extra Model SP-10 barrel.

The first 5,000 SP-10s were assigned special serialization (LE89 prefix) - no premiums exist at this time, however.

This model is NOT a re-designed Ithaca Mag-10 and the parts are NOT interchangeable. The SP-10 is a new design.

✳ *Model SP-10 Camo* - 23 (Turkey Model, mfg. 1999-2000, reintroduced 2007 with Williams Firesights), or 26 in. VR barrel, choice of Mossy Oak (disc. 1996), full coverage Mossy Oak Break-Up (mfg. 1997-2004), full coverage Mossy Oak Obsession or Duck Blind (new 2007), regular or thumbhole (Turkey only) stock, R3 recoil pad (became standard 2005), or Bottomland (mfg. 1994-96) camo finish. New 1993.

MSR $1,981	$1,500	$1,150	$975	$875	$775	$675	$575

Add $9 for Magnum Waterfowl with 100% Mossy Oak Duck Blind camo and special waterfowl choke tubes (new 2007).

Add $110 for Turkey Magnum with 100% Mossy Oak Obsession camo and thumbhole stock (new 2007).

Subtract 10% for disc. camo finishes.

✳ *Model SP-10 Magnum Synthetic* - features lightweight black synthetic stock and forearm, matte non-reflective metal finish, 26 in. barrel only, 10 3/4 lbs. Mfg. 2000-2004.

	$995	$875	$785	$675	$575	$550	$475

Last MSR was $1,331.

GRADING - PPGS™	100%	98%	95%	90%	80%	70%	60%

✳ *Model SP-10 Turkey Camo NWTF 25th Anniversary* - 12 ga., limited mfg. to commemorate the 25th Anniversary of the NWTF during 1998, Truglo fiberoptic sights. Mfg. 1998 only.

	$1,050	$925	$775	N/A	N/A	N/A	N/A

Last MSR was $1,225.

✳ *Model SP-10 Turkey Combo* - includes choice of either 26 or 30 VR regular barrel and extra 22 in. deer barrel with rifle sights. Mfg. 1991-94.

	$1,295	$1,125	$925	$775	$700	$650	$625

Last MSR was $1,132.

MODEL 11-96 EURO LIGHTWEIGHT - 12 ga. only, steel receiver with distinctive slight hump over chamber, 26 or 28 in. 6mm VR Rem Choke barrel, checkered walnut stock and forearm, receiver panel engraving, approx. 7 lbs. Mfg. 1996 only.

	$715	$615	$550	$475	$395	$335	$295

Last MSR was $852.

MODEL 105 CTi - 12 ga. only, 3 in. chamber, skeletonized titanium receiver with carbon fiber shell, gas operated, 4 shot mag., TriNyte receiver coating, bottom feed and ejection, overbored 26 or 28 in. carbon fiber VR barrel with three ProBore chokes, rotary bolt lock-up, checkered walnut stock with rate reduction recoil system (up to 50% reduction), target grade roller sear trigger, R3 recoil pad, utilizing oil filled cylinder in stock, includes hardshell case, 7 lbs. New 2006.

MSR $1,548		$1,225	$1,000	$875	$775	$675	$600	$525

Shotguns: Semi-Auto, Model 1100 & Variations

3 in. shells (12 or 20 ga.) may be shot in Magnum receivers only, regardless of what the barrel markings may indicate (the ejection port is larger in these Magnum models with "M" suffix serialization). Model 1100 serial numbers on the receiver started with the number 1001. All but the early guns also have a prefix letter. All Model 1100 Remington shotguns were serial numbered in blocks of numbers. Each serial number has a suffix and the following indicates the meaning: V = 12 ga. standard, M = 12 ga. Mag., W = 16 ga., X = 20 ga., N = 20 ga. Mag., K = 20 ga. lightweight, U = 20 ga. lightweight Mag., J = 28 ga., H = .410 bore.

Add $877 for custom shop Etchen stock and forearm installed on new Model 1100s (new 2000).

SPORTSMAN 12 AUTO - 12 ga. only, 2 3/4 in. chamber, 28 or 30 in. VR barrel, similar to Model 1100 action, hardwood stock and forearm, 7 3/4 lbs. Mfg. 1985-86 only.

	$300	$260	$220	$195	$170	$160	$150

Last MSR was $405.

Add 10% for Rem Chokes (mfg. 1986 only).

MODEL 1100 FIELD - 12 (disc. 1987), 16 (mfg. 1964-1980), or 20 (new 1964) ga., 26, 28, or 30 in. barrels, various chokes, gas operated, checkered pistol grip stock and forearm, "cut" checkering and receiver scroll markings became standard in 1979, Rem Chokes became standard 1987 (introduced 1986 as $40 option), VRs became standard in 1985 on this model, 20 ga. lightweight frame became standard 1972, prices assume VR and Rem Chokes. Mfg. 1963-1988.

	$350	$295	$265	$225	$200	$185	$170

Last MSR was $545.

Add 25% for 16 ga.
Subtract $40 if without VR.
Subtract $45 if without Rem Chokes.

The Model 1100 20 ga. Standard (12 ga. frame) was disc. in 1969 (mahogany wood stock and forearm - advertised as a Lightweight), except for Skeet A & B grades. This model was produced only in a Lightweight or Mag. 20 (3 in. chamber), 28 ga., or .410 bore, before the release of the Model 11-87.

The Model 1100 left-hand, with the ejection port on the left side of the receiver was introduced in 1972 in both 20 and 12 ga., with either VR or plain barrels. The 20 ga. left-hand model was disc. in 1977.

GRADING - PPGS™	100%	98%	95%	90%	80%	70%	60%

MODEL 1100 SPECIAL FIELD - 12, 20 ga., or .410 (limited mfg., disc.) bore, 21 (disc. 1993) or 23 (new 1994) in. VR barrel, various chokes, gas operated, checkered straight grip stock, VR standard, high gloss wood finish (1991 only) or satin wood finish. Rem Chokes became standard in 1987. Mfg. 1983-1999.

	$510	$415	$325	$265	$230	$210	$180

Last MSR was $665.

Subtract 10% if without Rem Chokes.
Add 15%-20% for .410 bore.

Two hundred .410 bore models were mfg. for National Shooting Supplies in Houston, TX.

MODEL 1100 SAM WALTON SPECIAL EDITION - 12 or 20 ga., manufactured for Wal-Mart stores at a lower price point with standard features and wood, 5,000 mfg. in both 12 and 20 ga., serialization was almost matching with the exception of the 12 or 20 after the prefix being different (an example being SMW12134 and SMW201234). Mfg. late 2001 only.

	$395	$350	$300	$260	$230	$200	$175

MODEL 1100 CLASSIC FIELD - 12 (new 2006), 16, 20 (new 2004), 28 (new 2006) ga. or .410 bore (new 2006), 2 3/4 in. chamber, 25 (.410 bore or 28 ga. only), 26 or 28 in. VR light contoured barrel with Rem Choke, non-embellished receiver with blue finish, satin (disc.) or gloss finished American walnut stock and forearm, 7 lbs. Mfg. 2003-2006.

	$675	$550	$475	$400	$350	$300	$275

Last MSR was $834.

Add $34 for 28 ga. or .410 bore.

MODEL 1100 "1 OF 3,000" FIELD - 12 ga. only, limited edition, serial numbered 1-3,000, deluxe walnut, gold washed etched hunting scenes on receiver, 28 in. modified VR barrel. Mfg. 1980.

	$1,100	$900	$600	$500	$425	$350	$300

MODEL 1100 SMALL GAUGE - 28 ga. or .410 bore, 25 in. barrel, scaled down receiver, skeet and field fixed choke, VR standard. Mfg. 1969-94.

	$550	$475	$425	$365	$300	$275	$250

Last MSR was $647.

MODEL 1100 LW-20 (LIGHTWEIGHT) - 20 ga. only, 2 3/4 in. chamber, lightweight scaled down receiver, mag. tube, and barrel, similar to 28 ga./.410 bore frame, standard length ejection port, with mahogany stock, 26 or 28 in. barrel, 6 1/2 lbs. Mfg. 1970-76.

	$510	$415	$325	$265	$230	$210	$180

Subtract 10% if w/o VR.

Remington introduced a lightweight 20 ga. Model 1100 in 1961, with standard frame, mahogany stock and forearm. This model was disc. in Dec., 1969.

MODEL 1100 LT-20 - 20 ga. only, variation of Model 1100 LW-20, 2 3/4 in. chamber, has opened ejection port and barrel extension similar to 12 ga. (long), lightened receiver, 23, 26 (disc., gloss wood only) or 28 (disc., satin wood only) in. barrel, VR became standard 1985, hi-gloss (disc.) or satin finish walnut stock and forearm, 6 1/2 lbs. Mfg. 1977-95.

	$510	$415	$325	$265	$230	$210	$180

Last MSR was $665.

Subtract 10% if without VR.
Subtract $34 for gloss walnut.

Rolled scroll receiver engraving became standard on 20 ga. in 1998.

MODEL 1100 LT-20 YOUTH - 20 ga. only, similar to Model 1100 Lightweight, except stock is 1 in. shorter and 21 in. barrel only. Disc. 1998.

	$500	$415	$325	$265	$230	$210	$180

Last MSR was $659.

GRADING - PPGS™	100%	98%	95%	90%	80%	70%	60%

✳ *Model 1100 LT-20 Youth Camo NWTG* - 20 ga. only, features 100% Mossy Oak break up camo finish, Truglo fiberoptic sights, 6 1/2 lbs. Mfg. 1998 only.

| | $495 | $415 | $325 | $265 | $230 | $210 | $180 |

Last MSR was $652.

MODEL 1100 LT-20 MAG. (LIGHTWEIGHT MAGNUM) - chambered for 3 in. 20 ga. Mag., 20 (disc.), 26 (disc.), or 28 in. barrel, Rem Chokes became standard 1987. Introduced 1977, disc. 1998.

| | $500 | $415 | $325 | $265 | $230 | $210 | $180 |

Last MSR was $659.

Subtract 10% if without VR.

MODEL 1100 MAGNUM DUCK GUN - similar to 1100, in 12 (disc. 1987) or 20 ga., 3 in. chamber, recoil pad, VR became standard 1984, Rem Chokes became standard 1987. Mfg. 1963-88.

| | $400 | $325 | $280 | $260 | $220 | $200 | $180 |

Last MSR was $533.

Add $80 for left-hand model (disc. 1986).
Subtract $40 if without VR.
Subtract $45 if without Rem Chokes.

✳ *Model 1100 Magnum Duck Gun Special Purpose (SP)* - 12 ga. only, low luster finish on stock and forearm, sand blasted metal parts. Mfg. 1985-86 only.

| | $395 | $350 | $295 | $265 | $235 | $200 | $180 |

Last MSR was $550.

Add $40 for Rem Chokes

MODEL 1100 DEER GUN - 12 (disc. 1987) or 20 ga., 20 (disc.), 21 in. (20 ga. only) or 22 (disc.) in. imp. cyl. barrel with rifle sights. Disc. 1996.

| | $435 | $345 | $270 | $225 | $200 | $185 | $165 |

Last MSR was $584.

Add $80 for left-hand model (disc. 1986).
Add $117 for 21 in. fully rifled cantilever deer barrel.

✳ *Model 1100 Deer Gun Special Purpose (SP)* - similar to Model 1100 Deer Gun, except has low luster finish on stock and forearm, sandblasted metal parts. Mfg. 1986 only.

| | $335 | $295 | $275 | $255 | $220 | $200 | $180 |

Last MSR was $495.

MODEL 1100 SYNTHETIC (INCLUDING LT-20) - 12, 16 (new 2003), or 20 (LT-20) ga., 2 3/4 in. chamber, 26 (20 ga. only) or 28 (12 ga. only) in. VR barrel with Rem Choke, checkered black synthetic stock and forearm, matte metal finish, 7-7 1/2 lbs. Mfg. 1996-2004.

| | $430 | $340 | $275 | $225 | $195 | $165 | $140 |

Last MSR was $549.

Add $157-$296 (factory MSR) per extra barrel (2 3/4 in. chamber only), depending on configuration.

✳ *Model 1100 Synthetic Deer* - 12 or 20 (LT-20) ga., 21 in. fully rifled barrel with choice of cantilever scope mount (12 ga. only, became standard 2004 in 12 ga.) or rifle sight (20 ga. only), 7 or 7 1/2 lbs. New 1997-2004.

| | $495 | $375 | $300 | $240 | $210 | $180 | $155 |

Last MSR was $629.

Subtract approx. $50 for rifle sights.

✳ *Model 1100 LT-20 Synthetic Youth* - features 21 in. VR barrel, matte black synthetic stock and forearm. Mfg. 1999-2004.

| | $430 | $340 | $275 | $225 | $195 | $165 | $140 |

Last MSR was $549.

Add $63 for Youth Turkey Camo - includes 3 in. chamber and 100% Realtree Advantage or Skyline Excel (new 2003) camo on stock and forearm.

GRADING - PPGS™	100%	98%	95%	90%	80%	70%	60%

MODEL 1100 TACTICAL - 12 ga. only, 3 in. chamber, choice of Speedfeed IV pistol grip or black synthetic stock and forearm, 6 (Speedfeed IV) or 8 (22 in. barrel only) shot mag., 18 (Speedfeed IV with fixed IC choke) or 22 (synthetic with Rem Chokes with Hi-Viz sights) in. VR barrel, OD Green metal finish, R3 recoil pad, approx. 7 1/2 lbs. Disc. 2006.

	$640	$575	$515	$450	$400	$350	$295

Last MSR was $759.

Add $40 for 22 in. barrel.

MODEL 1100 TAC-2/TAC-4 - 12 ga., 2 3/4 in. chamber, 18 or 22 in. barrel, blasted black oxide metal finish, black synthetic stock with (Tac-2) or w/o (Tac-4) pistol grip, fixed (18 in.) or Rem Chokes, 6 or 8 shot mag., single bead sight, sling swivels, R3 recoil pad with Limbsaver, 7 1/2 - 7 3/4 lbs. New 2007.

MSR $860	$715	$635	$550	$500	$450	$400	$350

Add $68 for Tac-4 with 4 shot mag. and 22 in. barrel.

MODEL 1100 G3 - 12 or 20 ga., 3 in. chamber, steel receiver with titanium PVD coating, all internal operating parts feature a nickel plated Teflon coating, pressure compensated overbored 26 or 28 in. VR barrel with five ProBore chokes, two-piece RealWood semi-fancy carbon fiber laminated wood stock and forearm with high gloss finish and machine cut checkering, "R" insignia on pistol grip cap, R3 recoil pad, satin finished receiver, includes high grade travel case, 6 3/4 - 7 5/8 lbs. New 2006.

MSR $1,239	$1,045	$915	$775	$675	$575	$500	$450

Add $90 for left-hand action (new 2008).

MODEL 1100 COMPETITION - 12 ga. only, 2 3/4 in. chamber with .735 bore diameter, 30 in. barrel with 10mm target style rib and five ProBore choke tubes, receiver and internal parts are nickel/Teflon finished, high gloss semi-fancy adj. or non-adj. American walnut stock and forarm, R3 recoil pad, 8 lbs. New 2006.

MSR $1,529	$1,225	$1,065	$925	$800	$700	$600	$500

Add $163 for adj. comb stock.

MODEL 1100 COMPETITION MASTER - 12 ga. only, 2 3/4 in. chamber, designed for 3 gun matches in practical shooting, 22 in. VR barrel with fiberoptic front sight and Rem Choke, 8 shot mag., grey synthetic stock and forearm, features R3 recoil pad, matte black finish, 8 lbs. Mfg. 2003-2004.

	$775	$600	$525	$465	$435	$395	$350

Last MSR was $932.

MODEL 1100 TOURNAMENT SKEET - 12 or 20 (LT-20 variation disc. 1995) ga., 26 in. skeet bored or Rem Choke barrel, optional Cutts Compensator available from Jan. 1964 to Dec. 1976. Mfg. 1963-1994, mfg. 1996-97, reintroduced 2003 in 12 ga. only, 8 lbs.

MSR $1,084	$895	$675	$550	$475	$400	$350	$300

Add 5% for left-hand model (disc. 1986).

MODEL 1100 SMALL GAUGE SKEET - 28 ga. or .410 bore, 25 or 26 (disc.) in. VR barrel, 6 1/2-7 1/4 lbs. Mfg. 1969-94.

	$550	$450	$415	$375	$300	$265	$230

Last MSR was $692.

2 1/2 in. chamber is standard on the .410 bore (Skeet only).

MODEL 1100 SKEET MATCHED PAIR - 28 ga. and .410 bore, walnut stock and forearm. 5,067 cased Skeet sets were mfg. 1969 and 1970 only.

	$1,250	$995	$875	$765	$635	$530	$455

GRADING - PPGS™	100%	98%	95%	90%	80%	70%	60%

MODEL 1100 SPORTING - 12 (new 2000), 20 (new 1998, LT variation new 2006), 28 ga., or .410 bore (new 2004), 25 (28 ga. only, disc. 2003), 27 (small gauge only, new 2004) or 28 (20 ga. only) in. VR barrel with Rem Chokes, 12 ga. has lightweight 28 in. VR target barrel, high gloss checkered deluxe walnut stock and forearm, 6 1/2 - 8 lbs. New 1996.

MSR $1,084	$895	$685	$575	$475	$400	$350	$300

Add $45 for 28 ga. or .410 bore.

MODEL 1100 PREMIER SPORTING - 12, 20, 28 ga., or .410 bore, 2 3/4 in. chamber, 27 or 28 in. VR barrel with ProBore chokes, nickel finished receiver with gold inlays, high gloss finish select walnut stock and forearm, 6 1/2 - 8 lbs. New 2008.

MSR $1,385	$1,150	$975	$825	$700	$600	$500	$450

Add $56 for 28 ga. or .410 bore.

MODEL 1100 TA TRAP - 12 ga., 30 in. barrel, recoil pad on regular stock, available in left- or right-hand. Mfg. 1979-86.

	$410	$330	$295	$270	$230	$210	$190

Last MSR was $570.

Add 5% for Monte Carlo stock.
Add $50 for left-hand model.

MODEL 1100 TB TRAP - 12 ga., 30 in. VR full choke barrel, special trap stock, select wood. Mfg. 1963-81.

	$475	$400	$325	$300	$245	$210	$190
Monte Carlo stock	$495	$415	$340	$310	$280	$235	$220

MODEL 1100 TOURNAMENT TRAP - 12 ga., 30 in. VR full choke barrel, special trap stock, extra select wood. Mfg. 1979-86.

	$550	$495	$425	$365	$325	$285	$250

Last MSR was $675.

Add 5% for Monte Carlo stock.

MODEL 1100 CLASSIC TRAP - 12 ga. only, features 30 in. VR light contour target barrel, high gloss checkered walnut Monte Carlo stock and forearm, high polish blue, receiver features fine line engraving and gold inlays, 8 1/4 lbs. New 2000.

MSR $1,129	$915	$725	$600	$500	$400	$325	$250

MODEL 1100 150TH ANNIVERSARY - limited mfg. in 1966 only.

	$400	$340	$290	N/A	N/A	N/A	N/A

MODEL 1100 BICENTENNIAL - 12 ga. only, configurations include Trap, Skeet, and Trade, mfg. to commemorate U.S. Bicentennial (1776-1976).

Trap or Skeet	$450	$375	$325	N/A	N/A	N/A	N/A
Trade	$375	$295	$225	N/A	N/A	N/A	N/A

In 1976, the 1100 Bicentennial Trap retailed for $320 ($330 w/ Monte Carlo stock), the Skeet retailed for $285, and the Trade retailed for $270.

MODEL 1100 DUCKS UNLIMITED - "DU" in serial number.

Remington has offered many variations of the Model 1100 specifically manufactured according to individual DU chapter specifications. The price of a DU 1100 varies substantially from the "DU point of purchase" to real market conditions. When contemplating a DU gun it is always important to know how many of that particular variation were manufactured. The Remington factory normally has this information unless the special DU work was subcontracted elsewhere.

While most DU guns are good vehicles for fund raising, their collectibility to date has been minimal. Actual market conditions indicate that unless production is truly limited, most DU firearms sell very close to the models they were derived from. Also, any collectibility that does exist is for 100% guns new in the box with warranty papers. Used DU guns have values comparable to the standard model from which they were derived.

In addition to regular DU guns, Remington has also produced special editions including the 1981 Atlantic Flyway (12 ga., 3 in. Mag. configuration, dinner gun, marked "Atlantic Flyway Edition") and a 1981 DU Lt. 20 ga. (marked "Ducks Unlimited Special"), and 12 ga. (dinner gun - 2,400 mfg. each), and a 1973 dinner gun (500 mfg., marked "Chesapeake"). These were rarer DU shotguns, and current values could vary significantly.

GRADING - PPGS™	100%	98%	95%	90%	80%	70%	60%

MODEL 1100 D-GRADE (TOURNAMENT) - custom order only, any gauge. New 1963.

MSR POR	N/A	$2,900	$2,075	N/A	N/A	N/A	N/A

The last published MSR on this model was $4,532 in 2007.

MODEL 1100 F-GRADE (PREMIER) - custom order only, any gauge. New 1963.

MSR POR	N/A	$6,000	$4,400	N/A	N/A	N/A	N/A

The last published MSR on this model was $8,799 (2007).

MODEL 1100 F-GRADE W/GOLD (GOLD PREMIER) - with gold inlay, custom order only. New 1963.

MSR POR	N/A	$5,550	$3,600	N/A	N/A	N/A	N/A

Note: Grades differ in quality, grade of wood, amount of engraving, and gold inlays.
The last published MSR on this model was $11,999 (2007).

Shotguns: Semi-Auto, Model 11-87 & Variations

Add $887 for custom shop Etchen stock and forearm installed on new Model 11-87s (new 2000).

Remington MSRs on extra barrels (3 in. chamber standard) for the following currently manufactured models range from $221-$368 per barrel, depending on configuration.

MODEL 11-87 SPORTSMAN - 12 or 20 ga., 3 in. chamber, 100% camo or black synthetic stock, vent. rib, 21 (fully rifled with cantilever, 12 ga. only), 26 or 28 in. barrel with Rem Chokes. New 2005.

MSR $757	$615	$525	$425	$350	$285	$245	$225

Add $110 for 21 in. fully rifled barrel with cantilever scope mount.
Add $110 for 100% Mossy Oak New Break-Up camo.
Add $13 for NRA Edition with Mossy Oak New Break-Up on stock and forearm (12 ga. only, disc. 2006).

This model is available in a 20 ga. Youth configuration with 21 in. barrel at no extra charge.

✳ *Model 11-87 Sportsman Synthetic ShurShot* - 12 ga., synthetic ShurShot, Realtree Hardwoods HD camo stock, 21 in. fully rifled barrel, otherwise similar to Model 11-87 Sportsman. New 2008.

MSR $994	$875	$775	$675	$600	$500	$400	$350

✳ *Model 11-87 Sportsman Youth* - 20 ga., 3 in. chamber, 21 in. VR barrel with Rem Chokes, features 13 in. LOP, Mossy Oak New Break-Up 100% camo coverage. New 2008.

MSR $818	$725	$625	$550	$475	$400	$350	$295

MODEL 11-87 PREMIER - 12 or 20 (new 1999, LT-20) ga. (3 in. chamber), 26, 28, 30 (12 ga. only, new 2000) or 32 (disc. 1996) in. VR Rem Choked barrel, successor to Model 1100, gas compensating action adaptable to all loads, stainless steel magazine tube, polished blue finish, high gloss or satin (current mfg. is in 12 ga./28 in. barrel only) finished and checkered walnut stock and forearm, a high gloss wood finish option became available in 1991 at N/C, and is now standard, fine line receiver engraving (referred to as embellished receiver) became standard during 1999, solid recoil pad, 8 1/8 - 8 3/8 lbs. Mfg. 1987-2006.

		$685	$525	$435	$375	$315	$275	$250

Last MSR was $860.

Add $84 for 21 in. fully rifled cantilever deer barrel.
Add $67 for left-hand action (12 ga. only).
Note: Model 11-87 Premier barrels are not interchangeable with Model 1100 barrels.

✳ *Model 11-87 Premier Upland Special* - 12 or 20 ga., 3 in. chamber, 23 in. (light contour barrel on 12 ga.) VR barrel, straight grip satin finished checkered walnut stock and forearm, high polish metal with engraving, 6 1/2 or 7 1/4 lbs. Mfg. 2000-2006.

		$685	$525	$435	$375	$315	$275	$250

Last MSR was $860.

MODEL 11-87 PREMIER 3 1/2 IN. SUPER MAGNUM - 12 ga. only, 3 1/2 in. chamber, 28 in. VR barrel with Rem Chokes, blue high polish non-embellished receiver and barrel, checkered high gloss walnut stock and forearm or 100% Mossy Oak Break-Up camo (disc. 2004) coverage, 8 1/4 lbs. Mfg. 2001-2006.

	$750	$600	$525	$450	$375	$325	$275

Last MSR was $932.

Add approx. 10% for camo (disc. 2004).

MODEL 11-87 SP (SPECIAL PURPOSE) - 12 ga. only, 3 in. chamber, 26, 28, or 30 (disc.) in. VR Rem Choked barrel, parkerized metal with satin finish wood stock and forearm, vent. recoil pad, included camouflaged nylon sling, 8 1/4 lbs. Mfg. 1987-2003.

	$590	$465	$395	$350	$315	$275	$250

Last MSR was $765.

MODEL 11-87 SP (SPECIAL PURPOSE) 3 1/2 IN. SUPER MAGNUM - 12 ga. only, 3 1/2 in. chamber, non-reflective black matte finish on barrel and receiver, 26 or 28 in. VR barrel with Rem Choke, satin finished stock and forearm, approx. 8 1/8 lbs. Mfg. 2000-2005.

	$725	$525	$450	$375	$325	$300	$280

Last MSR was $912.

MODEL 11-87 POLICE - 12 ga. only, 18 in. barrel, improved cylinder choke, synthetic stock, parkerized finish, choice of bead or rifle sights, 7 shot extended mag., designed for police/law enforcement.

Remington does not publish consumer retail pricing for this police/law enforcement model. Secondary prices for this model will be slightly higher than for current pricing on the Model 11-87 SPS.

MODEL 11-87 SPS (SPECIAL PURPOSE SYNTHETIC) - see individual sub-models listed below.

✴ *Model 11-87 SPS 3 In. Magnum* - similar to Model 11-87 SP 3 in. Mag., except is supplied with black synthetic stock and forearm. Disc. 2004.

	$610	$475	$400	$360	$315	$275	$250

Last MSR was $791.

✴ *Model 11-87 SPS Camo (Special Purpose Synthetic Camo)* - 12 ga. only, 3 in. chamber, 21 (mfg. 1999-2005), 26 or 28 (disc. 1998) in. VR barrel with Rem Choke, available in Mossy Oak Bottomland (disc. 1996), Mossy Oak Obsession (new 2006) or Mossy Oak Break-Up (mfg. 1997-2005) finish. Mfg. 1994-2006.

	$765	$575	$450	$375	$325	$300	$280

Last MSR was $963.

✴ *Model 11-87 SPS Waterfowl* - 12 ga., 3 in. chamber, 100% Mossy Oak New Shadow Grass camo coverage, 28 in. VR barrel with Hi-Viz front sight (interchangeable), includes sling and swivels, 8 1/4 lbs. Mfg. 2004-2006.

	$825	$625	$525	$450	$400	$350	$300

Last MSR was $999.

✴ *Model 11-87 SPS-BG Camo (Special Purpose Synthetic Big Game)* - 12 ga. only, 21 in. plain barrel with rifle sights and Rem Choke. Mfg. 1994 only.

	$555	$425	$350	$290	$250	$225	$200

Last MSR was $692.

✴ *Model 11-87 SP/SPS (Special Purpose Deer Gun)* - 12 ga. only, 3 in. chamber, 21 in. IC or Rem Choked (Model SP, mfg. 1989-2003) or fully rifled (new 1993, became standard 2004) barrel with iron sights, parkerized metal with matte finished wood or black synthetic (Model SPS, new 1993) stock and forearm, vent. recoil pad, includes camouflaged nylon sling, 7 1/4 lbs. Mfg. 1987-2005.

	$695	$525	$450	$395	$350	$300	$250

Last MSR was $908.

Subtract 10% for fixed choke barrel or if w/o cantilever (became standard 2005) scope mount. Rem Chokes were standard on this model between 1989-1992.

GRADING - PPGS™	100%	98%	95%	90%	80%	70%	60%

✳ *Model 11-87 SP Thumbhole Deer Gun* - 12 ga., features grey laminate thumbhole wood stock and forearm, 21 in. rifled barrel with cantilever scope mount, 8 lbs. Mfg. 2006-2007.

	$925	$825	$725	$625	$550	$500	$425

Last MSR was $1,135.

✳ *Model 11-87 SPS-T (Special Purpose Turkey)* - 12 ga. only, 3 in. chamber, 21 in. VR barrel with Rem Choke, available in flat black (disc. 2000) or 100% camo treatment in Mossy Oak (disc. 1996), Mossy Oak Break Up (new 1999), Realtree X-tra Brown (mfg. 1997 only), or Greenleaf (disc. 1996), TruGlo rifle sights became standard in 2002 (Model SPS-T Turkey Gun RS/TG). Disc. 2003.

	$765	$550	$460	$385	$335	$300	$280

Last MSR was $963.

Add $324 for Leupold Gilmore red dot sights, Monte Carlo stock and superfull choke tube (mfg. 2000 only).
Subtract approx. $20 if w/o TruGlo rifle sights.

❖ **Model 11-87 SPS Turkey Camo NWTF** - 20 ga. only, features 100% Mossy Oak Break-Up camo finish, TruGlo fiberoptic sights, 6 1/2 lbs. Mfg. 1998 only.

	$675	$575	$450	$395	$325	$290	$265

Last MSR was $832.

MODEL 11-87 SPS 3 1/2 IN. SUPER MAGNUM - choice of 26 or 28 in. VR barrel with Rem Choke, black synthetic or 100% Mossy Oak Break-Up (disc. 2005) or Mossy Oak Obsession (new 2006) camo covered stock and forearm, approx. 8 1/8 lbs. Mfg. 2000-2007.

	$950	$825	$725	$575	$475	$400	$350

Last MSR was $1,076.

Add $99 for camo coverage.

✳ *Model 11-87 SPS-T 3 1/2 in. Super Magnum Turkey Camo* - 12 ga. only, 3 1/2 in. chamber, full coverage Mossy Oak Break-Up (disc. 2003) or Obsession (new 2005) camo treatment, 23 in. barrel with TruGlo rifle sights and Rem Choke tube, thumbhole stock became optional 2006, 8 1/8 lbs. Mfg. 2001-2007.

	$1,000	$875	$775	$675	$600	$525	$450

Last MSR was $1,175.

Add $66 for thumbhole stock (new 2006).

✳ *Model 11-87 SPS 3 1/2 in. Waterfowl* - 12 ga., 30 in. barrel with Hi-Viz sight system and Rem Chokes, 100% Mossy Oak Duck Blind camo coverage, Speed-feed synthetic stock, 8 1/4 lbs. Mfg. 2007.

	$1,025	$875	$775	$675	$600	$525	$450

Last MSR was $1,199.

MODEL 11-87 3 1/2 IN. SPORTSMAN SUPER MAGNUM - 12 ga. only, 28 in. VR barrel with Rem Chokes and Hi-Viz sights, 3 lbs. trigger pull, black synthetic stock and forearm with SuperCell recoil pad. New 2008.

MSR $846		$750	$675	$600	$550	$495	$450	$395

✳ *Model 11-87 3 1/2 in. Sportsman ShurShot Turkey* - 12 ga., features 100% RealTree AP Green HD camo coverage with skeletonized ShurShot stock, elevated Hi-Viz sights, extended choke tubes. New 2008.

MSR $972		$875	$750	$650	$575	$500	$450	$395

✳ *Model 11-87 3 1/2 in. Sportsman Super Mag. Waterfowl* - 12 ga., features 100% Mossy Oak Duck Blind camo coverage, Speedfeed stock with SuperCell recoil pad, Hi-Viz sights. New 2008.

MSR $972		$875	$750	$650	$575	$500	$450	$395

GRADING - PPGS™	100%	98%	95%	90%	80%	70%	60%

MODEL 11-87 3 1/2 IN. SUPER MAGNUM XCS (XTREME CONDITIONS) - 12 ga., 28 in. VR barrel with Rem Chokes, features choice of black synthetic Speedfeed stock and forearm, or Mossy Oak Duck Blind camo coverage, grey TriNyte PVD coating on receiver and barrel, nickel plated internal components. New 2008.

MSR $1,188 $1,000 $875 $775 $675 $600 $525 $450

Add $40 for Mossy Oak Duck Blind stock and forearm camo coverage.

This model is available from Remington Premier dealers only.

MODEL 11-87 SPORTING CLAYS - 12 ga. only, 26 (disc. 1996) or 28 in. VR barrel with extended Rem Chokes (knurled extension chokes allow for no-wrench field changes), specially balanced, satin finished walnut, top metal surfaces have fine matte finish, radiused recoil pad, twin bead sights on 5/16 wide VR, 7 1/2 lbs. Mfg. 1992-99.

     $675 $575 $450 $395 $325 $290 $265

Last MSR was $833.

＊ *Model 11-87 Sporting Clays NP* - 12 ga. only, features matte nickel plated receiver with engraving, satin finished checkered stock and forearm, 28 (new 1998) or 30 in. VR ported barrel with extended choke tubes, 7 3/4 lbs. Mfg. 1997-2001.

     $775 $650 $525 $450 $375 $325 $295

Last MSR was $948.

MODEL 11-87 PREMIER SKEET - 12 ga. only, 26 in. VR Rem Choked barrel, deluxe walnut with quality cut checkering, 7 3/4 lbs. Mfg. 1987-99.

     $650 $550 $475 $425 $375 $325 $275

Last MSR was $799.

Add approx. $70 for left-hand action.
Subtract 10% if without Rem Chokes.

MODEL 11-87 PREMIER TRAP - 12 ga. only, 30 in. raised VR Rem Choked barrel, deluxe walnut stock (Monte Carlo became standard in 1996) with quality cut checkering, 8 1/4 lbs. Mfg. 1987-99.

     $660 $565 $440 $385 $300 $275 $260

Last MSR was $833.

Subtract $30 if without Monte Carlo stock.
Add approx. $40 for left-hand action (disc. 1994).
Subtract 10% if without Rem Chokes.

MODEL 11-87 175TH ANNIVERSARY - 12 ga. only, 28 in. barrel with Rem - chokes, 175th Anniversary Model (1816-1991) with light engraving and high gloss wood finish. 4,606 1991 mfg. only.

     $515 $425 $335   N/A   N/A   N/A   N/A

Last MSR was $618.

MODEL 11-87 DALE EARNHARDT COMMEMORATIVE - 12 ga. only, features "7 Time Winston Cup Champion" tributary banner on right side with gold letters, 28 in. light contoured VR barrel, select checkered American walnut stock and forearm, serialization starts with DE3, 7 3/4 lbs. Mfg. 2003-2004.

     $800 $650 $575   N/A   N/A   N/A   N/A

Last MSR was $972.

MODEL 11-87 D-GRADE (TOURNAMENT) - custom order only, any gauge. New 1963.

MSR POR   N/A $2,900 $2,075   N/A   N/A   N/A   N/A

The last published MSR on this model was $4,532 (2007).

MODEL 11-87 F-GRADE (PREMIER) - custom order only, any gauge. New 1963.

MSR POR   N/A $6,000 $4,400   N/A   N/A   N/A   N/A

The last published MSR on this model was $8,799 (2007).

GRADING - PPGS™	100%	98%	95%	90%	80%	70%	60%

MODEL 11-87 F-GRADE W/GOLD (GOLD PREMIER) - with gold inlay, custom order only. New 1963.

	MSR POR	N/A	$5,550	$3,600	N/A	N/A	N/A	N/A

Note: Grades differ in quality, grade of wood, and amount of engraving.
The last published MSR on this model was $11,999 (2007).

100%	98%	95%	90%	80%	70%	60%	50%	40%	30%	20%	10%

SHOTGUNS: SINGLE BARREL

MODEL NO. 3 RIDER SINGLE BARREL - 12 ga., single barrel, 30 or 32 in. barrels, top lever break open, button release forend, plain pistol grip stock. Approx. 87,850 mfg. 1893-1903.

$325	$290	$260	$230	$200	$170	$140	$110	$85	$65	$50	$35

MODEL NO. 9 RIDER SINGLE BARREL - similar to No. 3, screw release forend, auto ejector. 65,698 mfg. 1902-10.

$375	$325	$290	$260	$230	$200	$170	$140	$110	$85	$65	$50

GRADING - PPGS™	100%	98%	95%	90%	80%	70%	60%

MODEL 90-T (TRAP) - 12 ga., 32 (disc. 1993) or 34 in. full choke VR barrel with fixed full choke, matte black receiver and wood around tang area, deluxe checkered stock and forearm, short throw top-lever release, elongated forcing cone, approx. 8 3/4 lbs. Mfg. 1992-97.

			$1,850	$1,550	$1,375	$1,175	$1,025	$925	$850

Last MSR was $3,199.

Add $50 for factory porting.

✳ *Model 90-T HPAR (High Post w/ adj. Rib)* - features high post, adj. rib. Mfg. 1994-97.

			$2,300	$1,875	$1,700	$1,550	$1,450	$1,325	$1,075

Last MSR was $3,992.

MODEL 310 SKEET - .32 Rimfire case loaded with No. 12 leadshot, break open single shot, .310 bore shotgun, used in conjunction with a self-operated trap set which threw half-size clay targets, entire set-up included gun, shooting booth, ammunition, and trap thrower, 5 1/2 lbs., mfg. circa late 1960s.

	Gun only	$425	$350	$300	$250	$195	$175	$150

Add 25%-75% depending on the amount of original accessories included.

This model was mfg. by CBC in Brazil, and imported into the U.S. as the .310 Skeet. This model was never mass produced, but test marketed for approx. 5 years in CT, NJ, PA, and TX primarily at amusement parks. It failed commercially due to lack of sales.

SHOTGUNS: SLIDE ACTION, DISC.

REMINGTON REPEATING SHOTGUN - 12 ga., hammerless, bottom ejection, takedown, plain barrel only, blue finish, sight notch on receiver top, marked "REMINGTON ARMS CO." with February 3rd, 1903 and May 18th, 1905 patent dates, walnut pistol grip stock and short forearm, hard rubber buttplate, 7 1/2 lbs., approx. 10,000 mfg. 1908-10.

			$295	$225	$200	$175	$150	$125	$110

Add 10% for 32 in. barrel.

There were 7 grades of this model (Numbers 0-6) that were originally priced from $27 to approx. $140. This model was renamed the Model 10 in 1911.

MODEL 10A SLIDE ACTION - 12 ga., 26-32 in. barrels, various chokes, takedown, plain pistol grip stock. Mfg. 1911-29.

			$300	$275	$200	$175	$150	$125	$110

Add 10% for 32 in. full choke barrel.
Add 35% for guns marked "Long Range" - beware of fakes.

GRADING - PPGS™	100%	98%	95%	90%	80%	70%	60%

MODEL 17A SLIDE ACTION - 20 ga., 26-32 in. barrel, various chokes, takedown, bottom ejection, 4 shot mag., plain grip stock. Approx. 48,000 mfg., 1917-33.

	100%	98%	95%	90%	80%	70%	60%
Plain barrel	$350	$275	$220	$195	$165	$140	$110
Solid. rib	$450	$375	$325	$290	$270	$250	$210

Grades range from "A" - "F" in suffix form, "F" being the highest. Large premiums are paid for mint condition, higher grade models.

MODEL 17R - 20 ga. only, security configuration, 20 in. cylinder bore barrel, 4 shot mag. Mfg. circa 1920s.

	100%	98%	95%	90%	80%	70%	60%
	$325	$265	$235	$200	$150	$120	$100

MODEL 29A SLIDE ACTION - 12 ga., 26-32 in. barrel, bottom ejection, various chokes, takedown, 5 shot mag., checkered pistol grip stock. Approx. 24,000 mfg., 1929-33.

	100%	98%	95%	90%	80%	70%	60%
	$325	$265	$235	$200	$150	$120	$100

Add 15% for solid rib, 25% for VR.

* *Model 29A Slide Action 32 in. Long Range barrel* - should be marked "Long Range" - beware of fakes.

	100%	98%	95%	90%	80%	70%	60%
	$525	$475	$425	$350	$250	$200	$180

Grades range from A - C and TA - TF, lowest to highest. Premiums exist for finer condition upper grades. The Model 29 was similar in appearance to the Model 10.

MODEL 29R - 12 ga. only, security configuration, 20 in. cylinder bore barrel, 5 shot mag. Mfg. circa 1920s.

	100%	98%	95%	90%	80%	70%	60%
	$375	$325	$265	$235	$200	$150	$120

MODEL 29S - "Trap Special" with trap style straight grip stock, matted or VR rib.

	100%	98%	95%	90%	80%	70%	60%
	$500	$450	$425	$375	$350	$325	$300

Add 20% for VR rib.

MODEL 31A SLIDE ACTION - 12, 16, or 20 ga., side ejection, 2 or 4 shot mag., 26-32 in. barrels, various chokes, takedown, pistol grip stock. Approx. 160,000 mfg., 1931-49.

	100%	98%	95%	90%	80%	70%	60%
Plain barrel	$395	$345	$300	$265	$225	$185	$150
Solid rib	$455	$385	$345	$300	$270	$230	$190
Vent. rib	$475	$415	$375	$320	$290	$250	$210

Add 15% for 20 ga.

Grades range from A - F suffixes. Higher grades will bring considerable premiums in excellent condition. TC suffix is Target Model. A Model 31L (lightweight) was mfg. 1948-1950 and while rare, demand dictates to subtract 20% for this variation. Early models will command a small premium in this model.

MODEL 31B "SPECIAL" - higher grade wood and hand checkered pistol grip stock and forearm.

	100%	98%	95%	90%	80%	70%	60%
	$650	$550	$440	$385	$360	$305	$275

MODEL 31R "RIOT" GRADE - features shortened barrel.

	100%	98%	95%	90%	80%	70%	60%
	$425	$365	$325	$295	$270	$230	$190

MODEL 31D TOURNAMENT - features scroll engraving.

	100%	98%	95%	90%	80%	70%	60%
	$1,600	$1,350	$1,100	$880	$715	$580	$525

MODEL 31E EXPERT - features scroll engraving with game scene on left side of receiver.

	100%	98%	95%	90%	80%	70%	60%
	$1,750	$1,500	$1,325	$1,100	$935	$880	$770

MODEL 31F PREMIER - features scroll engraving and game scenes on both sides of receiver. Introduced 1942.

	100%	98%	95%	90%	80%	70%	60%
	$2,950	$2,550	$2,200	$1,875	$1,600	$1,500	$1,300

Add 20% for 20 ga.

Note: Grades differ in quality, grade of wood, and amount of engraving. This model was also available with a Cutts compensator 1940-49, or a Poly Choke on special order from 1941-49.

GRADING - PPGS™	100%	98%	95%	90%	80%	70%	60%

MODEL 31TC TRAP - similar to 31A, with 12 ga. only, 30 or 32 in. VR barrel milled out of one piece of steel, full choke, trap stock and beavertail forend, pad.

	$875	$795	$675	$575	$450	$375	$300

Subtract 10% for lightweight receiver.

TC stands for Trap with C Grade wood.

MODEL 31S TRAP SPECIAL - solid rib barrel, plainer wood.

	$550	$500	$450	$400	$365	$345	$325

MODEL 31H HUNTER - similar to 31S, with sporter stock. Mfg. 1941-disc.

	$395	$350	$300	$275	$250	$220	$195

MODEL 31L LIGHTWEIGHT - features an alloy receiver, available in both field and skeet, introduced 1941.

	$350	$325	$300	$275	$250	$225	$200

MODEL 31 SKEET - similar to 31A, with 26 in. skeet bored barrel, standard solid rib, beavertail forend.

	100%	98%	95%	90%	80%	70%	60%
Plain barrel	$495	$450	$395	$365	$335	$265	$220
Vent. rib	$650	$550	$495	$425	$375	$340	$295

Subtract 10% for lightweight receiver.

Add 20% for 20 ga. with VR barrel.

SHOTGUNS: SLIDE ACTION, MODEL 870 & VARIATIONS

3 in. shells (12 or 20 ga.) may be shot in Magnum receivers only regardless of what the barrel markings may indicate (the ejection port is larger in these Magnum models with M suffix serialization).

Remington has manufactured many limited production runs for various distributors and wholesalers over the years. These shotguns are usually built to a specific configuration (gauge, stock, barrel length, finish, etc.), and are usually available until supplies run out. While these models are not included in this section, pricing in most cases will be similar to the base models from which they were derived.

Add $877 for custom shop Etchen stock and forearm installed on new Model 870s.

Add 25%-35% for 16 ga. on older mfg., if original condition is 95%+.

Remington MSRs on extra barrels (3 in. chamber is standard, except for Skeet barrel) for the following currently manufactured models range from $151-$369 per barrel, depending on configuration.

MODEL 870AP SLIDE ACTION - "Wingmaster," 12, 16, or 20 ga., 26, 28, or 30 in. barrel, 5 shot, various chokes, plain pistol grip stock. Mfg. 1950-63.

	100%	98%	95%	90%	80%	70%	60%
Plain barrel	$220	$195	$175	$165	$140	$120	$110
Vent. rib	$250	$220	$200	$195	$165	$150	$140

Add 15% for "Sungrain" blonde maple wood (mfg. 1959-1961).

MODEL 870ADL - deluxe checkered version of 870AP. Mfg. 1950-63.

	100%	98%	95%	90%	80%	70%	60%
Plain barrel	$250	$220	$200	$180	$165	$140	$120
Matted top barrel	$275	$250	$220	$210	$195	$165	$140
Vent. rib	$300	$275	$250	$225	$200	$175	$150

MODEL 870BDL - select walnut stock.

	100%	98%	95%	90%	80%	70%	60%
Plain barrel	$275	$250	$220	$200	$180	$165	$140
Vent. rib	$315	$290	$260	$240	$210	$195	$165

SPORTSMAN 12 PUMP - 12 ga. only (3 in. chamber), 28 or 30 in. barrel, recoil pad, VR standard, hardwood stock and forearm, Model 870 type action, 7 1/2 lbs. Mfg. 1984-86.

	$275	$235	$195	$175	$160	$150	$140

Last MSR was $270.

Add $35 for Rem Chokes.

GRADING - PPGS™	100%	98%	95%	90%	80%	70%	60%

MODEL 870 EXPRESS - 12, 16 (mfg. 2002-2006), 20 (new 1991), 28 ga. (disc., reintroduced 2002-2004), or .410 bore (disc., reintroduced 2002-2004), 3 in. chamber, 20, 25 (28 ga. or .410 bore only), 26, or 28 in. VR Rem Choked (12 or 20 ga., supplied with Mod. Rem Choke) barrel, parkerized metal, matte finished hardwood stock and forearm, solid recoil pad, 7 1/4 lbs. New 1987.

MSR $373	$295	$240	$200	$175	$155	$140	$130

Add $27 for 28 ga. or .410 bore.
Add $28 for left-hand action (12 ga., 28 in. barrel only, new 1998).

Various combination Express packages are available in both 12 and 20 ga. Retail prices range from $543-$648.

* *Model 870 Express Synthetic* - 12 or 16 ga. (disc. 2005), 26 or 28 in. VR barrel with one Rem Choke, features black synthetic stock and forearm. New 1994.

MSR $373	$295	$240	$200	$175	$155	$140	$130

❖ Model 870 Express Synthetic Deer - 12 or 20 ga., features 20 in. fully rifled barrel with rifle sights. New 2002.

MSR $416	$325	$245	$200	$175	$150	$135	$130

* *Model 870 Express Deer Gun* - 12 or 20 ga., 20 in. IC choked barrel or fully rifled barrel with rifle sights, Monte Carlo stock. Introduced in 1991.

MSR $373	$295	$240	$200	$175	$155	$140	$130

Add $87 for fully rifled cantilever barrel with Bushnell scope (12 or 20 ga., mfg. 2005).
Add $78 for cantilever scope system and IC Rem Choke (disc. 1991).
Add $43 for fully rifled barrel with rifle sights.
Add $115 for fully rifled cantilever barrel in 12 (23 in. barrel) or 20 (18 1/2 in. barrel) ga.

* *Model 870 Express ShurShot Deer* - 12 ga., 23 in. fully rifled barrel with cantilever scope mount, features black thumbhole ShurShot synthetic stock and forearm. New 2008.

MSR $547	$425	$375	$325	$275	$240	$210	$180

* *Model 870 Express Turkey* - 12 ga. only, choice of wood with flat finish, Realtree Advantage (mfg. 1998-2005), Skyline Excel (mfg. 2003-2005), or Mossy Oak Break-Up (new 2006) camo stock and forearm, 21 in. VR barrel with Rem. turkey choke, 7 1/4 lbs.

MSR $388	$300	$240	$200	$175	$150	$135	$130

Add $57 for standard camo stock and forearm.
Add $115 for ShurShot skeletonized stock and Mossy Oak Obsession stock and forearm.

* *Model 870 Express Youth* - 16 (mfg. 2004-2005) or 20 ga. only, 21 in. VR barrel with Rem Choke, 13 in. LOP with recoil pad, choice of RealTree Advantage (mfg. 1998-2005), Mossy Oak Break-Up (new 2006), or Skyline Excel (mfg. 2003-2005) camo or regular wood finish on stock and forearm, 6 lbs.

MSR $373	$295	$240	$200	$175	$155	$140	$130

Add $43 for Youth Deer Gun (fully rifled 20 in. barrel). New 1994.
Add $87 for Youth Turkey with choice of NWTF Jake's Skyline Excel camo (disc. 2005).
Add $72 for Youth Turkey with camo (disc. 2006, reintroduced 2008).

* *Model 870 Express Junior* - 20 ga., 18 3/4 in. VR barrel, features Mossy Oak Break-Up camo finish on stock and forearm, matte metal finish, 6 lbs. New 2006.

MSR $445	$360	$310	$270	$235	$200	$180	$160

* *Model 870 Express Synthetic HD (Home Defense)* - 12 or 20 (new 2007, 7 shot mag. only) ga., 18 in. cyl. choked barrel with bead front sight, black synthetic stock and forend. New 1991.

MSR $359	$275	$220	$180	$155	$140	$130	$125

Add $29 for 12 ga. 7 shot tube mag. or $38 for 20 ga. 7 shot tube mag.

* *Model 870 Express Combo* - 12 ga., includes 23 in. cantilever fully rifled and 28 in. Rem Choke vent. rib barrels, black synthetic stock. New 2008.

MSR $585	$460	$360	$275	$225	$185	$160	$145

This model is available through Remington Premier dealers only.

GRADING - PPGS™	100%	98%	95%	90%	80%	70%	60%

✱ *Model 870 Express Specialty* - 12 or 20 ga., 18 in. cylinder bore or Rem Choke barrel, folding or Knoxx Spec-Ops pistol grip stock, 2 or 7 shot mag extension. New 2008.

MSR $452	$365	$315	$270	$235	$200	$180	$160

Add $27 for 2 shot mag. extension with Knoxx Spec-Ops stock.
Add $53 for synthetic folding stock with 7 shot mag extension.
This model is available through Remington Premier dealers only.

MODEL 870 EXPRESS SUPER MAGNUM - 12 ga., 3 1/2 in. chamber, choice of checkered natural hardwood, black synthetic, or 100% camo stock and forearm, 23 (camo only), 26 (synthetic only), 28 (wood only), or 30 (mfg. 2007) in. VR barrel, matte or 100% camo finish metal, recoil pad, approx. 7 1/4 lbs. New 1998.

MSR $420	$335	$255	$210	$185	$160	$150	$140

Add $15 for synthetic non-camo Turkey Model with 23 in. barrel (mfg. 1999-2007).

Add $124 for 100% Skyline Fall Flight camo coverage (mfg. 2005).
Add $152 for Waterfowl Model w/ 100% camo coverage (new 2007).
Add $159 for combo package (includes 26 in. regular and 20 in. fully rifled deer barrel).

✱ *Model 870 Express Super Magnum Turkey Camo* - features Mossy Oak Break-Up (new 2006), 100% RealTree Advantage (disc. 2005) or Skyline Excel (mfg. 2003-2005) camo on metal and stock/forearm, 23 in. VR barrel only with Turkey extra full Rem Choke. New 1998.

MSR $555	$440	$350	$275	$225	$185	$160	$145

✱ *Model 870 Express Super Magnum Synthetic Camo* - 12 ga., 3 1/2 in. chamber, 23 or 26 in. VR barrel with Rem Choke, 100% Mossy Oak Break Up camo coverage, wood or synthetic stock and forearm. Mfg. 1999 only.

	$385	$320	$265	$240	$220	$200	$180

Last MSR was $532.

✱ *Model 870 Express Super Magnum Camo* - 12 ga., 26 in. vent. rib. barrel, Rem Choke, 100% Mossy Oak Break-Up camo coverage, sling swivels, Hi-Viz sights, camo sling. New 2008.

MSR $545	$430	$340	$275	$225	$185	$160	$145

This model is available through Remington Premier dealers only.

MODEL 870 SPS SUPER MAG TURKEY - 12 ga., 3 1/2 in. chamber, 23 in. rifle sighted barrel, 100% RealTree AP Green HD ShurShot thumbhole stock, SuperCell recoil pad, Wingmaster HD extended Rem Choke, black sling, sling swivels, TruGlo fiber optic sights. New 2008.

MSR $644	$550	$475	$400	$350	$300	$260	$220

MODEL 870 SPS SUPER MAG. MAX GOBBLER - 12 ga., 23 in. rifle sighted barrel, 100% RealTree APG HD camo Knoxx SpecOps stock, drilled and tapped, Williams Fire Sight fiber optic sights, R3 recoil pad, sling, Rem Chokes. New 2008.

MSR $819	$675	$550	$450	$350	$315	$275	$250

MODEL 870 WINGMASTER - 12 or 20 ga., 26 or 28 in. vent. rib. barrel, Rem Chokes, high gloss semi-fancy Claro walnut stock, engraved receiver with pheasant and duck scenes, gold trigger, silver grip cap with raised Remington "R" logo. New 2008.

MSR $955	$795	$725	$650	$575	$500	$450	$395

This model is available through Remington Premier dealers only.

GRADING - PPGS™	100%	98%	95%	90%	80%	70%	60%

MODEL 870 FIELD WINGMASTER - 12, 16 (disc. 1980, reintroduced late 2001), 20 (LW-20), 28 (disc. late 1994, reintroduced 1999) ga., or .410 (disc. late 1994, reintroduced 1999) bore, various barrel lengths (26, 28, and 30 are current mfg.), incorporates twin slide rails, 3 in. chamber in 12 ga. became standard in 1985, Rem Chokes became standard in 1987, lightweight frame on 20 ga. was introduced 1972, checkered walnut stock and forearm, a choice of high gloss or satin (28 in. barrel only) wood finish became available in 1991, approx. 6 1/2 - 7 1/4 lbs. New 1964.

Plain barrel	$250	$225	$205	$190	$175	$160	$150

✳ *Model 870 Field Wingmaster with Vent. rib* - became standard in 1985.

MSR $773	$585	$475	$385	$315	$265	$215	$190

Subtract 10% without Rem Chokes.
Add $48 for left-hand model (12 ga. only, disc. 1994).
Add $80 for 20 in. fully rifled cantilever deer barrel (12 ga. - mfg. 1992-99 or 20 ga. - mfg. 1992-95).

Beginning 1998, rolled scroll engraving started to appear on 20 ga. guns only. During 2005, a Wingmaster Jr. was released in a LW-20 in 20 ga. with 12 in. LOP and 18 3/4 in. barrel at no extra charge.

✳ *Model 870 Field Wingmaster Small Gauge* - 28 ga. or .410 bore, scaled down 870 on lightweight smaller frame, 25 in. fixed (F or M, .410 bore only) or Rem Choke (28 ga. only, new 1999) barrel, VR became standard 1984, satin finished wood, 6-6 1/2 lbs. Mfg. 1969-94, reintroduced 1999.

MSR $808	$665	$530	$425	$350	$315	$275	$250

Add $63 for 28 ga.
Subtract 10% if w/o VR.

✳ *Model 870 Field Wingmaster Fiftieth Anniversary Classic Trap* - 12 ga. only, 2 3/4 in. chamber, features high polish blue fine line embellished receiver with gold inlays, 30 in. low profile light contour barrel, checkered high gloss semi-fancy walnut stock and forearm with cut checkering, 8 lbs. New 2000.

MSR $1,015	$815	$660	$500	$400	$350	$300	$285

✳ *Model 870 Field Wingmaster 100th Anniversary* - 12 ga., features "100th Anniversary of Pump Action Shotguns" embellished on left side of receiver with gold banners, fleur-de-lis laser engraved checkering on high gloss walnut stock and forearm. New 2008.

MSR $1,035	$830	$665	$500	$400	$350	$300	$285

✳ *Model 870 Field Wingmaster Dale Earnhardt Tribute* - 12 (mfg. 2005) or 20 (new 2006) ga, 28 in. VR barrel with Rem Chokes, special embellishments featuring Dale Earnhardt. Mfg. 2005-2006.

	$710	$575	$475	$400	$345	$300	$265

Last MSR was $820.

✳ *Model 870 Field Wingmaster NRA Edition* - 12 ga., 28 in. VR barrel, features NRA Heritage logo on receiver. Mfg. 2006.

	$495	$395	$325	$275	$220	$195	$175

Last MSR was $685.

WINGMASTER 3 1/2 IN. SUPER MAGNUM - 12 ga. only, 28 in. VR barrel with choke tubes, high polish blue with receiver engraving, high gloss walnut stock and forearm with cut checkering, 7 1/2 lbs. Mfg. 2000-2006.

	$610	$500	$410	$355	$300	$265	$250

Last MSR was $732.

MODEL 870 MAGNUM DUCK GUN - 3 in. chamber, 12 or 20 ga., 26, 28, or 30 in. full or mod. barrel, recoil pad, 3 in. chambers became standard on all Model 870s starting in 1985. Rem Chokes became standard 1987 (introduced 1986 as $40 option). New 1964.

Please refer to Model 870 Field Wingmaster prices.

GRADING - PPGS™	100%	98%	95%	90%	80%	70%	60%

MODEL 870 SPECIAL PURPOSE - 12 ga. only, differs only in that metal parts are sand blasted, choice of Mossy Oak Camo (new 1992), black synthetic, or checkered wood stock with low luster finish, 21 (Turkey barrel), 26, or 28 in. VR barrel. Rem Chokes were introduced 1986.
Add $75 for wood stock and forearm (disc. 1992).
Subtract 10% without Rem Chokes.

* *Model 870 Special Purpose Super Magnum Synthetic Camo* - 12 ga. only, 3 1/2 in. chamber, 26 or 28 in. VR barrel with Rem Choke, available in either Mossy Oak (disc. 1995), Bottomland (disc. 1996), full coverage Mossy Oak Break Up (mfg. 1997-2005) or Mossy Oak Obsession (new 2006) finish. Mfg. 1994-2007.

	$575	$475	$375	$300	$265	$225	$190

Last MSR was $741.

* *Model 870 Special Purpose SPS-T (Turkey) Super Magnum* - 12 ga. only, features 3 1/2 in. chamber, choice of 23, 26 (disc. 2004), or 28 (mfg. 2001-2004) in. VR barrel with Rem Chokes, fully camouflaged in Mossy Oak Break Up (disc. 2005) or Obsession (new 2005) pattern, choice of standard wood, thumbhole (new 2005), or synthetic (26 in. barrel only) stock. Mfg. 2000-2007.

	$575	$475	$375	$300	$265	$225	$190

Last MSR was $741.

Add $58 for thumbhole stock with TruGlo rifle sights and 100% Mossy Oak Obsession coverage (new 2005).
Add $18 for cantilever scope mount (mfg. 2001-2005) with Turkey super full choke tube.

Add approx. $330 if with Leupold Gilmore red dot sights and Turkey super full choke tube - 23 in. barrel only (mfg. 2000 only).
Add $58 for Maxx Gobbler model with 100% RealTree APG HD camo coverage, Knoxx Special Ops stock, and Williams Firesights (new 2007).

* *Model 870 Special Purpose SPS-BG Camo (Special Purpose Synthetic Big Game)* - 12 ga. only, 20 in. plain barrel with rifle sights and Rem Choke. Mfg. 1994 only.

	$350	$285	$235	$200	$170	$150	$130

Last MSR was $442.

* *Model 870 Special Purpose Deer* - 12 ga., 3 in. chamber, grey laminate thumbhole stock and forearm with R3 recoil pad, 23 in. fully rifled barrel with cantilever scope mount, 8 1/8 lbs. Mfg. 2006-2007.

	$650	$575	$525	$450	$400	$365	$335

Last MSR was $799.

* *Model 870 Special Purpose Synthetic ShurShot* - 12 ga., features 23 in. fully rifled barrel with cantilever scope mount, 3 lbs. trigger pull, ShurShot thumbhole stock with SuperCell recoil pad and extended forearm grip, RealTree Hardwoods HD camo on stock and forend. New 2008.

MSR $671	$575	$500	$450	$395	$350	$295	$250

* *Model 870 Special Purpose Turkey (SPS-T)* - 12 (disc. 2004) or 20 ga., 20 (new 2002) or 21 in. VR barrel with Rem Choke, available in flat black, Mossy Oak (disc. 1996, reintroduced 2002), Greenleaf (disc. 1996), or Realtree X-tra Brown (full SPS-T-camo, mfg. 1997 only) finish. Disc. 1999, reintroduced 2002-2005.

	$460	$365	$285	$250	$215	$180	$170

Last MSR was $621.

This model was also available 2002-2003 in a Youth Model with 1 in. shorter LOP.

GRADING - PPGS™	100%	98%	95%	90%	80%	70%	60%

✱ *Model 870 Special Purpose Deer Gun (SPS-Deer)* - 12 ga. only, 3 in. chamber, 20 in. Rem Choke barrel (disc. 1992) or fully rifled barrel with iron sights (new 1993), satin finished (disc. 1992) or black synthetic (new 1993) stock and forearm, matte black metal, 7 1/4 lbs. Mfg. 1989-99.

	$345	$275	$225	$195	$175	$160	$145

Last MSR was $436.

Add $28 for Cantilever deer barrel with Rem Choke (disc. 1996).
Add $60 for fully rifled Cantilever deer barrel.
Add $65 for Cantilever scope mount system (disc. 1992).

✱ *Model 870 Special Purpose Super Slug Deer (SPS Super Slug Deer)* - 12 or 20 (new 2004) ga., 3 in. chamber, 23 in. fully rifled cantilever barrel, matte black metal finish, black synthetic Monte Carlo stock and forearm, approx. 8 lbs. Mfg. 1999-2004.

$470	$375	$310	$255	$225	$195	$175

Last MSR was $580.

MODEL 870 SPECIAL PURPOSE MARINE MAGNUM - 12 ga. only, 3 in. chamber, 18 in. plain barrel bored cyl., features electroless nickel plating on all metal parts, supplied with 7 shot mag., R3 recoil pad became standard during 2004, sling swivels and Cordura sling, 7 1/2 lbs.

MSR $752		$590	$485	$410	$350	$300	$250	$200

Add $117 for XCS Marine Model with black TriNyte metal coating (new 2007).

MODEL 870 XCR (XTREME CONDITIONS) - 12 ga., 28 in. vent. rib. barrel, black synthetic or Mossy Oak Duck Blind (Waterfowl) camo coverage, Rem Choke, TriNyte PVD coating, Speedfeed stock, nickel plated internal parts. New 2008.

MSR $899		$675	$550	$425	$350	$315	$275	$250

Add $56 for Waterfowl model with camo.

This model is available through Remington Premier dealers only.

MODEL 870 LIGHTWEIGHT - 20 ga. only, lighter and shorter mahogany stock than magnum model, 23 in. barrel. Mfg. 1972-83.

	$270	$230	$210	$190	$175	$165	$155

Add $30 for VR.

MODEL 870 LIGHTWEIGHT (MAGNUM) - 20 ga., 3 in. chamber, 26 or 28 in. barrel, 6 lbs. Mfg. 1972-1994. Rem Chokes became standard 1987.

	$365	$320	$260	$225	$200	$175	$160

Last MSR was $460.

Subtract 10% without Rem Chokes.
Subtract $40 without VR.

MODEL 870 SPECIAL FIELD - 12 or 20 (LW-20) ga., lighter straight grip stock with solid recoil pad, 21 (disc. 1993) or 23 (new 1994) in. VR barrel, 6 1/4 or 7 lbs. New 1984. Rem Chokes became standard 1987 (introduced 1986 as $40 option). Disc. 1995.

	$380	$320	$265	$230	$210	$190	$175

Last MSR was $473.

Subtract 10% without Rem Chokes.

MODEL 870 BRUSHMASTER - 12 or 20 (disc.) ga., 20 in. barrel with imp. cyl. (disc.) or Rem Choke and rifle sights, 3 in. chamber standard for 1985, normal bluing with satin finished wood. Disc. 1994.

	$355	$310	$255	$225	$200	$175	$160

Last MSR was $452.

Add $43 for left-hand model.

GRADING - PPGS™	100%	98%	95%	90%	80%	70%	60%

MODEL 870 POLICE - 12 ga. only, 18 or 20 in. plain barrel, choice of blue or parkerized finish, bead or rifle (disc. 1995, 20 in. barrel only) sights, Police cylinder (disc.) or IC choke. Mfg. 1994-2006.

	$385	$315	$250	$200	$175	$160	$145

Last MSR was $492.

Add $13 for parkerized finish.
Add $44 for rifle sights (disc. 1995).

Remington also offers a Model 870P, 870P MAX, and 870P Synthetic for police/law enforcement, featuring Speedfeed, extended capacity magazines and improved cylinder chokes. While Remington does not publish consumer retail pricing for these police/law enforcement models, secondary prices for these guns will be slightly higher than for current pricing on the Model 870 Police.

MODEL 870 TACTICAL - 12 ga. only, 3 in. chamber, 18 or 20 in. fixed IC choke barrel, 6 or 7 (20 in. barrel only) shot mag., OD Green metal finish, black synthetic tactical or SpecOps adj. spring loaded stock with pistol grip, iron sights, approx. 7 1/2 lbs. Mfg. 2006.

	$515	$465	$425	$385	$350	$320	$290

Last MSR was $599.

Add $26 for SpecOps adj. stock.

MODEL 870 TAC-2/TAC-3 12 ga., 3 in. chamber, 18 or 20 in. barrel with fixed cylinder choke, black oxide metal finish, black synthetic stock and forearm, pistol grip with choice of Knoxx Special Ops folding stock (Tac-2 FS), Knoxx Special Ops tube stock or regular synthetic stock, 2 (Tac-2 w/18 in. barrel) or 3 (Tac-3 w/20 in. barrel) shot mag., bead sights, R3 recoil pad on fixed stock, approx. 7 lbs. New 2007.

MSR $587		$500	$450	$400	$350	$315	$275	$250

Add $94 for Tac-2 or Tac-3 w/folding stock.

MODEL 870 TACTICAL DESERT RECON - 12 ga., 18 or 20 in. barrel, Digital Tiger TSP Desert Camo stock and forend, special ported tactical extended Rem Choke tube, 2 or 3 shot, Speedfeed stock. New 2008.

MSR $719		$625	$525	$450	$395	$350	$295	$260

Add $66 for 20 in. barrel.

MODEL 870 RIOT - 12 ga. only, 18 or 20 in. barrel, choice of blue or parkerized metal finish. Disc. 1991.

	$295	$265	$225	$200	$170	$150	$130

Last MSR was $355.

Add $40 for police rifle sights (20 in. barrel only).

MODEL 870 D-GRADE (TOURNAMENT) - custom order only, any gauge. New 1950.

MSR POR		N/A	$2,900	$2,075	N/A	N/A	N/A	N/A

The last published MSR on this model was $4,532 (2007).

MODEL 870 F-GRADE (PREMIER) - custom order only, any gauge. New 1950.

MSR POR		N/A	$6,000	$4,400	N/A	N/A	N/A	N/A

The last published MSR on this model was $8,799 (2007).

MODEL 870 F-GRADE W/GOLD (GOLD PREMIER) - with gold inlays, custom order only. New 1950.

MSR POR		N/A	$5,550	$3,600	N/A	N/A	N/A	N/A

Note: Grades differ in quality, grade of wood, and amount of engraving. Prices also vary accordingly.

The last published MSR on this model was $11,999 (2007).

GRADING - PPGS™	100%	98%	95%	90%	80%	70%	60%

MODEL 870 DUCKS UNLIMITED - "DU" in serial number, disc.

	$335	$270	$195	N/A	N/A	N/A	N/A

Remington has offered many variations of the Model 870 specifically manufactured according to individual DU chapter specifications. The price of a DU 870 varies substantially from the "DU point of purchase" to real market conditions. When contemplating a DU gun it is always important to know how many of that particular variation were manufactured. The Remington factory normally has this information unless the special DU work was subcontracted elsewhere.

While most DU guns are good vehicles for fund raising, their collectibility to date has been minimal. Actual market conditions indicate that unless production is truly limited, most DU firearms sell very close to the model which they were derived from. Also, any collectability that does exist is for 100% guns new in the box with warranty papers. Used DU guns have values comparable to the standard model from which they were derived.

In addition to regular DU guns, Remington has also produced special editions including the 1982 Mississippi Edition (dinner gun) and a 1974 DU (dinner gun - first 500 mfg.).

MODEL 870 "WILDLIFE FOR TOMORROW" - 12 ga. only, side panels fine line laser etched with gold engraving, special wood, 2,000 mfg. for Wildlife Forever fundraiser 1996.

	$325	$250	$175	N/A	N/A	N/A	N/A

MODEL 870 150TH ANNIVERSARY - 12 ga. only, 2,534 mfg. 1966 only.

	$400	$325	$275	N/A	N/A	N/A	N/A

MODEL 870 BICENTENNIAL - 12 ga. only, configurations include Trap, Skeet, and Trade, mfg. to commemorate U.S. Bicentennial (1776-1976).

	100%	98%	95%	90%	80%	70%	60%
Trap or Skeet	$425	$350	$295	N/A	N/A	N/A	N/A
Trade	$375	$295	$225	N/A	N/A	N/A	N/A

In 1976, the 870 Bicentennial Trap retailed for $255 ($265 w/Monte Carlo stock), and the Skeet retailed for $220.

MODEL 870 SC SKEET - 12, 16 (disc. 1960), or 20 ga., 26 in. VR skeet bore barrel, C grade hand checkered wood stock. Mfg. 1950-79.

	$600	$445	$365	$280	$245	$210	$185

MODEL 870 SKEET MATCHED PAIR - includes .410 bore and 28 ga., 1,503 cased sets mfg. 1969 only.

	$1,150	$995	$895	$785	$655	$550	$465

MODEL 870 TA TRAP - 12 ga. trap model, deluxe walnut, VR. Add $15 for Monte Carlo stock. Mfg. 1978-86.

	$425	$375	$325	$275	$250	$225	$200

Last MSR was $430.

MODEL 870 TB TRAP - similar to 870, with 28 or 30 in. VR full choke barrel, trap stock, recoil pad. Mfg. 1950-81.

	$425	$375	$325	$275	$250	$225	$200

MODEL 870 TC TRAP - higher grade walnut and special VR, Rem Chokes became standard 1987. Mfg. 1950-79, reintroduced 1996-99.

	$600	$475	$400	$350	$275	$240	$220

Last MSR was $680.

Subtract 5% if w/o Monte Carlo stock.

Add 20% for early Model 870 TC Trap guns with hand cut checkering.

MODEL 870 COMPETITION TRAP - 12 ga. single shot competition model, reduced recoil, competition walnut stock with cut checkering, VR. 5,300 mfg. 1980-86.

	$550	$475	$395	$350	$315	$275	$250

Last MSR was $680.

MODEL 870 ALL AMERICAN TRAP - 30 in. full choke barrel, engraved receiver, triggerguard and barrel, deluxe trap stock. Approx. 1,000 mfg., 1972-76.

	$795	$700	$650	$605	$495	$440	$385

GRADING - PPGS™	100%	98%	95%	90%	80%	70%	60%

RENATO GAMBA
Please refer to the Gamba section in this text.

RENETTE, GASTINNE
Please refer to the Gastinne Renette section of this text.

REPUBLIC ARMS, INC.
Previous manufacturer 1997-2001, and located in Chino, CA.

PISTOLS: SEMI-AUTO

THE PATRIOT - .45 ACP cal., double action only, ultra compact with 3 in. barrel, 6 shot mag., black polymer frame with stainless steel slide (either brushed or with black Melonite coating, new 2000), locked breech action, checkered grips, 20 oz. New 1997.

$265	$230	$210	$185	$175	$165	$155

Last MSR $299.

REPUBLIC ARMS OF SOUTH AFRICA
Previous manufacturer located in Jeppestown, Union of South Africa. Previously imported until 2002 by TSF Ltd., located in Fairfax, VA.

PISTOLS: SEMI-AUTO

RAP 401 - 9mm Para. cal., 8 shot mag., otherwise similar to Rap-440. Importation 1999-circa 2002.

$495	$425	$375	$350	$325	$300	$275

RAP-440 - .40 S&W cal., compact double action, 3 1/2 in. barrel with high contrast 3-dot sights, last shot hold open, hammer drop safety/decocking lever, firing pin block safety, 7-shot mag., all steel construction, 31 1/2 oz., includes case, spare magazine, and lock. Imported 1998-circa 2002.

$545	$475	$425	$395	$375	$330	$300

Add $50 for Trilux tritium night sights.

SHOTGUNS: SLIDE ACTION

MUSLER MODEL - 12 ga., lightweight shotgun, polymer reinforced stock and forearm, action opening release lever, action locks open after the last round. Imported 1998-circa 2002.

$549	$475	$425	$395	$375	$330	$300

REXIO
Previous trademark of guns manufactured in Argentina beginning late 1999. Previously imported and distributed until 2002 by VAM Distribution Company, LLC, located in Wooster, OH.

PISTOLS: SINGLE SHOT

OUTFITTER RC-SERIES - various cals., including .45 LC/.410 bore, tip-up action, 6 or 10 in. barrel, synthetic SAA style grip and full forearm, opening release lever in front of triggerguard, transfer bar safety, with or w/o (.45 LC/.410 bore only) sights, manual locking safety, 2.2-3 lbs. Imported 2000-2002.

$185	$165	$145	$130	$120	$110	$100

Last MSR was $205.

REVOLVERS

RJ-22 SERIES - .22 LR cal., 9 shot, 4 or 6 in. VR barrel with full shroud, choice of wood or synthetic grips with finger grooves, adj. sights, 2.1-2.6 lbs. Imported 2000-2002.

$150	$135	$125	$115	$105	$100	$95

Last MSR was $170.

GRADING - PPGS™	100%	98%	95%	90%	80%	70%	60%

RJ-38 SERIES - .38 Spl. cal., 6 shot, 3 or 4 in. VR barrel with full shroud, choice of wood or synthetic grips with finger grooves, 1.8-2 lbs. Imported 2000-2002.

	$150	$140	$125	$115	$110	$105	$100

Last MSR was $170.

RS-22 SERIES - .22 LR or .22 Mag. cal., 8 (.22 Mag.) or 9 (.22 LR) shot, alloy or steel frame, blue finish, rubber grips with finger grooves, 4 or 6 in. VR barrel with full shroud, fixed or adj. sights, supplied with plastic case. Imported 2000-2002.

	$155	$140	$125	$115	$110	$105	$100

Last MSR was $175.

Add $12 for adj. sights.

* *RS-22 Series Stainless* - similar to RS-22 Series, except is stainless steel. Imported 2000-2002.

	$175	$150	$130	$120	$115	$110	$105

Last MSR was $200.

Add $12 for adj. sights.

RS-357 SERIES - .357 Mag. cal., 6 shot, alloy or steel frame, 3, 4, or 6 in. VR barrel with full shroud, fixed or adj. sights, supplied with plastic case. Imported 2000-2002.

	$155	$140	$125	$115	$110	$105	$100

Last MSR was $175.

Add $12 for adj. sights.

* *RS-357 Series Stainless* - similar to RS-357 Series, except is stainless steel. Imported 2000-2002.

	$175	$150	$130	$120	$115	$110	$105

Last MSR was $200.

Add $12 for adj. sights.

RHODE ISLAND ARMS COMPANY

Previous manufacturer located in Hope Valley, RI.

SHOTGUNS: O/U

MORRONE MODEL - 12 or 20 ga., 26 or 28 in. plain barrels, boxlock, extractors, single trigger, checkered straight or pistol grip stock. Mfg. 1949-1953, only 500 of these guns were mfg., 450 in 12 ga., and 50 in 20 ga., very few with VR, they are quite rare although collector interest is not overwhelming.

	$1,100	$880	$770	$660	$550	$495	$440

Add 20% for 20 gauge.
Add 20% for VR.

RIB MOUNTAIN ARMS, INC.

Previous rifle manufacturer circa 1992-2000, and located in Beresford and Sturgis, SD.

RIFLES: BOLT ACTION

MODEL 92 - .50 BMG cal., match grade barrel with muzzle brake, long action, walnut thumbhole stock, Timney trigger, approx. 28 lbs. Mfg. 1997-2000.

	$3,175	$2,725	$2,275	$2,000	$1,750	$1,575	$1,300

Last MSR was $3,475.

MODEL 93 - similar to Model 92, except has short action with removable shell holder bolt, approx. 25 lbs. Mfg. 1997-2000.

	$3,175	$2,725	$2,275	$2,000	$1,750	$1,575	$1,300

Last MSR was $3,475.

GRADING - PPGS™	100%	98%	95%	90%	80%	70%	60%

RICHLAND ARMS COMPANY

Previous importer (until 1986) located in Blissfield, MI. The models listed were made by various manufacturers located in either Italy or Spain.

SHOTGUNS

MODEL 80 LS SINGLE SHOT - 12, 20 ga., or .410 bore, 26 or 28 in. full choke barrel. Mfg. 1986 only.

$140	$120	$110	$100	$90	$80	$70

Last MSR was $162.

MODEL 711 MAGNUM SxS - 10 ga., 3 1/2 in. chamber, 12 ga., 3 in. chamber, 32 in. full and full, 30 in. full and full, 20, 28 ga., and .410 bore also available on special order, hammerless, boxlock, extractors, checkered, walnut stock, recoil pad. Mfg. 1963-85 in Spain.

10 gauge	$400	$325	$275	$250	$230	$210	$190
12 gauge	$340	$295	$265	$250	$230	$210	$190
20 gauge	$450	$340	$295	$260	$230	$210	$195

MODEL 707 DELUXE SxS - 12 or 20 ga., 3 in. chambers, 26, 28, or 30 in. barrels, various chokes, boxlock, extractors, double triggers, checkered stock and forend. Mfg. 1963-1972 in Spain.

$330	$300	$275	$250	$230	$210	$190

MODEL 200 FIELD GRADE SxS - 12, 16, 20, 28 ga., or .410 bore, 22, 26, and 28 in. barrels, various chokes, Anson & Deeley boxlock, extractors, double triggers, checkered stock, 6 lbs. 2 oz. - 7 lbs. 4 oz. Mfg. 1963-85 in Spain.

$330	$300	$275	$250	$230	$210	$190

Last MSR was $379.

Add 20% for 20 ga., or 50% for 28 ga. or .410 bore.

MODEL 202 ALL PURPOSE SxS - similar to Field, except 2 sets of barrels, 12 and 20 ga. only. Mfg. 1963-disc. in Spain.

$450	$400	$350	$300	$275	$250	$225

Add 20% for 20 ga., or 50% for 28 ga. or .410 bore.

MODEL 41 ULTRA O/U - 20, 28 ga., or .410 bore, 3 in. chambers (.410 bore only), single non-selective trigger, 26 or 28 in. barrels, extractors, VR, engraved silver finished receiver, select checkered walnut stock and forearm, 6 lbs. 2 oz. Importation disc. 1986.

$395	$350	$300	$260	$230	$200	$180

Last MSR was $298.

MODEL 747 O/U - 12 or 20 ga. only, 3 in. chambers, Greener crossbolt, boxlock action, VR and barrels, SST, extractors. Importation disc. 1986.

$475	$425	$350	$325	$310	$295	$280

Last MSR was $464.

MODEL 757 O/U - 12 ga., 3 in. chambers, boxlock action with Greener crossbolt, vent. barrels and rib, double triggers, extractors, walnut stock and forearm, 7 lbs. 4 oz. New 1986. Importation disc. 1986.

$325	$275	$225	$200	$185	$170	$155

Last MSR was $325.

Add 20% for multi-chokes (Model 7570).

MODEL 787 O/U - 12 ga. only, 3 in. chambers, boxlock action with silver finish, single trigger, vent. barrels and rib, extractors, walnut stock with recoil pad, is supplied with 5 interchangeable choke tubes, 7 1/4 lbs. Made 1986 only.

$495	$440	$380	$340	$310	$280	$250

Last MSR was $471.

GRADING - PPGS™	100%	98%	95%	90%	80%	70%	60%

MODEL 808 O/U - 12 ga., 26, 28, or 30 in. barrels, various chokes, boxlock, extractors, checkered stock. Mfg. 1963-1968 in Italy.

	$425	$375	$330	$315	$290	$270	$230

MODEL 810 O/U - 10 ga., 3 1/2 in. chambers, ST, extractors.

	$600	$550	$500	$460	$430	$395	$360

MODEL 828 O/U - 28 ga., single non-selective trigger, extractors, engraved, only 250 imported.

	$650	$550	$500	$450	$400	$350	$325

RIEDL RIFLE COMPANY

Previous single shot rifle manufacturer.

RIFLES: SINGLE SHOT

SINGLE SHOT RIFLE - many cals., 22-30 in. barrel, rack and pinion action, lever trigger guard activated, fully adj. trigger, select walnut stock, basically custom made.

	$495	$470	$440	$415	$385	$330	$305

* *Single Shot Rifle Stainless Barrel*

	$560	$535	$505	$480	$450	$395	$370

RIFLES, INC.

Current rifle manufacturer located in Pleasanton, TX. Previously located in Cedar City, UT. Dealer or direct consumer sales.

Riflemaker and custom gunsmith Lex Webernick has been manufacturing lightweight sporting rifles for 20 years.

RIFLES: BOLT ACTION

On the following models, the customer needs to supply the Remington or Winchester action.

CLASSIC - various cals., features stainless lapped barrel, matte stainless finish, laminated fiberglass stock with pillar glass bedding, approx. 6 1/2 lbs. New 1996.

MSR $2,300	$2,125	$1,650	$1,225	$1,085	$870	$765	$620

Add $100 for left-hand action.

LIGHTWEIGHT STRATA STAINLESS - various cals., lightened stainless Remington action, match grade barrel with slimbrake, matte stainless finish, 5 lbs. New 1996.

MSR $2,600	$2,400	$2,025	$1,650	$1,455	$1,195	$1,010	$835

Add $150 for left-hand action.

TITANIUM STRATA - various cals., based on lightened and blue printed Rem. 700 action, titanium receiver, 4 1/2 lbs. New 2002.

MSR $3,300	$2,950	$2,550	$2,000	$1,740	$1,495	$1,215	$1,000

LIGHTWEIGHT 70 - most cals. up to .375 H&H, features Winchester Model 70 stainless controlled round feeding blue printed action, match grade stainless steel barrel with muzzle brake, matte stainless finish, laminated Kevlar/boron/graphite stock with glass bedding, approx. 5 1/2 lbs. New 1997.

MSR $2,500	$2,300	$1,950	$1,600	$1,410	$1,160	$980	$800

Add $150 for left-hand action.

VARMINT/TARGET - similar to Classic, except has different stock design and dimensions, different barrel contour. Mfg. 1998-99.

	$1,800	$1,375	$1,075	$960	$775	$655	$550

Last MSR was $1,900.

Add $250 for Varmint brake.

GRADING - PPGS™	100%	98%	95%	90%	80%	70%	60%

MASTER SERIES - various cals. up to .300 Wby. Mag., designed for long range accuracy, blue printed Rem. Model 700 action, fiberglass stock, guaranteed to shoot 1/2 MOA. New 1998.

	MSR $2,750	$2,500	$2,075	$1,650	$1,455	$1,195	$1,010	$835

SIGNATURE SERIES - .300 Rem. Ultra Mag. cal., blue printed, Rem. M-700 stainless receiver, honed trigger assembly, 27 in. fluted match grade stainless steel barrel with matte finish, w/o sights, synthetic McMillan sporter stock, each gun is signed by Lex Webernick on the floorplate, guaranteed 1/2 MOA accuracy Limited mfg. 2000-2006.

		$2,600	$2,050	$1,700	$1,500	$1,235	$1,030	$855

Last MSR was $2,800.

Add $175 for slimbrake.
Add $150 for left-hand action.

SAFARI - .375 H&H, .416 Rem., or .458 Lott cal., Win. Model 70 action, features match grade barrel with slimbrake, matte stainless or black Teflon finish, various options are available. New 1996.

	MSR $2,950	$2,625	$2,100	$1,700	$1,450	$1,195	$1,010	$835

RIGANIAN, RAY (RIFLEMAKER)

Current custom riflemaker and gunsmith established in 1988 and located in Glendale, CA. Consumer direct sales.

RIFLES: BOLT ACTION

PEERLESS I - various cals., various blueprinted actions, McMillan fiberglass stock with Pachmayr decelerator recoil pad, various barrel lengths, matte black metal finish, custom order only.

	MSR $4,500	$4,500	$4,000	$3,500	$3,150	$2,750	$2,400	$2,100

PEERLESS II - various cals., various blueprinted actions, features California English XXX walnut stock, various barrel lengths, matte black metal finish, custom order only.

		$6,500	$5,750	$5,000	$4,300	$3,750	$3,150	$2,500

Last MSR was $6,500.

Add $1,400 for .375 H&H cal.
Add $2,100 for .416 Rem., .458 Lott, or .470 Capstick.
Other calibers such as .416 Rigby, .505 Gibbs, and .500 Jeffery are quoted on an individual basis.

PEERLESS II SPORTER - various cals., Win. Mod. 70 or Mauser 98 action, features California English XXX handcheckered walnut stock, ebony forend tip, steel grip cap, and cheekpiece, various match grade barrel lengths, matte black metal finish, custom order only.

	MSR $12,300	$12,300	$10,750	$9,250	$8,100	$7,200	$6,350	$5,500

Add $500 for Mag. cals.
Add $550 for Mauser 98 action.

PEERLESS II EXPRESS RIFLE - various cals., including .375 H&H, .416 Rem., or .458 Lott cals., similar features as the Sporter, extra deep Blackburn steel trigger guard and floorplate, 5 shot, custom made box mag. (.416 or .458 cal. only), quick detachable scope mount system, barrel band swivel base, front sight and bead, quarter rib with one standing leaf, custom order only.

	MSR $15,000	$15,000	$12,500	$11,000	$9,250	$8,100	$7,200	$5,000

Add $1,000 for .375 H&H cal. or higher on Granite Mt. actions.

GRADING - PPGS™	100%	98%	95%	90%	80%	70%	60%

RIGBY, JOHN & CO. (GUNMAKERS), INC.

Current trademark established during 1735, and previously manufactured in Dublin, Ireland from 1735-1897. Currently manufactured in Paso Robles, CA since 1997. Previously manufactured in London, England 1865-1996. Currently distributed domestically by John Rigby & Co. (Gunmakers), Inc., located in Paso Robles, CA. Previously imported by Griffin & Howe until 1998.

Original trade name was W. & J. Rigby circa 1820-1865, during the percussion era. Rigby has always been well-known for its dueling pistols. The first London Branch of J. Rigby was opened in 1865, and the Dublin Premises were closed during 1897. John Rigby became superintendent of the small arms factory at Enfield circa 1880, and was in charge of development for the .303 caliber rifle. The firm became a company in 1900, and has been responsible for many of the large caliber developments in both rifles and ammunition. During 1997, Rigby was acquired by an American investment group located in Paso Robles, CA.

Rigby is one of the world's finest weapons makers. A good portion of the guns they manufacture were custom built to customer specifications. They were chambered for the large black powder express cartridges used for dangerous game in Africa and Asia. The modern Rigby guns follow this same tradition.

Please contact the company directly for more information on the currently manufactured models listed, including delivery time.

We will list the modern Rigby Guns with approximate values but strongly urge that if purchase or sale is contemplated, a professional appraisal be utilized.

RIFLES

Current delivery time on the current rifles is approx. 10-12 months on sidelocks, and 6 months on boxlocks.

SINGLE SHOT STALKING RIFLE - .22 Hornet - .500 NE cals., Farquharson lever actuated falling block action, 24 in. barrel, extractor, checkered pistol grip stock, deluxe finish and engraving. Reintroduced 2000-2003.

$9,250	$8,500	$7,500	$6,500	$5,500	$4,500	$3,500

Last MSR was $9,750.

.350 MAGNUM MAGAZINE RIFLE - .350 Magnum cal. originally, most were rechambered to .375 H&H Mag. cal.

$3,995	$3,400	$2,950	$2,600	$2,300	$2,000	$1,700

AFRICAN (HEAVY) EXPRESS MAGAZINE RIFLE - various cals. include .300 H&H, .375 H&H, .416 Rigby, .458 Win. Mag., .500 Jeffrey (new 2003), or .505 Gibbs (disc. 2002), other calibers are available upon request, new double square bridge Mauser action (pre-1939), claw extraction bolt action, 3-5 shot mag., 20-28 in. barrel, exhibition grade checkered walnut, full pistol grip stock.

MSR $28,500	$25,000	$21,000	$16,750	$12,500	$9,950	$8,500	$7,500

Many options include wood upgrades, engraving, express sights, telescopic sight, case, or other details.

LIGHT STANDARD MAGAZINE RIFLE - similar to Heavy Express Magazine rifle, except in small cals.

MSR $14,500	$13,250	$11,250	$9,750	$8,500	$7,000	$6,000	$5,000

Many options include wood upgrades, engraving, express sights, telescopic sight, case, or other details.

BEST QUALITY SIDELOCK EJECTOR DOUBLE RIFLE - currently mfg. cals. include .375 H&H Flanged, .416/500 Flanged, .470 NE, .500 NE, or .577 NE, 3 leaf express sights, older cals. have included .22 LR, .275 Mag., .350 Mag., .416 Rigby, .458 Win. Mag., .465, or .470 NE cal., 24-28 in. barrels, case colored contoured and reinforced Greener sidelock action with cross bolt, deluxe finish and engraving.

MSR $45,500	$41,750	$37,500	$33,000	$27,250	$22,500	$18,500	$14,000

Many options include wood upgrades, engraving, express sights, telescopic sight, case, or other details.

GRADING - PPGS™	100%	98%	95%	90%	80%	70%	60%

BEST QUALITY BOXLOCK EJECTOR DOUBLE RIFLE - current production cals. include .375 H&H Flanged, .416/500 Flanged, .470 NE, .500 NE, or .577 NE cal., 22-26 in. barrels, Greener cross bolt Anson & Deeley action.

	100%	98%	95%	90%	80%	70%	60%
MSR $28,500	$25,500	$22,250	$18,250	$16,450	$13,250	$10,750	$8,750

Add $1,500 for .500 NE cal.
Add $3,000 for .577 NE cal.

SECOND QUALITY BOXLOCK EJECTOR DOUBLE RIFLE - similar to Best Quality, with less select wood and engraving. Disc.

		98%	95%	90%	80%	70%	60%
	$12,750	$10,750	$9,750	$8,750	$7,350	$6,350	$5,000

Subtract 35% without ejectors.
Values are for larger calibers, smaller cals. could have less value than listed.

SHOTGUNS: O/U

BEST QUALITY SIDELOCK - 12, 16 (new 2006) 20, 28 ga. or .410 bore, true sidelock action with double safety sears, configured for clay pigeon sports, live bird, or field use, all working parts are titanium nitrate coated, various length vent. barrels with VR, exhibition grade English walnut and various stock configurations, case colored, rust blue, or coin finished is standard, 100% small English scroll engraved. New 2000.

		98%	95%	90%	80%	70%	60%
MSR $47,500	$43,000	$36,500	$32,000	$28,000	$25,000	$22,000	$18,500

SHOTGUNS: SxS

HAMMER SHOTGUN - 12, 16, 20, 28 ga. or 410 bore, manual cocking hammers, rebounding firing pins and hammers, extractors only, exhibition grade English walnut, 70% English scroll engraving coverage, special order only.

		98%	95%	90%	80%	70%	60%
MSR $39,000	$35,000	$27,500	$20,000	$16,000	$12,000	$10,000	$8,000

BOXLOCK SHOTGUN - all gauges, barrel lengths and chokes to order, checkered stock to order, auto ejectors, double triggers.

✳ *Boxlock Shotgun Chatsworth Grade*

		98%	95%	90%	80%	70%	60%
	$4,500	$3,500	$3,000	$2,500	$2,000	$1,600	$1,200

✳ *Boxlock Shotgun Sackville Grade* - deluxe engraved.

		98%	95%	90%	80%	70%	60%
	$5,900	$5,000	$4,500	$3,750	$3,100	$2,650	$2,200

Add 20% for 20 ga.
Add 40% for 28 ga.
Add 60% for .410 bore.

SIDELOCK SHOTGUN - PRE-1997 PRODUCTION - all gauges, barrel lengths and chokes to specifications, double triggers, auto ejectors stocked to order.

✳ *Sidelock Shotgun - Pre-1997 Production Sandringham Grade*

		98%	95%	90%	80%	70%	60%
	$9,500	$7,500	$6,000	$5,000	$4,450	$3,775	$2,950

✳ *Sidelock Shotgun - Pre-1997 Production Regal Grade* - deluxe engraved.

		98%	95%	90%	80%	70%	60%
	$12,500	$10,000	$8,750	$7,500	$6,400	$5,250	$4,250

Add 20% for 20 ga.
Add 40% for 28 ga.
Add 60% for .410 bore.

BEST QUALITY SIDELOCK - CURRENT MFG. - 12, 16 (disc.), 20, 28 ga. or 410 bore, case colored or coin finished contoured hand detachable sidelock action, Krupp steel barrels, current engraving includes fine frame and border English scroll, also available with optional game scene engraving on both sidelocks.

		98%	95%	90%	80%	70%	60%
MSR $39,950	$36,250	$32,150	$26,750	$22,000	$18,000	$14,000	$12,000

RIZZINI & TANFOGLIO srl

Current longarm manufacturer established during 2005 and located in Brescia, Italy.

Rizzini & Tanfoglio combines two great names of Italian gunmaking into one company. Rizzini & Tanfoglio manufactures best quality shotguns and rifles, utilizing some of Europe's top engravers. Prices will vary depending on custom order features. For more information, please contact the company directly (see Trademark Index).

RIFLES

Calibers .375 H&H, .470 NE, .500 NE, and .600 NE are POR on the following models.

BOXLOCK SxS - various cals., choice of traditional or round body action, express sights, engraving quoted separately, custom order only.

Base price on this model is €26,240, including VAT tax.
Add €1,830 for round body action.

SIDELOCK SxS - various cals., traditional action only, express sights, engraving quoted separately, custom order only.

Base price on this model is €36,612, including VAT tax.

SHOTGUNS

Add 10% for 28 ga. or .410 bore.

HAMMER SxS - various gauges, choice of round or RT style round body action, rose and scroll engraving, custom order only.

Base price on this model is €21,967, including VAT tax.
Add €1,221 for RT style round body action.

BOXLOCK SxS - various gauges, choice of traditional English style or round body action, rose and scroll engraving, custom order only.

Base price on this model is €12,814, including VAT tax.
Add €4,882 for round body action.

401 SIDELOCK O/U - various gauges, Boss type locking system, chopper lump barrels, ST, best quality wood, engraving quoted separately, custom order only.

Base price on this model is €35,736, including VAT tax.

SIDELOCK SxS - various gauges, choice of English, special RT style, or round body action, engraving quoted separately, custom order only.

Base price on this model range approx. €29,900, including VAT tax.
Add €3,662 for special RT style action.
Add €4,882 for round body action.

RIZZINI, BATTISTA

Current manufacturer established during 1965, and located in Marcheno, Italy. Currently imported beginning 2008 by Rizzini USA, located in New Britain, CT., previously located in West Chester, PA, and by William Larkin Moore, located in Scottsdale, AZ. Previously located in Harpswell, ME. Previously imported in the U.S. 2002-2003 by SIG Arms, located in Exeter, NH, and by New England Arms Corp. located in Kittery Point, ME. Dealer direct sales.

RIFLES: O/U

The models listed below are available in 7x65R, 8x57 JRS, 9.3x74R, .30-06, .308 Win., .444 Marlin, or .30R Blaser cal.

EXPRESS 90L - 23 1/2 in. barrels, ST, ejectors, deluxe wood and features, standard dimensions, includes case, 7 3/4 lbs.

MSR $5,650	$5,300	$4,600	$4,000	$3,300	$2,800	$2,300	$1,950

GRADING - PPGS™	100%	98%	95%	90%	80%	70%	60%

EXPRESS 92EL - similar to Express 90, except has sideplates with more elaborate engraving, includes Nizzoli case, custom dimensions available, 7 3/4 lbs.

MSR $12,125		$10,750	$9,500	$7,850	$6,700	$5,600	$4,700	$3,900

WILD EXPRESS - various cals., low profile boxlock action, ejectors, ST, coin finished receiver with relief game scene engraving, oil finished, hand checkered pistol grip select walnut stock with cheekpiece and Schnabel forend. Importation began 2004.

MSR N/A		$5,200	$4,500	$3,950	$3,250	$2,750	$2,300	$1,950

SHOTGUNS: O/U

12 ga. models listed below have fixed chokes only.

ROUND BODY EL - all gauges, 26, 28, 29 or 30 in. solid rib barrels, ejectors, SST, coin finished or case colored steel frame, two frame sizes, fancy Turkish checkered walnut stock and forearm, five screw in flush chokes, scroll engraving, cased, approx. 6 lbs.

MSR $5,880		$5,500	$4,600	$3,550	$2,900	$2,300	$1,725	$1,425

Add $607 for 28 ga. or .410 bore (small frame).

ROUND BODY EM - all gauges, 26, 28, 29 or 30 in. vent. rib barrels, ejectors, SST, coin finished or case colored steel receiver, two frame sizes, fancy Turkish checkered walnut stock and forearm, five screw in flush chokes, scroll engraving, approx. 6 lbs. New 2007.

MSR $3,500		$3,150	$2,750	$2,400	$2,100	$1,700	$1,500	$1,250

Add $639 for 28 ga. or .410 bore (small frame).

OMNIUM EM - all gauges, blued frame with basic scroll engraving, two frame sizes, SST, ejectors, 24 1/2 - 30 in. VR barrels with choke tubes, cased, approx. 6 3/4 lbs. New 2004.

MSR N/A		$1,800	$1,525	$1,275	$1,050	$800	$700	$625

AURUM CLASSIC - 12, 16, 20, 28 ga. or .410 bore, boxlock action, three frame sizes, SST, ejectors, 24 1/2 - 30 in. VR barrels with choke tubes (except 16 ga.), case hardened receiver with light engraving, cased. New 1996.

MSR $2,375		$2,100	$1,750	$1,325	$1,100	$900	$700	$650

Add $515 for Aurum small action in 28 ga. or .410 bore.
Add $1,597 for Aurum small action combo (28 ga. & .410 bore).
Add $1,125 for Aurum Classic 20/28 ga. combo.

* *Aurum Classic Light* - 12 or 16 ga., nickel plated alloy frame, scroll engraving with gold inlays, cased, approx. 6 1/4 lbs. Imported 2000-2004, reintroduced 2007.

MSR $2,525		$2,250	$1,800	$1,350	$1,100	$900	$700	$650

* *Aurum Classic Teutonic* - all gauges, 24 1/2 - 30 in. VR barrels with five flush choke tubes, boxlock action, hand finished relief game scene engraving, oil finished checkered pistol grip stock and Schnabel forend, cased. Importation began 2004.

MSR $3,071		$2,675	$2,175	$1,850	$1,450	$1,150	$1,000	$850

ARTEMIS CLASSIC - all gauges, 24 1/2 - 30 in. VR barrels with five flush choke tubes, case hardened boxlock action with three frame sizes, hand finshed game scene engraved sideplates with gold inlays, ejectors, SST, oil finished checkered select walnut pistol grip stock and Schnabel forend, approx. 6 3/4 lbs. New 1996.

MSR $2,680		$2,375	$1,950	$1,425	$1,175	$950	$850	$750

Add $515 for Artemis small action in 28 ga. or .410 bore.
Add $1,808 for small action combo with 28 ga. and .410 bore barrels.

GRADING - PPGS™	100%	98%	95%	90%	80%	70%	60%

ARTEMIS DELUXE FIELD - all gauges, 24 1/2 - 30 in. VR barrels, engraved coin finished frame with sideplates, boxlock action in three frame sizes, ejectors, SST, oil finished hand checkered pistol grip select walnut stock with Schnabel forend, approx. 6 3/4 lbs.

MSR $5,880		$5,500	$4,600	$3,550	$2,900	$2,300	$1,725	$1,425

Add $475 for Aurum small action in 28 ga. or .410 bore.

ARTEMIS DELUXE SPORTING - 12 ga., coin finished action, sideplates with hand finished game scenes, SST, ejectors, extra select walnut stock, 28, 29 1/2, 30, or 32 in. barrels, 10mm rib, 5 extended chokes, cased. Importation began 2004.

MSR N/A		$6,950	$5,750	$4,500	$3,650	$2,850	$2,350	$2,100

ARTEMIS EL - top-of-the-line gun with hand engraving, three frame sizes. Importation disc. 2000, reintroduced 2004.

MSR N/A		$16,500	$14,250	$11,250	$9,500	$8,350	$7,100	$6,000

Add $3,750 for small action in 28 ga. or .410 bore.

MODEL BR 320 - 12 or 20 ga., 2 3/4 or 3 in. chambers, 28-34 in. barrels, fixed chokes, 10mm rib, color case hardened boxlock action, light engraving with Rizzini name in gold, SST, pistol grip stock with palm swell and round forend. New 2007.

MSR N/A		$3,000	$2,600	$2,150	$1,675	$1,375	$1,250	$1,100

MODEL BR 440/440 EL - 12 or 20 ga., 28-32 in. barrels with 5 chokes, removable trigger group, SST, blue frame, scroll (440) or hand (440 EL) engraving, checkered pistol grip select (440) or fancy (EL) walnut stock and forearm. New 2007.

MSR N/A		$6,450	$5,850	$5,250	$4,600	$3,850	$3,250	$2,350

Add $3,562 for Model BR440 EL.

780 FIELD SERIES - 10, 12, or 16 ga., boxlock action, DTs, extractors, checkered walnut stock and forearm. Importation disc. 1998.

		$1,075	$875	$750	$875	$595	$525	$450

Last MSR was $1,225.

Add $550 for 10 ga.
Add $150 for ejectors (Model S780 E).
Add $200 for SST with ejectors (Model S780 EM).
Add $350 for SST, ejectors, and upgraded wood (Model S780 EML).
A Model S780 EMEL was also available that is entirely hand-finished and engraved for $5,995.

✱ *780 Field Series Competition* - includes Skeet, Trap, and Sporting Clays configuration. Importation disc. 1998.

		$1,375	$1,050	$925	$825	$725	$625	$525

Last MSR was $1,600.

✱ *780 Field Series Small Gauge* - includes 20, 28, or 36 ga., DTs, ejectors. Importation disc. 1998.

		$1,275	$975	$875	$800	$725	$625	$525

Last MSR was $1,500.

Add $50 for SST (Model 780 EM).

S 780 EMEL - 12, 16, 20, 28 ga. or .410 bore, highly polished coin finish, 28 or 29 1/2 in. barrels, hand engraved ornamental motifs and game scenes, SST, ejectors, extra select hand checkered and polished walnut stock, includes Nizzoli case.

MSR $14,900		$13,000	$11,000	$9,250	$7,800	$6,800	$5,350	$4,850

Add $2,896 for small frame in 28 ga. or .410 bore.

782 EM FIELD SERIES - 12 or 16 ga., boxlock action with sideplates, SST ejectors, extractors, checkered walnut stock and forearm. Importation disc. 1998.

		$1,450	$1,150	$995	$875	$750	$675	$550

Last MSR was $1,700.

Add $450 for Slug variation (Model 782 EM Slug).
Add $350 for better engraving and wood (Model 782 EML).
A Model S7820 EMEL was also available that was entirely hand-finished and engraved for $12,000.

GRADING - PPGS™	100%	98%	95%	90%	80%	70%	60%

* *S 782 EMEL Field Series Deluxe* - all gauges, individually made per customer specifications, 27 1/2 in. VR barrels with choke tubes (except .410 bore), coin finished receiver with side plates featuring elaborate Bulino game scene engraving with gold inlays and fine scroll borders, deluxe English walnut, Nizzoli best leather case. Importation began 1994.

    MSR $15,450   **$13,750 $11,750 $10,350 $8,900 $7,500 $6,500 $5,500**

    Add $3,110 for small action in 28 ga. or .410 bore.

790 SERIES COMPETITION - 12 or 20 ga., choice of Trap, Skeet, or Sporting Clays configuration, features black frame outlined with gold line engraving. Importation disc. 1999.

            $1,725 $1,475 $1,300 $1,050 $925 $825 $695

                 Last MSR was $2,275.

    Subtract $150 for 20 ga. Trap.
    Subtract $50 for 20 ga. Skeet.
    Add $1,050 for 20 ga. Sporting (includes sideplates and quick detachable stock).

A Model 790 Trap EL was also available that was entirely hand-finished with 18Kt. gold and hand engraving - prices began at $5,650 in 12 ga., $5,200 in 20 ga.

* *790 Series Competition Small Gauge* - similar to 790 Competition Series, except in 20, 28, or 36 ga., SST and ejectors standard. Importation disc. 2000.

            $1,375 $1,150 $995 $875 $750 $675 $550

                 Last MSR was $1,750.

A Model 790 EMEL was also available that was entirely hand-finished with 18Kt. gold and hand engraving - prices began at $9,600.

* *S 790 EL Series Competition Sporting* - includes multichokes and case. Importation disc. 2000, reintroduced 2004 by special order only.

    MSR N/A   **$6,950 $5,850 $4,850 $4,000 $3,500 $3,000 $2,500**

* *S 790 EMEL Series Competition Deluxe* - all gauges, individually made per customer specifications, 27 1/2 in. VR barrels with choke tubes (except .410 bore), color case hardened or coin finished receiver with ornate ornamental engraving and Rizzini crest, deluxe English walnut, Nizzoli best leather case. Importation began 1994.

    MSR $11,950   **$9,650 $7,650 $6,500 $5,400 $4,350 $3,400 $2,600**

    Add $2,375 for small action in 28 ga. or .410 bore.

792 SMALL GAUGE MAG. SERIES - 20, 28, or 36 ga., Mag. chambers, SST, ejectors, includes engraved sideplates. Importation disc. 1998.

            $1,675 $1,325 $1,100 $895 $750 $675 $595

                 Last MSR was $2,000.

A Model 792 EMEL was also available that was entirely hand finished with 18Kt. gold and hand engraving - prices begin at $8,250.

S 792 EMEL - all gauges, individually made per customer specifications, 27 1/2 in. VR barrels with choke tubes (except .410 bore), coin finished receiver with side plates featuring upgraded Bulino game scene engraving and fine scroll borders, deluxe English walnut, Nizzoli leather case. Importation began 1994.

    MSR $12,700   **$10,500 $9,500 $7,750 $6,300 $5,150 $4,500 $3,950**

    Add $2,495 for small action in 28 ga. or .410 bore.

MODEL 2000 TRAP - 12 ga. only, includes nickel finished receiver with sideplates, gold trigger, VR barrels and rib. Importation disc. 1998.

            $1,675 $1,375 $1,275 $1,025 $925 $825 $695

                 Last MSR was $2,200.

A Model 2000 Trap EL was also available that was entirely hand finished with 18Kt. gold and hand engraving - prices began at $5,290.

GRADING - PPGS™	100%	98%	95%	90%	80%	70%	60%

MODEL 2000-SP - 12 ga. only, 26, 28, 30, or 32 in. overbored barrels with choke tubes, includes engraved sideplates, semi-fancy select walnut with quick detachable stock, cased. Imported 1994-98.

	$3,000	$2,700	$2,400	$1,975	$1,600	$1,300	$1,000

Last MSR was $3,650.

PREMIER SPORTING - 12 or 20 ga., 28, 29 1/2, 30, 32 or 34 in. multi-choke (5 extended chokes) barrels, hard cased, custom dimensions upon application. Imported 1994-2006.

	$2,600	$2,050	$1,650	$1,375	$1,100	$900	$750

Last MSR was $2,995.

PREMIER II - similar to Premier Sporting, except has blued receiver, European target style stock and beavertail foream, extra select walnut. Limited importation 2004 only.

	$2,950	$2,800	$2,275	$1,775	$1,450	$1,300	$1,075

Last MSR was $4,050.

VERTEX SPORTING - 12 ga., chromium finished action, light border and scroll engraving, ejectors, ST or SST, hand checkered oil finished select pistol grip walnut stock and forend, 28 - 32 in. barrels, SST, 10mm rib, long forcing cones, 5 extended chokes, cased. Importation began 2004.

MSR N/A	$2,100	$1,850	$1,650	$1,350	$1,150	$950	$850

S 2000 SPORTING - 12 ga., chromium finished action, 28 - 32 in. VR barrels, ejectors, SST, 10mm rib, long forcing cones, 5 extended chokes, sideplates with English scroll and border engraving, extra select checkered pistol grip walnut stock with palm swell, cased. Importation began 2004.

MSR N/A	$3,950	$3,550	$3,150	$2,600	$2,100	$1,675	$1,500

SPORTING EL - includes multi-chokes and case. Importation disc. 2000.

	$2,975	$2,850	$2,500	$2,225	$1,950	$1,675	$1,500

Last MSR was $3,750.

UPLAND EL - all gauges, 27 1/2 in. VR barrels with choke tubes (except .410 bore), case hardened receiver, deluxe walnut, hard case. Imported 1994-2003.

	$2,625	$2,400	$2,100	$1,800	$1,500	$1,200	$995

Last MSR was $2,800.

SHOTGUNS SxS

BR550 - 20 ga., scalloped boxlock action with coin finish or case colors, 26 1/2, 28, or 29 1/8 in. barrels, DT or SST, ejectors, fixed chokes, floral scroll engraving, checkered straight grip English style walnut stock. Importation began 2006.

MSR $3,400		$3,100	$2,750	$2,400	$2,100	$1,700	$1,500	$1,250

BR 552 - 20 ga., engraved boxlock action with sideplates, 26 1/2, 28, or 29 1/8 in. barrels, DT or SST, ejectors, fixed chokes, extensive floral scroll engraving, checkered pistol grip walnut stock. Importation began 2006.

MSR $3,715		$3,395	$2,900	$2,500	$2,150	$1,750	$1,500	$1,250

UPLAND EL - various gauges, standard dimensions only, deluxe engraving with premium grade checkered walnut stright grip stock and forearm.

MSR $5,260		$4,875	$4,400	$3,950	$3,500	$2,950	$2,400	$1,850

RIZZINI, EMILIO

Current shotgun manufacturer established during 1974, and located in Brescia, Italy. No current U.S. importation. Previously imported by Tristar Sporting Arms, Ltd., located in N. Kansas City, MO, and by Traditions, located in Old Saybrook, CT. (see Traditions section for listings). Some models were also previously imported by Armsport, Inc, located in Miami, FL.

Fausti Stefano srl acquired Emilio Rizzini in 1999.

All Emilio Rizzini shotguns are equipped with a patented Four Locks locking system.

GRADING - PPGS™	100%	98%	95%	90%	80%	70%	60%

Models listed were introduced during 1999. Most Emilio Rizzini field shotguns are available with internal choke tubes.

SHOTGUNS: O/U

CLASS MODEL - 12, 16, 20, 28 ga., or 410 bore, boxlock action with reinforced frame, hand engraving, select wood, ejectors, SST. Importation disc. 2000.

	$1,625	$1,400	$1,125	$975	$875	$750	$675

Last MSR was $1,870.

Add $70 for sideplates and case (Class SL Model).

CLASS DE LUXE MODEL - 12, 16, 20, 28 ga., or 410 bore, boxlock action with reinforced frame, hand finished game scene engraving with gold inlays, ejectors, SST, cased. Importation disc. 2000.

	$3,675	$3,325	$2,975	$2,625	$2,300	$1,950	$1,675

Last MSR was $4,185.

Add $170 for sideplates (Class SL De Luxe Model).

BRIXIAN DE LUXE - all gauges, top-of-the-line model, boxlock action with reinforced frame, master fine scroll engraving, ejectors, SST, deluxe English wood, individually made per customer's specifications, leather cased. Importation disc. 2000.

	$8,350	$7,600	$6,950	$5,700	$4,500	$3,650	$2,950

Last MSR was $8,975.

Add $1,986 for sideplates and best leather case (Brixian SL DE Luxe).

TR-I FIELD (NOVA I) - 12 or 20 ga., blue boxlock action, SST, extractors, 26 or 28 vent. barrels with 7mm VR and fixed chokes, checkered standard grade walnut stock and forearm, gold trigger, approx. 7 1/4 lbs. Imported 1998-2001.

	$585	$485	$430	$375	$330	$300	$275

Last MSR was $687.

✳ *TR-I Field Plus* - 12 or 20 (disc. 2004) ga., 3 in. chambers, includes choke tubes, 7mm vent. rib, Imported 2000-disc.

	$650	$575	$485	$435	$375	$330	$300

Last MSR was $779.

TR-II FIELD (NOVA II) - 12, 16 (fixed chokes, disc. 2004), 20 (disc. 2004), 28 (disc. 2004) ga. or .410 bore (fixed chokes, disc. 2004), similar to Nova I, except has choke tubes and ejectors. Mfg. 1998-2005.

	$795	$675	$575	$475	$415	$355	$300

Last MSR was $919.

Add $50 for 20, 28 ga., or .410 bore (disc. 2004).

TR-MAG. (NOVA MAG.) - 10 (mfg. 2000-2002) or 12 ga. only, 3 1/2 in. chambers, SST, ejectors or extractors (10 ga. only), 24 or 28 in. vent. barrels with 7mm VR and choke tubes, matte finished wood and metal or Mossy Oak/Shadowgrass camo wood finish (new 2000), 7 1/4 - 9 1/4 lbs. Impoprted 1998-2004.

	$665	$585	$475	$435	$375	$330	$300

Last MSR was $799.

Add $170 for camo (new 2000).
Add $368 for 10 ga. with camo (mfg. 2000-2002).

SHOTGUNS: O/U, COMPETITION SERIES

The following models were available in either Trap, Skeet, or Sporting Clays configuration. Sporting Clays models have 5 internal multi-chokes.

GRADING - PPGS™	100%	98%	95%	90%	80%	70%	60%

COMPACT MODEL - 12, 16, or 20 ga., boxlock action with reinforced frame, ejectors, SST, model and company name inlaid on black finished action, select checkered walnut stock and forearm, cased. Importation disc. 2000.

	$1,725	$1,650	$1,450	$1,100	$900	$775	$700

Last MSR was $2,135.

GARA MODEL - similar to Compact, except has hand engraving and wood upgrade. Importation disc. 2000.

	$3,100	$2,850	$2,600	$2,200	$1,800	$1,400	$1,250

Last MSR was $3,765.

Add $351 for Gara Cup Model (company logo inlaid in gold).
Add $1,022 for Gara SL Model (includes engraved sideplates).

GARA DE LUXE - top-of-the-line competition model, ornamental pattern engraved by master engraver, deluxe wood, best leather case. Importation disc. 2000.

	$6,100	$5,750	$5,250	$4,400	$3,500	$2,750	$2,450

Last MSR was $7,375.

SHOTGUNS: O/U, PREMIER SERIES

Last MSRs for the models listed below are as follows: Premier - $1,599, Premier Deluxe - $2,199, Premier SL - $1,899, Premier SL Deluxe - $2,399, Premier EL - $1,999, Premier EL Gold - $2,699, Premier ELX Gold - $3,199.

PREMIER SERIES - 12 or 20 ga., various configurations, oil finished stock and forearm, ST or DT, includes 3 choke tubes. Limited importation by Traditions 2003 only.

The Premier Series had limited importation during 2003 only, and MSRs ranged from $1,599-$3,199. Current values for these models range from 35%-75% of the values listed above, depending on condition.

SHOTGUNS: O/U, SPORTING CLAYS

TR-SC (NOVA SC) - 12 or 20 (mfg. 1999-2003) ga. only, 3 in. chambers, sporting clays model, silver finished boxlock action, gold SST, 28 or 30 in. vent. barrels with 10mm VR and mid-rib sight beads, fancy checkered walnut stock and forearm, approx. 7 1/2 lbs. Imported 1998-2005.

	$885	$775	$675	$575	$475	$395	$350

Last MSR was $1,047.

Add $80 for 20 ga. (mfg. 1999-2003).

TR-L - similar to Nova SC, except has stock dimensions for female shooter (13 1/2 LOP), was also available in 20 ga. until 2004, approx. 7 3/4 lbs. Imported 1999-2004.

	$890	$780	$680	$575	$450	$395	$350

Last MSR was $1,063.

TR-ROYAL - 12, 20 (disc. 2004), or 28 (disc. 2004) ga., 3 in. chambers, similar to the TR-SC, except has special dimension stock designed to reduce recoil, 28 or 30 in. VR barrels with 7mm-10mm tapered rib and rhino ported extended choke tubes, ejectors, silver finished boxlock action, deluxe checkered walnut stock and forearm, silver frame with gold accents, approx. 7 1/2 lbs. Imported 1999-2005.

	$1,075	$935	$825	$700	$600	$500	$400

Last MSR was $1,319.

TR-CLASS SL - 12 ga. only, 2 3/4 in. chambers, features select materials, silver finished boxlock action with engraved sideplates, ejectors, SST, 28 or 30 VR barrels with choke tubes, 7 3/4 lbs. Imported 1999-2002.

	$1,525	$1,275	$1,025	$900	$800	$700	$575

Last MSR was $1,775.

GRADING - PPGS™	100%	98%	95%	90%	80%	70%	60%

RIZZINI, F.LLI

Current manufacturer located in Magno V.T., Italy. Consumer direct sales. Some models were previously imported by New England Arms Corp. located in Kittery Point, ME, and by L. Michael Weatherby, located in Laguna Niguel, CA. Please contact the company directly for more information, including an individualized quotation and delivery time (see Trademark Index).

F.lli Rizzini manufactures some of the most technologically advanced rifles and shotguns in the world, approx. 11 guns per year.

RIFLES: SxS, CUSTOM

R1E SAFARI SIDELOCK EJECTOR - .375 H&H or .470 NE cal., every possible refinement, best quality double rifle, includes Purdey English scroll engraving and case. New 2005.

This model has a MSR of €88,000.

Delivery time on this model is approx. 2-4 years, depending on the engraver and amount of engraving.

R3-E SAFARI BOXLOCK - .444 Marlin cal. only, best quality boxlock double rifle, includes Purdey English scroll engraving and case. New 2005.

This model has a current MSR of €66,000.

Delivery time on this model is approx. 2-4 years, depending on the engraver and amount of engraving.

SHOTGUNS: O/U, OLDER MFG.

Zoli Rizzini manufactured an O/U boxlock with sideplates in most gauges, including 28 ga. and .410 bore. These guns were imported by Abercrombie & Fitch. They were available with or w/o ejectors, and single or double triggers. Prices can range from $1,250 - $3,750, depending on gauge and configuration, with the smaller gauges being worth more than the 12 or 20.

SHOTGUNS: SxS, CUSTOM, OLDER MFG.

In the past the Rizzini brothers collaborated with Rinaldo Zoli to make "spec" guns that were usually imported by Abercrombie & Fitch. These guns are normally marked on the water table "Zoli Rizzini". The Zoli Rizzini gun factory closed in 1971. These guns are not to be confused with the quality of current Rizzini F.lli mfg. Normally these older Field Grade models (non-ejector, boxlock action in 12, 16, 20, 28 ga. or .410 bore) sell in the $500-$1,200 range, with a 25% premium for 28 ga. or .410 bore. Deluxe Field Models with scalloped boxlock action ad ejectors are currently valued in the $1,500-$2,500 range with a 30% premium for 28 ga. or .410 bore. The Extra Lusso Model (top-of-the-line) currently sells in the $3,500 range in 12 ga., $4,750 in 28 ga., and $4,250 in .410 bore.

SHOTGUNS: SxS, CUSTOM, RECENT MFG.

Today's F.lli Rizzini shotguns are made to individual custom order only. Prices do not include engraving, and prices will be substantially more for famous name engravers such as Pedersoli, Fracassi and Torcoli. F.lli Rizzini makes their own barrels in house, and use their patented mechanisms.

Please contact the manufacturer directly for a quotation on special engraving options.

R2-E BOXLOCK EJECTOR - 12, 16, or 20 ga., select walnut, detachable bottom inspection plate, various barrel lengths, without engraving. Disc. 1995.

$10,500	$9,000	$8,000	$7,000	$6,200	$5,500	$4,750

Last MSR was $25,000.

✱ R2-E Boxlock Ejector 28 ga. or .410 bore. - otherwise similar to above. Disc. 1995.

$12,750	$11,500	$10,000	$8,750	$7,500	$6,250	$5,000

Last MSR was $27,500.

GRADING - PPGS™	100%	98%	95%	90%	80%	70%	60%

RI-E SIDELOCK EJECTOR - 12, 16, 20, 28 ga. or .410 bore, F.lli Rizzini patented sidelocks, select Circassian walnut, various barrel lengths, without engraving.
Add €6,500 for 28 ga. or .410 bore. Add €16,000 for extra barrels (same ga.).
Current MSR on this model is €61,500.
Current MSR on a pair of 12 & 20 ga. is €147,000 and €160,000 for a pair of 28 ga. & .410 bore.
Engraving on this model is quoted on a special order basis. Estimates may only be given at time of order. Only the best quality engravers are used for this model.

R3-E - best quality patented boxlock ejector model w/o engraving, Importation began 2000.
Add €5,500 for 28 ga. or .410 bore.
Add €16,000 for extra barrels (same ga.).
Current MSR on this model is €46,500.
Delivery time on this model is approx. 2-4 years. depending on engraver and amount of engraving.

RIZZINI, I. (ISIDORA)

Please refer to the Fair Tecni-Mec listing.

THE ROBAR COMPANIES, INC.

Current customizer established during 1986, and located in Phoenix, AZ.

Robar is a leader in custom metal finishing, including combination finishes. These include the Roguard black finish, NP3 surface treatment, and additional finishes including bluing, electroless nickel, Polymax camoflauge, and Polymax finish. Please contact Robar directly (see Trademark Index) for more information, including current prices on their lineup of firearms, custom metal and wood finishes, and customizing services, including shotguns.

PISTOLS: SEMI-AUTO

Robar offers customizing services on new Colt-style semi-auto .45 ACP pistols. Various configurations include the Super Deluxe Pistol Package, Robar Combat Master, or Basic Carry. These guns are built up from other makers including Springfield, Glock, and Browning to provide the configuration/modifications necessary.

RIFLES

Robar also offers customizing services, mainly on the Remington 700, and Ruger M-77 actions. Various configurations include: the SR60, SR90, Thunder Ranch, QR2, QR2-F, Robar RC 50 BMG, Hunter, Precision Hunter, and Varminter.

SHOTGUNS

Defensive shotguns are also customized from the Remington Model 870, and include the Robar Elite, Robar Defender, Robar S.O.F., and Thunder Ranch model

ROBERT HISSERICH COMPANY

Current custom rifle manufacturer located in Mesa, AZ. Previous company name was Stockworks. Consumer direct sales only.

RIFLES: BOLT ACTION

ROBERT HISSERICH BOLT GUN - various cals., features Weatherby Vanguard action, Pac-Nor stainless steel barrel, Pachmayr decelerator pad, hinged floor plate, black synthetic stock. Mfg. 2003 - disc.

	$1,795	$1,500	$1,250	$1,050	$875	$750	$625

GRADING - PPGS™	100%	98%	95%	90%	80%	70%	60%

LIGHTWEIGHT RIFLES SLR - various cals., Rem. long or short action, Kevlar/fiberglass MPI stock, match grade Pac-Nor barrel, straight flutes in bolt body, Timney trigger, straight line muzzle brake, pillar bedded action free floating barrel, "window" cuts in action for lightening, black oxide finish on carbon or stainless steel, English or Claro deluxe checkered stock, custom order only - allow 3-4 months. Approx. 4 3/4-5 lbs.

	$2,600	$2,300	$2,000	$1,800	$1,600	$1,400	$1,200

Add $200 for stainless steel.

SHARPSHOOTER - various cals., Win. Model 70 action with controlled feeding, precision long range hunting rifle with Schnieder stainless steel fluted barrel, laminated stock with ebony forend tip, titanium firing pin, pillar glass bedded with free floating barrel, includes Leupold 6.5-20x40mm scope, custom order only.

	$5,950	$5,100	$4,500	$3,900	$3,400	$2,850	$2,150

ROBERTS, J. & SON (GUNMAKERS) LTD.

Current manufacturer, import agent, and dealer established during 1950, and located in London, England.

Please contact J. Roberts & Son (Gunmakers) Ltd. directly for more information on their current inventory of custom rifles and shotguns, in addition to other services (see Trademark Index).

ROBERTSON

Current trademark manufactured by Boss & Co., Ltd. Manufacture is in Birmingham, England.

Please refer to the individual listings in the Boss section for this trademark.

ROBINSON ARMAMENT CO.

Current rifle manufacturer located in Salt Lake City, UT. Currently distributed by ZDF Import/Export, Inc., located in Salt Lake City, UT. Dealer and consumer direct sales.

RIFLES: SEMI-AUTO

M96 EXPEDITIONARY RIFLE/CARBINE - .223 Rem. cal., paramilitary modular design, unique action allows accessory kit to convert loading from bottom to top of receiver (available later in 2000), 16.2 (Recon Model, new 2001), 17 1/4 (carbine, new 2000) or 20 1/4 in. barrel with muzzle brake, stainless steel receiver and barrel, matte black finish metal, black synthetic stock and forearm, adj. sights, gas operated with adjustment knob, last shot hold open, rotating bolt assembly, 8 1/2 lbs. Mfg. 1999-2006.

	$1,495	$1,300	$1,100	$925	$850	$775	$700

Add $750 for rifle/carbine with top feed.

XCR MODEL - .223 Rem. or 6.8mm SPC cal., paramilitary design, 16 in. full floating barrel with 8 in. side and bottom Picatinny rails, open sights, and quick change barrel system, includes bolt hold open, side folding stock, two-stage trigger, uses M16 mags., 7 1/2 lbs. New 2006.

MSR $1,300		$1,200	$1,000	$850	$725	$600	$500	$450

Add $550 for 6.8mm SPC cal. conversion kit, including barrel bolt and 25 shot mag.
Add $200 for 6.8mm SPC cal.

ROCHE, CHRISTIAN

Current manufacturer located in Veauche, France.

Christian Roche manufactures quality side-by-side shotguns and double rifles. Since all orders are per individual specifications, the factory must be contacted directly to obtain a current price quotation and information (see Trademark Index).

ROCK ISLAND ARMORY

Previous WWII subcontractor of Springfield Model 1903 rifles located in Rock Island, IL. Please refer to Springfield Armory listing for more information.

GRADING - PPGS™	100%	98%	95%	90%	80%	70%	60%

ROCK-OLA MANUFACTURING CO.

Previous WWII subcontractor of M1 carbines located in Chicago, IL. Please refer to US M1 carbines/rifles under U.S. Military listing for more information.

ROCK RIVER ARMS, INC.

Current handgun and rifle manufacturer located in Colona, IL beginning 2004. Previously located in Cleveland, IL until 2003. Dealer and consumer direct sales.

PISTOLS: SEMI-AUTO

Rock River Arms makes a variety of high quality M-1911 based semi-autos. They specialize in manufacturing their own National Match frames and slides. Previous models included: the Standard Match (disc. 2003, last MSR was $1,150), Ultimate Match Achiever (disc. 2003, last MSR was $2,255), Matchmaster Steel (disc. 2001, last MSR was $2,355), Elite Commando (disc. 2005, last MSR was $1,725), Hi-Cap Basic Limited (disc. 2003, last MSR was $1,895), and the Doug Koenig Signature Series (disc. 2003, last MSR was $5,000, .38 Super cal.). Rock River Arms also offers additional options and parts.

BASIC LIMITED MATCH - 9mm Para., .38 Super, .40 S&W, or .45 ACP cal., blue, hard chrome, black "T", or black/green "T" duotone finish, 4 1/4, 5, or 6 in. barrel, National Match frame and slide with low mount Bomar hidden leaf rear sight, beveled mag well and choice of 20, 25, or 30 LPI checkered front strap, match Commander hammer and match sear, tuned and polished extrator and extended ejector, lowered and flared ejection port, beavertail grip safety, aluminum speed trigger, two piece recoil guide road and polished feed ramp, RRA dovetail front sight, serrated slide stop and ambidextrous safety, deluxe checkered grips.

MSR $1,770	$1,595	$1,350	$1,150	$950	$825	$700	$600

LIMITED MATCH - 9mm Para., .38 Super, .40 S&W, or .45 ACP cal., blue, hard chrome, black "T" or black/green duotone finish, National match frame with beveled mag well and choice of 20, 25, or 30 LPIS checkered front and rear strap, 4 1/4, 5, or 6 in. barrel with double slide serrations and RRA borders, low mount Bomar hidden leaf rear sight, RRA dovetail front sight, 40 LPI checkering under trigger guard, Match Commander hammer and match sear, aluminum speed trigger, beavertail grip safety with raised pad, extended mag. release button, tuned and polished feed ramp, deluxe checkered grips, two-piece recoil guide rod.

MSR $2,150	$1,950	$1,700	$1,500	$1,300	$1,100	$900	$750

NATIONAL MATCH HARDBALL - 9mm Para., .38 Super, .40 S&W, or .45 ACP cal., blue, hard chrome, black "T" or black/green "T" duotone finish, forged National Match frame with 4 1/4, 5, or 6 in. barrel, beveled mag well, choice of 20, 25, or 30 LPI checkered front strap, choice of rear or double slide serrations, aluminum speed trigger, milled in Bomar rear sight with hidden rear leaf, lowered and flared ejection port, polished feed ramp, tuned and polished extrator and extended ejector, checkered rosewood grips.

MSR $1,535	$1,395	$1,100	$900	$750	$650	$575	$500

BULLSEYE WADCUTTER - 9mm Para., .38 Super, .40 S&W, or .45 ACP cal., blue, hard chrome, black "T" or black/green "T" duotone finish, 7 shot mag., 4 1/4, 5, or 6 in. barrel, National Match frame with choice of RRR Slide mount, Bomar rib, Caspian frame mount, or Weigand 3rd Gen. frame mount, double slide serrations, choice of 20, 25, or 30 LPI checkered front strap, beavertail grip safety with raised pad, lowered and flared ejection port, Commander hammer and match sear, aluminum speed trigger, checkered rosewood grips.

MSR $1,690	$1,500	$1,295	$1,075	$925	$800	$700	$600

Add $35 for Caspian frame mount or Bo-Mar rib.

GRADING - PPGS™	100%	98%	95%	90%	80%	70%	60%

TACTICAL PISTOL - 9mm Para., .38 Super, .40 S&W, .45 ACP cal., blue, hard chrome, black "T" or black/green "T" duotone finish, 5 in. barrel with double slide serrations, RRA bar stock frame with integral light rail, choice of 20, 25, or 30 LPI checkered front strap, lowered and flared ejection port, RRA dovetail front sight with tritium inserts, Heinie rear sight with tritium inserts, optiona Novak rear sight, aluminum speed trigger, tuned and polished extractor, extended ejector, beavertail grip safety, tactical mag. catch, safety, standard recoil system, completely dehorned for carry, checkered rosewood grips, optional ambidextrous safety, optional Smith & Alexander magwell.

	MSR $1,965		$1,775	$1,525	$1,300	$1,100	$900	$750	$625

BASIC CARRY - .45 ACP cal., 5 in. National Match barrel with double slide serrations, parkerized finish, checkered rosewood grips, RRA forged National Match frame, choice of 20, 25, or 30 LPI checkered front strap, lowered and flared ejection port, RRA dovetail front sight, Heine rear sight, Match Commander hammer and match sear, aluminum speed trigger, beavertail grip safety, standard mag. catch, safety, and standard recoil system.

	MSR $1,555		$1,400	$1,100	$900	$750	$650	$575	$500

PRO CARRY - 9mm Para., .38 Super, .40 S&W, or .45 ACP cal., 4 1/4, 5, or 6 in. barrel with slide serrations, RRA National Match frame with choice of 20, 25, or 30 LPI checkered front strap, lowered and flared ejection port, RRA dovetail front sight with tritium inserts, Match Commander hammer, aluminum speed trigger, tuned and polished extractor, extended ejector, deluxe rosewood grips, choice of Heinie or Novak rear sight with tritium inserts, beavertail grip safety.

	MSR $1,795		$1,595	$1,350	$1,150	$950	$825	$700	$600

LIMITED POLICE COMPETITION - 9mm Para. cal., 5 in. National Match barrel, blue, hard chrome, black "T", or black/green "T" duotone finish, RRA forged National Match frame with beveled mag well with choice of 20, 25, or 30 LPI checkered front strap, double slide serrations, 3-position rear sight, choice of wide or narrow blade, RRA dovetail front sight, tall, thinned, and relieved for PPC, Smith & Alexander flat mag well, lowered and flared ejection port, Match Commander hammer and match sear, tuned and polished extractor and extended ejector, beavertail grip safety and flat checkered mainspring housing, deluxe checkered grips, ambidextrous safety, tuned and polished feed ramp, two-piece recoil guide rod.

	MSR $2,355		$2,050	$1,825	$1,600	$1,375	$1,250	$1,000	$775

UNLIMITED POLICE COMPETITION - 9mm Para. cal., forged 6 in. National Match barrel, RRA forged National Match frame with beveled mag well, choice of 20, 25, or 30 LPI checkered front strap, double slide serrations, similar configuration as Limited Police Competition.

	MSR $2,355		$2,050	$1,825	$1,600	$1,375	$1,250	$1,000	$775

LAR-15 - .223 Rem. cal., 7 or 10 1/2 in. barrel, A2 or A4 configuration, A2 flash hider, single stage trigger, Hogue rubber pistol grip, approx. 5 lbs.

	MSR $910		$795	$725	$650	$575	$500	$450	$395

Add $10 for aluminum free floating forearm or $45 for gas block sight base.

LAR-9 - similar to LAR-15, excpet is 9mm Para. cal., A1 flash hider, 4.8 - 5.2 lbs.

	MSR $1,045		$950	$850	$750	$650	$550	$450	$350

Add $10 for A4 handguard, $55 for aluminum free floating forearm with A2 front sight, or $70 for aluminum free floating handguard with gas block sight base.

RIFLES: SEMI-AUTO

Rock River Arms makes a variety of paramilitary style rifles/carbines patterned after the AR-15 in .223 Rem. cal. Previous models include the CAR UTE (disc. 2004, last MSR was $850), Tactical Carbine A2, M4 Entry (disc. 2003, last MSR was $875), and NM A2-DCM Legal (disc. 2005, last MSR was $1,265).

GRADING - PPGS™	100%	98%	95%	90%	80%	70%	60%

Beginning 2006, Rock River Arms released a series of paramilitary style rifles in 9mm Para. cal. Also during 2006, the company released a series of paramilitary style rifles in .308 Win. cal. A wide variety of options are available for each rifle. Base model assumes black furniture.

STANDARD A2 - .223 Rem. cal., forged A2 upper receiver, 20 in. Wilson chromemoly barrel, A2 flash hider, two-stage match trigger, A2 pistol grip, handguard, and buttstock, 8.6 lbs.

MSR $930	$850	$725	$625	$550	$485	$415	$320

STANDARD A4 - similar to Standard A2 model, except has forged A4 upper receiver, 8.2 lbs.

MSR $890	$800	$700	$600	$525	$465	$395	$295

NATIONAL MATCH A2 - .223 Rem. cal., forged A2 upper receiver, 20 in. Wilson heavy match stainless barrel, 20 shot mag., two-stage match trigger, A2 flash hider, A2 pistol grip and buttstock, free floating handguard, 9.7 lbs.

MSR $1,150	$1,025	$900	$775	$675	$575	$500	$415

NATIONAL MATCH A4 - .223 Rem. cal., similar to National Match A2 model, except has forged A4 upper receiver with NM carry handle, 9.7 lbs.

MSR $1,200	$1,075	$925	$825	$725	$625	$525	$450

CAR A2 - .223 Rem. cal., forged A2 upper receiver, 16 in. Wilson chromemoly barrel, A2 flash hider, two-stage match trigger, CAR length handguard, A2 pistol grip and buttstock, 7 1/2 lbs.

MSR $910	$815	$700	$600	$525	$465	$395	$295

CAR A4 - .223 Rem. cal., similar to CAR A2, except has forged A4 upper receiver, 7.1 lbs.

MSR $875	$795	$700	$600	$525	$465	$395	$295

MID-LENGTH A2 - .223 Rem. cal., forged A2 upper receiver, 16 in. Wilson chromemoly barrel, two-stage match trigger, mid-length handguard, A2 pistol grips and buttstock, 7 1/2 lbs.

MSR $910	$815	$700	$600	$525	$465	$395	$295

MID-LENGTH A4 - .223 Rem. cal., similar to Mid-Length A2 model, except has forged A4 upper receiver, 7.1 lbs.

MSR $875	$795	$700	$600	$525	$465	$395	$295

TACTICAL CAR A4 - .223 Rem. cal., forged A4 upper receiver, detachable tactical carry handle, 16 in. Wilson chromemoly barrel, A2 flash hider, two-stage match trigger, Hogue rubber pistol grip, R-4 handguard, six-position tactical CAR stock, 7 1/2 lbs.

MSR $1,000	$900	$775	$650	$575	$500	$435	$350

ELITE CAR A4 - .223 Rem. cal., similar to Tactical CAR A4, except has mid-length handguard, 7.7 lbs.

MSR $1,000	$900	$775	$650	$575	$500	$435	$350

TACTICAL CAR UTE2 - .223 Rem. cal., forged Universal Tactical Entry 2 upper receiver, 16 in. Wilson chromemoly barrel, A2 flash hider, two-stage match trigger, Hogue rubber pistol grip, R-4 handguard, six-position tactical CAR stock, 7 1/2 lbs.

MSR $985	$885	$775	$650	$575	$500	$435	$350

ELITE CAR UTE2 - .223 Rem. cal., similar to Tactical CAR UTE2, except has mid-length handguard, 7.7 lbs.

MSR $985	$895	$775	$650	$575	$500	$435	$350

ENTRY TACTICAL - .223 Rem. cal., forged A4 upper receiver, 16 in. Wilson chromemoly R-4 heavy barrel, detachable tactical carry handle, A2 flash hider, two-stage match trigger, Hogue rubber pistol grip, R-4 handguard with double heat shields, six-position tactical CAR stock, 7 1/2 lbs.

MSR $1,000	$900	$775	$650	$575	$500	$435	$350

TASC RIFLE - .223 Rem. cal., forged A2 upper receiver with lockable windage and elevation rear sight, 16 in. Wilson chromemoly barrel, A2 flash hider, two-stage match trigger, Hogue rubber pistol grip, A2 buttstock or six-position CAR tactical buttstock, choice of R-4 or mid-length handguard, approx. 7 1/2 lbs.

MSR $935	$850	$725	$625	$550	$485	$415	$320

    Add $15 for six-position collapsible stock.

PRO-SERIES GOVERNMENT - .223 Rem. cal., forged A4 upper receiver, 16 in. chrome lined Wilson chromemoly barrel, A2 flash hider, two-stage match trigger, flip-up rear sight, Hogue rubber pistol grip, six-position tactical CAR stock, Surefire M73 quad rail handguard, Surefire M951 WeaponLight light system, EOTech 552 Holosight red-dot optical sight, side mount sling swivel, 8.2 lbs.

MSR $2,275	$2,000	$1,750	$1,500	$1,300	$1,100	$900	$750

PRO-SERIES TASC - .223 Rem. cal., forged A2 upper reciever, chrome lined 16 in. Wilson chromemoly barrel, Smith vortex flash hider, two-stage match trigger, Winter trigger guard, A2 rear sight with lockable windage and elevation, Hogue rubber pistol grip, six-position tactical CAR stock, Surefire M85 mid-length quad rail, graphite fore grip, EOTech 511 Holosight red-dot optical sight, Midwest Industries A2 adj. cantilever sight mount, 8.7 lbs.

MSR $1,985	$1,800	$1,600	$1,400	$1,200	$1,000	$800	$675

PRO-SERIES ELITE - .223 Rem. cal., forged A4 upper receiver, chrome lined 16 in. Wilson chromemoly barrel, RRA tactical muzzle brake, flip front sight gas block assembly, two-stage match trigger, Winter trigger guard, Badger tactical charging handle latch, A.R.M.S. #40L low profile flip-up rear sight, ERGO sure-grip pistol grip, six-position tactical CAR stock, MWI front sling adapter, MWI CAR stock end plate adapter loop rear sling mount, Daniel Defense 12.0 FSPM quad rail handguard, SureFire M910A-WH vertical foregrip weaponlight, Aimpoint Comp M2 red-dot optical sight and QRP mount and spacer sight and mount, 9 1/2 lbs.

MSR $2,880	$2,550	$2,150	$1,800	$1,575	$1,250	$1,075	$950

VARMINT EOP (ELEVATED OPTICAL PLATFORM) - .223 Rem. cal., forged EOP upper receiver, 16, 18, 20, or 24 in. Wilson air gauged stainless steel bull barrel, Weaver style light varmint gas block with sight rail, two-stage match trigger, Winter trigger guard, knurled and fluted free floating aluminum tube handguard, Hogue rubber pistol grip, A2 buttstock, approx. 8.2 - 10 lbs.

MSR $1,065	$925	$800	$675	$600	$525	$450	$375

VARMINT A4 - .223 Rem. cal., similar to Varmint EOP, except has forged A4 upper receiver., 7.9-9.7 lbs.

MSR $1,040	$815	$785	$660	$575	$500	$435	$350

PREDATOR PURSUIT RIFLE - .223 Rem. cal., similar to Varmint A4, except has 20 in. Wilson heavy match stainless steel barrel, 8.1 lbs.

MSR $1,060	$925	$800	$675	$600	$525	$450	$375

COYOTE RIFLE - .223 Rem. cal., forged A4 upper receiver, 20 in. Wilson chromemoly HBar barrel, Smith vortex flash hider, Weaver style light varmint gas block with sight rail, two-stage match trigger, Winter trigger guard, Hogue rubber pistol grip, Hogue overmolded free float tube handguard, ACE ARFX skeleton stock, 8.4 lbs.

MSR $1,140	$1,000	$900	$775	$675	$575	$500	$415

LAR-6.8 A2/A4 - .6.8mm Rem. SPC cal., forged A2 or A4 upper receiver, 16 in. Wilson chromemoly barrel, A2 flash hider, two-stage match trigger, A2 pistol grip and buttstock, choice of CAR length or mid-length handguard, 7 1/2 lbs.

MSR $900	$815	$700	$600	$525	$465	$395	$295

    Add $15 for A4 with six-position stock.
    Add $35 for A2 buttstock.

GRADING - PPGS™	100%	98%	95%	90%	80%	70%	60%

LAR-458 CAR A4 - .458 SOCOM cal., forged A4 upper receiver, 16 in. Wilson chromemoly bull barrel, A2 flash hider, Weaver style varmint gas block with sight rail, two-stage match trigger, knurled and fluted free floating aluminum tube handguard, A2 buttstock and pistol grip, 7.6 lbs.

MSR $1,065	$925	$800	$675	$600	$525	$450	$375

LAR-10 VARMINT A4 - .308 Win. cal., forged A4 upper reciever with forward assist and port door, 26 in. Wilson stainless steel bull barrel, Weaver type sight base gas block, two-stage match trigger, knurled and fluted free floating aluminum tube handguard, Hogue pistol grip, A2 buttstock, 11.6 lbs.

MSR $1,350	$1,200	$1,000	$925	$825	$725	$625	$525

LAR-10 STANDARD A2/A4 - .308 Win. cal., forged A2 or A4 upper receiver, with forward assist and port door, 20 in. Wilson chromemoly barrel, A2 flash hider, A2 front sight or A4 gas block with sight base, two-stage match trigger, A2 handguard, Hogue rubber pistol grip, A2 buttstock, 9.3 lbs.

MSR $1,100	$1,000	$895	$775	$675	$575	$500	$415

LAR-10 MID-LENGTH A2/A4 - .308 Win. cal., forged A2 or A4 upper receiver with forward assist and port door, 16 in. Wilson chromemoly barrel, A2 flash hider, A2 front sight or A4 gas block with sight base, two-stage match trigger, mid-length handguard, Hogue rubber pistol grip, six-position tactical CAR stock, approx. 8 lbs.

MSR $1,100	$1,000	$895	$775	$675	$575	$500	$415

LAR-9 CAR A2/A4 - 9mm Para. cal., forged A2 or A4 upper receiver, 16 in. Wilson chromemoly barrel, A1 flash hider, standard single stage trigger, CAR length handguard, A2 pistol grip, six-position tactical CAR stock, approx. 7 lbs.

MSR $1,035	$815	$785	$660	$575	$500	$435	$350

Add $25 for A2 buttstock.

ROCKY MOUNTAIN ARMS CORP.

Previous manufacturer of mini revolvers circa mid-1960s, and located in Salt Lake City, UT.

REVOLVERS

MINI REVOLVER - .22 Short cal., 5 shot, stainless steel, locking bolt is in top strap, bolt cam on left side of hammer, supplied with black velveteen case.

	$275	$225	$150	$120	$105	$90	$80

When RMAC went out of business, production was resumed by North American Arms Corp., then after another company change, Freedom Arms started production.

ROCKY MOUNTAIN ARMS, INC.

Current firearms manufacturer located in Longmont, CO since 1991.

Rocky Mountain Arms is a quality specialty manufacturer of rifles and pistols. All firearms are finished in a Dupont Teflon-S industrial coating called Bear Coat.

PISTOLS: SEMI-AUTO

BAP (BOLT ACTION PISTOL) - .308 Win., 7.62x39mm, or 10mm Rocky Mountain Thunderer (10x51mm) cal., features 14 in. heavy fluted Douglas Match barrel, Kevlar/graphite pistol grip stock, supplied with Harris bipod and black nylon case. Mfg. 1993 only.

	$1,425	$1,275	$1,100	$950	$825	$700	$575

Last MSR was $1,595.

1911A1-LH - .40 S&W or .45 ACP cal., specifically designed for left-handed shooters, featuring left side ejection port and right side controls, gold cup size, stainless steel construction, hand fitted parts, integral ramp barrel, Millett adj. sights, test target. Mfg. 1991-93.

	$1,295	$995	$750	$640	$535	$450	$390

Last MSR was $1,395.

Add $100 for Bo-Mar sights.

GRADING - PPGS™	100%	98%	95%	90%	80%	70%	60%

BACKUP PLUS - .45 ACP cal., hand tuned AMT Back-up pistol, black DuPont Teflon-S finish, Tritium front night sight. Mfg. 1995-97.

| | $575 | $515 | $450 | $400 | $360 | $330 | $300 |

Last MSR was $650.

22K PISTOLS - .22 LR cal., AR style pistols featuring 7 in. barrel, choice of matte black or NATO Green Teflon-S finish, will use Colt conversion kit, choice of carrying handle or flattop upper receiver, 10 or 30 shot mag., includes black nylon case. Mfg. 1993 only.

| | $475 | $425 | $375 | $350 | $325 | $295 | $275 |

Last MSR was $525.

Add $50 for flattop receiver with Weaver style bases.

PATRIOT PISTOL - .223 Rem. cal., AR style pistol featuring 7 in. match barrel with integral Max Dynamic muzzle brake, 21 in. overall, available with either carrying handle upper receiver and fixed sights or flattop receiver with Weaver style bases, fluted upper receiver became an option in 1994, accepts standard AR-15 mags, 5 lbs. Mfg. 1993-94 (per C/B), reintroduced 2005.

| MSR $3,000 | $2,850 | $2,500 | $2,250 | $2,000 | $1,750 | $1,500 | $1,250 |

KOMRADE - 7.62x39mm cal., includes carrying handle upper receiver with fixed sights, floating 7 in. barrel, Teflon red or black finish, 5 lbs., 5 shot mag. Mfg. 1994-95.

| | $1,825 | $1,650 | $1,425 | $1,200 | $975 | $850 | $775 |

Last MSR was $1,995.

RIFLES: BOLT ACTION

PROFESSIONAL SERIES - .223 Rem., .30-06, .308 Win., or .300 Win. Mag. cal., bolt action rifle utilizing modified Mauser action, fluted 26 in. Douglas premium heavy match barrel with integral muzzle brake, custom Kevlar-Graphite stock with off-set thumbhole, test target. Mfg. 1991-95.

| | $2,050 | $1,650 | $1,275 | $995 | $850 | $725 | $600 |

Last MSR was $2,200.

Add $100 for .300 Win. Mag. cal.
Add $300 for left-hand action.

PRAIRIE STALKER - .223 Rem., .22-250 Rem., .30-06, .308 Win., or .300 Win. Mag. cal., choice of Remington, Savage, or Winchester barreled action, includes Choate ultimate sniper stock, lapped bolt and match crown, Bear Coat all-weather finish, includes factory test target. Limited mfg. 1998 only.

| | $1,595 | $1,350 | $1,150 | $950 | $875 | $775 | $675 |

Last MSR was $1,795.

＊*Prairie Stalker Ultimate* - similar to Prairie Stalker, except custom barrel and caliber specifications are customer's choice. Limited mfg. 1998 only.

| | $2,200 | $1,875 | $1,625 | $1,400 | $1,200 | $1,000 | $895 |

Last MSR was $2,495.

PRO-VARMINT - .22-250 Rem., or .223 Rem. cal., RMA action, 22 in. heavy match barrel with recessed crown, Bear Coat metal finish, Choate stock with aluminum bedding. Mfg. 1999-2002.

| | $995 | $875 | $800 | $725 | $650 | $575 | $450 |

Last MSR was $1,095.

POLICE MARKSMAN - .308 Win. or .300 Win. Mag. cal., similar to Professional Series, except has 40X-C stock featuring adj. cheekpiece and buttplate, target rail, Buehler micro-dial scope mounting system. Mfg. 1991-95.

| | $2,325 | $1,995 | $1,650 | $1,325 | $1,100 | $900 | $700 |

Last MSR was $2,500.

Add $100 for .300 Win. Mag. cal.
Add $400 for left-hand action.
Add $400 for illuminated dot scope (4-12x56mm).

GRADING - PPGS™	100%	98%	95%	90%	80%	70%	60%

* *Police Marksman II* - .308 Win. cal., RMA action, 22 in. heavy match barrel with recessed crown, Bear Coat metal finish, Choate stock with aluminum bedding. Mfg. 1999-2002.

	$995	$875	$800	$725	$650	$575	$450

Last MSR was $1,095.

PRO-GUIDE - .280 Rem., .35 Whelen, .308 Win., 7x57mm Mauser, or 7mm-08 Rem. cal., Scout Rifle design with 17 in. Shilen barrel, Bear Coat finish, approx. 7 lbs. Mfg. 1999-2002.

	$2,025	$1,800	$1,600	$1,425	$1,200	$1,000	$825

Last MSR was $2,295.

NINJA SCOUT RIFLE - .22 Mag. cal., takedown rifle based on Marlin action, black stock, 16 1/2 in. match grade crowned barrel, forward mounted Weaver style scope base, adj. rear sight, 7 shot mag. Mfg. 1991-95.

	$640	$575	$525	$460	$430	$390	$360

Last MSR was $695.

Add $200 for illuminated dot scope (1.5-4X) w/extended eye relief.

SCOUT SEMI-AUTO - .22 Mag. cal., patterned after Marlin action. Mfg. 1993-95.

	$650	$575	$495	$395	$350	$295	$260

Last MSR was $725.

Add $200 for illuminated dot scope (1.5-4X) w/extended eye relief.

RIFLES: SEMI-AUTO

M-SHORTEEN - .308 Win. cal., compact highly modified M1-A featuring 17" match crowned barrel, custom front sight, mod. gas system, hand honed action and trigger, custom muzzle brake. Mfg. 1991-94.

	$1,650	$1,425	$1,175	$995	$850	$725	$600

Last MSR was $1,895.

Add $200 for Woodland/Desert camo.

VARMINTER - .223 Rem. cal. only, AR-15 styled rifle with 20 in. fluted heavy match barrel, flattop receiver with Weaver style bases, round metal National Match hand guard with floating barrel, choice of NATO green or matte black Teflon-S finish, supplied with case and factory test target (sub-MOA). Mfg. 1993-94.

	$2,195	$1,800	$1,600	$1,400	$1,200	$1,000	$875

Last MSR was $2,495.

PATRIOT MATCH RIFLE - .223 Rem. cal., 20 in. Bull Match barrel, regular or milled upper and lower receivers, two-piece machined aluminum hand guard, choice of DuPont Teflon finish in black or NATO green, 1/2 MOA, hard case. Mfg. 1995-97, reintroduced 2005.

MSR $2,500		$2,350	$2,050	$1,700	$1,425	$1,200	$1,000	$895

SHOTGUNS: SLIDE ACTION

870 COMPETITOR - 12 ga., 3 in. chamber, security configuration with synthetic stock, hand-honed action, ghost ring adj. sights, "Bear Coat" finish, high visibility follower. Mfg. 1996-97.

	$695	$625	$550	$500	$450	$400	$360

Last MSR was $795.

GRADING - PPGS™	100%	98%	95%	90%	80%	70%	60%

ROCKY MOUNTAIN ELK FOUNDATION

Current national conservation organization with national headquarters located in Missoula, MT.

RIFLES: BOLT ACTION

RUGER NO. 1-A LIGHT SPORTER - .35 Whelen cal., features gold inlaid elk on right side of receiver and mountain scene with gold accents on left side, engraved by Adams & Son, blue finish, deluxe wood, 50 mfg. 1995 only.

	$2,395	$1,850	$1,475	N/A	N/A	N/A	N/A

Last MSR was $2,395.

SAUER MODEL 90 - .270 Win. or .30-06 cal., banquet offering only, total mfg. unknown.

	$1,375	$1,100	$925	N/A	N/A	N/A	N/A

ROGAK

Please refer to the L E S Incorporated listing in this text for more information on the Rogak Pistol.

ROGUE RIVER RIFLEWORKS

Current manufacturer located in Paso Robles, CA. Dealer and consumer direct sales.

RIFLES

Please contact the manufacturer directly, including current MSRs on these models.

BOLT ACTION MODEL - 7mm STW, .300 Win. Mag., .30-378 Wby. Mag., 8mm Rem. Mag., .375 H&H, .416 Rem. Mag., or .458 Win. Mag. cal., choice of Remington M-700 or Winchester M-70 action, Pac-Nor match grade barrel (with cryogenic treatment), engraved receiver, floorplate, and grip cap, jewelled bolt, exhibition grade checkered walnut stock with ebony forend cap. Limited mfg. beginning 1998.

MSR N/A	$9,500	$8,500	$7,500	$6,500	$5,500	$4,500	$3,250

LEVER ACTION MODEL - .243 Win., .260 Rem., 7mm-08 Rem., .308 Win., or .358 Win. cal., features rebuilt Winchester Model 88 action, match grade chrome moly barrel, exhibition grade walnut, choice of American classic or Mannlicher stock design. Limited mfg. beginning 1998.

MSR N/A	$4,650	$4,125	$3,675	$3,100	$2,600	$2,000	$1,700

SxS MODEL - .470 NE, .500 NE, or .577 NE cal., Anson & Deeley action, Purdey double locking lugs, Greener crossbolt, Southgate selective ejectors, quarter rib with rear sights, exhibition grade wood, case colored or coin finished receiver. Limited mfg. 1998-2000.

Prices started at $12,500 for .470 NE cal. A 12, 16, or 20 ga. shotgun barrel conversion kit was also available for $3,800.

RÖHM

Previous firearms manufacturer located in Sontheim an der Brenz, Germany. Limited importation into the U.S. Röhm still manufactures gas alarm pistols, mostly for European sales.

Röhm produced inexpensive revolvers for the U.S. marketplace during the late 1960s-1970s. Most of these guns were built as sub-contracts for U.S. companies and/or distributors (i.e., Hy-Score, a previous distributor located in Brooklyn, NY). Some of the models included are RG-7 through RG-88 (21 variations), Romo, Thalco, Valor, Vestpocket, Western Style, Zephyr, and others. Röhm also manufactured a few semi-auto pistols (RG-25 and RG-26) at approx. the same time. Currently, these guns are seen priced in the $35-$125 range, as the shooting value determines the price tag, not collector interest.

GRADING - PPGS™	100%	98%	95%	90%	80%	70%	60%

DERRINGERS

DERRINGER - .22 LR cal., blue, copy of Remington O/U derringer. Excellently made, but half-cock safety is old design and could fail if dropped.

	$150	$115	$95	$85	$75	$65	$55

ROHRBAUGH FIREARMS CORP.
Current manufacturer located in Deer Park, NY.

PISTOLS: SEMI-AUTO

R-9 - 9mm Para or .380 ACP (new 2007) cal., DAO, 2.9 in. barrel, free bored to reduce felt recoil, frame is 7075-T651 aluminum, stainless steel or black Stealth slide, 6 shot mag., parts cut from solid billets, all internal parts are stainless, short recoil locked breech with cam operated tilting barrel locking system, recessed hammer, carbon fiber grips, no sights, 12.8 oz. New 2003.

MSR $1,050	$935	$750	$640	$535	$430	$365	$315

Add $50 for black Stealth slide.

* *R9S Model* - similar to Model R-9, except has fixed iron sights. New 2004.

MSR $1,099	$975	$750	$640	$535	$430	$365	$315

Add $50 for black Stealth slide.

ROSS RIFLE COMPANY
Previous manufacturer located Quebec City, Canada circa 1900-1917.

The Ross rifle was the design of Sir Charles Henry Augustus Frederick Lockhart Ross (1872-1942), 9th Baronet of Balnagown, born in Scotland. He immigrated to Canada in 1897, and left in 1917, following government expropriation of his plant.

While still a student at England's Eton College in 1893, Ross patented his first rifle design, which never left the drawing board. His patent of 1897 was more practical, and reached limited production first in Hartford, CT, then shortly after by the Chas. Lancaster firm in England. Ross worked with J.A. Bennett in Hartford until 1905, and apparently supplied components to Charles Lancaster in London, England until just before WWI began in 1914. By 1903, the new Ross Plant in Quebec City had begun production of early commercial rifles.

Ross was responsible for developing the first commercially available high velocity round in 1906, the .280 Ross, which developed a muzzle velocity round in excess of 3,000 fps, supplied initially as the 1907 Scotch Deerstalker Model. Patterns were sent to Eley in England, who produced the early ammunition for Ross.

While early Ross Commercial Sporting Rifles could almost be considered to be "custom" rifles with many available variations, it would appear the the military rifle production was considered to be the "bread and butter" for the Ross Plant in Canada.

It must be recognized that while Ross provided the basic military designs for the MK I, MK II, and MK III variations, on-going military production was entirely at the mercy of a multitude of Canadian government inspectors, insisting upon almost daily alterations at several points. Overall lengths, weights, and even sights were decided by others.

Unfortunately, the Ross MK III was saddled with a similar Crown of Thorns as the low-numbered Springfield 1903 receivers. The reality was (and still is) that with considerable difficulty, a MK III bolt can be reversed 180 degrees in its sleeve, then with added brute force and ignorance, can be partially inserted in its receiver and fired, with highly unpleasant results. A complete mechanical inspection by a competent gunsmith who is familiar with Ross rifles is urged before firing one of these guns.

The author wishes to express his thanks to Mr. Barry DeLong for making the following information available.

GRADING - PPGS™	100%	98%	95%	90%	80%	70%	60%

RIFLES: BOLT ACTION

The values listed below are for specimens that have been unaltered except where noted.

MODEL 1897 SPORTER - .303 Brit. cal., 26 inch barrel, 5 round magazine, known as the "hammer model" because the bolt cocked the hammer as it traveled over it, clip loaded Mannlicher type magazine, bolt head design of solid, opposing locking lugs with vertical travel and horizontal locking. Hartford, CT version checkered walnut straight stock and a two leaf rear sight, Lancaster version has checkered walnut pistol grip stock, V notch rear sight and tang mounted peep sight. Mfg. 1897-1900.

This variation is encountered with such low frequency that consistent market pricing cannot be established.

MODEL 1900 SPORTER - similar to the Model 1897, except has no hammer and a coil mainspring and internal bolt striker. Mfg. 1900-01.

This variation is encountered with such low frequency that consistent market pricing cannot be established.

RIFLES: BOLT ACTION, CANADIAN PRODUCTION

Canadian production of Ross Rifles consisted of three basic centerfire actions and one rimfire. All four were produced in sporting and military configurations. Commerical rifles typically have a serial number on the left side of the barrel immediately ahead of the receiver. Military rifles are numbered on the right side of the stock - a three digit number from 1-999 over the year manufactured/accepted, followed initially by one letter, then two letters.

MARK I (MILITARY)/MODEL 1903 (SPORTING) - a modification of the Model 1900, "Patented 1903" on left side of receiver, slide button safety, slimmed and completely knurled bolt piece and thumbpiece mag. lifter, enclosed mag.

* *Mark I* - .303 Brit. cal., 28 in. barrel, walnut stock, overall length of 45 and 5/8th inches, H-type hinged rear sight adjustable to 2,200 yards with adjustments for windage and elevation.

$2,000	$1,750	$1,500	$1,250	$1,000	$900	$800

In 1905, the first 1000 rifles were delivered to the Royal Northwest Mounted Police in Regina, Saskatchewan. The early Mk Is used the Ross Mk I and Mk I* rear sight. Most were retrofitted with the Ross Mk II sight. The early nosecaps were formed from sheet metal. Those specimens with the original Mk I or Mk I* sight and original nosecap would bring a premium with values up to $3,500 for a top condition specimen.

* *Model 1903 Sporter* - .303 British (most common), .256 Mannlicher, or .370 Express cal., 26 or 28 in. barrel, walnut checkered stock, two leaf English style rear sight, 5 round magazine. Very scarce with manufacture in Hartford, CT, London, and Quebec. Slight variations based on manufacture location.

$2,000	$1,600	$1,250	$1,000	$850	$700	$600

Add 50% for .256 Mannlicher cal.
Add 50% for .370 Express cal.

MARK II (MILITARY)/MODEL 1905 (SPORTING) - "1905 Patented" on left side of receiver, action is cocked on opening, bolt action camming to initiate cartridge extraction, did not have bolt knurled thumbpiece, improved extractor added to later Model 1905 variations. Mfg. beginning 1906.

* *Mark II (Not Including MKII**)* - .303 Brit. cal., 28 in. round barrel, walnut stock, same basic rifle design with modifications, identified by Roman numeral and number on left of star stamped above serial number in stock.

$750	$675	$600	$550	$500	$450	$425

* *Mark II Original (No Star)* - .303 Brit. cal., Ross MKII or MKIII sight, early model with flat buttplate and "stepped" nosecap (similar to MKI rifles).

$1,000	$900	$800	$700	$600	$550	$500

GRADING - PPGS™	100%	98%	95%	90%	80%	70%	60%

* *Mark II 2** - .303 Brit. cal., 30 1/2 in. heavy barrel and receiver bridge mounted rear sight, military issue, but primarily a target rifle, final military model had no barrel sight and one piece top wood, scarce variation and seldom seen.

	$1,700	$1,500	$1,325	$1,175	$950	$850	$750

* *Mark II 3** - .303 Brit. cal., 28 in. barrel, most common example, includes 20,000 sold to U.S. and marked with flaming bomb proof.

	$1,000	$800	$650	$600	$550	$500	$450

The scarce U.S. sub-variation is shortened by 7/8 in. and has rechambered barrel. This model is seldom seen and commands a premium.

* *Mark II 4** - .303 Brit. cal., 28 in. barrel, similar to MKII 3*, except has earlier Ross MKIII sight fitted (flattop sight), many were converted to a 3*.

	$650	$625	$600	$550	$500	$450	$400

* *Mark II 5** - .303 Brit. cal., 28 in. barrel, seldom encountered variation that has the Sutherland "H" type sight variation with short wood between receiver and sight.

	$850	$750	$650	$600	$525	$475	$400

* *Model 1905 M Sporter* - .303 Brit. cal., 28 in. barrel, illustrated in 1906 catalog only, Enfield barrel sight. Very few known.

	$1,250	$1,100	$950	$850	$775	$700	$625

* *Model 1905 R Sporter* - .303 Brit. cal., 26 or 28 in. barrel, no checkering on stock, originally fitted with Winchester semi-buckhorn sight.

	$750	$675	$625	$575	$525	$475	$400

* *Model 1905 E Sporter* - .303 Brit. or .35 WCF cal., 22, 24, 26 or 28 in. barrel, built up on MKII** receiver, fine-thread heavy barrel, checkered pistol grip wood. Several different multi-leaf "express" sights found on this model.

	$1,250	$1,000	$850	$750	$625	$550	$500

Add 25% for .35 WCF cal.

* *Mark II** Commercial Target Model* - .303 Brit. cal., 30 1/2 in. barrel, identical to the Military 2* rifle but typically found with commercial finish on wood and no sling swivels, target sight on bridge over receiver and serial number on barrel.

	$2,000	$1,600	$1,200	$1,000	$900	$850	$800

Add $500 for Presentation Target Rifle w/o inscription.

This model won almost all rifle matches from 1908 to 1913. A Presentation Target Rifle with deluxe wood and finish, and with a sterling silver medallion in stock was offered in several catalogs, but is seldom encountered. Values increase for a model with an engraved inscription, depending on documentation.

MODEL 1907 & 1905/1910 MATCH TARGET RIFLE - between the MKII (1905) and the MKIII (1910), two important and scarce rifles were built and sold on a modified MKII action with threaded, not solid, locking lugs.

* *Model 1907 "Scotch Deer Rifle Stalking Pattern"* - .280 Ross cal., 26 or 28 in. barrel, 4 shot mag., walnut pistol grip checkered stock, finely finished for Canadian/U.S. market, usually fitted with steel buttplate. For British/Colonial market, many were supplied "in the white" to British gunmakers for completion, usually found UK proofed, finer finish on steel and wood with checkered walnut butt.

	$2,200	$2,000	$1,700	$1,500	$1,250	$1,100	$1,000

Add $500+ if English customized and cased.

This model was a favorite in England circa 1908-1912. English gunmakers such as Cogswell & Harrison, Gibbs, Westley Richards and others offered this model and the Model 1910 in their catalogs. These guns are usually found restocked, rebarrel and refinished, with custom sights and occasionally cased.

GRADING - PPGS™	100%	98%	95%	90%	80%	70%	60%

✳ *Model 1905/Model 1910 Match Target Model* - .280 Ross cal., single-shot with 30 1/2 in. barrel, tangent rear sight on heel of butt and optical hooded front sight, free-floated barrel, can be found in early (tapered forend) and later (deep forend with finger grooves) versions. Very scarce and none found blued (left in the white).

	$2,750	$2,500	$2,250	$2,000	$1,900	$1,800	$1,750

MKIII (MILITARY)/MODEL 1910 (SPORTER) RIFLE - replaced the previously used solid lugs which traveled vertically, has the "triple thread, interrupted-screw, double-bearing cam bolt" with the bolt head traveling horizontally.

It is these models where the report of "bolt blowbacks" have occurred. The bolt on these models, could, with some difficulty be rotated 180 degrees and hence not close completely. If fired in this situation, the bolt could blow back and potentially injure the shooter. Sporters were produced in three grades: R (economy), E (military box magazine and checkered wood) and the top of the line - the M-10.

✳ *MKIII/MKIII B Military* - .303 Brit. cal., 30 1/2 in. barrel, slight changes only through the production run, early models had stamped sheet metal nosecaps, later ones were forged, models found with British proofs were likely in the trenches in France and WWII Homeguard. For the Mk III B, the only change from Canadian issue is the front and rear sight.

	$1,500	$1,250	$1,000	$950	$800	$700	$625

✳ *Military Match Target Model* - .280 Ross cal., 26 in. barrel, box mag. (same as M-10 Sporter with flat floorplate), light walnut stocks with a commercial finish and a Ross MK III battle sight, recalibrated for .280 Ross cal. Mfg. circa 1912. Extremely scarce.

	$5,000	$4,500	$3,750	$3,000	$2,500	$2,000	$1,500

In 1912, Ross built what he considered the perfect military rifle. A suspected total of 25 rifles were built on the commercial line and all known examples are serial numbered in the 10,200 range.

✳ *Model R-10* - .303 Brit. cal., 26 or 28 in. barrel, no checkering, Winchester semi-buckhorn rear sight, miltary five shot box mag., plain steel uncheckered rifle buttplate.

	$800	$700	$600	$550	$500	$425	$400

There is the possibility that Ross used previously rejected military components in these rifles. This is a fairly plain rifle, but seldom encountered.

✳ *Model E-10* - .303 Brit. or .35 WCF cal., 26 or 28 in. barrel, checkered straight grain walnut stock, M-10 pattern checkering on bottom of pistol grip, military box mag, several different express sights can be found on this model. Scarce.

	$1,000	$800	$700	$650	$600	$550	$500

Add 25% for .35 WCF cal.

✳ *Model M-10* - .280 Ross cal., 24, 26 or 28 in. barrel, enclosed four shot double row mag., beautifully finished, pistol grip checkered walnut, grip cap screwed to pistol grip, flat floorplate, 0 to 500 yard sight on barrel, some are equipped with Porter "pop up" sight on the rear receiver bridge.

	$1,500	$1,200	$1,000	$800	$700	$600	$500

Add $100-$200 for rifles with Porter aperture sight or factory option Lyman 48S sight.

✳ *Mark III Homeguard Model* - .303 Brit. cal., identical to the Canadian issued Mk III Military Model but appears to have superior finish and fit on wood and metal, serial number will be found on the barrel just ahead of the receiver, issue stamps may (or may not) be stamped in the stock, considered to be commercial, not military. Less than 1,000 mfg.

	$1,500	$1,250	$1,100	$950	$850	$750	$650

MODEL 1912 CADET

✳ *Model 1912 Cadet Commercial* - serial number on the left side of the barrel, ahead of the receiver.

	$500	$475	$450	$400	$375	$350	$300

GRADING - PPGS™	100%	98%	95%	90%	80%	70%	60%

✳ *Model 1912 Cadet Military* - serial number stamped in stock over year of acceptance, preceeded by a letter, usually multiple "CC" (Cadet Corps) stamps also.

	$500	$475	$450	$400	$375	$350	$300

✳ *Model 1912 Cadet Leftovers* - so called because models were assembled after factory expropriation, no serial numbers, proofs, or stamps in metal or wood.

	$400	$375	$350	$325	$300	$275	$250

ROSSI

Current trademark manufactured by Amadeo Rossi S.A., located in Sao Leopoldo, Brazil. Currently imported exclusively by BrazTech, International beginning late 1998, located in Miami, FL. Previously imported by Interarms, located in Alexandria, VA.

ROSSI
F I R E A R M S

PISTOLS: SINGLE SHOT

ROCKET SINGLE SHOT - .22 LR, .22 Hornet, .22-250 Rem., .220 Swift, .223 Rem., .30-30 Win., .357 Mag., .44 Mag., or .45 LC cal., break open single shot action. Limited importation 2000 only.

	$135	$120	$110	$100	$90	$80	$75

Last MSR was $149.

Add $36 for stainless steel.

REVOLVERS: DOUBLE ACTION

All discontinued models in this section were only imported by Interarms, not Braztech. Braztech is the exclusive North American importer for Rossi firearms.

MODEL 31 - .38 Spl., 5 shot, 4 in. medium barrel, target trigger and hammer, 22 oz. Disc. 1985.

	$120	$105	$95	$85	$75	$70	$65

Last MSR was $139.

Add $5 for nickel.

MODEL 51 - .22 LR cal., 6 shot, 6 in. barrel, blue only, adj. sights. Disc. 1985.

	$125	$110	$100	$90	$85	$80	$75

Last MSR was $149.

✳ *Model 51 Sportsman 511 Stainless* - .22 LR cal. only, stainless steel, 4 in. barrel, with matted rib, adj. rear sight, 6 shot, hardwood stocks, 30 oz. Imported 1986-90 only.

	$190	$160	$125	$100	$85	$70	$65

Last MSR was $235.

MODEL 68 - .38 Spl. cal., 5 shot, 2 or 3 in. barrel, blue or nickel (3 in. barrel only), choice of wood or rubber grips with 2 in. barrel. Disc. 1998.

	$165	$135	$100	$90	$80	$70	$65

Last MSR was $225.

MODEL 69 - .32 S&W cal., 6 shot, 3 in. barrel, walnut grips. Disc. 1985.

	$120	$105	$95	$85	$75	$70	$65

Last MSR was $139.

Add $5 for nickel finish.

MODEL 70 - .22 LR cal, 6 shot, 3 in. barrel. Disc. 1985.

	$120	$105	$95	$85	$75	$70	$65

Last MSR was $139.

Add $5 for nickel finish.

MODEL 84 STAINLESS - .38 Spl. cal., 6 shot, 3 or 4 in. solid raised rib barrel, standard service sights, checkered hardwood grips, 27 1/2 oz. Imported 1985-86 only.

	$190	$155	$125	$100	$85	$70	$65

Last MSR was $205.

GRADING - PPGS™	100%	98%	95%	90%	80%	70%	60%

MODEL 88 STAINLESS - .38 Spl. cal., 5 shot, stainless steel construction, 2 or 3 in. barrel, hardwood or rubber (2 in. barrel only) grips, 21 oz. Disc. 1998.

	$195	$145	$110	$90	$75	$70	$65

Last MSR was $255.

* *Model 88 Stainless Lady Rossi* - .38 Spl., 2 in. barrel, stainless steel, slim round grips. Imported 1995-98.

	$215	$175	$150	$120	$105	$90	$80

Last MSR was $285.

MODEL 89 STAINLESS - .32 S&W cal. only, 6 shot, 3 in. barrel. Imported 1985-86. Reintroduced 1989-90.

	$175	$135	$115	$90	$75	$60	$55

Last MSR was $215.

MODEL 94 - .38 Spl. cal., 6 shot, 3 or 4 in. barrel, blue finish only, 27 1/2 oz. Imported 1985-1988.

	$160	$140	$120	$110	$95	$85	$75

Last MSR was $185.

MODEL R351 - .38 Spl.+P cal., 5 shot, 2 in. barrel, blue finish, combat rubber grips, supplied with key lock, 24 oz. Importation began 1999.

MSR $344	$290	$245	$200	$165	$145	$130	$115

MODEL R352 - similar to Model R351, except is stainless steel. Importation began 1999.

MSR $398	$350	$285	$235	$175	$145	$130	$115

MODEL R461 - .357 Mag.+P cal., 6 shot, 2 in. barrel, blue finish, combat rubber grips, supplied with key lock, 26 oz. Importation began 1999.

MSR $344	$290	$245	$200	$165	$145	$130	$115

MODEL R462 - similar to Model R461, except is stainless steel. Importation began 1999.

MSR $376	$295	$235	$175	$145	$130	$115	$105

MODEL 515(M) STAINLESS - .22 LR or .22 Mag. (Model 515M) cal., double action, 6 shot, classic kit gun design, stainless steel with shrouded ejector rod, adj. rear sights, checkered custom wood grips, 4 in. barrel, 30 oz. Imported 1992 only.

	$195	$145	$110	$90	$75	$70	$65

Last MSR was $248.

MODEL 515 STAINLESS - .22 Mag. cal., similar to 515(M), supplied with 2 pairs of grips (checkered wood and rubber wraparound). Imported 1994-98.

	$210	$165	$140	$110	$95	$85	$75

Last MSR was $270.

MODEL 518 STAINLESS - .22 LR cal., otherwise similar to Model 515 Stainless. Disc. 1998.

	$195	$155	$135	$110	$95	$80	$75

Last MSR was $255.

MODEL 677 FS - .357 Mag. cal., 6 shot, 2 in. heavy barrel, enclosed ejector rod, rubber combat grips, matte blue finish, 26 oz. Imported 1997-98.

	$215	$160	$135	$110	$95	$80	$70

Last MSR was $260.

MODEL 720 STAINLESS - .44 Spl. cal., choice of hammer or hammerless (new 1994) design, 3 in. ribbed barrel, double action, 5 shot with fluted or unfluted cylinder, full ejector rod shroud, adj. rear sight, rubber combat grips, stainless, 27 1/2 oz. Imported 1992-98.

	$220	$180	$155	$125	$110	$90	$80

Last MSR was $290.

GRADING - PPGS™	100%	98%	95%	90%	80%	70%	60%

✳ *Model 720C Stainless* - similar to Model 720 Stainless, except hammerless.

	$220	$180	$155	$125	$110	$90	$80

Last MSR was $290.

MODEL 851 - .38 Spl.+P cal., 4 in. barrel, 6 shot, integral key lock, rubber grips. Importation began 2001.

MSR $344	$290	$245	$200	$165	$145	$130	$115

MODEL 851 STAINLESS - .38 Spl. cal., 3 (disc. 1994) or 4 in. VR barrel, 6 shot, walnut grips, adj. rear sight, 27 1/2 oz. Mfg. 1985-98.

	$195	$155	$135	$110	$95	$80	$75

Last MSR was $255.

This model was previously designated the Model 85 Stainless.

MODEL 877 FS STAINLESS - .357 Mag. cal., 6 shot, small frame, 2 in. barrel with full ejector rod housing, rubber combat grips, 26 oz. Mfg. 1996-98.

	$220	$175	$150	$120	$105	$90	$80

Last MSR was $290.

MODEL 951 - .38 Spl. cal., 6 shot, 3 or 4 in. VR barrel, blue finish only, 27 1/2 oz. Imported 1985-90.

	$190	$155	$135	$120	$110	$100	$90

Last MSR was $233.

This model was previously designated the Model 95.

MODEL 971 - .357 Mag. cal., 4 in. solid rib barrel with internal ejector shroud, 6 shot, adj. rear sight, blue only, hardwood grips, 36 oz. Imported 1988-98.

	$200	$160	$145	$135	$125	$115	$105

Last MSR was $255.

✳ *Model 971 Stainless* - .357 Mag. cal., 2 1/2 (new 1992), 4, or 6 in. solid rib barrel with full shroud, 6 shot, combat style rubber grips, adj. rear sight, 35.4 - 40 1/2 oz. Imported 1989-98.

	$220	$175	$145	$135	$125	$115	$105

Last MSR was $290.

✳ *Model 971 Compensated* - .357 Mag. cal., stainless steel, 3 1/4 in. compensated barrel, 32 oz. Imported 1993-98.

	$220	$175	$145	$135	$125	$115	$105

Last MSR was $290.

MODEL 971 VRC STAINLESS - .357 Mag. cal., stainless steel, 6 shot, choice of 2 1/2, 4, or 6 in. barrel with 8-port vented rib compensator and full-length ejector shroud, combat rubber grips, adj. rear sight, 30-39 oz. Mfg. 1996-98.

	$295	$220	$175	$135	$115	$100	$85

Last MSR was $340.

MODEL 971 (NEW MFG.) - .357 Mag. cal., 4 in. barrel, 6 shot, rubber grips, adj. sights, integral key lock. Importation began 2001.

MSR $398	$350	$285	$235	$175	$145	$130	$115

MODEL 972 - similar to Model 971, except is stainless steel, 6 in. barrel only. Importation began 2001.

MSR $452	$400	$350	$295	$250	$200	$150	$125

CYCLOPS (MODEL 988 STAINLESS) - .357 Mag. cal., 6 or 8 shot, 8 or 10 3/4 (ported or unported, new 1998) in. full shroud barrel with 8 compensation ports, black rubber grips, 51 oz. Imported 1997-98.

	$385	$300	$230	$175	$140	$125	$105

Last MSR was $429.

Add $50 for unported 10 3/4 in. barrel.
Add $60 for ported 10 3/4 in. barrel.

GRADING - PPGS™	100%	98%	95%	90%	80%	70%	60%

RIFLES

For current information on Rossi mfg. Puma rifles imported by Legacy, please refer to the Puma section.

MODEL 65/92 SRC LEVER ACTION - .38 Spl./.357 Mag., .44 Spl./.44 Mag., .44-40 WCF (mfg. 1995-98), or .45 LC (mfg. 1995-98) cal., patterned after Win. Model 92, 16 (.38 Spl./.357 Mag. only), 20 (blue or stainless) or 24 (new 1997, half round/half octagon) in. barrel, 5-5 3/4 lbs. Importation disc. 1998.

	$285	$220	$165	$125	$110	$100	$90

Last MSR was $360.

Add approx. $70 for 24 in. half-round, half-octagon barrel.

This model in .44 Spl./.44 Mag., .44-40 WCF, or .45 LC cal. is sometimes known as the Model 65. This model was also available in matte blue finish at no extra charge.

MODEL 62 SA SLIDE ACTION - .22 LR cal., copy of Win. 1890 "gallery" model, rifle (23 in. barrel) or carbine (16 1/2 in. barrel) available, takedown action, blue or nickel finish, round or octagon barrel, 12 or 13 shot tube mag. Importation disc. 1998.

	$185	$145	$115	$95	$85	$80	$75

Last MSR was $240.

Add $10 for nickel finish.
Add $10 for octagon barrel.

* *Model 62 SA Slide Action Stainless* - similar to regular model, except is stainless steel. Imported 1986 only.

	$165	$145	$120	$100	$85	$70	$65

Last MSR was $192.

MODEL 62 SAC CARBINE - similar to Model 62 SA, except has 16 1/2 in. carbine barrel with full length mag. tube (12 shot), 4 1/4 lbs. Imported 1988-98.

	$185	$145	$115	$95	$85	$80	$75

Last MSR was $240.

Add $10 for nickel finish.

* *Model 62 SAC Carbine Stainless* - similar to Model 62 SAC Carbine, except is stainless steel. Imported 1998 only.

	$215	$165	$125	$100	$85	$70	$65

Last MSR was $280.

MODEL 59 - .22 Mag. version of Model 62 SA, 10 shot mag., 5 1/2 lbs. Importation disc. 1998.

	$220	$170	$130	$120	$110	$100	$90

Last MSR was $280.

ROCKET SINGLE SHOT - .22 LR, .22 Hornet, .22-250 Rem., .220 Swift, .223 Rem., .30-30 Win., .357 Mag., .44 Mag., or .45 LC cal., action and other specifications similar to Model S12 shotgun. Limited importation 2000 only.

	$160	$145	$130	$115	$100	$90	$80

Last MSR was $179.

Add $30 for stainless steel.

FIELD GRADE SINGLE SHOT - .17 HMR cal. (new 2003), .22-250 Rem. (new 2005), .22 LR (disc. 2003), .22 Mag. (disc. 2003), .223 Rem. (new 2002), .243 Win. (new 2002), .270 Win. (new 2004), .30-06 (new 2004), .308 Win. (new 2004), .357 Mag./.38 Spl. (disc. 2003), .44 Mag. (disc. 2003), 7.62x39mm (new 2005), or .410/.45 LC (disc. 2003) cal., 23 in. lightweight tapered or heavy (new 2005) barrel with fully adj. sights, choice of matte blue with natural wood or matte stainless steel (disc. 2004, except for Youth Model) with black wood finish, manual safety, extractor (centerfire) or ejector (rimfire), Monte Carlo stock became an option in 2002, 4 3/4 - 6 1/4 lbs. Importation began 2001.

GRADING - PPGS™	100%	98%	95%	90%	80%	70%	60%

✳ *Field Grade Single Shot Rimfire* - .17 HMR cal., 18 1/2 (Youth) or 23 in. matte finished blue or stainless steel barrel, natural (matte blue) or black (stainless steel) finished wood. Disc. 2006.

	$140	$115	$95	$80	$70	$60	$60

Last MSR was $175.

Add $47 for stainless steel.
Subtract $11 for Youth Model.

✳ *Field Grade Single Shot Centerfire* - centerfire cals., 22 (Youth) or 23 in. barrel, matte blue metal, natural wood finish.

MSR $250		$200	$175	$145	$125	$110	$95	$80

Add $9 for heavy barrel.

SHOTGUNS: SxS

OVERLUND - 12, 20 ga., or .410 bore, exposed hammers, 20 (Coach Model), 26, or 28 in. barrels, double triggers. Importation disc. 1988.

	$275	$230	$185	$155	$140	$125	$115

Last MSR was $332.

SQUIRE - 12, 20 ga., or .410 bore, hammerless, 20, 26 or 28 in. barrels, double triggers, raised matted rib, beavertail forearm, pistol grip, hardwood stock, 3 in. chambers. Imported 1985-90.

	$300	$245	$195	$160	$150	$140	$130

Last MSR was $350.

SHOTGUNS: SINGLE SHOT

MODEL S12/S20/S41 - 12, 20 ga., or .410 bore, 3 in. chamber, lightweight break open action with exposed hammer, ejector, uncheckered hardwood stock and forearm with sling swivels, blue action and 22 (Youth) or 28 (Standard) in. barrel, supplied with trigger lock, 4 lbs. 13 oz Importation began 1999.

MSR $125		$100	$90	$80	$70	$60	$50	$45

Add $89 for 12 ga. Slug gun with 23 in. fully rifled barrel with adj. TruGlo sights (new 2004).
Add $43 for 12 ga. Turkey Model w/ 3 1/2 in. chamber, fiber optic sights and removable choke (new 2007).

This model is also available as a Youth Model in .20 ga. or .410 bore (.410 bore weighs approx. 4 lbs.) - prices are the same as listed.

MATCHED PAIR RIMFIRE/CENTERFIRE - includes choice of 12, 20 ga., or .410 bore single shotgun barrel and interchangable .22 LR, .223 Rem. (new 2002), .243 Win. (new 2002), .270 Win. (new 2003), .30-06 (new 2003), .308 Win. (new 2003) cal. rifle barrel with fully adj. front sight, manual safety. Importation began 2000.

✳ *Matched Pair Rimfire*

MSR $170		$135	$115	$95	$85	$70	$60	$60

Add $40 for .17 HMR cal.
Add $83 for stainless steel (.410 bore and .22 LR or .17 HMR cal. only).

Add $40 for .410 bore and .17 HMR rifle barrel.
Add $24 for matched pair carrying case.

✳ *Matched Pair Youth Trifecta* - includes 22 in. 20 ga. barrel with bead sight, 18 1/2 in. .22 LR barrel with adj. fiber optic sights, and 22 in. .243 Win. cal. barrel with adj. sights, blue metal finish, black synthetic stock with removable cheekpiece. New 2007.

MSR $319		$260	$230	$200	$180	$160	$150	$140

GRADING - PPGS™	100%	98%	95%	90%	80%	70%	60%

✻ *Matched Pair Centerfire* - includes 12 or 20 ga. barrel and choice of .22-250 Rem. (new 2005, Youth only), .223 Rem., .243 Win., .270 Win., .30-06, or .308 Win. cal., 22 (Youth only) or 28 in. shotgun barrel, 22 (Youth only) or 23 (full size) in. rifle barrel.

	MSR $298	$235	$200	$175	$150	$135	$115	$100

Add $24 for matched pair carrying case.

This model is also available in Youth Model in 20 ga. with .22-250 Rem., .223 Rem., .243 Win., or .308 Win. cal. rifle barrel.

ROTA, LUCIANO

Current manufacturer located in Brescia, Italy. No current U.S. importation. Previously imported and distributed 2002-2005 by Tristar, located in N. Kansas City, MO, and by New England Arms Corp., located in Kittery Point, ME.

SHOTGUNS: SxS

The Models 105 and 106 were imported exclusively by New England Arms, and the Model 411 was imported exclusively by Tristar.

MODEL 105 - most gauges, 26-32 in. barrels, boxlock action with sideplates, floral scroll engraving, choice of case colored or coin finished receiver, fixed chokes (any combination), extractors, Circassian checkered walnut stock and forearm. Importation disc. 2004.

	$1,325	$1,075	$875	$750	$650	$550	$500

Last MSR was $1,595.

Add $100 for 28 ga. or .410 bore.
Add $50 for ST, or $175 for multichokes.
Add $500 for hand engraving.

MODEL 106 - all gauges, Anson & Deeley type engraved boxlock action, DT or ST, ejectors, extractors, Circassian checkered walnut stock and forearm, case colored action. Importation disc. 2004.

	$1,225	$950	$775	$675	$550	$500	$450

Last MSR was $1,395.

Add $100 for 28 ga. or .410 bore.
Add $155 for 10 ga.
Add $50 for ST, or $175 for multichokes.
Add $300 for hand engraving.

✻ *Model 106 Slug Gun* - 12 or 20 ga., similar to Model 106, except has 25 in. barrels with express rib and folding leaf sights, with or w/o sideplates, tapered front ramp sight, choke tubes. Importation disc. 2004.

	$1,325	$1,075	$875	$750	$650	$550	$500

Last MSR was $1,595.

Add $200 for hand engraving.
Add $400 for sideplates.

MODEL 411 SERIES - various configurations, all models include boxlock action, checkered walnut stock and forearm, and have either color case hardened or coin finished frame. Importation by Tristar began 2003.

✻ *Model 411 Series Field* - 12, 16, 20, 28 ga. or .410 bore, DTs, splinter forearm, 3 choke tubes included except for fixed chokes on 16, 28 ga. and .410 bore, extractors, 6 1/4-7 1/4 lbs.

	$775	$675	$550	$500	$450	$400	$350

Last MSR was $849.

✻ *Model 411 Series D Field* - 12, 20, 28 ga. or .410 bore, straight grip English stock with ST, ejectors, 6 1/4-7 1/4 lbs.

	$995	$875	$775	$650	$525	$400	$350

Last MSR was $1,110.

GRADING - PPGS™	100%	98%	95%	90%	80%	70%	60%

✳ *Model 411 Series F Field* - 12, 20, 28 ga. or .410 bore, engraved coin finished action with sideplates, gold ST, ejectors, straight grip English stock, 6 1/4-7 1/4 lbs.

	$1,475	$1,250	$995	$875	$775	$650	$525

Last MSR was $1,608.

✳ *Model 411 Series R Field* - 12 or 20 ga., 20 in. fixed choke barrels bored cyl./cyl., DTs, extractors, designed for cowboy competition, approx. 6 1/2 lbs. Disc. 2003.

	$675	$550	$500	$450	$400	$350	$295

Last MSR was $745.

ROTTWEIL

Current manufacturer located in Rottweil, Germany. Previously imported on a limited basis by RUAG Ammotec, USA located in Closter, NJ, and by Rottweil Competition, located in Orange, CA.

SHOTGUNS

PARAGON - 12 ga. only, new design featuring boxlock action, 11 different stock configurations, detachable and interchangeable trigger action, trigger and sear safety, ejectors (switchable to extractors), various barrel lengths (30 in. standard) and rib combinations, cased. Limited importation 1993-99.

	$6,950	$6,500	$5,750	$4,850	$3,950	$3,000	$2,500

Last MSR was $7,500.

Add $850 for Trap Model.
Add $3,150 per extra set of barrels.

✳ *Paragon Sporting Clays Deluxe* - 30 in. barrels only, features better quality wood and engraving. Limited importation.

	$6,950	$6,500	$5,750	$4,850	$3,950	$3,000	$2,500

Last MSR was $7,500.

MODEL 650 FIELD O/U - 12 ga. only, 28 in. barrels with VR, ejectors, single trigger, select checkered walnut, multi-choked with 6 choke tubes, lightly engraved, coin finished receiver. Importation disc. 1986.

	$750	$650	$595	$550	$500	$460	$435

Last MSR was $850.

MODEL 72 FIELD O/U - 12 ga. only, 28 in. vent. barrels and rib, sand blasted receiver, select walnut with checkered stock and forearm, single trigger, ejectors. Importation disc. 1987.

	$1,850	$1,650	$1,450	$1,200	$1,000	$850	$700

Last MSR was $2,295.

MODEL 72 AMERICAN SKEET O/U - 12 ga. only, 26 3/4 in. barrels, VR, ejectors, select French walnut, marginal engraving on sand blasted receiver, single trigger, 7 1/2 lbs. Importation disc. 1987.

	$1,850	$1,650	$1,450	$1,200	$1,000	$850	$700

Last MSR was $2,295.

This model was distributed exclusively by Paxton Arms, located in Dallas, TX.

MODEL 72 AAT SINGLE BARREL TRAP - 12 ga. only, adj. American trap (AAT) barrel features adj. point of impact, 34 in. barrel bored full, high VR. Importation disc. 1986.

	$1,400	$1,200	$1,000	$850	$700	$650	$600

Last MSR was $2,295.

MODEL 72 AT O/U - 12 ga. only, 32 in. IM & F barrels, VR, sand blasted receiver, checkered select walnut stock and forearm, non-adj. point of impact, single trigger, ejectors. Importation disc. 1987.

	$1,850	$1,650	$1,450	$1,200	$1,000	$850	$700

Last MSR was $2,295.

GRADING - PPGS™	100%	98%	95%	90%	80%	70%	60%

MODEL 72 AAT COMBINATION - 12 ga. only, comes with 2 single barrels (32 and 34 in.) that have adj. impact points. Importation disc. 1986.

	$2,450	$2,100	$1,850	$1,600	$1,450	$1,250	$995

Last MSR was $2,850.

✴ *Model 72 AAT Combination* - supplied with 1 single adj. barrel and 32 in. O/U barrels.

	$2,450	$2,100	$1,850	$1,600	$1,450	$1,250	$995

Last MSR was $2,850.

MODEL 72 AAT 3-BARREL SET - 12 ga. only, supplied with 2 single barrels (32 and 34 in.) with adj. impact points and 1 set of 32 in. O/U barrels bored IM & F. Importation disc. 1986.

	$2,850	$2,600	$2,300	$2,000	$1,800	$1,600	$1,400

Last MSR was $3,250.

MODEL 72 INTERNATIONAL TRAP - 12 ga. only, O/U 30 in. barrels bored IM & F with extra high rib. Importation disc. 1987.

	$1,850	$1,650	$1,450	$1,200	$1,000	$850	$700

Last MSR was $2,295.

MODEL 72 INTERNATIONAL SKEET - 12 ga. only, 26 3/4 in. barrels, VR, select walnut stock and forearm. Importation disc. 1987.

	$1,850	$1,650	$1,450	$1,200	$1,000	$850	$700

Last MSR was $2,295.

ROYAL AMERICAN SHOTGUNS

Previously imported by Royal Arms International, located in Woodland Hills, CA circa 1985-87.

SHOTGUNS

MODEL 100 O/U - 12 or 20 ga., 2 3/4 in. chambers, double triggers, extractors, vent. rib and barrels. Imported 1985-87 only.

	$325	$265	$240	$220	$200	$180	$170

Last MSR was $390.

Add $40 for 3 in. chambers, single trigger, and auto ejectors.

MODEL 600 BOXLOCK SxS - 12, 20, 28 ga., or .410 bore, sideplates, silver finished receiver, 3 in. chambers, single trigger, auto ejectors. Imported 1985-87 only.

	$365	$295	$265	$235	$210	$195	$180

Last MSR was $420.

Subtract 25% for double triggers and 2 3/4 in. chambers.

MODEL 800 SIDELOCK SxS - 12, 20, 28 ga., or .410 bore, sidelocks with sideplates, silver finished receiver, 3 in. chambers, single trigger, checkered straight grip stock with select walnut, auto ejectors. Imported 1985-87 only.

	$775	$650	$595	$550	$500	$460	$435

Last MSR was $899.

RUBY

Previous trademark manufactured by Gabilondo, located in Eibar, Spain.

RUGER

See Sturm, Ruger, & Co. section in this text.

RUKO SPORTING GOODS, INC.

Previous importer (non-exclusive) located in Buffalo, NY that imported Arms Corp. of the Philippines firearms circa 1990-95. Ruko Sporting Goods, Inc. (previously Ruko Products) firearms were manufactured by the Arms Corporation of the Philippines. In 1991, Ruko Products, Inc. became the exclusive domestic importer for arms manufactured by Arms Corp. of the Philippines. These firearms were marked "Ruko-Armscor" on the barrels.

Please refer to the Armscor section for current importation, as well as previous importation by Armscorp Precision, Inc. and Ruko Products, Inc.

RUSSIAN AMERICAN ARMORY COMPANY

Current importer located in Scottsburg, IN.

RIFLES AND SHOTGUNS

Russian American Armory Company is an import company for both Izhmash and Molot, located in Russia. Current product/model lines include Saiga semi-auto rifles and shotguns, Vepr. rifles, in addition to a line of bolt action rifles, including the LOS/BAR Series, CM-2 Target rifle, and Sobol hunting model. For current U.S. availability and pricing, please contact the company for more information (see Trademark Index).

RUSSIAN SERVICE PISTOLS AND RIFLES

Previously manufactured at various Russian military arsenals (including Tula).

HANDGUNS

MODEL TT30 & TT33 TOKAREV AUTOMATIC - 7.62x25mm Tokarev cal., design borrowed from Colt 1911, Petter-type unitized trigger/hammer assembly, 8 shot, 4 1/2 in. barrel, blue. Mfg. 1930-54.

$600	$500	$400	$350	$300	$250	$200

Add 20% for matching mag.
Add 100% for TT30 Model.

Values listed assume original condition - no recent imports with importer markings.

✱ *Model TT Tokarev Automatic Recent Import* - 7.62x25mm Tokarev cal., must be stamped by importer, Russian Arsenal mfg., currently imported by Century Arms International, Inc. and others.

No MSR	$140	$110	$90	$80	$70	$60	$50

NAGANT REVOLVER - 7 shot, cylinder comes forward to seal barrel.

$260	$225	$185	$165	$135	$115	$100

Add 10% for pre-communist Imperial marked.

"GRU" marked gun (Armed Forces Intelligence) has shorter barrel and grip frame. While rarer, there is a slight premium being asked.

MAKAROV MD - 9mm Makarov (9x18mm) cal., 8 shot mag. fed double action, 3.7 in. barrel, mfg. circa 1952, standard Russian Service pistol 1957-2003.

$450	$400	$350	$300	$250	$200	$150

Recent imports or commercial models with adj. rear sight are currently selling in the $175 range.

RIFLES

Original Soviet Mosin-Nagant bolt action rifles/carbines include: M1891 rifle, M1891 Dragoon, M1891/30 Rifle, M1891/30 Sniper Model, M1910 Carbine, M1938 Carbine, and the M1944 Carbine. Values for these older original military configurations will approximate values listed for the original mfg. Mosin-Nagant.

TOKAREV M1938 & M1940 (SVT) SEMI-AUTO - 7.62x54R cal., SVT M40 is the more common variation, while the SVT M38 sniper is very rare, 10 shot mag., first Russian military semi-auto, large quantities manufactured beginning 1938, but original surviving specimens in excellent condition are now very scarce.

SVT M38	$2,950	$2,600	$2,400	$1,900	$1,600	$1,400	$1,200
SVT M40	$1,200	$1,000	$800	$700	$600	$500	$425

GRADING - PPGS™	100%	98%	95%	90%	80%	70%	60%

MOSIN-NAGANT BOLT ACTION - various cals., bolt action, many produced under various military contracts, including Remington, New England Westinghouse, and Sako, prices assume recent importation.

	100%	98%	95%	90%	80%	70%	60%
Original mfg.	$250	$225	$185	$165	$145	$130	$120
Recent imports	$125	$100	$90	$80	$70	$65	$60

Add $40% for laminate stock.

RPD SEMI-AUTO - 7.62x39mm cal., converted from belt fed to semi-auto only, closed bolt, milled receiver, includes 50 shot mag., recent importation.

100%	98%	95%	90%	80%	70%	60%
$3,795	$3,495	$2,950	$2,600	$2,300	$2,000	$1,750

RUTTEN HERSTAL

Previous firearms manufacturer of O/U shotguns located in Herstal, Belgium. Previously imported by Labanu, Inc. located in Ronkonkoma, NY.

For more information and current pricing on both new and used Rutten airguns, please refer to the *Blue Book of Airguns* by Dr. Robert Beeman & John Allen (also online).

SHOTGUNS: O/U

MODEL RM 100 - 12 ga., 3 in. chambers, VR multi-choke barrels, ejectors, checkered walnut stock and forearm, hard case. Imported 1995-98.

100%	98%	95%	90%	80%	70%	60%
$875	$775	$675	$575	$500	$450	$400

Last MSR was $1,095.

MODEL RM 285 - similar to Model RM 100, except has engraved side plates and silver engraved receiver, select walnut with Schnabel forearm, hard case. Imported 1995-98.

100%	98%	95%	90%	80%	70%	60%
$1,025	$850	$725	$600	$500	$450	$400

Last MSR was $1,295.

S SECTION

S.A.C.M.

Previous company located in Cholet, France. S.A.C.M. stands for Societe Alsacienne de Construction Mechanique.

GRADING - PPGS™	100%	98%	95%	90%	80%	70%	60%

PISTOLS: SEMI-AUTO

FRENCH MODEL 1935A - 7.65mm Long cal., 8 shot, 4.3 in. barrel, blue, fixed sights, checkered stocks, used by French troops in WWII and Indochina 1945-1954. Mfg. 1935-45.

	$250	$220	$205	$180	$165	$150	$140

Add 50% for Nazi WWII mfg. (Waffenamt proofed).

SAE

Previous importer located in Miami, FL. SAE stands for Spain America Enterprises Inc. SAE imported Felix Sarasqueta shotguns from Spain until circa 1988.

SHOTGUNS: O/U

MODEL 70 - 12 or 20 ga., 3 in. chambers, boxlock action, single trigger, ejectors, 26 in. VR barrel, European checkered walnut stock and forearm, standard finish is blue, Model 70 multi-choke has silver finished action with Florentine engraving and low gloss stock finish. Imported 1988 only.

	$400	$275	$260	$245	$230	$215	$195

Last MSR was $598.

Add $120 for multi-chokes (27 in. barrel).

MODEL 66C - 12 ga. only, 26 in. Skeet or 30 in. F&M VR barrels, boxlock with engraved sideplates including 24Kt. gold inlays, Monte Carlo deluxe stock and beavertail forearm. Imported 1988 only.

	$950	$725	$650	$575	$495	$450	$395

Last MSR was $1,544.

SHOTGUNS: SxS

MODEL 210S - 12, 20 ga., or .410 bore, 3 in. chambers, boxlock action, double triggers, extractors, silver finished receiver with light engraving, approx. 7 lbs. Imported 1988 only.

	$420	$280	$260	$245	$230	$215	$195

Last MSR was $638.

MODEL 340X - 12 or 20 ga., sidelock action, 26 in. barrels with 2 3/4 in. chambers, H&H boxlock action, case hardened finish with moderate scroll engraving, straight grip select walnut stock and forearm with high gloss finish. Imported 1988 only.

	$700	$550	$495	$460	$430	$395	$375

Last MSR was $1,170.

MODEL 209E - 12, 20 ga., or .410 bore, H&H type sidelock action, 26 or 28 in. barrels with 2 3/4 in. chambers, hand engraved coin finished receiver, select checkered walnut stock and forearm, double triggers. Imported 1988 only.

	$925	$700	$650	$575	$495	$450	$395

Last MSR was $1,490.

S.A.M.

Please refer to Shooter Arms Manufacturing Incorporated.

S.I.A.C.E.

Current shotgun and rifle manufacturer located in Gardone V.T., Italy. S.I.A.C.E. also offers an extensive variety of gunsmithing services. Currently imported by Dewing's Fly & Gun Shop, located in W. Palm Beach, FL, Cherry's Fine Guns, located in Greensboro, NC, Kebco LLC, located in Silver Spring, MD, and Don's Sport Shop, located in Scottsdale, AZ. Previously imported on a private label basis by Dakota Arms, located in Stugis, SD, and by New England Arms Corp., located in Kittery Point, ME.

RIFLES: SxS

Add 40% per set of small gauge shotgun barrels with additional forearm.

MODEL ALASKA - 7x65R, 9.3x74R, .30-06, .45-70 Govt., or .444 Marlin cal., rounded scalloped boxlock with hand engraving, sideplates, figured Turkish walnut with skipline checkering, extractors and DT. Limited importation beginning 2002.

Current MSR on this model is €3,960.

Add €1,310 for the Alaska Lusso model or €3,040 for Alaska Lusso EL model with sideplates.

Add €450 for ejectors.

MODEL YUKON - 8x57JRS, .30-06, .45-70 Govt., or .444 Marlin cal., exposed hammers, sidelock action, Bulino style hand engraving, figured Turkish walnut. Limited importation beginning 2002.

Current MSR on this model is €4,050.

Add €1,410 for the Yukon Lusso model.

SHOTGUNS: O/U

600T LUSSO EL - 12, 20, 24, 28, 32 ga. or .410 bore, ST or DT, sideplates with fine hand engraving, multichokes (12 or 20 ga.).

Current MSR on this model is €6,000.

EVOLUTION - 12 or 20 ga., Boss type locking system, detachable trigger group, engraving available on request.

Current MSR on this model is €13,650, w/o engraving.

SHOTGUNS: SxS

MODEL GARDONE HAMMER GUN - 12, 16, 20, 28 ga., or .410 bore, scalloped boxlock with different round frame sizes for each gauge, ejectors, DT, full coverage best hand engraving, checkered deluxe Turkish walnut and custom dimensions. Imported 2000-2004.

$3,650	$3,125	$2,700	$2,250	$1,850	$1,450	$1,250

Last MSR was $3,995.

This model was imported by New England Arms only.

MODEL VINTAGE HAMMER GUN - 12, 16, or 20 ga., sidelock, case hardened or coin finished receiver with border edged engraving, top tang safety, DT, extractors, monobloc barrels.

$2,625	$2,000	$1,425	$1,100	$850	$700	$550

Last MSR was $2,950.

MODEL ETON HAMMER GUN - 12, 16, 20, 28 ga., or .410 bore, 2 3/4 in. chambers standard, DT, extractors, monobloc barrels, case colored or coin finished receiver with scroll engraving, Turkish walnut, straight or pistol grip stock with splinter or semi-beavertail forearm. Imported 2000-2004.

$3,650	$3,125	$2,700	$2,250	$1,850	$1,450	$1,250

Last MSR was $3,995.

Add $1,250 for ejectors and self cocking system (Model Eton Deluxe).

GRADING - PPGS™	100%	98%	95%	90%	80%	70%	60%

MODEL 350G LUSSO/SUPER LUSSO HAMMER GUN (AURORA) - 12, 20, 24 (disc.), 28, 32 (disc.) ga., or .410 bore, back action sidelock, case hardened or coin finished receiver with finely engraved rose and scroll patterns, DT, extractors (Lusso) or ejectors (Super Lusso), top tang safety.

   Current MSR on the Model 350G Lusso Model is €6,180.
   Current MSR on the Model 350G Super Lusso Model is €8,000.
   Add €3,640 for 28 ga. or .410 bore.
   Add €910 for ST, €390 for beavertail forearm, or €360 for multichokes.
This model became part of the Juno Series.

MODEL 370B HAMMER GUN (CONCORDIA) - 12, 16 (disc.), 20, 24 (disc.), 28 or 32 (disc.) ga., or .410 bore, scalloped frame back action sidelock, silver or case hardened receiver with fine scroll engraving, top tang safety, select checkered Turkish walnut, prices include custom dimensions.

   Current MSR on this model is €7,600.
   Add €3,640 for 28 ga. or .410 bore.

MODEL 371Q JUNO HAMMER GUN - 12, 16, 20, 24, 28, 32 ga., or .410 bore, sidelock, available with self cocking and ejectors, silver or case colored receiver, best quality rose and scroll engraving, DT or ST, top tang safety, select checkered Turkish walnut, prices include custom dimensions.

	$5,525	$4,750	$3,950	$3,150	$2,450	$1,875	$1,450

MODEL 475P BIS EL - 12, 20, 28 ga. or .410 bore, hammerless, Anson & Deely boxlock with sideplates and pins, ST or DT, ejectors, straight grip checkered walnut stock, coin finished receiver with light scroll scene engraving.

   Current MSR on this model is €4,000.
   Add €830 for .410 bore.
   Add €450 for ST.

MODEL 475P SUPERLIGHT - 12, 20, 28 ga. or .410 bore, hammerless, scalloped boxlock action with scroll engraving, ejectors, DT, checkered straight grip English stock with splinter forearm, 5.4 - 6 lbs.

   Current MSR on this model is €4,420. Superlight EL Model (sideplates) is €5,270.
   Add €800 for .410 bore.

MODEL 900 HAMMERLESS - 12 or 20 ga., deluxe hammerless model with H&H style sidelock action, ejectors, demibloc barrels, DT or ST, briar walnut stock and forend.

   Current MSR on this model is €13,000, w/o engraving.
This model is available in other gauges by request.

SKB SHOTGUNS

Currently manufactured by the new SKB Arms Company located in Tokyo, Japan. Currently imported and distributed by G.U. Inc. located in  Omaha, NE. SKB has been manufacturing firearms since 1855. Dealer sales.

Previously imported by Ithaca. In 1987, importation resumed on most SKB models. While the model numbers have changed, quality is similar to those models imported previously by Ithaca. In most cases, the newer models are derived closely from their previous counterparts. Listings below will differentiate older, disc. models from currently imported models. SKB also manufactures other models and variations of O/Us and semi-autos (Models 1900 and 3000 Field) shotguns that are not imported into the U.S.

SHOTGUNS: O/U

MODEL 85 TARGET SUPER SPORT (TSS) - 12, 20, 28 ga. or .410 bore, monobloc barrel construction, 2 different frame sizes, Greener crossbolt, nondetachable trigger assembly, silver nitride receiver finish, polished blue barrels, available in Sporting Clays, Skeet, or Trap configuration (including sets), Mag-na-ported barrels, Hi-Viz competition front sight, available with or w/o adj. comb stock (Graco CTS systems), matte wood finish. New 2002.

GRADING - PPGS™	100%	98%	95%	90%	80%	70%	60%

✳ *Model 85 TSS Sporting Clays* - choice of fixed or adj. comb stock, 28, 30, or 32 in. VR barrels, 8.5mm (28 ga. or .410 bore) or 12mm (12 or 20 ga.) stepped VR, 7 1/2-8 1/2 lbs. New 2002.

MSR $2,199	$1,850	$1,525	$1,225	$950	$875	$800	$725

  Add $90 for .410 bore.
  Add $230 for adj. comb on stock.
  Add $190 for pigeon porting by Mag-na-port.
  Add $400 for high grade wood (limited availability, new 2003).

❖ **Model 85 TSS Sporting Clays 2 Gauge Set** - includes 2 sets of barrels in different gauges. New 2002.

MSR $3,549	$3,000	$2,525	$2,050	$1,800	$1,600	$1,400	$1,200

  Add $230 for adj. comb on stock.
  Add $380 for pigeon porting by Mag-na-port.
  Add $470 for high grade wood (limited availability).

❖ **Model 85 TSS Sporting Clays 3 Gauge Set** - includes 20 ga., 28 ga. and .410 bore and 30 in. barrels, includes aluminum case. New 2002.

MSR $5,349	$4,650	$4,200	$3,600	$3,150	$2,750	$2,450	$2,000

  Add $230 for adj. comb on stock.
  Add $550 for high grade wood (limited availability, new 2004).

✳ *Model 85 TSS Skeet* - choice of fixed or adj. comb stock, 28, 30, or 32 in. VR barrels, 8.5mm (28 ga. or .410 bore) or 9.5mm (12 ga.) sloped VR, 7 lbs. 6 oz.-8 lbs. 6 oz. New 2002.

MSR $2,199	$1,850	$1,525	$1,225	$950	$875	$800	$725

  Add $90 for .410 bore.
  Add $230 for adj. comb on stock.
  Add $400 for high grade wood (limited availability, new 2003).

❖ **Model 85 TSS Skeet 3 Gauge Set** - includes 20 ga., 28 ga. and .410 bore and 28 in. barrels, includes aluminum case. New 2002.

MSR $5,349	$4,650	$4,200	$3,600	$3,150	$2,750	$2,450	$2,000

  Add $230 for adj. comb on stock.
  Add $550 for high grade wood (limited availability, new 2004).

✳ *Model 85 TSS Trap O/U* - choice of 30 or 32 in. barrels, fixed or adj. comb standard or Monte Carlo stock, 8 3/4 lbs. New 2002.

MSR $2,199	$1,850	$1,525	$1,225	$950	$875	$800	$725

  Add $230 for adj. comb.
  Add $190 for pigeon porting by Mag-na-port.

✳ *Model 85 TSS Trap Un-Single* - 12 ga. only, bottom un-single, 32 or 34 in. barrel with adj. rib, fixed or adj. comb stock, standard or Monte Carlo stock, 8 3/4 lbs. New 2002.

MSR $2,499	$2,100	$1,750	$1,375	$1,050	$975	$850	$750

  Add $200 for adj. comb on stock.
  Add $400 for high grade wood (limited availability, new 2003).
  Add $114 for pigeon porting by Mag-na-port.

❖ **Model 85 TSS Un-Single Combo** - includes bottom un-single barrel and extra 30 or 32 in. VR O/U barrels. New 2002.

MSR $3,489	$2,975	$2,450	$2,000	$1,750	$1,500	$1,250	$1,000

  Add $210 for adj. comb on stock.
  Add $400 for high grade wood (limited availability, new 2003).
  Add $300 for pigeon porting by Mag-na-port.
  Add $210 for combo with 13 1/2 in. LOP stock (adj. comb only).

MODEL 500 - 12, 20, 28 ga., or .410 bore, field grade, selective ejectors, VR, SST, 26 in. imp. cyl. and mod., 28 in. full and mod., and 30 in. full and mod. barrels, checkered stock. Prices below assume 50% engraving coverage and gold SST. Mfg. in Japan by SKB 1966-79.

	$525	$440	$395	$365	$330	$300	$275

GRADING - PPGS™	100%	98%	95%	90%	80%	70%	60%

Add 15% for 20 ga.
Add 25% for 28 ga. or .410 bore.
Add 10%-15% for fully engraved frame with pheasant, or duck/quail and dog game scene if in 98%+ condition.
Subtract 10% if w/o gold trigger.
Subtract 15%-25% if less than 50% engraving coverage.

The Model 500 varied quite a bit during the course of production in the amount of factory engraving (engraved animals or not), the quality of wood, style of checkering, and also had either silver or gold trigger. This model should also be checked carefully for hairline cracks in the buttstock, where it joins the receiver. Also, beware of bluing wear on frame bottom, and on the front and back of the triggerguard.

* *Model 500 Magnum* - 12 ga., 3 in. Mag., field grade, similar to Model 500, except 3 in. Mag. chambers.

	$550	$450	$410	$385	$355	$320	$290

MODEL 505 FIELD - 12, 20, or 28 (disc.) ga., blue (new 1998) or silver nitride engraved frame (disc. 1997), 3 in. chambers, 26 or 28 in. barrels (supplied with choke tubes), single selective trigger, ejectors, matte finished (new 2006) or high gloss (disc. 2005) checkered walnut stock with recoil pad and forearm, 6 3/4 - 7 3/4 lbs.

MSR $1,429	$1,225	$975	$800	$700	$550	$500	$450

Add $500 for combo package (disc.).
The combo package included either 12/20 ga. barrels with Inter-chokes or 28 ga./.410 bore barrels.

* *Model 505 Sporting Clays* - 28 or 30 in. multi-choke barrels, blue frame with light engraving, dimensioned for Sporting Clays competition, 1997 importation features Schnabel forearm, semi-wide channeled rib, and lengthened forcing cones, approx. 8 1/4 lbs. Older importation, in addition to new model imported 1997-2002.

	$1,100	$885	$765	$650	$525	$460	$420

Last MSR was $1,299.

* *Model 505 Trap* - 12 ga., 30 or 32 in. choke tube barrels with or without Monte Carlo stock, high rib.

	$875	$725	$650	$525	$475	$430	$395

Last MSR was $995.

Add $400 for O/U Trap Combo.
The above Combo includes one set of O/U Trap barrels and a top single Trap barrel.

* *Model 505 Skeet* - 12, 20, 28 ga., or .410 bore, 28 in. barrels with multi-chokes.

	$875	$725	$650	$525	$475	$430	$395

Last MSR was $995.

* *Model 505 3-Ga. Skeet Set* - includes 20, 28 ga., and .410 bore fitted 28 in. barrel sets with individual forends, aluminum case.

	$1,925	$1,575	$1,350	$1,200	$1,125	$950	$875

Last MSR was $2,195.

MODEL 585 FIELD - 12, 20, 28 ga., or .410 (new 1995) bore, silver nitride engraved receiver, 3 in. chambers, 26 or 28 in. barrels (supplied with choke tubes), similar to 505 Series, except has .735 diameter bore on 12 ga. models and includes lengthened forcing cones with extended length "Competition Series" Inter-Choke System designed to improve shot patterns and reduce recoil, SST, ejectors, high gloss (disc. 2005), matte finished (new 2006), or checkered walnut stock with recoil pad and forearm (Youth/Ladies model is also available with 13 1/2 LOP), 6 lbs. 10 oz.-7 lbs. 11 oz. Importation began 1992.

MSR $1,699	$1,425	$1,200	$1,000	$850	$725	$600	$550

Add $80 for 28 ga. or .410 bore.
Add $200 for Gold Package featuring choice of silver or blue receiver, gold plated trigger, and 2 gold game scenes with Schnabel forearm - new 1998.

GRADING - PPGS™	100%	98%	95%	90%	80%	70%	60%

✳ **Model 585 Field Set** - includes 12/20 ga., 20/28 ga., 28 ga./.410 bore, 26 or 28 (new 1994) in. VR barrels with SKB Inter-choke system, silver nitride receiver with finely engraved scroll game scenes, low profile receiver, crossbolt locking system, SST, ejectors, manual safety, checkered high gloss (disc. 2005) or matte finish (new 2006) American walnut stock and forearm.

MSR $2,749	$2,375	$2,000	$1,700	$1,350	$1,100	$975	$850

Add $80 for 20/28 ga. set or 28 ga./.410 bore set.

Add approx. $340 for Gold Package featuring choice of silver or blue (disc. 2004) receiver, gold plated trigger, and 2 gold game scenes with Schnabel forearm - new 1998.

✳ **Model 585 Medallion** - 12 or 20 ga., 3 in. chambers, features two inlaid medallions in gold or bronze finish (medallion artwork by Ron Van Gilder and Rocky Capece), very limited production. Mfg. 2000-2005.

	$1,610	$1,275	$1,025	$900	$800	$700	$600

Last MSR was $1,819.

✳ **Model 585 Upland** - 12, 20, or 28 ga., 3 in. chambers for 12 and 20 ga., features straight grip stock with recoil pad and 26 in. VR barrels, Schnabel forearm, 6 lbs. 10 oz.-7 lbs. 10 oz. Mfg. 1997-2005.

	$1,285	$975	$775	$625	$525	$475	$425

Last MSR was $1,549.

Add $90 for 28 ga.

Add $200 for Gold Package featuring choice of silver or blue receiver, gold plated trigger, and 2 gold game scenes with Schnabel forearm - mfg. 1998-2005.

✳ **Model 585 Trap** - 12 ga., 30 or 32 in. choke tube barrels with or w/o Monte Carlo stock, high rib. Disc. 2002.

	$1,310	$975	$800	$600	$500	$450	$395

Last MSR was $1,619.

Add $200 for Gold Package featuring choice of silver or blue receiver, gold plated trigger, and 2 gold game scenes with Schnabel forearm - mfg. 1998-2002.

Add $800 for O/U Trap Combo or $1,100 for O/U Trap Combo with Gold Package.

The above Combo includes one set of O/U Trap barrels and a top single Trap barrel.

✳ **Model 585 Skeet** - 12, 20, 28 ga., or .410 bore, 28 or 30 (12 ga. only - new 1994) in. barrels with multi-chokes. Disc. 2002.

	$1,310	$975	$800	$600	$500	$450	$395

Last MSR was $1,619.

Add $60 for 28 ga. or .410 bore.

Add $200 for Gold Package featuring choice of silver or blue receiver, gold plated trigger, and 2 gold game scenes with Schnabel forearm - mfg. 1998-2002.

✳ **Model 585 3-Ga. Skeet Set** - includes 20, 28 ga., and .410 bore fitted 28 in. barrel with individual forend, aluminum case. Disc. 2002.

	$3,175	$2,550	$2,000	$1,700	$1,525	$1,400	$1,300

Last MSR was $3,779.

Add $450 for Gold Package featuring choice of silver or blue receiver, gold plated trigger, and 2 gold game scenes with Schnabel forearm - mfg. 1998-2002.

✳ **Model 585 Sporting Clays** - 12, 20, 28 ga. or .410 bore, 3 in. chambers (12 and 20 ga.), 28 or 30 in. multi-choke barrels, dimensioned for Sporting Clays competition, narrow rib (3/8 in.) became available 1994. Disc. 2002.

	$1,410	$1,050	$850	$635	$530	$475	$425

Last MSR was $1,679.

Add $60 for 28 ga. or .410 bore.

Add $200 for Gold Package featuring choice of silver or blue receiver, gold plated trigger, and 2 gold game scenes with Schnabel forearm - mfg. 1998-2002.

GRADING - PPGS™	100%	98%	95%	90%	80%	70%	60%

❖ **Model 585 Sporting Clays Set** - includes 2 sets of barrels (12 ga. - 30 in., 20 ga. - 28 in.), cased. Mfg. 1996-2002.

	$2,135	$1,775	$1,495	$1,200	$1,050	$925	$825

Last MSR was $2,419.

Add $300 for Gold Package featuring choice of silver or blue receiver, gold plated trigger, and 2 gold game scenes with Schnabel forearm - mfg. 1998-2002.

＊ *Model 585 Waterfowler* - 12 ga. only, 3 in. chambers, oil finished stock and forearm, matte finished barrel and receiver. Imported 1995-2000, reintroduced 2005.

	$1,285	$975	$775	$625	$525	$475	$425

Last MSR was $1,549.

＊ *Model 585 Youth/Ladies* - 12 or 20 ga., 26 or 28 (12 ga. only) in. VR barrels, features 13 1/2 in. LOP, barrels have .735 in. bores with lengthened forcing cones. New 1994.

MSR $1,699		$1,425	$1,200	$975	$850	$725	$600	$550

Add $200 for Gold Package featuring choice of silver or blue receiver, gold plated trigger, and 2 gold game scenes with Schnabel forearm - new 1998.

MODEL 585 150th ANNIVERSARY - 12 or 20 ga., 3 in. chambers, silver nitride engraved receiver with gold game scenes, matte finished metal, 26 or 28 in. barrels, matte finish high grade black American walnut stock with finger groove forend, 6 lbs. 12 oz. - 7 lbs. 14 oz. 150 mfg. 2005 only.

	$1,685	$1,425	$1,175	N/A	N/A	N/A	N/A

Last MSR was $1,999.

A total of 150 of this model was manufactured - 70 in 12 ga. w/28 in. barrels, 25 in 12 ga. w/26 in. barrels, 30 in 20 ga. w/28 in. barrels, and 25 in 20 ga. w/26 in. barrels.

MODEL 600 FIELD GRADE - similar to Model 500, except silver-plated frame and select wood and fully engraved.

	$950	$825	$700	$525	$475	$430	$395

Add 20% for 20 ga.

An unknown quantity of Model 600s were mfg. with blue receivers - a small premium may be asked.

MODEL 600 MAGNUM - similar to Model 600 Field, except chambered for 3 in. Mag., 12 ga. Mfg. 1969-72 by SKB.

	$975	$850	$700	$525	$475	$430	$395

MODEL 600 TRAP GRADE - similar to Model 600 Field Grade, except 12 ga. only, trap stock, recoil pad, select wood.

	$995	$850	$700	$525	$475	$430	$395

MODEL 600 DOUBLES GUN - similar to Model 600 Trap, except choked for 21 yd. and 30 yd. targets. Mfg. 1973-75.

	$995	$850	$700	$525	$475	$430	$395

MODEL 600 SKEET GRADE - 12, 20, 28 ga., or .410 bore, 26 or 28 in. barrels, bored S&S, otherwise similar to Model 600 Trap.

	$995	$850	$700	$525	$475	$430	$395
28 ga. or .410 bore.	$1,425	$1,175	$900	$750	$650	$550	$450

MODEL 600 SKEET GRADE COMBO SET - similar to Model 600 Skeet, except fitted with matched set of 20, 28 ga., and .410 bore barrels, in fitted case.

	$2,650	$2,250	$1,875	$1,550	$1,325	$1,175	$1,025

MODEL 605 FIELD - similar to Model 505 Deluxe Field except has silver finished engraved receiver with better walnut. Importation disc. 1992.

	$1,075	$850	$750	$675	$575	$500	$450

Last MSR was $1,195.

Add $500 for extra set of barrels (Combo).

✳ *Model 605 Trap* - 12 ga., 30 or 32 in. choke tube barrel with or without Monte Carlo stock, high rib.

	100%	98%	95%	90%	80%	70%	60%
	$1,075	$850	$750	$675	$575	$500	$450

Last MSR was $1,195.

Add $400 for O/U Trap Combo.
The above Combo includes one set of O/U Trap barrels and a top single Trap barrel.

✳ *Model 605 Skeet* - 12, 20, 28 ga., or .410 bore, 28 in. barrels with multi-chokes.

	100%	98%	95%	90%	80%	70%	60%
	$1,100	$850	$750	$675	$575	$500	$450

Last MSR was $1,195.

✳ *Model 605 3-Ga. Skeet Set* - includes 20, 28 ga., and .410 bore fitted 28 in. barrel sets with individual forends, aluminum case.

	100%	98%	95%	90%	80%	70%	60%
	$2,175	$1,650	$1,400	$1,250	$1,125	$950	$875

Last MSR was $2,395.

✳ *Model 605 Sporting Clay* - 28 or 30 in. multi-choke barrels, dimensioned for Sporting Clay competition.

	100%	98%	95%	90%	80%	70%	60%
	$1,110	$850	$750	$675	$575	$500	$450

Last MSR was $1,245.

✳ *Model 605 DU Sponsor Gun* - mfg. for DU chapters - dinner auction gun, 850 mfg. in 12 ga. (1990) and 850 mfg. in 20 ga. (1991). Features gold inlays and presentation case.

DU sponsor gun values are usually hard to ascertain in the secondary marketplace. Currently, prices seem to range between $1,200-$1,400.

MODEL 680 ENGLISH - similar to Model 600 Field, except English style stock, select walnut and fine scroll engraving. Mfg. 1973-76.

	100%	98%	95%	90%	80%	70%	60%
	$1,300	$1,150	$975	$850	$725	$650	$600

Add 20% for 20 ga.

MODEL 685 FIELD - similar to Model 585 Deluxe Field, except has silver finished engraved receiver with gold inlays and better walnut, engine turned monobloc. Imported 1992-1995.

	100%	98%	95%	90%	80%	70%	60%
	$1,325	$950	$795	$675	$575	$500	$450

Last MSR was $1,549.

✳ *Model 685 Field Set* - includes 12/20, 20/28 ga., 28 ga./.410 bore 26 or 28 (new 1994) in. VR barrels with SKB Inter-choke system (on 12, 20, and 28 ga.), silver nitride receiver with finely engraved scroll game scenes, low profile receiver, crossbolt locking system, SST, ejectors, manual safety, checkered high gloss American walnut stock and forearm.

	100%	98%	95%	90%	80%	70%	60%
	$1,850	$1,650	$1,500	$1,350	$1,275	$1,100	$1,000

Last MSR was $2,149.

✳ *Model 685 Trap* - 12 ga., 30 or 32 in. choke tube barrels with or w/o Monte Carlo stock, high rib.

	100%	98%	95%	90%	80%	70%	60%
	$1,365	$975	$825	$700	$600	$525	$450

Last MSR was $1,595.

Add $600 for O/U Trap Combo.
The above Combo includes one set of O/U Trap barrels and a top single Trap barrel.

✳ *Model 685 Skeet* - 12, 20, 28 ga., or .410 bore, 28 or 30 (12 ga. only - new 1994) in. barrels with multi-chokes.

	100%	98%	95%	90%	80%	70%	60%
	$1,365	$975	$825	$700	$600	$525	$450

Last MSR was $1,595.

GRADING - PPGS™	100%	98%	95%	90%	80%	70%	60%

✳ *Model 685 3-Ga. Skeet Set* - includes 20, 28 ga., and .410 bore fitted 28 in. barrels sets with individual forends, aluminum case.

	$2,550	$2,175	$1,875	$1,675	$1,450	$1,275	$1,125

Last MSR was $2,949.

✳ *Model 685 Sporting Clays* - 28 (all gauges), 30 (12 ga. only), or 32 (12 ga. only) in. multi-choke barrels, dimensioned for Sporting Clays competition, 3/8 in. narrow rib became available 1994. Importation disc. 1995.

	$1,365	$975	$825	$700	$600	$525	$450

Last MSR was $1,595.

✳ *Model 685 Sporting Clays Set* - includes one set of 12 ga. (28, 30, or 32 in. VR barrels) and 20 ga. (28 in. only) or one set of 32 and 28 in. barrels in 12 ga only. Imported 1994-95.

	$2,000	$1,675	$1,500	$1,350	$1,200	$1,025	$895

Last MSR was $2,295.

MODEL 700 TRAP GRADE - 12 ga., similar to Model 600 Trap, except more engraving, better grade wood, wide rib. Mfg. 1969-75.

	$820	$770	$740	$685	$630	$595	$565

MODEL 700 DOUBLES GUN - 12 ga., similar to Model 700 Trap, except choked for 21 yd. and 30 yd. targets. Mfg. 1973-75.

	$795	$770	$740	$685	$630	$595	$565

MODEL 700 SKEET GRADE - 12 ga., similar to Model 700 Doubles, only bored S&S, available in 12 or 20 ga.

	$840	$770	$740	$685	$620	$585	$555

MODEL 785 FIELD - 12, 20, 28 ga., or .410 bore, silver nitride engraved receiver, 3 in. chambers, 26 or 28 in. barrels (supplied with choke tubes), similar to 585 Series, except has chrome lined bores on all models and also includes lengthened forcing cones with extended length "Competition Series" Inter-Choke System designed to improve shot patterns and reduce recoil, SST, ejectors, checkered walnut stock with recoil pad and forearm, 6 lbs. 10 oz.-7 lbs. 11 oz. Imported 1995-2002.

	$1,900	$1,650	$1,400	$1,150	$1,000	$900	$800

Last MSR was $2,119.

Add $80 for 28 ga. or .410 bore.

✳ *Model 785 Field Set* - includes 12/20, 20/28 ga., 28 ga./.410 bore, 26 or 28 in. VR barrels with SKB Inter-Choke system (on 12 and 20 ga.), silver nitride receiver with finely engraved scroll game scenes, low profile receiver, crossbolt locking system, SST, ejectors, manual safety, checkered high gloss American walnut stock and forearm. Importation disc. 2002.

	$2,680	$2,300	$1,925	$1,600	$1,500	$1,375	$1,275

Last MSR was $3,019.

Add $100 for 20/28 ga. set or 28 ga./.410 bore set.

✳ *Model 785 Medallion* - 12 or 20 ga., 3 in. chambers, features three inlaid medallions in gold or bronze finish (medallion artwork by Ron Van Gilder and Rocky Capece), very limited production. Mfg. 2000-2005.

	$2,075	$1,750	$1,450	$1,175	$1,050	$925	$825

Last MSR was $2,389.

✳ *Model 785 Trap* - 12 ga., 30 or 32 in. choke tube barrels with or w/o Monte Carlo stock, high rib. Importation disc. 2002.

	$1,940	$1,625	$1,365	$1,125	$995	$895	$800

Last MSR was $2,199.

Add $880 for O/U Trap Combo.
The above Combo includes one set of O/U Trap barrels and a top single Trap barrel.

GRADING - PPGS™	100%	98%	95%	90%	80%	70%	60%

* *Model 785 Skeet* - 12, 20, 28 ga., or .410 bore, 28 or 30 (12 ga. only) in. barrels with multi-chokes. Importation disc. 2002.

	$1,940	$1,625	$1,365	$1,125	$995	$895	$800

Last MSR was $2,199.

Add $40 for 28 ga. or .410 bore.

* *Model 785 3-Ga. Skeet Set* - includes 20, 28 ga., and .410 bore fitted 28 in. barrel sets with individual forends, aluminum case. Importation disc. 2002.

	$3,835	$2,975	$2,350	$2,000	$1,600	$1,400	$1,295

Last MSR was $4,439.

* *Model 785 Sporting Clays* - 12, 20, or 28 ga., 28 in. (all gauges), 30 in. (12 ga. only), or 32 in. (12 ga. only) multi-choke barrels, dimensioned for Sporting Clays competition with 12mm narrow rib. Importation disc. 2002.

	$2,000	$1,675	$1,375	$1,150	$995	$895	$800

Last MSR was $2,269.

Add $80 for 28 ga.

❖ **Model 785 Sporting Clays Set** - includes 2 sets of barrels (12 ga. - 30 in., 20 ga. - 28 in.). Imported 1996-2002.

	$2,775	$2,450	$2,125	$1,825	$1,625	$1,400	$1,200

Last MSR was $3,149.

MODEL 800 TRAP GRADE - 12 ga., similar to Model 700 Trap, except more engraving, better grade wood, wide rib. Limited mfg. 1969-1975.

	$1,150	$875	$775	$675	$575	$500	$425

MODEL 800 SKEET GRADE - 12 or 20 ga., skeet chokes. Mfg. 1969-1975.

	$1,200	$1,000	$895	$795	$680	$595	$565

MODEL 880 CROWN GRADE - 12, 20, 28 ga., or .410 bore, coin finished receiver, extensively engraved with sideplates, SST, ejectors, select walnut with fleur-de-lis scroll style checkering, double crossbolt action. Limited mfg. Disc. 1980.

	$2,000	$1,825	$1,625	$1,300	$1,150	$975	$890

Add 25% for 28 ga. or .410 bore.

MODEL 885 - available in either Field, Skeet, or Trap configuration, coin finished receiver featuring fine scroll engraving with game scenes, boxlock action with sideplates, beginning 1992, the 885 Series in 12 ga. features lengthened forcing cones, .735 bore, and a competition series of extended length multi-chokes. Imported 1988-94.

* *Model 885 Field* - 12, 20, 28 ga., or .410 bore, field dimensions, 26 or 28 in. barrels include choke tubes. Imported 1989-94.

	$1,600	$1,200	$975	$825	$725	$650	$595

Last MSR was $1,895.

* *Model 885 Trap* - 12 ga., 30 or 32 in. barrels with multi-chokes, standard or Monte Carlo stock.

	$1,650	$1,200	$975	$850	$750	$650	$595

Last MSR was $1,949.

Add $700 for O/U Trap Combo.
The above Combo includes one set of O/U Trap barrels and a top single Trap barrel.

* *Model 885 Skeet* - 12, 20, 28 ga., or .410 bore, 28 or 30 (12 ga. only - new 1994) in. barrels with multi-chokes.

	$1,650	$1,200	$975	$850	$750	$650	$595

Last MSR was $1,949.

GRADING - PPGS™	100%	98%	95%	90%	80%	70%	60%

✳ *Model 885 Field Set* - includes 12/20, 20/28 ga., 28 ga./.410 bore 26 or 28 (new 1994) in. VR barrels with SKB Inter-Choke system (on 12 and 20 ga.), silver nitride receiver with finely engraved scroll game scenes, low profile receiver, crossbolt locking system, SST, ejectors, manual safety, checkered high gloss American walnut stock and forearm.

	$2,450	$2,150	$1,750	$1,500	$1,250	$1,075	$925

✳ *Model 885 3-Ga. Skeet Set* - includes 20, 28 ga., and .410 bore fitted 28 in. barrel sets with individual forends, aluminum case.

	$3,200	$2,700	$2,300	$1,975	$1,725	$1,500	$1,400

Last MSR was $3,595.

✳ *Model 885 Sporting Clays* - 28 (all gauges), 30 (12 ga. only), or 32 (12 ga. only) in. multi-choke barrels, dimensioned for Sporting Clays competition, 3/8 in. narrow rib became available 1994.

	$1,650	$1,200	$975	$850	$750	$650	$595

Last MSR was $1,949.

MODEL 5600 - 12 ga. only, available as Trap or Skeet model only, VR (Trap only) and vent. barrels (Skeet only), no engraving, select walnut. Disc. 1980.

	$575	$495	$450	$420	$390	$360	$330

MODEL 5700 - available as Trap or Skeet model only, silver nitride receiver, fully engraved with game scenes, select walnut, VR. Disc. 1980.

	$1,550	$1,325	$1,100	$900	$775	$650	$575

MODEL 5800 - available as Trap or Skeet model only, more deluxe engraving, select walnut. Disc. 1980.

	$1,800	$1,550	$1,325	$1,100	$900	$775	$650

SHOTGUNS: SxS

Models 100, 150, 200, 280, 300, 400, and 480 were available in 12 and 20 ga. only, featured 25-30 in. barrels, and all had boxlock actions. More expensive models differ in the amount of engraving, grade of walnut, and style of checkering, beavertail forearm, 6 1/4-7 lbs. Disc. 1980.

Add approx. 10% for NIB condition on the following models.

MODEL 100 - 12 or 20 ga., Mag. model also, SST, extractors, blue only.

	$695	$595	$490	$395	$350	$300	$250

Add 20% for 20 ga.
Add 10%-15% for fully engraved receiver with pheasant, or duck/quail and dog game scene if in 98%+ condition.
Subtract 15%-25% if w/ less than 50% engraving coverage.
The Model 100 varied quite a bit during the course of production in the amount of factory engraving (engraved animals or not), the quality of wood, style of checkering, and also had either silver or gold trigger. This model should also be checkered carefully for hairline cracks in the buttstock, where it joins the receiver. Also, beware of bluing wear on receiver bottom, and on the front and back of the triggerguard.

MODEL 150 - similar to Model 100, except scroll engraving, beavertail forearm. Mfg. 1972-74 by SKB.

	$695	$550	$485	$395	$350	$300	$275

Add 20% for 20 ga.

MODEL 200 - 12 or 20 ga., Mag. model also, SST, ejectors, boxlock, scalloped frame, lightly engraved coin finished receiver.

	$995	$895	$795	$695	$650	$490	$425

Add 20% for 20 ga.

GRADING - PPGS™	100%	98%	95%	90%	80%	70%	60%

MODEL 200 (RECENT MFG.) - similar to original Model 200, SST, ejectors, pistol grip stock, recoil pad. Imported 1987-1988 only.

	$995	$895	$795	$695	$650	$490	$425

Last MSR was $895.

Add 20% for 20 ga.

This model was supplied with 3 factory choke-tubes.

✳ *Model 200E (English)* - similar to New Model 200, except has straight grip stock. Importation disc. 1988.

	$1,050	$950	$825	$725	$600	$500	$425

Last MSR was $895.

Add 30% for 20 ga.

MODEL 280 ENGLISH - 12 or 20 ga., Mag. model also, SST, AE, lightly engraved blue receiver, straight grip.

	$1,095	$995	$885	$775	$675	$585	$495

Add 30% for 20 ga.

MODEL 300 - 12 or 20 ga., Mag. model also, SST, AE, lightly engraved coin finished receiver.

	$995	$895	$795	$685	$575	$485	$425

Add 30% for 20 ga.

MODEL 385 FIELD - 12 (new 1998), 20 or 28 ga., scalloped boxlock action with silver nitride receiver, engraved scroll and game scene designs, SST, ejectors, automatic safety, semi-fancy gloss finished American walnut, English or pistol grip stock, beavertail or satin finished splinter forearm, limited quantities. Imported 1992-2004.

	$1,750	$1,425	$1,050	$850	$725	$600	$525

Last MSR was $2,049.

✳ *Model 385 Field Sporting Clays* - 12, 20 (new 2000), or 28 (new 2000) ga., 3 in. chambers (12 ga.), 28 or 30 (new 2003) in. barrels with raised VR and double bead sights, pistol grip stock, approx. 7 1/2 lbs. Imported 1998-2004.

	$1,850	$1,425	$1,050	$875	$750	$650	$550

Last MSR was $2,159.

❖ **Model 385 Field Sporting Clays Set** - includes a pair of 20 and 28 ga., 28 or 30 (new 2003) in. barrels. Imported 1999-2004.

	$2,575	$2,100	$1,750	$1,475	$1,200	$1,050	$975

Last MSR was $3,059.

✳ *Model 385 Field Set* - includes a pair of 20 and 28 ga., 26 in. barrels, choice of pistol grip or English straight stock. Imported 1997-2004.

	$2,475	$2,100	$1,750	$1,475	$1,200	$1,050	$975

Last MSR was $2,929.

✳ *Model 385 Field DU Commemorative* - features gold inlaid mallards on both receiver sides and gold inlaid DU duck head on receiver bottom, includes hard shell case, and signed letter from SKB president, DU proofmarks, limited mfg. - 200 sets in 1992.

	$3,950	$2,750	$1,950	N/A	N/A	N/A	N/A

Last MSR was $5,000.

This model was a DU "Collectors Series" gun.

MODEL 400 - 12 or 20 ga., Mag. model also, boxlock, SST, AE, moderately engraved coin finished receiver with sideplates.

	$1,395	$1,295	$1,195	$950	$795	$695	$585

Add 30% for 20 ga.

GRADING - PPGS™	100%	98%	95%	90%	80%	70%	60%

MODEL 400 (RECENT MFG.) - similar to original Model 400, SST, ejectors, recoil pad, choke tube system. Imported 1987-88 only.

	$1,395	$1,295	$1,195	$950	$795	$695	$585

Last MSR was $1,195.

Add 30% for 20 ga.

* *Model 400E (English)* - similar to New Model 400, except has engraved side-plates and straight grip stock. Importation disc. 1989.

	$1,595	$1,495	$1,395	$1,195	$995	$795	$675

Last MSR was $1,195.

Add 30% for 20 ga.

MODEL 480 ENGLISH - 12 or 20 ga., Mag. model also, SST, AE, moderately engraved coin finished receiver, straight grip. Limited mfg.

	$1,675	$1,525	$1,395	$1,195	$995	$795	$675

Add 30% for 20 ga.

MODEL 485 FIELD - 12 (new 1998), 20, or 28 ga., coin finished boxlock action with engraved upland game scene side plates, 26 or 28 in. barrels with raised VR, checkered gloss finished American walnut stock and beavertail forearm, ejectors, SST, satin finish and splinter forearm became available in 20 or 28 ga. during 2002, approx. 7 lbs. Imported 1997-2004.

	$2,400	$2,050	$1,725	$1,425	$1,250	$995	$850

Last MSR was $2,769.

* *Model 485 Field Set* - includes a pair of 20 and 28 ga., 26 or 28 in. barrels, choice of pistol grip or English straight stock, very limited production. Imported 1998-2004.

	$3,400	$2,825	$2,300	$2,000	$1,675	$1,375	$1,150

Last MSR was $3,949.

SHOTGUNS: SEMI-AUTO

MODEL 300 STANDARD - 12 or 20 ga., 3 in. chamber, recoil operated, 26 in. imp. cyl., 28 in. mod. or full plain barrel, 30 in. full, checkered pistol grip stock. Mfg. 1968-72.

	$295	$255	$205	$165	$155	$145	$140

MODEL XL 300 - 12 or 20 ga., 2 3/4 (12 ga.) or 3 (20 ga.) in. chamber, gas operated, white alloy receiver with light game scene etching, 4 shot mag., 26-30 in. plain barrel.

	$325	$285	$235	$200	$185	$165	$150

MODEL 1300 UPLAND - 12 or 20 ga., 3 in. chamber, 22, 26, or 28 in. VR barrel with multi-chokes, matte black receiver, checkered walnut stock and forearm. Importation resumed 1988-96.

	$450	$385	$340	$300	$270	$240	$210

Last MSR was $495.

This model was previously designated the Model XL-300. The new Model 1300 was available in Slug configuration with 22 in. barrel/iron sights at no extra charge. Recent Model 1300s have a magazine cutoff system on front left side of frame.

MODEL 900 STANDARD - 12 or 20 ga., 3 in. chamber, similar to Model 300 standard, except has vent. rib. barrel. Mfg. 1968-1972.

	$325	$285	$235	$200	$185	$165	$150

XL 900 - similar to XL 300, except has vent. rib barrel and no recoil pad, 6 1/4 lbs.

	$365	$325	$275	$250	$230	$190	$175

XL 900 MR - 12 ga. only, gas operated, 26-30 in. barrel, 5 shot, alloy receiver, engraved game bird scroll work on receiver, shoots both 2 3/4 and 3 in. shells by interchanging barrels. Disc. 1980.

	$325	$280	$260	$240	$225	$190	$175

GRADING - PPGS™	100%	98%	95%	90%	80%	70%	60%

XL 900 TRAP GRADE - similar to XL 900 MR, 12 ga. only, scroll engraved black chrome receiver, 30 in. imp. mod. or full barrel, trap style stock, straight or Monte Carlo, recoil pad. Mfg. 1980-disc.

	$395	$350	$320	$305	$275	$265	$260

XL 900 SKEET GRADE - similar to XL 900 MR, except scroll engraved black chrome receiver, 26 in. barrel, skeet stock. Mfg. 1972-disc.

	$400	$350	$320	$305	$275	$265	$260

XL 900 SLUG GUN - similar to XL 900 MR, except 24 in. slug barrel, rifle sights, no rib. Mfg. 1972-disc.

	$350	$310	$280	$265	$250	$220	$200

MODEL 1900 - 12 or 20 ga., 3 in. chamber, 22, 26, or 28 in. VR barrel with multi-chokes, deluxe outdoor field scene etched on receiver, gold trigger, approx. 1,000-2,000 mfg. per year. Importation disc. 1996.

	$485	$430	$395	$360	$330	$295	$260

Last MSR was $545.

This model was previously designated the Model XL 900. The Model 1900 was available in Slug configuration with 22 in. barrel and iron sights or Trap Model at no extra charge. Recent Model 1900s have a magazine cutoff system on front left side of frame.

MODEL 3000 - 12 or 20 ga., 3 in. chamber, gas operated, (shoots both 2 3/4 and 3 in. shells interchangeably) with semi-squareback styling, elaborate game scenes etched on both sides of receiver, deluxe checkered walnut stock and forearm. Imported 1988-90.

	$545	$475	$415	$380	$350	$315	$285

Last MSR was $597.

Add $125 for Trap model (2 3/4 in. chamber).

This model has not previously been imported in this configuration.

SHOTGUNS: SINGLE BARREL, TRAP

MODEL 505 TRAP - 12 ga., 32 or 34 in. barrel with multi-chokes, regular or Monte Carlo stock.

	$875	$725	$650	$525	$475	$430	$395

Last MSR was $995.

MODEL 605 TRAP - 12 ga., 32 or 34 in. barrel with multi-chokes.

	$1,075	$850	$750	$675	$575	$500	$450

Last MSR was $1,195.

CENTURY TRAP - 12 ga., 32 or 34 in. VR barrel, engraved, auto ejector, full choke, checkered walnut stock. Mfg. 1973 and 1976.

	$550	$525	$470	$440	$385	$360	$320

This model was imported by Ithaca.

CENTURY II TRAP - improved trap stock version of Century, Monte Carlo stock.

	$600	$550	$495	$470	$415	$385	$350

This model was imported by Ithaca.

SHOTGUNS: SLIDE ACTION

MODEL 7300 - 12 or 20 ga., 2 3/4 or 3 in. chambers, blue only, French walnut stock-hand checkered, twin action slide bars. Disc. 1980.

	$295	$250	$225	$200	$180	$165	$150

MODEL 7900 - trap or skeet variation of the Model 7300.

	$350	$310	$265	$235	$200	$180	$160

SKS

SKS designates a semi-auto rifle design originally developed by the Russian military, and manufactured in Russia by both Tula Arsenal (1949-1956) and by Izhevsk Arsenal from 1953-1954. Currently manufactured in Russia, China, and many other countries. Previously manufactured in Russia, China (largest quantity), N. Korea, East Germany, Romania, Albania, Yugoslavia, and North Vietnam.

SKS DEVELOPMENT & HISTORY

SKS (Samozaryadnyi Karabin Simonova) - developed by Sergei Gavrilovich Simonov in the late 1940s to use the 7.62 cartridge of 1943 (7.62x39mm). The SKS is actually based on an earlier design developed by Simonov in 1936 as a prototype self-loading military rifle. The SKS was adopted by the Soviet military in 1949, two years after the AK-47, and was originally intended as a complement to the AK-47s select-fire capability. It served in this role until the mid-to-late 1950s, when it was withdrawn from active issue and sent to reserve units and Soviet Youth "Pioneer" programs. It was also released for use in military assistance programs to Soviet Bloc countries and other "friendly" governments. Much of the original SKS manufacturing equipment was shipped to Communist China prior to 1960. Since then, most of the SKS carbines produced, including those used by the Viet Cong in Vietnam, have come from China.

Like the AK-47, the Simonov carbine is a robust military rifle. It, too, was designed to be used by troops with very little formal education or training. It will operate reliably in the harshest climatic conditions, from the Russian arctic to the steamy jungles of Southeast Asia. Its chrome-lined bore is impervious to the corrosive effects of fulminate of mercury primers and the action is easily disassembled for cleaning and maintenance.

The SKS and a modified sporter called the OP-SKS (OP stands for Okhotnichnyi Patron) are the standard hunting rifles for a majority of Russian hunters. It is routinely used to take everything from the Russian saiga antelope up to and including moose, boar, and brown bear. The main difference between the regular SKS and the OP variant is in the chamber dimensions and the rate of rifling. The OP starts as a regular SKS, then has the barrel removed and replaced with one designed to specifically handle a slightly longer and heavier bullet.

Prior to the "smal weapon" ban, hundreds of thousands of SKS carbines were imported into the U.S. The SKS was rapidly becoming one of the favorites of American hunters and shooters. Its low cost and durability made it a popular "truck gun" for those shooters who spend a lot of time in the woods, whether they are ranchers, farmers, or plinkers. While the Russian made SKS is a bonafide curio and relic firearm and legal for importation, the Clinton administration suspended all import permits for firearms having a rifled bore and ammunition from the former Soviet Union in early 1994. In order to get the ban lifted, the Russian government signed a trade agreement, wherein they agreed to deny export licenses to any American company seeking SKS rifles and a variety of other firearms and ammunition deemed politically incorrect by Clinton & Gore. The BATF then used this agreement as a reason to deny import licenses for any SKS from any country.

Most of the SKS carbines imported into the U.S. came from the Peoples Republic of China. They were a mix of refurbished military issue, straight military surplus, and even some new manufacture. Quality was rather poor. Compared to the SKS Chinese carbines, only a few Russian made SKSs ever made it into the U.S. All are from military stockpiles and were refurbished at the Tula Arms Works, probably the oldest continuously operating armory in the world. Recently, more SKS carbines have been imported from the former Yugoslavia by Century International Arms. These carbines carry the former Soviet Bloc designation of "Type 58" and feature milled receivers. Quality is generally good, and values are comparable to other Russian/European SKS imports. Values for unmodified Russian and Eastern European made SKS carbines (those with the original magazines and stock) are higher than the Chinese copies.

The most collectible SKS is East German mfg., and SKS rifles mfg. in N. Korea and N. Vietnam are also quite rare in the U.S.

Over 600 million SKS carbines have been manufactured in China alone, by over 45 different manufacturers, in addition to the millions manufactured in other former Soviet Bloc

GRADING - PPGS™	100%	98%	95%	90%	80%	70%	60%

countries. The Simonov carbine was the best selling semi-auto rifle in America (and other countries) during 1993-94, and remains a popular choice for plinking, hunting, and protection in the new millennium.

RIFLES: SEMI-AUTO

SKS - 7.62x39mm Russian cal., Soviet designed, original Soviet mfg. as well as copies mfg. in China, Russia, Yugoslavia, and many other countries, gas operated weapon, 10 shot fixed mag., wood stock (thumbhole design on newer mfg.), with or w/o (newer mfg.) permanently attached folding bayonet, tangent rear and hooded front sight, no current importation from China, Russia, or the former Yugoslavia.

	100%	98%	95%	90%	80%	70%	60%
Original Mfg.	$275	$250	$220	$200	$185	$175	$170
Chinese Mfg.- thumbhole stock	$195	$175	$140	$120	$100	$85	$70

From late 1993 until the Crime Bill was enacted during September of 1994, runaway demand escalated SKS prices on recent Chinese exports to the $195-$250 range. Earlier Russian manufacture at the time was selling for $250-$325, but prices fell once the glut of Chinese imports arrived. However, as supply began equaling demand, prices fell off to their current levels. With interest waning and a current stable marketplace, SKS pricing has become more predictable, and knowledgeable shooters and collectors are now seeking out earlier Russian-made SKSs, as these guns have the most quality and best fit/finish (not Chinese overall poor quality). During the 1990s, there were many lawsuits as a result of imported SKS models going full auto, and as a result, prices have gone down slightly.

This model may also be listed under those importers/distributors who import this model and are listed in this text.

SOG INTERNATIONAL INC.

Current importer located in Lebanon, OH.

SOG International Inc. imports a wide variety of surplus military firearms, in addition to currently manufactured guns. Please contact the company directly for more information regarding current model availability and pricing (see Trademark Index).

S.P.S.

Current handgun manufacturer established circa 1997, and located in Ripollet, Barcelona, Spain.

S.P.S. manufactures a variety of semi-auto pistols based on the M1911 design, and many configurations are available, including competition, standard, and compact models in .38 Super, .40 S&W and .45 ACP cal. Please contct the company directly for more information, including U.S. availability and pricing (see Trademark Index).

SSK INDUSTRIES

Previous Class II manufacturer located in Wintersville, OH.

SSK Industries is no longer manufacturing complete guns, but maintains a wide variety of gunsmithing services.

SSK Industries previously manufactured complete rifles and suppressors for police, military, and civilian use (where legal in accord with ATF regulations). Their custom shop worked on virtually anything 20mm or smaller.

SSK Industries used Thompson Center flatside frames and applied an industrial hard chrome finish. Most SSK handguns and rifles were extensively customized in exotic calibers, finishes, and various engraving options. Receivers and barrels could be purchased separately - values below are for complete assembled pistols.

SSK has also manufactured various limited editions including the Handgun Hunters International (HHI) Models 1, 2, and 3. Issue prices on these guns were $1,100 (Model 3), $1,200 (Model 2), and $1,300 (Model 1). Only 50 were mfg. total in 1987. SSK also customized a Ruger Super Redhawk (.44 Mag. or .45 LC cal.). This variation came with either a scoped 7 1/2 in. octagon barrel (Beauty Model) or a 6 in. bull barrel with muzzle brake (Beast Model). Prices started at $1,430 - add $245 extra for .45 LC cal.

GRADING - PPGS™	100%	98%	95%	90%	80%	70%	60%

PISTOLS: SINGLE SHOT

Values listed are for basic models with no options or special features.

SSK-CONTENDER - over 150 cals. available from .17 Bee to .50-70, various custom barrels available, basically, this is a custom order only gun.

	$1,500	$1,375	$1,250	$1,125	$1,000	$900	$825

Individual barrels were available starting at $268.
An arrestor muzzle brake was available on special order.
This model included barrel, frame, stocks, and sights as standard equipment.

SSK-XP100 - various cals. between .17 and .50, includes TSOB mount and rings.

	$1,700	$1,500	$1,300	$1,150	$1,025	$925	$850

The .50 cal. XP100 (12.9 X 50.8 JDJ) came with SSK muzzle brake, scope, dies, and new reinforced fiberglass stock - retail price was $1,700.

RIFLES

Values listed are for basic models with no options or special features. In addition, SSK also custom manufactured a bolt action rifle available in almost any caliber and configuration - prices started at approx. $2,000 and can go as high as $6,000, depending on the customer's individual special orders. SSK also has developed a 6.5mm, 7mm, or .30 cal. upper unit conversion for AR-15s and M-16s utilizing heavy sub-sonic "Whisper" ammunition. SSK also manufactured a line of .50 BMG cal. rifles available in either Brown or Sako action.

SSK TCR 87 - .14 through .600 cals., Nitro Express cals. are also available, features Thompson Center TRC 87 receiver, and SSK custom barrels, muzzle brakes, and exotic finishes were available at extra cost.

	$1,700	$1,500	$1,300	$1,150	$1,025	$925	$850

SSK RUGER NO. 1 - many cals. including .577 NE (optional), custom order rifle based on a Ruger No. 1 frame.

	$2,000	$1,800	$1,600	$1,400	$1,250	$1,100	$1,000

SSK BOLT ACTION - various cals., ground up custom order rifle.

	$2,500	$2,250	$1,800	$1,600	$1,400	$1,250	$1,100

STI INTERNATIONAL

Current manufacturer established during 1993, and located in Georgetown, TX. Distributor and dealer sales.

In addition to manufacturing the pistols listed, STi International also makes frame kits in steel, stainless steel, aluminum, or titanium - prices range between $405-$717.

PISTOLS: SEMI-AUTO

The beginning numerals on all STi pistols designate the barrel length, and most of the following models are listed in numerical sequence.

3.4 BLS9/BLS40 - 9mm Para. or .40 S&W cal., blue finish, Govt. length grips, Heine low mounted sights, single stack mag., 30 oz. Mfg. 1999-2005.

	$765	$650	$565	$460	$400	$360	$330

Last MSR was $889.

3.4 LS9/LS40 - 9mm Para. or .40 S&W cal., blue finish, Commander length grips, single stack mag., Heine low mounted sights, 28 oz. New 1999.

MSR $789	$665	$575	$525	$450	$400	$350	$325

3.4 ESCORT - 9mm Para. or .45 ACP cal., 1911 forged aluminum Commander style frame, 3.4 in. ramped bull barrel, slide with rear cocking serrations, Duracoat finish with blue slide, undercut trigger guard, stippled front strap, rosewood grips, STi hi-ride beavertail grip safety, fixed Novak style 3-dot sights, 22.8 oz. New 2007.

MSR $1,024	$925	$825	$725	$650	$575	$500	$425

GRADING - PPGS™	100%	98%	95%	90%	80%	70%	60%

3.9 FALCON - .38 Super, .40 S&W, or .45 ACP cal., STi standard frame, 3.9 in. barrel, size is comparable to Officers Model, adj. rear sight. Limited mfg. 1993-98.

		$1,875	$1,375	$1,175	$925	$850	$775	$675

Last MSR was $2,136.

3.9 STINGER - 9mm Para. or .38 Super cal., black frame, designed for IPSC and USPSA competition, 38 oz. New 2005.

MSR $2,773		$2,500	$2,225	$1,975	$1,750	$1,575	$1,375	$1,150

3.9 V.I.P. - .45 ACP cal. only, aluminum frame, STi modular polymer frame, stainless steel slide, 3.9 in. barrel with STi Recoilmaster muzzlebrake, 10 shot double stack mag., STi fixed sights, 25 oz. Mfg. 2001-2006.

		$1,450	$1,275	$1,025	$950	$850	$750	$650

Last MSR was $1,653.

3.9 GUARDIAN - .45 ACP cal., 1911 Commander style blue frame, 3.9 in. ramped bull barrel, stainless slide with polished sides, stippled front strap, undercut trigger guard, rosewood grips, fixed 3-dot sights, 32.4 oz. New 2007.

MSR $1,024		$925	$825	$725	$650	$575	$500	$425

4.15 TACTICAL - 9mm Para., .40 S&W, or .45 ACP cal., blue steel, fixed sights, short trigger, ambidextrous safety, 34 1/2 oz. New 2004.

MSR $1,922		$1,725	$1,475	$1,250	$1,000	$875	$800	$675

4.15 RANGER II (3.9 RANGER) - .45 ACP cal. only, Officer's Model with 3.9 (Ranger, disc. 2004) or 4.15 (Ranger II, new 2005) in. barrel and 1/2 in. shortened grip frame, 6 shot mag., blue steel frame with stainless steel slide, single stack mag., low mount STI/Heinie sights, 29 oz. New 2001.

MSR $1,029		$885	$750	$640	$550	$450	$400	$350

4.15 DUTY CT - 9mm Para. .40 S&W or .45 ACP cal., 5 in. bull barrel, matte blue finish, intergral tactical rail, flat top slide with rear cocking serrations, ramped front sight, fixed rear sight, 36.6 oz. New 2006.

MSR $1,286		$1,100	$950	$825	$700	$600	$525	$450

4.3 HAWK - various cals., 4.3 in. barrel, STi standard frame (choice of steel or aluminum), 27 or 31 oz. Mfg. 1993-1999.

		$1,725	$1,275	$1,075	$875	$800	$700	$600

Last MSR was $1,975.

4.3 NIGHT HAWK - .45 ACP cal., 4.3 in. barrel, STi wide extended frame, blue finish, 33 oz. Limited mfg. 1997-99.

		$1,875	$1,375	$1,175	$925	$850	$775	$675

Last MSR was $2,136.

5.0 SPARROW - .22 LR cal. only, unlocked blow back action, STi standard extended frame, 5.1 in. ramped bull barrel, fixed sights, blue finish, 30 oz. Limited mfg. 1998-99 only.

		$1,025	$900	$800	$700	$600	$500	$400

Last MSR was $1,090.

5.0 EDGE - 9mm Para., 10mm Norma, .40 S&W, or .45 ACP cal., designed for limited/standard IPSC competition, STi wide extended frame, wide body with staggered stack mag., blue finish, 39 oz. New 1998.

MSR $1,874		$1,650	$1,400	$1,200	$950	$850	$750	$625

5.0 DUTY ONE - 9mm Para., .40 S&W, or .45 ACP cal., ramped bull barrel, checkered wood grips, 38 oz. New 2005.

MSR $1,286		$1,100	$950	$825	$700	$600	$525	$450

GRADING - PPGS™	100%	98%	95%	90%	80%	70%	60%

5.0 EXECUTIVE - .40 S&W cal. only, STi long/wide frame, 10 shot double stack mag., stainless construction, grey nylon polymer grips and square trigger-guard, hard chrome finish with black inlays, fiberoptic front and STi adj. rear sights, approved for IPSC standard and USPSA limited edition, 38 oz. New 2001.

MSR $2,464		$2,150	$1,825	$1,525	$1,300	$1,050	$900	$800

✱ *5.0 Executive IPSC 30th Commemorative* - 9mm Para., .40 S&W, or .45 ACP cal., ramped bull barrel, two-tone hard chrome finish, special engraved slide with "IPSC 30th Anniversary" on side, 39 oz. Mfg. 2005-2006.

		$2,500	$2,225	$1,975	N/A	N/A	N/A	N/A

Last MSR was $2,775.

✱ *5.0 Executive Special Edition* - 9mm Para., .40 S&W, or .45 ACP cal., ramped bull barrel, 24Kt. gold on all steel surfaces, checkered black grips, "Special Edition" engraved on slide, 39 oz. Mfg. 2005-2006.

		$2,625	$2,325	$2,000	N/A	N/A	N/A	N/A

Last MSR was $2,930.

5.0 TROJAN - 9mm Para., .40 S&W, .40 Super, or .45 ACP, standard Govt. length grips, single stack mag., stainless steel available 2006, 36 oz. New 1999.

MSR $1,024		$885	$750	$625	$550	$450	$400	$350

Add $288 for .40 Super with .45 ACP conversion kit.
Add $412 for stainless steel.

5.0 SPARTAN - .45 ACP cal., 1911 Govt. steel frame, parkerized finish, bald front strap, hand checkered double diamond wood grips, front and rear slide serrations, STi long curved trigger, 5 in. chrome ramped bushing barrel, STi high ride beavertail grip safety, fiber optic front sights, adj. rear sights, 35.3 oz. New 2007.

MSR $660		$625	$550	$500	$450	$400	$375	$350

5.0 RANGEMASTER - 9mm Para. or .45 ACP cal., black frame, ramped bull barrel, STI Recoilmaster guide rod, 38 oz. New 2005.

MSR $1,440		$1,275	$1,050	$875	$750	$625	$525	$475

5.0 RANGEMASTER II - similar to Rangemaster, except does not have extended frame dust cover. Mfg. 2006.

		$1,175	$965	$850	$725	$625	$525	$475

Last MSR was $1,344.

5.0 EAGLE - various cals., 5.1 in. barrel, STi standard frame (choice of steel or aluminum) govt. model full-size, wide body with staggered stack mag., adj. rear sight, 31 or 35 oz.

MSR $1,794		$1,550	$1,325	$1,065	$850	$825	$725	$600

Add $266 for .40 Super with .45 ACP conversion kit.

5.0 TACTICAL - 9mm Para., .40 S&W, or .45 ACP cal., blue steel, fixed sights, short trigger, ambidextrous safety, 39 oz. New 2004.

MSR $1,922		$1,725	$1,475	$1,250	$1,000	$875	$800	$675

✱ *5.0 Tactical Lite* - similar to 5.0 Tactical, except stainless slide, alloy frame, fixed sights, 34 1/2 oz. Mfg. 2004-2005.

		$1,800	$1,525	$1,300	$1,050	$900	$825	$700

Last MSR was $2,002.

5.0 TRUSIGHT - 9mm Para., .40 S&W, or .45 ACP cal., 5 in. ramped bull barrel with expansion chamber, black glass filled nylon polymer grip with aluminum magwell, Dawson fiber optic front sight, adj. rear sight, blue finish with polished slide, 39 oz. New 2006.

MSR $1,985		$1,795	$1,525	$1,275	$1,050	$900	$825	$700

GRADING - PPGS™	100%	98%	95%	90%	80%	70%	60%

5.0 LEGEND - 9mm Para., .40 S&W, or .45 ACP cal., STi modular steel long wide frame, 5 in. tri-top barrel with sabertooth cocking serrations, hard chrome slide with black inlay and polished sides, blue finish, black glass filled nylon polymer grips with hard chrome magwell, Dawson fiber optic front sights, adj. rear sight, 38 oz. New 2007.

MSR $2,670		$2,300	$1,950	$1,725	$1,450	$1,200	$1,000	$900

LEGACY MODEL - 45 ACP cal., 5 in. ramped STI bushing barrel, PVD finish, polished black flat top slide with rear cocking serrations, front strap checkering, custom cocobolo grips, ambidextrous thumb safety, ramped front sight, 36 oz. New 2006.

MSR $1,929		$1,750	$1,500	$1,250	$1,000	$900	$825	$700

LSA LAWMAN - .45 ACP cal., 1911 Govt. style, 5 in. barrel, hammer forged carbon steel frame, designed for IPSC, USPSA, and IDPA competion, 36 oz. New 2005.

MSR $1,344		$1,150	$950	$825	$700	$575	$500	$450

SENTINEL - 9mm Para., .40 S&W, or .45 ACP cal., 1911 Govt. forged frame, 5 in. barrel, flattop slide with rear cocking serrations, matte blue finish, front strap 30 LPI checkering, checkered steel D&T mainspring housing and flared magwell, STi competition front sights, adj. rear sight, thick rosewood gripos, 38.3 oz. New 2007.

MSR $1,598		$1,395	$1,200	$1,025	$875	$750	$625	$550

5.1 LIMITED - while advertised during 1998, this model never went into production.

Last MSR was $1,699.

5.5 EAGLE - various cals., features STi standard frame, 5 1/2 in. compensated barrel, 44 oz. Limited mfg. 1994-98.

		$2,100	$1,750	$1,475	$1,200	$995	$895	$775

Last MSR was $2,399.

5.5 TRUBOR COMPETITOR (COMPETITOR) - .38 Super cal. only, standard frame, classic slide with front and rear serrations, square hammer, compensator, double stack, match sear, STi "Alchin" style blast deflector mount, Tru-Bor compensator became standard 2005, C-more rail scope, wide ambidextrous and grip safeties, 42 1/2 oz. New 1999.

MSR $2,639		$2,275	$1,925	$1,700	$1,450	$1,200	$995	$875.

5.5 GRANDMASTER - .38 Super cal. standard, custom order gun with any variety of options available, double stack mag., 42 oz. New 2001.

MSR $3,371		$3,075	$2,650	$2,275	$1,900	$1,650	$1,425	$1,200

6.0 HUNTER - 10mm cal. only, 6 in. barrel, STi super extended heavy frame with single stack mag., blue finish, 51 oz. Only 2 mfg. 1998, disc. 2000.

		$2,250	$1,875	$1,650	$1,425	$1,200	$995	$895

Last MSR was $2,485.

Add $350 for Leupold 2X scope with terminator mount.

6.0 EAGLE - various competition cals., features STi super extended heavy frame, 6 in. barrel, blue finish, wide body with staggered stack mag., 42 oz. New 1998.

MSR $1,894		$1,700	$1,450	$1,275	$1,025	$875	$800	$725

Add $267 for .40 Super with .45 ACP conversion kit.

6.0 TROJAN - similar to Trojan 5.0, except has 6 in. barrel and single stack mag., 36 oz. New 2000.

MSR $1,344		$1,150	$950	$825	$700	$575	$500	$450

Add $143 for .40 Super with .45 ACP conversion kit.

6.0 TARGETMASTER - 9mm Para. or .45 ACP cal., black frame, ramped bull barrel, two piece steel guide rod, 40 oz. New 2005.

MSR $1,440		$1,275	$1,050	$875	$750	$625	$525	$475

GRADING - PPGS™	100%	98%	95%	90%	80%	70%	60%

6.0 .450 XCALIBER - .450 cal., single stack mag., V-10 barrel and slide porting, stainless grip and thumb safeties, adj. rear sight. Limited mfg. 2000-2002.

| | $1,000 | $850 | $750 | $650 | $525 | $450 | $395 |

Last MSR was $1,122.

6.0 .450+ XCALIBER - .450+ cal., otherwise similar to Xcaliber 6.0 .450, except has 6 in. frame with patented polymer grip and staggered stack mag. Limited mfg. 2000-2002.

| | $1,775 | $1,575 | $1,350 | $1,175 | $995 | $875 | $775 |

Last MSR was $1,998.

REVOLVERS

TEXICAN SAA - .45 LC cal., blue finish, color case hardened frame and hammer, 5 1/2 in. barrel, 6 shot, hard rubber grips with STi logo, floating firing pin, fixed sights, 36 oz. New 2007.

| MSR $1,260 | | $1,100 | $975 | $850 | $725 | $600 | $500 | $400 |

RIFLES: SEMI-AUTO

STi 10/22 FORCE - .22 LR cal., aluminum receiver, 21 in. Lothar Walther barrel, black synthetic Hogue stock, 7 lbs. Mfg. 2003-2006.

| | $975 | $850 | $725 | $625 | $500 | $400 | $350 |

Last MSR was $1,103.

S.W.D., INC.

Previous manufacturer located in Atlanta, GA.

Similar models have previously been manufactured by R.P.B. Industries, Inc. (1979-82), and met with BATF disapproval because of convertibility into fully automatic operation. "Cobray" is a trademark for the M11/9 semiautomatic pistol.

CARBINES

SEMI-AUTO CARBINE - 9mm Para. cal., same mechanism as M11, 16 1/4 in. shrouded barrel, telescoping stock.

| | $550 | $495 | $450 | $400 | $325 | $275 | $235 |

PISTOLS: SEMI-AUTO

COBRAY M-11/NINE mm - 9mm Para. cal., fires from closed bolt, 3rd generation design, stamped steel frame, 32 shot mag., parkerized finish, similar in appearance to Ingram Mac 10.

| | $475 | $395 | $350 | $300 | $295 | $275 | $250 |

This model was also available in a fully-auto variation, Class III transferable only.

REVOLVERS

LADIES HOME COMPANION - .45-70 Govt. cal., double action design utilizing spring wound 12 shot rotary mag., 12 in. barrel, steel barrel and frame, 9 lbs. 6 oz. Mfg. 1990-94.

| | $650 | $525 | $400 | $360 | $335 | $310 | $290 |

SHOTGUNS: SINGLE SHOT

TERMINATOR - 12 or 20 ga., paramilitary design shotgun with 18 in. cylinder bore barrel, parkerized finish, ejector. Mfg. 1986-88 only.

| | $95 | $80 | $70 | $60 | $55 | $50 | $45 |

Last MSR was $110.

GRADING - PPGS™	100%	98%	95%	90%	80%	70%	60%

SWS 2000

Current rifle manufacturer located in Krefeld, Germany. Currently imported by Euro-Imports, located in Yoakum, TX.

RIFLES

SWS 2000 manufactures a variety of sporting and tactical style rifles in a variety of configurations. Please contact the importer directly for more information, including pricing and U.S. availability (see Trademark Index).

SABATTI s.p.a.

Current manufacturer located in Gardone, Italy with history tracing back to 1674. No current U.S. importation. Sabatti sub-contracts some of its models for private label. Previous limited importation by European American Armory located in Sharpes, FL.

In 1960, the sons of Antonio Sabatti formed the current company, and manufacture currently includes good quality O/U and SxS shotguns, O/U combination and double rifles, bolt action and semi-auto rifles, and slide action and single shot shotguns. Sabatti should be contacted directly (see Trademark Index) regarding more information and domestic availability on their extensive firearms lineup.

SABRE

Current trademark of shotguns previously imported by Mitchell's Mausers, located in Fountain Valley, CA.

SHOTGUNS: SEMI-AUTO

SABRE - 12 ga. only, gas operated, 18 1/2 (w/o VR), 22, or 28 in. VR barrel with choke tubes, choice of black fiberglass or checkered walnut stock and forearm, configurations include Hunting, Turkey, Deer Hunter, and Police, mfg. in Turkey. Importation disc. 2007.

	100%	98%	95%	90%	80%	70%	60%
	$435	$375	$325	$275	$235	$210	$190

Last MSR was $495.

Add $50 for Police model.

SABRE DEFENCE INDUSTRIES LLC.

Current manufacturer established in 2002, with production headquarters located in Nashville, TN, with sales offices located in Middlesex, U.K. This company was previously known as Ramo, which was founded in 1977. Sabre Defence is also the U.S. distributor for Sphinx pistols.

RIFLES: SEMI-AUTO

Sabre Defence Industries manufactures many variations of the AR-15 paramilitary design rifle for civilians, law enforcement, and military. Please contact the U.S. office directly for more information, including civilian models and current pricing (see Trademark Index).

SACO DEFENSE INC.

Previous firearms manufacturer located in Saco, ME. Saco Defense was purchased by General Dynamics in July of 2000, and continues to produce guns for military defense contracts. This company was previously owned by Colt's Manufacturing Company, Inc. during late 1998-2000.

In the past, Saco Defense utilized their high-tech manufacturing facility to produce guns for Magnum Research, Weatherby (contract ended Sept., 2001), and others.

SAFARI ARMS

Previous trademark manufactured in Olympia, WA. M-S Safari Arms, located in Phoenix, AZ, was started in 1978 as a division of M-S Safari Outfitters. In 1987, Safari Arms was absorbed by Olympic Arms. Safari Arms manufactured 1911 style pistols since the acquisition of M-S Safari Arms in 1987. In Jan. 2004, the Safari Arms name

GRADING - PPGS™	100%	98%	95%	90%	80%	70%	60%

was discontinued and all 1911 style pistols are now being manufactured by Olympic Arms. Please refer to the Olympic Arms section for currently manufactured models.

Safari Arms previously made the Phoenix, Special Forces, Camp Perry, and Royal Order of Jesters commemoratives in various configurations and quantities. Prices average in the $1,500 range except for the Royal Order of Jesters ($2,000).

SCHUETZEN PISTOL WORKS

Schuetzen Pistol Works is the current custom shop of Olympic Arms. Some of the pistols made by Safari Arms had the "Schuetzen Pistol Works" name on them (c. 1994-96). Until Jan. 2004, all pistols were are marked with the Safari Arms slide marking. All pistols, however, have been marked "Safari Arms" on the frame. The pistols formerly in this section have been moved to the PISTOLS: SEMI-AUTO category.

PISTOLS: SEMI-AUTO

Safari Arms manufactured mostly single action, semi-auto pistols derived from the Browning M1911 design with modifications. Please refer to Olympic Arms listing for currently manufactured pistols.

GI SAFARI - .45 ACP cal., patterned after the Colt Model 1911, Safari frame, beavertail grip safety and commander hammer, parkerized matte black finish, 39.9 oz. Mfg. 1991-2000.

	$500	$455	$395	$350	$295	$275	$250

Last MSR was $550.

CARRYCOMP - similar to MatchMaster, except utilizes W. Schuemann designed hybrid compensator system, 5 in. barrel, available in stainless steel or steel, 38 oz. Mfg. 1993-99.

	$1,030	$875	$750	$600	$500	$425	$375

Last MSR was $1,160.

❋ *CarryComp Enforcer* - similar to Enforcer, except utilizes W. Schuemann designed hybrid compensator system, available in stainless steel or steel, 36 oz. Mfg. 1993-96.

	$1,175	$1,025	$875	$750	$600	$500	$425

Last MSR was $1,300.

CARRIER - .45 ACP cal. only, reproduction of the original Detonics ScoreMaster, except has upgraded sights, custom made by Richard Niemer from the Custom Shop. New 1999-2001.

	$750	$625	$575	$500	$450	$400	$350

Last MSR was $750.

RENEGADE - .45 ACP cal., left-hand action (port on left side), 4 1/2 (4-star, disc. 1996) or 5 (new 1994) in. barrel, 6 shot mag., adj. sights, stainless steel construction, 36-39 oz. Mfg. 1993-98.

	$955	$800	$700	$600	$525	$450	$395

Last MSR was $1,085.

Add $50 for 4-star (4 1/2 in. barrel, disc.).

RELIABLE - similar to Renegade, except has right-hand action. Mfg. 1993-98.

	$730	$620	$525	$450	$425	$400	$375

Last MSR was $825.

Add $60 for 4-star (4 1/2 in. barrel, disc.).

GRIFFON PISTOL - .45 ACP cal., 5 in. stainless steel barrel, 10 shot mag., standard govt. size with beavertail grip safety, full-length recoil spring guide, commander style hammer, smooth walnut grips, 40 1/2 oz. Disc. 1998.

	$855	$725	$650	$575	$500	$450	$395

Last MSR was $920.

GRADING - PPGS™	100%	98%	95%	90%	80%	70%	60%

BLACK WIDOW - .45 ACP cal., 3.9 in. barrel, hand contoured front gripstrap, schrimshawed ivory Micarta grips with Black Widow emblem, 6 shot mag., 27 oz. Inventory was depleted 1988.

	$565	$510	$460	$430	$400	$375	$350

Last MSR was $595.

BILL OF RIGHTS BICENTENNIAL MATCHED SET - includes the MatchMaster Pistol and ServiceMatch Rifle, features beryllium receivers and special engraving. Disc.

	$8,950	$6,500	$4,750	N/A	N/A	N/A	N/A

Last MSR was $7,400.

PARTNER - .22 LR cal., formerly the Whitney Wolverine, 8 shot mag., black plastic grips, non-adj. sights. Advertised beginning late 1997.

While advertised since 1997, this gun was not manufactured commercially.

MODEL 81 TARGET PISTOL - .38 Spl. or .45 ACP cal., 5 in. barrel, hand contoured front gripstrap, 2 lbs. 10 oz. Disc. 1987.

	$775	$695	$550	$440	$410	$375	$350

Last MSR was $875.

Add $50 for Deluxe Model (with Herrett adj. grips).

✳ *Model 81L Target Pistol* - .38 Spl. or .45 ACP, 6 in. barrel, 2 lbs. 13 oz. Disc. 1987.

	$850	$775	$695	$550	$440	$410	$375

Last MSR was $975.

Add $50 for Deluxe Model (with Herrett adj. grips).

✳ *Model 81 NM Target Pistol* - .38 Spl. or .45 ACP cal., similar frame as Model 81, except has flat front gripstrap, 5 in. barrel, 2 lbs. 5 oz. Disc. 1987.

	$775	$695	$550	$440	$410	$375	$350

Last MSR was $875.

✳ *Model 81BP Target Pistol* - .38 Spl. or .45 ACP cal., 6 in barrel, contoured front gripstrap, faster cycle time, 2 lbs. 9 oz. Disc. 1987.

	$875	$775	$695	$550	$440	$410	$375

Last MSR was $995.

✳ *Model 81 Target Pistol Silueta* - .45 ACP or .38/.45 Wildcat cal., 10 in. extended barrel, designed for silhouette shooting, 2 lbs. 14 oz. Disc. 1987.

	$875	$775	$695	$550	$440	$410	$375

Last MSR was $1,050.

PISTOLS: SINGLE SHOT

ULTIMATE/UNLIMITED - various cals., bolt action target pistol, 14 15/16 in. barrel, black finished metal, laminated stock. Disc. 1987.

	$850	$775	$695	$550	$440	$410	$375

Last MSR was $975.

SAFARI CLUB INTERNATIONAL

SCI is an international hunting and conservation organization with headquarters located in Tucson, AZ.

Although Safari Club International (SCI) is not a manufacturer or importer, this organization is responsible for special and limited editions similar to the one listed. Additionally, SCI also has one custom-built rifle manufactured for each annual SCI convention with an auction determining the price of the rifle.

Model	Manufacturer	Qty.	Year	Issue Price
SPECIAL/LIMITED EDITIONS				
Super Grade 25th Anniversary	Winchester	200	1997	$1,395

GRADING - PPGS™	100%	98%	95%	90%	80%	70%	60%

SAIGA

Current trademark manufactured by Izhmash, located in Izhevsk, Russia. Currently imported by Russian American Armory Company, located in Scottsburg, IN. Previously imported by European American Armory Corp., located in Sharpes, FL.

RIFLES: SEMI-AUTO

For current pricing information and availability on Saiga semi-auto rifles, including the Saiga .223 Rem., Saiga 7.62mm, Saiga 100 Series, Saiga 9 and Saiga .308, please contact the importer directly.

SAIGA RIFLE - .223 Rem. or .308 Win. cal., Kalashnikov type action, black synthetic or hardwood (new 2003, only available in .308 Win. cal.) stock and forearm, 16.3-22 in. barrel length, matte black metal, 7-8 1/2 lbs. Imported 2002-2004, reintroduced 2006.

MSR $275	$260	$230	$200	$180	$160	$140	$120

    Add $75 for .308 Win. cal.
    Add $40 for wood stock.

✳ *Saiga Rifle 7.62x39mm Cal.* - 7.62x39mm cal., 16.3 or 20 1/2 in barrel, otherwise similar to Saiga Rifle. Imported 2002-2004, reintroduced 2006.

MSR $275	$260	$230	$200	$180	$160	$140	$120

SAIGA 100 - .223 Rem., .30-06, .308 Win., or 7.62x39mm cal., hunting configuration with black synthetic stock, 3 or 10 shot mag., 22 in. barrel with open sights, 7.7 lbs. Importation began 2006.

MSR $350	$325	$285	$250	$225	$200	$180	$165

SHOTGUNS: SEMI-AUTO

SAIGA SHOTGUN - 12 or 20 ga., 3 in. chamber, 5 shot detachable box mag., Kalashnikov type action, black synthetic stock and forearm, 19-22 in. barrel length, matte black metal, 6.7-7.8 lbs. Imported 2002-2004, reintroduced 2006.

MSR $435	$375	$335	$300	$275	$250	$225	$200

    Add $20 for 12 ga.
    Add $40 for choke tubes (12 ga. only).

✳ *Saiga Shotgun .410 Bore* - .410 bore, 19 or 21 in barrel, 4 shot detachable box mag., otherwise similar to Saiga Shotgun, approx. 6.6 lbs. Imported 2002-2004, reintroduced 2006.

MSR $235	$210	$195	$180	$160	$140	$130	$120

SAKO, LTD.

Current rifle manufacturer established circa 1921 and located in Riihimäki, Finland. Current models are presently being imported by Beretta USA, located in Accockeek, MD. Previously imported by Stoeger Industries, Inc. located in Wayne, NJ, Garcia, and Rymac.

During 2000, Sako, Ltd. was purchased by Beretta Holding of Italy. All currently produced Sakos are imported by Beretta USA Corp. located in Accokeek, MD.

Beginning 2000, most Sako rifles (except the Action I in .223 Rem. cal.) are shipped with a Key Concept locking device. This patented system uses a separate key to activate an almost invisible lock which totally blocks the firing pin and prevents bolt movement.

PISTOLS: SEMI-AUTO

Less than 200 Triace pistols were imported into the United States.

TRIACE - .22 Short, .22 LR, or .32 S&W Wadcutter cal., target pistol incorporating unique action, competition walnut grips with thumbrest and adj. heel, blue finish with chrome accents. Imported 1985-86 only.

	$1,300	$1,150	$950	$825	$700	$600	$500

Last MSR was $1,395.

GRADING - PPGS™	100%	98%	95%	90%	80%	70%	60%

* *Triace Pistol Kit* - consists of Triace frame, .22 Short, .22 LR, and .32 S&W barrels. Cased with accessories. Imported 1985-86 only.

	$2,500	$2,200	$2,000	$1,500	$1,300	$1,175	$1,025

Last MSR was $2,385.

RIFLES: BOLT ACTION, DISC.

Sako used FN Mauser-style long actions under the Sako name circa 1951-1960. Serial numbers started with 100,001. During 1962, Sako introduced its L61R action, but older FN long actions remained at the factory. Sako also manufactured commercial Mauser actioned rifles for Weatherby and others. Previous importation for these FN actioned Sakos included Firearms International.

Add 10%-15% for popular Mag. cals. on rifles listed.
Note: Prices are for pre-1972 Sako rifles, unless stated otherwise. Pre-1972 Sakos utilize the L-46, L-461, L-579, L-57, and L-61 R actions.
Subtract approx. 25% for post-1972 models.

DELUXE - various cals., Monte Carlo stock, skipline checkering, long, medium, or short actions, contrasting pistol grip cap and forend tip, engraved floorplate.

	$1,045	$925	$775	$625	$450	$425	$385

STANDARD SPORTER - long, medium, and short actions.

	$850	$725	$625	$500	$450	$410	$375

HEAVY BARREL MODEL - long, medium, and short actions.

	$850	$725	$625	$500	$450	$410	$375

FULL STOCK MODELS - 20 in. carbine barrel (all actions), 23 1/2 in. barrel on rifle (short & medium actions).

* *Full Stock Model Finnbear* - long L-61 R action.

	$1,100	$975	$800	$725	$550	$475	$425

* *Full Stock Model Forester* - medium L-579 action.

	$1,050	$925	$775	$700	$525	$450	$400

* *Full Stock Model Vixen* - short L-461 action.

	$1,050	$925	$775	$700	$525	$450	$400

L-46 action pre-Vixen Sakos had detachable mags.

MAUSER ACTION (FN) - .270 Win. or .30-06 cal., long action. Mfg. 1950-57.

	$695	$500	$400	$345	$310	$280	$260

MAGNUM MAUSER (FN) - 8x60S, 8.2x57mm, .300 H&H, or .375 H&H cal.

	$745	$635	$580	$495	$450	$410	$375

MODEL 74 - various cals.

	$650	$575	$450	$375	$340	$320	$290

MODEL 78 - .22 LR, .22 Mag., or .22 Hornet cal., detachable mag., same size as short action Standard Model. Importation disc. 1986.

	$480	$395	$340	$310	$280	$265	$250

Last MSR was $647.

Add $30 for .22 Hornet cal.

FINNSPORT MODEL 2700 - available in long (AIII) action only, .270 Win., .300 Win. Mag. cals., select checkered walnut. Disc. 1985.

	$750	$675	$600	$560	$510	$475	$430

Last MSR was $910.

FINNWOLF - .243 Win. or .308 Win. cal., lever action, LV63 action, 4 shot mag. early model, 3 shot mag. later model. Mfg. 1962-1974.

	$895	$775	$550	$500	$440	$410	$375

Add 15% for early model with 4 shot mag.

GRADING - PPGS™	100%	98%	95%	90%	80%	70%	60%

✱ *Finnwolf Sako Collectors Association* - .243 Win. or .308 Win. cal., gold lettering on left side of breech, approx. 175 mfg. in 1982.

	$2,995	**$1,750**	**$1,050**	**N/A**	**N/A**	**N/A**	**N/A**

The 100% value on this model refers to NIB unfired condition with factory papers.

ANNIVERSARY MODEL - 7mm Rem. Mag. cal. only, 1,000 mfg.

	$2,750	**$1,625**	**$975**	**N/A**	**N/A**	**N/A**	**N/A**

The 100% value on this model refers to NIB unfired condition with factory papers.

RIFLES: BOLT ACTION, RECENT PRODUCTION

Beginning late 2001, Sako established a custom shop, which allows the consumer to select from a wide variety of finishes, options, and special orders, including individual stock dimensions. Please contact Beretta USA for more information regarding the Sako custom shop.

All Sako left-handed models are available in medium or long action only.

Some older model TGR rifles (Models TRG-S, TRG-22, and TRG-42) have experienced firing pin breakage. Ser. no. ranges on these U.S. distributed rifles are 202238 - 275255 and 973815 - 998594. Please contact Beretta USA directly (str@berettausa.com or 800-803-8869) for a replacement firing pin assembly if you have a rifle within these serial number ranges.

FINNFIRE - .22 LR cal., 22 in. regular or heavy (new 1996) or 23 (Sporter/Varmint and Target) in. cold-hammer forged free-floating barrel, M-P94S action, single stage adj. trigger, 50 degree bolt lift, 2 position safety, European walnut pistol grip or adj. Target competition (new 2003) stock, cocking indicator, available in Hunter, Target (new 2003)/Sporter (new 1999), or Varmint configuration, 5 or 10 shot mag., integral 11mm dovetail (for scope mounting), with (new 1996) or w/o open sights, 5 3/4 (Target/Sporter) lbs. Imported 1994-2005.

	$850	**$725**	**$625**	**$525**	**$450**	**$400**	**$350**

Last MSR was $1,044.

Add $45 for Varmint Model with heavy barrel.
Add $125 for Target/Sporter Model with 10 shot mag. and adj. competition stock.

QUAD - .17 HMR, .17 Mach 2, .22 LR, or .22 Mag. cal., 22 in. barrel, black synthetic stock with ambidextrous palm swell and adj. buttpad, interchangeable rimfire barrels, 50 degree bolt lift, blued finish, 5 shot mag., no sights, 5 3/4 lbs. Mfg. 2005-2007.

	$760	**$650**	**$575**	**$500**	**$425**	**$375**	**$325**

Last MSR was $925.

Quad 2-Barrel Combo - .17 HMR and .22 LR cal., includes two interchangeable barrels, fitted aluminum case. New 2008.

MSR $1,750	**$1,500**	**$1,250**	**$1,000**	**$875**	**$775**	**$700**	**$625**

✱ **Quad 4-Barrel Combo** - includes four interchangeable rimfire barrels in cals. .17 HMR, .17 Mach 2, .22 LR, and .22 Mag. New 2005.

MSR $2,150	**$1,800**	**$1,525**	**$1,200**	**$975**	**$850**	**$775**	**$700**

HUNTER LIGHTWEIGHT RIFLE - available in short action (AI) in .17 Rem., .222 Rem., or .223 Rem. cal., medium action (AII) in .22-250 Rem., .243 Win., .308 Win., or 7mm-08 Rem. cal., or long action (AIII) in .25-06 Rem., .270 Win., .280 Rem., .30 - 06, .270 Wby. Mag. (disc. 1996), 7mm Wby. Mag. (disc. 1996), 7mm Rem. Mag., .300 Win. Mag., .300 Wby. Mag., .338 Win. Mag., .340 Wby. Mag. (disc. 1996), .375 H&H, or .416 Rem. Mag. (new 1991) cal., 21 1/4, 21 3/4, or 22 in. barrel, classic styled stock with choice of oil (disc. 1996) or matte lacquer finish, finely checkered French walnut. Disc. 1997.

	$850	**$685**	**$550**	**$490**	**$460**	**$430**	**$410**

Last MSR was $1,050.

Add $35 for long action.
Add $50-$70 for Mag. cals.
Add approx. $80 for left-hand action (available in all Mag. cals. - mfg. 1994-96).

GRADING - PPGS™	100%	98%	95%	90%	80%	70%	60%

❋ *Hunter Lightweight Rifle Carbine (Handy)* - available in medium action in .22-250 Rem. (disc. 1990), .243 Win. (new 1991), .308 Win. (new 1991) cal. or long action in .25-06 Rem. (disc. 1990), 7mm Rem. Mag. (disc. 1990), .338 Win. Mag. cal., or .375 H&H (new 1990) cal., 18 1/2 in. barrel with iron sights, oil or lacquer finished deluxe walnut stock with checkering, approx. 7 lbs. Mfg. 1986-91.

	$725	$650	$600	$490	$460	$430	$410

Last MSR was $945.

Add $50-$65 for long action (Mag. cals.).

FINNLIGHT - .243 Win, .25-06 Rem., .260 Rem. (new 2006), .270 Win., .270 WSM (new 2004), .280 Rem. (disc. 2007), .30-06, .308 Win., .300 Win. Mag., .300 WSM (new 2003), .338 Win. Mag., 6.5x55mm, 7mm-08 Rem., 7mm WSM (mfg. 2005-2007), or 7mm Rem. Mag. cal., stainless steel action with four sizes, 20 1/4, 20 7/8, or 24 3/8 in. stainless steel free-floating fluted barrel, alloy triggerguard/mag. bottom, black synthetic stock, 4 or 5 shot detachable mag., no sights, 6 1/2 lbs. Importation began 2001.

MSR $1,600	$1,295	$995	$775	$650	$550	$450	$390

Add $50 for WSM cals.

LONG RANGE HUNTING MODEL - available in long action in .25-06 Rem., .270 Win., .300 Win. Mag., or 7mm Rem. Mag. cal., 26 in. heavy barrel only w/o sights. Mfg. 1996-97.

	$1,030	$785	$625	$545	$495	$465	$440

Last MSR was $1,275.

Add $15 for Mag. cals.

FIBERCLASS MODEL - available in medium action (disc. 1992) in .22-250 Rem., .243 Win., .308 Win., or 7mm-08 cal., or long action in .25-06 Rem., .270 Win., .280 Rem., .30-06, 7mm Rem. Mag., .300 Win. Mag., .338 Win. Mag., .375 H&H, or .416 Rem. Mag. (new 1991) cal., has black fiberglass stock. Disc. 1996.

	$1,170	$930	$785	$725	$630	$560	$510

Last MSR was $1,388.

Add $17-$37 for Mag. cals.
Subtract $40 for medium action cals. (disc. 1992).
Add $80 for left-hand action (disc. 1989).

❋ *FiberClass Model Carbine (Handy)* - available in medium action in .243 Win. or .308 Win. cal. and long action in .25-06 Rem. (disc.), .270 Win. (disc.), .30-06, 7mm Rem. Mag. (disc.), .300 Win. Mag. (disc.), .338 Win. Mag., or .375 H&H (new 1991) cal., 18 1/2 in. barrel with fiberglass stock. Mfg. 1986-91.

	$995	$895	$775	$725	$630	$560	$510

Last MSR was $1,239.

Add $50-$65 for Mag. cals.

LAMINATED RIFLE - available in short action (disc. 1989), medium action in .22-250 Rem., .243 Win., .308 Win., or 7mm-08 Rem. cal., or long action in .25-06 Rem., .270 Win., .280 Rem., .30-06, 7mm Rem. Mag., .300 Win. Mag., .338 Win. Mag., .375 H&H, or .416 Rem. Mag. (new 1991) cal., features laminated wood stock. Mfg. 1988-95.

	$985	$790	$635	$550	$495	$460	$430

Last MSR was $1,200.

Add $35 for short action.
Add $55 for long action.
Add $75-$95 for Mag. cals.
Add approx. $100 for left-hand action (disc.).

The left-hand action was available in .270 Win., .280 Rem., .30-06, 7mm Rem. Mag., .300 Win. Mag., .338 Win. Mag., .375 H&H, or .416 Rem. Mag. cal.

MODEL TRG-21 - .308 Win. cal., bolt action, 25 3/4 in. barrel, new design features modular synthetic stock construction with adj. cheekpiece and buttplate, stainless steel barrel, cold hammer forged receiver, and resistance free bolt, 10 shot detachable mag., 10 1/2 lbs. Imported 1993-99.

	$2,300	$2,000	$1,800	$1,600	$1,400	$1,200	$975

Last MSR was $2,699.

MODEL TRG-22 - .308 Win. cal., bolt action, 26 in. barrel, updated TRG-21 design featuring adj. modular synthetic stock (green, desert tan, or all black) construction with adj. cheekpiece and buttplate, competition trigger, choice of blue (disc. 2002) or phosphate (new 2002) metal finish, stainless steel barrel, cold hammer forged receiver, and resistance free bolt, 10 shot detachable mag., approx. 10 1/4 lbs. Importation began 2000.

MSR $2,775	$2,325	$1,925	$1,750	$1,500	$1,250	$1,000	$875

Add $1,225 for folding stock.

MODEL TRG-41 - .338 Lapua Mag. cal., similar to Model TRG-21, except has long action and 27 1/8 in. barrel, 7 3/4 lbs. Imported 1994-99.

	$2,700	$2,425	$2,150	$1,850	$1,625	$1,400	$1,200

Last MSR was $3,099.

MODEL TRG-42 - .300 Win. Mag. or .338 Lapua Mag. cal., updated TRG-41 design featuring long action and 27 1/8 in. barrel, choice of black composite/blue finish, desert tan, or green composite/phosphate (new 2002) finish, 5 shot mag., 11 1/4 lbs. Importation began 2000.

MSR $2,775	$2,325	$1,925	$1,750	$1,500	$1,250	$1,000	$875

Add $475 for green or desert tan (new 2008) stock with phosphate metal finish.

MODEL TRG-S - available in medium action (disc. 1993) in .243 Win. or 7mm-08 cal., or long action in .25-06 Rem. (Mfg. 1994-98), .270 Win. (disc. 2000), 6.5x55mm Swedish (disc. 1998), .30-06 (disc.), .308 Win. (disc. 1995), .270 Wby. Mag. (disc. 1998), 7mm Wby. Mag. (Mfg. 1998), 7mm Rem. Mag. (disc.), .300 Win. Mag. (disc.), .300 Wby. Mag. (mfg. 1994-99), .30-378 Wby. Mag. (new 1998, 26 in. barrel only), .338 Win. Mag. (disc. 1999), .338 Lapua Mag. (new 1994), .340 Wby. Mag. (disc. 1998), 7mm STW (26 in. barrel only, disc. 1999), .375 H&H (disc. 1998), or .416 Rem. Mag. (disc. 1998) cal., black synthetic stock, Sporter variation derived from the Model TRG-21, 22 (disc.), 24 (Mag. cals. only, disc.), or 26 in. barrel, 3 or 5 shot detachable mag., fully adj. trigger, 60 degree bolt-lift, matte finish, 8 1/8 lbs. Imported 1993-2004.

	$765	$615	$525	$475	$440	$415	$380

Last MSR was $896.

MANNLICHER CARBINE - available in short action (disc. 1989), medium action in .243 Win. or .308 Win. cal., or long action in .25-06 Rem. (disc. 1991), .270 Win., .30-06, 7mm Rem. Mag. (disc. 1991), .300 Win. Mag. (disc. 1991), .338 Win. Mag., or .375 H&H cal., 18 1/2 in. barrel, two-piece full Mannlicher style stock, open sights. Disc. 1996.

	$1,030	$785	$625	$545	$495	$465	$440

Last MSR was $1,275.

Add $35 for long action.
Add $60-$75 for Mag. cals.

PPC MODEL - 22 PPC or 6 mm PPC cal., 21 3/4 or 23 3/4 (Benchrest Model) in. barrel, single shot in Benchrest Model, 4 shot mag. in Hunter or Deluxe Model, checkered walnut stock, Deluxe Model has rosewood pistol grip and forearm caps plus skip line checkering, matte lacquer finish on Hunter and Deluxe, oiled finish on Benchrest, 6 1/4 or 8 3/4 (Benchrest Model with heavy barrel) lbs. Imported 1989-97.

	$1,250	$950	$750	$650	$600	$540	$500

Last MSR was $1,535.

Add $320 for Deluxe Hunter Model (disc. 1993).
Add $85 for Benchrest Model (disc. 1993).

GRADING - PPGS™	100%	98%	95%	90%	80%	70%	60%

VARMINT RIFLE - available in short action (AI) in .17 Rem., .222 Rem., or .223 Rem., and medium action (AII) .22-250 Rem., .243 Win., .308 Win., or 7mm-08 cal., 22 3/4 in. heavy barrel, no sights. Disc. 1997.

	$1,025	$795	$615	$545	$475	$430	$400

Last MSR was $1,240.

CLASSIC GRADE - .243 Win., .270 Win., .30-06, or 7mm Rem. Mag. cal., short (AI, disc. 1992), medium (AII), or long (AIII) action, classic styled stock, finely checkered French walnut with matte lacquer finish. Disc. 1985, reintroduced 1992-97.

	$895	$745	$600	$545	$475	$430	$400

Last MSR was $1,050.

Add $50 for Mag. cal.
Add $35 for long action.
Add $120-$135 for left-hand action (disc. 1994) (.270 Win. or 7mm Rem. Mag cal. only).
In 1992, the Classic Grade was once again imported into the U.S. in .243 Win., .270 Win., .30-06, or 7mm Rem. Mag. cal.

DELUXE LIGHTWEIGHT RIFLE - available in short action (AI) in .17 Rem., .222 Rem., or .223 Rem. cal., medium action (AII) in .22-250 Rem., .243 Win., .308 Win., or 7mm-08 Rem. cal., or long action (AIII) in .25-06 Rem., .270 Win., .280 Rem., .30 - 06, 7mm Rem. Mag., .300 Win. Mag., .300 Wby. Mag., .338 Win. Mag., .375 H&H, or .416 Rem. Mag. (new 1991) cal., 21 1/4, 21 3/4, or 22 in. barrel, deluxe quality skipline checkered walnut stock with rosewood forend tip. Disc. 1997.

	$1,185	$965	$750	$650	$595	$540	$500

Last MSR was $1,475.

Add $35 for long action.
Add $50-$70 for Mag. cals.
Add $150-$175 for left-hand action (disc. 1994, available in long action only).

SAFARI GRADE - available in long (AIII) action only, .300 Win. Mag. (disc. 1989), .338 Win. Mag., .375 H&H, or .416 Rem. Mag. (new 1991) cal., deluxe walnut with sculptured cheekpiece, 22 in. barrel, 4 shot mag., open sights, sling swivels. Disc. 1996.

	$2,235	$1,785	$1,475	$1,250	$1,050	$900	$795

Last MSR was $2,765.

SUPER DELUXE - a limited edition rifle available on special order only, various cals. are available in the short (AI), medium (AII), and long (AIII) actions, presentation grade walnut with both checkering and carving, rosewood forend tip. Disc. 1997.

	$2,400	$1,825	$1,475	$1,250	$1,050	$900	$795

Last MSR was $3,100.

SAKO 75 HUNTER - available in 5 action sizes, .17 Rem. (mfg. 1998-2002), .222 Rem. (mfg. 1998-2002), .223 Rem. (new 1998), .22-250 Rem., .243 Win., .308 Win., 7mm-08 Rem., .25-06 Rem., .260 Rem. (new 2005), .270 Win., .270 WSM (new 2004), .280 Rem. (disc. 2004), .30-06, .270 Wby. Mag. (disc. 2001), 6.5x55mm (new 2005), 7mm Rem. Ultra Mag. (mfg. 2002-2003), 7mm Wby. Mag. (disc. 2003), 7mm STW (disc. 2003), 7mm WSM (new 2005), 7mm Rem. Mag., .300 WSM (new 2004), .300 Win. Mag., .300 Wby. Mag. (disc. 2003), .300 Rem. Ultra Mag. (mfg. 2000-2003), .338 Win. Mag., .340 Wby. Mag. (disc. 2003), .375 H&H, or .416 Rem. Mag. (disc. 2001) cal., hammer forged 22-24 3/8 in. barrel, utilizes 3 locking lugs, mechanical ejector, 5 bolt sliding guides with 70 degree bolt lift, 3-position rear tang safety, available with top loading fixed mag. (hinged floorplate, .300 Rem. Ultra Mag., .416 Rem. Mag., and 7mm Rem. Ultra mag. cals. only), or detachable staggered 4-6 shot mag., checkered walnut stock, no sights, approx. 7 3/4 lbs. Mfg. 1997-2007.

	$1,125	$900	$725	$625	$550	$500	$450

Last MSR was $1,375.

Add $100 for .375 H&H cal.
This model was also available in left-hand action in .270 Win. or .30-06 cal. at no extra charge.

GRADING - PPGS™	100%	98%	95%	90%	80%	70%	60%

SAKO 75 DELUXE - similar cals. as Sako 75 Hunter, features hinged floorplate and deluxe walnut stock with gloss finish, skipline checkering, and rosewood forend and pistol grip caps, custom stock bedding and iron sights available on .375 H&H or .416 Rem. Mag. cals., approx. 7 3/4 lbs. Mfg. 1997-2007.

	$1,700	$1,450	$1,200	$925	$750	$625	$550

Last MSR was $2,050.

Add $125 for .416 Rem. Mag.

SAKO 75 KING RANCH - .270 Win., .30-06, or .300 WSM cal., 22 7/8 or 24 3/8 (.300 WSM cal. only) in. barrel, similar to Sako 75 Deluxe, except has King Ranch "W" stock checkering and gold-filled "W" emblem on floorplate. Mfg. 2006-2007.

	$2,050	$1,650	$1,325	$1,050	$875	$750	$625

Last MSR was $2,475.

SAKO 75 STAINLESS SYNTHETIC - available in .22-250 Rem., .243 Win., .25-06 Rem., .260 Rem. (new 2005), .270 Win., .270 WSM (new 2004), .30-06, .308 Win., .300 Win. Mag., .300 Wby. Mag. (mfg. 1999-2003), .300 WSM (new 2004), .300 Rem. Ultra Mag. (mfg. 2000-2003), 7mm-08 Rem. (new 1998), 7mm STW (mfg. 1998-2003), 7mm WSM (new 2006), 7mm Rem. Mag., 7mm Rem. Ultra Mag. (mfg. 2002-2003), .338 Win. Mag., or .375 H&H cal., 3-4 shot detachable mag. (except for floorplate with Rem. Ultra Mag. cals.), features black composite stock with soft rubber grip inserts in pistol grip and forearm area, matte stainless steel metal, 7 3/4 lbs. Mfg. 1997-2007.

MSR $1,425		$1,150	$900	$750	$640	$535	$450	$390

SAKO 75 STAINLESS WALNUT - .270 Win., .30-06, .300 Win. Mag., .300 Wby. Mag., .338 Win. Mag., 7mm STW, or 7mm Rem. Mag. cal., features checkered walnut stock and forearm. Imported 1999-2002.

	$1,050	$840	$685	$575	$485	$400	$350

Last MSR was $1,239.

Add $35 for Mag. cals.

SAKO 75 GREY WOLF - .22-250 Rem., .223 Rem., .243 Win., .25-06 Rem., .260 Rem., .270 Win., .30-06, .308 Win., .270 WSM, .300 WSM, 7mm WSM, or 7mm-08 Rem. cal., available in 4 frame sizes and 3 barrel lengths. Mfg. 2005-2007.

	$1,225	$925	$800	$700	$600	$525	$450

Last MSR was $1,550.

SAKO 75 VARMINT - .17 Rem. (disc. 2003), .22-250 Rem., .222 Rem. (disc. 2002), .223 Rem., 22PPC (mfg. 1999-2003), or 6mmPPC (mfg. 1999-2003) cal., 23 5/8 in. heavy barrel w/o sights and beavertail forend, 5 or 6 shot detachable mag., 8 5/8 lbs. Mfg. 1998-2005.

	$1,400	$1,000	$850	$725	$650	$575	$500

Last MSR was $1,628.

SAKO 75 VARMINT W/SET TRIGGER - similar to Sako 75 Varmint, except is also available in .204 Ruger, .243 Win., .260 Rem., or .308 Win. cal., set trigger. Mfg. 2005-2007.

	$1,575	$1,275	$975	$800	$700	$600	$500

Last MSR was $1,850.

SAKO 75 STAINLESS VARMINT LAMINATED - .22-250 Rem., .222 Rem. (disc. 2002), .223 Rem., 22PPC (disc. 2003), 6mmPPC (disc. 2003), or 7mm-08 Rem. (new 2002) cal., similar to Sako 75 Varmint, features stainless steel action and barrel, brown laminated wood stock, 9 lbs. Mfg. 1999-2005.

	$1,475	$1,175	$875	$765	$635	$530	$455

Last MSR was $1,794.

GRADING - PPGS™	100%	98%	95%	90%	80%	70%	60%

SAKO 75 STAINLESS VARMINT LAMINATED W/SET TRIGGER - similar to Sako 75 Stainless Varmint Laminated, except is also available in .204 Ruger, .243 Win., .260 Rem., or .308 Win. cal., set trigger. Mfg. 2005-2007.

	$1,675	$1,375	$1,025	$850	$725	$600	$500

Last MSR was $1,950.

SAKO 75 CUSTOM DELUXE - .270 Win. or .30-06 cal., extra grade deluxe oil finished walnut stock with rosewood forend tip and pistol grip cap, 7 3/4 lbs. Imported late 2003-2007.

	$3,750	$3,250	$2,575	$2,175	$1,850	$1,550	$1,350

Last MSR was $4,325.

This model was available through Sako showcase dealers only.

SAKO 75 SINGLE SHOT - .22-250 Rem. (disc. 2005), .243 Win. (disc. 2005), 7mm-08 Rem. (disc. 2005), 6mmPPC (disc. 2005), or .308 Win. cal., medium III action, stainless steel action and barrel, heavy free floating fluted barrel w/o sights, 9 lbs. Mfg. 2004-2007.

	$2,850	$2,375	$2,125	$1,850	$1,550	$1,350	$1,150

Last MSR was $3,450.

SAKO 75 80TH ANNIVERSARY - .375 H&H cal., limited edition rifle featuring Mauser style claw extractor, premium grade checkered walnut with ebony forend tip, cold hammer forged match grade barrel has 1/4 rib with open sights, 5 shot internal mag. with hinged floorplate, includes Swarovski PV-1 scope and case, only 80 rifles (serial numbered 200101-200180) mfg. 2001-2007.

	$16,500	$14,000	$11,000	$9,000	N/A	N/A	N/A

Last MSR was $19,550.

SAKO 75 SUPER DELUXE - a limited edition rifle available special order only, presentation grade walnut with both checkering and carving, rosewood forend tip.
Limited availability precludes accurate pricing on this model.

SAKO 85 HUNTER - various cals. between .22-250 - .375 H&H, 3 lug bolt, available in 5 action sizes, checkered walnut stock and forearm, 22 1/2 or 24 3/8 in. blue barrel, blue action, 4-5 shot detachable mag., short claw extractor on bolt, two-position safety, adj. trigger, guaranteed 1 MOA 5 shot groups, approx. 7 1/2 lbs., mfg. to celebrate Sako's 85th anniversary during 2006. Importation began 2006.

MSR $1,700		$1,400	$1,100	$875	$775	$675	$575	$525

Add $50 for .370 Sako Mag., .375 H&H, or WSM cals.

SAKO 85 STAINLESS SYNTHETIC - similar to Sako 85 Hunter, except has black synthetic stock with overmolded grips and matte stainless steel barrel/action, FinSoft recoil reduction system. Importation began 2007.

MSR $1,575		$1,275	$975	$775	$675	$575	$525	$475

Add $50 for WSM cals.

SAKO 85 GREY WOLF - similar to Sako 85 Stainless Synthetic, except has checkered grey laminate stock, no recoil pad. Importation began 2007.

MSR $1,575		$1,275	$975	$775	$675	$575	$525	$475

Add $50 for WSM cals.

SAKO 85 VARMINT - .204 Ruger, .22-250 Rem., .223 Rem., .243 Win., or .308 Win. cal., two action sizes, 23 5/8 in. heavy blue (walnut stock) or stainless barrel w/o sights, set trigger, unchecked walnut or laminate stock. Importation began 2008.

MSR $1,800		$1,475	$1,150	$900	$800	$700	$600	$550

Add $75 for laminate stock w/stainless barrel.

GRADING - PPGS™	100%	98%	95%	90%	80%	70%	60%

SALERI, W.R. di SALERI WILLIAM & C. snc

Current longun manufacturer established in 1998 located in Gardone, Italy. Previously imported by MacGregor Wing and Clay, located in Cary, NC, and by S.R. Lamboy, located in Victor, NY.

RIFLES AND SHOTGUNS

W.R. Saleri manufactures high quality boxlock O/U shotguns (Continental model, in both a standard and round scalloped frame with detachable locks) and single barrel rifles (Viper model). Please contact the company directly for more information, including pricing and availability (see Trademark Index).

SAMCO GLOBAL ARMS, INC.

Current importer and distributor located in Miami, FL. Dealer sales.

Samco Global Arms currently imports a variety of foreign and domestic surplus military rifles, including various contract Mausers, Loewe, Steyr, Czech, Lee Enfield, Mosin-Nagant, etc. Most of these guns offer excellent values to both shooters and collectors. Please contact the company directly for current availability and pricing, as its inventory changes weekly (see Trademark Index).

SAN SWISS ARMS AG

Current company established during late 2000, with headquarters located in Neuhausen, Switzerland. Most SAN Swiss firearms/trademarks are currently imported into the U.S. by Sig Sauer (SIG Arms until 2007).

During the end of 2000, SIG Arms AG was purchased by SAN Swiss Arms AG, a newly formed company. Unchanged are the 141 years of expertise in the development and manufacture of firearms for the military, law enforcement, and civilian market. Also firmly in place is the group of companies that represent numerous renowned brands and products. This new group currently includes four independently operational companies - Blaser Jadgwaffen GmbH located in Isny, Germany, J.P. Sauer & Sohn GmbH located in Eckernförde, Germany, Sig Sauer (U.S.A.) located in Exeter, NH, and SAN Swiss Arms AG (headquarters), located in Neuhausen, Switzerland. Current trademarks include: Blaser, Mauser Magnum rifles (current mfg. by Blaser), Sauer rifles, and Sig-Sauer pistols. Please refer to these individual listings for current information and pricing.

SARASQUETA, FELIX

Previous manufacturer located in Eibar, Spain. Previously imported and distributed by SAE (Spain America Enterprises), Inc. located in Miami, FL.

SHOTGUNS: O/U

MODEL MERKE - 12 ga. only, boxlock action, 22 or 27 in. separated barrels, single non-selective trigger, blue only, extractors, recoil pad. Imported 1986 only.

$255	$215	$200	$190	$180	$170	$160

Last MSR was $291.

SARASQUETA, J.J.

Previous manufacturer located in Eibar, Spain. Imported until 1984 by American Arms, Inc. located in Overland Park, KS.

SHOTGUNS: SxS

MODEL 107 E - 12, 16, or 20 ga., ejectors, various barrel lengths, checkered walnut stock and forearm, double triggers.

$360	$290	$270	$255	$240	$215	$200

Last MSR was $435.

MODELS 119E-132E-1882E - more deluxe versions of Model 107E.

$470	$375	$340	$315	$285	$255	$230

Last MSR was $570.

GRADING - PPGS™	100%	98%	95%	90%	80%	70%	60%

MODEL 130 E - more deluxe version of Model 119 E.

	$800	$635	$590	$555	$515	$480	$450

Last MSR was $960.

MODEL 131 E - action similar to Model 107 E, except has deluxe engraving.

	$1,050	$845	$770	$710	$665	$620	$585

Last MSR was $1,250.

MODEL 1882 E LUXE - double triggers, moderate engraving, otherwise similar to Model 107 E.

	$825	$660	$615	$565	$520	$480	$450

Last MSR was $990.

✻ *Model 1882 E Luxe w/ gold inlays* - SST, extensive engraving.

	$1,120	$920	$850	$790	$740	$695	$650

Last MSR was $1,320.

✻ *Model 1882 E Luxe w/silver inlays* - SST, extensive engraving.

	$1,055	$855	$795	$740	$700	$660	$630

Last MSR was $1,260.

MODEL 150 E - 12 or 16 ga., single trigger, ejectors, select walnut and extensive engraving.

	$1,285	$1,035	$960	$895	$835	$770	$695

Last MSR was $1,500.

✻ *Model 150 E Trap* - similar to Model 150 E, except trap dimensions on stock.

	$1,360	$1,125	$1,010	$940	$875	$790	$720

Last MSR was $1,600.

SARASQUETA, VICTOR

Previous manufacturer located in Eibar, Spain. Trademark was sold to Diarm S.A. circa 1986.

SHOTGUNS:SxS

MODEL 3 BOXLOCK - 12, 16, or 20 ga., all standard barrel lengths and chokes, boxlock, double triggers, checkered English style stock and forearm.

	100%	98%	95%	90%	80%	70%	60%
Extractors	$445	$395	$350	$295	$250	$215	$185
Auto ejectors	$575	$515	$450	$375	$300	$250	$225

HAMMERLESS SIDELOCK - 12, 16, 20, 28 ga., or .410 bore, SxS, barrel length and choke to order, straight English style stock, models differ as to amount of engraving, grade of wood, and overall quality as follows:

Add 25% for 28 ga.
Add 30% for .410 bore.

MODEL 4 - extractors.

	$620	$550	$525	$495	$450	$415	$360

MODEL 4E - auto ejectors.

	$680	$605	$580	$550	$505	$470	$415

MODEL 203 - extractors.

	$650	$570	$545	$515	$475	$435	$380

MODEL 203E - auto ejectors.

	$710	$625	$600	$570	$530	$490	$435

MODEL 6E

	$800	$715	$690	$660	$615	$580	$525

MODEL 7E

	$855	$770	$745	$715	$670	$635	$580

GRADING - PPGS™	100%	98%	95%	90%	80%	70%	60%
MODEL 10E							
	$1,735	$1,595	$1,485	$1,405	$1,320	$1,240	$1,100
MODEL 11E							
	$1,870	$1,680	$1,595	$1,515	$1,430	$1,350	$1,265
MODEL 12E							
	$2,145	$1,900	$1,790	$1,705	$1,570	$1,430	$1,375

SARCO, INC.

Current importer and wholesaler located in Stirling, NJ.

Sarco Inc. imports a wide variety of foreign and domestic surplus military style rifles and shotguns that offer excellent values for the shooter. Please contact the company directly, as inventory changes constantly (see Trademark Index).

SARDIUS

Please refer to the Sirkis Industries section in this text.

SARRIUGARTE, FRANCISO S.A.

Previous manufacturer located in Elgoibar, Spain. Previously part of the Diarm S.A. Group which was imported and distributed by American Arms, Inc. located in North Kansas City, MO.

SARSILMAZ

Current manufacturer established during 1880, and located in Istanbul, Turkey. Pistols currently imported by Armalite, Inc., located in Geneseo, IL. Previously distributed 2000-2003 by PMC, located in Boulder City, NV. Previously imported and distributed until 2000 by Armsport, Inc. located in Miami, FL.

SHOTGUNS

Sarsilmaz manufactures a variety of shotguns in O/U, semi-auto, and slide action configurations. Some of these models have been imported in the past in limited quantities. Currently, Sarsilmaz is manufacturing some models for Bernardelli. Please contact the factory directly for more information regarding U.S. availability and pricing (see Trademark Index).

SAUER, J.P., & SOHN

Current manufacturer located in Eckernförde, Germany since 1751 (originally Prussia). Currently imported by JP Sauer USA, located in Palm Beach, FL.

Previously manufactured in Suhl pre-WWII. Previously imported and warehoused 1995-2007 by SIG Arms, located in Exeter, NH. Rifles were previously imported until 1995 by the Paul Company Inc. located in Wellsville, KS and until 1994 by G.U., Inc. located in Omaha, NE.

In 1972, J.P. Sauer & Sohn entered into a cooperative agreement with SIG. During 2000, SAN Swiss Arms AG purchased SIG Arms AG, including the J.P. Sauer & Sohn trademark. Production remains in Eckernförde, Germany.

DRILLINGS & COMBINATION GUNS

SAUER MODEL 3000 DRILLING - available in either 16 ga./.30-06, 6.5x57R, 7x57R, 7x65R or 12 ga./.222 Rem. (disc.), .243 Win., .30-06, 6.5x57R, 7x57R, 7x65R, or 9.3x74R cal., Greener crossbolt and double barrel lug locking, cocking indicators, front set trigger, automatic safety, walnut pistol grip stock with hog-back and cheekpiece, Grade III scroll engraving, 7 1/4 lbs. Importation disc. 1999.

$4,300	$3,600	$3,100	$2,675	$2,200	$1,800	$1,400

Last MSR was $4,600.

This model was also previously imported by Weatherby and Colt - please refer to separate listings for more information.

GRADING - PPGS™	100%	98%	95%	90%	80%	70%	60%

✳ *Sauer Model 3000 Drilling Luxury Grade* - similar to Model 3000 standard, except select root timber and extensive engraving featuring two animals. Importation disc. 1999.

	100%	98%	95%	90%	80%	70%	60%
	$5,550	$4,875	$4,400	$3,875	$3,475	$3,000	$2,575

Last MSR was $6,100.

COMBO BBF 54 O/U - standard grade combination gun, 16 ga./.222 Rem., .243 Win., 6.5x57R, 7x57R, 7x65R, or .30-06 cals., ejectors, double triggers with front set trigger, moderate engraving on coin finished receiver, Greener crossbolt with double barrel lugs, 6 lbs. Importation disc. 1986.

	$2,200	$2,060	$1,760	$1,565	$1,380	$1,250	$1,125

Last MSR was $2,495.

✳ *Combo BBF 54 O/U Luxury Grade* - similar to Combo BBF 54, except game scene engraved and deluxe crotch walnut.

	$2,450	$2,200	$2,000	$1,785	$1,600	$1,475	$1,300

Last MSR was $2,745.

LUFTWAFFE SURVIVAL DRILLING - 12 or 16 ga. (65mm) SxS over 9.3x74R, 28 in. barrels, large eagle swastika on stock and breech end of right barrel. Originally mfg. for Luftwaffe pilots during WWII.

	$15,000	$13,000	$11,000	$8,000	$7,000	$6,000	$5,000

Subtract 40% if w/o original aluminum case or accessories.

SAUER MODEL 3000E DRILLING - see listing under Colt Sauer Drilling.

PISTOLS: SEMI-AUTO

MODEL 1913 POCKET AUTOMATIC - .32 ACP cal., 7 shot, 3 in. barrel, fixed sights, blue, black rubber grips. Mfg. 1913-30.

	$295	$225	$185	$165	$155	$145	$135

MODEL 1913 25 AUTOMATIC - .25 ACP cal., 7 shot, 2 1/2 in. barrel, fixed sights, blue, black rubber grips. Mfg. 1913-30.

	$325	$250	$200	$175	$150	$140	$135

MODEL 28 - .25 ACP cal., 7 shot, 3 in. barrel, fixed sights, blue, black rubber grips. Mfg. 1930-38.

	$300	$240	$185	$170	$155	$145	$135

BEHÖRDEN "AUTHORITY" M1930 MODEL - .32 ACP cal., 3 in. barrel, blue only, black plastic grips.

	$325	$240	$200	$175	$150	$145	$135

Add $1,000 for very rare alloy frame example.

MODEL 38 H DOUBLE ACTION AUTOMATIC - .22 LR (extremely rare), .32 ACP, or .380 ACP (rare) cal., 3 1/4 in. barrel, fixed sights, blue, plastic grips. Mfg. 1938-45.

	100%	98%	95%	90%	80%	70%	60%
.32 ACP	$500	$425	$375	$325	$275	$250	$225
.380 ACP	$3,500	$2,750	$2,000	$1,500	$1,250	$995	$775
.22 LR	$4,500	$3,000	$2,200	$1,600	$1,250	$995	$775

Add 100% for early high polish guns.
Add 10% for Waffenamt proofing.
Add 15%-25% for police markings.
Add 60% for alloy frame.

REVOLVERS: SA/DA

Sauer manufactured .38 cal. double action revolvers circa 1960-1985, and also licensed other manufacturers, including Armi San Paolo. Most had blue finish and walnut grips. Current values range from $150-$295, depending on condition.

GRADING - PPGS™	100%	98%	95%	90%	80%	70%	60%

RIFLES: BOLT ACTION

SAUER PRE-WWII BOLT ACTION RIFLE - most popular European cals. and .30 - 06, 22 or 24 in. barrel, raised solid rib, Krupp steel, double-set triggers, folding 3 leaf express sight, checkered sporter stock. Mfg. pre-WWII.

	$1,395	$1,250	$1,050	$875	$750	$625	$550

MODEL 90 STANDARD - .22-250 Rem., .222 Rem. (only 3 mfg.), .243 Win., .25-06 Rem., 6.5x55mm, .270 Win., .30-06, .308 Win. (late mfg.), .300 Win. Mag., .300 Wby. Mag., 7mm Rem. Mag., .375 H&H, or .458 Win. Mag. cal., 24 in. barrel, 3 or 4 shot detachable mag., satin, oil finished checkered walnut stock with Monte Carlo cheekpiece and rosewood forend cap, 2 stage set trigger, free floated barrel, approx. 7 1/2 lbs. Importation disc.

	$1,000	$875	$750	$625	$550	$500	$450

Last MSR was $1,175.

Early importation rifles came standard with a half stock and barrel band, and also had European sling swivels with milled stops. In 1989, this model's design changed to look more like the Colt Sauer rifle (w/o sights, gloss finished stock and set trigger was removed). During 1985-1989, Sauer exported to Sigarms 2,300 Model 90 rifles, 1,100 of these were in Mag. cals.

* *Model 90 Standard Stutzen* - .22-250 Rem., .222 Rem. (3 mfg.), or .243 Win., Mannlicher style full stock, not available in European or Mag. cals. Importation disc. 1989.

	$1,200	$995	$850	$750	$650	$475	$500

Last MSR was $1,225.

* *Model 90 Standard Safari* - .458 Win. Mag cal., 23.62 in. barrel, 10 1/2 lbs. Imported 1986-88 only.

	$1,250	$950	$850	$750	$650	$575	$500

Last MSR was $1,675.

MODEL 90 SUPREME (LUX) - .243 Win., .25-06 Rem., 6.5x55 Swedish, .270 Win., .30 - 06, .300 Win. Mag., .300 Wby. Mag., 7mm Rem. Mag., .338 Win. Mag., or .375 H&H cal., similar to Model 90, satin finished deluxe stock with Monte Carlo cheekpiece and rosewood forearm and pistol grip caps, gold trigger, no sights, 7.1-7.7 lbs. Importation 1987-98.

	$1,995	$1,750	$1,500	$1,300	$1,050	$875	$775

Last MSR was $1,350.

Add approx. 60% for Grade I engraving, 100% for Grade II, 125% for Grade III, and 160% for Grade IV.

* *Model 90 Supreme (Lux) Safari*
While advertised, this model had limited importation. MSR was set at $1,795.

* *Model 90 Supreme (Lux) Stutzen*
While advertised, this model had little importation. MSR was set at $1,200.

MODEL 200 BOLT ACTION - available in 15 cals. between .243 Win. and .375 H&H, short and medium actions only, 23.62 in. unique interchangeable barrels, 6 lug bolt, easily detachable stock and forearm, optional set trigger, detachable mag. with hidden release button, 7.7 lbs. Production disc. 1993.

	$1,225	$925	$800	$700	$600	$525	$450

Last MSR was $1,395.

Add $100 for 7mm Rem. Mag. or .300 Win. Mag. cal.
Add $300 for extra interchangeable barrel.

During 1986-89, Sauer exported to Sigarms 4,170 Model 200 rifles, 1,370 of these were in Mag. cals.

GRADING - PPGS™	100%	98%	95%	90%	80%	70%	60%

✱ *Model 200 Bolt Action Lightweight* - similar to Model 200, only with alloy receiver, 6.6 lbs.

	$1,225	$925	$800	$700	$600	$525	$450

Last MSR was $1,395.

Add $150 for left-hand version.

✱ *Model 200 Bolt Action Lux* - similar to Model 200, except has deluxe walnut, rosewood forend tip and pistol grip cap, marmorized bolt and gold trigger.

	$1,395	$1,175	$925	$800	$700	$600	$525

Last MSR was $1,595.

✱ *Model 200 Bolt Action Lux American* - similar to Model 200 Lux, except has high gloss Monte Carlo stock, 24 in. barrel, jeweled bolt, and gold trigger.

	$1,395	$1,175	$925	$800	$700	$600	$525

Last MSR was $1,595.

Add $150 for left-hand version.

✱ *Model 200 Bolt Action Lux European* - similar to Model 200 Lux, except has European configured stock with Schnabel forearm, 26 in. barrel.

	$1,395	$1,175	$925	$800	$700	$600	$525

Last MSR was $1,595.

Add $95 for left-hand version.

✱ *Model 200 Bolt Action Carbon Fiber* - similar to Model 200, except has carbon fiber stock. Imported 1987-88 only.

	$800	$700	$625	$565	$500	$465	$430

Last MSR was $1,200.

MODEL 202 SUPREME (LUX) - .22-250 Rem. (new 2001), .243 Win. (disc. 1998, resumed 2000), .25-06 Rem., .270 Win., .30-06, .308 Win., 6.5x55mm Swedish (disc. 2000), or 7x64mm (disc. 1997) cal., steel receiver, modular design allowing barrel change within 2 minutes, dual safety, 2 piece figured walnut stock, cocking indicator, detachable 3-5 shot mag., takedown with interchangeable barrels, right- or left-hand action, 7 1/2 lbs. Imported 1994-2004.

	$2,500	$2,250	$2,000	$1,750	$1,500	$1,300	$1,050

Last MSR was $3,400.

Add $300 for left-hand action (.30-06 cal. only).
Add $900 per extra barrel in non-Mag. cals.
Also available in left-hand action in .270 Win. (disc. 2000) or .30-06 cal.

✱ *Model 202 Supreme (Lux) Magnum* - .300 Win. Mag., .300 Wby. Mag., .338 Win. Mag. (disc. 1997), .375 H&H, 7mm Rem. Mag., 6.5x68mm (importation disc. 1997), or 8x68mm (importation disc. 1997) cal., converts to 7 cals., 7.7 lbs. Imported 1994-2004.

	$2,750	$2,350	$2,100	$1,800	$1,550	$1,350	$1,150

Last MSR was $3,600.

Add $200 for .375 H&H cal.
Was also available until 2000 in left-hand action in .300 Win. Mag. or 7mm Rem. Mag. cal.

MODEL 202 CLASSIC (STANDARD) - similar to Model 202 Synthetic, except has checkered walnut stock and forearm, 7.7 lbs. Importation began 2001.

MSR N/A		$2,075	$1,300	$1,050	$900	$775	$675	$600

Add $200 for Mag. cals., $400 for .375 H&H cal.
Add $900 for interchangeable standard cal. barrel, or $1,000 for Mag. cal. barrel.

MODEL 202 SYNTHETIC - .22-250 Rem. (new 2001), .243 Win. (new 2001), .25-06 Rem., .270 Win., .30-06, .308 Win., .300 Win. Mag., 7mm Rem. Mag. (new 2000), .300 Wby. Mag., .375 H&H (disc. 2005), or 6.5x55mm Swedish (disc. 2000) cal., features black synthetic stock, 24 or 26 in. barrel w/o sights, 7.7 lbs. Importation began 1999.

MSR N/A		$1,750	$1,200	$995	$875	$750	$675	$600

Add $200 for Mag. cals., $400 for .375 H&H cal.
Add $900 for interchangeable standard cal. barrel, or $1,000 for Mag. cal. barrel.

GRADING - PPGS™	100%	98%	95%	90%	80%	70%	60%

MODEL 202 LIGHTWEIGHT - .22-250 Rem., .243 Win., .25-06 Rem., .270 Win., .30-06, .308 Win., and various metric cals., 24 in. fluted barrel w/o sights, aluminum alloy receiver with integral Weaver rail, Ilaflon (disc.) or Teflon coated metal, black synthetic stock, 6 1/2 lbs. Importation began 2001.

MSR N/A	$2,600	$1,500	$1,225	$975	$800	$700	$600

MODEL 202 VARMINTER - .22-250 Rem., .243 Win., or .25-06 Rem. cal., 24 in. match grade fluted bull barrel with no sights, 3 shot mag., matte black finish, adj. cheekpiece on checkered Turkish walnut stock, 9 1/2 lbs. Imported 2001-2005.

	$2,950	$1,500	$1,225	$975	$800	$700	$600

Last MSR was $3,400.

MODEL 202 TAKEDOWN - available in many standard and Mag. cals., 2 or 4 shot mag., takedown action allows disassembly within seconds, point of impact remains constant, open sights on .375 H&H Mag. cal., 6 bolts connect forend with action, and can be detached by pressing a button, deluxe checkered walnut, round or flat bolt handle, approx. 8.8 lbs. Importation began 2003.

MSR N/A	$4,500	$3,500	$2,600	$2,225	$1,875	$1,550	$1,300

Add $200 for Mag. cals.
Add $3,001 for Model 202 Takedown Hatari with Grade III wood and Ilaflon coating (.375 H&H, .416 Rem., .404 Jeffrey, or .458 Lott cal.).

MODEL 202 SUPER GRADE

While advertised in 1994, this model was never imported. MSR was set at $1,020.

MODEL 202 HUNTER MATCH

While advertised in 1994, this model was never imported. MSR was set at $1,495.

MODEL 202 ALASKA

While advertised in 1994, this model was never imported. MSR was set at $1,335.

MODEL 205 TR TARGET - 6.5x55mm or .308 Win. cal., true left-hand variation, 200 meter diopter sights, modular design allows changing single components including caliber, free floating barrel with vent. forearm, 5 shot mag., interchangeable barrel systems, 12.1 lbs. Imported 1994-97.

	$1,775	$1,575	$1,400	$1,250	$1,100	$950	$825

Last MSR was $1,900.

SSE 3000 PRECISION RIFLE - .308 Win. cal., very accurate, law enforcement counter Sniper Rifle, built to customer specifications.

	$4,845	$3,655	$3,200	$2,850	$2,500	$2,275	$2,000

SSG 2000 - available in .223 Rem., 7.5mm Swiss, .300 Wby. Mag., or .308 Win. (standard) cal., bolt action, 4 shot mag., no sights, deluxe sniper rifle featuring thumbhole style walnut stock with stippling and thumbwheel adj. cheekpiece, 13 lbs. Importation disc. 1986.

	$2,480	$2,260	$1,950	$1,700	$1,500	$1,300	$1,100

Last MSR was $2,850.

This model was available in .223 Rem., .300 Wby. Mag., or 7.5mm cal. by special order only.

SSG 3000 - .223 Rem., 22 1/2 in. barrel, Parker-Hale bipod, 2-stage match trigger, includes 2 1/2-10x52mm Zeiss scope, 200 mfg. for Swiss police.

	$12,000	$10,000	$8,500	$7,000	$6,750	$5,500	$4,250

SSG 3000 PRECISION TACTICAL RIFLE (CURRENT MFG.) - .308 Win. cal., modular design, ambidextrous McMillan tactical stock with adj. comb, 23.4 in. barrel with muzzle brake, 5 shot detachable mag., supplied in 3 different levels, Level I does not have bipod or scope, cased, 12 lbs. New 2000.

MSR $3,999	$3,500	$3,100	$2,650	$2,250	$1,850	$1,500	$1,325

Add $1,500 for Level II (includes Leupold Vari-X III 3.5-10x40mm duplex scope and Harris bipod, disc.).
Add $2,300 for Level III (includes Leupold Mark 4 M1 10x40mm Mil-Dot scope and Harris bipod, disc.).
Add $1,500 for .22 conversion kit (disc.).

GRADING - PPGS™	100%	98%	95%	90%	80%	70%	60%

SHOTGUNS

MODEL 60 SXS - various gauges, boxlock action, DT, extractors, checkered walnut stock and forearm, this model was the standard model of its period.

	$975	$875	$750	$650	$550	$450	$395

Add 20% for 20 ga.

ROYAL MODEL SXS - 12, 16 or 20 ga., 26, 28, or 30 in. barrels, various chokes, boxlock, scalloped engraved frame, cocking indicators, SST, auto ejectors, Krupp steel barrel, checkered pistol grip stock. Mfg. 1955-77.

	$1,650	$1,375	$1,210	$1,100	$880	$770	$660

Add 20% for 20 ga.

ARTEMIS SXS - 12 ga., 28 in. barrels, mod. and full choke, H&H type sidelock, SST, auto ejector, Krupp steel, checkered pistol grip stock. Mfg. 1966-77.

* *Artemis SxS Grade I* - fine line engraved.

	$5,500	$4,620	$3,850	$3,520	$3,080	$2,640	$2,200

* *Artemis SxS Grade II* - extensive engraving.

	$6,600	$5,500	$4,840	$4,235	$3,850	$3,300	$3,080

GRADE 380 SXS

	$4,500	$4,000	$3,500	$3,000	$2,500	$2,200	$1,500

GRADE F-40 SXS

Rarity factor precludes accurate price evaluation.

MODEL F-45 SXS

	$12,000	$10,500	$9,000	$8,000	$6,500	$5,000	$3,200

MODEL F-60 SXS

	$23,000	$20,000	$17,000	$14,000	$12,000	$9,000	$5,000

MODEL 66 O/U FIELD GUN - 12 ga., 28 in. mod. and full, Krupp steel barrels, H&H type sidelocks, SST, auto ejectors, checkered pistol grip stock, available in three grades of engraving. Mfg. 1966-75.

Grade I	$2,200	$1,760	$1,540	$1,320	$1,100	$880	$770
Grade II	$3,080	$2,420	$1,980	$1,650	$1,430	$1,210	$990
Grade III	$3,850	$3,300	$2,860	$2,420	$1,980	$1,650	$1,320

MODEL 66 O/U SKEET GUN - similar to Field Gun, with 26 in. VR skeet bored barrel and vent. forearm. Mfg. 1966-75.

MODEL 66 O/U TRAP GUN - similar to 66 Skeet, with 30 in. barrels, full and full, or mod. and full choke, trap style stock.

Grade I	$2,090	$1,760	$1,540	$1,320	$1,100	$880	$770
Grade II	$3,080	$2,420	$1,980	$1,650	$1,430	$1,210	$880
Grade III	$3,850	$3,300	$2,860	$2,420	$1,980	$1,650	$1,320

SAUER/FRANCHI STANDARD GRADE O/U - 12 ga. only, double triggers, checkered walnut stock and forearm, SST, blue finish only, sling swivels, VR. Importation disc. 1986.

	$375	$340	$315	$290	$275	$260	$245

Last MSR was $785.

* *Sauer/Franchi Standard Regent Grade O/U* - similar to Standard grade, except has single trigger and lightly engraved silver finished receiver. Importation disc. 1986.

	$475	$395	$350	$310	$290	$275	$265

Last MSR was $825.

GRADING - PPGS™	100%	98%	95%	90%	80%	70%	60%

❋ *Sauer/Franchi Standard Favorit Grade O/U* - similar to Regent Grade, except has elaborate scroll engraving on coin finished receiver, gold-plated trigger. Importation disc. 1986.

	$550	$495	$450	$420	$385	$350	$300

Last MSR was $875.

❋ *Sauer/Franchi Standard Diplomat Grade O/U* - similar to Favorit Grade, except has more elaborate scroll engraving and with model name gold filled on receiver sides and barrel, extra grain French walnut, cased.

	$875	$750	$625	$550	$495	$460	$435

Last MSR was $1,520.

SAUER/FRANCHI SPORTING S O/U - 12 ga. only, 28 in. barrels, ejectors, SST, select European walnut with checkered stock and forearm, 10mm VR, plain silver finished receiver with model name gold filled on both sides. Importation disc. 1986.

	$800	$700	$600	$500	$450	$420	$395

Last MSR was $1,375.

SAUER/FRANCHI MODEL TRAP O/U - similar to Sporting S, except has 29 in. barrels, trap chokes and stock dimensions. Importation disc. 1986.

	$875	$750	$625	$550	$495	$460	$435

Last MSR was $1,375.

SAUER/FRANCHI MODEL SKEET O/U - similar to Sporting S, except has skeet chokes. Importation disc. 1986.

	$875	$750	$625	$550	$495	$460	$435

Last MSR was $1,375.

SAVAGE ARMS, INC.

Current manufacturer located in Westfield, MA since 1959, with sales offices located in Suffield, CT. Previously manufactured in Utica, NY - later manufacture was in Chicopee Falls, MA. Dealer and distributor sales.

This company originally started in Utica, NY in 1894. The Model 1895 was initially manufactured by Marlin between 1895-1899. The company was renamed Savage Arms Co. in 1899. After WWI, the name was again changed to the Savage Arms Corporation. Savage moved to Chicopee Falls, MA circa 1946 (to its Stevens Arms Co. plants). In the mid-1960s the company became The Savage Arms Division of American Hardware Corp., which later became The Emhart Corporation. This division was sold in September 1981, and became Savage Industries, Inc. located in Westfield, MA (since the move in 1960). On November 1, 1989, Savage Arms Inc. acquired the majority of assets of Savage Industries, Inc.

Savage Arms, Inc. will offer service and parts on their current line of firearms only (those manufactured after Nov. 1, 1995). These models include the 24, 99, and 110 plus the imported Model 312. Warranty and repair claims for products not acquired by Savage Arms, Inc. will remain the responsibility of Savage Industries, Inc. For information regarding the repair and/or parts of Savage Industries, Inc. firearms, please refer to the Trademark Index in the back of this text. Parts for pre-1989 Savage Industries, Inc. firearms may be obtained by contacting the Gun Parts Corporation located in West Hurley, NY (listed in Trademark Index). Savage Arms, Inc. has older records/info. on pistols, the Model 24, older mfg. Model 99s, and Model 110 only. A factory letter authenticating the configuration of a particular specimen may be obtained by contacting Mr. John Callahan (see Trademark Index for listings and address). The charge for this service is $30.00 per gun, and $25.00 per gun for Models 1895, 1899, and 99 rifles. Please allow 6 weeks for an adequate response.

For more Savage model information, please refer to the Serialization section in the back of this text.

Please refer to the *Blue Book of Modern Black Powder Arms* by John Allen (also online) for more information and prices on Savage's lineup of modern black powder models. For more information and current pricing on both new and used Savage airguns, please refer to the *Blue Book of Airguns* by Dr. Robert Beeman & John Allen (also online).

Black Powder Reproductions & Replicas by Dennis Adler is also an invaluable source for most black powder reproductions and replicas, and includes hundreds of color images on most popular makes/models, provides manufacturer/trademark histories, and up-to-date information on related items/accessories for black powder shooting - www.bluebookinc.com

COMBINATION GUNS

All Model 24s are under the domain of Savage Arms, Inc.

Add 20% for .22 Mag. cal. on models listed below, where applicable.

MODEL 24 O/U - .22 LR over .410 bore, open rifle sight, visible hammer, break open, plain pistol grip stock. Mfg. 1950-65.

	100%	98%	95%	90%	80%	70%	60%
	$450	$395	$325	$275	$230	$210	$180

This model featured top lever opening, except on the Models 24S and 24MS.

MODEL 24B-DL - 22 LR or .22 Mag. over .410 bore.

	$500	$450	$375	$325	$265	$215	$165

MODEL 24S - similar to Model 24, with 20 ga. or .410 bore barrel, side lever, dovetail for scope. Mfg. 1964-71.

	$395	$350	$315	$275	$250	$225	$190

MODEL 24MS - similar to Model 24S, with .22 Mag. barrel. Mfg. 1964-71.

	$600	$550	$450	$400	$350	$275	$225

MODEL 24DL - similar to Model 24S, with top lever, satin chrome frame and checkered stock. Mfg. 1962-69.

	$395	$350	$315	$275	$250	$225	$190

MODEL 24MDL - similar to Model 24DL, with .22 Mag. barrel and chrome frame. Mfg. 1962-69.

	$495	$450	$400	$350	$275	$225	$185

MODEL 24FG - similar to Model 24DL, w/o Monte Carlo stock, with top lever. Mfg. 1972-disc.

	$450	$395	$325	$275	$230	$210	$180

Action was changed to under lever opening in front of trigger guard circa 1980.

MODEL 24 FIELD - .22 LR or .22 Mag. over 20 ga. or .410 bore, under lever opening in front of trigger guard introduced circa 1980, lightweight field version, 24 in. separated barrels, 3 in. chambers, 6 3/4 lbs. Disc. 1989.

	$395	$350	$315	$275	$250	$225	$190

Last MSR was $209.

MODEL 24F (PREDATOR) - choice of .17 HMR (new 2004), .22 Hornet, .222 Rem. (disc. 1989), .223 Rem., or .30-30 Win. (12 ga. only) cal., over 12, 20 ga., or .410 bore (mfg. 1998-2000), 3 in. chamber, 24 in. barrels, 12 ga. barrel is available either with fixed choke or choke tube, wood (disc.) or matte black Dupont Rynite synthetic stock, hammer block safety, DTs, approx. 8 lbs. Mfg. 1989-2007.

	$585	$450	$345	$290	$235	$200	$180

Last MSR was $698.

Add $31 for 12 ga.
Add $55 for .410 bore adaptor (12 ga. only, disc. 2000).
Add $14 for Camo Rynite stock (disc., Model 24F-T, Turkey Model-12 ga./.22 Hornet or .223 Rem. cal. only).

GRADING - PPGS™	100%	98%	95%	90%	80%	70%	60%

MODEL 24V - similar to Model 24, in .22 Hornet (disc. 1984), .222 Rem. (new 1967), .223 Rem., .30-30 Win., .357 Max., or .357 Mag.(disc.), 20 ga., 3 in. chamber, 24 in. barrels, single trigger, 7 lbs. Mfg. 1967-1989.

	$495	$425	$375	$325	$275	$250	$225

Action was changed to under lever opening in front of trigger guard circa 1980.

MODEL 24D - .22 LR or .22 Mag. over .410 bore or 20 ga., black or case hardened frame, game scene decoration was eliminated in 1974, forearm not checkered after 1976. Introduced 1971.

	$450	$395	$325	$275	$230	$210	$180

Action was changed to under lever opening in front of trigger guard circa 1980.

MODEL 24C CAMPER'S COMPANION - nickel finish, .22 LR over 20 ga., 20 in. barrel cylinder bore, buttplate opens to store ten .22 LR cartridges and one 20 ga. shell in buttstock, carrying case, 5 3/4 lbs. Mfg. 1972-88.

	$525	$450	$400	$325	$275	$235	$200

Last MSR was $239.

Add 10% for nickel finish (Model 24CS - shipped with pistol grip stock also).
Action was changed to under lever opening in front of trigger guard circa 1980.

MODEL 24 VS - similar to Model 24CS, only .357 Mag. over 20 ga., nickel finish, accessory pistol grip stock is included.

	$595	$550	$475	$400	$350	$275	$225

MODEL 2400 O/U - 12 ga. full choke barrel over .222 Rem. or .308 Win. rifle barrel, 23 1/2 in. barrels, folding leaf sight, solid rib, dovetailed for scope mount, checkered Monte Carlo stock. Mfg. by Valmet 1975-1980.

	$695	$625	$575	$525	$495	$440	$415

MODEL 389 - 12 ga. with 3 in. chamber over choice of .308 Win. or .222 Rem., choke tubes standard, hammerless, double triggers, checkered walnut stock and forearm with recoil pad. Mfg. 1988-90 only.

	$850	$775	$675	$550	$450	$375	$325

Last MSR was $919.

PISTOLS: BOLT ACTION

MODEL 501F SPORT STRIKER - .22 LR cal., left-hand bolt, right side ejection, 10 in. button rifled barrel with scope blocks, 10 shot mag., grey fiberglass/graphite composite stock, 4 lbs. Mfg. 2000-2005.

	$235	$200	$180	$165	$145	$130	$125

Last MSR was $245.

Add $46 for XP package (Model 501FXP, includes scope and mounts).

MODEL 502F SPORT STRIKER - similar to Model 501F Sport Striker, except is .22 Mag. cal., and 5 shot mag. Mfg. 2000-2005.

	$295	$260	$220	$195	$180	$160	$140

Last MSR was $269.

MODEL 503F SPORT STRIKER - similar to Model 501F Sport Striker, except available in .17 HMR cal., 4 lbs. Mfg. 2003-2005.

	$295	$260	$225	$185	$165	$155	$140

Last MSR was $295.

✱ *Model 503FSS Sport Striker* - similar to Model 503F Sport Striker, except is stainless steel. Mfg. 2003-2004.

	$325	$285	$240	$200	$150	$125	$110

Last MSR was $335.

GRADING - PPGS™	100%	98%	95%	90%	80%	70%	60%

MODEL 510F STRIKER CENTERFIRE - .22-250 Rem. (disc. 2002), .223 Rem. (new 1999), .243 Win., .260 Rem. (mfg. 1999-2000), .308 Win., or 7mm-08 Rem. cal., left-hand short bolt action with right-hand ejection, 14 in. free floating unported barrel, 2 shot internal box mag., blue barrel action, black composite stock with grooved forend and wide bottom swell, drilled and tapped, 5 lbs. Mfg. 1998-2003.

	$475	$425	$360	$325	$295	$275	$250

Last MSR was $469.

MODEL 516FSS STRIKER - similar to 510F Striker, except has stainless steel barreled action. Mfg. 1998-2000.

	$495	$450	$375	$335	$300	$280	$260

Last MSR was $462.

✴ *Model 516FSAK Striker* - .243 Win., .270 WSM (mfg. 2003-2004), .300 WSM (new 2003), .308 Win., 7mm WSM (disc. 2004), or 7mm-08 Rem. cal., similar to 516FSS Striker, except has adj. muzzle brake (AMB), 14 in. ported barrel. Mfg. 1998-2005.

	$650	$575	$500	$450	$400	$350	$300

Last MSR was $621.

✴ *Model 516FSAK Striker Camo* - .300 WSM cal., similar to 516FSAK Striker, except has camo treatment stock. Mfg. 2002 only.

	$650	$575	$500	$450	$400	$350	$300

Last MSR was $538.

MODEL 516BSAK/BSS SUPER STRIKER - similar cals. to Model 510F Striker, features dual pillar bedded short action and custom designed thumbhole laminate grey stock, stainless steel frame and fluted 14 in. barrel with adj. muzzle brake (AMB), new ESP (Engineered Step Performance) adj. two-stage trigger, approx. 5 lbs. Mfg. 1999-2001.

	$725	$650	$575	$500	$450	$400	$350

Last MSR was $618.

Subtract approx. $50 if w/o muzzle brake (Model 516BSS, disc. 2000).

PISTOLS: SEMI-AUTO

MODEL 1907 AUTO PISTOL - .32 ACP or .380 ACP cal., 9 (.380 ACP) or 10 (.32 ACP) shot mag., 3 13/16 (.32 ACP) or 4 5/16 (.380 ACP) in. barrel, blue, fixed sights, metal (early mfg. in .32 ACP only until ser. no. 10,980) or hard rubber grips, exposed cocking piece. Mfg. 1910-17.

.32 ACP	$550	$425	$300	$200	$150	$125	$100
.380 ACP	$650	$525	$400	$300	$250	$200	$150

Add 40% for original box with instructions (beware of recent reproductions).
Add large premiums for factory nickel, silver, or gold finish (rare).

There were three different types of pearl grips: the early variation was a snap-on with an S/A logo, screw-on with an indian head logo, and the flared 1917 with no logo. Asking prices for the grips alone are in the $250-$1,000 range (this also applied to the Model 1915 Hammerless and Model 1917 Automatic).

MODEL 1915 HAMMERLESS - similar to Model 1907, with grip safety and no visible cocking piece. Mfg. 1915-17.

.32 ACP	$900	$750	$500	$400	$300	$225	$200
.380 ACP	$1,000	$850	$600	$450	$300	$250	$200

Add 40% with original box and instruction manual.

MODEL 1917 AUTOMATIC - similar to Model 1907, with spur cocking piece and trapezoidal grips. Mfg. 1920-28.

.32 ACP	$425	$300	$200	$150	$130	$110	$100
.380 ACP	$500	$400	$350	$300	$250	$200	$150

GRADING - PPGS™	100%	98%	95%	90%	80%	70%	60%

Add 40% with original box and instruction manual.

M1907 U.S. ARMY TEST TRIAL .45 ACP - .45 ACP cal., large version of Model 1907, exposed hammer. Approx. 400 mfg. 1907-11 for military trials.

	$10,000	$8,500	$7,500	$6,500	$5,000	$4,500	$4,000

Add 250% for experimental M1910 and M1911.
Add 100% if in original condition.
Most pistols were repurchased from the government, reconditioned (many reblued), and resold to the public as commercial models.

PISTOLS: SINGLE SHOT

MODEL 101 - .22 LR cal., 5 1/2 in. barrel, single action, adj. sight, swing out barrel, blue, wood grips. Mfg. 1960-68.

	$225	$200	$135	$100	$80	$70	$60

RIFLES: DISC, CENTERFIRE & RIMFIRE

Savage made a wide variety of inexpensive, utilitarian rifles that, to date, have attracted mostly shooting interest, but little collector interest. A listing of these models may be found in the back of this text under "Serialization."

Whenever Savage made an engineering change on a model, it was usually designated with a letter suffix after the model number. These letters were added to the basic model numbers as the changes were made. The engineering changes could be dimensional on any part, cosmetic, or a total component redesign. The letter suffixes indicated to the company what changes were incorporated into that variation. Most model suffixes are preceeded with a dash. These alphabetical suffix variations are no listed separately in this section, but values will be similar to the base model, unless denoted otherwise.

MODEL 1895 - .303 Savage cal. only, lever action, mfg. in either carbine (22 in.), rifle (26 in.), or musket (30 in.) variations, round (scarce) or octagon barrel that has Marlin proofmark under the forend, open top, solid breech, side ejecting, 6 shot rotary mag., some had unfired shots indicator. Originally mfg. by Marlin, marked "Savage Repeating Arms Co. Utica, N.Y. U.S.A. Pat. Feb. 7, 1893", approx. 6,000 mfg. 1895-99, early models had hole in top of bolt - later ones were smooth.

	N/A	$6,000	$5,300	$4,500	$3,800	$3,100	$2,600

Values assume rifle configuration - add a 150%+ premium for the carbine (rare) and musket (rare) and for unfired shots indicator.

MODEL 1895 ANNIVERSARY - a replica of the original M1895, .308 Win. cal., 24 in. octagon barrel, engraved receiver, brass-plated lever, straight stock, Schnabel forend, medallion in stock, brass crescent buttplate. Mfg. 9,999 in 1970 only, to commemorate Savage's 75th year.

	$550	$400	$300	N/A	N/A	N/A	N/A

Last MSR was $195 and mfg. by Savage Arms, Division of Emhart.

MODEL 1899 - improvement of Model 1895 with squared-off front end of breech bolt and cocking indicator as opposed to viewing hole indicator. Early Model 1899s have oblong cocking indicator located on the top of the breech bolt. In approx. 1908, this was changed to a pin on the upper tang. A wide variety of special order features were available including special length barrels (up to 30 in.), pistol grip stocks, checkering, woods, plating, grades of engraving, sights, etc., all of which can command a moderate to sizeable premium.

Add 20% for .25-35 WCF, .32-40 WCF, or .38-55 WCF cal.
Add approx. 100% for fancy checkered deluxe grade wood or 30% for checkered plain grain wood on models below that apply.

In 1905 Savage broadened the variety of this model and added the 1899A2, CD, BC, AB, Excelsior, Leader, Crescent, Victor, Rival, Premier, and Monarch (top-of-the-line model). Prices at the time ranged from $21 to $250 - quite a range. Any factory engraved Savage 99 is rare (less than 1,000 mfg. to date) with values having to be computed one gun at a time.

Engraved Model 1899s range from $2,500-$75,000+, depending on the level of engraving and original condition. Because of this, the above values assume standard rifle with no engraving options (Grades A through G).

All Model 1899s and 99s fall within the domain of Savage Arms, Inc.

Rifles under ser. no. 90,000 should be inspected before firing for possible receiver cracking at rear left corner.

From 1899-circa 1950, Model 1899s had serial numbers stamped on buttplate, buttstock, and forearm. A factory drilled and tapped Model 1899 has the model nomenclature moved to the left side.

* ***Model 1899A Rifle*** - .303 Savage, .30-30 Win., .25-35 WCF, .32-40 WCF, .38-55 WCF, or .300 Sav., 26 in. round barrel, straight grip stock, crescent or steel shotgun butt, takedown added 1909. Mfg. 1899-1927, Short rifle (22 in.) mfg. 1899-1922.

	$1,100	$1,000	$800	$700	$625	$550	$495

* ***Model 1899B Rifle*** - .303 Savage, .30-30 Win., .25-35 WCF, .32-40 WCF, or .38 - 55 WCF, 26 in. octagon barrel, straight grip stock, crescent or steel shotgun butt. Mfg. 1899-1915.

	$1,200	$1,050	$875	$750	$650	$575	$500

Add 25% for .25-35 WCF, .32-40 WCF. and .38-55 WCF.

* ***Model 1899C Rifle*** - .303 Savage, .30-30 Win., .25-35 WCF, .32-40 WCF, or .38 - 55 WCF, 26 in. half octagon barrel, straight grip, crescent or steel shotgun butt. Mfg. 1899-1915.

	$1,400	$1,250	$1,100	$975	$825	$750	$675

Add 25% for .25-35 WCF, .32-40 WCF, or .38-55 WCF.

* ***Model 1899-D Military Rifle (Musket)*** - .30-30 Win. or .303 Savage cal., 28 or 30 in. round barrel with two barrel bands, straight grip stock with bayonet lug.

	$4,000	$3,675	$3,350	$2,925	$2,525	$2,050	$1,600

* ***Model 1899-F Carbine*** - various cals., three cataloged variations, first variation w/small barrel band is controversial as to whether or not it exists, all variations have sling ring and carbine butt.

	$2,000	$1,800	$1,600	$1,400	$1,075	$925	$800

Add approx. 25% for Winchester calibers.
Add 10% for .30-30 Win. cal.
Add 150% for small barrel band variation.

* ***Model 1899H Rifle*** - .22 Hi-Power, .25-35 WCF, .30-30 Win., or .303 Savage cal., 20 in. featherweight barrel, straight grip, steel or hard rubber shotgun butt, takedown added in 1909. Mfg. 1905-15.

	$1,200	$1,000	$800	$675	$625	$500	$400

Add 10% for .22 Hi-Power.
Add 20% for .25-35 WCF.

* ***Model 1899 .250-3000 Rifle*** - takedown frame only, pistol grip checkered stocks with corrugated steel butt, fine cross-checkered trigger (unique to this model). Mfg. 1914-21.

	$1,250	$1,050	$840	$685	$575	$465	$400

MODEL 99A - .30-30 Win., .300 Sav., or .303 Sav. cal., lever action, 24 in. barrel, open sight, hammerless, straight grip stock, crescent butt. Mfg. 1920-36.

	$975	$850	$725	$625	$525	$450	$375

MODEL 99A RECENT PRODUCTION - similar to original, with .243 Win., .250 Sav., .300 Sav., .308 Win., or .375 Win. (1981 only, approx. 1,500 mfg.) cal., 20 or 22 in. barrel, tang safety, conventional butt. Mfg. 1971-81.

	$475	$425	$360	$325	$300	$275	$250

Add 10% for .375 Win. or .250 Sav. cal.

GRADING - PPGS™	100%	98%	95%	90%	80%	70%	60%

MODEL 99B - takedown version of original Model 99A, 24 (introduced 1926-27) or 26 (initial standard barrel length) in. barrel. Mfg. 1920-34.

	$1,200	$1,050	$840	$685	$575	$465	$400

MODEL 99H CARBINE - .250-3000 Sav., .30-30 Win., .300 Sav. (scarce) or .303 Sav. cal., solid frame, carbine type stock. Mfg. 1923-40.

	$995	$795	$630	$525	$400	$350	$300

Add 30% for .250 Sav. and .300 Sav. cal.

There were four variations of this model - the latter three had barrel bands. This variation did not have a saddle ring.

MODEL 99E - .22 Hi Power, .250-3000 Sav., .30-30 Win., .300 Sav., or .303 Sav. cal., 20, 22 or 24 in. barrel, solid frame, straight stock. Mfg. 1922-34.

	$895	$750	$625	$500	$400	$350	$300

Add 15% for .22 Hi Power or .250 Sav. cal.

MODEL 99E CARBINE - .243 Win., .250 Sav., .300 Sav., or .308 Win. cal., 22 in. barrel, checkered pistol grip stock, 5 shot rotary mag. Mfg. 1960-82.

	$600	$550	$500	$450	$375	$300	$250

Last MSR was $343.

Add 25% for early Schnabel forearm.

MODEL 99F FEATHERWEIGHT - similar to pre-war Model 99E, except takedown and 1/2 pound lighter, also mfg. with .410 bore shotgun barrel. Mfg. 1920-40.

	$1,200	$1,000	$850	$725	$675	$625	$550

Add 35% for .410 bore shotgun barrel.
Add 10% for cut checkering.
Add 10% for .22 HP or .250 Sav. cal.

MODEL 99F - .243 Win., .250-3000 Sav., .284 Win., .300 Sav., .308 Win., or .358 Win. cal., solid frame, checkered pistol grip stock. Mfg. 1955-73.

	$750	$630	$525	$465	$400	$300	$250

Add 35% for .250-3000 Sav., .358 Win., or .284 Win. cal.

This model, in many cases, had the receiver marked "99M".

MODEL 99G - similar to Model 99E pre-war, with checkered pistol grip stock and takedown. Mfg. 1922-41.

	$1,100	$950	$850	$750	$675	$575	$500

Add 10% for .250 Sav. cal.

MODEL 99EG - similar to Model 99G, with solid frame and no checkering. Mfg. 1935-41.

	$795	$685	$600	$525	$400	$350	$300

MODEL 99EG POST-WAR - .243 Win., .250 Sav., .300 Sav., .308 Win., or .358 Win. cal., checkered stock. Mfg. 1946-60.

	$575	$525	$450	$395	$340	$295	$260

Add 50% for .358 Win. or .250 Sav. cal.

MODEL 99R PRE-WAR - .250-3000 Sav., .303 Sav., or .300 Sav. cal., 22 or 24 in. barrel, large pistol grip stock and forearm. Mfg. 1932-42.

	$695	$625	$525	$400	$350	$325	$300

Add 35% for .250-3000 Sav. cal.

MODEL 99R POST-WAR - .250-3000 Sav., .300 Sav., .308 Win., .358 Win., or .243 Win. cal., similar to Pre-War, 24 in. barrel only, swivel studs. Mfg. 1946-60.

	$600	$500	$450	$400	$350	$325	$300

Add 35% for .250-3000 Sav. or .358 Win. cal.

MODEL 99RS PRE-WAR - similar to Model 99R Pre-War, with Lyman aperture sight, swivels and sling. Mfg. 1932-42.

	$850	$700	$600	$500	$450	$400	$350

GRADING - PPGS™	100%	98%	95%	90%	80%	70%	60%

MODEL 99RS POST-WAR - similar to Model 99R Post-War, with Redfield receiver sight. Mfg. 1946-58.

	$700	$600	$500	$400	$350	$325	$300

MODEL 99T - 20 or 22 in. barrel, solid frame, lightweight, checkered pistol grip stock. Mfg. 1935-40.

	$1,050	$950	$850	$700	$500	$400	$300

MODEL 99K - engraved receiver and fancy wood stock, Lyman aperture sight and folding middle sight. Mfg. 1926-40.

	$3,750	$3,500	$3,000	$2,750	$2,500	$2,200	$1,875

MODEL 99DL - .243 Win., .250-3000 Sav., .284 Win., .300 Sav., .308 Win., or .358 Win. cal., Monte Carlo stock and sling swivels. Post-war mfg. 1960-73.

	$700	$600	$500	$400	$350	$325	$300

    Add 10% for cut checkering.
    Add 35% for .250-3000 Sav. cal.
    Add 35% for .284 Win. or .358 Win. cal.

MODEL 99C - similar to Model 99F Post-War, available in .22-250 Rem. (rare), .243 Win., .284 Win. (disc.), 7mm-08 (disc.), or .308 Win. cal., 22 in. barrel, Monte Carlo stock with cut checkering and recoil pad, top tang safety, cocking indicator, open sights, detachable 4 shot mag., 7 3/4 lbs. Mfg. 1965, 1995-97.

	$500	$450	$400	$350	$300	$275	$250

Last MSR was $629.

    Add 50% for .22-250 cal.
    Add 25% for .284 Win.
    Add 25% for 7mm-08 cal.

MODEL 99CD - similar to Model 99C, with Monte Carlo cheekpiece stock. Mfg. 1975-81.

	$550	$500	$400	$325	$300	$275	$250

MODEL 99-358 (BRUSH GUN) - .358 Win. cal., recoil pad. Mfg. 1977-80.

	$1,100	$1,000	$900	$800	$700	$600	$550

MODEL 99-375 (BRUSH GUN) - .375 Win. cal., recoil pad, fluted forearm. Mfg. 1980 only.

	$1,300	$1,200	$1,050	$950	$875	$800	$725

MODEL 99PE - elaborately engraved and plated receiver, tang, and lever, fancy wood with hand cut checkering. Mfg. 1966-70.

	$1,800	$1,600	$1,400	$1,200	$1,000	$850	$700

This model had the receiver marked "99M".

MODEL 99DE CITATION - similar to Model 99PE, except with less engraving and pressed checkering. Mfg. 1968-70.

	$1,200	$1,050	$900	$800	$700	$600	$500

This model had the receiver marked "99M".

MODEL 99M - while the receivers on Models 99F, 99PE, and 99DE were marked "99M" this is not a model designation. Rather, the "M" barrel designation indicated Monte Carlo stock.

MODEL 1903 STANDARD SLIDE ACTION - .22 S, L, or LR cal., 24 in. barrel, open sights, box mag., pistol grip stock. Mfg. 1903-1922.

	$675	$550	$450	$375	$300	$250	$200

  ❋ *Model 1903 Standard Slide Action Grade EF* - features "B" grade checkering on fancy English walnut stock, Savage #22B front sight, and #21B micrometer open rear sight.

	$875	$750	$700	$650	$600	$550	$500

GRADING - PPGS™	100%	98%	95%	90%	80%	70%	60%

✻ *Model 1903 Standard Slide Action Expert Grade* - features "A" grade engraving on receiver, "B" grade checkering on fancy American walnut stock, standard sights.

	$1,950	$1,750	$1,600	$1,500	$1,200	$1,000	$800

✻ *Model 1903 Standard Slide Action Grade GH* - features "A" grade checkering on plain American walnut stock, no engraving, #22B front sight, and #21B micrometer open rear sight.

	$800	$700	$600	$550	$500	$450	$300

✻ *Model 1903 Standard Slide Action Gold Medal* - features animal ornamentation on receiver, less elaborate checkering on plain American walnut stock, standard sights.

	$1,050	$900	$800	$700	$650	$600	$400

MODEL 1909 SLIDE ACTION - similar to Model 1903, with 20 in. round barrel. Mfg. 1909-1915.

	$750	$650	$500	$450	$400	$325	$250

MODEL 1904 SINGLE SHOT - .22 S, L, or LR cal., bolt action, 18 in. barrel, straight stock. Mfg. 1904-17.

	$175	$140	$125	$100	$85	$65	$50

MODEL 1905 SINGLE SHOT - similar to Model 1904, except 24 in. barrel, takedown. Mfg. 1905-19.

	$175	$140	$125	$100	$85	$65	$50

MODEL 1911 BOLT ACTION - .22 S only, bolt action, 20 shot tubular mag. in buttstock, 20 in. barrel. Limited mfg. 1911-12.

	$400	$325	$295	$240	$195	$150	$115

MODEL 1912 AUTOLOADER - .22 LR cal., semi-auto, 20 in. barrel, takedown, straight stock. Mfg. 1912 16.

	$750	$650	$500	$400	$300	$250	$200

MODEL 1914 SLIDE ACTION - .22 S, L, and LR cal., 24 in. octagon barrel, plain pistol grip stock. Mfg. 1914-26.

	$450	$400	$325	$250	$215	$170	$130

MODEL 19 NRA BOLT ACTION - .22 LR cal., 25 in. barrel, adj. aperture sight, 5 shot, military stock. Approx. 50,000 mfg. 1919-32.

	$275	$225	$200	$175	$150	$125	$110

Between 1943-45 approx. 6,000 Model 19s were made under military contract - add 15%.

MODEL 19 BOLT ACTION TARGET - .22 LR cal., 25 in. barrel, speed lock, adj. aperture sight, target stock. Mfg. 1933-46.

	$300	$250	$200	$175	$150	$125	$110

MODEL 19L - similar to Model 19, with Lyman receiver sight. Mfg. 1933-42.

	$330	$275	$195	$140	$120	$110	$100

MODEL 19M - similar to Model 19, with 28 in. heavy barrel and scope bases. Mfg. 1933-42.

	$330	$275	$195	$165	$140	$120	$110

MODEL 19H - similar to Model 19, except .22 Hornet. Mfg. 1933-42.

	$550	$495	$330	$220	$175	$165	$155

MODEL 1920 BOLT ACTION - Mauser type action, .250-3000 Sav. or .300 Sav. cal., 22 or 24 in. barrel, open sights, 5 shot, checkered pistol grip, Schnabel forend. Mfg. 1920-31.

	$500	$450	$375	$325	$300	$250	$200

Add 10% for .250-3000 Sav. cal.

GRADING - PPGS™	100%	98%	95%	90%	80%	70%	60%

MODEL 1920-1926 - similar to Model 1920, with 24 in. barrel, Lyman aperture sight, Mfg. 1926-31.

	$450	$400	$350	$300	$275	$250	$225

Add 10% for .250-3000 cal.

MODEL 1922 - .22 LR cal., predecessor of the Model 23A, mfg. 1922.

	$250	$220	$165	$140	$110	$95	$85

MODEL 23A BOLT ACTION RIFLE - .22 LR cal., 23 in. barrel, open sights, plain pistol grip stock, Schnabel forend. Mfg. 1923-33.

	$250	$200	$185	$140	$100	$85	$70

MODEL 23AA - improved version of Model 23A, with speedlock and checkered stock. Mfg. 1933-42.

	$300	$250	$195	$150	$130	$100	$80

MODEL 23B - .25-20 WCF cal., same configuration as Model 23A, 25 in. barrel, full forearm. Mfg. 1923-42.

	$300	$250	$200	$175	$140	$125	$100

MODEL 23C - .32-20 WCF, similar to Model 23B. Mfg. 1923-42.

	$350	$300	$225	$175	$150	$125	$100

MODEL 23D - with .22 Hornet, similar to Model 23B. Mfg. 1933-47.

	$375	$325	$275	$240	$225	$185	$140

MODEL 25 SLIDE ACTION - .22 S, L, or LR cal., 24 in. octagon barrel, open sight, takedown, hammerless, tube mag., plain pistol grip stock. Mfg. 1925-29.

	$350	$300	$250	$200	$175	$125	$75

MODEL 40 BOLT ACTION RIFLE - .250-3000 Sav., .300 Sav., .30-30 Win., or .30-06 cal., 22 or 24 in. barrel, open sight, 4 shot mag., plain pistol grip stock, Schnabel forend. Mfg. 1928-40.

	$350	$300	$250	$225	$200	$175	$150

Add 10% for .250-3000 Sav. cal.

MODEL 45 SUPER - similar to Model 40, with Lyman receiver sight and checkered stock. Mfg. 1928-40.

	$385	$325	$275	$225	$200	$175	$150

MODEL 29 SLIDE ACTION - .22 S, L, or LR cal., 22 in. barrel, octagon until 1940, round on post-WWII, open sights, checkered pistol grip stock on pre-war, plain on late model. Mfg. 1929-67.

Pre-war	$350	$275	$225	$200	$175	$150	$125
	$300	$250	$200	$165	$150	$135	$125

MODEL 3 SINGLE SHOT - .22 S, L, or LR cal., bolt action, 26 in. barrel, 24 in. barrel on post-war, open sights, plain grip stock. Mfg. 1930-47.

	$85	$65	$55	$40	$30	$30	$30

MODEL 3S - similar to Model 3, with aperture sight. Mfg. 1930-47.

	$100	$85	$70	$55	$40	$30	$30

MODEL 3ST - similar to Model 3S, with swivels and sling. Mfg. 1930-47.

	$110	$90	$85	$70	$45	$35	$30

MODEL 4 BOLT ACTION REPEATER - .22 S, L, or LR cal., 24 in. barrel, open sight, takedown, 5 shot, checkered pistol grip stock on pre-war, plain stock on post-war. Mfg. 1933-65.

	$110	$85	$70	$55	$40	$30	$30
Pre-war	$120	$95	$85	$65	$50	$40	$30

MODEL 4S - similar to Model 4, with aperture sight. Mfg. 1933-42.

	$120	$90	$75	$65	$55	$40	$30

GRADING - PPGS™	100%	98%	95%	90%	80%	70%	60%

MODEL 4M - similar to Model 4, except .22 Mag. Mfg. 1961-65.

	$110	$85	$70	$55	$45	$30	$30

MODEL 5 - similar to Model 4, with tubular mag. Mfg. 1938-64.

	$110	$85	$70	$55	$45	$30	$30

MODEL 5S - similar to Model 5, with aperture sight. Mfg. 1936-42.

	$120	$95	$85	$65	$55	$40	$30

MODEL 6 AUTOLOADER - .22 S, L, or LR cal., 24 in. barrel, tubular mag., take-down, checkered pistol grip stock on pre-war, plain stock on post-war. Mfg. 1938-68.

	$140	$110	$95	$85	$65	$55	$40
Pre-war	$150	$120	$105	$95	$75	$65	$50

MODEL 6S - similar to Model 6, with aperture sight. Mfg. 1938-42.

	$150	$120	$105	$95	$75	$65	$45

MODEL 7 AUTOLOADER - similar to Model 6, with box mag. Mfg. 1939-51.

	$140	$110	$95	$65	$55	$55	$40
Pre-war	$150	$120	$105	$95	$75	$65	$50

MODEL 7S - similar to Model 7, with aperture sight. Mfg. 1938-42.

	$150	$120	$105	$95	$75	$65	$45

MODEL 60 AUTOLOADER - .22 LR cal., 20 in. barrel, leaf sight, tubular mag., checkered Monte Carlo walnut stock. Mfg. 1969-72.

	$95	$85	$70	$55	$45	$35	$30

MODEL 90 AUTOLOADING CARBINE - similar to Model 60, with 16 1/2 in. barrel, plain carbine stock, with barrel band.

	$95	$85	$70	$55	$45	$35	$30

MODEL 88 AUTOLOADER - similar to Model 60, except has walnut finished hardwood stock. Mfg. 1969-72.

	$85	$85	$55	$45	$40	$35	$30

MODEL 63/63K SINGLE SHOT - .22 S, L, or LR cal., bolt action, 18 in. barrel, open sights, trigger locks with key (only on Model 63K), full length pistol grip walnut finished hardwood stock, Model 63s were mfg. 1964-69, Model 63Ks were mfg. 1970-72.

	$80	$65	$55	$45	$40	$35	$30

MODEL 63KM - .22 Mag. cal., similar to Model 63K.

	$115	$90	$80	$70	$60	$50	$40

MODEL 219 SINGLE SHOT - .22 Hornet, .25-20 WCF, .32-20 WCF, or .30-30 Win. cal., 26 in. barrel, open sight, hammerless, break open, top lever, plain pistol grip stock. Mfg. 1938-65.

.30-30 Win. cal.	$195	$160	$135	$110	$100	$90	$80

Add 15% for all other cals.

MODEL 219L - similar to Model 219, with side lever. Mfg. 1965-67.

	$135	$85	$70	$55	$45	$35	$30

MODELS 221, 222, 223, 227, 228, AND 229 - single shot, similar to Model 219, only supplied with additional shotgun barrel, interchangeable, different model numbers are for different cals., gauges, and barrel lengths, all have been disc.

	$130	$100	$85	$75	$65	$50	$45

SAVAGE/STEVENS MODEL 65 - please refer to listing under Stevens section.

MODEL 34M - similar to Model 34, chambered for .22 Mag. Mfg. 1969-73.

	$90	$70	$55	$45	$35	$30	$30

GRADING - PPGS™	100%	98%	95%	90%	80%	70%	60%

MODEL 35 - .22 LR cal., bolt action, 22 in. barrel, 5 shot detachable mag., open sights, hardwood Monte Carlo stock. Disc. 1985.

	$90	$80	$65	$50	$35	$30	$30

Last MSR was $100.

MODEL 36 - .22 LR cal., single shot, otherwise similar to Model 35. Mfg. 1983-84.

	$90	$80	$65	$50	$35	$30	$30

MODEL 46 - similar to Model 34, with tubular mag. Mfg. 1969-73.

	$90	$70	$55	$45	$35	$30	$30

MODEL 65M - .22 Mag. cal., similar to Model 65.

	$95	$75	$65	$55	$45	$35	$30

SAVAGE/FOX MODEL FB-1 - .22 LR cal., bolt action, 24 in. barrel, hooded front sight, Williams adj. rear, premium walnut stock with rollover cheekpiece, rosewood tip and forend cap, fancy cut checkering. Mfg. 1981 only.

	$225	$185	$165	$140	$120	$100	$80

SAVAGE/STEVENS MODEL 72 "CRACKSHOT" - please refer to listing under Stevens section.

SAVAGE/STEVENS MODEL 73 - similar to Model 63, w/o Monte Carlo stock. Mfg. 1964-69.

	$125	$100	$85	$65	$55	$40	$35

SAVAGE/STEVENS MODEL 89 SINGLE SHOT - please refer to listing under Stevens section.

MODEL 340 BOLT ACTION - .22 Hornet, .222 Rem., .223 Rem., or .30-30 Win. cal., 22 and 24 in. barrel, open sights, 4 or 5 shot mag., 7 1/2 lbs., plain pistol grip stock. Mfg. 1950-85.

	$225	$195	$170	$160	$150	$140	$130

Last MSR was $257.

EL 340C - similar to Model 340, with aperture sight, checkered stock, and sling swivels. Mfg. 1952-60.

	$235	$205	$180	$165	$155	$145	$135

MODEL 340V - .225 Win. cal., varmint configuration, 24 in. barrel. Limited mfg. in late 1960s.

	$295	$265	$235	$205	$180	$165	$150

MODEL 340S DELUXE - similar to Model 340, with aperture sight, checkered stock, sling swivels. Mfg. 1952-60.

	$300	$265	$235	$200	$185	$165	$150

MODEL 342 AND 342S - .22 Hornet cal., similar to Model 340. Mfg. 1950-55.

	$300	$265	$235	$200	$185	$165	$150

MODEL 982DL/MDI - .22 LR (DL) or .22 Mag. (MDI) cal., bolt action, 22 in. barrel, ramp front sight, folding leaf rear sight, checkered American walnut stock with Monte Carlo comb, matte receiver finish. Mfg. 1981 only.

	$195	$175	$150	$125	$100	$85	$65

Add 20% for .22 Mag. cal.

RIFLES: RIMFIRE, CURRENT PRODUCTION

Savage introduced a new line of Rimfire rifles during 1996. Recent Savage nomenclature usually involves alphabetical suffixes which mean the following: B - Brown laminated wood stock, BT - laminated thumbhole stock, F - composite/synthetic stock, G - hardwood stock, L - left-hand, S/SS - stainless steel, T - Target (aperture rear sight), V - Long Range (Varmint w/ heavy barrel), XP - package gun (scope, sling, and rings/base), Y - Youth/Ladies Model (shortened dimensions). Hence, the Model Mark II-GLY designates a Mark II model with hardwood stock, left-hand action in a Youth configuration. A Model 93 Series with

GRADING - PPGS™	100%	98%	95%	90%	80%	70%	60%

BTVSS suffix indicates a laminated thumbole stock with heavy barrel in stainless steel.

Subtract 10% if w/o AccuTrigger (became standard on most rimfire rifles 2006, except Model 64 and Model 200).

CUB (G) - .17 Mach 2 (mfg. 2005 only), .22 LR cal., single shot Youth Model with 16 1/8 in. barrel and shortened hardwood stock, traditional safety, aperture rear sight, Accutrigger became standard 2006, 4 1/2 lbs. New 2003.

MSR $199	$150	$120	$100	$80	$70	$65	$60

Add 10% for .17 Mach 2 cal. (mfg. 2005).

❋ *Cub Target* - .22 LR cal., similar to Cub Model, except has ergonomic thumbhole stock. New 2007.

MSR $248	$195	$150	$120	$100	$90	$80	$70

Add $13 for pink stock (new 2008).

MARK I-G SERIES BOLT ACTION - .22 S-L-LR, or LR shot (Mark I - GSB) cal., single shot, self-cocking, 19 (Mark I-GY, Youth Model) or 20 3/4 in. barrel, checkered hardwood stock, AccuTrigger became standard 2006, approx. 5 lbs. New 1996.

MSR $209	$165	$130	$100	$85	$75	$65	$60

Add $35 for Youth Color (mfg. 2002-2005) or $31 for Camo Youth (mfg. 2002-2004).
Add $7 for scope (Model Mark I-GYXP only, mfg. 2002-2004).

This Model was also available with left-hand action (Mark I-GL, disc. 2003), Youth Model (Mark I-GY), Youth Color (Mark I-GLY, features blue/green/grey laminate stock, new 2002), Camo Youth (Mark I-Y Camo, mfg. 2002-2004), or with smooth bore barrel (Mark I-GSB).

❋ *Mark I-FVT Series Bolt Action* - similar to Mark I-G, except has synthetic stock, 20 3/4 in. heavy barrel and aperture target sights, 5 1/4 lbs. New 2005.

MSR $367	$285	$210	$160	$130	$100	$90	$80

MARK II-F SERIES BOLT ACTION - .17 Mach 2 (new 2004) or .22 LR cal., features checkered black synthetic stock, 20 3/4 in. barrel, blue barrel, 10 shot mag., AccuTrigger became standard 2006, 5 lbs. New 1998.

MSR $191	$150	$125	$100	$85	$75	$65	$60

Add $7 for Mark II-FXP package (includes 4x15mm scope, disc. 2005).
Add $45 for .17 Mach 2 cal.

❋ *Mark II Series Bolt Action Camo* - .22 LR cal. only, similar to Mark II-F, Realtree Hardwoods HD full camo stock treatment. New 2002.

MSR $233	$185	$150	$120	$95	$80	$75	$65

Add $167 for Mark II XP Camo package with 3-9x32mm scope (new 2008).

❋ *Mark II Series Bolt Action FSS* - .17 Mach 2 (mfg. 2004-2005) or .22 LR cal., 20 3/4 stainless steel barrel with sights, black graphite/polymer stock with checkering, dovetailed receiver, 5 lbs. New 1997.

MSR $258	$200	$155	$150	$90	$70	$65	$60

Add 10% for .17 Mach 2 cal.

❋ *Mark II Series Bolt Action FV/FVT* - .17 Mach 2 (new 2004) or .22 LR cal., features 21 in. heavy barrel with target sights (FVT) or w/o sights (FV), black synthetic stock, 5 shot detachable mag., Weaver style bases included, 6 lbs. New 1998.

MSR $259	$200	$155	$150	$90	$70	$65	$60

Add $116 for Model FVT with target sights (new mid-2005).
Add $6 for .17 Mach 2 cal.
Add $60 for Mark II-FVSS (stainless) in .17 Mach 2 cal. (mfg. 2005).
Add $33 for Mark II-FVXP package (includes 4x32mm scope, disc. 2004, reintroduced 2006).

GRADING - PPGS™	100%	98%	95%	90%	80%	70%	60%

✻ *Mark II Series Bolt Action G* - .17 Mach 2 (mfg. 2004-2005) or .22 LR cal., similar to Mark I-G Series, except has detachable 10 shot mag., approx. 5 lbs. New 1996.

MSR $209	$170	$135	$100	$85	$75	$65	$60

    Add $64 for Mark II-GV (mfg. 2005).
    Add $7 for Mark II-GXP package (includes 4x15mm scope, disc. 2004).
    Add $7 for Mark II-GLXP package (left-hand, includes 4x15mm scope, disc. 2004).

This Model is also available with left-hand action (Mark II-GL), Youth Model (Mark II-GY), Youth Model Left-Hand (Mark II-GLY), Varmint Left Hand (Mark II GLV, disc. 2005) at no additional charge.

✻ *Mark II Series Bolt Action BV/LV* - .17 Mach 2 (mfg. 2005) or .22 LR cal., features 21 in. blue heavy barrel, 5 shot mag., no sights, grey or brown laminated hardwood stock with (Mark II LV, disc. 2004) or w/o (Mark II BV) cut checkering, 6 1/2 lbs. New 1997.

MSR $322	$260	$210	$175	$145	$120	$105	$100

    Add 10% for Mark II BVSS (stainless) in .17 Mach 2 cal. - grey finish only, mfg. 2005.

✻ *Mark II Series Bolt Action BTVS* - .22 LR cal., 21 in. heavy stainless barrel w/o sights, features brown laminated thumbhole stock with vent. forend, stainless steel action, 7 1/2 lbs. New 2007.

MSR $421	$350	$290	$250	$215	$180	$160	$140

✻ *Mark II Series Bolt Action Classic* - .22 LR cal., 21 (disc.) or 24 in. matte blue barrel, 5 shot detachable box mag., hinged floorplate, checkered pistol grip walnut stock, no sights. New 2007.

MSR $520	$440	$385	$330	$280	$225	$175	$150

    Add $33 for MK Classic T with target sights (new 2008).

MODEL 64 SERIES SEMI-AUTO - .22 LR cal., 20 1/4 in. barrel with adj. rear sight, 10 shot detachable mag., choice of black synthetic (Model 64F) or checkered hardwood (Model 64G) stock, thumb operated rotary safety, Accu-Trigger not available, 5 1/2 lbs. New 1996.

MSR $175	$145	$120	$95	$75	$70	$65	$60

    Add $9 for Model 64-GXP package (includes 4x15mm scope, disc. 2005).

✻ *Model 64F/64FV Semi-Auto* - .22 LR cal., similar to Model 64, except has black graphite/polymer checkered stock, 20 1/4 regular or 21 (Model 64FV, mfg. 1998-2004) heavy barrel, not available w/Accu-Trigger, 5 or 6 lbs. New 1997.

MSR $146	$120	$100	$85	$75	$70	$65	$60

    Add $48 for Model 64FV with heavy barrel (disc. 2004).
    Add $5 for Model 64-FXP package (includes unmounted 4x15mm scope).
    Add $63 for Model 64-FVXP package (includes 4x32mm scope, new 2006).

✻ *Model 64FSS Semi-Auto* - similar to Model 64F, except has stainless steel barrel and action with checkered black synthetic graphite/polymer stock, 5 lbs. New 2002.

MSR $222	$175	$135	$105	$80	$70	$65	$60

✻ *Model 64FVSS Semi-Auto* - similar to Model 64FSS, except has 21 in. heavy barrel, 6 lbs. Mfg. 2002-2004.

	$190	$150	$115	$100	$85	$70	$65

Last MSR was $240.

✻ *Model 64F Semi-Auto Camo* - similar to Model 64F, except has Realtree Hardwoods HD, camo finish and 20 in. barrel, 5 lbs. New 2003.

MSR $195	$150	$125	$100	$80	$70	$65	$60

✻ *Model 64BTV* - .22 LR cal., features laminated stock, rear aperture sight and 21 in. heavy barrel. New 2008.

MSR $331	$270	$210	$155	$130	$100	$90	$80

MODEL 93 SERIES MAGNUM BOLT ACTION - .22 Win. Mag. cal., 20 3/4 in. barrel with adj. rear sight, 5 shot detachable mag., checkered right- or left-hand (Model 93 GL) hardwood Monte Carlo stock, AccuTrigger became standard 2006, 5 3/4 lbs. New 1996.

✳ *Model 93 G/GL Series Magnum Bolt Action*

MSR $241	$185	$150	$120	$95	$75	$70	$65

✳ *Model 93F/FV Series Magnum Bolt Action* - features 20 3/4 blue regular (F) or heavy (FV) barrel with checkered black synthetic graphite polymer stock, 5 lbs. New 1998.

MSR $229	$180	$145	$115	$90	$75	$70	$65

Add $32 for Model 93FV with heavy barrel (new 2006).

✳ *Model 93FSS Series Magnum Bolt Action* - similar to Model 93G, except has stainless steel barrel and action with checkered black synthetic graphite/polymer stock, 5 lbs. New 1997.

MSR $291	$235	$190	$140	$105	$85	$70	$65

✳ *Model 93FVSS Series Magnum Bolt Action* - similar to Model 93FSS, except has 21 in. heavy barrel with recessed crown and button rifling, drilled and tapped, Weaver bases included, 6 lbs. New 1998.

MSR $331	$265	$200	$150	$115	$85	$70	$65

Add $30 for Model 93FVSSXP package (includes 4x32mm scope and mounts).

✳ *Model 93F Camo Series Magnum Bolt Action* - similar to Model 93G, except has Realtree Hardwoods HD camo finish. Mfg. 2003-2004.

	$180	$150	$110	$90	$75	$70	$65

Last MSR was $211.

This model is still available as a package, including a 3-9x40mm scope - MSR is $414.

✳ *Model 93 BTVS Series Magnum Bolt Action* - similar to Model 93FVSS, except has brown laminated thumbhole stock, stainless steel action and 21 in. heavy barrel w/o sights. New 2007.

MSR $428	$350	$295	$255	$215	$180	$160	$140

✳ *Model 93 Classic* - .22 Win. Mag., features 24 in. regular or heavy high luster blue barrel with or w/o aperture rear sight, 5 shot detachable box mag., with (Model 93 Classic-T) or w/o sights. New 2008.

MSR $534	$450	$390	$335	$280	$230	$190	$170

Add $35 for heavy barrel with apeture rear sight (Model 93 Classic-T).

MODEL 93R17 SERIES BOLT ACTION - .17 HMR cal., black synthetic or hardwood stock and forearm, 20 3/4 or 21 in. barrel, otherwise similar to Model 93 Series, AccuTrigger became standard 2006, 5 lbs. New 2003.

✳ *Model 93R17F Series Bolt Action* - synthetic stock.

MSR $236	$185	$145	$115	$90	$75	$70	$65

Add $46 for Model 93R17FXP package (includes 3-9x40mm scope, new 2006).

✳ *Model 93R17BV/BVSS/BTVS Series Bolt Action* - features laminated hardwood stock, steel (BV) or stainless steel (BVSS) action, with (BTVS) or w/o target sights, 6 lbs. New 2003.

MSR $392	$320	$225	$170	$135	$115	$100	$80

Add $36 for Model BTVS with target sights (new 2006).
Add $22 for Model BV (new 2006).

✳ *Model 93R17 Series Bolt Action Camo* - similar to Model 93R17F, except has Realtree Hardwoods HD camo finish. New 2003.

MSR $278	$230	$185	$135	$100	$85	$70	$65

Add $136 for 93R17 XP camo package with 3-9x40mm scope (new 2008).

✳ *Model 93R17FSS Series Bolt Action* - similar to Model 93R17F, except has stainless steel barrel and action with checkered black synthetic graphite/polymer stock, 5 lbs. New 2003.

MSR $291	$240	$195	$135	$105	$85	$70	$65

GRADING - PPGS™	100%	98%	95%	90%	80%	70%	60%

✴ *Model 93R17FV Series Bolt Action* - similar to Model 93R17F, except has heavy stainless steel barrel. New 2003.

MSR $265		$215	$170	$130	$100	$85	$70	$65

✴ *Model 93R17FVSS Series Bolt Action* - similar to Model 93FSS, except has 21 in. heavy barrel with recessed crown and button rifling, drilled and tapped, Weaver bases included, 6 lbs. New 2003.

MSR $331		$260	$200	$150	$110	$95	$80	$75

✴ *Model 93R17GV/GLV Series Bolt Action* - similar to Model 93R17 F, except has checkered hardwood stock with varmint barrel, GLV is left-hand model, 6 lbs. New 2003.

MSR $264		$215	$175	$130	$100	$85	$70	$65

Add $47 for Model 93R17GVXP package (includes 3-9x40mm scope, new 2006).

✴ *Model 93R17 Classic Series Bolt Action* - .17 HMR cal., features 24 in. high luster blue barrel, 5 shot detachable box mag., walnut stock, no sights, 6 1/2 lbs. New 2007.

MSR $534		$450	$390	$335	$280	$230	$190	$170

Add $35 for target barrel with apeture rear sight (new 2008).

MODEL 900 SERIES - .22 LR cal., single (Target/Silhouette Model) or 5 shot (Biathlon Model), 21 or 25 (Target Model) in. free floated barrel, uncheckered hardwood stock, right- or left-hand action, approx. 8 lbs. Mfg. 1996-2001.

✴ *Model 900B Series Biathlon* - blonde stock, supplied with five 5-shot mags., includes shooting rail and barrel snow cover, aperture rear sight. Mfg. 1996-97.

			$445	$395	$350	$300	$265	$230	$200

Last MSR was $498.

This model was also available with left-hand action (Model 900B-LH, new 1997).

✴ *Model 900S Series Silhouette* - brown hardwood stock, heavy 21 in. barrel with muzzle crown, scope bases installed, w/o sights. Mfg. 1996-97.

			$300	$265	$230	$200	$180	$160	$140

Last MSR was $346.

This model was also available with left-hand action (Model 900S-LH, mfg. 1997).

✴ *Model 900TR Series Target* - features aperture sights, shooting rail with hand stop, 25 in. barrel. Disc. 2001.

			$395	$325	$280	$235	$200	$180	$160

Last MSR was $448.

This model was also available with left-hand action (Model 900TR-LH, new 1997).

RIFLES: CENTERFIRE, CURRENT/RECENT PRODUCTION

The 110 Series was first produced in 1958. Beginning in 1992, Savage Arms, Inc. began supplying this model with a master trigger lock, earmuffs, shooting glasses (disc. 1992), and test target.

Beginning 1994, all Savage rifles employ a laser etched bolt featuring the Savage logo. During 1996, Savage began using pillar bedded stocks for many of their rifles.

Recent Savage nomenclature usually involves alphabetical suffixes which mean the following: B - laminated wood stock, BT - laminated thumbhole stock, C - detachable box mag., F - composite/synthetic stock, G - hardwood stock, H - hinged floorplate, K - standard muzzle brake, AK - adj. muzzle brake with fluted barrel, L - left-hand, LE - Law Enforcement, NS - no sights, P - police (tactical) rifle, SB - smooth bore, SE - safari express, SS - stainless steel, SS-S - stainless steel single shot, T - Target (aperture rear sight), U - high luster blue, blue metal finish and/or stock finish, V - Long Range (Varmint w/ heavy barrel), XP - package gun (scope, sling, and rings/base), Y - Youth/Ladies Model. Hence, the Model 111FCNS designates a 111 Series firearm with synthetic stock, detachable magazine, and no sights. Likewise, a Model 11FYCXP3 indicates a Model 11 Series with synthetic stock, youth dimensions, detachable magazine, is a packaged gun which includes scope. A 2 digit model number (10) designates new short action. A 3 digit model number (110) indicates long action.

During 2003, Savage released its new patented AccuTrigger, which allows the consumer to adjust the trigger pull from the outside of the rifle from 1 1/2 lbs. - 6 lbs. using a proprietary tool. The AccuTrigger also has almost no trigger creep and is infinitely adjustable. Initially, it was released in all Varmint, LE, and heavy barrel long range rifles, and during 2004, the AccuTrigger became standard on nearly all Savage centerfire rifles, except the Model 11 and 11FCXP3 and 10/110G Package guns. During 2007, Savage began offering target actions with AccuTrigger, right bolt, and choice of left or right port ejection with .223 Rem. bolt head - MSR is $446-$460.

Whenever possible, the models within this category have been listed in numerical sequence.

Subtract approx. 10% on models listed below w/o AccuTrigger (became standard on all centerfire rifles in 2004).

MODEL 10 PREDATOR - .204 Ruger, .22-250 Rem., .223 Rem., or .243 Win. (new 2008) cal., 22 in. barrel, laminate stock, 100% Mossy Oak Brush patterned camo, no sights, includes scope blocks, 7 1/4 lbs. New 2007.

MSR $760	$650	$500	$400	$325	$300	$275	$250

Add $39 for Model 10XP Predator package, which includes scope (new 2008).

MODEL 10FCM SCOUT - .308 Win. or 7mm-08 Rem. (disc. 2002) cal., 20 in. barrel with removable ghost ring rear sight, one-piece barrel mount (allows long scope eye relief), 4 shot detachable mag., satin blue action with large ball bolt handle, black synthetic dual pillar bedded stock, includes swivel set and sling, tripod became standard 2007, 6 1/8 lbs. Mfg. 1999-2003, reintroduced 2007.

MSR $646	$545	$465	$385	$340	$300	$280	$265

MODEL 10FM (SIERRA) - .243 Win., .308 Win., .270 WSM (new 2003), .300 WSM (new 2002), or 7mm-08 Rem. (new 1999) cal., short action, lightweight, features black synthetic stock with dual pillar bedding, button rifling and recessed crown, 20 (Sierra, standard weight, new 1999) or 24 (heavy only, disc. 1998) in. barrel, w/o sights, 6 lbs. Mfg. 1998-2004.

	$435	$360	$290	$245	$210	$175	$160

Last MSR was $511.

This model was also available in left-hand action (disc.).

MODEL 10FCM (SIERRA) - .243 Win., .270 WSM, .300 WSM, .308 Win., or 7mm-08 Rem cal., 20 in. barrel, synthetic stock, short action, detachable box mag., no sights, 6 1/4 lbs. Mfg. 2005-2006.

	$440	$350	$295	$265	$225	$190	$165

Last MSR was $540.

MODEL 10 50TH ANNIVERSARY - .300 Savage cal., short action, hinged floorplate. New 2008.

MSR $1,724	$1,475	$1,250	$1,050	$875	$750	$650	$595

MODEL 10 LAW ENFORCEMENT SERIES - .223 Rem., .260 Rem. (mfg. 1999-2001), .308 Win., or 7mm-08 (mfg. 1999-2001) cal., short action, tactical/law enforcement model, checkered black synthetic stock, features 20 (new 2006) or 24 in. heavy barrel w/o sights, AccuTrigger became standard 2003, 8 lbs. Mfg. 1998-2007.

	$505	$395	$320	$275	$230	$190	$165

Last MSR was $621.

✳ Model 10FP - .223 Rem. or .308 Win. cal., 20 or 24 in. barrel, black McMillan synthetic stock. New 1998.

MSR $678	$545	$430	$340	$285	$235	$190	$165

This model is also available in left-hand action (Model 10FLP, 24 in. barrel only).

GRADING - PPGS™	100%	98%	95%	90%	80%	70%	60%

❊ *Model10FP Duty* - similar to Model 10FP, except has open iron sights. Mfg. 2002 only.

	100%	98%	95%	90%	80%	70%	60%
	$435	$355	$290	$250	$215	$180	$165

Last MSR was $525.

❊ *Model10FP 20 In. (LE1/LE1A)* - .223 Rem. (LE1A only, disc. 2007) or .308 Win. cal., similar to Model 10FP, except has 20 in. heavy barrel with no sights, choice of standard (LE1, disc. 2005) or Choate (LE1A) stock (folding only, new 2006). New 2002.

MSR $936	$775	$625	$500	$435	$365	$300	$275

    Subtract 20% for standard stock (LE1).

❊ *Model10FP 26 In. (LE2/LE2A)* - .223 (LE2A only) or .308 Win. cal., similar to Model 10FP-LE1/LE1A, except has 26 in. heavy barrel and choice of standard (LE2, disc. 2005) or Choate stock (LE2A). Mfg. 2002-2006.

	$625	$500	$400	$360	$330	$300	$275

Last MSR was $754.

    Subtract 20% for standard stock.

❊ *Model10FP McMillan (LE2B)* - .308 Win. cal., short action, features McMillan tactical fiberglass stock with stippled grip areas, 4 shot mag., 26 in. heavy barrel. Mfg. 2003-2006.

	$860	$725	$625	$525	$425	$325	$265

Last MSR was $1,033.

❊ *Model 10FP HS Precision* - .308 Win. cal., 24 in. barrel, features H-S Precision stock. Mfg. 2006 only.

	$720	$585	$475	$425	$350	$300	$275

Last MSR was $864.

❊ *Model10FPCPXP/10FPXP (LE/LEA)* - .308 Win. cal. only, short action, features skeletonized synthetic stock, 24 (new 2006) or 26 (disc. 2005) in. barrel w/o sights, H-S Precision stock became standard 2006, LEA has Choate stock, LE has standard stock (disc. 2005), includes Burris (disc.) or Leupold (new 2004) 3.5-10x50mm scope with flip covers and sling, 4 shot internal (FPXP, disc. 2006) or detachable (FPCPXP, new 2007) mag., Harris bipod, aluminum case, 10 1/2 lbs. New 2002.

MSR $2,539	$2,050	$1,675	$1,300	$1,025	$900	$825	$750

    Subtract 20% LE standard stock or 10% for Choate stock (Model 10FPXP-LEA package).

❊ *Model 10FCP H-S Precision* - .308 Win. cal., 24 in. barrel, features H-S Precision stock, detachable box mag. New 2007.

MSR $1,028	$885	$775	$700	$600	$500	$400	$325

❊ *Model 10FCP Choate* - .308 Win. cal., 24 in. barrel, features Choate stock, detachable box mag. Mfg. 2007 only.

	$700	$575	$475	$425	$350	$300	$275

Last MSR was $833.

❊ *Model 10FCP McMillan* - .308 Win. cal., 24 in. barrel, features McMillan stock, detachable box mag. New 2007.

MSR $1,242	$995	$850	$700	$600	$500	$400	$350

MODEL 10GY - .223 Rem., .243 Win., or .308 Win. cal., ladies/youth model with shorter checkered hardwood stock and 22 in. barrel with open sights. Disc. 2007.

	$455	$360	$295	$240	$200	$175	$160

Last MSR was $541.

    This model is still available as a 10GYXP3 package which includes scope, bipod, and case. MSR is $633.

MODEL 11B HUNTER - .204 Ruger, .22-250 Rem., .223 Rem., .243 Win., or .308 Win. cal., short action, 22 in. barrel with no sights, hinged floorplate. New 2008.

MSR $735	$625	$525	$460	$400	$350	$300	$250

GRADING - PPGS™	100%	98%	95%	90%	80%	70%	60%

MODEL 11F HUNTER - .22-250 Rem., .223 Rem., .243 Win., .260 Rem. (mfg. 1999-2000), .270 WSM (new 2003), .308 Win., .300 RSUM (mfg. 2003), .300 WSM (new 2002), 7mm RSUM (mfg. 2003), 7mm WSM (mfg. 2003-2005, reintroduced in 2007 in left-hand only), or 7mm-08 Rem. (new 1999) cal., short action, dual pillar bedding, checkered black synthetic stock, 22 or 24 (WSM cals. only) in. blue barrel with open sights, 6 3/4 lbs. New 1998.

MSR $564	$470	$370	$310	$250	$200	$175	$160

> Subtract $9 if w/o sights (Model 11FNS, disc. 2004).
> Add $23 for WSM cals. (left-hand only).

This model is also available in left-hand action (Model 11FL).

MODEL 11FCNS/FHNS (11FC) - .204 Ruger (new 2008), .22-250 Rem., .223 Rem. (new 2008), .243 Win., .260 Rem. (disc. 2000), .270 WSM (new 2005), .308 Win., .300 WSM (new 2005), 7mm WSM (new 2005, FHNS only beginning 2008), or 7mm-08 Rem. cal., 22 in. blue barrel and action, fixed (disc. 2004), detachable box mag. (new 2005, Model FCNS), or hinged floorplate (new 2006, Model FHNS), dual pillar bedded black synthetic stock, 6 3/8 lbs. Mfg. 1999-2001, reintroduced 2003.

MSR $591	$485	$385	$310	$250	$200	$175	$160

> Add $23 for WSM cals.

This model is also available in left-hand action (Model 11FLC, disc. 2001, other cals. still available).

MODEL 11FYXP3 - .223 Rem. (new 2003), .243 Win., 7mm-08 Rem. (new 2003) cal., similar to 11F Hunter, except is Youth Model with 12 1/2 LOP, includes 3-9x40mm scope, 6 1/2 lbs. New 2002.

MSR $593	$485	$375	$310	$240	$210	$185	$170

MODEL 11FYCXP3 YOUTH PACKAGE - .243 Win. cal., short action, detachable 4 shot box mag., Youth model w/shorter dimensions, AccuTrigger not available, includes scope, 6 1/2 lbs. New 2006.

MSR $499	$380	$325	$275	$250	$225	$200	$175

MODEL 11FYCAK - .243 Win., 7mm-08 Rem., or .308 Win. cal., 22 in. barrel, detachable box mag., Youth Model with shortened LOP. New 2006.

MSR $652	$525	$400	$340	$300	$270	$235	$200

MODEL 11FXP3 - see listing later in this category, combined with Model 111FXP3 package.

MODEL 11G/11GCNS HUNTER - similar to 11F Hunter, except has wood stock with pressed fleur-de-lis checkering, detachable box mag became standard in 2005 (Model 11GCNS). New 1998.

MSR $582	$480	$375	$300	$230	$200	$180	$165

> Add $31 for Model 11GCNS (new 2005, not available in .223 Rem.).
> Add $25 for .270 WSM or .300 WSM cals. (11GCNS Model only).
> Subtract $10 if w/o sights (Model 11GNS, disc. 2004).

This model is also available in left-hand action (Model 11GL).

MODEL 11GC - .22-250 Rem., .243 Win., .260 Rem. (disc. 2000), .308 Win. or 7mm-08 Rem. cal., detachable mag., hardwood stock, open sights, 22 in. barrel, blue finish, 6 3/8 lbs. Mfg. 1999-2001.

	$375	$310	$270	$230	$200	$175	$160

Last MSR was $441.

This model is also available in left-hand action (Model 11GLC).

MODEL 12 - .204 Ruger, .22-250 Rem., .223 Rem., or 6mm Norma BR cal., 26 in. barrel, short action, detachable box mag. New 2008.

MSR $1,208	$985	$850	$750	$650	$575	$500	$425

GRADING - PPGS™	100%	98%	95%	90%	80%	70%	60%

MODEL 12 VARMINTER LOW PROFILE - .204 Ruger (new 2005), .22-250 Rem., .223 Rem., .243 Win. (new 2007), .300 WSM (new 2007), or .308 Win. (new 2007) cal., choice of repeater or single shot (.204 Ruger, .22-250 Rem., or .223 Rem. cals. only), right-hand bolt, smaller ejection port on left side of receiver, 2 or 4 shot detachable box mag., 26 in. fluted stainless heavy barrel and action, AccuTrigger standard, low profile brown laminated stock with extra wide beavertail forend, short action, 10 lbs. New 2004.

MSR $934	$775	$625	$475	$400	$350	$300	$280

  Add $38 for .300 WSM cal.
  Subtract $41 for single shot.

During 2005, this model became available in left-hand action at no extra charge in select cals.

MODEL 12 LONG RANGE PRECISION VARMINTER - .204 Ruger, .22-250 Rem., .223 Rem., or 6mm Norma BR (new 2008) cal., single shot, right-hand bolt, left port ejection, stainless short action, 26 in. X-Tra heavy fluted free floating barrel, black synthetic H-S Precision varmint stock with molded alloy bedding system, drilled and tapped, target Accu-Trigger, oversized bolt handle, swivel studs, 12 lbs. New 2005.

MSR $1,167	$950	$825	$715	$600	$500	$400	$350

During 2005-2006, this model was available in left-hand action at no extra charge.

MODEL 12 VARMINTER THUMBHOLE (12BTCSS) - .204 Ruger, .22-250 Rem., or .223 Rem. cal., 26 in. heavy barrel, short action, detachable box mag. New 2008.

MSR $981	$850	$775	$675	$600	$525	$450	$375

MODEL 12BVSS - .22-250 Rem., .223 Rem., .243 Win. (mfg. 2002-2006), .300 WSM (mfg. 2003-2006), or .308 Win. (disc. 1999, reintroduced 2001-2006) cal., short action, right bolt, left port ejection, 26 in. heavy fluted stainless barrel w/o sights, dual pillar bedding, brown laminated wood stock with flat beavertail forend, Accu-Trigger became standard 2003, 9 lbs. New 1998.

MSR $847	$695	$550	$450	$375	$325	$285	$250

This model was also available in left-hand action in cals. .22-250 Rem. and .223 Rem. at no extra charge (mfg. 2004, Model 12BLVSS).

✳ *Model 12BVSS-S* - .220 Swift (new 2004), .22-250 Rem., .223 Rem., or .308 Win. cal., similar to Model 12BVSS, except is single shot, AccuTrigger became standard 2003. Mfg. 1998-2001, mfg. 2002-2005.

	$600	$490	$395	$335	$290	$245	$215

Last MSR was $721.

✳ *Model 12BVSS-SXP* - similar to Model 12BVSS, except not available in .243 Win. cal., target style heavy prone laminate stock with Wundhammer palm swell and black forend cap, 26 in. fluted stainless barrel w/o sights, includes 6-18x37mm scope and black aluminum hard case, 12 lbs. Mfg. 2002-2004.

	$1,050	$895	$775	$665	$560	$465	$410

Last MSR was $1,225.

MODEL 12FV/FVY - .204 Ruger (new 2005), .22-250 Rem., .223 Rem., .243 Win. (new 2002), or .308 Win. (new 1999) cal., short action, right bolt, left ejection port, features 26 in. regular barrel with low luster bluing, black synthetic stock with dual pillar bedding, 5 shot top loading mag., drilled and tapped, AccuTrigger became standard 2003, 9 lbs. New 1998.

MSR $620	$495	$395	$325	$275	$235	$200	$175

This model was also available as a Youth Model (Model 12FVY, available in .22-250 Rem. and .223 Rem. cal. only, mfg. 2003-2004). This model is also available in left-hand action (Model 12FLV, disc. 2001, reintroduced during 2004, not available in .243 Win. or .308 Win. cal.).

GRADING - PPGS™	100%	98%	95%	90%	80%	70%	60%

MODEL 12FVSS - .22-250 Rem., .223 Rem., .270 WSM (new 2003), .300 WSM (new 2003), or .308 Win. cal., short action, right-hand bolt, left ejection port, features 26 in. fluted heavy stainless free floating barrel w/o sights, black checkered synthetic stock with dual pillar bedding, drilled and tapped, AccuTrigger became standard 2003, 9 lbs. New 1998.

MSR $776	$645	$495	$395	$335	$300	$275	$240

Add $31 for WSM cals.

This model was also available in left-hand action (Model 12FLVSS, not available in WSM cals., disc. 2004).

✳ *Model 12FVSS-S* - similar to Model 12FVSS, except is single shot and not available in .308 Win. cal. Mfg. 1998-2001.

	$480	$405	$335	$275	$235	$200	$175

Last MSR was $549.

✳ *Model 12VSS/12VSS-S* - .22-250 Rem., .223 Rem., or .308 Win. cal., available in long (12VSS) or short (12VSS-S, mfg. 2003-2004, not available in .308 Win. cal.) action, semi-skeletonized Choate adj. black synthetic stock with cheekpiece, 24 (disc. 2004) or 26 in. fluted stainless barrel, blue stainless steel receiver, 4 shot mag., drilled and tapped receiver, AccuTrigger became standard 2003, 11 1/4 lbs. Mfg. 2000-2006.

	$700	$595	$495	$425	$375	$315	$270

Last MSR was $865.

MODEL 12 F/TR - .308 Win. cal., short action, single shot, 30 in. stainless steel barrel, target features, target Accu-Trigger, oversize bolt handle, no sights, 12 1/2 lbs. New 2007.

MSR $1,193	$975	$840	$715	$625	$550	$475	$400

MODEL 12 F CLASS - 6.5x284mm Norma or 6mm Norma BR (new 2008) cal., short action, single shot, 30 in. stainless steel barrel, target features, ergonomic grey laminate stock, oversize bolt handle, no sights, 13 lbs. New 2007.

MSR $1,265	$1,025	$875	$750	$650	$575	$500	$425

MODEL 14 CLASSIC/AMERICAN CLASSIC - .204 Ruger (new 2008), .22-250 Rem., .223 Rem. (new 2008), .243 Win., .270 WSM, .300 WSM, .325 WSM (new 2007), .308 Win., or 7mm-08 Rem. cal., 22 or 24 in. barrel, detachable box mag. (American Classic, right or left (new 2008) hand action) or hinged floorplate (Classic, new 2006), no sights, checkered walnut stock and black forend tip, high polish blue, AccuTrigger standard, 7 or 7 1/2 lbs. New 2005.

MSR $735	$600	$475	$385	$325	$275	$250	$225

Add $32 for Classic Model with hinged floorplate.
Add $27 for WSM cals.

MODEL 14 EURO CLASSIC - .22-250 Rem., .243 Win., or .308 Win. cal., 22 in. barrel, detachable box mag., AccuTrigger standard, open sights with adj. rear sight on barrel, checkered walnut stock with cheekpiece, 7 1/2 lbs. New 2006.

MSR $809	$675	$525	$450	$375	$325	$275	$250

MODEL 16BSS WEATHER WARRIOR - .270 WSM (new 2003), .300 WSM, .300 RSUM (disc. 2002), 7mm WSM (new 2003), or 7mm RSUM (disc. 2002) cal., 24 in. barrel w/o sights, 2 or 3 shot mag., brown laminated stock with cut checkering, stainless action and barrel, 7 3/4 lbs. Mfg. 2002-2003.

	$560	$460	$355	$290	$250	$215	$185

Last MSR was $668.

MODEL 16FCSS WEATHER WARRIOR - .243 Win., .260 Rem. (disc. 2000), .308 Win., or 7mm-08 Rem. cal., stainless steel barreled action with 22 in. barrel, detachable mag., dual pillar bedded black synthetic stock, 6 3/4 lbs. Mfg. 1999-2001.

	$460	$395	$325	$265	$230	$195	$170

Last MSR was $532.

This model was also available in left-hand action at no additional charge (Model 16FLCSS).

MODEL 16FCSAK WEATHER WARRIOR - .243 Win., .270 WSM, .300 WSM, .308 Win., 7mm-08 Rem., or 7mm WSM cal., short action, 22 or 24 in. fluted barrel with adj. muzzle brake, detachable box mag., no sights. Mfg. 2005 only.

$560	$495	$415	$350	$315	$275	$245

Last MSR was $661.

MODEL 16FSS - .204 Ruger (new 2005), .22-250 (new 2003), .223 Rem., .243 Win., .260 Rem. (mfg. 1999-2000), .270 WSM, .308 Win., .300 WSM (new 2002), .300 RSUM (mfg. 2002-2003), 7mm WSM (mfg. 2003-2007), 7mm RSUM (mfg. 2002-2003), or 7mm-08 Rem. (new 1999) cal., short action, stainless steel 22 or 24 (WSM and RSUM cals only) in. barreled action w/o sights, checkered black synthetic stock with dual pillar bedding, 6 3/4 lbs. New 1998.

MSR $640	$515	$440	$385	$315	$275	$230	$200

Add $25 for WSM cals.

Also available in left-hand action at no additional charge (Model 16FLSS).

* *Model 16FCSS* - similar to Model 16FSS, except features detachable box mag., not available in .204 Ruger or .223 Rem. cal. until 2008, also available in 7mm WSM. New 2005.

MSR $676	$545	$450	$365	$310	$265	$235	$200

Add $28 for WSM cals.

* *Model 16FHSS* - similar to Model 16FCSS, except has hinged floorplate. New 2006.

MSR $676	$545	$450	$365	$310	$265	$235	$200

Add $25 for WSM cals.

This model is also available in left-hand action at no additional charge (Model 16FLHSS, new 2007).

* *Model 16FHSAK* - .243 Win., .270 WSM, .300 WSM, or .308 Win. cal., 22 or 24 in. barrel, similar to Model 16FHSS, except has adj. muzzle brake. New 2006.

MSR $739	$600	$465	$385	$320	$275	$250	$225

Add $28 for WSM cals.

MODEL 16FXP3 PACKAGE - .204 Ruger (new 2005), .22-250 Rem. (new 2003), .223 Rem., .243 Win., .270 WSM (new 2003), .300 RSUM (mfg. 2003), .308 Win., .300 WSM, .325 WSM (new 2007), 7mm WSM (new 2003), or 7mm RSUM (mfg. 2003) cal., short action, stainless action and 22 or 24 in. stainless barrel w/o sights, checkered black synthetic stock, includes nickel finished 3-9x40mm scope and mounts, supplied with sling, approx. 6 1/2 lbs. New 2002.

MSR $695	$575	$450	$375	$335	$300	$270	$225

Add $26 for WSM cals.

MODEL 25 LIGHTWEIGHT VARMINTER - .204 Ruger or .223 Rem. cal., 22 (Classic) or 24 in. barrel, short action, detachable box mag., with (Varminter-T) or w/o (Varminter) target features. New 2008.

MSR $588	$485	$400	$325	$275	$235	$210	$185

Add $28 for 22 in. barrel (Model 25 Classic).
Add $47 for Model 25 Lightweight Varminter-T.

MODEL 40 SINGLE SHOT - .22 Hornet or .223 Rem. (disc. 2004) cal., single shot action, varmint configuration featuring 24 in. heavy contour barrel and brown laminate stock with full beavertail forend, AccuTrigger became standard 2003, 7 3/4 lbs.

MSR $519	$410	$330	$270	$230	$210	$185	$160

MODEL 99C LEVER ACTION - .243 Win. or .308 Win. cal., detachable box mag., checkered Monte Carlo stock and forearm, high gloss bluing, 22 in. barrel with adj. rear sight, drilled and tapped, 7 3/4 lbs. Reintroduced 1996-97 only.

$585	$500	$450	$400	$360	$330	$300

Last MSR was $665.

MODEL 99-CE (CENTENNIAL EDITION) - .300 Sav. cal. only, limited edition featuring fully engraved nickel receiver and lever, 24Kt. gold-plated receiver figures, trigger, and safety, deluxe hand checkered walnut stock and forearm, 1,000 mfg. 1996-97 only, serial numbered AS0001-AS1000.

	$1,500	$1,100	$750	N/A	N/A	N/A	N/A

Last MSR was $1,660.

MODEL 110 SPORTER BOLT ACTION - .243 Win., .270 Win., .308 Win., or .30 - 06 cal., 22 in. barrel, open sight, 4 shot, checkered pistol grip stock. Mfg. 1958-63.

	$375	$325	$275	$250	$225	$200	$185

MODEL 110-MC - similar to Model 110, with Monte Carlo stock. Mfg. 1959-69.

	$385	$325	$275	$250	$225	$200	$185

MODEL 110-M - similar to Model 110MC, except 7mm Rem. Mag., .264 Win. Mag., .300 Win. Mag., or .338 Win. Mag. cal., recoil pad. Mfg. 1963-69.

	$395	$335	$285	$250	$225	$200	$185

MODEL 110-C/CL - various cals., push-button detachable mag., walnut stock. Mfg. 1966-85.

	$425	$365	$325	$295	$275	$250	$225

MODEL 110-D - .22-250 Rem. (disc.), .223 Rem., .243 Win., .25-06 Rem. (disc.), .270 Win., .308 Win. (disc.), .30-06, 7mm Rem. Mag., .300 Win. Mag. (disc.), or .338 Win. Mag. cal., similar to Model 110B, hinged floorplate (1972-75 only), checkered walnut stock, removable and adj. rear sight, 7 1/2 lbs. Mfg. 1966-88.

	$350	$300	$275	$250	$225	$190	$170

Last MSR was $409.

Add $80 for left-hand version.

MODEL 110-E - .22-250 Rem., .223 Rem., .243 Win., .270 Win., 7mm Rem. Mag., .308 Win., or .30-06 cal., 22 or 24 (Mag. only) in. barrel, open sights, unchecked hardwood Monte Carlo stock, blind internal magazine with floorplate, 7 lbs. Mfg. 1963-88.

	$350	$300	$275	$250	$225	$190	$170

Last MSR was $325.

Subtract $16 without sights.

MODEL 110-F - .22-250 Rem., .223 Rem., .243 Win., .250 Sav. (new 1993), .25-06 Rem. (new 1993), .308 Win., .30-06, .270 Win., 7mm-08 Rem. (new 1993), 7mm Rem. Mag., .300 Sav. (new 1993), .300 Win. Mag., or .338 Win. Mag. (new 1991) cal., 22 or 24 (Magnum) in. barrel, black DuPont Rynite stock with swivel studs and recoil pad, adj. rear sight, drilled and tapped for scope mounts, 4 or 5 shot mag., 6 3/4 lbs. Mfg. 1989-1993.

	$335	$300	$265	$235	$210	$195	$180

✻ *Model 110-FNS* - similar to Model 110-F, except has no sights. Mfg. 1991-93.

	$325	$285	$250	$225	$200	$190	$175

✻ *Model 110-FXP3* - .22-250 Rem. (new 1992), .223 Rem. (new 1992), .243 Win., .270 Win., .30-06, .308 Win. (new 1992), 7mm Rem. Mag., or .300 Win. Mag. cal., similar to Model 110-F except is without sights and has integral Weaver type scope bases. Mfg. 1989-93.

	$415	$370	$325	$285	$250	$225	$195

MODEL 110-GY - .223 Rem. (Mfg. 1993-99), .243 Win. (disc. 1999), .270 Win. (new 1994), .300 Sav. (disc. 1995), or .308 Win. (mfg. 1994-99) cal., 22 in. barrel, youth/ladies variation with shortened classic stock, open sights, 6 1/2 lbs. Mfg. 1991-2000.

	$350	$300	$260	$220	$195	$175	$160

Last MSR was $395.

GRADING - PPGS™	100%	98%	95%	90%	80%	70%	60%

MODEL 110-WLE - .250-3000 Sav., .300 Sav., or 7x57mm Mauser cal. Mfg. 1991-93.

	$425	$390	$360	$320	$280	$250	$225

Approx. 1,000 of each cal. were mfg. in this model.

* *Model 110-WLE 1 of 1,000* - 7x57mm Mauser, features select walnut stock with Monte Carlo cheekpiece, high luster blue finish with laser etched Savage logo on bolt body, drilled and tapped, 1,000 mfg. beginning 1992, 7 3/4 lbs. Mfg. 1992-93 only.

	$415	$370	$325	$285	$250	$225	$195

MODEL 110-FM SIERRA ULTRA LIGHT - .243 Win. (disc. 1998), .270 Win., .30 - 06, or .308 Win. (disc. 1998) cal., features 20 in. high gloss barrel w/o sights, black graphite/fiberglass-filled stock with non-glare finish, drilled and tapped, 6 1/4 lbs. Mfg. 1996-2000.

	$380	$325	$270	$230	$205	$175	$160

Last MSR was $449.

MODEL 110-FP LAW ENFORCEMENT (TACTICAL POLICE) - .223 Rem. (disc. 1998), .25-06 Rem. (new 1995), .300 Win. Mag. (new 1995), .30-06 (mfg. 1996-2006), .308 Win. (disc. 1998), or 7mm Rem. Mag. (mfg. 1995-2007) cal., long action, 24 in. heavy barrel pillar bedded tactical rifle, all metal parts are non-reflective, 4 shot internal mag., black Dupont Rynite stock, right- or left-hand (new 1996) action, tapped for scope mounts, AccuTrigger became standard 2003, 8 1/2 lbs. Mfg. 1990-2001, reintroduced 2003.

MSR $678	$575	$465	$360	$310	$265	$240	$210

Also available in left-hand action at no additional charge (mfg. 1996-2001, Model 110-FLP).

MODEL 110-G - .22-250 Rem., .223 Rem., .243 Win., .250 Sav. (new 1992), .25-06 Rem. (new 1992), .300 Sav. (new 1993), .308 Win., .30-06, .270 Win., 7mm-08 Rem. (new 1992), 7mm Rem. Mag., or .300 Win. Mag. cal., top loading internal box mag., 22 or 24 in. barrel, adj. iron sights, checkered hardwood stock, approx. 7 lbs. Mfg. 1989-93.

	$325	$285	$250	$225	$200	$190	$175

Subtract $10-$20 if without sights (Model 110-GNS).

* *Model 110-GC* - .270 Win., .30-06, 7mm Rem. Mag., or .300 Win. Mag. cal., features detachable 3 or 4 shot mag., 22 or 24 in. barrel, checkered hardwood stock, adj. sights, 6 3/4 lbs. Mfg. 1992-93.

	$410	$325	$275	$240	$210	$180	$165

Add $20 for Mag. cals.

* *Model 10GXP3/110-GXP3 Package* - .22-250 Rem., .223 Rem., .243 Win., .250 Savage (disc. 1995), .25-06 Rem., .270 Win., .270 WSM (new 2003), .300 Sav. (disc. 1995), .30-06, .300 RSUM (mfg. 2002-2003), .308 Win., 7mm-08 Rem. (disc. 1995, reintroduced 1999), 7mm WSM (mfg. 2003-2007), 7mm Rem. Mag., 7mm RSUM (mfg. 2003), .300 WSM (new 2005), .300 Rem. Ultra Mag. (mfg. 2002-2006), or .300 Win. Mag. cal., short (10GXP3) or long (110-GXP3) action, similar to Model 110-G, except has no sights, includes 3-9x32 scope, rings, bases, QD swivels, and deluxe rifle sling, includes integral Weaver type scope bases. New 1989.

MSR $633	$515	$410	$340	$280	$240	$220	$190

Add $25 for WSM cals. (Model 10GXP3 only).

Also available in left-hand action at no additional charge (Model 10GLXP3/110-GLXP3).

* *Model 110-GCXP3 Package* - .270 Win., .30-06, .300 Win. Mag., or 7mm Rem. Mag. cal., 22 or 24 in. barrel, checkered hardwood stock, detachable box mag., package includes 3-9x32 scope, rings, bases, QD swivels, and deluxe rifle sling, 7 1/4 lbs. Disc. 2001.

	$445	$375	$315	$275	$235	$190	$175

Last MSR was $524.

Was also available in left-hand action at no additional charge (Model 110-GLCXP3 - disc. 2000).

GRADING - PPGS™	100%	98%	95%	90%	80%	70%	60%

✴ *Model 110-GL* - .30-06, .270 Win., or 7mm Rem. Mag. cal., left-hand variation of the Model 110 - G. Mfg. 1989-93.

	$325	$265	$225	$200	$180	$165	$150

✴ *Model 110-GLNS* - similar to Model 110-GL, except has no sights. Mfg. 1991-1993.

	$320	$260	$220	$200	$180	$165	$150

MODEL 110-K - .243 Win., .270 Win., or .30-06 cal., laminated camouflage stock. Mfg. 1986-88.

	$335	$280	$240	$185	$155	$135	$115

Last MSR was $399.

MODEL 110-S - .308 Win. or 7mm-08 Rem. (disc.) cals., silhouette model, 22 in. heavy barrel, Wundhammer swell pistol grip with stippling, no sights, 4 shot mag., 8 lbs. 10 oz. Disc. 1985.

	$340	$290	$255	$225	$205	$190	$175

Last MSR was $385.

MODEL 110-V - .22-250 Rem. or .223 Rem. cal. only, varmint model, 26 in. heavy barrel, no sights, 5 shot mag., stippled walnut Wundhammer pistol grip stock, 9 1/4 lbs. Disc. 1989.

	$370	$315	$265	$230	$205	$190	$175

Last MSR was $439.

MODEL 110-GV - .22-250 Rem. or .223 Rem. cal., varmint variation, 24 in. medium barrel, no sights, checkered hardwood stock with rubber butt pad, drilled and tapped for scope, 8 1/4 lbs. Mfg. 1989-93.

	$380	$285	$250	$225	$200	$190	$175

MODEL 110-B - similar to Model 110E, except available in .243 Win., .270 Win. or .30-06 cal., select stock and pistol grip cap, features blind mag., walnut Monte Carlo stock. Reintroduced 1989 with laminate stock (Model 110-B Laminate). Mfg. 1978-79.

	$360	$300	$265	$235	$205	$190	$175

This model was also available in left-hand action (Model 110-BL).

MODEL 110-B LAMINATE - similar to Model 110-B, except is available in .300 Win. Mag. or .338 Win. Mag. cal. also, has brown laminate hardwood stock with iron sights, approx. 7 1/2 lbs. Mfg. 1989-91.

	$385	$310	$250	$225	$200	$190	$180

Last MSR was $477.

MODEL 110-P PREMIER GRADE - similar to Model 110B, with select French walnut stock, skip checkered, rosewood forend and pistol grip cap, sling swivels, 7mm Mag. has recoil pad. Mfg. 1964-70.

	$440	$330	$310	$275	$250	$220	$195
7mm Mag.	$460	$350	$330	$305	$275	$240	$220

MODEL 110-PE PRESENTATION GRADE - similar to Model 110P, with engraved receiver, floorplate and triggerguard. Mfg. 1968-70.

	$660	$550	$525	$470	$440	$415	$385
7mm Mag.	$690	$580	$550	$495	$470	$440	$415

MODEL 111B HUNTER - .25-06 Rem., .270 Win. or .30-06 cal., long action, 22 in. barrel with no sights, hinged floorplate. New 2008.

MSR $735	$625	$525	$460	$400	$350	$300	$250

MODEL 111 CHIEFTAIN ACTION - .243 Win., .270 Win., 7x57mm, 7mm Mag., or .30-06 cal., 22 in. barrel, 24 in. barrel (Mag. cals.), leaf sight, 4 shot detachable mag., checkered walnut Monte Carlo stock, pistol grip cap, sling swivels. Mfg. 1974-78.

	$375	$350	$300	$250	$225	$200	$175
Mag. cals.	$395	$375	$325	$295	$275	$225	$195

GRADING - PPGS™	100%	98%	95%	90%	80%	70%	60%

MODEL 111-F - similar to Model 111-G, except has black graphite/fiberglass stock (with non-glare finish) and was also available in .338 Win. Mag. (disc. 2005) cal., long action, 22, 24, or 26 (disc. 2003) in. barrel, solid recoil pad, 6 1/2 lbs. New 1994.

MSR $564	$475	$385	$320	$250	$215	$185	$170

Subtract $8 if w/o sights (Model 111-FNS, not available in .300 Rem. Ultra Mag. or 7mm Rem. Ultra Mag. cals., disc. 2002).

This model is also available in left-hand (Model 111-FL).

✱ *Model 111-FC* - .270 Win., .30-06, .300 Win. Mag., or 7mm Rem. Mag. cal., 22 or 24 in. barrel, detachable box mag., black graphite/fiberglass stock, 6 1/2 lbs. Mfg. 1994-2003.

	$400	$340	$285	$230	$195	$175	$160

Last MSR was $468.

This model was also available with left-hand action (Model 111-FLC).

✱ *Model 111-FCNS* - .25-06 Rem., .270 Win., .30-06, .300 Win. Mag., .338 Win. Mag., or 7mm Rem. Mag. cal., features detachable box mag., 22 or 24 in. barrel, no sights, approx. 6 1/2 lbs. New 2005.

MSR $591	$485	$385	$310	$250	$210	$180	$160

✱ *Model 111-FHNS* - similar to Model 111-FCNS, except has hinged floorplate. New 2006.

MSR $591	$485	$385	$310	$250	$210	$180	$160

MODEL 111FYCAK - .270 Win.or .30-06 cal., 22 in. barrel, detachable box mag., long action, Youth Model with shortened LOP. New 2006.

MSR $652	$525	$400	$340	$300	$270	$235	$200

MODEL 111-FAK EXPRESS - .270 Win., .30-06, .300 Win. Mag., .338 Win. Mag., or 7mm Rem. Mag. cal., 22 in. barrel with adj. muzzle brake, black or black matte graphite/fiberglass-filled stock, w/o sights, 6 3/4 lbs. Mfg. 1996-98.

	$390	$340	$285	$240	$200	$180	$165

Last MSR was $450.

MODEL 11/111-FCXP3 PACKAGE - .243 Win. (Model 11FCXP3), .270 Win., .30-06, .300 Win. Mag. (disc. 2001, reintroduced 2005), or 7mm Rem. Mag. (disc. 2001, reintroduced 2005) cal., 4 shot detachable box mag., checkered black synthetic stock, 22 or 24 in. barrel, package includes bore sighted 3-9x32mm scope, rings, bases, QD swivels, and deluxe rifle sling, not available w/Accu-Trigger, 6 1/2 lbs. New 1994.

MSR $499	$380	$325	$275	$250	$225	$200	$175

This model was also available with left-hand action (Model 111-FLCXP3 - disc. 2000).

MODELS 11FXP3 & 111-FXP3 PACKAGES - .204 Ruger (new 2005), .22-250 Rem., .223 Rem., .243 Win., .250 Savage (disc. 1996), .25-06 Rem., .270 WSM (new 2003), .270 Win., .300 Sav. (disc. 1996), .30-06, .308 Win., .300 Rem. Ultra Mag. (mfg. 2003-2004), .300 Win. Mag., .300 WSM (new 2002), .338 Win. Mag., 7mm WSM (mfg. 2003-2007), 7mm RSUM (mfg. 2003), 7mm Rem. Mag., 7mm Rem. Ultra Mag. (mfg. 2002-2003), or 7mm-08 Rem. (disc. 1996, reintroduced 1999-2001) cal., short (11FXP3) or long (111-FXP3) action, 22 or 24 in. barrel, black graphite/fiberglass composite stock, non-glare finish, package consists of bore sighted 3-9x32 scope, rings, bases, QD swivels, and deluxe rifle sling, approx. 7 1/4 lbs. New 1994.

MSR $601	$500	$400	$325	$275	$225	$200	$185

Add $25 for WSM cals. (Model 11FXP3 only).

This model was also available with left-hand action (Model 11FLXP3/111-FLXP3, disc. 2002).

GRADING - PPGS™	100%	98%	95%	90%	80%	70%	60%

MODEL 111-G - .22-250 Rem. (disc. 1998), .223 Rem. (disc. 1998), .243 Win. (disc. 1998), .250 Savage (disc. 1996), .25-06 Rem., .270 Win., .300 Sav. (disc. 1996), .30-06, .308 Win. (disc. 1998), .300 Win. Mag. (disc. 2007), .300 Rem. Ultra Mag. (mfg. 2002-2003), .338 Win. Mag. (disc. 1993 - not available with wood stock), 7mm-08 Rem. (disc. 1996), 7mm Rem. Ultra Mag. (mfg. 2002-2003), or 7mm Rem. Mag. (disc. 2007) cal., long action, walnut finished hardwood stock with cut checkering and vent. recoil pad, open sights, top tang safety with red dot indicator, 22, 24, or 26 (disc. 2005) in. barrel, drilled and tapped, 6 3/8 or 7 lbs. New 1994.

MSR $582	$490	$385	$310	$270	$230	$210	$180

Subtract $10 w/o sights (Model 111-GNS, not available in .300 Rem. Ultra Mag. or 7mm Rem. Ultra Mag. cals., disc. 2004).

This model is also available in left-hand (Model 111-GL, not available in 7mm Rem. Ultra Mag.).

✱ *Model 111-GC* - .270 Win., .30-06, .300 Win. Mag., or 7mm Rem. Mag. cal., 22 or 24 in. barrel, detachable box mag., walnut finished hardwood stock with cut checkering and vent. recoil pad. Mfg. 1994-2001.

$385	$325	$275	$240	$210	$175	$160

Last MSR was $441.

This model was also available with left-hand action (Model 111-GLC - disc. 2000).

✱ *Model 111-GCNS* - .25-06 Rem., .270 Win., .30-06, .300 Win. Mag., or 7mm Rem. Mag. cal., features detachable box mag., no sights, 22 or 24 in. barrel, approx. 7 lbs. New 2005.

MSR $613	$500	$400	$325	$275	$235	$210	$185

MODEL 112V VARMINT RIFLE - .220 Swift, .222 Rem., .223 Rem. (new 1976), .22-250 Rem., .243 Win., or .25-06 Rem. cal., single shot, bolt action, 26 in. heavy barrel, no sights, heavy select walnut stock, checkered, swivels. Mfg. 1975-78.

$350	$325	$300	$275	$250	$235	$225

MODEL 112 VARMINTER LOW PROFILE - .25-06 Rem. or .300 Win. Mag. cal., stainless long action, right-hand bolt, smaller ejection port on left side of receiver, 26 in. heavy fluted free floating barrel, low profile laminated stock with extra-wide beavertail forend, drilled and tapped, AccuTrigger, oversized bolt handle, 4 shot internal box mag., swivel studs, 10 lbs. Mfg. 2006 only.

$665	$545	$435	$370	$325	$260	$225

Last MSR was $806.

MODEL 112 R - .22-250 Rem., .25-06 Rem., or .243 Win. cal., similar to Model 112V, except has 4 shot mag. Disc. 1980.

$340	$305	$275	$250	$230	$210	$175

MODEL 112-BV - .22-250 Rem. or .223 Rem. cal., alloy steel construction, 26 in. barrel with recessed muzzle, 4 shot mag., brown laminate stock with ambidextrous Wundhammer style pistol grip, 9 1/2 lbs. Mfg. 1993 only.

$475	$430	$365	$315	$285	$250	$215

MODEL 112-BVSS LONG RANGE - .22-250 Rem. (disc. 1998), .223 Rem. (disc. 1998), .25-06 Rem. (new 1996), .30-06 (new 1996), .308 Win. (mfg. 1996-98), .300 Win. Mag. (new 1996), or 7mm Rem. Mag. (new 1996) cal., 4 shot, pillar bedded laminate wood stock with Wundhammer palm swell, right-hand bolt, smaller ejection port on left side of receiver, 26 in. stainless steel fluted barrel, bolt handle and trigger guard, recessed muzzle, AccuTrigger became standard 2003, 10 1/2 lbs. Mfg. 1994-2005.

$595	$470	$390	$325	$280	$235	$200

Last MSR was $721.

GRADING - PPGS™	100%	98%	95%	90%	80%	70%	60%

* *Model 112-BVSS-S Long Range* - .220 Swift, .223 Rem. (disc. 1998), .22-250 Rem. (disc. 1998), or .300 Win. Mag. (new 1996) cal., single shot, 26 in. stainless steel fluted barrel, with target features, 10 1/2 lbs. Mfg. 1994-2001.

| | $510 | $420 | $360 | $295 | $255 | $220 | $190 |

Last MSR was $595.

MODEL 112-BT COMPETITION GRADE - .223 Rem. or .308 Win. cal., laminated pillar bedded wood stock with adj. cheek rest and Wundhammer palm swell, vent. forend, 5 shot internal mag., alloy steel receiver with 26 in. matte black finished heavy stainless steel barrel w/o sights, drilled and tapped receiver, approx. 10 7/8 lbs. Mfg. 1994-2001.

| | $930 | $810 | $705 | $625 | $550 | $495 | $400 |

Last MSR was $1,049.

* *Model 112-BT-S Competition Grade* - .300 Win. Mag. cal., single shot, otherwise similar to Model 112 - BT Competition Grade. Mfg. 1995-2001.

| | $930 | $810 | $705 | $625 | $550 | $495 | $400 |

Last MSR was $1,049.

MODEL 112-FV - .22-250 Rem. or .223 Rem. cal., varmint variation with 26 in. heavy barrel, with or w/o iron sights, 4-shot mag., black Rynite synthetic stock with recoil pad, 8 7/8 lbs. Mfg. 1991-98.

| | $360 | $300 | $260 | $235 | $200 | $175 | $160 |

Last MSR was $410.

* *Model 112-FVS* - similar to Model 112-FV, except is single shot with solid bottom receiver and is available in .220 Swift (new 1993) cal. Mfg. 1992-93 only.

| | $375 | $340 | $295 | $265 | $235 | $210 | $195 |

* *Model 112-FVSS (Long Range)* - .22-250 Rem. (disc. 1998), .223 Rem. (disc. 1998), .25-06 Rem. (new 1995), .30-06 (new 1996), .308 Win. (mfg. 1996-98), .300 Win. Mag. (new 1995), or 7mm Rem. Mag. (new 1995) cal., alloy receiver with 26 in. fluted stainless steel barrel, 4 shot mag., black synthetic pillar bedded sporter stock w/o sights, 8 7/8 lbs. Mfg. 1993-2002.

| | $495 | $425 | $360 | $295 | $255 | $220 | $190 |

Last MSR was $569.

This model was also available with left-hand action (Model 112-FLVSS, mfg. 1996-2002, not available in .30-06 cal.).

* *Model 112-FVSS-S* - .220 Swift, .22-250 Rem. (disc. 1998), .223 Rem. (disc. 1998), or .300 Win. Mag. (new 1996) cal., single shot variation, pillar bedded stock, 8 7/8 lbs. Mfg. 1994-2001.

| | $480 | $415 | $355 | $300 | $270 | $230 | $200 |

Last MSR was $549.

MODEL 114 CLASSIC/AMERICAN CLASSIC - .270 Win., .30-06, .300 Win. Mag., or 7mm Rem. Mag. cal., features detachable box mag. (American Classic) or hinged floorplate (Classic, new 2006), long action, drilled and tapped, satin lacquer American walnut with ebony forend and wraparound checkering, right or left (new 2008) action, no sights, 7 or 7 1/2 lbs. New 2005.

| MSR $735 | $600 | $465 | $385 | $325 | $275 | $250 | $225 |

Add $32 for Classic Model with hinged floorplate.

MODEL 114 EURO CLASSIC - .270 Win. or .30-06 cal., 22 in. barrel, detachable box mag., AccuTrigger standard, checkered walnut stock with cheekpiece, high polished blued action/barrel, 7 3/4 lbs. New 2006.

| MSR $809 | $675 | $525 | $450 | $375 | $325 | $275 | $250 |

GRADING - PPGS™	100%	98%	95%	90%	80%	70%	60%

MODEL 114-C (CLASSIC) 114-CU (CLASSIC ULTRA) - .270 Win., .30-06, .300 Win. Mag., or 7mm Rem. Mag. cal., 22 or 24 in. barrel, features high gloss classic American black walnut stock with cut checkering, fitted grip cap, and recoil pad, removable 3 or 4 shot staggered box mag., available with deluxe adj. sights (Model 114-CU, disc. 1995) or w/o sights (Model 114-C, new 1996), approx. 7 1/8 lbs. Mfg. 1991-2000.

	$485	$410	$355	$300	$270	$230	$200

Last MSR was $556.

MODEL 114-U - similar to Model 114-C, except is also available in 7mm STW (disc. 2002) cal., 3 shot internal mag, no sights, approx. 7 lbs. Mfg. 1999-2004.

	$490	$415	$350	$285	$250	$230	$200

Last MSR was $569.

MODEL 114-CE (CLASSIC EUROPEAN) - same cals. as the Model 114-C, except also available in 7x64mm Brenneke cal., features oil finished stock with Schnabel forend and skip-line checkering, high luster bluing, 22 or 24 in. barrel with adj. rear sight, 7 1/8 lbs. Mfg. 1996-2001.

	$480	$400	$350	$285	$260	$235	$200

Last MSR was $554.

MODEL 116-BSS WEATHER WARRIOR - .270 Win., .30-06, .300 Win. Mag., .300 Rem. Ultra Mag., or 7mm Rem. Mag. cal., long action, brown wood laminate stock with cut checkering, stainless steel action and tapered barrel, 2-4 shot internal mag., 24 or 26 in. barrel, 7-7 3/4 lbs. Mfg. 2001-2002.

	$560	$480	$410	$345	$295	$250	$220

Last MSR was $644.

MODEL 116-FSS - .22-250 Rem. (mfg. 1992 only), .223 Rem. (mfg. 1992-98), .243 Win. (mfg. 1993-98), .270 Win., .30-06, .308 Win. (disc. 1998), 7mm Rem. Mag., 7mm STW (mfg. 2001-2002), 7mm Rem. Ultra Mag. (mfg. 2002-2003), .300 Win. Mag., .300 Rem. Ultra Mag. (mfg. 2001-2006), .338 Win. Mag., or .375 H&H (mfg. 2002, reintroduced 2007) cal., short (disc.) or long (new 2001) action, features black Dupont Rynite synthetic stock, stainless steel metal parts, drilled and tapped for scope mounting, 22, 24, or 26 (disc. 2005) in. barrel, 3 or 4 shot mag., 6 3/4 lbs. New 1991.

MSR $640		$525	$440	$365	$300	$250	$225	$200

Add $145 for .375 H&H cal. (iron sights only).

This model is also available with left-hand action (Model 116-FLSS, not available in .375 H&H).

✶ Model 116-FCSS - .270 Win., .30-06, 7mm Rem. Mag., .300 Win. Mag., .338 Win. Mag. (new 2005) cal., otherwise similar to Model 116-FSS, except has detachable 3 or 4 shot box mag. with recessed push-button release, 22 or 24 in. barrel, 6 1/2 lbs. Mfg. 1992-2001, reintroduced 2005.

MSR $676		$555	$475	$375	$320	$280	$240	$210

Subtract $21 for left-hand action (Model 116-FLCSS, disc. 2005).

✶ Model 116-FHSS/116FHSAK - .270 Win., .30-06, 7mm Rem. Mag., .300 Win. Mag., or .338 Win. Mag., 22 or 24 in. free floating barrel, drilled and tapped stainless action, hinged floorplate, AccuTrigger, muzzle brake (FHSAK), 3 or 4 shot mag., black synthetic stock, 6 1/2 - 7 1/2 lbs. New 2006.

MSR $676		$555	$475	$375	$320	$280	$240	$210

Add $63 for Model FHSAK with muzzle brake.

This model is also available in left-hand action (Model 116-FLHSS, new 2007).

✶ Model 116-FSK (Kodiak) - similar cals. as Model 116-FCSS, except also available in .338 Win Mag. cal., stainless steel construction, 22 in. barrel with recoil arrester, cocking indicator, 3 shot mag., black synthetic sporter stock, no sights, 6 1/2 lbs. Mfg. 1993-2000.

	$495	$430	$370	$325	$290	$260	$230

Last MSR was $569.

This model was also available with left-hand action (Model 116-FLSK).

GRADING - PPGS™	100%	98%	95%	90%	80%	70%	60%

MODEL 116-US (ULTRA STAINLESS) - .270 Win., .30-06, 7mm Rem. Mag., or .300 Win. Mag. cal., 24 in. barrel, checkered walnut stock and forearm with ebony tip, no sights, 7 1/8 lbs. Mfg. 1995-98.

	$625	$550	$500	$450	$400	$360	$330

Last MSR was $700.

MODEL 116-SE (SAFARI EXPRESS) - .300 Win. Mag. (disc. 2002), .300 Rem. Ultra Mag. (mfg. 2002), .338 Win. Mag. (disc. 2001), .375 H&H (mfg. 2000-2002), .425 Express (mfg. 1995 only), or .458 Win. Mag. cal., stainless steel receiver and 24 in. barrel with adj. muzzle brake, controlled round feeding, select grade checkered walnut stock with solid recoil pad and ebony forend, 3-leaf express sights, 8 1/2 lbs. Mfg. 1994-2004.

	$895	$775	$685	$625	$575	$535	$475

Last MSR was $1,045.

MODEL 116-FSAK - .270 Win., .30-06, .300 Win. Mag., .300 Rem. Ultra Mag. (new 2001), .338 Win. Mag., .375 H&H (mfg. 2002 only), 7mm STW (mfg. 2001-2002), 7mm Rem. Ultra Mag. (mfg. 2002 only), or 7mm Rem. Mag. cal., short (disc.) or long (new 2001) action, features 22 in. fluted stainless steel barrel with adj. muzzle brake, 6 1/2 lbs. Mfg. 1994-2004.

	$530	$465	$390	$340	$295	$265	$235

Last MSR was $619.

This model was also available with left-hand action (Model 116-FLSAK, not available in 7mm STW, 7mm Rem. Ultra Mag., or .375 H&H cals.).

MODEL 116-FCSAK - .270 Win., .30-06, .300 Win. Mag., .338 Win. Mag. (new 2005), or 7mm Rem. Mag. cal., features push-button activated detachable box mag., 22 or 24 (new 2005) in. fluted barrel with adj. muzzle brake, 6 1/2 lbs. Mfg. 1994-2000, reintroduced 2005.

	$560	$495	$415	$350	$315	$275	$245

Last MSR was $661.

This model was also available with left-hand action (Model 116-FLCSAK).

MODEL 116FXP3 PACKAGE - .270 Win., .30-06, .300 Rem. Ultra Mag. (disc. 2003), .300 Win. Mag., .338 Win. Mag., 7mm STW (disc. 2002), 7mm Rem. Mag., or 7mm Rem. Ultra Mag. (disc. 2003) cal., stainless long action 22, 24, or 26 in. stainless barrel w/o sights, checkered black synthetic stock, includes nickel finished 3-9x40 scope and mounts, supplied with sling, approx. 6 1/2 - 7 lbs. New 2002.

MSR $695	$575	$455	$375	$335	$300	$270	$225

MODEL 170 PUMP RIFLE - .30-30 Win. or .35 Rem. (rare) cal., 22 in. barrel, folding leaf sight, 3 shot tube mag., checkered pistol grip stock. Mfg. 1970-81.

	$225	$195	$165	$145	$110	$90	$65

Add 20% for .35 Rem. cal.

This model was mfg. by Emhart.

MODEL 170C - .30-30 Win. cal. only, similar to 170, 18 1/2 in. barrel. Mfg. 1974-81.

	$250	$225	$195	$175	$160	$140	$120

SHOTGUNS: DISC.

Most Savage shotguns (except the Model 312 Series) fall under the domain of Savage Industries, Inc. Savage made a wide variety of inexpensive, utilitarian shotguns that, to date, have attracted mostly shooting interest, but little collector interest. A listing of these models may be found in the back of this text under "Serialization."

The models listed are grouped by configuration, and are not in numerical sequence.

GRADING - PPGS™	100%	98%	95%	90%	80%	70%	60%

MODEL 420 O/U - 12, 16, or 20 ga., 26-30 in. barrel, various chokes, boxlock, double trigger, extractors, plain pistol grip stock. Mfg. 1937-43.

	$385	$305	$275	$250	$210	$195	$155
Single trigger	$440	$360	$330	$305	$265	$220	$195

MODEL 430 O/U - similar to Model 420, with checkered stock and solid rib, recoil pad.

	$440	$360	$305	$275	$240	$220	$195
Single trigger	$495	$415	$360	$320	$285	$265	$220

MODEL 220 SINGLE BARREL - 12, 16, 20, 28 ga., or .410 bore, 26-32 in. barrel, various chokes, hammerless, plain pistol grip stock. Mfg. 1938-65.

$125	$100	$85	$75	$65	$50	$40

MODEL 220P - similar to Model 220, with poly choke, not made in .410 bore.

$90	$65	$55	$45	$35	$30	$30

MODEL 220 AC - similar to Model 220, with Savage adj. choke.

$100	$85	$65	$55	$45	$35	$30

MODEL 220L - similar to Model 220, with sidelever. Mfg. 1965-72.

$90	$65	$55	$45	$35	$30	$30

MODEL 720 AUTOLOADER STANDARD - 12 or 16 ga., Browning A-5 style semi-auto action, 26-32 in. barrels, various chokes, checkered pistol grip stock. Mfg. 1930-49.

$225	$180	$165	$155	$140	$120	$110

MODEL 720 RIOT - see the "Trench/Riot Shotgun" category in the T section for more Information and prices.

MODEL 726 SEMI-AUTO UPLAND SPORTER - similar to Model 720, except 2 shell mag. Mfg. 1931-49.

$275	$195	$165	$155	$140	$120	$110

MODEL 740C SKEET GUN - similar to Model 726, with Cutts Compensator and skeet stock, 24 1/2 in. barrel. Mfg. 1936-49.

$305	$230	$200	$175	$155	$140	$120

MODEL 745 LIGHTWEIGHT - similar to Model 720, with alloy receiver, 12 ga. only, 28 in. barrel. Mfg. 1940-49.

$275	$195	$165	$155	$140	$120	$110

MODEL 755 STANDARD SEMI-AUTO - 12 or 16 ga., 26, 28, or 30 in. barrel, various chokes, rounded-off receiver, checkered pistol grip stock. Mfg. 1949-58.

$265	$180	$160	$150	$140	$120	$110

MODEL 755SC - similar to Model 755, with Savage Super Choke.

$275	$195	$165	$155	$140	$120	$110

MODEL 775 LIGHTWEIGHT SEMI-AUTO - similar to Model 755, with alloy receiver. Mfg. 1950-65.

$275	$195	$180	$165	$150	$140	$120

MODEL 775SC - similar to Model 775, with Savage Super Choke.

$285	$205	$195	$175	$160	$150	$130

MODEL 750 SEMI-AUTO - 12 ga., Browning patterned semi-auto, 26 or 28 in. barrels, various chokes, checkered pistol grip stock. Mfg. 1960-69.

$275	$195	$165	$155	$140	$120	$110

MODEL 750SC - similar to Model 750, with Savage Super Choke.

$285	$205	$175	$165	$150	$130	$120

MODEL 750AC - similar to Model 750, with poly choke.

$285	$205	$175	$165	$150	$130	$120

GRADING - PPGS™	100%	98%	95%	90%	80%	70%	60%

MODEL 21 SLIDE ACTION - similar to Model 28, except stock has no checkering. Mfg. 1920-28.

	$300	$265	$235	$190	$165	$150	$130

MODEL 28 SLIDE ACTION - 12, 16, or 20 ga., patterned after the Winchester Model 12. Mfg. 1927-34.

	$300	$265	$235	$190	$165	$150	$130

This model was available in either standard configuration (Models 28A and 28B), Riot (28C), Trap (28D), or Special (28S).

MODEL 30 SLIDE ACTION - 12, 16, 20 ga., or .410 bore, 26, 28, or 30 in. barrels, various chokes, VR, plain pistol grip stock. Mfg. 1958-70.

	$220	$175	$155	$140	$120	$100	$85
Checkered Late Model	$230	$185	$165	$150	$130	$110	$95

MODEL 30AC - similar to Model 30, with adj. choke, checkered wood, 12 ga. only. Mfg. 1959-70.

	$240	$200	$175	$160	$145	$120	$100

MODEL 30T TRAP AND DUCK GUN - similar to Model 30, with 30 in. full barrel, 12 ga. only, Monte Carlo stock and pad. Mfg. 1963-70.

	$230	$185	$165	$150	$130	$110	$90

MODEL 30FG TAKEDOWN ACTION - 12, 20 ga., or .410 bore, 26, 28, or 30 in. barrel, various chokes, checkered pistol grip stock. Mfg. 1970-75.

	$175	$155	$130	$110	$95	$85	$70

MODEL 30T TAKEDOWN TRAP - 12 ga. only, 30 in. full barrel, Monte Carlo stock with pad. Mfg. 1970-73.

	$195	$175	$155	$140	$110	$100	$85

MODEL 30AC TAKEDOWN - similar to Model 30FG, with adj. choke, 12 or 20 ga., 26 in. barrel. Mfg. 1971-72.

	$200	$180	$165	$150	$120	$110	$90

MODEL 30 TAKEDOWN SLUG GUN - similar to Model 30FG, with 32 in. cylinder bore barrel, rifle sights. Mfg. 1971-disc.

	$195	$175	$160	$140	$110	$100	$85

MODEL 30D TAKEDOWN - similar to Model 30FG, with VR, engraved receiver and pad. Mfg. 1971-disc.

	$200	$180	$165	$150	$120	$110	$90

MODEL 67 SLIDE ACTION - see listing under Stevens Section.

FOX MODELS B, B-SE, AND STEVENS 311 (REFER TO FOX & STEVENS) - see listings under Fox and Stevens Sections.

SAVAGE/FOX MODEL FA-1 - 12 ga., 2 3/4 in. chamber, semi-auto, gas operated, walnut stock and forend, cut checkering, 28 or 30 in. vent. rib barrel. Mfg. 1981-82 in Japan.

	$250	$215	$185	$160	$140	$120	$100

SAVAGE/FOX MODEL FP-1 - 12 ga., similar to Model FA-1, except is slide action. Mfg. 1981-82 in Japan.

	$175	$150	$125	$100	$85	$70	$60

MODEL 242 O/U - .410 bore, single exposed hammer, single trigger, barrel selector lever, full chokes. Mfg. 1977-81.

	$350	$300	$260	$230	$200	$175	$150

MODEL 440/440B O/U - 12 or 20 ga., 26, 28, or 30 in. barrels, various chokes, boxlock, ST (Model 440) or SST (Model 440B), extractors, checkered pistol grip stock, VR. Imported from Italy 1968-72.

	$495	$440	$415	$385	$330	$305	$250

GRADING - PPGS™	100%	98%	95%	90%	80%	70%	60%

MODEL 440T - similar to Model 440, 12 ga., 30 in. barrel only, imp mod. or full choke, wide VR, trap style stock, pad. Mfg. 1969-72.

	$550	$470	$440	$415	$385	$360	$330

MODEL 444 DELUXE - similar to Model 440, with auto ejectors, select walnut. Mfg. 1969-72.

	$550	$470	$440	$415	$385	$360	$330

MODEL 550 SxS - 12 or 20 ga., 26, 28, or 30 in. barrels (made by Valmet - rare), various chokes, boxlock, auto ejectors, single trigger, checkered pistol grip stock. Mfg. 1971-73.

	$275	$220	$195	$165	$150	$130	$110

KIMEL KAMPER SINGLE SHOT - 20 ga. or .410 bore, 3 in. chamber, 18 1/2 in. barrel, pistol grip hardwood stock and forearm, butt trap holds 3 shells, bottom opening, exposed hammer. Mfg. 1979-c.1981

	$175	$150	$135	$120	$105	$90	$75

MODEL 312 SERIES O/U - 12 ga. only, boxlock action, 3 in. chambers, vent. barrels, satin chrome finished receiver, checkered walnut stock and forearm, SST, choke tubes, approx. 7 lbs. Mfg. 1990-93.

The Model 312 Series falls under the domain of Savage Arms, Inc.

✳ *Model 312 Series O/U Field* - 26 or 28 in. VR barrels with choke tubes.

	$585	$520	$485	$435	$395	$360	$330

✳ *Model 312 Series O/U Trap* - 30 in. barrels only, Monte Carlo stock with recoil pad.

	$615	$550	$500	$460	$415	$375	$330

✳ *Model 312 Series O/U Sporting Clays* - 28 in. barrels only with 7 choke tubes provided, recoil pad.

	$595	$530	$485	$435	$395	$360	$320

MODEL 330 O/U - 12 or 20 ga., 26, 28, or 30 in. barrels, various chokes, boxlock, SST, extractors, checkered pistol grip stock. Mfg. by Valmet 1969-1980.

	$495	$440	$385	$335	$275	$250	$220

Add 25% for extra set of barrels.

MODEL 333T - similar to Model 330, with 30 in. VR barrels bored imp. mod. and full choke, trap stock with pad. Mfg. by Valmet 1972-1980.

	$550	$470	$415	$385	$360	$305	$275

MODEL 333 O/U - 12 or 20 (rare) ga., 26, 28, or 30 in. VR barrels, various chokes, boxlock, SST, auto ejectors, checkered pistol grip stock. Mfg. by Valmet 1973-1980.

	$650	$575	$500	$450	$400	$375	$330

Add 25% for extra set of barrels.
Add 30% for 20 ga.

SHOTGUNS: RECENT MFG.

Currently manufactured Stevens shotguns can be found in the Stevens section.

MODEL 210F SLUG WARRIOR BOLT ACTION (MASTER SHOT) - 12 ga. only, 3 in. chamber, built on Model 100 action with controlled round feeding, 24 in. rifled barrel (1:35 twist), 2 shot detachable mag., 60 degree bolt lift, Realtree camo finished (new 2003) or black synthetic stock with checkering and recoil pad, top tang safety, no sights, 7 1/2 lbs. New 1997.

MSR $587	$475	$385	$335	$275	$220	$200	$180

Add $46 for camo finish (Model 210F Camo).
Add $41 for Turkey configuration with 24 in. barrel and camo coverage (Model 210FT Camo, mfg. 2005-2006).

GRADING - PPGS™	100%	98%	95%	90%	80%	70%	60%

∗ Model 210FT Slug Warrior Bolt Action - similar to Model 210F, except has Advantage camo stock and mag., 24 in. smooth bore barrel accepts Win. style choke tubes. Mfg. 1997-2000.

	$410	$350	$305	$265	$235	$215	$195

Last MSR was $466.

MILANO O/U - 12, 20, 28 ga., or .410 bore, ejectors, 28 in. chrome lined vent. rib barrels, satin nickel finished boxlock action, satin finished Turkish walnut stock and forearm with laser engraved checkering, rubber recoil pad, Schnabel forend, SST, fiber optic front sight with brass mid-rib sight, ventilated rib, includes three choke tubes (except for .410 bore), elongated forcing cones, 6 1/4 - 7 1/2 lbs., imported from Italy. New mid-2006.

MSR $1,714	$1,475	$1,250	$995	$900	$800	$700	$600

SAVIN, J.C.

Current manufacturer located in St. Etienne, France. J.C. Savin manufactures only best quality shotguns and rifles per individual order. Annual production is approx. 25 long guns. Please contact the factory directly for domestic availability and current pricing.

RIFLES: DOUBLE, CUSTOM

Available in either O/U or SxS sidelock or Anson & Deeley boxlock. Available in various cals. (.30 - .577 NE), 24 or 26 in. barrels.

SHOTGUNS: DOUBLE, CUSTOM

Available in either O/U or SxS sidelock configuration, 12 or 20 ga., DT or ST, premier quality. A SxS round action Dixon model with trigger plate is also available in 12 or 20 ga.

SAXONIA

Previous manufacturer located in Schwarzenberg, Germany.

Saxonia manufactured good quality semi-auto pistols, security/combat shotguns, and bolt action sniper rifles in various configurations. These guns had very little or no importation in the U.S.

SCATTERGUN TECHNOLOGIES INC. (S.G.T.)

Current manufacturer located in Berryville, AR since 1999. Previously located in Nashville, TN 1991-1999. Distributor, dealer, and consumer sales.

During 1999, Wilson Combat purchased Scattergun Technologies. S.G.T. manufactures practical defense, tactical, and hunting shotguns in 12 ga. only, utilizing Remington Models 870 and 11-87 (disc.) actions in various configurations as listed. All shotguns feature 3 in. chamber capacity and parkerized finish.

SHOTGUNS: SEMI-AUTO

Add $15 for short stock on models listed.
Add $125 for Armor-Tuff finish on models listed.

K-9 MODEL - 12 ga., 18 in. barrel, adj. ghost ring sight, 7 shot mag., side saddle, synthetic buttstock and forearm. Disc. 2003.

	$1,100	$875	$775	$665	$560	$465	$410

Last MSR was $1,325.

SWAT MODEL - 12 ga., similar to K-9 Model, except has 14 in. barrel and forearm with 11,000 CP flashlight. Disc. 2003.

	$1,400	$1,150	$895	$785	$655	$550	$465

Last MSR was $1,750.

This model was available for military and law enforcement only.

URBAN SNIPER MODEL - 12 ga., 18 in. rifled barrel, scout optics, 7 shot mag., side saddle, synthetic buttstock, forearm and bipod. Disc. 1999.

	$1,225	$1,075	$950	$835	$685	$585	$485

Last MSR was $1,390.

GRADING - PPGS™	100%	98%	95%	90%	80%	70%	60%

SHOTGUNS: SLIDE ACTION

On the following models, Armor-Tuff finish became standard during 2003.

Add $15 for short stock on models listed.
Subtract approx. $100 if w/o Armor Tuff finish.

STANDARD MODEL - 12 or 20 ga., 18 in. barrel, adj. ghost ring sight, 7 shot mag., side saddle, synthetic buttstock and forearm with 11,000 CP flashlight.

MSR $1,150	$975	$875	$725	$610	$515	$425	$375

PROFESSIONAL MODEL - 12 ga., similar to Standard Model, except has 14 in. barrel and 6 shot mag.

MSR $1,175	$995	$875	$725	$610	$515	$425	$375

This model is available for military and law enforcement only.

EXPERT MODEL - 12 ga., 18 in. barrel with mod. choke, nickel/Teflon finished receiver, adj. ghost ring sight, forearm incorporates 11,000 CP flashlight. Mfg. 1997-2000.

	$1,200	$995	$775	$665	$560	$465	$410

Last MSR was $1,350.

ENTRY MODEL - 12 ga., 12 1/2 in. barrel with mod. choke, adj. ghost ring sights, 5 shot mag., side saddle, synthetic buttstock and nylon strap assisted forearm with 5,000 CP flashlight. Disc.

	$995	$800	$600	$495	$430	$365	$315

Last MSR was $1,125.

This model was available for military and law enforcement only.

COMPACT MODEL - 12 1/2 in. barrel with mod. choke, adj. ghost ring sight, 5 shot mag., synthetic buttstock and forearm. Mfg. 1994-99.

	$575	$510	$420	$360	$315	$260	$225

Last MSR was $635.

This model was available for military and law enforcement only.

PRACTICAL TURKEY MODEL - 20 in. barrel with extra full choke, adj. ghost ring sight, 5 shot mag. for 3 in. shells, synthetic buttstock and forearm. Mfg. 1995-99.

	$545	$500	$465	$405	$350	$290	$250

Last MSR was $595.

LOUIS AWERBUCK SIGNATURE MODEL - 18 in. barrel with fixed choke, adj. ghost ring sight, 5 shot mag., side saddle, wood buttstock with recoil reducer and forearm. Mfg. 1994-99.

	$625	$490	$385	$325	$275	$230	$200

Last MSR was $705.

F.B.I. MODEL - similar to Standard Model, except has 5 shot mag. Disc. 1999.

	$715	$625	$490	$420	$370	$305	$265

Last MSR was $770.

MILITARY MODEL - 18 in. barrel with vent. handguard and M-9 bayonet lug, adj. ghost ring rear sight, 7 shot mag., synthetic stock and grooved corncob forearm. Mfg. 1997-98.

	$625	$490	$385	$325	$275	$230	$200

Last MSR was $690.

PATROL MODEL - 18 in. barrel, adj. ghost ring sight, 5 shot mag., synthetic buttstock and forearm. Disc. 1999.

	$545	$500	$465	$405	$350	$290	$250

Last MSR was $595.

GRADING - PPGS™	100%	98%	95%	90%	80%	70%	60%

BORDER PATROL MODEL 20 - 12 or 20 ga., similar to Patrol Model, except has 7 shot mag., black synthetic stock and forearm, choice of 18 or 20 in. barrel.

MSR $875	$750	$650	$550	$460	$395	$335	$285

Add $35 for 20 ga.

BORDER PATROL MODEL 21 - similar to Border Patrol Model 20, except has 14 in. barrel and 6 shot mag.

MSR $900	$775	$675	$550	$460	$395	$335	$285

This model is available for military and law enforcement only.

CONCEALMENT MODEL 00 - 12 1/2 in. barrel with fixed choke, 5 shot mag., bead sight, grooved wood forearm and pistol grip. Disc. 1998.

	$490	$395	$280	$230	$200	$170	$145

Last MSR was $550.

This model is available for military and law enforcement only.

CONCEALMENT MODEL 01 - similar to Concealment Model 00, except has synthetic finger-grooved combat forearm and pistol grip. Disc. 1993.

	$475	$395	$295	$235	$205	$175	$150

Last MSR was $525.

This model is available for military and law enforcement only.

CONCEALMENT MODEL 02 - similar to Concealment Model 00, except has Pachmayr forearm and pistol grip. Disc. 1993.

	$495	$415	$315	$255	$225	$190	$165

Last MSR was $555.

This model is available for military and law enforcement only.

CONCEALMENT MODEL 03 - similar to Concealment Model 01, except has synthetic nylon strap assisted forearm with 5,000 CP flashlight. Disc. 1993.

	$550	$455	$350	$285	$250	$215	$185

Last MSR was $625.

BREACHING MODEL - similar to Concealment Model 00, except has standoff device. Disc. 1998.

	$450	$390	$340	$275	$240	$200	$175

Last MSR was $500.

This model is available for military and law enforcement only.

SCHALL

Previous manufacturer located in Hartford, CT.

Schall provided parts and repair service for Fiala pistols, and produced additional repeating pistols with the Schall name between 1930-36.

PISTOLS

REPEATING HANDGUN - .22 LR cal., 10 round mag. fed manual repeating action, tapered 7 1/2 in. barrel with fixed sights and blue finish, walnut ribbed grips, usually marked "Schall & Co./New Haven, Conn. USA", some have no markings.

	$475	$445	$410	$375	$315	$280	$210

Subtract 50% if not in working order.

SCHEIRING GmbH

Current custom rifle manufacturer located in Ferlach, Austria.

H. Scheiring manufactures best quality rifles (including O/U, SxS, and Stalking variations) per individual customer special order. Scheiring was a member of the Ferlach Guild until it was dissolved in 2004. The factory should be contacted directly for more information regarding current models and domestic availability (see Trademark Index).

SCHELLER SPEZIALWAFFEN

Previous manufacturer located in Suhl, Germany that specialized in bolt action rifles.

SCHERZ, MICHAEL

Please refer to Gila River Gun Works.

SCHILLING, FA. ALFRED

Current rifle manufacturer and gunsmith established in 1898, and located in Zella-Mehlis, Germany. Currently imported by Sundog Firearms, located in Kimberly, OR.

RIFLES: CUSTOM

Current owner Jorg Schilling manufactures high quality hunting and target rifles in many configurations, in addition to providing gunsmithing services, including traditional case color hardening, bluing, restoration of damascus barrels and engravings. All guns are custom order and include the standard Schilling bolt action rifle, the single shot rifle, the falling block rifle, and the Aydt target model. Please contact the importer for more information, including an individual price quotation, delivery time and availability (see Trademark Index).

SCHMIDT-RUBIN RIFLES

Please refer to the Swiss Military listing in this section.

SCHMITT FRERES

Previous manufacturer located in Saint Etienne, France.

This manufacturer produced copies of 1894 patent Darne R model guns until 1956. While higher grades do exist, they do not command the prices given for the later patent (1909) Darne-produced guns. Lower grade guns will be priced in the same range as Soleihac and lower grade Darne R models.

SCHUERMAN ARMS., LTD.

Current bolt action rifle manufacturer located in Desert Hills, AZ. Previously located in Scottsdale, AZ. Consumer direct sales.

RIFLES: BOLT ACTION

MODEL SA40 - various cals., including WSMs (disc.), WSSMs (disc.), and Rem. Ultra Mags., right or left-hand action features three rotating locking lugs in short throw bolt, 70 degree bolt lift, 20-26 in. matte stainless steel barrel and action, trigger safety, controlled round feeding, fully enclosed case head, three-position safety, choice of detachable mag., hinged floorplate, or blind box mag., laminated fiberglass sporter style stock. New 2001.

MSR $4,250	$4,250	$3,600	$3,200	$2,700	$2,400	$2,100	$1,800

SCHUETZEN PISTOL WORKS

Schuetzen Pistol Works is the in-house custom shop of Olympic Arms. Schuetzen Pistol Works has been customizing Safari Arms and Olympic Arms 1911 style pistols since 1997. For currently manufactured pistols, please refer to the Olympic Arms listing. For discontinued models, please refer to the Safari Arms listing.

SCHUETZEN RIFLES

A Schuetzen Rifle is a special single-shot target rifle. During the time span 1875-1945 this target configuration rifle was very popular with competition shooters. Many of these guns had elaborate locking systems, top quality sights, double-set triggers, heavy barrels, palm and thumbrests, sculptured cheekpiece, Swiss style buttplate, etc. Rather than list all the various domestic and European makers (there are hundreds), it should be noted that, since there are so many combinations of options for this configuration, most guns have to be examined and appraised individually. Most non-major trademarks sell in the $900 - $2,750 range, depending on features and condition. A famous trademark specimen (Ballard, Stevens, Winchester, etc.) in a rare model with superior original condition can bring over $15,000. Schuetzen Rifles are a field in themselves and a knowledgeable dealer/collector should be consulted before buying or selling one of these guns.

GRADING - PPGS™	100%	98%	95%	90%	80%	70%	60%

SCHULTZ & LARSEN

Previous manufacturer located in Otterup, Denmark circa 1911.

RIFLES: BOLT ACTION

NO. 47 MATCH RIFLE - .22 LR cal., single shot, 28 in. heavy barrel, target sights, set trigger, free rifle stock.

	$660	$550	$495	$440	$385	$360	$330

M61 MATCH RIFLE - .22 LR cal., single shot, 28 in. heavy barrel, target sights, set trigger, free rifle stock, palm rest.

	$895	$825	$740	$680	$600	$550	$500

M62 MATCH RIFLE - various cals., single shot, 28 in. heavy barrel, target sights, set trigger, free rifle stock, palm rest.

	$995	$875	$780	$700	$620	$550	$500

MODEL 54 FREE RIFLE - any American centerfire standard caliber, plus 6.5x55mm, 27 in. heavy barrel, target sights, free rifle stock.

	$825	$745	$690	$605	$550	$495	$440

MODEL 54J SPORTING RIFLE - .244 Rem., .270 Win., .30-06, 6.5x55mm, or 7x61 Sharpe and Hart cal., 3 shot, 24 in. barrel, checkered Monte Carlo stock, no sights. Mfg. 1954-1957.

	$650	$550	$470	$415	$360	$330	$300

MODEL 60 - 7x61S&H cal. only, improved Model 54J, mfg. 1957-1960.

	$675	$575	$475	$425	$375	$330	$300

MODEL 65 -.308 Norma Mag., .358 Win. Mag., or 7x61 S&H cal., improved Model 60, replaced by the Model 68DL, mfg. 1960-1967.

	$675	$575	$475	$425	$375	$330	$300

MODEL 68 DL - .22-250 Rem., .243 Win., 6mm Rem., .264 Win. Mag., .270 Win., .30-06, .308 Win., 7x61 S&H, 7mm Rem. Mag., 8x57JS, .300 Win. Mag., .308 Norma Mag., .338 Win. Mag., .358 Norma Mag., or .458 Win. Mag. cal., 24 in. barrel, Bofors Steel receiver, bolt has 4 rear locking lugs, select French walnut, adj. trigger, no sights except for .458 Mag. Mfg. 1967-mid-1980s.

	$725	$650	$575	$525	$495	$460	$430

SHOTGUNS: O/U

Schultz & Larsen also manufactured a very limited quantity of O/U shotguns, including a 20 ga. boxlock. Current pricing reflects shooting value more than collectibility.

SCHWABEN ARMS GMBH

Current manufacturer located in Rottweil, Germany.

Schwaben Arms GmbH manufactures an extensive lineup of quality paramilitary rifles and carbines, primarily patterned after H&K models. Both commercial and military/law enforcement is available. Please contact the factory directly for U.S. availability and pricing (see Trademark Index).

SCOTT, W.C., LTD.

Previous manufacturer established during 1834 and located in Birmingham, England. All operations ceased during 1991.

Established in 1834 by William Scott, located in Birmingham, England, and remained in the family until 1897. At this time, Scott merged with P. Webley & Son to form Webley & Scott Revolver and Arms Co., Ltd. (later changed to Webley & Scott Ltd.). Even though Scott family members were no longer associated with this new company, the Scott gun - line was continued with the trademark intact until 1935. Thereafter, only a few guns were marked Scott. In 1979, Webley & Scott ceased manufacture of all firearms. A new company, W. & C. Scott, was formed in 1980 utilizing mostly employees of Webley & Scott. W. & C. Scott remained part of its parent company, Harris & Shel-

GRADING - PPGS™	100%	98%	95%	90%	80%	70%	60%

don (also had controlling interest in Hardy and Churchill trademarks), until 1985 when Scott was purchased by Holland & Holland. Manufacture of Scott guns decreased substantially after the merger, and in September 1991, W. & C. Scott ceased operation altogether. During its 157 years of production, Scott and Webley & Scott produced approximately, 150,000 double guns, 10,000 rifles (either double or bolt-action) and thousands of single guns and single rifles.

SHOTGUNS: SxS

All W.C. Scott Shotguns were discontinued in 1990. W.C. Scott also manufactured many hammer guns that vary in price from $250-$2,500, depending on grade and original condition.

KINMOUNT - 12, 16, 20, or 28 ga., boxlock action, ejectors, deluxe checkered walnut, scroll engraving.

$6,500	$5,750	$5,000	$4,500	$4,000	$3,000	$2,500

Last MSR was $11,000.

Add 20% for 28 ga. or .410 bore.
Add 10% for SNT.

BOWOOD - 12, 16, 20, or 28 ga., boxlock action, ejectors, deluxe checkered walnut, extensive scroll engraving.

$7,500	$6,500	$5,750	$5,000	$4,500	$4,000	$3,500

Last MSR was $12,500.

Add 20% for 28 ga. or .410 bore.
Add 10% for SNT.

CHATSWORTH - 12, 16, 20, or 28 ga., top-of-the-line boxlock action, ejectors, deluxe checkered walnut, extensive scroll engraving.

$8,750	$7,500	$6,500	$5,750	$5,000	$4,500	$4,000

Last MSR was $14,000.

Add 20% for 28 ga. or .410 bore.
Add 10% for SNT.

BLENHEIM - 12 bore only, upgraded models, custom-made to individual specifications, originally priced per individual order.

Specimen rarity precludes percentage grading pricing. Individual appraisals have to be secured on this model.

SEARCY, B. & CO.

Current rifle manufacturer established in 1975 and located in Boron, CA.

RIFLES: CUSTOM

B. Searcy & Co. manufactures a unique stainless steel double rifle in a variety of calibers. Current models include: Classic ($16,000 - MSR), Deluxe Grade ($19,500 - MSR), Under Lever Model ($19,500 - MSR), Back Action Sidelock ($22,000 - MSR), .577 NE Boxlock (MSR - $22,500), .577 NE Sidelock ($55,000 - MSR), .600 NE Boxlock ($35,000 - MSR), .700 NE Boxlock ($85,000 - MSR). Previous models included the PH Boxlock Model w/ ejectors (disc. 2008, $12,000 last MSR), .600 NE Sidelock (last MSR was $35,000), and the .700 NE Sidelock (last MSR was $50,000).

B. Searcy also manufactures a bolt action rifle - starting price is $15,000, and many options are available. Additionally, a stalking rifle is available - base price is $8,500 or $12,500 for takedown model.

Please contact the company directly (see Trademark Index) for current model information and availability.

SEARS, ROEBUCK AND CO.

Catalog merchandiser that, in addition to selling major trademark firearms, also private labeled many configurations of firearms (mostly longarms) under a variety of trademarks and logos (i.e., J.C. Higgins, Ted Williams, Ranger, etc.). Sears discontinued the sale of all firearms circa 1980, and the Ted Williams trademark was stopped circa 1978.

A general guideline for Sears Roebuck and related labels (most are marked "Sears, Roebuck and Co." on left side of barrel) is that values are generally lower than those of the major factory models from which they were derived. Remember, 99% of Sears Roebuck and related label guns get priced by their shootability factor in today's competitive marketplace, not collectibility. An extensive crossover listing (see Storebrand Cross-Over List) has been provided in the back of this text for linking up the various Sears Roebuck models to the original manufacturer with respective "crossover" model numbers.

SECURITY INDUSTRIES

Previous manufacturer located in Little Ferry, NJ.

REVOLVERS

MODEL PSS 38 DOUBLE ACTION - .38 Spl. cal., 5 shot cylinder, 2 in. barrel, stainless steel, fixed sights, wood grips. Mfg. 1973-78.

	$175	$150	$140	$130	$125	$110	$100

MODEL PM357 - .357 Mag. cal., similar to Model PSS 38, 2 1/2 in. barrel. Mfg. 1975-disc.

	$225	$175	$165	$150	$140	$125	$110

MODEL PPM 357 - .357 Mag. cal., 5 shot, 2 in. barrel, spurless hammer until 1977, new models have spur. Mfg. 1965-disc.

	$225	$175	$165	$150	$140	$125	$110

SEDCO INDUSTRIES, INC.

Previous manufacturer located in Lake Elsinore, CA until 1991.

PISTOLS: SEMI-AUTO

MODEL SP-22 - .22 LR cal., single action, 2 1/2 in. barrel, rotary safety, serrated slide, nickel, satin nickel (new 1990), or black metal finish, simulated pearl grips in white, blue, grey, or pink, 11 oz. Mfg. 1989-90 only.

	$60	$55	$50	$45	$40	$35	$35

Last MSR was $69.

SEDGLEY, R.F., INC.

Previous manufacturer located in Philadelphia, PA.

RIFLES: BOLT ACTION

SPRINGFIELD SPORTING RIFLE - .218 Bee, .220 Swift, .22-3000, .22-4000, .22 Hornet, .25-35 WCF, .250-3000 Sav., .257 Roberts, .270 Win., 7x57mm Mauser, or .30-06 cal., ´03 Springfield bolt action, 24 in. barrel, Lyman receiver sight, checkered pistol grip stock, pre-WWII.

	$1,250	$1,125	$995	$875	$750	$625	$495

SPRINGFIELD CARBINE SPORTER - similar to Rifle, with 20 in. barrel, and full length stock.

	$1,450	$1,250	$1,125	$995	$875	$750	$625

SEECAMP, L.W. CO., INC.

Current handgun manufacturer located in Milford, CT. Dealer direct sales only.

Ludwig (Louis) Wilhelm Seecamp (1901-1989), after whom the company was named, was trained as a master gunsmith in the technical academy system of pre-WW II Germany. Having survived the Eastern Front in an elite Gebirgsjaeger (Mountain Troops) unit, he brought his family to the United States in 1959 by way of Canada. From 1959 until his retirement in 1971, he was the gun designer for O.F. Mossberg.

L.W. Seecamp Co, Inc. was founded in 1973 as a family business specializing in Ludwig's patented double action conversion of the venerable 1911 semi-auto pistol (Colt

.45). This conversion, done during a period when the single-action versus double-action controversy was at its peak, resulted in the first commercially available DA .45 autoloaders anywhere in the world. Nearly 2000 such DA conversions were done from the early 70s to the early 80s.

PISTOLS: SEMI-AUTO

All Seecamp pistols are hand machined and fitted from stainless steel. Manufacture has always emphasized quality over quantity - this explains why values can exceed the company's retail pricing.

LWS .25 ACP MODEL - .25 ACP cal., double action, 2 in. barrel, 7 shot mag., stainless steel, matte finish, no sights, 12 oz. Approx. 4,000 mfg. 1981-85.

	100%	98%	95%	90%	80%	70%	60%
	$400	$325	$275	$225	$195	$165	$140

Last MSR was $275.

LWS 32 MODEL - .32 ACP cal., (mfg. recommends .32 ACP Win. Silvertip ammo only), double action, 2.06 in. barrel, stainless steel, 6 shot mag., no sights, 11 1/2 oz. Mfg. began Jan. 1985.

MSR $425	$425	$375	$350	$285	$250	$215	$185

Add $100 for California edition (with trigger mounted safety).

This model is available in either a matte or polished finish. The polished finish carries a slight premium. Extreme back order situation coupled with high demand may result in higher prices than listed above.

MATCHED PAIR - includes both .25 ACP and .32 ACP pistols with the same serial number, approx. 200 sets were mfg. before the BATF stopped this practice.

	$1,200	$1,000	$850	$740	$620	$515	$440

This set contained a matte finished .25 ACP and a polished .32 ACP.

LWS-380 MODEL - .380 ACP cal. (mfg. recommends .380 ACP Win. Silvertip ammo only), identical in appearance to the LWS 32 Model, 2.06 in. barrel, double action only, delayed blowback mechanism, polished stainless steel, checkered black glass filled nylon grips, no sights, 11 1/2 oz. Very limited production beginning 2000.

MSR $850	$850	$775	$650	$540	$465	$385	$335

SEITZ

Previous manufacturer located in Portland, OR circa mid-1980s-1993.

SHOTGUNS: SINGLE BARREL TRAP

SINGLE BARREL TRAP GUN - 12 ga. only, single barrel, various barrel lengths, pull or release trigger, only 45 guns mfg.

	$18,500	$16,000	$13,000	$10,000	$8,500	$7,700	$6,950

SEMMERLING

Current trademark owned by American Derringer Corp., located in Waco, TX. Previously manufactured by Semmerling Corporation, located in Boston, MA from 1978-1982. Less than 600 LM-4 pistols were originally mfg. by the Semmerling Corporation.

PISTOLS: SLIDE ACTION

LM-4 PISTOL - .45 ACP cal., 2 in. barrel, blue, smallest .45 ACP repeater available, slide is worked manually with thumb on serrated slide-top, extremely high quality, hand fitted and choice of finishes include chrome, electroless nickel, or high polish blue.

	100%	98%	95%	90%	80%	70%	60%
Chrome	$2,950	$2,600	$2,300	$2,100	$1,950	$1,725	$1,600
Electroless nickel	$3,200	$2,950	$2,600	$2,300	$2,100	$1,950	$1,725
High polish blue	$4,950	$4,500	$4,000	$3,600	$3,200	$2,800	$2,500

The original U.S. Army contract pistol mfg. by Semmerling in Boston sold for $5,000. Earlier mfg. by Lichtman will also command a premium over values listed.

At a recent 2007 Rock Island Auction Co. auction a 99.8% condition chrome finish example, ser. no. 217, mfg. by Semmerling in Boston sold for $5,750.

GRADING - PPGS™	100%	98%	95%	90%	80%	70%	60%

✳ LM-4 Pistol (Current Mfg.) - .45 ACP cal., 2 in. barrel, thumb activated slide mechanism, matte stainless steel (disc.) or blue finish, 24 oz. Limited mfg. by special order only since 1998.

The 2003 MSR on this model was $2,655.

Please contact American Derringer directly for a price quotation on this special order model.

SENTINEL ARMS

Previous importer of Arsenal Bulgaria pistols and rifles.

SERBU FIREARMS, INC.

Current manufacturer located in Tampa, FL.

RIFLES: SINGLE SHOT

SINGLE SHOT MODEL - .50 BMG cal., single shot bolt action, 22 (carbine) or 29 (rifle) in. match grade barrel with muzzle brake, AR-15 style trigger and safety, Picatinny rail, parkerized finish, 17-22 lbs.

	100%	98%	95%	90%	80%	70%	60%
MSR $2,195	$2,195	$1,850	$1,650	$1,450	$1,250	$1,175	$975

Add $25 for "Have a Nice Day" engraving on Shark muzzle brake.
Add $120 for bi-pod.

SERENGETI RIFLES, INC.

Current custom rifle manufacturer and stock maker located in Kalispell, MT.

RIFLES: BOLT ACTION, CUSTOM

Serengeti Rifles Inc. manufactures a complete line of high-quality, custom-order bolt action rifles, including the Standard African ($7,369 MSR), Dangerous Game African ($8,249 MSR), Montanan ($6,269 MSR), Red Mist ($6,269 MSR), TigerCat ($6,869 MSR), and the Walkabout ($6,269 MSR). A number of options are available. Additionally, Serengeti Rifles manufactures its own line of proprietary actions and high quality walnut stocks. Please contact the company directly for more information, including options, availability and delivery time (see Trademark Index.)

C. SHARPS ARMS CO. INC.

Current manufacturer located in Big Timber, MT.

C. Sharps Arms Co. Inc. currently distributes smokeless powder replicas of C. Sharps rifles/carbines and the Winchester Model 1885 single shot. They are able to shoot both smokeless and black powder loads. Most models are available in the following cals.: .38-55, .40-50, .40-65, .40-70, .40-90, .45-70, .45-90, .45-100, .45-110, .45-120, .50-70, .50-90, .50-100, and .50-140. All models are authentically reproduced and high quality.

RIFLES: REPRODUCTIONS, SHARPS BLACK POWDER

Because each rifle is a special order, there are many options available which would be added to the base price shown. Please contact the company directly for availability (see Trademark Index).

NEW MODEL 1874 BRIDGEPORT SPORTING RIFLE

	100%	98%	95%	90%	80%	70%	60%
MSR $1,570	$1,570	$1,450	$1,400	$1,350	$1,300	$1,200	$1,100

In addition to the 1874 Sporting Model, a custom long range target rifle or Schuetzen short range target rifle is available in this model.

NEW MODEL 1874 HARTFORD SPORTING RIFLE

100%	98%	95%	90%	80%	70%	60%
$1,700	$1,575	$1,475	$1,400	$1,350	$1,300	$1,200

Last MSR was $1,775.

NEW MODEL 1874 CARBINE HUNTER

100%	98%	95%	90%	80%	70%	60%
$1,450	$1,395	$1,300	$1,250	$1,200	$1,150	$1,100

Last MSR was $1,495.

GRADING - PPGS™	100%	98%	95%	90%	80%	70%	60%

CUSTOM NEW MODEL 1874 BOSS GUN - features 34 in. No. 1 heavy tapered octagon barrel, vernier tang sight, straight grip stock with cheekrest and steel shotgun butt.

This gun is custom order only. Please contact the factory to obtain a quotation on this model.

NEW MODEL 1875 SPORTING RIFLE - similar to New Model 1875 Classic, except has receiver with round crown.

MSR $1,385	$1,325	$1,225	$1,100	$975	$900	$825	$750

NEW MODEL 1875 TARGET SPORTING RIFLE - .38-55, .40-65, .40-70 Sharps Straight, .45-70 Govt., or .45-90 cal., 30 in. heavy tapered round barrel American walnut stock with pistol grip, black buttplate, color case receiver, drilled and tapped, single trigger, 11 lbs. Limited mfg. 2004 only.

$1,075	$975	$925	$850	$795	$725	$650

Last MSR was $1,137.

NEW MODEL 1875 CLASSIC RIFLE - receiver with octagon top, 26, 28, or 30 in. tapered full octagon barrel, straight grip stock with steel toe plate, 9 1/2 lbs. New 1992.

MSR $1,185	$1,125	$995	$900	$850	$750	$700	$650

NEW MODEL 1875 CARBINE - features 24 in. tapered round barrel. Mfg. 1996-98.

$875	$750	$675	$600	$500	$450	$375

Last MSR was $810.

NEW MODEL 1875 SADDLE RIFLE - receiver with octagon top, 26 in. barrel only. Disc. 1998.

$925	$850	$775	$700	$625	$550	$460

Last MSR was $910.

NEW MODEL 1875 BUSINESS RIFLE - receiver with round top, 28 in. heavy tapered round barrel. Disc. 1998.

$875	$775	$700	$625	$550	$500	$450

Last MSR was $810.

Add $50 for barrel sights.

CUSTOM NEW MODEL 1877 -.44-90, .45-70 Govt., .45-90, or .45-100 cal., 32 or 34 in. tapered round barrel, presentation grade American or English walnut stock, checkered pistol grip and forend, ebony forend tip, classic long range sights, 10 lbs. Limited production 2004 only.

$5,250	$4,750	$4,450	$4,100	$3,750	$3,450	$3,100

Last MSR was $5,500.

NEW MODEL 1885 HIGHWALL - .22 LR, .22 Hornet, .219 Zipper, .30-40 Krag, .32-40, .348 Win., .38-55 WCF, .40-65, .405 Win., .444 Marlin, or .45-70 cal., patterned after the Winchester Model 1885 single shot, falling block action, case colored receiver and small parts, 26-30 in. octagon barrel. New 1992.

MSR $1,350	$1,050	$900	$775	$650	$550	$475	$410

Add $200 for New Model 1885 Highwall Classic rifle (crescent buttplate and satin grey receiver finish, disc.).

SHARPS, CHRISTIAN

Previously manufactured by Sharps Rifle Manufacturing Company circa 1851-1855 and located in Windsor, VT. Also manufactured in Hartford, CT under same name between 1855-1874. Reorganized as Sharps Rifle Company in 1876 with production resuming in Hartford (1876 only) and Bridgeport, CT from 1877-1881.

100%	98%	95%	90%	80%	70%	60%	50%	40%	30%	20%	10%

HANDGUNS

REVOLVER, PERCUSSION - made 1850s in Philadelphia, production about 2000, 3 in. octagonal tip-up barrel with rib, .25 caliber, 6 shot.

N/A	N/A	$3,950	$3,650	$3,500	$3,250	$3,150	$3,000	$2,500	$2,250	$2,050	$1,500

PEPPERBOX PISTOL - also marked Sharps and Hankins, 4-shot breech-loading, .32, .30, or .22 rimfire cal., firing pin rotates, brass frame with silver plating, or case-hardening on iron frame.

* *Pepperbox Pistol First Model* - 5 variations, 2 1/2 in. barrel. Scarcer variations can be worth up to 150% more.

N/A	N/A	$750	$700	$650	$600	$550	$525	$500	$450	$425	$400

* *Pepperbox Pistol Second Model* - 5 variations, 3 in. barrel. Scarcer variations can be worth up to 150% more.

N/A	N/A	$750	$700	$650	$600	$550	$525	$500	$450	$425	$400

* *Pepperbox Pistol Third Model* - Sharps and Hankins markings, .32 rimfire short, 4 variations, 3 1/2 in. barrel. Premium for scarcer variations.

N/A	N/A	$800	$750	$700	$650	$600	$550	$500	$450	$400	$350

* *Pepperbox Pistol Fourth Model* - 4 variations, 2 1/2, 3, or 3 1/2 in. barrel, bird's head grip, .32 rimfire long. Premium for scarcer variations.

N/A	N/A	$925	$900	$850	$800	$760	$725	$700	$650	$625	$500

RIFLES: BREECH LOADING

The earliest Sharps rifles and carbines were made for Christian Sharps by A.S. Nippes, in Mill Creek, PA circa 1850, and a year later by Robbins and Lawrence Co. of Windsor, VT. Not until 1856 did the Sharps Rifle Co. of Hartford, CT begin to manufacture its own guns.

MODEL 1849 RIFLE - .36 or .44 cal., percussion breechloader, 30 in. barrels and brass patchboxes were standard, serial numbered 1 and up, very few examples exist, less than 100 mfg. These are the first of all Sharps long guns, there is no fixed value range. Depending on condition, they could range from $5,000 to $50,000+.

MODEL 1850 RIFLE - .36 or .44 cal., incorporated the Maynard tape primer on the right side of the breech, features similar to Model 1849, approx. 150 mfg. by A.S. Nippes, very rare. Values only slightly less than Model 1849.

MODEL 1851 CARBINE - .52 cal. percussion, 21 5/8 barrel, hammer mounted inside frame, Maynard tape primer. Approx. 1,800 mfg. by Robbins and Lawrence, 200 went to U.S. Government - these will bring a premium.

N/A	N/A	$14,000	$12,500	$11,000	$9,500	$9,000	$8,500	$8,000	$5,350	$4,840	$4,400

MODEL 1852 CARBINE - this design became standard for all the Sharps for the next two decades, first to be called "slant breech," established Christian Sharps as a major gun manufacturer. Approx. 5,000 mfg. by Robbins and Lawrence, U.S. military markings will command a premium.

N/A	N/A	$8,000	$7,500	$6,500	$6,000	$5,000	$4,000	$3,800	$3,500	$3,000	$2,800

MODEL 1853 CARBINE - .52 cal., very similar to Model 1852, with walnut stock and brass patchbox, Sharps patented pellet primer feed, ser. no. range 9,000-19,000.

N/A	N/A	$8,000	$7,300	$6,500	$5,350	$4,500	$4,000	$3,800	$3,500	$3,000	$2,500

Approx. 10,000 mfg. by Robbins and Lawrence 1854-1858, an additional 3,000 rifles mfg. - subtract 25%.

MODEL 1855 CARBINE - .52 cal., U.S. military model, all with Maynard tape primer, this was the period during which Robbins and Lawrence failed, and Sharps Rifle Co. took over production. 800 mfg.

N/A	N/A	$11,500	$10,900	$9,500	$9,000	$8,750	$8,600	$8,500	$8,000	$7,500	$6,000

100%	98%	95%	90%	80%	70%	60%	50%	40%	30%	20%	10%

Sharps "New Model"

Manufactured in Hartford, CT by Sharps Rifle Manufacturing Co. circa 1859-1866. Visibly different from earlier models because of straight breech and pellet priming feature built into lock plate. Approx. 115,000 were built, all in .52 cal. breechloading paper cartridge. Carbines had 22 in. barrels, rifles came standard with 30 in. round barrels. After ser. nos. reached 100,000, a "C" prefix was used in the number - i.e. C500 represents ser. no. 100,500.

MODEL 1859 CARBINE - standard with all-iron furniture and patchbox, first 3,000 had brass instead of iron, ser. no. range 30,000-75,000. Approx. 33,000 mfg.

N/A	N/A	$10,500	$9,500	$9,000	$7,000	$5,000	$4,500	$4,000	$3,500	$3,000	$2,500

MODEL 1863 CARBINE - made with and w/o iron patchbox, ser. no. range 75,000 - 140,000. Approx. 65,000 mfg. - those with patchbox will bring a premium.

N/A	N/A	$8,800	$7,700	$6,500	$6,000	$5,500	$5,000	$4,500	$4,000	$3,500	$3,000

MODEL 1865 CARBINE - made w/o patchbox, ser. no. range 140,000-145,000. Only 5,000 mfg.

N/A	N/A	$9,000	$8,000	$7,500	$6,500	$5,500	$5,000	$4,500	$4,000	$3,500	$3,000

MODEL 1859 RIFLE - iron patchbox only, long forearm fastened with three barrel bands, approx. 4,300 mfg. in carbine ser. range with lug on barrel for attachment of saber bayonet. Approx. 600 were mfg. with 36 in. long barrel - these will command a premium.

N/A	N/A	$13,000	$10,000	$9,000	$7,500	$7,000	$6,000	$4,000	$3,500	$3,000	$2,500

COFFEE MILL MODEL - experimental variation buttstock with a grinding device and detachable handle that was fitted to several Model 1859 & 1863 Carbines. Designed to provide a quick and easy method for cavalry troops in the field to process coffee beans or corn for meals. Field trials are believed to have been in Trenton, NJ circa 1863. Very few originals known - no official records indicating government acceptance. Originals are extremely rare and values could range from $10,000-$50,000.

Buyer beware! Many fakes exist.

MODEL 1863 RIFLE - adapted for socket bayonet, shared ser. range with carbine. Approx. 6,000 mfg.

N/A	N/A	$9,500	$9,000	$7,500	$6,500	$5,500	$4,500	$3,500	$3,000	$2,800	$2,500

MODEL 1865 RIFLE - only 1,000 mfg. in carbine ser. range.

N/A	N/A	$11,500	$10,500	$8,600	$7,500	$6,000	$5,500	$5,000	$4,500	$4,000	$3,500

Sharps Cartridge Conversions

In 1867, the U.S. government decided to convert their percussion Sharps carbines and rifles to the new .50/70 metallic cartridge. Approx. 31,000 carbines and 1,000 rifles were converted by the Sharps Co. Any original, six groove barrels that were worn beyond specification had a groove liner installed. Those barrels meeting specs. remained unaltered. All buttstocks were stamped on the left side with "D.F.C." in a ribbon cartouche, the initials for the principal sub-inspector, David F. Clark. Damaged buttstocks were all replaced with the plain (no patchbox) Model 1865 buttstock, regardless of the model of the carbine; however, many of the old style buttplates with notches for patchboxes were retained.

.50/70 CARBINES - most had relined three groove barrels, approx. 31,000 remodeled. Those found with original six groove barrels will command a slight premium, as will those Model 1859s & Model 1863s with original patchbox buttstocks.

N/A	N/A	$6,000	$5,000	$4,500	$4,200	$4,000	$3,750	$3,500	$3,000	$2,750	$2,500

.50/70 RIFLES - all had three groove relined barrels, approx. 1,000 converted in 1867. More rare, but do not command any higher prices than their carbine counterparts.

100%	98%	95%	90%	80%	70%	60%	50%	40%	30%	20%	10%

SPRINGFIELD/SHARPS MODEL 1870-1871 - approx. 1,000 rifles and 300 carbines altered by Springfield Armory to fire .50/70 metallic cartridge, in addition to those done by Sharps Co., rifle barrels 35 1/2 in., carbine barrels 22 in., receivers color case hardened, all other metal parts bright finish, own ser. range, and numbered on receiver tang and left side of barrel.

* *Springfield/Sharps Model 1870-1871 Rifles*

N/A	N/A	$6,000	$5,000	$4,500	$4,200	$4,000	$3,700	$3,500	$3,250	$3,000	$2,500

* *Springfield/Sharps Model 1870-1871 Carbines*

N/A	N/A	$8,000	$7,850	$7,500	$7,250	$7,000	$6,500	$6,250	$6,000	$5,500	$5,000

Sharps Metallic Cartridge Models

MODEL 1874 - mfg. in several configurations and a variety of calibers, designed to fire metallic cartridges and was not a conversion from percussion parts, made famous for its deadly accuracy at long distances and became known as the "Buffalo Rifle" of its day. Mfg. in Hartford, CT circa 1874-76, and in Bridgeport, CT circa 1881.

* *Model 1874 Sporting Model* - .40, .44, .45 or .50 cal., variety of barrel lengths and weights, many special order features. Approx. 6,500 mfg.

N/A	N/A	$15,000	$11,000	$9,500	$8,500	$8,250	$8,000	$7,750	$7,500	$7,200	$7,000

* *Model 1874 Business Rifle* - no frills version of the 1874 Sporting, with shorter, round barrel and open sights.

N/A	N/A	$9,500	$8,500	$7,500	$6,750	$5,500	$5,250	$5,000	$4,750	$4,500	$4,250

* *Model 1874 Military Rifle* - .45/70 or .50/70 cal., long forearm and three barrel bands. Approx. 1,700 mfg.

N/A	N/A	$8,000	$7,750	$7,500	$7,000	$6,500	$6,000	$5,000	$4,500	$4,000	$3,500

* *Model 1874 Military Carbine* - most in .50/70 cal., very similar to previous Sharps carbines. Less than 500 mfg.

N/A	N/A	$8,500	$8,250	$8,000	$7,750	$7,500	$7,000	$6,000	$5,500	$5,000	$4,500

* *Model 1874 Meachan Type Conversion* - most in .45/70 cal., very similar to Business Rifle, with both round and octagon barrels, mfg. from Civil War Sharps carbine actions and surplus, as well as new parts by several commercial firms in the 1880s after Sharps Rifle Co. closed. Sharps Co. assembled several hundred of these from 1879-1881 from existing parts on hand.

N/A	N/A	$7,500	$6,800	$6,000	$5,250	$5,175	$5,000	$4,750	$4,500	$4,250	$4,000

While of lesser quality than the Model 1874, these rifles were widely used on the Western frontier and have become very desirable to today's firearms collectors.

MODEL 1878 SHARPS-BORCHARDT - many cals. and barrel lengths, single trigger, hammerless action designed by Hugo Borchardt, carbines, military, sporting, and target rifles were all mfg., but sales suffered from a bolt and lever action market glut. Less than 9,000 mfg. by Sharps Rifle Co. in Bridgeport, CT c. 1878-81.

N/A	N/A	$6,000	$5,750	$5,500	$5,250	$5,175	$5,000	$4,750	$4,500	$4,250	$4,000

Special order or deluxe models with other than standard features will command a premium.

GRADING - PPGS™	100%	98%	95%	90%	80%	70%	60%

SHARPS-LEE - material for 1,300 rifles was purchased in 1879 but little work was done on the U.S. Navy order for 300 rifles before Sharps ceased operations Oct. 18, 1880. Only a few hand-made tool room models for demonstration purposes were completed.

	N/A	$10,000	$8,000	$6,000	$4,750	$4,250	$3,500

Add 50% for carbine or factory sporting rifle.

GRADING - PPGS™	100%	98%	95%	90%	80%	70%	60%

SHERIDAN PRODUCTS INCORPORATED

Previous manufacturer located in Racine, WI.

PISTOLS: SINGLE SHOT

KNOCKABOUT - .22 S-L-LR cal., 5 in. barrel, checkered plastic grips, fixed sights. Mfg. 1953-60.

$195	$150	$110	$100	$85	$75	$60

SHILEN RIFLES, INCORPORATED

Previous manufacturer located in Enis, TX circa 1975-mid 1980s.

RIFLES: BOLT ACTION

Older Shilen rifles have become very desirable for target shooters and other accuracy enthusiasts. Because of their small quantities of manufacture (approx. 3,350 mfg.) and new-found demand, prices have gone up considerably on this trademark. Originally, the Sporters retailed in the $600-$700 range, but at the end, prices were in the $3,500 range.

DGA SPORTER - .17 Rem., .223 Rem., .22-250 Rem., .220 Swift, 6mm Rem., .243 Win., .250 Savage, .257 Roberts, .284 Win., .308 Win., or .358 Win. cal., 3 shot mag., 24 in. barrel, no sights, claro walnut stock.

$1,475	$1,175	$950	$800	$675	$575	$495

DGA VARMINTER - similar to Sporter, except 25 in. medium heavy barrel.

$1,395	$1,100	$900	$775	$650	$575	$495

DGA SILHOUETTE RIFLE - similar to Varminter, .308 Win. cal. only.

$1,395	$1,100	$900	$775	$650	$575	$495

DGA BENCHREST RIFLE - single shot, choice of cals., 26 in. heavy or medium barrel, no sights, choice of fiberglass or walnut stock, thumbhole available.

$1,450	$1,200	$950	$800	$650	$575	$495

Actions for this model are currently selling in the $450 - $550 range.

SHILOH SHARPS RIFLE MANUFACTURING COMPANY

Current manufacturer located in Big Timber, MT since 1983. Previously manufactured by Shiloh Products, a division of Drovel Tool Company of Farmingdale, NY, 1976-1983. Dealer or consumer direct sales.

For more information on Shiloh's lineup of black powder reproductions and replicas, please refer to the *Blue Book of Modern Black Powder Arms* by John Allen (also online).

RIFLES: REPRODUCTIONS

The Shiloh Rifle Mfg. Co. is currently manufacturing quality replicas of Sharps rifles and carbines. Models include: 1874 #2 Creedmor Silhouette Rifle ($2,535 MSR), 1874 Military Carbine ($1,657 MSR), 1874 Business Rifle ($1,657 MSR), 1874 Creedmor Target Rifle ($2,535 MSR), 1874 Quigley Buffalo Rifle ($3,041 MSR), 1874 Long Range Express ($1,754 MSR), 1874 Sporter #3 ($1,657 MSR), 1874 Sporter #1 ($1,754 MSR), 1874 Montana Roughrider ($1,754 MSR), 1874 Saddle Rifle ($1,707 MSR), 1874 Hartford Model ($1,869 MSR), and the 1874 Military ($1,920 MSR). Please contact Shiloh Rifle Mfg. Co. directly regarding availability and the current waiting period (see Trademark Index.)

SHOOTERS ARMS MANUFACTURING INCORPORATED

Current manufacturer established in 1992, and located in Cebu, the Philippines. Currently imported by Century International Arms, located in Delray Beach, FL, and Pacific Arms Corp. in Modesto, CA.

Shooter Arms Manufacturing Inc. makes semi-auto pistols, including the Elite, Commodore, Military, GI, Chief, Scout, Falcon, Raven, Omega, and Alpha. Previous models have included the React, React-2, Military Enhanced, GI Enhanced, and Elite Sport.

GRADING - PPGS™	100%	98%	95%	90%	80%	70%	60%

Shooters Arms Manufacuring Inc. also manufactures a revolver, the Protector, and previously manufactured slide action shotguns. Please contact the importers directly for more information, including pricing and U.S. availability (see Trademark Index).

SIDEWINDER

Previous trademark manufactured by D-Max, Inc. located in Bagley, MN circa 1993-96. Dealer or consumer sales.

REVOLVERS

SIDEWINDER - .45 LC or 2 1/2/3 in. .410 bore shotshells/slugs, 6 shot, stainless steel construction, 6 1/2 or 7 1/2 in. bull barrel (muzzle end bored for removable choke), Pachmayr grips, transfer bar safety, adj. rear sight, unique design permits one cylinder to shoot above listed loads, cased with choke tube, 3.8 lbs. Mfg. 1993-96.

$695	$575	$475	$415	$360	$300	$255

Last MSR was $775.

SIG ARMS AG

Current Swiss company (SIG) established during 1860 in Neuhausen, Switzerland. P 210 pistols are currently imported and distributed by Sig Sauer (formerly SIG Arms, Inc.), established in 1985, located in Exeter, NH. Previously located in Herndon, VA and Tysons Corner, VA.

During late 2000, SIG Arms AG was purchased by SAN Swiss Arms AG, a newly formed company. This new group includes four independently operational companies - Blaser Jadgwaffen GmbH, J.P. Sauer & Sohn GmbH, Sig Sauer (U.S.A.), and SAN Swiss Arms AG. Please refer to these individual listings for current information and pricing.

PISTOLS: SEMI-AUTO

SIG Custom Shop variations of the P 210 were also available in three configurations - United We Stand ($8,990 last MSR) and two variations of the 50 Year Jubilee ($4,995 or $5,999 last MSR).

> **Add $1,473 for .22 LR conversion kit on the following models (not available on the P 210-8).**

TRAILSIDE/TRAILSIDE COMPETITION - please refer to the Hämmerli section for more information and current pricing on these models.

P 210 - 9mm Para. or 7.65mm Para. (disc.) cal., single action, 4 3/4 in. barrel, 8 shot mag., standard weapon of the Swiss Army, 2 lbs.

Originally mfg. in 1947, this pistol was first designated the SP 47/8 and became the standard military pistol of the Swiss Army in 1949. Later designated the P 210, this handgun has been mfg. continuously for over 55 years.

　✳ *P 210 Danish Army M49* - Danish Army version of the Model P 210, approx. 25,000 mfg.

$1,675	$1,375	$1,050	$900	$750	$625	$550

　✳ *P 210-1* - polished finish, walnut grips, special hammer, fixed sights. Importation disc. 1986.

$2,350	$1,950	$1,500	$1,250	$975	$850	$750

Last MSR was $1,861.

　✳ *P 210-2* - matte finish, field or contrast (recent mfg.) sights, plastic (disc.) or wood grips. Limited importation 1987-2002.

$1,675	$1,375	$1,050	$900	$750	$625	$550

Last MSR $1,680.

> **Add 20% for early high polish guns.**
> **Add 20% for West German Police Contract models with unique loaded indicator on slide. Approx. 5,000 mfg. in "D" prefix serial range.**

GRADING - PPGS™	100%	98%	95%	90%	80%	70%	60%

✳ *P 210-5* - matte finish, heavy frame, micrometer target sights, 150mm or 180mm (disc.) extended barrel, hard rubber (disc.) or wood (current mfg.) grips, bottom (EU) or push-button side mounted (U.S.) mag. release, very limited mfg. Limited importation since 1997.

MSR N/A	$2,250	$2,150	$1,675	$1,350	$1,125	$1,000	$895

Add $124 for side mounted mag. release.

✳ *P 210-6* - matte blue finish, fixed (current importation) or micrometer sights, 120mm barrel, checkered walnut grips, bottom (EU) or push-button side mounted (U.S.) mag. release.

MSR N/A	$1,850	$1,700	$1,500	$1,300	$1,125	$1,000	$895

✳ *P 210-7* - .22 LR or 9mm Para. cal., regular or target long barrel, limited importation. Disc.

	$3,375	$2,950	$2,600	$2,300	$1,950	$1,600	$1,275

✳ *P 210-8* - features heavy frame, target sights, and wood grips. Special order only. Limited importation 2001-2003.

	$3,750	$3,250	$2,650	$2,300	$1,950	$1,600	$1,275

Last MSR was $4,289.

✳ *P 210 Deluxe Models* - various models differ in the amount of engraving, gold inlays, carved wood grips, presentation cases, and other special order features available from the factory.

Please contact SIG directly for more information, including availability and pricing.

RIFLES: BOLT ACTION

SHR 970 - .25-06 Rem., .270 Win., .280 Rem., .30-06, .308 Win., .300 Win. Mag. or 7mm Rem. Mag. cal., steel receiver, standard model featuring easy takedown (requires single tool) and quick change 22 or 24 (Mag. cals. only) in. barrel, detachable 3 or 4 shot mag., 65 degree short throw bolt, 3 position safety, standard medium gloss walnut stock with checkering, ultra-fast lock time, nitrided bore, no sights, includes hard carry case, approx. 7.3 lbs. Mfg. 1998-2002.

	$475	$395	$350	$325	$295	$275	$250

Last MSR was $550.

Add $395 for extra barrel.

✳ *SHR 970 Synthetic* - similar to SHR 970, except has checkered black synthetic stock with stippled grip. Mfg. 1999-2002.

	$445	$375	$325	$295	$275	$250	$230

Last MSR was $499.

STR 970 LONG RANGE - .308 Win. or .300 Win. Mag. cal., inlcudes stippled black McMillan composite stock with precision bedding blocks, 24 in. fluted heavy barrel with integral muzzle brake and non-reflective Ilaflon metal coating, cased, 11.6 lbs. Mfg. 2000-2002.

	$875	$795	$675	$575	$525	$475	$425

Last MSR was $899.

RIFLES: SEMI-AUTO

PE-57 - 7.5 Swiss cal. only, semi-auto version of the Swiss military rifle, 24 in. barrel, includes 24 shot mag., leather sling, bipod and maintenance kit. Importation disc. 1988.

	$5,250	$4,650	$3,950	$3,400	$2,950	$2,500	$2,000

Last MSR was $1,745.

The PE-57 was previously distributed in limited quantities by Osborne's located in Cheboygan, MI.

GRADING - PPGS™	100%	98%	95%	90%	80%	70%	60%

SIG-AMT RIFLE - .308 Win. cal., semi-auto version of SG510-4 auto paramilitary design rifle, roller delayed blowback action, 5, 10, or 20 shot mag., 18 3/4 in. barrel, wood stock, folding bipod. Mfg. 1960-1988.

	100%	98%	95%	90%	80%	70%	60%
	$3,875	$3,250	$2,675	$2,300	$2,000	$1,750	$1,500

Last MSR was $1,795.

SG 550/551 - .223 Rem. cal. with heavier bullet, Swiss Army's semi-auto version of newest paramilitary design rifle (SIG 90), 20.8 (SG 550) or 16 in. (SG 551 Carbine) barrel, some synthetics used to save weight, 20 shot mag., diopter night sights, built-in folding bipod, 7.7 or 9 lbs.

	100%	98%	95%	90%	80%	70%	60%
Sig 550 (Rifle)	$8,500	$7,750	$7,000	$6,250	$5,500	$4,950	$4,500
Sig 551 (Carbine)	$10,500	$9,500	$8,875	$8,000	$7,250	$6,500	$5,600

Last MSR was $1,950.

This model has been banned from domestic importation due to 1989 Federal legislation.

SIG 556 Please refer to the Sig Sauer section.

SIG-HÄMMERLI

Previously manufactured by Hämmerli Ltd. in Lenzburg, Switzerland.

PISTOLS: SEMI-AUTO

P240 TARGET PISTOL - .32 S&W Long Wadcutter or .38 Mid-range (disc.) cal., single action, 5 shot mag., 5.9 in. barrel, blue finish, thumbrest walnut grips, adj. sights and trigger, 3 lbs. Importation mostly disc. 1986.

	100%	98%	95%	90%	80%	70%	60%
	$1,475	$1,225	$1,000	$875	$775	$700	$660

Last MSR was $1,350.

Add $100 for Morini adj. grips.

.38 Mid-range cal. is very desirable in this model - healthy (and inconsistent) premiums are being asked.

✱ *P240 Target Pistol .22 Conversion Unit*

	100%	98%	95%	90%	80%	70%	60%
	$550	$495	$400	$335	$290	$245	$215

Last MSR was $595.

SIG SAUER

Current firearms trademark manufactured by SIG Arms AG (Schweizerische Industrie-Gesellschaft) located in Neuhausen, Switzerland. Currently imported, manufactured (some models), and distributed by Sig Sauer, Inc., established in 2007, and located in Exeter, NH. Previously imported and distributed from 1985-2006 by Sigarms, Inc. located in Exeter, NH. Previously located in Herndon, VA and Tysons Corner, VA.

During late 2000, SIG Arms AG (including Sig Sauer) was purchased by SAN Swiss Arms AG, a newly formed company. This new group includes four independently operational companies - Blaser Jadgwaffen GmbH, J.P. Sauer & Sohn GmbH, Sig Sauer (U.S.A.), and SAN Swiss Arms AG. Current trademarks include: Blaser, Mauser, Sauer rifles, Sig rifles, and Sig Sauer pistols. Please refer to these individual listings for current information and pricing.

On Oct. 1, 2007, SIG Arms changed its corporate name to Sig Sauer. Sig Sauer is the largest member of a worldwide business group of firearms manufacturers that includes J.P. Sauer & Sohn GmbH (Germany), Blaser GmbH (Germany), and Swiss Arms SG (Switzerland).

PISTOLS: SEMI-AUTO

Beginning 2001, add approx. $20 for all handguns that are MA compliant (include loaded chamber indicator). Pistols that are NY compliant (includes empty shell casing) are priced the same as the models listed.

The Sigarms Custom Shop, located in Exeter, NH, has recently been established, and offers a wide variety of custom shop services, including action enhancement, full servicing, DA/SA conversions, trigger and hammer modifications, barrel replacement, and many refinishing options. Please contact Sigarms Custom Shop directly for more information and current pricing on these services.

During 2005, the Sigarms Custom Shop produced 12 limited editions, including the P229 Rail (January), P245 w/nickel accents and Meprolight night sights (February), P220 .45 ACP Rail (March), P239 Satin Nickel w/Hogue rubber grips (April), GSR 1911 Reverse Two-Tone (May), P229 Satin Nickel Reverse Two-Tone (June), P232 Rainbow Titanium (July), P226 Rail (August), P220 Sport Stock (September), P239 w/ extra .357 SIG cal. barrel (October), P228 Two-Tone (November), and the P226 package w/ Oakley glasses (December).

Early SIG Sauer pistols can be marked either with the Herndon or Tysons Corner, VA barrel address, and can also be marked "W. Germany" or "Germany". Earlier mfg. had three proofmarks on the bottom front of the slide, with a fourth on the frame in front of the serial number. Early guns with these barrel markings will command a slight premium over prices listed below, if condition is 98%+. Current mfg. has Exeter, NH barrel address.

P 210 - please refer to listing under SIG heading.

MOSQUITO - .22 LR cal., compact design similar to P226, 3.98 in. barrel, polymer frame, 10 shot mag., SA/DA, decocker, ambidextrous manual safety, Picatinny rail on bottom of frame, internal locking device, adj. rear sight, molded composite grips, black, nickel (new 2007), blue, or reverse two-tone (new 2007) finish, 24.6 oz. New 2005.

MSR $343	$300	$265	$235	$200	$185	$170	$155

    Add $15 for nickel or reverse two-tone finish.
    Add $43 for threaded barrel.
    Add $72 for long slide with barrel weight (black finish only, new 2007, Sporter model).

MODEL P220 - .22 LR (disc.), .38 Super (disc.), 7.65mm (disc.), 9mm Para. (disc 1991), or .45 ACP cal., 7 (.45 ACP, disc.) or 8 shot mag., full size, SAO, regular double action or double action only (.45 ACP cal. only), 4.4 in. barrel, decocking lever safety, choice of matte blue (disc. 2006), black nitron (new 2007), stainless steel (mfg. 2001-2007), K-Kote (disc. 1999), electroless nickel (disc. 1991), two-tone with nickel finished slide, or Ilaflon (mfg. 2000 only) finish, lightweight alloy frame, black plastic grips, optional DAK trigger system (DAO with 6 1/2 lb. trigger pull) available during 2005 only, tactical rail became standard 2004 at no extra charge (blue or stainless only), approx. 30.4 or 41.8 (stainless steel) oz. New 1976.

MSR $929	$815	$700	$600	$500	$450	$400	$350

    Add $40 for DAK trigger system (limited mfg. 2005).
    Add $71 for Siglite night sights.
    Add $100 for P220 SAO Model (single action only).
    Add $306 for Crimson Trace laser grips w/night sights.
    Add $129 for two-tone (nickel slide) finish.
    Add $95 for stainless steel frame & slide mfg. 2001-2007).
    Add $40 for Ilaflon finish (disc. 2000).
    Add $45 for factory K-Kote finish (disc. 1999).
    Add $70 for electroless nickel finish (disc. 1991).
    Add $359 for .22 LR conversion kit (current mfg.) or $680 for older mfg. .22 LR conversion kit.
    Subtract 10% for "European" Model (bottom mag. release - includes 9mm Para. and .38 Super cals.).

Values are for .45 ACP cal. and assume American side mag. release (standard 1986).

This model was also available as a Custom Shop Limited Edition during July, 2004 (MSR was $800 and November, 2004 (MSR was $861).

✱ *Model P220 Combat* - features flat Dark Earth finish, alloy frame, Nitron stainless slide, corrosion resistant parts, 8 shot mag., M1913 Picatinny rail, Siglite night sights, with (Combat TB) or w/o (Combat) threaded barrel. New 2007.

MSR $1,143	$1,000	$900	$800	$700	$600	$500	$400

    Add $143 for Combat TB Model w/threaded barrel.

GRADING - PPGS™	100%	98%	95%	90%	80%	70%	60%

✳ *Model P220 Elite* - .45 ACP cal., similar to P220, except has short reset trigger, DA/SA or SAO, two-tone (limited mfg.), black Nitron finish, or stainless steel, 8 shot mag., ergonomic beavertail, Picatinny rail, front cocking serrations, custom shop wood grips or checkered aluminum (platinum Elite) grips. New 2007.

MSR $1,143	$1,000	$900	$800	$700	$600	$500	$400

Add $143 for stainless steel.
Add $72 for platinum Elite with aluminum grips.

✳ *Model P220 Carry Elite* - .45 ACP cal., similar to P220 Elite, except is compact model. New 2007.

MSR $1,143	$1,000	$900	$800	$700	$600	$500	$400

Add $143 for stainless steel.

✳ *Model P220 Carry* - .45 ACP cal., compact model w/full size frame, 3.9 in. barrel, 8 shot single stack mag., DA/SA, DAK, or SAO, black Nitron or two-tone finish, Siglite night sights, Picatinny rail, black polymer or custom shop brown (Carry SAS) wood grips. New 2007.

MSR $929	$815	$700	$600	$500	$450	$400	$350

Add $71 for Siglite night sights.
Add $129 for two-tone finish.
Add $100 for SAO trigger.
Add $164 for P220 Carry SAS model.

✳ *Model P220 Carry Equinox* - similar to P220 Carry, except has two-tone accented slide with nitron finish, Truglo TFO front sight, Siglite rear sight, black wood grips w/custom shop logo. New 2007.

MSR $1,143	$1,000	$900	$800	$700	$600	$500	$400

✳ *Model P220 Compact* - .45 ACP cal., compact beavertail frame, 3.9 in. barrel, 6 shot mag., DA/SA or SAO, black Nitron or two-tone finish, Siglite night sights, black polymer or custom shop wood (Compact SAS) grips. New 2007.

MSR $1,000	$875	$750	$650	$550	$450	$375	$325

Add $58 for two-tone finish.
Add $93 for P220 Compact SAS model.

✳ *Model P220 Equinox* - similar to P220, except has two-tone accented slide with nitron finish, Truglo TFO front sight, Siglite rear sight, black wood grips w/ custom shop logo. New 2007.

MSR $1,143	$1,000	$900	$800	$700	$600	$500	$400

✳ *Model P220 Match* - .45 ACP cal., similar to P220, except has 5 in. cold hammer forged barrel, DA/SA or SAO, ambidextrous safety, two-tone finish, adj. sights, black polymer or custom shop wood (Super Match) grips. New 2007.

MSR $1,115	$985	$900	$800	$700	$600	$500	$400

Add $271 for Super Match model.

✳ *Model P220 NRALE* - .45 ACP cal., features NRA Law Enforcement logo and the words "NRA Law Enforcement" engraved in 24Kt. gold, cocobolo grips with NRA medallions, gold trigger and appointments. Limited production of 1,000, including P226 NRALE 2002-2003.

	$850	$650	$495	N/A	N/A	N/A	N/A

Last MSR was $911.

✳ *Model P220 Sport* - .45 ACP cal., features 4.8 in. heavy compensated barrel, stainless steel frame and slide, 10 shot mag., target sights, improved trigger pull, single or double action, 46.1 oz. Imported 1999-2000, reintroduced 2003-2005.

	$1,375	$975	$800	$695	$585	$485	$415

Last MSR was $1,600.

GRADING - PPGS™	100%	98%	95%	90%	80%	70%	60%

MODEL P225 - 9mm Para. cal., regular double action or double action only, similar to P220, shorter dimensions, 3.85 in. barrel, 8 shot, thumb actuated button release mag., fully adj. sights, 28.8 oz. Disc. 1998.

	$595	$525	$450	$425	$395	$350	$310

Last MSR was $725.

Add $45 for factory K-Kote finish.
Add $105 for Siglite night sights.
Add $45 for nickel finished slide (new 1992).
Add $70 for electroless nickel finish (disc. 1991).

This model was also available as a Custom Shop Limited Edition during March, 2004. MSR is $803.

MODEL P226 - .357 SIG (new 1995), 9mm Para. (disc. 1997, reintroduced 1999), or .40 S&W (new 1998) cal., full size, choice of double action or double action only (new 1992) operation, 10 (C/B 1994), 12 (new mid-2005, .357 SIG or .40 S&W cal.) or 15* (9mm Para. cal. only) shot mag., 4.4 in. barrel, alloy frame, currently available in blackened stainless steel (Nitron finish became standard 2000), two-tone, or nickel (disc. 2002) finish (stainless slide only), tactical rail became standard 2004, choice of traditional DA or DAK trigger system (DAO with 6 1/2 lb. trigger pull, not available in all stainless) available beginning 2005, high contrast sights, automatic firing pin block safety, 31.7 or 34 oz. New 1983.

MSR $929	$815	$700	$600	$500	$450	$400	$350

Add $71 for Siglite night sights.
Add $71 for .357 SIG cal. (includes night sights).
Add $306 for Crimson Trace laser grips w/Siglite night sights (mfg. 2007).
Add $95 for stainless steel frame and slide (mfg. 2004-2005).
Add $129 for two-tone finish (nickel finished stainless steel slide) w/night sights.
Add $45 for K-Kote (Polymer) finish (mfg. 1992-97, 9mm Para. only).
Add $70 for electroless nickel finish (disc. 1991).

This model is also available in double action only (all finishes) at no extra charge.
This model was also available as a Custom Shop Limited Edition during Feb., 2004 (MSR was $1,085). A limited edition P226 America with blue titanium and gold finishes was also available from SIG's Custom Shop (MSR was $7,995).
This model is also available as the P226R Tactical, sold exclusively by Ellet Bros distribtors - no pricing information is available.

✻ Model P226 Jubilee - 9mm Para. cal., limited edition commemorating SIG's 125th anniversary, features gold-plated small parts, carved select walnut grips, special slide markings, cased. Mfg. 1985 only.

	$1,495	$1,175	$950	$835	$685	$585	$485

Last MSR was $2,000.

✻ Model P226 NRALE - .40 S&W cal., features NRA Law Enforcement logo and the words "NRA Law Enforcement" engraved in 24Kt. gold, cocobolo grips with NRA medallions, gold trigger and appointments. Limited production of 1,000, including P220 NRALE, 2002-2003.

	$850	$650	$495	N/A	N/A	N/A	N/A

Last MSR was $911.

✻ Model P226 Sport - 9mm Para. cal., features 5.6 in. match or heavy compensated barrel, stainless steel frame and slide, 10 shot mag., target sights, improved trigger pull, single or double action, rubber grips, 48.8 oz. Mfg. 2003-2005.

	$1,375	$975	$800	$695	$585	$485	$415

Last MSR was $1,600.

GRADING - PPGS™	100%	98%	95%	90%	80%	70%	60%

✻ *Model P226 Elite* - .45 ACP cal., similar to P226, except has short reset trigger, DA/SA or SAO, two-tone (disc.), black Nitron finish, or stainless steel, 8 shot mag., ergonomic beavertail, Picatinny rail, front cocking serrations, custom shop wood grips. New 2007.

MSR $1,143	**$1,000**	**$900**	**$800**	**$700**	**$600**	**$500**	**$400**

Add $143 for stainless steel.
Add $72 for platinum Elite with aluminum grips.

✻ *Model P226 Tactical* - similar to P226, black Nitron finish, Picatinny rail, threaded barrel, post and dot contrast Siglite night sights. New 2007.

MSR $1,186	**$1,025**	**$915**	**$800**	**$700**	**$600**	**$500**	**$400**

✻ *Model P226 ST* - 9mm Para., .40 S&W, or .357 Mag. cal., 4.4 in. barrel, white stainless slide and frame, blue barrel, Picatinny rail, 10 shot mag., 38.8 oz.
While advertised during 2006, this model has not gone into production.

✻ *Model P226 Equinox* - .40 S&W cal., 4.4 in. barrel, two-tone Nitron stainless steel slide, lightweight black anodized alloy frame, nickel accents, 10 or 12 shot mag., Truglo tritium front sight, rear Siglite night sight, Picatinny rail, grey laminated wood grips, 34 oz., mfg. by the Custom Shop. New 2006.

MSR $1,143	**$1,000**	**$900**	**$800**	**$700**	**$600**	**$500**	**$400**

✻ *Model P226 Special Editions* - 9mm Para. or .40 S&W (Cops Commemorative only) cal., engraved, variations include Blackwater (black Nitron finish, Siglite night sights, and wood grips), Navy (black Nitron finish, phosphate components and anchor engraving), or Cops Commemorative (Siglite night sights and wood grips).

MSR $972	**$850**	**$750**	**$650**	**$550**	**$450**	**$400**	**$350**

Add $207 for Blackwater version.

MODEL P226 X-FIVE - 9mm Para. or .40 S&W cal., SA, adj. trigger, 5 in. stainless steel barrel and slide, ambidextrous thumb safety, all stainless construction with magwell, low profile adj. sights, 14 (.40 S&W) or 19 (9mm Para.) shot mag., available in blue, two-tone, stainless or black Nitron finish, checkered walnut grips, includes 25 meter test target, checkered front grip strap, 47.2 oz. New mid-2005.

MSR $2,786	**$2,450**	**$2,150**	**$1,750**	**$1,450**	**$1,250**	**$1,000**	**$850**

✻ *Model P226 X-Five Competition* - 9mm Para. or .40 S&W cal., similar to X-Five, except has black polymer grips. New 2007.

MSR $2,000	**$1,750**	**$1,475**	**$1,250**	**$1,000**	**$850**	**$700**	**$650**

✻ *Model P226 X-Five Allround* - 9mm Para. or .40 S&W cal., adj. sights, ergonomic beavertail grip, DA/SA, stainless slide and frame, black polymer grips. Mfg. 2007.

	$1,395	**$1,175**	**$925**	**$800**	**$675**	**$575**	**$500**

Last MSR was $1,600.

✻ *Model P226 X-Five Tactical* - 9mm Para. cal., black Nitron finish, contrast sights, lightweight alloy frame, Picatinny rail, single action trigger, ergonomic beavertail grips. New 2007.

MSR $1,715	**$1,500**	**$1,250**	**$1,000**	**$850**	**$750**	**$650**	**$575**

MODEL P228 - 9mm Para., choice of double action or double action only (new 1992) operation, compact design, 3.86 in. (compact) barrel, 10 (C/B 1994) or 13* (reintroduced 2004) shot mag., automatic firing pin block safety, high contrast sights, alloy frame, choice of blue, Nitron (new 2004), nickel (mfg. 1991-97), or stainless steel (new 2004) slide, or K-Kote (disc. 1997) finish, 29.3 oz. Mfg. 1990-97, reintroduced 2004-2006.

	$700	**$600**	**$500**	**$450**	**$400**	**$350**	**$310**

Last MSR was $840.

Add $50 for Siglite night sights.
Add $45 for K-Kote (Polymer) finish (disc. 1997).
Add $45 for nickel finished slide (1991-97).
Add $70 for electroless nickel finish (disc. 1991).
This model was also available in double action only (all finishes) at no extra charge.
This model was also available as a Custom Shop Limited Edition during April, 2004 (MSR was $800).

GRADING - PPGS™	100%	98%	95%	90%	80%	70%	60%

MODEL P229 - .357 SIG (new 1995), 9mm Para. (mfg. 1994-96, reintroduced 1999), or .40 S&W cal., compact size, 3.9 in. barrel, similar to Model P228, except has blackened Nitron or satin nickel (disc.) finished stainless steel slide with aluminum alloy frame, 10 (C/B 1994), 12* (.357 SIG or .40 S&W cal. only), or 13 (9mm Para. cal. only, new 2005) shot mag., choice of traditional DA or DAK trigger system (DAO with 6 1/2 lb. trigger pull) available beginning 2005, tactical rail became standard in 2004 (Nitron finish only), includes lockable carrying case, 31.1 or 32.4 oz. New 1991.

MSR $929	$815	$700	$600	$500	$450	$400	$350

Add $71 for Siglite night sights.
Add $306 for Crimson Trace laser grips w/Siglite night sights (new 2007).

Add $129 for two-tone finish (nickel finished stainless steel slide) with night sights.
This model was also available in double action only at no extra charge.
This model was also available as a Custom Shop Limited Edition during June, 2004 (MSR was $873), during August, 2004 (MSR was $916) and during Dec., 2004 (MSR was $844).

* *Model P229 Elite* - .45 ACP cal., similar to P229, except has short reset trigger, DA/SA or SAO, two-tone (disc.), black Nitron finish, or stainless steel, 8 shot mag., ergonomic beavertail, Picatinny rail, front cocking serrations, custom shop wood grips. New 2007.

MSR $1,143	$1,000	$900	$800	$700	$600	$500	$400

Add $72 for platinum Elite with aluminum grips.
Add $143 for stainless steel.

* *Model P229 Equinox* - .40 S&W cal., 4.4 in. barrel, two-tone Nitron stainless steel slide, lightweight black anodized alloy frame, nickel accents, 10 or 12 shot mag., Truglo tritium front sight, rear Siglite night sight, Picatinny rail, grey laminated wood grips, 34 oz., mfg. by the Custom Shop. New 2007.

MSR $1,143	$1,000	$900	$800	$700	$600	$500	$400

* *Model P229 Sport* - .357 SIG or .40 S&W (new 2003) cal., features 4.8 in. match or heavy (disc. 2000) compensated barrel, stainless steel frame and slide, target sights, improved trigger pull, single or double action, 43.6 oz. Mfg. 1998-2000, reintroduced 2003-2005.

	$1,375	$975	$800	$695	$585	$485	$415

Last MSR was $1,600.

* *Model P229 SAS* - .40 S&W cal., 3.86 in. barrel, 12 shot mag., DAK trigger, smooth dehorned stainless steel slide, Siglite night sights, contrast rear sight, light-weight black hard anodized frame, rounded trigger guard, checkered wood grips, designed for snag-free profile for concealed carry, 32 oz. Mfg. by Custom Shop June, 2005 - 2007.

	$865	$775	$675	$575	$500	$425	$350

Last MSR was $1,020.

* *Model P229 HE (Heritage Fund)* - .40 S&W cal., 10 shot, 3.9 in. barrel, slide marked "10th Anniversary P229", frame marked "1992-2002", gold engraving and accents, brushed stainless steel, gold trigger, cocobolo Hogue grips with NSSF Heritage Fund medallion, includes wood display case. Limited mfg. late 2001-2004.

	$1,195	$750	$600	N/A	N/A	N/A	N/A

Last MSR was $1,299.

MODEL P230 - .22 LR (disc.)-10 shot, .32 ACP-8 shot, .380 ACP-7 shot, or 9mm Ultra (disc.) cal., 7 shot, 3.6 in. barrel, regular double action or double action only, blue, composite grips, 17.6 oz. Mfg. 1976-96.

	$425	$375	$300	$270	$240	$215	$190

Last MSR was $510.

Add $35 for stainless slide (.380 ACP only).

GRADING - PPGS™	100%	98%	95%	90%	80%	70%	60%

✳ *Model P230 SL Stainless* - similar to Model P230, except stainless steel construction, 22.4 oz. Disc. 1996.

	$480	$400	$375	$315	$270	$230	$200

Last MSR was $595.

MODEL P232 - .380 ACP cal., choice of double action or double action only, 3.6 in. barrel, 7 shot mag., aluminum alloy frame, compact personal size, blue or two-tone stainless slide, automatic firing pin block safety, composite grips, 17.6 oz. New 1997.

MSR $629	$550	$475	$395	$350	$295	$250	$200

Add $60 for Siglite night sights (mfg. 2001-2006).

Add $156 for night sights and two-tone finish (new 2007).

✳ *Model P232 Stainless* - similar to Model P232, except stainless steel construction, natural finish, 22.4 oz. New 1997.

MSR $858	$750	$625	$475	$400	$350	$300	$275

Subtract approx. 10% if w/o Siglite night sights and Hogue grips (standard beginning 2007).

MODEL P239 - .357 SIG, 9mm Para., or .40 S&W (new 1998) cal., compact personal size, double action or double action only, black Nitron or two-tone stainless steel slide and aluminum alloy frame, firing pin block safety, 3.6 in. barrel, 7 or 8 (9mm Para. only) shot mag., fixed sights, approx. 29 oz. New 1996.

MSR $800	$700	$600	$525	$425	$350	$300	$275

Add $72 for Siglite night sights.
Add $305 for Crimson Trace laser grips and night sights (mfg. 2007).
Add $129 for two-tone stainless slide with night sights.
Add $72 for .357 SIG cal. with night sights.

This model was also available as a Custom Shop Limited Edition during May, 2004 (MSR was $673).

✳ *Model P239 SAS* - 9mm Para. (new 2008) or .40 S&W cal., 3.6 in. barrel, 7 shot mag., DAK trigger, smooth dehorned stainless steel slide, Siglite night sights, contrast rear sight, light-weight black hard anodized frame, rounded trigger guard, checkered/carved wood grips, designed for snag-free profile for concealed carry, 29 1/2 oz. Mfg. by Custom Shop beginning June, 2005.

MSR $1,029	$900	$750	$625	$550	$475	$425	$350

MODEL P245 - .45 ACP cal., compact model featuring 3.9 in. barrel, traditional double action, includes 6 and 8 shot mag., blue, two-tone (disc. 2005), Ilaflon (mfg. 2000 only), or K-Kote (disc. 1999) finish, approx. 30 oz. Mfg. 1999-2006.

	$695	$585	$495	$440	$400	$350	$310

Last MSR was $840.

Add $75 for Siglite night sights.
Add $56 for two-tone or K-Kote finish (disc.).
Add $50 for Ilaflon finish (mfg. 2000 only).

P250 - 9mm Para., .357 SIG, .40 S&W or .45 ACP cal., DAO, choice of 4.7 (full size), 3.9 (Compact), or 3.1 (Subcompact) in. barrel, steel frame with black polymer grip shell (three different sizes), features modular syntheticframe with fire control assembly, 10 (.45 ACP), 17 (.357 SIG or .40 S&W) or 20 (9mm Para.) shot mag., ambidextrous catch lever, black Nitron or two-tone finish, night sights, integrated accessory rail, converts into various calibers by changing slides, grip modules, and magazine, 27.6 oz. New mid-2008.

MSR $699	$625	$550	$500	$450	$400	$350	$300

Add $50 for .45 ACP cal. or two-tone finish.
Add $529 for 9mm Para, .357 SIG, or .40 S&W caliber change package (includes slide assembly, grip module, and magazine), or $556 for .45 ACP package.

GRADING - PPGS™	100%	98%	95%	90%	80%	70%	60%

✻ P250 Compact - similar to P250 Full Size, except has 3.9 in. barrel, 8 (.45 ACP), 13 (.357 SIG or .40 S&W) or 16 (9mm Para.) shot mag., 24.6 oz. New mid-2008.

MSR $699		$625	$550	$500	$450	$400	$350	$300

✻ P250 Subcompact - similar to P250 Compact, except has 3.1 in. barrel, 6 (.45 ACP), 9 (.357 SIG or .40 S&W) or 12 (9mm Para.) shot mag., 22.6 oz. New mid-2008.

MSR $699		$625	$550	$500	$450	$400	$350	$300

GSR 1911 REVOLUTION - .45 ACP cal., single action, 5 in. match grade barrel, choice of white (disc.), standard blue, two-tone, reverse two-tone (new 2007), XO Black (new 2007), or black Nitron finished stainless steel, includes two 8 shot mags., with or w/o under frame Picatinny rail, firing pin safety, front and rear strap checkering, Novak sights, checkered wood (all stainless) or synthetic (blued stainless) grips, approx. 41 oz. Mfg. in Exeter, NH. New 2004.

MSR $1,115		$975	$850	$725	$625	$550	$475	$395

Add $28 for black Nitron finish.
Add $28 for Target Model with adj. target night sights (new 2007).
Add $114 for TTT Model with two-tone finish, black controls, and adj. combat night sights.
Add $271 for STX Model with two-tone finish, flattop, adj. combat night sights and magwell.
Add $100 for platinum Elite with aluminum grips (new 2008).
Subtract $40 for reverse two-tone finish (mfg. 2007).
Subtract $157 for XO Model with black finish, Novak contrast sights, and black ergo-grips (new 2007).

The abbreviation GSR on this model stands for Granite Series Revolution.

REVOLUTION CARRY - similar to GSR, except is carry configuration with short stainless slide, 4 in. barrel, stainless steel frame or black Nitron finish, Novak night sights, 8 shot mag., custom wood grips. New 2007.

MSR $1,115		$975	$850	$725	$625	$550	$475	$395

Add $28 for black Nitron finish.

REVOLUTION COMPACT - .45 ACP cal., short slide and compact frame, 6 shot, stainless or black Nitron finish, 4 in. barrel, available in three variations, Compact, Compact C3 (black hard coat anodized alloy frame, stainless slide and rosewood grips), or Compact RCS (dehorning and anti-snag treatment, black Nitron or two-tone finish and rosewood custom shop grips). New 2007.

MSR $1,115		$975	$850	$725	$625	$550	$475	$395

Add $27 for black Nitron finish.
Add $120 for RCS Model.
Add $28 for C3 Model.

MODEL SIG PRO SP2009 - 9mm Para. cal., otherwise identical to SP2340, 28 oz. Mfg. 1999-2005.

			$510	$450	$355	$290	$260	$220	$195

Last MSR was $640.

Add $60 for Siglite night sights.
Add $31 for two-tone finish.

MODEL SIG PRO SP2022 - 9mm Para., .357 SIG, or .40 S&W cal., 10, 12 or 15 (9mm Para. cal. only) shot mag., 3.85 in. barrel, polymer frame, Picatinny rail, Nitron, blue, or two-tone (disc. 2005) stainless steel slide, black Nitron finish, convertible DA/SA to DAO, optional interchangeable grips, 26.8 (9mm Para.) or 30 oz. Mfg. 2004-2007.

		$495	$440	$355	$290	$260	$220	$195

Last MSR was $613.

Subtract 10% if w/o Siglite night sights (became standard 2007).

GRADING - PPGS™	100%	98%	95%	90%	80%	70%	60%

MODEL SIG PRO SP2340 - .357 SIG, or .40 S&W cal., features polymer frame and one-piece Nitron finished stainless steel or two-tone (new 2001) finished slide, 3.86 in. barrel, includes two interchangeable grips, 10 shot mag., approx. 30.2 oz. Mfg. 1999-2005.

	$510	$450	$355	$290	$260	$220	$195

Last MSR was $640.

Add $60 for Siglite night sights.
Add $31 for two-tone finish.

RIFLES: BOLT ACTION

Please refer to listing in J.P. Sauer & Sohn section.

RIFLES: SEMI-AUTO

SIG 556 - 5.56 NATO cal., gas operated w/rotary bolt, paramilitary design, 16 in. barrel with muzzle brake, polymer forearm, alloy trigger casing, choice of SIG quad-rail (SWAT Model) or tri-rail, integrated Picatinny rails, two-stage trigger, collapsible or collapsible/folding tube stock, Magpul CTR Carbine stock type (SWAT) or M4 style stock (556ER or 556 Holo), 30 shot AR-15 type mag., 7.8-8.7 lbs. New 2007.

MSR $1,565		$1,375	$1,125	$1,000	$900	$800	$700	$600

Add $435 for quad-rail system (SWAT Model).
Add $78 for Holo model with holographic sight.
Add $189 for collapsible stock.
Subtract $200 if w/o iron sights (became standard 2008).

SIG 556 DMR - similar to Model 556, except has 24 in. heavy barrel w/o sights, adj. Magpul PRS stock, vented synthetic forearm, Picatinny rail on bottom of forearm and top of receiver, includes tactical bipod, 12 lbs. New 2008.

MSR $2,286		$2,000	$1,750	$1,550	$1,375	$1,150	$1,000	$900

SHOTGUNS: O/U

The following Aurora shotguns were mfg. by Battista Rizzini, located in Marcheno, Italy.

L.L. BEAN NEW ENGLANDER SERIES - 12, 20, 28 ga., or .410 bore. Imported 2001-2004.

	$1,895	$1,575	$1,325	$1,100	$950	$800	$675

AURORA TR20 FIELD (APOLLO) - 12, 20, 28 ga., or .410 bore, 3 in. chambers except for 28 ga., 26 or 28 in. VR barrels with choke tubes, satin finished low profile boxlock receiver, monobloc construction, removable hinge pins, gold SST, ejectors, deluxe checkered round pistol grip walnut stock and forearm, 6-7 lbs. Mfg. 2000-2005.

	$1,995	$1,750	$1,475	$1,265	$1,050	$925	$800

Last MSR was $2,250.

* *Aurora TR20U Field (Apollo)* - similar to Apollo/Aurora TR20 Field, except has straight English stock (Upland Model) and color case hardened receiver. Mfg. 2000-2005.

	$1,995	$1,750	$1,475	$1,265	$1,050	$925	$800

Last MSR was $2,250.

AURORA TR30 FIELD (APOLLO) - similar to Apollo/Aurora TR20 Field, except has color case hardened receiver with sideplates. Mfg. 2000-2005.

	$2,275	$1,900	$1,675	$1,375	$1,150	$975	$850

Last MSR was $2,650.

GRADING - PPGS™	100%	98%	95%	90%	80%	70%	60%

AURORA TR40 GOLD/SILVER (APOLLO) - similar to Apollo/Aurora TR30 Field, except receiver and sideplates are engraved and have multiple gold bird inlays, choice of color case hardened (Gold Series) or silver receiver (Silver Series) finish, deluxe checkered walnut stock and forearm. Mfg. 2000-2005.

	$2,575	$2,125	$1,850	$1,575	$1,350	$1,100	$950

Last MSR was $3,050.

✳ *Aurora TR40U Gold/Silver (Apollo)* - similar to Apollo/Aurora TR40 Gold/Silver, except has straight English grip stock and silver finished receiver only. Imported 2000 only.

	$2,250	$1,950	$1,725	$1,500	$1,300	$1,000	$825

Last MSR was $2,595.

AURORA TT25 COMPETITION (APOLLO) - 12 or 20 ga., 3 in. chambers, features include polished 5 in. forcing cones and American stock dimensions with palm swell and Schnabel forearm, oil finished checkered walnut stock and forearm, matte finished 28, 30, or 32 (12 ga. only) in. VR barrels, 6 3/4 or 7 1/4 lbs. Mfg. 2000-2005.

	$2,475	$2,000	$1,750	$1,500	$1,300	$1,075	$950

Last MSR was $2,950.

AURORA TT45 COMPETITION - 12 or 20 ga., 28, 30, or 32 (12 ga. only) in. VR barrels. Imported 2001-2005.

	$2,745	$2,250	$1,925	$1,700	$1,500	$1,300	$1,100

Last MSR was $3,350.

SA 3 - 12 or 20 (new 1998) ga., 3 in. chambers, scalloped coin finished monobloc boxlock action with game scene engraving, field or Sporting Clays (new 1998) configuration, 26, 28, or 30 (Sporting Clays only) in. separated barrels with VR and choke tubes, ejectors, SST, checkered walnut stock and forearm, approx. 7 lbs. Mfg. 1997-98 only.

	$1,175	$925	$775	$650	$550	$475	$400

Last MSR was $1,335.

SA 5 - 12 or 20 ga., 3 in. chambers, features coin finished boxlock action with hand engraved detachable side plates, ejectors, SST, select checkered walnut stock and forearm, field or Sporting Clays (new 1998) configuration, 26 1/2, 28, or 30 (Sporting Clays only) in. barrels with VR and choke tubes, supplied with lockable case, 6 or 7 lbs. Mfg. 1997-99.

	$2,175	$1,775	$1,450	$1,225	$1,075	$900	$775

Last MSR was $2,670.

Add $130 for Sporting Clays Model (12 ga. only, 28 or 30 in. barrels).

SILE DISTRIBUTORS

Previous distributor, importer, and previous manufacturer located in New York, NY.
In addition to distributing a wide variety of firearms and related accessories (including the mfg. of stocks and grips), Sile Distributors also had some firearms "private labeled" to their specifications.

SILMA SPORTING GUNS

Current manufacturer established during 1949 and located in Brescia, Italy. No current U.S. importation. Previously distributed and imported beginning 2000 on a limited basis by Legacy Sports, International, LLC, located in Alexandria, VA (Model 70 EJ variations only). All Silma shotguns, double rifles, and combination models are high quality and utilize premium materials in their manufacture.
Please contact the factory directly (see Trademark Index) for current domestic model availability and pricing.

GRADING - PPGS™	100%	98%	95%	90%	80%	70%	60%

RIFLES

Currently, Silma offers one O/U double rifle (Model EX 70 N). This is also available in a combination gun (12 ga. x various cals.). Not currently imported.

SHOTGUNS

In addition to the Model 70 EJ and Superlight models listed, Silma also manufactures other Model 70 configurations. Models 70 and 80 are O/U hunting models available in either 12, 20 ga., or .410 bore. They are available with double triggers standard, extractors or ejectors (extra cost), with or without sideplates, or in superlight configuration. Competition models (including T.J. 70, T.S. 81, Cobra T1, T2, or T3) are also available for trap, skeet, or sporting clays events. Two side-by-side models (AS/70 N and AS/70 EJ) are also available.

MODEL 70 EJ STANDARD O/U - 12 or 20 ga., 3 or 3 1/2 (12 ga. only) in. chambers, similar to Model 70 EJ Deluxe, except has standard grade walnut, 6.9-7.6 lbs. Importation began 2001.

MSR N/A	$775	$625	$525	$475	$425	$375	$335

Add $72 for 12 ga. with 3 1/2 in. chambers.

MODEL 70 EJ DELUXE O/U - 12, 20, 28 ga., or .410 bore, 3 (12 and 20 ga. only) or 3 1/2 in. chambers, 28 in. VR barrels with either multichokes (12 ga. only) or fixed chokes, engraved coin finished boxlock receiver, gold ST (disc.) or SST (standard beginning 2004), deluxe checkered walnut stock and forearm, 6.9-7.6 lbs. Importation began 2001.

MSR N/A	$865	$775	$700	$625	$575	$525	$475

Add $73 for 12 ga. with 3 1/2 in. chambers.
Add $124 for 28 ga. or .410 bore.

MODEL 70 EJ SUPERLIGHT O/U - 12 or 20 ga., 3 in. chambers, similar to Model 70 EJ Deluxe, except has separated barrels and lightweight aluminum frame, 5.6 lbs. Importation began 2001.

MSR N/A	$1,025	$875	$750	$650	$550	$495	$450

MODEL 70 EJ CLAYS - 12 ga., 3 in. chambers, 28 in. vent. barrels with VR and three choke tubes, non-automatic safety, satin silver finish, competition style, oil finished checkered stock and forearm, mechanical SST, 7.9 lbs. Importation began 2003.

MSR N/A	$1,060	$925	$800	$675	$575	$495	$450

SIMILLION, GENE

Current custom rifle maker located in Gunnison, CO. Consumer direct sales.

RIFLES: BOLT ACTION, CUSTOM

EXTREME HUNTER RIFLE - various cals., customer supplied Winchester Model 70 Classic action, match grade barrel, McMillan fiberglass stock, 8 1/2-10 lbs. New 2003.

MSR $6,600	$6,250	$5,000	$4,250	$3,300	$2,500	$2,100	$1,850

Add $800 for Mag. cals through .338.
Add $1,100 for heavy Mags. cals. .375 H&H and greater.

CLASSIC HUNTER RIFLE - various cals., new Winchester Model 70 Classic action, options include LOP, caliber, and barrel length, deluxe walnut, custom made to individual customer specifications. Disc. 2004.

	$6,950	$5,750	$5,150	$4,500	$3,750	$3,000	$2,500

Last MSR was $7,500.

Add $1,000 for Mag. cals. up to .375 H&H.
Add $1,500 for heavy Mag. cals. .375 H&H. and larger.

GRADING - PPGS™	100%	98%	95%	90%	80%	70%	60%

PREMIER MODEL 70 RIFLE - various cals., mostly Winchester new Model 70 action (others available), custom made to individual customer specifications, finest materials and workmanship, individually tested.

MSR $12,800		$11,500	$9,250	$8,250	$7,250	$6,250	$5,250	$4,250

Add $1,000 for Mag. cals. up to .375 H&H.
Add $1,700 for heavy Mag. cals. .375 H&H and larger.

PREMIER MODEL 98 RIFLE - various cals., Granite Mountain Arms Model 98 short or long action, custom made to individual customer specifications, exhibition grade walnut, ebony forend tip, swivel bases, solid steel grip cap, wide variety of custom options. New 2005.

MSR $13,600		$12,000	$9,500	$8,450	$7,350	$6,250	$5,250	$4,250

Add $300 for standard length action, or $2,000 for long Magnum action.
Add $3,900 for scope sighted rifle with long Mag. action.

SIMSEK

Previous shotgun manufacturer located in Turkey.

Simsek manufactured shotguns in O/U, SxS, and semi-auto configurations. They had very limited importation into the U.S.

SIMSON

Previous firearms and airgun manufacturer established in 1856 and located in Suhl, Germany.

Simson & Co. began building guns and gun barrels circa 1856, and continued its enterprise until 1936, when Hitler's dictatorship forced the Simson family to flee the country. The factory continued to build firearms, bicycles, and cars until 1945, when the Soviets took over and the factory was integrated into a Russian state motorcycle company. In 1952, the USSR returned the control of the factory to the GDR. Production of sporting arms, prams, and bicycles slowly resumed, with the main focus on motorcycle manufacture. The company struggled during the 1980s to modernize the production and the facility, but the company finally ceased operations in late 2002, and bankruptcy was declared in Feb., 2003. Collectibility for Simson firearms is mostly for pre-1936 mfg.

Simson made a wide variety of rifles and shotguns, including some private labels. A comprehensive listing of everything Simson made would be nearly impossible, as most of its guns were not imported in the U.S. on a regular basis, and much of the company's history was destroyed after the Russians occupied Suhl after WWII. A general rule for evaluating Simson firearms is to determine the overall desirability of the configuration which takes into consideration the following - action type (boxlock or sidelock), caliber/gauge, ejectors or extractors, plain or engraved frame, special features, cocking indicators, overall eye appeal, and of course, original condition. Each Simson's unique mix of these factors determines the value, and as a result, each gun must be appraised individually. A good pricing guideline is to compare a Simson with other major European trademarks such as Krieghoff and Merkel, determine the value on those, and use them as a comparison.

SIRKIS INDUSTRIES, LTD.

Previous manufacturer located in Ramat-Gan, Israel. Previously imported and distributed by Armscorp of America, Inc. located in Baltimore, MD.

PISTOLS: SEMI-AUTO

S.D. 9 - 9mm Para. cal., double action mechanism, frame is constructed mostly of heavy gauge sheet metal stampings, 3.07 in. barrel, parkerized finish, loaded chamber indicator, 7 shot mag., plastic grips, 24 1/2 oz. Imported under the Sirkis and Sardius trademarks between 1986-90.

	$375	$295	$250	$200	$190	$180	$170

Last MSR was $350.

GRADING - PPGS™	100%	98%	95%	90%	80%	70%	60%

RIFLES

MODEL 35 MATCH RIFLE - .22 LR cal. only, single shot bolt action, 26 in. full floating barrel, select walnut, match trigger, micrometer sights. Disc. 1985.

	$650	$625	$595	$550	$510	$460	$420

Last MSR was $690.

MODEL 36 SNIPER RIFLE - .308 Win. cal. only, gas operated action, carbon fiber stock, 22 in. barrel, flash suppressor, free range sights. Disc. 1985.

	$670	$580	$520	$475	$430	$390	$350

Last MSR was $760.

SKORPION

Please refer to Armitage International, Ltd. in the "A" section of this text.

SMITH-CORONA

Previous WWII subcontractor of 1903 Springfield rifles located in Syracuse, NY.
Please refer to the Springfield Armory listing for more information.

SMITH, L.C.

Current trademark manufacture beginning late 2004 by Marlin Firearms Company, located in North Haven, CT. Previous trademark manufactured 1878-1888 by W.H. Baker & Co and L.C. Smith Maker located in Syracuse, NY, also manufactured 1890-1950 by Hunter Arms Company and L.C. Smith Gun Co. in Fulton, NY, and from 1968-1972 by Marlin Firearms Company, located in New Haven, CT.

The L.C. Smith sidelock shotgun with its famous rotary locking bolt is considered an "American Best" and is recognized as one of America's most prestigious and collectible shotguns. Recently released records indicate that L.C. Smith sold more medium to high grade models than Parker Bros., and collector interest has been very high. The *Blue Book of Gun Values* strongly recommends an expert appraisal when contemplating a purchase of a higher grade L.C. Smith, particularly in 90%+ original condition.

Grading an L.C. Smith. The price guide in this book is based on the percentage of factory finish remaining (PFFR). However, due to the sheer age of most of these guns, the original finish especially case colors have faded over time. Therefore, most Smith collectors generally make the following adjustments to the PFFR when converting to NRA Modern Standards.

NRA PFFR
EXC = 95% BBW & 66% CCC
VG = 90% BBW & 50% CCC
GOOD = 80% BBW & 33% CCC
FAIR = 40% BBW & 0% CCC
NOTE 1. BB is barrel rust blue; W is wood finish and condition; CCC is case color coverage.
NOTE 2. Bold vivid case colors in addition to coverage, will command a substantial premium.
L.C. Smith shotguns with a second set of barrels and forend serial numbered to the gun will add 40% to the value. Barrels only 33%.
Guns that are mechanically factory original, but have been expertly restored (barrels, receivers, and wood) have less collector interest. Therefore, these expertly restored guns should be valued at approx. 80% of the highest value listed for a particular model in this section, assuming the restored gun exhibits little, if any wear.
Collector interest in Syracuse and Fulton damascus barreled models, both hammer and hammerless, is on the rise, and any damascus barrel gun should be examined closely by an expert gunsmith before use.
The L.C. Smith Collectors Association offers a variety of services as well as a collector newsletter. Readers may reach the organization through the website: www.lcsmith.org., or by phone: 513-842-7572.
The Cody Firearms Museum in Cody, WY, has records available for the following L.C. Smith and Hunter Arms Co. shotguns: Hunter Arms Company factory records 1890-1919, production and shipping records 1918-1946 (including Fulton guns), and L.C. Smith Gun Co. records

100%	98%	95%	90%	80%	70%	60%	50%	40%	30%	20%	10%

1946-1950 ("FWS" prefix). Please contact the Cody Firearms Museum directly for historical research on these periods of manufacture (see Trademark Index).

SHOTGUN-RIFLES: BAKER 3-BARREL, HAMMER-DAMASCUS, SYRACUSE MFG. 1878-1888

The ser. no. range is 1-1,600, and estimated total guns produced is 1,186. Values are based on NRA Antique condition.

QUALITY NO. 1

100%	98%	95%	90%	80%	70%	60%	50%	40%	30%	20%	10%
N/A	N/A	N/A	N/A	$1,250	$1,100	$1,025	$950	$775	$600	$475	$325

QUALITY NO. 2

| N/A | N/A | N/A | N/A | $1,400 | $1,200 | $1,050 | $1,000 | $850 | $700 | $525 | $350 |

QUALITY NO. 3

| N/A | N/A | N/A | N/A | $1,700 | $1,500 | $1,350 | $1,250 | $1,100 | $900 | $675 | $475 |

QUALITY NO. 4

| N/A | N/A | N/A | N/A | $1,900 | $1,650 | $1,500 | $1,400 | $1,350 | $1,150 | $875 | $600 |

QUALITY NO. 5

| N/A | N/A | N/A | N/A | $2,500 | $2,250 | $2,000 | $1,750 | $1,625 | $1,500 | $1,250 | $995 |

SHOTGUNS: SXS, BAKER HAMMER-DAMASCUS, SYRACUSE MFG. 1878-1884

The ser. no. range is 50-10,000, and estimated total guns produced is 8,305. Values are based on NRA Antique Conditions.

QUALITY A

100%	98%	95%	90%	80%	70%	60%	50%	40%	30%	20%	10%
N/A	N/A	N/A	N/A	$500	$450	$375	$350	$275	$200	$150	$100

QUALITY B

| N/A | N/A | N/A | N/A | $650 | $550 | $485 | $450 | $350 | $250 | $175 | $125 |

QUALITY C

| N/A | N/A | N/A | N/A | $850 | $700 | $625 | $550 | $425 | $300 | $200 | $150 |

QUALITY D

| N/A | N/A | N/A | N/A | $950 | $750 | $675 | $600 | $475 | $350 | $250 | $175 |

QUALITY E

| N/A | N/A | N/A | N/A | $1,250 | $950 | $750 | $700 | $550 | $450 | $325 | $225 |

QUALITY F

| N/A | N/A | N/A | N/A | $1,700 | $1,250 | $1,000 | $900 | $750 | $600 | $450 | $325 |

SHOTGUNS: SxS, L.C. SMITH SIDELOCK, HAMMER-DAMASCUS, MFG. 1884-1932

L.C. Smith hammer guns have become very popular with collectors and shooters and this popularity has coinsided with the availability of commercially mfg'ed black powder loads. The vast majority of these guns had damascus barrels which have also experienced a similar renaissance in recent years. The values shown are based on damascus barrels in 90% original condition, without pitting, reboring or polishing out. All damascus barreled guns should be examined by an expert gunsmith before being shot.

Serial number ranges for bar action (1884-1902) Syracuse guns: 10,000-17,999 and Fulton guns: 22,500-29,999; 50,500-58,000; 79,000-89,999. Serial number range for back action (1902-1932) Fulton guns: 125,000-180,925.

QUALITY F - available w/royal fluid steel barrels 1901.

100%	98%	95%	90%	80%	70%	60%	50%	40%	30%	20%	10%
N/A	N/A	$1,750	$1,550	$1,375	$1,100	$900	$700	$550	$400	$300	$200

QUALITY E

| N/A | N/A | $2,200 | $1,800 | $1,500 | $1,250 | $950 | $775 | $600 | $450 | $325 | $225 |

	100%	98%	95%	90%	80%	70%	60%	50%	40%	30%	20%	10%

QUALITY D

100%	98%	95%	90%	80%	70%	60%	50%	40%	30%	20%	10%
N/A	N/A	$3,000	$2,500	$1,850	$1,500	$1,000	$795	$625	$475	$350	$250

QUALITY C

N/A	N/A	$4,000	$3,300	$2.475	$1,850	$1,100	$850	$675	$525	$375	$275

QUALITY B

N/A	N/A	$6,000	$4,000	$2,750	$2,100	$1,250	$1,050	$800	$650	$450	$325

QUALITY A - approx. 104 mfg.

N/A	N/A	$10,000	$7,500	$5,500	$3,500	$2,500	$2,000	$1,500	$1,250	$1,000	$750

QUALITY AA - approx. 50 mfg.

N/A	N/A	$12,500	$9,500	$7,500	$5,500	$4,500	$4,000	$3,000	$2,500	$2,000	$1,500

SHOTGUNS: SxS, L.C. SMITH SIDELOCK, HAMMERLESS-DAMASCUS, MFG. 1886-1895

The L.C. Smith "Syracuse style" hammerless guns in both 10 and 12 gauge have become extremely popular with serious collectors. The vast majority of these guns had damascus barrels and the values shown are based on damascus barrels in 90% original condition, without pitting, reboring or polishing out. The Syracuse style guns are all over 100 years old and should therefore, be graded pursuant to NRA Antique Conditions.

Serial number range for Syracuse guns: 16,000-16,999, 18,000-20,999, 22,000-23,500.
Serial number range for Fulton guns: 30,000-40,334 and 500-1,683 (ejector).

> Add $500 for auto ejectors on all grades values at $1,500+.
> Add 33% to values less than $1,500.
> Add $500 for gold dog on triggerguard or $1,000 on lockplates.

QUALITY 0 - new 1895.

N/A	N/A	$1,750	$1,550	$1,375	$800	$700	$500	$450	$400	$350	$300

QUALITY 1 - new 1892.

N/A	N/A	$2,200	$1,800	$1,500	$1,000	$900	$700	$600	$500	$400	$350

QUALITY 2

N/A	N/A	$2,850	$2,200	$1,850	$1,500	$1,150	$900	$750	$600	$450	$300

QUALITY 3

N/A	N/A	$3,500	$2,700	$2,100	$1,800	$1,300	$1,100	$825	$650	$475	$325

QUALITY 4 - approx. 330 mfg.

N/A	N/A	$4,500	$3,500	$2,600	$2,050	$1,400	$1,100	$850	$675	$500	$350

QUALITY 5 - approx. 138 mfg.

N/A	N/A	$6,000	$5,000	$4,000	$3,000	$2,500	$2,000	$1,150	$900	$700	$600

QUALITY 6 - approx. 47 mfg., disc. 1892.

N/A	N/A	$12,500	$11,000	$10,000	$8,000	$6,500	$5,500	$4,500	$3,500	$2,000	$1,000

QUALITY 7 - approx. 35 mfg.

N/A	N/A	$16,500	$15,000	$13,500	$10,500	$8,500	$7,500	$6,500	$5,500	$3,000	$2,000

SHOTGUNS: SxS, L.C. SMITH/HUNTER ARMS, SIDELOCK, HAMMERLESS, FLUID STEEL BARRELS, MFG. 1892-1913

Pre-1913 guns - All values listed are for hammerless 10 and 12 ga. guns with fluid steel barrels (except A-1 Grade). Guns were manufactured in the following gauges on regular weight frames in 8 ga. and 10 ga., and regular and light frames in 12, 16, and 20 ga. Guns with damascus barrels are of almost equal value if the damascus barrels are in 90% original condition, without pitting, reboring or polished out. L.C. Smith shotguns are rare and were all made to exacting standards. Collector interest can be high, and guns in 90%+ original condition are very hard to evaluate and the values shown are meant as a guide only. It is important to note that 16 ga. guns are almost as rare as 20 ga., and that collector interest and values for these gauges are approaching parity.

> Add 50% for 20 ga. on all grades.
> Add 33% for 16 ga. on all grades.

100%	98%	95%	90%	80%	70%	60%	50%	40%	30%	20%	10%

Add $500 for auto ejectors on all grades with values of $1,500+, or 33% for values less than $1,500.

Add $500 for Hunter SST on all grades with values of $1,500+, or 33% for values less than $1,500.

HAMMERLESS GRADES

00 - approx. 58,000 mfg.

N/A	N/A	$1,600	$1,350	$1,100	$850	$650	$550	$500	$450	$400	$350

0 - approx. 30,000 mfg.

N/A	N/A	$1,900	$1,650	$1,400	$1,000	$800	$700	$600	$550	$500	$450

1 - approx. 10,000 mfg.

N/A	N/A	$2,100	$1,950	$1,450	$1,050	$950	$850	$750	$650	$550	$500

2 - approx. 13,000 mfg.

N/A	N/A	$2,900	$2,500	$2,150	$1,650	$1,450	$1,350	$1,250	$1,150	$1,050	$850

3 - approx. 4,000 mfg.

N/A	N/A	$4,000	$3,250	$2,750	$2,200	$1,850	$1,750	$1,650	$1,550	$1,450	$1,150

PIGEON - approx. 1,200 mfg.

N/A	N/A	$5,500	$4,500	$4,000	$3,000	$2,500	$2,000	$1,850	$1,750	$1,650	$1,350

4 - approx. 455 mfg.

N/A	N/A	$7,000	$5,800	$4,800	$3,800	$3,300	$2,800	$2,600	$2,500	$2,400	$2,000

A1 - Syracuse style frames, damascus barrels only, approx. 740 mfg.

N/A	N/A	$7,000	$5,800	$4,800	$3,800	$3,300	$2,800	$2,600	$2,500	$2,400	$2,000

5 - approx. 485 mfg.

N/A	N/A	$9,500	$7,500	$6,000	$5,000	$4,000	$3,600	$3,500	$3,400	$3,300	$2,800

MONOGRAM - approx. 131 mfg.

N/A	N/A	$14,500	$12,000	$10,000	$8,000	$7,000	$6,000	$5,500	$5,000	$4,500	$4,000

A2 - approx. 210 mfg.

N/A	N/A	$16,500	$14,000	$12,000	$9,500	$7,500	$7,000	$6,500	$6,000	$5,000	$4,500

A3 - approx. 18 mfg.

N/A	N/A	$40,000	$32,500	$25,000	$20,000	$17,500	$15,000	$13,000	$12,000	$10,000	$9,000

SHOTGUNS: SxS, L.C. SMITH/HUNTER ARMS, SIDELOCK, HAMMERLESS, FLUID STEEL BARRELS, MFG. 1913-1950

Post 1913 guns - Values shown are for hammerless 12 ga. guns with fluid steel barrels. Guns were manufactured in 12, 16, 20 ga. and .410 bore on either regular or lightweight frames. Guns with damascus barrels are of almost equal value if the damascus barrels are in 90%+ original condition, without pitting, reboring or polished out. L.C. Smith shotguns are rare and were all made to exacting standards. Collector interest can be high, and guns in 90%+ original condition are very hard to evaluate and the values shown are meant as a guide only. It is important to note that 16 ga. guns are almost as rare as 20 ga., and that collector interest and values for these gauges are approaching parity.

Add 50% for 20 ga. on all grades.

Add 33% for 16 ga. on all grades.

Add 300% for .410 bore on Field Grades.

Add 400% for .410 bore on Grades Ideal and higher.

Add $500 for auto ejectors on all grades with values of $1,500+, or 33% for values less than $1,500.

Add $500 for Hunter SST on all grades with values of $1,500+, or 33% for values less than $1,500.

Add $500 for vent. rib. on all grades with values of $1,500+, or 33% for values less than $1,500.

100%	98%	95%	90%	80%	70%	60%	50%	40%	30%	20%	10%

HAMMERLESS GRADES

FIELD - approx. 195,000 mfg.

100%	98%	95%	90%	80%	70%	60%	50%	40%	30%	20%	10%
N/A	N/A	$1,600	$1,350	$1,150	$850	$650	$550	$500	$450	$425	$375

IDEAL - approx. 26,000 mfg.

| N/A | N/A | $2,300 | $1,950 | $1,650 | $1,200 | $950 | $800 | $700 | $650 | $500 | $450 |

SKEET SPECIAL - includes AE, SST, and BTF, approx. 770 mfg.

| N/A | N/A | $3,500 | $3,000 | $2,650 | $2,200 | $2,000 | $1,900 | $1,800 | $1,700 | $1,500 | $1,350 |

PREMIER SKEET - includes AE, SST, and BTF, approx. 510 mfg.

| N/A | N/A | $3,500 | $3,000 | $2,650 | $2,200 | $2,000 | $1,900 | $1,800 | $1,700 | $1,500 | $1,375 |

TRAP - approx. 3,400 mfg.

| N/A | N/A | $2,700 | $2,300 | $2,000 | $1,500 | $1,200 | $1,000 | $900 | $800 | $650 | $550 |

SPECIALTY - approx. 6,700 mfg.

| N/A | N/A | $3,500 | $3,100 | $2,700 | $2,200 | $1,900 | $1,800 | $1,700 | $1,600 | $1,400 | $1,200 |

EAGLE - approx. 580 mfg.

| N/A | N/A | $7,000 | $5,800 | $4,800 | $4,000 | $3,500 | $3,000 | $2,700 | $2,500 | $2,200 | $1,900 |

CROWN - approx. 890 mfg.

| N/A | N/A | $9,500 | $7,500 | $6,000 | $5,000 | $4,000 | $3,600 | $3,500 | $3,400 | $3,300 | $2,800 |

MONOGRAM - approx. 140 mfg.

| N/A | N/A | $14,500 | $12,000 | $10,000 | $8,000 | $7,000 | $6,000 | $5,500 | $5,000 | $4,300 | $4,000 |

PREMIER - approx. 28 mfg.

| N/A | N/A | $40,000 | $32,500 | $25,000 | $20,000 | $17,500 | $15,000 | $13,000 | $12,000 | $10,000 | $9,000 |

DELUXE - approx. 30 mfg.

| N/A | N/A | $60,000 | $52,500 | $45,000 | $35,000 | $30,000 | $25,000 | $23,000 | $21,000 | $19,000 | $18,000 |

SHOTGUNS: SINGLE BARREL TRAP, BOXLOCK, HAMMERLESS, MFG. 1917-1950

The L.C. Smith single barrel trap is considered one of America's best made guns, and awards for both the guns and shooters are legendary, including Olympic medals and world titles. Collector interest can be high, and an expert appraisal is recommended on guns in 80%+ condition. Single barrel trap models were 12 ga. only, with 32 or 34 in. barrel, boxlock, auto ejector, checkered pistol grip stock and recoil pad. Approx. 2,650 were mfg. between 1917-1951.

OLYMPIC - approx. 662 mfg.

100%	98%	95%	90%	80%	70%	60%	50%	40%	30%	20%	10%
N/A	N/A	$2,500	$2,000	$1,500	$1,000	$800	$750	$700	$600	$550	$500

SPECIALITY - approx. 1,861 mfg.

| N/A | N/A | $3,000 | $2,500 | $2,000 | $1,350 | $1,150 | $1,100 | $1,050 | $1,000 | $800 | $650 |

EAGLE - approx. 56 mfg.

| N/A | N/A | $5,000 | $4,000 | $3,500 | $2,500 | $1,750 | $1,400 | $1,250 | $1,200 | $1,000 | $900 |

CROWN - approx. 88 mfg.

| N/A | N/A | $7,500 | $6,000 | $5,000 | $4,000 | $2,500 | $2,000 | $1,800 | $1,600 | $1,500 | $1,400 |

MONOGRAM - approx. 15 mfg.

| N/A | N/A | $12,500 | $10,500 | $9,000 | $7,000 | $6,000 | $5,000 | $4,500 | $4,000 | $3,500 | $3,000 |

PREMIER - approx. 2 mfg.

Extreme rarity precludes accurate pricing on this model.

DELUXE - approx. 3 mfg.

Extreme rarity precludes accurate pricing on this model.

100%	98%	95%	90%	80%	70%	60%	50%	40%	30%	20%	10%

SHOTGUNS: SxS, HUNTER ARMS, FULTON BOXLOCK, HAMMERLESS, FLUID STEEL, MFG. 1915-1945

These models have been unduly maligned over the years, being referred to as cheap box-locks, and are not to be confused with actual L.C. Smith sidelock shotguns. In reality, these models are high quality, inexpensive boxlocks built with quality similar to field grade L.C. Smiths. The receiver, forend iron, trigger guard and triggers were all machined (not stamped) from forgings. These models have excellent durability and there is collector interest. Manufactured in 12, 16, 20 ga. and .410 bore with 26, 28, 30, or 32 in. barrels.

> Add 50% for 20 ga.
> Add 33% for 16 ga.
> Add 250% for .410 bore.
> Add $150 for non-selective single trigger.

FULTON - plain checkered stock with half pistol grip.

N/A	N/A	$600	$550	$500	$400	$300	$250	$225	$200	$175	$150

FULTON SPECIAL - checkered stock with full pistol grip, decorated frame.

N/A	N/A	$700	$650	$600	$500	$400	$350	$325	$300	$275	$250

HUNTER SPECIAL - similar to Fulton Special, except has L.C. Smith rotary locking bolt system.

N/A	N/A	$825	$775	$700	$600	$500	$450	$425	$400	$375	$350

SHOTGUNS: SxS, L.C. SMITH/MARLIN, SIDELOCK, HAMMERLESS, FLUID STEEL, MFG. 1968-1973

The Marlin Firearms Company reintroduced the L.C. Smith trademark in 1968. These models are considered real L.C. Smiths, not copies, and collector interest is increasing. The following Marlin-manufactured shotguns with an "FWM" prefix that were manufactured through 1971 can be researched by the Cody Firearms Museum.

FIELD - 12 ga., 28 in. barrels, aluminum vent. rib, F/M chokes, extractors, double triggers, checkered pistol grip stock.

N/A	N/A	$800	$700	$600	$500	$475	$450	$425	$400	$375	$350

DELUXE - 12 ga., 28 in. barrels, Simmons floating vent. rib, F/M chokes, extractors, double triggers, select walnut PG stock, beavertail forearm.

N/A	N/A	$1,100	$1,000	$900	$750	$675	$650	$625	$500	$450	$400

GRADING - PPGS™	100%	98%	95%	90%	80%	70%	60%

SHOTGUNS: O/U, L.C. SMITH/MARLIN, CURRENT MFG. BEGINNING 2005

MODEL LC12 - 12 ga., 28 in. vent. rib barrels with choke tubes, SST, ejectors, fleur-de-lis checkered walnut pistol grip stock with fluted comb, recoil pad, bead front sight, approx. 7 1/4 lbs. Mfg. for Marlin in Italy beginning 2005.

MSR $1,254	$1,025	$885	$765	$625	$525	$450	$400

MODEL LC20 - 20 ga., 26 in. vent. rib barrels with choke tubes, otherwise similar to LC12, approx. 6 3/4 lbs. Mfg. for Marlin in Italy beginning 2005.

MSR $1,254	$1,025	$885	$765	$625	$525	$450	$400

SHOTGUNS: SxS, L.C. SMITH/MARLIN, CURRENT MFG. BEGINNING 2005

MODEL LC12-DB - 12 ga., boxlock action patterned after the first generation L.C. Smith action, 28 in. vent. rib barrels with choke tubes, single trigger, ejectors, detachable sideplates, semi-beavertail forearm, fleur-de-lis checkered walnut pistol grip stock with fluted comb, recoil pad, bead front sight, approx. 6 1/4 lbs. Mfg. for Marlin in Italy beginning 2005.

MSR $1,962	$1,650	$1,425	$1,250	$1,125	$900	$750	$625

GRADING - PPGS™	100%	98%	95%	90%	80%	70%	60%

MODEL LC20-DB - 20 ga., 26 in. vent. rib barrels with choke tubes, otherwise similar to Model LC12-DB, approx. 6 lbs. Mfg. for Marlin in Italy beginning 2005.

MSR $1,962 $1,650 $1,425 $1,250 $1,125 $900 $750 $625

MODEL LC28-DB/LC410-DB - 28 ga. or .410 bore, 26 in. vent. rib barrels with three choke tubes, scaled down version of the Model LC20-DB, gold game scenes on sides and bottom of receiver, approx. 5 lbs. Mfg. for Marlin in Italy beginning 2007.

MSR $1,484 $1,250 $1,075 $925 $825 $725 $625 $550

SMITH & WESSON

Current manufacturer located in Springfield, MA, 1857 to date. Partnership with H. Smith & D.B. Wesson 1856-1874. Family owned by Wesson 1874-1965. S&W became a subsidiary of Bangor-Punta from 1965-1983. Between 1983-1987, Smith & Wesson was owned by the Lear Siegler Co. On May 22, 1987, Smith & Wesson was sold to Tomkins, an English holding company. During 2001, Tomkins sold Smith & Wesson to Saf-T-Hammer, an Arizona-based safety and security company.

Smith & Wessons have been classified under the following category names - TIP-UPS, TOP-BREAKS, SINGLE SHOTS, EARLY HAND EJECTORS (Named Models), NUMBERED MODEL REVOLVERS (Modern Hand Ejectors), SEMI-AUTOS, RIFLES, and SHOTGUNS.

Each category is fairly self-explanatory. Among the early revolvers, Tip-ups have barrels that tip up so the cylinder can be removed for loading or unloading, whereas Top-breaks have barrels & cylinders that tip down with automatic ejection.

Hand Ejectors are the modern type revolvers with swing out cylinders. In 1958, S&W began a system of numbering all models they made. Accordingly, the Hand Ejectors have been divided into two sections - the Early Hand Ejectors include the named models introduced prior to 1958. The Numbered Model Revolvers are the models introduced or continued after that date, and are easily identified by the model number stamped on the side of the frame, visible when the cylinder is open. The author wishes to express his thanks to Mr. Sal Raimondi, Jim Supica, Rick Nahas, and Roy Jinks, the S&W Historian, for their updates and valuable contributions.

For more information and current pricing on both new and used Smith & Wesson airguns, please refer to the *Blue Book of Airguns* by Dr. Robert Beeman & John Allen (also online). Factory special orders, such as ivory or pearl grips, special finishes, engraving, and other production rarities will add premiums to the values listed. After 1893, all ivory and pearl grips had the metal S&W logo medallions inserted on top.

TIP-UPS

Spur-trigger rimfires, these include the earliest S&W revolvers, made 1857-1881. A latch at the bottom front of the frame allows the hinged barrel to be tipped up and the cylinder removed for loading and unloading. These pistols are listed in order of model number (1, 1 1/2, 2).

MODEL NO. 1 FIRST ISSUE TIP-UP - .22 Short cal., single action, 7 shot non-fluted cylinder, 3 3/16 in. octagon barrel, bottom break, spur trigger, silver-plated brass frame, blue barrel and cylinder, square rosewood grips, circular sideplate, cross-section of frame is oval with rounded frame sides. Approx. 11,500 mfg. 1857-60.

✳ *Model No. 1 First Issue Tip-Up First Type* - serial range approx. 1-200.

Extreme rarity factor of this model precludes accurate pricing - a nice condition model can easily exceed $10,000.

✳ *Model No. 1 First Issue Tip-Up Second Type* - serial range approx. 200-1130.

Extreme rarity factor of this model precludes accurate pricing - a nice condition model can easily exceed $10,000.

100%	98%	95%	90%	80%	70%	60%	50%	40%	30%	20%	10%

✳ *Model No. 1 First Issue Tip-Up Third Type* - serial range approx. 1130-3000.

| N/A | N/A | $8,000 | $7,000 | $5,500 | $5,000 | $4,500 | $3,000 | $2,500 | $2,000 | $1,500 | $1,000 |

✳ *Model No. 1 First Issue Tip-Up Fourth Type* - serial range approx. 3000-4200.

| N/A | $3,500 | $3,000 | $2,000 | $1,800 | $1,650 | $1,600 | $1,500 | $1,350 | $1,200 | $1,000 | $900 |

✳ *Model No. 1 First Issue Tip-Up Fifth Type* - serial range approx. 4200-5500.

| N/A | $3,500 | $3,000 | $2,000 | $1,800 | $1,650 | $1,600 | $1,500 | $1,350 | $1,200 | $1,000 | $900 |

✳ *Model No. 1 First Issue Tip-Up Sixth Type* - serial range approx. 5,500-11,500.

| N/A | $2,000 | $1,900 | $1,800 | $1,600 | $1,500 | $1,400 | $1,300 | $1,100 | $900 | $800 | $750 |

MODEL NO. 1 SECOND ISSUE TIP-UP - similar to First Issue, except flat-sided frame and irregular-shaped sideplate. 114,900 mfg. 1860-1868. Serial range approx. 11,500 - approx. 126,000.

| $1,500 | $1,000 | $700 | $650 | $600 | $575 | $550 | $500 | $450 | $400 | $350 | $300 |

An early sideplate variation with 2 patent dates on cylinder occurred in the serial range 11,500-12,100. The second sideplate variation with 2 patent dates occurred in the serial range 12,100-20,000.

✳ *Model No. 1 Second Issue Tip-Up Second Quality*

Extreme rarity precludes accurate pricing on this model. May bring double or triple values over the Model No. 1 Second Issue Tip-Up. Beware of fakes!

MODEL NO. 1 THIRD ISSUE TIP-UP - similar to Second Issue, except fluted cylinder, round barrel, and birdshead grip. 131,163 mfg. 1868-82. This model has its own serial range no. 1-131,163. Mfg. 1868-1882.

✳ *Model No. 1 Third Issue Tip-Up 3 3/16 in. Barrel Model.* - will have markings on top of barrel.

| $1,500 | $1,000 | $600 | $500 | $425 | $375 | $350 | $300 | $250 | $225 | $200 | $175 |

✳ *Model No. 1 Third Issue Tip-Up Short Barrels 2 11/16 - 2 3/4 in.* - will have markings on side of barrel.

| $900 | $850 | $775 | $720 | $680 | $640 | $600 | $560 | $520 | $480 | $440 | $400 |

MODEL NO. 1 1/2 OLD MODEL (MODEL 1 1/2 FIRST ISSUE) - .32 rimfire cal., single action, 3 1/2 or 4 (rare) in. octagon barrel, 5 shot non-fluted cylinder, bottom break, spur trigger, blue or nickel, rosewood grips, square butt. 26,300 mfg. 1865-68. Serial range 1-approx. 26,300.

| $1,200 | $800 | $600 | $500 | $425 | $350 | $275 | $250 | $225 | $210 | $195 | $185 |

Early production had 2 patent dates with the barrel markings (approx. serial range 1-15,500). Later production had 3 patent dates (approx. serial range 15,501-26,300).

✳ *Model No. 1 1/2 Old Model 4 in. Barrel*

Extreme rarity precludes accurate pricing on this model. May bring double or triple values over the Model No. 1 1/2 Old Model. Watch for fakes (i.e. stretched barrels).

✳ *Model 1 1/2 Old Model Transitional* - octagon barrel with birdshead grips, serial range 27,200-28,800, rare.

| $3,000 | $2,500 | $1,800 | $1,500 | $1,350 | $1,275 | $1,200 | $1,125 | $1,075 | $1,000 | $950 | $900 |

MODEL NO. 1 1/2 NEW MODEL (MODEL 1 1/2 SECOND ISSUE) - similar to First Issue, with birdshead grips and round barrel, fluted cylinder. 100,800 mfg. 1868-75. Serial range 26,301-127,100.

✳ *Model No. 1 1/2 New Model Short Barrel Model* - barrel markings on side, length varies from 2 1/2-2 3/4 in. (scarce).

Extreme rarity precludes accurate pricing on this model. May bring double or triple values over the Model No. 1 1/2 New Model. Beware of fakes!

✳ *Model No. 1 1/2 New Model 3 1/2 in. Barrel Model*

| $900 | $750 | $500 | $400 | $350 | $300 | $225 | $200 | $180 | $165 | $150 | $135 |

MODEL NO. 2 ARMY TIP-UP - .32 rimfire long cal., similar in appearance to No. 1 1/2 First Issue, except 6 shot cylinder, different barrel lengths, used as a sidearm during Civil War. 77,155 mfg. 1861-74. Serial number range 1-77,155.

100%	98%	95%	90%	80%	70%	60%	50%	40%	30%	20%	10%

✱ Model No. 2 Army Tip-Up 5 or 6 in. Standard Model

$3,000	$2,500	$1,500	$1,000	$900	$800	$700	$625	$525	$450	$400	$375

Premiums exist for early 2 pin models under ser. no. 3,000. Large premiums will be asked for 4 in. barrel - beware of fakes!

TOP-BREAKS

These revolvers have a latch just in front of the hammer, which locks the barrel to the frame. When the action is opened, the barrel & cylinder tip down, with an automatic extractor ejecting the shells. Mfg. 1870-1940, they include single action (spur-trigger or trigger guard), double action, and safety hammerless designs. They are listed in order of frame size. Model 1 1/2 is the smallest or .32 cal. pocket sized frame; Model 2 is the medium or .38 cal. belt sized frame; Model 3 is the large holster or .44 cal. frame. Within each frame size, they are listed by action type - SA, DA, or Hammerless, as applicable.

Changes from one Top-Break model type to another are not necessarily definitive at a specific serial number. Therefore, an overlap of serial numbers from one model to another may be observed.

.32 SINGLE ACTION (MODEL 1 1/2 CENTERFIRE) - .32 S&W cal., spur trigger, top break, rebounding hammer, auto extraction, 3, 3 1/2, 6 (rare), 8 (rare) or 10 (rare) in. barrel. 97,599 mfg. 1878-1892. Serial range 1-97,599.

✱ .32 Single Action Later Model - with strain screw, remainder of serial range.

$750	$500	$400	$350	$300	$275	$250	$225	$210	$200	$190	$150

Add 10%-15% for early models under ser. no. 6,000 w/o strain screw.
Add 50%-100% for factory original 6, 8, or 10 in. barrel, depending on the original condition factor.

.32 DOUBLE ACTION FIRST MODEL - .32 S&W cal., 5 shot fluted cylinder, 3 in. round barrel, square edged side plate, blue or nickel finish, black rubber grips, one of the rarest of all S&Ws. Only 30 mfg. 1880. Serial range 1-30.

Extreme rarity precludes accurate pricing on this model.

.32 DOUBLE ACTION SECOND MODEL - similar to First Model, except irregular shaped sideplate, 3, 3 1/4, 4, 5, or 6 in. barrel, 22,142 mfg. 1880-82. Serial range 31-22,172.

$475	$425	$380	$340	$300	$260	$220	$180	$150	$120	$100	$90

.32 DOUBLE ACTION THIRD MODEL - similar to Second Model, except without groove around cylinder. 22,232 mfg. 1882-83. Serial range 22,173-43,405.

$475	$425	$380	$340	$300	$260	$220	$180	$150	$120	$100	$90

.32 DOUBLE ACTION FOURTH MODEL - similar to Third Model, except rounded triggerguard, pinned front sight. 239,600 mfg. 1883-1909. Serial range 43,406-approx. 282,999.

$345	$305	$270	$240	$210	$185	$160	$135	$115	$100	$90	$85

An 8 or 10 in. barrel on this model will command a premium.

.32 DOUBLE ACTION FIFTH MODEL - similar to Fourth Model, except integral front sight. 44,641 mfg. 1909-19. Serial range approx. 282,300-327,641.

$375	$335	$300	$270	$240	$215	$190	$165	$135	$120	$105	$90

.32 SAFETY HAMMERLESS FIRST MODEL (LEMON SQUEEZER) - .32 S&W cal., double action only, 5 shot fluted cylinder, 2, 3 (most common), 3 1/4, 3 1/2, or 6 (rare) in. round barrel, blue or nickel, black rubber grips. This model was officially called the New Departure. 91,417 mfg. 1888-1902. Serial range 1-91,417.

Short 2 in. barrel versions known as "Bicycle model" will bring 25% to 50% premium on all Safety Hammerless models. Six inch barrels will bring a premium as well.

✱ .32 Safety Hammerless First Model Standard - 2, 3, 3 1/4, or 3 1/2 in. barrel.

$500	$475	$450	$425	$400	$375	$350	$325	$275	$235	$185	$150

100%	98%	95%	90%	80%	70%	60%	50%	40%	30%	20%	10%

.32 SAFETY HAMMERLESS SECOND MODEL - 2, 3, 3 1/4, 3 1/2, or 6 in. barrel, similar to First Model with pinned front sight and T-shaped latch. 78,500 mfg. 1902-09. Serial range 91,418-170,000.

100%	98%	95%	90%	80%	70%	60%	50%	40%	30%	20%	10%
$450	$425	$400	$375	$350	$325	$300	$275	$235	$200	$165	$130

.32 SAFETY HAMMERLESS THIRD MODEL - 2, 3, 3 1/4, 3 1/2, or 6 in. barrel, usually has forged front sight. 73,000 mfg. 1909-37. Serial range 163,082-242,981 (with some overlap from the Second Model).

100%	98%	95%	90%	80%	70%	60%	50%	40%	30%	20%	10%
$450	$425	$400	$375	$350	$325	$300	$275	$235	$200	$165	$130

.38 SINGLE ACTION FIRST MODEL (BABY RUSSIAN) WITH SPUR TRIGGER - .38 S&W cal., 5 shot fluted cylinder, 3 1/4, 4, 5, or 6 in. barrel, blue with wood grips, nickel with "S&W" monogram hard black or red rubber grips. 25,548 mfg. 1876-77. Serial range 1-25,548.

✳ *.38 Single Action First Model Standard*

100%	98%	95%	90%	80%	70%	60%	50%	40%	30%	20%	10%
$1,750	$700	$600	$500	$400	$350	$325	$300	$275	$250	$225	$200

Substantial premiums will be asked for "Aldrich" safety models (first 50-100 guns). Add a slight premium for ser. nos. under 1,500 with filler screws on right side of frame.

.38 SINGLE ACTION SECOND MODEL - similar to above, except very short ejector housing under barrel, cal. and cylinder same as above, 3 1/4, 4, 5, 6, 8, or 10 in. barrel, grips same as above. 108,225 mfg. 1877-1891. Serial range 1-108,255.

✳ *.38 Single Action Second Model Standard*

100%	98%	95%	90%	80%	70%	60%	50%	40%	30%	20%	10%
$700	$500	$375	$285	$250	$225	$210	$200	$190	$185	$180	$150

✳ *.38 Single Action Second 8 or 10 in. Barrel*

Extreme rarity precludes accurate pricing on this model.

.38 SINGLE ACTION THIRD MODEL (MODEL OF 1891) - similar to above, except has trigger guard, cal. and cylinder same as above, 3 1/4, 4, 5, or 6 in. barrel (also accepts the single shot barrel), blue or nickel finish with "S&W" monogram, hard black rubber grips. 26,850 mfg. 1891-1911. Serial range 1-28,107 which also includes the serial number range of the Single Shot First Model in .22 LR, .32 S&W, or .38 S&W cal. and the .38 S.A. Mexican Model described below. Barrel marked "Model of 1891".

100%	98%	95%	90%	80%	70%	60%	50%	40%	30%	20%	10%
$2,600	$2,300	$1,800	$1,525	$1,275	$1,075	$950	$850	$775	$700	$625	$550

Add 50%-75% for single shot barrel with matching serial number.

.38 SINGLE ACTION MEXICAN MODEL - essentially same as above, except has inserted spur trigger, .38 S&W cal., 5 shot fluted cylinder, 3 1/4, 4, 5, or 6 in. barrel, blue or nickel finish, "S&W" monogram checkered hard rubber or walnut grips. Features unique to this model are flat sided hammer, half cock notch, and "inserted" spur trigger assembly (not integral with frame). This model would also accept the single shot barrel, limited mfg. 1891-1911. Approx. 2,000 mfg. in ser. no. range 1-28107. Watch out for fakes (and conversions)!

100%	98%	95%	90%	80%	70%	60%	50%	40%	30%	20%	10%
N/A	$4,000	$3,500	$2,750	$2,000	$1,650	$1,400	$1,250	$1,150	$1,050	$975	$950

Add 50%-75% for single shot barrel with matching serial number.

.38 DOUBLE ACTION FIRST MODEL - .38 S&W cal., 5 shot fluted cylinder, 3 1/4 or 4 in. barrel, blue or nickel finish, "S&W" monogram checkered hard rubber grips. 4,000 mfg. 1880. Serial range 1-4,000.

100%	98%	95%	90%	80%	70%	60%	50%	40%	30%	20%	10%
$900	$850	$750	$650	$550	$475	$400	$325	$250	$200	$175	$150

.38 DOUBLE ACTION SECOND MODEL - .38 S&W cal., cylinder same as above, 3 1/4, 4, 5, or 6 in. barrel, blue or nickel finish, "S&W" monogram checkered hard rubber grips in black or red. 115,000 mfg. 1880-84. Serial range approx. 4,001-approx. 119,000.

100%	98%	95%	90%	80%	70%	60%	50%	40%	30%	20%	10%
$500	$350	$250	$225	$200	$185	$170	$165	$160	$145	$135	$125

100%	98%	95%	90%	80%	70%	60%	50%	40%	30%	20%	10%

.38 DOUBLE ACTION THIRD MODEL

.38 S&W cal., cylinder same as above, 3 1/4, 4, 5, 6, 8, or 10 in. barrel, blue or nickel finish, "S&W" monogram hard rubber grips. 203,700 mfg. 1884-95. Serial range approx. 119,001-322,700.

$500	$350	$225	$200	$190	$175	$160	$155	$150	$140	$125	$115

✱ *.38 Double Action Third Model 8 or 10 in. Barrel*

Extreme rarity precludes accurate pricing on this model.

A 2 in. variation, while extremely rare, was manufactured in the Third Model, Fourth Model, Fifth Model, and Perfected Models listed. Large premiums do exist ($850-$1,500) - watch for fakes!

.38 DOUBLE ACTION FOURTH MODEL

.38 S&W cal., cylinder same as above, 3 1/4, 4, 5, or 6 in. barrel, blue or nickel finish, "S&W" monogram checkered hard rubber grips, also offered in an extended square butt target style. 216,300 mfg. 1895-1909. Serial range 322,701-539,000.

$450	$300	$230	$200	$185	$170	$155	$150	$145	$135	$120	$110

.38 DOUBLE ACTION FIFTH MODEL

.38 S&W cal., cylinder, barrel, and grip specifications same as above with the additional availability of an extended square butt target style walnut grip as an accessory. 15,000 mfg. 1909-11. Serial range approx. 539,001-554,077.

$500	$465	$425	$375	$325	$285	$250	$225	$200	$180	$150	$125

.38 DOUBLE ACTION PERFECTED MODEL

.38 S&W cal., 2 (extremely rare - watch for fakes), 3 1/4, 4, 5, or 6 in. barrel, cylinder change in frame incorporates rolled I frame revolver and lockwork, trigger guard is integral part of frame, and side plate is on right side, not left side. The last of the S&W break open revolvers. 59,400 mfg. 1909-20. Serial range 1-59,400. Identified by having both top latch and side latch.

$875	$550	$475	$425	$360	$315	$275	$250	$225	$200	$170	$150

✱ *.38 Double Action Perfected Model Top Latch Only* - as above, except no side latch - rare.

Add a substantial premium for triggerguard with integral frame.

Extreme rarity precludes accurate pricing on this model.

.38 SAFETY HAMMERLESS FIRST MODEL (.38 NEW DEPARTURE)

.38 S&W cal., 5 shot fluted cylinder, 3 1/4, 4, 5, or 6 in. barrel, blue or nickel finish, "S&W" monogram checkered hard rubber grips, features "Z-Bar" latch. Approx. 5,000 mfg. in 1887. Serial range 1-5,001.

$1,325	$875	$775	$600	$525	$475	$415	$360	$315	$275	$250	$175

Add 25% for blue finish.

✱ *.38 Safety Hammerless First Model 6 in. Barrel*

Extreme rarity precludes accurate pricing on this model.

.38 SAFETY HAMMERLESS SECOND MODEL

.38 S&W cal., cylinder same as above, 3 1/4, 4, 5, or 6 in. barrel, finish and grips same as above. 37,350 mfg. 1887-90. Serial range approx. 5,001-42,483.

$600	$465	$425	$375	$325	$285	$250	$225	$200	$180	$150	$125

U.S. MARTIALLY MARKED - 100 purchased by Govt. in 1890, serial range 41,333 - 41,470, serial numbers in Second Model range, but are true Third Models.

Extreme rarity precludes accurate pricing on this model. Beware of fakes!

.38 SAFETY HAMMERLESS THIRD MODEL

.38 S&W cal., cylinder same as above, 3 1/4, 4, 5, or 6 in. barrel, finish and grips same as above. 73,500 mfg. 1890-1898. Serial range 24,284-116,002.

$500	$375	$330	$300	$275	$250	$225	$200	$175	$150	$135	$110

.38 SAFETY HAMMERLESS FOURTH MODEL

.38 S&W cal., cylinder, barrel lengths, finishes and grips same as above. 104,000 mfg. 1898-1907. Serial range 116,003 to approx. 220,000.

$375	$280	$240	$205	$190	$165	$155	$145	$135	$125	$115	$100

A 2 in. barrel in this variation is rare (Bicycle Model).

100%	98%	95%	90%	80%	70%	60%	50%	40%	30%	20%	10%

.38 SAFETY HAMMERLESS FIFTH MODEL - .38 S&W cal., cylinder same as above, 2, 3 1/4, 4, 5, or 6 in. barrel, blue or nickel finish, "S&W" monogram checkered hard rubber or checkered walnut grips. 41,500 mfg. 1907-40. Serial range 220,000-261,493.

$450	$350	$240	$205	$190	$165	$155	$145	$135	$125	$115	$100

* *.38 Safety Hammerless Fifth Model 2 in. Barrel*
Extreme rarity precludes accurate pricing on this model - will bring a premium.

MODEL 3 AMERICAN FIRST MODEL (SINGLE ACTION) - .44 S&W American or .44 rimfire Henry cal., single action, 6 shot fluted cylinder, 6, 7, or 8 in. round barrel, blue or nickel finish, walnut grips. 8,000 mfg. 1870-72. Serial range 1-approx. 8,000. Serial number overlaps on the variations below are known to exist.

Slight premiums will be asked for models with vent. hole in bottom rear barrel (approx. first 1,500). Original barrel lengths other than 8 in. are worth a premium - beware of cut barrels.

* *Model 3 American First Model Standard* - without hole in extractor.

N/A	$8,000	$4,500	$3,500	$3,000	$2,500	$2,150	$1,850	$1,650	$1,450	$1,250	$1,100

* *Model 3 American First Model Transitional* - includes locking notch on hammer, with small trigger pin, serial range 6,700-8,000.

N/A	$8,000	$4,600	$3,600	$3,100	$2,650	$2,250	$2,150	$1,850	$1,650	$1,450	$1,200

* *Model 3 American First Model .44 Rimfire Henry* - limited mfg. Watch for fakes!

N/A	$8,250	$7,000	$6,000	$5,000	$4,000	$3,750	$3,500	$3,250	$3,000	$2,750	$2,500

* *Model 3 American First Model U.S. Marked* - approx. 1,000 mfg., 800 in blue, and 200 in nickel finish. All nickel plated revolvers are serial numbered above 1,950 - watch for fakes.

N/A	$15,000	$10,750	$9,100	$8,100	$7,250	$6,500	$5,900	$5,375	$4,850	$4,450	$4,000

* *Model 3 American First Model Nashville Police* - very rare, only 32 manufactured. Scarcity precludes accurate pricing - beware of fakes.

MODEL 3 AMERICAN SECOND MODEL - .44 S&W American or .44 rimfire Henry cal., single action, 6 shot fluted cylinder, mechanism allows the hammer to lock the barrel latch in place, larger trigger pin, 5 1/2, 6, 6 1/2, 7, or 8 in. barrel, blue or nickel, walnut grips. 19,635 mfg. 1872-1874, serial range approx. 8,000-32,800 which includes commercial version of Model 3 Russian First Model.

* *Model 3 American Second Model Standard* - .44 S&W American cal., 8 in. barrel.

N/A	$7,000	$3,750	$3,250	$2,750	$2,250	$2,150	$1,850	$1,650	$1,450	$1,250	$1,100

Add 35% for 5 1/2, 6, 6 1/2, or 7 in. barrel.
Add 30% if factory cut for stock or 50% if with original shoulder stock.
608 were factory cut for shoulder stock.

* *Model 3 American Second Model Standard .44 Rimfire Henry* - 6, 7, or 8 in. barrel, non-locking hammer below approx. serial number 25,000. 3,014 mfg.

N/A	$8,000	$4,750	$3,750	$3,525	$3,050	$2,650	$2,250	$2,150	$1,850	$1,650	$1,450

MODEL 3 FIRST MODEL RUSSIAN (OLD OLD MODEL RUSSIAN) - .44 S&W Russian, 5 1/2, 6, 7, or 8 in. barrel, Russian contract revolvers had 8 in. barrels, blue finish, and Cyrillic barrel markings, commerical mfg. had blue or nickel finish, walnut grips, looks similar to First and Second Model American. 5,165 mfg. 1871-1874 for commercial sale and 20,014 for Russian Contract (separate ser. no. range). Serial range 6,000-32,800, see Model 3 Second Model American.

* *Model 3 First Model Russian Commercial Version* - 4,665 mfg.

N/A	$5,000	$4,000	$3,250	$2,750	$2,250	$2,150	$1,850	$1,650	$1,450	$1,250	$1,100

* *Model 3 First Model Russian Reject Russian Contract* - approx. 500 mfg., can be determined by the barrel, latch, and cylinder having a full serial number, rather than assembly numbers.

N/A	$5,000	$4,000	$3,250	$2,750	$2,250	$2,150	$1,850	$1,650	$1,450	$1,250	$1,100

* *Model 3 First Model Russian Russian Contract* - 20,014 mfg., rare, most sent to Russia, Cyrillic marked. Serial range 1-approx. 20,014.

N/A	N/A	$6,750	$5,975	$5,125	$4,450	$3,800	$3,350	$2,950	$2,600	$2,250	$2,000

100%	98%	95%	90%	80%	70%	60%	50%	40%	30%	20%	10%

MODEL 3 SECOND MODEL RUSSIAN (OLD RUSSIAN) - 2nd and 3rd Model Russians have an extreme knuckle at the top of backstrap and trigger guard spur, 85,200 mfg. in all variations between 1873-78, 7 in. barrel, small screw in top-strap of frame, features longer ejector housing and "Russian Model" marking on top of barrel. Ser. nos. started at 32,800.

* *Model 3 Second Model Russian Commercial Version* - 6,200 mfg.

| N/A | $3,750 | $3,000 | $2,375 | $2,000 | $1,750 | $1,500 | $1,300 | $1,100 | $995 | $895 | $795 |

* *Model 3 Second Model Russian .44 Rimfire Henry* - approx. 500 mfg.

| N/A | $5,500 | $5,000 | $4,500 | $4,000 | $3,525 | $3,050 | $2,650 | $2,250 | $2,150 | $1,850 | $1,650 |

* *Model 3 Second Model Russian Contract* - approx. 70,000 mfg. for Russian Military contract, Cyrillic markmarkings, rare in U.S.

| N/A | N/A | $3,150 | $2,850 | $2,525 | $2,275 | $2,100 | $1,950 | $1,800 | $1,650 | $1,500 | $1,350 |

* *Model 3 Second Model Turkish Model* - 1,000 mfg. in their own serial number range in .44 Rimfire, features rimfire hammer, but the cylinder is chambered for .44 Russian. This is probably the rarest and most valuable variation.

| N/A | N/A | $5,750 | $5,100 | $4,650 | $4,150 | $3,650 | $3,250 | $2,900 | $2,675 | $2,475 | $2,250 |

This model was converted to rimfire from .44 S&W Russian cal.

* *Model 3 Second Model Japanese Contract* - may be marked with an anchor.

| N/A | N/A | $3,200 | $2,600 | $2,300 | $2,050 | $1,825 | $1,650 | $1,500 | $1,375 | $1,250 | $1,175 |

MODEL 3 THIRD MODEL RUSSIAN - commonly called the "New Model Russian" and is similar to old model, except has shorter extractor housing, 6 1/2 in. barrel, front sight is forged as an integral part of barrel instead of an interchangeable part, large knurled screw in top-strap of frame, shorter ejector housing, butt is usually marked with an "1874" in a square, approx. 60,600 mfg. 1874-78. Values are similar to old model for comparable variations. In addition, the Tula Arsenal in Russia also mfg. 300,000-400,000 pistols for domestic use and Ludwig & Loewe in Germany mfg. 100,000.

* *Model 3 Third Model Russian Commercial Version* - approx. 13,500 mfg.

| N/A | $3,750 | $3,000 | $2,375 | $2,000 | $1,750 | $1,500 | $1,300 | $1,100 | $995 | $895 | $795 |

* *Model 3 Third Model Russian .44 Rimfire Henry*

| N/A | $5,000 | $4,500 | $4,000 | $3,525 | $3,050 | $2,650 | $2,250 | $2,150 | $1,850 | $1,650 | $1,500 |

* *Model 3 Third Model Russian Contract* - 41,138 mfg. Cyrillic marking.

| N/A | $3,500 | $3,200 | $2,900 | $2,650 | $2,400 | $2,200 | $2,000 | $1,775 | $1,575 | $1,325 | $1,100 |

* *Model 3 Third Model Russian Ludwig & Loewe, & Tula Copies* - copies mfg. for the Russian government.

| N/A | $2,800 | $2,500 | $2,250 | $2,000 | $1,800 | $1,625 | $1,475 | $1,350 | $1,225 | $1,100 | $950 |

Add 30% for Tula copies.

* *Model 3 Third Model Turkish Contract* - 5,000 mfg., utilizes .44 Russian cylinder - chambered for .44 Rimfire.

| N/A | $4,000 | $3,700 | $3,425 | $3,100 | $2,850 | $2,575 | $2,325 | $2,025 | $1,700 | $1,425 | $1,200 |

* *Model 3 Third Model Japanese Contract* - 1,000 made.

| N/A | $3,800 | $3,150 | $2,300 | $2,000 | $1,750 | $1,500 | $1,300 | $1,225 | $1,100 | $950 | $800 |

MODEL 3 SCHOFIELD FIRST MODEL - .45 S&W cal., single action, 7 in. barrel, 6 shot fluted cylinder, blue finish only, walnut grips, ser. no. range 1-3035. 3,035 mfg. 1875.

* *Model 3 Schofield First U.S. Issue* - 3,000 mfg.

| N/A | $15,000 | $9,000 | $6,000 | $4,500 | $4,000 | $3,600 | $3,400 | $3,200 | $3,000 | $2,600 | $2,250 |

* *Model 3 Schofield First Commercial Model (not U.S. marked)* - 35 were produced without U.S. markings, very rare - beware of fakes - there could be more phony ones than real ones.

Extreme rarity factor of this model precludes accurate pricing.

100%	98%	95%	90%	80%	70%	60%	50%	40%	30%	20%	10%

✳ *Model 3 Schofield First Wells Fargo and Company* - barrel cut to approx. 5 in. with Wells Fargo markings.

N/A	N/A	N/A	N/A	$7,000	$5,100	$4,550	$4,175	$3,750	$3,350	$3,050	$2,750

Warning - Beware of fakes! There may be more fake Wells Fargo Schofields than authentic ones. While most fakes are usually poor quality, others may be quite impressive.
Many Schofields are found with cut 5 in. barrels and no Wells Fargo marking - these will bring approx. 66% of uncut values, or if they have fake WF markings, then their value is 1/2 of the uncut values.

MODEL 3 SCHOFIELD SECOND MODEL - ser. no. range 3036-8969. Mfg. 1876-1877.

✳ *Model 3 Schofield Second Standard Model* - "U.S." on butt.

N/A	$14,000	$8,000	$5,500	$4,500	$4,000	$3,600	$3,400	$3,200	$3,000	$2,600	$2,250

✳ *Model 3 Schofield Second Commercial Model* - blue or nickel finish, 650 mfg.

N/A	$9,500	$7,000	$5,000	$4,500	$4,000	$3,600	$3,400	$3,200	$3,000	$2,600	$2,250

✳ *Model 3 Schofield Second Wells Fargo and Company* - barrel cut to 5 in. with Wells Fargo markings.

N/A	N/A	N/A	N/A	$7,000	$5,100	$4,550	$4,175	$3,750	$3,350	$3,050	$2,750

Warning - Beware of fakes! There may be more fake Wells Fargo Schofields than authentic ones. While most fakes are usually poor quality, others may be quite impressive. Many Schofields are found with cut 5 in. barrels and no Wells Fargo marking - these will bring approx. 66% of uncut values, or if they have fake WF markings, then their value is 1/2 of the uncut values.

NEW MODEL NO. 3 - features very short extractor housing under the barrel, knuckle on backstrap is less pronounced than Russian Models, single action, round butt. 35,796 mfg. between 1878-1912.

Slight premiums will be asked for cut shoulder stock ($750-$1,250), target sights (standard non-target models only).
Add a premium for barrel lengths other than 6 1/2 in. (beware of .44 DA barrels!), and for calibers other than .44 Russian, .32-44, or .38-44.
Add a premium for .44 Target variation if all numbers match (usually found in the 25,000 - 35,796 ser. no. range).

Early production had rack and gear extractor (serial number range 1-13,500), and will bring a slight premium over the later mfg. Also, premiums do exist for all but 6 and 6 1/2 in. barrel lengths; premiums for unusual chamberings.

✳ *New Model No. 3 Commercial Version*

$8,500	$5,000	$2,850	$2,000	$1,800	$1,625	$1,475	$1,325	$1,175	$995	$795	$695

✳ *New Model No. 3 Japanese Navy Model* - Japan purchased approx. 1/3 of total production.

Add 50% for Japanese characters on ejector housing. Japanese anchor brings only a small premium, if any.

✳ *New Model No. 3 Australian Model* - 7 in. barrel, detachable stock, for Australian Colonial Police, broad arrow marking on both pistol and stock, stocks were originally numbered to the matching pistol, but are seldom seen with matching numbers today, approx. 250 mfg., usually found in the low 12,000-low 13,000 ser. no. range.

Add a substantial premium if with shoulder stock.
Original holsters for this model are extremely scarce. Holster is a double flap type which will holster the gun with or w/o shoulder stock attached. There is also a seaprate holster for shoulder stock when it is not attached to the gun. All types are scarce, and have Broad Arrow stamp.

✳ *New Model No. 3 Argentine Model* - unknown total production, marked "Ejercito Argentina" (very rare).

Add a premium over the Commercial Version.

✳ *New Model No. 3 State of Maryland Model* - "U.S." marked, serial number range 7,126-7,405.

Add a premium over the Commercial Version.
Add a premium for Revenue Cutter Service (Coast Guard) model, identifiable only by ser. no.

100%	98%	95%	90%	80%	70%	60%	50%	40%	30%	20%	10%

NEW MODEL NO. 3 FRONTIER - .44-40 WCF cal., single action, 4, 5, or 6 1/2 in. barrel, blue or nickel finish, walnut or hard rubber grips, ser. no. range 1-2072. 2,072 mfg. 1885-1908.

    ✱ *New Model No. 3 Frontier Japanese Purchase* - 786 converted to .44 Russian cal., cylinder should measure 1 9/16 in., in the Frontier serial range of 1-2,072.

| N/A | $5,000 | $3,000 | $2,250 | $1,800 | $1,625 | $1,475 | $1,325 | $1,175 | $995 | $795 | $695 |

    ✱ *New Model No. 3 Frontier Standard Model* - .44-40 WCF cal.

| $9,000 | $6,000 | $3,500 | $3,000 | $2,500 | $2,250 | $2,000 | $1,850 | $1,600 | $1,400 | $1,250 | $1,100 |

NEW MODEL NO. 3 - .38-40 WCF - separate ser. range, only 74 mfg., ser. no. 1-74. Mfg. 1900-1907.

    Extreme rarity factor of this model precludes accurate pricing.

NEW MODEL NO. 3 TARGET MODEL - .32-44 S&W or .38-44 S&W cal., target sights, ser. no. range 1-4333. 4,333 mfg. between 1887-1910.

| $6,500 | $3,250 | $2,500 | $2,250 | $1,925 | $1,700 | $1,500 | $1,350 | $1,100 | $950 | $800 | $700 |

NEW MODEL NO. 3 TURKISH - .44 rimfire cal., 5,461 mfg. 1879-1888, in separate serial number series.

| N/A | $7,000 | $4,675 | $4,350 | $4,050 | $3,750 | $3,450 | $3,150 | $2,850 | $2,550 | $2,275 | $1,950 |

.44 CAL. DOUBLE ACTION FIRST MODEL - .32-44 (rare), .38-44 (rare), .38 Military (rare), .44 S&W Russian (most common), and .455 (rare) cal., caliber markings on later production for .44 S&W Russian is ".44 Smith & Wesson", 6 shot fluted cylinder, 4, 5, 6, or 6 1/2 in. barrel, blue or nickel finish, "S&W" monogram checkered hard rubber or walnut grips. Walnut grips with "S&W" inlays will be found after 1900. 53,668 mfg. 1881-1913. Serial range 1-54,668.

    Add 100% for cals. other than .44 S&W Russian with target sights on sub-models listed.

    ✱ *.44 Cal. Double Action First Model Standard*

| $4,500 | $1,900 | $1,500 | $1,275 | $1,000 | $925 | $825 | $695 | $650 | $575 | $475 | $375 |

    ✱ *.44 Cal. Double Action First Model Wesson Favorite* - similar to Standard Model, but in 5 in. barrel only with special front sight, blue nickel finish, patent markings are on the cylinder rather than on the barrel, grooved barrel rib, external and internal lightening cuts to reduce weight. Approx. 1,000 mfg. 1882-83. Serial number within the .44 Double Action First Model range, approx. 8,900-10,100.

| N/A | $10,000 | $8,000 | $7,000 | $5,500 | $4,500 | $3,600 | $3,200 | $2,825 | $2,500 | $2,275 | $2,000 |

    Add 30-40% for blue finish.

.38 WIN. DOUBLE ACTION - .38-40 WCF cal., 4, 5, 6, or 6 1/2 in. barrel, only 276 mfg. in separate ser. range 1-276. Mfg. 1900-1910.

| N/A | $6,000 | $5,000 | $4,000 | $3,000 | $2,500 | $2,000 | $1,750 | $1,500 | $1,300 | $1,225 | $1,125 |

.44 DOUBLE ACTION FRONTIER - .44-40 WCF cal., 4, 5, 6, or 6 1/2 in. barrel, only 15,340 mfg. in separate ser. range 1-15,340. Mfg. 1886-1913.

| $4,500 | $1,900 | $1,500 | $1,275 | $1,000 | $925 | $825 | $695 | $650 | $575 | $475 | $375 |

    Add 100% for factory target sights.

.44 DOUBLE ACTION WESSON FAVORITE - .44 S&W Russian cal., ser. no. range 8900-10100. Approx. 1,000 mfg. 1882-1883.

| N/A | N/A | $10,000 | $8,200 | $7,500 | $6,500 | $6,000 | $5,000 | $4,000 | $2,500 | $2,000 | $1,500 |

SINGLE SHOTS

FIRST MODEL (MODEL OF 1891) - .22 LR (862 mfg.), .32 S&W (229 mfg.), or .38 S&W (160 mfg.) cal., 6, 8, or 10 in. barrel marked "Model of 1891", blue or nickel, hard rubber extension grips, single action trigger. 1,251 mfg. 1893-1905, ser. range (same as Third Model 38 Single Action) 1-28,107. Serial number is located on the front strap.

    ✱ *First Model .22 LR* - approx. 862 mfg.

| N/A | $2,350 | $2,150 | $1,825 | $1,650 | $1,375 | $1,150 | $925 | $750 | $550 | $425 | $325 |

    Add a premium for .32 S&W or .38 S&W cals.

100%	98%	95%	90%	80%	70%	60%	50%	40%	30%	20%	10%

SECOND MODEL .22 LR - similar to First Model, but will not accommodate a revolver cylinder, flatsided frame (does not have recoil shield) 6 (rare) or 10 in. barrel, single action trigger, black hard rubber extension grips, 4,617 mfg. 1905-09. Ser. range 1-4,617 (ser. no. located on front gripstrap).

| N/A | $2,000 | $1,825 | $1,650 | $1,425 | $1,250 | $1,075 | $875 | $700 | $500 | $400 | $300 |

THIRD MODEL .22 (PERFECTED MODEL) - similar to Second Model, except is built on "I" solid frame with integral trigger guard, side plate on right side, made in both single or double action, checkered walnut extension grips. 6,949 mfg. 1909-1923. Serial range 4,618-11,641 (ser. no. located on front gripstrap).

| N/A | $2,000 | $1,825 | $1,650 | $1,425 | $1,250 | $1,075 | $875 | $700 | $500 | $400 | $300 |

Add 30% for Olympic Model in extra short .22 LR rifle chamber.

STRAIGHT LINE TARGET SINGLE SHOT - .22 LR cal., single shot, 10 in. barrel, sideswing barrel, blue, target sights, smooth walnut grips, shaped like an autoloader. 1,870 mfg. 1925-36. Ser. range 1-1,870. Values below assume steel case and accessories.

| N/A | $2,950 | $2,500 | $1,975 | $1,800 | $1,525 | $1,275 | $1,025 | $800 | $550 | $475 | $300 |

Subtract 30% w/o case and accessories.

EARLY HAND EJECTORS (NAMED MODELS)

Named Models. 1896-1958. Listed in order by caliber, except where newer mfg. might also include model number. These will NOT have any model number stamped on the frame. Several were continued after 1958 as Numbered Models, so be sure to check that section as well.

MODEL .22 HAND EJECTOR (LADYSMITH) - originally chambered for .22 S&W (same as .22 Long) cal., 7 shot fluted cylinder, small frame, available in blue or nickel finish, nicknamed "Ladysmith" due to its small size. Over 26,000 mfg. between 1902-21.

* *Model .22 Hand Ejector First Model* - .22 L cal., 3 or 3 1/2 in. barrel, serial numbered 1-4,575, checkered hard rubber grips, round butt. 4,575 mfg. 1902-1906. Serial range 1-4,575. Identifiable by frame mounted cylinder release lever.

| N/A | $2,500 | $2,000 | $1,500 | $1,250 | $975 | $800 | $650 | $550 | $475 | $435 | $390 |

* *Model .22 Hand Ejector Second Model* - .22 L cal., 3 or 3 1/2 in. barrel, distinguishable from first model in that cylinder locking device was placed on barrel bottom, locking both ends. 9,400 mfg. 1906-10. Serial range 4,576-13,950.

| N/A | $2,500 | $2,000 | $1,500 | $1,250 | $975 | $800 | $650 | $550 | $475 | $435 | $390 |

* *Model .22 Hand Ejector Third Model* - .22 L cal., 2 1/2, 3, 3 1/2, or 6 in. barrel, smooth walnut grips with "S&W" medallion inlays, square butt. 12,200 mfg. 1910-21. Serial range 13,951-26,154.

| N/A | $2,500 | $2,000 | $1,500 | $1,250 | $975 | $800 | $650 | $550 | $475 | $435 | $390 |

Add 85% for 6 in. barrel with target sights.
Add 95% for 6 in. barrel with plain sights.

.22/.32 HAND EJECTOR (ALSO KNOWN AS .22/32 BEKEART MODEL) - .22 LR cal., 6 shot fluted cylinder, 6 in. barrel, blue, checkered walnut grips with "S&W" medallions, extension style square butt, there were several hundred thousand of the standard .22/.32 Hand Ejector mfg. The first 3,000 mfg. will be found with a separate ser. no. (1-3,000) stamped into the bottom of the wood grips. This model was cataloged as the .22/.32 heavy frame target unit in 1931. Mfg. 1911-1941.

* *.22/.32 Hand Ejector Bekeart Model* - will be found with separate identification number on bottom of its wooden grip. Serial numbers for early Bekeart models start at 138,226.

| N/A | $1,575 | $1,325 | $1,075 | $875 | $750 | $650 | $550 | $450 | $350 | $275 | $200 |

Add a premium for ser. no. 1-1,000 ("True Bekearts").
Slight premiums are charged over the values listed for early production in lower ser. no. range 1,001-3,000.
This model was specifically mfg. for a San Francisco retailer, Philip Bekeart. Originally, Mr.

100%	98%	95%	90%	80%	70%	60%	50%	40%	30%	20%	10%

Bekeart ordered 1,000 guns to his specifications, S&W mfg. 5,000. While the first 1,000 revolvers in ser. no. range 138,226 with grip numbered 1-1,000 are accepted as "True Bekearts", only 292 were actually delivered to Philip Bekeart.

⁕ **.22/.32 *Hand Ejector Standard Model*** - mfg. approx. 1913-53, continued as the Model 35.

$750	$600	$500	$425	$350	$325	$275	$225	$175	$135	$115	$100

.22/.32 KIT GUN - similar to Standard .22/32 Hand Ejector Model, except has 2 or 4 in. barrels, round or square butt. Mfg. 1935-53, serial number overlaps occur within this model, continued as the Model 34.

N/A	$2,675	$2,250	$1,800	$1,650	$1,375	$1,150	$925	$725	$500	$425	$275

Pre-war kit guns in ser. no. range approx. 525,670 to 536,684 will bring a 300%-400% premium over above values, if in better condition. Mfg. 1935-1941.
Early post-war kit guns in ser. no. range approx. 536,684 to 590,000 will bring a 200% premium over above values, if in better condition. Mfg. 1946-1952.

⁕ **.22/.32 *Kit Gun 1953-1957 "Pre-Model 34" Production*** - improved I- or J- frame, continued in 1957 as the Model 34.

N/A	$675	$500	$425	$350	$300	$250	$200	$175	$160	$140	$120

Early alloy frame airweight kit guns (pre-Model 43), will bring values similar to the steel frame pre-Model 34.

K-22 OUTDOORSMAN - .22 LR cal., 6 shot, 6 in. round barrel, K-frame, blue, adj. target sights, walnut grips, serial numbers in the 600,000 range with the .38 M&P. Mfg. 1931-40.

N/A	$2,050	$1,850	$1,625	$1,375	$1,100	$875	$625	$425	$300	$250	$200

PRE-WAR K-22 MASTERPIECE - similar to K-22 Outdoorsman, but has micro click rear sight, short action, round barrel w/o rib. 1,067 mfg. in 1940 with serial number in the .38 Hand Ejector range, 682,420-696,952.

N/A	$4,650	$4,350	$3,800	$3,200	$2,650	$2,000	$1,400	$1,100	$775	$500	$350

POST-WAR K-22 MASTERPIECE - similar to pre-war K-22, ribbed barrel, ser. no. started with "K" prefix, pre-Model 17, mfg. 1946-1957, then continued as the Model 17.

N/A	$775	$725	$650	$575	$500	$425	$325	$250	$200	$175	$150

.32 HAND EJECTOR FIRST MODEL (MODEL OF 1896) - .32 S&W Long cal., 6 shot fluted cylinder, 3 1/4, 4 1/4, or 6 in. barrel, blue or nickel, black rubber grips, round butt, cylinder stop is mounted in frame top-strap, patent markings are on cylinder, rather than on barrel. 19,712 mfg. 1896-1903. Serial range 1-19,712.

$1,000	$775	$650	$600	$550	$525	$475	$425	$400	$375	$335	$300

Add 10% for short hammer variation.

.32 HAND EJECTOR SECOND MODEL (MODEL OF 1903) - .32 S&W Long cal., 6 shot fluted cylinder, 3 1/4, 4 1/4, or 6 in. barrel, blue or nickel, black rubber grips. 19,425 mfg. 1903-04. Serial range 1-19,425.

N/A	$1,575	$1,325	$1,075	$875	$750	$650	$550	$450	$350	$275	$200

⁕ **.32 *Hand Ejector Second Model (Model of 1903 - 1st Change)*** - rubber grips. 31,700 mfg. 1904-06. Serial range 19,426-51,126.

N/A	$1,850	$1,625	$1,375	$1,100	$875	$625	$425	$300	$250	$200	$175

⁕ **.32 *Hand Ejector Second Model (Model of 1903 - 2nd Change)*** - rubber grips. 44,373 mfg. 1906-09. Serial range 51,127-95,500.

N/A	$650	$575	$475	$375	$300	$275	$250	$225	$200	$175	$150

⁕ **.32 *Hand Ejector Second Model (Model of 1903 - 3rd Change)*** - rubber grips. 624 mfg. 1909-10. Serial range 95,501-96,125.

N/A	$650	$575	$475	$375	$300	$275	$250	$225	$200	$175	$150

⁕ **.32 *Hand Ejector Second Model (Model of 1903 - 4th Change)*** - rubber grips. 6,374 mfg. 1910. Serial range 96,126-102,500.

N/A	$650	$575	$475	$375	$300	$275	$250	$225	$200	$175	$150

100%	98%	95%	90%	80%	70%	60%	50%	40%	30%	20%	10%

✳ *.32 Hand Ejector Second Model (Model of 1903 - 5th Change)* - rubber grips.

| N/A | $650 | $575 | $475 | $375 | $300 | $275 | $250 | $225 | $200 | $175 | $150 |

.32 HAND EJECTOR THIRD MODEL - .32 S&W Long cal., 6 shot fluted cylinder, 3 1/4, 4 1/4, or 6 in. barrel, blue or nickel finish, grips of checkered hard rubber with "S&W" monogram, round butt. 271,531 mfg. 1917-1942. Serial range approx. 263,001-534,532.

| N/A | $650 | $575 | $475 | $375 | $300 | $275 | $250 | $225 | $200 | $175 | $150 |

Add 50% for pre-war mfg.

.32 HAND EJECTOR POST WWII (PRE-MODEL 30) - .32 S&W Long cal., 6 shot, 2, 3, 4, or 6 in. barrel, blue or nickel, fixed sights, walnut or rubber grips. Mfg. 1946-1976.

| N/A | $600 | $500 | $400 | $300 | $275 | $250 | $225 | $200 | $175 | $150 | $125 |

This model was designated Model 30 after 1958.

.32 REGULATION POLICE - .32 S&W cal., 6 shot, 2, 3, 4, or 6 in. barrel, square butt, walnut grips, fixed sights, blue or nickel. Mfg. 1917-1957.

| N/A | $650 | $575 | $475 | $375 | $300 | $275 | $250 | $225 | $200 | $175 | $150 |

Add 300% for Regulation Police Target (6 in. barrel only, blue).
Subtract 25% for post-war manufacture.

.32-20 WCF HAND EJECTOR FIRST MODEL - .32-20 WCF cal., 6 shot fluted cylinder, 4, 5, 6, or 6 1/2 in. barrel, blue or nickel, case hardened trigger and hammer, hard rubber with "S&W" monogram or non-monogrammed walnut grips, round butt style.

| N/A | $2,800 | $2,450 | $2,100 | $1,850 | $1,500 | $1,200 | $950 | $750 | $550 | $350 | $250 |

.32-20 WCF HAND EJECTOR SECOND MODEL (MODEL OF 1902) - .32-20 WCF cal., 6 shot fluted cylinder, 4, 5, or 6 1/2 in. barrel, blue or nickel, grips of hard rubber with "S&W" monogram or round butt walnut, 4,499 mfg. 1902-05. Serial range 5,312-9,811.

| N/A | $1,850 | $1,625 | $1,375 | $1,100 | $875 | $625 | $425 | $300 | $250 | $200 | $175 |

✳ *.32-20 WCF Hand Ejector Second Model (Model of 1902 - 1st Change)* - grip also available in checkered walnut. 8,313 mfg. 1903-05. Serial range 9,812-18,125.

| N/A | $1,850 | $1,625 | $1,375 | $1,100 | $875 | $625 | $425 | $300 | $250 | $200 | $175 |

.32-20 WCF HAND EJECTOR (MODEL OF 1905) - .32-20 WCF cal., (revolvers manufactured until approx. 1916 were marked .32 Winchester, .32 WCF between 1916-1928, and late production was marked .32/20), cylinder and barrel specifications same as above, with round or square butt grip. 4,300 mfg. 1905-06. Serial range 18,126-22,426.

| N/A | $1,850 | $1,625 | $1,375 | $1,100 | $875 | $625 | $425 | $300 | $250 | $200 | $175 |

Add 75% for Target Models.

✳ *.32-20 WCF Hand Ejector (Model of 1905 - 1st Change)* - 4, 5, 6, or 6 1/2 barrel, blue or nickel, grips same as above, round or square butt. 11,073 mfg. 1906-07. Serial range 22,427 to approx. 33,500.

| N/A | $1,850 | $1,625 | $1,375 | $1,100 | $875 | $625 | $425 | $300 | $250 | $200 | $175 |

✳ *.32-20 WCF Hand Ejector (Model of 1905 - 2nd Change)* - caliber, cylinder, barrel and grip specifications same as above. 11,699 mfg. 1906-07. Serial range 33,501-45,200.

| N/A | $1,850 | $1,625 | $1,375 | $1,100 | $875 | $625 | $425 | $300 | $250 | $200 | $175 |

✳ *.32-20 WCF Hand Ejector (Model of 1905 - 3rd Change)* - caliber and cylinder same as above, 4 or 6 in. barrel, finish and grips same as above. 20,499 mfg. 1909-15. Serial range approx. 45,201-65,700.

| N/A | $1,850 | $1,625 | $1,375 | $1,100 | $875 | $625 | $425 | $300 | $250 | $200 | $175 |

100%	98%	95%	90%	80%	70%	60%	50%	40%	30%	20%	10%

* *.32-20 WCF Hand Ejector (Model of 1905 - 4th Change)* - caliber and cylinder same as above, 4, 5, or 6 in. barrel, finish and grips same as above. 78,983 mfg. 1915-40. Serial range 65,701-144,684.

N/A	$1,850	$1,625	$1,375	$1,100	$875	$625	$425	$300	$250	$200	$175

.38 MILITARY & POLICE FIRST MODEL (MODEL OF 1899) - .38 S&W Special cal., early Army & Navy models were marked "S&W .38 MIL.", civilian guns and standard models are 2-line barrel marked ".38 S&W SPECIAL & U.S. SERVICE CTG'S" with the "Maltese Cross" emblem stamped both before and after the caliber, these models are also referred to as .38 Hand Ejectors, 6 shot fluted cylinder, 4, 5, or 6 1/2 in. barrel, blue or nickel finish, "S&W" monogram checkered hard rubber or checkered walnut grips with walnut grips exhibiting an impressed circle at top, left plain for civilian issue, marked with inspector's initials for military issue. 20,975 mfg. 1899-1902. Serial range 1-20,975.

On these models, barrel markings are somewhat confusing, generally marked .38 S&W Spl. & U.S. Service cartridge, Military Issue is typically marked .38 Military. Fixed sights are referred to as Military & Police Models while target sights are referred to as .38 Hand Ejectors.

* *.38 Military & Police First Model Standard* - Civilian Issue

N/A	$1,850	$1,625	$1,375	$1,100	$875	$625	$425	$300	$250	$200	$175

Add 100%-200% for target sights, depending on condition.

* *.38 Military & Police First Model U.S. Navy* - 1,000 revolvers in .38 S&W Spl. cal. with 6 in. barrel, blue, checkered walnut grips, delivered in 1900. Stamped on butt "U.S.N." with an anchor and inspector's initials. All in S&W serial range 5,001-6,000. U.S. Navy serial range 1-1,000.

N/A	$3,600	$3,300	$2,875	$2,500	$1,975	$1,550	$1,100	$825	$685	$550	$425

* *.38 Military & Police First Model U.S. Army* - 1,000 revolvers in .38 Military cal. with 6 in. barrel, blue, checkered walnut grips, inspector's initials "K.S.M." on right grip panel with "J.T.T.1901" on left grip panel. Stamped on butt "U.S. ARMY/MODEL 1899". S&W serial range 13,001-14,000.

N/A	$3,600	$3,300	$2,875	$2,500	$1,975	$1,550	$1,100	$825	$685	$550	$425

.38 MILITARY & POLICE SECOND MODEL (MODEL OF 1902) - .38 S&W Special and .38 Military cal., civilian standard model barrels have a s-line marking ".38 S&W SPECIAL & U.S. SERVICE CTG'S" with the "Maltese Cross" emblem stamped both before and after the caliber, 6 shot, fluted cylinder, 4, 5, 6, and 6 1/2 in. barrels, blue or nickel, "S&W" monogram checkered hard rubber or checkered walnut grips. 12,827 mfg. 1902-03. Serial range 20,976-33,803.

* *.38 Military & Police Second Model Standard* - civilian issue, all in .38 S&W Special cal.

N/A	$1,475	$1,275	$1,150	$900	$775	$650	$525	$400	$300	$250	$200

Add 100%-200% for target sights, depending on condition.

* *.38 Military & Police Second Model U.S. Navy* - 1,000 revolvers in .38 United States Service caliber with 6 in. barrel, delivered in 1902. Stamped on butt "U.S.N." with "J.A.B.", anchor, and arrow through horizontal "S" and "No." (Naval Ser. No. designation), ser. no. range is 1,001 - 2,000.

N/A	$4,425	$4,100	$3,600	$3,200	$2,750	$2,150	$1,650	$1,300	$1,000	$800	$600

.38 MILITARY & POLICE SECOND MODEL - 1ST CHANGE - .38 S&W Special cal., 6 shot fluted cylinder, 4, 5, or 6 1/2 in. barrel, blue or nickel, "S&W" monogram checkered hard rubber or checkered walnut grips, rounded butt style. 28,645 mfg. 1903-05. Serial range 33,804-62,449.

Add 100%-200% for target sights, depending on condition.

* *.38 Military & Police Second Model 1st Change Standard Round Butt* - hard rubber grips, round butt.

N/A	$1,475	$1,275	$1,150	$900	$775	$650	$525	$400	$300	$250	$200

100%	98%	95%	90%	80%	70%	60%	50%	40%	30%	20%	10%

✱ .38 Military & Police Second Model 1st Change Standard Square Butt - checkered walnut grips or square butt to frame style. All will have serial numbers over the 58,000 range.

N/A	$1,275	$1,150	$900	$775	$650	$525	$400	$300	$250	$200	$175

.38 MILITARY & POLICE (MODEL OF 1905) - .38 S&W Special cal., 6 shot fluted cylinder, 4, 5, or 6 1/2 in. barrel, blue or nickel finish, "S&W" monogram checkered hard rubber (round butt) or checkered walnut (square butt) grips. 10,800 mfg. 1905-06. Serial range 62,450-73,250.

N/A	$1,400	$1,225	$1,050	$850	$775	$650	$525	$400	$300	$250	$200

Add 50% for Target Model.

.38 MILITARY & POLICE (MODEL OF 1905 - 1ST CHANGE) - .38 S&W Special cal., 6 shot fluted cylinder, 4, 5, 6, or 6 1/2 in. barrel, blue or nickel finish, grips same as above. 73,648 mfg. (including Model 1905 2nd change), exact quantity of both models has not been determined. The first change mfg. in 1906-08. Serial range 73,251 - unknown.

N/A	$1,400	$1,225	$1,050	$850	$775	$650	$525	$400	$300	$250	$200

Add 50% for Target Model.

.38 MILITARY & POLICE (MODEL OF 1905 - 2ND CHANGE) - .38 S&W Special cal., cylinder barrel lengths, finishes and grip styles same as above. 73,648 (including Model 1905 1st change) mfg. Exact quantity unknown. The second change mfg. in 1908-09. Serial range unknown-146,899.

N/A	$1,400	$1,225	$1,050	$850	$775	$650	$525	$400	$300	$250	$200

Add 50% for Target Model.

.38 MILITARY & POLICE (MODEL OF 1905 - 3RD CHANGE) - .38 S&W Special cal., 6 shot fluted cylinder, 4, 5, or 6 in. barrel, finishes and grip styles same as above. 94,803 mfg. 1909-15. Serial range 146,900-241,703.

N/A	$1,400	$1,225	$1,050	$850	$775	$650	$525	$400	$300	$250	$200

Add 50% for Target Model.

.38 MILITARY & POLICE (MODEL OF 1905 - 4TH CHANGE) - .38 S&W Special cal., 6 shot fluted cylinder, 2, 4, 5, or 6 in. barrel, finishes and grip styles same as above. 458,296 mfg. 1915-42. Serial range 241,704-approx. 1,000,000.

N/A	$1,400	$1,225	$1,050	$850	$775	$650	$525	$400	$300	$250	$200

Add 50% for Target Model.

GRADING - PPGS™	100%	98%	95%	90%	80%	70%	60%

.38 CHIEFS SPECIAL TARGET - original finish satin blue (military post-war type), early production (1955-1956), found sporadically in the 55,000 - 57,000 ser. no. range, polished blue finish from 1957-1959 (approx. 149,000 - 150,000 range).

	$850	$725	$575	$475	$395	$325	$275

.38 REGULATION POLICE - .38 S&W cal., 6 shot, 2, 3, 4, or 6 in. barrel, square butt, walnut grips, fixed sights, blue or nickel. Mfg. 1917-57.

Pre-war	$750	$650	$550	$450	$300	$250	$200
Post-war	$475	$400	$325	$275	$225	$170	$145

Add 300% for Regulation Police Target (6 in. barrel only, blue).

VICTORY MODEL - .38 Spl. (post-WWII commercial sales only), .38 S&W Spl. (U.S. government sales only), or .38 S&W (Lend-Lease arms to Allied Forces only) cal., 2 (rare) or 4 in. barrel, mfg. in accordance with British/American Lend-Lease agreement of WWII, parkerized finish, most with "V" prefix, approx. 240,000 mfg. 1942-1945.

U.S. Govt. Models	$750	$650	$525	$450	$400	$350	$325
Lend-lease mfg.	$700	$600	$500	$450	$400	$350	$325
Post WWII Commercial	$700	$600	$500	$450	$400	$350	$325

Post-WWII Victory models sold commercially went through the Defense Supply Commission, and had no U.S. markings. These models will bring a premium. Be careful of fake markings.

GRADING - PPGS™	100%	98%	95%	90%	80%	70%	60%

U.S. AIR FORCE LIGHTWEIGHT (U.S. MODEL M 13)

.38 Spl. cal., aluminum cylinder and frame, "USAF" marked back strap, K frame, 6 shot. Most were destroyed by the government. Perhaps S&W's most faked revolver!

	100%	98%	95%	90%	80%	70%	60%
	$1,800	$1,625	$1,375	$1,100	$875	$625	$425

The 5 shot, J-frame, "Baby Aircrewman" will bring a premium, depending on condition, (usually $5,000 when documented as an original.)

This model was based on the S&W .38 Military & Police Airweight (later became the Model 12). This model was purchased in large quantities from 1951 to 1957 only. While S&W never assigned a model number to this variation, M 13 is marked on the top strap and thus misnomered as the Model 13. In 1954, a conventional steel cylinder replaced the aluminum cylinder on the civilian model only because of cracking.

.357 MAGNUM FACTORY REGISTERED

.357 Mag. cal., this model could be custom ordered with any barrel length from 3 1/2 - 8 3/4 in., adj. sights, checkered walnut grips, hand fitted and registered to the buyer by a number found on the inside of the yoke, ser. no. with "REG" prefix. This practice was disc. 1939 (approx. 5,500 were mfg.) due to the tremendous demand for the .357 Mag. revolver. Mfg. 1935-39.

	100%	98%	95%	90%	80%	70%	60%
	$8,000	$6,500	$5,500	$4,500	$3,750	$2,750	$2,150

Add $1,300 for rare registration certificate.
Add 20% for non-standard barrel lengths.

Common barrel lengths were 3 1/2, 4, 5, 6 1/2, and 8 3/4 in.
Be wary of fakes - it is highly recommended to get a factory letter when buying, selling, or trading this model. This is perhaps S&W most collectible revolver currently, and prices have risen significantly in the past several years.

.357 MAGNUM PRE-WAR NON-REGISTERED

similar to above, but not registered. 1,142 mfg. 1938-1941.

	100%	98%	95%	90%	80%	70%	60%
	$6,500	$5,500	$4,500	$3,750	$2,750	$2,150	$1,800

.357 MAGNUM POST-WAR (PRE-MODEL 27)

ser. no. had "S" prefix, 3 1/2, 5, 6, 6 1/2, or 8 3/8 in. barrel. Mfg. 1950-1957.

	100%	98%	95%	90%	80%	70%	60%
	$1,325	$1,175	$900	$800	$675	$550	$425

Add 10% for 8 3/8 in. barrel.

.44 HAND EJECTOR FIRST MODEL (.44 HAND EJECTOR NEW CENTURY OR .44 TRIPLE LOCK)

.38-40 WCF, .44 S&W Special (standard), .44-40 WCF, .44 S&W Russian, .45 LC, or .455 Mark II cal., 4, 5, 6 1/2, or 7 1/2 in. barrel, non-monogrammed checkered walnut grips and square butt on early production, gold monogram inlay on later production. 15,375 mfg. 1908-17. Serial range 1-15,375 (overlapping occurs between the 1st and 2nd models, and there is some ser. no. duplication with the .455 Mark II).

∗ *.44 Hand Ejector First Model Special Caliber* - .38-40 WCF, .44 Russian, .44-40 WCF, .45 LC (marking, only 21 mfg.), or .455 Mark II (commercial) cal.

Due to the rarity of these calibers, prices could be 200% or more above Standard Model values.

100%	98%	95%	90%	80%	70%	60%	50%	40%	30%	20%	10%

∗ *.44 Hand Ejector First Model Conversion* - .455 Mark II cal.

100%	98%	95%	90%	80%	70%	60%	50%	40%	30%	20%	10%
N/A	$4,650	$4,250	$3,700	$3,250	$2,750	$2,150	$1,500	$995	$750	$500	$325

Only 808 factory conversions of .44 Special to .455 cal. were mfg. and sold to the British government.

∗ *.44 Hand Ejector First Model Standard* - .44 S&W Special cal.

100%	98%	95%	90%	80%	70%	60%	50%	40%	30%	20%	10%
$2,750	$1,525	$1,325	$1,100	$1,000	$900	$800	$715	$630	$545	$460	$400

Add 100% for factory target sights.

∗ *.44 Hand Ejector First Model British Target Triple Lock* - .455 cal., 6 1/2 or 7 1/2 in. barrel, with drift adj. sights (not screw operated) for shooting at Bisley, England, typically unmarked for cal., very few mfg.

100%	98%	95%	90%	80%	70%	60%	50%	40%	30%	20%	10%
$3,200	$2,950	$2,675	$2,350	$1,875	$1,650	$1,450	$1,275	$1,130	$985	$840	$695

100%	98%	95%	90%	80%	70%	60%	50%	40%	30%	20%	10%

.44 HAND EJECTOR 2ND MODEL - .44 S&W Special cal. as standard, .38-40 WCF, .44-40 WCF, or .45 LC cal., 4, 5, 6, or 6 1/2 in. barrel, blue or nickel finish, checkered walnut grips of square butt style, with or w/o "S&W" monogram inlays. 34,624 mfg. 1914-37. Ser. range 15,376-approx. 60,000.

✱ *.44 Hand Ejector 2nd Model Standard Caliber* - .44 S&W Special cal.

N/A	$2,375	$2,050	$1,850	$1,500	$1,200	$900	$625	$475	$350	$250	$200

Add 50% for factory target sights.

✱ *.44 Hand Ejector 2nd Model Special Calibers* - .38-40 WCF, .44-40 WCF, or .45 LC cal.

Due to the rarity of these calibers, prices could be 200% or more above Standard Model values.

.44 HAND EJECTOR THIRD MODEL (MODEL 1926 HAND EJECTOR THIRD MODEL) - .44 S&W Special cal., very rare in .44-40 WCF or .45 LC cal., 6 shot fluted cylinder, 4, 5, or 6 1/2 in. barrel, finishes and grips same as above, same ser. range as the Second Model .44 Hand Ejectors, approx. 4,976 mfg. pre-war. Ser. range 28,358-S62,489.

✱ *.44 Hand Ejector Third Model Standard* - .44 S&W Special Cal.

N/A	$3,675	$3,300	$2,950	$2,600	$2,200	$1,750	$1,250	$850	$575	$450	$300

There is also a post-war variation of this model mfg. 1946-49 in the ser. range S62,490-S74,000 (approx. 1,432 mfg. 1946-49). These transitional guns have hammer block safeties but long actions. The values are about 2/3 of the pre-war models.

✱ *.44 Hand Ejector Third Model 1926 Target* - pre-war, target sights, blue only, otherwise same as above. Mfg. 1926-41.

N/A	$3,675	$3,300	$2,950	$2,600	$2,200	$1,750	$1,250	$850	$575	$450	$300

There is also a post-war variation of this model mfg. 1946-49 in the ser. range S62,490-S74,000. These transitional guns have hammer block safeties but long actions. The post-war Target Model has a barrel rib and 1950s style micrometer rear sight. The values are similar to those listed.

GRADING - PPGS™	100%	98%	95%	90%	80%	70%	60%

.44 MAGNUM PRE-MODEL 29 (5 SCREW) - .44 Mag. cal., 5 screw, can be discerned by 3 visible screws on right sideplate, 1 hidden under the grip, and 1 in front of the trigger guard. Approx. 6,500 mfg. during 1956-58.

	$3,000	$2,675	$2,150	$1,800	$1,550	$1,200	$995

This model was cataloged in 4 and 6 1/2 in. barrel. The 4 in. is rare. Also, a rare variation in this model is a 5 in. barrel. Only 500 were mfg. in 5 screw Pre-Model 29 variation with bright blue finish, diamond target stocks, and wood case.

.44 MAGNUM PRE-MODEL 29 (4 SCREW) - similar to 5 screw model, except has four screws total, top plate screw was eliminated. Mfg. 1957-1958.

	$2,250	$2,000	$1,700	$1,475	$1,200	$1,000	$875

Add 40% for nickel finish.

.45 HAND EJECTOR (MODEL OF 1917) - .45 Auto Rim, or .45 ACP (in half moon clip) cal., 6 shot, 5 1/2 in. barrel, fixed sights, satin blue on military - high gloss blue on commercial, smooth walnut on military, checkered walnut on commercial models. Early military revolvers have concentric groove cut inside of hammer (approx. serial range 1-15,000).

✱ *.45 Hand Ejector Military* - 175,000 mfg., 1917-19.

	$1,850	$1,675	$1,450	$1,200	$1,000	$875	$750

Add 25% for early military mfg. with concentric groove cut inside of hammer.

Military overruns (unissued guns) were sold to the civilian market. Be sure to properly identify.

✱ *.45 Hand Ejector Commercial* - mfg. 1920-1941.

	$2,450	$2,200	$1,925	$1,725	$1,500	$1,250	$1,000

GRADING - PPGS™	100%	98%	95%	90%	80%	70%	60%

✳ .45 Hand Ejector Brazilian Contract of 1937 - Brazilian shield on right side, 25,000 originally sold to Brazil, 14,000 were imported.

	$1,450	$1,275	$1,075	$875	$750	$625	$500

Add 100% for older "non-import."

Post-war Commercial Model 1917s will bring similar values as the pre-war Commercial models.

There was also a "1917 Army" commercial mfg. May 14, 1946-July 25, 1947 (approx. 991 mfg.). Denoted by hammer block safety and ser. no. "S" prefix.

100%	98%	95%	90%	80%	70%	60%	50%	40%	30%	20%	10%

.455 HAND EJECTOR FIRST MODEL - .455 Mark II cal., ser. range 1-5,000 in its own range, English or Canadian proof.

N/A	$1,750	$1,550	$1,325	$1,150	$975	$885	$765	$675	$600	$540	$480

Add 25% for commerically sold revolvers.

Subtract 20%-40% for conversion to American caliber.

.455 HAND EJECTOR SECOND MODEL - ser. range 5,001-74,755, generally British or Canadian proofed.

N/A	$1,350	$1,175	$1,000	$875	$750	$650	$550	$450	$350	$250	$200

Add 25% for commerically sold revolvers.

Subtract 20%-40% for conversion to American caliber.

GRADING - PPGS™	100%	98%	95%	90%	80%	70%	60%

NUMBERED MODEL REVOLVERS (MODERN HAND EJECTORS)

Smith & Wesson handguns manufactured after 1958 are stamped with a model number on the frame under the cylinder yoke. The number is visible when the cylinder is open. All revolvers manufactured by S&W from 1946-58 were produced without model numbers.

To determine which variation a particular revolver is in the following section, simply swing the cylinder out to the loading position and notice the model number inside the yoke. The designation Mod. and a two- or three-digit number followed by a dash and another number designates which engineering change was underway when the gun was manufactured. Hence, a Mod. 48-3 is a Model 48 in its 3rd engineering change (and should be indicated when ordering parts). Usually, earlier variations are the most desirable to collectors unless a particular improvement is rare. The same rule applies to semi-auto pistols, and the model designation is usually marked on the outside of the gun.

Beginning 1994, S&W started providing synthetic grips and drilled/tapped receiver for scope mounting on certain models.

S&W revolvers are generally categorized by frame size. Frame sizes are as follows: J-frame (small), K-frame (medium), L-frame (medium), N-frame (large), and X-frame (extra large). All currently manufactured S&W revolvers chambered for .38 S&W Spl. cal. will also accept +P rated ammunition.

Add 10%-15% for those models listed that are pinned and recessed (pre-1981 mfg.), if in 90% or better condition.

Earlier mfg. on the following models with lower engineering change numbered suffixes are more desirable than later mfg. (i.e., a Model 10-1 is more desirable than a Model 10-14).

MODEL 10 (.38 M&P POST-WWII) - .38 Spl. +P cal., 6 shot, K-frame, round or square butt (4 in. barrel only starting 1992), fixed sights, 2 (disc. 1996), 3 (disc.), 4 (standard - disc. or heavy), 5 (disc.), or 6 (disc.) in. barrels, current mfg. utilizes Uncle Mike's combat grips, 36 oz.

MSR $687		$500	$345	$255	$195	$140	$120	$100

Add $12 for nickel finish (disc. 1991, 4 in. barrel only).

The Model 10 is currently available in 4 in. heavy barrel only (a 4 in. heavy barrel nickel square butt variation was disc. in 1992).

To date, there have been 14 engineering changes in this model.

GRADING - PPGS™	100%	98%	95%	90%	80%	70%	60%

MODEL 11 (.38/200 M&P) - .38 S&W cal. only, similar to Model 10, limited production. Mfg. 1938-1965.

| | | $1,100 | $975 | $850 | $700 | $550 | $400 | $200 |

There were 4 engineering changes in this model.

MODEL 12 (.38 M&P AIRWEIGHT) - similar to Model 10, only alloy frame, 2 or 4 in. barrel. Disc. 1986.

| | | $500 | $400 | $350 | $275 | $225 | $200 | $180 |

Last MSR was $320.

Add $40 for nickel finish (disc.).
There were 4 engineering changes in this model.

MODEL 13 (.357 MAG. M&P) - .357 Mag. cal., 6 shot, fixed sights, 3 (round butt, disc. 1996) or 4 (square butt) in. heavy barrel. Disc. 1998.

| | | $375 | $325 | $260 | $200 | $185 | $175 | $165 |

Last MSR was $411.

Add $20 for nickel finish (disc. 1986).
There were 5 engineering changes in this model.

∗ *Model 13 M & P - N.Y. State Police* - .357 Mag. cal., 4 in. barrel, blue, fixed sights, 1,200 were mfg. for the N.Y. State Police and are marked 10-6. All 1,200 were recalled by S&W and exchanged for Model 28s.

| | | $475 | $400 | $325 | $250 | $200 | $175 | $150 |

MODEL 14 (K-38 TARGET MASTERPIECE) - .38 Spl. cal., 6 or 8 3/8 (new 1959) in. barrel, target model, blue only. Mfg. 1947-1981.

| | | $500 | $375 | $300 | $275 | $245 | $220 | $195 |

Add $100 for single action.
There were 4 engineering changes on this model.

MODEL 14 K-38 FULL-LUG - .38 Spl. cal., 6 in. full lug barrel, adj. rear sight, combat style Morado wood square butt grips, blue finish, 47 oz. Mfg. 1991-1999.

| | | $475 | $375 | $300 | $275 | $245 | $220 | $195 |

Last MSR was $498.

There were 3 engineering changes on this model.

MODEL 15 (K-38 COMBAT MASTERPIECE) - .38 Spl. cal., adj. sights, 6 shot, square butt, 2 (disc.), 4, 6 (mfg. 1986-91), or 8 3/8 (new 1986, disc.) in. barrel. Disc. 1999.

| | | $500 | $375 | $300 | $275 | $245 | $220 | $195 |

Last MSR was $450.

Add $31 for TT or TH (disc. 1991).
Add $11 for 8 3/8 in. barrel (disc.).
Add $20 for nickel finish (disc. 1987).
Add 300% for USAF marked (mfg. 1965).
There were 9 engineering changes on this model.

MODEL 16 (K-32 MASTERPIECE) - .32 S&W Long cal., 6 in. barrel, adj. sights, checkered walnut, blue. Only 3,630 mfg., 1947-74.

| | | $1,350 | $1,150 | $995 | $875 | $750 | $625 | $525 |

There were 3 engineering changes to this model.

∗ *Model 16 Post-War K-32 (Pre-Model 16)* - mfg. 1946-1957.

| | | $3,000 | $2,700 | $2,400 | $2,100 | $1,800 | $1,500 | $1,325 |

∗ *Model 16 Post-War* - mfg. 1957-1974.

| | | $2,500 | $2,250 | $1,950 | $1,700 | $1,500 | $1,250 | $1,000 |

GRADING - PPGS™	100%	98%	95%	90%	80%	70%	60%

MODEL 16-4 MASTERPIECE (FULL LUG) - .32 H&R Mag. cal., K-frame, 6 shot, 4 (mfg. 1990-91 only), 6, or 8 3/8 (disc. 1991) in. barrel, square butt, blue finish only, TH and TT. Mfg. 1990-92.

	$750	$650	$550	$450	$350	$250	$200

Last MSR was $419.

Add 5%-10% for 8 3/8 in. barrel.

MODEL 17 (K-22 MASTERPIECE) - .22 LR cal., blue only, 6 shot, 4 (mfg. 1986-93), 6 (current mfg.), or 8 3/8 (disc. 1992) in. barrel. Disc. 1993, reintroduced 1996, disc. 1998.

	$575	$475	$350	$275	$235	$210	$200

Last MSR was $508.

Add $39 for full lug 6 in. long barrel (w/ TT & TH, disc.).
Add $50 for full lug 8 3/8 in. long barrel (w/ TT & TH, disc. 1992).
There were 5 engineering changes in this model.

MODEL 17 FULL LUG - .22 LR cal., 6 (mfg. 1990-95) or 10 (mfg. 1996-99) shot, 4, 6, or 8 3/8 full lug barrel, steel (6 shot) or alloy (10 shot) cylinder.

	$475	$425	$360	$325	$265	$235	$180

There were 3 engineering changes in this model.

MODEL 17-2 PROTOTYPE MERCOX DART PROJECTILE GUN - .530 Dart Projectile, .22 Ramset blank gas generator, 12 in. barrel, blue finish only, 25 prototype units mfg. 1966 only.

	$3,950	$3,250	$2,750	N/A	N/A	N/A	N/A

Add $500 for handmade Safariland holster.
Add $100-$500 depending on variation of projectile (six known).

MODEL 18 .22 COMBAT MASTERPIECE - .22 LR cal., combat style adj. sights, 4 in. barrel, blue only. Disc. 1985.

	$650	$550	$450	$375	$300	$275	$275

Last MSR was $352.

Add $30 for TT and TH.
There were 4 engineering changes to this model.

MODEL 19 .357 COMBAT MAGNUM - .357 Mag. cal. (some variations found in .38 Spl.), K frame, adj. sights, 2 1/2 (round butt, disc. 1998), 4 (square butt), or 6 (square butt, disc. 1996) in. barrel, bright blue or nickel (disc. 1992) finish, drilled/tapped receiver and synthetic grips became standard 1994. Disc. 1999.

	$475	$350	$300	$275	$245	$220	$195

Last MSR was $457.

Add $9 for 4 in. or $14 for 6 in. (disc. 1996) barrel.
Add $35 for white outline rear sight (disc. 1994).
Add $20 for nickel finish - disc. 1991.
Add $60 for TS, TT, TH, RR, and WO - disc. 1991 (6 in. barrel only).
This model was supplied with a round butt on 2 1/2 in. barrel. The 2 1/2 and 6 in. barrels (blue finish) were disc. in 1991 along with the 4 and 6 in. nickel variations.
There were 8 engineering changes to this model.

MODEL 20 HEAVY DUTY (.38/44 HEAVY DUTY) - .38 Spl. cal., 6 shot, 4, 5, or 6 1/2 in. barrel lengths, N frame, fixed sights, walnut grips, blue or nickel, walnut grips. Mfg. 1930-1941 and re-introduced 1946 (with "S" prefix starting at serial 62,930), became the Model 20 in 1957.

	100%	98%	95%	90%	80%	70%	60%
.38/44 H.D. Pre-war	$1,950	$1,750	$1,500	$1,300	$1,075	$875	$700
Pre-Model 20 (1950-57 mfg.)	$1,125	$975	$825	$700	$575	$500	$425
Post-war (1958-1966 mfg.)	$2,250	$1,875	$1,600	$1,350	$1,100	$900	$750

Add 40% for 6 1/2 in. barrel.
Early post-war models had pre-war long action (ser. range S62,489-approx. S74,000).
There were two engineering changes in this model.

MODEL 21 (.44 HAND EJECTOR FOURTH MODEL - MODEL OF 1950 MILITARY) - .44 S&W cal., 6 shot, 4, 5, or 6 1/2 in. barrel, large frame, blue, walnut grips, fixed sights, 1,200 mfg. scattered throughout serial range S75,000-S263,000. Mfg. 1950-1966.

	$2,950	$2,500	$2,000	$1,200	$950	$750	$600

Add 50% for 6 1/2 in. (rare).
There were 3 engineering changes for this model.

MODEL 21-4 "THUNDER RANCH" - .44 Spl., 4 in. barrel, 24Kt. gold plated Thunder Ranch insignia, blue, nickel, or case colored finish. Mfg. 2004-2005.

	$750	$675	$600	$525	$450	$375	$300

Last MSR was $958.

MODEL 22 (.45 HAND EJECTOR MODEL OF 1950 MILITARY) - .45 Auto Rim (disc. 1966) or .45 ACP cal., same specifications as 1917 Army, except redesigned hammer block, short action, fixed sights. Approx. 1,200 mfg. 1950-1966, reintroduced 2008 as part of S&W's Classic Firearms series.

Current Mfg. MSR $972	$725	$575	$495	$450	$400	$365	$325
1950-1966 Mfg.	$2,000	$1,750	$1,500	$1,100	$900	$800	$700

Add $100 for nickel finish on current mfg.
Add $158 for case colored frame on current mfg.
There were 2 engineering changes for this model during 1950-1966.

MODEL 22, MODEL OF 1917 - .45 ACP cal., 6 shot, N frame, 5 1/2 in. barrel, case colored frame, blue or nickel finish, pinned half-moon service front sight, Altamont wood grips, lanyard ring, carbon steel frame and cylinder, part of S&W's Classic Firearms series, 37.2 oz. New 2008.

MSR $1,011	$755	$585	$495	$450	$400	$365	$325

Add $79 for nickel finish.
Add $174 for case colored frame.

MODEL 23 (.38-44 OUTDOORSMAN) - .38 Spl. cal., similar to Model 20 in .38 Spl., except with adj. sights, blue only, featured ribbed 6 1/2 in. barrel standard. Mfg. 1930-1967.

Pre-war	$2,500	$2,250	$1,950	$1,700	$1,500	$1,250	$1,000
Post-war (1946-49)	$1,750	$1,550	$1,350	$1,150	$950	$775	$625
Pre-Mod. 23 (1950-57)	N/A	$3,750	$3,500	$3,150	$2,850	$2,500	$2,150
Numbered Mod. 23	$2,500	$2,250	$1,950	$1,700	$1,500	$1,250	$1,000

Early post-war models had long action with barrel rib and micrometer sights (ser. range S62,489-approx. S74,000). There were 4,761 pre-war revolvers, 2,036 post-war transitional, and 6,039 styled after the 1950 model.
The "44" in this model's name refers to the size frame, not the caliber. This variation became designated the Model 23 after 1958.
There were 2 engineering changes for this model.

MODEL 24 (.44 HAND EJECTOR FOURTH MODEL - 1950 TARGET) - .44 Spl., redesigned hammer, short action, 6 1/2 in. ribbed barrel standard, satin blue or bright blue, micrometer sights, serialization begins at approx. S75,000. 5,050 mfg. 1950-67.

	$2,450	$2,000	$1,650	$1,400	$1,175	$800	$600

Add 20% for bright blue.
Add 40% for 4 in. barrel.
Add 50% for 5 in. barrel.
There were 2 engineering changes for this model.

MODEL 24 - .44 Spl., 4, 5, 5 1/2 (rare), or 6 1/2 in. barrel, bright blue only, checkered Goncalo Alves target grips (without speedloader cutout), barrel and frame not pinned, 7,500 mfg. 1983.

* *Model 24 4 in. barrel.* - 2,625 mfg.

	$650	$550	$450	$425	$400	$375	$325

GRADING - PPGS™	100%	98%	95%	90%	80%	70%	60%

＊ *Model 24 6 1/2 in. barrel.* - 4,875 mfg.

	100%	98%	95%	90%	80%	70%	60%
	$600	$500	$400	$375	$350	$325	$275

Last MSR was $359.

This model's serialization is triple alpha - 4 numeric (i.e. ABC0123).

＊ *Model 24 Lew Horton Special* - .44 Spl., 3 in. barrel, round butt, adj. sights, blue finish, includes special fitted holster.

	$395	$335	$275	$240	$210	$185	$160

Subtract 10% without holster.

MODEL 24 (CURRENT MFG.) - .44 Spl. cal., N frame, 3 (Lew Horton only) or 6 1/2 in. barrel, choice of blue or nickel finish, carbon steel frame and cylinder, square butt wood grips, part of S&W's Classic Firearms series. New 2008.

MSR $988	$735	$585	$495	$450	$400	$365	$325

Add $55 for nickel finish (6 1/2 in. barrel only).

MODEL 25 (1955 TARGET MODEL) - .45 ACP, .45 Auto Rim or .45 LC (earlier mfg.) cal., N frame, blue finish only, target grips, 6 (later mfg.) or 6 1/2 (earlier mfg.) in. barrel. Disc. approx. 1985.

	$700	$600	$500	$400	$350	$300	$235

Last MSR was $347.

Add $150 for 6 1/2 in. barrel (early mfg. with pinned barrel).
Add 300% for .45 LC cal.

After 1957, the Model 25 in .45 ACP cal was designated Model 25-2, with trigger guard screw eliminated.

There were 13 engineering changes to this model.

＊ *Model 25 Lew Horton Special* - .45 ACP cal., 3 in. barrel, adj. sights, blue finish, only 100 mfg.

	$500	$450	$375	$300	$260	$230	$200

MODEL 25 - .45 LC cal., 4, 6, or 8 3/8 in. barrel, blue or nickel finish (no extra charge - disc. 1987). Disc. 1991.

	$475	$325	$250	$215	$200	$190	$180

Last MSR was $429.

Add 5%-10% for 8 3/8 in. barrel.

MODEL 25 (CURRENT MFG.) - .45 ACP cal., 6 shot, N frame, 3 (Lew Horton) or 6 1/2 in. barrel, blue or nickel finish, square butt wood grips, carbon steel frame and cylinder, red ramp front sight, part of S&W's Classic Firearms series. New 2008.

MSR $988	$735	$585	$495	$450	$400	$365	$325

Add $55 for nickel finish (6 1/2 in. barrel only).

MODEL 26 (.45 HAND EJECTOR MODEL OF 1950 TARGET) - .45 ACP, or .45 LC cal., adj. sights, thin ribbed barrel, 2,768 mfg. 1950-1960.

	$4,500	$4,000	$3,500	$2,750	$2,000	$1,500	$1,000

＊ *Model 26-1 Georgia Highway Patrol Commemorative* - .45 Colt cal., blue finish, 5 in. barrel, marked "1937 Georgia State Patrol 1987", mfg. 1988.

	$1,350	$1,175	$950	N/A	N/A	N/A	N/A

MODEL 27 - .357 Mag. cal., N-frame, 3 1/2 (disc. 1977), 4 (disc. 1991), 5 (disc. 1977), 6, 6 1/2, or 8 3/ 8 (disc. 1991) in. barrel, blue or nickel (disc. 1987) finish. Disc. 1994.

4 screw	$850	$775	$700	$575	$450	$325	$225
3 screw	$700	$600	$475	$325	$250	$200	$175

Last MSR was $486.

Add $28 for white outline rear sight - (disc. 1991).
Add $8 for 8 3/8 in. barrel - (disc. 1991).
There were 7 engineering changes to this model.

GRADING - PPGS™	100%	98%	95%	90%	80%	70%	60%

* *Model 27 3 1/2 and 5 in. barrel* - disc.

	$525	$450	$375	$325	$275	$250	$225

* *Model 27 (Current Mfg.)* - .357 Mag. cal., N frame, 4 or 6 1/2 in. barrel, blue or nickel finish, part of S&W's Classic Firearms series. New 2008.

MSR $1,003	$750	$585	$495	$450	$400	$365	$325

Add $71 for nickel finish.
Add $40 for 6 1/2 in. barrel.

MODEL 28 HIGHWAY PATROLMAN - .357 Mag. cal., "Highway Patrol" utility model, dull or brushed nickel (very rare) finish, adj. sights, standard grips, blue only, 4 or 6 in. barrel, mfg. 1954-1986.

1954-1957 mfg.	$850	$775	$700	$575	$450	$325	$225
1957-1986 mfg.	$450	$400	$350	$300	$275	$250	$225

Last MSR was $306.

Add $20 for TS.
Add 30% for 5 screw variation (pre-Model 28).
Add 300% for brushed nickel finish (beware of fakes).
There were 3 engineering changes to this model.

MODEL 29 .44 MAGNUM (5 SCREW) - please refer to listing under Early Hand Ejectors, Named Models.

MODEL 29 .44 MAGNUM (4 SCREW) - .44 Mag. cal., 4 screw, can be discerned by 2 exposed screws on lower right sideplate (one is concealed by the right grip, and one in front of the trigger guard). Mfg. began 1957 after approx. ser. no. S175,000 and was disc. 1961.

	$1,650	$1,450	$1,250	$1,000	$875	$775	$675

MODEL 29-1 & LATER VARIATIONS (3 SCREW) - .44 Mag. cal., 4, 6 1/2, or 8 3/8 in. barrel, eliminated top screw on sideplate and 1 screw in front of trigger guard. Disc. 1999.

M29-1	$3,450	$3,050	$2,600	$2,200	$1,700	$1,400	$1,100
M29-2	$800	$700	$600	$500	$425	$375	$325
M29-3 & higher	$550	$495	$450	$400	$365	$335	$300

Last MSR was $574.

Add $12 for 8 3/8 in. barrel.
Add $11 for nickel finish (disc. 1991).

Add $45 for combat grips with scope mount - disc. 1991 (8 3/8 in. barrel only).
Subtract $40 if without case.
Older .44 Magnum Pre-Model 29 mfg. (4 & 5 screw variations) will appear under the previous subheading: "EARLY HAND EJECTORS (NAMED MODELS)."
The "S" serial number prefix was used on this model until 1968, at which time the law required a new numbering system, and the serial number prefix was changed to "N". The "S" prefix originally designated the additional hammer block safety.
There were 9 engineering changes to this model.

MODEL 29 CLASSIC - .44 Mag. cal., 5, 6 1/2, or 8 3/8 in. full lug barrel, blue only, round butt with Hogue conversion square butt grips, interchangeable front sights with white outline rear sight, frame is drilled and tapped to accept scope mounts, blue finish only. Mfg. 1990-94.

	$600	$500	$400	$380	$325	$300

Last MSR was $591.

Add $8 for 8 3/8 in. barrel.

* *Model 29 Classic DX* - similar to Model 29 Classic, except supplied with 2 sets of grips, 6 1/2 or 8 3/8 in. barrel, 5 interchangeable front sights, numbered test target, 51-54 oz. Mfg. 1991-92.

	$850	$750	$650	$550	$500	$450	$400

GRADING - PPGS™	100%	98%	95%	90%	80%	70%	60%

MODEL 29 SILHOUETTE - .44 Mag. cal., 10 5/8 in. barrel, adj. front and rear sights, bright blue only, Goncalo Alves target stocks. Mfg. 1983-91.

| | $650 | $575 | $500 | $425 | $350 | $295 | $260 |

Last MSR was $536.

MODEL 29 MAGNACLASSIC - .44 Mag. cal., 7 1/2 in. full lug, ported barrel, high polish bright bluing, round butt, interchangeable front sight, supplied with cherry wood display case mfg. in England, 3,000 mfg. in 1990 only.

| | $900 | $850 | $775 | $625 | $500 | $450 | $395 |

Last MSR was $999.

MODEL 29 CLASSIC HUNTER - .44 Mag. cal., 6 in. barrel with full length barrel lug, non-fluted cylinder, Hogue grips, four position adj. front sight. Mfg. late 1980s.

| | $575 | $475 | $395 | $335 | $290 | $260 | $240 |

MODEL 29 50TH ANNIVERSARY - .44 Mag. cal., N-frame, blue finish, 6 1/2 in. barrel, 6 shot, 24Kt. gold anniversary logo medallion on rear frame signifying 50th anniversary, checkered African cocobolo grips, red ramp front sight, adj. outline rear sight, includes mahogany presentation case. Limited mfg. 2006.

| | $1,075 | $950 | $825 | N/A | N/A | N/A | N/A |

Last MSR was $1,129.

MODEL 29 (CURRENT MFG.) - .44 Mag. cal., N frame, 6 shot, 3 (Lew Horton), 4 (Talo, blue finish only), or 6 1/2 in. barrel, Altamont walnut (61/2 in. only), square butt wood (3 in. only), or custom Hogue monogrip (4 in. only), adj. or white outline rear sight, black or red ramp front sight, blue or nickel finish, part of S&W's Classic Firearms series, 39.3 - 48 1/2 oz.

| MSR $980 | | $730 | $575 | $495 | $450 | $400 | $365 | $325 |

> Add $55 for nickel finish.
> Add $166 for 6 1/2 in. barrel.

MODEL 30 - .32 S&W cal., improved I frame and J frame, 6 shot, 2, 3, 4, or 6 in. barrel, square butt, walnut grips, fixed sights, blue or nickel finish. Mfg. 1948-1976.

| | $475 | $325 | $245 | $220 | $195 | $175 | $165 |

There was one engineering change to this model.

MODEL 31 - .32 S&W Long cal., improved I frame and J frame, fixed sights, 2, 3 or 4 (disc.) in. barrel, blue only. Disc. 1991.

| | $450 | $300 | $245 | $220 | $195 | $175 | $165 |

Last MSR was $365.

> Add 25% for early flatlatch models.
> There were 3 engineering changes to this model.

MODEL 32 (.38 TERRIER) - .38 S&W cal., 5 shot, 2 in. barrel, walnut or rubber grips, blue or nickel, fixed sights, built on .32 frame. Mfg. 1948-1974.

| | $400 | $365 | $275 | $175 | $150 | $135 | $125 |

MODEL 032 - .32 Mag. cal., 6 shot, alloy J frame, blue, scarce, mfg. 1992 only.

| | $525 | $450 | $325 | $250 | $200 | $150 | $75 |

MODEL 33 (.38 REGULATION POLICE) - .38 S&W cal., 5 shot, 2, 3, 4 in. barrel, square butt, walnut grips, fixed sights, blue or nickel finish, improved I frame and J frame. Mfg. 1958-1974.

| | $400 | $325 | $250 | $200 | $160 | $135 | $125 |

MODEL 34 - .22 LR cal., adj. sights in J frame, improved I frame and J frame, 6 shot, 2 or 4 in. barrel, round or square butt, blue or nickel (disc. 1986) finish. Disc. 1991. This model was reissued for 2-3 years.

| | $450 | $340 | $295 | $225 | $185 | $175 | $165 |

Last MSR was $366.

> Add $25 for nickel finish.
> Add 25% for early flatlatch models.
> There were 2 engineering changes to this model.

GRADING - PPGS™	100%	98%	95%	90%	80%	70%	60%

MODEL 35 (.22/32 TARGET MODEL OF 1953) - similar to Standard .22/.32 Hand Ejector Model, except micrometer rear sight, 6 in. barrel, improved I and J frame, target grips. Mfg. 1953-74.

	$725	$650	$525	$400	$300	$250	$200

MODEL 36 (.38 CHIEFS SPECIAL) - .38 Spl. cal., 5 shot, J frame, round or square (disc. 1991) butt, 1 7/8 in. regular or 3 in. (heavy only, disc. 1994, reintroduced 2008) barrel, case colored frame (new 2008), blue or nickel (disc. 1992, reintroduced 2008) finish. Disc. 1999, reintroduced 2008 as part of S&W Classic Firearms series.

MSR $735	$525	$400	$350	$300	$250	$200	$185

Add $23 for nickel finish or 3 in. barrel.
Add $150 for case colored frame (new 2008).
Add 25% for early small trigger guard and grips (below ser. no. 2,500).

Note: 1st models with high polish blue and diamond grips will bring premiums when mint in original box.

There were 10 engineering changes to this model through 1999.

MODEL 36 TARGET - similar to Model 50, 2 in. barrel, square butt, usually marked 36-1 with target sights, mfg. started 1955.

	$850	$725	$650	$575	$500	$400	$350

MODEL 36 LADYSMITH (36LS) - .38 Spl. +P cal., 5 shot, J-frame, 1 7/8 in. standard or 3 (disc. 1991) in. standard or heavy barrel, blue finish only, Combat Dymondwood grips are anatomically designed for women (round butt on 1 7/8 in., wood combat grips on 3 in.), fixed sights, redesigned double action, 20-23 oz., Morocco grained (disc. 1991) or soft side jewelry case. Mfg. 1990-2008.

	$475	$350	$285	$225	$185	$180	$175

Last MSR was $672.

MODEL 37 CHIEFS SPECIAL AIRWEIGHT - similar to Model 36 Chiefs Special, except alloy frame and 1 7/8 or 3 (disc. 1988) in. barrel, J-frame, blue or nickel (disc. 1995) finish, barrels are marked "Airweight", no internal lock, 15 oz.

	$450	$350	$250	$210	$190	$180	$175

Last MSR was $602.

Add $16 for nickel finish (disc.).
There were 3 engineering changes to this model.

MODEL 38 BODYGUARD AIRWEIGHT - .38 S&W Spl. cal., 5 shot, alloy frame, round butt, shrouded hammer, 2 in. barrel, blue or nickel (disc. 1996) finish. Disc. 1998.

	$450	$350	$300	$250	$200	$185	$175

Last MSR was $462.

Add $15 for nickel finish (disc. 1996).
There were 3 engineering changes for this model.

MODEL 40 CENTENNIAL - .38 S&W Spl. cal., 1 7/8 (new 2008) or 2 (disc. 1974) in. barrel, double action only, fully concealed hammer, grip safety, smooth walnut grips, case colored frame, blue or nickel finish. Mfg. 1952-1974, reintroduced 2008 as part of S&W's Classic Firearms series.

MSR $790	$575	$475	$400	$325	$290	$250	$225

Add $32 for nickel finish.
Add $166 for case colored frame.

This model commands a premium for the first series with no letter prefix. After 1968, "L" prefix series began.

MODEL 42 CENTENNIAL AIRWEIGHT - .38 S&W Spl. cal., aluminum variation of Model 40 Centennial, mfg. began 1953. Disc. 1974.

Blue	$575	$500	$425	$395	$325	$300	$265
Nickel	$1,250	$1,100	$950	$875	$775	$675	$550

GRADING - PPGS™	100%	98%	95%	90%	80%	70%	60%

MODEL 042 - .38 Spl. cal., 5 shot, blue finish, alloy frame. Mfg. 1992 only.

	$450	$350	$300	$275	$225	$175	$100

MODEL 43 (.22/32 KIT GUN AIRWEIGHT) - .22 LR cal., 3 1/2 in. barrel, round or square butt, adj. sights, aluminum frame and cylinder, mfg. 1955-74.

	$500	$350	$300	$265	$240	$200	$165

MODEL 45 (.22 MILITARY & POLICE) - .22 LR cal. only, originally mfg. as training gun, not cataloged. Mfg. 1948-1978.

	$1,925	$1,700	$1,500	$1,275	$1,000	$800	$600

There were 3 engineering changes to this model.

MODEL 48 (K-22 MRF MASTERPIECE) - .22 Mag cal., 4, 6 or 8 3/8 in. barrel, blue only. Disc. 1986.

	$475	$395	$350	$300	$250	$200	$170

Last MSR was $320.

  Add $15 for 8 3/8 in. barrel.
  Add $15 for TT, TH, and TS (disc.).
There were 4 engineering changes to this model.

MODEL 49 BODYGUARD - similar to Model 38, only steel frame, 2 in. barrel, blue or nickel (disc.) finish. Disc. 1996.

	$450	$350	$300	$250	$225	$200	$175

Last MSR was $409.

  Add $25 for nickel finish (disc.).
  There were 3 engineering changes to this model.

MODEL 50 (.38 CHIEFS SPECIAL TARGET) - .38 S&W Spl. cal., Chiefs Special Target, mfg. from 1955 in 2 in. (see Model 36 Target listing and .38 Chiefs Special Target under Early Hand Ejectors) or 3 (211 mfg. beginning 1973) in. barrels, target sights, most were unmarked for model number, approx. 1,100 mfg. The other variation was designated Model 36 Target.

	$750	$650	$525	$425	$350	$300	$250

The Model 50 designation was not used until 1970.

MODEL 51 - .22 Mag. cal. only, variant of the .22/32 kit gun, 3 1/2 in. barrel, 6 shot, adj. rear sight, blue or nickel, walnut stocks. Disc. 1974.

	$500	$400	$350	$300	$275	$250	$200

MODEL 53 .22 REM. JET - .22 Jet cal. with S, L, or LR inserts, 6 shot, 4, 6, or 8 3/8 in. barrel, blue, walnut grips, adj. sights. Mfg. 1960-74.

4 screw	$900	$775	$650	$550	$470	$385	$360
3 screw	$725	$600	$550	$500	$425	$375	$350

  Add 10% for 8 3/8 in. barrel.
  Add $200 for extra matching .22 LR cylinder.
  There was one engineering change to this model.

MODEL 56 "USAF" - .38 Spl. cal., 2 in. barrel marked "U.S." on backstrap. 15,205 mfg. 1963 only.

	$7,500	$5,750	$5,000	$4,500	$3,500	$2,900	$2,200

MODEL 57 - .41 Mag. cal., N Target frame, 6 shot, 4 (disc. 1991), 6 or 8 3/8 (disc. 1991) in. barrel, blue or nickel finish, micrometer rear sight, special oversize Goncalo Alves grips, shrouded extractor rod, "S" ser. no. prefix 1964-68, changed to "N" prefix during 1969, 44-52 oz. Mfg. 1964-1993.

	$650	$575	$475	$400	$350	$300	$250

Last MSR was $466.

  Add 10-20% for "S" prefix serialization.
  Add 10% for nickel finish if NIB.
  Add 5% for 8 3/8 in. barrel.
  Add 10% for pinned barrel and recessed cylinder.
There were 4 engineering changes to this model.

GRADING - PPGS™	100%	98%	95%	90%	80%	70%	60%

MODEL 58 - .41 Mag cal., M&P, fixed sights, 4 in. barrel, blue or nickel finish. Mfg. 1964-1977.

	$800	$750	$650	$575	$500	$400	$300

Add 10% for nickel finish or "S" serial number prefix.

MODEL 60 .38 SPL. CHIEFS SPECIAL - .38 S&W Spl., stainless version of Chiefs Special, 2 or 3 in. full lug barrel. Disc. 1996.

	$450	$350	$300	$250	$200	$150	$120

Last MSR was $458.

Subtract $25 for 2 in. barrel.

Add 30% for early Model 60s without letter prefix and bright satin finish.

The full lug barrel option began in 1990 with limited mfg. It had been tested for +P ammo and features an adj. rear sight - 24 1/2 oz.

There were 16 engineering changes to the base model in two calibers.

MODEL 60 .357 MAG. CHIEFS SPECIAL - .357 Mag. cal., 2 1/8, 3 (new 1997), or 5 (new 2005) in. barrel, round butt, stainless steel, J-frame, Uncle Mike's Combat or wood (5 in. barrel only) grips, 22 1/2 - 30 oz. New 1996.

MSR $727		$515	$375	$295	$245	$200	$165	$140

Add $31 for 3 in. full lug barrel with adj. sight (new 1997) or $71 for 5 in. barrel (new 2005).

MODEL 60LS (LADYSMITH) - .38 S&W Spl. +P or .357 Mag. (disc.) cal., 5 shot, 2 in. regular (disc. 1996), 2 1/8 (new 1997), or 3 in. heavy (disc. 1991) barrel, J-frame, frosted stainless steel finish, Combat Dymondwood grips are ana-tomically designed for women (round butt on 2 in., wood combat grips on 3 in.), fixed sights, redesigned double action, 20-23 oz, Morocco grained (disc. 1991) or soft side jewelry case. New 1990.

MSR $727		$515	$375	$295	$245	$200	$165	$140

MODEL 60 PRO SERIES - .38 S&W Spl. cal., 3 in. barrel, SA/DA, 5 shot, J-frame, adj. rear sight, matte stainless finish, stainless steel frame and cylinder, Pro Series features include chamfered charge holes, pinned ramp with night sight and ergonomic high hand hold oversized laminate grip, 23.4 oz. New mid-2007.

MSR $782		$570	$475	$400	$325	$290	$250	$225

MODEL 63 .22/32 KIT GUN - .22 LR cal., J frame, stainless kit gun, 2 or 4 in. barrel, 19 oz. Disc. 1998.

	$450	$350	$300	$250	$200	$150	$125

Last MSR was $476.

There were three engineering changes to this model.

MODEL 63 (CURRENT MFG.) - 22 LR cal., 8 shot, J frame, stainless steel frame and cylinder, SA/DA, 5 in. barrel, adj. black blade rear sight, black ramp front sight, black rubber grips with finger grooves, part of S&W's Classic Firearms series, 28.8 oz. New 2008.

MSR $766		$525	$400	$325	$275	$225	$200	$185

MODEL 64 M & P - .38 Spl. +P cal., satin stainless Model 10, 6 shot, 2 (disc. 2005), 3 (disc.) or 4 in. barrel, K-frame, 3 (square butt disc. 1992) and 4 in. (square butt only) barrels are heavy, current production uses Uncle Mike's combat grips, 30 1/2 - 36 oz.

MSR $687		$450	$325	$240	$190	$155	$130	$110

There have been 7 engineering changes to this model.

MODEL 65 - .357 Mag. cal., stainless version of Model 13, K-frame, has 3 (round butt, disc. 2000) or 4 (square butt) in. heavy barrels, satin stainless steel, current production uses Uncle Mike's grips, fixed sights, 35 oz. Disc. 2004.

	$400	$350	$300	$250	$200	$175	$150

Last MSR was $563.

There have been 7 engineering changes to this model.

GRADING - PPGS™	100%	98%	95%	90%	80%	70%	60%

MODEL 65 LADYSMITH - .357 Mag. cal., K-frame, 3 in. barrel with round butt, glass beaded stainless finish, soft side jewelry case, smooth Dymondwood combat grips, 32 oz. Mfg. 1992-2004.

	$400	$325	$230	$180	$145	$125	$105

Last MSR was $618.

MODEL 66 COMBAT MAGNUM - .357 Mag. cal., K-frame, satin stainless version of Model 19, has 2 1/2, 3 (disc., only 2,500 mfg.), 4, or 6 (disc.) in. barrel, current production uses Uncle Mike's Combat grips, 32-39 oz. Disc. 2004.

	$475	$350	$230	$180	$145	$125	$105

Last MSR was $614.

Add $11 for 2 1/2 in. barrel.
Add $29 for 6 in. barrel (disc.).
Add $48 for TH and TT with 4 (disc. 1991) or 6 in. barrel only (disc. 1999).
Note: Several models of the Model 66 were made - such features as an all-stainless steel rear sight and a recessed cylinder will bring a slight premium if NIB. There have been 6 engineering changes to this model.

MODEL 67 COMBAT MASTERPIECE - .38 S&W Spl.+P cal., K-frame, stainless version of Model 15, has 4 in. barrel, current production uses Uncle Mike's Combat grips, 36 oz. Disc. 1988, reintroduced 1991.

MSR $751		$485	$375	$250	$195	$115	$125	$110

1991 mfg. included square butt and red ramp front sight insert.
There have been 5 engineering changes to this model.

MODEL 68 - .38 S&W Spl. cal., similar in appearance to the Model 66, except is in .38 Spl. cal., 6 in. barrel, approx. 7,500 mfg.

	$750	$625	$495	$425	$375	$315	$270

Add 10% for CHP markings.
This model was originally ordered by CA Highway Patrol (usually has "OHB" overstamp).

MODEL 73 - .38 Spl. cal., C frame.
A general price range for this model is $2,250-$5,000.
Most copies of this model were destroyed by S&W in 1973. Few examples have survived.

MODEL 242 AIRLITE Ti CENTENNIAL - .38 Spl.+P cal., L-frame, 7 shot, similar to Model 296. Mfg. 1990 only.

	$500	$400	$300	$240	$210	$180	$155

MODEL 296 AIRLITE Ti CENTENNIAL - .44 S&W Spl. cal., L-frame, 5 shot, 2 1/2 barrel, similar to Model 242 in construction materials, alloy frame and titanium cylinder, Uncle Mike's Boot grips, 18.9 oz. Mfg. 1999-2002.

	$650	$525	$400	$300	$250	$215	$185

Last MSR was $754.

MODEL 317 AIRLITE/KIT GUN - .22 LR cal., J-frame, 8 shot, 1 7/8 or 3 (new 1998, Hi-Viz sights became standard in 2001, Model 317 Kit Gun) in. barrel, combination of aluminum alloy and stainless steel construction, brushed aluminum finish, round butt, choice of synthetic or Dymondwood Boot (disc. 1998) grips, fixed sights, 10 1/2 oz. New 1997.

MSR $695		$525	$360	$250	$195	$150	$130	$105

Add $63 for 3 in. barrel.
Add $33 for Dymondwood Boot grips (disc.).
There have been three engineering changes to this model.

✱ *Model 317 Airlite LadySmith* - .22 LR cal., 1 7/8 in. barrel only, includes Dymondwood Boot grips, 9.9 oz. Mfg. 1998-2002.

	$445	$320	$220	$170	$135	$120	$100

Last MSR was $596.

MODEL 325 PD-AIRLITE Sc - .45 ACP cal., 2 1/2 (disc. 2006) or 4 in. barrel, otherwise similar to Model 329 PD, approx. 21 1/2 - 25 oz. Mfg. 2004-2007.

	$800	$625	$485	$400	$335	$300	$275

Last MSR was $1,067.

MODEL 325 NIGHTGUARD - .45 ACP cal., two-piece 2 1/2 in. barrel, alloy frame with stainless cylinder, black alloy finish, 6 shot, N-frame, SA/DA, rubber grips, fixed sight with front night sight. New 2008.

MSR $1,044	$795	$625	$485	$400	$335	$300	$275

MODEL 327 PD-AIRLITE Sc - .357 Mag., 8 shot, N-frame, 4 in. two-piece barrel, wood grips, Scandium frame with titanium cylinder, blue/black finish. New 2008.

MSR $1,153	$875	$675	$525	$425	$350	$315	$285

MODEL 327 NIGHTGUARD - .357 Mag. cal., two-piece 2 1/2 in. barrel, alloy frame with stainless cylinder, black alloy finish, 8 shot, N-frame, SA/DA, rubber grips, fixed sight with front night sight. New 2008.

MSR $1,044	$795	$625	$485	$400	$335	$300	$275

MODEL 329 PD-AIRLITE Sc - .44 Mag. cal., 4 in barrel, N-frame, 6 shot, Scandium frame and titanium cylinder with matte black metal finish, wood Ahrends grips with finger grooves, and Hogue rubber mongrip, Hi-Viz front sight, approx. 26 oz. New 2003.

MSR $1,153	$875	$675	$525	$425	$350	$315	$285

MODEL 329 NIGHTGUARD - .44 Mag. cal., two-piece 2 1/2 in. barrel, alloy frame with stainless cylinder, black alloy finish, 6 shot, N-frame, SA/DA, rubber grips, fixed sight with front night sight. New 2008.

MSR $1,044	$795	$625	$485	$400	$335	$300	$275

MODEL 331 AIRLITE Ti CHIEFS SPECIAL - .32 H&R Mag. cal., J-frame, 6 shot, 1 7/8 in. barrel with stainless steel liner, features titanium cylinder and aluminum alloy frame, barrel shroud, and yoke, fixed sights, Uncle Mike's or Dymondwood Boot (disc.) wood grips, two-tone matte stainless/grey finish approx. 12 oz. Mfg. 1999-2003.

	$575	$450	$375	$335	$300	$275	$250

Last MSR was $716.

Add $24 for Dymondwood Boot grips (mfg. 1999 only).

MODEL 332 AIRLITE Ti CENTENNIAL - .32 H&R Mag. cal., J-frame, similar Model 331 Airlite Ti, except is hammerless and double action only, recent production used Uncle Mike's Boot grips, 12 oz. Mfg. 1999-2003.

	$575	$455	$390	$345	$310	$280	$250

Last MSR was $734.

Add $24 for Dymondwood Boot grips (mfg. 1999 only).

MODEL 337 AIRLITE Ti CHIEFS SPECIAL - .38 S&W Spl.+P cal., J-frame, 5 shot, 1 7/8 in. barrel, similar design as the Model 331, 11.9 oz. Mfg. 1999-2003.

	$565	$435	$375	$335	$310	$280	$250

Last MSR was $716.

Add $24 for Dymondwood Boot grips (mfg. 1999 only).

MODEL 337 AIRLITE Ti KIT GUN - .38 S&W Spl.+P cal., J-frame, 5 shot, 3 1/8 in. barrel with Hi-Viz front sight (new 2001), choice of Dymondwood or Uncle Mike's combat grips, approx. 13 oz. Mfg. 2000-2003.

	$600	$460	$385	$345	$315	$285	$250

Last MSR was $779.

MODEL 337 PD AIRLITE Ti CHIEFS SPECIAL - .38 S&W Spl.+P cal., J-frame, 5 shot, 1 7/8 in. barrel, black/grey finish, black Hogue Bantam grips, 10.7 oz. Mfg. 2000-2003.

	$580	$450	$385	$340	$310	$280	$250

Last MSR was $740.

GRADING - PPGS™	100%	98%	95%	90%	80%	70%	60%

MODEL 340 AIRLITE Sc CENTENNIAL - .357 Mag. cal., J-frame, 5 shot, 1 7/8 in. barrel only, Scandium alloy frame, barrel shroud, and yoke, titanium cylinder, two-tone matte stainless/grey finish, hammerless, Hogue Bantam grips, 12 oz. New 2001.

	MSR $1,019		$775	$575	$475	$400	$340	$295	$250

MODEL 340 PD AIRLITE Sc CENTENNIAL - similar to Model 340 Airlite Sc, except has black/grey finish, 12 oz. New 2000.

	MSR $1,019		$775	$575	$475	$400	$340	$295	$250

    Add $16 for Hi-Viz front sight (disc. 2008).

MODEL 340 M & P - .357 Mag. cal., 5 shot, J-frame, DAO, concealed hammer, 1 7/8 in. barrel, includes XS sights (24/7 tritium night and intergral U-notch), Scandium alloy frame with stainless steel cylinder, matte black finish, synthetic or Crimson Trace laser grips, 13.3 oz. New 2007.

	MSR $869		$595	$500	$365	$310	$255	$200	$175

    Add $253 for Crimson Trace laser grips.

MODEL 342 AIRLITE Ti CENTENNIAL - .38 S&W Spl.+P cal., similar to Model 337, except is hammerless and double action only, matte stainless/grey finish, Uncle Mike's Boot grips, 12 oz. Mfg. 1999-2003.

			$575	$445	$390	$345	$310	$280	$250

Last MSR was $734.

    Add $24 for Dymondwood Boot grips (mfg. 1999 only).

MODEL 342 PD AIRLITE Ti CENTENNIAL - .38 S&W Spl.+P cal., J-frame, 5 shot, double action only, aluminum alloy frame with titanium cylinder and stainless steel 1 7/8 in. barrel, hammerless, black/grey finish, Hogue Bantam grips, 10.8 oz. Mfg. 2000-2003.

			$595	$460	$390	$340	$310	$280	$250

Last MSR was $758.

MODEL 351 PD AIRLITE Sc CHIEFS SPECIAL (CENTENNIAL) - .22 Mag. cal., J-frame, 1 7/8 in. barrel, 7 shot, black finish, aluminum (new 2007) or Scandium (disc. 2006) alloy frame and cylinder, wood grips, 10.6 oz. New 2004.

	MSR $758		$495	$375	$265	$220	$190	$170	$155

MODEL 357 PD - .41 Rem. Mag. cal., 6 shot, 4 in. barrel, N frame, Scandium alloy frame with titanium cylinder, matte black finish, unckeckered wood grips with finger grooves, Hi-Viz front sight, adj. V-notch rear sight, 27 1/2 oz. Mfg. mid-2005-2007.

			$815	$575	$475	$400	$340	$300	$275

Last MSR was $1,067.

MODEL 360 AIRLITE Sc CHIEFS SPECIAL - .357 Mag. cal., J-frame, 5 shot, 1 7/8 in. barrel, Scandium alloy frame with titanium cylinder, matte stainless/grey finish, Hogue Bantam grips, fixed sights, 12 oz. New 2001.

	MSR $1,019		$775	$575	$475	$400	$340	$295	$250

MODEL 360 PD AIRLITE Sc CHIEFS SPECIAL - similar to Model 360 Airlite Sc Chiefs Special, except has matte stainless/grey finish, 12 oz. New 2002.

	MSR $940		$695	$525	$435	$365	$325	$280	$250

    Add $16 for Hi-Viz front sight.

MODEL 360 AIRLITE Sc KIT GUN - .357 Mag. cal., J-frame, 5 shot, 3 1/8 in. barrel with Hi-Viz front sight, Scandium alloy frame with titanium cylinder, matte stainless/grey finish, Uncle Mike's Combat grips, 14 1/2 oz. Mfg. 2001-2007.

			$695	$525	$435	$365	$325	$280	$250

Last MSR was $940.

GRADING - PPGS™	100%	98%	95%	90%	80%	70%	60%

MODEL 360 M & P CHIEFS SPECIAL - .357 Mag. cal., 5 shot, J-frame, SA/DA, 1 7/8 in. barrel, includes XS sights (24/7 tritium night and intergral U-notch), Scandium alloy frame with stainless steel cylinder, matte black finish, synthetic grips, 13.3 oz. New 2007.

MSR $869	$600	$500	$360	$310	$250	$200	$175

MODEL 386 AIRLITE Sc MOUNTAIN LITE - .357 Mag. cal., L-frame, 7 shot, 2 1/2 (new 2007) or 3 1/8 (disc. 2006) in. stainless barrel with Hi-Viz front sight, Scandium alloy frame with titanium cylinder, two-tone matte stainless/grey finish, Hogue Bantam grips, 18 1/2 oz. Mfg. 2001-2007.

	$650	$510	$420	$365	$325	$295	$265

Last MSR was $869.

MODEL 386 PD AIRLITE Sc - .357 Mag. cal., L-frame, 7 shot, 2 1/2 in. stainless barrel with adj. black rear sight, Scandium alloy frame with titanium cylinder, black/grey finish, Hogue Bantam grips, 17 1/2 oz. Mfg. 2001-2005.

	$665	$500	$415	$355	$315	$285	$250

Last MSR was $872.

Add $22 for Hi-Viz front sight (disc. 2005).

MODEL 386 Sc/S - .357 Mag., 7 shot, 2 1/2 in. barrel, L-frame, synthetic finger groove grips, matte black finish, Scandium alloy frame with stainless steel cylinder, red ramp front sight, adj. rear sight, 21.2 oz. New mid-2007.

MSR $948	$695	$550	$440	$375	$330	$295	$265

MODEL 386 NIGHTGUARD - .357 Mag. cal., two-piece 2 1/2 in. barrel, alloy frame with stainless cylinder, black alloy finish, 7 shot, L-frame, SA/DA, rubber grips, fixed sight with front night sight. New 2008.

MSR $980	$725	$540	$450	$375	$325	$285	$250

MODEL 396 AIRLITE Ti MOUNTAIN LITE - .44 S&W Spl. cal., L-frame, 5 shot, 3 1/8 in. barrel with stainless liner and Hi-Viz front sight, aluminum alloy frame with titanium cylinder, matte stainless/grey finish, Hogue Bantam grips, 18 oz. Mfg. 2001-2004.

	$625	$475	$400	$355	$315	$285	$250

Last MSR was $812.

There has been one engineering change to this model.

MODEL 396 NIGHTGUARD - .44 Spl. cal., two-piece 2 1/2 in. barrel, alloy frame with stainless cylinder, black alloy finish, 5 shot, L-frame, SA/DA, rubber grips, fixed sight with front night sight. New 2008.

MSR $980	$725	$540	$450	$375	$325	$285	$250

MODEL 431 CENTENNIAL AIRWEIGHT - .32 H&R Mag cal., J-frame, 6 shot, 2 in. barrel, blue finish. New mid-2004-2005.

	$425	$375	$300	$260	$230	$200	$180

Last MSR was $450.

MODEL 432 CENTENNIAL AIRWEIGHT - .32 H&R Mag cal., J-frame, DAO, 6 shot, 2 in. barrel, blue finish. New mid-2004-2005.

	$450	$365	$310	$265	$235	$200	$180

Last MSR was $469.

Add $263 for Crimson Trace laser grips (new 2005).

MODEL 442 CENTENNIAL AIRWEIGHT - .38 S&W Spl.+P cal., J-frame, 5 shot, double action only, 1 7/8 in. barrel only with fixed sights, hammerless, aluminum alloy/steel frame, blue or nickel (disc. 1995) finish, round butt, current production uses Uncle Mike's Boot grips, 15 oz. New 1993.

MSR $545	$415	$335	$255	$210	$185	$170	$150

Add $15 for nickel finish (disc.).

There have been two engineering changes to this model.

GRADING - PPGS™	100%	98%	95%	90%	80%	70%	60%

MODEL 460 V/XVR - .460 S&W Mag. cal., 5 shot, X-frame, SA/DA, 5 (V) or 8 3/8 (XVR) in. barrel with Hi-Viz sights, stainless steel frame with matte finish (approx. 16 mfg. in blue/black finish), similar in design to the Model 500, approx. 70 oz. New 2005.

    MSR $1,319   **$1,025**   **$865**   **$750**   **$650**   **$560**   **$465**   **$410**

MODEL 500 - .500 S&W Mag. cal., X-frame, 5 shot, DA, two-piece 4 (new 2004) or 8 3/8 in. ported barrel and full shroud, stainless steel, recoil compensator, new Sorbathane Hogue wraparound rubber finger groove grips, micrometer click adj. rear sight, red ramp (4 in. barrel) or interchangeable front sight blades (8 3/8 in. barrel only), frame is drilled and tapped, 56 or 72 1/2 oz. (with 8 3/8 in. barrel). New 2003.

    MSR $1,248   **$975**   **$800**   **$700**   **$600**   **$500**   **$425**   **$395**

    Add $71 for 4 in. barrel.

    Add $71 for Hi-Viz sights (8 3/8 in. barrel only, new 2005).

✳ *Model 500 SCI "Big 5" Master's Edition* - features hand engraving by S&W master engraver Wayne D´Angelo, with 24Kt. gold inlays of the African Big 5 animals, ivory grips, includes presentation case, serial numbered SCI001-SCI005. Limited mfg. 2004.

    $10,000 **$8,000** **$6,000** **N/A**   **N/A**   **N/A**   **N/A**

                                 Last MSR was $10,000.

✳ *Model 500 SCI "Big 5" Limited Edition* - features roll engraving, with 24Kt. gold inlays of the African Big 5 animals, ivory grips, includes presentation case, serial numbered SCI0006-SCI0300. Limited mfg. 2004.

    $3,000 **$2,250** **$1,500** **N/A**   **N/A**   **N/A**   **N/A**

                                 Last MSR was $3,000.

MODEL 520 (OLDER MFG.) - .357 Mag. cal., 4 in. barrel, fixed sights, N-frame, originally ordered for N.Y. State Police but never purchased. Approx. 3,000 mfg. with box during 1980 only.

    $925   **$800**   **$700**   **$575**   **$450**   **$350**   **$275**

MODEL 520 (CURRENT MFG.) - .357 Mag. cal., L-frame, two-piece, semi-lug 4 in. barrel, 7 shot, adj. rear sight, wood grips with finger grooves, matte black finish, carbon steel frame with titanium cylinder, Hi-Viz front sight, 37.9 oz. Mfg. mid-2005-2006.

    $495   **$425**   **$375**   **$330**   **$295**   **$265**   **$235**

                                 Last MSR was $731.

MODEL 544 - please refer to the Commemorative section.

MODEL 547 M & P - 9mm Para. cal., 3 or 4 in. heavy barrel, 6 shot, round (3 in. barrel) or square (4 in. barrel) butt, blue only, 32 oz. Disc. 1985.

    $775   **$675**   **$575**   **$450**   **$350**   **$275**   **$225**

                                   Last MSR was $317.

MODEL 581 (DISTINGUISHED SERVICE MAGNUM) - .357 Mag. cal., L-Frame, fixed sights, 4 in. barrel, 6 shot, blue or nickel finish, 38 oz. Disc. 1992.

    $600   **$525**   **$450**   **$375**   **$300**   **$250**   **$200**

                                   Last MSR was $335.

    Add $20 for nickel (mfg. 1980-88).

MODEL 586 (DISTINGUISHED COMBAT MAGNUM) - .357 Mag. cal., L-Frame, 4, 6, or 8 3/8 (disc. 1991) in. barrel, adj. sights, blue or nickel (disc. 1991) finish. Disc. 1999.

    $650   **$550**   **$450**   **$375**   **$300**   **$250**   **$200**

                                   Last MSR was $494.

    Add 5%-10% for nickel finish (disc.).

    Add $4 for white outlined rear sight (disc. 1994).

    Add $5 for 6 in. barrel.

    Add $22 for 8 3/8 in. barrel (disc. 1991).

    Add $35 for adj. front sight - disc. 1991 (6 in. barrel only, new 1986).

There have been 7 engineering changes to this model.

GRADING - PPGS™	100%	98%	95%	90%	80%	70%	60%

MODEL 610 CLASSIC - 10mm Norma or .40 S&W cal., N-frame, 6 shot, adj. sights, 4 (new 2001) 5 (disc. 2000) or 6 1/2 (disc. 2000) in. full lug barrel, stainless steel construction, fluted or unfluted (4 or 6 1/2 in. barrel only) cylinder, round butt, adj. rear sight, current production uses Hogue rubber grips, target hammer optional, 50 oz., approx. 5,000 mfg. 1990 only, reintroduced 1998-2004.

	$650	$525	$425	$350	$295	$245	$215

Last MSR was $833.

There have been three engineering changes to this model.

MODEL 617 (K-22 MASTERPIECE STAINLESS) - .22 LR cal., K-frame, stainless steel variation of the Model 17 (K-22 Masterpiece), 6 (6 in. full lug barrel only beginning 1999) or 10 (new 1997) shot, 4, 6, or 8 3/8 (disc. 2002) in. full lug barrel, satin stainless finish, combat trigger and Hogue rubber grips are standard on current production, semi-target, 41-52 1/2 oz. New 1990.

MSR $837	$550	$415	$265	$200	$175	$135	$115

Add $16 for 4 or 6 in. barrel with 10 shot, or $54 for 8 3/8 in. barrel (disc. 2002).

In 2000, this model includes target hammer with 8 3/8 in. barrel. 4 and 6 in. barrels were standard during a limited production period in 1991.

MODEL 619 - .357 Mag. cal., L-frame, 7 shot, two-piece 5 in. barrel, stainless steel with satin finish, rubber grips, fixed sights, 37 1/2 oz. Mfg. 2005-2006.

	$450	$375	$275	$225	$185	$150	$125

Last MSR was $646.

MODEL 620 - .357 Mag. cal., 4 in. barrel, similar to Model 619, except has white outline rear sight and red ramp front sight, 38 oz. New 2005.

MSR $814	$565	$445	$375	$310	$260	$220	$190

MODEL 624 .44 TARGET - .44 S&W Spl. cal., 6 shot, 4 or 6 1/2 in. barrel, 42 oz. Mfg. 1986-1987 only.

	$475	$395	$325	$250	$195	$165	$140

Last MSR was $449.

Add $14 for 6 1/2 in. barrel.

MODEL 625 - .45 ACP or .45 Colt (disc.) cal., N-frame, stainless variation of the Model 25-2, 6 shot, 3 (disc. 1991), 4 (disc. 1991, reintroduced 2002), or 5 in. barrel, round butt, choice of matte or satin (mfg. 2005-2007) stainless finish, ramp front (3 or 4 in. barrel) or Patridge front (5 in. barrel) sight, full lug barrel, Pachmayr (disc.) or Hogue rubber combat grips, 45 oz. New 1988.

MSR $988	$650	$550	$475	$375	$275	$240	$215

Add $40 for Model 625-JM w/Jerry Miculek initialled wood grips (mfg. 2007).

Approx. 1,500 of the 5 in. barrel models had the frame stamped "625-2", roll engraved barrel with ".45 CAL MODEL OF 1988" barrel inscription, and a ramp front sight. Laser engraving replaced roll engraving in 1989.

There have been 10 engineering changes for this model.

MODEL 627 - .357 Mag. cal., also known as "Model of 1989" (stamped on barrel), N-frame, smooth combat grips, S&W medallion logo, round butt, unfluted cylinder, full underlug 5 1/2 in. barrel. Disc.

	$700	$600	$500	$425	$325	$265	$230

This model evolved into a Performance Center model.

MODEL 627 (CURRENT MFG.) - .357 Mag. cal., 8 shot, SA/DA, 4 in. barrel, N-frame, adj. rear sight, red ramp front sight, stainless steel frame, rubber finger groove grips, 42 oz. New 2008.

MSR $916	$700	$575	$400	$350	$300	$275	$250

MODEL 627 PRO SERIES - similar to Model 627, except has Pro Series features, including custom barrel with recessed precision crown and chamfered charge holes. New 2008.

MSR $964	$720	$575	$495	$450	$400	$365	$325

GRADING - PPGS™	100%	98%	95%	90%	80%	70%	60%

MODEL 629 - .44 Mag./.44 S&W Spl. cal., N-frame, 6 shot, similar to Model 29, available with 4, 6, or 8 3/8 (disc. 2002) in. barrel, satin stainless finish, current production uses Hogue rubber combat grips, 41 1/2 - 49 1/2 oz. New 1979.

	MSR $948	$650	$575	$495	$375	$325	$275	$215

Add $47 for fully shrouded 5 in. barrel (disc.) or $39 for 8 3/8 in. barrel (disc.).

Add $52 for combat grips with barrel scope mount (cut across barrel rib) - disc. 1991 (8 3/8 in. barrel only).

Add $198 for Model 629 ES (Emergency Survival) kit with blankets, knife, compass, whistle, signal mirror, fire starter, tinder, chain saw, "Bear Attacks of the Century" book and waterproof storm case.

During 1978, approx. 100 pre-production revolvers were made with pinned barrels and recessed cylinders, serial range is N629,062-N629,200, includes wood box. Prices range from $650-$750, depending on condition.

✻ *Model 629 Classic* - satin stainless steel variation of the Model 29 Classic, 5, 6 1/2 (with or w/o PowerPort), or 8 3/8 in. barrel, current production uses Hogue rubber combat grips, 49 1/2 - 53 1/2 oz. New 1990.

MSR $995	$695	$575	$450	$375	$325	$275	$200

Add $16 for Powerport.

Add $27 for 6 1/2 in. barrel with white outline on rear sight (disc.).

Add $54 for Hi-Viz front sight, 6 1/2 in. barrel only (disc.).

Add $245 for Crimson Trace laser grips (Model 629CT, mfg. 2006).

✻ *Model 629 Classic DX* - similar to Classic, except is supplied with 2 sets of grips (Hogue combat square and Morado wood round buttstocks), 6 1/2 or 8 3/8 in. barrel, satin stainless finish, 5 interchangeable front sights, numbered test target, 51-54 oz. Mfg. 1992-2002.

	$650	$550	$510	$440	$385	$320	$275

Last MSR was $986.

Add $32 for 8 3/8 in. barrel.

✻ *Model 629 Magna Classic* - .44 Mag. cal., similar to Model 29, 3,000 mfg. during 1990 only.

	$900	$825	$750	$640	$535	$450	$390

Last MSR was $999.

MODEL 631 - .32 H&R Mag. cal., 6 shot, 2 (fixed sight) or 4 (adj. sight) in. barrel, combat stocks, round butt only, approx. 5,500 mfg. 1990-1992.

	$500	$425	$350	$275	$200	$150	$125

Last MSR was $386.

MODEL 631 LADYSMITH - .32 H&R Mag. cal., 2 in. barrel only, rosewood stocks.

	$400	$350	$300	$250	$195	$150	$125

Last MSR was $400.

MODEL 632 CENTENNIAL - .32 H&R Mag. cal., 2 or 3 (mfg. 1991 only) in. barrel, stainless/alloy construction, fully concealed hammer, J frame, Santoprene combat grips, fixed sights, 15 1/2 oz. Mfg. 1991-1992.

	$500	$450	$350	$250	$195	$165	$140

Last MSR was $410.

Add 20% for 3 in. barrel.

MODEL 637 CHIEFS SPECIAL AIRWEIGHT - .38 S&W Spl.+P cal., J-frame, 5 shot, matte finish, alloy frame with 1 7/8 in. satin stainless steel barrel and cylinder, current production uses Uncle Mike's Boot grips, 15 oz., 560 mfg. during 1991, reintroduced 1996.

MSR $545		$385	$290	$270	$180	$140	$120	$105

Add $16 for Carry Combo configuration (new 2004).

Add $243 for Crimson Trace laser grips (new 2005).

GRADING - PPGS™	100%	98%	95%	90%	80%	70%	60%

MODEL 638 BODYGUARD AIRWEIGHT - .38 S&W Spl.+P cal., J-frame, 5 shot, alloy frame, 1 7/8 in. stainless steel barrel and cylinder, shrouded hammer, round butt, Uncle Mike's Boot grips, 15 oz. 1,200 mfg. during 1990 only, reintroduced 1998.

MSR $545	$385	$290	$270	$180	$140	$120	$105

MODEL 640 CENTENNIAL - .357 Mag./.38 S&W Spl.+P or .38 S&W Spl. (disc.) cal., J-frame, 5 shot, double action only, 1 7/8 (mfg. 1998-2001), 2 1/8 (new 1991), or 3 (disc. 1992) in. barrel, hammerless, current production uses Uncle Mike's Combat grips, satin stainless finish, round butt, 23 oz. New 1991.

MSR $727	$515	$365	$265	$210	$170	$145	$120

MODEL 642 CENTENNIAL AIRWEIGHT - .38 S&W Spl.+P cal., J-frame, 5 shot, 1 7/8, 2 (disc. 1997), or 3 (disc. 1991) in. barrel, alloy frame with stainless steel cylinder and barrel, combat grips, hammerless, satin stainless finish, fixed rear sight, 15 oz. Mfg. 1990-1992, reintroduced 1996.

MSR $545	$385	$290	$270	$180	$140	$120	$105

✱ *Model 642 CT Centennial Airweight* - similar Model 642 Centennial Airweight, except has Crimson Trace laser grips. New 2004.

MSR $798	$595	$425	$325	$250	$220	$200	$180

MODEL 642 LADYSMITH AIRWEIGHT - .38 S&W Spl.+P cal., J-frame, 5 shot, 1 7/8 in. barrel, stainless steel/alloy construction, smooth wood grips, satin stainless finish, includes soft side carry or jewelry case, 14 1/2 oz. New 1996.

MSR $711	$545	$365	$245	$190	$145	$125	$105

MODEL 646 - .40 S&W cal., 4 in. barrel, stainless steel, 6 shot, titanium cylinder. Limited mfg. during 2000 and 2003.

	$525	$450	$365	$310	$265	$225	$200

MODEL 647 - .17 HMR cal., K-frame, 6 shot, stainless steel, 8 3/8 in. barrel with full lug, Hogue rubber grips with finger grooves, Patridge rear with adj. front sight, 52 oz. Mfg. 2003-2004.

	$550	$475	$375	$315	$270	$225	$200

Last MSR was $697.

MODEL 648 - .22 Mag. cal., K-frame, 6 in. full lug barrel, combat grips, square butt, combat trigger, semi-target hammer. Mfg. 1989-1996.

	$450	$325	$250	$195	$165	$140	$120

Last MSR was $464.

MODEL 648-2 - .22 Mag. cal., K-frame, 6 shot, stainless steel, 6 in. barrel with full lug, Hogue rubber grips with finger grooves, Patridge rear with adj. front sight, 45 oz. Mfg. 2003-2005.

	$525	$345	$240	$185	$160	$135	$115

Last MSR was $703.

MODEL 649 BODYGUARD - .357 Mag./.38 S&W Spl.+P or .38 S&W Spl. (disc.) cal., J-frame, otherwise similar to Model 49 Bodyguard, except is satin stainless steel, 1 7/8 (mfg. 1998 only), 2 (disc. 1997), or 2 1/8 (new 1998) in. barrel, shrouded hammer, current production uses Uncle Mike's Combat grips, 23 oz. New 1986.

MSR $727	$545	$365	$245	$190	$145	$125	$105

There have been five engineering changes to this model.

MODEL 650 - .22 Mag. cal., service kit gun, stainless steel, 3 in. heavy barrel, J-frame, fixed sights. Mfg. 1983-1987.

	$500	$425	$325	$250	$200	$150	$125

Last MSR was $305.

GRADING - PPGS™	100%	98%	95%	90%	80%	70%	60%

MODEL 651 KIT GUN - .22 Mag. cal., target kit gun, stainless steel, 4 in. barrel, J-frame, adj. sights. Mfg. 1983-87, re-released in late 1990, disc. 1998.

	$500	$425	$325	$250	$200	$150	$125

Last MSR was $478.

This model could be ordered with a factory fitted optional .22 LR cylinder until 1987 (last mfg. sug. retail was $295 for the cylinder alone). This variation with the extra cylinder is very desirable.

MODEL 657 - .41 Mag. cal., N-frame, 4 (disc.), 6 (disc. 2000), 7 1/2 (new 2001), or 8 3/8 (disc. 1992) in. barrel, satin stainless steel, current production uses Hogue rubber combat grips, approx. 53 oz. New 1986.

MSR $869	$550	$425	$315	$250	$215	$185	$165

There have been 5 engineering changes to this model.

MODEL 681 DISTINGUISHED SERVICE MAGNUM - .357 Mag. cal., stainless steel, 4 in. barrel, L-Frame. Mfg. 1980-1992.

	$425	$350	$275	$225	$175	$140	$125

Last MSR was $412.

1991 mfg. includes square butt.

MODEL 686 DISTINGUISHED COMBAT MAGNUM - .357 Mag./.38 S&W Spl.+P cal., L-Frame, similar to Model 586, except 2 1/2 (new 1990), 4, 6 (with or w/o PowerPort), or 8 3/8 (disc. 2002) in. barrel, fixed (disc.) or adj. sights, current production uses Hogue rubber grips, 35-51 oz. New 1980.

MSR $830	$550	$425	$325	$250	$200	$165	$140

Add $23 for PowerPort 6 in. barrel.

✳ *Model 686 Distinguished Combat Magnum Plus* - .357 Mag./.38 S&W Spl.+P cal., L-frame, 7 shot, 2 1/2, 3 (new 2007), 4, or 6 in. barrel, synthetic or Hogue rubber grips, stainless steel, round (2 1/2 in. barrel only) or square butt, white outline rear sight on 4 or 6 in. barrel, 34 1/2 - 43 oz. New 1996.

MSR $853	$565	$415	$285	$230	$190	$160	$135

MODEL 686SSR - .357 Mag. cal., 6 shot, L-frame, 4 in. barrel, SA/DA, interchangeable front sight, adj. rear sight, satin stainless finish, checkered wood grips, stainless steel frame and cylinder, Pro Series model featuring forged hammer and trigger, custom barrel with recessed crown, bossed mainspring, and tuned action, 38.3 oz. New 2007.

MSR $964	$705	$555	$440	$375	$330	$295	$265

MODEL 696 - .44 S&W Spl. cal., L-frame, 5 shot, 3 in. barrel with full shroud, Hogue rubber (disc. 2000) or Uncle Mike's Combat grips, satin stainless steel, adj. rear sight, 36 oz. Mfg. 1997-2002.

	$485	$315	$250	$195	$165	$140	$120

Last MSR was $620.

MODEL 940 CENTENNIAL - 9mm Para. cal., fully concealed hammer, 2 or 3 (disc. 1992) in. barrel, fixed rear sight, Santoprene combat grips, 23-25 oz. Mfg. 1991-1998.

	$450	$375	$300	$250	$200	$175	$150

Last MSR was $493.

PISTOLS: SEMI-AUTO

Listed in order of model number (except .32 and .35 Automatic Pistols). Alphabetical models will appear at the end of this section.

To understand S&W 3rd generation model nomenclature, the following rules apply. The first two digits (of the four digit model number) specify caliber. Numbers 39, 59, and 69 refer to 9mm Para. cal. The third digit refers to the model type. 0 means standard model, 1 is for compact, 2 is for standard model with decocking lever, 3 is for compact variation with decocking lever, 4 is for standard with double action only, 5 designates a compact model in

100%	98%	95%	90%	80%	70%	60%	50%	40%	30%	20%	10%

double action only, 6 indicates a non-standard barrel length, 7 is a non-standard barrel length with decocking lever, and 8 refers to non-standard barrel length in double action only. The fourth digit refers to the material(s) used in the fabrication of the pistol. 3 refers to an aluminum alloy frame with stainless steel slide, 4 designates an aluminum alloy frame with carbon steel slide, 5 is for carbon steel frame and slide, 6 is a stainless steel frame and slide, and 7 refers to a stainless steel frame and carbon steel slide. Hence, a Model 4053 refers to a pistol in .40 S&W cal. configured in compact version with double action only and fabricated with an aluminum alloy frame and stainless steel slide. This model nomenclature does not apply to 2 or 3 digit model numbers (i.e., Rimfire Models and the Model 52).

When applicable, early variations of some of the older semi-auto models listed in this category will be more desirable than later mfg.

.32 AUTOMATIC PISTOL - .32 ACP cal., 7 shot mag., 3 1/2 in. barrel, blue with "S&W" monogram inlaid plain walnut grip. 957 mfg. 1924-1936. Serial range starting with S/N 1.

N/A	$2,500	$2,000	$1,750	$1,500	$1,250	$1,000	$800	$700	$600	$500	$400

.35 AUTOMATIC PISTOL (MODEL 1913) - .35 S&W Auto cal., 7 shot mag., 3 1/2 in. barrel, blue or nickel w/ "S&W" monogram inlaid in plain walnut grips. 8,350 mfg. 1913-1921. Serial range starting with no. 1.

N/A	$875	$775	$625	$525	$450	$375	$325	$275	$235	$200	$185

A slight premium might exist for the first model (up to ser. no. 3,125).

GRADING - PPGS™	100%	98%	95%	90%	80%	70%	60%

MODEL 22A SPORT SERIES - .22 LR cal., single action, 10 shot mag., aluminum alloy frame, stainless steel slide, choice of 4 in. standard, 5 1/2 in. standard or bull, or 7 in. standard barrel with raised solid rib, adj. rear and Hi-Viz (5 1/2 in. bull barrel only, new 2001) sights, 2-piece black polymer (hard or soft) or Dymondwood (5 1/2 bull barrel only) grips, blue, two-tone (new 2006, 5 1/2 in. barrel only), or camo (new 2004, 5 1/2 in. barrel only) finish, 28-39 oz. New 1997.

MSR $284		$215	$180	$140	$115	$100	$85	$75

Add $16 for 4 in. barrel or blue/black finish.
Add $48 for 5 1/2 in. barrel.
Add $16 for 7 in. standard barrel.
Add $127 for 5 1/2 in. bull barrel with camo finish (disc. 2007).
Add $114 for 5 1/2 in. bull barrel with Dymondwood target grips (disc. 2005).
Add $48 for 5 1/2 in. bull barrel with Hi-Viz sights (new 2001) and two-tone finish.
Add $71 for 5 1/2 in. bull barrel with 2 piece target grips and thumbrest (disc. 2000).

MODEL 22S SPORT SERIES - .22 LR cal., single action, 10 shot mag., aluminum alloy frame, stainless steel slide, choice of 5 1/2 standard or bull (disc. 2005) or 7 (disc. 2004) in. standard barrel with raised solid rib, adj. rear and Hi-Viz (5 1/2 in. bull barrel only, new 2001) sights, 2-piece black polymer (hard or soft) or Dymondwood (5 1/2 in. bull barrel only) grips, satin stainless finish, 41-48 oz. Mfg. 1997-2007.

		$325	$255	$210	$170	$140	$125	$110

Last MSR was $419.

Add $40 for 7 in. standard barrel with thumbrest soft-touch grips (disc. 2004).
Add $83 for 5 1/2 in. bull barrel with Dymondwood target grips (disc. 2004).
Add $102 for 5 1/2 in. bull barrel with Hi-Viz sights (mfg. 2001-2004).
Add $44 for 5 1/2 in. bull barrel with 2 piece target grips and thumbrest (disc. 2000).

MODEL 39 STEEL FRAME - 9mm Para. cal., 8 shot, 4 in. barrel, long ejector, walnut stocks, blue, adj. rear windage only sight, double action, walnut grips, 927 mfg. during 1966 only in 3 ser. no. ranges.

		$1,495	$1,325	$1,125	$975	$850	$735	$650

GRADING - PPGS™	100%	98%	95%	90%	80%	70%	60%

MODEL 39 ALLOY FRAME - 9mm Para. cal., alloy frame, this model was unmarked up to ser. no. approx. 2,600, early guns had a short safety lever, checkered walnut grips, blue or nickel finish. Mfg. started 1954.

	$400	$350	$315	$260	$210	$175	$140

Add $35 for nickel finish.

Collectors report an approx. ser. no. range 1,001-105,000 with long ejector.

This model was the first commercially mfg. 9mm Para. double action semi-auto in the U.S.

MODEL 39 ALLOY FRAME EARLY MFG. (PRE-39) - short safety, first group of 298 were produced for military inspection, various markings include "Quantico, VA", approx. ser. no. range 1,001-2,600. Mfg. 1954-55.

	$1,495	$1,325	$1,125	$975	$850	$735	$650

Add 50% for early manufacture original military trial guns.

MODEL 39-2 ALLOY FRAME (LATER PRODUCTION) - 7.65mm (.30 Luger) or 9mm Para. cal., double action, 8 shot mag., 4 in. barrel, checkered walnut grips, adj. sight, alloy frame, approx. 1971, the 39-2 was introduced as an improved version. Mfg. 1970-82.

	100%	98%	95%	90%	80%	70%	60%
9mm Para.	$395	$365	$325	$260	$240	$220	$200
7.65mm cal.	$1,375	$1,250	$1,100	$950	$825	$700	$625

Add 10% for nickel finish.

The .30 Luger cal. (7.65mm) was mfg. for the European marketplace only. Very hard to find in the U.S.

MODEL 41/41-1 .22 RF - .22 S (disc., Model 41-1) or LR cal., match target pistol, single action, 10 shot mag., adj. Patridge sights, checkered walnut grips with thumbrest, 5 (disc.), 5 1/2 (heavy), 7 (standard) or 7 3/8 (disc. 2004) in. barrel, blue finish only, 41 oz. New 1957.

MSR $1,209	$835	$660	$495	$395	$350	$300	$275

Add $100 for 5 1/2 in. barrel with extended sight (disc.).

Add $35 for 7 3/8 in. barrel with muzzle brake (disc.).

Add 125% for .22 Short cal. with counterweight and muzzle brake (disc.).

Add 15%-40% for early variations with cocking indicator (disc. 1978).

There are several disc. barrels on the Model 41, including a 5 in. standard weight with extended sight, 7 3/8 in. with muzzle brake, and 5 1/2 in. heavy barrel with extended sight. Factory engraving Model 41s with cocking indicator in NIB condition are currently selling in the $2,500 range.

MODEL 44 - 9mm Para. cal., single action design, S&W's rarest semi-auto pistol, approx. 10 mfg.

Original examples are typically seen in the $10K-$15K range, depending on condition.

MODEL 46 - .22 LR cal., 5, 5 1/2, or 7 in. barrel, blue, nylon grips, adj. sights. Mfg. 4,000, 1957-1966.

	$725	$600	$500	$400	$300	$260	$225

This model is similar to the Model 41, but does not have high polish bluing, and has brown plastic grips.

MODEL 52-A - .38 AMU cal., same action as Model 39, 4 in. barrel. Originally mfg. for U.S. Army Marksman Training Unit, 87 mfg.

	$3,750	$3,250	$2,750	$2,250	$1,950	$1,600	$1,300

MODEL 52 - .38 S&W Spl. Wadcutter only, similar action to Model 39, except incorporates a set screw locking out the double action, 5 in. barrel, 5 shot mag. Approx. 3,500 mfg. 1961-63.

	$950	$850	$775	$675	$575	$475	$395

MODELS 52-1 & 52-2 - .38 Spl. Mid-Range Wadcutter cal. only, single action semi-auto, 5 in. barrel, adj. sights, checkered walnut grips, blue only, 5 shot mag.

	$950	$850	$775	$675	$575	$475	$395

Last MSR was $908.

The Model 52-1 was mfg. 1963-1971, and the Model 52-2 was mfg. 1971-93.

GRADING - PPGS™	100%	98%	95%	90%	80%	70%	60%

MODEL 59 - similar to Model 39, except has 14 shot mag., black nylon grips. Disc. 1981.

	$475	$400	$350	$275	$250	$225	$215

Add $35 for nickel finish.
Add $150 for smooth (ungrooved) grip frame.

MODEL 61 ESCORT - .22 LR cal., 5 shot, semi-auto, blue or nickel, 2 1/2 in. barrel, plastic grips, mfg. 1970-74.

Blue finish	$350	$250	$225	$175	$150	$140	$110
Nickel finish	$395	$275	$235	$185	$155	$140	$110

MODEL 147-A - 9mm Para. cal., 14 shot, steel frame, 4 in. barrel, black plastic grips, adj. sights for windage only, similar to Model 59, except has steel frame, 112 mfg. 1979 only.

	$1,550	$1,375	$1,050	$875	$800	$725	$650

This model was originally marked Model 47 for export, prefix and suffix were added. Ser. nos. were stamped, and are crude by today's standard.

MODEL 410 - .40 S&W cal., traditional double action, steel slide with alloy frame, blue finish, 4 in. barrel, 10 or 11 shot mag., single side safety, 3-dot sights, straight backstrap with synthetic grips, 28 1/2 oz. Mfg. 1996-2007.

	$525	$370	$275	$230	$195	$175	$165

Last MSR was $687.

Add $21 for Hi-Viz front sight (disc. 2003).

✱ *Model 410S* - similar to Model 410, except has stainless steel slide with alloy frame, 28 1/2 oz. Mfg. 2003-2007.

	$545	$375	$275	$245	$205	$175	$165

Last MSR was $711.

Add $237 for Crimson Trace laser grips (new 2005).

MODEL 411 - .40 S&W cal., 4 in. barrel, 11 shot mag., fixed sights, blue finish, aluminum alloy frame, manual safety. Mfg. 1993-95.

	$475	$400	$350	$325	$295	$280	$265

Last MSR was $525.

MODEL 422 .22 RF (FIELD) - .22 LR cal., single action, 4 1/2 or 6 in. barrel, aluminum frame with steel slide, 10 shot mag., fixed sights, black plastic or wood grips, matte blue finish, 22 oz. Mfg. 1987-1996.

	$195	$165	$130	$115	$105	$100	$95

Last MSR was $235.

✱ *Model 422 Target* - .22 LR cal., single action, 4 1/2 or 6 in. barrel, aluminum frame with steel slide, 10 shot mag., adj. rear sight, checkered walnut grips, matte blue finish, 22 oz. Mfg. 1987-1996.

	$250	$200	$165	$135	$115	$105	$95

Last MSR was $290.

MODEL 439 - 9mm Para. cal., double action, 4 in. barrel, blue or nickel finish, alloy frame, 8 shot mag., checkered walnut grips, 30 oz. Disc. 1988.

	$475	$35	$325	$275	$240	$225	$210

Last MSR was $472.

Add $34 for nickel finish (disc. 1986).
Add $26 for adj. sights.

MODEL 457 COMPACT - .45 ACP cal., traditional double action, alloy frame and steel slide, 3 3/4 in. barrel, single side safety, 3-dot sights, 7 shot mag., straight backstrap, blue finish only, black synthetic grips, 29 oz. Mfg. 1996-2006.

	$525	$365	$270	$225	$195	$175	$165

Last MSR was $681.

GRADING - PPGS™	100%	98%	95%	90%	80%	70%	60%

✳ *Model 457S Compact* - similar to Model 457, except has stainless steel slide with alloy frame, 29 oz. Mfg. 2003-2006.

| | $545 | $390 | $280 | $245 | $200 | $175 | $165 |

Last MSR was $710.

MODEL 459 - 9mm Para. cal., 14 shot version of Model 439, checkered nylon stocks, limited mfg. with squared-off triggerguard with serrations. Disc. 1988.

| | $450 | $400 | $350 | $300 | $275 | $255 | $240 |

Last MSR was $501.

> Add $26 for adj. sights.
> Add $44 for nickel finish (disc. 1986).

✳ *Model 459 Brushed Finish* - 9mm Para. cal., 14 shot, 4 in. barrel, dull finish, fixed sights, special grips made to F.B.I. or police specs., 803 mfg.

| | $700 | $625 | $550 | $440 | $385 | $330 | $300 |

Pricing assumes proper F.B.I. documentation (be wary).

MODEL 469 "MINI" - 9mm Para. cal., double action, alloy frame, 12 shot finger extension mag., short frame, bobbed hammer, 3 1/2 in. barrel, sandblast blue or satin nickel finish, ambidextrous safety standard (1986), molded Delrin black Grips, 26 oz. Disc. 1988.

| | $475 | $35 | $325 | $275 | $240 | $225 | $210 |

Last MSR was $478.

MODEL 539 - 9mm Para. cal., double action, steel frame, 8 shot, 4 in. barrel, blue or nickel. Approx. 8,300 mfg. Disc. 1983.

| | $550 | $475 | $415 | $375 | $350 | $325 | $300 |

> Add $35 for nickel finish.
> Add $30 for adj. rear sight.

MODEL 559 - 9mm Para. cal., double action, steel frame, 14 shot mag., 4 in. barrel, blue or nickel. Approx. 1,700 mfg. Disc. 1983.

| | $600 | $525 | $450 | $375 | $275 | $250 | $225 |

> Add $35 for nickel finish.
> Add $30 for adj. rear sight.

MODEL 622 .22 RF (Field) - .22 LR cal., single action, 4 1/2 or 6 in. barrel, stainless/alloy construction, 10 shot mag., fixed sights, black plastic grips, 21 1/2 or 23 1/2 oz. Mfg. 1990-96.

| | $220 | $175 | $160 | $125 | $110 | $95 | $85 |

Last MSR was $284.

✳ *Model 622 Target* - .22 LR cal., single action, 4 1/2 or 6 in. barrel (VR was an option in 1996 only), stainless steel construction, 10 shot mag., adj. rear sight, checkered walnut grips, 21 1/2 or 23 1/2 oz. Mfg. 1990-96.

| | $275 | $225 | $175 | $135 | $115 | $100 | $85 |

Last MSR was $337.

MODEL 639 STAINLESS - 9mm Para. cal., similar to Model 439-only stainless steel, 8 shot mag., ambidextrous safety became standard 1986, 36 oz. Disc. 1988.

| | $475 | $400 | $350 | $300 | $250 | $200 | $165 |

Last MSR was $523.

> Add $27 for adj. sights.

MODEL 645 STAINLESS - .45 ACP cal. only, 5 in. barrel, 8 shot mag., squared-off trigger guard, black molded nylon grips, ambidextrous safety, fixed sights, 37 1/2 oz. New 1986. Disc. 1988.

| | $550 | $475 | $400 | $350 | $300 | $250 | $200 |

Last MSR was $622.

> Add approx. 25% for the approx. 150 Model 645 "Interim" pistols were mfg. in 1988 only.
> Add $27 for adj. sight.

GRADING - PPGS™	100%	98%	95%	90%	80%	70%	60%

MODEL 659 STAINLESS - 9mm Para. cal., similar to Model 459-only stainless steel, 14 shot mag., ambidextrous safety became standard 1986, 39 1/2 oz. Disc. 1988.

	$475	$400	$350	$300	$250	$215	$180

Last MSR was $553.

Add approx. 30% for the approx. 150 Model 659 "Interim" pistols were mfg. in 1988 only. Add $27 for adj. sights.

MODEL 669 STAINLESS - 9mm Para. cal., smaller version of Model 659 with 12 shot finger extension mag., 3 1/2 in. barrel, fixed sights, molded Delrin grips, ambidextrous safety standard, 26 oz. Mfg. 1986-88 only.

	$450	$375	$300	$250	$195	$165	$140

Last MSR was $522.

Add approx. 30% for the approx. 150 Model 669 "Interim" pistols were mfg. in 1988 only.

MODEL 745 IPSC - .45 ACP cal., single action, 5 in. barrel, stainless steel frame with steel slide, hammer, and trigger, checkered walnut stocks, fixed rear sight, 38 3/4 oz. Mfg. 1987-90.

	$700	$575	$450	$350	$275	$235	$200

Last MSR was $699.

Early guns had optional "IPSC" markings. Later, these markings became standard.

MODEL 908 COMPACT - 9mm Para. cal., compact variation of the Model 909/910, 3 1/2 in. barrel, 3-dot sights, 8 shot mag., straight backstrap, 24 oz. Mfg. 1996-2007.

	$495	$355	$275	$230	$195	$175	$165

Last MSR was $648.

* *Model 908S Compact* - similar to Model 908, except has stainless steel slide with alloy frame, 24 oz. Mfg. 2003-2007.

	$495	$355	$275	$230	$195	$175	$165

Last MSR was $648.

Add $24 for carry combo variation (includes Kydex carry holster, new 2004).

MODEL 909 - 9mm Para. cal., 4 in. barrel, traditional double action, large frame, 9 shot mag., fixed sights, single side safety, alloy frame and steel slide, curved backstrap with black synthetic grips, 27 oz. Mfg. 1994-96.

	$450	$375	$300	$250	$210	$190	$175

Last MSR was $443.

MODEL 910 - similar to Model 909, except has 10 or 15 shot mag., 28 oz. Mfg. 1994-2007.

	$455	$345	$270	$230	$195	$175	$165

Last MSR was $616.

Add $22 for Hi-Viz front sight (disc. 2003).

* *Model 910S* - similar to Model 910, except has stainless steel slide with alloy frame, 28 oz. Mfg. 2003-2007.

	$460	$345	$270	$225	$195	$175	$165

Last MSR was $624.

MODEL 915 - 9mm Para. cal., 4 in. barrel, fixed sights, 10 (C/B 1994) or 15* shot mag., manual safety, aluminum alloy frame, blue finish. Mfg. 1993-94.

	$425	$350	$275	$225	$205	$190	$175

Last MSR was $467.

MODEL 1006 STAINLESS - 10mm cal., double action semi-auto, stainless steel construction, 5 in. barrel, exposed hammer, 9 shot mag., fixed or adj. sights, ambidextrous safety. Mfg. 1990-93.

	$675	$575	$425	$350	$300	$245	$215

Last MSR was $769.

Add $27 for adj. rear sight.

GRADING - PPGS™	100%	98%	95%	90%	80%	70%	60%

MODEL 1026 STAINLESS - 10mm cal., 5 in. barrel, traditional double action, features frame mounted decocking lever, 9 shot mag., straight backstrap. Mfg. 1990-91 only.

	$675	$575	$425	$350	$300	$245	$215

Last MSR was $755.

MODEL 1046 STAINLESS - 10mm cal., 5 in. barrel, fixed sights, double action only, 9 shot mag., straight backstrap. Mfg. 1991 only.

	$675	$575	$425	$350	$300	$245	$215

Last MSR was $747.

MODEL 1066 STAINLESS - 10mm cal., 4 1/4 in. barrel, 9 shot mag., straight backstrap, ambidextrous safety, traditional double action, fixed sights. Mfg. 1990-92.

	$650	$550	$425	$350	$300	$245	$215

Last MSR was $730.

Add $75 for Tritium night sights - disc. 1991 (Model 1066-NS).
Only 1,000 Model 1066-NSs were manufactured.

MODEL 1076 STAINLESS - similar to Model 1026 Stainless, except has 4 1/4 in. barrel. Mfg. 1990-93.

	$700	$625	$550	$450	$350	$300	$245

Last MSR was $778.

MODEL 1086 STAINLESS - similar to Model 1066 Stainless, except is double action only.

	$725	$600	$475	$375	$300	$250	$210

Last MSR was $730.

MODEL SW1911 - .45 ACP cal., patterned after the Colt M1911, large frame, SA, 5 in. barrel, 8 shot single stack mag., alloy (disc. 2006), steel or stainless steel frame, steel slide, matte, blue/black (new 2005) or Clear Coat finish, patented S&W firing pin safety release activated by the grip safety, pinned-in external extractor, Wolff springs throughout, Texas Armament match trigger, Hogue rubber (standard) or wood (new 2004) grips, McCormick hammer and thumb safety, Briley barrel bushing, two Wilson magazines, full-length heavy guide rod, high profile Wilson beavertail safety, dot, adj. rear black blade, or Novak Lo-Mount Carry sights, 39 oz. New 2003.

MSR $1,051	$840	$620	$450	$395	$350	$300	$275

Add $71 for rear adj. sights.
Add $269 for Doug Koenig Model w/two-tone finish and adj. rear sight (disc. 2007).

✳ *Model SW1911 Stainless* - features stainless steel frame and slide, checkered wood or black synthetic grips, 39.4 oz.

MSR $1,035	$825	$615	$450	$395	$350	$300	$275

Add $118 for adj. sights.
Add $93 for matte finish with black blade front sights (disc. 2006).
Add $300 for wood grips and adj. sights.
Add $71 for tactical lower frame rail w/wood grips (new 2006).
Add $269 for Crimson Trace laser grips (new 2005).

✳ *Model SW1911 PD (Sc)* - similar to Model SW1911, except has 4 1/4 or 5 (new 2007) in. barrel with small Scandium alloy frame, 8 shot, black finish, and wood grips. New 2004.

MSR $1,130	$900	$675	$475	$425	$385	$350	$325

Add $237 for Crimson Trace laser grips.
Add $126 for Gunsite model with gold bead front sight.
Add $39 for tactical lower rail.

GRADING - PPGS™	100%	98%	95%	90%	80%	70%	60%

SW1911 PRO SERIES - .45 ACP cal., SA, 8 shot mag., 5 in. barrel, Novak front and rear sights, checkered wood grips, stainless steel frame and slide, satin stainless finish, Pro Series features include 300 LPI front strap checkering, hand polished barrel feed ramp, crisp 4 1/2 lb. trigger pull, full length guide rod, oversized external extractor, double sided frame safety, precision crowned muzzle, 41 oz. New mid-2007.

MSR $1,383	$1,095	$950	$825	$700	$600	$500	$425

MODEL 2206 STAINLESS .22 RF (FIELD) - .22 LR cal., similar to Model 622 Field, except all stainless steel components, black plastic grips, 6 in. barrel with standard (disc. 1995) or adj. rear sight, 35 or 39 oz. Mfg. 1990-96.

	$290	$225	$175	$135	$115	$100	$85

Last MSR was $385.

Subtract $58 if w/o adj. sights.

✳ *Model 2206 Stainless Target* - similar to Model 2206 Stainless, except has adj. target sight, target stocks, and is drilled and tapped. Mfg. 1994-96.

	$360	$275	$225	$175	$140	$125	$105

Last MSR was $433.

MODEL 2213 STAINLESS .22 RF "SPORTSMAN" - .22 LR cal., single action, 3 in. barrel, alloy frame with stainless steel slide, 8 shot mag., 2 dot fixed rear sight, black plastic molded grips, 18 oz., includes holster/carry case. Mfg. 1992-99.

	$255	$200	$160	$130	$115	$100	$85

Last MSR was $340.

MODEL 2214 .22 RF "SPORTSMAN" - .22 LR cal., similar to Model 2213, except has alloy frame with blue carbon steel slide with matte black finish, and no case. Mfg. 1991-99.

	$230	$185	$160	$150	$140	$130	$120

Last MSR was $292.

MODEL 3904 - 9mm Para. cal., double action semi-auto, aluminum alloy frame, 4 in. barrel with fixed bushing, 8 shot mag., Delrin one piece wraparound grips, exposed hammer, ambidextrous safety, beveled magazine well, extended squared-off triggerguard, adj. or fixed rear sight, 3-dot sighting system, 28 oz. Mfg. 1989-91.

	$450	$385	$350	$325	$300	$280	$265

Last MSR was $541.

Add $25 for adj. rear sight.

MODEL 3906 STAINLESS - stainless steel variation of the Model 3904, 35 1/2 oz. Mfg. 1989-91.

	$510	$435	$375	$315	$270	$230	$200

Last MSR was $604.

Add $28 for adj. rear sight.

MODEL 3913 COMPACT STAINLESS - stainless steel variation of the Model 3914, 25 oz. Mfg. 1990-99.

	$535	$440	$365	$305	$260	$220	$190

Last MSR was $662.

✳ *Model 3913NL Compact Stainless* - similar to Model 3913 Ladysmith, except does not have Ladysmith on the slide. Disc. 1994.

	$550	$475	$395	$350	$295	$250	$220

Last MSR was $622.

GRADING - PPGS™	100%	98%	95%	90%	80%	70%	60%

✱ *Model 3913 LS Compact Stainless (Ladysmith)* - similar to Model 3913 Stainless, except is matte stainless with white Delrin grips and mag. does not have finger extension, includes case, 25 oz. Mfg. 1990-2006.

	$710	$525	$400	$335	$290	$245	$215

Last MSR was $901.

MODEL 3913TSW TACTICAL - 9mm Para. cal., traditional double action, compact frame, 3 1/2 in. barrel, 8-shot mag., Novak low mount 2-dot sights, stainless steel slide, aluminum alloy frame, matte stainless finish, straight black backstrap synthetic grips, 24.8 oz. Mfg. 1998-2006.

	$690	$520	$400	$335	$290	$245	$215

Last MSR was $876.

MODEL 3914 COMPACT - 9mm Para. cal., double action semi-auto, aluminum alloy frame, 3 1/2 in. barrel, hammerless, 8 shot finger extension mag., fixed sights only, ambidextrous safety, blue finish, straight backstrap grip, 25 oz. Mfg. 1990-95.

	$495	$425	$350	$325	$295	$280	$265

Last MSR was $562.

This model was also available with a single side manual safety at no extra charge - disc. 1991 (Model 3914NL).

✱ *Model 3914 Compact LadySmith* - similar to Model 3914, except has Delrin grips, 25 oz. Mfg. 1990-91 only.

	$485	$415	$365	$305	$260	$220	$190

Last MSR was $568.

MODEL 3953 COMPACT STAINLESS - 9mm Para. cal., double action only, aluminum alloy frame with stainless steel slide, compact model with 3 1/2 in. barrel, 8 shot mag. Mfg. 1990-99.

	$535	$440	$365	$305	$260	$220	$190

Last MSR was $662.

MODEL 3953TSW - similar to Model 3913TSW, except is double action only, 24.8 oz. Mfg. 1998-2002.

	$615	$475	$380	$320	$275	$230	$200

Last MSR was $760.

MODEL 3954 - similar to Model 3953, except has blue steel slide. Mfg. 1990-92.

	$475	$395	$350	$325	$295	$280	$265

Last MSR was $528.

MODEL 4003 STAINLESS - .40 S&W cal., traditional double action, 4 in. barrel, 11 shot mag., white dot fixed sights, ambidextrous safety, aluminum alloy frame with stainless steel slide, one piece Xenoy wraparound grips, straight gripstrap, 28 oz. Mfg. 1991-93.

	$575	$495	$395	$330	$285	$240	$215

Last MSR was $698.

✱ *Model 4003TSW Stainless* - similar to Model 4003 Stainless, but has aluminum alloy frame, 10 shot mag., stainless steel slide, S&W tactical features, including equipment rail and Novak Lo-Mount Carry sights, traditional double action only, satin stainless finish, 28 1/2 oz. Mfg. 2000-2004.

	$700	$600	$500	$450	$400	$360	$330

Last MSR was $940.

MODEL 4004 - .40 S&W cal., similar to Model 4003, except has aluminum alloy frame with blue carbon steel slide. Mfg. 1991-92.

	$540	$460	$375	$325	$295	$280	$265

Last MSR was $643.

GRADING - PPGS™	100%	98%	95%	90%	80%	70%	60%

MODEL 4006 STAINLESS - .40 S&W cal., 3 1/2 (Shorty Forty) or 4 in. barrel, 10 (C/B 1994) or 11* shot mag., satin stainless finish, exposed hammer, Delrin one piece wraparound grips, 3-dot sights, 38 1/2 oz. Mfg. 1990-99.

	$655	$545	$400	$335	$290	$245	$215

Last MSR was $791.

Add $31 for adj. rear sight.
Add $115 for fixed Tritium night sights (new 1992).
The bobbed hammer option on this model was disc. in 1991.

✻ *Model 4006TSW Stainless* - similar to Model 4006 Stainless, but has aluminum alloy frame and stainless steel slide, S&W tactical features, including equipment rail, traditional double action only, 37.8 oz. Mfg. 2000-2004.

	$700	$600	$500	$450	$400	$360	$330

Last MSR was $963.

Add $38 if w/o Novak Low Carry (NLC) mount sights.
Add $133 for night sights (disc.).

MODEL 4013 COMPACT STAINLESS - .40 S&W cal., semi-auto, standard double action, 3 1/2 in. barrel, 8 shot mag., fixed sights, ambidextrous safety, alloy frame. Mfg. 1991-96.

	$595	$485	$385	$330	$295	$280	$265

Last MSR was $722.

MODEL 4013TSW TACTICAL - .40 S&W cal., semi-auto, standard double action, 3 1/2 in. barrel, 9 shot mag. with reversible mag. catch, aluminum alloy frame with stainless steel slide, satin stainless finish, black synthetic grips, fixed 3-dot Novak Lo-Mount Carry sights, ambidextrous safety, 26.8 oz. Mfg. 1997-2006.

	$825	$630	$450	$385	$335	$280	$235

Last MSR was $1,021.

MODEL 4014 COMPACT - similar to Model 4013, except is steel with blue finish. Mfg. 1991-93.

	$550	$475	$425	$375	$330	$300	$275

Last MSR was $635.

MODEL 4026 STAINLESS - .40 S&W cal., traditional double action with frame mounted decocking lever, 10 (C/B 1994) or 11* shot mag., fixed sights, curved backstrap, 36 oz. Mfg. 1991-93.

	$625	$525	$400	$335	$290	$245	$215

Last MSR was $731.

MODEL 4040 PD - .40 S&W cal., compact frame using Scandium, 3 1/2 in. barrel, Hogue rubber grips, Novak Lo-Mount Carry 3-dot sights, matte black finish, 25.6 oz. Mfg. 2003-2005.

	$625	$525	$400	$335	$290	$245	$215

Last MSR was $840.

MODEL 4043 STAINLESS - .40 S&W cal., double action only, aluminum alloy frame with stainless steel slide, 4 in. barrel, 10 (C/B 1994) or 11* shot mag., one piece Xenoy wraparound grips, straight backstrap, white-dot fixed sights, 30 oz. Mfg. 1991-99.

	$635	$510	$390	$325	$280	$240	$210

Last MSR was $772.

✻ *Model 4043TSW Stainless* - double action only, similar to Model 4043 Stainless, but has S&W tactical features, including equipment rail, 28 1/2 oz. Mfg. 2000-2002.

	$650	$550	$425	$350	$290	$245	$215

Last MSR was $886.

GRADING - PPGS™	100%	98%	95%	90%	80%	70%	60%

MODEL 4044 - .40 S&W cal., similar to Model 4043, except has carbon steel slide. Mfg. 1991-92.

	$540	$460	$375	$325	$295	$280	$265

Last MSR was $643.

MODEL 4046 STAINLESS - similar to Model 4006 Stainless, except is double action only, 4 in. barrel only. Mfg. 1991-99.

	$655	$540	$400	$335	$290	$245	$215

Last MSR was $791.

Add $115 for Tritium night sights (new 1992).

* *Model 4046TSW Stainless* - double action only, similar to Model 4046 Stainless, but has S&W tactical features, including equipment rail, 37.8 oz. Mfg. 2000-2002.

	$700	$625	$500	$455	$400	$360	$330

Last MSR was $907.

Add $133 for night sights.

MODEL 4053 COMPACT STAINLESS - double action only variation of the Model 4013. Mfg. 1991-97.

	$625	$525	$400	$335	$290	$245	$215

Last MSR was $734.

MODEL 4053TSW (TACTICAL) - .40 S&W cal., double action only, 3 1/2 in. barrel, 9 shot mag. with reversible mag. catch, alloy frame with stainless steel slide, satin stainless finish, black synthetic grips, fixed sights, ambidextrous safety, 26.8 oz. Mfg. 1997-2002.

	$730	$580	$425	$360	$315	$260	$225

Last MSR was $886.

MODEL 4054 - double action only variation of the Model 4014. Mfg. 1991-92.

	$650	$550	$425	$350	$290	$245	$215

Last MSR was $629.

MODEL 4056TSW (TACTICAL) - .40 S&W cal., double action only, 3 1/2 in. barrel, 9 shot mag. with reversible mag. catch, alloy frame with stainless steel slide, satin stainless finish, black synthetic grips, fixed sights, ambidextrous safety, 37 1/2 oz Mfg. 1997-2000.

	$675	$575	$450	$350	$290	$245	$215

Last MSR was $844.

MODEL 4505 - .45 ACP cal., carbon steel variation of the Model 4506, fixed or adj. rear sight. 1,200 mfg. 1991 only.

	$650	$550	$425	$350	$290	$245	$215

Last MSR was $660.

Add $27 for adj. rear sight.

MODEL 4506 STAINLESS - .45 ACP cal., 5 in. barrel, 8 shot mag., combat triggerguard, exposed hammer, fixed or adj. rear sight, straight backstrap (curved is optional), Delrin one-piece grips, 40 1/2 oz. Mfg. 1990-99.

	$680	$550	$410	$345	$300	$250	$220

Last MSR was $822.

Add $33 for adj. rear sight.

Approx. 100 Model 4506s left the factory mismarked Model 645 on the frame. In NIB condition they are worth $700.

MODEL 4513TSW - 45 ACP cal., traditional double action, compact frame, 3 3/4 in. barrel, 7 shot mag., 3-dot Novak Lo-Mount Carry sights, stainless steel slide, aluminum alloy frame, satin stainless finish, 28.6 oz. Mfg. 1998-2004.

	$725	$625	$475	$395	$340	$285	$240

Last MSR was $980.

GRADING - PPGS™	100%	98%	95%	90%	80%	70%	60%

MODEL 4516 COMPACT STAINLESS - .45 ACP cal., hammerless compact varia-tion of the Model 4506, 3 3/4 in. barrel, 7 shot mag., ambidextrous safety, fixed rear sight only, 34 oz. Mfg. 1990-97.

	$650	$525	$400	$335	$290	$245	$215

Last MSR was $787.

Original model is marked 4516 while later mfg. changed slide legend to read 4516-1. Original mfg. is more collectible and slight premiums are being asked.

MODEL 4526 STAINLESS - similar to Model 4506 Stainless, except has frame mounted decocking lever. Mfg. 1990-91 only.

	$675	$550	$425	$350	$290	$245	$215

Last MSR was $762.

MODEL 4536 STAINLESS - similar to Model 4516 Compact, except has frame mounted decocking lever only. Mfg. 1990-91 only.

	$675	$550	$425	$350	$290	$245	$215

Last MSR was $762.

MODEL 4546 STAINLESS - similar to Model 4506 Stainless, except is double action only. Mfg. 1990-91 only.

	$675	$550	$425	$350	$290	$245	$215

Last MSR was $735.

MODEL 4553TSW - similar to Model 4513TSW, except is double action only. Mfg. 1998-2002.

	$755	$595	$450	$385	$335	$280	$235

Last MSR was $924.

MODEL 4556 STAINLESS - .45 ACP cal., features double action only, 3 3/4 in. barrel, 7 shot mag., fixed sights. Mfg. 1991 only.

	$675	$550	$425	$350	$290	$245	$215

Last MSR was $735.

MODEL 4563TSW - .45 ACP cal., traditional double action only, 4 1/4 in. barrel, 8 shot mag., aluminum alloy frame with stainless steel slide, satin stainless fin-ish, includes S&W tactical features, including equipment rail and Novak 3-dot sights, synthetic black straight backstrap grips, 30.6 oz. Mfg. 2000-2004.

	$750	$625	$450	$390	$340	$280	$235

Last MSR was $977.

MODEL 4566 STAINLESS - .45 ACP cal., traditional double action with ambidex-trous safety, 4 1/4 in. barrel, 8 shot mag. Mfg. 1990-99.

	$650	$550	$410	$345	$300	$250	$220

Last MSR was $822.

* *Model 4566TSW Stainless* - similar to Model 4566, except has ambidextrous safety, 39.1 oz. Disc. 2004.

	$725	$600	$450	$390	$340	$280	$235

Last MSR was $1,000.

MODEL 4567-NS STAINLESS - similar to Model 4566 Stainless, except has Tri-tium night sights, stainless steel frame and carbon steel slide. 2,500 mfg. in 1991 only.

	$650	$550	$425	$350	$290	$245	$215

Last MSR was $735.

MODEL 4576 STAINLESS - .45 ACP cal., features 4 1/4 in. barrel, frame mounted decocking lever, fixed sights. Mfg. 1990-92.

	$635	$535	$410	$345	$300	$250	$220

Last MSR was $762.

GRADING - PPGS™	100%	98%	95%	90%	80%	70%	60%

MODEL 4583TSW - similar to Model 4563TSW, except is double action only, 30.6 oz. Mfg. 2000-2002.

	$700	$575	$450	$380	$330	$275	$230

Last MSR was $921.

MODEL 4586 STAINLESS - .45 ACP cal., 4 1/4 in. barrel, double action only, 8 shot mag. Mfg. 1990-99.

	$695	$575	$425	$345	$300	$250	$220

Last MSR was $822.

∗ *Model 4586TSW Stainless* - similar to Model 4566TSW, except is double action only, 39.1 oz. Mfg. 2000-2002.

	$700	$600	$445	$380	$330	$275	$230

Last MSR was $942.

MODEL 5903 - 9mm Para. cal., double action semi-auto, 4 in. barrel, stainless steel slide and alloy frame, exposed hammer, 10 (C/B 1994) or 15* shot mag., adj. (disc. 1993) or fixed rear sight, ambidextrous safety. Mfg. 1990-97.

	$650	$575	$475	$395	$365	$325	$300

Last MSR was $701.

Add $30 for adj. rear sight (disc).

∗ *Model 5903TSW* - 9mm Para. cal., traditional double action, aluminum alloy frame with stainless slide, satin stainless finish, includes S&W tactical features, such as equipment rail and Novak Lo-Mount Carry sights, black synthetic grips with curved backstrap, 28.9 oz. Mfg. 2000-2004.

	$725	$580	$430	$385	$330	$275	$250

Last MSR was $892.

MODEL 5904 - similar to Model 5903, except has steel slide and blue finish, 26 1/2 oz. Mfg. 1989-98.

	$535	$445	$360	$330	$300	$280	$265

Last MSR was $663.

Add $30 for adj. rear sight (disc. 1993).

MODEL 5905 - 9mm Para. cal., similar to Model 5904, except has carbon steel frame and slide. Approx. 5,000 mfg. 1990-91 only.

	$650	$575	$500	$440	$375	$335	$300

MODEL 5906 STAINLESS - stainless steel variation of the Model 5904, 37 1/2 oz. Mfg. 1989-99.

	$615	$500	$400	$335	$290	$245	$215

Last MSR was $751.

Add $37 for adj. rear sight.
Add $115 for Tritium night sights.

∗ *Model 5906TSW Stainless* - traditional double action only, similar to Model 5906 Stainless, but has S&W tactical features, including equipment rail, 38.3 oz. Mfg. 2000-2004.

	$650	$575	$475	$350	$300	$265	$235

Last MSR was $915.

Add $44 if w/o NLC sight.
Add $132 for night sights (disc.).

MODEL 5924 - 9mm Para. cal., 4 in. barrel, features frame mounted decocking lever, 15 shot mag., 37 1/2 oz. Mfg. 1990-91 only.

	$625	$550	$475	$375	$335	$300	$280

Last MSR was $635.

MODEL 5926 STAINLESS - stainless variation of the Model 5924. Disc. 1992.

	$600	$525	$425	$350	$295	$250	$210

Last MSR was $697.

GRADING - PPGS™	100%	98%	95%	90%	80%	70%	60%

MODEL 5943 STAINLESS - 9mm Para. cal., double action only, 4 in. barrel, aluminum alloy frame with stainless steel slide, straight backstrap, 15 shot mag. Mfg. 1990-91 only.

| | $550 | $465 | $390 | $325 | $280 | $235 | $205 |

Last MSR was $655.

* *Model 5943-SSV Stainless* - similar to Model 5943 Stainless, except has 3 1/2 in. barrel, Tritium night sights. Mfg. 1990-91 only.

| | $625 | $550 | $475 | $395 | $330 | $285 | $240 |

Last MSR was $690.

* *Model 5943TSW Stainless* - double action only, aluminum alloy frame with stainless steel slide, includes S&W tactical features, equipment rail, and Novak Lo-Mount Carry sights, 28.9 oz. Mfg. 2000-2002.

| | $650 | $575 | $450 | $375 | $325 | $280 | $265 |

Last MSR was $844.

MODEL 5944 - similar to Model 5943 Stainless, except has blue finish slide. Mfg. 1990-91 only.

| | $625 | $550 | $475 | $400 | $350 | $300 | $280 |

Last MSR was $610.

MODEL 5946 STAINLESS - 9mm Para. cal., double action only, one piece Xenoy wraparound grips, all stainless steel variation of the Model 5943, 39 1/2 oz. Mfg. 1990-99.

| | $615 | $500 | $400 | $335 | $290 | $245 | $215 |

Last MSR was $751.

* *Model 5946TSW Stainless* - 9mm Para. cal., double action only, includes S&W tactical features, equipment rail, and Novak Lo-Mount Carry sights, 38.3 oz. Mfg. 2000-2002.

| | $725 | $600 | $450 | $375 | $315 | $260 | $225 |

Last MSR was $863.

MODEL 6904 COMPACT - 9mm Para. cal., compact variation of the Model 5904, 3 1/2 in. barrel, 10 (C/ B 1994) or 12* shot finger extension mag., fixed rear sight, 26 1/2 oz. Mfg. 1989-97.

| | $550 | $475 | $400 | $350 | $325 | $300 | $280 |

Last MSR was $625.

MODEL 6906 COMPACT STAINLESS - stainless steel variation of the Model 6904, 26 1/2 oz. Mfg. 1989-99.

| | $585 | $470 | $380 | $320 | $275 | $235 | $200 |

Last MSR was $720.

Add $116 for Tritium night sights (new 1992).

MODEL 6926 STAINLESS - 9mm Para. cal., 3 1/2 in. barrel, standard double action, features frame mounted decocking lever, aluminum alloy frame with stainless slide, 12 shot mag. Mfg. 1990-91 only.

| | $650 | $575 | $450 | $375 | $315 | $270 | $230 |

Last MSR was $663.

MODEL 6944 - 9mm Para., double action only, 3 1/2 in. barrel, 12 shot mag., aluminum alloy frame with blue steel slide. Mfg. 1990-91 only.

| | $600 | $525 | $450 | $375 | $325 | $300 | $280 |

Last MSR was $578.

MODEL 6946 STAINLESS - similar to Model 6944, except has stainless steel slide, semi-bobbed hammer, 26 1/2 oz. Mfg. 1990-99.

| | $675 | $575 | $475 | $375 | $315 | $270 | $230 |

Last MSR was $720.

GRADING - PPGS™	100%	98%	95%	90%	80%	70%	60%

MODEL CS9 CHIEFS SPECIAL - 9mm Para. cal., compact design with traditional double action, hammerless, 3 in. barrel, 7 shot mag., alloy frame/stainless slide or stainless steel construction (disc. 2000), Hogue wraparound rubber grips, 3-dot Novak low mount sights, 20.8 oz. Mfg. 1999-2006.

	$600	$460	$380	$325	$270	$230	$195

Last MSR was $777.

MODEL CS40 CHIEFS SPECIAL - .40 S&W cal., similar to Model CS9, except has 3 1/4 in. barrel, 24.2 oz. Mfg. 1999-2002.

	$575	$435	$375	$315	$275	$230	$195

Last MSR was $717.

MODEL CS45 CHIEFS SPECIAL - .45 ACP cal., similar to Model CS40, except has 6 shot mag., matte finished stainless steel slide, 23.9 oz. Mfg. 1999-2006.

	$660	$485	$410	$335	$285	$230	$195

Last MSR was $826.

SIGMA MODEL SW9F SERIES - 9mm Para. cal., double action only, 4 1/2 in. barrel, fixed sights, polymer frame and steel slide, striker firing system, blue finish only, 10 (C/B 1994) or 17* shot mag., 26 oz. Mfg. 1994-96.

	$475	$400	$350	$325	$295	$280	$265

Last MSR was $593.

Add $104 for Tritium night sights.

* *Sigma Model SW9C Series Compact* - similar to Sigma Model SW9F, except has 4 in. barrel, 25 oz. Mfg. 1996-98.

	$450	$355	$325	$295	$280	$265	$240

Last MSR was $541.

* *Sigma Model SW9M Series Compact* - features 3 1/4 in. barrel, 7 shot mag., fixed channel rear sight, grips integral with frame, satin black finish, 18 oz. Mfg. 1996-98.

	$300	$270	$240	$220	$195	$175	$160

Last MSR was $366.

SIGMA MODEL SW9VE/GVE (SW9E/SW9P/SW9G/SW9V) - 9mm Para. cal., DAO, features 4 in. standard or ported (SW9P, mfg. 2001-2003) barrel, 10 or 16 (new late 2004) shot mag., 3-dot sighting system, grips integral with grey (disc. 2000), Nato green (SW9G, disc. 2003) or black polymer frame, black (SW9E, mfg. 1999-2002) or satin stainless steel (SW9VE) slide, 24.7 oz. New 1997.

MSR $450		$360	$310	$240	$200	$180	$165	$150

Add $8 for Allied Forces model w/melonite slide (new 2007).
Add $380 for SW9VE/SW40VE Allied Forces model w/emergency kit, including space blankets, emergency food, first aid kit, crank radio/flashlight, multi-tool, and pocket survival pack, cased (new 2007).
Add $48 for SW9P or SW9G with night sights (disc. 2003).
Add $210 for Tritium night sights (disc. 2000).

The Enhanced Sigma Series Model SW9VE was introduced during 1999, after the SW9V was discontinued.

SIGMA MODEL SW40F SERIES - .40 S&W cal., double action only, 4 1/2 in. barrel, fixed sights, polymer frame, blue finish only, 10 (C/B 1994) or 15* shot mag., 26 oz. Mfg. 1994-98.

	$450	$355	$325	$295	$280	$265	$240

Last MSR was $541.

Add $104 for Tritium night sights (disc. 1997).

* *Sigma Model SW4OC Series Compact* - similar to Sigma Model SW40F, except has 4 in. barrel, 26 oz. Mfg. 1996-98.

	$450	$355	$325	$295	$280	$265	$240

Last MSR was $541.

GRADING - PPGS™	100%	98%	95%	90%	80%	70%	60%

SIGMA MODEL SW40VE/SW40P/SW40G/SW40GVE (SW40E/SW40V) - .40 S&W cal., features 4 in. standard or ported (SW40P, mfg. 2001-2005) barrel, 10 or 14 (new mid-2004) shot mag., 3-dot sighting system, grips integral with grey (disc. 2000), Nato green (SW40G) or black polymer frame, black slide with melonite finish (SW40E, mfg. 1999-2002) or satin stainless steel slide, 24.4 oz. New 1997.

MSR $450	$360	$310	$240	$200	$180	$165	$150

Add $8 for Allied Forces model w/melonite slide, new 2007.
Add $210 for Tritium night sights (disc.).
Add $145 for Model SW40P or SW40G (includes night sights, disc. 2005).
Add $380 for SW9VE/SW40VE Allied Forces model w/emergency kit, including space blankets, emergency food, first aid kit, crank radio/flashlight, multi-tool, and pocket survival pack, cased (new 2007).

The Enhanced Sigma Series Model SW40VE was introduced during 1999, after the SW40V was discontinued.

MODEL SW99 - 9mm Para., .40 S&W, or .45 ACP (new 2003) cal., traditional double action, 9 (.45 ACP cal.), 10 shot mag., similar to the Walther P99, black polymer frame with black stainless slide and barrel, 4, 4 1/8 (.40 S&W cal. only), or 4.25 (.45 ACP cal. only, new 2003) in. barrel, black finish, ambidextrous mag. release, frame equipment groove, interchangeable backstraps, decocking lever, cocking indicator, adj. 3-dot or night sights, 25.4 (9mm Para cal.) or 28 1/2 oz. Mfg. 2000-2004.

	$565	$485	$430	$380	$340	$300	$275

Last MSR was $667.

Add $123 for night sights.
Add $41 for .45 ACP cal. (new 2003).

* *Model SW99 Compact* - similar to SW99, except is compact version, not available in .45 ACP cal., 3 1/2 in. barrel, 8 (.40 S&W cal.) or 10 (9mm Para cal.) shot mag. with finger extension, approx. 23 oz. Mfg. 2003-2004.

	$565	$485	$430	$380	$340	$300	$275

Last MSR was $667.

SIGMA MODEL SW357 - .357 SIG cal., 4 in. barrel, 10 shot mag., black finish, stainless steel. Mfg. 1998 only.

	$525	$450	$375	$325	$250	$195	$165

SIGMA MODEL SW380 - .380 ACP cal., double action only, 3 in. barrel, fixed sights, polymer frame and steel slide, striker firing system, blue finish only, 6 shot mag., shortened grip, 14 oz. Mfg. 1996-2000.

	$285	$245	$210	$190	$180	$170	$160

Last MSR was $358.

MODEL SW990L - 9mm Para., .40 S&W, or .45 ACP cal., DAO, 9 (.45 ACP cal. only), 10 (all cals. except .45 ACP), 12 (.40 S&W cal.) or 16 (9mm Para.) shot mag., similar to the Walther P99, black polymer frame with black stainless melonite slide and barrel, 4 (9mm Para. cal. only), 4 1/8 (.40 S&W cal. only), or 4.25 (.45 ACP cal. only) in. barrel, black finish, approx. 25 oz. Mfg. 2005-2006.

	$610	$515	$450	$400	$350	$300	$275

Last MSR was $729.

Add $44 for .45 ACP cal.

* *Model SW990L Compact* - similar to SW990L, except is compact version with small polymer frame, not available in .45 ACP cal., 3 1/2 in. barrel, 8 (.40 S&W cal.) or 10 (9mm Para cal.) shot mag. with finger extension, approx. 23 oz. Mfg. 2005-2006.

	$610	$515	$450	$400	$350	$300	$275

Last MSR was $729.

GRADING - PPGS™	100%	98%	95%	90%	80%	70%	60%

MODEL M&P - 9mm Para., .40 S&W, .357 SIG, or .45 ACP (new 2007) cal., DAO, 3 1/2 (new 2007, compact model), 4 (new 2008, .45 ACP cal. only, compact Model 45C), 4 1/4, 4 1/2 (new 2007, .45 ACP cal. only), or 5 (new 2008, 9mm Para. cal. only) in. black melonite finished stainless steel barrel and slide with twin scalloped slide serrations, large black Zytel polymer frame reinforced with stainless steel chasis, matte black or dark Earth brown (.45 ACP cal. only, new 2007) finish, 10, 12, 15, or 17 shot mag., ramp front sights, Novak Lo-Mount Carry rear sight, 6 1/2 lbs. trigger pull, 18 degree grip angle, Picatinny rail in front of trigger guard, three interchangable grip sizes, 24 1/4-29 1/2 oz. New 2006.

MSR $656	$485	$395	$330	$285	$250	$220	$180

    Add $104 for night sights (new 2007, full size models only).
    Add $252 for Crimson Trace laser grips (new 2008).
    Add $39 for .45 ACP cal.
    Add $63 for Model 45C (compact) with 4 in. barrel.

ENGRAVING OPTIONS FOR CURRENT PRODUCTION HANDGUNS

The prices listed are for original factory finished guns with no extra engraving. The listings below show most recent factory engraving costs. These prices should be added to the cost of each engraved production gun to determine the correct value.

CLASS "C" ENGRAVING - 1/3 METAL COVERAGE
    Pistols - add $1,108.
    For J Frame - add $876.
    10 5/8 in. N Frame - add $1,343.
    2-5 in. K, L, or N Frame - add $1,130.
    6-8 3/8 in. K, L, or N Frame - add $1,285.

CLASS "B" ENGRAVING - 2/3 METAL COVERAGE
    Pistols - add $1,448.
    For J Frame - add $1,430.
    10 5/8 in. N Frame - add $1,672.
    2-5 in. K, L, or N Frame - add $1,477.
    6-8 3/8 in. K, L, or N Frame - add $1,599.

CLASS "A" ENGRAVING - FULL COVERAGE
    Pistols - add $1,761.
    For J Frame - add $1,501.
    10 5/8 in. N Frame - add $2,006.
    2-5 in. K, L, or N Frame - add $1,814.
    6-8 3/8 in. K, L, or N Frame - add $1,919.

SPECIAL ENGRAVING - Also available with custom artwork: inlays, seals, scenes, lettering - prices quoted on request. Please call 1-800-331-0852, ext. 216 - a free color brochure on custom engraving services is available.

LASERSMITH ENGRAVING - laser etching was available 1989-90 only. This process involved a digitally-controlled laser producing a variety of designs, logos, commemorative messages, or autograph on the metal surface(s). Some of these designs were made exclusively for major firearms distributors. Others were custom designed for clubs or organizations. Retail prices started at just under $18 and went as high as $150+, depending on the amount and complexity of the laser etching. To date, premiums are not being paid for these "rarer" variations.

S&W COMMEMORATIVES/SPECIAL EDITIONS

During the course of a year, I receive many phone calls and letters on special editions and limited editions that do not appear in this section. Many of these are listed separately under the Davidson's or Lew Horton sections. It should be noted that a commemorative issue is a gun that has been manufactured, marketed, and sold through the auspices of the specific trademark (in this case S&W). During the past several decades, hundreds of limited edi-

GRADING - PPGS™	100%	Issue Price	Qty. Made

tions have been ordered through various police agencies, state highway patrol units, and other law enforcement organizations. Many of these variations do not have the special suffix serialization (and may not have had a retail price when issued). Since most of these special editions/commemoratives were made for a specific organization, regional demand has a lot to do with determining values (a Model 27 special edition mfg. for a sheriff's dept. in Arkansas will not bring a premium in California). For this reason, most of these guns will not appear in this section and you should contact the factory to learn more about the provenance of these special editions. Remember - values on these models can vary A LOT from one region to another and an averaged "national" single price is almost impossible. While these guns do have special interest, they do not have the collectibility or desirability of many of the standard models listed.

The variations listed represent the only factory S&W Commemoratives manufactured to date. Anything else will be a special or limited edition made for a organization, company, or special event.

MODEL 19 TEXAS RANGER - .357 Mag., with or without knife, approx. 8,000 with knife, approx. 2,000 without, cased. Mfg. 1973 only.

	$595	$250	10,000

Values are for model with knife.

* *Model 19 Texas Ranger Deluxe* - approx. 50 mfg. with a serial numbers divisible by 10, cased.

	$2,500	N/A	50

125TH ANNIVERSARY COMMEMORATIVE - .45 LC cal., plain variation was called Model 25-3, 10,000 mfg. total in 1977, cased with nickel silver medallion, and Roy Jinks's book, "125th Anniversary of Smith & Wesson."

	$595	$350	10,000

* *125th Anniversary Commemorative Deluxe* - Model 25-4, approx. 50 mfg. with S&W prefix serial numbers divisible by 10, cased, sterling silver medallion, and a leather-bound "History of Smith & Wesson" book by Roy Jinks.

	N/A	N/A	50

MODEL 26-1 GEORGIA STATE PATROL COMMEMORATIVE - .45 ACP cal. Mfg. 1988.

	$1,275	N/A	800

MODEL 29 ELMER KEITH COMMEMORATIVE - .44 Mag. cal., 4 in. barrel, standard and deluxe editions, approx. 2,500 total mfg.

Standard	$850	N/A	2,500
Deluxe	$1,500	N/A	100

50TH ANNIVERSARY OF THE .357 MAGNUM - Model 27, both standard and deluxe editions. Mfg. 1985.

Standard	$450	N/A	2,500
Deluxe	$1,600	N/A	N/A

MODEL 544 TEXAS WAGON TRAIN COMMEMORATIVE - .44-40 WCF cal. only, 6 shot, 5 in. barrel, bright blue finish, adj. sights, 4,782 mfg. 1986 to commemorate the Texas Sesquicentennial (1836-1986). Special markings on frame and barrel, smooth Goncalo commemorative grips, ser. no. TWT0001-TWT7800 (estimated). Made 1986 only.

	$500	N/A	7,800

S&W PERFORMANCE CENTER HANDGUNS

The Performance Center (PC) of Smith & Wesson got its start in 1990 from the efforts of two Master Gunsmiths, Paul Liebenburg and John French. The Performance Center is today managed by Tom Kelly and has grown to about 26 employees, all of which are engaged in the handgun shooting sports, a condition of being in the Center. The Performance Center generally does not take production guns and improve them. These handguns are built from scratch. Using two CNC machines, the Performance Center turns out about 400+ guns a month. There is no inventory of PC products. They are pre-sold before they are made. Once a new design is made and prototyped, it is shown to distributors of specialty guns. The distributor is given an exclusive on a particular model and those handguns are sold through the distributor's network of retailers. Currently, the major distributors ordering PC products include: Lew Horton, RSR Group, Camfour, and Talo Dist. The Performance Center delivers limited production runs, unique design and special feature firearms, and also provides gunsmithing services to existing S&W standard products.

While we have tried to list all the Performance Center guns in this section, it is possible that you may find some models listed with their corresponding numbered model in the Semi-Auto Pistols and Numbered Model Revolvers section in this text. Models are listed in the general order of the model number upon which they are based, with descriptions of each gun. At the end of the model descriptions, you may find a collected listing of variations, changes, and/or product codes for PC guns based on a particular model. In the Serialization section in the back of this text, a listing of all Performance Center guns in order of Product Code number has been provided.

During the past 10 years, all PC guns have been marked with the Performance Center trademark on the frame. The product codes are only on the shipping container or box. The 170XXX Performance Center product code indicates a handgun that has been designed and made from scratch by the Performance Center, while the 178XXX code indicates an exisiting product/SKU that has been improved/changed.

Pricing of Performance Center Handguns

Whenever possible, original PC model MSRs have been provided. In some cases, the distributor never posted an MSR on a particular PC model. N/As designate that more research is under way to find out more about the original MSRs, if they exist, and will be included in future editions and our online services.

As a general rule, the easiest way to determine values for Performance Center handguns is to look at the current pricing of the models from which they are derived. In other words, on a PC Model 442 Ultralight, check the standard Model 442 pricing in this text, and use the MSR - 100% price range to establish a base price, assuming the condition is NIB. Depending on the desirability of the PC configuration, such as finishes, barrel lengths, styling, special orders/features (i.e., laser or hand engraving, precious metal inlays, ivory or exotic wood grips, etc.), special sights, and other production variances from the standard model, premiums may exist over the 100% or current MSR values listed for the standard model. If a particular PC model has an original MSR that's significantly higher than the standard model, the buyer and seller are going to have to interpolate a possible premium which both feel comfortable with.   It is important to note that PC models are essentially limited runs of custom guns, which sell out in a relatively short period of time, and only resurface sporadically in the secondary marketplace. Many can be found in NIB or Excellent condition. Also, dealer or retail pricing is very rarely published on these models, making values difficult to determine for the secondary marketplace. PC gun values can form a bell curve, with the peak being around $1,000. Semi-auto pistols generally sell for more than revolvers. Elaborate engraving, custom shop options, and the desirability of the configuration make all the difference when determining the value of an S&W Performance Center handgun.

Heritage Series From Lew Horton & Performance Center Handguns

Beginning in 2001, Lew Horton Dist and the Performance Center manufactured a series of specials from Smith & Wesson called "The Heritage Series." These were produced over a period of 2 years which include case color Models (10 & 24) and other models no longer manufactured and were very popular over the last century. This series included Models 10, 15, 17, 19, 24, 25, 29, and the Model of 1917 in various finishes. Each had a gold color antique style box unique to the Heritage series, with a picture of Horace Smith and Daniel Wesson on the top with blue metal corners and a modern end label. All guns were shipped with a fired case from the gun by ser. no. in a small sealed envelope signed by the shooter, along with a trigger lock or cable lock. Mfg. 2001-2003.

PERFORMANCE CENTER REVOLVER VARIATIONS

SCHOFIELD MODEL OF 2000 - .45 S&W (.45 Schofield) cal., 6 shot, 7 in. barrel, SA, this 3rd Model Schofield is a modern top break, features the design concepts of the original Model 3 Schofield and incorporates the technical and engineering advantages of the last 125 years, modern hammer block safety, case colored hammer, smooth case colored trigger, 1st edition latches, fixed notch rear and pinned half moon post front sights, walnut grips, carbon steel frame w/ polished blue finish, 40 oz., 12 1/2 in. overall, Serial prefix of "GWS" for Col. George W. Schofield. Mfg. began in Jan., 2000.

Last MSR was $1,800.

Product Code: 170146.

✻ *Schofield Model of 2000 w/ Nickel Finish* - .45 S&W (.45 Schofield) cal., 7 in. barrel, nickel finish, "US" stamped on the butt with ser. no., black pinned round blade front sight with Mod 3 Schofield 1875" on the right side, case colored hammer, latch and trigger guard, shipped in the Heritage Series box. Mfg. began in Nov. 2001.

Last MSR was $1,520.

Product Code: 170209FC.

✻ *Schofield Model of 2000 Wells Fargo Editions* - .45 S&W (.45 Schofield) cal., 5 in. barrel, blue or nickel finish, black pinned round blade front sight, case colored hammer, latch and trigger guard, similar to other editions with "US" on butt with ser. no., marked ".45 S&W" on left side of barrel, and "Schofield Pat. Apr. 22d 1873" on right side, shipped in Heritage Series box. Mfg. beginning Nov. 2001.

Last MSR was $1,500.

Product Code: 170207FC (nickel), 170208FC (blue).

LEW HORTON MODEL 10 - .38 S&W Spl. cal., DA, case colored square butt frame and yoke, blue 4 1/4 in. tapered barrel, blue cylinder and thumb piece finish, brown laminated magna style wood grips with silver medallions, limited production from Lew Horton Dist. "Heritage Series", serial prefix of CRS0001-CRS0080, model stampings of 10-7 and 10-9 have been observed, 80 were scheduled for manufacture with a square butt frame and another 70 on a round butt frame with square butt grips, does not have Performance Center trademark, 1st shipments of square butt frames were in May 2001.

Last MSR was $790.

Product Code: 178006FC.

MODEL PC-13 - .357 Mag. cal., DA, 6 shot, 3 in. Magna ported barrel, fixed rear w/ramp front sight, Eagle Secret Service boot or Uncle Mike's grips on a K-frame, matte blue finish with beveled cylinder latch, trigger, and charge holes, shrouded extractor rod, trigger has an overtravel stop, 400 mfg., distributed by Lew Horton during 1995.

Last MSR was $760.

Product Code: 170059 (eagle grips) or 170063 (Uncle Mike's grips).

MODEL 14 PPC - .38 Spl. cal., DA, 4 in. full lug barrel, precision crowned muzzle, custom duty action, polished forcing cone, shipped to a law enforcement distributor in Mississippi for the National Police Shooting Championships, received by the MS Highway Patrol and L.A.P.D. pistol teams, accurized by the Performance Center, not for retail trade. Limited production of less than 100 units 1995-96.

Last MSR was N/A.

Product Code: 170154.

LEW HORTON HERITAGE SERIES MODEL 15-8 - .38 Spl. cal., special case colored frame and yoke, 4 in. blue barrel, blue cylinder, ramp on ramp base front sight with micrometer click rear sight, drilled and tapped, smooth trigger with checked hammer spur, round butt frame with wood laminated checkered grips, marked ".38 Smith & Wesson Special CTG" on right side of barrel and "Smith & Wesson" on the left, Performance Center logo under the thumbpiece, ser. no. prefix CSC0164 (example), shipped in a Heritage Series box with metal corners. Mfg. Aug., 2001.

Last MSR was $922.

Product Code: 17009FC.

LEW HORTON HERITAGE SERIES MODEL 15-8 - .38 Spl. cal., similar to previous model, except has bright nickel finish, wood laminate grips on round butt 3 screw frame, ser. prefix NSC0170 (example). Mfg. Sept. 2001.

Last MSR was $922.

Product Code: 178008FC.

LEW HORTON HERITAGE SERIES MCGIVERN MODEL 15-9 - .38 S&W Spl. cal., 6 in. barrel, new Model 15-9 frame with integral frame lug, commemorates Ed McGivern's world speed records in 1934, commemorative plate details McGivern's records of 5 shots in 2/5 of a second and 5 shots in 9/20 of a second at the Armory in Lewiston, MT, 6 shot with Patridge front sight and McGivern gold bead, micrometer click rear sight, round butt frame, period Altamont fancy checkered service grips, color case hardened, nickel, or blue finish, McGivern speed record sideplate attached just like on McGivern's original gun, shipped in Heritage Series box. Mfg. 2001.

Last MSR was $1,059.

Product Code: 170217FC (nickel), 170216FC (case colored), or 170199FC (blue).

MODEL 17-8 KT22 - .22 LR cal., DA, 6 shot, all blue finish or case colored frame with blue barrel and cylinder, counter bored cylinder with a nominal length of 1.62 in., round butt frame built on new K-frame (-8) with CNC machining, built-in frame lug, floating firing pin, drilled and taped, Non-Magna Wood grips with the Diamond insert around the screw with S&W medallions held in place with RTV, Patridge front sight on a pinned raised boss with an adjustable rear sight on a round barrel, smooth trigger with a pinned stop, checked hammer, frame is fitted with a standard non-MIM thumbpiece and 4 screw sideplate, blue finish, serial numbers w/ LRM prefix on the butt and in two places on the frame under the grips, Performance Center logo under the thumbpiece, supplied with fired case serial numbered to the frame in a small manila envelope, shipped in "Heritage Series" box. Distributed by Lew Horton, 2003.

Last MSR was $1,040.

Product Code: 170198FC (blue) or 170212FC (case colored).

MODEL 19 PERFORMANCE CENTER K COMP - .38 Spl./.357 Mag. cal., DA, blue matte finish, Target K-frame w/ round butt, 6 shot fluted cylinder with counterbores, 3 in. full lug ported barrel, blue matte finish, smooth combat trigger, set back tritium night rear sight on post, black blade adjustable front sight, contoured thumbpiece, rubber combat grips, 36 oz. Mfg. 1994 and 2000.

Last MSR was $800.

Product Code: 170025 (1994 mfg.) and 170163 (2000 mfg.).

LEW HORTON HERITAGE SERIES MODEL 24-5 - 44 Spl. cal., case colored frame, blue 6 1/2 in. barrel, blue cylinder, 4 screw sideplate, round butt frame, ball detent lockup at yoke, traditional thumpiece, diamond checkered walnut grips with S&W monogram, PC trademark under thumbpiece, ser. prefix "CSH". 150 mfg. May 2001.

Last MSR was $1,110.

Product Code: 170185FC.

❋ *Lew Horton Heritage Series Model 24-5* - similar to previous model except has all blue finish, ser. prefix of BCBxx66. Mfg. Sept. 2001.

Last MSR was $1,050.

Product Code: 170189FC.

MODEL 25-10 "HAND EJECTOR" 2001 - .45 LC cal., 6 in. tapered barrel with shrouded extractor, pinned gold bead Patridge front sight with black blade micrometer click rear sight, 1955 Hand Ejector features built on the most modern N-frame design, yoke has a ball detent front lockup with the normal extractor rod lock, sideplate is made with 4 screws, traditional thumbpiece opening, cylinder modified with chamfered charge holes, wood grips with S&W medallions, bright blue finish, supplied with Certificate signed by the Performance Center manager, shipped with aluminum PC locking gun case, 42 oz., approx. 150 mfg. Distributed by Sports South, Inc. 2001.

Last MSR was N/A.

Product Code: 170179FC.

MODEL 25-11 - 45 LC cal., 6 1/2 in. blue barrel, case colored frame, adj. rear sight, 6 shot fluted cylinder, 4 screw frame stamped Model 25-11, ser. prefix "GBP", marked "45 Colt CTG" on right side of barrel, shipped in Heritage Series gold box. 150 mfg. July 2001.

Last MSR was $1,150.

Product Code: 170186FC.

MODEL 25-11 - 45 LC cal., 6 1/2 in. barrel, all blue finish, adj. rear sight, 6 shot fluted cylinder, 4 screw frame stamped Model 25-11, ser. prefix "BAK", marked "45 Colt CTG" on right side of barrel, shipped in Heritage Series gold box. Mfg. July 2001.

Last MSR was $1,150.

Product Code: 170196FC.

LEW HORTON HERITAGE SERIES MODEL OF 1917 - 45 ACP cal., 5 1/2 in. barrel, blue finish, fixed rear sight, lanyard ring and half moon clips, 4 screw frame, marked Model 25-12, 6 shot fluted cylinder, marked ".45 ACP" on right side of barrel and "S&W D.A. 45" on left, PC logo under thumbpiece, ser. no. prefix "NCS00", shipped in Heritage Series gold box. 150 mfg. Aug. 2001.

Last MSR was $1,050.

Product Code: 170197FC.

❋ *Lew Horton Heritage Series Model of 1917* - similar to Lew Horton Heritage Series Model of 1917, except has case colored finish. 150 mfg. Sept., 2001.

Last MSR was $1,050.

Product Code: 170211FC.

❋ *Lew Horton Heritage Series Model of 1917 Military* - similar to Lew Horton Heritage Series Model of 1917, except has dull military-style finish.

Last MSR was $1,050.

Product Code: 170218FC.

MODEL 27-7 - .357 Mag. cal., 8 shot, 100 with 4 in. barrel with black ramp front sight, 100 with 6 1/2 in. barrel with black Patridge front sight, Magna combat grips, 42-45 oz. Distributed by Bangers.

Last MSR was N/A.

Product Code: 170166 (4 in.) or 170167 (6 1/2 in.).

"CLASSIC SERIES" MODEL 27 - .357 Mag. cal., the last 6 shot Model 27s were mfg. with frame and barrels from 50th Anniversary Commemoratives with recessed cylinder from "outnumbered," "AVU" ser. prefix. 14 were mfg. and sold through Lew Horton in June 1999.

Last MSR was N/A.

Product Code: 170151.

MODEL 28 - .357 Mag., red ramp front sight with white outline rear sight, 4 in. barrel with recessed cylinder, during 2000, approx. five Model 28s were stamped with the Performance Center trademark, ser. no. N951647 Model 28-2 was a salesmens' example was discovered during 2004.

Extreme rarity precludes accurate pricing on this model.

MODEL 29 "AMERICAN PRIDE" - .44 Mag. cal., first ever carbon steel Performance Center Hunter model, Hi-Viz interchangeable front sight, high polish blue finish, unique barrel design with removable scope base, 4 screw sideplate, checkered wood grips with American Pride logo, internal key lock. Mfg. 2005.

Last MSR was N/A.

Product Code: 170253.

MODEL 29-9 HERITAGE SERIES - .44 Mag. cal., 6 1/2 in. barrel, blue finish, adj. rear sight, 6 shot fluted cylinder, 4 screw frame stamped "Model 29-9", extractor shroud, PC logo under thumbpiece, target grips, shipped in Heritage Series gold box. Mfg. 2002.

Last MSR was $1,045.

Product Code: 170213FC.

✳ *Heritage Series Model 29-9 Lew Horton* - similar to Model 29-9 Heritage Series, except has nickel finish, serial prefix is BBR. Mfg. 2002.

Last MSR was $1,045.

Product Code: 170214FC.

MODEL 41 - "Classic 41", approx. 10 mfg.

Last MSR was N/A.

Product Code: 170108.

MODEL 60 ET COMP - .38 Spl.+P cal., 3 in. ported full lug barrel, dovetail front and adj. rear sight, round butt frame, contoured thumbpiece, rosewood laminate or pearl inlaid synthetic grips, blue hard case, approx. 300 mfg. Distributed by Lew Horton, 1993.

Last MSR was $795.

Product Code: 170029.

MODEL 66 F COMP - .357 Mag. cal., 3 in. full lug barrel w/ compensator, dovetailed tritium front night sight, tuned action, round butt w/ rubber grips, counterbored cylinder, contoured cylinder latch, "LHF" serial number prefix, approx. 300 mfg. Distributed by Lew Horton, 1993.

Last MSR was N/A.

Product Code: 170024.

MODEL 66 THE SUPER K - .357 Mag. cal., 3 in. specially contoured barrel with 2 port magna porting, white synthetic grip with S&W medallions, Performance Center Tuned action and overtravel trigger stop. Distributed by Lew Horton, 1997.

Last MSR was N/A.

Product Code: 170090.

MODEL 66 F-COMP - .357 Mag. cal., 3 in. full lug ported barrel with drift adj. dovetailed ramp front sight and micrometer click rear sight, 6 shot cylinder with chamfered charge holes, front sight set behind barrel port, glass bead finish, shipped with walnut combat grips and an additional Hogue Bantam monogrip, released during 2003 at the SHOT Show.

Last MSR was $798.

Product Code: 170024FC.

MODEL 67 F-COMP - .38 Spl. cal., 6 shot, SA/DA, 3 in. full lug Power Port barrel, adj. front and rear sights, stainless steel frame, matte black finish, synthetic finger groove grips, 35 oz. New mid-2007.

MSR $1,217	$950	$800	$700	$600	$525	$450	$400

Product code: 17034.

GRADING - PPGS™	100%	98%	95%	90%	80%	70%	60%

MODEL 325 THUNDER RANCH - .45 ACP cal., SA/DA, 6 shot, large frame, interchangeable front sight, adj. rear sight, Scandium alloy frame with stainless steel cylinder, matte black finish, rubber finger groove grips, 31 oz. New 2008.

MSR $1,311	$1,055	$895	$750	$625	$525	$425	$375

Product code: 170316.

MODEL 327 Sc - .357 Mag., 8 shot, 2 or 5 (mfg. 2006-2007) in. barrel with titanium shroud, black finish with natural grey titanium cylinder, Scandium alloy N-frame, teardrop color case hammer and trigger with overtravel stop, Ahrens cocobolo round butt grips with finger grooves (2 in. barrel only) or Hogue rubber (5 in. barrel only) grips, small lanyard pin, PC logo under thumbpiece, fixed or adj. sights, shipped with black PC marked gun rug made by Allen with internal pouch, 2 full moon clips, special ser. no. range, released during 2004 at the SHOT Show.

MSR $1,296	$995	$825	$700	$600	$525	$450	$400

   Add $16 for 5 in. barrel with adj. sights.

Product Code: 170245FC (black), 170269 (5 in. barrel), or 170251FC (clear).

MODEL 327 Sc JERRY MICULEK - similar to Model 327 Sc, 5 in. barrel, 8 shot, unfluted titanium cylinder with adj. sights, orange Hi-Viz fiber optic sights, unique new two-piece barrel design, Jerry Miculek signature grip and extra Hogue rubber grips. Mfg. 2005.

Last MSR was $1,149.

MODEL 327 TRR8 - .357 Mag. cal., 8 shot, 5 in. barrel, large frame, interchangeable front sight, adj. V-notch rear sight, Scandium alloy with titanium alloy cylinder, synthetic finger groove grips, black finish, equipment rail, 35.3 oz. New mid-2007.

MSR $1,311	$1,055	$895	$750	$625	$525	$425	$375

Product code: 170269.

MODEL 329-1 AIRLITE PD - .44 Mag. cal. DA, round butt Scandium alloy N-frame, 6 shot titanium cylinder, painted red ramp front sight, serrated and ported 3 in. barrel, adj. black blade front sight, Ahrends cocobolo finger groove wood grips, includes extra Hogue rubber grip, checked teardrop hammer and smooth combat trigger, marked ".44 MAGNUM" on left side of barrel and "PERFORMANCE CENTER" on right, clear or black matte finish, internal key lock, PC logo under thumbpiece, shipped with PC aluminum double lock carry case. Mfg. 2003.

Last MSR was $1,100.

Product Code: 170233 (clear) or 170232FC (black).

All Model 329-1 Airlites were recalled by S&W during July, 2004.

MODEL 442 THE ULTRALIGHT - .38 S&W Spl. cal., similar to Model 442 Centennial, it has been reported (and photographed) that a few (approx. 10) with an alloy cylinder were made for the U.S. Secret Service as prototypes but were never sold or released to the general public. These prototypes have no markings on the sideplate, and have a matte blue finish. One observed Ser. no. prefix is "BSS". Both fluted cylinders and non-fluted cylinders are reported to have been mfg. These cylinders passed the 5000 round test with no failures, using +P ammo. Built on the original "J" frame. This variation is actually lighter than the Ti series because of the all alloy cylinder. Mfg. 1997.

Last MSR was N/A.

This model was never offered for commercial sale.
Product Code: 170023.

GRADING - PPGS™	100%	98%	95%	90%	80%	70%	60%

MODEL 460 XVR - .460 S&W Mag. cal., capable of shooting both the .45 Colt and .454 Casull cartridges, 5 shot, similar to Model 500, stainless frame, cylinder, and one-piece 3 1/2, 6 1/2, 7 1/2, 10 1/2 or 12 (new 2008) in. stainless steel barrel with interchangeable green Hi-Viz front sight, integral Weaver style scope mount, Hogue dual density monogrip with S&W monogram, barrel mounted recoil reducer, glass bead finish, Uncle Mike's detachable sling and swivels, 82 1/2 oz. New 2006.

MSR $1,541	$1,225	$1,025	$875	$775	$700	$625	$550

Add $102 for 12 in. barrel.

Product Code: 170262.

Lew Horton ordered a number of 3 1/2 in. models - product code is 170268FC.

The 6 1/2 in. barrel does not have sling mounts.

In late summer, 2005, a 7 1/2 in. barrel version was manufactured for Ellett Bros. distrobutors with black finish, stainless steel cylinder, muzzle brake and shoulder sling. This model included a Lothar-Walther custom rifle barrel and a special ser. no. (EBD0001-EBD0500).

MODEL 460 AIRWEIGHT - .38 S&W Spl. cal., DA only, alloy J-frame w/ round butt, 5-shot fluted steel cylinder, fully concealed hammer, 2 in. steel Magna Ported barrel, fixed sight, blue matte finish, Eagle Secret Service grips, smooth trigger, Performance Center logo laser etched on the sideplate, does not have the standard S&W trademark on the frame. Shipped in a Performance Center blue plastic case, ser. no. prefix "SDE", 15.8 oz. approx. 450 mfg. 1994.

Last MSR was $595.

Product Code: 170055.

MODEL 500 MAGNUM HUNTER (NEW 2004) - .500 S&W Magnum cal., X-frame, 5 shot, fluted cylinder, 6 1/2 (Compensated Hunter, mfg. 2004 only), 7 1/2, or 10 1/2 in. tapered lug barrel, with recoil compensator and integral Weaver base, Hogue mono-grip, stainless steel, glass bead finish with flash chromed hammer and trigger, adj. white outline rear sight, includes black nylon sling, swivels, and soft case, 82 oz.

MSR $1,525	$1,225	$1,025	$875	$775	$700	$625	$550

Product Code: 170231 (10 1/2 in.), 170246FC (6 1/2 in.), 170299 (7 1/2 in.).

MODEL 586 L COMP - .357 Mag. cal., 3 in. full lug ported barrel with Tritum Dot front and Micrometer click rear sight, Altamont Rosewood grips, 7 shot cylinder recessed for moon clips, black or blue finish, shipped with locking aluminum case & Master Gun Lock, first blue finish revolver in 7 shot offered by S&W, 37 1/2 oz. Distributed by Camfour, 2000 and 2004.

Last MSR was N/A.

Product Code: 170170 (2000 mfg.) or 170248FC (2004 mfg.).

MODEL 610 - 10mm cal., 6 1/2 in. barrel.

Last MSR was N/A.

Product Code: 170109.

MODEL 617 - .22 LR cal., new profile barrel for export, only 327 mfg. 1995 and 1999.

Last MSR was N/A.

Product Code: 170122 or 170066 (235 were mfg. in 1995 for export only).

MODEL 625-6 FLUTED HUNTER - .45 Colt cal., 6 in. ported barrel, chamfered cylinder, red ramp dovetailed front sight, round butt frame, serrated backstrap & forestrap, will accept Weaver style scope mount on the integral rail system, removable of weights and spacers internal to the barrel with a small allen wrench, ser. no. prefix "LHD", most were sent to Germany with about 50 remaining in the U.S. Distributed by Lew Horton, 1997.

Last MSR was N/A.

Product Code: 170081.

MODEL 625-6 HUNTER - .45 Colt cal., 6 in. ported slabside barrel, non-fluted cylinder, marked "45 Colt CTG". Mfg. 1997.

Last MSR was N/A.

Product Code: 170085.

MODEL 625-6 "V COMP" - .45 ACP cal., 4 in. slabside barrel with a removable compensator or a replacement muzzle to protect the crown, 6 shot non-fluted cylinder has a ball-detent lockup in the yoke, Millett dovetailed red ramp front and micrometer click rear sight, Hogue Combat wood grips, semi-target hammer, smooth combat trigger w/ overtravel stop, shipped w/ double combo lock aluminum carry case, 43 oz. Distributed by RSR, 1999.

Last MSR was $925.

Product Code: 170136.

MODEL 625-7 LIGHT HUNTER - .45 Colt cal., 6 in. ported match grade barrel with integral Weaver style base rail, ball detent lockup, fluted cylinder w/ chamfered charge holes, Millet dovetail front sight, forged and flash chromed trigger and hammer, satin stainless finish, Hogue wood combat grips, shipped with aluminum PC carry case, 43 oz. Distributed by RSR, 1999.

Last MSR was N/A.

Product Code: 170132.

MODEL 625-5 JERRY MICULEK DESIGN -.45 ACP cal., 5 1/4 in. barrel, Patridge front w/ gold bead and adj. black blade rear sight, reduced cylinder freebore, 6 shot fluted cylinder w/ chamfered charge holes, deep cut broached rifling, hand honed bore, satin stainless finish, "Jerry Miculek" Hogue Laminate combat grips, lockable aluminum case, 42 oz. Distributed by Camfour, 2001.

Last MSR was $899.

Product Code: 170176.

MODEL 625-10 -.45 ACP cal., 6 shot, 2 in. barrel, Scandium N-frame, fixed V-notch rear sight with serrated and dovetailed ramp front sight, Eagle wood and Hogue rubber grips, stainless steel cylinder, glass bead finish, barrel marked ".45 ACP", includes PC locking case, 24 oz. Distributed by Lew Horton Sept., 2003.

Last MSR was $925.

Product Code: 170266FC (clear) or 170252FC (black).

MODEL 625-11 - .45 LC cal., 1 1/8 in. barrel, 6 shot, aluminum/Scandium N frame, fixed sight, V-notch rear sight, serrated and dovetailed black ramp front sight with white dot, Eagle woodd grip, includes extra Hogue rubber grip, stainless steel cylinder, flame shield inserted above barrel, chamfered charge holes, smooth trigger and checked teardrop hammer, Performance Center locking case, 25 oz. 103 mfg. for Lew Horton during Oct. 2005.

Last MSR was $1025.

Product Code: 170266FC.

MODEL 627-2 STAINLESS - .357 Mag./.38 Spl. cal., DA, stainless steel version of the Model 27, 8 shot cylinder, 5 in. tapered barrel, interchangeable front sights, drilled & tapped for scope mount, chamfered charge holes, flash chrome teardrop hammer, radiused smooth combat trigger with overtravel stop pin, Hogue hardwood combat grips, new thumbpiece, engraved ".357 Magnum 8 More" on barrel, floating firing pin, 44 oz. Distributed by Lew Horton, 1997-98.

Last MSR was $1,000.

Product Code: 170089.

MODEL 627 1998 LEW HORTON SPECIAL "HUNTER STYLE" - .357 Mag. cal., 6 1/2 in. magna ported slabside barrel, fluted cylinder w/ beveled edges, contoured thumb latch, integral scope mount and weight system, adj. sights, rosewood grips.

Last MSR was $1,025.

Product Code: 170102.

GRADING - PPGS™	100%	98%	95%	90%	80%	70%	60%

MODEL 627PC 1998 LEW HORTON SPECIAL - .357 Mag. cal., 8 shot, 6 in. barrel. ser. no. prefix "LHV", engraved ".357 Magnum 8 times" with floating firing pin.

Last MSR was N/A.

MODEL 627-2 1998 LEW HORTON SPECIAL - .357 Mag. cal., 8 shot cylinder, 6 1/2 in. tapered barrel, interchangeable front sights, flash chrome teardrop hammer, radiused smooth combat trigger with overtravel stop pin.

Last MSR was $1,025.

MODEL 627-3 "V-COMP JERRY MICULEK SPECIAL" - 8 shot cylinder, 5 in. barrel, removable compensator, removable/interchangeable cap to protect the rifling, smooth combat trigger w/ overtravel stop pin, TH, drift adj. red ramp front sight, micrometer click rear sight. "Jerry Miculek" design Hogue wooden grips, locking aluminum case, 47 oz. Distributed by RSR, 2000.

Last MSR was N/A.

On July 24th 1999, Jerry Miculek set a world record for firing an S&W 8 shot revolver. The results were: 8 Shots on 1 target in 1.00 seconds and 8 Shots on 2 targets in 1.06 seconds. Both records set using a Model 627 from the Performance Center.
Product Code: 170142.

MODEL 627-3 HUNTER - .357 Mag. cal., 8 shot unfluted cylinder, ball detent lockup, 2 5/8 in. barrel, full length extractor, Millett red ramp drift adj. front sight, micrometer click white outline rear sight, Eagle wood boot grips, flash chromed custom teardrop hammer, smooth combat trigger, glass bead stainless steel finish, aluminum double lock carry case, 37.6 oz., 450 mfg. Distributed by Lew Horton, 1999-2000.

Last MSR was $1,025.

Product Code: 170095.

MODEL 627-PC - .357 Mag. cal., 8 shot, 2 5/8 in. barrel, Millet red ramp drift adj. front sight with micrometer click white outline rear sight, Eagle wood boot grips, flash chromed custom teardrop hammer, smooth combat trigger, full length extractor, stainless steel with glass bead finish, shipped with aluminum double lock carrying case, 37.6 oz. Approx. 302 mfg. 1999-2000.

Last MSR was $1,025.

Product Code: 170133.

MODEL 627-4 - .38 Super cal., 8 shot, black non-fluted cylinder, 5 1/2 in. barrel, angled cut removable compensator and cap, red/white/blue Jerry Miculek designed grip, Patridge front sight with adj. black outline rear sight, chrome teardrop hammer and chrome trigger with overtravel stop, stainless steel, glass bead finish, drilled and tapped. Mfg. for Banger's 2002.

Last MSR was N/A.

Product Code: 170205.

MODEL 627-5 - .357 Mag. cal., 5 in. tapered and countoured barrel with fluted cylinder, 8 shot, floating firing pin, interchangeable front sight with black blade rear sight, Hogue rubber grips, trigger overtravel stop, internal lock system, new frame design, shipped with black PC marked gun rug, released during 2003.

MSR $1,272		$1,000	$775	$650	$475	$425	$375	$335

Product Code: 170210.

* *Model 627-5* - .357 Mag. cal., 8 shot, 5 in. full lug barrel, removable cap and crown, wood grips with extra Hogue grip, fluted cylinder, black drift adj. front sight, black rear sight, marked ".357 Magnum-V8" on left side of barrel and "Performance Center" on right, floating firing pin, internal lock system, new frame design, ser. no. prefix "VCM". Limited mfg. 2004.

$875	$600	$525	$475	$425	$375	$335

Last MSR was $1,106.

Product Code: 170237FC.

GRADING - PPGS™	100%	98%	95%	90%	80%	70%	60%

MODEL 627 V-COMP - .357 Mag. cal., 8 shot, 5 in. barrel, SA/DA, adj. front and back sights, stainless steel/alloy frame with two-tone matte or satin stainless finish, synthetic rubber or wood laminate finger groove grips, chrome tear drop hammer, 47 oz. New 2008.

MSR $1,533	$1,225	$1,025	$875	$775	$700	$625	$550

Product code: 170296.

MODEL 629 CARRY COMP - .44 Mag. cal., 6 shot, 3 in. barrel, adj. orange dovetail front sight, stainless steel frame and cylinder, matte stainless finish, fixed notch rear sight, large frame, wood combat grips with finger grooves, 38 oz. New mid-2007.

MSR $1,217	$950	$800	$700	$600	$525	$450	$400

Product code: 170279.

MODEL 629 STEALTH HUNTER - .44 Mag. cal., 6 shot, SA/DA, 7 1/2 in. barrel, stainless steel frame and cylinder, matte black finish, adj. front and rear sight, synthetic finger groove grips, 56 oz. New mid-2007.

MSR $1,596	$1,250	$1,035	$875	$775	$700	$625	$550

Product code: 170323.

MODEL 629-3: CARRY COMP STAINLESS - .44 Mag. cal., 3 in. barrel, integral compensator, dovetailed interchangeable red ramp front sight, fixed rear sight, beveled cylinder, semi-target hammer, smooth combat trigger, N-frame, round butt, Goncalo Alves grips w/ finger grooves, contoured thumbpiece, 42 oz. Distributed by Lew Horton, 1992.

Last MSR was $1,000.

Product Code: 170012.

MODEL 629-3 CLASSIC HUNTER I - .44 Mag. cal., fluted cyl. Distributed by Lew Horton, 1992.

Last MSR was $1,234.

Product Code: 170008.

MODEL 629-3: THE CLASSIC HUNTER II .44 Mag. cal., unfluted cyl., 6 in. slab-side barrel, approx. 600 mfg. Distributed by Lew Horton, 1992.

Last MSR was $1,234.

Product Code: 170197.

MODEL 629-3: CARRY COMP II - .44 Mag. cal., 3 in. barrel, adj. rear sight, compensator system, unfluted Classic Hunter style cylinder, hard case, approx. 100 mfg. Distributed by Lew Horton, 1993.

Last MSR was $1,000.

Product code: 170026.

MODEL 629-4: .44 MAGNUM LIGHT HUNTER - .44 Mag. cal., 6 in. Magna ported slabside barrel, non-fluted cylinder, round butt frame, scope broaching, recessed crown, radiused smooth trigger w/ stop, serial number range RSR3500-RSR4000, 500 mfg. Distributed by RSR.

Last MSR was N/A.

May 1995. Two additional variations also made for Lew Horton Dist.
Product Code: 170056.

MODEL 629-4: THE CLASSIC HUNTER III - .44 Mag. cal., 6 in. slab side barrel, integral variable weight system, Weaver scope mount rail system, Magna ported, non fluted chamfered cylinder, red ramp dovetail front sight, ser. no. prefix "LHK". Distributed by Lew Horton, 1996.

Last MSR was $1,234.

Product Code: 170046.

MODEL 629 "THE AVENGER" - .44 Mag. cal., 3 in. Dual Magna-port barrel, unfluted cylinder, 26 Mfg.

Last MSR was N/A.

Product code: 170058.

MODEL 629 MAGNUM HUNTER PLUS - .44 Mag. cal., 7 1/2 in. slabside barrel, Magna ported, integral Weaver Scope Rail, unfluted cylinder. Distributed by RSR, 1996.

Last MSR was N/A.

Product Code: 170065.

MODEL 629-4 TROPHY WHITE TAIL - .44 Mag. cal., 6 1/2 in. ported barrel, dove-tailed front sight, adj. rear sight, target hammer, smooth trigger with stop, chambered cylinder, contoured thumbpiece, Hogue Grips with S&W trade-mark, two deer scene laser etched on the sideplate, with "Trophy Whitetail" etched on the barrel's right side, drilled and tapped for scope mount, Perfor-mance Center logo on the frame, ser. no. range is ZAN0001-ZAN0200. 200 mfg. Distributed by Zanders Sports, 1997.

Last MSR was N/A.

Product Code: 170050.

MODEL 629-4 "SCOPE ONLY" MASTER HUNTER - .44 Mag. cal., 7 1/2 in. barrel, non-fluted cylinder, drilled and tapped for scope mount only w/ rear cutout for a standard rear sight, smooth barrel without a rib, satin stainless finish, Per-formance Center logo, ser. no. prefix "MHS". Mfg. 1997.

Last MSR was N/A.

Product Code: 170087.

MODEL 629-4 "COMPED HUNTER" - .44 Mag. cal., 6 in. barrel, Weaver integral base, fully adj. micrometer click rear sight, dovetailed Millett red ramp front sight, removable 4 port compensator, w/ replacement muzzle, glass bead fin-ish, stainless steel, N-frame, round butt, Altamont wood grips, unfluted cylin-der with chamfered charge holes, ball detent lock up, flash chromed and radiused hammer, smooth combat trigger with stop, "CMH" ser. no. prefix, 58.9 oz. Distributed by RSR, 1998.

Last MSR was $1,080.

Product Code: 170100.

MODEL 629-4 "3" CARRY COMP" - .44 Mag. cal., dovetailed front sight w/ bright red stripe, unfluted cylinder, Magna ported, w/ trigger stop. Mfg. 1998.

Last MSR was N/A.

MODEL 629-4 - .44 Mag. cal., 6 1/2 in. barrel, removable muzzle brake with replaceable end cap, rosewood grips. Distributed by Lew Horton, 1998.

Last MSR was N/A.

Product code: 170124.

MODEL 629-5 "V-COMP" - .44 Mag. cal., 4 in. slabside barrel with removable compen-sator, muzzle cap, non-fluted cylinder, ball-detent lockup in the yoke, flash chromed semi-target hammer, smooth combat trigger w/ overtravel stop, dovetail red ramp front sight, micrometer click rear sight, Hogue wood combat grips w/ S&W Mono-gram, aluminum carry case, 43 oz. Distributed by RSR in 1999.

Last MSR was N/A.

Product code: 170137.

MODEL 629-5 DEFENSIVE REVOLVER - .44 Mag. cal., 2 5/8 in. barrel, ball detent lockup system in the yoke, 6 shot non-fluted cylinder, flash chromed teardrop hammer and smooth combat trigger, Millett dovetailed red ramp front sight, micrometer click rear sight, Hogue wood combat grips, glass bead stainless steel finish, aluminum carry case with the Performance Center logo, 39.6 oz. Distributed by Lew Horton, 1999-2000.

Last MSR was $1,026.

Product code: 170135.

MODEL 629-5 "THE EXTREME HUNTER" - .44 Mag./.44 S&W Special cal., 12 in. barrel, 6 shot fluted cylinder, Wilson rubber combat grips, round butt frame, Uncle Mike's swivels and sling, long under extension to support the long barrel and front swivel mount, dovetailed Patridge front sight, Wilson Silhouette rear sight, glass bead stainless steel finish, new design frame with floating firing pin and MIM hammer and trigger, Waller 21 in. gun rug, ser. no. prefix "AMH", 65 oz. Distributed by Lew Horton, 2000.

Last MSR was $1,201.

Product code: 170157.

MODEL 629-5 "STEALTH HUNTER" - .44 Mag. cal., 7 1/2 in. Magna ported Hunter style barrel, 6 shot unfluted flat black cylinder with ball detent lockup and chamfered charge holes, integral Weaver style rib and counterbored muzzle, adj. Millett red ramp drift front sight, white outline micrometer adj. rear sight, Hogue black rubber monogrip with the S&W trademark, black smooth trigger with a rubber stop, black tapered hammer spur, NATO green stainless steel frame and barrel, black contrasting screws, grip, cylinder, thumbpiece, hammer, and trigger, Performance Center aluminum case, ser. no. prefix "FBS", approx. 50 oz. Distributed by Camfour, 2000-2001.

Last MSR was $1,200.

Product code: 170171.

MODEL 629-5 "COMPENSATED HUNTER" - .44 Mag. cal., 7 1/2 in. ported barrel, glass bead finish, stainless steel, fixed compensator, 6 shot fluted cylinder w/ chamfered charge holes, ball detent lock-up, adj. front sight w/ orange ramp insert, adj. micrometer black blade rear sight, removable stainless steel scope mount, rosewood laminate grips, extra Hogue monogrip, round butt frame, lockable Performance Center aluminum case, 52.2 oz. Distributed by Talo, 2001.

Last MSR was $1,104.

Product code: 170181.

MODEL 629-5 "44 MAGNUM LIGHT HUNTER" - .44 Mag. cal., all black Birdsong finish, barrel is cut for scope mount with Weaver rail, unfluted cylinder, gold bead front sight, Hogue monogrip, ser. no. prefix "DEL". Mfg. 2002.

Last MSR was N/A.

Product code: 170194.

MODEL 629 LIGHT HUNTER (NEW 2003) - .44 Mag. cal., large frame, 6 shot, 7 1/2 in. barrel with integral muzzle brake, stainless steel, tapered ejector rod housing, wood combat grips, includes scope rail, 52.2 oz. New 2003.

MSR $1,304	$1,050	$895	$750	$625	$525	$425	$375

Product code: 170181.

MODEL 640 CARRY COMP - .38 Spl.+P cal., 2 in. ported barrel, adj. front sight, fixed rear sight, radiused hammer and trigger, 150 mfg. w/ rosewood grips, 150 mfg. w/ Bader mother-of-pearl inlaid fingergroove grips, blue plastic case w/ Performance Center logo, 23 oz. Distributed by Lew Horton. Mfg. 1993.

Last MSR was $750.

Product code: 170042.

MODEL 640 "PAXTON QUIGLEY" - 38 Spl. cal., 2 5/8 in. barrel, integral compensator, dovetailed adj. front sight, tuned by the S&W Performance Center, laminated wood grips w/ mother-of-pearl inlaid heart, Boyt tapestry case and letter of authenticity from Paxton Quigley, author of *Armed & Female*. Limited production of 250. Distributed by Lew Horton, 1994.

Last MSR was $725.

Product codes: 170014 (3 in.) or 170043 (2 in.).

MODEL 640 RSR SPECIAL - .357 Mag. cal., 2 1/8 in. Magna-Ported barrel, 5 shot non-fluted cylinder, glass bead stainless steel finish, concealed hammer, J-frame, round butt, Heritage walnut grips, chrome smooth combat trigger, pinned black ramp front sight, square notch rear sight, 25 oz. Mfg. 1996.

. Last MSR was N/A.

Product code: 170073.

MODEL 640 LEW HORTON - .357 Mag. cal., 5 shot, 2 1/8 in. ported barrel, dove-tail front sight with tritium insert on black post, matte stainless finish, Performance Center tuned action, Pachmayr Decelerator grips, chrome smooth combat trigger. Mfg. 1996.

Last MSR was $839.

At least one Model 640 is known to have been chambered in .38 Super caliber for test purposes by the Performance Center. Product code: 170068.

MODEL 640 "LEW HORTON .357 MAGNUM" - .357 Mag. cal., 2 1/8 in. Quad Port barrel, glass bead finish. Mfg. 1999.

Last MSR was $851.

Product code: 170078.

MODEL 646 - .40 S&W cal., 4 in. ribbed slabside barrel, SA/DA, 6 shot fluted titanium cylinder, adj. Patridge front sight, micrometer adj. rear sight, drilled and tapped for scope mount, smooth combat trigger, round butt, L-target frame, "Performance Center" on the left side and "40 S&W" on the right side, frosted glass bead stainless finish, Performance Center trademark on the frame, Altamont wood combat grips, 2 sets of half moon clips and extraction tool, Performance Center aluminum case with Performance Center trademark, ser. no. prefix "RDA", 36 oz. Mfg. 2000.

Last MSR was $845.

Product code: 170165.

MODEL 647-1 VARMINTER - .17 HMR cal., stainless steel K-frame, 12 in. Walther barrel, Weaver scope rail, includes bipod adapter, black Patridge front sight with adj. black blade rear sight, glass bead satin stainless finish, wood target square grips, internal trigger lock system, black Allen soft zipper case, distributed by Camfour and Hill Country.

Last MSR was $1,200.

Product code: 170229FC.

MODEL 657 DEFENSIVE REVOLVER - .41 Mag. cal., 2 5/8 in. barrel, 6 shot non-fluted cylinder, ball detent lockup, full length extractor, round butt, N-frame, adj. Millett red ramp front sight, micrometer adj. white outline rear sight, flash chromed teardrop hammer, chromed trigger with travel overstop, Hogue combat grips, glass bead stainless steel finish, aluminum carry case, 39.6 oz. Distributed by Lew Horton, 1999.

Last MSR was $1,001.

Product code: 170134.

MODEL 657 HUNTER - .41 Mag. cal., 6 in. Magna-Ported barrel, integral weaver base, N-frame, round butt, 6 shot unfluted cylinder, ball detent lockup, adj. Millett red ramp front sight, adj. rear sight, 48 oz. Distributed by RSR, 1995-99.

Last MSR was N/A.

Product code: 170062.

MODEL 681-4 LEW HORTON SPECIAL - .357 Mag. cal., 3 in. Quadra-port barrel, 7 shot chamfered cylinder, trigger overtravel stop, fixed sight, ser. no. prefix "LHB", 300 mfg. Distributed by Lew Horton, 1996.

Last MSR was $700.

Product code: 170080.

MODEL 681-5 SPECIAL FOR CAMFOUR - .357 Mag. cal., 3 in. or 4 in. full lug barrel, 7 shot fluted cylinder, adj. black ramp front sight, Quad Porting, glass bead stainless steel finish, laminate checkered wood and Hogue Bantam Monogrip, 7 shot moon clips, chamfered cylinder charge holes, Performance Center case. Distributed by Camfour, 2001.

Last MSR was N/A.

Product code: 170172 (4 in.) or 170178 (3 in.).

MODEL 686 MAG COMP - .357 Mag. cal., 3 in. barrel, integral compensator, adj. front red ramp sight, white outline rear sight, radiused full lug barrel, radiused hammer, radiused combat trigger w/ overtravel stop, Uncle Mike's grips, Performance Center logo, contoured thumbpiece, full-length extractor rod, 350 mfg. Distributed by Lew Horton, 1992.

Last MSR was $1,000.

Product code: 170010.

MODEL 686 CARRY COMP - .357 Mag. cal., 4 in. barrel, integral compensator, dovetailed front sight w/ interchangeable post or red ramp, white outline rear sight, Uncle Mike's grips. Distributed by Lew Horton.

Last MSR was $1,000.

Product code: 170016.

MODEL 686 PPC REVOLVER - .357 Mag. cal., 6 in. barrel, custom underlug, integral barrel port.

Last MSR was N/A.

MODEL 686 CARRY COMP - .357 Mag. cal., 6 in. barrel, integral port, replaceable front sight, Hogue grips, semi-target hammer, smooth combat trigger, full underlug contour.

Last MSR was $1,099.

Product code: 170009.

MODEL 686 COMPETITOR - .357 Mag. cal., 6 in. barrel, fluted cylinder w/ radiused charge holes, integral scope base, 6 ounce variable underweight, dovetailed front post, black blade rear sight, Hogue grips, semi-target hammer, smooth combat trigger, 52-58 oz. Distributed by Lew Horton.

Last MSR was $1,100.

Product code: 170015.

MODEL 686 ACTION REVOLVER - .357 Mag. cal., 6 in. match grade barrel, barrel compensator.

Last MSR was N/A.

MODEL 686 HUNTER - .357 Mag. cal., similar to the Model 686 Competitor, except wood grips. 200 mfg.

Last MSR was $1,153.

Product code: 170021.

MODEL 686 PLUS - .357 Mag. cal., 6 in. tapered barrel, 7 shot fluted cylinder, machined for full moon clips w/ chamfered charge holes, L-frame drilled and tapped for scope mount, round butt, Altamont wood grips, flash chromed semi-target hammer and smooth combat trigger, gold bead Patridge front sight, micrometer adj. white outline rear sight, satin stainless steel finish, 44 oz. Distributed by Lew Horton, 1998.

Last MSR was $929.

Product code: 170103.

MODEL 686-4 WITH ADJUSTABLE SIGHTS - .357 Mag. cal., 2 1/2 in. barrel, Magna Port, 7 shot cylinder, wood grips. Mfg. 1998.

Last MSR was N/A.

Product code: 170077.

GRADING - PPGS™	100%	98%	95%	90%	80%	70%	60%

MODEL 686 - .38 Super cal., 4 in. tapered lug barrel, interchangeable red ramp front sight, adj. black rear sight, Ahrend's cocobolo finger groove grips, stainless steel, glass bead finish, 6 shot, unfluted cylinder, L-frame, internal key lock system, accepts full moon clips, includes PC aluminum carry case, 37 oz. Distributed by Banger's 2003.

Last MSR was N/A.

Product code: 170225.

MODEL 940 SPECIAL - .356 TSW cal., ported barrel, dovetail front sight, barrel markings are ".356 TSW" on the right and "Smith & Wesson" on the left side. S/N prefix "APC". Limited Production of 300. Distributed by Lew Horton, 1994.

Last MSR was $575.

Product code: 170047.

This model has also been referred to as the "Pocket Rocket."

MODEL 942 AIRWEIGHT 9MM CENTENNIAL - 9mm cal., 2 in. ported barrel, one was made as a prototype using a Model 642-1 alloy frame, stainless steel cylinder, S/N CAN1706. Built as a T&E prototype, it was shipped to Firearms Journalist Wiley Clapp in 1999 for test and evaluation.

Last MSR was N/A.

MODEL M&P R8 - .357 Mag. cal., 8 shot, SA/DA, 5 in. two-piece barrel, large frame, Scandium alloy frame, stainless steel cylinder, interchangeable dot front sight, adj. V-notch rear sight, accessory rail, 36.3 oz. New mid-2007.

MSR $1,311	$1,055	$895	$750	$625	$525	$425	$375

Product code: 170292.

PERFORMANCE CENTER RIFLE VARIATIONS

M&P RIFLE - .223 Rem. cal., 10 shot mag., 20 in. stainless steel barrel, full length, skeletonized stock, free-floating black matte anodized forend, two-stage mtch trigger, billet aluminum upper and lower receiver, hard coat black or camo anodized finish, includes rifle case. New 2008.

MSR $1,841	$1,575	$1,350	$1,125	$900	$800	$700	$600

Add $171 for camo.

Product code: 178016 (black) or 178015 (camo).

PERFORMANCE CENTER SEMI-AUTO PISTOL VARIATIONS

MODEL 845 BULLSEYE - .45 ACP cal., full target version of the Model 745, Bo-Mar low-profile sights, beavertail, checkered front strap, fitted barrel bushing, Hi-Impact plastic grips, 8-round magazine, extra recoil spring, S/N prefix "MPC" (1995) "SDN" (1998). Distributed by Lew Horton.

Last MSR was $1,496.

Product code: 170064.

MODEL 945 PERFORMANCE CENTER .45 MATCH PISTOL - .45 ACP cal., 5 in. barrel, titanium coated spherical barrel bushing, 8 round mag., Performance Center markings, post front sight, adj. Bo-Mar rear sight, checkered two-piece laminated wood grips, bead blast stainless steel finish, ambidextrous frame mounted thumb safety, grip safety as part of the short beavertail, Master trigger lock, "Performance Center" marked foam-filled aluminum case starting in 1999, 43.5 oz. (1998) 42 oz. (1999 and later mfg.) Mfg. 1998-2000.

✳ *Model 945 Performance Center .45 Match Pistol 170104* - 5 in. barrel, stainless steel, 8 shot, 43.5 oz. Mfg. 1998.

Last MSR was $1,618.

✳ *Model 945 Performance Center .45 Match Pistol 170147* - 5 in. barrel, two-tone or blue finish, lightened trigger, grip safety, Bo-Mar rear sight, post front sight, stainless steel, ambidextrous frame mounted safety, 42 oz. Distributed by RSR. Mfg. 1998, 1999-2000.

Last MSR was N/A.

✳ *Model 945 Performance Center .45 Match Pistol 170152* - 4 in. barrel, black finish, 8 shot mag., post front and Novak 2 Dot Lo- Mount Carry rear sight, frame mounted safety, titanium coated spherical bushing, 20 LPI checkering front and back strap, extended magazine catch, checkered two-piece wood grips, stainless steel, grip safety, S/N prefix "PCZ", 36 oz. Distributed by Camfour, 2000.

Last MSR was N/A.

✳ *Model 945 Performance Center .45 Match Pistol 170153* - 4 in. barrel, post front and Novak 2 Dot Lo-Mount carry rear sight, grip safety, checkered two piece wood grips, lightened trigger, bead blast stainless steel finish, frame mounted safety, S/N prefix "PCZ", 36 oz. Distributed by RSR, 2000.

Last MSR was N/A.

✳ *Model 945 Performance Center .45 Match Pistol 170169* - 3 3/4 in. barrel, white dot dovetail front and Novak 2 Dot Lo-Mount Carry rear sight, grip and single side mounted safety, 7 round mag., checkered laminate wood grips, lightened trigger, black finish alloy frame, stainless steel slide, S/N Prefix "CMF", 28 oz. Distributed by Camfour, 2000.

Last MSR was N/A.

✳ *Model 945 Performance Center .45 Match Pistol 170177* - 3 1/4 in. barrel, white dot dovetail front and Novak 2 Dot Lo-Mount Carry rear sight, beavertail grip and single-side mounted safety, 6 round mag., checkered Hogue laminated wood grips, alloy frame with clear glass bead stainless steel slide, Performance Center carry case, 2 mags., 24.5 oz. Distributed by Camfour, 2001.

Last MSR was N/A.

✳ *Model 945 Performance Center .45 Match Pistol 170180* - .40 S&W cal., 3 3/4 in. barrel, white dot dovetail front and Novak 2 Dot Lo Mount Carry rear sight, beavertail grip and single-side mounted safety, 7 round mag., checkered Hogue laminated wood grips, alloy frame w/ glass bead finish stainless steel slide, Performance Center carry case, 2 mags., 25.7 oz. Distributed by Sports South, 2001.

Last MSR was N/A.

✳ *Model 945 Performance Center .45 Match Pistol 170184* - 3 1/4 in. glass bead black barrel, white dovetail front and Novak 2 Dot Lo-Mount Carry rear sight, grip and single side mounted safety, 6 round mag., checkered Hogue laminated wood grips, alloy frame with stainless steel slide, lightened trigger, S/N prefix "PCZ", 24 oz. Distributed by RSR, 2001.

Last MSR was N/A.

MODEL 945-1 - .45 ACP cal., 8 shot mag., SA, 5 in. barrel, features scalloped slide serrations, black or two-tone finish, checkered front and rear gripstrap, checkered wood panel grips, stainless steel, adj. rear sight, target trigger and bobbed hammer, 40 1/2 oz., released during 2003, reintroduced 2005.

MSR $2,157	$1,675	$1,200	$1,024	$900	$800	$725	$650

Product codes: 170173 (two-tone) and 170300 (black).

MODEL 952 (MFG. 2000) - 9mm Para. cal., 5 in. match grade black finish stainless steel barrel, titanium coated spherical barrel bushing, 9 round mag., loaded chamber indicator, dovetail post front and adj. Wilson rear sight, carbon steel frame and slide, two-piece wood grip panels w/ alloy backstrap, slide mounted decocking lever, marked "Performance Center 952" with small "mm" in the curl of the 9, Performance Center case, 200 mfg., 41 oz. Distributed by Bangers, 2000.

Last MSR was N/A.

Product code: 170168.

GRADING - PPGS™	100%	98%	95%	90%	80%	70%	60%

MODEL 952-1 - 9mm Para. cal., 5 in. barrel, 9 shot mag., SA, checkered wood panel grips, black finish, steel frame with stainless steel barrel, released during 2003.

Last MSR was $1,515.

Product code: 170220.

MODEL 952-2 (NEW 2004) - 9mm Para. cal., 5 or 6 (mfg. 2004, reintroduced 2007) in. barrel, blue finish, 9 shot mag., checkered wood grips, stainless steel frame, wide spur hammer, firing pin block safety, wide smooth trigger with frame stop, adj. dovetailed black post front sight and Wilson adj. black rear sight, released during 2004.

MSR $2,157	$1,675	$1,200	$1,024	$900	$800	$725	$650

Add $387 for 6 in. barrel.

Product code: 170244 (5 in.) or 170247 (6 in.).

MODEL 1911 (NEW 2004) - .38 Super (new 2005) or .45 ACP cal., 5 in. barrel, single action, black finish, 8 or 10 (.38 Super cal.) shot mag., dovetailed black front sight with adj. micro-click black rear sight, checkered laminate wood grips, stainless steel or stainless melonite (new 2005) frame/barrel, glass bead finish, full length guide rod, ambidextrous frame mounted safety, 30 LPI front strap checkering, hand lapped and polished fitted barrel, frame and slide, unique front and rear serrations, includes two magazines, 41 oz., released during 2004.

MSR $2,402	$1,850	$1,300	$1,075	$950	$825	$700	$625

Add $15 for .38 Super cal. (stainless steel only, new 2005).
Subtract $166 for stainless steel frame/slide.

Product code: 170243 and variations.

✱ *Model 1911 (2005)* - .45 ACP cal., two additional variations of this model were produced during 2005, stainless steel with glass bead satin finish, 8 shot mag., 5 in. barrel, Doug Koenig speed hammer, lightweight match trigger with over travel stop, black dovetail front sight with black micro adj. rear sight, laminate fully checkered front grip, oversized external extractor, full length guide rod and oversized mag. well extension, custom front and rear slide serrations, ambidextrous frame safety, shipped with two 8 shot mags, other variation had high polished flats on the slide and barrel.

Last MSR was N/A.

Product code: 170258 and 170261.

MODEL 3566 - .356 TSW (9x21.5 mm) cal., 3 1/2 (approx. 200 mfg. Compact), 4 1/4 (Tactical), or 5 in. (.356 TSW Limited) match grade barrel, titanium barrel bushing, stainless frame, matte blue and hand rubbed stainless finish, oversize frame rails, 12 shot (Compact) or 15 shot (Limited) mag., adj. trigger, fitted slide and barrel, adj. Bo-Mar sights, checkered front strap, extended mag. well, Hogue rubber grips w/S&W logo or plastic panel grips, Performance Center trademark on the right side of the slide, S/N prefix "TSW". Distributed by Lew Horton, 1993.

Last MSR was $1,000-$1,350.

Product code: 170027 (3 1/2 in., 12 shot Compact), 170032 (5 in., 15 shot Limited), 170037/39 (exported models), or 170052(4 1/4 in., 12 shot Tactical).

THE SHORTY 9 MKIII - 9mm cal., match grade barrel w/ hand fitted titanium bushing, over-size slide rails, ambidextrous safety, Performance Center action tune job, adj. Novak Lo-Mount sights, included Zippo lighter with Performance Center logo. Distributed by Lew Horton, 1997.

Last MSR was $1,024.

9 RECON - 9mm cal., 3 1/2 in. match grade barrel, titanium coated spherical barrel bushing, double stack 12 + 1 mag., white dot front and Novak 2 Dot Lo-Mount rear sight, traditional DA trigger, hand lapped oversize rails, ambidextrous spring loaded decocker, 20 LPI checkering on the front strap, Hogue wraparound rubber grips, compact frame, two-tone finish with a clear anodized alloy frame and a carbon steel blue slide, aluminum carry case, 27.2 oz. Distributed by RSR, 1999-2000.

Last MSR was N/A.

Product code: 170140.

S&W 4006 SHORTY FORTY - .40 S&W cal., 3 1/2 in. Bar-Sto barrel, spherical bushing, bobbed hammer, Novak Lo-Mount carry sights, 9-round single stack magazine, alloy frame, grips and frame stamped with Performance Center logo, beveled trigger, adj. front dovetail sight, oversize slide rails, 500 mfg., 27 oz. Distributed by Lew Horton, 1992, 1993, and 1995.

Last MSR was $1,500.

 ✻ *S&W 4006 Shorty Forty Tactical* - .40 S&W cal., full size companion to Shorty Forty, 5 in. barrel. Distributed by Lew Horton, limited production 1993.

Last MSR was $1,500.

Product code: 170020.

 ✻ *S&W 4006 Shorty Forty Compensated* - .40 S&W cal., compensator mounted on ported barrel. Distributed by Lew Horton.

Last MSR was $1,700.

 ✻ *S&W 4006 Shorty Forty MK III* - third variation S/N prefix "PCW". Mfg. 1995.

Last MSR was $949.

Product code: 170011.

 ✻ *S&W 4006 Shorty Forty MKIII 1997* - ambidextrous safety, low mount adj. sights, hand fitted titanium barrel bushing, precision checkered front strap, hand honed double action S/N prefix "KPC". Distributed by Lew Horton.

Last MSR was $1,025.

Product code: 170061.

 ✻ *S&W 4006 Shorty Forty Performance Center .40 S&W Tactical* - .40 S&W cal., 5 in. match grade barrel, fixed tritium night front and Novak 2-dot rear sight, stainless steel frame w/ carbon steel slide materials, tactical black matte slide w/ satin stainless frame finish, 10 round mag., box cut frame and slide rails for 100% contact, balanced slide, ambidextrous decocker, 41.6 oz. Distributed by RSR, 1997.

Last MSR was $1,146.

Product code: 170091.

 ✻ *S&W 4006 Shorty Forty Performance Center Compact* - .40 S&W cal., 4 1/4 in. barrel. Mfg. August, 1994.

Last MSR was N/A.

Product code: 170054.

MODEL 4006 SHORTY FORTY Y2000 - .40 S&W cal., 3 1/2 in. barrel, white dovetail front sight, Novak Lo-Mount Carry 2 Dot rear sight, aluminum frame with stainless slide, 9 round mag., two-tone black finish, Performance Center aluminum case. Distributed by Camfour 2000.

Last MSR was N/A.

Product code: 170164.

PERFORMANCE CENTER 40 RECON - .40 S&W cal., 4 1/4 in. match grade barrel w/ compensator, titanium coated spherical barrel bushing, white dot post front and all black Novak Lo-Mount rear sight, 7 round magazine, ambidextrous spring loaded decocker, Hogue wraparound rubber grip, stainless steel material with matte black finish, laser etched with "40 RECON Performance Center" on the left side. Distributed by RSR, 1998.

Last MSR was N/A.

Product code: 170099.

100%	98%	95%	90%	80%	70%	60%	50%	40%	30%	20%	10%

PERFORMANCE CENTER 45 RECON - .45 ACP cal., 4 1/4 in. match grade ported barrel, titanium coated spherical barrel bushing, white dot post front and black Novak Lo-Mount rear sight, ambidextrous spring loaded decocker, Hogue wraparound rubber grip, 7 round magazine, stainless steel construction, stainless or matte black finish, laser etched "45 RECON Performance Center" on the left side, aluminum carry case, S/N prefix "SFF", 27.8 oz. Distributed by RSR, 1998.

Last MSR was $1022.

Product code: 170098 (matte black), 170141 (stainless finish), or 170128 (includes Recon SWAT knife).

PERFORMANCE CENTER 45 CQB PISTOLS (CLOSE QUARTERS BATTLE) - .45 ACP cal., 4 in. match grade barrel, two variations offered in 1998, Novak Lo-Mount Dot front and Novak Lo-Mount 2 Dot rear sight, 7 round mag., straight backstrap grip, stainless steel slide, titanium coated spherical barrel bushing, alloy frame with a matte black finish (Model CQB-AL) or stainless steel frame with a matte stainless (Model CQB-SS) finish, ".45 C.Q.B. Performance Center" laser etched on the slide's left side. Distributed by Lew Horton, 1998-1999.

Last MSR was $1,235.

Product code: 170106 (alloy) or 170105 (stainless).

THE SHORTY .45 - .45 ACP cal., match grade barrel, ambidextrous safety, adj. sights, hand fitted titanium barrel bushing, oversize frame and slide rails, precision checkered front strap, hand honed double action. Mfg. 1997.

Last MSR was $1,146.

Product code: 170075.

THE .45 LIMITED - 45 ACP cal., match grade barrel, SA trigger, oversize precision cut frame and slide rails, hand fitted titanium barrel bushing, and slide lock, adj. sights, oversize mag. well, tuned action, Zippo lighter with Perf. Center logo. Distributed by Lew Horton, 1997.

Last MSR was $1,470.

MODEL 5906 PC-9 - 9mm cal., 3 1/2 in. titanium spherical barrel bushing, 15 shot mag., blue slide with satin stainless frame, smooth trigger, bobbed hammer, dovetail front and Novak Lo-Mount fixed rear sight, 27 oz. Distributed by Lew Horton.

Last MSR was N/A

✻ *Model 1911 (2005)* - .38 Super cal., another variation of the original 2004 model, part of Doug Koenig Professional Series, 5 in. barrel, satin stainless steel finish, 10 shot mag., Dou Koenig speed hammer, competition match trigger with over trasvel stop, black dovetail front sight, Doug Koenig logo on smooth black Micarta grips, oversized external extractor, full length guide rod, competition mag. well, 30 LPI front strap checkering. Mfg. 2005.

Last MSR was N/A.

Product code: 170257.

RIFLES

S&W in 1984 disc. importation of all Howa manufactured rifles. Mossberg continued importation utilizing leftover S&W parts in addition to fabricating their own.

MODEL 320 REVOLVING RIFLE - .320 S&W cal., 6 shot cylinder, 16, 18, or 20 in. round barrel, hard rubber grips, detachable shoulder stock, blue or nickel (rare, add a premium) finish. 977 mfg. 1879-87.

✻ *Model 320 Revolving Rifle 16 or 20 in. barrel* - 239 mfg. with 16 in., and 224 with 20 in. barrel.

100%	98%	95%	90%	80%	70%	60%	50%	40%	30%	20%	10%
N/A	$15,000	$12,000	$10,000	$8,700	$8,100	$7,675	$7,000	$6,375	$5,600	$4,800	$3,850

✻ *Model 320 Revolving Rifle 18 in. barrel* - 514 mfg.

100%	98%	95%	90%	80%	70%	60%	50%	40%	30%	20%	10%
N/A	$13,500	$11,000	$9,750	$9,350	$8,700	$8,100	$7,675	$7,000	$6,375	$5,600	$4,800

GRADING - PPGS™	100%	98%	95%	90%	80%	70%	60%

MODEL A BOLT ACTION RIFLE - .22-250 Rem., .243 Win., .270 Win., .308 Win., .30 - 06, 7mm Mag., or .300 Win. Mag. cal., 23 3/4 in. barrel, folding leaf sight, checkered Monte Carlo stock with rosewood forend tip and pistol grip cap. Mfg. 1969-72.

	$385	$330	$305	$275	$220	$195	$165

MODEL B - similar to Model A, in .243 Win., .270 Win., or .30-06 cal., 20 3/4 in. barrel, Schnabel forend.

	$425	$305	$275	$250	$195	$165	$140

MODEL C - similar to Model B, with cheekpiece.

	$425	$305	$275	$250	$195	$165	$140

MODEL D - similar to Model C, with full length stock.

	$550	$385	$360	$305	$250	$220	$195

MODEL E - similar to Model D, with no cheekpiece.

	$550	$385	$360	$305	$250	$220	$195

Note: These rifles were made for S&W by Husqvarna in Sweden.

MODEL 1500 MOUNTAINEER - .222 Rem., .22-250 Rem., .223 Rem, .243 Win, .25-06 Rem., .270 Win, .30-06, or .308 Win. cal., bolt action, 22 in. barrel 5-6 shot mag., no sights, walnut stock, approx. 7 lbs. 10 oz. New 1983.

	$300	$250	$245	$210	$195	$175	$160

Add $27 for sights.

✳ *Model 1500 Mountaineer Magnum* - 7mm Rem. Mag. or .300 Win. Mag. cal.

	$325	$275	$260	$225	$200	$180	$160

MODEL 1500 DELUXE - same cals. as standard 1500, Monte Carlo stock, skip-line checkering, select walnut, no sights. New 1983.

	$350	$300	$260	$220	$200	$180	$160

Add $20 for 7mm Mag. and .300 Win. Mag.

MODEL 1500 DELUXE VARMINT - .222 Rem, .22-250 Rem., or .223 Rem. cal., heavy 24 in. barrel, skip-line checkering, no sights. New 1983-disc..

	$375	$325	$275	$225	$200	$180	$160

Add $15 for parkerized finish.

MODEL 1700 LS "CLASSIC HUNTER" - .243 Win, 270 Win, or .30-06 cal., 22 in. barrel, removable 5 shot mag., solid recoil pad, no sights, Schnabel forend, finely checkered. New 1983.

	$400	$350	$315	$265	$240	$220	$195

MODEL M&P15 SEMI-AUTO RIFLE SERIES - .223 Rem. cal., gas operated semi-auto, AR-15 style design with 16 in. chrome lined barrel with muzzle brake or 20 in. barrel, 10 (M&P15PC or M&P15FT) or 30 shot mag., one piece (OR), fixed position (FT), skeletonized (PC) or six position CAR collapsible stock, hard coat black anodized finish, the Model M&P15 features detachable carrying handle, A2 post front sight, adj. dual aperture rear sight, and thinned handguard, M&P15A features a receiver Picatinny rail and adj. rear folding battle sight with ribbed handguard, M&P15T features extended Picatinny rail on receiver and barrel, in addition to RAS on both sides and bottom of barrel, adj. front and rear folding battle sights, supplied with hard carry case, approx. 6 3/4 lbs. New 2006.

MSR $1,304	$1,095	$950	$850	$750	$650	$575	$500

Add $16 for M&P15A.
Add $450 for M&P15T or M&P15FT.
Add $111 for M&P15X (new 2008, A2 post front sight, folding rear sight).
Add $935 for M&P15PC w/flattop, skeletonized stock, two-stage trigger, and 20 in. barrel (mfg. 2007 only).
Subtract $290 for M&P15OR.

GRADING - PPGS™	100%	98%	95%	90%	80%	70%	60%

I-BOLT RIFLE - .25-06, .270 Win., .30-06, 7mm Rem. Mag., or .300 Win. Mag., short or long action, 23 or 25 in. barrel, black synthetic, Realtree camo synthetic, or Monte Carlo walnut (new 2008) stock, blue carbon steel or stainless steel action and barrel, Picatinny rail integral with frame, approx. 7 lbs. New mid-2007.

	100%	98%	95%	90%	80%	70%	60%
MSR $699	$575	$500	$425	$375	$325	$275	$225

    Add $53 for camo.
    Add $194 for checkered walnut stock (new 2008).
    Add $131 for stainless steel action and barrel and black synthetic stock (new 2008).
    Add $201 for stainless steel action and barrel and synthetic stock with camo finish.

SHOTGUNS

S&W in 1984 disc. importation of all Howa manufactured shotguns. Mossberg continued importation utilizing leftover S&W parts in addition to fabricating their own.

MODEL 916 SLIDE ACTION SHOTGUN - 12, 16, or 20 ga., 20, 26, 28, or 30 in. barrels, various chokes, plain pistol grip stock, solid frame. Mfg. by S&W in Springfield, MA. 1972-disc.

	$175	$150	$140	$130	$120	$110	$100

* *Model 916 Slide Action Shotgun Vent. rib and pad*

	$200	$175	$155	$145	$135	$130	$120

MODEL 916T SLIDE ACTION - similar to 916, except barrels can be interchanged.

	$195	$170	$155	$145	$135	$130	$125

* *Model 916T Slide Action Vent. rib and pad*

	$225	$200	$180	$170	$155	$145	$135

MODEL 96 SLIDE ACTION - various gauges, disc.

	$125	$110	$100	$90	$75	$70	$65

MODEL 1000 P SLIDE ACTION - 12 ga., various barrel lengths, chokes, VR.

	$350	$305	$270	$230	$210	$190	$170

    This model is the same as the Model 3000.

MODEL 1000 AUTOLOADER - 12 or 20 ga., 22-30 in. barrels, various chokes, gas operated, vent rib, engraved alloy receiver, checkered pistol grip stock. Mfg. 1972-1984.

	$350	$325	$295	$260	$240	$220	$200

    Add $30 for multi-choke tubes.
    Add approx. $125 for slug barrel.

* *Model 1000 Autoloader Waterfowler* - 3 in. chamber, parkerized finish, Magnum 28 or 30 in. barrel, multi-chokes, steel receiver, "M" suffix, camo sling and swivels.

	$500	$450	$375	$340	$310	$275	$255

* *Model 1000 Autoloader Super 12* - handles all loads interchangeably, top-of-the-line model during its time.

	$500	$450	$400	$360	$330	$300	$280

    Add $50 for multi-choke.

* *Model 1000 Autoloader Target* - 12 or 20 ga., skeet, super skeet, and trap models available. Super skeet has 15 barrel muzzle vents to reduce recoil. Trap model has multi-choke tubes, Monte Carlo select walnut stock and forend. Both alloy and steel receivers available in Skeet model, Trap is steel only.

Skeet/Super Skeet	$400	$390	$335	$260	$235	$215	$190
Trap (Model 1000T)	$595	$525	$450	$375	$325	$285	$235

Note: Shotguns made for S&W by Howa Machinery, Ltd., Japan. This line was picked up by Mossberg after S&W discontinued them - these models may be more desirable.

GRADING - PPGS™	100%	98%	95%	90%	80%	70%	60%

MODEL 1012 SEMI-AUTO - 12 ga., 3 in. chamber, 24, 26, 28, or 30 in. barrel with vent. rib and 5 flush choke tubes, micro coated twin piston gas operated, checkered satin walnut, black synthetic, or synthetic stock with 100% Max-4 or APG camo treatment, includes four-piece shim kit, approx. 6 1/2 lbs., mfg. in Turkey. Importation began 2007.

	MSR $644	$525	$475	$425	$395	$350	$300	$275

  Add $35 for satin finished walnut stock and forearm.
  Add $91 for 100% camo coverage.

* *Model 1012 Super Semi-Auto* - similar to Model 1012, except has 3 1/2 in. chamber, not available with walnut stock and forearm, approx. 7.3 lbs. Importation began 2007.

	MSR $784	$650	$575	$525	$475	$425	$395	$360

  Add $98 for full camo coverage.

MODEL 1020 SEMI-AUTO - 20 ga., 3 in. chamber, otherwise similar to Model 1012, single piston gas operation, approx. 6 lbs.

	MSR $644	$525	$475	$425	$395	$350	$300	$275

  Add $35 for satin finished walnut stock and forearm.
  Add $91 for 100% camo coverage.
  Subtract $21 for Model 1020SS w/short stock and 24 in. barrel.

MODEL 3000 SLIDE ACTION - 12 or 20 ga., 3 in. chambers, 22-30 in. barrels, walnut stock and forend, 6 1/4-7 1/2 lbs.

		$350	$305	$270	$230	$210	$190	$170

  Add $30 for multi-choke tubes.
  Subtract $40 for slug gun (rifle sights on 22 in. barrel).

This model was also available in a "Waterfowler" variation - values are approx. the same as listed.

MODEL 3000 POLICE - 12 ga. only, blue or parkerized finish, many combinations of finishes, stock types, and other combat accessories were available for this model, 18 or 20 in. barrel.

		$325	$255	$215	$185	$170	$155	$140

  Add $125 for folding stock.

ELITE GOLD GRADE I SxS - 20 ga., 3 in. chamber, scalloped boxlock action, 26 or 28 in. barrels with fixed chokes, ejectors, ST, Grade III checkered walnut straight grip English or pistol grip stock, color case hardened frame with light scroll engraving, 6.5-6.7 lbs., mfg. in Turkey. Importation began 2007.

	MSR $2,380	$1,975	$1,750	$1,525	$1,350	$1,150	$950	$775

ELITE SILVER GRADE I O/U - 12 ga., scalloped boxlock action, 26, 28, or 30 in. VR barrels with 5 flush choke tubes, ST, ejectors, color case hardened frame with light scroll engraving, Grade III checkered walnut pistol grip stock, solid recoil pad, engine turned internal barrel parts, 7.6-7.8 lbs., mfg. in Turkey. Importation began 2007.

	MSR $2,380	$1,975	$1,750	$1,525	$1,350	$1,150	$950	$775

SMITHSON, J.P.

Current custom rifle manufacturer located in Orem, UT.

  J.P. Smithson specializes in custom bolt action rifles. Please contact him directly for more information, including model availability and pricing (see Trademark Index).

SNAKE CHARMER

Currently manufactured by Verney-Carron USA, Inc. located in Clay Center, KS a joint venture of Verney-Carron SA located in Saint-Etienne, France (please refer to the separate Verney-Carron listing) and Y.B.E., Inc. located in Clay Center, KS (distributor of Hastings barrels and choke tubes). Distributor sales only.

GRADING - PPGS™	100%	98%	95%	90%	80%	70%	60%

SHOTGUNS: SINGLE SHOT

SNAKE CHARMER II - .410 bore only, stainless steel, break open single shot, black molded plastic stock and forend, shell holder in stock, also available as Night Charmer (disc. 1988) and Sea Charmer (disc. 1988), 3 1/2 lbs.

MSR $216	$180	$160	$145	$130	$115	$100	$90

Add $10 for Night Charmer (disc. 1988).
Add $18 for Sea Charmer (disc. 1988).
Subtract $18 for black carbon steel barrel (New Generation Model).

SOCIETA SIDERURGICA GLISENTI

Previous manufacturer located in Brescia, Italy. Also see the Italian Military Arms listing.

PISTOLS: SEMI-AUTO

GLISENTI MODEL 1910 - 9mm Glisenti cal., 7 shot, 4 in. barrel, fixed sights, blue, checkered wood, rubber or plastic grips, Italian service pistol. Mfg. 1910-WWII.

	$750	$625	$450	$325	$275	$225	$200

Warning: While some Glisentis may chamber and fire the 9mm Para. cartridge, it is extremely dangerous to do so.

SODIA, FRANZ

Current manufacturer established during 1871, and located in Salzburg, Austria since 1961. Previously located in Ferlach, Austria.

LONG GUNS: CUSTOM

Sodia arms are superb and are often excellently engraved and inlaid. Sodia is famous for its high quality long arms in many configurations. Current models include: Model 557 Mountain Carbine O/U combination gun, Model 557 Super De Luxe O/U combination gun, Model 270 AD Drilling, Model 30 Drilling, Model 160 EJ Safari SxS double rifle, Model 260 EJ SxS double rifle, Model 158 AN Drilling, Model 360 EJ SxS double rifle, Model 560 EJ Safari SxS double rifle, Model 150 HH single barrel rifle, in addition to a bolt action model in many calibers. Please contact the company for more information, inlcuding U.S. availability, delivery time, and a custom quotation.

To determine current values on older Franz Sodia rifles and shotguns, it is very importation to consider the overall desirability of the gun's configuration (i.e., boxlock or sidelock action, caliber/gauge, special features, amount and quality of engraving (including gold inlays), type and quality of wood, checkering/carving, eye appeal, and original condition factor). All Franz Sodia guns are hand crafted, and need to be evaluated individually to determine value and shootability.

SOKOLOVSKY CORPORATION SPORT ARMS (SCSA)

Previous manufacturer until 1990 located in Sunnyvale, CA.

PISTOLS: SEMI-AUTO

SOKOLOVSKY .45 AUTOMASTER - .45 ACP cal. only, stainless steel, single action, 6 in. barrel, 6 shot mag., adj. Millet sights, unique action, is free of external devices, 55 oz. Mfg. 1984-90.

	$2,700	$2,200	$1,850	$1,620	$1,335	$1,115	$930

Last MSR was $3,300.

Total production on this model is 50 pistols.

GRADING - PPGS™	100%	98%	95%	90%	80%	70%	60%

SOLEIHAC ARMURIER

Previous manufacturer located in Saint Etienne, France.

This manufacturer produced copies of 1894 patent Darne R model guns until 1950. The guns produced were generally simple and less expensive than other manufacturers' sliding breech guns. Most unmarked sliding breech guns were probably manufactured by Soleihac Armurier. Quality and pricing will be similar to low grade (Halifax and RIO model) Darne guns in average condition.

SOMMER + OCKENFUSS GmbH

Previous manufacturer located in Baiersbronn, Germany until 2002. Previously imported by Lothar Walther Precision Tool, located in Cumming, GA. Previously imported by Intertex Carousels Corporation during 1998-2000, and located in Pineville, NC.

Sommer + Ockenfuss also produced a bolt adapter to convert the Remington 700 bolt action into a straight pull repeater, enabling the addition of a firing pin safety and firing chamber lock.

PISTOLS: SEMI-AUTO

P21 - .224 HV, 9mm Para., or .40 S&W cal., 3.11 (Combat) or 3.55 (Police) in. rotating barrel, SA/DA operation, release grip safety uncocks the hammer, keyed slide lock blocks firing pin and slide, 10 shot mag., approx. 24 oz. Mfg. 2001.

$550	$495	$450	$415	$375	$340	$310

Last MSR was $608.

Add approx. $320 for conversion slide assemblies.

RIFLES: SLIDE ACTION

SHORTY - most popular cals., unique slide action rifle in bullpup configuration featuring a straight line design with a grip safety pistol grip which also works the slide assembly, stainless or black coated barrel, compact 6-lug bolt with a locking surface of 0.263 sq. in., with or w/o sideplates inlet into walnut or black synthetic (new 1999) stock. Imported 1998-2002.

  * *Shorty Wilderness Rifle* - match trigger, polymer stock, and stainless steel barrel.

$1,495	$1,275	$1,100	$995	$925	$850	$750

Last MSR was $1,660.

Add $310 for .375 H&H or .416 Rem. Mag. cal. (Shorty Safari).
Add $200 for walnut stock (Shorty American Hunter).
Add $210 for sight mounts.
Add $88 for recoil brake.

  * *Shorty Marksman Rifle* - similar to Wilderness Rifle, except has choice of black coated or fluted heavy match barrel and recoil brake.

$1,875	$1,675	$1,450	$1,275	$1,100	$995	$850

Last MSR was $2,020.

Add $80 for .308 Win. or .300 Win. Mag. (fluted barrel), $420 for .338 Lapua Mag. with black coated barrel, or $710 for .338 Lapua Mag. with fluted stainless barrel.
Add $80 for stainless barrel.
Add $210 for sight mount, $168 for bipod, $210 for Spigot stock cap.

There were also deluxe variations, limited editions, and Marksman's packages ($4,100-$4,860 MSR) available in this model.

SPARTAN GUN WORKS

Spartan Gun Works is a trademark of Remington Arms Company, Inc. Select long gun configurations are imported from Russia beginning 2004.

Remington refers to these firearms as part of its ISP (International Sourced Product) line.

GRADING - PPGS™	100%	98%	95%	90%	80%	70%	60%

COMBINATION GUNS

SPR94 - choice of 12 ga. over .223 Rem., .30-06 (disc. 2006) or .308 Win. (disc. 2006) cal., or .410 bore over .17 HMR (disc. 2006), .22 LR or .22 Mag. cal., .22 cal., 3 in. chamber, DT, boxlock action, 24 in. barrels with rifle sights, extractors, checkered walnut stock and forearm with recoil pad, sling swivels, separated barrels grouped for scope, approx. 7 1/2 lbs. Importation began 2006.

✱ *SPR94 .410 Bore/Rimfire*

MSR $392	$330	$275	$235	$210	$180	$170	$160

✱ *SPR94 12 ga./Centerfire*

MSR $661	$525	$465	$410	$360	$315	$280	$260

RIFLES

SPR18 SINGLE SHOT - .223 Rem., .243 Win., .270 Win., .30-06, .308 Win. or 7.62x39mm cal., break open single shot with opening lever on rear of trigger guard, 23 1/2 in. spiral cut fluted barrel, choice of blue or nickel finished frame, adj. sights and scope rail, walnut stock with recoil pad and forearm, 6 3/4 lbs. Importation began 2006.

MSR $277	$225	$190	$165	$140	$125	$110	$100

Add $28 for scope and case (blue finish only, disc. 2006).
Add $49 for nickel finish.

SPR22 SxS - .30-06 or .45-70 Govt. cal., boxlock action, blue metal finish, sling swivels, 23 1/2 in. monobloc barrels with iron sights, DT, extractors, top opening lever, checkered walnut stock and forearm with recoil pad, 7 1/2 lbs. Limited importation 2006 only.

	$585	$535	$475	$425	$385	$350	$325

Last MSR was $699.

SHOTGUNS

SPR100 SINGLE SHOT - 12, 20 ga., or .410 bore, 3 in. chamber, 24 (Youth only), 26 (20 ga.) or 28 (12 ga.) in. barrel with or w/o VR and fixed choke, trigger guard opening lever, blue or nickel plated steel action with selectable ejector or extractor, cocking indicator, crossbolt safety, hardwood stock and forearm, 5.8-6 lbs. Importation began 2004.

MSR $118	$90	$80	$65	$55	$45	$40	$35

Add $9 for standard Youth model (.410 bore or 20 ga.).
Add $86 for SPR100 Max with nickel receiver (also available in Youth Model).

✱ *SPR100 Single Shot Sporting* - 12 or 20 ga., nickel receiver, includes choke tubes and recoil pad, Monte Carlo walnut stock and forearm. Importation began 2006.

MSR $300	$235	$190	$160	$140	$120	$100	$90

SPR210 SxS - 12, 16 (disc. 2007), 20, 28 ga., or .410 bore, 3 in. chambers except for 16 and 28 ga., boxlock action, SST, ejectors, 26 or 28 in. barrels with choke tubes (N/A on 28 ga. or .410 bore), tang safety, blued or nickel frame, VR, checkered walnut stock and forearm with recoil pad, 6.8-7 lbs. Importation began 2004.

MSR $479	$390	$330	$280	$250	$225	$200	$185

Add $82 for 28 ga. or .410 bore (fixed chokes only).
Add $52 for nickel frame (12 or 20 ga. only).
Add $8 for hammerless cowboy gun in 12 or 20 ga. only with 20 in. barrels (disc. 2007).

GRADING - PPGS™	100%	98%	95%	90%	80%	70%	60%

SPR220 SxS - 12 or 20 ga., 3 in. chambers, boxlock action, DT, extractors, 20 (cowboy only), 26 or 28 in. barrels with choke tubes, tang safety, blue or nickel frame, checkered walnut stock and forearm, 6.8-7 lbs. Importation began 2004.

MSR $392	$325	$275	$240	$210	$185	$140	$120

Add $169 for hammers.
Subtract $50 for cowboy gun with hardwood stock and forearm, 12 ga. only and fixed cylinder chokes.
Add $29 for hammerless cowboy gun with nickel finished frame, 12 or 20 ga. with choke tubes.
Subtract $20 for 2 3/4 in. chambers on cowboy gun.

SPR310 O/U - 12, 20, 28 ga., or .410 bore, 3 in. chamber except for 28 ga., boxlock action with monobloc barrels, SST, ejectors, 26 or 28 in. VR barrels with choke tubes (N/A on 28 ga. or .410 bore), tang safety, blue or nickel plated frame, checkered walnut stock and forearm with rubber recoil pad, 7.3-7.4 lbs. Importation began 2004.

MSR $598	$485	$415	$365	$320	$295	$250	$225

Add $88 for 28 ga. or .410 bore.
Add $54 for nickel frame.
Add $70 for nickel frame with bird scene engraving.
Add $172 for nickel Sporting Model (12 or 20 ga. only, new 2006).

SPR320 O/U - 12, 16, 20, 28 ga., or .410 bore, 3 in. chamber except for 16 and 28 ga., boxlock action with monobloc barrels, DT, extractors, 26 or 28 in. VR barrels with choke tubes (N/A on 28 ga. or .410 bore), tang safety, blued finish, checkered walnut stock and forearm with rubber recoil pad, 7.3-7.4 lbs. Limited importation 2004-2005.

	$350	$295	$250	$215	$185	$165	$145

Last MSR was $419.

SPR453 SEMI-AUTO - 12 ga. only, 3 1/2 in. chamber, gas operated, choice of matte black or new Mossy Oak Break-Up (disc.) camo finish, black synthetic or camo stock and forearm, 24, 26, or 28 in. VR barrel with four extended choke tubes, dual extractors on bolt face, approx. 8 1/8 lbs. Importation began 2006.

MSR $497	$400	$350	$300	$265	$230	$200	$185

Add $56 for 100% new Mossy Oak Break-Up camo finish (disc. 2006).

SPECIAL WEAPONS LLC

Previous paramilitary rifle manufacturer 1999-2002, and located in Mesa, AZ. Previously located in Tempe, AZ.

Special Weapons LLC closed its doors on Dec. 31, 2002. Another company, Special Weapons, Inc., is handling the warranty repairs on Special Weapons LLC firearms (see Trademark Index).

CARBINES: SEMI-AUTO

OMEGA 760 - 9mm Para. cal., reproduction of the S&W Model 76, 16 1/4 in. partially shrouded barrel, fixed wire stock, 30 shot mag., 7 1/2 lbs. Limited mfg. 2002.

	$495	$450	$425	$395	$375	$350	$325

Last MSR was $575.

SW-5 CARBINE - 9mm Para. cal., paramilitary configuration styled after the HK-94 (parts interchangeable), stainless steel receiver, plastic lower housing, 16 1/4 in. stainless steel barrel, A2 style black synthetic stock with wide forearm, 10 shot mag. (accepts high capacity HK-94/MP-5 mags also), approx. 6 3/4 lbs. Mfg. 2000-2002.

	$1,475	$1,225	$1,025	$875	$800	$750	$695

Last MSR was $1,600.

GRADING - PPGS™	100%	98%	95%	90%	80%	70%	60%

SW-45 CARBINE - .45 ACP cal., otherwise similar to SW-5 Carbine. Mfg. 2000-2002.

	$1,550	$1,275	$1,050	$895	$825	$775	$725

Last MSR was $1,700.

RIFLES: SEMI-AUTO

SW-3 - .308 Win. cal., paramilitary configuration styled after the HK-91 (parts interchangeable), tooled receiver, metal steel lower trigger housing, 17.71 stainless steel barrel, A2 style stock, approx. 10 lbs. Mfg. 2000-2002.

	$1,425	$1,175	$995	$850	$800	$750	$695

Last MSR was $1,550.

✳ *SW-3 SP* - similar to SW-3, except has PSG-1 style trigger assembly, 22 in. custom target barrel and Weaver rail welded to top. Mfg. 2000-2002.

	$2,250	$1,975	$1,700	$1,500	$1,250	$1,050	$895

Last MSR was $2,500.

SPENCER REPEATING RIFLES CO.

Manufactured by Spencer Repeating Rifle Company located in Boston, MA between 1860-1868. Spencer manufactured approximately 144,000 rimfire rifles and carbines, of which approximately 107,000 were contracted to the United States Government during the Civil War.

The brainchild of young Christopher Miner Spencer, more than 13,500 Spencer M1860 Army rifles, 800 M1860 Navy rifles, and 48,000 M1860 Army carbines saw action during the Civil War. In late 1864, the Chief of Ordnance directed modifications, including reducing the bore from .52 to .50 caliber, and shortening the barrel from 22 inches to 20 inches. The new carbine was designated the Spencer M1865 carbine. Nearly 19,000 were produced by the Spencer Repeating Rifle Company, and another 30,500 by the Burnside Rifle Company, although all were delivered too late to see action in the Civil War. Model 1865 carbines and refurbished M1860 carbines became the mainstay of America's troops on the Western Frontier until replaced by "Trap-Door" Springfield carbines after 1873.

The author wishes to express his thanks to Mr. Roy Marcot for providing most of the information listed.

100%	98%	95%	90%	80%	70%	60%	50%	40%	30%	20%	10%

RIFLES: LEVER ACTION

SMALL-FRAME MILITARY CARBINES AND SPORTING RIFLES - fewer than four dozen prototype small-frame .38 rimfire cal. sporting rifles and .44 rimfire cal. military carbines were made by Christopher Spencer in Hartford between 1860 and 1861. They are exceedingly rare, and only a few are in private hands.

N/A	$16,000	$15,000	$13,000	$11,000	$9,000	$8,500	$7,500	$7,000	$6,000	$5,000	$4,500

MODEL 1860 NAVY RIFLES - the rarest of production Spencer firearms, 803 Spencer Model 1860 Navy rifles with sword-type bayonets were produced for the U.S. Navy Bureau of Ordnance between 1862 and 1863.

N/A	$14,000	$13,500	$12,000	$11,000	$9,000	$8,500	$7,500	$7,000	$6,000	$5,500	$5,000

Add $1,000 for correct Collins produced sword-type bayonet.

MODEL 1860 ARMY RIFLES - between 1863 and 1864, the Spencer factory in Boston produced 11,471 Spencer M1860 Army rifles for the Federal Ordnance Department, another 200 for the U.S. Navy, and approximately 2,000 for private purchase. All were issued with Pattern M1855 angular bayonets which fit only these rifles.

N/A	$11,000	$10,500	$10,000	$8,000	$6,500	$5,000	$4,000	$3,000	$2,500	$2,000	$1,800

Add $450 for correct angular bayonet.

100%	98%	95%	90%	80%	70%	60%	50%	40%	30%	20%	10%

MODEL 1860 CARBINES - beginning in October 1863, the Spencer factory began delivering the first of 45,733 Spencer M1860 carbines to the Ordnance Department for use by Federal cavalrymen. As many as 3,000 additional M1860 carbines went to private purchasers, and also saw action in the war. Because Spencer carbines were so important to the Federal war effort, nearly all saw hard use during the last 18 months of fighting. This resulted in very few weapons available today in excellent condition, and fewer yet with case colors remaining on the receiver.

N/A	$11,000	$10,500	$10,000	$7,500	$6,000	$4,500	$3,750	$2,750	$2,000	$1,800	$1,500

Subtract 25% for Springfield Armory reconditioned Spencer Model 1860 carbines (after the war).

MODEL 1865 CARBINES - in 1865 and 1866, the Spencer factory delivered 18,959 Spencer M1865 carbines to the Federal Ordnance Department. Concurrently, the Burnside Rifle Company of Providence, Rhode Island manufactured and delivered 30,502 Spencer M1865 carbines to the Ordnance Department.

N/A	$6,000	$5,000	$4,000	$3,000	$2,750	$2,500	$2,000	$1,750	$1,500	$1,200	$1,000

MODEL 1865 ARMY RIFLES - as many as 3,000 Spencer M1865 Army rifles were made by the Spencer factory in 1865. While none were ordered by the U.S. Army Ordnance Department, 2,000 went to the Commonwealth of Massachusetts National Guard, and another 1,000 went to Canadian troops and to private purchasers.

N/A	$6,000	$5,000	$4,000	$3,000	$2,750	$2,500	$2,000	$1,750	$1,500	$1,200	$1,000

SPRINGFIELD ARMORY RIFLE MUSKET CONVERSION OF SPENCER CARBINES - in 1871, General Dyer, Chief of Ordnance, directed that 1,109 Spencer M1865 carbines be converted to two-band muskets. Each was fitted with Springfield .50 caliber barrels which held the standard M1855 pattern bayonet.

N/A	$6,500	$6,000	$5,000	$4,000	$3,000	$2,750	$2,500	$2,250	$2,000	$1,750	$1,500

MODEL 1867 ARMY RIFLES AND CARBINES - in 1867, the Spencer factory produced approx. 1,000 M1867 Army rifles and 12,000 carbines. All were intended for private domestic or foreign military sales.

N/A	$4,000	$3,000	$2,500	$2,000	$1,900	$1,750	$1,500	$1,400	$1,200	$1,000	$900

NEW MODEL ARMY RIFLES AND CARBINES - in their final year of production, 1868, the Spencer Repeating Rifle Company produced approx. 1,000 Army rifles and 5,000 carbines. These too, were intended for private domestic or foreign military sales.

N/A	$4,000	$3,000	$2,500	$2,000	$1,900	$1,750	$1,500	$1,400	$1,200	$1,000	$900

SPORTING RIFLES - between 1864-68, the Spencer factory produced approximately 2,000 sporting rifles for the civilian trade. The initial 200 or so were made from surplus military M1860 Army rifle receivers. Thereafter, approximately 1,800 sporting rifles were made expressly as such. The majority chambered the Spencer 56-46 bottleneck rimfire cartridge, but a small number were produced in .50 caliber, chambering 56-50 and the 56-52 cartridges. Spencer sporting rifles missing the rear tang sight are worth approximately 25% less than those listed.

N/A	$10,000	$9,500	$9,000	$8,000	$6,500	$5,000	$3,500	$3,000	$2,500	$2,000	$1,500

Factory engraved rifles are known, and will command a substantial premium.

SPHINX SYSTEMS LTD.

Current manufacturer established in 1876, and presently located in Matten b. Interlaken, Switzerland. Currently distributed by Sabre Defence Industries, LLC, located in Nashville, TN. Previously imported by Rocky Mountain Armoury, located in Silverthorne, CO. Previously manufactured by Sphinx Engineering S.A. located in Porrentruy, Switzerland. Previously imported by Sphinx U.S.A., located in Meriden, CT until 1996. Previously imported by Sile Distributors located in New York, NY.

GRADING - PPGS™	100%	98%	95%	90%	80%	70%	60%

PISTOLS

MODEL AT-380 - .380 ACP cal., semi-auto double action only, 3.27 in. barrel, stainless steel frame, two-tone finish, 10 shot mag. with finger extension, checkered walnut grips. Disc. 1996.

$435	$375	$350	$325	$295	$275	$250

Last MSR was $494.

Add $20 for black finish.
Add $71 for N/Pall finish.

MODEL 2000S STANDARD - 9mm Para. or .40 S&W (new 1993) cal., semi-auto in standard double action or double action only, 4.53 in. barrel, stainless steel fabrication, 10 (C/B 1994), 15* (9mm Para.), or 11* (.40 S&W) shot mag., checkered walnut grips, fixed sights, 35 oz. Importation disc. 2002

$965	$750	$625	$525	$450	$410	$375

Add $117 for .40 S&W cal.

  ✳ *Model 2000PS Standard Police Special* - similar to Model 2000S, except has compact slide and 3.66 in. barrel.

$850	$625	$525	$450	$410	$380	$350

Add $40 for .40 S&W cal.
Add $87 for N/Pall finish.

  ✳ *Model 2000P Standard Compact* - similar to Model 2000 Standard, except has 3.66 in. barrel and 13 shot mag., 31 oz.

$850	$625	$525	$450	$410	$380	$350

Add $40 for .40 S&W cal.
Add $87 for N/Pall finish.

  ✳ *Model 2000H Standard Sub-Compact* - similar to Model 2000 Compact, except has 3.34 in. barrel and 10 shot mag., 26 oz. Disc. 1996.

$850	$625	$525	$450	$410	$380	$350

Last MSR was $940.

Add $40 for .40 S&W cal.
Add $87 for N/Pall finish.

MODEL 2000 MASTER - 9mm Para., 9x21mm, or .40 S&W cal., single action only, two-tone finish only, designed for Master's stock class competition.

$1,795	$1,350	$1,100	$995	$895	$775	$650

Last MSR was $2,035.

MODEL AT-2000 (NEW MODEL) - 9mm Para. or .40 S&W cal., 4.53 in. barrel, 10 shot mag., machined slide with electro deposited finish, decocking mechanism. Limited mfg. 2004-2005.

$1,825	$1,675	$1,450	$1,225	$1,000	$800	$675

Last MSR was $1,995.

MODEL AT-2000CS COMPETITOR - 9mm Para., 9x21mm, or .40 S&W cal., single or double action, competition model featuring many shooting improvements including 5.3 in. compensated barrel, 10 (C/B 1994), 11* (.40 S&W), or 15* shot mag., Bo-Mar adj. sights, two-tone finish. Imported 1993-96.

$1,725	$1,275	$1,050	$950	$850	$750	$675

Last MSR was $1,902.

Add $287 for Model AT-2000C (includes Sphinx scope mount).
Add $1,538 for AT-2000K conversion kit (new 1995).
Add $1,490 for Model AT-2000CKS (competition kit to convert AT-2000 to comp. pistol, disc. 1994).

GRADING - PPGS™	100%	98%	95%	90%	80%	70%	60%

MODEL 2000 COMPETITION - similar to Model 2000 Master, except is SA only and includes more advanced competitive shooting features, Bo-Mar sights, top-of-the-line competition model. Imported 1993-96.

	$2,475	$1,925	$1,725	$1,500	$1,250	$1,050	$895

Last MSR was $2,894.

Add $78 for Model AT-2000GM (includes Sphinx scope mount).

MODEL 3000 SERIES - 9mm Para., 9x21mm (disc.), .40 S&W, or .45 ACP cal., SA/DA, available in standard (4.53 in. barrel), tactical (3 3/4 in. barrel), or competition (4.53 in. barrel, adj. sights), configuration, choice of manual safety or decocker, titanium upper/lower frame with stainless slide, stainless steel slide with titanium lower frame or stainless steel frame/slide, front/rear gripstrap stipling or grooved, two-tone finish, approx. 40 oz. New 2001.

MSR $2,350		$2,275	$2,000	$1,800	$1,575	$1,375	$1,150	$850

Add $350 for titanium frame with stainless steel slide.
Add $800 for stainless steel slide with titanium upper/lower frame (disc.).
Add $75 for tactical model.
Add $350 for competition model.

SPHINX COMPETITION MODELS - currently available in either an Open (extended barrel with 3 port compensator and Aimpoint scope), Modified (2 port compensator and rear sight optics), or Standard.

Please contact the distributor directly for more information on these models, including U.S. availability and pricing.

SPHINX .45 ACP - .45 ACP cal., SA/DA, steel construction, 3 3/4 in. barrel, double slide serrations, blue finish, 10 shot mag., fixed Trijicon night sights, black polymer grips, decocker mechanism, approx. 43 oz. New 2007.

MSR $2,990		$2,850	$2,500	$2,150	$1,850	$1,500	$1,250	$1,000

SPIDER FIREARMS

Current rifle manufacturer located in St. Cloud, FL.

RIFLES: SINGLE SHOT

FERRET 50 - .50 BMG cal., single shot bolt action, A2 style buttstock and pistol grip, Picatinny rail, choice of 18, 29, or 36 in. barrel, matte black finish, perforated handguard with bipod, includes muzzle brake. New 2003.

MSR $2,693		$2,325	$2,000	$1,800	$1,600	$1,400	$1,200	$1,000

Add $163 for 29 in. barrel or $217 for 36 in. barrel.
Add $394-$448 for stainless steel barrel, depending on length.
Add $330-$380 for stainless super match barrel (disc.).

SUPERCOMP FERRET - similar to Ferret 50, except also available in .408 CheyTac and .338 Lapua cal., features solid steel construction, fixed scope rails, 29 or 36 Lothar Walther stainless Supermatch barrels, adj. 1 lb. competition style trigger, two-axis cheekrest, and detachable rear monopod. New 2004.

MSR $3,172		$2,950	$2,600	$2,300	$2,000	$1,750	$1,600	$1,450

Add $162 for .50 BMG cal.

SPITFIRE

See listing under JSL (Hereford) in this text.

SPORT-SYSTEME DITTRICH

Current manufacturer established in 2003 and located in Kulmbach, Germany. No current importation.

Sport-Systeme Dittrich manufactures high quality semi-auto reproductions of famous military weapons, including the MP38 (BD 38), Sturmgewehr 44 (BD 44) and the Gerät Neumünster (BD 3008). Please contact the company directly for more information, including pricing and U.S. availability (see Trademark Index).

SPRINGER'S ERBEN, JOHANN

GRADING - PPGS™	100%	98%	95%	90%	80%	70%	60%

Current manufacturer and retailer established in 1836, and located in Vienna, Austria.

Joh. Springer's Erben is one of the leading retailers for hunting and sporting guns and rifles, shooting supplies, security equipment, and related accessories in Austria. Additionally, Springer's manufactures custom made long guns in a variety of configurations on a limited basis. PLease contact the company directly for more information, including U.S. availability and an individualized price quotation based on the configuration (see Trademark Index).

SPRINGFIELD ARMORY

America's first federal armory located in Springfield, MA. Production began in 1795 and an Act of Congress made it an official federal arsenal in 1872. Not associated with the private firm of the same name located in Geneseo, IL.

In recent years, collectors have realized that military specimens in 90%-100% original condition are very rare and desirable. Since the supply of these guns is limited, values listed for these condition factors may actually be a little under current market values, especially auction pricing. On Springfields and other U.S. military long arms, the importance of the wood being original, unsanded, and with crisp, clear cartouches cannot be overstated.

CARBINES/RIFLES, SINGLE SHOT

MODEL 1870 ROLLING-BLOCK RIFLE, U.S.N. - .50 cal. centerfire, 32 5/8 in. barrel, not serial numbered, 22,013 mfg.

	N/A	$2,500	$2,200	$1,950	$1,500	$1,100	$900

MODEL 1871 ROLLING-BLOCK RIFLE, U.S.A. - .50 cal. centerfire, 36 in. barrel, not serial numbered, 10,001 mfg.

	N/A	$2,150	$1,750	$1,350	$1,000	$900	$750

MODEL 1873 RIFLE "TRAPDOOR" - .45-70 Govt. cal., 32 5/8 in. barrel, 2 bands. Approx. 73,000 mfg. between 1873-77.

$2,500	$2,200	$1,800	$1,500	$1,150	$775	$650

Subtract 40% if stock cartouche faint or absent.

MODEL 1884 RIFLE "TRAPDOOR" - .45-70 Govt. cal., 32 5/8 in. barrel, 2 bands. Approx. 232,000 mfg. between 1885-1890.

$2,250	$1,850	$1,450	$975	$725	$625	$525

Subtract 40% if stock cartouche faint or absent.

MODEL 1873 CARBINE - 22 in. barrel, half stock, single barrel band/stacking swivel, 20,000 made, but semi-scarce.

	N/A	$6,000	$5,250	$4,250	$3,250	$2,750	$2,250

Add up to 50% for Pre-Custer serial numbers below 43,700 (pre-1876 mfg.).
Subtract 50% for faint or no stock cartouche.

MODEL 1873 CADET RIFLE - .45-70 Govt. cal., 29 1/2 in. barrel, stacking swivel, no sling swivels.

$2,500	$2,000	$1,475	$1,100	$925	$775	$650

Subtract $100 for variation with sling-swivels.
Subtract 25-35% if restocked with buttplate and hole drilled for cleaning tools.

MODEL 1875 OFFICER'S RIFLE FIRST TYPE - .45-70 Govt. cal., 477 mfg. between 1875 and 1886, 26 in. barrel, single barrel band. Not serial numbered, some dated, non-issue.

	N/A	$39,000	$34,000	$27,000	$23,000	$17,500	$15,000

Subtract 15-20% for types 2 and 3.
Approx. 25 rifles were mfg. prior to the standardization of this model.

MODEL 1877 RIFLE - .45-70 Govt. cal., mfg. 3,943.

	N/A	$3,000	$2,650	$2,250	$1,875	$1,625	$1,325

MODEL 1877 CARBINE - .45-70 Govt. cal., 22 in. barrel, "C" rear sight to 1,200

GRADING - PPGS™	100%	98%	95%	90%	80%	70%	60%

yards. Mfg. 2,946.

	N/A	$4,750	$4,250	$3,850	$3,300	$2,850	$2,450

MODEL 1877 CADET RIFLE - .45-70 Govt. cal., 29 1/2 in. barrel. 1,050 mfg.

	N/A	$2,000	$1,400	$1,100	$950	$900	$800

MODEL 1879 RIFLE - .45-70 Govt. cal., approx. 140,000 mfg.

	$1,800	$1,400	$1,150	$950	$850	$700	$650

MODEL 1879 CARBINE - .45-70 Govt. cal., no stacking swivel. Approx. 15,000 mfg.

	N/A	$3,500	$2,850	$2,300	$1,950	$1,500	$1,000

MODEL 1879 CADET RIFLE - .45-70 Govt. cal., stacking swivel but no sling swivels. 5,000 mfg.

	$2,000	$1,600	$1,150	$950	$775	$650	$600

MODEL 1880 - .45-70 Govt. cal., combination triangular, sliding type, bayonet-ramrod. 1,001 mfg.

	N/A	$2,800	$2,200	$1,950	$1,650	$1,325	$1,050

MODEL 1881 FORAGER - 20 ga., 1,376 mfg. 1881-85. Be cautious when purchasing.

	N/A	$2,600	$2,250	$1,800	$1,500	$1,300	$1,150

MODEL 1875 SPRINGFIELD LEE VERTICAL ACTION - 32 1/2 in. barrel, 143 rifles in .45-70 US Govt cal. were manufactured at Springfield Armory in 1875, as per 1874 Congressional appropriation of $10,000. Rifles were issued to companies of the 1st and 20th Infantry Regiments for field trials. Rifles were withdrawn, declared surplus and purchased by Bannerman's who later sold them in his catalog for $36.

	N/A	N/A	$9,000	$7,000	$6,000	$5,000	$3,000

PISTOLS: SEMI-AUTO

M1911 MILITARY MFG. SPRINGFIELD ARMORY - approx. 30,000 mfg. 1914-1915, blue finish.

	N/A	$5,950	$4,600	$3,500	$3,000	$2,500	$2,000

Serialization is 72,751-83,855, 102,597-107,596, 113,497-120,566, and 125,567-133,186. Most mint/100% specimens encountered in this model have been refinished - be careful.

RIFLES: BOLT ACTION, KRAG-JORGENSEN

Please refer to Krag-Jorgensen section for models and pricing.

RIFLES: BOLT ACTION, MODEL 1903 & VARIATIONS

On Springfields and other U.S. military long arms, the importance of the wood being original, unsanded, and with crisp, clear cartouches cannot be overstated.

Values listed for Model 1903s assume 100% original guns. Values listed for Model 1922s assume 100% original blued guns.

U.S. MODEL 1903 SPRINGFIELD - .30-06 cal., bolt action, mfg. by Springfield Armory and Rock Island Arsenal, 24 in. barrel. Mfg. 1903-30.

* *U.S. Model 1903 Springfield Pre-WWI Mfg.* - values below represent original rifles.

	$7,000	$6,000	$5,000	$4,000	$3,000	$2,250	$1,850

Subtract 80% if reworked.

* *U.S. Model 1903 Springfield Serialized 800,000 - 1,275,767* - double heat treated receiver.

	$4,950	$4,000	$3,300	$2,750	$2,500	$2,100	$1,650

* *U.S. Model 1903 Springfield Serialized 1,275,768 +* - nickel steel receiver.

	$4,950	$4,000	$3,300	$2,750	$2,500	$2,100	$1,650

GRADING - PPGS™	100%	98%	95%	90%	80%	70%	60%

MODEL 1903 MARK I - .30-06 cal., similar to U.S. Model 1903 Springfield, except altered for the Pedersen device, a slot is milled into the left side of receiver to act as an ejection port for use of the semi-auto bolt insert, value without device.

	$4,950	$4,000	$3,500	$1,800	$1,200	$1,000	$850

1903-A1 - .30-06 cal., similar to U.S. Model 1903 Springfield, except type C pistol grip stock. Mfg. 1930-39. In 1941 Remington mfg. approx. 350,000.

	$4,500	$4,000	$3,500	$1,800	$1,200	$1,000	$850

   ✻ *1903-A1 Remington produced*

	$4,500	$4,000	$3,500	$1,800	$1,200	$1,000	$850

1903-A1 NATIONAL MATCH

	$5,000	$4,500	$3,500	$2,000	$1,200	$1,000	$850

1903-A3 - .30-06 cal., similar to 1903, with production modifications, aperture rear sight, no finger groove in forestock, lower quality finish, stamped floorplate and barrel band. Mfg. WWII by Remington and Smith Corona.

	$1,000	$800	$700	$500	$400	$330	$300

   Add 25% for Smith Corona mfg.

1903-A3 NATIONAL MATCH - 200 mfg., known as the "unmatched" match rifle.

	$3,700	$3,350	$3,000	$2,600	$2,200	$1,875	$1,625

1903-A4 SNIPER - .30-06 cal., with M73B1 or M84 scope in Redfield mount, no front sight.

	$5,000	$4,500	$3,800	$2,500	$1,800	$1,000	$700

   Subtract 25% if reworked with parkerized small parts.

1903 MARINE SNIPER - .30-06 cal., includes 8X Unertl scope.

	$6,250	$5,500	$4,150	$3,000	$2,500	$2,000	$1,800

   If this model is verified as an original, large premiums (double or triple) are currently being asked on values listed.

1903 NRA NATIONAL MATCH - .30-06 cal., similar to 1903, with hand selected and custom fit parts, produced for target shooting. "NRA" and flaming bomb proofed on trigger guard. 1915 date.

	$5,000	$4,500	$3,500	$2,400	$1,500	$995	$850

1903 SPORTER - .30-06 cal., similar to National Match, with sporter stock and Lyman sight.

	$5,400	$4,800	$3,500	$1,800	$1,200	$925	$825

1903 MATCH STYLE T - .30-06 cal., similar to Sporter, with heavy barrel, globe sight, target bases, 26, 28, or 30 in. barrel.

   Excellent original condition specimens have been seen with asking prices in the $8,500-$10,000+ range.

1903 FREE RIFLE TYPE A - .30-06 cal., similar to Style T, with 28 in. barrel, and Swiss hook butt.

   Excellent original condition specimens have been seen with asking prices in the $8,500-$10,000+ range.

1903 FREE RIFLE TYPE B - .30-06 cal., similar to Type A, with double-set triggers, cheekpiece stock, modified firing pin.

   Excellent original condition specimens have been seen with asking prices in the $8,500-$10,000+ range.

MODEL 1922-M1 - .22 LR cal., Target Rifle, 5 shot mag., 24 in. barrel, modified 1903, Lyman receiver sight, sporter stock, issued 1927.

	$2,950	$2,500	$2,000	$1,500	$1,000	$625	$550

MODEL 1922 NRA VARIATION - not tapped for scope, without forend grooves.

	$2,950	$2,500	$2,250	$1,925	$1,725	$1,500	$1,250

GRADING - PPGS™	100%	98%	95%	90%	80%	70%	60%

M2 .22 TARGET RIFLE - similar to 1922 M1, except improved lock time, adj. head space bolt design.

| | $1,800 | $1,500 | $1,200 | $1,000 | $700 | $600 | $550 |

RIFLES: SEMI-AUTO

Please refer to the U.S. Military section for more information on previously manufactured military and commercial M1 carbines and Garands.

SPRINGFIELD ARMORY (MFG. BY SPRINGFIELD INC.)

Current trademark manufactured by Springfield Inc., located in Geneseo, IL. Springfield Inc. has also imported a variety of models. This company was named Springfield Armory, Geneseo, IL until 1992.

Springfield Inc. manufactures commercial pistols and rifles, including reproductions of older military handguns and rifles.

COMBINATION GUNS

M6 SCOUT RIFLE - .22 LR, .22 Mag. (disc.), or .22 Hornet cal. over smoothbore .410 bore w/ 3 in. chamber, O/U Survival Gun, 14 (legal transfer needed) or 18 1/4 in. barrels, parkerized or stainless steel (new 1995), approx. 4 lbs. Disc. 2004.

| | $175 | $145 | $115 | $90 | $75 | $70 | $65 |

Last MSR was $215.

Add $34 for stainless steel.
Add $24 for lockable Marine flotation plastic carrying case.
Older mfg. does not incorporate a trigger guard while newer production has a trigger guard.

M6 SCOUT PISTOL/CARBINE - .22 LR or .22 Hornet cal. over .45 LC/.410 bore, 16 in. barrels, parkerized or stainless steel. Mfg. 2002-2004.

| | $185 | $160 | $125 | $95 | $80 | $70 | $65 |

Last MSR was $223.

Add $24 for stainless steel.
Add $134-$149 per interchangeable 10 in. barrel assembly.
This model is also available with an optional detachable stock ($49-$59 MSR, not legal with a rifled barrel less than 16 in. or smoothbore less than 18 in.).

M6 SCOUT PISTOL - .22 LR or .22 Hornet cal. over .45 LC/.410 bore, 10 in. barrels, parkerized or stainless steel. Mfg. 2002-2004.

| | $165 | $135 | $110 | $85 | $75 | $70 | $65 |

Last MSR was $199.

Add $24 for stainless steel.
Add $134-$149 per interchangeable 16 in. carbine barrel.

PISTOLS: SEMI-AUTO

OMEGA PISTOL - .38 Super, 10mm Norma, or .45 ACP cal., single action, ported slide, 5 or 6 in. interchangeable ported or unported barrel with Polygon rifling, special lockup system eliminates normal barrel link and bushing, Pachmayr grips, dual extractors, adj. rear sight. Mfg. 1987-90.

| | $775 | $650 | $575 | $495 | $425 | $360 | $295 |

Last MSR was $849.

Add $663 for interchangeable conversion units.
Add $336 for interchangeable 5 or 6 in. barrel (including factory installation).
Each conversion unit includes an entire slide assembly, one mag., 5 or 6 in barrel, recoil spring guide mechanism assembly, and factory fitting.

OMEGA MATCH - same cals. as Omega, except has low profile combat sights, 8 shot mag., and beveled mag. well. Mfg. 1991-92 only.

	$925	$775	$660	$535	$460	$420	$385

Last MSR was $1,103.

Pistols: Semi-Auto - P9 Series

MODEL P9 - 9mm Para., 9x21mm (new 1991) .40 S&W (new 1991), or .45 ACP cal., patterned after the Czech CZ-75, selective double action design, blue (standard beginning 1993), parkerized (standard until 1992), or duotone finish, various barrel lengths, checkered walnut grips. Mfg. in U.S. starting 1990.

✳ *Model P9 Standard* - 4.72 in. barrel, 15 shot (9mm Para.), 11 shot (.40 S&W), or 10 shot (.45 ACP) mag., parkerized finish standard until 1992 - blue finish beginning 1993, 32.16 oz. Disc. 1993.

	$430	$375	$335	$295	$275	$240	$215

Last MSR was $518.

Add $61 for .45 ACP cal.
Add $182 for duotone finish (disc. 1992).
Subtract $40 for parkerized finish.

In 1992, Springfield added a redesigned stainless steel trigger, patented sear safety which disengages the trigger from the double action mechanism when the safety is on, lengthened the beavertail grip area offering less "pinch," and added a two-piece slide stop design.

✳ *Model P9 Stainless* - similar to P9 Standard, except is constructed from stainless steel, 35.3 oz. Mfg. 1991-93.

	$475	$425	$350	$285	$250	$215	$185

Last MSR was $589.

Add $50 for .45 ACP cal.

✳ *Model P9 Compact* - 9mm Para. or .40 S&W cal., 3.66 in. barrel, 13 shot (9mm Para.) or 10 shot (.40 S&W) mag., shorter slide and frame, rounded triggerguard, 30 1/2 oz. Disc. 1992.

	$395	$350	$300	$275	$250	$225	$200

Last MSR was $499.

Add $20 for .40 S&W cal.
Add $20-$30 for blue finish depending on cal.
Add $78 for duotone finish.

✳ *Model P9 Sub-Compact* - 9mm Para. or .40 S&W cal., smaller frame than the P9 Compact, 3.66 in. barrel, 12 shot (9mm Para.) or 9 shot (.40 S&W) finger extension mag., squared-off triggerguard, 30.1 oz. Disc. 1992.

	$395	$350	$300	$275	$250	$225	$200

Last MSR was $499.

Add $20 for .40 S&W cal.
Add $20-$30 for blue finish depending on cal.

✳ *Model P9 Factory Comp* - 9mm Para., .40 S&W, or .45 ACP cal., 5 1/2 in. barrel (with compensator attached), extended sear safety and mag. release, adj. rear sight, slim competition checkered wood grips, choice of all stainless (disc. 1992) or stainless bi-tone (matte black slide), dual port compensated, 15 shot (9mm Para.), 11 shot (.40 S&W), or 10 shot (.45 ACP) mag., 33.9 oz. Mfg. 1992-93.

	$595	$525	$450	$420	$390	$360	$330

Last MSR was $699.

Add $36 for .45 ACP cal.
Add $75-$100 for all stainless finish.

✳ *Model P9 Ultra IPSC (LSP)* - competition model with 5.03 in. barrel (long slide

GRADING - PPGS™	100%	98%	95%	90%	80%	70%	60%

ported), adj. rear sight, choice of parkerized (standard finish until 1992 when disc.), blue (disc. 1992), bi-tone (became standard 1993), or stainless steel (disc. 1992) finish, extended thumb safety, and rubberized competition (9mm Para. and .40 S&W cals. only) or checkered walnut (.45 ACP cal. only) grips, 15 shot (9mm Para.), 11 shot (.40 S&W), or 10 shot (.45 ACP) mag., 34.6 oz. Disc. 1993.

	$555	$475	$415	$350	$300	$275	$250

Last MSR was $694.

Add $30 for .45 ACP cal.

✳ *Model P9 Ultra LSP Stainless* - stainless steel variation of the P9 Ultra LSP. Mfg. 1991-92.

	$675	$525	$425	$360	$315	$260	$225

Last MSR was $769.

Add $30 for .40 S&W cal.
Add $90 for .45 ACP cal.

✳ *Model P9 World Cup* - see listing under 1911-A1 Custom Models heading.

Pistols: Semi-Auto - R-Series

PANTHER MODEL - 9mm Para., .40 S&W, or .45 ACP cal., semi-auto single or double action, 3.8 in. barrel, hammer drop or firing pin safety, 15 shot (9mm Para.), 11 shot (.40 S&W), or 9 shot (.45 ACP) mag., Commander hammer, frame mounted slide stop, narrow profile, non-glare blue finish only, walnut grips, squared-off triggerguard, 29 oz. Mfg. 1992 only.

	$535	$450	$395	$350	$300	$275	$250

Last MSR was $609.

FIRECAT MODEL - 9mm Para. or .40 S&W cal., single action, 3 1/2 in. barrel, 3-dot low profile sights, all steel mfg., firing pin block and frame mounted ambidextrous safety, 8 shot (9mm Para.) or 7 shot (.40 S&W) mag., checkered combat style triggerguard and front/rear gripstraps, non-glare blue finish, 35 3/4 oz. Mfg. 1992-93.

	$495	$425	$375	$330	$295	$275	$250

Last MSR was $569.

BOBCAT MODEL - while advertised in 1992, this model was never mfg.

LINX MODEL - while advertised in 1992, this model was never mfg.

Pistols: Semi-Auto - Disc. 1911-A1 Models

MODEL 1911-A1 STANDARD MODEL - .38 Super, 9mm Para., 10mm (new 1990), or .45 ACP cal., patterned after the Colt M1911-A1, 5.04 (Standard) or 4.025 (Commander or Compact Model) in. barrel, 7 shot (Compact), 8 shot (.45 ACP), 9 shot (10mm), or 10 shot (9mm Para. and .38 Super) mag., walnut grips, parkerized, blue, or duotone finish. Mfg. 1985-90.

	$400	$360	$330	$300	$280	$260	$240

Last MSR was $454.

Add $35 for blue finish.
Add $80 for duotone finish.
This model was also available with a .45 ACP to 9mm Para. conversion kit for $170 in parkerized finish, or $175 in blue finish.

✳ *Model 1911-A1 Standard Defender Model* - .45 ACP cal. only, similar to Standard 1911-A1 Model, except has fixed combat sights, beveled mag. well, extended thumb safety, bobbed hammer, flared ejection port, walnut grips, factory serrated front strap and two stainless steel magazines, parkerized or blue finish. Mfg. 1988-90.

	$485	$435	$375	$340	$300	$280	$260

Last MSR was $567.

Add $35 for blue finish.

GRADING - PPGS™	100%	98%	95%	90%	80%	70%	60%

＊*Model 1911-A1 Standard Commander Model* - .45 ACP cal. only, similar to Standard 1911-A1 Model, except has 3.63 in. barrel, shortened slide, Commander hammer, low profile 3-dot sights, walnut grips, parkerized, blue, or duotone finish. Mfg. in 1990 only.

	$450	$415	$350	$325	$285	$260	$245

Last MSR was $514.

Add $30 for blue finish.
Add $80 for duotone finish.

＊*Model 1911-A1 Standard Combat Commander Model* - .45 ACP cal. only, 4 1/4 in. barrel, bobbed hammer, walnut grips. Mfg. 1988-89.

	$435	$385	$325	$295	$275	$250	$230

Add $20 for blue finish.

＊*Model 1911-A1 Standard Compact Model* - .45 ACP cal. only, compact variation featuring shortened Commander barrel and slide, reduced M1911 straight grip-strap frame, checkered walnut grips, low profile 3-dot sights, extended slide stop, combat hammer, parkerized, blue, or duotone finish. Mfg. 1990 only.

	$450	$415	$350	$325	$285	$260	$245

Last MSR was $514.

Add $30 for blue finish.
Add $80 for duotone finish.

＊*Model 1911-A1 Standard Custom Carry Gun* - .38 Super (special order only), 9mm Para., 10mm (new 1990), or .45 ACP cal., similar to Defender Model, except has tuned trigger pull, heavy recoil spring, extended thumb safety, and other features. Mfg. 1988-disc.

	$860	$725	$660	$535	$460	$420	$385

Last MSR was $969.

Add $130 for .38 Super Ramped, 10mm was POR.

＊*Model 1911-A1 Standard National Match Hardball Model* - .38 Super (disc.), 9mm Para. (disc.), or .45 ACP cal., National Match barrel and bushing, specially fitted frame and slide, Bo-Mar adj. rear sight, Herrett walnut grips, plastic cased. Mfg. 1988-90.

	$780	$650	$565	$515	$460	$415	$385

Last MSR was $897.

This model was made specifically for DCM competition shooting.

＊*Model 1911-A1 Standard Bullseye Wadcutter Model* - .45 ACP cal. only, designed for wadcutter loads only, 5 or 6 (ported or unported) in. barrel, Bo-Mar rib mounted on slide, checkered gripstraps, match trigger, beavertail grip safety, polished feed ramp and throated barrel. Mfg. 1989-disc.

	$1,415	$1,200	$1,025	$925	$825	$750	$675

Last MSR was $1,599.

Add $25 for 6 in. barrel.
Add $80 for 6 in. ported barrel.

＊*Model 1911-A1 Standard Trophy Master Competition Pistol* - .38 Super, 9mm Para. (disc.), 10mm (new 1990), or .45 ACP cal., competition model which includes low profile combat sights, ambidextrous safety, long match trigger, bobbed hammer, Pachmayr wraparound grips. Mfg. 1988-90.

	$1,300	$1,100	$950	$875	$800	$730	$660

Last MSR was $1,443.

Add $130 for .38 Super with supported chamber, 10mm was POR.

* *Model 1911-A1 Standard Trophy Master Competition Expert Model* - .38 Super, 9mm Para. (disc.), 10mm (new 1990), or .45 ACP cal., mfg. for IPSC competition shooting, dual chamber compensator system on match barrel, blue finish, ambidextrous thumb safety, beveled and polished mag. well, lowered and flared ejection port, wraparound Pachmayr grips, shock buffer, includes 2 mags. and plastic carrying case. Mfg. 1988-90.

$1,664	$1,450	$1,225	$1,025	$950	$890	$850

Last MSR was $1,664.

Add $130 for .38 Super with supported chamber, 10mm was POR.
This model was an improved variation of the Master Grade Competition Pistol "A."

* *Model 1911-A1 Standard Trophy Master Competition Distinguished Model* - similar to Expert Model, except has brushed hard chrome finish, checkered gripstraps and trigger guard, top-of-the-line competition model. Mfg. 1988-1990.

$2,000	$1,675	$1,450	$1,225	$1,025	$950	$875

Last MSR was $2,275.

Add $130 for .38 Super with supported chamber, 10mm was POR.
Subtract $130 for "B" Model.
This model was an improved variation of the Master Grade Competition Pistol "B-1."

Pistols: Semi-Auto - 1911-A1 (90s Series)

The initials "PDP" refer to Springfield's Personal Defense Pistol series.
Beginning in 2000, Springfield Armory started offering a Loaded Promotion package on their 1911-A1 pistol line. Many of these features and options are found on the FBI's Hostage Rescue Teams (HRT) pistol contract with Springfield Armory. Standard features of this Loaded Promotion package are hammer forged premium air-gauged barrel, front and rear cocking serrations, Novak patented low profile sights or Bo-Mar type adj. sights, extended thumb safety, tactical beavertail, flat mainspring housing, Cocobolo grips, High Hand grip, lightweight match trigger, full length guide rod, and machine beveled mag. well. This promotion includes all pistols except the Mil-Spec Model 1911 A-1.
In 2001, Springfield's Custom Loaded 1911-A1 Series pistols came equipped standard with Springfield's integral locking system, carry bevel, hammer forged premium air-gauged barrel, front and rear cocking serrations, Novak patented low profile sights (some models come equipped with Tritium sights or Bo-Mar type adj. sights), extended thumb safety, tactical beavertail, flat mainspring housing, cocobolo grips, high hand grip, lightweight adj. match trigger, full length guide rod, machine beveled magwell, and a "loaded" coupon ($600 consumer savings). These Custom Loaded features will vary by model. All models with less than a 5 in. and all alloy pistols supplied with ramped, fully supported barrels.
Beginning 2002, every Springfield pistol is equipped with a patented integral locking system (I.L.S., keyed in the rear gripstrap) at no extra charge.

PDP DEFENDER MODEL - .40 S&W (disc. 1992) or .45 ACP cal., standard pistol with slide and barrel shortened to Champion length (4 in.), tapered cone dual port compensator system, fully adj. sights, Videcki speed trigger, rubber grips, Commander style hammer, serrated front strap, parkerized (disc. 1992), duotone/bi-tone, or blue (disc. 1993) finish. Mfg. 1991-1998.

$850	$735	$630	$550	$495	$450	$425

Last MSR was $992.

* *PDP Defender Model Factory Comp* - .38 Super (disc.) or .45 ACP cal. only, entry level IPSC gun, featuring 5 5/8 in. barrel with compensator attached, adj. rear sight, Videki speed trigger, checkered walnut grips, beveled mag. well, 10 shot (.38 Super) or 8 shot (.45 ACP) mag., blue finish only, 40 oz. Mfg. 1991-2000.

900	$685	$585	$500	$450	$420	$390

Last MSR was $1,049.

GRADING - PPGS™	100%	98%	95%	90%	80%	70%	60%

✳ *PDP Defender Model High Capacity Factory Compensated* - .38 Super (disc.) or .45 ACP cal. only, blue finish. Mfg. 1995-2000.

	$955	$795	$655	$575	$500	$450	$395

Last MSR was $1,109.

MODEL 1911-A1 90s EDITION (CUSTOM LOADED) - .38 Super, 9mm Para., 10mm (disc. 1991), .40 S&W, or .45 ACP cal., patterned after the Colt M1911-A1, except has linkless operating system, 5.04 (Standard) or 4 (Champion or Compact Model) in. barrel, 7 shot (Compact), 8 shot (.40 S&W or .45 ACP Standard), 9 shot (9mm Para., 10mm, or .38 Super), or 10 shot (.38 Super) mag., checkered walnut grips, parkerized (.38 Super beginning 1994 or .45 ACP beginning 1993), blue or duotone (disc. 1992) finish. New 1991.

✳ *1911-A1 90s Edition Mil-Spec* - .38 Super or .45 ACP cal., blue (disc.), parkerized, bi-tone (new 2004), or OD Green (new 2004) finish, 3-dot Hi-Viz fixed combat sights, includes belt holster and extra set of grips, 35.6 oz.

MSR $660	$540	$420	$360	$315	$285	$265	$235

Add $17 for blue finish (disc. 2001).
Add $21 for OD Green or bi-tone finish (mfg. 2004 only).
Add $123 for .38 Super cal. (until 2003).
Add $594 for .38 Super cal. in High Polish Nickel (Acusport exclusive beginning 2004).

❖ *1911-A1 90s Edition Mil-Spec Stainless Steel* - similar to Mil-Spec Model, except is .45 ACP cal. only and stainless steel, includes belt holster and extra set of grips. New 2003.

MSR $724	$580	$465	$370	$315	$270	$230	$200

✳ *1911-A1 90s Edition Mil-Spec Operator* - .45 ACP cal. only, similar to Mil-Spec 1911-A1, except has Picatinny light mounting system forged into lower front of frame, parkerized finish only. Disc. 2002.

	$615	$475	$425	$365	$325	$285	$255

Last MSR was $756.

✳ *1911-A1 90s Edition Loaded Operator* - .45 ACP cal. only, similar to full size service model, except has Picatinny light mounting platform forged into lower front of frame, checkered hardwood (disc. 2003) or plastic grips, OD Green with black bi-tone Armory Kote finish, Novak low mount tritium (disc.) or Trijicon night sights. New 2002.

MSR $1,254	$1,000	$825	$675	$600	$475	$400	$350

✳ *1911-A1 90s Edition Lightweight Operator* - .45 ACP cal. only, 5 in. barrel. New 2006.

This model is POR.

✳ *1911-A1 90s Edition Standard or Lightweight Model* - .45 ACP cal. (current mfg.), Standard model has parkerized, blue, or OD Green with Armory Kote (new 2002) finish, Custom Loaded features became standard in 2001, Lightweight Model was introduced 1995 with either matte (disc. 2002), bi-tone (new 2003) or blue (mfg. 1993-disc.) finish, current mfg. is w/ either Novak low mount or Trijicon night sights, 28.6 or 35.6 oz.

MSR $869	$700	$535	$450	$375	$325	$285	$255

Add $65 for Lightweight Model (with Trijicon night sights).
Subtract approx. 10%-25% if w/o Custom Loaded features (new 2001), depending on condition.
Subtract $31 for parkerized finish with Novak tritium sights.

✳ *1911-A1 90s Edition Stainless Standard Model* - 9mm Para. (new 1994), .38 Super (disc.), .40 S&W (mfg. 2001-2002), or .45 ACP cal., 7 (.45 ACP cal.), 8 (.40 S&W), or 9 (9mm Para.) shot mag., Custom Loaded features became standard in 2001, wraparound rubber (disc.) or checkered hardwood grips, Novak Lo-Mount or Bo-Mar type (mfg. 1996-2001) sights, beveled mag. well, 39.2 oz. New 1991.

MSR $902	$735	$560	$470	$415	$360	$300	$255

Add $74 for 9mm Para. cal., or $32 for .40 S&W cal. (disc.).

GRADING - PPGS™	100%	98%	95%	90%	80%	70%	60%

Add $2 for Tactical Model with combat features and black stainless steel (new 2005).
Add $50 for Bo-Mar type sights (disc. 2001).
Add $202 for long slide variation in .45 Super cal. with V16 porting and Bo-Mar sights (disc.).

✴ *1911-A1 90s Edition Stainless Super Tuned Standard* - .45 ACP cal. only, super tuned by the Custom Shop, 7 shot mag., 5 in. barrel, Novak fixed low mount sights, 39.2 oz. Mfg. 1997-99.

	$875	$750	$600	$495	$430	$365	$315

Last MSR was $995.

✴ *1911-A1 90s Edition Target Model* - 9mm Para. or .45 ACP cal., includes Custom Loaded features, stainless steel or black stainless steel (new 2003), with (.45 ACP cal. only) or w/o V12 ported barrel, adj. sights, 38 oz. New 2001.

MSR $966		$820	$600	$495	$430	$375	$315	$270

Add $158 for black stainless steel with adj. Trijicon sights.

Subtract approx. $15 for non-ported V12 barrel.

✴ *1911-A1 90s Edition Trophy Match* - .40 S&W (mfg. 2001-2005) or .45 ACP cal. only, top-of-the-line pistol featuring improved trigger pull, adj. rear sight, match grade barrel and bushing, Custom Loaded features became standard in 2001, choice of Armory Kote (.40 S&W cal. only, new 2001), stainless steel, bi-tone (disc.), or blue finish, 35.6 oz. New 1994.

MSR $1,452		$1,200	$935	$715	$600	$550	$475	$425

Add $10 for bi-tone finish (disc.).
Add $8 for High Capacity Trophy Match (disc.).
Subtract $100 for blue finish (disc.).

✴ *1911-A1 90s Edition Standard High Capacity* - 9mm Para. (disc.) or .45 ACP cal., 5 in. barrel, blue (disc. 2001) or matte parkerized (new 1996) finish with plastic grips, 3-dot fixed combat sights, 10 shot (except for law enforcement) mag. Mfg. 1995-2003.

	$635	$540	$475	$425	$375	$335	$295

Last MSR was $756.

Add $50 for blue finish (disc.).

✴ *1911-A1 90s Edition Stainless High Capacity* - similar to Standard High Capacity, except is stainless steel. Mfg. 1996-2000.

	$675	$540	$475	$425	$375	$335	$295

Last MSR was $819.

✴ *1911-A1 90s Edition XM4 High Capacity Model* - 9mm Para. or 45 ACP cal., features widened frame for high capacity mag., blue (mfg. 1993 only) or stainless finish only. Mfg. 1993-94.

	$595	$550	$500	$435	$385	$340	$300

Last MSR was $689.

MODEL 1911-A1 LONG SLIDE CUSTOM LOADED STAINLESS - .45 ACP or .45 Super (mfg. 2001 only) cal., 6 in. ported (disc. 2004) or unported barrel, 7 shot mag., checkered wood grips, adj. sights, 41 oz. New 2001.

MSR $1,097		$915	$715	$575	$480	$410	$350	$300

Add $72 for ported barrel (V16, disc. 2004).
Add $403 for Trophy Match Model (disc. 2004).

MODEL 1911-A1 GI - .45 ACP cal., 5 in. barrel, parkerized, OD Green Armory Kote finish or stainless steel, 7 (standard) or 13 (high capacity) shot mag., low profile military sights, diamond checkered walnut grips with U.S. initials, includes belt holster, 36 oz. New 2004.

MSR $564		$480	$385	$340	$300	$260	$240	$220

Add $44 for stainless steel.
Add $53 for high capacity magazine (parkerized finish, new 2005).

GRADING - PPGS™	100%	98%	95%	90%	80%	70%	60%

1911-A1 TACTICAL RESPONSE (TRP SERIES) - .45 ACP only, 5 in. standard or bull (Operator Model only) barrel, 7 shot mag., matte Armory Kote finish or stainless steel, checkered rosewood grips, Trijicon (new 2006), Novak or Hi-Viz (disc., Operator Model only) 3-dot Tritium (disc. 2001) sights, 36 oz. New 1999.

MSR $1,606	$1,325	$1,075	$865	$735	$625	$575	$500

Add $83 for Operator Model with integral light mounting rail and adj. night sights.

1911-A1 COMMANDER MODEL - .45 ACP cal. only, similar to Standard 1911-A1 Model, except has 3.63 in. barrel, shortened slide, Commander hammer, low profile 3-dot sights, walnut grips, parkerized, blue, or duotone finish. Mfg. 1991-92.

	$425	$365	$330	$300	$275	$250	$225

✱ *1911-A1 Commander Model Combat* - .45 ACP cal. only, 4 1/4 in. barrel, bobbed hammer, walnut grips. Mfg. 1991 only.

	$425	$365	$330	$300	$275	$250	$225

1911-A1 CHAMPION MODEL - .380 ACP (Model MD-1, mfg. 1995 only) or .45 ACP cal., similar to Standard Model, except has 4 in. barrel and shortened slide, blue (disc. 2000) or parkerized (Mil-Spec Champion, new 1994) finish, Commander hammer, checkered walnut grips, 3-dot sights (Novak night sights became standard 2001), 7 shot mag., 33 1/2 oz. Mfg. 1992-2002.

	$695	$500	$400	$350	$325	$295	$275

Last MSR was $856.

Add $30 for Ultra Compact slide (mfg. 1997-98).
Add $79 for ported Champion V10 with Ultra Compact slide (disc.).
Subtract approx. 10%-25% if w/o Custom Loaded features (new 2001), depending on condition.
Subtract approx. $150 for .380 ACP cal. (Model MD-1, disc.).

✱ *1911-A1 Champion Model (Custom Loaded)* - .45 ACP cal. only, stainless steel or Lightweight bi-tone with OD Green finish (new 2004). New 1992.

MSR $952	$765	$575	$440	$380	$350	$325	$295

Add $119 for Ultra Compact slide (mfg. 1997-98).
Add $52 for ported Champion V10 with Ultra Compact slide (disc. 2000).
Subtract $39 for Lightweight Champion with bi-tone OD Green finish (new 2004).
Subtract approx. 10%-25% if w/o Custom Loaded features (new 2001), depending on condition.

✱ *1911-A1 Champion Model Lightweight Operator* - .45 ACP cal., 4 in. barrel. New 2006.

This model is POR.

✱ *1911-A1 Champion Model GI Model* - .45 ACP cal., parkerized or blued slide with black anodized frame (Lightweight Model, new 2005), low profile military sights, diamond checkered wood grips with U.S. initials, includes belt holster, 34 oz. New 2004.

MSR $564	$480	$385	$335	$295	$260	$240	$220

✱ *1911-A1 Champion Model TRP* - .45 ACP cal., 4 in. barrel, otherwise similar to TRP Tactical Response. Mfg. 1999-2001.

	$1,045	$875	$700	$600	$500	$450	$395

Last MSR was $1,249.

✱ *1911-A1 Champion Model Lightweight* - .45 ACP cal., aluminum frame, matte metal finish, night sights became standard during 2001. New 1999.

	$700	$495	$395	$345	$310	$275	$240

Last MSR was $867.

Subtract approx. 10%-25% if w/o Custom Loaded features (new 2001), depending on condition.

GRADING - PPGS™	100%	98%	95%	90%	80%	70%	60%

✳ *1911-A1 Champion Model Comp PDP* - .45 ACP cal. only, compensated version of the Champion Model, blue. Mfg. 1993-98.

	$780	$690	$600	$550	$500	$450	$395

Last MSR was $869.

✳ *1911-A1 Champion Model Super Tuned* - .45 ACP cal., super tuned by the Custom Shop, 7 shot mag., 4 in. barrel, blue or parkerized finish, Novak fixed low mount sights, 36.3 oz. Mfg. 1997-99.

	$850	$725	$575	$500	$450	$400	$365

Last MSR was $959.

Add $30 for blue finish.

✳ *1911-A1 Champion Model XM4 High Capacity* - 9mm Para. or .45 ACP cal., high capacity variation. Mfg. 1994 only.

	$615	$555	$500	$430	$375	$315	$270

Last MSR was $699.

1911-A1 COMPACT MODEL - .45 ACP cal. only, compact variation featuring shortened 4 in. barrel and slide, reduced M1911-A1 curved gripstrap frame, checkered walnut grips, low profile 3-dot sights, 6 or 7 shot mag., extended slide stop, standard or lightweight alloy (new 1994) frame, combat hammer, parkerized, blue, or duotone (disc. 1992) finish, standard or lightweight (new 1995) configuration, 27 or 32 oz. Mfg. 1991-96.

	$415	$355	$300	$275	$250	$225	$200

Last MSR was $476.

Add $66 for blue finish.
Add $67 for Compact Lightweight Model (matte finish only).

✳ *1911-A1 Compact Model Stainless* - stainless steel variation of the Compact Model. Mfg. 1991-96.

	$495	$420	$350	$285	$250	$215	$185

Last MSR was $582.

✳ *1911-A1 Compact Model Lightweight* - .45 ACP cal., forged alloy frame, matte metal finish, 6 shot mag., Novak night sights became standard 2001. Mfg. 1999-2003.

	$585	$495	$425	$375	$325	$295	$275

Last MSR was $733.

Subtract approx. 10%-25% if w/o Custom Loaded features (new 2001), depending on condition.

❖ **1911-A1 Compact Model Lightweight Stainless** - similar to Compact Lightweight, except is stainless steel. Disc. 2001.

	$725	$550	$475	$415	$360	$300	$255

Last MSR was $900.

Subtract approx. 10%-25% if w/o Custom Loaded features (new 2001), depending on condition.

✳ *1911-A1 Compact Model Comp Lightweight* - compensated version of the Compact Model, bi-tone or matte finish, regular or lightweight alloy (new 1994) frame. Mfg. 1993-98.

	$775	$685	$600	$550	$500	$450	$395

Last MSR was $869.

✳ *1911-A1 Compact Model High Capacity* - blue or stainless steel, 3-dot fixed combat sights, black plastic grips, 10 shot (except for law enforcement) mag. Mfg. 1995-96 only.

	$540	$465	$425	$395	$360	$330	$295

Last MSR was $609.

Add $39 for stainless steel.

GRADING - PPGS™	100%	98%	95%	90%	80%	70%	60%

✷ *1911-A1 Compact Model High Capacity PDP Comp* - .45 ACP cal. only, features compensated 3 1/2 in. barrel, 10 shot (except law enforcement) mag., blue finish only. Mfg. 1995-96 only.

	$830	$725	$625	$550	$495	$450	$425

Last MSR was $964.

1911 A-1 ULTRA COMPACT (CUSTOM LOADED) - .380 ACP (lightweight only, mfg. 1995 only), 9mm Para. (new 1998, lightweight stainless only), or .45 ACP cal., 3 1/2 in. barrel, bi-tone (.45 ACP only, disc.), matte (.380 ACP, MD-1), or parkerized (Mil-Spec Ultra Compact) finish, 6, 7 (.380 ACP cal.) or 8 (9mm Para. cal.) shot mag., Custom Loaded features and night sights became standard in 2001, 24 or 30 oz. Mfg. 1995-2003.

	$680	$485	$380	$325	$295	$265	$235

Last MSR was $837.

Add $12 for V10 porting.
Add $12 for Novak Tritium sights (not available on 9mm Para cal.).
Add $110 for bi-tone finish (disc.).
Subtract $50 for MD-1 variation (.380 ACP only).
Subtract approx. 10%-25% if w/o Custom Loaded features (new 2001), depending on condition.

✷ *1911 A-1 Ultra Compact Mil-Spec* - .45 ACP cal., parkerized (disc.) or blued (new 2004) finish, similar to full size Mil-Spec Model, 6 shot mag., checkered grips, 3-dot fixed Hi-Viz combat sights. Mfg. 2001-2002, reintroduced 2004 only.

	$550	$475	$425	$375	$325	$275	$225

Last MSR was $641.

Subtract approx. 10%-25% if w/o Custom Loaded features (new 2001), depending on condition.

✷ *1911 A-1 Ultra Compact Stainless* - 9mm Para. (disc. 2004) or .45 ACP cal., stainless steel, Novak Trijicon night sights became standard 2001. New 1998.

MSR $952	$800	$575	$460	$395	$340	$280	$235

Add $17 for 9mm Para cal. (lightweight, disc. 2004).
Subtract approx. 10%-25% if w/o Custom Loaded features (new 2001), depending on condition.

✷ *1911 A-1 Ultra Compact Lightweight* - .45 ACP cal., aluminum frame, matte metal finish, night sights became standard 2001. Mfg. 1999-2001.

	$695	$495	$395	$345	$310	$275	$240

Last MSR was $867.

Subtract approx. 10%-25% if w/o Custom Loaded features (new 2001), depending on condition.

✷ *1911 A-1 Ultra Compact V10 Lightweight Ported* - .45 ACP cal., bi-tone finish. Mfg. 1999-2001.

	$750	$550	$425	$365	$335	$300	$275

Last MSR was $737.

❖ **1911 A-1 Ultra Compact V10 Lightweight Stainless** - 9mm Para. or .45 ACP (exclusive) cal., similar to Ultra Combat Lightweight, except is stainless steel, Novak low mount sights. Mfg. 1999-2002.

	$725	$525	$425	$365	$335	$300	$275

Last MSR was $870.

Add $31 for night sights (.45 ACP cal. only).
Subtract approx. 10%-25% if w/o Custom Loaded features (new 2001), depending on condition.

GRADING - PPGS™	100%	98%	95%	90%	80%	70%	60%

* *1911 A-1 Ultra Compact High Capacity* - 9mm Para. (disc.) or .45 ACP cal., parkerized (Mil-Spec) or blue (disc.) finish, and stainless steel (disc.) construction, 10 shot mag., 3-dot fixed combat (disc.) or Novak Lo-Mount (new 2002) sights, black plastic grips. Mfg. 1996-2002.

	$735	$525	$425	$365	$325	$300	$275

Last MSR was $909.

> **Add $98 for stainless steel.**
> **Add $145 for stainless steel with V10 ported barrel (disc.).**
> **Subtract approx. 10%-25% if w/o Custom Loaded features (new 2001), depending on condition.**

* *1911 A-1 Ultra Compact V10 Ported* - .45 ACP cal. only, 3 1/2 in. specially compensated barrel/slide, blue (disc.), bi-tone, or parkerized (Mil-Spec Ultra Compact) finish, Novak Lo-Mount or 3-dot combat sights, 30 oz. Mfg. 1995-2002.

	$690	$485	$395	$345	$310	$275	$240

Last MSR was $853.

> **Subtract approx. 10%-25% if w/o Custom Loaded features (new 2001), depending on condition.**

* *1911 A-1 Ultra Compact V10 Super Tuned Ported* - .45 ACP cal. only, super tuned by the Custom Shop, 3 1/2 in. ported barrel, bi-tone finish or stainless steel (exclusive), Novak fixed Lo-Mount sights, 32.9 oz. Mfg. 1997-99.

	$925	$775	$600	$525	$475	$425	$385

Last MSR was $1,049.

> **Add $70 for stainless steel (exclusive).**

1911-A1 MICRO COMPACT - .45 ACP cal. only, 3 in. tapered barrel w/o bushing, matte finish, checkered grips, 6 shot mag., Novak low mount Tritium sights. Mfg. 2002 only.

	$625	$475	$375	$325	$295	$265	$235

Last MSR was $749.

* *1911 A-1 Micro Compact Lightweight Custom Loaded* - similar to Micro Compact 1911 A-1, except also available in .40 S&W (disc.) cal., bi-tone, OD Green (mfg. 2003 only), or black Armory Kote (mfg. 2003-2004) finish with forged steel slide (grey) and aluminum alloy frame (blue), checkered cocobolo grips, Trijicon night sights, 24 oz. New 2002.

MSR $1,220	$1,000	$865	$760	$650	$550	$450	$375

> **Add $64 for Operator Model with XML X-treme mini light.**

* *1911 A-1 Micro Compact Lightweight Stainless Custom Loaded* - .45 ACP cal. only, similar to Micro Compact 1911 A-1 Custom Loaded, except is stainless or black stainless steel slide. Mfg. 2003.

	$825	$725	$595	$490	$425	$365	$315

Last MSR was $993.

* *1911 A-1 Micro Compact GI* - .45 ACP cal., parkerized finish, checkered diamond walnut grips with U.S. initials, includes belt holster, 32 oz. New 2004.

MSR $608	$515	$440	$375	$340	$295	$265	$240

GULF VICTORY SPECIAL EDITION - .45 ACP cal., special edition featuring presentation grade blue finish, gold etching on slide and other gold-plated small parts, includes specially padded and embroidered storage case with jacket patch, window decal, and cloisonne medallion honoring all U.S. Armed Forces. Mfg. 1991-92.

	$750	$600	$475	$415	$360	$300	$255

Last MSR was $869.

Pistols: Semi-Auto - 1911-A1 Custom Models

In addition to the models listed, Springfield also custom builds other configurations of Race Guns that are available through Springfield dealers. Prices range from $2,245-$2,990.

> **Add $100 for all cals. other than .45 ACP.**

GRADING - PPGS™	100%	98%	95%	90%	80%	70%	60%

CUSTOM CARRY GUN - .45 ACP (other cals. available upon request) cal., similar to Defender Model, except has tuned trigger pull, 7 shot mag., heavy recoil spring, extended thumb safety, available in blue or phosphate (disc.) finish. New 1991.

MSR $1,499		$1,325	$1,050	$875	$750	$650	$550	$475

CUSTOM OPERATOR - .45 ACP cal. New 2001.

MSR $2,495		$2,150	$1,725	$1,375	$1,075	$950	$825	$725

BASIC COMPETITION - .45 ACP (other cals. available upon request) cal., Bo-Mar adj. rear sight, blue finish, checkered walnut grips. New 1994.

MSR $1,600		$1,400	$1,075	$900	$775	$675	$550	$475

PROFESSIONAL MODEL - .45 ACP cal., FBI contract model, black finish, with or w/o light rail. New 1999.

MSR $2,395		$2,050	$1,675	$1,350	$1,075	$950	$825	$725

PPC TROPHY MATCH - 9mm Para. cal. New 2004.

MSR $1,395		$1,200	$1,000	$825	$700	$625	$525	$450

NRA PPC DISTINGUISHED - .45 ACP (other cals. available upon request) cal., designed to comply with NRA PPC competitive rules/regulations, factory test target, custom carrying case. New 1995.

MSR $1,950		$1,700	$1,400	$1,050	$925	$775	$675	$575

Add $145 for PPC 1500 Model.

1911-A1 CUSTOM COMPACT - .45 ACP cal. only, carry or lady's model with shortened slide and frame, compensated, fixed 3-dot sights, Commander style hammer, Herrett walnut grips, other custom features, blue only.

		$1,615	$1,325	$1,100	$950	$850	$750	$675

Last MSR was $1,815.

1911-A1 CUSTOM CHAMPION - similar to Custom Compact, except is based on Champion model with full size frame and shortened slide.

		$1,615	$1,325	$1,100	$950	$850	$750	$675

Last MSR was $1,815.

NATIONAL MATCH HARDBALL - .45 ACP cal. only, National Match barrel and bushing, specially fitted frame and slide, blue only, Bo-Mar adj. rear sight, Herrett walnut grips, plastic cased.

MSR $1,535		$1,350	$1,040	$900	$775	$650	$550	$475

This model is made specifically for DCM competition shooting.

BULLSEYE WADCUTTER - .45 ACP (other cals. available upon request) cal., specifically designed for wadcutter loads, Bo-Mar rib mounted on slide top, 5 or 6 in. barrel.

MSR $1,725		$1,525	$1,250	$995	$875	$750	$650	$575

ENTRY LEVEL WADCUTTER - .38 Super, .40 S&W, 10mm, or .45 ACP cal., 5 in. barrel, standard competition features.

		$925	$800	$700	$600	$550	$475	$425

Last MSR was $1,049.

Add $200 for .38 Super cal.
Add $391 for 10mm or .40 S&W cal.

This model featured supported chambers in all cals. except .45 ACP.

TROPHY MASTER "COMPETITION" - .45 ACP (other cals. available upon request) cal., competition model which includes low profile combat sights, ambidextrous safety, long match trigger, bobbed hammer, Pachmayr wraparound grips. Disc. 1996.

		$1,420	$1,125	$950	$875	$800	$725	$650

Last MSR was $1,598.

GRADING - PPGS™	100%	98%	95%	90%	80%	70%	60%

EXPERT - .45 ACP (other cals. available upon request) cal., mfg. for IPSC competition shooting, dual chamber compensator system on match barrel, duotone finish.

MSR $1,985	$1,775	$1,500	$1,225	$995	$850	$750	$675

Subtract $160 for Limited Class variation.

This model is an improved variation of the Trophy Master Competition Model.

DISTINGUISHED - similar to Expert Model, except has brushed hard chrome finish, checkered gripstraps and triggerguard, top-of-the-line competition model.

MSR $2,825	$2,475	$2,050	$1,650	$1,275	$995	$850	$750

Subtract $130 for Limited Class variation.

CUSTOM HIGH CAPACITY LTD - new 2004.

MSR $2,395	$2,050	$1,675	$1,350	$1,075	$950	$825	$725

OPERATOR LIGHTWEIGHT - .45 ACP cal., 3 in. barrel, bi-tone finish, XML mini-light, includes Novak Trijicon night sights. Limited mfg. 2005.

	$1,050	$925	$800	$700	$600	$500	$400

Last MSR was $1,247.

OPERATOR TACTICAL RESPONSE - .45 ACP cal., 5 in. barrel, black Armory Kote finish, adj. Trijicon night sights. Limited mfg. 2005.

	$1,395	$1,075	$900	$775	$675	$575	$475

Last MSR was $1,639.

LOADED OPERATOR - .45 ACP cal., 5 in. barrel, OD Green or black Armory Kote finish and slide, Novak or Trijicon night sights. Limited mfg. 2005.

	$1,025	$900	$800	$700	$600	$500	$400

Last MSR was $1,218.

LEATHAM TROPHY MATCH - .40 S&W cal., 5 in. barrel, high capacity model, Armory Kote finish. New 2005.

This model is available POR - please contact the company directly.

LEATHAM LEGEND SERIES These models are available exclusively through Davidson's. Please refer to the Davidson's section for pricing.

DISTINGUISHED BIANCHI/COMPETITION STEEL - new 2004.

MSR $2,995	$2,650	$2,375	$2,000	$1,625	$1,250	$995	$850

FULL HOUSE RACE GUN - .45 ACP cal., high capacity frame, chrome finish only. New 1998.

MSR $3,085	$2,700	$2,300	$2,000	$1,725	$1,500	$1,350	$1,200

Add $150 for STI/SV style frame.

P9 WORLD CUP - 9mmx21 or .40 S&W cal., state-of-the-art competition pistol, based on factory P9 Race gun, hard chrome finish only.

	$2,550	$2,100	$1,775	$1,500	$1,250	$975	$795

Last MSR was $2,935.

Pistols: Semi-Auto - XD Series

All XD pistols were originally shipped with two magazines. Beginning 2005, high capacity magazines are legal for civilian sales in those states that permit high cap. mags. During 2006, all XD pistols are shipped with the XD Gear System, consisting of belt holster, double magazine pouch, magazine loader, two magazines and cable lock.

X-TREME DUTY (XD MODELS) - 5 IN. TACTICAL - 9mm Para., .357 SIG, .40 S&W, .45 ACP (new 2006), or .45 GAP (new 2005) cal., cold hammer forged 5 in. barrel, 9 (.45 GAP), 10, 12 (.40 S&W or .357 SIG), or 15 (9mm Para.) shot mag., lightweight polymer frame, matte black, bi-tone, or OD Green finish, steel slide, single action striker fired with U.S.A. trigger system, firing pin and loaded chamber indicators, dual recoil spring system, integral accessory rails

GRADING - PPGS™	100%	98%	95%	90%	80%	70%	60%

standard on frame, ambidextrous mag. release, grip safety, front and rear slide serrations, approx. 23 oz. New 2002.

MSR $573	$485	$425	$385	$345	$300	$265	$235

Add $29 for bi-tone finish (.45 GAP cal. only, new 2005).
Add $29 for .45 ACP cal. (new 2006).
Add $89 for Trijicon or Heinie (disc.) tritium Slant Pro sights (N/A in .45 GAP or .45 ACP).

* *XD Tactical Pro* - limited mfg. 2003 only.

	$875	$775	$675	$575	$475	$400	$350

Last MSR was $1,099.

X-TREME DUTY (XD MODELS) - 4 IN. SERVICE

X-TREME DUTY (XD MODELS) - 4 IN. SERVICE - 9mm Para., .357 SIG, .40 S&W, .45 ACP (new 2006), or .45 GAP (new 2005) cal., cold hammer forged 4 in. ported or unported barrel, 9 (.45 GAP), 10 (.45 ACP), 12 (.40 S&W or .357 SIG), or 15 (9mm Para.) shot mag., lightweight polymer frame, matte black, bi-tone (new 2003) or OD Green finish, steel slide, single action striker fired with U.S.A. trigger system, firing pin and loaded chamber indicators, dual recoil spring system, integral accessory rails standard on frame, ambidextrous mag. release, grip safety, front and rear slide serrations, approx. 23 oz. New 2002.

MSR $536	$460	$400	$350	$300	$265	$235	$200

Add $30 for V10 ported barrel (black or OD Green finish, not available in .45 ACP or .45 GAP cal.).
Add approx. $30 for bi-tone finish.
Add $90 for Trijicon or Heinie tritium Slant Pro night sights (9mm Para., .357 SIG or .40 S&W cal.).

X-TREME DUTY (XD MODELS) - 3 IN. SUB-COMPACT

X-TREME DUTY (XD MODELS) - 3 IN. SUB-COMPACT - 9mm Para. or .40 S&W (new 2004) cal., cold hammer forged 3 in. barrel, 9 (.40 S&W) or 10 (9mm Para.) shot mag., lightweight polymer frame, bi-tone (new 2004, 9mm Para. cal. only), matte black or OD Green finish, steel slide, single action striker fired with U.S.A. trigger system, firing pin and loaded chamber indicators, dual recoil spring system, integral accessory rails standard on frame, ambidextrous mag. release, grip safety, front and rear slide serrations, 20 1/2 oz. New 2003.

MSR $536	$460	$400	$350	$300	$265	$235	$200

Add $30 for bi-tone finish.

Add $90 for Trijicon or Heinie tritium Slant Pro night sights.
Add $100 for X-treme mini light.

PISTOLS: SINGLE SHOT, 1911-A2 SASS SERIES

1911-A2 SASS - various cals., single shot break open action featuring interchangeable barrels, Pachmayr grips, adj. front and rear sights, blue finish only, 61-66 oz. Mfg. 1990-1992.

* *1911-A2 SASS 10 3/4 in. barrel* - .22 LR, 7mm BR, .243 Win., .357 Mag., or .44 Mag. cal.

	$650	$560	$495	$450	$420	$390	$360

Last MSR was $749.

Add $399 per interchangeable conversion unit (includes barrel).

* *1911-A2 SASS 15 in. barrel* - .22 LR, .223 Rem., .243 Win. (new 1991), 7mm BR, 7mm-08 Rem., .308 Win., or .358 Win. cal.

	$650	$560	$495	$450	$420	$390	$360

Last MSR was $749.

Add $399 per interchangeable conversion unit (includes barrel).

RIFLES: BOLT ACTION

MAUSER M98 - 7x57mm Mauser cal., surplus rifles with standard military dimensions and features. Importation disc. 1989.

GRADING - PPGS™	100%	98%	95%	90%	80%	70%	60%

✻ Mauser M98 Hunting/Utility Grade

	$70	$50	$45	$45	$40	$40	$35

Last MSR was $75.

✻ Mauser M98 Collector Grade

	$105	$90	$80	$70	$60	$50	$40

Last MSR was $116.

✻ Mauser M98 Premium Grade

	$170	$150	$130	$115	$100	$90	$80

Last MSR was $194.

CZ 98 HUNTER CLASSIC - .243 Win., .270 Win., .30-06, .308 Win., 6.5x55mm, 7x57 Mauser, 7x64mm, 7.29x57mm, .300 Win. Mag., or 7mm Rem. Mag. cal., features Mauser 98 Large Ring action, mfg. by CZ in the Czech Republic and Springfield Armory, controlled feeding, 24 in. hammer forged barrel, adj. trigger, choice of walnut or synthetic stock, 7.7 lbs. Limited mfg. 1995 only.

	$345	$315	$285	$260	$240	$220	$195

Last MSR was $411.

Add $38 for walnut stock.

RIFLES: SEMI-AUTO, MILITARY DESIGN

Many models listed below are CA legal, since they do not have a muzzle brake. MSRs are typically the same as those guns available with a muzzle brake.

M1 CARBINE - .30 Carbine cal., features new receiver on older military M1 GI stocks. Disc.

	$375	$325	$285	$260	$240	$220	$195

M1 GARAND AND VARIATIONS - .30-06, .270 Win. (disc. 1987), or .308 Win. cal., semi-auto, 24 in. barrel, gas operated, 8 shot mag., adj. sights, 9 1/2 lbs.

✻ M1 Garand Rifle - .30-06 or .308 Win. cal., mfg. with original U.S. government issue parts, with new walnut stock, 8 shot mag., 24 in. barrel, 9 1/2 lbs. Limited mfg. beginning 2002.

MSR $1,437		$1,175	$1,025	$900	$750	$650	$575	$475

Add $30 for .308 Win. cal.

✻ M1 Garand Standard Model - supplied standard with camo GI fiberglass stock.

	$725	$650	$575	$525	$485	$450	$425

Last MSR was $761.

Subtract $65 if with GI stock.

✻ M1 Garand National Match - walnut stock, match barrel and sights.

	$850	$775	$700	$650	$600	$550	$495

Last MSR was $897.

Add $240 for Kevlar stock.

✻ M1 Garand Ultra Match - match barrel and sights, glass bedded stock, walnut stock standard.

	$950	$850	$725	$675	$610	$550	$500

Last MSR was $1,033.

Add $240 for Kevlar stock.

✻ M1-D Sniper Rifle - .30-06 or .308 Win. cal., limited quantities, with original M84 scope, prong type flash suppressor, leather cheek pad and slings.

	$950	$850	$725	$675	$610	$550	$500

Last MSR was $1,033.

✻ M1 Garand Tanker Rifle - similar to T-26 authorized by Gen. MacArthur at the

GRADING - PPGS™	100%	98%	95%	90%	80%	70%	60%

end of WWII, 18 1/4 in. barrel, .30-06 or .308 Win. cal., GI stock standard.

	$725	$675	$600	$525	$460	$380	$335

Last MSR was $797.

Add $23 for walnut full stock.

* **D-Day M1 Garand Rifle** - .30-06 cal., 24 in. barrel, gas operated, military square post front sights, engraved stock, two 8 shot mags., leather sling, cleaning kit, includes wooden crate and limited edition lithograph print, 9 1/2 lbs. 1,944 mfg. 2004-2005.

	$1,375	$1,250	$1,125	$900	$800	$700	$600

Last MSR was $1,490.

BM 59 - .308 Win. cal., mfg. in Italy and machined and assembled in the Springfield Armory factory, 19.32 in. barrel, 20 shot box mag., 9 1/2 lbs.

* **BM 59 Standard Italian Rifle** - with grenade launcher, winter trigger, tri-compensator, and bipod.

	$1,750	$1,400	$1,200	$1,000	$895	$850	$800

Last MSR was $1,950.

* **BM 59 Alpine Rifle** - with Beretta pistol grip type stock.

	$2,025	$1,625	$1,350	$1,150	$1,000	$925	$850

Last MSR was $2,275.

This model was also available in a Paratrooper configuration with folding stock at no extra charge.

* **BM 59 Nigerian Rifle** - similar to BM 59, except has Beretta pistol grip type stock.

	$2,075	$1,650	$1,375	$1,150	$1,000	$925	$850

Last MSR was $2,340.

* **BM 59 E Model Rifle**

	$1,975	$1,595	$1,325	$1,125	$975	$900	$825

Last MSR was $2,210.

M1A RIFLES - .243 Win. (disc.), .308 Win., or 7mm-08 Rem. (1991 mfg. only) cal., patterned after the original Springfield M14 - except semi-auto, walnut or fiberglass stock, 22 in. steel or stainless steel barrel, fiberglass handguard, "New Loaded" option (see separate listing) beginning 2001 includes NM air gauge barrel, trigger group, front and rear sights, and flash supressor or Springfield proprietary muzzle brake, 9 lbs.

* **M1A Standard/Basic Model** - above specifications, choice of Collector (original GI stock, disc. 2001), birch (disc. 2003), walnut (M1A Standard Model beginning 1993), Mossy Oak camo finished (new 2003), black fiberglass (M1A Basic Model), camo fiberglass (disc.), GI wood (disc. 1992), and brown (disc.) or black laminated (M1A Standard Model mfg. 1996-2000) stock, regular or National Match (disc.) barrel.

MSR $1,531		$1,285	$1,100	$940	$835	$725	$625	$525

Add $104 for new walnut stock.
Add $21 for Mossy Oak camo finished stock.
Add $12 for black fiberglass stock.
Add $59 for birch stock (disc. 2003).
Add $44 for stainless steel barrel (disc.), $74 for bipod and stabilizer (disc.) or $159 for brown laminated stock (disc.), $59 for National Match barrel (disc.), $155 for National Match barrel and sights (disc.), $200 for folding stock (disc. 1994).
Subtract $58 for camo fiberglass stock (disc.).

Standard (entry level model) stock configuration for 1996 was black or camo fiberglass.

GRADING - PPGS™	100%	98%	95%	90%	80%	70%	60%

* **M1A E-2** - standard stock is birch. Disc.

	$975	$825	$745	$650	$590	$550	$495

Last MSR was $842.

Add $30 for walnut stock.
Add $120 for Shaw stock with Harris bipod.

* **M1A Bush Rifle** - .308 Win. cal., 18 in. shrouded barrel, 8 lbs. 12 oz., collector GI, walnut, Mossy Oak camo finished (new 2003), black fiberglass folding (disc. 1994 per C/B), and black fiberglass (disc.) or laminated black (disc.) stock. Disc. 1999, reintroduced 2003 only.

	$1,300	$985	$845	$725	$625	$525	$475

Last MSR was $1,529.

Add $29 for walnut stock (disc.), $15 for black fiberglass stock (disc.), $86 for black laminated stock (disc.), $235 for National Match variation (disc.), and $525 for Super Match variation (disc.)

* **M1A National Match** - National Match sights, steel or stainless steel (new 1999) barrel, mainspring guide, flash suppressor, and gas cylinder, special glass bedded oil finished match stock, tuned trigger, walnut stock became standard in 1991, 9 lbs.

MSR $2,113		$1,775	$1,275	$995	$825	$725	$625	$550

Add $32 for stainless steel barrel.
Add $155 for heavy composition stock (disc.).
Add $250 for either fiberglass or fancy burl wood stock (disc.).
.243 Win. and 7mm-08 Rem. cals. are also available at extra charge.

* **M1A Super Match** - similar to National Match, except has air-gauged Douglas or Hart (disc.) heavy barrel, oversized walnut or fiberglass super match stock, and modified operating rod guide, rear lugged receiver beginning 1991, approx. 11 1/2 lbs.

MSR $2,651		$2,250	$1,600	$1,200	$995	$850	$750	$650

Add $149 for stainless steel Douglas barrel.
Add $250 for Krieger or Hart barrel (disc.).
Add $605 for McMillan black or Marine Corps camo fiberglass stock.
Add $200 for fancy burl walnut (disc.) stock.
.243 Win. and 7mm-08 Rem. cals. are also available at extra charge.

M1A LOADED STANDARD - .308 Win. cal., 22 in. National Match steel or stainless steel barrel, features shooting upgrades such as National Match trigger assembly, front and rear sights, and National Match flash suppressor, 10 shot mag., black fiberglass, Collector GI walnut (disc. 2000), or new walnut stock, approx. 9 1/2 lbs. New 1999.

MSR $1,688		$1,435	$1,125	$915	$750	$650	$575	$525

Add $107 for new walnut stock.
Add $198 for stainless steel barrel and walnut stock.
Add $92 for stainless steel barrel.
Add $348 for extended cluster rail with black fiberglass stock and National Match stainless steel barrel (new 2006).
Add $100 for Collector GI walnut (disc. 2000).

M1A "GOLD SERIES" - .308 Win. cal., heavy walnut competition stock, gold medal grade heavy Douglas barrel. Mfg. 1987 only.

	$1,944	$1,750	$1,375	$1,150	$975	$850	$740

Last MSR was $1,944.

Add $126 for Kevlar stock, add $390 for special Hart stainless steel barrel, add $516 for Hart stainless steel barrel with Kevlar stock.

GRADING - PPGS™	100%	98%	95%	90%	80%	70%	60%

M1A SCOUT SQUAD - .308 Win. cal., 18 in. barrel, choice of GI Collector (disc. 1998), new walnut, black fiberglass, Mossy Oak camo finished, or black laminated (disc. 1998) stock, muzzle stabilizer standard, supplied with Scout mount and handguard, approx. 9 lbs. New 1997.

MSR $1,658	$1,410	$1,065	$900	$775	$650	$575	$500

Add $122 for walnut stock.
Add $45 for Mossy Oak camo finish.

M1A SOCOM - .308 Win. cal., 16 1/4 in. barrel with muzzle brake, black fiberglass stock with steel buttplate, upper handguard has been cut out for sight rail, 10 shot mag., tritium front sight with ghost ring aperture rear sight, two-stage military trigger, 8.9 lbs. New 2004.

MSR $1,818	$1,525	$1,200	$985	$850	$750	$675	$600

Add $260 for urban camo stock with cluster rail (new 2005).
Add $231 for Generation II black fiberglass stock with cluster rail (new 2005) or $305 for extended cluster rail (new 2007).

M21 TACTICAL - .308 Win. cal., Garand action, 22 in. barrel, tactical variation of the Super Match mfg. with match grade parts giving superior accuracy, adj. cheekpiece stock, 11.6 lbs. New 1990.

MSR $3,180	$2,725	$2,200	$1,825	$1,575	$1,275	$1,050	$875

Add $375 for Krieger stainless barrrel.

M25 "WHITE FEATHER" TACTICAL - .308 Win. cal., Garand action, includes black fiberglass M3A McMillan stock, 22 in. Kreiger heavy carbon barrel standard, Rader trigger, White Feather logo and Carlos Hathcock II signature, 10 shot box mag., includes Harris bipod, 12 3/4 lbs. New 2001.

MSR $4,963	$4,375	$3,500	$2,950	$2,425	$1,925	$1,600	$1,250

SAR-3 - .308 Win. cal., licensed copy of the pre-import ban HK-91, predecessor to the SAR-8, mfg. in Greece.

$995	$825	$750	$675	$600	$550	$500

SAR-8 - .308 Win. cal., patterned after the H & K Model 91, recoil operated delayed roller lock action, fluted chamber, rotary adj. rear aperture sight, 18 in. barrel, recent mfg. incorporated a cast aluminum receiver with integrated Weaver rail, pistol grip, slim forearm, and green furniture (for law enforcement only), supplied with walnut (disc. 1994) or black fiberglass thumbhole sporter stock, 10 (C/B 1994) or 20 (disc. 1994) shot detachable mag., 8.7 lbs. Mfg. in U.S. starting 1990, disc. 1998.

$1,015	$835	$750	$675	$600	$550	$500

Last MSR was $1,204.

SAR-8 parts are interchangeable with both SAR-3 and HK-91 parts.

* *SAR-8 Tactical Counter Sniper Rifle* - .308 Win. cal., tactical sniper variation of the SAR-8. Mfg. 1996-98.

$1,325	$1,000	$825	$725	$650	$575	$525

Last MSR was $1,610.

SAR-48 MODEL - .308 Win. cal., authentic model of the Belgian semi-auto FAL/LAR rifle, 21 in. barrel, adj. gas operation, 20 shot mag., walnut or stock, adj. sights, sling, and mag. loader. Mfg. 1985-89.

$1,675	$1,475	$1,200	$1,050	$925	$850	$775

This model was available in the Israeli configuration with heavy barrel, bipod, flash hider, and flip-up buttplate - add approx. 20%. The SAR-48 was disc. in 1989 and reintroduced as the Model SAR-4800 in 1990.

* *SAR-48 Bush Rifle* - similar to SAR-48 model, except has 18 in. barrel.

$1,750	$1,550	$1,250	$1,075	$950	$850	$775

* *SAR-48 .22 Cal.* - .22 LR cal., variation of the Sporter Model. Disc. 1989.

$725	$660	$595	$540	$495	$450	$400

Last MSR was $760.

SAR-4800 SPORTER MODEL - .223 Rem. (new 1997) or .308 Win. cal., authentic model of the Belgian semi-auto FAL/LAR rifle, 18 (.223 Rem. cal. only) or 21 in. barrel, adj. gas operation, 10 (C/B 1994) or 20 (disc.) shot mag., walnut (disc.) or black fiberglass thumbhole sporter stock, adj. sights, sling, and mag. loader. Mfg. 1990-98.

$1,080	$915	$785	$675	$625	$575	$525

All SAR - 4800 parts are interchangeable with both SAR-48 and FN/FAL parts. This model is an updated variation of the pre-WWII FN Model 49.

* *SAR-4800 Bush Rifle Sporter Model* - similar to standard model, except has 18 in. barrel.

$1,085	$900	$795	$695	$640	$595	$550

Last MSR was $1,216.

DR-200 SPORTER RIFLE - while advertised, this model never went into production. ($687 was planned MSR).

STAG ARMS

Current rifle manufacturer located in New Britain, CT.

RIFLES: SEMI-AUTO

Stag Arms offers four variations of a paramilitary style semi-auto rifle in .223 Rem. cal., available with both right and left hand ejection ports. All rifles are available in post-ban configuration for restricted states. Models include: the Model 1 carbine ($949 MSR, $989 MSR for M1L), the Model 2 carbine ($925 MSR, $949 MSR for M2L), the Model 3 carbine ($895 MSR, $920 for Model 3L), the Model 4 rifle ($1,015 MSR, $1,095 for Model 4L), the Model 5 ($1,045 MSR), and the Model 6 ($1,055 MSR).

Please contact the company directly for more information (see Trademark Index).

STALLARD ARMS

Current manufacturer of 9mm Para. pistols located in Mansfield, OH since 1991. Distributed by MKS Supply, Inc. located in Dayton, OH.

Please refer to the I li-Point listing in this text.

STANDARD ARMS & STANDARD ARMS MFG. CO.

Previous manufacturer that started production in Wilmington, DE, in Sept., 1909, and closed in 1912. The company was restarted in 1913 as Standard Arms Mfg. Co., and closed in April, 1914.

Nearly 5,000 rifles were manufactured at the actual factory. At the time the plant closed, approx. 2,200 rifles were in various stages of production, and a supply of parts remained. These were primarily purchased by Numrich Arms, made into complete rifles, and sold. Total production (Standard Arms, Standard Arms Mfg. Co. & those assembled by Numrich Arms) reached approx. 7,000 rifles. The highest known serial number is 9012. Within serialization, it is noted that large blocks of numbers were abandoned, and this is thought to be due to changes and improvements made during production. In addition, as the factory folded with a large number of rifles in partial stages of production, it is often not possible to determine which rifles were actually made and completed at the factory, and which were completed outside the factory at a later date.

Many special order options were available, such as checkering, pistol grip, deluxe grades of woods, special sights, etc. Several grades of engraving were available, including Rocky Mountain, Adirondack, Sierra, and Selkirk. Lower priced "etched" models were also available and less frequently encountered than engraved models. A .50 caliber "Camp Carbine" was offered in smooth bore, slide action only. Approx. 25-30 were manufactured and utilized a special cartridge similar to the .50-70 shot cartridge. These are rarely encountered, although they are known to exist in collections.

GRADING - PPGS™	100%	98%	95%	90%	80%	70%	60%

RIFLES: SEMI-AUTO

MODEL G AUTOLOADER - .25-35 WCF, .30-30 Win., .25 Rem., .30 Rem., or .35 Rem. cal., bottom loading box mag., 22 in. barrel, open sight, straight stock. This was the first gas operated rifle in the U.S.A. Gas port can be closed and gun will function as a slide action. Mfg. 1910.

	$475	$400	$300	$275	$250	$225	$200

Subtract 10% for slide action only (Model M).

STANDARD ARMS OF NEVADA, INC.

Previous manufacturer 1999-2000, and located in Reno, NV.

PISTOLS: SEMI-AUTO

SA-9 - 9mm Para. cal., double action only, sub-compact design, 10 shot mag., 3.1 in. barrel, black polymer frame with matte black steel slide, 14 oz. Mfg. 1999-2000.

	$220	$190	$175	$165	$150	$140	$130

Last MSR was $249.

STANDARD 380 - while advertised, this model never went into production. MSR was $176.

STANDARD PRODUCTS CO.

Previous WWII subcontractor of M1 carbines located in Port Clinton, OH.
Please refer to US Military carbines/rifles listing for more information.

STAR, BONIFACIO ECHEVERRIA S.A.

Previous manufacturer located in Eibar, Spain. Star, Bonifacio Echeverria S.A. closed its doors on July 28th, 1997, due to the intense financial pressure the Spanish arms industry experienced during the late 1990s. Previously imported by Interarms, located in Alexandria, VA.

PISTOLS: SEMI-AUTO

MODEL H - similar to Model HN, except 7.65mm, 7 shot.

	$350	$250	$170	$120	$100	$90	$75

MODEL HN - .380 ACP cal., 6 shot, 2 3/4 in. barrel, blue, fixed sights, plastic grips. Mfg. 1934-41.

	$375	$265	$180	$120	$100	$90	$75

MODEL I - .32 ACP cal., 9 shot, 4 3/4 in. barrel, blue, fixed sights, plastic grips. Mfg. 1934-36.

	$350	$250	$170	$120	$100	$85	$70

MODEL IN - similar to Model I, except .380 ACP, 8 shot, 4 3/4 in. barrel, blue.

	$395	$265	$180	$125	$105	$90	$75

MODEL 1920 - 9mm Bergmann Bayard or .38 Super cal., easily identified by unusual safety located on left rear slide. Issued to Spanish Guardia Civil.

	$650	$525	$400	$300	$250	$200	$175

MODEL 1921 - 9mm Bergmann Bayard cal., this model was fitted with a grip safety that was later dropped when standardizing the Model A production. Issued to Spanish Guardia Civil.

	$600	$500	$400	$300	$250	$200	$175

MODEL 1922 - designation for the early Model A. Issued to Spanish Guardia Civil.

	$450	$300	$240	$215	$180	$145	$135

MODEL A - .38 Super cal., modified Government Colt, 5 in. barrel, no grip safety, blue, checkered wood grips. Mfg. 1934-disc.

	$325	$275	$240	$215	$180	$145	$135

Add 50% for Spanish Air Force issue if in original box.

GRADING - PPGS™	100%	98%	95%	90%	80%	70%	60%

MODEL A CARBINE - usually 7.63mm cal., unusual variation, slotted with tangent rear sight and extended barrel.

	$2,500	$2,000	$1,500	$1,200	$1,000	$800	$600

Add $500 for original stock (different from MB and MMS stock).

MODEL B - similar to Model A, but 9mm Para. cal. Mfg. 1934-75.

	$400	$300	$250	$200	$150	$140	$115

Add 50% for post-war German police if with 2 matching magazines.
Add 150% if Waffenamt proofed (WaA251).

MODEL M - similar to Model A, except has large frame, available in 9mm Bergmann Bayard, 9mm Para., 8 shot, and .45 ACP, 7 shot, 5 in. barrel, blue, fixed sights, checkered wood or plastic grips.

	$375	$300	$250	$215	$185	$160	$140

Add 100% for early variation with ser. no. under 4,835.

MODEL P - .45 ACP cal. only, similar to Model A, except has large frame, 7 shot mag. Mfg. 1934-75.

	$375	$300	$250	$215	$185	$160	$140

Add 100% for early variation with ser. no. under 5,112.

MODELS SUPER A (9mm Largo), M (9mm Largo), & P (.45 ACP) - similar to Models A, M, & P, except has loaded chamber indicator, mag. safety, and easier takedown feature. Mfg. 1946-89.

	$395	$325	$215	$180	$160	$145	$125

Last MSR was $340.

Add 100% for Super M and 150% for Super P.
The Super A was a Spanish Service pistol. Recent imports in 80% condition were available in the $150 range.

MODEL SUPER B - 9mm Para. cal., similar to Model B, except has loaded chamber indicator, mag. safety and easier takedown feature, choice of blue or Starvel finish on Model B, late production models are poorly polished and have parkerized small parts. Importation disc. in 1990.

	$350	$295	$225	$200	$150	$140	$120

Last MSR was $330.

Add $30 for Starvel finish.

SUPER TARGET MODEL - similar to Star Super, but target sights, extended trigger guard, modified trigger. Rare.

	$1,500	$1,250	$1,000	$800	$600	$500	$400

MODEL MB - 9mm Para. cal., late production Model M cut for shoulder stock, mag. safety.

	$2,250	$1,750	$1,250	$800	$650	$500	$400

Add $300 for shoulder stock.
Add 20% to rig if matching stock.

MODEL MMS - 7.63mm cal., late production Model M cut for shoulder stock, mag. safety.

	$1,950	$1,600	$1,200	$800	$650	$500	$400

Add $300 for shoulder stock.
Add 20% to rig for matching stock.

MODEL SI - .32 ACP cal., 8 shot, 4 in. barrel, blue, without grip safety, small version of Government .45 in appearance, plastic grips. Mfg. 1941-65.

	$225	$190	$160	$135	$115	$100	$80

GRADING - PPGS™	100%	98%	95%	90%	80%	70%	60%

MODEL S - similar to Model SI, except .380 ACP cal., 9 shot, mfg. 1941-1965. Importation of these Police contract models was disc. 1991.

	$250	$200	$160	$135	$115	$100	$80

Last MSR was $237.

Add $30 for Starvel finish.
Add 100% for guns issued to the Spanish Air Force with original box and 2 matching mags.
In 1989, Interarms imported factory reconditioned used Spanish Police Contract Model S pistols - these guns were available in either blue or Starvel finish and were supplied with a plastic box with accessories.

MODELS SUPER SI AND S - similar to Model S, with Super Star improvements. Mfg. 1946-1972.

	$275	$230	$210	$195	$165	$140	$120

MODEL SUPER SM - similar to Model Super S, except adjustable sight and wood grips. Mfg. 1973-81.

	$350	$295	$220	$200	$175	$145	$125

MODEL CO POCKET - .25 Auto cal., 2 3/4 in. barrel, blue, fixed sights, plastic grips. Mfg. 1929-56.

	$275	$195	$165	$145	$120	$110	$90

MODEL CU STARLET - .25 Auto cal., 2 3/8 in. barrel, alloy frame, fixed sights, plastic grips, blue, or chrome slide, frame anodized in black, blue, green, grey, or gold. Mfg. 1957-72.

	$250	$200	$165	$145	$120	$110	$90

Minor changes prompted a model redesignation as CK during 1973.

MODEL D - .380 ACP cal., small steel frame version of the Model A with several minor variations, 40,416 mfg. 1922-47.

	$550	$475	$400	$350	$300	$250	$200

MODEL DK (STARFIRE) - .380 ACP cal., 3 1/8 in. barrel, fixed sights, plastic stocks, finished in same color availability as Model CU. Mfg. 1957-1972, U.S. import ceased as of 1968 due to Federal GCA legislation.

	$400	$350	$295	$255	$225	$180	$155

Add 10% for unusual alloy colors.
Minor changes prompted a redesignation as DKL (.380 ACP) 1972 and DKI (.32 ACP) 1972.

MODEL HK LANCER - similar to Model Starfire, except .22 LR cal. Mfg. 1955-68.

	$275	$225	$200	$175	$150	$120	$110

MODEL F - .22 LR cal., 10 shot, 4 in. barrel, fixed sights, blue, plastic grips. Mfg. 1942-67.

	$325	$225	$140	$110	$95	$85	$55

MODEL FS - similar to Model F, except 6 in. barrel, adj. sights. Mfg. 1942-67.

	$325	$225	$150	$120	$100	$90	$65

MODEL F OLYMPIC RAPID FIRE - .22 Short cal., 9 shot, 7 in. barrel, adj. sight, aluminum slide, barrel weights and muzzle brake, blue, plastic grips. Mfg. 1942-67.

	$500	$400	$300	$200	$155	$140	$130

MODEL FR - restyled Model F, with "squared" barrel, adj. sight and slide stop. Mfg. 1967-72.

	$325	$225	$150	$120	$100	$90	$65

Add 15% for chrome finish.

MODELS FR SPORT AND MODEL FR TARGET - similar to Model FR, except FR Sport has 150mm barrel, and the Model FR Target has 180mm barrel, 65,534 mfg. 1967-83.

	$350	$250	$150	$120	$100	$90	$65

Add 15% for chrome finish.

MODEL FM - similar to Model FR, except heavier frame, web ahead of trigger guard, 4 1/2 in. barrel. 8,799 mfg. 1972-83.

$325	$250	$200	$150	$100	$90	$65

MODEL BKS STARLIGHT - 9mm Para. cal., 8 shot, 4 1/4 in. barrel, plastic grips. Mfg. 1970-81.

Blue						
$265	$230	$210	$180	$160	$145	$130

Add 10% for chrome finish.

MODEL BM - 9mm Para. cal., single action, 8 shot mag., 4 in. barrel, steel frame, Colt 1911 action, blue, chrome (disc. 1989), or Starvel (new 1990) finish, plastic grips, 35 oz. Importation disc. 1991.

$285	$245	$205	$180	$165	$155	$145

Last MSR was $415.

Add $30 for Starvel or chrome (disc. 1990) finish.
Add 150% for Navy issue with escutcheon grips.

MODEL BKM - identical to Model BM, except lightweight duraluminum frame, blue finish only, 26 oz. Importation disc. 1991.

$310	$270	$225	$200	$180	$170	$155

Last MSR was $415.

MODEL PD - .45 ACP cal., 6 shot mag., single action, 4 in. barrel, adj. rear sight, blue or Starvel (new 1990) finish only, walnut grips, alloy frame, 25 oz. Mfg. 1975-importation disc. 1991.

$345	$290	$250	$215	$195	$170	$160

Last MSR was $475.

Add $20 for Starvel finish (new 1990).
Add 20% for late variation with 30M rear sight.

MODEL 28 - 9mm Para. cal., double action, 15 shot mag., 4 1/4 in. barrel, blue finish only, advanced design, 40 oz. Mfg. 1983 and 1984 only.

$400	$335	$325	$275	$250	$225	$200

Note: Model 28 is interesting since no screws were used in its manufacture. Hammer assembly (including spring, cocking lever, sear, disconnector and ejector) is housed under removable backstrap.

MODEL 30M - 9mm Para. cal. only, successor to the Model 28, double action, 4.33 in. barrel, 15 shot mag., blue finish only, adj. rear sight, checkered wraparound plastic grips, steel frame, 40 oz. New 1985. Importation disc. 1991.

$350	$295	$275	$255	$235	$215	$195

Last MSR was $495.

MODEL 30 PK DURAL FRAME - similar to Model 30M, except slightly shorter duraluminum frame, 3.86 in. barrel, 30 oz. Disc. 1989.

$350	$295	$270	$250	$225	$210	$195

Last MSR was $580.

MODEL 31P (STEEL FRAME)/31PK (DURAL FRAME) - 9mm Para. (disc. 1993) or .40 S&W (new 1990) cal., compact variation utilizing double action, features Acculine barrel (3.86 in.), 14 shot mag., ambidextrous safety with decocking lever, blue or Starvel finish, all steel construction, 39.4 oz. Imported 1990-94.

$350	$295	$270	$250	$225	$210	$195

Last MSR was $398.

Add $30 for Starvel finish (disc. 1993).
Prices are the same for Model 31PK Dural Frame (imported 1990-93).

GRADING - PPGS™	100%	98%	95%	90%	80%	70%	60%

MODEL M40 FIRESTAR - .40 S&W cal., single action, 6 shot mag., 3.39 in. Accu-line barrel, checkered rubber grips, compact design utilizing all steel construction, 3-dot sighting system with adjustable rear sight, blue, Starvel, or nickel (new 1997) finish, 30.35 oz. Mfg. 1990-disc.

	$295	$250	$200	$180	$165	$150	$135

Last MSR was $306.

Add $17 for nickel finish.
Add $20 for Starvel finish.

✱ *Model M40 Firestar Plus* - similar to M40 Firestar, except incorporates alloy frame, new grip design, ambidextrous easy-view safety, and fast button release 10 shot mag. Advertised initially during 1995.

This model was never released for commercial sale.

MODEL M43 FIRESTAR - 9mm Para. cal., 7 shot mag., otherwise similar to Model M40 Firestar. Disc.

	$295	$265	$235	$200	$185	$170	$155

Last MSR was $296.

Add $17 for nickel finish.
Add $20 for Starvel finish.

✱ *Model M43 Firestar Plus* - similar to M43 Firestar, except incorporates alloy frame, new grip design, ambidextrous easy-view safety, and fast button release 10 shot double stack mag. Mfg. 1995-97.

	$325	$265	$235	$200	$185	$170	$155

Last MSR was $351.

Add $12 for nickel finish.
Add $25 for Starvel finish.

MODEL M45 FIRESTAR - .45 ACP cal., single action, ultra compact design featuring 4 barrel lugs, steel frame and slide, 3.6 in. reverse taper Acculine barrel, 6 shot mag., black synthetic grips, blue or Starvel finish, 35 oz. Mfg. 1992-97.

	$350	$300	$250	$200	$185	$170	$155

Last MSR was $351.

Add $12 for nickel finish.
Add $20 for Starvel finish.

✱ *Model M45 Firestar Plus* - similar to M45 Firestar, except incorporates alloy frame, new grip design, ambidextrous easy-view safety, and fast button release 10 shot mag. Advertised during 1995.

This model was never released for commercial sale.

MEGASTAR - 10mm or .45 ACP cal., larger variation of the Firestar featuring 4.6 in. barrel and 12 (.45 ACP) or 14 (10mm) shot mag., 47.6 oz. Imported 1992-94.

	$450	$375	$350	$325	$295	$275	$250

Last MSR was $653.

Add $29 for Starvel finish.

ULTRASTAR - 9mm Para. or .40 S&W (new 1996) cal., compact double action design, 3.57 in. barrel, 9-shot mag., blue steel metal, triple dot sights, steel internal mechanism, polymer exterior construction, 26 oz. Mfg. 1994-97.

	$325	$295	$235	$200	$175	$165	$155

Last MSR was $296.

STEEL CITY ARMS, INC.

Previous manufacturer located in Pittsburgh, PA until 1990. In 1991, the name was changed to Desert Industries, Inc. and manufacture was moved to Las Vegas, NV. Very few guns exist with Steel City markings.

GRADING - PPGS™	100%	98%	95%	90%	80%	70%	60%

PISTOLS: SEMI-AUTO

DOUBLE DEUCE - .22 LR cal. only, double action, matte finish stainless steel, 2 1/2 in. barrel, 7 shot mag., uncheckered rosewood grips, 18 oz. Mfg. 1984-90.

	$265	$230	$200	N/A	N/A	N/A	N/A

Last MSR was $290.

Various select hardwood stocks were also available at extra cost ($20-100).

STEINKAMP MASCHINENBAU GmbH & Co. KG

Current manufacturer located in Espelkamp, Germany. No current U.S. importation. Steinkamp manufactures a unique combination rifle/shotgun in three different configurations. Please contact the company directly for more information, including pricing and domestic availability (see Trademark Index).

STEERING GEAR (GRAND RAPIDS & SAGINAW LOCATIONS)

Previous WWII subcontractor of M1 carbines located in Saginaw and Grand Rapids, MI. Saginaw Steering Gear was a division of General Motors Corp.

Please refer to US Military carbines/rifles listing for more information.

STERLING

Previous manufacturer located in Gasport and Lockport (1978-1986), NY until 1986.

PISTOLS

Rather than list individual models, the following generalizations will help in ascertaining values for this trademark. Models 300, 302 and 402 will average between $75 and $150 if in 70%+ condition, Models 283, 284, 285 (Husky), and 286 (Trapper) are semi-auto .22 cal. pistols with various barrel lengths - values will range between $90-$150. Models 400 (.380 ACP), PPL (.380 ACP short barrel), and 450 (.45 ACP, prototype only - no mfg.) usually range between $150-$275.

STERLING ARMAMENT, LTD.

Previous manufacturer established c. 1900, and located in Dagenham, Essex, England. Previously imported and distributed by Cassi Inc. located in Colorado Springs, CO until 1990.

CARBINES: SEMI-AUTO

AR-180 - please refer to Armalite section for more information and pricing on this model.

STERLING MK 6 - 9mm Para. cal., blowback semi-auto with floating firing pin, shrouded 16.1 in. barrel, side mounted mag., folding stock, 7 1/2 lbs. Disc. 1989.

	N/A	$1,750	$1,500	$1,400	$1,200	$1,000	$795

Last MSR was $650.

PISTOLS: SEMI-AUTO

PARAPISTOL MK 7 C4 - 9mm Para. cal., 4 in. barrel, semi-auto paramilitary design pistol, crinkle finish, same action as MK. 6 Carbine, fires from closed bolt, 10, 15, 20, 30, 34 or 68 shot mag., 5 lbs. Disc. 1989.

	N/A	$1,500	$1,400	$1,200	$1,000	$800	$700

Last MSR was $600.

Add $50 per 30 or 34 shot mag., $125 for 68 shot mag.

PARAPISTOL MK 7 C8 - 9mm Para. cal., similar to C4, except has 7.8 in. barrel, 5 1/4 lbs. Disc. 1989.

	N/A	$1,500	$1,400	$1,250	$1,050	$900	$750

Last MSR was $620.

Add $50 per 30 or 34 shot mag., $125 for 68 shot mag.

GRADING - PPGS™	100%	98%	95%	90%	80%	70%	60%

STEVENS, J., ARMS COMPANY

J. Stevens Arms Company was founded in 1864 at Chicopee Falls, MA as J. Stevens & Co. In 1886 the name was changed to J. Stevens Arms and Tool Co. In 1916, the plant became New England Westinghouse, and tooled up for Mosin-Nagant Rifles. In 1920, the plant was sold to the Savage Arms Corp. and manufactured guns were marked "J. Stevens Arms Co." This designation was dropped in the late 1940s, and only the name "Stevens" has been used up to 1990. Beginning in 1999, Savage Arms, Inc. began manufacturing/importing Stevens trademarked guns again, including rifles and shotguns.

Depending on the remaining Stevens factory data, a factory letter authenticating the configuration of a particular specimen may be obtained by contacting Mr. John Callahan (see Trademark Index for listings and address). The charge for this service is $20.00 per gun - please allow 6 weeks for an adequate response.

For more Stevens model information, please refer to the Serialization section in the back of this text.

COMBINATION GUNS

MODEL 22-410 - .22 LR cal. over .410 bore, selector on right side of frame, Tenite stock. Introduced mid-1939-disc.

$425	$375	$300	$250	$200	$165	$140

PISTOLS

NO. 10 TARGET SINGLE SHOT - .22 LR cal., 8 in. barrel, blue, adj. sights, rubber grips, squared-off like an automatic pistol, tip up action. Mfg. 1919-39.

$220	$200	$185	$165	$140	$120	$100

NO. 35 TARGET SINGLE SHOT - .22 LR or .25 Rimfire cal., 6, 8, 10, or 12 1/4 in. barrel, blue, walnut grips. Mfg. 1907-39.

$350	$300	$265	$220	$200	$185	$165

NO. 35 "OFF-HAND" SHOTGUN - .410 smoothbore cal., 8 or 12 1/4 in. barrel. Mfg. 1923-35.

$350	$300	$250	$225	$200	$150	$125

If this model is not currently registered with the ATF, it cannot be legally owned, and is subject to seizure.

NO. 35 "OFF-HAND" AUTOSHOT - similar to Off-Hand Shotgun. Mfg. 1929-34.

$300	$250	$225	$200	$150	$125	$100

RIFLES

Stevens made a wide variety of inexpensive, utilitarian rifles that, to date, have attracted mostly shooting interest, but little collector interest. A listing of these models may be found in the back of this text under "Serialization."

TIP-UP RIFLES - .22 S, .22 LR, .25 Stevens, .32, .38, or .44 Long RF or CF, variations No. 1 - No. 15 feature various weights, wood styles, sights, and other differences, later series has full loop at rear triggerguard, circa 1870s-95.

* *Tip-Up Rifle Basic Model No. 1 without forearm*

$500	$475	$425	$375	$300	$250	$200

* *Tip-Up Rifle Model 101* - .44 shot cartridge, built on the No. 12 Marksman action, lever action opening, straight grip stock, 26 in. barrel. Mfg. 1914-20.

$250	$225	$195	$175	$150	$125	$100

NO. 12 MARKSMAN - .22 LR, .25 Long or .32 rimfire cal., boys type single shot with traditional Stevens profile, operated with underlever that allows barrel to tip up for loading, 22 in. round tapered barrel, walnut stock and forend, silver blade front sight and "V" block rear sight, knurled thumbscrew for take-down. Mfg. 1912-1933.

$425	$350	$275	$240	$215	$185	$160

GRADING - PPGS™	100%	98%	95%	90%	80%	70%	60%

NO. 14 1/2 LITTLE SCOUT - .22 RF cal., 18 or 20 in. barrel, rolling breech block action, iron sights. Mfg. 1909-36.

	$425	$350	$275	$240	$215	$185	$160

STEVENS/SPRINGFIELD MODEL 15/120 - .22 S, L, or LR, bolt action single shot, one piece integral barrel and receiver, manually operated cocking piece at rear of bolt, birch hardwood stock, open rear and bead front sight, thousands mfg. for companies such as Sears, Montgomery Wards, J.C. Penny, Cotter & Co., etc. Mfg. 1936-1971.

	$200	$185	$165	$135	$115	$95	$80

POCKET RIFLES - detachable serially numbered nickel-plated stock, variations found within each frame size.

✳ *Pocket Rifle Small Frame* - .22 cal. (various issues).

	$450	$400	$350	$300	$275	$235	$200

✳ *Pocket Rifle Small Frame Without Stock*

	$300	$250	$200	$150	$125	$100	$80

✳ *Pocket Rifle Medium Frame* - .22, .32, .38, .44 cals. (various issues).

	$500	$450	$400	$350	$300	$250	$200

✳ *Pocket Rifle Medium Frame Without Stock*

	$300	$250	$200	$150	$125	$100	$75

✳ *Pocket Rifle Large Frame* - .22 to .44 cals.

	$600	$550	$500	$450	$400	$350	$300

✳ *Pocket Rifle Large Frame Without Stock*

	$425	$375	$325	$275	$225	$200	$175

MODEL 44 IDEAL SINGLE SHOT - .22 LR through .44-40 WCF cals., rolling block, lever action, takedown, 24 or 26 in. barrels, straight grip stock and forearm. Mfg. 1894-1932.

	$650	$600	$550	$500	$425	$325	$300

Subtract 20% for Rimfire cals.

MODEL 44 1/2 IDEAL SINGLE SHOT - similar to Model 44, except .22 LR through .44-40 WCF cals., falling block, lever action, takedown, 24 or 26 in. barrels, straight grip stock and forearm, action redesigned 1903. Mfg. 1903-16.

	$950	$850	$750	$625	$500	$425	$350

Subtract 10% for rimfire cals.

MODELS 45-54 SINGLE SHOTS - .22 LR through .44-40 WCF cals., rolling and falling block receivers, lever action, takedown, deluxe versions of the Models 44 and 44 1/2, many special order features, including double-set triggers, types of finish, engraving, length and weight of barrels, stock configuration could be special ordered. The higher grade Schuetzens and Stevens-Pope are very collectible and command premiums. These models have to be taken one at a time for determining value. Therefore, no prices are shown. Mfg. 1896-1916.

MODEL 200 BOLT ACTION - .22-250 Rem., .223 Rem., .243 Win., .25-06 Rem., .270 Win., .30-06, .308 Win., .300 Win. Mag., 7mm-08 Rem., or 7mm Rem. Mag. cal., short or long action, no sights, 3 or 4 shot internal mag., AccuTrigger not available on this model, 22 or 24 in. barrel, checkered synthetic stock and forend with pillar bedding, Stevens laser etched on bolt, 6 1/2 lbs. New 2005.

MSR $346	$275	$235	$200	$180	$165	$150	$135

MODEL 300 BOLT ACTION - .22 LR cal., 20 3/4 in. barrel, AccuTrigger not available, 10 shot detachable mag., grey checkered synthetic stock, adj. rear sight, swivel studs, approx. 5 lbs. New 2006.

MSR $160	$130	$115	$90	$75	$65	$55	$45

Add $7 for 4x15mm scope.

GRADING - PPGS™	100%	98%	95%	90%	80%	70%	60%

MODEL 305 BOLT ACTION - .22 Win. Mag. cal., similar to Model 300 bolt action, except has 22 in. barrel and 5 shot mag. New 2006.

MSR $209	$175	$145	$125	$100	$85	$70	$55

MODEL 310 BOLT ACTION - .17 HMR cal., similar to Model 305 bolt action, except has 21 in. standard or heavy barrel w/o sights. New 2006.

MSR $213	$175	$155	$125	$100	$85	$70	$55

Add $31 for heavy barrel.

MODEL 315 BOLT ACTION YOUTH - .22 LR cal., single shot, uncheckered hardwood stock, shortened Youth dimensions, 19 in. barrel, 5 lbs. New 2006.

MSR $175	$135	$115	$90	$75	$65	$55	$45

CADET BOLT ACTION - .22 LR cal., does not have AccuTrigger, single shot mini-Youth Model with 16 in. barrel, shortened hardwood stock, fixed sights w/rear aperture sight, 4 1/2 lbs. New 2006.

MSR $179	$140	$115	$95	$80	$70	$65	$60

MODEL 322 BOLT ACTION (INCLUDING A, B, C, & S) - .22 Hornet cal., otherwise similar to Model 325. Mfg. 1947-50.

	$450	$395	$335	$275	$225	$185	$150

The Model 322S had an aperture sight.

MODEL 325 BOLT ACTION (INCLUDING A, B, C) - .30-30 Win. cal., 4 shot detachable mag. Introduced 1947. Disc. 1950.

	$375	$335	$275	$225	$185	$150	$135

NO. 414 ARMORY MODEL - .22 LR or .22 Short cal. only, lever action, 26 in. barrel, single shot, Lyman aperture sight. Mfg. 1912-32.

	$450	$400	$375	$330	$290	$250	$220

MODEL 416 - .22 LR cal., bolt action, 25 in. medium barrel, 5 shot mag. Disc.

	$140	$120	$110	$100	$90	$80	$70

This model was also mfg. as a U.S. military training rifle. Can be denoted by "U.S. Property" on rear of bolt housing. Healthy premiums exist for this variation. Originally, 10,000 were mfg. at a cost of $22.42 each.

NO. 417 WALNUT HILL MODEL - .22 LR, .22 Short, and .22 Hornet cal., lever action, 28 or 29 in. extra heavy barrel, target stock with full pistol grip, beavertail forend, made in 0-3 suffix variations (different sights). Mfg. 1932-47.

	$875	$675	$525	$475	$440	$395	$360

NO. 417 1/2 WALNUT HILL MODEL - similar to No. 417, except available in .25 rimfire also. Mfg. 1932-40.

	$875	$675	$525	$475	$440	$395	$360

NO. 418 WALNUT HILL MODEL - .22 LR or .22 Short only, 26 in. barrel, pistol grip stock, semi beavertail forearm. Mfg. 1932-40.

	$950	$825	$700	$600	$500	$400	$360

NO. 425 HIGH POWER LEVER ACTION RIFLE - .25, .30, .32, or .35 Rem. cals., 22 in. round barrel with 2/3 length mag. tube, side ejection, blue only, plain walnut stock and forearm, originally designed by John Redfield. Approx. 26,000 mfg. 1910-17.

	$650	$595	$535	$465	$400	$350	$295

Variations of the No. 425 include the No. 430 (deluxe checkered stock and forearm), No. 435 (extra fancy checkered stock and forearm with engraved designs on receiver borders and lever), or No. 440 (best quality checkered walnut with fully engraved game scenes, and engraved forearm tip and lever). Values range respectively from $450-$950, $650-$1,400, and $1,000-$2,950.

STEVENS FAVORITE NO.'S 17-29 - .22 LR, .25 RF or .32 RF cal., 24 in. barrel most common, other lengths available, Rocky Mountain front sight, straight grip stock, small tapered forearm. Mfg. 1894-1935.

	$450	$395	$300	$195	$165	$145	$125

Add 35% for octagon barrels.

MODEL 1915 FAVORITE - .22 LR, .25 or .32 cal., redesigned of original Steve's Favorite, action slightly heavier and stronger, blue takedown frame, walnut stock and foreaarm, other internal changes, similar outward appearance, marked "SVG" after 1920, offered as the No. 27 with full octagon barrel, the No. 17 with round barrel, and the No. 20 with smooth bore barrel, 4 1/2 lbs. Mfg. 1915-1940.

	$450	$395	$300	$195	$165	$145	$125

STEVENS FAVORITE (CURRENT MFG.) - .17 HMR (Model 30R17, mfg. 2004-2005), .22 LR (Model 30G), or .22 Mag. (Model GM, mfg. 2002-2005) cal., choice of solid or takedown (new 2004) action, lever action falling block with inertia firing pin, 20 in. round or 21 (disc.) in. half octagon (Model 30G) or full octagon (Model GM) barrel, uncheckered wood stock and forearm, open sights, 4 1/4 lbs. New mfg. began in late 1998 by Savage Arms, Inc., limited availability beginning 2007.

MSR $291	$235	$190	$150	$125	$100	$80	$65

Add $38 for .22 Mag. cal. (mfg. 2002-2005).
Add $64 for .17 HMR cal. (mfg. 2004-2005).
Add $25 for takedown action (.22 LR or .17 HMR cal. only).

STEVENS MODEL 65 - .22 LR cal., bolt action, 20 in. barrel, open sights, 5 shot mag., checkered walnut stock. Mfg. 1969-disc.

	$90	$70	$55	$45	$35	$30	$30

NO. 70 "VISIBLE LOADING" SLIDE ACTION RIFLE - .22 S, L, or LR cal., exposed hammer, 22 in. barrel, open sights, straight grip stock, tube mag., grooved slide handle. Other variations with different barrel lengths and sights will command slight premiums.

	$550	$475	$400	$350	$300	$250	$200

MODEL 71 "STEVENS FAVORITE" COMMEMORATIVE - .22 LR cal., replica of original, 22 in. octagon barrel, plain straight stock, medallion inlaid, crescent butt. 1,000 mfg. in 1971.

	$250	$195	$150	N/A	N/A	N/A	N/A

Last MSR was $75.

SIDE LEVER CRACKSHOT - .22 RF or .32 RF cal., boys type single shot rifle, breech block is operated by a small lever on the side of the frame, side lever opening, 20 in. round barrel with fixed sights. Mfg. 1900-1913.

	$295	$235	$195	$150	$100	$60	$50

NO. 26 CRACKSHOT - .22 RF or .32 RF cal., boys type single shot rifle, under lever opening, 18 in. round barrel, hardwood straight grip stock and forend, open sights. Mfg. 1913-41.

	$295	$235	$195	$150	$100	$60	$50

MODEL 72 CRACKSHOT - .22 LR cal., single shot falling block action, 22 in. octagon barrel, open sights, color case hardened frame, straight stock. Mfg. 1972-89.

	$145	$125	$110	$100	$90	$80	$70

Last MSR was $165.

MODEL 74 - similar to Model 72 Crackshot, except has round barrel. Mfg. 1972-89.

	$140	$120	$110	$100	$90	$80	$70

Last MSR was $165.

GRADING - PPGS™	100%	98%	95%	90%	80%	70%	60%

MODEL 987 - .22 LR cal. only, semi-auto, 15 shot tube mag., 20 in. barrel, hardwood Monte Carlo stock, adj. rear sight, 6 lbs. Disc. 1989.

	$95	$80	$70	$60	$50	$40	$45

Last MSR was $119.

MODEL 83/083 BOLT ACTION - .22 S, L, LR, .22 Mag., or .25 Stevens rimfire cal., 24 in. round barrel, chrome bolt and trigger, walnut pistol grip stock, single shot, gold bead front and open rear sights (Model 83) or hooded front with interchangeable inserts and #105 rear apeture and folding middle sight (Model 083), 5 lbs. Mfg. 1935-1942.

	$175	$150	$125	$100	$85	$70	$60

Add 15% for .22 Mag., or 30% for .25 Stevens cal.

MODEL 87 SEMI-AUTO - .22 LR cal., tube mag., round tapered barrel, over 1.8 million made in numerous variations, including the Model 6, 76, 87, 187, 188, 60, 90, 88, 388, 887 and many others under brand names for Sears, Montgomery Ward, Western Auto, CIL, Coast to Coast, etc., model numbers include letter suffix added as changes were made. Introduced in 1938, and continued through the early 1980s.

	$150	$130	$110	$90	$70	$60	$50

MODEL 89 LEVER ACTION - .22 LR cal., single shot, 18 1/2 in. barrel, Martini type action, Western style lever, straight stock. Mfg. 1976-disc.

	$85	$65	$60	$50	$45	$40	$35

SHOTGUNS

Stevens made a wide variety of inexpensive, utilitarian shotguns that, to date, have attracted mostly shooting interest, but little collector interest. A listing of these models may be found in the back of this text under "Serialization."

NO. 20 FAVORITE - .22 RF or .32 RF smooth bore, 24 in. barrel, smooth bore variation of the No. 17 rifle.

	$250	$225	$200	$165	$125	$95	$75

NO. 26 1/2 CRACKSHOT - .22 RF or .32 RF smooth bore, smooth bore variation of the No. 26 rifle.

	$225	$200	$175	$135	$110	$85	$65

MODEL 67 SLIDE ACTION - 12, 20 ga., or .410 bore, all are 3 in. chambered, steel receiver, 5 shot, upper receiver safety, 6 1/4-7 1/2 lbs. Recent mfg. by Stevens. Disc. 1989.

	$200	$180	$170	$155	$145	$135	$125

Last MSR was $229.

Add $30 for choke tubes (with VR).
Add $10 for VR only.

✳ *Model 67 Slide Action VTR-K Camo* - 12 or 20 ga., 28 in. VR barrel with choke tubes, laminated camo stock. Mfg. 1986-88.

	$250	$220	$190	$170	$155	$145	$135

Last MSR was $295.

✳ *Model 67 Slide Action Slug Model* - 12 ga. only, 21 in. barrel, rifle sights. Disc. 1989.

	$200	$165	$140	$110	$100	$90	$80

Last MSR was $245.

✳ *Model 67 Slide Action VRT-Y* - 20 ga. only, 22 in. VR barrel with choke tubes, youth model with smaller stock dimensions. Mfg. 1987-88.

	$205	$170	$140	$110	$100	$90	$80

Last MSR was $259.

GRADING - PPGS™	100%	98%	95%	90%	80%	70%	60%

MODEL 69-RXL SLIDE ACTION - 12 ga. only, law enforcement version of the Model 67, 18 1/4 in. cylinder bore barrel with recoil pad, 6 1/2 lbs. Disc. 1989.

	$200	$165	$140	$110	$100	$90	$80

Last MSR was $245.

MODEL 77 SLIDE ACTION W/ J, K, M, OR SC SUFFIX - 12 ("J" suffix), 16 ("K" suffix), or 20 ("M" suffix) ga. or .410 bore, "SC" designates Super Choke. Mfg. 1955-1971.

	$175	$160	$140	$120	$100	$80	$60

MODEL 94 - 12, 16, 20, 28 ga., or .410 bore, single shot breakopen, hammer, 6 1/4 lbs. Mfg. 1929-disc.

	$95	$85	$75	$60	$50	$45	$40

Last MSR was $92.

MODEL 124 BOLT ACTION - 12 ga. only, straight pull action, 28 in. barrel, 3 shot, Tenite buttstock and forearm, circa 1950.

	$215	$190	$175	$155	$145	$135	$125

NO. 200 SLIDE ACTION - 20 ga., 3 in. chamber, tube mag., 26, 28, 30, or 32 in. barrel, take-down, 5 shot, 6 1/2 lbs., c. 1910.

	$225	$190	$180	$150	$125	$95	$85

MODEL 240 O/U - .410 bore, split hammers, double trigger.

	$350	$300	$250	$220	$190	$170	$155

MODEL 311 SxS - 12, 16, 20 ga., or .410 bore, 3 in. chambers, double triggers, extractors, VR. Disc. 1989.

	$275	$235	$200	$175	$160	$145	$130

Last MSR was $309.

Add 30% for .410 bore.
Add 20% for 16 or 20 ga.
Add 200% for early models in .410 bore w/walnut stocks and case colors.

* *Model 311-R SxS* - 12 ga. only, similar to Model 311, except has 18 1/4 in. cylinder bore barrels for law enforcement use, 3 in. chambers, 6 3/4 lbs. Disc. 1989.

	$245	$205	$185	$150	$140	$125	$115

Last MSR was $309.

MODEL 315 SxS - 12, 16, 20 ga., or .410 bore, DT, extractors, hammerless, case colored frame, walnut stock and forearm, model identification is on top lever, this model also was mfg. under various trade names, including Riverside and Springfield.

	$225	$185	$150	$140	$125	$115	$100

MODEL 411 SxS - 12, 20 ga. (disc. 2004) or .410 bore (disc. 2004), 28 in. monobloc barrels with choke tubes, boxlock action with laser engraved sideplates, SST, checkered walnut stock and splinter forearm, approx. 6 1/4 lbs., mfg. in Russia. Imported 2004-2005.

	$380	$330	$280	$235	$200	$180	$160

Last MSR was $438.

MODEL 512 GOLD WING 0/U - 12, 20, 28 ga., or .410 bore, boxlock action, 2 3/4 (28 ga.) or 3 in. chambers, 26 or 28 in. VR barrels, choke tubes (except for .410 bore), ST, Turkish walnut pistol grip stock, Schnabel forearm, fleur-de-lis checkering, blue receiver with light relief engraving and gold pheasant inlays. New 2007.

MSR $649	$525	$450	$400	$365	$335	$300	$265

MODEL 520 SLIDE ACTION - this model was designed by John M. Browning, slight humpback in receiver.

	$190	$180	$150	$125	$95	$85	$75

GRADING - PPGS™	100%	98%	95%	90%	80%	70%	60%

MODEL 520-30 TRENCH/RIOT MILITARY SHOTGUNS - see the "Trench/Riot Shotgun" category in the T section for more information and prices.

MODEL 530A SxS - 12, 16, 20 ga. or .410 bore, 2 3/4 in. chambers, boxlock action similar to Model 311, DT, extractors, 28 in. barrels, F/Mod. chokes, handcut checkered walnut stock, splinter forearm, case colored hardened finish, light engraving with dog, no ser. no.

| | $275 | $235 | $200 | $175 | $160 | $145 | $130 |

Add 30% for .410 bore.
Add 20% for 16 or 20 ga.

MODEL 620 SLIDE ACTION - an improved version of the Model 520 with streamlined receiver.

| | $275 | $240 | $215 | $180 | $160 | $135 | $100 |

MODEL 620 TRENCH/RIOT MILITARY SHOTGUNS - see the "Trench/Riot Shotgun" category in the T section for more information and prices.

MODEL 675 SLIDE ACTION - 12 ga. only, 24 in. VR multi-choked barrel with iron sights (including removable rear ramp), hardwood stock with recoil pad, 6 1/2 lbs. Mfg. 1987-88.

| | $250 | $220 | $190 | $170 | $155 | $145 | $135 |

Last MSR was $295.

MODEL 9478 - 10, 12, 20 ga., or .410 bore, single shot break open, inertia firing pin, external hammer. Mfg. 1978-85.

| | $95 | $85 | $75 | $60 | $50 | $45 | $40 |

FOX/STEVENS MODEL B SxS - please refer to this listing in the A.H. Fox section.

FOX/STEVENS MODEL B-SE SxS - please refer to this listing in the A.H. Fox section.

STEYR AUSTRIAN MILITARY

Previously manufactured for the Austrian military in Steyr, Austria.

RIFLES: BOLT ACTION

MODEL 95 RIFLE - 8x56R Mannlicher cal., straight pull bolt action, 30 in. barrel, adj. sights, military full stock.

| | $295 | $265 | $225 | $195 | $170 | $135 | $100 |

MODEL 90 CARBINE - similar to Model 95, except 19 1/2 in. barrel.

| | $395 | $360 | $315 | $275 | $225 | $175 | $125 |

STEYR DAIMLER PUCH A.G.

Previous manufacturer located in Steyr, Austria 1911 to circa 1960.

PISTOLS

POCKET AUTO - .25 ACP or .32 ACP cal., tip up barrel, mag. fed. Disc.

| | $400 | $300 | $250 | $200 | $175 | $150 | $125 |

Add 10% for .32 ACP cal.

ROTH STEYR AUTO (MODEL 1907) - 8mm Steyr cal.

| | $1,500 | $1,250 | $1,000 | $750 | $600 | $500 | $450 |

Add 30% for "Budapest" markings.

STEYR-HAHN MODEL 1911 AUTOMATIC - 9mm Steyr cal., 8 shot, 5.1 in. barrel, fixed magazine top loaded by stripper clip, blue, checkered wood grips. Mfg. 1911-19. In 1938, the Germans confiscated and converted a quantity of these to 9mm Para., "08" was stamped on the left side of these guns.

| | $650 | $550 | $450 | $350 | $300 | $250 | $200 |

Add 100% if marked "08" or with Rumanian Crest.

GRADING - PPGS™	100%	98%	95%	90%	80%	70%	60%

MODEL SP - .32 ACP cal., semi-auto, trigger cocking mechanism, very rare. Mfg. in 1959 only.

	$750	$650	$550	$500	$450	$400	$350

STEYR MANNLICHER

Currently manufactured by Steyr-Mannlicher AG & Co. KG in Austria. Founded in Steyr, Austria by Joseph Werndl circa 1864. Currently imported beginning mid-2005 by Steyr Arms, Inc., located in Cumming, GA. Previously imported 2004-mid-2005 by Steyr USA, located in West Point, MS. Previously imported 2002-2003 by Dynamit Nobel, located in Closter, NJ. Previously imported and distributed until 2002 by Gun South, Inc. (GSI) located in Trussville, AL.

Note: also see Mannlicher Schoenauer in the M section for pre-WWII models.

For more information and current pricing on both new and used Steyr airguns, please refer to the *Blue Book of Airguns* by Dr. Robert Beeman & John Allen (also online).

PISTOLS: SEMI-AUTO

MODEL GB - 9mm Para. cal., double action, 18 shot mag., gas delayed blowback action, non-glare checkered plastic grips, 5 1/4 in. barrel with Polygon rifling, matte finish, steel construction, 2 lbs. 6 oz. Importation disc. 1988.

Commercial	$675	$600	$525	$450	$400	$350	$300
Military	$795	$725	$650	$600	$525	$450	$400

Last MSR was $514.

In 1987, Steyr mfg. a military variation of the Model GB featuring a phosphate finish - only 937 were imported into the U.S.

MODEL SPP - 9mm Para. cal., single action semi-auto, delayed blow back system with rotating 5.9 in. barrel, 15 or 30 shot mag., utilizes synthetic materials and advanced ergonomics, adj. sights, grooved receiver for scope mounting, matte black finish, 44 oz. Limited importation 1992-93.

	$800	$675	$600	$550	$495	$450	$400

Last MSR was $895.

MODEL M SERIES - 9mm Para., .357 SIG, or .40 S&W cal., features first integrated limited access key lock safety in a semi-auto pistol, 3 different safety conditions, black synthetic frame, 10 shot mag., matte black finish, loaded chamber indicator, triangle/trapezoid sights, 28 oz. Limited importation 1999-2002.

	$440	$395	$360	$330	$300	$275	$250

Last MSR was $610.

Add $65 for night sights.

M-A1 SERIES - .357 SIG (M357 A-1), 9mm Para. (M9 A-1), or .40 S&W (M40 A-1) cal., DAO, updated Model M with Picatinny rail on lower front of frame, redesigned grip frame, trigger safety and lockable safety system, black polymer frame with matte black finished slide, 3 1/2 (not available in .357 SIG cal.) or 4 in. barrel, 10, 12 (.40 S&W or .357 SIG) or 15 (9mm Para.) shot mag., white outlined triangular sights, approx. 27 oz. Importation began 2004.

MSR $669	$550	$475	$425	$375	$325	$295	$275

Add $23 for right angle sights with Trilux (disc.)
Add $40 for night sights.

MODEL S - similar to Model M, except has 3 1/2 in. barrel and shorter grip frame, 10 shot mag., 22 1/2 oz. Limited importation 2000-2002.

	$475	$435	$385	$350	$325	$300	$280

Last MSR was $610.

GRADING - PPGS™	100%	98%	95%	90%	80%	70%	60%

RIFLES: BOLT ACTION, RECENT PRODUCTION

Current production guns are now called Steyr-Mannlicher models. For models manufactured 1903 - 1971, please refer to the Mannlicher Schoenauer Sporting Rifles section in this text. All known calibers are listed for each model. Caliber offerings varied often throughout the 28 year run of the Steyr-Mannlicher, stock designs evolved, and sights and magazine styles changed. The only truly rare caliber is the 6mm Rem., which was always special order. Next in North American rarity is the .25-06. Certain additional European calibers are rare in the USA because they were not imported due to lack of popularity - 5.6x57mm, 6.5x57mm, 6x62mm Freres, 6.5x65mm, and 9.3x62mm.

All four action lengths, SL, L, M, S, were offered in numerous deluxe variations with engraving and stock carving on special order blued metal and highly polished engraved actions. Stock carving is heavy and elegant.

A major irritant for hardcore Steyr-Mannlicher collectors is the continued misidentification of Luxus models by online sellers. First, a standard USA version Luxus has the word "Luxus" engraved on the left side of the receiver. A Luxus also has a steel box magazine instead of a rotary plastic one and a rotary shotgun style safety, although some apparently early Luxus models exist with the sliding side safety.

Pricing shows the result of continued cost increases at Steyr, which finally caused the end of the production run and redesign to the SBS-96 model to save costs, regain competition, and take advantage of improved safety features.

ZEPHYR 22 - .22 LR cal., features full length Mannlicher stock, single- or double-set triggers, open sights, checkered walnut stock with horn cap, sling swivels. Mfg. circa 1955-71.

	$1,350	$1,200	$1,000	$850	$725	$600	$525

MODEL M72 - 5.6x57mm, .243 Win., .270 Win., 7x57mm, 7x64mm, .30-06, or 308 Win. cal., available in rifle and full stock carbine versions, single and double set triggers, 5 shot rotary mag., this is a hybrid design resembling the original Mannlicher-Schoenauer with features from the new (1968) Steyr-Mannlicher Sporter to reduce costs. Mfg. 1973-circa 1980.

	$875	$795	$725	$650	$575	$500	$460

Last MSR was $525

✳ *Model 72 (Model S & S/T Mag.)* - 6.5x68mm, 8x68mm, 9.3x64mm, 7mm Rem. Mag., .300 Win. Mag., .375 H&H, or .458 Win. Mag., 4 shot rotary mag., half stock, 25.6 in. barrel, DT or optional ST, S/T Model has heavy tropical barrel, which was also optional in 23.6 inches, and only offered in 9.3x64mm, .375 H&H, or .458 Win. Mag. Mfg. 1973-1975.

	$1,750	$1,600	$1,450	$1,300	$1,150	$1,000	$900

Note: some rare catalogs show S and S/T Magnum action versions, though none appear to have been imported into the USA.

MODEL SL - .222 Rem., .222 Rem. Mag., .223 Rem, .22-250 Rem, or 5.6x50mm cal., available in carbine (20 in. barrel); rifle (23.6 in. barrel); and heavy barrel (25.6 in. barrel) with double set or single trigger and 5 shot rotary mag., 6.27 lbs. Mfg. 1968-1996.

	$1,400	$1,100	$900	$700	$600	$495	$450

Last MSR was $2,540.

✳ *Model SL Carbine Model* - same calibers as SL rifle, 20 in. barrel with full stock, early models possess slimmer stock design, 38 1/2 inches overall, 6.16 lbs. (some list 5.95 lbs.)

	$1,600	$1,200	$1,000	$900	$700	$650	$500

Last MSR was $2,450.

GRADING - PPGS™	100%	98%	95%	90%	80%	70%	60%

✶ *Model SL Varmint Rifle* - same calibers as SL rifle, 25.6 in. barrel, two heavy barrel varmint versions with either traditional heavy stock and heavy barrel or square forearm vented stock, double set or single trigger, no sights, 7.92 lbs.

	$1,625	$1,325	$900	$800	$650	$550	$500

Last MSR was $2,450.

MODEL L - 5.6x50mm, 5.6x57mm, .22-250, .243 WCF, 6mm Rem., or .308 Win. cal., available in carbine (20 in. barrel), rifle (23.6 in. barrel), and heavy barrel (25.6 in. barrel) varmint rifle, double set and single trigger, 5 shot rotary mag., 6.38 lbs. Mfg. 1968-1996.

	$1,500	$1,300	$900	$750	$675	$600	$540

Last MSR was $2,250.

This model is most often seen in .243 Win. and .308 Win. - special order calibers included 6mm Rem. and .22-250 Rem.

✶ *Model L Carbine Model* - same calibers as L rifle, 20 in. barrel with full stock, early models possess a slimmer stock design, 38 1/2 inches overall, approx. 6.2 lbs.

	$1,600	$1,300	$995	$825	$700	$600	$540

Last MSR was $2,450.

✶ *Model L Varmint Rifle* - same calibers as L rifle, 25.6 in. barrel, two heavy barrel varmint versions with either traditional stock and heavy barrel square forearm vented stock, double set or single trigger, no sights, 7.92 lbs.

	$1,600	$1,325	$875	$800	$650	$550	$500

Last MSR was $2,450.

✶ *Model L Luxus* - same calibers as L, stock design, magazine, and safety are different from other Steyr-Mannlichers, full or half stock with better checkering, rotary thumb safety, single set trigger, and in-line, non-rotary 3 shot steel magazine, open sights, available in full stock and half-stock versions. Mfg. 1980-1996.

	$1,700	$1,450	$1,100	$950	$800	$700	$650

Last MSR was $2,950 or $3,150.

✶ *Model L Luxus Carbine (Full Stock)* - similar to L Luxus rifle, except has full stock and 20 in. barrel. Disc. 1996.

	$1,800	$1,500	$1,200	$1,000	$800	$700	$650

Last MSR was $3,150.

MODEL M - 6x62mm Freres, .25-06 Rem., 6.5x55mm, 6.5x57mm, 6.5x65mm, .270 Win., 7x57mm, 7x64mm, .30-06, 7.5x55mm Swiss, 8x57mm, or 9.3x62mm cal., available in carbine (20 in. barrel), and rifle (23.6 in. barrel), double set and single trigger, 5 shot rotary mag. Mfg. 1968-1996.

	$1,500	$1,300	$900	$700	$650	$600	$540

Last MSR was $2,250.

Add $400 for left-hand action.

Special order and unlisted calibers varied and included .25-06, 6.5x55mm, and 7.5x55mm.

✶ *Model M Carbine Model* - 6.5x55mm, 6.5x57mm, .270 Win., .30-06, 8x57mm, or 9.3x62mm cal., full stock, 20 in. barrel, 7.26 lbs.

	$1,600	$1,400	$900	$825	$700	$600	$540

Last MSR was $2,450.

✶ *Model M Luxus* - same calibers as Model M, stock design, magazine, and safety are different from other Steyr-Mannlichers, full or half stock with better checkering, rotary thumb safety, single set trigger, and in-line, non-rotary, 3 shot steel mag., open sights, 7.7 lbs. Mfg. 1980-1996.

	$1,750	$1,500	$1,200	$900	$800	$700	$650

Last MSR was $2,950.

GRADING - PPGS™	100%	98%	95%	90%	80%	70%	60%

✱ *Model M Luxus Carbine (Full Stock)* - similar to Model M Luxus, except with full stock and 20 in. barrel. Disc. 1996.

	$1,900	$1,650	$1,300	$950	$825	$700	$650

Last MSR was $3,150.

✱ *Model M "1000 Year City of Steyr Commemorative" Luxus Carbine* - .30-06 cal., deluxe full stock, gold inlayed on receiver and trigger guard, single set trigger, in-line, non-rotary, 3 shot steel mag., open sights, approx 7.7 lbs. Mfg. 1980-1983.

	$3,650	$2,850	$2,400	N/A	N/A	N/A	N/A

Last MSR was $4,200.

MODEL ML-79 - .270 Win., 6.5x57mm (Europe), 7x57mm, 7x64mm, or .30-06 cal., apparently the European predecessor of the Luxus, extremely rare in the USA, marked on the receiver as ML-79, has the magazine and stock design of the Luxus with the sliding side safety of the standard Steyr-Mannlicher Sporter. Mfg. 1977-1979.

Extreme rarity factor precludes accurate pricing on this model.

PROFESSIONAL RIFLE - 6.5x55mm, .270 Win., 7x57mm, 7x64mm, .30-06, 7.5x55mm Swiss, 8x57mm, or 9.3x62mm cal., brown (disc. 1970) or green (new 1970) synthetic half stock, double set trigger, sights optional. Mfg. 1968-1993.

	$1,000	$800	$700	$600	$550	$500	$400

Last MSR was $995.

The 6.5x55mm cal. Professionals were totally unknown in the USA until a small lot was imported by GunSouth in the mid-1990s.

JAGDMATCH - .222 Rem., .243 Win., or .308 Win. cal., match rifle for European sports competition, special receiver Steyr SSG match type, laminated half stock only, 23.6 in. barrel, 5 shot rotary mag., single or double set trigger, 8 1/2 lbs.

	$1,600	$1,200	$1,000	$800	$725	$625	$550

Last MSR was $2,450.

MODEL S - 6.5x68mm, .257 Wby., .264 Win. Mag., 7mm Rem. Mag., .300 H&H, .300 Win. Mag., 8x68mm, .338 Win. Mag., 9.3x64mm, or .375 H&H cal., 25.6 in. barrel with half stock, 4 shot rotary mag.shot, double set or single trigger, optional with reserve magazine in butt-stock, 8.4 lbs. Mfg. 1968-1996.

	$1,600	$1,200	$1,000	$800	$725	$625	$550

Last MSR was $2,745.

✱ *Model S/T (Tropical Model)* - 9.3x64mm, .375 H&H, .458 Win. Mag. cal., 25.6 in. barrel with half stock, 4 shot rotary mag., reserve magazine in buttstock, double set or single trigger, 9.02 lbs. Mfg. 1968-1996.

	$1,750	$1300	$1,000	$800	$700	$600	$550

Last MSR was $2,850.

✱ *Model S Luxus* - same calibers as S, stock design, magazine, and safety are different from other Steyr-Mannlichers, full or half stock with better checkering, rotary thumb safety, single set trigger, in-line, non-rotary, 3 shot steel mag., open sights, 8 lbs. Mfg. 1980-1996.

	$1,950	$1,700	$1,500	$1,400	$1,200	$1,000	$800

Last MSR was $3,250.

MANNLICHER (STEYR) ULTRA LIGHT - .222 Rem., .223 Rem., .243 Win., .308 Win., or 7mm-08 Rem. cal., bolt has 4 locking lugs and a 70 degree bolt throw, 3-position roller tang safety, 19 in. fluted barrel, Weaver rail, 4 shot detachable mag., checkered European walnut stock with rosewood pistol grip and forend caps, approx. 6 lbs. Importation began 2004.

MSR $2,414	$2,100	$1,825	$1,475	$1,200	$1,050	$925	$800

GRADING - PPGS™	100%	98%	95%	90%	80%	70%	60%

MANNLICHER/STEYR SCOUT - .223 Rem. (new 2000), .243 Win. (mfg. 2000 only, reintroduced 2005), .308 Win., 7mm-08 Rem. (new 2000), or .376 Steyr (mfg. 1999-2000, reintroduced 2005) cal., designed by Jeff Cooper, features grey, black synthetic Zytel or camo (.308 Win. cal. only beginning 2005) stock, 19 1/4 in. fluted barrel, Picatinny optic rail, integral bipod, Package includes Steyr or Leupold (disc. 2005) M8 2.5x28 IER scope with factory Steyr mounts, and luggage case. New 1998.

MSR $2,186	$1,925	$1,700	$1,450	$1,200	$1,050	$900	$775

Add $53 for camo.
Add $414 for Steyr Scout Package with Steyr or Leupold (disc. 2004) scope, mounts and luggage case.

* **Steyr Scout Jeff Cooper** - .223 Rem., .308 Win. or .376 Steyr (disc. 2000, reintroduced 2005) cal., grey synthetic Zytel stock with Jeff Cooper logo and integral bipod, certificate of authenticity with test target, Package (disc. 2004) included Leupold M8 2.5x28 IER scope with factory Steyr mounts, and luggage case. New 1999.

MSR $2,600	$2,300	$2,000	$1,750	$1,425	$1,175	$1,050	$900

Add approx. 15% for Steyr Scout Package with Leupold scope, mounts and luggage case (disc. 2004).

* **Steyr Scout** - .243 Win. cal., similar to Jeff Cooper Package, except does not include scope, mounts, or case. Mfg. 1999-2002.

	$1,525	$1,350	$1,200	$1,050	$900	$750	$625

Last MSR was $1,969.

Add $100 for .376 Steyr cal. (black stock only, disc. 2000).
Add $100 for Jeff Cooper grey stock.

* **Steyr Scout Tactical** - .223 Rem. (new 2000) or .308 Win. cal., similar to Steyr Scout, except has black synthetic stock with removable spacers, oversized bolt handle, and emergency ghost ring sights. Mfg. 1999-2002.

	$1,600	$1,400	$1,250	$1,050	$900	$750	$625

Last MSR was $2,069.

❖ **Steyr Scout Tactical Stainless** - similar to Steyr Scout Tactical, except has stainless steel barrel. Mfg. 2000-2002.

	$1,650	$1,425	$1,150	$1,025	$830	$710	$590

Last MSR was $2,159.

MANNLICHER/SBS PROHUNTER MODEL - .222 Rem. (new 2004), .223 Rem. (new 2004), .243 Win., .25-06 Rem., .260 Rem. (mfg. 2000-2004), .270 Win., .280 Rem. (new 2000), .30-06, .308 Win., 7mm-08 Rem., 6.5x55mm, 6.5x57mm (disc. 1999), 7x64mm (disc. 1999), or 9.3x62mm (disc. 1999) cal., features safe bolt system (SBS), detachable mag., black synthetic or camo (new 2000) stock, matte blue finish, 23.6 in. barrel without sights. New 1997.

MSR $991	$895	$775	$650	$525	$465	$400	$350

Add $109 for camo stock (new 2000).
Add $152 for heavy barrel (.308 Win. cal. only, disc. 2005).

* **SBS ProHunter Model Magnum** - .270 WSM (new 2004), .300 WSM (new 2004), .300 Win. Mag., 7mm WSM (new 2004), 7mm Rem. Mag., 6.5x68mm (disc. 1999), or 8x68S (disc. 1999) cal., similar to SBS ProHunter Model, except has 23.6 in. or 25.6 (disc.) in. barrel. New 1997.

MSR $991	$895	$775	$650	$525	$465	$400	$350

Add $109 for camo stock (new 2000).
Add $152 for heavy barrel (.300 Win. Mag. only, disc.).
Add $150 for metric cals (disc.).

✳ *SBS ProHunter Model SS* - similar to SBS ProHunter, except has stainless steel barrel with matte finish. New 2000.

MSR $1,001	$850	$700	$600	$495	$430	$365	$315

Add $129 for camo stock (.270 Win. or .30-06 cal.).

❖ **SBS ProHunter Model SS Magnum** - similar to SBS ProHunter Magnum, except has stainless steel barrel with matte finish. New 2000.

MSR $1,195	$1,050	$850	$700	$600	$495	$430	$375

Add $100 for camo stock (.300 Win. Mag. or 7mm Rem. Mag. cal. only).
Add $165 for black finish (7mm Rem. Mag. cal. only, mfg. 2005).

✳ *SBS ProHunter Model .376 Steyr* - .376 Steyr cal. only, 20 in. barrel with iron sights, black synthetic or camo (new 2000) stock, matte blue finish. Mfg. 1999-2004.

	$695	$600	$500	$450	$395	$350	$300

Last MSR was $799.

Add $60 for camo.

✳ *SBS ProHunter Model Compact (Youth/Ladies) Rifle* - .243 Win., .260 Rem. (new 2000) 7mm-08 Rem., or .308 Win. cal., shortened stock with 2 butt spacers for adj. length, 20 in. barrel with iron sights, matte blue finish. Mfg. 1999-2002.

	$710	$640	$570	$500	$450	$395	$350

Last MSR was $819.

✳ *SBS ProHunter Model Compact (Youth/Ladies) SS* - similar to ProHunter Compact, except has stainless steel barrel with matte finish. Mfg. 2000-2002.

	$780	$675	$600	$495	$430	$365	$315

Last MSR was $909.

✳ *SBS ProHunter Model Mountain Rifle* - .243 Win., .25-06 Rem., .260 Rem. (new 2000), .270 Win., .270 WSM (mfg. 2004), .30-06, .300 WSM (mfg. 2004), .308 Win., .376 Steyr (new 2005), 7mm-08 Rem., 7mm WSM (mfg. 2004), or 6.5x55mm (new 2000) cal., 20 in. barrel, no sights, matte blue finish, black or camo (mfg. 2000-2002) synthetic stock, detachable mag. New 1999.

MSR $991	$895	$775	$650	$525	$465	$400	$350

✳ *SBS ProHunter Model Mountain Rifle SS* - similar to ProHunter Mountain Rifle, except has stainless steel barrel with matte finish. New 2000.

MSR $1,195	$1,050	$850	$700	$600	$495	$430	$375

Add $129 for camo stock (.243 Win., .270 Win. or .30-06 cal. only).

✳ *SBS ProHunter Model Tactical* - .308 Win. cal., features 20 in. barrel and 10 shot mag. Limited mfg. 2005.

	$850	$700	$575	$500	$450	$400	$350

Last MSR was $983.

SBS FORESTER MODEL - similar to SBS Pro Hunter Model, except has wood stock and standard blue finish. Mfg. 1997-2002, reintroduced 2005.

	$925	$800	$700	$600	$525	$425	$350

Last MSR was $1,051.

✳ *SBS Forester Model Mountain Rifle* - .243 Win. (disc. 2002), .25-06 Rem., .260 Rem. (new 2000), .270 Win. (disc. 2002, reintroduced 2005), .30-06 (disc. 2002), .308 Win. (disc. 2002), 7mm-08 Rem., 6.5x55mm (mfg. 2000-2002) cal., 20 in. barrel, no sights, matte blue finish, checkered walnut stock, detachable mag. Mfg. 1999-2002, reimported 2004-2005.

	$925	$800	$700	$600	$525	$425	$350

Last MSR was $1,051.

GRADING - PPGS™	100%	98%	95%	90%	80%	70%	60%

✳ *SBS Forester Model Magnum* - .300 Win. Mag., 7mm Rem. Mag., 6.5x68mm (disc. 1999), or 8x68S (disc. 1999) cal., similar to SBS Forester Model, except has 25.6 in. barrel. Mfg. 1997-2002.

	$720	$635	$565	$510	$450	$395	$350

Last MSR was $829.

CLASSIC MANNLICHER (SBS) HALF STOCK (AMERICAN) - .222 Rem., .223 Rem., .243 Win., .25-06 Rem., .260 Rem. (disc. 2002), .270 Win., .280 Rem. (disc. 2002), .30-06, .308 Win., 7mm-08 Rem., 6.5x55mm, 6.5x57mm, 6.5x58mm, 7x64mm, or 8x57JRS cal., features deluxe checkered walnut stock with full pistol grip and forend cap, deep blue finish, 23.6 in. barrel with exterior hammer forged swirls, with or w/o sights. New 2000.

MSR $2,132	$1,850	$1,575	$1,225	$1,025	$875	$750	$650

Add $113 for open sights.

✳ *SBS Classic Mannlicher Half Stock Magnum* - .270 WSM (new 2004), .300 WSM (new 2004), .300 Win. Mag., 7mm WSM (new 2004) or 7mm Rem. Mag. cal., 25.6 in. barrel. New 2000.

MSR $2,132	$1,850	$1,575	$1,225	$1,025	$875	$750	$650

Add $113 for open sights.

✳ *SBS Classic Mannlicher Half Stock Mountain* - similar cals. as SBS Classic Mannlicher Full Stock, features 20 in. barrel with open sights. New 2006.

MSR $2,269	$2,050	$1,625	$1,250	$1,025	$875	$750	$650

SBS CLASSIC MANNLICHER FULL STOCK - various cals., similar to SBS Classic Mannlicher Half Stock, except has deluxe full length stock and 20 in. barrel with sights. New 2000.

MSR $2,458	$2,175	$1,800	$1,500	$1,150	$950	$825	$675

✳ *SBS Classic Mannlicher Goiserer* - .270 Win., .30-06, or .308 Win. cal., similar to Classic Mannlicher Half Stock, except has iron sights and 20 in. barrel, 4 shot mag. Mfg. 2003-2005.

	$1,725	$1,325	$1,100	$950	$775	$675	$575

Last MSR was $2,014.

CLASSIC MANNLICHER ANTIQUE - various cals., 20 or 23 in. barrel with open sights, choice of half-stock or Mannlicher full stock. New 2006.

MSR $4,580	$4,100	$3,675	$3,200	$2,800	$2,400	$2,000	$1,650

Add $440 for Mannlicher full stock.

SBS TACTICAL - .308 Win. cal. only, 20 in. barrel w/o sights, features oversized bolt handle and high capacity 10 shot mag. with adapter, matte blue finish. Mfg. 1999-2002.

	$840	$735	$625	$550	$500	$450	$395

Last MSR was $969.

✳ *SBS Tactical Heavy Barrel* - .300 Win. Mag. (new 2000) or .308 Win. cal., features 20 (carbine, new 2000, .308 Win. only) or 26 in. heavy barrel w/o sights and oversized bolt handle, matte blue finish or stainless steel (carbine only, new 2000). Mfg. 1999-2002.

	$865	$745	$635	$550	$500	$450	$395

Last MSR was $1,019.

Add $30 for .300 Win. Mag. cal.
Add $40 for stainless steel.

✳ *SBS Tactical McMillan* - similar to SBS Tactical Heavy Barrel, except has custom McMillan A - 3 stock with adj. cheekpiece and oversized bolt handle, matte blue finish. Mfg. 1999-2002.

	$1,465	$1,245	$1,035	$850	$725	$600	$550

Last was $1,699.

Add $30 for .300 Win. Mag. cal.

GRADING - PPGS™	100%	98%	95%	90%	80%	70%	60%

* SBS Tactical CISM - .308 Win. cal., 20 in. heavy barrel w/o sights, laminated wood stock with black lacquer finish, adj. cheekpiece and buttplate, 10 shot detachable mag., vent. forend. Mfg. 2000-2002.

	$3,050	$2,650	$2,300	$1,950	$1,600	$1,300	$1,150

Last MSR was $3,499.

This model was also available as a Swiss contract CISM Match in 7.5x55mm cal. with match diopter sights and 23 1/2 in. barrel. Only 100 were imported. NIB Prices are in the $1,850 range.

STEYR ELITE (SBS TACTICAL) - .223 Rem. or .308 Win. cal., 20 (carbine, disc.), 22.4 (new 2006) or 26 (disc. 2005) in. barrel with full length Picatinny spec. mounting rail, oversize bolt handle, two 5 shot detachable mags. (with spare buttstock storage), adj. black synthetic stock, matte blue finish or stainless steel. New 2000.

MSR $2,833		$2,475	$2,025	$1,625	$1,275	$1,050	$875	$775

MANNLICHER SBS EUROPEAN MODEL - .243 Win., .25-06 Rem., .270 Win., .30-06 (disc. 1998), .308 Win., 7mm-08 Rem., 6.5x55mm, 6.5x57mm, 7x64mm, 7.5x55mm, or 9.3x62mm cal., features safe bolt system (SBS), 23.6 in. barrel with sights, checkered walnut stock and forearm. Mfg. 1997-99.

	$2,300	$1,850	$1,600	$1,325	$1,100	$925	$850

Last MSR was $2,795.

* Mannlicher SBS European Model Magnum - .300 Win. Mag., 7mm Rem. Mag., 6.5x68mm, or 8x68S cal., 25.6 in. barrel with sights, checkered walnut stock and forearm. Mfg. 1997-99.

	$2,375	$1,900	$1,625	$1,350	$1,100	$925	$850

Last MSR was $2,895.

* Mannlicher SBS European Model - "Goiserer" - similar to Mannlicher SBS European Model, except has 20 in. barrel. Mfg. 1997-99.

	$2,500	$2,000	$1,650	$1,350	$1,100	$925	$850

Last MSR was $2,995.

* Mannlicher SBS European Model - Full Stock - similar to Mannlicher SBS European Model, except has full-length Mannlicher stock. Mfg. 1997-99.

	$2,500	$2,000	$1,650	$1,350	$1,100	$925	$850

Last MSR was $2,995.

MODEL SSG - .243 Win. (disc., PII Sniper only) or .308 Win cal., for competition or law-enforcement use. Marksman has regular sights, detachable rotary mag., teflon coated bolt with heavy duty locking lugs, synthetic stock has removable spacers, parkerized finish. Match version has heavier target barrel and "match" bolt carrier, can be used as single shot. Extremely accurate.

* Model SSG 69 Sport (PI Rifle) - .243 Win. or .308 Win. cal., 26 in. barrel with iron sights, 3 shot mag., black or green ABS Cycolac synthetic stock.

MSR $1,989		$1,775	$1,500	$1,225	$1,000	$850	$725	$650

Add 15% for walnut stock (disc. 1992, retail was $448).

* Model SSG PII/PIIK Sniper Rifle - .22-250 Rem. (new 2004), .243 Win. (disc.) or .308 Win. cal., 20 in. heavy (Model PIIK) or 26 in. heavy barrel, no sights, green or black synthetic Cycolac or McMillan black fiberglass stock, modified bolt handle, choice of single or set triggers.

MSR $1,989		$1,775	$1,550	$1,300	$1,050	$875	$750	$625

Add $111 for rifle sights.
Add 15% for walnut stock (disc. 1992, retail was $448).

GRADING - PPGS™	100%	98%	95%	90%	80%	70%	60%

✳ *Model SSG PIII Rifle* - .308 Win. cal., 26 in. heavy barrel with diopter match sight bases, H-S Precision Pro-Series stock in black only. Importation 1991-93.

	$2,300	$1,875	$1,425	$1,050	$825	$700	$600

Last MSR was $3,162.

✳ *Model SSG PIV (Urban Rifle)* - .308 Win. cal., carbine variation with 16 1/2 in. heavy barrel and flash hider (disc.), ABS Cycolac synthetic stock in green or black. Imported 1991-2002, reimported beginning 2004.

MSR $2,456	$2,175	$1,825	$1,500	$1,250	$1,025	$875	$750

✳ *Model SSG Jagd Match* - .222 Rem., .243 Win., or .308 Win. cal., hunting rifle that features checkered wood laminate stock, 23.6 in. barrel, Mannlicher sights, double-set triggers, supplied with test target. Mfg. 1991-92.

	$1,550	$1,050	$950	$800	$675	$600	$540

Last MSR was $1,550.

✳ *Model SSG Match Rifle* - .308 Win. only, 26 in. heavy barrel, brown ABS Cycolac stock, Walther Diopter sights, 8.6 lbs. Mfg. disc. 1992.

	$2,000	$1,500	$1,225	$925	$800	$700	$600

Last MSR was $2,306.

Add $437 for walnut stock.

✳ *Model SPG-T* - .308 Win. cal., Target model. Mfg. 1993-98.

	$3,225	$2,850	$2,550	$2,200	$1,850	$1,500	$1,200

Last MSR was $3,695.

✳ *Model SPG-CISM* - .308 Win. cal., 20 in. heavy barrel, laminated wood stock with adj. cheekpiece and black lacquer finish. Mfg. 1993-99.

	$2,995	$2,600	$2,300	$1,950	$1,700	$1,450	$1,200

Last MSR was $3,295.

✳ *Model SSG Match UIT* - .308 Win. cal. only, 10 shot steel mag., special single set trigger, free floating barrel, Diopter sights, raked bolt handle, 10.8 lbs. Disc. 1998.

	$3,000	$2,500	$2,000	$1,800	$1,500	$1,200	$1,000

Last MSR was $3,995.

UIT stands for Union Internationale de Tir.

✳ *Model SSG 04* - .308 Win. or .300 Win. Mag. cal., 20 (disc. 2005) or 23.6 heavy hammer forged barrel with muzzle brake, two-stage trigger, matte finished metal, black synthetic stock, adj. bipod, 8 (.300 Win. Mag.) or 10 (.308 Win.) shot mag., Picatinny rail, adj. buttstock, 10.1 lbs. Importation began 2004.

MSR $2,717	$2,400	$2,050	$1,750	$1,350	$1,050	$875	$750

HS-50 - .460 Steyr or .50 BMG cal., bolt action, 33 in. barrel with muzzle brake, includes Picatinny rail and bipod. Importation began 2004.

MSR $4,275	$3,895	$3,500	$3,150	$2,850	$2,500	$2,250	$2,000

RIFLES: SEMI-AUTO

AUG S.A. - .223 Rem. cal., semi-auto paramilitary design rifle, blowback operation, design incorporates use of advanced plastics, integral Swarovski scope or Picatinny rail (24 in. heavy barrel only), 16, 20, or 24 in. barrel, bullpup configuration, black stock, 30 shot mag., 7.9 lbs. Importation resumed mid-2006.

MSR $1,568	$1,395	$1,250	$1,100	$1,000	$900	$825	$750

Add $142 for 24 in. heavy barrel with Picatinny rail and bipod.

Until the Aug S.A. is imported again in sufficient quantities, values will probably be closer to pre-2006 levels, which were $2,950 in 100% condition down to $1,400 in 60% condition.

GRADING - PPGS™	100%	98%	95%	90%	80%	70%	60%

✴ *AUG S.A. Commercial* - similar to AUG S.A., grey (3,000 mfg. circa 1997), green, or black finish.

	100%	98%	95%	90%	80%	70%	60%
SP receiver (Stanag metal)	$2,950	$2,750	$2,450	$2,150	$1,750	$1,575	$1,400
Grey finish	$3,150	$2,875	$2,600	$2,250	$1,825	$1,625	$1,450
Green finish (last finish)	$3,400	$2,975	$2,700	$2,300	$1,875	$1,675	$1,500
Black finish	$4,125	$3,750	$3,300	$2,950	$2,750	$2,500	$2,250

Last MSR was $1,362 (1989) for Green finish.

MODEL MAADI AKM - 7.62x39mm cal., copy of Soviet AKM paramilitary design rifle, 30 shot mag., open sights.

	100%	98%	95%	90%	80%	70%	60%
	$2,250	$2,000	$1,800	$1,600	$1,450	$1,250	$1,125

SHOTGUNS

MODEL 300 SxS - boxlock, cocking indicators, DT, pistol grip stock with cheekpiece, 28 in. barrels, selector switch to change from extractors to ejectors, sling swivels, light scroll engraving. Mfg. circa mid 1920s - late 1930s, scarce.

	100%	98%	95%	90%	80%	70%	60%
	N/A	N/A	$1,500	$1,300	$1,100	$925	$700

STOCK, FRANZ
Previous manufacturer located in Berlin, Germany.

PISTOLS: SEMI-AUTO

.22 LR PISTOL - .22 LR cal. Mfg. in Germany 1920-40.

	100%	98%	95%	90%	80%	70%	60%
	$295	$250	$225	$175	$125	$100	$75

.25 ACP PISTOL - .25 ACP or .32 ACP cal. Mfg. in Germany 1920-40.

	100%	98%	95%	90%	80%	70%	60%
	$295	$225	$175	$150	$100	$90	$80

STOCKWORKS
Please refer to Robert Hisserich Co. section.

STOEGER INDUSTRIES, INC.

Current importer/trademark established in 1924, and currently located in Accokeek, MD. Previously located in Wayne, NJ, until 2000. Stoeger Industries, Inc. was purchased by Beretta Holding of Italy in 2000, and is now a division of Benelli USA. Please refer to the IGA listing for currently imported Stoeger shotgun models.

Stoeger has imported a wide variety of firearms during the past seven decades. Most of these guns were good quality and came from known makers in Europe (some were private labeled). Stoeger carried an extensive firearms inventory of both house brand and famous European trademarks - many of which were finely made with beautiful engraving, stock work, and other popular special order features. As a general rule, values for Stoeger rifles and shotguns may be ascertained by comparing them with a known trademark of equal quality and cal./ga. Certain configurations will be more desirable than others (i.e. a Stoeger .22 caliber Mannlicher with double-set triggers and detachable mag. will be worth considerably more than a single shot target rifle). Perhaps the best reference works available on these older Stoeger firearms (not to mention the other trademarks of that time) are the older Stoeger catalogs themselves - quite collectible in their own right. You are advised to purchase these older catalogs (some reprints are also available) if more information is needed on not only older Stoeger models, but also the other firearms being sold at that time.

PISTOLS: SEMI-AUTO

PRO SERIES 95 - .22 LR cal., target pistol with choice of either 5 1/2 or 7 1/4 VR, fluted, or bull barrel, adj. rear sight, adj. trigger, push-button takedown, Pachmayr rubber grips, gold accents, 10 shot mag., 45-47 oz. Mfg. 1995-96.

GRADING - PPGS™	100%	98%	95%	90%	80%	70%	60%

✳ Pro Series 95 5 1/2 in. bull barrel

	$440	$375	$335	$300	$275	$250	$225

Last MSR was $495.

✳ Pro Series 95 5 1/2 in. VR barrel

	$515	$425	$365	$325	$285	$255	$225

Last MSR was $595.

✳ Pro Series 95 7 1/4 in. fluted barrel

	$455	$385	$340	$300	$275	$250	$225

Last MSR was $525.

COUGAR - 9mm Para. or .40 S&W cal., SA/DA operation, 3.6 in. barrel, matte black finish, 11 (.40 S&W) or 15 (9mm Para.) shot mag., ambidextrous safety, 3-dot sights, blue finish, checkered plastic grips, blowback action with rotating bolt, removeable front sight, mfg. in Turkey. Importation began 2007.

MSR $449	$375	$325	$285	$250	$225	$200	$180

SHOTGUNS: RECENT IMPORTATION

Please refer to the IGA section for currently imported Stoeger O/U, SxS, semi-auto, and single shot shotguns.

STONER RIFLE

Please refer to the Knight's Manufacturing Company listing in this text.

STRAYER TRIPP INTERNATIONAL

Please refer to the STI International listing in this section.

STRAYER-VOIGT, INC.

Current manufacturer of Infinity pistols located in Grand Prairie, TX. See the Infinity listing for more information.

STREET SWEEPER

Previously manufactured by Sales of Georgia, Inc. located in Atlanta, GA.

SHOTGUNS

STREET SWEEPER - 12 ga. only, 12 shot rotary mag., paramilitary configuration with 18 in. barrel, double action, folding stock, 9 3/4 lbs. Restricted sales following the ATF classification as a "destructive device." Mfg. 1989-approx. 1995.

	$895	$825	$725	$625	$550	$500	$450

Unless this model was registered with the ATF before May 1st, 2001, it is subject to seizure with a possible fine/imprisonment.

STURM, RUGER & CO., INC.

Current manufacturer with production facilities located Newport, NH and Prescott, AZ. Previously manufactured in Southport, CT 1949-1991 (corporate and administrative offices remain at this location). A second factory was opened in in Newport, NH in 1963, and still produces single action revolvers, rifles and shotguns.

Sturm, Ruger & Co. was founded in 1949 by Alexander Sturm and William B. Ruger to manufacture .22 cal. semi-auto pistols. The original factory was in a wooden structure located across from the train depot in Southport, CT. By 1959, the company moved into a larger modern factory not too far from the original buildings. The product line quickly expanded to a Target Model, single action revolvers, rifles, DA revolvers and shotguns.

From four separate factories, Ruger has manufactured and shipped over 20 million guns. The two Southport, CT facilities are no longer utilized. Guns are manufactured at the two large modern facilities located in Newport, NH and Prescott, AZ. Ruger is America's largest small arms maker, and offers a complete line of firearms for sports-

GRADING - PPGS™	100%	98%	95%	90%	80%	70%	60%

men, law enforcement, and military.

Mr. Alex Sturm passed away in November 1951. On July 6, 2002, the legendary William B. Ruger, Sr. passed away in his home in Prescott, AZ.

Beginning 1996, all handguns are supplied with a case and lock.

Please refer to the *Blue Book of Modern Black Powder Arms* by John Allen (also online) for more information and prices on Sturm Ruger black powder models.

Black Powder Reproductions & Replicas by Dennis Adler is also an invaluable source for most black powder reproductions and replicas, and includes hundreds of color images on most popular makes/models, provides manufacturer/trademark histories, and up-to-date information on related items/accessories for black powder shooting - www.bluebookinc.com

RUGER COLLECTIBILITY OVERVIEW

For the past two decades Ruger collecting has become very popular and as a result, many of the early pistols, revolvers and rifles are actively sought after. Some models and sub-models were produced in such small quantities that they were not cataloged. The engraving project in the mid-1950s produced 275 ornamented guns which are regarded as the holy grail of Ruger collecting.

Ruger firearms fall into three categories identified by the time frames they were produced; 1949-1963, 1963-1973 and those made from 1973 to date. In most instances the earliest time frame encompasses the rarest and most collectable specimens; certain of these guns command the highest prices.

The 100% condition pricing structure in this text assumes a gun that is new, or in mint condition with the original box and all paperwork included. Of course guns that are in lesser condition sometimes have the packaging and consideration should be afforded when establishing prices for them.

All Ruger firearms produced in 1976 were marked MADE IN THE 200th YEAR OF AMERICAN LIBERTY, collectors refer to them as "Liberty Models". Some guns that fall into this category will sell for a slight premium.

Some guns of all models can have special markings, "S" denoting sold as seconds, "D" duplicate numbered, "U" used, US on guns shipped to the military. A star designates a single cylinder. Foreign proof marks and ATF marked guns appear occasionally. A premium will be added to specimens featuring any of the markings. The premium will sometimes equal the amount of the basic price of the gun.

In 2002 the Ruger Studio of Art & Decoration was established and master engraver Paul Lantuch was designated as the director. Examples of engraved guns were produced from basic traditional engraving patterns to masterpieces valued at upwards of $50,000 and more.

PISTOLS: SEMI-AUTO, RIMFIRE

Many distributors and customizers have produced special/limited editions on this popular series of .22 cal. pistols. Individual companies should be contacted for current pricing and special order features/prices.

After 1999, all .22 cal. pistols were fitted with Ruger logo medallions with red background.

"RED EAGLE" - approx. 27,000 mfg. 1949-1952, distinguishable by recessed red enamel eagle in left-hand grip, most production occurred prior to Alexander Sturm's death (1951).

	100%	98%	95%	90%	80%	70%	60%
Standard Auto	$750	$600	$500	$400	$265	$235	$200
Target w/ 6 7/8 in. barrel	$675	$595	$525	$425	$375	$350	$300

Add $2,000 in 100% condition factor only for early 4 3/4 in. Red Eagle with wood "salt cod" box.

Produced until early 1952. Serialized approx. 0001 - 25,300 and 30001 to 35000 with Mark I Auto occupying blocks from 15,000-16,999 and 25,000-25,300.

GRADING - PPGS™	100%	98%	95%	90%	80%	70%	60%

STANDARD MODEL (POST RED EAGLE) - .22 LR cal., 9 shot, 4 3/4 in. or 6 in. barrel, blue, fixed sights, checkered wood or rubber grips with black or silver eagle medallion, ser. no. above 33,000. Mfg. 1952-1982.

	$295	$240	$175	$145	$115	$95	$80

Variations marked "HECHO EN MEXICO" are rare. Specimens in any condition have sold for as much as $1,500.

✴ *Standard Model (Post Red Eagle) Stainless Steel 1 of 5,000*

	$395	$350	$300	N/A	N/A	N/A	N/A

❖ **Standard Model (Post Red Eagle) Stainless Steel 1 of 5,000 w/California Freedom Inscription** - engraved "CAL. FREEDOM '82" on chamber, donated by Ruger to the California Citizens Against the Gun Initiative in 1982, and raffled to NRA members and CA gun owners, known ser. no. range is 17-03379 to 17-04792. 26 mfg., including one prototype.

	$725	$650	$575	N/A	N/A	N/A	N/A

MARK I TARGET - similar to Standard, except has 5 1/2 in. heavy barrel, 5 1/4 in. tapered (scarce) barrel, or 6 7/8 in. heavy tapered barrel, adj. rear sights, target sight. Mfg. 1951-82.

	$375	$325	$275	$225	$185	$150	$135
U.S. Marked (6 7/8 in.)	$775	$675	$575	$450	$325	$200	$165
5 1/4 in. tapered bbl.	$795	$700	$600	$475	$350	$225	$175

Add $100 for Ruger addressed muzzle brake.

MARK II STANDARD - .22 LR cal., 4 3/4 or 6 in. barrel, checkered black Delrin synthetic grips, blue finish, 10 shot mag., approx. 2 1/4 lbs., ser. nos. start at 18-00001. Mfg. 1982-2004.

	$225	$175	$135	$115	$110	$100	$95

Last MSR was $299.

✴ *Mark II Standard Stainless Steel* - variation of the Mark II Standard. Disc. 2004.

	$295	$215	$175	$135	$115	$100	$85

Last MSR was $390.

Serial numbers start approx. at 211-00001 and thereafter are intermixed with the blue model.

MARK II STANDARD 50TH ANNIVERSARY - .22 LR cal., features blue receiver machined to same contour as original production, stainless steel bolt with Ruger medallion on rear, 50th Anniversary Ruger crest on top of frame in front of ejection port, black grips with Ruger medallion in red background, lockable red case. Approx. 35,000 mfg. 1999 only.

	$300	$250	$200	$125	$115	$110	$100

Last MSR was $287.

MARK II TARGET - .22 LR cal., blued steel, 4 (mfg. 1996-99) bull, 5 1/4 (disc. 1994), 5 1/2 bull, 6 7/8 standard, 6 7/8 bull, or 10 in. bull barrel, single action, 2 5/8 - 3 1/4 lbs. depending on barrel. Disc. 2004.

	$295	$245	$205	$165	$130	$120	$110

Last MSR was $365.

Add $16 for 4 in. bull barrel.
Add $8 for 10 in. bull barrel.

✴ *Mark II Target Stainless Steel* - stainless variation of the Mark II Target, includes choice of 5 1/4 (disc. 1994), 5 1/2 bull, 6 7/8 standard, 6 7/8 bull, or 10 in. bull barrel. Disc. 2004.

	$355	$280	$210	$160	$130	$115	$95

Last MSR was $460.

Add $6 for 10 in. bull barrel.

GRADING - PPGS™	100%	98%	95%	90%	80%	70%	60%

MARK II MODEL 22/45 - .22 LR cal. only, Zytel frame is patterned after the Model 1911 .45 ACP Govt, 4, 4 3/4, 5 1/4 (Target, disc.), or 5 1/2 in. bull barrel, 10 shot mag. (push-button release), fixed (4 3/4 in. barrel only) or adj. sights, 28-35 oz. Mfg. 1993-2004.

* *Mark II Model 22/45 Blue Finish* - 4 in. regular barrel with adj. sights (Model P4, new 1997) or 5 1/2 in. bull barrel with adj. sights (Model P512). Mfg. 1994-2004.

	$225	$190	$165	$135	$125	$115	$100

Last MSR was $290.

* *Mark II Model 22/45 Stainless* - 4 3/4 in. regular barrel with fixed sights (Model KP4, new 1997), 5 1/4 in. tapered barrel (Model KP514 disc. 1994) or 5 1/2 in. bull barrel with adj. sights (Model KP512). Disc. 2004.

	$250	$210	$190	$165	$135	$125	$115

Last MSR was $315.

Add $65 for adj. sights (5 1/2 in. bull barrel only).

GOVERNMENT TARGET MODEL (MK678G) - commercial variation of the government training model without "U.S." markings, 6 7/8 in. bull barrel, adj. rear sight, blue finish, black plastic grips, 46 oz., individually test targeted. Mfg. 1987-2004.

	$350	$280	$210	$180	$155	$140	$125

Last MSR was $445.

* *Government Target Model (MK678G) Military "U.S." Marked* - blue finish, adj. sights, 6 7/8 in. bull barrel, U.S. marking on chamber, issued to U.S. military personnel, must be factory verified, ser. no. range 210-00001 - 210-18500. Disc. 1999.

	$750	$650	$450	$400	$360	$330	$300

Last MSR was $600.

* *Government Target Model (MK678G) Competition Slabside* - .22 LR cal., stainless steel, black polymer grips, 6 7/8 in. slabside barrel, adj. sights, drilled and tapped, includes two magazines. Mfg. 1992-2004.

	$400	$320	$235	$185	$145	$125	$105

Last MSR was $555.

* *Government Target Model (MK678G) Stainless Foreign Military Contract* - .22 LR cal., stainless steel, black phosphate finish, black polymer grips, with blackened Ruger medallion, 5 1/2 in. bull barrel (KMK512B) with narrow aperture rear sight and thin front sight blade, contract overrun of 84 pistols sold to domestic market, ser. no. range 212-89651 - 213-52645.

	$675	$575	$500	$450	$400	$350	$300

MARK III STANDARD - .22 LR cal., 4 3/4 or 6 in. barrel, the Mark III action is an evolution of the Mark II design, featuring a relocated mag. release button on the left side of the grip, behind the triggerguard, recontoured ejection port and tapered bolt ears, blue finish, loaded chamber indicator, internal lock, 10 shot mag. with disconnect, checkered composition grip panels, approx. 35 oz. New 2005.

MSR $342		$260	$210	$160	$125	$110	$100	$95

MARK III TARGET - .22 LR cal., 5 1/2 in. bull or 6 7/8 in. tapered barrel, adj. rear sight, operating mechanism is the same as the Mark III Standard, blue finish, checkered composition grip panels, approx. 42 oz. New 2005.

MSR $405		$315	$250	$210	$190	$165	$140	$125

* *Mark III Target (KMKIII) Stainless* - similar to Mark III Target, except has stainless steel construction, 5 1/2 in. bull barrel, 42 oz. New 2005.

MSR $512		$400	$315	$250	$190	$150	$125	$105

GRADING - PPGS™	100%	98%	95%	90%	80%	70%	60%

✳ *Mark III Target Government Competition* - features 6 7/8 in. slab sided bull barrel and brown laminated grip panels, 45 oz. New 2005.

MSR $589	$460	$385	$325	$265	$230	$210	$195

MARK III HUNTER - .22 LR cal., stainless steel construction, 6 7/8 in. target crowned fluted barrel, checkered cocobolo grips, V-notch rear sight blade, Hi-Viz front sights with interchangeable LitePipes, drilled and tapped, 41 oz. New 2005.

MSR $602	$485	$415	$360	$320	$275	$230	$195

MARK III 22/45 - .22 LR cal., Zytel frame is patterned after the Model 1911 .45 ACP Gov´t, push button mag. release, 4 (2,000 mfg., disc. 2005), 4 1/2, or 5 1/2 in. bull barrel, fixed dot or adj. sights, blue finish, tapered bolt ears, approx. 31 oz. New 2005.

MSR $314	$240	$185	$145	$125	$115	$100	$95

Add $2 for adj. rear sight.

✳ *Mark III 22/45 Hunter* - .22 LR cal., similar to Mark III 22/45, except has fluted barrel, green case, scope base adapter, six interchangeable Litepipes and lock. New 2007.

MSR $517	$400	$325	$250	$200	$160	$140	$120

✳ *Mark III 22/45 Stainless* - .22 LR cal., similar to Mark III 22/45, except is stainless steel, 5 1/2 in. bull barrel only with adj. rear sight, 35 oz. New 2005.

MSR $422	$315	$250	$185	$160	$145	$130	$125

"FRIENDS OF NRA" MK6 - .22 LR cal., high polish blue finish, NRA logo, faux ivory grips, "NATIONAL RIFLE ASSOCIATION" in gold on left side barrel, ser. no. range 221-78058 to 221-89364, 650 mfg. for NRA auction events in the U.S. during 1997.

	$525	$450	$400	N/A	N/A	N/A	N/A

"FRIENDS OF NRA" KMK6 - .22 LR cal., stainless steel with black enamel type ornamentation highlights, two-line "Limited Edition" appearing on one side of the barrel, two-line "NATIONAL RIFLE ASSOCIATION" on other side of barrel with NRA logo on rear of bolt, ser. no. range 223-76165 to 224-33634, 750 mfg. for NRA auction events in the U.S. during 2001.

	$525	$450	$400	N/A	N/A	N/A	N/A

KMK4 "ONE OF ONE THOUSAND" - .22 LR cal., stainless steel, produced as a commemoration of the last 1,000 Mark II pistols mfg. before the introduction of the Mark III series, ser. no. range 226-17150 to 226-18143.

	$350	$300	$250	N/A	N/A	N/A	N/A

PISTOLS: SEMI-AUTO, CENTERFIRE

LCP (LIGHTWEIGHT COMPACT PISTOL) - .380 ACP cal., DAO, hammerless, black glass filled nylon frame with molded checkering, blued steel slide, 2 3/4 in. barrel, 6 shot mag., .82 in. wide, black Ruger logos inset in grip panels, includes external locking device, 9.4 oz. New 2008.

MSR $330	$275	$240	$210	$180	$160	$150	$140

P85 - 9mm Para. cal., double action, 4 1/2 in. barrel, aluminum frame with steel slide, 3-dot fixed sights, 15 shot mag., ambidextrous safety or decocking levers, oversized trigger, polymer grips, matte black finish, decocking and DAO models were introduced during 1990, 2 lbs. Mfg. 1987-1990.

	$350	$295	$265	$235	$215	$200	$185

Last MSR was $410.

Subtract $30 if without case and extra mag.

Any P85 models without the "MKIIR" stamp on either the left or right side of the safety must be returned to the factory for a free safety modification.

GRADING - PPGS™	100%	98%	95%	90%	80%	70%	60%

✻ *KP85* - stainless variation of the P85. Mfg. 1990 only.

	$375	$315	$280	$230	$200	$165	$140

Last MSR was $452.

Subtract $30 if without case and extra mag.
Variants included a decocking or double action only version at no extra charge.

P85 MARK II - 9mm Para. cal., double action, 4 1/2 in. barrel, aluminum frame with steel slide, 3-dot fixed sights, 15 shot mag., ambidextrous safety beginning in 1991, oversized trigger, polymer grips, matte black finish, 2 lbs. Mfg. 1990-1992.

	$350	$295	$265	$235	$215	$200	$185

Last MSR was $410.

Subtract $30 if without case and extra mag.
Decocker and DAO models are not available in the Mark II series.

✻ *KP85 Mark II* - stainless variation of the P85. Mfg. 1990-1992.

	$375	$315	$280	$230	$200	$165	$140

Last MSR was $452.

Subtract $30 if without case and extra mag.
Variants included a decocking or double action only version at no extra charge.

P89 - 9mm Para. cal., improved variation of the P85 Mark II, 10 (C/B 1994) or 15 (new late 2005) shot mag., ambidextrous safety or decocker (Model P89D), blue finish, 32 oz. Mfg. 1992-2007.

	$380	$330	$280	$250	$215	$200	$185

Last MSR was $475.

Variants were available in a decocking (P89DC) or double action only (P-89DAO, disc. 2004) version at no extra charge.

KP89 STAINLESS - stainless variation of the P89, also available in double action only (disc.). Mfg. 1992-2007.

	$425	$360	$305	$250	$215	$200	$185

Last MSR was $525.

Add $45 for convertible 7.65mm Luger cal. barrel (Model KP89X, approx. 5,750 mfg. during 1994 only).

P90 - .45 ACP cal., similar to KP90 Stainless, except has blue finish, 8 shot mag., 33 1/2 oz.

MSR $557	$450	$375	$315	$260	$215	$200	$185

Add $50 for tritium night sights (disc. 2006).
P90 models were produced in a variety of models for law enforcement or government contracts and will be found with any combination of safety model, decocker or double action only with fingergroove tactical rubber grip and/or tritium night sights.

KP90 STAINLESS - .45 ACP cal., double action, 4 1/2 in. barrel, oversized trigger, aluminum frame with stainless steel slide, 8 shot single column mag., ambidextrous safety (KP90) or decocking (KP90D), polymer grips, 3-dot fixed sights, ser. no. began approx. 660-12800. New 1991.

MSR $599	$465	$395	$335	$275	$225	$200	$185

Add $50 for tritium night sights (disc. 2006).
This model was previously available in a double action only variation (KP90C, disc. 1992). KP90 models were produced in a variety of models for law enforcement or government contracts and will be found with any combination of safety model, decocker or double action only with fingergroove tactical rubber grip and/or tritium night sights.

KP91 STAINLESS - .40 S&W cal., similar to Model KP90 Stainless, except is not available with external safety and has 11 shot double column mag. Mfg. 1991-1994.

	$385	$335	$295	$240	$210	$180	$155

Last MSR was $489.

This model was available in a decocking variation (KP91D) or double action only (KP91DAO). Approx. 39,600 of all models were mfg. before being discontinued in favor of the tapered slide KP944 model.

P93D BLUE - similar to KP93 Stainless, except has blue finish, ambidextrous decocker, 31 oz. Mfg. 1998-2004.

	100%	98%	95%	90%	80%	70%	60%
	$395	$330	$285	$240	$215	$200	$185

Last MSR was $495.

Add $50 for tritium night sights.

P93 models were produced in a variety of models for law enforcement or government contracts and will be found with any combination of decocker model or double action only with fingergroove tactical rubber grip and/or tritium night sights.

P93 CHICAGO POLICE SPECIAL CONTRACT - produced in the late 1990s for a Chicago Police Department contract, this P93 was ordered with a special P89M rollmark on the slide so that those who were concerned about having a "compact" pistol would not be alerted to the fact that it was indeed a P93. Extremely rare in civilian hands.

Extreme rarity precludes accurate pricing on this model, and should be examined for authenticity. NIB specimens have been noted at $500.

KP93 STAINLESS - 9mm Para. cal., compact variation with 3 9/10 in. tilting barrel - link actuated, matte blue or REM (new 1996) finish, 3-dot sights, 10 (C/B 1994) or 15* shot mag., available with ambidextrous decocking or double action only, 31 oz. Mfg. 1994-2004.

	100%	98%	95%	90%	80%	70%	60%
	$450	$370	$315	$260	$220	$200	$185

Last MSR was $575.

Add $50 for tritium night sights.

KP93 models were produced in a variety of models for law enforcement or government contracts and will be found with any combination of decocker model or double action only with fingergroove tactical rubber grip and/or tritium night sights.

P94 BLUE - similar to KP94 Stainless, except has blue finish. Mfg. 1998-2004.

	100%	98%	95%	90%	80%	70%	60%
	$395	$330	$285	$240	$215	$200	$185

Last MSR was $495.

Add $50 for tritium night sights.

P94 models have been produced in a variety of models for law enforcement or government contracts and will be found with any combination of safety model, decocker or double action only with fingergroove tactical rubber grip and/or tritium night sights.

KP94 STAINLESS - 9mm Para. cal., available with ambidextrous safety, matte blue or REM (new 1996) finish, ambidextrous decocker, or double action only, 10 (C/B 1994), or 15* (9mm Para.) shot mag., 33 oz. Mfg. 1994-2004.

	100%	98%	95%	90%	80%	70%	60%
	$450	$370	$315	$260	$220	$200	$185

Last MSR was $575.

Add $50 for tritium night sights.

KP94 models have been produced in a variety of models for law enforcement or government contracts and will be found with any combination of safety model, decocker or double action only with fingergroove tactical rubber grip and/or tritium night sights.

P95PR - 9mm Para. cal., available in ambidextrous decocker (D/DPR suffix), ambidextrous safety (new 2001) or double action only configuration (DAO suffix, disc.), polymer frame, 3.9 in. barrel, fixed sights, blue finish, 10 or 15 (new late 2005) shot mag., lower Picatinny rail became standard in 2006, 27 oz. New 1997.

	100%	98%	95%	90%	80%	70%	60%
MSR $393		$315	$265	$230	$195	$165	$150	$135

Add $50 for tritium night sights (disc. 2006).

During 2006, this model's nomenclature changed from P95 to P95PR to reflect the Picatinny style rail.

P95 models have been produced in a variety of models for law enforcement or government contracts and will be found with any combination of safety model, decocker or double action only with fingergroove tactical rubber grip and/or tritium night sights. The P95DAO double action only model was disc. 2004.

GRADING - PPGS™	100%	98%	95%	90%	80%	70%	60%

KP95PR STAINLESS - stainless variation of Model P95PR. New 1997.

MSR $424	$345	$290	$245	$190	$165	$140	$120

During 2006, this model's nomenclature changed from KP95 to KP95PR to reflect the Picatinny style rail.

P97D - .45 ACP cal., ambidextrous decocker, 8 shot mag., blue finish, 30 1/2 oz. Mfg. 2002-2004.

	$370	$315	$275	$235	$215	$200	$185

Last MSR was $460.

Add $50 for tritium night sights.

KP97 STAINLESS - .45 ACP cal., similar to KP95 Stainless, except has 8 shot mag., 27 oz. Mfg. 1999-2004.

	$395	$315	$265	$235	$215	$200	$185

Last MSR was $495.

Add $50 for tritium night sights.

P345 - .45 ACP cal., ambidextrous safety or decocker (KP345DPR), black polymer frame with matte stainless or blue stainless steel slide, 4.2 in. barrel with fixed sights, polyurethane grips, slimmer profile frame, 8 shot single column mag., with or w/o Picatinny rail, loaded chamber indicator, 29 oz. New 2005.

MSR $544	$440	$385	$325	$270	$225	$210	$195

Add $29 for stainless steel w/o Picatinny rail (KP345) or $37 for stainless steel slide with Picatinny rail (KP345PR).

P944 - .40 S&W cal., similar to P93, ambidextrous safety, blue finish, 34 oz. New 1999.

MSR $525	$420	$345	$290	$240	$215	$200	$185

Add $50 for tritium night sights (disc. 2006).

P944 models have been produced in a variety of models for law enforcement or government contracts and will be found with any combination of safety model, decocker or double action only with fingergroove tactical rubber grip and/or tritium night sights.

KP944 STAINLESS - similar to P944, except is stainless steel, also available as decocker (KP944D). New 1999.

MSR $610	$475	$390	$330	$270	$230	$195	$170

Add $50 for tritum night sights (disc. 2006).

KP944 models have been produced in a variety of models for law enforcement or government contracts and will be found with any combination of safety model, decocker or double action only with fingergroove tactical rubber grip and/or tritium night sights. The KP944DAO double action only model was disc. 2004.

SR9 - 9mm Para cal., striker fired ignition, semi-double action trigger pull, 4 1/8 in. barrel, 10 or 17 shot mag., reversible backstrap, low profile 3-dot sights, glass filled nylon frame, choice of black stainless or brushed stainless steel, stainless steel slide, Picatinny rail, ambidextrous safety, 26 1/2 oz. New late 2007.

MSR $525	$450	$400	$350	$315	$275	$240	$210

Add $40 for black stainless finish.

REVOLVERS: SINGLE ACTION, OLD MODELS

Note: The following Rugers are known as "Old Models" (mfg. 1953-early 1973) and are instantly recognized by the three screws through the frame and the four clicks emitted upon cocking. They are now actively sought by collectors and some shooters who desire the smoother operation they afford.

Due to the Ruger Company's safety conversion program, many old model single action revolvers may be found without their original lockwork. If these original parts are not included with the revolver, deduct $85 for any Single-Six model, $110 for any Blackhawk model and $140 for the Super Blackhawk model. If your revolver has not had the safety conversion installed, please contact Sturm, Ruger & Company, Inc. and they will provide shipping instructions.

SINGLE SIX REVOLVER .22 LR cal., 4 5/8, 5 1/2 or 9 1/2 in. barrel, fixed sights, rubber grips, blue finish. Mfg. 1953-1973.

> Add $475 for Factory stag XR3 grips.
> Add $1,100 for Factory ivory XR3 grips.

> After 1962, only the 5 ½ gun was available as an LR only model (RSS5W). Walnut grips became standard equipment in 1961 and from 1961 to 1962 hard rubber grips were available only as an option on this model. Genuine stag and ivory grips were also available as an accessory for the XR3 grip frame and due to their rarity, authentication by an expert is necessary. XR3 grip frame changed to XR3-RED in 1962.

✳ *Single Six Revolver Flat loading gate* - 5 1/2 in. barrel only, approx. 60,000 mfg. from 1953-1957. Four variations.

	100%	98%	95%	90%	80%	70%	60%
	$750	$600	$475	$325	$200	$160	$150

> Add $300 for those serial numbered under 2000 with a non-serrated front sight.

✳ *Single Six Revolver 5 1/2 or 6 1/2 in. barrel, XR-3 grip frame* - with round loading gate, serial numbered up to approximately 194000.

	100%	98%	95%	90%	80%	70%	60%
	$450	$350	$250	$200	$120	$110	$100

> Subtract $50 (98% condition or better) for 5-1/2 in. barrel with XR3-RED frame (produced from approximately 194000 to 833352 and 20-00001 to 21-56105.

❖ Single Six Revolver Early 4 5/8 in. Barrel, XR-3 grip frame - .22 LR single cylinder, ser. no. range 126,600-189,000. Mfg. 1959-1963.

	100%	98%	95%	90%	80%	70%	60%
	$650	$550	$450	$300	$250	$200	$175

> A 4 5/8 in. gun of this variety originally shipped with an extra .22 Mag. cylinder will command a premium of at least $80 on this model (mfg. 1961-1962, ser. no. range 173000 to 189000).

❖ Single Six Revolver Early 9 1/2 in. Barrel, XR-3 grip frame - .22 LR only single cylinder, ser. no. range 139,000-175,500. Mfg. 1959-1962.

	100%	98%	95%	90%	80%	70%	60%
	$600	$500	$400	$300	$250	$200	$175

> A 9 1/2 in. gun of this variety originally shipped with an extra .22 Mag. cylinder will command a premium of at least $80 on this model (mfg. 1961-1962, ser. no. range 164000 to 193700).

✳ *Single Six Revolver Factory Engraved Model RSSE*

> Subtract $650 if w/o presentation case.

> Approx. 260 factory cased, engraved Single Six models were mfg. Seldom seen and among the rarest of Ruger revolvers, prices have been reported up to $6,500 for one of the more common Jerred patterns. The Jerred engraved blue grip frame (25 made) is currently valued in the $7,500 range, the Jerred engraved polished grip frame is currently valued at $6,500, and the Spanish engraved (22 made) is currently valued at $10,000. These values are for NIB, unfired examples.

✳ *Single Six Revolver .22 Mag.* - 6 1/2 in. barrel only, mfg. only three years, serial numbered between 300000-340100, left side of frame rollmarked in two lines with "RUGER SINGLE-SIX WIN..22RF MAG.CAL.". The last few thousand of this variety were fitted with XR3-RED grip frame.

	100%	98%	95%	90%	80%	70%	60%
	$450	$350	$250	$175	$165	$160	$150

> Add $30 if revolver was originally shipped as a convertible with extra .22 LR cylinder.
> A very few Mag. only Single-Sixes (not magnum marked) were produced after 340200. These are very rare and authentication through factory letter (as RSSMW) is necessary - add $75.

SINGLE SIX CONVERTIBLE - similar to Single Six, except .22 LR and .22 Mag. interchangeable cylinders, redesigned grip frame (XR-3 red), wood grips, 4 5/8, 5 1/2, 6 1/2, or 9 1/2 in. barrel with 4 5/8 in. being the rarest. Mfg. 1962-1972.

✳ *Single Six Convertible 5 1/2, 6 1/2 in. barrel*

	100%	98%	95%	90%	80%	70%	60%
	$450	$350	$250	$170	$120	$110	$100

> Ser. no. range for 5 ½ in. barrel begins about 194000.
> Ser. no. range for 6 ½ in. barrel begins about 340200.

GRADING - PPGS™	100%	98%	95%	90%	80%	70%	60%

✱ *Single Six Convertible 4 5/8 or 9 1/2 in. barrel*

| | $550 | $450 | $350 | $250 | $175 | $160 | $150 |

Ser. no. range for 4 5/8 in. barrel begins about 428000.
Ser. no. range for 9 ½ in. barrel begins about 360000.

LIGHTWEIGHT SINGLE SIX - similar to Single Six, except alloy frame, XR3 grip frame, 4 5/8 in. barrel, made 1956-1958. 200,000-212,000 serial range, can have alloy or steel cylinder.

| | $700 | $600 | $500 | $400 | $250 | $175 | $150 |

✱ *Lightweight Single Six Tri-color* - silver colored aluminum cylinder frame, ser. no. range 200,000-205,250.

| | $850 | $775 | $675 | $550 | $425 | $300 | $225 |

✱ *Lightweight Single Six Blue Alloy* - all blue with black anodized aluminum cylinder frame, alloy cylinder, ser. no. range 205,8238-207,300

| | $1,000 | $850 | $750 | $650 | $525 | $375 | $275 |

✱ *Lightweight Single Six Blue Steel* - steel cylinder, with black anodized aluminum cylinder frame, ser. no. range 206,200-212,534.

| | $650 | $550 | $475 | $400 | $325 | $250 | $175 |

✱ *Lightweight Single Six Tri-color* - "S" (seconds) marked (verified).

| | $1,350 | $1,100 | $875 | $725 | $600 | $475 | $350 |

SUPER SINGLE SIX CONVERTIBLE - similar to Single Six Convertible, except adj. sights. 5 ½ or 6 ½ barrel lengths std., Mfg. 1964-1972.

| | $450 | $350 | $250 | $155 | $140 | $120 | $105 |

Two of the most sought after rarities that exist in this model include a 4 5/8 barreled variety with prices ranging between $1,400 and $1,800. Another is a factory nickel finish 6 1/2 in. barrel revolver which can fetch $1,800-$2,500. Factory authentication recommended on both of these varieties.

BLACKHAWK SINGLE ACTION "FLATTOP" - .357 Mag. cal., 6 shot, 4 5/8, 6 1/2, or 10 in. barrel, flattop cylinder strap, adj. sight, blue, black rubber or walnut grips. Approx. 42,700 mfg. between 1955-1962.

	100%	98%	95%	90%	80%	70%	60%
4 5/8 in. barrel	$900	$750	$500	$400	$250	$225	$200
6 1/2 in. barrel	$1,000	$750	$550	$375	$350	$300	$250
10 in. barrel	$1,650	$1,350	$995	$850	$700	$600	$500

BLACKHAWK SINGLE ACTION - .30 Carbine, .357 Mag., .41 Mag., or .45 LC cal., this model is the 1962 variation with protected rear sight, ramp front sight, and 4 5/8 (.357 Mag., .41 Mag. or .45 Colt), 6 1/2 (.357 Mag. or .41 Mag.), or 7 1/2 (.30 Carbine or .45 LC) in. barrel.

	100%	98%	95%	90%	80%	70%	60%
.30 Carbine	$500	$400	$300	$215	$180	$160	$140
.357 Mag.	$500	$400	$300	$200	$170	$150	$130
.41 Mag.	$700	$500	$400	$300	$225	$185	$165
.45 Colt	$850	$600	$425	$325	$250	$200	$175
.357 Mag. w/brass frame	$750	$550	$450	$350	$275	$225	$200
.41 Mag. w/brass frame	$1,000	$750	$650	$550	$450	$350	$250
.45 Colt w/brass frame	$925	$700	$600	$500	$400	$300	$225

Add $500 for a .41 Mag. with brass frame and 4 5/8 in. barrel.

Note that the values listed above for revolvers with brass grip frames must be for guns that have been factory authenticated.

BLACKHAWK CONVERTIBLE - similar to Blackhawk, with extra cylinder, .357 Mag. and 9mm Para., or .45 LC and .45 ACP cals.

	100%	98%	95%	90%	80%	70%	60%
.357 Mag./9mm Para.	$650	$450	$300	$250	$225	$195	$175
.45 LC/.45 ACP	$1,000	$750	$600	$500	$325	$295	$275

Add $200 for .357/9mm Para with non-prefix serial number (103000 to 141000). Factory authentication necessary.

This model did not feature a brass grip frame.

BLACKHAWK FLATTOP .44 MAGNUM - similar to .357 Mag. cal. Blackhawk Flattop, except heavier frame and cylinder, .44 Mag., 6 1/2, 7 1/2, or 10 in. barrel. Approx. 29,900 mfg. between 1956-1963.

	100%	98%	95%	90%	80%	70%	60%
6 1/2 in. barrel	$1,250	$800	$625	$500	$350	$300	$250
7 1/2 in. barrel	$1,500	$950	$725	$625	$550	$475	$400
10 in. barrel	$1,950	$1,375	$950	$825	$700	$600	$500

Distinguishable from Super Blackhawk by fluted cylinder and rounded triggerguard.

SUPER BLACKHAWK - .44 Mag. cal., 6 1/2 (rare) or 7 1/2 in. barrel, larger grip frame and square back triggerguard, unfluted cylinder, adj. sights, walnut grips. Mfg. 1959-72.

	100%	98%	95%	90%	80%	70%	60%
	$650	$550	$450	$350	$200	$185	$175

For original two-piece black and red S47 box, add $110.

✳ *Super Blackhawk Early Variations*

	100%	98%	95%	90%	80%	70%	60%
Brass grip frame	$900	$700	$650	$600	$500	$400	$300
Dragoon frame 6 1/2 in. bbl.	$1,100	$700	$650	$600	$500	$400	$300
Dragoon frame white cardboard case/sleeve	$1,500	$1,000	$800	$700	$600	$500	$400
Dragoon frame, mahogany cased	$1,250	$850	$750	$650	$500	$400	$300
Long frame, mahogany cased	$1,850	$1,200	$1,000	$900	$800	$700	$650

For those 80- prefix guns that are factory verified as S47B, add $700 to the 98% - mint prices.
For a factory verified S47B with non-prefix serial number, add $1,500 to 98% - mint prices.
Note that the price listed above for the Brass grip frame model is for a revolver which is "unverifiable" from the factory.

OLD MODEL BEARCAT - .22 LR cal., 6 shot, 4 in. barrel, alloy frame, brass anodized trigger guard, blue, simulated wood grips w/o medallion on early models, models mfg. after 1963 had oil filled walnut with insert eagle medallion, 17 oz. Mfg. 1958-1970.

	100%	98%	95%	90%	80%	70%	60%
	$450	$350	$275	$225	$200	$180	$170
w/ alphabetical prefix	$500	$400	$325	$275	$250	$230	$215

Add 100%+ for blue anodized aluminum triggerguard variation (73,200-76,400 ser. no. range).
Numerous variations exist within this model incorporating production changes.

OLD MODEL SUPER BEARCAT - similar to Bearcat, except steel frame, made with brass anodized aluminum trigger guard (early model), or blue steel guard, 25 oz. Mfg. 1971-74.

	100%	98%	95%	90%	80%	70%	60%
	$450	$350	$250	$225	$200	$180	$165

HAWKEYE SINGLE SHOT - .256 Mag. cal., single shot, round cylinder replaced by rectangular rotating breech block, 8 1/2 in. barrel, blue, walnut grips, adj. sight, very rare, 45 oz., approx. 3,300 mfg. Mfg. 1963-64 only.

	100%	98%	95%	90%	80%	70%	60%
	$2,250	$1,600	$1,200	$800	$600	$550	$500

REVOLVERS: SINGLE ACTION, NEW MODELS

The following single actions are known as "New Models." They have 2 pins through the frame and cock without the clicks associated with Ruger's Old Model mechanism. The changeover occurred as a result of incorporating safety features. The "New Models" have a transfer bar similar to those found on modern double action revolvers and do not accidentally discharge if dropped. Manufacture started 1973. During certain years of manufacture, Ruger's changes in production on certain models (cals., barrel markings, barrel lengths, etc.) have created rare variations that are now considered premium niches. These areas of low manufacture will add premiums to the values listed on standard models. Beginning 1996, Ruger started supplying all New Model revolvers with a case and lock.

GRADING - PPGS™	100%	98%	95%	90%	80%	70%	60%

SINGLE SIX CONVERTIBLE - .22 S, L, or LR cal., includes interchangeable .22 Mag. cylinder, 4 5/8 (rare), 5 1/2, or 6 1/2 in. barrel, fixed Vaquero style sights, blue finish, approx. 34 oz. New 1994.

	100%	98%	95%	90%	80%	70%	60%
MSR $492	$415	$350	$300	$250	$215	$185	$160
4 5/8 in. barrel	$675	$525	$450	$375	$300	$250	$200

Add $11 for adj. rear sight.

* *Single Six Convertible Stainless Steel* - similar to Single Six Convertible, except is stainless steel. Mfg. 1994-97, reintroduced 1999 only.

		98%	95%	90%	80%	70%	60%
	$350	$255	$185	$165	$150	$140	$130

Last MSR was $415.

Add a premium for extremely rare 4 5/8 in model (only 3 known to have been produced).

* *Single Six Convertible 50th Anniversary* - similar to Single Six Convertible, 4 5/8 in. barrel only, cocobolo wood grips special high polish, and "50th Anniversary 1953-2003" Ruger logo, includes red plastic case. Mfg. 2003 only.

		98%	95%	90%	80%	70%	60%
	$325	$240	$190	$170	$155	$145	$135

Last MSR was $425.

SUPER SINGLE SIX "STAR" MODEL - .22 LR cal., so named because of star stamped on bottom of frame, blue or stainless, single cylinder (not convertible). Mfg. 1974-75 only.

	100%	98%	95%	90%	80%	70%	60%
Blue 5 1/2 or 6 1/2 in. bbl.	$470	$400	$350	$295	$275	$250	$225
Blue 9 1/2 in. bbl. (rare)	$595	$500	$450	$400	$350	$300	$250
Blue 4 5/8 in. bbl.(very rare)	$800	$750	$700	$625	$550	$475	$395
Stainless 5 1/2 or 6 1/2 in. bbl.	$495	$300	$250	$195	$165	$140	$120
Stainless 9 1/2 in. bbl.	$565	$450	$400	$335	$290	$245	$215
Stainless 4 5/8 in. bbl.(rare)	$600	$550	$500	$430	$375	$315	$270
Stainless 4 5/8 in. bbl rollmarked Liberty	$1,000	$875	$750	N/A	N/A	N/A	N/A

Only 300 Stainless 4 5/8 in. barrels were rollmarked "Liberty".

* *Super Single Six "Arrow" Model* - similar to Star Model, except produced with an arrow stamp (also looks to be in the shape of a house) on bottom of frame. Blue models only. Models SSR4, SSR5, SSR6 and SSR9. Mfg. 1986 only.

	100%	98%	95%	90%	80%	70%	60%
	$385	$335	$265	N/A	N/A	N/A	N/A

Add $200 for 4 5/8 in. or 9 ½ in. barrel.

SUPER SINGLE SIX HIGH GLOSS STAINLESS - 5 1/2 (disc. 1996) or 6 1/2 in. barrel, features high gloss stainless steel finish, simulated ivory grips became standard 1997. Mfg. 1994-97.

	100%	98%	95%	90%	80%	70%	60%
	$400	$300	$195	$145	$120	$110	$95

Last MSR was $425.

A model with simulated ivory grips (GKNR6-I) was also offered in 1996 for one year only. Last MSR was $425. Add 8% to pricing shown above.

COLORADO CENTENNIAL SUPER SINGLE SIX - 15,000 mfg. 1975 only, includes walnut case with medallion insert, stainless steel grip frame, 6 1/2 in. barrel, issue price was $250.

	100%	98%	95%	90%	80%	70%	60%
	$500	$350	$250	N/A	N/A	N/A	N/A

Although a single example has yet to be uncovered, rumors persist of a few of this model having the "MADE IN THE 200th YEAR OF AMERICAN LIBERTY" rollmark on the barrel in addition to the standard Colorado Centennial/US Bicentennial rollmark and the Sturm, Ruger & Co., Inc. rollmark.

GRADING - PPGS™	100%	98%	95%	90%	80%	70%	60%

SUPER SINGLE SIX - .17 HMR cal., 6 shot, 6 1/2 in. barrel with special crown, blue finish with adj. barrel sights, smooth rosewood grips, 35 oz. New 2003.

MSR $503	$425	$350	$300	$250	$215	$185	$160

✳ *Super Single Six Stainless Steel Hunter* -.22 LR or .22 Mag. cal., similar to Super Single Six, except stainless steel, 7 1/2 in. barrel, black laminate grips, includes Ruger scope rings, 45 oz. Mfg. 2004-2006.

	$475	$345	$290	$230	$200	$170	$145

Last MSR was $617.

SUPER SINGLE SIX CONVERTIBLE - .22 LR cal., includes interchangeable .22 Mag. cylinder, 4 5/8, 5 1/2, 6 1/2, or 9 1/2 in. barrel, 6 shot, similar to old Super Single Six, except has new interlocking safety mechanism previously described, adj. rear sight, 33 oz (w/5 1/2 in. barrel). New 1973.

MSR $503	$425	$350	$300	$250	$215	$185	$160

✳ *Super Single Six Convertible Stainless Steel* - similar to Super Single Six, except stainless steel construction, 4 5/8 (disc. 1976), 5 1/2, 6 1/2, or 9 1/2 (disc. 1975-rare) in. barrel.

MSR $567	$450	$400	$300	$200	$145	$120	$110
4 5/8 or 9 1/2 in. bbl	$595	$550	$500	$450	$400	$325	$250

Add 5% for "Friends of NRA" model KNR6-NRA issue of 750 produced in 2000.

✳ *Super Single Six Convertible Stainless Steel Hunter* - similar to Super Single Six Stainless Steel, except has 7 1/2 in. barrel, black laminate grips, integral scope mounts with one inch rings. New 2004.

MSR $711	$550	$425	$335	$265	$225	$190	$170

✳ *Super Single Six Convertible Hunter 17 HMR/17 Mach 2 Stainless* - includes .17 HMR and .17 Mach 2 cylinders, 6 shot, stainless steel, 7 1/2 in. barrel, black laminated wood grips, integral scope mounts with one inch rings, 45 oz. Mfg. 2005-2006.

	$530	$410	$330	$270	$230	$195	$170

Last MSR was $695.

NEW MODEL SUPER SINGLE SIX SSM - similar to original Super Single-Six except .32 H&R Mag. cal., 4 5/8, 5 1/2, 6 1/2 or 9 1/2 in. barrel, blue frame, 6 shot, adj. sights, wood grips, 32-35 oz. Mfg 1984 to 1994.

	$550	$500	$450	$400	$350	$300	$250

Add 20% if frame is marked "SSM" (5-1/2 in. and 6-1/2 in. most common although only one in 4 5/8" with this marking believed to have been produced).

NEW MODEL .32 H&R MAG. (SUPER SINGLE SIX SSM) - .32 H&R Mag. cal., 4 5/8 or 5 1/2 in. barrel, case colored frame or high gloss stainless steel (new 2001), 6 shot, fixed sights, choice of steel XR3-RED grip frame (later shortened) with faux ivory, bird's head with black Micarta grips (new 2002) or regular grips (simulated ivory became standard 2001), 32-35 oz. Mfg. 2001-2004, reintroduced 2006.

	$500	$320	$255	$210	$175	$160	$150

Last MSR was $535.

Add $41 for stainless steel or bird's head grip frame.
Add $40 for faux ivory or black micarta grips.
Subtract $41 for slim rosewood grips (disc.).

BLACKHAWK - .30 Carbine (disc. 1996, reintroduced 1998), .357 Mag., .41 Mag. (disc. 1996, reintroduced 1999), or .45 LC cal., similar to old Model Blackhawk, with new interlocking safety mechanism, 6 shot, 4 5/8, 6 1/2, or 7 1/2 in. (.30 Carbine and .45 LC only) barrel, 40-44 oz. New 1973.

MSR $525	$395	$295	$245	$210	$175	$155	$130

New Model .357 Mag. Blackhawks are serial numbered 32-00001 on up. New Model .45 LC Blackhawks are serial numbered 46-00001 on up. New Model .30 Carbine Blackhawks are serial numbered 51-00001 on up and the earliest .41 Blackhawks were serial numbered 41-00001 on up only to be included within the 46- prefix beginning in 1980.

GRADING - PPGS™	100%	98%	95%	90%	80%	70%	60%

✳ *Blackhawk Buckeye Special* - .32-20 WCF/.32 H&R Mag. cal., 6 1/2 in. barrel. Mfg. 1989.

	$650	$500	$400	$250	$220	$200	$180

Add 10% for limited edition Buckeye Special in .32/.32-20 cal. (mfg. for Buckeye Sports in 1990).

✳ *Blackhawk Stainless Steel* - .357 Mag. or .45 LC (new 1993) cal., 4 5/8, 5 1/2 (.45 LC only), 6 1/2 (.357 Mag. only) or 7 1/2 (.45 LC only) in. barrel.

MSR $642	$530	$375	$295	$250	$240	$200	$180

Add approx. 75% for .357 Mag./9mm Para. convertible pistols (300 were made in this model).

The 5 ½ in. .45 LC is very scarce in stainless, but is still being produced by Ruger in very limited quantity, so pricing above is still reflective of the model.

✳ *Blackhawk High Gloss Stainless Steel* - .357 Mag. or .45 LC cal., 4 5/8, 6 1/2 (.357 Mag. only), or 7 1/2 (.45 LC only) in. barrel, features high gloss stainless steel finish. Mfg. 1994-96.

	$395	$295	$250	$195	$165	$140	$120

Last MSR was $443.

All models are considered rare.

BLACKHAWK 50th ANNIVERSARY MATCHED SET - includes one .44 Mag. and one .357 Mag. revolver, 4 5/8 (.357 Mag.) and 6 1/2 in. barrel with gold roll-mark "50 Years of .44 Magnum", black checkered grips with medallions, matched serial numbers, collector's wood case. New 2007.

MSR $1,350	$1,175	$995	$875	N/A	N/A	N/A	N/A

50th ANNIVERSARY BLACKHAWK - .357 Mag. or .44 Mag. cal., 4 5/8 (mfg. 2005 only) or 6 1/2 (new 2006) in. barrel, flattop frame, smaller, pre-1962 XR-3 grip frame with checkered hard rubber grips with black Ruger medallions, cylinder indexing aligns loading gate cutout with cylinder borings, unobtrusive internal lock, "50th YEAR BLACKHAWK 1955-2005" gold rollmark, supplied with red case. Mfg. 2005-2006.

	$500	$365	$320	$280	$260	$240	$220

Last MSR was $605.

BLACKHAWK CONVERTIBLE - similar to New Model Blackhawk, except interchangeable cylinders, .357 Mag./9mm Para., .44 Mag./.44-40 WCF (disc.), or .45 LC/.45 ACP (disc. 1985, reintroduced 1999) cal., 4 5/8, 5 1/2 (.45 Colt/.45 ACP only), or 6 1/2 in. barrel.

MSR $599	$465	$375	$325	$265	$230	$200	$175

Add 30% for disc. convertible cals.

BLACKHAWK-SRM .357 REM. MAXIMUM - similar to New Model Blackhawk, except is chambered for .357 Rem. Maximum, 7 1/2 or 10 1/2 in. barrels available, target sights, 53 oz., 11,500 mfg. 1982-84 - production suspended due to unresolvable engineering problems.

	$650	$500	$400	$325	$300	$250	$225

SUPER BLACKHAWK - .44 Mag. cal., 4 5/8 (new 1994), 5 1/2 (new 1987), 7 1/2 or 10 1/2 (bull) in. barrel, 6 shot, blue finish, unfluted cylinder except for 5 1/5 in. barrel, walnut grips, similar to old model in appearance, but has new action, steel ejector housing was introduced in 2000, 45-55 oz. New 1973.

MSR $631	$475	$350	$275	$220	$180	$160	$150

Add $11 for 10 1/2 in. bull barrel (not cased).

The new model started with serial number 81-00001.

✳ *Super Blackhawk Stainless Steel* - stainless variation of the Super Blackhawk.

MSR $647	$500	$385	$270	$215	$180	$140	$120

Add $27 for 10 1/2 in. bull barrel (not cased).
Add $16 for hunter grip frame with laminate grip panels (disc.).

GRADING - PPGS™	100%	98%	95%	90%	80%	70%	60%

✴ *Super Blackhawk High Gloss Stainless Steel* - high gloss stainless steel finish, not available in 10 1/2 in. bull barrel. Mfg. 1994-96.

	$450	$350	$250	$195	$165	$140	$120

Last MSR was $450.

✴ *Super Blackhawk Stainless Hunter* - 7 1/2 in. ribbed barrel only, choice of standard or Bisley configuration, black laminated wood grips, includes scope rings and integral scope mounts (new 2002). Mfg. 1992-95, reintroduced 2002.

MSR $759	$675	$550	$400	$335	$280	$230	$200

A special edition of this model with wood grain laminated grips and lockable plastic case was available through Davidson's - retail was $639.

VAQUERO - .357 Mag. (new 1997), .44-40 WCF (new 1994), .44 Mag. (new 1994), or .45 LC cal., 6 shot, 4 5/8, 5 1/2, or 7 1/2 (not available in .357 Mag.) in. barrel, color case hardened frame, blue steel frame, barrel, and cylinder, steel ejector housing became standard in 2000, transfer bar hammer safety, smooth rosewood, smooth bird's head (mfg. 2001 only) or black Micarta bird's head, (.45 LC cal. only, 4 3/4 in. barrel, new 2002), or simulated ivory (new 1996) grips, patterned after the Colt SAA, fixed sights, 39-41 oz. Mfg. 1993-2004.

	$495	$330	$265	$225	$195	$170	$160

Last MSR was $555.

Add $40 for simulated ivory grips (new 1996).
Add approx. $150 for simulated ivory grips and engraved cylinder (mfg. 1998-99).

✴ *Vaquero High Gloss Stainless Steel* - high gloss stainless steel finish, black Micarta bird's head grips became optional 2002. Mfg. 1994-2004.

	$495	$330	$265	$225	$195	$170	$160

Last MSR was $555.

Add $40 for simulated ivory grips (new 1996).

✴ *Vaquero Bird's Head* - .357 Mag. or .45 Colt cal., 3 3/4 (.357 Mag.) or 4 5/8 (.45 Colt) in. barrel, color case hardened frame or high polish stainless steel bird's head frame, choice of black Micarta or simulated ivory (new 2003) grips. Disc. 2004.

	$495	$360	$295	$245	$210	$185	$165

Last MSR was $595.

NEW VAQUERO - .357 Mag. or .45 LC cal., 4 5/8, 5 1/2, or 7 1/2 (.45 LC cal. only) in. barrel, 6 shot, redesigned using a slimmer pre-1962 XR-3 style grip frame, smaller cylinder frame allows loading gate cutout to align with cylinder borings, color case hardened frame with blued gripstraps, barrel, and cylinder, recontoured hammer, new hammerspring, beveled cylinder, checkered hard rubber grips, crescent-shaped ejector rod head, 37-41 oz. New 2005.

MSR $640	$500	$395	$315	$260	$225	$200	$175

Add $445 for standard Grade 1 engraving (new 2006) or $1,395 for consecutive pair with standard Grade 1 engraving (new 2006)

✴ *New Vaquero High Gloss Stainless* - similar to New Vaquero, except is stainless steel. New 2005.

MSR $640	$500	$395	$315	$260	$225	$200	$175

Add $445 for standard Grade 1 engraving (new 2006) or $1,395 for consecutive pair with standard Grade 1 engraving (new 2006)

NEW VAQUERO COWBOY PAIR - .45 LC cal., 5 1/2 in. barrel, includes two consectively numbered and engraved revolvers with presentation case, 500 sets mfg. 2007.

	$3,450	$3,150	$2,850	N/A	N/A	N/A	N/A

Last MSR was $3,863.

GRADING - PPGS™	100%	98%	95%	90%	80%	70%	60%

BISLEY VAQUERO - .357 Mag. (new 1999, 5 1/2 in. barrel only), .44 Mag. or .45 LC cal., 4 5/8 (new 1999) or 5 1/2 in. barrel, case colored frame with blue steel grips, barrel, and cylinder, steel ejector housing became standard in 2000, fixed sights, approx. 40 oz. Mfg. 1998-2004.

	$495	$340	$275	$230	$200	$180	$160

Last MSR was $555.

Add $40 for simulated ivory grips.

* *Bisley Vaquero Stainless* - similar to Bisley Vaquero, except is stainless steel. Disc. 2004.

	$495	$345	$280	$235	$200	$180	$160

Last MSR was $575.

Add $40 for simulated ivory grips.

BISLEY MODEL - .22 LR (disc.), .32 H&R Mag. (disc. 1996), .357 Mag. (disc. 2007), .41 Mag. (disc. 1996), .44 Mag., or .45 LC cal., 6 shot, incorporates Bisley features (flattop frame, raked hammer, longer grip frame), 6 1/2 (.22 LR or .32 H&R Mag. only) or 7 1/2 in. barrel, fixed (disc. 1992, except for .32 H&R Mag.) or adj. sights, available with fluted/unfluted or roll-marked/unmarked (disc.) cylinders, satin blue finish only, Goncalo Alves smooth grips. New 1986.

* *Bisley Model .22 LR or .32 H&R Mag.*

	$450	$325	$250	$210	$180	$160	$150

Last MSR was $475.

Add $50 for .32 H&R Mag. (disc. 1996).

* *Bisley Model .357 Mag., .41 Mag., .44 Mag. or .45 LC*

MSR $663	$515	$395	$310	$250	$200	$180	$160

* *Bisley Model Shootist* - .22 LR cal., special limited edition, stainless steel, 4 5/8 in. barrel, adj. sights, marked "In Memory of Our Friend, Tom Ruger, The Shootist", inscribed with the name of the recipient on backstrap, only 52 mfg. 1994.

	$1,500	$1,250	$995	$880	$715	$610	$515

NEW BEARCAT - .22 LR cal., includes interchangeable .22 Mag. cyl. (disc. 1996), frame slightly longer than old Bearcat, 4 in. barrel, transfer bar hammer safety, blue finish, smooth rosewood grips, fixed sights, 24 oz. New 1994.

MSR $486	$385	$330	$270	$215	$140	$125	$115

Add $110 for LR cylinder without firing pin groove.

* *New Bearcat Stainless Steel* - similar to New Bearcat, except is matte stainless steel. New 2002.

MSR $524	$445	$340	$265	$235	$200	$180	$160

Add $110 for LR cylinder without firing pin groove.

* *New Bearcat Convertible* - similar to New Bearcat, except has convertible cylinder, early production, recalled by the factory.

	$1,100	$1,000	$900	$785	$655	$550	$465

The .22 Mag. cylinder was recalled to the factory in 1994. It is estimated that at least 60% of the 1,000 New Bearcat Convertibles produced had their .22 Mag. cylinders returned to the factory due to the recall.

REVOLVERS: DOUBLE ACTION

During certain years of manufacture, Ruger's changes in production on certain models (cals., barrel markings, barrel lengths, etc.) have created rare variations that are now considered premium niches. These areas of low manufacture will add premiums to the values listed on standard models.

SPEED SIX (MODELS 207, 208 and 209) - .38 Spl., .357 Mag., or 9mm Para. cal., 2 3/4 or 4 in. barrel, fixed sights, checkered walnut grips, round butt, blue finish, some guns have factory speed hammer (no hammer spur). Mfg. 1973-88. Model 207 and 208 disc. 1988.

	$400	$300	$200	$170	$160	$150	$140

Last MSR was $292.

Add $100 for 9mm Para. (Model 209 disc. 1984).

* *Speed Six Models 737 and 738* - stainless steel versions of Models 207 and 208, .357 Mag and .38 Spl. cals., 2 3/4 or 4 in. barrel. Disc. 1988.

	$425	$325	$220	$175	$140	$125	$105

Last MSR was $320.

* *Speed Six Model 739* - stainless steel, 9mm Para. Disc. 1984.

	$450	$350	$230	$180	$145	$125	$105

SECURITY SIX (MODEL 117) - .357 Mag. cal., 6 shot, 2 3/4, 3 (late production only), 4, 4 (heavy), or 6 in. barrel, adj. sights, checkered walnut grips, square butt. Mfg. 1970-1985.

	$350	$225	$195	$185	$160	$150	$140

Last MSR was $309.

Add $15 for target grips.

Note that beginning late in the 150- serial number prefix, the grip frame was changed to have a more outward "highback" shape. Revolvers with the earlier "lowback" grip frame are generally considered more collectible. All revolvers having fixed sights and square butt grip frame with "lowback" shape to the backstrap were also marked "SECURITY-SIX". Only when the new highback gripframe came out were the fixed sight and square butt revolvers marked "SERVICE-SIX".

500 of this model were mfg. for the California Highway Patrol during 1983 (.38 Spl. cal.) in stainless steel only. They are distinguishable by a C.H.P. marking. Other Security Six Model 117 special editions have been made for various police organizations - premiums might exist in certain regions for these variations.

* *Security Six Model 717* - stainless steel version of Model 117. Disc. 1985.

	$350	$255	$230	$180	$145	$125	$105

Last MSR was $338.

POLICE SERVICE SIX - .357 Mag, .38 Spl., or 9mm Para. cal., blue finish only, square butt, fixed sights, checkered walnut grips.

* *Police Service Six Model 107* - .357 Mag, 2 3/4 or 4 in. barrel, fixed sights. Disc. 1988.

	$400	$300	$250	$190	$180	$170	$165

Last MSR was $287.

* *Police Service Six Model 108* - .38 Spl., 4 in. barrel, fixed sights. Disc. 1988.

	$300	$220	$200	$190	$180	$170	$165

Last MSR was $287.

* *Police Service Six Model 109* - 9mm Para., 4 in. barrel, fixed sights. Disc. 1984.

	$300	$230	$205	$195	$185	$180	$175

POLICE SERVICE SIX STAINLESS STEEL - stainless construction, 4 in. barrel only, fixed sights, checkered walnut grips.

* *Police Service Six Stainless Steel Model 707* - .357 Mag., square butt. Disc. 1988.

	$300	$235	$210	$160	$130	$115	$100

Last MSR was $310.

* *Police Service Six Stainless Steel Model 708* - .38 Spl., square butt. Disc. 1988.

	$300	$235	$210	$160	$130	$115	$100

Last MSR was $310.

GRADING - PPGS™	100%	98%	95%	90%	80%	70%	60%

GP-100 - .357 Mag./.38 Spl. cal., 3 (new 1990, fixed sights, .357 Mag. only), 4, or 6 (.357 Mag. only) in. standard or heavy barrel, 6 shot, strengthened design intended for constant use with all .357 Mag. ammunition, rubber cushioned grip panels with polished Goncalo Alves wood inserts, fixed (mfg. 1989-2006) or adj. sights (standard beginning 2007) with white outlined rear and inter-changeable front, 35-46 oz. depending on barrel configuration. New 1986.

	MSR $598	$480	$365	$295	$240	$200	$185	$170

* *GP-100 Stainless Steel* - similar to GP-100, .357 Mag. cal. only, stainless steel. New 1987.

	MSR $640	$510	$385	$300	$235	$200	$170	$140

Add $20 for adj. sights (3 in. barrel only).

* *GP-100 High Gloss Stainless Steel* - .357 Mag. only, high gloss stainless steel finish, adj. sights, 3 or 4 in. heavy barrel. Mfg. 1996 only.

	$485	$375	$295	$250	$195	$165	$140

Last MSR was $457.

Fixed sights were cataloged but not known to have been produced in this model.

SP-101 STAINLESS STEEL - .22 LR (6 shot - mfg. 1990-2004), .32 H&R (6 shot - new 1991), .327 Federal (6 shot - new 2007), .38 Spl. (5 shot), 9mm Para. (5 shot - mfg. 1991-2000), or .357 Mag. (5 shot - new 1991) cal., 2 1/4, 3 1/16, or 4 (mfg. 1990-2007) in. barrel, small frame variation of the GP - 100 Stain-less, fixed or adj. (new 1996) sights, 25-34 oz. New 1989.

	MSR $572	$460	$345	$270	$215	$175	$140	$120

Add $100 for .357 Mag. models with "125 GR. BULLET" rollmarked on barrel lug.
Add $100 for 9mm Para. caliber.
Add $50 for .22 LR caliber.
Add $242 for Crimson Trace laser grips (new 2008).

The .327 Federal caliber configuration will also shoot .32 H&R Mag., .32 S&W, and .32 S&W Long cartridges.

The first few thousand SP-101s in .38 Special had green grip inserts. Also, approximately 3,000 total of the earliest KSP-321 and KSP-331 .357 Mag. models were rollmarked with "125 GR. BULLET" on the barrel under the caliber designation (serial range 570-59359 to 570-67976).

Ruger introduced adj. sights in 1996 available in .22 LR or .32 H&R cal. only.

Ruger introduced a .357 Mag./2 1/4 in. (new 1993) or .38 Spl./2 1/4 (new 1994) in. configura-tion featuring a spurless hammer, double action only.

SP-101 barrel lengths are as follows: .22 cal. is available in 2 1/4 or 4 in. standard or heavy barrel, .32 H&R is available in 3 1/16 or 4 (new 1994) in. heavy barrel, .38 Spl. is available in 2 1/4 or 3 1/16 in. length only, 9mm Para. is available in 2 1/4 (new 1992) or 3 1/16 in. only, and .357 Mag. is available in 2 1/4 or 3 1/16 in. only.

* *SP-101 Stainless Steel High Gloss* - .38 Spl. (disc. 1996), 9mm Para. (disc. 1996), or .357 Mag. cal., similar to SP-101 Stainless Steel, except has high gloss stainless steel finish. Mfg. 1996-97.

	$485	$400	$325	$250	$195	$165	$140

Last MSR was $443.

Add $60 for 9mm Para. cal.

Estimated 100 produced in .38 Spl, 1,500 produced in .357 mag. and an unknown quantity in 9mm (very rare). Serial range 571-81675 to 572-44777.

Ruger introduced adj. sights in 1996 available in .22 LR or .32 H&R cal. only.

REDHAWK - .357 Mag. (disc. 1985), .41 Mag. (disc. 1991), or .44 Mag. cal., 6 shot, redesigned large frame, 5 1/2 and 7 1/2 (disc. 2005) in. barrel, blue fin-ish, square butt, smooth hardwood grips, 49-54 oz.

	MSR $766	$600	$450	$360	$285	$225	$180	$165

Add $40 for scope rings (disc. 2005).

.357 Mag. and .41 Mag. cals. will bring collector premiums if NIB.

GRADING - PPGS™	100%	98%	95%	90%	80%	70%	60%

✳ *Redhawk Stainless Steel* - .44 Mag or .45 LC (mfg. 1998-2005, reintroduced 2008, 4 in. barrel only) cal., stainless steel construction, 4 (new 2007), 5 1/2, or 7 1/2 in. barrel, choice of regular or Hogue (4 in. barrel only) grips, 49-54 oz.

MSR $836	$650	$500	$375	$300	$265	$230	$210

    Add $52 for scope rings.

This model was also available as a KRH-35, and is marked both "Redhawk" and ".357 Magnum". Mfg. was circa 1984-1991.

The 7 1/2 in. barrel was available with or w/o integral scope mounting system.

SUPER REDHAWK STAINLESS - .44 Mag., .454 Casull (new 1999), or .480 Ruger (mfg. 2001-2007) cal., 6 shot, 7 1/2 or 9 1/2 in. barrel, fluted (.44 Mag. cal. only) or non-fluted cylinder, choice of regular or high gloss (mfg. 1997-2004) stainless steel, adj. rear sight, cushioned grip panels (GP-100 style), stainless steel scope rings, 53-58 oz. New late 1987.

MSR $888	$700	$625	$525	$440	$360	$320	$285

    Add $75 for early .44 Mag. with "SUPER REDHAWK" rollmarked on both sides of cylinder frame extension, serial range 550-00500 to at least 550-00659.

    Add $75 for .454 Casull or .480 Ruger cal.

.44 Mag. cal. has stainless steel satin finish and calibers .454 Casull and .480 Ruger have stainless steel Target Grey finish.

✳ *Super Redhawk Stainless Alaskan* - .44 Mag. (new 2008), .454 Casull or .480 Ruger (disc. 2007), 6 shot, 2 1/2 in. barrel, includes Hogue monogrips and unfluted cylinder, 42 oz. New 2005.

MSR $963	$765	$575	$425	$350	$315	$285	$260

RIFLES: BOLT ACTION, RIMFIRE

MODEL 77/17 - .17 Mach 2 (disc. 2006) or .17 HMR cal., 22 in. barrel, blue finish, rotary mag., checkered walnut or black laminate (new 2003, .17 HMR cal. only) stock, 6 - 7 1/4 lbs. New 2002.

MSR $732	$550	$425	$340	$270	$230	$210	$190

✳ *Model 77/17 Stainless* - similar to Model 77/17, except has target grey finish stainless steel action/barrel, 22 (disc. 2005) or 24 in. barrel (new 2006), 9 (HMR) or 10 shot mag., black laminate stock became standard 2006. New 2002.

MSR $812	$650	$465	$340	$270	$230	$195	$170

MODEL 77/22-R/RS - .22 LR cal. only, 10 shot rotary mag., 20 in. barrel, all steel construction, 3 position safety, checkered walnut stock, blue finish, non-adj. trigger, available with either optional iron sights (RS suffix, disc. 2004) or plain barrel (no sights) with scope rings (included), 2.7 millisecond lock time on trigger, 6 lbs. 2 oz. New 1984.

MSR $732	$550	$425	$340	$270	$230	$210	$190

    Add $25 for iron sights (disc. 2004).

    Add 125% if w/o 77/22 roll mark or with green laminated stock.

✳ *Model 77/22-RP/RSP All-Weather Stainless* - similar to Model 77/22, except has stainless steel metal with matte black DuPont Zytel synthetic stock, 5 lbs. 14 oz. New 1989.

MSR $732	$550	$425	$340	$270	$230	$210	$190

    Add $25 for iron sights (disc. 2004).

✳ *Model 77/22-VBZ Varmint Stainless Laminated* - similar to Model 77/22, except stainless steel (target grey finish became standard 2005), heavy stainless barrel, laminated brown hardwood stock. New 1995.

MSR $812	$625	$460	$365	$280	$245	$210	$180

GRADING - PPGS™	100%	98%	95%	90%	80%	70%	60%

MODEL 77/22-RM/RSM MAG. - similar to Model 77/22-R/RS, except in .22 Win. Mag. cal., 9 shot rotary mag., blue finish, checkered walnut stock, approx. 6 lbs. New 1990.

MSR $732	$550	$425	$340	$270	$230	$210	$190

   Add $25 for iron sights (disc. 2004, RSM suffix).

✳ *Model 77/22-RMP/RSMP Mag. All-Weather Stainless* - similar to Model 77/22-RM/RSM Mag., except has stainless steel metal with matte black Dupont Zytel synthetic stock. New 1990.

MSR $732	$550	$425	$340	$270	$230	$210	$190

   Add $25 for iron sights (disc. 2005).

✳ *Model 77/22-VMBZ Mag. Varmint Stainless Laminated* - similar to Model 77/22 RM/RSM Mag., except stainless steel (target grey finish became standard 2005), 24 in. heavy stainless barrel, laminated brown hardwood stock, 7 1/2 lbs. New 1993.

MSR $812	$625	$460	$365	$280	$245	$210	$180

RIFLES: BOLT ACTION, CENTERFIRE

During certain years of manufacture, Ruger's changes in production on certain models (cals., barrel markings, barrel lengths, etc.) have created rare variations that are now considered premium niches. These areas of low manufacture will add premiums to the values listed on standard models.

   Earlier mfg. had flat-bolt handle or hollow round bolt, and will bring $150+ premium, depending on configuration.

   Early (pre-1972) mfg. with flat-bolt handle are desirable in the rarer cals. and will command a 100% premium if in 98%+ original condition.

MODEL 77/22-RH/RSH HORNET - .22 Hornet cal., features lengthened receiver, detachable 6 shot rotary mag. (not interchangeable with other 77/22 mags.), 20 in. blue barrel, checkered American walnut stock, includes scope rings, 6 1/4 lbs. New 1994.

MSR $732	$550	$425	$340	$270	$230	$210	$190

   Add $20 for iron sights (disc. 2002).

✳ *Model 77/22-VHZ Hornet Varmint Stainless Laminated* - similar to Model 77/22 Hornet, stainless steel action, 24 in. heavy stainless barrel (target grey finish became standard 2005), no sights, laminated brown hardwood stock, 7 1/2 lbs. New 1995.

MSR $812	$625	$460	$365	$280	$245	$210	$180

MODEL 77/44 - .44 Mag. cal., 18 1/2 in. barrel, rotary mag., plain birch or checkered walnut stock, open sights, 6 lbs. Mfg. 1998-2004.

$510	$380	$310	$270	$245	$200	$175

Last MSR was $635.

✳ *Model 77/44 Stainless* - .44 Mag. cal., black synthetic stock, stainless steel construction, open sights. Mfg. 1999-2004.

$510	$380	$310	$270	$245	$200	$175

Last MSR was $635.

MODEL 77R - .22-250 Rem., .220 Swift, 6mm Rem. (disc.), .243 Win. (disc.), .250 Savage (disc.), .257 Roberts, .25-06 Rem., .270 Win., 7x57mm, 7mm-08 (disc.), 6.5mm Rem. Mag. (scarce), 7mm Rem. Mag., .280 Rem., .284 Win., .308 Win. (disc.), .30-06, .300 Win. Mag., .338 Win Mag., .350 Rem. Mag., or .358 Win. cal., long or short action, blue finish, 5 shot mag., 3 shot in Mag. cals., 22 or 24 in. barrel, available with integral bases or round top, some models supplied with sights, stock is checkered walnut with red rubber buttplate, approx. 7 lbs. Mfg. 1968-92.

$450	$395	$325	$265	$245	$200	$200

Last MSR was $558.

   Add 10-15% for .284 cal.
   Add 20%-30% for .350 Rem. Mag. cal.

GRADING - PPGS™	100%	98%	95%	90%	80%	70%	60%

❋ *Model 77 RL* - .22-250 Rem. (disc.), .243 Win., .250 Sav., .257 Roberts, .270 Win., .30-06, or .308 Win. cal., ultra light variation weighing 6 lbs., black forearm tip. Disc. 1992.

	$445	$375	$325	$270	$250	$225	$205

Last MSR was $592.

❋ *Model 77 RS* - .243 Win., .250 Sav., 6mm Rem., 6.5mm Rem. Mag., 7x57mm, .25-06 Rem. (disc.), 270 Win., .280 Rem., .284 Win., .30-06, .308 Win., 7mm Rem. Mag., 300 Win. Mag., .338 Win. Mag, .35 Whelen, .350 Rem. Mag., or .358 Win. cal., similar to Model 77R, except has open sights. Disc. 1992.

	$500	$425	$350	$300	$265	$230	$210

Last MSR was $616.

Add 30% for .284 Win.
Add 50% for .35 Whelen, .358 Win., or .350 Rem. Mag. cal.

❋ *Model 77PL* - .25-06 Rem., .270 Win., .30-06, .300 Win., .338 Win. Mag., 7mm Rem. Mag., or 7x57mm cal., differs from R Model in that it has a round top, drilled to take Redfield scope mounts, w/o sights.

	$420	$395	$325	$265	$245	$200	$200

❋ *Model 77ST* - .25-06 Rem., .257 Roberts, 7x57mm, .300 Win. Mag., .338 Win. Mag., 7mm Rem. Mag., .30-06, or .270 Win. cal., differs from RS Model in that is has round top drilled to take Redfield scope mounts with iron sights on barrel.

	$460	$425	$350	$300	$265	$230	$210

❋ *Model 77V Varmint* - .22-250 Rem., .220 Swift, .243 Win. (disc.), 6mm Rem. (disc.), .25-06 Rem., .280 Rem., .308 Win., or .30-06 cal., 24 in. heavy barrel (26 in. on .220 Swift), drilled and tapped for target bases, approx. 9 lbs. Mfg. 1968-92.

	$430	$395	$325	$265	$245	$210	$200

Last MSR was $574.

❋ *Model 77 RS African* - similar to Model 77R, except in .458 Win. Mag. cal. Disc. 1991.

	$600	$500	$400	$365	$335	$315	$300

Last MSR was $680.

This model was supplied standard with a steel triggerguard and steel floor plate.

❋ *Model 77 RSC* - similar to Model 77 RS African, except has Circassian walnut stock (C suffix). Mfg. 1976-78.

	$800	$650	$500	$450	$400	$365	$335

❋ *Model 77 RLS* - .243 Win. (disc. 1989), .270 Win., .30-06, or .308 Win. cal. (disc. 1989), ultra light, 18 1/2 in. barrel, open sights, 6 lbs. Mfg. 1987-93.

	$445	$395	$310	$280	$260	$230	$210

Last MSR was $592.

❋ *Model 77 RSI* - .22-250 Rem. (disc. 1991), .243 Win. .250-3000 Sav. (reintroduced 1990), .270 Win., .30-06, .308 Win. (disc. 1991), 7x57mm (rare), or 7mm-08 Rem. cal., International Mannlicher (full length stock) with 18 1/2 in. barrel and open sights (includes scope rings), approx. 7 lbs. Disc. 1993.

	$550	$400	$325	$295	$265	$230	$210

Last MSR was $623.

Add 20% for 7mm-08 cal.

MODEL 77R MARK II SERIES - various cals. as listed in the submodels below, evolutionary design of the Ruger Model 77R featuring slenderized proportioning, 3 position swing-back safety, new trigger, trigger guard and floor plate latch, stainless steel bolt with Mauser extractor design, various barrel lengths, integral base receiver, hand checkered American walnut stock, includes scope rings, various weights. New 1989.

The Hawkeye Model was introduced during 2007, and please refer separate model listings.

GRADING - PPGS™	100%	98%	95%	90%	80%	70%	60%

✳ *Model 77R Mark II* - .204 Ruger (new 2004), .220 Swift (new 1995), .22-250 Rem. (new 1993), .223 Rem. (new 1992), .243 Win., .25-06 Rem. (new 1993), .257 Roberts (new 1993), .260 Rem. (new 1999), .270 Win. (new 1993), .270 WSM (new 2004), .280 Rem. (new 1993), 6mm Rem., 6.5x55mm Swedish (new 1993), 7x57mm (new 1993), .30-06 (new 1993), .308 Win., 7mm WSM (new 2004), 7mm Rem. Mag. (new 1993), 7mm RSUM (new 2002), .300 Win. Mag. (new 1993), .300 WSM (new 2004), .300 RSUM (new 2002), .338 Win. Mag. (new 1993). or .350 Rem. Mag. (new 2004) cal., checkered walnut stock is standard, 22 or 24 in. barrel, standard model of the new Mark II Series, approx. 7 lbs. Disc. 2006.

	$480	**$395**	**$325**	**$285**	**$245**	**$200**	**$200**

Last MSR was $695.

✳ *Model 77 LR Mark II* - .25-06 Rem., .270 Win., .30-06, .300 Win. Mag. or 7mm Rem. Mag. cal., left-hand variation of the Model 77R. Mfg. 1991-2007.

	$515	**$415**	**$335**	**$295**	**$245**	**$200**	**$200**

Last MSR was $749.

✳ *Model 77 RL Mark II* - .223 Rem., .243 Win., .257 Roberts (new 1993), .270 Win. (new 1993), .30-06 (mfg. 1993-2004, reintroduced 2006), or .308 Win. cal., 20 in. barrel, black forend tip, ultra light variation weighing approx. 6 lbs. New 1990.

MSR $837	**$640**	**$475**	**$370**	**$280**	**$245**	**$210**	**$180**

✳ *Model 77 RLFP Mark II Stainless* - .204 Ruger, .223 Rem. (new 2005), .243 Win., .270 Win. or .30-06 cal., 20 in. barrel, black synthetic stock, ultralight variation of the Model 77, w/o sights, 6 1/2 lbs. New 1999.

MSR $779	**$540**	**$435**	**$345**	**$295**	**$245**	**$200**	**$200**

✳ *Model 77 RS Mark II* - 6mm Rem., .243 Win., .25-06 Rem. (new 1993), .270 Win. (new 1993), .30-06 (new 1993), .308 Win., 7mm Rem. Mag. (new 1993), .300 Win. Mag. (new 1993), .338 Win Mag. (new 1993), or .458 Win. Mag. (mfg. 1994-98) cal., 22 or 24 in. barrel, similar to Model 77R, except has open sights. Mfg. 1990-2004.

	$555	**$435**	**$355**	**$310**	**$270**	**$230**	**$210**

Last MSR was $780.

✳ *Model 77 CR Mark II Compact* - .223 Rem., .243 Win., .260 Rem., .308 Win., or 7mm-08 Rem. cal., features 16 1/2 in. barrel, checkered walnut stock, includes scope rings, no sights, approx. 5 3/4 lbs. New 2002.

MSR $779	**$540**	**$435**	**$345**	**$295**	**$245**	**$200**	**$200**

❖ **Model 77 CRBBZ Mark II Compact Stainless** - stainless variation of the Model 77 CR Compact, black laminate stock. New 2002.

MSR $837	**$575**	**$465**	**$350**	**$295**	**$255**	**$225**	**$205**

✳ *Model 77 FRBBZ Mark II Frontier* - .243 Win., .308 Win., .300 WSM (disc. 2006), or 7mm-08 Rem. cal., compact design features 16 1/2 in. barrel, and shortened grey laminate stock, barrel cantilever allows scope to be mounted over barrel in front of action, blue finish, includes scope rings and Weaver style scope base adapter. New 2005.

MSR $831	**$595**	**$460**	**$365**	**$315**	**$275**	**$230**	**$210**

❖ **Model 77 FRTG Mark II Frontier Stainless** - .338 Federal (new 2007), .358 Win. (new 2008), .325 WSM (disc. 2007), other cals. similar to Frontier model disc. 2007, stainless variation of the Model 77 FRBBZ Frontier, target grey finish stainless steel barrel/action. New 2006.

MSR $936	**$725**	**$625**	**$525**	**$400**	**$335**	**$290**	**$245**

✳ *Model 77 RSI Mark II* - .243 Win., .270 Win., .30-06, or .308 Win. cal., International Mannlicher (full length stock) with 18 1/2 in. barrel and open sights (includes scope rings), approx. 7 lbs. New 1993.

MSR $911	**$715**	**$625**	**$525**	**$400**	**$335**	**$290**	**$245**

✱ **Model 77 RLS Mark II** - .243 Win. or .308 Win. cal., ultra light, 18 1/2 in. barrel, open sights. Mfg. 1990 only.

	$460	$375	$310	$280	$260	$230	$210

Last MSR was $564.

✱ **Model K77 RFP Mark II All-Weather Stainless** - .204 Ruger (new 2005), .22-250 (new 1996), .223 Rem., .243 Win., .25-06 Rem. (new 1999), .260 Rem. (new 1999), .270 Win., .270 WSM (new 2004), .280 Rem. (new 1993), 7.62x39mm (disc. 2000), .30-06, .308 Win., .325 WSM (New 2006), .350 Rem. Mag. (new 2006), 7mm-08 Rem. (new 2005), 7mm Rem. Mag., 7mm WSM (new 2004), 7mm RSUM (new 2002), .300 Win. Mag., .300 WSM (new 2004), .300 RSUM (new 2002), or .338 Win. Mag. (new 1992) cal., 22 or 24 in. barrel, similar to Model 77R Mark II except has stainless steel metal with matte black DuPont Zytel synthetic stock, no sights. Mfg. 1990-2006.

	$480	$395	$325	$285	$245	$200	$185

Last MSR was $695.

✱ **Model K77 RSFP Mark II All-Weather Stainless** - .223 Rem. (new 2002), .243 Win., .270 Win., .30-06, 7mm Rem. Mag., .300 Win. Mag., or .338 Win. Mag. cal., otherwise similar to Model K77 RFP All-Weather Stainless, except has open sights. Disc. 2004.

	$525	$425	$355	$285	$250	$215	$185

Last MSR was $780.

✱ **Model K77 RBZ Mark II Satin Stainless** - .22-250 Rem. (new 1999), .223 Rem., .243 Win., .270 Win., .280 Rem. (disc. 2006), .30-06, .308 Win., 7mm Rem. Mag., .300 Win. Mag., .338 Win. Mag., or .350 Rem. Mag. (disc. 2005) cal., features brown wood laminate stock with sling swivels, 22 or 24 in. barrel without sights, approx. 7 5/16 lbs. New 1997.

MSR $837	$575	$465	$350	$295	$255	$225	$205

✱ **Model K77 RSBZ Mark II** - .243 Win., .270 Win., .30-06, .300 Win. Mag., .338 Win. Mag., or 7mm Rem. Mag. cal., 22 or 24 in. barrel, laminated stock, open sights, includes scope rings, approx. 7 3/8 lbs. Disc. 2004.

	$515	$470	$355	$285	$250	$215	$185

Last MSR was $825.

✱ **Model K77 VT (VBZ) Mark II** - .22 PPC (disc. 1996), .204 Ruger (new 2004), .220 Swift (disc. 2006), .22-250 Rem., .223 Rem., .243 Win., .25-06 Rem., .308 Win., or 6mm PPC (disc. 1996) cal., 26 in. heavy barrel, features stainless steel construction, target grey finish became standard 2005, laminated stock, approx. 9 3/4 lbs. New 1993.

MSR $935	$725	$625	$525	$400	$335	$290	$245

This model's nomenclature changed from VBZ to VT during 1994.

✱ **Model 77 LRBBZ Mark II Stainless** - .25-06 Rem. (new 2004), .270 Win., .30-06, 7mm Rem. Mag., or .300 Win. Mag. cal., left-hand action, 22 in. barrel, uncheckered grey laminated stock, includes scope rings. New 1999.

MSR $837	$575	$465	$350	$295	$255	$225	$205

MODEL 77 RSM - .375 H&H, .416 Rigby, or .458 Lott (new 2002) cal., 23 in. barrel, 3 or 4 (.375 H&H cal.) shot mag., premium grade Circassian walnut with hand cut checkering and ebony forend tip, integral barrel and sighting quarter rib with two folding sights, approx. 9 1/2 lbs. New 1990.

MSR $2,334	$1,850	$1,350	$1,075	$950	$825	$725	$675

MODEL 77 RS EXPRESS - .270 Win., .30-06, 7mm Rem. Mag., .300 Win. Mag., or .338 Win. Mag. (new 1994) cal., 22 or 24 in. barrel, 3 or 4 shot mag., similar construction to Model 77RSM with premium grade wood and other materials, 7 1/2 lbs. Mfg. 1991-2002.

	$1,250	$875	$815	$750	$700	$675	$595

Last MSR was $1,625.

GRADING - PPGS™	100%	98%	95%	90%	80%	70%	60%

MODEL HM77R HAWKEYE SERIES - various cals., newest variation of the M77, featuring one-piece stainless bolt, new LC6 trigger, rotating Mauser type feed extractor, slimmer profile, checkered American walnut stock with solid red recoil pad, matte bluing on barrel and action, redesigned steel floorplate and latch, left-hand available in certain cals. beginning 2008, includes scope rings, various weights. New 2007.

✳ *Model HM77R Hawkeye* - .204 Ruger, .22-250 Rem., .223 Rem., .243 Win., .25-06 Rem., .257 Roberts (disc. 2007), .270 Win., .280 Rem. (new 2008), .30-06, .308 Win., 7mm Rem. Mag., 7mm-08 Rem., .300 Win. Mag., .338 Win. Mag., .338 Federal (new 2008) or .358 Win. (new 2008) cal., newest variation of the M77, featuring one-piece stainless bolt, rotating Mauser type feed extractor, slimmer profile, checkered American walnut stock with solid red recoil pad, matte bluing on barrel and action, new LC6 trigger, redesigned steel floorplate and latch, includes scope rings. New 2007.

MSR $779	$540	$435	$345	$295	$245	$200	$200

✳ *Model HM77 Hawkeye All-Weather Stainless* - similar cals. as RFP Mark II All-Weather Stainless, except not available in WSM, matte finish stainless steel, black checkered synthetic stock, no sights, similar Hawkeye features as the HM77R. New 2007.

MSR $779	$540	$435	$345	$295	$245	$200	$200

✳ *Model HM77 RBH* - .30-06 cal., 22 in. blue or stainless steel barrel, brown Hogue overmolded stock. New 2008.

MSR $821	$575	$450	$365	$315	$275	$230	$210

✳ *Model HM77 RGH* - .270 Win. cal., 22 in. blue or stainless steel barrel, green Hogue overmolded stock. New 2008.

MSR $821	$575	$450	$365	$315	$275	$230	$210

✳ *Model HM77 Hawkeye Alaskan* - .375 Ruger cal., 20 in. stainless steel barrel with choice of Diamondblack corrosion resistant coating or stainless Hawkeye matte finish, open sights, black Hogue overmolded stock with recoil pad. New 2007.

MSR $1,139	$935	$815	$735	$650	$575	$525	$475

✳ *Model HM77 Hawkeye African* - .375 Ruger cal., matte blue finish, 23 in. alloy steel barrel, checkered American walnut stock and forearm. New 2007.

MSR $1,139	$935	$815	$735	$650	$575	$525	$475

This model is also available in left-hand action at no extra charge.

RIFLES: LEVER ACTION

MODEL 96 CARBINE - .17 HMR (new 2002), .22 LR (disc. 2003), .22 Mag., or .44 Mag. (disc. 2007) cal., 18 1/2 in. barrel with single barrel band, uncheckered hardwood stock with curved buttplate, 10 (.17 HMR or .22 LR), 9 (.22 Mag.), or 4 (.44 Mag.) shot detachable rotary mag., crossbolt safety on trigger guard, adj. rear sight, .44 Mag. has case hardened lever, rimfire receivers are drilled and tapped while the .44 Mag. has an integral base receiver with scope rings (became standard 1997), approx. 5 1/4 - 6 lbs. New 1996.

MSR $451	$345	$260	$215	$180	$150	$135	$125

Add $174 for .44 Mag. cal. with scope rings (disc. 2007).

RIFLES: SEMI-AUTO

During certain years of manufacture, Ruger's changes in production on certain models (cals., barrel markings, barrel lengths, etc.) have created rare variations that are now considered premium niches. These areas of low manufacture will add premiums to the values listed on standard models. The Model 10/22 has been mfg. in a variety of limited production models including a multi-colored or green laminate wood stock variation (1986), a brown laminate stock (1988), a Kittery Trading Post Commemorative (1988), a smoke or tree bark

GRADING - PPGS™	100%	98%	95%	90%	80%	70%	60%

laminate stock (1989), a Chief AJ Model, Wal-Mart (stainless with black laminated hardwood stock - 1990), etc. These limited editions will command premiums over the standard models listed, depending on the desirability of the special edition.

Note: All Ruger Rifles, except Stainless Mini-14, all Mini-30s, and Model 77-22s were made during 1976 in a "Liberty" version. Add $50-$75 when in 100% in the original box condition.

10/17 CARBINE - .17 HMR cal., steel receiver, birch stock only, 18 1/2 in. barrel, otherwise similar to 10/22 Standard Carbine. Limited mfg. 2004 only.

	$425	$335	$265	$225	$185	$165	$150

Last MSR was $510.

While advertised, very few of this model were manufactured.

10/22 COMPACT - .22 LR cal., similar to 10/22 Standard Carbine, except has 16 1/2 in. barrel with hardwood stock.

MSR $298	$235	$175	$130	$105	$80	$60	$55

10/22 STANDARD CARBINE - .22 LR cal., 10 shot rotary mag., 18 1/2 in. barrel, birch, black synthetic (new 1999), or optional deluxe hand checkered walnut stock, folding rear sight, approx. 5 lbs. New 1964.

MSR $261	$210	$175	$125	$100	$80	$60	$55

Add 10% for uncheckered walnut stock (mfg. 1964-1980 and 1987-1989).
Add $84 for deluxe checkered walnut sporter stock (Model 10/22 DSP).

✳ *10/22RB Standard Carbine Stainless* - similar to 10/22 Standard Carbine, except has stainless barrel and choice of birch or black synthetic (new 1997) stock. New 1992.

MSR $308	$230	$190	$135	$105	$85	$65	$55

✳ *10/22 Standard Carbine 40th Anniversary* - similar to 10/22 Standard Carbine, except includes 40th Ruger anniversary medallion. Mfg. 2004 only.

	$225	$165	$125	$100	$85	$65	$55

Last MSR was $279.

10/22 RIFLE - similar to 10/22 Standard Carbine, except has 20 in. barrel with hardwood stock. Mfg. 2004-2006.

	$220	$165	$125	$105	$80	$60	$55

Last MSR was $275.

10/22-T TARGET MODEL - .22 LR cal., features brown laminated American hardwood stock, blue hammer-forged spiral finish barrel, w/o sights, 7 1/2 lbs. New 1996.

MSR $470	$380	$310	$235	$185	$145	$125	$105

✳ *K10/22-T Target Model Stainless* - similar to 10/22T Target Model, except is stainless steel. New 1998.

MSR $518	$415	$325	$255	$195	$165	$140	$120

✳ *K10/22-TNZ Target Model Stainless* - features 20 in. barrel w/o sights, stainless steel action and barrel, laminated thumbhole stock with slanted forend, 7 lbs. Mfg. 2001-2002.

	$450	$375	$300	$240	$210	$180	$155

Last MSR was $649.

10/22 FINGERGROOVE SPORTER - similar to 10/22 Standard, except Monte Carlo stock and beavertail forearm. Mfg. 1966-71.

	$475	$400	$325	$275	$225	$200	$175

Add 100% for checkered stock in NIB condition.

10/22 INTERNATIONAL (OLD PRODUCTION) - similar to 10/22 Standard, except walnut full stock Mannlicher style. Mfg. 1966-69.

	$650	$550	$475	$425	$375	$350	$325

Add 50% for checkered stock.

GRADING - PPGS™	100%	98%	95%	90%	80%	70%	60%

10/22RBI INTERNATIONAL (NEW PRODUCTION) - features Mannlicher style international birch full stock. Mfg. 1994-2003.

	$220	$180	$135	$105	$95	$80	$65

Last MSR was $279.

✳ *K10/22RBI International (New Production) Stainless* - stainless variation of the 10/22RBI International. Disc. 2003.

	$275	$190	$140	$110	$100	$80	$75

Last MSR was $299.

10/22 CANADIAN CENTENNIAL - 2,000 mfg. in 1967.

	$450	$400	$350	N/A	N/A	N/A	N/A

Last MSR was $100.

10/22 MAGNUM - .22 Mag. cal., steel receiver, longer and heavier bolt, 10 shot rotary mag., 18 1/2 in. barrel, uncheckered birch stock, blue metal, folding rear sight, 6 1/2 lbs. Mfg. 1999-2006.

	$550	$425	$365	$300	$260	$230	$200

Last MSR was $536.

RUGER/REMINGTON CANADIAN CENTENNIAL MATCHED NO. 3 SET - includes a Remington Model 742 in .308 Win. cal. and a Ruger 10/22 Sporter with special commemorative appointments, cased. 1,000 sets mfg. 1967 only.

	$700	$525	$425	N/A	N/A	N/A	N/A

✳ *Ruger/Remington Canadian Centennial Matched No. 2 Set* - 70 sets mfg. 1967 only.

	$950	$775	$550	N/A	N/A	N/A	N/A

✳ *Ruger/Remington Canadian Centennial Matched No. 1 Special Deluxe Set* - 30 sets mfg. 1967 only.

	$1,150	$895	$675	N/A	N/A	N/A	N/A

MODEL 44 STANDARD CARBINE - .44 Mag. cal., 4 shot mag., 18 1/2 in. barrel, blowback action, folding sight, curved butt. Mfg. 1961-85.

	$500	$350	$325	$295	$275	$250	$225

Last MSR was $332.

✳ *Model 44 Standard Carbine Deerstalker* - approx. 3,750 mfg. with "Deerstalker" marked on rifle until Ithaca lawsuit disc. manufacture (1962).

	$925	$850	$725	$600	$550	$475	$400

✳ *Model 44 Standard Carbine 25th Year Anniversary* - mfg. 1985 only, limited production, has medallion in stock.

	$650	$525	$400	N/A	N/A	N/A	N/A

Last MSR was $495.

MODEL 44RS - similar to 44, but has aperture sight and swivels.

	$600	$550	$500	$450	$400	$350	$300

MODEL 44 FINGERGROOVE SPORTER - Monte Carlo stocked version of 44 Standard. Mfg. until 1971.

	$750	$650	$550	$500	$450	$400	$350

Add 100% for factory checkered stock.

MODEL 44 INTERNATIONAL - similar to Standard, except full length Mannlicher style stock. Mfg. until 1971.

	$825	$700	$625	$550	$475	$400	$350

Add 50% for factory checkered stock.

MODEL 99/44 DEERFIELD CARBINE - .44 Mag. cal., 4 shot rotary mag., 18 1/2 in. barrel with folding aperture rear sight, rotating bolt with dual front locking lugs, blue finish only, uncheckered hardwood stock, includes intergral scope mounts and rings, 6 1/4 lbs. Mfg. 2000-2006.

	$540	$450	$410	$375	$335	$300	$260

Last MSR was $702.

RUGER CARBINE - 9mm Para. (PC9) or .40 S&W (PC4) cal., 16 1/4 in. barrel, 10 (PC4) or 15 (PC9) shot detachable mag., black synthetic stock, matte metal finish, with or w/o sights, with fully adj. rear sight or rear receiver sight, crossbolt safety, 6 lbs. Mfg. 1998-2006.

	$510	$415	$360	$310	$265	$240	$215

Last MSR was $623.

Add $24 for adj. rear receiver sight.

Beginning 2005, this model came standard with an adjustable ghost ring apeture rear sight and protected blade front sight.

MINI-14 - .223 Rem. or .222 Rem. (disc.) cal., 5 (standard mag. starting in 1989), 10 (disc.), or 20* shot detachable mag., 18 1/2 in. barrel, gas operated, blue finish, apeture rear sight, military style stock, approx. 6 3/4 lbs. Mfg. 1974-2004.

	$535	$445	$365	$320	$275	$240	$215

Last MSR was $655.

Add 20% for .222 Rem. cal.
Add $300 for folding stock (disc. 1989).
Add 25% for Southport Model with gold bead front sight.

Due to 1989 Federal legislation and public sentiment, the Mini-14 was shipped with a 5 shot detachable mag. only. This model was also available as a Mini-14 GB (primarily used for law enforcement), and was equipped with a flash hider and bayonet lug (blue or stainless, current value is approx. $1,000 if in 95%+ original condition).

✳ *Mini-14 Stainless* - mini stainless steel version, choice of wood or black synthetic (new 1999) stock. Disc. 2004.

	$565	$445	$380	$320	$275	$230	$200

Last MSR was $715.

Add 20% for .222 Rem. cal.
Add $200 for folding stock (disc. 1990).

MINI-14 RANCH RIFLE - .223 Rem. cal., 5 (standard mag. starting in 1989), 10 (disc.), or 20* shot detachable mag., 18 1/2 in. barrel, hardwood stock, folding rear sight, receiver cut for factory rings, similar to Mini-14, supplied with scope rings, adj. ghost ring aperture rear sight, protected front sight, and flat style recoil pad (became standard 2005), approx. 6 1/2 lbs. New 1982.

MSR $830		$635	$500	$450	$400	$350	$315	$275

Add $260 for Mini 14 NRA-ILA Limited Edition with 16 1/8 in. barrel and black Hogue overmolded stock (ltd. mfg. beginning 2008).

Due to 1989 Federal legislation and public sentiment at the time, the Mini-14 Ranch Rifle is now being shipped with a 5 shot detachable mag. only.

✳ *Mini-14 Stainless Ranch Rifle* - .223 Rem. or 6.8mmSPC (new 2007) cal., stainless steel construction, choice of wood or black synthetic (new 1999) stock, 6 3/4 lbs. New 1986.

MSR $894		$695	$550	$425	$350	$325	$300	$250

Add $200 for folding stock (disc. 1990).

✳ *Mini-14 Target Ranch Rifle* - .223 Rem. cal., 22 in. stainless steel heavy barrel, ergonomic black or grey laminated thumbhole or Hogue overmolded stock, stainless scope rings, otherwise similar to Mini-14 Stainless Ranch Rifle. New 2007.

MSR $1,035		$845	$725	$600	$525	$450	$400	$350

GRADING - PPGS™	100%	98%	95%	90%	80%	70%	60%

MINI-THIRTY - 7.62x39mm Russian cal., 18 1/2 in. barrel, 5 shot detachable mag., hardwood stock, includes scope rings, 7 lbs. 3 oz. Mfg. 1987-2004.

	$540	$450	$405	$375	$335	$300	$260

Last MSR was $695.

* *Mini-Thirty Stainless* - stainless steel variation of the Mini-Thirty, adj. ghost ring aperture rear sight and protected front sight became standard 2005. New 1990.

MSR $894	$695	$550	$425	$350	$325	$300	$250

XGI - while advertised, this model was never shipped commercially because it could not maintain Ruger accuracy standards.

MSR was originally targeted at $425.

RIFLES: SINGLE SHOT

During certain years of manufacture, Ruger's changes in production on certain models (cals., barrel markings, barrel lengths, etc.) have created rare variations that are now considered premium niches. These areas of low manufacture will add premiums to the values listed on standard models.

Non-prefix rifles are known in .222, .22-250, .243, 6mm, .25-06, .270, .280, 7mm Rem. Mag., 7x57, .300 Win. Mag., .30-06, .308, .375 H&H., 45-70 and .458 cal.

Calibers 6.5mm Rem., .264 Win. Mag., 7x65R, .300 H&H and .338 were also rumored or cataloged during the 1966-1968 time period but are not known to have been produced.

One rifle chambered in .225 Win. is known to be in the factory collection.

In addition to the calibers listed above, the Number 1 during this time period could be ordered with nearly any combination of barrel length and weight (22" light weight or 26" medium weight barrel). The .375 H&H and .458 were available with a 24" heavy weight barrel and most in .45-70 were produced with a 22" medium weight barrel.

For all but the .375 H&H, .45-70 and .458, the 1966-1968 period rifles could also be ordered with any combination of no sights/open sights/target blocks or either Alex Henry or Semi-Beavertail forearm.

Pre-1969, non-prefix rifles will command a 30%-50% premium (ser. no. 1-8XXX).

NO. 1-A LIGHT SPORTER - similar to No. 1-B Standard, .204 Ruger (mfg. 2005-2006), .22 Hornet (disc., 355 mfg.), .223 Rem. (rare), .243 Win., .270 Win., 7mm-08 (rare), 7x57mm, or .30-06 cal., 22 in. barrel, folding sight on quarter rib, ramp front sight, no rings, Alexander Henry forearm, front swivel in barrel band, 7 1/4 lbs. New 1966.

MSR $1,093	$875	$600	$500	$400	$325	$275	$250

The "A" suffix designates an Alexander Henry classic forearm with light barrel.

NO. 1-AB - various cals., .204 Ruger cal. (new 2006), 22 in. barrel, checkered walnut stock and forearm. Mfg. 1967-68, 1982-83, and 2006.

MSR $1,093	$875	$600	$500	$400	$325	$275	$250

NO. 1-B STANDARD - falling block action with curved Farquharson lever, popular cals. include .204 Ruger (new 2004), .218 Bee (disc. 2006), .22 Hornet (mfg. 1988-2006), .22-250 Rem. (disc. 2006), .220 Swift (disc. 2006), .223 Rem., .257 Roberts (disc. 2003), .243 Win. (disc. 2006), 6mm Rem (disc. 2003), .25-06 Rem., .270 Win., .280 Rem. (disc. 2003), .30-06, .308 Win. (new 2002), 6.5mm Rem. Mag. (disc.), 7x57 (disc.), 7mm Rem. Mag., .270 Wby. Mag. (mfg. 1990-2006), .300 Wby. Mag. (mfg. 1990-2006), .300 Win. Mag., or .338 Win. Mag. (disc. 2006) cal., 22 or 26 in. barrel, quarter rib with integral scope bases, supplied with rings and no sights, checkered stock and semi beavertail forearm, approx. 8 1/4 lbs. New 1966.

MSR $1,093	$875	$600	$500	$400	$325	$275	$250

Add 50% for 6.5mm Rem. Mag. or 30% for 7x57 cal.

The "B" suffix designates semi-beavertail forearm with medium barrel and is available in all cals. under .375 H&H.

GRADING - PPGS™	100%	98%	95%	90%	80%	70%	60%

NO. 1-H TROPICAL RIFLE - similar to Medium Sporter, except .375 H&H, .404 Jeffery (mfg. 1993-95), .416 Rem. (mfg. 1993-2003), .416 Rigby (new 1991), .450/400 NE (new 2007), .458 Lott (new 2004), .458 Win. Mag., or .405 Win. (new 2004) cal., 24 in. heavy barrel, open sights, approx. 9 lbs.

MSR $1,093	$875	$625	$525	$425	$350	$295	$260

Add 100% for .404 Jeffrey cal. (rare).
Add 200% for .45-70 Govt. cal. (rare, mfg. 1976).

NO. 1-RSI INTERNATIONAL - .243 Win. (disc. 2006), .270 Win., 7x57mm, or .30-06 cal., features 20 in. lightweight barrel with full length Mannlicher stock, includes swivels and open sights, 7 1/4 lbs.

MSR $1,130	$895	$635	$515	$395	$325	$260	$230

NO. 1-S MEDIUM SPORTER - .218 Bee (disc. 2003), 7mm Rem. Mag. (disc. 2003), 9.3x74R (new 2007), .45-70 Govt., .300 Win. Mag. (disc. 2003), or .338 Win. Mag. (disc. 2003) cal., similar to Light Sporter, 22 (.45-70 Govt. cal. only) or 26 in. medium barrel, open sights, 7 1/4-8 lbs.

MSR $1,093	$875	$600	$500	$400	$325	$275	$250

✳ *No. 1-S Medium Sporter 50th Anniversary* - .45-70 Govt. cal. only, engraved action with gold inlays, including the Ruger logo and 50 years, William B. Ruger signature on receiver bottom, checkered Circassian walnut stock and forearm. 1,500 mfg. 1999 only.

	$1,950	$1,500	$1,300	$1,100	$995	$850	$700

Last MSR was $1,950.

NO. 1-V VARMINT - similar to No. 1-B Standard, except .22 PPC (mfg. 1993-96), .22-250 Rem., .220 Swift (disc.), .223 Rem., .243 Win. (disc.), .25-06 Rem., 6mm Rem. (disc. 2005), 6mm PPC (mfg. 1993-96), 7mm Rem. (disc.), .280 Rem. (disc.) or .300 Win. Mag. (disc.) cal., 24 or 26 (.220 Swift only) in. heavy barrel, without rib, checkered walnut stock and forearm, target scope blocks, 9 lbs. New 1970.

MSR $1,093	$875	$600	$500	$400	$325	$275	$250

Add 20% for .22 PPC cal.

NO. 1 K1-B-BBZ STAINLESS - various cals. and configurations, satin stainless steel action and barrel, grey laminate hardwood stock with black recoil pad, drilled and tapped rear quarter rib w/o sights. New 2001.

✳ *No. 1 K1-B-BBZ Stainless Standard* - .243 Win., .25-06 Rem., .270 Win. (new 2004), .30-06, .308 Win. (mfg. 2002-2006), .300 Win. Mag., 7mm STW (disc. 2004), or 7mm Rem. Mag. cal., 26 in. barrel, 8 lbs. New 2001.

MSR $1,130	$895	$635	$515	$395	$325	$260	$230

✳ *No. 1 K1-H-BBZ Stainless Tropical* - .375 H&H, .416 Rigby (mfg. 2002-2006), .405 Win. (mfg. 2004, reintroduced 2006), .458 Win. (mfg. 2005-2006), or .458 Lott (mfg. 2002-2004, reintroduced 2007) cal., 24 in. barrel, 9 lbs. New 2001.

MSR $1,130	$895	$635	$515	$395	$325	$260	$230

✳ *No. 1 K1-S-BBZ Stainless Sporter* - .45-70 Govt. cal. only, 22 in. barrel with iron sights, 7 1/4 lbs. New 2001.

MSR $1,130	$895	$635	$515	$395	$325	$260	$230

✳ *No. 1 K1-V-BBZ Stainless Varmint* - .204 Ruger (new 2004), or .22-250 Rem. cal. only, 24 in. barrel, 9 lbs. New 2001.

MSR $1,130	$895	$635	$515	$395	$325	$260	$230

NO. 3 CARBINE - same basic action as No. 1, except simpler lever design, uncheckered stock, available in .22 Hornet, .30-40 Krag, .45-70 Govt. (only cal. available 1986), .223 Rem., .44 Mag., or .375 Win. cal., 22 in. barrel, folding sight. Mfg. 1972-87.

	$700	$550	$450	$350	$250	$200	$150

Last MSR was $284.

Add 20% for .44 Mag. or .375 Win. cal.

GRADING - PPGS™	100%	98%	95%	90%	80%	70%	60%

RUGER/LYMAN 1878 CENTENNIAL RIFLE - .45-70 Govt. cal., 101 sets mfg. in Grade I and 1,000 in Grade II. Grade I has hand engraving, custom stock, 28 in. D weight barrel, tubular 4X Lyman Century scope, ser. nos. L-001-1878 to L-101-1978. Grade II had photo engraved frame, ser. nos. L-78-0001 to L-101-1978. Mfg. 1978 only.

	100%	98%	95%	90%	80%	70%	60%
Grade I	$1,750	$1,425	$1,050	$850	$725	$600	$525
Grade II	$2,500	$2,000	$1,200	$900	$800	$700	$600

One William Lyman commemorative cased rifle was also mfg., preceeding Grades I & II. This model was auctioned off at the 1978 NRA Show.

SHOTGUNS: O/U

RED LABEL - 12, 20, or 28 (new 1994) ga., 3 in. chambers (except 28 ga.), various barrel lengths and choke (including skeet) combinations, boxlock, SST, 26 or 28 in. VR barrels, auto ejectors, choice of checkered pistol grip or English straight grip (new 1992, Red Label English Field) stock, stainless steel frame became standard on 12 ga. 1985 (not available in 20 ga.), choke tubes became optional in 1988, standard 1990, 6-7 3/4 lbs. New 1977.

✳ *Red Label Standard Grade*

MSR $1,899	$1,425	$1,100	$875	$750	$625	$500	$450

    Add $622 for .410 bore Briley conversion tube set for 28 ga. only (disc. 2005).
    Subtract 15%-20% without choke tubes.

During late 1994, some 12 and 20 ga. Red Label boxes were marked "EZ", indicating the new easy-opening feature (this is not mechanically spring-assisted, but rather works on tight machining tolerances). All Red Label shotguns have the "EZ"-opening feature beginning 1995. Earlier all-steel 12 ga. models (approx. 500 mfg.) with short field tubes could command 10%-15% premiums over values listed from collectors interested in acquiring this variation. 20 ga. models w/o choke tubes are blue only.

✳ *Red Label All Weather Stainless* - 12 ga. only, stainless steel (disc.) or target grey stainless steel (new 2003) receiver and barrels, checkered black synthetic stock and forearm, 26, 28, or 30 in. VR barrels with choke tubes, 7 1/2 lbs. Mfg. 1999-2006.

			$1,275	$975	$800	$700	$600	$500	$450

Last MSR was $1,702.

✳ *Red Label Sporting Clays* - 12 or 20 (mfg. 1994-2007) ga., features 30 in. separated barrels, choice of walnut or synthetic (12 ga. only) stock, Briley chokes with forcing cones back bored to .744 in., 3/8 in. VR with middle bead, sporting clays recoil pad, approx. 7 1/2 lbs. New 1992.

MSR $1,899	$1,425	$1,100	$875	$750	$625	$500	$450

❖ **Red Label Sporting Clays Engraved** - available in 12 ga. only with 1/3 engraving pattern. Mfg. 1997.

		$2,500	$2,200	$1,900	$1,650	$1,300	$1,000	$850

Last MSR was $3,068.

✳ *Red Label English Field* - 12, 20, or 28 (new 1995) ga., similar to Red Label, except has English style straight grip stock. Mfg. 1992-2000.

		$965	$775	$685	$600	$550	$500	$450

Last MSR was $1,276.

✳ *Red Label Engraved (Current Mfg.)* - 12, 20, or 28 ga., 26, 28, or 30 (disc. 2004) in. barrels, 4 different gold inlay options depending on ga., with receiver scroll engraving, pheasant standard on 12 ga., grouse on 20 ga., and woodcock on 28 ga., available in Standard Model, All Weather Stainless (disc. 2004), and Sporting Clays (disc. 2004) configurations. New 2001.

MSR $2,117	$1,595	$1,275	$925	$750	$625	$500	$450

GRADING - PPGS™	100%	98%	95%	90%	80%	70%	60%

✳ *Red Label Hand Engraved (1997-2000 Mfg.)* - available in 12 (167 or 168 made), 20 (55 or 56 made), or 28 (73 to 75 made) ga., available in 2/3 "C" coverage, 1/3 "B" coverage or dit-dot border "A" pattern coverage (pattern engraving standard). Only the earliest hand engraved guns had circassian walnut buttstock and forearm. Later guns were produced with circassian walnut buttstock and black walnut forearm or have buttstock and forearm of black walnut for both pieces. The contracted engravers of this series were John J. Adams, Sr., John J. Adams, Jr., Carmine Lombardy, Alvin White, Andrew Bourbon and Jon Ashford. Mfg. 1997-2000.

	$2,200	$1,900	$1,650	$1,300	$1,000	$850	$725

Last MSR was $2,552.

> **Add $190 for 1/3 engraving coverage.**
> **Add $532 for 2/3 engraving coverage (12 ga. only, disc.).**
> 28 ga production quantities: KRL-2826A (27); KRL-2827A (24); KRL-2826B (19); KRL-2827B (1 or 2); KRL-2826C (1); KRL-2827C (1 or 2).
> 20 ga. production quantities: KRL-2029B (40); KRL-2030B (11); KRL-2029C (3 or 4); KRL-2030C (1).
> 12 ga. production quantities: KRL-1227A (18); KRL-1226B (44); KRL-1227B (88 or 89); KRL-1236B (1); KRL-1226C (10) and KRL-1227C (6)
> In all, only 295 to 299 Red Label shotguns of these special hand engraved models were produced.

✳ *Red Label 50th Anniversary Engraved* - 12, 20, or 28 ga., 26 or 28 in. barrels, engraved with receiver scroll engraving, 3 different gold inlay options (depending on ga.) on right side of receiver and Ruger 50th Anniversary logo on left side of receiver. Mfg. 1999 only. Probably not more than 1,500 of each model produced.

	$1,350	$1,125	$850	N/A	N/A	N/A	N/A

RED LABEL "WOODSIDE" - 12 ga. only, 3 in. chambers, 26, 28, or 30 (Sporting Clays Model only with special chokes, new 1996) in. barrels, straight or pistol grip stock, features premium checkered walnut, satin nickel finish, unique stock design permitting wood to fill-in where frame boxlock action would normally be, hand-engraving available at extra cost, 7 1/2-8 lbs. Mfg. 1995-2002.

	$1,525	$1,250	$1,000	$800	$625	$550	$500

Last MSR was $1,889.

✳ *Red Label "Woodside" Engraved* - available in 2/3 "C" coverage, 1/3 "B" coverage or dit-dot border "A" pattern coverage (pattern engraving standard) with pistol grip and 26 or 28 in. barrels. Only the earliest hand engraved guns had circassian walnut buttstock and forearm. Later guns were produced with circassian walnut buttstock and black walnut forearm or have buttstock and forearm of black walnut for both pieces The contracted engravers of this series were John J. Adams, Sr., John J. Adams, Jr., Carmine Lombardy, Alvin White, Andrew Bourbon and Jon Ashford. Mfg. 1997-2000.

	$2,200	$2,050	$1,725	$1,350	$1,050	$875	$750

Last MSR was $2,805.

> **Add $190 for 1/3 engraving coverage.**
> **Add $532 for 2/3 engraving coverage.**
> Production quantities: KWS-1226A (44); KWS-1227A (17); KWS-1226B (8); KWS-1227B (6); KWS-1226C (1) and KWS-1227C (5).

WILDLIFE FOREVER SPECIAL EDITION - 12 ga. only, limited edition to celebrate the 50th anniversary of Wildlife Forever, features Baron & Son engraving with gold pheasant and mallard inlays on receiver sides, 300 mfg. 1993 only.

	$1,595	$900	$775	N/A	N/A	N/A	N/A

Last MSR was $1,595.

> **Add $125 for hard case.**

GRADING - PPGS™	100%	98%	95%	90%	80%	70%	60%

SHOTGUNS: SxS

GOLD LABEL SxS - 12 ga. only, 3 in. chambers, 28 in. barrels with solid rib and choke tubes, rounded stainless boxlock action, SST, blue barrel finish, ejectors, choice of deluxe 22 LPI checkered English straight grip or pistol grip stock and splinter forearm, approx. 6 1/2 lbs. New late 2002.

MSR $3,226	$2,650	$2,225	$1,850	$1,625	$1,250	$1,050	$925

SHOTGUNS: SINGLE BARREL

TRAP MODEL - 12 ga., 34 in. stainless barrel with straight grooves and 2 choke tubes, fully adj. high post rib, engraved stainless receiver with gold Ruger name, adj. deluxe checkered walnut stock, beavertail forearm, adj. trigger, 9 lbs. Approx. 300 mfg. 2000-2003.

	$3,500	$3,000	$2,500	$2,000	$1,500	$1,300	$1,200

Last MSR was $2,850.

SUHLER JAGDGEWEHR MANUFAKTUR GmbH

Previous manufacturer and firearms restorer located in Suhl, Germany.

Suhler Jagdgewehr manufactured a variety of SxS shotguns, in addition to restoring both antique and historical guns.

SUNDANCE INDUSTRIES, INC.

Previous manufacturer located in Valencia, CA.

DERRINGERS

POINT BLANK DERRINGER - .22 LR cal., O/U design, double action, 3 in. barrels, black matte finish, 8 oz. Mfg. mid-1994-2002.

	$80	$60	$50	$45	$40	$35	$30

Last MSR was $99.

PISTOLS: SEMI-AUTO

MODEL A-25 - .25 ACP cal., single action design, 2 7/16 in. barrel, 7 shot mag., rotary safety, lower grip push button mag. release, satin nickel (disc.), bright chrome, or black teflon finish, choice of simulated pearl with different colors or grooved black grips, serrated slide. Mfg. 1989-2002.

	$65	$55	$45	$40	$35	$30	$25

Last MSR was $79.

LADY LASER/LASER 25 - .25 ACP cal., similar to Model A-25, except has factory installed and sighted 5mW Laser sight with no exposed wiring or switch, polished chrome or black finish (Laser 25 only), dual safety switch. Mfg. 1995-2002.

	$195	$160	$135	$115	$95	$80	$70

Last MSR was $220.

The Laser Lady was disc. during 1998.

MODEL BOA - similar to Model A-25, except has patented squeeze grip safety. Mfg. 1990-2002.

	$75	$60	$50	$45	$40	$35	$30

Last MSR was $95.

GRADING - PPGS™	100%	98%	95%	90%	80%	70%	60%

SUPER SIX LIMITED

Previous manufacturer located in Brookfield, WI until 1992.

REVOLVERS

GOLDEN BISON SERIES - .45-70 Govt. cal., 6 shot revolver, 8 or 10 1/2 in. octagon barrel, large size (overall length 15-17 1/2 in.), manganese bronze frame, crossbolt manual safety, smooth hardwood grips, approx. 6 lbs. 177 total mfg. (including special/limited editions). Disc. approx. 1992.

	$1,675	$1,475	$1,275	$1,000	$875	$775	$675

Last MSR was $1,895.

Low serialization specimens (ser. nos. 1-15) have asking prices of $2,250-$2,950.

✳ *Golden Bison Series Centennial Limited Edition* - features special engraving and case. 20 total mfg.

	$2,950	$2,275	$1,675	N/A	N/A	N/A	N/A

Last MSR was $3,995.

SUPER SIX LLC

Previous manufacturer located in Milwaukee, WI from 1999-2004.

During late 1998, Super Six LLC purchased the previous trademark of Super Six Limited. This trademark had very limited manufacture.

SUPER SIX CLASSIC, LLC

Current trademark manufactured by Defense Supply & Manufacturing, located in Fort Atkinson, WI.

REVOLVERS

Defense Supply & Manufacturing currently offers the Super Six Bison Bull and the Super Six Golden Bison Bull in .45-70 Govt. cal. Current MSR is $1,295. Please contact the company directly for more information, including prices for available options and delivery time (see Trademark Index).

SUPERIOR AMMUNITION

Previous custom rifle and current ammunition manufacturer located in Sturgis, SD. Consumer direct sales only.

RIFLES: BOLT ACTION

SUPERIOR CLASSIC LIGHTWEIGHT - various cals. up to .375 H&H, Rem. Mod. 700, Win. Mod. 70 Classic, or Dakota Mod. 76 action, blind box mag. or hinged floorplate, approx. 5 3/4 lbs.

	$1,850	$1,650	$1,350	$1,100	$900	$750	$625

Last MSR was $2,000.

SUPERIOR VARMINT MODEL - various smaller cals., Rem. Mod. 700, Dakota Varmint, or Searcy action, stainless match grade barrel, heavy or light variations.

	$1,900	$1,725	$1,400	$1,125	$900	$750	$625

Last MSR was $2,100.

SUPERIOR PROFESSIONAL MODEL - various large cals. up to .470 Capstick, only available in Win. Mod. 70 Classic or Dakota Mod. 76 action, blind box mag. (optional) or hinged floorplate.

	$2,350	$2,050	$1,850	$1,600	$1,350	$1,150	$900

Last MSR was $2,500.

SUPERIOR ARMS

GRADING - PPGS™	100%	98%	95%	90%	80%	70%	60%

Current manufacturer established in 2004 and located in Wapello. IA. Currently distributed by Professional Gunsmithing, located in Wapello, IA, RB Precision, located in Preemption, IL, Boom to Zoom, located in Marshfield, WI, and Haynes Inc., located in Clinton, IN.

PISTOLS: SEMI-AUTO

Superior Arms manufactured complete AR-style semi-auto pistols, with either an A4 flattop or A2 carry handle, and 10 1/2 or 11 1/2 in. barrel.

RIFLES: CUSTOM

Superior Arms manufactures a wide variety of customized semi-auto rifles in A2 and A4 style configurations, with many options available. Prices start at $800 for the 16 in. carbine A4 and go up accordingly depending on the number of options. Please contact the distributor directly for more information on delivery and availability (see Trademark Index).

SURVIVAL ARMS, INC.

Previous manufacturer established in 1990 located in Orange, CT. Previously located in Cocoa, FL, until 1995.

In 1990, Survival Arms, Inc. took over the manufacture of AR-7 Explorer rifles from Charter Arms located in Stratford, CT.

RIFLES: SEMI-AUTO

AR-7 EXPLORER RIFLE - .22 LR cal., takedown or normal wood stock, takedown barreled action stores in Cycolac synthetic stock, 8 shot mag., adj. sights, 16 in. barrel, black matte finish on AR-7, silvertone on AR-7S, camouflage finish on AR-7C, 2 1/2 lbs. Disc.

	$150	$125	$100	$85	$75	$65	$55

Last MSR was $150.

Add 20% for takedown action.

AR-20 SPORTER - similar to AR-22, except has shrouded barrel, tubular stock with pistol grip, 10 or 20 shot mag. Mfg. 1996-98.

	$195	$165	$140	$120	$105	$95	$80

Last MSR was $200.

AR-22/AR-25 - .22 LR cal., 16 in. barrel, black rifle features pistol grip with choice of wood or metal folding* stock, includes 20 (1995 only) or 25 (disc. 1994) shot mag. Disc. 1995.

	$175	$150	$125	$100	$80	$70	$60

Last MSR was $200.

Subtract $50 for wood stock model.

SVENDSEN, ERL, F.A. MFG. CO.

Previous manufacturer located in Itasca, IL.

DERRINGERS

LITTLE ACE - .22 S cal., patterned after the Ethan Allen "HIDE-A-WAY", bronze frame, blue steel barrel with case hardened hammer and spur trigger.

	$85	$75	$70	$65	$60	$55	$50

4-ACES - .22 S cal., 4 barrel derringer with rotating firing pin and spur trigger, bronze frame with blue rifled steel barrels and case hardened parts.

	$175	$150	$135	$120	$105	$90	$75

SWING

GRADING - PPGS™	100%	98%	95%	90%	80%	70%	60%

Previously manufactured by Schutzen Bohme GmbH located in Rintein, Germany.

RIFLES: BOLT ACTION

SWING BOLT ACTION - .308 Win. cal., target bolt action rifle with thumbhole stock and vented forearm, target sights, 30 in. barrel, 12.1 lbs. Mfg. 1994.

	$850	$750	$650	$575	$500	$450	$395

SWISS MILITARY

Previously manufactured Swiss military rifles.

RIFLES: BOLT ACTION

The models below were manufactured by Schmidt-Rubin, unless otherwise indicated.

MODEL 1889 - usually encountered between 85%-95% condition.

	$350	$325	$285	$260	$230	$210	$185

MODEL 1911 - available in either carbine or rifle configuration.

	$450	$325	$200	$185	$170	$160	$150

Add 125% for carbine configuration.

MODEL 1931

	$650	$600	$525	$450	$285	$250	$225

Add 500% for sniper variations.
Subtract 30% if import marked.

VETTERLI - .41 Swiss or 10.4mm Swiss cal., not mfg. by Schmidt-Rubin.

	$495	$450	$400	$360	$320	$285	$250

SYMES & WRIGHT LTD.

Previous manufacturer located in London, England.

Symes & Wright Ltd. manufactured approx. 25 best quality shotguns and double rifles annually. Values must be determined after evaluating each firearm individually.

SZECSEI & FUCHS FINE GUNS GmbH

Current long gun manufacturer established in 1986, and located in Innsbruck, Austria. North American headquarters are located in Windsor, Canada.

Szecsei & Fuchs manufactures extremely high quality and unique long guns, including combination guns, drillings, bolt action and double rifles, and SxS shotguns. The company is well known for its unique magazine fed SxS double rifle, which utilizes a single bolt to load/unload both chambers. Many options are available, including a titanium bolt trigger system. Please contact the North American office directly for more information on their current models (virtually anything is possible), including pricing, availability, delivery time, and U.S. pricing.

RIFLES: BOLT ACTION

DOUBLE BARREL REPEATER - various cals., unique action allows single bolt to chamber both barrels from one twin column detachable titanium mag., titanium bolt face, right or left hand, various engraving and wood options available. Base weight is approx. 13 lbs.

Please contact the company directly for a price quotation.

NOTES

T SECTION

TG INTERNATIONAL

Current importer located in Knoxville, TN.

TG International imports a variety of firearms, including a sporterized Mosin-Nagant rifle, an FPK Dragunov ($710 MSR), a TOZ-78 bolt action rimfire target rifle ($160 MSR), and a TOZ-99 semi-auto rimfire rifle ($199 MSR). Pistols include a P-64 Makarov produced by Radom, a PA-63 PPK copy in 9mm Makarov cal., and FEG pistols in 9mm and .32 ACP. Please contact the company directly for more information, pricing, and current availability (see Trademark Index).

TNW, INC.

Current rifle manufacturer located in Vernonia, OR. Consumer direct sales.

RIFLES: SEMI-AUTO

TNW makes a belt-fed semi-auto variation of the original Browning M2 HB machine gun in .50 BMG cal. Price is POR. They also made a semi-auto Model 1919 A4 in .30-06 or .308 Win. cal. Retail pricing was in the $2,050 range. TNW also manufactures a variation of the German MG-34 semi-auto, and a M230 conversion for the M1919 A4 machine gun. Please contact the company directly for more information regarding these semi-auto working replicas (see Trademark Index).

TACONIC FIREARMS, LTD.

Previous rifle manufacturer located in Cambridge, NY until 2003.

GRADING - PPGS™	100%	98%	95%	90%	80%	70%	60%

RIFLES: BOLT ACTION, CUSTOM

TACONIC 98 ULTIMATE MOUNTAIN HUNTER - various cals., features double square bridge, titanium alloy M-98 action, XXX Grade English or Circassian walnut, stainless or chrome moly barrel, matte finished metal, available with a variety of options, base prices are listed below.

	$5,750	$5,100	$4,500	$4,000	$3,500	$3,000	$2,500

Last MSR was $5,995.

TACTICAL RIFLES

Current rifle manufacturer located in Dade City, FL.

RIFLES

Tactical Rifles makes a complete lineup of bolt action and semi-auto tactical rifles. Current models include the Tactical Long Range ($2,950 MSR), Tactical Para w/ folding stock ($3,550 MSR), Tactical Long Range Magnum ($3,550 MSR), Tactical M40 ($2,795 MSR), Tactical M21 ($4,595 MSR), Dow Custom AR10 (disc. 2004, $2,695 last MSR), Dow FAL15 (disc. 2007, $1,895 last MSR), Tactical AR15 ($2,295 MSR), Tactical Special Varmint ($2,495 MSR), and the Tactical M4C ($1,885 MSR). Please contact the company for more information (see Trademark Index).

TACTICAL WEAPONS

Current law enforcement/military division of FNH USA, located in McLean, VA.

Tactical Weapons currently manufactures machine guns only for law enforcement/military.

GRADING - PPGS™	100%	98%	95%	90%	80%	70%	60%

TALON INDUSTRIES, INC.

Previous pistol manufacturer located in Ennis, MT until 2001.

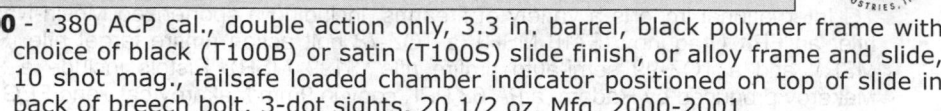

PISTOLS: SEMI-AUTO

T100 - .380 ACP cal., double action only, 3.3 in. barrel, black polymer frame with choice of black (T100B) or satin (T100S) slide finish, or alloy frame and slide, 10 shot mag., failsafe loaded chamber indicator positioned on top of slide in back of breech bolt, 3-dot sights, 20 1/2 oz. Mfg. 2000-2001.

	$115	$95	$85	$75	$65	$55	$50

Last MSR was $135.

T200 - 9mm Para. cal., otherwise similar to Model T100. Mfg. 2000-2001.

	$145	$125	$100	$90	$75	$65	$55

Last MSR was $170.

TANFOGLIO, FRATELLI, S.r.l.

Current pistol and parts manufacturer located in Gardone, Italy. Currently imported by European American Armory, located in Sharps, FL. Previously imported by K.B.I., located in Harrisburg, PA, and also by Excam, F.I.E., and others.

Tanfoglio manufactures a wide variety of high quality semi-auto pistols, including the Witness Series, which are currently imported by European American Armory Corp. (please refer to EAA section). Tanfoglio also manufactures a proprietary line of pistols, including competition models and the Raptor single shot, which has been mostly distributed in Europe.

TANNER, ANDRÉ

Previous manufacturer located in Switzerland. Previously imported and distributed by Mandall Shooting Supplies, Inc. located in Scottsdale, AZ, and by Osborne's located in Cheboygan, MI.

Tanner rifles are noted for their superior accuracy and limited production - less than 150 were mfg. annually.

RIFLES: BOLT ACTION

300 METER MATCH RIFLE - 7.5 Swiss (special order) or 7.62mm cal. only, single shot, top-of-the-line 300 meter match rifle incorporating all match shooting features including deluxe palm rest, aperture sights. Importation disc.

	$4,650	$3,995	$3,400	$2,775	$2,250	$1,900	$1,600

Last MSR was $4,900.

Add $100 for adj. cheekpiece.
Subtract $190 for repeating model with similar features.

* *300 Meter Match Rifle UIT Standard* - similar to Model 300, except is without palm rest and adj. Swiss buttplate, 10 shot mag., aperture sights. Importation disc.

	$4,450	$3,850	$3,350	$2,750	$2,225	$1,925	$1,600

Last MSR was $4,700.

Add $100 for adj. cheekpiece.

SUPERMATCH MODEL 50 M - .22 LR cal. only, 50 meter free rifle, deluxe palm rest, adj. buttplate, thumbhole stock. Importation disc.

	$3,600	$3,200	$2,850	$2,450	$2,050	$1,800	$1,600

Last MSR was $3,900.

Add $100 for adj. cheekpiece.

TAR-HUNT CUSTOM RIFLES, INC.

Current custom rifled shotgun manufacturer established in 1990, and located in Bloomsburg, PA. Dealer and consumer direct sales.

GRADING - PPGS™	100%	98%	95%	90%	80%	70%	60%

SHOTGUNS: BOLT ACTION

The following models are available in left-hand action at no additional charge.

DSG (DESIGNATED SLUG GUN) - 12 or 16 ga., based on Rem. 870, non-removable custom fit Shaw 23 in. rifled slug barrel with muzzle brake, includes Leupold two-piece windage bases which accept any standard rings, available in Express Mag., Wingmaster Mag., or Express Super Mag. configurations.

MSR $840	$795	$725	$650	$550	$475	$400	$350

Add $356 for Wingmaster Mag.
Add $69 for left hand.

PROFESSIONAL MODEL RSG-12 - 12 (RSG-12) ga., 2 3/4 or 3 (new 2003) in. chamber, bolt action slug gun featuring 21 1/2 or 23 (new 2003) in. Shaw barrel and 2 lug bolt, 1 round down in mag. (new 1998), matte black finish, McMillan fiberglass stock with Pachmayr Decelerator rifle pad, receiver drilled and tapped for standard Leupold windage bases (included, new 1997), muzzle brake became standard 1994, various finish options, 7 3/4 lbs. New 1991.

MSR $2,715	$2,475	$2,200	$1,875	$1,525	$1,275	$1,050	$900

Add $100 for left-hand action.

✳ *Professional Model RSG-12 Combo Slug Gun* - includes standard Professional RSG-12 Slug Gun and a second benchrest McMillan heavy weight stock. Mfg. 1994-2004.

$2,250	$1,900	$1,575	$1,250	$1,000	$850	$750

Last MSR was $2,175.

✳ *Professional Model RSG-12/RSG-20 10th Anniversary* - 12 or 20 ga., hand selected actions and barrels, Jewell custom adj. trigger, NP-3 nickel/Teflon metal finish, black McMillan stock with Pachmayr Decelerator pad. Only 25 mfg. during 2000 only, reintroduced 2005.

$2,150	$1,875	$1,525	$1,275	$1,050	$900	$800

Last MSR was $2,395.

MATCHLESS MODEL RSG-12 - upgraded variation featuring 400 grit polished gloss metal finish and the McMillan regular or "Fiber" grain stock (wood grain finish, disc. 2000). Mfg. 1995-2004.

$2,175	$1,925	$1,600	$1,300	$1,100	$950	$850

Last MSR was $2,495.

PEERLESS MODEL RSG-12 - upgraded variation featuring NP-3 (nickel/Teflon) metal finish by Robar of Phoenix, AZ, McMillan regular or "Fiber" grain stock (wood grain finish, disc. 2000). Mfg. 1995-2004.

$2,725	$2,350	$1,900	$1,600	$1,400	$1,200	$1,000

Last MSR was $3,075.

ELITE MODEL RSG-16 - 12 ga., 2 3/4 in. chamber, 23 in. Shaw rifled barrel, and 2 lug bolt, 1 shot mag., matte black finish, black McMillan fiberglass stock with Pachmayr decelerator pad, drilled and tapped for Rem. 700 long action style bases. Mfg. 2003-2004.

$2,150	$1,875	$1,525	$1,275	$1,050	$900	$800

Last MSR was $2,395.

MOUNTAINEER MODEL RSG-20 - 20 (RSG-20) ga., 2 3/4 in. chamber, features 21 in. Shaw rifled barrel and 2 lug bolt, one shot mag., matte black finish only, McMillan fiberglass stock with Pachmayr Decelerator pad, receiver drilled and tapped for Rem. Mod. 700 long action style bases, muzzle brake standard, 6 1/2 lbs. Mfg. 1997-2004.

$2,150	$1,875	$1,525	$1,275	$1,050	$900	$800

Last MSR was $2,395.

GRADING - PPGS™	100%	98%	95%	90%	80%	70%	60%

RSG-TACTICAL (SNIPER) MODEL - 12 ga. only, similar to RSG-12, except has M-86 McMillan fiberglass black tactical stock with Pachmayr Decelerator pad and heavy barrel. Mfg. 1992-98.

	$1,495	$1,250	$995	$875	$750	$700	$650

Last MSR was $1,595.

Add $150 for Bipod.

BLOCK CARD MODEL - 12 ga., 2 3/4 in. chamber, various barrel lengths, cartage type chokes, special McMillan fiberglass stock, Pachmayr Decelerator pad, fluted barrels optional, special chambers, weighted stocks optional, single shot actions. Disc.

	$1,625	$1,425	$1,125	$900	$800	$750	$700

Last MSR was $1,775.

TATE GUNMAKERS LLC

Current shotgun manufacturer established 1995 and located in Ione, CA. Consumer direct sales.

SHOTGUNS: SxS

Dale Tate, formerly of J. Purdey & Sons, makes custom order shotguns per individual customer specifications in 10, 12, 16, 20, or 28 ga. Current SxS models include: Vintager Model w/ hammers, Concours Model w/ hammers, and the Tate Model w/ hammers. All models are POR. Hammerless models include the Tate Model, which is also POR, w/ optional engraving available. Tate Gunmakers also specializes in gun repair and restoration. Prices are quoted per individual work order. Please contact the company directly for more information, including delivery time and pricing (see Trademark Index).

TAURUS INTERNATIONAL MFG., INC.

Currently manufactured by Taurus Forjas S.A., located in Porto Alegre, Brazil. Currently imported by Taurus International Mfg., Inc. located in Miami, FL since 1982. Beginning 2007, Taurus Tactical, a separate entity, was created for law enforcement/military sales and service. Distributor sales only.

All Taurus products are known for their innovative design, quality construction, and proven value, and are backed by a lifetime repair policy.

Taurus order number nomenclature is as follows: the first digit followed by a dash refers to type (1 = pistol, 2 = revolver, 3 = rifle/carbine, 5 = magazines, accessories, or grips, and 10 = scope mount bases), the next 2 or 3 digits refer to model number, the next digit refers to type of hammer (0 = exposed, 1 = concealed), the next digit refers to barrel length, the last digit refers to finish (1 = blue, 9 = stainless), and the suffix at the end refers to special features (T = total titanium, H = case hardened, M = matte finish, UL = Ultra-Lite, C = compensator [ported], G = gold accent, R = rosewood grips, PRL = mother-of-pearl grips, and NS = night sights). Hence, 2-941029UL refers to a Model 941 Ultra-Lite revolver in .22 Mag. cal. with an exposed hammer and a 2 in. barrel in stainless steel.

PISTOLS: SEMI-AUTO

From 1990-92, certain models became available with a Laser Aim LA1 sighting system that included mounts, rings (in matching finish), a 110 volt AC recharging unit, a 9 volt DC field charger, and a high impact custom case.

Taurus incorporated their keyed Taurus security system on most models during 2000, except the PT-22 and PT-25, and this is now available with all models. When the security system is engaged (via a keyed button on the bottom of rear grip strap), the pistol cannot be fired, cocked, or disassembled, and the gun's manual safety cannot be disengaged. This security key also works for the revolvers.

Add approx. $30 for the Deluxe Shooter's Pack option (included extra mag. and custom case) on the 92, 99, 100, and 101 Series (disc. 2000).

GRADING - PPGS™	100%	98%	95%	90%	80%	70%	60%

PT-22 - .22 LR cal., double action only, tip-up 2 3/4 in. barrel, 8 shot mag., fixed sights, blue, nickel (new 1995), blue/nickel (mfg. 1997-2000), Duo-tone (new 2000), or deluxe blue/gold (new 1997) finish, wood (new 1999), mother-of-pearl (new 2000, deluxe blue/gold finish only), black pearl (new 2006), or rosewood grips, 12.3 oz. New 1992.

MSR $248		$190	$170	$155	$135	$120	$105	$85

   Add $18 for blue/gold or nickel/gold finish with rosewood or $35 for blue/gold or nickel/gold finish with black pearl (new 2006) or mother-of-pearl grips.
   Add $18 for pink pearl grips with blue or nickel finish or $35 for pink pearl grips with blue/nickel and gold finish (Model PP-22).

PT-24/7 - 9mm Para., .40 S&W, or .45 ACP (new 2005) cal., DAO, large black polymer frame with blued steel or satin stainless steel slide, 4 in. barrel with 3-dot sights, grips have Ribber grip overlays, 10, 12 (.45 ACP cal.), 15 (.40 S&W cal.), or 17 (9mm Para. cal.) shot mag., built-in Picatinny rail system on bottom of frame, includes 3 safeties, 27 1/2 oz. Mfg. late 2004-2005.

		$450	$400	$350	$310	$250	$200	$180

Last MSR was $578.

   Add $16 for stainless steel.

PT-24/7 PRO FULL SIZE - 9mm Para., .40 S&W, or .45 ACP cal., SA first shot, and follows continually in SA mode, large black polymer frame with blued steel, titanium (9mm Para. cal. only), or satin stainless steel slide, 4 in. barrel with Heinie front and slant pro rear sight, Ribber grips (.45 ACP cal.) or Ribber overmold grips (grip inlays), 10, 12 (.45 ACP cal.), 15 (.40 S&W cal.), or 17 (9mm Para. cal.) shot mag., built-in Picatinny rail system on bottom of frame, includes 3 safeties, 27.2 oz. New 2006.

MSR $452		$385	$345	$295	$250	$215	$170	$150

   Add $15 for stainless steel or $171 for titanium.

This model uses a SA trigger mechanism. However, if a cartridge does not fire, a DA feature allows the shooter a second firing pin strike via the DA trigger pull. If the cartridge still does not fire, then extraction by slide operation will insert a fresh round while reverting to the SA model automatically.

✳ *PT-24/7 Pro Long Slide* - similar to Full Size 24/7-Pro, except has 5 in. barrel, similar mag. capacities, 29.1 oz. New 2006.

MSR $481		$415	$365	$320	$275	$225	$185	$165

   Add $16 for stainless steel.

✳ *PT-24/7 Pro Compact* - similar to Full Size 24/7-Pro, except has 3 1/3 in. barrel, similar mag. capacities, not available in .45 ACP cal. New 2006.

MSR $452		$385	$345	$295	$250	$215	$170	$150

   Add $15 for stainless steel or $171 for titanium.

PT-24/7 OSS - 9mm Para., .40 S&W, or .45 ACP cal., similar operating system as PT-24/7 Pro Full Size, including SA/DA trigger system, choice of tan or black frame, 5 1/4 in. match grade barrel with Novak sights and under Picatinny rail, 10, 12, 15, or 17 shot mag., ambidextrous decocking safety, blued steel slide with front and rear serrations, approx. 32 oz. New 2007.

MSR $623		$475	$425	$365	$325	$260	$215	$190

   Add $63 for Novak low-mount night sights.

PT-25 - .25 ACP cal., similar to PT-22, except has 9 shot mag., 12.3 oz. New 1992.

MSR $248		$190	$170	$155	$135	$120	$105	$85

   Add $18 for blue/gold or nickel/gold finish with rosewood or $35 for blue/gold or nickel/gold finish with mother-of-pearl grips.
   Add $18 for pink pearl grips with blue or nickel finish or $35 for pink pearl grips with blue/nickel and gold finish (Model PP-25).

GRADING - PPGS™	100%	98%	95%	90%	80%	70%	60%

PT-38S - .38 Super cal., 4 1/4 in. barrel, DA/SA utilizes Model PT-945 alloy frame, choice of blue, stainless steel, or stainless/gold finishes, 3-dot fixed sights, 10 shot mag., checkered rubber (standard) or smooth faux mother-of-pearl grips, 30 oz. New 2005.

MSR $625	$465	$415	$360	$320	$260	$210	$185

Add $16 for stainless steel slide.
Add $81 for stainless steel slide, gold accents, and faux mother-of-pearl grips.

PT-58 - .380 ACP cal., similar to PT-99AF, except in .380 ACP cal., 4 in. barrel, 10 (C/B 1994) or 12* shot mag. Mfg. 1988-96.

	$325	$280	$245	$200	$175	$145	$130

Last MSR was $429.

Add $32 for satin nickel finish (disc. 1994).
Beginning 1993, the PT-58 utilized the Taurus Tri-Position safety system which features hammer-drop or "cocked-and-locked" options.

＊*PT-58SS (Stainless Steel)* - similar to PT-58, except is stainless steel. Mfg. 1992- 96.

	$385	$345	$295	$250	$215	$170	$150

Last MSR was $470.

PT-58 HC PLUS - .380 ACP cal., medium frame, similar to PT-58, except has 19 shot mag., ambidextrous safety, fixed sights, 18.7 oz. New 2006.

MSR $602	$450	$400	$350	$310	$250	$200	$180

Add $15 for stainless steel slide.

PT-91AF - .41 Action Express cal., action similar to PT-92AF, except is in .41 AE cal., 10 shot mag., 34 oz. Imported 1990 only.

	$365	$320	$275	$230	$195	$160	$140

Last MSR was $446.

Add $36 for satin nickel finish.
Add $25 for shooter's pack (includes custom case and extra mag.).

PT-92(AF) - 9mm Para. cal., semi-auto double action, design similar to Beretta Model 92 SB-F, exposed hammer, ambidextrous safety, 5 in. barrel, 10 (C/B 1994), 15*, or 17 (new late 2004) shot mag., smooth Brazilian walnut (disc.) or checkered rubber (new 1999) grips, blue, nickel (disc.), or stainless steel finish, fixed or night (mfg. 2000-2004) sights, 34 oz.

MSR $542	$425	$370	$320	$275	$225	$185	$165

Add $40 for satin nickel finish (disc. 1994).
Add $415 for Laser Aim Sight (disc. 1991).
Add $78 for night sights (disc. 2004).
Add $266 for blue or stainless conversion kit to convert 9mm Para. to .22 LR (mfg. 1999-2004).

＊*PT-92SS (Stainless Steel)* - similar to PT-92AF, except is combat matte (new 2006, high cap. mag. only) or regular stainless steel. New 1992.

MSR $559	$435	$390	$340	$295	$240	$195	$175

Add $78 for night sights (disc. 2004).

＊*PT-92 Deluxe* - choice of blue/gold (disc. 2004) or stainless steel with gold finish, rosewood, or mother-of-pearl (new 2000) grips. New 1999.

MSR $613	$485	$400	$315	$260	$225	$200	$190

Add $17 for mother-of-pearl grips.
Subtract approx. $15 for blue/gold finish (disc. 2004).

＊*PT-92AFC* - compact variation of the Model PT-92AF, 4 in. barrel, 10 (C/B 1994) or 13* shot mag., fixed sights. Disc. 1996.

	$335	$285	$235	$225	$200	$190	$180

Last MSR was $449.

Add $38 for satin nickel finish (disc. 1993).

GRADING - PPGS™	100%	98%	95%	90%	80%	70%	60%

❋ *PT-92AFC (Stainless Steel)* - similar to PT-92AFC, except stainless steel. Mfg. 1993-96.

	$400	$310	$260	$200	$170	$145	$125

Last MSR was $493.

PT-99 (AF) - 9mm Para. cal., similar to Model PT-92AF, except has adj. rear sight, 10 or 17 shot mag., 34 oz.

MSR $559	$435	$360	$290	$245	$215	$195	$180

Add $45 for satin nickel finish (disc. 1994).
Add $266 for blue or stainless conversion kit to convert 9mm Para. to .22 LR (mfg. 1999-2004) or .40 S&W (mfg. 2000-2004).

This action is similar to the Beretta Model 92SB-F.

❋ *PT-99SS (Stainless Steel)* - similar to PT-99, except is fabricated from stainless steel. New 1992.

MSR $575	$450	$375	$310	$245	$210	$180	$155

PT-100 - .40 S&W cal., semi-auto, standard double action, 5 in. barrel, 10 (C/B 1994), 11* (reintroduced late 2004) shot mag., safeties include ambidextrous manual, hammer drop, inertia firing pin, and chamber loaded indicator, choice of blue, satin nickel (disc. 1994), or stainless steel finish, smooth Brazilian hard wood (disc.) or rubber grips, 34 oz. Mfg. 1992-97, reintroduced 2000.

MSR $542	$425	$350	$285	$235	$210	$195	$180

Add $40 for satin nickel finish (disc. 1994).
Add $78 for night sights (mfg. 2000-2004).
Add $266 for blue or stainless conversion kit to convert .40 S&W to .22 LR cal. (disc. 2004).

❋ *PT-100SS (Stainless Steel)* - similar to PT-100, except is fabricated from stainless steel. Mfg. 1992-96, reintroduced 2000.

MSR $559	$435	$360	$290	$245	$215	$195	$180

Add $78 for night sights (disc. 2005).

❋ *PT-100 Deluxe* - choice of blue/gold (disc. 2004) finish or stainless steel with gold, rosewood, or mother-of-pearl grips. New 2000.

MSR $613	$485	$430	$375	$330	$280	$230	$200

Add $17 for mother-of-pearl grips.
Subtract approx. $15 for blue/gold finish (disc. 2004).

PT-101 - .40 S&W cal., similar to PT-100, except has adj. rear sight., 11 shot mag. became standard during late 2004, 34 oz. Mfg. 1992-96, reintroduced 2000.

MSR $559	$435	$380	$330	$285	$235	$190	$170

Add $266 for blue or stainless conversion kit to convert .40 S&W to .22 LR cal. (disc. 2004).
Add $45 for satin nickel finish (disc. 1994).

❋ *PT-101SS (Stainless Steel)* - similar to PT-101, except is stainless steel. Mfg. 1992-96, reintroduced 2000.

MSR $575	$450	$400	$350	$310	$250	$200	$180

PT-111 MILLENNIUM - 9mm Para. cal., double action only, 3 1/4 in. barrel with fixed 3-dot sights, black polymer frame with steel slide, striker fired, 10 shot mag. with push-button release, 18.7 oz. Mfg. 1998-2004.

	$355	$310	$265	$225	$190	$155	$135

Last MSR was $422.

Add $78 for night sights (new 2000).
Add $47 for pearl or burl walnut grips (limited mfg. 2003).

❋ *PT-111 Millennium Stainless* - similar to Model PT-111, except has stainless steel slide. Mfg. 1998-2004.

	$360	$315	$270	$225	$190	$155	$135

Last MSR was $438.

Add $78 for night sights (new 2000).
Add $46 for pearl or burl walnut grips (limited mfg. 2003).

GRADING - PPGS™	100%	98%	95%	90%	80%	70%	60%

✳ *PT-111 Millennium Titanium* - similar to Model PT-111, except has titanium slide and night or 3-dot (new 2004) sights. Mfg. 2000-2004.

	$415	$365	$320	$275	$225	$185	$165

Last MSR was $508.

Add $78 for night sights.

PT-111 MILLENNIUM PRO - 9mm Para. cal., similar to Model PT-111 Millennium, 10 or 12 (new late 2004) shot mag., except has improved ergonomics, Posi-Traction slide serrations, recessed magazine release, manual safety lever, trigger block mechanism, firing pin block, and lightweight frame, 18.7 oz. New 2003.

MSR $419	$345	$300	$260	$220	$185	$155	$135

Add $78 for night sights (disc. 2004).

✳ *PT-111 Millennium Pro Stainless* - similar to Model PT-111 Millennium Pro, except has stainless steel slide. New 2003.

MSR $436	$365	$325	$275	$230	$195	$160	$140

Add $78 for night sights (mfg. 2004).

✳ *PT-111 Ti Millennium Pro Titanium* - similar to Model PT-111 Millennium Pro, except has titanium slide, 16 oz. New 2005.

MSR $592	$475	$425	$365	$325	$265	$215	$190

PT-132 MILLENNIUM - .32 ACP cal., double action only, 3 1/4 in. barrel, black polymer frame, manual safety, 10 shot mag., fixed 3-dot (disc. 2002) or adj. (new 2003) sights, blue steel slide, 18.7 oz. Mfg. 2001-2004.

	$355	$315	$265	$225	$190	$155	$135

Last MSR was $422.

✳ *Model PT-132 Millennium Stainless* - similar to Model PT-132, except has stainless steel slide. Mfg. 2001-2004.

	$360	$315	$265	$225	$190	$155	$135

Last MSR was $438.

PT-132 MILLENNIUM PRO - .32 ACP cal., similar to Model PT-132 Millennium, except has improved ergonomics, Posi-Traction slide serrations, recessed magazine release, manual safety lever, trigger block mechanism, firing pin block, adj. rear sight, and lightweight frame, 19.9 oz. Mfg. 2003, reintroduced 2005.

MSR $419	$345	$285	$230	$190	$155	$135	$120

✳ *PT-132 Millennium Pro Stainless* - similar to Model PT-132 Millennium Pro, except has stainless steel slide. Mfg. 2003, reintroduced 2005.

MSR $436	$365	$285	$230	$190	$155	$135	$120

PT-138 MILLENNIUM - .380 ACP cal., double action only, 3 1/4 in. barrel, black polymer frame, manual safety, 10 shot mag., fixed 3-dot sights, blue steel slide, 18.7 oz. Mfg. 1999-2004.

	$355	$290	$235	$190	$155	$135	$120

Last MSR was $422.

Add $78 for night sights (mfg. 2000-2003).

✳ *Model PT-138 Millennium Stainless* - similar to Model PT-138, except has stainless steel slide. New 1999.

	$360	$290	$235	$190	$155	$135	$120

Add $78 for night sights (mfg. 2000-2003).

PT-138 MILLENNIUM PRO - .380 ACP cal., similar to Model PT-138 Millennium, 10 or 12 shot (new 2005) mag. except has improved ergonomics, Posi-Traction slide serrations, recessed magazine release, manual safety lever, trigger block mechanism, firing pin block, adj. rear sight, and lightweight frame, 18.7 oz. Mfg. 2003, reintroduced 2005.

MSR $419	$345	$285	$230	$190	$155	$135	$120

Add $78 for night sights (disc. 2003).

GRADING - PPGS™	100%	98%	95%	90%	80%	70%	60%

* PT-138 Millennium Pro Stainless - similar to Model PT-138 Millennium Pro, except has stainless steel slide. Mfg. 2003, reintroduced 2005.

MSR $436	$365	$285	$230	$190	$155	$135	$120

PT-140 MILLENNIUM - .40 S&W cal., double action only, 3 1/4 in. barrel, black polymer frame, manual safety, 10 shot mag., fixed 3-dot sights, blue steel slide, 18.7 oz. Mfg. 1999-2004.

	$375	$335	$280	$240	$200	$165	$150

Last MSR was $461.

Add $78 for night sights (new 2000).
Add $47 for pearl or burl walnut grips (mfg. 2003).

* PT-140 Millennium Stainless - similar to Model PT-140, except has stainless steel slide. Mfg. 1999-2004.

	$380	$340	$285	$240	$200	$165	$150

Last MSR was $476.

Add $78 for night sights (new 2000).
Add $46 for pearl or burl walnut grips (mfg. 2003).

PT-140 MILLENNIUM PRO - .40 S&W cal., similar to Model PT-140 Millennium, except has improved ergonomics, Posi-Traction slide serrations, recessed magazine release, manual safety lever, trigger block mechanism, firing pin block, and lightweight frame, 23 1/2 oz. New 2003.

MSR $436	$365	$320	$275	$230	$195	$160	$140

Add $78 for night sights (disc. 2004).

* PT-140 Millennium Pro Stainless - similar to Model PT-140 Millennium Pro, except has stainless steel slide. New 2003.

MSR $453	$375	$335	$280	$240	$200	$165	$150

Add $78 for night sights (disc. 2004).

PT-145 MILLENNIUM - .45 ACP cal., otherwise similar to Model PT-140 Millennium, 23 oz. Mfg. 2000-2003.

	$400	$350	$300	$260	$215	$175	$155

Last MSR was $484.

Add $79 for night sights (new 2000).

* PT-145 Millennium Stainless - similar to Model PT-140, except has stainless steel slide. Mfg. 1999-2003.

	$400	$350	$300	$260	$200	$165	$150

Last MSR was $500.

Add $78 for night sights (new 2000).

PT-145 MILLENNIUM PRO - .45 ACP cal., similar to Model PT-145 Millennium, except has improved ergonomics, Posi-Traction slide serrations, recessed magazine release, manual safety lever, trigger block mechanism, firing pin block, and lightweight frame, 22.2 oz. New 2003.

MSR $436	$365	$320	$275	$230	$195	$160	$140

Add $78 for night sights (disc. 2004).

* PT-145 Millennium Pro Stainless - similar to Model PT-145 Millennium Pro, except has stainless steel slide. New 2003.

MSR $453	$375	$335	$280	$240	$200	$165	$150

Add $78 for night sights (mfg. 2000-2004).

PT-400 - .400 Cor-Bon cal., similar to Model PT-940, except has 4 1/4 in. ported barrel and 8 shot mag., 29 1/2 oz. Mfg. 1999 only.

	$415	$365	$320	$275	$225	$185	$165

Last MSR was $523.

* PT-400 Stainless - similar to Model PT-400, except has stainless steel slide. Mfg. 1999 only.

	$415	$365	$320	$275	$225	$185	$165

Last MSR was $539.

GRADING - PPGS™	100%	98%	95%	90%	80%	70%	60%

PT-609 - 9mm Para cal., DA/SA, 3 1/4 in. barrel with titanium slide, fixed sights, grey polymer grips, lower rail on frame, 13 shot mag., 16.3 oz. New 2007.

MSR $608	$485	$435	$375	$330	$280	$230	$200

PT-745 COMPACT MILLENNIUM PRO - .45 ACP cal., DAO, compact variation of Millennium Pro with 3 1/4 in. barrel, 6 shot mag. with finger extension, matte blue steel slide, loaded chamber indicator, black polymer grip frame, Desert Tan grips were added 2006, 20.8 oz. New 2005.

MSR $436	$365	$320	$275	$230	$195	$160	$140

✳ *PT-745 Compact Millenium Pro Stainless* - similar to PT-745 Compact Millennium Pro, except has stainless steel slide. New 2005.

MSR $453	$375	$330	$280	$240	$200	$165	$150

MODEL 809 - 9mm Para. cal., similar design to the PT-24/7 OSS, 4 in. barrel, SA/DA with Strike Two capability, Novak sights, 17 shot mag., blue or stainless, front and rear slide serrations, lower Picatinny rail. New 2007.

MSR $623	$495	$445	$385	$335	$290	$235	$200

Add $18 for stainless steel slide.

MODEL 840 - .40 S&W cal., similar design to the PT-24/7 OSS, 4 in. barrel, SA/DA with Strike Two capability, Novak sights, 15 shot mag., blue or stainless, front and rear slide serrations, lower Picatinny rail. New 2008.

MSR $623	$495	$445	$385	$335	$290	$235	$200

Add $18 for stainless steel slide.

MODEL 845 - .45 ACP cal., similar design to the PT-24/7 OSS, 4 in. barrel, SA/DA with Strike Two capability, Novak sights, 12 shot mag., blue or stainless, front and rear slide serrations, lower Picatinny rail. New 2008.

MSR $623	$495	$445	$385	$335	$290	$235	$200

Add $18 for stainless steel slide.

PT-908 - 9mm Para. cal., compact version of the PT-92 with 3.8 in. barrel and 8 shot mag., fixed sights, blue or nickel finish. Mfg. 1993-97.

	$330	$290	$250	$210	$180	$150	$130

Last MSR was $435.

✳ *PT-908D SS (Stainless Steel)* - similar to Model PT-908, except is stainless steel. Mfg. 1993-97.

	$385	$345	$295	$250	$215	$170	$150

Last MSR was $473.

PT-909 - 9mm Para. cal., DA/SA, 4 in. barrel with Picatinny rail on bottom of frame, 10 or 17 shot mag., blue finish, fixed rear sight, alloy medium frame with steel slide, checkered rubber grips, 28.2 oz. New 2006.

MSR $584	$455	$400	$350	$310	$250	$200	$180

Add $18 for stainless steel slide.

PT-911 COMPACT - 9mm Para. cal., single or double action, 4 in. barrel, 10 or 15 (new late 2004) shot mag., checkered rubber grips, fixed sights, 28.2 oz. New 1997.

MSR $584	$455	$400	$350	$310	$250	$200	$180

Add $79 for night sights (disc. 2004).

✳ *PT-911 Compact SS (Stainless Steel)* - stainless variation of the PT-911 Compact.

MSR $602	$485	$365	$295	$235	$200	$185	$170

Add $78 for night sights (disc. 2004).

✳ *PT-911 Compact Deluxe* - choice of blue/gold finish or stainless steel with gold, rosewood, or mother-of-pearl grips. New 2000.

MSR $633	$495	$395	$315	$260	$225	$210	$200

Add $17 for stainless steel with gold or mother-of-pearl grips.

GRADING - PPGS™	100%	98%	95%	90%	80%	70%	60%

PT-917 COMPACT - 9mm Para. cal., DA/SA, 4 in. barrel with fixed sights, rubber grips, 19 shot mag., medium frame, blue finish or stainless steel, 31.8 oz. New 2007.

MSR $542		$450	$400	$350	$310	$250	$200	$180

Add $17 for stainless steel.

PT-922 - .22 LR cal., sport model with 10 shot mag., 6 in. tapered barrel and adj. sights, medium frame, blue finish, angled synthetic grip frame with Taurus medallions on bottom, 25 oz. Limited mfg. 2004.

		$285	$240	$210	$180	$155	$130	$115

Last MSR was $370.

PT-938 COMPACT - .380 ACP cal., DA/SA, 3 3/4 in. barrel, ambidextrous safety, 10 or 15 (new late 2004) shot mag., blue finish with alloy frame and steel slide, rubber grips, fixed sights, 34 oz. Mfg. 1997-2005.

		$410	$360	$315	$270	$220	$180	$160

Last MSR was $516.

✱ *PT-938 Compact SS (Stainless Steel)* - stainless slide variation of the PT-938 Compact with matte stainless finish.

		$420	$370	$320	$275	$225	$185	$165

Last MSR was $531.

PT-940 - .40 S&W cal., compact version of the PT-100 with 3 5/8 in. barrel and 10 shot mag., fixed sights, 28.2 oz. New 1996.

MSR $584		$455	$400	$350	$310	$250	$200	$180

Add $79 for night sights (disc. 2004).

✱ *PT-940 SS (Stainless Steel)* - similar to PT-940, except is stainless steel. New 1996.

MSR $602		$475	$425	$365	$325	$265	$215	$190

Add $80 for night sights.

✱ *PT-940 Deluxe* - choice of blue/gold or stainless steel with gold finish, rosewood, or mother-of-pearl grips. New 2000.

MSR $633		$495	$445	$385	$335	$290	$235	$200

Add $17 for stainless steel with gold with rosewood grips or for mother-of-pearl grips.

PT-945 - .45 ACP cal., DA/SA, 4 1/4 in. ported (mfg. 1997-2003) or unported barrel, 8 shot single stack mag., ambidextrous 3 position safety, chamber loaded indicator, 3-dot sights, 29 1/2 oz. New 1995.

MSR $625		$510	$460	$405	$350	$300	$245	$215

Add $78 for night sights (disc. 2004).
Add $39 for ported barrel (disc. 2003).

✱ *PT-945 SS (Stainless Steel)* - stainless steel variation of the PT-945. New 1995.

MSR $641		$520	$465	$415	$360	$310	$250	$220

Add $78 for night sights (disc. 2004).
Add $39 for ported barrel (disc. 2003).

✱ *PT-945 Deluxe* - choice of blue/gold (disc. 2004) or stainless steel finish, mother-of-pearl (new 2000), or rosewood grips. New 1999.

MSR $691		$545	$485	$425	$375	$325	$265	$235

Add $15 for mother-of-pearl grips.
Subtract approx. $15 for blue/gold finish.

PT-957 - .357 SIG cal., compact model with 3 5/8 in. ported (available only with night sights or in 957 Deluxe beginning 2002) or non-ported (new 2002) barrel and slide, 10 shot mag., ambidextrous 3-position safety, blue finish, checkered rubber grips, fixed sights, 28 oz. Mfg. 1999-2003.

		$425	$375	$325	$275	$225	$185	$165

Last MSR was $523.

Add $90 for night sights.
Add $40 for ported barrel (disc. 2002).

GRADING - PPGS™	100%	98%	95%	90%	80%	70%	60%

* **PT-957 SS (Stainless Steel)** - stainless steel variation of the PT-957. Mfg. 1999-2003.

$430	$380	$330	$275	$225	$185	$165

Last MSR was $539.

> **Add $40 for ported (disc. 2001) barrel, or $130 for ported barrel and night sights (disc. 2003).**

* **PT-957 Deluxe** - choice of blue/gold or stainless steel with gold finish, rosewood, or mother-of-pearl grips. Mfg. 2000-2002.

$475	$425	$365	$325	$265	$215	$190

Last MSR was $610.

> **Add $15 for stainless steel.**
> **Add $15 for mother-of-pearl grips.**

PT-1911 - .38 Super (mfg. 2006), 9mm Para. (mfg. 2006), .40 S&W (mfg. 2006) or .45 ACP cal., SA, 5 in. barrel, choice of Heinie front and rear sights or Picatinny rail, 8 (.40 S&W or .45 ACP) or 9 (.38 Super or 9mm Para.) shot mag., blue or Duo-tone (new 2008) finish, choice of steel or aluminum (new 2008) frame with steel slide, checkered diamond pattern wood grips, bobbed hammer, front and rear serrations on slide, accurized hand tuned action, 32 oz. New mid-2005.

MSR $719	$575	$500	$450	$395	$340	$275	$240

> **Add $97 for stainless steel slide.**
> **Add $31 for Picatinny rail.**
> **Add $76 for aluminum frame or Duo-tone finish.**

* **PT-1911 Compact** - .45 ACP cal., only, similar to PT-1911, except has 4 1/4 in. barrel, 6 shot mag. Mfg. 2006 only.

$490	$440	$385	$335	$290	$235	$200

Last MSR was $599.

> **Add $20 for stainless steel slide.**

REVOLVERS: RECENT PRODUCTION

From 1990-1992, certain models became available with a Laser Aim LA1 sighting system that included mounts, rings (in matching finish), a 110 volt AC recharging unit, a 9 volt DC field charger, and a high impact custom case.

The following Taurus revolvers have been listed in numerical order. All currently manufactured revolvers listed are rated for +P ammunition.

Tracker model nomenclature refers to a heavy contoured barrel with full shroud, porting, and with or w/o VR.

All currently manufactured Taurus revolvers are equipped with their patented Taurus Security System, introduced in 1998, which utilizes an integral key lock on the back of the hammer, locking the action.

> **Add approx. $45 for scope base mount on currently produced models that offer this option.**
> **Add $31 for carrying case on Raging Bull & Raging Hornet Models listed (disc. 2006).**

MODEL GAUCHO SA - .357 Mag. (new 2006), .44-40 WCF (mfg. 2006), or .45 LC cal., SA Western style revolver, large frame, 4 3/4 (new 2006), 5 1/2, 7 1/2 (new 2006), or 12 (mfg. 2006) in. barrel, fixed sights, four click action, choice of all blue, blue/color case hardened, matte stainless, or polished stainless steel, 36.7 oz (5 1/2 in. barrel). Mfg. 2005-2007.

$425	$375	$325	$275	$225	$185	$165

Last MSR was $520.

> **Add $16 for stainless steel or blue/color case hardened finish.**
> **Add $26 for 12 in. barrel (mfg. 2006).**

GRADING - PPGS™	100%	98%	95%	90%	80%	70%	60%

MODEL 17C - .17 HMR or .17 Mach 2 (mfg. 2004-2006) cal., small frame, 8 shot, 2, 4 or 5 in. barrel, blue only, adj. sights, full underlug on 4 and 5 in. barrels, soft rubber grips, 24-27 1/2 oz. Mfg. 2003-2007.

	$295	$255	$220	$185	$160	$135	$120

Last MSR was $391.

❋ *Model 17C Ultra-Lite* - ultra light hammer forged frame, 2 in. barrel, available in matte blue (disc. 2004, reintroduced 2006) or bright stainless steel, 18 1/2 oz. Mfg. 2003-2006.

	$340	$300	$260	$220	$185	$155	$135

Last MSR was $453.

Subtract $47 for matte blue finish.

❋ *Model 17CSS (Stainless Steel)* - similar to Model 17C, except is polished (disc.) or matte stainless steel, 5 in. barrel disc. 2006. Mfg. 2003-2007.

	$330	$290	$250	$210	$180	$150	$130

Last MSR was $439.

MODEL 17-IB (INSTANT BACKUP) - .17 HMR or .17 Mach 2 cal., small steel frame, 1 3/4 in. barrel, concealed hammer, blue finish, 8 (.17 HMR) or 9 (.17 Mach 2) shot, DA/SA, checkered rubber grips, adj. rear sight, transfer bar safety, 22.2 oz. Mfg. 2005-2007.

	$295	$255	$220	$185	$160	$135	$120

Last MSR was $391.

❋ *Model 17 Instant Backup Stainless* - .17 HMR or .17 Mach 2 cal., similar to Model 17 Instant Backup, except is matte stainless steel. Mfg. 2005-2007.

	$330	$290	$250	$210	$180	$150	$130

Last MSR was $439.

MODEL 17 TRACKER - .17 HMR cal., compact frame, 7 shot, adj. sights, 6 1/2 or 8 3/8 (mfg. 2004 only) in. Tracker VR barrel, blue (mfg. 2004-2005, reintroduced 2007 only), duo-tone (mfg. 2004 only, 6 1/2 in. barrel only) finish or matte stainless steel, 41 or 45 oz. New 2003.

MSR $453		$325	$285	$245	$210	$180	$150	$130

Subtract approx. 10% for blue finish (disc. 2007)..

MODEL 17-12 SILHOUETTE - .17 HMR cal., compact frame, features 12 in. barrel, adj. sights, includes scope mount. Mfg. 2003-2004.

	$320	$280	$240	$210	$180	$150	$130

Last MSR was $430.

MODEL 21T TRACKER - .218 Bee cal., compact frame, 7 shot, 6 1/2 in. Tracker barrel with VR, matte stainless steel, adj. sights. Mfg. 2003-2004.

	$325	$285	$245	$210	$180	$150	$130

Last MSR was $438.

MODEL 22H SS RAGING HORNET - .22 Hornet cal., large frame, 8 shot, stainless steel construction, 10 in. VR barrel with full shroud, fully adj. sights, scope mount bases included, contoured rubber grips, 50 oz. Mfg. 1999-2004.

	$795	$695	$600	$525	$465	$390	$295

Last MSR was $898.

MODEL 30C SS RAGING THIRTY HUNTER - .30 Carbine cal., large frame, 8 shot, 10 in. heavy VR barrel with full shroud and adj. sights, matte stainless steel, includes scope mounts and full moon clips, 50 oz. Mfg. 2003-2004.

	$795	$695	$600	$525	$465	$390	$295

Last MSR was $898.

MODEL 30S SILHOUETTE/HUNTER - .30 Carbine cal., large frame, 8 shot, double action, 12 in. VR barrel with partial shroud, matte stainless steel, adj. trigger tension and trigger stop, includes scope mounts, 50 oz. Mfg. 2003-2004.

$625	$550	$485	$425	$375	$310	$255

Last MSR was $743.

MODEL 44 - .44 Mag. cal., 6 shot, large frame, integral porting compensator, exposed or concealed (3 in. barrel only, mfg. 1997-98) hammer, bright blue finish, adj. sights, rubber grips, 3 (mfg. 1997-98), 4, 6 1/2 (VR), or 8 3/8 (VR) in. ported or non-ported (disc. 2002) barrel, 45-57 oz. Mfg. 1994-2004.

$400	$350	$300	$260	$215	$175	$155

Last MSR was $500.

Add $23 for 6 1/2 or 8 3/8 in. ported barrel.
Subtract approx. 10% for non-ported barrel.

✳ *Model 44SS (Stainless Steel)* - similar to Model 44, except matte finished stainless steel. New 1994.

MSR $617	$495	$445	$385	$335	$290	$235	$200

Add $16 for 6 1/2 or 8 3/8 in. ported barrel.
Add $46 for 3 in. ported barrel with fixed sights and round butt grips (mfg. 1996-97).

✳ *Model 44 Silhouette* - similar to Model 44, except has 12 in. VR non-ported barrel and adj. trigger tension and trigger stop, includes scope base mounts. Mfg. 2003-2004.

$485	$435	$375	$330	$280	$230	$200

Last MSR was $602.

MODEL 44C TRACKER - .44 Mag. cal., 5 shot, blue or stainless steel, 4 in. ported barrel, adj. rear sight, Ribber grips, 34 oz. New 2005.

MSR $552	$440	$390	$340	$295	$240	$195	$175

Add $48 for stainless steel.

MODEL 45-410 JUDGE (44-TEN TRACKER) - .45 LC/.410 shotshell, 2 1/2 or 3 (new 2008) in. chamber) cal., SA/DA, 5 shot, 2 1/2 (disc.), 3 (new 2007), or 6 /12 in. barrel, blue or stainless, fiber optic front sight, Ribber grips, compact frame, 32 oz. New 2006.

MSR $519	$425	$375	$325	$275	$225	$185	$165

Add $39 for 3 in. cylinder.
During late 2007, this model's nomenclature changed to the Model 45-410 Judge.

✳ *Model 45-410 Judge Stainless (44-Ten Tracker Stainless)* - similar to Model 45-410, except is matte stainless steel. New 2006.

MSR $569	$465	$420	$365	$325	$260	$210	$185

Add $39 for 3 in. cylinder.

✳ *Model 45-410 Judge Ultra-Lite* - similar to Model 45-410 Judge, except has alloy frame, choice of blued steel or stainless steel cylinder. New 2008.

MSR $589	$480	$430	$375	$330	$280	$230	$200

Add $50 for stainless steel barrel and cylinder.

MODEL 45 RAGING BULL - .45 LC cal., 6 shot, 6 1/2 or 8 3/8 in. VR ported barrel, adj. sights, soft rubber grips, 53 or 63 oz. Mfg. 1999-2001.

$475	$425	$365	$325	$265	$215	$190

Last MSR was $575.

✳ *Model 45 .45 LC Raging Bull Stainless* - similar to Model 45 Raging Bull, except is stainless steel. Disc. 2001.

$530	$470	$415	$365	$310	$250	$220

Last MSR was $630.

GRADING - PPGS™	100%	98%	95%	90%	80%	70%	60%

MODEL 65 - .357 Mag./.38 Spl. cal., medium frame, double action, 6 shot, fixed sights, 2 1/2 (mfg. 1993-97), 3 (disc. 1992) or 4 in. full underlug barrel, blue finish, checkered walnut (disc.) or rubber (new 1999) grips, 38 oz. Disc. 1997, reintroduced 1999.

MSR $419	$320	$280	$245	$200	$175	$145	$130

    Add $15 for satin nickel finish (disc.).

❋ *Model 65SS (Stainless Steel)* - similar to Model 65, except is matte finished stainless steel. Mfg. 1993-97, reintroduced 1999.

MSR $469	$360	$320	$275	$230	$195	$160	$140

MODEL 66 - .357 Mag./.38 Spl. cal., medium frame, double action, 6 (disc. 2001) or 7 (new 1999) shot, 2 1/2 (mfg. 1993-97), 3 (disc. 1992), 4, or 6 in. barrel, checkered walnut (disc. 1999) or rubber (new 2000) grips, blue finish, adj. sights, 38-40 oz. Disc. 1997, reintroduced 1999.

MSR $469	$360	$320	$275	$230	$195	$160	$140

    Add $15 for satin nickel finish (disc.).
    Add $10 for 4 or 6 in. compensated (66CP) barrel (mfg. 1993-94).

❋ *Model 66SS (Stainless Steel)* - similar to Model 66, but in stainless steel. Mfg. 1987-97, reintroduced 1999.

MSR $519	$410	$360	$315	$270	$220	$180	$160

    Add $10 for 4 or 6 in. compensated (66CP) barrel (mfg. 1993-94).

❋ *Model 66 Silhouette/Hunter* - .357 Mag./.38 Spl. cal., 7 shot, 12 in. barrel with adj. sights, rubber grips, adj. trigger tension and stop became standard 2003, includes scope mount. Mfg. 2001-2004.

	$330	$290	$250	$210	$180	$150	$130

                      Last MSR was $430.

❋ *Model 66 Silhouette/Hunter SS (Stainless Steel)* - similar to Model 66 Silhouette/Hunter, except is matte finished stainless steel. Mfg. 2001-2004.

	$380	$340	$290	$245	$210	$170	$150

                      Last MSR was $477.

MODEL 73 - .32 Long cal. only, double action, 6 shot, 3 in. heavy barrel only, checkered walnut grips, 20 oz. Disc. 1992.

	$190	$170	$155	$135	$120	$105	$85

                      Last MSR was $223.

    Add $20 for satin nickel finish.

MODEL 76 - .32 H&R Mag. cal., double action, 6 shot, 6 in. heavy barrel with solid rib, fully adj. rear sight, transfer bar safety, checkered hard wood grips, blue only, 34 oz. Mfg. 1991-94.

	$240	$200	$185	$160	$140	$120	$100

                      Last MSR was $308.

MODEL 80 - .38 Spl. cal. only, double action, 6 shot, 3 or 4 in. barrel, checkered walnut grips, fixed sights, 30 oz. Disc. 1996.

	$190	$170	$155	$135	$120	$105	$150

                      Last MSR was $252.

    Add $15 for satin nickel finish (disc. 1992).

❋ *Model 80SS (Stainless Steel)* - similar to Model 80, except stainless steel. Mfg. 1993-97.

	$245	$205	$190	$160	$140	$120	$100

                      Last MSR was $313.

MODEL 82 - .38 Spl. cal. only, medium frame, double action, 6 shot, 3 (disc. 1998) or 4 in. heavy barrel, checkered walnut (disc.) or rubber (new 1999) grips, full underlug, fixed sights, 34 oz.

MSR $403	$300	$260	$220	$190	$170	$140	$125

    Add $15 for satin nickel finish (disc.).

GRADING - PPGS™	100%	98%	95%	90%	80%	70%	60%

✳ *Model 82SS (Stainless Steel)* - similar to Model 82, except is polished stainless steel. New 1993.

MSR $453		$340	$300	$260	$220	$185	$155	$135

MODEL 83 - .38 Spl. cal. only, double action, 6 shot, 4 in. heavy barrel, checkered walnut grips, adj. sights, 34 1/2 oz. Disc. 1998.

		$220	$190	$175	$150	$130	$115	$95

Last MSR was $278.

Add $13 for satin nickel finish.

✳ *Model 83SS (Stainless Steel)* - similar to Model 83, except stainless steel. Mfg. 1993-98.

		$250	$210	$190	$165	$145	$120	$100

Last MSR was $324.

MODEL 85 - .38 Spl. cal. only, small frame, double action, 5 shot, 2 or 3 (disc. 2001, reintroduced 2006) in. heavy ported (new 1997) or unported barrel, hammer forged frame, exposed hammer, checkered walnut (disc. 2000) or soft rubber boot grips, fixed sights, 21-24 1/2 oz.

MSR $403		$310	$270	$235	$195	$175	$145	$130

Add $16 for ported barrel (disc. 2003).
Add $20 for satin nickel finish (3 in. barrel only, disc. 1992).
Subtract $15 for Hy-Lite magnesium grey finish.

✳ *Model 85SS (Stainless Steel)* - stainless version of Model 85.

MSR $453		$340	$300	$260	$220	$185	$155	$135

Add $16 for ported barrel (mfg. 1997-2003).

✳ *Model 85 Special Edition/Deluxe* - features blue finish with gold trim or stainless/gold trim, ported 2 in. barrel, rosewood or mother-of-pearl grips, includes integral key lock. New 1998.

MSR $445		$335	$295	$255	$215	$185	$155	$135

Add $24 for mother-of-pearl grips.
Add $24 for stainless/gold trim.

✳ *Model 85 Ultra-Lite* - ultra-lightweight version of Model 85 using an alloy frame, 17 oz.

MSR $388		$300	$260	$220	$190	$170	$140	$125

❖ **Model 85SSUL Ultra-Lite Stainless** - matte stainless variation of the Model 85 Ultra-Lite, 17 oz.

MSR $411		$310	$270	$235	$195	$175	$145	$130

Add $291 for Crimson Trace grips.

❖ **Model 85 Ultra-Lite Deluxe** - ported barrel, choice of blue/gold or stainless/gold, mother-of-pearl (new 2000) or rosewood grips, 17 oz. New 1999.

MSR $478		$355	$315	$270	$225	$190	$155	$135

Add $10 for stainless/gold.
Add $25 for mother-of-pearl grips with blue finish or $33 for mother-of-pearl grips in stainless/gold.

✳ *Model 85CH (Blue or Stainless)* - similar to Model 85, except has Brazilian hardwood combat (disc. 2000) or soft rubber grips and spurless concealed hammer that fits flush with the frame, 2 in. barrel, double action only, 21 oz. Mfg. 1992-2004.

		$285	$245	$215	$180	$155	$130	$115

Last MSR was $375.

Add $16 for ported barrel (disc. 2003).
Add $47 for polished stainless steel.

GRADING - PPGS™	100%	98%	95%	90%	80%	70%	60%

✴ *Model 85 Titanium Ultra-Lightweight* - features titanium barrel and cylinder and choice of matte aluminum or stainless steel (disc. 2001) small frame, fixed sight, rubber grips, choice of hammer or concealed hammer (Police Model 85), 17 oz. New 1999.

MSR $584	$480	$390	$325	$255	$225	$190	$165

Add $94 for Crimson Trace laser grips.

✴ *Model 85T* - similar to Model 85, except 100% titanium construction, 2 in. ported barrel only, choice of bright spectrum blue, matte spectrum blue, matte spectrum gold, stealth grey (mfg. 2000 only), or shadow grey (new 2000) finish, 15.4 oz. Mfg. 1999-2006.

	$530	$470	$415	$360	$310	$250	$220

Last MSR was $625.

Add $39 for blue and gold titanium finish and mother-of-pearl grips (disc. 2004, reintroduced 2006).

MODEL 86 CUSTOM TARGET - .38 Spl. cal. only, double action target model, 6 shot, 6 in. barrel, specially contoured smooth walnut grips, adj. rear sight, blue only, 34 oz. Disc. 1994.

	$270	$230	$200	$175	$150	$125	$110

Last MSR was $352.

This model was available in either single or double action with adj. counterweight and interchangeable front sight inserts.

MODEL 94 - .22 LR cal., small frame, double action, 9 shot, 2 (new 1997), 3 (mfg. 1991-98), 4, or 5 (new 1996) in. barrel, full underlug on 4 or 5 in. barrel, blue finish, adj. rear sight, target features, 25 oz. New 1989.

MSR $369	$275	$235	$205	$175	$150	$125	$110

✴ *Model 94 Ultra-Lite* - ultra light hammer forged frame, 2 in. barrel, available in matte blue or bright stainless steel, 18 oz. New 1999.

MSR $403	$310	$270	$235	$195	$175	$145	$130

Add $50 for matte stainless steel construction.

✴ *Model 94SS (Stainless Steel)* - stainless version of Model 94. New 1990.

MSR $419	$320	$280	$245	$200	$175	$145	$130

MODEL 96 TARGET SCOUT - .22 LR cal. only, double action, 6 shot, 6 in. barrel, checkered walnut grips, same features as Model 86, 34 oz. Disc. 1998.

	$275	$235	$205	$175	$150	$125	$110

Last MSR was $376.

MODEL 218 RAGING BEE - .218 Bee cal., large frame, 8 shot, 10 in. heavy VR barrel with full shroud and adj. sights, matte stainless steel, includes scope mounts, 50 oz. Mfg. 2003-2004.

	$795	$695	$600	$525	$465	$390	$295

Last MSR was $898.

MODEL 218 SILHOUETTE/HUNTER - .218 Bee cal., large frame, 7 shot, double action, 12 in. VR barrel with partial shroud, matte stainless steel, rubber boot grips, adj. trigger tension and trigger stop, includes scope mounts, 49.8 oz. Mfg. 2003-2004.

	$400	$350	$300	$260	$215	$175	$155

Last MSR was $461.

MODEL 415SS - .41 Mag. cal., compact frame, 5 shot, similar to Model 415T, except has matte stainless steel construction, Ribber grips, 30 oz. New 1999.

	$435	$385	$335	$285	$235	$190	$170

Last MSR was $508.

GRADING - PPGS™	100%	98%	95%	90%	80%	70%	60%

MODEL 415T - .41 Mag. cal., compact frame, 5 shot, all titanium construction, 2 1/2 in. ported barrel with fixed sights, choice of bright spectrum blue (disc. 2001), matte spectrum blue (disc. 2001), matte gold (mfg. 1999 only), stealth grey (mfg. 2000 only), or shadow grey (new 2000) finish, Ribber grips. Mfg. 1999-2003.

	$500	$450	$400	$350	$300	$245	$210

Last MSR was $602.

MODEL 415 - .41 Mag. cal., 5 shot, 2 1/2 in. barrel, stainless steel, compact frame, fixed sights, Ribber grips, 30 oz. New 2006.

MSR $469	$360	$320	$275	$230	$195	$160	$140

MODEL 416 SS RAGING BULL - .41 Mag., large frame, 6 shot, 6 1/2 or 8 3/8 in. ported heavy barrel with VR and adj. sights, matte stainless steel, rubber grips, 53 or 63 oz. New 2003.

MSR $706	$575	$500	$450	$395	$340	$275	$240

MODEL 425 SS TRACKER - .41 Mag. cal., compact frame, 5 shot, similar to Model 415T, 4 in. ported barrel with full shroud, adj. sights with red inserts, Ribber grips, stainless steel with matte finish, 34.8 oz. New 2000.

MSR $569	$465	$420	$365	$325	$260	$210	$185

MODEL 425T TRACKER - similar to Model 425 Tracker, except is all titanium construction, choice of stealth grey (mfg. 2000 only) or matte shadow grey finish, 4 or 6 in. barrel, adj. sights, 24.3 oz. Mfg. 2000-2006.

	$625	$550	$485	$425	$375	$310	$255

Last MSR was $766.

MODEL 431 - .44 Spl. cal., 5 shot, 2 (new 1995), 3, or 4 in. barrel, blue only, fixed sights. Mfg. 1993-97.

	$220	$190	$175	$150	$130	$115	$95

Last MSR was $286.

✳ *Model 431SS (Stainless Steel)* - similar to Model 431, except stainless steel. Mfg. 1993-97.

	$285	$240	$210	$180	$155	$130	$115

Last MSR was $368.

MODEL 441 - similar to Model 431, except has 3, 4, or 6 in. barrel, adj. sights. Mfg. 1993-97.

	$240	$200	$185	$160	$140	$120	$100

Last MSR was $313.

✳ *Model 441SS (Stainless Steel)* - similar to Model 441, except is stainless steel. Mfg. 1993-97.

	$350	$310	$265	$225	$190	$155	$135

Last MSR was $468.

MODEL 444 RAGING BULL - .44 Mag. cal. only, large frame, 6 shot, 6 1/2 or 8 3/8 in. VR ported barrel with full shroud, soft rubber grips, 53 or 63 oz. New 1999.

MSR $641	$525	$465	$410	$360	$310	$250	$220

✳ *Model 444 Raging Bull Stainless* - similar to Model 444, except is matte stainless steel. New 1999.

MSR $706	$575	$500	$450	$395	$340	$275	$240

✳ *Model 444 Raging Bull Ultra-Lite Multi* - .44 Mag. cal., 6 shot, 2 1/2 or 4 in. barrel, blue alloy or stainless steel Raging Bull style frame with titanium cylinder, rubber grips with finger grooves and insert cushion, fiber optic front sight, 28.3 oz. New 2005.

MSR $666	$545	$480	$420	$370	$320	$260	$230

Add $65 for stainless steel frame.
Add $15 for 4 in. barrel with adj. rear sight.

GRADING - PPGS™	100%	98%	95%	90%	80%	70%	60%

MODEL 445 - .44 Spl. cal., compact frame, 5 shot, 2 in. ported (new 1999) or standard barrel, fixed sights, blue or stainless, Ribber or rubber grips, 28 oz. Mfg. 1997-2003.

	$280	$240	$210	$180	$155	$130	$115

Last MSR was $359.

Add $16 for ported barrel (new 1999).

✳ *Model 445 Concealed Hammer* - similar to Model 445, except w/o hammer, ported or unported barrel. Mfg. 1999-2003.

	$280	$240	$210	$180	$155	$130	$115

Last MSR was $359.

Add $16 for ported barrel.

✳ *Model 445 Concealed Hammer Stainless* - similar to Model 445 Concealed Hammer, except is stainless steel. Mfg. 1999-2003.

	$310	$270	$235	$195	$175	$145	$130

Last MSR was $406.

Add $16 for ported barrel.

✳ *Model 445 SS (Stainless Steel)* - stainless variation of the Model 445. Mfg. 1997-2003.

	$310	$270	$235	$195	$175	$145	$130

Last MSR was $406.

Add $16 for ported barrel.

✳ *Model 445 Ultra-lite Stainless* - features ported 2 in. barrel and matte stainless steel. Mfg. 1999-2002.

	$370	$330	$280	$240	$200	$165	$150

Last MSR was $500.

✳ *Model 445 Ultra-lite Concealed Carry* - features stainless steel or titanium frame, ported 2 in. barrel, walnut combat grips. Mfg. 2002 only.

	$370	$330	$280	$240	$200	$165	$150

Last MSR was $500.

Add $100 for titanium construction.

MODEL 445T - .44 Spl. cal., 5 shot, all titanium construction, 2 in. ported barrel with fixed sights, choice of bright spectrum blue, matte spectrum blue, matte gold (mfg. 1999 only), stealth grey (new 2000), or shadow grey (new 2000) finish, Ribber grips. Mfg. 1999-2002.

	$500	$450	$400	$350	$300	$245	$210

Last MSR was $600.

MODEL 450 - .45 LC cal., 5 shot, compact frame, similar to Model 450T, except is matte stainless steel, also available in Ultra-Lite variation, Ribber grips, 20 (Ultra Lite) or 28 oz. Mfg. 1999-2005.

	$425	$375	$325	$275	$225	$185	$165

Last MSR was $492.

Add $31 for Ultra-Lite Model.

MODEL 450T - .45 LC cal., 5 shot, all titanium construction, 2 in. ported barrel with fixed sights, choice of bright spectrum blue, matte spectrum blue, matte gold (mfg. 1999 only), stealth grey (new 2000), or shadow grey (new 2000) finish, Ribber grips. Mfg. 1999-2002.

	$500	$450	$400	$350	$300	$245	$210

Last MSR was $600.

GRADING - PPGS™	100%	98%	95%	90%	80%	70%	60%

MODEL 454 CASULL RAGING BULL - .454 Casull cal., large frame, single or double action, 5 shot, front and rear cylinder locks, bright blue or case colored (new 1999) finish, 2 1/4 (mfg. 2005-2006), 5 (case colored, disc. 2000), 6 1/2 or 8 3/8 in. full lug ported barrel with integral VR, soft black rubber grips with recoil absorbing insert, micrometer adj. rear sight, transfer bar ignition, integral key lock, 53-63 oz. New 1998.

MSR $877	$735	$645	$570	$485	$425	$360	$280

Add $96 for case colored frame (disc. 2000).
Subtract $53 for 2 1/4 in. ported barrel.

✱ *Model 454 Casull Raging Bull Stainless* - similar to Model 454 Casull Raging Bull, except is stainless steel, 2 1/2 (new 2007), 5, 6 1/2 or 8 3/8 in. barrel, satin (6 1/2 in. barrel only, disc. 2000) or matte (new 1999) stainless finish. New 1998.

MSR $925	$785	$675	$595	$525	$450	$385	$290

Add $17 for 5, 6 1/2, or 8 3/8 in. barrel.

✱ *Model 454 Casull Raging Bull Silhouette* - similar to Model 454 Casull Raging Bull Stainless, except has 12 in. non-ported barrel with adj. sights, adj. trigger tension and trigger stop. Mfg. 2003-2004.

	$725	$640	$565	$485	$425	$360	$280

Last MSR was $859.

MODEL 455 TRACKER - .45 ACP cal., compact frame, 5 shot, 2, 4 or 6 in. ported barrel, adj. rear sight, matte stainless steel, includes 5 Stellar full moon clips, Ribber grips. Mfg. 2002-2004.

	$450	$400	$350	$310	$250	$200	$180

Last MSR was $523.

✱ *Model 455 Tracker Titanium* - similar to Model 455 Tracker, except has titanium construction with shadow gray finish. Mfg. 2004 only.

	$525	$465	$410	$360	$310	$250	$220

Last MSR was $625.

MODEL 460 TRACKER - .45 LC cal., compact frame, 5 shot, 4 or 6 1/2 in. VR ported barrel, adj. sights, matte stainless steel. Mfg. 2003-2004.

	$445	$395	$345	$295	$240	$195	$175

Last MSR was $516.

✱ *Model 460T Tracker* - similar to Model 460 Tracker, except has titanium construction, 4 VR or non-VR 6 1/2 in. barrel. Mfg. 2003-2004.

	$565	$495	$440	$385	$335	$270	$235

Last MSR was $688.

MODEL 465 RAGING BULL - .460 S&W Mag. cal., 2 1/2, 4, 6 1/2, or 10 in. ported barrel, matte stainless steel construction, fixed or adj. sights, soft rubber grips. Mfg. 2006.

	$750	$650	$575	$500	$440	$375	$290

Last MSR was $880.

MODEL 480 RUGER RAGING BULL - .480 Ruger cal., large frame, 5 shot, 5 (limited mfg.), 6 1/2, or 8 3/8 in. VR barrel, matte stainless finish only, otherwise similar to Model 454 Casull, 51-63 oz. Mfg. 2001-2005.

	$525	$465	$410	$360	$310	$250	$220

Last MSR was $641.

MODEL 500 - .500 S&W Mag. cal., 5 shot, 2 1/2 (fixed sights only, new 2006), 4 (new 2006), 6 1/2 (new 2006), or 10 in. ported barrel with adj. sights, adj. rear sight, soft rubber cushioned grips, stainless steel only, 68-72 oz. Mfg. mid-2005-2007.

	$775	$665	$585	$515	$450	$385	$290

Last MSR was $934.

Subtract $17 for 2 1/2 in. barrel.

MODEL 605 - .357 Mag. cal., small frame, 5 shot, 2 in. unported (new 2002), 2 1/4 (disc. 2005) or 3 (mfg. 1996-98, reintroduced 2006) in. barrel, blue steel, 4 port compensated barrel (2 1/4 in. only) with fixed sights, exposed or concealed (Model 605CH, mfg. 1997-2005, 2 1/4 in. barrel) hammer, full barrel shroud, oversized finger grooved rubber grips, 24 1/2 oz. New 1995.

MSR $403	$300	$260	$220	$190	$170	$140	$125

    Add $16 for ported barrel (disc. 2003).
    Add $291 for Crimson Trace laser grips.

✳ *Model 605 SS (Stainless Steel)* - stainless variation of the Model 605.

MSR $453	$325	$285	$245	$210	$180	$150	$130

    Add $16 for ported barrel (disc. 2003).

✳ *Model 605T Titanium* - similar to Model 605, except is titanium with shadow grey finish. Mfg. 2005-2006.

$535	$475	$420	$365	$315	$250	$220

Last MSR was $625.

MODEL 606 - .357 Mag. cal., 6 shot, 2 or 2 1/4 in. uncompensated or compensated barrel, exposed or concealed hammer, fixed sights. Mfg. 1997-98.

$235	$200	$185	$160	$140	$120	$100

Last MSR was $296.

    Add $19 for ported barrel (2 in. only).

✳ *Model 606 SS (Stainless Steel)* - stainless variation of the Model 606. Disc. 1998.

$260	$220	$195	$170	$150	$125	$110

Last MSR was $344.

    Add $20 for ported barrel (2 in. only).

MODEL 607 - .357 Mag. cal., 7 shot, 4 or 6 1/2 (VR) in. compensated barrel, adj. rear sight, Santoprene synthetic grips, 44 oz. Mfg. 1995-97.

$335	$295	$250	$215	$185	$150	$130

Last MSR was $447.

    Add $18 for 6 1/2 in. VR barrel.

✳ *Model 607SS (Stainless Steel)* - stainless variation of the Model 607. Mfg. 1995-97.

$375	$335	$285	$240	$200	$165	$150

Last MSR was $508.

    Add $20 for 6 1/2 in. VR barrel.

MODEL 608 - .357 Mag. cal., large frame, 8 shot, 3 (mfg. 1997-98), 4, 6 1/2(VR), 8 3/8 (VR, new 1997) in. barrel with integral compensator, rubber finger grooves, exposed or concealed (new 1997, 3 in. barrel) hammer, adj. sights, 44-56 oz. Mfg. 1996-2004.

$355	$315	$270	$225	$190	$155	$135

Last MSR was $469.

    Add $15 for 6.5 or 8 3/8 in. VR ported barrel.

✳ *Model 608SS (Stainless Steel)* - stainless variation of the Model 608. New 1996.

MSR $584	$440	$390	$340	$295	$240	$195	$175

    Add $25 for 6 1/2 or 8 3/8 in. VR barrel.

MODEL 617 - .357 Mag. cal., compact frame, 7 shot, double action, 2 in. regular or ported barrel, fixed sights, exposed or concealed (Model 617CH, disc. 2005) hammer, rubber (disc. 2006) or Ribber (new 2007) grips, 28.3 oz. New 1998.

MSR $436	$350	$310	$265	$225	$190	$155	$135

    Add $15 for ported barrel (disc. 2003).

GRADING - PPGS™	100%	98%	95%	90%	80%	70%	60%

✳ *Model 617SS (Stainless Steel)* - similar to Model 617, except is polished stainless steel. Mfg. 1998-2007.

	$360	$320	$275	$230	$195	$160	$140

Last MSR was $472.

    Add $15 for ported barrel (disc. 2003).

✳ *Model 617 ULT* - similar to Model 617, except is 5 shot, aluminum alloy receiver and titanium cylinder, matte stainless finish, 2 in. regular or ported barrel, soft rubber grips. Mfg. 2001-2002.

	$455	$410	$355	$315	$255	$205	$185

Last MSR was $530.

    Add $15 for ported barrel.

✳ *Model 617T* - .357 Mag. cal., compact frame, 7 shot, all titanium construction, 2 in. ported barrel with fixed sights, choice of bright spectrum blue, matte spectrum blue (disc. 2001), matte gold (mfg. 1999 only), stealth grey (mfg. 2000 only), or shadow grey (new 2000) finish, Ribber grips, 19.9 oz. Mfg. 1999-2006.

	$550	$485	$425	$375	$325	$265	$235

Last MSR was $680.

MODEL 627 SS TRACKER - .357 Mag. cal., compact frame, 7 shot, 4 or 6 1/2 (new 2001, VR) in. ported barrel with adj. sights, and heavy full underlug, stainless steel with matte finish, Ribber grips, 28.8 or 40 oz. New 2000.

MSR $570		$440	$390	$340	$295	$240	$195	$175

✳ *Model 627T Tracker* - .357 Mag. cal., 7 shot, all titanium construction, 4 or 6 1/2 (new 2001, non-VR) in. ported barrel with adj. sights, choice of stealth grey (disc. 2001) or shadow grey finish, Ribber grips, 24.3 or 28 oz. Mfg. 2000-2006.

	$610	$535	$475	$420	$375	$295	$250

Last MSR was $766.

MODEL 650 CIA - .357 Mag. cal., small frame, 5 shot, double action only, hammerless, 2 in. barrel with fixed sights, soft rubber boot grips, blue finish, 24.2 oz. New 2001.

MSR $411		$310	$270	$235	$195	$175	$145	$130

✳ *Model 650 CIA SS (Stainless Steel)* - similar to Model 650 CIA, except is matte stainless steel. New 2001.

MSR $461		$345	$300	$265	$225	$185	$155	$135

MODEL 651 PROTECTOR - .357 Mag. cal., small frame, 5 shot, 2 in. barrel, single or double action, shrouded zero profile hammer, soft rubber boot grips, 25 oz. New 2003.

MSR $411		$310	$270	$235	$195	$175	$145	$130

✳ *Model 651T Protector* - similar to Model 651 CIA Protector, except is shadow grey titanium construction, 17.3 oz. Mfg. 2004-2006.

	$510	$460	$400	$350	$300	$245	$210

Last MSR was $625.

✳ *Model 651 Protector SS (Stainless Steel)* - similar to Model 651 Protector, except is matte stainless steel. New 2003.

MSR $461		$345	$300	$265	$225	$185	$155	$135

MODEL 669 - similar to Model 66 except has fully shrouded 4 or 6 in. barrel, blue finish, 37 oz. Disc. 1998.

	$260	$220	$195	$170	$150	$125	$110

Last MSR was $344.

    Add $10 for VR barrel (mfg. 1989-1992).
    Add $400 for Laser Aim Sight (offered 1990-1992).
    Add $19 for compensated (669CP) barrel (new 1993).

GRADING - PPGS™	100%	98%	95%	90%	80%	70%	60%

✳ *Model 669SS (Stainless Steel)* - similar to Model 669, but in stainless steel. Disc. 1998.

	$325	$285	$250	$200	$175	$145	$130

Last MSR was $421.

Add $21 for compensated (669CP) barrel (new 1993).

MODEL 689 - similar to Model 669, except has VR. Disc. 1998.

	$265	$225	$200	$175	$150	$125	$110

Last MSR was $358.

Add $390 for Laser Aim Sight (mfg. 1990-91 only).

✳ *Model 689SS (Stainless Steel)* - similar to Model 669, but in stainless steel. Disc. 1999.

	$340	$300	$260	$220	$185	$155	$135

Last MSR was $435.

MODEL 731 SS ULTRA-LITE - .32 H&R Mag. cal., small frame, double action, 6 shot, aluminum frame with matte stainless steel cylinder, 2 in. ported barrel, fixed sights, rubber boot grips, 17 oz. New 1998.

MSR $469		$360	$320	$275	$230	$195	$160	$140

✳ *Model 731T* - .32 H&R Mag. cal., small frame, 6 shot, all titanium construction, 2 in. ported barrel with fixed sights, bright blue (disc. 1999), matte blue, shadow grey (new 2003) or matte gold (disc. 1999) finish, rubber grips. Mfg. 1999, reintroduced 2003-2004.

	$455	$410	$355	$315	$255	$205	$185

Last MSR was $531.

Subtract $64 for matte blue finish.

MODEL 741 - .32 H&R Mag. cal., 6 shot, 3 or 4 in. barrel, blue only, adj. sights. Mfg. 1993-94.

	$210	$185	$165	$145	$125	$110	$90

Last MSR was $254.

✳ *Model 741SS (Stainless Steel)* - similar to Model 741, except is stainless steel. Mfg. 1993-94.

	$275	$235	$200	$175	$150	$125	$110

Last MSR was $342.

MODEL 761 - .32 H&R Mag. cal., 6 shot, 6 in. barrel, blue only, adj. sights. Mfg. 1993-94.

	$250	$210	$190	$165	$145	$120	$100

Last MSR was $326.

MODEL 817 ULTRA-LITE - .38 Spl. cal., compact frame, 7 shot, 2 in. ported (disc. 2002) or unported solid rib barrel, soft rubber (disc. 2006) or Ribber (new 2007) grips, bright blue finish, 21 oz. New 1999.

MSR $436		$340	$300	$260	$220	$185	$155	$135

Add $20 for ported barrel (disc. 2002).

✳ *Model 817 Ultra-Lite Stainless* - similar to Model 817 Ultra-Lite, except is stainless steel. New 1999.

MSR $486		$370	$330	$280	$240	$200	$165	$150

Add $20 for ported barrel (disc. 2003).

MODEL 827 - .38 Spl. cal., 7 shot, 4 in. heavy SR barrel, fixed sights, rubber grips, 36 1/2 oz. Mfg. 1999 only.

	$240	$200	$185	$160	$140	$120	$100

Last MSR was $317.

GRADING - PPGS™	100%	98%	95%	90%	80%	70%	60%

✴ *Model 827 Stainless* - similar to Model 827, except is stainless steel. Mfg. 1999 only.

| | $280 | $240 | $210 | $180 | $155 | $130 | $115 |

Last MSR was $364.

MODEL 850 CIA - .38 Spl. cal., small frame, 5 shot, hammerless, double action only, 2 in. barrel with fixed sights, rubber boot grips, blue finish, approx. 23 oz. New 2001.

| MSR $411 | $310 | $270 | $235 | $195 | $175 | $145 | $130 |

✴ *Model 850 CIA SS (Stainless Steel)* - similar to Model 850 CIA, except is matte stainless steel. New 2001.

| MSR $461 | $345 | $300 | $265 | $225 | $185 | $155 | $135 |

✴ *Model 850 CIA Ultra Lite* - similar to Model 850 CIA, except is ultralight variation with adj. sight. Mfg. 2005, reintroduced 2008.

| MSR $419 | $320 | $280 | $245 | $200 | $175 | $145 | $130 |

Add $47 for aluminum frame with stainless steel slide (disc.).

✴ *Model 850T CIA* - .38 Spl. cal., similar to Model 850 CIA, except has shadow grey finish and all titanium construction, spectrum blue/titanium gold finish and mother-of-pearl grips optional 2005. New 2001.

| MSR $666 | $530 | $470 | $415 | $365 | $315 | $250 | $220 |

Add $47 for blue and gold finish with mother-of-pearl grips (disc. 2006).

MODEL 851 PROTECTOR - .38 Spl. cal., small frame, 5 shot, 2 in. full underlug barrel, double action only, shrouded hammer, rubber boot grips, 25 oz. New 2003.

| MSR $411 | $310 | $270 | $235 | $195 | $175 | $145 | $130 |

✴ *Model 851 Protector SS (Stainless Steel)* - similar to Model 851 Protector, except is matte stainless steel. New 2003.

| MSR $461 | $345 | $300 | $265 | $225 | $185 | $155 | $135 |

✴ *Model 851 Protector Ultra-Lite* - similar to Model 851 Protector, except is Ultra-Lite model with blue finish and intergral adj. sight. New 2003.

| MSR $445 | $340 | $300 | $260 | $220 | $185 | $155 | $135 |

✴ *Model 851 Protector Ultra-Lite Aluminum/Titanium* - similar to Model 851 Protector Ultra-Lite, except is aluminum/stainless steel or aluminum/titanium. New 2003.

| MSR $495 | $410 | $360 | $315 | $270 | $220 | $180 | $160 |

Add $89 for aluminum/titanium construction.

✴ *Model 851 Protector Titanium* - similar to Model 851 Protector, except is shadow grey titanium. Mfg. 2003-2004, reintroduced 2006.

| | $525 | $465 | $410 | $360 | $310 | $250 | $220 |

Last MSR was $625.

Add $39 for spectrum blue/titanium gold finish and mother-of-pearl grips (disc. 2004).

MODEL 905 - 9mm Para cal., small frame, 5 shot, rubber boot grips, exposed or concealed (CH Model, disc. 2005) hammer, fixed sights, includes 5 Stellar full moon clips, 21 oz. New 2003.

| MSR $411 | $310 | $270 | $235 | $195 | $175 | $145 | $130 |

✴ *Model 905SS (Stainless Steel)* - similar to Model 905, except is stainless steel. New 2003.

| MSR $461 | $345 | $300 | $265 | $225 | $185 | $155 | $135 |

✴ *Model 905 Ultra-Lite* - ultra light frame, blue finish. Mfg. 2003-2004.

| | $310 | $270 | $235 | $195 | $175 | $145 | $130 |

Last MSR was $414.

GRADING - PPGS™	100%	98%	95%	90%	80%	70%	60%

❖ **Model 905 Ultra-Lite Stainless** - matte stainless variation of the Model 905 Ultra-Lite. Mfg. 2003-2004.

	$380	$340	$290	$245	$210	$170	$150

Last MSR was $461.

MODEL 941 - .22 Mag. cal., small frame, 8 shot, 2 (new 1997), 3 (disc. 1998), 4, or 5 in. barrel, blue only, adj. sights, full underlug on 4 and 5 in. barrels, soft rubber or wood (disc. 2000, 5 in. barrel only) grips, 24-27 1/2 oz. New 1993.

MSR $386	$295	$250	$215	$185	$160	$135	$120

✳ *Model 941 Ultra-Lite* - ultra light hammer forged frame, available in matte blue or bright stainless steel, 2 in. barrel standard beginning 2007, 18 1/2 oz. New 1999.

MSR $419	$320	$280	$245	$200	$175	$145	$130

Add $50 for matte stainless steel construction (2 in. barrel only).

✳ *Model 941SS (Stainless Steel)* - similar to Model 941, except is polished stainless steel. New 1993.

MSR $436	$340	$300	$260	$220	$185	$155	$135

MODEL 970 TRACKER - .22 LR cal., compact frame, double action, 7 shot, 6 1/2 in. heavy barrel with VR and adj. rear sight, Ribber grips, matte stainless steel or blue finish (new 2007), 45.6 oz. New 2001.

MSR $403	$300	$260	$220	$190	$170	$140	$125

Add $50 for matte stainless steel.

MODEL 971 TRACKER SS (STAINLESS STEEL) - .22 Mag. cal., otherwise similar to Model 970 Tracker, 45.2 oz. Mfg. 2001-2004, reintroduced 2006.

MSR $453	$325	$285	$245	$210	$180	$150	$130

MODEL 980 SILHOUETTE/HUNTER SS (STAINLESS STEEL) - .22 LR cal., compact frame, 7 shot, double action, 12 in. heavy barrel with adj. rear sight, Ribber grips, adj. trigger tension and trigger stop, includes scope mount, 56.8 oz. Mfg. 2001-2004.

	$335	$300	$260	$220	$185	$155	$135

Last MSR was $414.

MODEL 981 SILHOUETTE/HUNTER SS (STAINLESS STEEL) - .22 Mag. cal., otherwise similar to Model 980 Silhouette SS, 56.2 oz. Mfg. 2001-2004.

	$350	$310	$265	$225	$190	$155	$135

Last MSR was $430.

RIFLES: LEVER ACTION

MODEL 62 LA RIFLE/CARBINE - 22 LR cal., blue finish, 16 1/2 (mfg. 2006 only) or 23 in. barrel, uncheckered walnut hardwood stock, adj. rear sight, 11 or 12 shot tube mag., 4 1/2 lbs. Mfg. 2006-2007.

	$280	$240	$210	$175	$155	$140	$125

Last MSR was $329.

✳ *Model 62 Rifle/Carbine Stainless* - similar to Model 62 Rifle/Carbine, except is polished stainless steel, 4 1/2 lbs. Mfg. 2006-2007.

	$295	$250	$210	$175	$155	$140	$125

Last MSR was $349.

RIFLES: SEMI-AUTO

MODEL 63 - 22 LR cal., patterned after the Winchester Model 63, 10 shot tube mag., blue finish, takedown design, 23 in. round barrel with adj. rear sight, 4 1/2 lbs. Imported 2003-2007.

	$285	$240	$210	$185	$155	$140	$125

Last MSR was $329.

Add $33 for tang sight (mfg. 2005-2006).
Add $30 for scope mount (new 2007).

✳ *Model 63 Stainless* - similar to Model 63, except is stainless steel. Mfg. 2003-2007.

	100%	98%	95%	90%	80%	70%	60%
	$295	$250	$210	$185	$155	$140	$125

Last MSR was $349.

Add $33 for tang sight (mfg. 2005-2006).

MODEL 73 - .22 Mag. cal., similar to Model 63, except mag. has less capacity. Imported late 2003-2004.

	$270	$235	$200	$175	$155	$140	$125

Last MSR was $311.

✳ *Model 73 Stainless* - similar to Model 73, except is stainless steel. Imported 2003-2004.

	$290	$250	$210	$185	$160	$145	$130

Last MSR was $342.

MODEL 173 - .17 HMR cal., similar to Model 73. Imported late 2003-2004.

	$290	$250	$210	$185	$160	$145	$130

Last MSR was $342.

✳ *Model 173 Stainless* - similar to Model 173, except is stainless steel. Imported 2003-2004.

	$300	$260	$210	$185	$160	$145	$130

Last MSR was $358.

RIFLES: SLIDE ACTION

Add $30 for Weaver style scope base mount.
Add $14 for Taurus Rimfire Recharger (2 pack w/o ammo, new 2002).

MODEL 62 RIFLE/CARBINE - .22 LR or .22 Mag. (disc. 2000) cal., patterned after the Win. Model 62, 16 1/2 (carbine) or 23 (rifle) in. barrel with open adj. sights, 11 or 12 shot tube mag., includes switchable manual firing pin block safety on top of receiver and integral Taurus Security System lock on hammer, uncheckered hardwood stock and grooved forearm, blue or case colored receiver, approx. 4 1/2 lbs. Imported 1999-2007.

	$265	$230	$195	$170	$160	$140	$125

Last MSR was $299.

Add $34 for rear tang sight (new 2002).

✳ *Model 62 Rifle/Carbine Stainless* - similar to Model 62 Rifle/Carbine, except is stainless steel. Mfg. 2000-2007.

	$275	$240	$200	$150	$125	$110	$95

Last MSR was $319.

Add $78 for rear tang sight (mfg. 2002-2004).

✳ *Model 62 Rifle/Carbine "Upstart" Youth/Adult Combo* - similar to Model 62 Rifle/Carbine, except is available with both youth (shortened LOP), and adult stocks. Imported 2002-2004.

	$270	$235	$200	$150	$125	$110	$95

Last MSR was $311.

Add $16 for stainless steel.

MODEL 72 RIFLE/CARBINE - .22 Mag. cal., 10 or 11 shot tube mag., blue or case colored receiver, similar to Model 62 Rifle/Carbine, 4 1/2 lbs. Imported 2001-2007.

	$285	$240	$210	$185	$155	$140	$125

Last MSR was $329.

Add $34 for rear tang sight (new 2002).
Add $20 for case colored receiver.

Beginning 2001, this model's nomenclature changed from Model 62 to Model 72 (.22 Mag. cal. only).

GRADING - PPGS™	100%	98%	95%	90%	80%	70%	60%

✻ *Model 72 Rifle/Carbine Stainless* - similar to Model 72 Rifle/Carbine, except is stainless steel, 80 oz. Imported 2001-2007.

	$295	$250	$210	$185	$155	$140	$125

Last MSR was $349.

Add $34 for rear tang sight (new 2002).

MODEL 172 RIFLE/CARBINE - .17 HMR cal., 16 1/2 (carbine, disc. 2005) or 23 (rifle) in. barrel with adj. sights, 4 1/2 oz. Imported 2003-2006.

	$280	$240	$200	$175	$155	$140	$125

Last MSR was $327.

✻ *Model 172 Rifle/Carbine Stainless* - similar to Model 172 Rifle/Carbine, except is stainless steel. Imported 2003-2006.

	$290	$245	$205	$180	$160	$140	$125

Last MSR was $342.

THUNDERBOLT RIFLE/CARBINE - .357 Mag./.38 Spl. or .45 LC cal., 20 (carbine) or 26 in. (rifle) round barrel with full mag., patterned after the Colt Lightning rifle, 11 (carbine) or 13 (rifle) shot tube mag., choice of case colored or blue finish, short stroke action, uncheckered hardwood stock and forearm, hammer drop release button hidden in the hammer, solid metal curved crescent butt-plate, long horn adj. rear sight, 8 lbs. New 2006.

MSR $705	$515	$400	$325	$260	$225	$195	$180

Add $43 for case colors.

✻ *Thunderbolt Rifle/Carbine Stainless* - similar to Thunderbolt Rifle/Carbine, except is polished stainless steel. New 2006.

MSR $813	$675	$575	$515	$435	$350	$300	$250

TAYLOR, F.C. FUR CO.

Previous company which marketed animal trap guns circa 1921-1941.

PISTOLS: SINGLE SHOT

.22 CAL. TAYLOR FUR GETTER - .22 LR cal., designed to shoot animal at close range once trigger mechanism has been activated (usually with bait attached to a lever). Mfg. by O.F. Mossberg for Taylor, ser. range 1-3,100.

	N/A	$1,050	$900	$800	$700	$600	$550

Add 10%-15% for low ser. no. with two-piece swiveling stake.

.38 CAL. TAYLOR FUR GETTER - .38 cal., mfg. on 1914 patent of C.D. Lovelace, believed to have been mfg. by Hopkins & Allen, markings cast in top of frame (brass) with iron barrel - all bearing the 1914 patent date.

	N/A	$850	$775	$700	$625	$550	$475

Add 10%-15% premium for alloy frame with top plate attached with two screws and uncracked frame.

TAYLOR'S & CO., INC.

Current importer and distributor established during 1988, and located in Winchester, VA.

Taylor's & Co. is an Uberti importer and distributor of both black powder and firearms reproductions, in addition to being the exclusive U.S. distributor for Armi Sport, located in Brescia, Italy. Taylor's is also a distributor for Bond Arms - please refer to the Bond Arms section.

For more information and up-to-date pricing regarding current Taylor's & Co., Inc. black powder models, please refer to the *Blue Book of Modern Black Powder Arms* by John Allen. This book features hundreds of color photographs and support text of the most recent black powder models available, as well as complete pricing and reference guides.

Black Powder Reproductions & Replicas by Dennis Adler is also an invaluable source for most black powder reproductions and replicas, and includes hundreds of color images on most popular makes/models, provides manufacturer/trademark histories, and up-to-date information on related items/accessories for black powder shooting - www.bluebookinc.com

GRADING - PPGS™	100%	98%	95%	90%	80%	70%	60%

REVOLVERS: REPRODUCTIONS, CONVERSIONS

MODEL 1871-1872 OPEN TOP - .38 Spl., .38 LC, .44 Colt, .44 Spl., .45 Schofield, or .45 LC cal., 4 3/4, 5 1/2, or 7 1/2 in. barrel, choice of Early (1851 Navy size grips) or Late (1860 Army grips, 7 1/2 in. barrel only), Model frame, steel or nickel finish, brass backstrap and triggerguard. New 2007.

MSR $420	$365	$330	$295	$260	$230	$190	$150

Add $50 for Late Model frame with 1860 Army size grips.
Add $5 for .45 Schofield.

MODEL 1871 C. MASON - .38 Spl., .38 LC, .44 Colt, .44 Spl., .45 LC or .45 Schofield, 4 3/4, 5 1/2, 7 1/2, or 8 in. barrel, choice of 1851 Navy or 1860 Army frame, steel backstrap and triggerguard. New 2007.

MSR $440	$380	$340	$300	$260	$230	$190	$150

Add $30 for 1860 Army frame.
Add $5 for .45 Schofield.

REVOLVERS: REPRODUCTIONS, SAA

CATTLEMAN VARIATIONS - available in .32-20 WCF, .357 Mag., .38-40 WCF, .44 Spl., .44-40 WCF, .45 ACP (new 2003), or .45 LC cal., 4 3/4, 5 1/2, and 7 1/2 in. barrel lengths, brass (New Model frame) or steel (Old Model frame) backstrap and trigger guard, mfg. by Uberti. New 2002.

✻ *Cattleman Variations Steel backstrap and trigger guard* - choice of new or old model frame, old model frame not available in .357 Mag. cal.

MSR $435	$370	$300	$240	$200	$175	$165	$150

Add $49 for charcoal blue finish (.357 Mag. or .45 LC cal. only).
Add $180 for convertible cylinder (.45 LC/.45 ACP in 5 1/2 in. barrel only).
Add $5 for all cals. except for .45 LC.

✻ *Cattleman Variations Brass backstrap and trigger guard* - .357 Mag., or .45 LC cal.

MSR $485	$425	$335	$265	$225	$185	$165	$140

✻ *Cattleman Variations Millenium* - .45 LC cal., 4 3/4 in. barrel, brass backstrap and trigger guard. New 2000.

MSR $365	$300	$265	$225	$200	$175	$155	$125

✻ *Cattleman Variations Engraved* - .45 LC cal. only, 4 3/4 or 5 1/2 in. barrel, features unique photo engraving on frame, cylinder, and barrel (Taylor´s exclusive), choice of blue (new 2006), colored case hardened, or white heat treated finish with charcoal blue screws. New 2003.

MSR $725	$600	$475	$400	$350	$295	$265	$235

Add $64 for white finish.

✻ *Cattleman Variations "TR" Presidential* - .45 LC cal. only, 5 1/2 in. barrel, features unique photo engraving on frame, cylinder, and barrel (Taylor´s exclusive), white heat treated finish with charcoal blue screws, simulated ivory, wood, or black hard rubber grips. Mfg. 2005-2006.

	$565	$450	$375	$315	$275	$240	$215

Last MSR was $685.

Add $30 for black grips, or $100 for simulated ivory grips.

CATTLEMAN QUICK DRAW - .45 LC cal., 4, 4 3/4, 5 1/2, or 7 1/2 in. barrel, choice of Old or New Model frame. New 2006.

MSR $400	$350	$295	$260	$230	$210	$175	$150

Add $40 for Old Model frame.

GRADING - PPGS™	100%	98%	95%	90%	80%	70%	60%

CATTLEMAN ISLAND GIRL QUICK DRAW - .38 Spl., 4 3/4 in. barrel, nickel finish with one-piece white checkered polymer grips, fire blued screws, beveled cylinder, Ruger style coil spring. New 2006.

MSR $710	$595	$525	$465	$400	$345	$275	$240

CATTLEMAN SHERIFF BIRDSHEAD - .357 Mag. or .45 LC cal., 3 1/2 or 4 3/4 in. barrel, patterned after the Colt 1877 Thunderer, choice of Old or New Model frame, case colored frame, smooth walnut birdshead grips. New 1997.

MSR $500	$425	$335	$265	$230	$200	$180	$165

Add $79 for nickel finish (.357 Mag. cal. only, with 4 3/4 in. barrel).

CATTLEMAN BISLEY - .357 Mag., .38-40 WCF or .45 LC cal., patterned after the Colt Bisley Model, 4 3/4, 5 1/2, or 7 1/2 in. barrel, case colored New Model frame, wood grips. New 1997.

MSR $500	$425	$335	$265	$230	$200	$180	$165

STALLION 1873 - .38 Spl. cal., 3 1/2, 4 3/4, or 5 1/2 in. barrel, scaled down SAA with small frame, standard or birdshead smooth grips, steel backstrap and trigger guard. Mfg. 1999-2004, reintroduced 2006.

MSR $415	$365	$315	$250	$200	$165	$145	$130

Add $70 for birdshead grips.

OUTFITTER - .357 Mag. or .45 LC cal., solid stainless construction with two-piece walnut grips, 4 3/4, 5 1/2, or 7 1/2 in. barrel. New 2003.

MSR $535	$465	$425	$350	$300	$250	$215	$185

NEW VAUQUERO "HANDLEBAR DOC SIGNATURE SERIES" - .357 Mag. or .45 LC cal., color case hardened blue or stainless steel frame, 4 5/8, 5 1/2, or 7 1/2 in. barrel, checkered black grips with white "HD" medallions, "Handlebar Doc Series" etched on barrel, Taylor's exclusive. New 2005.

MSR $676	$575	$500	$450	$385	$340	$275	$240

NEW MODEL BLACKHAWK - .357 Mag. cal., 4 5/8 in. barrel, flattop frame with adj. rear sight and pre-1962 XR3 grip frame, choice of blue or stainless, hard rubber grips with Handlebar Doc white medallions. New 2006.

MSR $675	$575	$500	$450	$395	$340	$275	$240

SMOKE WAGON - .38 Spl., .357 Mag., .44-40 WCF, or .45 LC cal., 4 3/4 or 5 1/2 in. barrel, blue finish with case color hardened frame, checkered wood grips, low profile hammer, wider style sights. New 2008.

MSR $495	$450	$395	$365	$335	$300	$275	$250

Add $125 for deluxe edition, which features custom tuned action.

REVOLVERS: REPRODUCTIONS, SCHOFIELD

1875 NO. 3 NEW MODEL RUSSIAN - .38 Spl., .44 Russian, .44-40 WCF, or .45 LC cal., 6 shot, top-break action, 3 1/2, 5, (6 1/2 special order only with case colored trigger guard), or 7 in. barrel with solid rib, automatic extraction, blue finish with smooth walnut grips. New 2007.

MSR $830	$750	$650	$550	$450	$375	$325	$275

Add $40 for 6 1/2 in. barrel with lanyard ring and trigger guard spur.

RIFLES: REPRODUCTIONS, LEVER ACTION

HENRY RIFLE - .44-40 WCF or .45 LC cal., brass or steel frame, 24 1/2 in. barrel, 13 shot mag., available in brass, case colored, or in-the-white finish, with or w/o sling swivels.

MSR $1,050	$900	$750	$650	$525	$425	$360	$320

Add $91 for charcoal blue barrel finish.
Add $120 for steel frame.
Add $83 for in-the-white finish.
Add $50 for sling swivels.
Add $120 for transition model with hinged loading port (new 2006).
Add $153 for standard engraving.

GRADING - PPGS™	100%	98%	95%	90%	80%	70%	60%

1866 YELLOWBOY RIFLE/CARBINE - .32-20 WCF, .38 Spl., .44-40 WCF, or .45 LC cal., 18 (Trapper), 19 (carbine), 20 (rifle) or 24 1/4 (rifle) in. barrel. New 2002.

	MSR $925	$825	$700	$550	$450	$375	$325	$295

Add $5 for rifle.
Add $15 for Trapper model with 18 in. barrel.

1873 CARBINE - .32-20 WCF, .357 Mag. or .45 LC cal., steel receiver, 18 1/2 in. octagon (Trapper, not available in .32-20 WCF cal.) or 19 in. round barrel, blued steel receiver w/o saddle ring. New 2002.

	MSR $995	$865	$735	$575	$450	$400	$350	$325

Add $35 for Trapper model with straight stock or $105 for Trapper with pistol grip checkered stock.

1873 SPORTING RIFLE - .32-20 WCF (disc. 2004, reintroduced 2007), .357 Mag., .38-40 WCF (disc. 2004, reintroduced 2007), .44-40 WCF, or .45 LC cal., case hardened receiver, 18 in. half-octagon (Short Rifle), 20 in. half-octagon, 24 1/4 in. octagon or 30 (Deluxe) in. octagon barrel. New 2002.

	MSR $995	$875	$750	$600	$475	$425	$375	$350

Add $175 for Special Sporting Rifle.
Add $125 for Deluxe Model.
Add $15 for 24 1/4 in. full octagon or $35 for octagon barrel.

1876 SPORTING RIFLE - .40-60, .45-60, .45-75, or .50-95 cal., 28 in. octagon barrel, case colored frame. New 2006.

	MSR $1,255	$1,000	$825	$700	$550	$450	$400	$350

1892 CARBINE/RIFLE - .32-20 WCF (disc. 2006), .32 H&R Mag. (disc. 2006), .38-40 WCF, .38 Spl., .357 Mag., .44 S&W (disc. 2006), .44-40 WCF, or .45 LC cal., choice of 20 or 24 1/2 round (new 2005) or octagon barrel, solid (.32-20 WCF, .38-30 WCF, or .44 S&W cal. only) frame or takedown action.

	MSR $845	$750	$675	$600	$525	$450	$400	$350

Add $104 for takedown action.
Subtract $25 for large loop lever (new 2007).

RIFLES: REPRODUCTIONS, SINGLE SHOT

1865 SPENCER CARBINE/RIFLE (160 SERIES) - .44 Russian (limited mfg., disc. 2006), .44-40 WCF (new 2005), .45 Schofield, or .56-50 (rifle only) cal., reproduction of the Civil War Spencer carbine, case colored receiver, lock, and hammer, 20 or 30 (rifle, new 2005) in. barrel, 7-9 shot mag., walnut stock and forearm, includes slings, mfg. by Armi-Sport. Importation began 2002.

	MSR $1,285	$1,075	$950	$825	$700	$600	$500	$400

Add $215 for rifle.

1874 SHARPS SPORTING RIFLE - .40-65 (disc. 2006), .45-70 Govt., .45-90, or .45-120 cal., 30, 32, or 34 in. barrel, single or double set triggers, case colored for white finished frame, with or w/o pewter accents.

	MSR $965	$860	$750	$625	$525	$450	$375	$300

Add $45 for double triggers with Schnabel forend, or $155 for double triggers with Hartford style pewter forearm tip.
Add $300 for 34 in. barrel.
Add $225 for pistol grip stock with buckhorn sight or $295 for pistol grip stock and heavy barrel (disc. 2006).

Taylor's also imports engraved models of the 1874 Sporting Rifle in either .45-70 Govt. or .45-120 cal., including standard engraving ($2,040 MSR) and hand engraving with gold medallions ($2,975 MSR).

GRADING - PPGS™	100%	98%	95%	90%	80%	70%	60%

1874 SHARPS QUIGLEY - .45-70 Govt. or .45-120 cal., 32 or 34 in. octagon barrel, exact reproduction of rifle used in the "Quigley Down Under" movie, with patchbox, includes Hartford style pewter forearm tip.

MSR $1,265	$1,050	$900	$800	$700	$575	$475	$400

1874 SHARPS CAVALRY CARBINE - .45-70 Govt. or .50-70 (mfg. 2005-2006) cal., patterned after Sharps Cavalry carbine, 22 in. barrel, color case hardened frame.

MSR $920		$825	$725	$600	$525	$450	$375	$300

Add approx. 10% for .50-70 cal.

1874 SHARPS INFANTRY/BERDAN MODEL - .45-70 Govt. cal., 30 in. barrel, musket configuration with 3 barrel bands and patchbox. Disc. 2006.

		$925	$775	$625	$500	$425	$375	$350

Last MSR was $1,045.

Add $45 for Berdan model with DT.

1885 LOW/HIGH WALL - .17 HMR (new 2005), .17 Mach 2 (new 2005), .22 LR, .32-20 WCF, .38-40 WCF, .38-55 WCF, or .45-70 Govt. (High Wall only) cal., 30 or 32 (High Wall only) in. octagon barrel, case colored receiver, straight (High Wall) or checkered pistol grip (Low Wall) walnut stock and forearm. New 1999.

MSR $850		$750	$650	$575	$500	$450	$400	$350

Add $178 for High Wall with checkered pistol grip stock.
Add $50-$70 for Low Wall, depending on caliber.

RIFLES: REPRODUCTIONS, SLIDE ACTION

LIGHTNING SLIDE ACTION - .357 Mag., .44-40, or .45 LC cal., 20 in. round (carbine only) 24 1/4, or 26 in. octagon barrel, case colored frame, straight grip walnut stock with checkered forearm. New 2007.

MSR $1,099		$925	$750	$650	$525	$425	$375	$325

Add $21 for 26 in. round barrel.
Subtract $54 for 20 in. round barrel carbine.

TECHNO ARMS (PTY) LIMITED

Previous manufacturer located in Johannesburg, S. Africa circa 1994-1996. Previously imported by Vulcans Forge, Inc. located in Foxboro, MA.

SHOTGUNS: SLIDE ACTION

MAG-7 SLIDE ACTION SHOTGUN - 12 ga. (60mm chamber length), 5 shot detachable mag. (in pistol grip), 14, 16, 18, or 20 in. barrel, straight grip or pistol grip stock, matte finish, 8 lbs. Imported 1995-96.

		$795	$675	$625	$550	$500	$450	$400

Last MSR was $875.

TELO, RENATO

Current manufacturer located in Brescia, Italy. No current U.S. importation.

Renato Telo manufactures best quality long guns. To date, this trademark has had very little importation into the U.S. Please contact the factory directly for more information, including models, availability, delivery time and U.S. pricing (see Trademark Index).

TERRIER ONE

Previous trademark distributed by Serrifile located in Lancaster, CA.

REVOLVERS

TERRIER ONE - .32 S&W cal., double action, 2 1/4 in. barrel, 5 shot, nickel-plated, 17 oz. Mfg. 1984-87.

		$45	$35	$30	$25	$25	$25	$25

Last MSR was $55.

GRADING - PPGS™	100%	98%	95%	90%	80%	70%	60%

TESRO SPORTWAFFEN GMBH & CO. KG

Current manufacturer located in Bächingen, Germany. Previously located in Nieder-stotzingen, Germany. No current U.S. importation.

Tesro currently manufactures the target models TS22 (.22 LR cal.) and TS32 (.32 S&W Wadcutter cal.) with ergonomic grips and target features. Tesro also manufactures air pistols and air rifles. Please contact the company directly for more information regarding U.S. availability and pricing (see Trademark Index).

TEXAS ARMS

Previous manufacturer located in Waco, TX, until circa 1999.

DERRINGERS: O/U

DEFENDER - .357 Mag., .38 Spl., 9mm Para., .44 Mag., .45 ACP, or .45 LC cal./.410 bore shotshell, SS, features 3 in. interchangeable octagon barrels, spur trigger, shell ejector for rimmed cartridges, rebounding hammer and retracting firing pins, crossbolt safety, bead blasted grey finish, 16-21 oz. Mfg. 1993-c.1999.

	$275	$235	$200	$175	$160	$145	$130

Last MSR was $310.

Add $100 per interchangeable set of barrels.

TEXAS GUNFIGHTERS

Previous importer located in Irving, TX circa 1988-1990.

REVOLVERS: SINGLE ACTION

SHOOTIST EDITION - .45 LC cal., patterned after the Colt SAA, 4 3/4 in. barrel, nickel-plated black powder frame, one piece walnut grips, mfg. by A. Uberti of Italy. New 1988.

✳ *Shootist Edition Standard Model* - 1,000 total mfg., cased.

	$625	$525	$440	N/A	N/A	N/A	N/A

Last MSR was $649.

✳ *Shootist Edition 1 of 100* - 100 total mfg., fully engraved, genuine mother-of-pearl one-piece grips, cased.

	$1,275	$1,050	$775	N/A	N/A	N/A	N/A

Last MSR was $1,395.

This model was also supplied with an extra set of walnut grips.

TEXAS LONGHORN ARMS, INC.

Previous manufacturer located in Richmond, TX circa 1988-1997.

REVOLVERS

SINGLE-ACTION - various cals., patterned after Colt's SAA, except the ejection port has been moved to left side of frame enabling left-hand loading, mfg. from 4140 steel, 1-piece grip, adj. trigger, case-hardened and blue, entirely handmade, supplied with lifetime warranty. Models included the Texas Border Patrol (last MSR was $1,595), South Texas Army (last MSR was $1,595), Texas Flattop (last MSR was $1,595), Grover's Northpaw (last MSR was $685), and Grover's Improved Number Five (last MSR was $1,195). Special editions and sets were also advertised (ranging from $1,500 MSR - $7,650 MSR), but very few were actually built. Mint examples are currently in the $1,350-$1,500 range, except for Grover's Northpaw, which is in the $650 range. While production plans called for 1,000 of each model to be manufactured, very few pistols were actually made.

GRADING - PPGS™	100%	98%	95%	90%	80%	70%	60%

THOMAS

Previous trademark manufactured by Alexander James Ordnance, Inc. located in Covina, CA.

Please refer to listing under A.J. Ordnance in this text.

THOMPSON & CAMPBELL

Current rifle manufacturer located in Rosshire, Scotland. No current U.S. importation. Consumer direct sales.

RIFLES: BOLT ACTION

Thompson & Campbell manufactures high quality bolt action rifles featuring the patented Inver action, which utilizes a rear extension plate and reinforcement rod that is inletted into the stock for additional strength. Individual models include the Inver, Cromie, the Islay, and Jura (Mannlicher configuration). Thompson & Campbell manufactures approx. 20-24 rifles annually. Please contact the factory directly for more information, current pricing, and delivery times.

THOMPSON CARBINES & PISTOLS

Auto-Ordnance Corporation

See Auto Ordnance Corp. section of this book.

THOMPSON/CENTER ARMS CO., INC.

Current manufacturer established during 1967, and located in Rochester, NH. Distributor and dealer sales.

During 2006, Thompson/Center was purchased by Smith & Wesson. Thompson/Center also has created a custom shop to enable customers to create custom pistols, rifles, shotguns, and muzzleloaders. Please contact the factory for availability and an individualized quotation.

Please refer to the *Blue Book of Modern Black Powder Arms* by John Allen (also online) for more information and prices on Thompson/Center's lineup of modern black powder models.

Black Powder Reproductions & Replicas by Dennis Adler is also an invaluable source for most black powder reproductions and replicas, and includes hundreds of color images on most popular makes/models, provides manufacturer/trademark histories, and up-to-date information on related items/accessories for black powder shooting - www.bluebookinc.com

PISTOLS: SINGLE SHOT

Caution: older and newer TC components do not interchange safely. Although parts will fit, they may not function properly. Special ordering of barrels, frames, and calibers started in 1988. Values below are for complete guns - including frame and barrel.

PRO-HUNTER - various cals., 15 in. fluted stainless steel barrel with adj. sights, hardwood or composition grips. New 2006.

MSR $748	$600	$525	$450	$400	$350	$325	$295

Add $30 for hardwood grips.
Add $8 for .204 Ruger cal.

G2 CONTENDER - various rimfire and centerfire cals., including .17 Mach 2 (new 2005), .204 Ruger (new 2004) and .375 JDJ (new 2004), 12 or 14 in. barrel with adj. sights, blued finish, walnut finger groove grip and forearm, replacement for the Contender model, will accept older Contender barrels w/o frame alteration, automatic hammer block safety with built-in interlock, hammer recocking w/o breaking open the gun, opening has been made easier, approx. 3 1/2 lbs. New late 2002.

MSR $608	$485	$435	$365	$290	$255	$220	$195

Add $7 for 14 in. barrel.
Add approx. $12 for 22 LR cal.
Add $22 for .17 HMR or 17 Mach 2 cal.
Add $47 for .45 LC/.410 bore.
Add $260-$322 per additional barrel, depending on length and caliber.

Currently, a G2 Contender frame assembly only retails for $313.

GRADING - PPGS™	100%	98%	95%	90%	80%	70%	60%

* *G2 Contender Stainless* - various cals., similar to G2 Contender, except is stainless steel with black rubber grips, 14 in. barrel only. New 2006.

MSR $677	$550	$485	$435	$365	$290	$255	$220

CONTENDER - .22 LR, .22 Rem., 5mm Rem., .218 Bee, .22 Hornet, .22 Jet, .221 Fireball, .222 Rem., .25-35 WCF, .256 Mag., .30 Carbine, .30-30 Win., .38 Spl., .357 Mag., .17 Ackley Bee, .17 Bumblebee, .17 Hornet, .17K Hornet, .17 Rem., .300 Whisper (new 1994), .30 Herrett, .357 Herrett, .357-44 B&D, 7x30 Waters, .32 H&R Mag., .32-20 WCF, 6mm TCU, 6.5mm TCU, or 9mm Para. cal., barrels are interchangeable, 8 3/4 (disc.), 10, or 14 in. barrel, hinged break open, triggerguard action lever, blue, .44, .357 Mag., and .45 Colt available with detachable choke for hot shot cartridges, VR, 10 in. barrel available, 10 in. bull barrel, adj. sights, checkered walnut grip and forearm. Mfg. 1967-2000.

The Contender action was made in 3 variations, and a wide variety of changes were made to grips, stocks, sights, etc. during 1967-2000. These production variances do not necessarily add premiums to values listed.

* *Contender Bull Barrel* - available in 13 cals. between .17 Rem. and .45 Win. Mag., 10 in. round barrel only.

			$380	$295	$220	$190	$170	$160	$150

Last MSR was $510.

Add $22 for .45 Colt/.410 bore with internal chokes.
Add $11 for .22 LR match grade chamber (new 1996).
Add approx. $230-$267 per additional barrel.

* *Contender Armour Alloy II Bull Barrel* - 7 cals. between .22 LR and .30-30 Win., similar to regular Bull Barrel, except has Armour Alloy II satin finish which is harder than stainless steel. Mfg. 1986-89.

			$320	$285	$230	$180	$170	$155	$130

Last MSR was $415.

Add $5 for .45 Colt/.410 bore internal choke.

* *Contender Vent. Rib* - .357 Mag. (disc.), .44 Mag. (disc.) or .45 Colt/.410 bore, 10 in. VR barrel only, adj. front and flip-up rear sight, internal choke became standard in 1985.

			$400	$300	$225	$185	$170	$160	$150

Last MSR was $533.

* *Contender Armour Alloy Vent. Rib* - .45/.410 internal choke, has Armour Alloy II satin finish which is harder than stainless steel. Mfg. 1986-disc.

			$350	$295	$230	$180	$170	$155	$130

Last MSR was $435.

* *Contender Stainless Steel* - various cals., 10 in. bull barrel. Mfg. 1993-2000.

			$435	$315	$220	$190	$170	$160	$150

Last MSR was $578.

Add approx. $240 per additional barrel.
Add $5 for .45/.410 with adj. sights.
Add $20 for .45/.410 with VR.

* *Contender Octagon Barrel* - .22 LR, .22 Mag. (disc.), .22 Hornet (disc.), .22K Hornet (disc.), .222 Rem. (disc.), or .357 Mag. (disc.) cal., 10 in. barrel. Disc. 1998.

			$355	$260	$200	$180	$170	$160	$150

Last MSR was $474.

* *Contender Match Grade Barrel* - .22 LR cal. only, choice of 10 or 14 in. match barrel. Mfg. 1992-98.

			$350	$265	$200	$180	$170	$160	$150

Last MSR was $460.

Add $10 for 14 in. barrel.

GRADING - PPGS™	100%	98%	95%	90%	80%	70%	60%

CONTENDER SHOOTERS PACKAGE - .22 LR Match, .223 Rem., .30-30 Win., or 7-30 Waters cal., includes blue frame and 14 in. barrel w/o sights, 2.5-7X scope, composite grips and forend, Weaver style base and rings, pistol case. Mfg. 1998-2000.

	$650	$575	$550	$450	$400	$360	$330

Last MSR was $754.

CONTENDER SUPER (14 & 16 IN.) - 13 cals. available from .17 Rem. - .45 Win. Mag. (disc.), 14 or 16 in. bull barrel only, special grips, beavertail forearm, adj. sight, 3 1/2 lbs. Disc. 1997.

	$360	$265	$200	$180	$170	$160	$150

Last MSR was $474.

> Add $5 for 16 in. barrel.
> Add $31 for .17 Rem. cal. (new 1992).
> Add $10 for .45-70 Govt. cal. in 16 in. barrel only with muzzle brake (new 1992).
> Add approx. $224 per additional barrel.
> Add $31 for VR barrel (.45 LC/.410 bore only).

Thompson Center will also make special order guns in different cals. other than those listed above. If factory work, these pistols will be worth a premium.

✳ *Contender Super Stainless* - various cals., choice of 14 or 16 in. barrel. Mfg. 1993-97.

	$385	$275	$215	$165	$130	$120	$100

Last MSR was $505.

> Add $5 for 16 in. barrel.
> Add $25 for .45-70 Govt. bull barrel with muzzle tamer.
> Add $30-$35 for .45 LC/.410 bore with internal choke.
> Add approx. $240 per additional barrel.

✳ *Contender Super Armour Alloy II* - 5 cals. between .22 LR and 7mm Rem. Mag., similar to regular Super Contender, except has Armour Alloy II satin finish which is harder than stainless steel. Mfg. 1986-89.

	$355	$295	$240	$185	$160	$135	$115

Last MSR was $425.

SUPER CONTENDER (14 & 16 IN.) - various cals. between .22 LR - .45-70 Govt., wood grips with rear stippling, 14 or 16 in. bull barrel (with or w/o VR), adj. sights, blue finish only. Mfg. 1999-2000.

	$410	$345	$285	$255	$220	$195	$170

Last MSR was $520.

> Add $35 for 14 in. VR barrel.
> Add $5 for 16 in. tapered barrel.

✳ *Super Contender Stainless* - similar to Super Contender, except is only available in 14 in. barrel. Mfg. 1999-2000.

	$430	$320	$215	$165	$135	$120	$100

Last MSR was $578.

> Add $35 for VR barrel.
> Add $22 for .45/.410 ga. barrel.

CONTENDER HUNTER PACKAGE - .223 Rem., .7-30 Waters, .30-30 Win., .35 Rem., .357 Rem. Max. (disc. 1994), .375 Win. Mag. (new 1992), .44 Mag., or .45-70 Govt. cal., special 12 (disc.) or 14 (new 1992) in. barrel with muzzle brake, 2.5 power scope with lighted reticle, walnut grip has nonslip rubber insert to cushion recoil, includes studs, swivels, sling, and deluxe carrying case, approx. 4 lbs. Mfg. 1990-97.

	$695	$575	$495	$430	$365	$315	$275

Last MSR was $798.

GRADING - PPGS™	100%	98%	95%	90%	80%	70%	60%

CONTENDER 25TH ANNIVERSARY - .22 LR cal. only, 10 in. octagon barrel, laser etched anniversary logo on receiver sides and barrel, checkered stock and forearm, limited mfg. in 1992 only.

	$610	$535	$465	$410	$360	$315	$275

Last MSR was $700.

* *Contender 25th Anniversary Cased Set* - cased set with 5 barrels including .22 LR, .22 Mag., .22 Jet, .22 Hornet, and .38 Spl. cal., 50 sets mfg. 1992 only.

	$1,850	$1,550	$1,225	$1,050	$900	$775	$650

Last MSR was $1,975.

ENCORE - various cals. between .22 LR and .480 Ruger (new 2002), features walnut grip with finger grooves and forend, blue finish, 10 (disc. 1999), 12 (new 1999), or 15 in. barrel with adj. sights, VR barrel on .45 LC/.410 bore, hammer block safety with bolt interlock, 4-4 1/2 lbs. New 1998.

MSR $626	$500	$440	$375	$310	$265	$230	$200

Add $8 for 15 in. barrel.
Add $228 for extra 10 in. (disc.), $268-$294 for extra 12 in. barrel, or $370-$332 for extra 15 in. barrel, depending on caliber.
Add $29 for .45 LC/.410 bore barrel, depending on barrel length.
Add approx. $300 for .270 Win. or .308 cal.

Encore pistol barrels ARE NOT interchangeable with Contender pistol barrels.
Currently, an Encore frame assembly only retails for $385.
Values are for base caliber - most calibers will add to base price approx. 5%.

* *Encore Stainless* - .22-250 Rem., .223 Rem., .243 Win., .30-06, .308 Win., 7mm-08 Rem., .44 Mag., .45 LC/.410 bore, or .480 Ruger (mfg. 2003) cal., black synthetic finger groove grips and forearm. New 1999.

MSR $685	$550	$415	$295	$215	$185	$160	$145

Add $23 for .480 Ruger cal. (mfg. 2003).
Add $9 for 15 in. barrel.

* *Encore Hunter Package* - .22-250 Rem., .270 Win., or .308 Win. cal., features 15 in. barrel w/o sights and 2.5-7X scope, Weaver base and rings, composite grip and forend, includes case. Mfg. 1998-2005.

	$730	$620	$575	$465	$400	$360	$330

Last MSR was $859.

RIFLES: BOLT ACTION

ICON - .22-250 Rem., .243 Win., .270 Win., .30-06, .300 Win. Mag., .308 Win., .30 TC, or 7mm Rem. Mag. cal., medium or long action, black synthetic (medium action), Realtree camo (medium action), checkered American walnut (long action only), or choice of Ultra Wood pistol grip stock and forearm, 24 in. barrel, hinged floor plate on long action, cocking indicator, adj, trigger, detachable 3 shot mag. on medium action, interlocked bedding system, butterknife jeweled bolt handle, 60 degree bolt lift, Weaver style base, guaranteed to shoot 1 in. or less at 100 yards, 7 1/2 lbs. New 2007.

MSR $1,106	$995	$875	$750	$625	$500	$450	$395

Subtract $96 for synthetic stock with Weathershield dull nickel finish (medium action) only).
Subtract $14 for camo stock.

RIFLES: SEMI-AUTO

SILVER LYNX - .22 LR cal., 20 in. match grade barrel with adj. fiber optic open sights, 5 shot mag., stainless steel action and barrel, black composite stock with Monte Carlo cheekpiece, 5 1/2 lbs. Mfg. 2004-2005.

	$340	$295	$240	$200	$165	$145	$120

Last MSR was $423.

GRADING - PPGS™	100%	98%	95%	90%	80%	70%	60%

CLASSIC - .17 Mach 2 (new 2006) or .22 LR cal., blowback action, all steel construction, 5 (new 2003) or 8 (disc. 2002) shot mag., 22 in. match grade barrel with muzzle crown, adj. rear sight, blue finish, uncheckered Monte Carlo walnut stock, 5 1/2 lbs. New 2000.

MSR $504	$395	$335	$285	$240	$195	$160	$140

CLASSIC BENCHMARK TARGET - same action as Classic, 18 in. heavy target barrel, brown laminated hardwood Monte Carlo target stock, matte finish blue, 10 shot mag., no sights, receiver is drilled and tapped, 6.8 lbs. New 2003.

MSR $518	$425	$350	$270	$235	$215	$175	$150

MODEL R55 - .17 Mach 2 cal., blue or stainless steel, 20 in. barrel, brown laminate or black composite stock, fiberoptic sights. New 2005.

MSR $518	$425	$350	$275	$240	$220	$200	$175

> Add $65 for stainless steel.
> Add $50 for all-weather SST.

RIFLES: SINGLE SHOT

ENCORE RIFLE - available in many rimfire and centerfire cals. between .17 Mach 2 (new 2005) and .45-70 Govt., interchangeable standard 24 or heavy 26 in. barrel, automatic hammer block, trigger guard opening lever, choice of black synthetic (new 1999), Realtree camo (new 2005), Realtree Hardwoods HD camo, or American walnut uncheckered forearm and Monte Carlo stock with pistol grip, adj. rear sight, approx. 7 lbs. New 1997.

MSR $645	$530	$415	$320	$250	$200	$180	$170

> Add $43 for walnut stock and forearm.
> Add $58 for camo.
> Add $35 for .17 Mach 2 cal.
> Add $286 per extra blue finish barrel.

Encore rifle barrels ARE NOT interchangeable with Contender Carbine barrels.
Currently, an Encore frame, including buttstock and forearm starts at $334 MSR.

* *Encore Rifle Stainless* - similar to Encore Rifle, except has black synthetic stock and forearm or Realtree/Realtree Hardwoods HD (new 2005) camo treatment, and is stainless steel. New 1999.

MSR $736	$595	$425	$295	$245	$205	$180	$170

> Add $320 per extra barrel.
> Add $58 for camo.

* *Encore Rifle Katahdin Carbine* - .444 Marlin (disc. 2003), .450 Marlin, or .45-70 Govt. cal., 18 in. barrel with muzzle tamer, blue steel, black composite stock and forearm, fiber optic sights, drilled and tapped, 6 lbs., 10 oz. Mfg. 2002-2005.

	$490	$370	$255	$235	$195	$180	$170

Last MSR was $617.

> Add $292 for extra barrel.

* *Encore Rifle Hunter Package* - .300 Win. Mag., or .308 Win. cal., includes 3-9x40mm scope, Weaver style base and rings, and hard case. Mfg. 2002-2005.

	$770	$640	$585	$475	$400	$360	$330

Last MSR was $905.

PRO HUNTER RIFLE - various cals., 28 in. barrel only, stainless steel, features recoil reducing Flex Tech stock and choice of black, Hardwoods camo, with or w/o thumbhole. New 2006.

MSR $810	$665	$595	$525	$450	$400	$350	$300

> Add approx. $67 for camo.

GRADING - PPGS™	100%	98%	95%	90%	80%	70%	60%

CONTENDER CARBINE - available in 15 cals. between .17 Rem. and .44 Rem. Mag., also .410 bore (3 in.), Contender action with pistol grip full stock and forearm, 21 in. interchangeable barrel, drilled for scope mounts, iron sights standard. Mfg. 1986-2000.

	$415	$315	$255	$215	$190	$175	$160

Last MSR was $540.

Add $31 for .17 Rem. cal. (disc. 1997).
Add $21 for .410 bore barrel. (disc. 1997).
Add approx. $244 per extra barrel.
Add $11 for match grade .22 LR barrel.
Subtract $36 for Youth Model (16 1/4 in. barrel w/o VR - disc. 1998).
Add $175 for Survival Carbine System (disc. - includes Rynite stock, 16 1/4 .223 Rem. barrel, extra .45 Colt/.410 barrel, and soft camo cordura case).

✳ *Contender Carbine Rynite* - similar to Contender Carbine, except has Rynite stock and forend. Mfg. 1990-93.

	$335	$270	$220	$195	$180	$165	$155

Last MSR was $425.

Add $30 for .17 Rem. cal.
Add $10 for match grade barrel.
Add $25 for 21 in. VR smooth bore .410 bore barrel.

✳ *Contender Carbine Stainless* - various cals., 21 in. barrel, choice of walnut (disc. 1993) or Rynite synthetic stock. Mfg. 1993-2000.

	$415	$310	$230	$200	$185	$165	$155

Last MSR was $546.

Add $35 for walnut stock (disc.).
Add $11 for .22 LR match barrel (new 1995).
Add $26 for .410 smooth bore barrel with screw-in full choke (disc.).
This model was also available in a Youth Model with walnut stock at no extra charge (disc. 1993).

HUNTER RIFLE MODEL - single shot, top lever break open action w/ interchangeable barrels, .22 Hornet, .223 Rem., .22-250 Rem., .243 Win., .270 Win., 7x57mm, .30-06, .308 Win., .375 H&H (new 1992), or .416 Rem. Mag. (new 1992) cal., 23 in. barrel, 6 lbs. 14 oz., checkered walnut stock, choice of medium or light sporter weight barrel. New 1983 and improved in 1987. Available in left-hand at no extra charge. Disc. 1992.

	$500	$415	$350	$295	$265	$240	$220

Last MSR was $595.

Add $20 for .375 H&H or .416 Rem. Mag. cal.
Add approx. $275 per extra rifle barrel.

✳ *Hunter Rifle Model Deluxe* - similar to Hunter Model, except features double triggers and upgraded walnut stock and forearm. Mfg. 1992 only.

	$550	$450	$375	$325	$285	$250	$225

Last MSR was $675.

Add $20 for .375 H&H or .416 Rem. Mag. cal.

✳ *Hunter Rifle Model Shotgun* - same action as Hunter Rifle, except is supplied with 12 ga. barrel (field choke with 3 1/2 in. chamber or slug with 3 in. chamber and iron sights) or 10 ga. barrel (3 1/2 in. chamber). Disc. 1992.

	$500	$415	$350	$295	$265	$240	$220

Last MSR was $595.

Add $275 per additional shotgun barrel.

TCR ´83 ARISTOCRAT - similar to Hunter Model, except stock has cheekpiece and forearm is checkered, stainless steel, double set triggers. Disc. 1986.

	$425	$370	$345	$290	$260	$235	$215

Last MSR was $475.

Add $175 for each additional barrel(s) (including 12 ga. slug).

GRADING - PPGS™	100%	98%	95%	90%	80%	70%	60%

SHOTGUNS: SINGLE SHOT

ENCORE SHOTGUN - 12 (new 2004) or 20 (disc. 2005) ga., 3 in. chamber, action based on Encore pistol with trigger guard release for barrel opening, 26 in. VR barrel with three choke tubes, recoil pad. New 1998.

MSR $825	$695	$600	$500	$400	$325	$250	$200

Add $337 (20 ga.) or $358 (12 ga.) per additional shotgun barrel with choke tubes. Subtract $23 for 20 ga.

＊*Encore Shotgun Slug Gun* - 12 or 20 ga. only, 3 in. chamber, 24 or 26 (20 ga. only) in. rifled barrel with fiberoptic sights, walnut stock and forearm. Mfg. 2000-2005.

	$570	$475	$385	$315	$250	$225	$200

Last MSR was $684.

Subtract $27 for 20 ga.

＊*Encore Shotgun Turkey Gun* - 12 (disc. 2005) or 20 ga., 3 in. chamber, 24 in. smoothbore barrel with screw-in turkey choke tube, 100% Realtree Hardwoods (new 2003) or Advantage Timber (mfg. 2002 only) camo coverage, and fiberoptic sights. New 2002.

MSR $825	$715	$600	$520	$415	$325	$275	$225

Add $71 for muzzleloading barrel (disc. 2003).

＊*Encore Shotgun Katahdin Turkey Gun* - 12 ga., 3 in. chamber, 20 in. barrel with turkey choke tube, composite stock with Realtree Hardwoods HD camo pattern, fiberoptic sights. Limited mfg. 2005.

	$590	$510	$410	$325	$275	$225	$200

Last MSR was $748.

THUNDER-FIVE

Current trademark manufactured by MIL Inc., located in Piney Flats, TN. Previous company name was Holston Enterprises, Inc. Various distributors. Previously manufactured by Mil, Inc. located in Piney Flats, TN. Previously distributed by C.L. Reedy & Associates, Inc. located in Jonesborough, TN.

While previously advertised as the Spectre Five (not mfg.), this firearm was re-named the Thunder-Five.

REVOLVERS

THUNDER-FIVE - .45 LC cal./.410 bore with 3 in. chamber or .45-70 Govt. cal. (mfg. 1994-98), single or double action, unique 5 shot revolver design permits shooting .45 LC or .410 bore shotshells interchangeably, 2 in. rifled barrel, phosphate finish, external ambidextrous hammer block safety, internal draw bar safety, combat sights, hammer, trigger, and trigger guard, Pachmayr grips, includes padded plastic carrying case, 48 oz., serialization starts at 1,101. New 1992.

MSR $545	$495	$450	$400	$375	$350	$325	$300

Sub-caliber sleeve inserts were available until 1998 for 9mm Para., .357 Mag./.38 Spl., and .38 Super cals.

TIKKA

Current trademark imported by Beretta U.S.A. Corp., located in Accokeek, MD. Previously imported until 2000 by Stoeger Industries, located in Wayne, NJ. Tikka rifles are currently manufactured by Sako, Ltd. located in Riihimäki, Finland. Previously manufactured by Oy Tikkakoski Ab, of Tikkakoski, Finland (pre-1989).

During 2000, Tikka was purchased by Beretta Holding of Italy. All currently produced Tikkas are imported by Beretta U.S.A. Corp., located in Accokeek, MD.

Also see listings under Ithaca combination guns and bolt action rifles for older models.

GRADING - PPGS™	100%	98%	95%	90%	80%	70%	60%

COMBINATIONS GUNS: O/U

Previously manufactured in Jyvaskyla, Finland. In 1989, under a joint venture agreement, the 412 O/U shooting system was manufactured in Italy. Older models may be found in the Valmet trademark section of this text.

During 1993, the new models of the 512S series replaced the older 412S series. Separate listings have not been provided, since they are almost identical in most respects.

> Add $745-$765 for extra shotgun barrels (includes screw-in chokes), $810 for extra shotgun/rifle combo, and $1,040 for double rifle barrels.

MODEL 512S/412S SHOOTING SYSTEM - interchangeable barrel assemblies permit a double rifle, shotgun/rifle, and O/U shotgun configuration, user installed interchangeable barrels, monobloc locking, rifle barrel positioning by adjustment, SST, extractors or ejectors, checkered walnut stock and forend, cocking indicators, blue finish.

⁂ *Model 512S Field Grade* - 12 ga. only, 3 in. chambers, auto ejectors, screw-in choke tubes (includes 5), 26 or 28 in. barrels, matte nickel finish. New 1986-importation disc. 1997, reintroduced 2000 only.

$1,050	$750	$595	$550	$475	$440	$400

Last MSR was $1,134.

> Subtract 10% if w/o choke tubes.
> Add $45 for Sporting Clays Model (new 2000).

The Premium Grade became standard issue beginning 1995. This model was reintroduced in 2000 only, and new features included back boring and ported barrels (Sporting Clays Model only).

⁂ *Model 412ST Trap* - 12 ga., Monte Carlo stock, 30 in. barrels, screw-in chokes standard.

$1,125	$925	$725	$650	$580	$540	$475

Last MSR was $1,325.

This variation was made by Valmet in Finland.

⁂ *Model 412ST Premium Grade Trap* - similar to Model 412ST Trap, except has better walnut and checkering.

$1,425	$1,000	$875	$750	$625	$580	$515

Last MSR was $1,665.

This variation was made by Valmet in Finland.

⁂ *Model 512S Sporting Clays* - 12 ga. only, sporting clays configuration with 28 or 30 (new 1994) in. VR barrels and choke tubes. Imported 1992-97.

$1,160	$950	$735	$650	$580	$540	$475

Last MSR was $1,360.

⁂ *Model 512S Combination Gun* - combination rifle/shotgun, 12 ga, 3 in. chambers, 24 in. barrels, under rifle barrel has choice of .222 Rem., .30-06, or .308 Win. cal., extractors. Importation disc. 1997.

$1,425	$1,025	$775	$675	$600	$525	$475

Last MSR was $1,770.

⁂ *Model 512S Double Rifle* - .30-06 (new 1994), .308 Win. (new 1994), 9.3x74R cal., 24 in. barrels, extractors. Importation disc. 1997.

$1,525	$1,125	$825	$750	$625	$550	$500

Last MSR was $1,890.

RIFLES: BOLT ACTION

About 3,000 rifles sold under the Tikka name have been recalled following catastrophic failures, but a small number of guns sold in the American market remain in the hands of consumers who have apparently not heard about the recall. A weakness in the stainless steel used to manufacture rifles during 2003-2004 has lead to ruptured barrels. Consumers are urged to contact the Tikka Recall Center at 800-503-8869 with your rifle's serial number to find out if your firearm is affected.

NEW GENERATION RIFLE (MODELS 595/695) - .22-250 Rem., .223 Rem., .243 Win., .270 Win., .30-06, .308 Win., 7mm Rem. Mag, .300 Win. Mag., or .338 Win Mag. cal., 22 1/2 (non-Mag.) or 24 1/2 (Mag. cals.) in. barrel, detachable 3 (standard) or 5 (optional) shot mag., forged and milled action in two lengths, checkered walnut stock, 7-7 1/2 lbs. Sako mfg. 1989-94.

	$725	$600	$550	$500	$450	$400	$360

Last MSR was $835.

Add $25 for Mag. cals.

Cals. .22-250 Rem., .308 Win., and .300 Win. Mag. were introduced in late 1989.
This model's nomenclature also included the Models 595 (short actions with cals. up to .308 Win. cal.) and 695 (long action, including Mag. cals.).

PREMIUM GRADE MODEL - same cals. as New Generation Rifle, stock is select walnut with rollover cheek-piece and rosewood pistol grip cap and forend tip, high polished barrel blue. Imported 1989-94.

$860	$715	$600	$550	$500	$450	$400

Last MSR was $1,030.

Add $40 for Mag. cals.

VARMINT MODEL - .22-250 Rem., .223 Rem., .243 Win., or .308 Win. cal., 24 1/2 in. heavy barrel, no sights. Mfg. 1991-94.

$895	$750	$625	$550	$500	$450	$400

Last MSR was $1,090.

T3 HUNTER - .22-250 Rem., .223 Rem., .243 Win., .25-06 Rem., .270 Win., .270 WSM, .30-06, .308 Win., 6.5x55mm, 7mm-08 Rem. (new 2006), 7mm Rem. Mag., .300 WSM, .300 Win. Mag., .338 Federal, or .338 Win. Mag. cal., cold hammer forged 22 7/16-24 3/8 in. barrel, similar action as the Whitetail Hunter, choice of checkered walnut or black synthetic stock (disc. 2003), 3-4 shot detachable mag., 2 position rear safety, designed by Giugiaro of Italy, approx. 6 3/4 lbs. Importation began mid-2003.

MSR $625	$550	$495	$450	$395	$350	$300	$275

Add $15 for WSM cals.
Subtract 10% for synthetic stock.

∗ *T3 Deluxe* - similar cals. as T3 Hunter, oil finished deluxe Tripartiti checkered walnut stock with rosewood forend tip and pistol grip cap. Mfg. 2006-2007.

$895	$725	$600	$550	$500	$450	$400

Last MSR was $1,075.

∗ *T3 Lite* - similar to T3 Hunter, except has TrueBody glass fiber reinforced polymer black stock, adj. buttplate, approx. 6 1/4 lbs. Importation began 2004.

MSR $525	$475	$425	$385	$350	$295	$275	$250

Add $15 for WSM cals.

∗ *T3 Lite Stainless* - similar to T3, except has stainless action and barrel, available with black synthetic stock only. Importation began mid-2003.

MSR $600	$500	$450	$400	$350	$300	$275	$250

Add $15 for WSM cals.
Add $25 for left-hand action.

∗ *T3 Camo Stainless* - similar to T3 Lite Stainless, except has Realtree HD Hardwoods camo stock finish. Mfg. 2006-2007.

$650	$575	$495	$425	$350	$300	$260

Last MSR was $795.

GRADING - PPGS™	100%	98%	95%	90%	80%	70%	60%

✳ **T3 Laminated Stainless** - .243 Win., .25-06 Rem., .270 Win., .270 WSM, .30-06, .300 WSM, .300 Win. Mag., .308 Win., 7mm Rem. Mag., or .338 Win. Mag., similar to T3 Stainless, except has stainless action and barrel, available with grey matte laminated hardwood stock, approx. 6 3/4 lbs. Importation began 2004.

MSR $850	$725	$625	$525	$450	$400	$350	$300

Add $25 for WSM cals.

✳ **T3 Big Boar Synthetic** - .30-06, .308 Win. or .300 WSM cal., black synthetic stock, 19 in. barrel, features Giugiaro design, 6.1 lbs. Imported 2005-2007.

	$585	$515	$460	$400	$350	$300	$275

Last MSR was $695.

✳ **T3 Varmint** - .22-250 Rem., .223 Rem., or .308 Win. cal., choice of steel or stainless steel action/barrel, 23 3/8 in. heavy barrel, adj. stock mfg. from reinforced copolymer polypropylene, 3-6 shot detachable mag., 8 lbs. Importation began 2004.

MSR $800	$725	$650	$575	$475	$400	$365	$330

✳ **T3 Super Varmint** - .22-250 Rem., .223 Rem., or .308 Win. cal., 23 3/8 in. heavy stainless barrel, 3 or 4 shot mag., laminated synthetic stock with adj. comb, Picatinny rail, extra swivel stud, adj. trigger. Imported 2005-2007.

	$1,250	$1,000	$800	$695	$585	$485	$415

Last MSR was $1,425.

✳ **T3 Tactical** - .223 Rem. or .308 Win. cal., T3 action, 20 or 24 (disc. 2007) in. barrel, 5 shot mag., adj. comb, Picatinny rail, 7 1/4 lbs. Importation began 2004.

MSR $1,400	$1,195	$975	$875	$775	$675	$575	$500

WHITETAIL HUNTER/SYNTHETIC (BATTUE) - .22-250 Rem. (new 1995), .223 Rem. (new 1995), .243 Win. (new 1995), .25-06 Rem.(new 1995), .270 Win., .30-06, .308 Win. (not available in synthetic), 6.5x55mm Swedish (new 2002), 7mm Rem. Mag., 7mm-08 Rem. (new 1999), .300 Win. Mag., or .338 Win. Mag. cal., 20 1/2 (disc. 1994), 22 1/2 (new 1995), or 24 1/2 (new 1995, Mag cals. only), in. barrel, 3 or 5 (optional) shot detachable mag., choice of wood or black synthetic (new 1996) stock, no sights (Hunter Model), or open sights on raised rib (disc., Battue Model), approx. 7 1/4 lbs. Mfg. 1991-2002.

	$525	$450	$390	$350	$325	$300	$275

Last MSR was $615.

Add $30 for Mag. cals.
Add $60 for carved elk or deer game scene stock (mfg. 1996-97).

✳ **Whitetail Hunter/Synthetic Left Hand** - similar cals. as Whitetail Hunter, left-hand action. Importation disc. 2003.

	$590	$530	$460	$395	$360	$325	$295

Last MSR was $680.

Add $30 for Mag. cals.

✳ **Whitetail Hunter/Synthetic/Battue Stainless** - similar cals. as Whitetail Hunter, except not available in 6.5x55mm Swedish cal., black synthetic stock only and satin finished stainless steel, 7 1/4 lbs. Mfg. 1997-2002.

	$590	$530	$460	$395	$360	$325	$295

Last MSR was $680.

Add $30 for Mag. cals.

GRADING - PPGS™	100%	98%	95%	90%	80%	70%	60%

✳ *Whitetail Hunter/Synthetic Stainless Laminate* - .25-06 Rem., .270 Win., .30-06, .300 Win. Mag., or 7mm Rem. Mag. cal., similar to Whitetail Hunter Stainless, except has grey laminate wood stock and forend with checkering, satin finished stainless steel, 3 shot detachable mag., 7 1/4 lbs. Imported 2002-2003.

	$650	$565	$500	$430	$375	$315	$270

Last MSR was $745.

Add $30 for Mag. cals.

✳ *Whitetail Hunter/Synthetic Deluxe* - similar cals. as Whitetail Hunter, gloss finished deluxe checkered walnut stock and forearm with rollover cheekpiece. Imported 1999-2003.

	$650	$565	$500	$460	$400	$360	$330

Last MSR was $745.

Add $30 for Mag. cals.

CONTINENTAL VARMINT MODEL - .17 Rem. (mfg. 2000-2002), .22-250 Rem., .223 Rem., or .308 Win. cal., heavy 26 in. barrel w/o sights, adj. trigger, quick release 3 shot detachable mag., integral scope mount rails, checkered walnut stock with beavertail forend, recoil pad spacer system, 8 1/8 lbs. Mfg. 1996-2003.

	$615	$520	$460	$400	$350	$325	$300

Last MSR was $720.

CONTINENTAL LONG RANGE HUNTER - .25-06 Rem. (disc. 2002), .270 Win. (disc. 2002), 7mm Rem. Mag., or .300 Win. Mag. cal., heavy 26 in. barrel w/o sights, checkered walnut stock and forend, 8 3/8 lbs. Mfg. 1996-2003.

	$640	$540	$475	$415	$365	$325	$300

Last MSR was $750.

Subtract 5% for non-Mag. cals. (disc. 2002).

TARGET (SPORTER) MODEL - .22-250 Rem., .223 Rem., .308 Win., 7mm-08 Rem. (new 2002), 6.5x55mm Swedish (new 2003) cal., 23 3/8 in. barrel w/o sights, competition style stock with adj. buttplate and cheekpiece, detachable 5 shot mag., stippled pistol grip and forend, 9 lbs. Mfg. 1998-2003.

	$845	$765	$660	$580	$515	$450	$395

Last MSR was $950.

This model was designated the Tikka Sporter until 2003.

TIMBERWOLF

Previous trademark manufactured by I.M.I. (Israel Military Industries) located in Israel. Previously imported and distributed by Action Arms located in Philadelphia, PA until 1994.

RIFLES: SLIDE ACTION

TIMBERWOLF - .357 Mag. or .44 Mag. (disc.) cal., slide action, straight grip shotgun style stock with adj. drop, blue or satin chrome finish, takedown, 18 1/2 in. barrel, 10 shot tube mag., sear locking and firing pin safeties, integral scope base, approx. 5 1/2 lbs. Imported 1989-93.

	100%	98%	95%	90%	80%	70%	60%
.357 Mag.	$295	$260	$230	$195	$180	$160	$145
.44 Mag. (blue only)	$450	$400	$360	$335	$300	$275	$250

Last MSR was $299.

Add $80 for satin chrome finish.

This model was designed by Evan Whilden, and imported/distributed by Action Arms Ltd. Springfield Armory imported 1,000 .44 Mag. Timberwolf models during 1990-91.

TIME PRECISION ARMS

Current custom riflemaker located in New Milford, CT. Previously located in Brookfield, CT. Consumer direct sales.

GRADING - PPGS™	100%	98%	95%	90%	80%	70%	60%

RIFLES: BOLT ACTION

Time Precision rifles feature SLV/ALV actions and are available in over 30 different types, in cals. from .22 LR - .416 Rigby, prices range from $900-$1,146. All guns are made per individual custom order, but are basically available in 3 different configurations - Hunting, Benchrest, and Target rifles. Base prices begin at $2,576 and $2,316 for .22 Sporter with a wide range of special order options. Please contact the company directly regarding delivery times and other information (see Trademark Index).

TIPPMAN ARMS CO.

Previous manufacturer located in Fort Wayne, IN.

Tippman Arms manufactured 1/2 scale semi-auto working models of famous machine guns. All models were available with an optional hardwood case, extra ammo cans, and other accessories. Mfg. 1986-1987 only.

RIFLES: REPRODUCTIONS, SEMI-AUTO

MODEL 1919 A-4 - .22 LR cal. only, copy of Browning 1919 A-4 Model, belt fed, closed bolt operation, 11 in. barrel, includes tripod, 10 lbs.

	$3,125	$2,950	$2,700	$2,350	$2,000	$1,725	$1,500

Last MSR was $1,325.

MODEL 1917 - .22 LR cal. only, copy of Browning M1917, watercooled, belt fed, closed bolt operation, 11 in. barrel, includes tripod, 10 lbs.

	$6,375	$6,000	$5,500	$5,000	$4,350	$3,750	$3,250

Last MSR was $1,830.

MODEL .50 HB - .22 Mag. cal. only, copy of Browning .50 cal. machine gun, belt fed, closed bolt operation, 18 1/4 in. barrel, includes tripod, 13 lbs.

	$6,625	$6,400	$5,950	$5,400	$4,950	$4,500	$4,000

Last MSR was $1,929.

TISAS

Current trademark of semi-auto pistols manufactured by Trabzon Gun Industry Corp., located in Ankara, Turkey. No current U.S. importation.

PISTOLS: SEMI-AUTO

Trabzon manufactures good quality semi-auto pistols with white and black chrome slides in .380 ACP, 7.65mm, 9mm Para., and .45 ACP cal. Prices range from $285-$325 (FOB Turkey). Please contact the company directly for more information, including pricing and availability (see Trademark Index).

TOKAREV

See Russian Service Pistols and Rifles section.

TOLLEY, J & W

Current trademark owned by F.J. Wiseman & Co., Ltd., located in Staffordshire, England.

J.W. Tolley was renowned for big bore wildfowl guns, as well as Express and Big Game rifles. Current double rifles are built to order. Please contact the company directly for a price quotation, available options, and delivery time (see Trademark Index).

RIFLES: SxS

J & W TOLLEY BOXLOCK - various cals. and options, custom made to order.
  Base price for this model is £15,000.

J & W TOLLEY SIDELOCK - various cals. between .375 H&H - .600 NE, true H&H style action, custom made to order, approx. 12-18 months delivery time.
  Base price on this model is £27,000.

GRADING - PPGS™	100%	98%	95%	90%	80%	70%	60%

TOMPKINS

Previous pistol trademark manufactured through licensed production to Varsity Manufacturing Co., located in Springfield, MA circa 1947-1953. Also manufactured by Walter Woodman in limited quantities after 1953.

PISTOLS: SINGLE SHOT

TOMPKINS PRECISION PISTOL - 22 LR cal., single shot pistol utilizing flexible sear mechanism and trap door style breech block, checkered walnut grips with full length forend, adj. sights, approx. 200 mfg. through 1953, late mfg. will be marked WE Woodman (approx. 2 dozen) on top receiver, instead of AH Tompkins.

$1,100	$900	$750	$600	$500	$400	$350

TORNADO

Currently manufactured by AseTekno located in Helsinki, Finland.

RIFLES: BOLT ACTION

TORNADO MODEL - .338 Lapua Mag. cal., unique straight line design with free floating barrel, 5 shot mag., pistol grip assembly is part of frame, limited importation into the U.S.

The factory should be contacted directy regarding domestic availability and pricing (see Trademark Index).

TOZ

Current manufacturer established in 1712, and located in Tula, Russia. Limited U.S. pistol importation by Larry's Guns, located in Portland, ME. Previously imported by Tula Firearms, located in San Diego, CA. TOZ is an abbreviation for Tulsky Oruzheiny Zavod. Dealer sales.

TOZ manufactures a wide variety of quality O/U, SxS, single shot, and semi-auto shotguns, in addition to pistols, rifles and combination guns. TOZ also provides a complete line of custom services, including elaborate inlays (gold, silver, and platinum) and wood carving. Please contact the importer directly for more information on the TOZ pistol. For more information on TOZ long guns, please refer to the Tula Arms Plant section.

PISTOLS: SINGLE SHOT

TOZ-35 FREE PISTOL - .22 LR cal., employs virtually every shooting refinement possible in a single shot target pistol, fully adj. target grips (with or w/o Rink laminate grip and forestock), limited mfg.

No MSR	$1,299	$1,050	$900	$800	$725	$650	$575

TRADEWINDS

Previous importer located in Tacoma, WA.

RIFLES

HUSKY MODEL 5000 - .22-250 Rem., .243 Win., .270 Win., .308 Win., or .30-06 cal., bolt action, 23 3/4 in. barrel, adj. sight, removable mag., hand-checkered walnut stock.

$325	$310	$290	$250	$225	$200	$175

NORAHAMMER 900 SERIES - .270 Win., .308 Win., or .30-06 cal., similar to Husky Model, 20 1/2 in. barrel, 6 lbs., 8 oz.

$325	$310	$290	$250	$225	$200	$175

MODEL 311-A - .22 LR cal., bolt action, 5 shot, 22 1/2 in. barrel, folding leaf rear sight, walnut checkered stock.

$180	$170	$150	$130	$120	$100	$85

GRADING - PPGS™	100%	98%	95%	90%	80%	70%	60%

MODEL 260-A - .22 LR cal., semi-auto, 5 shot, 22 1/2 in. barrel, 3 leaf folding sight, checkered walnut stock.

		100%	98%	95%	90%	80%	70%	60%
		$200	$190	$175	$150	$130	$120	$100

SHOTGUNS: SEMI-AUTO

MODEL H-170 - 12 ga., 2 3/4 in. chamber, 26 in. mod. or 28 in. full, recoil operated action, alloy receiver, 5 shot, tube mag., VR, checkered walnut stock.

$275	$265	$250	$225	$200	$180	$150

TRADITIONS PERFORMANCE FIREARMS

Current importer located in Old Saybrook, CT. Distributor and dealer sales.

Currently, the company offers two proprietary single shot rifles, the Outfitter and Tip-Up models, in addition select single

shot (Pedersoli mfg.) rifles and accessories. Traditions previously imported a wide variety of Stefano Fausti shotguns until 2007, Emilio Rizzini shotguns from Italy, a semi-auto shotgun, and a line of Uberti mfg. black powder models. Please contact the company directly for more information (see Trademark Index).

Please refer to the *Blue Book of Modern Black Powder Arms* by John Allen (also online) for more information and prices on Traditions' extensive lineup of modern black powder models.

Black Powder Reproductions & Replicas by Dennis Adler is also an invaluable source for most black powder reproductions and replicas, and includes hundreds of color images on most popular makes/models, provides manufacturer/trademark histories, and up-to-date information on related items/accessories for black powder shooting - www.bluebookinc.com

RIFLES

Traditions currently imports the Pedersoli 1874 Sharps rifle, Remington Rolling Block sporting rifle, and a Springfield Trapdoor carbine. Prices start from $1,029 for the Remington rolling block reproduction in .45-70 Govt. cal. The Springfield Trapdoor carbine has a $1,397 MSR, with 22 in. barrel and blued frame/barrel. The 1874 Sharps Standard rifle has a MSR of $1,324, $1,545 for the Deluxe Sharps rifle (add $59 for pistol grip stock), $2,796 for the Deluxe hand engraved Sharps rifle, and $2,060 for the Quigley model. Traditions also imported Uberti black powder guns until 2002, including the Henry, Model 1866, and Model 1873. Prices ranged from $669-$969, depending on the model.

OUTFITTER - .243 Win., .270 Win., .30-06, .308 Win., or .444 Marlin cal., 24 in. Wilson rifled barrel, drilled and tapped, black synthetic (with or w/o thumbhole), or Mossy Oak Treestand camo stock, sling swivels, tip-up action, opening lever in front of trigger guard, fiber optic front sight, single shot, recoil pad, dual safety system. New 2008.

MSR $543	$425	$375	$325	$275	$225	$200	$175

Add $56 for camo.
Add $22 for thumbhole stock.
Add $192 for Outfitter centerfire/muzzleloader combo which includes extra .50 cal. 28 in. barrel using a 209 primer for detonation.

TIP-UP .45-70 Govt. cal., 24 in. nickel or blue Wilson barrel, steel frame, fiber optic front sight, adj. rear sight on barrel, cross-bolt rear block safety in trigger group, transfer bar safety, black synthetic (with or w/o thumbhole) or Mossy Oak Treestand camo stock, drilled and tapped. New 2008.

MSR $464	$395	$350	$300	$265	$230	$200	$175

Add $20 for nickel finish.
Add $56 for camo.
Add $22 for thumbhole stock.

GRADING - PPGS™	100%	98%	95%	90%	80%	70%	60%

SHOTGUNS: O/U

CLASSIC FIELD SERIES - 12, 16 (disc. 2002), 20, 28 ga., or .410 bore, boxlock action, vent. barrels, vent. recoil pad, various configurations. Mfg. by Fausti, imported 2000-2006.

* *Classic Field Series Hunter* - 12 or 20 ga., 3 in. chambers, 26 or 28 in. VR barrels with 3 choke tubes included, blue (disc.) or matte silver finished frame, SST, extractors, checkered walnut stock and forearm, blue finish, 6 lbs. 7 oz. - 7 lbs. 4 oz.

	$795	$675	$575	$500	$450	$400	$375

Last MSR was $899.

Subtract 5% for blue finish.

* *Classic Field Series I* - 12, 20, 28 ga., or .410 bore, 3 in. chambers (except for 28 ga.), 26 or 28 in. VR barrels with fixed chokes, gold SST, extractors, coin finished frame with etched engraving, checkered walnut stock and forearm, blue finish, 6 lbs. 5 oz. - 7 lbs. 4 oz.

	$750	$625	$535	$500	$450	$395	$375

Last MSR was $849.

Add $50 for 28 ga. or .410 bore.

* *Classic Field Series II* - 12, 16 (mfg. 2001 only), 20, 28 ga., or .410 bore, 3 in. chambers (12 and 20 ga. only), 26 or 28 in. VR barrels with 3 choke tubes (except 28 ga. and .410 bore) included, coin finished frame with etched engraving, gold SST, ejectors, checkered walnut stock and forearm, blue finish, 6 lbs. 5 oz. - 7 lbs. 4 oz.

	$895	$775	$675	$575	$525	$475	$425

Last MSR was $1,039.

Add $10 for 28 ga. or .410 bore.

* *Classic Field Series II Combo* - 20 ga. frame, includes 20 ga. and .410 bore 26 in. barrels with extra forearm, cased. Mfg. 2004-2007.

	$1,395	$1,175	$995	$900	$825	$750	$675

Last MSR was $1,649.

* *Classic Field Series III Gold* - 12 or 20 (new 2003) ga., 3 in. chambers, 26 or 28 in. VR barrels with 3 choke tubes included, gold SST, ejectors, coin finished frame with 3 gold engraved pheasants, deluxe checkered walnut stock and forearm, blue finish, protective gun sock and molded hard gun case became standard 2002, approx. 7 lbs. 5 oz.

	$1,125	$925	$825	$700	$600	$550	$495

Last MSR was $1,299.

Add $100 for 20 ga.

CLASSIC UPLAND SERIES - 12 or 20 ga., boxlock action, gold SST, vent. recoil pad, various configurations. Mfg. by Fausti, protective gun sock and molded hard gun case became standard 2002. Imported 2000-2004.

* *Classic Upland Series II* - 3 in. chambers, 24 or 26 in. VR barrels with 3 choke tubes included, blue engraved frame, straight English grip walnut stock with Schnabel forearm, 6 lbs. 3 oz. - 7 lbs. 3 oz.

	$995	$850	$725	$650	$575	$500	$425

Last MSR was $1,119.

* *Classic Upland Series III* - 3 in. chambers, 26 in. VR barrels with 3 choke tubes included, blue engraved frame with gold pheasant inlays, checkered pistol grip walnut stock with Schnabel forearm, 7 lbs. 3 oz.

	$1,300	$1,075	$950	$825	$725	$625	$525

Last MSR was $1,519.

GRADING - PPGS™	100%	98%	95%	90%	80%	70%	60%

CLASSIC SERIES SPORTING CLAYS II - 12 ga. only, 28, 30 or 32 (new 2005) in. wide VR ported barrels with 4 extended choke tubes, SST, ejectors, coin finished frame with perimeter engraving, checkered walnut stock with Schnabel forearm, approx. 8 lbs.

	$1,115	$915	$800	$700	$600	$500	$400

Last MSR was $1,299.

✳ *Classic Series Sporting Clays III* - 12 or 20 ga., 28 or 30 in. wide VR ported barrels, SST, ejectors, extended choke tubes, hand finished silver engraved frame with gold inlays, premium checkered walnut stock with Schnabel forearm, protective gun sock and molded hard gun case, approx. 7 1/2 -8 lbs. Imported 2002-2007.

	$1,400	$1,175	$1,025	$900	$775	$675	$575

Last MSR was $1,649.

Add $50 for 20 ga.

REAL 16 SERIES - 16 ga., features proportioned 16 ga. receiver, 26 in. VR barrels with choke tubes, gold SST, silver engraved frame with or w/o gold snipes on sides, ejectors, checkered semi-gloss walnut stock with shock absorbing recoil pad and forearm, 6 3/4 lbs. Mfg. by Fausti. Imported 2004-2007.

	$1,150	$900	$800	$700	$600	$500	$425

Last MSR was $1,249.

Add $250 for gold receiver inlays with hardshell case.

MAG. HUNTER (350 SERIES) - 12 ga. only, 3 1/2 in. chambers, SST, ejectors, vent. recoil pad, various configurations.

✳ *Mag. 350 Series Hunter II* - 28 in. vent. barrels with VR, matte black metal finish, matte finished checkered walnut stock and forearm, 3 choke tubes, sling swivels, 7 lbs. 2 oz. Importation disc. 2002.

	$700	$630	$575	$530	$480	$425	$400

Last MSR was $799.

✳ *Mag. Hunter II Field* - 12 ga., 28 in. barrels, checkered walnut stock and forearm with sling swivels, matte finished engraved black frame, SST, ejectors. Imported 2005-2007.

	$895	$800	$700	$600	$525	$475	$425

Last MSR was $1,039.

✳ *Mag. Hunter II Waterfowl* - 12 ga., 28 in. vent. barrels with VR, engraved matte black frame with Realtree Max-4 (new 2006) Advantage Wetlands (disc. 2005) wood and barrel coverage, 3 choke tubes, sling swivels, 7 1/4 lbs.

	$1,050	$900	$750	$650	$550	$475	$400

Last MSR was $1,199.

✳ *Mag. Hunter II Turkey* - 12 ga., 24 or 26 in. vent. barrels with VR, engraved matte black frame with Mossy Oak Breakup wood and barrel coverage, 3 choke tubes, sling swivels, approx. 7 lbs.

	$1,050	$900	$750	$650	$550	$475	$400

Last MSR was $1,199.

GOLD WING SERIES - 12 ga. only, boxlock action with patented 4 lock system, 28 in. barrels with choke tubes, choice of case colored or silver finished frame, checkered oil finished pistol grip stock with recoil pad and forearm, ST, approx. 7 1/2 lbs. Mfg. by E. Rizzini. Imported 2004 only.

✳ *Gold Wing Series II Silver* - silver finished frame with engraving.

	$1,575	$1,350	$1,025	$900	$800	$700	$600

Last MSR was $1,759.

GRADING - PPGS™	100%	98%	95%	90%	80%	70%	60%

✳ *Gold Wing Series III Silver* - similar to Gold Wing II Silver, except has gold snipes inlaid on frame, upgraded walnut stock and forearm.

	$1,925	$1,650	$1,350	$1,025	$925	$825	$725

Last MSR was $2,289.

Add $220 for engraved silver finished sideplates (Gold Wing SL III Silver) with gold bird inlays.
Add $250 for engraved silver finished sideplates (Gold Wing SL III) case colored frame with gold inlays.

SHOTGUNS: SxS

ELITE SERIES - 12, 20, 28 ga., or .410 bore, boxlock action, 3 in. chambers (except 28 ga.), fixed or multichoke tubes. Mfg. by Fausti, importation began 2000.

✳ *Elite Field Hunter* - 12 or 20 ga. only, 26 in. barrels with 4 choke tubes, gold SST, blue finish with etched engraving, checkered walnut stock and forearm, approx. 6 or 6 1/2 lbs. Importation disc. 2002.

	$890	$785	$700	$575	$525	$475	$425

Last MSR was $999.

✳ *Elite Hunter* - 12 or 20 ga. only, 26 or 28 in. barrels with 3 screw-in chokes, ST, extractors, coin finished frame with engraving, checkered walnut stock and forearm. Imported 2003-2007.

	$1,185	$975	$850	$750	$650	$550	$450

Last MSR was $1,399.

✳ *Elite Field I* - 12, 20, 28 ga. or .410 bore, 26 in. barrels with fixed chokes, DT or ST, extractors, coin finished frame with etched engraving, checkered walnut stock and forearm, 5 lbs. 12 oz.-6 lbs. 8 oz.

	$950	$800	$700	$600	$550	$500	$425

Last MSR was $1,099.

Add $150 (DT) or $200 (ST) for 28 ga. or .410 bore.
Add $150 for ST.

✳ *Elite Field III* - 28 ga. or .410 bore only, 26 in. barrels with fixed chokes, DT or gold SST, ejectors, coin finished frame with multiple gold inlays, deluxe checkered straight grip walnut stock and forearm, approx. 6 1/4 lbs. Importation disc. 2002.

	$1,825	$1,550	$1,275	$1,000	$875	$750	$625

Last MSR was $2,099.

Subtract approx. $100 for DT.

UPLANDER SERIES - 12 or 20 ga., 26 or 28 in. barrels with choke tubes, boxlock action with or w/o sideplates and engraving, DT or ST, checkered oil finished straight grip English stock and splinter forearm. Mfg. by E. Rizzini. Imported 2004 only.

✳ *Uplander Series II Silver* - silver finished frame with engraving, 6 3/4 lbs.

	$1,825	$1,575	$1,225	$975	$875	$775	$700

Last MSR was $2,129.

✳ *Uplander Series III Silver* - similar to Uplander II Silver, except has gold snipes inlayed on engraved frame, upgraded walnut stock and forearm, includes long trigger guard.

	$2,400	$1,975	$1,675	$1,375	$1,100	$975	$875

Last MSR was $2,889.

✳ *Uplander Series IV Silver* - similar to Uplander III Silver, except has gold game birds on engraved sideplates, includes long trigger guard.

	$2,995	$2,500	$2,150	$1,775	$1,500	$1,275	$1,100

Last MSR was $3,439.

SHOTGUNS: SEMI-AUTO

AL 2100 SERIES - 12 or 20 ga., 3 in. chamber, various VR barrel lengths, lightweight alloy receiver, gas operation, choke tubes in most models. Imported from Europe 2000-2004.

∗ *AL 2100 Series ALS Field Model* - checkered walnut stock and forearm, blue metal, multichokes, also available in Youth Model, 5 lbs. 10 oz. - 6 lbs. 5 oz.

$295	$265	$235	$200	$185	$170	$155

Last MSR was $349.

∗ *AL 2100 Series ALS Hunter Model* - similar to ALS Field Model, except has black synthetic stock and forearm, not available in Youth Model, approx. 6 1/4 lbs.

$275	$245	$215	$185	$170	$155	$140

Last MSR was $319.

∗ *AL 2100 Series ALS Hunter Combo* - includes 26 or 28 in. VR barrel and choice of 24 in. rifled slug barrel and walnut or synthetic stock and forearm. Importation began 2002.

$435	$385	$340	$305	$275	$250	$225

Last MSR was $499.

Add $30 for cantilever scope mount.
Add $30 for walnut stock and forearm.

∗ *AL 2100 Series ALS Slug Hunter Model* - similar to ALS Hunter Model, except is 12 ga. only, 24 in. rifled barrel with choice of rifle sights or cantilever scope mount, Turkish walnut or black synthetic stock and forearm. Importation began 2002.

$300	$270	$235	$200	$185	$170	$155

Last MSR was $359.

Add $30 for cantilever scope mount or walnut stock and forearm.

∗ *AL 2100 Series ALS Turkey/Waterfowl Hunter Model* - 21 (Turkey Model with Mossy Oak Breakup, disc. 2001), 26 (Turkey) or 28 (Waterfowl Model with Advantage Wetlands) in. barrel, 100% camo coverage.

$315	$280	$240	$200	$185	$170	$155

Last MSR was $379.

∗ *AL 2100 Series ALS Home Security Model* - 12 ga. only, 20 in. barrel bored IC, black synthetic stock and forearm, bead sights, 6 lbs. Importation began 2002.

$275	$245	$215	$185	$170	$155	$140

Last MSR was $319.

TRENCH/RIOT SHOTGUNS

The following is a chronological listing beginning with WWI of the various U.S. commercial Riot and military Trench and Riot shotguns mfg. to date.

The publisher wishes to express thanks to the late Pat Redmond and Rick Crosier for the information in this section.

Some 100% values have been intentionally omitted in this section as they are seldom seen or sold.

Values listed below are for original, unmodified shotguns with proper parts markings, and unsanded wood with crisp stock cartouches.

All Trench/Riot shotguns listed are in 12 ga. only.

GRADING - PPGS™	100%	98%	95%	90%	80%	70%	60%

SHOTGUNS: MILITARY TRENCH, WWI

WINCHESTER MODEL 1897 MILITARY TRENCH GUN - high-polish commercial blue finish, solid frame with 6 row ventilated handguard for bayonet attachment, walnut high comb stock with hard rubber buttplate (no cartouches in stock). Guns used by the U.S. Army for trench warfare in WWI, originally did not have military markings. A "U.S." and ordnance bomb were hand stamped on the right side of the receiver on trench guns kept in the Army's inventory after the war. Military markings were added in the 1920s to about 10% of the total production. Serial range 650,000-695,000.

	100%	98%	95%	90%	80%	70%	60%
Trench Gun	N/A	$3,500	$2,400	$1,400	$1,000	$800	$700
Trench Gun w/ military markings	N/A	$5,800	$4,350	$3,000	$1,800	$1,500	$1,250

REMINGTON MODEL 10 MILITARY TRENCH GUN - high polish commercial blue finish with wood handguard on top of barrel, separate bayonet adaptor attaches to front of barrel for bayonet attachment. "U.S." and ordnance bomb marked on left side receiver, stock is unmarked. Extremely rare and hard to find complete and in original condition. Trench gun barrel length is 22 in. as compared to 20 in. Riot gun. Prices quoted only for complete guns with wood handguard and bayonet adaptor. Serial range 160,000-165,000.

	100%	98%	95%	90%	80%	70%	60%
Trench Gun	N/A	$10,000	$8,500	$4,800	$3,500	$2,000	$1,800
Riot Gun	N/A	$1,900	$1,500	$1,200	$650	$500	$400

SHOTGUNS: MILITARY RIOT/TRENCH, WWII

ITHACA MODEL 37 MILITARY SHOTGUNS - rarest of all Trench shotguns, high polish commercial blue finish, "RLB" and ordnance bomb marking on left side of receiver, ordnance bomb on barrel, stocks not proofed, blue vent. handguard for bayonet attachment, only 1,420 Trench guns were ordered in 1941. Ithaca supplied mostly long barrel martially marked shotguns. Serial range 49,000-62,000.

	100%	98%	95%	90%	80%	70%	60%
Trench Gun	N/A	$12,000	$10,000	$7,500	$4,000	$3,250	$2,350
Riot Gun	N/A	$3,000	$2,500	$2,000	$1,000	$750	$600
Long Barrel	N/A	$1,850	$1,500	$1,000	$750	$600	$500

REMINGTON MODEL 31 MILITARY SHOTGUNS - commercial blue finish (high polish and flat blue finishes noted). Can be marked "U.S. Property" on receiver and/or barrel. Some examples noted with only ordnance mark on stock. Serial range 39,500-60,500.

	100%	98%	95%	90%	80%	70%	60%
Riot Gun	N/A	$1,800	$1,500	$1,000	$750	$650	$500
Long Barrel	N/A	$1,200	$1,000	$650	$500	$400	$300
Trainer w/ comp.	N/A	$1,300	$1,100	$750	$600	$500	$400

REMINGTON MODEL 11 MILITARY SHOTGUNS - this is the most commonly found military shotgun. Examples of 5 shot and 3 shot Sportsman Model. Examples with plain or engraved receivers and plain or fancy checkered wood. Military marked with "U.S." and ordnance bomb on receiver and barrel. Later models are marked "Military Finish". These shotguns all have highly polished commercial blue finish and ordnance marked stocks. Serial range 450,000-500,000 and 700,000-711,000.

	100%	98%	95%	90%	80%	70%	60%
Riot Guns	N/A	$1,000	$650	$450	$400	$350	$300
Long Barrel	N/A	$850	$500	$350	$300	$250	$200

✱ *Remington Model 11 Military Shotgun Riot* - this configuration was sold by the government as surplus as late as the 1970s and can occasionally be found NIB with packing materials and instruction manual. Mint in factory box - $2,500.

GRADING - PPGS™	100%	98%	95%	90%	80%	70%	60%

SAVAGE MODEL 720 MILITARY SHOTGUNS - appears identical to Remington Model 11. This was mfg. by Stevens/Savage in very limited quantities, plain and engraved receivers noted with high quality commercial blue finish. Stocks are unmarked and must have ramp sights to be original. Watch for altered guns made into Riots. Serial range 69,000-90,000.

	100%	98%	95%	90%	80%	70%	60%
Riot Gun	N/A	$2,500	$1,850	$1,250	$925	$750	$600
Long Barrel	N/A	$1,000	$800	$750	$500	$350	$300

STEVENS MODEL 620 MILITARY SHOTGUNS - this was the current model being sold by Stevens and has a commercial blue finish, but not of the same quality as the other companies. Trench guns are equipped with handguards that have a definite purple/reddish color to the front and dark blue vent. shroud. Model 620s are much rarer than 520s and have "U.S." and ordnance bomb on receiver, ordnance bomb on barrel and unmarked stock. Serial range 1,000-30,000.

	100%	98%	95%	90%	80%	70%	60%
Trench Gun	N/A	$3,500	$2,800	$1,700	$1,200	$800	$600
Riot Gun	N/A	$900	$750	$450	$400	$350	$250
Long Barrels	N/A	$500	$400	$250	$200	$175	$150

STEVENS 520-30 MILITARY SHOTGUNS - this model was resurrected due to available machinery and is the most commonly found Trench gun. Riot guns in mint condition are hard to find. Same finish as Model 620, "U.S." and ordnance bomb on receiver, ordnance bomb on barrel and no proofing on stocks, except for reworks. Trench gun has same style handguard as Model 620. Serial range 30,000-70,000.

	100%	98%	95%	90%	80%	70%	60%
Trench Gun	N/A	$3,000	$2,000	$1,500	$800	$600	$500
Riot Gun	N/A	$1,000	$750	$350	$300	$250	$200
Long Barrels	N/A	$500	$400	$225	$175	$150	$125

STEVENS SINGLE & DOUBLE BARREL MILITARY SHOTGUNS - these guns were procured by the government from distributors and gun dealers. "U.S." and oversized flaming bomb hand stamped on left side receiver.

	100%	98%	95%	90%	80%	70%	60%
Single Barrel	N/A	$750	$600	$400	$350	$300	$250
Double Barrel	N/A	$950	$800	$600	$400	$350	$300

WINCHESTER MODEL 97 MILITARY SHOTGUNS - takedown model, high polish commercial blue finish, finger groove walnut stock with hard rubber buttplate. All early riot and trenchguns have "WB" and crossed cannons cartouches on the left side of stock, left side of receiver is machined marked "U.S." with or w/o ordnance bomb. All "WB" trenchguns have a 6 row ventilated handguard. All 97s will have ordnance bomb on top of barrel. Around serial range 950,000, receivers were all marked on left side with a machined "U.S." and ordnance bomb proofs, ventilated handguard was changed to a 4 row, "GHD" and ordnance bomb cartouches on left side of stock. During this transition, a very few examples with 6 row handguards have been found. Serial range 920,000-960,000.

	100%	98%	95%	90%	80%	70%	60%
Riot Gun w/ WB	N/A	$1,800	$1,500	$800	$600	$500	$400
Trench Gun w/ WB	N/A	$5,000	$3,950	$2,850	$1,500	$1,200	$1,000
Trench Gun w/ GHD	N/A	$4,800	$3,550	$2,700	$1,800	$1,200	$1,000
Long Barrel	N/A	$1,500	$1,200	$800	$650	$500	$400

WINCHESTER MODEL 12 MILITARY SHOTGUNS - takedown model with improved hammerless receiver. These were made to supplement Model 97 production. Riot guns and Trench guns share same serial range. Finished in high polished commercial blue, Trench guns (only) were the only WWII shotguns to have factory parkerized finishes. All Model 12s have "U.S." and ordnance bomb on right side of receiver, ordnance bomb on barrel and ordnance mark and inspector initials on left side of stock. Trench guns have 4 row vent. handguards.

GRADING - PPGS™	100%	98%	95%	90%	80%	70%	60%

* *Winchester Model 12 Military Shotgun Blue finish* - serial range 926,000-1,030,000.

	100%	98%	95%	90%	80%	70%	60%
Trench Gun	N/A	$5,000	$3,800	$2,200	$1,600	$1,400	$1,000
Riot Gun	N/A	$1,850	$1,500	$750	$650	$500	$400
Long Barrel	N/A	$1,200	$1,000	$750	$600	$450	$350

* *Winchester Model 12 Military Shotgun Parkerized finish* - serial range 1,030,000-1,040,000.

	100%	98%	95%	90%	80%	70%	60%
Trench Gun	N/A	$5,000	$3,800	$3,000	$2,000	$1,500	$1,200

WINCHESTER MODEL 37 MILITARY SHOTGUNS - high polish, commercial blue, single barrel, procured from Winchester. "U.S." and ordnance bomb proofmarks were applied to left side of receiver. Winchester records show shipment of 5,410 guns to the military - very few examples of this model have ever been found.

	100%	98%	95%	90%	80%	70%	60%
Single Barrel	N/A	$2,000	$1,500	$1,200	$1,000	$750	$500

SHOTGUNS: MILITARY RIOT/TRENCH, VIETNAM

ITHACA MODEL 37 - parkerized finish with "U.S." marks on right side of receiver. Receiver and barrel are also marked "P". Serial range, applied on gun upside-down, is from S1,000-S23,500. Used in the Vietnam era. A very few original Trench guns with parkerized handguards have been noted.

	100%	98%	95%	90%	80%	70%	60%
Riot Gun	N/A	$2,000	$1,500	$800	$600	$500	$400
Trench Gun	N/A	$4,500	$3,500	$2,500	$2,000	$1,800	$1,200

SAVAGE 77E - parkerized finish with sling swivels and red rubber buttpad. "U.S." marked on right side of receiver and military "P" proofmark on receiver and barrel. Hard to find in excellent condition.

	100%	98%	95%	90%	80%	70%	60%
Riot Gun	N/A	$1,000	$750	$400	$300	$250	$225

WINCHESTER MODEL 1200 - parkerized barrel, mag. tube, and bayonet adapter with U.S. marking on barrel. Aluminum receiver with black or matte type finish, "U.S." is marked under serial number. Very rare as few examples have been released by the government due to its continued use by military forces.

	100%	98%	95%	90%	80%	70%	60%
Trench Gun	N/A	$3,500	$2,750	$1,375	$850	$600	$500

SHOTGUNS: RIOT/TRENCH GUN, COMMERCIAL SALES

WINCHESTER MODEL 12 RIOT - thousands mfg. late 1930s-1960s.

	100%	98%	95%	90%	80%	70%	60%
	N/A	$550	$450	$395	$350	$295	$240

WINCHESTER MODEL 97 - commercial high polish blue, changed from solid frame to takedown in 1935. Trench guns made through 1945 and Riot gun mfg. continued until 1960s.

* *Winchester Model 97 Solid Frame* - Serial range 700,000+.

	100%	98%	95%	90%	80%	70%	60%
Trench Gun	N/A	$2,500	$2,000	$1,500	$1,200	$1,000	$750
Riot Gun	N/A	$1,000	$900	$750	$600	$500	$300

* *Winchester Model 97 Takedown* - Serial range 800,000+.

	100%	98%	95%	90%	80%	70%	60%
Trench Gun	N/A	$2,500	$2,000	$1,300	$1,100	$900	$600
Riot Gun	N/A	$800	$700	$600	$500	$400	$300

REMINGTON MODEL 10 - commercial high polish blue, sold in the 1920s to various government and banking agencies.

	100%	98%	95%	90%	80%	70%	60%
Riot Gun	N/A	$400	$350	$300	$275	$250	$200

REMINGTON MODEL 11 - made in 1930s for law enforcement use.

	100%	98%	95%	90%	80%	70%	60%
Riot Gun	N/A	$400	$350	$300	$275	$250	$200

MODEL 31R RIOT GUN - similar to 31A, with 20 in. barrel.

	100%	98%	95%	90%	80%	70%	60%
	N/A	$300	$200	$175	$150	$130	$110

GRADING - PPGS™	100%	98%	95%	90%	80%	70%	60%

ITHACA MODEL 37 - parkerized models made in 1960s for police agencies and commercial sales.

	100%	98%	95%	90%	80%	70%	60%
Trench Gun	N/A	$1,200	$900	$700	$600	$500	$400
Riot Gun	N/A	$275	$250	$225	$175	$150	$125

U.S. MILITARY SHOTGUN ACCESSORIES

WWI BAYONETS - military acceptance proofs, leather scabbards, and two variations of attachments to belt, two-toned blue handle and parkerized blade.

❋ *WWI Bayonet Winchester 1917 date*
Prices range from $150-$400, depending on original condition.

❋ *WWI Bayonet Remington 1917-1918 dates*
Prices range from $125-$300, depending on original condition.

LEATHER SLING - WWI dates, w/ brass hardware.
Prices range from $75-$150, depending on original condition. Mint condition will bring $400.

SHOTGUN SHELL POUCHES

❋ *Shotgun Shell Pouch 32 round with sling*
Prices range approx. $500, depending on original condition. Mint condition prices are approx. $1,200

❋ *Shotgun Shell Pouch 12 round dated 1921-1922*
Prices range approx. $400, depending on original condition.

WWII BAYONETS - same as from WWI, but have plastic scabbard w/ large ordnance bomb, or original WWI leather scabbard.
Prices range approx. $125-$300, depending on original condition.

LEATHER SLING - WWII dates, w/ steel hardware.
Prices range from $50-$125, depending on original condition. Mint condition will bring $400.

SHOTGUN SHELL POUCHES - 12 round pouches with contract dates from 1960s-1990s.
Prices range from $50-$125.

SHOTGUN SHELL POUCHES - 12 round pouches dated 1942-45, various manufacturers, watch for recent 1943 JQMD fake pouches - they have extreme two-tone colors.
Prices range approx. $350, depending on original condition.

VIETNAM BAYONETS - new contracts to supplement large quantities of shotguns being sent to Vietnam, black plastic handles, green plastic scabbards, marked "M-1917".
Gen. Cut - mfg. by General Cutlery prices range from $150-$250.
CA mfg. by Canadian Arsenal prices range from $150-$300.

TRIPLE ACTION LLC
Previous gun design firm located in Logan, UT.

PISTOLS: SINGLE SHOT

Triple Action LLC planned to manufacture a .50 BMG single shot pistol with 13.2 in. barrel, with muzzle brake and nitrogen recoil controller. Only a few prototypes were manufactured. Construction materials included titanium and aircraft grade aluminum, and the weight was 10 or 12 lbs.

TRISTAR SPORTING ARMS, LTD.
Current importer established in 1994, and located in N. Kansas City, MO. Distributor and dealer sales.

REPRODUCTIONS: REVOLVERS, SAA

REGULATOR - .357 Mag. (disc. 2005) or .45 LC cal., 4 3/4 or 5 1/2 in. barrel,

GRADING - PPGS™	100%	98%	95%	90%	80%	70%	60%

choice of brass or steel backstrap/trigger guard, two-piece smooth walnut grips. Mfg. by Uberti.

	$385	$335	$295	$260	$225	$200	$180

Last MSR was $455.

Add $34 for Regulator DLX with steel backstrap/trigger guard (.45 LC only).

STALLION - .17 HMR/.17 Mach 2 cal., 5 1/2, 7 1/2 (mfg. 2005 only), or 9 (mfg. 2005 only) in. barrel. Mfg. by Uberti. Imported 2005-2006.

	$395	$350	$300	$265	$235	$200	$180

Last MSR was $459.

Add $94 for Stallion DLX with steel backstrap/trigger guard (mfg. 2005 only).

REPRODUCTIONS: RIFLES

HENRY LEVER ACTION - .44-40 WCF (disc 2005) or .45 LC cal., brass frame only, 18 1/2 (Trapper, disc. 2005) or 24 1/4 (rifle) in. barrel, 9.4 lbs. Mfg. by Uberti.

	$1,125	$875	$750	$625	$525	$425	$325

Last MSR was $1,359.

MODEL 1866 LEVER ACTION - .38 Spl. (disc. 2005), .44-40 WCF (disc. 2005) or .45 LC cal., 19 (Yellowboy), 20 (disc. 2005), or 24 1/4 in. barrel, 7.2 (Yellowboy) or 8.4 (rifle) lbs. Mfg. by Uberti.

	$840	$700	$600	$500	$450	$400	$350

Last MSR was $999.

Add $110 for Sport configuration (20 or 24 1/4 in. barrel).

MODEL 1873 SPORT LEVER ACTION - .44-40 WCF (disc. 2005) or .45 LC cal., 24 1/4 or 30 (disc. 2005) in. barrel, 8.4 lbs. Mfg. by Uberti.

	$1,075	$800	$675	$575	$500	$425	$325

Last MSR was $1,259.

Add $45 for 30 in. barrel (disc. 2005).

MODEL 1885 SINGLE SHOT HIGH WALL - .45-70 Govt. cal., 28 in. barrel. Mfg. by Uberti, importation disc. 2005.

	$725	$595	$535	$475	$400	$325	$250

Last MSR was $852.

MODEL 1874 SHARPS - .45-70 Govt. cal., 28, 32, or 34 (disc. 2006) in. barrel, double set triggers, adj. rear sight, case hardened frame, approx. 10 lbs. Mfg. by Pedersoli. Importation disc. 2004, resumed 2006.

MSR $959		$825	$725	$625	$525	$450	$400	$350

Add $60 for Bridgeport Model with higher sideplate (disc. 2006).

RIFLES: BOLT ACTION

PEE-WEE .22 - .22 LR cal., single shot, manual cocking bolt, 16 1/2 in. barrel, steel construction, blue finish with adj. rear leaf sight, 12 in. LOP, uncheckered walnut stock with Monte Carlo, 2 3/4 lbs. Limited mfg. 1998 only.

	$170	$140	$130	$120	$110	$100	$90

Last MSR was $189.

SHOTGUNS: LEVER ACTION

MODEL 1887 - 12 ga. only, patterned after the Winchester Model 1887, "WRA Co." logo on left side of receiver, 30 in. barrel, 5 shot tube mag., blue finish, 2-piece walnut forearm and rounded pistol grip stock, 8 lbs. Limited importation 1997-98.

	$535	$475	$435	$400	$360	$330	$295

Last MSR was $599.

GRADING - PPGS™	100%	98%	95%	90%	80%	70%	60%

SHOTGUNS: O/U

MODEL 300 - 12 ga. only, 3 in. chambers, under-lug action, double triggers, extractors, etched engraving, standard checkered Turkish walnut stock and forearm, 26 or 28. in. VR barrels with fixed chokes. Imported 1994-98 from Turkey.

	$375	$330	$300	$275	$250	$225	$200

Last MSR was $429.

MODEL 333 FIELD GRADE - 12 or 20 ga., 3 in. chambers, engraved boxlock frame with satin finish, SST, ejectors, fancy grade Turkish walnut with hand-cut checkering, 26 (12 ga. only), 28, or 30 in. VR barrels, supplied with 5 choke tubes, approx. 7 1/2 lbs. Imported from Turkey 1994-98.

	$735	$625	$550	$500	$450	$400	$360

Last MSR was $800.

* *Model 333 Field Grade Sporting Clays* - similar to Model 333 Field Grade, except has sporting recoil pad, elongated forcing cones, 28 or 30 in. ported barrels with extended stainless steel choke tubes, 7 3/4 lbs. Imported from Turkey 1994-97.

	$825	$725	$625	$550	$500	$450	$400

Last MSR was $900.

* *Model 333SCL Ladies Sporting Clays* - similar to Model 333 Sporting Clays, except is fitted with special ladies stock, 28 in. barrels only with four choke tubes. Imported from Turkey. Disc. 1997.

	$825	$725	$625	$550	$500	$450	$400

Last MSR was $900.

MODEL 330 - 12 or 20 ga., 3 in. chambers, etched satin finished frame, SST, extractors, fixed chokes, checkered standard Turkish walnut stock and forearm, approx. 7 1/2 lbs. Imported from Turkey 1994-99.

	$475	$415	$375	$325	$295	$280	$265

Last MSR was $549.

* *Model 330D* - similar to Model 330, except has ejectors and three choke tubes. Imported from Turkey 1994-99.

	$615	$525	$495	$450	$400	$360	$330

Last MSR was $689.

SILVER HUNTER - 12 or 20 ga., 3 in. chambers, under-lug action, SST, extractors, silver receiver with etched engraving, standard checkered Turkish walnut stock and forearm, 26 or 28. in. VR barrels with choke tubes, 7 lbs. Imported from Spain 2002-2004.

	$615	$500	$450	$400	$365	$335	$300

Last MSR was $737.

SILVER II - 12, 16, or 20 ga., similar to Silver Hunter, except has ejectors, approx. 7.4 lbs. Imported from Spain 2002-2006.

	$740	$550	$480	$420	$365	$335	$300

Last MSR was $915.

SILVER CLASSIC - 12 or 20 (new 2002) ga., similar to Silver II, except has case colored receiver and long forcing cones. Imported from Spain 2002-2004.

	$750	$625	$525	$465	$415	$365	$315

Last MSR was $899.

GRADING - PPGS™	100%	98%	95%	90%	80%	70%	60%

SILVER SPORTING - 12 ga., similar to Silver II, except has 3 in. chambers and 28 or 30 in. ported barrels with broadway VR, 7 lbs., 6 oz. Imported from Spain 2002-2004.

	$750	$625	$525	$465	$415	$365	$315

Last MSR was $899.

WS/OU MAGNUM - 12 ga., 3 1/2 in. chambers, ejectors, SST, 28 in. VR barrels with choke tubes, 100% Skyline Excel camo (new 2003) coverage (except frame) or matte black metal and checkered black finished walnut stock and forearm. 7 lbs. 2 oz. Imported 2002-2004.

	$650	$550	$475	$425	$395	$375	$350

Last MSR was $779.

Add $84 for Skyline Excel camo coverage.

HUNTER - 12 or 20 ga., 26 or 28 in. VR barrels with choke tubes, blued boxlock action, SST, extractors, checkered walnut stock and forearm, 6-7 1/4 lbs. Importation began 2006.

MSR $499	$425	$365	$325	$275	$235	$200	$180

✻ *Field Hunter* - similar to Hunter, except has auto ejectors and vent. recoil pad, 6-7 1/4 lbs. Importation began 2007.

MSR $579	$475	$400	$350	$300	$250	$200	$180

✻ *Hunter Lite* - similar to Hunter, except has lightweight construction with silver alloy frame, 5 1/2 or 6 lbs. Importation began 2006.

MSR $529	$440	$380	$325	$285	$240	$200	$180

SHOTGUNS: SxS

MODEL 311 - 12 or 20 ga., 3 in. chambers, Greener boxlock action, 26 or 28 in. barrels, standard checkered Turkish walnut stock and forearm, DTs, supplied with five choke tubes, white chrome frame finish, extractors. Imported 1994-97 from Turkey.

	$535	$475	$435	$400	$360	$330	$295

Last MSR was $599.

✻ *Model 311R* - 12 or 20 ga., 20 in. cylinder bore barrels designed for cowboy re-enactment shooting or home defense, other features similar to Model 311. Imported from Turkey. Disc. 1997.

	$375	$325	$300	$275	$250	$225	$200

Last MSR was $429.

MODEL 411 - 12, 16 (mfg. 1999-2004), 20 (disc. 2004), 28 (disc. 2004) ga., or .410 bore (disc. 2004), 3 in. chambers (except 28 ga.), 26 or 28 (12 ga. only) in. barrels with (12 and 20 ga.) or w/o (28 ga. or .410 bore) choke tubes, boxlock action, DT, extractors, steel shot compatible, case colored frame, checkered walnut stock and forearm with recoil pad, 6 1/2-7 1/4 lbs, mfg. by Luciano Rota (R.F.M.). Imported 1998-2005.

	$710	$650	$575	$525	$450	$400	$350

Last MSR was $849.

✻ *Model 411D* - similar to Model 411, except not available in 16 ga., features engraved case colored frame, single trigger, ejectors, and English style stock, 6 1/2-7 1/4 lbs. Imported 1999 - 2005.

	$915	$800	$700	$600	$500	$400	$325

Last MSR was $1,110.

GRADING - PPGS™	100%	98%	95%	90%	80%	70%	60%

* *Model 411F* - 12, 20 (disc. 2004), 28 (disc. 2004) ga., or .410 bore (disc. 2004), 3 in. chambers (except 28 ga.), silver engraved sideplates, gold SST, English straight stock with cut checkering, ejectors, choke tubes (except for 28 ga. and .410 bore), 6 1/2-7 1/4 lbs. Imported 2000-2005.

	$1,425	$1,200	$995	$850	$725	$650	$575

Last MSR was $1,608.

* *Model 411R Coach Gun* - 12 or 20 ga., 3 in. chambers, hammerless, 20 in. fixed choke (C/C) barrels, case colored frame, DT, extractors, 6-6 1/2 lbs. Imported 1999-2003.

	$650	$575	$525	$475	$425	$375	$325

Last MSR was $745.

This model was designed for both cowboy competition shooting and quail hunting.

GENTRY - 12, 16, 20, 28 ga. or .410 bore, 3 in. chambers, engraved coin finished boxlock action with sideplates, SST, extractors, 20 (Gentry Coach Model, 12 or 20 ga. only), 26, or 28 in. barrels with matted rib and three choke tubes (fixed chokes on 16, 20 ga. and .410 bore) checkered pistol grip stock and semi-beavertail forearm, approx. 6 1/2 lbs. Imported 2003-2006.

	$775	$600	$500	$440	$380	$325	$275

Last MSR was $929.

Add $16 for 28 ga. or .410 bore.
Subtract $14 for Gentry Coach Model (hammerless, disc. 2003).

BRITTANY - 12, 16 (new 2006), 20, 28 (new 2006) ga. or .410 bore (disc. 2006), 3 in. chambers, boxlock action, case colored frame, SST, ejectors, 26 in. barrels with matted rib and three choke tubes, checkered straight grip stock and semi-beavertail forearm, 6.2 - 7.4 lbs. Importation began 2003.

MSR $1,150	$950	$775	$650	$525	$450	$400	$350

Add $30 for 28 ga. or .410 bore.

* *Brittany Classic* - 12, 16, 20, 28 ga. or .410 bore, similar to Brittany, except has upgraded features, including fancy checkered pistol grip walnut stock and forearm with oil finish, engraved frame. Importation began 2007.

MSR $1,150	$950	$775	$650	$525	$450	$400	$350

Add $30 for 28 ga. or .410 bore.

BRITTANY SPORTING - 12 or 20 ga., 3 in. chambers, boxlock action with sideplates, engraved case colored frame, SST, ejectors, 28 in. barrels with matted rib and three choke tubes, checkered pistol grip stock and semi-beavertail forearm, approx. 6 3/4 lbs. Imported 2003-2005.

	$875	$725	$625	$525	$475	$425	$375

Last MSR was $1,049.

DERBY CLASSIC - 12 or 20 ga., 3 in. chambers, true sidelock case colored action, DT, ejectors, checkered straight grip stock and splinter forearm, 7 3/4 lbs. Mfg. by Zabala Hermanos in Spain 2002-2005.

	$1,300	$1,075	$900	$775	$675	$600	$525

Last MSR was $1,550.

YORK - 12 or 20 ga., boxlock action, 26 or 28 in. barrels with choke tubes, approx. 7 lbs. Imported during 2006.

	$525	$450	$400	$350	$300	$260	$230

Last MSR was $609.

GRADING - PPGS™	100%	98%	95%	90%	80%	70%	60%

SHOTGUNS: SEMI-AUTO

PHANTOM SERIES - 12 ga. only, 3 or 3 1/2 (Phantom Field/Synthetic Mag. only) in. chamber, various VR (except Phantom HP) barrel lengths with choke tubes, available in Field (blue metal finish, gold accents, and checkered walnut stock and forearm), Synthetic (black non-glare matte metal and flat black synthetic stock and forearm), or HP (home security with open sights, matte finished metal, and synthetic stock and forearm), 6 lbs. 13 oz.-7 lbs. 6 oz. Italian mfg., limited importation 2001-2002.

	$385	$350	$315	$285	$265	$245	$225

Last MSR was $425.

Subtract $44 for Phantom Synthetic.
Add $74 for 3 1/2 in. Mag. (Field).
Add $44 for Mag. Synthetic.

TSA SERIES (DIANA SERIES) - 12, 20, or 28 (disc. 2003) ga., 3 or 3 1/2 in. chamber, various VR barrel lengths with choke tubes, available in Marine (19 in. barrel), Field (blue metal finish, gold accents, and checkered walnut stock and forearm), Synthetic (black non-glare matte metal and flat black synthetic stock and forearm), Slug (24 in. rifled barrel with iron sights), or camo model (100% camo coverage), 6 3/4 - 7 1/2 lbs. Importation began 2003.

MSR $399		$340	$310	$285	$255	$225	$200	$185

Add $30 for Field Grade.
Add $30 for 20 ga. (disc.) or Youth Model with synthetic stock, or $60 for Youth with walnut stock.
Add $200 for Synthetic Model with 3 1/2 in. chamber.
Add $200 for camo model with 3 1/2 in. chamber.
Add $100 for camo model with 3 in. chamber.
Add $25 for Slug Model (24 in. rifled barrel, disc. 2004).
Add $34 for Marine Model with 19 in. barrel and choke tubes (mfg. 2004).

This model is designed by CD Europe of Italy and manufactured in Turkey.

SHOTGUNS: SLIDE ACTION

DIANA SERIES - 12 or 20 ga., 3 or 3 1/2 in. chamber, choice of Field, camo Mag., or black synthetic configuration, dual slide rails, 20, 24, or 28 (VR) in. barrel with choke tubes, 5 shot mag., crossbolt safety behind trigger, 6-7 lbs. Imported 2004 only.

	$160	$140	$120	$100	$90	$80	$70

Last MSR was $188.

Add $51 for Field or synthetic Mag.
Add $31 for synthetic stock/forearm.
Add $147 for Mag. camo in 12 ga., or $94 for Mag. w/o camo.

TROMIX CORPORATION

Current rifle manufacturer established in 1999, and located in Broken Arrow, OK. Dealer or consumer direct sales.

RIFLES: SEMI-AUTO

Tromix manufactures AR-15 style rifles. Tromix lower receivers bear no caliber designation. Serialization begins at TR-0001.

The models listed below are also available with many custom options - please contact the company directly for availability and pricing (see Trademark Index).

TR-15 SLEDGEHAMMER - .44 Rem. Mag. (disc. 2001), .440 Cor-Bon Mag., .458 SOCOM, .475 Tremor, or .50 AE cal., 16 3/4 in. barrel, other lengths and weights available by custom order. Mfg. 1999-2006.

	$1,175	$975	$850	$775	$700	$650	$600

Last MSR was $1,350.

TR-15 TACKHAMMER - various cals., 24 in. bull barrel, other lengths and weights available by custom order. New 1999.

	MSR $1,350	$1,175	$975	$850	$775	$700	$650	$600

TROY INDUSTRIES, INC.

Current paramilitary rifle customizer and accessories manufacturer located in Lee, MA.

RIFLES: SEMI-AUTO

Troy Industries customizes paramilitary style rifles manufactured by Small Arms & Munitions. Please contact the company directly for more information, including options, availability, and pricing (see Trademark Index).

TRUVELO ARMOURY

Current manufacturer located in Midrand, South Africa. Truvelo Armoury is a division of Truvelo Manufacturers (Pty) Ltd. No current U.S. importation.

Truvelo Armoury manufactures a variety of barrels and firearms, including the Neostead shotgun, the BXP 9mmP Tactical pistol, hunting rifles, and sporting rifles in 7.62x51mm, .338 Lapua, or 12.7x99mm, as well as military rifles in 14.5mm or 20x82mm cal. The newest addition is the Raptor Infantry rifle and carbine in 5.56 NATO cal. Prices range from $5,200 - $20,000. Please contact the factory directly (see Trademark Index) for more information, including delivery time and availability..

TULA ARMS PLANT

Current manufacturer established during 1712, and located in Tula, Russia. Long gun importation by SSME Deutschwaffen, Inc., located in Plant City, FL. Previously distributed by Tulsky Souvenir, LLC, located in San Diego, CA.

Currently, Tula is increasing importation of sporting arms to western countries. For more information and current pricing on the wide variety of firearms produced by this world-famous manufacturing facility, please contact the importer directly (see Trademark Index).

TULA HISTORY

The Tula Arms Plant is one of the world's oldest and largest gun manufacturing facilities. Plant construction began on Feb. 15, 1712, under the decree of Peter the Great. By 1720, this new plant had supplied the Russian Army with 22,000 flintlock pistols and light infantry/ dragoon shotguns. By 1749, Tula was engaged in the production of cold steel used for knives, sabres, swords, etc.

Many great names and inventors have been associated with the famous Tula Arms Plant, including Ivan Pushkin, Ivan Lyalin, Ivan Polin, Sergei Ivanovich Mosin, I. Nagant, F.V. Tokarev, etc. Many famous designs and models have originated from the Tula plant over the years, including the Model 1891 Mosin-Nagant rifle, Model 1910 Maxim-type machine gun, many TOZ sporting rifles, SVT-38 WWII semi-auto rifle, Nagant revolver, SKS rifles and many different styles and variations of commercial and military machine guns.

RIFLES

Currently, SSME Deutsche Waffen Inc. is importing a line of TOZ .22 LR cal. bolt action and semi-auto rifles, including the TOZ-78-01 ($300-$400 MSR), TOZ-78-04L ($325-$425 MSR), TOZ-78-05 ($375 MSR), and the TOZ-99 semi-auto ($387-$493 MSR). Most models are available with scopes. Additionally, SSME imports a TOZ-122 bolt action rifle in .223 Rem., .30-06, 9.3x62mm, or .308 Win. cal. ($550 MSR). Please contact the company for more information on options and availability (see Trademark Index).

SHOTGUNS

Currently, SSME Deutsche Waffen Inc. is importing the TOZ-34ER O/U (MSR $550), TOZ-87 12 ga. semi-auto (MSR $518), TOZ-120-12MV-1E O/U in 12 ga. (MSR $695), and the TOZ-200-12M-2 O/U in 12 ga. (new 2005, MSR $695). Some options are available, including gold triggers, extractors or ejectors, fixed chokes and cheekpiece. Please contact the company for more information on option pricing and availability (see Trademark Index).

TURKISH FIREARMS CORPORATION

Please refer to the Huglu section in this text.

DOUG TURNBULL RESTORATION, INC.

Current firearms restoration company established circa 1990 and located in Bloomfield, NY, which specializes in the accurate recreation of historic metal finishes on period firearms, from initial polishing to final finishing. These finishes include bone charcoal color case hardened, charcoal bluing, and Nitre bluing.

Turnbull Restoration has performed extensive restoration work on Colt 1911s, A.H. Foxes, Parkers, L.C. Smiths, and lever action Winchesters (including upgrades and antique finishes to duplicate natural aging). These guns have been provided with documentation.

Please contact the company directly for more information and pricing on the wide variety of services available (see Trademark Index).

REVOLVERS: SAA

Turnbull Restoration has reworked current Colt SAAs to look like a pre-1920 SAA. These guns have special factory assigned serial numbers beginning with 000DT. The retail price is $2,200, not including many options. Additionally, the company produced a special run of Colt SAAs in .45 LC, 5 1/2 in. barrel configuration, which are serial numbered EHBM01-EHBM50. These guns have color case hardened frames with charcoal bluing, long flutes (1st Generation), beveled cylinder, and ejector housing. Retail price was $2,150.

A portion of the proceeds from many of the guns listed in this section benefit the Doug Turnbull Firearms Conservation Laboratory at the National Firearms Museum.

GEORGE PATTON SERIES COLT SAA - .45 LC cal., patterned after Patton's original factory engraved SAA, 4 3/4 in. barrel, Helfricht style engraving by John Adams & Son, ivory grips with carved eagle on left and "GSP" monogram on right, silver plated finish, ser. nos. GP01-GP10. 10 mfg. 2003 - sold out early 2004.

$5,500	$4,250	$2,995	N/A	N/A	N/A	N/A	

Last MSR was $5,500.

CATTLE BRAND COLT SAA - .45 LC cal., 5 1/2 in. barrel, two-piece ivory grips with blind screw hole, 3/4 engraving coverage by John Adams & Son, bone color case hardening and charcoal blue (ser. nos. CB01B-CB10B) or silver plated (ser. nos. CB01S-CB10S) finish, guns sold in sets of two, owner's personal cattle brand or initials can be scrimshawed on one side of grips, includes fitted hardwood case. Mfg. 2003-2004.

MSR on this model was $7,995.

THEODORE ROOSEVELT COLT SAA - .44-40 WCF cal., 7 1/2 in. barrel, one-piece ivory grips with carved "TR" monogram on right grip and buffalo on left grip, black powder style frame, Nimschke style pattern engraving by John Adams & Son, gold-plated hammer, cylinder, and ejector rod housing, rest of gun silver plate, ser. nos. TR01-TR25, includes French style fitted monogrammed case and factory letter. 25 mfg. 2003.

MSR on this model was $7,500.

COWBOY CLASSIC SAA - .45 LC cal. standard, other cals. available, 4 3/4, 5 1/2, or 7 1/2 in. barrel, hard rubber grips standard with many options available, bone charcoal color case hardening and carbona bluing, ser. no. range 001DT-999DT. New 2004.

Current MSR is $1,150.

RIFLES

Turnbull Restoration also announced the introduction of its Big Bore Classics line during late 2003, utilizing either new or original Winchester and Browning Model 1886 receivers. Chamberings include: .45-70, .45-90, .450 Alaskan (new 2005), .50-110 (.50 Express), and .50 Alaskan. Many metal options and wood choices are available - please contact the company directly for more information on these custom rifles.

Turnbull Restoration introduced its own .475 Turnbull proprietary rifle cartridge during 2007. This caliber can be used on one of the company's modified Winchester Model 1886.

THEODORE ROOSEVELT WINCHESTER MODEL 1876 - exact duplicate of the rifle carried by Roosevelt, copied from the original model, historically accurate, including measurements, dimensions and specifications, 25 mfg. beginning 2006.

This model is for sale exclusively through the NRA Foundation. Current MSR is $28,000, and price includes display case. A portion of the proceeds will benefit the Doug Turnbull Firearms Conservation Laboratory at the National Firearms Museum.

U SECTION

U.S. ARMS COMPANY

Previous manufacturer located in Riverhead, NY.

GRADING - PPGS™	100%	98%	95%	90%	80%	70%	60%

REVOLVERS: SINGLE ACTION

ABILENE .357 MAG. - 6 shot, 4 5/8, 5 1/2, or 6 1/2 in. barrel, adj. sights, transfer bar ignition, smooth walnut grips, blue finish only. Mfg. 1976-83.

	$325	$275	$240	$200	$185	$170	$155

✻ *Abilene .357 Mag. Stainless Steel* - similar to Abilene, only in stainless steel.

	$350	$285	$240	$200	$185	$170	$155

ABILENE .44 MAG. - 7 1/2 and 8 1/2 in. barrel, unfluted cylinder blue finish only, otherwise similar to .357 Mag.

	$325	$265	$240	$220	$200	$165	$150

✻ *Abilene .44 Mag. Stainless Steel* - similar to Abilene .44 Mag., only stainless steel.

	$375	$330	$290	$235	$210	$180	$155

U.S. GENERAL TECHNOLOGIES, INC.

Previous manufacturer located in S. San Francisco, CA circa 1994-96.

RIFLES: SEMI-AUTO

P-50 SEMI-AUTO - .50 BMG cal., includes 10 shot detachable mag., folding bipod, muzzle brake, matte black finish. Mfg. 1995-96.

	$5,600	$4,950	$4,475	$3,975	$3,500	$3,050	$2,600

Last MSR was $5,995.

U.S. HISTORICAL SOCIETY

Previous organization which marketed historically significant firearms reproductions until April, 1994. Located in Richmond, VA. Most firearms were manufactured by the Williamsburg Firearms Manufactory and the Virginia Firearms Manufactory.

On April 1, 1994, the Antique Arms Divison of the U.S. Historical Society was acquired by America Remembers located in Mechanicsville, VA. America Remembers affiliates include the Armed Forces Commemorative Society, American Heroes & Legends, and the United States Society of Arms and Armor. Issues that were not fully subscribed are now available through America Remembers (please refer to listing in A section).

The information listed below represents current information up until America Remembers acquired the Antique Arms Division of the U.S. Historical Society.

Please refer to the *Blue Book of Modern Black Powder Arms* by John Allen (also online) for more information and prices on U.S. Historical Society's modern black powder models.

Model	Manufacturer	Qty.	Year	Issue Price
HANDGUNS: SPECIAL EDITIONS				
✻ *Secret Service Museum Edition*	Uberti	500	1988	$2,750
✻ *Secret Service Investigator´s Edition*	Uberti	1,000	1988	$1,250
✻ *George Jones SAA*	N/A	950	1993	$1,675
✻ *Richard Petty Silver Edition SAA*	N/A	1,000	1992	$1,675

Model	Manufacturer	Qty.	Year	Issue Price
✳ King Richard Hand Engraved Colt .45 SAA	Colt	100	1993	$4,500
✳ Charlton Heston SAA	N/A	500	1993	$1,850
✳ Hopalong Cassidy Cowboy Edition SAA	N/A	950	1993	$1,675
✳ Hopalong Cassidy Premier Colt Edition	Colt	100	1993	$4,500
✳ Mel Torme Colt SAA	Colt	100	1992	$4,500
✳ Roy Rogers Cowboy Edition SAA	N/A	2,500	1990	$1,350
✳ Roy Rogers Premier Edition SAA	N/A	250	1990	$4,500
✳ U.S. Marshals Wyatt Earp SAA	Armi San Marco	2,500	1991	$1,250
✳ National Cowboy Hall of Fame SAA	N/A	1,000	1992	$1,600
✳ Interpol Colt SAA	Colt	154	1991	$4,500
✳ Eisenhower .45 Auto	Springfield	1,000	1992	$1,675
✳ "Don´t Give Up the Ship" Model .45 Auto	Colt	1,997	1993	$1,485
✳ American Eagle Colt .45 Auto	Colt	2,500	1993	$1,950

REVOLVERS: MINIATURE SPECIAL EDITIONS

✳ SA Army Presidential Edition	Uberti	1,500	1988	$1,550
✳ SA Army Classic Edition	Uberti	1,500	1988	$575

SHOTGUNS: SPECIAL EDITIONS

✳ Chuck Yeager Tribute	Bertuzzi	100	1989	$12,500
✳ Arnold Palmer Tribute	Renato Telo	100	1990	$9,750
✳ Christopher Columbus Tribute	Antonio Zoli	200	1991	$12,500

U.S. MILITARY HANDGUNS

Please refer to listings in the Colt (includes subcontracted variations of the M1911 and M1911A1) and Smith & Wesson sections.

U.S. MILITARY LONG ARMS

Also see listings under Colt, Enfield, Krag-Jorgensen, Springfield Armory, and Winchester. U.S. Military Trench and Riot guns may be found under the "Trench/Riot Shotguns" category in the T section of this text.

100%	98%	95%	90%	80%	70%	60%	50%	40%	30%	20%	10%

CARBINES: SEMI-AUTO

Values are for original unmodified carbines, with proper parts makers, unsanded wood, and crisp stock cartouches.

U.S. M1 CARBINE (MILITARY & COMMERCIAL) - .30 Carbine cal., 18 in. barrel, 15 or 30 shot box mag., wood stocked, two- or four-position aperture rear, blade front sight with protective ears, with or without bayonet lug. This weapon was designed by Winchester for the U.S. government, over 6 million were produced by 12 different companies: Plainfield mfg. after WWII was for civilian sales. It is a gas operated lightweight carbine which was also used by other countries' armed forces. Makers and values as follows. Some variations have the type III barrel band.

✳ **Carbines: Semi-Auto, Reworks & Commercial Mfg.** - includes carbines that have been factory reworked at U.S. arsenals.

Underwood	$850	$675	$495	$400	$350	$300	$275
S.G. Saginaw	$825	$650	$475	$400	$350	$300	$275

GRADING - PPGS™	100%	98%	95%	90%	80%	70%	60%
Quality Hardware	$850	$675	$495	$415	$370	$325	$295
Nat´l Postal Meter	$950	$775	$525	$425	$375	$325	$295
IBM	$950	$775	$525	$425	$370	$325	$295
Standard Products	$800	$650	$495	$415	$370	$325	$295
Inland	$850	$675	$495	$415	$370	$325	$295
SG Grand Rapids	$950	$775	$525	$425	$375	$325	$295
Winchester	$1,150	$850	$750	$550	$425	$350	$325
Irwin Pedersen	$1,700	$1,400	$995	$850	$775	$675	$580
Rockola	$995	$925	$700	$525	$425	$350	$325
Plainfield (Commercial only)	$195	$175	$160	$150	$140	$130	$120

Recent imports can usually be denoted by visible import markings and/or alterations to original finish.

An Inland presentation carbine with white stock was also mfg. in limited quantities for military service organizations (i.e. V.F.W., American Legion, etc.). Values for original guns are currently in the $1,750-$2,000 range.

* Carbines: Semi-Auto, Original Type I - includes original carbines with flip rear sight and no bayonet lug.

	100%	98%	95%	90%	80%	70%	60%
Underwood	$2,125	$1,675	$1,250	$1,000	$875	$750	$675
S.G. Saginaw	$2,050	$1,600	$1,200	$950	$825	$700	$650
Quality Hardware	$2,125	$1,675	$1,250	$1,000	$875	$750	$675
Nat´l Postal Meter	$2,375	$1,950	$1,325	$1,050	$950	$800	$750
IBM	$2,375	$1,950	$1,325	$1,050	$950	$800	$750
Standard Products	$2,000	$1,625	$1,250	$1,050	$925	$800	$750
Inland	$2,125	$1,675	$1,250	$1,000	$875	$750	$675
SG Grand Rapids	$2,375	$1,950	$1,325	$1,050	$950	$800	$750
Winchester	$2,875	$2,200	$1,875	$1,375	$1,075	$875	$800
Irwin Pedersen	$4,250	$3,500	$2,500	$2,125	$1,925	$1,675	$1,425
Rockola	$2,500	$2,275	$1,750	$1,300	$1,050	$875	$800

Subtract 30% for original finish guns that have been changed back to the original configuration by switching parts.

* Carbines: Semi-Auto, Original Type II - includes original carbines with adj. rear sight and no bayonet lug.

	100%	98%	95%	90%	80%	70%	60%
S.G. Saginaw	$1,825	$1,450	$1,050	$875	$775	$650	$600
Quallity Hardware	$1,875	$1,650	$1,075	$875	$775	$650	$600
IBM	$2,100	$1,700	$1,150	$925	$825	$715	$650
Standard Products	$1,750	$1,425	$1,050	$875	$775	$650	$600
Inland	$1,875	$1,475	$1,075	$875	$775	$650	$600
SG Grand Rapids	$2,100	$1,700	$1,150	$925	$825	$715	$650
Winchester	$2,525	$1,875	$1,650	$1,200	$925	$775	$700
Irwin Pedersen	$3,750	$3,050	$2,175	$1,875	$1,700	$1,475	$1,275
Rockola	$2,175	$2,025	$1,550	$1,150	$925	$775	$700

Subtract 30% for original finish guns that have been changed back to the original configuration by switching parts.

* Carbines: Semi-Auto, Original Type III - includes original carbines with adj. rear sight and bayonet lug.

	100%	98%	95%	90%	80%	70%	60%
Inland	$1,700	$1,350	$1,000	$800	$700	$600	$550
Winchester	$2,300	$1,700	$1,500	$1,100	$850	$700	$650

Subtract 30% for original finish guns that have been changed back to the original configuration by switching parts.
Subtract 50% for modified guns with adj. sight and bayonet lug.

M1 A1 PARATROOPER CARBINE - .30 Carbine cal., mfg. by Inland - WWII production, folding stock, crossed cannon proofed on bottom, 140,000 mfg. 1942-1945. Stock folds to 26 1/2 in. overall.
Beware of after-market fakes.

* **M1 A1 Paratrooper Carbine Type I** - values assume original guns with flip rear sight and no bayonet lug.

	100%	98%	95%	90%	80%	70%	60%
	$4,500	$4,000	$3,250	$2,500	$2,150	$1,750	$1,450

* **M1 A1 Paratrooper Carbine Type II** - values assume original guns with adj. rear sight and no bayonet lug.

	100%	98%	95%	90%	80%	70%	60%
	$4,200	$3,800	$2,700	$2,100	$1,750	$1,450	$1,150

* **M1 A1 Paratrooper Carbine Type III** - values assume original guns with adj. rear sight and bayonet lug.

	100%	98%	95%	90%	80%	70%	60%
	$3,200	$2,800	$2,150	$1,750	$1,500	$1,250	$1,000

RIFLES: SEMI-AUTO

On original (non-reworked) variations listed, it is absolutely critical that rifles have not been rebuilt and must have original cartouche stock.

Values are for original unmodified rifles, with proper parts makers, unsanded wood, and crisp stock cartouches. Without original wood and non-original parts, values drop to rework prices. Beware of fake stock cartouches.

M1 GARAND - .30-06 cal., semi-auto, 8 shot en bloc clip fed, gas operated, adj. aperture sight, wooden stock. Made 1937-57 by Springfield, Winchester, H&R, and International Harvester.

* **M1 Garand Reworks** - includes reworked rifles at U.S. Arsenals.

	100%	98%	95%	90%	80%	70%	60%
	$1,250	$1,050	$900	$800	$700	$600	$500

* **M1 Garand Early Type I** - identified by gas trap barrel up to ser. no. 50,000, all were mfg. by Springfield.

	100%	98%	95%	90%	80%	70%	60%
	$1,875	$1,575	$1,350	$1,200	$1,050	$900	$750

Some early original gas trap Type I guns with rare features are bringing up to $40,000.

* **M1 Garand Type II** - identified by gas port barrel and ser. no. over 50,000.

	100%	98%	95%	90%	80%	70%	60%
	$1,450	$1,200	$1,035	$925	$800	$695	$575

* **M1 Garand Pre-WWII Winchester Mfg.**

	100%	98%	95%	90%	80%	70%	60%
	$3,750	$3,150	$2,700	$2,400	$2,100	$1,800	$1,500

* **M1 Garand Pre-WWII Springfield Mfg.**

	100%	98%	95%	90%	80%	70%	60%
	$3,750	$3,150	$2,700	$2,400	$2,100	$1,800	$1,500

* **M1 Garand WWII Mfg.** - serialization starts at approx. 400,000.

	100%	98%	95%	90%	80%	70%	60%
	$5,000	$4,200	$3,600	$3,200	$2,800	$2,400	$2,000

* **M1-C or M1-D Garand Sniper** - with scope and mounts (beware of fakes and rewelds with boxes and papers). M1-D values assume paperwork for values listed.

	100%	98%	95%	90%	80%	70%	60%
M1-D	$3,800	$3,400	$2,800	$2,200	$1,725	$1,350	$1,150
M1-C	N/A	N/A	$3,650	$3,250	$2,850	$2,500	$2,150

Top values require original DCM shipping box, paperwork, and all listed accessories.

M1 GARAND NATIONAL MATCH - target version of the Garand, using National Match barrel and sights, glass bedding, etc. Must have serialized N.M. paperwork for prices listed below.

	100%	98%	95%	90%	80%	70%	60%
	$2,800	$2,500	$1,800	$1,400	$1,000	$800	$650

GRADING - PPGS™	100%	98%	95%	90%	80%	70%	60%

U.S. ORDNANCE

Current rifle manufacturer located in Reno, NV.

RIFLES: SEMI-AUTO

U.S. Ordnance manufactures semi-auto reproductions (BATF approved) of the .303 Vickers (MSR was $4,500 w/o tripod), M-60/M-60E3 (MSR is POR), M60E4/Mk43 (MSR POR, new 2004), Browning M-1919 (last MSR was $1,995), and the M-1919A4 (last MSR was $2,095). These belt-fed variations are machined to military specifications, and have a 5-year warranty. Please contact the company directly for more information on these semi-auto reproductions (see Trademark Index).

USAS 12

Previous trademark manufactured by International Ordnance Corporation located in Nashville, TN circa 1992-95. Previously manufactured (1990-91) by Ramo Mfg., Inc. located in Nashville, TN. Previously distributed by Kiesler's Wholesale located in Jeffersonville, IN until 1994. Originally designed and previously distributed in the U.S. by Gilbert Equipment Co., Inc. located in Mobile, AL. Previously manufactured under license by Daewoo Precision Industries, Ltd. located in South Korea.

SHOTGUNS: SEMI-AUTO

USAS 12 - 12 ga. only, gas operated action available in either semi- or fully auto versions, 18 1/4 in. cylinder bore barrel, closed bolt, synthetic stock, pistol grip, and forearm, carrying handle, 10 round box or 20 drum (disc.) mag., 2 3/4 in. chamber only, parkerized finish, 12 lbs. Mfg. 1987-95.

$1,050	$925	$850	$750	$650	$575	$500

Last MSR was $995.

Add $250+ for extra 20 shot drum magazine (banned by the BATF).

Values above are for a semi-auto model. This model is currently classified as a destructive device and necessary federal transfer paperwork must accompany a sale.

U.S.R.A.

Previous organization (United States Revolver Association) that established certain rules for target pistol shooting. Target pistols were manufactured by Harrington & Richardson - please refer to the Handgun section under Harrington & Richardson.

Readers interested in obtaining more information about specific U.S.R.A. pistols, or with information to share, are encouraged to contact Mr. L. Richard Littlefield (see Trademark Index).

UBERTI, A. S.r.l.

Current firearms, black powder, and accessories manufacturer established in 1959 and located in Serezzo, Italy. Currently imported and distributed by Stoeger Industries (beginning 2003), located in Accokeek, MD, Taylor's & Co, located in Winchester, VA, Cimarron F.A. & Co, located in Fredricksburg, TX, E.M.F., located in Santa Ana, CA, Navy Arms, located in Martinsburg, WV, Cabela's (certain models only), located in Sidney, NE, and Dixie Gun Works, located in Union City, TN. Previously imported by Tristar Sporting Arms, located in N. Kansas City, MO, and until Dec. 31st, 2002 by Uberti USA, Inc., located in Lakeville, CT.

In late 1999, Beretta purchased Aldo Uberti & Co. S.r.l.

The current importers listed above import Uberti guns with their own importer stamp. However, all guns will also have the Uberti name listed as the manufacturer. Please refer to the individual importers for additional information on Uberti firearms.

For more information and up-to-date pricing regarding current Aldo Uberti black powder models, please refer to the *Blue Book of Modern Black Powder Arms* by John Allen.

Black Powder Reproductions & Replicas by Dennis Adler is also an invaluable source for most black powder reproductions and replicas, and includes hundreds of color images on most popular makes/models, provides manufacturer/trademark histories, and up-to-date information on related items/accessories for black powder shooting - www.bluebookinc.com.

GRADING - PPGS™	100%	98%	95%	90%	80%	70%	60%

PISTOLS: REPRODUCTIONS, SINGLE SHOT

1871 ROLLING BLOCK TARGET PISTOL - available in .22 LR, .22 Mag., .22 Hornet (disc. 2004), .357 Mag. (disc. 2002) or .45 LC (Navy Model with open sights only, mfg. 1992-95) cal., 9 1/2 in. half-round, half-octagon barrel, case colored frame and backstrap, brass trigger guard. Imported 2002-2006.

		$385	$300	$250	$210	$175	$155	$135

Last MSR was $480.

REVOLVERS: DOUBLE ACTION

INSPECTOR MODEL - .32 S&W or .38 Spl. cal., 3, 4, or 6 in. barrels, double action, blue or chrome finish. Imported 1985-89.

		$390	$295	$245	$210	$170	$145	$125

Last MSR was $406.

Add $35 for target sights.
Add $25 for chrome plating.

REVOLVERS: REPRODUCTIONS, SA/SAA & VARIATIONS

Factory engraving and other embellishments or finishes (including antique charcoal blue, white steel, nickel, etc.) may be special ordered by contacting the importer(s) directly.

Add $85 for antique patina finish.
Add $45 for antique charcoal blue finish on all Cattleman variations.
Add $130 for silver plating.
Add $40 for white finish.
Add $85 for nickel plating (not available on Schofield).
Add $85 for select grade walnut one-piece fitted grips (disc.), $250 or $575 (solid silver) for Army/Navy Tiffany grips.
Add $45 for checkered grips.
Add $50 for stag horn grips (disc.), $150 for black buffalo grips (disc.), or $350 for mother-of-pearl grips (disc.).
Add $650-$1,450 for Cattleman engraving, depending on amount, and if with gold inlays.

COLT 1851 NAVY CONVERSION - .38 Spl. cal. only, 4 3/4, 5 1/2, or 7 1/2 in. barrel, patterned after original 1851 Navy, brass backstrap and trigger guard. Importation began 2007.

MSR $519		$425	$365	$310	$265	$230	$200	$170

REMINGTON 1858 NEW ARMY CONVERSION - .45 LC cal., 8 in. barrel, brass backstrap and trigger guard. Importation began 2007.

MSR $529		$430	$365	$310	$265	$230	$200	$170

COLT 1860 ARMY CONVERSION - .38 Spl. or .45 LC cal., 4 3/4 (.38 Spl. cal. only), 5 1/2, 7 1/2, or 8 in. barrel, patterned after original 1860 Army, blued steel backstrap and trigger guard. Importation began 2007.

MSR $549		$450	$385	$330	$280	$250	$220	$180

COLT 1871 RICHARDS/MASON CONVERSION - .38 Spl., .38 LC, .44 Colt (8 in. barrel only), or .45 Schofield cal., choice of brass (New Model) or steel BS/TG (Old Model), 5 1/2, 7 1/2, or 8 in. round or octagon barrel, one-piece walnut grips, approx. 2.6 lbs. Imported 2002 only.

		$385	$350	$315	$275	$250	$225	$200

Last MSR was $450.

COLT 1871-1872 OPEN TOP EARLY/LATE MODEL - .38 Spl., .38 LC (disc. 2002), .44 Russian (disc. 2002), .44 Colt (disc. 2002), .44 LC (disc. 2002), .44 Spl. (disc. 2002), .45 Schofield (disc. 2002), or .45 LC cal., open top frame, 4 3/4 (Early Model only), 5 1/2 (Early Model only) or 7 1/2 in. octagon barrel, Army (Late Model) or Navy (Early Model) size grips. Imported 2002, reintroduced 2007.

MSR $519		$425	$365	$310	$265	$230	$200	$170

Subtract $20 for Early Model Navy.

GRADING - PPGS™	100%	98%	95%	90%	80%	70%	60%

1873 CATTLEMAN SAA & VARIATIONS - available in .22 LR (disc. 1990), .22 Mag. (disc. 1990), .32-20 WCF (mfg. 2001-2003), .357 Mag., .38 Spl. (disc. 2003), .38-40 WCF (mfg. 1989-2003), .44 Spl. (disc. 2003), .44-40 WCF, or .45 LC cal., 3 3/4 (.45 LC only, disc.), 4 (.45 LC only, disc.), 4 3/4, 5 1/2, and 7 1/2 in. barrel lengths, brass or steel backstrap and trigger guard, Old Model (with cylinder pin retainer) or New Model (with plunger) frame, 2.3 lbs. (with 5 1/2 in. barrel). New 2002.

∗ *1873 Cattleman SAA with Steel Backstrap and Trigger Guard* - choice of New or Old Model frame, case colored or nickel finished, charcoal blue barrel/cylinder also available on Old Model.

MSR $519	$425	$365	$310	$265	$230	$200	$170

Add $90 for nickel finish (New Model, .45 LC cal. only).
Add $110 for Old West Model (Old Model, not available in .44-40 WCF cal.) finish.
Add $270 for Cattleman Cody model with nickel finish and faux ivory grips (new 2005, .45 LC cal. only).
Add $270 for Cattleman Frisco model with charcoal blue finish with pearl grips (new 2005, .45 LC cal. only).
Add $55 for walnut grips.
Add $160 for faux ivory, black buffalo horn, or faux pearl grips (new 2006).
Add $60 for charcoal blue barrel, cylinder, and grip frame/trigger guard (.45 LC cal. only).
Add $130 for stainless steel construction (.45 LC cal. only).
Add $75 for convertible cylinder (.45 LC/.45 ACP, .22 LR/.22 Mag. in 5 1/2 in. barrel only, disc. 2002).

❖ **1873 Cattleman SAA Sheriff's Model w/SB & TG** - .44-40 WCF or .45 LC cal., 3 or 4 in. barrel. Importation disc. 2002.

	$345	$265	$210	$175	$160	$150	$135

Last MSR was $410.

∗ *1873 Cattleman SAA with Brass Backstrap and Trigger Guard* - .357 Mag., .38-40 WCF (mfg. 2001-2002), .44 Mag. (mfg. 2001-2002), .44 Spl. (mfg. 2001-2002), .44-40 WCF, or .45 LC cal., 3 3/4 (.45 LC only, disc.), 4 (.45 LC only, disc.), 4 3/4, 5 1/2, or 7 1/2 in. barrel.

MSR $489	$395	$335	$285	$225	$185	$160	$150

Add $51 for convertible cylinder (.45 LC/.45 ACP, disc. 2002).

❖ **1873 Cattleman SAA Sheriff's Model w/SB & TG** - .44-40 WCF or .45 LC cal., 3 or 4 in. barrel. Importation disc. 2002.

	$310	$240	$190	$165	$150	$140	$135

Last MSR was $359.

∗ *1873 Cattleman SAA Target Model* - similar to standard Cattleman Model, only fully adj. rear blade sight, brass backstrap. Importation disc. 1990.

	$315	$245	$200	$185	$170	$150	$135

Last MSR was $335.

Add $25 for steel backstrap and trigger guard.
Add $60 for stainless steel construction (disc.).

CATTLEMAN U.S. SAA CAVALRY - .45 LC cal. only, 7 1/2 in. barrel, Old Model frame, charcoal blue finish.

MSR $629	$540	$450	$375	$310	$250	$215	$190

CATTLEMAN ARTILLERY SAA - .45 LC cal. only, 5 1/2 in. barrel, Old Model frame, charcoal blue finish.

MSR $629	$540	$450	$375	$310	$250	$215	$190

CATTLEMAN MILLENIUM SAA - .357 Mag. or .45 LC cal., 4 3/4 in. barrel, matte finished metal, brass backstrap and trigger guard, New Model frame only. Imported 2000-2006.

	$260	$215	$190	$165	$150	$130	$120

Last MSR was $300.

GRADING - PPGS™	100%	98%	95%	90%	80%	70%	60%

1873 CATTLEMAN HOMBRE SAA - .45 LC or .357 Mag. cal., 4 3/4 in. barrel, New Model frame, matte blue finish, walnut grips. Importation began 2007.

MSR $429	$340	$285	$250	$225	$200	$180	$160

CATTLEMAN GUNFIGHTER SAA - .45 LC cal., 4 3/4, 5 1/2, or 7 1/2 in. barrel, steel backstrap and trigger guard, matte metal finish, black checkered synthetic grips, New Model frame. New 2005.

MSR $479	$400	$350	$300	$260	$230	$210	$180

CATTLEMAN CHISHOLM SAA - .45 LC cal. only, 4 3/4, 5 1/2, or 7 1/2 in. barrel, New Model frame only with matte metal finish and two-piece walnut grips. Importation began 2006.

MSR $539	$450	$400	$330	$280	$240	$210	$180

CATTLEMAN DESPERADO SAA - .45 LC cal. only, choice of 4 3/4, 5 1/2, or 7 1/2 in. barrel, features New Model frame only with nickel finish and black buffalo horn grips. Importation began 2006.

MSR $789	$650	$550	$425	$350	$300	$270	$250

CATTLEMAN FLAT-TOP SAA ("FIRST ISSUE") - .357 Mag. (mfg. 2001-2002), .38-40 WCF (disc. 2002), .44-40 WCF, or .45 LC cal., 4 3/4, 5 1/2, or 7 1/2 in. barrel, choice of regular (disc. 2002) or flattop receiver. Imported 1997-2004.

	$365	$310	$240	$195	$175	$160	$150

Last MSR was $430.

CATTLEMAN BIRD'S HEAD SAA - .357 Mag. (new 2001), .44 Spl. (disc. 2002), .44-40 WCF (disc. 2004), or .45 LC cal., 3 (Sheriff's Model, .44-40 WCF or .45 LC cal. only, disc.), 3 1/2, 4, 4 3/4, or 5 1/2 in. barrel, patterned after the Colt 1877 Thunderer, case colored frame, checkered (disc.) or smooth walnut birdshead grips, choice of Old or New Model frame. New 1997.

MSR $539	$450	$400	$330	$280	$240	$210	$180

CATTLEMAN BISLEY SAA - .357 Mag., .38-40 WCF (disc. 2002), .44 Spl. (disc. 2002), .44-40 WCF (disc. 2004), or .45 LC cal., patterned after the Colt Bisley Model, 4 3/4, 5 1/2, or 7 1/2 in. barrel, case colored frame, wood grips, New Model frame. New 1997.

MSR $569	$475	$415	$350	$300	$260	$220	$180

* *Cattleman Bisley Flattop SAA* - similar to Cattleman Bisley, except has flattop frame with fixed or target (.44-40 WCF - disc. or .45 LC cal., 7 1/2 in. barrel only) sights. Importation disc. 2004.

	$365	$310	$240	$195	$175	$160	$150

Last MSR was $435.

Add $25 for target sights (disc.).

CATTLEMAN BUNTLINE SAA - .22 LR/.22 Mag. combo (disc. 2000), .357 Mag., .44-40 WCF, .44 Mag. (mfg. 2001-2002), or .45 LC cal., 12 (mfg. 2001-2002, .45 LC only) or 18 in. barrel, New Model frame with steel or brass backstrap cut for shoulder stock, choice of field sights with round frame or target sights on flattop frame. Importation disc. 1989, re-introduced 1993.

MSR $569	$475	$415	$350	$300	$260	$220	$180

Add $70 for Target model with extended front and adj. rear blade sight.
Subtract $56 for brass backstrap and trigger guard (disc. 2002).

* *Cattleman Buntline SAA Carbine* - similar to Cattleman Buntline, 18 in. barrel, includes non-detachable shoulder stock with brass hardware and lanyard ring. Importation disc. 1989, re-introduced 1993-95.

	$390	$310	$245	$200	$175	$160	$150

Last MSR was $475.

Add $34 for target sights.
Add $34 for .22 LR/.22 Mag. combo. (disc. 1989).
Add $175 for detachable shoulder stock.

CATTLEMAN SAA REVOLVER CARBINE - .357 Mag. (disc. 2002), .44-40 WCF (disc. 2002), or .45 LC cal., 18 (new 2004) or 19 (disc. 2003) in. barrel, fixed stock with brass rifle buttplate, New Model frame, finger rest extension on trigger guard, choice of quick detachable mounts or target sights, 4.4 lbs. New 1997.

MSR $729	$625	$550	$425	$350	$300	$260	$240

Add $70 for target sights on flattop frame.

BUCKHORN SAA - .44 Mag., .44 Spl. (disc.), or .44-40 WCF (disc.) cal., 4 3/4, 5 1/2 (new 2002) 6 (disc.), or 7 1/2 in. barrel, brass or steel backstrap. Importation disc. 2002.

✳ *Buckhorn SAA New Model Frame* - steel or brass backstrap and triggerguard.

	$345	$265	$210	$175	$160	$150	$135

Last MSR was $410.

   Add $69 for convertible cylinder.
   Add $40 for Target Model (disc.).
   Subtract $51 for New Model frame (brass BS & TG).

✳ *Buckhorn SAA Buntline* - .44-40 WCF (disc.) or .44 Mag. cal., 18 in. barrel, includes non-detachable shoulder stock with brass hardware and lanyard ring. Importation disc. 1989, resumed 2001-2002.

	$375	$310	$240	$195	$175	$160	$150

Last MSR was $455.

   Add $40 for target sights.
   Add $40 for extra .44-40 WCF cylinder combo (disc.).
   Add $122 for detachable shoulder stock (disc.).
   Subtract $45 for New Model frame (brass BS & TG).

STALLION 1873 COLT SAA - .22 LR/.22 Mag. cal. combo only, 4 3/4, 5 1/2, or 6 1/2 in. barrel, case hardened frame, 1-piece walnut grip, 2.4 lbs. Importation disc. 1989.

	$300	$210	$195	$170	$155	$140	$120

Last MSR was $325.

   Add $27 for steel backstrap and trigger guard.
   Add $26 for Target Model.

✳ *Stainless 1873 Colt SAA Stallion* - similar to standard Stallion, except is stainless steel. Importation disc. 1989.

	$370	$275	$225	$175	$140	$125	$105

Last MSR was $425.

STALLION 1873 SAA STEEL BS/TG - .22 LR (new 2000) or .38 Spl. cal., 3 1/2 (disc. 2002), 4 3/4 (disc. 2002), or 5 1/2 in. barrel, smaller, scaled-down SAA case colored New Model frame, approx. 32 oz. New 1999.

MSR $449	$385	$325	$285	$250	$225	$195	$165

   Add $30 for .38 Spl. cal.
   Add $50 for target sights.
   Add $39 for Target Model (38 Spl. cal. only, not available with 3 1/2 in. barrel, disc. 2002).
   Add $55 for .22 LR/.22 Mag. combo (disc. 2002).

✳ *Stallion 1873 SAA Brass BS/TG* - .22 LR cal. only, 5 1/2 in. barrel.

MSR $429	$365	$310	$260	$220	$185	$165	$140

   Add $50 for target sights.
   Add $39 for dual cylinder (.22 LR/.22 Mag., disc. 2002).
   Add $39 for Target Model (disc.), or $90 for Target Model with dual cylinder (disc.).

GRADING - PPGS™	100%	98%	95%	90%	80%	70%	60%

1875 REMINGTON ARMY/FRONTIER SA - .357 Mag. (disc. 2002), .44-40 WCF (disc. 2002), .45 ACP (mfg. 1992-2002, extra cylinder only), or .45 LC cal., 5 1/2 (Frontier configuration, disc. 1995, resumed 2001) or 7 1/2 (Outlaw configuration) in. barrel, brass (disc.) or steel (new 1993) trigger guard, case colored frame, two-piece walnut grips, approx. 2.6 lbs. Imported 2002, reimported beginning 2005.

MSR $539		$450	$400	$330	$280	$240	$210	$180

Add $42 for convertible cylinder (.45 LC/.45 ACP, disc.).

Add $90 for nickel finish and walnut grips in Outlaw configuration only (new 2006).

* *1875 Remington SA Carbine* - same cals. as Outlaw 1875, 18 in. barrel, includes non-detachable shoulder stock with brass hardware and lanyard ring. Importation disc. 1989.

		$425	$285	$230	$200	$185	$180	$175

Last MSR was $440.

Add $110 for nickel plating.

1890 REMINGTON POLICE SA - .357 Mag., .44-40 WCF (disc. 2002), .45 ACP (mfg. 1993-2002, dual cylinder only), or .45 LC cal., 5 1/2, or 7 1/2 (disc. 1995) in. barrel, blue finish with lanyard ring, brass (disc. 2002) or steel (new 1993) trigger guard, two-piece walnut grips, 2.6 lbs. Imported 2002, reimported beginning 2005.

MSR $549		$455	$400	$330	$280	$240	$210	$180

Add $42 for dual cylinder (disc.).

PHANTOM MODEL SAA - .357 or .44 Mag. cal. only, 10 1/2 in. barrel for silhouette use. Imported 1985-89.

	$475	$395	$325	$290	$260	$230	$215

Last MSR was $509.

1874 SCHOFIELD RUSSIAN SA - .44 Russian cal., 6 shot, top-break, 6 (disc.), 6 1/2 (new 2002) or 7 (new 2002) in. barrel. Imported 2000-2002.

	$675	$585	$475	$425	$365	$300	$275

Last MSR was $800.

1875 SCHOFIELD SA - .44-40 WCF or .45 LC cal., 3, 5, or 7 in. barrel. Imported 2000-2002.

	$635	$550	$465	$400	$350	$300	$275

Last MSR was $750.

RUSSIAN NEW MODEL NO. 3 SA - .44 Russian or .45 LC (new 2006) cal., 6 1/2 in. barrel, features trigger guard finger extension, steel frame, top-break, 6 shot with automatic extraction, Cyrillic barrel stamping, case colored opening mechanism and trigger guard, 2.7 lbs. Importation began 2005.

MSR $1,049	$875	$750	$625	$550	$475	$425	$350

Add $350 for nickel finish with faux ivory grips (.45 LC cal. only).

1875 NO. 3 SECOND MODEL TOP BREAK SA - .38 Spl. (new 2006), .44-40 WCF or .45 LC cal., patterned after the Schofield break-open action, 3 1/2, 5, or 7 in. barrel, 6 shot, blue or nickel (new 2005) finish, walnut or pearl (new 2006) grips, case colored opening lever and trigger guard, available in First or Second Model, approx. 2 1/2 lbs. Importation began 2005.

MSR $999	$850	$725	$625	$525	$425	$350	$300

Add $370 for nickel finish with pearl grips (not available in .44-40 WCF cal.).

* *1875 No. 3 Second Model Top Break Premium* - 45 LC cal. only, 6 shot, faux pearl or walnut grips, blue or nickel finish, extensive scroll engraving with blue screws (nickel) or gold-lined border (blue), available from World Class dealers only. Importation began 2007.

MSR $2,999	$2,550	$2,100	$1,800	$1,500	$1,200	$900	$700

Add $140 for blue finish with faux pearl grips.

GRADING - PPGS™	100%	98%	95%	90%	80%	70%	60%

RIFLES: REPRODUCTIONS, LEVER ACTION

Values for finishes and special options reflect most recent pricing available.

> **Add $140 for antique patina finish.**
> **Add $80 for charcoal blue finish.**
> **Add $75 for white finish.**
> **Add $235 for silver plating.**
> **Add $210 for nickel plating.**
> **Add $90 for checkered wood, $210 for select wood, or $475 for deluxe wood.**
> **Add $850-$3,500 for hand-engraving options, depending on the amount of engraving and gold inlays.**

1860 HENRY RIFLE/CARBINE - .44-40 WCF or .45 LC (rifle only) cal., iron, brass or steel (.44-40 WCF only, disc. 2002) frame, 10 or 13 shot mag., 24 1/4 in. barrel on rifle, 22 1/2 in. barrel on carbine (disc. 2002), available in modern gun blue, charcoal blue, white, or chrome finish, approx. 9 lbs.

MSR $1,329	$1,100	$900	$700	$600	$525	$475	$425

> **Add $90 for steel or iron frame.**

The carbine was disc. in 1989, re-introduced 1992-2002.

* *1860 Henry Carbine Trapper* - similar to above, except has 16 1/2 (disc. 2002) or 18 1/2 in. barrel. New 1990.

MSR $1,329	$1,100	$900	$700	$600	$525	$475	$425

* *1860 Henry Rifle/Carbine 1 of 1,000* - disc.

	$1,450	$1,150	$975	$850	$700	$575	$425

1866 YELLOWBOY CARBINE - .22 LR (disc. 1989), .22 Mag. (disc. 1989), .38 Spl., .44-40 WCF, or .45 LC cal., brass receiver, 10 shot mag., 19 in. round barrel, 7.4 lbs. Importation disc. 1995, resumed 2002.

MSR $1,079	$900	$775	$625	$525	$450	$400	$350

* *1866 Yellowboy Carbine Trapper* - .22 LR, .38 Spl., or .44-40 WCF cal., 16 in. barrel. Importation disc. 1989.

	$650	$475	$395	$340	$285	$260	$235

Last MSR was $686.

* *1866 Yellowboy Carbine Indian* - .22 LR, .22 Mag., .32-20 WCF (new 2002), .38 Spl., .44-40 WCF, or .45 LC (new 1996) cal., 19 in. barrel. Imported 2002 only.

	$670	$535	$430	$360	$310	$275	$240

Last MSR was $760.

> **Subtract $50 without brass tacks (disc.).**

* *1866 Yellowboy Carbine Red Cloud Commemorative* - same cals., special engraving and brass tacks in forearm and stock. Importation officially disc. 1989.

	$720	$600	$475	$400	$350	$330	$300

Last MSR was $850.

1866 SPORTING RIFLE - .22 LR (mfg. 2001-2002), .22 Mag. (mfg. 2001-2002), .32-20 WCF (mfg. 2002), .38 Spl., .38-40 WCF (mfg. 2002), .44-40 WCF, or .45 LC (new 1996) cal., brass receiver, 10 or 13 shot mag., 20 (short rifle, new 2001) round (new 1993, carbine only) or 24 1/4 in. octagon barrel, 8.2 lbs.

MSR $1,129	$925	$795	$650	$550	$450	$400	$350

* *1866 Sporting Rifle Deluxe Uberti Model* - .44-40 WCF cal., features high polished receiver with fire-blue small parts, ladder rear sight. Imported 1995.

	$895	$675	$525	N/A	N/A	N/A	N/A

Last MSR was $895.

This model was sold exclusively by Cherry's, located in Greensboro, NC.

* 1866 Sporting Rifle "L.D. Nimschke" Special Edition - .44-40 WCF cal., receiver, buttplate, and forend cap feature recreations of Nimschke scroll engraving by Giovanelli of Italy, silver plated, deluxe walnut, optional 2nd Edition of Nimschke pattern book by R.L. Wilson ($100), only 300 mfg. beginning 1995. Disc.

	$1,495	$1,000	$650	N/A	N/A	N/A	N/A

Last MSR was $1,495.

This model was sold exclusively by Cherry's, located in Greensboro, NC.

* 1866 Sporting Rifle Yellowboy Indian Rifle - .22 LR (disc. 1989), .22 Mag. (disc. 1989), .38 Spl., or .44-40 WCF cal., 24 1/4 in. barrel. Importation disc. 1989, reintroduced 1993-95.

	$700	$560	$475	$385	$300	$260	$235

Last MSR was $800.

1866 MUSKET - .44-40 WCF or .45 LC cal., features 27 in. barrel with barrel bands. Imported 1999-2002.

	$810	$600	$500	$425	$360	$320	$280

Last MSR was $910.

1873 CARBINE - .22 LR (disc. 1991), .22 Mag. (disc. 1991), .32-20 WCF (mfg. 2001-2005), .357 Mag., .38 Spl. (disc. 1991) .38-40 (mfg. 2002), .44-40 WCF, or .45 LC (new 1992) cal., 10 shot mag., steel receiver, 19 in. round barrel with forearm barrel bands, 7.4 lbs.

MSR $1,199	$975	$825	$700	$575	$475	$425	$375

Add $35 for case colored frame (disc.).

* 1873 Carbine Trapper - .357 Mag., .44-40 WCF, or .45 LC cal. only, 16 1/8 in. barrel. Importation disc. 1990.

	$750	$600	$500	$425	$360	$320	$280

Last MSR was $750.

1873 SPORTING RIFLE - .32-20 WCF (mfg. 2001-2002), .357 Mag. (new 1995), .38-40 WCF (mfg. 2002), .44-40 WCF (new 1995), or .45 LC cal., case hardened receiver, 10 or 13 short mag., 20 in. octagon (new 1990, Short Rifle), 24 1/4 in. octagon, half-round/half-octagon, or 30 (mfg. 1990-2002) in. octagon barrel, can be drilled and tapped for Uberti rear tang aperture sight (new 1993), 8.2 lbs.

MSR $1,249	$1,000	$850	$725	$600	$500	$450	$400

Add approx. $100 for Deluxe model with hand checkered pistol grip stock and forearm (disc.).
Add $130 for Special Sporting/Deluxe Model with hand-checkered pistol grip stock/forearm and 24 1/2 in. half-round, half-octagon barrel.

Add $17 for 30 in. barrel (.44-40 WCF or .45 LC cal. only, disc. 2002).
Add $77 for Deluxe Model with 30 in. barrel (disc. 2002).

MODEL 1873 125th ANNIVERSARY - .44-40 WCF cal., special anniversary offering featuring engraved gold plated metal with fire blue receiver and small parts, long rifle configuration with deluxe pistol grip and forearm. 125 mfg. 1998 only, marketed exclusively by Cherry's.

	$3,250	$2,500	$1,750	N/A	N/A	N/A	N/A

Last MSR was $3,500.

1873 MUSKET - .44-40 WCF or .45 LC cal., features 30 in. round barrel with barrel bands. Imported 1999-2002.

	$875	$700	$575	$450	$375	$325	$300

Last MSR was $999.

GRADING - PPGS™	100%	98%	95%	90%	80%	70%	60%

1876 CENTENNIAL RIFLE - .40-60 WCF, .45-60 WCF, .45-75 WCF, or .50-95 WCF cal., 28 in. octagon barrel, blue finish and case hardened frame, full mag., iron sights, walnut stock and forearm. Importation began 2008.

	MSR $1,569	$1,325	$1,125	$900	$775	$675	$575	$500

RIFLES: REPRODUCTIONS, SINGLE SHOT

1871 ROLLING BLOCK TARGET CARBINE/RIFLE - available in .22 LR, .22 Mag., .22 Hornet (disc. 2004), or .357 Mag. (disc.) cal., 22 in. round (carbine) or 26 in. octagon barrel, color case hardened receiver and hammer, brass trigger guard, open sights, approx. 5 lbs. Disc. 2007.

		$440	$350	$295	$240	$200	$175	$155

Last MSR was $535.

Add $65 for rifle model.

1874 SHARPS RIFLE/CARBINE - .45.70 Govt. cal., patterned after the 1874 Sharps action, 22 in. (carbine, new 2007) or 28-34 in. octagon barrel, available in standard, special, deluxe, Down Under, Adobe Walls (disc.), Buffalo Hunter, or Long Range configuration. Importation began 2006.

	MSR $1,459	$1,275	$1,075	$875	$725	$650	$575	$495

Add $270 for special model (32 in. barrel).
Add $110 for Cavalry carbine with 22 in. barrel and barrel band.
Add $1,290 for deluxe model (34 in. barrel with AA grade walnut).
Add $760 for Buffalo Hunter model.
Add $790 for either Down Under or $820 for Long Range (34 in. half-round, half-octagon barrel) model.
Add $550 for Adobe Walls configuration (disc.).

✳ *1874 Sharps Rifle Premium* - .45-70 Govt. cal., 32 in. barrel, AAA grade walnut stock, elaborate scroll engraving with buffalo gold inlays. Importation began 2007.

	MSR $4,199	$3,600	$3,150	$2,700	$2,300	$1,950	$1,700	$1,425

SPRINGFIELD TRAPDOOR CARBINE/RIFLE - .45-70 Govt. cal., choice of 22 (carbine) or 32 1/2 (rifle) in. round barrel, case colored receiver, uncheckered walnut stock and forearm. Importation began 2006.

	MSR $1,429	$1,250	$1,050	$875	$725	$650	$575	$495

Add $240 for rifle configuration.

1885 WINCHESTER CARBINE/RIFLE - .22 Hornet (mfg. 2004), .30-30 Win. (disc. 2004), .38-55 WCF (disc. 2002), .40-65 WCF (disc. 2002), .44 Mag. (mfg. 2004), .44-40 WCF (disc. 2002), .45 LC (disc. 2004), .45-70 Govt., .45-90 WCF (disc. 2002, reintroduced 2005) or .45-120 (disc. 2002, reintroduced 2005) cal., Low Wall (disc. 2004) or High Wall, 28 (carbine, High Wall only, .45-70 Govt. cal. only) round, 30 (rifle), or 32 in. octagon barrel, case colored receiver, straight grip walnut stock and forearm, 7.7 or 9.9 lbs. New 1999.

	MSR $1,049	$900	$750	$650	$550	$450	$395	$350

Add $120-$130 for Special Sporting (Deluxe) Model with checkered pistol grip and aperture sights, depending on barrel length.
Add $40 for 32 in. barrel.
Subtract $60 for 28 in. carbine barrel.

RIFLES: REPRODUCTIONS, SLIDE ACTION

COLT LIGHTNING CARBINE/RIFLE - .357 Mag. or .45 LC cal., patterned after the Colt Lightning carbine/rifle, available with 20 (carbine or short rifle) or 24 1/4 (rifle) in. barrel, choice of blue or case colored frame finish, uncheckered walnut stock and forearm. Importation began 2006.

	MSR $1,179	$995	$800	$675	$525	$450	$400	$375

Add $50 for rifle variation.
Add $30 for case colored frame (rifle only).

GRADING - PPGS™	100%	98%	95%	90%	80%	70%	60%

SHOTGUNS: SxS

DOUBLE BARREL - 12 ga. only, 2 3/4, 3, or 3 1/2 in. chambers, 20, 21 1/2 , 24, or 26 in. barrels, exposed hammers, checkered walnut pistol grip stock and forearm. Imported 1999-2001.

$875	$700	$575	$450	$375	$325	$300

Last MSR was $999.

UGARTECHEA, ARMAS

Current manufacturer located in Eibar, Spain. Currently being imported by Aspen Outfitting Co., located in Aspen, CO, and by Lion Country Supply, located in Port Matilda, PA.

Currently, Aspen Outfitting Co. exclusively imports Models 116, 119, 1000, 1030, 1042, and the AOC/SG boxlock. Lion Country Supply exclusively imports Models 30, 40, 40 NEX, 75, 75EX, and 110.

SHOTGUNS: SxS, BOXLOCK

MODEL AOC/SG - 12, 16, 20, 28 ga., or .410 bore, 2 3/4 in. chambers, Anson & Deeley boxlock action with extra polishing and fitting of parts, scalloped action shaping, 28 in. chopper lump barrels, IC/M choke, front bead sight, concave rib, DT w/ articulating front trigger, southgate auto ejectors, auto safety, free floating firing pins, engraved receiver with border scroll, upgraded European straight grip walnut stock and splinter forend with plunger release, inlaid forend screw escutcheon, hand-checkered buttstock, initial shield, case hardened action finish, long tang trigger guard with comfort roll, upgraded wood finish. Importation began in 1999.

MSR $3,250	$2,850	$2,500	$2,200	$1,950	$1,750	$1,575	$1,425

Add $300 for 28 ga. or $600 for .410 bore.

This model is imported exclusively by Aspen Outfitting Company.

UPLAND CLASSIC GRADE I (MODEL 30) - 12, 16, 20, 28 ga., or .410 bore, Anson & Deeley boxlock action, DT, concave rib, extractors, case colored receiver, hand-checkered straight grip walnut stock and splinter forend.

MSR N/A	$950	$875	$750	$600	$475	$400	$325

Add $100 for 28 ga.
Add $150 for .410 bore.

This model is imported exclusively by Lion Country Supply.

UPLAND CLASSIC GRADE II (MODEL 40) - 12, 16, 20, or 28 ga., Anson & Deeley boxlock action, DT, coin finished and engraved receiver, hand-checkered straight grip walnut stock and splinter forend.

MSR N/A	$1,075	$950	$875	$750	$600	$475	$400

Add $100 for 28 ga.

This model is imported exclusively by Lion Country Supply.

UPLAND CLASSIC GRADE III (MODEL 40 NEX) - 12, 16, 20, or 28 ga., Anson & Deeley boxlock action, DT or SST, case colored and engraved receiver, hand-checkered straight grip walnut stock and splinter forend.

MSR N/A	$1,400	$1,200	$1,000	$875	$750	$600	$500

Add $200 for SST.
Add $100 for 28 ga.

This model is imported exclusively by Lion Country Supply.

GRADING - PPGS™	100%	98%	95%	90%	80%	70%	60%

BILL HANUS BIRDGUN - 16, 20, 28 ga., or .410 bore (6 mfg.), boxlock action, 26 in. barrels bored SK1/SK2, Churchill raised rib, SNT, ejectors, lightly engraved case colored receiver, tang and lever, checkered straight grip walnut stock and semi-beavertail forearm, oil finish, lifetime operational warranty, 5 1/4-6 1/2 lbs. Approx. 200 mfg. Imported 1989-circa 1992.

	$1,425	$1,250	$1,050	$880	$750	$635	$540

Last MSR was $1,695.

Add $100 for 28 ga.
Add $150 for .410 bore.
Add 15% for optional fitted luggage case.

BILL HANUS BIRDGUN CLASSIC - 20, 28 ga., or .410 bore (4 mfg.), similar to Birdgun Model, except has double triggers with hinged front trigger, 27 in. barrels, splinter forearm and English leather handguard. Imported 1989-circa 1992.

	$1,355	$1,220	$1,035	$880	$750	$635	$540

Last MSR was $1,595.

Add 15% for optional fitted luggage case.
Add $100 for 28 ga.
Add $200 for .410 bore.

SHOTGUNS: SxS, SIDELOCK

Ugartechea sidelocks are best quality guns. Currently, Lion Country Supply stocks the Upland Classic Series. Additionally, custom orders are available through Aspen Outfitting and Lion Country Supply.

UPLAND CLASSIC GRADE IV - 12, 16, or 20 ga., best quality true sidelock with intercepting sears, DT or SST with hinged front trigger, case colored or coin finished receiver with English style scroll engraving, auto ejectors, upgraded wood with hand rubbed oil finish.

MSR N/A	$2,000	$1,700	$1,475	$1,200	$1,000	$875	$750

Add $200 for SST (20 ga. only).
This model is imported exclusively by Lion Country Supply.

UPLAND CLASSIC GRADE V (MODEL 110) - 12, 16, 20, or 28 ga., best quality round body game gun, true sidelock with intercepting sears, DT or SST with hinged front trigger, case colored or coin finished receiver with English style scroll engraving, auto ejectors, upgraded wood with hand rubbed oil finish.

MSR N/A	$2,675	$2,300	$1,900	$1,600	$1,350	$1,100	$925

Add $200 for SST.
Add $100 for 28 ga.
This model is imported exclusively by Lion Country Supply.

MODEL 75/75EX - 12, 16, or 20 ga., case colored finish with minimal engraving, oil finished deluxe walnut stock and forearm. Importation began 1999.

MSR N/A	$1,900	$1,750	$1,575	$1,425	$1,275	$1,150	$975

Add $200 for SST.

MODEL 116 - 12, 16, 20, 28 ga., or .410 bore, sidelock action, antique silver finish with elaborate floral engraving, deluxe oil finished walnut stock and forearm.

MSR $7,250	$6,800	$5,900	$4,500	$3,875	$3,250	$2,600	$2,000

Add $525 for 28 ga. or $750 for .410 bore.
This model is imported exclusively by Aspen Outfitting Company.

MODEL 119 - 12, 16, 20, 28 ga., or .410 bore, sidelock action with coin finish or case hardened frame, Purdey style engraving, deluxe oil finished walnut stock and forearm.

MSR $7,550	$7,125	$6,150	$4,650	$3,950	$3,350	$2,650	$2,000

Add $600 for 28 ga. or $900 for .410 bore.
This model is imported exclusively by Aspen Outfitting Company.

GRADING - PPGS™	100%	98%	95%	90%	80%	70%	60%

MODEL 1000 - 12, 16, 20, or 28 ga., sidelock action with coin finish or case hardened frame, Churchill style deep relief engraving, deluxe oil finished walnut stock and forearm.

MSR $9,350	$8,750	$7,950	$6,250	$5,250	$4,500	$3,750	$3,000

Add $450 for 28 ga.

This model is imported exclusively by Aspen Outfitting Company.

MODEL 1030 - 12, 16, or 20 ga., coin finished or case hardened frame, Woodward style scalloped fences and engraving. Importation began 1994.

MSR $9,675	$9,000	$8,150	$6,400	$5,350	$4,500	$3,750	$3,000

This model is imported exclusively by Aspen Outfitting Company.

MODEL 1042 - 12, 16, or 20 ga., sidelock action, coin finished or case hardened frame, exquisite full coverage fine scroll engraving, deluxe oil finished walnut stock and forearm.

MSR $11,500	$10,750	$8,750	$7,500	$6,500	$5,500	$4,500	$3,750

This model is imported exclusively by Aspen Outfitting Company.

SPECIAL MODELS - available in all gauges with game scene engraving and/or gold inlays to customer specifications. POR only. Please contact Aspen Outfitting Company (see Trademark Index).

UGARTECHEA, IGNACIO

Previous manufacturer located in Eibar, Spain. Previously imported exclusively by Aspen Outfitting Company, located in Aspen, CO.

Ignacio Ugartechea was founded in 1922 and is the oldest maker of side-by-side sidelock and boxlock shotguns in Spain (please refer to Armas Ugartechea for current information). From 1970 until the Parker-Hale name was sold in 1990 to Navy Arms, Ugartechea manufactured the popular line of Anson & Deeley boxlocks imported by Precision Sports in Cortland, NY. Precision Sports continued to import these guns under the Classic "600" name until 1994. Previously imported by Precision Sports, Inc. located in Cortland, NY until 1994. Previously imported by Exel Arms in Gardener, MA until 1987 as the Exel Model 200 series.

Due to space considerations, the individual Ignacio Ugartechea models have not been listed. Please refer to older print editions or our online services (free of charge) for more information on these previously imported models. The importation of Parker-Hale shotguns was disc. in 1993. Please contact Apsen Outfitting Company for more information on older Ignacio Ugartechea models.

ULTIMATE

Please refer to Camex-Blaser USA in the C section.

ULTRA LIGHT ARMS, INC.

Previous manufacturer located in Granville, WV. Ultra Light Arms, Inc. was purchased by C.F. Holding Corp. in 1999.

PISTOLS: BOLT-ACTION

MODEL 20 HUNTERS PISTOL - various cals., 14 in. Douglas heavy barrel, 5-shot mag., Kevlar graphite reinforced stock in choice of 4 colors, Timney trigger, left- or right-hand bolt, approx. 4 lbs. Mfg. 1987-89.

$1,295	$1,150	$975	$850	$700	$640	$575

Last MSR was $1,600.

MODEL 20 REB - popular cals. from .22-250 Rem. through .308 Win. (other cals. on request), 14 in. Douglas #3 barrel, 5 shot mag., composite Kevlar graphite reinforced stock, green, brown, black, or camo Dupont Imron paint, Timney adj. trigger, includes hard case, 4 lbs. Mfg. 1994-95, reintroduced 1998 only.

$1,475	$1,200	$1,000	$875	$750	$625	$500

Last MSR was $1,600.

GRADING - PPGS™	100%	98%	95%	90%	80%	70%	60%

RIFLES: BOLT ACTION

ULTRA LIGHT RIFLE - caliber to customer specs., various actions, 2-position 3-function safety in top of stock, Timney trigger, Douglas 22 or 24 in. barrel, no sights, graphite reinforced stock with recoil pad, matte finish standard, other finishes at extra cost. Many special order features and services were available on these models, 4 3/4-5 3/4 lbs. Mfg. 1985-1999.

MODEL 20 - many cals. available between .17 Rem. and .358 Win., short action, Kevlar stock.

	$2,225	$1,675	$1,225	$950	$800	$700	$640

Last MSR was $2,500.

Add $100 for left-hand action.

✳ *Model 20 RF* - .22 LR cal., convertible from repeater to single shot, 22 in. Douglas premium barrel, DuPont composite stock with Imron paint (some color options available), no sights, drilled and tapped, 5 1/4 lbs. Mfg. 1983-1999.

	$750	$650	$550	$475	$400	$350	$300

Last MSR was $800.

Add $50 for repeater action.

The first 100 pre-production rifles in this model were marked "1-of-100" consecutively, with owner's initials.

MODEL 24 - .25-06 Rem., .270 Win., .280 Rem. (mfg. 1992 only), .30-06, or 7mm Exp. cal., long action, Kevlar stock, 5 1/4 lbs. Disc. 1999.

	$2,325	$1,775	$1,300	$995	$825	$700	$640

Last MSR was $2,600.

Add $100 for left-hand action.

MODEL 28 MAGNUM - .264 Win. Mag., .300 Win. Mag., .338 Win. Mag., 7mm Rem. Mag., or .416 Rigby (mfg. 1992 only) cal., Kevlar stock, 5 3/4 lbs. Disc. 1999.

	$2,625	$1,975	$1,550	$1,225	$950	$700	$600

Last MSR was $2,900.

Add $100 for left-hand action.

MODEL 40 MAGNUM - .300 Wby. Mag. or .416 Rigby cal., otherwise similar to Model 28 Series. Mfg. 1993-99.

	$2,625	$1,975	$1,550	$1,225	$950	$700	$600

Last MSR was $2,900.

Add $100 for left-hand action.

ULTRAMATIC

Previous trademark with manufacture located in Enzesfeld, Austria. Ultramatic Productions, GmbH, changed its name to Wolf Sporting Pistols in 1997.

PISTOLS: SEMI-AUTO

ULTRAMATIC PISTOL - 9mm Para. cal., double action semi-auto, various barrel lengths, competition model with muzzle brake. Disc. approx. 1996.

	$1,150	$975	$850	$700	$640	$575	$500

UMAREX SPORTWAFFEN GmbH & Co. KG.

Current firearms, airguns, air soft, and signal pistol manufacturer established 1972 with headquarters located in Arnsberg, Germany. Umarex purchased Walther during 1996, and also manufactures ammunition, optics, and accessories. During 2006, Umarex purchased Hämmerli, and production equipment was moved from Lenzburg, Switzerland to Ulm, Germany. Please refer to the Hämmerli and Walther listings for currently imported firearms.

For more information on currently manufactured Umarex airguns, including many major U.S. trademark mfg. under license, please refer to the *Blue Book of Airguns* by Dr. Robert Beeman & John Allen (also online).

GRADING - PPGS™	100%	98%	95%	90%	80%	70%	60%

UNDERWOOD-ELLIOT-FISHER CORP.

Previous WWII subcontractor of M1 carbines located in Chicago, IL.
Please refer to U.S. Military rifles/carbines section.

UNERTL ORDNANCE COMPANY, INC.

Previous manufacturer circa 2004-2006 and located in Las Vegas, NV.

Unertl Ordnance Company manufactured a .45 ACP cal. semi-auto pistol in various configurations, including MEU (SOC) $2,795 last MSR, UCCP $2,195 last MSR, and the DLX $2,195 last MSR. The company also manufactured the UPR bolt action sniper rifle in .308 Win. cal. MSR was $5,900.

UNIQUE-ALPINE

Current manufacturer established 1923 and located in Erding, Germany. Previously located in Patin, France circa 2005-2006. The company name was changed from Unique to Unique-Alpine. Previously located in Hendaye, France until 2001. Previously imported by Nygord Precision Products located in Prescott, AZ.

Currently, Unique is manufacturing target, sniper, and bolt action rifles in addition to shotguns. These models are not currently being imported into the U.S. Please contact the company directly for more information, including current model availability and pricing (see Trademark Index).   In addition to the models listed below, Unique also manufactured additional models that were not imported into the U.S., but distributed mostly in Europe (Models I.S., DES 2000U, DES 69U, T3000 rifle, T/SM, T, and X51).

PISTOLS: SEMI-AUTO

Unique pistols were supplied with leatherette case, weights are additional.

KRIEGSMODELL L - 7.65mm cal., 9 shot, 3.2 in. barrel, blue, plastic grips, fixed sights. Mfg. 1940-45, during German occupation of France, has German acceptance marks.

	$325	$250	$220	$200	$180	$160	$140

MODEL RR - .22 LR or 7.65mm cal., post-war commercial version of Kreigsmodell, higher quality finish. Mfg. 1951-disc.

	$180	$170	$155	$130	$120	$110	$90

Add 15% for .22 LR.

MODEL B/CF - 7.65mm cal., 9 shot, or .380 auto cal., 8 shot, 4 in. barrel, blue, plastic thumbrest grips. Mfg. 1954-disc.

	$205	$195	$175	$155	$145	$130	$110

MODEL D6 - .22 LR cal., 10 shot, 6 in. barrel, adj. sights, blue, plastic grips. Mfg. 1954-disc.

	$300	$250	$200	$160	$145	$135	$120

MODEL D2 - similar to D6, except 4 1/2 in. barrel.

	$300	$250	$200	$160	$145	$135	$120

MODEL L - .22 LR cal., 10 shot, 7.65mm cal., 7 shot, and .380 ACP cal., 6 shot, 3.3 in. barrel, fixed sights, steel and alloy frame offered, plastic grips. Mfg. 1955-disc.

	$250	$200	$150	$130	$115	$100	$90

Add $500 for .22 LR cal. pistol-rifle combination.

MODEL MIKROS POCKET - .22 Short and .25 ACP cal., 6 shot, fixed sights, blue, plastic grips, steel or alloy frame. Mfg. 1957-disc.

	$200	$155	$140	$120	$100	$90	$75

MODEL DES/32U - .32 S&W Wadcutter cal., 5.9 in. barrel, dry firing device, ergonomically designed French walnut grips with adj. hand rest, 5 or 6 shot mag., 40.2 oz.

	$1,350	$1,225	$1,025	$900	$775	$625	$500

GRADING - PPGS™	100%	98%	95%	90%	80%	70%	60%

MODEL DES/69 MATCH - .22 LR cal. target pistol, wraparound grips, adj. features. Imported 1986-1988.

	$995	$850	$725	$625	$550	$490	$445

Last MSR was $1,198.

Add $62 for left-hand model.

MODEL DES/69U STANDARD MATCH - .22 LR cal., 5 shot mag., 5.9 in. barrel, adj. rear sight, adj. target stippled stocks, blue finish only. Imported 1969-1999.

	$1,150	$995	$875	$750	$625	$500	$450

Last MSR was $1,250.

Add $30 for left-hand model.

MODEL DES/96U - .22 LR cal., replacement for the Model DES/69U, top loading model, thinner grips, features gold-plated slide. Mfg. 1996-2002.

	$1,350	$1,225	$1,025	$900	$775	$625	$500

MODEL DES/823-U RAPID FIRE MATCH - .22 Short cal., 5 shot, 6 in. barrel, adj. sight, adj. trigger, adj. walnut target grips, squared barrel assembly, dry fire mechanism. Imported 1974-1988.

	$1,100	$850	$725	$625	$550	$490	$445

Last MSR was $1,300.

Add $60 for left-hand model.

MODEL 2000-U - .22 Short cal. only, specifically designed for rapid fire U.I.T. competition, 5.9 in. barrel, ergonomic styled grips with adj. hand rest, 5 shot mag. (inserted in top), 43.4 oz. Importation disc. 1995.

	$1,300	$1,050	$925	$775	$625	$500	$450

Last MSR was $1,450.

Add $30 for left-hand model.

RIFLES: BOLT ACTION

T66 MATCH RIFLE - .22 LR cal., single shot, bolt action, 25 1/2 in. barrel, micro rear and globe front sight, full target stock. Mfg. 1966-disc.

	$425	$410	$390	$350	$300	$280	$250

MODEL F 11 - .22 LR cal., military trainer, adj. sights, target walnut stock. Limited importation.

	$560	$435	$350	$285	$260	$240	$220

Last MSR was $695.

MODEL T DIOPTRA - .22 LR or .22 Mag. cal., bolt action Sporter with 23.6 in. barrel and adj. rear sight, 5 (.22 Mag. only) or 10 shot mag., grooved receiver for scope, checkered French walnut Monte Carlo stock, approx. 6.4 lbs. Importation disc. 1995.

	$795	$700	$600	$525	$450	$375	$300

Last MSR was $890.

MODEL T/SM - .22 LR or .22 Mag cal., bolt action Target variation with 20 1/2 in. barrel, no sights, 5 (.22 Mag. only) or 10 shot mag., stippled pistol grip stock and forearm, right- or left-hand action, 6.6 lbs. Importation disc. 1995.

	$850	$735	$625	$525	$450	$375	$300

Last MSR was $960.

Add $50 for left-hand action.

MODEL T/STANDARD UIT - .22 LR cal., designed for UIT competition, single shot, aperture sights, adj. cheekpiece and buttplate on stippled walnut stock, right- or left-hand action, 10.8 lbs. Importation disc. 1995.

	$1,350	$1,125	$975	$850	$725	$625	$525

Last MSR was $1,450.

Add $50 for left-hand action.

GRADING - PPGS™	100%	98%	95%	90%	80%	70%	60%

MODEL 2000 FREE RIFLE - .22 LR cal., Free Rifle variation of the Model T/Standard UIT.

	$2,600	$2,250	$1,875	$1,500	$1,250	$1,000	$850

TPG1 V2 - .243 Win., .308 Win., or .300 Win. Mag. cal., modular construction with hardcoated aluminum receiver available in various colors, paramilitary synthetic stock with ergonomic thumbhole grip, adj. cheekpiece and buttplate, 23.6 or 25.6 in. fluted barrel with or w/o muzzle brake, Picatinny rail, 5 shot detachable mag., bipod, approx. 12 1/4 lbs.

Please contact the company directly for more information, including pricing and U.S. availability (see Trademark Index).

UNITED SPORTING ARMS, INC.
Previous manufacturer located in Tombstone and Tucson, AZ and Post Falls, ID.

UNITED SPORTING ARMS HISTORY

The Seville and El Dorado line of single actions began life in 1972 as the "Abilene". It was during that year that Sig Himmelman built the prototype and formed United States Arms of Riverhead, NY. IN 1976, the company split, with Sig and Forrest Smith reorganizing as United Sporting Arms of Hauppauge, NY, manufacturing the blue model Seville and the stainless El Dorado. The El Dorado was an important model, because it was the first time that an all stainless .44 Mag. was available to the general public. United States Arms continued to produce the Abilene in Riverhead until Mossberg acquired the line in 1979. Production was moved to New Haven, CT and ceased in 1983.

In 1979, United Sporting Arms established a second facility in Tombstone, AZ. Sevilles weren't manufactured in Tombstone, but were assembled from parts shipped from Hauppage. Only a few hundred models were produced before operations were moved to Bisbee, AZ. While most models were blue, the Silver Seville was a Tombstone variant, with stainless backstrap and high blue finish.

The Bisbee operation was short lived too, and during mid-1979, Sig Himmelman relocated the western operations of United Sporting Arms to Tucson. By 1980, the company had split again into El Dorado Arms of Hauppauge and Sporting Arms Inc. of Tucson. These were separate companies with their own lines of revolvers. Stainless El Dorados were produced in NY and the blue/stainless Sevilles came from Arizona.

While El Dorado Arms primarily built .44 Mags., Sporting Arms Inc. expanded the line with many new chamberings. In 1982, the company unveiled the stretch-frame Seville in .357 Maximum. A couple of .375 Super Mags were also produced before the company was sold and the name changed to United Sporting Arms in 1983. That same year, El Dorado Arms closed shop.

The Tucson facility continued until folding in late 1985. Many unique variants were produced between 1983-1985, including .454 Mag., .375 SuperMag, Sheriff's models, and silhouette guns.

During 1986, United Sporting Arms was reformed in Post Falls, ID, but operations could not be sustained. Only 200 (approx.) guns were produced in this location, and quality was sub par compared to earlier Seville models.

By 1988, Forrest Smith and Russell Wood resurrected El Dorado Arms, basing production in Chimney Rock, NC. During 1988-1998, the company manufactured hand fitted and tuned single actions. Both standard frame and stretch platforms were offered, as well as a rimfire model. Production was low, but quality was very high.

The publisher would like to thank Mr. Rick Maples for providing the above information.

REVOLVERS: SINGLE ACTION

SEVILLE - .357 Mag., .41 Mag., .44 Mag., or .45 LC cal., single action revolver, 4 5/8, 5 1/2, 6 1/2, or 7 1/2 in. barrels, adj. sights, smooth walnut grips.

	$395	$350	$315	$280	$260	$240	$220

Last MSR was $435.

GRADING - PPGS™	100%	98%	95%	90%	80%	70%	60%

✳ *Seville Stainless steel* - all stainless version of the Seville.

	$395	$350	$315	$280	$260	$240	$220

Last MSR was $435.

✳ *Seville Silver* - similar to Seville, except has blue barrel, and high polish stainless steel grip frame.

	$425	$370	$330	$290	$270	$245	$225

Last MSR was $460.

✳ *Seville Stainless .357 Maxi* - available in 5 1/2 or 7 1/2 in. barrel only.

	$575	$475	$395	$335	$290	$245	$215

Last MSR was $465.

✳ *Seville Stainless .375 USA* - only in 7 1/2 in. barrel.

	$625	$525	$425	$360	$315	$260	$225

Last MSR was $490.

✳ *Seville Stainless .454 Mag.* - only in 7 1/2 in. barrel, 5 shot.

	$700	$600	$500	$430	$375	$315	$270

Last MSR was $595.

Note: In late 1986, some .454 Mags. were made up from parts purchased from the manufacturer. Unfortunately, while the exterior appearance might seem normal, they were not involved with any type of factory quality control program. As a result, shooting these non-factory revolvers could be dangerous, and careful inspection should be made before purchasing/ shooting this particular specimen.

✳ *Seville Eldorado Stainless* - .44 Mag., 4 5/8, 5 1/2, 6 1/2, 7 1/2, or 10 1/2 in. barrel, adj. sights.

	$700	$600	$500	$430	$375	$315	$270

SILVER SEVILLE SILHOUETTE - .357 Mag., .41 Mag., or .44 Mag. cal., single action revolver, 10 1/2 In. barrel, adj. sights, Pachmayr grips, blue barrel finish with stainless grip frame.

	$445	$370	$330	$295	$270	$250	$230

Last MSR was $485.

✳ *Silver Seville Silhouette Stainless steel* - stainless version of the Silver Seville Silhouette.

	$425	$370	$330	$290	$270	$245	$225

Last MSR was $460.

✳ *Silver Seville Silhouette Stainless .357 Maxi* - available in 10 1/2 in. barrel only.

	$575	$475	$395	$335	$290	$245	$215

Last MSR was $480.

✳ *Silver Seville Silhouette Stainless .375 USA* - available in 10 1/2 in. barrel only.

	$625	$525	$425	$360	$315	$260	$225

Last MSR was $515.

✳ *Silver Seville Silhouette Stainless .454 Mag.* - available in 10 1/2 in. barrel only, 5 shot.

	$700	$600	$500	$430	$375	$315	$270

Last MSR was $620.

SHERIFF MODEL - .357 Mag., .38 Spl., .44 Spl., .44 Mag., or .45 LC cal., single action revolver, 3 1/2 in. barrel, adj. sights, smooth walnut grips.

	$395	$350	$315	$280	$260	$240	$220

Last MSR was $435.

✳ *Sheriff Model Stainless steel* - stainless version of the Sheriff Model.

	$395	$350	$315	$280	$260	$240	$220

Last MSR was $435.

GRADING - PPGS™	100%	98%	95%	90%	80%	70%	60%

UNITED STATES FIREARMS MANUFACTURING COMPANY, INC.

Current manufacturer established during 1995 and located in Hartford, CT. Previously located at Colt's original old armory in Hartford, CT. Previous company name was United States Patent Firearms Manufacturing Company until 1997. Distributed exclusively beginning 2008 by Acusport.

PISTOLS: SEMI-AUTO

1910 COMMERCIAL MODEL - .45 ACP cal., 5 in. barrel, high polish Armory blue, hand checkered fancy walnut grips, 7 shot mag., fire blue appointments, 1905 patent dates, grip safety, checkered thumb safety, round 1905 fire blue hammer with hand cut checkering, original Colt 1910 rollmarks on both sides of slide. New 2006.

MSR $1,895	$1,650	$1,425	$1,275	$1,075	$925	$800	$700

1911 MILITARY MODEL - .45 ACP cal., 5 in. barrel, military polish Armory blue, hand checkered standard walnut grips, 7 shot mag., fire blue appointments, 1905 patent dates, grip safety, small contoured checkered thumb safety, spur hammer with hand cut checkering, original Colt 1911 military rollmarks on both sides of slide, including choice on right side of U.S. Navy or U.S. Army. New 2006.

MSR $1,895	$1,650	$1,425	$1,275	$1,075	$925	$800	$700

1911 SUPER 38 - .38 Super cal., features original 1911 Super 38 metal finishes and blue appointments, 1905 patent dates, grip safety, small thumb safety and spur hammer. New 2007.

MSR $1,895	$1,650	$1,425	$1,275	$1,075	$925	$800	$700

REVOLVERS: SAA

USFA also has a custom shop offering the following levels of engraving: Armory Grade A ($880 MSR), Armory Grade B ($985 MSR), Armory Grade C ($1,245 MSR), Armory Grade D ($1,500 MSR), Master Grade A ($1,100 MSR), Master Grade B ($2,465 MSR), Master Grade C ($3,575 MSR) or Master Grade D ($4,895 MSR).

COLT 1851 RICHARDS NAVY CONVERSION - .38 Spl. only, 7 1/2 in. barrel with ejector, Old Armoury Bone case hardened frame, gate, hammer, and conversion ring, Dome Blue barrel, cylinder, and ejector housing, smooth walnut grips.

	$1,175	$950	$825	$700	$600	$500	$400

Last MSR was $1,300.

SINGLE ACTION ARMY PREMIUM GRADE - .22 LR (mfg. 1996-2001), .22 Mag. (mfg. 1996-2001), .32-20 (new 1998), .357 Mag. (disc. 1998), .38 Spl. (new 2004), .38-40 WCF, .41 Colt (mfg. 1999-2003), .44 Spl. (new 2004), .44-40 WCF, .45 ACP (disc. 2006), or .45 LC cal., 3 (no ejector), 4 (no ejector), 4 3/4, 5 1/2, 7 1/2, or 10 (new 1997) in. barrel, original screw cylinder release, white sided hammer standard beginning 2005, choice of Dome Blue, Dome Blue/Old Armoury Bone Case, or nickel finish, checkered U.S. hard rubber grips.

MSR $1,085	$975	$850	$725	$625	$525	$450	$375

Add $200 for nickel finish.

The barrel marking for this revolver is "U.S.F.A. MFG. Co. HARTFORD CT. U.S.A."

✳ *SAA Flattop Target* - similar to SAA, except has flattop receiver with target sights, full Dome Blue finish is standard. Mfg. 1997-2002, reintroduced 2004.

MSR $1,495	$1,295	$1,125	$975	$800	$700	$600	$500

Add $55 for Dome Blue/Old Armory Bone Case finish (disc.).
Add $179 for Armory Blue/Old Armory Bone Case finish (disc.).
Add $219 for nickel finish (disc.).
Add $165 for full Armory Blue finish.
Add $199 for case colored frame and hammer.

✳ *SAA U.S. Pre-War* - similar cals. as the SAA Premium, except also available in .41 Colt, most historically correct and accurate pre-war SAA reproduction available. New 2000.

MSR $1,345	$1,225	$1,075	$875	$775	$625	$525	$450

✳ *SAA New Buntline Special* - .45 LC cal. only, 16 in. barrel, includes correct skeleton shoulder stock, ser. numbered 28,8xx and up. Mfg. 2000-2002.

	$1,850	$1,675	$1,500	$1,250	$1,000	$900	$800

Last MSR was $2,199.

Add $396 for nickel finish.

CUSTER BATTLEFIELD GUN - .45 LC cal., 7 1/2 in. barrel, has Orville W. Ainsworth inspector cartouche on one-piece walnut grips, antique patina finish, script barrel legend with slanted cross at each end, ser. range 200-14,343. New 2006.

MSR $1,485	$1,325	$1,150	$950	$850	$725	$625	$525

PATRIOT SERIES - .30 Carbine or .45 ACP cal., 5 1/2 (.45 ACP) or 7 1/2 (.30 Carbine) in. barrel with lanyard loop, Old Armory Bone case colored frame, Dome Blue (.30 Carbine) or Armory Blue (.45 ACP) finish, Automatic Colt Pistol rollmark. New 2005.

MSR $1,280	$1,125	$925	$800	$650	$525	$450	$400

Add $210 for .45 ACP cal.

GOVERNMENT INSPECTOR SERIES - .45 LC cal., exact recreations of guns inspected by government inspectors, including Henry Nettleton, Orville Ainsworth, David Clark, and Rinaldo Carr, exact cartouche stampings and hand-stamped markings, 5 1/2 or 7 1/2 in. barrel, historically correct, one-piece walnut grips, Old Armory Bone case color hardened frame, Armory Blue, antique, or nickel finish. New 2005.

MSR $1,485	$1,325	$1,150	$950	$825	$700	$600	$500

Add $40 for antique finish.
Add $134 for nickel finish (disc. 2007).

BISLEY MODEL SAA - same cals. as SAA, 4 3/4, 5 1/2, 7 1/2, or 10 (disc.) in. barrel, patterned after the Colt Bisley Model, smooth walnut grips, standard or target configuration, choice of Bone Case/Dome Blue, Bone Case/Armory Blue, or nickel finish. Disc. 1998, reintroduced 2000-2002, again in 2004.

MSR $1,525	$1,350	$1,150	$950	$825	$700	$600	$500

Add $200 for Armory Blue/Old Armory Bone Case finish.
Add $200 for nickel finish.
Add $145 for Bisley Target variation.

BIRDSHEAD MODEL SAA - same cals. as SAA, patterned after the Colt Model 1877 Thunderer, 3 1/2, 4, or 4 3/4 in. barrel with ejector, case colored frame. Mfg. 1997-2002.

	$975	$825	$725	$625	$525	$425	$325

Last MSR was $1,150.

Add $149 for nickel finish.

CHINA CAMP - various cals., designed for competition shooting, silver steel competition finish with two-piece hard rubber grips. Mfg. 2000-2003.

	$975	$850	$725	$625	$525	$425	$325

Last MSR was $1,200.

SHERIFF'S MODEL - similar cals. as the SAA, 2 1/2, 3, 3 1/2, or 4 in. barrel w/o ejector rod housing, U.S. hard rubber grips, choice of bone case/blue or nickel finish. New 2004.

MSR $1,200	$1,050	$900	$775	$700	$600	$525	$450

Add $200 for nickel finish.

GRADING - PPGS™	100%	98%	95%	90%	80%	70%	60%

RODEO - .32-20 WCF (mfg. 2005-2006), .38 Spl., .38-40 WCF (mfg. 2005-2006), .44-40 WCF (disc. 2006), .44 Spl. (mfg. 2005-2006), or .45 LC, 4 3/4, 5 1/2, or 7 1/2 (new 2004) in. barrel, matte blue finish, fixed firing pin, square notch rear sight, hard rubber or Tru-Ivory grips, white sided hammer became standard 2005, entry level cowboy action shooting model. New 2002.

	MSR $745	$660	$575	$500	$450	$400	$350	$315

Add $131 for Rodeo Heritage Model with Tru-Ivory grips (disc. 2005).
Add $358 for Rodeo Race Groove (limited mfg. 2006).

COWBOY - .38 Spl. or .45 LC cal., 4 3/4, 5 1/2, or 7 1/2 in. barrel, full Dome Blue metal finish, U.S. brown hard rubber grips, cross pin frame, square notch rear and square front blade sights. New 2007.

	MSR $945	$850	$750	$675	$600	$525	$450	$375

GUNSLINGER - .32-20 WCF, .38-40 WCF, .38 Spl., .44-40 WCF, .44 Spl., or .45 LC cal., 4 3/4, 5 1/2, or 7 1/2 in. barrel, cross-pin frame, cowboy action aged bluing, hard rubber grips, antique finish, square notch rear and front blade sights. New 2005.

	MSR $1,045	$925	$775	$650	$525	$450	$375	$300

Add $70 for black powder frame (disc. 2006).

OMNI-POTENT SIX SHOOTER - various cals., 4 3/4, 5 1/2, or 7 1/2 in. barrel, choice of case colored, Old Armory Bone Case or Armory blue finish, checkered Bisley style walnut grips with round butt and lanyard loop. Mfg. 2000-2002, reintroduced 2004.

	MSR $1,485	$1,325	$1,150	$950	$825	$700	$600	$500

Add approx. $200 for nickel finish.
Add $240 for Omni-Target Model with raised adj. sights.

OMNI-POTENT SNUBNOSE - various cals., 2, 3, or 4 in. barrel, full Armory blue or nickel finish, checkered Bisley style walnut grips with round butt and lanyard loop. Mfg. 2000-2002, reintroduced 2004.

	MSR $1,345	$1,150	$925	$800	$650	$550	$475	$400

Add $200 for nickel finish.

PLINKER - .22 LR or .22 Mag. cal., 4 3/4, 5 1/2, or 7 1/2 in. barrel, Old Armoury Bone Case/Dome Blue finish, U.S. hard rubber grips, square notch rear and square front blade sights, includes extra .22 Mag. cylinder. New 2004.

	MSR $1,085	$975	$875	$750	$650	$550	$475	$400

Add $410 for Target Model with adj. sights and Dome Blue finish.

HUNTER - .17 HMR cal., 7 1/2 in. barrel, matte blue finish, adj. rear sight, replaceable front blade sight, drilled and tapped, U.S. hard rubber grips, 3 1/2 lbs. Limited mfg. 2004-2005.

		$750	$650	$550	$475	$400	$325	$275

Last MSR was $839.

RIFLES: REPRODUCTIONS, LEVER ACTION

STANDARD LIGHTNING MAGAZINE RIFLE - .38-40 WCF, .44-40 WCF, or .45 LC cal., patterned after the Colt Lightning rifle, 26 in., round, half-round or octagon barrel, 15 shot mag., straight grip uncheckered walnut stock and small checkered forearm.

	MSR $1,480	$1,325	$1,150	$950	$825	$700	$600	$500

Add $270 for octagon barrel.
Add $245 for half-round/half-octagon barrel.
Nickel finish is POR.

GRADING - PPGS™	100%	98%	95%	90%	80%	70%	60%

* **Standard Lightning Deluxe Rifle** - similar to Standard, except has deluxe checkered semi-pistol grip stock and forearm, choice of 26 in. octagon, round or half-round, half-octagon barrel with half mag.

	MSR $2,559	$2,225	$1,950	$1,750	$1,500	$1,250	$1,000	$875

Add $100 for half-round, half-octagon barrel.

STANDARD LIGHTNING MAGAZINE CARBINE - similar to Lightning Rifle, except has 16 (Trapper) or 20 in. round barrel and 8 (Trapper, new 2006) or 12 shot mag.

	MSR $1,480	$1,325	$1,150	$950	$825	$700	$600	$500

Add $515 for Lightweight Baby Carbine with 20 in. special tapered barrel and lightweight forearm with special checkering.
Add $675 for Trapper Model with 16 in. special taper barrel and checkering.
Add $270 for checkered stock and forearm.

STANDARD LIGHTNING COWBOY RIFLE/CARBINE - .38-40 WCF, .44-40 WCF, or .45 LC cal., 20 in. (carbine) or 26 (rifle) in. round barrel with ladder (carbine) or buckhorn rear sight, matte blue metal and matte wood finish. Disc. 2006.

	$1,175	$1,025	$900	$800	$700	$600	$500

Last MSR was $1,345.

UNIVERSAL FIREARMS

Previous manufacturer 1958-1987 and located in Hialeah, FL. Previous company name was Bullseye Gunworks, located in Miami, FL. The company moved to Hialeah, FL in 1958 and began as Universal Firearms.

Universal Firearms M1 carbines were manufactured and assembled at the company's facility in Hialeah starting in the late 1950s. The carbines of the 1960s were mfg. with available surplus GI parts on a receiver subcontracted to Repp Steel Co. of Buffalo, NY. The carbines of the 1970s were mfg. with commercially manufactured parts due to a shortage of GI surplus. In 1983, the company was purchased by Iver Johnson Arms of Jacksonville, AR, but remained a separate division as Universal Firearms in Hialeah until closed and liquidated by Iver Johnson Arms in 1987.

PISTOLS: SEMI-AUTO

MODEL 3000 ENFORCER PISTOL - .30 Carbine cal., walnut stock, 11 1/4 in. barrel, 17 3/4 in. overall, 15, and 30 shot. Mfg. 1964-83. Also see listing under Iver Johnson.

	100%	98%	95%	90%	80%	70%	60%
Blue finish	$325	$275	$235	$200	$185	$170	$160
Nickel-plated	$350	$295	$250	$235	$220	$200	$185
Gold-plated	$350	$275	$250	$225	$200	$185	$165
Stainless	$425	$350	$275	$225	$195	$165	$140

Add $50 for Teflon-S finish.

RIFLES: SEMI-AUTO, CARBINES

MODEL 440 VULCAN - .44 Mag. cal., slide action, 18 1/4 in. barrel with adj. rear and front ramp sight, 5 shot detachable mag.

	$325	$275	$230	$195	$175	$150	$135

1000 MILITARY - .30 Carbine cal., "G.I." copy, satin blue, birch stock, 18 in. barrel. Disc.

	$300	$265	$235	$200	$180	$170	$160

MODEL 1003 - 16, 18, or 20 in. barrel, .30 M1 copy, blue finish, adj. sight, birch stock, 5 1/2 lbs. Also see listing under Iver Johnson.

	$300	$265	$235	$200	$180	$170	$160

Last MSR was $203.

* **Model 1010** - nickel finish, disc.

	$325	$275	$240	$210	$180	$155	$120

GRADING - PPGS™	100%	98%	95%	90%	80%	70%	60%

✳ Model 1015 - gold electroplated, disc.

	100%	98%	95%	90%	80%	70%	60%
	$325	$275	$250	$215	$185	$160	$130

Add $45 for 4X scope.

1005 DELUXE - .30 Carbine cal., custom Monte Carlo walnut stock, high polish blue, oil finish on wood.

	$350	$315	$275	$250	$225	$200	$180

1006 STAINLESS - .30 Carbine cal., stainless steel construction, birch stock, 18 in. barrel, 6 lbs.

	$375	$300	$265	$240	$220	$195	$175

Last MSR was $234.

1020 TEFLON - .30 Carbine cal., Dupont Teflon-S finish on metal parts, black or grey color, Monte Carlo stock.

	$350	$275	$250	$215	$185	$160	$130

1256 "FERRET" - .256 Win. Mag. cal., M1 Action, satin blue, birch stock, 18 in. barrel, 5 1/2 lbs.

	$300	$265	$235	$200	$175	$165	$155

Last MSR was $219.

2200 LEATHERNECK - .22 LR cal., recoil operated action, birch stock, satin blue, 18 in. barrel, 5 1/2 lbs.

	$240	$190	$180	$170	$160	$145	$135

5000 PARATROOPER - .30 Carbine cal., metal folding extension, walnut stock, 16 or 18 in. barrel.

	$450	$375	$325	$285	$250	$225	$200

Last MSR was $234.

5006 PARATROOPER STAINLESS - similar to 5000, only stainless with 18 in. barrel only.

	$525	$425	$350	$285	$250	$215	$185

Last MSR was $281.

1981 COMMEMORATIVE CARBINE - .30 Carbine cal., "G.I Military" model, cased with accessories. Mfg. for 40th Anniversary 1941-81.

	$650	$490	$400	N/A	N/A	N/A	N/A

SHOTGUNS

All Universal shotguns were disc. after 1982.

MODEL 7312 O/U - 12 ga., 30 in. full and mod., VR barrel, boxlock, vent. barrel spacer, SST, auto ejectors, barrels ported to reduce recoil, engraved, color case hardened receiver, trap or skeet style, checkered select stock.

	$1,650	$1,540	$1,485	$1,430	$1,320	$1,210	$1,045

MODEL 7412 O/U - similar to 7312, without ejectors, blue and silver receiver.

	$1,430	$1,210	$1,155	$1,100	$9,900	$880	$825

MODEL 7712 O/U - 12 ga., 26 or 28 in. barrel, VR, non-selective single trigger, extractors, light engraving, checkered pistol grip stock.

	$440	$415	$385	$360	$330	$275	$220

MODEL 7812 O/U - similar to 7712, with auto ejectors and more engraving.

	$605	$580	$550	$525	$470	$415	$385

MODEL 7912 O/U - similar to 7812, with selective single trigger and gold damascene engraving.

	$1,210	$1,155	$1,100	$1,045	$965	$880	$825

MODEL 7112 SxS - 12 ga., 26 or 28 in. barrels, various chokes, boxlock, extractors, engraved case hardened frame, checkered pistol grip stock.

	$330	$305	$275	$250	$195	$165	$140

GRADING - PPGS™	100%	98%	95%	90%	80%	70%	60%

DOUBLE WING SxS - 10, 12, 20 ga., or .410 bore, 26, 28, or 30 in. barrels, various chokes, double triggers, boxlock, extractors, checkered pistol grip stock.

	100%	98%	95%	90%	80%	70%	60%
	$330	$305	$275	$250	$195	$165	$140
10 gauge	$385	$360	$330	$305	$250	$220	$165

MODEL 7212 SINGLE BARREL TRAP - 12 ga., 30 in. full, Simmons type VR, engraved case colored frame, vent. barrel to reduce recoil, boxlock, auto ejector, select checkered trap style stock.

$1,100	$990	$935	$880	$770	$715	$605

USELTON ARMS INC

Current manufacturer located in Madison, TN.

PISTOLS: SEMI-AUTO

Uselton Arms Inc. manufactures M1911-style semi-auto pistols. Models included the Compact Classic Companion, Compact Classic, Carry Classic, Tactical Cobra Coat, Uselton National Match, and the Ultra Compact Classic. Base price for all models is $1,999, and goes up depending on options.

RIFLES: BOLT ACTION

Uselton also offers a Warbird Mountain Lite bolt action rifle in 7.82 Warbird cal., with stainless steel long action and choice of Kevlar or laminate thumbhole stock. Additionally, the Warbird is offered in a Tactical configuration with lightweight stock. Please contact the company directly for more information, including pricing and delivery time (see Trademark Index).

UZI

Current trademark manufactured by Israeli Military Industries (IMI). No commercial U.S. importation currently. During 1996-1998, Mossberg imported the Uzi Eagle pistols. These models were imported by UZI America, Inc., subsidiary of O.F. Mossberg & Sons, Inc. Previously imported by Action Arms, Ltd., located in Philadelphia, PA until 1994.

Serial number prefixes used on Uzi Firearms are as follows: "SA" on all 9mm Para. semi-auto carbines Models A and B; "45 SA" on all .45 ACP Model B carbines; "41 SA" on all .41 AE Model B carbines; "MC" on all 9mm Para. (only cal. made) semi-auto mini-carbines; "UP" on 9mm Para. semi-auto Uzi pistols, except Eagle Series pistols; "45 UP" on all .45 semi-auto Uzi pistols (disc. 1989). There are also prototypes or experimental Uzis with either "AA" or "AAL" prefixes - these are rare and will command premiums over values listed below.

CARBINES: SEMI-AUTO

CARBINE MODEL A - 9mm Para. cal., semi-auto, 16.1 in. barrel, parkerized finish, 25 shot mag., mfg. by IMI 1980-1983 and ser. range is SA01,001-SA037,000.

$1,650	$1,475	$1,325	$1,125	$975	$875	$750

Approx. 100 Model As were mfg. with a nickel finish. These are rare and command considerable premiums over values listed above.

CARBINE MODEL B - 9mm Para., .41 Action Express (new 1987), or .45 ACP (new 1987) cal., semi-auto carbine, 16.1 in. barrel, baked enamel black finish over phosphated (parkerized) base finish, 16 (.45 ACP), 20 (.41 AE) or 25 (9mm Para.) shot mag., metal folding stock, includes molded case and carrying sling, 8.4 lbs. Mfg. 1983 - until Federal legislation disc. importation 1989 and ser. range is SA037,001-SA073,544.

$1,500	$1,325	$1,200	$1,000	$950	$850	$750

Last MSR was $698.

Subtract approx. $150 for .41 AE or .45 ACP cal.
Add $150 for .22 cal. conversion kit (new 1987).

GRADING - PPGS™	100%	98%	95%	90%	80%	70%	60%

Add $215 for .45 ACP to 9mm Para./.41 AE conversion kit.
Add $150 for 9mm Para. to .41 AE (or vice-versa) conversion kit.
Add $215 for 9mm Para. to .45 ACP conversion kit.

MINI CARBINE - 9mm Para. cal., similar to Carbine except has 19 3/4 in. barrel, 20 shot mag., swing-away metal stock, scaled down version of the regular carbine, 7.2 lbs. New 1987. Federal legislation disc. importation 1989.

	100%	98%	95%	90%	80%	70%	60%
	$2,375	$2,175	$1,850	$1,600	$1,350	$1,150	$995

Last MSR was $698.

PISTOLS: SEMI-AUTO

UZI PISTOL - 9mm Para. or .45 ACP cal. (disc.), semi-auto pistol, 4 1/2 in. barrel, parkerized finish, 10 (.45 ACP) or 20 (9mm Para.) shot mag., supplied with molded carrying case, sight adj. key and mag. loading tool, 3.8 lbs. Importation disc. 1993.

	100%	98%	95%	90%	80%	70%	60%
	$975	$850	$795	$750	$700	$650	$600

Last MSR was $695.

Add $285 for .45 ACP to 9mm Para./.41 AE conversion kit.
Add $100 for 9mm Para. to .41 AE conversion kit.
Add approx. 30%-40% for two-line slide marking "45 ACP Model 45."

UZI EAGLE SERIES - 9mm Para., .40 S&W, or .45 ACP cal., semi-auto double action, various configurations, matte finish with black synthetic grips, 10 shot mag. Mfg. 1997-1998.

* *Uzi Eagle Series Full-Size* - 9mm Para. or .40 S&W cal., 4.4 in. barrel, steel construction, decocking feature, Tritium sights, polygonal rifling. Imported 1997-98.

	100%	98%	95%	90%	80%	70%	60%
	$485	$440	$400	$365	$335	$330	$275

Last MSR was $535.

* *Uzi Eagle Series Short Slide* - 9mm Para., .40 S&W, or .45 ACP cal., similar to Full-Size Eagle, except has 3.7 in. barrel. Imported 1997-98.

	100%	98%	95%	90%	80%	70%	60%
	$485	$440	$400	$365	$335	$330	$275

Last MSR was $535.

Add $31 for .45 ACP cal.

* *Uzi Eagle Series Compact* - 9mm Para. or .40 S&W cal., available in double action with decocking or double action only, 3 1/2 in. barrel. Imported 1997-98.

	100%	98%	95%	90%	80%	70%	60%
	$485	$440	$400	$365	$335	$330	$275

Last MSR was $535.

* *Uzi Eagle Series Polymer Compact* - similar to Compact Eagle, except has compact polymer frame. Imported 1997-98.

	100%	98%	95%	90%	80%	70%	60%
	$485	$440	$400	$365	$335	$330	$275

Last MSR was $535.

V SECTION

VM HY-TECH LLC
Current rifle manufacturer located in Phoenix, AZ. Dealer and direct sales.

GRADING - PPGS™	100%	98%	95%	90%	80%	70%	60%

RIFLES

VM15 - .223 Rem. or 9mm Para. cal., AR-15 style, semi-auto, unique side charging on left side of receiver operated by folding lever allowing easy replacement of scopes, 16, 20, or 24 in. fluted and ported Wilson barrel, aluminum free-floating hand guard, forged lower receiver, A-2 style buttstock with pistol grip, black finish. New 2002.

MSR N/A		$800	$750	$675	$600	$550	$500	$400

Add $34 for side-charging loading (new 2005).
Add $310 for 9mm Para. cal.

VM-50 - .50 BMG cal., single shot, 18, 22, 30, or 36 in. Lothar Walther barrel with muzzle brake, aluminum stock, includes bipod, black finish, 22-29 lbs. New 2004.

MSR N/A		$2,000	$1,775	$1,600	$1,475	$1,350	$1,225	$1,075

Add $40 - $120 for 22-36 in. barrel.

VAIL, ROY
Previous custom shotgun and rifle maker located in Warwick, NY circa 1950s - early 1970s.

Roy Vail was a top quality custom gunmaker who manufactured approx. 150 custom shotguns and 200 custom rifles. Francotte actions were typically used on his SxSs, and he would add the wood, engraving inlays, and checkering. Secondary values are difficult to establish, and each gun must be evaluated individually for its overall desirability factor, which includes configuration, condition, embellishments, and quality of wood and checkering.

VALKYRIE ARMS LTD.
Current manufacturer located in Olympia, WA. Dealer sales.

Valkyrie Arms Ltd. manufactures semi-auto copies of the M3A1, Browning 1919, and DeLisle Commando Carbine. Models include: M3-A1 SA Grease Gun ($950 MSR), Browning M1919-SA ($2,850 last MSR), Delisle Commando Carbine ($1,995 MSR), DeLisle 2000 (bolt action, $1,695 MSR), Sten MKII/MKIII ($645 last MSR), and the DeLisle Sporter Carbine ($650 MSR). For more information, including availability, please contact the company directly (see Trademark Index).

VALMET
Current trademark manufactured in Brescia, Italy by Marocchi CD Europe. Currently imported by Network Retailing LLC, located in Canby, OR. Previously imported 2004-2005 by Tristar, located in N. Kansas City, MO.

RIFLES: O/U

FINNCLASSIC 512 SC RIFLE/COMBO - .30-06, .308 Win. cal., 12 ga. (3 1/2 in. w/ choke tube) over .222 Rem. for combo, 23 1/2 in. barrels, SST, rifle has cocking indicators, boxlock action, checkered Monte Carlo walnut stock and forearm, 7.7 (combo) or 8 1/4 lbs.

MSR $1,475		$1,300	$1,050	$925	$825	$725	$625	$525

Add $375 for double rifle configuration.

GRADING - PPGS™	100%	98%	95%	90%	80%	70%	60%

SHOTGUNS: O/U

FINNCLASSIC 512 - 12 or 20 ga., 3 in. chambers, boxlock action, blue (Field), chrome, or matte nickel finished receiver, choice of Sporting (12 ga. only, 28, 30, or 32 in. VR barrels with 11mm VR), Youth/Ladies (shorter LOP), or Field, 7.4 lbs.

MSR $1,250	$1,035	$900	$775	$675	$600	$525	$450

> Add $70 for Ultralight variation.
> Add $245 for bright chrome metal finish.
> Add $22 for Sporting Clays configuration with 5 choke tubes (disc.).
> Add $314 for Youth/Ladies model (disc.).

VALMET, INC.

Previous manufacturer located in Jyvaskyla, Finland. Previously imported by Stoeger Industries, Inc. located in South Hackensack, NJ.

The Valmet line was discontinued in 1989 and replaced by Tikka (please refer to the Tikka section in this text) in 1990.

RIFLES: SEMI-AUTO

Magazines for the following models are a major consideration when purchasing a Valmet semi-auto rifle, and prices can run anywhere from $85 (.223 Rem.) up to $250 (.308 Win.). Model 76 .308 mags. will function in a Model 78, but not vice versa.

HUNTER MODEL - .223 Rem., .243 Win., .30-06 (scarce) or .308 Win. cal., gas operated semi-auto, Kalashnikov action, 20 1/2 in. barrel, checkered walnut stock and forearm, matte finished metal, 5, 9, or 20 shot mag., 8 lbs. New 1986, Federal legislation disc. importation 1989.

	$895	$795	$700	$625	$550	$500	$450

Last MSR was $795.

M-62S PARAMILITARY DESIGN RIFLE - 7.62x39 Russian, semi-auto version of Finn M-62, 15 or 30 shot mag., 16 5/8 in. barrel, gas operated, rotary bolt, adj. rear sight, tube steel or wood stock. Mfg. 1962-disc.

	$2,250	$2,000	$1,650	$1,375	$1,175	$975	$875

> Add approx. $200 for tube stock.

M-71S - similar to M-62S, except .223 Rem. cal., stamped metal receiver, reinforced resin or wood stock.

	$1,650	$1,450	$1,325	$1,175	$975	$875	$775

MODEL 76 - .223 Rem., 7.62x39mm, or .308 Win. cal., gas operated semi-auto paramilitary design rifle, 16 3/4 in. or 20 1/2 (.308 only) in. barrel, 15 or 30 (7.62x39mm only) shot mag., parkerized finish. Federal legislation disc. importation 1989.

Plastic Stock	$1,300	$1,075	$875	$750	$675	$575	$450
Wood Stock	$1,600	$1,300	$1,025	$875	$700	$575	$450

Last MSR was $740.

> Add approx. 10% for folding stock.
> Add 100% for 7.62x39mm cal. with wood stock.
> Add 20% for wood stock in .308 Win. cal.

MODEL 78 - .223 Rem., 7.62x39mm, or .308 Win. cal., similar to Model 76, except has 24 1/2 in. barrel, wood stock and forearm, and barrel bipod, 11 lbs. New 1987. Federal legislation disc. importation 1989.

	$1,750	$1,525	$1,375	$1,175	$950	$825	$700

Last MSR was $1,060.

> Add 10% for 7.62x39mm cal.

MODEL 82 BULLPUP - .223 Rem. cal., limited importation.

	$1,675	$1,425	$1,200	$995	$775	$650	$525

GRADING - PPGS™	100%	98%	95%	90%	80%	70%	60%

SHOTGUNS/RIFLES: O/U

LION MODEL - 12 ga., 26, 28, or 30 in. barrels, various chokes, boxlock, SST, checkered stock. Mfg. 1947-68.

	$415	$370	$340	$320	$305	$275	$240

MODEL 412 O/U SHOOTING SYSTEM - interchangeable barrel assemblies permit a double rifle, shotgun/rifle, and O/U shotgun configuration, user-installed interchangeable barrels, monobloc locking, rifle barrel positioning by adjustment, SST, extractors or ejectors, checkered walnut stock and forend, cocking indicators, blue finish. Importation on all models was disc. 1989.

Add $100 for synthetic stock on all 412 models.

✳ *Model 412S O/U Shooting System Field Grade* - 12 ga. was standard, auto ejectors, screw-in choke tubes, matte nickel finish. Imported 1986-89.

	$855	$670	$580	$540	$475	$440	$400

Last MSR was $999.

Add 15% for 20 ga.

✳ *Model 412S O/U Shooting System Field and Target* - 12 ga. only, 2 3/4 and 3 in. chambers, ejectors. Disc. 1988.

	$775	$660	$580	$540	$475	$440	$400

Last MSR was $874.

✳ *Model 412ST O/U Shooting System Trap and Skeet* - 12 ga., Monte Carlo stock on Trap model, 28 in. barrels on Skeet model, screw-in chokes standard.

	$1,040	$875	$695	$650	$580	$540	$475

Last MSR was $1,215.

✳ *Model 412ST O/U Shooting System Premium Grade Target* - similar to Model 412ST Trap and Skeet, except has better walnut and checkering. Imported 1987-89.

	$1,355	$1,050	$865	$750	$640	$580	$515

Last MSR was $1,550.

✳ *Model 412S O/U Shooting System Combination Gun* - combination, 12 ga, 3 in. chamber over choice of .222 Rem., .223 Rem., .243 Win., .30-06, or .308 Win. cal., extractors.

	$1,025	$850	$675	$600	$550	$475	$440

Last MSR was $1,615.

✳ *Model 412S O/U Shooting System Double Rifle* - .243 Win. (disc. 1987), .30-06, .308 Win. (disc. 1987), .375 H&H Mag. (disc. 1987), or 9.3x73R cal., extractors, 24 in. barrels.

	$1,060	$895	$725	$650	$580	$540	$475

Last MSR was $1,275.

Add $100 for 9.3x74R cal. or .375 H&H Mag. cal.

This model in .30-06 cal. has extractors only while in 9.3x74R cal. ejectors are standard.

✳ *Model 412K O/U Shooting System Double Rifle* - .30-06 or .308 Win. cal. only, 24 in. separated barrels, extractors. Importation disc. 1986.

	$800	$660	$580	$540	$475	$440	$400

Last MSR was $899.

✳ *Model 412 O/U Shooting System Engraved* - satin finish, receiver extensively bank note engraved in choice of 4 patterns, select Triple-X wood hand-checkered - choice of field or target, available in any Valmet model.

This model had limited availability and prices were on request from the manufacturer.

✳ *Model 412 O/U Shooting System Extra Barrel Assemblies* - $505-$605 each for shotgun (includes screw-in chokes), $579 each for shotgun/rifle combo, $660 each for double rifle (add $100 for ejectors).

GRADING - PPGS™	100%	98%	95%	90%	80%	70%	60%

VALTRO

Current manufacturer established during 1988 and located in Brescia, Italy. Currently imported by Valtro USA, located in Hayward, CA. Previously located in San Rafael, CA.

Valtro manufactures both excellent quality slide action and semi-auto shotguns, in addition to a very high quality semi-auto pistol, and a variety of signal pistols. Please contact the importer directly for more product information and availability (see Trademark Index listing).

PISTOLS: SEMI-AUTO

1998 A1 .45 ACP - .45 ACP cal., forged National Match frame and slide, 5 in. barrel, deluxe wood grips, 8 shot mag., ambidextrous safety, blue finish, flat checkered mainspring housing, front and rear slide serrations, beveled mag. well, speed trigger, 40 oz., lifetime guarantee. Very limited importation beginning 1998.

MSR N/A	$5,500	$5,200	$4,950	$4,650	$4,250	$3,850	$3,500

SHOTGUNS: SLIDE ACTION

TACTICAL 98 SHOTGUN - 12 ga. only, 18 1/2 or 20 in. barrel featuring MMC ghost ring sights and integral muzzle brake, 5 shot mag., internal chokes, receiver sidesaddle holds 6 exposed rounds, pistol grip or standard stock, matte black finish, lightweight. Imported 1998 - disc.

	$790	$630	$525	$475	$425	$400	$360

PM5 12 ga., 20 in. barrel, 7 shot mag., black synthetic stock with matte black finish, available with or w/o ghost ring sights, optional folding stock. Limited importation beginning 2006.

MSR N/A	$995	$900	$800	$725	$650	$575	$500

VARBERGER

Previous rifle manufacturer located in Varberg, Sweden. Previously imported by Hill Country Wholesale, Inc.

VARBERGER PRECISION PRODUCTS AB

located in Austin, TX, and distributed by Paul & Associates, located in Wellsville, KS until late 1995.

RIFLES: BOLT ACTION

MODEL 711 GRADE 1 - available in 19 cals. between .22 PPC and .358 Norma, bolt action design featuring specially designed and manufactured receiver, rotary mag., 6 lug engine-turned bolt, and stock featuring metal retainer plate, individually test-fired. Imported 1994-98.

	$950	$850	$750	$650	$550	$450	$375

Last MSR was $1,080.

MODEL 717 GRADE 1 MAGNUM - available in 11 Mag. cals. between .257 Wby. Mag. and .375 H&H. Imported 1994-98.

	$980	$875	$765	$650	$550	$450	$375

Last MSR was $1,130.

MODEL 757 GRADE 2 DELUXE - deluxe variation of the Model 711. Imported 1994-98.

	$1,775	$1,500	$1,250	$995	$895	$795	$695

Last MSR was $2,035.

Add $45 for Mag. cals.

MODEL 77 GRADE 3 PREMIER - top-of-the-line model. Imported 1994-98.

	$1,995	$1,675	$1,350	$1,050	$925	$795	$695

Last MSR was $2,375.

Add $65 for Mag. cals.

GRADING - PPGS™	100%	98%	95%	90%	80%	70%	60%

VARNER SPORTING ARMS, INC.
Previous manufacturer located in Marietta, GA circa 1988-1989.

RIFLES: SINGLE SHOT

VARNER FAVORITE HUNTER - .22 LR cal., patterned after J. Stevens Favorite Model, 1/2 round - 1/2 octagon 21 1/2 in. takedown barrel, blue frame, walnut stock and forearm, aperture rear sight, 5 lbs. Mfg. 1988-89.

	$325	$270	$220	$185	$150	$130	$110

Last MSR was $369.

✳ *Varner Favorite Hunter Deluxe* - similar to Favorite Hunter, except has case colored frame and lever, and deluxe walnut stock and forearm. Mfg. 1988-89.

	$450	$375	$285	$225	$175	$150	$135

Last MSR was $500.

✳ *Varner Favorite Hunter Presentation Grade* - includes target hammer and trigger, AAA quality checkered stock and forearm, includes takedown case. Mfg. 1988-89.

	$480	$400	$310	$250	$195	$170	$155

Last MSR was $569.

PRESENTATION ENGRAVED - previously available in a No. 1 Grade for $649, a No. 2 for $779, or a No. 3 for $1,099.

VECTOR ARMS, INC.
Current paramilitary rifle and parts manufacturer located in N. Salt Lake, UT.

RIFLES: SEMI-AUTO

Vector Arms offers the following semi-auto paramilitary style rifles currently: V-53 (semi-auto version of the HK53 - $1,350 MSR), V-93 (semi-auto version of the HK33 - $1,104 MSR), Uzi full size post-ban ($595 MSR), and the RPD (drum or belt fed - $1,999 MSR). Please contact the company directly for more information on these rifles, including availability (see Trademark Index).

VEGA
Current shotgun manufacturer located in Istanbul, Turkey. Currently imported by Adco Sales, located in Woburn, MA.

Vega manufactures Diamond shotguns for Adco Sales. Please refer to the Adco Sales section for more information.

VEKTOR
Current trademark established during 1953 as part of LEW (Lyttelton Engineering Work). In 1995, Vektor became a separate division of Denel of South Africa.

Vektor has been manufacturing a wide variety of firearms configurations, including semi-auto pistols, bolt action and slide action rifles, as well as military arms for South African law enforcement for quite some time.

PISTOLS: SEMI-AUTO

All Vektor pistols feature polygonal rifling, excluding the Z88.

MODEL CP1 - 9mm Para. cal., 4 in. barrel, compact model with unique aesthetics and ergonomic design allowing no buttons or levers on exterior surfaces, hammerless, striker firing system, black or nickel finished slide, 10 shot mag., approx. 25 1/2 oz. Imported 1999-disc.

	$440	$400	$360	$330	$300	$280	$260

Last MSR was $480.

Add $20 for nickel slide finish.
This model was recalled due to design problems.

GRADING - PPGS™	100%	98%	95%	90%	80%	70%	60%

MODEL Z88 - 9mm Para. cal., double action, patterned after the M92 Beretta, 5 in. barrel, steel construction, black synthetic grips, 10 shot mag., 35 oz. Importation began 1999.

	$550	$495	$450	$400	$360	$330	$295

Last MSR was $620.

MODEL SP1 - 9mm Para. cal., double action, 5 in. barrel with polygonal rifling, wraparound checkered synthetic grips, matte blue or normal black finish, 2.2. lbs. Importation began 1999.

	$535	$485	$445	$395	$360	$330	$295

Last MSR was $600.

Add $30 for natural anodized or nickel finish.
Add $230 for Sport Pistol with compensated barrel.

✻ *Model SP1 Compact (General's Model)* - similar to Model SP1, except is compact variation with 4 in. barrel, 25.4 oz. Importation began 1999.

	$575	$510	$460	$410	$360	$330	$295

Last MSR was $650.

✻ *Model SP1 Sport Pistol/Tuned* - similar to Model SP1, except has is available with tuned action or target pistol features. Importation began 1999.

	$1,050	$900	$775	$650	$525	$400	$350

Last MSR was $1,200.

Add $100 for Target Pistol with dual color finish.

MODEL SP2 - .40 S&W cal., otherwise similar to Model SP1. Importation began in 1999.

	$575	$510	$460	$410	$360	$330	$295

Last MSR was $650.

Add $190 for 9mm Para. conversion kit.

✻ *Model SP2 Compact (General's Model)* - similar to Model SP2, except is compact variation. Importation began 1999.

	$575	$510	$460	$410	$360	$330	$295

Last MSR was $650.

✻ *Model SP2 Competition* - competition variation of the Model SP2 featuring 5 7/8 in. barrel, additional magazine guide, enlarged safety levers and mag. catch, and straight trigger, 35 oz. Importation began 2000.

	$850	$775	$675	$575	$510	$460	$395

Last MSR was $1,000.

STOCK GUN - 9mm Para. cal., normal black finish. Importation began 2000.

	$850	$775	$675	$575	$510	$460	$395

Last MSR was $1,000.

ULTRA MODEL - 9mm Para. or .40 S&W (new 2000) cal., top-of-the-line double action with most performance features, optional Lynx (disc. 1999) or Tasco (new 2000) scope. Importation began 1999.

	$1,950	$1,700	$1,500	$1,300	$1,100	$900	$700

Last MSR was $2,150.

Subtract $150 if w/o Tasco scope.

RIFLES: BOLT-ACTION

K98 - standard cals are .243 Win., .270 Win., .30-06, .308 Win., 7x57mm Mauser, 7x64 Bren., Mag. cals. include .300 Win. Mag., .300 H&H, .416 Rigby, .470 Capstick, .458 Win. Mag., or 9.3x62mm, 5 shot staggered mag., non-rotating long extractor, positive bolt stop, checkered walnut stock, hammer forged barrel, iron sights on Mag. cals. only. Importation began 2000.

MSR N/A	$995	$850	$775	$675	$575	$510	$460

Last MSR was $1,149.

Add $100 for Mag. cals.

GRADING - PPGS™	100%	98%	95%	90%	80%	70%	60%

RIFLES: SLIDE ACTION

H5 - .223 Rem. cal., 18 or 22 in. barrel, rotating bolt, uncheckered forearm and thumb-hole stock with pad, includes 4X scope with long eye relief, 9 lbs., 7 oz.-10 1/4 lbs. Importation began 2000.

MSR N/A	$775	$650	$575	$510	$460	$410	$350

Last MSR was $850.

VEPR. RIFLES

Currently manufactured by Molot JSC (Vyatskie Polyany Machine Building Factory) located in Russia. Currently imported by ZDF Import/Export, Inc., located in Salt Lake City, UT. Previously imported during 2004 by European American Armory, located in Sharps, FL.

RIFLES: SEMI-AUTO

VEPR HUNTER (VEPR II) CARBINE/RIFLE - .223 Rem., .270 Win. (new 2004), .30-06 (new 2004), .308 Win., or 7.62x39mm (new 2001) cal., features Vepr.'s semi-auto action, 16 (.223 Rem. or 7.62x39mm cal.), 20 1/2 (carbine, .308 Win. only, disc.), 21.6 or 23 1/4 (disc.) in. barrel with adj. rear sight, scope mount rail built into receiver top, standard or optional thumbhole checkered walnut stock with recoil pad and forend, paddle mag. release, 5 or 10 shot mag., approx 8.6 lbs.

MSR N/A	$1,000	$850	$675	$475	$375	$325	$275

SUPER VEPR - .308 Win. cal., thumbhole stock. Limited importation 2001-2007.

Last 100% value on this gun was $950.

VERNEY-CARRON

Current manufacturer of shotguns and rifles established during 1820, and located in St. Etienne, France. Currently imported by Verney-Carron USA, Inc., located in Clay Center, KS. Previously distributed until 2002 by the Graystone Group, located in Chicago, IL. Previously imported by Yellow Brick Entreprises, located in Clay Center, KS during 1998 only.

VERNEY-CARRON HISTORY

The company was established during 1820 by Claude Verney-Carron, whose ancestors were "Faiseur de fusils" - gunmakers since at least 1650. Verney-Carron is proud to reflect on six generations of family ownership, and is the largest French manufacturer of hunting shotguns and rifles. Please contact the manufacturer directly for more information, including current model availability and domestic pricing regarding these fine firearms (see Trademark Index).

In 2000, Verney-Carron SA and Y.B.E., Inc. located in Clay Center, KS (distributor of Hastings barrels & choke tubes) established a joint venture, Verney-Carron USA, Inc., located in Clay Center, KS. This joint venture purchased Sporting Arms Manufacturing, Inc., the manufacturer of the Snake Charmer II shotgun. During 2001, Sporting Arms Manufacturing was dissolved, and the Snake Charmer II is now manufactured by Verney-Carron USA, Inc. Please refer to the separate Snake Charmer listing.

In 2002, Verney-Carron SA established, with Club Interchasse SAS another joint venture, Ligne Verney-Carron SAS, located in Bourges, France to develop and sell hunting clothes and accessories.

In 2004, Verney-Carron SA purchased 100% of Ets. Demas SAS (please refer to the seperate Demas listing) maker of fine handcrafted shotguns and double rifles (SxS or O/U).

RIFLES

Current models include the Sagittaire O/U (with or w/o sideplates, not imported), the Impact Plus bolt action with vent. quarter rib, front and rear sight ($2,100 MSR), Impact Plus take-down ($2,700 MSR), Azur boxlock SxS double rifle in .470 NE ($12,250 MSR), AD110 combination gun (20 ga./.300 Win. mag., $7,650 MSR), as well as the semi-auto Impact NT Rifle (approx. $1,600). All of these rifles are currently equipped for the easy mounting of an Optimum Infallible sight system.

GRADING - PPGS™	100%	98%	95%	90%	80%	70%	60%

SHOTGUNS

Verney-Carron makes a wide variety of shotgun models and configurations, including the Super 9 O/U (with or w/o sideplates, many options are available, base price is $3,300), Sagittaire O/U ($1,235 MSR), V12 semi-auto (not imported), AD210 20 ga. SxS ($8,250 MSR), 1050 Atelier ($8,576 MSR), Sagittaire Polynox O/U 12 ga. Mag. ($1,935 MSR), Sagittaire Hastings 20 ga. O/U ($1,700 MSR), and the J.E.T. SxS (not imported).

VERONA

Previous trademark of shotguns manufactured by F.A.I.R., located in Brescia, Italy. Previously imported until late 2005 by B.C. Outdoors, located in Boulder City, NV.

COMBINATION GUNS

LX1001 EXPRESS COMBO - .223 Rem., .243 Win., .270 Win., .30-06. or .308 Win. over 20 ga., 2 3/4 in. chambers, 26 in. barrels, vent. rib, ejectors, sling swivel, checkered oil finished walnut stock with Bavarian cheekpiece, includes screw chokes, leather canvas hard case, approx. 6 lbs.

$2,250	$1,900	$1,500	$1,200	$975	$875	$800

Last MSR was $2,583.

SHOTGUNS: O/U

LX501 HUNTING MODEL - 12, 20, 28 ga. or .410 bore, 2 3/4 (28 ga.) or 3 in. chambers, 28 in. barrels, gold plated SST, ejectors, blue steel receiver with light engraving, checkered walnut stock, black rubber recoil pad, 6-7 lbs.

$725	$650	$575	$525	$475	$425	$375

Last MSR was $791.

Add $44 for 28 ga. or $23 for .410 bore.

✱ *LX501 Hunting Model Two Barrel Set* - includes choice of 20 and 28 ga., or 28 ga. and .410 bore, 28 in. barrels. Imported 2002-2005.

$1,200	$1,050	$925	$850	$775	$700	$625

Last MSR was $1,379.

LX680 SERIES - 12 or 20 ga., 2 3/4 or 3 in. chambers, available in Sporting or Trap configuration, 29, 30, 32, or 34 in. ported or unported barrels, Interchokes, available in Sporting Clays, Skeet, or Competition Trap configurations, gold SST, silver alloy receiver with light engraving, vent. rib, adj. comb, 6 1/4-8 lbs.

$925	$825	$725	$650	$575	$500	$450

Last MSR was $1,043.

Add $468 for Gold Trap configuration.
Add $1,222 for Gold Trap combo.

LX692 SERIES - 12, 20, 28 ga. or .410 bore, 2 3/4 (28 ga.) or 3 in. chambers, available in Skeet, Sporting, or Trap configuration, 28 in. barrels, gold plated SST, ejectors, steel receiver with engraved sideplates and gold bird inlays, oil finished hand-checkered walnut stock and Schnabel forend, black rubber recoil pad, 6-7 lbs.

$925	$825	$725	$650	$575	$500	$450

Last MSR was $1,043.

Add $468 for Gold Trap configuration.
Add $1,222 for Gold Trap combo.

LX702 SERIES - 12 or 20 ga., 3 in. chambers, available in Skeet, Sporting, or Trap configuration, 28 in. barrels, hand-rubbed Turkish walnut stock and forend, color case hardened receiver and sideplates, engraving with gold inlaid bird hunting scenes, 6-7 lbs.

$1,300	$1,100	$900	$775	$650	$575	$500

Last MSR was $1,447.

GRADING - PPGS™	100%	98%	95%	90%	80%	70%	60%

LX980 SERIES - 12 ga., 2 3/4 in. chambers, available in Trap, Skeet or Sporting configuration, 30 or 32 in. ported barrels, oil finished Montecarlo Turkish walnut stock and forend with adj. comb, color case hardened receiver, wide competition rib, removable competition trigger assembly, includes deluxe case, 7 1/2 lbs.

		$3,150	$2,700	$2,325	$2,000	$1,650	$1,325	$1,175

Last MSR was $3,527.

Add $249 for Gold Competition Skeet or Trap configuration.

SHOTGUNS: SEMI-AUTO

SX401 HUNTING SERIES - 12 ga. only, 3 in. chamber, 28 in. barrel, 5 shot mag., Turkish walnut stock, lightweight aluminum aircraft alloy receiver, sling swivels, approx. 6 3/4 lbs.

$375	$335	$300	$275	$250	$225	$200

Last MSR was $427.

SX405 HUNTING SERIES - 12 ga. only, 3 in. chamber, 22, 24, 26, or 28 in. barrel, 5 shot mag., black synthetic, Realtree Wetland or Hardwood camo finished stock, lightweight aluminum aircraft alloy receiver, sling swivels, approx. 6 1/2 lbs.

$315	$285	$265	$245	$225	$200	$175

Last MSR was $352.

Add $88 for camo finish.
Add $138 for 22 in. slug barrel.
Subtract $17 for 26 in. barrel.

✻ *SX405 Hunting Series Combo* - includes 22 in. slug and 26 in. barrels.

$450	$400	$360	$330	$300	$275	$250

Last MSR was $503.

SX801 SERIES - 12 ga. only, 2 3/4 in. chamber, 28 or 30 in. ported barrel, available in Sporting or Gold Sporting configuration, vent. rib, Hi-Viz front sight, black anodized receiver, gold trigger, includes four extended Trulock chokes, oil finished Turkish Montecarlo stock, approx. 6 3/4 lbs.

$775	$700	$625	$550	$500	$450	$395

Last MSR was $868.

Add $197 for Gold Sporting model with adj. comb.

VICKERS LIMITED

Previous manufacturer located in Crayford/Kent, England.

RIFLES: SINGLE SHOT, TARGET

JUBILEE SINGLE SHOT TARGET RIFLE - Martini type action, .22 LR cal., 28 in. heavy barrel, target sights, one-piece pistol grip, target stock, pre-WWII.

$440	$330	$305	$275	$250	$220	$165

EMPIRE MODEL - similar to Jubilee, with 27 or 30 in. barrel, straight grip stock.

$415	$310	$285	$260	$220	$195	$150

VICTOR ARMS CORPORATION

Previous manufacturer located in Houston, TX.

Victor Arms Corporation manufactured limited quantities of a .22 LR upper unit for the AR-15. It works by removing the standard .223 upper, and replacing it with the V22 upper assembly and magazine. Additionally, a complete protoype gun was also manufactured.

VICTORY ARMS CO. LIMITED

Previously manufactured in prototype format only by Modern Manufacturing Company located in Phoenix, AZ.

PISTOL: SEMI-AUTO

MODEL MC5 - while a few prototypes were mfg. for trade shows (circa 1991-92), this model was never commercially manufactured. Last advertised retail was $465.

VIERLINGS

The German word Vierling denotes a four barrel long arm configuration mostly manufactured in Germany and Austria.

This configuration of long arm has four barrels, usually a mixture of centerfire/rimfire caliber barrel(s) and shotgun barrel(s). Some Vierlings may also have all-shotgun barrels or all-rifle barrels (rare). Vierlings typically have two triggers, both single-set. Barrel selectors are usually on the top tang. In order to reduce weight, quite a few have actions made from high grade aluminum with steel reinforcements in critical areas. This unusual configuration is mostly of German mfg., although there are a few Austrian specimens also (the gunmakers of Ferlach still custom-make this model). All Vierlings are mfg. one at a time, with fabrication being very complicated, lengthy, and expensive. Perhaps the most rare Vierling configuration is a gun with four shotgun barrels. As a result, every Vierling must be appraised individually - most older manufactured specimens, however, are priced in the $4,500-$10,000 range, depending on the desirability of the configuration, and overall condition. Recently and currently manufactured special order Vierlings are priced from $8,500-$40,000 range, depending on features, engraving, and other options.

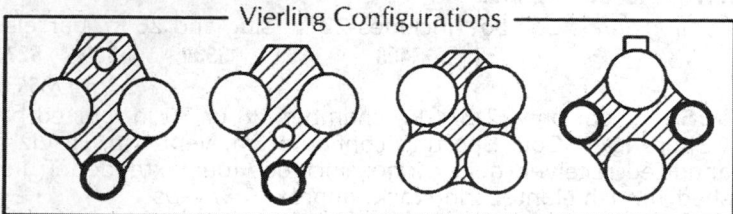

Vierling Configurations

VI-MA SNC.

Current rifle and shotguns manufacturer located in Brescia, Italy. No current U.S. importation.

Vi-Ma manufactures a high quality single shot boxlock rifle with unique sliding breech, available in various cals between .222 Rem. - .375 H&H. Three variations are available, and include the Pegaso, Pegaso L and Pegaso XL. Vi-Ma also manufactured a line of shotguns. Please contact the company directly for more information, including pricing and U.S. availability (see Trademark Index).

VIRGIN VALLEY CUSTOM GUNS

Previous manufacturer of custom bolt action rifles located in Hurricane, UT until 2005.

RIFLES: BOLT ACTION

Virgin Valley offered custom barrels, stocks, wildcat chamberings, and many other options and riflesmithing services.

SAFARI RIFLE - various big game cals., choice of Dakota Mod. 76, Mauser, or Win. Mod. 70 action, individually custom ordered.

VIRGINIAN

This trademark can be located under the Interarms section in this text.

VIS

Currently manufactured by the F.B. Radom arsenal in Radom, Poland. Please refer to the Radom section in this text.

VOERE (AUSTRIA)

Current manufacturer established during 1965, and located in Kufstein, Austria. No current U.S. importation.

Voere of Austria is not associated with the Voere trademark of Germany which was taken over by Mauser-Werke after going bankrupt. Voere manufactures a complete line of quality rimfire semi-auto and centerfire bolt-action/semi-auto rifles. Their caseless ammunition released in 1991 was a unique step in the development of ammunition. More information on this trademark, including current models, U.S. availability, and U.S. pricing, can be obtained by contacting the company directly (see Trademark Index for information).

RIFLES

Values listed below are in euros, w/o tax.

MODEL K98 VOERE-KESSLER BOLT ACTION - various cals., Mauser 98 action, wing type, 3 position or cocking safety, 21 1/2 in. barrel, select hand-checkered walnut stock with bavarian cheekpiece, rosewood pistol grip cap. New 2004.

> The current European MSR on this model is €2780.

MODEL VEC 91 BOLT ACTION - 5.7 UCC or 6mm UCC caseless ammo, unique ignition system requires electrical impulse to activate semi-conducting primer that ignites propellant (2 small batteries are housed in the pistol grip capable of igniting 5,000 shots), 5 shot detachable mag., 20 in. free floating barrel, twin forward locking lugs, 2-stage electrical trigger adj. from 1/2 oz. to 7 lbs, 55 grain bullet achieves 3,300 fps with no loss in accuracy over normal mechanical primer ignited cartridges, 6 lbs. New 1992.

> The current European MSR on this model is €2,388.

Unfortunately, BATF import certificates have made it very expensive to bring UCC caseless ammunition in small quantities into this country. This model is currently being distributed in Europe and other countries.

MODEL 20-02 XXL BOLT ACTION - various dangerous game cals., Magnum action, two locking lugs, checkered high grade walnut stock, iron sights, approx. 8 lbs. New 2003.

> The current European MSR on this model is €6,400 for the base model.

MODEL 20-03 LBW BOLT ACTION - various cals., interchangeable barrels, three lug fluted bolt, uncocking safety, walnut or rubber coated stock, 6 1/2 lbs. New 2003.

> The current European MSR on this model is € 950 for the base model, €1,300 for the Luxus model, and €2,200 for the Deluxe Takedown.

MODEL 2155 BOLT ACTION - various cals., K-98 Mauser action, 20 in. barrel, tang safety, no sights.

> The current MSR on this model is €750 for the base model.
> Add €59 for Mag. cals. (7mm Rem. Mag. or .300 Win. Mag.).

MODEL 2165 BOLT ACTION DELUXE - same cals. as Model 2155, European traditional style K-98 Mauser bolt action, 22 in. barrel, detachable 5 shot mag., hand-checkered deluxe walnut.

> The current European MSR on this model is €1,069.
> Add €59 for Mag. cals. (24 in. barrel).

MODEL 2185 SERIES MATCH/SPORTER SEMI-AUTO - .30-06, .308 Win. or 7x64mm cal., gas operated, free-floating barrel, 3 or 5 shot detachable mag., manual safety, iron sights, laminate wood, 11 lbs.

> The current European MSR on this model is €3,349.
> Add $1,500 for position style rifle (includes adj. cheekpiece, buttplate, and bottom sling rail, and Voere special scope base).

Other calibers are available on special order only. Sporter model has adj. aperture rear sight with post front sight.

GRADING - PPGS™	100%	98%	95%	90%	80%	70%	60%

MODEL 2185 SEMI-AUTO HUNTING RIFLE - 9.3x62mm, other cals. available upon special request, checkered stock and forend, iron sights.

> The current European MSR on this model is €1,740.
> Add €61 for Mannlicher full stock with 20 in. carbine barrel.
> Add €87 for Europe model with hinged bottom plate.

AMERICAN CUSTOM CLASSIC BOLT ACTION - .22-250 Rem., .243 Win., .270 Win., 7x57mm, 7x64mm, .30-06, or .308 Win. cal., K-98 Mauser action, 3 position safety, hinged floorplate, deluxe walnut with hand-rubbed oil finish and checkering. Mfg. 1996 only.

	$1,575	$1,450	$1,300	$1,150	$995	$850	$675

Last MSR was $1,795.

> Add $50 for Mag. cals. (.300 Win. Mag., .338 Win. Mag., 7mm Rem. Mag., or 9.3x64mm).
> Add $100 for .375 H&H or .458 Win. Mag. cal.

.22 SEMI-AUTO - .22 LR cal., open (disc.) or closed bolt design, 10 shot mag., checkered hardwood stock, adj. rear sight and trigger. Limited importation.

	$585	$535	$460	$400	$350	$300	$250

Last MSR was $645.

> Add $50 for Deluxe Model.

VOERE (GERMAN)

Previous manufacturer located in Vohrenvach, Germany. Voere was absorbed by Mauser-Werke circa 1986, and most of the company machinery was moved to Oberndorf during that time. Voere of Germany should not be confused with the current Austrian firm of the same name.

Voere of Germany manufactured a wide variety of rifles in many configurations, including both bolt action and semi-auto (closed and open bolt) .22 cal. rifles. Bolt action centerfire rifles were also produced in many styles and calibers, including some private label contracts with such firms as Shikar, Frankonia, Akah, and others. While not considered as highly collectible today, most German Voere rifles were noted for their quality craftsmanship and above-average accuracy. Secondary values today depend on the desirability of the rifle configuration (stock design, finish, caliber, etc.) and original condition, but most .22 cal. rifles sell in the $125 - $300 range, while centerfire rifles are typically priced in the $225 - $375 range, if complete with magazines.

VOLQUARTSEN CUSTOM, LTD.

Current pistol and rifle customizer and manufacturer located in Carroll, IA. Dealer sales.

PISTOLS: SEMI-AUTO, CONVERSION

Volquartsen manufactures a wide variety of custom pistols based on the Ruger Mark II and III action. Prices range from $799 - $1,256, depending on the configuration. Please contact the company directly for more information on these conversions.

CHEETAH - .17 HMR, .17 Mach 2 (disc. 2005), .22 LR, or .22 Mag. cal., titanium 7 in. (.22 LR cal. only) or 10 in. barrel, 9 or 10 shot mag., synthetic finger groove stock with ambidextrous grip, CNC aluminum frame, Weaver style mount, available with black, blue, red, green, or silver stock, 46 oz. Mfg. 2003-2006.

	$875	$775	$700	$625	$575	$525	$475

Last MSR was $972.

PREDATOR - .17 HMR or .22 Mag. cal., choice of brown laminate wood grips (disc. 2006) or black McMillan grips, 12 in. stainless steel bull barrel, wedge locking block system, includes scope mount. New 2005.

MSR $1,353	$1,175	$950	$850	$750	$675	$625	$550

> Add $220 for barrel only.
> Subtract approx. $300 if w/o black McMillan grips (became standard 2007).

GRADING - PPGS™	100%	98%	95%	90%	80%	70%	60%

RIFLES: SEMI-AUTO

Current Volquartsen stock configurations include: brown synthetic, grey synthetic, Hogue, McMillan Sporter, and McMillan thumbhole stock. Base values below represent standard Hogue synthetic stock.

Add approx. $97 for grey/brown synthetic stock.
Add approx. $404 for McMillan Sport or thumbhole stock on the models listed below.

STANDARD 17 HMR - .17 HMR cal., similar to Standard 22 LR, similar configurations as the .22 Mag model, 18 1/2 (standard) or 20 in. fluted and compensated stainless steel bull barrel.

MSR $1,167	$1,025	$885	$775	$675	$575	$500	$400

Add $70 for Deluxe model with Hogue stock.
Add $10 for Lightweight model.
Add $107 for radial flute or Snake model.
Add $300 for VX5000 Lightweight.
Add $658 for VG-1 model with fluted and compensated barrel.

STANDARD 17 MACH 2 - .17 Mach 2 cal., otherwise similar to Standard 17 HMR. New 2006.

MSR $1,077	$950	$850	$735	$650	$550	$450	$350

Add $88 for Deluxe model with Hogue stock.
Add $7 for Lightweight model.
Subtract $29 for Super Lightweight.
Add $177 for Snake model.
Add $319 for VX5000 Lightweight.

STANDARD 22 LR - .22 LR cal., similar to .22 Mag., stainless steel receiver, available in same configurations as .22 Mag, except not available in VG-1 or radial flute versions

MSR $1,029	$925	$825	$725	$650	$550	$450	$350

Add $95 for Deluxe or $8 for Lightweight model with Hogue stock.
Add $163 for Snake model.
Add $351 for VX5000 Lightweight.

STANDARD 22 MAG. - .22 Mag. cal., choice of standard (18 1/2 in. stainless steel), deluxe (20 in. fluted), or lightweight (16 1/2 in. aluminum) barrel, Monte Carlo laminated wood or Hogue Overmolded composite stock, available in Standard, Lightweight, Snake, radial flute, Deluxe, Signature Series (top-of-the-line), VG-1, and VX5000 models. approx. 7 1/2 lbs.

MSR $1,167	$1,025	$885	$775	$675	$575	$500	$400

Add $70 for Deluxe model with Hogue stock.
Add $10 for Lightweight model.
Add $107 for radial flute or Snake model.
Add $300 for VX5000 Lightweight.
Add $658 for VG-1 model with fluted and compensated barrel.

SIGNATURE SERIES - .17 HMR or .22 Mag. cal., top-of-the-line model, many options are available.

MSR $3,716	$3,400	$3,025	$2,600	$2,300	$1,925	$1,675	$1,350

FUSION TAKE DOWN MODEL - .17 HMR or .22 Mag. cal., features interchangeable barrels from/to .17 HMR and .22 Mag. cals., black finished alloy receiver, 18 3/8 in. barrel with muzzle brake, Picatinny rails on top of receiver and bottom of barrel shroud, 9 shot rotary mag., 6 1/2 lbs. Limited mfg. 2004, reintroduced 2006.

MSR $1,489	$1,325	$1,100	$900	$775	$650	$550	$450

Add $281 for barrel only.

EVOLUTION MODEL - .204 Ruger or .223 Rem. cal., gas operated, stainless steel receiver with Picatinny scope mount system machined into top of receiver, trigger guard and bolt, brown laminate stock with extended Monte Carlo checekpiece, 20 in. standard barrel, 10 shot AR-15 style mag., 10 lbs. New 2005.

MSR $2,117	$1,925	$1,600	$1,300	$1,050	$875	$725	$650

GRADING - PPGS™	100%	98%	95%	90%	80%	70%	60%

VOLUNTEER ENTERPRISES

Previous manufacturer located in Knoxville, TN.

Volunteer Enterprises became Commando Arms after 1978.

CARBINES

COMMANDO MARK III CARBINE - .45 ACP cal., semi-auto, blowback action, 16 1/2 in. barrel, aperture sight, stock styled after the Auto-Ordnance "Tommy Gun." Mfg. 1969-1976.

	$425	$365	$315	$280	$225	$195	$160
Vertical grip	$440	$365	$320	$280	$225	$195	$160

COMMANDO MARK 9 - similar to Mark III in 9mm Para. cal.

	$440	$375	$325	$285	$230	$195	$160
Vertical grip	$440	$365	$320	$280	$225	$195	$160

VOUZELAUD

Previous manufacturer located in France. Previously imported by Waverly Arms Co. located in Suffolk, VA.

SHOTGUNS: SxS

MODEL 315 E - 12, 16 or 20 ga., boxlock, 28 in. barrels, auto ejectors, straight grip French walnut stock, double triggers, case colored receiver, light engraving. Importation disc. 1987.

Values generally range between $1,350-$2,000 for this model.

MODEL 315 EL - similar to Model 315 E, except has satin finish receiver engraved with bouquets of fine English scrollwork, trigger guard and forearm also engraved. Importation disc. 1987.

Add $600 for 28 ga. or .410 bore (Model 315 EL-S, special order only).

Values generally range between $1,475-$2,250 for this model.

MODEL 315 EG - 12, 16 or 20 ga., sidelock, 28 in. barrels, selective ejectors, double triggers, extensive scroll engraving on coin finish receiver, English style stock of extra fancy French walnut. Importation disc. 1987.

Values generally range between $1,750-$2,750 for this model.

MODEL 315 EGL-S - same general features as the Model 315 EGL, except monobloc barrel construction, extensive game scene engraving, and grand deluxe walnut stock and forearm with extra fine hand-checkering. Importation disc. 1987.

Last MSR was $5,895.

Values generally range between $1,950-$2,950 for this model.

VULCAN ARMAMENT, INC.

Current rifle manufacturer established in 2003 and located in Inver Grove Heights, MN.

RIFLES

Vulcan Arms makes a wide variety of bolt action and AR-15 styled semi-auto rifles, including configurations for military and law enforcement. Please contact the factory directly for more information, including a listing of various configurations, options, and availability (see Trademark Index).

W SECTION

WAFFENFABRIK HEIN

Current bolt action rifle manufacturer located in Tekoa, WA.

RIFLES

Hein is known for its N-Series rifle action. Current bolt action rifles include Palouse Custom Trophy ($2,900 MSR) and the Palouse Custom Classic ($4,700 MSR). A single shot rifle, the Model C-97 is POR. Please contact the company directly for more information, including availability and delivery time (see Trademark Index).

WAFFENSTUBE GUGGI

Current long gun manufacturer and custom order stock carver established during 1981, and located in Graz, Austria. No current U.S. importation.

Waffenstube Guggi manufactures custom order sidelock combination guns, single barrel and SxS rifles, bolt action rifles, and shotguns. They also perform outstanding stock carving and checkering services. Please contact the company directly for more information and an individual price quotation (see Trademark Index).

WAFFEN GLATZ

Current manufacturer located in Erlendorf, Austria.

Johann Glatz manufactures high quality rifles, including a stalking rifle, a bolt action, and a drilling. All guns are custom order. Please contact him directly for an individualized price quotation (see Trademark Index).

WAFFEN JUNG GMBH

Current rifle manufacturer located in Lohmar, Germany. No current U.S. importation.

Waffen Jung GmbH manufactures a high quality Stutzen style Rominten edition bolt action rifle, in addition to a takedown model, Mauser sporter, and Mauser Magnum sporter bolt action rifles. All guns are custom order. Please contact the company directly for more information, including U.S. availability.

WAFFEN VERATSCHNIG

Previous manufacturer located in Ferlach, Austria.

Waffen Veratschnig manufactured a variety of high grade, made to individual special order rifles, shotguns, combination guns, drillings, and vierlings. A wide variety of engraving scenes, wood carvings, and other special features were available at extra cost. Very few models were actually imported into the U.S.

WALTHER

Current manufacturer located in Ulm, Germany, 1953 to date. Currently imported and distributed beginning 2002 by Smith & Wesson, located in Springfield, MA. Walther target pistols and target rifles are distributed by Champions Choice  located in La Vergne, TN. Some target, competiton and service pistols were also imported by Earl's Repair Service, Inc., located in Tewksbury, MA. Previously imported and distributed 1998-2001 by Walther USA LLC, located in Springfield, MA, and by Interarms located in Alexandria, VA. Previously manufactured in Zella-Mehlis, Germany 1886 to 1945. Walther was sold to Umarex Sportwaffen GmbH circa 1994, and company headquarters are located in Arnsberg, Germany.

The calibers listed in the Walther Pistol sections are listed in American caliber designations. The German metric conversion is as follows: .22 LR - 5.6mm, .25 ACP - 6.35mm, .32 ACP - 7.65mm, and .380 ACP - 9mm kurz. The metric caliber designations in most cases will be indicated on the left slide legend for German mfg. pistols listed in the Walther section.

For more information and current pricing on both new and used Walther airguns, please refer to the *Blue Book of Airguns* by Dr. Robert Beeman & John Allen (also online).

GRADING - PPGS™	100%	98%	95%	90%	80%	70%	60%

PISTOLS: SEMI-AUTO, PRE-WAR

MODEL 1 - .25 ACP cal., 2.1 in. barrel, fixed sights, blue, checkered hard rubber grips, pre-WWI, 13.1 oz. Mfg. 1908-1909.

	100%	98%	95%	90%	80%	70%	60%
	$750	$650	$550	$450	$350	$250	$200

MODEL 2 - .25 ACP cal., 2.1 in. barrel, fixed sights, blue, hard rubber grips, pop-up rear sight on early models, fixed on late models, 9 3/4 oz. Mfg. 1902-1909.

	$600	$500	$400	$275	$185	$135	$125

This model can usually be distinguished by its knurled barrel ring.

✳ *Model 2 Early* - differentiated by its pop-up rear sight.

	$1,500	$1,250	$1,000	$750	$675	$550	$425

Beware of fakes!

MODEL 3 - .32 ACP cal., 2.6 in. barrel, blue, fixed sights, hard rubber grips, ejection port on left side, 16 1/2 oz. Mfg. 1910-1913.

	$3,000	$2,500	$2,000	$1,500	$1,000	$750	$500

MODEL 4 - .32 ACP cal., 8 shot, 3 1/2 in. barrel, blue, hard rubber grips, ejection port on left side, 19.4 oz. Mfg. 1910-28.

	$500	$400	$325	$250	$200	$150	$100

Add 10% for WWI "Eagle" proofs.

MODEL 5 - better quality version of Model 2, fixed rear sight, 9.71 oz. Mfg. 1913-1915.

	$600	$500	$400	$275	$145	$135	$125

MODEL 6 - 9mm Para. cal., 4 7/8 in. barrel, blue, hard rubber grips, ejection port on right side, 34 oz. Approx. 1,000 mfg. 1915-17. Some are Imperial proofed.

	$8,500	$6,500	$5,500	$4,000	$3,000	$2,500	$2,000

MODEL 7 - .25 ACP cal., 3 in. barrel, blue, fixed sights, hard rubber grips, ejection port on right side, 12 oz. Mfg. 1917-18.

	$675	$550	$465	$385	$285	$200	$125

MODEL 8 - .25 ACP cal., 2 7/8 in. barrel, blue or nickel finish, fixed sights, black checkered plastic grips with round medallions, 12.7 oz. Mfg. 1920-43.

	$700	$575	$475	$325	$240	$150	$125

Add 25% for nickel.
Add 10% for "Eagle N" proofing.
Add 25% for engraved slide.

MODEL 9 VEST POCKET - .25 ACP cal., engineering revision of Model 1, 2 in. barrel, blue finish standard, upward ejection, 6 shot bottom release mag., fixed sights, black checkered plastic grips with round medallions, safety lever on left frame side behind trigger, 9 oz. Mfg. 1921-45.

	$650	$575	$495	$395	$285	$160	$140

Add 40% for engraved slide, 20% for nickel.
Add 10% for "Eagle N" proofing.

MODEL PP DOUBLE ACTION - .22 LR, .25 ACP, .32 ACP, or .380 ACP cal., PP designates "Polizei Pistole," 3 7/8 in. barrel, blue, fixed sights, plastic grips. Mfg. 1929-1945. Crown N proof until 1939. Eagle N Nazi commercial proof until 1945.

	100%	98%	95%	90%	80%	70%	60%
.22 LR cal.	$1,200	$975	$800	$675	$550	$450	$375
.25 ACP cal.	$3,750	$3,225	$2,75	$2,10	$1,600	$1,300	$1,075
.32 ACP cal.	$700	$600	$450	$375	$275	$225	$200
.380 ACP cal.	$1,350	$1,075	$80	$700	$600	$550	$500

Add 15% for alloy frame.

Original nickel finished Model PPs are very rare; this precludes accurate price evaluation. Values assume original guns without import markings. Recently imported WWII/surplus police used guns are stamped on the frame or receiver, indicating the current importer and address - subtract 20%-30% from values listed for these recent imports.

GRADING - PPGS™	100%	98%	95%	90%	80%	70%	60%

✳ *Model PP .32 ACP Bottom Release Magazine* - safety rotates 90 degrees.

	$1,500	$1,200	$800	$650	$550	$425	$395

✳ *Model PP .380 ACP Bottom Release Magazine* - safety rotates 90 degrees.

	$1,950	$1,650	$1,250	$900	$700	$600	$500

✳ *Model PP Pre-War Persian Proofed* - 9mm kurz BMR.

	$2,000	$1,800	$1,600	$1,450	$1,250	$995	$825

Subtract 75% for recent imports which have been relisted.

✳ *Model PP Pre-War Verchromt* -.32 ACP cal. or .380 ACP cal.

	$2,500	$1,850	$1,400	$1,200	$800	$700	$600

Add 50% for .380 ACP cal.

✳ *Model PP Pre-War Stoeger* - .32 ACP cal. only.

	$2,000	$1,450	$1,000	$750	$675	$525	$400

✳ *Model PP Nairobi* - Chas. Heyer.

	$1,800	$1,450	$1,000	$750	$675	$525	$400

✳ *Model PP Aluminum Frame* - safety rotates 90 degrees.

	$795	$675	$525	$400	$275	$235	$200

✳ *Model PP Allemagne* - French Comm.

	$1,400	$1,075	$825	$720	$600	$425	$325

MODEL PP WARTIME PRODUCTION - mfg. 1940-1945, "Eagle N" Proof (Nazi commercial nitro proof after April 1940) or "Crown N" proof (German commercial proofmark used until April, 1940) found on pre-WWII military production. Variations are listed either by proofmarks or frame/slide markings.

✳ *Model PP "Waffenamt" Proofed* - .32 ACP or .380 ACP cal., "Eagle N," military acceptance marking.

	100%	98%	95%	90%	80%	70%	60%
.32 ACP cal. Milled finish	$750	$625	$450	$350	$250	$220	$200
.380 ACP cal.	$2,500	$2,000	$1,000	$700	$600	$550	$500

Add 25%-50% if Waffenamt proofed, depending on condition (late war PPs are sometimes encountered with Walther marked beechwood grips).

✳ *Model PP Eagle N Proofed* - .22 LR or .32 ACP cal., with lanyard loop.

	100%	98%	95%	90%	80%	70%	60%
.32 ACP cal.	$650	$550	$425	$350	$250	$200	$150
.22 LR cal.	$950	$850	$700	$650	$495	$450	$395

Add 50% to .32 ACP cal., Waffenamt proofed PPs that are hi-gloss finish (all .380s are hi-gloss).

In most cases, the .380 ACP cal. has the bottom mag. release.

After WWII, the French added a lanyard to the left side of the grip. Subtract 25% for this alteration.

✳ *Model PP Eagle C & F Marked (Nazi Police)* - .32 ACP cal., "Eagle F or C" proofed on left side of frame.

	$850	$725	$650	$525	$450	$380	$300

Add 25% if Eagle C marked. All hi-gloss are early productions.

✳ *Model PP RFV Marked* - .32 ACP cal., "Crown N." Mfg. for "Reichsfinanzverwaltung" Reich Finance Administration.

	$1,100	$850	$650	$500	$400	$325	$225

✳ *Model PP RJ Marked* - .32 ACP cal., "Crown N." Mfg. for "Reichsjustizministerium" Reich Justice Ministry.

	$1,200	$1,000	$800	$500	$450	$325	$225

✳ *Model PP SA Marked* - .22 LR or .32 ACP cal., "Crown N." Mfg. for SA (Sturm Abteilung - group leaders) of the Nazi party.

	$2,500	$1,975	$1,550	$1,200	$900	$600	$425

Add 20% for .22 LR.

Rare SA markings may bring as much as 50% more over values listed.

There are 28 SA groups.

GRADING - PPGS™	100%	98%	95%	90%	80%	70%	60%

✳ *Model PP NSKK Marked* - .32 ACP cal., "Crown N" or "Eagle N" proofed. Mfg. for "National- sozialistischer Kraftfahrkorps" Nazi Party Transport Corps, rare.

	$3,300	$2,250	$1,950	$1,250	$925	$750	$600

✳ *Model PP RRZ Proofed* - .32 ACP cal., mfg. for for "Reichsrundfunkzentrale" Reich Radio Broadcasting - only 3 known.

	$3,700	$3,100	$2,550	$2,450	$2,200	$2,000	$1,850

✳ *Model PP PDM Marked* - .32 ACP cal., "Crown N," for "Polizeidirektion München" Munich Police Department, all have bottom mag. release.

	$1,750	$1,425	$1,050	$700	$550	$450	$400

✳ *Model PP AC Marked* - .32 ACP cal., replaced Walther Banner during 1945, "Eagle N."

	$500	$400	$300	$250	$200	$150	$125

Some are mismatched (assembled at factory by GIs after the factory was captured). Subtract 20% if mismatched.

✳ *Model PP Czech. Contract* - stamped "Rampant Lion".

	$1,125	$900	$800	$700	$600	$500	$400

✳ *Model PP Panagraph Slide*

	$850	$750	$695	$630	$550	$385	$275

✳ *Model PP Danish Rplt.*

	$995	$925	$825	$775	$700	$625	$400

MODEL PP LIGHTWEIGHT - aluminum alloy version.
> Add 20% to Standard Model prices.
> Add 20%-40% for original nickel finish (very rare).
> Add 25% for early hi-gloss finish.

MODEL PPK PRE-WAR PRODUCTION - .22 LR, .25 ACP, .32 ACP, or .380 ACP cal., PPK designates "Polizei Pistole Kriminal," 3 1/4 in. barrel, blue, gold, nickel, or chrome silver, fixed sights, plastic grips. Mfg. 1931-40.

	100%	98%	95%	90%	80%	70%	60%
.22 LR cal.	$2,200	$1,300	$950	$750	$650	$525	$400
.25 ACP cal.	$7,500	$4,550	$3,800	$3,400	$2,800	$2,100	$1,475
.32 ACP cal.	$950	$700	$600	$500	$400	$300	$250
.380 ACP cal.	$4,500	$2,500	$1,750	$1,500	$900	$700	$500

> Add 60% for bottom release mag (.32 ACP cal.).

MODEL PPK WARTIME PRODUCTION - mfg. 1940-1945, "Eagle N" proofed after April 1940, "Crown N" proofs appear on pre-1940 production with frame/slide markings. Variations are listed either by proof-marks, frame/slide markings, or type of finish.

✳ *Model PPK Commercial "Eagle N" Proofed* - .22 LR, .32 ACP, or .380 ACP cal., Nazi Eagle over N (standard Nazi commercial acceptance proof).

	100%	98%	95%	90%	80%	70%	60%
.22 LR cal.	$1,800	$1,300	$900	$750	$525	$460	$420
.32 ACP cal.	$950	$700	$450	$350	$300	$250	$225
.380 ACP cal.	$3,750	$2,900	$2,200	$1,500	$1,000	$750	$550

This variation is normally encountered with semi-polished, exterior metal showing milling marks to various degrees.

✳ *Model PPK Waffenamt Proofed With High Polish*

	$2,000	$1,500	$1,200	$700	$500	$400	$300

✳ *Model PPK Eagle C Marked* - .32 ACP cal., "Crown N - Eagle C," mfg. for Nazi Police.

	$1,400	$1,000	$850	$600	$500	$400	$300

> Add 25% for high polish finish.

GRADING - PPGS™	100%	98%	95%	90%	80%	70%	60%

✳ *Model PPK Eagle F Marked* - .32 ACP cal., "Crown N - Eagle F," Nazi Police, all have the light weight aluminum frame.

	$1,650	$1,200	$900	$650	$500	$400	$300

✳ *Model PPK RZM Marked* - .32 ACP cal., "Crown N," proof-marking for "Reich-szeugmeisterei" Reich Party Purchasing Office.

	$2,500	$1,800	$1,300	$850	$500	$400	$300

✳ *Model PPK Party Leader* - .32 ACP cal., named because grips (brown or black plastic) have the German eagle holding a Swastika, "Crown N" or "Eagle N" proofed, honor weapon awarded 3rd Reich political leaders, rare. Beware of fake grips (especially black color), as reproductions have been made recently. Unfortunately, the grips on a Party Leader (mfg. 1936-41) are the only distinguishing feature on this very desirable configuration.

	$4,750	$3,900	$2,450	$2,000	$1,600	$1,250	$1,000

✳ *Model PPK RZM With Party Leader Grips* - .32 ACP cal., RZM marked, "Crown N" proofed.

	$6,000	$5,000	$3,000	$2,350	$1,650	$1,250	$1,000

✳ *Model PPK RFV Marked* - .32 ACP cal., "Crown N." Mfg. for "Reichsfinanzverwaltung" Reich Finance Administration.

	$1,800	$1,500	$1,000	$750	$800	$700	$675

✳ *Model PPK PDM Marked* - .32 ACP cal., "Crown N." Mfg. for "Polizeidirektion München" Police Dept. Munich. All have the bottom mag. release.

	$2,000	$1,600	$1,100	$800	$600	$500	$395

✳ *Model PPK DRP Marked* - .32 ACP cal., "Crown N." Mfg. for "Deutsche Reichspost" German Postal Service.

	$1,500	$1,200	$1,000	$600	$420	$350	$260

✳ *Model PPK Panagraph Slide*

	$925	$775	$675	$525	$450	$375	$300

✳ *Model PPK Verchromt* - .32 ACP or 380 ACP cal., differentiated by dull silver satin type finish.

	$3,000	$2,500	$2,000	$1,000	$800	$650	$500

Add 50% for .380 ACP cal.

✳ *Model PPK "K" Suffix* - "K" beneath ser. no.

	$1,200	$1,000	$850	$500	$300	$275	$250

✳ *Model PPK "W" Suffix* - .32 ACP cal., "Crown N" proofed, "W" suffix ser. no.

	$850	$650	$475	$375	$300	$275	$250

✳ *Model PPK Early 90 Degree Safety*

	$950	$700	$525	$425	$325	$260	$195

✳ *Model PPK Early Bottom Release Mag.*

	$1,800	$1,500	$1,000	$800	$700	$600	$500

✳ *Model PPK PPK Marked PP*

	$2,650	$2,150	$1,850	$1,600	$1,400	$1,180	$900

✳ *Model PPK 7-Digit Ser. No.*

	$1,200	$1,000	$850	$600	$550	$400	$300

✳ *Model PPK Dural Frame* - .22 LR, .32 ACP, or .380 ACP cal., chrome finish (very rare), "Eagle N."

	$1,200	$900	$700	$525	$400	$325	$275

Add 200% for .380 ACP.
Add 100% for .22 LR cal.
Add 100% for early production with high-gloss finish (brown cast and green cast).

✳ *Model PPK Czech. Contract* - Rampant Lion stamped.

	$1,250	$1,000	$750	$625	$550	$425	$325

GRADING - PPGS™	100%	98%	95%	90%	80%	70%	60%

✳ *Model PPK Danish Rplt.*

	$1,250	$900	$750	$625	$550	$425	$325

✳ *Model PPK Allemagne* - French Commercial - rare.

	$1,500	$1,200	$1,000	$800	$550	$425	$325

MODEL PPK LIGHTWEIGHT - aluminum alloy version.
Add 20% to .32 cal. commercial price listing.

SPORT MODEL 1926 - .22 S or LR cal. (known as Standard Model in Germany).

	$1,275	$975	$850	$725	$600	$550	$495

1932 OLYMPIA MODEL - .22 S or LR cal., 10 shot, 6 or 9 in. barrel, target sights, one-piece grip, introduced in 1928 and used in 1932 Olympics. Marketed by Stoeger and Chas. Heyer-Nairobi.

	$2,200	$1,650	$1,250	$1,000	$800	$700	$600

Add 20% for longer barrel.

OLYMPIA SPORT MODEL - .22 LR cal., 7.4 in. barrel, adj. target sights, blue, wood grips, 4 barrel weights available. Mfg. 1936-40.

	$1,500	$1,200	$1,000	$900	$800	$700	$600

Add 20% for weight set.

1936 OLYMPIA "JÄGERSCHAFTS" HUNTING MODEL - similar to Sport, with 4 in. barrel. Mfg. 1936-40. Also seen with Eagle N proofs.

	$2,200	$1,650	$1,250	$1,000	$800	$700	$600

OLYMPIA RAPID FIRE MODEL - .22 Short cal. only, 7.4 in. barrel, blue, adj. sight, wood grip, has alloy slide. Mfg. 1936-40.

	$1,600	$1,200	$995	$600	$520	$460	$380

1936 OLYMPIA FÜNFKAMPF MODEL - .22 Short or LR cal., 9 1/4 in. barrel, blue, adj. sight, wood grips, barrel weights, circa 1936.

	$2,500	$2,200	$1,750	$1,500	$1,200	$900	$750

MODEL HP COMMERCIAL DOUBLE ACTION - 9mm Para. cal., pre-war version of P-38, 5 in. barrel, fixed sight, blue, wood or plastic grips. Mfg. 1937-44. Many variations, including several different finishes.
See German WWII Military Pistols section for values on this model.

PISTOLS: SEMI-AUTO, POST-WAR

MODEL PP & VARIATIONS - .22 LR, .32 ACP, or .380 ACP cal., double action, specifications similar to pre-war PP, 3 7/8 in. barrel. Imported 1963-2000. German manufacture.

✳ *Model PP .380 ACP cal.* - 7 shot mag.

	$750	$600	$450	$350	$300	$275	$250

Last MSR was $999.

✳ *Model PP .32 ACP cal.* - 8 shot mag.

	$650	$500	$395	$295	$275	$250	$225

Last MSR was $999.

✳ *Model PP .22 LR cal.* - 10 shot mag., disc. 1984.

	$800	$650	$425	$375	$325	$300	$275

Last MSR was $783.

✳ *Model PP Blue Engraved* - .22 LR (disc.) or .380 ACP cal. Disc. 1984.

	$1,425	$1,125	$950	$835	$685	$585	$485

Last MSR was $1,650.

Add 5% for .22 LR cal.

GRADING - PPGS™	100%	98%	95%	90%	80%	70%	60%

✳ *Model PP Chrome Engraved* - .22 LR or .380 ACP cal. Disc. 1984.

	$1,450	$1,125	$900	$785	$655	$550	$465

Last MSR was $1,600.

Add $50 for .22 LR cal.

✳ *Model PP Silver Engraved* - .22 LR (disc.) or .380 ACP cal. Disc. 1984.

	$1,750	$1,200	$1,000	$885	$715	$610	$515

Last MSR was $1,948.

✳ *Model PP Gold Engraved* - .22 LR (disc.) or .380 ACP cal. Disc. 1984.

	$1,950	$1,500	$1,150	$1,025	$830	$710	$590

Last MSR was $2,053.

✳ *Model PP Manurhin* - .22 LR, .32 ACP, or .380 ACP cal. Disc. 1984.

	$525	$440	$350	$225	$180	$165	$150

Add 10% for .380 ACP cal.

✳ *Model PP 50th Anniversary Commemorative* - .22 LR., .32 ACP, or .380 ACP cal., gold-plated parts, hand-carved grips, presentation case. 500 imported to U.S. 1979. 800 mfg.

	$1,625	$1,175	$650	N/A	N/A	N/A	N/A

Last MSR was $1,700.

✳ *Model PP "100 Jahre" 1886-1986* - 7.65mm cal., 100th anniversary PP edition, primarily made for the German marketplace, inscription marked on right side of slide.

	100%	98%	95%	90%	80%	70%	60%
Plastic Grips	$1,050	$750	$625	N/A	N/A	N/A	N/A
Extended Wood Grips	$1,150	$850	$675	N/A	N/A	N/A	N/A

✳ *Model PP Last Edition* - supplied with fitted hard case, certificate; and video Walther history, 400 mfg. in .32 ACP cal., 100 mfg. in .380 ACP cal., 500 total mfg. in Germany 1999 only.

	$1,350	$1,050	$900	N/A	N/A	N/A	N/A

Add $100 for .380 ACP cal.

This model was the last of the PP, PPK, PPK/S models to be manufactured when Germany stopped production in 1999.

PP SPORT - double action, thumbrest grips, round hammer with spur, adj. rear sight, 6.1 or 8.1 in. barrel, 25.6 or 27.2 oz. Mfg. 1953-70.

	100%	98%	95%	90%	80%	70%	60%
Manurhin Mfg.	$775	$675	$625	$550	$495	$425	$350
Mark II (1955-1957)	$875	$725	$650	$600	$545	$500	$450
Walther Mfg.	$975	$825	$700	$625	$575	$525	$450

Subtract 10% if not marked.

Add $75 for barrel weight, $100 for factory case, 20% for factory nickel, 5% for single action.

✳ *PP Sport "C" Model C* - mfg. for competition shooting, single action, 7 5/8 in. barrel, spur hammer.

	$950	$825	$725	$675	$575	$525	$450

MODEL PP SUPER - .380 ACP cal., 3.6 in. barrel, 7 shot, fixed sights, plastic grips, blue, 1,000 mfg. in .380 ACP cal., 26.8 oz. Mfg. 1973-79.

	$975	$750	$550	$395	$285	$250	$235

✳ *Model PP Super Ultra/Police* - 9x18mm cal., recently imported West German police trade-ins, approx. 4,000 mfg.

	$475	$400	$350	$300	$275	$250	$225

✳ *Model PP Super Super-Cutaway*

	$795	$650	$550	N/A	N/A	N/A	N/A

GRADING - PPGS™	100%	98%	95%	90%	80%	70%	60%

MODEL PPK - similar to pre-war PPK, .22 LR, .32 ACP, or .380 ACP cal., 3.31 in. barrel. Mfg. post-war-1999, U.S. import stopped by GCA 68 on W. German and French production.

	100%	98%	95%	90%	80%	70%	60%
.32 ACP Cal.	$775	$550	$425	$350	$325	$295	$275
.22 LR Cal.	$1,075	$750	$600	$525	$450	$375	$325
.380 ACP Cal.	$1,075	$750	$600	$475	$425	$350	$300
Blue Engraved	$1,675	$1,300	$950	$835	$685	$585	$485
Silver Engraved	$1,950	$1,400	$1,000	$885	$715	$610	$515
Gold Engraved	$2,275	$1,675	$1,250	$1,100	$895	$785	$630

100% column assumes NIB condition - subtract 15% if not boxed.

MODEL PPK LAST EDITION - similar to PP Last Edition, but was never imported into the U.S. because of the GCA of 1968.

MODEL PPK LIGHTWEIGHT - similar to Standard, with dural frame, .22 LR or .32 ACP cal.

	$995	$725	$500	$375	$325	$295	$275

Add 20% for .22 LR cal.

MODEL PPK-1986 U.S. PRODUCTION - .380 ACP cal. only, 3.35 in. barrel, similar specifications as previous W. German and French manufacture, blue or bright nickel (new 1997) finish, 7 shot finger extension mag., black plastic grips, 21 oz. Made in the U.S. Mfg. 1986-2001.

	$450	$365	$320	$295	$270	$250	$225

Last MSR was $543.

Manufacture in the U.S. was under an exclusive licensing agreement with Walther of Germany.

✳ *Model PPK 1996 U.S. Production Stainless* - .32 ACP (new 1998) or .380 ACP cal., stainless steel construction. Mfg. 1986-2001.

	$450	$365	$320	$295	$270	$250	$225

Last MSR was $543.

MODEL PPK (CURRENT MFG.) - .32 ACP (stainless only beginning 2008) or .380 ACP cal., choice of blue or stainless steel, 6 (.380 ACP cal.) or 7 shot mag. Importation began 2006.

MSR $573	$470	$400	$345	$310	$275	$230	$200

✳ *Model PPK 75th Anniversary* - .380 ACP cal. only, blue finish scroll engraving on frame and slide, "75th Anniversary" script on frame, gold Walther banner and PPK on left side, smooth wood grips, includes wooden presentation case, 1,500 mfg. 2006.

	$875	$750	$675	N/A	N/A	N/A	N/A

Last MSR was $996.

MODEL PPK/E - .380 ACP cal., 3.4 in. barrel., high polish blue, 7 (.380 ACP) or 8 (.32 ACP) shot mag., 23 oz.

While advertised in America during 2000 with a MSR of $294, this model was distributed in Europe only, and was produced with the cooperation of F.E.G., located in Hungary. Only 6 were imported into the U.S. for the SHOT Show.

MODEL PPK/S & VARIATIONS - .22 LR, .32 ACP, or .380 ACP cal., similar to PPK, except has larger PP frame to meet import requirements of 1968, 3 1/4 in. barrel, production in W. Germany, Manurhin of France (disc. 1986), and in the U.S. (mfg. under license from Walther by Interarms), 10 (.22 LR) or 8 (.32 ACP and .380 ACP) shot, double action, fixed sights.

✳ *American Model PPK/S* - .380 ACP cal. only, blue finish, 8 shot, one finger extension and one flat bottom mag. Disc. 2001, reintroduced 2007.

MSR $573	$470	$400	$345	$310	$275	$230	$200

GRADING - PPGS™	100%	98%	95%	90%	80%	70%	60%

✴ *Model PPK/S Stainless* - .32 ACP (new 1998) or .380 ACP cal., American manufacture, two-tone finish also available in .380 ACP cal. only, introduced July of 1983.

MSR $573	$470	$400	$345	$310	$275	$230	$200

  Add $217 for Crimson Trace laser grips (.380 ACP cal. only, new 2008).

✴ *West German Model PPK/S* - .22 LR (disc. 1984), .32 ACP (disc. 1999), or .380 ACP (disc. 1999) cal.

.22 LR cal.	$850	$725	$595	$450	$375	$325	$300
.32 ACP cal.	$600	$525	$450	$400	$325	$295	$275
.380 ACP cal.	$750	$675	$550	$400	$325	$295	$275

✴ *American Model PPK/S Blue Engraved* - blue engraved. Disc. 1985.

	$875	$850	$800	$695	$585	$485	$415

Last MSR was $990.

✴ *American Model PPK/S Gold-Engraved Commemorative* - 500 total mfg. Disc. 1987.

	$1,000	$875	$700	N/A	N/A	N/A	N/A

Last MSR was $1,200.

✴ *American Model PPK/S Gold-Engraved* - disc. 1985.

	$975	$850	$700	$585	$500	$415	$365

Last MSR was $1,070.

✴ *West German Model PPK/S Blue Engraved* - inventory depleted 1990.

	$1,475	$1,050	$850	$740	$620	$515	$440

Last MSR was $1,550.

✴ *West German Model PPK/S Chrome Engraved* - importation disc. 1991.

	$1,525	$1,075	$950	$835	$685	$585	$485

Last MSR was $1,700.

✴ *West German Model PPK/S Silver Engraved* - disc. 1988.

	$1,675	$1,150	$975	$860	$700	$600	$500

Last MSR was $1,700.

✴ *West German Model PPK/S Gold Engraved* - disc. 1985.

	$1,950	$1,250	$1,000	$885	$715	$610	$515

Last MSR was $1,800.

MANURHIN PPK/S - see listings under Manurhin section.

MODEL PPS - 9mm Para. cal. or .40 S&W cal., 3.2 in. barrel, 5 (.40 S&W cal. only), 6, 7, or 8 (9mm Para. cal. only) shot single stack mag., black polymer frame, matte black metal finish, fixed sights, thinner profile than the PPK (1.04 in.), ambidextrous safety, removeable grip straps, striker fire action, pre-cocked, magazine extension, 6.1 lbs. trigger pull, 21 oz. Importation began 2008.

MSR $665	$550	$495	$450	$400	$365	$335	$295

MODEL TP - .22 LR or .25 ACP cal., updated version of Model 9, 6 shot, 2.6 in. barrel, concealed hammer, 12 oz. Mfg. 1961-71.

.22 LR cal.	$800	$625	$435	$350	$300	$260	$210
.25 ACP cal.	$725	$500	$350	$300	$250	$220	$185

MODEL TPH - .22 LR or .25 ACP cal., double action 2.8 in. barrel, 6 shot, alloy frame, blue, fixed sights, plastic grips, 11 1/2 oz. Mfg. 1968-98 in W. Germany, U.S. import stopped by GCA of 1968.

.22 LR cal.	$875	$650	$550	$475	$350	$300	$250
.25 ACP cal.	$975	$750	$600	$500	$400	$325	$275

  Subtract 10% on the 100% values if not boxed with all accessories.

TPH cutaways were also mfg. in small quantities for instructional use. Current pricing for a mint specimen is approx. $1,500.

100% price assumes NIB condition.

GRADING - PPGS™	100%	98%	95%	90%	80%	70%	60%

AMERICAN MODEL TPH - .22 LR or .25 ACP (new 1992) cal., blue finish or stainless steel, double action, black plastic grips, 6 shot mag., 2 1/4 in. barrel, 14 oz. Mfg. 1987-2000.

	$425	$350	$280	$250	$225	$200	$185

Last MSR was $460.

✳ *American Model TPH Stainless* - stainless steel fabrication. Disc. 2000.

	$440	$350	$280	$250	$225	$200	$185

Last MSR was $460.

MODEL P.38 & VARIATIONS - Please refer to listings under the P.38 entries in the P section. Only the currently imported Walther P.38 appears in this section.

✳ *Model P.38 (Current Importation)* - .22 LR, 7.65mm Luger, or 9mm Para. cal., currently imported by Earl's Repair Service.

Current MSR on a 9mm Para. alloy frame is $995, $1,995 for steel frame.

MODELS P1 & P4 - Please refer to listings under the P.38 entries in the P section.

MODEL P5 - 7.65mm Luger, 9mm Para., or 9x21mm cal., double action, alloy frame, frame mounted decocking lever, 3 1/2 in. barrel, adj. rear sight, blue finish only, 8 shot mag., auto safeties, 28 oz. New 1977-currently imported by Earl's Repair Service.

MSR $1,095		$975	$850	$800	$700	$650	$525	$475

P-5 cutaways were also mfg. in small quantities for instructional use. Current pricing for a mint specimen is approx. $2,000.

✳ *Model P5 Compact* - compact variation of P-5 with 3.1 in. barrel, 26 1/2 oz. Limited importation beginning 1987.

	$995	$850	$600	$525	$450	$425	$375

✳ *Model P5 Long* - special edition, 5.3 in. barrel, wood grips, 29.6 oz. 50 mfg. 1988 only.

	$3,750	$2,750	$2,000	N/A	N/A	N/A	N/A

✳ *Model P5 100th Year Commemorative* - marked "1886-1986 100 Jahre" with Walther banner, elaborate grip carving, presentation walnut case. Imported 1986-91.

	$2,650	$1,750	$1,100	N/A	N/A	N/A	N/A

Last MSR was $2,890.

P22 - .22 LR cal., 3/4 scale of the P99, 3.42 (standard) or 5 in. (target) barrel, hammer fired, black polymer frame with grooved and stippled grip, SA or DA, Weaver rails on top of front sight/carrying handle and bottom of forend, matte black finish, military green frame or nickel slide, or brushed chrome slide and anthracite frame finish, internal trigger lock with loaded chamber indicator and mag. disconnect, 10 shot mag., firing pin drop safety, safety key lock on right side of frame, interchangable backstrap, adj. rear sight, 15.2 or 18 1/2 (w/o mag.) oz. New 2001.

MSR $335		$285	$230	$200	$175	$155	$145	$125

Add $87 for target model with 5 in. barrel.
Add $55 for nickel finish.
Add $63 for brushed chrome slide and anthracite frame finish (new 2007).
Add $87 for laser sight (3.4 in. barrel in blue finish only).
Add $257 for red dot sight (mfg. 2006-2007).

Walther offered a limited P22 first edition which included two barrels, stabilizer assembly/frame extension for 5 in. barrel, and a blue plastic case. These were marked "Limited Edition P22" and 1,000 were mfg. Current value for a mint gun with all accessories is in the $375-$425 range.

A special edition two barrel set of this model was available exclusively through Davidson's during 2006 - MSR was $370.

SP22-M1 - .22 LR cal., 4 in. barrel, 10 shot, SA, polymer frame, stainless steel slide, target trigger, wide variety of options, including accessory rails, grips, and optics, 27 oz. New 2008.

MSR $370	$300	$250	$215	$190	$170	$150	$130

Add $162 for red dot sight.
Add $124 for laser sight.
Add $299 for adj. match grips.
Add $20 for Picatinny rail.
Add $55 for Truglo fiber optic sights.

✻ *SP22-M2* - .22 LR cal., similar to SP22-M1, except has 6 in. barrel, vertical cutouts under barrel in front of frame assembly. New 2008.

MSR $390	$315	$260	$220	$190	$170	$150	$130

✻ *SP22-M3* - .22 LR cal., similar to SP22-M2, except has upper and lower accessory rails. New 2008.

MSR $450	$390	$330	$280	$240	$200	$180	$155

✻ *SP22-M4* - .22 LR cal., 6 in. match grade barrel, ergonomic black stippled wood target grips, 10 shot mag., SA, match trigger, 32 1/2 oz. New 2008.

MSR $725	$625	$550	$475	$425	$375	$325	$275

MODEL P88 & VARIATIONS - 9mm Para. or 9x21mm cal., double action, alloy frame, 4 in. barrel, 15 shot button release mag., fully ambidextrous, decocking lever, matte finish, adj. rear sight, internal safeties, plastic grips, 31 1/2 oz. Mfg. 1987-93.

	$1,100	$925	$750	$600	$500	$450	$400

Last MSR was $1,129.

P88 cutaways were also mfg. in small quantities for instructional use. Current pricing for a mint specimen is approx. $2,000.

✻ *Model P88 Compact* - 9mm Para. or 9x21mm cal., 3.93 in. barrel, 14* (disc.) or 10 (C/B 1994) shot mag., 29 oz. Imported 1993-2003.

	$975	$800	$650	$550	$500	$475	$450

Last MSR was $900.

Add 25% for 14 shot mag.

✻ *Model P88 Champion* - 9mm Para. only, 6 in. barrel, SA only, 14* shot mag., 30.9 oz. Very limited mfg. 1992-disc.

	$2,350	$1,850	$1,500	$1,250	$995	$775	$625

✻ *Model P88 Competition* - similar to P88 Champion, except has 4 in. barrel, SA only, 14* shot mag., 28.2 oz. Very limited mfg. 1992-disc.

		$1,875	$1,500	$1,250	$995	$775	$625	$550

✻ *Model P88 Sport* - .22 LR cal. only, 6 in. barrel, SA only, 10 shot mag. Very limited mfg. 1995-disc.

	$2,450	$1,900	$1,550	$1,250	$995	$775	$625

P99 & VARIATIONS - 9mm Para., 9x21mm (limited importation 1996), or .40 S&W (new 1999) cal., 4 (9mm Para.) or 4.1 (.40 S&W) in. barrel, polymer frame, 10, 12 (.40 S&W cal. only), 15, or 16 (9mm Para. cal. only, disc. 2006) shot mag., standard, anti-stress (traditional double action, AS Model, new 2004), or quick action (QA, allowing consistent SA trigger performance) trigger, decocking, and internal striker safeties, cocking and loaded chamber indicators, choice of matte black, QPQ (mfg. 1999-2003) finished (silver colored) slide, or titanium coated (mfg. 2003-2006) finish, ambidextrous mag. release, ergonomic black, desert tan, or green (Military model, new 1999) synthetic grip with interchangeable backstrap, adj. rear sight, 25 oz. Importation began 1995.

MSR $740	$625	$550	$475	$425	$375	$325	$275

Add $139 for tritium sight set with green 3-dot system or $99 for white 3-dot metal sights.
Add $31 for titanium finish (disc. 2006).

Add $125 for 9x21mm cal.

Engraved P99s are also available in the following configurations in 9mm Para. cal. only - Grade I Arabesque ($3,700 MSR), Grade II Goldline ($4,200 MSR), Grade III Arabesque w/ gold ($4,660 MSR). Please contact Walther USA directly for more information about these engraved models.

✻ *P99 Compact* - 9mm Para. or .40 S&W cal., 3 1/2 in. barrel, 8 (.40 S&W cal.) or 10 shot mag. with finger extension, available in QA, AS, or DAO (disc. 2006), Weaver rail, compact frame, blue finish only, 20 oz. New 2004.

MSR $740	$625	$550	$475	$425	$375	$325	$275

✻ *P99 QSA* - 9mm Para. or .40 S&W cal., first introduced before the QA, slide marked with QSA inscription, large decocking plate. Very few mfg.

	$900	$750	$525	N/A	N/A	N/A	N/A

✻ *P99 2000 Commemorative* - 9mm Para. or .40 S&W cal., features high polish blue slide with laser inscription "Commemorative for the year 2000." Limited mfg. 1,000 (only 500 for the U.S.) of each cal. in 2000 only, cased with Walther videotape.

	$850	$650	$495	N/A	N/A	N/A	N/A

Last MSR was $840.

✻ *P99 La Chasse DU Engraved* - 9mm Para. or .40 S&W cal., similar to Model P-99 Military, except has laser engraved slide, wooden backstrap and green lanyard, luminescent sights, special case. Mfg. 1998-2000.

	$950	$800	$725	N/A	N/A	N/A	N/A

Last MSR was $1,078.

✻ *P99 La Chasse Engraved* - features choice of elaborate oak leaf, arabesque, or English style hand scroll engraving on polished slide. Mfg. 1998-2000.

	$1,995	$1,600	$1,400	N/A	N/A	N/A	N/A

Last MSR was $2,126.

✻ *P99 Canada Edition* - 9mm Para. cal. only, 105mm barrel, black finish only, scarce in the U.S., includes two 16 shot mags.

	$1,000	$750	$600	N/A	N/A	N/A	N/A

✻ *P99 Malta Special Edition* - special edition commemorating the Malta Arms Act of 2005, 99 mfg. 2005 only.

	$750	$625	$475	N/A	N/A	N/A	N/A

P990 - similar to P99, except is double action only, features Walther's constant pull trigger system, black, QPQ slide finish, or Military Model (green), 25 oz. Mfg. 1998-2003.

	$550	$475	$425	$385	$350	$325	$295

Last MSR was $644.

PISTOLS: SEMI-AUTO, TARGET

Walther target pistols are imported by Champions Choice located in La Vergne, TN. Previously imported by Interarms until 1993, Nygord Precision Products until 1996, and by Earl's Repair Service, located in Tewksbury, MA.

Add 10% to the values listed for left-hand stocks (available on most models).

MODEL GSP TARGET STANDARD - .22 LR cal., 4 1/2 in. barrel, single action, 5 shot mag. standard, 8 or 10 shot mag. optional, adj. sights, nickel, two-tone, or blue finish, walnut target grips, 2-stage trigger became optional in 1995, optional carrying case, 42.3 oz. Mfg. 1969-2001.

	$1,425	$1,225	$995	$650	$550	$475	$425

Last MSR was $1,450.

This model was available as a complete international package, including a GSP with .22 Short and .32 S&W Wadcutter conversion units, including triggers. MSR was approx. $3,100.

✳ *Model GSP Target Junior* - similar to GSP Target, except has slimmer 4 1/4 in. barrel design, smaller walnut grips, 40.1 oz. Importation disc. 1992.

	100%	98%	95%	90%	80%	70%	60%
	$1,450	$1,350	$995	$775	$600	$500	$425

Last MSR was $1,810.

✳ *Model GSP-C Target* - similar to Model GSP Target, except in .32 S&W Wadcutter, and 4 1/4 in. barrel, 49.4 oz. Mfg. 1971-2001.

$1,475 $1,025 $800 $650 $550 $475 $425

Last MSR was $1,595.

> Add $1,095 for OSP-2000 .22 Short conversion unit.
> Add $995 for GSP .22 LR cal. conversion unit.
> Add $1,195 for GSP-C .32 S&W Wadcutter conversion unit.

✳ *Model GSP Target Expert* - .22 LR cal. only, similar to GSP Standard, except for recoil compensation system located in barrel weight, sight radius has been changed, and sights are located further to the rear of the gun, modified frame (cut on an angle) behind the trigger area, stippled blonde/blue ergonomic laminated wood grips, 42.3 oz. New 2001.

MSR $2,375 $2,000 $1,700 $1,350 $1,050 $900 $800 $725

✳ *Model GSPC Target Expert* - similar to Model GSP Expert, except available in .32 S&W Wadcutter cal., 45.1 oz. Mfg. 2001-2005.

$2,275 $1,695 $1,100 $850 $675 $575 $495

Last MSR was $1,695.

✳ *Model GSP Target Atlanta* - .22 LR cal., special edition for the 1996 Olympic Games, Atlanta inscribed on right side of bolt housing, black laminate grips, titanium plated bolt, otherwise same as GSP Target Standard.

$1,800 $1,450 $1,000   N/A   N/A   N/A   N/A

✳ *Model GSP Target 25th Year Commemorative Special Limited Edition* - .22 LR cal., aluminum carrying case, options included two-tone finish, laminated Canadian black birch grip, titanium plated bolt, special 70 g. barrel weight with "25 Jahre GSP" engraved, adj. front sight, two-stage trigger, 3 lbs. 1,000 mfg. 1994.

$2,500 $2,150 $1,850   N/A   N/A   N/A   N/A

This model was only available from Earl's Repair Service.

✳ *Model GSP-C Target 25th Year Commemorative Special Limited Edition* - similar to GSP 25th Year Commemorative, except in .32 S&W Wadcutter, engraved 65 g. barrel weight, 1,000 mfg. as complete pistols or conversion units. Mfg. 1996 only.

$1,995 $1,600 $1,250   N/A   N/A   N/A   N/A

✳ *Model GSP Target Special Anniversary Pistol/Rifle Combination* - only 50 sets mfg. for 2000, includes scope, pistol, and rifle conversion kit, includes carry case. Disc.

$5,000 $3,750 $2,750   N/A   N/A   N/A   N/A

Last MSR was $5,500.

This combo was only available from Earl's Repair Service.

✳ *Model GSP Target Rifle Conversion Kit* - .22 LR cal., unique conversion allows inserting a GSP action in a rifle stock, includes 16 3/4 in. (18 1/4 with GSP compensator) stainless barrel, black, brown, camo, or Walther blue, laminate stock, right or left-hand, 5, 8, or 10 shot mag. New 1996.

MSR $995 $995 $850 $725 $610 $515 $425 $375

> Add $155 with Super Match stock.
> Add $300 for Super Match Kit.
> Add $75 for left-hand stock.

This rifle conversion kit is only available from Earl's Repair Service, Inc.

GRADING - PPGS™	100%	98%	95%	90%	80%	70%	60%

MODEL KSP 200 - .22 LR cal., semi-auto target pistol with adj. laminated ergonomic grips, target trigger and sights, two-tone slide finish, mfg. in cooperation with Baikal. Mfg. 2000-2004.

	$500	$450	$415	$385	$350	$325	$295

Last MSR was $575.

MODEL OSP - similar to GSP, in .22 Short cal. Mfg. 1961-1994 for international competition (meets ISU and NRA regs.), 3.35 (new 1994, current model is OSP 2000) or 4 1/4 in. barrel, 44.4 oz.

MSR $1,275	$1,275	$1,025	$800	$650	$550	$475	$425

Add $520 for extended sight radius and semi-wraparound grip (Model OSP 2000).

MODEL SSP EXPERT - .22 LR cal., 6 in. barrel, lightweight construction, black synthetic ergonomic grips in three different sizes, pneumatic buffer, cocking indicator, extended rear sight, 5 shot mag., 34 oz. Importation began 2006.

MSR $2,795	$2,425	$2,100	$1,825	$1,600	$1,400	$1,200	$975

FREE PISTOL - .22 LR cal., single shot, electronic trigger, 11.8 in. heavy barrel, advanced target design with fully adj. grips and sights, 49.4 oz. Mfg. 1977-91.

	$1,450	$1,200	$1,000	$850	$675	$575	$500

Last MSR was $2,140.

HÄMMERLI-WALTHER - see Hämmerli.

REVOLVERS

MODEL R99 - .357 Mag. cal., 6 shot, double action, 3 in. barrel, adj. rear sight, blue or stainless steel, unique Duo-grip allows for different hand sizes (2 grips included), 28 1/2 oz. Mfg. by Smith & Wesson 1999 only for the European market with no U.S. importation.

This model was basically a variation of the S&W Models 19 (blue) or 66 (stainless).

RIFLES: DISC.

MODEL B - .30-06 cal., bolt action, post-war mfg., 22 in. barrel. Disc.

	$775	$625	$500	$400	$300	$250	$200

Add 20% for double-set triggers.

MODEL 1 AUTOLOADING - .22 LR cal., Carbine model, autoloading, detachable mag., 20 1/2 in. barrel, 5 or 9 (optional) shot mag., could be used as bolt action or semi-auto, checkered pistol grip, walnut sporter stock, 5 1/2 lbs.

	$895	$800	$700	$600	$500	$400	$300

MODEL 2 AUTOLOADING - .22 LR cal., similar to Model 1, except has 24 1/2 in. barrel, finger grooved forearm, tangent sight, adj. trigger, checkered sporter stock, pre-war, 7 lbs.

	$995	$875	$775	$625	$500	$400	$300

MODEL V CHAMPION - micrometer adj. sight and checkered pistol grip stock.

	$775	$625	$500	$400	$300	$250	$200

MODEL DSM 34 - .22 LR cal., single shot, military stock, tangent sight. Pre-war and wartime mfg.

	$1,000	$650	$550	$500	$450	$375	$300

Add 50% for stamp in stock.
Add 20% for AS stamp in stock.

MODEL KKM INTERNATIONAL MATCH - .22 LR cal., single shot bolt action, 28 in. heavy barrel, adj. aperture sight, adj. hook butt, thumbhole stock, accessory rail, post-war mfg.

	$880	$770	$715	$660	$550	$495	$440

GRADING - PPGS™	100%	98%	95%	90%	80%	70%	60%

MODEL KKM-S - similar to KKM, with adj. cheekpiece.

	$935	$825	$770	$715	$605	$550	$495

MODEL KKJ SPORTER - .22 LR cal., bolt action, 5 shot, 22 1/2 in. barrel, open sight, checkered sporter stock, post-war.

	$1,250	$995	$650	$550	$450	$385	$330

Add 20% for double-set triggers.

MODEL KKJ-MA - .22 Mag. cal.

	$1,250	$1,100	$775	$650	$550	$450	$385

MODEL KKJ-HO - .22 Hornet cal., repeater or single shot (Model KKJ-E).

	$1,450	$1,225	$825	$700	$575	$450	$385

Add 20% for double-set triggers.

MODEL KKW - .22 LR cal., single shot, military stock, tangent sight, pre-war and wartime mfg.

	$750	$600	$420	$300	$260	$220	$195

Add 50% for SA stamp on stock.

MODEL SSV VARMINT - .22 LR cal., single shot bolt action, 25 1/2 in. barrel, no sights, Monte Carlo pistol grip stock, post-war mfg.

	$700	$600	$525	$495	$415	$360	$330
.22 Hornet	$825	$725	$600	$550	$475	$415	$385

MODEL UIT BV UNIVERSAL - .22 LR cal., single shot bolt action, 25.6 in. heavy barrel, adj. aperture sight, target stock with palm rest, adj. butt, meets ISU regs., 11 lbs. Disc. 1990.

	$1,325	$1,050	$850	$700	$635	$580	$530

Last MSR was $1,700.

This model was previously known as the Model UIT Special.

GX-1 - similar to Model UIT Match, 25 in. barrel with fully adj. free rifle stock, all accessories included, 16 1/2 lbs. Importation disc. 1991.

	$1,895	$1,375	$1,125	$885	$860	$775	$680

Last MSR was $2,350.

MODEL KK/MS SILHOUETTE - .22 LR cal. only, designed for silhouette shooting, no sights, thumbhole stock with adj. butt, fully stippled forend and stock grip, front barrel weight, 23.6 in. barrel, 16.3 lbs. Imported 1984-91.

	$975	$795	$625	$560	$495	$435	$395

Last MSR was $1,175.

RUNNING BOAR MODEL 500 - similar to KK/MS, no sights, thumbhole stock with adj. wood buttplate and cheekpiece, 23.6 in. barrel, 8.4 lbs. Disc. 1990.

	$1,195	$900	$675	$575	$500	$435	$395

Last MSR was $1,300.

MODEL WA-2000 - .300 Win. Mag. (55 mfg., standard) or .308 Win. (92 mfg., optional) cal., ultra-deluxe semi-auto, 25.6 in. barrel, 5 or 6 shot mag., optional extras include aluminum case, spare mags., integral bipod, adj. tools and leather sling, regular or night vision scope, special order only, 16 3/4 lbs. Disc. 1988.

	$36,000	$32,000	$29,000	$27,000	$25,000	$22,500	$20,000

A 7.5 Swiss cal. conversion kit was also optional on this model.

MODEL UIT MATCH - similar to Model UIT, except with improved stock design which includes fully stippled lower forearm and pistol grip, 25.6 in. barrel, 8.6 lbs. Importation disc. 1993.

	$1,125	$925	$800	$660	$610	$555	$510

Last MSR was $1,400.

GRADING - PPGS™	100%	98%	95%	90%	80%	70%	60%

* Model UIT-E Match - electronic trigger, 25.6 in. barrel, 10.4 lbs. Disc. 1986.

	$1,350	$940	$860	$770	$670	$630	$560

Last MSR was $1,250.

MODEL PRONE 400 - similar to UIT Match, with Prone style competition stock and no sights. Disc.

	$750	$635	$580	$525	$415	$360	$305

RIFLES: CURRENT/RECENT MFG.

Except for the G22 and GSP rifles, the following models are available from Champion's Choice.

MODEL G22 SEMI-AUTO - .22 LR cal., bullpup design with thumbhole stock, fire control and mag. integrated in rear of stock, black synthetic, carbon fiber, or camo (disc. 2006) stock, adj. sliding sights, right or left-hand controls and ejection, blue or military green finish, Weaver style rails, 20 in. barrel, 10 shot mag., approx. 6 lbs. New 2004.

MSR $456		$375	$330	$285	$230	$200	$185	$170

Add $36 for scope or $64 for laser or $104 for red-dot sights.
Add $56 for carbon fiber stock (disc. 2007) or $50 for camo stock (disc. 2006).

MODEL KK200 - .22 LR cal., available in standard rifle laminated stock, power match, and sport configurations, top-of-the-line competition model, 19.7 in. barrel, 11.57 lbs.

MSR N/A		$1,995	$1,675	$1,375	$1,050	$850	$725	$600

Add approx. $1,000 for machined KK200 Power Match Model with nickel plated stippled stock and forend, 25 1/2 in. barrel, 13 lbs. (limited mfg. 1995).
Add approx. $500 for KK200 S (sport configuration).
Add $265 for electronic trigger on Power Match or Sport Models.

MODEL KK300 - similar to Model KK200, except has target or adj. aluminum competition stock. Importation began 2006.

MSR N/A		$2,625	$2,350	1,900	$1,600	$1,300	$995	$750

Add $1,200 for adj. aluminum competition stock.

MODEL KK CLUB SPORT RIFLE - .22 LR cal. New 2000.

MSR N/A		$525	$450	$400	$350	$275	$260	$230

MODEL GSP RIFLE - .22 LR cal., utilizes GSP sport pistol action, 16 3/4 in. stainless fluted barrel, through engraved compensator, laminated "silhouette style" thumbhole stock, 5 shot standard, 8 or 10 shot optional, optics or scope optional, 8.55 lbs. Imported 1996-2007.

	$2,400	$2,100	$1,800	$1,500	$1,250	$1,125	$1,000

Last MSR was $2,590.

This model was only available from Earl's Repair Service.

SHOTGUNS: SxS

MODEL WSF - 12 or 16 ga., checkered walnut stock, double triggers, boxlock, sling swivels, 28.4 in. barrel. Introduced 1932-disc.

	$725	$575	$425	$325	$275	$240	$200

MODEL WSFD - 12 or 16 ga., cheekpiece, checkered walnut stock, double triggers, boxlock, sling swivels, 6.3 (16 ga.) or 6.6 (12 ga.) lbs. Introduced 1932-disc.

	$925	$725	$575	$450	$400	$350	$300

SHOTGUNS: SEMI-AUTO

WALTHER SEMI-AUTO - 12 ga. only, 2 3/4 in. chamber, 25 1/2 in. barrel, crossbolt safety, checkered walnut stock and forearm. Mfg. in Zella-Mehlis 1921-1931.

	$950	$875	$775	$650	$550	$450	$375

GRADING - PPGS™	100%	98%	95%	90%	80%	70%	60%

WALTHER, FRENCH-MADE BY MANURHIN

Previously manufactured in Mulhouse, France. Previously imported 1984-86 by Matra-Manurhin International, Inc. located in Alexandria, VA.

PISTOLS: SEMI-AUTO

Manufacture of these Walther PP type pistols commenced in Mulhouse, France in 1951. They were marked "MANURHIN" on the slide until 1954. Since then they were designated Walther MKII. They were imported into the USA by Interarms up to 1983.

In 1984, following a disagreement regarding the use of the Walther trademark, a few pistols were manufactured using the standard Walther slide legend, w/o the "under license of" above the legend. Additionally, the Manurhin name, logo, and the words "Made in France" were stamped on the heel of the gun in very small letters. Following this French production, pistols were made in Germany and marked Walther, or made in France and marked Manurhin. Manurhin briefly set up an office in New York to do its own importation, and later moved to Florida.

In 1984, Manurhin was imported directly with no Interarms logo or Walther trademark appearing on Models PP and PPK/S. Importation was discontinued 1986, when all production resumed in Ulm, Germany.

MODEL PP - .22 LR, .32 ACP, or .380 ACP cal., 3 7/8 in. barrel, 10 shot mag. (.22 LR), 8 shot mag. (.32 ACP), 7 shot mag. (.380 ACP), blue only, all steel construction, double action with positive hammer block safety, 24 oz.

$450	$350	$300	$230	$205	$185	$170

Last MSR was $419.

Add 20% for .22 LR or .380 ACP cal.
Add $46 for Durgarde finish.

✳ *Model PP Collector* - blue finish, special engraving. Imported 1986 only.

$465	$415	$350	$285	$250	$215	$185

Last MSR was $529.

✳ *Model PP Presentation* - blue finish, special ornamentation. Imported 1986 only.

$720	$650	$500	$430	$375	$315	$270

Last MSR was $819.

✳ *Model PP Interarms Import*

$395	$325	$285	$235	$200	$170	$145

This model was also available with various engraving options in either blue, nickel, or gold finish - prices ranged from $222 - $540.

PP SPORT - .22 LR cal. only, double action, 6.1 or 8.1 in. barrel, blue finish only, precision adj. sights, contoured plastic grips with thumbrest, 25 oz. New Manurhin design beginning 1985-disc.

$545	$485	$430	$385	$325	$290	$270

Last MSR was $635.

✳ *PP Sport-C* - similar to PP Sport, except is single action.

$540	$475	$415	$370	$310	$280	$260

Last MSR was $635.

MODEL PPK - .22 LR, .32 ACP, or .380 ACP cal., 3 1/4 in. barrel, 10 shot mag.-.22 LR, 8 shot mag.-.32 ACP, 7 shot mag.-.380 ACP, blue only, all steel construction, double action with positive hammer block safety, 23 oz.

$550	$475	$425	$375	$350	$325	$300

Add 20% for .22 LR or .380 ACP cal.

GRADING - PPGS™	100%	98%	95%	90%	80%	70%	60%

MODEL PPK/S - .22 LR, .32 ACP, or .380 ACP cal., 3 1/4 in. barrel, 10 shot mag.-.22 LR, 8 shot mag.-.32 ACP, 7 shot mag.-.380 ACP, blue only, all steel construction, double action with positive hammer block safety, 23 oz.

	$400	$350	$300	$230	$205	$185	$170

Last MSR was $419.

Add 20% for .22 LR cal.

✳ *Model PPK/S Durgarde* - similar to Model PPK/S, only with bonded brushed chrome finish.

	$450	$400	$350	$300	$275	$250	$240

Last MSR was $465.

Add 20% for .22 LR cal.

✳ *Model PPK/S Collector* - blue finish, special engraving. Imported 1986 only.

	$465	$415	$350	$300	$275	$250	$225

Last MSR was $529.

✳ *Model PPK/S Presentation* - blue finish, special ornamentation. Imported 1986 only.

	$720	$650	$500	$430	$375	$315	$270

Last MSR was $819.

✳ *Model PPK/S Interarms Import*

	$395	$340	$300	$230	$205	$185	$170

Was also available with various engraving options in either blue, nickel, or gold finish - prices ranged from $222-$540.

WARNER ARMS CORPORATION

Previous manufacturer located in Norwich, CT.

PISTOLS: SEMI-AUTO

INFALLIBLE POCKET AUTO PISTOL - .32 ACP cal., 7 shot, 3 in. barrel, fixed sights, rubber grips. Mfg. 1917-19.

	$450	$350	$250	$150	$125	$100	$90

WATSON BROS.

Current long gun manufacturer established in 1885, and located in London, England.

Watson Bros. manufactures distinct round body actions with self-opening locks in both SxS and O/U shotgun configurations. Back action sidelock double rifles are also available. All guns are built to custom order. Please contact the factory directly (see Trademark Index) for more information including current pricing.

WEATHERBY

Current trademark manufactured and imported by Weatherby located Paso Robles, CA since 2006. Previously located in Atascadero, CA 1995-2006, and in South Gate, CA, 1945-1995. Weatherby began manufacturing rifles in the U.S. during early 1995. Dealer and distributor sales.

Weatherby is an importer and manufacturer of long arms. Earlier production was from Germany and Italy, and German mfg. is usually what is collectible. Rifles are currently produced in the U.S., while O/U shotguns are made in Japan and semi-autos are mfg. in Italy. Workmanship in all instances is excellent. Weatherby is well-known for their high-velocity proprietary rifle calibers.

Weatherby offers a research authentication service for Weatherby firearms. The cost is $50 per serial number ($75 for custom rifles, $100 for special editions and commemoratives), and includes a certificate signed by Roy Weatherby Jr. and company historian Dean Rumbaugh. Please contact the company directly for more information

GRADING - PPGS™	100%	98%	95%	90%	80%	70%	60%

regarding this service (see Trademark Index).

Early Weatherby rifles used a Mathieu Arms action in the 1950s - primarily since it was available in left-hand action. Right-handed actions were normally mfg. from the FN Mauser type.

DRILLINGS

WEATHERBY DRILLING - mfg. by J. P. Sauer during the late 1960s-early 1970s for Weatherby importation (marked Weatherby on right barrel), identical to Sauer Model 3000, except was not available in all metric cals. Disc.

	$2,850	$2,450	$2,100	$1,800	$1,500	$1,250	$1,000

PISTOLS: BOLT ACTION

SILHOUETTE PISTOL - .22-250 Rem. or .308 Win. cal., mfg. in Japan during late 1970s, 14 1/2 in. barrel, Lyman or Williams sights, fitted case. Only 50 were mfg. in .22-250 Rem. and 150 in .308 Win. cal. Disc. 1981.

	$3,750	$3,300	$2,750	$2,450	$2,100	$1,850	$1,650

MARK V CFP (CENTERFIRE PISTOLS) - .22-250 Rem., .223 Rem. (new 2000), .243 Win., 7mm-08 Rem., or .308 Win. cal., features 15 in. fluted stainless barrel with recessed crown, ambidextrous designed multi-layer brown laminate stock with finger grooves and swivel studs, blue Mark V lightweight action, no sights, 3 shot internal mag., 5 1/4 lbs. Mfg. 1997-2000.

	$935	$815	$735	$650	$600	$550	$500

Last MSR was $1,099.

✴ *Mark V CFP Accumark* - same cals. as Mark V CFP, features specially designed synthetic stock with Kevlar and other fibers, matte black finish with grey spider web pattern, 5 lbs. Limited mfg. 2000 only.

	$935	$815	$735	$650	$600	$550	$500

Last MSR was $1,099.

MARK V CFP (COMPACT FIRING PLATFORM) - .22-250 Rem., .223 Rem., .243 Win., or 7mm-08 Rem. cal., 16 in. unfluted matte blue barrel w/o sights, matte blue action, right hand Mark V one-piece bolt with 54 degree lift, tan Fibermark composite stock with black spider webbing and ambidextrous grip, 5 shot internal mag., Talley rings and bases became standard 2007, 5 1/4 lbs. New 2006.

MSR $1,611	$1,350	$1,095	$865	$725	$625	$525	$475

RIFLES: RIMFIRE

ACCUMARK CLASSIC & DELUXE BOLT ACTION - while these models were advertised in 1990 ($635 retail), they never went into production.

MARK XXII CLIP MAG OR TUBE FEED SEMI-AUTO - .22 LR cal., mag. feed, skip-line checkered walnut stock with or without rosewood forend and pistol grip cap, clip models have 5 or 10 shot detachable mag., 24 in. barrel, open V rear fold down sights, grooved alloy receiver, all XXIIs had a right side lever that allowed changing from semi-auto to single shot, tube feed model weighs approx. 6 lbs., 10 oz., clip model weighs 5 lbs., 13 oz. Approx. 100,000 mfg. 1964-1989.

Italian/Japanese mfg.	$495	$425	$360	$300	$240	$170	$140

Last MSR was $454.

> Add 5% for Italian models with rosewood.
> Subtract 10% for tube feed models if in 98%+ condition.
> Subtract 15% if trigger guard and floor plate is discolored (should be dark black like the receiver NOT turning gray; beware of refinished trigger guard/floor plates.
> Subtract 5% without original sling swivels.
> Subtract 5-10% for blonde colored wood and stocks with knots (usually JC or JT serial number prefix guns) and also stocks lacking figuring.

There were three different Japanese manufacturers between 1967-1999 (not domestically

GRADING - PPGS™	100%	98%	95%	90%	80%	70%	60%

imported after 1989). During this time, the type and quality of the wood and finish, safety switch, rear sight, trigger, floorplate design and magazines were just some of the many changes that occurred during this manufacturing period. Because of this, prices could fluctuate approx. 10%-20%, depending on what features have become more desirable today. A slight premium may be asked for U.S. mfg. Weatherby Mark XXII.

A Weatherby Mark XXII 4x50 scope was also marketed with these .22 cal rifles. The scope was made in Japan. It is a 4x28mm and not 4x50mm. The 4x was the magnification power. The 50 was a measure of the relative brightness or light gathering capabilities and not the diameter of the objective lens. If new in original box with papers the value is approx. $175.00. If used in good condition with original box, the value is approx. $140.00. If used without box, the value is approx. $45.00 to $100.00 (depending upon condition).

This model was originally mfg. in Italy by Beretta (there were no tube feed models made in Italy), followed by two different Japanese manufacturers, then production went to the U.S. briefly (Mossberg mfg.) and ended up back in Japan. This rifle was marketed for a stylish appearance and most buyers took good care of these guns and as a result, it is common to find these guns in 95% condition or better. Buyers beware, in recent years, there has been a wide difference between the "advertised prices" and the "actual selling prices" also many Italian XXIIs have been appearing that have been refinished.

MARK XXII BOLT ACTION - .17 HMR or .22 LR cal., features Anschutz action/barrel, 23 in. target grade barrel w/o sights, blue finish, deluxe checkered gloss finished Monte Carlo full pistol grip stock and forearm with rosewood caps, target type bolt handle with special cam cocking, 4 or 5 shot mag., adj. single stage trigger, supplied w/test target, approx. 6 1/2 lbs. New 2007.

MSR $917	$790	$660	$585	$500	$425	$375	$325

     Add $51 for .17 HMR cal.

RIFLES: BOLT ACTION, MARK V SERIES

Pre-Mark V production started in 1945 and ended in 1961. Initially, rifles were customized from customer supplied guns, and this ended circa 1949. Between 1949-1963, Weatherby manufactured rifles in Southgate from FN Mauser actions in various cals., including the Wby. Mag. cals. in .257, .270, 7mm, .300, and .375. From 1955-1959, Southgate also manufactured guns using the Mathieu left-hand action. Additionally, Schultz & Larson from Denmark was subcontracted to make rifles in .378 Wby. Mag. circa 1955-1962. Between 1956-1962, Southgate manufactured a .460 Wby. Mag. cal. using the Brevex Magnum action. Sako of Finland was also subcontracted circa 1957-1961 to produce rifles using a FN Mauser action. Initial Mark V production began in Southgate circa 1958-1959. During 1959-1973, J.P. Sauer of W. Germany was subcontracted to make the Mark V in a variety of calibers up to .460 Wby. Mag. These earlier pre-Mark V rifles will have a 20%-30% premium, depending on original condition and caliber.

In 1992, 24 in. barrels were disc. on most calibers of .300 or greater (including Models Mark V Deluxe, Fibermark, Lazermark, and Euromark). The Mark V action has also been manufactured in Japan.

All recently manufactured Weatherby Magnums in .30-378, .338-378, .378, .416, and .460 cal. are equipped with an Accubrake.

MARK V DELUXE - .22-250 Rem. (mfg. 1999-2004), .240 Wby. Mag. (disc. 1996, reintroduced 1999-2004, again beginning 2007), .243 Win. (mfg. 1999-2004, reintroduced 2007), .25-06 Rem. (mfg. 1999-2004), .257 Wby. Mag., .270 Win. (mfg. 1999-2004, reintroduced 2007), .270 Wby. Mag., .280 Rem. (mfg. 1999-2004), 7mm Wby. Mag., 7mm-08 Rem. (mfg. 1999-2004, reintroduced 2007), .30-06 (disc. 1996, reintroduced 1999-2004, again beginning 2007), .308 Win. (mfg. 1999-2004, reintroduced 2007), .300 Wby. Mag., .340 Wby. Mag., .375 H&H (mfg. 1993 only), .378 Wby. Mag., .416 Wby. Mag. or .460 Wby. Mag. cal., bolt action, 3-5 shot mag., 24 or 26 in. barrel, current mfg. has 9 locking lugs (Mag. cals.) or 6 locking lugs (standard cals. and .240 Wby. Mag.), deluxe skip line checkered pistol grip walnut stock with rosewood tipped forearm and pistol grip, no sights, 8 lbs. Left-hand actions (.270 Wby. Mag. and .300 Wby. Mag.) were available at no extra charge through 1997. Mfg. began 1957.

Add 15%-25% for German manufacture (J.P. Sauer) in calibers under .35 if condition is 95% or better.

✳ *Mark V Deluxe Short Action Cals.* - .22-250 Rem. (disc.), .243 Win., .240 Wby. Mag., .25-06 Rem. (disc.), .270 Win., .280 Rem. (disc.), .30-06, .308 Win., or 7mm-08 Rem. short action cals. Mfg. 1999-2004, reintroduced 2007.

	MSR $2,103		$1,625	$1,325	$1,000	$750	$625	$525	$475

✳ *Mark V Deluxe Wby. Mag. Cals.* - includes cals. between .257 Wby. Mag. - .340 Wby. Mag., 8 1/2 lbs.

| MSR $2,167 | $1,675 | $1,375 | $1,050 | $775 | $650 | $550 | $500 |

Add approx. $200 for .375 H&H cal. (disc. 1993).

✳ *Mark V Deluxe .30-378 or .378 Wby. Mag.* - .30-378 Wby. Mag. (mfg. 2006), .378 Wby. Mag., 26 (disc.) or 28 (with muzzle brake) in. barrel, 8 1/2 lbs.

MSR $2,551 $1,995 $1,425 $1,125 $800 $650 $550 $500

✳ *Mark V Deluxe .416 Wby. Mag.* - first new caliber (introduced 1989) since the .240 Mag. was released 1965, 26 (disc.) or 28 in. barrel, includes muzzle brake, 9 lbs.

MSR $2,551 $1,995 $1,425 $1,125 $800 $650 $550 $500

✳ *Mark V Deluxe .460 Wby. Mag.* - 24 (disc.), 26 (disc.) or 28 (new 2004) in. barrel, includes custom stock, integral muzzle brake, 10 lbs.

MSR $2,997 $2,375 $1,750 $1,300 $950 $800 $650 $575

This model is available in left-hand at no charge.

ACCUMARK (MAG. CALS.) - .240 Wby. Mag., .257 Wby. Mag., .270 Wby. Mag., .300 Win. Mag., .300 Wby. Mag., .30-378 Wby. Mag. (new 1997), .338-378 Wby Mag. (new 1998), 7mm STW (mfg. 1998-2004), 7mm Rem. Mag., 7mm Wby. Mag., or .340 Wby. Mag. cal., features Bell & Carlson hand laminated fiberglass stock with Pachmayr Decelerator pad, 2 or 3 shot mag., 26 or 28 (.30-378 or .338-378 Wby. Mag. cals. only) in. stainless steel fluted barrel, aluminum bedding plate, approx. 8 3/4 lbs. New 1996.

MSR $1,850 $1,475 $1,165 $950 $825 $725 $600 $550

Add $265 for .30-378 Wby. Mag. or .338-378 Wby. Mag. cals.
Add $72 for left-hand action (current mfg. is .257 Wby. and .300 Wby. Mag. only, other cals. available 1999-2004, reintroduced 2006).

✳ *Accumark (Reg. Cals.)* - .22-250 Rem., .223 Rem. (mfg. 2000-2004), .243 Win., .25-06 Rem., .270 Win., .280 Rem. (disc.), 7mm-08 Rem. (disc.), .30-06, or .308 Win. cal., features hand laminated fiberglass stock with Pachmayr Decelerator pad, 24 in. fluted stainless barrel w/o sights, 7 1/4 lbs. Mfg. 1998-2004, reintroduced 2007.

MSR $1,785 $1,450 $1,125 $900 $800 $700 $600 $550

CLASSICMARK I - available in 9 Wby. Mag. cals. in addition to .270 Win., 7mm Rem. Mag., .30-06, or .375 H&H cal., oil finished American Claro walnut stock with no cheekpiece and ebony forend cap, 1 in. solid recoil pad, panel point checkering. Mfg. 1992-93.

$1,075 $750 $625 $525 $475 $450 $410

Last MSR was $1,295.

Add $15 for 26 in. barrel.
Add $130 for .375 H&H cal.

✳ *Classicmark I .300 or .340 Wby. Mag.* - 26 in. barrel only, right- or left-hand action, 8 1/2 lbs.

$1,095 $775 $625 $525 $475 $450 $410

Last MSR was $1,323.

GRADING - PPGS™	100%	98%	95%	90%	80%	70%	60%

* *Classicmark I .378 Wby. Mag.* - 26 in. barrel only, right- or left-hand action, 8 1/2 lbs.

| | $1,125 | $795 | $625 | $525 | $475 | $450 | $410 |

Last MSR was $1,356.

* *Classicmark I .416 Wby. Mag.* - 26 in. barrel only, right- or left-hand action, integral muzzle brake.

| | $1,150 | $825 | $650 | $550 | $495 | $460 | $430 |

Last MSR was $1,411.

* *Classicmark I .460 Wby. Mag.* - 26 in. barrel only, includes custom stock, integral muzzle brake, 10 lbs. No extra charge for left-hand.

| | $1,250 | $900 | $675 | $575 | $525 | $475 | $430 |

Last MSR was $1,573.

CLASSICMARK II - available in 9 Wby. Mag. cals. in addition to .270 Win., 7mm Rem. Mag., or .30-06, similar to Classicmark I, except has deluxe American walnut with 22 LPI multiple point checkering, steel grip cap, satin finished wood and metal, guaranteed 1 1/2 in. or less 3 shot grouping at 100 yards, right-hand action only. Mfg. 1992 only.

| | $1,525 | $1,175 | $975 | $800 | $650 | $600 | $550 |

Last MSR was $1,775.

Add $28 for 26 in. barrel.

* *Classicmark II .300 or .340 Wby. Mag.* - 26 in. barrel only.

| | $1,550 | $1,175 | $975 | $800 | $650 | $600 | $550 |

Last MSR was $1,803.

* *Classicmark II .378 Wby. Mag.* - 26 in. barrel only.

| | $1,700 | $1,250 | $1,000 | $800 | $650 | $600 | $550 |

Last MSR was $1,976.

* *Classicmark II .416 Wby. Mag.* - 26 in. barrel only, integral muzzle brake.

| | $1,875 | $1,375 | $1,050 | $825 | $650 | $600 | $550 |

Last MSR was $2,128.

* *Classicmark II .460 Wby. Mag.* - 26 in. barrel only, includes custom stock, integral muzzle brake, 10 lbs.

| | $1,925 | $1,400 | $1,050 | $825 | $650 | $600 | $550 |

Last MSR was $2,207.

* *Classicmark II Safari Classic* - .375 H&H cal., 24 in. barrel only, right-hand action, limited edition featuring custom action, quarter rib express and front ramp sights, barrel band swivel and engraved floor plate, stock similar to Classicmark II. Mfg. 1992 only.

| | $2,300 | $1,850 | $1,650 | $1,450 | $1,300 | $1,175 | $995 |

Last MSR was $2,693.

EUROMARK - available in most cals. as the Sporter Model, also includes .378 Wby. Mag. and .416 Wby. Mag., differs from Mark V Deluxe in that it has an oil finished, hand checkered, deluxe American claro walnut stock with ebony pistol grip cap and forend tip, low luster bluing, and solid black recoil pad. Mfg. 1986-92, re-introduced 1995-2002.

| | $1,410 | $975 | $740 | $585 | $475 | $450 | $410 |

Last MSR was $1,819.

Add $312 for either .378 Wby. Mag. or .416 Wby. Mag. cal.

* *Euromark .460 Wby. Mag.* - 24 or 26 in. barrel, includes custom stock, internal muzzle brake, no extra charge for left-hand. Disc. 1992.

| | $1,450 | $1,100 | $925 | $775 | $650 | $600 | $550 |

Last MSR was $1,708.

GRADING - PPGS™	100%	98%	95%	90%	80%	70%	60%

FIBERMARK - available in .240 Wby. Mag., .257 Wby. Mag., .270 Wby. Mag., .30-06, 7mm Wby. Mag., .300 Wby. Mag., or .340 Wby. Mag. cal., black non-glare fiberglass with wrinkle finish stock, metal has non-glare matte finish, 24 or 26 in. barrel, available in right (disc. 1991) or left-hand action, 7 1/4 lbs. Mfg. 1983-92.

	$1,195	$875	$725	$600	$525	$475	$450

Last MSR was $1,376.

Add $118 for .300 or .340 Mag. cal.
This model was available in left-hand action (22 in. barrel) in .270 Win. or .30-06 cal. only.

FIBERMARK (CURRENT MFG.) - available in many cals. between .22-250 Rem. - .375 H&H, Mag. cals. only beginning 2005, 2 (.30-378 Wby. Mag. only) or 3 shot internal mag., pillar bedded black composite Monte Carlo stock of Aramid cross-directional fibers, matte blue metal, 24, 26 (Mag. cals. only), or 28 (.30-378 Wby. Mag. cal. only) in. steel barrel, 6 3/4-8 1/2 lbs. New 2001.

MSR $1,377	$1,095	$840	$675	$500	$400	$350	$325

Add $276 for .30-378 Wby. Mag. cal.

✻ *Fibermark Mark V Stainless* - similar to Mark V Fiberglass, except has stainless steel action and barrel with matte finish. Mfg. 2001-2004.

	$1,075	$775	$650	$540	$465	$385	$335

Last MSR was $1,334.

Add $98 for Mag. cals.
Add $301 for .30-378 Wby. Mag. cal.

LAZERMARK - various cals., differs from the Mark V Deluxe in that stock and forearm have been laser carved, 3 shot mag., 24 (disc.) or 26 in. barrel, 8 1/2 lbs. New 1985.

MSR $2,360	$1,925	$1,300	$915	$725	$575	$475	$450

✻ *Lazermark .378 Wby. Mag. or .416 Wby. Mag.* - first new caliber (introduced 1989) since the .240 Mag. was released 1965, includes muzzle brake. Disc. 2002.

	$1,850	$1,300	$1,025	$825	$650	$575	$525

Last MSR was $2,266.

✻ *Lazermark .460 Wby. Mag.* - 24 (disc. 2000), 26 (disc. 2000), or 28 in. barrel, includes custom stock, internal muzzle brake, no extra charge for left-hand. Disc. 2002.

	$2,150	$1,500	$1,200	$925	$650	$600	$550

Last MSR was $2,661.

✻ *Lazermark Varmintmaster* - .22-250 Rem. or .224 Varmintmaster cal., 24 or 26 in. barrel. Disc. 1991.

	$1,085	$815	$675	$575	$500	$460	$425

Last MSR was $675.

Add $25 for 26 in. barrel.
Not available in left-hand action.

ULTRAMARK (OLDER MFG.) - .240 Wby. Mag., .257 Wby. Mag., .270 Wby. Mag., .30-06, 7mm Wby. Mag., .300 Wby. Mag., .378 Wby. Mag. (mfg. 1989 only), or .416 Wby. Mag. (mfg. 1989 only) cal., fancy American walnut, individually hand-bedded, high luster finish, customized action, 24 or 26 in. barrel, basket weave checkering (including pistol grip). Imported 1989-90 only.

	$1,125	$925	$800	$700	$630	$590	$550

Last MSR was $1,315.

Add $25 for 26 in. barrel.
Add $220 for .378 Wby. Mag. cal. (26 in. barrel only).
Add $325 for .416 Wby. Mag. cal. (26 in. barrel only).

GRADING - PPGS™	100%	98%	95%	90%	80%	70%	60%

WEATHERMARK - available in various Wby. Mag. cals. from .240 (disc. 1996) to .340 and .257 Roberts (disc. 1994), .270 Win., 7mm Rem. Mag., .300 Win. Mag., .30-06, .338 Win. Mag., or .375 H&H (disc.) cal., design is similar to Classicmark II, except is fitted with black checkered composite stock, satin finish black metal, 22 (disc. 1995, .270 Win. or .30-06 only), 24, or 26 in. barrel, right-hand only, 7 1/2 lbs. Mfg. 1992-94.

	$685	$540	$475	$400	$360	$330	$300

Last MSR was $799.

SYNTHETIC (MAG. CALS.) - .240 Wby. Mag., .257 Wby. Mag., .270 Wby. Mag., .300 Wby. Mag., .30-378 Wby. Mag. (new 1998), .300 Win. Mag., .338 Win. Mag. (disc. 2004), .338-378 Wby. Mag. (new 2001), .340 Wby. Mag., 7mm Wby. Mag., 7mm Rem. Mag., 7mm STW (mfg. 2001-2004), or .375 H&H cal., 24, 26, or 28 in. barrel, 2 or 3 shot mag., features lightweight black synthetic stock, bead blasted matte metal finish, approx. 8 lbs. New 1997.

MSR $1,219	$975	$775	$595	$475	$375	$335	$300

Add $220 for .30-378 Wby. Mag. or .338-378 Wby. Mag. cal. (28 in. barrel only).

✳ *Synthetic (Standard Cals.)* - .22-250 Rem., .243 Win., .25-06 Rem., .270 Win., .280 Rem., .30-06, .308 Win., or 7mm-08 Rem. cal., 4 or 5 shot mag., features raised comb, matte black injection mold synthetic stock, no sights, 20 (carbine, .243 Win., .308 Win., or 7mm-08 Rem., disc. 2002) or 24 in. barrel, approx. 6 1/2 lbs. New 1997.

MSR $1,155	$915	$745	$565	$460	$350	$330	$300

✳ *Synthetic Fluted* - .257 Wby. Mag., .270 Wby. Mag., .300 Wby. Mag., .300 Win. Mag., 7mm Wby. Mag., or 7mm Rem. Mag. cal., features 24 or 26 in. fluted barrel, black synthetic stock with Monte Carlo cheekpiece, approx. 7 1/2 lbs. Mfg. 1997-98.

	$785	$635	$550	$495	$450	$395	$350

Last MSR was $949.

✳ *Synthetic Weathermark Alaskan Model* - same cals. as Weathermark, similar to Weathermark, except has non-glare electroless nickel-plated metal parts, right- or left-hand (mfg. 1992 only) action. Mfg. 1992-94.

	$750	$635	$560	$495	$450	$400	$360

Last MSR was $875.

Add $37 for Wby. Mag. cals.
Add $164 for .375 H&H cal.
Add $375 for left-hand action (disc.).

SYNTHETIC STAINLESS MODEL (MAG. CALS.) - same cals. as Synthetic, except not available in .338-.378 Wby. Mag. or 7mm STW, features bead blasted matte stainless construction, synthetic Monte Carlo stock. Mfg. 1995-2004.

	$1,075	$775	$600	$495	$430	$365	$315

Last MSR was $1,282.

Add $200 for .30-378 Wby. Mag. (28 in. barrel only).

✳ *Synthetic Stainless (Standard Cals.)* - .22-250 Rem., .243 Win., .240 Wby. Mag., .25-06 Rem., .270 Win., .280 Rem., .30-06, .308 Win., or 7mm-08 Rem. cal., features raised comb, matte black injection molded synthetic stock, no sights, 20 (carbine, .243 Win., .308 Win., or 7mm-08 Rem. cal.) or 24 in. stainless barrel and action, approx. 6 1/2 lbs. Mfg. 1997-2004.

	$975	$725	$575	$480	$410	$350	$295

Last MSR was $1,166.

GRADING - PPGS™	100%	98%	95%	90%	80%	70%	60%

✻ *Synthetic Fluted Stainless* - .257 Wby. Mag., .270 Wby. Mag., .300 Wby. Mag., .300 Win. Mag., 7mm Wby. Mag., or 7mm Rem. Mag., features 24 or 26 in. fluted stainless barrel and action, black synthetic stock with Monte Carlo cheekpiece, approx. 7 1/2 lbs. Mfg. 1997-98.

	$1,025	$925	$825	$720	$600	$500	$425

Last MSR was $1,149.

EUROSPORT - various cals., features hand-rubbed satin oil finished claro walnut stock with low luster blue metal work. Mfg. 1995-2002.

	$915	$695	$595	$510	$450	$395	$350

Last MSR was $1,143.

MARK V SLS (STAINLESS LAMINATE SPORTER) - .257 Wby. Mag., .270 Wby. Mag., .300 Wby. Mag., .300 Win. Mag., .338 Win. Mag., .340 Wby. Mag., 7mm Wby. Mag., or 7mm Rem. Mag. cal., 24 or 26 (Wby. Mag. cals. only) in. barrel, features grey laminate stock with recoil pad, stainless steel with matte blue finish, approx. 8 1/2 lbs. Mfg. 1997-2002.

	$1,125	$915	$700	$585	$500	$415	$365

Last MSR was $1,393.

SPORTER (LONG ACTION) - .240 Wby. Mag. (mfg. 1996 only), .257 Wby. Mag., .270 Wby. Mag., 7mm Wby. Mag., 7mm Rem. Mag., .270 Win. (mfg. 1996 only), .30-06 (disc. 1996), .300 Wby. Mag., .300 Win. Mag., .338 Win. Mag. (disc. 2004), .340 Wby. Mag., or .375 H&H (disc. 2002) cal., 24 or 26 in. barrel, similar features as the Mark V, except has checkered walnut stock without forearm or pistol grip caps, 3 shot mag., low luster metalwork, vent. recoil pad, no sights, approx. 8 lbs. New 1993.

MSR $1,430	$1,150	$875	$700	$575	$450	$400	$375

✻ *Sporter Standard Action* - .22-250 Rem., .243 Win., .240 Wby. Mag., .25-06 Rem., .270 Win., .280 Rem., .30-06, .308 Win., or 7mm-08 Rem. cal., features raised comb, checkered walnut stock, 54 degree bolt lift, no sights, 24 in. barrel, approx. 6 3/4 lbs. Mfg. 1997-2004.

	$1,000	$775	$650	$525	$450	$400	$375

Last MSR was $1,249.

ULTRA LIGHT WEIGHT - .243 Win., .240 Wby. Mag., .257 Wby. Mag. (new 1999), .25-06 Rem., .270 Win., .270 Wby. Mag. (new 1999), .280 Rem., .300 Wby. Mag. (new 1999), .300 Win. Mag. (new 1999), 7mm-08 Rem., 7mm Rem. Mag. (new 1999), 7mm Wby. Mag. (new 1999), .30-06, .308 Win., or .338-06 A-Square (mfg. 2001-2003) cal., 3 or 5 shot mag., features 24 or 26 in. barrel and lightweight synthetic stock, 5 3/4 or 6 3/4 lbs. New 1998.

MSR $1,789	$1,450	$1,150	$960	$800	$700	$600	$550

Add $88 for long action Mag. cals. (new 1999).
Add $160 for left-hand action (.257 Wby. Mag., .270 Wby. Mag. (disc.), .300 Wby. Mag., .300 Win. Mag. (disc.), 7mm Rem. Mag. (disc.), or 7mm Wby. Mag. (disc.).

WHITETAIL - .257 Sav. cal., limited edition features deluxe high grade Claro walnut, hand checkered bolt knob and engraved floorplate, 22 in. #1 contoured barrel, 6 lbs. Mfg. 1993 only.

	$1,150	$925	$775	$665	$560	$465	$410

Last MSR was $1,366.

SVR (SPECIAL VARMINT RIFLE) - .22-250 Rem. or .223 Rem. cal., features 22 in. free-floating Kreiger barrel, 4 or 5 shot mag., black Monte Carlo composite stock with grey spider webbing, aluminum bedding block, Pachmayr decelerator pad, 7 1/4 lbs. Mfg. 2003-2005.

	$925	$675	$600	$500	$450	$395	$350

Last MSR was $1,176.

GRADING - PPGS™	100%	98%	95%	90%	80%	70%	60%

SPM (SUPER PREDATORMASTER) - .22-250 Rem., .223 Rem., .243 Win., .308 Win., or 7mm-08 Rem. cal., features 24 in. Criterion button rifled barrel with flutes, black spider webbing on tan Accumark type stock with slim forend and CNC aluminum bedding block, Pachmayr Decelerator pad, 6 1/2 lbs. Mfg. 2001-2004.

	$1,375	$1,125	$925	$800	$650	$600	$550

Last MSR was $1,670.

SVM (SUPER VARMINTMASTER) - .220 Swift (single shot only, disc., reintroduced 2005 only), .22-250 Rem., .223 Rem., .243 Win., .308 Win. (disc. 2004), or 7mm-08 Rem. (disc. 2004) cal., features 26 in. Criterion button rifled fluted barrel with crown, 4 or 5 shot mag., available as repeater or single shot, black spider webbing on tan Accumark type stock with beavertail forend and CNC aluminum bedding block, Pachmayr Decelerator pad, approx. 8 1/2 lbs. New 2000.

MSR $1,862	$1,525	$1,225	$975	$835	$675	$600	$550

SPECIAL VARMINTMASTER - .22-250 Rem. or .223 (new 2008), similar to Super Varmintmaster, except has 22 in. barrel. New 2007.

MSR $1,200	$995	$860	$725	$600	$500	$400	$350

SBGM (SUPER BIG GAME MASTER) - various cals. between .240 Wby. Mag. - .338-06 A-Square (disc.), 24 or 26 (Mag. cals. only) in. Criterion hand-lapped fluted Krieger barrel, barreled action is bedded to a specially-designed, hand-laminated, raised comb, Monte Carlo composite stock (a combination of Aramid, graphite and unidirectional fibers, and fiberglass) with black spiderweb patterning, Pachmayr Decelerator pad, 6 3/4 lbs. New 2002.

	$1,375	$1,125	$925	$775	$650	$600	$550

Last MSR was $1,670.

Add $66 for Mag. cals.

TRR (THREAT RESPONSE RIFLE) - .223 Rem., .308 Win., .300 Win. Mag. (disc. 2002), .300 Wby. Mag. (disc. 2002), .30-378 Wby. Mag. (disc. 2002), or .338-.378 Wby. Mag. (disc. 2002) cal., 22 in. barrel, 5 shot mag., Mark V action with black finished metal and black hybrid composite stock, various barrel lengths, optional Picatinny style ring and base system, 8 1/2-10 1/2 lbs. Mfg. 2002-2005.

	$1,400	$1,150	$925	$800	$650	$600	$550

Last MSR was $1,737.

Add $52 for .300 Win. Mag. or .300 Wby. Mag. cals. (disc. 2002).
Add $208 for .30-378 Wby. Mag. or .338-378 Wby. Mag. cals. (disc. 2002).

VARMINTMASTER - .22-250 Rem. or .224 Varmintmaster (disc. 1994) cal., 24 (disc. 1991) or 26 in. barrel, 6 1/2 lbs. Disc. 1995.

	$1,075	$775	$625	$525	$475	$450	$410

Last MSR was $1,297.

Not available in left-hand action.

1976 BICENTENNIAL MARK V - .257 Wby. Mag., .270 Wby. Mag., 7mm Wby. Mag., or .300 Wby Mag. cal., 1,000 mfg. in 1976 only.

	$1,495	$1,150	$895	N/A	N/A	N/A	N/A

Last MSR was $2,000.

1984 MARK V OLYMPIC COMMEMORATIVE - .257 Wby. Mag., .270 Wby. Mag., 7mm Wby. Mag., or .300 Wby. Mag. cal., special gold accenting, extra-fancy walnut stock with burnished brass oval depicting the Olympic "Star In Motion" emblem inlay. Mfg. 1984, only 1,000 mfg. at $2,000 retail.

	$1,000	$895	$700	N/A	N/A	N/A	N/A

GRADING - PPGS™	100%	98%	95%	90%	80%	70%	60%

MARK V 35TH ANNIVERSARY COMMEMORATIVE - .257 Wby. Mag., .270 Wby. Mag., 7mm Wby. Mag., or .300 Wby. Mag. cal., limited mfg. 1980, 1,000 produced total.

	$1,000	$895	$700	N/A	N/A	N/A	N/A

MARK V 40TH ANNIVERSARY COMMEMORATIVE - .257 Wby. Mag. (35 mfg.), .270 Wby. Mag. (35 mfg.), 7mm Wby. Mag. (35 mfg.), or .300 Wby. Mag. (95 mfg.) cal. Limited mfg. 1985, 200 produced total.

	$1,000	$895	$700	N/A	N/A	N/A	N/A

ULTRAMARK (NEW MFG.) - .257 Wby. Mag. or .300 Wby. Mag. cal., fancy checkered American walnut stock with rosewood forend and pistol grip caps, individually hand-bedded, high gloss finish, customized blue action, 26 in. barrel, 8 1/2 lbs. New 2007.

MSR $2,836	$2,285	$2,025	$1,750	$1,500	$1,300	$1,100	$900

RIFLES: BOLT ACTION, CUSTOM SHOP

OUTFITTER CUSTOM - various cals. between .243 Win. - .338-06 A-Square (disc.), 24 or 26 in. barrel, features ultra lightweight bolt action with titanium nitride hardcoating and a desert camo stock. New 2001.

MSR $2,635	$2,115	$1,750	$1,375	$1,075	$850	$700	$600

Add $61 for Mag. cals.

OUTFITTER KREIGER CUSTOM - same cals. as Outfitter Custom, 24 or 26 in. barrel, ultra lightweight action with Kreiger ultra lightweight contoured barrel with cut rifling, trued receiver and bolt face, lapped locking lugs, titanium nitride coating, desert camo stock. Mfg. 2001-2002.

	$2,995	$2,550	$2,175	$1,800	$1,500	$1,250	$995

Last MSR was $3,499.

Add $50 for Mag. cals.

DANGEROUS GAME RIFLE (CUSTOM) - .300 Win. Mag. (mfg. 2002-2004), .300 Wby. Mag. (new 2002), .338 Win. Mag. (mfg. 2002-2004), .340 Wby. Mag. (new 2002), .375 H&H, .375 Wby. Mag., .378 Wby. Mag., .416 Rem. Mag., .416 Wby. Mag., .458 Win. Mag., .458 Lott (new 2005), or .460 Wby. Mag. cal., 24 or 26 in. barrel with express sights (rear is adj.), black fiberglass stock with CNC machined aluminum bedding block and Pachmayr Decelerator pad, black oxide metal finish, 8 3/4 or 9 1/2 (.460 Wby. Mag.) lbs. New 2001.

MSR $3,157	$2,615	$2,125	$1,750	$1,375	$1,075	$875	$700

Add $174 for .378 Wby. Mag. or .416 Wby. Mag., and $270 for .460 Wby. Mag. cal.
Add $295 for snow or desert camo stock with titanium nitride coating.

CUSTOM GRADE - various cals. from .240 Wby. Mag. to .340 Wby. Mag., 24 or 26 in. barrel, super fancy walnut stock featuring No. 7 style inlays, floorplate is engraved "Weatherby Custom", 6-8 months delivery time. Disc. 2001.

	$4,250	$2,750	$2,050	$1,650	$1,450	$1,300	$1,175

Last MSR was $5,099.

TRCM (THREAT RESPONSE CUSTOM MAGNUM) - .300 Win. Mag., .300 Wby. Mag., .30-378 Wby. Mag., or .338-.378 Wby. Mag. cal., Mark V action with ergonomic, fully adjustable composite stock, black finished metal, various barrel lengths, optional Picatinny style ring and base system. New 2002.

MSR $2,946	$2,325	$1,700	$1,225	$950	$725	$650	$575

Add $176 for .30-378 Wby. Mag. or .338-378 Wby. Mag. cals.
Add $499 for desert camo stock with titanium nitride coating.

GRADING - PPGS™	100%	98%	95%	90%	80%	70%	60%

SAFARI GRADE CUSTOM - .257 Wby. Mag. (new 2000), .270 Wby. Mag. (new 2000), .300 Wby. Mag., .340 Wby. Mag., .375 H&H (new 2000), .375 Wby. Mag. (disc. 2006), .378 Wby. Mag., .416 Wby Mag., .416 Rem. Mag. (new 2007), .458 Lott (new 2007), .460 Wby. Mag., or 7mm Wby. Mag. (new 2000) cal., custom order only, various options available, 6-8 month delivery.

MSR $6,171	$5,400	$3,250	$2,125	$1,725	$1,500	$1,300	$1,150

    Add $244 for .378 Wby. Mag. or .416 Wby. Mag. cal.
    Add $92 for .416 Rem. Mag. or .458 Lott cal.
    Add $724 for .460 Wby. Mag. cal.

ROYAL ULTRAMARK CUSTOM - same cals. as Crown Custom, custom order only, features high grade fancy Claro walnut with checkering with rosewood pistol grip cap and forend, damascene bolt and follower, engraved receiver and floorplate, select 24Kt. gold and nickel plating, 26 in. barrel. New 2002.

MSR $5,095	$4,450	$3,400	$2,275	$1,800	$1,600	$1,475	$1,200

CROWN CUSTOM MODEL - .257 Wby. Mag., .270 Wby. Mag., .300 Wby. Mag., .340 Wby. Mag., or 7mm Wby. Mag. cal., custom order only, engraved barrel, receiver, and scope mount, top-of-the-line model.

MSR $8,150	$6,995	$4,200	$3,250	$2,575	$1,950	$1,600	$1,350

RIFLES: BOLT ACTION, VANGUARD SERIES

All currently manufactured Vanguard rifles are shipped with a factory three shot target, guaranteeing 1.5 in. accuracy at 100 yards.

VANGUARD - .243 Win., .25-06 Rem., .270 Win., .30-06, .308 Win., 7mm Rem. Mag., .264 Win. Mag., or .300 Win. Mag. cal., mfg. circa late 1960s-early 1970s.

	$435	$375	$325	$295	$260	$230	$200

    Add 10% for .264 Win. Mag. cal.

VANGUARD SYNTHETIC (NEW MFG.) - .22-250 Rem., .223 Rem., .243 Win., .25-06 Rem. (new 2007), .257 Wby. Mag., .270 Win., .270 WSM (new 2005), .30-06, .308 Win., .300 WSM, .300 Win. Mag., .300 Wby. Mag., .338 Win. Mag., 7mm-08 Rem. (new 2008), or 7mm Rem. Mag. cal., choice of matte black metal or satin stainless steel action/barrel, black synthetic stock, includes many Mark V features, including one-piece fluted bolt with 3 gas ports, 2 locking lugs, and 90-degree bolt lift, 3 or 5 shot mag., 24 in. barrel, adj. trigger, each gun supplied with 3 shot factory target, approx. 7 1/2 lbs. Domestic mfg. beginning 1997.

MSR $525	$445	$400	$335	$300	$265	$230	$200

    Add $18 for WSM cals.
    Add $155 for Vanguard package (includes Bushnell Banner 3-9x40mm scope mounted and bore sighted, Uncle Mike's nylon sling, and Plano molded case, new 2005).
    Add $148 for stainless steel action/barrel.
    Add $263 for Vanguard stainless package (disc. 2006).

VANGUARD SPORTER - same cals. as Vanguard Synthetic, features checkered walnut stock with rosewood forend tip, satin finish and checkering, matte blue metal, 24 in. barrel, 3 or 5 shot mag., 7 3/4 lbs. New 2005.

MSR $689	$560	$475	$420	$355	$315	$270	$240

    Add $141 for matte stainless steel action/barrel (Sporter SS).
    Add $23 for WSM cals.

VANGUARD DELUXE - .257 Wby. Mag., .270 Win., .30-06, .300 Win. Mag. (new 2007), .300 Wby. Mag., or 7mm Rem. Mag. (new 2007) cal., 24 in. barrel w/o sights, features high gloss walnut Monte Carlo stock with rosewood forend tip and pistol grip cap, high gloss bluing, 3 or 5 shot mag., 7 3/4 lbs. New 2006.

MSR $931	$795	$665	$545	$455	$400	$350	$295

    Add $133 for matte stainless steel action/barrel (Deluxe SS, disc. 2006).

GRADING - PPGS™	100%	98%	95%	90%	80%	70%	60%

VANGUARD BACK COUNTRY CUSTOM - .257 Wby. Mag., .270 Win., .30-06, .300 Win. Mag., or .300 Wby. Mag., features stainless steel action and 24 in. fluted barrel, Ultralight composite stock with spider webbing and Pachmayr Decelerator pad, 6 3/4 lbs. New 2008.

MSR $1,065	$875	$725	$575	$450	$375	$335	$300

VANGUARD SAGE COUNTRY CUSTOM - available in various cals. between .22-250 Rem. - .338 Win. Mag., injection molded stock with desert camo, 24 in. barrel, low density recoil pad. New 2008.

MSR $630	$540	$450	$400	$350	$325	$300	$275

Add $23 for .270 WSM or .300 WSM cals.

VANGUARD VARMINT SPECIAL - .204 Ruger (new 2007), .22-250 Rem., .223 Rem., or .308 Win. cal., features checkered hand laminated tan Monte Carlo composite stock with aluminum bedding plate, 22 in. barrel w/o sights, 5 shot mag., 8 1/4 lbs. New 2006.

MSR $620	$535	$450	$395	$345	$315	$270	$240

Add $51 for .204 Ruger (new 2007).

VANGUARD COMPACT - .22-250 Rem., .223 Rem. (new 2008), .243 Win., .308 Win. or 7mm-08 Rem. (new 2006) cal., 20 in. barrel, shortened 12 1/2 LOP, 5 shot mag., matte black hardwood stock, 6 3/4 lbs. New 2005.

MSR $620	$535	$450	$395	$345	$315	$270	$240

VANGUARD SUB-MOA - same cals. as Vanguard Synthetic, matte finished steel or stainless steel action and 24 in. barrel, choice of light tan or charcoal Monte Carlo Fiberguard stock with Pachmayr Decelerator pad, no sights, guaranteed to shoot a three shot .99 in. group at 100 yards, 3 or 5 shot mag., 7 3/4 lbs. New 2005.

MSR $877	$740	$635	$550	$480	$425	$375	$325

Add $142 for stainless steel action/barrel.
Add $29 for WSM cals.

VANGUARD SUB-MOA VARMINT - .204 Ruger (new 2007), .22-250 Rem., .223 Rem., or .308 Win. cal., features hand laminated composite stock with over-sized vented forend and CNC machined aluminum bedding plate, Pachmayr decelerator pad, three sling swivels, 22 in. barrel, 5 shot mag., 8 1/4 lbs. New 2006.

MSR $952	$795	$675	$560	$475	$425	$375	$325

Add $51 for .204 Ruger cal.

VANGUARD CLASSIC I - .223 Rem., .243 Win., .270 Win., 7mm-08 Rem., 7mm Rem. Mag., .30-06, or .308 Win. cal., checkered walnut stock with satin finish, black buttpad, 24 in. barrel, 3 (7mm Rem. Mag.) or 5 shot mag., No. 1 barrel contour, approx. 7 lbs. 5 oz. Mfg. 1989-93.

	$480	$375	$325	$295	$260	$230	$200

Last MSR was $549.

This model was the replacement for the Vanguard VGS and VGL.

VANGUARD CLASSIC II - .22-250 Rem., .243 Win., .270 Wby. Mag., .270 Win., 7mm Rem. Mag., .30-06, .300 Win. Mag., .300 Wby. Mag., or .338 Win. Mag. cal., 24 in. No. 2 barrel contour, 3 or 5 shot mag., custom checkered deluxe walnut stock with pistol grip cap and black forend cap, solid black recoil pad, matte finished metal, approx. 7 3/4 lbs. Mfg. 1989-92.

	$675	$550	$475	$425	$395	$360	$330

Last MSR was $750.

This model was also available in a No. 3 barrel contour in .22-250 Rem. cal. only.

GRADING - PPGS™	100%	98%	95%	90%	80%	70%	60%

VANGUARD VGD - .22-250 Rem., .243 Win., .25-06 Rem., .270 Win., 7mm Rem. Mag., .30-06, or .300 Win. Mag. cal., bolt action, checkered deluxe walnut stock with rosewood tip forearm and pistol grip, 24 in. barrel, no sights, 5 shot mag. (except 3 shot for .300 Win. Mag.), high luster bluing, about 8 lbs. Disc. 1988.

	$525	$425	$365	$330	$300	$275	$255

Last MSR was $600.

Not available in left-hand action.

VANGUARD VGX DELUXE - .22-250 Rem., .243 Win., .270 Win., .270 Wby. Mag., .300 Win. Mag., .300 Wby. Mag., .30-06, .338 Win. Mag., or 7mm Rem. Mag. cal., 24 in. barrel, Monte Carlo stock with skipline checkering, high gloss wood and metal, rosewood grip cap and forend tip. Mfg. 1989-1993.

	$625	$550	$475	$425	$395	$360	$330

Last MSR was $699.

VANGUARD VGS - same cals. as Vanguard VGX, bolt action, checkered satin finished walnut stock, 24 in. barrel, no sights, approx. 8 lbs. Disc. 1988.

	$415	$355	$295	$265	$245	$220	$200

Last MSR was $467.

Not available in left-hand action.

VANGUARD VGL - .223 Rem., .243 Win., .270 Win., 7mm Rem. Mag., .30-06, or .308 Win. cal., lightweight bolt action, checkered walnut stock, 5 shot mag. (6 on .223 Rem.), 20 in. barrel, no sights, 6 1/2 lbs. Disc. 1988.

	$415	$355	$295	$265	$245	$220	$200

Last MSR was $467.

Not available in left-hand action.

VANGUARD WEATHERGUARD - same cals. as Classic I, replacement for Fiberguard, wrinkle black finished synthetic stock, entry level Weatherby, similar specs. as Classic I, approx. 8 lbs. Mfg. 1989-1993.

	$440	$350	$320	$290	$260	$230	$200

Last MSR was $499.

VANGUARD ALASKAN - same cals. as Classic I, features electroless nickel metal plating, no sights. Mfg. 1993-1994.

	$625	$550	$475	$425	$395	$360	$330

Last MSR was $699.

VANGUARD FIBERGUARD - .223 Rem., .243 Win., .270 Win., 7mm Rem. Mag., .30-06, or .308 Win. cal., 20 in. barrel, green fiberglass stock, 3 to 6 shot mags., no sights, blue metal parts, approx. 6 1/2 lbs. Disc. 1988.

	$500	$450	$395	$355	$285	$255	$220

Last MSR was $560.

Not available in left-hand action.

SHOTGUNS: O/U

Weatherby shotguns are currently mfg. by Fausti of Italy. Previous manufacture was by SKB of Japan. Japanese manufacture utilized the IMC choke system (integral multi-choke), which allows interchangeability with Briley choke tubes.

REGENCY FIELD GRADE - 20 ga. Mag. (new 1968) or 12 ga., checkered stock, VR, engraved side plates, SST, early importation beginning in 1967 was from Italy, later mfg. was switched to Japan.

	$1,250	$895	$800	$700	$600	$550	$500

Add 10-15% for early Italian mfg. (note proofmarks).

GRADING - PPGS™	100%	98%	95%	90%	80%	70%	60%

REGENCY TRAP GRADE - 12 ga., checkered trap stock, engraved, VR, SST. Imported from Italy.

	$900	$800	$700	$600	$550	$500	$475

OLYMPIAN STANDARD - 12 and 20 ga., lightly engraved sideplates. Disc. 1980.

	$850	$775	$725	$625	$525	$450	$400

OLYMPIAN SKEET - 26 or 28 in. barrel.

	$885	$775	$725	$625	$525	$450	$400

OLYMPIAN TRAP - 30 or 32 in. barrel, VR.

	$850	$775	$725	$625	$525	$440	$400

ATHENA GRADE III CLASSIC FIELD - 12, 20, or 28 (new 2001) ga., 2 3/4 (28 ga. only) or 3 in. chambers, 26 or 28 in. barrels, features oil finished Claro walnut stock with rounded pistol grip and slender forearm, gold SST (push button on trigger), silver grey nitride sideplates with rose and scroll engraved gold pheasant and quail hunting scenes, gold "W" on opening lever, 6 1/2-8 lbs. Mfg. 1999-2007.

	$2,125	$1,725	$1,375	$1,100	$900	$750	$625

Last MSR was $2,510.

ATHENA D'ITALIA III - 12 or 20 ga., 3 in. chambers, vented 26 or 28 in. VR barrels with choke tubes, ejectors, four-lock boxlock action with chrome plated sideplates with gold game bird scenes, SST (tang operated), checkered oil finished walnut stock and forearm, pierced top lever, trigger guard features Weatherby flying "W", 6 1/2 - 8 lbs. New 2008, mfg. by Fausti.

MSR $2,299	$1,950	$1,675	$1,325	$1,050	$875	$750	$675

ATHENA GRADE IV FIELD - 12, 20, 28 (mfg. 1989-1993) ga., or .410 (mfg. 1989-1993) bore, 3 in. chambers, 26 or 28 in. VR barrels with or without choke tubes, boxlock with Greener Crossbolt, SST, ejectors, high luster finish on hand checkered claro walnut stock (full pistol grip with rosewood cap) and forearm, recoil pad, engraved sideplates with satin nickel finish, vent. barrels and rib, multi-chokes became standard (except .410 bore) 1986 and 1992 (28 ga.), 6 1/2-8 lbs. Mfg. 1982-2002.

	$2,085	$1,525	$1,150	$925	$750	$600	$525

Last MSR was $2,549.

Subtract 10% if without choke tubes.
This model was redesignated the Grade IV in 1989.

* *Athena Grade IV Field Skeet & Trap Models* - 12 (Trap only) or 20 ga., special stock dimensions, target sights. Disc. 1992.

	$1,675	$1,275	$1,000	$875	$725	$600	$525

Last MSR was $1,965.

Skeet models are available in fixed choke only.

* *Athena Grade IV Field Single Trap Model* - 12 ga., 32 or 34 in. barrel with multi-choke feature. Disc. 1992.

	$1,675	$1,275	$1,000	$875	$725	$600	$525

Last MSR was $1,975.

* *Athena Grade IV Field Trap Combo* - 12 ga., includes a set of O/U barrels and oversingle barrel with multi-choke feature. Disc. 1992.

	$2,300	$1,900	$1,605	$1,300	$995	$800	$675

Last MSR was $2,616.

* *Athena Grade IV Field Master Skeet Set* - 12 ga., includes 6 fitted full length Briley tubes with integral extractors (20, 28 ga., and .410 bore), cased. Imported 1988-91.

	$3,100	$2,650	$2,150	$1,900	$1,775	$1,625	$1,525

GRADING - PPGS™	100%	98%	95%	90%	80%	70%	60%

ATHENA D'ITALIA IV - similar to Athena D'Italia III, except also available in 28 ga. New 2008, mfg. by Fausti.

| MSR $2,299 | $2,100 | $1,775 | $1,400 | $1,100 | $900 | $775 | $700 |

Add $300 for 28 ga.

ATHENA GRADE V CLASSIC FIELD - 12 or 20 ga., 3 in. chambers, similar to Grade IV, except has more elaborate engraving w/o gold inlays, gold SST, and better walnut, 6 1/2 - 8 lbs. Mfg. by SKB 1989-2007.

| | $2,375 | $1,900 | $1,600 | $1,300 | $1,100 | $925 | $850 |

Last MSR was $2,773.

In 1993, Weatherby changed the styling of this gun to incorporate European shooting features including an oil finished, round knob stock and slim forearm, tight rose-and-scroll engraving, and matted VR.

ATHENA D'ITALIA V - 12 or 20 ga., vented 26 or 28 in. VR barrels with choke tubes, ejectors, four-lock boxlock action with chrome plates sideplates featuring intricate rose and scroll engraving, raised and engraved hingepin, extra select checkered oil finished walnut stock and forearm, 7 1/2 - 8 lbs. New 2008, mfg. by Fausti.

| MSR $3,599 | $3,000 | $2,650 | $2,300 | $1,950 | $1,650 | $1,350 | $1,175 |

ORION UPLAND CLASSIC FIELD - 12 or 20 ga., 3 in. chambers, features high luster checkered Claro walnut stock and forearm, blue frame, gold SST, gold Weatherby flying W on triggerguard, rounded checkered pistol grip stock and slender forearm, ejectors, 26 or 28 in. VR barrels with choke tubes, 6 1/2 - 8 lbs. Mfg. 1999-2007.

| | $1,225 | $1,050 | $875 | $675 | $550 | $500 | $450 |

Last MSR was $1,500.

ORION I FIELD - 12 or 20 ga., 3 in. chambers, 26, 28, or 30 (12 ga. only) in. VR barrels with multi-chokes, SST, ejectors, checkered walnut full pistol grip stock and forearm, recoil pad, blue receiver with engraved upland and waterfowl scenes, 6 1/2-8 lbs. Mfg. 1989-2002.

| | $1,240 | $1,040 | $860 | $675 | $575 | $525 | $475 |

Last MSR was $1,539.

* *Orion I Field Ducks Unlimited* - 12 ga. (sponsor gun in 1986) or 20 ga. (sponsor gun in 1987), deluxe walnut with gold duck scenes, blue frame, multi-chokes, includes presentation case.

| | $1,395 | $1,100 | $875 | N/A | N/A | N/A | N/A |

ORION D'ITALIA I - 12 or 20 ga., 3 in. chambers, vented 26 or 28 in. VR barrels, ejectors, high lustre checkered walnut stock and forearm, blue boxlock action with game and floral engraving, engraved forearm iron and hinge pin, trigger guard has Weatherby flying "W" engraved in gold, 6 1/2 - 8 lbs. New 2008, mfg. by Fausti.

| MSR $1,499 | $1,275 | $1,050 | $875 | $750 | $675 | $600 | $525 |

ORION II FIELD - 12, 20, 28 ga., or .410 bore, 3 in. chambers (except 28 ga.), boxlock with Greener Crossbolt, SST, ejectors, walnut with high-gloss finish, silver nitride receiver with light engraving. Multi-chokes became standard 1986. Field Grade disc. 1993.

| | $1,075 | $875 | $750 | $625 | $550 | $500 | $450 |

Last MSR was $1,207.

Subtract 10% without choke tubes on older models.
Subtract $14 for Skeet grade (12 and 20 ga., fixed chokes only).
This model was redesignated Grade II in 1989. In 1993, the Standard Field Models in this variation were discontinued (Classic Grade took its place) - only Field and Sporting Clays variations are now available.

GRADING - PPGS™	100%	98%	95%	90%	80%	70%	60%

✳ *Orion II Field Classic* - 12, 20, or 28 ga., multi-choked barrels with matted VR, features rounded pistol grip stock and oil finished Claro walnut stock and forearm, gold SST, ejectors, waterfowl and upland game scenes on silver grey nitride finish, 6 1/2 - 8 lbs. Mfg. 1993-2007.

		$1,500	$1,225	$950	$775	$625	$550	$495

Last MSR was $1,873.

ORION II FIELD/CLASSIC SPORTING - 12 ga. only, Sporting Clays configuration, early mfg. was blue finish, current mfg. is silver nitride finish, choice of Field Sporting (with rosewood pistol grip cap and grooved upper forearm) or Classic Field Sporting (rounded pistol grip and smaller forearm), acid etched engraving, rounded recoil pad, matte finish VR, lengthened forcing cones. Mfg. 1991-2002.

		$1,400	$1,115	$925	$725	$625	$565	$515

Last MSR was $1,753.

ORION D'ITALIA II - 12, 20, or 28 ga., vented 26, 28, or 30 (12 ga. only) in. VR barrel, ejectors, fancy grade checkered walnut stock and forearm, hard chrome receiver with game and floral engraving, engraved forearm iron and hinge pin, trigger guard has Weatherby flying "W" engraved in gold, 6 1/2 - 8 lbs. New 2008, mfg. by Fausti.

MSR $1,599		$1,350	$1,100	$900	$775	$700	$625	$550

Add $78 for 28 ga.

SUPER SPORTING CLAYS (SSC) - 12 ga. only, 3 in. chambers, 28, 30, or 32 in. vented barrels with 12mm target VR and gas ports, choke tubes, fully adj. trigger, satin oil finished sporter style pistol grip stock with Schnabel forearm, Pachmayr Decelerator pad, approx. 8 lbs. Mfg. 1999-2007.

		$1,875	$1,525	$1,200	$900	$750	$650	$575

Last MSR was $2,378.

ORION D'ITALIA SC (SPORTING CLAYS) - 12 ga., 28, 30, or 32 in. ported barrels, ejectors, four-lock boxlock action, satin oil finished checkered walnut stock with adj. comb, pistol grip, and Schnabel forend, chrome plated receiver with engraved Weatherby logo, trigger guard has gold engraved flying "W", 8 lbs. New 2008, mfg. by Fausti.

MSR $2,299		$1,950	$1,750	$1,500	$1,275	$1,050	$925	$800

ORION III FIELD - 12 or 20 ga. only, similar to Grade II, except has silver grey receiver with custom engraving including mallard and pheasant game scenes, multi-chokes standard. Mfg. 1989-2002.

		$1,545	$1,225	$965	$795	$675	$600	$525

Last MSR was $1,917.

✳ *Orion III Field Classic* - 12 or 20 ga., multi-choked 26 or 28 in. VR barrels, features rounded pistol grip stock and oil finished Claro walnut stock and forearm, extensive engraving on silver grey nitride finish with gold game scene inlays, matted VR, 7 1/4-8 lbs. Mfg. 1993-2007.

		$1,800	$1,375	$1,025	$825	$700	$600	$525

Last MSR was $2,258.

✳ *Orion III Field English* - 12 or 20 ga., 3 in. chambers, features straight grip stock and silver grey nitride receiver with engraving and gold inlays, approx. 6 1/2 lbs. Mfg. 1997-2002.

		$1,595	$1,300	$1,075	$875	$700	$625	$550

Last MSR was $1,998.

ORION D'ITALIA III - similar to Orion D'Italia II, except has better walnut and gold inlays. New 2008, mfg. by Fausti.

MSR $1,975		$1,675	$1,475	$1,250	$1,050	$925	$800	$675

GRADING - PPGS™	100%	98%	95%	90%	80%	70%	60%

SHOTGUNS: SxS

Current manufacture is by Fausti of Italy. SxS manufacture utilized the IMC choke system (integral multi-choke), which allows interchangeability with Briley choke tubes. Importation was disc. during 2003, and reintroduced during 2005.

ORION - 12, 20, 28 ga. or .410 bore, 3 in. chambers standard except for 28 ga., ejectors, case colored boxlock action, gold SST, 18 LPI checkered half-round pistol grip Turkish walnut stock and semi-beavertail forearm, 26 or 28 in. barrels, solid pad, 6 3/4-7 lbs., approx. 400 mfg. (including Athena) in Spain by Abolla 2002-2003.

	$960	$845	$735	$625	$525	$450	$395

Last MSR was $1,149.

ORION D'ITALIA SBS - 12 or 20 ga., 3 in. chambers, SST, 26 (20 ga. only) or 28 (12 ga. only) in. back bored barrels with choke tubes, coin finished boxlock action, gloss finished checkered pistol grip stock and beavertail forearm, Weatherby flying "W" in gold on trigger guard, 6 3/4 - 7 1/4 lbs. New 2008, mfg. by Fausti.

MSR $2,099		$1,775	$1,525	$1,300	$1,100	$900	$800	$700

ATHENA - 12 or 20 ga. 3 in. chambers, ejectors, case colored engraved boxlock action with sideplates, gold SST, 22 LPI checkered straight grip select Turkish walnut stock and splinter forearm, 26 or 28 in. barrels with IMC choke system (interchangeable with Briley), solid pad, 6 3/4-7 lbs., approx. 400 (including Orion) mfg. in Spain by Abolla 2002-2003.

	$1,285	$1,025	$865	$750	$650	$550	$475

Last MSR was $1,599.

ATHENA D´ITALIA - 12, 20, or 28 ga., 2 3/4 (28 ga. only) or 3 in. chambers, engraved coin finished Anson & Deeley boxlock action with sideplates, double locking system, monobloc barrels with ejectors and stainless steel choke tubes, DTs, oil finished English straight grip select walnut stock and slim forearm with new Scottish checkering, gold "W" on triggerguard, supplied with hardshell takedown case, 6 3/4 - 7 1/4 lbs. Mfg. by Fausti of Italy. New 2005.

MSR $2,925		$2,475	$2,175	$1,865	$1,600	$1,350	$1,125	$875

Add $140 for 28 ga.

* *Athena D'Italia PG* - 12, 20, or 28 ga., similar boxlock action, except has more engraving, gold SST, deluxe checkered walnut rounded pistol grip stock and semi-beavertail forearm, 6 3/4 - 7 1/4 lbs. Mfg. by Fausti of Italy. New 2006.

MSR $3,599		$3,000	$2,600	$2,200	$1,850	$1,500	$1,300	$1,200

Add $126 for 28 ga.

* *Athena D'Italia Deluxe* - 12, 20, or 28 ga., coin finished boxlock action with sideplates featuring Bulino style game scene engraving and gold inlays by A. Posilini (hand signed), relief engraved shoulders, AAA straight grip 24 LPI checkered Turkish walnut stock with wood buttplate and splinter forearm, gold SST, ejectors, 6 3/4 - 7 1/4 lbs. Mfg. by Fausti of Italy. New 2006.

MSR $7,625		$6,900	$6,400	$5,600	$4,700	$4,000	$3,250	$2,500

Add $164 for 28 ga.

SHOTGUNS: SEMI-AUTO

Previous manufacture was by ITI of Italy until 2007, and utilized the IMC choke system (integral multi-choke), which allows interchangeability with Briley choke tubes. Beginning 2008, all semi-autos are manufactured in Turkey.

Add $359 for interchangeable SAS rifled 22 in. slug barrel (mfg. 2004-2007).

GRADING - PPGS™	100%	98%	95%	90%	80%	70%	60%

CENTURION FIELD GRADE - 12 ga., VR, checkered stock, gas operation, walnut full pistol grip stock. Mfg. 1972-81.

	$300	$280	$250	$240	$230	$210	$190

CENTURION TRAP GRADE - 12 ga., checkered stock, VR.

	$335	$300	$250	$240	$230	$210	$190

CENTURION DE LUXE - 12 ga., VR, checkered stock, lightly engraved.

	$375	$350	$310	$275	$250	$235	$210

Add 20% for deluxe wood.

✻ *Centurion De Luxe DU* - mfg. 1980 for DU chapters.

	$550	$375	$325	N/A	N/A	N/A	N/A

MODEL 82 - 12 ga. only, 2 3/4 or 3 in. chamber, gas operation, alloy receiver, VR, deluxe walnut, multi-chokes became standard in 1985, Trap Grade was disc. 1984. Mfg. 1983-89.

	$395	$350	$315	$280	$250	$235	$210

Last MSR was $500.

Subtract $30 without multi-chokes.
Subtract $35 for Trap Grade (disc. 1984).

✻ *Model 82 Buckmaster* - 22 in. barrel choked skeet, rifle sights, 7 1/2 lbs. Disc. 1989.

	$395	$350	$315	$280	$250	$235	$210

Last MSR was $500.

MODEL SAS FIELD - 12 ga., 3 in. chamber, self-compensating gas operated mechanism, high grade satin oil finished checkered Claro walnut stock and forearm, includes stock shim system, Weatherby outlined in gold on right side of receiver, 26, 28 (disc. 2001, reintroduced 2005), or 30 (12 ga. only. disc. 2001) in. VR barrel with Briley choke tubes, 6 3/4-7 3/4 lbs., mfg. in Italy. Mfg. 1999-2007.

	$775	$640	$560	$480	$400	$350	$300

Last MSR was $926.

✻ *Model SAS Field Sporting Clays* - similar to SAS Field, except has choice of 26 (disc. 2004), 28, or 30 (new 2005) in. ported VR barrel with extended choke tubes, Includes molded plastic case, 7 - 7 3/4 lbs. Mfg. 2002-2005.

	$850	$725	$625	$525	$425	$375	$325

Last MSR was $999.

✻ *Model SAS Field Synthetic* - similar to Model SAS Field, except has black synthetic stock and forearm. Mfg. late 2000-2007.

	$745	$615	$530	$465	$415	$350	$300

Last MSR was $879.

✻ *Model SAS Field Camo* - 12 ga. only, 24 (Mossy Oak Breakup only, new 2001) 26, or 28 (Shadow Grass only) in. VR barrel with 5 extended Briley choke tubes, Hi-Viz front sight, 100% camo coverage in either Mossy Oak Breakup (disc. 2006), Shadow Grass (disc. 2006), Skyline Fall Flight (new 2007), or Skyline Apparition Excel (new 2007), 7 1/4 - 7 3/4 lbs. Mfg. late 2000-2007.

	$810	$685	$580	$475	$400	$350	$300

Last MSR was $977.

✻ *Model SAS Field Slug Gun* - 12 ga. only, 3 in. chamber, 22 in. rifled barrel w/o sights, includes cantilever base, checkered Monte Carlo walnut stock and forearm with sling swivels, 7 3/4 lbs. Mfg. 2003-2007.

	$825	$695	$585	$475	$400	$350	$300

Last MSR was $987.

GRADING - PPGS™	100%	98%	95%	90%	80%	70%	60%

SA-08 UPLAND - 12 or 20 ga., 3 in. chamber, gas action with dual valves for light or heavy loads, 26 or 28 in. VR barrel with choke tubes, matte black receiver with Weatherby in gold on right side, oil finished checkered stock and forearm, 6-6 3/4 lbs., mfg. in Turkey. New 2008.

MSR $669	$565	$495	$425	$350	$315	$285	$250

This model is also available as a SA-08 Youth in 20 ga. with 12 1/2 LOP at no extra charge.

SHOTGUNS: SLIDE ACTION

PATRICIAN FIELD GRADE - 12 ga., checkered stock, VR. Mfg. 1972-81.

	$275	$230	$210	$190	$180	$160	$140

PATRICIAN TRAP GRADE - 12 ga., checkered stock, VR.

	$295	$250	$225	$200	$185	$175	$165

PATRICIAN DE LUXE - 12 ga., checkered stock, lightly engraved, fancy wood, VR.

	$325	$275	$250	$215	$195	$175	$165

MODEL 92 - 12 ga. only, 2 3/4 and 3 in. chambers, ultra-short slide action w/ twin rails, 26-30 in. VR barrels, engraved black alloy receiver, checkered pistol grip walnut stock and forearm. Mfg. 1982-89.

	$325	$275	$250	$225	$200	$185	$175

Last MSR was $400.

Subtract 10% for Trap grade (disc. 1984).
Subtract 10% if fixed choke (multi-chokes became standard 1985) barrel.

✳ *Model 92 Buckmaster* - 22 in. skeet bore barrel, rifle sights, 7 1/2 lbs. Disc. 1987.

	$345	$285	$260	$240	$220	$200	$185

Last MSR was $400.

PA-08 UPLAND - 12 ga., 3 in. chamber, 26 or 28 in. VR ribbed barrel with choke tubes, dual slide bar action, matte black metal, checkered low lustre walnut stock and forearm, 6 1/2 lbs. New 2008.

MSR $349	$295	$265	$235	$200	$185	$170	$155

PA-08 KNOXX STRUTTER X - 12 ga., 24 in. VR barrel with choke tubes, features adj. Knoxx reduction system with pistol grip, fiber optic sights, drop out trigger system, choice of matte black metal finish and black synthetic stock and forearm or 100% Apparition Excel camo coverage, 7 lbs., mfg. in Turkey. New 2008.

MSR $499	$425	$350	$300	$260	$220	$200	$180

Add $80 for 100% camo coverage.

PA-08 HD - 12 ga., 3 in. chamber, 18 in. barrel with fixed IC choke, features black synthetic Knoxx SpecOps adj. stock with pistol grip, extended mag. (5 shot capacity), 7 lbs., mfg. in Turkey. New 2008.

MSR $499	$425	$350	$300	$260	$220	$200	$180

WEAVER ARMS CORPORATION

Previous manufacturer located in Escondido, CA circa 1984-1990.

CARBINES

NIGHTHAWK CARBINE - 9mm Para. cal., semi-auto paramilitary design carbine, fires from closed bolt, 16.1 in. barrel, retractable shoulder stock, 25, 32, 40, or 50 shot mag. (interchangeable with Uzi), ambidextrous safety, parkerized finish, 6 1/2 lbs. Mfg. 1987-90.

	$675	$600	$525	$450	$375	$325	$300

Last MSR was $575.

GRADING - PPGS™	100%	98%	95%	90%	80%	70%	60%

PISTOLS: SEMI-AUTO

NIGHTHAWK PISTOL - 9mm Para. cal., closed bolt semi-auto, 10 or 12 in. barrel, alloy upper receiver, ambidextrous safety, black finish, 5 lbs. Mfg. 1987-90.

	$800	$700	$625	$550	$475	$425	$350

Last MSR was $475.

WEBLEY & SCOTT, LIMITED

Current firearms and airguns manufacturer located in West Midlands, England, with history dating back to 1790. Previously located in Birmingham, England. Currently imported and distributed beginning late 2007 by Legacy Sports International, located in Reno, NV.

For more information and current pricing on both new and used Webley & Scott airguns, please refer to the *Blue Book of Airguns* by Dr. Robert Beeman & John Allen (also online).

HISTORY OF WEBLEY & SCOTT

Webley & Scott is one the oldest names in the UK gun industry, being able to trace its origins back to 1790 when William Davies started making bullet moulds in his small factory in Birmingham, England. In this early period Birmingham flourished as the greatest manufacturing centre of firearms in the world. Yet the only official proof house was in London, then in 1813 the world famous Birmingham Proof House was established by an Act of Parliament.

In 1827 14 year old Philip Webley was apprenticed to Benjamin Watson a, Gun Lock filer. Having completed his apprenticeship he joined up with his brother in 1835 and formed Webley Brothers - Percussioners, Gun Lock & c.makers in Weaman Street, next door to William Davis. Philip began courting Caroline Davis, who following the death of her father three years earlier was running the family business alongside her mother. When the pair married in 1838 the two firms amalgamated. Over the next sixty years P. Webley and Sons prospered and grew, sons Thomas and Henry joining the company.

During the 1850s they began manufacturing percussion cap and ball revolvers. This was a time of unrest across the globe with the Crimea War, Indian Mutiny and the American Civil War and it created great demand for Webley's products. During the last quarter of the 19th century saw the introduction of firstly muzzle loaders, then breech loading rifle and the change from black powder to smokeless powder. In 1887 the company took over the well known firm of Tipping & Lawden of Constitution Hill, Birmingham, England and in the same year saw the award of the first of many Government contracts for the supply of revolvers from its new, modern and automated factory. Philip Webley died in 1888 aged 76 leaving the firm in the hands of his sons. In 1896 they built a second factory in Weaman Street for the production of rifles, notably the Martini-Henry Target Rifle.

W & C Scott was founded in 1832 by the brothers William and Charles Scott, who had moved to Birmingham from their native Suffolk and by the mid 1840s were gaining a reputation for the production of high quality double guns. Two of William's sons, William Middleditch and James Charles joined the company and it was renamed as W & C Scott & Sons, and in 1855 moved to larger premises at 94-95 Bath Street, Birmingham. In 1864 the continued success of the company necessitated a move to larger premises and the building of the world famous Premier Gun Works on Lancaster Street, Birmingham.

The Scott brothers were true innovators with many patents to their name, some of them truly historic. One of the earliest was the Scott spindle in connection was the top lever, this is still used today by makers of high grade breech loaders. They introduced the block safety catch for hammerless guns and later still the double catch hammerless lock which is still in use today.

William Middleditch was a brilliant engineer, having his first patent filed in 1865 and in 1878 he became the first man to design and patent a successful sidelock shotgun. This shotgun was manufactured under royalty arrangements by a number of firms, including Holland and Holland. He retired from the firm in 1894 and James became head of the company until he too retired at the time of the amalgamation of the three companies in 1897.

The amalgamation in 1897 of the three companies created a new public company registered under the name Webley and Scott Revolver and Arms Co Ltd, with a total capital of £335,000. Thomas Webley became Managing Director, Martin Scott, Richard Ellis, William Henry Ellis and Albert Ellis became departmental managers. Webley revolvers and Scott shotguns were popular and the new company prospered.

Over the 20th Century many forces came to bear on the company such as the 1920 Firearms Act that virtually barred individuals from owning handguns, the compulsory purchase of the Weaman Street factory for a road widening scheme and a general increase in competition from abroad. The company changed hands several times and in 1965 the company took over the gunmakers W.W. Greener who had moved to Birmingham in 1844.

The company diversified, producing parts for cars, airguns and general engineering components. At the end of the 1970's the production of shotguns was terminated at Webley and Scott and a seperate company was formed, W&C Scott (Gunmakers) Limited. In January 1985, this entire business was sold to the world famous shotgun makers Holland and Holland. Holland and Holland had been one of the companies which originally bought firearms "in the white" from Webley and Scott. Shortly after being acquired by Holland & Holland, firearms manufacture was discontinued while airgun production resumed.

In 2006 Webley & Scott was purchased by AGS, and once again began making shotguns under the name Webley & Scott.

To list all the types and models of guns and rifles produced by the company over the centuries would fill a separate book, but some of the more famous are the Webley falling block rifles, the Scott Imperial Premier Sidelock Hammerless shotgun and the Model 700 Boxlock Hammerless Sporting Shotgun.

Historical information courtesy of Webley & Scott.

PISTOLS: SEMI-AUTO

MODEL 1903 - .38 cal., experimental model.
Extreme rarity precludes accurate pricing on this model.

MODEL 1904 - .455 cal., limited production, 10-15 mfg.
Extreme rarity precludes accurate pricing on this model.

MODEL 1905 - 7.65mm-.32 cal., ser. no. range 1-22,309, approx. 13,000+ mfg. from 1906-1909.

$1,500	$1,300	$1,100	$750	$600	$400	$300

MODEL 1906 - .45 cal., never reached serial production.
Extreme rarity precludes accurate pricing on this model.

MODEL 1907 - 6.35mm cal., .25 cal. hammer model, ser. no. range 7,060-163,109, approx. 50,000 mfg. from 1906-1939.

$1,000	$900	$800	$700	$600	$500	$400

MODEL 1908 - .32 cal., ser. no. range 22,310-163,709, approx. 90,000 mfg. from 1909-1940.

$750	$650	$550	$450	$350	$250	$200

MODEL 1909 - 9mm Browning Long cal., ser. no. range 16,000-116,8873, approx. 1,700 mfg. from 1909-1915.

$2,000	$1,900	$1,800	$1,700	$1,600	$1,500	$1,400

MODEL 1910 - .380 ACP cal., ser. no. range 55,047-156,175, less than 2,000 mfg. from 1910-1932.

$2,000	$1,900	$1,800	$1,700	$1,600	$1,500	$1,400

MODEL 1910 - .38 ACP cal., ser. no. range 40,000-66,664, less than 1,000 mfg. from 1909-1911.

$3,500	$3,000	$2,500	$2,000	$1,750	$1,500	$1,400

METROPOLITAN POLICE MODEL - .32 cal., ser. no. range 57,000-163,382, approx. 15,000 mfg. from 1911-1940.

$1,500	$1,400	$1,300	$1,000	$750	$500	$400

GRADING - PPGS™	100%	98%	95%	90%	80%	70%	60%

MODEL 1911 - .22 LR cal., single shot target pistol, 4 1/2 or 9 in. barrel, ser. no. range 58,536-156,398, less than 1,400 mfg. from 1911-1932.

	$2,000	$1,900	$1,800	$1,700	$1,600	$1,500	$1,400

Add 100%-200% for shoulder stock or sets with both barrel lengths.

MODEL 1912 - 6.35mm cal., .25 cal. hammerless version of the Model 1907, ser. no. range 41,000-161,859, approx. 15,000 mfg. from 1909-1938.

	$1,500	$1,400	$1,300	$1,000	$750	$500	$400

NAVY MODEL .455 MKI - .455 auto cal. version of the Model 1913, government contract, ser. no. range 1-8,000, approx. 500 were Australian contract, commercial production probably never reached 1,000 with number 158919 being finished in Dec. 1933. Mfg. 1913-1919.

	$2,000	$1,900	$1,800	$1,700	$1,600	$1,500	$1,400

ROYAL HORSE ARTILLERY MODEL .455 MKI - .455 Webley auto cal., ser. no. range 2,501-8,050, less than 500 mfg. 1913-1919.

	$7,000	$6,000	$5,000	$4,500	$4,000	$3,700	$3,600

Add 100%-200% for shoulder stock.

MODEL 1921 - .32 cal., Improved Model, Webley's final attempt at modernizing the .32 auto, ser. no. range 106,000-160,000, less than 4,500 mfg. from 1921-1940.

	$3,500	$3,300	$3,000	$2,500	$2,000	$1,800	$1,700

MODEL 1922 - 9mm cal., also known as the New Military & Police Model, the African Model, and the Romanian Model, ser. no. range 130,000-160,000, less than 1,900 mfg. from 1920-1932.

	$4,500	$4,000	$3,500	$3,000	$2,500	$2,000	$1,900

"HUMANE KILLER" MODEL - .32 cal., single shot variation based on the .32 auto cal. models, designed specifically for the humane put-down of livestock, used by vets, the Royal Society for the Prevention of Cruelty to Animals, and the Ministry of Agriculture and Fisheries, ser. no. range 100,000-200,000, less than 1,000 mfg. 1920-1940.

	$1,000	$900	$800	$700	$550	$450	$350

PISTOLS: SINGLE SHOT

SINGLE SHOT MODELS - usually found in .22 LR cal., tip-up 10 3/8 in. barrel, target model, checkered walnut grips, early model grip terminates with steel weight to provide balance, also provides a means to attach a shoulder stock on some models, original model is improved with thumbrest as part of the wood grip, by the 1950s, thumbrest is expanded. pronounced and plastic, large grip has room for steel weight at the bottom.

	$1,500	$1,400	$1,300	$1,200	$1,100	$1,000	$900

Add 200%-300% for special order .32 S&W or .38 S&W cals.

M1911 TARGET MODEL - .22 LR cal., developed as companion piece for the Metropolitan Police .32 cal. service semi-auto, interchangeable 4 1/2 or 9 in. barrel, shoulder stock, could be ordered with both barrels, ser. no. range 58536 - 156398. Approx. 1,400 mfg. 1911-1932.

	$2,000	$1,900	$1,800	$1,700	$1,600	$1,500	$1,400

Add 150% - 200% four shoulder stock or sets with both barrel lengths.

WEBLEY PERCUSSION MODELS

The first patents for the Webley revolver were issued to brothers James and Phillip Webley in the months of February and March of 1853. Prior to 1853 and up to 1867, Webely revolvers went through a period of development, including the percussion system, the pinfire, rimfire, and finally, the more common centerfire system. Webley made the early Webley pistols, other makers in England, and on the continent made pistols to the Webley design.

GRADING - PPGS™	100%	98%	95%	90%	80%	70%	60%

The early percussion revolvers were of the open frame design similar to the Colt 1851 or 1860. Of particular note would be the three single action Lockspur models. The Longspur was easily identified by its overly long hammer spur, made in a pocket, holster and belt model, with barrel lengths from 3 1/2 to 7 inches, and in calibers from 48 ga. to 120 ga.

FIRST MODEL LONGSPUR - barrel hinged to frame, sides of frame obscure hammer except for spur, and no attached rammer, ser. no. range 131-388. Mfg. 1853-1855.

Extreme rarity preclues accurate pricing on this model.

SECOND MODEL LONGSPUR - barrel still hinged to frame, hammer more visible, also featured rammer attached to frame, ser. no. range 199-969. Mfg. 1855-1857.

Extreme rarity precludes accurate pricing on this model.

THIRD MODEL LONGSPUR - barrel not hinged to frame but attached via barrel over cylinder pin and is secured with thumb screw to frame with screw through cylinder pin, compound rammer is attached to barrel side, ser. no. range 985-1602. Mfg. 1857-1867.

Extreme rarity precludes accurate pricing on this model.

WEDGE FRAME MODELS - between 1857 and 1859, Webley developed the "wedge frame" as a transition between the "open frame" of the longspur and the final "solid frame" percussion pistol which would develop into the solid frame cartridge pistols that would become a hallmark of the Webley brand. This model met with great success with numerous guns being produced during a short time, most were made with attached ram under barrel or side barrel, five or six shot cylinder, numerous calibers and barrel lengths. Few examples have survived. Mfg. 1857-1859.

Extreme rarity precludes accurate pricing on this model.

SOLID FRAME MODELS - the development of the solid frame percussion revolver offered a rigidity in frame design that would last into the modern revolver, few of the percussion revolvers with the solid frame were produced by Webley because of the development of more modern cartridge systems. Final development of the Webley solid frame revolver culminates with the arrival in 1867 of Webely's RIC No. 1, the model officially adopted by the Royal Irish Constabulary in Jan. 1868, presented to George A. Custer in 1869, and the model produced by Webley until the 1930s in one form or another.

Extreme rarity factor of solid frame percussion, pinfire, and rimfire models precludes accurate pricing.

REVOLVERS

WEBLEY-FOSBERY AUTOMATIC MODELS - .455 cal., 6 shot, hinged frame, 4, 6, or 7 1/2 in. barrel, blue or nickel finish, walnut or hard rubber grips, ser. no. range 1-less than 5,000. Mfg. 1901-1924.

✳ *Webley-Fosbery Automatic Model First 1901* - ser. nos. under 300, production prior to Dec. 1901.

	100%	98%	95%	90%	80%	70%	60%
	$8,000	$7,000	$6,000	$5,000	$4,000	$3,500	$3,000

✳ *Webley-Fosbery Automatic Model 1902* - .38 Webley auto cal., 8 shot, ser. no. range mid 200-mid 1,300, extremely rare, less than 800 mfg. 1902-1903.

This model is extremely rare, and values may exceed 200% - 400% of values for the Model 1901 or the Model 1903.

✳ *Webley-Fosbery Automatic Model First 1903* - .455 cal., 6 shot, large and small frame, ser. nos. between 100 and 4930.

	100%	98%	95%	90%	80%	70%	60%
	$6,500	$5,500	$4,500	$4,000	$3,500	$3,000	$2,500

GRADING - PPGS™	100%	98%	95%	90%	80%	70%	60%

R.I.C. MODELS - .320, .380, .442, .450, .455, .476, .44 Win., .45 Colt, or .45 ACP cal., adopted by the Royal Irish Constabulary in Jan., 1868, recognized world-wide and produced in one variation or another from 1867-1939.

⁎ *R.I.C. Model No. 1* - .442 or .455 cal., first of the series was offered .442 cal. with 4 1/2 barrel, later No. 1 New Model was offered in .455 cal., ser. nos. exceeded 60,300 by Oct., 1884.

	$1,000	$900	$800	$700	$600	$500	$400

⁎ *R.I.C. Model No. 2* - .320, .380, .442, or .450 cal., 2 to 4 in. barrels, ser. nos. reached 100139 by 1914.

	$1,000	$900	$800	$700	$600	$500	$400

⁎ *R.I.C. Model No. 3* - typically found in .442 cal., 2 to 4 in. barrels, ser. nos. range from single digits to 15,000, 16,000, 30,000 and 70,000, 4 in. barrel variation was chosen as the official police weapon of the Queensland Govt. in Australia.

	$1,000	$900	$800	$700	$600	$500	$400

⁎ *R.I.C. Model 83* - .320, .380, .450, or .455 cal., 2 1/4, 2 1/2, 3, or 3 1/2 in. barrel, ser. no. 102,634. Mfg. until 1939.

	$900	$800	$700	$600	$500	$400	$300

⁎ *M. P. Model* - .450 cal., introduced after the R.I.C. New Model No. 1, 6 shot, adopted by the London Metropolitan Police in 1883 and remained in service until 1911.

	$900	$800	$700	$600	$500	$400	$300

WEBLEY NO. 1 1/2 MODEL - .442 or .450 cal., 4 1/4 in. octagon barrel, limited examples of ser. nos. 28,000 and 60,000 have been observed.

	$1,000	$900	$800	$700	$600	$500	$400

WEBLEY NO. 2 BULL DOG PATTERN - .320, .380, .442, .450, or .500 cal., short (2-3 in.) barrel, designed and manufactured by Webley as pocket models for civilians, with model names such as British Bulldog, The Pug, The Ulster Bull-dog, or The Tower Bulldog, all share same serial number range (exceeding 100,000).

	$900	$800	$700	$600	$500	$400	$300

WEBLEY NO. 5 EXPRESS MODEL - .360, .380, .450, .455, or .476 cal., include the large caliber military version and the small caliber civilian version, early military versions were based on the R.I.C. No. 1 frame with 6 in. barrel and came in .450 or .455 cal., New Model Express had new birdshead grip frame, .455 cal., and 5 1/2 in. barrel, military versions also included a single action in .476 cal., with 5 1/2 in. barrel issued to the Cape Mounted Rifles in 1881, civilian version offered in .360 or .380 cal., with a 2 1/2 - 4 1/2 in. barrel being the most common, ser. nos. range from the low 1000 to excess of 10000000.

	100%	98%	95%	90%	80%	70%	60%
Large Cals. (Military)	$2,000	$1,900	$1,800	$1,700	$1,200	$900	$600
Small Cals. (Civilian)	$1,000	$900	$800	$700	$600	$500	$400

Cased, engraved, or unusual examples will command a premium.

REVOLVERS: HINGED FRAME, CENTERFIRE

WOODS PATTERN - .450 cal., 6 shot, double action, 5 in. barrel, mfg. circa 1870. Extreme rarity precludes accurate pricing on this model.

WEBLEY NO. 4 PRYSE PATTERN - .32, .38, .44, .450, .455, .476, or 7.577 cal., double action, 3 to 5 3/4 in. barrel, numerous makers produced this model from the mid 1870s, Webley production covered a ser. no. range from 364 to 81,035.

	$2,500	$2,000	$1,500	$1,000	$800	$700	$600

Webley-marked models may command premiums over other makers. Cased, engraved, or inscribed examples will also command a premium.

GRADING - PPGS™	100%	98%	95%	90%	80%	70%	60%

WEBLEY IMPROVED GOVT. - .455 cal., 5 3/4 in. barrel, 6 shot, birdshead grips, blue or nickel finish, identified as the "Kaufmann" pattern. Mfg. circa early 1880s.

✳ *Webley Improved Govt. First Pattern* - Kaufmann numbers 33-121.

	$2,500	$2,000	$1,500	$1,000	$800	$700	$600

✳ *Webley Improved Govt. Second Pattern* - Kaufmann numbers 165-1228.

	$2,500	$2,000	$1,500	$1,000	$800	$700	$600

✳ *Webley Improved Govt. Third Pattern* - Kaufmann numbers 1245-1316.

	$2,500	$2,000	$1,500	$1,000	$800	$700	$600

WEBLEY IMPROVED GOVT. MODEL 1886 - .455 or .476 cal., 6 shot "church steeple" cylinder, 6 in. barrel, birdshead grips, ser. no. range 1467-1876. Mfg. circa mid 1880s.

	$2,500	$2,000	$1,500	$1,000	$800	$700	$600

WEBLEY GOVT. MODEL 1889 - .455 or .476 cal., 6 shot "church steeple" cylinder, 6 in. barrel, flared or birdshead grips, ser. no. range 1982-3933. Mfg. circa late 1880s.

	$2,500	$2,000	$1,500	$1,000	$800	$700	$600

WEBLEY GOVT. MODEL 1891 - .450 or .476 cal., 6 shot "church steeple" cylinder, 7 1/2 in. barrel, flared grips, ser. no. range 4100-4200. Approx. 200 mfg. circa early 1890s.

	$3,500	$3,000	$2,500	$2,000	$1,500	$1,400	$1,300

WEBLEY GOVT. MODEL 1892 - .450, .455, or .476 cal., 6 shot "church steeple" cylinder, 7 1/2 in. barrel, flared grips, blue or nickel finish, ser. no. range 4197-6499. Mfg. circa early 1890s.

	$3,000	$2,500	$2,000	$1,500	$1,400	$1,300	$1,200

WEBLEY GOVT. MODEL 1893 - .450 or .455 cal., 6 shot "church steeple" cylinder, 7 1/2 in. barrel, flared grips, ser. no. range 5000-6000. Mfg. circa early 1890s.

	$3,300	$2,800	$2,300	$1,800	$1,700	$1,600	$1,500

WEBLEY GOVT. ARMY (TARGET) MODEL 1896 - .450, .455, or .476 cal., 6 (Army) or 7 1/2 (Target) in. barrel, birdshead (Army) or flared (Target) grips, ser. no. range 10000-23000. Mfg. circa late 1890s.

	$2,300	$2,000	$1,700	$1,500	$1,000	$700	$500

Cased, engraved, or inscribed examples will command a premium.

WEBLEY W.S. NEW MODEL ARMY - .455 cal., 4, 6, or 7 1/2 (Target) in. barrel, ser. no. range 88056-454229. Mfg. early 1900s to 1935.

	$1,800	$1,400	$1,000	$900	$800	$700	$600

Add 75%-100% for cased Target models with accessories.

WEBLEY WILKINSON MODELS - .450/.455, or .455/.476 cal., during production of the Webley No. 4 Model, Webley associated with Henry Wilkinson to produce the Wilkinson retailed revolvers which were well-made and finished, barrels were typically 5 3/4 or 6 in., with Target models in 7 1/2 in. Mfg. 1884-1914.

✳ *Webley Wilkinson Model First 1884 Small Hinge Pattern* - Wilkinson numbers 7896-8301.

	$3,500	$3,000	$2,500	$2,000	$1,800	$1,600	$1,500

✳ *Webley Wilkinson Model Second 1888 Large Hinge Pattern* - Wilkinson numbers 8357-8741.

	$3,500	$3,000	$2,500	$2,000	$1,800	$1,600	$1,500

✳ *Webley Wilkinson Model 1892* - Wilkinson numbers 8788-9385.

	$3,500	$3,000	$2,500	$2,000	$1,800	$1,600	$1,500

GRADING - PPGS™	100%	98%	95%	90%	80%	70%	60%

❋ *Webley Wilkinson Model 1900* - Wilkinson numbers W467-W967.

	$3,500	$3,000	$2,500	$2,000	$1,800	$1,600	$1,500

❋ *Webley Wilkinson Model 1905* - Wilkinson numbers W1102-W2977.

	$3,000	$2,500	$2,000	$1,500	$1,300	$1,100	$1,000

❋ *Webley Wilkinson Model 1910* - transitional model, Wilkinson numbers around 3000. Mfg. between 1905-1911.

	$4,500	$4,000	$3,500	$3,000	$2,500	$2,000	$1,500

❋ *Webley Wilkinson Model 1911* - Wilkinson numbers 3104-4400.

	$3,000	$2,500	$2,000	$1,500	$1,300	$1,100	$1,000

WEBLEY MARK II POCKET MODEL - .380 cal., 3 or 4 in. barrel, 6 shot, blue or nickel finish, folding trigger, ser. no. range 1-808. Mfg. circa early 1890s.

	$1,000	$900	$800	$700	$600	$500	$400

WEBLEY MARK III POCKET MODEL - .380 cal., 3, 4, 6 (Target) or 10 (Target) in. barrel, 6 shot, blue or nickel finish, ser. no. range 1656-55627. Mfg. circa mid-1890s.

	$1,000	$900	$800	$700	$600	$500	$400

WEBLEY MARK III POCKET MODEL - .320 cal., 3 in. barrel, 6 shot, blue or nickel finish, ser. no. range 10000-22000. Mfg. circa early 1900s.

	$1,000	$900	$800	$700	$600	$500	$400

WEBLEY W.P. - .32 S&W or .320 cal., 2 or 3 in. barrel, 6 shot, hammerless or hammer type, blue or nickel finish, ser. no. range 1000-8527. Mfg. circa early 1900s to mid-1930s.

	$1,000	$900	$800	$700	$600	$500	$400

WEBLEY MARK IV - .22 LR (scarce), .32 (scarce), .38 S&W, or .38 cal., 3, 4, 5 or 6 (Target) in. barrel, 6 shot, wartime production exceeded 125,000, commerical production approx. 50,000. Mfg. early 1920s to late 1970s.

	$450	$400	$350	$300	$250	$200	$150

Add 75%-100% for .22 LR or .32 cal.

REVOLVERS: SERVICE MODELS

Mark I-V Service Models were very similar, but some were made with longer barrels.

Many service Webleys were modified to use .45 ACP cal. ammo - this will decrease their value by 50% or more.

Cased, engraved, or inscribed examples have also been seen (usually in the commercial/ non-military variation), and will bring a premium over values listed.

MARK I SERVICE - .455 cal., single/double action, 4 in. barrel, fixed sights, blue finish, top break 6 shot, service and commercial ser. no. range 4-39,436. Mfg. 1894-1897.

	$800	$750	$700	$625	$500	$400	$300

MARK II SERVICE - .455 cal., single/double action, 4 in. barrel, fixed sights, blue finish, top break 6 shot, service and commercial ser. no. range 41,675-63,584. Mfg. 1894-1897.

	$850	$800	$750	$675	$550	$450	$350

MARK III SERVICE - .455 cal., single/double action, 4 in. barrel, fixed sights, blue finish, top break 6 shot, ser. no. range 12-10,808 and 75,966-79,256. Mfg. 1894-1897.

	$900	$850	$800	$725	$600	$500	$400

MARK IV SERVICE - .455 cal., single/double action, 4 in. barrel, fixed sights, blue finish, top break 6 shot, "Boer War" model, ser. no. range 79,462-129,185. Mfg. 1899-1914.

	$750	$700	$650	$575	$500	$400	$300

GRADING - PPGS™	100%	98%	95%	90%	80%	70%	60%

MARK V SERVICE - .455 cal., single/double action, 4 in. barrel, fixed sights, blue finish, top break 6 shot, ser. no. range 129,942-159,724 and 173,015-193,025. Mfg. 1914-1915.

	$750	$700	$650	$575	$500	$400	$300

MARK VI SERVICE - .455 cal., single/double action, 6 in. barrel, fixed sights, blue finish, top break 6 shot, ser. no. range 214,000-445,999. Mfg. 1915-1919.

	$600	$550	$500	$425	$350	$250	$200

Add approx. 300% - 400% for rare shoulder stock and bayonet.

MARK VI SERVICE (LATER MFG.) - .455 cal., single/double action, 6 in. barrel, fixed sights, blue finish, top break 6 shot, ser. no. range 450,000-454,000. Mfg. by Enfield circa 1922-1935.

	$900	$800	$700	$600	$500	$300	$250

MARK VI TARGET - .22 cal., otherwise similar to Mark VI Service.

	$1,200	$1,000	$900	$800	$700	$600	$500

SHOTGUNS: O/U

Currently, Webley & Scott has a line of private label O/U shotguns manufactured for them in Turkey. Current models include: the 900 Series and the Junior .410. No current U.S. importation. Please contact Webley & Scott directly for more information (see Trademark Index).

SHOTGUNS: SxS, DISC.

MODEL 700 - 12 or 20 ga., boxlock, case hardened receiver, minimum engraving, single trigger. Mfg. 1949-80.

	$3,000	$2,600	$2,200	$1,850	$1,550	$1,200	$995

Subtract $50 for double trigger.

MODEL 701 - similar to Model 700 but fanciest walnut, most engraving. Mfg. 1949-80.

	$3,500	$3,150	$2,600	$2,300	$1,995	$1,675	$1,350

This model is hard to differentiate from the Model 702.

MODEL 702 - similar to Model 700 but middle grade. Mfg. 1949-80.

	$3,250	$2,800	$2,400	$2,200	$1,700	$1,425	$1,175

Subtract $75 for double trigger.

MODEL 712 - 12 ga., specifically designed for the American market.

	$2,500	$2,250	$1,875	$1,600	$1,350	$1,100	$895

MODEL 720 - 20 ga.

	$4,500	$3,995	$3,500	$3,100	$2,600	$2,150	$1,625

MODEL 728 - same action as the Model 700, except is 28 ga. and designed specifically for the American market, only 40 were mfg. 1966-68.

	$5,000	$4,500	$4,000	$3,500	$2,800	$2,350	$1,800

SHOTGUNS: SxS, CURRENT MFG.

Currently, Webley & Scott imports a line of 700 Series SxS shotguns that are manufactured in Turkey. Current models imported into the U.S. by Legacy Sports include the 712 (MSR $3,477, 12 ga.), 720 (MSR $3,477, 20 ga.), and the 728 (MSR $3,644, 28 ga.).

SHOTGUNS: SEMI-AUTO

Currently, Webley & Scott has a line of private label semi-auto shotguns manufactured for them in Turkey. Current models include: the 812 (12 ga.), 820 (20 ga.) and 828 (28 ga.). No current U.S. importation. Please contact Webley & Scott directly for more information (see Trademark Index).

GRADING - PPGS™	100%	98%	95%	90%	80%	70%	60%

WEIHRAUCH SPORT GmbH

Current firearms and airguns manufacturer located in Mellrichstadt, Germany. Currently imported exclusively by E.A.A.., located in Sharpes, FL.

Weihrauch manufactures a compete line of single and double action revolvers, including target models, in addition to bolt action hunting and target rifles. Please contact the importer directly for more information, including model availability and pricing (see Trademark Index).

For more information and current pricing on both new and used Weihrauch airguns, please refer to the *Blue Book of Airguns* by Dr. Robert Beeman & John Allen (also online).

REVOLVERS: ARMINIUS

Currently manufactured Arminius revolvers are not individually listed, since they are not imported into the U.S. There are, however, many models, including combat, sport, and target variations. Calibers include .22 LR, .22 Mag., .32 S&W Wadcutter, .357 Mag., and .38 Spl. Please refer to Arminius listing for older models, or contact the company directly regarding U.S. availability and pricing (see Trademark Index).

RIFLES: BOLT ACTION

Currently, Weihrauch manufactures the HW 660 Match Series Target rifles, the HW 60 J and HW 66 Series hunting rifles. These models are not currently imported into the U.S. Please contact the company directly for more information, including pricing and availability.

MODEL HW 60 TARGET - .22 LR cal., target rifle featuring adj. sights, 26 3/4 in. barrel, single shot, match walnut stock, and other match features, aperture sights, 10.8 lbs. Importation disc. 1995.

$625	$550	$450	$395	$350	$295	$275

Last MSR was $705.

Add $220 for left-hand action (disc.).

MODEL HW 60J - .22 LR or .222 Rem. cal., sporter model with checkered walnut stock. Importation disc. 1992.

$525	$465	$435	$395	$345	$300	$260

Last MSR was $585.

Add $304 for .222 Rem. cal.

MODEL HW 66 RIFLE - .22 Hornet or .222 Rem. cal., match grade bolt action rifle. Imported 1989-90 only.

$575	$495	$395	$325	$285	$250	$215

Last MSR was $688.

Add $78 for double-set triggers.
Add $55 for stainless steel barrel (.22 Hornet).

MODEL HW 660 MATCH - .22 LR cal., match rifle variation featuring adj. stock comb with vent. forend, with or w/o aperture sights, 10.8 lbs. Imported 1991-2005.

$850	$725	$600	$500	$400	$350	$300

Last MSR was $999.

Add $160 for laminate stock (new 1998).
Subtract $160 if w/o Anschütz aperture sights.

WELLS

Previous custom rifle manufacturer located in Prescott, AZ.

RIFLES: BOLT ACTION

Wells manufactured a custom rifle based on a Mauser double square bridge action, using the finest materials available. Action prices started at $5,500, and stocks were priced from $5,500 on up. Many custom features and options were available, including engraving by Rachel Wells. Delivery time was approximately 24 months. Additionally, Wells also had a complete barrel manufacturing facility, specializing in cut rifle barrels in almost every caliber.

100%	98%	95%	90%	80%	70%	60%	50%	40%	30%	20%	10%

WESSON, FRANK

Previous manufacturer located in Worcester, MA 1854 to 1865, and Springfield, MA circa 1865-1875.

PISTOLS: SINGLE SHOT

SMALL FRAME FIRST MODEL - .22 cal., tip up action, 3 1/2 in. 1/2 octagon barrel, brass frame, spur trigger, rosewood grips, round frame, irregular sideplate. Mfg. 2500, 1859-62.

$605	$550	$495	$440	$385	$330	$275	$220	$195	$165	$140	$110

SMALL FRAME SECOND MODEL - similar to First Model, with flat sided frame and circular sideplate. Mfg. 12,000, 1862-80.

$550	$495	$440	$385	$330	$305	$250	$195	$165	$110	$105	$85

MEDIUM FRAME FIRST MODEL - .30 S or L, .32 S rimfire cal., 4 in. 1/2 octagon barrel, iron frame, same as Small Frame in other respects, narrow hinge and short trigger. Mfg. 1000, 1859-62.

$525	$470	$415	$360	$305	$275	$220	$195	$165	$110	$105	$85

MEDIUM FRAME SECOND MODEL - similar to First Model Medium Frame, with wider hinge and longer trigger. Mfg. 1000, 1862-70.

$495	$440	$385	$330	$275	$250	$220	$195	$165	$110	$105	$85

RIFLES: SINGLE SHOT

NO. 1 LONG RANGE - .44-100 and .45-100 standard cal., side hammer, falling block lever actuated, 34 in. octagon barrel, aperture rear sight on upper tang, select checkered pistol grip stock. Less than 50 mfg., circa 1870-80.

$4,950	$4,675	$4,400	$3,850	$3,575	$3,080	$2,860	$2,475	$2,200	$2,035	$1,760	$1,540

NO. 2 HUNTING RIFLE - similar to No. 1, with finger loop lever. Less than 100 mfg.

$4,400	$4,180	$3,850	$3,520	$3,025	$2,750	$2,420	$2,255	$2,035	$1,925	$1,760	$1,540

NO. 1 SPORTING RIFLE - .38-100, .40-100, .45-100 standard cal., similar to No. 2, with center hammer, less than 25 mfg.

$4,400	$4,180	$3,850	$3,520	$3,025	$2,750	$2,420	$2,255	$2,035	$1,925	$1,760	$1,540

RIFLES: SINGLE SHOT, TIP UP

SMALL FRAME TIP UP - .22 Rimfire cal., 6 in. 1/2 octagon barrel, brass frame, spur trigger, rosewood grips. Approx. 500 mfg., 1865-75.

$605	$550	$525	$495	$470	$440	$415	$360	$330	$275	$220	$165

If without stock-subtract 25%.

MEDIUM FRAME TIP UP - .22, .30, or .32 rimfire cals, 10 or 12 in. barrel, same as small frame, with exceptions noted and larger frame. Approx. 1,000 mfg., 1862-70.

$605	$550	$525	$495	$470	$440	$415	$360	$330	$275	$220	$165

If without stock-subtract 25%.

MODEL 1870 SMALL FRAME FIRST TYPE - similar to Small Frame Tip Up, except barrel rotates on its axis to load, detachable stock. Approx. 3,000 mfg., 1870-90.

$550	$495	$470	$440	$415	$385	$360	$305	$275	$220	$195	$165

If without stock-subtract 25%.

MODEL 1870 SMALL FRAME SECOND TYPE - full octagon barrel.

$525	$470	$440	$415	$385	$360	$330	$275	$250	$195	$165	$140

MODEL 1870 SMALL FRAME THIRD TYPE - iron frame, push-button half cock.

$495	$440	$415	$385	$360	$330	$305	$250	$220	$165	$140	$110

100%	98%	95%	90%	80%	70%	60%	50%	40%	30%	20%	10%

MODEL 1870 MEDIUM FRAME FIRST TYPE - similar to Small Frame, except in size and availability of .32 cal. Approx. 5,000 mfg., 1870-93.

$525	$495	$470	$440	$415	$385	$360	$305	$275	$250	$195	$165

Subtract 25% if without stock.

MODEL 1870 MEDIUM FRAME SECOND TYPE - external push-button half cock and iron frame.

$440	$415	$385	$330	$305	$275	$220	$195	$165	$140	$110	$90

Subtract 25% if without stock.

MODEL 1870 MEDIUM FRAME THIRD TYPE - has three screws in iron frame.

$440	$415	$385	$330	$305	$275	$220	$195	$165	$140	$110	$90

Subtract 25% if without stock.

MODEL 1870 LARGE FRAME FIRST TYPE - .32, .38, .42, or .44 rimfire cal., 15-24 in. barrels, similar to smaller frame models, auto extractor. Approx. 500 mfg., 1870-80.

$825	$770	$715	$660	$605	$550	$525	$495	$440	$385	$305	$275

Subtract 25% if without stock.

MODEL 1870 LARGE FRAME SECOND TYPE - similar to First Type, with standard sliding extractor.

$825	$770	$715	$660	$605	$550	$525	$495	$440	$385	$305	$275

Subtract 25% if without stock.

WESSON & HARRINGTON

Previous trademark of special/limited editions manufactured by H&R 1871, LLC 1995-2001. During 2000, Marlin Firearms Co. purchased the assets of H&R 1871, Inc., and the name was changed to H&R 1871, LLC. Production of Wesson & Harrington products was at the factory located in Gardner, MA.

RIFLES: SINGLE SHOT

Please refer to the H & R 1871 section for earlier Wesson & Harrington Buffalo Classic & Target Models.

GRADING - PPGS™	100%	98%	95%	90%	80%	70%	60%

SHOTGUNS: SINGLE SHOT

WESSON & HARRINGTON NWTF LONG TOM CLASSIC - 12 ga., top lever break open action, 32 in. FC barrel, case hardened frame, checkered straight grip walnut stock and forearm, 7 1/2 lbs. Mfg. 1995-2001.

		$300	$240	$195	$150	$125	$110	$95

Last MSR was $350.

DAN WESSON FIREARMS

Current trademark manufactured by Dan Wesson Firearms beginning 2005, and located in Norwich, NY. Distributed beginning 2005 by CZ-USA, located in Kansas City, KS. Previously manufactured by New York International Corp. (NYI) located in Norwich, NY 1997-2005. Distributor and dealer sales.

PISTOLS: SEMI-AUTO

Until 2005, Dan Wesson manufactured a complete line of .45 ACP 1911 style semi-auto pistols. Previously manufactured models include: Seven (last MSR was $999), Seven Stainless (last MSR was $1,099), Guardian (last MSR was $799), the Guardian Deuce (last MSR was $799), the Dave Pruit Signature Series (last MSR was $899), and the Hi-Cap (last MSR was $689).

GRADING - PPGS™	100%	98%	95%	90%	80%	70%	60%

PATRIOT 1911 SERIES - .45 ACP or 10mm (Commander slide and frame only) cal., 4 1/4 (Commander) or 5 in. stainless steel match barrel, 1911 Series 70 action, features new external extractor, fitted parts, and many high-end components by McCormick, Ed Brown, Nowlin, etc., each gun shipped with test target, variations include Patriot Expert (blue or stainless, Bo-Mar style target sights), Patriot Marksman (blue or stainless, fixed sights), AAA cocobolo double diamond checkered grips with gold medallions, 2.3 lbs. Mfg. 2001-2005.

	$825	$750	$650	$550	$475	$425	$375

Last MSR was $929.

Add $20 for 5 in. Patriot with blued action.
Add $70 for 5 in. barrel in stainless steel.
Add $30 for checkered front grip strap.
Add $70 for bobtail frame.

KO3 PANTHER SERIES - .45 ACP cal., full size, 5 in. barrel, Series 70 pistol with cast alloy frame, features new external extractor, Chip McCormick beavertail with Commander style hammer, forged conventional round top slide, fixed rear sight, matte bead blasted frame and slide top, slide sides are polished, blue or stainless, Hogue rubber grips. Disc.

	$595	$525	$450	$415	$385	$350	$325

Add $20 for stainless steel.

PM POINTMAN SERIES - .45 ACP or 10mm cal., full size, 5 in. target barrel, features Chip McCormick beavertail with Commander style hammer, forged conventional round top slide, high target rib or low profile Clark style sights with adj. white outline or Bo-Mar rear sight, blue or stainless, PM1-S is standard gun, checkered exotic hardwood grips. Disc. 2005.

	$725	$650	$575	$500	$425	$385	$350

Last MSR was $809.

Add $50 for checkered front grip strap.
Add $50 for high or Ausi rib (Model PMA-S).
Add $100 for blue finish with Clark/Bo-Mar rib and sights (Model PMA-B, disc.).

POINTMAN SEVEN - .45 ACP or 10mm cal., 5 in. barrel, features stainless steel frame and slide, patterned after the Colt Series 70 semi-auto, 7 shot mag., double slide serrations, many target features, diamond checkered cocobolo grips, 38 oz. New 2005.

MSR $1,096	$995	$885	$775	$700	$600	$500	$400

Add $32 for 10mm cal.

PM3-P MINOR SERIES - .45 ACP cal., full size, 5 in. barrel, Series 70 pistol with cast alloy frame, Chip McCormick beavertail with Commander style hammer, forged conventional round top slide, fixed rear sight, matte bead blasted frame and slide top, slide sides are polished, blue or stainless, checkered exotic hardwood grips. Disc.

	$515	$450	$415	$385	$350	$325	$295

GLOBAL - .45 ACP or 10mm cal., 5 or 6 in. barrel, full size frame, steel or stainless steel, choice of accessory light rail or full length dust cover. Disc. 2005.

	$1,000	$900	$800	$700	$600	$475	$350

Last MSR was $1,149.

RZ-10 RAZORBACK SPECIAL EDITION - 10mm cal., full size, 5 in. barrel, Series 70 pistol with forged stainless frame and slide, Bo-Mar adj. rear sight, match barrel, bushing, and link, match grade trigger, sear, hammer, and beavertail, checkered synthetic or rubber (new 2006) grips, limited mfg. 2002-2004, and resumed in 2006.

MSR $1,128	$1,000	$885	$775	$700	$600	$500	$450

GRADING - PPGS™	100%	98%	95%	90%	80%	70%	60%

COMMANDER CLASSIC BOBTAIL - .45 ACP or 10mm cal., 4 1/4 in. barrel, features stainless steel frame and slide, patterned after the Colt Series 70 semi-auto, Ed Brown Bobtail mainspring housing, many target features, diamond checkered cocobolo grips, 34 oz. New 2005.

	MSR $1,128	$1,000	$885	$775	$700	$600	$500	$450

Add $31 for 10mm cal.

VALOR - .45 ACP cal., black ceramic coated finish, slimline VZ grips, adj. night sights. New 2008.

MSR $1,600	$1,395	$1,150	$925	$825	$725	$625	$550

SS CUSTOM - .40 S&W cal., stainless steel construction, fiber optic front sight, ambidextrous safety, shark grips. New 2008.

MSR $1,475	$1,275	$1,050	$900	$775	$650	$550	$475

REVOLVERS: DOUBLE ACTION

Dan Wesson has also manufactured a variety of revolver packages that were available by special order only.

MODEL 44-AGS (ALASKAN GUIDE SPECIAL) - .445 SuperMag. cal., 6 shot, stainless steel, compensated 4 in. heavy barrel with VR and full ejector shroud, black Teflon metal finish, rubber wraparound finger groove grips, fully adj. sights. Mfg. 2002-2004, resumed 2006-2007.

$1,075	$950	$850	$725	$650	$550	$475

Last MSR was $1,295.

MODEL 715 SMALL FRAME SERIES - .357 Mag. cal., 6 shot, stainless steel, 2 1/2, 4, 6, 8, or 10 in. heavy barrel with VR and full ejector shroud, rubber wraparound finger groove grips, interchangeable barrels. Mfg. 2002-2004.

$625	$550	$475	$425	$375	$325	$275

Last MSR was $709.

Add $50 for 4 in., $90 for 6 in., $150 for 8 in., or $190 for 10 in. barrel.
This model was also available as a pistol pack with 4 barrels and case. MSR was $1,699.

MODEL 741 LARGE FRAME SERIES - .44 Mag. cal., 6 shot, stainless steel, 4, 6, 8, or 10 in. heavy barrel with VR and full ejector shroud, rubber wraparound finger groove grips, raked hammer, interchangeable barrels. Mfg. 2002-2004.

$725	$650	$575	$500	$450	$400	$350

Last MSR was $829.

Add $30 for 6 in., $110 for 8 in., or $170 for 10 in. barrel.

MODEL 7445 SUPERMAG FRAME SERIES - .445 SuperMag. cal., 6 shot, stainless steel, 4, 6, 8, or 10 in. heavy barrel with VR and full ejector shroud, rubber wraparound finger groove grips, interchangeable barrels. Mfg. 2002-2004, resumed 2006-2007.

$965	$875	$775	$675	$600	$525	$450

Last MSR was $1,070.

MODEL 7460 - .45 ACP, .45 Auto Rim., .445 Super Mag., .45 Win. Mag., or .450 Rowland cal., mfg. 1999-disc.

$800	$725	$650	$575	$500	$450	$400

RIFLES: BOLT ACTION

COYOTE CLASSIC - .22 LR or .22 Mag. cal., 22 3/4 in. tapered barrel, 6 or 10 shot mag., checkered hardwood stock and forend, adj. rear sight. Limited mfg. 2002 only.

$200	$180	$160	$145	$130	$115	$100

Last MSR was $239.

GRADING - PPGS™	100%	98%	95%	90%	80%	70%	60%

COYOTE TARGET - .22 LR or .22 Mag. cal., 18 3/8 in. heavy bull barrel, 6 or 10 shot mag., uncheckered target hardwood stock with high cheekpiece, w/o sights. Limited mfg. 2002 only.

	$230	$200	$175	$155	$145	$135	$125

Last MSR was $279.

WESSON FIREARMS CO. INC.

Previous manufacturer located in Palmer, MA 1992-95. Previously located in Monson, MA until 1992. In late 1990, ownership of Dan Wesson Arms changed (within the family), and the new company was renamed Wesson Firearms Co., Inc.

REVOLVERS: DOUBLE ACTION

As a guideline, the following information is provided on Wesson Firearms frames. The smallest frames are Models 738P and 38P. Small frame models include 22, 722, 22M, 722M, 32, 732, 322, 7322, 8-2, 708, 9-2, 709, 14-2, 714, 15-2, and 715-2. Large frames include 41, 741, 44, 744, 45, and 745. SuperMag frame models include 40, 740, 375 (disc.), 414 (new 1995), 7414 (new 1995), 445, and 7445. Small frames are sideplate design, while large frames are solid frame construction. Dan Wesson revolvers were mfg. with solid rib barrels as standard equipment.

MODEL 11 - .357 Mag. cal., 6 shot, 2 1/2, 4, or 6 in. interchangeable barrels, fixed sights, blue, interchangeable grips, exposed barrel nut. Mfg. 1970-71 only.

	$200	$175	$160	$150	$140	$130	$120

Add $60 per extra barrel.

MODEL 12 - similar to Model 11, with adj. sights. Mfg. 1970-71 only.

	$245	$200	$175	$160	$150	$140	$130

MODEL 14 - similar to Model 11, with recessed barrel nut. Mfg. 1971-75.

	$225	$185	$170	$160	$150	$140	$130

MODEL 8 - similar to Model 14, except .38 Spl. cal.

	$200	$170	$155	$145	$135	$125	$115

MODEL 15 - similar to Model 14, with adj. sights. Mfg. 1971-75.

	$245	$200	$155	$145	$135	$125	$115

MODEL 9 - similar to Model 15, except .38 Spl. cal. Mfg. 1971-75.

	$245	$200	$155	$145	$135	$125	$115

MODEL 22 - .22 LR cal., double action, 6 shot, adj. sights, 2 1/2, 4, 6, 8, or 10 in. (disc. 1987) barrel, disc. 1995.

	$285	$225	$200	$190	$180	$170	$160

Last MSR was $357.

Add approx. $9 for each additional barrel length, $21 for VR, $57 for vent. heavy rib shroud.

✳ *Model 22 Pistol Pac* - includes 2 1/2, 4, 6, and 8 in. barrel assemblies, extra grip, 4 additional front sight blades, and aluminum case. Disc. 1995.

	$520	$400	$360	$330	$300	$275	$260

Last MSR was $653.

Add $103 for full shroud VR barrels.
Add $227 for heavy full shroud VR barrels.

✳ *Model 22 Silhouette* - .22 LR cal., choice of 10 in. vent. or heavy vent. barrel, single action only, combat style grip, narrow rear sight blade and Patridge front. Mfg. 1992-95.

	$395	$325	$295	$275	$260	$245	$230

Last MSR was $474.

Add $18 for vent. heavy barrel.

GRADING - PPGS™	100%	98%	95%	90%	80%	70%	60%

MODEL 22M - .22 Mag. cal., otherwise similar to Model 22. Disc. 1994.

	$290	$230	$200	$190	$180	$170	$160

Last MSR was $349.

✱ Model 22M Pistol Pac - includes 2 1/2, 4, 6, and 8 in. barrel assemblies, extra grip, 4 additional front sight blades, and aluminum case. Disc. 1994.

	$500	$400	$360	$330	$300	$275	$260

Last MSR was $637.

Add $101 for full shroud VR barrels.
Add $191 for heavy full shroud VR barrels.

MODEL 32 - .32 H&R Mag. cal., 2 1/2, 4, 6, or 8 in. barrel, adj. rear sight, interchangeable colored front sight blades, blue finish, checkered target grips. Mfg. 1986-95.

	$285	$225	$200	$190	$180	$170	$160

Last MSR was $357.

Add $21 for VR barrel shroud (Model 32-V), $57 for VR heavy barrel shroud (Model 32-VH), approx. $9 for each additional barrel length over 2 1/2 in.

✱ Model 32 Pistol Pac - includes 2 1/2, 4, 6, and 8 in. barrel assemblies, extra grip, 4 additional front sight blades, and aluminum case. Disc. 1995.

	$520	$400	$360	$330	$300	$275	$260

Last MSR was $653.

Add $103 for full shroud VR barrels.
Add $227 for heavy full shroud VR barrels.

MODEL 38P - .38+P cal., 5 shot, 6 1/2 in. barrel, fixed sights, wood or rubber grips, 24.6 oz. Mfg. 1992-93.

	$230	$190	$170	$150	$135	$120	$110

Last MSR was $285.

MODEL 322 - .32-20 WCF cal., 2 1/2, 4, 6, or 8 in. barrel, adj. rear sight, interchangeable colored front sight blades, blue finish, checkered target grips. Mfg. 1991-95.

	$285	$225	$200	$190	$180	$170	$160

Last MSR was $357.

Add $21 for VR barrel shroud (Model 322-V), $57 for VR heavy barrel shroud (Model 322-VH), approx. $9-$30 for each additional barrel length over 2 1/2 in.

✱ Model 322 Pistol Pac - includes 2 1/2, 4, 6, and 8 in. barrel assemblies, extra grip, 4 additional front sight blades, and aluminum case. Disc. 1995.

	$520	$400	$360	$330	$300	$275	$260

Last MSR was $653.

Add $103 for full shroud VR barrels.
Add $227 for heavy full shroud VR barrels.

MODEL 14 - .357 Mag. cal., 2 1/2, 4, 6, or 8 (disc. 1994) in. interchangeable barrels, fixed sights, blue. Mfg. 1975-95.

	$215	$170	$150	$140	$130	$120	$110

Last MSR was $274.

Add approx. $7 for each additional barrel length.

✱ Model 14 Fixed Barrel - .357 Mag. cal., 2 1/2 or 4 in. (fixed sight Service Model) barrel, satin blue finish. Mfg. 1993-95.

	$225	$175	$150	$140	$130	$120	$110

Last MSR was $289.

Add $7 for 4 in. barrel.

GRADING - PPGS™	100%	98%	95%	90%	80%	70%	60%

✳ *Model 14 PPC* - .357 Mag. cal., extra heavy 6 in. bull shroud barrel with removable underweight, Hogue Gripper grips, Aristocrat sights. Mfg. 1992 only.

	$675	$550	$450	$375	$330	$300	$275

Last MSR was $780.

✳ *Model 14 Pistol Pac* - includes 2 1/2, 4, and 6 in. barrel assemblies, extra grip and aluminum case. Disc. 1994.

	$390	$325	$300	$275	$260	$245	$230

Last MSR was $463.

MODEL 8 - similar to Model 14, except .38 Spl. cal. Disc. 1995.

	$220	$170	$150	$140	$130	$120	$110

Last MSR was $274.

Add approx. $6 for each additional barrel length.

✳ *Model 8 PPC* - .38 Spl. cal., extra heavy 6 in. bull shroud barrel with removable underweight, Hogue Gripper grips, Aristocrat sights. Mfg. 1992 only.

	$675	$550	$450	$375	$330	$300	$275

Last MSR was $780.

MODEL 15 - similar to Model 14, except adj. sights, available with 2, 4, 6, 8, 10, 12, or 15 in. barrels. Disc. 1995.

✳ *Model 15 2 in. barrel*

	$285	$225	$200	$190	$180	$170	$160

Last MSR was $346.

Add approx. $8-$13 for each additional barrel length over 2 inches, $22 for VR barrel (Model 15V), or $60 for VR heavy barrel shroud (Model 15HV).

✳ *Model 15 Target Fixed Barrel* - .357 Mag. cal., 3, 4, 5, or 6 in. barrel, high bright blue finish. Mfg. 1993-95.

	$270	$220	$190	$175	$150	$125	$110

Last MSR was $322.

Add approx. $9 for each barrel length over 3 in.
Add approx. $80 for compensated barrel (4, 5, or 6 in. - new 1994).

MODEL 15 GOLD SERIES - .357 Mag. cal., 6 or 8 in. VR heavy slotted barrel, "Gold" stamped shroud with Dan Wesson signature, smoother action (8 lb. double action pull), 18kt. gold-plated trigger, white triangle rear sight with orange-dot Patridge front sight, exotic hardwood grips. Mfg. 1989-94.

	$425	$380	$340	$300	$260	$225	$185

Last MSR was $544.

✳ *Model 15 Pistol Pac* - includes 2 1/2, 4, 6, and 8 in. barrel assemblies, extra grip, 4 additional front sight blades, and aluminum case. Disc. 1995.

	$500	$395	$360	$330	$300	$275	$260

Last MSR was $629.

Add $104 for full shroud VR barrels.
Add $214 for heavy full shroud VR barrels.

MODEL 9 - similar to Model 15, except .38 Spl. cal. Use same add-ons as in Model 15. Disc. 1995.

	$346	$285	$225	$200	$190	$180	$170

Last MSR was $346.

This model was also available in a Pistol Pac - same specifications and values as the Model 15 Pistol Pac.

GRADING - PPGS™	100%	98%	95%	90%	80%	70%	60%

MODEL 375 SUPERMAG - .375 Super Mag. cal., 4, 6, 8, or 10 in. VR barrel, adj. rear sight, interchangeable front and rear sight blades, bright blue finish, smooth target grips. Mfg. 1986-94.

	$650	$575	$500	$450	$400	$365	$335

Last MSR was $498.

Add approx. $15 for each barrel length after 6 in., $39 for slotted shroud (Model 375-V8S, 8 in. barrel only), $10-$12 for VR heavy shroud (Model 375-VH).

MODEL 40 (.357 SUPERMAG) - .357 Super Mag. cal. (.357 Max.), double action, 6 shot, 4, 6, 8, or 10 in. barrel VR. Disc. 1995.

	$650	$575	$500	$450	$400	$365	$335

Last MSR was $502.

Add $87 for slotted barrel shroud (8 in. barrel only), $22-$129 for heavy VR barrel, approx. $33 for each additional barrel length.

MODEL 41 - .41 Mag. cal., double action, 6 shot, 4, 6, 8, or 10 in. barrel VR. Disc. 1995.

	$375	$305	$265	$250	$230	$215	$200

Last MSR was $447.

Add approx. $20 for heavy barrel shroud, approx. $15 for each additional barrel length.

✳ *Model 41 Pistol Pac* - includes 6 and 8 in. VR barrel assemblies, extra grip, 2 additional front sight blades, and aluminum case. Disc. 1995.

	$555	$430	$380	$330	$300	$275	$260

Last MSR was $678.

Add $53 for full shroud VR barrels.

MODEL 414 SUPERMAG - .414 Super Mag. cal., 4, 6, 8, or 10 in. VR barrel, adj. rear sight, interchangeable front and rear sight blades (optional), bright blue finish, smooth target grips. Mfg. 1995 only.

	$650	$575	$500	$450	$400	$365	$335

Last MSR was $519.

Add approx. $14 for each barrel length after 4 in., $58 for slotted shroud (Model 414-V8S, 8 in. barrel only), approx. $23 for VR heavy rib shroud.

MODEL 44 - .44 Mag. cal., double action, similar to Model 41, adj. sights. Disc. 1995.

	$375	$305	$265	$250	$230	$215	$200

Last MSR was $447.

Add approx. $20 for heavy barrel shroud, approx. $15 for each additional barrel length.

✳ *Model 44 Target Fixed Barrel* - .44 Mag. cal., 4, 5, 6, or 8 in. barrel, high bright blue finish. Mfg. 1994-95.

	$375	$305	$265	$250	$230	$215	$200

Last MSR was $447.

Add approx. $4 for each barrel length over 3 in.

✳ *Model 44 Pistol Pac* - includes 6 and 8 in. VR barrel assemblies, extra grip, 4 additional front sight blades, and aluminum case. Disc. 1995.

	$555	$430	$380	$330	$300	$275	$260

Last MSR was $678.

Add $53 for full shroud VR barrels.

MODEL 45 - .45 LC cal., 4, 6, 8, or 10 in. VR barrel, same frame as Model 44V, blue finish. Mfg. 1988-95.

	$375	$305	$265	$250	$230	$215	$200

Last MSR was $447.

Add $20 for VR heavy barrel shroud, approx. $15 for each additional barrel length.

GRADING - PPGS™	100%	98%	95%	90%	80%	70%	60%

* **Model 45 Pistol Pac** - includes 6 and 8 in. VR barrel assemblies, extra grip, 2 additional front sight blades, and aluminum case. Disc. 1995.

| | $555 | $430 | $380 | $330 | $300 | $275 | $260 |

Last MSR was $678.

Add $53 for full shroud VR barrels.

MODEL 45 PIN GUN - .45 ACP cal., competition pin gun model with 5 in. vent. or heavy vent. barrel configuration, blue steel, two stage Taylor forcing cone, 54 oz. Mfg. 1993-95.

| | $575 | $495 | $440 | $395 | $350 | $300 | $250 |

Last MSR was $654.

Add $9 for VR heavy shroud barrel.

MODEL 445 SUPERMAG - .445 Super Mag. cal., 4, 6, 8, or 10 in. VR barrel, adj. rear sight, interchangeable front and rear sight blades (optional), bright blue finish, smooth target grips. Mfg. 1991-95.

| | $650 | $575 | $500 | $450 | $400 | $365 | $335 |

Last MSR was $519.

Add approx. $14 for each barrel length after 4 in., $58 for slotted shroud (Model 445-V8S, 8 in. barrel only), approx. $23 for VR heavy rib shroud.

HUNTER SERIES - .357 Super Mag., .41 Mag., .44 Mag., or .445 Super Mag. cal., 7 1/2 in. barrel with heavy shroud, Hogue rubber finger grooved and wood presentation grips, choice of Gunworks iron sights or w/o sights with Burris base and rings, non-fluted cylinder, with or w/o compensator, approx. 4 lbs. Mfg. 1994-95.

| | $750 | $575 | $475 | $400 | $360 | $330 | $300 |

Last MSR was $805.

Add $32 for compensated barrel.
Add $33 for scope mounts (w/o sights).

REVOLVERS: STAINLESS STEEL - Models 722, 722M, 709, 715, 732, 7322, 741V, 744V, and 745V were available in a pistol pack including 2 1/2, 4, 6, and 8 in. solid rib barrel assemblies, extra grip, 4 additional sight blades, and fitted carrying case. Last published retail prices were $712 and $785 for the standard and stainless steel models, respectively. VR or full shroud barrels were optional and were approx. priced $103 and $210, respectively.

MODEL 722 - stainless version of Model 22, use same add-ons for various barrel options. Disc. 1995.

| | $335 | $255 | $205 | $150 | $125 | $110 | $95 |

Last MSR was $400.

* **Model 722 Silhouette** - .22 LR cal., choice of 10 in. vent. or heavy vent. barrel, single action only, combat style grip, narrow rear sight blade and Patridge front. Mfg. 1992-95.

| | $410 | $340 | $295 | $240 | $210 | $180 | $155 |

Last MSR was $504.

Add $28 for heavy vent. barrel.

MODEL 722M - .22 Mag cal., otherwise similar to Model 722, use same add-ons for various barrel options. Disc. 1994.

| | $320 | $270 | $230 | $175 | $140 | $125 | $105 |

Last MSR was $391.

MODEL 708 - .38 Spl. cal., similar to Model 8. Add approx. $6 for each additional barrel length. Disc. 1995.

| | $265 | $200 | $170 | $135 | $115 | $100 | $85 |

Last MSR was $319.

GRADING - PPGS™	100%	98%	95%	90%	80%	70%	60%

✳ *Model 708 Action Cup/PPC* - .38 Spl. cal., extra heavy 6 in. bull shroud barrel with removable underweight, Hogue Gripper grips, mounted Tasco Pro Point II on Action Cup, Aristocrat sights on PPC. Mfg. 1992 only.

	$725	$650	$550	$460	$395	$335	$285

Last MSR was $857.

Add $56 for Action Cup Model with Tasco Scope.

MODEL 709 - .38 Spl. cal., target revolver, adj. sights. Also available in special order 10, 12 (disc.), or 15 (disc.) in. barrel lengths. Disc. 1995.

	$310	$255	$205	$150	$125	$110	$95

Last MSR was $376.

Add approx. $10 for each additional longer barrel length, approx. $19 for VR, approx. $56 for heavy VR.

MODEL 714 (INTERCHANGEABLE OR FIXED) - .357 Mag. cal., fixed sight Service Model with 2 1/2, 4, or 6 in. barrel, brushed stainless steel. Mfg. 1993-95.

	$260	$200	$160	$125	$110	$95	$85

Last MSR was $319.

Add approx. $6 for 4 or 6 in. barrel.
Subtract $6 for fixed barrel (2 1/2 or 4 in. barrel only).

✳ *Model 714 Action Cup/PPC* - .357 Mag. cal., extra heavy 6 in. bull shroud barrel with removable underweight, Hogue Gripper grips, mounted Tasco Pro Point II on Action Cup, Aristocrat sights on PPC. Mfg. 1992 only.

	$725	$650	$550	$460	$395	$335	$285

Last MSR was $857.

Add $56 for Action Cup Model with Tasco Scope.

MODEL 715 INTERCHANGEABLE - .357 Mag. cal., 2 1/2, 4, 6, 8, or 10 in. barrel with adj. rear sight, brushed stainless steel. Mfg. 1993-95.

	$310	$255	$205	$150	$125	$110	$95

Last MSR was $376.

Add approx. $10 for each additional longer barrel length, approx. $19 for VR, approx. $56 for heavy VR.

✳ *Model 715 Fixed Target* - .357 Mag. cal., 3, 4, 5, or 6 in. fixed barrel, adj. rear sight. Mfg. 1993-95.

	$280	$210	$170	$135	$115	$100	$85

Last MSR was $345.

Add approx. $70 for compensated barrel (4, 5, or 6 in. - new 1994).

MODEL 732 - .32 H&R Mag. cal., similar to Model 32, except is stainless steel. Mfg. 1986-95.

	$335	$255	$205	$150	$125	$110	$95

Last MSR was $400.

Add $22 for VR barrel shroud (Model 732-V), $53 for VR heavy barrel shroud (Model 732-VH), approx. $9 for each additional barrel length over 2 1/2 in.

MODEL 738P - .38 +P cal., 5 shot, 6 1/2 in. barrel, fixed sights, wood or rubber grips, 24.6 oz. Mfg. 1992-95.

	$275	$210	$175	$135	$115	$100	$85

Last MSR was $340.

MODEL 7322 - .32-20 WCF cal., similar to Model 322, except is stainless steel. Mfg. 1991-95.

	$335	$255	$205	$150	$125	$110	$95

Last MSR was $400.

Add $22 for VR barrel shroud (Model 7322-V), $53 for VR heavy barrel shroud (Model 7322-VH), approx. $9 for each additional barrel length over 2 1/2 in.

GRADING - PPGS™	100%	98%	95%	90%	80%	70%	60%

MODEL 740V - .357 SUPERMAG - .357 Max. cal., 4, 6, 8, or 10 in. barrel, adj. rear sight with interchangeable front and rear blades, high polished finish, smooth target grips. Mfg. 1986-95.

	$650	$575	$500	$450	$400	$365	$335

Last MSR was $567.

Add approx. $20 for each additional barrel length after 4 in., $78 with vent. slotted shroud (only avail. with 8 in. barrel), $20 for VR heavy barrel shroud (Model 740-VH).

MODEL 741V - .41 Mag. cal., similar to Model 41V. Disc. 1995.

	$420	$325	$270	$225	$195	$165	$140

Last MSR was $524.

Add approx. $20 for heavy VR, approx. $13 for each barrel length over 4 in.

MODEL 744V - .44 Mag. cal., similar to Model 44V. Disc. 1995. - limited mfg.

	$430	$345	$285	$235	$200	$170	$145

Last MSR was $524.

Add approx. $20 for heavy VR, $13 for each barrel length over 4 in.

✱ *Model 744V Target Fixed Barrel* - .44 Mag. cal., 4, 5, 6, or 8 in. barrel, brushed stainless steel. Mfg. 1994-95.

	$395	$315	$265	$215	$185	$155	$130

Last MSR was $493.

Add approx. $4 for each barrel length over 3 in.

✱ *Model 744 Commemorative*

	$595	$475	$325	N/A	N/A	N/A	N/A

MODEL 745V - .45 LC cal., similar to Model 45, except in stainless steel. Disc. 1995.

	$430	$345	$285	$235	$200	$170	$145

Last MSR was $524.

Add $20 for heavy full shroud VR barrels, $13 for each additional barrel length.

MODEL .45 PIN GUN - .45 ACP cal., similar to Model .45 Pin Gun, except is stainless steel. Mfg. 1993-95.

	$625	$525	$425	$360	$315	$260	$225

Last MSR was $713.

Add $49 for VR heavy rib shroud.

MODEL 7414 SUPERMAG - .414 Super Mag. cal., 4, 6, 8, or 10 in. VR barrel, adj. rear sight, interchangeable front and rear sight blades (optional), bright blue finish, smooth target grips. Mfg. 1995 only.

	$650	$575	$500	$450	$400	$365	$335

Last MSR was $596.

Add approx. $14 for each barrel length after 4 in., $74 for slotted shroud (Model 7414-V8S, 8 in. barrel only), approx. $25 for VR heavy rib shroud.

MODEL 7445 SUPERMAG - .445 Super Mag. cal., 4, 6, 8, or 10 in. VR barrel, adj. rear sight, interchangeable front and rear sight blades (optional), high polished finish, smooth target grips. Mfg. 1991-95.

	$650	$575	$500	$450	$400	$365	$335

Last MSR was $596.

Add approx. $17 for each barrel length after 6 in., $74 for slotted shroud (Model 7445-VH8S, 8 in. barrel only), approx. $25 for VR heavy rib shroud, approx. $40 for VR heavy shroud and interchangeable sights (Model 7445-VH).

SUPER RAM SILHOUETTE - .357 Max., .414 Super Mag., or .44 Mag. cal., silhouette variation featuring modified Iron Sight Gun Works rear sight, Allen Taylor throated barrel, factory trigger job, 4 lbs. Mfg. 1995 only.

	$775	$650	$550	$375	$315	$270	$230

Last MSR was $807.

Add $43 for .414 Super Mag. cal.

GRADING - PPGS™	100%	98%	95%	90%	80%	70%	60%

HUNTER SERIES - .357 Super Mag., .41 Mag., .44 Mag., or .445 Super Mag. cal., 7 1/2 in. barrel with heavy shroud, Hogue rubber finger grooved and wood presentation grips, choice of Gunworks iron sights or w/o sights with Burris base and rings, non-fluted cylinder, with or w/o compensator, approx. 4 lbs. Mfg. 1994-95.

	100%	98%	95%	90%	80%	70%	60%
	$795	$675	$500	$445	$385	$350	$300

Last MSR was $849.

Add $32 for compensated barrel.
Add $32 for scope mounts (w/o sights).

WESTERN ARMS COMPANY

Previous manufacturer located in Ithaca, NY.

SHOTGUNS: SxS

WESTERN LONG RANGE - 12, 16, 20 ga., or .410 bore, 26-32 in. barrels, mod. and full choke, boxlock, extractors, double or single trigger, plain pistol grip stock, Western Arms Co. was a division of Ithaca Gun. Mfg. 1929-46.

	$275	$225	$200	$175	$150	$125	$100

* *Western Long Range Single Trigger*

	$325	$275	$250	$225	$200	$150	$125

WESTERN FIELD

Previous trademark used on Montgomery Ward rifles and shotguns.

The Western Field trademark has appeared literally on hundreds of various models (shotguns and rifles) sold through the Montgomery Ward retail network. Most of these models were manufactured through subcontracts with both domestic and international firearms manufacturers. Typically, they were "spec." guns made to sell at a specific price to undersell the competition. Most of these models were derivatives of existing factory models with less expensive wood and perhaps missing the features found on those models from which they were derived. To date, there has been very little interest in collecting Western Field guns, regardless of rarity. Rather than list Western Field models, a general guideline is that values generally are under those of their "1st generation relatives." As a result, prices are ascertained by the shooting value of the gun, rather than its collector value. See Store Brand Crossover List located in the back of this text.

WESTLEY RICHARDS & CO. LTD.

Currently manufactured by Westley Richards and Co., Ltd., Birmingham, England 1812 to date. In 1995, Westley Richards opened their own agency in the US, which is currently located in Bozeman, MT. Previously located in Springfield, MO. Originally William Westley Richards was located in Birmingham, England.

Note: Westley Richards guns are essentially custom ordered - only 40-45 guns are made annually. They make many weapons that are impossible to list and evaluate, except on an individual basis. Professional appraisal is necessary upon purchase or sale.

To obtain a quotation for a new Westley Richards shotgun, an inquiry should be submitted to the manufacturer or importer (see Trademark Index).

WESTLEY RICHARDS & CO. HISTORY

There seems to be a lot of confusion regarding W. Richards, W. R. Richards, William Richards, and other generic derivatives of the famous English gunmaker, Westley Richards. Part of the problem is that there are seventeen registered firms in England, including several in London, who have made guns by the name of Richards. A genuine Westley Richards gun never has the first name abbreviated, and the London address is usually found on the rib panel. Further compounding the problem, a previous Belgian gunmaker, identifiable by W. Richards on the locks or rib, had many shotguns exported into the United States,

GRADING - PPGS™	100%	98%	95%	90%	80%	70%	60%

which are commonly confused with the real London maker. These Belgian guns are commonly hammer guns with damascus twist barrels most frequently encountered in either 10, 12, or 16 ga. The easiest way to determine this maker is to recognize the Liege proofmarks on the barrel flats and chamber length given in millimeters. Most of these Belgian guns sell in the $275-$650 range, depending on condition and configuration.

RIFLES

MSR values for currently manufactured rifles are listed in English pounds. On older rifles, a knowledgeable appraisal/evaluation should be procurred before buying.

FIXED LOCK (BOXLOCK) DOUBLE RIFLE - .470 NE or .500 NE; standard features include type 'C' doll's head, disc set strikers, two triggers, automatic ejectors, chopper lump barrels, quarter rib, express sights, ramp foresight, standard walnut stock, and traditional scroll engraving.

✳ *Fixed Lock Double Rifle Current Mfg.*
    Current MSR for the base model is £26,750.
    Add £3,250 for traditional scroll engraving.
The values listed represent the standard model without additional options (of which there are a wide array).

✳ *Fixed Lock Double Rifle Older & Recent Mfg.*

	100%	98%	95%	90%	80%	70%	60%
	N/A	$29,500	$25,000	$22,000	$20,000	$18,000	$16,000

HAND DETACHABLE LOCK (DROPLOCK) DOUBLE RIFLE - nearly all calibers available; standard features include type 'C' doll's head, disc set strikers, hand detachable locks, two triggers, automatic ejectors, manual or automatic safety, chopper lump barrels, quarter rib, express sight.

✳ *Hand Detachable Lock Double Rifle Current Mfg.*
    Current MSR for the base model is £39,500.
    Add £4,000 for .577 NE or .600 NE cal.
    Add £1,500 for sideplates.
    Add £3,250+ for engraving.
The values listed represent the standard model without additional options (of which there are a wide array).

✳ *Hand Detachable Lock Double Rifle Older & Recent Mfg.*

	100%	98%	95%	90%	80%	70%	60%
	N/A	$40,000	$34,000	$29,000	$25,000	$21,500	$16,750

    Add 20% for Mag. cals. .460NE or higher.

SIDELOCK DOUBLE RIFLE - nearly all calibers available, standard features include type 'C' doll's head, disc set strikers, two triggers, automatic ejectors, scroll engraving standard, manual or automatic safety, chopper lump barrels, quarter rib, express sight.
    Current MSR for the base model is £49,500.
    Add £5,000 for .577NE or .600NE cal.
    Add £6,000 for optional engraving.
The values listed represent the standard model without additional options (of which there are a wide array).

BOLT ACTION MAGAZINE RIFLE - nearly all calibers available; choice of standard, magnum, or short action, adjustable trigger, Model 70 style 3 postion safety, express sight, ramp foresight.

✳ *Bolt Action Magazine Rifle Current Mfg.*
    Current MSR for the base model is £7,750.
    Add £900-£2,750 for engraving.
The values listed represent the standard model without additional options (of which there are a wide array).

✳ *Bolt Action Magazine Rifle Older & Recent Mfg.*

	100%	98%	95%	90%	80%	70%	60%
	N/A	$11,000	$9,000	$7,750	$6,750	$5,750	$4,750

GRADING - PPGS™	100%	98%	95%	90%	80%	70%	60%

SHOTGUNS: PRE-WWII MFG.

Add 50% for 20 ga.
Add 100% for 28 ga.
Add $1,500 for cased extra set of locks.

OVUNDO O/U - detachable lock boxlock, optional sideplates. Disc.

	$18,000	$15,000	$12,500	$9,750	$8,500	$7,250	$6,000

MODELE DE GRANDE LUXE - SxS - scalloped receiver, detachable locks, profuse scroll & game scene engraving. Disc.

	$15,000	$13,000	$11,000	$9,750	$8,500	$7,250	$6,000

MODEL DE LUXE - SxS - scalloped receiver, detachable locks, fine scroll & game scene engraving. Disc.

	$11,000	$9,500	$8,500	$7,500	$6,000	$5,500	$5,000

HAMMERLESS EJECTOR PLAIN QUALITY - SxS - scalloped receiver, Anson & Deeley fixed locks.

	$6,000	$5,000	$4,000	$3,500	$3,000	$2,500	$2,000

"B" QUALITY EJECTOR - SxS - boxlock with plain (unscalloped) receiver, light scroll engraving. Disc.

	$5,000	$4,000	$3,500	$3,000	$2,500	$2,250	$2,000

SHOTGUNS: O/U, RECENT MFG.

BEST QUALITY O/U - available in 20 ga. only. 2 1/2 or 2 3/4 in. chambers, standard features include Westley Richards top lever, automatic ejectors, automatic safety, two triggers or Westley Richards patent single trigger, hand detachable locks, hinged coverplate, sideplates with inspection port, chopper lump barrels.

Current MSR on the base model is £37,500.

The values listed represent the standard model without additional options (of which there are a wide array)

SHOTGUNS: SxS, RECENT MFG.

MSR values for currently manufactured rifles are listed in English pounds. For used values, an appraisal/evaluation should be procured before buying.

CONNAUGHT MODEL - 12, 20, or 28 ga., Anson & Deeley scalloped boxlock action, scroll engraving, 26 or 28 in. barrels, ejectors, about 6 1/2 lbs. Disc.

	$9,250	$8,000	$6,600	$5,600	$4,800	$4,000	$3,400

Last MSR was $10,900.

HAND DETACHABLE LOCK (DROPLOCK) - available in 12, 16, 20, 28 ga. or .410, 2 3/4 in. or 3 in. chambers, standard features include model 'C' doll's head, Westley Richards top lever, automatic ejectors, automatic safety, two triggers, hand detachable locks, hinged coverplate, chopper lump barrels.

✻ *Hand Detachable Lock (Droplock) Current Mfg.*

Current MSR for the base model is £28,250.
Add £1,000 for 28 ga. or .410 bore.
Add £3,250 for SST.
Add £2,950 for spare detachable locks.
The values listed represent the standard model without engraving and additional options (of which there are a wide array).

✻ *Hand Detachable Lock (Droplock) Older & Recent Mfg.*

	N/A	$21,000	$17,500	$14,250	$11,000	$9,500	$7,750

Add 50% for 20 ga.
Add 100% for .410 bore or for 28 ga.
Only six .410 best quality boxlocks have been mfg. to date.

GRADING - PPGS™	100%	98%	95%	90%	80%	70%	60%

BEST QUALITY SIDELOCK - 12, 16, 20, 28 ga., or .410 bore, 2 3/4 in. or 3 in. chambers, standard features include Best London sidelock action, assisted opening system, automatic ejectors, automatic safety, two triggers, chopper lump barrels, scroll engraving standard.

✽ *Best Quality Sidelock Current Mfg.*
    Current MSR for the base model is £37,500.
    Add £1,750 for 28 ga. or .410 bore.
    Add £2,100 for SNT or £3,250 for SST.

The values listed represent the standard model without engraving and additional options (of which there are a wide array).

✽ *Best Quality Sidelock Older & Recent Mfg.*

	100%	98%	95%	90%	80%	70%	60%
	N/A	$27,500	$24,000	$21,500	$17,500	$13,750	$9,950

    Add 50% for 20 ga.
    Add 100% for 28 ga. or for .410 bore.
    Add $1,000 for SST.

Most specimens in this model were custom ordered, so each gun should be evaluated individually.

WHITNEY ARMS COMPANY

Previous manufacturer located in New Haven, CT, 1798-1886.

Whitney Arms Company began firearms production in 1798. Eli Whitney Sr. & Eli Whitney Jr. were prominent figures and prolific producers in the arms manufacturing world for a great many years, and their production plant in New Haven is credited as being the first major manufacturer of commercial firearms in America. The Whitneys produced a tremendous variety of firearms under family ownership for approximately 90 years before selling the company to Winchester in 1888. Numerous long arms, starting with the Whitney 1798 U.S. Contract Musket, and moving forward through various other flintlock, percussion, rimfire, and centerfire rifles, handguns, and shotguns, contributed to the vast broadness of the Whitney line. The Whitney name saw collaboration with Burgess, Kennedy, Morse, Tiesing, Howard, Cochran, Scharf, and many others. Many of the early Whitney rifles, such as the historic 1798 Flintlock muskets, are rare and highly collectible, commanding substantial premiums when found in original configuration, and not converted to percussion. The Whitney lever action repeaters are also quite popular among collectors. A fair number remain in circulation.

The author wishes to express his thanks to Mr. Steve Engleson for providing the following information on Whitney Arms Company.

100%	98%	95%	90%	80%	70%	60%	50%	40%	30%	20%	10%

RIFLES: LEVER ACTION

WHITNEY-KENNEDY LEVER ACTION MAGAZINE RIFLES - a repeating rifle with loading port on right side, top ejection, approx. 15,000 mfg. between 1879-1886, barrels are typically marked "Whitney Arms Co." or "Whitneyville Armory" with some variations having the Kennedy name included, often referred to as the Kennedy rifle, two basic frame styles, large and small caliber, frame sizes were the same, but internal parts and configuration had several differences, both frame styles also available in carbines and muskets, two other basic variations were the standard loop lever, a serpentine or "S" shaped finger lever, ser. nos. were sequential from 1-5,000, and from there a letter prefix was added, these appeared from "A" through "S", with numbers 1-999 following.

✽ *Whitney-Kennedy Lever Action Magazine Rifles Large Caliber* - .40-60 WCF, .45-60 WCF, .45-75 WCF, and .50-95 Express cal., 26 or 28 in. round or octagon barrels, walnut stocks, crescent steel buttplate, full magazine capacity of 9 rounds in standard rifle.

100%	98%	95%	90%	80%	70%	60%	50%	40%	30%	20%	10%
N/A	N/A	$4,000	$3,700	$3,500	$3,300	$3,000	$2,700	$2,500	$2,100	$1,950	$1,500

    Add 300% for .50-95 Express cal. (extremely rare).
    Add 10% for .45-75 cal. (rare).

100%	98%	95%	90%	80%	70%	60%	50%	40%	30%	20%	10%

Add 50% for carbine or musket.

Add 100% for half-round, half-octagon barrel.

Add 20% for nonprefix (early) serial numbers.

Add 10% for serpentine lever.

✳ *Whitney-Kennedy Lever Action Magazine Rifles Small Caliber* - .44-40 WCF, .38-40 WCF, and .32-20 WCF cal., 24 in. round or octagon barrel, walnut stock and crescent buttplate, full magazine capacity of 13 rounds in standard rifle.

100%	98%	95%	90%	80%	70%	60%	50%	40%	30%	20%	10%
N/A	N/A	$3,200	$2,900	$2,700	$2,500	$2,200	$2,000	$1,800	$1,600	$1,300	$1,100

Add 50% for carbine or musket (extremely rare).

Add 100% for half-round, half-octagon barrel.

Add 20% for half-magazine.

Add 20% for 26 or 28 in. barrel.

Add 20% for .38-40 WCF and .32-20 WCF cals.

1878 BURGESS REPEATING RIFLE - .45-70 Govt. cal., standard sporting rifle, 28 in. octagon or round barrel, loading port on right side, serpentine shaped lever, walnut stock, blue receiver and full magazine capacity of 9 rounds, typically w/o Whitney markings, barrels marked "G.W. Morse Patented Oct. 28th 1856", and tangs are marked "A. Burgess Patented Jan. 7th 1873", several variations, including the first, second, and third models, as well as military carbines and muskets.

100%	98%	95%	90%	80%	70%	60%	50%	40%	30%	20%	10%
N/A	N/A	$5,000	$4,500	$4,000	$3,500	$3,000	$2,700	$2,500	$2,300	$2,100	$1,950

Add 300% for the first model top loader (few made and most converted by the factory to side-loader).

Add 100% for military carbine or musket (certain variations will command a higher premium).

Add 30% for first or second model.

Values shown are for the most typically encountered variation, the third model sporting rifle. This model was also known as the Whitney-Burgess-Morse lever action repeating rifle, mfg. through a license agreement with Andrew Burgess, total production of approx. 2,000 were made between 1878-82.

WHITNEY FIREARMS COMPANY

Previous manufacturer from 1956-1959 located in Hartford, CT.

GRADING - PPGS™	100%	98%	95%	90%	80%	70%	60%

PISTOLS: SEMI-AUTO

WOLVERINE OR LIGHTNING - .22 Auto cal., unique futuristic Jetsons appearance, 10 shot, 4 5/8 in. barrel, plastic grips, aluminum alloy frame and barrel shroud, blue model is more common (approx. 13,000 mfg.), nickel is rare (approx. 900 mfg.). Mfg. 1955-62.

	100%	98%	95%	90%	80%	70%	60%
Blue finish	$495	$425	$350	$300	$260	$230	$200
Nickel finish	$950	$850	$600	$500	$400	$350	$300

WHITWORTH

This trademark can be found in the Interarms section of this text.

WICHITA ARMS, INC.

Current manufacturer located in Wichita, KS. Distributor, dealer, and consumer direct sales.

PISTOLS

WICHITA INTERNATIONAL PISTOL (WIP) - available in 8 cals. between .22 LR and .357 Mag., single shot, break open action, stainless steel, adj. sights, 10 or 14 in. barrel, adj. sights or scope mounts, smooth walnut stocks and forearm. Disc. 1994.

	100%	98%	95%	90%	80%	70%	60%
	$680	$465	$350	$285	$250	$215	$185

Last MSR was $775.

Add $100 for 14 in. barrel.

GRADING - PPGS™	100%	98%	95%	90%	80%	70%	60%

WICHITA CLASSIC PISTOL - assorted cals. to .308 Win., 11 1/4 in. barrel, action has left-hand bolt for shooting with right hand, deluxe walnut, custom made, 3 lbs. 15 oz. Disc. 1997.

	$3,280	$2,550	$2,150	$1,865	$1,715	$1,295	$1,075

Last MSR was $3,495.

✱ *Wichita Classic Pistol Engraved* - similar to Wichita Classic, except is extensively engraved.

MSR $5,250	$5,250	$3,750	$2,750	N/A	N/A	N/A	N/A

WICHITA SILHOUETTE PISTOL (WSP) - .308 Win. or 7mm/IHMSA cal., adj. trigger and sights, 14 15/16 in. barrel, center grip walnut stock, rear grip, 4 1/2 lbs. Left-hand action for shooting with right hand. Disc. 1994.

	$1,520	$1,050	$850	$740	$620	$515	$440

Last MSR was $1,800.

WICHITA MAGAZINE PISTOL - .308 Win. or 7mm/IHMSA cal., fiberthane (disc. 1987) or walnut (new 1988) stock, choice of MK-40, Silhouette, or Classic configuration, 13 in. barrel, adj. trigger, multi-range sights, 4 1/2 lbs. Disc. 1994.

	$1,250	$875	$700	$585	$500	$415	$365

Last MSR was $1,550.

✱ *Wichita Magazine Pistol Classic* - features octagon barrel, AAA walnut stock, 11 1/4 in. barrel, 3 lbs. 15 oz. Disc. 1994.

	$2,975	$2,450	$2,000	$1,740	$1,495	$1,215	$1,000

Last MSR was $3,400.

WICHITA BENCH PISTOL - .222 Rem., 6 PPC, or .22 Cheetah cal., uses WBR 1200 action, rear grip, 18 in. stainless steel Douglas barrel. Mfg. 1994-98.

	$1,875	$1,500	$1,250	$1,100	$895	$785	$630

Last MSR was $1,875.

RIFLES: BOLT ACTION

WICHITA CLASSIC RIFLE (WCR) - .17-222, .17-222 Mag., .222 Rem., .222 Mag., 223 Rem., 6x47mm, and other cals. up to and including .308 Win. cal., bolt action, single shot, select walnut, 21 in. octagon barrel, Canjar trigger, no sights, 7 lbs. Disc. 1997.

MSR $3,495	$3,275	$2,500	$2,150	$1,865	$1,715	$1,295	$1,075

Add $175 for left-hand action.

✱ *Wichita Classic Rifle Varmint (WVR)* - similar to WCR, except available only in Varmint cals. (up to and including .308 Win.) and round barrel. Disc. 1997.

	$2,500	$1,795	$1,375	$1,215	$985	$855	$685

Last MSR was $2,695.

Add $175 for left-hand action.

✱ *Wichita Classic Rifle Silhouette (WSR)* - available in most cals., grey fiberthane stock, 24 in. match grade barrel, 2 oz. Canjar trigger, no sights, 9 lbs. Disc. 1995.

	$2,475	$1,775	$1,375	$1,215	$985	$855	$685

Last MSR was $2,650.

Add $175 for left-hand action.

✱ *Wichita Classic Rifle Magnum* - Mag. cals., stainless steel only. Disc. 1984.

	$1,725	$1,300	$1,175	$1,040	$845	$735	$600

WICKLIFFE RIFLES

Previously manufactured by Triple S Development located in Wickliffe, OH.

RIFLES: SINGLE SHOT

MODEL 76 STANDARD - falling block action, most popular cals., 22 or 26 in. barrel, no sights, select walnut pistol grip, 2 piece stock. Mfg. 1976-disc.

	$395	$350	$325	$300	$275	$250	$225

MODEL 76 DELUXE GRADE - similar to Standard, in .30-06 cal. only, 22 in. barrel, fancy wood, silver pistol grip cap.

	$460	$415	$385	$360	$320	$290	$250

MODEL 76 COMMEMORATIVE - similar to Deluxe, except etched receiver, U.S. silver dollar inlaid in stock, presentation case. Mfg. 100, 1976.

	$1,100	$825	$550	$495	$440	$330	$305

STINGER - similar to Model 76 Standard, in .22 Hornet or .223 Rem. cal., lightweight 22 in. barrel.

	$395	$350	$325	$300	$275	$250	$225

STINGER DELUXE - similar to 76 Deluxe, in .22 Hornet or .223 Rem. cal., lightweight 22 in. barrel.

	$460	$415	$385	$360	$325	$290	$250

TRADITIONALIST - similar to Standard 76, in .30-06 or .45-70 Govt. cal., 24 in. barrel.

	$395	$350	$325	$300	$275	$250	$225

KODIAK COMMEMORATIVE - similar to Model 76 Deluxe, .338 Win. Mag. cal., 26 in. barrel, etched receiver.

	$650	$550	$475	$425	$375	$325	$275

WIENER WAFFENFABRIK

Previous manufacturer located in Vienna, Austria.

PISTOLS: SEMI-AUTO

LITTLE TOM - 6.35mm (.25 ACP) or 7.65mm (.32 ACP) cal., 2 1/2 (.25 ACP) or 3 1/2 (.32 ACP) in. barrel, DA, designed by Alois Tomiska, small quantities mfg. in Czechoslovakia circa 1908-1918, later production in Austria circa 1919-1925.

.25 ACP cal.	$500	$450	$400	$350	$300	$250	$200
.32 ACP cal.	$600	$550	$500	$450	$400	$350	$300

Values assume Austrian production. Czech production will bring a premium. The .32 ACP cal. model is more scarce.

WIFRA

Please refer to W.R. Saleri listing in the S section.

WILD WEST GUNS

Current custom gunsmith and manufacturer established in 1992 and located in Anchorage, AK. Dealer and consumer direct sales.

PISTOLS: SEMI-AUTO

Wild West Guns previously manufactured a customized M1911 style semi-auto model called the ShadowLite package - 1997 retail was $2,495.

RIFLES: BOLT ACTION

SUMMITLITE - various short action cals., Rem. or Win. action, fluted match grade barrel, lightweight configuration with scaled down synthetic stock, 4 1/2 lbs.

MSR $3,495	$3,125	$2,750	$2,400	$2,100	$1,800	$1,600	$1,200

Add $175 for stainless steel, $199 for thumbhole stock, or $220 for left-hand action.

GRADING - PPGS™	100%	98%	95%	90%	80%	70%	60%

PROGUIDE - .375 H&H, .416 Rem., .458 Win., or .458 Lott cal., Win. controlled feed action, slab side barrel with muzzle brake and quarter rib, parkerized finish, camo or black synthetic stock with Pachmayr decelerator pad.

MSR $3,995	$3,650	$3,250	$2,850	$2,500	$2,200	$1,800	$1,600

Add $175 for stainless steel or $220 for left-hand action.

RIFLES: LEVER ACTION

ALASKAN COPILOT RIFLE - .30-30 Win. (disc. 1999), .357 Mag. (disc. 1999), .44 Mag. (disc. 1999), .444 Marlin (disc. 1999), .45-70 Govt., .457 Mag. (new 2000), or .50 Alaskan (new 2000) cal., 16 1/2, 18 1/2, or 20 in. barrel with ghost ring rear sight, features customized Marlin lever action with takedown conversion, various finishes, ported barrel, matte blue or parkerized finish, includes soft case. New 1996.

MSR $1,995	$1,800	$1,475	$1,125	$900	$675	$625	$575

Add $250 for .50 Alaskan cal. package.
Add $200 for Marlin 1895 XLR Model in stainless.
Subtract approx. 20% for older disc. cals.

* *Alaskan CoPilot Rifle Limited* - .457 Mag. or .45-70 Govt. cal., takedown action, features most of Wild West Guns custom shop options, includes hard case. Only 150 to be mfg. beginning 2001 with custom ser. nos.

	$2,995	$2,650	$2,150	$1,750	$1,500	$1,300	$1,100

Last MSR was $2,995.

ALASKAN GUIDE - .457 Mag. or .50 Alaskan cal., similar to Alaskan CoPilot, except is non-takedown, has 18 1/2 in. ported barrel with fiberoptic front sight, ghost ring rear sight, parkerized finish, straight style stock and recoil control porting. New 1997.

MSR $1,395	$1,225	$1,025	$875	$800	$700	$600	$495

Add $250 for .50 Alaskan cal. package.
Add $125 for stainless steel.
Add $200 for Marlin 1895 XLR Model in stainless.

MASTER GUIDE - .457 Mag., .45-70 Govt., or .50 Alaskan cal., takedown action.

MSR $1,895	$1,700	$1,400	$1,100	$900	$675	$625	$575

Add $250 for .50 Alaskan cal. package.
Add $125 for stainless steel.

MODEL 04 - .454 Casull or .500 S&W cal., stainless steel CNC machined frame, takedown or solid rifle, 16 1/2, 18 1/2, or 20 in. barrel, walnut, laminate or synthetic stock, ghost ring sights, Pachmayr decelerator pad. Limited mfg. 2005.

	$1,350	$1,150	$975	$860	$700	$600	$500

Last MSR was $1,499.

Add $300 for synthetic stock.
Add $400 for takedown.

WILDEY, INC.

Current manufacturer located in Warren, CT. Previously located in New Milford, CT until 1999.

Originally, the company was named Wildey Firearms Co., Inc. located in Cheshire, CT. At that time, serialization of pistols was 45-0000. When Wildey, Inc. bought the company out of bankruptcy from the old shareholders, there had been approximately 800 pistols mfg. To distinguish the old company from the present company, the serial range was changed to 09-0000 (only 633 pistols with the 09 prefix were produced). These guns had the Cheshire, CT address. Pistols produced by Wildey, Inc., New Milford, CT are serial numbered with 4 digits (no numerical prefix).

CARBINES: SEMI-AUTO

WILDEY CARBINE - .44 Auto Mag., .45 Wildey Mag., .45 Win. Mag., or .475 Wildey Mag. cal., features 18 in. barrel with forearm and detachable skeleton walnut stock, polished or matte stainless steel. New 2003.

MSR $3,110	$2,700	$2,225	$1,750	$1,500	$1,235	$1,030	$855

Add $237 for matte stainless steel finish.

PISTOLS: SEMI-AUTO

Add $585-$1,950 per interchangeable barrel assembly, depending on barrel length and finish.

WILDEY AUTO PISTOL - .45 Win. Mag., .45 Wildey Mag., or .475 Wildey Mag., gas operated, 5, 6, 7, 8, 10, or 14 in. VR barrel, selective single shot or semi-auto, 3 lug rotary bolt, fixed barrel (interchangeable), polished stainless steel construction, 7 shot, double action, adj. sights, smooth or checkered wood grips, designed to fire proprietary new cartridges specifically for this gun including the .45 Win. Mag. cal., 64 oz. with 5 in. barrel.

Add $560-$1,148 per interchangeable barrel.

* *Wildey Survivor Model* - .357 Mag., .44 Auto Mag. (new 2003), .45 Win. Mag., 45 Wildey Mag., or .475 Wildey Mag. cal., 5, 6, 7, 8, 10, 12, 14 (new 2000), or 18 (new 2003) in. VR barrel, polished stainless steel finish. New 1990.

MSR $1,571	$1,375	$1,025	$800	$665	$560	$465	$410

Add $26 - $125 for 5 in. - 12 in. barrel, depending on length, and $1,206 for 18 in. silouhette model.

Add $26 for .45 Wildey Mag. or .475 Wildey Mag. cal.
The .475 Wildey cal. is derived from a factory cartridge.

* *Wildey Survivor Guardsman* - similar to Survivor Model, except has squared-off trigger guard, same options apply to this model as for the Survivor model. New 1990.

MSR $1,571	$1,375	$1,025	$800	$665	$560	$465	$410

* *Wildey Hunter Model* - .45 Win. Mag., .45 Wildey Mag., or .475 Wildey Mag. cal., 5, 6, 7, 8, 10, 12, 14 (new 2000) or 18 (new 2003) in. VR barrel, matte finish on all metal parts, adj. sights. New 1990.

MSR $1,829	$1,575	$1,225	$950	$810	$670	$565	$475

Add $15 - $582 for 8 in. - 14 in. barrel, depending on length, or $1,210 for 18 in. silouhette model.
Add $25 for .45 Wildey Mag. or .475 Wildey Mag. cal.
.475 Wildey Mag. is available in 8, 10, or 12 in. barrel only.

* *Wildey Hunter Guardsman* - similar to Hunter Model, except has squared-off trigger guard, same options apply to this model as for the Hunter model. New 1990.

MSR $1,829	$1,575	$1,225	$950	$810	$670	$565	$475

Add $100 for 12 in. barrel.
Add $625 for 14 in. barrel.
Add $1,175 for 18 in. silhouette barrel.

* *Wildey Presentation Model* - same specifications as Hunter Guardsman model, except is engraved with hand-checkered or smooth stocks.

	$2,500	$2,000	$1,600	$1,410	$1,160	$980	$800

Last MSR was $2,000.

WILDEY AUTO PISTOL OLDER MFG. .475 Wildey Mag. cal. was available in 8 or 10 in. barrel only.

* *Older Wildey Serial Nos. 1-200.*

	$1,900	$1,700	$1,550	$1,365	$1,125	$950	$775

Last MSR was $2,180.

Add $20 for 8 or 10 in. barrel.

GRADING - PPGS™	100%	98%	95%	90%	80%	70%	60%

* *Older Wildey Serial Nos. 201-400.*

	100%	98%	95%	90%	80%	70%	60%
	$1,750	$1,550	$1,400	$1,235	$1,000	$870	$700

Last MSR was $1,980.

Add $20 for 8 or 10 in. barrel.

* *Older Wildey Serial Nos. 401-600.*

	$1,650	$1,375	$1,250	$1,100	$895	$785	$630

Last MSR was $1,780.

Add $20 for 8 or 10 in. barrel.

* *Older Wildey Serial Nos. 601-800.*

	$1,450	$1,200	$1,000	$885	$715	$610	$515

Last MSR was $1,580.

Add $20 for 8 or 10 in. barrel.

* *Older Wildey Serial Nos. 801-1,000.*

	$1,100	$925	$800	$695	$585	$485	$415

Last MSR was $1,275.

Add $25 for 8 or 10 in. barrel.

* *Older Wildey Serial Nos. 1,001-2,489.*

	$1,025	$850	$750	$640	$535	$450	$390

Last MSR was $1,175.

Add $20 for 8 or 10 in. barrel.

WILKES, JOHN GUNMAKERS LTD.

Previous manufacturer established circa 1833, and located in Arundel, England Previously imported and distributed 2004-2007 by John Wilkes Gunmakers Ltd., located in Colorado Springs, CO, and from 2001-2004 by First National Gun Banque, located in Colorado Springs, CO.

RIFLES

A boxlock double rifle started at $14,750 and the sidelock double rifle started at $44,500. Disc. 2007.

SOLID BOLT ACTION - various cals., bolt action, made of one piece of steel (action and barrel), 30 degree bolt lift.

Base price for this model was $10,500.
A Signature Model limited edition (20 mfg.) was available for $22,500.

SHOTGUNS: O/U, SIDELOCK

O/U SIDELOCK BEST MODEL CLASSIC - 20 ga. only, unique sideplate locks w/o "V" springs (plungers instead), ST or DT, best quality wood and worksmanship, Brazier "solid solid," mono solid (new 2004), monobloc, or chopper lump barrels, lifetime warranty, special order only. Imported 2001-2007.

	$22,500	$17,750	$14,500	$12,250	$11,000	$10,000	$9,250

Last MSR was $22,500

Add $3,000 for "solid solid" barrels.
Add $2,500 per pair of additional locks.

* *O/U Sidelock Best Model Classic Special Series*

Prices for the Special Series started at $32,950 with "solid solid" barrels.

SHOTGUNS: SxS

John Wilkes manufactured a sidelock model in all gauges. Boxlock models were also available, with the best quality model had a last MSR of $10,500.

WILKINSON ARMS

Previous trademark established circa 1996 and manufactured by Ray Wilkinson circa 1996-1998 (limited production), and by Northwest Arms located in Parma, ID circa 2000-2005.

GRADING - PPGS™	100%	98%	95%	90%	80%	70%	60%

CARBINES

LINDA CARBINE - 9mm Para cal., 16 3/16 in. barrel, aluminum receiver, pre-ban configuration (limited supplies), fixed tubular stock with wood pad, vent. barrel shroud, aperture rear sight, small wooden forearm, 18 or 31 shot mag., beginning 2002, this model came standard with many accessories, 7 lbs. Mfg. circa 1996-2005.

	100%	98%	95%	90%	80%	70%	60%
	$1,295	$1,075	$850	$725	$600	$500	$425

Last MSR was $1,800.

Only 2,200 Linda Carbines were marked "Luger Carbine" on the receiver. The last 1,500 distributed by Northwest Arms include a longer stock, and matched bolt and barrel (Rockwell 57).

✳ *Linda Carbine L2 Limited Edition* - mfg. from the last 600 of the original 2,200 pre-ban Linda Carbines, includes many upgrades and accessories. Mfg. 2002-2005.

Last MSR was $4,800.

There isn't enough activity in the secondary marketplace to accurately predict values on this limited ed. Linda carbine.

TERRY CARBINE - 9mm Para. cal., blowback semi-auto action, 31 shot mag., 16 3/16 in. barrel, closed breech, adj. sights, 7 lbs. Disc.

	100%	98%	95%	90%	80%	70%	60%
With black P.V.C. stock	$475	$395	$325	$295	$260	$230	$200
With maple stock	$625	$525	$400	$350	$340	$325	$300

PISTOLS: SEMI-AUTO

SHERRY MODEL - .22 LR cal., 2 1/2 in. barrel, aluminum frame, fully machined steel slide, trigger group, and bolt insert, available in various colors, 9 1/4 oz. Mfg. 2000-2005.

	100%	98%	95%	90%	80%	70%	60%
	$245	$200	$160	$140	$125	$110	$100

Last MSR was $280.

Add $25 for gold anodized frame.
Add $20 for collector's edition.
Add $100 for Robar coating.

DIANE MODEL - .25 ACP cal., 6 shot, 2 1/8 in. barrel, fixed sight, matte blue, plastic grips. Disc.

	100%	98%	95%	90%	80%	70%	60%
	$150	$125	$95	$80	$65	$55	$50

LINDA MODEL - 9mm Para. cal., blowback action firing from closed bolt, 8.3 in. barrel, 31 shot mag., PVC pistol grip, maple forearm, Williams adj. rear sight. Disc.

	100%	98%	95%	90%	80%	70%	60%
	$675	$625	$550	$475	$425	$350	$295

WILLIAM & SON

Current firearms manufacturer and luxury retailer established in 1999, and located in London, England. Previous company name was William R. Asprey. William R. Asprey is the 7th generation of the renowned Asprey family who established their first business in 1781. William & Son continues the family tradition of building best quality English guns.

A competent appraisal is highly suggested for used Asprey and William & Son rifles and shotguns, as all guns have been built to custom order, and older guns need to be appraised individually based on condition, gauge, engraving, and possible accessories. Deluxe game scene engraving is available by quotation only.

Prices do not include English VAT.

GRADING - PPGS™	100%	98%	95%	90%	80%	70%	60%

RIFLES: BOLT ACTION

BOLT ACTION MAGAZINE RIFLE - standard cals. include .243 Win., .270 Win., .308 Win., or .375 H&H, Mauser or Mannlicher action, 3/4 rib with standard and two-folding leaf rear sight, best quality pistol grip walnut stock with traditional cheekpiece, custom order only, Magnum or short action and scopes are priced upon individual quotation only.

> Current MSR on this model is £15,500.
> Add £1,350 for cals. above .375 H&H.
> **Prices reflect base model, and include leather case with accessories.**

RIFLES: SxS, SIDELOCK

SxS DOUBLE RIFLE - various cals. up to .700, sidelock ejector with engraved reinforced action, pinless lockplates, best quality walnut, folding leaf rear sight on 3/4 rib, custom order only - prices below reflect base models, and include leather case with accessories. Limited mfg.

> Add £3,400 for detachable scope mounts.

* *SxS Double Rifle cals. to .300*
> Current MSR on this model is £69,000.

* *SxS Double Rifle cals. .375 H&H to .470 NE*
> Current MSR on this model is £74,500.

* *SxS Double Rifle cals. .500/465*
> Current MSR on this model is £74,500.

* *SxS Double Rifle .577NE*
> Current MSR on this model is £82,000.

* *SxS Double Rifle .600 and .700 Bore*
> Prices are POR.

SHOTGUNS: O/U, SIDELOCK

SIDELOCK MODEL - 12, 16, or 20 ga., best quality sidelock ejector model, DTs, scroll engraving standard, best quality checkered walnut, custom order only - prices below reflect base model, and include leather case with accessories.

> Current MSR on this model is £42,500.
> Add £650 for pistol grip stock.
> Add £3,250 for ST.
> Add £1,200 for pinless locks.

SHOTGUNS: SxS, SIDELOCK

SIDELOCK MODEL - available in 12 ga. - .410 bore, best quality sidelock ejector model, scroll engraving standard, DTs, best quality checkered walnut, custom order only.

> Current MSR on this model is £36,500.
> Add £3,250 for ST.
> Add £1,200 for pinless locks.

Pricing reflects base model, and include leather case with accessories.

WILLIAM DOUGLAS & SONS

Previous manufacturer located in Staffordshire, England. Limited U.S. importation by Cape Outfitters located in Cape Girardeau, MO until circa 2004.

RIFLES: SxS

EXPRESS RIFLE - .375 H&H cal., H&H type back action sidelock with bolster fences, DTs, ejectors, 24 in. regulated barrels, folding leaf rear sight, oil finished European walnut stock with 20 LPI checkering, light engraving, case hardened action.

$19,750	$15,250	$11,000	$8,750	$7,400	$6,200	$5,300

GRADING - PPGS™	100%	98%	95%	90%	80%	70%	60%

BOXLOCK EXPRESS RIFLE - .470 NE or .500 NE (new 1998) cal., Anson & Deeley action with DT (front trigger is articulated), case colored action with deep blue small parts, 24 in. regulated barrels, checkered European walnut stock and forearm with oil finish, light border engraving.

	$12,975	$9,950	$9,000	$8,250	$7,500	$6,750	$6,000

Add $1,000 for .500 NE cal.

* *Boxlock Express Rifle Deluxe* - includes better walnut and fully engraved receiver.

	$15,650	$12,750	$10,750	$9,500	$8,750	$7,500	$6,750

SHOTGUNS: SxS

WILLIAM DOUGLAS BOXLOCK - 16, 20, or 28 ga., 2 3/4 in. chambers, case colored receiver, chopper lump barrels, DT, 26 or 28 in. barrels. Importation began 2000.

MSR N/A	$4,650	$4,200	$3,750	$3,250	$2,750	$2,250	$1,750

Add $800 for ST.

WILLIAM EVANS LIMITED

Current manufacturer of long arms established during 1883, and located in London, England.

William Evans Limited, Gun & Rifle Makers, have been manufacturing high quality shotguns and rifles for over 100 years. Most William Evans shotguns and double rifles must be appraised individually since they were all custom ordered initially. All new guns must be ordered from the factory directly. All prices are FOB England, less VAT. Please contact William Evans (refer to the Trademark Index) for more information, including any special orders.

RIFLES

MSR values for currently manufactured rifles are listed in English pounds, and used prices are not listed, since these models are only infrequently encountered in today's marketplace.

BEST QUALITY SIDELOCK DOUBLE RIFLE - various cals., traditional bold scroll-engraved sidelock action, many options available, custom order only.

* *Best Quality Sidelock Double Rifle Current Mfg.*
   Current MSR on this model is £55,000.
   Add £15,000 for .500 NE-.577 NE cals.
   Cals. .600 NE and above are POR.

BOLT ACTION MAGAZINE RIFLE - various cals., Mauser standard or Magnum action, many options available, custom order only.

* *Bolt Action Magazine Rifle Current Mfg.*
   Current MSR on this model is £9,000.
   Add £7,000 for Mauser Magnum action.

SHOTGUNS: O/U & SxS

BEST QUALITY O/U SIDELOCK - 12, 16, 20, 28 ga. or .410 bore, best quality sidelock gun with DT, bold scroll engraving standard, custom order only.

* *Best Quality O/U Sidelock Current Mfg.*
   Current MSR on this model is £54,000.
   Add £14,000 for 28 ga. or .410 bore.

BEST QUALITY SxS SIDELOCK - 12, 16, 20, 28 ga. or .410 bore, best quality sidelock gun with DT, bold scroll engraving standard, custom order only.

* *Best Quality SxS Sidelock Current Mfg.*
   Current MSR on this model is £37,000.
   Add £5,000 for 28 ga. or .410 bore.

WILLIAM LARKIN MOORE

Current importer and dealer established in 1968, and located in Scottsdale, AZ.

William Larkin Moore imports a variety of high grade quality shotguns and double rifles. Currently, the company imports Arrieta, Art Manifacttura Armi, Pedro Arrizabalaga, Armas Garbi, Chapuis Armes, Famars, Lebeau-Courally, B. Rizzini, and F.lli Rizzini, and is the sole U.S. importer for F.lli Piotti. Please refer to the individual listings for information on current models and pricing (see Trademark Index).

WILLIAM POWELL & SON (GUNMAKERS) LTD.

Current manufacturer established in 1802, and located in Birmingham, England. The company is still controlled by the descendants of William Powell I. No current U.S. importation. Previously imported 1999-2002 by John Higgins, located in Richmond Hill, GA, and by Bells Legendary Countrywear located in New York, NY, until 1999. The Heritage Series was introduced into the U.S. in 1984.

William Powell & Sons celebrated their 200th anniversary during 2002, and are one of England's oldest premier gunmakers. Please contact the factory directly for more information. They have a fine catalog, which includes a lineup of accessories and clothing.

SHOTGUNS: SxS

Current MSRs are shown in pounds (£), and do not include VAT.

Add 10% for 16, 20, 28 ga. or .410 bore on models listed.

NO. 1 SIDELOCK EJECTOR - 12, 16, 20 ga., or .410 (disc.) bore, chopper lump barrels, extra choice French walnut, DTs, many special orders available. Gold inlays, deep relief carved action fences, can be obtained in self opener.

✳ *No. 1 Sidelock Ejector Current Mfg.*
Current MSR on this model is £42,688.
Add £4,005 for assisted opening action.
Add £3,327 for SNT.

✳ *No. 1 Sidelock Ejector Recent & Older Mfg.*

N/A	$39,500	$34,000	$28,750	$23,250	$17,500	$14,750

NO. 3 BOXLOCK EJECTOR - 12, 16, 20 ga., or .410 (disc.) bore, chopper lump barrels, scalloped boxlock action, extra choice French walnut, many special orders available.

✳ *No. 3 Boxlock Ejector Current Mfg.*
Current MSR on this model is £23,168.

✳ *No. 3 Boxlock Ejector Recent & Older Mfg.*

N/A	$27,000	$21,000	$16,000	$9,900	$7,500	$6,250

MODEL NO. 4 BOXLOCK EJECTOR - similar to Number 3, but has dovetail lump barrels and less engraving.
Current MSR on this model is £20,155.
Add £2,131 for SNT.

✳ *Model No. 4 Boxlock Ejector Older Mfg.*

N/A	$23,000	$16,500	$10,250	$7,950	$6,600	$5,400

MODEL 6 BOXLOCK EJECTOR - disc. 1988.

$2,750	$2,450	$2,050	$1,700	$1,400	$1,150	$900

HERITAGE NO. 1 SIDELOCK EJECTOR MKII - 12 or 20 ga., 2 3/4 in. chambers, chopper lump barrels, choice of game scene or bouquet and scroll engraving, DTs. Mfg. 1984-2000.

$8,710	$12,750	$10,750	$9,000	$7,800	$6,700	$5,500

Last MSR was £8,710.

HERITAGE NO. 2 SIDELOCK MARK 11 - similar to Heritage No. 1, except has less engraving and lesser grade walnut, easy opening action.

GRADING - PPGS™	100%	98%	95%	90%	80%	70%	60%

✴ *Heritage No. 2 Sidelock Mark 11 Current Mfg.*
   Current MSR on this model is £4,775.
   Add £1,495 for traditional scroll engraving.

✴ *Heritage No. 2 Sidelock Mark 11 Recent & Older Mfg.*

	N/A	$5,900	$5,200	$4,750	$4,375	$3,675	$3,100

HERITAGE "CONSORT" SIDELOCK EJECTOR - 12, 20, or 28 ga., 2 3/4 in. chambers chopper lump barrels, round body action, full bouquet and scroll engraving. New 1998.

✴ *Heritage "Consort" Sidelock Ejector Current Mfg.*
   Current MSR on this model is £7,895.

✴ *Heritage "Consort" Sidelock Ejector Recent & Older Mfg.*

	N/A	$8,200	$6,850	$6,000	$5,000	$4,250	$3,500

HERITAGE DE LUXE BOXLOCK DETACHABLE LOCK - features detachable locks, choice of traditional scroll or game scene engraving, ejectors. Disc. 1999.

$21,485	$16,750	$13,750	$11,000	$8,500	$7,250	$5,950

Last MSR was $21,485.

HERITAGE ROUND ACTION EJECTOR - features unscalloped, rounded boxlock action with fine English scrollwork throughout, DTs. Disc. 1999.

$15,785	$12,000	$9,600	$7,800	$6,600	$5,400	$4,500

Last MSR was $15,785.

WILSON COMBAT

Current firearms manufacturer, customizer, and supplier of custom firearms parts and accessories established in 1978, and located in Berryville, AR.

PISTOLS

Wilson Combat makes a complete range of high quality, semi-auto pistols styled after the M1911 Colt. Current models include: the CQB Series ($2,250-$2,610 MSR), CQB Compact (approx. $2,300 MSR), Classic ($2,345-$2,585 MSR), Compact Carry Comp (approx. $3,000 MSR), Protector ($2,295-$2,380 MSR), KZ Series ($1,325-$1,410 MSR), Classic Super Grade ($3,995-$4,095 MSR), Classic Stainless (approx. $2,450 MSR), Tactical Super Grade ($3,895 MSR), Stealth ($2,495-$2,930 MSR), Professional Series ($2,245-$3,030 MSR), Elite Professional ($3,015-$3,165 MSR), and the Tactical Elite (approx. $3,000 MSR). Please contact the company directly for more information, including a wide variety of options and features.

RIFLES

Wilson Combat makes three basic configurations patterned after the Colt AR-15. They include: the Urban Tactical Rifle ($1,599-$1,910 MSR), M4 Tactical Carbine ($1,575-$1,884 MSR), and the Super Sniper Model ($1,799-$1,924 MSR). Please contact the company directly for more information, including a wide variety of options and features.

SHOTGUNS

Please refer to Scattergun Technologies for complete listing of shotguns and accessories.

WINCHESTER

WINCHESTER®

Current trademark established in 1886 in New Haven, CT. Currently manufactured by Miroku of Japan since circa 1992, Herstal, Belgium (O/U shotguns since 2004), and in Columbia, SC (Model 70 only beginning 2008). Previously manufactured in New Haven, CT, 1866-2006, and by U.S. Repeating Arms from 1981-2006 through a licensing agreement from Olin Corp. to manufacture shotguns and rifles domestically using the Winchester Trademark. Corporate offices are located in Morgan, UT. Olin

Corp. previously manufactured shotguns and rifles bearing the Winchester Hallmark at the Olin Kodensha Plant (closed 1989) located in Tochigi, Japan, Coboung, Ontario, Canada, and also in European countries. In 1992, U.S. Repeating Arms was acquired by GIAT located in France. In late 1997, the Walloon region of Belgium acquired controlling interest of both Browning and U.S. Repeating Arms.

For more information and current pricing on both new and used Winchester airguns and current black powder models, please refer to the *Blue Book of Airguns* by Dr. Robert Beeman & John Allen, and the *Blue Book of Modern Black Powder Arms* by John Allen (also online).

WINCHESTER OVERVIEW

Note: Winchester Rifles are a field in themselves. Models Henry, 1866, 1873, 1876, 1885, 1886, 1892, 1894, and 1895 all were produced with a multitude of special order options. Special orders included front and rear special sights, half or 2/3 magazines, takedown, various barrel lengths (barrel lengths from 14 to 36 inches could be special ordered for many models), configurations, and weights, special metal finishes, deluxe wood (either checkered or carved) in a variety of finishes, an impressive range of engraving options, different butt plates, etc. All of these special orders act independently and interdependently to determine the correct value of a particular Winchester. Some of the finest rifles ever made are special order Winchesters engraved by the Ulrichs, G. Young, L.D. Nimschke, and others. For these reasons a Model 92 Winchester can range in price from $200 to over $500,000 - quite a price range for one model alone! When contemplating a purchase on the higher dollar range, qualified and professional opinions should be secured, preferably from at least 2 sources. Unfortunately many fakes and upgraded (non-original) guns have surfaced in the last 10 years with the sudden increase in prices. Winchesters shown in this section are priced assuming a standard model with no special orders. Any special orders will further add to the prices shown. Caliber rarities must also be considered. Many of the early Winchesters are broken down by year of manufacture. Refer to the "Model Serialization" section in this book.

A factory letter specifying original shipping information by serial number will certainly help solidify values shown on older out of production Winchester rifles and shotguns. A listing has been provided by model number with serialization range which can be historically researched by the Winchester Museum now located in Cody, WY. To use this outstanding service, make sure the model and its serial number fall within the ranges listed. Simply mail in your informational request with serial number, model, and caliber to the Cody Firearms Museum, 720 Sheridan Ave. in Cody, WY, 82414. There is a $55 charge for this service, so please contact them directly for the fee regarding researching your particular firearm(s). Research results will include (if available) specimen caliber, barrel length, any special orders or finishes, return(s) to the factory, as well as any additional provenance contained by interpolating existing factory shipping ledgers. I would recommend a trip to the Buffalo Bill Historical Center as it contains the most comprehensive collection of projectile arms (including Chinese specimens that date back 2,000 years) and Americana housed under one roof in this country.

With the recent price appreciation of most upper condition Winchester rifles, excellent original condition has become so expensive that the many special order features Winchester offered do not cost that much more. However, on lesser condition guns that are much less expensive, these same special order features will cost more percentage-wise since the condition factor does not cost a premium.

Model 1866 Lever Action Rifle - ser. no. range 125,000-170,101.
Approx. 33 specimens have been researched outside of this ser. no. range.
Model 1873 Lever Action Rifle - ser. no. range 1-720,496.
Approx. 160 specimens have been researched outside of this ser. no. range.
Model 1876 Lever Action Rifle - ser. no. range 1-63,871.
Model 1883 Bolt Action Rifle (Hotchkiss Repeater) - ser. no. range 1-84,555.
May be referred to as Model 1879, 1880, or 1883.
Model 1885 Single Shot Rifle or Shotgun - ser. no. range 1-109,999.
Not available in ser. nos. 74,459-74,556. Also known as High and Low Wall.
Model 1886 Lever Action Rifle - ser. no. range 1-156,599.
Not available in ser. nos. 135,125-135,144 and 146,000-150,799.

Model 1887 & 1901 Lever Action Shotguns - ser. no. range 1-72,999.
Model 1890 Slide Action Rifle - ser. no. range 1-329,999.
Not available in ser. nos. 10,809-10,884, 20,000-29,999, 32,629-32,698, 37,599-37,627, 234,061- 234,140, and 234,142-234,160.
Model 1892 Lever Action Rifle - ser. no. range 1-379,999.
Not available in ser. nos. 374,851-376,100.
Model 1893 Slide Action Shotgun - ser. no. range 1-34,050.
Model 1894 Lever Action Rifle - ser. no. range 1-353,999.
Model 1895 Lever Action Rifle - ser. no. range 1-59,999.
Model "Lee" Bolt Action Rifle - ser. no. range 1-19,999.
Model 1897 Slide Action Shotgun - ser. no. range 34,051-377,999.
Model 1903 Semi-Auto .22 Cal. Rifle - ser. no. range 1-39,999.
Model 1905 Semi-Auto Rifle - ser. no. range 1-29,078.
Model 1906 Slide Action Rifle - ser. no. range 1-79,999.
Model 1907 Semi-Auto Rifle - ser. no. range 1-9,999.
Winchester factory data on models produced between approx. 1907-1961 is almost non-existent (except Custom Shop mfg.) since there was a fire at the Winchester factory in 1961.
A NOTE ON WINCHESTER FINISHES: It is very important to understand that there is a big value difference between a Model 1873 with 90% bright blue as opposed to a gun that has patina finish (turning brown). A bright blue specimen might bring several times more, because it is closer to the way it originally left the factory - with bright bluing. "Brown" guns are simply not as desirable as guns that show little or no use and retain bright blue finish.

GRADING EXPLANATION FOR WINCHESTER LEVER ACTIONS

A combination of grading systems is being used exclusively for Winchester Models Henry, 1866, 1873, and 1876 in this section to assist the reader in ascertaining the value of a particular specimen more accurately. They work as follows - the top pricing line contains three value ranges (Above Average, Average, or Below Average) which have been created to encompass most of the specimens commonly encountered within these models.
Since there is a drastic value difference between 95%-50% bright blue and 30% dull patina/fading finish on older Winchesters, a traditional grading/value line has been included to give you examples of values from 100% down to 10% providing you a better perspective of the top end of the marketplace.
The three value groupings include "Below Average," "Average," and "Above Average" condition rifles. These value ranges indicate the following conditions:

BELOW AVERAGE VALUE RANGE - a specimen with no finish remaining, perhaps some parts have been replaced, deteriorated metal may be lightly pitted with faint barrel/frame markings, rounded edges of wood and metal, wood showing much wear with possible repairs or cracks, must be in working order.

AVERAGE VALUE RANGE - a specimen with all original parts, exhibits gun metal patina finish, metal mostly smooth (perhaps lightly pitted), principal lettering and markings legible throughout, wood showing honest wear with little finish remaining (may have small cracks and other imperfections), good working order.

ABOVE AVERAGE VALUE RANGE - a specimen featuring unpolished brass (on Henrys and Model 1866s) or plum brown patina with traces of bluing in protected areas (on all steel frame models), sharp corners, crisp barrel markings, traces of original finish remaining, metal should exhibit nice patina or older flaking finish, wood should have some original stock varnish remaining and minor handling marks and dings, good bore, perfect working order with no replacement parts.

VALUES FOR 10%-100% CONDITION FACTORS - this includes the entire range of condition factors from 10% - 100% in many cases. N/As indicate that the condition factor is so infrequently encountered, it does not have a value. Normally, below average value ranges will approximately correspond to the 20%-30% pricing line values, average value range represents 30%-40%, and above average can range from 40%-60%, depending on the model. Typically, over 50% refers to a rifle which exhibits over 30% bright bluing/case colors or unpolished brass on the frame.

100%	98%	95%	90%	80%	70%	60%	50%	40%	30%	20%	10%

PISTOLS: SINGLE SHOT

SINGLE SHOT PISTOL - .22 LR cal., bolt action, walnut, brass, or pot metal grips, 9 in. barrel with open sights, no two are exactly alike, and quality can run from very good to crude, ser. nos. under 20.

Prices on this model typically range from $3,750 - $4,950, depending on original condition.

RIFLES: LEVER ACTIONS - 1860-1964

For the following lever action rifles, multiple special order features that add value are not cumulative (i.e., do not add 30% for an octagon barrel to the premium for a Deluxe rifle). Also, as a general rule, premiums for calibers, options, and special order features become less important on the following lever action models in over 90% original condition (i.e., do not add a 50% premium for .44-40 WCF on a Model 1892 rifle if original condition is over 90%).

HENRY RIFLE - .44 rimfire, 15 shot, 24 in. barrel with integral slotted tube mag. and loading lever, blue barrel, brass or iron frame. Approx. 13,000 total production, mfg. 1860-1866.

Add at least 25%, and possibly a lot more for factory engraving, depending on amount and condition (these specimens should have fancy wood).

Because almost all Henrys have little or no original finish left, values are in ranges rather than in separate condition factors.

* **Henry Rifle Iron Frame Model** - frame made of iron, round type buttplate, without lever latch, adj. sporting type rear leaf sight, serial numbers are in three digits only. Total production is believed to be less than 300.

$60,000 - $95,000 (Above Ave.) $40,000 - $60,000 (Average) $25,000 - $40,000 (Below Ave.)

100%	98%	95%	90%	80%	70%	60%	50%	40%	30%	20%	10%
N/A	N/A	N/A	$100,000	$85,000	$75,000	$62,500	$50,000	$40,000	$30,000	$20,000	$15,000

* **Henry Rifle First Model** - approx. 3,500 mfg., generally serialized below 3,500, with or without lever latch, perch belly stock and slotted receiver for rear sight.

$37,000 - $27,000 (Above Ave.) $18,000 - $27,000 (Average) $15,000 - $18,000 (Below Ave.)

100%	98%	95%	90%	80%	70%	60%	50%	40%	30%	20%	10%
N/A	N/A	N/A	$60,000	$50,000	$40,000	$30,000	$22,000	$17,000	$13,500	$10,000	$7,500

* **Henry Rifle Martial Marked** - contracted by U.S. military for Civil War use, denoted by "C.G.C." inspector markings on upper barrel breech and stock, approx. 1,900 with serialization scattered.

$30,000 - $45,000 (Above Ave.) $20,000 - $30,000 (Average) $15,000 - $20,000 (Below Ave.)

100%	98%	95%	90%	80%	70%	60%	50%	40%	30%	20%	10%
N/A	N/A	N/A	$80,000	$70,000	$60,000	$50,000	$40,000	$30,000	$20,000	$15,500	$12,000

This rifle was the most revolutionary shoulder weapon introduced in the Civil War.

* **Henry Rifle Late Model** - similar to first model, except buttplate heel has pointed profile, lever latch became standard and receiver is not slotted for rear sight, serial numbers over approx. 3,500, most commonly encountered Henry with approx. 8,000 mfg.

$18,000 - $25,000 (Above Ave.) $10,000 - $18,000 (Average) $7,500 - $10,000 (Below Ave.)

100%	98%	95%	90%	80%	70%	60%	50%	40%	30%	20%	10%
N/A	N/A	N/A	$45,000	$37,500	$30,000	$24,000	$18,000	$13,000	$10,000	$7,500	$6,000

MODEL 1866 - .44 rimfire or centerfire (4th Model only), 24 in. barrel, blue barrel with brass frame, differs from Henry in that it has a wood forearm, frame cartridge loading port, and separate tube mag. Total production reached 170,101 for all models, mfg. 1866-98.

* **Model 1866 First Model Rifle** - "Improved Henry" action, .44 cal. rimfire, without forend cap, serialization is concealed on lower tang inside buttstock, serial range is from mid-12,000 to mid-15,000 (in Henry serial range sequence).

$18,000 - $25,000 (Above Ave.) $14,000 - $18,000 (Average) $10,000 - $14,000 (Below Ave.)

100%	98%	95%	90%	80%	70%	60%	50%	40%	30%	20%	10%
N/A	N/A	$60,000	$55,000	$50,000	$45,000	$40,000	$32,500	$25,000	$17,500	$10,000	$5,500

Buyer beware - watch for fakes!

	100%	98%	95%	90%	80%	70%	60%	50%	40%	30%	20%	10%

✳ *Model 1866 Carbine First Model* - same action as Rifle, only with 20 in. barrel, 2 barrel bands and saddle ring.

$7,000 - $10,000 (Above Ave.) $5,000- $7,000 (Ave.) $3,000 - $5,000 (Below Ave.)

N/A	N/A	$25,000	$22,000	$20,000	$17,500	$15,000	$12,000	$9,000	$6,000	$4,000	$2,000

✳ *Model 1866 Rifle Second Model* - "New Model" with redesigned frame, with Henry barrel markings, serial number inside on the earlier guns after ser. no. 19,000, outside lower tang beneath lever (approx. after ser. no. 20,000).

$5,000 - $8,000 (Above Ave.) $3,500 - $5,000 (Average) $2,000 - $3,500 (Below Ave.)

N/A	N/A	$30,000	$26,500	$23,000	$19,000	$16,000	$13,000	$10,000	$7,750	$5,500	$4,250

✳ *Model 1866 Carbine Second Model* - frame and other changes similar to Second Model Rifle.

$4,000 - $5,000 (Above Ave.) $3,000 - $4,000 (Average) $2,000 - $3,000 (Below Ave.)

N/A	N/A	$25,000	$21,000	$18,000	$16,000	$14,000	$12,500	$9,500	$6,500	$4,000	$2,000

✳ *Model 1866 Rifle Third Model* - block style serial numbers usually located behind trigger, improved frame. Serial numbered approx. 25,000-149,000.

$4,000 - $6,000 (Above Ave.) $3,000 - $4,000 (Average) $2,000 - $3,000 (Below Ave.)

N/A	N/A	$25,000	$21,000	$18,000	$16,000	$14,000	$12,500	$9,500	$6,500	$4,000	$2,000

✳ *Model 1866 Carbine Third Model* - same changes as Model 1866 Third Model Rifle, 20 in. barrel with 2 bands.

$4,000 - $6,000 (Above Ave.) $3,000 - $4,000 (Average) $2,000 - $3,000 (Below Ave.)

N/A	N/A	$20,000	$18,500	$16,000	$14,000	$12,000	$10,000	$7,250	$5,000	$3,750	$2,500

✳ *Model 1866 Musket Third Model* - 27 in. round barrel, 24 in. magazine, 3 barrel bands.

$4,000 - $5,000 (Above Ave.) $3,000 - $4,000 (Average) $2,000 - $3,000 (Below Ave.)

N/A	N/A	$20,000	$18,500	$16,000	$14,000	$12,000	$10,000	$7,250	$5,000	$3,750	$2,500

✳ *Model 1866 Rifle/Carbine/Musket Fourth Model* - .44 cal., twin rimfire and centerfire, script style serial number on lower tang near lever latch, improved frame, serial range approx. 149,000-170,101.

$4,000 - $5,000 (Above Ave.) $3,000 - $4,000 (Ave.) $2,000 - $3,000 (Below Ave.)

N/A	N/A	$20,000	$18,500	$16,000	$14,000	$12,000	$10,000	$7,250	$5,000	$3,750	$2,500

Subtract 20% for steel buttplate and forend cap on rifle.

This rifle is usually found with steel buttplate and forend cap.

MODEL 1873 - .32-20 WCF, .38-40 WCF, or .44-40 WCF cal., iron frame with sideplates, frame loading port, 20 or 24 in. round or octagon barrel, rifles have forearm caps and carbines have forearm bands, tube mag., blue finish with case hardened parts, oil finished stock, serial numbered on lower tang, 720,610 mfg. between 1873-1919.

Add 60%-100% for Deluxe Model 1873 with color case hardened frame, depending on original condition.

Since early Model 1873s were only made in .44 cal., no caliber markings are present. After the introduction of additional calibers, the barrels were stamped just in front of the receiver and on the brass elevator with the caliber.

Model 1873s are serial numbered sequentially on the lower tang. On guns serial numbered 80,000 to 170,000, an "A" followed the number. From 170,000 to 190,000, either "A" or "B" may be found, while after 200,000, usually "B" was used. The letter does not seem to have any definite meaning. The earliest guns had no marking on the upper tang, but were marked "Model 1873" on the lower tang next to the ser. no. up to number 350, after which "Model 1873" is marked on the upper tang, where it remained through the model run.

✳ *Model 1873 First Model Rifle* - serial numbers approx. 1-30,000, sliding thumbprint dust cover on 2 guides that are integral part of upper frame, absence of any cal. marking.

$1,800 - $3,000 (Above Ave.) $1,200 - $1,800 (Average) $800 - $1,200 (Below Ave.)

N/A	N/A	$14,000	$11,500	$10,250	$7,750	$6,250	$3,850	$2,700	$1,500	$900	$600

100%	98%	95%	90%	80%	70%	60%	50%	40%	30%	20%	10%

❋ *Model 1873 Carbine First Model* - 20 in. round barrel with carbine style forearm band. Distinctive curved buttplate, with saddle ring.

$2,750 - $3,500 (Above Ave.)   **$1,750 - $2,400 (Average)**   **$1,000 - $1,650 (Below Ave.)**

100%	98%	95%	90%	80%	70%	60%	50%	40%	30%	20%	10%
N/A	N/A	$16,500	$13,750	$11,000	$8,250	$6,250	$4,500	$3,250	$2,250	$1,500	$850

❋ *Model 1873 Musket First Model* - 30 in. round barrel, 27 in. mag. with 3 barrel bands, approx. 500 mfg.

$2,650 - $3,750 (Above Ave.)   **$2,150 - $2,650 (Average)**   **$1,100 - $2,150 (Below Ave.)**

100%	98%	95%	90%	80%	70%	60%	50%	40%	30%	20%	10%
N/A	N/A	$9,500	$8,250	$7,250	$6,000	$5,000	$4,000	$3,000	$2,000	$1,250	$750

❋ *Model 1873 Rifle Second Model* - improved dust cover featuring slides on center rail on rear section of frame top which is held in place by two screws, serial range 31,000-90,000.

$1,500 - $2,200 (Above Ave.)   **$1,000 - $1,500 (Average)**   **$600 - $1,000 (Below Ave.)**

100%	98%	95%	90%	80%	70%	60%	50%	40%	30%	20%	10%
N/A	N/A	$8,000	$7,150	$6,000	$5,850	$4,000	$3,000	$2,200	$1,500	$850	$500

❋ *Model 1873 Carbine Second Model* - changes similar to 1873 Second Model Rifle, with 20 in. round barrel and 2 barrel bands.

$1,800 - $2,500 (Above Ave.)   **$1,200 - $1,800 (Average)**   **$800 - $1,200 (Below Ave.)**

100%	98%	95%	90%	80%	70%	60%	50%	40%	30%	20%	10%
N/A	N/A	$12,000	$10,500	$9,000	$7,750	$6,500	$5,250	$4,000	$2,750	$1,450	$650

❋ *Model 1873 Musket Second Model* - changes similar to 1873 Second Model Rifle, with 30 in. barrel and 3 barrel bands.

$1,800 - $2,500 (Above Ave.)   **$1,400 - $1,800 (Ave.)**   **$1,000 - $1,400 (Below Ave.)**

100%	98%	95%	90%	80%	70%	60%	50%	40%	30%	20%	10%
N/A	N/A	$5,000	$4,500	$3,950	$3,400	$2,950	$2,500	$1,950	$1,450	$1,100	$825

❋ *Model 1873 Rifle Third Model* - dust cover rail integral with frame, serial 90,000-end of production.

$1,500 - $2,000 (Above Ave.)   **$1,000 - $1,500 (Average)**   **$750 - $1,000 (Below Ave.)**

100%	98%	95%	90%	80%	70%	60%	50%	40%	30%	20%	10%
N/A	N/A	$6,500	$5,500	$4,750	$3,950	$3,300	$2,750	$2,100	$1,475	$950	$500

Add 20% for .44-40 WCF cal.

Add 30% for octagon barrel for .44-40 WCF cal. only.

❋ *Model 1873 Carbine Third Model* - changes similar to 1873 Rifle Third Model, with 20 in. barrel and 2 barrel bands.

$1,800 - $2,250 (Above Ave.) $ **1,200 - $1,800 (Average)**   **$800 - $1,200 (Below Ave.)**

100%	98%	95%	90%	80%	70%	60%	50%	40%	30%	20%	10%
N/A	N/A	$10,000	$9,250	$8,500	$7,500	$6,400	$5,000	$3,750	$2,250	$1,500	$750

Add 10% for .32-20 WCF cal.

❋ *Model 1873 Musket Third Model* - 30 in. round barrel and 3 barrel bands.

$1,500 - $2,000 (Above Ave.)   **$1,200 - $1,500 (Average)**   **$800 - $1,200 (Below Ave.)**

100%	98%	95%	90%	80%	70%	60%	50%	40%	30%	20%	10%
N/A	N/A	$4,650	$4,250	$3,700	$3,100	$2,650	$2,250	$1,700	$1,250	$900	$775

❋ *Model 1873 .22 Rimfire Rifle* - .22 S, L, or Extra L (very rare) cal., 24 in. barrel, no loading gate, the first .22 caliber repeater, 19,552 produced, mfg. 1884-1904. Made in rifle configuration only.

$1,500 - $2,000 (Above Ave.)   **$1,000 - $1,450 (Average)**   **$700 - $1,000 (Below Ave.)**

100%	98%	95%	90%	80%	70%	60%	50%	40%	30%	20%	10%
N/A	N/A	$8,000	$7,250	$6,500	$5,850	$4,900	$3,950	$3,000	$2,000	$1,000	$650

Add 30% for takedown model.

The takedown mechanism is unique in that a pin is driven out of the receiver, and is very prone to wear.

❋ *Model 1873 Trapper's Carbine* - all features similar to .22 rimfire model, except available with 14, 15, or 16 in. barrel.

$4,000 - $4,750 (Above Ave.)   **$3,000 - $3,950 (Average)**   **$1,800 - $2,450 (Below Ave.)**

100%	98%	95%	90%	80%	70%	60%	50%	40%	30%	20%	10%
N/A	N/A	$20,000	$18,500	$16,000	$14,000	$12,000	$10,000	$7,250	$5,000	$3,750	$2,500

Other barrel lengths were also available on this model, but are much rarer.

❋ *Model 1873 "One of One Thousand"* - special care taken in manufacture to guarantee better accuracy, markings on top of breech designate model, deluxe walnut, extremely rare, barrel marked "One of One Thousand" in most cases, 136 mfg. Original cost was $100.

100%	98%	95%	90%	80%	70%	60%	50%	40%	30%	20%	10%

Values can range from $65,000 - $225,000, depending on condition. A factory letter is a must for any "One of One Thousand" Winchester. Watch for fake letters.

Note: Rarity of the "One of One Thousand" and the "One of One Hundred" models has made unethical upgrading of this model fairly common. Use extreme caution in purchasing.

* *Model 1873 "One of One Hundred"* - similar to "One of One Thousand" only rarer, 8 mfg. Sold new for $20 over the list price of a similarly equipped Model 1873.

Values can range from $100,000 - $350,000, depending on condition. A factory letter is a must for any "One of One Hundred" Winchester. Watch for fake letters.

MODEL 1876 - .40-60 WCF, .45-60 WCF, .45-75 WCF (first caliber offered), or .50-95 Express cal., 22, 26, or 28 in. round or octagon barrel, similar but larger frame than Model 1873, tube mag., rifles have forearm caps while carbines have forearm bands, crescent butt, blue finish, straight grip stock, 63,871 mfg. between 1876-97.

Add 75%-150% for Deluxe Model 1876s with color case hardened frames, depending on original condition.

The Model 1876 was also called the Centennial Model since its introduction coincided with the U.S. Centennial Exposition held in Philadelphia, PA in 1876. Popularity for this model decreased ten years later when the more powerful and advanced Model 1886 was introduced.

1876 Deluxe Models with 90%+ original case colors are extremely rare.

* *Model 1876 Rifle First Model* - serial numbered approx. 1-5,000, distinguishable by no dust cover on frame top.

$2,750 - $3,500 (Above Ave.) $2,000 - $2,750 (Average) $1,500 - $2,000 (Below Ave.)

| N/A | N/A | $12,500 | $11,250 | $10,000 | $8,750 | $7,500 | $6,250 | $4,950 | $3,650 | $2,300 | $1,600 |

* *Model 1876 Carbine First Model* - 22 in. round barrel, one barrel band, saddle ring, full-length forearm giving a musket appearance.

$3,000 - $4,000 (Above Ave.) $2,500 - $3,000 (Average) $2,000 - $2,500 (Below Ave.)

| N/A | N/A | $12,500 | $11,250 | $10,000 | $8,750 | $7,500 | $6,250 | $4,950 | $3,650 | $2,300 | $1,600 |

* *Model 1876 Musket First Model* - 32 in. round barrel with 1 band, scarce model because no foreign military contracts.

$5,500 - $6,200 (Above Ave.) $4,000 - $5,500 (Average) $3,000 - $4,000 (Below Ave.)

| N/A | N/A | $21,500 | $18,000 | $15,250 | $13,750 | $11,750 | $9,000 | $7,000 | $4,900 | $3,350 | $2,350 |

* *Model 1876 Rifle Second Model* - "Thumbprint" dust cover rail held on by screw, serial range 5,000-30,000.

$2,250 - $3,000 (Above Ave.) $1,600 - $2,250 (Average) $1,000 - $1,600 (Below Ave.)

| N/A | N/A | $10,000 | $8,500 | $7,250 | $6,000 | $5,000 | $4,000 | $3,250 | $2,500 | $1,500 | $1,000 |

Add 35% for .50-95 WCF cal.

* *Model 1876 Carbine Second Model* - changes similar to Model 1876 Rifle Early Second Model, with 22 in. round barrel and full length forearm giving a musket appearance.

$2,500 - $3,500 (Above Ave.) $1,500 - $2,500 (Average) $1,200 - $1,500 (Below Ave.)

| N/A | N/A | $15,000 | $12,000 | $8,950 | $7,000 | $5,700 | $4,500 | $3,350 | $2,250 | $1,600 | $1,100 |

* *Model 1876 Musket Second Model* - changes similar to Model 1876 Rifle Early Second Model, with 32 in. round barrel and carbine forend tip.

$5,000 - $6,000 (Above Ave.) $4,000 - $5,000 (Average) $3,000 - $4,000 (Below Ave.)

| N/A | N/A | $15,000 | $13,500 | $10,750 | $9,750 | $8,750 | $8,000 | $6,500 | $4,500 | $2,500 | $1,500 |

* *Model 1876 Rifle Third Model* - dust cover rail integral with frame, serial range 30,000-end of production.

$2,250 - $3,000 (Above Ave.) $1,600 - $2,250 (Average) $1,000 - $1,600 (Below Ave.)

| N/A | N/A | $10,000 | $8,500 | $7,250 | $6,000 | $5,000 | $4,000 | $3,250 | $2,500 | $1,500 | $1,000 |

Add 25% for .50-95 WCF cal.

100%	98%	95%	90%	80%	70%	60%	50%	40%	30%	20%	10%

✱ **Model 1876 Carbine Third Model** - frame similar to Model 1876 Rifle Third Model, with 22 in. round barrel and full-length forearm giving a musket appearance.

$2,500 - $3,500 (Above Ave.)   **$1,500 - $2,500 (Average)**   **$1,200 - $1,500 (Below Ave.)**

N/A	N/A	$15,000	$12,000	$8,950	$7,000	$5,700	$4,500	$3,350	$2,250	$1,600	$1,100

✱ **Model 1876 Musket Third Model** - frame similar to Model 1876 Rifle Third Model, with 32 in. round barrel.

$4,000 - $5,000 (Above Ave.)   **$3,000 - $4,000 (Average)**   **$2,000 - $3,000 (Below Ave.)**

N/A	N/A	$13,000	$11,500	$10,250	$8,850	$7,600	$6,325	$5,000	$3,700	$2,350	$1,650

✱ **Model 1876 "One of One Thousand"** - special care taken in manufacture to guarantee better accuracy, markings on top of breech designate model, deluxe walnut, extremely rare, 54 mfg. Original cost was $100.

Values can range from $75,000 - $250,000, depending on condition. A factory letter is a must for any "One of One Thousand" Winchester. Watch for fake letters.

Values are not listed because too few original specimens are bought or sold to accurately establish pricing. A factory letter is a must for any "One of One Thousand" Winchester.

Note: Rarity of the "One of One Thousand" and the "One of One Hundred" models has made unethical upgrading of this model fairly common. Use extreme caution in purchasing.

✱ **Model 1876 "One of One Hundred"** - similar to "One of One Thousand" only rarer, 8 mfg. Sold new for $20 over the list price of a similarly equipped Model 1876.

Values can range from $125,000 - $500,000, depending on condition. A factory letter is a must for any "One of One Hundred" Winchester. Believe it or not, watch for fake letters.

Values are not listed because too few original specimens are bought or sold to accurately establish pricing. A factory letter is a must for any "One of One Hundred" Winchester.

✱ **Model 1876 Northwest Mounted Police Carbine** - .45-75 WCF cal. only, 22 in. barrel, "NWMP" or "MP" marking may appear on stock (with wear, this cartouche may not be visible - the majority were not marked) approx. 1,600 mfg., factory records can only verify 150.

$5,250 - $6,500 (Above Ave.)   **$4,150 - $5,250 (Average)**   **$3,100 - $4,150 (Below Ave.)**

N/A	N/A	$16,500	$13,750	$11,000	$9,000	$7,750	$6,250	$5,250	$4,250	$3,500	$2,750

Above average specimens in this model should have traces of blue. Be very wary of the stock cartouche since these buttstocks were sold as surplus back in the 1920s. A letter of authenticity is a good idea on this model.

MODEL 1886 - .33 WCF, .38-56 WCF, .38-70 WCF (830 mfg.), .40-65 WCF, .40-70 WCF (629 mfg.), .40-82 WCF, .45-70 Govt., .45-90, .50-110 Express, or .50-100-450 (234 mfg.) cal. available, Browning's first high power lever action design distinguishable by vertical locking bars, .45-70 Govt. most popular cal., 26 in. round or octagon barrel, tube mag., steel forend cap, straight grip stock. Approx. 159,990 mfg. between 1886-1935.

On the following Model 1886 variations add the percentages for special order features and/or configuration.

Add 20% for octagon barrel.

Add 30% for octagon barrel with takedown (not on Lightweight).

Add 25% for .45-70 Govt. or .45-90 cal.

Add 100% for .50-110 or 200% for .50-100-450 cal.

Add 100%-150% for case colored receivers on standard guns only (pre-1902 mfg.), depending on original condition.

Add 200%-300% for Deluxe Model (pistol grip checkered walnut stock and case colored receiver), depending on original condition.

The Model 1886 had case hardening standard on the frame, buttplate, and forend cap until 1901 (approx. 122,000 serial range) when the standard finish became blue.

✱ **Model 1886 Rifle**

N/A	N/A	$6,250	$5,750	$5,000	$4,500	$3,950	$3,250	$2,250	$1,850	$1,550	$1,250

100%	98%	95%	90%	80%	70%	60%	50%	40%	30%	20%	10%

✷ *Model 1886 Carbine* - same general specifications as Rifle, except 22 in. round barrel and saddle ring, solid frame only.

| N/A | N/A | $15,000 | $12,750 | $10,500 | $8,950 | $7,500 | $6,000 | $5,000 | $4,350 | $3,500 | $2,750 |

Add 40% for full stock carbine (very rare).

.33 WCF cal. is the rarest caliber in this model.

✷ *Model 1886 Musket* - 30 in. round barrel, full-length military style forearm, military sights, only 350 mfg., very rare.

| N/A | N/A | $17,000 | $15,000 | $12,000 | $9,950 | $7,750 | $6,350 | $5,000 | $3,950 | $3,250 | $2,500 |

Most specimens encountered in this variation are in very good condition - a pitted musket is almost never encountered.

✷ *Model 1886 Lightweight Rifle* - .45-70 Govt. or .33 WCF cal. only, 22 (.45-70 Govt. cal.) or 24 (.33 WCF cal.) in. round nickel steel tapered barrel, half mag., rubber shotgun buttplate.

❖ **Model 1886 .33 caliber**

| N/A | N/A | $4,500 | $4,000 | $3,200 | $2,600 | $2,200 | $1,800 | $1,500 | $1,250 | $1,000 | $600 |

❖ **Model 1886 .45-70 Govt. caliber**

| N/A | N/A | $5,500 | $5,000 | $4,550 | $3,750 | $3,300 | $2,975 | $2,650 | $2,300 | $1,850 | $1,450 |

Since lightweight rifles were fairly late production, all specimens are blue and in very good condition usually.

MODEL 1892 RIFLE - .25-20 WCF, .32-20 WCF, .38-40 WCF, or .44-40 WCF cal., 24 in. round or octagon barrel, blue, tube mag., forend cap, crescent butt. Approx. 1,000,000 mfg. between 1892-1941.

| N/A | N/A | $3,000 | $2,575 | $1,900 | $1,550 | $1,150 | $1,050 | $875 | $700 | $575 | $475 |

Add 75% for .44-40 WCF cal.

Add 25% for .38-40 WCF cal.

Add 25% for Takedown Model.

Add approx. 150% - 200% for fancy pistol grip checkered wood (Deluxe Model).

A short rifle configuration was also available in this model with special order short barrels under 16 inches, 12 in. being the rarest. These guns are very rare (most went to South America) and prices typically range $2,750-$8,000, depending on original condition.

✷ *Model 1892 Rifle Antique* - .25-20 WCF, .32-20 WCF, .38-40 WCF, or .44-40 WCF cal., 24 in. round or octagon barrel, blue, tube mag., forend cap, crescent butt, ser. no. range under 168,000. Mfg. 1892-1898.

| N/A | N/A | $4,325 | $3,175 | $2,575 | $2,250 | $1,725 | $1,550 | $1,300 | $1,035 | $875 | $675 |

Add 100% for .44-40 WCF cal.

Add 25% for .38-40 WCF cal.

Add 25% for Takedown Model.

Add 150%-200% for Deluxe Model with fancy pistol grip checkered wood, depending on original condition.

MODEL 1892 CARBINE - 20 in. round barrel, 2 barrel bands and saddle ring.

| N/A | N/A | $3,750 | $3,175 | $2,475 | $1,850 | $1,575 | $1,275 | $1,100 | $950 | $800 | $700 |

Add 40% for .44-40 WCF cal. or 15% for .38-40 WCF cal.

MODEL 1892 TRAPPER'S CARBINE - all features similar to standard SRC, except has a 12, 14, 15, 16, or 18 in. barrel, so called Trapper's Model because it was handy for trappers who had to carry a powerful but lightweight repeating rifle.

| N/A | N/A | $9,250 | $8,000 | $6,325 | $5,250 | $4,200 | $3,600 | $2,950 | $2,200 | $1,775 | $1,150 |

Most 1892 Trapper's Carbines are in the 15 in., .44-40 WCF cal. configuration. Most of the 1892 Trapper's Carbine were shipped to South America or Australia. This variation is almost never encountered over 30% condition - most are brown guns. Check federal laws regarding 12, 14 and 15 inch barrels.

MODEL 1892 MUSKET - 30 in. round barrel, full length military style forearm with military style rear sight.

| N/A | N/A | $18,000 | $15,750 | $12,500 | $10,500 | $8,500 | $6,750 | $5,250 | $4,250 | $3,350 | $2,600 |

Add $1,500 - $2,000 for correct bayonet.

100%	98%	95%	90%	80%	70%	60%	50%	40%	30%	20%	10%

MODEL 1894 RIFLE - .25-35 WCF, .30-30 Win. (.30 WCF), .32-40 WCF, .32 Spl., or .38-55 WCF cal., most common (and popular) is .30-30 Win. cal., tube mag., 24 or 26 in. round or octagon barrel was standard, blue, straight grip stock, just before ser. no. 500,000 the barrel marking was changed to include model nomenclature, tang marking between 700,00 and 1,100,000 may or may not include "18", after 1,100,000 model nomenclature removed from tang. Over 5,000,000, mfg. 1894-2006, newer Model 94 mfg. may be found in the RIFLES: MODEL 94 LEVER ACTION - POST 1964 PRODUCTION section.

  ✳ *Model 1894 Rifle 1894-1898 Mfg.* - antique mfg., pre-148,000 ser. no.

| N/A | $4,500 | $3,875 | $3,250 | $2,650 | $2,250 | $1,800 | $1,600 | $1,275 | $1,100 | $900 | $750 |

     Add 20% for takedown variation.
     Add 75%-150% for deluxe models, depending on original condition.
     Add approx. 25% for cals. other than .30-30 Win. or .32 Spl.

The Model 1894 Winchester has the distinction of being the world's most popular rifle. Deluxe models will command substantial premiums on models listed.

  ✳ *Model 1894 Rifle 1899-1929 Mfg.* - Model 94s built 1899-1929.

| N/A | $3,250 | $2,800 | $2,300 | $1,850 | $1,500 | $1,200 | $950 | $800 | $675 | $550 | $475 |

     Add 25% for takedown variation.
     Add 100%-200% for Deluxe Model with fancy pistol grip checkered wood, depending on original condition.
     Add approx. 50% for cals. other than .30-30 Win. or .32 Spl.

The Model 1894 Winchester has the distinction of being the world's most popular rifle. Deluxe models will command substantial premiums on models listed.

MODEL 1894 TRAPPER'S CARBINE - all features similar to the standard SRC, except with a 14, 15, or 16 in. barrel.

| N/A | N/A | $6,500 | $5,750 | $4,650 | $4,000 | $3,400 | $2,750 | $2,150 | $1,650 | $1,350 | $1,000 |

The large majority of this variation are encountered in .30-30 Win. cal. with 15 in. barrel. Any other caliber or barrel length will create a premium. Most of these carbines are brown and rusty. Rarely, if ever, encountered with very much finish remaining.
Note: Check federal laws on legality of 14 and 15 in. barrels.

MODEL 1894 SADDLE RING CARBINE - 20 in. round barrel.

| N/A | N/A | $2,100 | $1,775 | $1,450 | $1,150 | $1,000 | $900 | $775 | $625 | $500 | $450 |

     Add 40% for any cal. other than .30-30 Win. or .32 Spl.

Carbines with special order features such as pistol grip, deluxe wood, checkering, etc. can bring even greater premiums than the rifle.

  ✳ *Model 1894 Saddle Ring Carbine Antique* - 20 in. round barrel, antique mfg., pre-148,000 ser. no.

| N/A | N/A | $3,200 | $2,750 | $2,300 | $1,800 | $1,550 | $1,400 | $1,175 | $925 | $750 | $675 |

     Add 40% for any cal. other than .30-30 Win. or .32 Spl.

Carbines with special order features such as pistol grip, deluxe wood, checkering, etc. can bring even greater premiums than the rifle.

  ✳ *Model 1894 Saddle Ring Carbine Eastern* - features long forearm, early stock design, early style carbine post front sight, and without saddle ring, mfg. late 1920s-early 1930s.

| N/A | N/A | $1,800 | $1,700 | $1,575 | $1,350 | $1,175 | $1,000 | $850 | $700 | $575 | $450 |

MODEL 1894 1940-1964 PRODUCTION CARBINE - 1940-1964 mfg. without saddle ring, barrel is marked Model 94.

| $825 | $725 | $600 | $500 | $450 | $400 | $350 | $300 | $275 | $250 | $225 | $200 |

     Add 50% for .25-35 WCF cal.

Some WWII carbines with special U.S. markings will bring a premium over prices listed.

MODEL 1895 RIFLE FLATSIDE - .30 US (most common), .38-72, or .40-72 cal., early model, distinguishable in that frame does not have fluting or ridge contouring, serial range approx. 1-5000.

| N/A | N/A | $5,250 | $4,850 | $4,400 | $3,950 | $3,500 | $3,050 | $2,600 | $2,200 | $1,600 | $1,100 |

     Add 30% for octagon barrel on cals. .38-72 or .40-72.

100%	98%	95%	90%	80%	70%	60%	50%	40%	30%	20%	10%

MODEL 1895 RIFLE - .30-03, .30-06, .30-40 Krag, .303 Brit., .35 Win., .38-72, .40- 72, .405 Win., or 7.62mm Russian cal., 24-28 in. barrel, blue action, box mag., straight grip stock, 425,881 mfg. from 1896-1931.

N/A	N/A	$4,500	$4,000	$3,600	$3,150	$2,750	$2,350	$1,925	$1,450	$1,000	$750

Add 30% for octagon barrel.
Add 60% for .405 Win. cal.
Add 25% for takedown model.
Add 100%-200% for Deluxe Model with fancy pistol grip checkered wood, depending on condition.

The Model 1895 was a Browning design incorporating the first box type mag. in a lever action repeating rifle. .30 US is the most commonly encountered cal. in this model. A large Russian military contract was secured in 1915 with chambering for the 7.62mm Russian cartridge (over 293,000 mfg. or over 66% of total production).

MODEL 1895 CARBINE - .30 US (.30/40 Krag Army - most common cal.), .30-03, .30-06, or .303 Brit. cal., 22 in. round barrel, military style top handguard wood and military sights, with or without saddle ring.

N/A	N/A	$4,200	$3,800	$3,475	$3,050	$2,700	$2,200	$1,800	$1,375	$1,000	$825

Add 20% for caliber other than .30 U.S.
Add 50% for U.S. government marked.

MODEL 1895 FLATSIDE MUSKET - early models have serial range under 5,000, no flutes on frame, .30-40 Krag only.

Rarity on this model means only a few specimens in several museums.

MODEL 1895 MUSKET - .30-03, .30-06, or .30-40 Krag cal., 28 in. round barrel with hand guard over barrel, military sights.

N/A	N/A	$5,500	$4,950	$4,400	$3,950	$3,475	$3,050	$2,600	$2,125	$1,600	$1,100

Add 10%-15% if U.S. Govt. marked.

MODEL 1895 NRA MUSKET - .30-03, .30-06, or .30-40 Krag cal., similar to Standard Musket grade with 24 or 30 in. barrel, 1901 Krag style rear sight. NRA approved for official NRA competition.

N/A	N/A	$4,400	$3,950	$3,475	$3,050	$2,650	$2,000	$1,825	$1,400	$1,000	$750

Add 30% if U.S. government marked.

MODEL 1895 RUSSIAN MUSKET - 7.62mm Russian cal., over 293,000 mfg. for Imperial Russian Govt., mfg. 1915-16, various Russian Ordnance stamps should be present.

N/A	N/A	$4,000	$3,600	$3,150	$2,750	$2,350	$1,900	$1,550	$1,275	$1,050	$875

MODEL 53 RIFLE - .25-20 WCF, .32-20 WCF, or .44-40 WCF cal., 22 in. round barrel, 1/2 tube mag. holding 6 cartridges, solid frame or takedown, blue finish, pistol grip or straight grip stock, serial numbered both separately and within the Model 92 range. Mfg. 24,916 between 1924-32.

N/A	N/A	$1,925	$1,725	$1,500	$1,250	$1,100	$850	$675	$550	$475	$350

Add 50% for .44-40 WCF cal.
Add 25% for Takedown Model.

MODEL 55 RIFLE - .25-35 WCF, .30-30 Win., or .32 Win. Spl. cal., lever action design, solid frame and takedown, 24 in. round barrel, shotgun style buttstock with serrated steel buttplate, tube mag., holds 3 cartridges. Approx. 20,500 mfg. between 1924-1932. Serial numbered independently to approx. 2,865, then serialized with Model 1894 production on underside of receiver. Simply could not compete with the Model 1894.

N/A	$2,000	$1,750	$1,500	$1,250	$1,000	$900	$750	$650	$550	$425	$325

Add 100% for .25-35 WCF cal.
Add 150%-200% for Deluxe Model with fancy pistol grip checkered wood, depending on condition.
Add 20% for Takedown Model.

100%	98%	95%	90%	80%	70%	60%	50%	40%	30%	20%	10%

MODEL 64 RIFLE - .219 Zipper, .25-35 WCF, .30-30 Win., or .32 Win. Spl. cal., 20 or 24 in. round barrel, with standard 26 in. on the .219 Zipper, blue metal, pistol grip stock, revamped Model 55 action with increased mag. capacity, 66,783 mfg. between 1933-1957 and 1972-73 (over 8,250 mfg. in .30-30 Win. cal. only - these last two years with minor changes).

N/A	$1,000	$875	$750	$675	$600	$550	$500	$450	$400	$350	$300

Add 100% for 20 in. barrel (sometime referred to as Carbine).
Add 200% for .25-35 WCF cal. (rare).
Add 300% for .219 Zipper cal. (very rare).
Add 75%-100% for Deluxe Model with fancy pistol grip checkered wood, depending on condition.

Many of this variation now have extra holes drilled on the top of the receiver to accept scope mounts - subtract 50% for this alteration. The Model 64 is usually found in excellent condition. Model 64 1972-73 mfg. may be found in the post-'64 section.

MODEL 65 RIFLE - .218 Bee (introduced 1939), .25-20 WCF, or .32-20 WCF cal., 22 in. round barrel (except .218 Bee - 24 in.), 1/2 tube mag. holding 7 cartridges, blue with pistol grip stock. Mfg. 5704 between 1933-1947.

N/A	$4,500	$4,000	$3,575	$3,125	$2,725	$2,300	$1,975	$1,650	$1,375	$1,100	$950

While the .25-20 WCF cal. is the rarest, the .218 Bee has the most demand.
The Model 65 was a design evolved from the Model 53. The Model 65 was not tapped on receiver side for scope mounts. As a rule, most specimens are in either pretty nice or refinished condition.

MODEL 71 RIFLE - .348 Win. cal., 2/3 tube mag. holding 4 cartridges, improved Model 1886 frame, blue metal with pistol grip stock, 20 or 24 in. barrel, short or long tang. Mfg. 47,254 between 1935-1957.

N/A	$2,000	$1,800	$1,675	$1,500	$1,300	$1,100	$975	$875	$800	$725	$650

Add 30%-40% for early variation long tang, depending on condition.
Add 100% for Deluxe Model with fancy pistol grip checkered wood, depending on condition.
Add 150% for short rifle with 20 in. barrel.
Add $250 for bolt peep sight.

MODEL 88 RIFLE AND CARBINE - see listing under RIFLES: LEVER ACTION - POST-1964 PRODUCTION section.

RIFLES: SINGLE SHOT

MODEL 1885 - available in most popular rimfire and centerfire cals. between .22 S-L-LR and .50, falling block trigger guard activated action, John Browning's first high power single shot rifle design, many variations were made and we will list the standard types. Over 139,725 mfg. between 1885-1920.

This design was originally mfg. as the Model 1878 by the Browning Brothers in Ogden, UT, in the early 1880s. Fewer than 600 were mfg. - see the Browning section for values.

* *Model 1885 Sporting Rifle Low Wall* - 24 or 26 in. round or octagon barrel was standard, open sights, solid frame, standard trigger.

N/A	N/A	$1,500	$1,350	$1,200	$1,100	$975	$825	$700	$550	$400	$300

Add 30% for centerfire cal.
Add 50% for case colored frame, if in 95%+ original condition.

* *Model 1885 Sporting Rifle High Wall* - 30 in. barrel, standard trigger, open sights, solid frame. Available in various size and weight barrels numbered (in front of forearm) from lightest to heaviest: 1, 2, 3, 3 1/2 (introduced 1910), 4, and 5. Case hardened frames standard until 1901 when bluing became standard, three different frames depending on caliber. Heavier barrels in rare calibers will bring a premium.

N/A	N/A	$3,300	$2,825	$2,500	$2,225	$2,000	$1,725	$1,500	$1,325	$1,100	$875

Add 50% for 20 ga. shotgun.
Add 50% for Takedown Model.
Add 25% for No. 5 barrel.
Add 50%-100% for Deluxe Model with fancy pistol grip checkered wood and case colored receiver, depending on original condition.
Add 10% for set trigger.
Add 30% for .405, .45, and .50 caliber.

100%	98%	95%	90%	80%	70%	60%	50%	40%	30%	20%	10%

✳ *Model 1885 Schuetzen Rifle* - high wall, 30 in. octagon barrel, double-set triggers, spur lever, aperture sight, Schuetzen style stock, adj. palm rest and buttplate.

| N/A | N/A | $7,000 | $6,000 | $5,000 | $4,250 | $3,650 | $3,200 | $2,850 | $2,500 | $2,250 | $1,875 |

Add 30% for Takedown frame.
Add 50% for case colored frame, if in 95%+ original condition.
Prices are for factory original guns only. Since this model had many shooting alterations performed by various aftermarket suppliers of its time, perhaps only 10% of remaining specimens are unaltered (or 100% factory).

✳ *Model 1885 High Wall Musket* - usually found in .22 LR cal.

| N/A | N/A | $1,400 | $1,275 | $1,100 | $975 | $850 | $750 | $650 | $550 | $475 | $400 |

Add 100% for .45-70 Govt. or .45-90 cal.

✳ *Model 1885 Low Wall Musket (Winder Musket)* - low wall, 3rd model, .22 Short or LR (most common), 28 in. barrel, standard trigger and lever, military style stock and sights, grooved forearm, one barrel band.

| N/A | N/A | $1,200 | $1,050 | $925 | $800 | $700 | $600 | $500 | $400 | $300 | $250 |

MODEL 1885 (RECENT MFG.) - please refer to the RIFLES: SINGLE SHOT, POST 1964 MFG. section for these listings.

MODEL 1900 SINGLE SHOT - .22 S and L cal., bolt action, 18 in. round barrel, blue metal, open sights, one-piece straight grip gumwood stock without fitted buttplate, takedown, not serial numbered. Approx. 105,000 mfg. between 1899-1902.

| N/A | N/A | $1,000 | $825 | $625 | $400 | $300 | $200 | $165 | $145 | $125 | $110 |

Add 100% for later models marked M1900 on barrel, and Win. stamped butt.
This model is usually encountered with flaked frames.

MODEL 1902 SINGLE SHOT - similar to 1900, bolt action, with minor improvements. Distinguishable by specially shaped extended trigger guard. Not serial numbered. Approx. 640,299 mfg. between 1902-1931.

| N/A | $500 | $400 | $300 | $200 | $150 | $125 | $100 | $90 | $80 | $70 | $60 |

Chambering included .22 cal. Extra Long in 1914 (interchangeable with S&L)

THUMB TRIGGER MODEL 99 - similar to 1902, with button behind cocking piece used to fire with thumb instead of trigger, not serial numbered. Approx. 75,433 were mfg. between 1904-1923.

| N/A | $2,250 | $2,000 | $1,750 | $1,500 | $1,200 | $1,000 | $800 | $700 | $600 | $400 | $350 |

MODEL 1904 SINGLE SHOT - improved version of 1902, 21 in. round barrel, chambering included .22 Extra Long in 1914, not serial numbered. Approx. 302,859 mfg. between 1904-31.

| N/A | $450 | $400 | $350 | $300 | $200 | $175 | $160 | $150 | $125 | $100 | $90 |

✳ *Model 1904-A Single Shot* - introduced 1927 with new sear bar and chambered for .22 LR.

| N/A | $450 | $350 | $300 | $250 | $200 | $175 | $150 | $125 | $100 | $90 | $80 |

MODEL 47 - .22 S, L, or LR cal., single shot bolt action, 25 in. round barrel, unique bolt design, uncheckered walnut stock, 5 1/4 lbs., approx. 43,000 (not serial numbered) mfg. during 1948-54.

| $350 | $300 | $250 | $200 | $180 | $150 | $140 | $130 | $125 | $120 | $115 | $110 |

MODEL 52 - please refer to listings in the Rifles: Bolt Action section.

MODEL 55 - .22 cal. only, top loading single shot, bottom ejection, 22 in. round barrel, open sporting sights, not serial numbered. Over 45,000 mfg. between 1958-61.

| $200 | $175 | $160 | $130 | $115 | $100 | $95 | $85 | $75 | $70 | $65 | $60 |

MODEL 58 SINGLE SHOT - similar to Models 1902 and 1904, .22 LR cal., 18 in. round barrel, open sights, takedown. Approx. 38,992 mfg. between 1928-31.

$1,000 $875 $775 $650 $550 $375 $250

MODEL 59 SINGLE SHOT - improved Model 58 with 23 in. round barrel and pistol grip stock with buttplate. Approx. 9,200 mfg. between 1930-31.

$925 $800 $725 $625 $425 $325 $250

This model was disc. due to lack of sales.

MODEL 60 - .22 S, L, or LR cal., improved Model 59, 23 in. round barrel increased to 27 in. 1933. Approx. 160,754 mfg. between 1930-34.

$350 $325 $300 $250 $200 $180 $150

Add 20% for 23 in. barrel.

MODEL 60A SPORTER - .22 S, L, or LR cal., sporter variation of Model 60, pistol grip walnut stock. Disc.

$450 $400 $350 $300 $250 $200 $180

MODEL 60A TARGET - similar to Model 60 with Lyman 55W aperture rear sight, heavier target stock, and 27 in. round tapered barrel. Approx. 6,118 mfg. between 1932-39.

$550 $500 $450 $425 $350 $300 $250

MODEL 67/67A - .22 S, L, LR or .22 WRF (introduced 1935) cal., 20 in. (Boys Rifle), 24 (miniature target boring), and 27 in. (sporting or smooth bore) round barrels, same basic action as the Model 60, not serial numbered. Approx. 383,000 mfg. between 1934-63.

$275 $235 $200 $150 $120 $90 $80

Add 30% for Boys rifle.
Add 150% for .22 WRF cal.
Add 100%-150% for smooth bore, depending on condition.

MODEL 677 - same basic specifications as Model 67, except no iron sights or sight cuts in barrel, not serial numbered, supplied with Win. 5-A scope, .22 WRF is scarce. Approx. 2,240 mfg. between 1937-39.

$2,100 $1,800 $1,675 $1,100 $800 $600 $400

MODEL 68 - .22 LR or .22 WRF cal., bolt action single shot, similar to Model 67, walnut stock, supplied with aperture sight (no rear sight), not serial numbered. Approx. 100,000 mfg. between 1934-46.

$300 $250 $195 $150 $115 $85 $65

Add 200% for .22 WRF cal.

MODEL 121 SINGLE SHOT RIFLE - .22 LR cal., bolt action, 20 3/4 in. barrel, open sights, plain pistol grip stock. Mfg. 1967-73.

$115 $85 $70 $55 $45 $35 $30

MODEL 121Y SINGLE SHOT RIFLE - similar to 121, with shorter stock.

$115 $85 $70 $55 $45 $35 $30

MODEL 121 DELUXE - similar to 121, with ramp front sight and sling swivels.

$125 $90 $75 $60 $50 $40 $35

MODEL 310 SINGLE SHOT - .22 LR cal., bolt action, 22 in. barrel, open sights, checkered pistol grip stock, swivels. 13,544 mfg. 1972-1975.

$200 $175 $140 $100 $80 $70 $60

WINGO "ICE PALACE" RIFLE - 5mm shot cartridge, 22 in. round barrel with vent. rib, modified lever action Martini type single shot, walnut Monte Carlo stock and forearm, marked "WINGO" on both sides of receiver, mfg. in England for Winchester "Ice Palace" shooting center, electrical cord extends from the magazine connecting to a target throwing device which threw black clay mini-pigeons, approx. 20 mfg.

$2,750 $2,500 $2,250 $2,000 $1,750 $1,600 $1,450

Add approx. 33% if with electric cables, operating trap mechanism, and at least 50 rounds of 5mm ammo and mini-pigeons.

100%	98%	95%	90%	80%	70%	60%	50%	40%	30%	20%	10%

RIFLES: BOLT ACTION

MODEL 1883 (HOTCHKISS REPEATER) - .45-70 Govt. cal., designed by Benjamin D. Hotchkiss, unique tube mag. located in buttstock attached to receiver, up-turn/pull- back bolt action, 26 in. round or octagon barrel standard on rifle. Over 84,000 mfg. between 1879-1889. Carbine extremely rare in Third Model (20 in. barrel).

> Subtract 25% for carbine configuration (24 in. round barrel with one band), or musket (32 in. round barrel with cleaning rod and two barrel bands).
> Add 25% for Deluxe Model with fancy pistol grip checkered wood.

✳ *Model 1883 First Style* - approx. 6,419 mfg. with magazine cut off and safety control incorporated into one unit.

| N/A | N/A | $2,500 | $2,150 | $1,800 | $1,500 | $1,350 | $1,200 | $1,050 | $900 | $850 | $800 |

✳ *Model 1883 Second Style* - approx. 16,102 mfg., magazine cut off on right receiver top, safety on left side.

| N/A | N/A | $2,500 | $2,150 | $1,800 | $1,500 | $1,350 | $1,200 | $1,050 | $900 | $850 | $800 |

✳ *Model 1883 Third Style* - most commonly encountered Hotchkiss, 2-piece stock, approx. 62,034 mfg. 1883-1899.

| N/A | N/A | $2,150 | $1,800 | $1,500 | $1,350 | $1,200 | $1,050 | $900 | $850 | $750 | $650 |

The Model 1883 Hotchkiss was the first bolt action designed for the U.S. military .45-70 Govt. cartridge. On the First and Second models, inspect wood directly below bolt and left frame side for cracks, breaks, or older repairs as it is frequently encountered on these early models with thin wrists.

LEE STRAIGHT PULL RIFLE - 6mm Lee (.236 U.S.N. cal.), 5 shot non-detachable box mag., 24 (Sporting Rifle) or 28 (Musket) in. barrel, folding leaf sight, blue metal, military style full stock, mfg. 1897-1902, Navy Issue Model is the Musket with "236 U.S.N." on barrels. Approx. 20,000 mfg. (including 15,000 Muskets for the U.S. Navy military contract) between 1895-1902 with parts clean up occurring in 1916.

✳ *Lee Straight Pull Rifle U.S.N. Military Musket*

| N/A | $2,750 | $2,350 | $2,000 | $1,750 | $1,500 | $1,250 | $1,100 | $1,000 | $875 | $750 | $625 |

✳ *Lee Straight Pull Rifle Sporting* - similar to Musket, with 24 in. barrel, sporter style stock. Approx. 1,700 mfg. 1897-1902.

| N/A | $3,000 | $2,650 | $2,300 | $2,000 | $1,750 | $1,500 | $1,250 | $1,050 | $975 | $875 | $800 |

This design was originally patented by James Paris Lee and assigned to the Lee Arms Company. Winchester obtained manufacturing rights to produce this model for the U.S Navy military contract 1895-1902.

MODEL 43 - .218 Bee, .22 Hornet, .25-20 WCF, or .32-20 WCF cal., dubbed "Poor Man's Model 70," 24 in. round tapered barrel, box type mag. Approx. 62,617 mfg. between 1949-1957.

| $725 | $600 | $525 | $450 | $400 | $350 | $300 | $250 | $200 | $175 | $150 | $125 |

> Add 75% for Deluxe Model with fancy checkered wood.
> Add 100% for .32-20 WCF and .25-20 WCF cal.
> Add 35% for .218 Bee cal.

> Subtract 60% if non-factory drilled and tapped (early models).

On Models 52, 54, 56, 57, 58, 59, 60, 60A, 67, 677, 68, 69, 69A, 697, and 70 values in 50% or less original condition have been omitted since values in those conditions will approximate the 60% price. This reflects the fact that while these lower condition specimens are not as desirable to collectors, they are still sought after as shooters.

GRADING - PPGS™	100%	98%	95%	90%	80%	70%	60%

MODEL 52 TARGET - .22 S (rare) or LR cal., 5 shot mag., 28 in. standard or heavy barrel (1st cataloged 1933), target sights and target style stock, speedlock trigger feature was introduced in 1929. Approx. 125,233 Model 52s in all variations were mfg. between 1919-79.

	100%	98%	95%	90%	80%	70%	60%
	$825	$750	$650	$550	$500	$450	$400
With speedlock	$700	$625	$575	$525	$475	$425	$350

Barrel drilling and tapping for scope blocks was not standard until ser. no. 5200.

✳ *Model 52A Target* - similar to Model 52, except all "A" suffix Model 52s have a speedlock action. Values are similar to Model 52 Target. In terms of rarity, it seems the "E" suffix is probably the scarcest (also the most poorly mfg.), followed by the "A" suffix variation.

MODEL 52A HEAVY BARREL - similar to Standard Target, with heavy barrel.

$1,050	$900	$775	$675	$550	$450	$400

MODEL 52-B TARGET - extensively redesigned action, improved stock design, offered with a variety of sights. Approx. mfg. 1940-47.

$1,225	$1,100	$1,000	$900	$750	$650	$550

MODEL 52-B HEAVY BARREL - similar to 52-B, with heavy barrel, with adj. sling swivel as to position of front swivel, and single shot adapter became available.

$1,325	$1,200	$1,100	$1,000	$900	$800	$700

MODEL 52-B BULL GUN - extra heavy weight barrel.

$1,650	$1,500	$1,300	$1,000	$900	$800	$650

MODEL 52 SPORTER (SPORTING RIFLE) - 24 in. round lightweight barrel with front sight cover, sporting type select walnut stock with cheekpiece, hard rubber pistol grip cap, black plastic tipped forearm, checkered steel buttplate, 5 shot mag. is standard, about 7 1/4 lbs. Mfg. 1934-1958. There is some controversy as to whether any of the Model 52 Sporters were drilled and tapped per factory worksmanship. Be cautious of "factory" drilled and tapped receivers on all model 52s, as there are many "gunsmith" Sporters that have been made with turned down, shortened target barrels.

✳ *Model 52 Sporter* - advertised approx. 1936.

$4,500	$3,750	$2,750	$2,250	$1,650	$1,400	$1,100

✳ *Model 52A Sporter* - introduced approx. 1937, receiver and locking lug were strengthened.

$4,250	$3,700	$3,250	$2,500	$2,250	$2,000	$1,500

✳ *Model 52B Sporter* - introduced approx. 1940.

$4,500	$3,600	$2,750	$2,250	$1,650	$1,400	$1,100

✳ *Model 52B (1993 Re-issue) Sporter* - .22 LR cal., patterned after the original Model 52B and includes steel buttplate, 24 in. barrel w/o sights, Micro Motion trigger with adjustment screw on bottom plate, high-polish blue, 5 shot mag., checkered 52B style stock with ebony forend tip, 7 lbs. Mfg. by Miroku in Japan 1993-2002.

$600	$525	$450	$400	$360	$330	$300

Last MSR was $662.

✳ *Model 52C Sporter* - introduced 1947 with adj. Micro Motion trigger, approx. 500-1,000 mfg., 2 screws in trigger guard.

$5,000	$4,500	$3,750	$2,850	$2,250	$1,650	$1,400

A few Model 52 Sporters & Targets were mfg. with stainless steel barrels (17,XXX-27,XXX serial range) - these guns will command a premium over values shown. Stainless steel barrels were also offered by Winchester as after market parts.

GRADING - PPGS™	100%	98%	95%	90%	80%	70%	60%

MODEL 52-C STANDARD TARGET - "Micro Motion" trigger and "Marksman" stock, single shot adaptor, 5 or 10 shot mag. was avail., standard barrel, otherwise similar to 52-B. Mfg. 1947-61.

	$1,300	$1,200	$1,100	$1,000	$800	$600	$500

MODEL 52-C HEAVY TARGET - similar to Standard Target, with heavy barrel.

	$1,350	$1,250	$1,100	$1,000	$800	$700	$650

MODEL 52-C BULL TARGET - extra heavy (bull) barrel model of Heavy Target 52-C. Mfg. approx. 1947-1961.

	$1,800	$1,500	$1,300	$1,200	$1,100	$1,000	$900

MODEL 52-D TARGET - improved version of 52-C with free-floating standard or heavy barrel and adj. bedding device, all 52-Ds were single shot.

	$1,300	$1,150	$1,000	$900	$800	$700	$600

MODEL 52-D INTERNATIONAL MATCH - similar to 52-D, with free rifle stock, accessory rail. Mfg. 1969-1975.

	$1,500	$1,300	$1,075	$900	$775	$650	$525

Previous Model 52s had ser. no. suffixes - either A, B, C, or D" After approx. 1975, rifles started appearing with an "E" serial prefix. Both Model 52 International and Prone could have factory stocks that were not Winchester mfg.

MODEL 52-D PRONE - similar to International Match, with prone style stock. Mfg. 1960-75.

	$1,400	$1,250	$1,075	$850	$725	$600	$550

MODEL 52-E INTERNATIONAL PRONE - similar to 52-D, with prone stock, removable roll over cheekpiece. Mfg. 1975-1980.

	$1,400	$1,250	$1,075	$900	$775	$650	$525

MODEL 54 HIGH POWER SPORTER - .270 Win., 7x57mm, 7.65x57mm Mauser (rare), .30-30 Win., .30-06, 9x57mm Mauser (rare) cal., 5 shot mag., 24 in. barrel, open sights, checkered pistol grip stock. Mfg. 1925-30. Approx. 50,145 Model 54s were mfg. in all variations between 1925-36.

	$1,150	$1,000	$900	$800	$700	$600	$500

Rare cals. will add premiums to the values listed. This model was also mfg. with a stainless steel barrel during the late 1920s-early '30s with premiums also being asked.

MODEL 54 CARBINE - Introduced 1927, similar to Rifle, with 20 in. barrel, plain stock.

	$1,500	$1,200	$1,000	$900	$800	$650	$500

MODEL 54 IMPROVED SPORTER - .22 Hornet, .220 Swift, .250-3000, .257 Robts., .270, 7x57mm, or .30-06 cal., 5 shot mag., 24 or 26 in. barrel, one piece firing pin, checkered pistol grip stock. Mfg. 1930-36.

	$1,375	$1,200	$1,000	$900	$800	$700	$600

Rare cals. will add premiums to the values listed.

MODEL 54 CARBINE IMPROVED - similar to Rifle, with 20 in. barrel.

	$1,750	$1,500	$1,250	$1,000	$875	$750	$650

MODEL 54 SUPER GRADE - introduced 1934, similar to Sporter, with better wood and black forend tip and pistol grip cap.

	$3,000	$2,650	$2,250	$1,775	$1,525	$1,375	$1,200

Rare calibers will command considerable premiums (i.e. this variation in 7x57mm cal. will sell for $2,500 in mint condition).

MODEL 54 SPORTING SNIPER'S RIFLE - introduced 1929, similar to Sporter, with 26 in. heavy barrel, .30-06 only, aperture sight.

	$2,400	$1,850	$1,500	$1,300	$1,100	$1,000	$900

GRADING - PPGS™	100%	98%	95%	90%	80%	70%	60%

MODEL 54 NATIONAL MATCH - introduced 1935, similar to Standard, with Lyman sights and Marksman stock.

	$1,650	$1,350	$1,100	$1,000	$850	$725	$600

MODEL 56 SPORTER - .22 S or LR cal., 5 or 10 shot box mag., 22 in. round barrel, open sights, plain pistol grip stock. Approx. 8,297 mfg. between 1926-29.

	$1,650	$1,350	$1,100	$1,000	$850	$725	$600

Approx. 1,000 mfg. in .22 Short cal.

MODEL 57 TARGET - .22 S (disc. 1930) or LR cal., 22 in. barrel with barrel band, open sights, stock cutaway for aperture sight on left side, drilled and tapped receiver, heavy target uncheckered pistol grip walnut stock, 5 (standard) or 10 shot mag., left side push-button mag. release, checkered steel buttplate approx. 5 lbs. Approx. 18,600 were mfg. between 1927-1936.

	$775	$700	$625	$525	$475	$425	$375

MODEL 69 & 69A - .22 S, L, or LR cal., 5 or 10 shot repeater, 25 in. barrel, aperture or open rear sight, not serial numbered. Approx. 355,000 mfg. between 1935-63.

	$425	$365	$300	$235	$150	$100	$85

Add 40% for Target Model.
Add 20% for grooved receiver (Model 69A only).
Add 5% for chrome plated bolt handle and trigger guard.

The Model 69 was cocked by the closing motion of the bolt and had a non-swept back bolt handle, whereas the 69A was cocked by the opening motion of the bolt and had a swept back bolt handle. Number 97B rear aperture sight and 80A hooded front target sights and standard open sights were offered on both the Model 69 and 69A.

MODEL 72/72A - .22 LR and Gallery Model (.22 short only), tube mag., bolt action, 25 in. round, tapered barrel, aperture or open rear sight, not serial numbered. Over 161,000 mfg. between 1938-59.

	$450	$375	$300	$250	$115	$100	$85

Add 30% for Target Model.
Add 100% for Gallery Model (mfg. 1939-1942) - rare.
Add 20% for grooved receiver (Model 72A only).
Add 5% for chrome plated bolt handle and trigger guard.

The Model 72 and 72A both cocked on opening. The Model 72A has a swept back bolt handle and some minor internal mechanical improvements. Same open sight options as Models 69/69A.

MODEL 75 TARGET - .22 LR, 5 or 10 shot mag., 28 in. barrel, target sights, slight variation used by Government in WWII. Approx. 88,715 Model 75 Target and Model 75s were mfg. between 1938-58.

	$550	$475	$425	$350	$300	$275	$250

Add 25% for Olympic sights.
Add 20% for original Winchester leather sling.

MODEL 75 SPORTER - similar to Target, except 24 in. tapered barrel, detachable mag., non-target sights and select checkered walnut.

	$1,375	$1,100	$875	$725	$650	$600	$500

Add 20%-25% for "grooved" receiver allowing "tip-off" scope mounts.

MODEL 131 - .22 S, L, and LR, 7 shot mag.

	$225	$200	$175	$150	$125	$95	$75

MODEL 141 - .22 S, L, and LR, butt loading tube mage.

	$225	$200	$175	$150	$125	$95	$75

MODEL 320 RIFLE - .22 LR cal., similar to Single Shot Model 310, with 5 shot mag. Mfg. 1972-74.

	$325	$325	$300	$265	$235	$185	$150

GRADING - PPGS™	100%	98%	95%	90%	80%	70%	60%

MODEL 325 RIFLE - .22 Mag. cal., otherwise similar to Model 320, limited mfg. 1972-74.

	$375	$350	$325	$300	$250	$200	$100

MODEL 670 RIFLE - another economy version of the model 70, .225 Win., .243 Win., .270 Win, .308 Win., or .30-06 cal., 22 in. barrel, open sights, no hinged floorplate, pistol grip stock. Mfg. 1967-73.

	$300	$250	$220	$195	$175	$165	$140

MODEL 670 CARBINE - similar to 670, with 19 in. barrel, not available in .308 Win. Mfg. 1967-70.

	$300	$250	$220	$195	$175	$165	$140

MODEL 670 MAGNUM - similar to 670, with reinforced stock, .264 Mag., 7mm Mag., or .300 Win. Mag. cal. Mfg. 1967-70.

	$330	$275	$255	$220	$205	$195	$165

MODEL 697 - .22 WRF cal., same general specifications as the Model 69, except no iron sights or sight cuts in barrel and no ramp or sight cover. Telescope bases attached to barrel were standard.

	$2,200	$1,975	$1,650	$1,375	$1,100	$875	$725

MODEL 770 - .22-250 Rem., .222 Rem., .243 Win., .270 Win., .30-06, or .308 Win. cal., 22 in. barrel, open sights, no floorplate or forend tip. Mfg. 1969-71.

	$375	$335	$300	$275	$250	$225	$200

MODEL 770 MAGNUM - similar to Standard, in .264 Mag., 7mm Mag., or .300 Win. Mag. cal., recoil pad. Mfg. 1969-71.

	$395	$350	$315	$285	$260	$240	$220

MODEL 777 - .30-06 cal., bolt action, 4 shot mag., mfg. by Nikko in Japan during 1979-80 for sale to Winchester subsidiaries in Australia, Germany, Italy, and Scandinavia, only 3 were shipped to the U.S., checkered Monte Carlo stock with Wundhammer swell grip, lightweight barrel, engraved action, "Winchester" is cast on the left side of the receiver near the top, approx. 1,000 mfg. with 250 in .30-06 cal. - 750 mfg. in different cal. and sold elsewhere, 8 1/2 lbs.

	$1,850	$1,675	$1,500	$1,350	$1,200	$1,100	$1,00

WILDCAT - .22 LR cal., 21 in. regular or heavy (Target/Varmint model) barrel with or w/o adj. sights, detachable 5 or 10 shot mag., checkered hardwood stock and forend (Target or Sporter configuration), sling swivels, includes one 5 round and three 10 shot mags., two-stage trigger, 4 1/2 or 5 1/2 (Target/Varmint) lbs. Importation from Russia began 2007.

MSR $269	$220	$180	$135	$115	$95	$85	$75

Add $30 for Wildcat Target/Varmint variation with heavy barrel and beavertail forend (no sights).

100%	98%	95%	90%	80%	70%	60%	50%	40%	30%	20%	10%

RIFLES: SEMI-AUTO

MODEL 1903 - .22 Win. Auto rimfire cal., 10 shot tube mag., 20 in. round barrel, open sights, straight grip stock cut out for partial magazine filling. Approx. 126,000 mfg. between 1903-1932.

N/A	$1,500	$1,325	$1,025	$900	$775	$650	$550	$475	$400	$325	$250

Add 100% for deluxe checkered model.

First U.S. semi-auto rifle designed for a special .22 cal. rimfire cartridge. Regular .22 cal. rimfire will not function or chamber properly in this model. The earliest models up to around ser. no. 5,000 were mfg. w/o a safety. Watch for fake boxes.

	100%	98%	95%	90%	80%	70%	60%	50%	40%	30%	20%	10%

MODEL 1905 - .32 Win. or .35 Win. cal., 5 or 10 shot box mag., 22 in. round barrel, open sights, straight or plain pistol grip stock. Approx. 29,113 mfg. between 1905-20.

N/A	$725	$650	$575	$525	$465	$400	$365	$330	$300	$275	$250

MODEL 1907 - .351 Win. cal., 5 or 10 shot box mag., 20 in. round barrel, open sights, plain pistol grip stock, an improved version of the Model 1905. Approx. 58,490 mfg. between 1907-57.

N/A	$675	$595	$525	$450	$375	$325	$295	$265	$230	$195	$175

MODEL 1910 - .401 Win. cal., 4 shot box mag., 20 in. barrel, open sight, plain pistol grip stock. Mfg. 20,786 between 1910-36.

N/A	$850	$750	$625	$550	$500	$450	$400	$365	$330	$300	$275

Add 50% for Fancy Sporting Rifle (special checkered walnut).

MODEL 55 - please refer to listing in Rifles: Single Shot.

MODEL 63 - .22 LR cal., styling similar to Model 1903, takedown, 10 shot tube mag., 20 (disc. 1936) or 23 in. barrel, open sights, plain pistol grip stock. Approx. 174,692 mfg. between 1933-58.

$1,275	$1,100	$975	$850	$750	$675	$550	$425	$350	$300	$265	$235

Add 20% for grooved receiver variation (WFF)

Add 100%-150% for 20 in. barrel (carbine) depending on condition.

The Model 63 was introduced to take advantage of the new .22 LR cartridge, which the older Model 1903 couldn't chamber.

Watch for fake boxes and hanging tags on this model, especially with rifles in over 95%+ original condition.

GRADING - PPGS™	100%	98%	95%	90%	80%	70%	60%

MODEL 63 GRADE I - RECENT PRODUCTION - .22 LR cal., similar to original Model 63, 10 shot mag., 23 in. barrel, checkered walnut stock and forearm, blue finish with engraved receiver, 6 1/4 lbs. Mfg. 1997-98.

		$675	$600	$550	$500	$430	$375	$315

Last MSR was $678.

✱ *Model 63 High Grade - Recent Mfg.* - .22 LR cal., similar to original Model 63, 10 shot mag., deluxe checkered walnut stock and forearm, blue finish with engraved gold animals and accents on receiver, 6 1/4 lbs. 1,000 mfg. 1997 only.

		$1,050	$875	$750	N/A	N/A	N/A	N/A

Last MSR was $1,083.

MODEL 74 - .22 S or LR (introduced in 1940) cal., tubular mag. in stock, pop-out bolt assembly. Approx. 406,574 mfg. between 1939-1955. Distinguishable by squared-off rear receiver.

		$295	$250	$215	$175	$150	$125	$70

Add 25% for .22 Short cal. (mfg. 1939-1952).

Add 25% for pre-WWII mfg.

MODEL 77 - .22 LR cal., detachable box mag. or tubular mag. under barrel. Over 217,000 mfg. between 1955-62.

		$250	$225	$200	$175	$110	$100	$70

Add $50 for tube mag.

MODEL 100 RIFLE - .243 Win., .284 Win., or .308 Win. cal., 4 shot detachable mag., 22 in. round barrel with open sights, gas operated, basket weave pattern impressed on stock, pistol grip cap. Over 262,000 mfg. 1961-73 with some production occurring in Japan.

		$550	$500	$450	$400	$300	$250	$230

The pre-1964 .284 Win. cal. with cut checkering was made for less than one year (WFF, ser. range 72,XXX with no letter suffix or prefix).

GRADING - PPGS™	100%	98%	95%	90%	80%	70%	60%

✳ *Model 100 Rifle Pre-1964 Mfg.*

	$650	$575	$500	$450	$400	$300	$250

Add $50 for .243 Win. cal.
Add $250 for .284 Win. cal.

MODEL 100 CARBINE - similar to rifle, with 19 in. barrel, plain pistol grip stock, barrel band. Mfg. 1967-1973.

	$725	$600	$500	$425	$375	$300	$250

Add $50 for .243 Win. cal.
Add $300 for .284 Win. cal.

MODEL 190 RIFLE - .22 S, L, or LR cal., semi-auto, 15 shot LR tube mag., alloy receiver, uncheckered walnut finished hardwood stock, 20 1/2 (Carbine Model) or 24 (Rifle Model) in. barrel, approx. 2,150,000 (including the Model 290 listed also) during 1967-1980.

	$175	$150	$125	$100	$85	$75	$65

MODEL 290 DELUXE RIFLE - similar to 190, with select Monte Carlo stock. Mfg. 1965-1973.

	$225	$200	$175	$150	$115	$100	$90

MODEL 490 RIFLE - .22 LR cal., 5 shot mag., 22 in. barrel, folding sight, checkered one piece stock. Mfg. 1975-1980.

	$295	$250	$225	$185	$155	$145	$130

SUPER X GRADE I (SXR) - .30-06, .270 WSM, .300 WSM, or .300 Win. Mag. cal., gas operated action with multi-lug rotating bolt locking system, blued alloy receiver, 22 (.30-06 cal.) or 24 in. blue barrel w/o sights, 3 or 4 shot detachable box mag., enlarged trigger guard with cross bolt safety, walnut stock and raked forearm featuring unique circle pattern checkering on stock and forearm for grip, removable trigger assembly, approx. 7 1/4 lbs. New 2006.

MSR $899	$750	$675	$575	$500	$425	$350	$295

Add $20 for Mag. cals.

SUPER X GRADE II - similar to Super X Grade I, except also available in .325 WSM cal., deluxe wood ergonomic stock with adj. LOP recoil system, with or w/o TruGlo fiber optic sight system, 7 1/2 lbs. Mfg. 2007 only.

	$725	$650	$575	$500	$425	$375	$325

Last MSR was $864.

Add $28 for Mag. cals.
Add $68 for adj. LPA Sights with TruGlo fiber optic elements (.300 Win. Mag. or .325 WSM cal. only).

100%	98%	95%	90%	80%	70%	60%	50%	40%	30%	20%	10%

RIFLES: SLIDE ACTION, DISC.

MODEL 1890 - .22 S, L, LR, or WRF rimfire, cals. are non-interchangeable (don't shoot a .22 S in a gun chambered for .22 L) and the barrel is marked for single cal. only, visible hammer, solid-frame (first 15,000) or takedown, 24 in. octagonal barrel, case hardened receivers until 1901, model nomenclature changed to Model 90 circa 1919 at approx. ser. no. range 640,000. Approx. 849,000 mfg. between 1890-1932.

✳ *Model 1890 First Model Solid Frame* - color case hardened receiver, mfg. 1890-1892.

N/A	$11,000	$9,000	$7,850	$6,750	$5,000	$4,500	$3,850	$3,325	$2,750	$2,250	$1,375

Add 20% for .22 L or WRF cal.

✳ *Model 1890 Second Model Takedown Frame* - color case hardened receiver, takedown feature was added in 1892 after over 15,000 solid frames had been made, approx. ser. no. range 15,500-326,000. Mfg. 1892-1907.

N/A	$7,250	$5,000	$3,850	$3,000	$2,500	$1,900	$1,650	$1,100	$875	$550	$385

100%	98%	95%	90%	80%	70%	60%	50%	40%	30%	20%	10%

* Model 1890 Takedown w/ Blue Finish - most commonly encountered Model 1890, post-1901 manufacture.

N/A	$3,000	$2,000	$1,250	$825	$650	$550	$450	$385	$335	$300	$250

Add 50% for .22 LR cal. (mfg circa 1919-1932, starting at ser. no. approx. 610,000).

.22 LR cal. accounted for approx. 10% of the total production on this model.

Deluxe model will bring premiums over values listed. There were also a limited amount of guns mfg. with stainless steel barrels which will add to values of post-1901 mfg.

The Model 1890 was Winchester's first slide action repeating rifle. It replaced the Model 1873 .22 cal. It was an excellent and inexpensive .22 rifle that rapidly became the universal firearm used in shooting galleries. Even though production reached approx. 849,000 units, most guns were heavily used and specimens existing today in 98%+ condition are rare. Check carefully for rebarreling (notice proofmarks on barrel).

MODEL 1906 - .22 S, L, or LR, 20 in. round barrel, tube mag., visible hammer, open sights, straight stock with shotgun buttplate. Approx. 848,000 mfg. between 1906-1932.

N/A	N/A	$1,500	$925	$675	$550	$450	$350	$275	$250	$200	$175

Add 20% for non-grooved forearm.

Add 20% for .22 S cal. only.

This model is seldom encountered in over 90% original condition - original mint specimens can top $2,000.

Model nomenclature was changed to the Model 06 circa 1918.

* Model 1906 Expert - similar to Model 1906, except has a pistol grip stock and different shaped slide handle, finish choices included blue, nickel trimmed receiver, guard, and bolt, or full nickel trimmed, .22 S cal. only until approx. 70,000, mfg. 1917-1925.

N/A	N/A	$1,900	$1,400	$1,200	$975	$750	$600	$475	$350	$275	$225

MODEL 61 HAMMERLESS - .22 S, L, LR, or WRF cal., 24 in. round or octagon barrel (disc. 1947, with rifling or smooth bore, i.e. Routledge), tube mag., open sights, plain grip stock. Approx. 350,000 mfg. between 1932-1963.

$1,150	$995	$875	$725	$550	$475	$375	$325	$275	$225	$200	$185

Add up to 150% for single cal. barrel marking (S or LR, Short is very rare).

Add $300 for pre-war mfg. w/small forearm.

Add 20% for grooved receiver.

Add 20% for pre-WWII rust blue metal finish.

Pre-war manufacture has small forearm. "WRF" marked round barrel is rare - front of receiver must be marked "W.R.F."

Watch for fake boxes and hanging tags on this model, especially with rifles in over 95%+ original condition. Mint original pre-war Model 61s in the proper picture box are selling in the $3,250-$3,500 range. Post-war boxed Model 61s (Kraft box) are selling in the $2,000-$2,250 range.

* Model 61 WRF - .22 WRF cal. only, front of the receiver, bottom side, must be stamped "WRF", octagon barrel mfg. 1932-1946, and round barrel mfg. 1947-1950.

$2,500	$2,375	$2,250	$2,000	$1,750	$1,250	$1,000	$750	$575	$475	$400	$250

Add 40% for round barrel.

Mint original pre-war WRF Model 61s in the proper picture box are selling in the $3,500-$3,800 range. Post-war boxed WRF Model 61s (Kraft box) are selling in the $3,250-$3,500 range.

* Model 61 Octagon - .22 S, LR, or WRF cal., octagon barrel variation of the Model 61. Disc. approx. 1947.

$3,000	$2,700	$2,400	$1,900	$1,650	$1,375	$1,050	$850	$725	$525	$500	$450

Add up to 100% for single cal. barrel marking (S or LR, Short is very rare).

* Model 61 Magnum - similar to Standard 61, but chambered for .22 Win. Mag., three variations include two barrel marking differences and the third has an additional letter "A" stamped on the bottom of the trigger guard assembly, indicating a factory update. Mfg. 1960-1963.

$1,700	$1,600	$1,400	$1,100	$900	$750	$650	$550	$450	$375	$325	$275

Add $600-$1,000 for rare "WMRF" barrel marking.

Mint original rifles in the proper Kraft box are currently selling for approx. $2,600.

100%	98%	95%	90%	80%	70%	60%	50%	40%	30%	20%	10%

* *Model 61 Smoothbore* - .22 cal. shot cartridge only, 24 in. round smoothbore barrel, three variations include the Routledge bore with 3/8 in. muzzle bore diameter and matted frame top (approx. 75 mfg. in the 45,000-47,000 ser. range), second variation is referred to as the Winchester Counter Bore (bore is slightly larger than a .22 cartridge), third variation is the Straight Smoothbore with bore diameter the same as the .22 cartridge.

100%	98%	95%	90%	80%	70%	60%	50%	40%	30%	20%	10%
$3,500	$3,200	$2,950	$2,600	$2,100	$1,800	$1,500	$1,250	$1,000	$750	$500	$400

Add 100% for Routledge bore.

Mint original boxed guns are currently selling for $4,500-$6,000 for the Winchester Counter Bore and Straight Smoothbore, and $8,000-$10,000 for the Routledge Bore.

MODEL 62/62A VISIBLE HAMMER - modern version of 1890, will shoot calibers interchangeably, 23 in. round tapered or octagon barrel. Over 409,000 mfg. between 1932-1958.

100%	98%	95%	90%	80%	70%	60%	50%	40%	30%	20%	10%
$1,500	$950	$675	$475	$375	$300	$250	$200	$185	$170	$155	$130

Add 50% for Gallery model (Gallery style loading port).
Add 30% for pre-WWII mfg.

Pre-war model is 62, distinguishable by small forearm. The Model 62-A was introduced 1940 at approx. serial number 99,200 with minor changes. Model 62A single cal. barrel markings do not add premiums. .22 Short only models without the Winchester roll die receiver marking are more scarce than the so-called "Gallery Rifle" - mint specimens without the roll die marking are approx. $1,000. Gallery variations of these models will also command sizable premium.

Watch for fake boxes and hanging tags on this model, especially with rifles in over 95%+ original condition.

GRADING - PPGS™	100%	98%	95%	90%	80%	70%	60%

MODEL 270 - .22 LR cal., tube mag., 20 1/2 in. barrel, checkered walnut pistol grip stock. Mfg. 1963-73.

	100%	98%	95%	90%	80%	70%	60%
	$175	$150	$135	$120	$100	$80	$70

* *Model 270 Plastic Forearm Variation*

	100%	98%	95%	90%	80%	70%	60%
	$150	$135	$120	$100	$80	$70	$60

* *Model 270 Deluxe* - similar to 270, with select wood, Monte Carlo stock. Mfg. 1965-73.

	100%	98%	95%	90%	80%	70%	60%
	$250	$200	$150	$110	$80	$70	$60

MODEL 275 - similar to 270, in .22 Mag.

	100%	98%	95%	90%	80%	70%	60%
	$200	$175	$150	$135	$100	$80	$70

* *Model 275 Deluxe* - similar to 270 Deluxe, in .22 Mag.

	100%	98%	95%	90%	80%	70%	60%
	$275	$225	$175	$140	$110	$80	$70

RIFLES: LEVER ACTION - POST 1964 PRODUCTION

Due to an engineering change in 1992, all Model 94s and variations (not including the 9422 models) had a crossbolt safety in the upper rear of the receiver which prevented the hammer from contacting the firing pin.

MODEL 64 1972-1974 MODEL - .30-30 Win. cal., lever action, 5 shot, 2/3 tube mag., 24 in. barrel, open sight, plain pistol grip stock. Mfg. 1972-74.

	100%	98%	95%	90%	80%	70%	60%
	$450	$400	$350	$300	$250	$200	$150

MODEL 88 RIFLE (1955-1963 MFG.) - pre-´64 version with diamond cut checkering, no barrel band, 22 in. barrel. Mfg. 1955-63. Total production for all varieties of the Model 88 Lever Action was approx. 284,000 units.

	100%	98%	95%	90%	80%	70%	60%
.308 Win. (1955-1963)	$1,100	$950	$700	$550	$450	$400	$350
.243 Win. (1956-1963)	$1,395	$1,250	$1,100	$950	$825	$750	$550
.358 Win. (1956-1962)	$3,750	$3,350	$2,750	$2,100	$1,800	$1,400	$1,100
.284 Win. (Intro-1963)	$2,850	$2,550	$2,300	$2,100	$1,650	$1,150	$850

GRADING - PPGS™	100%	98%	95%	90%	80%	70%	60%

MODEL 88 RIFLE (1964-1973 MFG.) - .243 Win., .284 Win. or .308 Win. cal., 1964 model with impressed basket weave checkering, no barrel band, 22 in. barrel. Mfg. 1964-1973.

	100%	98%	95%	90%	80%	70%	60%
.308 Win.	$925	$650	$475	$400	$350	$275	$225
.243 Win.	$1,100	$800	$550	$500	$450	$400	$300
.284 Win.	$1,575	$1,200	$950	$800	$725	$550	$495

MODEL 88 CARBINE - introduced 1968, no checkering, one-piece stock, barrel band, 19 in. barrel. Mfg. 1968-73.

	100%	98%	95%	90%	80%	70%	60%
.308 Win. (1968-1973)	$1,225	$1,100	$850	$725	$525	$450	$395
.243 Win.	$1,650	$1,350	$1,200	$1,025	$925	$800	$650
.284 Win.	$2,800	$2,425	$2,175	$1,925	$1,550	$1,275	$950

MODEL 150 - .22 LR, 20 1/2 in. barrel, tube mag., hammerless, uncheckered hardwood stock and forearm, sling swivels, approx. 47,400 mfg. 1967-74.

	100%	98%	95%	90%	80%	70%	60%
	$125	$110	$95	$70	$60	$50	$40

MODEL 250 - .22 LR, 20 1/2 in. barrel, tube mag., hammerless, checkered pistol grip stock. Mfg. 1963-73.

	100%	98%	95%	90%	80%	70%	60%
	$175	$150	$125	$110	$95	$70	$60

✳ *Model 250 Deluxe* - similar to Model 250, with select wood and sling swivels. Mfg. 1965-71.

	100%	98%	95%	90%	80%	70%	60%
	$250	$200	$160	$115	$95	$70	$60

MODEL 255 - .22 Mag., otherwise similar to Model 250. Mfg. 1964-70.

	100%	98%	95%	90%	80%	70%	60%
	$235	$200	$175	$150	$135	$110	$85

✳ *Model 255 Deluxe* - .22 Mag., with select wood and swivels. Mfg. 1965-73.

	100%	98%	95%	90%	80%	70%	60%
	$300	$260	$215	$165	$150	$135	$100

MODEL 1886 GRADE I - .45-70 Govt. cal., 26 in. octagon barrel. Mfg. 1997-98.

	100%	98%	95%	90%	80%	70%	60%
	$995	$900	$850	$750	$650	$600	$500

Last MSR was $996.

✳ *Model 1886 High Grade* - .45-70 Govt. cal., features gold-line receiver engraving with multiple gold animals, polished blue, deluxe checkered walnut stock and forearm with metal cap, 1,000 mfg. 1997 only.

	100%	98%	95%	90%	80%	70%	60%
	$1,625	$1,325	$1,050	N/A	N/A	N/A	N/A

Last MSR was $1,588.

MODEL 1886 TAKEDOWN - .45-70 Govt. cal., features original takedown action design, uncheckered semi-pistol grip walnut stock with crescent buttplate, 26 in. octagon barrel with buckhorn rear sight, forend has ebony cap, 9 1/4 lbs. Mfg. 1999 only.

	100%	98%	95%	90%	80%	70%	60%
	$1,100	$950	$825	$695	$650	$550	$450

Last MSR was $1,140.

MODEL 1886 EXTRA LIGHT GRADE I - .45-70 Govt. cal., 22 in. round tapered barrel, shotgun buttplate, half magazine, high polish receiver and barrel bluing, open sights, uncheckered walnut stock and forearm, 7 1/4 lbs. 3,500 mfg. 2000-2001.

	100%	98%	95%	90%	80%	70%	60%
	$1,150	$925	$775	N/A	N/A	N/A	N/A

Last MSR was $1,152.

✳ *Model 1886 Extra Light High Grade* - similar to Model 1886 Extra Light Grade I, except features engraved elk and whitetail deer and game scenes on blue receiver, extra fancy checkered walnut stock and forearm, 7 1/4 lbs. 1,000 mfg. 2000-2001.

	100%	98%	95%	90%	80%	70%	60%
	$1,350	$975	$850	N/A	N/A	N/A	N/A

Last MSR was $1,440.

GRADING - PPGS™	100%	98%	95%	90%	80%	70%	60%

MODEL 1892 GRADE I - .357 Mag. (new 1998), .44-40 WCF (new 1998), or .45 LC cal., similar to original Model 1892 Winchester, 24 in. round barrel, top tang mounted manual hammer stop, blue finish with etched receiver engraving, gold trigger, satin finished walnut straight grip stock and forend with metal cap, 6 1/4 lbs. Mfg. 1997-99.

	$725	$600	$475	$400	$350	$295	$250

Last MSR was $744.

✳ *Model 1892 Grade I Short Rifle* - .44 Mag. cal., features 20 in. round barrel with full mag., uncheckered staight grip walnut stock with crescent buttplate, buckhorn rear sight, high polish blue finish only, 6 lbs. Mfg. 1999-2000.

	$750	$625	$500	$425	$375	$325	$275

Last MSR was $752.

✳ *Model 1892 High Grade* - .45 LC cal., features gold accents and receiver game scene, 1,000 mfg. 1997 only.

	$1,250	$1,050	$795	N/A	N/A	N/A	N/A

Last MSR was $1,285.

MODEL 1892 JOHN WAYNE HIGH GRADE - .44-40 WCF cal., 18 1/2 in. barrel, 9 shot, silver nickel nitride receiver with engraved John Wayne portrait, initials, and flowing banner with "Courage, Strength, Grit" on right side, two portraits and banner with "John Wayne American 1907-2007" on left side, blue loading gate and action screws, ladder style adj. rear sight, saddle ring, blue hammer and trigger, large loop lever, uncheckered walnut stock, limited mfg. of 4,000, first 1,000 offered as match set with Custom Grade.

MSR $1,999		$1,895	$1,750	$1,500	N/A	N/A	N/A	N/A

MODEL 1892 JOHN WAYNE CUSTOM GRADE - .44-40 WCF cal., 18 1/2 in. barrel with gold signature, 9 shot, blue receiver with engraved John Wayne portrait, initials, and flowing banner with "Courage, Strength, Grit" on right side, two portraits and banner with "John Wayne American 1907-2007" on left side, blue loading gate and action screws, ladder style adj. rear sight, saddle ring, blue hammer and trigger, large loop lever, checkered Grade 5/6 satin walnut stock and forearm, limited mfg. of 1,000.

MSR $3,499		$3,250	$2,750	$2,325	N/A	N/A	N/A	N/A

MODEL 1895 GRADE I - .270 Win. (disc. 1999), .30-06 (mfg. 1998-99), or .405 Win. (new 2000) cal., similar to original Model 1895 Winchester, checkered straight grip stock and Schnabel forearm, 24 in. round barrel, 4 shot mag., top tang safety, blue finish, 8 lbs. Mfg. 1997-2002, .405 Win. cal. reintroduced 2004.

.270 Win. or .30-06 cal.	$1,000	$875	$750	$650	$575	$525	$450
.405 Win. cal.	$1,150	$1,000	$875	$750	$650	$600	$525

Last MSR was $1,116. Last MSR was $1,045 on .270 Win. and .30-06 cals.

MODEL 1895 LIMITED EDITION - .30-06, similar to original Model 1895 Winchester, blue receiver, 24 in. round barrel, 4 shot mag. (box mag.), uncheckered woodstock and forearm, rear buckhorn sight, 2 piece cocking lever, 8 lbs. 4,000 mfg. 1995-97.

	$875	$625	$500	N/A	N/A	N/A	N/A

Last MSR was $853.

✳ *Model 1895 Limited Edition High Grade* - .30-06 (mfg. 1995-99) or .405 Win. (mfg. 2000-2002) cal., same general specifications as the Model 1895 Limited Edition, features older No. 3 engraving pattern with double scenes, gold borders with multiple gold inlays, deluxe checkered walnut stock and forearm. 4,000 mfg. 1995-2002.

	$1,575	$1,150	$900	N/A	N/A	N/A	N/A

Last MSR was $1,532.

Add 20% for .405 Win. cal.

GRADING - PPGS™	100%	98%	95%	90%	80%	70%	60%

RIFLES: MODEL 94 LEVER ACTION, 1964-2006 MFG.

100th Anniversary Model 1894s (mfg. 1994) are marked "1894-1994" on the receiver. During 2003, Winchester discontinued the crossbolt receiver safety, and introduced the new top tang safety.

U.S. Repeating Arms closed its New Haven, CT manufacturing facility on March 31, 2006, and an auction was held on Sept. 27-28, 2006, selling the production equipment and related assets. As a result, 95%-100% asking prices on many of the following models may be higher than listed, and there are reports of consumers paying over 50% above retail values for some of the rarer variations, including calibers. Remember, most of these recently discontinued Model 94s are not rare, and the only way they can keep going up in value is if there is a continued long-term increase in demand. Don't rule out the possibility that Olin could license the Winchester trademark to another company, which means production could start all over again, even though it wouldn't be at the famous old factory in New Haven. CT. All previous MSRs listed are from the Winchester 2006 price sheet. On some of the following models, N/As may be listed for the 100% value - this means there isn't a single value for this gun, and refer to the price range listed underneath as a model note.

The Modle 94s listed below w/crossbolt safety (1992-2006 mfg.) are not as desirable as those models w/o the crossbolt safety manufactured pre-1992, unless a rare variation, configuration and/or caliber is involved.

MODEL 94 STANDARD RIFLE - .30-30 Win., .32 Win. Spl. (disc. 1973, reintroduced 1992), 7-30 Waters (new 1989), or .44 Mag. (mfg. circa late 1960s-1970s) cal., lever action, 6 or 7 (24 in. barrel only) shot tube mag., 20 or 24 (mfg. 1987-88 only) in. round barrel, open sights, straight walnut stock, barrel band on forearm. Angled ejection became standard 1982, 6 1/2 lbs. Mfg. 1964-1997.

	N/A	$350	$295	$250	$200	$175	$150

Last MSR was $363.

Add 25% for 7-30 Waters cal.

A survey of recent sales indicates a price range of $375-$450 for NIB specimens.

MODEL 94 TRADITIONAL (DELUXE WALNUT) - .30-30 Win., .44 Mag. (new 1999), or .480 Ruger Big Bore (mfg. 2002-2003) cal., similar to Standard Rifle, except has plain (new 1998, not available in .44 Mag. cal.) or checkered walnut stock and forearm, 6 (.30-30 Win. cal.) 10 (.480 Ruger cal.), or 11 (.44 Mag. cal.) shot mag., 6 1/4 lbs. Mfg. 1988-2004.

	$325	$250	$200	$165	$150	$140	$135

Last MSR was $436.

Add $34 for Traditional-CW Model (w/ checkered stock and forearm).
Add $57 for .44 Mag. cal. (Traditional-CW Model with checkered stock, mfg. 1999-2004).
Add for .480 Ruger Big Bore cal. (mfg. 2002-2003) - $43 (Traditional) or $105 (Traditional-CW).
Add $55 for 1.5 - 4.5X scope with low mounts (disc.).

MODEL 94 LEGACY ROUND - .30-30 Win., .357 Mag. (new 1997), .44 Mag. (new 1997), or .45 LC (new 1997) cal., 7 (.30-30 Win. cal. only) or 12 shot mag., features pistol grip checkered walnut stock and forearm, 20 (disc. 1999) or 24 (new 1997) in. round barrel, 6 3/4 lbs. Mfg. 1995-2006.

	N/A	$450	$300	$225	$175	$150	$135

Last MSR was $497.

Subtract $15 for 20 in. barrel.

A survey of recent sales indicates a price range of $550-$750 for NIB specimens.

GRADING - PPGS™	100%	98%	95%	90%	80%	70%	60%

✳ *Model 94 Legacy Round 26 In.* - .30-30 Win. or .38-55 Win. cal., 7 shot mag., adj. Marble's rear tang sight, similar to Model 94 Legacy Round, except features blue or color case hardened receiver and 26 in. round barrel, 7 lbs. Mfg. 2004-2006.

	N/A	$575	$425	$350	$300	$250	$200

Last MSR was $783.

Add 15% for case colored receiver.

A survey of recent sales indicates a price range of $650-$800 for NIB specimens, and add a slight premium for .38-55 WCF cal.

MODEL 94 LEGACY OCTAGON - .30-30 Win. or .38-55 Win. cal., 7 shot mag., adj. Marble's rear tang sight, features crescent buttplate, blue or color case hardened receiver and 26 in. octagon barrel, 7 1/4 lbs. Mfg. 2004-2006.

	N/A	$600	$450	$375	$325	$300	$275

Last MSR was $882.

Add 20% for case colored receiver.

A survey of recent sales indicates a price range of $700-$900 for NIB specimens, and add a slight premium for .38-55 WCF cal.

MODEL 94 RANGER - .30-30 Win. only, 20 in. barrel, uncheckered hardwood stock and forearm, 6 shot mag., 6 1/4 lbs. Mfg. 1985-2006.

	N/A	$300	$250	$200	$175	$150	$125

Last MSR was $386.

Add approx. 15% for 4x32 scope with see-through mounts (disc. 1999).

A survey of recent sales indicates a price range of $350-$450 for NIB specimens.

✳ *Model 94 Ranger Compact* - .30-30 Win. or .357 Mag. cal., 16 in. barrel, uncheckered hardwood stock with 12 1/2 LOP with recoil pad, post-style front sight, 5 (.30-30 Win. cal.) or 9 shot mag., 5 7/8 lbs. Mfg. 1998-2004.

	N/A	$375	$275	$200	$175	$150	$125

Last MSR was $402.

A survey of recent sales indicates a price range of $450-$700 for NIB specimens.

MODEL 94 TRAILS END - .357 Mag., .44-40 WCF (mfg. 1998-99), .44 Mag., or .45 LC cal., similar to standard rifle, except has 11 shot tube mag., 20 in. barrel, choice of standard or large loop lever (disc. 1998), crossbolt safety, 6 1/2 lbs. Mfg. 1997-2006.

	N/A	$575	$475	$300	$225	$175	$150

Last MSR was $480.

Add approx. $20 for large loop lever (disc. 1998).

A survey of recent sales indicates a price range of $650-$800 for NIB specimens.

✳ *Model 94 Trails End Takedown* - similar to Model 94 Trails End, except has takedown action. Limited mfg. 2006.

$500	$450	$375	$315	$270	$230	$210

Last MSR was $559.

✳ *Model 94 Trails End Octagon* - similar to Model 94 Trails End, except has octagon barrel, choice of blue or case colored receiver finish, 6 3/4 lbs. Mfg. 2004-2006.

	N/A	$650	$525	$400	$300	$250	$200

Last MSR was $757.

Add 15% for case colored receiver.

A survey of recent sales indicates a price range of $700-$950 for NIB specimens.

GRADING - PPGS™	100%	98%	95%	90%	80%	70%	60%

MODEL 94 TRAILS END HUNTER ROUND - .25-35 Win., .30-30 Win., or .38-55 Win. cal., 20 in. round barrel, 6 shot mag., uncheckered walnut stock and forearm, shotgun buttplate, 6 1/2 lbs. Mfg. 2005-2006.

	N/A	$575	$450	$325	$250	$175	$150

Last MSR was $480.

A survey of recent sales indicates a price range of $650-$800 for NIB specimens, with a premium for .25-35 WCF or .38-55 WCF cal.

∗ *Model 94 Trails End Hunter Round Takedown* - similar to Model 94 Trails End Hunter Round, except has takedown action. Limited mfg. 2006.

	$500	$450	$375	$295	$250	$215	$190

Last MSR was $559.

∗ *Model 94 Trails End Hunter Octagon* - similar to Model 94 Trails End Hunter, except has blued (new 2006) or case colored receiver and octagon barrel, crescent buttplate. Mfg. 2005-2006.

	N/A	$650	$500	$375	$295	$265	$245

Last MSR was $757.

    Add 15% for case colored receiver.

A survey of recent sales indicates a price range of $700-$950 for NIB specimens, with a premium for .25-35 WCF or .38-55 WCF cal.

MODEL 94 SHORT HUNTER TAKEDOWN - .30-30 Win., .44 Mag., or .450 Marlin cal., takedown action, 18 in. barrel, 6 or 10 (.44 Mag. only) shot mag., uncheckered walnut stock, XS ghost ring sight, 6 lbs. Limited mfg. 2006.

	$500	$450	$375	$275	$260	$220	$200

Last MSR was $587.

MODEL 94 PACK RIFLE - .30-30 Win. or .44 Mag. cal., 18 in. barrel, 4 or 5 shot 3/4 mag., over-dimension walnut stock and forearm cap w/o checkering, removable hood sight, 6 1/4 lbs. Mfg. 2000-2001.

	N/A	$300	$250	$200	$175	$150	$140

Last MSR was $496.

A survey of recent sales indicates a price range of $375-$500 for NIB specimens.

MODEL 94 TIMBER CARBINE - .444 Marlin (disc. 2001) or .450 Marlin (new 2004) cal., 18 in. ported barrel with 4 (.450 Marlin cal. only) or 5 (disc. 2001) shot 2/3 mag., top tang safety, checkered semi-pistol grip stock and forearm, blue finish only, adj. XS ghost ring rear sight (new 2004), hooded front sight (disc. 2001) or ramp style front sight, 6 lbs. Mfg. 1999-2001, reintroduced 2004-2006.

	N/A	$650	$525	$400	$300	$250	$200

Last MSR was $623.

A survey of recent sales indicates a price range of $700-$950 for NIB specimens.

∗ *Model 94 Timber Carbine Scout* - .30-30 Win. or .44 Mag. cal., similar to Model 94 Timber Carbine, 18 in. non-ported barrel with rail base, 4 (.30-30 Win.) or 8 (.44 Mag.) shot mag., XS ghost ring sights, uncheckered walnut stock and forearm, 6 lbs. Mfg. 2005-2006.

	N/A	$550	$425	$325	$250	$175	$150

Last MSR was $623.

A survey of recent sales indicates a price range of $600-$750 for NIB specimens.

∗ *Model 94 Timber Carbine Scout Takedown* - similar to Model 94 Timber Scout, except has takedown action and Pachmayr recoil pad. Limited mfg. 2006.

	$575	$475	$360	$330	$295	$265	$245

Last MSR was $699.

GRADING - PPGS™	100%	98%	95%	90%	80%	70%	60%

MODEL 94 WIN-TUFF RIFLE - .30-30 Win. cal., similar to Model 94 Rifle, except has laminated hardwood stock and forearm with checkering. Drilled and tapped for scope mounts. Mfg. 1987-disc.

	$300	$230	$180	$165	$150	$140	$135

Last MSR was $404.

MODEL 94 BLACK SHADOW - .30-30 Win. or .44 Mag./.44 Spl. cal., 20 or 24 (.30- 30 Win. cal. only) in. barrel, 4 or 5 shot mag., non-glare finish, features black composite synthetic stock with recoil pad and Fuller forearm, approx. 6 1/4 lbs. Mfg. 1998-2000.

	N/A	$450	$300	$225	$175	$150	$135

Last MSR was $381.

A survey of recent sales indicates a price range of $550-$750 for NIB specimens.

✳ *Model 94 Black Shadow Big Bore* - .444 Marlin cal., 20 in. barrel only, otherwise similar to Model 94 Black Shadow, 6 1/2 lbs. Mfg. 1998-2000.

	$495	$425	$325	$250	$200	$175	$150

Last MSR was $394.

MODEL 94 TRAPPER - .30-30 Win., .357 Mag. (mfg. beginning 1992), .44 Mag./.44 Spl. (new 1985), or .45 LC (new 1985) cal., 16 in. barrel, side ejection, walnut stock, 5 (.30-30 Win. cal.) or 9 shot tube mag., blue finish, dovetailed front sight, 6 lbs. Disc. 2006.

	N/A	$550	$425	$325	$250	$175	$150

Last MSR was $470.

A survey of recent sales indicates a price range of $600-$750 for NIB specimens.

✳ *Model 94 Trapper Compact* - .357 Mag. cal., similar to Model 94 Trapper, except has 12 1/2 LOP stock. Limited mfg. 2006.

	N/A	$600	$450	$375	$325	$300	$275

Last MSR was $486.

A survey of recent sales indicates a price range of $700-$900 for NIB specimens.

MODEL 94 BIG BORE - .307 Win. (disc. 1998), .356 Win. (disc. 1998), or .375 Win. (disc. 1987), or .444 Marlin (new 1998) cal., angled ejection port provides scope mounting, checkered walnut Monte Carlo stock with recoil pad, 20 in. barrel, 6 shot mag., sling swivels, 6 1/2 lbs. New 1983.

	N/A	$600	$450	$375	$325	$300	$275

Last MSR was $465.

Add 25% for .356 Win. or .375 Win. cal.

A survey of recent sales indicates a price range of $700-$900 for NIB specimens.
Also mfg. in a top eject (pre-USRA). This model had an "XTR" suffix until 1989.

MODEL 94 HERITAGE CUSTOM 1 OF 100 - .38-55 WCF cal., special edition for the NSSF Heritage Fund, features Winchester's historic No. 2 pattern hand engraved with 24Kt. gold inlays and individually signed by the engraver, deluxe spade checkered straight grip stock and forearm with metal cap, 1/2 round, 1/2 octagon 26 in. barrel, 6 3/4 lbs. Mfg. 2002-2003.

	$4,750	$3,150	$1,600	N/A	N/A	N/A	N/A

Last MSR was $5,200.

MODEL 94 HERITAGE CUSTOM 1 OF 1000 - .38-55 WCF cal., special edition for the NSSF Heritage Fund, features Winchester's historic No. 3 engraving pattern with 24Kt. gold inlays, deluxe spade checkered straight grip stock and forearm with metal cap, 1/2 round, 1/2 octagon 26 in. barrel, 6 3/4 lbs. Mfg. 2002 only. While 1,000 rifles were scheduled to be manufactured, only 2 were built, signed by engraver, with factory letter, ser. no. HER0001 and HER0002.

Last MSR was $1,883.

Extreme rarity precludes accurate pricing on this model.

GRADING - PPGS™	100%	98%	95%	90%	80%	70%	60%

MODEL 94 HERITAGE EDITION 1 OF 1,000 - 1,000 scheduled to be mfg., only 255 actually built.

Extreme rarity factor precludes accurate pricing on this model.

MODEL 94 CUSTOM LIMITED EDITION - .44-40 WCF (mfg. 2000 only) or .38-55 WCF (new 2001) cal., features case colored receiver and 24 in. octagon match (.44-40 WCF cal. only) or 1/2 round, 1/2 octagon (.38-55 WCF cal. only) barrel with satin bluing, full (.44-40 WCF only) or 3/4 mag. tube, spade checkered straight grip walnut stock and forearm with metal cap, 7 1/4 (.38-55 WCF cal.) or 7 3/4 lbs. Only 75 mfg. in .44-40 WCF cal. 2000-2002.

	$2,100	$1,775	$1,650	N/A	N/A	N/A	N/A

Last MSR was $2,393.

MODEL 94 NEW GENERATION CUSTOM - .30-30 Win. cal., fancy pistol grip stock and long forearm with spade checkering, high lustre bluing with custom scroll engraving and hand engraved gold moose on right side of frame and gold doe/buck on left, new tang safety, 20 in. barrel. Limited mfg. 2003-2004.

	$2,550	$2,100	$1,775	N/A	N/A	N/A	N/A

Last MSR was $2,995.

MODEL 94 LIMITED EDITION CENTENNIAL - .30-30 Win. cal., crossbolt safety, manufactured to commemorate the 100th anniversary of the Model 94 in 1994.

✳ *Model 94 Limited Edition Centennial Grade I* - features No. 9 style Winchester engraving pattern (rolled) on both sides of receiver, 26 in. half-round half-octagonal barrel, pistol grip stock and forearm with cut checkering, half mag., open sights, crescent buttplate, 12,000 mfg. 1994.

	$995	$800	$650	N/A	N/A	N/A	N/A

Last MSR was $811.

✳ *Model 94 Limited Edition Centennial High Grade* - features No. 6 style Winchester engraving pattern (rolled) on both sides of receiver with gold outlines and 2 gold animals (mountain sheep and deer), Lyman No. 2 tang mounted rear sight, F-style checkering and carving, deluxe walnut, 26 in. half-round half-octagonal barrel, half-mag., crescent buttplate, 3,000 mfg. 1994.

	$1,850	$1,450	$1,150	N/A	N/A	N/A	N/A

Last MSR was $1,272.

✳ *Model 94 Limited Edition Centennial Custom High Grade* - .30 WCF cal., features No. 5 style Winchester engraving pattern (hand-executed) on both sides of greyed receiver, etched by Baron Technology, gold outline panel scenes featuring caribou and pronghorns, Lyman No. 2 upper tang sight, F-style checkering and carving, 26 in. half-round half-octagonal barrel, half-mag., crescent buttplate, 94 mfg. in 1994.

	$4,950	$4,300	$3,750	N/A	N/A	N/A	N/A

Last MSR was $4,684.

MODEL 94 XTR - .30-30 Win. or 7-30 Waters (new 1985) cal., 20 or 24 (7-30 Waters only) in. barrel, checkered select walnut, hooded front sight (except 7-30 Waters which has dovetailed front blade), 6 1/2 lbs. Disc. 1988.

	N/A	$550	$425	$325	$250	$175	$150

Last MSR was $285.

Add $100 for 7-30 Waters cal. rifle.

A survey of recent sales indicates a price range of $600-$750 for NIB specimens.
The XTR nomenclature was disc. 1988.

GRADING - PPGS™	100%	98%	95%	90%	80%	70%	60%

✳ *Model 94 XTR Deluxe* - .30-30 Win. cal. only, deluxe American walnut stock and lengthened forearm with fancy checkering, 20 in. barrel with deluxe script, rubber buttpad. Mfg. 1987-88 only.

	N/A	$575	$450	$325	$250	$175	$150

Last MSR was $426.

A survey of recent sales indicates a price range of $600-$750 for NIB specimens.

MODEL 94 .44 MAG. S.R.C. - .44 Mag., top eject, 20 in. barrel, SRC. Mfg. 1967-1972.

	N/A	$450	$300	$225	$175	$150	$135

A survey of recent sales indicates a price range of $550-$750 for NIB specimens.

MODEL 94 CLASSIC SERIES - .30-30 Win. cal., 20 or 26 in. octagon barrel. Approx. 47,000 mfg. 1967-1970.

	N/A	$400	$275	$225	$175	$150	$135

A survey of recent sales indicates a price range of $475-$650 for NIB specimens.

MODEL 94 ANTIQUE CARBINE - similar to Standard, with case hardened scroll-engraved receiver, gold-plated saddle ring. Mfg. 1964-83.

	N/A	$350	$275	$200	$175	$150	$140

A survey of recent sales indicates a price range of $375-$450 for NIB specimens.

MODEL 94 WRANGLER - .32 Win. Special, top ejection, only 7,947 mfg. Disc.

	N/A	$400	$275	$225	$175	$150	$135

A survey of recent sales indicates a price range of $450-$600 for NIB specimens.

MODEL 94 WRANGLER II - .32 Win. Special (disc. 1984) or .38-55 WCF cal., angle ejection, 16 in. barrel, oversized hoop-shaped lever, roll-engraved receiver, 5 shot mag., 6 1/8 lbs. Made 1983-85 only.

	N/A	$350	$275	$200	$175	$150	$140

Last MSR was $275.

A survey of recent sales indicates a price range of $375-$450 for NIB specimens.

MODEL 94 WRANGLER LARGE LOOP - .30-30 Win., .44 Mag., or .45 LC (new 1999) cal., 16 in. barrel, has large loop lever, uncheckered walnut stock and forearm, blue finish, open sights, 6 lbs. Mfg. 1992-99.

	N/A	$350	$275	$200	$175	$150	$140

Last MSR was $400.

A survey of recent sales indicates a price range of $375-$400 for NIB specimens.

MODEL 9417 TRADITIONAL - .17 HMR cal., 11 shot mag., 20 1/2 in. barrel, checkered straight grip stock and forearm, full mag., 6 lbs. Limited mfg. 2003-2004.

	N/A	$500	$375	$225	$175	$150	$135

Last MSR was $515.

A survey of recent sales indicates a price range of $575-$600 for NIB specimens.

MODEL 9417 LEGACY - .17 HMR cal., 11 shot mag., 22 1/2 in. barrel, checkered pistol grip grip stock and longer forearm, 6 lbs. Limited mfg. 2003-2004.

	N/A	$500	$375	$225	$175	$150	$135

Last MSR was $551.

A survey of recent sales indicates a price range of $575-$600 for NIB specimens.

MODEL 9422 XTR CLASSIC - same general specifications as Model 9422 XTR Standard, except has 22 1/2 in. barrel and non-checkered, satin finished, pistol grip walnut stock and extended forearm, stock also has fluted comb with crescent steel buttplate, curved finger lever, 6 1/2 lbs. Mfg. 1985-87.

$500	$450	$425	$400	$325	$250	$200

Last MSR was $301.

GRADING - PPGS™	100%	98%	95%	90%	80%	70%	60%

MODEL 9422 XTR TRADITIONAL (STANDARD WALNUT) - .22 LR or .22 Mag. cal., takedown, 20 1/2 in. round barrel, 15 shot (LR) or 11 shot (Mag. cal.) mag., grooved forged steel receiver, checkered straight grip, checkered high gloss (disc.) or satin weather resistant finish (new 1988) walnut stock and forearm, regular or large loop (mfg. 1998-99) lever, sights, 6 lbs. Mfg. 1972-2004.

	N/A	$450	$300	$225	$175	$150	$135

Last MSR was $479.

Add $25 for large loop lever (disc. 1999).
Add approx. 15% for .22 Mag. cal.
A survey of recent sales indicates a price range of $550-$625 for NIB specimens.
This model had an "XTR" suffix until 1989. Earlier mfg., including pre-XTR and early XTR rifles, had no checkering - these guns will command slight premiums over values listed.

MODEL 9422 LEGACY - .22 LR or .22 Mag. (new 1999) cal., features 22 1/2 in. barrel with deluxe checkered semi-pistol grip stock, 11 (.22 Mag.) or 15 shot non-full length mag., 6 lbs. Mfg. 1998-2004.

	N/A	$500	$375	$225	$175	$150	$135

Last MSR was $512.

Add 15% for .22 Mag. cal.
A survey of recent sales indicates a price range of $575-$650 for NIB specimens.

MODEL 9422 SPECIAL EDITION TRADITIONAL TRIBUTE - .22 LR or .22 WMR cal., 20 1/2 in. round barrel, features a Winchester horse and rider engraved on right side of receiver, and Model 9422 Tribute banner on left, checkered straight grip walnut stock and forearm, 6 lbs. while 9,422 were scheduled to be mfg. 2005-2006, this production total was not achieved.

$475	$425	$350	$275	$225	$195	$175

Last MSR was $516.

Add 10% for .22 WMR cal.

MODEL 9422 SPECIAL EDITION LEGACY TRIBUTE - .22 LR or .22 WMR cal., similar to Model 9422 Special Edition Traditional, except has 22 1/2 in. barrel and pistol grip stock with crescent recoil pad, although 9,422 were scheduled to be mfg 2005-2006, production total was not achieved.

$650	$575	$475	$375	$300	$265	$235

Last MSR was $551.

Add 10% for .22 WMR cal.

MODEL 9422 HIGH GRADE TRADITIONAL TRIBUTE - .22 LR or .22 WMR cal., 20 1/2 in. round barrel, features silver banner with Model 9422 Tribute on left receiver side and horse and rider on right side, etched engraving on blued receiver, checkered straight grip walnut stock and forearm, 6 lbs. Although 9,422 were scheduled to be mfg. 2005-2006, production total was not achieved.

$1,125	$975	$850	$750	$675	$550	$450

Last MSR was $1,050.

Add 10% for .22 WMR cal.

MODEL 9422 HIGH GRADE LEGACY TRIBUTE - .22 LR or .22 WMR cal., similar to High Grade Traditional Tribute, except has 22 1/2 in. barrel and crescent recoil pad, pistol grip stock, 6 lbs. Although 9,422 were scheduled to be mfg. 2005-2006, production total was not achieved.

$1,175	$1,000	$875	$775	$675	$550	$450

Last MSR was $1,085.

Add 5% for .22 WMR cal.

GRADING - PPGS™	100%	98%	95%	90%	80%	70%	60%

MODEL 9422 CUSTOM TRIBUTE - .22 LR cal., 20 1/2 in. barrel, features engraved silver plated receiver with gold inlaid Model 9422 Tribute banner on left side of receiver and gold horse and rider on right, engine turned bolt and extractor, gold plated trigger, select walnut with fleur-de-lis checkering on straight grip stock and forearm, 6 lbs. 222 mfg. by the Custom Shop 2005.

	$2,575	$1,900	$1,475	N/A	N/A	N/A	N/A

Last MSR was $2,313.

MODEL 9422 TRAPPER - .22 LR or .22 Mag. (new 1998), 16 1/2 in. barrel, checkered walnut stock and forearm, 11 (.22 LR) or 8 (.22 Mag.) shot tube mag., 5 3/4 lbs. Mfg. 1996-2000.

	N/A	$450	$300	$225	$175	$150	$135

Last MSR was $437.

Add 10% for .22 Mag. cal.

A survey of recent sales indicates a price range of $475-$625 for NIB specimens.

MODEL 9422 WIN-CAM - .22 Win. Mag. only, similar to 9422 XTR Standard, except has checkered greenish laminated hardwood stock and forearm. Mfg. 1987-1997.

	N/A	$500	$375	$225	$175	$150	$135

Last MSR was $424.

A survey of recent sales indicates a price range of $575-$650 for NIB specimens.

MODEL 9422 WINTUFF - .22 LR or .22 Mag., 20 1/2 in. barrel, checkered laminated brown hardwood stock and forearm, 6 1/4 lbs. Mfg. 1988-1999.

	$375	$275	$225	$190	$175	$160	$145

Last MSR was $423.

Add 10% for .22 Mag. cal.

MODEL 9422 HIGH-GRADE .22 LR cal., features engraved receiver with raccoon and coonhound, deluxe checkered walnut stock and forearm. Mfg. 1995-96 only.

	$475	$425	$350	$265	$220	$190	$160

Last MSR was $489.

MODEL 9422 HIGH GRADE SERIES II - .22 LR cal., 20 1/2 in. barrel, features high grade walnut stock and forearm with cut checkering, engraved receiver includes dog and squirrels, 6 lbs. Mfg. 1998-99.

	$495	$425	$325	$250	$195	$165	$140

Last MSR was $504.

MODEL 9422 25TH ANNIVERSARY GRADE I - .22 LR cal., features deluxe checkered walnut stock and forearm, engraved receiver with Winchester Horse and Rider, 2,500 mfg. 1997 only, inventory remained through 1999.

	$650	$475	$350	N/A	N/A	N/A	N/A

Last MSR was $606.

MODEL 9422 25TH ANNIVERSARY HIGH GRADE - .22 LR cal., features extra-deluxe checkered walnut stock and forearm, high gloss blue and engraved receiver with Winchester Horse and Rider, featuring silver borders and lever accents, 250 mfg. 1997 only.

	$1,400	$1,175	$995	N/A	N/A	N/A	N/A

Last MSR was $1,348.

RIFLES: BOLT ACTION - PRE-1964 MODEL 70

The Pre-'64 Model 70 Bolt Action Rifle (advertised by Winchester throughout much of its production history as "The Rifleman's Rifle") was produced from 1936 through 1963. Collectors recognize three major manufacturing periods: "Pre-War" (1936-1941); "Transition" (1946-1948); and "Latter" (1949-1963). There were only eighteen (18) original chamberings, these are: .22 Hornet, .220 Swift, .243 Win., .250 Savage (.250-3000), .257 Roberts,

.264 Win. Mag., .270 Win., 7x57mm Mauser, .300 Savage, .300 H&H, .300 Win. Mag., .30-06 (.30 Govt. '06 Springfield - approx. 80% of total mfg. by cal.), .308 Win. (standard in Featherweight Style only), .338 Win. Mag., .35 Rem., .358 Win. (in Featherweight Style only), .375 H&H, and .458 Win. Mag. (in Super Grade AFRICAN Style only). It is important to note that every caliber was not available during each manufacturing period. Any other caliber encountered (including 7.65mm Argentine and 9x57mm Mauser) may be regarded as either special ordered or non-original. Magazine capacities are as follows: "Standard Calibers" (including .22 Hornet) five (5) rounds; "H&H Magnums" (.300 & .375) four (4) rounds; and "Winchester Short Magnums" (.264, .300, .338, .458) three (3) rounds. The rifle was produced in a myriad of styles and variations - most of which are covered individually. Unfortunately, a veritable "cottage industry" has developed involving the alteration, "upgrading," and/or outright faking of these guns. Be careful when contemplating a purchase of any rare Model 70 (and get a receipt describing the purchase accurately).

MODEL 70 PRE-WWII PRODUCTION STANDARD GRADE - 12 standard cals., 5 shot mag., 4 shot mag. on Magnums, 24, 25, or 26 in. barrel, open sights, checkered walnut pistol grip stock, ser. range is 1-31,675. Mfg. 1937-1941.

	100%	98%	95%	90%	80%	70%	60%
Standard Cals.	$1,585	$1,450	$1,300	$1,000	$775	$675	$595
.22 Hornet	$2,775	$2,450	$2,125	$1,700	$1,375	$1,125	$900
.220 Swift	$1,950	$1,800	$1,500	$1,025	$875	$750	$625
.257 Roberts	$3,000	$2,600	$2,400	$1,650	$1,325	$1,000	$750
.270 Win.	$2,000	$1,850	$1,600	$1,125	$875	$750	$625
.300 H&H	$2,500	$2,250	$1,875	$1,550	$1,250	$1,000	$750
.375 H&H	$3,400	$3,000	$2,700	$2,075	$1,700	$1,425	$1,125
7x57mm Mauser	$5,000	$4,500	$3,750	$3,450	$2,800	$2,500	$2,000
.250-3000 Savage	$4,375	$4,000	$3,750	$3,450	$3,125	$2,500	$2,075

Add approx. 80% for Super Grades in common cals.

Values listed assume original, unaltered specimens - modifications/alterations to either the metal or wood surfaces can reduce prices by large amounts. All pre-war Model 70s have only 2 holes drilled in the front of the receiver (none in the back). An extra set of "holes" can decrease value as much as 50%. Some pre-WWII Model 70s have a "D" suffix indicating a doubled up serial number - this variation will command a premium because of its rarity. The Model 70 is one gun for which caliber ranks before condition in terms of desirability. Specimens encountered in under 60% condition will not decrease in price substantially since almost any shooter is worth $500-$600.

There are more fakes than legitimate specimens in cals. 7x57mm and .250-3000 Savage!

Rare cals. such as the .300 Savage, .35 Rem., 7.65mm, and 9x57mm Mauser are seldom encountered, and their scarcity precludes accurate price evaluation. Cals. 7.65mm and 9x57mm Mauser were special order only and were made up from leftover Model 54 barrels. Also, the original factory box, papers, and hanging tag will add 25%-30% to the values listed. Believe it or not, there are getting to be a lot of fake Model 70 boxes that have been intentionally aged. Carefully screen NIB (watch the hanging tag also) specimens in this model for possible expert refinishing.

MODEL 70 CARBINE (MFG. 1936-1946) - available in most cals. during its period, 20 in. barrel, short rifle variation of the Pre-´64 Model 70 (Winchester never officially used the "Carbine" terminology). If original, front sight base will be an integral part of the barrel. All carbines were disc. shortly after WWII. Beware of fakes.

Add 60%-85% for carbine variations mfg. 1936-1946 with 20 in. barrel in .22 Hornet (watch for fakes with cut off barrels, rechambered "K" models, and examine the front sight carefully), .250-3000 Savage, .257 Roberts, .270 Win., 7mm, or .30-06 (most common) cal.

MODEL 70 TRANSITION (MFG. 1946-1948) - several of the post-war Model 70s mfg. between 1946-48 exhibit the pre-war receiver characteristics and have a transition safety. This variation is more rare than normal models, ser. no. range is 60,000-100,000.

Add 10%-20% above values for post-Transitional models.

On this Transitional Model, the receiver bridge may or may not be factory drilled.

GRADING - PPGS™	100%	98%	95%	90%	80%	70%	60%

MODEL 70 STANDARD GRADE (1946-1963 PRODUCTION)

- 18 standard cals. including .22 Hornet, .220 Swift, .243 Win., .250 Savage (.250-3000), .257 Roberts, .264 Win. Mag., .270 Win., 7x57mm Mauser, .300 Savage, .300 H&H, .300 Win. Mag., .30-06, .308 Win., .338 Win. Mag., .35 Rem., .358 Win., and .375 H&H, 5 shot mag., 4 shot mag. on Magnums, 24, 25, or 26 in. barrel, open sights, checkered walnut pistol grip stock, ser. range is 52,549-581,471. Mfg. 1946-1963.

	100%	98%	95%	90%	80%	70%	60%
Standard cals.	$1,300	$1,075	$1,000	$850	$600	$550	$500
.22 Hornet	$2,100	$1,900	$1,700	$1,600	$1,200	$950	$850
.220 Swift	$1,800	$1,600	$1,500	$1,000	$775	$600	$550
.243 Win.	$1,375	$1,200	$1,100	$800	$700	$600	$550
.257 Roberts	$2,500	$2,000	$1,800	$1,500	$1,050	$750	$600
.270 Win.	$1,450	$1,200	$1,000	$700	$600	$575	$550
.300 H&H	$2,000	$1,775	$1,425	$1,000	$825	$650	$575
.300 Win. Mag.	$2,400	$2,275	$2,000	$1,500	$1,200	$1,000	$850
.338 Win. Mag.	$1,975	$1,750	$1,600	$1,225	$950	$825	$725
.375 H&H	$3,000	$2,700	$2,500	$1,975	$1,750	$1,650	$1,325

Add 10% for .300 H&H or .375 H&H if rear receiver is not drilled and tapped.
Add 20% for stainless steel barrel in .300 H&H or .270 Win. cal.

Values listed assume original, unaltered specimens - modifications/alterations to either the metal or wood surfaces can reduce prices by large amounts. Most post-war Model 70s are drilled on top of the receiver (2 holes in front and 2 holes in back) to accept scope mounts (except early .300 and .375 H&H cals.). Pre-1962 mfg. Model 70s are desirable since Winchester implemented manufacturing techniques that lowered the quality beginning in 1964.

Rare cals. such as the .250-3000, .300 Savage, .308 Win. (extremely rare, so watch for fakes), .35 Rem., and 7x57mm Mauser are seldomly seen or sold. Premiums depend on the rarity of the caliber and original condition.

Believe it or not, there are getting to be a lot of fake Model 70 boxes that have been intentionally aged. Carefully screen NIB (watch the hanging tag also) specimens in this model.

MODEL 70 SUPER GRADE

- similar to Standard Model, except has deluxe wood, black pistol grip cap and forend tip, all Super Grades have a raised cheekpiece with deluxe wraparound checkering, and Super Grade marked floorplate. Disc. 1960.

	100%	98%	95%	90%	80%	70%	60%
.375 H&H	$6,000	$5,000	$4,000	$3,500	$3,000	$2,500	$2,250

A general rule for Super Grades is that if you add 100% to the standard grade in similar cals., values should be rather close. For .375 H&H cal., values are listed.

Later Model 70 Super Grades have jeweled action components and rust blued barrels.

MODEL 70 SUPER GRADE AFRICAN

- .458 Win. Mag. only, front swivel base relocated and attached to bottom of barrel, nearly all possess one or two visible stock crossbolts (usually covered with Bakelite). Most have all action components (bolt body, extractor, extractor ring and magazine follower) jeweled (i.e., engine turned), rust blued barrel. 1,226 mfg. 1956-63.

	100%	98%	95%	90%	80%	70%	60%
	$7,000	$6,000	$5,500	$4,500	$4,000	$3,500	$2,750

While other Super Grades were disc. approx. 1960, the "AFRICAN" continued in that style until the end of all production. Normal attrition and collectors owning more than one contribute to extreme rarity. Retains considerable "shooter" value in lesser external conditions. Watch for cracked and/or repaired stocks.

MODEL 70 FEATHERWEIGHT

- lightened version of Standard, .243 Win., .264 Win. Mag. (Westerner, mfg. 1962-1963), .270 Win., .308 Win., .30-06, or .358 Win. cal., 22 (standard) or 26 (Westerner only) in. barrel, aluminum trigger guard and floorplate, ser. range is 206,626-581,471. Mfg. 1952-1963.

	100%	98%	95%	90%	80%	70%	60%
.243 Win.	$1,500	$1,350	$1,000	$800	$625	$550	$500
.264 Mag. (Westerner)	$1,850	$1,600	$1,400	$1,250	$1,100	$900	$800
.270 Win.	$1,600	$1,400	$1,250	$1,100	$900	$800	$700
.30-06	$875	$750	$550	$500	$475	$450	$400
.308 Win.	$1,000	$900	$800	$650	$500	$450	$425

GRADING - PPGS™	100%	98%	95%	90%	80%	70%	60%
.358 Win.	$2,800	$2,500	$2,200	$2,000	$1,800	$1,500	$1,300

Add 25% for .30-06, .308 Win., .243 Win., .358 Win. or .270 Win. cal. models with aluminum buttplate.

The .358 Win. cal. is rare because Winchester had problems with this cal. Many of them were exchanged for other calibers, and the result is that original guns are rare in this cal.

MODEL 70 SUPER GRADE FEATHERWEIGHT - .243 Win., .270 Win., .30-06, or .308 Win. cal. only, because of inconsistencies of Super Grade action component jeweling (i.e., engine turning), a simple stock and hinged floorplate change can create an "instant" Super Grade Featherweight (check stock carefully for wood filling near area of Standard Super Grade rear sight "boss" in barrel channel), all Super Grade Featherweights have a raised cheekpiece with wraparound "fish tail" checkering, all have rust blued barrels, less than 1,000 mfg.

	100%	98%	95%	90%	80%	70%	60%
	$5,000	$4,500	$4,000	$3,500	$3,000	$2,500	$2,250

This is perhaps the rarest variation of the Pre-´64 Model 70 - beware of fakes.

MODEL 70 NATIONAL MATCH - similar to Standard, with target stock and scope bases, .30-06 only. Disc. 1960.

	100%	98%	95%	90%	80%	70%	60%
	$2,750	$2,500	$2,250	$2,000	$1,800	$1,600	$1,400

MODEL 70 TARGET - similar to Model 70 Standard, in .243 Win. or .30-06 cal. (mfg. 1955-1963), earlier pre-´51 Target guns were available in virtually any cal. (i.e., .22 Hornet, .220 Swift, etc.), 24 in. medium weight barrel and target stock. Disc. 1963.

Add 50%-75% over standard values if condition is over 90%. 60% condition will be priced the same.

MODEL 70 BULL GUN - similar to Standard Model 70, with 28 in. heavy barrel, .300 H&H or .30-06 cal. only, .30-06 cal is much rarer.

	100%	98%	95%	90%	80%	70%	60%
.300 H&H cal.	$3,800	$3,525	$3,300	$2,850	$2,425	$2,200	$1,800
.30-06	$4,175	$3,850	$3,525	$3,300	$2,975	$2,750	$2,325

MODEL 70 VARMINT - similar to Standard Model 70, in .220 Swift or .243 Win. cal., 26 in. heavy barrel, scope bases, varmint style stock. Mfg. 1956-63.

	100%	98%	95%	90%	80%	70%	60%
	$1,650	$1,425	$1,275	$1,050	$875	$775	$650

Add 60% for .220 Swift cal.

Less than 900 were mfg. in .220 Swift cal. Stainless steel barrels are also encountered in this model with 3 different types of finishes.

MODEL 70 ALASKAN - similar to Standard Model 70, in .300 Win. Mag. (mfg. 1963 only with 25 in. barrel - known as Alaskan), .338 Win. Mag., or .375 H&H cal., 24 (Westerner Alaskan) or 25 in. barrel, recoil pad. Mfg. 1960-63.

	100%	98%	95%	90%	80%	70%	60%
.375 H&H	$3,500	$3,000	$2,500	$2,000	$1,500	$1,300	$1,200
.300 or .338 Win. Mag.	$2,500	$2,200	$2,000	$1,700	$1,550	$1,300	$1,100

RIFLES: BOLT ACTION - MODEL 70, 1964-2006 MFG.

Beginning 1994, Winchester began using the Classic nomenclature to indicate those models featuring a pre-1964 style action with controlled round feeding.

U.S. Repeating Arms closed its New Haven, CT manufacturing facility on March 31, 2006, and an auction was held on Sept. 27-28, 2006, selling the production equipment and related assets. As a result, 95%-100% asking prices on many of the following models may be higher than listed, and there are reports of consumers paying over 50% above retail values for some of the rarer variations and/or calibers. Remember, most of these recently discontinued Model 70s are not rare, and the only way they can keep going up in value is if there is a continued long-term increase in demand. In late 2007, Olin announced that an updated Model 70 with M.O.A. trigger system would be reintroduced during 2008, and be built by FN Manufacturing, located in Columbia, SC. For these newer models, please refer to the Rifles: Bolt Action - Model 70, 2007-Current Mfg.

All previous MSRs listed are from the Winchester 2006 price sheet. On some of the following models, N/As may be listed for the 100% value - this means there isn't a single value for this gun, and refer to the price range listed underneath as a model note.

WSM cals. will bring an approx. 10% premium, and WSSM cals. will bring an approx. 15% premiums on most of the following models, if in 95%+ condition.

GRADING - PPGS™	100%	98%	95%	90%	80%	70%	60%

MODEL 70 STANDARD - .22-250 Rem., .222 Rem., .225 Win., .243 Win., .25-06 Rem., .270 Win., .308 Win., or .30-06 cal., 5 shot, 22 or 24 in. heavy barrel, open sight, Monte Carlo stock, swivels. Mfg. 1964-1980.

	$550	$425	$350	$325	$300	$240	$200

Add 75%-100% for .225 Win. cal., depending on condition.

MODEL 70 MAGNUM - .264 Win. Mag., 7mm Rem. Mag., .300 H&H Mag., .300 Win. Mag., .338 Win. Mag., .375 H&H, or .458 Win. Mag. cal., 24 in. barrel.

	$595	$495	$425	$395	$350	$300	$275

Add 25%-35% for .375 H&H or .458 Win. Mag. (African Model) cal.

MODEL 70 SUPER GRADE - various cals., deluxe wood with ebony forend cap, Super Grade appears on the floorplate. Disc.

	$795	$650	$575	$500	$475	$450	$425

MODEL 70 DELUXE - .243 Win., .270 Win., .30-06, or .300 Win. Mag. cal., 22 in. barrel, open sight, hand-checkered, black forend tip. Mfg. 1964-71.

	$625	$525	$435	$375	$350	$265	$215

The Model 70 Deluxe was redesignated the Standard Model 70 in 1972.

MODEL 70 TARGET RIFLE 1964-1971 - .308 Win. or .30-06 cal., 24 in. heavy barrel, no sights, target bases, heavy target style stock with hand stop. Disc. 1971.

	$775	$650	$600	$525	$425	$400	$325

MODEL 70 INTERNATIONAL ARMY MATCH 1971 - .308 Win. cal., 5 shot, 24 in. heavy barrel, no sights, adj. trigger, ISU stock with forearm, accessory rail, adj. butt. Disc. 1971.

	$875	$795	$725	$650	$550	$525	$450

MODEL 70 MANNLICHER 1969-1971 - .243 Win., .270 Win., .30-06, or .308 Win. cal., 19 in. barrel, open sight, full-length Monte Carlo stock with steel forend cap. Disc. 1971.

	$850	$725	$650	$600	$550	$475	$425

MODEL 70A - economy version of 1972 type Model 70, same cals., no hinged floorplate or forend tip. Mfg. 1972-78.

	$400	$350	$315	$275	$240	$200	$165

MODEL 70A MAGNUM - similar to Model 70A, except in Mag. cals. but not .375 H&H or .458. Mfg. 1972-78.

	$425	$365	$325	$275	$240	$200	$165

MODEL 70 FEATHERWEIGHT - .22-250 Rem., .223 Rem., .243 Win., .25-06 Rem. (disc. 1993), .257 Robts. (disc.), .270 Win., .280 Rem., 6.5x55mm Swedish (new 1991), 7x57mm Mauser (disc.), .30-06, .308 Win., 7mm-08 Rem. (new 1992), 7mm Rem. Mag. (mfg. 1991-92 only), or .300 Win. Mag. (mfg. 1991-92 only) cal., bolt action, both short and medium action, 5 shot mag., 22 in. barrel (24 in. with .300 Win. Mag.), checkered walnut stock, with or w/o sights, approx. 6 1/2 lbs. Mfg. 1981-94.

	N/A	$550	$400	$350	$300	$275	$250

Last MSR was $562.

A survey of recent sales indicates a price range of $650-$900 for NIB specimens.
In 1981, during U.S.R.A. takeover transition, guns were distinguishable by the U.S.R.A. trademark on the recoil pad. Some collectors will pay a premium for Win. marked pads. Cals. .257 Robts. and 7x57mm Mauser were disc. 1985.
This model had an "XTR" suffix until 1989.

MODEL 70 CLASSIC FEATHERWEIGHT - .22-250 Rem. (new 1994), .223 Rem. (mfg. 1994 only), .243 Win. (new 1994), .270 Win., .280 Rem. (disc. 2000), .30-06, .308 Win. (new 1994), 6mm Rem. (limited mfg. circa 1995), 6.5x55mm Swedish (new 1997), or 7mm-08 Rem. (new 1994) cal., 22 in. barrel, 5 shot mag., blue action, features claw-controlled round feeding action bedded into standard grade walnut stock, jewelled bolt, knurled bolt handle, includes rings and bases, approx. 7 lbs. Mfg. 1992-2006.

	N/A	$550	$400	$350	$300	$275	$250

Last MSR was $762.

A survey of recent sales indicates a price range of $650-$900 for NIB specimens.

* *Model 70 Classic Featherweight WSM* - .270 WSM (new 2002), .300 WSM, .325 WSM (new 2005) or 7mm WSM (new 2002) cal., controlled round feeding, 24 in. round barrel, 3 shot internal mag., approx. 7 1/4 lbs. Mfg. 2001-2006.

	N/A	$600	$450	$375	$300	$275	$250

Last MSR was $792.

Add $39 for left-hand action (new late 2003, not available in .325 WSM cal.).
A survey of recent sales indicates a price range of $700-$950 for NIB specimens.

* *Model 70 Classic Featherweight Super Short WSSM* - similar to Model 70 Classic Featherweight, except available in .223 WSSM, .243 WSSM, and .25 WSSM (new 2004) cals., 22 in. barrel, 3 shot mag., 6 lbs. Mfg. 2003-2006.

	N/A	$600	$450	$375	$300	$275	$250

Last MSR was $814.

A survey of recent sales indicates a price range of $700-$950 for NIB specimens.

* *Model 70 Classic Featherweight BOSS* - similar to Model 70 Classic Featherweight, except has 22 in. barrel with BOSS. Mfg. 1996 only.

	$650	$525	$400	$350	$325	$295	$275

Last MSR was $735.

* *Model 70 Classic Featherweight Stainless (Recent Mfg.)* - same calibers as Classic Featherweight, WSM, and WSSM models, 22 or 24 in. stainless barrel and action, no sights, three position safety, controlled round feed, Pachmayr Decelerator pad on WSM models, 3 shot mag., cut checkering with Schnabel forend, 6-7 1/4 lbs. Mfg. 2005-2006.

	N/A	$650	$475	$400	$325	$275	$250

Last MSR was $806.

A survey of recent sales indicates a price range of $750-$950 for NIB specimens.

* *Model 70 Classic Featherweight Stainless* - .22-250 Rem., .243 Win., .270 Win., .30-06, .308 Win., .300 Win. Mag. (disc. 1998), or 7mm Rem. Mag. cal., 22 or 24 (Mag. cals. only) in. stainless barrel, checkered walnut stock, 3 or 5 shot mag., approx. 7-7 1/2 lbs. Mfg. 1997-99.

	N/A	$550	$400	$350	$300	$275	$250

Last MSR was $746.

A survey of recent sales indicates a price range of $650-$900 for NIB specimens.

* *Model 70 Classic Featherweight All-Terrain* - .270 Win., .30-06, .300 Win. Mag. or 7mm Rem. Mag. cal., 22 or 24 in. matte finish stainless steel barrel/ receiver, black fiberglass/graphite stock with checkering, with (1996-1997 only) or without BOSS, 3 or 5 shot mag., 7 1/4 lbs. Mfg. 1996-98.

	N/A	$550	$400	$350	$300	$275	$250

Last MSR was $672.

Add 20% for BOSS (disc. 1997).
A survey of recent sales indicates a price range of $650-$900 for NIB specimens.

GRADING - PPGS™	100%	98%	95%	90%	80%	70%	60%

✻ *Model 70 Classic Featherweight Win-Tuff Rifle* - .22-250 Rem., .223 Rem., .243 Win., .270 Win., .30-06, or .308 Win. cal., features brown laminated, checkered stock with Schnabel forend, includes base and rings, pistol grip cap, 7 lbs. Mfg. 1988-90. Reintroduced 1992-93.

	$500	**$450**	**$400**	**$350**	**$300**	**$280**	**$260**

Last MSR was $572.

✻ *Model 70 Classic Featherweight Special* - .243 Win. cal., features custom fitted stock, hand-honed action, barrel, and bolt/follower, custom shop proofstamp, select American walnut with rounded pistol grips, no sights. Only 50 mfg.

	$750	**$650**	**$550**	**$475**	**$425**	**$380**	**$340**

This model is distinguishable by the Super Grade floorplate marking.

MODEL 70 XTR EUROPEAN FEATHERWEIGHT - 6.5x55 Swedish Mauser cal., 22 in. barrel, 5 shot mag., rifle sights, 6 3/4 lbs. Made 1986 only.

	$450	**$400**	**$365**	**$330**	**$305**	**$280**	**$260**

Last MSR was $460.

MODEL 70 LIGHTWEIGHT RIFLE - .22-250 Rem. (disc. 1992), .223 Rem., .243 Win., .270 Win., .280 Rem. (mfg. 1988-92), .30-06, or .308 Win. cal., 22 in. barrel, checkered walnut stock, no sights, 6 1/2 lbs. Mfg. 1987-1995.

	N/A	**$450**	**$325**	**$275**	**$235**	**$210**	**$190**

Last MSR was $513.

A survey of recent sales indicates a price range of $500-$700 for NIB specimens.

✻ *Model 70 Lightweight Rifle Win-Tuff* - .22-250 Rem. (mfg. 1988-89), .223 Rem. (new 1989), .243 Win. (new 1988), .270 Win. .30-06 or .308 Win. (new 1989) cal., similar to Model 70 Lightweight Rifle, except has laminated brown hardwood stock with checkering. Mfg. 1987-92.

	N/A	**$400**	**$300**	**$255**	**$230**	**$210**	**$190**

Last MSR was $471.

A survey of recent sales indicates a price range of $450-$650 for NIB specimens.

✻ *Model 70 Lightweight Rifle Win-Cam* - .270 Win. or .30-06 cal., greenish laminated hardwood stock with checkering, 22 in. barrel. Mfg. 1987-disc.

	$450	**$400**	**$350**	**$300**	**$255**	**$230**	**$210**

Last MSR was $471.

This model was previously designated Featherweight before 1989.

MODEL 70 LIGHTWEIGHT CARBINE - .22-250 Rem., .222 Rem. (scarce), .223 Rem., .243 Win., .250 Savage (new 1986), .308 Win., .270 Win., or .30-06 cal., bolt action, 5 shot mag., both short and medium action, 20 in. barrel, checkered walnut stock, no sights, approx. 6 lbs. Mfg. 1984-87.

	N/A	**$450**	**$325**	**$275**	**$235**	**$210**	**$190**

Last MSR was $395.

Add $15 for open sights.
A survey of recent sales indicates a price range of $500-$700 for NIB specimens.

MODEL 70 SPORTER - .22-250 Rem. (mfg. 1989-1993), .223 Rem. (mfg. 1989-93), .243 Win. (mfg. 1989-93), .25-06 Rem. (mfg. 1985-87 and reintroduced 1990), .264 Win. Mag., .270 Win., .270 Wby. Mag. (new 1988), .30-06, .300 Win. Mag., .300 Wby. Mag. (new 1989), .300 H&H (mfg. 1989- 1992), .308 Win. (mfg. 1986-89), .338 Win. Mag., or 7mm Rem. Mag. cal., 24 in. barrel, 3 or 5 shot mag., custom Sporter styling, Monte Carlo cheek piece, detachable sling swivels, 7 3/4 lbs. Disc. 1994.

	N/A	**$500**	**$375**	**$335**	**$295**	**$275**	**$250**

Last MSR was $556.

Add approx. 5% for iron sights (.270 Win., .30-06, .300 Win. Mag., or 7mm Rem. Mag. only).
A survey of recent sales indicates a price range of $600-$850 for NIB specimens.
This model had an "XTR" suffix until 1989.

GRADING - PPGS™	100%	98%	95%	90%	80%	70%	60%

✳ *Model 70 Sporter Win-Tuff* - .270 Win., .30-06, 7mm Rem. Mag., .300 Win. Mag., .300 Wby. Mag., or .338 Win. Mag., similar to Model 70 Sporter, except has checkered brown laminate stock with sling swivels, solid recoil pad, 24 in. barrel, approx. 7 3/4 lbs. Mfg. 1992 only.

	100%	98%	95%	90%	80%	70%	60%
	$495	$450	$395	$325	$300	$280	$260

Last MSR was $572.

MODEL 70 CLASSIC SPORTER III (LT) - .25-06 Rem., .264 Win. Mag. (disc. 2000), .270 Win., .270 Wby. Mag. (disc. 1998), .270 WSM (new 2004), .30-06, .300 Win. Mag., .300 WSM (new 2004), .300 Wby. Mag. (disc. 2000), .325 WSM (new 2005), .338 Win. Mag., 7mm STW (mfg. 1997-2002), 7mm WSM (new 2004), or 7mm Rem. Mag. (disc. 2005) cal., similar to Model 70 Sporter, except features controlled round feeding, 3 (Mag. cals. only) or 5 shot internal mag., 24 or 26 in. barrel, checkered walnut stock, blue finish, stock was redesigned by David Miller in 1999 (denoted by "LT" Model suffix), approx. 7 3/4-8 lbs. Mfg. 1994-2006.

	N/A	$550	$400	$350	$300	$275	$250

Last MSR was $742.

    Add 10% for Mag. cals.
    Add 10% for left-hand action (new 1997).
    Add 10% for iron sights - disc. 1998 (available in .270 Win., .30-06, .300 Win. Mag., .338 Win. Mag., or 7mm Rem. Mag.).
A survey of recent sales indicates a price range of $650-$900 for NIB specimens.
This model's nomenclature was changed from Model 70 Classic Sporter LT to Model 70 Classic Sporter III during 2005. Sporter III improvements include a trimmer forend and stock, Pachmayr Decelerator pad, and a more open pistol grip.

✳ *Model 70 Classic Sporter Stainless* - .270 Win., .30-06, .300 Win. Mag., .338 Win. Mag., or 7mm Rem. Mag. cal., 24 or 26 in. barrel with (1997 only) or without BOSS, checkered walnut stock, controlled round feeding, 3 or 5 shot mag., right- or left-hand action, approx. 7 3/4 lbs. Mfg. 1997-98.

	$700	$625	$550	$450	$375	$325	$275

Last MSR was $716.

    Add 10% for BOSS.
    Add 5% for left-hand action.

✳ *Model 70 Classic Sporter BOSS* - .25-06 Rem. (disc. 1996), .270 Win., .30-06, .264 Win. Mag. (disc. 1996), 7mm STW (new 1997), 7mm Rem. Mag., .270 Wby. Mag. (mfg. 1996 only), .300 Win. Mag., .300 Wby Mag. (mfg. 1996 only), or .338 Win. Mag. cal., 24 or 26 in. barrel with BOSS, 3 or 5 shot mag., checkered walnut stock, approx. 7 3/4 lbs. Mfg. 1995-98.

	N/A	$550	$400	$350	$300	$275	$250

Last MSR was $728.

    Add approx. 10% for left-hand action (new 1997).
A survey of recent sales indicates a price range of $650-$900 for NIB specimens.

✳ *Model 70 Classic Sporter Laredo* - .300 Win Mag., 7mm STW (mfg. 1997-98), or 7mm Rem. Mag. cal., features claw extraction and controlled round feeding, 26 in. round or fluted (new 1998) barrel with (.300 Win. Mag and 7mm Rem. Mag. disc. 1997) or without BOSS. Mfg. 1996-99.

	$750	$650	$550	$450	$350	$295	$275

Last MSR was $794.

    Add approx. 20% for BOSS (disc. 1998).
    Add approx. $130 for fluted barrel.

GRADING - PPGS™	100%	98%	95%	90%	80%	70%	60%

✳ *Model 70 Classic Sporter Safari Express* - .375 H&H, .416 Rem. Mag., or .458 Win. Mag. cal., features Express style rear sight with standing blade, redesigned stock with negative drop and Pachmayr decelerator recoil pad, trigger guard and floorplate are one assembly, 3 shot mag., controlled round feed, 24 in. barrel with barrel band swivel attachment, checkered walnut stock and forearm, 8 1/2 lbs. Mfg. 1999-2006.

	N/A	$1,000	$775	$625	$550	$475	$425

Last MSR was $1,149.

A survey of recent sales indicates a price range of $1,200-$1,600 for NIB specimens.

✳ *Model 70 Classic Sporter Super Express Mag.* - .375 H&H, .416 Rem. Mag. (new 1994), or .458 Win. Mag. cal., 3 shot mag., claw extractor controlled round feeding (new 1993), open sights, 22 or 24 in. (.375 H&H or .416 Rem. Mag.) barrel, 8 1/2 lbs. Disc. 1998.

	N/A	$1,000	$775	$625	$550	$475	$425

Last MSR was $865.

A survey of recent sales indicates a price range of $1,100-$1,500 for NIB specimens.
This model had an "XTR" suffix until 1989.

MODEL 70 CLASSIC LAMINATED WSM - .270 WSM, .300 WSM, .325 WSM (new 2005) or 7mm WSM cals., claw extractor controlled round feed, brown laminate stock, 24 in. barrel w/o sights, one inch deluxe recoil pad, blued receiver and barrel, 3 shot mag., 7 3/4 lbs. Mfg. 2003-2005.

	N/A	$500	$425	$375	$325	$300	$275

Last MSR was $810.

A survey of recent sales indicates a price range of $600-$800 for NIB specimens.

MODEL 70 DBM (DETACHABLE BOX MAGAZINE) - .22-250 Rem. (mfg. 1993 only), .223 Rem. (mfg. 1993 only), .243 Win. (new 1993), .270 Win., .30-06, .308 Win. (mfg. 1993 only), 7mm Rem. Mag., or .300 Win. Mag. cal., checkered walnut stock and forend, features 3 shot detachable box mag., 24 or 26 in. barrel with or without sights, includes bases and rings or iron sights (new 1993, optional) in .30-06, .300 Win. Mag., or 7mm Rem. Mag., 7 3/4 lbs. Mfg. 1992-94.

	N/A	$500	$375	$335	$295	$275	$250

Last MSR was $598.

Add $35 for iron sights.

A survey of recent sales indicates a price range of $600-$800 for NIB specimens.

MODEL 70 CLASSIC DBM - .22-250 Rem., .243 Win., .270 Win., .284 Win., .30-06, .308 Win., .300 Win. Mag., or 7mm Rem. Mag. cal., similar to Model 70 DBM, except has controlled round feeding, 24 or 26 in. barrel. Mfg. 1994 only.

Most cals.	N/A	$500	$375	$335	$295	$275	$250
.284 Win. (less than 200 mfg.)	$825	$725	$600	$525	$400	$350	$295

Last MSR was $619.

Add $50 for iron sights (.270 Win., .30-06, .300 Win. Mag., or 7mm Rem. Mag.).

A survey of recent sales indicates a price range of $600-$800 for NIB specimens.

✳ *Model 70 Classic DBM-S* - .270 Win., .30-06, .300 Win. Mag., or 7mm Rem. Mag. cal., similar to Model 70 DBM, except has black synthetic stock, this model became a Classic series in 1994 (featuring controlled round feeding). Mfg. 1993-94.

	N/A	$500	$375	$335	$295	$275	$250

Last MSR was $619.

A survey of recent sales indicates a price range of $600-$800 for NIB specimens.

MODEL 70 STAINLESS - .270 Win., .30-06, 7mm Rem. Mag., .300 Win. Mag., or .338 Win. Mag., features matte finished stainless steel receiver barrel and bolt, black synthetic composite stock, 22 (.270 Win. or .30-06 only, disc. 1992) or 24 in. barrel, approx. 6 3/4 lbs. Mfg. 1992-94.

	100%	98%	95%	90%	80%	70%	60%
	$550	$475	$395	$350	$300	$280	$260

Last MSR was $616.

MODEL 70 CLASSIC STAINLESS - .22-250 Rem. (disc. 1999), .223 Rem. (disc. 1994), .243 Win. (disc. 1998), .270 Win., .270 WSM (mfg. 2002), .30-06, .308 Win. (disc. 1998), .270 Wby. Mag. (mfg. 1997 only), .300 Win. Mag., .300 Wby. Mag. (disc. 2000), .300 Rem. Ultra Mag. (disc. 2002), .300 WSM (mfg. 2001-2003), .338 Win. Mag., .375 H&H, 7mm STW (mfg. 2001-2002), 7mm WSM (mfg. 2002), or 7mm Rem. Mag. (disc. 2003, reintroduced 2004) cal., features controlled round feeding, 22 (disc. 2001), 24, or 26 in. barrel, black synthetic composite stock, 3, 5, or 6 shot mag., without sights except for .375 H&H cal., 6 3/4-7 1/2 lbs. Mfg. 1994-2005.

	100%	98%	95%	90%	80%	70%	60%
	$700	$600	$475	$375	$300	$265	$225

Last MSR was $817.

Add $30 for Mag. cals., or $125 for .375 H&H cal.

✳ *Model 70 Classic Stainless BOSS* - .22-250 Rem. (disc. 1996), .243 Win. (disc. 1996), .270 Win., .30-06, .308 Win. (disc. 1996), .270 Wby. Mag. (mfg. 1997 only), .300 Win. Mag., .300 Wby. Mag. (mfg. 1996-97), .338 Win. Mag., or 7mm Rem. Mag. cal., 22, 24, or 26 in. barrel with BOSS, black synthetic stock, 6 3/4-7 1/2 lbs. Mfg. 1995-98.

	100%	98%	95%	90%	80%	70%	60%
	$725	$650	$550	$425	$375	$325	$275

Last MSR was $788.

MODEL 70 CLASSIC LAMINATED STAINLESS - .270 Win., .30-06, .300 Win. Mag., .338 Win. Mag., or 7mm Rem. Mag. cal., 24 or 26 (Mag. cals. only) in. barrel without sights, checkered grey/black laminate stock with sporter style dimensions, stainless action and barrel, 3 or 5 shot mag., approx. 8 lbs. Mfg. 1998-99.

	100%	98%	95%	90%	80%	70%	60%
	$725	$650	$550	$425	$375	$325	$275

Last MSR was $753.

A survey of recent sales indicates a price range of $650-$900 for NIB specimens.

✳ *Model 70 Classic Laminated Stainless Camo* - similiar to Model 70 Classic Stainless, except has Mossy Oak Treestand stock finish composite stock, not available in .338 Win. Mag. cal. approx. 7 1/4 lbs. Mfg. 1998 only.

	100%	98%	95%	90%	80%	70%	60%
	$725	$650	$550	$425	$375	$325	$275

Last MSR was $745.

MODEL 70 COYOTE STAINLESS LAMINATED - various standard, WSSM, or WSM cals., push feed (non-WSM/WSSM cals.) or controlled round feed (WSM/WSSM cals. only) action, 24 in. medium heavy stainless steel sporter barrel, uncheckered brown or grey (new 2006) laminate stock with reverse taper on forend, 3 (WSM cals. only), 5, or 6 (.223 Rem. or .204 Ruger only) shot mag., 8 3/4 lbs. Mfg. 2000-2006.

	100%	98%	95%	90%	80%	70%	60%
	N/A	$550	$400	$350	$300	$275	$250

Last MSR was $689.

Add 10% for WSM cals.
Add 15% for WSSM cals.

A survey of recent sales indicates a price range of $650-$800 for NIB specimens.

GRADING - PPGS™	100%	98%	95%	90%	80%	70%	60%

MODEL 70 COYOTE LAMINATED BLUE - .223 Rem., .270 WSM, .300 WSM, .325 WSM, 7mm WSM, .223 WSSM, .243 WSSM, or .25 WSSM cal., similar to Model 70 Coyote Laminated Stainless, except has blued barrel/receiver finish. Mfg. 2005 only.

	N/A	$525	$400	$350	$300	$275	$250

Last MSR was $689.

Add 10% for WSM cals.
Add 15% for WSSM cals.
A survey of recent sales indicates a price range of $600-$750 for NIB specimens.

MODEL 70 COYOTE OUTBACK STAINLESS LAMINATED - various standard, Mag., or WSM cals., grey laminate stock with three oval holes in buttstock and four in forend, matte finished stainless receiver and 24 in. fluted barrel w/o sights, 3-6 shot mag., controlled round push feeding, approx. 7 3/4 lbs. Limited mfg. 2006.

$995	$850	$700	$550	$450	$375	$325

Last MSR was $1,016.

Add 10% for WSM and standard Mag. cals.

MODEL 70 COYOTE LITE - similar cals. as Model 70 Coyote Laminated Blue, except also available in .22-250 Rem., .243 Win., and .308 Win. (new 2006) cal., features 24 in. blued steel (WSSM cals. only) or stainless steel fluted barrel/action, controlled round feed action, floorplate, carbon fiber/fiberglass composite Bell & Carlson stock with vented forend, Pachmayr Decelerator pad, 7 1/2 lbs. Mfg. 2005-2006.

	N/A	$600	$450	$375	$300	$275	$250

Last MSR was $889.

Add 10% for WSM cals.
A survey of recent sales indicates a price range of $650-$800 for NIB specimens.

MODEL 70 CLASSIC SM (SYNTHETIC MATTE) - .22-250 Rem. (mfg. 1993 only), .223 Rem. (mfg. 1993 only), .243 Win. (mfg. 1993 only), .270 Win., .30-06, .308 Win. (mfg. 1993 only), 7mm Rem. Mag., .300 Win. Mag., .338 Win. Mag., or .375 H&H (new 1993) cal., features black composite stock with checkering and sling swivels, 22 (.22-250 Rem., .223 Rem., .243 Win., or .308 Win. - mfg. 1993 only), 24, or 26 in. barrel with matte metal finish, 3 or 5 shot, approx. 7 1/2 lbs. Mfg. 1992-96.

	N/A	$525	$400	$350	$300	$275	$250

Last MSR was $620.

Add 10% for Mag. cals.
A survey of recent sales indicates a price range of $600-$800 for NIB specimens.
Until 1993, this model was called the Model 70 SSM. In 1994, this model became the Model 70 Classic SM featuring controlled round feeding.

MODEL 70 CLASSIC SM BOSS - .270 Win., .30-06, 7mm Rem. Mag., .300 Win. Mag., or .338 Win. Mag. cal., 24 or 26 in. barrel with BOSS, 3 or 5 shot, approx. 7 1/4 lbs. Mfg. 1995-96 only.

	N/A	$550	$425	$350	$300	$275	$250

Last MSR was $735.

A survey of recent sales indicates a price range of $600-$800 for NIB specimens.

MODEL 70 CLASSIC COMPACT - .243 Win., .308 Win. (disc. 2003), or 7mm-08 Rem. cal., features 12 1/2 in. LOP, 20 in. barrel and shallow profile, pre-64 type action, 4 shot mag., checkered walnut stock and forearm, blue action and barrel, 6-6 1/2 lbs. Mfg. 1998-2006.

	N/A	$550	$425	$350	$300	$275	$250

Last MSR was $762.

A survey of recent sales indicates a price range of $600-$800 for NIB specimens.

GRADING - PPGS™	100%	98%	95%	90%	80%	70%	60%

MODEL 70 VARMINT - same general specifications as standard Sporter, .22-250 Rem., .223 Rem., .225 Win., .243 Win., or .308 Win. cal., 26 in. heavy barrel with cold hammer forged rifling and counter-bored at muzzle, no sights, 5 shot mag., target scope bases, 7 3/4 lbs. Mfg. 1964-1993.

	N/A	$450	$325	$275	$235	$210	$190

Last MSR was $720.

Add 50% for .225 Win. cal.

A survey of recent sales indicates a price range of $550-$700 for NIB specimens. This model had an "XTR" suffix 1978-89.

* *Model 70 Varmint Heavy (HBV)* - .220 Swift (mfg. 1994-98), .22-250 Rem., .222 Rem. (mfg. 1997-98), .223 Rem., .243 Win., or .308 Win. cal., push-feed style action, 26 in. heavy stainless fluted (new 1997) or plain barrel (counter-sunk muzzle) without sights, features black synthetic beavertail H&S Precision stock with aluminum bedding block, 10 3/4 lbs. Mfg. 1993-99.

	N/A	$550	$425	$350	$300	$275	$250

Last MSR was $795.

Add approx. $125 for fluted barrel.

A survey of recent sales indicates a price range of $600-$800 for NIB specimens.

MODEL 70 SHB (SYNTHETIC HEAVY BARREL) - .308 Win. cal., features checkered black composite stock, 26 in. barrel with matte metal finish, jeweled bolt, 9 lbs. Mfg. 1992 only.

	$525	$450	$375	$325	$300	$280	$260

Last MSR was $563.

MODEL 70 WINLIGHT - .25-06 Rem., .270 Win., .280 Rem. (new 1987), .30-06, 7mm Rem. Mag., .300 Win. Mag., .300 Wby. Mag., or .338 Win. Mag. cal., McMillan fiberglass stock, thermoplastic receiver bedding, blue metal parts, 22 or 24 (Mag. cals. only) in. barrel, 3 or 4 shot mag., no sights, approx. 6 1/2 lbs. Mfg. 1986-90.

	$625	$550	$475	$425	$350	$300	$250

Last MSR was $637.

MODEL 70 RANGER RIFLE - .22-250 Rem. (new 1999), .223 Rem. (new 1992), .243 Win. (new 1991), .270 Win., .30-06, or 7mm Rem. Mag. cal., push-feed action, 22 or 24 in. barrel, 3 (7mm Rem. Mag.), 5, or 6 shot mag., plain hardwood stock without checkering, open sights, approx. 7 lbs. Disc. 1999.

	N/A	$300	$250	$225	$200	$180	$160

Last MSR was $503.

A survey of recent sales indicates a price range of $400-$500 for NIB specimens.

* *Model 70 Ranger Rifle Compact (Ladies/Youth)* - .22-250 Rem. (mfg. 1999 only), .223 Rem. (disc. 1989, reintroduced 1997, disc. 1998), .243 Win., .308 Win. (new 1991), or 7mm-08 Rem. (mfg. 1997-98, reintroduced 2000) cal., push-feed action, 20 (disc. 1992) or 22 (new 1993) in. barrel, 5 or 6 shot mag., shorter hardwood stock dimensions, open sights, 6 1/2 lbs. Disc. 2000.

	N/A	$325	$265	$235	$200	$180	$160

Last MSR was $528.

A survey of recent sales indicates a price range of $425-$525 for NIB specimens.

MODEL 70 STEALTH - .22-250 Rem., .223 Rem., .308 Win. cal., push-feed style action, 26 in. heavy barrel w/o sights, non-glare matte metal finish, Accu Block black synthetic stock with full length aluminum bedding block, 5 or 6 shot mag., 10 3/4 lbs. Mfg. 1999-2003.

	N/A	$595	$475	$425	$350	$325	$295

Last MSR was $800.

A survey of recent sales indicates a price range of $600-$800 for NIB specimens.

GRADING - PPGS™	100%	98%	95%	90%	80%	70%	60%

MODEL 70 STEALTH II - .22-250 Rem., .223 WSSM, .243 WSSM, .25 WSSM, or .308 Win. cal., push-feed style action, 26 in. heavy barrel w/o sights, matte blue finish, redesigned black synthetic stock with aluminum pillar bedding, 3 or 5 shot mag., 10 lbs. Mfg. 2004-2006.

	N/A	$600	$500	$440	$385	$340	$300

Last MSR was $886.

Add 10% for WSSM cals.

A survey of recent sales indicates a price range of $650-$850 for NIB specimens.

MODEL 70 BLACK SHADOW - .270 Win., .30-06, .300 Win. Mag., or 7mm Rem. Mag cal., push-feed action, 3 (Mag. cals.) or 5 shot internal mag., 24 or 26 (Mag. cals.) in. barrel w/o sights, matte receiver and barrel finish, black composite stock with conventional floorplate mag., 7 1/4 lbs. Mfg. 1998-2003.

	N/A	$300	$250	$225	$200	$180	$165

Last MSR was $523.

Add approx. 10% for Mag. cals.

A survey of recent sales indicates a price range of $400-$500 for NIB specimens.

MODEL 70 CLASSIC/CAMO ULTIMATE SHADOW - .223 WSSM (new 2004), .243 WSSM (new 2004), .25 WSSM (new 2004), .270 WSM, .300 WSM, .325 WSM (new 2005) or 7mm WSM cal., features controlled round feed, black or Dura-Touch armor coated Mossy Oak New Break-Up camo finished molded synthetic stock with rubber grip inserts and new recoil pad, matte black metal, 3 shot mag., 24 in. blued steel or stainless steel barrel, 6 3/4 lbs. Mfg. 2003-2005.

	N/A	$550	$475	$425	$365	$335	$300

Last MSR was $817.

Add 10% for WSM cals. or 15% for WSSM cals.
Add 10% for stainless steel action.
Add approx. $100 Mossy Oak New Break-Up camo finish.

A survey of recent sales indicates a price range of $600-$700 for NIB specimens.

MODEL 70 SUPER SHADOW - various cals., similar to Classic Ultimate Shadow, except has oval dot texture gripping surface on pistol grip and forearm, blue finish, controlled round push feed action, available in either short or super short action, blind mag., 22 (.223 WSSM, .243 WSSM, or .25 WSSM cal.) or 24 in. barrel w/o sights, 6 (WSSM cals.) or 6 3/4 lbs. Mfg. 2003-2006.

	N/A	$325	$265	$235	$200	$180	$165

Last MSR was $525.

Add 10% for WSM and Mag. cals. or 15% for WSSM cals.

A survey of recent sales indicates a price range of $400-$550 for NIB specimens.

MODEL 70 SHADOW ELITE STAINLESS - various standard, WSM, and Mag. cals., short or long action, features lightweight black synthetic stock with rubberized overmolding gripping surfaces on pistol grip and forearm, and Dura-Touch Armor coating, WinSorb recoil pad, 24 or 26 in. stainless fluted barrel, no sights, except .375 H&H cal., controlled round feed action, 3 or 5 shot mag., 6 3/4 - 7 3/4 lbs. Limited mfg. 2006.

$650	$525	$400	$325	$275	$235	$200

Last MSR was $739.

Add 10% for WSM and standard Mag. cals.
Add approx. $125 for .375 H&H cal.

✱ *Model 70 Shadow Elite Stainless Camo* - similar to Model 70 Shadow Elite Stainless, except available in Mossy Oak Break-Up camo. Limited mfg. 2006.

$725	$550	$475	$400	$350	$300	$250

Last MSR was $808.

Add 10% for standard Mag. and WSM cals.
Add $125 for .375 H&H cal.

GRADING - PPGS™	100%	98%	95%	90%	80%	70%	60%

MODEL 70 PRO SHADOW - various standard, WSM, and Mag. cals., short or long action, 22 or 24 in. blue barrel, black synthetic stock with Dura-Touch Armor coating and oval-dot gripping surfaces, controlled round push feed, 3 or 5 shot mag., 6 1/2 - 7 lbs. Limited mfg. 2006.

	N/A	$375	$325	$275	$250	$225	$190

Last MSR was $594.

    Add 10% for standard Mag. and WSM cals.
A survey of recent sales indicates a price range of $450-$600 for NIB specimens.

✱ *Model 70 Pro Shadow Stainless* - similar to Model 70 Pro Shadow, except has stainless barrel/action. Limited mfg. 2006.

	N/A	$425	$375	$350	$325	$250	$225

Last MSR was $638.

    Add 10% for standard Mag. and WSM cals.
    Add $125 for .375 H&H cal.
A survey of recent sales indicates a price range of $500-$650 for NIB specimens.

MODEL 70 CLASSIC SUPER GRADE III - .25-06 Win. (new 2001), .270 Win. (mfg. 1991-2003), .270 WSM (new 2004), .30-06 (new 1991), 7mm STW (230 mfg. 1999 only), 7mm WSM (new 2004), 7mm Rem. Mag. (disc. 1998, reintroduced 2000-2003), .264 Win. Mag. (limited mfg. 2000 only), .300 WSM (new 2004), .300 Win. Mag. (disc. 2003, reintroduced 2005), .325 WSM (new 2005), or .338 Win. Mag. cal., 24 or 26 in. barrel, 3 (Mag. cals.) or 5 shot mag., jewelled bolt, stainless steel extractor for true claw controlled round feeding and ejecting, three-position safety, checkered satin finish walnut stock with wood cheekpiece, black forend tip, bases and rings included, approx. 7 3/4 - 8 lbs. Mfg. 1990-2006.

	N/A	$900	$775	$625	$500	$425	$350

Last MSR was $1,036.

    Add 10% for WSM and Mag. cals.
A survey of recent sales indicates a price range of $1,100-$1,500 for NIB specimens.
This model was designated the Model 70 Super Grade until 1995. During 1999, this model was redesigned to include a new Express style rear sight with standing blade, negative stock drop, Pachmayr Decelerator pad, one-piece floorplate and full barrel band swivel attachment. This model was on its third generation of design improvements (now called the Super Grade III) with trimmer sporter style stock, steel stock crossbolt, and inlaid swivel studs.

✱ *Model 70 Classic Super Grade III RMEF* - .300 WSM or .325 WSM (new 2005) cal., similar to Model 70 Classic Super Grade, except is Rocky Mountain Elk Foundation special edition, includes Super Grade Stock with ebony forend and Pachmayr decelerator pad, special RMEF emblem on grip cap, 26 in. barrel, 8 lbs. Limited mfg. 2003-2006.

	N/A	$975	$850	$675	$550	$475	$375

Last MSR was $1,183.

A survey of recent sales indicates a price range of $1,250-$1,600 for NIB specimens.
This model was redesignated the Super Grade III RMEF in 2005.

✱ *Model 70 Classic Super Grade III BOSS* - similar to Model 70 Classic Super Grade, except has BOSS. Mfg. 1995-97.

$895	$725	$600	$475	$400	$350	$300

Last MSR was $956.

MODEL 70 SUPER GRADE CENTENNIAL - .30-06 cal., deluxe checkered walnut stock, black forend cap, controlled round feed with engraved "1906-2006 - 100 Years of .30-06 Springfield" on bolt face, 24 in. blue steel barrel, 3 shot mag., polished engraved floorplate with special gold and nickel accents, 8 lbs. 306 mfg. 2005-2006.

$1,275	$1,050	$875	N/A	N/A	N/A	N/A

Last MSR was $1,259.

GRADING - PPGS™	100%	98%	95%	90%	80%	70%	60%

MODEL 70 50TH ANNIVERSARY MODEL - .300 Win. Mag., 24 in. barrel, deluxe walnut stock, engraving and special motifs on metal surfaces, serial numbered 50 ANV 1 - 50 ANV 500, 7 3/4 lbs. 500 mfg. 1987 only.

	$1,425	$1,175	$950	N/A	N/A	N/A	N/A

Last MSR was $939.

RIFLES: BOLT ACTION - POST 1964 MODEL 70 CUSTOM GRADES

MODEL 70 CUSTOM GRADE - various cals., old style Model 70 action, semi-fancy American walnut checkered stock, engine turned bolt and follower, hand honed internal parts. Mfg. 1988-89 only.

	$1,550	$1,300	$1,000	$850	$725	$650	$550

Last MSR was $1,172.

MODEL 70 XTR FEATHERWEIGHT ULTRA GRADE "1 OF 1,000" - .270 Win., bolt action, extensively engraved, finely checkered deluxe French walnut, with mahogany presentation case.

	$2,450	$1,925	$1,550	N/A	N/A	N/A	N/A

Last MSR was $5,000.

MODEL 70 CLASSIC CUSTOM GRADE - .264 Win. Mag. (new 1994), .270 Win., .30-06, 7mm Rem. Mag., .300 Win. Mag., .300 Wby. Mag. (new 1994) or .338 Win. Mag. cal., 24 or 26 in. barrel, similar to Model 70 Super Grade, but must be special ordered through the Custom Gun Shop, and includes many custom features including semi-fancy walnut with satin finish and hand-honed internal parts. Mfg. 1990-94.

	$1,775	$1,375	$1,075	$900	$800	$725	$650

Last MSR was $1,757.

A Model 70 Collector Grade is also a variation of this model that was mfg. in the Custom Gun Shop - this model was priced on request only.

* *Model 70 Classic Custom Grade Featherweight* - .22-250 Rem. (new 1994), .223 Rem. (new 1994), .243 Win. (new 1994), .270 Win., .280 Rem., .30-06, .308 Win. (new 1994), 7mm-08 Rem. (new 1994) cal., 22 in. barrel, includes Featherweight features, controlled round feeding, higher grade wood. Mfg. 1992-94.

	$1,775	$1,375	$1,075	$900	$800	$725	$650

Last MSR was $1,757.

* *Model 70 Classic Custom Grade Sharpshooter I/II* - .22-250 Rem. (new 1993), .223 Rem. (mfg. 1993-94), .30-06, .308 Win., or .300 Win. Mag. cal., includes specially designed McMillan A-2 (disc. 1995) or H-S Precision heavy target stock, Schneider (disc. 1995) or H-S Precision (new 1996) 24 (.308 Win. cal. only) or 26 in. stainless steel barrel, choice of blue or grey finish starting 1996. Mfg. 1992-98.

	$1,950	$1,500	$1,050	$900	$850	$750	$675

Last MSR was $1,994.

Subtract $100 if without stainless barrel (pre-1995).

This model was designated the Sharpshooter II in 1996 (features H-S Precision stock and stainless steel barrel).

This model was also available in left-hand action beginning 1998 (.30-06 and .330 Win. Mag. cals. only).

* *Model 70 Classic Custom Grade Sporting Sharpshooter I/II* - .270 Win. (disc. 1994), 7mm STW, or .300 Win. Mag. cal., 1/2-minute of angle sporting version of the Custom Sharpshooter, custom shop only, Sharpshooter II became standard in 1996. Mfg. 1993-98.

	$1,875	$1,425	$1,000	$875	$825	$750	$675

Last MSR was $1,875.

This model was also available in left-hand action in 1998.

GRADING - PPGS™	100%	98%	95%	90%	80%	70%	60%

✴ *Model 70 Classic Custom Grade Sporting Sharpshooter* - .220 Swift cal., 26 in. Schneider barrel, controlled round feeding, available with either McMillan A-2 or Sporting synthetic (disc. 1994) stock. Mfg. 1994-95 only.

	$1,775	$1,375	$1,075	$900	$800	$725	$650

Last MSR was $1,814.

✴ *Model 70 Classic Custom Grade Express* - .300 Petersen (mfg. 1995 only), .375 H&H, .375 JRS (mfg. 1992-96), 7mm STW (mfg. 1993-94), .416 Rem. Mag., .458 Win. Mag., or .470 Capstick (disc. 1995) cal., 24 in. (22 in. on .458 Win. Mag.) barrel, features claw controlled round feeding, deluxe walnut with satin finish and checkering, 3-leaf express (disc. 1995) or pre-64 style adj. rear sight (new 1996), high luster metal finish, bolt and follower are engine turned, available by special order through the custom gun shop only. Mfg. 1990-98.

	$2,500	$2,000	$1,650	$1,375	$1,125	$1,000	$895

Last MSR was $2,512.

Subtract $200 for 7mm STW cal.

In 1994, the model nomenclature was changed from Model 70 Custom Grade Express, and in 1996 it was changed from Model 70 Classic Express.

MODEL 70 CUSTOM ULTIMATE CLASSIC - .25-06 Rem., 6.5x55mm Swedish (new 2001), .270 Win., .280 Rem. (mfg. 1996, reintroduced 1999), .30-06, 7mm STW (disc. 2006), .264 Win. Mag. (disc. 2006), .270 Wby. Mag. (disc. 1996), .35 Whelen (new 1998), 7mm Rem. Mag., 7mm Rem. Ultra Mag., .300 Win. Mag., .300 Wby. Mag., .300 H&H (mfg. 1996-99), .300 Rem. Ultra Mag. (new 2000), .338 Win. Mag., .338-06 (mfg. 1999-2001), .338 Rem. Ultra Mag. (new 2001), .340 Wby. Mag. (mfg. 1998), .375 H&H (1995 only), .416 Rem. Mag. (1995 only), or .458 Win. Mag. (1995 only) cal., controlled round feeding, engine turned bolt, checkered fancy walnut stock, choice of 22 (.458 Win. Mag. only), 24 or 26 in. tapered round full-fluted, 1/2 round, 1/2 octagonal, or full octagonal tapered stainless barrel, one inch black decelerator recoil pad, choice blue or stainless barreled action, 3 or 5 shot mag., includes bases/rings except on some Mag. cals., approx. 7 3/4 lbs., except for large disc. cals., includes hard case. Mfg. 1995-2006.

	$2,615	$2,050	$1,550	$1,275	$995	$850	$750

Last MSR was $3,060.

Add $100 for stainless steel barrel, $110 for fluted round barrel, or $235 for full or half octagon barrel.

Add approx. 15% for .375 H&H and larger Mag. cals (disc. 1995).

This model was previously designated the Model 70 Ultimate Classic until 2000, and was changed to the Model 70 Classic Custom Ultimate Classic.

Left-hand action (new 1997) was available in all current cals.

MODEL 70 CLASSIC CUSTOM SHORT ACTION - .243 Win. (disc. 2000, reintroduced 2002 only), .257 Roberts, .260 Rem. (disc. 2006), .270 WSM (new 2002), .284 Win. (new 2006), .308 Win., .358 Win., .300 WSM (new 2001), .325 WSM (new 2005), 7mm-08 Rem., 7mm WSM (new 2002), or .450 Marlin (mfg. 2001-2004) cal., 22 (disc. 2002) or 24 (new 2003) in. match grade tapered stainless or chrome-moly barrel with cut rifling, controlled round feed, no sights, deluxe high gloss checkered walnut stock and forend, one inch black decelerator recoil pad, satin matte blue finished action and barrel, 3-5 shot mag., approx. 7 1/2 lbs. Mfg. 2000-2006.

	$2,400	$1,850	$1,500	$1,250	$1,050	$875	$750

Last MSR was $2,866.

Left-hand action was available on this model.

MODEL 70 CLASSIC CUSTOM FEATHERWEIGHT - .223 WSSM (mfg. 2004), .243 WSSM (mfg. 2004), .25 WSSM (mfg. 2004), .243 Win. (new 2006), .25-06 Rem. (new 2006), .270 Win., .280 Rem. (new 2004), .284 Win. (new 2006), .30-06, .308 Win. (new 2006), 6.5x55mm Swedish (new 2006), or 7mm-08 Rem. (mfg. 2003) cal., 5 shot mag., Featherweight stock with Schnabel forend, match grade 22 in. barrel w/o sights, matte blue or stainless action/barrel, 7 1/4 lbs. Mfg. 2003-2006.

$2,400 $1,850 $1,500 $1,250 $1,050 $875 $750

Last MSR was $2,866.

MODEL 70 CLASSIC CUSTOM CARBON - .25-06 Rem., .270 WSM, .300 WSM, .338 Win. Mag., or 7mm WSM cal., satin stainless action, features 24 or 26 in. carbon fiber barrel with Shilen stainless barrel liner, controlled round feed, reinforced black composite stock, 6 1/2 - 7 lbs. Mfg. 2003-2004.

$2,775 $2,125 $1,650 $1,325 $1,050 $900 $800

Last MSR was $3,233.

MODEL 70 CLASSIC CUSTOM EXTREME WEATHER - .25-06 Rem. (disc. 2001), .270 Win. (disc. 2000), .270 WSM (new 2004), .30-06, .300 Win. Mag., .300 Rem. Ultra Mag. (new 2001), .300 WSM (new 2004), .308 Win. (new 2004), .325 WSM (new 2005), .338 Win. Mag., 7mm WSM (new 2004), 7mm Rem. Mag., or .375 H&H (new 2001) cal., controlled round feed, matte finished stainless action and match grade 22 lightweight (.375 H&H only), 24, or 26 in. fluted stainless barrel w/o sights, black McMillian fiberglass stock with cheekpiece and 1 in. decelerator pad, 3 or 5 shot mag., available in either right- or left-hand action, approx. 7 1/2 lbs. Mfg. 2000-2005.

$2,135 $1,725 $1,425   N/A   N/A   N/A   N/A

Last MSR was $2,576.

MODEL 70 CUSTOM EXTREME LIGHTWEIGHT WEATHER II - various standard, WSM, and Mag. cals., 22, 24, or 26 in. fluted Krieger barrel w/o sights, black lightweight McMillan Hunter's Edge fiberglass stock with Pachmayr Decelerator recoil pad, 3 or 5 shot mag., matte finished stainless steel action/barrel, 6 1/4 - 7 lbs. Limited mfg. 2006.

$2,350 $1,825 $1,500   N/A   N/A   N/A   N/A

Last MSR was $2,800.

This model was also available with left hand action, except in WSM cals.

MODEL 70 CUSTOM STAINLESS LAMINATE - .270 WSM, .300 WSM, .325 WSM, or 7mm WSM cal., choice of brown or black/grey featherweight stock with Pachmayr Decelerator recoil pad, controlled round feed, 24 in. stainless sporter barrel w/o sights, engine turned bolt, 8 lbs. Limited mfg. 2006.

$1,950 $1,675 $1,300   N/A   N/A   N/A   N/A

Last MSR was $2,332.

MODEL 70 CLASSIC CUSTOM MANNLICHER - .260 Rem., .308 Win., or 7mm-08 Rem. cal., features full length checkered walnut stock, smooth tapered barrel and blue action, 19 in. barrel w/o sights (sights optional), 4 shot internal mag., approx. 6 3/4 lbs. Mfg. 1999-2000.

$2,250 $1,800 $1,400 $1,200 $950 $800 $700

Last MSR was $2,595.

This model was designated the Model 70 Custom Mannlicher until 2000.

MODEL 70 CUSTOM MAPLE - .270 Win., .284 Win., .30-06, or .308 Win. cal., features gloss finished checkered hand-made fiddleback curly maple stock with black forend cap, custom shop pistol grip cap, right or left hand blue or stainless steel action, 24 in. sporter barrel w/o sights, 7 3/4 lbs. Limited mfg. 2006.

$3,700 $3,150 $2,750 $2,300 $1,850 $1,500 $1,250

Last MSR was $4,355.

GRADING - PPGS™	100%	98%	95%	90%	80%	70%	60%

MODEL 70 CUSTOM CONTINENTAL HUNTER - .270 Win., .284 Win., .30-06, or .308 Win. cal., features gloss finished Claro walnut stock with round pistol grip and Schnabel forend, Niedner style steel buttplate, controlled round feed, 22 in. Krieger stainless or blue sporter barrel w/o sights, right or left hand action, 4 or 5 shot mag., 6 3/4 lbs. Limited mfg. 2006.

	$4,450	$3,950	$3,500	$3,000	$2,500	$2,000	$1,550

Last MSR was $5,226.

MODEL 70 CLASSIC CUSTOM SAFARI EXPRESS - .340 Wby. Mag. (disc. 1999), .358 STA (disc. 2000), .375 H&H, .375 Rem. Ultra Mag. (new 2001), .404 Jeffrey (mfg. 2004), .416 Rem. Mag., .416 Rigby (mfg. 2001), .458 Win. Mag., .458 Lott, or .470 Capstick (new 2002) cal., features honed internal parts, engine turned bolt and follower, adj. Dietrich Apel Express rear and front sights, deluxe checkered walnut stock and forend, 22 (.458 Win. Mag. & .458 Lott) or 24 in. barrel with sling stud, 3 shot mag., approx. 9 1/4 lbs. Mfg. 1999-2006.

	$2,775	$2,150	$1,600	$1,300	$975	$825	$725

Last MSR was $3,252.

Add $490 for .416 Rigby cal. (mfg. 2001 only).

Beginning in 2000, this model was available in left-hand action in all cals. except .470 Capstick.

This model was designated the Model 70 Custom Safari Express until 2000.

MODEL 70 WSM CUSTOM NORTH AMERICAN BIG GAME SERIES - .270 WSM, .300 WSM, or 7mm WSM cal., controlled round feed, checkered XXX American walnut stock with Schnabel forend, Pachmayr decelerator recoil pad, engraved receiver, trigger guard, and floorplate, high lustre bluing. Only 125 of each edition (Whitetail Deer - .270 WSM, Elk - .300 WSM, and Antelope - 7mm WSM) mfg. 2004-2005 with matching serial numbers.

	$2,600	$2,150	$1,600	$1,300	$995	$875	$775

Last MSR was $3,030.

This model was sold in sets only (all 3 calibers.)

MODEL 70 CLASSIC CUSTOM AFRICAN EXPRESS - .340 Wby. Mag. (disc. 1999), .358 STA (disc. 2000), .375 H&H, .416 Rem. Mag., .416 Rigby (mfg. 2001 only), .458 Win. Mag., .458 Lott, or .470 Capstick (mfg. 2001 only) cal., features drop down floorplate, increasing mag. capacity to 4, checkered fancy English walnut stock with black decelerator pad and ebony pistol grip and forend caps, adj. Dietrich Apel Express rear and front sights, 22 (.458 Win. Mag. only) or 24 in. barrel with sling stud, approx. 9 1/2 lbs. Mfg. 1999-2006.

	$4,150	$3,350	$2,850	$2,400	$1,875	$1,450	$1,250

Last MSR was $4,867.

Add $437 for .416 Rigby cal. (disc. 2001).

Beginning in 2000, this model was available in left-hand action in all cals. except .458.

This model was designated the Model 70 Custom African Express until 2000.

MODEL 70 CLASSIC CUSTOM TAKE-DOWN - .300 Rem. Rem. Ultra Mag., .300 Win. Mag. (new 2002), .375 H&H, .416 Rem. Mag., or 7mm Rem. Mag. cal., all stainless construction with blue Teflon finish, take-down receiver/barrel assembly, brown synthetic stock and forearm, .75 MOA guaranteed for take-down action assembly/reassembly, 24 (.375 H&H or .416 Rem. Mag. cal. only) or 26 (fluted only) in. barrel, 3 shot internal mag., 8 1/2 - 9 lbs. Limited mfg. 2001-2006.

	$3,150	$2,675	$2,300	N/A	N/A	N/A	N/A

While advertised beginning in 1998 with a MSR of $2,495, this model was finally produced during 2001. This model was only available from the Bass Pro Shops.

GRADING - PPGS™	100%	98%	95%	90%	80%	70%	60%

MODEL 70 ULTRA GRADE - .270 Win. cal., gold line engraved, includes wood display case, 500 mfg.

	$2,500	$1,975	$1,550	$1,200	$900	$600	$425

Last MSR was $5,000.

MODEL 70 CUSTOM 100TH ANNIVERSARY .30-06 - 30-06 cal., 22 in. blue sporter barrel with "100th Anniversary Custom 1 of 100" engraved in gold, 5 shot mag., semi-fancy checkered American walnut stock with recoil pad, single steel crossbolt, controlled round feed action, gold and nicekl engraved floorplate with WWI Allied soldiers and sport hunter with whitetail deer, 7 1/4 lbs. 100 mfg. 2006.

	$2,275	$1,775	$1,500	N/A	N/A	N/A	N/A

Last MSR was $2,660.

MODEL 70 CUSTOM SPECIAL "70 YEARS OF THE MODEL 70" - .270 Win., .30-06, or .300 Win. Mag. cal., 24 or 26 (.300 Win. Mag. only) in. blue barrel with "one of Seventy" engraved in gold, semi-fancy checkered walnut stock with inletted sling swivel bases, controlled round feed action, each caliber has special engraved floorplate, 7 1/2 - 7 3/4 lbs. 70 of each caliber mfg. 2006.

	$2,175	$1,725	$1,425	N/A	N/A	N/A	N/A

Last MSR was $2,547.

MODEL 70 COLLECTOR GRADE - various cals., this variation was a special order through the Winchester Custom Shop and values will vary per individual gun.

MODEL 70 CUSTOM BUILT - various cals., this variation was a special order through the Winchester Custom Shop and values will vary per individual gun.

MODEL 70 EXHIBITION GRADE - various cals., fancy checkered American walnut stock with hardwood forend tip. Mfg. 1988-89 only.

	$1,850	$1,475	$975	N/A	N/A	N/A	N/A

Last MSR was $2,192.

RIFLES: BOLT ACTION - MODEL 70, 2007-CURRENT MFG.

In late 2007, Olin announced that its famous Winchester Model 70 would be reintroduced with a new M.O.A. trigger system, and manufactured by FN Manufacturing located in Columbia, SC.

MODEL 70 FEATHERWEIGHT DELUXE - .243 Win., .270 Win., 7mm-08 Win., .30-06, .308 Win., .300 Win. Mag., .270 WSM, .300 WSM, or .325 WSM cal., pre-64 style controlled round feeding, new M.O.A. trigger system adj. from 3-5 lbs., blade type ejector, 3 or 5 shot mag., 22 or 24 in. hammer forged blue barrel w/o sights, one-piece trigger guard and hinged mag. floorplate, satin finished Grade II fleur-de-lis checkered walnut stock with Schnabel forend, jeweled bolt, knurled bolt handle, 3-position safety, Pachmayr Decelerator recoil pad, 6 1/2 - 7 lbs. New 2008.

MSR $999	$825	$675	$575	$500	$425	$350	$295

Add $50 for Mag. cals.

During the first of manufacture (2008), this model featured an engraved custom one-piece floor plate with "2008 Model 70 Limited Edition".

MODEL 70 SPORTER DELUXE - .270 Win., .30-06, .300 Win. Mag., .270 WSM, .300 WSM, or .325 WSM cal., similar to Featherweight Deluxe, 3 or 5 shot mag., 24 or 26 (.300 Win. Mag. only) in. barrel, satin finished Grade II walnut stock with cheekpiece and cut checkering, Pachmayr Decelerator recoil pad, 7 1/2 - 7 3/4 lbs. New 2008.

MSR $999	$825	$675	$575	$500	$425	$350	$295

Add $50 for Mag. cals.

During the first of manufacture (2008), this model featured an engraved custom one-piece floor plate with "2008 Model 70 Limited Edition".

GRADING - PPGS™	100%	98%	95%	90%	80%	70%	60%

MODEL 70 SUPER GRADE - .30-06 or .300 Win. Mag. cal., similar to Model 70 Sporter Deluxe, except has fancy grade checkered walnut stock and forearm and rosewood forend tip. New 2008.

MSR $1,149	$925	$700	$600	$525	$450	$395	$350

Add $50 for .300 Win. Mag. cal.

During the first of manufacture (2008), this model featured an engraved custom one-piece floor plate with "2008 Model 70 Limited Edition".

MODEL 70 EXTREME WEATHER SS - .270 Win., .30-06, .308 Win., .270 WSM, .300 WSM, or .325 WSM cal., 3 or 5 shot mag., stainless steel action, 22, 24, or 26 (.300 Win. mag. cal. only) in. free floating, stainless steel fluted barrel, Bell & Carlson synthetic stock with alloy skeletal bedding block and cheekpiece, M.O.A. trigger system, one-piece trigger guard and mag. frame, no sights, 7 - 7 1/4 lbs. New 2008.

MSR $1,149	$925	$700	$600	$525	$450	$395	$350

Add $50 for Mag. cals.

During the first of manufacture (2008), this model featured an engraved custom one-piece floor plate with "2008 Model 70 Limited Edition".

RIFLES: O/U

DOUBLE XPRESS RIFLE - .30-06, .257 Roberts, .270 Win., 7x57M, 7x57R, 7x65R, or 9.3x74R cal., 23 1/2 in. O/U barrels, iron sights with claw scope mounts, ejectors, fully engraved satin finish receiver with game scene engraving, walnut specially hand checkered, sling swivels, 8 1/2 lbs. Mfg. 1984-85 only.

	$3,500	$3,150	$2,500	$2,150	$1,800	$1,600	$1,400

Last MSR was $2,995.

In 1984, Aero Marine located in Birmingham, AL special ordered 200 deluxe double rifles in 7x57mm Mauser cal. They featured better engraving and game scenes with bottom of receiver marked Jaeger. Of the 200, 100 were rifles with 90 being standard grade and 10 being deluxe. The other 100 were supplied with an extra set of O/U shotgun barrels. Sales were slow on these special guns and eventually they were liquidated to another wholesaler. Recently, prices are in the $2,250-$3,000 range for the rifle alone and $3,000-$3,750 for the Combo.

RIFLES: SINGLE SHOT, POST 1964 MFG.

MODEL 1885 LOW WALL GRADE I .22 LR CAL. - .22 LR cal., features 24 1/2 in. half-round, half-octagon barrel with buckhorn rear sights, uncheckered straight grip walnut stock and forearm, crescent buttplate, blue finish only, 8 lbs. 2,400 mfg. late 1999-2001.

	$735	$625	$525	$450	$400	$350	$300

Last MSR was $828.

* *Model 1885 Low Wall High Grade* - similar to Model 1885 Low Wall Grade I, except features frame engraving, 24Kt. squirrel/cottontail scenes, fancy walnut stock and forearm with cut checkering. 1,100 mfg. late 1999-2001.

	$1,050	$875	$750	$650	$550	$450	$350

Last MSR was $1,180.

MODEL 1885 LOW WALL - .17 HMR (disc. 2006) or .17 Mach 2 (new 2005) cal., 24 in. octagon barrel, checkered straight grip walnut stock and Schnabel forearm, open sights, 8 lbs. Mfg. 2003-2006.

	$875	$700	$575	$500	$450	$400	$350

Last MSR was $1,014.

GRADING - PPGS™	100%	98%	95%	90%	80%	70%	60%

MODEL 1885 HIGH WALL - .22-250 Rem. (new 2006), .223 Rem. (new 2006), .270 WSM, .300 WSM, .325 WSM (new 2006), or 7mm WSM cal., 28 in. full octagon barrel without sights, checkered walnut stock with recoil pad and Schnabel forearm, adj. trigger, Pachmayr Decelerator pad, blued receiver, 8 1/2 lbs. Mfg. 2005-2006.

	$915	$725	$600	$525	$475	$425	$375

Last MSR was $1,085.

MODEL 1885 HIGH WALL CENTENNIAL HUNTER - .30-06 cal., features gold embellished .30-06 seal on right side of engraved receiver, special barrel inscription, 28 in. octagon barrel, 8 1/2 lbs. Limited mfg. 2006.

	$1,375	$1,150	$875	N/A	N/A	N/A	N/A

Last MSR was $1,617.

100%	98%	95%	90%	80%	70%	60%	50%	40%	30%	20%	10%

SHOTGUNS: 1879-1963

BREECH LOADING SxS - 10 or 12 ga., imported from England for sales through the Winchester New York City office only, exposed hammers, available in 5 grades ranging from Class D - Class A and Match gun (lowest to highest). Higher grades were mfg. by W.C. Scott & Sons, C.G. Bonehill, W.C. McEntree, Richard Redmond, and H. & E. Hammond Gun Mfg.'s. Approx. 10,000 were imported between 1879-84.

Prices vary greatly due to condition and grade. Prices can range from $350 (poor condition Class D) to over $5,500 (95%+ condition specimen in Class A or Match gun).

This side by side model was the first shotgun bearing the Winchester name sold in the U.S. Identifiable by "Winchester Repeating Arms Co., New Haven, Connecticut, USA" marking on barrel rib top.

MODEL 1887 LEVER ACTION - 10 or 12 ga., 4 shot tube mag., 30 or 32 in. full choke fluid steel barrels, plain pistol grip stock, first Browning patent shotgun mfg. by Winchester, first lever action repeating shotgun mfg. domestically. Mfg. 1887-1901. Approx. 64,855 mfg.

N/A	$3,500	$3,000	$2,700	$2,400	$2,000	$1,700	$1,200	$1,000	$800	$700	$600

Standard frame finish on this model was color case hardening. Premiums exist for original bright case colored specimens. 10 ga. began production with serial number 22148. Also mfg. in Riot configuration (20 in. cylinder bore barrel). Gauges were chambered for 2 5/8 in. (12 ga.) and 2 7/8 in. (10 ga.). A very small amount was also made up in .70-150 cal. - add a significant premium.

* *Model 1887 Lever Action Deluxe* - damascus barrel, checkered stock, and other special order features.

N/A	$7,500	$6,000	$5,000	$4,000	$2,800	$2,200	$1,800	$1,500	$1,200	$1,000	$800

MODEL 1893 SLIDE ACTION - 12 ga., 30 (standard) and 32 in. barrel, black powder only. First Winchester shotgun with sliding forearm action, first Browning slide action patent, disc. 1897 after run of some 34,050. Note: chambered for 2 5/8 shells only, damascus barrels were available at extra cost, as were fancy stocks.

N/A	$950	$850	$750	$675	$600	$525	$485	$425	$375	$325	$275

This gun had limited sales because mechanical weaknesses developed when shooting smokeless powder. Winchester offered a brand new shotgun of the customer's choice when they returned their Model 1893.

MODEL 1897 SLIDE ACTION - 12 or 16 ga. (introduced 1900), improved Model 1893 action, 26-32 in. barrels, visible hammer, various chokes, takedown or solid frame, plain pistol grip stock. Over 1,024,700 mfg. between 1897-1957.

$900	$750	$595	$500	$450	$350	$250	$225	$195	$175	$150	$125

Add 50% for 16 ga.

Early 16 ga. Model 1897s were chambered for 2 9/16 in. shotshells, and are not as valuable

100%	98%	95%	90%	80%	70%	60%	50%	40%	30%	20%	10%

because of the 2 3/4 in. shell length currently manufactured. This model was marked "Model 1897" on the slide action rails until circa 1912 (approx. ser. no. 500,000). After approx. ser. no. 500,000, the marking was moved to the barrel and changed to Model 97. The Model 1897 was the first Winchester shotgun chambered for 2 3/4 in. smokeless ammunition. This model was also manufactured with a damascus barrel for a short period of time, and is rare.

MODEL 1897 RIOT GUNS - see the "Trench/Riot Shotgun" category in the T section for more information and prices.

MODEL 1897 TRENCH GUNS - see the "Trench/Riot Shotgun" category in the T section for more information and prices.

This model changed its stock configuration after WWI.

MODEL 1897 TRAP - higher grade version of Standard, checkered stock, could have black diamond inlay in stock until 1919 (Black Diamond Trap), breech block marked "Trap" until approx. 1926. Mfg. 1897-1931.

N/A	$2,250	$2,000	$1,800	$1,600	$1,300	$1,000	$750	$600	$450	$400	$350

✳ *Model 1897 Trap Black Diamond Trap* - distinguishable by diamond ebony inlays in stock pistol grip.

N/A	$2,250	$2,000	$1,750	$1,500	$1,250	$1,125	$925	$725	$600	$495	$350

MODEL 1897 PIGEON - higher grade version of Standard 97, should have engraved pigeon behind hammer on frame, breech block marked "Pigeon", most exhibit black diamond stock inlays until 1919. Mfg. 1897-1939.

N/A	$10,000	$8,500	$7,500	$6,000	$4,500	$3,500	$3,000	$2,000	$1,500	$1,000	$800

MODEL 1901 - 10 ga. only, strengthened Model 1887 action to accept smokeless powder, lever action, standard barrel 32 in., blue barrel and frame, 5 shot mag. 13,500 mfg. between 1901-1920, starting with serial number 64,856.

N/A	$3,500	$3,200	$3,000	$2,500	$2,000	$1,800	$1,500	$1,250	$800	$700	$500

Add 50% for Deluxe Grade (checkered wood).

This shotgun was chambered for 2 7/8 in. smokeless powder ammunition.

MODEL 1911 SL AUTOLOADER - 12 ga., recoil operated, 26 or 28 in. barrel, various chokes, pistol grip laminated birch stock. Mfg. 1911-1921, with some production occuring between 1921-1928, 103,246 produced, action had design problems, nicknamed "Head Buster."

$675	$600	$550	$500	$450	$350	$275	$200	$150	$140	$130	$120

Values assume original wood without splitting, repair, or replacement. The Model 1911 was Winchester's first semi-auto shotgun. It did not prove to be satisfactory partly because the design had to avoid infringing the patents for Browning's famous A-5 model. Interestingly enough, this was a design which Winchester originally had helped Browning patent.

MODEL 36 SINGLE SHOT - 9mm Rimfire cal., long shot, short shot, and ball, 18 in. round barrel, single shot bolt action, guns were not serial numbered, one-piece plain stock and forearm, special shaped trigger guard, 2 3/4 lbs. Approx. 20,000 mfg. between 1920-27.

N/A	$1,700	$1,500	$1,300	$1,050	$895	$750	$595	$495	$395	$295	$195

GRADING - PPGS™			100%	98%	95%	90%	80%	70%	60%

MODEL 12 SLIDE ACTION - 12 (introduced 1914), 16 (introduced 1914), 20 (initial ga., mfg. 1912, 2 1/2 in. chamber mfg. until 1927), or 28 (introduced 1937) ga., 25 (20 ga. only, mfg. 1912-14), 26, 28, 30, or 32 in. standard, nickel, or stainless steel (scarce) barrel with or without rib (matted, solid, or VR), 2 9/16 (early 16 or 20 ga., until 1927, at ser. no. 464,565), 2 3/4 (became standard 1927) or 3 in. chamber, 6 shot, blue metal, various chokes, hammerless, plain pistol grip or straight walnut stock and forearm, marked Model 1912 from 1912-1919, approx. ser. no. 172,000. Mfg. 1912-1976.

12 ga.	$700	$550	$450	$375	$325	$275	$225
16 ga.	$800	$625	$495	$425	$350	$300	$275

GRADING - PPGS™	100%	98%	95%	90%	80%	70%	60%
20 ga.	$1,100	$900	$725	$650	$575	$500	$450
28 ga.	$5,500	$4,750	$4,250	$3,850	$3,400	$2,850	$2,500

Subtract 50% if with factory Cutts compensator.
The following add-ons DO NOT apply to 28 ga. values.
Add 40%-50% for Win. solid rib.
Add 50%-60% for Win. milled VR.
Add 10% for pre-WWII mfg.
Add 60% for each extra barrel(s).
Add 40%-50% for Win. special VR (offset barrel proofmark).

"Y" prefix appears on Model 12s built 1964-1980 - see listing under Post-64 Models.

Special order features on field guns have captured much collector interest in recent years. Combinations of these features can add a considerable percentage to the base values listed. Rare special orders on rare variations are very desirable and prices can double and more if the combination is right. As is the case with most other collectible shotguns at this time, Model 12s with open choked barrels in shorter lengths are A LOT more desirable (and expensive) than a specimen with a 30 in. full choke barrel (most common). Values listed are for standard configuration (28 or 30 in. full choke barrel with no rib). For most Model 12s, values for condition factors less than 60% will approximate the 60% price, because of shooter demand. Premiums must be added for the rarer open choked barrels in shorter length on all gauges.

Original gauge can be determined by removing the buttstock and observing the gauge marking on the stock screw boss.

"Donut" post Winchester VRs are more desirable than the rectangular post.

Recently, some non-original, re-stamped 28 ga. barrels have been added to 16 or 20 ga. frames "creating" a more desirable (and expensive) gun to unsuspecting buyers. Roll die markings are getting better and better so be very cautious when considering a non-Cutts 28 ga. (as in get a receipt specifying originality). 28 ga. ser. no. range is approx. 720,XXX to 1,857,XXX. 28 ga. Model 12s were available with both 2 3/4 (common) or 2 7/8 (infrequent) in. chamber. Believe it or not, there are getting to be a lot of fake Model 12 boxes that have been intentionally aged. Carefully screen NIB (watch the hanging tag also) specimens in this model.

Editor's Note: The Model 12 Winchester was produced continuously from 1912-1980. Over 2,027,500 were produced both in standard and deluxe (Pigeon) grades. Pigeon grades were first listed in 1914 and disc. during the war (1941). Reintroduced in 1948, they were disc. permanently in 1964, after which the Super Pigeon Grade became available only on a custom order basis from Winchester's Custom Gun Shop. These guns are worth 50-300% premiums depending on gauge, barrel lengths, stock options, engraving patterns, etc.

With an attrition rate of 33%, Model 12s with rare features 50 years ago will only be much rarer today (and expensive). 28 ga. guns were built between 1934 and 1960. Gauge rarity in increasing order is 12 ga., 16 ga., 20 ga., .410 bore (Model 42), and 28 ga. Serialization breakdown by year of manufacture is provided under the "Model Serialization" section of this book. When collecting Model 12s, ser. nos. on the underside of receiver (forward end), should match ser. no. on bottom rear of Mag. tube. Stainless steel barrel Model 12s were mostly mfg. in the late 1920s - early 1930s (65X,XXX serial range). Values typically range between $1,250 - $3,000, and are very rare in over 95% original condition, as the bluing typically flaked off the stainless steel barrel.

Nickel steel Model 12s have become more popular in recent years, and some collectors are actually specializing on nickel steel Model 12s only.

MODEL 12 FEATHERWEIGHT
- similar to Standard, except with alloy guard and different takedown system. Mfg. 1959-62. "F" suffix after ser. no.

$550	$500	$450	$400	$325	$275	$225

MODEL 12 RIOT GUNS
- see the "Trench/Riot Shotgun" category in the T section for more information and prices.

MODEL 12 MILITARY TRENCH GUNS
- see the "Trench/Riot Shotgun" category in the T section for more information and prices.

MODEL 12 HEAVY DUCK GUN
- 12 ga., 3 in. chamber, 30 or 32 in. barrel, solid rubber recoil pad, 1/2 in. shorter pull than regular Model 12. Mfg. 1935-63.

$1,100	$925	$800	$700	$600	$525	$425

Add 60% for solid rib.
Add 50% for 32 in. barrel.

GRADING - PPGS™	100%	98%	95%	90%	80%	70%	60%

✳ *Model 12 Heavy Duck Gun Vent. rib* - factory Winchester or 2 different rib styles mfg. by Simmons, notice barrel proof marking - rare.

	100%	98%	95%	90%	80%	70%	60%
	$2,950	$2,750	$2,250	$2,000	$1,600	$1,350	$1,250

MODEL 12 SKEET GUN - 12, 16, 20, or 28 ga., 26 in. barrel, skeet choke, checkered pistol grip stock, pre-WWII. Mfg. 1933-1976.

	$1,825	$1,400	$1,100	$925	$725	$600	$550

Add 30% for solid rib.
Add 75% for Win. Special VR.
Add 100% for Win. milled VR.
Subtract 50% for Factory-Cutts compensator.
16 gauge - rarity will command a premium.
Add 150% for 20 ga.
Add 500% for 28 ga.
Add approx. 20%-25% for brown plastic Hydrocoil stock, 12 ga. only.
Add approx. 40%-50% for white plastic Hydrocoil stock (approx. 50 mfg, 12 ga. only).

MODEL 12 TRAP GUN - various gauges, full choke barrel, deluxe straight or pistol grip stock, solid recoil pad. Mfg. 1938-64.

	$1,625	$1,300	$1,075	$950	$750	$625	$600

Add 60% for milled VR.
Add approx. 20% for brown plastic Hydrocoil stock.
Add approx. 50% for white plastic Hydrocoil stock (approx. 50 mfg).
While plain barreled variation is rare, it is not as desirable.

MODEL 12 SUPER FIELD GRADE - 12, 16, or 20 ga., features 26, 28, or 30 in. matted rib barrel, deluxe walnut with checkered pistol grip stock and forearm, mfg. 1955-59.

	$1,850	$1,650	$1,425	$1,250	$1,050	$850	$700

Add 60% for 20 ga.
Add 40% for 16 ga.

MODEL 12 "BLACK DIAMOND" TRAP - various configurations, straight or pistol grip stock, features a small ebony diamond inlaid on each side of the pistol grip, 30 or 32 in. barrel with solid rib.

	$3,000	$2,650	$2,200	$1,850	$1,600	$1,400	$1,200

Add 50% for milled VR.

MODEL 12 TOURNAMENT GRADE - 12 ga. only, straight grip stock, small checkered forearm, usually stamped "Tourn" in wood on buttstock under buttplate. Mfg. 1914-1930.

	$2,750	$2,400	$2,150	$1,850	$1,600	$1,250	$1,000

MODEL 12 PIGEON GRADE - finer and more deluxe version of Model 12, many variations. Mfg. 1914-41 and 1948-64, engine turned breech block and shell follower, usually with engraved pigeon on bottom rear of mag. tube.

	$3,750	$3,400	$2,950	$2,400	$1,900	$1,500	$1,200
28 ga.	$8,000	$6,750	$5,750	$5,000	$4,300	$3,750	$3,250

Add 25% for VR.
Add 100% for 20 ga.
Beware of potential fakes (i.e., inspect the engraved pigeon carefully if engraved on gun, and also note the quality and finish of the extra grade wood).

MODEL 20 - .410 bore, single shot, hammer, boxlock, 26 in. full choke (a few guns have been observed with cylinder choking), 6 pounds. Mfg. 23,616 between 1919-1924.

	$875	$750	$600	$475	$350	$225	$200

While most Model 20s have 2 1/2 in. chambers, late parts cleanup guns could be chambered for 3 in. also.

✻ *Model 20 Winchester Junior Trap Shooting Outfit* - includes shotgun, midget hand trap, 150 .410 bore shells, 100 clay targets and accessories, cased.

$3,850	$3,500	$3,200	$3,000	$2,700	$2,500	$2,200

Prices for this model assume all accessories are included - if not, subtract substantially. Just the shotshell boxes and accessories from this outfit are worth $2,500+ in nice condition.

MODEL 21 - 12, 16, 20, 28 ga., or .410 bore, boxlock action, after years in the design stage, production began in 1929 with guns being shipped to the warehouse in 1930 and first offered in Winchester's 1931 price list. Regular production continued for thirty years, through 1959. Approx. 32,500 mfg. 1931-1988. Approx. 1,100 were mfg. by the Custom Shop (including Custom, Pigeon, and Grand American Grades) during 1960-1982. Factory records for these models (early mfg. is sketchy) are available by contacting the Cody Firearms Museum located in Cody, WY.

	100%	98%	95%	90%	80%	70%	60%
12 ga.	$6,950	$6,150	$5,500	$4,950	$4,500	$4,000	$3,750
16 ga.	$8,500	$7,850	$7,000	$6,500	$6,000	$5,500	$5,000
20 ga.	$9,450	$8,650	$7,500	$7,000	$6,500	$6,000	$5,500

Add $1,250 for VR.
Add 25% for 3 in. chambers (Duck Gun, 12 ga. only).
Add 10%-20% for "Deluxe" marked guns, depending on original condition.
Subtract approx. 30% for double triggers w/ extractors.
Subtract 20% for double triggers with ejectors (normally encountered with splinter forearm).

The early guns were plain, standard 12 gauge models with double triggers and extractors. Later in 1931, 16 and 20 gauge chamberings became available, as did selective single trigger and automatic ejectors.

By the end of 1933 the Model 21 skeet gun had been introduced as had Tournament, Trap, and Custom Built grades. By about this time options included fancier wood, beavertail or semi-beavertail foreends, checkered butts (standard on skeet guns) or skeleton steel buttplates, recoil pads and almost any variation the customers might desire. Metal finishes on a Model 21 are unusual in that they have salt blue frames and rust blue barrels - this explains the difference in coloration between these metal surfaces.

The Tournament Grade was dropped in 1936 and the Trap Grade in 1940. A Standard Grade Trap Gun was added in 1941. The early Custom Built Grade was dropped in 1942 and the Deluxe Grade was added. This grade included as standard many of the previously available extra cost options.

Relatively few guns were produced in chamberings smaller than 20 gauge. 28 gauge first appeared in the 1936 catalog, although a few were probably produced before that. Winchester records are unclear as to the total but it is generally believed that fewer than 100 original factory guns were made. In addition, a number of original 20 gauge guns have been modified at the factory or elsewhere with factory 28 gauge barrels. These latter guns are just as valuable if the conversion was done at the Winchester Custom Gun Shop. Authenticity of the original guns should be established by factory letter.

.410 bore guns were first listed in 1955 but, again, some had been produced earlier, one having been built for John Olin in 1950. Throughout Winchester history all the rules seem to have had exceptions and nowhere is this more apparent than with respect to the Model 21 which, after all, has been pretty much a custom gun from the very beginning. Factory records and tallies among dealers indicate the existence of 40 to 50 original factory guns. As in the case of the 28 gauge, extra barrels were available and at least some of those have been added to original 20 gauge guns.

The 3 inch Magnum 12 gauge Duck gun (stamped "Duck" on floor plate) was offered in Winchester catalogs from 1940 through 1952. Selective single triggers and automatic ejectors were standard as were the solid red Winchester recoil pads and 30 in. or 32 in. barrels. Some cases of non-factory upgrading of 2 3/4 or 3 inch Magnum guns have been reported. If authenticity is important to the buyer, a factory letter should be requested.

With respect to such letters, in cases where records may be missing or incomplete, the resultant letters may be less conclusive than desired. In some instances, consultation with, or a written appraisal from an authoritative collector arms dealer might be helpful.

Six standard patterns of engraving and several stock checkering and carving styles evolved during the production years. Values added by these and other embellishments such as pre-

GRADING - PPGS™	100%	98%	95%	90%	80%	70%	60%

cious metal inlays are beyond the scope of this work.

The following retail prices are for a standard field gun with average wood, beavertail forearm, ejectors, and single selective trigger with no alterations.

✳ *Model 21 Skeet Gun* - available in Standard, Tournament, and Trap grades. Introduced 1933.

Add 10% depending on grade.

✳ *Model 21 Trap Gun* - introduced 1940, Trap Grade disc. same year, unaltered specimens will bring premium - add 10-25%.

✳ *Model 21 3 Inch Duck Gun* - introduced 1940, must be so stamped (observe the 3 in. marking very carefully).

As can be seen, values are partly based on a certain interdependence between options. Higher grade guns, of course, will bring somewhat higher prices, although much of their increased value results from the many "options" being included as standard features.

Buyers or sellers with limited experience should always seek expert advice or appraisals in dealing with a Model 21. This is especially true with regard to higher grade guns and those with extra ornamentation.

✳ *Model 21 .410 Bore* - retail prices for original guns may be expected to range between $37,500 and $50,000 for mechanically sound guns depending on quality of finish. Non-original guns with add-on factory barrels would probably be reduced by one-third.

✳ *Model 21 28 Ga.* - factory original guns will probably bring from $25,000 to $30,000 and, as with the 410s, 20 gauge guns modified to 28 gauge with factory barrels would be worth approx. the same if done at the factory.

Refinishing or Restoration: There is disagreement as to the effects of refinishing a Model 21. Many shooters and at least some collectors prefer a professionally refinished gun to a badly worn one. Higher grade guns restored by a master craftsman may approach factory original guns in value.

MODEL 21: RECENT PRODUCTION - refer to listing under SHOTGUNS: RECENT PRODUCTION SxS.

MODEL 24 SxS - 12, 16, or 20 ga., boxlock, hammerless, double triggers. Introduced 1940, disc. 1957 after approx. 116,280 mfg.

	100%	98%	95%	90%	80%	70%	60%
	$825	$725	$625	$475	$350	$275	$225

Add 20% for 16 ga.
Add 40% for 20 ga.

MODEL 25 SLIDE ACTION - 12 ga. only, non-takedown version of the Model 12, 26 or 28 in. barrel. 87,937 mfg. between 1949-1954.

	100%	98%	95%	90%	80%	70%	60%
	$550	$475	$400	$350	$300	$250	$200

MODEL 37 SINGLE SHOT - 12, 16, 20, 28 ga., or .410 bore, top-lever break-open action, all barrels are full choke. Note on pricing that there is a big difference between a 100% gun without a box and NIB condition. Not serial-numbered. Over 1,015,000 mfg. between 1936-63.

	100%	98%	95%	90%	80%	70%	60%
12 gauge	$450	$325	$250	$200	$125	$100	$90
16 gauge	$450	$325	$250	$200	$125	$100	$90
20 gauge	$495	$395	$325	$250	$150	$110	$90
28 gauge	$2,500	$1,825	$1,325	$995	$725	$575	$450
.410 bore	$575	$425	$375	$325	$275	$165	$110

If models are truly NIB, add $125-$175 to 100% condition values only, depending on gauge.
Add 20% for "Red Letter" models.
Add 15% for 32 in. barrel (12, 16, or 20 ga. only).

Most 28 ga. Model 37s have the "Red Letter."

GRADING - PPGS™	100%	98%	95%	90%	80%	70%	60%

✱ *Model 37 Single Shot Youth/Boys/Red Dot* - 20 ga. only, 26 in. barrel marked Mod. Choke on barrel, solid red factory pad, identifiable by red dot inset into metal that is visible when hammer is cocked.

	N/A	$375	$300	$250	$195	$145	$110

MODEL 40 SEMI-AUTO - 12 ga. only, long recoil action, 28 or 30 in. barrel, walnut stock, skeet model also, poorly designed, many recalled by Winchester. Approx. 12,000 mfg. 1940-41.

	$825	$675	$550	$450	$400	$300	$225

MODEL 41 BOLT ACTION - .410 bore, 2 1/2 in. chamber until 1933 when it changed to 3 in., bolt action, single shot, 24 in. round barrel bored F, one-piece plain walnut stock and forearm, not serialized, approx. 22,145 were mfg. 1920-34.

	$650	$575	$500	$450	$375	$300	$250

Add 15% for 3 in. chamber.

This model is rarely encountered with over 80% original condition.

MODEL 42 SLIDE ACTION - first pump specifically designed for the .410 bore, hammerless, 2 1/2 (introduced 1935) or 3 in. chamber, 26 or 28 in. barrel, plain walnut pistol grip stock with circular grooved forearm (modified 1947), invented by William Roemer, approx. 6 1/2 - 7 lbs. Approx. 164,800 mfg. in 4 grades between 1933-63.

Add 35% to any Model 42 chambered for 2 1/2 in. shells.

Special order features on field guns have captured much collector interest in recent years. Combinations of these features can add a considerable percentage to the base values listed. Special orders on rare variations are very desirable, and prices can double, or more than double, if the combination is right.

✱ *Model 42 Slide Action Standard Grade* - 26 or 28 in. plain, solid rib or vent. rib barrel, plain walnut straight or pistol grip stock, walnut grooved forearm. Mfg. 1933-63.

	$1,850	$1,650	$1,500	$1,400	$1,200	$1,000	$900

Add 25% for pre-war.
Add 75% for solid rib.
Add 150% for factory vent. rib.

✱ *Model 42 Slide Action Skeet Grade* - 26 or 28 in. plain, solid rib or vent. rib barrel, select checkered walnut straight grip or pistol grip stock and checkered forearm extension, 4 different chokes (full, modified, skeet, or cylinder) during pre-war (approx. ser. no. 1-52,000), post-war (approx. ser. no. 52,000-164,000) had same chokes available through 1953, when cylinder choke was dropped, and improved cylinder was added.

	$4,000	$3,500	$3,000	$2,600	$2,400	$2,100	$1,800

Add 50% for vent. rib.

Above values are for solid rib.

✱ *Model 42 Slide Action Trap Grade* - first variation had small checkered forearm with one diamond in center, field choke (full, modified, or cylinder), second variation has large checkered forearm with 2 diamonds in center, both variations had 26 or 28 in. plain or solid rib barrel, select checkered walnut straight grip (one closed diamond on underside of grip) or pistol grip (one closed diamond on each side of grip) stock, usually choked skeet, stamped "TRAP" at bottom of receiver under the ser. no. Only 231 mfg.

	$14,000	$11,500	$8,500	$7,500	$6,500	$5,500	$5,000

✱ *Model 42 Slide Action Deluxe Grade* - same configurations as Trap Grade, 20 LPI checkering, most are fitted with special vent. rib after 1954 in 3 styles: round post-donut base, round post, and rectangle post, pre-1954 mfg. had plain or solid rib barrel, 1946-1950 mfg. may have "DELUXE" stamp under ser. no. on receiver. Mfg. 1946-63.

GRADING - PPGS™	100%	98%	95%	90%	80%	70%	60%
❖ **Model 42 Slide Action Deluxe Grade Solid Rib**							
	$8,500	$8,000	$6,500	$6,000	$5,250	$3,850	$3,250
❖ **Model 42 Slide Action Deluxe Grade Vent. Rib (factory)**							
	$10,000	$9,000	$7,500	$6,500	$5,000	$4,250	$3,750

✴ *Model 42 Slide Action Pigeon Grade* - same configurations as Deluxe Grade, except has pigeon engraved on underside of mag. tube, most were factory engraved, very few mfg.

Must be appraised individually. Before purchasing any factory engraved Model 42, it is advised that a reputable dealer/collector be consulted.

MODEL 50 SEMI-AUTO - 12 or 20 ga., 3 shot, recoil-operated (non-recoiling barrel), 26-30 in. barrels, VR optional, steel frame or Feather Weight Model (aluminum receiver, FTW) introduced 1958. Over 196,000 mfg. between 1954-61, starting with serial number 1,000.

	$650	$525	$450	$400	$350	$300	$250

Add $100 for VR (Simmons installed).
Add $50 for Feather Weight Model (denoted by "A" suffix in ser. no.).
Add $150 for 20 ga.
Add 100% for Trap or Skeet Model.
Add 200%-350% for Pigeon Grade ("PIGEON" stamped on receiver, near ser. no.).

MODEL 59 SEMI-AUTO - 12 ga. only, 3 shot, short recoil operation, Win-lite (steel and fiberglass) ribless barrels, 26-30 in. barrel lengths, alloy receiver inscribed with hunting scenes, Versalite (first interchangeable choke tubes) option introduced 1961, 6 1/2 lbs. 82,085 mfg. between 1960-65.

	$750	$625	$500	$400	$300	$250	$200

Add 30% for barrel with all three choke tubes.

Inspect carefully for either cracked receiver (by bolt handle cutout and over serial numbers), or separating fiberglass on end of barrel. Winchester also mfg. 20 and 14 gauges experimentally in this model, which are extremely rare and expensive.

✴ *Model 59 Semi-Auto Pigeon Grade* - mfg. 1962-1965.

	$3,000	$2,500	$2,000	$1,600	$1,200	$1,000	$800

SHOTGUNS: POST-1964

Winchester introduced WinChokes in 1969.

Shotguns: Post-1964, Lever Action

MODEL 9410 TRADITIONAL - .410 bore, 2 1/2 in. chamber, lever action based on the Model 94 rifle, 24 in. round barrel with cylinder bore or standard Invector chokes (new 2003), 9 shot tube mag., iron sights with TruGlo front and modified V adj. rear, checkered straight grip walnut stock and forearm, top tang safety became standard in 2003, approx. 6 3/4 lbs. Mfg. 2001-2006.

	N/A	$650	$550	$425	$325	$250	$200

Last MSR was $626.

Subtract approx. $50 if w/o Invector chokes.
A survey of recent sales indicates a price range of $700-$950 for NIB specimens.

✴ *Model 9410 Traditional Semi-Fancy* - similar to Model 9410 Traditional, except has checkered semi-fancy walnut stock and standard Invector choke system. Mfg. 2004.

	N/A	$825	$675	$550	$425	$350	$300

Last MSR was $789.

A survey of recent sales indicates a price range of $750-$1,000 for NIB specimens.

GRADING - PPGS™	100%	98%	95%	90%	80%	70%	60%

✳ *Model 9410 Traditional Packer* - cylinder bored or standard Invector chokes (new 2003, includes 3 chokes), 20 in. barrel, 5 shot, 2/3 mag., open sights, checkered semi-pistol grip walnut stock and forearm with sling swivel studs, also available in Packer Compact Model (12 1/2 in. LOP, new 2003), 6 1/4 - 6 1/2 lbs. Mfg. 2002-2006.

	N/A	$650	$550	$425	$325	$250	$200

Last MSR was $647.

Subtract approx. $50 if w/o standard Invector chokes (includes 3).
A survey of recent sales indicates a price range of $700-$950 for NIB specimens.

✳ *Model 9410 Traditional Ranger* - similar to Model 9410 Traditional, except has uncheckered hardwood stock and forearm, 24 in. barrel with fixed cylinder bore barrel, 6 3/4 lbs. Mfg. 2003-2006.

	N/A	$525	$425	$300	$250	$225	$200

Last MSR was $532.

✳ *Model 9410 Traditional TS Custom Case Colored* - similar to Model 9410 Traditional, features case colored receiver, lever, crescent buttplate, lower tang, and barrel bands, deluxe straight grip checkered walnut stock and extended forearm, matte bluing, 24 in. round barrel, gold trigger, top safety, 7 lbs. Mfg. 2005 only.

	N/A	$1,450	$1,200	$1,050	$875	$725	$595

Last MSR was $1,418.

A survey of recent sales indicates a price range of $1,650-$2,000 for NIB specimens.

Shotguns: Post-1964, Semi-Auto

Winchester introduced WinChokes in 1969.

MODEL 140 RANGER SEMI-AUTO - 12, 16, or 20 ga., entry level model. Disc.

	$275	$250	$220	$200	$175	$155	$140

MODEL 1400 SEMI-AUTO - 12, 16, or 20 ga., 26, 28, or 30 in. barrel, 2 3/4 in. chamber, alloy receiver, various chokes, gas operated, 2 shot mag., checkered pistol grip stock. Mfg. 1964-1981.

	$275	$250	$220	$200	$175	$155	$140
Vent. rib	$315	$265	$240	$220	$195	$165	$150

Add 33% for Winchester recoil reduction system (mfg. 1964-1970).

Note: In 1968 the model 1400 series was modified. The action release was improved and the checkering redesigned. From 1968-72, they were designated MKII, which was then dropped. The values for the later guns mfg. from 1968-73 may run approx. 10% higher - values shown are for guns mfg. from 1965-68. Left hand was also available, and was disc. in 1973.

NEW MODEL 1400 WALNUT - 12 or 20 ga., 2 3/4 in. chamber, 22 (disc.), 26 (mfg. 1991-93), or 28 in. VR barrel, checkered walnut stock and forearm, WinChokes standard, 3 shot mag., rotary bolt system, 7-7 1/2 lbs. Mfg. 1989-94.

	$350	$290	$260	$240	$220	$190	$165

Last MSR was $419.

Add $15 for limited mfg. 1993 Quail Unlimited Model (2,500 mfg. 1993).

MODEL 1400 CUSTOM HIGH GRADE - 12 ga. only, 28 in. VR WinChoke barrel, special order only through the Custom Gun Shop, features deluxe hand checkered walnut and special engraving. Mfg. 1991-92.

	$1,295	$995	$750	N/A	N/A	N/A	N/A

Last MSR was $1,695.

MODEL 1400 SKEET GRADE - similar to 1400, 12 or 20 ga., with 26 in. VR barrel, skeet bore, select skeet style stock. Mfg. 1965-73.

	$425	$350	$300	$275	$220	$195	$165

GRADING - PPGS™	100%	98%	95%	90%	80%	70%	60%

MODEL 1400 TRAP GRADE - similar to 1400, with 30 in. full choke VR barrel, select trap style stock. Mfg. 1965-73.

	$360	$330	$305	$275	$220	$195	$165

MODEL 1400 DEER GUN - similar to 1400, with 22 in. barrel, rifle sights, 12 ga. only. Mfg. 1965-74.

	$265	$240	$220	$200	$175	$165	$140

MODEL 1400 SLUG HUNTER - 12 ga. only, 22 in. smooth bore cyl. or rifled Sabot choke-tubed barrel, drilled and tapped for scope, includes bases or iron sights, 7 1/4 lbs. Mfg. 1990-92.

	$355	$310	$270	$250	$225	$195	$165

Last MSR was $420.

MODEL 1400 RANGER - 12 or 20 ga., gas operation, alloy receiver, 22 cyl. deer, 26 (mfg. 1991-93), or 28 in. WinChoke barrel, checkered walnut finished hardwood stock and forearm, VR became standard 1985, 7 1/4 lbs. Disc. 1994.

	$285	$235	$200	$180	$160	$140	$120

Last MSR was $377.

Add $53 for deer combo. (includes extra 22 in. cyl. bore barrel).
Subtract $40 without VR.

MODEL 1500 XTR - 12 or 20 ga., 2 3/4 inch only, 28 inch barrel, plain or VR, Win-Choke tubes, gas operation. Mfg. 1978-82.

	$300	$260	$240	$220	$200	$180	$160

SUPER X MODEL 1 - 12 ga., 26, 28, or 30 in. VR barrel, various chokes, steel receiver, gas operated - self compensating, checkered pistol grip stock and forearm. Mfg. 1974-81.

	$500	$450	$400	$350	$300	$250	$225

SUPER X MODEL 1 SKEET - similar to Standard, with 26 in. skeet bore barrel, select skeet style stock. Mfg. 1974-81.

	$695	$595	$500	$475	$450	$425	$400

Add 20% if NIB condition.

SUPER X MODEL 1 TRAP - similar to Standard, with 30 in. barrel, imp. mod. or full choke, select trap style stock.

	$595	$550	$475	$425	$415	$395	$350

Add 20% if NIB condition.

SUPER X MODEL 1 CUSTOM TRAP OR SKEET - 12 ga. only, limited production from the Custom Shop, deluxe checkered walnut stock and forearm, extensive scroll engraving on receiver, built to custom order. Limited mfg. 1987-92.

	$1,295	$925	$725	N/A	N/A	N/A	N/A

* *Super X Model 1 Custom Trap or Skeet Engraved* - features number 5 engraving pattern with 7 gold inlays. Disc.

	$2,395	$1,900	$1,350	N/A	N/A	N/A	N/A

Last MSR was $1,295.

Add $700 for factory gold inlays (8 flying ducks).

SUPER X2 3 IN. MAGNUM FIELD - 12 ga. only, 3 in. chamber, self-adjusting gas operation, 26 or 28 in. VR back-bored barrel with Invector chokes, 5 shot mag., choice of checkered walnut or black synthetic stock and forearm with recoil pad, high gloss blue or matte metal finish, approx. 7 1/4 - 8 lbs. Mfg. 1999-2004.

	$750	$650	$575	$525	$465	$400	$325

Last MSR was $874.

✳ *Super X2 3 in. Magnum Field Light* - 26 or 28 in. VR back-bored barrel with Invector Plus chokes, alloy receiver, checkered pistol grip walnut stock and forearm, 6 1/2 - 6 3/4 lbs. Mfg. 2005-2006.

	$835	$710	$600	$560	$500	$450	$375

Last MSR was $945.

✳ *Super X2 3 in. Magnum Field Sporting Clays* - 28 or 30 in. VR back-bored barrel with Invector chokes, adj. stock using spacers, includes 2 gas pistons, checkered walnut or Signature Red Dura-Touch finished (new 2003) hardwood stock and forearm, approx. 8 lbs. Mfg. 2001-2007.

	$875	$730	$610	$560	$500	$450	$375

Last MSR was $999.

Add $16 for Signature Red Dura-Touch finish on stock and forearm.

✳ *Super X2 3 in. Magnum Field Sporting Clays Signature II* - features red anodized alloy receiver and forearm cap, black metallic paint on stock and forearm, two gas pistons provided, adj. stock spacers provided, 28, 30 or 32 (mfg. 2005 only) in. barrel, approx. 8 lbs. Mfg. 2005-2006.

	$885	$735	$625	$575	$500	$450	$375

Last MSR was $1,015.

✳ *Super X2 3 in. Magnum Field Composite* - features black composite stock and forearm with Dura-Touch armor coating, matte metal finish, includes sling swivel studs, 26 or 28 in. VR barrels with three Invector chokes, approx. 7 3/4 lbs. Mfg. 2004-2005.

	$775	$665	$585	$525	$465	$400	$325

Last MSR was $908.

✳ *Super X2 3 in. Magnum Field Rifled Deer* - 22 in. rifled barrel with cantilever scope base and Tru-Glo sights (rear sight folds down), black synthetic stock and forearm, 7 1/4 lbs. Mfg. 2002-2005.

	$800	$675	$585	$530	$455	$395	$325

Last MSR was $957.

✳ *Super X2 2 3/4 in. Magnum Field Practical MK I* - similar to Super X2 Practical MKII, except is 2 3/4 in. chamber, has regular TruGlo iron sights, and does not have Dura-Touch, cylinder standard Invector choke, 8 lbs. Mfg. 2003-2007.

	$960	$800	$675	$575	$500	$465	$435

Last MSR was $1,116.

✳ *Super X2 3 in. Magnum Field Practical MK II* - home defense configuration featuring black composite stock and forearm, black metal finish, 22 in. barrel with standard Invector choke system and removable LPA ghost ring sights, 8 shot extended mag., includes sling swivels, Dura-Touch armor coated composite finish became standard during 2003, 8 lbs. Mfg. 2002-2006.

	$1,075	$885	$715	$635	$550	$495	$440

Last MSR was $1,287.

Subtract 10% if w/o Dura-Touch finished stock and forearm.

SUPER X2 3 1/2 IN. MAG. COMPOSITE - 12 ga. only, 3 1/2 in. chamber, similar to Super X2, black synthetic stock and forearm with vent. recoil pad, Dura-Touch armor coated stock/forearm treatment became standard during 2003 for all models, 24 (disc. 2000), 26, or 28 in. VR back-bored barrel with Invector chokes, 7 1/2-8 lbs. Mfg. 1999-2005.

	$885	$725	$625	$565	$500	$450	$375

Last MSR was $1,027.

✳ *Super X2 3 1/2 In. Mag. Composite Universal Hunter* - similar to Super X2 3 1/2 In. Mag., except has full coverage Mossy Oak Break-Up camo composite stock and forearm, 26 in. VR barrel with 3 Invector Plus chokes, including optional extended extra full (standard beginning 2006), TruGlo sights, 7 3/4 lbs. Mfg. 2002-2007.

	$1,050	$875	$700	$600	$515	$455	$375

Last MSR was $1,252.

Subtract approx. 5% for standard Invector Plus chokes.

✳ *Super X2 3 1/2 In. Mag. Composite Greenhead* - similar to Super X2 3 1/2 In. Mag., except has green Dura-Touch stock and forearm for enhanced durability and feel during cold/wet conditions, 28 in. VR barrel, matte metal finish, 8 lbs. Mfg. 2002-2005.

	$900	$740	$620	$565	$500	$450	$375

Last MSR was $1,036.

✳ *Super X2 3 1/2 In. Mag. Composite Turkey* - similar to Super X2 3 1/2 In. Mag., except has 24 in. VR barrel with TruGlo sights and extra full turkey choke tube, matte finish only, 7 1/2 lbs. Mfg. 1999-2002.

	$880	$730	$615	$555	$495	$450	$375

Last MSR was $1,018.

During 2001-2002, this model incorporated a "Team NWTF" logo on the stock.

✳ *Super X2 3 1/2 In. Mag. Composite Camo Turkey (NWTF)* - similar configuration as regular Turkey, except has 100% Mossy Oak Break-Up camo treatment and TruGlo sights, 7 1/2 lbs. Mfg. 2000-2007.

	$1,035	$850	$700	$550	$495	$425	$375

Last MSR was $1,236.

Beginning in 2001, this model incorporates a "Team NWTF" logo on the stock.

✳ *Super X2 3 1/2 In. Mag. Composite Camo Waterfowl* - similar to Super X2 3 1/2 In. Mag., except has 100% Mossy Oak Shadow Grass treatment, 28 in. VR back-bored barrel with Invector chokes, 8 lbs. Mfg. 1999-2005.

	$1,000	$840	$685	$565	$495	$425	$375

Last MSR was $1,185.

SUPER X3 3 IN. MAGNUM WALNUT FIELD - 12 ga. only, 3 in. chamber, self-adjusting Active Valve gas operation, 26 or 28 in. VR barrel with Invector Plus chokes, variable checkered walnut stock with second generation Pachmayr Decelerator pad, adj. LOP, alloy receiver and mag. tube, grey Perma-Cote Ultra Tough or Dura-Touch Armor coating (current) surface finish, approx. 7 lbs. New 2006.

MSR $1,079	$925	$825	$725	$625	$575	$500	$450

✳ *Super X3 3 in. Magnum Classic Field* - similar to 3 in. Walnut Field, except has traditional diamond pattern checkering and non-adj. Decelerator recoil pad. New 2008.

MSR $1,079	$925	$825	$725	$625	$575	$500	$450

✳ *Super X3 3 in. Flanigun Exhibition/Sporting* - features black composite stock and forearm with Dura-Touch armor coating and red annodized frame and forearm cap, 28 in. VR barrel with Invector Plus chokes, 7 1/4 lbs. New 2008.

MSR $1,349	$1,095	$925	$800	$675	$575	$500	$425

✳ *Super X3 3 in. Magnum Field Composite* - similar to 3 in. Field, features black composite stock and forearm, alloy receiver, 26 or 28 in. barrel with Invector Plus chokes, approx. 6 3/4 lbs. New 2006.

MSR $1,029	$875	$775	$650	$550	$500	$450	$375

GRADING - PPGS™	100%	98%	95%	90%	80%	70%	60%

❋ *Super X3 3 in. Magnum Field Cantilever Deer* - 12 ga., 22 in. rifled barrel with Weaver style cantilever scope base and Tru-Glo sights, alloy receiver, black synthetic stock and forearm, 7 1/4 lbs. New 2006.

MSR $1,079	$925	$825	$725	$625	$575	$500	$450

SUPER X3 3 1/2 IN. MAGNUM COMPOSITE - 12 ga. only, 3 1/2 in. chamber, features black composite stock and forearm, alloy receiver, grey Perma-Cote Ultra Tough (disc.) or Dura-Touch Armor coating (current) surface finish, 26 or 28 in. VR barrel with Invector Plus chokes, approx. 7 1/4 lbs. New 2006.

MSR $1,149	$975	$800	$650	$575	$500	$450	$375

❋ *Super X3 3 1/2 In. Magnum Composite Waterfowl* - similar to Super X3 3 1/2 In. Mag., except has 100% Mossy Oak New Shadow Grass (disc.) or Mossy Oak New Duck Blind (new 2007) treatment, 26 or 28 in. barrel, 7 - 7 1/4 lbs. New 2006.

MSR $1,329	$1,095	$900	$725	$575	$500	$450	$425

❋ *Super X3 3 1/2 In. Magnum Composite All Purpose Field* - similar to Super X3 3 1/2 In. Mag., except has 100% Mossy Oak New Break-Up camo treatment, 26 or 28 in. barrel, 6 3/4 - 7 lbs. New 2006.

MSR $1,329	$1,095	$900	$725	$575	$500	$450	$425

❋ *Super X3 3 1/2 in. Mag. NWTF Cantilever Extreme Turkey* - 12 ga., 24 in. cantilever barrel with extra-full extended turkey choke tube, composite stock with full Mossy Oak New Break-Up camo treatment and Dura-Touch Armor coating, Active Valve system, Pachmayr Decelerator recoil pad, steel sling swivels, includes TruGlo dexlue red dot scope and Weaver style mount, approx. 7 1/2 lbs. New 2008.

MSR $1,399	$1,125	$950	$825	$700	$575	$500	$425

Shotguns: Single Barrel

MODEL 370 - 12, 16, 20, 28 ga., or .410 bore, 28-32 in. full choke plain barrel, replaced the Model 37, top lever break open, exposed hammer, plain pistol grip stock. Approx. 221,578 mfg. between 1968-73.

	$150	$125	$100	$90	$85	$80	$75

Add 20%-75% for 28 ga. and .410 bore, depending on original condition.

The Model 370 was mfg. in Winchester's Canadian plant in Cobourg, Ontario.

MODEL 370 YOUTH - similar to 370, with 26 in. barrel, 12 1/2 in. stock, with recoil pad.

	$145	$110	$95	$85	$80	$75	$70

MODEL 37A - replaced the Model 370, roll engraved receiver, gold trigger. Approx. 391,168 mfg. between 1973-80 in the Winchester plant in Cobourg, Ontario.

	$140	$110	$95	$85	$75	$65	$55

Add 10% for 36 in. goose barrel.
Add 50% for 28 ga. and 75% for .410 bore.

MODEL 37A YOUTH - similar to 37A, except 20 ga. or .410 bore with 12 1/2 in. LOP stock.

	$145	$110	$95	$85	$80	$75	$70

MODEL 840 - various gauges, mfg. in Canada until 1980.

	$140	$110	$95	$85	$75	$65	$55

MODEL 1370 SLAGBLASTER - 12 ga., 26 in. heavy barrel, shoots special Winchester/Western CE8Z industrial ammunition with extended 3 oz. zinc slug (rare), industrial sale only - used to clean slag from steel kilns, 9 lbs. Mfg. in Canada, disc.

	$750	$700	$650	$575	$525	$450	$400

GRADING - PPGS™	100%	98%	95%	90%	80%	70%	60%

SHOTGUNS: SLIDE ACTION, 1964-CURRENT

Winchester introduced WinChokes in 1969.

U.S. Repeating Arms closed its New Haven, CT manufacturing facility on March 31, 2006. There may be some speculation on recently manufactured Model 1300 shotguns. All Model 1300 last MSRs listed are from the Winchester 2006 price sheet, and 60%-100% values reflect today's marketplace with no speculation.

MODEL 12 SUPER PIGEON GRADE - 12 ga., slide action, 26, 28, or 30 in. barrel, VR, any choke, hand honed action, engine turned breech block and loading flap, "B" checkering and No. 5 engraving, custom order grade walnut stock. Limited production between 1964-72.

	$3,750	$3,275	$2,650	$2,275	$1,995	$1,650	$1,400

Subtract 20% for Super Pigeon Grades mfg. 1984-85 (480 total).

MODEL 12 FIELD GRADE - 12 ga., slide action, 26, 28, or 30 in. VR barrel, various chokes, jeweled bolt, hand checkered, checkered select walnut stock. Mfg. 1972-75, "Y" ser. no. prefix.

	$750	$650	$600	$550	$500	$450	$400

In 1984, Y series Model 12s were once again available through a private contract with U.S.R.A. Co. which included engraving on Grades 1A-1C and 2-5. These guns were available in either Field, Trap, or Skeet configurations. Since there was no manufacturer's suggested retail, Model 12 values shown are established by analyzing the sales of the two private contractors - no more of these variations are available.

✳ **Model 12 Field Grades 1-A, 1-B, & 1-C** - light engraving depicting dogs or ducks. Disc.

	$1,425	$1,250	$1,025	$875	$785	$695	$600

Last MSR was $1,375.

✳ **Model 12 Field Grades 2 & 3** - engraving features large duck and dog game scenes on receiver flats. Disc.

	$1,875	$1,650	$1,500	$1,300	$1,150	$900	$800

Last MSR was $1,695.

✳ **Model 12 Field Grade 4** - more elaborate game scene engraving than Grades 2 & 3. Disc.

	$2,200	$1,875	$1,600	$1,400	$1,200	$1,050	$950

Last MSR was $1,995.

✳ **Model 12 Field Grade 5** - elaborate game scene engraving with style B checkering. Disc.

	$2,750	$2,300	$1,900	$1,600	$1,350	$1,200	$995

Last MSR was $2,450.

Also available with gold inlays - add $1,000 to values.

✳ **Model 12 Field Grade 3 Barrel Set** - grade 5 engraving with gold inlays and two extra barrels. Disc.

	$5,995	$5,495	$4,795	$4,295	$3,995	$3,495	$2,795

Last MSR was $6,000.

MODEL 12 SKEET GRADE - similar to Field Grade, with 26 in. VR skeet bore barrel, skeet style stock, with recoil pad. Mfg. 1972-75.

	$1,195	$995	$895	$750	$650	$550	$500

See listings under Model 12 Field Grade for engraved values.

MODEL 12 TRAP GRADE - similar to Field grade, with 30 in. VR full choke barrel, trap style stock, straight or Monte Carlo, recoil pad. Mfg. 1972-80.

	$1,095	$950	$850	$750	$650	$500	$450

See listings under Model 12 Field Grade for engraved values.

GRADING - PPGS™	100%	98%	95%	90%	80%	70%	60%

MODEL 12 DU - 800 mfg. during 1975 for auction at Ducks Unlimited chapter banquets.

Current values for this model in NIB condition range from $3,500-$4,000.

MODEL 12 LIMITED EDITION

✽ *Model 12 Limited Edition Grade I 20 Ga.* - 20 ga. only, 2 3/4 in. chamber only, reproduction of the famous Winchester Model 12 with slight design improvements, 26 in. VR barrel bored modified, 5 shot mag., high post floating rib, walnut stock and forearm with semi-gloss finish, takedown, 7 lbs. 4,000 mfg. by Miroku 1993-95.

	100%	98%	95%	90%	80%	70%	60%
	$995	$825	$650	N/A	N/A	N/A	N/A

Last MSR was $879.

✽ *Model 12 Limited Edition Grade IV 20 Ga.* - similar specifications to Grade I, except has select walnut checkered 22 lines per inch with high gloss finish, extensive game scene engraving including multiple gold inlays. 1,000 mfg. 1993-95.

	100%	98%	95%	90%	80%	70%	60%
	$1,500	$1,250	$995	N/A	N/A	N/A	N/A

Last MSR was $1,431.

MODEL 42 HIGH GRADE LIMITED EDITION - .410 bore, 26 in. full choke VR barrel, features Grade V-VI wood with special scroll and gold border engraving, 850 mfg. 1993 only.

	100%	98%	95%	90%	80%	70%	60%
	$1,850	$1,425	$1,100	N/A	N/A	N/A	N/A

Last MSR was $1,617.

MODEL 120 RANGER - 12, 16, or 20 ga., entry level model, VR and WinChokes. Disc.

	100%	98%	95%	90%	80%	70%	60%
	$200	$180	$165	$140	$110	$100	$90

MODEL 1200 FIELD GRADE - 12, 16, or 20 ga., 26, 28, or 30 in. barrel, alloy receiver, various chokes, checkered pistol grip stock, pad. Mfg. 1964-1981.

	100%	98%	95%	90%	80%	70%	60%
	$200	$180	$165	$140	$110	$100	$90
Vent. rib	$220	$205	$195	$165	$140	$110	$100
WinChoke	$240	$215	$200	$190	$180	$160	$140

Add 33% for Winchester recoil reduction system (mfg. 1966-1970).

MODEL 1200 MAGNUM - similar to 1200, chambered for 12 or 20 ga., 3 in. magnum shells. Mfg. 1964-80.

	100%	98%	95%	90%	80%	70%	60%
	$210	$190	$175	$165	$140	$110	$100
Vent. rib	$240	$215	$200	$185	$150	$140	$110

MODEL 1200 SKEET GUN - similar to 1200, 12 or 20 ga., 26 in. VR barrel, skeet bore, 2 shot mag. and select style stock. Mfg. 1965-74.

	100%	98%	95%	90%	80%	70%	60%
	$325	$275	$235	$200	$165	$140	$120

MODEL 1200 TRAP GUN - similar to 1200, with 12 ga., VR, 30 in. full choke barrel, select trap style stock. Mfg. 1965-74.

	100%	98%	95%	90%	80%	70%	60%
	$295	$275	$300	$195	$165	$140	$120
WinChoke	$330	$305	$275	$250	$220	$165	$140

MODEL 1200 DEER GUN - similar to 1200, with 22 in. barrel, rifle sights, 12 ga. only. Mfg. 1965-74.

	100%	98%	95%	90%	80%	70%	60%
	$250	$200	$165	$110	$100	$85	$75

MODEL 1200 POLICE STAINLESS - 12 ga. only, 18 in. barrel, 7 shot mag. Disc.

	100%	98%	95%	90%	80%	70%	60%
	$250	$195	$165	$125	$105	$90	$75

MODEL 1200 DEFENDER - 12 ga. only, 18 in. cylinder bore barrel, 7 shot mag., 6 lbs. Disc.

	100%	98%	95%	90%	80%	70%	60%
	$250	$200	$180	$155	$140	$125	$110

GRADING - PPGS™	100%	98%	95%	90%	80%	70%	60%

MODEL 1300 FEATHERWEIGHT - 12 or 20 ga., 3 in. chamber, takedown, 26 (new 1991) or 28 in. barrel, 5 shot, plain or VR (became standard 1990), WinChoke tubes, checkered walnut stock and grooved forearm, alloy frame, recoil pad, 6 3/4 - 7 1/8 lbs. Mfg. 1978-93.

	$300	$260	$230	$195	$175	$160	$145

Last MSR was $374.

Subtract $30 without VR.

This model had an "XTR" suffix until 1989. Older Model 1300 Featherweights had roll-engraving but no premiums are being asked at this time.

MODEL 1300 WALNUT FIELD - 12 or 20 (disc. 1994) ga., 3 in. chamber, 26 or 28 in. VR barrel with WinChokes (includes 3), checkered satin (disc. 2003) or gloss finished (new 2004) walnut stock and forearm, approx. 7 1/4 - 7 1/2 lbs. Mfg. 1994-2006.

	$350	$250	$200	$160	$140	$120	$110

Last MSR was $444.

Beginning 2003, Winchester started engraving "Speed Pump" on receiver on all Model 1300 variations.

✱ *Model 1300 Walnut Black Shadow Field* - 12 or 20 (new 1996) ga., 3 in. chamber, 26 or 28 in. (12 ga. only) VR WinChoke barrel, black composite stock and forearm, 6 3/4 - 7 1/4 lbs. Mfg. 1995-2006.

	$275	$210	$170	$135	$120	$110	$95

Last MSR was $357.

✱ *Model 1300 Walnut Field Sporting* - 12 ga., 3 in. chamber, 24 (compact) or 28 in. VR barrel with 5 WinChokes, satin finished checkered walnut full length or compact (13 in. LOP) stock and forearm with radiused recoil pad, Tru-Glo front sight, matte metal finish, 6 3/4 or 7 1/2 lbs. Mfg. 2002-2006.

	$350	$255	$205	$165	$135	$120	$110

Last MSR was $444.

✱ *Model 1300 Walnut Field Advantage Camo* - 12 ga. only, 28 in. barrel with choke tubes, full coverage. Advantage Camo. Mfg. 1997.

	$340	$265	$235	$195	$165	$145	$125

Last MSR was $432.

✱ *Model 1300 Walnut Field New Shadow Grass* - 12 ga. only, 26 or 28 in. VR barrel with 3 WinChokes, features 100% Mossy Oak New Shadow Grass camo coverage, approx. 7 lbs. Mfg. 2004-2006.

	$365	$275	$215	$180	$150	$130	$115

Last MSR was $472.

MODEL 1300 UPLAND SPECIAL FIELD - 12 or 20 (new 2000) ga., 3 in. chamber, features gloss finished (new 2004) or satin finished (disc. 2003) checkered straight grip walnut stock and forearm, solid recoil pad, 24 in. VR barrel with choke tube, blue only, 6 3/4 lbs. Mfg. 1999-2006.

	$350	$255	$205	$165	$135	$120	$110

Last MSR was $444.

MODEL 1300 CUSTOM HIGH GRADE - while advertised, this model never went into production. Advertised retail was $1,395.

MODEL 1300 WATERFOWL - 12 ga. only, 3 in. chamber, 28 or 30 (disc.) in. VR barrel, matte finished metal, choice of low luster walnut finish or brown Win-Tuff wood, recoil pad, includes camo sling and swivels, WinChokes standard, 7 lbs. Mfg. 1984-91.

	$295	$260	$235	$200	$180	$165	$150

Last MSR was $367.

MODEL 1300 TURKEY GUN - 12 ga. only, 3 in. chamber, 22 in. VR barrel, Win-Choked, walnut stock and forearm with low luster finish, metal surfaces have matte finish, supplied with camouflaged fabric sling, 6 3/8 lbs. Mfg. 1985-88.

$290	$265	$235	$200	$180	$165	$150

Last MSR was $348.

* *Model 1300 Turkey Gun Win-Cam* - similar to Model 1300 Turkey Gun, except has greenish laminated hardwood stock and forearm. Mfg. 1987-93.

$350	$295	$250	$200	$180	$165	$150

Last MSR was $435.

* *Model 1300 Turkey Gun Win-Cam Combo Pack* - 12 ga., supplied with 22 and 30 in. VR non-glare finished barrels, greenish laminated hardwood stock and forearm, camo sling, matte finished metal. Mfg. 1987-88 only.

$375	$330	$290	$260	$230	$200	$185

Last MSR was $425.

* *Model 1300 Turkey Gun Ladies-Youth Win-Cam Turkey Gun* - 20 ga. only, 3 in. chamber, 22 in. VR barrel, green camo laminate shortened stock and forearm, includes sling and National Wild Turkey Federation engraving, 6 lbs. Mfg. 1992 only.

$340	$295	$250	$200	$180	$165	$150

Last MSR was $411.

* *Model 1300 Turkey Gun Win-Cam NWTF Series I-IV* - 12 or 20 ga., Series I was released 1989 (12 ga. only) and included special receiver engraving featuring National Wild Turkey Federation motifs, Series II was released 1990 with a choice of either 12 (disc.) or 20 ga. Ladies/Youth model, Series III was released 1991-92, Series IV was released 1993. Disc. 1994.

$365	$300	$250	$200	$180	$165	$150

Last MSR was $458.

MODEL 1300 TURKEY - SYNTHETIC STOCK - 12 or 20 (mfg. 1996-99, Black Shadow only) ga., 3 in. chamber, 22 in. VR barrel with choke tube, choice of 2 color Realtree camo patterns on synthetic stock and forearm, full camo coverage available in Realtree or Advantage (new 1996), or non-glare black (Black Shadow) finish on all surfaces, approx. 6 3/4 lbs. Mfg. 1994-2000.

* *Model 1300 Turkey Synthetic Stock Black Shadow Finish* - disc. 2000.

$260	$195	$160	$135	$120	$110	$95

Last MSR was $328.

* *Model 1300 Turkey Synthetic Stock Mossy Oak Break-Up* - 12 ga. only, 3 in. chamber, 22 in. VR barrel with TruGlo sights, high density X-full turkey tube, 100% Mossy Oak coverage on wood and metal, 6 3/4 lbs. Mfg. 2000 only.

$375	$295	$260	$225	$200	$185	$170

Last MSR was $459.

This model was also available with iron sights and rifled sabot choke tube for deer hunting - add approx. $30.

* *Model 1300 Turkey Synthetic Stock RealTree/Advantage Camo Finish* - available with stock and forearm, RealTree only or full coverage camo. Disc. 1998.

$290	$240	$180	$150	$130	$115	$100

Last MSR was $370.

Add $62 for full coverage camo.
Add $40 for full coverage without sling (disc. 1997).
Add $40 for smoothbore barrel (Advantage full camo only).

MODEL 1300 UNIVERSAL HUNTER/TURKEY - 12 ga. only, 3 in. chamber, 26 in. VR barrel with 3 WinChokes, full coverage standard or New Mossy Oak Break-Up (new 2003) camo, with or w/o Tru-Glo 3-dot sights, composite stock and forearm, 7 lbs. Mfg. 2002-2006.

$400	$350	$300	$255	$200	$165	$140

Last MSR was $517.

    Subtract 5% if w/o TruGlo sights (Hunter Model).

MODEL 1300 NWTF TURKEY MODELS - 12 ga. only, 3 in. chamber, 18 (Short Turkey, new 2002) or 22 in. barrel, choice of Black Shadow (black synthetic stock and forearm with non-glare metal finish and extra full choke tube, mfg. 2001 only), Turkey Superflauge with full coverage TreBark Superflauge (mfg. 2001) or Mossy Oak Break-Up camo with TruGlo sights, Buck & Tom Super-flauge with full coverage TreBark Superflauge (mfg. 2001) or Mossy Oak Break-Up (new 2002) camo with 2 choke tubes including rifled sabot, or Short Turkey (18 in. barrel with rifled sights and full coverage Mossy Oak Break-Up camo) configurations, "Team NWTF" logo printed on stock, 6 3/4 lbs. Mfg. 2001-2006.

$425	$360	$260	$225	$175	$150	$125

Last MSR was $514.

    Subtract approx. $160 for Black Shadow configuration.
    Add $42 for Buck & Tom Superflauge configuration.

MODEL 1300 LADIES-YOUTH - 20 ga. only, 3 in. chamber, 22 in. VR barrel, short-ened stock dimensions, walnut stock with recoil pad and rear positioned, grooved forearm, 6 1/4 lbs. Mfg. 1992 only.

$315	$260	$220	$180	$165	$150	$135

Last MSR was $355.

MODEL 1300 SLUG HUNTER - 12 ga. only, 3 in. chamber, 22 in. rifled or smooth bore barrel with iron sights, checkered stock and forearm, satin walnut finish or brown laminate stock (Win-Tuff). Supplied with camo fabric sling and rings and bases. Mfg. 1988-disc.

$360	$300	$250	$200	$180	$165	$150

Last MSR was $445.

    Add $10 for smooth bore barrel with Sabot rifled tubes (disc. 1992).
    Add $4 for "Whitetails Unlimited" Model (new 1991).

MODEL 1300 WALNUT DEER - 12 ga. only, 3 in. chamber, 22 in. rifled barrel, non- glare metal surfaces, rifle sights, checkered walnut stock with recoil pad and forearm, 7 1/4 lbs. Mfg. 1994-99.

$350	$285	$255	$225	$200	$185	$170

Last MSR was $429.

✱ *Model 1300 Walnut Deer Black Shadow* - 12 or 20 (mfg. 1996-97, reintroduced 2000) ga., 3 in. chamber, 22 in. smoothbore (12 ga. only, disc. 2003) or rifled (new 1996) barrel with IC WinChoke, matte black stock, forearm, and metal parts, rifle sights, drilled and tapped receiver, approx. 6 3/4 lbs. Mfg. 1994-2006.

$300	$225	$175	$150	$125	$115	$95

Last MSR was $382.

    Add $44 for Cantilever scope mount, available in 12 ga. only (new 2000).
    Add $77 for deer combo package that includes 22 in. cyl. bore (disc. 1998) or rifled (new 2000) barrel and 28 in. VR WinChoke barrels.
    Subtract approx. $25 for smoothbore barrel (disc. 2003).

✳ *Model 1300 Walnut Deer Ranger* - 12 or 20 (Ranger regular or compact) ga., 3 in. chamber, 22 in. rifled barrel with rifle or TruGlo sights, smaller dimensions on 20 ga. Deer Ranger Compact (13 in. LOP, disc. 2005), brown composite stock and forearm, non-glare finish, 6 3/4 lbs. Mfg. 2000-2006.

	$305	$230	$170	$145	$125	$110	$100

Last MSR was $396.

✳ *Model 1300 Walnut Deer Full Advantage Camo* - 12 ga. only, 3 in. chamber, choice of 22 in. rifled or smoothbore barrel, entire gun is in Full Advantage camo pattern, drilled and tapped receiver, iron sights, 7 lbs. Mfg. 1995-98.

	$350	$295	$260	$225	$200	$185	$170

Last MSR was $432.

Subtract $22 for smoothbore barrel.

MODEL 1300 RANGER - 12 or 20 ga., 3 in. chamber, 22 cyl. or rifled (deer only, disc.), 24 1/8 cyl. (disc. deer barrel), 26 (mfg. 1991-98), 28, or 30 (disc. 1992) in. plain or VR barrel, walnut finished hardwood stock, alloy receiver, approx. 7 1/4 lbs. Mfg. 1983-2004.

	$285	$215	$170	$135	$120	$110	$95

Last MSR was $367.

Subtract $40 without VR or WinChokes.

This model was also available in a deer combination package which included either a 22 in. rifled or smoothbore deer barrel and a 28 in. VR WinChoke barrel in either 12 or 20 ga. (disc.). - add approx. 25% to values listed.

✳ *Model 1300 Ranger Gloss* - 12 or 20 ga., 3 in. chamber, 26 or 28 in. VR barrel, gloss finished checkered hardwood stock and forearm, 7 1/4 - 7 1/2 lbs. Limited mfg. 2006.

	$300	$225	$180	$140	$125	$110	$95

Last MSR was $391.

❖ **Model 1300 Ranger Gloss Compact** - similar to Model 1300 Ranger Gloss, except has 22 or 24 in. barrel and 13 in. LOP. Limited mfg. 2006.

	$285	$215	$170	$135	$120	$110	$95

Last MSR was $366.

✳ *Model 1300 Ranger Ladies/Youth Model* - 20 ga. only, 3 in. chamber, 22 in. VR barrel, shorter stock dimensions - 13 in. LOP and rearward positioned forearm. Disc. 1998.

	$285	$235	$200	$170	$150	$125	$110

Last MSR was $309.

Subtract $40 if without WinChoke and VR.

✳ *Model 1300 Ranger Compact* - 12 or 20 ga., 3 in. chamber, features shorter dimensions (13 LOP), 22 (20 ga. only) or 24 (12 ga. only) in. VR barrel with WinChoke and TruGlo sights, uncheckered hardwood stock and grooved forearm, blue only, approx. 6 3/4 lbs. Mfg. 1999-2005.

	$300	$225	$175	$140	$120	$110	$95

Last MSR was $391.

MODEL 1300 CAMP DEFENDER - 12 ga. only, 3 in. chamber, 8 shot mag., 22 in. barrel with rifle sights and WinChoke, choice of black synthetic (disc. 2000) or hardwood (new 2001) stock and forearm, matte metal finish, 6 7/8 lbs. Mfg. 1999-2004.

	$300	$230	$180	$150	$125	$110	$100

Last MSR was $392.

GRADING - PPGS™	100%	98%	95%	90%	80%	70%	60%

MODEL 1300 DEFENDER - 12 or 20 (disc. 1996, reintroduced 2001) ga., 3 in. chamber, available in Police (disc. 1989), Practical (new 2005), Marine, and Defender variations, 18 or 24 (mfg. 1994-98) in. cyl. bore barrel, 5 (disc. 1998), 7 (disc. 1998), or 8 shot mag., matte metal finish, choice of hardwood (disc. 2001), composite (matte finish), or pistol grip (matte finish, 12 ga. only) stock, TruGlo sights became standard 1999, 5 3/4 - 7 lbs. Disc. 2006.

	$270	$210	$160	$130	$110	$95	$85

Last MSR was $341.

   Add $13 for short pistol grip and full length stocks.
   Add approx. $100 for Combo Package (includes extra 28 in. VR barrel - disc. 1998).

✳ *Model 1300 Defender NRA* - 12 or 20 ga., 18 in. barrel, composite stock with removable TruGlo fiber optic sight, 8 shot mag., features NRA medallion on pistol grip, also available in 12 ga. combo with pistol grip stock, 6 1/4 - 6 1/2 lbs. Limited mfg. 2006.

	$285	$215	$175	$140	$120	$110	$95

Last MSR was $364.

   Add $13 for combo with pistol grip and full length stock.

✳ *Model 1300 Defender Practical* - 12 ga. only, 3 in. chamber, 8 shot mag., 22 in. barrel with TruGlo adj. open sights, designed for practical shooting events, black synthetic stock and forearm. Mfg. 2005.

	$300	$230	$170	$145	$125	$110	$100

Last MSR was $392.

❖ **Model 1300 Defender Practical NRA** - 12 ga. only, 3 in. chamber, 8 shot mag., 22 in. barrel with TruGlo sights, black synthetic stock and forearm, Winchoke system, adj. open sights, NRA logo grip cap, 6 1/2 lbs. Limited mfg. 2006.

	$315	$240	$180	$150	$130	$110	$100

Last MSR was $414.

✳ *Model 1300 Defender Stainless Coastal Marine* - 12 ga. only, 18 in. cyl. bore stainless steel barrel and mag. tube, a Sandstrom 9A phosphate coating was released late 1989 to give long lasting corrosion protection to all receiver and internal working parts, Dura-Touch armor coating stock treatment added 2004, 6 shot mag., synthetic pistol grip (disc. 2001) or full black stock configuration, approx. 6 3/8 lbs. Mfg. 2002-2005.

	$465	$380	$275	$225	$195	$165	$140

Last MSR was $575.

❖ **Model 1300 Defender Stainless Coastal Marine NRA** - 12 ga. only, 18 in. nickel plated stainless steel barrel, anodized aluminum alloy receiver and plated parts for corrosion resistance, Dura-Touch Armor coating on composite stock, 7 shot mag., sling swivel studs, removable TruGlo fiber optic front sight, 6 1/2 lbs. Limited mfg. 2006.

	$480	$390	$280	$230	$200	$165	$140

Last MSR was $598.

✳ *Model 1300 Lady Defender* - 20 ga. only, 3 in. chamber, choice of synthetic regular or pistol grip stock, 4 (disc. 1996) or 7 shot mag., 18 in. cyl. bore barrel (new 1996), 5 3/8 lbs. Disc. 1998.

	$235	$190	$150	$120	$105	$90	$80

Last MSR was $290.

SPEED PUMP FIELD - 12 ga., 3 in. chamber, side ejection, four lug rotary bolt, 26 or 28 in. VR barrel with Invector Plus chokes, choice of gloss finished checkered walnut or black synthetic stock and forearm, approx. 7 1/4 lbs. Mfg. by Miroku beginning 2008.

MSR $349	$295	$250	$215	$200	$185	$170	$155

   Add $50 for checkered walnut stock and forearm.

GRADING - PPGS™	100%	98%	95%	90%	80%	70%	60%

SPEED PUMP DEFENDER - 12 ga., 3 in. chamber, side ejection, 5 shot mag., features 18 in. plain barrel with fixed cylinder choke, black composite stock with non-glare finish and ribbed forearm. Mfg. by Miroku beginning 2008.

MSR $299	$240	$210	$190	$170	$150	$135	$120

SHOTGUNS: O/U - RECENT PRODUCTION

Model 101 dates of manufacture and serialization data can be found in the SERIALIZATION section in the back of this text.

In November of 1987 Olin/Winchester disc. the Model 101. Classic Doubles (listed separately in this text) imported this model under their own trademark until approx. 1990. With the discontinuance of the Model 101 and its many variations, both dealers and collectors have created a lot more demand for this model recently. As a result, prices have escalated and the scramble is on to try and pick off those rare and desirable variations. Since there have been a lot of limited editions and production changes in the 101 O/U series, it could very well be that this model might become very collectible in upcoming years (as happened to the Model 12).

Note: Model 101 and Model 96 Xpert guns were made by Olin Kodensha located in Tochigi, Japan.

Add 10% for the following Model 101s listed in this section, if in NIB condition.

MODEL 91 - 12 ga. only, mfg. by Laurona in Spain for international sales including Europe, SST, ejectors optional, VR, distinguishable by black chrome finish on metal parts. Disc.

Prices hard to evaluate because of limited importation domestically. In some regions they are bought as medium priced field guns ($550-$650), while in others they are sold as a rare Winchester O&U ($900-$1,100).

MODEL 96 XPERT FIELD GRADE - 12 or 20 ga., similar action to Model 101, 3 in. chambers, auto ejectors, SST, various barrel lengths and chokes, action similar to 101, no engraving, checkered pistol grip stock and forearm. Mfg. 1976-82.

	$875	$775	$850	$550	$475	$425	$375

Add 10% for 20 ga.

This model has become known as the "Poor Man's 101."

MODEL 96 XPERT SKEET GRADE - 2 3/4 in. chambers, similar to Field Grade, with 27 in. skeet barrels, skeet style stock. Mfg. 1976-82.

	$925	$850	$725	$600	$500	$450	$410

Add 10% for 20 ga.

MODEL 96 XPERT TRAP GRADE - 12 ga. only, 2 3/4 in. chambers, similar to Field, 30 in. imp. mod. and full or full and full choke, trap style stock. Mfg. 1976-82.

	$875	$775	$650	$550	$475	$425	$375

MODEL 99 - 12 ga., DT, no engraving. Disc.

	$700	$575	$525	$470	$430	$395	$360

MODEL 101 FIELD VARIATION - 12, 20 ga., or .410 bore, 26, 28, or 30 in. barrels, various chokes, boxlock, auto ejectors, SST, engraved receiver, checkered American walnut pistol grip stock. Mfg. 1963-87. Values assume WinChokes (standard since 1983) - subtract $60 if without.

* *Model 101 Field Variation Older production* - checkered walnut stock and forearm, ejectors, SST, blue metal with light engraving on receiver, various barrel lengths, w/o choke tubes.

	$995	$850	$725	$625	$585	$550	$500

Add 50% for 28 ga. or .410 bore.

Add 20% for 20 ga.

GRADING - PPGS™	100%	98%	95%	90%	80%	70%	60%

✳ *Model 101 Field Variation 25th Anniversary Model* - 12 ga., 32 in. F/M barrels, 2 3/4 in. chambers, engraved "1 of 101" with silver inlays, cased. Mfg. 1988.

	$3,500	$3,150	$2,750	$2,300	$1,950	$1,600	$1,200

Last MSR was $3,500.

✳ *Model 101 Field Variation Special* - 12 ga., 3 in. chambers, VR, 27 in. barrels with WinChokes, blue receiver with scroll engraved ejectors, 7 lbs. Disc. 1987.

	$1,350	$1,225	$995	$875	$775	$695	$600

Last MSR was $1,185.

✳ *Model 101 Field Variation Lightweight* - 12 or 20 ga., similar to regular Field Grade, except has coin finished receiver, vent. barrels, and solid rubber recoil pad, 6 1/2 - 7 lbs. Disc. 1987.

	$1,475	$1,295	$1,195	$975	$875	$675	$595

Last MSR was $1,425.

Add 20% for 20 ga.

✳ *Model 101 Field Variation Waterfowl Model* - 12 ga. only, 3 in. chambers, 30 or 32 (disc.) in. WinChoked barrels, VR, matte blue receiver with moderate engraving, low gloss walnut stock with vent. recoil pad, 7 3/4 lbs. Disc. 1987.

	$1,895	$1,700	$1,500	$1,250	$1,050	$800	$700

Last MSR was $1,570.

✳ *Model 101 Field Variation Grade 2 Barrel Hunting Set* - 12 or 20 ga. barrels, both with WinChokes, 26 in. barrels - 20 ga., 28 in. barrels - 12 ga., scroll engraved, blue receiver with game scene engraving and borders, cased. Mfg. 1984-87.

	$3,200	$2,795	$2,500	$2,395	$2,200	$1,795	$1,695

Last MSR was $2,345.

✳ *Model 101 Field Variation Quail Special* - 12, 20 (disc.1984), 28 (new 1987) ga., or .410 bore (new 1987), 25 1/2 in. WinChoke barrels, 6 3/4 lbs. - 12 ga., straight grip stock, vent. barrels and rib, coin finished receiver with game scene engraving, 500 of each ga. were mfg. Imported 1984-86.

	100%	98%	95%	90%	80%	70%	60%
12 ga.	$2,900	$2,495	$2,250	$1,995	$1,750	$1,550	$1,450
20 ga.	$3,500	$3,100	$2,650	$2,200	$1,850	$1,750	$1,650
28 ga.	$5,250	$4,500	$3,950	$3,600	$3,200	$2,700	$2,500
.410 bore	$4,500	$3,850	$3,250	$2,800	$2,350	$1,900	$1,800

Last MSR was $1,950.

All 28 ga. models are baby frames.

✳ *Model 101 Field Variation National Wild Turkey Federation Commemorative* - features golden turkeys on receiver sides, 27 in. VR barrels with choke tubes, only 300 mfg.

	$3,250	$2,400	$1,850	N/A	N/A	N/A	N/A

Original issue price was $1,950.

✳ *Model 101 Field Variation American Flyer Live Bird* - 12 ga. only, 28 or 29 1/2 (new 1988) in. separated barrels with special competition VR, blue frame with gold wire borders and pigeon inlay, 8 - 8 1/2 lbs. Imported 1987 only.

	$2,595	$2,275	$1,950	$1,775	$1,600	$1,425	$1,300

Last MSR was $2,910.

Add $925 for Combo Model (with extra set of 28 & 29 1/2 in. barrels with WinChokes - 45 mfg.).
Add $265 for 29 1/2 in. barrel with WT4 choke tubes.
Approx. 200 of this model were mfg.

MODEL 101 MAGNUM - similar to 101 Field, 12 or 20 ga., 3 in. Mag. chambering, recoil pad, 30 in. barrels, full and mod., or full and full choke. Mfg. 1966-81.

	$1,200	$1,000	$875	$725	$650	$575	$500

Add 20% for 20 ga.

GRADING - PPGS™	100%	98%	95%	90%	80%	70%	60%

MODEL 101 SKEET VARIATION - similar to 101 Field, with 26 1/2 (12 or 20 ga.) or 28 (28 ga. or .410 bore) in. skeet bored barrels, skeet style stock. Mfg. 1966-84.

	$1,200	$1,000	$825	$770	$700	$650	$595

Add 50% for 28 ga. or .410 bore.
Add 30% for 20 ga.

MODEL 101 THREE GAUGE SKEET SET - similar to Skeet 101, with 20, 28 ga., and .410 bore barrels, cased. Mfg. 1974-84.

	$3,800	$3,475	$3,150	$2,850	$2,600	$2,250	$1,900

MODEL 101 TRAP VARIATION - 12 ga. only, 30 or 32 in. barrels with normal or wide VR, imp. mod. and full or full and full chokes, trap style stock. Mfg. 1966-84.

	$1,320	$1,100	$935	$825	$715	$660	$605

MODEL 101 SINGLE BARREL TRAP - similar to O/U Trap, with 32 or 34 in. F or IM choke barrel, Monte Carlo trap style stock. Mfg. 1967-71.

	$880	$660	$550	$495	$385	$360	$330

Add 100% for an extra O/U barrel (Trap Set).

MODEL 101 PIGEON GRADE (XTR) - 12, 20, 28 ga. or .410 bore (disc. 1986), vent. O/U barrels, deluxe engraved silver receiver version of 101, select checkered wood. Mfg. 1974-87.

* *Model 101 Pigeon Grade Lightweight Field Model* - lightweight variation, Win-Chokes standard, 28 ga. baby frame has 27 in. barrels, 6 1/2 - 7 lbs. Disc. 1987.

	100%	98%	95%	90%	80%	70%	60%
12 ga.	$2,195	$2,000	$1,800	$1,450	$1,350	$1,250	$1,150
20 ga.	$2,700	$2,350	$2,000	$1,800	$1,700	$1,600	$1,500
28 ga. standard	$3,750	$3,300	$2,800	$2,500	$2,200	$2,100	$1,700
28 ga. baby frame	$4,650	$4,250	$3,800	$3,350	$2,750	$2,500	$2,400
.410 bore	$3,500	$3,250	$2,925	$2,500	$2,200	$2,100	$1,700

Last MSR was $1,950.

Subtract 5% if without WinChokes (available in all gauges).

* *Model 101 Pigeon Grade Lightweight recent mfg.* - 20 ga. only, 27 in. barrels only with WinChokes, previously manufactured guns that have been photo-chemically engraved and gold plated, 101 (total mfg.) shotguns were sold by Guns Unlimited Inc. located in Omaha, NE 1995-96.

	$2,495	$2,200	$2,000	$1,800	$1,600	$1,500	$1,300

Last MSR was $1,795.

* *Model 101 Pigeon Grade Lightweight two barrel set* - includes either 12/20 ga. with WinChokes (28 in. barrels on 12 ga. and 27 in. on 20 ga.) or 28 ga./.410 bore (27 in. barrels, 28 ga. has WinChokes; .410 bore has fixed M/F chokes), 250 sets mfg. serial numbered HS1-HS250. Disc. 1986.

	$3,595	$3,350	$2,950	$2,750	$2,300	$2,150	$1,900

Last MSR was $2,500.

Add 30% for 28 ga./.410 bore combo.

* *Model 101 Pigeon Grade 3 barrel set* - coin finished Pigeon Grade frame, approx. 250 mfg.

	$4,750	$4,350	$3,900	$3,400	$2,750	$2,450	$2,250

* *Model 101 Pigeon Grade Featherweight* - 12 or 20 ga., English straight stock, 25 1/2 in. barrels bored IC/IM, 6 1/2 - 6 3/4 lbs. Disc. 1987.

	$1,950	$1,750	$1,450	$1,275	$950	$850	$750

Last MSR was $1,580.

Add 20% for 20 ga.
Add 20% for WinChokes.

GRADING - PPGS™	100%	98%	95%	90%	80%	70%	60%

❋ *Model 101 Pigeon Grade Skeet* - 12, 20, 28 ga., or .410 bore.

	$1,500	$1,275	$1,100	$995	$880	$770	$715

Add 25% for 20 ga.
Add 50% for 28 ga. or .410 bore.

❋ *Model 101 Pigeon Grade Trap (Disc.)* - 12 ga. only, vent. barrels and rib, coin finish receiver with fine scroll engraving, engraved pigeon on floorplate, Win-Choke standard, 8 1/4 lbs. Disc. 1985.

	$1,475	$1,275	$1,050	$900	$800	$725	$650

Last MSR was $1,475.

Subtract 15% if w/o WinChokes.

❋ *Model 101 Pigeon Grade Super* - 12 ga. only, blue receiver with elaborate engraving including multiple gold inlays, extra select walnut with fleur-de-lis checkering on stock and forearm, WinChoke standard, 7 1/2 lbs. Imported 1985-87 only.

	$4,500	$4,150	$3,500	$2,900	$2,500	$2,150	$1,920

Last MSR was $4,590.

MODEL 101 PIGEON GRADE TRAP (CURRENT) - 12 ga., 2 3/4 in. chambers, engraved nickel finished action, choice of 30 or 32 in.10mm VR ported barrels with Invector Plus choking and TruGlo interchangeable fiber optic front sights, checkered Grade III/IV walnut with adj. comb, adj. trigger shoe, approx. 7 1/2 lbs., includes ABS hard case. Mfg. in Belgium. New 2008.

MSR $2,149	$1,900	$1,625	$1,400	$1,200	$995	$850	$725

Add $230 for adj. comb.

MODEL 101 DIAMOND GRADE - Trap or Skeet O/U, 12 (Trap only), 20, 28 ga., or .410 bore, vent. barrels and rib, WinChoke standard on Trap - add $75 on Skeet model (disc.1986), select hand checkered walnut, engraved satin-finish receiver. Trap model has extra high VR. Skeet model has raised rib and muzzle vents.

❋ *Model 101 Diamond Grade Standard Trap* - 12 ga. only, 30 or 32 in. vent. barrels, 8 3/4 - 9 lbs. Disc. 1987.

	$1,620	$1,440	$1,230	$1,075	$900	$780	$640

Last MSR was $1,860.

❋ *Model 101 Diamond Grade Unsingle Trap* - 12 ga. only, lower single barrel, 32 or 34 in. barrel, extended rib.

Add $60 for WinChoke. Disc. 1986.

	$1,700	$1,525	$1,250	$995	$895	$830	$740

Last MSR was $1,760.

❋ *Model 101 Diamond Grade Oversingle Trap* - 12 ga. only, WinChokes, 34 in. upper barrel only, 8 1/2 lbs. Imported 1986-87 only.

	$1,985	$1,695	$1,545	$1,395	$1,200	$995	$895

Last MSR was $2,145.

❋ *Model 101 Diamond Grade Oversingle Combo* - includes one set of O/U barrels and an oversingle barrel, cased. Imported 1987 only.

	$3,075	$2,750	$2,525	$2,300	$2,000	$1,750	$1,625

Last MSR was $3,550.

Add $275 for ATA Trap set.

❋ *Model 101 Diamond Grade Trap Combo* - 12 ga. only, includes a set of 30 or 32 in. vent. O/U barrels and a 32 or 34 in. high ribbed unsingle (lower) barrel, standard or Monte Carlo stock, approx. 9 lbs. Disc. 1987.

	$2,570	$2,320	$1,975	$1,800	$1,600	$1,400	$1,200

Last MSR was $2,940.

GRADING - PPGS™	100%	98%	95%	90%	80%	70%	60%

✴ *Model 101 Diamond Grade Standard Skeet* - 12, 20, 28 ga., or .410 bore, 27 1/2 in. vent. barrels and competition rib, 6 1/2 - 7 1/4 lbs. Disc. 1987.

	$1,650	$1,465	$1,240	$1,075	$900	$780	$640

Last MSR was $1,950.

> **Add 30% for 28 ga. or .410 bore.**
> **Add 20% for 20 ga.**
> Certain design features may increase/decrease the values of this model.

✴ *Model 101 Diamond Grade Four Gauge Skeet Set* - includes 12, 20, 28 ga., and .410 bore 27 1/2 in. separated barrel assemblies, cased. Imported 1985-87 only.

	$4,850	$4,025	$3,650	$3,200	$2,800	$2,500	$2,150

Last MSR was $5,025.

✴ *Model 101 Diamond Grade Sporting Clay* - 12 ga. only, marked Diamond Sporter, 28 in. barrels with WinChokes, designed for Sporting Clay competition. Disc. 1987.

	$2,050	$1,700	$1,400	$1,100	$925	$795	$650

Last MSR was $1,965.

MODEL 101 SPORTING - CURRENT MFG. (SELECT) - 12 ga., 28, 30, or 32 in. lightweight ported barrels, 2 3/4 in. chambers, ejectors, Invector-Plus chokes with 5 Signature extended choke tubes, traditional 101 styling with low profile blue engraved receiver, high-gloss Grade II/III walnut stock and forearm, adj. SST, Pachmayr Decelerator pad, 10mm runway rib, white mid-bead and Tru-Glo front sight, 7 1/4 - 7 1/2 lbs. Mfg. by FN in Belgium. New 2007.

MSR $2,329	$1,950	$1,650	$1,300	$1,025	$900	$800	$700

Select was dropped from this model's nomenclature beginning 2008.

MODEL 101 FIELD - CURRENT MFG. (SELECT) - 12 ga., 26 or 28 in. lightweight barrels, 3 in. chambers, ejectors, Invector-Plus flush chokes with three choke tubes, blue receiver with deep relief engraving, high-gloss Grade II/III walnut stock and forearm, adj. SST, vented Pachmayr Decelerator pad, 10mm runway rib, brass bead front sight, 7 1/4 - 7 1/2 lbs. Mfg. by FN in Belgium. New 2007.

MSR $1,899	$1,625	$1,375	$1,175	$995	$875	$775	$675

Select was dropped from this model's nomenclature beginning 2008.

501 GRAND EUROPEAN - Trap or Skeet, 12 or 20 (Skeet only) ga., 27, 30, or 32 in. barrels, extra select hand checkered walnut with oil finish, Schnabel forearm, extensive scroll engraving on satin-finished receiver, vent. barrels and rib. Mfg. 1981-86.

	$2,195	$1,995	$1,895	$1,795	$1,595	$1,395	$1,195

Last MSR was $1,720.

> **Add 20% for 20 ga. Skeet.**

✴ *501 Grand European Featherweight* - 20 ga. only, straight grip stock, 25 1/2 in. VR barrels, 5 3/4 lbs. Disc. 1986.

	$3,150	$2,750	$2,500	$2,175	$1,900	$1,700	$1,500

Last MSR was $1,720.

PRESENTATION GRADE - 12 ga. only, available in both Trap and Skeet models, blue action extensively engraved with gold inlays, special crotch walnut, 27 (Skeet) or 30 in. vent. barrels, hand checkered, silver wire borders on perimeter of receiver. Imported 1984-87 only.

	$3,950	$3,395	$3,075	$2,400	$2,000	$1,800	$1,600

Last MSR was $3,840.

> **Subtract 10% for Trap Model.**

GRADING - PPGS™	100%	98%	95%	90%	80%	70%	60%

SHOTGUN/RIFLE COMBINATION - combination 12 ga. and .222 Rem., .223 Rem., .243 Win., .270 Win., .30-06, .308 Win., .300 Win. Mag., 5.6x57R, 6.5x55mm, 7x65R, 7x57 Mauser, or 9.3x74R cal. rifle, O/U, 25 in. barrels, top barrel is WinChoked, Grand European engraving and finish, 8 1/2 lbs. Mfg. 1983-85.

	$2,795	$2,475	$2,100	$1,875	$1,650	$1,550	$1,425

Last MSR was $2,550.

Add 50% for .300 Win. Mag. or 6.5x55mm cal.

This model was advertised in .222 Rem., .223 Rem., 6.5x55mm, or .300 Win. Mag. cal., but very few 6.5x55mm or .300 Win. Mag. cals. have been encountered to date.

MODEL 1001 FIELD GRADE - 12 ga. only, 3 in. chambers, boxlock action, 28 in. VR (8mm) barrel with WinPlus chokes, blue metal featuring 40% engraving coverage, Grade I stock and forearm, high luster finish, mfg. in Italy by Marocchi 1993, disc. 1998.

	$975	$795	$725	$650	$595	$550	$495

Last MSR was $1,099.

✳ *Model 1001 Field Grade Sporting Clays* - 12 ga. only, 2 3/4 in. chambers, 28 or 30 in. VR (10mm) vent. barrels with WinPlus chokes, full engraving (includes scroll and flying W with clay bird), silver nitrate receiver with remaining parts blue, Grade II-III stock and forearm, satin finish, mfg. in Italy by Marocchi 1993, disc. 1998.

	$1,075	$925	$795	$725	$650	$595	$550

Last MSR was $1,253.

✳ *Model 1001 Field Grade Sporting Clays Lite* - 12 ga. only, 3 in. chambers, blue finish, 28 in. VR barrels with WinPlus chokes, checkered walnut stock and forearm, gold SST, 7 lbs. Mfg. 1995-98.

	$1,000	$795	$725	$650	$595	$550	$495

Last MSR was $1,153.

MODEL G5500 SPORTER - 12 ga. only, marked Sporter, 28 or 30 in. barrels with fixed chokes (bored IC/M, IM/F, or XF/F) or WinChokes.

	$1,795	$1,475	$1,275	$1,075	$900	$780	$640

Add 20% for WinChokes.

MODEL G6500 SPORTER - 12 ga. only, marked Sporter, barrels and chokes same as G5500.

	$2,295	$1,925	$1,625	$1,400	$1,225	$1,050	$900

Add 20% for WinChokes.

SELECT FIELD (SUPREME) - 12 ga. only, 3 in. chambers, low profile boxlock action with dual tapered locking lugs positioned between the barrels, SST, ejectors, game scene engraved receiver, 26 (new 2001) or 28 in. 6mm VR back-bored barrels with Invector Plus choking (high polish barrels became standard in 2005), redesigned barrels in 2003, checkered walnut stock and forearm, blue action and barrels, barrel selector on safety switch, approx. 7 lbs. Mfg. 2000-2005.

	$1,265	$1,025	$900	$800	$700	$600	$500

Last MSR was $1,498.

During 2004, this model's nomenclature was changed from Supreme Select Field to Select Field.

SELECT WHITE FIELD TRADITIONAL/EXTREME - 12 ga. only, 3 in. chambers, 26 or 28 in. barrels, engraved low profile silver nitride receiver, walnut stock with oval (Extreme) or standard (Traditional) checkering, Invector-Plus choke system, 7 - 7 1/4 lbs., mfg. by Miroku. Limited mfg. 2006.

	$1,295	$1,050	$900	$800	$700	$600	$500

Last MSR was $1,533.

GRADING - PPGS™	100%	98%	95%	90%	80%	70%	60%

SELECT ELEGANCE (SUPREME) - 12 ga. only, 3 in. chambers, grey game scene engraved low profile receiver with dual locking pin design, choice of regular checkered (Traditional Elegance) or oval checkered (Extreme Elegance, new 2004) Grade III walnut stock and Schnabel forearm, 26 or 28 in. non-ported barrels with Invector Plus choke system (high polish barrels became standard in 2005), includes red hardshell case, approx. 7 lbs., mfg. by Miroku. Mfg. 2003-2006.

	$1,950	$1,625	$1,275	$995	$875	$775	$675

Last MSR was $2,320.

SELECT MIDNIGHT - 12 ga. only, 3 in. chambers, 26 or 28 in. barrels, high gloss blued receiver with gold bird accents on both sides and bottom, satin finished Grade II/II walnut stock with oval checkering pattern, deluxe recoil pad, approx. 7 lbs., limited mfg. by Miroku 2006 only.

	$1,995	$1,650	$1,300	$1,025	$900	$800	$700

Last MSR was $2,380.

SUPREME SELECT SPORTING - 12 ga. only, 2 3/4 in. chambers, features satin finished bi-tone receiver w/o engraving, 28 or 30 in. 10mm VR back-bored barrels with porting, redesigned barrels in 2003, SST with adj. trigger shoe system, sharply checkered walnut stock and Schnabel style forearm, approx. 7 1/2 lbs. Mfg. 2000-2003.

	$1,200	$995	$900	$800	$700	$600	$500

Last MSR was $1,406.

SELECT ENERGY SPORTING - 12 ga. only, 2 3/4 in. chambers, 28, 30, or 32 in. ported and vented side rib high polish barrels with Invector Plus chokes (high polish barrels became standard in 2005), marked "Select Energy Sporting" on contrasting chrome finished receiver, 10mm VR, select American walnut stock with oval checkering and palm swell, with or w/o adj. cheekpiece, adj. trigger shoe, TruGlo front sight, approx. 7 1/2 lbs., mfg. by Miroku 2004-2006.

	$1,635	$1,425	$1,125	$965	$855	$750	$650

Last MSR was $1,950.

Add $165 for adj. comb stock.

SELECT ENERGY TRAP - 12 ga. only, 2 3/4 in. chambers, 30 or 32 in. VR barrels with Invector Plus chokes (high polish barrels became standard in 2005), similar features as the Select Energy Sporting, features oval checkering on stock and forearm, palm swell, TruGlo front sight, Monte Carlo or adj. comb stock with solid recoil pad, approx. 7 1/2 lbs., made by FN in Belgium. Mfg. 2004-2007.

	$1,635	$1,425	$1,125	$965	$855	$750	$650

Last MSR was $1,948.

Add $164 for adj. comb stock.

SELECT PLATINUM SPORTING - 12 ga. only, 2 3/4 in. chambers, 28, 30, or 32 in. ported barrels, ejectors, oil finished Grade II/III checkered walnut stock and forearm, Invector-Plus chokes and five Signature extended choke tubes, silver nitride receiver with light game scene engraving, adj. SST system, 10mm runway rib, mid-bead and TruGlo competition front sight, includes hard case, approx. 7 - 7 1/2 lbs. Mfg. by FN in Belgium. New 2007.

MSR $2,625	$2,200	$1,925	$1,650	$1,400	$1,200	$1,000	$875

SELECT PLATINUM FIELD - 12 ga. only, 3 in. chambers, 26 or 28 in. barrels, ejectors, oil finished Grade II/III checkered walnut stock and Schnabel forearm, Invector-Plus chokes and three Signature extended choke tubes, adj. SST, silver nitride receiver with deep relief engraving, includes hard case, 7 - 7 1/2 lbs. Mfg. by FN in Belgium. New 2007.

MSR $2,359	$1,975	$1,650	$1,300	$1,025	$900	$800	$700

GRADING - PPGS™	100%	98%	95%	90%	80%	70%	60%

SELECT DELUXE FIELD - 12 ga. only, 3 in. chambers, 26, 28, or 30 in. barrels, ejectors, oil finished Grade II checkered walnut stock and forearm, Pachmayr Decelerator pad, adj. SST, Invector-Plus chokes and three Signature flush choke tubes, silver nitride receiver with engraving, includes hard case, 7 - 7 1/2 lbs. Mfg. by FN in Belgium. New 2007.

MSR $1,607	$1,350	$1,100	$925	$825	$725	$625	$525

SHOTGUNS: RECENT PRODUCTION SxS

Values for recently manufactured side-by-sides assume NIB condition - subtract 10%-15% if without box, warranty card, and original shipping container (with packing materials).

MODEL 21: RECENT/CURRENT MFG. - between 1960-1987, Model 21 production was limited to high grades, built to special order only, and 1987 was the last year Winchester carried Model 21 pricing in its catalog. On custom shop guns mfg. 1960-1969, there is no Winchester name on the barrels, but the Winchester proofmark is on the water table, along with a designation "Model 21" or "New Haven, CT" plus the ser. no. On Model 21s produced from 1969-1988, the water tables are stamped as already noted, and the designation "Model 21 - Winchester" is stamped on the top of the left barrel adjacent to the rib, next to the receiver. Connecticut Shotgun Manufacturing Company is currently manufacturing Model 21 shotguns (marked "Model 21" only), including Grades 21-1, 21-5, 21-6, Grand American, and the Royal Exhibition. These guns are not marked "Winchester", are not finished in the Winchester custom shop, and will not letter from the Cody Firearms Museum. Please refer to the Connecticut Shotgun Manufacturing Company listing for more information regarding these newer custom Model 21s. Also refer to previously mfg. Winchester Model 21 listings under SHOTGUNS: 1879-1963.

    Add 25% for 16 or 20 ga.
    Add $1,500 for vent. rib.

✳ *Model 21 Custom Built* - standard model with no engraving.

	$8,000	$7,000	$5,000	N/A	N/A	N/A	N/A

Last MSR was $8,100.

✳ *Model 21 Custom Grade* - includes No. 6 engraved receiver and VR.

	$12,500	$10,500	$9,000	N/A	N/A	N/A	N/A

Last MSR was $11,080.

✳ *Model 21 Pigeon Grade* - single set of barrels, No. 6 engraved, w/o gold inlays, 37 mfg. total in 12, 16, and 20 ga.

	$21,000	$19,000	$16,000	N/A	N/A	N/A	N/A

✳ *Model 21 Grand American Grade* - includes 2 sets of barrels with forearms, No. 6 engraved with gold inlays, cased.

	$28,500	$23,000	$19,500	N/A	N/A	N/A	N/A

Last MSR was $22,745.

✳ *Model 21 Grand American Small Gauge* - 28 ga. or .410 bore.

	$39,000	$31,000	$24,500	N/A	N/A	N/A	N/A

Last MSR was $34,460.

    Add 25% for 28 ga./.410 bore combo.

✳ *Model 21 Grand American ("1 of 8" set)* - includes 20, 28 ga., and .410 bore VR barrels. Only 4 of 8 sets actually mfg.

	N/A	$65,000	$45,000	N/A	N/A	N/A	N/A

Last MSR was $55,000.

✳ *Model 21 Grand Royal (2 barrel set)* - the highest grade of Model 21s ever produced, originally made in a .410 bore 2 barrel set for John Olin, only 4 others were ever manufactured, and all were 2 barrel sets.

Extreme rarity precludes accurate pricing on this model.

GRADING - PPGS™	100%	98%	95%	90%	80%	70%	60%

MODEL 22 - 12 ga. only, subcontracted by Winchester and manufactured in Spain by Laurona circa 1975 for international sales including Europe, field configuration only with 28 in. barrels, DT, oil finished checkered walnut stock and semi-beavertail forearm, matted rib, black-chrome finish on metal parts, hand engraved receiver, limited mfg.

		100%	98%	95%	90%	80%	70%	60%
		$1,200	$995	$825	$700	$600	$525	$475

MODEL 23 XTR - 12 or 20 ga., 3 in. chambers, 25 1/2, 26, 28, or 30 in. barrels, various chokes, single trigger, VR, auto ejectors, scroll engraved, silver grey satin finish, blue barrel, checkered select walnut stock and forearm, first commercial gun to employ interchangeable chokes. Mfg. 1978-disc.

Grade 1	$1,900	$1,750	$1,600	$1,350	$1,100	$950	$800

Add 20% for 20 ga.
Subtract 10% for fixed chokes.

* *Model 23 Pigeon Grade* - standard weight model, 6 1/2-7 lbs, coin finished receiver with scroll engraving. WinChoke option became standard in 1986. Disc. 1986.

	$2,300	$2,100	$1,850	$1,600	$1,300	$1,100	$900

Last MSR was $1,460.

Add 20% for 20 ga.
Subtract 10% if w/o WinChokes.

* *Model 23 Pigeon Grade Lightweight* - 25 1/2 in. barrels only bored IM/IC (12 ga.) or IC/M (20 ga.) or with WinChokes, 6 1/4 - 6 3/4 lbs., coin finished receiver with scroll engraving. English stock. Disc. 1986.

	$2,495	$2,150	$1,925	$1,750	$1,250	$1,000	$800

Last MSR was $1,420.

Add 15% for 20 ga.
Subtract 10% if w/o WinChokes.

* *Model 23 Pigeon Grade Ducks Unlimited* - only 500 mfg. 1981, "SPO" serial no. suffix, cased.

	$2,295	$2,075	$1,750	$1,525	$1,250	$1,050	$950

* *Model 23 Golden Quail Series* - 12 ga. (1986), 20 ga. (1984), 28 ga. (1985), or .410 bore (1987), 25 1/2 in. solid rib barrels bored IC/M, mono-blocks are marked "IC/M" but the barrels are marked "Q1/Q2", coin finished receiver with one gold inlay on floorplate, beavertail forearm, straight grip English stock with recoil pad. Only 500 mfg. each year per gauge. Disc. 1987.

12 ga.	$2,775	$2,500	$2,150	$1,850	$1,475	$1,325	$1,200
20 ga.	$3,100	$2,700	$2,300	$1,975	$1,750	$1,475	$1,350
28 ga. (20 ga. frame)	$4,350	$3,950	$3,650	$3,300	$2,900	$2,450	$2,100
410 bore (small frame)	$4,350	$3,950	$3,650	$3,300	$2,900	$2,450	$2,100

Last MSR was $1,950.

* *Model 23 Light Duck* - limited edition, 500 mfg., introduced 1985, blue receiver and barrels, select walnut, 20 ga., 28 in.- F&F, 8 1/2 lbs.

	$2,895	$2,400	$2,075	$1,775	$1,350	$1,100	$975

Last MSR was $1,660.

* *Model 23 Heavy Duck* - limited edition, 500 mfg. 1984 only, blue receiver and barrels, select walnut, 12 ga., 30 in.- F&F, 8 1/2 lbs.

	$2,550	$2,050	$1,700	$1,375	$1,075	$975	$895

* *Model 23 Custom 2 Barrel Set* - interchangeable 20 and 28 ga. 26 in. barrels, blue engraved receiver with gold inlays, "B" checkering on stock and forearm, leather cased with accessories, only 500 sets mfg. 1986. Disc. 1987.

	$5,975	$5,325	$4,975	$4,075	$3,525	$3,375	$3,075

Last MSR was $4,625.

GRADING - PPGS™	100%	98%	95%	90%	80%	70%	60%

MODEL 23 GRANDE CANADIAN - 12 or 20 ga., 25 1/2 in. barrels with fixed chokes, coin finished receiver with oak leaf engraving and one gold leaf inlay on receiver bottom, English AAA select walnut stock with beavertail forearm, 51 mfg. in 12 ga., 450 mfg. in 20 ga., approx. 50 two-gun sets were also offered with cases (approx. ser. nos. 1-51).

	100%	98%	95%	90%	80%	70%	60%
	$2,850	$2,400	$1,950	$1,700	$1,500	$1,250	$1,125
Cased set	$6,750	$6,050	$5,150	$4,450	$4,000	$3,450	$3,000

Add 20% for 20 ga.

MODEL 23 CUSTOM - 12 ga. only, 27 in. WinChoke barrels, high luster bluing, no engraving, SST, ejectors, solid red rubber recoil pad, 7 lbs. Imported 1987 only.

	100%	98%	95%	90%	80%	70%	60%
	$2,600	$2,295	$1,950	$1,550	$1,275	$1,175	$995

Last MSR was $1,975.

MODEL 23 CLASSIC SERIES - 12, 20, 28 ga., or .410 bore, 26 in. VR barrels, single trigger, deluxe hand-checkered walnut stock and beavertail forearm, solid recoil pad, brass nameplate, gold inlay on bottom of receiver, ebony inlay in forearm, 5 3/4-7 lbs. Imported 1986-87 only.

	100%	98%	95%	90%	80%	70%	60%
12 ga.	$2,650	$2,375	$2,100	$1,825	$1,400	$1,250	$1,150
20 ga.	$2,950	$2,550	$2,225	$1,900	$1,675	$1,395	$1,295
28 ga. (small frame)	$5,750	$5,250	$4,250	$3,750	$3,250	$2,850	$2,450
.410 bore (small frame)	$4,250	$3,900	$3,450	$3,250	$3,050	$2,750	$2,400

Last MSR was $1,975.

100% values assume NIB for this model.

The 28 ga. on this model features a smaller frame, and was the only 28 ga. small frame produced in the Model 23 Series.

WINCHESTER COMMEMORATIVES: U.S. PRODUCTION

During the course of a year, I receive many phone calls and letters on Winchester special editions and limited editions which do not appear in this section. It should be noted that a factory commemorative issue is a gun that has been manufactured, marketed, factory cataloged, and sold through the auspices of the specific trademark. There have literally been hundreds of special and limited editions which, although mostly made by Winchester (some were subcontracted), were not marketed or retailed by Winchester. These guns are NOT Winchester commemoratives and for the most part, do not have the desirability factor that the factory commemoratives have. Special/limited editions are not listed in this text, because there is limited collector interest. Remember, the least your special/limited edition can be worth is a little more than the standard edition value. Do not concentrate on the rarity, you will be disappointed.

Typically, special and limited editions are made for distributors (these sub-contracts are the most common), an organization, state, special event, personality, etc. and are typically sold and marketed through a distributor to dealers, or a company/individual to those people who want to purchase them. These special editions may or may not have a retail price and often times, since demand is regional, values decrease rapidly in other areas of the country. Desirability is the key to determining values on these editions.

As a reminder on commemoratives, especially for the beginning collector, here are a few facts applicable to all manufacturers of commemoratives. Commemoratives are current production guns designed as a reproduction of an historically famous gun model, or as a tie-in with historically famous persons or events. They are generally of very excellent quality and often embellished with select woods and finishes such as silver, nickel, or gold plating. Obviously, they are manufactured to be instant collectibles and to be pleasing to the eye. As with firearms in general, not all commemorative models have achieved collector status, although most enjoy an active market - especially during the past four years. Consecutive-numbered pairs as well as collections based on the same serial number will bring a premium. Remember that handguns usually are in some type of wood presentation case,

GRADING - PPGS™	100%	Issue Price	Qty. Made

and that rifles may be cased or in packaging with graphics styled to the particular theme of the collectible.

The original factory packaging and papers should always accompany the firearm as they are necessary to realize full value at the time of sale. All commemorative firearms should be absolutely new, unfired, and as issued since any obvious use or wear removes it from collector status and lowers its value significantly. Many owners have allowed their commemoratives to sit in their boxes and plastic bags (could be serious if there is moisture where storage occurs) for years without inspecting them for corrosion or oxidation damage. Periodic inspection should be implemented to insure no damage occurs - this is important, since even light "freckling" created from touching the metal surfaces can reduce values significantly. A fired gun with obvious wear or without its original packaging can lose as much as 50% of its normal value - many used commemoratives get sold as "fancy shooters" with little, if any, premiums being asked.

The values listed reflect actual prices paid recently in various areas of the U.S. In some regions it may be possible to purchase a Winchester 94 commemorative made in substantial quantity for a slight premium over a standard production Winchester 94. Because of this, prices could fluctuate over 25% depending on the geographic location of purchase or sale.

A final note on commemoratives: One of the characteristics of commemoratives/special editions is that over the years of ownership, most of the original amount manufactured stays in the same NIB condition. Thus, if supply always is constant and in one condition, demand has to increase before price appreciation can occur. Many commemorative dealers have told me that recent changes in overseas currency rates have made domestic guns less expensive to own - for Europeans especially. For this reason, more commemoratives are being sold overseas resulting in less supply for the domestic market. After 43 years of commemorative/special edition production, many models performance records can be accurately analyzed and the appreciation (or depreciation) can be compared against other purchases of equal vintage. You be the judge.

U.S. Repeating Arms had announced in 1990 that they would once again resume the production of factory commemorative firearms.

1964 WYOMING DIAMOND JUBILEE 94 CARBINE - ser. no. range WJ1- WJ1500.

	$795	$100	1,501

1966 CENTENNIAL '66 RIFLE - no ser. no. prefix or suffix.

	$595	$125	N/A

1966 CENTENNIAL '66 CARBINE - total mfg. of both the rifle and carbine was 102,309, no ser. no. prefix or suffix.

	$595	$125	102,309

Add $50-$75 over individual prices for consecutively serial numbered rifle and carbine set.

1966 NEBRASKA CENTENNIAL 94 RIFLE - ser. no. range NC1- NC2500.

	$795	$100	2,500

1967 CANADIAN '67 CENTENNIAL RIFLE - no ser. no. prefix or suffix.

	$595	$125	N/A

1967 CANADIAN '67 CENTENNIAL CARBINE - total mfg. of both the rifle and carbine was 90,301, no ser. no. prefix or suffix.

	$595	$125	90,301

Add $50-$75 over individual prices for consecutively serial numbered rifle and carbine set.

1967 ALASKAN PURCHASE CENTENNIAL CARBINE - ser. no. range AP1-AP1500.

	$795	$125	1,501

1968 ILLINOIS SESQUICENTENNIAL 94 CARBINE - ser. no. range IS1- IS37468.

	$495	$110	37,468

GRADING - PPGS™	100%	Issue Price	Qty. Made
1968 BUFFALO BILL RIFLE "1 OF 300" PRES. - ser. no. range WCF1- WCF300.			
	$2,750	$1,000	300
1968 BUFFALO BILL RIFLE - ser. no. range WC1- WC112923.			
	$595	$130	N/A
1968 BUFFALO BILL CARBINE - total mfg. of both the rifle and carbine was 112,923, ser. no. range WC1- WC112923.			
	$595	$130	112,923
Add $50-$75 over individual prices for consecutively serial numbered rifle and carbine set.			
1969 GOLDEN SPIKE CARBINE - ser. no. range GS1- GS69996.			
	$595	$120	69,996
1969 THEO. ROOSEVELT RIFLE - ser. no. range TR1- TR52386.			
	$595	$135	N/A
1969 THEO. ROOSEVELT CARBINE - total mfg. of both the rifle and carbine was 52,386, ser. no. range TR1- TR52386.			
	$595	$135	52,386
1970 COWBOY COMMEMORATIVE CARBINE - ser. no. range CB1- CB27549.			
	$595	$125	27,549
1970 COWBOY CARBINE "1 OF 300" - ser. no. range NCHF1- NCHF300.			
	$2,750	$1,000	300
1970 LONE STAR RIFLE - ser. no. range LS1- LS38385.			
	$595	$140	N/A
1970 LONE STAR CARBINE - total mfg. of both the rifle and carbine was 38,385, ser. no. range LS1- LS38385.			
	$595	$140	38,385
1971 NRA CENTENNIAL MUSKET - ser. no. range NRA1- NRA47380, not all shipped.			
	$595	$150	23,400
1971 NRA CENTENNIAL RIFLE - ser. no. range NRA1- NRA47380, not all shipped.			
	$595	$150	21,000
1974 TEXAS RANGER CARBINE - ser. no. range RA151- RA5000.			
	$695	$135	4,850
1974 TEXAS RANGER PRESENTATION - ser. no. range RA1- RA150.			
	$2,750	$1,000	150
1976 U.S. BICENTENNIAL CARBINE - ser. no. range USA1- USA19999.			
	$695	$325	19,999
1977 WELLS FARGO - ser. no. range WFC1- WFC19999.			
	$595	$350	19,999
1977 "LIMITED EDITION I" - ser. no. range 77L1- 77L1500.			
	$1,500	$1,500	1,500
1977 LEGENDARY LAWMEN - ser. no. range LL1- LL19999.			
	$695	$375	19,999
1978 ANTLERED GAME CARBINE - ser. no. range AG1- AG19999.			
	$695	$375	19,999
1979 LEGENDARY FRONTIERSMAN RIFLE - ser. no. range LF1- LF19999.			
	$695	$425	19,999
1979 "LIMITED EDITION II" - ser. no. range 78L1- 78L1500.			
	$1,500	$1,750	1,500
1979 MATCHED SET OF 1000 - ser. no. range MC1- MC1000 and MR1- MR1000.			
	$2,250	$3,000	1,000
1980 BAT MASTERSON CARBINE - ser. no. range BM1- BM8000.			
	$795	$650	8,000

GRADING - PPGS™	100%	Issue Price	Qty. Made

1980 "OLIVER WINCHESTER" - ser. no. range OFW1- OFW1999.

| | $750 | $375 | 19,999 |

1981 U.S. BORDER PATROL - ser. no. range BP1- BP1000.

| | $595 | $1,195 | 1,000 |

1981 U.S. BORDER PATROL - MEMBERS MODEL - ser. no. range USBP1- USBP800.

| | $595 | $695 | 800 |

1981 JOHN WAYNE - ser. no. range JW1- JW49000.

| | $1,495 | $600 | 49,000 |

Optional accessories were also available for this model: the gun rack with leather insert is currently selling for approx. $300 and the leather scabbard is trading for $250.

1981 "DUKE" - ser. no. range DUKE1- DUKE1000.

| | $3,500 | $2,250 | 1,000 |

1981 JOHN WAYNE "1 OF 300" SET - ser. no. range JWM1- JWM300 and JWMD1- JWMD300.

| | $6,500 | $10,000 | 300 |

1982 GREAT WESTERN ARTIST I CANADIAN - no ser. no. prefix or suffix.

| | $1,500 | $2,200 | 999 |

1982 GREAT WESTERN ARTIST II CANADIAN - no ser. no. prefix or suffix.

| | $1,500 | $2,200 | 999 |

1982 ANNIE OAKLEY - ser. no. range AOK1- AOK6000.

| | $850 | $699 | 6,000 |

1982 OKLAHOMA DIAMOND JUBILEE - ser. no. range ODJ-1 - ODJ-1001.

| | $1,395 | $2,250 | 1,001 |

1982 AMERICAN BALD EAGLE - SILVER - ser. no. range ABE1984- ABE4784.

| | $695 | $895 | 2,800 |

1982 AMERICAN BALD EAGLE - GOLD - ser. no. range ABE1782- ABE1983.

| | $4,000 | $2,950 | 200 |

1983 CHIEF CRAZY HORSE - ser. no. range CCH1- CCH19999.

| | $795 | $600 | 19,999 |

1984 WINCHESTER-COLT COMMEMORATIVE SET - 1 each of the Model 1894 Carbine and Colt Peacemaker, serial numbered 1 WC-4440 WC., .44-40 WCF cal., elaborate gold etching, cased.

| | $2,250 | $3,995 | 2,300 |

Approx. 2,300 sets were actually put together in this combination. Some sets were split up with individual prices being discounted (Colt SAAs have been trading in the $700-$800 range).

1985 BOY SCOUTS 75TH ANNIVERSARY - Model 9422 action, .22 cal., rifle configuration, 6 1/4 lbs.

＊ *1985 Boy Scouts 75th Anniversary* - 15,000 mfg., serial numbered BSA 1 - BSA 15,000, roll engraved, antique pewter receiver, hooded front sight.

| | $1,000 | $495 | 15,000 |

＊ *1985 Eagle Scouts 75th Anniversary* - 1,000 mfg., serial numbered EAGLE 1 - EAGLE 1,000, receiver has triple level gold etching, select American walnut stock and forearm, gold-plated lever, hammer, and forearm cap.

| | $6,000 | $1,710 | 1,000 |

1985 MODEL 94 TEXAS SESQUICENTENNIAL - .38-55 WCF cal., available in carbine or rifle.

＊ *1985 Model 94 Texas Sesquicentennial Rifle* - 24 in. round barrel, elaborate gold etching, includes Bowie knife, oak cased, 586 mfg, ser. no. range TSR1- TSR586.

| | $2,400 | $2,995 | 1,500 |

GRADING - PPGS™	100%	Issue Price	Qty. Made

* 1985 Model 94 Texas Sesquicentennial Carbine - 18 1/2 in. round barrel, gold finished receiver and barrel bands, roll engraved receiver, 2,600 mfg., serial numbered TEX 1 -TEX 2600.

	$695	$695	15,000

* 1985 Model 94 Texas Sesquicentennial Rifle/Carbine Set - includes one each of the Model 94 rifle and carbine, Bowie knife, 150 mfg., ser. no. range Carbine: TEXM1- TEXM150 and Rifle: TSRM1- TSRM150.

	$6,250	$7,995	150

1986 120TH ANNIVERSARY MODEL 94 CARBINE - .44-40 WCF cal. only, 20 in. barrel, large loop type finger lever, crescent buttplate, deluxe checkered walnut stock and forearm, extensive gold etching on barrel and framesides, 1,000 mfg. ser. no. WRA001-WRA1000.

	$895	$995	1,000

1986 STATUE OF LIBERTY MODEL 94 - Model 94 rifle in .30-30 Win. cal. with octagon barrel, extensive C. Giovanelli scroll engraving with multiple 22Kt. gold inlays, deluxe walnut with fine checkering, also includes 29 in. hand-carved wooden statue of the Statue of Liberty, serial numbers can range from SL001-SL100, while 100 were scheduled to be produced, only 62 were mfg. on a special order basis only, and the customer could pick out the serial number. This model is a USRAC factory commemorative.

	$8,750	$6,500	62

1986 MODEL 94 DU - .30-30 Win. cal., approx. 2,800 rifles were mfg. in the U.S. Since each Model 94 DU was bid on for ownership, prices will vary from points of origin. An average bid price seems to be in the $700-$995 range with lower and completing set ser. nos. selling at premiums. Serial numbered DU-86 0001 on up.

This model is not a factory commemorative, but rather a trade gun commissioned by Ducks Unlimited.

1987 U.S. CONSTITUTION 200TH ANNIVERSARY - ser. no. range N/A.

	$14,000	$12,000	17

This model was distributed exclusively by Cherry's, located in Greensboro, NC.

1988 WINCHESTER ARMS COLLECTOR'S ASSOCIATION CASED SET - includes Colt SAA and Winchester Model 1894 in cased set, features special embellishments and W.A.C.A. emblems and medallions. 100 sets were advertised, but only 22 were sold, ser. no. range N/A.

	$2,995	$2,695	22 sets

1990 WYOMING CENTENNIAL .30-30 - ser. no. range N/A.

	$1,495	$895	500

This model was distributed exclusively by Cherry's, located in Greensboro, NC.

1991 125TH ANNIVERSARY .30-30 - ser. no. range N/A.

	$6,000	$4,995	61

This model was distributed exclusively by Cherry's, located in Greensboro, NC.

1992 KENTUCKY BICENTENNIAL .30-30 - Winchester Model 94 with true charcoal case coloring, engraving depicts important KY graphics, serial numbered KY001- KY500.

	$1,495	$995	500

This model was distributed exclusively by Cherry's, located in Greensboro, NC.

1992 ARAPAHO .30-30 - features gold-plated receiver with etched Indian scenes on both sides, checkered semi-fancy American walnut stock, ser. no. range N/A.

	$1,495	$895	500

This model was distributed exclusively by Cherry's, located in Greensboro, NC.

GRADING - PPGS™	100%	Issue Price	Qty. Made

1993 NEZ PERCE MODEL 94 CARBINE - features nickel finished receiver and barrel bands, extensively etched receiver, checkered semi-fancy American walnut stock and forearm, serial numbered NEZ 001-NEZ 600.

$1,495	$950	600	

This model was distributed exclusively by Cherry's, located in Greensboro, NC.

1995 FLORIDA SESQUICENTENNIAL 94 CARBINE - features motifs from Florida, including alligator scene and space shuttle launch, 24kt. gold-plated receiver, 500 mfg. ser. numbered FL001-FL500 during 1995 only.

$1,495	$1,195	500	

This model was distributed exclusively by Cherry's, located in Greensboro, NC.

1997 EARP BROTHERS MODEL 94 CARBINE - features engraving motifs with multi-colored cameos of the characters involved in the Tombstone OK Corral gunfight, gold-plated hammer, trigger, and barrel bands, crossbolt safety. 250 Mfg. 1997 only, ser. no. range N/A.

$1,495	$1,195	250	

This model was distributed exclusively by Cherry's, located in Greensboro, NC.

WINCHESTER COMMEMORATIVES: NON-DOMESTIC - 1970 TO DATE

1970 NORTH WEST TERRITORIES (CANADIAN) - ser. no. range NWT501-NWT3106.

$850	$150	2,500	

1970 NORTHWEST TERRITORIES DELUXE (CANADIAN) - ser. no. range NWT1-NWT500.

$1,100	$250	500	

1973 YELLOW BOY (SOLD IN EUROPE ONLY) - ser. no. range YB1- YB4903.

$1,150	$150	4,903	

1973 M.P.X. (MADE ESPECIALLY FOR A MOVIE) - ser. no. range MPX1- MPX32.

$4,995	$78	32	

1973 R.C.M.P. (CANADIAN) - ser. no. range RCMP1- RCMP10442, not all shipped.

$795	$190	9,500	

1973 R.C.M.P. MEMBERS ISSUE (CANADIAN) - ser. no. range MP1- MP5100, not all shipped.

$795	$190	4,850	

1973 R.C.M.P. PRESENTATION - (CANADIAN) - ser. no. range RCMP1P-RCMP10P.

$9,995	N/A	10	

1974 APACHE (CANADIAN) - ser. no. range AC1- AC10200, not all shipped.

$795	$150	8,600	

1975 KLONDIKE GOLD RUSH (CANADIAN) - ser. no. range KGR1- KGR10200.

$795	$230	10,200	

1975 K.G.R. (DAWSON CITY ISSUE) - (CANADIAN) - ser. no. range D1KGR-D25KGR.

$8,500	N/A	25	

1975 COMANCHE (CANADIAN) - ser. no. range CC1- CC11511.

$795	$230	11,511	

1976 SIOUX (CANADIAN) - ser. no. range SU1- SU12000, not all shipped.

$795	$280	10,000	

1976 LITTLE BIG HORN (CANADIAN) - ser. no. range LBH1- LBH11000.

$795	$230	11,000	

1977 CHEYENNE (CANADIAN) - .44-40 WCF Cal., ser. no. range CH1- CH13000, not all shipped.

$795	$300	11,225	

GRADING - PPGS™	100%	Issue Price	Qty. Made

1977 CHEYENNE (CANADIAN) - .22 LR Cal., ser. no. range CHF1- CHF8221, not all shipped.

	$750	$320	5,000

1978 CHEROKEE (CANADIAN) - .30-30 Win. Cal., ser. no. range CK1- CK9000.

	$795	$385	9,000

1978 CHEROKEE (CANADIAN) - .22 LR Cal., ser. no. range CHF1- CHF4286, not all shipped.

	$750	$385	3,950

1978 ONE OF ONE THOUSAND (SOLD IN EUROPE ONLY) - no ser. no. prefix or suffix.

	$7,995	$5,000	250

This model was not advertised in the U.S.

1980 ALBERTA DIAMOND JUBILEE (CANADIAN) - ser. no. range ADJ301- ADJ3000.

	$795	$650	2,700

1980 A.D.J. DELUXE PRESENTATION (CANADIAN) - ser. no. range ADJ1- ADJ300.

	$1,495	$1,900	300

1980 SASKATCHEWAN DIAMOND JUBILEE (CANADIAN) - ser. no. range SDJ301- SDJ3000.

	$795	$695	2,700

1980 S.D.J. DELUXE PRESENTATION (CANADIAN) - ser. no. range SDJ1- SDJ300.

	$1,495	$1,995	300

1981 CALGARY STAMPEDE (CANADIAN) - ser. no. range CS1- CS1000.

	$1,250	$2,200	1,000

1981 CANADIAN PACIFIC CENTENNIAL (CANADIAN) - ser. no. range CPC301- CPC3000.

	$695	$800	2,700

1981 CANADIAN PACIFIC CENTENNIAL PRESENTATION (CANADIAN) - ser. no. range CPC1- CPC300.

	$1,100	$2,200	300

1981 CANADIAN PACIFIC (EMPL.) - (CANADIAN) - ser. no. range CP1- CP2000.

	$695	$800	2,000

1981 JOHN WAYNE (CANADIAN) - ser. no. range CJW1- CJW1000.

	$1,495	$995	1,000

1986 SECOND SERIES EUROPEAN 1 OF 1,000 - mfg. for European sales only 1986, ser. no. range N/A.

	$6,500	$6,000	150

1992 ONTARIO CONSERVATION - this model was marketed in Canada only, ser. no. range N/A.

	$1,495	$1,195	400

WINSLOW ARMS COMPANY

Previous manufacturer located in Camden, SC.

RIFLES: BOLT ACTION

WINSLOW BOLT ACTION SPORTING RIFLE - offered with various actions, FN Supreme, Mark X Mauser, Rem. 700 and 788, Sako, and Win. 70, offered in all popular calibers from .17 Rem. to .458 Mag., standard calibers have 24 in. barrels and 3 shot magazines, magnum calibers have 26 in. barrels and 2 shot magazines, two style stocks, "Bushmaster Conventional," slender pistol grip and beavertail forearm, "Plainsmaster," full curl, hooked pistol grip and flat wide forearm, both are Monte Carlo with cheekpieces, recoil pads and swivels,

GRADING - PPGS™	100%	98%	95%	90%	80%	70%	60%

walnut, maple, and myrtle are used with rosewood forend tip and pistol grip cap, rifle comes in 8 basic grades, custom embellishments can increase values greatly, discretion must be used, values are for basic models.

COMMANDER GRADE

	$1,750	$1,500	$1,275	$1,025	$850	$725	$600

REGAL GRADE

	$1,875	$1,625	$1,300	$1,050	$875	$750	$625

REGENT GRADE

	$1,995	$1,675	$1,350	$1,100	$925	$800	$675

REGIMENTAL GRADE

	$2,750	$2,350	$2,050	$1,750	$1,500	$1,250	$1,000

CROWN GRADE

	$3,000	$2,500	$2,175	$1,850	$1,575	$1,325	$1,100

ROYAL GRADE

	$3,450	$2,950	$2,500	$2,150	$1,750	$1,500	$1,250

IMPERIAL GRADE

	$3,850	$3,500	$3,050	$2,700	$2,375	$2,000	$1,750

EMPEROR GRADE

	$6,200	$5,650	$5,000	$4,400	$3,700	$3,000	$2,350

WISCHO JAGD-UND SPORTWAFFEN GmbH & CO. KG

Current European firearms and airgun importer located in Erlangen, Germany. Wischo makes a complete line of shotguns, rifles, pistols, and revolvers. No current U.S. importation. Please contact the factory directly for more information regarding model lineup, availability, and pricing (see Trademark Index).

WISEMAN, BILL AND CO.

Current custom rifle and pistol manufacturer located in College Station, TX. Wiseman/McMillan also manufactures rifle barrels and custom stocks.

PISTOLS

SILHOUETTE PISTOL - various cals., Sako action, 14 in. Wiseman/McMillan fluted stainless barrel, 5 or 7 shot magazine, laminate or fiberglass (new 1999) pistol grip stock, no sights, 4 1/2-5 1/2 lbs. Limited mfg. 1989-2002.

	$1,295	$1,000	$900	$800	$750	$700	$650

Last MSR was $1,295.

Subtract $200 for fiberglass stock.

RIFLES: BOLT ACTION

Add 11% excise tax to prices shown for new manufacture. Some models listed have very limited production.

HUNTER MODEL - available in various cals., Sako action, similar to TSR2, stainless steel barrel by Wiseman/McMillan, laminate stock, teflon finished metal parts, Pachmayr Decelerator pad, sling swivels.

MSR $3,395	$3,395	$2,750	$2,350	$1,850	$1,425	$1,150	$925

HUNTER DELUXE - similar to Hunter Model except has TSR1 action and custom checkering.

MSR $3,995	$3,995	$3,500	$3,000	$2,500	$1,900	$1,450	$1,100

Add $500 for detachable mag.

MAVERICK - similar to Hunter but with black fiberglass stock. Disc. 2003.

	$1,995	$1,575	$1,200	$1,050	$900	$775	$675

Last MSR was $1,995.

GRADING - PPGS™	100%	98%	95%	90%	80%	70%	60%

VARMENTER - similar to Hunter but with thumbhole stock. Disc. 2003.

	$2,395	$1,925	$1,500	$1,250	$1,025	$875	$775

Last MSR was $2,395.

TEXAS SAFARI RIFLE (TSR) - various cals., choice of hidden mag. (no floorplate), standard floorplate or 4 shot detachable mag., regular or 2/3 position tang safety, stainless steel fluted or non-fluted barrel with or w/o integral muzzle brake, synthetic stock. New 1996.

MSR $2,295	$2,295	$1,725	$1,250	$1,050	$830	$710	$590

Add $500 for 4 shot detachable mag. (TSR1).
Add $395 for extra magazine concealed in stock.
Add $195 for 2 or 3 position tang safety.
Add $195 for fluted barrel or muzzle brake.
Add $195 for extra straight in-line feed magazine.

TSR TACTICAL - .300 Win. Mag., .308 Win., or .338 Lapua Mag., 5 shot inline, detachable mag., or standard floorplate, synthetic stock with adj. cheekpiece, stainless steel fluted barrel with integral muzzle brake, guaranteed 1/2 minute of angle. Mfg. 1996-2003.

	$2,795	$2,200	$1,700	$1,500	$1,235	$1,030	$855

Last MSR was $2,795.

Add $195 for fluted barrel.
Add $195 for muzzle brake.
Add $150 for 3 position safety.

WOLF SPORTING PISTOLS

Previous trademark of pistols manufactured in Vienna, Austria. Previously imported and distributed by J R Distributing, located in Moorpark, CA until 1999.

Wolf pistols were noted for their features, quality construction, and were based on the M 1911 type action.

WOODWARD, JAMES AND SONS

Previously mfg. in London, England. Acquired by James Purdey & Sons in January 1949. In 1996, James Purdey & Sons once again started manufacturing a best quality Woodward shotgun.

SHOTGUNS: DOUBLE AND SINGLE BARREL

Woodward made one of the world's finest shotguns. They were formally acquired by J. Purdey and Sons on January 1, 1949. Most of the long guns they made were custom built and grading and pricing should be done individually. It is strongly recommended to get competent professional appraisals when contemplating a Woodward purchase or sale.

All new prices do not include VAT.

BEST QUALITY SxS SHOTGUN - custom-built in all gauges, barrel lengths and chokes, sidelock, auto ejectors, stocked to specifications, pre-WWII and new mfg. circa 1996-2003.

	$29,950	$26,000	$23,000	$19,950	$17,000	$14,250	$12,000

Last MSR was £40,100 (20 ga. only).

Add 50% for 20 ga.
Add 100% for 28 ga.
Add 150% for .410 bore.
Add $1,000 for SST

BEST QUALITY O/U SHOTGUN - custom-built in all gauges, barrel lengths, and chokes, VR, sidelock, auto ejectors, stocked to customer specifications, pre-WWII and new mfg. by special order only beginning 1996.

✳ *Best Quality O/U Shotgun - 1996-Current Mfg.* - 12, 16, 20, 28 ga., or .410 bore. This model is POR. The last posted MSR was £55,000.

GRADING - PPGS™	100%	98%	95%	90%	80%	70%	60%

✻ *Best Quality O/U Shotgun - Pre-WWII Mfg.*

	N/A	$35,000	$31,500	$27,500	$23,000	$19,000	$16,000

Add 75% for 20 ga.
Add 125% for 28 ga.
.410 bore - 2 mfg., too rare to accurately predict. Big Buck$!
Add $1,000 for ST.

BEST QUALITY SINGLE BARREL TRAP GUN - 12 ga. only, limited mfg. pre-WWII only.

	$12,750	$10,000	$8,950	$7,725	$6,500	$5,750	$4,900

WYOMING ARMS MFG. CORP.

Previous manufacturer located in Thermopolis, WY. Very small quantities of Parker pistols were mfg.

PARKER PISTOLS: STAINLESS STEEL

STANDARD PISTOL - 9mm Para., 10mm, .40 S&W, or .45 ACP cal., 3 3/8, 5, or 7 in. barrel, 7 (.45 ACP), 8 (10mm & .40 S&W), or 9 (9mm Para.) shot mag., Millett adj. sights, grooved synthetic grips, 29-39 oz. Disc. 1992.

	$350	$300	$250	$195	$165	$140	$120

Last MSR was $399.

Add $50 for 7 in. barrel.

.357 MAG. - .357 Mag. cal., single action semi-auto, 7 in. barrel, adj. sights, 8 shot mag., lifetime warranty, 44 oz. Disc. 1992.

	$425	$350	$300	$240	$210	$180	$155

Last MSR was $479.

St. Francis and the Wolf (Gubbio, Italy)
courtesy Clint H. Schmidt

IF YOU WORK WITH YOUR HANDS, YOU ARE A WORKER.

IF YOU WORK WITH YOUR HANDS AND YOUR HEAD, YOU ARE A CRAFTSMAN.

IF YOU WORK WITH YOUR HANDS, HEAD AND HEART, YOU ARE AN ARTIST.

- ST. FRANCIS OF ASSISI

NOTES

Y-Z SECTION

YILDIZ SILAH SANAYI

Current shotgun manufacturer located in Burdur, Turkey. Currently imported exclusively by Academy Sports (multiple locations).

SHOTGUNS

Yildiz Silah Sanayi manufactures good quality O/U, SxS, semi-auto, slide action and single barrel shotguns, using a wide variety of wood, engraving, and configurations. Please contact the importer directly for more information on pricing and U.S. availability (see Trademark Index).

Z-B RIFLE

Previous trademark of rifles manufactured by Brno & Uhersky Brod, located in Czechoslovakia.

GRADING - PPGS™	100%	98%	95%	90%	80%	70%	60%

RIFLES: BOLT ACTION

Z-B MAUSER VARMINT RIFLE - .22 Hornet cal., short Mauser bolt action, 23 in. barrel, double set triggers, 3 leaf sight, checkered pistol grip stock (also known as Brno Hornet).

	100%	98%	95%	90%	80%	70%	60%
	$825	$745	$690	$605	$550	$470	$415

ZDF IMPORT EXPORT INC.

Current importer located in Salt Lake City, UT, since 1995.

RIFLES: SEMI-AUTO

Please refer to Robinson Armament listing.

Z-HAT CUSTOM

Current custom rifle manufacturer located in Casper, WY.

RIFLES: CUSTOM

Z-Hat Custom builds four basic rifles, with a variety of options and special features, based on a customer supplied action. The Hunter starts at $2,549, the Pro Stalker starts at $2,735, the Varmint Hunter starts at $2,598, and the Mountaineer starts at $3,398. Please contact the company directly for more information, including available options, pricing, and delivery time (see Trademark Index).

Z-M WEAPONS

Current rifle manufacturer and pistol components maker located in Bernardston, MA. Dealer and consumer direct sales.

PISTOLS: SEMI-AUTO

STRIKE PISTOL - .38 Super, .40 S&W, or .45 ACP cal., several configurations available, with or without compensator. Limited mfg. 1997-2000.

	100%	98%	95%	90%	80%	70%	60%
	$2,375	$1,825	$1,700	$1,400	$1,150	$995	$750

Last MSR was $2,695.

RIFLES: SEMI-AUTO

LR 300 & VARIATIONS - .223 Rem. cal., modified gas system using AR-15 style action, features pivoting skeletal metal stock, 16 1/4 in. barrel, flattop receiver, matte finish, aluminum or Nylatron handguard, 7.2 lbs. New 1997.

MSR $2,208	$2,100	$1,800	$1,550	$1,300	$1,100	$900	$750

Add $23 for Nylatron handguard.
Add $50 for Military/Law Enforcement model.
Add $75 for Military/Law Enforcement model with Nylatron handguard.

GRADING - PPGS™	100%	98%	95%	90%	80%	70%	60%

ZABALA HERMANOS, S.A.

Current manufacturer established in 1932 and located in Eibar, Spain. Z. Hermanos is currently private labeling shotguns for KBI, Inc. (Charles Daly SxSs only) and Tristar, located in N. Kansas City. Previously imported and distributed by American Arms located in Kansas City, MO, until 2000, and by Galef Shotguns.

SHOTGUNS

Zabala Hermanos manufactures good quality boxlock SxS shotguns (Models 213 €370 - €430 MSR, Kestrel €370 MSR, Berri €380 - €510 MSR, Vencedor Magnum (sideplates) €550 - €590 MSR, Sporting Magnum €535 MSR, and the Anthea Magnum €560 - €600, O/U shotguns (XL 90 Series €445 - †690 MSR, Suprema Magnum †510 MSR, and Century Classic Magnum €530 MSR) and sidelock SxS shotguns (Vencedor Model €720 - €758 MSR). To date, the company has produced over 600,000 long guns, and remains family owned. For more information regarding this trademark, (including availability) please contact the manufacturer directly (see Trademark Index).

ZANARDINI

Current manufacturer established in 1946, and located in Brescia, Italy. Currently imported by S.O.G. Arms, located in Hacienda Heights, CA. Several U.S. firms have stocked a few Zanardini models in the past, but not the complete line.

All rifles and shotguns are custom-built. For current information and up-to-date pricing, please contact the importer directly (see Trademark Index).

The values listed represent older importation.

COMBINATION GUNS: O/U

Zanardini is currently offering the Model 2000 Deluxe Super Light (with or w/o new loading system), and the Boxer Model with H&H style sidelocks.

PRINCESS - super light variation.

	100%	98%	95%	90%	80%	70%	60%
	$4,400	$3,850	$3,300	$2,800	$2,400	$2,000	$1,600

Last MSR was $5,085.

BOXER MODEL - H&H styled sidelocks, top-quality engraving.

	$11,000	$9,250	$8,000	$7,000	$6,000	$5,000	$4,150

Last MSR was $12,500.

BOXER 4-LOCKS MODEL

	$8,200	$7,300	$6,400	$5,500	$4,600	$3,750	$3,000

Last MSR was $9,200.

402 STRAUSS - top-of-the-line combination gun with best quality engraving and wood.

	$18,000	$16,000	$14,000	$12,000	$10,000	$8,000	$6,000

RIFLES

FUCHS A FOLDING RIFLE - double lock system.

MSR $5,000	$4,550	$3,750	$3,000	$2,600	$2,250	$1,675	$1,250

PRINZ A 401 SUPER DELUXE SINGLE SHOT - internal and external hammers.

MSR $35,000	$30,500	$26,000	$20,000	$17,500	$15,000	$12,500	$11,000

✳ *Prinz B 401 Super Deluxe Single Shot*

MSR $21,000	$18,000	$15,500	$13,000	$10,750	$8,750	$6,400	$4,400

✳ *Prinz C 401 Super Deluxe Single Shot Standard*

MSR $7,200	$6,400	$5,600	$4,800	$4,200	$3,700	$3,250	$2,800

403 OXFORD SxS - 9.3x74R and smaller cals.

MSR $7,700	$6,800	$6,000	$5,400	$4,900	$4,300	$3,750	$3,150

GRADING - PPGS™	100%	98%	95%	90%	80%	70%	60%

✱ *403 Oxford SxS Larger cals.* - .375 H&H Mag., .458 Win. Mag., or .470 Nitro cal.

	100%	98%	95%	90%	80%	70%	60%
MSR $15,200	$13,500	$12,000	$10,500	$9,000	$7,750	$6,500	$5,650

Add approx. 135% for .470 Nitro cal.

EXPRESS RIFLE SxS - .470 NE cal., boxlock action, ST, checkered walnut stock (with cheekpiece), express sights. Other cals. available upon special order.

MSR $18,000	$16,500	$14,000	$12,000	$10,000	$8,750	$7,500	$6,250

409 BRISTOL SxS - H & H style sidelock, ejectors, ST or DT.

MSR $42,000	$37,500	$32,000	$28,000	$23,000	$19,000	$17,500	$15,000

407 OXFORD SL SxS - Anson & Deeley scalloped reinforced boxlock action, ejectors, ST or DT.

MSR $29,900	$26,000	$22,000	$18,250	$16,000	$14,000	$12,000	$10,000

KONIG SIDELOCK O/U - 7.65R or 9.3x74R cal., H&H style sidelock, ejectors.

MSR $54,000	$46,000	$40,000	$34,000	$27,000	$22,000	$19,000	$17,000

KONIG BOXLOCK O/U - Anson & Deely boxlock.

MSR $30,000	$27,000	$22,000	$18,000	$15,000	$12,500	$10,000	$8,000

SHOTGUNS: SxS

Models listed are available in 12, 16, 20, 28 ga., or .410 bore, magnum chambers in 20 and 12 ga.

HAMMER LONDON MODEL SxS - features external hammers.

	$18,250	$16,250	$14,250	$12,250	$10,250	$8,750	$7,250

Last MSR was $21,500.

HAMMERLESS LONDON MODEL SxS - 12 or 20 ga.

Prices on this model range from $22,000-$29,995 depending on engraving.

DONAU STANDARD MODEL SxS - boxlock action.

MSR $21,000	$18,500	$16,000	$14,000	$12,000	$10,000	$8,000	$6,000

DONAU SIDELOCK SxS - H&H style sidelock action.

Prices on this model range from $34,000 - $36,000, depending on engraving.

PRESTIGE TRAP AND SKEET SxS

MSR $5,200	$4,750	$4,000	$3,400	$2,800	$2,400	$2,000	$1,600

HASE CACCIA MONTECATINI SxS - boxlock action, double set triggers, extractors.

MSR $2,100	$1,850	$1,600	$1,400	$1,200	$1,050	$900	$700

Add 30% for ejectors.

HORN MODEL SxS - boxlock action, double set triggers, extractors.

MSR $2,250	$1,950	$1,700	$1,500	$1,250	$1,100	$950	$775

Add 40% for ejectors.

ZANOTTI, ARMORIA

Current manufacturer established during 1625, and located in Bologna, Italy. Previously located in Brescia, Italy. Currently imported beginning 2008 by Zanotti USA, located in Houston, TX. Previous company names were Zanotti 1625 and Fabio Zanotti. Previously imported and distributed by New England Arms Corp. located in Kittery Point, ME until 1999. Zanotti became part of the Renato Gamba Group in 1985.

Zanotti is one of the world's oldest quality shotgun manufacturers. Values on discontinued guns listed are for previous importation (ended approx. 2000). Current values may have gone up due to the devaluation of the dollar against the euro.

Currently, Zanotti is manufacturing a SxS double rifle and a SxS shotgun on a custom order basis only. Please contact the importer directly for an individualized price quotation.

GRADING - PPGS™	100%	98%	95%	90%	80%	70%	60%

SHOTGUNS: O/U

MODEL 725 - 28 ga. or .410 bore only, scalloped case hardened shallow frame, DT or ST, ejectors, game scene and scroll engraving, custom built to individual specifications.

$6,000	$4,500	$3,650	$3,000	$2,450	$2,000	$1,875

Last MSR was $7,000 (circa 2000).

CASSIANO - 12, 20, 28 ga., or .410 bore, Boss style shallow action, best quality gun built to individual specifications. Prices started at $27,500 and went up accordingly.

SHOTGUNS: SxS

Add $500 for ST.
Add $250 for beavertail forearm.
Add $650 for leather case.

MODEL 625 BOXLOCK

$6,275	$5,500	$4,250	$3,150	$2,500	$2,000	$1,750

Last MSR was $7,000 (circa 2000).

MODEL 626 BOXLOCK - scroll, game scene, or combination engraving.

$7,000	$6,000	$4,450	$3,375	$2,750	$2,175	$1,900

Last MSR was $7,995 (circa 2000).

MODEL GIACINTO - hammer gun.

$5,875	$5,300	$4,000	$2,950	$2,400	$1,900	$1,650

Last MSR was $6,500 (circa 2000).

MODEL MAXIM SIDELOCK

$10,750	$8,600	$7,450	$6,200	$5,200	$4,600	$3,850

Last MSR was $12,000 (circa 2000).

MODEL EDWARD SIDELOCK

$13,000	$9,900	$8,700	$7,000	$5,875	$5,000	$4,000

Last MSR was $15,000 (circa 2000).

MODEL CASSIANO I SIDELOCK

$15,500	$13,250	$9,900	$8,700	$7,000	$5,875	$5,000

Last MSR was $17,500 (circa 2000).

MODEL CASSIANO II

$17,750	$15,500	$13,250	$9,900	$8,700	$7,000	$5,875

Last MSR was $20,000 (circa 2000).

CASSIANO EXECUTIVE - prices varied per individual order, top-of-the-line model. Prices started at $20,000.

ZASTAVA ARMS

Current manufacturer established in 1853, and located in Serbia. Currently, certain models are imported by Remington, located in Madison, NC, and by EAA, located in Rockledge, FL. KBI previously imported certain models and actions until 2005. Previously distributed by Advanced Weapons Technologies, located in Athens, Greece, and by Nationwide Sports Distributors, located in Southampton, PA. Previously imported by T.D. Arms, followed by Brno U.S.A., circa 1990.

Zastava Arms makes a wide variety of quality pistols, rifles, and sporting shotguns. Currently, Zastava Arms has been subcontracted by Remington Arms Co. to make certain bolt action rifle models.

GRADING - PPGS™	100%	98%	95%	90%	80%	70%	60%

HANDGUNS: SEMI-AUTO

MODEL CZ99 - 9mm Para. or .40 S&W cal., double action, 15 shot, 4 1/4 in. barrel, short recoil, choice of various finishes, SIG locking system, hammer drop safety, ambidextrous controls, 3-dot Tritium sighting system, alloy frame, firing pin block, loaded chamber indicator, squared-off trigger guard, checkered dark grey polymer grips, 32 oz.

$450	$395	$365	$330	$300	$285	$265

Last MSR was $495.

While a latter Z9 was advertised, it was never commercially imported. All guns were CZ99 or CZ40.

Zastava CZ99 configurations (with finishes) included matte blue with synthetic grips (500 imported), commercial blue with synthetic grips (750 imported), military "painted finish" with synthetic grips (1,000 imported), matte blue finish with checkered wood grips (115 imported), high polish blue with checkered grips (115 imported), and military "painted finish" with wood grips (2 prototypes only).

MODEL CZ999 SCORPION - 9mm Para. cal., similar to CZ99, except has indicator for the last three rounds in the magazine, fire selector for pistol and revolver mode.

This pistol was imported by K.B.I. as the ZDA model. Please refer to the Charles Daly semi-auto pistol section.

MODEL CZ40 - .40 S&W cal., 55 prototypes were imported for testing, but most had a feeding problem due to improper magazine design, mag. design changes were planned, but were cancelled due to the Serbian/Croatian war.

Suggested retail was $495.

RIFLES: BOLT ACTION

Since 1881, Zastava Arms has remained loyal to Mauser system with all the innovations that followed for the past century. Today, Zastava arms produces sporting rifles, based on Mauser system, in many calibers. Barrels for sporting rifles are made of high quality chrome-vanadium steel, by cold forging. Various versions of sporting rifles made by Zastava arms provide a choice of three types of triggering mechanism, three types of stock, assembly of optical sights and different styles engravings.

MODEL CZ22 - .22 LR, .22 Mag. or .22 Hornet cal., 35 of each cal. imported circa 1990. Suggested retail was $275.

$225	$195	$175	$150	$135	$120	$110

Add 15% for .22 Mag. or .22 Hornet cal.

MODEL CZ99 PRECISION - .22 LR or .22 Mag. cal., rotating bolt.

Please refer to the Remington Model Five listing in the Remington section.

MODEL LK M70 - .22-250 Rem., 6mm Rem., 6.5x57mm, 7x57mm, 8x57mm, .270 Win., 7x64mm, .30-06, .25-06 Rem., 6.5x55mm, 9.3x62mm, .243 Win., .308 Win., .264 Win. Mag., 7mm Rem. Mag., .300 Win.Mag., .375 H&H, or .458 Win.Mag. cal., sporting rifle, Mauser action. Previously imported by Interarms, American Arms and K.B.I.

Please refer to the Remington Model 798 listing in the Remington section.

MODEL LK M85 - .22 Hornet, .222 Rem., .222 Rem. Mag., .22-250 Rem., .223 Rem., or 7.62x39mm cal., sporting rifle with mini-Mauser system. Previously iomported by Interarms, American Arms and K.B.I.

Please refer to the Remington Model 799 listing in the Remington section.

ZIEGENHAHN & SOHN OHG

Current custom gun manufacturer established in 1923, and located in Zella-Mehlis, Germany. Currently imported by New England Custom Gun Service, Ltd., located in Plainfield, NH, and by Heirloom Armes, located in Howard Lake, MN.

Ziegenhahn & Sohn manufactures high quality, classic Anson & Deeley boxlock "Big Five" double rifles with Holland & Holland pattern sidelocks and ejectors, and sidelocks

GRADING - PPGS™	100%	98%	95%	90%	80%	70%	60%

in calibers up to .500 NE., with larger calibers also available upon request. Ziegenhahn & Sohn also manufactures high quality shotguns, drillings, and combination guns with a variety of custom order options, including traditional bone charcoal color case hardening. Please contact the importer directly for current pricing, availability, and delivery time.

Ziegenhahn currently is building the Krieghoff Essencia SxS in 20 ga. with back action - please refer to the Krieghoff section for more information.

ZEPHYR

Previous Stoeger trademark of guns manufactured in Spain, and imported by Stoegers circa 1930s-1972.

RIFLES

Stoeger's has imported a wide variety of bolt action rifles during the past 60 years. Rather than list the many models individually, each Zephyr rifle should be compared to a gun of equal caliber, quality, and features to ascertain an approximate value range.

SHOTGUNS: SxS

WOODLANDER II - 12 or 20 ga., various chokes, boxlock, double triggers, extractors, engraved, checkered pistol grip stock.

	100%	98%	95%	90%	80%	70%	60%
	$495	$440	$385	$360	$305	$275	$250

UPLANDER (4E) - 12, 16, 20, 28 ga., or .410 bore, sidelock action, double triggers, ejectors, engraved.

	$775	$695	$640	$585	$570	$480	$440

STERLINGWORTH II - similar to Woodlander, with sidelock action.

	$825	$725	$660	$605	$580	$525	$495

VICTOR SPECIAL - 12 ga., 25, 28, or 30 in. barrels, various chokes, double triggers, extractors, checkered pistol grip stock.

	$440	$385	$330	$305	$250	$220	$195

UPLAND KING - 12 or 16 ga., sidelock, single trigger, VR, ejectors, fully engraved.

	$1,000	$900	$800	$725	$650	$600	$550

THUNDERBIRD - 10 ga. Mag, 32 in. barrels, double triggers, French walnut, engraved.

	$850	$750	$625	$550	$510	$490	$475

Add $175 for ejectors.

SHOTGUNS: SINGLE SHOT

HONKER - 10 ga. Mag., 36 in. VR barrel, lightly engraved.

	$500	$460	$420	$350	$310	$290	$270

VANDALIA TRAP - 12 ga. Trap Model, 32 in. barrel, engraved.

	$700	$620	$575	$525	$475	$425	$390

ZOLI, ANGELO

Previous manufacturer located in Brescia, Italy. Previously imported and distributed exclusively by Angelo Zoli USA located in Addison, IL. Mfg. 1985-87.

Angelo Zoli went out of business in December, 1987 and was taken over by the Italian Bank of Brescia in 1989. Many people tend to confuse the shotguns of Angelo and Antonio Zoli (it is hard to determine which manufacturer made a gun marked "A. Zoli"). There is no correlation between these trademarks and Antonio Zoli DOES NOT have parts for these earlier Angelo Zoli long arms. Even though both trademarks may indicate "A. ZOLI" for a barrel address, they are mostly discernable by the model listings under both headings in this section.

GRADING - PPGS™	100%	98%	95%	90%	80%	70%	60%

COMBINATION GUNS

AIRONE - 12 ga./.30-06 or .308 Win. cal., boxlock with false sideplates, double triggers, checkered walnut stock and forearm, swivels. Disc. 1987.

	$1,450	$1,275	$1,050	$900	$800	$700	$600

CONDOR - similar to Airone, except does not have false sideplates. Disc. 1987.

	$1,295	$1,050	$725	$675	$525	$400	$300

RIFLES: SxS

LEOPARD EXPRESS - .30-06, .308 Win., .375 H&H Mag., or 7x65R cal., boxlock action, double triggers, checkered walnut stock and forearm. Disc. 1987.

	$1,325	$1,150	$975	$725	$600	$425	$300

Last MSR was $1,529.

SHOTGUNS: O/U

SNIPE - .410 bore, 3 in. chambers, 26 or 28 in. barrels, single trigger. Disc. 1987.

	$230	$200	$185	$170	$155	$145	$135

Last MSR was $265.

TEXAS - all gauges, 26 or 28 in. barrels, double triggers, folding design, lever action. Disc. 1987.

	$250	$220	$200	$185	$170	$155	$145

Last MSR was $291.

DOVE - .410 bore only, 3 in. chambers, 26 or 28 in. barrels, single trigger. Disc. 1987.

	$260	$230	$200	$185	$170	$155	$145

Last MSR was $306.

FIELD SPECIAL - 12, 20, or 28 ga., 3 in. chambers, various barrel lengths and chokings, single trigger. Disc. 1987.

	$450	$400	$360	$330	$300	$270	$240

Last MSR was $699.

PIGEON MODEL - 12 or 20 ga., 3 in. chambers, various barrel lengths, single trigger. Disc. 1987.

	$350	$295	$270	$250	$220	$195	$175

Last MSR was $394.

Add $60 for 20 ga.

STANDARD MODEL - 12 or 20 ga., 3 in. chambers, various barrel lengths and chokings, single trigger. Disc. 1987.

	$395	$345	$320	$300	$280	$260	$245

Last MSR was $459.

SILVER SNIPE - 12 or 20 ga., 3 in. chambers on the 20 ga., single trigger, ejectors, light engraving. Disc. 1987.

	$675	$585	$530	$485	$440	$400	$375

Last MSR was $739.

Add $50 for multi-chokes (12 ga. only).

This model was distributed by Euroarms of America, Inc.

CONDOR MODEL - 12 ga. skeet model, 28 in. barrels, SST, ejectors, wide VR, engraved silver finished receiver, recoil pad. Disc. 1987.

	$795	$700	$640	$585	$530	$485	$440

Last MSR was $895.

This model was distributed by Mandall Shooting Supplies, Inc.

GRADING - PPGS™	100%	98%	95%	90%	80%	70%	60%

TARGET MODEL 208 - 12 ga. only, available in either Trap, Skeet, or Monotrap configuration. Disc. 1987.

| | $895 | $775 | $550 | $475 | $300 | $275 | $200 |

Last MSR was $996.

Add $494 for Monotrap II 208 Model.

TARGET MODEL 308 - 12 ga. only, available in either Trap, Skeet, or Monotrap configuration. Disc. 1987.

| | $1,375 | $1,125 | $800 | $725 | $650 | $525 | $475 |

Last MSR was $1,581.

Add $76 for multi-chokes.
Add $824 for Monotrap II 308 Model.

SPECIAL MODEL - 12 ga. only, 3 in. chambers, various barrel lengths and chokings, SST. Disc. 1987.

| | $465 | $395 | $355 | $325 | $290 | $270 | $250 |

Last MSR was $528.

Add $120 for multi-chokes.

DELUXE MODEL - similar to Special Model, except better wood and engraving. Disc. 1987.

| | $645 | $550 | $495 | $450 | $400 | $360 | $320 |

Last MSR was $730.

Add $80 for multi-chokes.

PRESENTATION MODEL - 12 ga. only, includes sideplates. Disc. 1987.

| | $740 | $630 | $575 | $495 | $450 | $395 | $350 |

Last MSR was $842.

Add $42 for multi-chokes.

ANGEL MODEL - 12 ga. only, field grade, SST, ejectors, wide VR, engraved receiver, recoil pad. Disc. 1987.

| | $850 | $775 | $450 | $400 | $325 | $275 | $200 |

This model was distributed by Mandall Shooting Supplies, Inc.

ST. GEORGE'S TARGET - 12 ga. only, trap or skeet gun, SST, fixed choke. Disc. 1987.

| | $900 | $725 | $525 | $425 | $350 | $250 | $200 |

Last MSR was $1,024.

✳ *St. George's Competition* - 12 ga. only, includes 30 in. O/U barrels and single barrel multi-choke. Disc. 1987.

| | $1,995 | $1,750 | $1,000 | $900 | $800 | $650 | $550 |

Last MSR was $1,627.

PATRICIA MODEL - .410 bore only, 3 in. chambers, 28 in. barrels, SST. Disc. 1987.

| | $1,175 | $1,010 | $675 | $600 | $525 | $450 | $375 |

Last MSR was $1,345.

Add $121 for case.

SHOTGUNS: SxS

QUAIL SPECIAL - .410 bore, 3 in. chambers, single trigger, 28 in. barrels. Disc. 1987.

| | $205 | $185 | $170 | $150 | $125 | $110 | $100 |

Last MSR was $243.

FALCON II - .410 bore, 3 in. chambers, 26 or 28 in. barrels, double triggers. Disc. 1987.

| | $205 | $185 | $170 | $150 | $125 | $110 | $100 |

Last MSR was $246.

GRADING - PPGS™	100%	98%	95%	90%	80%	70%	60%

SILVER HAWK - 12 or 20 ga., double trigger, engraved.

| | $420 | $395 | $360 | $330 | $300 | $280 | $260 |

SILVER SNIPE - 12 or 20 ga., various barrel lengths, VR, single trigger, engraved.

| | $485 | $440 | $400 | $360 | $330 | $300 | $280 |

PHEASANT - 12 ga. only, 3 in. chambers, 28 in. barrels only, single trigger. Disc. 1987.

| | $370 | $320 | $300 | $280 | $260 | $240 | $220 |

Last MSR was $428.

ALLEY CLEANER - 12 or 20 ga., 3 in. chambers, 20 in. barrels, riot configuration, SST. Disc. 1987.

| | $575 | $495 | $460 | $420 | $390 | $350 | $310 |

Last MSR was $649.

Add $65 for multi-chokes.

CLASSIC - 12 or 20 ga., 3 in. chambers, 26-30 in. barrels, ST. Disc. 1989.

| | $995 | $875 | $750 | $650 | $550 | $475 | $400 |

Last MSR was $706.

Add $80 for multi-chokes.

SHOTGUNS: LEVER ACTION

APACHE - 12 ga. only, 3 in. chambers, 20 in. barrel, SST. Disc. 1987.

| | $410 | $355 | $275 | $225 | $175 | $125 | $100 |

Last MSR was $473.

Add $80 for multi-chokes.

SHOTGUNS: SINGLE BARREL

DIANO I - 12, 20 ga., or .410 bore, 3 in. chambers, top lever single barrel action, folding configuration, VR. Disc. 1987.

| | $115 | $95 | $85 | $80 | $75 | $70 | $65 |

Last MSR was $129.

DIANO II - similar to Diano I, except has bottom lever opening. Disc. 1987.

| | $115 | $95 | $85 | $80 | $75 | $70 | $65 |

Last MSR was $129.

LONER I - similar to Diano I. Disc. 1987.

| | $95 | $80 | $75 | $65 | $55 | $45 | $35 |

Last MSR was $109.

LONER II - similar to Diano II. Disc. 1987.

| | $95 | $80 | $75 | $65 | $55 | $45 | $35 |

Last MSR was $109.

SHOTGUNS: SLIDE ACTION

PUMP ACTION - 12 ga. only, available in riot, field, or deer (slug) barrel configurations, 3 in. chamber, hunter model has multi-chokes standard. Disc. 1987.

| | $290 | $245 | $205 | $185 | $170 | $150 | $125 |

Last MSR was $329.

ZOLI, ANTONIO

Current manufacturer established in 1945, and located in Brescia, Italy. Currently imported by and distributed beginning 2006 by Antonio Zoli America, located in Canandaigua, NY. Previously located in Weston, FL. O/U rifles were previously imported by Cape Outfitters, located in Cape Girardeau, MO. Previously imported and distributed (1990-91 only) by European American Armory Corp. located in Hialeah,

GRADING - PPGS™	100%	98%	95%	90%	80%	70%	60%

FL. Prior to 1990, A. Zoli was imported and distributed exclusively by Antonio Zoli U.S.A., Inc. located in Fort Wayne, IN.

Antonio Zoli firearms are totally unrelated to those guns of Angelo Zoli (guns marked "A. Zoli" make it hard to determine the correct manufacturer). Parts are not interchangeable and warranties from Antonio Zoli firearms DO NOT apply to Angelo Zoli guns.

COMBINATION GUNS

COMBINATO - 12 or 20 ga. over .243 Win. or .222 Rem. cal., boxlock action, game scene engraved frame with silver finish, double triggers, folding rear sight, skipline checkering, with sling swivels. Importation disc. 1993.

	$1,750	$1,500	$1,300	$1,100	$950	$775	$600

Last MSR was $1,995.

✱ *Combinato Set* - includes one set of either 20 or 12 ga. barrels and an additional rifle/shotgun barrel set, same cals. as Combinato, cased. Importation disc. 1993.

	$2,400	$2,150	$1,850	$1,600	$1,400	$1,200	$995

Last MSR was $2,700.

SAFARI DELUXE - similar to Combinato, except has sideplates with elaborate game scene engraving. Importation disc. 1993.

	$4,850	$4,400	$3,950	$2,100	$2,675	$2,400	$2,225

Last MSR was $5,200.

Add approx. 50% for Safari Deluxe 2 (includes 2 sets of shotgun barrels).

EXPRESS ELE3 SET - includes one set of .30-06 cal. O/U barrels, one set of 20 ga./.243 Win. cal. barrels, one set of 20 ga./20 ga. barrels, special order, elaborate game scene engraving, includes German claw mount 4X scope and case. Disc.

	$7,950	$7,250	$6,500	$5,750	$5,000	$4,500	$3,950

RIFLES: BOLT ACTION

AZ 1900C - .243 Win., .270 Win., 6.5x55mm, .30-06, .308 Win., 7mm Rem. Mag., or .300 Win. Mag. cal., 21 or 24 (Mag. cals.) in. barrel, checkered walnut stock with weatherproof stock finish, sling swivels, iron sights, 7.4 lbs. Importation disc. 1993.

	$1,100	$850	$740	$660	$585	$500	$450

Last MSR was $1,295.

Add approx. 10% for AZ 1900 Deluxe (better walnut).
Add 60% for AZ 1900 Super Deluxe (select walnut and moderate engraving).
Add approx. 10% for Model AZ 1900 DL (photo engraved receiver and floorplate).

MODEL AZ 1900M - .243 Win., 6.5x55mm, .270 Win., .30-06, or .308 Win. cal., 21 in. barrel, composite stock is composed of fiberglass, Kevlar, and graphite and features baked on walnut wood grain finish with checkering, drilled and tapped receiver. Imported 1991 only.

	$725	$625	$550	$495	$450	$415	$375

Last MSR was $840.

Add approx. 10% for Model AZ 1900M DL (photo engraved receiver and floorplate).

RIFLES: O/U

EXPRESS - 7x65R, 7x57mm, .30-06, .308 Win., or 9.3x74R cal., 25.6 in. barrels, hand checkered walnut stock with cheekpiece, set trigger for bottom barrel, extractors. Importation disc. 1993.

	$3,875	$3,250	$2,900	$2,600	$2,200	$1,950	$1,650

Last MSR was $4,400.

Add $600 for E Model (with ejectors).

GRADING - PPGS™	100%	98%	95%	90%	80%	70%	60%

EXPRESS EM - 7x65R, .30-06, .308 Win., or 9.3x74R cal., mechanical single trigger, ejectors. Importation disc. 1990, reintroduced 1992 only.

	100%	98%	95%	90%	80%	70%	60%
	$4,850	$3,975	$3,300	$2,900	$2,600	$2,200	$1,900

Last MSR was $5,300.

Add $2,395 for De Luxe Model (disc.).
Add $7,200 for E3 De Luxe Model (disc.).
The Express E3 De Luxe Model includes 2 extra sets of barrels - 1 set is shotgun (20 ga. - 2 3/4 or 3 in. chambers).

Z EXPRESS - 9.3x74R, .30-06, or 8x57mm cal., 22 in. barrel with open sights, standard features include Boss locking system, ejectors, monolithic forged frame, hand detachable mecahnical trigger, express rib with folding sights, oil finished Turksih walnut stock, scope mount and rings, includes aluminum case. Importation began 2008.

MSR $6,000		$5,500	$5,000	$4,500	$4,000	$3,500	$3,000	$2,500

Add $2,900 for interchangeable 20 or 28 ga. shotgun barrels.

Z EXPRESS AFRICAN - .450-400 Hornady Nitro cal., otherwise similar to Z Express Model.

MSR $10,500		$9,750	$8,500	$7,250	$6,000	$5,000	$4,000	$3,350

Z AMBASSADOR EL - similar to Z Express Model, except has better quality wood and more engraving. Importation began 2008.

MSR $11,000		$10,000	$8,750	$7,500	$6,250	$5,250	$4,250	$3,500

Add $2,900 for interchangeable 20 or 28 ga. barrels.

Z AMBASSADOR AFRICAN - similar to Z Express African Model, except has extra select walnut and more elaborate engraving. Importation began 2008.

MSR $15,500		$14,250	$12,500	$10,500	$8,750	$7,500	$6,250	$5,250

Add $2,900 for interchangeable 20 or 28 ga. barrels.

Z CUSTOM GRADE - Zoli's top-of-the-line double rifle, custom order only.
Base price on this model starts at $25,000.

RIFLES: SxS

SAVANA E - 7x65R, .30-06, .308 Win., or 9.3x74R cal., boxlock action, ejectors. Importation disc. 1990.

		$5,850	$4,850	$3,975	$3,300	$2,800	$2,350	$2,000

Last MSR was $6,600.

Add $400 for Savana EM Model (single trigger).

✳ *Savana E Deluxe* - similar to Savana E, except has elaborate game scene engraving. Importation disc. 1990.

		$7,750	$7,100	$6,500	$6,000	$5,500	$5,000	$4,600

Last MSR was $8,295.

SHOTGUNS: O/U, RECENT PRODUCTION

All newer manufactured Z guns from Antonio Zoli feature a detachable posi-lock trigger system, and ultra high quality barrels.

Please contact the importer directly for pricing on available options for currently manufactured shotguns (see Trademark Index).

GOLDEN SNIPE - 12 or 20 ga, various barrel lengths, VR, single trigger, ejectors, engraved.

		$560	$520	$475	$430	$395	$360	$330

DELFINO - 12 or 20 ga., 3 in. chambers, 26 or 28 in. barrels, ejectors, VR, single non-selective trigger, blue frame with delicate engraving, walnut pistol grip stock and forearm. Disc.

		$500	$425	$375	$325	$295	$280	$265

GRADING - PPGS™	100%	98%	95%	90%	80%	70%	60%

RITMO HUNTING - 12 ga. only, 3 in. chambers, 26 or 28 in. vent. barrels and rib, SST, ejectors, select checkered walnut, blue frame and barrels with moderate engraving, recoil pad, 7 1/4 lbs. Disc.

	$575	$510	$465	$410	$370	$350	$335

RITMO PIGEON GRADE IV - 12 ga. only, live pigeon gun, 28 in. barrels, SST, ejectors, superbly engraved silver finished receiver, extra fine checkering on deluxe walnut, vent. barrels and rib, cased, 7 1/2 lbs. Disc.

	$1,250	$1,100	$950	$800	$675	$600	$550

M85 RITMO TRAP OR SKEET - 12 ga. only, 28 in. (Skeet only), 30, or 32 in. barrels, ejectors, SST, special stock dimensions, engraved blue receiver, select checkered walnut stock and forearm, cased, 7 3/4 lbs. Disc.

	$595	$500	$465	$440	$415	$395	$370

This model was also available in a single barrel trap model at no extra charge.

✳ *M85 Ritmo Trap Combination* - 12 ga. only, supplied with O/U and single barrel sets, various barrel lengths, cased. Disc.

	$995	$895	$800	$700	$620	$575	$500

SILVER FALCON - 12 or 20 ga., 3 in. chambers, boxlock action, SST, ejectors, 26 or 28 in. barrels with multi-chokes, coin finished receiver with engraving, checkered Turkish walnut stock and forearm with weatherproof finish. Importation disc. 1991.

	$1,050	$600	$500	$400	$350	$300	$250

Last MSR was $1,695.

WOODSMAN - 12 ga. only, 3 in. chambers, 23 in. vent. barrels are designed to shoot rifle slugs at 55 yards and to accept 5 interchangeable choke tubes, SST, ejectors, quarter rib on barrels with pop-up rifle sights, checkered Circassian walnut stock and forearm with swivels (waterproof finish).

	$1,200	$1,000	$875	$750	$650	$550	$400

Last MSR was $1,895.

✳ *Woodsman Combo* - includes 2 sets of barrels (3 in. chambers) with Zoli interchangeable choke system.

	$1,800	$1,550	$1,400	$1,200	$1,050	$925	$800

Last MSR was $2,320.

MODEL Z-90 TARGET MODEL - 12 ga. only, boxlock action, adj. SST, black competition receiver, deluxe checkered Turkish walnut stock with recoil pad and forearm, vent. barrels and rib, SST, ejectors.

✳ *Model Z-90 Target Model Trap Gun* - 29 1/2 or 32 in. barrels with screw-in chokes and raised VR, Monte Carlo stock, blue finish. Importation disc. 1993.

	$1,700	$1,450	$1,050	$825	$775	$625	$500

Last MSR was $2,495.

✳ *Model Z-90 Target Model Mono Trap Gun* - 32 or 34 in. barrel with screw-in chokes and raised VR, Monte Carlo stock. Importation disc. 1993.

	$1,650	$1,450	$1,125	$850	$775	$625	$500

Last MSR was $2,495.

✳ *Model Z-90 Target Model Combo Trap Set* - includes O/U trap barrels as well as Mono trap barrel on same receiver, available as 30/32 in. sets or 32/34 in. sets. Imported 1991-92.

	$1,800	$1,750	$1,650	$925	$825	$750	$500

Last MSR was $2,700.

✳ *Model Z-90 Target Model Skeet Gun* - 28 in. barrels only with screw-in chokes. Importation disc. 1993.

	$1,800	$1,300	$1,200	$995	$850	$700	$600

Last MSR was $2,495.

GRADING - PPGS™	100%	98%	95%	90%	80%	70%	60%

✳ *Model Z-90 Target Model Sporting Clays Gun* - 28 in. barrels with screw-in chokes, coin finished receiver with engraved sideplates, separated barrels, Schnabel forend, solid recoil pad. Importation disc. 1990.

	$1,700	$1,450	$1,200	$995	$850	$700	$600

Last MSR was $2,495.

Z SPORT - 12 or 20 (new 2008) ga., various barrel lengths to 32 in., 3 choke tubes, choice of blue or French grey receiver finish, border engraved with gold logo, fancy oil finished checkered Turkish walnut stock, detachable posi-lock trigger system, includes hard case with tools. Importation began 2007.

MSR $5,200		$4,800	$4,350	$3,500	$3,000	$2,650	$2,150	$1,750

Add $400 for adj. stock.
Add $1,950 for 20/28 ga. combination set.

✳ *Z Sport Extra* - similar to Z Sport, except has 80% engraving coverage in bold English scroll and checkered extra fancy Turkish walnut. Importation began 2007.

MSR $6,500		$5,995	$5,250	$4,500	$3,950	$3,400	$2,750	$2,150

Add $400 for adj. stock.
Add $2,100 for 20/28 ga. combination set.

Z AMBASSADOR ROUND BODY SPORTING - 12 or 20 ga., 28, 30, or 32 in. barrels with 6 choke tubes, Boss coin finished action, hand engraved with deep floral scroll and 24Kt. shield logo, exhibition grade oil finished Turkish walnut stock with hand checkering, includes leather hard case. Limited importation 2007.

	$7,500	$6,500	$5,500	$4,750	$4,000	$3,300	$2,750

Last MSR was $8,690.

Z AMBASSADOR EL SPORTING - similar to Round Body Sporting, except has 100% deep scroll engraving and three Bulino style game scenes, hand carved oil finished exhibition grade Turkish walnut stock with hand-cut checkering, includes leather hard case, tools, parts kits, and snap caps. Importation began 2007.

MSR $9,950		$9,250	$8,500	$7,500	$6,500	$5,500	$4,500	$3,500

Add $3,050 for 20/28 ga. combination set (new 2008).

EXPEDITION - 12 or 20 ga., 28, 30, or 32 in. barrels with 5 flush choke tubes, engraved action with Z gun logo in deep relief, oil finished fine checkered Turkish pistol grip walnut stock, includes hard case and tools. Limited importation 2007.

	$4,250	$3,500	$3,000	$2,650	$2,150	$1,750	$1,450

Last MSR was $4,775.

Add $1,100 for Extra Game model with 80% coverage in bold English scroll and checkered extra fancy Turkish walnut.

Z AMBASSADOR EL ROUND BODY GAME GUN - 12 or 20 ga., 28, 30, or 32 in. barrels with 6 choke tubes, Boss coin finished action, hand engraved with deep floral scroll and 24Kt. shield logo, exhibition grade oil finished Turkish walnut pistol grip or straight English stock with hand checkering, includes leather hard case. Limited importation 2007.

	$7,500	$6,500	$5,500	$4,750	$4,000	$3,300	$2,750

Last MSR was $8,690.

Z AMBASSADOR EL GAME GUN - similar to Round Body Game, except has 100% deep scroll engraving and three game scenes with birds in flight, hand carved oil finished exhibition grade Turkish walnut pistol grip or straight English stock with hand-cut checkering, includes leather hard cases. Limited importation 2007.

	$8,750	$7,500	$6,500	$5,500	$4,750	$4,000	$3,300

Last MSR was $9,500.

GRADING - PPGS™	100%	98%	95%	90%	80%	70%	60%

Z SKEET - 12 ga., 28 or 29 1/2 in. barrels with 4 Skeet chokes, adj. trigger or NST, adj. comb Monte Carlo Turkish walnut stock, includes hard plastic luggage case. Importation began 2007.

MSR $5,700		$5,250	$4,650	$4,100	$3,600	$3,100	$2,600	$2,250

Add $1,100 for Z Extra Skeet SK Model.

Z AMBASSADOR BT SKEET - similar to Z Skeet, except has Ambassador features, includes Americase. Limited importation 2007.

	$7,500	$6,500	$5,500	$4,750	$4,000	$3,300	$2,750

Last MSR was $8,690.

Z AMBASSADOR EL SKEET - similar to Z Skeet, except has Ambassador features, includes leather case. Importation began 2007.

MSR $9,950		$9,250	$8,500	$7,500	$6,500	$5,500	$4,500	$3,500

PALOMA ROUND BODY GAME GUN - 12 or 20 ga., rounded and sculpted frame with 100% deep ornamental scroll engraving with cameo game scene, hand detachable mechanical trigger, best quality Turkish walnut stock, includes aluminum case, tools and accessories. Importation began 2008.

MSR $7,500		$6,850	$5,750	$4,950	$4,250	$3,600	$3,000	$2,350

Add $2,000 for 20/28 ga. combination set.

SHOTGUNS: SxS, RECENT PRODUCTION

UPLANDER - 12 or 20 ga., 3 in. chambers, 25 in. barrels with fixed chokes (IC/M), ST, ejectors, color case hardened receiver, English style checkered Circassian walnut stock and forearm with oil or polyurethane finish. Importation disc. 1990.

	$750	$625	$560	$520	$485	$450	$425

Last MSR was $1,295.

SILVER FOX - 12 or 20 ga., 3 in. chambers, 26 or 28 (12 ga. only) in. barrels with fixed chokes, ST, ejectors, hand engraved silver finished receiver with "AZ" in gold, straight grip checkered Circassian walnut stock and forearm. Importation disc. 1990.

	$1,400	$1,300	$1,200	$995	$875	$750	$625

Last MSR was $2,995.

ARIETE M3 - 12 ga. only, 26 or 28 in. barrels, matted rib, single non-selective trigger, ejectors, blue receiver with fine scroll engraving, cased. Disc.

	$550	$475	$400	$360	$330	$310	$285

EMPIRE - 12 or 20 ga. Mag., 27 or 28 in. barrels, moderate engraving, coin finished receiver. Disc.

	$1,100	$1,075	$975	$875	$795	$725	$650

Add $100 for 3 in. Mag. chambers.

This model was distributed by Euroarms of America, Inc.

VOLCANO RECORD - 12 ga. only, 28 in. barrels, H&H type sidelocks, ejectors, SST, treble Purdey locks, silver finished receiver with elaborate engraving, best quality fine checkered walnut, special order only. Disc.

	$4,100	$4,000	$3,800	$3,400	$2,950	$2,650	$2,300

＊*Volcano Record ELM* - 12 ga. only, built to individual customer specifications, best quality H&H style sidelock. Disc.

	$10,750	$9,800	$8,800	$7,100	$6,850	$6,200	$4,400

This model was distributed by Euroarms of America, Inc.

CUSTOM SERIES - SxS, individual custom order only, every refinement is used in the construction of these extremely rare and expensive shotguns. The Volcano Extra Lusso shotgun is probably the most elaborate Antonio Zoli shotgun with the recent list price being $58,850.

TRADEMARK INDEX

Having originally made its humble beginning back in the 10th edition, published in 1989, the original Trademark Index section listed pertinent contact information for over 200 companies. At that time, most companies did not even have a fax number yet! The fax machine had just been introduced, and most companies wouldn't spend $1,100-$1,300 at the time to buy one. Up until then, it was either mail, telephone, telex, or smoke signals if there was no wind. The Trademark Index originally started because I was frustrated trying to find contact information on the multitudes of firearms and related companies, both domestic and foreign, without having to go through a pile of brochures, business cards, and magazines. Back then, there was no Internet, no email, and no contact management programs, and a fax machine was considered a luxury. Finding useful, up-to-date information was difficult.

The Trademark Index wasn't something that was planned. All of a sudden, one March afternoon, the light bulb came on, and it was approximated that this new section would initially take no more than 4-8 hours of computer time. Four days later, after a virtual non-stop frenzy of WP activity, it was decided that the section was finally good enough to publish.

Since then, the Trademark Index has grown significantly each year, and continues to be the only up-to-date and accurate contact information published for firearms manufacturers, trademarks, importers, distributors, repair and service centers, and auction houses. Gathering this information has required scouring every firearms booth at both domestic and foreign trade shows. Additionally, hundreds of hours have been spent updating this section, and we feel confident that the information listed below is the most up-to-date and accurate we can provide, especially with the ever-changing emails, website addresses, and area codes.

Previously published annually, this Trademark Index is now available online at no charge. Also, the Trademark Index information is now revised and updated quarterly, and this Trademark Index online will now be the most up-to-date contact information available for the firearms industry. Since all of us want to be better informed, if you have new or additional information that would be helpful to update this continually changing section, please send in your potential contributions to us by email or fax, and we will enter them into our database immediately. Creating and maintaining this Trademark Index database is a big job, and we only have one goal – to make it the best and most up-to-date available.

Even more so than last year, you will note additions and substantial changes regarding website and email listings – this may be your best way of obtaining up-to-date model and pricing information directly from some current manufacturers, importers, and/or distributors. When online with the various company's websites, it's not a bad idea to look at the date of last web update, as this will tell you how current the online information really is.

Previous readers will note that contact information for the black powder and airgun industries is no longer included in this *Blue Book of Gun Values* Trademark Index (it's large enough the way it is). For a complete listing of companies and contact information for these two separate industries, please refer to the respective Trademark Indexes in the *Blue Book of Modern Black Powder Arms* and the *Blue Book of Airguns*, also available online at no charge.

If parts are needed for older, discontinued makes and models (even though the manufacturer/trademark is current), it is recommended you contact either Numrich Gun Parts Corp. located in West Hurley, NY, or Jack First, Inc. located in Rapid City, SD for domestic availability and prices. For current manufacturers, it is recommended that you contact an authorized warranty repair center or stocking gun shop, unless a company/trademark has an additional service/parts listing. In Canada, please refer to the Bowmac Gunpar Inc. listing. Remember, most of the people you come in contact with to request customer service questions or parts/service will probably be busy, so have patience and respect their time.

If you should require additional assistance in "tracking" any of the current companies listed in this publication (or perhaps, current companies that are not listed), please contact us and we will try to help you regarding these specific requests. Again, the most up-to-date Trademark Index for the firearms, black powder, and airguns industries will be posted on our website: **www.bluebookinc.com.** We hope you appreciate this service – no one else in the industry has anything like it.

ADC
Armi Dallera Custom
Via Michelangelo, 64
I-25063 Gardone, VT (BS) ITALY
Phone/Fax No.: 011-39-0308911562
Website: www.adccustom.com
Email: info@adccustom.com

AMT
Crusader Gun Company, Inc.
5200 Mitchelldale, Ste. E17
Houston, TX 77092
Phone No.: 800-272-7816
Fax No.: 713-681-5665
Website: www.highstandard.com

AMOSKEAG AUCTION COMPANY, INC.
250 Commercial Street, Unit 3011
Manchester, NH 03101
Phone No.: 603-627-7383
Fax No.: 603-627-7384
Website: www.amoskeagauction.com

ANGLO AMERICAN SPORTING AGENCY
P.O. Box 331
Corona del Mar, CA 92625
Phone No.: 949-644-9557
Fax No.: 949-644-9558
Website: www.angloamericansport.com
Email: angloamericansport@earthlink.net

AR-7 INDUSTRIES L.L.C.
Please refer to Armalite, Inc. listing.

ATA ARMS
Importer - please refer to K.B.I. listing.
Importer - please refer to Tristar listing.
Factory - ATA AV Tufekleri San. Ve Tic. Ltd. STI.
Yukari Dudullu Imes Sanayi Sitesi
B Blok 201 Sk. No. 8 34788
Umraniye, Istanbul, TURKEY
Fax No.: 011-90-216-466-4571
Website: www.ataarms.com.tr
Email: info@ataarms.com.tr

AWA USA
2280 W. 80th Street, Ste. 2
Hialeah, FL 33016
Phone No.:305-828-1982
Fax No.: 305-828-1066
Website: www.awaguns.com
Email: info@awaguns.com
Factory - AWA USA
Branch Office
Via De Gusperi
I-25013 Carpenedolo (BS) ITALY
Fax No.: 011-390-30-9966322

A-SQUARE COMPANY
Glenrock, WY
Website: www.asquarecompany.com

AYA
Importer/Distributor – please refer to New England Custom Gun Service, Ltd. listing
Importer/Distributor - please refer to Fieldsport listing
Importer - please refer to Anglo American Sporting Agency listing.
Importer - H.G. Lomas Gunmakers, Inc.
54 W. Rhine St.
P.O. Box 565
Elkhart Lake, WI 53020
Phone No.: 920-876-3745
Email: hughlomas@yahoo.com
Importer/Distributor and AYA Warranty Service & Repairs
John F. Rowe
4213 Oakcrest Ave.
Enid, OK 73702
Phone No.: 405-233-5942
Phone No.: 405-233-4038
Retailer - Bill Hanus Birdguns LLC
(Bill Hanus models only)
P.O. Box 533
Newport, OR 97365
Phone No.: 541-265-7433
Fax No.: 541-265-7400
Website: www.billhanusbirdguns.com
U.K. Importer/Distributor - A.S.I.
Alliance House, Snape, Saxmundham
Suffolk, ENGLAND IP17 1SW
Fax No.: 011-44-1728-688950
Email: info@a-s-i.co.uk
Factory - AYA – Aguirre Y Aranzabal, S.A.L.
Avda. Otaol, 25-3
P.O. Box 45
20600 Eibar (Guipuzcoa) SPAIN
Fax No.: 011-34-943100133
Website: www.aya-fineguns.com
Email: aya@aya-fineguns.com

ABBIATICO & SALVINELLI (FAMARS)
Please refer to Famars di Abbiatico & Salvinelli listing.

ACCU-TEK
Factory - Excel Industries, Inc.
4510 Carter Court
Chino, CA 91710
Toll Free Phone No.: 888-442-6096
Phone No.: 909-627-2404
Fax No.: 909-627-7817
Website: www.accu-tekfirearms.com
Email: email@accu-tekfirearms.com

ACCURACY INTERNATIONAL LTD.
Importer - Tac Pro Shooting Center
35100 North State Hwy.
Mingus, TX 76463-6405
Phone No.: 254-968-3112
Fax No.: 254-968-5857
Website: www.tacproshootingcenter.com
Email: email@tacproshootingcenter.com
Factory
P.O. Box 81, Portsmouth
Hampshire, ENGLAND PO3 5SJ
Fax No.: 011-44-23-9269-1852
Website: www.accuracyinternational.com
Email: ai@accuracyinternational.org

ADAMY, GEBR. JADGWAFFEN
Importer - please refer to New England Custom Gun Service, Ltd. listing.
Factory - Adamy-Jadgwaffen
Bochsenmacher-Handwerkshetrieh
Windeweg 3, Suhl D-98527 GERMANY
Fax No.: 011-49-3681-709076
Website: www.adamy-jagdwaffen.de
Email: info@adamy-jagdwaffen.de

ADCO SALES INC.
4 Draper Street
Woburn, MA 01801-4522
Phone No.: 781-935-1799
Fax No.: 781-935-1011
Website: www.diamondguns.com
Website: www.adcosales.com
Email: questions@adcosales.com

ADVANTAGE ARMS, INC.
Conversion Kits for Glocks & 1911 Pistols
25163 W. Stanford
Valencia, CA 91355
Phone No.: 888-617-4666
Website: www.advantagearms.com
Email: gunkits@advantagearms.com

AKKAR
Importer - please refer to K.B.I. listing.
Akkar Silah Sanayi Ltd.
Orhanli Merkez Mh.
34956 Tuzla, Istanbul TURKEY
Fax: 011-90-216-394-4373
Website: www.akkarsilah.com
Email: akkar@akkarsilah.com

ALEXANDER ARMS LLC
U.S. Army - Radford Arsenal
P.O. Box 1
Radford, VA 24143
Phone No.: 540-639-8356
Fax No.: 540-639-8353
Website: www.alexanderarms.com
Email: sales@alexanderarms.com

ALFA PROJ. spol. s.r.o.
Importer - Trail Blazin' Innovations
8711 Belle Glen Dr.
Houston, TX 77099-1502
Phone No.: 281-530-3916
Fax No.: 281-530-1275
Website: www.tbicatalog.com
Email: tbifred@aol.com
Factory
Zabrdovicka 11
615 00 Brno CZECH REPUBLIC
Fax No.: 011-420-545-120-622
Website: www.alfa-proj.cz
Email: prodej@alfa-proj.cz

ALMAR
S. Alamanos & Co. O.E.
44 Kyprou Str. 16452 Argiroupolis
Athens GREECE
Fax No.: 011-30-210-9935117
Website: www.alamanosoe.gr

AMERICA REMEMBERS
10226 Timber Ridge Dr.
Ashland, VA 23005
Phone No.: 804-550-9616
Fax No.: 804-550-9603
Website: www.americaremembers.com
Email: america.remembers@comcast.net

AMERICAN CUSTOM GUNMAKERS GUILD
22 Vista View Dr.
Cody, WY 82414-9606
Phone/Fax No.: 307-587-4297
Website: www.acgg.org
Email: acgg@acgg.org

AMERICAN DERRINGER CORPORATION
127 N. Lacy Dr.
Waco, TX 76705
Phone No.: 254-799-9111
Fax No.: 254-799-7935
Website: www.ladyderringer.com
Website: www.amderringer.com
Email: amderr@aol.com

AMERICAN HISTORICAL FOUNDATION
10195 Maple Leaf Court
Ashland, VA 23005
Phone No.: 804-550-7851
Fax No.: 804-550-0923
Website: www.ahffirearms.com
Email: ahffirearms@comcast.net

AMERICAN HUNTING RIFLES, INC.
1711 Mountain View Orchard Road
Corvallis, MT 59828
Phone No.: 406-363-8033
Website: www.hunting-rifles.com
Email: wayne@hunting-rifles.com

AMERICAN LEGACY FIREARMS
P.O. Box 369
Ft. Collins, CO 80522
Phone No.: 877-887-4867
Fax No.: 970-221-0614
Website: www.americanlegacyfirearms.com
Email: alfirearms@msn.com

ANSCHÜTZ

Sporting Rifle Importer & Factory Service
Merkel USA, Inc.
7661 Commerce Lane
Trussville, AL 35173
Phone No.: 205-655-8299
Fax No.: 205-655-7078
Website: www.merkel-usa.com
Importers/Distributors - Target Rifles
Please refer to Gunsmithing Inc. listing.
Please refer to Champion's Choice lising.
Champions Shooter's Supply
P.O. Box 303
New Albany, OH 43054
Phone No.: 614-855-1603
Fax No.: 614-855-1209
Website: www.championshooters.com
Repair - Target Rifles
Please refer to Gunsmithing Inc. listing.
Repair/Warranty/Gunsmithing Services
10-Ring-Service, Inc.
2227 West Lou Drive
Jacksonville, FL 32216
Phone No.: 904-724-7419
Fax No.: 904-724-7149
Factory - ANSCHÜTZ, J.G. GmbH & Co. KG
Daimlerstrasse 12
D-89079 Ulm, GERMANY
Fax No.: 011-49-731-40125-205
Website: www.anschuetz-sport.com
Email: anschuetz@anschuetz-sport.com

ANZIO IRONWORKS

1905 16th Street North
St. Petersburg, FL 33704
Phone No.: 727-895-2019
Fax No.: 727-827-4728
Website: www.anzioironworks.com
Email: anzioshop@hotmail.com

ARCUS

Importer - please refer to Century International Arms listing.

ARMALITE, INC.

P.O. Box 299
Geneseo, IL 61254
Phone No.: 309-944-6939
Fax No.: 309-944-6949
Website: www.armalite.com
Email: info@armalite.com
Law Enforcement Support Only
P.O. Box 340
Campbellsburg, KY 40011
Phone No.: 502-532-0300
Fax No.: 502-532-0775
Email: toppc@armalite.com

ARMAMENT TECHNOLOGY

(Repair only - no current mfg.)
3045 Robie St., Suite 113
Halifax, N.S. CANADA B3K 4P6
Phone No.: 902-454-6384
Fax No.: 902-454-4641
Website: www.armament.com

LA ARMERIA DE MADRID

Infanta Maria Teresa, 15
ES-28016 Madrid SPAIN
Fax No.: 011-91-564-6289
Web site: www.armeriademadrid.com
Email: correo@armeriademadrid.com

ARMES DE CHASSE LLC

6311 Granby Street, Ste. 436
Norfolk, VA 23505
Phone No.: 757-747-0096
Fax No.: 757-747-0019

ARMI SALVINELLI

Importer - please refer to Cherry's listing.
Factory
via Zanardelli, 210
I-25060 Marcheno, Brescia ITALY
Fax No.: 011-39-030-861-285
Website: www.armisalvinelli.com
Email: info@armisalvinelli.com

ARMI SPORT SNC DI CHIAPPIA SILVIA & C.

Distributor - please refer to K.B. I. listing.
Distributor - please refer to Cimarron listing.
Distributor - please refer to E.M. F. listing.
Distributor - please refer to I.A.R. listing.
Distributor - please refer to Traditions listing.
Distributor - please refer to Taylor's & Co., Inc. listing.
Factory
via Milano 2
I-25020 Azzano Mella (BS) ITALY
Fax No.: 011-39-030-9749232
Website: www.armichiappa.com
Email: info@armichiappa.com

ARMINIUS

Please refer to Herman Weihrauch Revolver GmbH listing.

ARMORY USA, L.L.C.

8777 Tallyho Road
Houston, TX 77061
Phone No.: 713-944-3551
Fax No.: 713-944-3581
Website: www.globaltrades.com

ARMS MORAVIA LTD.

Factory
Nadrazni 22
Ostrava 2, CZ-70200
CZECH REPUBLIC
Fax No.: 011-420-69-611-2202

ARMSCOR (ARMS CORPORATION OF THE PHILIPPINES)

Importer & Distributor - Armscor Precision International
5329 S. Cameron St., Ste. 110
Las Vegas, NV 89118
Phone No.: 702-362-7750
Fax No.: 702-362-5019
Email: apiusa@earthlink.com
Factory office - Arms Corp. of the Philippines
Parang Marikina 1800
Metro Manila, PHILIPPINES
Phone No.: 632-942-5936
Fax No.: 632-942-0862
Website: www.armscor.com.ph
Email: armscor@info.com.ph

Executive office - Arms Corp. of the Philippines
6th Floor, Strat 100 Bldg., Emerald Ave.
Ortigas Center, Pasig City, 1600 The Phillipines
Fax No.: 632-634-3906
Email: squires@cnl.net

ARMSAN
Importer - please refer to Mossberg listing.
Factory - Armsan SilahSan. ve Tic.A.S.
Inkilap Mah. Alemdag Cad. Site Yolu Sok. no. 3
34768 Umraniye-Istanbul TURKEY
Fax No.: 011-90-216-630-2288
Website: www.armsan.com

ARMSPORT LLC
Colt and Remington cartridge conversions
P.O. Box 254
Eastlake, CO 80614
Phone No.: 303-451-7212
Website: www.armsportllc.com
Email: RLMillington@armsportllc.com

ARRIETA, S.L.
Importer & Distributor - please refer to Quality Arms listing.
Importer - please refer to Griffin & Howe listing.
Importer - please refer to William Larkin Moore listing.
Importer - please refer to Orvis listing.
Importer - plesae refer to Wingshooting Adventures listing.
Factory - Arrieta, Manufacturas, S.L.
Morkaiko 5
E-20870 Elgoibar (Guipuzcoa) SPAIN
Fax No.: 011-34-943-743154
Email: marrietasl@euskalnet.net

ARRIZABALAGA, PEDRO
Importer - please refer to Harry Marx Hi-Grade Imports listing.
Importer - please refer to William Larkin Moore listing.
Factory - Arrizabalaga, Pedro, S.A.
Errekatxu, 5
E-20600 Eibar (Gipuzkoa) SPAIN
Fax No.: 011-34-943-201743
Website: www.pedroarrizabalaga.net

ARSENAL, BULGARIA
Importer - please refer to Arsenal Inc. listing.
Factory - Arsenal 2000 JSCo.
100, Rozova Dolina St.
6100 Kazanlack, BULGARIA
Fax No.: 011-359-431-50001
Website: www.arsenal2000-bg.com
Email: arsenal2000@arsenal2000-bg.com

ARSENAL INC.
5015 West Sahara Ave., Ste. 125
Las Vegas, NV 89146-3407
Phone No.: 888-539-2220
Fax No.: 702-643-8860
Website: www.arsenalinc.com
Email: support@arsenalinc.com

ARSENAL USA LLC
Please refer to Armory USA LLC listing.

ART MANIFACTTURA ARMI
Importer - please refer to William Larkin Moore listing.
Factory
Via Madonnina 89
Gardone, VT, Brescia
I-25063 ITALY
Phone/Fax No.: 011-030-861-591
Web site: www.armi-art.com
Email: armi-art@intred.it

ASPEN OUTFITTING CO.
315 East Dean St.
Aspen, CO 81611
Phone No.: 800-784-2140
Fax No.: 970-920-3706
Website: www.aspenoutfitting.com
Email: contact@aspenoutfitting.com

ATKIN, GRANT & LANG
Broomhill Leys, Windmill Road, Markyate
St. Albans, Hertfordshire AL3 8LP ENGLAND
Fax No.: 011-44-1582-842318
Website: www.atkingrantandlang.co.uk
Email: AtkinGrant.Lang@btinternet.com

ATKIN, HENRY
Factory - please refer to Atkin, Grant & Lang listing.

AUSTRALIAN INTERNATIONAL ARMS
North American Importer - Marstar Canada
R.R. #1, Vankleek Hill
Ontario, CANADA K0B 1R0
Phone No.: 888-744-0066
Fax No.: 613-678-2359
Website: www.marstar.ca
Factory
P.O. Box 526
Ashgrove, Brisbane,
Queensland, AUSTRALIA 04060
Fax No.: 011-61-7-3366-7661

AUTO-ORDNANCE CORP.
Please refer to the Kahr Arms listing.
Website: www.tommygun.com
Website: www.tommygunshop.com

AXTELL RIFLE COMPANY
Distributor - The Riflesmith Inc.
353 Mill Creek Road
Sheridan, MT 59749
Phone/Fax No.: 406-842-5814
Website: www.riflesmith.com
Email: riflesmith@riflesmith.com

BAER, LES
Please refer to the Les Baer Custom listing.

BAIKAL
Importer - U.S. Sporting Goods
P.O. Box 719
Sharpes, FL 32959
Phone No.: 321-639-4842
Baikal Factory
Izhevsky Mekhanichesky Zavod
8, Promyshlennaya str.
Izhevsk, 426063 RUSSIA
Fax No.: 011-95-007-341-2765830
Website: www.baikalinc.ru
Email: worldlinks@baikalinc.ru

BALLARD ARMS, LLC
113 West Yellowstone Avenue
Cody, Wyoming 82414
Phone No.: 307-587-4914
Fax No.: 307-527-6097
Website: www.ballardrifles.com

BANSNER'S ULTIMATE RIFLES L.L.C.
P.O. Box 839
261 East Main Street
Adamstown, PA 19501
Phone No.: 717-484-2370
Fax No.: 717-484-0523
Website: www.bansnersrifle.com
Email: bansner@ptd.net

BARRETT FIREARMS MANUFACTURING, INC.
P.O. Box 1077
Murfreesboro, TN 37133
Phone No.: 615-896-2938
Fax No.: 615-896-7313
Website: www.barrettrifles.com
Email: mail@barrettrifles.com

WERNER BARTOLOT
Egger Strasse 5
A-9620 Hermagor, AUSTRIA
Fax No.: 011-43-0428225205
Website: www.jagdwaffe.at
Email: office@jagdwaffe.at

BATTAGLIA, MAURO
Via Dismano, 181
Santo Stefano di Ravenna ITALY
Phone/Fax No.: 011-39-0544-497-879
Website: www.maurobattaglia.com

BECAS
Factory - Molot JSC
Vyatskie Polyany Machine Building Plant
135 Lenin St., Vyatski Polyany
RUS-612960 Krov Region, RUSSIA
Fax No.: 011-007-83334-61832
Website: www.molot.biz
Email: molot_ves@list.ru

BEEMAN PRECISION AIRGUNS
5454 Argosy Dr.
Huntington Beach, CA 92649-1039
Toll Free Phone No.: 800-227-2744
Fax No.: 714-890-4808
Website: www.beeman.com

BEEMILLER
Please refer to Hi-Point Firearms listing.

BENELLI
Importer - Benelli USA
17603 Indian Head Highway
Accokeek, MD 20607-2501
Phone No.: 301-283-6981
Fax No.: 301-283-6988
Website: www.benelliusa.com
Email: benusa1@aol.com
Pistol/Airgun Importer - please refer to Larry's Guns listing.
Warranty Repair Address - Benelli USA Corp.
901 Eight Street
Pocomoke, MD 21851

Factory - Benelli Armi S.p.A.
Via della Stazione, 50
I-61029 Urbino (PU) ITALY
Fax No.: 011-39-0722-307-207
Website: www.benelli.it

BERETTA, PIETRO
Importer - Beretta U.S.A. Corp
17601 Beretta Drive
Accokeek, MD 20607
Fax No.: 301-283-0435
Website: www.berettausa.com
Beretta Premium Grades
Beretta Gallery
718 Madison Avenue
New York, NY 10021
Phone No.: 212-319-3235
Fax No.: 212-207-8219
Beretta Gallery
41 Highland Park Village
Dallas, TX 75205
Phone No.: 214-559-9800
Fax No.: 214-559-9805
Factory - Fabbrica d'Armi Pietro Beretta S.p.A
Via Pietro Beretta 18
25063 Gardone Val Trompia
Brescia, ITALY
Fax No.: 011-39-30-834-1421
Website: www.beretta.it

WAYNE BERGQUIST CUSTOM PISTOLS
5760 Shirley Street, Unit #21
Naples, FL 34109
Phone No.: 239-594-1573
Fax No.: 239-597-8259
Website: www.naplesflguns.com

BERNARDELLI, VINCENZO
Via Grandi, 10
Torbole Casaglia
I-25030 Brescia, ITALY
Fax No.: 011-39-030-215-0963
Website: www.bernardelli.com
Email: bernardelli@bernardelli.com

BERSA
Master Distributor – Eagle Imports, Inc.
1750 Brielle Ave., Unit B-1
Wanamassa, NJ 07712
Phone No.: 732-493-0333
Fax No.: 732-493-0301
website: www.bersafirearmsusa.com
Email: billstroh12@aol.com
Factory - Bersa S.A.
Castillo 312
(1704) Ramos Mejia, ARGENTINA
Fax No.: 011-54-1-656-2093

BERTUZZI
Distributor - please refer to Dewing's listing.
Factory - Bertuzzi, F.lli
Via Alessandro Volta, 65
I-25063 Gardone V.T. (BS) ITALY
Fax No.: 011-39-030-8912188

BETTINSOLI, TARCISIO Srl

Importer - see Franchi listing (private label models).
European Distributor - Bignami S.p.A.
via Lahn, 1
I-39040 Ora (Bolzano), ITALY
Fax No: 011-39-471-810899
Web site: www.bignami.it
Factory
Via I Maggio, 116
Zanano di Sarezzo, Brescia, I-25068 ITALY
Fax No.: 011-39-030-890-0240
Email: info@bettinsoli.it

BILL HANUS BIRDGUNS LLC

P.O. Box 533
Newport, OR 97365
Phone No.: 541-265-7433
Fax No.: 541-265-7400
Website: www.billhanusbirdguns.com

BLAND, THOMAS & SONS GUNMAKERS LTD.

Woodcock Hill, Inc.
P.O. Box 363
192 Spencers Road
Benton, PA 17814
Phone No.: 570-864-3242
Fax No.: 570-864-3232
Website: www.woodcockhill.com
Email: bland@epix.net

BLASER

Importer & Distributor - Blaser USA, Inc.
220 G Log Canoe Circle
Stevensville, MD 21666
Phone No.: 410-604-1495
Fax No.: 410-604-1498
Website: www.blaser-usa.com
Factory - Blaser Jagdwaffen GmbH
Ziegelstadel 1
D-88316 Isny im Allgau, GERMANY
Fax No.: 011-49-75-62702 43
Website: www.blaser.de

H. BLEIKER FEINMECHANIK/SPORTWAFFEN

Neufeldstrasse 1
CH – 9606 Bütschwil, SWITZERLAND
Phone No.: 011.41.71.982.8210
Fax No.: 011.41.71.982.8219
Website: www.bleiker.ch
Email: hbleiker@bleiker.ch

BLOW

Factory - ÜCYILDIZ SILAH SANAYI TIC LTD. STI
Bostanci Cad. Yol Sokak No. 14/A
Y. Dudullu/Ümraniye/Istanbul 34775 TURKEY
Fax No.: 011-90-216-527-6705
Website: www.voltranarms.com
Email: blow@voltranarms.com

BLUEGRASS ARMORY

P.O. Box 1293
Richmond, KY 40476
Phone/Fax No.: 859-625-0874
Website: www.bluegrassarmory.com
Email: support@bluegrassarmory.com

BOBCAT WEAPONS INC.

Please refer to Red Rock Arms listing.

BOND ARMS, INC.

P.O. Box 1296
204 Alpha Lane
Granbury, Texas 76048
Phone No.: 817-573-4445
Fax No.: 817-573-5636
Website: www.bondarms.com
Email: info@bondarms.com

BOROVNIK, LUDWIG KG

Bahnofstrasse 7
A-9170 Ferlach, AUSTRIA
Fax No.: 011-43-0-4227-4349
Email: borovnik@ferlachjagdwaffen.at

BOSIS, LUCIANO

Distributor - please refer to Dewing's listing.
Importer - British Sporting Arms, Ltd.
3684 Route 44
Millsbrook, NY 12545
Phone No.: 845-677-8303
Fax No.: 845-677-5756
Website: www.bsaltd.com/bsa_home.html
Email: info@bsaltd.com
Factory
via G. Marconi 32
I-25039 Travagliato, Brescia, ITALY
Phone/Fax No.: 011-39-030-660-413
Website: www.bosis.com
Email: info@bosis.com

BOSS & CO., LTD.

16 Mount Street
London, ENGLAND W1K 2RH
Phone No.: 011-44-020-7493-1127
Fax No.: 011-44-020-7493-0711
Website: www.bossguns.com
Email: mail@bossguns.com

BOSWELL, CHARLES

Importer - Chris Batha
43 Pinckney Colony Road
Okatie, SC 29902
Phone No.: 866-254-2406
Website: www.chrisbatha.com
Email: chrisbatha@aol.com

BOWEN, BRUCE & COMPANY

3541 Mayer Ave.
Sturgis, SD 57785
Phone No.: 605-347-3133
Website: www.bbguns.net
Email: Bbowen999@aol.com

BOWMAC GUNPAR INC.

Canadian Parts Supplier
69 Iber Rd., Unit 101
Stittsville, Ontario CANADA K2S 1E7
Phone No.: 800-668-2509
Phone No.: 613-831-8548
Fax No.: 613-831-0530

BRAZIER, JOSEPH, LTD.
Distributor & Importer - Joseph Brazier Ltd./Karl Lippard, Gunmaker
P.O. Box 60719
Colorado Springs, CO 80960
Phone No.: 719-444-0786
Fax No.: 719-444-0786
Website: www.josephbrazier.com
Website: www.karllippard.com

BREDA MECCANICA BRESCIANA
Importer - please refer to Legacy Sports International listing.
Factory
Via Lunga, 2
I-25126 Brescia ITALY
Fax No.: 011-39-030-3791-330
Website: www.bredafucili.com

RYAN BREEDING CUSTOM RIFLES
4573 W. Saddle Ridge Dr.
Nampa, ID 83687
Phone No.: 208-288-2158
Website: www.rbbigbores.com
Email: ryan@rbbigbores.com

BRENZOVICH FIREARMS TRAINING CENTER
22301 Old Texas
Ft. Hancock, TX 79839
Phone/Fax No.: 915-764-2030
Website: www.brenzovich.com
Email: GunChamp@aol.com

BRETTON-GAUCHER
Factory
17 rue Victor Grignard
Z1 de Montreynaud
F-42 026 St. Etienne FRANCE
Fax No.: 011-33-477419572
Website: www.bretton-gaucher.com
Email: info@bretton-gaucher.com

BRIGNOLI, SILVIO
via Alfieri 6
I-25063 Gardone VT, Brescia ITALY
Fax No.: 011-39-030-8910498
Web site: www.brignoliarmi.com
Email: info@brignoliarmi.com

BRILEY MANUFACTURING INC.
1230 Lumpkin Rd.
Houston, TX 77043
Phone No.: 713-932-6995 (Technical)
Phone No.: 800-331-5718 (Orders only)
Fax No.: 713-932-1043
Website: www.briley.com

BRNO ARMS
Factory - ZBROJOVKA BRNO, a.s.
Lazaretni 7
615 00 Brno, CZECH REPUBLIC
Fax No.: 011-42(0)-545-152-288
website: www.zbrojovkabrno.com

BROCKMAN'S CUSTOM GUNSMITHING
445 Idaho St.
Gooding, Idaho 83330
Phone No.: 208-934-5050
Fax No.: 208-934-5284
Website: www.brockmansrifles.com
Email: Brockman@brockmansrifles.com

A.A. BROWN & SONS GUNMAKERS
1 Snake Lane, Alvechurch
Brimingham, B48 7NT ENGLAND
Fax No.: 011-44-1214452113
Website: www.aabrownandsons.com
Email: robin@aabrownandsons.com

DAVID MCKAY BROWN GUNMAKERS, LTD.
U.S. Agent - please refer to Griffin & Howe listing.
Importer - please refer to Wingshooting Adventures listing.
Factory
32 Hamilton Road, Bothwell
Glasgow, SCOTLAND (U.K.) G71 8NA
Fax No.: 011-44-141-1698-854207
Website: www.mckaybrown.com
Email: info@mckaybrown.com

ED BROWN CUSTOM, INC.
(Rifles Only)
PO Box 492
43825 Muldrow Trail
Perry, MO 63462
Phone No.: 573-565-3261
Fax No.: 573-565-2791
Website: www.edbrown.com
Email: edbrown@edbrown.com

ED BROWN PRODUCTS, INC.
(Pistols only)
PO Box 492
43825 Muldrow Trail
Perry, MO 63462
Phone No.: 573-565-3261
Fax No.: 573-565-2791
Website: www.edbrown.com
Email: edbrown@edbrown.com

BROWN PRECISION, INC.
P.O. Box 270 W
7786 Molinos Avenue
Los Molinos, CA 96055
Phone No.: 530-384-2506
Fax No.: 530-384-1638
Website: www.brownprecision.com
Email: info@brownprecision.com

BROWNING
Administrative Headquarters
One Browning Place
Morgan, UT 84050-9326
Phone No.: 801-876-2711
Product Service: 800-333-3288
Fax No.: 801-876-3331
Website: www.browning.com or www.browningint.com
Custom Shop U.S. Representative
Mr. Ron McGhie
Email: ronm@browning.com
Browning Parts and Service
3005 Arnold Tenbrook Rd.
Arnold, MO 63010-9406
Phone No.: 800-322-4626
Fax No.: 636-287-9751
Historical Research (Browning Arms Co. marked guns only)
Browning Historian
One Browning Place
Morgan, UT 84050-9326
Fax No.: 801-876-3331
Website: www.browning.com

BRUCHET
Please refer to Darne listing.

BRUEGGER & THOMET
Importer - please refer to D.S.A. listing
Factory
Thun, SWITZERLAND

BUL TRANSMARK LTD.
Importer – please refer to KBI listing.
Factory - Bul Transmark Ltd.
10 Rival Street
Tel-Aviv 67778, ISRAEL
Fax No.: 011-972-3-687-4853
Website: www.bultransmark.com
Email: info@bultransmark.com

BUTTERFIELD & BUTTERFIELD (AUCTIONS)
Main Gallery & Corporate Office
220 San Bruno Ave.
San Francisco, CA 94103
Phone No.: 415-861-7500
Fax No.: 415-861-8951
Website: www.butterfields.com

BUSHMASTER FIREARMS
P.O. Box 1479
999 Roosevelt Trail
Windham, ME 04062
Phone No.: 800-883-6229
Fax No.: 207-892-8068
Website: www.bushmaster.com
Email: info@bushmaster.com

BÜYÜK HUGLU
Büyük Huglu Av Tüfekleri San. Tic. Ltd. Stl.
Huglu-Beysehir, Konya TURKEY
Fax No.: 011-90-332-516-1182
Website: www.buyukhuglu.com
Email: info@buyukhuglu.com

C Z (CESKA ZBROJOVKA)
Firearms & Airguns Importer - CZ-USA
P.O. Box 171073
Kansas City, KS 66117-0073
Phone No.: 913-321-1811
Toll Free No.: 800-955-4486
Fax No.: 913-321-2251
Website: www.cz-usa.com
Email: info@cz-usa.com
Website: www.safariclassics.com (custom rifles only)
Administration Offices - Ceska Zbrojovka
Svatopluka Cecha 1283
CZ-68827 Uhersky Brod
CZECH REPUBLIC
Fax No.: 011-420-63363-3811
Website: www.czub.cz
Email: info@czub.cz

CZ (STRAKONICE)
Factory - CZ Stojirna s.r.o.
Tovarni 202
CZ-386 01 Strakonice CZECH REPUBLIC
Email: cz_strojirna@pvtnet.cz

CBC
Av. Humberto de Campos 3220
09426 900 Ribeirao Pires SP BRAZIL
Fax No.: 011-55-11-4822-8323
Website: www.cbc.com.br

CABELAS INC.
One Cabela Dr.
Sidney, NE 69160
Phone No.: 800-237-4444
Fax No.: 800-496-6329
website: www.cabelas.com

RENATO CAEM
Factory
via Indipendenza 55
25060 Marcheno, Brescia, ITALY
Phone/Fax No.: 011-39-030-861142

CAESAR GUERINI, s.r.l.
Importer - Caesar Guerini USA LLC
700 Lake Street
Cambridge, MD 21613
Phone No.: 410-901-1131
Fax No.: 410-901-1137
Website:www.gueriniusa.com
Email: info@gueriniusa.com
Factory
Via Parte, 33
I-25060 Marcheno Brescia, ITALY
Fax No.: 011-39-030-896-6147
Website: www.caesarguerini.it
Email: info@caesarguerini.it

CASPIAN ARMS, LTD.
75 Cal Foster Dr.
Wolcott, VT 05680
Phone No.: 802-472-6454
Fax No.: 802-472-6709
Website: www.caspianarms.com
Email: caspianarm@aol.com

CAVARLY ARMS CORPORATION
723 W. Commerce Ave. Ste. A
Gilbert, AZ 85233
Phone No.: 480-833-9685
Fax No.: 480-497-4002
Website: www.cavalryarms.com
Email: scout@cavalryarms.com

CENTURY INTERNATIONAL ARMS, INC.
430 Congress Ave., Ste. 1
Delray Beach, FL 33445
Phone No.: 800-527-1252
Phone No.: 561-265-4530
Fax No.: 561-265-4520
Website: www.centuryarms.com
Email: support@centuryarms.com

CHAMPIONS CHOICE, INC.
201 International Blvd.
LaVergne, TN 37086
Phone No.: (Orders Only) 800-345-7179
Phone No.: 615-793-4066
Fax No.: 615-793-4070
Email: champchoice@nashville.com

CHAMPLIN FIREARMS, INC.
P.O. Box 3191
Enid, OK 73702
Phone No.: 580-237-7388
Fax No.: 580-242-6922
Website: www.champlinarms.com
Email: info@champlinarms.com

CHAPPARAL ARMS
Importer - please refer to Charter 2000 listing.
Meerspinstrasse 28
D-67435 Neustadt an der Weinstrasse
GERMANY
Fax No.: 011-49-6321-968668
Website: www.chapparal-arms.de

CHAPUIS ARMES
Importer - Please refer to William Larkin Moore listing.
Importer - Please refer to Evolution USA
Importer - Please refer to Heirloom Armes listing.
Factory - Chapuis Armes
Z.I. La Gravoux, BP 15
F-42380 St. Bonnet le Chateau, FRANCE
Fax No.: 011-33-4-77-501070
Website: www.chapuis-armes.com
Email: info@chapuis-armes.com

CHARTER 2000, INC.
U.S. Marketer - MKS Supply, Inc.
8611-A North Dixie Drive
Dayton, OH 45414
Phone No.: 877-425-4867
Fax No.: 937-454-0503
Email: mkshpoint@aol.com
Factory
273 Canal St.
Shelton, CT 06484
Phone No.: 203-922-1652
Fax No.: 203-922-1469
Website: www.charterfirearms.com

CHERRY'S FINE GUNS
3408-N West Wendover Avenue
Greensboro, NC 27407
Phone No.: 336-854-4182
Fax No.: 336-854-4184
Website: www.cherrys.com
Email: fineguns@cherrys.com

CHEYTAC
Representatives - Cheytac Associates LLC
792 Ridge Road
Lansing, NY 14882
Phone No.: 888-807-8611
Fax No.: 607-533-8553
Factory
185 Arco Ave.
Arco, ID 83213
Toll Free: 888-807-8611
Phone No.: 208-527-8614
Fax No.: 208-527-3328
Website: www.cheytac.com

CHIPMUNK RIFLES
Please refer to Crickett Rifle listing.

CHRISTENSEN ARMS
192 East 100 North
Fayette, UT 84630
Phone No.: 435-528-7999
Fax No.: 435-528-5773
Website: www.christensenarms.com
Email: sales@christensenarms.com

CHRISTIE'S (AUCTIONS)
Rockefeller Center
20 Rockefeller Plaza
New York, NY 10020
Phone No.: 212-636-2000
Fax No.: 212-636-2399
Website: www.christies.com

E.J. CHURCHILL (GUNMAKERS)
U.S. Agent - please refer to Fieldsport listing.
Factory
Park Lane, Lane End, High Wycombe
Buckinghamshire, HP14 3NS ENGLAND
Phone No.: 011-44-1494-883066
Fax. No.: 011-44-1494-883215
Website: www.ejchurchill.com
Email: info@ejchurchill.com

CIMARRON, F.A. CO., INC.
105 Winding Oaks
Fredericksburg, TX 78624-0906
Phone No.: 830-997-9090
Fax No.: 830-997-0802
Website: www.cimarron-firearms.com
Email: cimarron@fbg.net

CLARK CUSTOM GUNS, INC.
336 Shootout Lane
Princeton, LA 71067
Phone No.: 318-949-9884
Toll Free Order No.: 888-458-4126
Fax No.: 318-949-9829
website: www.clarkcustomguns.com
Email: clarkguns@prysm.net

COBB MANUFACTURING, INC.
Please refer to Bushmaster listing.

COBRA
Please refer to Tristar listing.

COBRA ENTERPRISES OF UTAH, INC.
1960 S. Milestone Drive, Ste. F
Salt Lake City, UT 84104
Phone No.: 801-908-8300
Fax No.: 801-908-8301
Website: www.cobrapistols.com
Email: info@cobrapistols.net

CODY FIREARMS MUSEUM
720 Sheridan Ave.
Cody, WY 82414
Historical Research Phone No.: 307-578-4031
Website: www.bbhc.org

COGSWELL & HARRISON LTD.
Heathcliffe, Parkers Lane
Maidens Green, Bracknell
Berkshire, ENGLAND
Phone No.: 011-44-1344885091
Fax No.: 011-44-1344890906
Website: www.cogswell.co.uk
Email: cogswellandharrison@barclays.net

COLE GUNSMITHING
21 Bog Hollow Rd.
Harpswell, ME 04079
Phone No.: 207-833-5027
Fax No.: 207-833-5677
Website: www.colegun.com

COLT
Colt's Manufacturing Company LLC
P.O. Box 1868
Hartford, CT 06144-1868
Phone No.: 800-962-COLT
Fax No.: 860-244-1449
Website: www.coltsmfg.com
Colt Defense LLC (Law Enforcement & Rifles)
P.O. Box 118
Hartford, CT 06141
Phone No.: 860-232-4489
Fax No.: 860-244-1442
Website: www.colt.com
Historical Research - Colt Archive Properties LLC
P.O. Box 1868
Hartford, CT 01644-1868
If mailing in a request, make sure the proper research fee is enclosed (please refer to appropriate Colt section for current fees and related information).
1st and 2nd Generation phone service only
Phone no: 800-962-COLT
(Ask for Historical Dept. Research fees start at $150.)
Colt Cavalry & Artillery Revolver Authentication Service
Mr. John Kopec, Historian
Phone: 530-222-4440
Email: coltauthenticity@aol.com

COMANCHE
Master Distributor – SGS Imports Int'l, Inc.
1750 Brielle Ave., Unit B-1
Wanamassa, NJ 07712
Phone No.: 732-493-0302
Fax No.: 732-493-0301
Email: sodinimike@earthlink.net

COMPETITOR CORPORATION
26 Knight Street, Unit 3
P.O. Box 352
Jaffrey, NH 03452
Phone No.: 603-532-9483
Fax No.: 603-532-8209
Website: www.competitor-pistol.com
Email: Competitorcorp@aol.com

CONCO ARMS INTERNATIONAL
P.O. Box 159
Emmaus, PA 18049
Phone/Fax No.: 610-967-5477

CONNECTICUT SHOTGUN MANUFACTURING COMPANY
100 Burritt Street
New Britain, CT 06503-4004
Phone No.: 860-225-6581
Fax No.: 860-832-8707
Website: www.connecticutshotgun.com
Email: Galazan@msn.com

CONQUEST
MK Vertriebs-Gesellschaft
Am Tairnbacher Weg 14
Dielheim D-69234 GERMANY
Fax No.: 011-49-06222-7721-35

COOPER FIREARMS OF MONTANA, INC.
P.O. Box 114
4004 Hwy. 93 North
Stevensville, MT 59870
Phone No.: 406-777-0373
Fax No.: 406-777-5228
Website: www.cooperfirearms.com
Email: cooper@bigsky.net

CORTONA
Importer - Kalispell Case Line
P.O. Box 267
Cusick, WA 99119
Phone No.: 800-398-0338
Website: www.cortonashotguns.com
Factory - please refer to F.A.I.R. listing

COSMI, AMERICO & FIGLIO s.n.c.
Distributor - please refer to Dewing's Fly & Gun listing.
Importer - Pacific Sporting Arms
850 W. Foothill Blvd. No. 20
Azuza, CA 91702
Phone No.: 626-633-1002
Fax No.:626-633-1113
Website: www.pacificsportingarms.com
Factory
Via Flaminia 307
I-60020 Torrette di Ancona, ITALY
Fax No.: 011-39-071-887-008
Website: www.cosmi.net
Email: cosmi@cosmi.net

CRICKETT RIFLE
Keystone Sporting Arms
RD2 Box 20
Milton, PA 17847
Phone No.: 570-742-2777
Fax No.: 570-742-1455
Website: www.crickett.com
Email: crickett@sunlink.net

D'ARCY ECHOLS & CO.
P.O. Box 421
98 West 300 South
Millville, UT 84326
Phone No.: 435-755-6842
Fax No.: 435-753-2367

DGS, INC.
404 N. Jackson
Casper, WY 82601
Phone No.: 307-237-2414
Email: dalest42@msn.com

DPMS FIREARMS, LLC
3312 12th Street SE
St. Cloud, MN 56304
Phone No.: 320-258-4448
Fax No.: 320-258-4449
Website: www.dpmsinc.com
Email: dpms@dpmsinc.com

DSA, INC.
P.O. Box 370
Barrington, IL 60011
Phone No.: 847-277-7258
Fax No.: 847-227-7259
Website: www.dsarms.com
Email: dsarms@earthlink.net

DAEWOO
Importer - please refer to Century International Arms listing.

DAKOTA ARMS, INC.
1310 Industry Road
Sturgis, SD 57785
Phone No.: 605-347-4686
Fax No.: 605-347-4459
Website: www.dakotaarms.com
Email: info@dakotarms.com

DAKOTA SINGLE ACTION REVOLVERS
Importer - please refer to E.M.F. Company listing.

DALVAR OF U.S.A.
Please refer to the Radom listing.

DALY, CHARLES: CURRENT MFG.
Importer - please refer to K.B.I., Inc. listing.
Website: www.charlesdaly.com

DARNE S.A.
Importer - Geoffroy Gournet
Phone No.: 610-559-0710
Website: www.darneusa.com
Email: DarneUSA@yahoo.com
Factory - Bruchet Darne
4 ter, rue de la Convention
F-42100 Saint Etienne, FRANCE
Phone No.: 011-33-477-370096
Email: darne.fusil.bruchet@wanadoo.fr

DAUDSONS ARMOURY
Industrial Estate, Kohat Road
Peshawar, 25210 PAKISTAN
Fax No.: 011-92-91-276059
Web site: www.daudsons.org
Email: info@daudsons.org

DAVID MILLER CO.
3131 E. Greenlee Rd.
Tucson, AZ 85716
Phone No.: 520-326-3117
Fax No.: 520-327-7672

DAVIDSON'S
6100 Wilkinson Dr.
Prescott, AZ 86301-6162
Phone No.: 800-367-4867
Fax No.: 928-776-0344
Website: www.galleryofguns.com

DEHANN SHOTGUNS LTD.
4660 E. 267 N.
Rigby, ID 83442
Phone No.: 208-538-6744
Website: www.DHshotguns.com
Email: info@DHshotguns.com

DEMAS, Ets
Importer & Sales - please refer to Verney-Carron listing.
Factory - Atelier Demas
11, rue Agricol Perdiguier
F-42000 St. Etienne, FRANCE
Fax No.: 011-33-477-813437
Website: www.demas.fr
Email: demas@demas.fr

J.C. DEVINE, INC. (AUCTIONS)
P.O. Box 413
20 South Street
Milford, NH 03055
Phone No.:603-673-4967
Fax No.: 603-672-0328
Website: www.jcdevine.com
Email: jcdevine@empire.net

DEWING'S FLY & GUN SHOP
123 Datura Street
West Palm Beach, FL 33401-5601
Phone: 561-659-2321
Web site: www.dewings.com
Email: dewing@bellsouth.net

DICKSON & MACNAUGHTON
21 Frederick Street
Edinburgh, Scotland UK EH2 2NE
Fax No.: 011-44-131-225-3658
Website: www.dicksonandmacnaughton.com

JOHN DICKSON & SON
Please refer to the Dickson & MacNaughton listing.

DIXIE GUN WORKS
P.O. Box 130
Union City, TN 38281
Phone No.: 731-885-0700
Fax No.: 731-885-0400
Website: www.dixiegunworks.com
Email: info@dixiegunworks.com

DLASK ARMS CORP.
202B 1546 Derwent Way
Delta, British Columbia, V3M 6M4 CANADA
Phone No.: 604-527-9942
Fax No.: 604-527-9982
Website: www.dlask.com
Email: dlask@telus.net

DOUBLESTAR CORPORATION
Box 430
Winchester, KY 40391
Phone No.: 859-745-1757
Fax No.: 859-745-4638
Website: www.star15.com
Website: www.jtdistributing.com
Email: sales@star15.com

DOWNSIZER CORPORATION
P.O. Box 710316
Santee, CA 92072-0316
Phone No.: 619-448-5510
Website: www.downsizer.com

DUCKS UNLIMITED, INC.
One Waterfowl Way
Memphis, TN 38120-2351
Phone No.: 901-758-3825
Fax No.: 901-758-3850
website: www.ducks.org

DUMOULIN, ERNEST S.P.R.L.
Importer - please refer to Empire Rifle Company listing.
Factory
Rue du Bouxthay 41
B-4041 Vottem-Herstal, BELGIUM
Fax No.: 011-32-41-228-89-69
Website: www.dumoulin-herstal.com
Email: contact@dumoulin-herstal.be

DUMOULIN, HENRI & FILS
Factory - Dumoulin, Henri & Fils
60 rue Hubert Streel
Herstal 4432, BELGIUM
Fax No.: 011-31-492-523-937
Email: aukesyh@hotmail.com

DUMOULIN HERSTAL S.A.
Importer - please refer to Empire Rifle Company listing.
Factory
13 Rue du Tige
B-4040 Herstal, BELGIUM
Fax No.: 011-32-41-228-89-69
Website: www.dumoulin-herstal.com
Email: contact@dumoulin-herstal.be

DYNAMIT NOBEL
Factory - Dynamit Nobel Ammo Tec GmbH
Kronacher Strasse 63
Furth D-90765 GERMANY
Fax No.: 011-49-180-279-7797
Email: RWS@dynamit-nobel.com

E.D.M. ARMS
421 Business Ctr. Ct.
Redlands, CA 92374
Phone No.: 909-798-2770
Fax No.: 909-798-2889
Website: www.edmarms.com
Email: edm.arms@verizon.net

E.M.F. COMPANY
1900 E. Warner Ave., Suite 1-D
Santa Ana, CA 92705
Phone No.: 949-261-6611
Fax No.: 949-756-0133
Website: www.emf-company.com
Email: sales@emf-company.com

EAGLE ARMS
Please refer to Armalite listing.

EFFEBI snc
Factory
Via Rossa, 4
I-25062 Concesio (BS) ITALY
Fax No.: 011-39-030-218-0414
Website: www.effebisnc.it
Email: info@effebisnc.it

EGE SPORTING ARMS
Ataurk Mah. Gazi Bulv No. 24
Kemalpasa Izmir TURKEY TR-35170
Fax No.: 011-90-232-877-1362
website: www.egesilah.com
Email: info@egesilah.com

EGO ARMAS, S.A.
Victor Sarasqueta, 1-4
Apartado 56
E-20600 Eibar (Guipuzcoa) SPAIN
Fax No.: 011-34-43-120463

EMPIRE RIFLE COMPANY LLC
36 Jenney Road, P.O. Box 406
Meriden, NH 03770
Phone No.: 603-469-3152
Fax No.: 603-619-8918
Website: www.empirerifles.com
Email: info@empirerifles.com

ENTRÉPRISE ARMS INC.
5321 Irwindale Ave.
Baldwin Park, CA 91706-2025
Phone No.: 626-962-8712
Fax No.: 626-962-4692
Websites: www.entreprise.com

ERHARDT, DENNIS
4508 North Montana Ave.
Helena, MT 59602
Phone No.: 406-442-4533

ERN, MAX
Importer - please refer to New England Custom Gun listing.
Bergische Landstrasse 87
Leverkusen-Schlebusch D-51375 GERMANY
Fax No.: 011-49-0214-505860
Email: Max.Ern@t-online.de

ESCALADE
Importer - please refer to Mitchell's Mausers listing.

ESCORT
Importer – please refer to Legacy Sports International listing.
Factory - Hatsan Arms Company
Izmir - Ankara Karayolu 28. km. No. 289
Kemalpasa 35170, Izmir - TURKEY
Fax No.: 011-90-232-878-9102-878-9723
Website: www.hatsan.com.tr
Email: info@hatsan.com.tr

ESSEX ARMS (Parts)
Box 345
Island Pond, VT 05846
Phone No.: 802-723-4313
Fax No.: 802-723-6203

EUROARMS OF AMERICA
208 East Piccadilly Street
P.O. Box 3277
Winchester, VA 22604
Phone No.: 540-662-1863
Fax No.: 540-662-4464
Website: www.euroarms.net
Email: tell-us@euroarms.net

EUROARMS ITALIA s.r.l.
(formerly Armi San Paolo)
via Europa 172/A
I-25062 Concesio, (BS) ITALY
Fax No.: 011-39-30-218-0365
Website: www.euroarms.net
Email: info@euroarms.net

EUROPEAN AMERICAN ARMORY CORP.
P.O. Box 560746
Rockledge, FL 32959
Phone No.: 321-639-4842
Fax No.: 321-639-7006
Website: www.eaacorp.com
Email: eaacorp@eaacorp.com

EVOLUTION USA
P.O. Box 154
White Bird, ID 83554
Phone No.: 208-983-9208
Fax No. 208-983-0944
Website: www.evo-rifles.com
Email: evorifles@wildblue.net

EXCEL INDUSTRIES, INC.
4510 Carter Court
Chino, CA 91710
Phone No.: 909-627-2404
Fax No.: 909-627-7817
Website: www.excelarms.com
Email: info@excelarms.com

F.A.I.R. S.r.l.
Importer - please refer to Savage listing.
Importer - please refer to Cortona listing.
Importer - please refer to Dewing's listing.
Factory - Fabbrica Armi Isidoro Rizzini
Via Gitti, 41
I-25060 Marcheno (BS) ITALY
Fax No.: 011-39-030-861-0179
Website: www.fair.it
Email: info@fair.it

F.A.V.S.
Factory – Fabbrica Armi Valle Susa
Via Nazionale Moncenisio 35
10050 Villar Focchiardo (To) ITALY
Fax No.: 011-39-964-5496
Website: www.favsarmi.com
Email: info@favsarmi.com

FAS
Factory
Domino via Galilei
1-20010 Cornaredo, ITALY
Fax No.: 011-39-02-9364-9570
Website: www.fasdomino.com
Email: info@fasdomino.com

FEG
Importer - SSME Deutsche Waffen, Inc.
408 W. Renfro St. #107J
Plant City, FL 33566
Phone No.: 813-754-8668
Fax No.: 813-659-3361
Website: www.ssmedwi.com
Email: ssmedwi@verizon.net
Factory - FEGARMY
1095 Budapest, Soroksari ut 158
Levelcim: H-1440 Budapest Pf. 6 HUNGARY
Fax No.: 011-361-280-6669

FIAS
Please refer to the Sabatti Armi listing.

FN HERSTAL S.A.
Importer - FNH USA, Inc.
P.O. Box 697
McLean, VA 22101
Phone No.: 703-288-1292
Fax No.: 703-288-1730
Website: www.fnhusa.com
Email: info@fnhusa.com
Military Only
P.O. Box 896
McLean, VA 22101
Phone No.: 703-288-3500
Fax No.: 703-288-4505
Factory - F.N. Herstal S.A.
Voie de Liege, 33
Herstal, Belgium B4040
Fax No.: 011-324-240-8679
Website: www.fnherstal.com

FABARM S.p.A.
Importer - please refer to Tristar listing.
Factory - Fabbrica Breciana Armi
Via Averolda 31, Zona Industriale
I-25039 Travagliato, Brescia ITALY
Fax No.: 011-39-030-686-3684
Website: www.fabarm.com

FABBRI s.n.c.
Importer - please refer to Dewing's listing.
Factory
Via Dante Alighieri, 29
I-25062 Concesio (BS) ITALY
Fax No.: 011-39-030-218-7301
Website: www.fabbri.it
Email: info@fabbri.it

FABRIQUE NATIONALE
Factory - Browning S.A.
Fabrique Nationale Herstal SA
Parc Industriel des Hauts Sarts
3me Ave. 25
B-4040 Herstal, BELGIUM
Fax No.: 011-32-42-40-5212

FALCO, s.r.l.
European Representative - please refer to Effebi listing.
Factory
via A. Gitti, 60
I-25060 Marcheno (Brescia) ITALY
Fax No.: 011-39-30-896-6413
Website: www.falcoarms.com
Email: info@falcoarms.com

FAMARS di ABBIATICO & SALVINELLI srl
Importer - please refer to William Larkin Moore listing.
Importer - please refer to Dewing's Fly & Gun Shop listing.
Importer - Chris Batha
43 Pinckney Colony Road
Okatie, SC 29902
Phone No.: 866-254-2406
Website: www.chrisbatha.com
Email: chrisbatha@aol.com
Importer – Robin Hollow Outfitters
Addieville East Farm
200 B Pheasant Dr.
Mapleville, RI 02839
Phone No.: 401-568-0331
Fax No.: 401-568-0264
Website: www.robinhollow.com
Email: RHOAddieville@aol.com
Factory
Via Valtrompia 16/18
I-25063 Gardone, V.T. Brescia ITALY
Fax No.: 011-39-030-891-2894
Website: www.famars.com
Email: info@famars.com

FANZOJ, JOHANN
Exclusive U.S. dealer - please refer to Dewing's Fly & Gun Shop listing.
Factory - Fanzoj Jagdwaffen GmbH
Greisgasse 3
9170 Ferlach, AUSTRIA
Fax No.: 011-43-4227-2867
Website: www.fanzoj.com
Email: jfanzoj@aon.at

FARQUHARSON
Please refer to Ballard Arms listing.

FAUSTI, STEFANO SRL
Importer - please refer to Weatherby listing.
Importer - please refer to Cabela's listing.
Factory
Via Martiri Dell'Indipendenza, 70
I-25060 Marcheno (Brescia) ITALY
Fax No.: 011-39-030-861-0155
Website: www.faustistefanoarms.com
Email: info@faustistefanoarms.com

FEATHER USA
600 Oak Avenue
P.O. Box 247
Eaton, CO 80615
Phone No.: 800-519-0485
Fax No.: 970-206-1958
Website: www.featherusa.com
Email: featherawi@aol.com

FEINWERKBAU
Importer - please refer to Brenzovich listing.
Factory - Westinger & Altenburger GmbH
Neckarstrasse 43
D-78727 Oberndorf GERMANY
Fax No.: 011-49-7423-814-223
Website: www.feinwerkbau.de
Email: info@feinwerkbau.de

FERLACHER WAFFEN PRÄZISIONSTECHNIK PRODUCTIONS GmbH & CO. KG.
Maschinenhausgasse 5
A-9170 Ferlach AUSTRIA
Fax No.: 011-43-4227-3714
Website: www.ferlacherpraezision.com
Email: office@ferlacherpraezision.com

FERLIB
Factory - Ferlib di Tanfoglio Ivano
via Parte 33
I-25060 Marcheno BS ITALY
Fax No. 011-39-030-896-6882
Website: www.ferlib.com
Email: info@ferlib.com

FERELL, ROGER
130 White Oak Ct.
Fayetteville, GA 30214-3885
Phone /Fax No.: 770-460-0533
Email: rogersgunworks@yahoo.com

FIELDSPORT
3313 W. South Airport Road
Traverse City, MI 49684
Phone No.: 616-933-0767
Phone No.: 616-933-0768
Website: www.fieldsportltd.com

FIREARMS INTERNATIONAL INC.
5200 Mitchelldale, Suite E-17
Houston, TX 77092
Phone No.: 713-462-4200
Fax No.: 713-681-5665
Website: www.highstandard.com
Email: info@highstandard.com

FIRESTORM
Master Distributor – SGS Imports Int'l, Inc.
1750 Brielle Ave., Unit B-1
Wanamassa, NJ 07712
Phone No.: 732-493-0302
Fax No.: 732-493-0301
Website: www.firestorm-sgs.com
Email: firestormsgs@aol.com

FIOCCHI OF AMERICA, INC.
(Ammunition & Components)
5030 Fremont Rd.
Ozark, MO 65721
Phone No.: 417-725-4118
Fax No.: 417-725-1039
Factory - Fiocchi Munizioni S.P.A.
Via Santa Barbara, 4
I-23900 Lecco ITALY
Fax No.: 011-039-0341473-203
Web site: www.fiocchigfl.it
Email: segreteria@fiocchigfl.it

FLODMAN GUNS SWEDEN
Skullman Enterprise AB
S-647 95 Akers Styckebruk
Jarsta SWEDEN
Fax No.: 011-46-159-30061
Website: www.flodman.com
Email: virve@flodman.com

A.H. FOX
Current mfg. only – please refer to Connecticut Shotgun Manufacturing Co. listing.
Older A.H. Fox Historical Research
Mr. John Callahan
53 Old Quarry Rd.
Westfield, MA 01085
$30-$40 gun research fee.

FRANCHI, LUIGI
Importer - please refer to Benelli USA listing.
Website: www.franchiusa.com
Factory - Franchi, Luigi, S.p.A.
via Artigiani 1
I-25063 Gardone, VT (Brescia) ITALY
Fax No.: 011-039-030-8341-899
Website: www.franchi.com
Email: info@franchi.com

FRASER, DANL. & CO.
Please refer to the Dickson & MacNaughton listing.

FREEDOM ARMS
P.O. Box 150
314 Hwy. 239
Freedom, WY 83120
Phone No.: 307-883-2468
Fax No.: 307-883-2005
Website: www.freedomarms.com
Email: freedom@freedomarms.com

FULTON ARMORY
8725 Bollman Place #1
Savage, MD 20763
Phone No.: 301-490-9485
Fax No.: 301-490-9547
Website: www.fulton-armory.com

GALAZAN
Please refer to Connecticut Shotgun Manufacturing Co. listing.

GALIL
No current U.S. importation - semi-auto rifle configuration was banned April, 1998.

GAMBA, RENATO
Exclusive Importer and Distributor – Renato Gamba U.S.A. Corp.
P.O. Box 615
Walnut, CA 91788-0615
Website: www.renatogambausa.com
Email: info@renatogambausa.com
U.S. Service Center
33 Claremont Road
Bernardsville, NJ 07924
Phone No.: 908-766-2287
Fax No.: 908-766-1068
Factory - Bremec srl
Via Artigiani, 91/93
I-25063 Gardone V.T. (Brescia), ITALY
Fax No.: 011-39-030-891-0265
Website: www.renatogamba.it
Email: infocomm@renatogamba.it

GARBI
Importer - please refer to William Larkin Moore & Co. listing.
Factory - Armas Garbi
Urki, 12-14
E-20600 Eibar, SPAIN

GARRAY RIFLES, LTD.
P.O. Box 29099
OK Mission RPO
Kelowna, BC CANADA V1W 4A2
Phone No.: 250-764-0712
Fax No.: 250-764-0728
Website: www.bgamag.com

GATEWAY PRECISION ARMS
8301 Crest Industrial Drive, Ste. C
Affton, MO 63123
Phone No.: 314-832-4005
Fax No.: 314-832-4006
Email: gatehose@mindspring.com

GATLING GUN COMPANY
Battery Gun Co.
Website: www.thebatteryguncompany.com
BWE Firearms
Longwood, FL 32750
Phone: (407) 592-3975
Website: www.bwefirearms.com
E-Mail: BWE@cfl.rr.com
New Zealand Gatling Gun Co.
Website: www.machineguns.co.nz
Manufacturer and distributor - Furr Arms
485 South Commerce Road
Orem, UT 84058
Phone No.: 801-226-3877

GAUCHER
Please refer to Bretton-Gaucher listing.

GAZELLE ARMS
Importer - EMA Distributors LLC
10809 Southern Loop Blvd. #7
Pineville, NC 28134
Phone: 1-866-GAZELLE
Factory - Hisar Avcilik & Doga Sporlasi San Ve Tic. Ltd. Sti.
Sokak No. 48
Konak/Izmir, 861
TR-35250 TURKEY
Fax No.: 011-90-0232-441-6667
Website: www.gazellearms.com
Email: gazellearms@gazellearms.com

GENTRY, DAVID - CUSTOM GUNMAKER
314 N. Hoffman
Belgrade, MT 59714
Phone No.: 406-388-GUNS
Website: www.gentrycustom.com

GIANI, VITTORIO (MAG)
Via Dante, 163
Ponte Zanano (BS), ITALY I-25068
Fax No.: 011-39-030-8908079
Website: www.mag.it
Email: info@mag.it

GIL, ANTONIO & CO.
Factory
C/Ibargain, 8-2
Eibar (Guipuzcoa), SPAIN 20600
Fax No.: 011-34-943-700699

GLOCK, INC.

Importer
6000 Highlands Pkwy.
Smyrna, GA 30082
Fax No.: 770-433-8719
Website: www.glock.com

Factory - Glock Ges.m.b.H.
Nelkengasse 3, POB 9
A-2232 Deutsch-Wagram AUSTRIA
Fax No.: 011-43-2247-90300312

GRAND POWER s.r.o.

Importer - please refer to STI International listing.
Lesna 1
974 01 Banska Bystrica
SLOVAK REPUBLIC
Fax No.: 011-421-48-414-8754
Website: www.grandpower.sk
Email: sales@grandpower.eu

GRANGER, G.

U.S. Agent - Jean-Jacques Perodeau
P.O. Box 3191
Woodring Municipal Airport
Enid, OK 73702
Phone No.: 580-237-7388
Fax No.: 580-242-6922

Factory
66 Cours Fauriel
F-42100 St. Etienne FRANCE
Fax No.: 011-33-0477-38-66-99

GRANITE MOUNTAIN ARMS, INC.

1725 W. Williams Drive, Ste. 24
Phoenix, AZ 85027
Phone No.: 623-434-3404
Website: www.granitemountainarms.com
Email: GMAHUNTER@aol.com

GRANT, STEPHEN

Factory - please refer to Atkin, Grant & Lang listing.

GREG MARTIN AUCTIONS

298 San Bruno Ave.
San Francisco, CA 94103
Phone No.: 800-509-1988
Phone No.: 415-522-5708
Fax No.: 415-522-5706
Website: www.gmartin-auctions.com
Email: info@gmartin-auctions.com

GREEN, ROGER

11611 E. Tom Sawyer Road
Evansville, WY 82636
Phone No.: 307-473-1112
Fax No.: 307-473-1516
Website: www.rogermgreen.com
Email: rmgreen@rogermgreen.com

GREENER, W. W.

Sales/Administration Offices
Poachers Pocket, Stoppers Hill, Brinkworth
Chippenham, Wiltshire, SN15 5AW ENGLAND
Fax No.: 011-44-1666-510898
Website: www.wwgreener.com
Email: sales@wwgreener.com

Factory
The Mews, Hagley Hall
Hagley DY9 9LG ENGLAND

GRIFFIN & HOWE

Store Location (Gunsmithing also)
33 Claremont Road
Bernardsville, NJ 07924
Phone No.: 908-766-2287
Fax No.: 908-766-1068
Website: www.griffinhowe.com
Email: prather@griffinhowe.com

Store Location
340 West Putnam Ave.
Greenwich, CT 06830
Phone No.: 203-618-0270
Fax No.: 203-618-0419
Website: www.griffinhowe.com

Shooting School & Events
270 Stanhope Rd.
Andover, NJ 07821
Phone No.: 973-398-4330

GRIFFON

European Distributor
Kung GmbH
Amtshausgasse 2
Liestal, Switzerland CH-4410
Fax No.: 011-41-061-922-1245

Manufacturer - Continental Weapons (Pty) Ltd.
2 Royal Palm Business Estate
Corner K101, West Roads
Midrand, Gauteng SOUTH AFRICA 1685
Fax No.: 011-27-11-312-2080
Website: www.cwl.co.za

GRULLA ARMAS, S.L.

Importer/Dealer - please refer to Fieldsport listing.
Importer/Dealer - please refer to Merkel USA listing.
Importer /Dealer– please refer to Harry Marx Hi-Grade Import listing.
Importer/Dealer - please refer to Lion Country Supply listing.
Importer/Dealer - Dale Decoys Den
5474 State Street
Albany, OH 45710
Phone No.: 614-698-5060
Website: www.dalesdecoyden.com

Factory - Grulla Armas
P.O. Box 453
Avda. de Otaola, 12
E-20600 Eibar (Guipuzcoa) SPAIN
Fax No.: 011-34-9-43-702133
Website: www.grullarmas.com
Email: usobiaga@grullaarmas.com

GRUND, KARL

Pfarrhofgasse 2
A-9170 Ferlach, AUSTRIA
Fax No.: 011-43-4227-2256
Website: www.jagdwaffen-juch-grund-ferlach.at

GRÜNIG & ELMIGER AG

U.S. representative - please refer to Gunsmithing, Inc. listing.
U.S. representative - please refer to Brenzovich listing.
U.S. representative - please refer to Champion's Choice listing.
Factory
Industriestr. 22
CH-6102 Malters SWITZERLAND
Fax No.: 011-041-499-9049
Website: www.gruenel.ch
Email: gruenel@gruenel.ch

GSI (GUN SOUTH INC.)
Please refer to Merkel USA listing.

G.U. INC.
Please refer to SKB Shotguns listing.

GUN 1
Please refer to Savage listing.

GUNCRAFTER INDUSTRIES
171 Madison 1510
Huntsville, AR 72740
Phone No.: 479-665-2466
Website: www.guncrafterindustries.com

GUNSMITHING INC.
30 West Buchanan Street
Colorado Springs, CO 80907
Phone No.: 800-284-8671
Fax No.: 719-632-3493
Website: www.nealjguns.com
Email: neal@nealjguns.com

HHF
Please refer to Huglu listing.

H & R 1871, LLC
Harrington & Richardson (post-1991 mfg. only)
60 Industrial Rowe
Gardner, MA 01440
Phone No.: 978-632-9393
Fax No.: 978-632-2300
Website: www.hr1871.com
Email: hr1871@hr1871.com

H-S PRECISION, INC.
1301 Turbine Dr.
Rapid City, SD 57703
Phone No.: 605-341-3006
Fax No.: 605-342-8964
Website: www.hsprecision.com

HABSBURG, LINIE
Griesgasse 3
A-9170 Ferlach Austria
Fax No.: 011-43-4227-533630
Website: www.linie-habsburg.com
Email: ferlach@liniehabsburg.com

HALO ARMS, LLC
P.O. Box 552
Phoenixville, PA 19460
Phone No.: 484-614-4860
Fax No.: 610-933-0186
Website: www.haloarms.com
Email: mail@haloarms.com

HAMBRUSCH JAGDWAFFEN GmbH
Importer - please refer to CONCO Arms International
Factory - Hambrusch Jagdwaffen Gesellschaft
Gartengasse 4
A-9170 Ferlach, AUSTRIA
Fax No.: 011-43-4227-4106
Website: www.ferlachguns.com
Email: hambrush@ferlachguns.com

HÄMMERLI AG
Importer, Sales & Service – please refer to
Larry's Guns Inc. listing.

Importer – please refer to Champion's Choice listing.
Importer - please refer to Brenzovich Firearms listing.
Importer - please refer to Gunsmithing, Inc. listing.
Repair/Gunsmithing Services – HÄMMERLI AG
10-Ring-Service, Inc.
2227 West Lou Drive
Jacksonville, FL 32216
Phone No.: 904-724-7419
Fax No.: 904-724-7149
Factory - please refer to Walther factory listing.

HARRISON & HUSSEY
Please refer to Cogswell & Harrison listing.

HARRY MARX HI-GRADE IMPORTS
8707 Monterey Road
P.O. Box 519
Gilroy, CA 95021
Phone No.: 408-846-1111 or 408-846-8500
Fax No.: 408-842-7270 or 408-842-9323
Website: www.higradeimports.com
Email: Hi-gradeimports@mindspring.com

HARTMANN & WEISS GmbH
Rahlstedter Bahnhofstr. 47
22143 Hamburg, GERMANY
Phone No.: 011-49-40-677-5585
Fax No.: 011-49-40-677-5592
Email: hartmannundweiss@t-online.de

HATFIELD GUN COMPANY LLC
1247 Rand Road
Des Plaines, IL 60016
Phone No.: 847-768-1000
Fax No.: 847-768-1001
Website: www.hatfield-usa.com
Email: info@hatfield-usa.com

HATFIELD'S
2028 Frederick Ave.
St. Joseph, MO 64501
Phone No.: 816-233-9106
Email: TLRiver@aol.com

HATSAN ARMS COMPANY
Importer - please refer to Legacy Sports International LLC listing.
Izmir-Ankara Karayolu 28.km. No. 289
Kemalpasa 35170 Izmir TURKEY
Fax No.: 011-90-232-878-9102
website: www.hatsan.com.tr
Email: info@hatsan.com.tr

KARL HAUPTMANN JAGDWAFFEN
Bahnhofstrasse 5
A-9170 Ferlach, AUSTRIA
Fax No.: 011-43-4227-3435
Website: www.hauptmann-rifles.com
Email: office@hauptmann-rifles.com

HASKELL MFG. INC.
Please refer to Hi-Point listing.

HECKLER & KOCH, INC.
Importer - Merkel USA
7661 Commerce Lane
Trussville, AL
Phone No.: 205-655-8299
Fax No.: 205-655-7078
Website: www.hk-usa.com

Factory - Heckler & Koch GmbH
Alte Steige 7
P.O. Box 1329
D-78727 Oberndorf Neckar GERMANY
Fax No.: 011-49-7423-7922-80
Website: www.heckler-koch.de

N.L. HEINEKE, INC.
201 South Second Street
Laramie, WY 82070
Phone No.: 307-745-8592
Fax No.: 307-745-4198
Website: www.nlheineke.com
Email: nlh@nlheineke.com

HEINIE SPECIALTY PRODUCTS
301 Oak Street
Quincy, IL 62301
Phone No.: 217-228-952
Fax No.: 217-228-9502
Website: www.heinie.com
Email: rheinie@heinie.com

HEIRLOOM ARMES
5996 5th St. SW
Howard Lake, MN 55349
Phone No.: 320-963-5551
Web site: www.heirloomarmes.com
Email: dln@lakedalelink.net

HELLIS, CHARLES
16 Saville Row
London W1X 1AE ENGLAND
Fax No.: 011-44-1727-834469
Website: www.hellis.com
Email: Info@hellis.com

HENRY, ALEX
Please refer to the Dickson & MacNaughton listing.

HENRY REPEATING ARMS COMPANY
110 8th St.
Brooklyn, NY 11215
Phone No.: 718-499-5600
Fax No.: 718-768-8056
Website: www.henry-guns.com
Email: info@henryrepeating.com

HERITAGE MANUFACTURING, INC.
4600 NW 135th St.
Opa Locka, FL 33054
Phone No.: 305-685-5966
Fax No.: 305-687-6721
Website: www.heritagemfg.com
Email: infohmi@heritagemfg.com

HERMANN HISTORICA AUCTIONS
Lindprunstrasse 16
D-80335 München GERMANY
Fax No.: 011-49-089-523-7103
Web site: www.hermann-historica.com
Email: contact@hermann-historica.com

HEYM AG
Importer - Double Gun Imports LLC
3416 Rosedale
Dallas, TX 75205
Phone No.: 214-606-2566
Website: www.heymusa.com
Email: info@heymusa.com

Factory - Heym Waffenfabrik AG
Am Aschenbach 2
D-98646 Gleichamberg GERMANY
Fax No.: 011-49-368-75-63222
Website: www.heym-waffenfabrik.de
Email: heym-waffenfabrik@t-online.de

HIENDLMAYER, KLAUS
Landshuter Strasse 59
D-84307 Eggenfelden GERMANY
Fax No.: 011-49-8721-6451
website: www.waffen-hiendlmayer.de
Email: K.Hiendlmayer@t-online.de

HI-POINT FIREARMS
U.S. Marketer - MKS Supply, Inc.
8611-A North Dixie Drive
Dayton, OH 45414
Phone No.: 877-425-4867
Fax No.: 937-454-0503
Website: www.hi-pointFirearms.com
Email: mkshpoint@aol.com

HIGH STANDARD MANUFACTURING CO.
5200 Mitchelldale, Ste. E17
Houston, TX 77092
Phone No.: 713-462-4200
Fax No.: 713-681-5665
Website: www.highstandard.com
Email: info@highstandard.com

HIGH TECH CUSTOMS
3109 N. Cascade Ave., Ste. 102
Colorado Springs, CO 80907
Phone No.: 719-667-1090
Fax No.: 719-632-4505
Website: www.htcustoms.com
Email: htcustoms@pcisys.net

HILL COUNTRY RIFLE COMPANY
5726 Morningside Dr.
New Braunfels, TX 78132
Phone No.: 830-609-3139
Fax No.: 830-625-4020
Website: www.hillcountryrifles.com
Email: sales@hillcountryrifles.com

GEORGE HOENIG INC.
4357 Frozen Dog Rd.
Emmett, ID 83617
Phone No.: 208-365-7716
Email: gnhoenig@msn.com

HOFER-JAGDWAFFEN, PETER
Kirchgasse 24
A-9170 Ferlach, AUSTRIA
Phone No.: 011-43-4227-3683
Fax No.: 011-43-4227-3683-30
Website: www.hoferwaffen.com
Email: peterhofer@hoferwaffen.com

P.L. HOLEHAN, INC.
5758 E. 34th St.
Tucson, AZ 85711
Phone No.: 520-745-0622
Fax No.: 520-745-2248
Email: plholehan@theriver.com
Web site: www.plholehancustomrifles.com

HOLLAND & HOLLAND LTD.
H&H - New York
10 East 40th Street, Ste. 1910
New York, NY 10016
Phone No.: 212-752-7755
Fax No.: 212-752-6975
Website: www.hollandandholland.com
Email: gunroomny@hollandandholland.com
Factory
Attn: Customer Service-BB
31-33 Bruton Street
London, ENGLAND W1X 8JS
Phone No.: 011-44-71-499 4411
Fax No.: 011-44-71-499 4544
Email: gunroomuk@hollandandholland.com

HOLLOWAY & NAUGHTON
Please refer to Premier English Shotguns, Ltd. listing.

HORTON, LEW, DIST. CO.
Please refer to Lew Horton Dist. Co. listing.

HOWA
*Importer – please refer to Legacy Sports
International, LLC listing.*

HUGLU
Importer – please refer to CZ-USA listing.
Factory - Huglu S.S. AV Tufekleri Kooperatifi
Antalya Cad. No. 58
TR-42710 Huglu-Reyashir-Konya TURKEY
Fax No.: 011-90-332-5161032
Website: www.huglu.com.tr
Email: export@huglu.com.tr
Warranty & Service – (Huglu USA guns only)
H-Legacy Shotguns, Ltd. Co.
4660 E. 267 N.
Rigby, ID 83442
Phone No.: 208-538-6744

I.A.B.
Importer - please refer to E.M.F. listing.
Importer - please refer to Dixie Gun Works listing.
Importer - please refer to Tristar listing.
Importer - Kiesler's Firearms
3300 Industrial Parkway
Jeffersonville, IN 47130
Phone No.: 812-288-5740
Factory - Industria Armi Bresciane
Via Matteotti, 311
I-25063 Gardone, Brescia ITALY
Phone/Fax No.: 011-39-030-891-2366
Website: www.iabarms.com
Email: info@iabarms.com

IAR, INC.
33171 Camino Capistrano
San Juan Capistrano, CA 92675
Phone No.: 949-443-3642
Fax No.: 949-443-3647
Website: www.iar-arms.com

I.O. INC.
P.O. Box 847
Monroe, NC 28111-0847
Phone No.: 866-882-1479
Fax No.: 704-225-8895
Website: www.ioinc.us
Email: uli@ioinc.us

IGA SHOTGUNS
Importer - please refer to Stoeger Industries, Inc. listing.

IBERIA FIREARMS
Please refer to Hi-Point listing.

INFINITY FIREARMS
Distributor - please refer to JP Enterprises listing.
Manufacturer - Strayer Voight, Inc.
3435 Roy Orr Blvd., Ste. 200
Grand Prairie, TX 75050
Phone No.: 972-513-1911
Fax No.: 972-513-0575
Website: www.sviguns.com
Email: info@sviguns.com
Factory - INTERTEX-Maschinenbau GmbH & Co.
Ludwigstrasse 24-28
D-73054 Eislingen GERMANY
Fax no.: 011-49-7161-98-40-5-50
Email: intertex@t-online.de

INTERARMS ARSENAL
Please refer to High Standard listing.

INTERSTATE ARMS CORP.
6G Dunham Road
Billerica, MA 01821
Phone No.: 800-243-3006
Phone No.: 978-667-7060
Fax No.: 978-671-0023
Website: www.interstatearms.com

INVESTARM, s.p.a.
Factory - Fabbrica D'Armi
via Zanardelli, 210
I-25060 Marcheno, Brescia ITALY
Fax No.: 011-39-030-861-285
Website: www.investarm.com
Email: info@investarm.com

ITHACA GUN COMPANY LLC
Repair & Service - please refer to Ithaca Guns USA, LLC listing.

ITHACA GUNS USA, LLC
420 N. Warpole St.
Upper Sandusky, OH 43351
Phone No.: 419-294-4113
Fax No.: 419-294-9433
Web site: www.ithacagunsusa.com
Email: service@ithacagunsusa.com

ISRAELI MILITARY INDUSTRIES
*U.S./Canadian importer & distributor - please refer to Magnum
Research, Inc. listing*
Factory
Website: www.imi-israel.com

IVER JOHNSON ARMS, INC.
1840 Baldwin Street, Unit 10
Rockledge, FL 32955
Phone No.: 321-636-3377
Fax No.: 321-632-7745
Website: www.iverjohnsonarms.com

IZHMASH
Importer - please refer to Russian American Armory listing.
Factory - Izhmash, Concern OJSC
3 Proyezd Deryabinia
Izhevsk, RUSSIA 426006
Fax No.: 011-73412-609-099
Website: www.izhmash.ru
Email: itc@izhmash.ru

J.B. CUSTOM INC.
3700 E. Pontiac Street
Fort Wayne, IN 46803
Phone No.: 260-417-2099
Fax No.: 260-422-1400
Website: www.jbcustom.com
Email: diamondjim@jbcustom.com

J.L.D. ENTERPRISES, INC.
Please refer to PTR 91 Inc. listing.

JP ENTERPRISES, INC.
P.O Box 378
Hugo, MN 55038
Phone No.: 651-426-9196
Fax No.: 651-426-2472
Website: www.jprifles.com
Email: service@jprifles.com

J R DISTRIBUTING
15634 Tierra Rejada Rd.
Moorpark, CA 93021
Fax No.: 805-529-2368

JAGD-UND SPORTWAFFEN SUHL GmbH
Distributor - please refer to Merkel USA listing.
Factory - please refer to Merkel listing.

JACK FIRST, INC.
Gun Parts/Accessories/Service
1201 Turbine Dr.
Rapid City, SD 57703
Phone No.: 605-343-9544
Fax No.: 605-343-9420

JACKSON RIFLES
Parton, Castle Douglas
Scotland DG7 3NL U.K.
Fax No.: 011-44-1644-470227
Website: www.jacksonrifles.com

JAMES D. JULIA, INC. (AUCTIONS)
P.O. Box 830, Rte. 201
Skowhegan Rd.
Fairfield, ME 04937
Phone No.: 207-453-7125
Fax No.: 207-453-2502
Website: www.juliaauctions.com

JANZ GmbH
Importer - please refer to Brenzovich listing.
Factory - JANZ-Technik und Labor GmbH
Lutjenburger Str. 84
D-23714 Malente/Holst. GERMANY
Fax No.: 011-49-4523-201655
Website: www.jtl.de/revolver
Email: info@jtl.de

JARRETT RIFLES, INC.
383 Brown Road
Jackson, SC 29831
Phone No.: 803-471-3616
Fax No.: 803-471-9246
Website: www.jarrettrifles.com
Email: info@jarrettrifles.com

JEFFERY, W.J. & CO., LTD.
Please refer to the J. Roberts & Son listing.

JIMENEZ ARMS
Distributor - Shining Star Investments LLC
860 Hembry St., Ste. 403
Lewisville, TX 75057
Phone No.: 866-906-7356
Fax No.: 972-906-7356
Website: www.shiningstardist.com
Email: Contact@shiningStarDist.com

JOHANNSEN RIFLES
Importer - please refer to New England Custom Gun Service listing.
Factory – Reimer Johannsen GmbH
Haart 49
D-24534 Neumünster GERMANY
Fax No.: 011-49-4321-29325
Website: www.johannsen-jagd.de
Email: info@johannsen-jagd.de

JOHNSON AUTOMATIC
Restorations only - Miltech Arms
P.O. Box 322
Los Altos, CA 94023
Phone No.: 650-948-3500
Fax No.: 408-255-7144
Website: www.miltecharms.com

JUST, JOSEF
Hauptplatz 18
A-9170, Ferlach, AUSTRIA
Fax No.: 011-41-04227-2273
Website: www.jagdwaffen-just.at
Email: office@jagdwaffen-just.at

K.B.I., INC.
P.O. Box 6625
5480 Linglestown Road
Harrisburg, PA 17112-0625
Phone No.: 717-540-8518
Fax No.: 717-540-8567
Website: www.kbi-inc.com
Website: www.charlesdaly.com
Website: www.charlesdalydefense.com
Email: sales@kbi-inc.com

KDF, INC.
2485 Highway 46 North
Seguin, TX 78155
Phone No.: 800-KDF-GUNS
Phone No.: 830-379-8141
Fax No.: 830-379-8144
Email: kdfinc@hotmail.com

KAHR ARMS
P.O. Box 220
Blauvelt, NY 10913
Phone No.: 508-795-3919
Fax No.: 508-795-7046
Website: www.kahr.com
Website: www.kahrshop.com

KARL LIPPARD, GUNMAKER
P.O. Box 60719
Colorado Springs, CO 80960
Phone No.: 719-444-0786
Fax No.: 719-444-0731
Website: www.karllippard.com

KEL-TEC CNC INDUSTRIES, INC.
1475 Cox Road
Cocoa, FL 32926
Phone No.: 321-631-0068
Fax No.: 321-631-1169
Website: www.kel-tec-cnc.com
Email: ktcustserv@kel-tec-cnc.com

KEMEN
Importer - please refer to Fieldsport listing.
Factory - Armas Kemen, S.L.
Ermuraranbide, 14 - Apartado n. 60
20870 Elgoibar (Guipuzcoa), SPAIN
Fax No.: 011-34-43-74-4401
Website: www.sport-kemen.com
Email: kemen@sport-kemen.com

KEPPELER TECHNISCHE ENTWICKLUNG GmbH
Friedrich-Reinhardt Strasse 4
D-74427 Fichtenberg, GERMANY
Fax No.: 011-49-07971-91-1243
Website: www.keppeler-te.de
Email: keppeler.te@t-online.de

KEYSTONE SPORTING ARMS
Please refer to Crickett Rifle listing.

KHAN
Importer - please refer to Mossberg listing.
Headquarters
Inkilap Mah. Alemdag Cad.
Site Yolu Sok. No: 3 34768
Umraniye/Istanbul, TURKEY
Fax No.: 011-90-216-632-7444
Website: www.khanshotguns.com
Email: info@khanshotguns.com

KIMAR SRL
Importer - please refer to IAR listing.
Importer - please refer to Traditions listing.
Importer - please refer to Taylor's listing.
Importer - Valor Corporation
1001 Sawgrass Corporate Parkway
Sunrise, FL 33323
Phone No.: 954-377-4925
Website: www.valorcorp.com
Email: sales@valorcorp.com
Factory
Via Milano 2
I-25020 Azzano, Mella (BS) ITALY
Fax No.: 011-39-030-974-9232
Website: www.kimar.com
Email: info@kimar.com

KIMBER
Corporate Offices - Kimber Mfg., Inc.
1 Lawton St.
Yonkers, NY 10705
Phone No.: 800-880-2418
Fax No.: 406-758-2223
Custom Shop Phone No.: 914-964-0742
Website: www.kimberamerica.com
Email: info@kimberamerica.com

KING'S GUN WORKS INC.
1837 West Glenoaks Blvd.
Glendale, CA 91201
Phone No.: 818-956-6010
Fax No.: 818-548-8606
Website: www.kingsgunworks.com
Email: kngswks@earthlink.net

KNIGHTS MANUFACTURING CO. (KMC)
701 Columbia Blvd.
Titusville, FL 32780
Phone No.: 321-607-9900
Fax No.: 321-268-1498
Website: www.knightarmco.com
Email: civiliansales@knightarmco.com

KOLAR ARMS
1925 Roosevelt Ave.
Racine, WI 53406
Phone No.: 262-554-0800
Fax No.: 262-554-9093
Website: www.kolararms.com
Email: info@kolararms.com

KORA BRNO
Factory - Kroko a.s.
Hybesova 46
CZ-602 00 Brno, Czech Republic
Fax No.: 011-420-5-43244346
Website: www.korabrno.cz
Email: kroko@brn.czn.cz

KORTH
Factory - Korth Vertriebsgesellschaft GmbH
Robert Bosch Strasse 4
D-23909 Ratzeburg, GERMANY
Fax No.: 011-49-45-4182479
Website: www.korthwaffen.de
Email: info@korthwaffen.de

KOSCHAT, JAKOB
12 November-Strasse 3
A-9170 Ferlach, AUSTRIA
Fax No.: 011-43-4227-2278
Website: www.jagdwaffen-ferlach.at
Email: koschat@jagdwaffen-ferlach.at

KRICO
Importer - Northeast Arms LLC
Presque Isle Road, P.O. Box 325
Fort Fairfield, ME 04742
Phone No.: 207-473-7698
Email: info@northeastarms.com
European Sales - please refer to Marocchi listing.

Factory - Krico Jagd-und Sportwaffen GmbH
Nurnberger Strasse 6
Pyrbaum, D-90602 GERMANY
Fax No.: 011-49-091-80-2661
Website: www.krico.de
Email: info@krico.de

KRIEGHOFF, H., GUN CO.
Importer - Krieghoff Intl., Inc.
P.O. Box 549
7528 Easton Rd.
Ottsville, PA 18942
Phone No.: 610-847-5173
Fax No.: 610-847-8691
Website: www.krieghoff.com
Email: info@krieghoff.com
Factory - H. Krieghoff GmbH
Boschstrasse 22
D-89079 Ulm, GERMANY
Fax No.: 011-49-731-40-18270
Website: www.krieghoff.de

KRISS-TDI
1776 K Street, 2nd Floor
Washington, DC 20006
Phone No.: 202-659-6888
Fax No.: 202-659-6887
Website: www.kriss-tdi.com

KUPEC, PAVEL PUSKASTVI s.r.o.
areal byv. kasaren Hurka c.6
530 12 Pardubice CZECH REPUBLIC
Fax No.: 011-42-0466-501-557
website: www.puskastvi.cz
Email: kupec@guns-info.cz

L.A.R. MANUFACTURING, INC.
4133 West Farm Road
West Jordan, UT 84088-4997
Phone No.: 801-280-3505
Fax No.: 801-280-1972
Website: www.largrizzly.com
Email: guns@largrizzly.com

LANBER ARMAS S.A.
Importer - Lanber U.S.A.
65 Westfield Industrial Park Rd.
Westfield, MA 01085
Phone No.: 800-545-6952
Fax No.: 413-568-9663
Website: www.lanberusa.com
Factory - ComLanber, S.A.
C/Zubiaurre 3
E-48250 Zaldibar (Vizcaya) SPAIN
Fax No.: 011-34-94-6827999
Website: www.lanber.net
Email: lanber@euskalnet.net

LANG, JOSEPH
Please refer to the Atkin, Grant & Lang Ltd. listing.

LAPORTE HOLDING
357, Allee du Val de Pome
F-06410 Biot, FRANCE
Fax No.: 011-33-493-657778
Website: www.swingtrap.com
Email: info@swingtrap.com

LARRY'S GUNS INC.
56 West Gray Road
Gray, ME 04039
Phone No: 207-657-4559
Fax No.: 207-657-3429
Website: www.larrysguns.com
Email: info@larrysguns.com

LAURONA
Factory - Armas Laurona S.A.L.
P.O. Box 260, Avda de Otaola, 25
E-20600 Eibar (Guipuzcoa) SPAIN
Fax No.: 011-34-943-700616
Website: www.laurona.com
Email: laurona@laurona.com

HARRY LAWSON LLC
3328 N. Richey Blvd.
Tucson, AZ 85716
Phone No.: 520-326-1117

LAZZERONI ARMS COMPANY
1415 South Cherry Ave.
Tucson, AZ 85713
Phone No.: 888-492-7247
Fax No.: 520-624-4250
Website: www.lazzeroni.com
Email: arms@lazzeroni.com

LEBEAU-COURALLY
Importer - please refer to William Larkin Moore & Co. listing.
Importer - please refer to Griffin & Howe listing.
Importer - please refer to Heirloom Armes listing.
Factory - Aug. Lebeau-Courally
386, rue Saint-Gilles
B-4000 Liege, BELGIUM
Fax No.: 011-32-41-52-2008
Website: www.lebeau-courally.com
Email: info@lebeau-courally.com

LEGACY SPORTS INTERNATIONAL LLC
4750 Longley Lane, Ste. 208
Reno, NV 89502
Phone No.: 775-828-0555
Fax No.: 775-828-0565
Website: www.legacysports.com

LEGEND RIFLES
Please refer to D'Arcy Echols & Co.

LEGION
Please refer to Izhmash listing.

LEITNER-WISE RIFLE CO.
7200-G Fullerton Road
Springfield, VA 22150
Phone No.: 703-455-8650
Fax No.: 703-455-8654
Website: www.lwrifles.com
Email: sales@lwrifles.com

LES BAER CUSTOM, INC.
Website: www.lesbaer.com
Email: info@lesbaer.com

LEW HORTON DISTRIBUTING CO.
Distributor Only
15 Walkup Dr., P.O. Box 5023
Westboro, MA 01581
Phone No.: 508-366-7400
Fax No.: 508-366-5332
Website: www.lewhorton.com
Email: 1horton@tiac.net

LEWIS MACHINE & TOOL COMPANY
1305 West 11th Street
Milan, IL 61264
Phone No.: 309-787-7151
Fax No.: 309-787-7193
Website: www.lewismachine.net

LINDER GUN COMPANY
P.O. Box 580
Sanbornville, NH 03872
Website: desertmoon.net/lindner.html
Email: lindner@lindnergun.com

LINEBAUGH, JOHN
P.O. Box 455
Cody, WY 82414
Phone No.: 307-645-3332
Website: www.customsixguns.com

LION COUNTRY SUPPLY
P.O. Box 480
Port Matilda, PA 16870
Phone No.: 800-662-5202
Fax No.: 814-684-5900
Website: www.ugartechea.com

LITTLE JOHN'S AUCTION SERVICE
1740 W. LaVeta Ave.
Orange, CA 92868
Phone No.: 714-939-1170
Fax No.: 714-939-7955
Website: www.littlejohnsauctionservice.com
Email: info@littlejohnsauctionservice.com

LITTLE SHARPS RIFLE MFG.
Mr. Aaron Pursley
8885 Coal Mine Road
Big Sandy, MT 59520
Phone No.: 406-378-3200
Mr. Ronald Otto
P.O. Box 336
Big Sandy, MT 59520
Phone No.: 406-378-3855
Website: www.littlesharps.com
Email: otto@ttc-cmc.net

LJUTIC INDUSTRIES, INC.
732 North 16th Ave., Ste. 22
Yakima, WA 98902
Phone No.: 509-248-0476
Fax No.: 509-576-8233
Website: www.ljuticgun.com
Email: ljuticgun@earthlink.net

LONE STAR RIFLE CO., INC.
11231 Rose Road
Conroe, TX 77303
Phone/Fax No.: 936-856-3363
Website: www.lonestarrifle.com
Email: dave@lonestarrilfe.com

LORENZO, CRESS
349 E. 100 S., Box 14
Minersville, UT 84752
Phone No.: 435-386-1428

SANDRO LUCCHINI
Importer - Springbrook Manufacturing Ltd.
3809 Ninth St. SE
Calgary, Alberta, T2G 3C7 CANADA
Phone No.: 403-243-3308
Fax No.: 403-243-3792
Website: www.springbrook.ca
Factory - Armi Italia di Lucchini Sandro
via Petrarca 47
I-25068 Sarezzo, Brescia, ITALY
Fax No.: 011-39-030-89-11573

MG ARMS, INC.
6030 Treaschwig
Spring, TX 77373
Phone No.: 281-821-8282
Fax No.: 281-821-6387
Website: www.mgarmsinc.com
Email: kerry@mgarmsinc.com

MKE
Factory
06330 Tandogan, Ankara TURKEY
Fax No.: 011-90-312-222-2241
Website: www.mkek.gov.tr

M.O.A. CORPORATION
285 Government Valley Road
Sundance, WY 82729
Phone No.: 307-283-3030
Website: www.moaguns.com
Email: moaguns@rangeweb.net

M.R. NEW SYSTEM ARMS
via Mazzini 30
I-13882 Cerrione ITALY
Fax No.: 011-39-15-671700
Website: www.newsystemarms.com
Email: info@newsystemarms.com

MTs ARMS
Factory - TsKIB SOO
Krasnoarmeyskiy Prospekt 17
R-300041 Tula, RUSSIA
Fax No.: 011-7-0872-31-5959
Email: tularms@tula.net

JAMES MacNAUGHTON & SONS
Please refer to the Dickson & MacNaughton listing.

MAG
Please refer to Vittorio Giani listing.

MAGNUM RESEARCH, INC.
7110 University Ave. NE
Minneapolis, MN 55432
Phone No.: 763-574-1868
Fax No.: 763-574-0109
Website: www.magnumresearch.com

MAGTECH AMMUNITION CO., INC.
6845 20th Ave. S., Ste. 120
Centerville, MN 55038
Phone No.: 651-762-8500
Fax No.: 651-429-9485
Website: www.magtechammunition.com
Email: sales@magtechammunition.com

MAJESTIC ARMS, LTD.
101A Ellis St.
Staten Island, NY 10307
Phone No.: 718-356-6765
Fax No.: 718-356-6835
Website: www.majesticarms.com
Email: majesticarms@juno.com

MAKAROV
Importer - please refer to Century International Arms listing.

MANDALL SHOOTING SUPPLIES
3616 N. Scottsdale Rd.
Scottsdale, AZ 85252
Phone No.: 602-945-2553
Fax No.: 602-949-0734
Email: mandallshooting@earthlink.net

MANU-ARM
43, avenue de la liberation
F-42340, Veauche, FRANCE
Fax No.: 011-33-0477-947936
Website: www.manuarm.fr
Email: manuarm@manuarm.fr

MANUFRANCE
6, Rue de Lodi
F-42000 St. Etienne 1 FRANCE
Fax No.: 011-33-0477-418830
Email: manufrance@wanadoo.fr

MANURHIN REVOLVERS
Factory - Manufacture d. Armes de tir Chapuis - M.A.T.C.H.
Z.I. La Gravoux, BP 15
F-42380 St. Bonnet le Chateau, FRANCE
Fax No.: 011-33-4-77-501070
Website: www.chapuis-armes.com
Email: info@chapuis-armes.com

MARCEL THYS & SONS
U.S. Agent - Jean-Jacques Perodeau
P.O. Box 3191
Woodring Municipal Airport
Enid, OK 73702
Phone No.: 580-237-7388
Fax No.: 580-242-6922
Factory
Rue de Villers, 8
B-4367 Crisne BELGIUM
Fax No.: 011-32-4-240-1718
Email: info@marcelthys.com

MARLIN FIREARMS COMPANY
100 Kenna Drive
P.O. Box 248
North Haven, CT 06473-0905
Phone No.: 203-239-5621
Fax No.: 203-234-7991
Website: www.marlinfirearms.com

MAROCCHI SHOTGUNS
Factory - C.D. Europe SRL
Via Galilei, 6
I-25068 Sarezzo (Brescia) ITALY
Fax No.: 011-39-030-890-0370
Web site: www.marocchiarms.com
Email: info@marocchiarms.com

MARTIN, ALEX
Please refer to the Dickson & MacNaughton listing.

MATCHGUNS srl
Distribution - Gehmann GmbH & Co. KG
Karlstrasse 40
Karlsruhe, GERMANY D-76133
Fax No.: 011-49-721-29888
Website: www.gehmann.com
Factory
Via cartiera 6/d
I-43010 Vigatto, Parma ITALY
Fax No: 011-39-0521-631973
Website: www.matchguns.com
Email: info@matchguns.com

MATCH GRADE ARMS & AMMUNITION
Please refer to MG Arms, Inc. listing.

MATEBA
Please refer to AWA USA listing.

MATHELON ARMES
Factory
Rue de l'Artisanat
Zone Industrielle Les Granges
F-74150 Rumilly FRANCE
Fax No.: 011-33-4-50-016786
website: www.mathelon-armes.com
Email: eric@mathelon-armes.com

MAUSER
Importer - please refer to Briley Manufacturing listing.
Factory - Mauser Jagdwaffen GmbH
Ziegelstadel 1
D-88316 Isny, GERMANY
Fax No.: 011-490-368-4750794
Website: www.mauser.com
Email: info@mauser.com

MAVERICK ARMS, INC.
Please refer to Mossberg listing.

MCCANN INDUSTRIES
132 South 162nd
Spanaway, WA 98387
Phone No. 253-537-6919
Fax No. 253-537-6993
Website: www.mccannindustries.com
Email: mccann.machine@worldnet.att.net

MCBROS RIFLE COMPANY
1638 W. Knudsen Dr.
Phoenix, AZ 85027
Phone No.: 623-582-9674
Fax No.: 623-581-3825
Website: www.mcmillanusa.com

MEDWELL & PERRETT LIMITED
Nicks Lane, Brome, Eye
Suffolk, ENGLAND IP23 8AN
Fax No.: 011-44-01379-870777
Email: nicky@medwellandperrett.com

MERKEL
Importer and Distributor - Merkel USA (GSI)
7661 Commerce Lane
Trussville, AL 35173
Phone No.: 205-655-8299
Fax No.: 205-655-7078
Website: www.merkel-usa.com
Factory - Merkel Jagd-und Sportwaffen GmbH
Schutzenstrasse 26
D-98527 Suhl, GERMANY
Fax No.: 011-49-3681-854-203
Website: www.merkel-waffen.de

MILLER ARMS
Please refer to Dakota Arms listing.

MILLER, DAVID
Please refer to David Miller Co. listing.

MIL-SPEC INDUSTRIES CORP.
(Parts only)
10 Mineola Avenue
Roslyn Heights, NY 11577
Phone No.: 516-625-5787
Fax No.: 516-625-0988
Website: www.milspecindustries.com
Email: info@mil-spec-industries.com

MIROKU FIREARMS MFG. CO.
537-1 Shinohara
Nangoku City Kochi-Pref, JAPAN
Fax No.: 011-81-88-863-3317

MITCHELL'S MAUSERS
P.O. Box 9295
Fountain Valley, CA 92728 -9295
Phone No.: 800-274-4124
Fax No.: 714-848-7208
Website: www.mauser.org
Email: customerservice@mauser.org

MODULO MASTERPIECE
via Torino 15/5
I-10154 Roletto, Torino, ITALY
Fax No.: 011-39-011-283322
Website: www.modulo-masterpiece.it
Email: info@modulo-masterpiece.it

MOLL, M.F.
Steins Strasse 101
D-41199 Moenchengladbach GERMANY
Phone No.: 011-49-2166997091
Fax No.: 011-49-216642253

MOLOT
Please refer to Becas and Vepr. listings.

MONTANA ARMORY, INC.
Please refer to C. Sharps Arms Co. Inc. listing.

MOORE, W.L. & CO.
Please refer to William Larkin Moore & Co. listing.

MORAVIA
Please refer to Arms Moravia listing.

MORINI
*Importer - please refer to Pilkington Competition Equipment LLC
listing.*
Factory - Morini Competition Arm SA
Casella Postale 92
CH-6930 Bedano SWITZERLAND
Fax No.: 011-41-91-9-45-1502
Website: www.morini.ch
Email: morini@bluewin.ch

MORTIMER, THOMAS
Please refer to the Dickson & MacNaughton listing.

MOSSBERG
O.F. Mossberg & Sons, Inc.
7 Grasso Ave., P.O. Box 497
North Haven, CT 06473-9844
Phone No.: 203-230-5300
Fax No.: 203-230-5420
Factory Service Center - OFM Service Department
Eagle Pass Industrial Park
Industrial Blvd.
Eagle Pass, TX 78853
Phone No.: 800-989-4867
Website: www.mossberg.com
Email: service@mossberg.com

MOUNTAIN RIFLERY, INC.
1775 North Elk Road
Pocatello, ID 83204
Phone No.: 208-234-7142
Website: www.mountainriflery.com

NATIONAL WILD TURKEY FEDERATION
P.O. Box 530
Edgefield, SC 29824
Phone No.: 803-637-3106
Fax No.: 803-637-0034
Website: www.nwtf.com

NAVY ARMS CO.
219 Lawn St.
Martinsburg, WV 25401
Phone No.: 304-262-9870
Fax No.: 304-262-1658
Website: www.navyarms.com
Email: info@navyarms.com

NELSON, P.V., (GUNMAKERS)
Folly Meadow, Hammersley Lane
Penn, High Wycombe,
Buckinghamshire, ENGLAND HP10 8HF
Phone/Fax No.: 011-44-49-4812836

NESIKA
Please refer to Dakota Arms listing.
Website: www.nesika.com

NEW ENGLAND CUSTOM GUN SERVICE LTD.
438 Willow Brook Rd.
Plainfield, NH 03781
Phone No.: 603-469-3450
Fax No.: 603-469-3471
Website: www.newenglandcustomgun.com
Email: bestguns@adelphia.net

NEW ENGLAND FIREARMS
60 Industrial Rowe
Gardner, MA 01440
Phone No.: 978-632-9393
Fax No.: 978-632-2300
Website: www.hr1871.com
Email: hr1871@tiac.net

NEW ULTRA LIGHT ARMS LLC
P.O. Box 340
214 Price Street
Granville, WV 26534
Phone No.: 304-292-0600
Fax No.: 304-292-9662
Website: www.newultralight.com

NIGHTHAWK CUSTOM
1306 W. Trimble Ave.
Berryville, AR 72616-4632
Phone No.: 877-268-4867
Fax No.: 870-423-4230
Website: www.nighthawkcustom.com
Email: info@nighthawkcustom.com

NOR-CAL PRECISION
2004 Elliot Dr.
American Canyon, CA 94503
Phone No.: 707-552-3810
Fax No.: 707-558-8977
Website: www.norcalprecision.com
Email: nor-cal@worldnet.att.net

NORINCO
Factory - China North Industries Corporation
12A Guang An Men Nan Jie
Beijing 100053 CHINA
Fax No.: 011-86-10-63547603
Website: www.norinco.com
Email: info@norinco.com.cn

NORINCO USA
P.O. Box 104801
Jefferson City, MO 65110
Phone No.: 573-634-2846
Fax No.: 573-634-2355
Website: www.norinco-usa.com

NORSMAN SPORTING ARMS & OUTFITTERS LLC
P.O. Box 500
1028 Second Ave., Ste. A-1
Havre, MT 59501
Phone No.: 406-262-2403
Email: norsmanarms@yahoo.com

NORTH AMERICAN ARMS, INC.
2150 South, 950 East
Provo, UT 84606-6285
Phone No.: 801-374-9990
Fax No.: 801-374-9998
Customer Service/Custom Shop: 800-821-5783
Website: www.naaminis.com

NOSLER, INC.
107 SW Columbia St.
Bend, OR 97702
Phone No.: 800-285-3701
Fax No.: 541-388-4667
Website: www.noslercustom.com

NOWLIN MFG. INC.
20622 4092 Rd., Unit B
Claremore, OK 74019
Phone No.: 918-342-0689
Fax No.: 918-342-0624
Website: www.nowlinguns.com
Email: nowlinguns@msn.com

NUMRICH GUN PARTS CORP.
Parts supplier only
226 Williams Lane
P.O. Box 299
W. Hurley, NY 12491
Phone No.: 866-686-7424
Fax No.: 877-486-7278
Website: www.e-gunparts.com
Email: info@gunpartscorp.com

OBERLAND ARMS
Duernhauser Str. 10
82392 Habach/Obb. GERMANY
Fax No.: 011-49-8847-697258
Website: www.oberlandarms.com

OHIO ORDNANCE WORKS, INC.
P.O. Box 687
Chardon, OH 44024
Phone No.: 440-285-3481
Fax No.: 440-286-8571
Website: www.ohioordnanceworks.com
Email: oow@ohioordnanceworks.com

OLD TOWN STATION LTD. (AUCTIONS)
P.O.B. 14040
Lenexa, KS 66285
Phone No.: 913-492-3000
Fax No.: 913-492-3022
Website: www.armsbid.com
Email: armsbid@aol.com

OLLENDORFF, PHILIPP
Eisack 169
A-6108 Scharnitz AUSTRIA
Phone/Fax No.: 011-43-5213-20133
Website: www.jagdwaffen-ollendorff.com
Email: info@jagdwaffen-ollendorff.com

OLYMPIC ARMS, INC.
624 Old Pacific Hwy. S.E.
Olympia, WA 98513
Phone No.: 800-228-3471
Fax No.: 360-491-3447
Website: www.olyarms.com
Email: info@olyarms.com

OMEGA WEAPONS SYSTEMS, INC.
Distributor - Defense Technology, Inc.
P.O. Box 482
Lake Forest, CA 92630
Phone No.: 949-830-8540
Fax No.: 949-830-1103
Factory
2918 E. Ginter
Tucson, AZ 85706
Phone No.: 520-889-8895
Fax No.: 520-741-9466
Website: www.omega-weapons-systems.com
Email: ddbell@flash.net

OMNI
Please refer to E.D.M. Arms listing.

OPTIMA
Please refer to Hatsan Arms Co. listing.

ORVIS
(Custom shotgun information only)
Historic Route 7A
Manchester, VT 05254
Phone No.: 802-362-2580
Fax No.: 802-362-3525
Website: www.orvis.com

PGW DEFENCE TECHNOLOGIES
Importer - LBVG
527 2nd Ave. N.
Glasgow, MT 59230
Factory
Website: www.pgwdti.com

M. PADRONE
Importer - Padrone USA
5108 Broadway, Ste. 200
San Antonio, TX 78209
Phone No.: 877-566-4867
Website: www.padroneusa.com
Factory
Marcheno, Brescia, ITALY

PALMETTO ARMS CO.
Factory
via Oberdan 70
Brescia, ITALY I-25125
Fax No.: 011-39-030-3700-960
Website: www.palmetto.it
Email: info@palmetto.it

PARA-ORDNANCE MANUFACTURING INC.
Importer - Para USA
1919 NE 45th Street, Ste. 215
Ft. Lauderdale, FL 33308-5136
Phone No.: 954-202-4440
Fax No.: 416-297-1289
Factory
980 Tapscott Rd.
Scarborough, Ontario
M1X 1C3 CANADA
Phone No.: 416-297-7855
Fax No.: 416-297-1289
website: www.paraord.com
Email: info@paraord.com

PARDINI, ARMI S.r.l.
Importer - please refer to Larry's Guns listing.
Factory
154/A via Italica
I-55043 Lido di Camaiore, (LU) ITALY
Fax No.: 011-39-0584-90122
Website: www.pardini.it
Email: info@pardini.it

PARKER (NEW MFG.)
Website: www.parkergunmakers.com
Email: Parker@Remington.com

PARKER BROS. GUNMAKERS
Charles Parker Business Park
50 High Street
Meriden, CT 06450
Phone No.: 203-206-7287
Website: www.parkerbrosmakers.com
Email: sales@parkerbrosmakers.com

PARKER REPRODUCTIONS
Parker Reproduction Div.
115 U.S. Hwy 202
Ringoes, NJ 08551
Phone No.: 908-284-2800
Fax No.: 908-284-2113

PATRIOT ORDNANCE FACTORY
23623 North 67th Ave.
Glendale, AZ 85310
Phone No.: 623-561-9572
Fax No.: 623-321-1680
Website: www.pof-usa.com
Email: sales@pof-usa.com

PEDERSOLI, DAVIDE & C. Snc
Distributor - please refer to Cherry's listing.
Distributor - please refer to Dixie Gun Works listing.
Importer - please refer to Cabela's listing.
Importer - please refer to Cimarron, F.A. & Co listing.
Importer - please refer to Navy Arms listing.
Service & Repair - please refer to VTI Gun Parts listing.
Factory
Via Artigiani 57
I-25063 Gardone V.T. (BS), ITALY
Fax No.: 011-39-030-891-1019
Website: www.davide-pedersoli.com

PENTHENY de PENTHENY, INC.
2352 Baggett Ct.
Santa Rosa, CA 95401
Phone/Fax No.: 707-237-6990

PERAZZI
Importer - Perazzi USA, Inc.
1010 W. Tenth St.
Azusa, CA 91702
Phone No.: 626-334-1234
Fax No.: 626-334-0344
Email: perazziusa@aol.com
Factory - Armi Perazzi S.p.A.
Via Fontanelle, 1
I-25080 Botticino Mattina Brescia ITALY
Fax No.: 011-39-030-269-2594
Website: www.perazzi.it
Email: info@perazzi.it

PERUGINI & VISINI
Factory
Via Camprelle 126
Nuvolera, Brescia I-25080 ITALY
Fax No.: 011-39-030-689-7821
Website: www.intred.it/perugini-visini
Email: info@perugini-visini.com

PETERS STAHL GmbH

Importer - Euro-Imports
412 Slayden St.
Yoakum, TX 77995
Phone/Fax No.: 361-293-9353
Email: mrbrno@yahoo.com
Factory
Stettiner Strasse 42
D-33106 Paderborn, GERMANY
Fax No.: 011-49-5251-75611
Website: www.peters-stahl.com
Email: info@peters-stahl.com

PFEIFER-WAFFEN

10-12 Schlossgraben
A-6800 Feldkirch, AUSTRIA
Fax No.: 011-43-5522-77660
website: www.pfeifer-waffen.at
Email: office@pfeifer-waffen.at

PHOENIX ARMS

4231 E. Brickell St.
Ontario, CA 91761
Phone No.: 909-937-6900
Fax No.: 909-937-0060

PIETTA, F.A.P. F.lli e C. Snc.

Various U.S. distributors and importers
Service & Repair - please refer to VTI Gun Parts listing.
Factory - PIETTA, F.A.P. F.lli e C. Snc.
Via Mandolossa 102
I-25064 Gussago (Brescia) ITALY
Fax No.: 011-39-030-373-7100
Website: www.pietta.it
Email: info@pietta.it

PILKINGTON COMPETITION EQUIPMENT LLC

P.O. Box 97, #2 Little Tree's Ramble
Monteagle, TN 37356
Phone No.: 931-924-3400
Fax No.: 931-924-3489
Website: www.pilkguns.com
Email: info@pilkguns.com

PIOTTI

Importer - please refer to William Larkin Moore & Co. listing.
Factory - Piotti, F.lli, S.n.c.
Via Cinelli, 10-12
I-25063 Gardone V.T. Brescia, ITALY
Fax No.: 011-39-030-891-6522
Website: www.piotti.com
Email: info@piotti.com

POINTER

Please refer to Legacy Sports International listing.

POLI, ARMI F.LLI

Importer - please refer to Anglo American Sporting Agency listing.
Importer - Deep River Sporting Clays
3420 Cletus Hall Road
Sanford , NC 27330
Phone No.: 919-774-7080
Fax No.: 919-708-5052
Website: www.deepriver.net

Factory - POLI, ARMI F.LLI
Casella Postale, 6
via Giacomo Matteotti 163
I-25063 Gardone, VT (BS), ITALY
Fax No.: 011-39-030-834-9413
Website: www.fpafratellipoli.com
Email: info@fpafratellipoli.com

POLI NICOLETTO & C. snc

via Matteotti, 311
I-25063 Gardone VT Brescia ITALY
Fax No.: 011-39-030-8910743
Website: www.polinicoletta.com
Email: info@polinicoletta.com

WAFFEN PRECHTL

Importer - please refer to Mitchell's Mauser's listing.
Factory
Auf der Aue 3
Birkenau, GERMANY D-69488
Fax No.: 011-49-6201-182-701

PRECISION SMALL ARMS, INC.

Distributor - please refer to Acusport listing.
Factory
P.O. Box 931
Aspen, CO 81612
Website: www.precisionsmallarms.com
Email: sales@precisionsmallarms.com

PREMIER ENGLISH SHOTGUNS LTD.

Turners Barn Farm, Kibworth Road
Three Gates, Illston-on-the-Hill, Leicestershire
LE7 9ER ENGLAND
Phone No.: 011-441-16-259-6592
Fax No.: 011-441-16-259-6574
Website: www.hollowaynaughton.co.uk
Email: afharvieon@hollowaynaughton.oo.uk

PTR 91 INC.

U.S. Representative - Vincent Pestilli & Associates
193 Sam Brown Hill Rd.
Brownfield, ME 04010
Phone No.: 207-935-3603
Fax No.: 207-935-3996
Email: vapame@pivot.net
Factory
P.O. Box 562
Unionville, CT 06085
Phone No.: 860-676-1776
Fax No.: 860-676-1880
Website: www.PTR91.com
Email: jldenter@aol.com

PUMA RIFLES

Importer – please refer to Legacy Sports International, LLC listing.

PURDEY, JAMES, & SONS, LTD.

Showroom
57-58 South Audley Street
London, W1K 2 ED ENGLAND
Phone No.: 011-44-20-7499-1801
Fax No.: 011-44-20-7355-3297
Website: www.purdey.com
Email: sales@james-purdey.co.uk

Q.S. PROGETTO MECCANICA s.a.s.
via S. Agostino, 9
I-23892, Bulcaigo (Lecco) - ITALY
Fax No.: 011-39-31861186
Web site: www.qsarmi.biz
Email: penna@qsarmi.biz

QIQIHAR HAWK INDUSTRIES CO., LTD.
15 Nanyuan Road, Qiqihar
Heilongjiang, CHINA 161005
Fax No.: 011-0452-2340633
Website: www.hawkindustries.com.cn

QUAIL UNLIMITED, INC.
31 Quail Run
PO Box 610
Edgefield, SC 29824
Phone No.: 803-637-5731
Fax No.: 803-637-0037
Website: www.qu.org
Email: National@qu.org

QUALITY ARMS, INC.
P.O. Box 19477
Houston, TX 77224
Phone No.: 281-870-8377
Fax No.: 281-870-8524
Website: www.arrieta.com
Email: Arrieta2@excite.com

QUALITY PARTS CO.
Please refer to Bushmaster Firearms, Inc. listing.

R.F.M.
Please refer to Rota, Luciano listing.

RBA
Factory - Renzo Bonora Armi
via 2 Argosto 1980 nr. 25
I-40057 Granarolo Emilia ITALY
Fax No.: 011-39-0517-66262
Email: rbaarms@dada.it

RND MANUFACTURING
14399 Mead Street
Longmont, CO 80504
Phone/Fax No.: 970-535-4458
Website: www.rndedge.com
Email: info@rndedge.com

RPA INTERNATIONAL LTD.
P.O. Box 441
Tonbridge, Kent, ENGLAND TN9 9DZ
Fax No.: 011-44-8458803232
Website: www.rpa-eng.com

RPM PISTOLS
Please refer to the Gateway Precision Arms listing.

RWS
Disc. firearms only - please refer to Dynamit Nobel listing.

RADOM
Importer (Current mfg.) - Dalvar of U.S.A.
1175 Sierra Verde Ranch
P.O. Box 31
Seligman, AZ 86337-0031
Website: www.dalvar.net
Email: dalvar_usa@juno.com

RED ROCK ARMS
P.O. Box 21017
Mesa, AZ 85277
Phone No.: 480-832-0844
Fax No.: 206-350-5274
Website: www.redrockarms.com
Email: info@redrockarms.com

REDOLFI F.LLI
via Brescia, 47/49
Manerbio (BS) ITALY
Fax No.: 011-39-0309385348
Website: www.redolfiarmi.com
Email: info@redolfiarmi.com

GARY REEDER CUSTOM GUNS
2601 E. 7th Ave.
Flagstaff, AZ 86004
Phone No.: 928-527-4100
Fax No.: 928-527-0840
website: www.reedercustomguns.com
Email: gary@reedercustomguns.com

REMINGTON ARMS CO., INC.
Consumer Services
870 Remington Drive
P.O. Box 700
Madison, NC 27025-0700
Phone No.: 800-243-9700
Fax No.: 336-548-7801
Website: www.remington.com
Email: info@remington.com
Repairs
14 Hoefler Ave.
Ilion, NY 13357
Phone No.: 800-243-9700
Fax No.: 336-548-7801

RIFLES, INC.
3580 Leal Rd.
Pleasanton, TX 78064
Phone No.: 830-569-2055
Fax No.: 830-569-2297
Website: www.riflesinc.com
Email: info@riflesinc.com

RIGANIAN, RAY (RIFLEMAKER)
324 N. Central Ave., Unit B
Glendale, CA 91203
Phone No.: 818-502-2678

RIGBY, JOHN & CO. (GUNMAKERS), INC.
500 Linne Rd., Ste. D
Paso Robles, CA 93446
Phone No.: 805-227-4236
Fax No.: 805-227-4723
Website: www.johnrigbyandco.com
Email: jrigby@johnrigbyandco.com

RIZZINI & TANFOGLIO srl
via Zanardelli 49/C
I-25060 Gardone, VT, Brescia ITALY
Fax No.: 011-39-030-8349140
Website: www.rizzinietanfoglio.it

RIZZINI, BATTISTA
Repair & Service - please refer to CT Shotgun Manufacturing listing.
Importer - Rizzini USA
100 Burritt Street
P.O. Box 1692
New Britain, CT 06053-1692
Phone No.: 860-225-6581
Fax No.: 8608328707
Website: www.rizziniusa.com
Factory - Rizzini srl
Via 2 Giugno, 7/7 bis
I-25060 Marcheno (Brescia), ITALY
Fax No.: 011-39-030-861-319
Website: www.rizzini.it
Email: info@rizzini.it

RIZZINI, EMILIO, s.n.c.
Factory - Fausti Stefano srl
Via Martiri Dell'Indipendenza, 70
I-25060 Marcheno (Brescia) ITALY
Fax No.: 011-39-030-861-0155
Website: www.emiliorizzini.com
Email: info@emiliorizzini.com

RIZZINI, F.LLI.
Factory
Via X Giornate N. 9
I-25063, Magno, VT, ITALY
Fax No.: 011-39-030-8911400
Website: www.fllirizzini.it
Email: fllirizzini@fastwebnet.it

ROBAR COMPANIES, INC.
21438 N. 7th Avenue
Phoenix, AZ 85027
Phone No.: 623-581-2648
Fax No.: 623-582-0059
Website: www.robarguns.com
Email: info@robarguns.com

ROBERT HISSERICH COMPANY
183A S. Los Alamos
Mesa, AZ 85204
Phone No.: 480-545-2994
Email: bhisserich@earthlink.net

ROBERTS, J. & SON (GUNMAKERS) LTD.
22 Wyvil Road, Vauxhall
London SW8 2TG ENGLAND
Fax No.: 011-44-0207-627-4442
Website: www.jroberts-gunmakers.co.uk
Email: shop@jroberts-gunmakers.co.uk

ROBERTSON
Please refer to Boss & Co., Ltd. listing.

ROBINSON ARMAMENT CO.
ZDF Import/Export
P.O. Box 16776
Salt Lake City, UT 84116-0776
Phone No.: 801-355-0401
Fax No.: 801-355-0402
Website: www.robarm.com
Email: ZDF@robarm.com

ROCHE, CHRISTIAN
12 Lotissement les Eglantiers
42 340 Veauche, FRANCE
Phone No.: 011-33-7793-3533
Fax No.: 011-33-7794-3533

ROCK ISLAND AUCTION COMPANY
1050 35th Ave.
Moline, IL 61265
Phone No.: 309-797-1500
Fax No.: 309-797-1655
Website: www.mgnteam.com
Email: riauction@aol.com

ROCK RIVER ARMS, INC.
1042 Cleveland Road
Colona, IL 61241
Phone No.: 309-792-5780
Fax No.: 309-792-5781
Website: www.rockriverarms.com
Email: rockriverarms@revealed.net

ROCKY MOUNTAIN ARMS, INC.
1813 Sunset Place, Unit D
Longmont, CO 80501
Phone No.: 800-375-0846
Fax No.: 303-678-8766
Website: www.rockymountainarms.us

ROCKY MOUNTAIN ELK FOUNDATION
2291 W. Broadway
Missoula, MT 59802
Phone No.: 406-523-4500
Fax No.: 406-523-4581
Website: www.rmef.org

ROGUE RIVER RIFLEWORKS
500 Linne Road, Ste. D
Paso Robles, CA 93446
Phone No.: 805-227-4236
Fax No.: 805-227-4723

ROHRBAUGH FIREARMS CORP.
P.O. Box 785
Bayport, NY 11705
Phone No.: 800-803-2233
Phone No.: 631-242-3175
Fax No.: 631-242-3183
Website: www.rohrbaughfirearms.com
Email: ecr@rohrbaughfirearms.com

ROOSEVELT AND DRAKE
418 Main Street
Murray, KY 42071
Phone No.: 270-436-5270
Fax No.: 270-436-5257
Website: www.drake.net

ROSSI
Importer - BrazTech International L.C.
16175 N.W. 49th Ave.
Miami, FL 33014
Phone No.: 305-474-0401
Fax No.: 305-624-3180
Website: www.rossiusa.com
Factory - Amadeo Rossi, S.A.
Rua Amadeo Rossi, 143
B-93030-220 Sao Leopoldo-RS BRAZIL
Email: rossi.firearms@pnet.com.br

ROTA, LUCIANO

Factory - R.F.M. di Rota Luciano
via Patrioti, 26
I-25068 Noboli di Sarezzo
V.T. (Brescia) ITALY
Fax No.: 011-49-30-801152

ROTTWEIL

Repair - Pylinski Arms
(Models 72, 720 & Paragon service)
967 Anderson Hwy.
Cumberland, VA 23040
Phone No.: 804-492-4082
Email: pylinskifarms@aol.com
Factory
Metzgasse 13
D-78628 Rottweil, GERMANY
Fax No.: 011-49-0741-949-4070

RUSSIAN AMERICAN ARMORY COMPANY

677 S. Cardinal Lane
Scottsburg, IN 47170
Phone No.: 877-752-2894
Fax No.: 812-752-7683
Website: www.raacfirearms.com
Email: info@raacfirearms.com

S.I.A.C.E.

Importer - please refer to Dewing's listing.
Importer - please refer to Cherry's listing.
Importer - Kebco LLC
P.O. Box 6272
Silver Spring, MD 20916-6272
Phone No.: 301-460-9563
Fax No.: 301-460-3370
Website: www.kebcollc.com
Email: info@kebcollc.com
Importer - Don's Sport Shop
7803 E. McDowell Road
Scottsdale, AZ 85257
Phone No.: 480-946-5313
Factory
Via Matteotti 127, C.P. 97
Gardone, VT, Brescia, ITALY I-25063
Fax No.: 011-39-030-891-1518
Website: www.siacearmi.com
Email: siace@libero.it

SKB SHOTGUNS

Importer - G.U. Inc.
4325 S 120th Street
Omaha, NE 68137
Phone No.: 402-330-4492
Fax No.: 402-330-8040
Website: www.skbshotguns.com
Email: skb@skbshotguns.com
Factory
Pacico Bldg. #601
Honokomagome 6-15-8
Tokyo, JAPAN 113-0021
Fax No.: 011-81-0339-430695
Website: www.shirstone.com/skb
Email: mail@shirstone.com

SOG INTERNATIONAL

P.O. Box 590
Lebanon, OH 45036-0590
Phone No.: 800-944-4867
Fax No.: 513-932-8928
Website: www.southernohiogun.com
Email: soginc@go-concepts.com

S.P.S

Can Roqueta 2
08291 Ripollet, Barcelona, SPAIN
Fax No.: 011-34-93-592-1258
Website: www.sps-dc.com
Email: custom@sps-dc.com

SSK INDUSTRIES

Gunsmithing services only
590 Woodvue Lane
Wintersville, OH 43953
Phone No.: 740-264-0176
Fax No.: 740-264-2257
Website: www.sskindustries.com
Email: info@sskindustries.com

STI INTERNATIONAL

114 Halmar Cove
Georgetown, TX 78628
Phone No.: 800-959-8201
Fax No.: 512-819-0465
Website: www.stiguns.com
Email: sales@stiguns.com

SWS 2000

Importer - please refer to Euro-Imports listing.
Dionysiusstrasse 64
D-47798 Krefeld GERMANY
Fax No.: 01149-215197-5516
Website: www.sws-2000.de
Email: info@sws-2000.de

SABATTI s.p.a.

Factory - Armi Sabatti s.p.a.
Via Alessandro Volta 90
I-25063 Gardone Valtrompia, (BS) ITALY
Fax No.: 011-39-030-891-2059
Website: www.sabatti.com
Email: info@sabatti.com

SABRE

Please refer to Mitchell's Mausers listing.

SABRE DEFENCE INDUSTRIES LLC

Sales Office
Sabre House, Belvue Road
Northolt, Middlesex, U.K. UB5 5QJ
Fax No.: 011-44020-8845-4814
Factory
450 Allied Drive
Nashville, TN 37211
Phone No.: 615-333-0077
Fax No.: 615-333-6229
Website: www.sabredefence.com

SAFARI CLUB INTERNATIONAL
4800 West Gates Pass Road
Tucson, AZ 85745
Phone No.: 888-724-4868
Fax No.: 520-622-1205
Website: www.safariclub.org
Membership email: huntsci@safariclub.org

SAIGA
Importer - please refer to Russian American Armory Company listing.

SAKO LTD.
Importer (USA) - please refer to Beretta USA listing.
Importer (CANADA) – Stoeger Canada Ltd.
1801 Wentworth St., Unit 16
Whitby, Ontario, L1N 8R6 CANADA
Phone No.: 905-436-9077
Fax No.: 905-436-9079
Email: stoeger@idirect.com
Factory - Sako, Limited
P.O. Box 149
FIN-11101 Riihimaki, FINLAND
Fax No.: 011-358-19-720446
Website: www.sako.fi
Email: export@sako.fi

SALERI, W.R. di WILLIAM & C. snc
Factory
Via Zanardelli, 231
Marcheno, Brescia ITALY
Fax No.: 011-39-030-8966322
Website: www.wrsaleri.it
Email: wrsaleri@wsaleri.it

SAMCO GLOBAL ARMS, INC.
6995 N.W. 43rd St.
Miami, FL 33166
Phone No.: 800-554-1618
Phone No.: 305-593-9782
Fax No.: 305-593-1014
Website: www.samcoglobal.com
Email: samco@samcoglobal.com

SAN SWISS ARMS AG
Industrieplatz, CH-8212 Neuhausen am Rheinfall SWITZERLAND
Fax No.: 011-41-052-674-6418
Website: www.swissarms.ch
Email: info@swissarms.ch

SARCO INC.
323 Union Street
Stirling, NJ 07980
Phone No.: 908-647-3800
Fax No.: 908-647-9413
Website: www.sarcoinc.com
Email: info@sarcoinc.com

SARSILMAZ
Importer - please refer to Armalite, Inc.
Factory
Nargileci Sk. Sarsilmaz is Merkezi Mercan 34450
Istanbul, TURKEY
Fax No.: 011-90212-51119-99
Website: www.sarsilmaz.com

SAUER, J.P. & SOHN
Importer - JP Sauer USA
340 Royal Palm Way, Ste. 101
Palm Beach, FL 33480
Phone No.: 561-837-8625
Fax No.: 561-837-8629
Website: www.JPSauerUSA.com
Factory – J.P. Sauer & Sohn GmbH
Sauerstrasse 2-6
D-24340 Eckernförde, GERMANY
Fax No.: 011-49-43-51-471-160
Website: www.sauer-waffen.de

SAVAGE ARMS, INC.
Sales & Marketing
118 Mountain Road
Suffield, CT 06078
Phone No.: 866-312-4119
Fax No.: 860-668-2168
Parts & Service
100 Springdale Road
Westfield, MA 01085
Phone No.: 413-568-7001
Fax No.: 413-562-7764
Website: www.savagearms.com
Older Savage Arms Historical Research
Mr. John Callahan
53 Old Quarry Rd.
Westfield, MA 01085
$30.00/gun research fee, $25.00 per gun for Models 1895, 1899, and 99 rifles.

SAVIN, J.C.
11 Place de la Cite
F-42220 Bourg Argental, FRANCE
Fax No.: 011-33-4-77-39-1855

SCATTERGUN TECHNOLOGIES INC.
Please refer to Wilson Combat listing.

SCHEIRING GmbH
Klagenfurter Strasse 19
A-9170 Ferlach AUSTRIA
Fax No.: 011-43-4227-287620
Email: waffen.scheiring@aon.at

SCHERZ, MICHAEL
Please refer to Gila River Gun Works.

FA. ALFRED SCHILLING
Importer - Sundog Firearms
Star Route 2
Kimberly, OR 97848
Phone No: 541-934-2117
Website: www.sundogfirearms.com
Email: sundog@oregontrail.net
Factory
Peter-Haseney Strasse 32
D-98544 Zella-Mehlis, GERMANY
Fax No.: 011-49-0362-486706
Website: www.Alfred-Schilling.de
Email: schilling@alfred-schilling.de

SCHUERMAN ARMS, LTD.
3322 W. Irvine Road
Desert Hills, AZ 85096
Phone No.: 623-465-5260
Fax No.: 480-465-5372
Website: www.schuermanarms.com
Email: info@schuermanarms.com

SCHUETZEN PISTOL WORKS, INC.
Please refer to Olympic Arms listing.

SCHUTZEN BOHME GmbH
Muhlenstrasse 6-8
31737 Rintein, GERMANY
Phone No.: 011-49-5751-44770
Fax No.: 011-49-5751-42490

SCHWABEN ARMS GmbH
Neckartal 95
D-78628, Rottweil, GERMANY
Fax No.: 011-49-0741-9429218
Website: www.schwabenarmsgmbh.de
Email: schwabenarmsgmbh@web.de

SCOTT, W. C., LTD.
Holland & Holland, Ltd. (Repairs)
Attn: Mr. P. C. Chismon
31-33 Bruton St.
London WiJ 6HH ENGLAND
Phone No.: 011-44-020-7499-4411
Fax No.: 011-44-020-7409-3283
Website: www.hollandandholland.com
Email: peter.chismon@holland-holland.co.uk

SEARCY, B. & CO.
P.O. Box 584
Boron, CA 93596
Phone No.: 760-762-6131
Fax No.: 760-762-0191
Website: www.searcyent.com
Email: searcy@ccis.com

SEECAMP, L.W. CO., INC.
280 Rock Lane
Milford, CT 06460
Phone No.: 203-877-7926
Fax No.: 203-877-3429
Website: www.seecamp.com
Email: info@seecamp.com

SEMMERLING
Please refer to American Derringer Corp. listing.

SERBU FIREARMS, INC.
6001 Johns Rd., Ste. 144
Tampa, FL 33634
Phone/Fax No.: 813-243-8899
Website: www.serbu.com

SERENGETI RIFLES, INC.
P.O. Box 9138
Kalispell, MT 59904
Phone No.: 406-756-2399
Fax No.: 406-756-0785
Website: www.serengetirifles.com
Email: larryt@serengetirifles.com

C. SHARPS ARMS CO. INC.
100 Centennial Dr.
P.O. Box 885
Big Timber, MT 59011
Phone No.: 406-932-4353
Fax No.: 406-932-4443
Website: www.csharpsarms.com
Email: csharps@ttc-cmc.net

SHILOH RIFLE MFG. CO.
P.O. Box 279
Big Timber, MT 59011
Phone No.: 406-932-4454
Fax No.: 406-932-5627
Website: www.shilohrifle.com

**SHOOTERS ARMS MANUFACTURING
INCORPORATED**
Importer - please refer to Century International Arms listing.
Importer - Pacific Arms Corp.
4813 Enterprise Way, Unit K
Modesto, CA 95356-8736
Phone No.: 209-545-2800
Fax No.: 209-545-2528
Factory
National Highway, Wireless
Mandaue City, Cebu, Phillipines
Fax No.: 011-6032-346-2331
Email: rhonedeleon@yahoo.com

SIG SAUER
18 Industrial Park Drive
Exeter, NH 03833
Phone No.: 603-772-2302
Fax No.: 603-772-9082
Customer Service Phone No.: 603-772-2302
Customer Service Fax No.: 603-772-4795
Law Enforcement Phone No.: 603-772-2302
Law Enforcement Fax No.: 603-772-1481
Website: www.sigarms.com
Factory - SIG - Schweizerische Industrie-Gesellschaft
Industrielplatz , CH-8212 Neuhausen am Rheinfall, Switzerland
Fax No.: 011-41-153-216-601

SILMA s.r.l.
Factory
Via I Maggio, 74
I-25060 Zanano di Sarezzo, (BS) ITALY
Fax No.: 011-39-030-890-0712
Website: www.silma.net
Email: info@silma.net

GENE SIMILLION GUNMAKER
220 S. Wisconsin
Gunnison, CO 81230
Phone/Fax No.: 970-641-1126
Email: Gsimillion@hotmail.com

SMITH, L.C.
Please refer to Marlin listing.

SMITH & WESSON
2100 Roosevelt Avenue
P.O. Box 2208
Springfield, MA 01102-2208
Phone No.: 800-331-0852
Website: www.smith-wesson.com
Service email only: qa@smith-wesson.com

Smith & Wesson Research
Attn: Mr. Roy Jinks, S&W Historian
P.O. Box 2208
Springfield, MA 01102-2208
Phone No.: 413-781-8300
Fax No.: 413-731-8980

SMITHSON, J.P.
1194 N. 240 E.
Orem, UT 84057
Phone No.: 801-224-2041

SNAKE CHARMER
Verney-Carron USA, Inc.
320 Court Street
Clay Center, KS 67432
Phone No.: 785-632-2184
Fax No.: 785-632-6554
Website: www.snake-charmer.net
Email: email@verney-carron.us

SODIA, FRANZ
Sodia Jagdwaffen & Bekleidungs GesmbH
Vogelweiderstrasse 55
5020 Salzburg AUSTRIA
Fax No.: 011-43-662-872123-20
Website: www.waffen-sodia.at
Email: office@waffen-sodia.at

SOLD USA (AUCTIONS)
1418 Industrial Drive
Matthews, NC 28105
Phone No.: 704-815-1500
Website: www.soldusa.com
Email: support@soldusa.com

SOTHEBY'S (AUCTIONS)
U.S. Office
1334 York Ave. at 72nd St.
New York, NY 10021
Phone No.: 212-606-7000
Fax No.: 212-606-7107
Website: www.sothebys.com
U.K. Office
34-35 New Bond Street at Bloomfield Place
London, WIA 2AA ENGLAND
Phone No.: 011-44-20-7293-5000
Fax No.: 011-44-20-7293-5989
Website: www.sothebys.com

SPARTAN GUN WORKS
Please refer to the Remington listing.

SPECIAL WEAPONS INC.
Warranty service & repair for Special Weapons LLC
Website: www.tacticalweapons.com

SPHINX SYSTEMS LTD.
Distributor - please refer to Sabre Defence Industries LLC listing.
Factory
Gsteigstrasse 12
CH-3800 Matten Interlaken SWITZERLAND
Fax No.: 011-41-033-821-1006
Website: www.sphinxarms.com
Email: info@sphinxarms.com

SPIDER FIREARMS
2005-B Murcott Dr.
St. Cloud, FL 34771-5826
Phone No.: 407-957-3617
Fax No.: 407-957-0296
Website: www.ferret50.com
Email" info@ferret50.com

SPORT-SYSTEME DITTRICH
Burghaiger Weg 20a
D-95326 Kulmbach, GERMANY
Fax No.: 011-49-09221-8213758
Website: www.ssd-weapon.com
Email: sportsysteme.dittrich@t-online.de

SPRINGER'S ERBEN, JOHANN
Website: www.springer-vienna.com

SPRINGFIELD ARMORY
Springfield Inc.
420 W. Main St.
Geneseo, IL 61254
Phone No.: 309-944-5631
Phone No.: 800-680-6866
Fax No.: 309-944-3676
Website: www.springfield-armory.com
Email: sales@springfield-armory.com
Custom Shop Email: customshop@springfield-armory.com

STAG ARMS
515 John Downey Dr.
New Britain, CT 06051
Phone No.: 860-229-994
Website: www.stagarms.com
Email: sales@stagarms.com

STALLARD ARMS
Please refer to Hi-Point listing.

STEINKAMP MASCHINENBAU GmbH & Co. KG
In der Tuetenbecke 14
D-32339 Espelkamp GERMANY
Fax No.: 011-49-05772-911161
Website: www.stkm.de
Email: info@stkm.de

STEVENS, J., ARMS COMPANY
Please refer to Savage Arms listing.
Older Stevens Historical Research
Mr. John Callahan
53 Old Quarry Rd.
Westfield, MA 01085
$20.00/gun research fee.

STEYR MANNLICHER
Importer - Steyr Arms, Inc.
P.O. Box 2609
Cumming, GA 30028
Phone No.: 770-888-4201
Fax No.: 770-888-4863
Factory - Steyr Mannlicher A.G. & Co. KG
Ramingtal 46
Steyr A-4401 AUSTRIA
Fax No.: 01143-7252-78621
Website: www.steyr-mannlicher.com
Email: office@steyr-mannlicher.com

STOEGER INDUSTRIES
17601 Indian Head Hwy.
Accokeek, MD 20607-2501
Phone No.: 301-283-6981
Fax No.: 301-283-6988
Website: www.stoegerindustries.com

STONER RIFLE
Factory – please refer to Knight's Manufacturing Co. listing.

STRAYER TRIPP INTERNATIONAL
Please refer to the STI Internation listing.

STURM, RUGER & CO., INC.
Headquarters
1 Lacey Place
Southport, CT 06490
Phone No.: 203-259-7843
Fax No.: 203-256-3367
www.ruger.com
Service Center for Pistols, PC4 & PC9 Carbines
200 Ruger Road
Prescott, AZ 86301-6181
Phone No.: 928-778-6555
Fax No.: 928-778-6633
Website: www.ruger-firearms.com
Service Center for Revolvers, Long Guns & Ruger Date of Manufacture
411 Sunapee Street
Newport, NH 03773
Phone No.: 603-865-2442
Fax No.: 603-863-6165

SUPER SIX CLASSIC LLC
Defense Supply & Manufacturing
639 Hilltop Trail
W. Fort Atkinson, WI 53539
Phone No.: 920-568-8299
Fax No.: 920-568-8259

SUPERIOR ARMS
Distributor - RB Precision, Inc.
P.O. Box 96
Preemption, IL 61276
Phone/Fax No.: 309-534-8175
Website: www.rbprecision.com
Distributor - Haynes, Inc.
131 Baker Lane
Clinton, IL 47842
Phone No.: 765-832-1953
Email: jon@haynes-inc.com
Distributor (including law enforcement) - Boom to Zoom LLC
East 4th St. & South Anton Ave.
Marshfield, WI 5449
Phone No.: 877-387-4611
Fax No.: 715-387-4668
Distributor (including law enforcement) - Professional Gunsmithing, Inc.
5435 Hwy. 99
Wapello, IA 52653
Phone No.: 563-766-2048
Email: Matt@superiorarms.com

Factory - Superior Arms
836 Weaver Blvd.
Wapello, IA 52653
Phone No.: 319-523-2016
Fax No.: 319-527-0188
Website: www.superiorarms.com
Email: sales@superiorarms.com

SZECSEI Et. FUCHS FINE GUNS GmbH
North America Office
450 Charles St.
Windsor, Ontario N8X 3Z1 CANADA
Phone No.: 519-966-1234
Factory
Bozner Platz 1
corner Wilhelm-Greil-Strasse
A-6020 Innsbruck AUSTRIA
Phone/Fax No.: 011-43-512-5872-67
Website: www.jagdwaffe.com
Email: fuchs@jagdwaffe.com

TG INTERNATIONAL
P.O. Box 787
Knoxville, TN 37777
Phone No.: 865-977-9707
Fax No.: 865-977-9728
Website: www.tnguns.com

TNW INC.
P.O. Box 311
Vernonia, OR 97064
Phone No.: 503-429-5001
Fax No.: 503-429-3505
Website: www.tnwfirearms.com
Email: tnwcorp@aol.com

TACTICAL RIFLES
19250 Hwy. 301
Dade City, FL 33523
Phone No.: 352-999-0599
Website: www.tacticalrifles.net
Email: info@tacticalrifles.net

TACTICAL WEAPONS
Please refer to FNH USA listing.

TANFOGLIO, FRATELLI, S.n.c
Importer - please refer to European American Armory listing.
Factory
Via Valtrompia 39/41
I-25063 Gardone V.T. (BS) ITALY
Fax No.: 011-39-030-891-0183
Website: www.tanfoglio.it
Email: info@tanfoglio.it

TAR-HUNT CUSTOM RIFLES, INC.
101 Dogtown Rd.
Bloomsburg, PA 17815-7544
Phone No.: 570-784-6368
Fax No.: 507-389-9150
Website: www.tar-hunt.com
Email: sales@tar-hunt.com

TATE GUNMAKERS LLC
2951 Curran Road
Ione, CA 95640
Phone No.: 949-644-9557 (office)
Phone No.: 209-763-9040 (workshop)
Fax No.: 949-644-9558
Website: www.angloamericansport.com
Email: angloamericansport@earthlink.net

TAURUS INTERNATIONAL MANUFACTURING INC.
16175 NW 49th Ave.
Miami, FL 33014-6314
Phone No.: 305-624-1115
Fax No.: 305-623-7506
Website: www.taurususa.com

TAYLOR'S & CO.
304 Lenoir Dr.
Winchester, VA 22603
Phone No.: 540-722-2017
Fax No.: 540-722-2018
website: www.taylorsfirearms.com
Email: info@taylorsfirearms.com

TELO, RENATO
Via Goldoni, 8
Gardone, VT, Brescia, ITALY I-25063
Fax No.: 011-39-030-831109

TESRO SPORTWAFFEN GmbH & Co. KG
Seehoffstrasse 14/b
D-89431 Bächingen GERMANY
Fax No.: 011-49-7325-919384
Website: www.tesro.de
Email: info@tesro.de

THOMPSON & CAMPBELL
Cromarty the Black Isle
Ross-shire IV11 8YB SCOTLAND
Fax No.: 011-44-1463-231-602
Website: www.rifle.co.uk
Email: reception@rifle.co.uk

THOMPSON/CENTER ARMS CO., INC.
P.O. Box 5002
Rochester, NH 03866
Customer Service Phone No.: 603-332-2333
Repair Only Phone No.: 603-332-2441
Fax No.: 603-332-5133
Website: www.tcarms.com
Email: tca@tcarms.com
Custom Shop - Fox Ridge Outfitters
P.O. Box 1700
Rochester, NH 03866
Phone No.: 800-243-4570

THUNDER 5
Factory - MIL Inc.
1345-B Enterprise Rd.
Piney Flats, TN 37686
Website: www.thunder5.com

TIKKA
Importer - please refer to Beretta U.S.A. Corp. listing.
Factory - please refer to Sako listing.
Website: www.tikka.fi

TIME PRECISION ARMS
4 Nicholas Square
New Milford, CT 06776
Phone No.: 860-350-8343
Fax No.: 860-350-6343
Email: timeprecision@aol.com

TISAS
Trabzon Gun Industry Corp.
De Gol Caddesi No. 13/1 Tandogan
Ankara TURKEY
Fax No.: 011-90-312-213-7806
Website: www.trabzonsilah.com
Email: sales@trabonsilah.com

TOLLEY, J & W
F.J. Wiseman & Co., Ltd.
262 Walsall Road, Bridgtown
Cannock, Staffordshire
WS11 0JL ENGLAND
Fax No.: 011-44-1543-574806
Email: fjwiseman@lineone.net

TORNADO
Factory - AseTekno OY
P.O. Box 94 Plkneentie 18
FIN-00511 Helsinki, Finland
Fax No.: 011-358-9-753-6463
Website: www.asetekno.fi
Email: jaakko.vottonen@asetekno.fi

TOZ
Pistol Importer - please refer to Larry's Guns listing.
Factory
1 a Sovetskaja Str.
RUS-300002 Tula, RUSSIA
Fax No: 011-70872-27-3439
Website: www.tulatoz.ru
Email: tozmarketing@home.tula.net

TRADITIONS PERFORMANCE FIREARMS
1375 Boston Post Road
P.O. Box 776
Old Saybrook, CT 06475
Phone No.: 860-388-4656
Fax No.: 860-388-4657
Website: www.traditionsfirearms.com
Email: info@traditionsfirearms.com

TRISTAR SPORTING ARMS LTD.
1816 Linn St.
N. Kansas City, MO 64116
Phone No.: 816-421-1400
Fax No.: 816-421-4182
Website: www.tristarsportingarms.com
Email: tristarsporting@sbcglobale.net

TROMIX CORPORATION
405 N. Walnut Ave. #8
Broken Arrow, OK 74012
Phone/Fax No.: 918-251-5640
Website: www.tromix.com
Email: tonyr@tromix.com

TROY INDUSTRIES, INC.
17 Main Street
Lee, MA 01238
Phone No.: 413-243-9315
Fax No.: 413-383-0339
Website: www.troyind.com
Email: info@troyind.com

TRUVELO MANUFACTURERS (PTY) LTD.
Factory – Truvelo Armoury
P.O. Box 14183
Lyttelton 0140 SOUTH AFRICA
Fax No.: 011-27-11-314-1409
Website: www.truvelo.co.za
Email: armoury@truvelo.co.za

TULA ARMS PLANT
Long Gun Importer - SSME Deutsche Waffen, Inc.
408 W. Renfro St. #107J
Plant City, FL 33566
Phone No.: 813-754-8665
Fax No.: 813-659-3361
Website: www.ssmedwi.com
Factory
1 a Sovetskaja Str.
RUS-300002 Tula, RUSSIA
Fax No: 011-70872-27-3439
Website: www.tulatoz.ru
Email: tozmarketing@home.tula.net

DOUG TURNBULL RESTORATION, INC.
6680 Rts. 5 & 20
Bloomfield, NY 14469
Phone No.: 585-657-6338
Fax No.: 585-657-7743
Website: www.turnbullrestoration.com
Email: info@turnbullrestoration.com

U.S. HISTORICAL SOCIETY
Please refer to America Remembers listing.

U.S.R.A. PISTOLS
(Information Only)
Mr. L. Richard Littlefield
P.O. Box 9
Jaffrey, NH 0342
Phone No.: 603-532-8004

U.S. ORDNANCE
P.O. Box 70425
Reno, NV 89570-0443
Phone No.: 775-356-1303
Fax No.: 775-356-1313
Website: www.usord.com

UBERTI, A. & C., S.r.l.
Importer - please refer Stoeger Industries listing.
Importer - please refer to Taylor's listing.
Importer - please refer to Dixie Gun Works listing.
Importer - please refer to Cabela's listing.
Importer - please refer to Cimarron, F.A. & Co listing.
Importer - please refer to E.M.F. Co. Inc. listing.
Importer - please refer to Navy Arms listing.
Service & Repair - please refer to VTI Gun Parts listing.

Factory - A. Uberti & C., S.r.l.
Via Artigiani 1
I-25063 Gardone, VT (BS) ITALY
Fax No.: 011-39-030-834-1801
Website: www.ubertireplicas.it
Email: info@ubertireplicas.it

UGARTECHEA, ARMAS
Importer - please refer to Aspen Outfitting Co. listing.
Importer - please refer to Lion Country Supply listing.
Factory
P.O. Box 21
E-20600, Eibar, SPAIN
Fax No.: 011-3443-121669

UMAREX SPORTWAFFEN GmbH & CO. KG
Donnerfeld 2
D-59757 Arnsberg GERMANY
Fax No.: 011-49-2932-638224
Website: www.umarex.de

UNIQUE-ALPINE
Postfach 15 55
D-85435 Erding GERMANY
Fax No.: 011-49-08122-9797-23
Website: www.unique-alpine.com

UNITED STATES FIRE ARMS MANUFACTURING COMPANY, INC.
Distributor - please refer to Acusport listing.
Factory
445 Ledyard Street
Hartford, CT 06114
Phone No.: 877-227-6901
Fax No.: 860-724-6809
Website: www.usfirearms.com
Email: Sales@usfirearms.com

USELTON ARMS INC.
1236 Northgate Bus. Parkway, Ste. A1
Madison, TN 37115
Phone No.: 615-865-0006
Fax No.: 615-865-1874
Website: www.useltonarmsinc.com

UZI
Trademark of IMI - no commercial importation.
Repair & Service - please refer to Vector Arms, Inc. listing.

VM HY-TECH LLC
2701 W. Grovers Ave., Ste. 100A
Phoenix, AZ 85053
Phone No.: 602-944-3956
Fax No.: 602-944-3953
Website: www.vmhytech.com
Email: info@vmhytech.com

VALKYRIE ARMS LTD.
120 State Ave. NE, No. 381
Olympia, WA 98501
Phone/Fax No.: 360-482-4036
Website: www.valkyriearms.com
Email: info@valkyriearms.com

VALMET
Importer - Network Retailing LLC
22700 S Central Point Rd
Canby, OR 97013
Phone No.: 503-263 3787
Fax No: 775-414 0833
e-mail: russ@vh2q.com
Factory - please refer to Marocchi listing.

VALTRO
Importer - Valtro USA
24800 Mission Blvd.
Hayward, CA 94544
Phone No.: 510-489-8477
Fax No.: 510-489-8477
Website: www.valtrousa.com
Factory - Valtro Europe s.r.l.
Via Capretti 12
I-25136 Brescia, ITALY
Fax No.: 011-39-030-2000869

VECTOR ARMS INC.
270 West 500 North
N. Salt Lake, UT 84054
Phone No.: 801-295-1917
Fax No.: 801-295-9316
Website: www.vectorarms.com
Email: vectorarms@att.net

VEGA
Importer - please refer to Adco Sales listing.
Tigcilar Sk. No. 2
34450 Mercan-Istanbul TURKEY
Fax No.: 011-90-212-512-0879
Website: www.vegaarms.com

VEKTOR
Denel
PO Box 8322
Centurion
0046 South Africa
Fax No.: 011-27-12-428-0651

VEPR. RIFLES
Importer - please refer to Robinson Armament listing.
Factory – MOLOT JSC
Vyatskie Polyany Machine Building Plant
135 Lenin St., Vyatski Polyany
RUS-612960 Kirov Region, RUSSIA
Fax No.: 011-007-83334-61832
Website: www.molot.biz

VERNEY-CARRON
Importer - Verney-Carron U.S.A., Inc.
320 Court Street
Clay Center, KS 67432-3169
Phone No.: 785-632-2184
Fax No.: 785-632-6554
Website: www.verney-carron.us
Email: email@verney-carron.us
Factory - Verney-Carron S.A.
54, Boulevard Thiers
Boite Postale 72
F-42002 St.-Etienne Cedex 1 FRANCE
Phone No.: 011-33-477-791500
Fax No.: 011-33-477-790702
Website: www.verney-carron.com
Email: email@verney-carron.com

VERONA
Factory - please refer to F.A.I.R. listing.

VI-MA s.n.c. di VIVENSI m. & C.
via Madonnina, 42
I-25060 Marcheno, VT (Brescia) ITALY
Fax No.: 011-39-030-8913519
Website: www.meccanicavima.it
Email: info@meccanicavima.it

VOERE
Factory - Voere Austria
Untere Sparchen 56
A-6330 Kufstein, AUSTRIA
Fax No.: 011-43-5372-65752
Website : www.voere.de
Email: marketing@voere.de

VOLQUARTSEN CUSTOM LTD.
P.O. Box 397
24276 240th St.
Carroll, IA 51401
Phone No.: 712-792-4238
Fax No.: 712-792-2542
Website: www.volquartsen.com
Email: info@volquartsen.com

VTI GUN PARTS
P.O. Box 509
Lakeville, CT 06039
Phone No.: 860-435-8068
Fax No.: 860-435-8146
Website: www.vtigunparts.com

VULCAN ARMAMENT, INC.
P.O. Box 2473
Inver Grove Heights, MN 55076-8473
Phone No.: 651-451-5956
Website: www.vulcanarms.com

WAFFENFABRIK HEIN
P.O. Box G10
Tekoa, WA 99033
Phone No: 509-284-2215
Website: www.rifleactions.com
Email: sales@rifleactions.com

WAFFFEN GLATZ
Erlendorf 55
9587 Rigersdorf bei Arnoldstein AUSTRIA
Website: www.waffen-glatz.at
Email: johann_glatz@utanet.at

WAFFEN HIENDLMAYER GmbH
Please refer to Klaus Hiendlmayer listing.

WAFFENSTUBE GUGGI
Wienerstrasse 9
A-8020 Graz AUSTRIA
Fax No.: 011-43-316-711878
Website: www.guggi-arms.com
Email: office@guggi-arms.com

WAFFEN JUNG GmbH
Am Alten Garten 7
53797 Lohmar, GERMANY
Fax No.: 011-0224618491
Website: www.waffenjung.de
Email: info@waffenjung.de

WALTHER
Importer – please refer to Smith & Wesson listing.
www.waltheramerica.com
Target pistol & rifle importer - please refer to Champion's Choice Inc. listing.
GSP/rifle conversion kits & factory repair station - Earl's Repair Service, Inc.
437 Chandler Street (rear)
Tewksbury, MA 01876
Phone No.: 978-851-2656
Fax No.: 978-851-9462
Website: www.carlwalther.com
Email: info@carlwalther.com
German Company Headquarters (Umarex)
Carl Walther Sportwaffen GmbH
Donnerfeld 2
D-59757 Arnsberg GERMANY
Fax No.: 011-49-29-32-638149
Website: www.carl-walther.de
Email: sales@carl-walther.de
Factory - Carl Walther, GmbH Sportwaffenfabrik
Postfach 4325
D-89033 Ulm/Donau, GERMANY
Fax No.: 011-49-731-1539170

WATSON BROS.
54 Redchuch Street,
City of London, ENGLAND
Website: www.watsonbrosgunmakers.com
Email: Michael.Louca@WatsonBrosGunMakers.com

WEATHERBY
1605 Commerce Way
Paso Robles, CA 93446
Technical Support: 805-227-2600
Service/Warranty: 800-227-2023
Fax No.: 805-237-0427
Website: www.weatherby.com

WEBLEY & SCOTT
Importer - SxS shotguns only - please refer to Legacy Sports listing.
Factory
Universe House
Key Industrial Park
Willenhall, West Midlands
WV13 3YA ENGLAND
Fax: 011-44-1902-722-880
Website: www.webleyandscott.co.uk
Email: info@webleyandscott.co.uk

WEIHRAUCH SPORT GmbH
Importer - please refer to E.A.A. listing.
Factory
Postfach 25
D-97638 Mellrichstadt, GERMANY
Fax No.: 011-49-9776-707679
Website: www.weihrauch-sport.de
Email: info@weihrauch-sport.de

DAN WESSON FIREARMS
Distributor - please refer to CZ-USA listing.
Factory
5169 Highway 12 South
Norwich, NY 13815
Phone No.: 607-336-1174
Fax No.: 607-336-2730
Website: www.danwessonfirearms.com

WESTLEY RICHARDS & CO., Ltd.
Importer - Westley Richards Agency USA
3810 Valley Commons Drive, Ste. 2
Bozeman, MT 59718
Phone No.: 406-586-1946
Fax No.: 406-586-3326
Factory
40 Grange Road
Bournbrook, Birmingham, ENGLAND B29 6AR
Fax No.: 011-44-121-414-1138
Website: www.westleyrichards.com

WICHITA ARMS, INC.
923 E. Gilbert
Wichita, KS 67211
Phone No.: 316-265-0661
Fax No.: 316-265-0760
Website: www.wichitaarms.com
Email: info@wichitaarms.com

WIFRA
Please refer to W.R. Saleri listing.

WILD WEST GUNS, INC.
7100 Homer Drive
Anchorage, AK 99518
Phone No.: 800-992-4570
Fax No.: 907-344-4005
Website: www.wildwestguns.com
Email: wildwestguns@alaska.net

WILDEY F.A. INC.
45 Angevine Road
Warren, CT 06754
Phone No.: 860-355-9000
Fax No.: 860-354-7759
Website: www.wildeyguns.com
Email: info@wildeyguns.com

WILLIAM & SON
10 Mount Street
London, W1K 2TY ENGLAND
Phone No.: 011-44-020-7493-8385
Fax No.: 011-44-020-7493-8386
Website: www.williamandson.com
Email: info@williamandson.com

WILLIAM LARKIN MOORE & CO.
16622 North 91st. St., #103
Scottsdale, AZ 85260
Phone No.: 480-951-8913
Fax No.: 480-951-3677
Website: www.williamlarkinmoore.com
Email: info@williamlarkinmoore.com

WILLIAM EVANS LIMITED
The Old Armoury
Bisley Camp, Brookwood
Woking, Surrey, GU24 0NY U.K.
Fax No.: 011-44-1483486580
Website: www.williamevans.com
Email: sales@williamevans.com

WILLIAM POWELL & SON (GUNMAKERS), Ltd.
Factory & Store
35-37 Carrs Lane
Birmingham B47SX ENGLAND
Phone No.: 011-44-121-643-8362
Fax No.: 011-44-121-631-3504
Website: www.william-powell.co.uk
Email: sales@william-powell.co.uk

WILSON COMBAT
2234 CR 719
P.O. Box 578
Berryville, AR 72616-0578
Phone No.: 800-955-4856
Fax No.: 870-545-3310
Website: www.wilsoncombat.com

WINCHESTER - U.S.REPEATING ARMS
Administrative Offices
275 Winchester Avenue
Morgan, UT 84050-9333
Customer Service Phone No.: 800-333-3288
Parts & Service Phone No.: 800-945-1392
Fax No.: 801-876-3737
Website: www.winchester-guns.com
Website: www.winchesterguns.com
Winchester Parts and Service
3005 Arnold Tenbrook Rd.
Arnold, MO 63010-9406
Phone No.: 800-322-4626
Fax No.: 636-287-9751

WINCHESTER/OLIN
Models 101 & 23 only (Disc.)
Attn: Shotgun Customer Service
427 N. Shamrock Street
East Alton, IL 62024
Fax No.: 618-258-3393
Website: www.winchester.com

WINGSHOOTING ADVENTURES
9516 Taft Street
Coopersville, MI 49404-9418
Phone No.: 616-837-9000
Fax No.: 616-837-9002

WISCHO JAGD-UND SPORTWAFFEN
Dresdener Strasse 30,
D-91058 Erlangen, GERMANY
Fax No.: 011-4991-31-300930
Website: www.wischo.com
Email: info@wischo.com

WISEMAN, BILL & CO.
18456 State Hwy. 6 South
College Station, TX 77845
Phone No.: 979-690-3456
Fax No.: 979-690-0156

WM. PETE HARVEY AUCTIONS
P.O. Box 280
Cataumet, MA 02534
Phone/Fax No.: 508-548-0660
Website: www.firearmsauctions.com

WOODWARD, JAMES AND SONS
Factory - please refer to Purdey, James, & Sons, Ltd. listing.

YILDIZ SILAH SANAYI
Importer - Academy Sports
Website: www.academy.com
Factory
Organize Sanayi Bolgesi 40, Sokak No. 13
TR-15100 Burdur TURKEY
Fax No.: 01190-0248-252-9569
Website: www.yildizshotgun.com

ZDF IMPORT EXPORT INC.
Please refer to Robinson Armament listing.

Z-HAT CUSTOM
4010 A. So. Poplar
PMB #72
Casper, WY 82601
Phone No.: 307-577-7433
Website: www.z-hat.com
Email: rifle.builder@z-hat.com

Z-M WEAPONS
203 South St.
Bernardston, MA 01337
Phone No.: 413-648-9501
Fax No.: 413-648-0219
Website: www.zmweapons.com
Email: zm@zmweapons.com

ZABALA HERMANOS, S.A.
Apartado do Corroos 97
20600 Eibar SPAIN
Fax No.: 011-34-943-768201
Website: www.zabalahermanos.com
Email: imanol@zabalahermanos.com

ZANARDINI
Importer - S.O.G. Arms
15902A Halliburton Road #267
Hacienda Heights, CA 91745
Phone No.: 626-968-3208
Fax No.: 626-961-7719
Factory - Zanardini, P. & C., S.n.c.
Via C. Goldoni, 34
I-25063 Gardone V.T. (Brescia), ITALY
Fax No.: 011-39-030-837180
Website: www.zanardini.com
Email: info@zanardini.com

ZANOTTI
Importer - Zanotti USA
Houston, TX
Phone No.: 281-414-2184
Website: www.zanottiusa.com
Email: management@zanottiusa.com
Factory
via Donato 78/A
40127 Bologna, ITALY
Website: www.zanottiarms.com
Email: staff@zanottiarms.com

ZASTAVA ARMS

Importer - please refer to Remington listing.
Importer - please refer to E.uropean American Armory listing.
Factory
Trg Topolivaca 4
34000 Kragujevac, SERBIA
Fax No.: 011-381-034-323683
Website: www.zastava-arms.co.yu
Email: zastavanp@ptt.yu

ZIEGENHAHN & SOHN OHG

Importer - please refer to New England Custom Gun Service, Ltd. listing.
Importer - please refer to Heirloom Armes listing.
Factory
Suhler Str. 9 A
D-98544 Zella-Mehlis GERMANY
Fax No.: 011-49-36-82-896-28
Website: www.ziegenhahn.de
Email: info@ ziegenhahn.de

ZOLI, ANTONIO

Not affiliated with Angelo Zoli.
Importer & Distributor - Antonio Zoli America
3630 East Ridge Run
Canandaigua, NY 114424
Phone No.: 585-394-2171
Fax No.: 585-394-1909
Email: zguns@rochester.rr.com
Service, Warranty & Custom Shop - please refer to Cole Gun-smithing listing.
Factory - Antonio Zoli S.r.l.
Via Zanardelli, 39
I-25063 Gardone V.T. (BS) ITALY
Fax No.: 011-39-030-891-1165
Website: www.zoli.it
Email: world@zoli.it

GLOSSARY

ACCOUTREMENT

All equipment carried by soldiers on the outside of their uniform, such as buckles, belts, or canteens, but not weapons.

ACTION

The heart of the gun, including receiver, bolt, or breechblock feeding and firing mechanism. See Boxlock, Rolling Block, or Sidelock.

ADJUSTABLE CHOKE

A device built into the muzzle of a shotgun enabling changes from one choke to another.

AIRGUN

A gun that utilizes compressed air or gas to launch the projectile.

APERTURE SIGHT

A rear sight assembly consisting of a hole or aperture located in an adjustable assembly through which the front sight and target are aligned.

ASSAULT RIFLE

Definition usually depends on if you're pro-gun or anti-gun. If you're pro-gun, it generally refers to a paramilitary style semi-auto rifle with certain features. If you're anti-gun, it can include almost anything, including sporter rifles from the turn of the 20th century.

AUTO LOADING/LOADER

See Semiautomatic.

BACKSTRAP

Those parts of the revolver or pistol frame that are exposed at the rear of the grip.

BARREL

The steel tube (may be a sleeve wrapped in a synthetic material) that a projectile travels through.

BARREL BAND

A metal band, either fixed or adjustable, around the forend of a gun that holds the barrel to the stock.

BARREL THROAT

The breech end of a barrel that is chambered and somewhat funneled for the passage of a bullet from cartridge case mouth into the barrel. Also known as a forcing cone.

BATTUE

A ramped fixed rear sight assembly located on the back of the barrel, allowing quick target acquisition.

BEAVERTAIL FOREND

A wider than normal forend.

BLUING

The chemical process of artificial oxidation (rusting) applied to gun parts so that the metal attains a dark blue or nearly black appearance.

BOLT

The removable stud that rises and falls from the frame to lock the cylinder with the firing chamber in correct alignment with the bore.

BORE

Internal dimensions of a barrel (smooth or rifled) that can be measured using the Metric system (i.e. millimeters), English system (i.e. inches), or by the Gauge system (see gauge). On a rifled barrel, the bore is measured across the lands. Also, it is a traditional English term used when referring to the diameter of a shotgun muzzle (gauge in U.S. measure).

BOXLOCK ACTION

Typified by Parker shotgun in U.S. and Westley Richards in England. Generally considered inferior in strength to the sidelock. Developed by Anson & Deeley, the boxlock is hammerless. It has two disadvantages. First, the hammer pin must be placed directly below knee of action, which is its weakest spot. Second, action walls must be thinned out to receive locks. These are inserted from below into large slots in the action body, which is then closed with a plate. Greener crossbolt, when made correctly, overcomes many of the boxlock weaknesses.

BREECH

That portion of a gun which contains the rear chamber portion of the barrel(s), action, the trigger or firing mechanism, and the magazine.

BREVETTE

French word which, in gun terminology, refers to a European copy (usually English, French, or Belgian) or patterned after a more famous design (i.e., Brevette Remington O/U derringer refers to a copy of the Remington O/U .41 cal. derringer).

BUCKHORN SIGHT

Open metallic rear sight with sides that curl upward and inward.

BULL BARREL

A heavier, thicker than normal barrel with little or no taper.

BUTTPLATE

A protective plate, usually steel, attached to the back of the buttstock.

BUTTSTOCK

See Stock.

CALIBER

The diameter of the bore (measured from land to land), usually measured in either inches or millimeters/centimeters. It does not designate bullet diameter.

CAMO (CAMOUFLAGE)

Refers to a patterned treatment using a variety of different colors/patterns that enables a gun to blend into a particular outdoors environment. In most cases, this involves a film or additional finish to be put on top of a gun's wood and/or metal parts (i.e. Mossy Oak Break-Up, Advantage Timber, Realtree Hardwoods, etc.).

CASE COLORS

See Color Case Hardening.

CAST OFF

The distance that a buttplate is offset to the right of the line of sight for a right-handed shooter. Especially important in shotgun stocks.

CAST ON

The same as Cast Off, except that the buttplate is offset to the left of the line of sight for a left-handed shooter.

CENTERFIRE

Self-contained cartridge where the detonating primer is located, in the center of the case head.

CHAMBER

Rear part of the barrel that has been reamed out so that it will contain a cartridge. When the breech is closed, the cartridge is supported in the chamber, and the chamber must align the primer with the firing pin, the bullet with the bore.

CHAMBER THROAT

The area in the barrel that is directly forward of the chamber and that tapers to bore diameter. Also called throat.

CHECKERING

A functional decoration consisting of pointed pyramids cut into the wood. Generally applied to the pistol grip and forend/forearm areas, affording better handling and control.

CHOKE

The muzzle constriction on a shotgun which controls the spread of the shot.

CHOKE TUBES

Interchangeable screw-in devices allowing different choke configurations (i.e., cylinder, improved cylinder, improved modified cylinder, modified, full). While most choke tubes fit flush with the end of the barrel, some choke tubes now also protrude from the end of the barrel. Most recently made shotguns usually include three to five choke tubes with the shotgun.

CHOPPER LUMP

A method of construction of barrels for double barreled, SxS shotguns in which the "lump" extending beneath the breech of the barrel is forged as an integral part of the barrel. When the barrels are assembled, the two lumps are carefully fitted on their mating surfaces and brazed solidly together into a single unti, into which locking and other functional recesses are cut.

CLIP

See Magazine.

COCKING INDICATOR

Any device for which the act of cocking a gun moves it into a position where it may be seen or felt, in order to notify the shooter that the gun is cocked. Typical examples are the pins found on some high-grade hammerless shotguns, which protrude slightly when they are cocked, and also the exposed cocking knobs on bolt-action rifles. Exposed hammers found on some rifles and pistols are also considered cocking indicators.

COLOR CASE HARDENING

A method of hardening steel and iron while imparting colorful swirls as well as surfaces figure. Normally, the desired metal parts are put in a crucible packed with a mixture of charcoal and finely ground animal bone to temperatures in the 800ºC - 900ºC range, after which they are slowly cooled. Then they are submerged into cold water, leaving a thin, colorful protective finish.

COMB

The portion of the stock on which the shooter's cheek rests.

COMBINATION GUN

Generally, a break-open shotgun-type configuration that is fitted with at least one shotgun barrel and one rifle barrel. Such guns may be encountered with either two or three barrels, and less frequently with as many as four or five, and have been known to chamber for as many as four different calibers.

COMPENSATOR

A recoil-reducing device that mounts on the muzzle of a gun to deflect part of the powder gases up and rearward. Also called a muzzle brake.

CRANE

In a modern solid-frame, swing-out cylinder revolver, the U-shaped yoke on which the cylinder rotates, and which holds the cylinder in the frame. The crane/yoke is the weakest part of a revolver's mechanism.

CRIMP

A turning in of the case mouth to affect a closure or to prevent the bullet from slipping out of the case mouth. Various crimps include: roll crimp, pie crimp, star or folded crimp, and rose crimp.

CROWNING

The rounding or chambering normally done to a barrel muzzle to insure that the mouth of the bore is square with the bore axis and that the edge is countersunk below the surface to protect it from impact damage. Traditionally, crowning was accomplished by spinning an abrasive-coated brass ball against the muzzle while moving it in a figure-eight pattern, until the abrasive had cut away any irregularities and produced a uniform and square mouth.

CROSSBOLT

A transverse locking rod/bar used in many SxS boxlock shotguns and a few rifles, which lock the standing breech and barrels. Originally designed by W.W. Greener, this term is also referred to as the Greener crossbolt.

CRYOGENIC TEMPERING

Computer controlled cooling process that relieves barrel stress by subjecting the barrel to a temperature of -310° F for 22 hours.

CURIO/RELIC

Firearms which are of special interest to collectors by reason of some quality other than is associated with firearms intended for sporting use or as offensive or defensive weapons. Must be older than 50 years.

CYLINDER

A rotating cartridge holder in a revolver. The cartridges are held in chambers and the cylinder turns, either to the left or the right, depending on the gun maker's design, as the hammer is cocked.

CYLINDER ARM

See Crane.

DAMASCENE

The decorating of metal with another metal, either by inlaying or attaching in some fashion.

DAMASCUS BARREL

A barrel made by twisting, forming and welding thin strips of steel around a mandrel.

DERRINGER

Usually refers to a small, concealable pistol with one or two short barrels.

DOUBLE ACTION

The principle in a revolver or auto-loading pistol wherein the hammer can be cocked and dropped by a single pull of the trigger. Most of these actions also provide capability for single action fire. In auto loading pistols, double action normally applies only to the first shot of any series, the hammer being cocked by the slide for subsequent shots.

DOUBLE ACTION ONLY

Hammer no longer cocks in single action stage (many new DAO models are hammerless).

DOUBLE-BARRELED

A gun consisting of two barrels joined either side-by-side or one over the other.

DOUBLE-SET TRIGGER

A device that consists of two triggers one to cock the mechanism that spring-assists the other trigger, substantially lightening trigger pull.

DOVETAIL

A flaring machined or hand-cut slot that is also slightly tapered toward one end. Cut into the upper surface of barrels and sometimes actions, the dovetail accepts a corresponding part on which a sight is mounted. Dovetail slot blanks are used to cover the dovetail when the original sight has been removed or lost; this gives the barrel a more pleasing appearance and configuration.

DRILLED & TAPPED

Refers to screw holes that are drilled into the top of a receiver/frame, allowing scope bases, blocks, rings, or other sighting devices to be rigidly attached to the gun.

DRILLING

German for triple, which is their designation for a three-barrel gun, usually two shotgun barrels and one rifle barrel.

EJECTOR

Automatic mechanical device used to eject empty cartridges from chamber(s) after firing.

ELECTROCIBLE

Unique reusable target designed like an aircraft propeller that causes it to spin and go in different directions. In competition, electrocibles come out of one of five boxes located 25 meters from the shooter, who must hit it before it crosses over the ring at 21 meters.

ENGINE TURNING

Machined circular polishing on metal, creating a unique overlapping pattern.

ENGLISH STOCK

A straight, slender-gripped stock.

ENGRAVING

The art of engraving metal in decorative patterns. Scroll engraving is the most common type of hand engraving encountered. Much of today's factory engraving is rolled on which is done mechanically. Hand engraving requires artistry and knowledge of metals and related materials.

ETCHING

A method of decorating metal gun parts, usually done by acid etching or photo engraving.

EXTRACTOR

A device which partially lifts the spent casing(s) from the breech area, allowing the empty shell(s) to be removed manually.

FALLING BLOCK

A single shot action where the breechblock drops straight down when the lever is actuated.

FIT AND FINISH

Terms used to describe over-all firearm workmanship.

FIRE CONTROL

Modern term referring to trigger mechanism and operating system - sometime detachable.

FIRING PIN

That part of a gun that strikes the cartridge primer, causing detonation.

FLOATING BARREL

A barrel bedded to avoid contact with any point on the stock.

FLOOR PLATE

Usually, a removable/hinged plate at the bottom of the receiver covering the magazine well.

FORCING CONE

Forward part of the chamber in a shotgun where the chamber diameter is reduced to bore diameter. The forcing cone aids the passage of shot into the barrel.

FOREARM

In this text, a separate piece of wood in front of the receiver and under the barrel used for hand placement when shooting. Forearms can get expensive - H&H currently prices a replacement forearm at £10,000 (that's $20,088!).

FOREND

Usually the forward portion of a one-piece rifle or shotgun stock (in this text), but can also refer to a separate piece of wood.

FRAME

The part of a firearm that the action (lock work), barrel, and stock/grip are connected to. Most of the time used when referring to a handgun or hinged frame long gun.

FREE RIFLE

A rifle designed for international-type target shooting. The only restriction on design is weight maximum 8 kilograms (17.6 lbs.).

FRONT STRAP

That part of the revolver or pistol grip frame that faces forward and often joins with the trigger guard. In target guns, notably the .45 ACP, the front strap is often stippled to give shooter's hand a slip-proof surface.

GAUGE/GA.

A unit of measure used to determine a shotgun's bore. Determined by the amount of pure lead balls equaling the bore diameter needed to equal one pound (i.e., a 12 ga. means that 12 lead balls exactly the diameter of the bore weigh one pound). In this text, .410 is referenced as a bore (if it was a gauge, it would be a 68 ga.).

GAUGE VS. BORE DIAMETER

10-Gauge = Bore Diameter of .775 inches or 19.3mm
12-Gauge = Bore Diameter of .729 inches or 18.2mm
16-Gauge = Bore Diameter of .662 inches or 16.8mm
20-Gauge = Bore Diameter of .615 inches or 15.7mm
28-Gauge = Bore Diameter of .550 inches or 13.8mm
68-Gauge = Bore Diameter of .410 inches or 12.6mm

GRIP

The handle used to hold a handgun, or the area of a stock directly behind and attached to the frame/receiver of a long gun.

GRIPS

Can be part of the frame or components attached to the frame used to assist in accuracy, handling, control, and safety of a handgun. Many currently manufactured semi-auto handguns have grips that are molded w/ checkering as part of the synthetic frame.

GRIPSTRAP(S)

Typically refers to the front and back metal that attaches to a handgun frame and supports the grips/stocks.

GROOVES

The spiral cuts in the bore of a rifle or handgun barrel that give the bullet its spin or rotation as it moves down the barrel.

HAMMER

A part of a gun's mechanism that creates it to fire. May or may not have a firing pin attached.

HAMMERLESS

Some "hammerless" firearms do in fact have hidden hammers, which are located in the action housing. Truly hammerless guns, such as the Savage M99, have a firing mechanism that is based on a spring-activated firing pin.

HALF COCK

A position of the hammer in a hammer activated firing mechanism that serves as a manual safety.

HEEL

Back end of the upper edge of the butt stock at the upper edge of the buttplate or recoil pad.

IN-THE-WHITE

Refers to a gun's finish w/o bluing, nickel, case colors, gold, etc. Since all metal surfaces are polished, the steel appears white, hence, "in-the-white" terminology.

JUXAPOSED

See Side-by-Side listing.

LAMINATED STOCK

A gunstock made of many layers of wood glued together under pressure. Together, the laminations become very strong, preventing damages from moisture, heat, and warping.

LANDS

Portions of the bore left between the grooves of the rifling in the bore of a firearm. In rifling, the grooves are usually twice the width of the land. Land diameter is measured across the bore, from land to land.

M1913 PICATINNY RAIL

Picatinny rail with standardized dimensions for mounting sights, scopes, or optics.

MAGAZINE (MAG.)

The container (may be detachable) which holds cartridges under spring pressure to be fed into the gun's chamber.

MAGNUM (MAG.)

A modern cartridge with a higher-velocity load or heavier projectile than standard.

MAINSPRING

The spring that delivers energy to the hammer or striker.

MANNLICHER STOCK

A full-length slender stock with slender forend extending to the muzzle (full stock) affording better barrel protection.

MICROMETER SIGHT

A finely adjustable target sight.

MONOBLOC

A form of construction and assembly for double barreled shotguns wherein the breeching and locking surfaces are cut into a single separate housing or "bloc" into which the breeches of the barrels are brazed or threaded. See also CHOPPER LUMP.

MONTE CARLO STOCK

A stock with an elevated comb used primarily for scoped rifles.

MUZZLE

The forward end of the barrel where the projectile exits.

MUZZLE BRAKE

A recoil-reducing device attached to the muzzle.

NEEDLE GUN

Ignition system invented by Johan Nikolas von Dreyse in 1829. This ignition system using a paper cartridge became obsolete with the invention of the metallic cartridge.

OVER-UNDER (Superposed)

A two-barrel gun in which the barrels are stacked one on top of the other.

PARALLAX

Occurs in telescopic sights when the primary image of the objective lens does not coincide with the reticle. In practice, parallax is detected in the scope when, as the viewing eye is moved laterally, the image and the reticle appear to move in relation to each other.

PARAMILITARY

Typically refers to a gun's configuration/styling resembling some military configurations. In this text, it refers mostly to semi-auto rifles that are styled/patterned after popular military models (i.e., AR-15/M16, AK-47, Galil, Uzi, FALs, etc.).

PARKERIZING

Matted rust-resistant oxides finish, usually matte or dull gray, or black in color, found on military guns.

PEEP SIGHT

Rear sights consisting of a hole or aperture through which the front sight and target are aligned.

PEPPERBOX

An early form of revolving repeating pistol, in which a number of barrels were bored in a circle in a single piece of metal resembling the cylinder of a modern revolver. Functioning was the same as a revolver, the entire cylinder being revolved to bring successive barrels under the hammer for firing. Though occurring as far back as the 16th century, the pepperbox did not become practical until the advent of the percussion cap in the early 1800s. Pepperboxes were made in a wide variety of sizes and styles, and reached their popularity peak during the percussion period. Few were made after the advent of practical metallic cartridges. Both single and double action pepperboxes were made. Single-barreled revolvers after the 1840s were more accurate and easier to handle and soon displaced the rather clumsy and muzzle-heavy pepperbox.

PERCH BELLY

Refers to a rifle's stock configuration where the bottom portion is curved rather than straight between the buttplate and pistol grip.

PICATINNY

Refers to a serrated flat rail typically located on the top of a frame/slide/receiver, but may also be located on the sides and bottom, allowing different optics/sights/accessories to be used on the gun. Developed at the U.S. Army's Picatinny arsenal.

PINFIRE

Self contained cartridge that is detonated by striking a small pin sticking through the side wall of the cartridge casing.

POLYGONAL

Circular rifling w/o hard edged lands and grooves.

POPE RIB

A rib integral with the barrel. Designed by Harry M. Pope, famed barrel maker and shooter, the rib made it possible to mount a target scope low over the barrel.

PROOFMARK

Proofmarks are usually applied to all parts actually tested, but normally appear on the barrel (and possibly frame), usually indicating the country of origin and circa of proof (especially on European firearms). In the U.S., there is no federalized or government proof house, only the manufacturer's in-house proofmark indicating that a firearm has passed its internal quality control standards per government specifications.

PRIMER

Small detonating cap fitted in the head of a centerfire cartridge case that when struck by a firing pin, ignites the powder charge.

PRIMER RING

Refers to a visible dark ring created by the primers in centerfire ammunition around the firing pin hole in the frame after much use.

RECEIVER

That part of a rifle or shotgun (excluding hinged frame guns) that houses the bolt, firing pin, mainspring, trigger group, and magazine or ammunition feed system. The barrel is threaded into the somewhat enlarged forward part of the receiver, called the receiver ring. At the rear of the receiver, the butt or stock is fastened. In semiautomatic pistols, the frame or housing is sometimes referred to as the receiver.

RELEASE TRIGGER

A trap shooting trigger that fires the gun when the trigger is released.

RELIC

See listing under Curio/Relic.

RIB

A raised sighting plane affixed to the top of a barrel.

RIFLING

The spirally cut grooves in the bore of a rifle or handgun. The rifling stabilizes the bullet in flight. Rifling may rotate to the left or the right, the higher parts of the bore being called lands, the cuts or lower parts being called the grooves. Many types exist, such as oval, polygonal, button, Newton, Newton-Pope, parabolic, Haddan, Enfield, segmental rifling, etc. Most U.S.-made barrels have a right-hand twist, while British gun makers prefer a left-hand twist. In practice, there seems to be little difference in accuracy or barrel longevity.

RIMFIRE

Self contained metallic cartridge where the priming compound is contained inside the rim of the cartridge case. Detonated by the firing pin(s) striking the bottom edge of the outside rim.

RINGS

See Scope Rings.

ROLLING BLOCK ACTION

Single shot action, designed in the U.S. and widely used in early Remington arms. Also known as the Remington-rider action, the breechblock, actuated by a lever, rotates down and back from the chamber. Firing pin is contained in block and is activated by hammer fall.

SAFETY

A mechanism(s) in/on a gun that prevents it from firing. Many different types and variations.

SAW HANDLE

Refers to distinctive squared off type of pistol grip design where stock makes right angle at top and is then attached to the frame.

SCHNABEL FOREND/FOREARM

The curved/carved flared end of the forend/forearm that resembles the beak of a bird (Schnabel in German). This type of forend is common on Austrian and German guns; was popular in the U.S., but the popularity of the Schnabel forend/forearm comes and goes with the seasons. A Schnabel forend is often seen on custom stocks and rifles.

SCOPE RINGS (BLOCKS/BASES)

Metal mounts used to attach a scope to the top of a gun's frame/receiver.

SEAR

The pivoting part in the firing or lock mechanism of a gun. The sear is linked to the trigger, and may engage the cocking piece or the firing pin.

SEMIAUTOMATIC

A pistol, rifle, or shotgun that is loaded manually for the first round. Upon pulling the trigger, the gun fires, ejects the fired round, cocks the firing mechanism, and feeds a fresh round from the magazine. The trigger must be released after each shot and pulled again to fire the next round.

SHORT ACTION

A rifle action designed for shorter cartridges.

SHOTSHELL

Self-contained round of ammunition used in shotguns, generally either brass and paper (older mfg.) or brass/steel and plastic (newer mfg.).

SIDE-BY-SIDE (JUXTAPOSED)

A two-barrel shotgun where the barrels are arranged side-by-side.

SIDE LEVER

Refers to opening mechanism lever on either left or right side of receiver/frame.

SIDELOCK

A type of action, usually long gun, where the moving parts are located on side of the lock plates, which in turn are inlet in the stock. Usually found only on better quality shotguns and rifles.

SIDEPLATES

Ornamental steel panels normally attached to a boxlock action to simulate a sidelock.

SINGLE ACTION

A firearms design which requires the hammer to be manually cocked for each shot. Also an auto loading pistol design which requires manual cocking of the hammer for the first shot only.

SINGLE TRIGGER

One trigger on a double-barrel gun. It fires both barrels individually by successive pulls.

SLING SWIVELS

Metal loops affixed to the gun on which a carrying strap is attached.

SPUR TRIGGER

A trigger mounting system that housed the trigger in an extension of the frame in some old guns. The trigger projected only slightly from the front of the extension or spur, and no trigger guard was used on these guns.

STOCK

Usually refers to the buttstock of a long gun, or that portion of a rifle or shotgun that comes in contact with the shooter's arm, and is attached to the frame/receiver.

STOCKS

Older terminology used to describe handgun grips (see Grips).

SUICIDE SPECIAL

A mass-produced variety of inexpensive single action revolvers and derringers, usually with a spur trigger. Produced under a variety of trade names, these guns earned their nickname by being almost as dangerous to shoot as to be shot at.

SUPERPOSED

Refers to an O/U barrel configuration.

TAKE DOWN

A gun which can be easily taken apart in two sections for carrying or shipping.

TANG (S)

Usually refers to the extension straps (upper and lower) of a rifle or shotgun receiver/frame to which the stock/grips are attached.

TOP LEVER

Refers to the opening lever mechanism on top of the upper frame/tang.

TOP STRAP

The upper part of a revolver frame, which often is either slightly grooved - the groove serving as rear sight - or which carries at its rearward end a sight that may be adjustable.

TRAP STOCK

A shotgun stock with greater length and less comb drop (Monte Carlo, in many cases) used for trap shooting, enabling a built in height lead when shooting.

TRIGGER

Refers to a release device in the firing system that starts the ignition process. Usually a curved, grooved, or serrated piece of metal that is pulled rearward by the shooter's finger, and then activates the sear or hammer.

TRIGGER GUARD

Usually a circular or oval band of metal, horn, or plastic that goes around the trigger to provide both protection and safety in shooting circumstances.

TWIST BARRELS

A process in which a steel rod (called a mandrel) was wrapped with skelps - ribbons of iron. The skelps were then welded in a charcoal fire to form one piece of metal, after which the rod was driven out to be used again. The interior of the resulting tube then had to be laboriously bored out by hand to remove the roughness. Once polished, the outside was smoothed on big grinding wheels, usually turned by water-power.

UNDER-LEVER

Action opening lever that is usually located below or in trigger guard, can also be side pivoting from forearm.

VENTILATED RIB

A sighting plane affixed along the length of a shotgun barrel with gaps or slots milled for cooling and lightweight handling.

VERNIER

Typically used in reference to a rear aperture (peep) sight. Usually upper tang mounted, and is adj. for elevation by means of a highly accurate vernier.

VIERLING

A German word designating a four-barrel gun.

WUNDHAMMER GRIP/SWELL

Originally attributed to custom gunsmith Louis Wundhammer, it consists of a bulge on the right side of the pistol grip that ergonomically fills the palm of a trigger hand.

YOKE

See Crane.

YOUTH DIMENSIONS

Usually refers to shorter stock dimensions and/or lighter weight enabling youth/women to shoot and carry a lighter, shorter firearm.

ABBREVIATIONS

*	Banned due 1994-2004 Crime Bill (may be current again)
A	Standard Grade Walnut
A2	AR-15 Style/Configuration w/fixed carry handle
A3	AR-15 Style/Configuration w/detachable carry handle
AA	Extra Grade Walnut
AAA	Best Quality Walnut
ACP	Automatic Colt Pistol
adj.	Adjustable
AE	Automatic Ejectors or Action Express
appts.	Appointments
AWB	Assault Weapons Ban
B	Blue
BAC	Browning Arms Company
BAN/CRIME BILL ERA	Mfg. between Nov. 1989 - Sept. 12, 2004
BB	Brass backstrap
BBL	Barrel
BMG	Browning Machine Gun
BOSS	Ballistic Optimizing Shooting System
BP	Buttplate or Black Powder
BPE	Black Power Express
BR	Bench Rest
BT	Beavertail
C/B 1994	Introduced because of 1994 Crime Bill
c.	Circa
cal.	Caliber
CB	Crescent Buttplate
CC	Case Colors
CCA	Colt Collectors Association
CF	Centerfire
CH	Cross Hair
CLMR	Colt Lightning Magazine Rifle
COMM.	Commeorative
COMP	Compensated/Competition
C-R	Curio-Relic
CYL/C	Cylinder
DA	Double Action
DAO	Double Action Only
DB	Double Barrel
DCM	Director of Civilian Marksmanship
DISC or disc.	Discontinued
DSL	Detachable Side Locks
DST	Double Set Triggers
DT	Double Triggers
DWM	DeutscheWaffen and Munitions Fabriken
EJT	Ejectors
EXC	Excellent
EXT	Extractors
F	Full Choke
F&M	Full & Modified
FA	Forearm
FBT	Full Beavertail Forearm
FDL	Fleur-de-lis
FE	Fore End
FFL	Federal Firearms License
FK	Flat Knob
FKLT	Flat Knob Long Tang
FIRSH	Free Floating Integrated Rail System Handguard
FM	Full Mag
FMJ	Full Metal Jacket
FN	Fabrique Nationale
FPS	Feet Per Second
g.	Gram

ga.	Gauge
gr.	Grain
GCA	Gun Control Act
GOVT	Government
H&H	Holland & Holland
HB	Heavy Barrel
HC	Hard Case
HMR	Hornady Magnum Rimfire
HP	Hollow Point
I	Improved
IC	Improved Cylinder
IM	Improved Modified
intro.	Introduced
IPSC	International Practical Shooting Confederation
ISSF	International Shooting Sports Federation
L	Long
lbs.	Pounds
LC	Long Colt
LEM	Law Enforcement Model
LOP	Length of Pull
LPI	Lines Per Inch
LR	Long Rifle
LT	Long Tang or Light
LTRK	Long Tang Round Knob
M (MOD.)	Modified Choke
M-4	Newer AR-15/M16 Carbine Style/Configuration
M&P	Military & Police
Mag.	Magnum Caliber
mag.	Magazine or Clip
MC	Monte Carlo
MFG or Mfg.	Manufactured/manufacture
MIL SPEC	Mfg. to Military Specifications
MK	Mark
MOA	Minute of Angle
MR	Matted Rib
MSR	Manufacturer's Suggested Retail
N	Nickel
N/A	Not Applicable or Not Available
NE	Nitro Express
NIB	New in Box
NM	National Match
no.	Number
NSST	Non Selective Single Trigger
O/U	Over and Under
OA	Overall
OAL	Overall Length
OB	Octagon Barrel
OBFM	Octagon Barrel w/full mag.
OBO	Or Best Offer
OCT	Octagon
oz.	Ounce
Para.	Parabellum
PFFR	Percentage of factory finish remaining
PG	Pistol Grip
POR/P.O.R.	Price on Request
POST-'89	Paramilitary mfg. after Federal legislation in Nov. 1989
POST-BAN	Refers to production after Sept. 12, 2004
PPC	Pindell Palmisano Cartridge
PPD	Post Paid
PRE-'89	Paramilitary mfg. before Federal legislation in Nov. 1989
PRE-BAN	Mfg. before September 13, 1994 per C/B or before Nov. 1989.
QD	Quick Detachable

RAS	Rail Adapter System		SxS	Side by Side
RB	Round Barrel/Round Butt		TBA	To be Announced
RCMP	Royal Canadian Mounted Police		TD	Take Down
REC	Receiver		TEN-T.	$ Amount of Federal deficit when Bush left office
REM	Remington			
REM. MAG.	Remington Magnum		TGT	Target
RF	Rimfire		TH	Target Hammer
RFM	Rim Fire Magnum		TS	Target Stocks
RK	Round Knob		TSOB	Scope mount rail Weaver type
RKLT	Round Knob Long Tang		TT	Target Trigger
RKST	Round Knob Short Tang		UIT	Union Internationale de Tir
RR	Red Ramp		UMC	Union Metallic Cartridge Co.
RSM	Remington Short Magnum		VG	Very Good
RSUM	Remington Short Ultra Magnum		VR	Ventilated Rib
S	Short		w/	with
S&W	Smith & Wesson		w/o	without
S/N	Serial Number		WBY	Weatherby
SA	Single Action		WC	Wad Cutter
SAA	Single Action Army		WCF	Winchester Center Fire
SAE	Selective Automatic Ejectors		WD	Wood
SB	Shotgun butt or Steel backstrap		WFF	Watch For Fakes
ser.	serial		WIN	Winchester
SG	Straight Grip		WO	White Outline
SK	Skeet		WRA	Winchester Repeating Arms Co.
sq.	Square		WRF	Winchester Rim Fire
SMG	Submachine Gun		WRM	Winchester Rimfire Magnum
SMLE	Short Magazine Lee Enfield Rifle		WSM	Winchester Short Magnum
SNT	Single Non-Selective Trigger		WSSM	Winchester Super Short Magnum
SPEC	Special		WSUM	Winchester Short Ultra Magnum
SPG	Semi-Pistol Grip		WW	World War
Spl.	Special		X (1X)	1X Wood Upgrade or Extra Full Choke Tube
SR	Solid Rib			
SRC	Saddle Ring Carbine		XX (2X)	2X Wood Upgrade or Extra Extra Full Choke Tube
SS	Single Shot or Stainless Steel			
SSA	Super Short Action		XXX (3x)	3X Wood Upgrade
SST	Single Selective Trigger			
ST	Single Trigger			

MUSEUMS

National Firearms Museum (NFM)

National Rifle Association
11250 Waples Mill Road
Fairfax, VA 22030
www.nrahq.org/museum
(Check website for special exhibits)
This is easily the best firearms museum east of the Mississippi, and if you are an NRA member, please take the time and stop by this well-appointed museum in the Washington, D.C., area - you won't be disappointed. Blue Book Publications, Inc. is proud to be a NRA Foundation supporter of the NFM, and has contributed over $70,000 to date for future museum acquisitions.

Buffalo Bill Historical
Center/Cody Firearms Museum

720 Sheridan Ave.
Cody, WY 82414
www.bbhc.org
(Check website for special exhibits)
The BBHC is actually five museums under one large roof - the Cody Firearms Museum, the Plains Indian Museum, Whitney Gallery of Western Art, the Buffalo Bill Museum, and the Draper Museum of Natural History. The BBHC is by far one of the best places on earth to learn about the American West, the Great Plains and early American history. Summer is the busiest time, so check their website for special events and exhibits. Please allow at least two days to take in everything this complex offers, or you will be making a mistake. Blue Book Publications, Inc. is also pleased to be a One of 1,000 Society sponsor of The Buffalo Bill Historical Center.

Ogden Union Station

2501 Wall Ave.
Ogden, UT 84401
www.theunionstation.org
This complex has five separate museums - the Browning Firearms Museum, the Browning-Kimball Car Museum, Eccles Rail Center, Union Station Natural History Museum and the Utah State Railroad Museum. Additionally, there are two art galleries. The Browning Firearms Museum celebrates the genius of John Browning, inventor of many legendary military and sporting firearms, many built in Ogden.

FIREARMS/SHOOTING ORGANIZATIONS

Listed below are the names and addresses of various firearms organizations/associations throughout the U.S. You are encouraged to join those organizations that pertain to your region and area of interest. As thorough as we try to be, every year we get back quite a bit of mail back from individual firearms associations that is undeliverable. So, if your club does not appear on the following pages or doesn't have a current address, please forward the correct information to us for inclusion in the next edition.

For the past 40 years, the NRA's affiliated Gun Collecting clubs (identified in the following listings with an *) have been a vital part of NRA's educational outreach programs. With over 100 of these clubs, there is one for almost every collecting interest and area. Collector affiliates are leaders in firearms safety programs for gun shows, and they sponsor some of the most popular and successful shows in the country. They participate in the NRA's Annual Meetings and Exhibits with spectacular displays of rare and historically important arms. Affiliates also sponsor the annual National Gun Show and the annual National Gun Collecting Seminar. An annual awards ceremony for collector affiliates is held every year at the NRA's Annual Meetings.

Academics for the Second Amendment (A2A)
Prof. J.E. Olson, President
Hamline University
P.O. Box 131254
St. Paul, MN 55113
Email: jolson@gw.hamline.edu

* Alabama Gun Collectors Association
Tom Campbell, Secretary/Treasurer
P.O. Box 307
Dolomite, AL 35061-0307
Phone: 205-491-1962
Website: www.agcagunshow.com
Email: AGCABham@aol.com
$20 Annual Membership

* Alamo Arms Collectors' Association
P.O. Box 680642
San Antonio, TX 78268-0642
James P. Duke, Secretary
Phone: 830-980-4746
George O. Stenzel, Treasurer
Phone: 210-523-5540
Email: aacanews@satx.rr.com
$20 yearly membership, meetings first Tuesday of each month

*Alaska Gun Collectors Association
P.O. Box 242233
Anchorage, Alaska 99524
Phone: 907-346-1075
Website: www.agca.net

American Custom Gunmakers Guild
Jan Billeb, Executive Director
22 Vista View Lane
Cody, WY 82414-9606
Phone: 307-587-4297
Website: www.acgg.org
Email: acgg@acgg.org
$95 Associate Membership Fee
$45 Gunsmithing Students
$180 Commercial Associate Membership Fee

* The American Thompson Association
Tracie Hill
P.O. Box 8710
Newark, OH 43058-8710
Phone: 740-345-9777
Website: www.nfatoys.com/tsmg/tata
$30 Annual Membership Dues

* American Single Shot Rifle Association
Rudi Prusok, Archivist
625 Pine Street
Marquette, MI 49855
Phone: 906-225-1828
Website: www.assra.com
Email: rprusok@nmu.edu
$35 Annual Membership (includes journal)

* American Society of Arms Collectors
J. William La Rue, Secretary
P.O. Box 50400
Albuquerque, NM 87181-0400
Phone: 505-299-7950
Website: www.americansocietyofarmscollectors.org
Invitation only
Dues: $200 annual

* Arkansas Gun Cartridge Collectors Club
Joe Burnett
P.O. Box 1015
Little Rock, AR 72203
Phone: 501-753-1970

* Ark - La - Tex Gun Collectors
Thomas L. Baird, President
9601 Blom Blvd.
Shreveport, LA 71118
Phone: 318-686-7101

* Arms Collectors of Georgia
Robert Messner
1554 Bubling Creek Rd.
Atlanta, GA 30319
Phone: 770-740-4908
Dues: $45 annual
Meetings 2nd Monday of each month

* Arms Collectors of Southwest Washington
James Hoeflein
P.O. Box 2622
Vancouver, WA 98668
Phone: 360-263-3447

* Association of Ohio Longrifle Collectors
Robin D. (Dan) Smith, Secretary
23003 St., Rt. 339
Beverly, OH 45715
Phone: 740-984-4896
$15 annual dues

* Bayou Gun Club of LA
Robert Eddy
P.O. Box 73402
Metairie, LA 70033
Phone: 504-455-7078

* **Browning Collectors Association**
Charles P. Wagner, Secretary
711 Scott Street
Covington, KY 41011
Phone: 859-431-1712
Website: www.browningcollectors.com

Buffalo Bill Historical Center
David Kennedy
The Robert W. Woodruff Curator
Cody Firearms Museum
720 Sheridan Ave.
Cody, WY 82414
Phone: 307-587-4771
Website: www.bbhc.org

* **C.A.D.A. (Collector Arms Dealer Association)**
P.O. Box 427
Thomson, IL 61285

California Rifle & Pistol Association, Inc.
271 Imperial Highway, Suite #620
Fullerton, CA 92835
Phone: 714-992-2772
Website: www.crpa.org

* **Central Penn Antique Arms Association**
John E. Holman Jr.
978 Thistle Road
Elizabethtown, PA 17022

* **Central States Gun Collectors Association**
Lois Schwade
633-3 Rd. Street SE
Mason City, IA 50401-4104
Phone: 641-424-9234

* **Central Wisconsin Gun Collectors Association**
Bruce D. Cook, President
10971 Clinic Road
Suring, WI 54174
Phone: 920-842-2083
Fax: 920-842-4203
Email: RamCook1@yahoo.com

* **Colt Collectors Association**
Karen Green, Secretary
P.O. Box 2241
Los Gatos, CA 95031
Website: www.coltcollectors.org
$40 Annual Membership Fee
$50 Annual Membership Fee (Canada)
$100 Annual Membership Fee (Foreign)

Contemporary Longrifle Association
P.O. Box 2097
Stauton, VA 24402
Phone: 540-886-6189
Website: www.longrifle.ws

* **Dakota Territory Gun Collectors Association**
Vicki Sandvig, Executive Secretary
Lenard Cave, President
P.O. Box 5053
West Fargo, ND 58078
Phone: 701-484-5010
$10 Annual Membership Fee
$150 Life Membership Fee

* **Delaware Antique Arms Collectors Association**
Robert Howard
P.O. Box 2966
Wilmington, DE 19805

* **Eastern Shores Arms Collectors**
Rodney Schwarm
P.O. Box 1836
Easton, MD 21601
Phone: 410-822-1555

* **Egyptian Collectors Association**
Bob Leckrone
Box 138
Centralia, IL 62801
Phone: 618-495-2572

The Firearms Coalition of Colorado
Steve Schreiner, President
P.O. Box 1454
Englewood, CO 80150-1454
Phone: 303-296-4867
Email: COGunIssues-subscribe@yahoogroups.com
$25 Annual Membership Fee

* **Forks of the Delaware Historical Arms Society, Inc.**
Mr. Howard A. Hoffman
3491 Linden St.
Bethlehem, PA 18017
Phone: 610-997-8613
Fax: 610-997-8614
Website: www.allentownshow.net
$20 Annual Membership Fee

* **Ft. Lee Arms Collectors**
Walter Dubas
50 Second Street
Clifton, NJ 07011
Phone: 914-796-2300

* **Garand Collectors Association**
James Spawn
P.O. Box 7498
N. Kansas City, MO 64116
Phone No.: 816-471-2005
Website: www.thegca.org

Georgia Arms Collectors
Michael Kindberg
P.O. Box 277
Alpharetta, GA 30009
Phone: 678-860-8600

German Gun Collectors Association
438 Willow Brook Rd
P.O. Box 385
Meriden, NH 03770
Phone: 603-469-3438
Fax: 603-469-3800
Website: www.germanguns.com
Email: jaeger@valley.net
$45 Annual Fee (U.S. & Canada)
$60 Annual Fee (Foreign)

Gibbs Military Collector's Club
219 Lawn St.
Martinsburg, WV 25401
Phone: 304-262-1651
Fax: 304-262-1658
Website: www.gibbsrifle.com
Email: support@gibbsrifle.com

* **Glock Collectors Association**
Colette Steck, Membership Secretary
P.O. Box 1063
Maryland Heights, MO 63043
Phone/Fax: 314-878-2061
Website: www.glockcollectors.com
Email: casteck@prodigy.net
$25 Annual Membership Fee, includes 3-4 journals

Golden Eagle Collectors Association
Chris Showler, Secretary
90 Will Sauer Road
Washoe Valley, NV 89704-8594

Great Lakes Military Collectors Association
P.O. Box 401
Maumee, OH 43537

Gun Owners Civil Rights Alliance/ Concealed Carry Reform Now!
Joseph E. Olson, President
P.O. Box 131254
St. Paul, MN 55113
Phone: 651-636-4465
Website: www.mnccrn.org
$30 Annual Membership Fee

Gun Owners of America
Larry Pratt, Executive Director
8001 Forbes Pl., Suite 102
Springfield, VA 22151
Fax: 703-321-8408
Website: www.gunowners.org
Email: goamail@gunowners.org
$20 Annual Membership Fee

* Hawaii Historic Arms Association
Sheldon Tyau
Box 1733
Honolulu, HI 96806
Phone: 808-955-9552

* High Standard Collectors Association
John Hanks
P.O. Box 1578
Decatur, IL 62525-1578
Website: www.highstandard.org
$20 Annual Dues

* Houston Gun Collectors Association
P.O. Box 741429
Houston, TX 77274-1429
Phone: 713-981-6463
Website: www.hgca.org
$60 Annual Dues

Indianhead Firearms Association
13810 25th Ave.
Chippewa Falls, WI 54729
Phone: 715-723-0860

Indian Territory Gun Collectors Association
8733 East 58 ORD
Catoosa, OK 74015
Phone: 918-266-4434

* International Ammunition Association
Robert P. Ruebel, Secretary
37752 880th Ave.
Olivia, MN 56277-2528
Phone: 320-523-2250
Website: www.cartridgecollectors.org
Email: rhruebel@rswb.coop
$35 Annual Dues (USA)
$40 Annual (Canada)
$55 Foreign
$25 Annual Dues (electronic copy of IAA Journal, worldwide)

* Iroquois Arms Collectors Association
Kenneth Keller, Secretary
Susann Keller, Show Secretary
214 70th St.
Niagara Falls, NY 14304

Jersey Shore Antique Arms Collectors
Steve Cassidy
P.O. Box 100
Bayville, NJ 08721-0100
$25 Annual Membership Fee

Kansas Cartridge Collectors Association
Vic Suelter
2185 E. Iron Drive
Lincoln, KS 67455

Kentuckiana Arms Collectors Association
Sally Harper, Secretary
P.O. Box 1776
Louisville, KY 40201
Phone: 502-425-2460
$20 Annual Membership Fee

* Kentucky Rifle Association
Attn: Ruth Collis
2319 Sue Ann Dr.
Lancaster, PA, 17602.

* Lancaster Muzzle Loading Rifle Association
James H. Frederick, Jr.
700 Prospect Road
Columbia, PA 17512

Lee County Gun Collectors Association of Ft. Myers, FL
P.O. Box 6168
Fort Myers Beach, FL 33932
Phone: 239-463-2840

* Long Island Antique Gun Collectors Association
Frederick R. Wilkens
35 Beach Street
Farmingdale, L.I., NY 11735
Phone: 516-249-5133
$40 Annual Membership Fee

* Mahoning Valley Gun Collectors Association
P.O. Box 86
Campbell, OH 44405
$15 annual dues

* Mannlicher Collectors Association
P.O. Box 10105
College Station, TX 77842
$25 Annual Dues
$34 Annual Foreign Dues
Website: www.mannlicher.org

* Marlin Firearms Collectors Association, Ltd.
P.O. Box 491
Clay Center, KS 67432-0491
$5 Initiation Fee
$20 Annual Membership Fee
$22 Canadian (U.S. funds)
$29 International (U.S. Funds)

* Maryland Arms Collectors Association (MACA)
Del Kuzemchak, Secretary
33 S. Main Street, P.O. Box 206
Loganville, PA 17342-0206
$35 Annual Membership Fee

Maryland Licensed Firearms Dealers Association, Inc.
Sanford Adams, Exc. Vice President
P.O. Box 10237
Baltimore, MD 21234-9998
Phone: 410-356-9485
Fax: 410-356-9486

* Massachusetts Arms Collectors
P.O. Box 111
Hingham, MA 02043
Phone: 781-749-2889

* Maumee Valley Gun Collectors Association
P.O. Box 492
Maumee, OH 43537
Website: www.mvgca.com

* Michigan Antique Arms Collectors
Les Scott
12499 Margaret Dr.
Fenton, MI 48430
Phone: 810-629-8024

* Midwest Gun Traders Inc.
Walter Butler
1304 Inwood Drive
Ft. Wayne, IN 46815
Phone: 219-426-3562

* Miniature Arms Collectors/ Makers Society, Ltd.
Bill Adrian, President
2502 Fresno Ln.
Plainfield, IL 60544-8470
Phone: 815-254-8692

* Minnesota Weapons Collectors
Alvin Olson
P.O. Box 605
Waseca, MN 56093
Phone: 507-833-5615
Website: www.mwca.org
Email: cartal@hickorytech.net
$25 Annual Membership

* Missouri Valley Arms Collectors Association, Inc. (MVACA)
Membership Secretary
P.O. Box 6013
Leawood, KS 66206
Phone: 913-649-4248
Website: www.mvacagunshow.com
$25 Annual Membership (age 21 and over)
$10 Annual Membership (under 21)

Mohave Arms Collectors Association
Keith Gilbert, VP
10130 Vock Canyon Place
Kingman, AZ 86409
Phone: 928-681-4476
$20 Annual Individual Membership
$30 Annual Family Membership

* Montana Arms Collectors Association
Dean E. Yearout, Sr.
1516 - 21st Ave. S.
Great Falls, MT 59405
Phone: 406-761-7280
$20 Annual Membership Fee
All new members receive embroidered arm patch

* Nat'l Automatic Pistol Collectors Association (N.A.P.C.A.)
Thompson D. Knox
Box 15738
St. Louis, MO 63163
Phone: 314-638-6505
Website: www.napca.net
$50 annual dues U.S.
$55 annual dues Canada
$65 Elsewhere

* National Mossberg Collectors Association
Victor Havlin
P.O. Box 487
Festus, MO 63028
$12 Annual Membership Fee
Phone: 636-937-6401
Website: www.mossbergcollectors.org

National Rifle Association (NRA)
11250 Waples Mill Rd.
Fairfax, VA 22030
Phone: 888-JOIN-NRA/800-NRA-3888
Fax: 703-267-3970
Website: www.nra.org
Email: membership@nrahq.org
$35 Regular Annual Membership Dues
$30 Annual Senior Membership
(65 years of age and older, also disabled vets)
$60 for two years
$85 for three years
$125 for five years
$750 Life Membership Dues
$375 Senior Life Membership (also disabled vets)
$15 Annual Junior Membership (18 years and younger)
$10 Annual Liberty Associate Membership (w/o magazine)

National Shooting Sports Foundation (NSSF)
11 Mile Hill Road
Newtown, CT 06470
Phone: 203-426-1320
Fax: 203-426-1245
Website: www.nssf.org

New Eastcoast Arms Collectors Associates, Inc., NEACA, Inc.
Cathy Petronis, Secretary
38 N. Main St.
P.O. Box 385
Mechanicville, NY 12118
Phone: 518-664-9743
Website: www.neaca.com
$30 annual dues
Promoters of Saratoga Springs & other NY arms fairs

* New Mexico Gun Collectors Association
Mr. Mark Covell, Show Host
P.O. Box 13687
Albuquerque, NM 87912
Phone: 505-262-1350
Website: www.nmgca.net
$25 Annual Dues
4 shows per year - Mar., June, Aug., Oct.

* New York State Arms Collectors
Sandy Ackerman-Klinger
346 Paul Street
Endicott, NY 13760
Phone: 607-748-1010

* North Carolina Gun Collectors
Scott Woller
P.O. Box 23570
Charlotte, NC 28227
Phone: 704-573-1686

* North Eastern Arms Collectors Assoc., Inc.
Thomas J. Mulligan
P.O. Box 306
Island Park, NY 11558
Email: Mulligun@aol.com
$30 Application Fee
$30 Annual Membership Fee

* Northern Florida Arms Collectors
Danny Brady
4471 Loveland Pass Dr.
Jacksonville, FL 32210
Phone: 904-613-9280

* Northern Indiana Gun Collectors
William Best
15237 W. 12th Road
Plymouth, IN 46563
Phone: 219-936-4431

* Northwest Montana Arms Collectors Association (NWMACA)
Paul Willis, Treasurer
P.O. Box 653
Kalispell, MT 59903-0653
Phone: 406-755-3980
Email: pswillis@centurytel.net

* Ohio Gun Collectors Association
Laura Knotts, Business Manager
P.O. Box 670406
Sagamore Hills, OH 44067-0406
Phone: 330-467-5733
Fax: 330-467-5793
Website: www.ogca.com
Email: ogca@ogca.com
$30.00 Annual Membership Fee
$10.00 Application Fee
Members and guests of members only

* Oregon Arms Collectors, Inc.
2221 NE Hoyt St.
Portland, OR 97232-2858
Phone: 503-254-5986
Website: members.tripod.com/~oregonarmscollectors/index.html
$20 Annual Membership Fee

* Palm Beach Historical Arms Association
Adolph Stuffer
6304 Silver Moon Lane
Greenacres, FL 33463

Parker Gun Collectors Association
Mr. Thomas Wooden
6 Jade Walk
Medfield, MA 02052
Website: www.parkergun.org

* Paso Del Norte Gun Collectors
James Foran
P.O. Box 31613
El Paso, TX 79930
Phone: 915-566-7968

* Penn Antique Gun Collectors Assn.
Ronald Gabel
P.O. Box 97
Slatington, PA 18080
Phone: 610-767-0356
Website: www.pagca.com
$30 Annual Membership Fee

* Penn Gun Collectors Assn.
Richard Vensel
5209 Norma Dr.
Pittsburgh, PA 15236
Phone: 412-655-3850

Peoples Rights Organization
4444 Indianola Ave.
Columbus, OH 43214-2226
Phone: 614-268-0122
Fax: 614-261-9981
Firearms Classes: 614-261-1601
Refuse to be a Victim Classes: 614-323-3102
Website: www.pro-training.info
Website: www.peoplesrights.org
Email: d-walker@juno.com
$30 Annual Membership Fee
$360 Lifetime Membership Fee

* Pioneer Gun Collectors Assn.
Jim Marten
4500 South Georgia
Amarillo, TX 79110
Phone: 806-352-5331

* Potomac Arms Collectors Association
P.O. Box 1812
Wheaton, MD 20915
Phone: 301-384-7177
$30 Annual Membership Fee

* Remington Society of America
Richard Shepler, President
P.O. Box 269
Duck River, TN 38454-0269
Phone: 931-583-0564
Website: www.remingtonsociety.com
Email: rjs@isdn.net
$45 New Annual Membership
$40 Renewal Membership
Foreign Memberships Available

* Ruger Collectors Association, Inc.
P.O. Box 240
Green Farms, CT 06838
Phone: 203-259-9498, Ext. 124
$30 Annual Membership Fee

SAAMI (Sporting Arms & Ammunition Manufacturers' Institute)
1145 19th St. NW, Ste. 700
Washington, DC 20036-3727
Website: www.saami.org

SASS (Single Action Shooting Society)
23255 La Palma Avenue
Yorba Linda, CA 92887
Phone: 714-694-1800
Fax: 714-694-1815
Website: www.sassnet.com
Email: SASS@sassnet.com

* St. Louis Antique Arms Collectors
11220 W. Florissant Ave.
Florissant, MO 63033

* Santa Barbara Historical Arms Association
Paul Doyle
P.O. Box 6291
Santa Barbara, CA 93160-6291
Phone/Fax: 661-299-6436
$40 Initiation
$25 Annual Membership Fee
Website: www.sbhaa.org

San Bernardino Valley Arms Collectors
Robert Walter
18710 Cajon Blvd.
San Bernardino, CA 92407
Los Alamos, NM 87544

San Fernando Valley Arms Collectors Association
Tom Barrabee, Secretary
10655 Olive Grove Ave.
Sunland, CA 91040
$20 Annual Membership Fee

San Gabriel Valley Arms Collectors
Gerald C. Knight, Secretary/Treasurer
1140 Daveric Drive
Pasadena, CA 91107-1740
Phone: 818-351-9368
$20 Annual Dues

* San Luis Obispo Historical Arms Society
P.O. Box 3554
San Luis Obispo, CA 93403

Second Amendment Foundation
James Madison Building
12500 NE Tenth Place
Bellevue, WA 98005
Phone: 425-454-7012
Fax: 425-451-3959
Member Services: 800-426-4302
Website: www.saf.org
Email: info@saf.org
Tax deductible membership dues $15.00
Tax deductible life membership dues $150

* Smith & Wesson Collectors Association
Michael G. Speers, Administrative Assistant
P.O. Box 357
Larned, KS 67550-0357
Phone: 620-285-6880
Email: swca357@hotmail.com
$60 first year dues
$50 renewal dues

L.C. Smith Collectors Association
Frank Finch, Executive Director
1322 Bay Avenue
Mantoloking, NJ 08738
Phone: 732-899-1498
Website: www.lcsmith.org
Email: FrankFinch@msn.com
$25 Annual Membership
$300 Life Membership

* Smoky Mountain Gun Collectors Assn.
Hugh Yarbro
244 Hi-Way Drive
Clinton, TN 37716
Phone: 865-457-0505

* South Carolina Arms Collectors Assn.
Bobby Oshields
P.O. Box 6611, Sta. B
Greenville, SC 29606
Phone: 863-233-8892

* South Jersey Arms Collectors
Ralph Fairley
6 Georgetown Road
Glassboro, NJ 08028
Phone: 609-881-0637

* Southeastern Antique Arms Collectors, Inc.
Donald Armstrong, Secretary
Doug Eberhart, President & Show Chairman
P.O. Box 1104
Alpharetta, GA 30009
One annual show per year the 3rd week in Feb.

* Southern California Arms Collectors Association, Inc.
Martin J. Miller, Jr.
P.O. Box 7432
Thousand Oaks, CA 91359-7432
$40 Annual Membership Fee
Phone: 805-373-0683

* Stark Gun Collectors
Terry Roan
3241 Riverside Ave. NW
Massillon, OH 44647
Phone: 330-833-2483

* Stratford Gun Collectors
Steve Varga
90 Meadow Park Drive
Milford, CT 06460

Swiss Gun Collectors Association
Max von Hausmann
P.O. Box 480
Barre, VT 05641
Phone: 802-479-0044
Fax: 802-479-3308
Website: www.swiss-guncollectors.com
Email: info@swiss-guncollectors.com

* Tennessee Military Collectors Assn.
William Price
P.O. Box 1006
Brentwood, TN 37024
$15 annual dues
Phone: 615-661-9379
Website: www.tmcaonline.org
Email: williamprice4@comcast.net

Texas Gun Collectors Association (TGCA)
Carolyn Mims
P.O. Box 701314
San Antonio, TX 78270

Texas Women's Shooting Sports
Judy Rhodes
11241 Ferndale Road
Dallas, TX 75238
Phone/Fax No.: 214-349-0045
Website: www.txdiva.com
Email: jr@txdiva.com

* Tri-State Gun Collectors, Inc.
Manette Sneary, Business Manager
P.O. Box 1201
Lima, OH 45802
Phone: 419-647-0067

* Tulsa Arms Collectors Association
Mr. Joe Wanenmacher, Secretary-Treasurer
P.O. Box 33201
Tulsa, OK 74153-1201
Phone: 918-492-0401

* Utah Gun Collectors
Carrol Cone
P.O. Box 711161
Salt Lake City, UT 84121
Phone: 801-944-9324

* Virginia Gun Collectors Association, Inc.
Wm. Addison Hurst R.Ph, President
P.O. Box 328
Manassas, VA 20108-0328
Phone: 540-882-3543
Email: HurstA@mediasoft.net

* Wabash Valley Gun Collectors
Roger Dorsett
2601 Willow Road
Urbana, IL 61801
Phone: 217-367-5452

Washington Arms Collectors, Inc.
Jennifer Masterjohn, WAC Administrator
P.O. Box 389
Renton, WA 98057-0389
Phone: 425-255-8410
Fax: 425-255-8946
Website: www.washingtonarmscollectors.org
Email: office@washingtonarmscollectors.org
$35 Membership Dues
$500 Life Membership Dues

* Weapons Collectors Society of Montana
Ed Spragg, Executive Secretary
71713 US Hwy 89
Belt, MT 59412
Phone: 406-277-4485
Website: www.wsofmt.com
Email: emspragg@3rivers.net
$20 Single Membership (NRA)
$25 Couples Membership (NRA)
$30 Single Membership (non-NRA)
$35 Couples Membership (non-NRA)

* Weatherby Collectors Association, Inc.
P.O. Box 478
Pacific, MO 63069
Phone: 636-239-0348
Website: www.weatherbycollectors.com
Email: WCAsecretary@aol.com
$30 Membership Fee
$500 Lifetime Membership Fee

* Westchester Collectors Club
Martin Fasack
54 Farm View Road
Pt. Washington, NY 11050
Phone: 516-627-8804

Williamette Valley Arms Collectors Association, Inc.
Bill Sheppard, Executive Secretary
P.O. Box 1299
Springfield, OR 97477-0152
Phone: 541-726-1801
$25 Membership Fee

* Winchester Arms Collectors Association
David P. Bichrest, Executive Secretary
P.O. Box 367
Silsbee, TX 77656-0367
Phone: 409-385-5768
Fax: 409-385-5726
Web site: www.winchestercollector.org

Winchester Arms Collectors Association, cont.
Email: david.Bichrest@winchestercollector.org
$40 annual dues U.S.A.
$50 annual dues Canada
$60 annual dues Foreign
$750 lifetime membership fee

Winchester Club of America
Morris Hallowell, Treasurer
P.O. Box 1445
Livingston, MT 59047
Email: morris@hallowellco.com
$35 U.S. Annual membership
$50 Foreign membership
$350 Life U.S. membership
$500 Life Foreign membership

* Wisconsin Gun Collectors Assn., Inc.
Robert Zellmer
P.O. Box 181
Sussex, WI 53089
Phone: 262-538-1316

* Wyoming Weapons Collectors
Pat Aldrich
P.O. Box 1784
Laramie, WY 82073
Phone: 307-742-4630

* Ye Conn Gun Guild
Peter Kuck
602 Park Road
W. Hartford, CT 06107

* Zumbro Valley Arms Collectors, Inc.
Floyd Baumler
P.O. Box 6621
Rochester, MN 55901
Phone: 507-289-9383

CONSERVATION ORGANIZATIONS

The following are not firearms associations, but are conservation organizations that may or may not have links to hunting/shooting sports. These organizations are dedicated to preserving wildlife and natural habitat. You are encouraged to contact these organizations to learn more.

Dove Sportsman's Society
31 Quail Run
P.O. Box 610
Edgefield, SC 29824
Phone: 803-637-5731
Fax: 803-637-0037
Website: www.dovesociety.org
Membership includes Dove Hunter magazine

Ducks Unlimited, Inc.
One Waterfowl Way
Memphis, TN 38120
Phone: 901 758 3825
Fax: 901-758-3850
Website: www.ducks.org

Foundation for North American Wild Sheep
Raymond Lee, President
720 Allen Ave.
Cody, WY 82414-9981
Phone: 307-527-6261
Website: www.fnaws.org
1 Yr. Membership $45; 3 Yrs. $120

The Mule Deer Foundation
404 East 4500 South, Ste. B10 Salt Lake City, UT 84107
Phone: 866-822-DEER
Fax: 801-747-3344
Website: www.muledeer.org
Email: membercoord@muledeer.org
$35 Annual Membership Fee, includes 6 issues of MDF magazine

The National Wild Turkey Federation
P.O. Box 530
Edgefield, SC 29824
Phone: 800-843-6983
Call for membership details.

North American Moose Foundation
Shannon James, Executive Director
P.O. Box 30
610 W. Custer, Ste. B
Mackay, ID 83251
Phone: 208-588-2939
Fax: 208-588-2980
Website: www.moosefoundation.org
Email: moose@atcnet.net
$1,000 Lifetime Membership

North American Pronghorn Foundation
P.O. Box 13813
Rawlins, WY 82301
Phone: 307-324-5238
Website: www.antelope.org

Pheasants Forever
1783 Buerkle Circle
White Bear Lake, MN 55110
Phone: 651-773-2000
Fax: 651-773-5500
Website: www.pheasantsforever.org
Email: contact@pheasantsforever.org
$30 Annual Membership Fee includes five issues of Pheasants Forever magazine

Quail Forever
1783 Buerkle Circle
White Bear Lake, MN 55110
Phone: 866-457-8245
Fax: 651-773-5500
Website: www.quailforever.org
Email: contact@quailforever.org
$30 Annual Membership, includes 4 issues of Quail Forever magazine

Quail Unlimited
31 Quail Run
P.O. Box 610
Edgefield, SC 29824
Phone: 803-637-5731
Fax: 803-637-0037
Website: www.qu.org

Email: national@qu.org
$30 Annual Membership includes bimonthly subscription to Quail Unlimited

The Ruffed Grouse Society
Ronald P. Burkert
451 McCormick Rd.
Coraopolis, PA 15108
Phone: 888-564-6747
Website: www.ruffedgrousesociety.org
Email: rgs@ruffedgrousesociety.org
$25 Annual Membership Fee
$50 Conservation Membership Fee
$100 Sustaining Membership Fee
$250+ Various Sponsor Membership Fee
All memberships include a subscription to Ruffed Grouse Society magazine.

Safari Club International & SCI Foundation
Mr. Mark Labarbera
4800 W. Gates Pass Rd.
Tucson, AZ 85745-9490
Phone: 520-620-1220
Website: www.safariclub.org
$55 Annual Membership Fee USA/CAN/MEX (includes subscription to monthly Safari magazine and bimonthly Safari Times newsletter)

Whitetails Unlimited
P.O. Box 720
2100 Michigan Street
Sturgeon Bay, WI 54235
Phone: 800-274-5471
Fax: 920-743-4658
Website: www.whitetailsunlimited.com
Email: nh@whitetailsunlimited.com

REFERENCE SOURCES

Adler, Dennis, *Colt Blackpowder Reproductions & Replicas.* Minneapolis, MN: Blue Book Publications, 1998.

Adler, Dennis, *Black Powder Reproductions & Replicas.* Minneapolis, MN: Blue Book Publications, Inc., 2008.

Adler, Dennis, *Colt Single Actions - From Patersons to Peacemakers.* Edison, NJ: Chartwell Books, 2007.

Adler, *Metallic Cartridge Conversions.* Iola, WI: Krause Publications, 2002.

Adler, Dennis, *Winchester Shotguns*, Edison, NJ: Chartwell Books, 2006.

Allen, John & Dennis Adler, The 4th Edition *Blue Book of Modern Black Powder Arms.* Minneapolis, MN: Blue Book Publications, Inc. 2004.

Allen, John, The 5th Edition *Blue Book of Modern Black Powder Arms.* Minneapolis, MN: Blue Book Publications, Inc., 2007.

Antaris, Leonardo, Dr., *Astra Automatic Pistols.* Sterling, CO: FIRAC Publishing Co., 1988.

Antaris, Leonardo, Dr., *Star Firearms*, Davenport, IA, Firac Publishing, 2002.

Bady, Donald B., *Colt Automatic Pistols.* Los Angeles, CA: Borden Publishing Co., 1973.

Baer, Larry L., *The Parker Book.* North Hollywood, CA: Beinfeld Publishing Co., 1974.

Ball, Robert., *Mauser Military Rifles of the World*, Iola, WI: Krause Publications, 1996.

Ball, Robert., *Remington Firearms: The Golden Age of Collecting*, WI: Krause Publications, 1995.

Barnes, Frank C., *Cartridges of the World.* Northbrook, IL: DBI Books, Inc., 1989.

Beeman, Robert, Dr. & John Allen, The 7th Edition *Blue Book of Airguns*, Minneapolis, MN: Blue Book Publications, Inc., 2008.

Belford, James N. and Dunlap, Jack, *Mauser Self Loading Pistol.* Alhambia, CA: Borden Publishing Co., 1969.

Bender, Roy G. III, *Mauser.* Houston, TX: Collector's Press, 1971.

Boothroyd, Geoffry & Susan M., *Boothroyd's Directory of British Gunmakers.* Amity, OR: Sand Lake Press, 1994.

Braceras, Saul, *Express Rifle - A Different Weapon.* Madrid, Spain: Valmayor Ediciones, S.L., 2007.

Breathed and Schroeder, *System Mauser.* Chicago, IL: Handgun Press, 1967.

Brophy, William S., *L.C. Smith Shotguns.* North Hollywood, CA: Beinfeld Publishing Co., 1977.

Brophy, William S., *Marlin Firearms.* Harrisburg, PA: Stackpole Books, 1989.

Butzer, David F., *The American Shotgun.* Middlefield, CT: Lyman Publications, 1973.

Buxton, Warren H., *The P-38 Pistol.* Volumes I,II & III. Los Alamos, NM: U.C. Ross Books.

Byron, David, *Gunmarks, Tradenames, Codemarks, and Proofs from 1870 to the Present.* New York, NY: Crown Publishers, 1979.

Carder, Charles, *Side by Sides of the World.* Delphos, OH: AVIL ONZE Publishing.

Carder, Charles, *Side by Sides of the World Y2K.* Delphos, OH: AVIL ONZE Publishing, 2000.

Condry, Ken, & Jones, Larry, *The Colt Commemoratives, 1961-1986.* Dallas, TX: Taylor Publishing Co., 1989.

Costanza, Sam, *World of Lugers. Volume I.* Mayfield Heights, OH: World of Lugers, 1977.

Eastman, Matt, *Browning, Sporting Arms of Distinction.* Fitzgerald, GA: Published by Author, 1994.

Ezell, Edward Clinton, *Handguns of the World.* Harrisburg, PA: Stackpole Books, 1981.

Ezell, Edward Clinton, *Small Arms of the World.* (12th Ed). Harrisburg, PA: Stackpole Books, 1983.

Dance, Tom, *High Standard; A Collector's Guide to the Hamden & Hartford Target Pistols.* Lincoln, RI: Andrew Mobray Publishers, 1991.

Flayderman, Norm, *Flayderman's Guide to Antique American Firearms*. Iola, WI: Gun Digest Books, 2007.

Gardner, Col. Robert, *Small Arms Makers*. New York, NY: Bonanza Books, 1963.

Grant, James. J., *Boys' Single Shot Rifles*. Prescott, AZ: Wolfe Publishing Company, 1991.

Groenewold, John, *Quackenbush Guns*. Mundelein, IL, published by author, 2000.

Gunther, Mullins, Price, and Cote', *The Parker Story. Vol. I*. Knoxville, TN: Parker Story Joint Venture Group, 1998.

Gunther, Mullins, Price, and Cote', *The Parker Story. Vol. II*. Knoxville, TN: Parker Story Joint Venture Group, 2000.

Hogg, Ian V., *Pistols of the World*, 4th Ed.

Houchins, John, *L.C. Smith - The Legend Lives*, Winston-Salem, NC: Published by Author, 2006.

Hill and Anthony, *Confederate Long Arms and Pistols*. Charlotte, NC: Confederate Arms, 1978.

Jinks, Roy G., *History of Smith & Wesson*. North Hollywood, CA: Beinfeld Publishing Co., 1977.

Karr and Karr, Jr., *Remington Handguns*. Stackpole Co., Second Edition, 1951.

Kenyon, Charles Jr., *Lugers at Random*. Chicago, IL: Handgun Press, 1969.

Kersten, Manfred, *Walther: A German Legend*, Long Beach, CA: Safari Press, Inc., 2001.

Kimmel, J., *Savage & Stevens Arms*. Portland, OR: Corey/Stevens Pub., Inc., 1990.

Kopec, Graham, and Moore, *A Study of the Colt Single Action Army Revolver*. Redding, CA: Kopec, Graham, and Moore Publishers, 2006.

Krasne, Jerry A., *Enyclopedia and Reference Catalog for Auto Loading Guns*. San Diego, CA: Triple K Manufacturing, 1989.

Leithe, Frederick, *Japanese Handguns*. California: Borden Publishing Co., 1968.

Madis, George, *The Model 12. Lancaster*, TX: Published by Author, 1981.

Madis, George, *The Winchester Book*. Lancaster, TX: Privately Published by Author, 1975.

Marcot, Roy, *Remington, America's Oldest Gunmaker*. Peoria, IL: Primedia Special Interest Publications, 1998.

Marcot, Roy & John Gyde, *Remington .22 Rimfire Rifles*. Creswell, OR: Remington Armory Press, 2007.

Maxwell, Samuel L., Sr., *Lever Action Magazine Rifles*. Published by Author, 1978.

Muderlak, Ed, *Parker Guns, The Old Reliable*. Long Beach, CA: Safari Press, 1997.

Murray, Douglas, *The Ninety-Nine*. Published by Author, 1985.

Nonte, Jr., George C., *Firearms Encyclopedia*. Outdoor Life: New York, NY, 1973.

Olson, Ludwig, *Mauser Bolt Action Rifles*. Montezuma, IA: F. Brownell & Son Publishers, Inc., 1976.

Price, Charlie & Parker Story Joint Venture Group, *Parker Gun Identification & Serialization*, Minneapolis, MN: Blue Book Publications, Inc. 2002.

Rankin, James L., *Walther. Vols. I, II, III*. Coral Gables, FL: Published by Author, 1976.

Rule, Roger C., *The Rifleman's Rifle*. Northridge, CA: Alliance Books, Inc., 1982.

Sellers, Frank, *American Gunsmiths*. Highland Park, NJ: The Gun Room Press, 1983.

Sellers, Frank, *Sharp's Firearms*. North Hollywood, Ca: Beinfeld Publishing Co., 1978.

Serven, editor, *The Collecting of Guns*. Bonanza Books, 1964.

Sharpe, Phillip B., *The Rifle in America*. Funk and Wagnalls, 1947.

Shooter's Bible. S. Hackensack, NJ: Published annually by Stoeger Industries.

Skennerton, Ian, *British Small Arms of World War II*, Labrador, Australia: self-published, 1988.

Skennerton, Ian, *The Lee Enfield Story*, Labrador, Australia: self-published, 1992.

Skennerton, Ian & Stamps, *.380 Enfield Revolver*, Labrador, Australia: self-published, 1992.

Skennerton, Ian, *Small Arms Identification Series. Vols. 1-17*. Labrador, Australia: self-published, 1993-2003.

Steindler, *Steindler's New Firearms Dictionary*. Phoenix, AZ: Stackpole Books, 1985.

Still, Jan C., *Axis Pistols. Marceline*, MO: Walsworth Publishing Co., 1986.

Still, Jan C., *Imperial Lugers*. Marceline, MO: Walsworth Publishing Co., 1991.

Still, Jan C., *Third Reich Lugers*. Marceline, MO: Walsworth Publishing Co., 1988.

Supica, Jim and Nahas, Richard, *Standard Catalog of Smith & Wesson*. Iola, WI: Krause Publications, 1996.

Supica, Jim, *Standard Catalog of Smith & Wesson. Vol. II*. Iola, WI: Krause Publications, 2001.

Supica, Jim and Nahas, Richard, *Standard Catalog of Smith & Wesson*, 3rd Ed. Iola, WI: Gun Digest Books, 2006.

Tanner, Hans, *Guns of the World*. Bonanza Books, 1972, 1977.

Tinker, Edward & Johnson, Graham, *Simson Lugers, Simson & Co, Suhl - The Weimar Years*. Galesburg, IL: Brad Simpson Publishing, 2007.

Trolard, Tom, *Winchester Commemoratives*. Plano, TX: Commemorative Investments Press, 1985.

Vanderlinden, Anthony, *Belgian Browning Pistols 1889-1949*, Greensboro, NC, Wet Dog Publications, 2001.

Vanderlinden, Anthony, & H.M. Shirley, *Browning Auto-5 Shotgun - The Belgian FN Production*, Greensboro, NC: Wet Dog Publications, 2003.

Webster, Donald B. Jr., *Suicide Specials*. Harrisburg, PA: Stackpole, Co., 1958.

West, Bill, *Browning Arms & History*. Santa Fe Springs, CA: Stockton Trade Press, Inc., 1972.

West, Bill, *Marlin and Ballard Firearms & History*. Norwalk, CA: Stockton Trade Press, Inc., 1977.

West, Bill, *Remington Arms & History*. Whittier, CA: Stockton Trade Press, Inc., 1970.

West, Bill, *Savage and Stevens Arms & History*. Whittier, CA: Stockton Trade Press, Inc., 1971.

Whitaker, Dean H., *Model 70 Winchester 1937-1964*. Dallas, TX: Taylor Publishing Co., 1978.

Wilkerson, Don, *Post-War Colt Single Action Army*. Published by Author, 1978.

Wilkerson, Don, *Post-War Colt Single Action Revolver, 1976-1986*. Dallas, TX: Taylor Publishing, 1986.

Wilkerson, Don, *Colt Scouts, Peacemakers, and New Frontiers in .22 Caliber*, Marceline, MO, Walsworth Publishing Co., 1993.

Wilkerson, Don, *Colt Single Action Army Revolver, Pre-War/Post-War Model*, Minneapolis, MN, Broughton Printing Inc., 1991.

Wilson, R.L., *The Colt Engraving Book*. Vols. I & II. New York, NY: Bannerman's Limited Edition, 2001.

Wilson, R.L., *The Book of Colt Firearms*. Minneapolis, MN: Blue Book Publications, Inc., 1993.

Wilson, R.L., *Colt, An American Legend*. New York, NY: Abbeville Press.

Wilson, R.L., *Colt Commemorative Firearms*. Geneseo, IL: Robert E.P. Cherry Publishing Co., 1973.

Wilson, R.L., *The Colt Heritage*. New York, NY: Simon and Schuster.

Wilson, R.L., *Silk & Steel*, New York: Random House. 2003

Wilson, R.L., *Winchester: An American Legend*, New York: Random House. 1991.

Wilson, R.L., *The World of Beretta: An International Legend*, New York: Random House. 2000.

Wilson, R.L., *Ruger & His Guns*. New York: Simon and Schuster. 1996.

Wirnsberger, Gerhard, *The Standard Directory of Proofmarks*. Jolex, Inc.

Wood, J.B., *Beretta Automatic Pistols*, The Collector's & Shooter's Comprehensive Guide. Harrisburg, PA: Stackpole Books, 1985.

Zhuk, A.B., *The Illustrated Encyclopedia of Handguns*. London: Greenhill Books. 1995.

PERIODICALS

American Firearms Industry - 150 SE 12th Street, Suite #200, Ft. Lauderdale, FL 33316. Phone No.: 954-467-9994. Membership is $55 per year. Trade publications and related material.

America's First Freedom - Published by the NRA. 11250 Waples Mill Rd., Fairfax, VA 22030. Phone No.: 800-672-3888. Subscription included in price of NRA Membership ($35). Published monthly.

American Cop - Published by FMG. 12345 World Trade Center Drive, San Diego, CA 92128. Phone No.: 858-605-0253. Published monthly.

American Gunsmith - P.O. Box 540638, Merrit Island, FL 32954. Phone No.: 321-459-1558. Published monthly. Subscription is $60 per year.

American Handgunner - Published by FMG. 12345 World Trade Center Drive, San Diego, CA 92128. Phone No.: 858-605-0253. Published bi-monthly. Subscription is $16.95 per year.

American Hunter - Published by the NRA. 11250 Waples Mill Rd., Fairfax, VA 22030. Phone No.: 800-672-3888. Subscription included in price of NRA Membership ($35). Published monthly.

American Rifleman - Published by the NRA. 11250 Waples Mill Rd., Fairfax, VA 22030. Phone No.: 800-672-3888. Subscription included in price of NRA Membership ($35). Published monthly.

Armi Magazine - Published by C.A.F.F. srl, via Sabatelli, Milano, Italy, I-20154, Phone No.: 011-39-02-3453-7504, Fax No.: 011-3902-3453-7513, www.armimagazine.it, Published monthly.

Australian Shooter - Published by the Sporting Shooters Association of Australia, Inc., P.O. Box 2520, Unley, SA 5061, AUSTRALIA. Fax No.: 011-61-8-8272-2945. Web site: www.ssaa.org.au. Subscription is $50 per year in Australia, $60 per year elsewhere, published monthly.

Bear Hunting - P.O. Box 457, Becker, MN, 55308, Subscription is $20 for 6 issues.

Big Game Adventures - P.O. Box 29099, OK Mission RPO, Kelowna, BC, Canada, V1W 4A2, Phone No.: 866-944-8382, Subscription is $24.95 per year, published quarterly.

Big Show Journal - N7450 Aanstad Road, P.O. Box 217, Iola, WI, 54945, Subscription is $14.95 per year, published 6 times per year.

Black's Wing & Clay - Published by the Ehlert Publishing Group. 6420 Sycamore Lane, Maple Grove, MN 55369. Phone No.: 800-848-6247. Published annually, $14.95.

Boar Hunter - 865 GW Turner Road, Baxley, GA, 31515, Phone No.: 888-297-2627, Fax No.: 912-366-8085, Subscription is $14.97 for 6 issues.

Buckmaster's Whitetail Magazine - P.O. Box 244022, Montgomery, AL, 36124-4022, Phone No.: 334-215-3337, Subscription is $26 per year with membership, published 6 times per year.

The Clay Pigeon - P.O. Box 1022, Milford, PA 18337. Phone No.: 570-296-5768, Fax No.: 570-296-9298. Subscription is $18 per year (11 issues).

Combat Handguns - Published by Harris Publications. 1115 Broadway, 8th Floor, New York, NY 10010. Phone No.: 212-807-7100, Fax No.: 212-807-1479. Subscription rate: $35 for 1 year (8 issues).

Deer & Deer Hunting - Published by Krause Publications, 700 E. State St., Iola, WI 54990. Phone No.: 715-445-2214. $19.95 per year, published 9 times per year.

Deutsches Waffen Journal - DWJ Verlags GmbH, Schmollerstrasse 31, Schwabisch Hall, D-74523, GERMANY, Phone No.: 011-49-791-956690, Fax No.: 011-49-791-95669-19, Web site: www.dwj.de, Email: info@dwj.de

Diana Armi, via E. Fermi, 24, Osmannoro, 50019 Sesto Fiorentino, Firenze, Italy, Fax No.: 011-39-055-303228050, www.edolimpia.it, various publications on shooting and shooting sports.

The Double Gun Journal - P.O. Box 550, East Jordan, MI 49727-9636. Phone No.: 231-536-7439, Fax No.: 231-536-7450. Published quarterly.

Ducks Unlimited - One Waterfowl Way, Memphis, TN 38120. Phone No.: 901-758-3825, Fax No.: 901-758-3850. Membership rate: $25 per year, includes 6 issues.

Eastman's Bowhunting Journal - P.O. Box 798, 1201 East 7th Street, Powell, WY, 82435, Subscription is $19.95 per year, published 6 times per year.

Eastman's Hunting Journal - P.O. Box 798, 1201 East 7th Street, Powell, WY, 82435, Subscription is $19.95 per year, published 6 times per year.

Field & Stream Magazine - P.O. Box 55652, Boulder, CO 80322. Phone No.: 800-289-0639 or 212-779-5000. Subscription rate $25 annually. Published monthly (12 issues).

Gazette de Armes - Paris, France.

Gray's Sporting Journal - Published by North American Publications, Inc. 735 Broad Street, Augusta, GA 30901. Phone No.: 706-722-6060. Subscription is $36.95 for 7 issues.

Gun Report - P.O. Box 38, Aledo, IL 61231, Phone No.: 309-582-5311. $33.00 per year (USA), published monthly.

Guns and Ammo - Published by Intermedia Outdoors. 6420 Wilshire Blvd., Los Angeles, CA 90048. Phone No.: 323-782-2000. Subscription is $25 per year, published monthly.

Gun List - Published by Krause Publications, 700 E. State St., Iola, WI 54990. Phone No.: 715-445-2214. $36.98 per year, published bi-weekly.

Gun Tests - 1510 Eldridge Parkway, Ste. 110-163, Houston, TX 77077, Phone No.: 800-829-9084, Subscription is $24 for 13 issues.

Gun Week - P.O. Box 488, Buffalo, NY 14209. Annual Subscription is $35. Published 3 times per month. Phone No.: 716-885-6408.

Gun World - Published by Y-Visionary Publishing, 265 S. Anita Drive, Ste. 120, Orange, CA, Phone No.: 800-999-9718, Subscription is $21.95 for 12 issues.

Guns Magazine - Published by FMG. 12345 World Trade Center Drive, San Diego, CA 92128. Phone No.:858-605-0252. Subscription is $19.95 per year (12 issues).

Gun Hunter - P.O. Box 244022, Montgomery, AL, 36124-4022, Phone No.: 334-215-3337, Subscription is $18.95 per year with membership, published 6 times per year.

Handguns Magazine - Published by Intermedia Outdoors. 6420 Wilshire Blvd., Los Angeles, CA 90048. Phone No.: 323-782-2000. Subscription is $20 per year, published monthly.

Handloader - Published by Wolfe Publishing Company, 2625 Stearman Rd., Ste. A, Prescott, AZ 86301, Phone No.: 800-899-7810, Subscription is $19.97 per year.

Knight & Hale's Ultimate Team Hunting - Published by Grandview Media, 3535 Grandview Parkway, 5th Floor, Ste. 500, Birmingham, AL, 35243, Phone No.: 888-431-2877, Subscription is $5.95, published twice a year.

Le Hussard - www.lehussard.fr. Published in Cedex, France.

Man at Arms - P.O. Box 460, Lincoln, RI 02865. Published bimonthly ($32 yearly). Phone No.: 401-726-8011.

Mossy Oak's Hunting the Country - Published by Grandview Media, 3535 Grandview Parkway, 5th Floor, Ste. 500, Birmingham, AL, 35243, Phone No.: 888-431-2877, Subscription is $9.95 for 4 issues.

Muzzle Blasts - Published by the National Muzzle Loading Rifle Association. P.O. Box 67, Friendship, IN 47021. Phone No.: 812-667-5131. Subscription is $35 per year, published monthly.

North American Hunter - 12301 Whitewater Dr., Minnetonka, MN 55343. Phone No.: 952-936-9333. Published 8 times per year (subscription included in membership).

North American Whitetail - Dept. NAW, P.O. Box 741, Marietta, GA, 30061, Subscription is $14.97 for 8 issues.

Outdoor Guide Magazine - 505 S. Ewing, St. Louis, MO 63103, Phone No.: 314-535-9786. Subscription is $12 for 6 issues.

Outdoor Life Magazine - Two Park Ave., New York, NY 10016. Phone No.: 800-365-1580 or 212-779-5000. Subscription is $15.97 for 9 issues.

Petersen's Hunting - Published by Intermedia Outdoors. 6420 Wilshire Blvd., Los Angeles, CA 90048. Phone No.: 323-782-2000. Subscription is $25 per year, published monthly.

Pheasants Forever - 1783 Buerkle Circle, White Bear Lake, MN 55110. Phone No.: 651-773-2000, Fax No.: 651-773-5500. Membership is $25 per year, includes 5 issues.

Pointing Dog Journal/Retriever Journal - Published by the Village Press, 2779 Aero Park Dr., Traverse City, MI 49686. Phone No.: 231-946-3712, Fax No.: 231-946-3289. Subscription is $25.95 for 8 issues.

Predator Extreme Magazine - Published by the Vulcan Outdoor Group. 1 Chase Corp. Dr., Ste. 300, Birmingham, AL 35244.

Quail Unlimited - P.O. Box 610 Edgefield, SC 29824. Phone No.: 803-637-5731, Fax No.: 803-637-0037. Membership is $25 per year, published bimonthly.

Rack - P.O. Box 244022, Montgomery, AL, 36124-4022, Phone No.: 334-215-3337, Subscription is $18.95 per year with membership, published 6 times per year.

Rifle - Published by Wolfe Publishing Company, 2625 Stearman Rd., Ste. A, Prescott, AZ 86301, Phone No.: 800-899-7810, Subscription is $19.97 per year.

Rifle Shooter - Published by Intermedia Outdoors. 6420 Wilshire Blvd., Los Angeles, CA 90048. Phone No.: 323-782-2000. Subscription is $20 per year, published bimonthly.

Safari Club International - 4800 W. Gates Pass Rd., Tucson, AZ 85745. Web site: www.safari-club.org. Publications: Safari Magazine, Safari Africa, Deer of the World, Sheep of the World, International Record Book of Trophy Animals, Record Book Field Edition.

Sendas de Caza - Published by Ediciones Valmayor, C/los Nardos 2, San Lorenzo de El Escorial, ES-28200, Madrid, Spain. Fax No.: 011-34-0918905287

Shoot Magazine - 1770 West State St. #340, Boise, ID, 83702, Phone No.: 800-342-0904, Subscription is $27.95, published 6 times per year.

Shooting Illustrated - Published by the NRA. 11250 Waples Mill Rd., Fairfax, VA 22030. Phone No.: 800-672-3888. Subscription included in price of NRA Membership ($35). Published monthly.

Shooting Industry - Published by FMG. 12345 World Trade Center Drive, San Diego, CA 92128. Phone No.: 858-605-0254, Subscription is $25 per year (USA). Published monthly.

Shooting Sports USA - Published by the NRA. 11250 Waples Mill Rd., Fairfax, VA 22030. Phone No.: 800-672-3888. Subscription included in price of NRA Membership ($35). Published monthly.

Shooting Sportsman - Published by Down East Enterprise, Inc., P.O. Box 1357, Camden, ME, 04843. Phone No.: 207-594-9544, Fax No.: 207-594-5144. Subscription is $30 for 6 issues.

Shooting Sports Retailer - 130 W. 42nd St., New York, NY 10036. Phone No.: 212-840-0660. Free to retailers. Published 6 times per year.

Shooting Times - Published by Intermedia Outdoors, Inc. 2 News Plaza, Peoria, IL 61614. Phone No.: 800-727-4353. Subscription is $28.

Shotgun News - Published by Intermedia Outdoors, Inc. 2 News Plaza, Peoria, IL 61614. Phone No.: 800-345-6923. Subscription is $30 yearly (36 issues).

Shotgun Sports Magazine - P.O. Box 6810, Auburn, CA 95604. Web site: www.shotgunsportsmagazine.com. Phone No.: 800-876-8920, Fax No.: 530-889-9106. Subscription is $32.95 per year (12 issues).

Sporting Classics - P.O. Box 23707, Columbia, SC 29224. Phone No.: 803-736-2424.

Sporting Clays Magazine - 5211 S. Washington Ave., Titusville, FL 32780. Phone No.: 800-376-2237. Subscription is $29.95 per year (USA). Published monthly.

Sporting Goods Business - 1 Penn Plaza, New York, NY 10119. $65 per year.

Sports Afield Magazine - 15621 Chemical Lane, Huntington Beach, CA, 92649. Web site: www.sportsafield.com. Phone No.: 714-373-4910, Fax No.: 714-894-4949. Subscription is $32.95 per year (9 issues).

Successful Hunter - Published by Wolfe Publishing Company, 2625 Stearman Rd., Ste. A, Prescott, AZ 86301, Phone No.: 800-899-7810, Subscription is $19.97 per year.

Turkey & Turkey Hunting - Published by Krause Publications, Inc. 700 E. State St., Iola, WI 54990. Phone No.: 715-445-2214. Published bimonthly for $14.95 (6 issues).

True West - Published by True West Publishing, Inc., P.O. Box 8008, Cave Creek, AZ, 85327, Phone No.: 888-687-1881, Subscription is $29.95 for 10 issues.

Varmint Hunter Magazine - Published by the Varmint Hunter's Association. 436 S. Pierre St., Pierre, SD, 57501. Phone No.: 605-224-6665, Fax No.: 605-224-6544, www.varminthunter.org. Subscription is $30 per year (4 issues).

Visier - International Waffen Magazine - Erich-Kastner-Strasse 2, D-56379, Singhofen, GERMANY. Phone No.: 011-49-2604-9780, Fax No.: 011-49-2604-978-703.

Waterfowl Magazine - Published by Waterfowl USA, P.O. Box 50, Edgefield, SC 29824. Phone No.: 803-637-5767. 6 issues per year.

Western Outdoors - 3197-E East Airport Dr., Costa Mesa, CA 92626. Phone No: 714-546-4370. Published 9 times per year for $14.95

Whitetail Journal - Published by Grandview Media, 3535 Grandview Parkway, 5th Floor, Ste. 500, Birmingham, AL, 35243, Phone No.: 888-431-2877, Subscription is $9.95 for 5 issues.

Wildfowl - Published by Intermedia Outdoors. 2 In-Fisherman Drive, Brainerd, MN 56425. Phone No.: 800-800-7724. Subscription is $25 for 6 issues. Published bimonthly.

Women & Guns - Published by Second Amendment Foundation, P.O. Box 488, Station C, Buffalo, NY 14209. $18 annual subscription. Published bimonthly.

STORE BRAND CROSS-OVER LIST

The following listing is provided as a cross-reference of Store Brands to original manufacturer and model number. Although not exhaustive, this list covers most major stores and chains that have had their name put on guns by other manufacturers. The values for the firearms listed on these pages are approximately 15% – 40% less than the original manufacturers' model(s).
Our thanks goes out to Numrich Gun Parts Corp., West Hurley, NY. They can be reached at (845) 679-4867.

House Brand	Model No.	Orig. Mfgr.	Orig. Model	House Brand	Model No.	Orig. Mfgr.	Orig. Model
Aldens	670	Springfield	67	Cotter & Co	75-45	Glenfield	75
Aldens	670	Savage	67	Cotter & Co	842	Springfield	840
				Cotter & Co	911	Springfield	511
Belknap	964A	Stevens	87N	Cotter & Co	918	Springfield	18
Belknap	B63	Springfield	947	Cotter & Co	948	Stevens	940
Belknap	B63	Savage	947B	Cotter & Co	948E	Savage	948E
Belknap	B63E	Savage	940E	Cotter & Co	949	Springfield	944
Belknap	B64	Savage	67	Cotter & Co	949C	Savage	940
Delknap	D65C	Springfield	745	Cottor & Co	949Y	Savage	944Y
Belknap	865C	Savage	745				
Belknap	B68	Savage	94C	C.I.L.	125	Anschutz	184
Belknap	B68D	Savage	94D	C.I.L.	212	Savage	7J
Belknap	B963	Springfield	120	C.I.L.	221	Savage	7J
Belknap	B963	Savage	120	C.I.L.	227	Savage	871
Belknap	B964	Savage	87J	C.I.L.	233	Savage	85N
Belknap	B967	Savage	87N	C.I.L.	266	Savage	187
				C.I.L.	470	Anschutz	520/61
Coast to Coast	180	Savage	58	C.I.L.	607	Savage	67
Coast to Coast	1800	Savage	18D	C.I.L.	607 TD	Savage	30 FLD GR.
Coast to Coast	182	Savage	18S	C.I.L.	621	Savage	30
Coast to Coast	184	Savage	951	C.I.L.	621 TD	Savage	30D
Coast to Coast	267	Savage	77	C.I.L.	710	Savage	311
Coast to Coast	285	Savage	7J	C.I.L.	725	Savage	FOX BDE
Coast to Coast	286	Savage	46	C.I.L.	830	Savage	340
Coast to Coast	288	Savage	87.I	C.I.L.	871	Savage	170
Coast to Coast	320	Savage	120	C.I.L.	950C.D	Savage	110C.D
Coast to Coast	367	Savage	30	C.I.L.	MKVII	H & R	865
Coast to Coast	40	Marlin	99C				
Coast to Coast	42	Marlin	70	Eastern Arms	101.1	Stevens	94B
Coast to Coast	650	Marlin	55	Eastern Arms	101.23	Savage	416
Coast to Coast	779	Mossberg	479				
Coast to Coast	843	Savage	340	Foremost See J.C.Penney			
Coast to Coast	843	Springfield	840				
Coast to Coast	843V2DS	Savage	340(.222)	Gamble Skogmo, Hiawatha			
Coast to Coast	843V3DS	Savage	340(.30/30)				
Coast to Coast	946	Stevens	940	Gamble Skogmo	130	Savage	30
Coast to Coast	946	Springfield	947	Gamble Skogmo	1300-567 VR	Savage	67-VR
Coast to Coast	946E	Stevens	940E	Gamble Skogmo	180N	Savage	87N
Coast to Coast	946Y	Stevens	940Y	Gamble Skogmo	189J	Savage	87J
				Gamble Skogmo	189N	Stevens	87N
Cotter & Co	10-40	Glenfield	10	Gamble Skogmo	521	Savage	120
Cotter & Co	10-40	Marlin	101	Gamble Skogmo	567	Savage	67
Cotter & Co	121	Stevens	120-15	Gamble Skogmo	S87	Savage	187
Cotter & Co	167	Springfield	67	Gamble Skogmo	594	Savage	944
Cotter & Co	167T	Savage	30	Gamble Skogmo	594Y	Savage	944Y
Cotter & Co	168	Savage	30	Gamble Skogmo	GU12-5517A	J.C.Higgins	60 & 66
Cotter & Co	168	Springfield	67VR				
Cotter & Co	287	Springfield	87J	Glenfield	10	Marlin	101
Cotter & Co	33	Marlin	336C	Glenfield	20	Marlin	80
Cotter & Co	410	Savage	110E	Glenfield	25	Marlin	80 W/swivels
Cotter & Co	424	Savage	24F	Glenfield	30A	Marlin	336
Cotter & Co	434	Savage	34	Glenfield	35	Marlin	336 .35 cal
Cotter & Co	474	Savage	170	Glenfield	50	Marlin	55
Cotter & Co	474	Springfield	174	Glenfield	60	Marlin	5
Cotter & Co	487T	Springfield	187	Glenfield	60	Marlin	99C
Cotter & Co	489	Savage	89	Glenfield	65	Marlin	99M1
Cotter & Co	60-50	Glenfield	60	Glenfield	70	Marlin	989M2
Cotter & Co	60-50	Marlin	99C	Glenfield	75	Marlin	989MI
Cotter & Co	645	Savage	745				
Cotter & Co	645C	Savage	745C	Globco	Mohawk	Russian	Tokarev
Cotter & Co	75-46	Marlin	99M1				

House Brand	Model No.	Orig. Mfgr.	Orig. Model	House Brand	Model No.	Orig. Mfgr.	Orig. Model
Hawthorn See Wards				Sears. Ranger. J.C. Higgins			
Hercules	50	Stevens	5100	J.C.Higgins	30	High Standard	30
				J.C.Higgins	101.1	Savage	94
Hiawatha See Gambles				J.C.Higgins	101.24	Savage	15-120
				J.C.Higgins	20	High Standard	200
J.C. Higgins See Sears				J.C.Higgins	42 DL	Marlin	80
				J.C.Higgins	52	Sako	L46
J.C. Penney common name, F - Foremost				J.C.Higgins	S4	Browning	FN-300
				J.C.Higgins	583.13 to.23	High Standard	10
J.C.Penney	2025	Marlin	80C	J.C.Higgins	583.2078-79	High Standard	20ga pump
J.C.Penney	2035	Marlin	80	J.C.Higgins	583.514-730	High Standard	20ga pump
J.C.Penney	2035	Glenfield	20	J.C.Higgins	6670H	Stevens	67H
J.C.Penney	2066	Marlin	49DL	J.C.Higgins	80	High Standard	101
J.C.Penney	2935	Marlin	336				
J.C.Penney	3040	Marlin	336	Ranger	101.2	Savage	238
J.C.Penney	3040	Glenfield	30A	Ranger	101.8	Stevens	83
J.C.Penney	4011	High Standard	FLIGHT KING	Ranger	104.7	H&R	120
J.C.Penney	6400	Savage	340	Ranger	105.20	H&R	120
J.C.Penney	6610	Savage	120	Ranger	120	Winchester	1200
J.C.Penney	6630	Glenfield	50	Ranger	30	Stevens	520A
J.C.Penney	6630	Marlin	66	Ranger	34A	Marlin	80.C,780
J.C.Penney	6647	Savage	944	Ranger	34A	Marlin	50-50E
J.C.Penney	6647	Springfield	944	Ranger	35A	Stevens	66A
J.C.Penney	6660	Glenfield	60	Ranger	36	Marlin	80 Adj. Trigger
J.C.Penney	6660	Marlin	99C	Ranger	400	Stevens	311
J.C.Penney	6670	Springfield	67H				
J.C.Penney	6670	Savage	67	Sears	101.1	Savage	94
J.C.Penney	6870	Savage	30	Sears	101.100	Savage	96/96Y
J.C.Penney	6870H	Savage	30H	Sears	101.10040	Savage	94
				Sears	101.10041	Savage	94
Katz	F-1282	Marlin	989M2	Sears	101.10080	Stevens	940
Katz	F-1282	Glenfield	70	Sears	101.1120	Savage	51 and 951
Katz	F-1287	Marlin	55	Sears	101.12	Stevens	39
Katz	F-1287	Glenfield	50	Sears	101.13	Stevens	86-7
				Sears	101.138	Savage	38A and 58A
Kresge	151	Boito	CBC	Sears	101.138	Springfield	18.410
				Sears	101.1380	Springfield	18,18C
K-Mart	151	Boito	CBC	Sears	101.1380	Stevens	58,C
				Sears	101.1381	Springfield	18,951 E,F
Marlin/new	780	Marlin/old	80	Sears	101.1381	Stevens	58,51, E,F
Marlin/new	781	Marlin/old	81	Sears	101.16	Savage	6,87
Marlin/new	782	Marlin/old	980	Sears	101.1610	Savage	540 DL
				Sears	101.1610	Savage	FOX BDL
New Haven	220K	Mossberg	320K-A	Sears	101.1610	Fox BST	EC,BD,BE,B-F
New Haven	240K	Mossberg	340K	Sears	101.1620-1670	Stevens	530,A;311,A,C
New Haven	246K	Mossberg	346K-A	Sears	101.1700	Savage	94
New Haven	250K	Mossberg	152K	Sears	101.1701	Fox BSE	C,D,Ser F,H
New Haven	250K8	Mossberg	350K-A	Sears	101.1701-C	Savage	BSE
New Haven	273	Mossberg	173	Sears	101.1710	Savage	FOX BDE
New Haven	273A	Mossberg	173A	Sears	101.1710	Savage	540 BDE
New Haven	283.D	Mossberg	183D	Sears	101.1750	Savage	94
New Haven	284	Mossberg	173	Sears	101.1760	Savage	94
New Haven	285	Mossberg	185D-C	Sears	101.19	Stevens	827-7
New Haven	290	Mossberg	190D-A	Sears	101.20	Stevens	15
New Haven	453	Mossberg	353	Sears	101.22	Stevens	87M(MUSKET)
New Haven	600AT	Mossberg	500A	Sears	101.25	Stevens	39A,59A,BandC
New Haven	600C	Mossberg	500C	Sears	101.2830	Savage	63-73
New Haven	600E	Mossberg	500E	Sears	101.2830	Savage	73
New Haven	679	Mossberg	472	Sears	101.3	Stevens	237
New Haven	740	Mossberg	640	Sears	101.3538830	Stevens	89
				Sears	101.4	Stevens	38
Otasco	30	Marlin	336	Sears	101.40	Springfield	947,D,Y
Otasco	30	Glenfield	30A	Sears	101.40	Stevens	940,D,Y,DY
Otasco	65	Glenfield	60	Sears	101.451	Marlin	336
Otasco	65	Marlin	99C	Sears	101.5	Stevens	37
				Sears	101.51004	Savage	94
Palmetto	11	Stevens	85,89	Sears	101.510070	Savage	94
				Sears	101.51009	Springfield	944,Yseries A
Premier	Trail Blazer	Stevens	29A	Sears	101.51013	Springfield	944,Yseries A
				Sears	101.51024	Savage	94
Revelation, see Western Auto							

House Brand	Model No.	Orig. Mfgr.	Orig. Model	House Brand	Model No.	Orig. Mfgr.	Orig. Model
Sears	101.510270	Savage	94	Sears	103.2850	Marlin	81
Sears	101.51044	Savage	94	Sears	103.2870	Marlin	56
Sears	101.510660	Stevens	9478	Sears	103.350	Marlin	M90
Sears	101.510660	Springfield	944,Y series A	Sears	103.360	Marlin	90
Sears	101.510670	Stevens	9478	Sears	103.4	Marlin	A1
Sears	101.510680	Stevens	9478	Sears	103.450	Marlin	336
Sears	101.512220	Stevens	5100,530,311	Sears	103.451	Marlin	336
Sears	101.512230	Stevens	5100,530,311	Sears	103.720	Marlin	59
Sears	101.51451	Springfield	67	Sears	103.740	Marlin	59
Sears	101.51452	Springfield	67	Sears	103.8	Marlin	100
Sears	101.51454	Springfield	67	Sears	10.19790	Marlin	80
Sears	101.51472	Springfield	67 Series B	Sears	11.2	Stevens	238
Sears	101.52701	Stevens	71,74 S/S	Sears	153.512350	Laurona	S/S
Sears	101.52772	Savage	34,65,34M.65M	Sears	153.512351	Laurona	S/S
Sears	101.52773	Savage	34,65,34M,65M	Sears	153.512360	Laurona	S/S
Sears	101.5350	Springfield	18.58	Sears	153.512361	Laurona	S/S
Sears	101.5350-D	Stevens	18D	Sears	153.512740	Laurona	71 O/U
Sears	101.53521	Savage	340	Sears	18	Mossberg	183K
Sears	101.53527	Savage	340	Sears	18AC	Savage	18C
Sears	101.5380	Savage	18/18AC.58	Sears	2C	Winchester	131
Sears	101.5380	Springfield	18,12,16,20ga.	Sears	20	High Standard	200
Sears	101.5380D	Stevens	18ADC	Sears	200	Winchester	1200
Sears	101.538840	Savage	34,65,34M,65M	Sears	200	Mossberg	G4
Sears	101.540	FOX	B-BST,BDL	Sears	201	Mossberg	80
Sears	101.5410	Springfield	18,58	Sears	202	Mossberg	80
Sears	101.5410D	Savage	18D	Sears	203	Mossberg	85
Sears	101.5410D	Springfield	18DS	Sears	204	Mossberg	83
Sears	101.54880	Stevens	80 Series A	Sears	205	Mossberg	73
Sears	101.54880	Springfield	187 Series A	Sears	206	Mossberg	70
Seem	101.64881	Marlin	980 DL,987	Sears	207	Mossberg	75
Sears	101.600	Stevens	39A,59A,B,C	Sears	209	Stevens	84-7
Sears	101.7	Stevens	311	Sears	21	High Standard	K2011
Sears	101.750	SpringField	18.410	Sears	210	Mossberg	85B
Sears	101.750	Savage	38A and 58A	Sears	211	Mossberg	83B
Sears	101.7C	Stevens	311-C	Sears	211	Stevens	86-7
Sears	101.8	Stevens	83	Sears	212	Mossberg	73D
Sears	102	Stevens	240	Sears	213	Mossberg	75B
Sears	102.25	Stevens	520A	Sears	215	Mossberg	85C
Sears	102.35	Savage	M521	Sears	216	Mossberg	83C
Sears	102.35	Savage	M29-D2	Sears	217	Mossberg	75C
Sears	103.13	Marlin	81	Sears	217	Stevens	87M (MUSKET)
Sears	103.16	Marlin	80	Sears	218	Mossberg	73C
Sears	103.18	Marlin	100	Sears	218	Stevens	22/410
Sears	103.181	Marlin	101	Sears	231	Stevens	83
Sears	103.1977	Marlin	101	Sears	232	Stevens	87-7
Sears	103.19770	Marlin	101	Sears	233	Stevens	87-7
Sears	103.19771	Marlin	101	Sears	234	Savage	234
Sears	103.19780	Marlin	101	Sears	238	Stevens	827-7
Sears	103.19790	Marlin	80	Sears	25	High Standard	A1041 .22 auto
Sears	103.19791	Marlin	80	Sears	273.2400	Winchester	190
Sears	103.19800	Marlin	80	Sears	273.27S10(2C)	Winchester	131
Sears	103.19801	Marlin	80	Sears	273.27520(2M)	Winchester	131
Sears	103.1981	Marlin	81	Sears	273.510770	Winchester	37A
Sears	103.19810	Marlin	81	Sears	273.510780	Winchester	37A
Sears	103.19811	Marlin	81	Sears	273.510790	Winchester	37A
Sears	103.1982	Marlin	81DL	Sears	273.53421	Winchester	100
Sears	103.19820	Marlin	81	Sears	277	Stevens	1S
Sears	103.19821	Marlin	81	Sears	278.28180	Cooey	64
Sears	103.19840	Marlin	56	Sears	281.512650	Antonio Zoli	O/U
Sears	103.19880	Marlin	57 LR-MAG.	Sears	281.512651	Antonio Zoli	O/U
Sears	103.19881	Marlin	57 LR-MAG.	Sears	281.512660	Antonio Zoli	O/U
Sears	103.19890	Marlin	57 LR-MAG.	Sears	281.512661	Antonio Zoli	O/U
Sears	103.2	Marlin	80	Sears	281.512750	Antonio Zoli	O/U
Sears	103.228	Marlin	80	Sears	282.510821	Boito	ERA Single Bbl
Sears	103.229	Marlin	81	Sears	282.510831	Boito	ERA Single Bbl
Sears	103.273	Marlin	782	Sears	282.510841	Boito	ERA Single Bbl
Sears	103.273	Marlin	980	Sears	282.5227740	CBC	122
Sears	103.274	Marlin	122	Sears	282.527740	FIE	122
Sears	103.275	Marlin	122	Sears	2C	Winchester	131
Sears	103.2751	Marlin	122	Sears	2T	Winchester	121,131,141
Sears	103.2840	Marlin	80	Sears	2/57	Stevens	66

House Brand	Model No.	Orig. Mfgr.	Orig. Model	House Brand	Model No.	Orig. Mfgr.	Orig. Model
Sears	2/58	Stevens	66	Sears 200	273.2160	Winchester	1200
Sears	30	High Standard	22 PUMP	Sears 200	273.2250	Winchester	1200
Sears	300	Winchester	1400	Sears 200	273.2251	Winchester	1200
Sears	31	J.C. Higgins	31	Sears 200	273.2280	Winchester	1200
Sears	33	J.C. Higgins	33	Sears 200	273.4310	Winchester	1200
Sears	34	J.C. Higgins	34	Sears 200	273.4320	Winchester	1200
Sears	340.530430	Ithaca	49SS	Sears 200	273.4340	Winchester	1200
Sears	35A	Stevens	66A	Sears 200	273.4350	Winchester	1200
Sears	36	Marlin	80	Sears 200	273.4410	Winchester	1200
Sears	375	Mossberg	45B	Sears 200	273.4420	Winchester	1200
Sears	377	Mossberg	42C	Sears 200	273.4450	Winchester	1200
Sears	381	Mossberg	46B	Seem 200	273.514010	Winchester	1200
Sears	382	Mossberg	46B	Sears 200	273.614010	Winchester	1200
Sears	384	Mossberg	45A	Sears 200	273.514011	Winchester	1200
Sears	385	Mossberg	45B	Sears 200	273.514020	Winchester	1200
Sears	387	Mossberg	42C	Seem 200	273.514040	Winchester	1200
Sears	388	Mossberg	42C	Sears 200	273.514050	Winchester	1200
Sears	389	Mossberg	42A OR 26C	Sears 200	273.514051	Winchester	1200
Sears	390	Mossberg	26C	Sears 200	273.514210	Winchester	1200
Sears	3T	Winchester	190	Sears 200	273.514220	Winchester	1200
Sears	41	Marlin	101	Sears 200	273,514250	Winchester	1200
Sears	41 DLA	Marlin	122	Sears 200	273.514251	Winchester	1200
Sears	42	Marlin	80	Sears 200	273.514810	Winchester	1200
Sears	42DL	Marlin	80	Sears 200	273.614820	Winchester	1200
Sears	42DLM	Marlin	980	Sears 200	273.514830	Winchester	1200
Sears	43	Marlin	81	Sears 200	273.514840	Winchester	1200
Sears	43DL	Marlin	81	Sears 200	273.515010	Winchester	1200
Sears	44DL	Marlin	57	Sears 200	273.515020	Winchester	1200
Sears	44DLM	Marlin	57M	Sears 200	273.515050	Winchester	1200
Sears	45	Marlin	336C	Sears 200	273.515051	Winchester	1200
Sears	46	Marlin	56	Sears 200	273.515080	Winchester	1200
Sears	46DL	Marlin	56	Sears 200	273.515090	Winchester	1200
Sears	4980	Stevens	94-2 W/PAD	Sears 200	273.515220	Winchester	1200
Sears	49.11830/30	Savage	99 A	Sears 200	273.515221	Winchester	1200
Sears	53	Winchester	70	Sears 200	273.515250	Winchester	1200
Sears	54	Winchester	94	Sears 200	273.515251	Winchester	1200
Sears	583.1	High Standard	N/A	Sears 200	273.515280	Winchester	1200
Sears	583,126	Sako	L46	Sears 200	273.515290	Winchester	1200
Sears	583.13	High Standard	N/A	Sears 200	273.515410	Winchester	1200
Sears	583.14	H & R	120	Sears 200	273.515420	Winchester	1200
Sears	583.15	H&R	121	Sears 200	273.515470	Winchester	1200
Sears	583.16	High Standard	10	Sears 200	273.515710	Winchester	1200
Sears	583.17	High Standard	N/A	Sears 200	273.515720	Winchester	1200
Sears	583.18	H & R	120	Sears 200	273.515920	Winchester	1200
Sears	583.2	H & R	M120	Sears 200	273.5310	Winchester	1200
Sears	583.20	High Standard	Flight King	Sears 200	273.5350	Winchester	1200
Sears	583.2085-87	High Standard	20ga pump	Sears 2T	273.27530	Winchester	141
Sears	583.21	H&R	M120	Sears 300	273.1310	Winchester	1400
Sears	583.25	H&R	M121	Sears 300	273.1320	Winchester	1400
Sears	583.3	H&R	M121	Sears 300	273.1350	Winchester	1400
Sears	583.4	High Standard	10	Sears 300	273.21550	Winchester	1400
Sears	583.7	High Standard	10	Sears 300	273.2500	Winchester	1400
Sears	583.91	H & R	121	Sears 300	273.2540	Winchester	1400
Sears	6C (Canada)	Winchester	Cooy 64,64B	Sears 300	273.32060	Winchester	1400
Sears	6C(American)	Winchester	490	Sears 300	273.32070	Winchester	1400
Sears	66	High Standard	66	Sears 300	273.521050	Winchester	1400
Sears	73	Savage	73	Sears 300	273.521051	Winchester	1400
Sears	870.528140	Voere	Clip .22	Sears 300	273.521080	Winchester	1400
Sears	92	Stevens	39	Sears 300	273.521090	Winchester	1400
Sears	93	Stevens	38	Sears 300	273.521160	Winchester	1400
Sears	94	Stevens	237	Sears 300	273.521161	Winchester	1400
Sears	95	Stevens	238	Sears 300	273.521250	Winchester	1400
Sears	97	Savage	94	Sears 300	273.521251	Winchester	1400
Sears	97AC	Savage	94AC	Sears 300	273.521260	Winchester	1400
Sears	98	Stevens	37	Sears 300	273.521280	Winchester	1400
Sears	98	Springfield	944	Sears 300	273.521290	Winchester	1400
Sears	M30	Stevens	M520	Sears 300	273.521580	Winchester	1400
Sears	mzm	Savage	34	Sears 300	273.521680	Winchester	1400
Sears 100	273.532141	Winchester	NM 94	Sears 300	273.521710	Winchester	1400
Sears 200	2732.5320	Winchester	1200	Sears 300	273.521770	Winchester	1400
Sears 200	273.2011	Winchester	1200	Sears 300	273.521780	Winchester	1400
Sears 200	273.21010	Winchester	1200	Sears 300	273.523251	Winchester	1400

House Brand	Model No.	Orig. Mfgr.	Orig. Model	House Brand	Model No.	Orig. Mfgr.	Orig. Model
Sears 300	273.52151	Winchester	1400	Western Auto	101.53521	Savage	340
Sears 3T-A	273.2390	Winchester	190-290	Western Auto	101.5380	Savage	18AC
Sears 3T-A	273.2400	Winchester	190-290	Western Auto	101.5380D	Savage	18DAC
Sears 3T-A	273.528110	Winchester	190-290	Western Auto	101.5410	Savage	18DS,S
Sears 3T-A	273.528111	Winchester	190-290	Western Auto	103	Savage	89
Sears 4T	273.2360	Winchester	270	Western Auto	103.13	Marlin	81
Sears 53A	273.532780	Winchester	70A	Western Auto	103.16	Marlin	80
Sears 54	273.2120	Winchester	NM 94	Western Auto	103.18	Marlin	80
Sears 54	273.532140	Winchester	NM 94	Western Auto	103.181	Marlin	101
Sears 54	273.53419	Winchester	NM 94	Western Auto	103.19780	Marlin	101
Sears 54	273.810	Winchester	NM 94	Western Auto	103.19790	Marlin	80
Sears 54	273.811	Winchester	NM 94	Western Auto	103.19800	Marlin	80
Sears 6C	273.28130	Winchester	490	Western Auto	103.1981	Marlin	81
Sears 6C	273.528131	Winchester	490	Western Auto	103.1982	Marlin	81DL
Sears 6C	273.528132	Winchester	490	Western Auto	103.19820	Marlin	81
Sears MI	273.27010	Winchester	121	Western Auto	103.19840	Marlin	56
Sears M5,M-5T	273.2340	Winchester	150-250	Western Auto	103.19880	Marlin	57
Sears M5,M-5T	273.2341	Winchester	150-250	Western Auto	103.19890	Marlin	57M
Sears M5,M-5T	273.2350	Winchester	150-250	Western Auto	103.1997	Marlin	101
Sears M5,M-5T	273.2351	Winchester	150-250	Western Auto	103.2	Marlin	80
Sears T.W. 73	273.532730	Winchester	670 Mag.	Western Auto	103.228	Marlin	80
Sears T.W. 73	23.31020	Winchester	New Mod 70	Western Auto	103.229	Marlin	81
Sears T.W. 73	273.1390	Winchester	MN 30-06	Western Auto	103.273	Marlin	980
Sears T.W. 73	273.1400	Winchester	MN 70 (.270)	Western Auto	103.274	Marlin	122
Sears T.W. 73	273.1830	Winchester	New Mod 70	Western Auto	103.2751	Marlin	122
Sears T.W. 73	273.1840	Winchester	New Mod 70	Western Auto	103.2840	Marlin	80
Sears T.W. 73	273.1850	Winchester	New Mod 70	Western Auto	103.2850	Marlin	81
Sears T.W. 73	273.1860	Winchester	New Mod 70	Western Auto	103.2870	Marlin	56
Sears T.W. 73	273.1870	Winchester	New Mod 70	Western Auto	103.360	Marlin	90
Sears T.W. 73	273.31010	Winchester	New Mod 70	Western Auto	103.450	Marlin	336
Sears T.W. 73	273.31060	Winchester	New Mod 70	Western Auto	103.451	Marlin	336
Sears T.W. 73	273.32020	Winchester	New Mod 70	Western Auto	103.720	Marlin	59
Sears T.W. 73	273.32030	Winchester	New Mod 70	Western Auto	103.740	Marlin	59
Sears T.W. 73	273.32040	Winchester	New Mod 70	Western Auto	105-2060	Marlin	780
Sears T.W. 73	273.532061	Winchester	New Mod 70	Western Auto	105-2060	Marlin	80
Sears T.W. 73	273.532071	Winchester	New Mod 70	Western Auto	107	Mossberg	640K
Sears T.W. 73	273.532081	Winchester	New Mod 70	Western Auto	107A	Mossberg	640
Sears T.W. 73	273.53403	Winchester	New Mod 70	Western Auto	110-2140	Marlin	81
Sears T.W. 73	273.53406	Winchester	New Mod 70	Western Auto	110-2140	Marlin	781
Sears T.W. 73	273.53409	Winchester	New Mod 70	Western Auto	115	Savage	46
Sears T.W. 73	273.32010	Winchester	Now Mod 70	Western Auto	115-2277	Marlin	57
				Western Auto	116-2276	Marlin	57M
Ted Williams	340.530430	Ithaca	49SS	Western Auto	117	Mossberg	402
				Western Auto	120-2220	Marlin	99
Shapleigh's	KING NITRO	Savage	15	Western Auto	125	Mossberg	353
				Western Auto	135	Savage	187
Simmons	411	Savage	540DL	Western Auto	135	Springfield	187A
Simmons	411	Savage	Fox BDE 20ga	Western Auto	150m	Marlin	49
Simmons	411E	Savage	540 BDE	Western Auto	150-2225	Marlin	49
Simmons	411E	Savage	Fox BDE 20ga	Western Auto	160	Springfield	187A
				Western Auto	160	Savage	80
Talo	12DL	Stevens	120	Western Auto	200-2280	Marlin	39A
Talo	176 VR	Springfield	67 VR	Western Auto	200-2282	Marlin	39A
Talo	176DL	Springfield	67	Western Auto	200-2550	Marlin	336
				Western Auto	200-2554	Marlin	336(.44MAG)
Western Auto,Revelation				Western Auto	205	Mossberg	472PCA
				Western Auto	210A	Mossberg	810AH
Revelation	300	Savage	30 D,E,F	Western Auto	220A	Mossberg	800A
Revelation	394 Series P	Stevens	94P	Western Auto	220AD	Mossberg	800AD
Revelation	76	High Standard	Double Nine	Western Auto	220B	Mossberg	800B
Revelation	R310	Mossberg	500AB	Western Auto	220BD	Mossberg	800BD
				Western Auto	220C	Mossberg	800C
Western Auto	100	Mossberg	321	Western Auto	220CD	Mossberg	800CD
Western Auto	101Y	Savage	73Y	Western Auto	225	Savage	340
Western Auto	101.1701	Savage	540BS	Western Auto	2280	Marlin	39A
Western Auto	101.171	Savage	540BD	Western Auto	2282	Marlin	39A Mountie
Western Auto	101.2830	Savage	73	Western Auto	230	Savage	340
Western Auto	101.52772	Savage	65M	Western Auto	250	Savage	110E
Western Auto	101.535D	Savage	18	Western Auto	250A	Savage	110D
Western Auto	101.53500	Savage	18D	Western Auto	250D	Savage	110
				Western Auto	260	Savage	170

House Brand	Model No.	Orig. Mfgr.	Orig. Model
Western Auto	260	Springfield	174
Western Auto	300	Springfield	67
Western Auto	300	Stevens	30
Western Auto	300A	Savage	30AC
Western Auto	300F	Stevens	77C
Western Auto	300H	Savage	30,HAC
Western Auto	300-300AC	Springfield	67
Western Auto	310	Mossberg	500
Western Auto	310A	Mossberg	500A
Western Auto	310AB	Mossberg	500AB
Western Auto	310B	Mossberg	500B
Western Auto	310C	Mossberg	500C
Western Auto	310E	Mossberg	500E
Western Auto	312	Mossberg	395
Western Auto	312AK	Mossberg	395K
Western Auto	312SB	Mossberg	395T
Western Auto	316	Mossberg	390
Western Auto	316BB	Mossberg	390T
Western Auto	316BK	Mossberg	390K
Western Auto	325B	Mossberg	385T
Western Auto	325BK	Mossberg	385K
Western Auto	330	Mossberg	183 & 183K
Western Auto	330B	Mossberg	183T
Western Auto	335-3725	Marlin	59
Western Auto	336	Springfield	951
Western Auto	350	Stevens	94
Western Auto	350A	Savage	94D
Western Auto	350M	Stevens	94
Western Auto	355	Stevens	947
Western Auto	355Y	Savage	94Y
Western Auto	355YE	Springfield	947YE
Western Auto	356Y	Springfield	944Y
Western Auto	360	Savage	540
Western Auto	360	Savage	FOX mod B
Western Auto	360C	Savage	540C
Western Auto	400	Stevens	745
Western Auto	400C	Savage	745C
Western Auto	420	High Standard	Supmatic C-011
Western Auto	425	High Standard	Supmatic C-120
Western Auto	460	Springfield	511
Western Auto	SD52A	Stevens	311
West Point	45	Marlin	60

Wards, Western Field, and Hawthorn

House Brand	Model No.	Orig. Mfgr.	Orig. Model
Hawthorn	110	Unknown	S shot SG
Hawthorn	580 EJN	Colt	Colteer/bolt
Hawthorn	814 EJN	Colt	Colteer/SS
Hawthorn	820B	Mossberg	340
Hawthorn	880	Colt	Colteer/semi
Hawthorn	880 EJN	Colt	Colteer/bolt
Wards	24M 419A	Mossberg	9
Wards	472	Noble	50
Wards	850	Mossberg	353
Wards Triumph	52	Stevens	315
Western Field	04M-489A	Mossberg	50
Western Field	04M-218A	Mossberg	73C
Western Field	04M-2117A	Mossberg	9
Western Field	04M-217A	Mossberg	75C
Western Field	04M-214A	Mossberg	85C
Western Field	04M-216A	Mossberg	83C
Western Field	I	Mossberg	RF-1
Western Field	10-SD247A	Stevens	94B (Tenite)
Western Field	14	Savage	39A
Western Field	14	Savage	59A
Western Field	14M-215A	Mossberg	85
Western Field	14M-497B	Mossberg	M42
Western Field	14M-488A	Mossberg	50
Western Field	15	Mossberg	80
Western Field	150	Mossberg	183K

House Brand	Model No.	Orig. Mfgr.	Orig. Model
Western Field	151X	Kessler	N/A
Western Field	155	Mossberg	173
Western Field	15A	Mossberg	83
Western Field	16	Mossberg	85
Western Field	160	Mossberg	385K
Western Field	16A	Mossberg	85
Western Field	17	Mossberg	73
Western Field	170	Mossberg	395K
Western Field	172	Mossberg	395K
Western Field	173	Mosaberg	395
Western Field	175	Mossberg	385K
Western Field	17A	Mossberg	73
Western Field	I8	Mossberg	75
Western Field	20	Mossberg	9R
Western Field	215A	Mossberg	85
Western Field	24M,488A	Mossberg	51
Western Field	30	Stevens	520
Western Field	31A	Mossberg	44
Western Field	31A	Mossberg	40
Western Field	32	Mossberg	21
Western Field	32	Mossberg	20
Western Field	33	Marlin	336
Western Field	35A	Mossberg	30
Western Field	36	Stevens	521
Western Field	36	Mossberg	10
Western Field	36B	Mossberg	25A
Western Field	36B	Mossberg	10
Western Field	36C	Mossberg	25A
Western Field	360	Mossberg	26C
Western Field	37	Mossberg	30
Western Field	39	Mossberg	25
Western Field	390A	Mossberg	26C
Western Field	40,D	Mossberg	44
Western Field	40	Marlin	101
Western Field	40N	Noble	40NA
Western Field	40M-215A	Mossberg	185
Western Field	41	Mossberg	45
Western Field	45	Marlin	989M2
Western Field	45	Mossberg	42
Western Field	45B	Mossberg	26C
Western Field	45C	Mossberg	25A
Western Field	46	Mossberg	42
Western Field	466	Mossberg	RA1
Western Field	469	Mossberg	RA1-Kit
Western Field	46A	Mossberg	42
Western Field	46C	Moseberg	42A
Western Field	46D	Mossberg	42C
Western Field	47	Mossberg	45A
Western Field	472	Noble	50
Western Field	47A,L	Mossberg	45A
Western Field	48	Mossberg	45A
Western Field	488A	Mossberg	51
Western Field	48A	Mossberg	45B
Western Field	48A	Mossberg	46MLB
Western Field	5-4	Mossberg	8-M4
Western Field	50	Glenfield	60
Western Field	502-26FR	Mossberg	500
Western Field	505	Mossberg	500
Western Field	509	Mossberg	500
Western Field	524	Mossberg	500
Western Field	534	Mossberg	500
Western Field	536	Mossberg	500
Western Field	539	Mossberg	500
Western Field	550A	Mossberg	500A
Western Field	550AS	Mossberg	500AB
Western Field	550B	Mossberg	500B
Western Field	550C	Mossberg	500B
Western Field	550E	Mossberg	500E
Western Field	550E	Mossberg	500E
Western Field	60	Savage	620A
Western Field	600ERI 12 GA	Remington	SPT 58
Western Field	60SB	Savage	620A

House Brand	Model No.	Orig. Mfgr.	Orig. Model	House Brand	Model No.	Orig. Mfgr.	Orig. Model
Western Field	679	Mossberg	472	Western Field	M172	Mossberg	395K
Western Field	710	Savage	110	Western Field	M175	Mossberg	385K
Western Field	72	Noble	50	Western Field	M23 NH402A	Stevens	820
Western Field	72C	Mossberg	472	Western Field	M35	Savage	520 POLY
Western Field	730	Mossberg	810AH	Western Field	M36	Savage	521
Western Field	732	Mossberg	810AH	Western Field	M60	Savage	620 DELUX
Western Field	734	Mossberg	810A	Western Field	M61	Savage	621 DELUX
Western Field	740	Marlin	336	Western Field	M72	Mossberg	472 PRA
Western Field	765	Mossberg	810A	Western Field	M734	Mossberg	810BH
Western Field	766	Mossberg	810B	Western Field	M771	Moseberg	472SBA
Western Field	767	Mossberg	800A	Western Field	M772	Mossberg	472PCA
Western Field	768	Mossberg	800A	Western Field	M7 75	Mossberg	800AD
Western Field	771	Mossberg	472BA	Western Field	M776	Mossberg	800BD
Western Field	772	Mossberg	472PCA	Western Field	M778	Mossberg	472BAS
Western Field	775	Mossberg	800AD	Western Field	M780	Mossberg	800A
Western Field	776	Mossberg	800BD	Western Field	M782	Mossberg	800B
Western Field	778	Mossberg	472BAS	Western Field	M808.C	Stevens	87,C,J
Western Field	780	Mossberg	800A	Western Field	M808N	Stevens	87N
Western Field	782	Mossberg	800B	Western Field	M80A	Savage	M29-D1
Western Field	79	Mossberg	472 PRA	Western Field	M815	Mossberg	320
Western Field	50	Savage	29	Western Field	M822	Mossberg	640K
Western Field	807A ECH	Colt	Colteer S.S.	Western Field	M85	Stevens	85
Western Field	808	Savage	87	Western Field	M-SD57	Stevens	87
Western Field	808C	Savage	87J	Western Field	SS 94B	Stevens	94C
Western Field	815	Mossberg	321	Western Field	SB033	Savage	520 W/POLY
Western Field	820B	Mossberg	340	Western Field	SB066	Savage	621 DELX POLY
Western Field	822	Mossberg	640K	Western Field	SB067	Savage	621 DELX COMP
Western Field	828	Mossberg	353	Western Field	S5112C	Savage	540C
Western Field	830	Mossberg	340K	Western Field	SB115	Savage	115
Western Field	832	Mossberg	341	Western Field	SB300,C	Stevens	311,C
Western Field	836	Savage	187N	Western Field	SB30A	Savage	520
Western Field	840	Mossberg	640	Western Field	SB311C	Savage	311C
Western Field	842	Mossberg	346K	Western Field	SB312	Savage	540D
Western Field	846	Mossberg	351C	Western Field	SB312	Savage-Fox	BDL
Western Field	850 855	Mossberg	353	Western Field	SB33	Savage	520 POLY
Western Field	852	Mossberg	341	Western Field	SB60A	Savage	620 DELUX
Western Field	865	Mossberg	402	Western Field	SB61A	Savage	621 DELUX
Western Field	880	Colt	Colteer Semi.	Western Field	SB620A	Stevens	620A
Western Field	894	Mossberg	430-432	Western Field	SB66	Savage	621 DELX POLY
Western Field	895	Mossberg	402	Western Field	SB712	Savage	84U
Western Field	9-2 3/4	Mossberg	9-2 1/2	Western Field	SB80A	Savage	29-DI
Western Field	93M	Mossberg	26C	Western Field	SB85TA	Stevens	85
Western Field	93M-213A	Mossberg	75B	Western Field	SB87,TA	Stevens	M87
Western Field	93M-2116A	Mossberg	9	Western Field	XNH 175	Marlin	55
Western Field	93M-212A	Mossberg	738	Western Field	XNH 565	Noble	60-66
Western Field	93M-211A	Mossberg	83B				
Western Field	93M-210A	Mossberg	85B	Widgeon	SA 650	Marlin	55 12 GA
Western Field	93M-497A	Mossberg	42C				
Western Field	93M-491A	Mossberg	465				
Western Field	93M-495A	Mossberg	45B				
Western Field	EMN 171	Marlin	50				
Western Field	EMN 176	Marlin	55				
Western Field	M-SD57	Stevens	M87				
Western Field	M025	Savage	520A				
Western Field	M040 0/U	Marlin	90				
Western Field	M040N	Stevens	820				
Western Field	M051	Stevens	515				
Western Field	M059	Stevens	M87				
Western Field	M060	Stevens	620				
Western Field	M080	Savage	29 & 75				
Western Field	M087	Stevens	M87				
Western Field	M10	Stevens	94 Short tang				
Western Field	M150	Mossberg	183T				
Western Field	M155	Mosaberg	183D				
Western Field	M160	Mossberg	385T				
Western Field	M170	Mossberg	395S				

SERIALIZATION

This section has once again been expanded to help you identify the year of manufacture on many popular manufacturers and trademarks. To use these tables, compare your serial number(s) to the correct manufacturer and model, and ascertain which bracket it falls into based on the year of manufacture and corresponding serial number. In several cases, caliber rarity can also be determined. Date codes are now also provided on some manufacturers and countries to allow you to determine the year of manufacture by the date code on the barrel or frame/receiver.

The publisher wishes to thank Galazan's and Dixie Gun Works for providing a portion of this serialization information.

AGUIRRE Y ARANZABAL (AYA) SERIALIZATION 1945 to 1994

From 1945 to 1994 AYA had manufactured over 600,000 shotguns of all models and grades with all serial numbers assigned in chronological order. For 1927-1944 year of manufacture date codes, see "Spanish Year Of MFG. Date Codes" in this section.

Years	Ser. # Start	Ser. # End
1945-1948	0001	19999
1949-1954	20000	71999
1955-1959	72000	115286
1960-1965	115287	222508
1966-1971	222509	378548
1972-1977	378549	481401
1978-1983	481402	576551
1984-1987	576553	599999
1988-1993	600000	602422
1994	602423	602642

Beginning 1995 the Spanish proof house implemented a new serial number system. The new system consists of four sets of digits separated by a hyphen. The firstr set is the manufactureres code, the second designates the type of firearm, the third set is the firearms chronological number, the fourth set shows the year of mfg.

AYA 1995-2006

Year	Ser. # Start	Ser. # End
1995	16-03-001-95	16-03-800-95
1996	16-03-001-96	16-03-755-96
1997	16-03-001-97	16-03-642-97
1998	16-03-001-98	16-03-677-98
1999	16-03-001-99	16-03-719-99
2000	16-03-001-00	16-03-758-00
2001	16-03-001-01	16-03-645-01
2002	16-03-001-02	16-03-645-02
2003	16-03-001-03	16-03-781-03
2004	16-03-001-04	16-03-703-04
2005	16-03-001-05	16-03-652-05
2006	16-03-001-06	16-03-750-06

BOSS & CO., LTD. SERIALIZATION

Year Starting	Serial Number
1830	680
1850	1400
1857	1600
1900	4700
1920	6618

Boss & Co. LTD. Cont.

Year Starting	Serial Number
1930	7730
1945	8711
1951	8912
1953	8920
1963	9219
1970	9559

BROWNING SERIALIZATION PRE-1976

Since 1968-1969 was a transition period in Browning serialization, firearms may be serialized with either 1968 or 1969 style markings.

A-5 (AUTOMATIC 5) SHOTGUN -12 ga.

Year	Ser. # Start	Ser. # End
1903	1	4121
1904	4122	15300
1905	15301	19920
1906	19921	22320
1907	22321	26970
1908	26971	30446
1909	30447	33431
1910	33432	35630
1911	35631	35925
1912	35926	38988
1913	38989	44250
1914	44251	47298
1915-1918	No Production	
1919	47719	47950
1920	47299	47718
1921	48951	53500
1922	53501	58150
1923	58151	62600
1924	62601	69300
1925	69301	79150
1926	79151	88000
1927	88001	106250
1928	106251	127650
1929	127651	154500
1930	154501	177100
1931	177101	182300
1932	182301	182788
1933	182789	183152
1934	183153	185560
1935	185561	191604
1936	191605	194535
1937	194536	199200
1938	199201	208400
1939	208401	218808
1940	218809	224596
1941-1943	No Production	
1944	Production limited to servicemen	
1945	Production limited to servicemen	

A-5 SHOTGUN -12 ga. cont.

Year	Ser. # Start	Ser. # End
1946	228729	240950
1947	240951	256500
1948	256501	274100
1949	274101	288550
1950	288551	316750
1951	316751	352050
1952	352051	387499
1953	387500	437400
1954	437401	447750
1955	447751	454700
1956	454701	459900
1957	459901	463700

In 1954 Browning added an alpha prefix to the serial number to differentiate between Lightweight and Standardweight guns.

Year	Std.12	Lt.Wt. 12
1953	H1-H6600	L1-L4450
1954	H6601-H39700	L4451-L45250
1955	H39701-H83450	L45251-L83600
1956	H83451-H100000	L83601-L99877
1956	M1-M35250	G1-G35450
1957	M35251-M86300	G35451-G85950
1958	M86301-M99999	G85951-G99663

1958-1976 Ser. No. sequence changed to include a one or two digit numeral followed by an alpha character.

Year	Std. Wt.	Lt. Wt.	Magnum
1958	8M	8G	8V
1959	9M	9G	9V
1960	0M	0G	0V
1961	1M	1G	1V
1962	2M	2G	2V
1963	3M	3G	3V
1965	5M	5G	5V
1966	6M	6G	6V
1964	4M	4G	4V
1967	7M	7G	7V
1968	8M	8G	8V
1969	69M	69G	69V
1970	Disc.	70G	70V
1971	Disc.	71G	71V
1972	Disc.	72G	72V
1973	Disc.	73G	73V
1974	Disc.	74G	74V
1975	Disc.	75G	75V
1976	Disc.	76G	76V

A-5 (AUTOMATIC 5) SHOTGUN -16 ga.

Year	Ser. # Start	Ser. # End
1909	1	3200
1910-1912	3201	15000
1913	15001	19000
1914-1918	No Production	
1919	19671	20500
1920	20501	22237
1921	22238	24050
1922	24051	26000
1923	26001	28400
1924	28401	35650
1925	35651	40010
1926	40011	51600
1927	51599	57900
1928	57901	65100
1929	65101	82750
1930	82751	90500
1931	90501	94000

A-5 SHOTGUN -16 ga. cont.

Year	Ser. # Start	Ser. # End
1932	94001	96072
1933	96073	96143
1934	96144	99500
1935	99501	103500
1936	103501	105850
1937	105851	111000
1938	111001	118200
1939	118201	126123
1940	126123	126175
1941-1943 No Production		
1944 Production limited to servicemen		
1945 Production limited to servicemen		
1946	128117	128646
1947	128647	130616
1947	X1001	X13666
1948	X13667	X23501
1949	X23502	X34600
1950	X34601	X43700
1951	X43701	X59400
1952	X59401	X77700
1953	X77701	X99999

In 1953 Browning changed the Ser. No. alphabetic character to differentiate between Lightweight (Sweet 16) & Standard weight guns.

Year	Std.16	Sweet 16
1953	R1-R3100	S1-S3700
1954	R3100-R20800	S3701-S24850
1955	R20801-R48750	S24851-S49350
1956	R48751-R74700	S49350-S72300
1957	R74701-R99999	S72301-S99908

1957-58 Prefix "T" for Standardweight and Prefix "A" for Sweet 16 numbers mixed, but range from 1-10900.
1958-1976 Ser. No. sequence changed to include a one or two digit numeral followed by an alpha character.

Year	Std.16	Sweet 16
1958	8R	8S
1959	9R	9S
1960	0R	0S
1961	1R	1S
1962	2R	2S
1963	3R	3S
1964	Disc.	4S
1965	Disc.	5S
1966	Disc.	6S
1967	Disc.	7S
1968	Disc.	8S
1969	Disc.	69S
1970	Disc.	70S
1971	Disc.	71S
1972	Disc.	72S
1973	Disc.	73S
1974	Disc.	74S
1975	Disc.	75S
1976	Disc.	Disc.

A-5 SHOTGUN - 20 ga.

Year	Lt.Wt. 20	Magnum 20
1958	8Z	Introduced in
1959	9Z	1967
1960	0Z	
1961	1Z	
1962	2Z	
1963	3Z	
1964	4Z	

A-5 SHOTGUN - 20 ga. cont.

Year	Lt.Wt. 20	Magnum 20
1965	5Z	
1966	6Z	
1967	7Z	7X
1968	68Z	68X
1969	69Z	69X
1970	70Z	70X
1971	71Z	71X
1972	72Z	72X
1973	73Z	73X
1974	74Z	74X
1975	75Z	75X
1976	76Z	76X

SUPERPOSED MODEL - O & U - 12 ga.

Year	Ser. # Start	Ser. # End
1931	1	2000
1932	2001	4000
1933	4001	6000
1934	6001	8000
1935	8001	10000
1936	10001	12000
1937	12001	14000
1938	14001	16000
1939	16001	17000
1939-1947	NO PRODUCTION	
1948	17001	17200
1949	17201	20000
1950	20001	21000
1951	21001	27000
1952	27001	33000
1953	33001	37000
1954	37001	43000
1955	43001	48000
1956	48001	54000
1957	54001	59000
1958	59001	68500
1959	68501	76500
1960	76501	86500
1961	86501	96500
1962	96501	99999
1962	1	6500
1962	S2 suffix after Ser. No.	
1963	S3 suffix after Ser. No.	
1964	S4 suffix after Ser. No.	
1965	S5 suffix after Ser. No.	
1966	S6 suffix after Ser. No.	
1967	S7 suffix after Ser. No.	
1968	S8 suffix after Ser. No.	
1969	S69 suffix after Ser. No.	
1970	S70 suffix after Ser. No.	
1971	S71 suffix after Ser. No.	
1972	S72 suffix after Ser. No.	
1973	S73 suffix after Ser. No.	
1974	S74 suffix after Ser. No.	
1975	S75 suffix after Ser. No.	
1976	S76 suffix after Ser. No.	
1976 to 1984	"P" or Presentation Models only	

SUPERPOSED MODEL - O & U - 20 ga.

Year	Ser. # Start	Ser. # End
1949	201	1700
1950	1701	2800
1951	2801	3200
1952	3201	5300
1953	5301	6700
1954	6701	8400
1955	8401	9400
1956	9401	10500
1957	10501	11500

SUPERPOSED MODEL - O & U - 20 ga. cont.

Year	Ser. No.	Prefix
1958	11501	14180
1959	14181	17060
1960	17061	20640
1961	20641	23820
1962	23821	27300

Serial number change to letter and number suffix.

1963	V3 suffix after Ser. No.
1964	V4 suffix after Ser. No.
1965	V5 suffix after Ser. No.
1966	V6 suffix after Ser. No.
1967	V7 suffix after Ser. No.
1968	V8 suffix after Ser. No.
1969	V69 suffix after Ser. No.
1970	V70 suffix after Ser. No.
1971	V71 suffix after Ser. No.
1972	V72 suffix after Ser. No.
1973	V73 suffix after Ser. No.
1974	V74 suffix after Ser. No.
1975	V75 suffix after Ser. No.
1976	V76 suffix after Ser. No.

SUPERPOSED MODEL - O & U - 28 ga. & .410 bore

Year	28 ga.	.410 bore
1960-1962	NOT AVAILABLE	
1963	F3	J3
1964	F4	J4
1965	F5	J5
1966	F6	J6
1967	F7	J7
1968	F8	J8
1969	F69	J69
1970	F70	J70
1971	F71	J71
1972	F72	J72
1973	F73	J73
1974	F74	J74
1975	F75	J75
1976	F76	J76

LIEGE O & U - Approximately 10,000 prouced

Year	Ser. No. Prefix
1973	73J prefix before Ser. No.
1974	74J prefix before Ser. No.
1975	75J prefix before Ser. No.

DOUBLE AUTOMATIC SHOTGUN

Year	Ser. # Start	Ser. # End
1952 -	N/A	
1959	N/A	
1960 -	N/A	
1971	N/A	

1st or both digits indicate last 2 digits in year of manufacture (i.e. - OA1947 - 1960 mfg., 70A245671 - 1970 mfg.)

HI-POWER (9mm) PISTOL

Year	Ser. # Start	Ser. # End
1945-1954 no data for the annual breakdown		
	1	72250
1955	72251	75000
1956	75001	77250
1957	77251	80000
1958	80001	85267
1959	85268	89687
1960	89688	93027

HI-POWER (9mm) PISTOL cont.

Year	Ser. # Start	Ser. # End
1961	93028	109145
1962	109146	113548
1963	113549	115822
1964	115823	T136538
1965	T136569	T146372
1966	T146373	T173285
1967	T173286	T213999
1968	T214000	T258000
1969	T258001	T261000

Serial Number code change to two digit year and "C" prefix indicating Hi-Power pistol.

	and 69C prefix before Ser. No.
1970	70C prefix before Ser. No.
1971	71C prefix before Ser. No.
1972	72C prefix before Ser. No.
1973	73C prefix before Ser. No.
1974	74C prefix before Ser. No.
1975	75C prefix before Ser. No.
1976	76C prefix before Ser. No.
1977 to date	New style serialization

BROWNING .380 ACP CAL.

Year	Ser. # Start	Ser. # End
1955 -	N/A	
1964	N/A	
1965	500000	598804
1966	598805	603890
1967	603891	619474
1968	619475	N/A
1969 -	N/A	

1970 Discontinued due to GCA of 1968. New model has longer barrel, adj. rear sight, modified grip.

1971	71N prefix before Ser. No.
1972	72N prefix before Ser. No.
1973	73N prefix before Ser. No.
1974	74N prefix before Ser. No.
1975	75N prefix before Ser. No.

.25 ACP CAL. BABY BROWNING

Year	Ser. # Start	Ser. # End
1955-1958	Records not available	
1959	181000	206349
1960	206350	230999
1961	231000	250999
1962	251000	278999
1963	279000	286099
1964	286100	308499
1965	308500	329999
1966	333000	367443
1967	367444	412999
1968	413000	479000
1969	Discontinued because of GCA of 1968	

.22 CAL. (Nomad-Challenger-Medalist)

Year	Nomad	Challenger	Medalist
1959	P9	U9	T9
1960	P0	U0	T0
1961	P1	U1	T1
1962	P2	U2	T2
1963	P3	U3	T3
1964	P4	U4	T4
1965	P5	U5	T5
1966	P6	U6	T6
1967	P7	U7	T7
1968	P8	U8	T8

.22 CAL. (Nomad-Challenger-Medalist), cont.

Year	Nomad	Challenger	Medalist
1969	P69	U69	T69
1970	P70	U70	T70
1971	P71	U71	T71
1972	P72	U72	T72
1973	P73	U73	T73
1974	Disc.	U74	T74
1975	Disc.	Disc.	Disc.

BOLT ACTION RIFLES
(Safari, Medallion, & Olympian Models)

Year	
1959 -	N/A
1962	No prefix (numeral-letter) before Ser. No. (i.e., only digits)
1963	3-single letter prefix or suffix by Ser. No.
1964	4-single letter prefix or suffix by Ser. No.
1965	5-single letter prefix or suffix by Ser. No.
1966	6-single letter prefix or suffix by Ser. No.
1967	7-single letter prefix or suffix by Ser. No.
1968	8-single letter prefix or suffix by Ser. No.
1969	Single letter (Y, Z, or L) followed by last 2 digits of year of mfg. Prefix only.
1970	"Y70" prefix
1971	"L71" prefix
1972	"Z72" prefix
1973	"Y73" prefix
1974	"Z74" prefix
1975	"L75" prefix

B.A.R.

Year	
1967	"M7" suffix after Ser. No.
1968	"M8" suffix after Ser. No.
1969	"M69" suffix after Ser. No.
1970	"M70" suffix after Ser. No.
1971	"M71" suffix after Ser. No.
1972	"M72" suffix after Ser. No.
1973	"M73" suffix after Ser. No.
1974	"M74" suffix after Ser. No.
1975	"M75" suffix after Scr. No.
1976	"M76" suffix after Ser. No.
1976 to date	New sequence with "RT" appearing in middle of Ser. No.

.22 AUTO RIFLE (Grades I, II, and III)

Year	
1956-Mid. 1961	"T" prefix = LR, "A" prefix = short
Mid. 1961	"A" changed to "E" prefix 5 digits or less.
1961	"1T" or "1A" or "1E" prefix before Ser. No.
1962	"2T" or "2E" prefix before Ser. No.
1963	"3T" or "3E" prefix before Ser. No.
1964	"4T" or "4E" prefix before Ser. No.
1965	"5T" or "5E" prefix before Ser. No.
1966	"6T" or "6E" prefix before Ser. No.
1967	"7T" or "7E" prefix before Ser. No.
1968	"8T" or "8E" prefix before Ser. No.
1969	"69T" or "69E" prefix before Ser. No.
1970	"70T" or "70E" prefix before Ser. No.
1971	"71T" or "71E" prefix before Ser. No.
1972	"72T" or "72E" prefix before Ser. No.
1973	Japan production

T-BOLT RIFLE (T1 and T2)

Year	
1965	"X5" suffix after Ser. No.
1966	"X6" suffix after Ser. No.
1967	"X7" suffix after Ser. No.
1968	"X8" suffix after Ser. No.

T-BOLT RIFLE (T1 and T2), cont.

Year	
1969	"X69" suffix after Ser. No.
1970	"X70" suffix after Ser. No.
1971	"X71" suffix after Ser. No.
1972	"X72" suffix after Ser. No.
1973	"X73" suffix after Ser. No.
1974	"X74" suffix after Ser. No.
1975	"X75" suffix after Ser. No.

BROWNING SERIALIZATION 1976-CURRENT

In 1975 Browning began using the two (2) letter code system (located in the middel of the serial number) for determining the year of manufacture. For example "PN" would be "89" inditacting 1989.

LETTER	NUMBER
Z	1
Y	2
X	3
W	4
V	5
T	6
R	7
P	8
N	9
M	10

E.J. CHURCHILL GUNMACKERS SER.

YEAR	GUN #
1891	156
1892	339
1893	384
1894	480
1895	569
1896	655
1897	761
1898	923
1899	1047
1900	1156
1924	2834
1957	6901

COLT'S FIREARMS SERIALIZATION

MODEL 1849 POCKET REVOLVER

Year	Ser. # Start	Ser. # End
1849	1	11999
1850	12000	15999
1851	16000	24999
1852	25000	54999
1853	55000	84999
1854	85000	99999
1855	100000	109999
1856	110000	129999
1857	130000	139999
1858	140000	149999
1859	150000	159999
1860	160000	183999
1861	184000	196999
1862	197000	222999
1863	223000	249999
1864	250000	269999

MODEL 1849 POCKET REVOLVER, cont.

Year	Ser. # Start	Ser. # End
1865	270000	279999
1866	280000	289999
1867	290000	299999
1868	300000	309999
1869	310000	319999
1870	320000	324999
1871	325000	329999
1872	330000	330999
1873	331000	340000

MODEL 1849 POCKET REVOLVER -LONDON BARREL ADDRESS

Year	Ser. # Start	Ser. # End
1853	1	999
1854	1000	4999
1855	5000	8999
1856	9000	11000

MODEL 1851 NAVY

Year	Ser. # Start	Ser. # End
1850	1	2499
1851	2500	9999
1852	10000	19999
1853	20000	34999
1854	35000	39999
1855	40000	44999
1856	45000	64999
1857	65000	84999
1858	85000	89999
1859	90000	92999
1860	93000	97999
1861	98000	117999
1862	118000	131999
1863	132000	174999
1864	175000	179999
1865	180000	184999
1866	185000	199999
1867	200000	203999
1868	204000	206999
1869	207000	209999
1870	210000	211999
1871	212000	213999
1872	214000	214999
1873	215000	215348

MODEL 1851 NAVY - LONDON BARREL ADDRESS

Year	Ser. # Start	Ser. # End
1853	1	3999
1854	4000	14999
1855	15000	40999
1856	41000	42000

MODEL 1860 ARMY

Year	Ser. # Start	Ser. # End
1860	1	1999
1861	2000	24999
1862	25000	84999
1863	85000	149999
1864	150000	152999
1865	153000	155999
1866	156000	161999
1867	162000	169999
1868	170000	176999
1869	177000	184999
1870	185000	189999
1871	190000	197999
1872	198000	198999
1873	199000	200500

MODEL 1861 NAVY

Year	Ser. # Start	Ser. # End
1861	1	4599
1862	4600	9999
1863	10000	16999
1864	17000	24999
1865	25000	27999
1866	28000	29999
1867	30000	30999
1868	31000	32999
1869	33000	33999
1870	34000	34999

MODEL 1861 NAVY, cont.

Year	Ser. # Start	Ser. # End
1871	35000	35999
1872	36000	36999
1873	37000	38843

MODEL 1862 POLICE

Year	Ser. # Start	Ser. # End
1861	1	8499
1862	8500	14999
1863	15000	25999
1864	26000	28999
1865	29000	31999
1866	32000	34999
1867	35000	36999
1868	37000	39999
1869	40000	41999
1870	42000	43999
1871	44000	44999
1872	45000	45999
1873	46000	47000

MODEL 1873 - SINGLE ACTION ARMY

(SAA) - PRE-WAR

Year	Caliber	Ser. # Start
1873	.45 Colt Caliber, Standard	1
1874	.450 Boxer	200
1875	.44 Rimfire series (own serials, 1-1863 made through 1880)	15000
1876	.476 Eley introduced	22000
1877		33000
1878	.44-40 introduced in quantity	41000
1879		49000
1880		53000
1881		62000
1882	Sheriff's model introduced	73000
1883	.22 rimfire introduced	85000
1884	.32-20 and .38-40 introduced	102000
1885	.41 Colt introduced	114000
1886	.38 Colt introduced	117000
1887	.32 Colt and .32 S&W introduced	119000
1888	Flattop Target S.A.A. began; no.	125000 126530
1889	.32 rimfire; ,32-44 S&W, .38 S&W; and .44 Russian introduced	128000
1890	.44 Smoothbore; .380 and .450 Eley; and .44 S&W introduced	130000
1891	.38-44 introduced	136000
1892	Transverse cylinder latch introduced, screw lock at front of frame dropped	144000
1893		149000
1894	Beginning of Bisley models	154000
1895		159000

MODEL 1873 - SINGLE ACTION ARMY

(SAA) - PRE-WAR cont.

Year	Caliber	Ser. # Start
1896		163000
1897		168000
1898		175000
1899		182000
1900	Revolvers built to handle smokeless powder	192000
1901		203000
1902		220000
1903		238000
1904		250000
1905		261000
1906		273000
1907		288000
1908		304000
1909		308000
1910		312000
1911		316000
1912	Discontinue Bisley model	321000
1913	S&W Special introduced	325000
1914		328000
1915	Long flute cylinders; range no. 330001 to 331480	329500
1916		332000
1917		335000
1918		337000
1919		337200
1920		338000
1921		341000
1922		343000
1923		344500
1924	.45 ACP introduced, requiring special cylinders	346400
1925		347300
1926		348200
1927		349800
1928		351300
1929		352400
1930	.38 Special introduced	353800
1931		354100
1932		354500
1933		354800
1934		355000
1935	.357 Magnum introduced	355200
1936		355300
1937		355400
1938		356100
1939		356600
1940	A few S.A.A. during and just after the war 357000 thru 357859	

1ST GENERATION COLT SINGLE ACTION ARMY - CALIBER BREAKDOWN

Caliber	S.A.A	Flattop Target	Bisley	Bisley Target
.22 Rimfire	107	93	0	0
.32 Rimfire	1	0	0	0
.32 Colt	192	24	160	44
.32 S&W	32	30	18	17
.32-44	2	9	14	17
.32-20	29,812	30	13,291	131
.38 Colt (through 1914)	1,011	122	412	96
.38 Colt (post-1922)	1,365	0	0	0
.38 S&W	9	39	10	5
.38 Colt Special	82	7	0	0

ST GENERATION COLT SINGLE ACTION ARMY – CALIBER BREAKDOWN, cont.

Caliber	S.A.A	Flattop Target	Bisley	Bisley Target
.38 S&W				
Special	25	0	2	0
.38-44	2	11	6	47
.357				
Magnum	525	0	0	0
.380 Eley	1	3	0	0
.38-40	38,240	19	12,163	98
41	16,402	91	3,159	24
.44				
Smoothbore	15	0	1	0
.44 Rimfire	1,863	0	0	0
.44 German	59	0	0	0
.44 Russian	154	51	90	62
.44 S&W	24	51	29	64
.44 S&W				
Special	506	1	0	0
.44-40	64,489	21	6,803	78
.45	150,683	100	8,005	97
.45				
Smoothbore	4	0	2	0
.45 ACP	44	0	0	0
.450 Boxer	729	89	0	0
.450 Eley	2,697	84	5	0
.455 Eley	1,150	37	180	196
.476 Eley	161	2	0	0
Total Quantities				
	310,386	914	44,350	976

COLT SINGLE ACTION ARMY –
POST-WAR PRODUCTION

Year	Ser. # Start	Ser. # End
"SA" suffix from 1956 to 1978,		
"SA" prefix 1978 to 1981		
1956	0001SA	8799SA
1957	8800SA	18499SA
1958	18500SA	23399SA
1959	23400SA	28499SA
1960	28500SA	33599SA
1961	33600SA	35649SA
1962	35650SA	37299SA
1963	37300SA	38499SA
1964	38500SA	39999SA
1965	40000SA	41499SA
1966	41500SA	43799SA
1967	43800SA	46299SA
1968	46300SA	48999SA
1969	49000SA	52599SA
1970	52600SA	59399SA
1971	59400SA	61699SA
1972	61700SA	64399SA
1973	64400SA	69399SA
1974	69400SA	73319SA
1975	NONE PRODUCED	
1976 (start of 3rd generation of production)		
	80000SA	82000SA
1977	82001SA	95999SA
1978	96000SA	99999SA
Mid-1978 Start of "SA" prefix on front of ser. no.		
1978	SA01000	SA14808
1979	SA14809	SA30254
1980	SA30255	SA46919
1981	SA46920	SA58627
1982	SA58628	SA65255
1983	SA65256	SA66495
1984	SA66496	C.S. PROD.

NEW FRONTIER SINGLE ACTION ARMY

Year	Ser. # Start	Ser. # End
1961	3000NF	3005NF
1962	3006NF	3849NF
1963	3850NF	4699NF
1964	4700NF	4974NF
1965	4975NF	5399NF
1966	5400NF	5674NF
1967	5675NF	5699NF
1968	5700NF	5899NF
1969	5900NF	5924NF
1970	5925NF	6874NF
1971	6875NF	7049NF
1972	7050NF	7074NF
1973	7075NF	7174NF
1974	7175NF	7264NF
1975	7265NF	7288NF

NEW FRONTIER SINGLE ACTION ARMY, cont.

Year	Ser. # Start	Ser. # End
1978	7501NF	N/A
REINTRODUCED IN SEPTEMBER		
1978	01001NF	04424NF
1979	04425NF	06274NF
1980	06275NF	11374NF
1981	11375NF	16584NF
1982	16584NF	DISC. 1982

MODEL 1911 AND 1911A1 – Commercial production Capital "C" prefix - .45 cal.

Year	Ser. # Start	Ser. # End
1912	C1	C1899
1913	C1900	C5399
1914	C5400	C16599
1915	C16600	C27599
1916	C27600	C74999
1917	C75000	C98999
1918	C99000	C105999
1919	C106000	C120999
1920	C121000	C126999
1921	C127000	C128999
1922	C129000	C133999
1923	C134000	C134999
1924	C135000	C139999
1925	C140000	C144999
1926	C145000	C150999
1927	C151000	C151999
1928	C152000	C154999
1929	C155000	C155999
1930	C156000	C158999
1931	C159000	C160999
1932	C161000	C164799
1933	C164800	C174599
1934	C174600	C177999
1935	C178000	C179799
1936	C179800	C183199
1937	C183200	C188699
1938	C188700	C189599
1939	C189600	C198899
1940	C198900	C199299
1941	C199300	C208799
1942	C208800	C215018
1943-1945: Commercial production interrupted by WWII		
1946	C221001	C222000
1947	C222001	C231999
1948	C232000	C238500
1949	C238501	C240000
1950	C240000	247701C
"C" SUFFIX STARTED WITH SER. NO. 240228		
1951	247701C	253179C
1952	253180C	259549C

MODEL 1911 AND 1911A1 – Comm. production Capital "C" prefix - .45 cal. cont.

Year	Ser. # Start	Ser. # End
1953	259550C	266349C
1954	266350C	270549C
1955	270550C	272549C
1956	272550C	276699C
1957	276700C	281999C
1958	282000C	283799C
1959	283800C	285799C
1960	285800C	287999C
1961	288000C	289849C
1962	289850C	291299C
1963	291300C	293799C
1964	293800C	295999C
1965	296000C	300299C
1966	300300C	308499C
1967	308500C	315599C
1968	315600C	324499C
1969	324500C	332649C
1970	332650C	336169C
Mid 1970 New	70G01001	70G05550
1971	70G05551	70G18000
1972	70G18001	70G34400
1973	70G34401	70G43000
1974	70G43001	70G73000
1975	70G73001	70G88900
1976	70G88901	70G99999
Mid-1976 New	01001G70	13900G70
1977	13901G70	45199G70
1978	45200G70	N/A

MODEL 1911 AND 1911A1 MILITARY PRODUCTION

Year	Ser. # Start	Ser. # End	Mfg.
1912	1	500	COLT
	501	1000	COLT USN
	1001	1500	COLT
	1501	2000	COLT USN
	2001	2500	COLT
	2501	3500	COLT USN
	3501	3800	COLT USMC
	3801	4500	COLT
	4501	5500	COLT USN
	5501	6500	COLT
	6501	7500	COLT USN
	7501	8500	COLT
	8501	9500	COLT USN
	9501	10500	COLT
	10501	11500	COLT USN
	11501	12500	COLT
	12501	13500	COLT USN
	13501	17250	COLT USN
1913	17251	36400	COLT
	36401	37650	COLT USMC
	37651	38000	COLT
	38001	44000	COLT USN
	44001	60400	COLT
1914	60401	72570	COLT
	72571	83855	SPRINGFIELD-

(THESE NUMBERS RESERVED FOR SPRINGFIELD)

	83856	83900	COLT
	83901	84400	COLT USMC
	84401	96000	COLT
	96001	97537	COLT USN
	97538	102596	COLT
	102597	107596	

SPRINGFIELD(RESERVED NO. RANGE)

1915	107597	109500	COLT
	109501	110000	COLT USN
	110001	113496	COLT
	113497	120566	SPRINGFIELD-

MODEL 1911 AND 1911A1 MILITARY PRODUCTION, cont.

Year	Ser. # Start	Ser. # End	Mfg.
(RESERVED FOR SPRINGFIELD)			
1915	120567	125566	COLT
	125567	133186	SPRINGFIELD-
(RESERVED FOR SPRINGFIELD)			
1916	133187	137400	COLT
1917	137401	151186	COLT
	151187	151986	COLT USMC
	151987	185800	COLT
	185801	186200	COLT USMC
	186201	209586	COLT
	209587	210386	COLT USMC
	210387	215386	COLT
FRAMES(RESERVED FOR RECEIVERS)			
	215387	216186	COLT USMC
	216187	216586	COLT
	216587	216986	COLT USMC
1918	216987	217386	COLT USMC
1918	217387	223952	COLT
	223953	223990	COLT USN
	223991	232000	COLT
	232001	233600	COLT USN
	233601	580600	COLT
	1	13152	REM. UMC
1919	13153	21676	REM. UMC
	580601	629500	COLT
	629501	717386	COLT
1924	700001	710000	COLT
1937	710001	712349	COLT USN
1938	712350	713645	COLT
1939	713646	717281	COLT USN
1940	717282	721977	COLT
1941	721978	756733	COLT
1942	756734	793657	COLT
	793658	797639	COLT USN
	797640	800000	COLT
	S800001	S800500	SINGER
	800501	801000	H&R
	801001	856100	COLT
1943	856101	958100	COLT
	**856101	856404	Replacement No
	**856405	916404	ITHACA
	**916405	1041404	REM. RAND
	1041405	1096404	US&S
	1088726	1208673	COLT
	1208674	1279673	ITHACA
	1279674	1279698	RE NO AA
	1279699	1441430	REM. RAND
	1441431	1471430	ITHACA
	1471431	1609528	REM. RAND
1944	1609529	1743846	COLT
	1743847	1816641	REM. RAND
	1816642	1890503	ITHACA
	1890504	2075103	REM. RAND
1945	2075104	2134403	ITHACA
	2134404	2244803	REM. RAND
	2244804	2380013	COLT
	2380014	2619013	REM. RAND
	2619014	2693613	ITHACA

** Denotes double issue ranges.

COLT SINGLE-ACTION MODEL NUMBERS

The author wishes to express thanks to Mr. Don Wilkerson for allowing the edited information published below from his 1986 Post-War Single-Action Revolver, 1976-1986 publication.

A working knowledge of model numbers for the various Colt single-action revolvers is a must for even a novice collector. Since the mid - 1970s Colt has placed the model number on the end label of the shipping cartons of virtually all their firearms. Many collectors and publications regularly use the model number to describe or differentiate between revolvers. Using the model number is an accurate and efficient method to delineate a particular variation. Example: .45 caliber revolver with a 4 3/4 in. barrel, blue and casehardened finish and eagle stocks can be described as a simple "P-1840."

Each Colt model is specified by an alphabetical letter and 4 numerical digits. The basic model number as it pertains to single-action revolvers can be broken down as follows:

MODEL P - basic type of frame. The letter "P" is used to delineate the single-action type of frame.

FIRST NUMERAL - "1" is the first model built on a particular type of frame. Numerals 2, 3, 4, etc.

COLT SINGLE-ACTION MODEL NUMBERS cont.

indicate later versions. These versions are not always numbered in numerical order and the same number has been used for different models at different times. A "1" denotes the basic standard single-action frame. A "2" denotes the new black powder frame available through the Colt Custom Gun Shop. A "3" has been used at various times to denote a non-standard frame or cylinder. The "4" is used to specify the New Frontier style of frame. Numbers such as "7" and "8" are frequently used to specify commemorative or special editions.

SECOND NUMERAL - specifies caliber. A "4" denotes .32-20, a "6" denotes .357 Magnum, a "7" denotes .44 Special, an "8" denotes .45 caliber, and a "9" specifies .44-40 caliber.*

THIRD NUMERAL - denotes barrel length. "3" is used to denote both a 3 inch and a 4 inch barrel. "4" is 4 3/4 inch or 5 inch, "5" is 5 1/2 inch, "7" is 7 1/2 inch, and "1" is 12 inch.*

FOURTH NUMERAL - is used to denote several different variations of the standard model. Some of the most common examples are: "1," "2," or "6" for nickel finish, "1" for full blue finish in the case of P-1871, and "2," "3," and "4" as used for the Sheriff's Model series to denote blue and casehardened finish, nickel finish, and Royal Blue and casehardened finish, respectively. The fourth numeral can also denote the type of stocks as in P-1673. The fourth numeral in the basic model designation must be used in conjunction with the preceding three numerals to determine its exact meaning. The fourth numeral is kind of a "catch-all" number. Many times this number serves only to differentiate a later model from a similar model assembled years earlier.

*The .32-20 caliber and the 5 inch barrel length are listed in the 1984 Colt Buyer's Guide, but as of this date neither have been produced.

STANDARD MODEL P REVOLVER CODES

The primary model numbers used by Colt for Model P revolvers produced since 1976 are as follows:

P-1640 - .357 Magnum, 4 3/4 in. barrel, blue finish, eagle stocks.
P-1641 - .357 Magnum, 4 3/4 in. barrel, nickel finish, wood stocks.
P-1650 - .357 Magnum, 5 1/2 in. barrel, blue finish, eagle stocks.
P-1656 - .357 Magnum, 5 1/2 in. barrel, nickel finish, wood stocks.
P-1670 - .357 Magnum, 7 1/2 in. barrel, blue finish, eagle stocks.
P-1673 - .357 Magnum, 7 1/2 in. barrel, blue finish, wood stocks.
P-1676 - .357 Magnum, 7 1/2 in. barrel, nickel finish, wood stocks.
P-1740 - .44 Special, 4 3/4 in. barrel, blue finish, eagle stocks.
P-1746 - .44 Special, 4 3/4 in. barrel, nickel finish, wood stocks.
P-1750 - .44 Special, 5 1/2 in. barrel, blue finish, eagle stocks.
P-1756 - .44 Special, 5 1/2 in. barrel, nickel finish, wood stocks.

STANDARD MODEL P REVOLVER CODES cont.

P-1770 - .44 Special, 7 1/2 in. barrel, blue finish, eagle stocks.
P-1776 - .44 Special, 7 1/2 in. barrel, nickel finish, wood stocks.
P-1716 - .44 Special, 12 in. barrel, nickel finish, wood stocks.
P-1840 - .45 Colt, 4 3/4 in. barrel, blue finish, eagle stocks.
P-1841 - .45 Colt, 4 3/4 in. barrel, nickel finish, wood stocks.
P-1850 - .45 Colt, 5 1/2 in. barrel, blue finish, eagle stocks.
P-1856 - .45 Colt, 5 1/2 in. barrel, nickel finish, wood stocks.
P-1870 - .45 Colt, 7 1/2 in. barrel, blue finish, eagle stocks.
P-1876 - .45 Colt, 7 1/2 in. barrel, nickel finish, wood stocks.
P-1813 - .45 Colt, 12 in. barrel, blue finish, eagle stocks.
P-1816 - .45 Colt, 12 in. barrel, nickel finish, wood stocks.
P-1940 - .44-40 caliber, 4 3/4 in. barrel, blue finish, eagle stocks.
P-1941* - .44-40 caliber, 4 3/4 in. barrel, nickel finish, wood stocks.
P-1950 - .44-40 caliber, 5 1/2 in. barrel, blue finish, eagle stocks.
P-1970 - .44-40 caliber, 7 1/2 in. barrel, blue finish, eagle stocks.
P-1976* - .44-40 caliber, 7 1/2 in. barrel, nickel finish, wood stocks.
P-1911 - .44-40 caliber, 12 in. barrel, nickel finish, wood stocks.

*These model numbers were used primarily for engraved or special ordered revolvers as the two models indicated were never produced as a regular model. "Blue finish" in the above chart denotes the standard blue finish, i.e., blue with case-hardened frame.

NEW FRONTIER MODEL

P-4671 - .357 Magnum, 7 1/2 in. barrel, nickel finish, wood stocks.
P-4750 - .44 Special, 5 1/2 in. barrel, Royal Blue finish, wood stocks.
P-4770 - .44 Special , 7 1/2 in. barrel, Royal Blue finish, wood stocks.
P-4840 - .45 Colt, 4 3/4 in. barrel, Royal Blue finish, wood stocks.

P-4850 - .45 Colt, 5 1/2 in. barrel, Royal Blue finish, wood stocks.
P-4870 - .45 Colt, 7 1/2 in. barrel, Royal Blue finish, wood stocks.

P-4940 - .44-40 caliber, 4 3/4 in. barrel, Royal Blue finish, wood stocks.

P-4970 - .44-40 caliber, 7 1/2 in. barrel, Royal Blue finish, wood stocks.

Note: The term "Royal Blue" in the New Frontier chart denotes a revolver with a casehardened frame and a Royal (high polish) Blue finish on the other major components.

SHERIFF'S MODELS

P-1932 - .44-40 caliber, 3 in. barrel, blue finish, eagle stocks.

P-1933* - .44-40/.44 Special, 3 in. barrel, nickel finish, wood stocks.

SHERIFF'S MODELS cont.

P-1934* - .44-40/.44 Special, 3 in. barrel, Royal Blue finish, wood stocks.

*Circa 1984 all Sheriff's Models are listed as single calibers: .44-40 or .45 caliber.

REVOLVERS WITH FULL BLUE FRAMES

Some of the "full blue" models have had more than one model number assigned to the same variation. As a result, a particular model may have been identified by different model numbers at different times. Following the model numbers and descriptions in this chart will be an approximate time frame during which that particular model was in use. No date following the description indicates that only one model number for that particular variation is known to the author (Don Wilkerson).

P-1640 - FB - .357 Magnum, 4 3/4 in. barrel, fluted cylinder, eagle stocks.

P-1650 - FB - .357 Magnum, 5 1/2 in. barrel, fluted cylinder, eagle stocks.

P-1740 - FB - .44 Special, 4 3/4 in. barrel, fluted cylinder, eagle stocks.

P-1750 - FB - .44 Special, 5 1/2 in. barrel, fluted cylinder, eagle stocks.

P-1770 - FB - .44 Special, 7 1/2 in. barrel, fluted cylinder, eagle stocks.

P-1770 - UB - .44 Special, 7 1/2 in. barrel, unfluted cylinder, eagle stocks.

P-3840 - .45 Colt, 4 3/4 in. barrel, both fluted and unfluted cylinders, eagle stocks (early to mid - 1982).

P-1840 - FB - .45 Colt, 4 3/4 in. barrel, fluted cylinder, eagle stocks (mid to late 1982 to date).

P-1840 - UB - .45 Colt, 4 3/4 in. barrel, unfluted cylinder, eagle stocks (mid to late 1982 to date).

P-1850 - FB - .45 Colt, 5 1/2 in. barrel, fluted cylinder, eagle stocks.

P-1850 - UB - .45 Colt, 5 1/2 in. barrel, unfluted cylinder, eagle stocks.

P-1871 - .45 Colt, 7 1/2 in. barrel, fluted cylinder, wood stocks (1977 to 1979).

P-1870 - FB - .45 Colt, 7 1/2 in. barrel, fluted cylinder, wood stocks (1982 to date).

P-1870 - UB - .45 Colt, 7 1/2 in. barrel, unfluted cylinder, wood stocks (1982 to date).

P-1871 - FB - .45 Colt, 12 in. barrel, fluted cylinder, eagle stocks.

FULL BLUE NEW FRONTIERS

P-4770 - FB - .44 Special, 7 1/2 in. barrel, fluted cylinder, wood stocks.

P-4870 - FB - .45 Colt, 7 1/2 in. barrel, fluted cylinder, wood stocks.

P-4870 - UB - .45 Colt, 7 1/2 in. barrel, unfluted cylinder, wood stocks.

MISCELLANEOUS MODEL NUMBERS

1750 - AA - .44 Special, 5 1/2 in. barrel, blue finish with nickel cylinder, eagle stocks.

1750 - AB - .44 Special, 5 1/2 in. barrel, blue finish with nickel cylinder with blue flutes, eagle stocks.

1840 - UC - .45 Colt, 4 3/4 in. barrel, blue finish, unfluted cylinder, eagle stocks.

1850 - UC - .45 Colt, 5 1/2 in. barrel, blue finish, unfluted cylinder, eagle stocks.

1870 - UC - .45 Colt, 7 1/2 in. barrel, blue finish, unfluted cylinder, eagle stocks.

Note: The term "blue finish" in this chart is the standard blue finish with a casehardened frame.

BLACK POWDER MODEL P REVOLVERS

P-2830 - .45 Colt, 3 in. barrel, blue finish.

P-2833 - .45 Colt, 3 in. barrel, nickel finish.

P-2834* - .45 Colt, 3 in. barrel, Royal Blue finish.

P-2836 - .45 Colt, 4 in. barrel, Royal Blue finish.

P-2837 - .45 Colt, 4 in. barrel, nickel finish.

P-2840 - .45 Colt, 4 3/4 in. barrel, blue finish.

P-2841 - .45 Colt, 4 3/4 in. barrel, nickel finish.

P-2847* - .45 Colt, 5 in. barrel, nickel finish.

P-2870 - .45 Colt, 7 1/2 in. barrel, blue finish.

P-2871 - .45 Colt, 7 1/2 in. barrel, nickel finish.

P-2940 - .44-40 caliber, 4 3/4 in. barrel, blue finish.

P-2941 - .44-40 caliber, 4 3/4 in. barrel, nickel finish.

P-2970 - .44-40 caliber, 7 1/2 in. barrel, blue finish.

P-2971 - .44-40 caliber, 7 1/2 in. barrel, nickel finish.

P-2437* - .32-20 caliber, 4 in. barrel, nickel finish.

P-2474* - .32-20 caliber, 7 1/2 in. barrel, Royal Blue finish.

*As of this writing these calibers have not been produced. The terms "blue finish" and "Royal" in this chart refer to Colt's standard single-action finish, i.e., casehardened frame with all components finished in either standard blue or Royal Blue.

MODEL 1077 LIGHTNING & THUNDERER DA

Year	Ser. # Start	Ser. # End
1877	1	2900
1878	3000	13499
1879	13500	18999
1880	19000	27999
1881	28000	33999
1882	34000	39999
1883	40000	47999
1884	48000	51499
1885	51500	52999
1886	53000	57499
1887	57500	62699
1888	62700	72499
1889	72500	73499
1890	73500	80499
1891	80500	85399
1892	85400	88999
1893	89000	94999
1894	95000	96999
1895	97000	101699
1896	101700	105199
1897	105200	107499
1898	107500	111499
1899	111500	115499
1900	115500	122699
1901	122700	130299
1902	130300	139999
1903	140000	148499
1904	148500	156199
1905	156200	158999
1906	159000	161999

MODEL 1877 LIGHTNING & THUNDERE DA, cont.

Year	Ser. # Start	Ser. # End
1907	162000	163999
1908	164000	164999
1909	165000	166849

MODEL 1878 SxS HAMMER SHOTGUN

1878	1	99
1879	100	2249
1880	2250	7849
1881	7850	11799
1882	11800	14999
1883	15000	17399
1884	17400	18549

MODEL 1883 SxS HAMMERLESS SHOTGUN

1885	18550	20349
1886	20350	21199
1888	22000	22499
1889	22500	22683
1883	1	249
1884	250	849
1885	850	1399
1886	1400	2199
1887	2200	3055
1888	3056	4057
1889	4058	4449
1890	4450	5349
1891	5350	6249
1892	6250	6749
1893	6750	7249
1894	7250	7549
1895	7550	8366

LIGHTNING SLIDE ACTION - SMALL FRAME

1887	1	999
1888	1000	7999
1889	8000	11749
1890	11750	14299
1891	14300	14699
1892	14700	15399
1893	15400	16599
1894	16600	19799
1895	19800	22999
1896	23000	25999
1897	26000	29599
1898	29600	35299
1899	35300	42799
1900	42800	52299
1901	52300	63299
1902	63300	73699
1903	73700	81999
1904	82000	89912

LIGHTNING SLIDE ACTION - MEDIUM FRAME

1884	1	3074
1885	3075	12649
1886	12650	20499
1887	20500	24999
1888	25000	32999
1889	33000	40999
1890	41000	49999
1891	50000	63199
1892	63200	65999
1893	66000	70999
1894	71000	75999
1895	76000	78999
1896	79000	80499
1897	80500	82499
1898	82500	83999
1899	84000	85799
1900	85800	87799
1901	87800	89299
1902	89300	89777

LIGHTNING SLIDE ACTION - LARGE FRAME

Year	Ser. # Start	Ser. # End
1887	1	999
1888	1000	2399
1889	2400	3799
1890	3800	5199
1891	5200	5699
1892	5700	5999
1893	6000	6299
1894	6300	6496

AR-15 - SPORTER MODELS

1963	SP00001	SP00023
SP00024-SP00100 Specials		
1964	SP00101	SP02500
1965	SP02501	SP05599
1966	SP05600	SP08249
1967	SP08250	SP10749
1968	SP10750	SP13999
1969	SP14000	SP14653
1970	SP15001	SP15473
1971	SP16001	SP19400
1972	SP19401	SP24200
1973	SP24201	SP32600
1974	SP32601	SP43800
1975	SP43801	SP55300
1976	SP55301	N/A

COLT BLACKPOWDER 2ND GENERATION SERIALIZATION

Model No.	Ser. # Range		Total	Start	End

MODEL 1851 NAVY

C-1121	4201	25100	20900	1971	1978
C-1122					

As above but at higher range of numbers Unk'n - 1978

MODEL 1851 NAVY, R. E. LEE

C-9001	251 REL	5000 REL	4750	-	1971

1851 NAVY, U. S. GRANT

C-9002	251 USG	5000 USG	4750	-	1971

MODEL 1851 GRANT-LEE PAIR

C-9003	01 GLP	250 GLP	250	-	1971

3rd MODEL DRAGOON

C-1770	20801	20826	25	1974	1978
Prototype	20901	24501	3601		
C-1770MN					
S/N As Above			20	1984	1984

MODEL 1851 NAVY

F-1100	24900	29150	4250	5/80	10/81
F-1101					
S/N As Above			300	10/81	11/81
W/Blank Cylinders					
F-1110	29151 S	29640 S	489	6/82	10/82
Stainless Steel					

MODEL 1860 ARMY

F-1200	201000	212835	7593	11/78	11/82
Rebated Cylinder					
F-1200 EBO					
S/N As Above			500	1979	1979
Butterfield					
F-1200 LNK					
S/N As Above			Unk'n	Unk'n	Unk'n
Electroless Nickel					
F-1200 MN					
S/N As Above			12	1984	1984

Model No.	Ser. # Range		Total	Start	End
MODEL 1860 ARMY cont.					
Nickel/Ivory					
F-1202					
S/N As Above			500	1979	1979
Limited Edition					
F-1203	207330	211250	2670	7/80	10/81
Fluted Cylinder					
F-1210	211263 S	212540 S	1278	1/82	4/82
Stainless Steel					
1861 NAVY					
F-1300	40000	43165	3166	9/80	10/81
1862 POCKET NAVY					
F-1400	48000	58850	5765	12/79	11/81
and skip odd no.					
F-1400MN					
S/N As Above			25	1984	1984
Nickel/Ivory					
F-1401					
S/N As Above			500	1979	1980
Limited Edition					
1862 POCKET POLICE					
F-1500	49000	57300	4801	1/80	9/81
and skip even no.					
F-1500 MN					
S/N As Above			25	1984	1984
Nickel/Ivory					
F-1501					
S/N As Above			500	1979	1980
Limited Edition					
1847 WALKER					
F-1600	1200	4120	2573	6/80	4/82
	32256	32500	245	5/81	9/81
1st MODEL DRAGOON					
F-1700	25100	34500	3878	1/80	2/82
2nd MODEL DRAGOON					
F-172 S/N As Above and Mix at Random for					
1st, 2nd & 3rd			2676	1/80	2/82
3rd MODEL DRAGOON					
F-140 S/N As Above and Mix at Random for					
1st, 2nd & 3rd		2856	1/80	2/82	
	31401	31450	50	10/81	11/81
F-1740 EGA Unk'n	Unk'n		200	1982	1982
(Garabaldi Model <- "GCA" prefix)					
BABY DRAGOON					
F-1760	16000	17851	1852	2/81	4/81
F-1761 S/N As Above			500	1979	1980
Limited Edition					
1860 ARMY					
F-9005 US 001/001 US to					
US 3025/3025 US			3025	9/77	1/80
Cavalry Commemorative (Two Gun Set)					
HERITAGE WALKER					
F-9006	01	1853	1853	6/80	6/81

JOHN DICKSON & SON SERIALIZATION

Year Starting	Serial Number
1812-1854	1-1500
1860	2000
1864	2500
1870	3000
1878	3500
1885	3933
1886	4000
1889	4889
1892	4500
1898	5000
1903	5500

A.H. FOX SERIALIZATION

GRADE A-F 12 GAUGE

Year Starting	Serial Number
1907	7500
1908	7600
1909	9900
1910	15000
1911	18700
1912	20000
1913	20700
1914	21500
1915	22000
1916	23200
1917	24300
1918	24700
1919	25000
1920	25900
1921	27000
1922	27900
1923	29000
1924	30000
1925	30900
1926	31600
1927	32000
1928	32900
1929	33850
1930	33900
1931	33999
1932	34100
1933	34200
1934	34300
1935	34400
1936	34500

GRADE A-F 16 GAUGE

Year Starting	Serial Number
1937	34750
1938	34900
1939	35150
1940	35280
1912	300075
1913	300200
1914	300400
1915	300600
1916	300700
1917	300750
1918	300800
1919	300900
1920	301100
1921	301300
1922	301500
1923	301800
1924	302000

GRADE A-F 16 GAUGE cont.

Year Starting	Serial Number
1925	302300
1926	302500
1927	302650
1928	302800
1929	303000
1930	303050
1931	303100
1932	303200
1933	303300
1934	303350
1935	303400
1936	303500
1937	303650
1938	303800
1939	303850
1940	303870
Highest no.	303875

GRADE A-F 20 GAUGE

Year Starting	Serial Number
1912	200100
1913	200250
1914	200500
1915	200700
1916	200800
1917	200900
1918	201000
1919	201300
1920	201500
1921	201600
1922	201800
1923	202000
1924	202200
1925	202400
1926	202500
1927	202800
1928	202950
1929	203100
1930	203150
1931	203200
1932	203300
1933	203350
1934	203500
1935	203700
1936	203750
1937	203800
1938	203830
1939	203900
1940	203970
Highest no.	203974

STERLINGWORTH 12 GAUGE

Year Starting	Serial Number
1910	53800
1911	59000
1912	63500
1913	66500
1914	74200
1915	75600
1916	77500
1917	79000
1918	82000
1919	84500
1920	89500
1921	92300
1922	94500
1923	97500
1924	99000
1925	100600
1926	105500
1927	113500

STERLINGWORTH 12 GAUGE cont.

Year Starting	Serial Number
1928	119000
1929	122600
1930	128500
1931	130000
1932	132000
1933	134000
1934	136000
1935	138000
1936	139000
1937	145000
1938	150000
1939	155000
1940	161500
Highest no.	161556

STERLINGWORTH 16 GA.

Year Starting	Serial Number
1913	351000
1914	351600
1915	352300
1916	353000
1917	353700
1918	354200
1919	355000
1920	356500
1921	357000
1922	357800
1923	358500
1924	359500
1925	359900
1926	360300
1927	362000
1928	364500
1929	366400
1930	367500
1931	368000
1932	368600
1933	369200
1934	369900
1935	372000
1936	373500
1937	374200
1938	374800
Highest no.	378481

STERLINGWORTH 20 GAUGE

Year Starting	Serial Number
1912	250100
1913	252000
1914	253000
1915	254500
1916	254600
1917	254700
1918	255000
1919	255300
1920	255800
1921	256100
1922	256400
1923	256800
1924	257200
1925	257700
1926	258200
1927	259300
1928	260500
1929	262000
1930	263600
1931	263800
1932	264000
1933	264300
1934	264600
1935	266500

STERLINGWORTH 20 GAUGE cont.

Year Starting	Serial Number
1936	268500
1937	270500
1938	270800
1939	271200
1940	271225
Highest no.	271304

SINGLE BARREL TRAP - GRADE J, K, L, M

Year Starting	Serial Number
1919	400090
1920	400250
1921	400275
1922	400300
1923	400325
1924	400350
1925	400375
1926	400385
1927	400395
1928	400400
1929	400410
1930	400415
1931	400425
1932	400500
1933	400525
1934	400540
1935	400568

STEPHEN GRANT SERIALIZATION

Year Starting	Serial Number
1867	2480
1870	3000
1875	3900
1880	4750
1885	5450
1890	6100
1895	6700
1896	6857
1900	7300

W. W. GREENER SERIALIZATION

Year Starting	Serial Number
1878	19304
1880	22860
1895	38917
1902	50911
1915	58536
1920	62621
1930	68635
1967	79259

HARRINGTON & RICHARDSON SERIALIZATION 1940 - 1982

The following serial numbered prefixes are related to the corresponding year of manufacture:

Year Starting	S.N. Prefix
1940	A
1941	B
1942	C

H&R SERIALIZATION, cont.

Year Starting	S.N. Prefix
1943	D
1944	E
1945	F
1946	G
1947	H
1948	I
1949	J
1950	K
1951	L
1952	M
1953	N
1954	P
1955	R
1956	S
1957	T
1958	U
1959	V
1960	W
1961	X
1962	Y
1963	Z
1964	AA
1965	AB
1966	AC
1967	AD
1968	AE
1969	AF
1970	AG
1971	AH(Snap on forecap)
1972	AJ
1973	AL
1974	AM
1975	AN
1976	AP
1977	AR(Striker Mech. Intr.)
1978	AS
1979	AT
1980	AU
1981	AX
1982	AY

H&R SINGLE BARREL SHOTGUNS

The following is a years of production listing for all Main Line single barrel shotguns produced by Harrington & Richardson with a cross reference to Deluxe and Youth variations.

MODEL	DATES	YEARS MFG.
1900	1901-1916	15 Years
1905 (Small Frame)		
	1906-1915	10 Years
1908	1909-1930	32 Years
1915 (Small Frame)		
	1916-1930	15 Years
No. 5	1931-1942	12 Years
No. 8	1931-1942	12 Years
48 (First use of the TOPPER name)		
	1943-1956	14 Years
188 (Deluxe variant of Model 48)		
	1943-1956	14 Years
148	1957-1961	5 Years
488 (Deluxe variant of Model 148)		
	1957-1961	5 Years
480 (Youth variant of Model 148)		
	1957-1961	5 Years
158	1962-1973	12 Years
198 (Deluxe variant of Model 158)		
	1962-1973	12 Years
490 (Youth variant of Model 158)		
	1962-1981	20 Years
058	1974-1981	8 Years

H&R SINGLE BARREL SHOTGUNS cont.

MODEL	DATES	YEARS MFG.
098 (Deluxe variant of Model 058)		
	1974-1981	8 Years
088 (Economy model)		
	1979-1986	5 Years
088 JR (Youth variant of Model 088)		
	1979-1986	5 Years
099 Deluxe 1982-1986		5 Years

HIGH STANDARD SERIALIZATION

The author wishes to express thanks to Mr. John J. Stimson, Jr. for the following information.
The serial numbers listed represent the highest serial number shipped for the year. Regular serial numbers began with 5,000 which was shipped October 15, 1932. Although it appears the guns were generally assembled in numerical sequence, the shipments were not and some guns may have remained in inventory for weeks, monthes, or even years between assenbly and shipment.

Year	Serial Number
1932	5,102
1933	6,567
1934	8,313
1935	11,651
1936	18,751
1937	30,026
1938	39,430
1939	50,619
1940	70,715
1941	91,986
1942	104,520
1943	115,423
1944	135,659
1945	145,817
1946	174,194
1947	233,402
1948	301,349
1949	326,123
1950	335,693
1951	356,899
1952	357,295
1953	442,984
1954	475,186
1955	508,613
1956	652,405
1957	776,129
1958	913,111
1959	1,044,802
1960	1,147,641
1961	1,224,652
1962	1,285,049
1963	1,353,764
1964	1,418,870
1965	1,507,541
1966	1,610,707
1967	1,853,513
1968	2,030,404
1969	2,172,356
1970	2,232,503
1971	2,828,293
1972	2,356,207
1973	2,424,175
1974	2,469,497

HIGH STANDARD, cont.

1975 is the last year of the regular serial number series (except for Sr. No. 2,500,811 shipped August 28, 1976) and marks the beginning of the letter prefix serialization.

Year	Sr. No.	Sr. No.	Sr. No.
1975	2,500,810	G 04,566	ML 06,747
1976		G 13,757	ML 23,065
1977	G 18,298	G 162,590	ML 29,707
1978	G 20,223		ML 41,270
1979			ML 63,483
1980	MLG 20,408		ML 81,629
1981	SH 18,446		ML 90,000
1982	SH 25,964		
1983	SH 31,558		
1984	SH 34,034		

HOLLAND & HOLAND SERIALIZATION

PARADOX SERIES

Year Starting	Serial Number
1885	11500
1886	N/A
1887	N/A
1888	11691
1889	11788
1890	11865
1891	11948
1895	15036
1892	15075
1895	15347
1900	15558
1903	15655
1905	15750
1906	15825
1907	15860
1911	15900
1914	15950
1919	19560
1922	15970
1930	15980
1956	15979

RECORDED DATES

Year Starting	Serial Number
March 1856	565(First Recorded Date)
October 1868	580
February 1857	584
August 1859	700
A gap in records	728-1059
1864	1060
1865	1101
1868	1352
1869	1439
1870	1578
1871	1769
1872	2002
1873	2401
1874	2759
1875	3174
1876	3649
1877	4179
1878	4774
1879	5274
1880	5819
1881	6382
1882	7009
1883	7473
1884	7904

Holland & Holland, cont. RECORDED DATES cont.

Year Starting	Serial Number
1885	8406
1886	8809
1887	8999
Unused	9000-10000
Missing	10000-10849
Rook Rifles	10850-10999
Normal Series	11000-11499
Paradox Guns	11500-11999
Normal Series	12000-12999
Rook Rifles	13000-13999
Normal Series	14000-14999
Paradox Guns	15000-15999
Normal Series	16000-16999
Normal Series	17000-17399
Rifles and Rook Rifles	17400-17999
Believed Unused	18000-18999
Rifles	19000-19999
Misc. Guns and Rifles	20000-21999
See separate lists	22000+

ROOK RIFLES

Year Starting	Serial Number
1887	10850-10999
Assumed 1888 records missing	11000-11499
1889	13106
1890	13465
1891	13566
1892	13674
1893	13885-13999
1894 Rrook/others rifles	17401
1899	17999

MAGAZINE RIFLES

Year Starting	Serial Number
1910	28000
1911	28100
1913	28199
1913	28300
1919	28399
1920-29	1-581
1930-33	582-880
1920-32	881-1181
1935-49	1182-1782
1949-60	1783-2179
1951-58	2180-2577
1952-62	2578-2977
1958-65	2978-3377
1964-74	3378-3783
1975-80	3784-4000
1981-87	4001-4250
1988-92	4251-4330

PLAIN GUNS

Year Starting	Serial Number
1907	26200
1908	26300
1909	26400
1909	26500
1910	26600
1911	26700
1912	26800
1913	26900
1913	26999
1913	28600
1914	28700
1914	28800
1915	28900
1915	28999

PLAIN GUNS, cont.

Year Starting	Serial Number
1915	29500
1915	29600
1916	29700
1919	29800
1919	29900
1919	30000
1920	30100
1922	30200
1924	30300
1925	30334
1925	31100
1926	31200
1928	31300
1929	31399
1929	32200
1931	32300
1933	32400
1935	32499
1935	34000
1936	34100
1937	34200
1939	34300
1949	34400
1953	34500
1956	34600
1961	34700
1975	34800

ROYAL GUNS

Year Starting	Serial Number
1899	22000
1900	22500
1902	23000
1903	23500
1906	25000
1907	25500
1910	25599
1910	27000
1911	27250
1912	27500
1913	27750
1914	27999
1914	29000
1915	29100
1919	29200
1920	29300
1920	29400
1921	29499
1921	30500
1922	30600
1922	30700
1924	30800
1925	30900
1926	30999
1926	31500
1927	31600
1927	31700
1928	31800
1929	31900
1929	32900
1934	32999
1934	33000
1935	33100
1936	33200
1937	33300
1937	33400
1939	33500
1946	33600
1948	33700
1950	33800
1952	33900
1954	33999
1954	36251

ROYAL GUNS cont.

Year Starting	Serial Number
1956	36300
1958	36400
1959	36500
1962	36600
1964	36700
1965	36800
1970	36900
1970	40006
1972	40100
1974	40200
1979	40300
1980	40400
1981	40500
1982	40530
1983	40560
1984	40590
1985	40650
1986	40770
1987	40820
1988	40880
1989	40920
1990	41000
1991	41075
1992	41150
1993	41210

ROYAL OVER & UNDER GUNS

Year Starting	Serial Number
1950	36000
1952	36010
1954	36020
1958	36029
1993	51001

SPORTING OVER & UNDER GUNS

Year Starting	Serial Number
1993	50500

CAVALIER GUNS

Year Starting	Serial Number
1986	50001
1989	50150
1992	50250

ROYAL DOUBLE RIFLES - .450 & .465

Year Starting	Serial Number
1910	28200
1914	28299
1914	28500
1919	28535
1921	30335
1921	30415
1925	31042
1925	31049
1927	32000
1941	32099

ROYAL DOUBLE RIFLES - .375

Year Starting	Serial Number
1911	28400
1920	28499
1920	30416
1925	30499
1925	31050
1927	31099
1927	32100
1933	32199

ROYAL DOUBLE RIFLES - .240 & Small Bores

Year Starting	Serial Number
1920	28566
1923	28599
1923	31000
1926	31041
1926	31400
1931	31450
1955	31499

ROYAL DOBLE RIFLES ALL CALIBRES

Year Starting	Serial Number
1933	35000
1939	35100
1950	35200
1953	35250
1956	35300
1963	35350
1968	35450
1975	35495
1977	35498
1980	35500
1981	35505
1984	35524
1985	35527
1988	35540
1989	35542
1990	35552
1991	35590

ITALIAN YEAR OF MFG. DATE CODES

Additional information regarding Italian Proof marks, and dates of manufacture can be found in *THE WORLD OF BERETTA An International Legend* by R. L. Wilson. www.bluebookinc.com to order.

THE WORLD OF BERETTA
AN INTERNATIONAL LEGEND

R. L. WILSON

All Dates Prior to 1954 Have Year in Digits.

Code	Year
I =	1945
II =	1946
III =	1947
IV =	1948
V =	1949
VI =	1950
VII =	1951
VIII =	1952
IX =	1953
X =	1954
XI =	1955
XII =	1956
XIII =	1957
XIV =	1958
XV =	1959
XVI =	1960
XVII =	1961
XVIII =	1962
XIX =	1963
XX =	1964
XXI =	1965

ITALIAN, cont.

Code	Year
XXII =	1966
XXIII =	1967
XXIV =	1968
XXV =	1969
XXVI =	1970
XX7 =	1971
XX8 =	1972
XX9 =	1973
XXX =	1974
AA =	1975
AB =	1976
AC =	1977
AD =	1978
AE =	1979
AF =	1980
AH =	1981
AI =	1982
AL =	1983
AM =	1984
AN =	1985
AP =	1986
AS =	1987
AT =	1988
AW =	1989
AZ =	1990
BA =	1991
BB =	1992
BC	1993
BD	1994
BF	1995
BH	1996
BI	1997
BL	1998
BM	1999
BN	2000
BP	2001
BS	2002
BT	2003
BU	2004
BZ	2005
CA	2006
CB	2007
CC	2008

ITHACA GUN CO. SERIALIZATION

BAKER MODEL ITHACA DOUBLES

Year Starting	Serial Number
1880-1885	2447
1886	4104
1887	7003
1888	8787
1889 (Jan.-Aug.)	10534

CRASS MODEL ITHACA DOUBLES

Year Starting	Serial Number
1892	17235-21999
1893	25421
1894	25759

CRASS MODEL ITHACA DOUBLES

Year Starting	Serial Number
1895	27762
1896	28713
1897	30222
1898	33026

CRASS MODEL ITHACA DOUBLES, cont.

Year Starting	Serial Number
1899	38399
1900	46627
1901	61609
1902	76599
1903	94108

FLUES MODEL ITHACA DOUBLE & SINGLE

Year Starting	Serial Number
1908	175000-182031
1909	192499
1910	205399
1911	216499
1912	230099
1913	242599
1914	256699
1915	268199
1916	276899
1917	289299
1918	299799
1919	315399
1920	343335
1921	356513
1922	361849
1923	372099
1924	390499
1925	398352
1926	398365

N.I.D. MODEL ITHACA DOUBLE

Year Starting	Serial Number
1925	425000-425299
1926	439199
1927	451099
1928	454530
1929	457299
1930	458399
1931	459139
1932	459162
1933	459195
1935	459637
1936	459649
1935	460799
1936	462399
1937	464699
1938	464827
1939	464850
1940	464899
1938	465199
1939	465999
1940	466999
1941	467146
1946	467199
1941	468099
1946	468699
1947	468794
1948	468799
1947	469949
1948	469979
1948	470099

CHARLES LANCASTER SERIALIZATION

Year Starting	Serial Number
1826	100
1830	600
1840	1200
1850	2100

CHARLES LANCASTER SERIALIZATION, cont.

Year Starting	Serial Number
1860	3200
1861	3400
1862	3540
1863	3693
1864	3805
1865	3914
1866	3999
1867	4087
1868	4183
1869	4271
1870	4328
1871	4401
1872	4477
1873	4562
1874	4644
1875	4714
1876	4769
1877	4833
1878	4892
1879	4924
1880	4949
1881	4982
1882	5079
1883	5186
1884	5359
1885	5497
1886	5627
1887	5764
1888	5926
1889	6136
1890	6406
1891	6671
1892	6988
1893	7189
1894	7360
1895	7548
1896	7709
1897	7940
1898	8132
1899	8353
1900	8529
1901	8700

JOSEPH LANG SERIALIZATION

Year Starting	Serial Number
1858	2085
1860	2332
1865	2970
1870	3916
1875	5180
1880	6000
1885	7031
1890	7546
1895	8150
1900	9100

MARLIN FIREARMS COMPANY SERIALIZATION

Approximate serialization for Marlin rifles from 1883 to 1906 including Models 1881, 1888, 1889, 1891, 1892, 1893, 1894, and 1897. Marlin did not assign a specific block of Ser. No. to these models, rather the models being produced that time were mixed. Using this list will place the year of manufacture plus or minus one year.

For a factor letter on an older Marlin firearm, contact the Buffalo Bill Historical center, Cody Firearms Museum, 720 Sheridan Ave., Cody, WY 82414. Web site www.bbhc.org or phone 307-587-4771. There is a $45 fee per serial number search.

Older Rifles Mfg.

Year	From #	To #
1883	4001	6700
1884	6701	8850
1885	8851	11300
1886	11301	15000
1887	15001	17800
1888	17801	21500
1889	21501	30000
1890	30001	45000
1891	45001	63250
1892	63251	80250
1893	80251	95750
1894	95751	115000
1895	115001	133000
1896	133001	144400
1897	144401	161200
1898	161201	175500
1899	175501	196000
1900	196001	213000
1901	213001	233300
1902	233301	262500
1903	262501	287300
1904	287301	310500
1905	310501	329000
1906	329001	355300

1948-1968 Mfg.

Year	Serial No. Prefix
1948	E
1949	F
1950	G
1951	H
1952	J
1953	K
1954	L
1955	M
1956	N
1957	P
1957-1958	R
1958-1959	S
1960	T
1960-Aug. 1961	U
1961-Aug. 1962	V
1963	W
1964	Y & Z
1965	AA

MARLIN 1948-1968 Mfg. cont.

Year	Serial No. Prefix
1966	AB
1967	AC
1968	AD

MAUSER BROOMHANDLES SERIALIZATION 1896 - late 1930

Ser. #	Date	Nature of Changes
before	1896	-The cone hammer used in place of spur hammer.
#25	1896	- "SYSTEM MAUSER" marked on top of the chamber.
before	1897	- The locking system changed from one to two lugs.
#200		- The barrel contour at the chamber is tapered instead of stepped.
#390	1897	- "WAFFENFABRIK MAUSER OBERNDORF A/N" marked on top of the chamber.
#975	1897	- The center section of the rear panel on the left side of the frame is not milled out (this feature appears earlier on a few 20-shot pistols). This area is sometimes used for special markings on contract pieces such as the Turkish and Persian.
#12,200 to #14,999	1898	- The large ring hammer replaces the cone hammer.
#21,000	1899	- There is no panel milling on either side of the frame.
		- A single lug bayonet type mount adopted for retaining the firing pin instead of the dovetail plate.
		- The trigger is mounted directly to the frame by two integral lugs rather than attached to a removable block.
		- The position of the serial number moved from the rear of the frame above the stock slot to the left side of the chamber.
#22,000	1900	- Two integral lugs used to mount the rear sight instead of a pin.
#29,000	1902	- Very shallow panels milled into the frame on both sides.*
#31,200	1903	- "WAFFENFABRIK MAUSER OBERNDORF A NECKAR" added to the right rear frame panel.*
#34,000	1904	- The depth of the frame panel milling increased.*
#35,000	1904	- The barrel extension side rails lengthened about a half inch.*
		- An additional lug for mounting added to the firing pin.*
		- The hammer changed to the small ring pattern.*
		- The safety mechanism altered to require that the lever be pushed up to engaged it instead of down.*
		- The center of the safety lever knob is no longer milled out.*
#38,000	1905	- The short extractor with two ribs replaces the long thin extractor.*
#100,000	1910	- The rifling changed from four groove to six groove.
	to	
#130,000	1911	
#270,000	1915	- "NS" (Neues Sicherung or New Safety) appears on the back of the hammer. The hammer must be moved back beyond the cocked position to engage the safety.
#440,000	1921	- The lanyard ring stud is rotated 90 degrees.
#501,000	1923	- The Mauser "banner" appears on the left rear frame panel.
#800,000	1930	- The Mauser banner is enlarged.
		- A step is added to the barrel contour just ahead of the chamber.

MAUSER BROOMHANDLES, cont.

Ser. #	Date	Nature of Changes
		- The safety is changed to allow the hammer to be dropped from a cocked position, without danger, by pulling the trigger (called Universal Safety).
		- The front of the grip frame widened to equal the rear part where the stock slot is.
#850,000	1932	- "D.R.P.u.A.P." (Deutsches Reich Patenten und Anderes Patenten) added below the inscription on the right rear frame panel.
#860,000	1932	- The lettering in the frame inscription is slanted forward.
#900,000	1934	- The serial number is moved to the rear of the barrel extension behind the sight.
		- The two grooves in each side of the barrel extension side rails are eliminated.

*These nine changes appear out of sequence on three small batches of guns (29,000 to 29,900, 40,000 to 41,000, and 42,600 to 43,900). Most of these pistols are of the "bolo" style, that is they have 3.9 inch barrels, small grips, six or 10-shot magazines and fixed or adjustable rear sights. A few of these pistols show non-standard barrel contours, barrel extension milling and hammer safety devices. Apparently the factory withheld these numbers from the regular production series and reissued them at later dates.

PARKER BROTHERS SHOTGUNS SERIALIZATION 1866 - 1942

Additional information regarding Parker shotgun is available in PARKER GUN IDENTIFICATION & SERIALIZATION compiled and edited by Charles E. Price & S.P. Fjestad available on www.bluebook-inc.com.

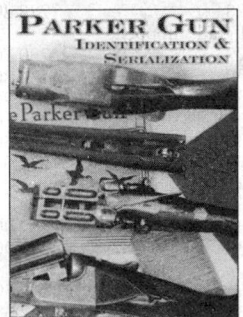

Year Starting	Serial Number
1866-1868	0-6,800
1868-1877	9,700
1877-1879	15,700
1880	17,600
1881	22,700
1882	27,300
1883	34,900
1884	36,000

PARKER BROTHERS, cont.

Year Starting	Serial Number
1885	46,450
1886	48,125
1887	56,650
1889	59,500
1890	61,350
1891	66,800
1892	71,600
1893	77,000
1894	80,300
1895	82,400
1896	85,200
1897	86,450
1898	89,350
1899	92,450
1900	97,300
1901	105,750
1902	113,100
1903	121,900
1904	129,200
1905	132,000
1906	138,300
1907	144,250
1908	148,250
1910	153,000
1911	157,050
1912	157,800

first year of Trojan grade

Year Starting	Serial Number
1913	165,000
1914	168,200
1915	171,500
1916	173,450
1917	175,650

first single barrel trap gun

Year Starting	Serial Number
1918	180,250
1919	184,900
1920	190,100
1921	195,000
1922	200,500

first Parker single trigger

Year Starting	Serial Number
1923	205,150
1924	207,150

first beaver tail forend

Year Starting	Serial Number
1925	214,400
1926	218,050

first ventilated rib, first .410

Year Starting	Serial Number
1927	222,650
1928	228,200

PH grade dropped

Year Starting	Serial Number
1929	230,700
1930	234,200
1931	235,950
1932	236,100
1933	236,300
1934	236,650

first skeet guns, takeover of factory by Remington

Year Starting	Serial Number
1935	237,000
1936	239,900

last regular catalog

Year Starting	Serial Number
1937	240,300
1938-1942	242,385

PIOTTI SERIALIZATION

Year Starting	Serial Number
1962	1
1962	515
1963	1285
1964	1913

PIOTTI SERIALIZATION, cont.

Year Starting	Serial Number
1965	2594
1966	2988
1967	3351
1968	3954
1969	4787
1970	5018
1971	5499
1972	5815
1973	6180
1974	6437
1975	6650
1976	6839
1977	7025
1978	7236
1979	7388
1980	7524
1981	7663
1982	7797
1983	7918
1984	8038
1985	8179
1986	8318
1987	8465
1988	8605
1989	8753
1990	8878
1991	8978
1992	9063

JAMES PURDEY & SONS, LTD. SERIALIZATION

Year	Serial Number
1814	974
1826	1149
1827	1324
1828	1549
1829	1874
1830	1999
1831	2247
1832	2421
1833	2497
1834	2697
1835	2773
1836	2848
1837	3098
1838	3223
1839	3298
1840	3473
1841	3623
1842	3698
1843	3848
1844	3998
1845	4048
1846	4098
1847	4223
1848	4348
1849	4473
1850	4599
1851	4720
1852	4844
1853	4944
1854	5093
1855	5167
1856	5267
1857	5443
1858	5542
1859	5747
1860	5997
1861	6271

JAMES PURDEY & SONS, LTD. cont.

Year Starting	Serial Number
1862	6422
1863	6671
1864	6871
1865	7121
1866	7420
1867	7646
1868	7896
1869	8246
1870	8322
1871	8646
1872	8821
1873	9096
1874	9288
1875	9505
1876	9648
1877	10153
1878	10440
1879	10800
1880	10900
1881	11082
1882	11342
1883	11669
1884	12036
1885	12171
1886	12530
1887	12875
1888	13150
1889	13468
1890	13662
1891	14000
1892	14520
1893	14851
1894	15134
1895	15362
1896	15726
1897	16095
1898	16420
1899	16736
1900	17078
1901	17227
1902	17547
1903	17849
1904	18148
1905	18400
1906	18686
1907	18987
1908	19272
1909	19546
1910	19813
1911	20147
1912	20400
1913	20770
1914	21086
1915	21332
1916	21465
1917	21541
1919	21574
1920	21892
1921	22111
1922	22312
1923	22491
1924	22896
1925	22937
1926	23283
1927	23284
1928	23551
1929	23854
1930	24139
1931	24387
1932	24567
1933	24647
1934	24743

JAMES PURDEY & SONS, LTD. cont.

Year Starting	Serial Number
1935	24920
1936	25130
1937	25325
1938	25526
1939	25711
1940	25783
1941	25793
1942	25813
1943	25844
1945	25851
1946	25901
1947	25990
1948	26051
1949	26128
1950	26206
1951	26275
1952	26349
1953	26423
1955	26531
1975	28003
1979	28546
1981	28569

REMINGTON DATE CODE DATA & SxS SHOTGUN SERIALIZATION

Firearms Identification (Code located on barrel, left side at frame) Month of Manufacture (Code letter corresponds to numeral underneath).

The following barrel code information is reliable when used to identify the month and year of manufacture of Remington rifles since Remington seldom replaced barrels. When used to date Remington shotguns, where the barrel is easily changed, make sure the barrel is original to the shotgun.

For example "KP" would be 5 (May) 1923, and "RYY" would be 11 (November) 1952.

B	L	A	C	K	P	O	W	D	E	R	X
1	2	3	4	5	6	7	8	9	10	11	12

Year of Manufacture and letter code

Year	Letter code
1921	M
1922	N
1923	P
1924	R
1925	S
1926	T
1927	U
1928	W
1929	X
1930	Y
1931	Z
1932	A
1933	B
1934	C
1935	D
1936	E
1937	F
1938	G
1939	H
1940	J
1941	K
1942	L
1943	MM

REMINGTON cont.

Year of Manufacture and letter code

Year	Code
1944	NN
1945	PP
1946	RR
1947	SS
1948	TT
1949	UU
1950	WW
1951	XX
1952	YY
1953	ZZ
1954	A
1955	B
1956	C
1957	D
1958	E
1959	F
1960	G
1961	H
1962	J
1963	K
1964	L
1965	M
1966	N
1967	P
1968	R
1969	S
1970	T
1971	U
1972	W
1973	X
1974	Y
1975	Z
1976	I
1977	O
1978	Q
1979	V
1980	A
1981	B
1982	C
1983	D
1984	E
1985	F
1986	G
1987	H
1988	I
1989	J
1990	K
1991	L
1992	M
1993	N
1994	O
1995	P
1996	Q
1997	R
1998	S
1999	T*
2000	U*
2001	V*
2002	W
2003	X
2004	Y
2005	Z
2006	A
2007	B
2008	C

Additional markings if present will indicate the following.

2	Part order replacement bbl.
3	Service section repair.
4	Returned as received.
5	Employee sale.

* Remington suspended barrel date code stamping circa August 1999 - October 2001, but did continue to mark shipping box end flaps with the date code.

The author wishes to express thanks to Mr. Charles Semmer for the following Remington SxS shotgun serialization information.

E. REMINGTON & SONS
WHITMORE MODELS

Model	Years	Ser. Block	Est. Total
1873	1873-1878	1-5000	5000
1875	1875-1877	1-3350	3350
1876	1876-1882	3350-5900	2250
1878	1878-1882	1-2400	2400
1879	1879-1888	W/ 1878	N/A

E. REMINGTON & SONS
MODELS 1882, 1883, 1885 AND 1887

Model	Years	Ser. Block	Est. Total
1882	1882-1888	1000-17000	16000
1883	1882-1884	W/ 1882	N/A
1885	1885-1886	16700-202003500	
1887	1886-1888	20200-237003500	

REMINGTON ARMS COMPANY
MODEL 1889 TOTAL Mfg. 134200

Year Starting	Serial Number
1888	W/ 1887
1889	30000-32199
1890	32200-36949
1891	36950-43012
1892	43013-49844
1893	49845-58879
1894	58880-66016
1895	66017-73571
1896	73572-76980
1897	76981-80389
1898	80390-89123
1899	89124-97714
1900	EST. 97715-105000
1900	EST. 200000-205934
1901	205935-221450
1902	221451-234803
1903	234804-240530
1904	240531-247581
1905	247582-251192
1906	251193-254394
1907	254395-257745
1908	257746-259246
1909	N/A
1910	259247-259262

REMINGTON ARMS COMPANY
MODEL 1900 TOTAL Mfg. 98508

Year Starting	Serial Number
1900	300000-305000
1901	305001-317502
1902	317503-337038
1903	337039-343893
1904	343894-350207
1905	350208-354620
1906	354621-363060
1907	363061-372117
1908	372118-377925
1909	377926-382072
1910	382073-398507
1911	398508

REMINGTON ARMS COMPANY
MODEL 1894 TOTAL Mfg. 41194

Year Starting	Serial Number
1894	100,000-100,660
1895	100,661-103,106
1896	103,107-104,144
1897	104,145-106,916
1898	106,917-110,895
1899	110,896-116,139
1900	116,140-120,932
1901	120,933-123,913
1902	123,914-127,017
1903	127,018-129,349
1904	129,350-131,263
1905	131,264-133,042
1906	133,043-134,627
1907	134,628-136,292
1908	136,293-137,319
1909	137,320-137,988
1910	137,989-141,194

REMINGTON ARMS COMPANY
MODEL 1894 REM. SPCL.
TOTAL Mfg. Aprox. 12, W/ 4 recorded

Year Starting	Serial Number
1902-1910	400000-400012

SAVAGE/STEVENS PRODUCTION DATA

The information below represents a listing of most Savage/Stevens rifles and shotguns mfg. in the past (some data has been approximated). Rather than list these models separately, they have been provided in this section for quick reference. Values on many of the models listed below typically range between $50-$175, depending on rarity and condition.

MODEL	DATES	APPROX.GUNS
1903	1912-20	13,000
1904	1912-32	62,000
1905	1912-15	6,500
1909	1912-15	3,500
1911	1912-15	22,500
1912	1913-15	12,000
1914	1914-26	49,500
19	1933-45	16,000
1920	1920-32	12,000
1922	1922-25	16,000
'23A	1924-45	88,000
'23B	1924-45	16,500
'23C	1924-42	14,500
'23D	1932-45	15,000
3	1931-45	121,000
4	1933-45	38,000
5	1936-45	22,000
6	1938-45	45,500
7	1939-45	6,000
40	1928-42	16,000
45	1928-42	6,000
1925	1925-32	36,000
29	1933-45	23,500
CS22	1926-45	87,500
219	1938-45	12,500
220	1937-45	50,000
420	1937-42	13,500
430	1937-42	11,000
1921	1921-32	13,000
1928	1928-32	6,500

MODEL	DATES	APPROX.GUNS
721	1930-32	12,000
FOX	1933-45	31,000
FX B	1940-45	20,000
No. 12	1912-35	166,500
14-1/2	1912-41	592,500
Fav.	1912-42	462,000
No. 26	1912-45	501,500
44+414	1912-35	23,000
No. 70	1912-31	295,500
No. 71	1930-34	10,000
No. 75	1928-34	19,000
15+425	1912-17	11,500
No. 35	1912-19	12,500
No. 35	1923-42	43,000
41-43	1912-18	18,500
No. 10	1919-34	9,500
85-89	1912-42	38,500
No. 93	1912-19	12,500
No. 97	1912-19	16,000
No. 101	1914-20	5,000
No. 105	1912-45	221,500
No. 107	1912-45	443,500
106-08	1916-35	56,500
No. 115	1912-31	23,000
No. 124	1949-55	----
No. 125	1912-23	5,000
180-85	1912-23	16,000
No. 958	1925-33	5,000
116-17	1926-35	5,000
946-48	1928-34	7,000
No. 215	1913-32	61,000
No. 235	1912-32	61,500
No. 315	1914-36	192,000
No. 385	1912-31	67,500
No. 345	1916-31	3,500
No. 311	1926-45	145,500
No. 330	1926-35	33,500
No. 335	1926-35	2,000
No. 520	1912-32	191,000
No. 521	1930-32	5,000
60&61	1930-34	6,500
620-21	1926-45	66,500
Mod. 30	1933-34	26,000
Mod. 31	1933-34	2,000
No. 15	1936-45	224,000
No. 11	1923-33	141,500
No. 95	1926-35	55,000
No. 52	1933-37	88,000
No. 55	1935-36	3,500
No. 54	1933-42	23,500
No. 56	1933-45	97,500
No. 57	1939-42	500
No. 58	1933-45	29,500
No. 37	1936-42	29,000
No. 38	1936-45	33,500
No. 39	1938-45	64,000
No. 59	1938-45	21,000
No. 76	1938-45	6,000
65-66	1929-45	174,000
No. 82	1936-37	35,500
No. 83	1936-42	159,000
No. 84	1936-45	99,500
No. 85	1939-43	14,000
No. 86	1936-43	82,500
No. 87	1938-45	200,000
No. 872	1940-42	3,500
NO. 89	1926-37	12,000
No. 94	1926-45	934,000
No. 96	1926-33	3,500
No. 416	1937-42	2,000
No. 417	1932-42	1,000
No. 418	1932-42	1,500

SAVAGE/STEVENS, cont.

SAVAGE/STEVENS, cont.

MODEL	DATES	APPROX.GUNS
No. 419	1932-36	1,000
No. 237	1936-43	16,000
No. 254	1936-42	1,000
No. 238	1936-45	40,000
No. 258	1936-45	11,000
102-04	1936-42	500
No. 116	1936-42	1,000
No. 944	1936-42	1,500
No. 600	1936-42	5,500
No. 900	1936-42	2,000
No. 515	1936-42	500
No. 5151	1936-42	95,000
No. 530	1936-42	8,000
No. 500	1936-42	500
22 410	1939-45	105,000
M.240	1940-45	20,500

SAVAGE MODEL NINETY-NINE SERIALIZATION

Serial Numbers At Year End:

10,000	1899
13,400	1900
19,500	1901
25,000	1902
35,000	1903
45,000	1904
53,000	1905
67,500	1906
73,500	1907
81,000	1908
95,000	1909
110,000	1910
119,000	1911
131,000	1912
146,500	1913
162,000	1914
175,500	1915
187,500	1916
193,000	1917
N/A	1918
212,500	1919
229,000	1920
237,500	1921
244,500	1922
256,000	1923
270,000	1924
280,000	1925
292,500	1926
305,000	1927
317,000	1928
324,500	1929
334,500	1930
338,500	1931
341,000	1932
344,500	1933
345,800	1934
350,800	1935
359,800	1936
N/A	1937
381,351	1938
388,640	1939
398,400	1940
416,000	1941
438,000	1946
464,000	1947
494,000	1948
528,000	1949
566,000	1950

L.C. SMITH SERIALIZATION

Existing L.C. Smith shotgun records include: Hunter Arms Company factory records circa 1890-1919, Hunter Arms Company shipping records circa 1918-1946, L.C. Smith Gun Company, 1946-1950 (FWS prefix), Marlin Firearms Company, 1969-71 (FWS prefix).

For a factor letter on an older Marlin firearm, contact the Buffalo Bill Historical center, Cody Firearms Museum, 720 Sheridan Ave. Cody, WY 82414. Web site www.bbhc.org or phone 307-587-4771. There is a $45 fee per serial number search.

L.C. Smith (Manufactured by Hunter Arms Co. 1890-1918).

Hammer Shotguns

GAUGE	YEAR	GUN
20	1907	5000-5131
20	1908	5379
20	1909	5677
20	1910	6238
20	1911	6593
20	1912	7076
20	1913	7521
20	1914	7828
20	1915	7935
20	1916	8149
20	1917	8250
10, 12, & 16	1894	50000-50867
10, 12, & 16	1895	51735
10, 12, & 16	1896	52602
10, 12, & 16	1897	55301
10, 12, & 16	1898	58000
10, 12, & 16	1900	79000-84943
10, 12, & 16	1901	89999
10, 12, & 16	1902	125000-129700
10, 12, & 16	1903	133039
10, 12, & 16	1904	137445
10, 12, & 16	1905	144409
10, 12, & 16	1906	150221
10, 12, & 16	1907	156901
10, 12, & 16	1908	159519
10, 12, & 16	1909	163160
10, 12, & 16	1910	166705
10, 12, & 16	1911	168761
10, 12, & 16	1912	171415
10, 12, & 16	1913	173371
10, 12, & 16	1914	175483
10, 12, & 16	1915	176091
10, 12, & 16	1916	176576
10, 12, & 16	1917	178522
10, 12, & 16	1918	179841

Hammerless Shotguns

GAUGE	YEAR	GUN
20	1907	1000-1204
20	1908	1329
20	1909	1788
20	1910	2587
20	1911	3615
20	1912	4630

L.C. Smith, cont.
Hammerless Shotguns cont.

GAUGE	YEAR	GUN
20	1913	4999
20	1913	10000-10786
20	1914	11451
20	1915	11873
20	1916	12361
20	1917	12666
20	1918	12753
10 & 12	1890	30000-32527
10 & 12	1891	34381
10 & 12	1892	36615
10 & 12	1893	37324
10 & 12	1894	38892
10 & 12	1895	40334
8, 10, 12, & 16	1896	40335-42219
8, 10, 12, & 16	1897	44104
8, 10, 12, & 16	1898	45999
16	1895	60000 60144
16	1896	60289
16	1897	60434
16	1898	60579
16	1899	60724
16	1900	60869
16	1901	61014
16	1902	61159
16	1903	61402
16	1904	61685
16	1905	62156
16	1906	62653
16	1907	63698
16	1908	64226
16	1909	65021
16	1910	65861
16	1911	66821
16	1912	67683
16	1913	68704
16	1914	69681
16	1915	69999
16	1915	400000-401758
10 & 12	1899	105210
10 & 12	1900	105917
10 & 12	1901	111681
10 & 12	1902	119035
10 & 12	1903	120767
10 & 12	1904	124419
10 & 12	1905	124999
10 & 12	1904	300000-300301
10 & 12	1905	305787
10 & 12	1906	311528
10 & 12	1907	318079
10 & 12	1908	322129
10 & 12	1909	329476
10 & 12	1910	333081
10 & 12	1911	336572
10 & 12	1912	341717
10 & 12	1913	345493
10 & 12	1914	350857
10 & 12	1915	352431
10 & 12	1916	355068
10 & 12	1917	359624
10 & 12	1918	361071
10, 12, & 16	1891	500-559
10, 12, & 16	1898	3173
10, 12, & 16	1901	6959

L.C. Smith, cont.
Hammerless Shotguns cont.

GAUGE	YEAR	GUN
10, 12, & 16	1902	9000
10, 12, & 16	1902	200000-200025
10, 12, & 16	1903	201758
10, 12, & 16	1904	203272
10, 12, & 16	1905	205098
10, 12, & 16	1906	207093
10, 12, & 16	1907	209368
10, 12, & 16	1908	210579
10, 12, & 16	1909	211885
10, 12, & 16	1910	213084
10, 12, & 16	1911	214246
10, 12, & 16	1912	215615
10, 12, & 16	1913	216939
10, 12, & 16	1914	218260
10, 12, & 16	1915	218829
10, 12, & 16	1916	219603
10, 12, & 16	1917	219750

1918-1950 (These serial numbers include all types of L.C. Smith, Fulton and Hunter Shotguns).

YEAR	GUN
1918	101-3850
1919	18252
1920	35228
1921	44566
1922	51985
1923	64187
1924	75897
1925	86695
1926	93841
1927	103900
1928	114817
1929	125347
1930	132827
1931	134242
1932	137779
1933	138371
1934	140146
1935	144296
1936	151123
1937	162670
1938	171179
1939	181701
1940	190280
1941	197124
1942	201794
1943	202959
1944	204084
1945	205423
1946	1-8595
1947	25661
1948	41825
1949	55608
1950	56800

SMITH & WESSON PERFORMANCE CENTER PRODUCT CODE INFO.

The following Smith & Wesson Performance Center product code information appear courtesy of Mr. Jim Supica and Mr. Richard Nahas. I would like to thank them for making these product codes available. For additional information on Smith & Wesson firearms, the *Standard Catalog of Smith & Wesson* by Jim Supica and Richard Nahas is highly recomended. This book is available through www.bluebookinc.com.

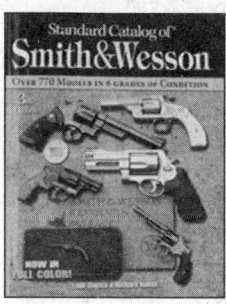

S & W PERFOMANCE CENTER PRODUCT CODES

170 = Designed/made from scratch
178 = Used existing Product / and improved

Code	Configuration
170002	M-5906
170008	M-626 HUNTER
170009	M-686 C. C. 6"
170010	M-686 C. C. 3"
170011	SHORTY 40
170012	M-629 3" MAG.COMP.
170014	M-640 3" C. C.
170015	M-686 6" COMPETITOR
170016	M-686 4" C. C.
170020	Tactical Forty
170021	M-686 6" HUNTER
170023	M-442 ULTRALITE
170024	M-66 3" F-COMP.
170025	M-19 3" K-COMP.
170026	M-629 3" UNFLUTED
170027	M-356 COMPACT
170028	S/S SHORTY 40
I70029	M-60 3"FL ET-COMP.
170030	SHORTY 9mm
170032	M-356 LIMITED
170033	M-40 LIMITED
170034	M-686 6" HUNTER (BRAZIL)
170035	M-I9 3" K-COMP (BRAZIL)
170036	M-52 PERF. CTR.
170037	M-356 BRILEY CHASSIS
170038	M-845 WISCHO LIMITED
170039	M-356 PARKER HALE
170040	M-9mm WISCHO LIMITED
170042	M-640 2" Carry Comp.
170043	M-64O 2" Carry Comp.
170044	M-9mm WISCHO LTD. (2TONE)
170046	M-629 6" HUNTER (UNFLUTED)
170047	M-356 2" Carry Comp.
170048	M-629-4 3" Quad Port
170049	M-629 5" Carry Comp
170050	M-629 6.5" Carry Comp.
170052	356 TSW 4 1/4" Stocking Dealer
170053	9mm 4 1/4" Stocking Dealer
170054	40 S&W 4 1/4" Stocking Dealer
170055	M-460 Airweight
170056	M-629 Light Hunter: Duplicate PC
170056	M-625 V Comp 4" : Duplicate PC
170057	M-9mm Horton Limited
170058	M-629 3" DBL Magna Ported

S & W PERFOMANCE CENTER PRODUCT CODES cont.

Code	Configuration
170059	M-13 3" FS DBL Port (Eagle)
170060	Shorty 40 Mark II
170061	Shorty 40 MK III
170062	M-657 .41 Mag Light Hunter
170063	M-13 3" FS Dbl Port (Uncle Mikes)
170064	M-845 HORTON LIMITED
170065	M-629 7.5" HUNTER PLUS
170066	M-617 WISCHO Target
170067	M-9mm Compact
170068	M-640-.357 J-COMP
170069	not active
170070	M-625 5"
170071	not active
170072	M-625 HUNTER (PORTLESS)
170073	M-640-357 2 1/8 FL GB (RSR)
170074	M-686 7SH 3" FL CARRY COMP.
170075	SHORTY 45
170076	SHORTY 40 MARK III-S
170077	M-686 7SH 2.5" FL MAGPORT
170078	M-640.357 2 I/8 FL QUAD GB
170079	M-686 7SH 6" Hunter
170080	M-681 3" Quad Port
170081	M-625 45LC Flutted Hunter
170082	M-686 6" Supertarget
170083	PPC 9mm Limited
170084	M-629 7.5" Hunter
170085	M-625 6" GB Hunter
170086	M-686 7Shot 6" GB Hunter
170087	M-629 7.5" Master Hunter/Scope only
170088	Shorty 45 MKII
170089	M-627 5" 8SH Lew Horton GB
170090	M-66 3" Contour Frame/ bbl
170091	40 S&W Tactical-RSR
170092	M-627 5" 8 Shot Ported
170093	9mm 4" DA/SA FS
170094	M-629 7.5" Master Hunter
170095	M-627 6" 8 Shot Hunter
170098	45 RECON 45 ACP
170099	Shorty 4006 RECON 40 S&W
170100	M-629 6" Compensated Hunter
170102	M-627 6.5" 8 Shot
170103	M-686 6" 7 Shot Profile Bbl
170104	M-945 5" Stainless
170105	CQB Stainless 45 ACP
170106	CQB Alloy 45 ACP
170109	M-610 6 1/2"
170110	Not Used
170111	M-686 6" 6 Shot Profile Bbl
170116	M-627 5" 8 Shot unfluted
170117	M-5906 5" 9mm LTD CS Slide (Wischo)
170118	M-4563 CQB Two Tone
170119	M-5906 5" 9mm/356Mag SuperPC
170120	M-629 44 6" 6 shot Competitor
170121	M-686 6" 6 shot Fluted Competitor
170122	M-617 New Profile Barrel
170123	M-627 5" Profile Barrel 6 Shot Fluted
170124	M-629 44 6.5" 6 shot flutted full lug comp & cap
170125	M-657 41 6.5" 6 shot flutted full lug comp & cap
170126	M-629 Compensated Hunter- New Frame/ Hammer
170128	.45 4515 RECON -RSR w/Knife
170129	M-4587 4.25"
170130	M-629 Classic 7 1/2" Barrel w/ Case
170131	M-29 Classic 7 1/2" Barrel w/Case
170132	M-625 6" 45 Long Colt Light Hunter Fluted GB
170133	M-627 2 5/8" 8 shot Defensive Revolver
170134	M-657 2 5/8" Defensive Revolver
170135	M-629 2 5/8" Defensive Revolver
170136	M-625 Light Hunter 6"
170137	M-629 V Comp 4" -RSR

S & W PERFOMANCE CENTER PRODUCT CODES cont.

Code	Configuration
170138	M-629 7 1/2" Light Hunter RSR
170139	M-4006
170140	9mm M-6906 RECON 3 1/2"
170141	45 RECON Black
170142	M-627-3 V-Comp Jerry Miculek Spcl. 5"
170143	M- 9mm Full Lug
170144	M-332 Never Made
170145	M-632 Never Made
170146	Schofield Model of 2000
170147	M-945 5" Blue 1998
170147	M-945 Two Tone 1999
170148	M-629 5" V-Comp RSR Special
170149	6" 629 Hunter Unfluted
170150	M-627 5 1/2" UnFluted RD
170151	M-27 Classic Series
170152	M-945 4" Black
170153	M-945 4" Stainless-RSR
170154	M-14 4"
170155	M-5906 5" 9mm 10 RDv Mag PPC
170156	M-945 3-3/4" RSR Special
170157	M-629 Extreme Hunter 12"
170158	M-629 12" w/sling
170159	M-629 8.5" Revolver w/sling
170160	M-657 12" Revolver w/sling
170161	M-657 12" Revolver w/sling
170162	M-657 8.5" Revolver w/sling
170163	M-19 K COMP Y2000
170164	M-4006 Shorty Forty -Y2000- Camfour
170165	M-646 4" 40 S&W
170166	M-27-7 8 Shot 4"
170167	M-27-7 8 Shot 6 1/2"
170168	M-952 9mm
170169	M-945 3 3/4" Black -Camfour
170170	M-586 L-Comp 3"
170171	M-629 7 1/2" Stealth Hunter
170172	M-681 4" Quad Port for Camfour
170173	M-945 5" RSR Special
170174	M-945 5" Two Tone RSR Special
170175	M-629 2 5/8" unfluted cyl
170176	M-625 5 1/4" 45 ACP for Camfour
170177	M-945 3 1/4" 45 ACP for Camfour
170178	M-681 3" Quad Port for Camfour
170179	M-25-10 6" for Sports South
170180	M-945 3 3/4" 40S&W for Sports South
170181	M-629 7 1/2" Compensated Hunter for TALO
170182	M-627 4" w/ Comp RSR Special
170183	M-627 4" w/ Comp RSR Special
170184	M-945 3 1/4" 45ACP for RSR
170185	M-24-5 6 1/2" Case Color Frame 44 Spl Heritage
170186	FC M-25-11 6 1/2" Case Color Frame 45 Colt Heritage
170187	M-25 44-40 6" 6 Sh AS WG Color Case Frame Heritage
170188	M-25 38-40 6" 6 Sh AS WG Blue
170189	M-24 44 Spl 6.5" AS WG All Blue Finish Heritage
170190	M-25 44-40 6" 6Sh AS WG Blue
170191	M-25 38-40 6" 6Sh AS WG Blue
170192	M-625 FL 5" 45 ACP 6 Sh AS IFS S
170193	M-629 7 1/2" Unfluted Green/ Black
170194	M-629 7-1/2" Black Unfluted
170195	M- 4006 4" SA/DA FS IDPA
170196	M-25 Colt 6" Taper Bbl 6 Sh Fluted Blue
170197	M-25-12 5 1/2" Fixed Sight Model of 1917 45ACP
170198	FC KT-22 6" 6 Sh Fluted Adj Blue Model 17-8 Heritage
170199	M-15-9 5" Blue
170200	M-681 357 3" FS WG 7 Sh Birdsong
170201	M-5906 6" Pistol
170202	M-952

S & W PERFOMANCE CENTER PRODUCT CODES cont.

Code	Configuration
170203	Mfg Purposes Only
170204	Mfg Purposes Only
170205	M-627 38 Super 8 shot
170206	M-586 357 GB 4-1/8"
170207	M-3 5" nickel
170208	M-3 5" blue
170209	M-3 Nickel Schofield 7" 45
170210	M-627-5 357 w/Internal Lock
170211	M-25-12 Case Colored, 45 ACP
170212	M-17-8 6" Heritage Series
170213	M-29 Heritage Series Blue
170214	M-29 Heritage Series Nickel
170215	M-29 Nickel ?
170216	M-15-9 Heritage Series 6" Blue (McGivern Model)
170217	M-15-9 Heritage Series 6" Nickel (McGivern Model)
170218	M-25 45ACP 5-1/2" 1917 w/Military Finish
170219	N/A
170220	N/A
170221	N/A
178001	N/A
178002	N/A
178003	N/A
178004	N/A
178005	M-29-5 8 3/8 RB TT TH RR WO B Wood Grips (SCR0002)
178006	FC M-10 4 1/4" Case Color Frame Square Butt w/FC
178007	N/A
178008	M-15-8 4" Nickel
178009	M-15-8 4" Heritage Series
A2D	Adj. 2-Dot Sight
AA	Aluminum Alloy Frame
AB	Adj. Black Sight
AMSF	Ambidextious Safety
AS	Adj. Rear Sight
ATS	Adj. Target Sight
AV	Adj. V Notch Sight
AWO	Adj. White Outline Sight
B	Blue
BB	Bead Blast Finish
BBL	Barrel
B/G	Black/Gray Finish
BK	Black Finish

PISTOL/REVOLVER FEATURE CODES
cont.

Code	Feature
BK/M	Black/Melonite Finish
BP	Black Polymer Grip
BPF	Black Polymer Frame
BULL	Bull Barrel
CB	Curved Backstrap Grip
CC	Clear Cote™ Finish
CS	Carbon Steel
CWG	Checkered Wood Grip
CWP	Checkered Wood Panel
DA	Double Action
DAO	Double Action Only
DBP	Dovetail Black Post
DFS	Dovetail Front Sight
DT	Drilled & Taped
ER	Equipment Rail
F2D	Fixed 2-Dot Sight
FN	Fixed Notch Sight
FNS	Fixed Tritium Night Sight (Fr. & Rr.)
FS	Fixed Sight
FV	Fixed V-Notch Sight
G	NATO Green
GB	Glass Bead Finish

PISTOL/REVOLVER FEATURE CODES
cont.

Code	Feature
GD	Green Dot
GY	Grey Finish
#SH	Magazine Capacity/Rds
HB	Heavy Barrel
HIVIS®	Light Gathering Sight
HR	Hogue Rubber Grip
HT	Hardwood Target Grip
HV	HIVIS® Front Sight
HWA	Hogue Wrap Around Rubber Grip
I	Integral or Interchangeable Sight
IB	Interchangeable Backstraps
IC	Integral Compensator
IFS	Interchangeable Front Sight
IL	Internal Lock
ISBR	Interchangeable Serrated Black Ramp Sight
LS	LadySmith®
M	Melonite Finish
MCA	Micrometer Click Adj.
MNSF	Manual Safety (Single Side)
MS	Matte Stainless
NG	Nato Green Polymer Grips
NLMC	Novak Lo-Mount Carry 2-Dot Sight
OD	Orange Dot
P	Partridge Sight
PBP	Pinned Black Partridge Sight
PBSR	Pinned Black Serrated Ramp Sight
PF	Polymer Frame
PP	PowerPort™ Ported Barrel
RB	Round Butt
RR	Red Ramp Sight
S	Stainless Finish
SA	Single Action
SB	Black Straight Backstrap Grip
SC	Scandium Alloy Frame
SG	Synthetic Grip
SNS	Satin Stainless Finish
SR	Serrated Ramp Sight
SS	Stainless Steel
STD	Standard Barrel
STG	Soft Touch Grip
T	Tritium
T2D	Tritium 2-Dot Rear Night Sight
TD	Tritium Dot Front Night Sight
TDA	Traditional Double Action
TR	Thumbrest
TS	Target Stock
UC	Unfluted Cylinder
UMB	Uncle Mike's Boot Grip
UMC	Uncle Mike's Combat Grip
UMR	Uncle Mike's Rubber Grip
VR	Vented Rib
WAS	Wilson Adj. Rear Sight
WC	Wood Combat Grip
WD	White Dot Sight
WG	Dymondwood® Grip
WO	White Outline Rear Sight
WT	Wooden Target Grip

SPANISH YEAR OF MFG. DATE CODES

The following Spanish year of manufacture information appears courtesy of Leonardo M. Antaris, M.D., author of Astra Automatic Pistols, and Star Firearms. For additional information regarding Spanish pistols, particularly Astras and Stars, see www.firac.us.

Code	Year
A	1927
B	1928
C	1929
CH	1930
D	1931
E	1932
F	1933
G	1934
H	1935
I	1936
J	1937
K	1938
L	1939
LL	1940
M	1941
N	1942
Ñ	1943
O	1944
P	1945
Q	1946
R	1947
S	1948
T	1949
U	1950
V	1951
X	1952
Y	1953
Z	1954
A1	1955
B1	1956
C1	1957
D1	1958
EI	1959
F1	1960
G1	1961
H1	1962
I1	1963
J1	1964
K1	1965
L1	1966
M1	1967
N1	1968
Ñ1	1969
O1	1970
P1	1971
Q1	1972
R1	1973
S1	1974
T1	1975
U1	1976
V1	1977
X1	1978
Y1	1979
Z1	1980
A2	1981
B2	1982

SPANISH DATE CODES cont.

Code	Year
C2	1983
D2	1984
E2	1985
F2	1986
G2	1987
H2	1988
I2	1989
J2	1990
K2	1991
L2	1992
M2	1993
N2	1994

Beginning in January 1995 the Spanish proof house implemented a new serial number system. Requirements included: 1) all guns, would be numbered in a new sequential series starting with the number 1 at the beginning of the year, 2) the serial number was to be followed by the last two digits of the production year, 3) each manufacturer was assigned a code to be stamped on every gun, and 4) weapons were to be marked as to type.

The new system consists of four sets of digits separated by a hyphen. The first set is the manufacturer's code, the second set designates the type of weapon, and the third set is the firearms chronological number irrespective of model, the fourth set shows the year of mfg.

The new weapons coding system includes, Carbines 01, Shotguns 03, Pistols 04, Revolvers 05, Rifles 06, Muzzleloaders 13, Short carbines 14, Submachine guns 15; etc.

STURM, RUGER & CO., INC.

Additional information regarding Sturm, Ruger & Co., Inc. firearms (including serialization) can be found in Ruger & His Guns; A History of the Man, the Company and Their Firearms by R.L. Wilson. www.bluebookinc.com to order.

WINCHESTER RIFLES SERIALIZATION

The following Winchester serial numbers appear courtesy of U.S. Repeating Arms, New Haven, CT. I would like to thank U.S. Repeating Arms and Mr. Pardee for making these production figures available.

Records at the factory indicate the following serial numbers were assigned to guns at the end of the calendar year.

For additional information including factory letters contact the Cody Firearms Museum. Factory letters are $55.

Buffalo Bill Historical Center
Attn: Cody Firearms Museum
720 Sheridan Ave.
Cody, WY 82414

In the spring of 2005, the Cody Firearms Museum began a research project involving the Winchester Repeating Arms Company production through the comparison of shipping and polishing room records. The little known polishing room records (used in many works of George Madis) are a collection of small notebooks that document Winchester firearms receiver serialization circa 1873 to 1964. These notebooks cover many, but do not cover all models or all eras of production. The data assembled from this research will be published over time to improve available information to collectors.

MODEL 1866

Year	Approx. Last No.
1866	12476 to 14813
67	15578
68	19768
69	29516
70	52527
71	88184
72	109784
73	118401
74	125038
75	125965
76	131907
77	148207
78	150493
79	152201
80	154379
81	156107
82	159513
1883	162376
84	163649
85	163664
86	165071
87	165912
88	167155
89	167401
90	167702
91	169003
92	NONE
93	169007
94	169011
95	NONE
96	NONE
97	169015
98	170100
99	DISCONTINUED

MODEL 1873

Year	Approx. Last No.
1873	1 to 126
74	2726
75	11325
76	23151
77	23628
78	27501
79	41525
80	63537
81	81620
82	109507
83	145503
84	175126
85	196221
86	222937
87	225922
88	284529
89	323220
90	363220

MODEL 1873, cont.

Year	Approx. Last No.
91	405026
92	441625
93	466641
94	481826
95	499308
96	507545
97	513421
98	525922
99	541328
1900	554128
01	557236
02	564557
03	573957
04	588953
05	602557
06	613780
07	NONE
08	NONE
09	630385
10	656101
11	669324
12	678527
13	684419
14	686510
15	688431
16	694020
17	698617
18	700734
19	702042

No last # available
20, 21, 22, 23, 720609

MODEL 1876

Year	Approx. Last No.
1876	1 to 1429
77	3579
78	7967
79	8971
80	14700
81	21759
82	32407
83	42410
1884	54666
85	58714
86	60397
87	62420
88	63539
89	NONE
90	NONE
91	NONE
92	63561
93	63670
94	63678
95	NONE
96	63702
97	63869
98	63871

MODEL 1885 SINGLE SHOT

Year	Approx. last No.
1885 -	1 to 375
86 -	6841
87 -	18328
88 -	30571
89 -	45019
90 -	NONE
91 -	53700
92 -	60371
93 -	69534
94 -	NONE
95 -	73771

MODEL 1885 SINGLE SHOT, cont.

Year	Approx. last No.
96 -	78253
97 -	78815
98 -	84700
99 -	85086
1900 -	88501
01 -	90424
02 -	92031
03 -	92359
04 -	92785
05 -	93611
06 -	94208
07 -	95743
08 -	96819
09 -	98097
10 -	98506
11 -	99012
12 -	NONE
13 -	100352

No further serial numbers were recorded until the end of 1923. Last No. known was: 139700

MODEL 1886

Year	Approx. Last No.
1886 -	1 to 3211
87 -	14728
88 -	28577
89 -	38401
90 -	49723
91 -	63601
92 -	73816
93 -	83261
94 -	94543
95 -	103708
96 -	109670
97 -	113997
98 -	119192
99 -	120571
1900 -	122834
01 -	125630
02 -	128942
03 -	132213
04 -	135524
05 -	138838
06 -	142249
07 -	145119
1908 -	147322
09 -	148237
10 -	150129
11 -	151622
12 -	152943
13 -	152947
14 -	153859
15 -	154452
16 -	154979
17 -	155387
18 -	156219
19 -	156930
20 -	158716
21 -	159108
22 -	159337

No further serial numbers were recorded until the discontinuance of the Model 1886 which was in 1935 - at - 159994.

MODEL 1890

Records on the Model 1890 are somewhat incomplete. Factory records indicate the following serial numbers were assigned to guns at the end of the calendar year beginning with 1908. Actual records on the firearms which were manufactured between 1890 and 1907 will be available from the "Cody Firearms Museum," located at the "Buffalo Bill Historical Center."

Year	Approx. Last No.
1908 -	330000 to 363850
09 -	393427
10 -	423567
11 -	451264
12 -	478595
13 -	506936
14 -	531019
15 -	551290
16 -	570497
17 -	589204
18 -	603438
19 -	630801
20 -	NONE
21 -	634783
22 -	643304
23 -	654837
24 -	664613
25 -	675774
26 -	687049
27 -	698987
28 -	711354
29 -	722125
30 -	729015
31 -	733178
32 -	734454

The Model 1890 was discontinued in 1932, however, a clean up of the production run lasted another 8+ years and included another 14 to 15000 guns. Our figures indicate approximately 849,000 guns were made.

MODEL 1892

Year	Approx. Last No.
1892 -	1 to 23701
93 -	35987
94 -	73508
95 -	106721
96 -	144935
97 -	159312
98 -	165431
99 -	171820
1900 -	183411
01 -	191787
02 -	208871
03 -	253935
04 -	278546
05 -	315425
06 -	376496
07 -	437919
08 -	476540
09 -	522162
10 -	586996
11 -	643483
12 -	694752
13 -	742675
14 -	771444
15 -	804622
16 -	830031
17 -	853819

MODEL 1892 cont.

Year	Approx. Last No.
18 -	870942
19 -	903649
20 -	906754
21 -	910476
22 -	917300
23 -	926329
24 -	938641
25 -	954997
26 -	973896
27 -	990883
28 -	996517
29 -	999238
30 -	999730
31 -	1000727
32 -	1001324

MODEL 1894

Records at the factory, and in some years, estimates, indicate the following serial numbers were assigned to guns at the end of the calendar year.

Year	Approx. Last No.
1894 -	1 to 14579
95 -	44359
96 -	76464
97 -	111453
98 -	147684
99 -	183371
1900 -	204427
01 -	233975
02 -	273854
03 -	291506
04 -	311363
05 -	337557
06 -	378878
07 -	430985
08 -	474241
1909 -	505831
10 -	553062
11 -	599263
12 -	646114
13 -	703701
14 -	756066
15 -	784052
16 -	807741
17 -	821972
18 -	838175
19 -	870762
20 -	880627
21 -	908318
22 -	919583
23 -	938539
24 -	953198
25 -	978523
26 -	997603
27 -	1027571
28 -	1054465
29 -	1077097
30 -	1081755
31 -	1084156
32 -	1087836
33 -	1089270
34 -	1091190
35 -	1099605
36 -	1100065
37 -	1100679
38 -	1100915
39 -	1101051

MODEL 1894, cont.

Year	Approx. Last No.
40 -	1142423
41 -	1191307
42 -	1221289
43 -	No Record Available
44 -	No Record Available
45 -	No Record Available
46 -	No Record Available
47 -	No Record Available
48 -	1500000
49 -	1626100
50 -	1724295
51 -	1819800
52 -	1910000
53 -	2000000
54 -	2071100
55 -	2145296
56 -	2225000
57 -	2290296
58 -	2365887
59 -	2410555
60 -	2469821
61 -	2500000
62 -	2551921
63 -	2586000
*1964	2700000 - 2797428
65 -	2894428
66 -	2991927
67 -	3088458
68 -	3185691
69 -	3284570
70 -	3381299
71 -	3557385
72 -	3806499
73 -	3929364
74 -	4111426
75 -	4277926
75 -	4463553
76 -	4463553
77 -	4565925
78 -	4662210
1979 -	4826596
80 -	4892951
81 -	5024957
82 -	5103248
83-	No Record Available
84-	5309432
85-	5362944
86-	5409249
87-	5463790
88-	5517897
89-	5574822
90-	5615397
91-	6008296

Model 1894 facts.

* The post-64 Model 94 began with serial number 2,700,000.

*Serial number 1,000,000 was presented to President Calvin Coolidge in 1927.

*Serial number 1,500,000 was presented to President Harry S. Truman in 1948.

*Serial number 2,500,000 and 3,000,000 were presented to the Winchester Gun Museum, now located in Cody, Wyoming.

Model 1894 facts cont.

*Serial number 3,500,000 was not constructed until 1979 and was sold at auction in Las Vegas, Nevada.

*Serial number 4,000,000 - whereabouts unknown at this time.

*Serial number 4,500,000 - shipped to Italy by Olin in 1978. Whereabouts unknown.

*Serial number 5,000,000 - in New Haven, not constructed as of March 1983.

MODEL 9422

Year	Approx. Last No.
1972 -	F48558
73 -	F121182
74 -	F169044
1975 -	F229666
76 -	F293472
77-	F323197
78-	F367976
79-	F398044
80-	F431532
81-	F489918
82-	F527632
83-	F531722
84-	F539305
85-	F550843
86-	F557835
87-	F571623
88-	F590039
89-	F605281
90-	F617848
91-	F633224
92-	F646000
93-	F658316
94-	F671391

MODEL 1895

Year	Approx. Last No.
1895 -	1 to 287
96 -	5715
97 -	7814
98 -	19871
99 -	26434
1900 -	29817
01 -	31584
02 -	35601
03 -	42514
04 -	47805
05 -	54783
06 -	55011
07 -	57351
08 -	60002
09 -	60951
10 -	63771
11 -	65017
12 -	67331
13 -	70823
14 -	72082
15 -	174233
16 -	377411
17 -	389106
18 -	392731
19 -	397250
20 -	400463
21 -	404075
22 -	407200
23 -	410289
24 -	413276

MODEL 1895 cont.

Year	Approx. Last No.
25 -	417402
26 -	419533
27 -	421584
28 -	422676
29 -	423680
30 -	424181
31 -	425132
32 -	425825

MODEL 1903

Year	Approx. Last No.
1903 -	# Not Available
04 -	6944
05 -	14865
1906 -	23097
07 -	31852
08 -	39105
09 -	46496
10 -	54298
11 -	61679
12 -	69586
13 -	76732
14 -	81776
15 -	84563
16 -	87148
17 -	89501
18 -	92617
19 -	96565
20 -	# Not Available
21 -	97650
22 -	99011
23 -	100452
24 -	101688
25 -	103075
26 -	104230
27 -	105537
28 -	107157
29 -	109414
30 -	111276
31 -	112533
32 -	112992

This model was discontinued in 1932, however, a clean up of parts was used for further production of approximately 2000 guns. Total production was approx. 126000 rifles through 1936.

MODEL 1905

Year	Approx. Last No.
1905 -	1 to 5659
06 -	15288
07 -	19194
08 -	20385
09 -	21280
10 -	22423
11 -	23503
12 -	24602
13 -	25559
14 -	26110
15 -	26561
16 -	26910
17 -	27297
18 -	27585
19 -	28287
20 -	29113

MODEL 1906

Year	Approx. Last No.
1906 -	1 to 52278
07 -	89147

MODEL 1906 cont.

Year	Approx. Last No.
08 -	114138
09 -	165068
10 -	221189
11 -	273355
12 -	327955
13 -	381922
14 -	422734
15 -	453880
16 -	483805
17 -	517743
18 -	535540
19 -	593917
20 -	NONE
21 -	598691
22 -	608011
23 -	622601
24 -	636163
25 -	649952
26 -	665484
1927 -	679892
28 -	695915
29 -	711202
30 -	720116
31 -	725978
32 -	727353

A clean up of production took place for the next few years with a record of production reaching approximately 729305.

MODEL 1907

Year	Approx. Last No.
1907 -	1 to 8657
08 -	14486
09 -	19707
10 -	23230
11 -	25523
12 -	27724
13 -	29607
14 -	30872
15 -	32272
16 -	36215
17 -	38235
18 -	39172
19 -	40448
20 -	No # Available
21 -	40784
22 -	41289
23 -	41658
24 -	42029
25 -	42360
26 -	42688
27 -	43226
28 -	43685
29 -	44046
30 -	44357
31 -	44572
32 -	44683
33 -	44806
34 -	44990
35 -	45203
36 -	45482
37 -	45920
38 -	46419
39 -	46758
40 -	47296
41 -	47957
42 -	48275
43 -	NONE
44 -	NONE
45 -	48281

MODEL 1907 cont.

Year	Approx. Last No.
46 -	48395
47 -	48996
48 -	49684
**49 -	50662
**50 -	51640
**51 -	52618
**52 -	53596
**53 -	54574
**54 -	55552
**55 -	56530
**56 -	57508
**57 -	58486

** Actual records on serial numbers stops in 1948. The serial numbers ending each year from 1948 to 1957 were derived at by taking the last serial number recorded (58486) and the last number from 1948, (49684) and dividing the years of production (9), which relates to 978 guns each year for the nine year period.

MODEL 1910

1910 -	1 to 4766
11 -	7695
12 -	9712
13 -	11487
14 -	12311
15 -	13233
16 -	13788
17 -	14255
18 -	14625
19 -	15665
20 -	No # Available
21 -	15845
22 -	16347
23 -	16637
24 -	17030
25 -	17281
26 -	17696
27 -	18182
28 -	18469
29 -	18893
30 -	19065
31 -	19172
32 -	19232
33 -	19281
34 -	19338
35 -	19388
36 -	19445

A cleanup of production continued into 1937 when the total of the guns was completed at approximately 20786

MODEL 1911 S.L.

Year	Approx. Last No.
1911 -	1 to 3819
12 -	27659
13 -	36677
14 -	40105
15 -	43284
16 -	45391
17 -	49893
18 -	52895
19 -	57337
20 -	60719
21 -	64109
22 -	69132
23 -	73186
24 -	76199
25 -	78611

MODEL 1911 S.L. cont.

The Model 1911 was discontinued in 1925. However, guns were produced for three years after that date to clean up production and excess parts. When this practice ceased there were approximately 82774 guns produced.

MODEL 52

Year	Approx. Last No.
1920 -	None indicated
21 -	397
22 -	745
23 -	1394
24 -	2361
25 -	3513
26 -	6383
27 -	9436
28 -	12082
29 -	14594
30 -	17253
31 -	21954
32 -	24951
33 -	26725
34 -	29030
35 -	32448
1936 -	36632
37 -	40419
38 -	43632
39 -	45460
40 -	47519
41 -	50317
42 -	52129
43 -	52553
44 -	52560
45 -	52718
46 -	56080
47 -	60158
48 -	64265
49 -	68149
50 -	70766
51 -	73385
52 -	76000
53 -	79500
54 -	80693
55 -	81831
56 -	96869
57 -	97869
58 -	98599
59 -	98899
60 -	102200
61 -	106986
62 -	108718
63 -	113583
64 -	118447
65 -	120992
66 -	123537
67 -	123727
68 -	123917
69 -	E 124107
70 -	E 124297
71 -	E 124489
72 -	E 124574
73 -	E 124659
74 -	E 124744
75 -	E 124828
76 -	E 125019
77 -	E 125211
78 -	E 125315

This Model was discontinued in 1978. A small clean up of production was completed in 1979 with a total of 125419.

MODEL 53

The Model 53 was serial numbered in both its own series (1 to slightly over 15,000) as well as within the Model 1892 series. Early guns predominate the Model 53 serial number series with Model 1892 series serial numbers appearing more frequently mid to late production.

This Model was discontinued in 1932, however, a clean up of production continued for 9 more years.

Year	Approx. Last No.
1924-	1 to 1488
25-	4350
26-	6882
27-	9180
28-	11139
29-	12873
30-	13794
31-	14416
32-	14623
33-	14727
34-	14817
35-	14976
36-	15047
37-	15078
38-	15092
39-	15099
1940-	15109
41-	15118

Total Production Approximately 24,916.

Records at the factory indicate the following serial numbers were assigned to guns at the end of the calendar year.

MODEL 54

Year	Approx. Last No.
1925 -	1 to 3140
26 -	8051
27 -	14176
28 -	19587
29 -	29104
30 -	32499
31 -	36731
32 -	38543
33 -	40722
34 -	43466
35 -	47125
36 -	50145

MODEL 55

Year	Approx. Last No.
1924 -	1 to 836
25 -	2783
26 -	4957
27 -	8021
28 -	10467
29 -	12258
30 -	17393
31 -	18198
32 -	19204
33 -	Clean up 20580

MODEL 61

Year	Approx. Last No.
1932 -	1 to 3532
33 -	6008
34 -	8554
35 -	12379
36 -	20615

MODEL 61 cont.

Year	Approx. Last No.
37 -	30334
38 -	36326
39 -	42610
40 -	49270
41 -	57493
42 -	59871
43 -	59872
44 -	59879
45 -	60512
46 -	71629
47 -	92297
48 -	115281
49 -	125461
50 -	135461
51 -	145821
52 -	156000
53 -	171000
54 -	186000
55 -	200962
56 -	216923
57 -	229457
58 -	242992
59 -	262793
60 -	282594
61 -	302395
62 -	322196
63 -	342001

This Model was discontinued in 1963. For some unknown reason there are no actual records available from 1949 through 1963. The serial number figures for these years are arrived at by taking the total production figure of 342001, subtracting the last known # of 115281, and dividing the difference equally by the amount of remaining years available (15).

MODEL 62

Year	Approx. Last No.
1932 -	1 to 7643
33 -	10695
34 -	14090
35 -	23924
36 -	42759
37 -	66059
38 -	80205
39 -	96534
40 -	116393
41 -	137379
42 -	155152
43 -	155422
44 -	155425
45 -	156073
46 -	183756
47 -	219085
48 -	252298
49 -	262473
50 -	272648
51 -	282823
52 -	293000
53 -	310500
54 -	328000
55 -	342776
56 -	357551
57 -	383513
58 -	409475

MODEL 63

Year	Approx. Last No.
1933 -	1 to 2667
34 -	5361

MODEL 63, cont.

Year	Approx. Last No.
35 -	9830
36 -	16781
37 -	25435
38 -	30934
39 -	36055
40 -	41456
41 -	47708
42 -	51258
43 -	51631
44 -	51656
45 -	53853
46 -	61607
47 -	71714
48 -	80519
49 -	88889
50 -	97259
51 -	105629
52 -	114000
53 -	120500
54 -	127000
55 -	138000
56 -	150000
57 -	162345
58 -	175223

MODEL 70

Year	Approx. Last No.
1935 -	1 to 19
36 -	2238
37 -	11573
38 -	17844
39 -	23991
40 -	31675
41 -	41753
42 -	49206
43 -	49983
1944 -	49997
45 -	50921
46 -	58382
47 -	75675
48 -	101680
49 -	131580
50 -	173150
51 -	206625
52 -	238820
53 -	282735
54 -	323530
55 -	361025
56 -	393595
57 -	425283
58 -	440792
59 -	465040
60 -	504257
61 -	545446
62 -	565592
63 -	581471

All post 64 Model 70s began with the serial number 700,000.

Year	Approx. Last No.
1964 -	740599
65 -	809177
66 -	833795
67 -	869000
68 -	925908
69 -	G941900
70 -	G957995
71 -	G1018991
72 -	G1099257
73 -	G1128731
74 -	G1175000
75 -	G1218700
76 -	G1266000

MODEL 70 cont.

Year	Approx. Last No.
77 -	G1350000
78 -	G1410000
79 -	G1447000
80 -	G1490709
81 -	G1537134
82-	G1632872
83-	G1656883
84-	G1782457
85-	G1783276
86-	G1808838
87-	G1845122
88-	G1893903
89-	G1950701
90-	G1987984
91-	G2037985

The control round feed Model 70 was reintroduced in 1990 as the Model 70 Classic at serial number G15000.

MODEL 70 CLASSIC

Year	Approx. Last No.
1990-	G16859
1991-	G23072
1992-	G26709

MODEL 71

Year	Approx. Last No.
1935 -	1 to 4
36 -	7821
37 -	12988
38 -	14690
39 -	16155
40 -	18267
41 -	20810
42 -	21959
43 -	22048
44 -	22051
45 -	22224
46 -	23534
47 -	25728
48 -	27900
49 -	29675
50 -	31450
51 -	33225
52 -	35000
53 -	37500
54 -	40770
55 -	43306
56 -	45843
57 -	47254

MODEL 74

Year	Approx. Last No.
1939 -	1 to 30890
40 -	67085
41 -	114355
42 -	128293
1943 -	NONE
44 -	128295
45 -	128878
46 -	145168
47 -	173524
48 -	223788
49 -	249900
50 -	276012
51 -	302124
52 -	328236
53 -	354348
54 -	380460
55 -	406574

MODEL 88

Year	Approx. Last No.
1955 -	1 to 18378
56 -	36756
57 -	55134
58 -	73512
59 -	91890
60 -	110268
61 -	128651
62 -	139838
63 -	148858
64 -	160307
65 -	162699
66 -	192595
67 -	212416
68 -	230199
69 -	H239899
70 -	H258229
71 -	H266784
72 -	H279014
73 -	H283718

MODEL 100

Year	Approx. Last No.
1961 -	1 to 32189
62 -	60760
63 -	78863
64 -	92016
65 -	135388
66 -	145239
67 -	209498
68 -	210053
69 -	A210999
70 -	A229995
71 -	A242999
72 -	A258001
73 -	A262833

WINCHESTER RIFLE AND SHOTGUN SERIAL NUMBER PREFIXES POST-1968

The following serial number prefixes are found on Winchester rifles and shotguns as a result of the Gun Control Act of 1968.

Model No. (s)	S.N. Prefix
Super X Model 1	M
Super X Model 1 (Ducks Unlimited)	IDU
12	Y
12 (Ducks Unlimited)	DU
21	W
22	WS
23	PWK
52	E
60 (Cooey)	C
40-70A-770-670	G
88	H
91	KS or WS
94	No Prefix used
94 Big Bore	BB
96	K
100	A
101	K
101 Pigeon Grade	PK
Bolt Action Rimfires	

Winchester ser. no. prefixes post-1968 cont.

121-131 & 141	Z
Rimfire 150-190-250-255-270	
275 & 290	B
Rimfire 300-310 & 320	D
370 & 37A	C
490	J
1200	L
1300	LX
1400	N
1500	NX
1500 (European)	NE
9422	F

WINCHESTER SHOTGUNS

Records at the factory indicate the following serial numbers were assigned to guns at the end of the calendar year.

MODEL 1887

Year	Approx. Last No.
1887 -	1 to 7431
88 -	22408
89 -	25673
90 -	29105
91 -	38541
92 -	49763
93 -	54367
94 -	56849
95 -	58289
96 -	60175
97 -	63952
98 -	64855

According to these records no guns were produced during the last few years of this model and it was therefore discontinued in 1901.

MODEL 1897

Year	Approx. Last No.
1897 -	1 to 32335
98 -	64668
99 -	96999
1900 -	129332
01 -	161665
02 -	193998
03 -	226331
04 -	258664
05 -	296037
06 -	334059
07 -	377999
08 -	413618
09 -	446888
1910 -	481062
11 -	512632
12 -	544313
13 -	575213
14 -	592732
15 -	607673
16 -	624537
17 -	646124
18 -	668383
19 -	691943
20 -	696183
21 -	700428
22 -	715902
23 -	732060

MODEL 1897 cont.

Year	Approx. Last No.
24 -	744942
25 -	757629
26 -	770527
27 -	783574
28 -	769806
29 -	807321
30 -	812729
31 -	830721
32 -	833926
33 -	835637
34 -	837364
35 -	839728
36 -	848684
37 -	856729
38 -	860725
39 -	866938
40 -	875945
41 -	891190
42 -	910072
43 -	912265
44 -	912327
45 -	916472
46 -	926409
47 -	936682
48 -	944085
49 -	953042
50 -	961999
51 -	970956
52 -	979913
53 -	988860
54 -	997827
55 -	1006784
56 -	1015741
57 -	1024700

Records on this Model are incomplete. The above serial numbers are estimated from 1897 thru 1903 and again from 1949 thru 1957. The actual records are in existence from 1904 through 1949

MODEL 1897 TRENCH/RIOT SHOTGUN

This information is provided by Mr. Pat Redmond, after many years of research and collecting. Reference a Winchester Repeating Arms Co. Memorandum dated September 1945. Trench, Riot, and Long Barrel Contract Dates 1/31/42 - 3/23/43, Contract Shipments 24829 shotguns.

Year	Ser. Nos.	Type	Configuration
1937	902117-903762	Mil.	Long Barrel
1939	911788-911813	Mil.	Trench Gun
1940	914087	Com.	Trench Gun
1940	924312	Com.	Trench Gun
1941	920235-956126	Mil.	Trench Gun
1942	930537-956216	Mil.	Trench Gun
1943	956628	Mil.	Trench Gun
1944	965482	Com.	Trench Gun
1944	966144	Com.	Trench Gun
1944	967371	Com.	Riot Gun
1949	993750	Com.	Riot Gun

MODEL 1901

Year	Approx. Last No.
1904 -	64,856 to 64,860
05 -	66453
06 -	67486
07 -	68424
08 -	69197
09 -	70009

MODEL 1901 cont.

Year	Approx. Last No.
10 -	70753
11 -	71441
12 -	72167
13 -	72764
14 -	73202
15 -	73509
1916 -	73770
17 -	74027
18 -	74311
19 -	74872
20 -	77000

MODEL 1911

Year	Approx. Last No.
1911	1-3819
1912	27659
1913	36677
1914	40105
1915	43284
1916	45391
1917	49843
1918	52895
1919	57337
1920	60719
1921	64109
1922	69132
1923	73186
1924	76199
1925	78611
1926-28 parts clean-up ending at.	82744

MODEL 12

Year	Approx. Last No.
1912 -	5308
13 -	32418
14 -	79765
15 -	109515
16 -	136412
17 -	159391
18 -	183461
19 -	219457
20 -	247458
21 -	267253
22 -	304314
23 -	346319
24 -	385196
25 -	423056
26 -	464564
27 -	510693
28 -	557850
29 -	600834
30 -	626996
31 -	651255
32 -	660110
33 -	664544
34 -	673994
35 -	686978
36 -	720316
37 -	754250
38 -	779455
39 -	814121
40 -	856499
41 -	907431
42 -	958303
43 -	975640
44 -	975727
45 -	990004
46 -	1029152
47 -	1102371
48 -	1176055

MODEL 12, cont.

Year	Approx. Last No.
49 -	1214041
50 -	1252028
51 -	1290015
52 -	1328002
53 -	1399996
54 -	1471990
55 -	1541929
56 -	1611868
57 -	1651435
58 -	1690999
59 -	1795500
60 -	1800000
61 -	1930999
62 -	1956990
63 -	1962001

A clean up of production took place from 1964 through 1966 with the ending serial # 1970875.

MODEL 12 TRENCH/RIOT SHOTGUN

This information is provided by Mr. Pat Redmond after many years of research and collecting. Reference a Winchester Repeating Arms Co. Memorandum dated September 1945. Trench/Riot and long barrel Contract Dates 4/1/42 - 3/21/44, Contract Shipments 61014 shotguns.

Blue Finish

Year	Ser. Nos.	Type	Configuration
1941	926558--956504	Mil.	Riot & Long Barrel
1942	961934-1001014	Mil.	Trench/Riot/Long
1943	996899-1028856	Mil.	Trench & Riot

Parkerized Finish

Year	Ser. Nos.	Type	Configuration
1943	1030000-1035214	Mil.	Trench Gun
1944	1035458	Mil.	Trench Gun
1944	1035525	Mil.	Trench Gun
1946	1071586	Com.	Riot Gun
1949	1740610	Com.	Riot Gun

NEW STYLE M/12

Year	Approx. Last No.
1972 -	Y200 011-Y2006396
73 -	Y2015662
74 -	Y2022061
75 -	Y2024478
76 -	Y2025482
77 -	Y2025874
78 -	Y2026156
79 -	Y2026399

MODELS 120/1200/1300

Year	Approx. Last No.
1972 -	L739617
73-	L828677
74-	L898065
75-	L967242
76-	L1063788
77-	L1163671
78-	L1202123
79-	L1235083
80-	L1269765

MODELS 120/1200/1300 cont.

Year	Approx. Last No.
81-	L1320354
82-	L1434776
83-	L1567997
84-	L1755346
85-	L1894542
86-	L1983657
87-	L2075117
88-	L2178816
89-	L2306558
90-	L2386211
91-	L2498813
92-	L2599825

MODEL 24

Year	Approx. Last No.
1939 -	1 to 8118
40 -	21382
41 -	27045
42 -	33670
43 -	NONE RECORDED
44 -	33683
45 -	34965
46 -	45250
47 -	58940
48 -	64417

There were no records kept on this model from 1949 until its discontinuance in 1958. The total production was approximately 116280.

MODEL 36

Approximately 20,000 Model 36 single shot 9mm shotguns were manufactured 1920-1927. These shotguns where not serial numbered.

MODEL 37

Approximately 1,000,000 Model 37 single shot shotguns were manufactured 1936-1963. These shotguns where not serial numbered.

MODEL 40

Year	Approx. Last No.
1939 -	1 to 2671
1940	10592
1941	13265
1942	18929

MODEL 42

Year	Approx. Last No.
1933 -	1 to 9398
34 -	13963
35 -	17728
36 -	24849
37 -	30900
38 -	34659
39 -	38967
40 -	43348
41 -	48203
42 -	50818
43 -	50822
44 -	50828
45 -	51168
46 -	54256
47 -	64853
48 -	75142

MODEL 42, cont.

Year	Approx. Last No.
49 -	81107
50 -	87071
51 -	93038
52 -	99000
53 -	108201
54 -	117200
55 -	121883
56 -	126566
57 -	131249
58 -	135932
59 -	140615
60 -	145298
61 -	149981
62 -	154664
63 -	159353

MODEL 50

Year	Approx. Last No.
1954 -	1 to 24550
55 -	49100
56 -	73650
57 -	98200
58 -	122750
59 -	147300
60 -	171850
61 -	196400

WINCHESTER MODEL 101 SERIALIZATION

12 gauge

Ser. No.	Mfg.Mo.	Year
50,000	10	1959
50,500	3	1960
51,000	5	1960
51,500	6	1960
52,000	9	1961
52,500	3	1962
53,000	4	1962
53,500	5	1962
54,000	8	1962
54,500	9	1962
55,000	10	1962
55,500	12	1962
56,000	1	1963
56,500	2	1963
57,000	3	1963
57,500	3	1963
58,000	4	1963
58,500	5	1963
59,000	6	1963
59,500	6	1963
60,000	7	1963
60,500	8	1963
61,000	8	1963
61,500	11	1963
62,000	11	1963
62,500	11	1963
63,000	12	1963

MODEL 101, cont. 12 gauge cont.

Ser. No.	Mfg.Mo.	Year
63,500	1	1964
64,000	1	1964
64,500	2	1964
65,000	3	1964
65,500	3	1964
66,500	3	1964
67,000	5	1964
67,500	5	1964
68,000	5	1964
68,500	5	1964
69,000	6	1964
69,500	6	1964
70,000	7	1964
70,500	7	1964
71,000	8	1964
71,500	9	1964
72,000	9	1964
72,500	10	1964
73,000	10	1964
73,500	11	1964
74,000	11	1964
74,500	12	1964
75,000	12	1964
75,500	1	1965
76,000	2	1965
76,500	2	1965
77,000	3	1965
77,500	4	1965
78,000	4	1965
78,500	4	1965
79,000	4	1965
79,500	4	1965
80,000	5	1965
80,500	6	1965
81,000	6	1965
81,500	6	1965
82,000	6	1965
82,500	8	1965
83,000	8	1965
83,500	8	1965
84,000	9	1965
84,500	9	1965
85,000	10	1965
85,500	10	1965
86,000	10	1965
86,500	10	1965
87,000	10	1965
87,500	10	1965
88,000	11	1965
88,500	11	1965
89,000	11	1965
90,000	12	1965
90,500	12	1965
91,000	12	1965
91,500	1	1966
92,000	1	1966
92,500	2	1966
93,000	2	1966
93,500	2	1966
94,000	3	1966

MODEL 101, cont. 12 gauge cont.

Ser. No.	Mfg.Mo.	Year
94,500	3	1966
95,000	5	1966
95,500	5	1966
96,000	6	1966
96,500	7	1966
97,000	7	1966
97,500	7	1966
98,000	8	1966
98,500	8	1966
99,000	9	1966
99,500	9	1966
100,000	10	1966
100,500	10	1966
101,000	10	1966
101,500	11	1966
102,000	11	1966
102,500	12	1966
103,000	1	1967
103,500	1	1967
104,000	2	1967
104,500	3	1967
105,000	4	1967
105,500	5	1967
106,000	5	1967
106,500	5	1967
107,000	9	1967
107,500	10	1967
108,000	10	1967
108,500	11	1967
109,000	11	1967
109,500	11	1967
110,000	12	1967
110,500	1	1968
111,000	2	1968
111,500	3	1968
112,000	3	1968
112,500	3	1968
113,000	3	1968
113,500	4	1968
114,000	5	1968
114,500	5	1968
115,000	6	1968
115,500	6	1968
116,000	7	1968
116,500	7	1968
117,000	9	1968
117,500	10	1968
118,000	1	1969
118,500	1	1969
119,000	2	1969
119,500	3	1969
120,000	4	1969
120,500	4	1969
121,000	4	1969
121,500	4	1969
122,000	5	1969
122,500	6	1969
123,000	6	1969
123,500	6	1969
124,000	7	1969

MODEL 101, cont. 12 gauge cont.

Ser. No.	Mfg.Mo.	Year
124,500	7	1969
125,000	7	1969
125,500	8	1969
126,000	8	1969
126,500	9	1969
127,000	9	1969
127,500	10	1969
128,000	11	1969
128,500	11	1969
129,000	11	1969
129,500	2	1970
130,000	2	1970
130,500	3	1970
131,000	3	1970
131,500	4	1970
132,000	4	1970
132,500	4	1970
133,000	4	1970
133,500	5	1970
134,000	5	1970
134,500	5	1970
135,000	6	1970
135,500	6	1970
136,000	6	1970
136,500	8	1970
137,000	8	1970
137,500	8	1970
138,000	8	1970
138,500	11	1970
139,000	12	1970
139,500	12	1970
140,000	12	1970
140,500	1	1971
141,000	2	1971
141,500	2	1971
142,000	2	1971
142,500	3	1971
143,000	3	1971
143,500	4	1971
144,000	4	1971
144,500	4	1971
145,000	4	1971
145,500	5	1971

MODEL 101, 20 gauge.

Ser. No.	Mfg.Mo.	Year
200,000	3	1966
200,500	3	1966
201,000	3	1966
201,500	3	1966
202,000	4	1966
202,500	4	1966
203,000	4	1966
203,500	5	1966
204,000	6	1966
204,500	6	1966
205,000	7	1966
205,500	8	1966
206,000	8	1966

MODEL 101, 20 gauge.

Ser. No.	Mfg.Mo.	Year
206,500	8	1966
207,000	9	1966
207,500	9	1966
208,000	9	1966
208,500	12	1966
209,000	2	1967
209,500	7	1967
210,000	10	1967
210,500	12	1967

MODEL 101, 28 ga. & .410 bore

Ser. No.	Mfg.Mo.	Year
211,000	1	1968
211,500	1	1968
212,000	10	1968
212,500	10	1968
213,000	10	1968
213,500	11	1968
214,000	12	1968
214,500	12	1968
215,000	1	1969
215,500	2	1969
216,000	5	1969
216,500	6	1969
217,000	9	1969
217,500	10	1969
218,000	11	1969

MODEL 101, 28 ga. & .410 bore, cont.

Ser. No.	Mfg.Mo.	Year
218,500	12	1969
219,000	12	1969
219,500	12	1969
220,000	12	1969
220,500	1	1970
221,000	1	1970
221,500	2	1970
222,000	3	1970
222,500	7	1970
223,000	9	1970
223,500	9	1970
224,000	9	1970
224,500	9	1970
225,000	10	1970
225,500	10	1970
226,000	11	1970
226,500	11	1970
227,000	11	1970
227,500	12	1970
228,000	12	1970
228,500	4	1971
229,000	4	1971
229,500	4	1971

PROOF MARKS

The proof marks shown below will assist in determining nationality of manufacturers when no other markings are evident. Since the U.S. has no proofing houses (as in England, France, Germany and other European countries), most U.S. manufacturers voluntarily proof their firearms with a specifed style of proofmark (i.e. the interlocked ©WPª synonymous with the Winchester trademark can be fired using modern smokeless powder) shells. Pre-1850 European firearms oftentimes do not exhibit any commercial proof marks and, with the exception of an occasional barrel address, they represent the single hardest bracket of firearms one can research properly. Captured weapons from major wars occasionally show two different nationalities of proofmarks. This is acceptable since the gun was proofed in a national proof house after original manufacture and again when the gun was exported to a different country as a military acquisition. Please refer to the References section in this text for proofmark source information.

AUSTRIAN PROOF MARKS

PROOF MARK	CIRCA	PROOF HOUSE	TYPE OF PROOF AND GUN
	since 1891	Vienna	provisional proof for multi barrel guns
	since 1891	Ferlach	provisional proof for multi barrel guns
	1892-1918	Prague	provisional proof for rifles
	1892-1918	Ferlach	black powder proof for rifles
	1892-1918	Prague	black powder proof for rifles
	1892-1918	Weipert	black powder proof for rifles
	1892-1918	Viena	black powder proof for rifles
	1918-1938	Ferlach	black powder proof for rifles
	1918-1938	Viena	black powder proof for rifles
	1938-1940	Ferlach	black powder proof for rifles
	1938-1940	Viena	black powder proof for rifles
	since 1945	Vienna	black powder proof for multi barrel guns
	since 1945	Ferlach	black powder proof for multi barrel guns
BH	since 1891	Bundesheer	preliminary proof for multi barrel guns

PROOF MARK	CIRCA	PROOF HOUSE	TYPE OF PROOF AND GUN
N^P_B	1891-1928	Budapest	smokeless powder proof for parabellum pistols
N^P_F	Since 1981	Ferlach	smokeless powder proof for parabellum pistols
N^P_P	1891-1931	Ferlach	smokeless powder proof for parabellum pistols
N^P_V	since 1891	Vienna	smokeless powder proof for parabellum pistols
N^P_W	1891-1931	Weipert	smokeless powder proof for parabellum pistols

BELGIAN PROOF MARKS

PROOF MARK	CIRCA	PROOF HOUSE	TYPE OF PROOF AND GUN
EL	since 1852	Liege	provisional black powder proof for breech loading guns and rifled barrels
	-	Liege-	double proof marking for unfurnished barrels
	-	Liege-	triple proof provisional marking for unfurnished barrels
E.L.G	since 1893	-Liege	definitive black powder proof for breech loading guns, small bore guns and handguns
	since 1853	Liege	View stamp and inspectors mark for firearms "Perron"
P.V	since 1924	-Liege	Nitro proof for rifled barrel and parabellum pistols
R	since 1852	-Liege	rifled arms defense for smokeless proof parabellum pistols
PV	-	-Liege	Superior nitro proof

BRITISH PROOF MARKS

PROOF MARK	CIRCA	PROOF HOUSE	TYPE OF PROOF AND GUN
	since 1856	London	provisional proof for barrels
	since 1856	Birmingham	provisional proof for barrels

PROOF MARK	CIRCA	PROOF HOUSE	TYPE OF PROOF AND GUN
	since 1637	London	definitive black powder proof for shotguns, muzzle loader barrels
	1811-1892	Liege	black powder proof for rifles
	1897-1923	Liege	black powder proof for rifles
	1891-1968	Liege	type EC. smokeless powder proof for rifles
	1898-1968	Liege	type Pt. smokeless powder proof for rifles
	1898-1968	Liege	smokeless powder proof for rifles
	since 1968	Liege	smokeless powder proof for rifles
	since 1904	London	definitive nitro proof for all guns - parabellum pistols
	since 1954	Birmingham	definitive nitro proof for barrel and action
	since 1904	Birmingham	black powder proof only for parabellum pistols
	1868-1925	London	definitive special super power proof for parabellum pistols
	1868-1925	Birmingham	voluntary special black powder proof
	1868-1925	London	reproof marking for black powder rifles
	1868-1925	Birmingham	reproof marking for black powder rifles
	1868-1925	Birmingham	definitive black powder proof for shotguns
	since 1904	Birmingham	definitive nitro proof for all guns
	since 1670	London	view mark
	since 1904	Birmingham	view mark

FRENCH PROOF MARKS

PARIS HOUSE	ST ETIENNE HOUSE	CIRCA	TYPE OF PROOF AND GUN
		since 1897	provisional proof unfinished short barreled guns
		1897	standard proof for finished guns
		1897	double proof finished and joined barrels
		1897	single barrel proof for non-assembled guns
		1897	finished black powder guns
		since 1962	black powder proof for rifles
R		1962-1972	final black powder proof for rifles
		1926-1962	final black powder proof for rifles
		since 1962	final black powder proof for rifles
		since 1900	smokeless powder proof for rifles
PJ		1896-1926	smokeless powder proof for rifles
PS		1896-1926	smokeless powder proof for rifles
PM		1896-1926	smokeless powder proof for rifles
PT		1900-1972	smokeless powder proof for rifles
P.T		1926-1972	smokeless powder proof for rifles
PT R		1962-1972	final smokeless powder proof for rifles
R		since 1962	final smokeless powder proof for rifles
R		since 1982	final smokeless powder proof for rifles

PARIS HOUSE	ST ETIENNE HOUSE	CIRCA	TYPE OF PROOF AND GUN
		1897	special proof for finished guns
		1897	ordinary smokeless powder proof
		1897	superior smokeless powder proo

GERMAN PROOF MARKS

Research continues for the inclusion of Pre-1950 German Proofmarks.

PROOF MARK	CIRCA	PROOF HOUSE	TYPE OF PROOF AND GUN
	since 1952	Ulm	
	since 1968	Hannover	
	since 1968	Kiel (W. German)	
	since 1968	Munich	
	since 1968	Cologne (W. German)	
	since 1968	Berlin (W. German)	
	since 1952	Ulm	voluntary proof for hand/long guns
	since 1952	Ulm	repair proof for major gun parts
	since 1952	Ulm	provisional black powder for shotgun & multi barreled rifles
	since 1952	Ulm	definitive nitro proof for all guns
	since 1952	Ulm	definitive black powder for smokeless ammo guns
	since 1952	Ulm	Flobert for special purpose guns signal, flare, gas, & stun guns
	since 1945	E. German, Suhl	smokeless powder proof
	since 1950	E. German, Suhl	1st black powder proof for rifled barrels
	since 1950	E. German, Suhl	nitro powder proof

PROOF MARK	CIRCA	PROOF HOUSE	TYPE OF PROOF AND GUN
R	since 1950	E. German, Suhl	repair proof
S	since 1950	E. German, Suhl	1st black powder proof for smooth bored barrels
U	since 1950	E. German, Suhl	inspection mark
W	since 1950	E. German, Suhl	choke-bore barrel mark

ITALIAN PROOF MARKS

PROOF MARK	CIRCA	PROOF HOUSE	TYPE OF PROOF AND GUN
	since 1951	Brescia	provisional proof for all guns
	since 1951	Gardone	provisional proof for all guns
PSF	since 1951	Gardone & Brescia	definitive proof for guns with smokeless powder
PSF FINITO	since 1951	Gardone & Brescia	finish proof for firearms ready for sale
P N	since 1951	Gardone & Brescia	1st black powder proof

SPANISH PROOF MARKS

PROOF MARK	CIRCA	PROOF HOUSE	TYPE OF PROOF AND GUN
P₂	since 1910	Eibar	provisional black powder proof for shotguns
EX	since 1910	Eibar	temporary black powder proof for shotguns
NF	since 1910	Eibar	final black powder proof for breech loading shotguns
BV	since 1910	Eibar	final smokeless powder proof for breech loading shotguns
SCH	since 1910	Eibar	re-enforced smokeless powder proof for breech loading shotguns
	since 1910	Eibar	provisional proof for shotguns
PC	since 1910	Eibar	final black powder proof for breech loading shotgun

PROOF MARK	CIRCA	PROOF HOUSE	TYPE OF PROOF AND GUN
	since 1923	Eibar	final and single black powder proof for double barreled muzzle loading shotun
	since 1923	Eibar	final and single black powder proof for single barrel smooth bored breechloading guns
	since 1923	Eibar	final black powder proof for double barreled breechloading rifles
	since 1923	Eibar	final black powder proof for single barrel breechloading rifles
E	since 1923	Eibar	reinforced voluntary proof for single proof for single and double barrel shotguns
	since 1923	Eibar	final proof of military-style rifle
	since 1923	Eibar	single and final proof of non-self loading pistols
	since 1923	Eibar	single and final proof for self loading pistols and revolvers
	since 1929	Eibar	admission proof for guns with old marks
	since 1929	Eibar	proof used in Barcelona for guns with old marks
	since 1929	Eibar	final proof for revolver
	since 1929	Eibar	proof for semiautomatic pistols
FE	since 1929	Eibar	special manufacturer's mark for guns made for foreign sales
AXIII	since 1929	Eibar	smokeless proof for shotgun barrels
CH	since 1929	Eibar	reinforced smokeless proof for shotgun barrels

ATF GUIDE

A listing has been provided below of Field Division offices for the ATF. You are encouraged to contact them if you have any questions regarding the legality of any weapons or their interpretation of existing laws and regulations. Remember, ignorance is no excuse when it involves Federal firearms regulations and laws. Although these various offices may not be able to help you with state, city, county, or local firearms regulations and laws, their job is to assist you on a Federal level.

U.S. Department of Justice
Bureau of Alcohol, Tobacco,
Firearms and Explosives:

Atlanta Field Division
2600 Century Parkway
Atlanta, Georgia 30345
(404) 417-2600
Fax: (404) 417-2601

Baltimore Field Division
31 Hopkins Plaza, 5th Floor
Baltimore, Maryland 21201
(443) 965-2000
Fax: (443) 965-2001

Boston Field Division
10 Causeway Street, Suite 791
Boston, Massachusetts 02222
(617) 557-1200
Fax: (617) 557-1201

Charlotte Field Division
6701 Carmel Road, Suite 200
Charlotte, North Carolina 28226
(704) 716-1800
Fax (704)716-1801

Chicago Field Division
525 West Van Buren Street,
 Suite 600
Chicago, Illinois 60607
(312) 846-7200
Fax: (312) 846-7201

Columbus Field Division
37 West Broad Street, Suite 200
Columbus, Ohio 43215-4167
(614) 827-8400
Fax: (614) 827-8401

U.S. Department of Justice
Bureau of Alcohol, Tobacco,
Firearms and Explosives
Dallas Field Division
1114 Commerce Street, Room
303
Dallas, TX 75242
(469) 227-4300
Fax: (469) 227-4330

Detroit Field Division
1155 Brewery Park Boulevard,
 Suite 300
Detroit, Michigan 48207-2602
(313) 259-8050
Fax: (313) 393-6054

Houston Field Division
15355 Vantage Parkway West,
 Suite 200
Houston, Texas 77032-1960
(281) 372-2900
Fax: (281) 372-2919

Kansas City Field Division
2600 Grand Avenue, Suite 200
Kansas City, Missouri 64108
(816) 559-0700
Fax: (816) 559-0701

Los Angeles Field Division
350 South Figueroa Street, Suite
 800
Los Angeles, California 90071
(213) 534-2450
Fax: (213) 534-2415

Louisville Field Division
600 Dr. Martin Luther King Jr.
 Place, Suite 322
Louisville, KY 40202
(502) 753-3400
Fax: (502) 753-3401

Miami Field Division
5225 NW 87 Avenue, Suite 300
Miami, FL 33178
(305) 597-4800
Fax: 305-597-4801

Nashville Field Division
5300 Maryland Way, Suite 200
Brentwood, Tennessee 37027
(615) 565-1400
Fax: 615-565-1401

New Orleans Field Division
111 Veterans Memorial BLVD.,
 Suite 1008
Heritage Plaza Building
Metairie, Louisiana 70005
(504) 841-7000
Fax: (504) 841-7039

New York Field Division
241 37th Street, 3rd Floor
Brooklyn, NY 11232
(718) 650-4000
Fax: (718) 650-4001

Philadelphia Field Division
The Curtis Center
601 Walnut Street, Suite 1000E
Philadelphia, Pennsylvania
 19106
(215) 446-4800
Fax: (215) 446-4811

Phoenix Field Division
201 E. Washington Street, Suite
 940
Phoenix, AZ 85004
(602) 776-5400
Fax: (602) 776-5429

San Francisco Field Division
5601 Arnold Road, Suite 400
Dublin, CA 94568
(925) 479-7500
Fax: (925) 829-7612

Seattle Field Division
915 2nd Avenue, Room 790
Seattle, Washington 98174-1093
(206) 389-5800
Fax: (206) 389-582

St. Paul Field Division
30 East Seventh Street , Suite
 1900
St. Paul, Minnesota 55101
(651) 726-0200
Fax: (651) 726-0201

Tampa Field Division
501 East Polk Street, Suite 700
Tampa, Florida 33602
(813) 202-7300
Fax: (813) 202-7301

Washington Field Division
1401 H. Street NW, Suite 900
Washington, DC 20226
(202) 648-8010
Fax: (202) 648-8001

SHOW TIME

Over the last 29 years, Blue Book Publications, Inc. has attended hundreds of domestic and international industry and consumer shows. This is where much of the new information is gathered, in addition to providing us an opportunity to annually meet industry leaders, contributing editors, and interested consumers. It's a party! Make sure that you check our website periodically: www.bluebookinc.com (click on Show Time) for the most up-to-date schedule. Also, don't miss S.P. Fjestad's Lethal Blogging!

Here's a listing of all the gun-related trade shows (both consumer and industry) we'll either be attending or exhibiting at during 2008 and early 2009. If you want to hook up with our content providers and meet the staff while on the show circuit, here's where we'll be. It is highly recommended that you try to attend some of these shows, as these are the best places to acquire up-to-date information on what you like and collect. In the past, we have had a lot of requests for either appointments or to meet some of our personnel. Keeping this in mind, if you would like to schedule some time to see us at any of these shows, please contact us directly before each show date, so that we can make arrangements.

April 4-6, 2008
Tulsa Gun & Knife Show
(consumer show, exhibiting)
Expo Center - Expo Square
Tulsa Fairgrounds
Friday - dealers only, Sat. 8-7pm, Sun. 8-4pm
Contact: Tulsa Gun Show, Inc.
PO Box 33201
Tulsa, OK 74153-1201
Phone: 918-492-0401
www.tulsagunshow.com
mail@tulsagunshow.com

April 12-15, 2008
EXA
(Italian trade show, exhibiting)
Brixia Expo
Brescia, Italy
www.exa.it

May 16-18, 2008
The 137th NRA Annual Meetings & Exhibits Show
(consumer show, exhibiting)
Expo Center
Lousville, KY
Contact: NRA
Phone: 800-694-9300
www.nraam.org

June 20-22, 2008
Duluth Gun Show
(consumer show, exhibiting)
Duluth Entertainment Convention Center
South Pioneer Hall
Sat. 9-5 p.m. Sun. 9-3 p.m.
$5.00 admission
Contact: Bob White
1920 Greysolon Rd
Duluth, MN 55812
Phone: 218-724-8387
Fax: 218-724-8740

July 25-27, 2008
Annual Kansas City National Summer Arms Show
(consumer show, exhibiting)
K.C.I. Expo-Center
Kansas City, MO
Contact: MVACA Show Committee
PO Box 33033
Kansas City, MO 64114
Phone: 913-642-2863
www.mvacagunshow.org

August 9-10, 2008
Minnesota Weapons Collectors & NRA National Gun Collectors Show
Minneapolis Convention Center
www.mwca.org

Oct. 17-19, 2008
Tulsa Gun & Knife Show
(consumer show, exhibiting)
Expo Center - Expo Square
Tulsa Fairgrounds
Sat. 8-7 PM, Sun. 8-5 PM
Contact: Tulsa Gun Show, Inc.
PO Box 33201
Tulsa, OK 74153-1201
Phone: 918-492-0401
www.tulsagunshow.com
mail@tulsagunshow.com

Dec. 13-14, 2008
Minnesota Weapons Collectors Show
(consumer show, exhibiting)
Rivercentre, St. Paul, MN
www.mwca.org

Jan. 15-18, 2009
Annual SHOT (Shooting, Hunting, Outdoor Trade) Show
(trade show only-no consumers, exhibiting)
Orlando Convention Center
Orlando, FL
www.shotshow.org

Jan. 21-25, 2009
SCI (Safari Club International) Annual Hunters Convention
(members only show, attending)
Reno-Sparks Convention Center
Reno, NV
www.safariclub.org

Jan. 23-25, 2009
Firearms Engravers Guild Annual Exhibition
(trade and consumer show)
Silver Legacy Hotel
Reno, NV
www.fega.com

April 4-5, 2009
Tulsa Gun & Knife Show
(consumer show, exhibiting)
Expo Center - Expo Square
Tulsa Fairgrounds
Sat. 8-7pm, Sun. 8-5pm
Contact: Tulsa Gun Show, Inc.
PO Box 33201
Tulsa, OK 74153-1201
Phone: 918-492-0401
www.tulsagunshow.com
mail@tulsagunshow.com

INDEX

A

B

D

I

J

K

L

T

P.S.

TOP TEN EMAILED GUN QUESTIONS

In the good ol' days, some shooters and gun collectors would mail us out of focus, blurry pictures with illegible handwritten letters going into detail about the questions they had. The great thing about email is that it allows some people to write even more badly than they speak. As you can see from the following, effective communication may not be going in the right direction.

10. RE: .22/45 over under pistol or darringer - I just bought this one, don't know if it is a pistol or a darringer, or the age of it, if you have any info on gun I would appreciate it, how old and is it safe, it was made in ducktown, tn. is all the information I have on gun how much is it worth, looks like it has never been fired could be old or new

9. RE: Army - I was looking at Blue Book online. I cannot find Army

8. RE: Guns - 1889 winchesrt leaver axion 3006what it werth

7. RE: Manufacturer - I got a 38 special revolver with c.a.l. georgia unit writin on it and it says it's a astra 960. I'm trying to find the maker of this gun. can you help.

6. RE: shells - I got this old worn out 20 guage H&R single shot that still shoots good. My buddi dropped off some 28 guage shells the other day. We put them in the 20 gauge, and they fit pretty close. How will they shoot?

5. RE: How old - I have a 22 calibar short made in Germany and the serial number is 339919. I'm trying to find out when this gun was made.

4. RE: gunsock - I would like to buy a gunsock for my husband for Christmas and need a price.

3. RE: rifle - I have a .22 rifle. Can you tell me what it worth

2. RE: Saddam's gun - What is the estimated value of the gun Saddam had on him when he was caught?

1. RE: Winchester - I bought a Winchester Remington 870 I was wondering how much they run for.